P9-DMV-114

Wife's Family Tree

Grandfather

Grandmother

their sisters/brothers

Father

his sisters/brothers

Wife

her sisters/brothers

Grandfather

Grandmother

their sisters/brothers

Mother

her sisters/brothers

Husband's Family Tree

Grandfather

Grandmother

their sisters/brothers

Father

his sisters/brothers

Husband

his sisters/brothers

Grandfather

Grandmother

their sisters/brothers

Mother

her sisters/brothers

The Ketubah *A Jewish Marriage Contract*

In Judaism, the *ketubah* (Hb, lit "her writing") is a unilateral marriage contract required from the groom. The wedding (Hb *kiddushin*, lit "sanctification") officially sanctifies and blesses this contract. The *ketubah* is read aloud during this ceremony just as in the giving of the law (Ex 24:7). The properly signed covenant document is received by the bride from the groom for her safekeeping. A personal *ketubah* is often written in an aesthetically beautiful way as an illuminated manuscript, which may be displayed alongside a wedding portrait as a work of art in ones home.

The *ketubah* is written in Aramaic, the legal language of Talmudic law, rather than in Hebrew. In the State of Israel, the *ketubah* is a legally binding and enforceable agreement. The document is signed by the groom and witnessed by two people who, in effect, attest to the groom's promises. The bride may sign but is not required to do so because she is the recipient of this commitment; yet it is a unilateral rather than a mutual agreement.

The responsibilities of the bridegroom are carefully listed in the *ketubah*:

- the bridegroom's responsibilities to his wife during their wedded life together—food, clothing, a home, and pleasure (i.e., her conjugal rights)—as he promises (in what is called the alimentation clause), . . . "I will work for you, honor, provide for, and support you, in accordance with the practice of Jewish husbands, who work for their wives, honor, provide for, and support them in truth";
- the wife's designation as the heir to the estate if he predeceases her; and,
- the man's provision of a financial settlement for his wife if he divorces her.

In the event of the husband's death or his pursuit of divorce, a lien is placed on all his property to provide her financial support. This lien obligates the husband personally, becoming a mortgage not only on his real estate but also on his personal assets.

These funds are called *mohar*, first the cash gift the groom gave to his bride's father but later an addition to the bride's dowry, ultimately serving as a minimal life insurance or divorce settlement. The *ketubah* also records the specific dowry arrangements (provided by the bride's father and representing her share of her family's inheritance) and the groom's acceptance of them. Additional funds (*mattan*) are promised voluntarily by the groom. If the marriage is dissolved, all three—*mohar*, dowry, and *mattan*—belong to the wife.

The *ketubah* stands as a monumental document protecting the rights of women. God's plan for the woman in marriage is manifested beautifully in this document in which the groom makes his commitments to his bride with no reciprocal commitment demanded from her.

A *ketubah* commemorating your marriage may be prepared on the opposite page. It should include the names of the fathers of the bride and groom. If either father is a Cohen or Levi (i.e., of priestly lineage), Jewish families also note this fact. The wedding ceremony's location is designated; if necessary, the closest waterway (e.g., river, sea, lake) may be included to be more precise. The date of the wedding is also essential. Since in Jewish tradition a new day begins at sunset, a wedding on a Friday evening, for example, would use Saturday's date. A Jewish couple records the month and year both in modern terms and as they correspond to the Hebrew calendar.

–Dorothy Kelley Patterson

"It is not good for man to be alone. I will make a helper who is like him."

Genesis 2:18

Wedding Date

Wedding Location

Name of the Groom

Name of the Groom's Father

Name of the Bride

Name of the Bride's Father

Scripture Challenge

The Groom's Pledge to the Bride

Signature of Groom

Signature of Bride

Signature of Witness

Signature of Witness

"Then Samuel took a stone and set it upright between Mizpah and Shen. He named it Ebenezer," explaining "The LORD has helped us to this point."

1 Sm 7:12

Samuel named this stone "Ebenezer" (Hb, "stone of help") to honor what Yahweh had done for the Israelites throughout their generations. This stone became a public and permanent reminder of God's grace poured out on generation after generation.

Believers need to be reminded to focus their lasting memories on what God has done, is doing, and will do in the lives of their families. To put the LORD God at the center of life and develop traditions and rituals that honor Him will create a godly legacy not only for this generation but also for the generations to come.

Family Milestones

Date/Location

Description

Date/Location

Description

Date/Location

Description

Date/Location

Description

Date/Location

Description

Date/Location

Description

Date/Location

Description

Date/Location

Description

Date/Location

Description

Date/Location

Description

Date/Location

Description

Date/Location

Description

My Spiritual Mothers

Name

Spiritual Gift

Scripture Passage

Name

Spiritual Gift

Scripture Passage

Name

Spiritual Gift

Scripture Passage

Name

Spiritual Gift

Scripture Passage

Name

Spiritual Gift

Scripture Passage

Name

Spiritual Gift

Scripture Passage

Name

Spiritual Gift

Scripture Passage

Name

Spiritual Gift

Scripture Passage

the Study Bible *for* WOMEN

HOLMAN CHRISTIAN STANDARD BIBLE®

the Study Bible *for* WOMEN

HOLMAN CHRISTIAN STANDARD BIBLE®

Dorothy Kelley Patterson, General Editor

Rhonda Harrington Kelley, Managing Editor

Editorial Committee:

CANDI FINCH, Section Editor: Genesis–Deuteronomy and Acts–Philemon

SHARON GRITZ, Section Editor: Hebrews–Revelation

SUSIE HAWKINS, Section Editor: Character Profiles

TAMRA HERNANDEZ, Section Editor: Job–Song of Songs and Matthew–John

LAUREN JOHNSON, Section Editor: Hosea–Malachi

STEFANA DAN LAING, Section Editor: Isaiah–Daniel

KATIE MCCOY, Section Editor: Joshua–Esther

NASHVILLE, TENNESSEE

The Study Bible for Women, designed by Jade Novak, typeset by TF Designs, Greenbrier, TN, proofread by Peachtree Editorial Services, Peachtree City, GA

Binding	*ISBN*
Printed Hardcover	978-1-5864-0098-9
Sky Blue/Deep Red LeatherTouch	978-1-5864-0088-0
Sky Blue/Deep Red LeatherTouch Indexed	978-1-5864-0086-6
Teal/Sage LeatherTouch	978-1-5864-0087-3
Teal/Sage LeatherTouch Indexed	978-1-5864-0085-9
Chocolate Genuine Leather	978-1-5864-0092-7
Chocolate Genuine Leather Indexed	978-1-5864-0094-1
Brown/Pink LeatherTouch	978-1-5864-0938-8
Brown/Pink LeatherTouch Indexed	978-1-5864-0939-5
Springlike LeatherTouch	978-1-4336-1662-4
Springlike LeatherTouch Indexed	978-1-4336-1661-7

Printed in South Korea
2 3 4 5 6 — 17 16 15 14
SWP

Table of Contents

The
Old Testament

The
New Testament

Introduction to *The Study Bible for Women*

Opening God's Word to women through a comprehensive study of Scripture prepared by women for women on subjects important to women is not really a modern phenomenon. The Apostle Paul placed within his discussion on church order a mandate for spiritually mature women to teach women who were new to the faith (Ti 2:3-5). In the modern era as well, women are devoting personal time and resources to diligent study of God's Word and woman-to-woman instruction.

The Study Bible for Women, together with the Old and New Testament volumes of *The Women's Evangelical Commentary*, completes a trilogy of unique tools for unlocking the riches of holy Scripture. These three volumes, without apology, are prepared primarily for women to use in personal study and preparation for teaching. In the Study Bible, women will find guidance for unfolding the clear meaning of Scripture as well as timely challenges to fashion their lives accordingly, written by believing sisters in the Lord who have a passion for woman-to-woman exposition and who are uniquely prepared to explain the Scriptures. The women who contributed to these volumes model disciplined reading of Scripture according to carefully defined hermeneutical boundaries, resulting in:

- distinctive exegesis that pulls out the meaning of the text rather than reading into the text their own personal opinions;
- sensitivity to apply Scripture to the particular needs and questions of women without using a feminist "gender lens";
- intuitive scholarship—the linking of discerning intuition with the discipline of scholarship;
- cultivation of mentoring friendships that offer common ground instead of polarity in the tasks of understanding and teaching the Bible; and
- creativity in connecting mind and heart, doctrine and practical service, firm biblical boundaries and relevant life applications.

Scripture provides all you need for "life and godliness," and *The Study Bible for Women* is the perfect tool for discovering this provision. Its specially designed features offer to any woman who comes to Scripture with an open heart and ready mind a catalyst for personal study of God's Word as well as resources for teaching other women how to read and study the Scriptures. The introduction to each of the Bible's 66 books answers basic fact questions about the book, explains what the book is about, offers good reasons for women to read it, and provides guidance for studying it effectively. Also included are a carefully selected key verse that captures one of the book's themes, a timeline situating people and main events in history, and a content outline that provides a helpful overview of the book and its structure. The study notes in the outer margins offer insights on difficult-to-understand passages and spotlight important truths. In addition, "threads" of specialized study are woven throughout—explanations of foundational doctrines, profiles of biblical women, relevant discussions of biblical womanhood, helpful word studies, and answers to hard questions prompted by the text of Scripture. At the end of each book is a devotional word of application, celebration, encouragement, or other means of allowing the Holy Spirit to write the particular truths of that book on your own heart.

Come to Scripture with a teachable heart ready to hear God speak, respond to Him in obedience, and find your place in His story. The godly woman will seek to conform her beliefs and behavior to Scripture, not pick and choose what Scripture is most agreeable to her own desires. Attentiveness to the Word of God, willingness to explore its depths, and eagerness to meet and enjoy fellowship with its divine Author will inspire your readiness to become a wise woman whose life is securely built on the rock of doing whatever the Lord says (Mt 7:24-25). May the Lord grant to each of you who uses this Study Bible a renewed commitment of personal time and the determination to pursue the riches found in serious study of God's Word—not only for yourself but also for the women you will teach as the Word is continually written on your heart.

Yours for a journey through God's Word,

Dorothy Kelley Patterson

How to Study the Bible

Dorothy Kelley Patterson

Scripture can become *within your life an illuminating and powerful reminder* that God speaks, acts, awaits, and loves you (2Pt 1:19-21). There are obvious qualifications for the serious student of God's Word:

- a personal relationship with Jesus Christ (Jn 16:13);
- a deep reverence for God's Word (Pr 1:7);
- a passion to know God's Word (2Tm 1:12; 3:14-17); and
- an utter dependence on the Holy Spirit to open His Word (Jn 14:26).

The Bible is inspired (Gk *theopneustos,* lit "God-breathed" or inspired of God, 2Tm 3:16); inerrant (without error); infallible (trustworthy in the sense that it cannot and will not lead you astray); immutable (without the constraints of time and unchanging). The first and foremost step in understanding Scripture is to read its words, not haphazardly but with purpose, not just a passage but the whole counsel of God. Before embarking on serious study of a focal passage, read the Bible in its entirety. Understand its flawless *unity* through the great central theme of the Lord's atonement and redemption. *This compilation of 66 books—all inspired by the Holy Spirit—has a common purpose of reconciling God to man.* The Bible not only makes you wise unto salvation (2 Tm 3:15), but its words also nurture and edify spiritually (2 Tm 3:16-17).

How Can I Read the Entire Bible?

Read through the Bible. You can begin in Genesis and read through to Revelation. Reading three chapters each weekday and five on Sunday is one option. Select various books at random or according to personal preference. Start and keep on reading—not for preparation to teach but to become familiar with Scripture—the broadest survey of the Bible as a whole in the shortest period of time. Reading does not take the place of day-in and day-out disciplined study, which alone provides a working knowledge of the Bible in all its parts. Anyone who dares to teach must never cease to learn.

As you read the Bible for personal study, keep a notebook without concern for form or style. Record your insights concerning the words of Scripture before researching what others have said as in my personal entry on the book of Micah:

(6:8) This challenge pricks my heart. God does not demand justice toward others but justness in our own personal actions of life. We are to be just and righteous personally. For others, He demands mercy, which is more than justice. For God, He demands still more—humility, the stripping away of any pride of our self-righteousness and own mercy to others!

Without prayer, your Bible study can degenerate into a dull and monotonous chore of trying to remember facts and people and places for head knowledge. On the other hand, if your personal devotional time consists of prayer alone, *you can move unconsciously toward believing that God's imprimatur is on whatever you want. However, bringing together the knowledge you gain about God's creation order, His plan of redemption, and His demands for holiness in life will enable you to achieve a helpful dialogue with God.*

How Do I Begin Personal Bible Study?

Spiritual formation or quiet time begins with setting apart a definite time for personal Bible study—not preparation time for research or teaching or writing but a communication time with God. Guard that time and use it wisely. Once the time is set and you are serious about personal study, you are ready to move into the biblical text. You should first read the book as a whole, not once but several times, hopefully reading through the book in one sitting. I emphasize a different aspect of study with each reading. For example, my first reading is to get *broad acquaintance* with the book, without making notes but underlining or highlighting key ideas, not trying to interrupt reading with explanations from others but listening for the Spirit's direction and application. My second reading is to determine how the book is divided or outlined and note in my journal recurring themes, terms of interest, and topics addressed.

At this point you are ready to read the book by sections and summarize as you read, documenting the flow of the book's message prayerfully and reverently. By reading the text without consulting other sources, under the tutelage of the Holy Spirit, you come to your own understanding of the text. Without being sidetracked, you are able to master the overall message of the words themselves.

What Should I Look for in This Personal Reading of the Text Itself?

Look for these elements:

- The principal or most important subject addressed
- Any outstanding lessons
- Verses for focus and memorizing
- Prominent people and places mentioned—are there any role models?
- References to the central message of Scripture—Christ and His atonement
- Practical applications to life and work
- Devotional thoughts for meditation

The most careful study of Scripture is verse-by-verse exegesis in which you move slowly and deliberately through the text without trying to sidestep difficult verses:

- Consider parallel passages expressing the same thought (e.g., "fears the Lord" as found in Pr 31:30 and also in 1Pt 3:1-4).
- See how one passage casts light on another (e.g., an understanding of the creation order in Gn 2 in explaining the relationship between men and women in the home, Eph 5:21-31; and in the church, 1Tm 2:9-15).
- Let the meaning of one passage further define another (e.g., love as defined in 1Co 13 and then further amplified in 1Jn 3:16).
- Develop original principles to be modified and explained in relation to some new set of circumstances (e.g., the relationship between women and men clearly established through generations but then in question because of cultural changes and now defined through an understanding of egalitarianism vs. complementarianism).

Resources play heavily into personal study—whether for your own edification or to help you in teaching others. Grammatical tools can also be helpful, such as diagramming sentences.

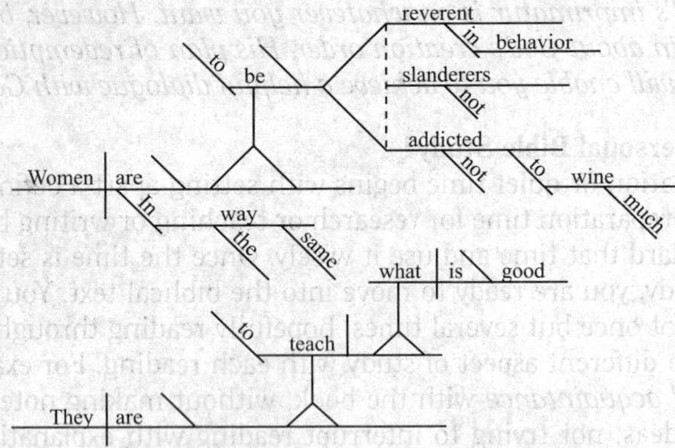

Also include literary evaluation (e.g., what genre—history, parable, prophecy, poetry, epistle or letter), consideration of figurative language (e.g., whether straightforward sharing of information or some figurative device), the meaning of key words (e.g., how they function in the sentence, significance of the word in the passage, other occurrences of the word in Scripture as found in a concordance), looking at the historical context (identifying author, determining date and place from which the book was written, identity and circumstances of recipients, and especially determining authorial intent, e.g., what the author meant by what he wrote).

What Kind of Sources Should I Use?

Sources are readily available. While the Bible is the primary source, the following are secondary sources that should be within every woman's reach for study:

- Find verses quickly and examine how the words are used throughout Scripture by using a **concordance** of the Bible (an unabridged desk copy).
- Detailed information about words, people, places, and events can be found in a **Bible dictionary**.
- An overview and general information on books of the Bible can be found in a **Bible handbook**.
- Pinpointing geographical locations, often together with a description of the history and significance of the place, is best done in a **Bible atlas**.
- **Translations** and **paraphrases** are helpful to express the best understanding of a passage.
- A **Harmony of the Gospels** is essential for any study of the four Gospels.
- **Charts** and **graphics** are helpful organizational and clarifying tools.
- **Bible commentaries** are essential for exegetical study. Perhaps you will begin with the *Women's Evangelical Commentary*—both Old Testament and New Testament volumes (see additional bibliographies at the end of each book in these commentaries).

Once you have worked your way systematically through the text you are ready to study its theological content. With the big picture, you can better understand the flow of the author's message. The most accurate interpretation is always found in comparing Scripture with Scripture:

- Obscure passages *must be interpreted in light of passages* that are crystal clear.
- Beware of trying to build a major doctrine on one, or even several, isolated verses.
- Understand doctrines by reviewing many verses and sections of Scripture.

- If, in your human evaluation, two doctrines appear to contradict each other, accept both, realizing that you will never understand the mind of God.
- Study brief passages in light of lengthier passages.
- Note that the New Testament helps to interpret the Old Testament and vice versa.
- Timeless principles are found behind timely manifestations of those principles.
- Systematic passages should take priority over incidental passages.
- Teaching or didactic passages make more clear symbolic or practical passages.
- Every part of Scripture must be viewed in light of its overall emphasis.

Application is the finale to your study of Scripture, but all practical lessons must be governed by disciplined and tested principles of hermeneutics. The Bible is a book of principles and not merely a catalog of solutions for every situation. Principles are clearly stated, but you must be sensitive to the spirit of God's Word since Scripture will not directly address every subject. The emphasis of Scripture is on inner commitment to holiness of life and obedience to God *rather than a pseudo-spiritual cloak of outward acquiescence to whatever seems relevant in your own thinking*. You must make a distinction between what the Bible records (e.g., slavery) and what it approves (e.g., male headship in the home and church). Express commands to individuals in Scripture are not necessarily the will of God for you, nor is a literal reproduction of a biblical situation necessary to determine God's will for you.

General Rules for Hermeneutics	
Regeneration (1Co 2:14)	You must have a personal relationship with Christ.
Authority (2Tm 3:16-17)	Accept the Bible as the authoritative Word of God.
Preparation (Ps 119:33-40)	Pray for and accept the Holy Spirit's instruction in understanding Scripture.
Organization (2Tm 2:15)	Read the Bible from beginning to end. Organize and summarize the section you want to study.
Natural Interpretation (2Tm 2:7)	Read the Bible in a natural way as any book, believing that God says what He means and means what He says.
Christocentric Interpretation (Lk 24:25-27)	Keep Christ at the center of the biblical message.
Contextual Consideration	You can prove anything by isolating verses. Maintain the integrity of the text by considering its meaning in context.
Common Sense (Mt 11:28-30)	The Bible was written to be understood by anyone who comes earnestly to learn from its message.
Pneumatic Guidance (Jn 16:13)	Only the Holy Spirit can ultimately give understanding of Scripture.

Personal study is definitely the first step in preparing to teach the Bible. You must discover what the passage really says and what it means by following good hermeneutical principles and by harmonizing the text with its context and with the whole of Scripture. You are then ready to make an outline and to prepare an introduction to draw your pupils into the study as well as a conclusion to persuade them to move to action. In the heart of your teaching, challenge your listeners to think and make practical applications to life.

The Christian Life

Rhonda Harrington Kelley

Are you a Christian? A Christian is anyone who has received by faith the salvation God has provided in Jesus Christ. *Salvation* is necessary because all have sinned against God (Rm 3:23). Salvation begins with *repentance*—turning away from sin and turning toward God, who alone has the power to save. You cannot earn salvation by doing good works for it is a gift of grace from God, accomplished through the death of His Son, Jesus Christ (Eph 2:8-9). When Jesus died on the cross, He paid the price to forgive all sin (Jn 3:16; Rm 5:8; 1Jn 2:2). Romans 6:23 says, "For the wages of sin is death, but the gift of God is eternal life in Christ Jesus our Lord." God's free gift of salvation—the exchange of your sin for His righteousness—must be accepted by faith (Rm 10:9-10). When you accept God's gift of salvation, you become a new creation (2Co 5:17). Salvation changes everything—your past, your present, and your future:

- *Justification* may be considered the past tense of salvation. Justification is God's declaration that you are righteous through the blood of Christ (Rm 4:3-25).
- *Sanctification* is the present tense of salvation, the process of growing in faith and in holiness since you are set apart by and for God (1Co 6:11).
- *Glorification* is the future tense of salvation. Glorification is the perfection of God's image and character in you when you enter His presence in heaven (2Co 3:18).

If you are a Christian, you are promised security in your salvation, but what is your present "new creation" life supposed to look like? What responsibilities do you have in maintaining a vibrant relationship with your Savior?

The Beginning. Your Christian life begins the moment you turn away from sin and, by faith, receive the salvation God has provided in the crucifixion and resurrection of His Son Jesus Christ. At that moment, the Holy Spirit makes Himself at home in your life, immediately beginning the remodeling process necessary for Christ to be seen in every aspect. Just as the Christian life does not begin when you are born, when you become a church member, or when you mistakenly think you have earned God's approval for doing good, so it does not continue on the basis of who you are, whom you know, where you go to church, or what you do. Just as there is nothing you can do to get rid of your sin and restore your relationship with God—Jesus sacrificed Himself to provide the forgiveness needed, so you cannot "live the Christian life" on your own terms. Relinquishing ownership and control of your life to Christ is just the beginning of the total life makeover.

The Ongoing Story. From that point on, your salvation is secure. Regardless of how sin-stained or sin-wrecked your life is when you entrust it to Christ, all is forgiven. However, you have a ruthless enemy who is determined to thwart God's renovation plans for your life by any means possible and keep you from telling anyone else the Good News. In Christ you have freedom from the addiction to sin and from consequent death (i.e., eternal separation from God). No longer are you the enemy's slave to do his bidding, but he strives to convince you otherwise. Scripture often talks about this war in terms of light and darkness. Christ's message is that "God is light, and there is absolutely no darkness in Him" (1Jn 1:5). Speaking to authentic Christians about their changed status, Ephesians 5:8 says, "For you were once darkness, but now you are light in the Lord" and commands, "Walk as children of light."

The power to "walk in the light as He [Jesus Christ] Himself is in the light" (1Jn 1:7a) is available in the Holy Spirit who is always with the Christian. Living the Christian life—walking in the light—is only possible by continually agreeing with the truth He reveals and letting Him exchange, change, and rearrange however He sees fit. The truth is found in the Bible. The power to obey the truth is in the Holy Spirit. The Christian whose mind is Scripture-saturated and whose will is Spirit-directed is equipped to grow in Christlikeness, but this growth also requires staying connected to the body of Christ, the local church. The Christian life is nurtured in your personal devotional life of Bible study and prayer but expressed in your relationships—both with your brothers and sisters in Christ and with non-Christians.

In the End. Until Jesus returns, the physical lives of Christians will end but not without hope. Jesus' resurrection validates His promise of eternal life to those who follow Him. The Christian life is best lived with the end (as described in Scripture) in mind (see 2Pt 3), not only looking forward to God's justice and the rewards of endurance but also looking for opportunities to proclaim the gospel (see 1Pt 4). From confession of faith into eternity, the Christian life is a reflection of Christ Himself, an extension of His work in the world, and a witness of salvation to those who are unsaved.

Introduction to the Holman Christian Standard Bible®

The Bible is God's written revelation to man. It is the only book that gives us entirely accurate and authenticated information about God, man's need, and God's provision for that need. It provides us with guidance for life and tells us how to receive eternal life. The Bible can do these things because it is God's inspired Word, inerrant in the original manuscripts.

The Bible describes God's dealings with the ancient Jewish people and the early Christian church. It tells us about the great gift of God's Son, Jesus Christ, who fulfilled Jewish prophecies of the Messiah. It tells us about the salvation He accomplished through His death on the cross, His triumph over death in the resurrection, and His promised return to earth. It is the only book that gives us completely reliable information about the future, about what will happen to us when we die, and about where history is headed.

Bible translation is both a science and an art. It is a bridge that brings God's Word from the ancient world to the world today. In dependence on God to accomplish this sacred task, Holman Bible Publishers presents the Holman Christian Standard Bible, an English translation of God's Word.

Textual base of the HCSB®

The textual base for the New Testament [NT] is the Nestle-Aland *Novum Testamentum Graece*, 27th edition, and the United Bible Societies' *Greek New Testament,* 4th corrected edition. The text for the Old Testament [OT] is the *Biblia Hebraica Stuttgartensia,* 5th edition.

Where there are significant differences among Hebrew [Hb] and Aramaic [Aram] manuscripts of the OT or among Greek [Gk] manuscripts of the NT, the translators have followed what they believe is the original reading and have indicated the main alternative(s) in footnotes. The HCSB uses the traditional verse divisions found in most Protestant Bibles.

Goals of this translation

The goals of this translation are:

- to provide English-speaking people across the world with an accurate, readable Bible in contemporary English
- to equip serious Bible students with an accurate translation for personal study, private devotions, and memorization
- to give those who love God's Word a text that has numerous reader helps, is visually attractive on the page, and is appealing when heard
- to affirm the authority of Scripture as God's Word and to champion its absolute truth against social or cultural agendas that would compromise its accuracy
- to continue making improvements to the translation in each printing

The name, Holman Christian Standard Bible, captures these goals: *Holman* Bible Publishers presents a *Bible* translation, for *Christian* and English-speaking communities, which will be a *standard* in Bible translations for years to come.

Why is there a need for another English translation of the Bible?

There are several good reasons why Holman Bible Publishers invested its resources in a modern language translation of the Bible:

1. <u>Each generation needs a fresh translation of the Bible in its own language.</u>

The Bible is the world's most important book, confronting each individual and each culture with issues that affect life, both now and forever. Since each new generation must be introduced to God's Word in its own language, there will always be a need for new translations such as the

HCSB. The majority of Bible translations on the market today are revisions of translations from previous generations. The HCSB is a new translation for today's generation.

2. English, one of the world's greatest languages, is rapidly changing, and Bible translations must keep in step with those changes.

English is the first truly global language in history. It is the language of education, business, medicine, travel, research, and the Internet. More than 1.3 billion people around the world speak or read English as a primary or secondary language. The HCSB seeks to serve many of those people with a translation they can easily use and understand.

English is also the world's most rapidly changing language. The HCSB seeks to reflect recent changes in English by using modern punctuation, formatting, and vocabulary, while avoiding slang, regionalisms, or changes made specifically for the sake of political or social agendas. Modern linguistic and semantic advances have been incorporated into the HCSB, including modern grammar.

3. Rapid advances in biblical research provide new data for Bible translators.

This has been called the "information age," a term that accurately describes the field of biblical research. Never before in history has there been as much information about the Bible as there is today—from archaeological discoveries to analysis of ancient manuscripts to years of study and statistical research on individual Bible books. Translations made as recently as the late 20th century do not reflect many of these advances in biblical research. The HCSB translators have taken into consideration as much of this new data as possible.

4. Advances in computer technology have opened a new door for Bible translation.

The HCSB has used computer technology and telecommunications in its creation perhaps more than any Bible translation in history. Electronic mail was used daily and sometimes hourly for communication and transmission of manuscripts. An advanced Bible software program, Accordance®, was used to create and revise the translation at each step in its production. A developmental copy of the translation itself was used within Accordance to facilitate cross-checking during the translation process—something never done before with a Bible translation.

Translation philosophy of the HCSB

Most discussions of Bible translations speak of two opposite approaches: formal equivalence and dynamic equivalence. Although this terminology is meaningful, Bible translations cannot be neatly sorted into these two categories any more than people can be neatly sorted into two categories according to height or weight. Holman Bible Publishers is convinced there is room for another category of translation philosophy that capitalizes on the strengths of the other two.

1. Formal Equivalence:

Often called "word-for-word" (or "literal") translation, the principle of formal equivalence seeks as nearly as possible to preserve the structure of the original language. It seeks to represent each word of the original text with an exact equivalent word in the translation so that the reader can see word for word what the original human author wrote. The merits of this approach include its consistency with the conviction that the Holy Spirit did inspire the very words of Scripture in the original manuscripts. It also provides the English Bible student some access to the structure of the text in the original language. Formal equivalence can achieve accuracy to the degree that English has an exact equivalent for each word and that the grammatical patterns of the original language can be reproduced in understandable English. However, it can sometimes result in awkward, if not incomprehensible, English or in a misunderstanding of the author's intent. The literal rendering of ancient idioms is especially difficult.

2. Dynamic or Functional Equivalence:

Often called "thought-for-thought" translation, the principle of dynamic equivalence rejects as misguided the desire to preserve the structure of the original language. It proceeds by extracting the meaning of a text from its form and then translating that meaning so that it makes the same impact on modern readers that the ancient text made on its original readers. Strengths of this approach include a high degree of clarity and readability, especially in places where the original is difficult to render word for word. It also acknowledges that accurate and effective translation requires interpretation. However, the meaning of a text cannot always be neatly separated from its form, nor can it always be precisely determined. A biblical author may have intended multiple meanings but these may be lost with the elimination of normal structures. In striving for readability, dynamic equivalence also sometimes overlooks and loses some of the less prominent elements of meaning. Furthermore, lack of formal correspondence to the original makes it difficult to verify accuracy and thus can affect the usefulness of the translation for in-depth Bible study.

3. Optimal Equivalence:

In practice, translations are seldom if ever purely formal or dynamic but favor one theory of Bible translation or the other to varying degrees. Optimal equivalence as a translation philosophy recognizes that form cannot always be neatly separated from meaning and should not be changed (for example, nouns to verbs or third person "they" to second person "you") unless comprehension demands it. The primary goal of translation is to convey the sense of the original with as much clarity as the original text and the translation language permit. Optimal equivalence appreciates the goals of formal equivalence but also recognizes its limitations.

Optimal equivalence starts with an exhaustive analysis of the text at every level (word, phrase, clause, sentence, discourse) in the original language to determine its original meaning and intention (or purpose). Then relying on the latest and best language tools and experts, the nearest corresponding semantic and linguistic equivalents are used to convey as much of the information and intention of the original text with as much clarity and readability as possible. This process assures the maximum transfer of both the words and thoughts contained in the original.

The HCSB uses optimal equivalence as its translation philosophy. When a literal translation meets these criteria, it is used. When clarity and readability demand an idiomatic translation, the reader can still access the form of the original text by means of a footnote with the abbreviation "Lit."

The gender language policy in Bible translation

Some people today are uncomfortable with the Bible's teachings on distinctive roles for men and women in family and church settings and desire to gloss over those distinctions. They seek to correct a perceived male bias in the biblical culture and the English language, including English translations of the Bible. For example, they seek to move away from traditional linguistic practices such as the generic use of "man" or "men," as well as "he," "him," and "his."

A group of Bible scholars, translators, and other evangelical leaders met in 1997 to respond to this issue as it affects Bible translation. This group produced the "Guidelines for Translation of Gender-Related Language in Scripture" (adopted May 27, 1997 and revised Sept. 9, 1997). The HCSB was produced in accordance with these guidelines.

The goal of the translators has not been to promote a cultural ideology but to faithfully translate the Bible. While the HCSB avoids using "man" or "he" unnecessarily, the translation does not restructure sentences to avoid them when they are in the text. For example, the translators have not changed "him" to "you" or to "them," neither have they avoided other masculine words such as "father" or "son" by translating them in generic terms such as "parent" or "child."

History of the HCSB

After several years of preliminary development, Holman Bible Publishers, the oldest Bible publisher in America, assembled an international, interdenominational team of 100 scholars, editors, stylists, and proofreaders, all of whom were committed to biblical inerrancy. Outside consultants and reviewers contributed valuable suggestions from their areas of expertise. An executive team of translators edited, polished, and reviewed the final manuscripts.

Traditional features found in the HCSB

In keeping with a long line of Bible publications, the HCSB has retained a number of features found in traditional Bibles:

1. Traditional theological vocabulary (such as *justification, sanctification, redemption*) has been retained since such terms have no translation equivalent that adequately communicates their exact meaning.
2. Traditional spellings of names and places found in most Bibles have been used to make the HCSB compatible with most Bible study tools.
3. Some editions of the HCSB will print the words of Christ in red letters to help readers easily locate the spoken words of the Lord Jesus Christ.
4. Nouns and personal pronouns that clearly refer to any person of the Trinity are capitalized.
5. Descriptive headings, printed above each section of Scripture, help readers quickly identify the contents of that section.
6. Two common forms of punctuation are used in the HCSB to help with clarity and ease of reading: an em dash (—) is used to indicate sudden breaks in thought or to help clarify long or difficult sentences. Parentheses are used infrequently to indicate words that are parenthetical in the original languages.

How certain names and terms are translated

1. The names of God

The HCSB OT consistently translates the Hebrew names for God as follows:

HCSB English:	Hebrew original:
God	*Elohim*
LORD	*YHWH* (*Yahweh*)
Lord	*Adonai*
Lord GOD	*Adonai Yahweh*
LORD of Hosts	*Yahweh Sabaoth*
God Almighty	*El Shaddai*

However, the HCSB OT uses Yahweh, the personal name of God in Hebrew, when a biblical text emphasizes Yahweh as a name: "His name is Yahweh" (Ps 68:4). Yahweh is also used in places of His self-identification as in "I am Yahweh" (Is 42:8). Yahweh is used more often in the HCSB than in most Bible translations because the word LORD in English is a title of God and does not accurately convey to modern readers the emphasis on God's personal name in the original Hebrew.

2. The uses of Christ and Messiah

The HCSB translates the Greek word *Christos* ("anointed one") as either "Christ" or "Messiah" based on its use in different NT contexts. The first use of "Messiah" in each chapter is also marked with a bullet (•) referring readers to the Bullet Note at the back of most editions.

3. Place-names

In the original text of the Bible, particularly in the OT, a number of well-known places have names different from the ones familiar to contemporary readers. For example, "the Euphrates" often appears in the original text simply as "the River." In cases like this, the HCSB uses the modern name, "the Euphrates River," in the text without a footnote.

4. Substitution of words in sentences

A literal translation of the biblical text sometimes violates standard rules of English grammar, such as the agreement of subject and verb or person and number. In order to conform to standard usage, the HCSB has often made these kinds of grammatical constructions agree in English without footnotes.

In addition, the Greek or Hebrew texts sometimes seem redundant or ambiguous by repeating nouns where modern writing substitutes pronouns or by using pronouns where we would supply nouns for clarity and good style. When a literal translation of the original would make the English unclear, the HCSB sometimes changes a pronoun to its corresponding noun or a noun to its corresponding pronoun without a footnote. For example, Jn 1:42 reads: "And he brought Simon to Jesus . . ." The original Greek of this sentence reads: "And he brought him to Jesus."

Special formatting features

The HCSB has several distinctive formatting features:

1. OT passages quoted in the NT are set in boldface type. OT quotes consisting of two or more lines are block-indented.
2. In dialogue, a new paragraph is used for each new speaker as in most modern publications.
3. Many passages, such as 1Co 13, have been formatted as dynamic prose (separate block-indented lines like poetry) for ease in reading and comprehension. Special block-indented formatting has also been used extensively in both the OT and NT to increase readability and clarity in lists, series, genealogies and other parallel or repetitive texts.
4. Almost every Bible breaks lines in poetry using automatic typesetting programs with the result that words are haphazardly turned over to the next line. In the HCSB, special attention has been given to break every line in poetry and dynamic prose so that awkward or unsightly word wraps are avoided and complete units of thought turn over to the next line. The result is a Bible page that is much more readable and pleasing to the eye.
5. Certain commonly occurring words needing special explanation (such as foreign, geographical, historical, or theological terms) are preceded by a superscripted bullet (•*Abba*) at their first occurrence in each chapter. These words are listed in alphabetical order at the back of the Bible under the heading HCSB Bullet Notes.
6. Italics are used in the text for a transliteration of Greek and Hebrew words ("*Hosanna!*" in Jn 12:13) and in footnotes for direct quotations from the biblical text and for words in the original languages (the footnote at Jn 1:1 reads: "The *Word* (Gk *Logos*) is a title for Jesus . . .").
7. Since the majority of English readers do not need to have numbers and fractions spelled out in the text, the HCSB uses a similar style to that of modern newspapers in using Arabic numerals for the numbers 10 and above and in fractions, except in a small number of cases, such as when a number begins a sentence.

Footnotes

Footnotes are used to show readers how the original biblical language has been understood in the HCSB.

1. OT Textual Footnotes

OT textual notes show important differences among Hebrew manuscripts and ancient OT versions, such as the Septuagint and the Vulgate. See the list of abbreviations on page xxvi for a list of other ancient versions used.

Some OT textual notes (like NT textual notes) give only an alternate textual reading. However, other OT textual notes also give the support for the reading chosen by the editors as well as for the alternate textual reading. For example, the HCSB text of Ps 12:7 reads:

You will protect us[C]
  from this generation forever.

The textual footnote for this verse reads:

[C] **12:7** Some Hb mss, LXX; other Hb mss read *him*

The textual note in this example means that there are two different readings found in the Hebrew manuscripts: some manuscripts read *us* and others read *him*. The HCSB translators chose the reading *us*, which is also found in the Septuagint (LXX), and placed the other Hebrew reading *him* in the footnote.

Two other kinds OT textual notes are:

Alt Hb tradition reads ___	a variation given by scribes in the Hebrew manuscript tradition (known as *Kethiv/Qere* readings)
Hb uncertain	when it is uncertain what the original Hebrew text was

2. NT Textual Footnotes

NT textual notes indicate significant differences among Greek manuscripts (mss) and are normally indicated in one of three ways:

Other mss read ______
Other mss add ______
Other mss omit ______

In the NT, some textual footnotes that use the word "add" or "omit" also have large square brackets before and after the corresponding verses in the biblical text. Examples of this use of square brackets are in Mk 16:9-20, Jn 5:3-4, and Jn 7:53–8:11.

3. Other Kinds of Footnotes

Lit _____	a more literal rendering in English of the Hebrew, Aramaic, or Greek text
Or _____	an alternate or less likely English translation of the same Hebrew, Aramaic, or Greek text
=	an abbreviation for "it means" or "it is equivalent to"
Hb, Aram, Gk	the actual Hebrew, Aramaic, or Greek word is given using equivalent English letters
Hb obscure	the existing Hebrew text is especially difficult to translate
emend(ed) to ____	the original Hebrew text is so difficult to translate that competent scholars have conjectured or inferred a restoration of the original text based on the context, probable root meanings of the words, and uses in comparative languages

In some editions of the HCSB, additional footnotes clarify the meaning of certain biblical texts or explain biblical history, persons, customs, places, activities, and measurements. Cross-references are given for parallel passages or passages with similar wording, and in the NT, for passages quoted from the OT.

Transliteration Charts

Greek Transliteration Chart

Greek	English	Greek	English	Greek	English
α	a	ι	i	ρ	r
β	b	κ	k	σ	s
γ	g	λ	l	τ	t
δ	d	μ	m	υ	u
ε	e	ν	n	φ	ph
ζ	z	ξ	x	χ	ch
η	ē	ο	o	ψ	ps
θ	th	π	p	ω	ō

Hebrew Transliteration Chart

Hebrew	English	Hebrew	English
א	ʾ	ל	l
בּ ב	b v	מ	m
ג	g	נ	n
ד	d	ס	s
ה	h	ע	ʿ
ו	w	פּ פ	p ph
ז	z	צ	ts
ח	ch	ק	q
ט	t	ר	r
י	y	שׂ שׁ	s sh
כ	k	ת	t
Vowels			
ְ	e, vocal shewa	ֵ	ē
ַ	a	ִ	i
ָ	a	ֹ	o
ָ	o	ֻ	u
ֶ	e	וּ	u

Table of Weights and Measures

Weights

Biblical Unit	Language	Biblical Measure	U.S. Equivalent	Metric Equivalent	Various Translations
Gerah	Hebrew	1/20 shekel	1/50 ounce	.6 gram	gerah; oboli
Bekah	Hebrew	1/2 shekel or 10 gerahs	1/5 ounce	5.7 grams	bekah; half a shekel; quarter ounce; fifty cents
Pim	Hebrew	2/3 shekel	1/3 ounce	7.6 grams	2/3 of a shekel; quarter
Shekel	Hebrew	2 bekahs	2/5 ounce	11.5 grams	shekel; piece; dollar; fifty dollars
Litra (pound)	Greco-Roman	30 shekels	12 ounces	.4 kilogram	pound; pounds
Mina	Hebrew/ Greek	50 shekels	1 1/4 pounds	.6 kilogram	mina; pound
Talent	Hebrew/ Greek	3,000 shekels or 60 minas	75 pounds/ 88 pounds	34 kilograms/ 40 kilograms	talent/talents; 100 pounds

Length

Biblical Unit	Language	Biblical Measure	U.S. Equivalent	Metric Equivalent	Various Translations
Hand-breadth	Hebrew	1/6 cubit or 1/3 span	3 inches	8 centimeters	handbreadth; three inches; four inches
Span	Hebrew	1/2 cubit or 3 hand-breadths	9 inches	23 centimeters	span
Cubit/ Pechys	Hebrew/ Greek	2 spans	18 inches	.5 meter	cubit/cubits; yard; half a yard; foot
Fathom	Greco-Roman	4 cubits	2 yards	2 meters	fathom; six feet
Kalamos	Greco-Roman	6 cubits	3 yards	3 meters	rod; reed; measuring rod
Stadion	Greco-Roman	1/8 milion or 400 cubits	1/8 mile	185 meters	miles; furlongs; race
Milion	Greco-Roman	8 stadia	1,620 yards	1.5 kilometers	mile

Commonly Used Abbreviations in the HCSB

A.D.	In the year of our Lord	Lat	Latin
aka	also known as	Lit/lit	Literally/literally
alt	alternate	LXX	Septuagint—an ancient translation of the Old Testament into Greek
a.m.	from midnight until noon	ms(s)	manuscript(s)
Ant.	Antiquities—a history of the Jewish people by Josephus	MT	Masoretic Text
Aq	Aquila	NT	New Testament
Aram	Aramaic	Orig	Origen
B.C.	before Christ	OT	Old Testament
c.	century	p., pp.	page, pages
ca	circa	p.m.	from noon until midnight
chap(s).	chapter(s)	pl	plural
cp.	compare	Ps(s)	Psalm(s)
d.	died	Sam	Samaritan Pentateuch
DSS	Dead Sea Scrolls	sg	singular
e.g.	for example	Sym	Symmachus
Eng	English	Syr	Syriac
esp.	especially	Tg	Targum
etc.	etcetera	Theod	Theodotian
ff.	following	v., vv.	verse, verses
Gk	Greek	Vg	Vulgate—an ancient translation of the Bible into Latin
Hb	Hebrew	vol(s).	volume(s)
i.e.	that is	vs.	versus
Jer	Latin translation of Psalms by Jerome		

The
Old Testament

Genesis

Timeline World Events Biblical Events	*2166–1991 BC* Life of Abraham	*2156–2029 BC* Life of Sarah	*2085 BC* Destruction of Sodom and Gomorrah	*2066–1886 BC* Life of Isaac

"In the beginning God . . ." (1:1a).

Who wrote Genesis?

Even though Genesis is anonymous, Moses is believed to have recorded the events in this book and the rest of the Pentateuch, the first five book of the OT. Elsewhere in the Old Testament, the Pentateuch is referenced as "the book of the Law of Moses" (Jos 8:31; 2Kg 14:6; Neh 13:1). The New Testament also notes Moses as the author (Mt 19:8; Lk 24:27; Jn 5:45-47; Ac 3:22; Rm 10: 5; Rv 5:3). Jesus did not specifically say that Moses wrote Genesis, but in the Lord's day the Jews regarded the Pentateuch (*Torah,* Hb, "law") as a whole unit. Jesus affirmed this truth (Mt 19:8; Mk 7:10; Lk 16:16-18; Jn 7:19).

Who were the recipients?

The book was written initially to the nation of Israel, especially the new generation who would be taking possession of the promised land.

When was Genesis written?

The events recorded in Genesis stretch historically from creation to the death of Joseph, a period of at least 2,500 years. Although the date of writing cannot be fixed with certainty, the date of Genesis must be within Moses' lifetime (ca 1525–1405 B.C.), with the time of the wilderness wandering just before the people entered the land of promise under Joshua as the most likely date for writing. Accepting the date of the exodus as ca 1445 B.C. then suggests ca 1400 B.C. as a reasonable date.

Where did it happen?

Beginning with the creation of the universe, the setting moves through history to the settling of the nation of Israel in the small but fertile Nile Delta region of Egypt.

What is Genesis about?

- *God as Creator*. The first glimpse of God in the Bible displays His power as Creator of the heavens and the earth and of mankind—male and female.
- *God as Redeemer*. When sin enters the world, God's nature demands punishment of sin because of His personal holiness.

Why should women read Genesis?

The purpose of the book of Genesis is to reveal the history and basic principles of God's relationship with His people. Particularly important for women are the opening chapters in which creation order is presented as the basis for biblical womanhood. The account of God's creation of the woman upholds her worth and reveals the divine design of her assignment as her husband's "helper" (2:18). Genesis provides the historical basis for the rest of the Pentateuch and of the entire Bible. Throughout the book of Genesis, you can see God's plan for the redemption of His people as He enters into covenant with them. Israel, as God's chosen people from whom the Messiah, "the seed" of the woman, 3:14-15) would come, was the conduit for God's redemptive work. Throughout Genesis, God is the covenant-making and covenant-keeping God.

How do you read Genesis?

The book of Genesis should be read as the definitive source of truth upon which the other 65 books of the canon are based. God presents Himself as *the* Creator of all who fashioned man and woman in His own image and commissioned them to rule over His creation. Genesis bears witness to the goodness of the created order and reveals why the world we inhabit is full of brokenness rather than perfection. The book also directs the reader's

>WORD|*study*

1:1 The Hebrew word translated God (Hb *ʾelohim*) is the plural form of *ʾEl* (or strictly *ʾeloah*, which in the Bible is used only in poetry), the Hebrew and Canaanite word for a divine or supernatural being. It can also be used of the supernatural, such as angels or other-world beings (e.g., 1Sm 28:13) or of the "gods" of other nations (used with a plural verb). The plural found he with a singular verb, however, is intensive. In Hebrew this phenomenon is a plural of majesty, suggesting the greatness of God, who is complex and wonderful beyond description. Although th author probably did not think in terms of a triunity (as shown by the plural word's use with a singular verb), a believer, with the help of the New Testament, may see this conclusion as implied b the plural form.

1:1 Created (Hb *baraʾ*) is only used of divine workmanship, always indicating the production of something new. The word is used three times in this account—the initial creation o matter (1:1), the creation of animal life (1:21), and the creation of man "in the image of God" (1:27)—each seen as a unique beginning.

1:6 The word expanse (Hb *raqiyaʿ*, "firmament") indicated "something trodden on and stamped out." In its verbal form, the word suggests "making thin like a piece of metal beaten into shape" as in the work of a craftsman and thus "spreading out, expanding." The implication is that the "expanse" is the handiwork of a craftsman (i.e., specifically designed and crafted b God, thus with an inherent permanence and perfection as worthy of Him).

1:10 He **called the dry land** "earth" (Hb *ʾerets*), a word originally referring to the whole earth, including the waters (Gn 1:1-2). It can mean "the earth" as opposed to "the heaven (1:1; 2:1,4), "land" as opposed to sea (1:10), or a particular area of "land " (2:12-13).

2026 BC	*2006–1859 BC*	*1915–1805 BC*	*1876 BC*
Isaac's marriage to Rebekah	Life of Jacob	Life of Joseph	Settlement of Jacob's family in Egypt

attention toward the future where the fulfillment of God's promises and prophecies is sure. Genesis is also the first book in the Pentateuch, the five books containing the Torah or God's law—God's instruction to His people for establishing the nation of Israel.

Genesis is a carefully structured book. This historical narrative has an initial section on the creation itself. Thereafter the book is divided by a recurring phrase (Hb *toledot*, "these are the generations"), marking changes in God's people as His covenant promises are faithfully passed from one generation to the next. One might say that Genesis is "the story behind" the God who drew the Israelites to Himself as His covenant people. The book also includes poetry, such as the passage where Adam introduces Eve (2:23) and the description of Jacob's blessing (49:2-27).

Outline

- I. The Creation (1:1–2:25)
- II. The Fall (3:1-24)
- III. The Generations of Adam (4:1–6:7)
- IV. The Generations of Noah (6:7–11:32)
- V. The Generations of Abraham (12:1–25:18)
  - A. God's Covenant with Abraham (12:1–13:4)
  - B. God's Faithfulness in Renewing His Covenant (13:5–17:27)
  - C. Abraham's Obedience in Responding to the Covenant (18:1–25:18)
- VI. The Generations of Isaac (25:19–35:29)
  - A. The Birth of Two Sons (25:19-34)
  - B. God's Covenant with Isaac (26:1-35)
  - C. God's Choice of Jacob (27:1–35:29)
- VII. The Generations of Esau (36:1-43)
- VIII. The Generations of Jacob and the Saving of Israel (37:1–50:26)
  - A. The Sowing of Conflict (37:1-11)
  - B. The Slavery of Joseph (37:12-36)
  - C. The Faithfulness of God to Joseph During His Rise to Power (38:1–41:57)
  - D. The Reunion of Joseph and His Brothers (42:1–45:15)
  - E. The Journey of Jacob to Egypt (45:16–48:22)
  - F. The Blessing of Jacob's Descendants (49:1-28)
  - G. The Death of Jacob and then of Joseph (49:29–50:26)

The Creation (1:1–2:25)

The Heavens and the Earth (1:1-19)

1 In the beginning God created the heavens and the earth.[A] 2 Now the earth was[B] formless and empty, darkness covered the surface of the watery depths, and the Spirit of God was hovering over the surface of the waters. 3 Then God said, "Let there be light," and there was light. 4 God saw that the light was good, and God separated the light from the darkness. 5 God called the light "day," and He called the darkness "night." Evening came and then morning: the first day.

6 Then God said, "Let there be an expanse[C] between the waters, separating water from water." 7 So God made the expanse and separated the water under the expanse from the water above the expanse. And it was so. 8 God called the expanse "sky."[D] Evening came and then morning: the second day.

9 Then God said, "Let the water under the sky be gathered into one place, and let the dry land appear." And it was so. 10 God called the dry land "earth," and He called the gathering of the water "seas." And God saw that it was good. 11 Then God said, "Let the earth produce vegetation: seed-bearing plants and fruit trees on the earth bearing fruit with seed in it according to their kinds." And it was so. 12 The earth produced vegetation: seed-bearing plants according to their kinds and trees bearing fruit with seed in it according

[A]1:1 Or *created the universe* [B]1:1-2 Or *When God began to create the sky and the earth,* 2 *the earth was* [C]1:6 The Hb word for *expanse* is from a root meaning "to spread out, stamp, beat firmly," which suggests something like a dome; Jb 37:16-18; Is 40:22. [D]1:8 Or *"heavens"*

Title In the Hebrew Bible every book of the Pentateuch originally received its title from its first word or phrase. The Hebrew title is *Berēʾshit* ("in the beginning"). "Genesis" is a transliteration of the title in the Septuagint (the Greek translation of the OT), meaning "origins" (Gk *geneseōs*). "Account" or "generations" (Hb *toledot*) is the key word associated with the structure of Genesis (Gn 2:4; 5:1; 6:9; 10:1).

1:1 In the beginning signifies the beginning of existence, of the universe, as these relate to mankind. It does not refer to the creation of the angelic or spiritual world, which is outside the scope of the physical universe.

1:2 God created the earth **formless and empty** that He might give it form and fill it. He covered it with water that He might produce from it what would be altered by His hand. There is no thought that it had "become" this way or was naturally so, nor were forces of chaos with which God had to contend at work. His creative handiwork was as He had determined it to be.

1:11-12 Light and shape and differentiation—the building blocks of life—are being put in place. God provided the sustenance that animals and man would require. Notice the stress on the diversity of the **vegetation** He produced: **seed-bearing plants and fruit trees on the earth bearing fruit with seed in it**. By creating plants with seeds, God ensured that these plants would reproduce and provide sustenance for generations to come.

1:14-19 From the fourth day, periods of **light** and **darkness** were determined by the action of sun and moon. These **lights** now marked the length of **days and years**. Henceforth the heavenly **lights** would rule ideas of time and seasons. Days and months and years resulted from their activity. They were the signs of God's continued provision. Later the rainbow became God's sign of their permanence for man (Gn 8:22; 9:12-17). Significantly, "naming" occurred in the first three days, and in days five and six the results of God's creative activity were blessed as living and reproductive; but the "lights" were neither named nor blessed. God did not give them names indicating their background nature. Unlike plants and animals, the lights of heaven were not living and were not under man's dominion. All thought of their being divine or of any importance other than as created objects is deliberately excluded. This truth will be important as Israel encounters nations who worship these celestial bodies.

1:20-23 God created two categories of **living creatures** (Hb *nephesh chayyah*) on the fifth day. The word *nephesh*, meaning "throat" (i.e., the source for breath) evolves to mean "the life within" and thus "living things." The whole phrase, therefore, is more literally "living things that have life." **God** spoke into being **the large sea-creatures** (Hb *tannin*, "sea monsters, vast fish") and **every living creature** that **swarms** [Hb *sharats*, "teem, multiply, abound"; cp. 9:7; Ex 1:7; Ezk 47:9] **in the water** and **birds** to populate **the sky**. The writer was aware of huge creatures in the sea. To many they must have seemed terrifying, but he knew that they were creatures of God. Many ancient myths spoke of semi-divine sea monsters, which caused distress and chaos (and the psalmists used the ideas pictorially to demonstrate God's control over creation, e.g., Pss 74:13; 148:7), but their role here had nothing to do with chaos or conflict. They were made by God, and, therefore, they are under His control and will.

1:24-25 On the sixth day of creation again **God** planned a diversity of **creatures** according **to their kinds**.

Days of Creation Genesis 1:1–2:3

Day	
Day One (1:2-5)	Light (day and night)
Day Two (1:6-8)	Expanse (sky)
Day Three (1:9-13)	Dry land (earth), seas, and vegetation
Day Four (1:14-19)	Sun and moon
Day Five (1:20-23)	Living creatures (every kind of sea-creature and every kind of bird)
Day Six (1:24-31)	Living creatures on the land as well as the man and the woman
Day Seven (2:1-3)	God's rest

to their kinds. And God saw that it was good. 13 Evening came and then morning: the third day.

14 Then God said, "Let there be lights in the expanse of the sky to separate the day from the night. They will serve as signs for festivals[A] and for days and years. 15 They will be lights in the expanse of the sky to provide light on the earth." And it was so. 16 God made the two great lights—the greater light to have dominion over the day and the lesser light to have dominion over the night—as well as the stars. 17 God placed them in the expanse of the sky to provide light on the earth, 18 to dominate the day and the night, and to separate light from darkness. And God saw that it was good. 19 Evening came and then morning: the fourth day.

The Living Creatures (1:20-25)

20 Then God said, "Let the water swarm with[B] living creatures, and let birds fly above the earth across the expanse of the sky." 21 So God created the large sea-creatures[C] and every living creature that moves and swarms in the water, according to their kinds. He also created every winged bird according to its kind. And God saw that it was good. 22 So God blessed them, "Be fruitful, multiply, and fill the waters of the seas, and let the birds multiply on the earth." 23 Evening came and then morning: the fifth day.

24 Then God said, "Let the earth produce living creatures according to their kinds: livestock, creatures that crawl, and the wildlife of the earth according to their kinds." And it was so. 25 So God made the wildlife of the earth according to their kinds, the livestock according to their kinds, and creatures that crawl on the ground according to their kinds. And God saw that it was good.

Mankind—Male and Female (1:26-2:25)

26 Then God said, "Let Us make man in Our image, according to Our likeness. They will rule the fish of

HARD QUESTION

Racism, Abortion, Euthanasia—What does the Bible say?

The importance of the concept of men and women as bearers of God's **image** speaks to the dignity and worth of each human being (1:26-27). No one person can be considered more like the Creator than another. In addition, every life, whether in the beginning stages or at the end of days, shares the same value before God. This fact should encourage Christians with two important truths:

- You should seek to protect life at every stage. The assault on human life—whether abortion or euthanasia—is an assault on the concept of mankind as bearers of God's image because abortion and euthanasia employ a logic that life in the embryonic stage or in the final stage is not as valuable. This lie is from the pit of hell.
- You should never hold to racist beliefs. All humans—not just a certain race—are created in God's image. Each person equally bears the image of God.

A 1:14 Or *for the appointed times* B 1:20 Lit *with swarms of* C 1:21 Or *created sea monsters*

the sea, the birds of the sky, the livestock, all the earth,[A] and the creatures that crawl[B] on the earth."

27 So God created man
in His own image;
He created him in the image
of God;
He created them male
and female.

Doctrine THE IMAGE OF GOD

The fact that men and women are created in the **image** (Hb *tselem*) and **likeness** (Hb *demut*) of God affirms that human beings represent God in a way unlike any other part of His creation (1:26-27). In what ways are humans like God? Four key areas of commonality help answer this question and illustrate exactly how men and women can be set apart from every other part of creation: moral, spiritual, mental, and relational. They share a moral aspect with God because they have an innate sense of right and wrong and a sense of accountability; in the spiritual commonality between man and God, there is an immaterial part of man that will survive after death. Man's ability to use abstract reasoning and logic and to have both an awareness of and the capacity to plan for the future illustrates a mental acumen that sets him apart from the rest of creation. Finally, interpersonal relationships between men and women, such as family systems and marriage, display a relational aspect of God beyond what any other part of God's creation can display.

28 God blessed them, and God said to
them, "Be fruitful, multiply, fill the
earth, and subdue it. Rule the fish
of the sea, the birds of the sky, and
every creature that crawls[C] on the
earth." 29 God also said, "Look, I have
given you every seed-bearing plant
on the surface of the entire earth
and every tree whose fruit contains
seed. This food will be for you, 30 for
all the wildlife of the earth, for every
bird of the sky, and for every creature that crawls on the earth—everything having the breath of life
in it. I have given every green plant
for food." And it was so. 31 God saw
all that He had made, and it was
very good. Evening came and then
morning: the sixth day.

2 So the heavens and the earth and
everything in them[D] were completed. 2 By the seventh[E] day God
completed His work that He had
done, and He rested[F] on the seventh
day from all His work that He had
done. 3 God blessed the seventh day
and declared it holy, for on it He
rested from His work of creation.[G]

Doctrine CREATION OF MANKIND

Four different Hebrew verbs are used for God's creative activity in Genesis 1–2:

- **Created** (Hb *bara'*, "made from nothing," 1:1) is used only of divine activity. In the context of Gn 1:1, this word means "made from nothing" (cp. Lat *ex nihilo*, "out of nothing"). Regarding man, whom God made "from the dust of the ground," *bara'* means "created" in the sense of "fashioned, shaped, or produced," 1: 27; 5:1-2; 6:7).
- **Made** (Hb *'asah*; 1:7,16,25-26; 2:18) is a common word meaning to "produce, create, render" from pre-existing materials.
- **Formed** (Hb *yatsar*, "fashioned," 2:7-8, 19—only these three times in Gn; cp. Ps 95:5; 139:16; Is 29:16; 43:1,7,21; 44:21,24) is used of the potter or craftsman shaping his material according to his purpose (cp. 1Ch 4:23; Is 44:9-12; 45:9; 46:11; 64:8). The writer uses this word to depict God's creative work as skillful.
- Another verb translated **made** (Hb *banah*, "build with careful planning"; cp. 11:4-5) appears for the first time in Scripture in 2:22 to convey God's active "building" of the woman.

The description of man's creation is twofold. In one sense, **man** (Hb *'adam*) is of the earth, **formed . . . out of the dust from the ground** (Hb *'adamah*) as were the animals (2:7,19). The Hebrew play on words in the name "Adam" is a reminder of his earthly source. On the other hand, his life was inbreathed by the breath of God, bringing him in touch with heaven. The fact that God **breathed the breath of life into his** [Adam's] **nostrils** (v. 7), which He did not do with the animals, demonstrated that this new life was intended to be seen as something unique, a "something other," which makes him distinctive from the rest of creation. He is not just an animal; he possesses something that comes directly from God, confirming the uniqueness of being in the image of God (1:26).

4 These are the records of the
heavens and the earth, concerning their creation at the time[H] that
the LORD God made the earth and
the heavens. 5 No shrub of the field
had yet grown on the land,[I] and
no plant of the field had yet
sprouted, for the LORD God had not
made it rain on the land, and there
was no man to work the ground.
6 But water would come out of the
ground and water the entire surface

Diversity in creation is not blind chance but results from the purpose of God. Note that His plan included animals that would later be domesticated as well as the "wild" animals. Man's good is clearly in mind as God filled **the earth** with animal life—from **the livestock** to **creatures that crawl**, including the tiny scavengers that clean up the world. All have their place in God's creation.

2:1-3 The description of the final day is solely in the writer's words. *God Himself does not act or speak.* The writer describes **the seventh day** as the culmination of the work of creation, as the day on which **God completed His work . . . and He rested**. Previously when God is said to have bestowed blessing, His words followed to explain the blessing, but there are no words of explanation here. The writer affirms the day as **blessed** and set apart by God because the day marked the completion of **His work**.

2:4 This verse is not the start of a record of another **creation**; rather, the creation account is reiterated and expanded as the emphasis moves from the overall summary of God's creative activity to a focus on the creation of the man and the woman. These verses are concerned with God's specific provision for His creation. Man is central to the account. God's provision for him included fruitful trees in a chosen place, abundant water, animals to provide a kind of companionship, and, finally, the one who was to be this man's suitable companion.

2:4-8 The creation account is reiterated and expanded as the emphasis moves from the overall summary of God's creative activity to a focus on the creation of the man and the woman. The phrase **the LORD God** (Hb *Yahweh 'Elohim*) is rare outside chapters 2 and 3 and is only found elsewhere in the Pentateuch for Yahweh as Creator (Ex 9:30), emphasizing that the *Elohim* of creation (referring to the transcendent power of the Creator) is Yahweh ("the one who is," or "the one who causes to be, " see Ex 3:14). *Yahweh*, God's covenant name, is a reminder of His personal relationship with those who rightly related themselves to Him.

[A]**1:26** Syr reads *sky, and over every animal of the land* [B]**1:26** Lit *scurry* [C]**1:28** Lit *and all scurrying animals that scurry* [D]**2:1** Lit *and all their host* [E]**2:2** Sam, LXX, Syr read *sixth* [F]**2:2** Or *ceased* [G]**2:3** Lit *work that God created to make* [H]**2:4** Lit *creation on the day* [I]**2:5** Or *earth*

2:9 God is concerned not only for man's palate but also with his aesthetic enjoyment. The **tree of life** and **the tree of the knowledge of good and evil** were actual trees in **the garden.** Only the latter tree was forbidden, giving man the responsibility of choosing to obey.

2:15 God gave the man work to do before the fall. "Work" carries the idea of service and provision; **watch** is indicative of guarding and protecting. The man was there to worship and obey God and to protect God's handiwork.

2:16-17 Entrusting this information to Adam vested him with leadership. **Knowledge** (Hb *da'at*, "discernment, wisdom"), from the verb "know" (Hb *yada'*), is not used here in the sense of intellectual understanding but of

of the land. 7 Then the LORD God
formed the man out of the dust
from the ground and breathed the
breath of life into his nostrils, and
the man became a living being.
8 The LORD God planted a garden
in Eden, in the east, and there He
placed the man He had formed. 9 The
LORD God caused to grow out of the
ground every tree pleasing in appearance and good for food, including the tree of life in the middle of
the garden, as well as the tree of the
knowledge of good and evil.
10 A river went[A] out from Eden to
water the garden. From there it divided and became the source of four
rivers.[B] 11 The name of the first is
Pishon, which flows through the entire land of Havilah,[C] where there is
gold. 12 Gold from that land is pure;[D]
bdellium[E] and onyx[F] are also there.
13 The name of the second river is
Gihon, which flows through the entire land of •Cush. 14 The name of the
third river is the Tigris, which runs
east of Assyria. And the fourth river
is the Euphrates.
15 The LORD God took the man and
placed him in the garden of Eden
to work it and watch over it. 16 And
the LORD God commanded the man,

[A]2:10 Or *goes* [B]2:10 Lit *became four heads* [C]2:11 Or *of the Havilah* [D]2:12 Lit *good*
[E]2:12 A yellowish, transparent gum resin [F]2:12 Identity of this precious stone uncertain

Biblical Womanhood The Judgment on the Woman

There are three popular views on how the judgment on the woman would affect her relationship to the man:

- The popular view among evangelical feminists is that the submission of a woman to a man comes as a direct consequence of the fall and thus is a punishment for sin and completely undesirable and even evil.
- Another view among evangelicals suggests that the husband's role of leadership and the wife's submission to her husband, which is part of the original plan in creation, are not a curse but a blessing intended to console the woman in her role as a mother.
- The third view, which is slightly nuanced from the second view and is most strongly supported in the Christian tradition and also heavily supported among scholars, suggests that the judgment brought upon the woman is a form of submission tainted by domination. Sin corrupted the headship of a husband over his wife and turned what God designed as a blessing into a burden. The woman then seeks to contend with her husband for the leadership in their relationship.

However, others hold that the "desire" of Gn 3:16 is not the desire of the woman to control and dominate her husband, which would have been a curse on the man; rather this comment is an explanation of the relationships as they will exist after the fall. The woman's desire to dominate or rule over the man is just the essence, character, and result of all sin against God. The woman would still possess the strong desire to be with the man. The contention that sin has corrupted both the willing submission of the wife and the loving headship of the husband is true, but it is a natural consequence of sin, not a result of God's judgment.

The judgments may be summarized:

- The serpent would "move" on his "belly" (v. 14).
- Satan would receive a death blow by the "seed" of the woman (v. 15).
- The man would have difficulty in getting "the ground" to yield fruit, i.e., his work (vv. 17-19).
- The woman would experience pain in childbearing, and God's plan for servant headship of the husband and gracious submission of the wife would be marred by the selfishness of both.

In other words, when the woman and the man chose to disobey God and thus forfeit living in the perfect place God had prepared for them, they did not thwart or destroy God's creation order and the perfect plan as set forth in Gn 2. Rather, their sin of disobedience would make the future more difficult. Work for the man was always part of God's plan (1:26-30; 2:15; Ex 20:9), but in a sinful world it would be done with difficulty (3:17-19). The continuing of generations through bearing children was also God's plan for the woman (1:28; 2:24; 3:20); but because of sin, conceiving and bearing a child would be accompanied by pain (3:16). The nature of the curse has no essential relationship to the nature of the sin committed, which at its root is disobedience, but rather the disobedience and its consequences distort and make more difficult God's plan.

God did not curse the man or the woman as He cursed the snake and the ground, but He did declare that they would experience painful consequences. From that point forward, as a constant reminder of what he had done, the man would have to toil in pain for his food, contending with "thorns and thistles." Then, the ground, which had been "cursed," would receive him. He would "return to" the dust. Thus the curse fully embraces him in the end. But the cursing of "the ground," and not the man, was God's indication that in mercy He delays punishment. The man will die, but not yet.

>WORD|*study*

2:18 Helper as his complement (Hb *'ēzer kenegdo*, lit. "helper corresponding to what is in front of him") conveys the sense of a helper "suitable" or "comparable" to man. This word *'ēzer* is never used to describe the man in his relationship to the woman. However, the same word is used to describe God's relationship to mankind (Ex 18:4; Dt 33:7; Ps 54:4). The word implies neither superiority nor inferiority; it is not about worth. Rather, it is descriptive of function. You do not lose worth in becoming a helper to someone. In fact, the function suggests the development of an endearing and productive relationship.

3:1 Serpent (Hb *nachash*) always refers to ordinary snakes or serpents in the Old Testament, with the exception of Is 27:1 and possibly Am 9:3. Nevertheless, these exceptions show that the Israelites were familiar with contemporary myths relating to "snakes" and "serpents," which were often looked upon as semi-divine creatures involved in evil. *Nachash* is also the root word for "enchantment" because enchanting was often synonymous with charming a snake. The fact that the writer also called the serpent "the most cunning" (Hb *'arum*, "crafty, shrewd, sensible"; cp. Jb 5:12; 15:5; Pr 12:23; 22:3) creature demonstrates that this animal is unusual. The text seems to communicate from the beginning that the snake is endowed with some sinister power, but nothing takes away from the man and woman the responsibility for their response to temptation.

"You are free to eat from any tree
of the garden, 17 but you must not
eat[A] from the tree of the knowledge
of good and evil, for on the day you
eat from it, you will certainly die."
18 Then the LORD God said, "It is not
good for the man to be alone. I will
make a helper as his complement."
19 So the LORD God formed out of the
ground every wild animal and every
bird of the sky, and brought each to
the man to see what he would call
it. And whatever the man called a
living creature, that was its name.
20 The man gave names to all the
livestock, to the birds of the sky,
and to every wild animal; but for
the man[B] no helper was found as
his complement. 21 So the LORD God
caused a deep sleep to come over the
man, and he slept. God took one of
his ribs and closed the flesh at that
place. 22 Then the LORD God made
the rib He had taken from the man
into a woman and brought her to
the man. 23 And the man said:

> This one, at last, is bone
> of my bone
> and flesh of my flesh;
> this one will be
> called "woman,"
> for she was taken from man.

24 This is why a man leaves his
father and mother and bonds with
his wife, and they become one flesh.
25 Both the man and his wife were
naked, yet felt no shame.

The Fall (3:1-24)

The Approach of Satan (3:1-7)

3 Now the serpent was the most
cunning of all the wild animals
that the LORD God had made. He said
to the woman, "Did God really say,
'You can't eat from any tree in the
garden'?"
2 The woman said to the serpent,
"We may eat the fruit from the trees
in the garden. 3 But about the fruit
of the tree in the middle of the garden, God said, 'You must not eat it
or touch it, or you will die.' "
4 "No! You will not die," the serpent said to the woman. 5 "In fact,
God knows that when[C] you eat it
your eyes will be opened and you
will be like God,[D] knowing good
and evil." 6 Then the woman saw
that the tree was good for food and
delightful to look at, and that it was
desirable for obtaining wisdom. So

HARD QUESTION

Fight or Flight— What to Do with Temptation?

Eve contemplated the tree and the fruit carefully, and no doubt she wrestled with her conscience as does every woman (3:6). The New Testament addresses this common struggle (see 1Jn 2:16). Eve saw that the fruit was **good for food** (the lust of the flesh), **delightful to look at** (the lust of the eyes), and **desirable for obtaining wisdom** (the pride of life). Herein lies the root of sin. The fruit looked wonderful and desirable.

learning gained by experience. To eat from this forbidden tree would be an act of rebellion. The text does not suggest anything inherently wrong with the tree's fruit.

2:19-20 In the Oriental culture, naming indicates authority over what is named. Up to this point, God had named everything; but Adam was given the task of naming the animals over which he would have dominion.

2:22-23 God made [Hb *banah*, "built"] **the rib** [Hb *tsēlaʿ*, "side"; see Ex 25:12; 1Kg 6:5] **. . . taken from the man into a woman**. The woman is formed from the man, indicating clearly that she is like him—the same **flesh** and blood (Gn 2:23), with equal worth, and also "in the image of God" (1:27). **The man** (Hb *'ish*) named the **woman** (Hb *'ishshah*, a name similar to his own) thus establishing his unique relationship to her. The naming is an act cementing a close relationship as well as revealing the man's status as being in authority over the woman. While she is subject to him, she is also his close companion. Here at last is one who, as his helper, would stand on a par with the man.

2:24-25 The marriage covenant is formalized between one man and one woman in the presence of God and witnesses:

- leaving father and mother, keeping natural and necessary family ties and responsibilities but essentially forming a new loyalty;
- bonding with each other in growing tender affection and faithful commitment;
- becoming one flesh, the physical union and most exclusive intimacy.

Husband and wife become one, bound in an absolutely monogamous, exclusive, and permanent relationship closer than any other and culminating with the physical union of their two bodies.

3:1-3 The serpent approached Eve and questioned God's instructions regarding the trees **in the . . . garden**. Disobedience began with questioning God. Instead of responding with God's words alone, Eve added her own caveat—that she and Adam could **not** even **touch** the tree of the knowledge of good and evil or they would **die**, making the prohibition appear unreasonable and even ridiculous. You must be careful not to prohibit what God's Word does not prohibit (as Eve's "you must not eat it *or touch it*," italics added) while preserving whatever God says without question ("Did God really say?").

A2:17 Lit *eat from it* B2:20 Or *for Adam* C3:5 Lit *on the day* D3:5 Or *gods*, or *divine beings*

3:9-12 God spoke directly to **the man**; He made the first move. In the same way, God initiated contact with sinful humanity through Jesus Christ. Unlike other religions in which man seeks God, Christianity is the story of God's reaching out to sinful humanity. God knew where Adam was, but He gave him a chance to express his sorrow and repentance. However, Adam sought to place the blame anywhere but on himself and pointed to **the woman** whom God had given to him.

3:13 Eve followed Adam's pattern and tried to pass the blame to **the serpent** for her sin. The results of Adam and Eve's sin have affected every living being from that moment onward.

3:14-15 As God's curse on **the serpent** was being pronounced, the reference clearly points to the coming of One who will defeat the Serpent. Verse 15 is identified by evangelicals as the *protevangelium* (Lat, lit "the first preaching of gospel" in the sense of "good news" pointing to Christ's coming). In generations to come, the gospel is made complete with the **seed** of Adam, the Messiah who will achieve the final victory. The Serpent will be defeated by Christ, the anointed

she took some of its fruit and ate
it; she also gave some to her husband, who was with her, and he ate
it. 7 Then the eyes of both of them
were opened, and they knew they
were naked; so they sewed fig leaves
together and made loincloths for
themselves.

The Pronouncement of Judgment by God (3:8-24)

8 Then the man and his wife heard
the sound of the LORD God walking in the garden at the time of the
evening breeze,[A] and they hid themselves from the LORD God among the
trees of the garden. 9 So the LORD
God called out to the man and said
to him, "Where are you?"
10 And he said, "I heard You[B] in the
garden and I was afraid because I
was naked, so I hid."
11 Then He asked, "Who told you
that you were naked? Did you eat
from the tree that I commanded you
not to eat from?"
12 Then the man replied, "The
woman You gave to be with me—she
gave me some fruit from the tree,
and I ate."
13 So the LORD God asked the woman, "What is this you have done?"
And the woman said, "It was the
serpent. He deceived me, and I ate."
14 Then the LORD God said to the
serpent:

Because you have done this,
you are cursed more than
any livestock
and more than
any wild animal.
You will move on your belly
and eat dust all the days
of your life.
15 I will put hostility
between you
and the woman,

[A]3:8 Lit *at the wind of the day* [B]3:10 Lit *the sound of You*

BIBLICAL WOMANHOOD Did God Establish Different Roles or Functions for Men and Women Before the Fall?

Complementarians (who believe men and women are created equal in essence before God but have distinct roles or functions) and egalitarians (who believe that men and women are equal in essence and may have the same functions or roles) differ greatly on their interpretation of the significance of the creation account (Gn 1–2) in regard to gender roles. However, just as each member of the Trinity is equal in essence—each member is fully God—yet each has a distinct function—God the Father, God the Son, and God the Holy Spirit. So, too, men and women, though equal in the image of God, have distinct roles assigned by God. These distinctions are revealed in many ways, and some even before the fall. The timing of these distinctions as being present before the fall or as the result of the fall becomes a watershed issue in the gender debate.

- Adam was created first, then Eve (Gn 2:7; 1Tm 2:13; 1Co 11).
- Eve was created as a helper for Adam (Gn 2:18,20).
- Adam named Eve (2:23; 3:20).
- Adam's name was used generically in reference to the human race (1:26).
- Adam was given his authority by God prior to Eve's creation (2:15).
- God spoke to Adam first after the fall (3:9).
- Adam, not Eve, represents the human race (1Co 15; Rm 5).
- The curse brought a distortion of previous roles, not the introduction of new roles (Gn 3:15-19).
- The creation order was embraced and affirmed in Christ's redemption (1Pt 3; Eph 5).

The fact that men and women have distinct functions does not mean that men are superior and women are inferior. The word "helper" used to define the woman's function is also used to describe what God does for His people. Men and women both are created in God's image (Gn 1:26-27) and share the responsibility of being God's representatives on earth. The influence of feminism on Christian thought has been tragic in leading women to think that in order to be "equal" with men they must have the same functions. What they do not understand is that different functions originate within the Godhead itself: Just as wives are under the authority of their husbands, so Jesus was under the authority of the Father (Jn 5:19; 6:38). God established distinct functions for men and women; the unique genders and respective roles reflect important truths about God. Jesus did not regard equality with God something to be grasped (Php 2:6), and neither should women desire to seek what they suppose to be "equality" at the cost of refusing God-ordained roles.

CHARACTER PROFILE

Eve Mother of All Living

Her Background	• The first woman created by God in His image (2:22) • The wife of Adam (2:23) • The mother of Cain and Abel (4:1-2)
Her Story	• She lived with her husband in the garden of Eden (2:8). • She was deceived by Satan's lie and disobeyed God (3:4-6; 1Tm 2:14). • She, with her husband, was evicted from the garden (3:23-24). • She expressed hope for the future with the birth of her son Cain (4:1).
Life Lessons	• Eve sinned against God and had to suffer painful consequences (3:16). • She took responsibility for her sin immediately (3:13). • She experienced the grace of God (3:21).

and between your •seed
and her seed.
He will strike your head,
and you will strike his heel.

16 He said to the woman:

I will intensify
your labor pains;
you will bear children
in anguish.
Your desire will be
for your husband,
yet he will rule over you.

17 And He said to Adam, "Because
you listened to your wife's voice and
ate from the tree about which I commanded you, 'Do not eat from it':

The ground is cursed
because of you.
You will eat from it
by means of painful labor[A]
all the days of your life.
18 It will produce thorns
and thistles for you,
and you will eat the plants
of the field.
19 You will eat bread[B]
by the sweat of your brow
until you return
to the ground,
since you were taken from it.
For you are dust,
and you will return to dust."

20 Adam named his wife Eve[C] because she was the mother of all the
living. 21 The LORD God made clothing out of skins for Adam and his
wife, and He clothed them.
22 The LORD God said, "Since man
has become like one of Us, knowing
good and evil, he must not reach
out, take from the tree of life, eat,
and live forever." 23 So the LORD God
sent him away from the garden
of Eden to work the ground from
which he was taken. 24 He drove man
out and stationed the •cherubim and
the flaming, whirling sword east of
the garden of Eden to guard the way
to the tree of life.

The Generations of Adam (4:1–6:7)

The Family of Adam (4:1-26)

4 Adam was intimate with his wife
Eve, and she conceived and gave
birth to Cain. She said, "I have had
a male child with the LORD's help."[D]
2 Then she also gave birth to his
brother Abel. Now Abel became a
shepherd of flocks, but Cain worked
the ground. 3 In the course of time
Cain presented some of the land's
produce as an offering to the LORD.
4 And Abel also presented an offering—some of the firstborn of his
flock and their fat portions. The LORD
had regard for Abel and his offering,

[A]3:17 Lit *it through pain* [B]3:19 Or *food* [C]3:20 Lit *Living*, or *Life* [D]4:1 Lit *the LORD*

One. "Seed" in the Old Testament can refer to a child or offspring or to one's descendants as a whole. Eve is **the mother of all the living** (v. 20), and the Messiah would come through her (see Gl 4:4). The conception of Jesus was miraculous: The seed came to Mary through the overshadowing of the Holy Spirit rather than through a man's sperm delivered to her womb; see Lk 1:35). The striking of **his heel** (Gn 3:15) refers to the sufferings of Christ, which proved merely a prelude to His ultimate victory and resurrection. The striking of the serpent's **head**, however, was clearly a mortal wound and thus prophetic of Satan's ultimate defeat.

3:16 The effect of the fall on the woman is that the privilege and blessing of producing **children** is accompanied by intense pain. However, in the mercy of God, despite what she has done, she has the blessing of producing children. That the bearing of a child is achieved *through much pain* is the punishment of God. The woman will **desire** (Hb *teshuqah*, "longing," seen only two other times in the Old Testament, [in Gn 4:7 where sin "longs" to master Cain and in Sg 7:10]) her **husband**, but the man's role of servant leadership over the woman can be distorted and manifest itself as autocratic and tyrannical. (See **Biblical Womanhood**, p. 6.)

3:21 Adam and Eve could no longer walk naked before God, for by their disobedience they had made themselves vulnerable, inadequate, and ashamed. Their clothing would always be a reminder of their loss of a wonderful relationship with God, while also a token of God's tender mercy in providing the covering they needed. The clothes were **of skins**, the Bible's first hint of death, which had been totally absent up to this point. Already a substitute was required. An animal died that man might be able to face God. Here appeared the beginnings of an understanding of substitution and sacrifice, which would lead to the final sacrifice.

4:1-14 The account of Cain and Abel specifically speaks of the first instance of the shedding of man's blood. The existence of daughters of Adam (4:17) and of other relatives is assumed, for Cain says **whoever finds me will kill me** (v. 14). So Cain and Abel should be seen as two among other children, mentioned because of the incident that occurred. They were not the only ones on the earth at the time.

4:3-7 Cain brought **some of the land's produce as an offering** to God. The cereal offering was an acknowledgment of God's blessing and an expression of human gratitude (Lv 6:20-23), although not expiation.

There is no reason to assume that the offering itself was unacceptable. It was the fruit of Cain's labor. Cain's offering is described very blandly in comparison with Abel's. The first fruits are not mentioned but described as presented **in the course of time**. Thus there may be a hint that Cain's "offering" was somewhat half-hearted, which seems more apparent when it is suggested that Cain had not done **right** and **sin** (Hb *chattaʾat*, appearing here for the first time in the OT) was **crouching at the door**. The metaphor personifies sin as a wild animal, lurking at "the door" of Cain's life with the intent of attacking and even enslaving him. Certainly Cain's offering appears to be carelessly prepared and late. But that the rejection of Cain's offering was related to his overall attitude of mind and heart seems certain. Cain had to be acceptable according to God's standards, not his own convenience.

4:8 Instead of acknowledging his own sinfulness and seeking atonement, Cain shed innocent blood as an expression of continued rebellion. If you allow a grievance to fester in your heart, the end may be tragic for you as well as others.

4:12 Cain was no longer able to **work the land**, the purpose for which he was created. He was driven into the desert. Note that Cain was cursed directly in contrast with the curse on the **ground** in chapter 3. He was banished to a place where the ground was totally unfruitful and driven there as a consequence of his sin. There was nowhere for him to go, for his blood would be sought by the whole family of men. The only safe place was the desert where nothing would grow and a man had to be constantly on the move in order to find food and water.

4:13 When **Cain** stated, **"My punishment is too great to bear!"**, he was only thinking of sin's consequences for himself. There was no repentance, only regret over what he had lost. How could he cope with a life of loneliness and wandering, always afraid of every kinsman?

4:15 God responded to **Cain** with His unceasing mercies. The words God spoke are in the form of a pronouncement. Cain is mentioned in the third person and not as "you." This is God's commitment to protect Cain. The promise made to Cain extends to all who will see God's **mark** and respond accordingly, not because of Cain but in light of a public statement of Yahweh's mercy. Notice the reference to **seven**, uniquely the number of divine perfection and completeness. Sevenfold **vengeance** was the totality of divine retribution. In the end, only God determined the sentence on Cain.

Understanding Sin

Definition: Any failure to conform to God's standards in act, attitude, or nature

Biblical Terms	Definition	References
Chataʾ (Hb)	To miss the mark, wrongdoing as failure, coming short (a common word for sin in the OT; identifies sinful acts and implies blameworthiness)	Gn 39:9; Neh 13:26; Ps 41:4
Pashaʿ (Hb)	Break off, rebel (often used to indicate a rebellion against rightful authority)	1Kg 12:19; Is 1:2; Hs 7:13
Maʿal (Hb)	Act overtly or treacherously, plot against (faithlessness or breach of trust)	Dt 32:51; Neh 1:8; Ezk 20:27
Hamartia (Gk)	Missing the mark or aim; shortcoming; failure to grasp (common word for sin in the NT)	Rm 5:12-21; 1Co 15:3; Jms 1:15
Asebeia (Gk)	Active irreligion; godlessness; deliberately withholding from God worship and service He is due	Rm 1:18; Ti 2:12; Jd 15
Anomos (Gk)	Lawlessness	1Co 9:21; 1Tm 1:9
Adikia (Gk)	Unrighteousness	Lk 13:27; Ac 1:18; Heb 8:12
Kakos (Gk)	Bad; worthless; inferior	Mt 21:41; Rm 1:30; Col 3:5
Ponēros (Gk)	Evil; corruption; wicked	Mt 5:37; Rm 12:9; Gl 1:4

Sin does not come from God (Dt 32:4; Jb 34:10; Jms 1:13); every human being has a choice concerning sin. You can either resist temptations or give in to them, but the choice is yours.

5 but He did not have regard for Cain and his offering. Cain was furious, and he looked despondent.[A]

6 Then the LORD said to Cain, "Why are you furious? And why do you look despondent?[B] 7 If you do what is right, won't you be accepted? But if you do not do what is right, sin is crouching at the door. Its desire is for you, but you must rule over it."

8 Cain said to his brother Abel, "Let's go out to the field."[C] And while they were in the field, Cain attacked his brother Abel and killed him.

9 Then the LORD said to Cain, "Where is your brother Abel?"

"I don't know," he replied. "Am I my brother's guardian?"

10 Then He said, "What have you done? Your brother's blood cries out to Me from the ground! 11 So now you are cursed, alienated, from the ground that opened its mouth to receive your brother's blood you have shed.[D] 12 If you work the ground, it will never again give you its yield. You will be a restless wanderer on the earth."

13 But Cain answered the LORD, "My punishment[E] is too great to bear! 14 Since You are banishing me today from the soil, and I must hide myself from Your presence and become a restless wanderer on the earth, whoever finds me will kill me."

15 Then the LORD replied to him, "In that case,[F] whoever kills Cain will suffer vengeance seven times over."[G] And He placed a mark on Cain so that whoever found him would not

[A] **4:5** Lit *and his face fell* [B] **4:6** Lit *why has your face fallen* [C] **4:8** Sam, LXX, Syr, Vg; MT omits *Let's go out to the field* [D] **4:11** Lit *blood from your hand* [E] **4:13** Or *sin* [F] **4:15** LXX, Syr, Vg read *Not so!* [G] **4:15** Or *suffer severely*

Numbers in Scripture

Number	Significance
1	• Indivisible unity (Gn 2:24; Eph 4:4-6) • Exclusivity (Ex 20:3; Dt 6:4; Mt 4:10; Jn 3:16-18) • Primacy ("first," Ex 4:22)
2	• Difference, division, separation (Gn 1:6,16; 25:23) • Partnership; additional help or strength (Ex 28:11-14; Ec 4:9-12; Jn 8:17-18)
3	Indivisible, immutable unity, as of God's triunity (Ec 4:12; Is 6:3; Mt 12:40; 28:19; Lk 24:46; Rv 4:8)
4	Creation—the earth and its four directions or "corners" (Rv 7:1)
6	Man, the extent of his labor (Ex 20:9,11; 21:2; 23:10; Rv 13:18)
7	Wholeness, completion, perfection, full development, rest; purity, holiness (Gn 2:2-3; Ex 13:6; 20:10-11; 50 times in Rv, e.g., 1:4)
10	Completeness; perfect order (Ex 20:1-17; 34:28; Rv 2:10)
12	Perfection of divinely appointed government (Gn 35:22; Mt 10:1; Rv 21:12)
40	Period of testing or judgment (Gn 7:4,12; Ex 34:28; Mt 4:2)

kill him. 16 Then Cain went out from
the LORD's presence and lived in the
land of Nod, east of Eden.
17 Cain was intimate with his wife,
and she conceived and gave birth
to Enoch. Then Cain became the
builder of a city, and he named the
city Enoch after his son. 18 Irad was
born to Enoch, Irad fathered Mehujael, Mehujael fathered Methushael,
and Methushael fathered Lamech.
19 Lamech took two wives for himself, one named Adah and the other
named Zillah. 20 Adah bore Jabal; he
was the father of the nomadic herdsmen.[A] 21 His brother was named Ju-
bal; he was the father of all who play
the lyre and the flute. 22 Zillah bore
Tubal-cain, who made all kinds of
bronze and iron tools. Tubal-cain's
sister was Naamah.
23 Lamech said to his wives:

Adah and Zillah,
hear my voice;
wives of Lamech,
pay attention to my words.
For I killed a man
for wounding me,
a young man for striking me.
24 If Cain is to be avenged
seven times over,
then for Lamech it will be
seventy-seven times!

25 Adam was intimate with his wife
again, and she gave birth to a son
and named him Seth, for she said,
"God has given[B] me another child in
place of Abel, since Cain killed him."
26 A son was born to Seth also, and
he named him Enosh. At that time
people began to call on the name of
•Yahweh.

The Godly Seed of Seth (5:1-32)

5 These are the family[C] records of
the descendants of Adam. On the
day that God created man,[D] He made
him in the likeness of God; 2 He created them male and female. When
they were created, He blessed them
and called them man.[D]
3 Adam was 130 years old when
he fathered a son in his likeness,
according to his image, and named
him Seth. 4 Adam lived 800 years
after the birth of Seth, and he fathered other sons and daughters.

Many scholars have debated the nature of Cain's "mark," which must have been something quite distinctive, yet something recognized and calling for deference; but Scripture is silent on this point. All would acknowledge the mark of God. On the one hand, that mark showed everyone that vengeance belonged to God alone; and on the other hand, the mark proved God's faithfulness and mercy to sinful man.

4:17 Cain established **a city**, which can refer either to an encampment of tents or to a regular city (Nm 13:19).

4:18-24 The lines of **Cain** (4:18-24) and **Seth** (4:25–5:32) are contrasted. Lamech's deviation from God's plan for marriage is another sign of man's continuing fall. Not much is known about the woman Naamah (Hb, "pleasant, loveliness," v. 22), but she must have been outstanding or notoriously beautiful to be included in the genealogy. Jewish tradition identifies her as the wife of Noah.

5:1-32 This section begins with a list of 10 patriarchs representing the whole line from **Adam** (v. 1) to **Noah** (v. 32) and is followed by a passage where God makes a covenant with man after a particularly devastating example of man's downward slide. In Genesis, this covenant is the central point around which the passage is built, ending this section with the colophon "these are the family records of Noah" (6:9). After the flood, another 10 patriarchs are listed from Noah to Abraham. Other ancient Near Eastern lists name 10 kings before the flood, and in some cases the seventh in line is seen as especially prominent, providing an easily recognized ancient pattern. The deliberate omission of names from genealogies is common throughout the Bible, with **fathered** (Hb *yalad*, "beget"; 5:3) simply portraying descent. For example, Matthew deliberately does this with the genealogy of Jesus to make a series of 14 (twice seven) generations. The number 10 suggests a complete series (thus Jacob could say your father has "changed my wages 10 times," 31:7, meaning many times). Numbers are prominent in ancient Near Eastern literature.

There is a pattern for the whole genealogy with the partial exception of Enoch. Repeated again and again is the formula **fathered . . . lived . . . after the birth of . . . fathered other sons and daughters . . . life lasted . . . died** (e.g., 5:6-8). So each was fruitful, each lived a long "life" and died. **Seth** is portrayed clearly as in the **image** and **likeness** of **Adam** (v. 3). Adam's death at **930 years**, which is 70 short of 1,000, could be seen as significant (vv. 4-5). Certainly in later times 1,000 years represented a full and perfect period, the ideal. But Adam does not

[A]4:20 Lit *the dweller of tent and livestock* [B]4:25 The Hb word for given sounds like the name "Seth." [C]5:1 Lit *written family* [D]5:1,2 Or *Adam*

5 So Adam's life lasted 930 years; then he died.

6 Seth was 105 years old when he fathered Enosh. 7 Seth lived 807 years after the birth of Enosh, and he fathered other sons and daughters. 8 So Seth's life lasted 912 years; then he died.

9 Enosh was 90 years old when he fathered Kenan. 10 Enosh lived 815 years after the birth of Kenan, and he fathered other sons and daughters. 11 So Enosh's life lasted 905 years; then he died.

12 Kenan was 70 years old when he fathered Mahalalel. 13 Kenan lived 840 years after the birth of Mahalalel, and he fathered other sons and daughters. 14 So Kenan's life lasted 910 years; then he died.

15 Mahalalel was 65 years old when he fathered Jared. 16 Mahalalel lived 830 years after the birth of Jared, and he fathered other sons and daughters. 17 So Mahalalel's life lasted 895 years; then he died.

18 Jared was 162 years old when he fathered Enoch. 19 Jared lived 800 years after the birth of Enoch, and he fathered other sons and daughters. 20 So Jared's life lasted 962 years; then he died.

21 Enoch was 65 years old when he fathered Methuselah. 22 And after the birth of Methuselah, Enoch walked with God 300 years and fathered other sons and daughters. 23 So Enoch's life lasted 365 years. 24 Enoch walked with God; then he was not there because God took him.

25 Methuselah was 187 years old when he fathered Lamech. 26 Methuselah lived 782 years after the birth of Lamech, and he fathered other sons and daughters. 27 So Methuselah's life lasted 969 years; then he died.

28 Lamech was 182 years old when he fathered a son. 29 And he named him Noah,[A] saying, "This one will bring us relief from the agonizing labor of our hands, caused by the ground the LORD has cursed." 30 Lamech lived 595 years after Noah's birth, and he fathered other sons and daughters. 31 So Lamech's life lasted 777 years; then he died.

32 Noah was 500 years old, and he fathered Shem, Ham, and Japheth.

The Rise of Wickedness (6:1-7)

6 When mankind began to multiply on the earth and daughters were born to them, 2 the sons of God saw that the daughters of mankind were beautiful, and they took any they chose as wives[B] for themselves. 3 And the LORD said, "My Spirit will not remain[C] with[D] mankind forever, because they are corrupt.[E] Their days will be 120 years." 4 The Nephilim[F] were on the earth both in those days and afterward, when the sons of God came to the daughters of mankind, who bore children to them. They were the powerful men of old, the famous men.

5 When the LORD saw that man's wickedness was widespread on the earth and that every scheme his mind thought of was nothing but evil all the time, 6 the LORD regretted that He had made man on the earth, and He was grieved in His heart. 7 Then the LORD said, "I will wipe off from the face of the earth mankind, whom I created, together with the animals, creatures that crawl, and birds of the sky—for I regret that I made them."

The Generations of Noah (6:8–11:32)

The Pronouncement of God's Judgment on the World (6:8–7:6)

8 Noah, however, found favor in the sight of the LORD.

9 These are the family records of Noah. Noah was a righteous man, blameless among his contemporaries; Noah walked with God. 10 And Noah fathered three sons: Shem, Ham, and Japheth.

11 Now the earth was corrupt in God's sight, and the earth was filled with wickedness.[G] 12 God saw how corrupt the earth was, for every creature had corrupted its way on the earth. 13 Then God said to Noah, "I have decided to put an end to every creature, for the earth is filled

[A]5:29 In Hb, the name Noah sounds like the phrase "bring us relief." [B]6:2 Or *women* [C]6:3 Or *strive* [D]6:3 Or *in* [E]6:3 Lit *flesh* [F]6:4 Possibly means "fallen ones"; traditionally, "giants"; Nm 13:31-33 [G]6:11 Or *injustice*

reach the ideal, for he had sinned. Thus a God-appointed time made him short by 70 years (the ideal time intensified by seven). The message is that God controls all things, even this. God made clear that the consequences of sin are far reaching, even beyond death.

5:24 Like Noah (6:9), Enoch is said to have **walked with God**. Every individual has two choices: the way of Enoch or the way of Lamech. They are mutually exclusive—no middle road (Ps 1; Mt 7:13-14).

5:27 **Methuselah** is the oldest person mentioned in the Bible, living **969 years**.

6:1-4 In the Old Testament the term **the sons of God** (Hb *benē ha-ʾelohim*) refers to heavenly beings (Jb 1:6 and context; 38:7; Ps 29:1; 89:7; Dn 3:25; Dt 32:8 in the LXX; see also Jdg 6–7; 1Pt 3:19-20; and 2Pt 2:4-6). See *Women's Evangelical Commentary: Old Testament*, pp. 21-22 for further explanation. However you interpret the phrase, something in the union displeased God and resulted in the destructive flood.

6:5-7 The depth to which mankind had sunk was abominable. The description is very emphatic. **Every scheme** of **his mind** was continually **evil**. This suggests much more than just sinning on the part of mankind. There is no goodness, no compassion, no altruism, no thoughtfulness, no unselfishness, no genuine love, nothing that makes life wholesome. Notice the contrast between 1:31 where "God saw all that He had made, and it was very good" with these verses where **the LORD regretted that He had made man on the earth**. It **grieved** Him **in His heart**—He was sad at what man had become. Thus unlike the false gods of other nations, Yahweh is concerned about man's condition.

6:8-12 Four characterizations of Noah's godliness set him apart, in contrast to the ungodliness of those in his world.

- Noah **found favor** [Hb *chēn*, "grace, condition of being acceptable"; cp. 39:21] **in the sight of the LORD**, in contrast to **the earth**, which had become **corrupt** [Hb *shachat*, "ruined, decayed" in a moral sense] **in God's sight**.
- He **was a righteous** [Hb *tsaddiq*, "just, lawful" in conduct, v. 9; 7:1; cp. Dt 32:4] **man**, not meaning that he achieved righteousness by his works or that he was justified before God on his own account but that he was obedient (he was "right with God" in being faithful to God's covenants and promises, and he habitually **did everything**

with wickedness[A] because of them; therefore I am going to destroy them along with the earth.

[14] "Make yourself an ark of gopher[B] wood. Make rooms in the ark, and cover it with pitch inside and outside. [15] This is how you are to make it: The ark will be 450 feet long, 75 feet wide, and 45 feet high.[C] [16] You are to make a roof,[D] finishing the sides of the ark to within 18 inches[E] of the roof. You are to put a door in the side of the ark. Make it with lower, middle, and upper decks.

[17] "Understand that I am bringing a flood—floodwaters on the earth to destroy every creature under heaven with the breath of life in it. Everything on earth will die. [18] But I will establish My covenant with you, and you will enter the ark with your sons, your wife, and your sons' wives. [19] You are also to bring into the ark two of all the living creatures, male and female, to keep them alive with you. [20] Two of everything—from the birds according to their kinds, from the livestock according to their kinds, and from the animals that crawl on the ground according to their kinds—will come to you so that you can keep them alive. [21] Take with you every kind of food that is eaten; gather it as food for you and for them." [22] And Noah did this. He did everything that God had commanded him.

7 Then the LORD said to Noah, "Enter the ark, you and all your household, for I have seen that you alone are righteous before Me in this generation. [2] You are to take with you seven pairs, a male and its female, of all the •clean animals, and two of the animals that are not clean, a male and its female, [3] and seven pairs, male and female, of the birds of the sky—in order to keep •offspring alive on the face of the whole earth. [4] Seven days from now I will make it rain on the earth 40 days and 40 nights, and I will wipe off from the face of the earth every living thing I have made." [5] And Noah did everything that the LORD commanded him.

[6] Noah was 600 years old when the flood came and water covered the earth.

God's Call to Noah (7:7–8:19)

[7] So Noah, his sons, his wife, and his sons' wives entered the ark because of the waters of the flood. [8] From the clean animals, •unclean animals, birds, and every creature that crawls on the ground, [9] two of each, male and female, entered the ark with Noah, just as God had commanded him. [10] Seven days later the waters of the flood came on the earth.

[11] In the six hundredth year of Noah's life, in the second month, on the seventeenth day of the month, on that day all the sources of the watery depths burst open, the floodgates of the sky were opened, [12] and the rain fell on the earth 40 days and 40 nights. [13] On that same day Noah along with his sons Shem, Ham, and Japheth, Noah's wife, and his three sons' wives entered the ark with him. [14] They entered it with all the wildlife according to their kinds, all livestock according to their kinds, the creatures that crawl on the earth according to their kinds, all birds, every fowl, and everything with wings according to their kinds. [15] Two of all flesh that has the breath of life in it entered the ark with Noah. [16] Those that entered, male and female of all flesh, entered just as God had commanded him. Then the LORD shut him in.

[17] The flood continued for 40 days on the earth; the waters increased and lifted up the ark so that it rose above the earth. [18] The waters surged and increased greatly on the earth, and the ark floated on the surface of the water. [19] Then the waters surged even higher on the earth, and all the high mountains under the whole sky were covered. [20] The mountains were covered as the waters surged above them more than 20 feet.[F] [21] Every creature perished—those that crawl on the earth, birds, livestock, wildlife, and those that swarm[G] on the earth, as well as all mankind.

[A] **6:13** Or *injustice* [B] **6:14** Unknown species of tree; perhaps pine or cypress [C] **6:15** Or *300 cubits long, 50 cubits wide, and 30 cubits high* [D] **6:16** Or *window*, or *hatch*; Hb uncertain [E] **6:16** Lit *to a cubit* [F] **7:20** Lit *surged 15 cubits* [G] **7:21** Lit *all the swarming swarms*

that God had commanded him, Gn 6:22; 7:5).

- He was **blameless** (Hb *tamim*, "innocent, perfect" in the sense of "having integrity," 6:9; cp. 17:1), meaning that he refused to enter into the excesses of **his contemporaries.**
- He **walked with God** (v. 9; cp. Enoch, 5:22), indicating that he knew God in the deepest sense as an honored friend and guide, as well as his Creator and Judge.

6:13-16 God confided in Noah His plans and gave him instructions on how to build **an ark** (Hb *tēvah*, "box" or "chest," also used of the water-proofed basket in which the baby Moses was hidden; v. 14; Ex 2:3-5). An opening in the side was necessary for entry and would require special sealing. Thus Yahweh "shut them in" (7:16). Interestingly, the ark apparently had no method of steering since it was made for only one purpose—preservation.

6:17 God outlined the method He would use to **destroy** the sinful world in which Noah lived through **a flood—floodwaters** blotting everything out. However, this terrible disaster was to be the beginning of a new relationship between mankind and God.

6:18 A **covenant**, which is permanent, would be established. Only eight people were to be saved from the flood. In contrast to Lamech of the line of Cain, Noah was monogamous.

7:4 Forty days and 40 nights is later significant as a period when, in special moments in history, men of God wait on God (Moses—Ex 24:18; Dt 9:9,18; Elijah—1Kg 19:8; and Jesus Himself—Mt 4:2).

7:7 There had been no rain, but in full obedience **Noah** and **his sons** carried out the task of entering **the ark**, a process for which God allotted **seven days**, during which Noah and his immediate family, as well as all the creatures, were to go aboard. This links the sons with their father in obedience to the Lord.

7:16 Noah's security did not depend on what he had done but on the faithfulness of God.

8:1 The Creator **God remembered** His creatures, a vivid way of stating that God acted in accordance with His plan and the commitments He made to Noah. As *Elohim*, He acted in order to preserve His creation. He had not forgotten or rejected them, for He was in control of the whole event; and He Himself had ensured that they would be safe throughout the voyage.

8:10-11 This seven-day period parallels the earlier seven days of preparation and introduces the moment when Noah knew that all was well. Again **seven** indicates the divinely perfect time. The fresh **olive leaf** was a sign that the earth was once again fruitful. However, Noah was too wise to try to leave the ark immediately. **The earth's surface** was still not habitable.

8:21 God spoke of **man's inclination** (Hb *yētser*, "imagination, purpose" with *lēv*, "heart"; cp. 1Ch 28:9; Is 26:3)—of his will or thoughts. God is concerned not just with man's actions but even with how he thinks. Often a good action disguises an evil thought. Man looks at the outward appearance, but God looks at the heart.

9:1-17 In this passage **God** is identified as *Elohim*, the Creator; He is beginning again and reinstating man as His representative on earth. God includes Noah's **sons** in His instructions. The destruction of man might have been seen as annulling man's position as God's representative. Thus God as Creator renewed the commission, which He had first given to man:

- Man is commanded to **be fruitful** and repopulate the world (9:1; cp. 1:28a).
- Man is to have **authority** over creation (9:2: cp. 1:28b).
- Man is given the right to **eat** of the flesh of **every living creature** as he had been given with **plants**, but not meat with blood in it (9:3-4; compare and contrast 1:29).
- Man's **life** is sacred because he is made in the **image** of **God**, and to take that life is to merit death (9:5-6).
- God reiterated the command to repopulate the world (9:7).
- **God** promised that the earth would **never again** be destroyed by a similar **flood**, affirmed by the appearance of the rainbow (vv. 9-17).

9:21 Sadly, Noah misused what God had given him and showed himself to be sinful and wicked in his own self-indulgence. Even the best of men can fall into temptation and sin. In a drunken state Noah lay naked in **his tent**, unaware of the impropriety of his situation. To be seen **naked** was a shameful thing ever since man's first

22 Everything with the breath of the spirit of life in its nostrils—everything on dry land died. 23 He wiped out every living thing that was on the surface of the ground, from mankind to livestock, to creatures that crawl, to the birds of the sky, and they were wiped off the earth. Only Noah was left, and those that were with him in the ark. 24 And the waters surged on the earth 150 days.

8 God remembered Noah, as well as all the wildlife and all the livestock that were with him in the ark. God caused a wind[A] to pass over the earth, and the water began to subside. 2 The sources of the watery depths and the floodgates of the sky were closed, and the rain from the sky stopped. 3 The water steadily receded from the earth, and by the end of 150 days the waters had decreased significantly. 4 The ark came to rest in the seventh month, on the seventeenth day of the month, on the mountains of Ararat.[B]

5 The waters continued to recede until the tenth month; in the tenth month, on the first day of the month, the tops of the mountains were visible. 6 After 40 days Noah opened the window of the ark that he had made, 7 and he sent out a raven. It went back and forth until the waters had dried up from the earth. 8 Then he sent out a dove to see whether the water on the earth's surface had gone down, 9 but the dove found no resting place for her foot. She returned to him in the ark because water covered the surface of the whole earth. He reached out and brought her into the ark to himself. 10 So Noah waited seven more days and sent out the dove from the ark again. 11 When the dove came to him at evening, there was a plucked olive leaf in her beak. So Noah knew that the water on the earth's surface had gone down. 12 After he had waited another seven days, he sent out the dove, but she did not return to him again. 13 In the six hundred and first year,[C] in the first month, on the first day of the month, the water that had covered the earth was dried up. Then Noah removed the ark's cover and saw that the surface of the ground was drying. 14 By the twenty-seventh day of the second month, the earth was dry.

15 Then God spoke to Noah, 16 "Come out of the ark, you, your wife, your sons, and your sons' wives with you. 17 Bring out all the living creatures[D] that are with you—birds, livestock, those that crawl on the ground—and they will spread over the earth and be fruitful and multiply on the earth." 18 So Noah, along with his sons, his wife, and his sons' wives, came out. 19 All wildlife, all livestock, every bird, and every creature that crawls on the earth came out of the ark by their groups.

God's Covenant with Noah (8:20–9:29)

20 Then Noah built an altar to the LORD. He took some of every kind of •clean animal and every kind of clean bird and offered •burnt offerings on the altar. 21 When the LORD smelled the pleasing aroma, He said to Himself, "I will never again curse the ground because of man, even though man's inclination is evil from his youth. And I will never again strike down every living thing as I have done.

22 As long as the earth endures,
seedtime and harvest,
cold and heat,
summer and winter,
and day and night
will not cease."

9 God blessed Noah and his sons and said to them, "Be fruitful and multiply and fill the earth. 2 The fear and terror of you will be in every living creature on the earth, every bird of the sky, every creature that crawls on the ground, and all the fish of the sea. They are placed under your authority.[E] 3 Every living creature will be food for you; as I gave the green plants, I have given you everything. 4 However, you must not eat meat with its lifeblood in it. 5 I will require the life of every animal and every man for your life and your blood. I will require the life of each man's brother for a man's life.

6 Whoever sheds man's blood,

[A]8:1 Or *spirit*; Gn 1:2 [B]8:4 Turkey or Armenia [C]8:13 = of Noah's life [D]8:17 Lit *creatures of all flesh* [E]9:2 Lit *are given in your hand*

his blood will be shed by man,
for God made man in
His image.
7 But you, be fruitful and multiply;
spread out over the earth and multiply on it."
8 Then God said to Noah and his
sons with him, 9 "Understand that
I am confirming My covenant with
you and your descendants after you,
10 and with every living creature that
is with you—birds, livestock, and
all wildlife of the earth that are with
you—all the animals of the earth
that came out of the ark. 11 I confirm
My covenant with you that never
again will every creature be wiped
out by the waters of a flood; there
will never again be a flood to destroy
the earth."

COVENANT

God declared the primary **covenant** (Hb *berit*), around which all history is written (9:8-17). All mankind is included in the covenant, as are the **living creatures**. Notice, however, that although the covenant is with **all flesh**, it is specifically communicated to Noah and his sons. They were appointed by God to have authority over His creation. The covenant is a solemn and binding commitment that God fashioned, assuring man of God's faithfulness. God determined the terms and conditions, and He is forever faithful to the covenants He makes. His faithfulness is not dependent on any response from man (Gn 3:15; 12:1-3; Ex 19:5; Dt 30:3; 2Sm 7:16). God has made seven covenants with mankind:

- The covenant with Adam (2:16-17);
- The covenant with Noah (9:8-17);
- The covenant with Abraham (12:1-3);
- The covenant with Moses (Ex 19:5);
- The covenant regarding the land (Dt 30:3-10);
- The covenant with David (2Sm 7:16); and
- The covenant concerning the millennial age (Jr 31:31-34; Heb 8:8).

12 And God said, "This is the sign
of the covenant I am making between Me and you and every living creature with you, a covenant
for all future generations: 13 I have
placed My bow in the clouds, and
it will be a sign of the covenant
between Me and the earth. 14 Whenever I form clouds over the earth
and the bow appears in the clouds,
15 I will remember My covenant between Me and you and all the living
creatures:[A] water will never again
become a flood to destroy every
creature. 16 The bow will be in the
clouds, and I will look at it and remember the everlasting covenant
between God and all the living
creatures[B] on earth." 17 God said to
Noah, "This is the sign of the covenant that I have confirmed between
Me and every creature on earth."
18 Noah's sons who came out of the
ark were Shem, Ham, and Japheth.
Ham was the father of Canaan.
19 These three were Noah's sons,
and from them the whole earth was
populated.
20 Noah, a man of the soil, was the
first to plant[C] a vineyard. 21 He drank
some of the wine, became drunk,
and uncovered himself inside his
tent. 22 Ham, the father of Canaan,
saw his father naked and told his
two brothers outside. 23 Then Shem
and Japheth took a cloak and placed
it over both their shoulders, and
walking backward, they covered
their father's nakedness. Their faces
were turned away, and they did not
see their father naked.
24 When Noah awoke from his
drinking and learned what his
youngest son had done to him, 25 he
said:

Canaan will be cursed.
He will be the lowest of slaves
to his brothers.

26 He also said:

Praise the LORD, the God
of Shem;
Canaan will be[D] his slave.
27 God will extend[E] Japheth;
he will dwell in the tents
of Shem;
Canaan will be his slave.

28 Now Noah lived 350 years after
the flood. 29 So Noah's life lasted 950
years; then he died.

The Descendants of Noah (10:1-32)

Japheth (10:1-5)

10 These are the family records of
Noah's sons, Shem, Ham, and

[A]9:15 Lit *and creatures of all flesh* [B]9:16 Lit *creatures of all flesh* [C]9:20 Or *Noah began to be a farmer and planted* [D]9:26 As a prophecy; others interpret the verbs in vv. 26-27 as a wish or prayer: *let Canaan be . . .* [E]9:27 In Hb, the name Japheth sounds like the word "extend."

sin (vv. 22-23; cp. 3:7). Noah again revealed sinful man's **nakedness** by his weakness in regard to **the wine**, another sign of disobedience to God (9:20,23). The flood has undone creation; then creation was renewed. But in this incident, Noah reenacted the fall, leaving himself naked and showing his enslavement to sin.

9:22 The emphasis on **Ham** as **the father of Canaan** (vv. 18 and 22) points to the birth of Canaan after the flood ended. Ham was not to blame for finding his father uncovered, but he was unwise not to deal discreetly with the situation. There was clearly something unpleasant about his behavior in contrast to **Shem and Japheth**, who acted with consideration toward their drunken **father** and preserved his dignity, thus avoiding any unpleasant thoughts and taking steps to avoid temptation.

9:24-27 Time may have elapsed between Noah's awareness of Ham's deed and the series of blessings and curses Noah voiced. Thus Ham may have died by then, which would explain why the curse is leveled at **Canaan**. Alternately, perhaps Noah wanted Ham to see the consequences he had brought, not only on himself but on his children. Certainly the Canaanites would later be renowned for their sexual depravity. Curses and blessings had a powerful effect on the lives of descendants. Ham was to be punished through the consequences for his behavior, which resulted in his son being **the lowest of slaves to his brothers**.

10:1-32 The family records of Noah's sons (often called the "table of nations")—the names of Noah's sons are noted in reverse order, **Japheth** (vv. 2-4), **Ham** (vv. 6-8), and finally **Shem** (vv. 21-29), in order to deal with the former before concentrating on the one who is central to the remaining narrative.

This "table of nations" demonstrates the descent of the nations from the sons of Noah with special emphasis on Shem, including important bits of information typical of ancient genealogies (10:9-10,25). Although lists of people and nations are known elsewhere, in many ways they are unique in the ancient world. This list was not a record of conquests. It was a deliberate attempt to demonstrate God's concern for the world and show that Yahweh was God over all. Its scope is quite remarkable and must reflect the knowledge of someone with wide sources of information uncommon in a non-seafaring country like Israel. Such knowledge would be available to a man in Moses' position in Egypt.

10:2-5 The Japhethites went to Europe and northern Asia.

10:6-20 The Hamites spread into Egypt, Ethiopia, Arabia, Asia Minor, and Canaan.

10:21-32 The descendants of **Shem** and **Eber** (of special importance because his name evolved into the term "Hebrew"; see 14:13; Ex 5:1-3) move into western Mesopotamia, Assyria, Arabia, and what is identified as the Middle East.

11:2 The land of Shinar is where Nimrod later came in search of glory and conquest (10:10; see also 1Ch 1:10; Mc 5:6). It is the name of Babylonia proper, the beginning of the symbol of Great **Babylon**, which is later seen as the ultimate in rebellion against God (Gn 11:9; see Rv 17–18).

11:4 The building of **a city** in this context is a sign of their efforts toward self-sufficiency and independence from God. These people were banding together to trust in their own strength rather than depending on Yahweh.

11:5-9 The rebellion of Babel was stopped by God's intervention, but since then God has allowed other people groups to apply the same principles in the construction of other great and powerful civilizations, with their capitals residing in influential cities. Examples include Memphis of the Egyptian Kingdom, Nineveh of the Assyrian Empire, Babylon of the Neo-Babylonian Empire, and Rome of

Japheth. They also had sons after
the flood.
2 Japheth's sons: Gomer, Magog,
Madai, Javan, Tubal, Meshech, and
Tiras. 3 Gomer's sons: Ashkenaz,
Riphath, and Togarmah. 4 And Javan's sons: Elishah, Tarshish, Kittim, and Dodanim.[A] 5 The coastland
peoples spread out into their lands.
These are Japheth's sons by their
clans, in their nations. Each group
had its own language.

Ham (10:6-20)

6 Ham's sons: Cush, Egypt, Put,
and Canaan. 7 Cush's sons: Seba,
Havilah, Sabtah, Raamah, and Sabteca. And Raamah's sons: Sheba and
Dedan.
8 Cush fathered Nimrod, who was
the first powerful man on earth. 9 He
was a powerful hunter in the sight
of the LORD. That is why it is said,
"Like Nimrod, a powerful hunter in
the sight of the LORD." 10 His kingdom started with Babylon, Erech,[B]
Accad,[C] and Calneh,[D] in the land
of •Shinar.[E] 11 From that land he
went to Assyria and built Nineveh,
Rehoboth-ir, Calah, 12 and Resen,
between Nineveh and the great city
Calah.
13 Mizraim[F] fathered Ludim, Anamim, Lehabim, Naphtuhim, 14 Pathrusim, Casluhim (the Philistines
came from them), and Caphtorim.
15 Canaan fathered Sidon his firstborn, then Heth, 16 the Jebusites, the
Amorites, the Girgashites, 17 the Hivites, the Arkites, the Sinites, 18 the
Arvadites, the Zemarites, and the
Hamathites. Afterward the Canaanite clans scattered. 19 The Canaanite
border went from Sidon going toward Gerar as far as Gaza, and going
toward Sodom, Gomorrah, Admah,
and Zeboiim as far as Lasha.
20 These are Ham's sons, by their
clans, according to their languages,
in their own lands and their nations.

Shem (10:21-32), i.e., the Hebrews

21 And Shem, Japheth's older
brother, also had sons. Shem was
the father of all the sons of Eber.
22 Shem's sons were Elam, Asshur,[G]
Arpachshad, Lud, and Aram.
23 Aram's sons: Uz, Hul, Gether,
and Mash.
24 Arpachshad fathered[H] Shelah, and

[A] **10:4** Some Hb mss, Sam, LXX read *Rodanim*; 1Ch 1:7 [B] **10:10** Or *Uruk* [C] **10:10** Or *Akkad* [D] **10:10** Or *and all of them* [E] **10:10** Or *in Babylonia* [F] **10:13** = Egypt [G] **10:22** Or *Assyria* [H] **10:24** LXX reads *fathered Cainan, and Cainan fathered*; Gn 11:12-13; Lk 3:35-36

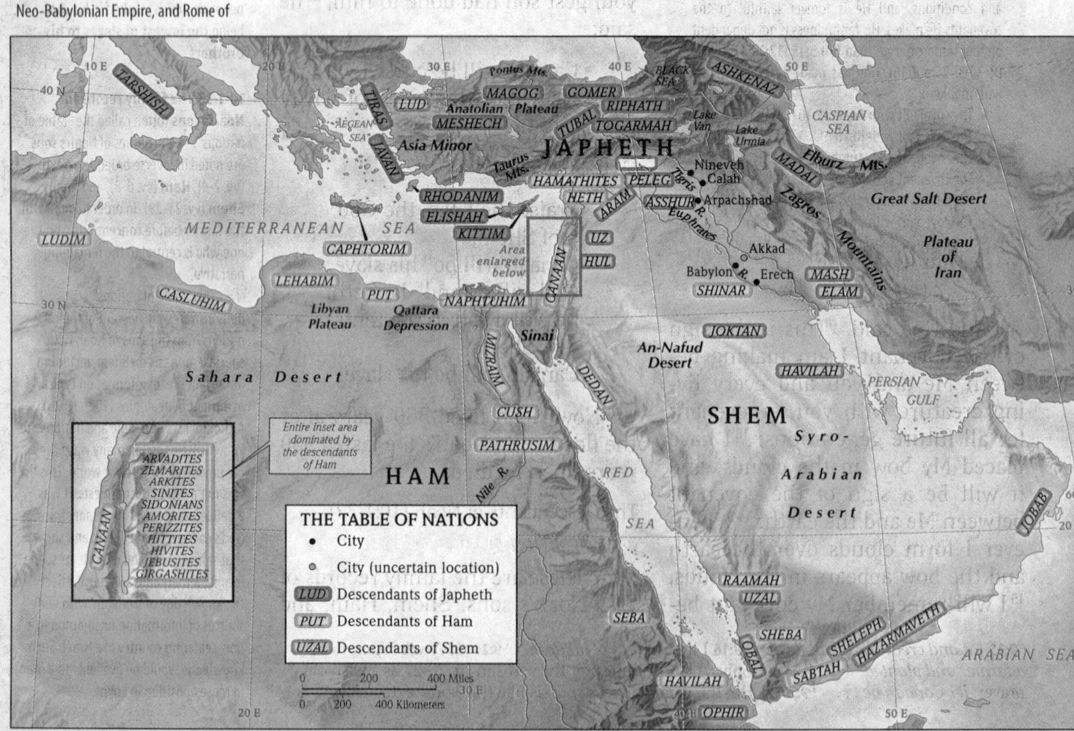

Shelah fathered Eber. [25]Eber had two sons. One was named Peleg, for during his days the earth was divided; his brother was named Joktan. [26]And Joktan fathered Almodad, Sheleph, Hazarmaveth, Jerah, [27]Hadoram, Uzal, Diklah, [28]Obal, Abimael, Sheba, [29]Ophir, Havilah, and Jobab. All these were Joktan's sons. [30]Their settlements extended from Mesha to Sephar, the eastern hill country.

[31]These are Shem's sons by their clans, according to their languages, in their lands and their nations.

[32]These are the clans of Noah's sons, according to their family records, in their nations. The nations on earth spread out from these after the flood.

The Confusion of Languages at Babel (11:1-32)

11 At one time the whole earth had the same language and vocabulary.[A] [2]As people[B] migrated from the east,[C] they found a valley in the land of •Shinar and settled there. [3]They said to each other, "Come, let us make oven-fired bricks." They used brick for stone and asphalt for mortar. [4]And they said, "Come, let us build ourselves a city and a tower with its top in the sky. Let us make a name for ourselves; otherwise, we will be scattered over the face of the whole earth."

[5]Then the LORD came down to look over the city and the tower that the •men were building. [6]The LORD said, "If they have begun to do this as one people all having the same language, then nothing they plan to do will be impossible for them. [7]Come, let Us go down there and confuse[D] their language[E] so that they will not understand one another's speech."[F] [8]So from there the LORD scattered them over the face of the whole earth, and they stopped building the city. [9]Therefore its name is called Babylon,[G] for there the LORD confused the language of the whole earth, and from there the LORD scattered them over the face of the whole earth.

[10]These are the family records of Shem. Shem lived 100 years and fathered Arpachshad two years after the flood. [11]After he fathered Arpachshad, Shem lived 500 years and fathered other sons and daughters. [12]Arpachshad lived 35 years[H] and fathered Shelah. [13]After he fathered Shelah, Arpachshad lived 403 years and fathered other sons and daughters. [14]Shelah lived 30 years and fathered Eber. [15]After he fathered Eber, Shelah lived 403 years and fathered other sons and daughters. [16]Eber lived 34 years and fathered Peleg. [17]After he fathered Peleg, Eber lived 430 years and fathered other sons and daughters. [18]Peleg lived 30 years and fathered Reu. [19]After he fathered Reu, Peleg lived 209 years and fathered other sons and daughters. [20]Reu lived 32 years and fathered Serug. [21]After he fathered Serug, Reu lived 207 years and fathered other sons and daughters. [22]Serug lived 30 years and fathered Nahor. [23]After he fathered Nahor, Serug lived 200 years and fathered other sons and daughters. [24]Nahor lived 29 years and fathered Terah. [25]After he fathered Terah, Nahor lived 119 years and fathered other sons and daughters. [26]Terah lived 70 years and fathered Abram, Nahor, and Haran.

[27]These are the family records of Terah. Terah fathered Abram, Nahor, and Haran, and Haran fathered Lot. [28]Haran died in his native land, in Ur of the Chaldeans, during his father Terah's lifetime. [29]Abram and Nahor took wives: Abram's wife was named Sarai, and Nahor's wife was named Milcah. She was the daughter of Haran, the father of both Milcah and Iscah. [30]Sarai was unable to conceive; she did not have a child.

[31]Terah took his son Abram, his grandson Lot (Haran's son), and his daughter-in-law Sarai, his son

[A]**11:1** Lit *one lip and the same words* [B]**11:2** Lit *they* [C]**11:2** Or *migrated eastward* [D]**11:7** Or *confound* [E]**11:7** Lit *lip* [F]**11:7** Lit *understand each man the lip of his companion* [G]**11:9** In Hb, the name Babylon sounds like the word "confuse." [H]**11:12-13** LXX reads *years and fathered Cainan.* [13]*After he fathered Cainan, Arphachshad lived 430 years and fathered other sons and daughters, and he died. Cainan lived 130 years and fathered Shelah. After he fathered Shelah, Cainan lived 330 years and fathered other sons and daughters, and he died*; Gn 10:24; Lk 3:35-36

the Roman Empire. In a way, each of these cities was the "Babel" of its day. Each embodied the spirit of rebellion and human glorification that began with Adam and Eve (3:6-7,11-13), who passed it to their son Cain (4:17), and is then continued here in Gn 11.

11:10-26 The genealogy that follows links **Abram** to **Shem**. Through Shem (9:26), God's man for the times would come. There is a chosen line reflected throughout chapters 1–11, and it leads to Abram. The patriarchs are listed with gradually decreasing ages, a further indication that man is fallen and will die and do so more quickly as the generations pass. The names are mainly of a Mesopotamian background. The line of patriarchs is probably to be seen as a selection of patriarchs numbering 10 to represent completeness rather than recording the full lineage, as with the list in chapter 5 and in the lists of kings of other nations.

11:27-28 Terah's family home was **Ur of the Chaldeans**. The family was not just semi-nomadic, wandering from place to place; they were inhabitants of Ur, although probably even at this stage with large herds and flocks. Ur of the Chaldeans was an important and highly sophisticated city of ancient origin, with access to good education. But these nomads were probably not city-dwellers (Dt 26:5). Ur's principal deity Nannar, the moon god, was probably worshiped by **Terah**. This worship included a number of degrading elements. Ur of the Chaldeans was destroyed around 1950 B.C., pointing to the fact that these events took place before then. Possibly God's command to Abram was also a warning of what was to happen to Ur. Later narrative (Gn 31:53), where the God of Abraham is distinguished from the god of **Nahor**, suggests that Nahor continued to worship his father's gods (see also Jos 24:2). Seemingly, he was not affected by his brother's conversion.

11:29-30 Interestingly, more details are given about **Nahor's wife . . . Milcah** than of **Sarai** except to note Sarai's barrenness. While clearly Sarai is an outstandingly beautiful woman (12:11,14), she bears the stigma of unfruitfulness. In her culture, the inability to produce children would have been a great tragedy for a couple, especially for the wife.

CHARACTER PROFILE

Sarah A Faithful Wife

Her Background
- She was the wife of Abraham (11:29).
- She immigrated to Canaan (12:5).
- She lived 127 years (23:1).

Her Story
- She was infertile (11:30; Rm 4:19).
- She was strong-willed and outspoken (Gn 21:8-11).
- She attempted to have a child through her maid Hagar (16:1-4).
- God promised her that she would produce a son (17:16).
- She gave birth to Isaac (21:2-3).
- She asked Abraham to send Hagar and Ishmael away (21:10).

Life Lessons
- Abraham and Sarah's marriage is an example of committed love.
- God's promises are kept on His timetable.
- Despite your mistakes, God is sovereign and His purposes will be accomplished.

Abram's wife, and they set out together from Ur of the Chaldeans to go to the land of Canaan. But when they came to Haran, they settled there. 32 Terah lived 205 years and died in Haran.

The Generations of Abraham (12:1–25:18)

God's Covenant with Abraham (12:1–13:4)

12 The Lord said to Abram:

Go out from your land,
your relatives,
and your father's house
to the land that I will
show you.
2 I will make you
into a great nation,
I will bless you,
I will make your name great,
and you will be a blessing.[A]
3 I will bless those
who bless you,
I will curse those
who treat you
with contempt,
and all the peoples[B] on earth
will be blessed[C] through you.[D]

4 So Abram went, as the Lord had told him, and Lot went with him. Abram was 75 years old when he left Haran. 5 He took his wife Sarai, his nephew Lot, all the possessions they had accumulated, and the people he had acquired in Haran, and they set out for the land of Canaan. When they came to the land of Canaan, 6 Abram passed through the land to the site of Shechem, at the oak of Moreh. At that time the Canaanites were in the land. 7 Then the Lord appeared to Abram and said, "I will give this land to your •offspring." So he built an altar there to the Lord who had appeared to him. 8 From there he moved on to the hill country east of Bethel and pitched his tent, with Bethel on the west and Ai on the east. He built an altar to •Yahweh there, and he called on the name of Yahweh. 9 Then Abram journeyed by stages to the •Negev.

10 There was a famine in the land, so Abram went down to Egypt to live there for a while because the famine in the land was severe. 11 When he was about to enter Egypt, he said to his wife Sarai, "Look, I know what a beautiful woman you are. 12 When the Egyptians see you, they will say, 'This is his wife.' They will kill me but let

[A]12:2 Or *great. Be a blessing!* [B]12:3 Lit *clans* [C]12:3 Or *will find blessing* [D]12:3 Or *will bless themselves by you*

12:1-3 Abram's dealings with God are built around covenants. **Abram** is called to venture into the unknown. The way ahead would be revealed to him as he took the path of obedience. His part was to trust and obey. This was a crucial moment in his life, determining not only his destiny but that of the world. God did not hold back on what was being demanded. Abram must leave his **land**. He must leave his **relatives**, those whom he knew and trusted. He must leave his position in the family hierarchy, his **father's house**, but in return he was promised a new **land**. He would become **a great nation**. He would experience God's special protection. He was to become **a blessing**. Indeed the whole earth would be blessed through what Abram did or rather what God did through him. The ideas are parallel. He must leave a land to receive a land. He must leave relatives in order to become part of a great nation. He must leave his close family so that all the **peoples on earth** might become his family. This was God's covenant. And Abram believed and obeyed.

12:4 The question of the basis of Abram's faith begs to be asked, though unfortunately the answer is not apparent. What originally turned his thoughts to Yahweh when his father Terah was a worshiper of other gods and most certainly reared his sons in the midst of idol worship? Joshua stated quite clearly to the people of Israel, "Long ago your ancestors, including Terah, the father of Abraham and Nahor, lived beyond the Euphrates River and worshiped other gods" (Jos 24:2). Furthermore Terah gave his son the name Ab-ram "my father is Ram." Why Abram turned from the gods his father worshiped to worship Yahweh is still a mystery. Yet the text clearly notes that when God called Abram out of Ur, Abram turned without hesitation to the true God and followed Him. Abram's age of **75 years** at his departure from Ur indicates that Terah was still alive when he left. Terah was 70 when he fathered Abram (11:26). Terah died at 205. He would have lived another 60 years after he and Abram left for Canaan (11:31-32).

12:10 Abram had been in Canaan for an extended time when severe **famine** occurred there. Canaan was always vulnerable to famine because it was totally dependent on rain, so Abram headed for **Egypt**, as would many others with herds to protect. Egypt exercised general control over the area during this period. There is no suggestion of wrongdoing about Abram's going to Egypt. On the contrary, he was justified on the grounds of the severity of the famine.

12:11-13 Because Abram feared that

you live. 13 Please say you're my sister so it will go well for me because of you, and my life will be spared on your account." 14 When Abram entered Egypt, the Egyptians saw that the woman was very beautiful. 15 Pharaoh's officials saw her and praised her to Pharaoh, so the woman was taken to Pharaoh's household. 16 He treated Abram well because of her, and Abram acquired flocks and herds, male and female donkeys, male and female slaves, and camels.

17 But the LORD struck Pharaoh and his household with severe plagues because of Abram's wife Sarai. 18 So Pharaoh sent for Abram and said, "What have you done to me? Why didn't you tell me she was your wife? 19 Why did you say, 'She's my sister,' so that I took her as my wife? Now, here is your wife. Take her and go!" 20 Then Pharaoh gave his men orders about him, and they sent him away with his wife and all he had.

13 Then Abram went up from Egypt to the •Negev—he, his wife, and all he had, and Lot with him. 2 Abram was very rich[A] in livestock, silver, and gold. 3 He went by stages from the Negev to Bethel, to the place between Bethel and Ai where his tent had formerly been, 4 to the site where he had built the altar. And Abram called on the name of •Yahweh there.

God's Faithfulness in Renewing His Covenant (13:5–17:27)

5 Now Lot, who was traveling with Abram, also had flocks, herds, and tents. 6 But the land was unable to support them as long as they stayed together, for they had so many possessions that they could not stay together, 7 and there was quarreling between the herdsmen of Abram's livestock and the herdsmen of Lot's livestock. At that time the Canaanites and the Perizzites were living in the land.

8 Then Abram said to Lot, "Please, let's not have quarreling between you and me, or between your herdsmen and my herdsmen, since we are relatives.[B] 9 Isn't the whole land before you? Separate from me: if you go to the left, I will go to the right; if you go to the right, I will go to the left."

10 Lot looked out and saw that the entire Jordan Valley as far as[C] Zoar was well watered everywhere like the LORD's garden and the land of Egypt. This was before the LORD destroyed Sodom and Gomorrah. 11 So Lot chose the entire Jordan Valley for himself. Then Lot journeyed eastward, and they separated from each other. 12 Abram lived in the land of Canaan, but Lot lived in the cities of the valley and set up his tent near Sodom. 13 Now the men of Sodom were evil, sinning greatly[D] against the LORD.

14 After Lot had separated from him, the LORD said to Abram, "Look from the place where you are. Look north and south, east and west, 15 for I will give you and your •offspring forever all the land that you see. 16 I will make your offspring like the dust of the earth, so that if anyone could count the dust of the earth, then your offspring could be counted. 17 Get up and walk around the land, through its length and width, for I will give it to you."

18 So Abram moved his tent and went to live near the oaks of Mamre at Hebron, where he built an altar to the LORD.

14 In those days Amraphel king of •Shinar, Arioch king of Ellasar, Chedorlaomer king of Elam,[E] and Tidal[F] king of Goiim[G] 2 waged war against Bera king of Sodom, Birsha king of Gomorrah, Shinab king of Admah, and Shemeber king of Zeboiim, as well as the king of Bela (that is, Zoar). 3 All of these came as allies to the Valley of Siddim (that is, the Dead Sea). 4 They were subject to Chedorlaomer for 12 years, but in the thirteenth year they rebelled. 5 In the fourteenth year Chedorlaomer and the kings who were with him came and defeated the Rephaim in Ashteroth-karnaim, the Zuzim in Ham, the Emim in Shaveh-kiriathaim, 6 and the Horites in the mountains of Seir, as far as El-paran by the

[A]**13:2** Lit *heavy* [B]**13:8** Lit *brothers* [C]**13:10** Lit *Valley as you go to* [D]**13:13** Lit *evil and sinful*
[E]**14:1** A region in southwest Iran [F]**14:1** The name Tidal may be related to the Hittite royal name *Tudhaliya*. [G]**14:1** Or *nations*

someone would kill him in order to have Sarai when they entered Egypt, Abram asked his wife Sarai to tell people that she was his **sister**. The statement was true; she was in fact his half-sister (20:12). Sarai submitted to Abram, even when he was wrong, placing herself under God's protection. The only reason a wife has to stand against her husband is in order to obey God (see Ac 5:29).

13:3-4 Relieved in his heart and full of praise to God for his preservation, Abram took his family back to the altar at **Bethel**; and there he led in worship. Bethel (a reference to the area, not the city) was considered his permanent "home." Even though Abram and his family were a nomadic tribe, whose main activity was herding and who thus had to seek pasturage continually, they could have a permanent home.

13:7-18 The greatness of Abram became apparent in his decision to let Lot make the first pick of land in which to settle. Lot made his choice to dwell among the cities of the plain. Bethel (the house of God) had been their center, but now Lot moved his center to **Sodom.** The wickedness of Sodom is set forth clearly (19:4-14). In fact, its name has become a synonym for gross immorality. Lot took up abode in Sodom and became an important man among them (19:2-3). Abram transferred the center of his activities from Bethel to **Hebron**, in the hill country of the south. There he established his main camp and built an altar for the worship of God. Trees indicate water, and Abram had chosen wisely to live near the **oaks of Mamre**. It was a reasonably safe part of the country and would enable his family to expand and grow.

14:1-12 The place Lot had chosen was indeed fruitful and close to the King's Highway, which extended from Damascus and the Euphrates southward to Elath at the Gulf of Aqabah. In ancient times, the King's Highway was a strategically important north-south trade route and is the corridor through which a major Jordanian highway has been built. This period at the beginning of the second millennium B.C. was a time when Mesopotamia was not one great powerful empire. Roving bands led by lesser kings would continually make their forays in an attempt to seize wealth and slaves. And the King's Highway was a convenient route.

The kings from the north came down and subjugated the cities near the Dead Sea in order to protect the trade route and exact tribute from those who traveled that route. The cities were sick of paying the tribute and rebelled (i.e., they withheld their tribute). **Chedorlaomer and the kings who were with him** swept down the wilderness. 7 Then they came back to invade En-mishpat (that is, Kadesh), and they defeated all the territory of the Amalekites, as well as the Amorites who lived in Hazazon-tamar.

8 Then the king of Sodom, the king of Gomorrah, the king of Admah, the king of Zeboiim, and the king of Bela (that is, Zoar) went out and lined up for battle in the Valley of Siddim 9 against Chedorlaomer king of Elam, Tidal king of Goiim, Amraphel king of Shinar, and Arioch king of Ellasar—four kings against five. 10 Now the Valley of Siddim contained many asphalt pits, and as the kings of Sodom and Gomorrah fled, some fell into them,[A] but the rest fled to the mountains. 11 The four kings took all the goods of Sodom and Gomorrah and all their food and went on. 12 They also took Abram's nephew Lot and his possessions, for he was living in Sodom, and they went on.

13 One of the survivors came and told Abram the Hebrew, who lived near the oaks belonging to Mamre the Amorite, the brother of Eshcol and the brother of Aner. They were bound by a treaty with[B] Abram. 14 When Abram heard that his relative had been taken prisoner, he assembled[C] his 318 trained men, born in his household, and they went in pursuit as far as Dan. 15 And he and his servants deployed against them by night, attacked them, and pursued them as far as Hobah to the north of Damascus. 16 He brought back all the goods and also his relative Lot and his goods, as well as the women and the other people.

17 After Abram returned from defeating Chedorlaomer and the kings who were with him, the king of Sodom went out to meet him in the Valley of Shaveh (that is, the King's Valley). 18 Then Melchizedek, king of Salem,[D] brought out bread and wine; he was a priest to God •Most High. 19 He blessed him and said:

Abram is blessed
by God Most High,
Creator[E] of heaven and earth,
20 and I give praise
to[F] God Most High
who has handed over
your enemies to you.

And Abram gave him a tenth of everything.

21 Then the king of Sodom said to Abram, "Give me the people, but take the possessions for yourself."

22 But Abram said to the king of Sodom, "I have raised my hand in an oath to •Yahweh, God Most High, Creator of heaven and earth, 23 that I will not take a thread or sandal strap or anything that belongs to you, so you can never say, 'I made Abram rich.' 24 I will take nothing[G] except what the servants have eaten. But as for the share of the men who came with me—Aner, Eshcol, and Mamre—they can take their share."

15 After these events, the word of the LORD came to Abram in a vision:

Do not be afraid, Abram.
I am your shield;
your reward will be
very great.

2 But Abram said, "Lord GOD, what can You give me, since I am childless and the heir of my house is Eliezer of Damascus?"[H] 3 Abram continued, "Look, You have given me no •offspring, so a slave born in[I] my house will be my heir."

A 14:10 Sam, LXX; MT reads *fell there* B 14:13 Lit *were possessors of a covenant of* C 14:14 Sam; MT reads *poured out* D 14:18 = Jerusalem E 14:19 Or *Possessor* F 14:20 Or *and blessed be* G 14:24 Lit *Nothing to me* H 15:2 Hb obscure I 15:3 Lit *a son of*

King's Highway, ignoring the rebels and demonstrating their contempt for the five cities. During the raid on the five kings, Lot was taken captive.

14:18 The sudden appearance of **Melchizedek, king of Salem** (i.e., "king of peace") is a surprise. If "Salem" is the same place as Jerusalem, although that is not certain, it is not on the expected return route from Damascus to Sodom, and Melchizedek had not previously been involved. Clearly Melchizedek was involved sufficiently to take the trouble to bring food to the returning troops. In the book of Hebrews, Melchizedek is described as a type of Christ (Heb 7:1-10), whose priesthood is not connected with Aaron. Many identify this appearance of Melchizedek as a Christophany or an appearance of the pre-incarnate Christ.

14:19-20 Here at the crux of the narrative is an unusual ceremony between Abram and Melchizedek, together with the king of Sodom. Abram apparently knew more about Melchizedek than is noted in the text. **Abram gave him a tenth of everything**, an allusion to the practice of tithing more than five centuries before Moses recorded the law. Abram introduced the concept of tithing; Moses commanded its observance (Dt 12:6); Christ affirmed its practice, while also acknowledging its distortion by the religious leaders, who had reduced the tithe to a ritual and used it in place of other spiritual responsibilities (Lk 11:42).

15:1 **After these events** (i.e., Abram's rescue of Lot) the Lord came to Abram, and Abram confessed his anxiety over Sarai's childlessness. The yearning of Abram's heart came out in these verses. Although he expressed disappointment, there was also a hint of hope that Yahweh would do something about his lack of an heir through Sarai.

15:2-3 The appointment of a **slave** (**Eliezer**) as heir, to be replaced if a son was born, is a practice well attested elsewhere. In return the slave or steward-adopted-as-a-son would ensure a suitable burial for his master. Similar situations are found, for example, in documents at fifteenth-century B.C. Nuzi and in Ur around 1800 B.C. An Old Babylonian letter from Larsa states that a childless man could adopt his own slave.

15:6 The word **believed** (Hb *'aman*) means "trust." One sense of **righteousness** is measuring up to God's standard, which is not the case here. Abraham's righteousness was a gift received by trusting God's word—not his human achievement.

>WORD|*study*

15:18 The brook [Hb *nahar*] of Egypt may not be the Nile (1Kg 8:65), the southernmost boundary of the land; it could be the Wadi el Arish just below Gaza, which reaches up toward the Gulf of Suez and the Gulf of Aqaba, thus excluding the absolute desert. But etymologically it would appear to speak of the Nile, for a "brook" (Hb *nachal*, "torrent; gully or watercourse that is dry except during rainfall"; cp. Gn 32:23) is a wadi, the stream arising after the rains, while a **river** (Hb *nahar*, used three times in the Hb text of 15:18) is a body of water with more permanence. There is no difficulty with seeing it as the southernmost part of the Nile in a general sense, not necessarily applied too literally. Either way the general boundary is clear. The land reached from **Egypt to the Euphrates**, two natural boundaries. In inscriptions, to Pharaoh's alarm, Sargon II reached the brook of Egypt and established a governor there (see 2Kg 24:7).

CHARACTER PROFILE

Hagar An Abused Woman

Her Background	• She was Sarah's Egyptian servant (16:1). • She was the mother of Ishmael (16:15). • She found an Egyptian wife for Ishmael (21:21).
Her Story	• She was a surrogate for Abraham's promised son since Sarah was infertile (16:3-4). • She was promised that she would be the mother of a great nation, paralleling God's promise to Abraham (15:4-5; 16:10). • She gave birth to Ishmael (16:15). • She was sent away by Sarah into the desert (16:6-7; 21:14). • God provided for her and her son; they settled in the wilderness (21:20-21).
Life Lessons	• Hagar experienced prejudice, injustice, abuse, and despair. • Yet God saw her and provided for her needs. • She responded in faith to God despite difficult circumstances.

4 Now the word of the LORD came to him: "This one will not be your heir; instead, one who comes from your own body[A] will be your heir." 5 He took him outside and said, "Look at the sky and count the stars, if you are able to count them." Then He said to him, "Your offspring will be that numerous."

6 Abram believed the LORD, and He credited it to him as righteousness.

7 He also said to him, "I am ·Yahweh who brought you from Ur of the Chaldeans to give you this land to possess."

8 But he said, "Lord GOD, how can I know that I will possess it?"

9 He said to him, "Bring Me a three-year-old cow, a three-year-old female goat, a three-year-old ram, a turtledove, and a young pigeon."

10 So he brought all these to Him, split them down the middle, and laid the pieces opposite each other, but he did not cut up the birds. 11 Birds of prey came down on the carcasses, but Abram drove them away. 12 As the sun was setting, a deep sleep fell on Abram, and suddenly great terror and darkness descended on him.

13 Then the LORD said to Abram, "Know this for certain: Your offspring will be foreigners in a land that does not belong to them; they will be enslaved and oppressed[B] 400 years. 14 However, I will judge the nation they serve, and afterward they will go out with many possessions. 15 But you will go to your fathers in peace and be buried at a ripe old age. 16 In the fourth generation they will return here, for the iniquity of the Amorites has not yet reached its full measure."[C]

17 When the sun had set and it was dark, a smoking fire pot and a flaming torch appeared and passed between the divided animals. 18 On that day the LORD made a covenant with Abram, saying, "I give this land to your offspring, from the brook of Egypt to the Euphrates River:[D] 19 the land of the Kenites, Kenizzites, Kadmonites, 20 Hittites, Perizzites, Rephaim, 21 Amorites, Canaanites, Girgashites, and Jebusites."

16 Abram's wife Sarai had not borne any children for him, but she owned an Egyptian slave named Hagar. 2 Sarai said to Abram, "Since the LORD has prevented me from bearing children, go to my slave; perhaps through her I can build a family." And Abram agreed to what Sarai said.[E] 3 So Abram's wife Sarai took Hagar, her Egyptian slave, and gave her to her husband

[A]15:4 Lit *loins* [B]15:13 Lit *will serve them and they will oppress them* [C]15:16 Lit *Amorites is not yet complete* [D]15:18 Lit *the great river, the river Euphrates* [E]16:2 Lit *Abram listened to the voice of Sarai*

This remarkable verse is the heart of the gospel. As Abram looked at the multiplicity of stars, he did not believe in the stars but in the faithfulness and goodness of God. All his disappointment and bitterness melted away, for he was reminded of Yahweh's promise and of the fact that He is faithful. And Yahweh saw his believing heart and accounted that faith to him as righteousness. By faith Abraham fulfilled all that was required of him in his covenant with God. No wonder Paul uses this verse as the rock on which his doctrine of justification by faith is founded (Gl 3:6).

15:12-16 When the sun was going down, **Abram** fell into a **deep sleep** (cp. 2:21; Jb 4:13; 33:15-16). This sleep is significant because Abram did not participate in the covenant ceremony. Therefore, the focus was not on him but on the promises of God (Gn 15:18; see Jr 34:18-20). The practice of establishing a covenant by dividing animals and walking through the parts originated in the ancient world, though Jeremiah had a close parallel (Jr 34:18). In this kind of ceremony each party was saying to the other, "May this happen to me if I don't fulfill my part of this covenant." Such an agreement was serious business. While there was not an exact correspondence between this traditional ceremony and what God was communicating to Abram, God purposefully used a picture that Abram knew well. God was telling Abram that He took seriously what He promised him and that the fulfillment of the promise was dependent on God alone. There is also a connection to the covenant made at Sinai by means of the reference to the **400 years** of bondage and subsequent exodus of Abram's descendants. Before the symbolic act, the words of the covenant must be spoken over the dead carcasses of the victims.

16:1-2 Sarai knew of God's covenant promises to Abram. But she had reached the age when she was physically unable to have a child. As time passed, she grieved over the shame of a barren womb. She had an **Egyptian** handmaid **Hagar**, probably one of those given to Abram by Pharaoh, and she proposed to Abram that he have a child by her handmaid and that they adopt the child as Abram's heir. A wife's servant, being her slave and not her husband's, could bear a child for the wife through her husband. Because the slave was hers, the child was hers also. If a natural son was born later, he could replace the adopted son according to the custom of the day.

Abram as a wife for him. This happened after Abram had lived in the
land of Canaan 10 years. 4 He slept
with[A] Hagar, and she became pregnant. When she realized that she
was pregnant, she treated her mistress with contempt. 5 Then Sarai
said to Abram, "You are responsible
for my suffering![B] I put my slave in
your arms,[C] and ever since she saw
that she was pregnant, she has treated me with contempt. May the LORD
judge between me and you."
6 Abram replied to Sarai, "Here,
your slave is in your hands; do whatever you want with her." Then Sarai
mistreated her so much that she ran
away from her.
7 The Angel of the LORD found her
by a spring of water in the wilderness, the spring on the way to Shur.
8 He said, "Hagar, slave of Sarai,
where have you come from and
where are you going?"
She replied, "I'm running away
from my mistress Sarai."
9 Then the Angel of the LORD said
to her, "You must go back to your
mistress and submit to her mistreatment."[D] 10 The Angel of the LORD also
said to her, "I will greatly multiply
your •offspring, and they will be too
many to count."
11 Then the Angel of the LORD said
to her:

You have conceived
and will have a son.
You will name him Ishmael,[E]
for the LORD has heard
your cry of affliction.
12 This man will be
like a wild donkey.
His hand will be
against everyone,
and everyone's hand will be
against him;
he will live at odds with[F] all
his brothers.

13 So she called the LORD who
spoke to her: The God Who Sees,[G]
for she said, "In this place, have I actually seen the One who sees me?"[H]
14 That is why she named the spring,
"A Well of the Living One Who Sees
Me."[I] It is located between Kadesh
and Bered.
15 So Hagar gave birth to Abram's
son, and Abram gave the name Ishmael to the son Hagar had. 16 Abram
was 86 years old when Hagar bore
Ishmael to him.

17 When Abram was 99 years old,
the LORD appeared to him, saying, "I am •God Almighty. Live in
My presence and be blameless. 2 I
will establish My covenant between
Me and you, and I will multiply you
greatly."
3 Then Abram fell facedown and
God spoke with him: 4 "As for Me,
My covenant is with you: you will
become the father of many nations.[J] 5 Your name will no longer
be Abram,[K] but your name will be
Abraham,[L] for I will make you the
father of many nations. 6 I will make
you extremely fruitful and will make
nations and kings come from you. 7 I
will keep My covenant between Me
and you, and your future •offspring
throughout their generations, as an
everlasting covenant to be your God
and the God of your offspring after
you. 8 And to you and your future
offspring I will give the land where
you are residing—all the land of Canaan—as an eternal possession, and
I will be their God."
9 God also said to Abraham, "As
for you, you and your offspring after
you throughout their generations
are to keep My covenant. 10 This is
My covenant, which you are to keep,
between Me and you and your offspring after you: Every one of your
males must be circumcised. 11 You
must circumcise the flesh of your
foreskin to serve as a sign of the
covenant between Me and you.[M]
12 Throughout your generations,
every male among you at eight days
old is to be circumcised. This includes a slave born in your house
and one purchased with money
from any foreigner. The one who is
not your offspring, 13 a slave born in
your house, as well as one purchased
with money, must be circumcised.

[A] **16:4** Lit *He came to* [B] **16:5** Or *May my suffering be on you* [C] **16:5** Lit *bosom* [D] **16:9** Lit *to mistreatment under her hand* [E] **16:11** = God Hears [F] **16:12** Or *live away from* [G] **16:13** Lit *her: You God Who Sees* [H] **16:13** Hb obscure [I] **16:14** Or *Beer-lahai-roi* [J] **17:4** Abraham was the father of the Israelites, Ishmaelites, Edomites, and Midianites. Spiritually, he is the father of all believers; Gl 3:7,29. [K] **17:5** = The Father Is Exalted [L] **17:5** = Father of a Multitude [M] **17:11** *You* in v. 11 is pl.

16:4 When Hagar **became pregnant**, she began to act in a superior way and to supplant her mistress and treat her **with contempt**, as if Sarai were now of little importance. She did not accept her responsibility to produce a child on Sarai's behalf.

16:6 Sarai then made her position clear by her harsh treatment of the **slave** who had tried to rise above her station. Although such treatment was in accordance with custom, Sarai cannot be excused for her unjust treatment of Hagar, who was a woman created equally in God's image. In the Code of Hammurabi the punishment for a servant girl who bore a child by her master and sought to take advantage of the situation was to be reduced again to the status of a slave.

17:1-4 Thirteen years after Ishmael's birth, Yahweh appeared to Abram when the patriarch was **99 years old**. The presence of Yahweh was so real and awe-inspiring that Abram **fell facedown** as before a great king (cp. 17:22, which authenticated this as a genuine theophany).

17:5 God's change of Abram's name indicated a new beginning. The name **Abram** is found in many contemporary ancient texts, often in the form *Abi-ram*, "my father is Ram - the exalted One." It may also mean "my father is exalted." The name "Ab-raham" is also similarly found and may mean "father of a multitude." The name change seems to be an alternative form rather than a new name, giving further evidence of God's determination to fulfill His promises to Abram.

17:6 More than one nation would come out of Abram and his seed, and the added promise was made of **kings**, rulers of peoples, reemphasizing the extension of the promise to many peoples so that there would be many tribes. To see this as a direct prophecy of the Davidic kingship is to miss the point, although later readers would read it so. This observation is the natural result of a man in Abram's position producing many tribes and peoples, including among his descendants many rulers. This prophecy reaches its final culmination when all nations come from Abraham's seed and culminate in the Messiah, Christ the King, through whom all the nations of the world are blessed (12:3).

17:7 God made explicit what had previously been implicit—that the **covenant** was with and included all the coming generations of Abraham's seed. God "established" the covenant. Abraham "kept" it (vv. 9-10).

17:10-16 Circumcision is not the making of a covenant but the response to a covenant already established by God; it was an act of obedience and faith (Dt 10:16; Jr 4:4; Col 2:11-12). Any

My covenant will be marked in your flesh as an everlasting covenant. 14 If any male is not circumcised in the flesh of his foreskin, that man will be cut off from his people; he has broken My covenant."

15 God said to Abraham, "As for your wife Sarai, do not call her Sarai, for Sarah[A] will be her name. 16 I will bless her; indeed, I will give you a son by her. I will bless her, and she will produce nations; kings of peoples will come from her."

17 Abraham fell facedown. Then he laughed and said to himself, "Can a child be born to a hundred-year-old man? Can Sarah, a ninety-year-old woman, give birth?" 18 So Abraham said to God, "If only Ishmael were acceptable to You!"[B]

19 But God said, "No. Your wife Sarah will bear you a son, and you will name him Isaac.[C] I will confirm My covenant with him as an everlasting covenant for his future offspring. 20 As for Ishmael, I have heard you. I will certainly bless him; I will make him fruitful and will multiply him greatly. He will father 12 tribal leaders, and I will make him into a great nation. 21 But I will confirm My covenant with Isaac, whom Sarah will bear to you at this time next year." 22 When He finished talking with him, God withdrew[D] from Abraham.

23 Then Abraham took his son Ishmael and all the slaves born in his house or purchased with his money—every male among the members of Abraham's household—and he circumcised the flesh of their foreskin on that very day, just as God had said to him. 24 Abraham was 99 years old when the flesh of his foreskin was circumcised, 25 and his son Ishmael was 13 years old when the flesh of his foreskin was circumcised. 26 On that same day Abraham and his son Ishmael were circumcised. 27 And all the men of his household—both slaves born in his house and those purchased with money from a foreigner—were circumcised with him.

Abraham's Obedience in Responding to the Covenant (18:1–25:18)

18 Then the LORD appeared to Abraham at the oaks of Mamre while he was sitting in the entrance of his tent during the heat of the day. 2 He looked up, and he saw three men standing near him. When he saw them, he ran from the entrance of the tent to meet them and bowed to the ground. 3 Then he said, "My lord,[E] if I have found favor in your sight, please do not go on past your servant. 4 Let a little water be brought, that you may wash your feet and rest yourselves under the tree. 5 I will bring a bit of bread so that you may strengthen yourselves.[F] This is why you have passed your servant's way. Later, you can continue on."

"Yes," they replied, "do as you have said."

6 So Abraham hurried into the tent and said to Sarah, "Quick! Knead three measures[G] of fine flour and make bread."[H] 7 Meanwhile, Abraham ran to the herd and got a tender, choice calf. He gave it to a young man, who hurried to prepare it. 8 Then Abraham took curds[I] and milk, and the calf that he had prepared, and set them before the men. He served[J] them as they ate under the tree.

9 "Where is your wife Sarah?" they asked him.

"There, in the tent," he answered.

10 The LORD said, "I will certainly come back to you in about a year's time, and your wife Sarah will have a son!" Now Sarah was listening at the entrance of the tent behind him. 11 Abraham and Sarah were old and getting on in years.[K] Sarah had passed the age of childbearing.[L] 12 So she laughed to herself: "After I have become shriveled up and my lord is old, will I have delight?"

13 But the LORD asked Abraham, "Why did Sarah laugh, saying, 'Can I really have a baby when I'm old?' 14 Is anything impossible for the LORD? At the appointed time I will come back

[A] **17:15** = Princess [B] **17:18** Lit *Ishmael would live in Your sight* [C] **17:19** = He Laughs [D] **17:22** Lit *went up*, or *ascended* [E] **18:3** Or *My Lord*, or *The Lord* [F] **18:5** Lit *may sustain your heart* [G] **18:6** Lit *three seahs*; about 21 quarts [H] **18:6** A round, thin, unleavened bread [I] **18:8** Or *butter* [J] **18:8** Lit *was standing by* [K] **18:11** Lit *days* [L] **18:11** Lit *The way of women had ceased for Sarah*

uncircumcised male who wished to join the covenant community at any age was required to be circumcised whether slave or free (vv. 12-13). Circumcision, a procedure in which the foreskin is removed from the male sexual organ the eighth day after birth (v. 12):

- distinguished Abraham's seed from Gentiles;
- reminded Israel of the nation's covenant with God;
- noted the necessity for purification and putting away evil.

17:15-16 Sarai (perhaps from the root meaning "contend") received a new name, **Sarah** ("princess"), though its meaning is not addressed as part of the covenant, in which she is an equal partner.

17:17 Abraham's faith faltered when he thought about having a son in his old age. The context suggests that he was incredulous. God understood Abraham's doubts and confirmed exactly what He had promised. Sarah would have a child of her own.

17:21 That the basic covenant for the chosen line was with **Isaac** is also made clear. Ishmael would produce a nation and be the father of rulers but not in the same way as Isaac.

18:1-15 The main purpose of the coming of **the LORD** (Hb *Yahweh*, the personal name of God) Himself was the confirmation of the covenant in respect to a son conceived by Sarah. The passage involves another theophany or perhaps Christophany (see 16:7; 32:24; Jos 5:13-15; Jdg 13:18). Although Abraham's visitors had the appearance of **men**, one was clearly identified as "the LORD," perhaps the pre-incarnate Christ, and He directed the conversation, including the announcement of the birth of Isaac (Gn 18:2,10-14); He was accompanied by two others who were heavenly messengers or "angels" (19:1). At this point Abraham did not know who they were. But he did recognize that their coming was important. God does at times choose to reveal Himself by means of some physical manifestation that is representative of His presence. Accordingly, God assured His people of His presence without suggesting that He had a physical form as did they. Abraham himself welcomed the men eagerly and with honor, providing full hospitality (18:4-8) as was important in the ancient Near East.

18:2 Bowing **to the ground** was a traditional way of showing deep respect (cp. 19:1; 33:3; 48:12).

18:11-15 The words **Sarah** overheard made her laugh **to herself**. The idea was preposterous. **Delight** (Hb *'eden*, "pleasure") refers to the joy when a child comes into the world (cp. Ps 113:9; Jn 16:21). Her laugh was a mark of unbelief. The promises previously given had been quite clear (Gn 17:19,21). Sarah was probably still not aware of who the visitors were. But her expression may have been enough to give away her cynicism. There was a poignancy in her words. Sarah had grown **old** (Hb *balah*, "worn out"; cp. Jos 9:13). She was beyond the possibility of a normal conception because of her post-menopausal age. But with God no one is ever too **old** to be used according to His purposes.

18:17 The Lord came to inform Abraham of what He was about to do and that He allowed him to be an intercessor ("one who goes between," vv. 23-24), emphasizing Abraham's unique position in God's sight. As one among the new people of God, Abraham was introduced to God's plan for the nations and given his first opportunity to influence wider events through intercession.

18:23-33 One of the marks of Abraham's character is that he was concerned for his neighbors and willing even to risk the displeasure of Yahweh in order to help them. Even while the men went toward Sodom, Abraham pleaded for the city as he stood on the mountainside looking down on the cities of the plain before him (19:27-28). For as he looked down on the doomed cities, how could he fail to be stirred? He knew that God is merciful and will not be unfair in His actions toward men. Thus he made God's mercy the basis of his plea (18:23-25).

19:1 Sitting in the **gate** of the city suggests Lot was involved with the "elders" who helped to rule **Sodom** (cp. Ru 4:1-2). Lot's presence there indicated his importance to the community. He was now well settled in Sodom and had put down his roots, regardless of the behavior of its inhabitants. The gate of the city was probably a tower gate, possibly with two gates (cp. 2Sm 18:24) so that there was a space between the gates, protecting the way into the city. During the day this area would be used for business and as a courtroom for trying local offenders. In the evening men, especially the elders of the city, would gather there.

19:2 The men were making clear that they had not come specifically to see Lot. They were there to check out the city. The test was genuine. Sodom was being given a chance, even though a slight one. Perhaps they were also testing Lot, who knew what a dangerous place Sodom's street was for strangers. To Lot's credit, he would not be restrained. In contrast to the men of the city, there was still much good in him. He did not realize that he was

to you, and in about a year she will have a son."

15 Sarah denied it. "I did not laugh," she said, because she was afraid.

But He replied, "No, you did laugh."

16 The men got up from there and looked out over Sodom, and Abraham was walking with them to see them off. 17 Then the Lord said, "Should I hide what I am about to do from Abraham? 18 Abraham is to become a great and powerful nation, and all the nations of the earth will be blessed through him. 19 For I have chosen[A] him so that he will command his children and his house after him to keep the way of the Lord by doing what is right and just. This is how the Lord will fulfill to Abraham what He promised him." 20 Then the Lord said, "The outcry against Sodom and Gomorrah is immense, and their sin is extremely serious. 21 I will go down to see if what they have done justifies the cry that has come up to Me. If not, I will find out."

22 The men turned from there and went toward Sodom while Abraham remained standing before the Lord.[B] 23 Abraham stepped forward and said, "Will You really sweep away the righteous with the wicked? 24 What if there are 50 righteous people in the city? Will You really sweep it away instead of sparing the place for the sake of the 50 righteous people who are in it? 25 You could not possibly do such a thing: to kill the righteous with the wicked, treating the righteous and the wicked alike. You could not possibly do that! Won't the Judge of all the earth do what is just?"

26 The Lord said, "If I find 50 righteous people in the city of Sodom, I will spare the whole place for their sake."

27 Then Abraham answered, "Since I have ventured to speak to the Lord—even though I am dust and ashes— 28 suppose the 50 righteous lack five. Will you destroy the whole city for lack of five?"

He replied, "I will not destroy it if I find 45 there."

29 Then he spoke to Him again, "Suppose 40 are found there?"

He answered, "I will not do it on account of 40."

30 Then he said, "Let the Lord not be angry, and I will speak further. Suppose 30 are found there?"

He answered, "I will not do it if I find 30 there."

31 Then he said, "Since I have ventured to speak to the Lord, suppose 20 are found there?"

He replied, "I will not destroy it on account of 20."

32 Then he said, "Let the Lord not be angry, and I will speak one more time. Suppose 10 are found there?"

He answered, "I will not destroy it on account of 10." 33 When the Lord had finished speaking with Abraham, He departed, and Abraham returned to his place.

19 The two angels entered Sodom in the evening as Lot was sitting at Sodom's •gate. When Lot saw them, he got up to meet them. He bowed with his face to the ground 2 and said, "My lords, turn aside to your servant's house, wash your feet, and spend the night. Then you can get up early and go on your way."

"No," they said. "We would rather spend the night in the square." 3 But he urged them so strongly that they followed him and went into his house. He prepared a feast and baked unleavened bread for them, and they ate.

4 Before they went to bed, the men of the city of Sodom, both young and old, the whole population, surrounded the house. 5 They called out to Lot and said, "Where are the men who came to you tonight? Send them out to us so we can have sex with them!"

6 Lot went out to them at the entrance and shut the door behind him. 7 He said, "Don't do this evil, my brothers. 8 Look, I've got two daughters who haven't had sexual relations with a man. I'll bring them out to you, and you can do whatever you want[C] to them. However, don't

[A] **18:19** Lit *known* [B] **18:22** Ancient Jewish tradition reads *while the Lord remained standing before Abraham* [C] **19:8** Lit *do what is good in your eyes*

CHARACTER PROFILE

Lot's Wife A Disobedient Woman

Her Background	• She married Lot, a prominent and wealthy man. • She lived in Sodom, a large, prosperous, but very wicked city in the Jordan Valley.
Her Story	• She and her family were warned by angels to flee Sodom (19:12-13). • As they fled, an angel commanded them not to look back at the city (19:17). • She disobeyed and was turned into a pillar of salt (19:26).
Life Lessons	• She did not take the angels' warning seriously and disregarded their command. • Neither she nor Lot had obedient hearts toward the Lord.

do anything to these men, because
they have come under the protection of my roof."
9 "Get out of the way!" they said,
adding, "This one came here as
a foreigner, but he's acting like a
judge! Now we'll do more harm to
you than to them." They put pressure on Lot and came up to break
down the door. 10 But the angels[A]
reached out, brought Lot into the
house with them, and shut the door.
11 They struck the men who were
at the entrance of the house, both
young and old, with a blinding light
so that they were unable to find the
entrance.
12 Then the angels[A] said to Lot, "Do
you have anyone else here: a son-
in-law, your sons and daughters, or
anyone else in the city who belongs
to you? Get them out of this place,
13 for we are about to destroy this
place because the outcry against its
people is so great before the LORD,
that the LORD has sent us to destroy
it."
14 So Lot went out and spoke to
his sons-in-law, who were going to
marry[B] his daughters. "Get up," he
said. "Get out of this place, for the
LORD is about to destroy the city!"
But his sons-in-law thought he was
joking.
15 At daybreak the angels urged
Lot on: "Get up! Take your wife
and your two daughters who are
here, or you will be swept away in
the punishment[C] of the city." 16 But
he hesitated. Because of the LORD's
compassion for him, the men
grabbed his hand, his wife's hand,
and the hands of his two daughters.
Then they brought him out and left
him outside the city.
17 As soon as the angels got them
outside, one of them[D] said, "Run for
your lives! Don't look back and don't
stop anywhere on the plain! Run to
the mountains, or you will be swept
away!"
18 But Lot said to them, "No, my
lords[E]—please. 19 Your servant has
indeed found favor in your sight, and
you have shown me great kindness
by saving my life. But I can't run
to the mountains; the disaster will
overtake me, and I will die. 20 Look,
this town is close enough for me to
run to. It is a small place. Please let
me go there—it's only a small place,
isn't it?—so that I can survive."
21 And he said to him, "All right,[F]
I'll grant your request[G] about this
matter too and will not demolish the
town you mentioned. 22 Hurry up!
Run there, for I cannot do anything

passing God's test and proving himself the only one who was righteous.

19:3 In Lot's favor, he persisted in his attempts to help the visitors, even though he did not know who they were. He had given hospitality to the strangers (and deliberately so), and hospitality then meant that he was responsible for protecting them. The laws of hospitality were strongly ingrained, and for the men of Sodom to ignore them completely is further evidence of their wickedness.

19:8 Lot was determined to do his best to save the visitors. He knew he could not appeal to the men of the city on the basis of conscience so he resorted to desperate devices. Under the laws of hospitality, Lot had an even greater duty to the strangers than to his own **daughters**. Homosexuality was definitely part of the perversion in Sodom. Lot had no illusions about his fellow-citizens, but he was doing what he could.

19:14-15 The text refers to the men whom Lot urged to escape the city's destruction as his **sons-in-law**, indicating that either Lot had other daughters who had already married or he had at home two virgin daughters who had been betrothed to these men (v. 8). If they were pledged to marry Lot's daughters, the effort made to include them as family members in the escape illustrates the binding nature of betrothal arrangements in early history. The serious nature of the marriage covenant, even before its consummation both in a public wedding and in the privacy of the nuptial bed, sheds light on the New Testament account of Joseph's initial plan to "divorce" Mary the mother of Jesus when he first learned of her pregnancy (Mt 1:18-21).

[A]19:10,12 Lit *men* [B]19:14 Lit *take* [C]19:15 Or *iniquity*, or *guilt* [D]19:17 LXX, Syr, Vg read *outside, they* [E]19:18 Or *My Lord*, or *My lords* [F]19:21 Or *Look!* [G]19:21 Lit *I will lift up your face*

19:23 In 14:2, Zoar (Hb "insignificance, small place") was called "Bela" (Hb "Destruction"). It may well have been that what was left following the destruction resulted in the change of its name to "insignificance." The writer saw the irony of the situation.

19:24-26 Later extrabiblical literature refers to a disaster in this area, but the sites of these cities are as yet unknown. Lot's wife may not have been a native Sodomite, but Sodom gripped her heart. Sin contaminates, grows, spreads, and then becomes all pervasive—and then God's judgment falls.

19:32 The daughters' immoral plan was not only an act of desperation but also the inevitable result of minds immersed in and perverted by a godless society. They felt totally estranged from the world outside. Yet the importance of seed to continue the family totally absorbed their minds. The firstborn had one fixation, to have a child; and she persuaded her sister to do the same. She saw hope only in her solutions. There was no thought of looking to God.

19:37-38 There is little doubt that these incestuous unions would later influence the attitude of the Israelites toward the **Moabites** and the **Ammonites**. This incident may have been partly the impetus for later prohibitions (Dt 23:3-6; Neh 13:1). Etymological conjectures suggest the name **Moab** means "of or from his father." **Ben-ammi** means "son of my kinship." Although Israel was initially required to spare these nations because of their common ancestry (Dt 2:9,19-21,37), a long history of hostility existed between Israel and these nations with incestuous origins. Interestingly, the union of Ruth the Moabitess with Boaz, the descendant of Judah, seemed to reconcile the alienated families of Lot and Abraham, respectively (Ru 4:13,18-22).

20:2 This incident compares with that in 12:10-20; but apart from the claim that Sarah is Abraham's sister, (see another instance, 20:12-13), and the taking of Sarah by another man, there are no similarities between the accounts. Each fits adequately into its respective setting. Sarah was a very beautiful woman, even in her old age.

20:3 The use of **God** rather than Yahweh in this passage is noteworthy. To Abimelech, Yahweh was not God, nor would God approach Abimelech as Yahweh, the covenant God. But Abimelech accepted that his dream came from a divine being. Abimelech's real crime is that he had taken a woman for the purpose of making her his wife without due inquiry as to her status. He

until you get there." Therefore the name of the city is Zoar.[A]

23 The sun had risen over the land when Lot reached Zoar. 24 Then out of the sky the LORD rained burning sulfur on Sodom and Gomorrah from the LORD. 25 He demolished these cities, the entire plain, all the inhabitants of the cities, and whatever grew on the ground. 26 But his wife looked back and became a pillar of salt.

27 Early in the morning Abraham went to the place where he had stood before the LORD. 28 He looked down toward Sodom and Gomorrah and all the land of the plain, and he saw that smoke was going up from the land like the smoke of a furnace. 29 So it was, when God destroyed the cities of the plain, He remembered Abraham and brought Lot out of the middle of the upheaval when He demolished the cities where Lot had lived.

30 Lot departed from Zoar and lived in the mountains along with his two daughters, because he was afraid to live in Zoar. Instead, he and his two daughters lived in a cave. 31 Then the firstborn said to the younger, "Our father is old, and there is no man in the land to sleep with us as is the custom of all the land. 32 Come, let's get our father to drink wine so that we can sleep with him and preserve our father's line." 33 So they got their father to drink wine that night, and the firstborn came and slept with her father; he did not know when she lay down or when she got up.

34 The next day the firstborn said to the younger, "Look, I slept with my father last night. Let's get him to drink wine again tonight so you can go sleep with him and we can preserve our father's line." 35 That night they again got their father to drink wine, and the younger went and slept with him; he did not know when she lay down or when she got up.

36 So both of Lot's daughters became pregnant by their father. 37 The firstborn gave birth to a son and named him Moab.[B] He is the father of the Moabites of today. 38 The younger also gave birth to a son, and she named him Ben-ammi.[C] He is the father of the Ammonites of today.

20 From there Abraham traveled to the region of the •Negev and settled between Kadesh and Shur. While he lived in Gerar, 2 Abraham said about his wife Sarah, "She is my sister." So Abimelech king of Gerar had Sarah brought to him.

3 But God came to Abimelech in a dream by night and said to him, "You are about to die because of the woman you have taken, for she is a married woman."[D]

4 Now Abimelech had not approached her, so he said, "Lord, would You destroy a nation even though it is innocent? 5 Didn't he himself say to me, 'She is my sister'? And she herself said, 'He is my brother.' I did this with a clear conscience[E] and •clean[F] hands."

6 Then God said to him in the dream, "Yes, I know that you did this with a clear conscience.[G] I have also kept you from sinning against Me. Therefore I have not let you touch her. 7 Now return the man's wife, for he is a prophet, and he will pray for you and you will live. But if you do not return her, know that you will certainly die, you and all who are yours."

8 Early in the morning Abimelech got up, called all his servants together, and personally[H] told them all these things, and the men were terrified.

9 Then Abimelech called Abraham in and said to him, "What have you done to us? How did I sin against you that you have brought such enormous •guilt on me and on my kingdom? You have done things to me that should never be done." 10 Abimelech also said to Abraham, "What did you intend when you did this thing?"

11 Abraham replied, "I thought, 'There is absolutely no •fear of God in this place. They will kill me be-

[A]**19:22** In Hb, the name Zoar is related to the phrase "small place" in v. 20; its original name was Bela; Gn 14:2. [B]**19:37** = From My Father [C]**19:38** = Son of My People [D]**20:3** Lit *is possessed by a husband* [E]**20:5** Lit *with integrity of my heart* [F]**20:5** Lit *cleanness of my* [G]**20:6** Lit *with integrity of your heart* [H]**20:8** Lit *in their ears*

cause of my wife.' 12 Besides, she really is my sister, the daughter of my father though not the daughter of my mother, and she became my wife. 13 So when God had me wander from my father's house, I said to her: Show your loyalty to me wherever we go and say about me: 'He's my brother.'"

14 Then Abimelech took sheep and cattle and male and female slaves, gave them to Abraham, and returned his wife Sarah to him. 15 Abimelech said, "Look, my land is before you. Settle wherever you want."[A] 16 And he said to Sarah, "Look, I am giving your brother 1,000 pieces of silver. It is a verification of your honor[B] to all who are with you. You are fully vindicated."

17 Then Abraham prayed to God, and God healed Abimelech, his wife, and his female slaves so that they could bear children, 18 for the LORD had completely closed all the wombs in Abimelech's household on account of Sarah, Abraham's wife.

21 The LORD came to Sarah as He had said, and the LORD did for Sarah what He had promised. 2 Sarah became pregnant and bore a son to Abraham in his old age, at the appointed time God had told him. 3 Abraham named his son who was born to him—the one Sarah bore to him—Isaac. 4 When his son Isaac was eight days old, Abraham circumcised him, as God had commanded him. 5 Abraham was 100 years old when his son Isaac was born to him.

6 Sarah said, "God has made me laugh, and everyone who hears will laugh with me."[C] 7 She also said, "Who would have told Abraham that Sarah would nurse children? Yet I have borne a son for him[D] in his old age."

8 The child grew and was weaned, and Abraham held a great feast on the day Isaac was weaned. 9 But Sarah saw the son mocking[E]—the one Hagar the Egyptian had borne to Abraham. 10 So she said to Abraham, "Drive out this slave with her son, for the son of this slave will not be a coheir with my son Isaac!"

11 Now this was a very difficult thing for[F] Abraham because of his son. 12 But God said to Abraham, "Do not be concerned[G] about the boy and your slave. Whatever Sarah says to you, listen to her, because your •offspring will be traced through Isaac. 13 But I will also make a nation of the slave's son because he is your offspring."

14 Early in the morning Abraham got up, took bread and a waterskin, put them on Hagar's shoulders, and sent her and the boy away.[H] She left and wandered in the Wilderness of Beer-sheba. 15 When the water in the skin was gone, she left the boy under one of the bushes. 16 Then she went and sat down nearby, about a bowshot away, for she said, "I can't bear to watch the boy die!" So as she sat nearby, she[I] wept loudly.

17 God heard the voice of the boy, and the[J] angel of God called to Hagar from heaven and said to her, "What's wrong, Hagar? Don't be afraid, for God has heard the voice of the boy from the place where he is. 18 Get up, help the boy up, and support him, for I will make him a great nation." 19 Then God opened her eyes, and she saw a well of water. So she went and filled the waterskin and gave the boy a drink. 20 God was with the boy, and he grew; he settled in the wilderness and became an archer. 21 He settled in the Wilderness of Paran, and his mother got a wife for him from the land of Egypt.

22 At that time Abimelech, accompanied by Phicol the commander of his army, said to Abraham, "God is with you in everything you do. 23 Swear to me by God here and now, that you will not break an agreement with me or with my children and descendants. As I have been loyal to you, so you will be loyal to me and to the country where you are a foreign resident."

24 And Abraham said, "I swear it." 25 But Abraham complained to

[A]20:15 Lit *Settle in the good in your eyes* [B]20:16 Lit *a covering of the eyes* [C]21:6 Isaac = He laughs; Gn 17:19 [D]21:7 Sam, Tg Jonathan; MT omits *him* [E]21:9 LXX, Vg add *Isaac her son* [F]21:11 Lit *was very bad in the eyes of* [G]21:12 Lit *Let it not be bad in your eyes* [H]21:14 To "send away" a woman = divorce her; Dt 24:1. To "send away" a slave = free her; Dt 15:13. [I]21:16 LXX reads *the boy* [J]21:17 Or *an*

was misled, but his peremptory action prevented him from learning the truth. But no man of ancient times would fail to see that what he had done, though accidental, was a crime.

20:11-13 Abraham might have been afraid, but now his deception has been revealed. He had thought there was no fear of God here, but events have proven he was totally wrong.

21:9 Though the word translated **mocking** can have a variety of meanings, it really indicates enjoying or amusing oneself. This could be totally innocent or at the expense of others (cp. its use in 19:14).

21:10-11 Sarah's swift and severe response suggests some inappropriate behavior by Ishmael, though she may well have overreacted because of her own jealousy.

21:12-13 God's approval of the plan must indicate that there were grounds for the expulsion (even granted that it was within His purpose).

21:14 The emphasis is on the expulsion of Hagar herself. Ishmael could not forget that Abraham sent his mother away. He grieved, not for himself—for he was possibly aware that he had committed some fault—but for her. The word for **boy** is neutral; it can be equally used to designate a young man.

21:15-18 The **water** ran out, and even the hardiest person cannot survive without water. Hagar could not bear to watch Ishmael die; yet she could not bear to leave him.

21:20-21 Ishmael soon learned to adapt to his surroundings and became a wilderness wanderer and a hunter both of man and beast as he lived out his precarious existence. The wilderness in which he established himself, and later his family, was the **Wilderness of Paran**, between Canaan and Egypt in the Sinai region near the Gulf of Aqabah. The hand of his mother continued to influence him as she selected a wife for him from Egypt. Throughout her life Hagar was a strong-minded, resourceful woman. Later a tribe called the Hagrites were connected with the tents of Edom and the Ishmaelites and with Moab (Ps 83:6). See also 1Ch 5:10,19 where they were connected with Jetur and Naphish, sons of Ishmael (Gn 25:15).

21:22 The names **Abimelech** and **Phicol** (Hb, "mouth of all") were titles assumed by the leader and military captain of the group.

21:31 **Beer-sheba** (Hb "the well of seven" or "well of the oath") reminded

Abimelech because of the water well that Abimelech's servants had seized.

26 Abimelech replied, "I don't know who did this thing. You didn't report anything to me, so I hadn't heard about it until today."

27 Abraham took sheep and cattle[A] and gave them to Abimelech, and the two of them made a covenant. 28 Abraham separated seven ewe lambs from the flock. 29 And Abimelech said to Abraham, "Why have you separated these seven ewe lambs?"

30 He replied, "You are to accept the seven ewe lambs from my hand so that this act[B] will serve as my witness that I dug this well." 31 Therefore that place was called Beer-sheba[C] because it was there that the two of them swore an oath. 32 After they had made a covenant at Beer-sheba, Abimelech and Phicol, the commander of his army, left and returned to the land of the Philistines.

33 Abraham planted a tamarisk tree in Beer-sheba, and there he called on the name of •Yahweh, the Everlasting God. 34 And Abraham lived as a foreigner in the land of the Philistines for many days.

22 After these things God tested Abraham and said to him, "Abraham!"

"Here I am," he answered.

2 "Take your son," He said, "your only son Isaac, whom you love, go to the land of Moriah, and offer him there as a •burnt offering on one of the mountains I will tell you about."

3 So Abraham got up early in the morning, saddled his donkey, and took with him two of his young men and his son Isaac. He split wood for a burnt offering and set out to go to the place God had told him about. 4 On the third day Abraham looked up and saw the place in the distance. 5 Then Abraham said to his young men, "Stay here with the donkey. The boy and I will go over there to worship; then we'll come back to you." 6 Abraham took the wood for the burnt offering and laid it on his son Isaac. In his hand he took the fire and the sacrificial knife,[D] and the two of them walked on together.

7 Then Isaac spoke to his father Abraham and said, "My father."

And he replied, "Here I am, my son."

Isaac said, "The fire and the wood are here, but where is the lamb for the burnt offering?"

8 Abraham answered, "God Himself will provide[E] the lamb for the burnt offering, my son." Then the two of them walked on together.

9 When they arrived at the place that God had told him about, Abraham built the altar there and arranged the wood. He bound his son Isaac[F] and placed him on the altar on top of the wood. 10 Then Abraham reached out and took the knife to slaughter his son.

11 But the Angel of the LORD called to him from heaven and said, "Abraham, Abraham!"

He replied, "Here I am."

12 Then He said, "Do not lay a hand on the boy or do anything to him. For now I know that you •fear God, since you have not withheld

HARD QUESTION

Why would God test Abraham?

Abraham was called by Yahweh to leave his home, his extended family, and his country to go to a new land, which God had prepared for him. His spiritual life was not smooth. He was not without testing. The very call itself was a test. The long wait for Isaac was a test. The incident of Sodom and Gomorrah was a test. But Abraham came through it all with his faith enhanced. Now he would face the greatest test of all. The ultimate test of faith would be administered by God and embraced by His servant Abraham, and the result would be supreme victory and an incomparable testimony. The event in this narrative (22:1-18) demonstrated that, whatever the cost, Abraham was willing to obey Yahweh and would not withhold from Him what he treasured most. Just as important is the testimony of God's faithfulness and providential care. God did not test Abraham to try to find the weak point at which His servant would fail, but rather He showed the testimony of His faithful child whose faith had matured.

both sides of the treaty made and sealed by the giving of the seven ewe lambs. The name was eventually applied to a city that still exists today (26:33).

21:32 This is the first mention of **Philistines** as being in the land. Some have doubted this on the grounds that the Philistines arrived later in the twelfth century B.C. in the wave of Sea Peoples, invading the coasts of Lebanon, ancient Phoenicia, and others, as well as sweeping down through the coastal plains of the Levant and troubling Egypt. As a ruling nation and a threat to others in Canaan, the presence of the Philistines commenced in the twelfth century B.C., but the peoples from whom they came were certainly in the ancient Near East before then. There is clear archaeological evidence of trade between Caphtor (home of the Philistines—see Gn 10:14; Jr 47:4; Am 9:7) and the mainland around this time, including trade with Ugarit, Hazor, and Egypt. A tablet from Mari (eighteenth century B.C.) records the sending of gifts from the king of Hazor to Kaptara (Caphtor). Therefore, trading by people from Caphtor, from whom came the Philistines, in Canaan on the route between Mesopotamia and Egypt around this time is not unlikely (Jr 47:4; Am 9:7). They were a sea people, and, in the time of Abraham, that name could easily apply to the people of Caphtor.

22:2 The land of Moriah is a region or range of mountains located just north of the ancient city of David (2Ch 3:1-2), in the territory where the temple would later be built. Abraham referred to the site, not as Moriah (which some translate as "the place of the appearance of Yahweh"), but as "The LORD Will Provide" (Hb *Yahweh yir'ēh*, v. 14). The emphasis that God was asking for the ultimate sacrifice—**your son, your only son Isaac, whom you love**—a spiritual test. The emphasis is not that he was the covenant son but that he was the only beloved son, the reminder of another only beloved Son who was sacrificed on our behalf. Isaac was not literally his "only son," but "the heir," the only son of the covenant marriage. Abraham was called to offer not only the person dearest to his heart but the one through whom all the covenant promises were to be fulfilled (17:19,21).

22:6-8 Abraham's confidence was in the Lord; Isaac's confidence was in understanding that his father could do him no harm.

22:11-13 The Angel of the LORD (Hb *Yahweh*) is clearly God Himself, for He says, **Now I know that you fear God, since you have not withheld your**

[A]**21:27** A covenant or treaty was regularly ratified by animal sacrifice (Gn 8:20–9:9; 15:9-17; Ex 24:8) and often involved an exchange of gifts (1Kg 15:19; Hs 12:1). The animals here could serve both purposes. [B]**21:30** Lit *that it* [C]**21:31** = Well of the Oath, or Seven Wells [D]**22:6** The same word is used in Jdg 19:29 and Pr 30:14. [E]**22:8** Lit *see* [F]**22:9** Or *Isaac hand and foot*

your only son from Me." 13 Abraham
looked up and saw a ram[A] caught in
the thicket by its horns. So Abraham
went and took the ram and offered
it as a burnt offering in place of his
son. 14 And Abraham named that
place The LORD Will Provide,[B] so today it is said: "It will be provided[C] on
the LORD's mountain."
15 Then the Angel of the LORD
called to Abraham a second time
from heaven 16 and said, "By Myself I
have sworn," this is the LORD's declaration: "Because you have done this
thing and have not withheld your
only son,[D] 17 I will indeed bless you
and make your •offspring as numerous as the stars of the sky and the
sand on the seashore. Your offspring
will possess the gates of their enemies. 18 And all the nations of the
earth will be blessed[E] by your offspring because you have obeyed My
command."
19 Abraham went back to his young
men, and they got up and went together to Beer-sheba. And Abraham
settled in Beer-sheba.
20 Now after these things Abraham
was told, "Milcah also has borne
sons to your brother Nahor: 21 Uz his
firstborn, his brother Buz, Kemuel
the father of Aram, 22 Chesed, Hazo,
Pildash, Jidlaph, and Bethuel."
23 And Bethuel fathered Rebekah.
Milcah bore these eight to Nahor,
Abraham's brother. 24 His concubine,
whose name was Reumah, also bore
Tebah, Gaham, Tahash, and Maacah.

23 Now Sarah lived 127 years;
these were all the years of her
life. 2 Sarah died in Kiriath-arba
(that is, Hebron) in the land of Canaan, and Abraham went to mourn
for Sarah and to weep for her.
3 Then Abraham got up from beside his dead wife and spoke to the
Hittites:[F] 4 "I am a foreign resident
among you. Give me a burial site
among you so that I can bury my
dead."[G]
5 The Hittites replied to Abraham,[H]
6 "Listen to us, lord.[I] You are God's
chosen one[J] among us. Bury your
dead in our finest burial place.[K]
None of us will withhold from you
his burial place for burying your
dead."
7 Then Abraham rose and bowed
down to the Hittites, the people of
the land. 8 He said to them, "If you
are willing for me to bury my dead,
listen to me and ask Ephron son of
Zohar on my behalf 9 to give me the
cave of Machpelah that belongs to
him; it is at the end of his field. Let
him give it to me in your presence,
for the full price, as a burial place."
10 Ephron was sitting among the
Hittites. So in the presence[L] of all
the Hittites who came to the •gate
of his city, Ephron the Hittite answered Abraham: 11 "No, my lord.
Listen to me. I give you the field,
and I give you the cave that is in it. I
give it to you in the presence[M] of my
people. Bury your dead."
12 Abraham bowed down to the
people of the land 13 and said to
Ephron in the presence[L] of the people of the land, "Please listen to me.
Let me pay the price of the field. Accept it from me, and let me bury my
dead there."
14 Ephron answered Abraham and
said to him, 15 "My lord, listen to
me. Land worth 400 •shekels of silver—what is that between you and
me? Bury your dead." 16 Abraham
agreed with Ephron, and Abraham
weighed out to Ephron the silver that
he had agreed to in the presence[L] of
the Hittites: 400 shekels of silver at
the current commercial rate. 17 So
Ephron's field at Machpelah near
Mamre—the field with its cave and
all the trees anywhere within the
boundaries of the field—became
18 Abraham's possession in the presence of all the Hittites who came to
the gate of his city. 19 After this, Abraham buried his wife Sarah in the cave
of the field at Machpelah near Mamre
(that is, Hebron) in the land of Canaan. 20 The field with its cave passed
from the Hittites to Abraham as a
burial place.

only son from Me (v. 12). God did not need to be convinced of Abraham's faithfulness. In His omniscience, He knew Abraham's heart. Rather, this experience gave Abraham the opportunity to demonstrate that faith to the world. Abraham's testimony was clear: He would hold nothing back from God, whatever the cost.

22:14 The naming of a place was an important matter in the ancient world, especially when it commemorated a theophany. Such a place became accepted as sacred. Here the naming was private. It would always be sacred to Abraham but would not be known to the world. **The LORD Will Provide** (Hb *Yahweh yir'eh*, "God sees") is a name that communicates clearly the fact that God sees your need before it becomes apparent to you, and He makes provision for what will be needed.

22:20-24 Milcah was the daughter of Haran, who had died young and she was married to Nahor (11:29) and bore him eight sons. The family generations were carefully laid out in preparation for obtaining a bride for Isaac. The continual emphasis was on Rebekah's relationship with Nahor in order to establish that she was a suitable wife for Isaac.

23:1-2 The specific reason for Sarah's presence in Hebron is not stated in the text. Abraham and his family were nomadic, especially when their herds prompted movement. Sarah is distinguished as the only woman whose age at death is recorded in Scripture. The mourning rites associated with death were considered very important, and paid mourners would often be employed (cp. Gn 50:10; Jr 9:17). The phrase **went to mourn for Sarah and to weep for her** thus refers to Abraham as coming to prepare for her funeral.

23:19-20 The record summarizes with satisfaction the successful conclusion of the transaction, noting that Abraham now owned property in the land promised to him for future generations. The parenthetical mention of **Hebron** is a typical scribal explanation added to explain to future generations the whereabouts of the site mentioned.

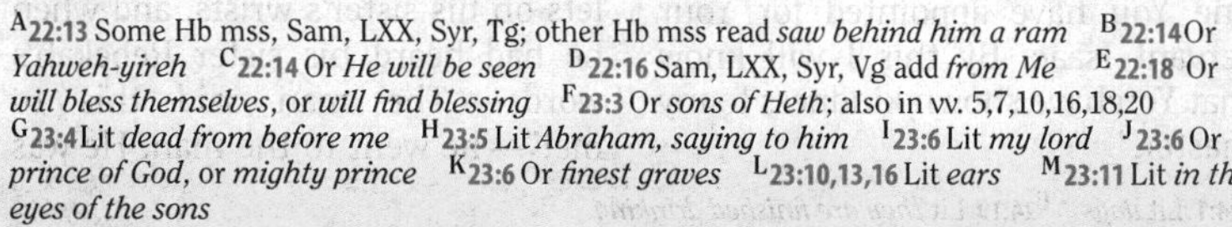

[A] **22:13** Some Hb mss, Sam, LXX, Syr, Tg; other Hb mss read *saw behind him a ram* [B] **22:14** Or *Yahweh-yireh* [C] **22:14** Or *He will be seen* [D] **22:16** Sam, LXX, Syr, Vg add *from Me* [E] **22:18** Or *will bless themselves*, or *will find blessing* [F] **23:3** Or *sons of Heth*; also in vv. 5,7,10,16,18,20 [G] **23:4** Lit *dead from before me* [H] **23:5** Lit *Abraham, saying to him* [I] **23:6** Lit *my lord* [J] **23:6** Or *prince of God*, or *mighty prince* [K] **23:6** Or *finest graves* [L] **23:10,13,16** Lit *ears* [M] **23:11** Lit *in the eyes of the sons*

24 Abraham was now old, getting
on in years,[A] and the LORD had
blessed him in everything. 2 Abraham said to his servant, the elder of
his household who managed all he
owned, "Place your hand under my
thigh, 3 and I will have you swear by
the LORD, God of heaven and God of
earth, that you will not take a wife
for my son from the daughters of
the Canaanites among whom I live,
4 but will go to my land and my family to take a wife for my son Isaac."
5 The servant said to him, "Suppose the woman is unwilling to follow me to this land? Should I have
your son go back to the land you
came from?"
6 Abraham answered him, "Make
sure that you don't take my son back
there. 7 The LORD, the God of heaven,
who took me from my father's house
and from my native land, who spoke
to me and swore to me, 'I will give
this land to your •offspring'—He
will send His angel before you, and
you can take a wife for my son from
there. 8 If the woman is unwilling to
follow you, then you are free from
this oath to me, but don't let my
son go back there." 9 So the servant
placed his hand under his master
Abraham's thigh and swore an oath
to him concerning this matter.
10 The servant took 10 of his master's camels and departed with all
kinds of his master's goods in hand.
Then he set out for Nahor's town
Aram-naharaim. 11 He made the
camels kneel beside a well of water
outside the town at evening. This
was the time when the women went
out to draw water.
12 "LORD, God of my master Abraham," he prayed, "give me success
today, and show kindness to my
master Abraham. 13 I am standing
here at the spring where the daughters of the men of the town are coming out to draw water. 14 Let the girl
to whom I say, 'Please lower your
water jug so that I may drink,' and
who responds, 'Drink, and I'll water
your camels also'—let her be the
one You have appointed for Your
servant Isaac. By this I will know
that You have shown kindness to my
master."
15 Before he had finished speaking, there was Rebekah—daughter
of Bethuel son of Milcah, the wife of
Abraham's brother Nahor—coming
with a jug on her shoulder. 16 Now
the girl was very beautiful, a young
woman who had not known a man
intimately. She went down to the
spring, filled her jug, and came up.
17 Then the servant ran to meet her
and said, "Please let me have a little
water from your jug."
18 She replied, "Drink, my lord."
She quickly lowered her jug to her
hand and gave him a drink. 19 When
she had finished giving him a drink,
she said, "I'll also draw water for your
camels until they have had enough
to drink."[B] 20 She quickly emptied
her jug into the trough and hurried
to the well again to draw water. She
drew water for all his camels 21 while
the man silently watched her to see
whether or not the LORD had made
his journey a success.
22 After the camels had finished
drinking, the man took a gold ring
weighing half a •shekel, and for her
wrists two bracelets weighing 10
shekels of gold. 23 "Whose daughter
are you?" he asked. "Please tell me,
is there room in your father's house
for us to spend the night?"
24 She answered him, "I am the
daughter of Bethuel son of Milcah,
whom she bore to Nahor." 25 She
also said to him, "We have plenty of
straw and feed and a place to spend
the night."
26 Then the man bowed down, worshiped the LORD, 27 and said, "Praise
the LORD, the God of my master
Abraham, who has not withheld His
kindness and faithfulness from my
master. As for me, the LORD has led
me on the journey to the house of
my master's relatives."
28 The girl ran and told her mother's household about these things.
29 Now Rebekah had a brother
named Laban, and Laban ran out to
the man at the spring. 30 As soon as
he had seen the ring and the bracelets on his sister's wrists, and when
he had heard his sister Rebekah's
words—"The man said this to
me!"—he went to the man. He was

[A]**24:1** Lit *days* [B]**24:19** Lit *they are finished drinking*

24:1-4 What seemed to be the end of an era with the death of Sarah and the aging of Abraham was really the springboard to the future advancement of the covenant promises. A portion of the land now belonged to the family of Abraham, and Isaac would be provided with a God-appointed bride who also came from the patriarchal line.

Sarah's death had reminded Abraham of his own mortality. Placing a **hand under** a **thigh**, also found among the Babylonians, was a recognized method of sealing an oath (cp. 24:2 with 47:29). The **thigh,** considered the seat of procreative power, was thus symbolic of the solemnity of the oath. The effect was to swear by the whole family since the procreative power and heritage is the source of the family. Abraham had a strong sense of family and understood God's command not to marry outside His chosen people (see Dt 7:1-4). The maintenance of the spiritual formation of the family is paramount. The Semitic line seemed designated for a godly tradition in contrast to the Canaanites, who were Hamites. Compare how Abraham married his half-sister and Nahor married his brother's daughter with the continual insistence on marriage within the extended familial group. Compare also Isaac's grief at the marriage of Esau outside the family (Gn 26:34-35). Yahweh was preserving the covenant with His people through whom His promises would be fulfilled. This truth is confirmed by the fact that Abraham did not have the same concern about the marriages of the sons borne to him by other wives. Isaac's wife had to know and trust Yahweh and thus share a common faith with her husband.

24:9-10 Ten **camels** would suggest great wealth. The town of **Nahor, Aram-naharaim** (lit "Aram between the two rivers," commonly known as Mesopotamia) was probably Haran (11:31; 27:43), undoubtedly associated with its most illustrious citizen. Haran, a center for moon worship, was situated on the river Balikh, a tributary of the upper Euphrates.

24:12-14 These all-important words form the basis of the agreement that the steward made with Yahweh, Abraham's covenant God, whom the steward reverently charged to act now to ensure the covenant succession. The servant outlined the terms by which he would understand Yahweh's response. God wants His children to interact with Him, even allowing them to challenge Him, with the understanding that in the end, the terms are always His. **Show kindness to my master Abraham** is again a reverent but solemn charge that God would act toward Abraham in accordance with His covenant promises. **Kindness** (Hb *chesed*; see

CHARACTER PROFILE

Rebekah A Chosen Wife

Her Background	• Her family lived in Haran and was part of Abraham's extended family there. • She was chosen by God to be Isaac's wife (24:14). • She was the mother of twin sons, Esau and Jacob, who were the progenitors of two nations (25:23).
Her Story	• She became pregnant with twins after years of infertility (25:21). • She favored Jacob, the younger son, over Esau, who was favored by Isaac (25:28). • She deceived her blind husband into giving Jacob the covenant blessing due the firstborn, stealing it from Esau (chap. 27).
Life Lessons	• Parental favoritism brings heartache, resentment, and estrangement. • Trusting God for your child's future will never involve manipulation or deceit.

standing there by the camels at the spring.

31 Laban said, "Come, you who are blessed by the LORD. Why are you standing out here? I have prepared the house and a place for the camels." 32 So the man came to the house, and the camels were unloaded. Straw and feed were given to the camels, and water was brought to wash his feet and the feet of the men with him.

33 A meal was set before him, but he said, "I will not eat until I have said what I have to say."

So Laban said, "Please speak."

34 "I am Abraham's servant," he said. 35 "The LORD has greatly blessed my master, and he has become rich. He has given him sheep and cattle, silver and gold, male and female slaves, and camels and donkeys. 36 Sarah, my master's wife, bore a son to my master in her[A] old age, and he has given him everything he owns. 37 My master put me under this oath: 'You will not take a wife for my son from the daughters of the Canaanites in whose land I live 38 but will go to my father's household and to my family to take a wife for my son.' 39 But I said to my master, 'Suppose the woman will not come back with me?' 40 He said to me, 'The LORD before whom I have walked will send His angel with you and make your journey a success, and you will take a wife for my son from my family and from my father's household. 41 Then you will be free from my oath if you go to my family and they do not give her to you—you will be free from my oath.'

42 "Today when I came to the spring, I prayed: LORD, God of my master Abraham, if only You will make my journey successful! 43 I am standing here at a spring. Let the virgin who comes out to draw water, and I say to her: Please let me drink a little water from your jug, 44 and who responds to me, 'Drink, and I'll draw water for your camels also'—let her be the woman the LORD has appointed for my master's son.

45 "Before I had finished praying silently, there was Rebekah coming with her jug on her shoulder, and she went down to the spring and drew water. So I said to her: Please let me have a drink. 46 She quickly lowered her jug from her shoulder and said, 'Drink, and I'll water your

[A]24:36 Sam, LXX read *his*

Word Study, p. 322) is a reference to covenant faithfulness and love. The test was then outlined.

24:15 Before he had finished speaking, there was an immediate response. Out to the well came Rebekah, a kinswoman of Abraham, specifically his great-niece. The family details refer back to the opening genealogy (22:23). The mention of her grandmother **Milcah** confirms that Rebekah descended from Nahor's wife, not his concubine (22:20-24). Though important as a member of a prominent family who doubtless had many household servants, Rebekah was not too important to carry a jug of water for her family.

24:16 The family of Terah appears to have produced beautiful women. Rebekah was attractive and pure, described as **a young woman who had not known a man intimately** (Hb *betulah*; see note on 1Kg 1:1-4). This description is important since part of God's covenant concerns the future lineage of Isaac. Though *betulah* specifically refers to a young woman still in her father's household, the traditional usage would overwhelmingly support sexual purity. In Rebekah's case, her purity was supported in the overall description of her in Scripture (see also Gn 24:43).

24:18-25 The well was a large, deep hole in the ground with steps leading down to the spring. Clearly there was a **trough** by the well for the watering of animals. Without hesitation Rebekah fulfilled the servant's requirements, which were included in the pact he had made with Yahweh. Ten camels would take a lot of satisfying, which was a testimony to her hospitable spirit, a character trait highly honored in the ancient world. However, she must also have been impressed with the evidence of wealth surrounding the servant.

Abraham's servant must have experienced a mounting excitement as he watched Rebekah carry out her watering service. The text says that **the LORD had made his journey a success**.

24:29-53 The responsibility for bringing the matter to its conclusion was rightly taken by Rebekah's brother **Laban**. The servant explained the terms and details of his commission, making clear in the meanwhile the splendid assets of the intended bridegroom. He was the son of Abraham and Sarah, both of whom were related to Nahor and well known to them. Moreover the wealth and success of Abraham was clear as well as the fact that Isaac was his heir, making him a worthy husband for Rebekah. The servant straightforwardly acknowledged that he was acting under oath. At this decisive turning point, Laban acknowledged that God had clearly taken control; and, therefore, he could not go against the Lord (vv. 50-53).

24:54-58 The detailing of arrangements was handled by Laban and Milcah, Rebekah's mother. Although most ancient Near Eastern marriages were arranged by the family, the contracts of some (Hurrians or Horites in Mesopotamia) required the bride's consent. Abraham must have been aware of this (v. 8). In the end Rebekah had a voice. She understood that the question concerned her immediate departure and agreed to go.

24:59-60 Rebekah, as a daughter of the family patriarch, was accompanied by a mature female attendant (a nurse who probably would have had responsibility for her upbringing from birth) and a number of young women to attend and watch over her.

24:62 No mention is made of the return to Abraham, which may have taken place before this incident; for Isaac was south of Beer-sheba in **the Negev region**, almost at the Egyptian border. After his father's death, Isaac went to live at **Beer-lahai-roi** (Hb, "A Well of the Living One Who Sees Me" or "The Well of Him Who Sees Me and Lives"; cp. 16:13-14), where the pregnant Hagar met the Angel of the Lord when she was returning to Egypt.

24:64-67 Rebekah had been traveling unveiled, but now modesty required that she veil herself to meet her betrothed for the first time, according to the ancient Near Eastern custom of unveiling after marriage. Rebekah took the place of Isaac's mother as the matriarch through whom God would fulfill His covenant. Whether she actually used Sarah's tent is really irrelevant, although it is very likely. The new position she received as Isaac's wife is of greatest importance. The phrase **brought her into the tent** is considered by some to be an idiom suggesting sexual intimacy, and the reference is greatly enriched with the statement **Isaac loved her**. Isaac was **comforted after his mother's death**. He missed his mother and found solace in the arms of Rebekah.

25:1-6 This chapter presents the transition from Abraham to Isaac. The exact time Abraham married Keturah is not explicitly stated. She was called a wife, but some commentators suggest that she was a concubine (see 1Ch 1:32), perhaps because she was not on the same footing with Sarah, who was the mother of Isaac. Polygamy was unacceptable to God and was fraught with sorrows for families. The descendants of both Keturah and of Hagar proved troublesome to Israel.

camels also.' So I drank, and she also watered the camels. 47 Then I asked her: Whose daughter are you? She responded, 'The daughter of Bethuel son of Nahor, whom Milcah bore to him.' So I put the ring on her nose and the bracelets on her wrists. 48 Then I bowed down, worshiped the LORD, and praised the LORD, the God of my master Abraham, who guided me on the right way to take the granddaughter of my master's brother for his son. 49 Now, if you are going to show kindness and faithfulness to my master, tell me; if not, tell me, and I will go elsewhere."[A]

50 Laban and Bethuel answered, "This is from the LORD; we have no choice in the matter.[B] 51 Rebekah is here in front of you. Take her and go, and let her be a wife for your master's son, just as the LORD has spoken."

52 When Abraham's servant heard their words, he bowed to the ground before the LORD. 53 Then he brought out objects of silver and gold, and garments, and gave them to Rebekah. He also gave precious gifts to her brother and her mother. 54 Then he and the men with him ate and drank and spent the night.

When they got up in the morning, he said, "Send me to my master."

55 But her brother and mother said, "Let the girl stay with us for about 10 days.[C] Then she[D] can go."

56 But he responded to them, "Do not delay me, since the LORD has made my journey a success. Send me away so that I may go to my master."

57 So they said, "Let's call the girl and ask her opinion."[E]

58 They called Rebekah and said to her, "Will you go with this man?"

She replied, "I will go." 59 So they sent away their sister Rebekah with the one who had nursed and raised her,[F] and Abraham's servant and his men.

60 They blessed Rebekah, saying to her:

Our sister, may you become
thousands upon
ten thousands.
May your offspring possess
the gates of their[G] enemies.

61 Then Rebekah and her female servants got up, mounted the camels, and followed the man. So the servant took Rebekah and left.

62 Now Isaac was returning from Beer-lahai-roi,[H] for he was living in the •Negev region. 63 In the early evening Isaac went out to walk[I] in the field, and looking up he saw camels coming. 64 Rebekah looked up, and when she saw Isaac, she got down from her camel 65 and asked the servant, "Who is that man in the field coming to meet us?"

The servant answered, "It is my master." So she took her veil and covered herself. 66 Then the servant told Isaac everything he had done.

67 And Isaac brought her into the tent of his mother Sarah and took Rebekah to be his wife. Isaac loved her, and he was comforted after his mother's death.

25 Now Abraham had taken another wife, whose name was Keturah, 2 and she bore him Zimran, Jokshan, Medan, Midian, Ishbak, and Shuah. 3 Jokshan fathered Sheba and Dedan. Dedan's sons were the Asshurim, Letushim, and Leummim. 4 And Midian's sons were Ephah, Epher, Hanoch, Abida, and Eldaah. All these were sons of Keturah. 5 Abraham gave everything he owned to Isaac. 6 And Abraham gave gifts to the sons of his concubines, but while he was still alive he sent them eastward, away from his son Isaac, to the land of the East.

7 This is the length of Abraham's life:[J] 175 years. 8 He took his last breath and died at a ripe old age, old and contented,[K] and he was gathered to his people. 9 His sons Isaac and Ishmael buried him in the cave of Machpelah near Mamre, in the field of Ephron son of Zohar the Hittite. 10 This was the field that Abraham bought from the Hittites. Abraham was buried there with his

[A] **24:49** Lit *go to the right or to the left* [B] **24:50** Lit *we cannot say to you anything bad or good* [C] **24:55** Lit *us a few days or 10* [D] **24:55** Or *you* [E] **24:57** Lit *mouth* [F] **24:59** Lit *with her wet nurse*; Gn 35:8 [G] **24:60** Lit *his* [H] **24:62** = A Well of the Living One Who Sees Me [I] **24:63** Or *pray*, or *meditate*; Hb obscure [J] **25:7** Lit *And these are the days of the years of the lives of Abraham that he lived* [K] **25:8** Sam, LXX, Syr read *full of days*

wife Sarah. 11 After Abraham's death, God blessed his son Isaac, who lived near Beer-lahai-roi.

12 These are the family records of Abraham's son Ishmael, whom Hagar the Egyptian, Sarah's slave, bore to Abraham. 13 These are the names of Ishmael's sons; their names according to the family records are: Nebaioth, Ishmael's firstborn, then Kedar, Adbeel, Mibsam, 14 Mishma, Dumah, Massa, 15 Hadad, Tema, Jetur, Naphish, and Kedemah. 16 These are Ishmael's sons, and these are their names by their villages and encampments: 12 leaders[A] of their clans.[B] 17 This is the length[C] of Ishmael's life: 137 years. He took his last breath and died, and was gathered to his people. 18 And they[D] settled from Havilah to Shur, which is opposite Egypt as you go toward Asshur. He[E] lived in opposition to[F] all his brothers.

The Generations of Isaac (25:19–35:29)

The Birth of Two Sons (25:19-34)

19 These are the family records of Isaac son of Abraham. Abraham fathered Isaac. 20 Isaac was 40 years old when he took as his wife Rebekah daughter of Bethuel the Aramean from Paddan-aram and sister of Laban the Aramean. 21 Isaac prayed to the LORD on behalf of his wife because she was childless. The LORD heard his prayer, and his wife Rebekah conceived. 22 But the children inside her struggled with each other, and she said, "Why is this happening to me?"[G] So she went to inquire of the LORD. 23 And the LORD said to her:

> Two nations are
> in your womb;
> two people will come
> from you and be separated.
> One people will be stronger
> than the other,
> and the older will serve
> the younger.

24 When her time came to give birth, there were indeed twins in her womb. 25 The first one came out red-looking,[H] covered with hair[I] like a fur coat, and they named him Esau. 26 After this, his brother came out grasping Esau's heel with his hand. So he was named Jacob.[J] Isaac was 60 years old when they were born.

27 When the boys grew up, Esau became an expert hunter, an outdoorsman,[K] but Jacob was a quiet man who stayed at home.[L] 28 Isaac loved Esau because he had a taste for wild game, but Rebekah loved Jacob.

29 Once when Jacob was cooking a stew, Esau came in from the field exhausted. 30 He said to Jacob, "Let me eat some of that red stuff, because I'm exhausted." That is why he was also named Edom.[M]

31 Jacob replied, "First sell me your birthright."

32 "Look," said Esau, "I'm about to die, so what good is a birthright to me?"

33 Jacob said, "Swear to me first." So he swore to Jacob and sold his birthright to him. 34 Then Jacob gave bread and lentil stew to Esau; he ate, drank, got up, and went away. So Esau despised his birthright.

God's Covenant with Isaac (26:1-35)

26 There was another famine in the land in addition to the one that had occurred in Abraham's time. And Isaac went to Abimelech, king of the Philistines, at Gerar. 2 The LORD appeared to him and said, "Do not go down to Egypt. Live in the land that I tell you about; 3 stay in this land as a foreigner, and I will be with you and bless you. For I will give all these lands to you and your •offspring, and I will confirm the oath that I swore to your father Abraham. 4 I will make your offspring as numerous as the stars of the sky, I will give your offspring all these lands, and all the nations of the earth will be blessed[N] by your offspring, 5 because Abraham listened to My voice and kept My mandate, My commands, My statutes, and My instructions." 6 So Isaac settled in Gerar.

[A]25:16 Or *chieftains* [B]25:16 Or *peoples* [C]25:17 Lit *And these are the years* [D]25:18 LXX, Vg read *he* [E]25:18 = Ishmael and his descendants [F]25:18 Or *He settled down alongside of* [G]25:22 Lit *If thus, why this I* [H]25:25 In Hb, the word red-looking sounds like "Edom"; Gn 32:3. [I]25:25 In Hb, the word hair sounds like "Seir"; Gn 32:3. [J]25:26 = He Grasps the Heel [K]25:27 Lit *a man of the field* [L]25:27 Lit *man living in tents* [M]25:30 = Red [N]26:4 Or *will bless themselves*

25:7-11 An account of Abraham's death and burial is followed by the administration of his estate. The description suggests a happy state of affairs between Ishmael and Isaac. The phrase **and he was gathered to his people** simply denoted burial. Abraham was buried in the promised land, having purchased a **field** and **cave** from **Ephron . . . the Hittite** (25:9-10).

25:21-22 Unlike his parents, Abraham and Sarah, who chose their own solution through a substitute womb, Isaac turned to prayer in the midst of his wife's infertility. After 20 years of barrenness, Rebekah conceived; but the birth was to be a difficult one, for she was having twins. In those days death in childbirth was a fairly common experience.

25:24-34 Jacob and Esau grew up as very different people. **Esau** (Hb, "the hairy one") was the outdoor type, interested in hunting and spending many days away from home. His nation Edom (Hb *'edom*, v. 30) provides a pun with *'adom* (Hb, "red," v. 25).

Jacob (Hb "grasps the heel, supplants") became an established farmer, tending the sheep and the crops and remaining in the family encampment. The brothers' struggles within the womb continued throughout their lives and between the nations they fathered—the Edomites and the Israelites.

Sadly both parents had their favorites. **Isaac** favored **Esau**, who brought him his favorite game dishes to enjoy. He overlooked and took for granted the fact that Jacob remained at home assisting with the necessary work. **Rebekah** may have favored **Jacob** because he was helpful in domestic affairs and more responsive to her love.

The conflict between the brothers began to escalate on an occasion when Esau's hunger got the better of him, and he sold his **birthright** to his brother. The seriousness of this transaction must not be underestimated. This transaction was carried out legally, not under duress, and it was established by an oath. The oath legally and permanently fixed the transfer of the birthright, which then legitimately belonged to Jacob. The birthright not only guaranteed the greater inheritance but also the headship of the family clan. In this case included the right to invoke "the blessing of Abraham" (see 28:4) and thus to receive the promises of the covenant (see 12:1-3; 17:6-8). The Nuzi Tablets (ca 1450 B.C.) from modern Iraq did allow the birthright to be sold or changed from one child to another *by the father*. However, Esau so despised his birthright that he bypassed his father because of his desire for instant gratification and sold the birthright himself.

26:5-11 The word translated **kept** (Hb *shamar*, "watch, preserve") has the idea of being a watchman or guard.

Thus, Isaac was to guard carefully everything the Lord commanded him. While the law had not yet been given, God provided an example of obedience and faith in Abraham. The law was not a prerequisite for a man to understand what constitutes obedience and disobedience.

Isaac was immediately obedient and did as God commanded by staying in **Gerar**. However, Isaac also erred when he lied to the men of Gerar, who asked about his wife Rebekah, by telling the men she was his sister. Isaac's father, Abraham, had done the same in that land with Sarah (20:1-17).

26:12-16 Often, someone's blessing will bring about envy in another's life, and Isaac's prosperity did so with the **Philistines**.

26:23-25 Isaac went to **Beer-sheba** (at the southern border of Canaan), where Abraham had made a treaty with Abimelech (21:22-34). **The Lord appeared** here to renew the covenant—first between Him and Abraham and now with the next generation, identifying Himself to Isaac as **the God of** his **father Abraham** and declaring that He would be with Isaac as well.

26:26-31 Isaac received a surprise visit from **Abimelech**, who saw that the Lord was with Isaac. As their fathers before them, Isaac and Abimelech made a **covenant** of peace.

26:34-35 While peace came to Isaac and Abimelech, another incident caused Isaac and Rebekah much grief. Their son **Esau** took foreign wives, a practice forbidden by God because it marred the set-apart nature of the covenant lineage. Esau had no sensitivity for preserving the spiritual heritage of the family. Just as Isaac married within the covenant family, so did Jacob. Later in the giving of the law God specifically forbade foreign wives (Dt 17:17). Neither did God ever condone polygamy, which Esau also embraced. From the beginning God's plan was one man and one woman, just as He had instituted with Adam and Eve (Gn 2:24). Despite this clear mandate from God, many of the patriarchs were polygamous, and thus their lives were fraught with discord. Esau disobeyed, too, and brought pain to his family. Esau's wives **made life bitter** (Hb *morat ruach*, "bitterness of spirit") and brought grief to Isaac and Rebekah since they were pagan Canaanite—Hittite—women.

27:1-4 The suspenseful narrative of the blessing of Jacob is marked with trickery, deceit, and favoritism. The true character of the players in this narrative comes through in their own words and

7 When the men of the place asked about his wife, he said, "She is my sister," for he was afraid to say "my wife," thinking, "The men of the place will kill me on account of Rebekah, for she is a beautiful woman." 8 When Isaac had been there for some time, Abimelech king of the Philistines looked down from the window and was surprised to see[A] Isaac caressing his wife Rebekah.

9 Abimelech sent for Isaac and said, "So she is really your wife! How could you say, 'She is my sister'?"

Isaac answered him, "Because I thought I might die on account of her."

10 Then Abimelech said, "What is this you've done to us? One of the people could easily have slept with your wife, and you would have brought •guilt on us." 11 So Abimelech warned all the people with these words: "Whoever harms this man or his wife will certainly die."

12 Isaac sowed seed in that land, and in that year he reaped[B] a hundred times what was sown. The Lord blessed him, 13 and the man became rich and kept getting richer until he was very wealthy. 14 He had flocks of sheep, herds of cattle, and many slaves, and the Philistines were envious of him. 15 The Philistines stopped up all the wells that his father's slaves had dug in the days of his father Abraham, filling them with dirt. 16 And Abimelech said to Isaac, "Leave us, for you are much too powerful for us."[C]

17 So Isaac left there, camped in the Valley of Gerar, and lived there. 18 Isaac reopened the water wells that had been dug in the days of his father Abraham and that the Philistines had stopped up after Abraham died. He gave them the same names his father had given them. 19 Then Isaac's slaves dug in the valley and found a well of spring[D] water there. 20 But the herdsmen of Gerar quarreled with Isaac's herdsmen and said, "The water is ours!" So he named the well Quarrel[E] because they quarreled with him. 21 Then they dug another well and quarreled over that one also, so he named it Hostility.[F] 22 He moved from there and dug another, and they did not quarrel over it. He named it Open Spaces[G] and said, "For now the Lord has made room for us, and we will be fruitful in the land."

23 From there he went up to Beer-sheba, 24 and the Lord appeared to him that night and said, "I am the God of your father Abraham. Do not be afraid, for I am with you. I will bless you and multiply your offspring because of My servant Abraham."

25 So he built an altar there, called on the name of •Yahweh, and pitched his tent there. Isaac's slaves also dug a well there.

26 Now Abimelech came to him from Gerar with Ahuzzath his adviser and Phicol the commander of his army. 27 Isaac said to them, "Why have you come to me? You hated me and sent me away from you."

28 They replied, "We have clearly seen how the Lord has been with you. We think there should be an oath between two parties—between us and you. Let us make a covenant with you: 29 You will not harm us, just as we have not harmed you but have only done what was good to you, sending you away in peace. You are now blessed by the Lord."

30 So he prepared a banquet for them, and they ate and drank. 31 They got up early in the morning and swore an oath to each other.[H] Then Isaac sent them on their way, and they left him in peace. 32 On that same day Isaac's slaves came to tell him about the well they had dug, saying to him, "We have found water!" 33 He called it Sheba.[I] Therefore the name of the city is Beer-sheba[J] to this day.

34 When Esau was 40 years old, he took as his wives Judith daughter of Beeri the Hittite, and Basemath daughter of Elon the Hittite. 35 They made life bitter[K] for Isaac and Rebekah.

[A]26:8 Or *and he looked and behold—* [B]26:12 Lit *found* [C]26:16 Or *are more numerous than we are* [D]26:19 Lit *living* [E]26:20 Or *Esek* [F]26:21 Or *Sitnah* [G]26:22 Or *Rehoboth* [H]26:31 Lit *swore, each man to his brother* [I]26:33 Or *Shibah* [J]26:33 = Well of the Oath [K]26:35 Lit *And they became bitterness of spirit*

God's Choice of Jacob (27:1–35:29)

27 When Isaac was old and his eyes were so weak that he could not see, he called his older son Esau and said to him, "My son."

And he answered, "Here I am."

2 He said, "Look, I am old and do not know the day of my death. 3 Take your hunting gear, your quiver and bow, and go out in the field to hunt some game for me. 4 Then make me a delicious meal that I love and bring it to me to eat, so that I can bless you before I die."

5 Now Rebekah was listening to what Isaac said to his son Esau. So while Esau went to the field to hunt some game to bring in, 6 Rebekah said to her son Jacob, "Listen! I heard your father talking with your brother Esau. He said, 7 'Bring me the game and make a delicious meal for me to eat so that I can bless you in the LORD's presence before I die.' 8 Now obey every order I give you, my son. 9 Go to the flock and bring me two choice young goats, and I will make them into a delicious meal for your father—the kind he loves. 10 Then take it to your father to eat so that he may bless you before he dies."

11 Jacob answered Rebekah his mother, "Look, my brother Esau is a hairy man, but I am a man with smooth skin. 12 Suppose my father touches me. Then I will be revealed to him as a deceiver and bring a curse rather than a blessing on myself."

13 His mother said to him, "Your curse be on me, my son. Just obey me and go get them for me."

14 So he went and got the goats and brought them to his mother, and his mother made the delicious food his father loved. 15 Then Rebekah took the best clothes of her older son Esau, which were in the house, and had her younger son Jacob wear them. 16 She put the skins of the young goats on his hands and the smooth part of his neck. 17 Then she handed the delicious food and the bread she had made to her son Jacob.

18 When he came to his father, he said, "My father."

And he answered, "Here I am. Who are you, my son?"

19 Jacob replied to his father, "I am Esau, your firstborn. I have done as you told me. Please sit up and eat some of my game so that you may bless me."

20 But Isaac said to his son, "How did you ever find it so quickly, my son?"

He replied, "Because the LORD your God worked it out for me."

21 Then Isaac said to Jacob, "Please come closer so I can touch you, my son. Are you really my son Esau or not?"

22 So Jacob came closer to his father Isaac. When he touched him, he said, "The voice is the voice of Jacob, but the hands are the hands of Esau." 23 He did not recognize him, because his hands were hairy like those of his brother Esau; so he blessed him. 24 Again he asked, "Are you really my son Esau?"

And he replied, "I am."

25 Then he said, "Serve me, and let me eat some of my son's game so that I can bless you." Jacob brought it to him, and he ate; he brought him wine, and he drank.

26 Then his father Isaac said to him, "Please come closer and kiss me, my son." 27 So he came closer and kissed him. When Isaac smelled[A] his clothes, he blessed him and said:

Ah, the smell of my son
is like the smell of a field
that the LORD has blessed.
28 May God give to you—
from the dew of the sky
and from the richness
of the land—
an abundance of grain
and new wine.
29 May peoples serve you
and nations bow down to you.
Be master over your brothers;
may your mother's sons
bow down to you.
Those who curse you
will be cursed,
and those who bless you
will be blessed.

30 As soon as Isaac had finished blessing Jacob and Jacob had left the presence of his father Isaac, his

[A] 27:27 Lit *smelled the smell of*

choices—their faults, insecurities, and favoritisms.

27:5-17 Some commentators argue that Rebekah exemplifies a woman's wisdom, knowing when to work behind the scenes to accomplish goals. However, trickery and deceit are in contradistinction to obedience to God's Word. A woman following Christ is to speak the truth rather than manipulate someone to achieve her own way as did Rebekah (see Pr 12:20). Heartache did come to Rebekah as her deception brought division to the family. The Bible tells Rebekah's story but without any commendation of her deceit and manipulation. Her description is not presented as an example for godly women to follow.

27:18-25 Jacob entered his father's room with an opportunity to tell the truth but instead continued with the lie, claiming to be Esau. Jacob did not claim God as his own yet but instead called Him **your** [referring to Isaac] **God**. Jacob was not committed to Yahweh at this point. He knew about the God of his father Isaac but had not entered into a relationship with Him. God had already determined that Jacob would be blessed, but Jacob's deceitfulness was never suggested or sanctioned by God.

27:26-29 Isaac blessed Jacob, whom he thought was Esau, promising blessing and leadership and calling for cursing on any who cursed him. These words are comparable to the Abrahamic covenant. Jacob was fruitful and became a strong nation himself (cp. 17:6; 28:3-4; 35:11-12). More specifically, the last line of the blessing was taken directly from the Abrahamic covenant (cp. 12:3), which was the first sign that the Abrahamic covenant would be passed on to Jacob. The blessing of Jacob was ultimately God's plan. However, God had a better way for this to come to fruition. Unlike his brother, Jacob had not taken wives from other lands and was thus a candidate for the blessing. Both Jacob and Esau were sinners. God made His choice based on His omniscience—neither brother "earned" the blessing. Jacob's deceit did have consequences in the form of brotherly conflict, but God's words never fall to the ground. The oracle given at birth came to its fulfillment in Jacob (25:23). Instead of trusting God, Rebekah and Jacob took things into their own hands and sought what seemed good to them, not waiting for God to do the work. Much strife is often caused when a believer is impatient.

27:30-40 Esau and Isaac quickly learned of the trickery of Jacob and Rebekah. Both were deeply wounded, Isaac for being deceived by his wife and son, and Esau for the loss of not only his birthright but his blessing as well. Esau took note of his brother's name, **Jacob** (Hb, "heel-grasper, supplanter"), and said that Jacob did indeed act accordingly. The word translated **cheated** (Hb *'aqav*, "follow at the heel" or figuratively "assail insidiously") is a pun on Jacob's name. Isaac was deeply troubled as he must answer his favorite son Esau and let him know that he indeed had given the blessing to Jacob. Esau, in desperation, asked his father for **one blessing**. At this point, Esau was ready to take anything he could get. Isaac complied; and while his blessing included fruitfulness from the earth, it also promised strife.

27:41 Esau was jealous and bitter over the loss of his birthright and blessing and the deceit of Jacob. He even thought about killing his brother. Envy and hatred destroy relationships. Anyone harboring such feelings must make every effort to rid herself of bitterness and wrath (Eph 4:31).

27:42-45 Rebekah received news of Esau's hatred and plan. Fearing for Jacob's life, she sent him on his way. Rebekah loved her child, as would any mother. She was willing to do anything to give him the best as well as to keep him from the worst. Her only option was to send Jacob away to her brother **Laban in Haran**. Rebekah experienced the consequences of her actions with death for Jacob at the hand of his brother Esau as a real possibility. Jacob would not return home for 20 years.

28:1-5 In order to prevent Jacob from erring as Esau had, Isaac charged Jacob to take a wife from the house of Laban. Isaac confirmed the covenant blessing of Abraham upon Jacob. The command and blessing in combination signified the importance of being set apart by God. Jacob was God's chosen vessel to carry out the blessing. Jacob was obedient, heeding his mother's warning and his father's charge; and he left for **Paddan-aram**, the home of Laban.

28:6-9 Esau reacted in an effort to please his parents, but he continued to fall short. Esau took a wife from Ishmael's family, which was still outside the covenant line. The foreign wives remained, and his moral judgment continued to be flawed as he expanded his polygamy.

28:10-15 **Jacob left Beer-sheba**, traveling to **Haran**, the home of Laban. En route, Jacob had a theophany, an encounter with God. This encounter was quite similar to Abraham's encounter with God when the covenant was given (see 12:7-8; 13:3-4). Jacob dreamed

brother Esau arrived from the hunt. 31 He had also made some delicious food and brought it to his father. Then he said to his father, "Let my father get up and eat some of his son's game, so that you may bless me."

32 But his father Isaac said to him, "Who are you?"

He answered, "I am Esau your firstborn son."

33 Isaac began to tremble uncontrollably. "Who was it then," he said, "who hunted game and brought it to me? I ate it all before you came in, and I blessed him. Indeed, he will be blessed!"

34 When Esau heard his father's words, he cried out with a loud and bitter cry and said to his father, "Bless me too, my father!"

35 But he replied, "Your brother came deceitfully and took your blessing."

36 So he said, "Isn't he rightly named Jacob?[A] For he has cheated me twice now. He took my birthright, and look, now he has taken my blessing." Then he asked, "Haven't you saved a blessing for me?"

37 But Isaac answered Esau: "Look, I have made him a master over you, have given him all of his relatives as his servants, and have sustained him with grain and new wine. What then can I do for you, my son?"

38 Esau said to his father, "Do you only have one blessing, my father? Bless me too, my father!" And Esau wept loudly.[B]

39 Then his father Isaac answered him:

Look, your dwelling place
  will be
away from the richness
  of the land,
away from the dew
  of the sky above.
40 You will live by your sword,
and you will serve
  your brother.
But when you rebel,[C]
you will break his yoke
  from your neck.

41 Esau held a grudge against Jacob because of the blessing his father had given him. And Esau determined in his heart: "The days of mourning for my father are approaching; then I will kill my brother Jacob."

42 When the words of her older son Esau were reported to Rebekah, she summoned her younger son Jacob and said to him, "Listen, your brother Esau is consoling himself by planning to kill you. 43 So now, my son, listen to me. Flee at once to my brother Laban in Haran, 44 and stay with him for a few days until your brother's anger subsides— 45 until your brother's rage turns away from you and he forgets what you have done to him. Then I will send for you and bring you back from there. Why should I lose you both in one day?"

46 So Rebekah said to Isaac, "I'm sick of my life because of these Hittite women. If Jacob marries a Hittite woman like one of them,[D] what good is my life?"

28 Isaac summoned Jacob, blessed him, and commanded him: "Don't take a wife from the Canaanite women. 2 Go at once to Paddan-aram, to the house of Bethuel, your mother's father. Marry one of the daughters of Laban, your mother's brother. 3 May •God Almighty bless you and make you fruitful and multiply you so that you become an assembly of peoples. 4 May God give you and your •offspring the blessing of Abraham so that you may possess the land where you live as a foreigner, the land God gave to Abraham." 5 So Isaac sent Jacob to Paddan-aram, to Laban son of Bethuel the Aramean, the brother of Rebekah, the mother of Jacob and Esau.

6 Esau noticed that Isaac blessed Jacob and sent him to Paddan-aram to get a wife there. When he blessed him, Isaac commanded Jacob, "Do not marry a Canaanite woman." 7 And Jacob listened to his father and mother and went to Paddan-aram. 8 Esau realized that his father Isaac disapproved of the Canaanite women, 9 so Esau went to Ishmael and married, in addition to his other wives, Mahalath daughter of Ishma-

[A]27:36 = He Grasps the Heel [B]27:38 Lit *Esau lifted up his voice and wept* [C]27:40 Hb obscure
[D]27:46 Lit *of these daughters of the land*

>WORD|*study*

28:17 Jacob's use of awesome (Hb *yarē'*) is appropriate. He had received a word from Almighty God. The word was meant to convey a sense of wonder, majesty, and reverence. Often in modern usage the word "awesome" is used nonchalantly for ordinary things. However, God is the one who is truly awesome.

el, Abraham's son. She was the sister of Nebaioth.

10 Jacob left Beer-sheba and went toward Haran. 11 He reached a certain place and spent the night there because the sun had set. He took one of the stones from the place, put it there at his head, and lay down in that place. 12 And he dreamed: A stairway was set on the ground with its top reaching heaven, and God's angels were going up and down on it. 13 •Yahweh was standing there beside him,[A] saying, "I am Yahweh, the God of your father Abraham and the God of Isaac. I will give you and your offspring the land that you are now sleeping on. 14 Your offspring will be like the dust of the earth, and you will spread out toward the west, the east, the north, and the south. All the peoples on earth will be blessed through you and your offspring. 15 Look, I am with you and will watch over you wherever you go. I will bring you back to this land, for I will not leave you until I have done what I have promised you."

16 When Jacob awoke from his sleep, he said, "Surely the LORD is in this place, and I did not know it." 17 He was afraid and said, "What an awesome place this is! This is none other than the house of God. This is the gate of heaven."

18 Early in the morning Jacob took the stone that was near his head and set it up as a marker. He poured oil on top of it 19 and named the place Bethel,[B] though previously the city was named Luz. 20 Then Jacob made a vow: "If God will be with me and watch over me on this journey, if He provides me with food to eat and clothing to wear, 21 and if I return safely to my father's house, then the LORD will be my God. 22 This stone that I have set up as a marker will be God's house, and I will give to You a tenth of all that You give me."

29 Jacob resumed his journey[C] and went to the eastern country.[D] 2 He looked and saw a well in a field. Three flocks of sheep were lying there beside it because the sheep were watered from this well. A large stone covered the opening of the well. 3 When all the flocks[E] were gathered there, the shepherds would roll the stone from the opening of the well and water the sheep. The stone was then placed back on the well's opening.

4 Jacob asked the men at the well, "My brothers! Where are you from?"

"We're from Haran," they answered.

5 "Do you know Laban grandson of Nahor?" Jacob asked them.

They answered, "We know him."

6 "Is he well?" Jacob asked.

"Yes," they said, "and here is his daughter Rachel, coming with his sheep."

7 Then Jacob said, "Look, it is still broad daylight. It's not time for the animals to be gathered. Water the flock, then go out and let them graze."

8 But they replied, "We can't until all the flocks have been gathered and the stone is rolled from the well's opening. Then we will water the sheep."

9 While he was still speaking with them, Rachel came with her father's sheep, for she was a shepherdess. 10 As soon as Jacob saw his uncle Laban's daughter Rachel with his sheep,[F] he went up and rolled the stone from the opening and watered his uncle Laban's sheep. 11 Then Jacob kissed Rachel and wept loudly.[G] 12 He told Rachel that he was her father's relative, Rebekah's son. She ran and told her father.

of **a stairway** (Hb *sullam*, "ladder"), which reached from the earth to the heavens. The stairway showed that activity was taking place between heaven and earth. Standing, Yahweh gave the blessing of Abraham to Jacob. The blessing was threefold—Jacob would receive the **land** on which he was sleeping; his offspring would be as **the dust of the earth**, and **all the peoples on earth would be blessed** through his **offspring**. The Lord also assured Jacob of His presence and faithfulness in fulfilling the promise. His dream provided assurance that despite his deceit he would receive the blessings of the Abrahamic covenant (13:14-16; 26:24; 35:10-13).

28:18-22 Because of God's awesomeness, Jacob renamed **the place Bethel** (Hb *Bēt'ēl*, "House of God"). The Canaanite name **Luz** identified the general district in which Jacob's special place was established. Jacob's vow to give **a tenth** back to God was the same as his grandfather Abraham had done before him (14:20); and to set his **stone** as a memorial by anointing it with **oil** showed his genuine devotion to God and confirmed his realization that all he had came from God. As Abraham before him, Jacob responded to God's presence with obedience (17:23-27) and with a tangible act of worship.

29:1-6 Jacob left Bethel and continued toward the house of Laban. Amazingly, he came upon the **well** used by his kin. According to some, Jacob's encounter with the **shepherds**, who were waiting for assistance with the massive **stone**, revealed his ignorance of the land's customs. Others point to the custom of waiting as being mere courtesy on the part of the shepherds, who would remove **the stone** only when all were present to avoid an unfair advantage in the use of a scarce water supply. In any case, the focus quickly moves to the arrival of **Rachel** with Laban's sheep.

29:13-17 Just as families are excited today when they see a relative, so was Laban when he ran to meet Jacob. This meeting, while happy, left a sense of wonder at what would occur next. During the time Jacob was a guest in Laban's home, his love grew steadily for Rachel, the younger daughter of Laban. **Rachel** [Hb, "ewe"] **was shapely** [Hb *to'ar*, "a beautiful form"; cp. "well-built," 39:6; "handsome," 1Sm 16:18; "form," Is 53:2] **and beautiful** (Hb *yapheh*, "fair, beautiful," cp. Gn 12:14; 2Sm 13:1; Sg 1:8) unlike her sister **Leah** (Hb, "wild cow") who **had ordinary** [Hb *rak*, "tender; weak, dull, infirm"] **eyes**. Leah's ordinary eyes mean one of several things: Her eyes lacked luster; they were diminished in the ability to see; or they were merely delicate.

[A]**28:13** Or *there above it* [B]**28:19** = House of God [C]**29:1** Lit *Jacob picked up his feet* [D]**29:1** Lit *the land of the children of the east* [E]**29:3** Sam, some LXX mss read *flocks and the shepherds* [F]**29:10** Lit *with the sheep of Laban his mother's brother* [G]**29:11** Lit *and he lifted his voice and wept*

29:18 Jacob's true devotion and affection for Rachel became clear when he agreed to work **seven years** for Rachel's hand in marriage. The seven years Jacob worked for Laban became Rachel's bride price (Hb *mohar*)—compensation to the bride's parents, not in the sense of payment for merchandise but more as proof of financial viability on the bridegroom. According to this custom in the ancient Near East, a man seeking a woman in marriage would pay the bride price before any ceremony could take place. According to Syrian records, assigning one's labor as payment was an acceptable alternative.

29:19-27 Laban acted as though he would follow through with his word as he held a wedding **feast**. Wedding feasts in the ancient Near East were a time of great celebration and joy, lasting for a week. Jacob had been fully expecting to receive Rachel as his wife. The feasting and most likely a dimly lit room had aided in the deception of Jacob. Leah may have readily agreed to any plot in order not to be ashamed that her younger sister had married before she had. But, also, she probably was not given a choice by her father but told to do as he directed. The man with the name meaning "deceiver" had himself been deceived. Jacob, frustrated at not having been given his true love in marriage, was confronted with a custom he knew all too well. In those days, the eldest customarily was given in marriage first, just as traditionally the older brother received the birthright and blessing, which Jacob had taken from Esau for himself. While Jacob knew this, Laban never specified which daughter he would give in marriage, even though Jacob specifically asked for Rachel. Laban, appearing somewhat generous but all the while ensuring himself of another laborer, allowed Jacob to complete the customary week with Leah and then take Rachel as well, while working yet another seven years for her. Traditionally in the ancient Near East the daughter was given something to take into the marriage. Money and slaves often made the daughter more valuable to a prospective husband. In the case of Leah and Rachel, Laban gave each a handmaid. To Leah he gave **Zilpah**, and to Rachel he gave **Bilhah**. These handmaids, while taking care of Leah and Rachel, took on an even greater role as pawns who became concubines in the struggle between the sisters for the love of Jacob and for children.

29:28-30 The next seven years were not like the first. Isaac and Rebekah's plan for Jacob to stay a few days had been crushed. Rebekah had intended for her son to be away only long enough for him to find a wife and for Esau's anger to cool (27:43). However, finding a wife and having a deceptive

CHARACTER PROFILE

Rachel A Beloved Wife

Her Background	• She was the beautiful daughter of Rebekah's brother, Laban, living in Haran (29:5-10). • She married Jacob after he was deceived into marrying her older sister Leah (29:28). • She was the mother of Joseph and Benjamin (30:22-24; 35:16-20).
Her Story	• Rachel was infertile, while Leah conceived easily, resulting in jealousy and resentment between the sisters (30:1). • She stole her father's household idols, perhaps in order to claim a family inheritance or as part of superstitious worship (31:19). • She gave birth to Joseph, favored son of Jacob (30:22-24). • She died while giving birth to Benjamin (35:18).
Life Lessons	• Unfulfilled dreams and expectations often result in bitterness and anger. • Physical attractiveness does not necessarily result in contentment.

13 When Laban heard the news
about his sister's son Jacob, he
ran to meet him, hugged him, and
kissed him. Then he took him to his
house, and Jacob told him all that
had happened.
14 Laban said to him, "Yes, you are
my own flesh and blood."[A]
After Jacob had stayed with him a
month, 15 Laban said to him, "Just
because you're my relative, should
you work for me for nothing? Tell
me what your wages should be."
16 Now Laban had two daughters:
the older was named Leah, and the
younger was named Rachel. 17 Leah
had ordinary[B] eyes, but Rachel was
shapely and beautiful. 18 Jacob loved
Rachel, so he answered Laban, "I'll
work for you seven years for your
younger daughter Rachel."
19 Laban replied, "Better that I give
her to you than to some other man.
Stay with me." 20 So Jacob worked
seven years for Rachel, and they
seemed like only a few days to him
because of his love for her.
21 Then Jacob said to Laban, "Give
me my wife, for my time is completed. I want to sleep with[C] her."
22 So Laban invited all the men of
the place to a feast. 23 That evening,
Laban took his daughter Leah and
gave her to Jacob, and he slept with
her. 24 And Laban gave his slave
Zilpah to his daughter Leah as her
slave.
25 When morning came, there was
Leah! So he said to Laban, "What is
this you have done to me? Wasn't
it for Rachel that I worked for you?
Why have you deceived me?"
26 Laban answered, "It is not the
custom in this place to give the
younger daughter in marriage before the firstborn. 27 Complete this
week of wedding celebration, and we
will also give you this younger one
in return for working yet another
seven years for me."
28 And Jacob did just that. He finished the week of celebration, and
Laban gave him his daughter Rachel
as his wife. 29 And Laban gave his
slave Bilhah to his daughter Rachel
as her slave. 30 Jacob slept with Rachel also, and indeed, he loved Rachel more than Leah. And he worked
for Laban another seven years.
31 When the LORD saw that Leah
was unloved, He opened her womb;
but Rachel was unable to conceive.
32 Leah conceived, gave birth to a
son, and named him Reuben,[D] for

[A]**29:14** Lit *my bone and my flesh* [B]**29:17** Lit *tender* [C]**29:21** Lit *to go to* [D]**29:32** = See, a Son; in Hb, the name Reuben sounds like "has seen my affliction."

>WORD|*study*

29:33 Leah was not just unloved (Hb *sanē'*, lit "hated") by Jacob but hated by him. Jacob's love for Rachel was apparently so intoxicating that in contrast his feelings for Leah seemed to be "hate." The sense of the word here seems to indicate more "rejection" or even "scorn." Of course, without doubt Leah was rejected from the greater honor due the first wife.

she said, "The LORD has seen my affliction; surely my husband will love me now."

33 She conceived again, gave birth to a son, and said, "The LORD heard that I am unloved and has given me this son also." So she named him Simeon.[A]

34 She conceived again, gave birth to a son, and said, "At last, my husband will become attached to me because I have borne three sons for him." Therefore he was named Levi.[B]

35 And she conceived again, gave birth to a son, and said, "This time I will praise the LORD." Therefore she named him Judah.[C] Then Leah stopped having children.

30 When Rachel saw that she was not bearing Jacob any children, she envied her sister. "Give me sons, or I will die!" she said to Jacob.

2 Jacob became angry with Rachel and said, "Am I in God's place, who has withheld children[D] from you?"

3 Then she said, "Here is my slave Bilhah. Go sleep with her, and she'll bear children for me[E] so that through her I too can build a family." 4 So Rachel gave her slave Bilhah to Jacob as a wife, and he slept with
her. 5 Bilhah conceived and bore Ja-
cob a son. 6 Rachel said, "God has vindicated me; yes, He has heard me and given me a son," and she named him Dan.[F]

[A]**29:33** In Hb, the name Simeon sounds like "has heard." [B]**29:34** In Hb, the name Levi sounds like "attached to." [C]**29:35** In Hb, the name Judah sounds like "praise." [D]**30:2** Lit *the fruit of the womb* [E]**30:3** Lit *bear on my knees* [F]**30:6** In Hb, the name Dan sounds like "has vindicated," or "has judged."

CHARACTER PROFILE

Leah An Unloved Wife

Her Background	• The daughter of Laban and sister to Rachel (29:16) • The first wife of Jacob (29:23) • The mother of Reuben, Simeon, Levi, Judah, Issachar, Zebulun, and Dinah
Her Story	• She married Jacob, who loved Rachel (29:20). • She was unattractive and unloved; yet she loved her husband (29:32). • She recognized God's gracious gift of children to her (29:32-35). • She produced six of Jacob's sons, who would be counted among the leaders of the 12 tribes of Israel (49:28). • The messianic lineage would be traced through the tribe of Judah; the priesthood would be established through the tribe of Levi (Nm 1:47-53; 3:1-11; Dt. 10:8-9).
Life Lessons	• Even though unloved by her husband, Leah found fulfillment and blessings through her sons. • God did not condone Jacob's behavior, but Leah wisely recognized that the Lord cared about her in the midst of her circumstances, even when the circumstances did not change.

father-in-law kept Jacob away much longer than expected. In addition, tension had become paramount, for Jacob loved Rachel more than Leah, which caused strife and struggle in the family for years. Mosaic law would later forbid a man from taking sisters in marriage when both women were still living (Lv 18:18). Note the tragedy resulting from polygamous unions:

- rivalry among wives and children (Gn 29:30,32);
- hatred (v. 31);
- envy (30:1);
- bitter anger (30:2);
- infighting (30:8); and
- bartering for sexual intimacy or virtual prostitution (30:15-16).

29:31-35 God allowed Leah to conceive even while Rachel was infertile. The names of the children are not strictly defined etymologically but rather express the innermost feelings of Leah as she gave birth to her sons:

- **Reuben** ("The LORD has seen my affliction");
- **Simeon** ("The LORD heard that I am unloved");
- **Levi** ("My husband will become attached to me").
- However, by Leah's fourth child, **Judah**, she gave the **praise** to God, realizing that God was the one who opens and closes the womb (see 30:2) and the one who ultimately deserved her loving devotion. While Leah would never be as physically attractive as Rachel, God had given her the beautiful gift of children.

30:1-6 Rachel saw her infertility and decided to act rather than waiting for God, who certainly saw her and had a plan for her life. Narratives regarding barren women are quite frequent in the Old Testament. For a woman to be unable to bear children in that culture was grievous because the people believed that children were evidences of God's blessing. Sarah (16:1), Rebekah (25:21), Hannah (1Sm 1:2), and Rachel all experienced a barren womb. Rachel, unlike the other wives, took her grief to the extreme. She was frustrated, angry, and bitter toward her husband Jacob. However, Jacob could not be blamed for her lack of children, for at that point Leah had already borne him four sons. Rachel was so upset that she even thought of death. Jacob wisely referred his wife to God for the cause of her barrenness. While Jacob and Rachel began with a captivating story of love, envy crept in and brought strife and bitterness to their relationship, which affected everything else in their lives. Rachel's desire to have children is a noble one, but Rachel was impatient and accusatory when God left her womb closed for a time. Rachel did not turn to the Lord in her greatest need. Much of her grief came through wrong choices and lack of confidence in the providences of Yahweh God.

Instead of accepting Jacob's words and waiting for God to act, Rachel, like Sarah, gave Jacob her maidservant. Rachel used the term **slave** (Hb *ʾamah*, "maidservant") in describing **Bilhah**. The same word described Hagar (21:10-15). Bilhah had been given to Rachel as part of the dowry from her father at the time of her marriage to Jacob (29:29). Jacob complied with his wife's decision, which certainly was not to his credit any more than in the case of Abraham, who made the same mistake and suffered greatly from its consequences. As with Sarah and Hagar, a servant could be provided as a surrogate for an infertile wife so that the children from that union would be acknowledged as her own.

30:7-8 Bilhah became Rachel's surrogate and **conceived**. Unlike Sarah, who was upset when Hagar became pregnant (16:5-6), **Rachel said, "God has vindicated me"**; hence the name of the child, **Dan** (Hb, "judged"). Rachel believed that God had **given** her **a son** and thus had rightly adjudicated the situation with her sister Leah. Rachel was further encouraged when **Bilhah . . . bore Jacob a second son**. She named him **Naphtali** (Hb, "my wrestlings"). At that moment, Rachel believed she had **won** the fight against Leah. However, the victory soon turned to defeat when Leah gave her maidservant **Zilpah** to Jacob. Zilpah would bear two sons for Jacob.

30:14-15 Once again the family of Jacob turned to trickery and cunning to get what their hearts desired. When Reuben, Leah's eldest son, brought home **mandrakes** (Hb *dudaʾim*, "love plants," related to the potato family), which were believed to be an aphrodisiac and fertility aid, a fight was inevitable. For Leah, the mandrakes were important because they might be used as a "love potion" on her husband in order to secure his affection (see Sg 7:13 in which the same word is used, pointing to their exotic smell). For Rachel, they were important because they were believed to promote conception. If these mandrakes were the same as those in Palestine today, they produced purple flowers with yellow fruit and a strong fragrance, as is evident in Sg 7:13. Rachel thus sought the mandrakes to assist her in her child-bearing desires.

30:16-21 The reason for Leah's hurt was because either her husband had denied her marital rights, or Rachel's usurpation as the favored wife had fully taken effect. Rachel played on Leah's desire for Jacob's affection and thus the trade was made—a night with Jacob for some mandrakes. Jacob, after coming in from working

The Children of Jacob

Mother	Son	Meaning of Name	Reference
Leah	Reuben	"see, a son"	29:32
	Simeon	"hearing with acceptance"	29:33
	Levi	"joined or attached to"	29:34
	Judah	"praised"	29:35
	Issachar	"there is reward or recompense"	30:18
	Zebulun	"exalted, honored"	30:20
	Dinah (daughter)	"judgment" or "judged," i.e., vindicated	30:21
Bilhah	Dan	"judge"	30:6
	Naphtali	"wrestling; my strife"	30:8
Zilpah	Gad	"good fortune; troop"	30:11
	Asher	"happy"	30:13
Rachel	Joseph	"Yahweh will add"	30:24
	Benjamin	"son of my right hand"	35:18

[7] Rachel's slave Bilhah conceived again and bore Jacob a second son. [8] Rachel said, "In my wrestlings with God,[A] I have wrestled with my sister and won," and she named him Naphtali.[B]

[9] When Leah saw that she had stopped having children, she took her slave Zilpah and gave her to Jacob as a wife. [10] Leah's slave Zilpah bore Jacob a son. [11] Then Leah said, "What good fortune!"[C] and she named him Gad.[D]

[12] When Leah's slave Zilpah bore Jacob a second son, [13] Leah said, "I am happy that the women call me happy," so she named him Asher.[E]

[14] Reuben went out during the wheat harvest and found some mandrakes in the field. When he brought them to his mother Leah, Rachel asked, "Please give me some of your son's mandrakes."

[15] But Leah replied to her, "Isn't it enough that you have taken my husband? Now you also want to take my son's mandrakes?"

"Well," Rachel said, "you can sleep with him tonight in exchange for your son's mandrakes."

[16] When Jacob came in from the field that evening, Leah went out to meet him and said, "You must come with me, for I have hired you with my son's mandrakes." So Jacob slept with her that night.

[17] God listened to Leah, and she conceived and bore Jacob a fifth son. [18] Leah said, "God has rewarded me for giving my slave to my husband," and she named him Issachar.[F]

[19] Then Leah conceived again and

[A] **30:8** Or *With mighty wrestlings* [B] **30:8** In Hb, the name Naphtali sounds like "my wrestling." [C] **30:11** Alt Hb tradition, LXX, Vg read *Good fortune has come* [D] **30:11** = Good Fortune [E] **30:13** = Happy [F] **30:18** In Hb, the name Issachar sounds like "reward."

bore Jacob a sixth son. 20 "God has given me a good gift," Leah said. "This time my husband will honor me because I have borne six sons for him," and she named him Zebulun.[A] 21 Later, Leah bore a daughter and named her Dinah.

22 Then God remembered Rachel. He listened to her and opened her womb. 23 She conceived and bore a son, and said, "God has taken away my shame." 24 She named him Joseph:[B] "May the LORD add another son to me."

25 After Rachel gave birth to Joseph, Jacob said to Laban, "Send me on my way so that I can return to my homeland. 26 Give me my wives and my children that I have worked for, and let me go. You know how hard I have worked for you."

27 But Laban said to him, "If I have found favor in your sight, stay. I have learned by •divination that the LORD has blessed me because of you." 28 Then Laban said, "Name your wages, and I will pay them."

29 So Jacob said to him, "You know what I have done for you and your herds. 30 For you had very little before I came, but now your wealth has increased. The LORD has blessed you because of me. And now, when will I also do something for my own family?"

31 Laban asked, "What should I give you?"

And Jacob said, "You don't need to give me anything. If you do this one thing for me, I will continue to shepherd and keep your flock. 32 Let me go through all your sheep today and remove every sheep that is speckled or spotted, every dark-colored sheep among the lambs, and the spotted and speckled among the female goats. Such will be my wages. 33 In the future when you come to check on my wages, my honesty will testify for me. If I have any female goats that are not speckled or spotted, or any lambs that are not black, they will be considered stolen."

34 "Good," said Laban. "Let it be as you have said."

35 That day Laban removed the streaked and spotted male goats and all the speckled and spotted female goats—every one that had any white on it—and every dark-colored one among the lambs, and he placed his sons in charge of them. 36 He put a three-day journey between himself and Jacob. Jacob, meanwhile, was shepherding the rest of Laban's flock.

37 Jacob then took branches of fresh poplar, almond, and plane wood, and peeled the bark, exposing white stripes on the branches. 38 He set the peeled branches in the troughs in front of the sheep—in the water channels where the sheep came to drink. And the sheep bred when they came to drink. 39 The flocks bred in front of the branches and bore streaked, speckled, and spotted young. 40 Jacob separated the lambs and made the flocks face the streaked and the completely dark sheep in Laban's flocks. Then he set his own stock apart and didn't put them with Laban's sheep.

41 Whenever the stronger of the flock were breeding, Jacob placed the branches in the troughs, in full view of the flocks, and they would breed in front of the branches. 42 As for the weaklings of the flocks, he did not put out the branches. So it turned out that the weak sheep belonged to Laban and the stronger ones to Jacob. 43 And the man became very rich.[C] He had many flocks, male and female slaves, and camels and donkeys.

31 Now Jacob heard what Laban's sons were saying: "Jacob has taken all that was our father's and has built this wealth from what belonged to our father." 2 And Jacob saw from Laban's face that his attitude toward him was not the same.

3 Then the LORD said to him, "Go back to the land of your fathers and to your family, and I will be with you."

4 Jacob had Rachel and Leah called to the field where his flocks were. 5 He said to them, "I can see from your father's face that his attitude toward me is not the same, but the God of my father has been with me.

in the fields, found he had been hired for the night by Leah. God listened to Leah, and she bore Jacob another son, **Issachar**. While Rachel and Leah believed the mandrakes would increase their fertility, ultimately God would be the giver of children. After the birth of Issachar, marital relations between Jacob and Leah appear to have been restored as Leah bore Jacob yet another son, **Zebulun**, bringing her total to six sons. Leah felt this would certainly bring some honor—the thing she most desired from her husband. Also a daughter, **Dinah** (Hb, "judgment"), was born to Leah.

30:22-24 God remembered Rachel in her barrenness, and she named her son **Joseph** (Hb, "he will **add**"). She was looking for God to be faithful in giving her more children. There is a lesson in the tragedies of Leah and Rachel: God is the one who is faithful in all things, and you need to trust Him even when He is not moving according to your personal desires and timetable.

30:29-35 Not the human scheming of Jacob but the divine blessing of God brought prosperity to Jacob and his family. Laban and his sons responded with envy, however. Laban's sons did not believe God had made Jacob prosper, but that Jacob deceived Laban in order to amass his wealth.

31:1-13 Jacob, already longing to return home with the new wealth he had accumulated, wanted to leave all the more when the jealousy of Laban and his sons became apparent. The pace of events quickened when **the LORD** told Jacob to go back to the **land of** his **fathers**. Jacob called **Rachel** (by listing Rachel first, Jacob may well have been conveying her importance in his life) and **Leah** to come to where the flocks were, probably for privacy, to discuss the situation. Fleeing his father-in-law was not something to be discussed around curious servants and jealous brothers. He needed to reason with his wives and see with whom they would side in this matter. Though the wives would not make the decision, Jacob explained the situation to them and let them voice their opinions. Jacob reinforced to his wives all the good he had done and all of the cheating their father had done. In the midst of the trouble with Laban, Jacob acknowledged that God was with him and, despite what Laban had been doing, had prospered him without letting Laban harm him. Interestingly, Jacob revealed that God was the One who told him to leave; Jacob was not leaving according to his own personal whim. God had reminded Jacob of the vow he had made at Bethel (28:13), and now the time had come to leave.

[A] **30:20** In Hb, the name Zebulun sounds like "honored." [B] **30:24** = He Adds [C] **30:43** Lit *The man spread out very much, very much*

31:14-16 Rachel and Leah finally agreed on something, both allying themselves with their husband Jacob. Both wives realized that God had blessed Jacob and that they and their children were provided with all they would ever need. They willingly submitted to their husband's leadership and supported his word from God saying, **So do whatever God has said to you**.

31:17-21 Jacob's ultimate goal was Canaan, but he headed first for **the hill country of Gilead,** a place to give his caravan rest. This mountain region was east of the Jordan River and thus a good stopping point. While this part of the narrative is short and the details are limited, one point is magnified. Rachel had stolen the **household idols** (Hb *teraphim*) from her father's house, indicating that Laban was not a worshiper of Yahweh. The small figurines were often used for divination purposes. While Rachel's theft might indicate that she, too, was a worshiper of these foreign gods, more likely she was after items she considered monetarily significant. The Nuzi Tablets (i.e., Hurrian law from contemporary Mesopotamia) link control of household idols with inheritance rights, supporting the view that Rachel's theft was prompted more by financial motives than spiritual belief. Even in the haste of this exodus, Rachel had felt so cheated by her father that she took the time to avenge herself by stealing something important to him—his household idols. After all, Rachel and Leah had agreed their father **spent** their **money** (v. 15). Rachel was getting potential financial gain, which she felt her father owed her because of his past deceptions.

31:34-35 Rachel's response to her father lacked respect. Rachel lied to her father by saying she was in the midst of her menstrual cycle and thus was unable to stand. Laban possibly would have considered Rachel and that upon which she sat as being unclean (see the later law recorded in Lv 15:19-24), and thus he did not touch her or the saddlebags upon which she sat and under which the idols were hidden.

31:43-55 While Jacob believed Laban owed him something because of his labor over the years, Laban believed that Jacob was indebted to him because of what he had given Jacob—his daughters and part of his flocks. Those things had flourished under Jacob, but Laban believed he was responsible for Jacob's success. The two men were at an impasse with these differing perspectives. Thus, Laban suggested a **covenant** be made. Covenants may be used to describe relationships between people or nations or between God and men. The stipulations in this covenant were that Jacob would do no harm

6 You know that I've worked hard[A]
for your father 7 and that he has
cheated me and changed my wages
10 times. But God has not let him
harm me. 8 If he said, 'The spotted
sheep will be your wages,' then all
the sheep were born spotted. If he
said, 'The streaked sheep will be
your wages,' then all the sheep were
born streaked. 9 God has taken away
your father's herds and given them
to me.

10 "When the flocks were breeding,
I saw in a dream that the streaked,
spotted, and speckled males were
mating with the females. 11 In that
dream the Angel of God said to
me, 'Jacob!' and I said, 'Here I am.'
12 And He said, 'Look up and see: all
the males that are mating with the
flocks are streaked, spotted, and
speckled, for I have seen all that Laban has been doing to you. 13 I am
the God of Bethel, where you poured
oil on the stone marker and made
a solemn vow to Me. Get up, leave
this land, and return to your native
land.'"

14 Then Rachel and Leah answered
him, "Do we have any portion or inheritance in our father's household?
15 Are we not regarded by him as outsiders? For he has sold us and has
certainly spent our money. 16 In fact,
all the wealth that God has taken
away from our father belongs to us
and to our children. So do whatever
God has said to you."

17 Then Jacob got up and put his
children and wives on the camels.
18 He took all the livestock and possessions he had acquired in Paddan-
aram, and he drove his herds to go
to the land of his father Isaac in
Canaan. 19 When Laban had gone to
shear his sheep, Rachel stole her father's household idols. 20 And Jacob
deceived[B] Laban the Aramean, not
telling him that he was fleeing. 21 He
fled with all his possessions, crossed
the Euphrates, and headed for[C] the
hill country of Gilead.

22 On the third day Laban was told
that Jacob had fled. 23 So he took his
relatives with him, pursued Jacob
for seven days, and overtook him
at Mount Gilead. 24 But God came
to Laban the Aramean in a dream
at night. "Watch yourself!" God
warned him. "Don't say anything to
Jacob, either good or bad."

25 When Laban overtook Jacob, Jacob had pitched his tent in the hill
country, and Laban and his brothers also pitched their tents in the
hill country of Gilead. 26 Then Laban
said to Jacob, "What have you done?
You have deceived me and taken
my daughters away like prisoners
of war! 27 Why did you secretly flee
from me, deceive me, and not tell
me? I would have sent you away with
joy and singing, with tambourines
and lyres, 28 but you didn't even let
me kiss my grandchildren and my
daughters. You have acted foolishly.
29 I could do you great harm, but last
night the God of your father said to
me: 'Watch yourself. Don't say anything to Jacob, either good or bad.'
30 Now you have gone off because
you long for your father—but why
have you stolen my gods?"

31 Jacob answered, "I was afraid,
for I thought you would take your
daughters from me by force. 32 If you
find your gods with anyone here, he
will not live! Before our relatives,
point out anything that is yours and
take it." Jacob did not know that Rachel had stolen the idols.

33 So Laban went into Jacob's tent,
then Leah's tent, and then the tents
of the two female slaves, but he
found nothing. Then he left Leah's
tent and entered Rachel's. 34 Now
Rachel had taken Laban's household
idols, put them in the saddlebag of
the camel, and sat on them. Laban
searched the whole tent but found
nothing.

35 She said to her father, "Sir, don't
be angry that I cannot stand up in
your presence; I am having my period." So Laban searched, but could
not find the household idols.

36 Then Jacob became incensed
and brought charges against Laban.
"What is my crime?" he said to Laban. "What is my sin, that you have
pursued me? 37 You've searched all
my possessions! Have you found
anything of yours? Put it here before my relatives and yours, and

[A]**31:6** Lit *worked with all my strength* [B]**31:20** Lit *And he stole the heart of* [C]**31:21** Lit *and set his face to*

let them decide between the two of
us. 38 I've been with you these 20
years. Your ewes and female goats
have not miscarried, and I have not
eaten the rams from your flock. 39 I
did not bring you any of the flock
torn by wild beasts; I myself bore
the loss. You demanded payment
from me for what was stolen by day
or by night. 40 There I was—the heat
consumed me by day and the frost
by night, and sleep fled from my
eyes. 41 For 20 years I have worked
in your household—14 years for
your two daughters and six years for
your flocks—and you have changed
my wages 10 times! 42 If the God of
my father, the God of Abraham, the
Fear of Isaac, had not been with
me, certainly now you would have
sent me off empty-handed. But God
has seen my affliction and my hard
work,[A] and He issued His verdict last
night."

43 Then Laban answered Jacob,
"The daughters are my daughters;
the sons, my sons; and the flocks,
my flocks! Everything you see is
mine! But what can I do today for
these daughters of mine or for the
children they have borne? 44 Come
now, let's make a covenant, you and
I. Let it be a witness between the
two of us."

45 So Jacob picked out a stone
and set it up as a marker. 46 Then
Jacob said to his relatives, "Gather
stones." And they took stones and
made a mound, then ate there by the
mound. 47 Laban named the mound
Jegar-sahadutha, but Jacob named it
Galeed.[B]

48 Then Laban said, "This mound
is a witness between you and me
today." Therefore the place was
called Galeed 49 and also Mizpah,[C]
for he said, "May the LORD watch
between you and me when we are
out of each other's sight. 50 If you
mistreat my daughters or take other
wives, though no one is with us, understand that God will be a witness
between you and me." 51 Laban also
said to Jacob, "Look at this mound
and the marker I have set up between you and me. 52 This mound is
a witness and the marker is a witness that I will not pass beyond this
mound to you, and you will not pass
beyond this mound and this marker
to do me harm. 53 The God of Abraham, and the gods of Nahor—the
gods of their father[D]—will judge between us." And Jacob swore by the
Fear of his father Isaac. 54 Then Jacob offered a sacrifice on the mountain and invited his relatives to eat a
meal. So they ate a meal and spent
the night on the mountain. 55[E] Laban
got up early in the morning, kissed
his grandchildren and daughters,
and blessed them. Then Laban left
to return home.

32 Jacob went on his way, and
God's angels met him. 2 When
he saw them, Jacob said, "This is
God's camp." So he called that place
Mahanaim.[F]

3 Jacob sent messengers ahead of
him to his brother Esau in the land
of Seir, the country of Edom. 4 He
commanded them, "You are to say to
my lord Esau, 'This is what your servant Jacob says. I have been staying
with Laban and have been delayed
until now. 5 I have oxen, donkeys,
flocks, male and female slaves. I
have sent this message to inform my
lord, in order to seek your favor.'"

6 When the messengers returned
to Jacob, they said, "We went to
your brother Esau; he is coming
to meet you—and he has 400 men
with him." 7 Jacob was greatly afraid
and distressed; he divided the people
with him into two camps, along
with the flocks, cattle, and camels.
8 He thought, "If Esau comes to one
camp and attacks it, the remaining
one can escape."

9 Then Jacob said, "God of my father Abraham and God of my father
Isaac, the LORD who said to me, 'Go
back to your land and to your family, and I will cause you to prosper,'
10 I am unworthy of all the kindness
and faithfulness You have shown
Your servant. Indeed, I crossed over
this Jordan with my staff, and now
I have become two camps. 11 Please
rescue me from the hand of my
brother Esau, for I am afraid of him;

[A] **31:42** Lit *and the work of my hands* [B] **31:47** *Jegar-sahadutha* is Aram, and *Galeed* is Hb; both names = Mound of Witness [C] **31:49** = Watchtower [D] **31:53** Two Hb mss, LXX omit *the gods of their father* [E] **31:55** Gn 32:1 in Hb [F] **32:2** = Two Camps

to Laban's daughters. Neither Laban nor Jacob could cross the boundary to harm one another. Only here in the Old Testament are **stones** used as part of verifying the treaty. Laban and Jacob, along with their relatives, set up stone pillars. The purpose of the pillars was twofold. First, they were to be a witness and reminder of the covenant agreement. Second, the pillars would mark the boundaries to the land of Laban and the land of Jacob. The place of the covenant agreement, marked by the heap of stones, was also given two names, signifying the difference in the people groups: **Jegar-sahadutha** (Aramaic equivalent of Galeed) by Laban and the Hebrew **Galeed** by Jacob, both meaning "Mound of Witness." **The God of Abraham and the gods of Nahor** were to be the witnesses and keepers of this covenant and ensure it was kept as the two men would be separated by great distances and not know whether or not the covenant was being kept. Both men took an oath. Jacob swore by the God of Abraham and Laban by his gods. The covenant was settled and sealed with a sacrifice by Jacob. **Jacob** and **his relatives** also **ate a meal** on the site, a custom often associated with covenants (see 26:30-31).

32:3-8 Jacob's travels had brought him to the outskirts of **Seir, the country of Edom**, and to a dreaded meeting with Esau. Over 20 years had passed since he stole Esau's blessing, but Jacob feared there would still be animosity between them. Therefore, Jacob sent messengers ahead to appease Esau with gifts. Apparently all went well with Esau as Jacob's servants returned with the news that Esau was coming to meet Jacob. However, Esau had **400 men with him**. Jacob prepared by dividing the family into two camps, hopefully allowing at least one camp to survive if Esau mounted an attack. God had promised Jacob that his descendants would become as numerous as the "dust of the earth" (28:14). Jacob soon realized that all his cunning and conniving could not get him out of this situation with Esau. God alone would be his salvation.

32:9-12 Jacob recalled what God had told him to do in the past and repeated that to the Lord, using God's full title, **God of my father Abraham and God of my father Isaac, the LORD.** The title in itself is a reminder of who God had been to Jacob's family in the past. Jacob recalled all of **the kindness and faithfulness** of God in the past and recognized that he was **unworthy** of God's beneficence to him. Just as the Lord's Prayer is an example of how believers ought to pray, the prayer of Jacob is also an excellent example of how to pray. One main focus of Jacob's prayer is his reminding God what He had said in the past. While God may not speak to you audibly, you have His Word, which still speaks truth, confronting you with the mandate to live for Him daily. Memorizing and praying Scripture is a reminder of what God has said and done in the past, and a way by which you let Him know that you desire His Word and trust Him to be faithful to His Word.

32:13-15 Jacob prepared a worthy **gift** for Esau, which included several varieties of livestock, all of which were extremely valuable for nomadic living. Certainly this gift was meant to appease Esau and also shows Jacob's anxiety over cheating his brother.

32:21-22 Jacob's life was marked by his struggles; and here is the climax in this unique encounter at the **ford of Jabbok**, a tributary of the Jordan River flowing through the Jordan Rift and southwest of Ramoth-gilead.

32:24-29 This portion of the narrative is shrouded in mystery. There is no explanation as to why Jacob and the **man**, who is not identified, are fighting, although he is obviously a messenger from God. Jacob and the man are resilient, as they fought all night until the dawn of a new day. The fact that Jacob was seeking a blessing implies that the man had the authority to render a blessing. Also, if the man could dislocate Jacob's **hip socket** with a strike or touch, he obviously could have defeated him at any time. The wrestling match serves as a metaphor for Jacob's life. The change of his **name** to **Israel** (Hb, lit "He struggled with God") is fitting as God wins Jacob's trust. The fighter not only has the authority to bless Jacob but also to change Jacob's name. In the ancient Near East, a person's name was believed to reveal the character of that person, and Jacob is the third person in Genesis whose name was changed at a pivotal point (see notes on Gn 17:5 and 17:15-16).

32:30-32 Before Jacob continued on his journey to meet Esau, he **named the place** of his wrestling match **Peniel** (Hb, "face of God") because he felt that he had struggled with God **face to face** and survived. As Jacob left **limping**, he was sure never to forget his encounter with God. It had marked him forever. Jacob had learned that God, not his own cunning resourcefulness, was the source of his blessings and well-being. Interestingly, the Jewish prohibition against eating the **thigh muscle that is at the hip socket** comes out of this life-changing incident as a way of honoring not only their ancestor Jacob, who became Israel, but also the Lord.

33:1-9 The experience at Peniel prepared Jacob to meet Esau humbly.

otherwise, he may come and attack
me, the mothers, and their children. 12 You have said, 'I will cause
you to prosper, and I will make your
•offspring like the sand of the sea,
which cannot be counted.'"
13 He spent the night there and
took part of what he had brought
with him as a gift for his brother
Esau: 14 200 female goats, 20 male
goats, 200 ewes, 20 rams, 15 30 milk
camels with their young, 40 cows,
10 bulls, 20 female donkeys, and 10
male donkeys. 16 He entrusted them
to his slaves as separate herds and
said to them, "Go on ahead of me,
and leave some distance between the
herds."
17 And he told the first one: "When
my brother Esau meets you and
asks, 'Who do you belong to? Where
are you going? And whose animals
are these ahead of you?' 18 then tell
him, 'They belong to your servant
Jacob. They are a gift sent to my lord
Esau. And look, he is behind us.'"
19 He also told the second one, the
third, and everyone who was walking
behind the animals, "Say the same
thing to Esau when you find him.
20 You are also to say, 'Look, your servant Jacob is right behind us.'" For
he thought, "I want to appease Esau
with the gift that is going ahead of
me. After that, I can face him, and
perhaps he will forgive me."
21 So the gift was sent on ahead of
him while he remained in the camp
that night. 22 During the night Jacob
got up and took his two wives, his
two female slaves, and his 11 sons,
and crossed the ford of Jabbok. 23 He
took them and sent them across the
stream, along with all his possessions.
24 Jacob was left alone, and a man
wrestled with him until daybreak.
25 When the man saw that He could
not defeat him, He struck Jacob's
hip socket as they wrestled and dislocated his hip. 26 Then He said to Jacob, "Let Me go, for it is daybreak."
But Jacob said, "I will not let You
go unless You bless me."
27 "What is your name?" the man
asked.
"Jacob," he replied.
28 "Your name will no longer be Jacob," He said. "It will be Israel[A] because you have struggled with God
and with men and have prevailed."
29 Then Jacob asked Him, "Please
tell me Your name."
But He answered, "Why do you
ask My name?" And He blessed him
there.
30 Jacob then named the place Peniel,[B] "For I have seen God face to
face," he said, "and I have been delivered." 31 The sun shone on him
as he passed by Penuel[C]—limping
because of his hip. 32 That is why,
to this day, the Israelites don't eat
the thigh muscle that is at the hip
socket: because He struck Jacob's
hip socket at the thigh muscle.[D]

33 Now Jacob looked up and saw
Esau coming toward him with
400 men. So he divided the children
among Leah, Rachel, and the two
female slaves. 2 He put the female
slaves and their children first, Leah
and her children next, and Rachel
and Joseph last. 3 He himself went
on ahead and bowed to the ground
seven times until he approached his
brother.
4 But Esau ran to meet him,
hugged him, threw his arms around
him, and kissed him. Then they
wept. 5 When Esau looked up and
saw the women and children, he
asked, "Who are these with you?"
He answered, "The children God
has graciously given your servant."
6 Then the female slaves and their
children approached him and bowed
down. 7 Leah and her children also
approached and bowed down, and
then Joseph and Rachel approached
and bowed down.
8 So Esau said, "What do you mean
by this whole procession[E] I met?"
"To find favor with you, my lord,"
he answered.
9 "I have enough, my brother,"
Esau replied. "Keep what you have."
10 But Jacob said, "No, please! If
I have found favor with you, take
this gift from my hand. For indeed,
I have seen your face, and it is like
seeing God's face, since you have accepted me. 11 Please take my present
that was brought to you, because

[A]32:28 In Hb, the name Israel sounds like "he struggled (with) God." [B]32:30 = Face of God [C]32:31 Variant of *Peniel* [D]32:32 Or *tendon* [E]33:8 Lit *camp*

God has been gracious to me and I
have everything I need." So Jacob
urged him until he accepted.
12 Then Esau said, "Let's move on,
and I'll go ahead of you."
13 Jacob replied, "My lord knows
that the children are weak, and I
have nursing sheep and cattle. If
they are driven hard for one day, the
whole herd will die. 14 Let my lord
go ahead of his servant. I will continue on slowly, at a pace suited to
the livestock and the children, until
I come to my lord at Seir."
15 Esau said, "Let me leave some of
my people with you."
But he replied, "Why do that?
Please indulge me,[A] my lord."
16 That day Esau started on his way
back to Seir, 17 but Jacob went on to
Succoth. He built a house for himself and stalls for his livestock; that
is why the place was called Succoth.[B]
18 After Jacob came from Paddan-
aram, he arrived safely at Shechem
in the land of Canaan and camped
in front of the city. 19 He purchased
a section of the field where he had
pitched his tent from the sons of
Hamor, Shechem's father, for 100
qesitahs.[C] 20 And he set up an altar
there and called it "God, the God of
Israel."[D]

34 Dinah, Leah's daughter whom
she bore to Jacob, went out to
see some of the young women of the
area. 2 When Shechem son of Hamor
the Hivite, a prince of the region,
saw her, he took her and raped her.
3 He became infatuated with Dinah,
daughter of Jacob. He loved the
young girl and spoke tenderly to
her.[E] 4 "Get me this girl as a wife," he
told his father Hamor.
5 Jacob heard that Shechem had
defiled his daughter Dinah, but
since his sons were with his livestock in the field, he remained
silent until they returned. 6 Meanwhile, Shechem's father Hamor
came to speak with Jacob. 7 Jacob's
sons returned from the field when
they heard about the incident and
were deeply grieved and angry. For
Shechem had committed an outrage against Israel by raping Jacob's
daughter, and such a thing should
not be done.
8 Hamor said to Jacob's sons, "My
son Shechem is strongly attracted
to your[F] daughter. Please give her to
him as a wife. 9 Intermarry with us;
give your daughters to us, and take
our daughters for yourselves. 10 Live
with us. The land is before you. Settle here, move about, and acquire
property in it."
11 Then Shechem said to Dinah's
father and brothers, "Grant me this
favor,[A] and I'll give you whatever you

[A] **33:15; 34:11** Lit *May I find favor in your eyes* [B] **33:17** = Stalls or Huts [C] **33:19** The value of this currency is unknown. [D] **33:20** Or El-Elohe-Israel [E] **34:3** Lit *spoke to her heart* [F] **34:8** The Hb word for "your" is pl, showing that Hamor is speaking to Jacob and his sons.

CHARACTER PROFILE

Dinah A Tragic Victim

Her Background	• She was the only daughter of Jacob. Leah was her mother (34:1) • She settled with her family near the city of Shechem (33:18).
Her Story	• She left the safety of the family home to find other young women (34:1-7). • She was seized and raped by Shechem, a prince of that region (34:2). • Shechem loved her and wanted to marry her (34:11). • Her rape was avenged by her brothers (34:24-29).
Life Lessons	• Dinah's rape led to a series of tragic events. • God's name was dishonored by Jacob's sons, who deceived and murdered the men of Shechem's city. • Certainly Dinah's life was scarred forever.

33:10-15 Just as Jacob wrestled with God and lived, he was now being delivered from Esau's once vengeful hands by the grace of God. Esau's face was **like seeing God's face.** Jacob's being accepted by his brother was more evidence of his acceptance with God. God had forgiven him; now Esau was forgiving him. The brothers were reconciled to each other because of God's graciousness.

33:16 Esau returned home to **Seir,** a mountainous region southeast of the Dead Sea, which would become Edom. There is not a mention of the brothers seeing each other again until the death of their father (36:29).

33:17 Jacob then pitched his tent and set up **stalls for his livestock** in a new camp called **Succoth** (Hb, lit "stalls, huts, shelters"), only a temporary stop.

33:18-20 Jacob journeyed to **Shechem,** a place that would darken the bright days of Jacob and his family. He purchased **a section of the field** where he could pitch his tent for **100 qesitahs,** an unknown amount that some commentators have suggested equaled 100 lambs. By purchasing a field, Jacob was establishing a more permanent dwelling for his nomadic tribe. Establishing **an altar** shows his deepening commitment to God and his desire for a more permanent settlement.

34:1-11 After such a wonderful encounter with Esau, tragedy struck. **Dinah** was **raped** by **Shechem son of Hamor.** Dinah's visit to Shechem to **see some of the young women of the area** was not wise. Customarily, women did not venture out alone. An escort was expected if she were traveling a distance. Certainly these cautions should have been considered in a pagan land. Nevertheless, while Dinah's behavior was not wise, she cannot be blamed for the rape. Nevertheless, Shechem acted out of his own lust when he saw Dinah. Some scholars have argued that the sex was consensual between Shechem and Dinah, but nothing in the Hebrew text suggests this interpretation.

Shechem violated the law by engaging in sexual intimacy with an Israelite as a foreigner and uncircumcised man, or by not going through the set of procedures leading to betrothal prior to the sexual encounter and afterward not admitting the crime or providing compensation to Dinah and her family. Shechem **took** her and raped her (Hb *shakav*, "lay," often used to describe forced sexual relations).

The reaction of a father whose daughter has just been raped is generally outrage and grief. Jacob's **silent** reaction is shocking. He may have been grieved within but waiting to act until his sons, who were fighters or warriors, were home. Also, sons—as with Laban and his father Bethuel—were very much involved in making family decisions and executing plans. By the time Hamor and Shechem approached Jacob with an offer, all of the brothers had returned, **deeply grieved and angry**.

34:12-17 Hamor and Shechem presented an offer that was hard to resist; Jacob had before him the opportunity for land, intermarriage, and a bride price of his choosing. Jacob knew quite a bit about the bride price (it had cost him 14 years of labor for his father-in-law Laban). Yet, he also knew God's prohibition concerning intermarriage.

For the sons and daughters of Israel to intermarry with the sons and daughters of Shechem, who practiced a different religion, would not be acceptable unless all from Shechem were converted (see Dt 7:3).

34:30-31 The sons returned home to find an enraged Jacob. What they had done was horrible and lacked proper forethought. Although Shechem's rape of Dinah was despicable, her brothers put themselves on the same level with the Hivites through their violence and pillaging.

35:4-8 Jacob set out toward **Bethel** to renew his covenant with God (28:13-22). Not one of the surrounding cities pursued them because the Lord put **a terror** upon them until they made it safely to **Luz (that is, Bethel)**. Jacob was obedient and built an altar, naming it **God of Bethel**. The return to Bethel was not one of complete happiness, however. Rebekah's nurse **Deborah** died and **was buried under the oak south of Bethel**, and Jacob **named it Oak of Weeping**. Depending on the social status of a mother, she might use a wet nurse to breastfeed her child; Deborah was the wet nurse who cared not only for Rebekah but likely for her children. Deborah was probably a maternal figure in Jacob's life. His weeping for her shows a deep emotional attachment, and mentioning her by name shows her significance.

35:16-20 Israel gathered his family and moved toward **Ephrath**, later known as Bethlehem. Rachel's pregnancy brings a heightened awareness in the text because she has only given birth once. **Difficult** labor was common. The midwife spoke comfort to Rachel, hoping that she would gather strength in birthing a son, the greatest blessing a mother could have. Her last words are evidence of the misery she experienced in giving birth—**Ben-oni** (Hb, "son of my sorrow"). Jacob instead found joy in this welcomed addition to the family

say. 12 Demand of me a high compensation[A] and gift; I'll give you whatever you ask me. Just give the girl to be my wife!"

13 But Jacob's sons answered Shechem and his father Hamor deceitfully because he had defiled their sister Dinah. 14 "We cannot do this thing," they said to them. "Giving our sister to an uncircumcised man is a disgrace to us. 15 We will agree with you only on this condition: if all your males are circumcised as we are. 16 Then we will give you our daughters, take your daughters for ourselves, live with you, and become one people. 17 But if you will not listen to us and be circumcised, then we will take our daughter and go."

18 Their words seemed good to Hamor and his son Shechem. 19 The young man did not delay doing this, because he was delighted with Jacob's daughter. Now he was the most important in all his father's house. 20 So Hamor and his son Shechem went to the •gate of their city and spoke to the men there.

21 "These men are peaceful toward us," they said. "Let them live in our land and move about in it, for indeed, the region is large enough for them. Let us take their daughters as our wives and give our daughters to them. 22 But the men will agree to live with us and be one people only on this condition: if all our men are circumcised as they are. 23 Won't their livestock, their possessions, and all their animals become ours? Only let us agree with them, and they will live with us."

24 All the able-bodied men[B] listened to Hamor and his son Shechem, and all the able-bodied men[C] were circumcised. 25 On the third day, when they were still in pain, two of Jacob's sons, Simeon and Levi, Dinah's brothers, took their swords, went into the unsuspecting city, and killed every male. 26 They killed Hamor and his son Shechem with their swords, took Dinah from Shechem's house, and went away. 27 Jacob's other sons came to the slaughter and plundered the city because their sister had been defiled. 28 They took their sheep, cattle, donkeys, and whatever was in the city and in the field. 29 They captured all their possessions, children, and wives and plundered everything in the houses.

30 Then Jacob said to Simeon and Levi, "You have brought trouble on me, making me odious to the inhabitants of the land, the Canaanites and the Perizzites. We are few in number; if they unite against me and attack me, I and my household will be destroyed."

31 But they answered, "Should he have treated our sister like a prostitute?"

35

God said to Jacob, "Get up! Go to Bethel and settle there. Build an altar there to the God who appeared to you when you fled from your brother Esau."

2 So Jacob said to his family and all who were with him, "Get rid of the foreign gods that are among you. Purify yourselves and change your clothes. 3 We must get up and go to Bethel. I will build an altar there to the God who answered me in my day of distress. He has been with me everywhere I have gone."

4 Then they gave Jacob all their foreign gods and their earrings, and Jacob hid them under the oak near Shechem. 5 When they set out, a terror from God came over the cities around them, and they did not pursue Jacob's sons. 6 So Jacob and all who were with him came to Luz (that is, Bethel) in the land of Canaan. 7 Jacob built an altar there and called the place God of Bethel[D] because it was there that God had revealed Himself to him when he was fleeing from his brother.

8 Deborah, the one who had nursed and raised Rebekah,[E] died and was buried under the oak south of Bethel. So Jacob named it Oak of Weeping.[F]

9 God appeared to Jacob again after he returned from Paddan-aram, and He blessed him. 10 God said to him:

Your name is Jacob;

[A]34:12 Or *bride-price*, or *betrothal present* [B]34:24 Lit *All who went out of the city gate* [C]34:24 Lit *all the males who went out of the city gate* [D]35:7 Or *El-bethel* [E]35:8 Lit *Deborah, Rebekah's wet nurse*; Gn 24:59 [F]35:8 Or *Allon-bacuth*

you will no longer be named
Jacob,
but your name will be Israel.

So He named him Israel. 11 God also
said to him:

I am •God Almighty.
Be fruitful and multiply.
A nation, indeed an assembly
of nations,
will come from you,
and kings will descend
from you.[A]
12 I will give to you the land
that I gave to Abraham
and Isaac.
And I will give the land
to your future descendants.

13 Then God withdrew[B] from him at
the place where He had spoken to
him.
14 Jacob set up a marker at the
place where He had spoken to
him—a stone marker. He poured a
drink offering on it and anointed it
with oil. 15 Jacob named the place
where God had spoken with him
Bethel.
16 They set out from Bethel. When
they were still some distance from
Ephrath, Rachel began to give birth,
and her labor was difficult. 17 During her difficult labor, the midwife
said to her, "Don't be afraid, for you
have another son." 18 With her last
breath—for she was dying—she
named him Ben-oni,[C] but his father
called him Benjamin.[D] 19 So Rachel
died and was buried on the way to
Ephrath (that is, Bethlehem). 20 Jacob set up a marker on her grave;
it is the marker at Rachel's grave to
this day.
21 Israel set out again and pitched
his tent beyond the Tower of Eder.[E]
22 While Israel was living in that region, Reuben went in and slept with
his father's concubine Bilhah, and
Israel heard about it.
Jacob had 12 sons:

23 Leah's sons were Reuben
(Jacob's firstborn),
Simeon, Levi, Judah,
Issachar, and Zebulun.
24 Rachel's sons were
Joseph and Benjamin.
25 The sons of Rachel's slave
Bilhah
were Dan and Naphtali.
26 The sons of Leah's slave
Zilpah
were Gad and Asher.

These are the sons of Jacob, who
were born to him in Paddan-aram.
27 Jacob came to his father Isaac
at Mamre in Kiriath-arba (that is,
Hebron), where Abraham and Isaac
had stayed. 28 Isaac lived 180 years.
29 He took his last breath and died,
and was gathered to his people, old
and full of days. His sons Esau and
Jacob buried him.

The Generations of Esau (36:1-43)

36 These are the family records
of Esau (that is, Edom). 2 Esau
took his wives from the Canaanite
women: Adah daughter of Elon the
Hittite, Oholibamah daughter of
Anah and granddaughter[F] of Zibeon
the Hivite, 3 and Basemath daughter
of Ishmael and sister of Nebaioth.
4 Adah bore Eliphaz to Esau, Basemath bore Reuel, 5 and Oholibamah
bore Jeush, Jalam, and Korah. These
were Esau's sons, who were born to
him in the land of Canaan.
6 Esau took his wives, sons, daughters, and all the people of his household, as well as his herds, all his
livestock, and all the property he
had acquired in Canaan; he went
to a land away from his brother
Jacob. 7 For their possessions were
too many for them to live together,
and because of their herds, the land
where they stayed could not support
them. 8 So Esau (that is, Edom) lived
in the mountains of Seir.
9 These are the family records of
Esau, father of the Edomites in the
mountains of Seir.

10 These are the names
of Esau's sons:
Eliphaz son of Esau's wife
Adah,
and Reuel son of Esau's wife
Basemath.
11 The sons of Eliphaz were
Teman, Omar, Zepho, Gatam,
and Kenaz.

and changed his name to **Benjamin** (Hb, "son of my right hand," a metaphor for a place of prominence because of the position's proximity to the action), showing his favor toward his new son. Jacob's changing his son's name reflects the importance of names in the ancient Near East.

35:21-22 Jacob continued with a heart of sorrow toward his father's house, settling at **Eder**. Here **Reuben** sinned gravely by sleeping with **his father's concubine Bilhah**. Reuben's act not only showed a lack of respect for his father but also possibly indicated an aggressive effort to become the next head of the family. While the consequences for his action are not seen in this passage, they are noted in 49:3-4.

35:23-26 Following the brief accounting of Reuben's grave actions is Jacob's genealogy. The wives and sons of Jacob are listed not in order of importance to Jacob but in the order he took his wives.

35:27-29 Finally, Jacob arrived at the home of his fathers, **Abraham and Isaac**. This notes the connection Jacob had with these patriarchs and shows a continuation of the covenant. Jacob's father Isaac died at the age of **180**. Statements of death for Isaac and Abraham follow a formula, which again connects Abraham, Isaac, and Jacob to the covenant. Both Abraham and Isaac take their **last breath** and die, **old and full of days**, and are **gathered to their people** (cp. 25:8).

36:1-43 After Isaac's death, Esau's family genealogy is given. Esau, who had gone his own way, was thereby separated from Abraham, Isaac, and Jacob. The genealogy is broken into four sections: wives; children; possessions; and the lands of Seir and Edom (vv. 20-43). Esau's disobedience to his parents is evident in the choosing of his wives, which included Canaanite, Hittite, and other foreign women who worshiped pagan gods. Three wives are listed: **Adah, daughter of Elon the Hittite; Oholibamah, daughter of Anah**; and **Basemath, daughter of Ishmael and sister of Nebaioth**. In another reference, Esau's wives are noted as Judith, the daughter of Beeri the Hizzite, and Basemath, the daughter of Elon the Hittite (26:34). Esau also married Mahalath, daughter of Ishmael and sister of Nebaioth (28:9). There are several possible explanations for the differences in these accounts:

The wives have alternate names, as did Esau himself—"Edom" (25:30).

Esau had more than three wives, but only the descendants of these three wives are listed (36:2-3).

Though not as large as Jacob's, Esau had a large family, too, with five sons. He had accumulated great

A 35:11 Lit *will come from your loins* B 35:13 Lit *went up* C 35:18 = Son of My Sorrow D 35:18 = Son of the Right Hand E 35:21 Or *beyond Migdal-eder* F 36:2 Sam, LXX read *Anah son*

possessions as well. **Their possessions were too many** for them **to live together**. In fact, because of Esau's large family, great possessions, and swelling herds, the family moved into the mountain range of **Seir**.

Esau's family was divided by his sons. Each family had a chief, as was common in that day. Edom was also ruled by **kings**, long before Israel demanded a king. While Abraham, Isaac, and Jacob were the fathers of the Israelites, Esau was the **father of the Edomites**. God's prophecy was fulfilled; from Rebekah's twins came two nations, Israel and Edom (see 25:23).

37:1-4 The family record of Jacob (Israel) begins the last section of the book of Genesis. It begins by describing Joseph, the central figure in the remaining chapters. At **17 years of age,** Joseph was considered a man, but his complaining, a sign of his immaturity, was causing friction among the brothers, which was further aggravated by Israel's partiality toward Joseph. Joseph not only was born to Israel in his old age but also was the son of Israel's beloved wife Rachel. Israel loved Joseph so much that he gave him a **robe of many colors**. There is some confusion over the exact meaning of this Hebrew phrase. Many translate the words as robe of many colors (Hb *kutonet passim*), which is easily understood as a beautiful coat. These words may also be translated "coat/dress with long sleeves," understanding the length of the sleeves as an indicator of wealth. Either way—whether because of the robe's beauty or considering its long sleeves a sign of wealth—the robe would awaken jealousy among the brothers. As Joseph felt and received love from his father, the other sons saw this love and became even more jealous so that **they hated** Joseph. Israel's favoritism brought strife to the family.

37:5-11 Joseph's **dream** is allegorical with the **sheaves** of Joseph's brothers bowing to Joseph's sheaf, which was standing. The dream did not deal with the brothers' current situation but was depictive of what would happen during the famine. The idea of Joseph ruling over his brothers drove them to hate Joseph **even more**. In the ancient Near East, dreams were of great importance, considered to be a communication of God. Before Joseph, God appeared to Abimelech (20:3), Jacob (31:10), and Laban (31:24) in dreams. Even after Joseph's time, God spoke in dreams to Gideon's men (Jdg 7:13); Solomon (1Kgs 3:5); Nebuchadnezzar (see Dn 2); and Joseph, the husband of Mary and the earthly father of Jesus (Mt 1:20). The brothers were even angrier to think that they as older brothers would receive one of the ultimate humiliations

12 Timna, a concubine
of Esau's son Eliphaz,
bore Amalek to Eliphaz.
These were the sons
of Esau's wife Adah.

13 These are Reuel's sons:
Nahath, Zerah, Shammah,
and Mizzah.
These were the sons
of Esau's wife Basemath.

14 These are the sons
of Esau's wife Oholibamah
daughter of Anah
and granddaughter[A]
of Zibeon:
She bore Jeush, Jalam,
and Korah to Edom.

15 These are the chiefs
of Esau's sons:
the sons of Eliphaz,
Esau's firstborn:
Chiefs Teman, Omar, Zepho,
Kenaz,
16 Korah,[B] Gatam, and Amalek.
These are the chiefs
of Eliphaz
in the land of Edom.
These are the sons of Adah.
17 These are the sons of Reuel,
Esau's son:
Chiefs Nahath, Zerah,
Shammah, and Mizzah.
These are the chiefs of Reuel
in the land of Edom.
These are the sons
of Esau's wife Basemath.

18 These are the sons
of Esau's wife Oholibamah:
Chiefs Jeush, Jalam,
and Korah.
These are the chiefs
of Esau's wife Oholibamah
daughter of Anah.
19 These are the sons of Esau
(that is, Edom),
and these are their chiefs.

20 These are the sons of Seir
the Horite,
the inhabitants of the land:
Lotan, Shobal, Zibeon, Anah,
21 Dishon, Ezer, and Dishan.
These are the chiefs
of the Horites,
the sons of Seir, in the land
of Edom.
22 The sons of Lotan were Hori
and Heman.
Timna was Lotan's sister.
23 These are Shobal's sons:
Alvan, Manahath, Ebal,
Shepho, and Onam.
24 These are Zibeon's sons:
Aiah and Anah.
This was the Anah who
found the hot springs[C]
in the wilderness
while he was pasturing
the donkeys of his father
Zibeon.
25 These are the children of Anah:
Dishon and Oholibamah
daughter of Anah.
26 These are Dishon's sons:
Hemdan, Eshban, Ithran,
and Cheran.
27 These are Ezer's sons:
Bilhan, Zaavan, and Akan.
28 These are Dishan's sons:
Uz and Aran.
29 These are the chiefs
of the Horites:
Chiefs Lotan, Shobal, Zibeon,
Anah,
30 Dishon, Ezer, and Dishan.
These are the chiefs
of the Horites,
according to their divisions,
in the land of Seir.

31 These are the kings who ruled
in the land of Edom
before any king ruled
over the Israelites:
32 Bela son of Beor ruled in Edom;
the name of his city
was Dinhabah.
33 When Bela died, Jobab
son of Zerah from Bozrah
became king in his place.
34 When Jobab died,
Husham from the land
of the Temanites
became king in his place.
35 When Husham died, Hadad
son of Bedad became king
in his place.
He defeated Midian
in the field of Moab;
the name of his city
was Avith.

[A]36:14 Sam, LXX read *Anah son* [B]36:16 Sam omits *Korah* [C]36:24 Syr, Vg; Tg reads *the mules*; Hb obscure

36 When Hadad died, Samlah
from Masrekah became king
in his place.
37 When Samlah died,
Shaul from Rehoboth
on the Euphrates River
became king in his place.
38 When Shaul died, Baal-hanan
son of Achbor became king
in his place.
39 When Baal-hanan
son of Achbor died, Hadar[A]
became king in his place.
His city was Pau,
and his wife's name
was Mehetabel
daughter of Matred daughter
of Me-zahab.
40 These are the names
of Esau's chiefs,
according to their families
and their localities,
by their names:
Chiefs Timna, Alvah, Jetheth,
41 Oholibamah, Elah, Pinon,
42 Kenaz, Teman, Mibzar,
43 Magdiel, and Iram.
These are Edom's chiefs,
according to their settlements
in the land they possessed.
Esau[B] was father
of the Edomites.

The Generations of Jacob and the Saving of Israel (37:1–50:26)

The Sowing of Conflict (37:1-11)

37 Jacob lived in the land where
his father had stayed, the land
of Canaan. 2 These are the family
records of Jacob.
At 17 years of age, Joseph tended
sheep with his brothers. The young
man was working with the sons of
Bilhah and Zilpah, his father's wives,
and he brought a bad report about
them to their father.
3 Now Israel loved Joseph more
than his other sons because Joseph
was a son born to him in his old age,
and he made a robe of many colors[C]
for him. 4 When his brothers saw
that their father loved him more
than all his brothers, they hated
him and could not bring themselves
to speak peaceably to him.
5 Then Joseph had a dream. When
he told it to his brothers, they hated
him even more. 6 He said to them,
"Listen to this dream I had: 7 There
we were, binding sheaves of grain
in the field. Suddenly my sheaf
stood up, and your sheaves gathered
around it and bowed down to my
sheaf."
8 "Are you really going to reign
over us?" his brothers asked him.
"Are you really going to rule us?" So
they hated him even more because
of his dream and what he had said.
9 Then he had another dream and
told it to his brothers. "Look," he
said, "I had another dream, and this
time the sun, moon, and 11 stars
were bowing down to me."
10 He told his father and brothers,
but his father rebuked him. "What
kind of dream is this that you have
had?" he said. "Are your mother
and brothers and I going to come
and bow down to the ground before
you?" 11 His brothers were jealous of
him, but his father kept the matter
in mind.

The Slavery of Joseph (37:12-36)

12 His brothers had gone to pasture
their father's flocks at Shechem.
13 Israel said to Joseph, "Your brothers, you know, are pasturing the
flocks at Shechem. Get ready. I'm
sending you to them."
"I'm ready," Joseph replied.
14 Then Israel said to him, "Go and
see how your brothers and the flocks
are doing, and bring word back to
me." So he sent him from the Valley
of Hebron, and he went to Shechem.
15 A man found him there, wandering in the field, and asked him,
"What are you looking for?"
16 "I'm looking for my brothers,"
Joseph said. "Can you tell me where
they are pasturing their flocks?"
17 "They've moved on from here,"
the man said. "I heard them say,
'Let's go to Dothan.'" So Joseph
set out after his brothers and found
them at Dothan.
18 They saw him in the distance,
and before he had reached them,
they plotted to kill him. 19 They said
to one another, "Here comes that
dreamer![D] 20 Come on, let's kill him

by having a younger brother rule over them. Joseph's telling of the second dream not only left his brothers filled with more bitterness. Even **his father** Israel was upset and **rebuked** Joseph. Jacob's rebuke (Hb *ga'ar*, "speak insultingly to," even "scream at") of Joseph's dream is indicative of his own disgust. In Ruth the same word is used by Boaz, but he is instructing his servants not to insult Ruth or take her to task for gathering grain (Ru 2:16).

37:14-20 When Joseph arrived at **Shechem** his brothers had moved to another place, and he was directed to **Dothan**. God's divine hand is seen through the man who directed Joseph to hardship on the one hand and to the saving of many lives on the other. The brothers saw Joseph at a distance and immediately began plotting his demise. Joseph's brothers were so full of jealousy and hate that murder seemed the only solution. They **plotted** [Hb *nakal*, "act fraudulently or treacherously, be deceitful, beguile"; cp. Nm 25:18; Ps 105:25; Mal 1:14] **to kill** their younger brother as one would an animal. With venomous words the brothers gave away their main point of contempt for Joseph—his dreams. They called him the **dreamer**. The sons of Jacob intended to murder their own brother as a way of ensuring that his dreams did not come to pass.

[A]36:39 Many Hb mss, Sam, Syr read *Hadad* [B]36:43 Lit *He Esau* [C]37:3 Or *robe with long sleeves* [D]37:19 Lit *comes the lord of the dreams*

37:29-36 When Reuben returned, he was surprised that the pit was empty. By fabricating a story about Joseph's death, the younger brothers came up with a scheme to make them appear blameless, while hopefully winning their father's favor since Joseph, at least in the mind of Jacob, would be dead. Just as Isaac fell for Jacob's deceit, so Jacob believed the trickery of his sons. Believing Joseph was mauled by a **vicious animal**, Jacob **mourned for his son many days**.

38:1-5 Some find the break in the Joseph narrative odd, but in fact the narrative shows the continuation of the Abrahamic covenant through Judah, the contrast between Judah and Joseph, and the moving of God's hand behind the scenes. After Joseph's brothers sold him into slavery, **Judah** moved away from **his brothers** and closer to Canaan. In this new settlement Judah saw **Shua**, a Canaanite, and took her as his wife. Already this conjures up images of Esau's disobedience in marrying foreign women. The Hebrew text implies a lustful relationship—Judah saw, took, and slept. Thus, the imagery given is one of Judah's turning away from the worship of Yahweh.

38:6-10 Judah selected **Tamar** as a wife for his firstborn **Er**. While Tamar's nationality is not noted, she may have been a Hebrew. Er was **evil** [Hb *ra'*, a word used to describe many illicit behaviors] **in the Lord's sight** and was put **to death**. As was the custom, Judah commanded **Onan**, his second-born, to perform his duty in what would be later known as levirate marriage (see Dt 25:5-10). Onan, however, was greedy and selfish, for the son who would come from such a union would not be considered his own son but the surviving son of Er and thus the firstborn of the firstborn—having a higher rank than he (Onan) when the inheritance of Judah was distributed. Instead of doing as his father commanded, Onan spilled his semen on the ground to ensure no conception occurred.

38:11 After the death of Judah's two eldest sons, he was left with his youngest son **Shelah**. Judah told Tamar that she must remain a widow until Shelah grew up. Judah may have believed that Tamar was the cause of his sons' deaths, and he did not want to lose his youngest. Tamar was sent to her father's house to wait. Normally, a widow continued to remain with the family of her father-in-law, so this was unusual and revealed Judah's doubts (see Ru 1). Tamar had been displaced and put in a precarious situation in which she might be left with no one to care for her.

38:12-19 Judah's wife Shua died, and

and throw him into one of the pits. We can say that a vicious animal ate him. Then we'll see what becomes of his dreams!"

21 When Reuben heard this, he tried to save him from them.[A] He said, "Let's not take his life." 22 Reuben also said to them, "Don't shed blood. Throw him into this pit in the wilderness, but don't lay a hand on him"—intending to rescue him from their hands and return him to his father.

23 When Joseph came to his brothers, they stripped off his robe, the robe of many colors that he had on. 24 Then they took him and threw him into the pit. The pit was empty; there was no water in it.

25 Then they sat down to eat a meal. They looked up, and there was a caravan of Ishmaelites coming from Gilead. Their camels were carrying aromatic gum, balsam, and resin, going down to Egypt.

26 Then Judah said to his brothers, "What do we gain if we kill our brother and cover up his blood? 27 Come, let's sell him to the Ishmaelites and not lay a hand on him, for he is our brother, our own flesh," and they agreed. 28 When Midianite traders passed by, his brothers pulled Joseph out of the pit and sold him for 20 pieces of silver to the Ishmaelites, who took Joseph to Egypt.

29 When Reuben returned to the pit and saw that Joseph was not there, he tore his clothes. 30 He went back to his brothers and said, "The boy is gone! What am I going to do?"[B] 31 So they took Joseph's robe, slaughtered a young goat, and dipped the robe in its blood. 32 They sent the robe of many colors to their father and said, "We found this. Examine it. Is it your son's robe or not?"

33 His father recognized it. "It is my son's robe," he said. "A vicious animal has devoured him. Joseph has been torn to pieces!" 34 Then Jacob tore his clothes, put •sackcloth around his waist, and mourned for his son many days. 35 All his sons and daughters tried to comfort him, but he refused to be comforted. "No," he said. "I will go down to •Sheol to my son, mourning." And his father wept for him.

36 Meanwhile, the Midianites sold Joseph in Egypt to Potiphar, an officer of Pharaoh and the captain of the guard.

The Faithfulness of God to Joseph During His Rise to Power (38:1–41:57)

38 At that time Judah left his brothers and settled near an Adullamite named Hirah. 2 There Judah saw the daughter of a Canaanite named Shua; he took her as a wife and slept with her. 3 She conceived and gave birth to a son, and he named him Er. 4 She conceived again, gave birth to a son, and named him Onan. 5 She gave birth to another son and named him Shelah. It was at Chezib that[C,D] she gave birth to him.

6 Judah got a wife for Er, his firstborn, and her name was Tamar. 7 Now Er, Judah's firstborn, was evil in the LORD's sight, and the LORD put him to death. 8 Then Judah said to Onan, "Sleep with your brother's wife. Perform your duty as her brother-in-law and produce •offspring for your brother." 9 But Onan knew that the offspring would not be his, so whenever he slept with his brother's wife, he released his semen on the ground so that he would not produce offspring for his brother. 10 What he did was evil in the LORD's sight, so He put him to death also.

11 Then Judah said to his daughter-in-law Tamar, "Remain a widow in your father's house until my son Shelah grows up." For he thought, "He might die too, like his brothers." So Tamar went to live in her father's house.

12 After a long time[E] Judah's wife, the daughter of Shua, died. When Judah had finished mourning, he and his friend Hirah the Adullamite went up to Timnah to the sheepshearers. 13 Tamar was told, "Your father-in-law is going up to Timnah to shear his sheep." 14 So she took off her widow's clothes, veiled her face, covered herself, and sat at the entrance to Enaim,[F] which is on the way to Timnah. For she saw that, though Shelah had grown up, she

[A]**37:21** Lit *their hands* [B]**37:30** Lit *And I, where am I going* [C]**38:5** LXX reads *She was at Chezib when* [D]**38:5** Or *He was at Chezib when* [E]**38:12** Lit *And there were many days* [F]**38:14** Or *sat by the mouth of the springs*

CHARACTER PROFILE

Tamar A Determined Widow

Her Background	• The wife of Er, firstborn son of Judah (38:6) • The mother of twin sons, Perez and Zerah (38:27-30)
Her Story	• She became a widow upon Er's death (38:7-11). • She was denied her legal right to an heir by Er's brother Onan, who refused to impregnate her (38:8-10). • She shrewdly deceived and trapped her father-in-law Judah into admitting she had been wronged (38:13-30).
Life Lessons	• Tamar did not accept her victimization but, right or wrong, sought a way to get what was rightfully hers. • She is listed in the genealogy of Christ, evidence of God's grace (Mt 1:3).

had not been given to him as a wife.
15 When Judah saw her, he thought
she was a prostitute, for she had covered her face.
16 He went over to her and said,
"Come, let me sleep with you," for
he did not know that she was his
daughter-in-law.
She said, "What will you give me
for sleeping with me?"
17 "I will send you a young goat
from my flock," he replied.
But she said, "Only if you leave
something with me until you send
it."
18 "What should I give you?" he
asked.
She answered, "Your signet ring,
your cord, and the staff in your
hand." So he gave them to her and
slept with her, and she got pregnant
by him. 19 She got up and left, then
removed her veil and put her widow's clothes back on.
20 When Judah sent the young goat
by his friend the Adullamite in order to get back the items he had left
with the woman, he could not find
her. 21 He asked the men of the place,
"Where is the cult prostitute who
was beside the road at Enaim?"
"There has been no cult prostitute
here," they answered.
22 So the Adullamite returned to
Judah, saying, "I couldn't find her,
and furthermore, the men of the
place said, 'There has been no cult
prostitute here.'"
23 Judah replied, "Let her keep the
items for herself; otherwise we will
become a laughingstock. After all,
I did send this young goat, but you
couldn't find her."
24 About three months later Judah
was told, "Your daughter-in-law,
Tamar, has been acting like a prostitute, and now she is pregnant."
"Bring her out!" Judah said. "Let
her be burned to death!"
25 As she was being brought out,
she sent her father-in-law this message: "I am pregnant by the man to
whom these items belong." And she
added, "Examine them. Whose signet ring, cord, and staff are these?"
26 Judah recognized them and said,
"She is more in the right[A] than I,
since I did not give her to my son
Shelah." And he did not know her
intimately again.
27 When the time came for her to
give birth, there were twins in her
womb. 28 As she was giving birth,
one of them put out his hand, and
the midwife took it and tied a scarlet
thread around it, announcing, "This
one came out first." 29 But then he
pulled his hand back, and his brother
came out. Then she said, "You have
broken out first!" So he was named
Perez.[B] 30 Then his brother, who had
the scarlet thread tied to his hand,
came out, and was named Zerah.[C]

39 Now Joseph had been taken
to Egypt. An Egyptian named

[A]38:26 Or *more righteous* [B]38:29 = Breaking Out [C]38:30 = Brightness of Sunrise; perhaps related to the scarlet thread

as soon as Judah had finished his time of mourning, he headed to **Timnah** (Hb, "allotted portion," v. 13), likely a reference to the village lying south of Hebron in the hill country about four miles east of Beit Nettif (see Jos 15:57). Tamar, aware of Judah's journey, was tired of being treated dishonestly and disrespectfully by her father-in-law. Thus, she decided to use her own means to carry on the Abrahamic line. She quickly changed from her widow's clothes and veiled herself. Appearing as a prostitute, she was propositioned by Judah. Had Judah been able to see beneath the veil, he would have recognized his desperate daughter-in-law, with whom he would not have had sexual relations because it was illegal. However, Judah did not know it was Tamar. She was clever in the items she requested from Judah—the equivalent to a modern driver's license (i.e., his legal identification). Once Tamar completed her mission, she returned to her widow's clothing, lying in wait until she was able to confront Judah with his actions. Judah was at the lowest point in his life. He had sold Joseph into slavery, married a foreign woman, broken his promise to Tamar, and now propositioned a prostitute.

38:20-26 Judah's embarrassment over his transaction with the **cult prostitute** is evident when, instead of going himself, he sent his friend with her payment. His main concern was the return of his things. Judah was even more humiliated when the **Adullamite** returned saying there was no cult prostitute there. About three months after the incident between Judah and the unknown "prostitute," Judah received word that Tamar was pregnant. Judah called for her death, the typical punishment for adultery. Judah's belongings from his bartering with the prostitute were returned to him with a message, **I am pregnant by the man to whom these items belong . . . Whose signet ring, cord, and staff are these?** Seeing his possessions, Judah understood that he was the father of the child. Judah declared Tamar **more in the right** (Hb *tsedaqah*, "just") than he because she was trying to fulfill levirate marriage, while he sought to dissuade the union of his youngest son to Tamar. With Judah's admission of guilt also comes a sign of repentance since he did not have sexual relations with his daughter-in-law again.

38:27-30 As Rebekah, Tamar had **twins in her womb**. Birth order was very important in the Hebrew tradition. The firstborn received certain rights and thus recording who was the elder child was of utmost importance. **Zerah** (Hb *zerach*, "brightness of sunrise") appeared to come forth first and a scarlet cord was tied to his hand.

However, **Perez** (Hb *perets*, "breaking out") broke through and became the firstborn. They were an influential pair as Zerah became head of a Judahite clan (1Ch. 2:6) and Perez was the ancestor of the King of kings, Jesus.

39:2-6a Chapter 39 resumes the Joseph narrative. In the midst of what seemed a desperate situation, **The Lord was with Joseph** becomes the theme of the entire Joseph narrative. Yahweh would bring about Joseph's success. Just as God was with Abraham, Isaac, and Jacob, so He would be with Joseph. The remark puts into perspective the unfortunate events that would befall Joseph. That the Lord was with Joseph was apparent even to those around him. Potiphar recognized the blessing upon Joseph and so entrusted to his authority everything in his house.

39:6b-10 Joseph was not only favored by God and successful in his duties. So strikingly **well-built and handsome** was Joseph that he captured the attention of Potiphar's wife.

39:11-15 When Joseph's attention was on his work in the home, Potiphar's wife seized her opportunity. **None of the household servants were there** in the house, and she aggressively commanded Joseph to sleep with her. The fact that none of the servants were in the house is important. If Joseph were to succumb to temptation, he would have done so when no one was watching. But God saw everything. Joseph so hurried to get out that he left his cloak in the temptress's hands. Joseph **ran** (Hb *nus*, "flee, escape") from temptation. The New Testament affirms fleeing from temptation and sexual immorality (see 1Co 6:18; 2Ti 2:22). Thus, Joseph is an excellent example of a man seeking to maintain purity and not pursue lusts. The theme of the garment runs throughout chapters 37, 38, and 39. The cloak is always evidence: the proof of Joseph's death by a wild animal, the evidence of Judah's misconduct, and the means by which Potiphar's wife accused Joseph of attempted rape. Humiliated and unfulfilled, Potiphar's wife screamed for the servants and portrayed Joseph as **a Hebrew** who came **to make fools of** us. She used a ploy to set the Egyptian servants against the Hebrew slave, Joseph. There might have been racial tensions already, and Potiphar's wife used this friction to her advantage.

39:16-20 The repetition of the lie reinforced how wicked Potiphar's wife was and how dire Joseph's situation was, though he was completely innocent of the charges.

39:21-23 But the Lord was with Joseph—even in the midst of his

Potiphar, an officer of Pharaoh and the captain of the guard, bought him from the Ishmaelites who had brought him there. 2 The LORD was with Joseph, and he became a successful man, serving[A] in the household of his Egyptian master. 3 When his master saw that the LORD was with him and that the LORD made everything he did successful, 4 Joseph found favor in his master's sight and became his personal attendant. Potiphar also put him in charge of his household and placed all that he owned under his authority.[B] 5 From the time that he put him in charge of his household and of all that he owned, the LORD blessed the Egyptian's house because of Joseph. The LORD's blessing was on all that he owned, in his house and in his fields. 6 He left all that he owned under Joseph's authority;[C] he did not concern himself with anything except the food he ate.

Now Joseph was well-built and handsome. 7 After some time[D] his master's wife looked longingly at Joseph and said, "Sleep with me."

8 But he refused. "Look," he said to his master's wife, "with me here my master does not concern himself with anything in his house, and he has put all that he owns under my authority.[E] 9 No one in this house is greater than I am. He has withheld nothing from me except you, because you are his wife. So how could I do such a great evil and sin against God?"

10 Although she spoke to Joseph day after day, he refused[F] to go to bed with her.[G] 11 Now one day he went into the house to do his work, and none of the household servants were there.[H] 12 She grabbed him by his garment and said, "Sleep with me!" But leaving his garment in her hand, he escaped and ran outside. 13 When she saw that he had left his garment with her and had run outside, 14 she called the household servants. "Look," she said to them, "my husband brought a Hebrew man to make fools of us. He came to me so he could sleep with me, and I screamed as loud as I could. 15 When he heard me screaming for help,[I] he left his garment with me and ran outside."

16 She put Joseph's garment beside her until his master came home. 17 Then she told him the same story: "The Hebrew slave you brought to us came to make a fool of me, 18 but when I screamed for help,[J] he left his garment with me and ran outside."

19 When his master heard the story his wife told him—"These are the things your slave did to me"—he was furious 20 and had him thrown into prison, where the king's prisoners were confined. So Joseph was there in prison.

21 But the LORD was with Joseph and extended kindness to him. He granted him favor in the eyes of the prison warden. 22 The warden put all the prisoners who were in the prison under Joseph's authority,[K] and he was responsible for everything that was done there. 23 The warden did not bother with anything under Joseph's authority,[L] because the LORD was with him, and the LORD made everything that he did successful.

40 After this, the Egyptian king's cupbearer and baker offended their master, the king of Egypt. 2 Pharaoh was angry with his two officers, the chief cupbearer and the chief baker, 3 and put them in custody in the house of the captain of the guard in the prison where Joseph was confined. 4 The captain of the guard assigned Joseph to them, and he became their personal attendant. And they were in custody for some time.[M]

5 The Egyptian king's cupbearer and baker, who were confined in the prison, each had a dream. Both had a dream on the same night, and each dream had its own meaning. 6 When Joseph came to them in the morning, he saw that they looked distraught. 7 So he asked Pharaoh's

[A] **39:2** Lit *and he was* [B] **39:4** Lit *owned in his hand* [C] **39:6** Lit *owned in Joseph's hand* [D] **39:7** Lit *And after these things* [E] **39:8** Lit *owns in my hand* [F] **39:10** Lit *did not listen to her* [G] **39:10** Lit *refused to lie beside her, to be with her* [H] **39:11** Lit *there in the house* [I] **39:15** Lit *me raise my voice and scream* [J] **39:18** Lit *I raised my voice and screamed* [K] **39:22** Lit *prison in the hand of Joseph* [L] **39:23** Lit *anything in his hand* [M] **40:4** Lit *custody days*

officers who were in custody with him in his master's house, "Why do you look so sad today?"

8 "We had dreams," they said to him, "but there is no one to interpret them."

Then Joseph said to them, "Don't interpretations belong to God? Tell me your dreams."

9 So the chief cupbearer told his dream to Joseph: "In my dream there was a vine in front of me. 10 On the vine were three branches. As soon as it budded, its blossoms came out and its clusters ripened into grapes. 11 Pharaoh's cup was in my hand, and I took the grapes, squeezed them into Pharaoh's cup, and placed the cup in Pharaoh's hand."

12 "This is its interpretation," Joseph said to him. "The three branches are three days. 13 In just three days Pharaoh will lift up your head and restore you to your position. You will put Pharaoh's cup in his hand the way you used to when you were his cupbearer. 14 But when all goes well for you, remember that I was with you. Please show kindness to me by mentioning me to Pharaoh, and get me out of this prison. 15 For I was kidnapped from the land of the Hebrews, and even here I have done nothing that they should put me in the dungeon."

16 When the chief baker saw that the interpretation was positive, he said to Joseph, "I also had a dream. Three baskets of white bread were on my head. 17 In the top basket were all sorts of baked goods for Pharaoh, but the birds were eating them out of the basket on my head."

18 "This is its interpretation," Joseph replied. "The three baskets are three days. 19 In just three days Pharaoh will lift up your head—from off you—and hang you on a tree.[A] Then the birds will eat the flesh from your body."[B]

20 On the third day, which was Pharaoh's birthday, he gave a feast for all his servants. He lifted up the heads of the chief cupbearer and the chief baker. 21 Pharaoh restored the chief cupbearer to his position as cupbearer, and he placed the cup in Pharaoh's hand. 22 But Pharaoh hanged[C] the chief baker, just as Joseph had explained to them. 23 Yet the chief cupbearer did not remember Joseph; he forgot him.

41 Two years later Pharaoh had a dream: He was standing beside the Nile, 2 when seven healthy-looking, well-fed cows came up from the Nile and began to graze among the reeds. 3 After them, seven other cows, sickly and thin, came up from the Nile and stood beside those cows along the bank of the Nile. 4 The sickly, thin cows ate the healthy, well-fed cows. Then Pharaoh woke up. 5 He fell asleep and dreamed a second time: Seven heads of grain, plump and ripe, came up on one stalk. 6 After them, seven heads of grain, thin and scorched by the east wind, sprouted up. 7 The thin heads of grain swallowed up the seven plump, ripe ones. Then Pharaoh woke up, and it was only a dream.

8 When morning came, he was troubled, so he summoned all the magicians of Egypt and all its wise men. Pharaoh told them his dreams, but no one could interpret them for him.

9 Then the chief cupbearer said to Pharaoh, "Today I remember my faults. 10 Pharaoh had been angry with his servants, and he put me and the chief baker in the custody of the captain of the guard. 11 He and I had dreams on the same night; each dream had its own meaning. 12 Now a young Hebrew, a slave of the captain of the guards, was with us there. We told him our dreams, he interpreted our dreams for us, and each had its own interpretation. 13 It turned out just the way he interpreted them to us: I was restored to my position, and the other man was hanged."

14 Then Pharaoh sent for Joseph, and they quickly brought him from the dungeon. He shaved, changed his clothes, and went to Pharaoh.

15 Pharaoh said to Joseph, "I have had a dream, and no one can interpret it. But I have heard it said about you that you can hear a dream and interpret it."

16 "I am not able to," Joseph answered

darkest hour. Joseph had been obedient to the Lord, faithful to his master, and had fled temptation. As in Potiphar's house, Joseph rose to a position of authority in the prison. Joseph was faithful in the little things, and God blessed him with more influence. Just as Potiphar was not concerned for his house (39:6), **the warden did not bother with anything under Joseph's authority**.

40:1-4 Joseph's authority did not include everyone. When the **cupbearer** and the **baker,** two men in Pharaoh's court, were thrown into prison, Joseph was assigned to them as a **personal attendant**.

40:5-15 Being a faithful servant, Joseph immediately recognized that his masters were **distraught**. Going beyond the call of duty and his job description, Joseph showed a deep concern for the well-being of the cupbearer and baker. The confidence they had in Joseph was shown as the two divulged their distress over their **dreams**. The reason for their worry was not because the dreams were nightmares but because the dreams were beyond their understanding. They needed an interpreter. Joseph replied that they should not look for an answer with men but with God. Joseph could only interpret their dreams because he walked with the Lord.

40:16-19 Joseph's favorable interpretation of the cupbearer's dream encouraged the baker to tell Joseph his dream. However, the baker was not to have restoration but execution. The fulfillment of both dreams would take place in **three days** (vv. 12-13,18-20).

41:1-13 The servants in Pharaoh's house were not the only dreamers; Pharaoh himself was troubled by dreams.

41:14-16 After being disappointed by his wise men and magicians, Pharaoh was willing to try anything, including turning to a Hebrew slave. Joseph was **sent for . . . brought . . . from the dungeon. . . . shaved, changed** since one had to be presentable to go before Pharaoh. While Pharaoh believed Joseph was the one who interpreted dreams, Joseph stated clearly that he was **not able**, but **God . . . will give Pharaoh a favorable answer**. Joseph's response to Pharaoh was a clear affirmation of the superiority of the God of Israel, whom he served, over the gods of the Egyptian "wise men" and "magicians" (41:8). Later Moses would repeat the same lesson (Ex 7–10).

[A] **40:19** Or *and impale you on a pole* [B] **40:19** Lit *eat your flesh from upon you* [C] **40:22** Or *impaled*

41:25-32 Unlike the magicians and wise men, Joseph had an answer: God was responsible for the dreams as the means of foretelling the events that were about to occur. **The dreams** meant **the same thing** and were allegorical for the seven years of plenty and the seven years of famine. Just as the gaunt cows ate the fat cows, so the famine would be so severe that an abundant harvest in Egypt would not be remembered. The repetition in the dreams is important, as Joseph pointed out that these events had been determined by God. Not only would these events take place but they would come **soon**. With no time to waste, Joseph presented a course of action to Pharaoh.

41:33-36 Joseph described the man who should care for the land of Egypt. He had to be **discerning and wise** and carry Pharaoh's authority. Joseph then proposed an agenda to save Egypt from the effects of famine by recommending that others be commissioned to take crops and store them for the famine (i.e., gathering grain as a tax). Of extreme importance was that Pharaoh's influence be prominent so that Egypt was unified in preparing for the famine and took seriously all that would happen so that the country would **not be wiped out by the famine**.

41:37-45 Joseph had shown himself to be wise, discerning, and filled with **God's spirit**; in essence, Pharaoh made Joseph his vizier, although his exact title is not stated. By presenting Joseph his **signet ring**, Pharaoh gave him supreme power. When Joseph rode in Pharaoh's **second chariot** (showing him to be second in command in the kingdom), the servants shouted ***Abrek!*** (Egyptian, "attention!" or Hb "kneel!"). In other words, respect for Joseph and his authority was demanded from the people of the land. As with Potiphar and with the prison warden, Joseph again had been given responsibility for his master's "home." Joseph was trusted with not only the life of Pharaoh but also with the lives of all Egyptians. Along with Joseph's new authority came a new name **Zaphenath-paneah** (Egyptian, "the god said let him live"). Pharaoh also gives **Asenath** [Egyptian, "she who belongs to Neith," an Egyptian goddess], **daughter of Potiphera, priest at On**, to Joseph as his wife. **On** was said to be the religious center for the solar deities. Why would Joseph, who had been so circumspect in honoring Yahweh and His law, marry the daughter of a pagan priest (24:3; 28:1; 34:16; see also Dt 7:3)? No comment is made in the text, but notably the names of his sons are Hebrew, suggesting that his wife may have adopted Joseph's faith.

41:46-53 Joseph's interpretation of

Pharaoh. "It is God who will give Pharaoh a favorable answer."[A]

[17] So Pharaoh said to Joseph: "In my dream I was standing on the bank of the Nile, [18] when seven well-fed, healthy-looking cows came up from the Nile and began to graze among the reeds. [19] After them, seven other cows—ugly, very sickly, and thin—came up. I've never seen such ugly ones as these in all the land of Egypt. [20] Then the thin, ugly cows ate the first seven well-fed cows. [21] When they had devoured them, you could not tell that they had devoured them; their appearance was as bad as it had been before. Then I woke up. [22] In my dream I had also seen seven heads of grain, plump and ripe, coming up on one stalk. [23] After them, seven heads of grain—withered, thin, and scorched by the east wind—sprouted up. [24] The thin heads of grain swallowed the seven plump ones. I told this to the magicians, but no one can tell me what it means."

[25] Then Joseph said to Pharaoh, "Pharaoh's dreams mean the same thing. God has revealed to Pharaoh what He is about to do. [26] The seven good cows are seven years, and the seven ripe heads are seven years. The dreams mean the same thing. [27] The seven thin, ugly cows that came up after them are seven years, and the seven worthless, scorched heads of grain are seven years of famine.

[28] "It is just as I told Pharaoh: God has shown Pharaoh what He is about to do. [29] Seven[B] years of great abundance are coming throughout the land of Egypt. [30] After them, seven years of famine will take place, and all the abundance in the land of Egypt will be forgotten. The famine will devastate the land. [31] The abundance in the land will not be remembered because of the famine that follows it, for the famine will be very severe. [32] Since the dream was given twice to Pharaoh, it means that the matter has been determined by God, and He will carry it out soon.

[33] "So now, let Pharaoh look for a discerning and wise man and set him over the land of Egypt. [34] Let Pharaoh do this: Let him appoint overseers over the land and take a fifth of the harvest of the land of Egypt during the seven years of abundance. [35] Let them gather all the excess food during these good years that are coming. Under Pharaoh's authority, store the grain in the cities, so they may preserve it as food. [36] The food will be a reserve for the land during the seven years of famine that will take place in the land of Egypt. Then the country will not be wiped out by the famine."

[37] The proposal pleased Pharaoh and all his servants. [38] Then Pharaoh said to his servants, "Can we find anyone like this, a man who has God's spirit[C] in him?" [39] So Pharaoh said to Joseph, "Since God has made all this known to you, there is no one as intelligent and wise as you are. [40] You will be over my house, and all my people will obey your commands.[D] Only with regard to the throne will I be greater than you." [41] Pharaoh also said to Joseph, "See, I am placing you over all the land of Egypt." [42] Pharaoh removed his signet ring from his hand and put it on Joseph's hand, clothed him with fine linen garments, and placed a gold chain around his neck. [43] He had Joseph ride in his second chariot, and servants called out before him, "*Abrek!*"[E] So he placed him over all the land of Egypt. [44] Pharaoh said to Joseph, "I am Pharaoh, but no one will be able to raise his hand or foot in all the land of Egypt without your permission." [45] Pharaoh gave Joseph the name Zaphenath-paneah and gave him a wife, Asenath daughter of Potiphera, priest at On.[F] And Joseph went throughout[G] the land of Egypt.

[46] Joseph was 30 years old when he entered the service of Pharaoh king of Egypt. Joseph left Pharaoh's presence and traveled throughout the land of Egypt.

[47] During the seven years of abundance the land produced outstanding harvests. [48] Joseph gathered all the excess food in the land of Egypt

[A] **41:16** Or *"God will answer Pharaoh with peace of mind."* [B] **41:29** Lit *Look! Seven* [C] **41:38** Or *the spirit of the gods*, or *a god's spirit* [D] **41:40** Lit *will kiss your mouth* [E] **41:43** Perhaps an Egyptian word meaning "Attention" or a Hb word meaning "Kneel." [F] **41:45** Or *Heliopolis* [G] **41:45** Or *Joseph gained authority over*

during the seven years and put it in
the cities. He put the food in every
city from the fields around it. 49 So
Joseph stored up grain in such
abundance—like the sand of the
sea—that he stopped measuring it
because it was beyond measure.
50 Two sons were born to Joseph
before the years of famine arrived.
Asenath daughter of Potiphera,
priest at On,[A] bore them to him.
51 Joseph named the firstborn
Manasseh, meaning, "God has made
me forget all my hardship in my father's house." 52 And the second son
he named Ephraim, meaning, "God
has made me fruitful in the land of
my affliction."
53 Then the seven years of abundance in the land of Egypt came to
an end, 54 and the seven years of famine began, just as Joseph had said.
There was famine in every country,
but throughout the land of Egypt
there was food. 55 Extreme hunger
came to all the land of Egypt, and
the people cried out to Pharaoh for
food. Pharaoh told all Egypt, "Go
to Joseph and do whatever he tells
you." 56 Because the famine had
spread across the whole country, Joseph opened up all the storehouses
and sold grain to the Egyptians, for
the famine was severe in the land of
Egypt. 57 Every nation came to Joseph in Egypt to buy grain, for the
famine was severe in every land.

The Reunion of Joseph and His Brothers (42:1–45:15)

42 When Jacob learned that there
was grain in Egypt, he said to
his sons, "Why do you keep looking
at each other? 2 Listen," he went on,
"I have heard there is grain in Egypt.
Go down there and buy some for us
so that we will live and not die." 3 So
10 of Joseph's brothers went down
to buy grain from Egypt. 4 But Jacob did not send Joseph's brother
Benjamin with his brothers, for he
thought, "Something might happen
to him."
5 The sons of Israel were among
those who came to buy grain, for
the famine was in the land of Canaan. 6 Joseph was in charge of the
country; he sold grain to all its people. His brothers came and bowed
down before him with their faces to
the ground. 7 When Joseph saw his
brothers, he recognized them, but
he treated them like strangers and
spoke harshly to them.
"Where do you come from?" he
asked.
"From the land of Canaan to buy
food," they replied.
8 Although Joseph recognized his
brothers, they did not recognize
him. 9 Joseph remembered his
dreams about them and said to
them, "You are spies. You have come
to see the weakness[B] of the land."
10 "No, my lord. Your servants have
come to buy food," they said. 11 "We
are all sons of one man. We are honest; your servants are not spies."
12 "No," he said to them. "You have
come to see the weakness of the
land."
13 But they replied, "We, your servants, were 12 brothers, the sons of
one man in the land of Canaan. The
youngest is now[C] with our father,
and one is no longer living."
14 Then Joseph said to them, "I
have spoken:[D] 'You are spies!' 15 This
is how you will be tested: As surely as
Pharaoh lives, you will not leave this
place unless your youngest brother
comes here. 16 Send one from among
you to get your brother. The rest of
you will be imprisoned so that your
words can be tested to see if they are
true. If they are not, then as surely
as Pharaoh lives, you are spies!" 17 So
Joseph imprisoned them together
for three days.
18 On the third day Joseph said
to them, "I •fear God—do this and
you will live. 19 If you are honest,
let one of you[E] be confined to the
guardhouse, while the rest of you go
and take grain to relieve the hunger
of your households. 20 Bring your
youngest brother to me so that your
words can be confirmed; then you
won't die." And they consented to
this.
21 Then they said to each other,
"Obviously, we are being punished
for what we did to our brother.
We saw his deep distress when he

Pharaoh's dreams came to pass. Not only was the land fruitful, but Joseph himself was blessed with two sons. Interestingly, Joseph named their sons despite the Israelite custom of the mother's assigning the names (see 4:25; Ex 2:10): **Manasseh** (Hb "He who makes [some]one forget") and **Ephraim** (Hb "He has made me fruitful"), showing Joseph's gratitude to God for His faithfulness and provision in the darkest hours.

41:54-57 Again, God was true to His word as a **famine**, far reaching and affecting every country, struck the land. The Egyptians turned to Pharaoh for help, and he in turn sent them to Joseph. This response from Pharaoh shows that he trusted the wisdom of Joseph, who showed kindness in that he opened all of the storehouses and sold food not only to Egyptians but to foreigners as well. Joseph's wisdom and faith in God were bringing life-giving sustenance to many.

42:1-4 The famine even reached as far as Canaan and the family of **Jacob**. He dispatched his sons to Egypt, and **10 of Joseph's brothers** made the journey. The same family dynamics were in play. **Benjamin**, seemingly the only remaining son of the beloved Rachel, was now the favored son. Jacob did not want to lose Benjamin as he had lost Joseph.

42:5-8 The lowliness of the brothers is contrasted with the greatness of Joseph. The sons of Israel were merely among those buying grain, while Joseph was in charge of selling the grain within the country. Joseph's dreams were fulfilled as his brothers bowed down to him (37:5-7,9). His second dream was similar but yet to be fulfilled. As with Pharaoh having similar dreams twice, Joseph's two dreams showed God's determination in the matter. The bowing of the brothers before Joseph would take place. Although Joseph recognized his brothers, the passage of time and the influence of Egyptian culture had changed Joseph's appearance so much that he remained unknown to them. Joseph was only 17 when the brothers sold him into slavery. Now he was in his late thirties (37:2).

42:17-20 Joseph was a man of his word, and the brothers were imprisoned for **three days**. This showed Joseph was serious about what he asked of them concerning the younger brother. Now that the sons of Israel knew Joseph was adamant about bringing their younger brother, they consented to his plan.

42:21-22 **Reuben** reiterated that he was not responsible because he

[A]**41:50** Or *Heliopolis* [B]**42:9** Lit *nakedness* [C]**42:13** Or *today* [D]**42:14** Lit *"That which I spoke to you saying* [E]**42:19** Lit *your brothers*

pleaded with us, but we would not listen. That is why this trouble has come to us."

22 But Reuben replied: "Didn't I tell you not to harm the boy? But you wouldn't listen. Now we must account for his blood!"[A]

23 They did not realize that Joseph understood them, since there was an interpreter between them. 24 He turned away from them and wept. Then he turned back and spoke to them. He took Simeon from them and had him bound before their eyes. 25 Joseph then gave orders to fill their containers with grain, return each man's money to his sack, and give them provisions for their journey. This order was carried out. 26 They loaded the grain on their donkeys and left there.

27 At the place where they lodged for the night, one of them opened his sack to get feed for his donkey, and he saw his money there at the top of the bag. 28 He said to his brothers, "My money has been returned! It's here in my bag." Their hearts sank. Trembling, they turned to one another and said, "What is this that God has done to us?"

29 When they reached their father Jacob in the land of Canaan, they told him all that had happened to them: 30 "The man who is the lord of the country spoke harshly to us and accused us of spying on the country. 31 But we told him: We are honest and not spies. 32 We were 12 brothers, sons of the same[B] father. One is no longer living, and the youngest is now[C] with our father in the land of Canaan. 33 The man who is the lord of the country said to us, 'This is how I will know if you are honest: Leave one brother with me, take food to relieve the hunger of your households, and go. 34 Bring back your youngest brother to me, and I will know that you are not spies but honest men. I will then give your brother back to you, and you can trade in the country.'"

35 As they began emptying their sacks, there in each man's sack was his bag of money! When they and their father saw their bags of money, they were afraid.

36 Their father Jacob said to them, "You have deprived me of my sons. Joseph is gone and Simeon is gone. Now you want to take Benjamin. Everything happens to me!"

37 Then Reuben said to his father, "You can kill my two sons if I don't bring him back to you. Put him in my care,[D] and I will return him to you."

38 But Jacob answered, "My son will not go down with you, for his brother is dead and he alone is left. If anything happens to him on your journey, you will bring my gray hairs down to •Sheol in sorrow."

43 Now the famine in the land was severe. 2 When they had used up the grain they had brought back from Egypt, their father said to them, "Go back and buy us some food."

3 But Judah said to him, "The man specifically warned us: 'You will not see me again unless your brother is with you.' 4 If you will send our brother with us, we will go down and buy food for you. 5 But if you will not send him, we will not go, for the man said to us, 'You will not see me again unless your brother is with you.'"

6 "Why did you cause me so much trouble?" Israel asked. "Why did you tell the man that you had another brother?"

7 They answered, "The man kept asking about us and our family: 'Is your father still alive? Do you have another brother?' And we answered him accordingly. How could we know that he would say, 'Bring your brother here'?"

8 Then Judah said to his father Israel, "Send the boy with me. We will be on our way so that we may live and not die—neither we, nor you, nor our children. 9 I will be responsible for him. You can hold me personally accountable![E] If I do not bring him back to you and set him before you, I will be •guilty before you forever. 10 If we had not wasted time, we could have come back twice by now."

warned them they should not do such a thing. The leadership of Reuben, however, ultimately was lost when he slept with his father's concubine (see 35:22). His brothers would not listen to him, nor would his father trust him with Benjamin's life (see 42:37-38). The ramifications of Reuben's sin were still felt years later. The episode shows the guilt of the brothers and their regret for what they had done to Joseph.

42:23-26 Instead of taking the eldest, Reuben, as one would think, Joseph had the second eldest **Simeon** bound, possibly because he learned Reuben had voiced objections to his brothers' plot against Joseph.

42:27-35 At the first sign of the money there was evidence of a change of heart among the brothers. Any hope for being considered men of integrity was taken away by the money in their bags. Joseph's brothers were truly **afraid**, for stealing could be punished by death.

42:36-38 **Sheol** refers to death. Losing another son of Rachel would be so serious that Jacob felt it would bring about his death.

43:1-10. Judah reminded his father that he was the head of the house, responsible for the family; thus, he must let Benjamin go with his brothers for the sake of the whole. Instead of offering his sons as Reuben had, Judah offered himself as the person who would be accountable for Benjamin's life.

43:11-14 Jacob could not refuse Judah's request due to the circumstances and so he relented. As with Esau, Jacob sought to appease Pharaoh's vizier by sending an impressive gift (32:13-15). The giving of a present was an ancient Near Eastern custom for approaching someone of rank. The money found in the sacks was also to be returned. Sending along Benjamin, Jacob entrusted all of his sons to **God Almighty** (Hb *ʾel shadday*) who is able to do the impossible.

43:15-26 The sons of Israel obeyed their father and returned to Egypt. When Joseph saw Benjamin was with them, he prepared a feast for them at his home. But the brothers thought it was a trick because of the money they had found in their bags. Their fear of being made slaves caused the brothers to approach the steward of Joseph's house. Surprisingly, the steward reassured the brothers, saying he received their money and that their God must have put the treasure in their bags. **Your God and the God of your father** refer to the brothers' Hebrew patriarchal heritage. Simeon was also returned to the brothers. Realizing

[A]42:22 Lit *Even his blood is being sought* [B]42:32 Lit *of our* [C]42:32 Or *today* [D]42:37 Lit *hand*
[E]43:9 Lit *can seek him from my hand*

11 Then their father Israel said to them, "If it must be so, then do this: Put some of the best products of the land in your packs and take them down to the man as a gift—some balsam and some honey, aromatic gum and resin, pistachios and almonds. 12 Take twice as much money with you. Return the money that was returned to you in the top of your bags. Perhaps it was a mistake. 13 Take your brother also, and go back at once to the man. 14 May •God Almighty cause the man to be merciful to you so that he will release your other brother and Benjamin to you. As for me, if I am deprived of my sons, then I am deprived."

15 The men took this gift, double the amount of money, and Benjamin. They made their way down to Egypt and stood before Joseph.

16 When Joseph saw Benjamin with them, he said to his steward,[A] "Take the men to my house. Slaughter an animal and prepare it, for they will eat with me at noon." 17 The man did as Joseph had said and brought them to Joseph's house.

18 But the men were afraid because they were taken to Joseph's house. They said, "We have been brought here because of the money that was returned in our bags the first time. They intend to overpower us, seize us, make us slaves, and take our donkeys." 19 So they approached Joseph's steward[B] and spoke to him at the doorway of the house.

20 They said, "Sir, we really did come down here the first time only to buy food. 21 When we came to the place where we lodged for the night and opened our bags of grain, each one's money was at the top of his bag! It was the full amount of our money, and we have brought it back with us. 22 We have brought additional money with us to buy food. We don't know who put our money in the bags."

23 Then the steward said, "May you be well. Don't be afraid. Your God and the God of your father must have put treasure in your bags. I received your money." Then he brought Simeon out to them. 24 The steward brought the men into Joseph's house, gave them water to wash their feet, and got feed for their donkeys. 25 Since the men had heard that they were going to eat a meal there, they prepared their gift for Joseph's arrival at noon. 26 When Joseph came home, they brought him the gift they had carried into the house, and they bowed to the ground before him.

27 He asked if they were well, and he said, "How is your elderly father that you told me about? Is he still alive?"

28 They answered, "Your servant our father is well. He is still alive." And they bowed down to honor him.

29 When he looked up and saw his brother Benjamin, his mother's son, he asked, "Is this your youngest brother that you told me about?" Then he said, "May God be gracious to you, my son." 30 Joseph hurried out because he was overcome with emotion for his brother, and he was about to weep. He went into an inner room to weep. 31 Then he washed his face and came out. Regaining his composure, he said, "Serve the meal."

32 They served him by himself, his brothers by themselves, and the Egyptians who were eating with him by themselves, because Egyptians could not eat with Hebrews, since that is abhorrent to them. 33 They were seated before him in order by age, from the firstborn to the youngest. The men looked at each other in astonishment. 34 Portions were served to them from Joseph's table, and Benjamin's portion was five times larger than any of theirs. They drank, and they got intoxicated with Joseph.

44 Then Joseph commanded his steward: "Fill the men's bags with as much food as they can carry, and put each one's money at the top of his bag. 2 Put my cup, the silver one, at the top of the youngest one's bag, along with his grain money." So he did as Joseph told him.

3 At morning light, the men were sent off with their donkeys. 4 They had not gone very far from the city when Joseph said to his steward,

that all was well and there was no trick, the brothers prepared their gift for the vizier.

43:27-31 The brothers again bowed before Joseph, reminiscent of Joseph's dreams as a young man. This time Joseph treated his brothers kindly, asking about their personal well-being as well as about their father. But Joseph was so overcome with emotion at seeing his own younger brother that he had to leave their presence and compose himself before the meal, showing the love Joseph had for his family, especially his younger brother. The word translated **overcome** (Hb *kamar*, "grow excited, grow hot, burn") is the same word used in the story of Solomon and the two women who claimed to be the mother of the one living baby (1Kg 3:26). The true mother of the baby was stirred to sacrifice to protect her baby and implored Solomon not to cut the baby in two. This mother felt an overwhelming love and bond for her baby; Joseph felt a special bond with Benjamin.

43:32-34 The meal shows how the group's hierarchy worked itself out. Joseph was served alone, while the Egyptians were served separately from the Hebrews. The Egyptians abhorred eating with the Hebrews because they were considered a lesser race. Joseph's brothers were astonished to see their seating according to birth order. Benjamin not only received the vizier's blessing but also the largest portion of food. What was true in real life was reflected at the table. Benjamin, as he was at home, was the favored one.

44:1-5 As his brothers slept off their intoxication, Joseph appeared very generous, filling their bags with food and returning their money. However, another test was on its way for the brothers as Joseph told the steward to put his silver **cup** in Benjamin's bag. Joseph's ploy was to see if the brothers would abandon their youngest brother as they did him. The brothers were stopped before they got too far away, and this time instead of mere accusation (42:27-35), they were indicted for stealing. As Joseph requested, the steward made clear the importance of the cup to Joseph, saying that it was used for **divination**. However, Scripture clearly condemns divination (Lv 19:26; Dt 18:10), and this most likely was also part of Joseph's scheme. Nowhere did Joseph use the movement of liquids to determine events; instead he relied upon God to interpret dreams.

[A] **43:16** Lit *to the one who was over his house* [B] **43:19** Lit *approached the one who was over the house*

44:6-13 The brothers were incredulous and made a case for their innocence, swiftly condemning to death the one who might have the cup and the others to servitude. However, the **steward** rejected the brothers' deal, saying **only the one who is found to have it** would be his **slave**. The brothers further proved their innocence by swiftly complying and opening their sacks. A sign of true brotherhood was shown when Benjamin was found to have the cup. The brothers **tore their clothes**, a sign of anguish. This time the sons of Jacob did not abandon their younger brother to servitude, and they returned with the steward.

44:14-17 Returning to Joseph's house, **Judah** appeared to be the spokesman for the brothers. Of the brothers, only Judah is specifically mentioned, setting up the dialogue that took place with the vizier, who was really his brother. Joseph's interrogation was meant to demean the brothers. Judah confessed their **iniquity** and put himself and his brothers into Joseph's service. However, Joseph would not have this and only accepted the servitude of the one with the cup.

44:18-34 The brothers could have resigned themselves to the situation and returned home to tell their elderly father, who would be heartbroken. Instead Judah gave a moving speech explaining how their father's life was **wrapped up with the boy's life**. Judah's discourse showed the compassion and concern he had for Jacob and Benjamin as well as revealing that Jacob was still mourning the loss of Joseph. After stating his responsibility for the boy, Judah offered himself as a substitute. Truly, Judah had changed since his selfishness with Tamar. He had become a selfless brother and son. Judah's primary concern was for his father. After seeing Jacob's grief over losing Joseph, Judah could not bear to see the **grief that would overwhelm** his **father** and most likely kill him.

45:1-8 Judah's moving speech proved to Joseph that his brothers had changed, and Joseph was overcome with emotion. Unlike the earlier times of his weeping, **Joseph could no longer keep his composure**. By having the Egyptians leave, Joseph could let his tears flow freely as well as reveal his true identity to his brothers in hopes of reconciliation. However, Joseph's weeping was so loud that the Egyptians heard it when they left, and thus word of the event reached Pharaoh's ears. His brothers were in shock and too **terrified** to **answer** Joseph. They feared revenge from the brother whom they had sold into slavery.

"Get up. Pursue the men, and when you overtake them, say to them, 'Why have you repaid evil for good?[A] 5 Isn't this the cup that my master drinks from and uses for •divination? What you have done is wrong!'"

6 When he overtook them, he said these words to them. 7 They said to him, "Why does my lord say these things? Your servants could not possibly do such a thing. 8 We even brought back to you from the land of Canaan the money we found at the top of our bags. How could we steal gold and silver from your master's house? 9 If any of us is[B] found to have it, he must die, and we also will become my lord's slaves."

10 The steward replied, "What you have said is right, but only the one who is found to have it will be my slave, and the rest of you will be blameless."

11 So each one quickly lowered his sack to the ground and opened it. 12 The steward searched, beginning with the oldest and ending with the youngest, and the cup was found in Benjamin's sack. 13 Then they tore their clothes, and each one loaded his donkey and returned to the city.

14 When Judah and his brothers reached Joseph's house, he was still there. They fell to the ground before him. 15 "What is this you have done?" Joseph said to them. "Didn't you know that a man like me could uncover the truth by divination?"

16 "What can we say to my lord?" Judah replied. "How can we plead? How can we justify ourselves? God has exposed your servants' iniquity. We are now my lord's slaves—both we and the one in whose possession the cup was found."

17 Then Joseph said, "I swear that I will not do this. The man in whose possession the cup was found will be my slave. The rest of you can go in peace to your father."

18 But Judah approached him and said, "Sir, please let your servant speak personally to my lord.[C] Do not be angry with your servant, for you are like Pharaoh. 19 My lord asked his servants, 'Do you have a father or a brother?' 20 and we answered my lord, 'We have an elderly father and a younger brother, the child of his old age. The boy's brother is dead. He is the only one of his mother's sons left, and his father loves him.' 21 Then you said to your servants, 'Bring him to me so that I can see him.' 22 But we said to my lord, 'The boy cannot leave his father. If he were to leave, his father would die.' 23 Then you said to your servants, 'If your younger brother does not come down with you, you will not see me again.'

24 "This is what happened when we went back to your servant my father: We reported your words to him. 25 But our father said, 'Go again, and buy us some food.' 26 We told him, 'We cannot go down unless our younger brother goes with us. So if our younger brother isn't with us, we cannot see the man.' 27 Your servant my father said to us, 'You know that my wife bore me two sons. 28 One left—I said that he must have been torn to pieces—and I have never seen him again. 29 If you also take this one from me and anything happens to him, you will bring my gray hairs down to •Sheol in sorrow.'

30 "So if I come to your servant my father and the boy is not with us—his life is wrapped up with the boy's life— 31 when he sees that the boy is not with us, he will die. Then your servants will have brought the gray hairs of your servant our father down to Sheol in sorrow. 32 Your servant became accountable to my father for the boy, saying, 'If I do not return him to you, I will always bear the •guilt for sinning against you, my father.' 33 Now please let your servant remain here as my lord's slave, in place of the boy. Let him go back with his brothers. 34 For how can I go back to my father without the boy? I could not bear to see the grief that would overwhelm my father."

45 Joseph could no longer keep his composure in front of all his attendants,[D] so he called out, "Send everyone away from me!" No one was with him when he revealed

[A] **44:4** LXX adds *Why have you stolen my silver cup?* [B] **44:9** Lit *If your servants are* [C] **44:18** Lit *speak a word in my lord's ears* [D] **45:1** Lit *all those standing about him*

his identity to his brothers. 2 But he
wept so loudly that the Egyptians
heard it, and also Pharaoh's household heard it. 3 Joseph said to his
brothers, "I am Joseph! Is my father
still living?" But they could not answer him because they were terrified
in his presence.

4 Then Joseph said to his brothers,
"Please, come near me," and they
came near. "I am Joseph, your brother," he said, "the one you sold into
Egypt. 5 And now don't be worried or
angry with yourselves for selling me
here, because God sent me ahead of
you to preserve life. 6 For the famine
has been in the land these two years,
and there will be five more years
without plowing or harvesting. 7 God
sent me ahead of you to establish
you as a remnant within the land
and to keep you alive by a great deliverance.[A] 8 Therefore it was not you
who sent me here, but God. He has
made me a father to Pharaoh, lord of
his entire household, and ruler over
all the land of Egypt.

9 "Return quickly to my father
and say to him, 'This is what your
son Joseph says: "God has made
me lord of all Egypt. Come down to
me without delay. 10 You can settle
in the land of Goshen and be near
me—you, your children, and grandchildren, your sheep, cattle, and all
you have. 11 There I will sustain you,
for there will be five more years of
famine. Otherwise, you, your household, and everything you have will
become destitute."' 12 Look! Your
eyes and my brother Benjamin's
eyes can see that it is I, Joseph, who
am[B] speaking to you. 13 Tell my father about all my glory in Egypt and
about all you have seen. And bring
my father here quickly."

14 Then Joseph threw his arms
around Benjamin and wept, and
Benjamin wept on his shoulder.
15 Joseph kissed each of his brothers
as he wept,[C] and afterward his brothers talked with him.

The Journey of Jacob to Egypt (45:16–48:22)

16 When the news reached Pharaoh's palace, "Joseph's brothers
have come," Pharaoh and his servants were pleased. 17 Pharaoh said to
Joseph, "Tell your brothers, 'Do this:
Load your animals and go on back
to the land of Canaan. 18 Get your
father and your families, and come
back to me. I will give you the best
of the land of Egypt, and you can eat
from the richness of the land.' 19 You
are also commanded, 'Do this: Take
wagons from the land of Egypt for
your young children and your wives
and bring your father here. 20 Do not
be concerned about your belongings, for the best of all the land of
Egypt is yours.'"

21 The sons of Israel did this. Joseph gave them wagons as Pharaoh
had commanded, and he gave them
provisions for the journey. 22 He
gave each of the brothers changes
of clothes, but he gave Benjamin
300 pieces of silver and five changes
of clothes. 23 He sent his father the
following: 10 donkeys carrying the
best products of Egypt and 10 female donkeys carrying grain, food,
and provisions for his father on the
journey. 24 So Joseph sent his brothers on their way, and as they were
leaving, he said to them, "Don't argue on the way."

25 So they went up from Egypt
and came to their father Jacob in
the land of Canaan. 26 They said,
"Joseph is still alive, and he is ruler
over all the land of Egypt!" Jacob
was stunned,[D] for he did not believe
them. 27 But when they told Jacob
all that Joseph had said to them,
and when he saw the wagons that
Joseph had sent to transport him,
the spirit of their father Jacob revived.

28 Then Israel said, "Enough! My
son Joseph is still alive. I will go to
see him before I die."

46 Israel set out with all that he
had and came to Beer-sheba,
and he offered sacrifices to the God
of his father Isaac. 2 That night God
spoke to Israel in a vision: "Jacob,
Jacob!" He said.

And Jacob replied, "Here I am."

3 God said, "I am God, the God of
your father. Do not be afraid to go
down to Egypt, for I will make you

Joseph saw God's hand in his coming to Egypt and assured his brothers that God had brought him to Egypt for three purposes: **to preserve life; to establish you** [Israel] **as a remnant within the land and to keep you alive by a great deliverance**; and to be **a father to Pharaoh . . . and ruler over all the land of Egypt**. Joseph did not fail to acknowledge that his brothers had sinned and were responsible for their wrong-doing, but he saw that God's plans for good had taken their sin into account and used it (see Rm 8:28).

45:9-15 Joseph requested that the family move to **Goshen** so that he could provide for them lest they **become destitute**. He urged them to convey to their father all they had experienced in Egypt and waste no time in moving the family to Goshen.

45:16-28 Pharaoh and his servants were pleased to hear of the reunion of Joseph and his brothers. Pharaoh offered the best in the land and even wagons to help transport the family. Joseph had served Pharaoh well, and now Joseph's family was reaping the rewards of their brother's faithful service. Pharaoh was perhaps concerned that Joseph's family would remain in Canaan for fear of losing their possessions, but Pharaoh reassured them that the best of Egypt was theirs. Joseph and Pharaoh followed through with their offer, but Joseph went above and beyond by giving his brothers clothes and money. There would be no retaliation, and thus the brothers could go home without fear.

46:1-7 Israel was leaving the promised land, the land of his fathers. Appropriately, the narrative begins with a reference to him as **Israel** since this trip the patriarch would make was not merely personal—rather, the venture of a nation. With the approval of God, the house of Jacob headed to Egypt. All their possessions were taken with them, being carried by **the wagons** of Pharaoh. The entire clan left Canaan until God would bring them back to their land as He said He would.

[A] **45:7** Or *keep alive for you many survivors* [B] **45:12** Lit *that my mouth is* [C] **45:15** Lit *brothers, and he wept over them* [D] **45:26** Lit *Jacob's heart was numb*

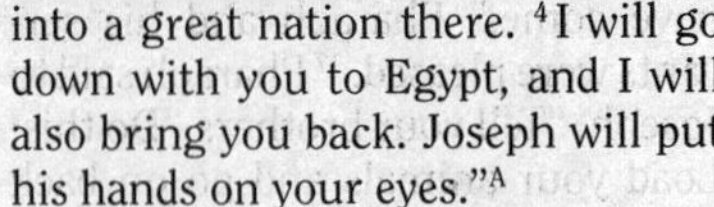

46:8-27 A genealogy of those who made the journey to Egypt is given. The listing is in order from Leah, Zilpah (Leah's handmaiden), Rachel, to Bilhah (Rachel's handmaiden). Of note is the mention of only **Rachel** as being **Jacob's wife** within this genealogy. The wording shows Jacob's love for Rachel as well as the favored status of her sons. Within the larger grouping of Jacob's wives, the sons are listed in order of birth. This microcosm of the descendants of Abraham, Isaac, and Jacob is indicative of the fulfillment of the prophecy that they would be like the sands on the seashore.

46:28-34 **Judah**, once the instigator of divisiveness among the brothers, had now become a leader of unity. Jacob sent him ahead to prepare for the family's arrival in **Goshen**, which was along the Nile delta. Unlike the reunion of Jacob and Esau, which built to the climax, the reunion of Joseph and Jacob was swift, with Joseph showing much more emotion than his father. God's hand was behind the uniting of brother with brother as well as father and son. Once the family reunion was over, Joseph, the grand administrator of Egypt, turned the attention of his family to how they were to present themselves to Pharaoh in order to receive the best response. Joseph's instructions were clever, as were the answers his family was prepared to give Pharaoh to ensure their receiving the land of Goshen. However, the speech also showed the prejudice the Egyptians had concerning shepherds.

into a great nation there. 4 I will go
down with you to Egypt, and I will
also bring you back. Joseph will put
his hands on your eyes."[A]
5 Jacob left Beer-sheba. The sons of
Israel took their father Jacob in the
wagons Pharaoh had sent to carry
him, along with their children and
their wives. 6 They also took their
cattle and possessions they had acquired in the land of Canaan. Then
Jacob and all his children went with
him to Egypt. 7 His sons and grandsons, his daughters and granddaughters, indeed all his •offspring,
he brought with him to Egypt.
8 These are the names of the Israelites, Jacob and his sons, who went
to Egypt:

Jacob's firstborn: Reuben.
9 Reuben's sons: Hanoch, Pallu,
Hezron, and Carmi.
10 Simeon's sons: Jemuel,
Jamin, Ohad, Jachin,
Zohar, and Shaul, the son
of a Canaanite woman.
11 Levi's sons: Gershon, Kohath,
and Merari.
12 Judah's sons: Er, Onan, Shelah,
Perez, and Zerah; but Er
and Onan died in the land
of Canaan.
Perez's sons: Hezron
and Hamul.
13 Issachar's sons: Tola, Puvah,[B]
Jashub,[C] and Shimron.
14 Zebulun's sons: Sered, Elon,
and Jahleel.
15 These were Leah's sons born
to Jacob in Paddan-aram,
as well as his daughter
Dinah. The total number
of persons:[D] 33.
16 Gad's sons: Ziphion, Haggi,
Shuni, Ezbon, Eri, Arodi,
and Areli.
17 Asher's sons: Imnah,
Ishvah, Ishvi, Beriah,
and their sister Serah.
Beriah's sons were Heber
and Malchiel.
18 These were the sons
of Zilpah—whom Laban
gave to his daughter
Leah—that she bore
to Jacob: 16 persons.
19 The sons of Jacob's wife Rachel:
Joseph and Benjamin.
20 Manasseh and Ephraim
were born to Joseph
in the land of Egypt.
They were born to him
by Asenath daughter
of Potiphera, a priest
at On.[E]
21 Benjamin's sons: Bela,
Becher, Ashbel, Gera,
Naaman, Ehi, Rosh,
Muppim, Huppim, and Ard.
22 These were Rachel's sons
who were born to Jacob:
14 persons.
23 Dan's son:[F] Hushim.
24 Naphtali's sons: Jahzeel,
Guni, Jezer, and Shillem.
25 These were the sons
of Bilhah, whom Laban
gave to his daughter
Rachel. She bore to Jacob:
seven persons.
26 The total number of persons
belonging to Jacob—
his direct descendants,[G]
not including the wives
of Jacob's sons—who came
to Egypt: 66.
27 And Joseph's sons
who were born to him
in Egypt: two persons.
All those of Jacob's household
who had come to Egypt:
70[H] persons.

28 Now Jacob had sent Judah ahead
of him to Joseph to prepare for his
arrival[I] at Goshen. When they came
to the land of Goshen, 29 Joseph
hitched the horses to his chariot
and went up to Goshen to meet his
father Israel. Joseph presented himself to him, threw his arms around
him, and wept for a long time.
30 Then Israel said to Joseph, "At
last I can die, now that I have seen
your face and know you are still
alive!"
31 Joseph said to his brothers and
to his father's household, "I will
go up and inform Pharaoh, telling
him: My brothers and my father's

[A]46:4 = Joseph will close your eyes after you die [B]46:13 Sam, Syr read *Puah*; 1Ch 7:1 [C]46:13 Sam, LXX; MT reads *Iob* [D]46:15 Lit *All persons his sons and his daughters* [E]46:20 Or *Heliopolis* [F]46:23 Alt Hb tradition reads *sons* [G]46:26 Lit *Jacob who came out from his loins* [H]46:27 LXX reads *75*; Ac 7:14 [I]46:28 Lit *to give directions before him*

household, who were in the land of Canaan, have come to me. 32 The men are shepherds; they also raise livestock. They have brought their sheep and cattle and all that they have. 33 When Pharaoh addresses you and asks, 'What is your occupation?' 34 you are to say, 'Your servants, both we and our fathers, have raised livestock[A] from our youth until now.' Then you will be allowed to settle in the land of Goshen, since all shepherds are abhorrent to Egyptians."

47 So Joseph went and informed Pharaoh: "My father and my brothers, with their sheep and cattle and all that they own, have come from the land of Canaan and are now in the land of Goshen."

2 He took five of his brothers and presented them before Pharaoh. 3 Then Pharaoh asked his brothers, "What is your occupation?"

And they said to Pharaoh, "Your servants, both we and our fathers, are shepherds." 4 Then they said to Pharaoh, "We have come to live in the land for a while because there is no grazing land for your servants' sheep, since the famine in the land of Canaan has been severe. So now, please let your servants settle in the land of Goshen."

5 Then Pharaoh said to Joseph, "Now that your father and brothers have come to you, 6 the land of Egypt is open before you; settle your father and brothers in the best part of the land. They can live in the land of Goshen. If you know of any capable men among them, put them in charge of my livestock."

7 Joseph then brought his father Jacob and presented him before Pharaoh, and Jacob blessed Pharaoh. 8 Then Pharaoh said to Jacob, "How many years have you lived?"[B]

9 Jacob said to Pharaoh, "My pilgrimage has lasted 130 years. My years have been few and hard, and they have not surpassed the years of my fathers during their pilgrimages." 10 So Jacob blessed Pharaoh and departed from Pharaoh's presence.

11 Then Joseph settled his father and brothers in the land of Egypt and gave them property in the best part of the land, the land of Rameses, as Pharaoh had commanded. 12 And Joseph provided his father, his brothers, and all his father's household with food for their dependents.

13 But there was no food in that entire region, for the famine was very severe. The land of Egypt and the land of Canaan were exhausted by the famine. 14 Joseph collected all the money to be found in the land of Egypt and the land of Canaan in exchange for the grain they were purchasing, and he brought the money to Pharaoh's palace. 15 When the money from the land of Egypt and the land of Canaan was gone, all the Egyptians came to Joseph and said, "Give us food. Why should we die here in front of you? The money is gone!"

16 But Joseph said, "Give me your livestock. Since the money is gone, I will give you food in exchange for your livestock." 17 So they brought their livestock to Joseph, and he gave them food in exchange for the horses, the herds of sheep, the herds of cattle, and the donkeys. That year he provided them with food in exchange for all their livestock.

18 When that year was over, they came the next year and said to him, "We cannot hide from our lord that the money is gone and that all our livestock belongs to our lord. There is nothing left for our lord except our bodies and our land. 19 Why should we die here in front of you—both us and our land? Buy us and our land in exchange for food. Then we with our land will become Pharaoh's slaves. Give us seed so that we can live and not die, and so that the land won't become desolate."

20 In this way, Joseph acquired all the land in Egypt for Pharaoh, because every Egyptian sold his field since the famine was so severe for them. The land became Pharaoh's, 21 and Joseph moved the people to the cities[C] from one end of Egypt to the other. 22 The only land he didn't acquire was the priests' portion, for it was given to them by Pharaoh. They lived off[D] the rations Pharaoh had given them; therefore they did not sell their land.

[A]46:34 Lit *fathers, are men of livestock* [B]47:8 Lit *many are the days of the years* [C]47:21 Sam, LXX, Vg read *and he made the people servants* [D]47:22 Lit *They ate*

47:1-6 The scene in Pharaoh's court was one of formalities, with Joseph presenting himself, five of his brothers, and then his father. Of note is the deference of the brothers to Joseph's instructions. In the past, they probably would have ignored Joseph's advice, but his wisdom and the favor of God upon him were now evident to all.

47:7-10 The meeting between Jacob and Pharaoh was like the interaction of two heads of state. Jacob was the elderly, stately father of a nation; and Pharaoh was the great, wealthy ruler of a nation. There was mutual respect in their conversation even though it was more relaxed than the formulated speech between Joseph's brothers and Pharaoh. For example, Jacob said, **my years** and not "your servant's years" when answering Pharaoh's question about his age.

47:11-12 Pharaoh was true to his words in chapter 45, as he gave Joseph's family **property in the best part of the land**. Joseph's provision for his family is astonishing. And his forgiveness is apparent in his actions; but as is shown later in chapter 50, even the kindness Joseph showed did not end his brothers' fears of revenge (see 50:16-18).

47:27-31 Even though the land was still famine-stricken, Jacob's family was bountifully blessed. God's promise was being fulfilled, even in the midst of the trial. Jacob was able to see this before he died. Joseph was still Jacob's favored son, the one whom he could trust. Thus, Joseph was called to his father's bedside for final instructions. The request of Jacob not to be buried in Egypt but with his fathers is a reminder that Egypt was not their home. God had prepared a land for them.

48:1-12 Joseph again went to the bedside of his father, together with Ephraim and Manasseh. Jacob had apparently been ill for a long time but now was **weaker**. Joseph's visit was not just to see his dying father. Jacob detailed all that **God Almighty** had promised him: fruitfulness, **many nations**, land. The promises had begun to come to fruition as Joseph's sons were evidence of the fruitfulness of the family. In the middle of Jacob's discourse, he in essence adopted Ephraim and Manasseh, ranking them with Reuben and Simeon and putting them on a par with those tracing their origin back to Jacob's own sons. Also of note is the mentioning of Ephraim before Manasseh, which hints at what happened when Jacob blessed them (see vv. 19-20). Joseph's bowing and presenting his sons before his father was basically a request for them to be blessed. Jacob was clearly happy about being able to see his grandsons, and he knew the opportunity was because of God's goodness and grace.

48:13-14 Joseph positioned his sons before Jacob in the order of their birth so that they might be blessed. **Manasseh**, the elder, was in the place of honor at Joseph's right. Jacob, however, crossed his arms so that his right hand was over **Ephraim**, the younger. Unlike when Jacob tricked Isaac, the ordained blessing of the younger is obvious, with no deceit involved.

48:15-16 Jacob began by blessing Joseph; there are three parts to the blessing, which is a form of poetry. First, Jacob acknowledged **the God** of his **fathers**, and **the God who has been my shepherd**, a poetic statement showing God as shepherd, which, though pictured here first, is continued throughout Scripture. God is portrayed as a shepherd in the Psalms (Ps 23:1; 80:1) and in the New Testament, culminating with Jesus calling Himself "the good shepherd" (Jn 10:14; see also Heb 13:20; 1Pt 2:25, 5:4). **The Angel** is most likely a reference to Jacob's wrestling match (see Gn 32:24-32). Second, Jacob called upon God to bless his grandsons and in essence asked that they be counted as part of the covenant that began with Abraham. To be called

[23] Then Joseph said to the people,
"Understand today that I have acquired you and your land for Pharaoh. Here is seed for you. Sow it in
the land. [24] At harvest, you are to give
a fifth of it to Pharaoh, and four-fifths
will be yours as seed for the field and
as food for yourselves, your households, and your dependents."
[25] And they said, "You have saved
our lives. We have found favor in
our lord's eyes and will be Pharaoh's
slaves." [26] So Joseph made it a law,
still in effect today in the land of
Egypt, that a fifth of the produce belongs to Pharaoh. Only the priests'
land does not belong to Pharaoh.
[27] Israel settled in the land of
Egypt, in the region of Goshen. They
acquired property in it and became
fruitful and very numerous. [28] Now
Jacob lived in the land of Egypt 17
years, and his life span was 147 years.
[29] When the time drew near for him
to die, he called his son Joseph and
said to him, "If I have found favor in
your eyes, put your hand under my
thigh and promise me that you will
deal with me in kindness and faithfulness. Do not bury me in Egypt.
[30] When I rest with my fathers, carry
me away from Egypt and bury me in
their burial place."
Joseph answered, "I will do what
you have asked."
[31] And Jacob said, "Swear to me."
So Joseph swore to him. Then Israel
bowed in thanks at the head of his
bed.[A]

48 Some time after this, Joseph
was told, "Your father is weaker." So he set out with his two sons,
Manasseh and Ephraim. [2] When Jacob was told, "Your son Joseph has
come to you," Israel summoned his
strength and sat up in bed.
[3] Jacob said to Joseph, "•God Almighty appeared to me at Luz in
the land of Canaan and blessed me.
[4] He said to me, 'I will make you
fruitful and numerous; I will make
many nations come from you, and I
will give this land as an eternal possession to your future descendants.'
[5] Your two sons born to you in the
land of Egypt before I came to you
in Egypt are now mine. Ephraim
and Manasseh belong to me just
as Reuben and Simeon do. [6] Children born to you after them will be
yours and will be recorded under
the names of their brothers with
regard to their inheritance. [7] When
I was returning from Paddan, to my
sorrow Rachel died along the way,
some distance from Ephrath in the
land of Canaan. I buried her there
along the way to Ephrath," (that is,
Bethlehem).
[8] When Israel saw Joseph's sons,
he said, "Who are these?"
[9] And Joseph said to his father,
"They are my sons God has given me
here."
So Jacob said, "Bring them to me
and I will bless them." [10] Now his
eyesight was poor because of old
age; he could hardly[B] see. Joseph
brought them to him, and he kissed
and embraced them. [11] Israel said to
Joseph, "I never expected to see your
face again, but now God has even
let me see your •offspring." [12] Then
Joseph took them from his father's
knees and bowed with his face to the
ground.
[13] Then Joseph took them
both—with his right hand Ephraim
toward Israel's left, and with his
left hand Manasseh toward Israel's
right—and brought them to Israel. [14] But Israel stretched out his
right hand and put it on the head of
Ephraim, the younger, and crossing
his hands, put his left on Manasseh's
head, although Manasseh was the
firstborn. [15] Then he blessed Joseph
and said:

The God before whom
my fathers Abraham
and Isaac walked,
the God who has been
my shepherd all my life
to this day,
[16] the Angel who has redeemed
me from all harm—
may He bless these boys.
And may they be called
by my name
and the names of my fathers
Abraham and Isaac,
and may they grow
to be numerous
within the land.

[A] **47:31** Or *Israel worshiped while leaning on the top of his staff* [B] **48:10** Lit *he was not able to*

[17]When Joseph saw that his father had placed his right hand on Ephraim's head, he thought it was a mistake[A] and took his father's hand to move it from Ephraim's head to Manasseh's. [18]Joseph said to his father, "Not that way, my father! This one is the firstborn. Put your right hand on his head."

[19]But his father refused and said, "I know, my son, I know! He too will become a tribe,[B] and he too will be great; nevertheless, his younger brother will be greater than he, and his offspring will become a populous nation."[C] [20]So he blessed them that day with these words:

The nation Israel will invoke
blessings by you, saying,
"May God make you
like Ephraim
and Manasseh,"
putting Ephraim
before Manasseh.

[21]Then Israel said to Joseph, "Look, I am about to die, but God will be with you and will bring you back to the land of your fathers. [22]Over and above what I am giving your brothers, I am giving you the one mountain slope[D] that I took from the hand of the Amorites with my sword and bow."

The Blessing of Jacob's Descendants (49:1-28)

49 Then Jacob called his sons and said, "Gather around, and I will tell you what will happen to you in the days to come.[E]

2 Come together and listen,
sons of Jacob;
listen to your father Israel:

3 Reuben, you are my firstborn,
my strength and the firstfruits
of my virility,
excelling in prominence,
excelling in power.
4 Turbulent as water, you will
no longer excel,
because you got
into your father's bed
and you defiled it—he[F] got
into my bed.

5 Simeon and Levi are brothers;
their knives are
vicious weapons.
6 May I never enter their council;
may I never join
their assembly.
For in their anger
they kill men,
and on a whim
they hamstring oxen.
7 Their anger is cursed, for it
is strong,
and their fury, for it is cruel!
I will disperse them
throughout Jacob
and scatter them
throughout Israel.

8 Judah, your brothers will
praise you.
Your hand will be
on the necks
of your enemies;
your father's sons
will bow down to you.
9 Judah is a young lion—
my son, you return
from the kill.
He crouches; he lies down
like a lion
or a lioness—who dares
to rouse him?
10 The scepter will not depart
from Judah
or the staff from between
his feet
until He whose right
it is comes[G]
and the obedience
of the peoples belongs
to Him.
11 He ties his donkey to a vine,
and the colt of his donkey
to the choice vine.
He washes his clothes in wine
and his robes in the blood
of grapes.
12 His eyes are darker than wine,
and his teeth are whiter
than milk.

13 Zebulun will live
by the seashore
and will be a harbor for ships,
and his territory will be
next to Sidon.

[A]**48:17** Or *he was displeased*; lit *head, it was bad in his eyes* [B]**48:19** Lit *people* [C]**48:19** Or *a multitude of nations*; lit *a fullness of nations* [D]**48:22** Or *Shechem*, Joseph's burial place; lit *one shoulder* [E]**49:1** Or *in the last days* [F]**49:4** LXX, Syr, Tg read *you* [G]**49:10** Or *until tribute comes to him*, or *until Shiloh comes*, or *until He comes to Shiloh*

by the same name as Abraham, Isaac, and Jacob would make them a part of the covenant and heirs to the promises given them. Last, Jacob blessed Joseph's sons in his reminder of God's promise that He would make Jacob's descendants **numerous**. Jacob blessed his grandsons in the same way.

48:17-20 After the first part of the blessing concluded, Joseph noticed his father's "mistake." Jacob's refusal to switch his hands again is one of reassurance that both would be great, and yet at the same time a declaration that the younger, **Ephraim**, would **be greater**.

48:21-22 Jacob's attention then returned to his favored son, Joseph. Both calamity and comfort were proclaimed—Jacob was **about to die**, but God would be with Joseph. Israel was displaced, but God would bring them back to the **land of** their **fathers**. The giving of the extra portion of land to Joseph is also concerned with the return to the land of promise, for **the one mountain slope** (Hb *Shechem*, lit "shoulder" or "back," and metaphorically "portion" as of land) would also be the burial place of Joseph (see Jos 24:32). Thus, chapter 48 serves as a reminder of the land of promise and of God who is faithful.

49:1-4 The scene with Jacob on his deathbed begins with parallelism as Jacob called his sons together. Most of chapter 49 is poetry with imagery and symbolism. **In the days to come** prefaces a prophetic statement. Jacob was about to pronounce the future of his sons. Jacob began by addressing his eldest son, **Reuben**. In Hebrew culture, as in the ancient world in general, the firstborn is seen as prominent. The same is true for Reuben. He was the **strength . . . firstfruits**, and **power** of Jacob. However, Reuben's sin still bore consequences. Because Reuben slept with his father's wife, he would **no longer excel**. The repetition of the sin shows the weight of its penalty and Jacob's disgust over the despicable act.

49:5-7 Simeon and Levi are the sons of Leah. Due to their savage revenge upon all of Shechem in response to the kidnapping and rape of their sister Dinah, they would be scattered. They were considered vicious fighters, easily angered, and full of **fury**. Their anger and cruelty were sin and, as evidenced here, were not to be imitated.

49:8-12 Judah, with the dismissal of his older **brothers** from the position of preeminence, now came to the forefront. His lineage would become the one of kings—the monarchs of the Davidic kingdom. His blessing was one of greatness and victory.

He would overcome his **enemies** and, like a successful **lion** after a hunt, would **return** triumphantly. However, the blessing and victory were not just for Judah himself but for future generations. Judah was given preeminence among his brothers until the coming of the Messiah. **Scepter** (Hb *shēvet*, "rod, staff, shepherd's crook," according to context; cp. Nm 24:17; Ps 23:4; Is 14:5) symbolizes rule over a kingdom. **Staff** (Hb *chaqaq*) is a verb, which, in the form of a participle can also be rendered "lawgiver, leader, commander," i.e., the one who decrees. **From between his feet** refers to procreation; Judah would continually produce leaders. **He whose right it is** (Hb *shiloh*, "tranquility, rest") translates a word that does not appear elsewhere as a title of the Messiah. It has been interpreted both as a reference to Shiloh (e.g., Jos 18:1), although the city has no particular messianic function, and as a verb form meaning "until he comes to who it (namely, the scepter) belongs." Gn 49:10-12 are messianic verses. They tell of the coming One from whom the **scepter** and **staff**, signs of authority, **will not depart**. Not only will Israel be obedient to Him, but all **peoples** shall be under Him. The blessing of Judah is of the highest praise. He is victorious, fruitful, but above all he has been blessed to be an ancestor of the coming Messiah.

49:13-15 Zebulun's territory did not touch the sea, yet the borders eventually would be extended there (Jos 19:10-16). Issachar's land was **pleasant**. He is depicted as a **donkey**, and the imagery of a beast of burden is used to show the hard work Issachar would perform.

49:16-18 Just as Dan's name is a word play on "judging," so he would **judge his people**. Verse 17 appears at first to suggest Dan would be violent and vengeful. However, taken in context with verse 18, the reference is to Dan's defeat of his enemies and his prosperity. All the tribes would prosper, but only because of the blessing and grace of the Lord.

49:19-21 Gad, Asher, and Naphtali would flourish but in different ways. **Gad** would triumph over his enemies. **Asher** would be able to produce wonderful, rich food. And finally, **Naphtali** would be fruitful with beautiful children.

49:22-26 The beginning of Joseph's blessing is a summary of his life thus far. Though attacked, he remained steady with God's help. For only the second time, God is referred to as the **Shepherd**. Joseph received all the **blessings** (Hb *berakah*, a term used among the brothers only with Joseph)—heaven's blessings, earthly

14 Issachar is a strong donkey
lying down between
the saddlebags.[A]
15 He saw that his resting place
was good
and that the land
was pleasant,
so he leaned his shoulder
to bear a load
and became a forced laborer.

16 Dan will judge his people
as one of the tribes of Israel.
17 He will be a snake by the road,
a viper beside the path,
that bites the horses' heels
so that its rider
falls backward.

18 I wait for Your salvation,
LORD.

19 Gad will be attacked by raiders,
but he will attack their heels.

20 Asher's[B] food will be rich,
and he will produce
royal delicacies.

21 Naphtali is a doe set free
that bears beautiful fawns.

22 Joseph is a fruitful vine,
a fruitful vine beside a spring;
its branches[C] climb
over the wall.[D]
23 The archers attacked him,
shot at him, and were hostile
toward him.
24 Yet his bow remained steady,
and his strong[E] arms
were made agile
by the hands
of the Mighty One of Jacob,
by the name of[F] the Shepherd,
the Rock of Israel,
25 by the God of your father
who helps you,
and by the •Almighty
who blesses you
with blessings
of the heavens above,
blessings of the deep
that lies below,
and blessings of the breasts
and the womb.
26 The blessings of your father
excel
the blessings of my ancestors[G]
and[H] the bounty
of the eternal hills.[I]
May they rest on the head of
Joseph,
on the crown of the prince
of his brothers.

27 Benjamin is a wolf; he tears
his prey.
In the morning he devours
the prey,
and in the evening he divides
the plunder."

28 These are the tribes of Israel, 12
in all, and this was what their father
said to them. He blessed them, and
he blessed each one with a suitable
blessing.

The Death of Jacob and Then of Joseph
(49:29–50:26)

29 Then he commanded them:
"I am about to be gathered to my
people. Bury me with my fathers in
the cave in the field of Ephron the
Hittite. 30 The cave is in the field
of Machpelah near Mamre, in the
land of Canaan. This is the field
Abraham purchased from Ephron
the Hittite as a burial site. 31 Abraham and his wife Sarah are buried
there, Isaac and his wife Rebekah
are buried there, and I buried Leah
there. 32 The field and the cave in it
were purchased from the Hittites."
33 When Jacob had finished instructing his sons, he drew his feet into
the bed and died. He was gathered
to his people.

50 Then Joseph, leaning over his
father's face, wept and kissed
him. 2 He commanded his servants
who were physicians to embalm his
father. So they embalmed Israel.
3 They took 40 days to complete this,
for embalming takes that long, and
the Egyptians mourned for him 70
days.

4 When the days of mourning were
over, Joseph said to Pharaoh's household, "If I have found favor with you,
please tell[J] Pharaoh that 5 my father
made me take an oath, saying, 'I
am about to die. You must bury me

[A] **49:14** Or *sheepfolds* [B] **49:19-20** LXX, Syr, Vg; MT reads *their heel.* [20] *From Asher* [C] **49:22** Lit *daughters* [D] **49:22** Hb obscure [E] **49:24** Lit *and the hands of his* [F] **49:24** Syr, Tg; MT reads *Jacob, from there* [G] **49:26** Or *of the mountains* [H] **49:26** Lit *to* [I] **49:26** Hb obscure [J] **50:4** Lit *please speak in the ears of*

there in the tomb that I made for
myself in the land of Canaan.' Now
let me go and bury my father. Then I
will return."
[6]So Pharaoh said, "Go and bury
your father in keeping with your
oath."
[7]Then Joseph went to bury his father, and all Pharaoh's servants, the
elders of his household, and all the
elders of the land of Egypt went with
him, [8]along with all Joseph's household, his brothers, and his father's
household. Only their children,
their sheep, and their cattle were left
in the land of Goshen. [9]Horses and
chariots went up with him; it was a
very impressive procession. [10]When
they reached the threshing floor of
Atad, which is across the Jordan,
they lamented and wept loudly, and
Joseph mourned seven days for his
father. [11]When the Canaanite inhabitants of the land saw the mourning
at the threshing floor of Atad, they
said, "This is a solemn mourning on
the part of the Egyptians." Therefore
the place is named Abel-mizraim.[A] It
is across the Jordan.
[12]So Jacob's sons did for him what
he had commanded them. [13]They
carried him to the land of Canaan
and buried him in the cave at Machpelah in the field near Mamre,
which Abraham had purchased as a
burial site from Ephron the Hittite.
[14]After Joseph buried his father, he
returned to Egypt with his brothers
and all who had gone with him to
bury his father.
[15]When Joseph's brothers saw that
their father was dead, they said to
one another, "If Joseph is holding a
grudge against us, he will certainly
repay us for all the suffering we
caused him."
[16]So they sent this message to
Joseph, "Before he died your father
gave a command: [17]'Say this to Joseph: Please forgive your brothers'
transgression and their sin—the
suffering they caused you.' Therefore, please forgive the transgression of the servants of the God of
your father." Joseph wept when
their message came to him. [18]Then
his brothers also came to him,
bowed down before him, and said,
"We are your slaves!"
[19]But Joseph said to them, "Don't
be afraid. Am I in the place of God?
[20]You planned evil against me; God
planned it for good to bring about
the present result—the survival of
many people. [21]Therefore don't be
afraid. I will take care of you and
your little ones." And he comforted
them and spoke kindly to them.[B]
[22]Joseph and his father's household remained in Egypt. Joseph
lived 110 years. [23]He saw Ephraim's
sons to the third generation; the
sons of Manasseh's son Machir were
recognized by[C,D] Joseph.
[24]Joseph said to his brothers, "I
am about to die, but God will certainly come to your aid and bring
you up from this land to the land
He promised Abraham, Isaac, and
Jacob." [25]So Joseph made the sons
of Israel take an oath: "When God
comes to your aid, you are to carry
my bones up from here."
[26]Joseph died at the age of 110.
They embalmed him and placed him
in a coffin in Egypt.

[A]**50:11** = Mourning of Egypt [B]**50:21** Lit *spoke to their hearts* [C]**50:23** Lit *were born on the knees of* [D]**50:23** Referring to a ritual of adoption or of legitimation; Gn 30:3

blessings, blessings of the womb—far more than his brothers. Despite human frailties and failures, Joseph had been faithful to God.

49:27 The picture of **Benjamin** as a ravenous wolf is rather surprising. In Genesis, Benjamin was only depicted as the youngest of Jacob's sons, one who needed care. But Jacob's blessing points to the tribe of warriors Benjamin would father. For example, Saul, the first king of Israel, was from the tribe of Benjamin.

49:29-33 For the second time, Jacob gave directions for his burial. Unlike the earlier instance, the commands were given to all his sons and not just to Joseph. Jacob would be buried with his first wife **Leah** and with his fathers, **Abraham**, **Isaac**, and their wives. As God had spoken to Jacob (46:4), so His promise would come true, and Jacob was making sure of it. On his deathbed Jacob was with his long lost son and knew his sons would return him to the land of promise to be buried.

50:1-14 Joseph's love for his father is evident in this chapter. Not only did he weep over his deceased father and kiss him, but he also gave special instructions to his physicians to embalm his father.

50:15-21 Jacob's death caused strife among his sons. Now, fearing Joseph would seek retribution without their father to stop him, the brothers were very nervous.

50:22-26 Joseph was indeed blessed with a fruitful life. He lived **110 years** and saw many of his grandchildren, great-grandchildren, and great-great-grandchildren. Joseph, as his forefathers, told his brothers that he would soon die. With this sorrow also came hope. Joseph was certain God would come to their aid, and He would also bring them to the land of promise. As Jacob had done, Joseph made his brothers swear an oath. Joseph, too, would be carried to the promised land to be buried there rather than in Egypt (see Jos 24:32). Thus Joseph died, while leaving the Israelites with the hope of a faithful God who would bring them out of Egypt.

GENESIS… WRITTEN ON MY *Heart*

The God who created you is the same God who is a covenant-keeping and promise-fulfilling God. Just as the Lord showed Himself faithful to Abraham, Isaac, and Jacob, He is more than able to bring about His plan for your life. You can trust Him to keep His Word to you.

Exodus

Timeline	1805 BC	1780–1540 BC	1529 BC	1526 BC
World Events / Biblical Events	Death of Joseph	Hyksos rule Egypt	Birth of Aaron	Birth of Moses

"I AM WHO I AM" (3:14a).

Who wrote Exodus?

The available evidence supports the conclusion that Moses was the author of Exodus.

Who were the recipients?

When Exodus was composed and recorded, the Israelites themselves were the immediate audience.

When was Exodus written?

Based on the proposed date for the historical events described in the book and on the assumption of Mosaic authorship, most of the book of Exodus was written between 1445 and 1405 B.C.

Where did it happen?

The events recorded in Exodus happened in Egypt, on the way out of Egypt, and at Mount Sinai.

What is Exodus about?

- *God as the personal God* who speaks and acts directly within history and creation.
- *God plans, promises, and proves faithful.* Keeping His covenant with Abraham, Isaac, and Jacob, even centuries after their deaths, God works with and through people to accomplish His purposes.
- *God is in control, and He is sovereign over history.* God is portrayed in Exodus as omnipotent, omniscient, and omnipresent.
- *God is holy and therefore jealous.* God does not tolerate sin but is determined to deal with sin Himself in order to redeem a people for His pleasure.
- *God delivers.* Exodus illustrates the power of the enemies of God's people but even more vividly their impotence before Yahweh, with whom none can contend.
- *God provides.* God is the One who provides for every need of the people who depend upon Him. He equips His people for everything He calls them to be and do.

Why should women read Exodus?

As one of the five books of the Torah (Hb "instruction," usually translated as "law"), Exodus has been considered part of the essential core of Jewish Scripture. Although Exodus has been integral to the identity of the nation of Israel and the Jewish people, it also establishes a spiritual and historical foundation for all believers. Every woman should be familiar with its context in order to make sense of the rest of Scripture. Especially in Exodus, Yahweh is like a husband who rescues His bride from slavery, gives her His own name as she agrees to be bound to Him in a covenant of marriage, and in love establishes boundaries of protection for her. Having done all this for her, He jealously guards her devotion to Him and tolerates no rivals. As God is holy, so must His people be holy and worship Him as He prescribes.

There are some significant women in the book of Exodus. Jochebed and Miriam have remained legendary in Hebrew history. Even lowly and seemingly insignificant midwives identified by their names (Shiphrah and Puah), together with Pharaoh's daughter, had strategic roles to play, illustrating clearly that even women in the shadows are important in God's plan.

How do you read Exodus?

Exodus is a largely narrative history written in prose. However, the larger story encompassing the book also contains a song (chap. 15), a body of laws (chaps. 20–23), a concise rehearsal of these laws as covenant obligations (34:10-27), and both the record and fulfillment of God's detailed instructions for building His tabernacle (chaps. 25–31; 35–40). One should read this book as a historical account that must be set in context with the rest of the Pentateuch.

Outline

I. Slavery: Living in the Land of Egypt (1:1–11:10)
  A. The Sons of Israel: Blessed but Oppressed (1:1-22)
  B. Moses: Rescued to Rescuer (2:1–4:31)
  C. Yahweh vs. Pharaoh (5:1–11:10)

II. Exodus: Deliverance from Slavery (12:1–15:21)
  A. Passover (12:1–13:16)
  B. Route of the Exodus (13:17–14:4)
  C. Egyptian Pursuit (14:5-14)
  D. Salvation of Yahweh (14:15-31)
  E. Song to Yahweh (15:1-21)

III. Journey to Sinai: Preparatory Testing Before the Covenant (15:22–17:16)
  A. Yahweh's Testing of the Israelites at Marah (15:22-27)
  B. Yahweh's Testing of the Israelites in the Wilderness of Sin (16:1-36)
  C. The Israelites' Testing of Yahweh at Rephidim (17:1-7)
  D. Amalek's Attack of Israel at Rephidim (17:8-16)

IV. The Covenant (18:1–24:18)
  A. Jethro's Visit (18:1-27)
  B. Covenant Mediation (19:1-25)
  C. God's Words: The Ten Commandments (20:1-26)

1486 BC	**1447 BC**	**1446 BC**	**1445 BC**
Moses' flight to Midian.	Moses at the burning bush	Israel's exodus from Egypt and receiving God's law at Sinai	Dedication of the tabernacle

Outline (continued)

The Sons of Israel: Blessed but Oppressed (1:1-22)

1 These are the names of the sons
of Israel who came to Egypt with
Jacob; each came with his family:

2 Reuben, Simeon, Levi,
and Judah;
3 Issachar, Zebulun,
and Benjamin;
4 Dan and Naphtali; Gad
and Asher.

5 The total number of Jacob's descendants[A] was 70;[B] Joseph was already in Egypt.
6 Then Joseph and all his brothers and all that generation died.
7 But the Israelites were fruitful,
increased rapidly, multiplied, and
became extremely numerous so that
the land was filled with them.
8 A new king, who had not known
Joseph, came to power in Egypt.
9 He said to his people, "Look, the
Israelite people are more numerous
and powerful than we are. 10 Let us
deal shrewdly with them; otherwise
they will multiply further, and if
war breaks out, they may join our
enemies, fight against us, and leave

[A]1:5 Lit *of people issuing from Jacob's loins* [B]1:5 LXX, DSS read *75*; Gn 46:27; Ac 7:14

>WORD|*study*

1:1 Throughout Exodus, Israelites are most frequently identified as **the sons of Israel** (Hb *benē yisrā'ēl*). The phrase usually refers to the people of Israel—both men and women, daughters as well as sons—and is therefore correctly translated "children of Israel" or "Israelites." However, as the story unfolds, a distinction between "sons" and "daughters" becomes important, and the repetition of this phrase in the Hebrew text lends unity to the various elements of the narrative.

Title Following the ancient Near Eastern custom for naming literary works, the first words of Exodus, "These are the names" (Hb *we'ēlleh shemot*), provide the Hebrew title, usually shortened to *Shemot*, "Names." "Exodus" (Gk *exodos*, "departure, exit, a going out") is the Latinized title of the Greek *tēs exodou* ("the exodus") found in the Septuagint (LXX) in Ex 19:1. The book of Exodus was part of an ongoing history of real people with real names, individuals to whom God had spoken and of whom God had promised to make a nation. The Greek title captured the central event and theme of the book, the departure of Israel from Egypt.

1:1 Chapter 1 presupposes the history recorded in Genesis. In many translations, as in the Hebrew text, the book's first word includes the conjunction, which in Hebrew is a radical prefixed to the word to form a connector in the sentence, "and" (Hb *waw*, a special usage often translated "now"), immediately connecting the Exodus narrative to the Genesis accounts of Joseph.

1:15-18 Pharaoh's instructions to the **midwives** led to a government-imposed system of infanticide or post-birth abortion—murder based on ethnicity, gender, and age. The practice, continuing throughout history, has acquired the terms "sex-selective infanticide" and "gendercide" but usually targets girls; it is believed to be part of the explanation for the unbalanced birth statistics in various countries of Asia and the Middle East. God's view is implicit —the midwives **feared** [Hb *yarē'*, "reverence, stand in awe of, honor, respect"] God, who overcame whatever circumstances had prevented these women from having their own children and gave them the desires of their hearts (v. 17; cp. Ps 37:4).

1:19-21 Confronted by their failure to follow orders, the midwives offered Pharaoh a believable excuse that exploited the king's concern for the difference in strength he had observed between the Hebrews and Egyptians. They described **the Hebrew women** as **vigorous** (Hb *chayeh*, "full of life, sustaining or preserving life," a *hapax legomenon* or word used only here in the OT), giving birth before the midwives' arrival.

1:22 Pharaoh reiterated the command to **let every daughter live.** Perhaps he envisioned the eventual assimilation of the girls but his concern about the rapidly increasing Hebrew population is the only certain motive to be gleaned from the biblical text.

2:1-2a Even without chapter divisions, the narrative clearly shifts perspective in 2:1, a simple statement about one seemingly insignificant, unnamed Israelite couple among thousands in Egypt. Several important facts may be noted:

- The Hebrew text called the **Levite woman** "a daughter of Levi," a dignifying and endearing way of expressing her heritage, as well as affirming that both Moses' father and mother were descendants of Levi.
- Marriage preceded pregnancy.
- The importance of this ancestry, supporting the priestly and intercessory roles of Moses and Aaron, became apparent when God set apart the tribe of Levi for spiritual leadership and as substitutes for the firstborn sons of Israel (Nm 3:11-13).

2:2b-3 Nothing unusual is indicated about Moses' parents or about his conception and birth. Given the socio-political context described in chapter 1, however, the reader is expected to recognize the dilemma of giving birth **to a son** and the risks of hiding him. Here the purpose of the narrative is to

>WORD|*study*

1:13-14 The root word for **work** (Hb, *avodah*) is used repeatedly as both noun and verb. This passage, when read aloud, conveys a heavy sense of weariness inflicted upon the Israelites. However, the same word also means "worship or service" rendered to God. Here, the labor was burdensome primarily because the work was imposed by a cruel taskmaster who aimed to keep the people in bondage and wear them out in the process. Freely performed service to God, on the other hand, is a labor of love and gratitude.

2:2-3 The only other appearance of the word for **basket** (Hb *tēvah*) in the Old Testament is in Genesis 6–9, where it is translated "ark." This word strongly suggests a parallel between the preservation of life in Noah's "ark" and the preservation of the life of Moses through whom God was going to rescue Israel. Those whose lives were saved from the floodwaters of judgment in "Noah's ark" represented a new start for mankind. Moses, whose life was saved from the Nile River (acting as the executioner of Pharaoh) likewise represented God's deliverance of Israel under his leadership and a new beginning for them as a nation. Neither the enormous wooden vessel bearing those under Noah's care nor Moses' infant-sized papyrus vessel possessed a steering mechanism; both "arks" were completely dependent on God's protection and guidance, although both "rescue missions" were also effected by men and women who honored Him with their obedience.

the country." 11 So the Egyptians
assigned taskmasters over the Israelites to oppress them with forced
labor. They built Pithom and Rameses as supply cities for Pharaoh.
12 But the more they oppressed
them, the more they multiplied and
spread so that the Egyptians came
to dread[A] the Israelites. 13 They
worked the Israelites ruthlessly
14 and made their lives bitter with
difficult labor in brick and mortar
and in all kinds of fieldwork. They
ruthlessly imposed all this work on
them.
15 Then the king of Egypt said
to the Hebrew midwives, one of
whom was named Shiphrah and
the other Puah, 16 "When you help
the Hebrew women give birth, observe them as they deliver.[B] If the
child is a son, kill him, but if it's
a daughter, she may live." 17 The
Hebrew midwives, however, •feared
God and did not do as the king of
Egypt had told them; they let the
boys live. 18 So the king of Egypt
summoned the midwives and asked
them, "Why have you done this and
let the boys live?"
19 The midwives said to Pharaoh,
"The Hebrew women are not like the
Egyptian women, for they are vigorous and give birth before a midwife
can get to them."
20 So God was good to the midwives, and the people multiplied and
became very numerous. 21 Since the
midwives feared God, He gave them
families. 22 Pharaoh then commanded all his people: "You must throw

[A]1:12 Or *Egyptians loathed* [B]1:16 Lit *birth, look at the stones*

HARD QUESTION

What if God does not give me a family of my own?

God rewarded the midwives who honored Him by giving them families (1:21). Throughout the Bible, families clearly are good gifts from God; they are blessings. Nevertheless, God is free to bless as He chooses, unrestrained and unrestricted by the demands or expectations of even the godliest woman. He knows your desires and cares about your longings, but He pursues His own plans. God would not be less than good if He had allowed the midwives to be executed or to remain single and/or childless, yet He chose to do what would bring the most glory to His name. How God dealt with the midwives represents His delight in revealing His power through the least expected channels (i.e., powerless people). This dramatic event showcases His view of the importance of radical obedience (cp. Jos 6:23; Mt 1:5; Heb 11:31). That God considered a family the reward for such life-threatening obedience reveals the value He attributes to family. Most likely a family—not fame, not money, but a family—was the greatest reward possible for these women. If you are tempted to be jealous of others because you *feel* that God has overlooked your obedience or *fear* that He has neglected to give you a family of your own, return to the midwives' example and the truths about God's character. The midwives were women who had made a profession of serving other women. Instead of withdrawing from society or becoming bitter or poisoned with envy, instead of blaming God or withering in despair, these women—in a poignant testimony that God provides for those who fear *Him*—exhibited strength to contribute to society, especially to the welfare of God's people. They exemplify the blessings of turning outward to see and meet the needs of others, a reliable antidote for discontentment and disappointment. God is good; you can be sure that He is always working for your good but even more so for the glory of His name and the fulfillment of His plans (Rm 8:28). Obey Him in all "the little things," invest in the lives of others, and delight in being a daughter of the King, a member of the family of God and the household of faith (Ps 68:6).

CHARACTER PROFILE

Shiphrah and Puah Obedient Midwives

Their Background	Midwives who served Egyptian and Hebrew women in giving birth (1:19)
Their Story	• They were commanded by Pharaoh to kill Hebrew baby boys, • Only the girls were to be allowed to live (1:16). • They disobeyed Pharaoh because they feared the Lord (1:17). • Because of their obedience, God gave them their own families (1:21).
Life Lessons	• The midwives courageously disobeyed Pharaoh, despite the possible consequences (Ex 1:15-19). • God rewarded their faithfulness (Ex 1:20-21).

every son born to the Hebrews[A] into the Nile, but let every daughter live."

Moses: Rescued to Rescuer (2:1–4:31)

Birth and Adoption (2:1-10)

2 Now a man from the family of Levi married a Levite woman.
2 The woman became pregnant and gave birth to a son; when she saw that he was beautiful,[B] she hid him for three months.
3 But when she could no longer hide him, she got a papyrus basket for him and coated it with asphalt and pitch. She placed the child in it and set it among the reeds by the bank of the Nile.
4 Then his sister stood at a distance in order to see what would happen to him.
5 Pharaoh's daughter went down to bathe at the Nile while her servant girls walked along the riverbank. Seeing the basket among the reeds, she sent her slave girl to get it.
6 When she opened it, she saw the child—a little boy, crying. She felt sorry for him and said, "This is one of the Hebrew boys."
7 Then his sister said to Pharaoh's

[A]1:22 Sam, LXX, Tg; MT omits *to the Hebrews* [B]2:2 Or *healthy*

introduce the key figure through whom God would fulfill His promise to come to the Israelites' aid (Gn 50:24); few details are provided. However, combining some facts scattered through Scripture can help modern readers flesh out these "minor characters" and appreciate them as real people. For example, "Amram" (Hb "High Father, Exalted People"), Moses' father (6:20), was the oldest of Kohath's four sons (6:18; Nm 3:19; 1 Ch 6:2,18; 23:12), and he "lived 137 years" (Ex 6:20). The Bible does not say how old he was when he married or when his children were born, but his age at death corroborates the description of God's blessing upon His people; most Egyptians did not live to be 50 years old. "Jochebed" (Hb, "Yah is glory or honor"), Moses' mother, was a sister of Amram's father (6:20; Nm 26:59). Considering the context of tremendous blessing in terms of fertility and longevity, one can reasonably (but not necessarily) infer that she was born into a large family and was still younger than her "nephew" Amram. Nm 26:59 adds that she was "a descendant of Levi, born to Levi in Egypt" and that she "bore to Amram: Aaron, Moses, and their sister Miriam." This list of her children is probably complete, particularly since it includes the daughter's name. After being "cared for in his father's home three months" (Ac 7:20), Moses' mother technically accepted Pharaoh's decree by leaving him "outside" (Ac 7:21), **by the bank of the Nile**. However, she **placed** the baby in a **basket** made of **papyrus** (Hb *gome'*, "reeds", "rushes") and **coated** with **asphalt and pitch** to make it waterproof.

2:4 Miriam was the **sister** who watched over Moses. The text does not provide her age at the time, but

BIBLICAL WOMANHOOD Midwifery

The text (1:15-18) does not explain why only two **Hebrew midwives** are named—**Shiphrah** (Hb "beautiful, fair") and **Puah** (Hb "girl"). These two may have been representatives or leaders through whom Pharaoh delivered his orders to the rest of the midwives. An Israelite population of more than a million undoubtedly required the services of many more midwives (cp. 12:37). Whether or not other midwives followed Pharaoh's directives, these two women demonstrated courageous civil disobedience. Pharaoh apparently did not prescribe the means of killing the babies, but his order would clearly require deception, betrayal, and denial of conscience. He apparently meant for the order to be carried out at the child's birth, for he instructed the midwives to **observe them as they deliver**—literally, "Look at/upon the stones" (Hb *'oven*), or "birthstools." The phrase refers to the posture of women in labor as they sat on a pair of stones or bricks spaced far enough apart for the midwife to handle the baby during childbirth. The Egyptian phrase "to sit on the bricks" was an idiom for giving birth. The pharaoh's familiarity with this practice suggests that the profession of midwifery was well-known. Depictions in ancient Egyptian art of a woman giving birth indicate that midwives may have worked in teams of two or three women. Whether they were Hebrew or Egyptian, working alone or in groups, the women were expected to fear the pharaoh enough to obey even such ghastly orders.

the understanding and behavior she displayed in her encounter with Pharaoh's daughter suggest a minimum age range of eight to ten years old.

2:7-9 The experience of breastfeeding secured an irrevocable bond between Jochebed and her son. Furthermore, during the earliest, formative years of his life, Moses was raised within his ethnic and religious culture, learning the language and values of God's people, and having opportunity to hear and sing the stories of the covenant. He was nurtured within the security of a family who loved and cherished him.

2:11 The New Testament describes Moses' faith as demonstrated by his refusing "to be called the son of Pharaoh's daughter" and in choosing to identify and "suffer with the people of God rather than to enjoy the short-lived pleasure of sin" (Heb 11:24-25).

2:17-18 This priest **Reuel** [Hb "friend of God," cp. Nm. 10:29], **had seven daughters**, all of whom appear to have been unmarried when they went together to the well **to water their father's flock**. Moses' response to the shepherds' behavior was consistent with how he responded to the beating of a fellow Hebrew and to the fighting of two Hebrew men. He proved to be a decisive man of action as he seized the opportunity to intervene and water the daughters' flock.

2:19-22 The daughters explained that **an Egyptian** had **rescued** (Hb *natsal*, "deliver, save, or snatch away from enemies"; cp. 3:8; 6:6; 18:9-10) them and added, **He even drew water for us**, complimenting Moses' gallantry. Their father's question displayed his willingness to offer hospitality to the foreigner. No mention is made about whether or not Reuel's wife was still living when Moses arrived. The text does not explain how long Moses stayed with Reuel before the man gave him **his daughter Zipporah** (Hb, "bird"), probably the oldest of the seven, to be his wife. When she **gave birth** to the couple's firstborn **son** is not evident either. The boy's name, **Gershom** (Hb "foreigner, sojourner, a stranger, one driven out"), reflected that he was born while his father was in exile. Moses may have also realized that he and his son were foreigners in other ways. His own people lived in bondage in a foreign country; as a Hebrew he had been living among strangers in a foreign country. His wife was a Midianite (or Cushite—see Nm 12:1), so his son was certainly of mixed ethnicity.

2:24-25 God heard [Hb *shama'*, "heed, listen to with interest"] **their groaning**—God neither ignores nor

>WORD|*study*

2:17-18 The phrase came to their rescue includes two verbs. The first (Hb *qum*, "arise, rise up, stand up," in the sense of making one's presence felt) is the same verb translated "came to power" in 1:8. The second (Hb *yasha'*, "deliver, help, save") is the first occurrence in Scripture of this verb, which usually designates an action performed exclusively by God, as in its only other appearance in the book (14:30). It is the root for the name Joshua and the Hebrew name of Jesus, *Yeshua* (Hb, "Savior, Deliverer"). Moses' action foreshadowed God's rescuing the Israelites from the Egyptians and then humanity from sin and death. Moses brought to the daughters' situation a man's strength and his particular intolerance for the oppression of those who cannot defend themselves; that the women were from a different ethnic group did not affect Moses' desire to act on their behalf.

daughter, "Should I go and call a
woman from the Hebrews to nurse
the boy for you?"
8 "Go," Pharaoh's daughter told her.
So the girl went and called the boy's
mother. 9 Then Pharaoh's daughter
said to her, "Take this child and nurse
him for me, and I will pay your wages." So the woman took the boy and
nursed him. 10 When the child grew
older, she brought him to Pharaoh's
daughter, and he became her son. She
named him Moses, "Because," she
said, "I drew him out of the water."[A]

Leadership Development (2:11-25)

11 Years later,[B] after Moses had
grown up, he went out to his own
people[C] and observed their forced labor. He saw an Egyptian beating a Hebrew, one of his people. 12 Looking all
around and seeing no one, he struck
the Egyptian dead and hid him in the
sand. 13 The next day he went out and
saw two Hebrews fighting. He asked
the one in the wrong, "Why are you
attacking your neighbor?"[D]
14 "Who made you a leader and
judge over us?" the man replied.
"Are you planning to kill me as you
killed the Egyptian?"
Then Moses became afraid and
thought: What I did is certainly
known. 15 When Pharaoh heard
about this, he tried to kill Moses.
But Moses fled from Pharaoh and
went to live in the land of Midian,
and sat down by a well.
16 Now the priest of Midian had
seven daughters. They came to draw
water and filled the troughs to water their father's flock. 17 Then some
shepherds arrived and drove them
away, but Moses came to their rescue and watered their flock. 18 When
they returned to their father Reuel[E]

[A] **2:10** The name Moses sounds like "drawing out" in Hb and "born" in Egyptian. [B] **2:11** Lit *And it was in those days* [C] **2:11** Lit *his brothers* [D] **2:13** Or *fellow Hebrew* [E] **2:18** Jethro's clan or last name was Reuel; Ex 3:1.

CHARACTER PROFILE

Zipporah A Wife with Attitude

Her Background	• One of seven daughters of Jethro, who lived in Midian (2:15-16) • The wife of Moses (2:21) • The mother of Gershom and Eliezer (2:22; 4:20; 18:2-4)
Her Story	• She and her sisters, when threatened at their father's well, were defended by Moses (2:16-17). • She was given to Moses in marriage (2:21). • She circumcised her own son (4:25-26). • She returned to her father with her sons while Moses was in Egypt (18:2).
Life Lessons	• Zipporah feared the Lord enough to obey Him even when her husband apparently failed to take seriously God's command (4:24-26). • Perceiving the danger to Moses' life, she determined to put him and her sons before her own interests and risked all to save her husband.

he asked, "Why have you come back so quickly today?"

19 They answered, "An Egyptian rescued us from the shepherds. He even drew water for us and watered the flock."

20 "So where is he?" he asked his daughters. "Why then did you leave the man behind? Invite him to eat dinner."

21 Moses agreed to stay with the man, and he gave his daughter Zipporah to Moses in marriage. 22 She gave birth to a son whom he named Gershom, for he said, "I have been a foreigner in a foreign land."[A]

23 After a long time, the king of Egypt died. The Israelites groaned because of their difficult labor, and they cried out; and their cry for help ascended to God because of the difficult labor. 24 So God heard their groaning, and He remembered His covenant with Abraham, Isaac, and Jacob. 25 God saw the Israelites, and He took notice.

Encounter with God (3:1–4:17)

3 Meanwhile, Moses was shepherding the flock of his father-in-law Jethro,[B] the priest of Midian. He led the flock to the far side of the wilderness and came to Horeb,[C] the mountain of God. 2 Then the Angel of the LORD appeared to him in a flame of fire within a bush. As Moses looked, he saw that the bush was on fire but was not consumed. 3 So Moses thought: I must go over and look at this remarkable sight. Why isn't the bush burning up?

4 When the LORD saw that he had gone over to look, God called out to him from the bush, "Moses, Moses!"

"Here I am," he answered.

5 "Do not come closer," He said. "Remove the sandals from your feet, for the place where you are standing is holy ground." 6 Then He continued, "I am the God of your father,[D] the God of Abraham, the God of Isaac, and the God of Jacob." Moses hid his face because he was afraid to look at God.

7 Then the LORD said, "I have observed the misery of My people in Egypt, and have heard them crying out because of their oppressors, and I know about their sufferings. 8 I have come down to rescue them from the power of the Egyptians and to bring them from that land to a good and

[A]**2:22** In Hb the name Gershom sounds like the phrase "a stranger there." [B]**3:1** Moses' father-in-law's first name was Jethro; Ex 2:18. [C]**3:1** = Desolation; another name for Mount Sinai; Dt 4:10,15; 18:16; Mal 4:4 [D]**3:6** Sam, some LXX mss read *fathers*; Ac 7:32

mocks your pain. When you cry out to Him with desperate willingness to do anything He says, you have His attention. **He remembered His covenant with Abraham, Isaac, and Jacob.** God had not forgotten His promises to Israel's patriarchs, but He affirmed His faithfulness to keep His promises and to effect justice on the basis of this prior commitment. **God saw the Israelites, and He took notice** (Hb *yada*ʿ, "know, perceive, recognize, acknowledge"). This implies the intimate, experiential knowledge of deep relationships. This word is also used to describe sexual intimacy between a man and a woman and here is practically synonymous with God's giving attention to "His covenant" with Israel. God "knew" the suffering of the "sons of Israel," not dispassionately as observing facts but with compassion for the agony of loved ones.

3:1 Whether his name or a title, **Jethro** ("His Abundance, Preeminence"), appearing for the first time, is a reference to Reuel—Moses' **father-in-law** and **the priest of Midian.**

3:6 God introduced Himself as **the God of your father**, presumably Amram, whose God was **the God of Abraham**, as was likely true of Jethro; **the God of Isaac,** the son of promise; **and the God of Jacob**, whose descendants were crying out for deliverance from their "difficult labor" (2:23). The statement revealed to Moses several important truths about God, who does not change:

BIBLICAL WOMANHOOD Liberation and Feminist Theology

A wide stream of feminist thought flows from the tenets of "liberation theology," which interprets God's liberation of the Israelites as a political paradigm or as a universal prescription for addressing injustice and oppression. God did deliver His people from political oppression and servitude (3:7-8), but liberation theology misinterprets God's Word by exalting His secondary concern for the earthly well-being of His children above His primary concern for their spiritual redemption. God did not rescue the Israelites merely to free them from bondage to an oppressive foreign power; instead, God led them to Mount Sinai where He bound them to *His* service by a covenant under which they would find true freedom.

Feminists who draw heavily from liberation theology typically label role expectations or limitations as evidences of the "oppression" of women, "bondage" from which women should be "liberated." Interest in liberating women *from* oppression often neglects to answer the question of what women should be liberated *for*. The heroic women of the exodus demonstrate that true liberation for women is found in fearing God, refusing to exalt any desire or person above Him.

Liberation theology also misapplies God's Word by exalting what humans can or should do about oppressive social and political structures above what God can and will do, in His own way, about every manifestation of humanity's captivity to and captivation by sin. To consider political freedom rather than liberation from sin as the ultimate good is to distort the central message of Scripture. In Exodus, God eloquently revealed His unchanging concern for the sufferings of His people and powerfully manifested His sovereignty in the mighty acts by which He liberated them from bondage. The unique events of their deliverance exemplify many truths about God and typify many truths about the ultimate liberation—from bondage to sin and death—wrought by Christ on the cross.

- He had kept the covenant made with Abraham in every generation to the present, including Moses' own father.
- His nature and character remain immutable and unchanging, even over hundreds of years.
- He makes Himself known in ways His people can understand.

3:13-14 Egypt's syncretistic religion boasted a plethora of gods with various names. Having grown up in the household of the pharaoh, believed to be the son of the chief god Amon-Re, and having married into the house of a Midianite priest, Moses' claim to be sent by **the God** of their **fathers** would be suspect, setting the stage for the momentous revelation of God's personal name. To bestow a name was to declare possession or control over the person or place being named, and to reveal one's name to another was to initiate deliberately a relationship; so it is significant that God named Himself before Moses.

3:15 Moses was instructed to identify **Yahweh** as the God of the patriarchs and to deliver a message of promise: **This is My name** [Hb *shēm*, "reputation, fame"] **forever**, which would give the Israelites hope for the future based on their past relationship with the God who was manifesting His activity in their present experience (cp. Jn 8:51-59). God expected **to be remembered in every generation** by this revealed name.

4:1-5 Given the extensive assurances God had just provided, Moses' continued objections exhibited doubt not only of himself but also of God. The questions betray a persistent fear of failure. God drew Moses' attention away from himself to consider his **staff** or rod, an essential piece of equipment for a herdsman in the wilderness. In Pharaoh's palace, a symbol of authority or power would have been a scepter or a staff such as Pharaoh's magicians held. Standing shoeless among the vegetation around Horeb, Moses was already vulnerable, and the staff was his only defense. Nevertheless, God commanded, and Moses obeyed. As instructed, Moses **threw it on the ground**.

>WORD|*study*

3:14 God replied with a mysterious name: I AM WHO I AM (Hb *ʾehyeh ʾasher ʾehyeh*, "I am that I am, I will be who I will be," from the verb *hayah*, "to be"). When written as a proper name, it is the "tetragrammaton" (Gk *tetra*, "four," and *grammata*, "letters") YHWH or "Yahweh" (Hb, probably "He Is, Existing One, He Who Brings into Being") with the addition of the most likely vowels. The original pronunciation of the name was lost when Jews avoided using it because they regarded it as too holy for sinful lips to speak. When Scripture was read aloud, the reader substituted *Adonay* (Hb "My Lord"). In extant Hebrew manuscripts, the consonants "YHWH" are written, but with the vowels of "Adonay"—so we do not even have a written representation of the full name. Later, scholars combined the vowels from *Adonay* with the consonants YHWH to form the hybrid transliterated in English as "YeHoWaH" or "JeHoVaH" (through German scholarship, for whom J is pronounced as English Y, and W is pronounced as English V). Translators of the Septuagint likewise substituted the Greek title for "Lord," *Kyrios*, in place of the divine name YHWH. English translations often signal the name *Yahweh* by writing the word "LORD" in capital letters to distinguish it from the actual word for "Lord," *Adonay*. **I AM** as God's name speaks of His eternal self-existence, continuous in history and transcending time; the existence of everyone and everything else is contingent upon Him, and knowledge of God is dependent on the extent to which He reveals Himself. He is the antithesis of the gods of Egypt (see chart, p. 73).

spacious land, a land flowing with
milk and honey—the territory of
the Canaanites, Hittites, Amorites,
Perizzites, Hivites, and Jebusites.
9 The Israelites' cry for help has come
to Me, and I have also seen the way
the Egyptians are oppressing them.
10 Therefore, go. I am sending you
to Pharaoh so that you may lead My
people, the Israelites, out of Egypt."
11 But Moses asked God, "Who am I
that I should go to Pharaoh and that
I should bring the Israelites out of
Egypt?"
12 He answered, "I will certainly be
with you, and this will be the sign to
you that I have sent you: when you
bring the people out of Egypt, you
will all worship[A] God at this mountain."
13 Then Moses asked God, "If I go
to the Israelites and say to them:
The God of your fathers has sent me
to you, and they ask me, 'What is His
name?' what should I tell them?"
14 God replied to Moses, "I AM
WHO I AM.[B] This is what you are to
say to the Israelites: I AM has sent
me to you." 15 God also said to Moses, "Say this to the Israelites: •Yah-
weh, the God of your fathers, the
God of Abraham, the God of Isaac,
and the God of Jacob, has sent me to
you. This is My name forever; this is
how I am to be remembered in every
generation.
16 "Go and assemble the elders of
Israel and say to them: Yahweh, the
God of your fathers, the God of Abraham, Isaac, and Jacob, has appeared
to me and said: I have paid close attention to you and to what has been
done to you in Egypt. 17 And I have
promised you that I will bring you
up from the misery of Egypt to the
land of the Canaanites, Hittites,
Amorites, Perizzites, Hivites, and
Jebusites—a land flowing with milk
and honey. 18 They will listen to what
you say. Then you, along with the elders of Israel, must go to the king of
Egypt and say to him: Yahweh, the
God of the Hebrews, has met with
us. Now please let us go on a three-
day trip into the wilderness so that
we may sacrifice to Yahweh our God.
19 "However, I know that the king
of Egypt will not allow you to go,
unless he is forced by a strong hand.
20 I will stretch out My hand and
strike Egypt with all My miracles
that I will perform in it. After that,
he will let you go. 21 And I will give
these people such favor in the sight
of the Egyptians that when you
go, you will not go empty-handed.
22 Each woman will ask her neighbor and any woman staying in her
house for silver and gold jewelry,
and clothing, and you will put them
on your sons and daughters. So you
will plunder the Egyptians."

4 Then Moses answered, "What if
they won't believe me and will
not obey me but say, 'The LORD did
not appear to you'?"
2 The LORD asked him, "What is
that in your hand?"
"A staff," he replied.
3 Then He said, "Throw it on the
ground." He threw it on the ground,
and it became a snake. Moses ran
from it, 4 but the LORD told him,
"Stretch out your hand and grab it
by the tail." So he stretched out his

[A]3:12 Or *serve* [B]3:14 Or *I AM BECAUSE I AM*, or *I WILL BE WHO I WILL BE*

Yahweh versus Egyptian Gods

Yahweh	Egyptian Gods
One; singular, no other	Many; plural; multiple
Self-existent	Emerging from and bound to the imagination, whim, superstitions, and mythologies of man
Speaks	Speechless—unable to speak audibly
Self-revealing; makes Himself known	Identities veiled in symbolic forms, requiring people with special powers to reveal
Unchanging identity	Evolving identities
Consistent over time	Shifting personalities and powers
Sovereign over all the earth	Localized, regional influence
Sovereign over life and death	Powerless to • create life, • grant fertility, • protect from death
Sovereign over the forces of nature	Identified with the forces of nature
Created man and woman in His image, to reflect His righteous and holy character	Created in the likeness of men, women, and animals and reflecting humanity's sinful nature
Absolute power	Power delineated in relation to other deities

hand and caught it, and it became
a staff in his hand. 5 "This will take
place," He continued, "so they will
believe that •Yahweh, the God of
their fathers, the God of Abraham,
the God of Isaac, and the God of Jacob, has appeared to you."
6 In addition the LORD said to him,
"Put your hand inside your cloak."
So he put his hand inside his cloak,
and when he took it out, his hand
was diseased, white as snow.[A] 7 Then
He said, "Put your hand back inside
your cloak." He put his hand back
inside his cloak, and when he took
it out,[B] it had again become like the
rest of his skin. 8 "If they will not believe you and will not respond to the
evidence of the first sign, they may
believe the evidence of the second
sign. 9 And if they don't believe even
these two signs or listen to what you
say, take some water from the Nile
and pour it on the dry ground. The
water you take from the Nile will become blood on the ground."
10 But Moses replied to the LORD,
"Please, Lord, I have never been
eloquent—either in the past or recently or since You have been speaking to Your servant[C]—because I am
slow and hesitant in speech."[D]
11 Yahweh said to him, "Who made
the human mouth? Who makes him
mute or deaf, seeing or blind? Is it
not I, Yahweh? 12 Now go! I will help[E]
you speak and I will teach you what
to say."
13 Moses said, "Please, Lord, send
someone else."[F]
14 Then the LORD's anger burned
against Moses, and He said, "Isn't
Aaron the Levite your brother? I
know that he can speak well. And
also, he is on his way now to meet
you. He will rejoice when he sees
you. 15 You will speak with him and
tell him what to say. I will help[G] both

[A] 4:6 A reference to whiteness or flakiness of the skin [B] 4:7 Lit *out of his cloak* [C] 4:10 = Moses
[D] 4:10 Lit *heavy of mouth and heavy of tongue* [E] 4:12 Lit *will be with you* [F] 4:13 Lit *send by the hand of whom You will send* [G] 4:15 Lit *be with*

4:6-8 God gave Moses a second sign to reinforce the first one. **The LORD** told Moses to **put his hand inside his cloak** (Hb *chēq*, "bosom"; cp. Nm 11:12).

4:9 A third sign would be available—**Nile** water poured on **dry ground** would become **blood**. The Nile was literally the "lifeline" of Egypt—the very existence of the nation depended on its regular rising and falling for their crops, drinking water, and every other use of water. To threaten the Nile was to threaten all of Egypt.

4:10-12 Still reluctant, Moses presented a fourth objection, claiming that he had **never been eloquent**—literally, "I am not a man of words." Moses' disavowal of all speaking ability was sweeping and emphatic; he even proceeded to describe the perceived obstacle: **I am slow** [Hb *kaved-peh*, "heavy of mouth"] **and hesitant in speech** [Hb *kaved lashon*, "heavy of tongue or language"].

4:13-17 Finally, Moses revealed how entrenched his fear was as he tested the limits of God's patience by trying to refuse the assignment. God met this final objection with His burning **anger**. Saying "no" to God's call does not release you from the task He has commissioned you to do. He promises His presence and whatever resources are needed, but He commands rather than negotiates your obedience.

4:24-26 Yahweh **confronted** Moses and was going to **put him to death** (Hb *mut*, "kill, execute") until **Zipporah** presented **her son's** circumcised **foreskin.** When she **threw** the foreskin **at Moses' feet**, the Lord **let him alone**; so a matter related to the circumcision of one of his sons was the source of peril. Which son Zipporah circumcised remains unclear, especially since the ages of the sons are unknown. The firstborn is the most likely candidate for this circumcision. The narrative suggests no hint of difficulty in Zipporah's conceiving a child shortly after she was married to Moses. Gershom, the firstborn, was probably an adult by this time. The natural sense of this text is that Zipporah performed the rite that Moses had neglected; circumcision was necessary to identify the son as a "son of Israel," a member of the covenant community and later qualified, therefore, to eat the Passover (Gn 17:9-14).

5:1-5 In obedience to God's directions (3:18), **Moses and Aaron** spoke directly with **Pharaoh**. The message was not their own—**Yahweh, the God of Israel** was directly confronting the king of Egypt with the command that would be put repeatedly before Pharaoh—**Let My people go** (Hb *shalach*, "give over, send away, dismiss, set free, cast out")—and with a reason for the order—to confirm moving allegiance from Pharaoh and the gods of Egypt to Israel's God.

5:6-11 Pharaoh's immediate reaction to God's demand was defiance. Assuming that the slaves had too much time on their hands for dreaming up such ridiculous requests, he determined to show them who was boss specifically by imposing **heavier work on the men.** The taskmasters relayed the new rules with an expression typically used to introduce important words: **This is what Pharaoh says.** Pharaoh refused to give the Israelites straw yet demanded that they meet the same quota. In contrast, the Lord does not give an assignment without supplying what is needed to fulfill it. Pharaoh told them, **Go get straw yourselves**. The Lord tells His servants, "Come to Me, all of you who are weary and burdened, and I will give you rest" (Mt 11:28).

5:19–6:1 Pharaoh's position worked as a shrewd ploy to turn the people against Moses and Aaron. They did bear the brunt of the foremen's frustration and fear, but God had prepared both the leaders and the people for this situation when He told them beforehand (4:21-23,28-31). Moses' prayer may seem irreverent to readers who know "the rest of the story," but God did not reprimand him. Moses took his distress to the right person—he poured out his complaint to God and received reassurance that God's

you and him to speak and will teach
you both what to do. 16 He will speak
to the people for you. He will be
your spokesman, and you will serve
as God to him. 17 And take this staff
in your hand that you will perform
the signs with."

Return to Egypt (4:18-31)

18 Then Moses went back to his
father-in-law Jethro and said to him,
"Please let me return to my relatives
in Egypt and see if they are still living."
Jethro said to Moses, "Go in peace."
19 Now in Midian the LORD told
Moses, "Return to Egypt, for all
the men who wanted to kill you are
dead." 20 So Moses took his wife and
sons, put them on a donkey, and returned to the land of Egypt. And Moses took God's staff in his hand.
21 The LORD instructed Moses,
"When you go back to Egypt, make
sure you do all the wonders before
Pharaoh that I have put within your
power. But I will harden his heart[A]
so that he won't let the people go.
22 Then you will say to Pharaoh: This
is what Yahweh says: Israel is My
firstborn son. 23 I told you: Let My
son go so that he may worship Me,
but you refused to let him go. Now I
will kill your firstborn son!"
24 On the trip, at an overnight
campsite, it happened that the LORD
confronted him and sought to put
him to death. 25 So Zipporah took a
flint, cut off her son's foreskin, and
threw it at Moses' feet.[B] Then she
said, "You are a bridegroom of blood
to me!" 26 So He let him alone. At
that time she said, "You are a bridegroom of blood," referring to the
circumcision.[C]
27 Now the LORD had said to Aaron,
"Go and meet Moses in the wilderness." So he went and met him at
the mountain of God and kissed him.
28 Moses told Aaron everything the
LORD had sent him to say, and about
all the signs He had commanded
him to do. 29 Then Moses and Aaron
went and assembled all the elders of
the Israelites. 30 Aaron repeated everything the LORD had said to Moses
and performed the signs before the
people. 31 The people believed, and
when they heard that the LORD had
paid attention to them and that He
had seen their misery, they bowed
down and worshiped.

Yahweh vs. Pharaoh (5:1–11:10)

The Challenge (5:1–6:27)

5 Later, Moses and Aaron went in
and said to Pharaoh, "This is what
•Yahweh, the God of Israel, says: Let
My people go, so that they may hold
a festival for Me in the wilderness."
2 But Pharaoh responded, "Who is
Yahweh that I should obey Him by
letting Israel go? I do not know anything about Yahweh, and besides, I
will not let Israel go."
3 Then they answered, "The God of
the Hebrews has met with us. Please
let us go on a three-day trip into the
wilderness so that we may sacrifice
to Yahweh our God, or else He may
strike us with plague or sword."
4 The king of Egypt said to them,
"Moses and Aaron, why are you
causing the people to neglect their
work? Get to your work!" 5 Pharaoh also said, "Look, the people of
the land are so numerous, and you
would stop them from working."
6 That day Pharaoh commanded
the overseers of the people as well
as their foremen: 7 "Don't continue
to supply the people with straw for
making bricks, as before. They must
go and gather straw for themselves.
8 But require the same quota of
bricks from them as they were making before; do not reduce it. For they
are slackers—that is why they are
crying out, 'Let us go and sacrifice
to our God.' 9 Impose heavier work
on the men. Then they will be occupied with it and not pay attention
to deceptive words."
10 So the overseers and foremen
of the people went out and said to
them, "This is what Pharaoh says:
'I am not giving you straw. 11 Go get
straw yourselves wherever you can
find it, but there will be no reduc-
tion at all in your workload.'" 12 So
the people scattered throughout
the land of Egypt to gather stubble
for straw. 13 The overseers insisted,

[A]**4:21** Or *will make him stubborn* [B]**4:25** Some interpret "feet" as a euphemism for genitals.
[C]**4:25-26** Zipporah appeased God on Moses' behalf by circumcising Gershom.

"Finish your assigned work each
day, just as you did when straw was
provided." 14 Then the Israelite foremen, whom Pharaoh's slave drivers
had set over the people, were beaten
and asked, "Why haven't you finished making your prescribed number of bricks yesterday or today, as
you did before?"
15 So the Israelite foremen went in
and cried for help to Pharaoh: "Why
are you treating your servants this
way? 16 No straw has been given to
your servants, yet they say to us,
'Make bricks!' Look, your servants
are being beaten, but it is your own
people who are at fault."
17 But he said, "You are slackers.
Slackers! That is why you are saying, 'Let us go sacrifice to the LORD.'
18 Now get to work. No straw will be
given to you, but you must produce
the same quantity of bricks."
19 The Israelite foremen saw that
they were in trouble when they were
told, "You cannot reduce your daily
quota of bricks." 20 When they left
Pharaoh, they confronted Moses and
Aaron, who stood waiting to meet
them.
21 "May the LORD take note of you
and judge," they said to them, "because you have made us reek in front
of Pharaoh and his officials—putting a sword in their hand to kill us!"
22 So Moses went back to the
LORD and asked, "Lord, why have
You caused trouble for this people? And why did You ever send
me? 23 Ever since I went in to
Pharaoh to speak in Your name
he has caused trouble for this
people, and You haven't delivered
6 Your people at all." 1 But the LORD
replied to Moses, "Now you are
going to see what I will do to Pharaoh: he will let them go because of
My strong hand; he will drive them
out of his land because of My strong
hand."
2 Then God spoke to Moses, telling
him, "I am •Yahweh. 3 I appeared to
Abraham, Isaac, and Jacob as •God
Almighty, but I did not reveal My
name Yahweh to them. 4 I also established My covenant with them
to give them the land of Canaan,
the land they lived in as foreigners. 5 Furthermore, I have heard the
groaning of the Israelites, whom
the Egyptians are forcing to work as
slaves, and I have remembered My
covenant.
6 "Therefore tell the Israelites: I
am Yahweh, and I will deliver you
from the forced labor of the Egyptians and free you from slavery to
them. I will redeem you with an
outstretched arm and great acts of
judgment. 7 I will take you as My
people, and I will be your God. You
will know that I am Yahweh your
God, who delivered you from the
forced labor of the Egyptians. 8 I will
bring you to the land that I swore[A] to
give to Abraham, Isaac, and Jacob,
and I will give it to you as a possession. I am Yahweh." 9 Moses told this
to the Israelites, but they did not listen to him because of their broken
spirit and hard labor.
10 Then the LORD spoke to Moses, 11 "Go and tell Pharaoh king of
Egypt to let the Israelites go from
his land."
12 But Moses said in the LORD's
presence: "If the Israelites will not
listen to me, then how will Pharaoh
listen to me, since I am such a poor
speaker?"[B] 13 Then the LORD spoke
to Moses and Aaron and gave them
commands concerning both the Israelites and Pharaoh king of Egypt
to bring the Israelites out of the land
of Egypt.
14 These are the heads of their fathers' families:

The sons of Reuben,
the firstborn of Israel:
Hanoch and Pallu, Hezron
and Carmi.
These are the clans
of Reuben.
15 The sons of Simeon:
Jemuel, Jamin, Ohad, Jachin,
Zohar, and Shaul, the son
of a Canaanite woman.
These are the clans
of Simeon.
16 These are the names
of the sons of Levi
according to their genealogy:
Gershon, Kohath, and Merari.
Levi lived 137 years.

[A]6:8 Lit *raised My hand* [B]6:12 Lit *I have uncircumcised lips*

sovereignty was intact. **The LORD** declared that **because of** His **strong hand** the pharaoh would not only **let** the Israelites **go** but would **drive them out,** a verb hinting at the nature of their final departure.

6:2-3 God continued to identify Himself and what He was doing for the sons of Israel. He declared His personal name, clearly and emphatically revealing Himself to Moses and to His people.

6:4 In the past, the patriarchs had lived in the promised land as **foreigners** (Hb *gēr*, "sojourner"; but now He was moving to fulfill *His* **covenant**, which *He* had **established** with Abraham, Isaac, and Jacob **to give them the land of Canaan**. To inhabit Canaan required leaving Egypt.

6:6 Next, because God is who He is and because He is faithful to His promises, He told Moses to **tell** the sons of Israel: **I will redeem you**. To "redeem" (Hb *ga'al*, "buy back, ransom") typically involved a transaction or exchange agreed upon by both parties or prescribed by law (e.g., Lv 25–27, Ru 4:1-8). When God is the subject of the verb "redeem," He is reclaiming what is rightfully His.

6:7 I will take [Hb *laqach*, "lay hold of, acquire, buy, select, choose, take possession of, seize; take in marriage; see Ex 2:1] **you as My people**, i.e., there will be a change of ownership. **I will be your God**—not only would God take to Himself the people of Israel as His own, but He would protect and provide for them and allow them to have a claim upon Him as well. **You will know** these truths from personal experience—**that I am Yahweh**, that I am **your God**, that I am the one who caused you to come out of Egyptian slavery.

6:8 I will give the land **to you as a possession**; like a husband providing a home for his bride, God would give His people a place of their own, a land they were to occupy and keep in the family from generation to generation (cp. Ezk 11:14-21; 33:24-26). **I am Yahweh**—the first statement in this passage and the last, establishing and sealing the surety of the promises spoken here.

6:9 Here is a sad but realistic report of the Israelites' response to God's word. They would not accept the hope offered **because of their broken** [Hb *qotser*, "shortness, impatience, anguish, grief, discouragement"] **spirit and hard** [Hb *qasheh*, "cruel, severe, difficult, harsh"; cp. 1:14; Dt 26:6; Is 14:3; 19:4] **labor**. Consumed with the darkness of their present circumstances, they failed to appreciate the light of truth about their future. Nevertheless, their lack of faith did not affect the promises God had already made to them.

6:14-27 Women included in the Israelite genealogy are: Amram's wife (and Moses' mother) **Jochebed** (v. 20; cp. Nm 26:59), Aaron's wife **Elisheba** (Ex 6:23), and Eleazar's wife, **one of the daughters of Putiel** (v. 25).

7:1-5 Pharaoh's obstinacy would serve as God's tool for making His plan work so that He would **bring** His **people** out **of Egypt** and make Himself known to **the Egyptians**. The latter constitutes an early missionary message in Scripture. Although the Lord chose Israel to be His own people, His overriding purpose has always been to make Himself known to all people.

7:7 The statement of each man's age provides an important piece of information for determining the chronology of the events recorded in Exodus and implicitly points out that Aaron's role was secondary to Moses even though Moses was the younger brother.

7:8-12 God demonstrated His omniscience to Moses and Aaron; He knew what Pharaoh would do before he did it. Pharaoh was confident that he was the supreme deity in Egypt, but God had prepared Moses and Aaron for the challenge. When the staff that Aaron threw down **became a serpent** (Hb *tannin*, "venomous snake, dragon"; cp. Ps 91:13; Is 27:1; Ezk 29:3; 32:2), Pharaoh's **wise men and sorcerers—the magicians of Egypt** replicated the **miracle**. The most important aspect of this scene was that Aaron's staff **swallowed** (Hb *bala*ʿ, "engulf, devour, completely consume," often eagerly or greedily) all the other serpents produced by **occult practices** (Hb *lahat*, "hidden or secret arts, enchantments, or magic"). Evil powers do exist; and they are powerful, but they are subject to the ultimate power of God.

CHARACTER PROFILE

Jochebed A Devoted Mother

Her Background	• A Levite, a slave in Egypt (2:1-10) • The wife of Amram (6:20) • The mother of Moses, Aaron, and Miriam (6:20; Nm 26:59)
Her Story	• She gave birth to Moses (Ex 2:1-10; 6:20; Nm 26:59). • She concealed him in a basket and placed it in the Nile because of Pharaoh's edict (2:3). • She sent her daughter Miriam to guard the baby (2:4). • She was asked by the princess who found the basket to nurse the baby (2:9). • She cared for her son in his young years and received wages from the princess (2:9).
Life Lessons	• Jochebed and her husband feared God more than Pharaoh (Heb 11:23). • She gave up her child in order for him to fulfill God's plan for his life (2:10).

17 The sons of Gershon:
Libni and Shimei,
by their clans.
18 The sons of Kohath:
Amram, Izhar, Hebron,
and Uzziel.
Kohath lived 133 years.
19 The sons of Merari:
Mahli and Mushi.
These are the clans
of the Levites
according to their genealogy.
20 Amram married
his father's sister Jochebed,
and she bore him Aaron
and Moses.
Amram lived 137 years.
21 The sons of Izhar:
Korah, Nepheg, and Zichri.
22 The sons of Uzziel:
Mishael, Elzaphan, and Sithri.
23 Aaron married Elisheba,
daughter of Amminadab
and sister of Nahshon.
She bore him Nadab
and Abihu, Eleazar
and Ithamar.
24 The sons of Korah:
Assir, Elkanah, and Abiasaph.
These are the clans
of the Korahites.
25 Aaron's son Eleazar married
one of the daughters of Putiel
and she bore him Phinehas.
These are the heads
of the Levite families
by their clans.

26 It was this Aaron and Moses
whom the LORD told, "Bring the Israelites out of the land of Egypt according to their divisions." 27 Moses
and Aaron were the ones who spoke
to Pharaoh king of Egypt in order to
bring the Israelites out of Egypt.

Credibility (6:28–7:13)

28 On the day the LORD spoke to
Moses in the land of Egypt, 29 He said
to him, "I am Yahweh; tell Pharaoh
king of Egypt everything I am telling you."
30 But Moses replied in the LORD's
presence, "Since I am such a poor
speaker,[A] how will Pharaoh listen to
me?"

7 The LORD answered Moses, "See,
I have made you like God to
Pharaoh, and Aaron your brother
will be your prophet. 2 You must
say whatever I command you; then
Aaron your brother must declare it
to Pharaoh so that he will let the Israelites go from his land. 3 But I will
harden Pharaoh's heart and multiply My signs and wonders in the
land of Egypt. 4 Pharaoh will not listen to you, but I will put My hand on
Egypt and bring the divisions of My

[A] 6:30 Lit *I have uncircumcised lips*

people the Israelites out of the land
of Egypt by great acts of judgment.
5 The Egyptians will know that I am
•Yahweh when I stretch out My hand
against Egypt, and bring out the Israelites from among them."
6 So Moses and Aaron did this; they
did just as the LORD commanded
them. 7 Moses was 80 years old and
Aaron 83 when they spoke to Pharaoh.
8 The LORD said to Moses and
Aaron, 9 "When Pharaoh tells you,
'Perform a miracle,' tell Aaron,
'Take your staff and throw it down
before Pharaoh. It will become a
serpent.'" 10 So Moses and Aaron
went in to Pharaoh and did just as
the LORD had commanded. Aaron
threw down his staff before Pharaoh
and his officials, and it became a serpent. 11 But then Pharaoh called the
wise men and sorcerers—the magicians of Egypt, and they also did
the same thing by their occult practices. 12 Each one threw down his
staff, and it became a serpent. But
Aaron's staff swallowed their staffs.
13 However, Pharaoh's heart hardened, and he did not listen to them,
as the LORD had said.

Ten Plagues (7:14–11:10)

Turning of water to blood (7:14-25)

14 Then the LORD said to Moses,
"Pharaoh's heart is hard: he refuses
to let the people go. 15 Go to Pharaoh in the morning. When you see
him walking out to the water, stand
ready to meet him by the bank of
the Nile. Take in your hand the staff
that turned into a snake. 16 Tell him:
Yahweh, the God of the Hebrews,
has sent me to tell you: Let My
people go, so that they may worship[A] Me in the wilderness, but so
far you have not listened. 17 This is
what Yahweh says: Here is how you
will know that I am Yahweh. Watch.
I will strike the water in the Nile
with the staff in my hand, and it will
turn to blood. 18 The fish in the Nile
will die, the river will stink, and the
Egyptians will be unable to drink
water from it."
19 So the LORD said to Moses, "Tell
Aaron: Take your staff and stretch
out your hand over the waters of

HARD QUESTION

Did Pharaoh have free will?

Three different words are used to describe Pharaoh's repeated response to God's demands and demonstrations of superior power. In 7:3, the LORD declared that He would **harden** (Hb *qashah*, "make obstinate or stubborn"; cp. Dt 2:30; Pr 28:14) Pharaoh's heart. In verse 13, his heart **hardened** (Hb *chazaq*, "tie or bind fast, hold or stick fast, make firm, strengthen, be undaunted, be resolute or obstinate"), a word with a range of meanings, any or all of which contribute different facets to our understanding of how God deals with the man who presumes to be a god. Also, Pharaoh hardened (Hb *kavad*, "made heavy or unresponsive") his own heart (8:15,32; 9:34). It is easy to question whether or not Pharaoh had free will in God's dealings with him (cp. Rm 9:18). To what extent was Pharaoh's response *determined* by God? Was he really free to choose to comply with God's terms, or was God's control so complete that Pharaoh really had no choice but to resist? Human freedom is within the framework of God's omnipotence and holiness, since He is the Creator and rightful owner of all there is.

The Exodus story demonstrates that only God is completely and utterly free as well as absolutely good and holy. Time and again, God, in His mercy, confronted Pharaoh with His rightful claim upon His people; yet Pharaoh determined to withstand Him. The Exodus story also illustrates the unyielding power of sin, personified in the obstinate pharaoh. Having chosen to pursue being like God instead of displaying God's image within His boundaries (Gn 3:1-7), all human beings are helplessly captive to sin. Pharaoh was no more willing to yield his delusion of deity to Yahweh than Israel was to keep the covenant (chap. 32), but God consistently held both Pharaoh and Israel accountable for their choices. Every opportunity to obey strengthened Pharaoh's resolve to win the contest. God is omniscient and knew not only how Pharaoh would respond but also what He would do with the man's resistance. Instead of zapping Pharaoh and his pantheon of false gods, Yahweh used him and all Egypt to serve as the stage upon which the Exodus drama would unfold, displaying His own glory for all the world to see. Pharaoh was both free and subject to God's control:

- *God* "hardened" Pharaoh's heart (7:3; 9:12; 10:1,20,27; 11:10; 14:4,8).
- *Pharaoh* "hardened" *his own* heart (8:15,32; 9:34).
- *Pharaoh* refused to humble himself (10:3), and *he* was stubborn (Hb, *qashah*, 13:15).
- Pharaoh's heart *was hardened* (passive voice) without indicating "by whom" (7:13,14,22; 8:19; 9:7,35).

Pharaoh chose to oppose God, whose confrontation with Pharaoh provoked but did not cause the king's choice. Pharaoh's obstinacy and the consequences thereof must have come to mind whenever God described His people's rebellion in similar terms (e.g., Ps 95:8).

7:14 Pharaoh's heart is hard (Hb *kavad lēv*, "unresponsive," lit "heavy of heart," in the sense of stubbornness, being slow or difficult to change one's mind; hardened, unmoved; cp. Is 1:4, "*weighed down* with iniquity"). **He refuses to let the people go.** Whether the attitude displayed is passive or aggressive, to "refuse" (Hb *ma'ēn*) to obey God's command constitutes defiance, a challenge to His authority.

7:15-21 God specified when, where, and how to approach the pharaoh, as well as what to say. Up front, Moses was to make clear who had sent him and whose command he was delivering. On the basis of Pharaoh's failure to take Him seriously, He announced what He would do to demonstrate His sovereignty. Pharaoh undoubtedly recognized **the staff** of Moses as having consumed those of his magicians, but when Aaron **raised the staff,** stretched **out** his **hand over the waters of Egypt,** and **struck the water in the Nile,** God's words were resounding in Pharaoh's ears: ***I* will strike** [Hb *nakah*; see 3:20] **. . . with the staff in *my* hand** (v. 17). As God predicted, the Nile and all water from it became **blood** (v. 21).

[A] **7:16** Or *serve*; Ex 4:23

Egypt—over their rivers, canals,[A] ponds, and all their water reservoirs—and they will become blood. There will be blood throughout the land of Egypt, even in wooden and stone containers."

20 Moses and Aaron did just as the LORD had commanded; in the sight of Pharaoh and his officials, he raised the staff and struck the water in the Nile, and all the water in the Nile was turned to blood. 21 The fish in the Nile died, and the river smelled so bad the Egyptians could not drink water from it. There was blood throughout the land of Egypt.

22 But the magicians of Egypt did the same thing by their occult practices. So Pharaoh's heart hardened, and he would not listen to them, as the LORD had said. 23 Pharaoh turned around, went into his palace, and didn't even take this to heart. 24 All the Egyptians dug around the Nile for water to drink because they could not drink the water from the river. 25 Seven days passed after the LORD struck the Nile.

Frogs (8:1-15)

8 [B] Then the LORD said to Moses, "Go in to Pharaoh and tell him: This is what •Yahweh says: Let My people go, so that they may worship Me. 2 But if you refuse to let them go, then I will plague all your territory with frogs. 3 The Nile will swarm with frogs; they will come up and go into your palace, into your bedroom and on your bed, into the houses of your officials and your people, and into your ovens and kneading bowls. 4 The frogs will come up on you, your people, and all your officials."

5 [C] The LORD then said to Moses, "Tell Aaron: Stretch out your hand with your staff over the rivers, canals, and ponds, and cause the frogs to come up onto the land of Egypt." 6 When Aaron stretched out his hand over the waters of Egypt, the frogs came up and covered the land of Egypt. 7 But the magicians did the same thing by their occult practices and brought frogs up onto the land of Egypt.

8 Pharaoh summoned Moses and Aaron and said, "Ask Yahweh to remove the frogs from me and my people. Then I will let the people go and they can sacrifice to Yahweh."

9 Moses said to Pharaoh, "You make the choice rather than me. When should I ask on behalf of you, your officials, and your people, that the frogs be taken away from you and your houses, and remain only in the Nile?"

10 "Tomorrow," he answered.

Moses replied, "As you have said, so you may know there is no one like Yahweh our God, 11 the frogs will go away from you, your houses, your officials, and your people. The frogs will remain only in the Nile." 12 After Moses and Aaron went out from Pharaoh, Moses cried out to the LORD for help concerning the frogs that He had brought against[D] Pharaoh. 13 The LORD did as Moses had said: the frogs in the houses, courtyards, and fields died. 14 They piled them in countless heaps, and there was a terrible odor in the land. 15 But when Pharaoh saw there was relief, he hardened his heart and would not listen to them, as the LORD had said.

Gnats (8:16-19)

16 Then the LORD said to Moses, "Tell Aaron: Stretch out your staff and strike the dust of the earth, and it will become gnats[E] throughout the land of Egypt." 17 And they did this. Aaron stretched out his hand with his staff, and when he struck the dust of the earth, gnats were on man and beast. All the dust of the earth became gnats throughout the land of Egypt. 18 The magicians tried to produce gnats using their occult practices, but they could not. The gnats remained on man and beast.

19 "This is the finger of God," the magicians said to Pharaoh. But Pharaoh's heart hardened, and he would not listen to them, as the LORD had said.

Swarms of flies (8:20-32)

20 The LORD said to Moses, "Get up early in the morning and present yourself to Pharaoh when you see him going out to the water. Tell

[A] **7:19** The Hb word refers specifically to the various branches and canals of the Nile River; Ex 8:5. [B] **8:1** Ex 7:26 in Hb [C] **8:5** Ex 8:1 in Hb [D] **8:12** Or *frogs, as he had agreed with* [E] **8:16** Perhaps sand fleas or mosquitoes

7:22-25 This first of God's 10 "plagues" against Egypt displayed His sovereignty over the river and water, which He had created, and it amounted to the defeat of Hapi, the Egyptian god of the Nile River, who was believed to be the source of life and of Egyptian identity. In addition, God visibly and experientially showed the Egyptians the effect of their slaughter of the Hebrew babies (cp. Gn 4:10; Ex 1:22). Blood that appeared outside the body represented injury and death; symbolically, the lives lost were manifested in the transformation of a life-sustaining river into life-choking blood (cp. 4:22-23). God's power to turn the water supply into blood demonstrated the people's dependence on Him. Water was, in effect, their lifeblood, and Yahweh, not the gods of Egypt, controlled it. Without Him, there would be nothing to drink. Life was in His hands—people would die if and when He so decided and by the means He chose. He was no territorial deity limited by the Hebrews' bondage or the borders of Goshen.

8:1-7 **The magicians** also **brought frogs up onto the land** but were powerless to get rid of them; in contrast, God could both bring up and make depart as many frogs as He pleased, and they would do His bidding.

8:8-15 By allowing Pharaoh to choose the time for his request to be granted, **Moses** gave him an opportunity to see for himself that **there is no one like Yahweh**, a God powerful enough not only to afflict and manipulate the Nile for His purposes but also to allow His enemy to choose the time for Him to end the plague upon Pharaoh's promise of cooperation. Unlike Egyptian gods who performed their "miracles" only at regular times (the rising and setting of the sun, the rising and falling of the Nile), the Israelite God could act according to His own timing. When Pharaoh asked for the frogs to be removed, he may have expected them to hop back to the Nile where they belonged. Instead, he was left with a mess, **heaps** of rotting frog carcasses. The natural order was restored, but for the Egyptians work multiplied to a loathsome proportion. The stench left by the bloody Nile with its dead fish and by the mounds of dead frogs was not soon forgotten. Pharaoh was believed to have power to maintain order, represented by the goddess Ma'at, in the Egyptian universe. Even though he had resorted to summoning **Moses and Aaron** to stop the frogs, when the plague passed, his resolve to withstand Yahweh's assaults was hardened.

8:16-19 God responded to Pharaoh's failure to keep his promise with a command to Aaron to **strike the dust of the earth**, the material from which He had created man (cp. Gn 2:7;

him: This is what Yahweh says: Let My people go, so that they may worship[A] Me. 21 But if you will not let My people go, then I will send swarms of flies[B] against you, your officials, your people, and your houses. The Egyptians' houses will swarm with flies, and so will the land where they live.[C] 22 But on that day I will give special treatment to the land of Goshen, where My people are living; no flies will be there. This way you will know that I, Yahweh, am in the land. 23 I will make a distinction[D] between My people and your people. This sign will take place tomorrow."

24 And the LORD did this. Thick swarms of flies went into Pharaoh's palace and his officials' houses. Throughout Egypt the land was ruined because of the swarms of flies. 25 Then Pharaoh summoned Moses and Aaron and said, "Go sacrifice to your God within the country."

26 But Moses said, "It would not be right[E] to do that, because what we will sacrifice to the LORD our God is detestable to the Egyptians. If we sacrifice what the Egyptians detest in front of them, won't they stone us? 27 We must go a distance of three days into the wilderness and sacrifice to the LORD our God as He instructs us."

28 Pharaoh responded, "I will let you go and sacrifice to the LORD your God in the wilderness, but don't go very far. Make an appeal for me."

29 "As soon as I leave you," Moses said, "I will appeal to the LORD, and tomorrow the swarms of flies will depart from Pharaoh, his officials, and his people. But Pharaoh must not act deceptively again by refusing to let the people go and sacrifice to the LORD." 30 Then Moses left Pharaoh's presence and appealed to the LORD. 31 The LORD did as Moses had said: He removed the swarms of flies from Pharaoh, his officials, and his people; not one was left. 32 But Pharaoh hardened his heart this time also and did not let the people go.

Death of livestock (9:1-7)

9 Then the LORD said to Moses, "Go in to Pharaoh and say to him: This is what •Yahweh, the God of the Hebrews, says: Let My people go, so that they may worship Me. 2 But if you refuse to let them go and keep holding them, 3 then the LORD's hand will bring a severe plague against your livestock in the field—the horses, donkeys, camels, herds, and flocks. 4 But the LORD will make a distinction between the livestock of Israel and the livestock of Egypt, so that nothing of all that the Israelites own will die." 5 And the LORD set a time, saying, "Tomorrow the LORD will do this thing in the land." 6 The LORD did this the next day. All the Egyptian livestock died, but none among the Israelite livestock died. 7 Pharaoh sent messengers who saw that not a single one of the Israelite livestock was dead. But Pharaoh's heart was hardened, and he did not let the people go.

Boils (9:8-12)

8 Then the LORD said to Moses and Aaron, "Take handfuls of furnace soot, and Moses is to throw it toward heaven in the sight of Pharaoh. 9 It will become fine dust over the entire land of Egypt. It will become festering boils on man and beast throughout the land of Egypt." 10 So they took furnace soot and stood before Pharaoh. Moses threw it toward heaven, and it became festering boils on man and beast. 11 The magicians could not stand before Moses because of the boils, for the boils were on the magicians as well as on all the Egyptians. 12 But the LORD hardened Pharaoh's heart and he did not listen to them, as the LORD had told Moses.

Hail (9:13-35)

13 Then the LORD said to Moses, "Get up early in the morning and present yourself to Pharaoh. Tell him: This is what Yahweh, the God of the Hebrews says: Let My people go, so that they may worship Me. 14 Otherwise, I am going to send all My plagues against you,[F] your officials, and your people. Then you will know there is no one like Me in all the earth. 15 By now I could have stretched out My hand and struck you and your people with a plague,

[A]**8:20** Or *serve* [B]**8:21** Or *insects* [C]**8:21** Lit *are* [D]**8:23** LXX, Syr, Vg; MT reads *will place deliverance* [E]**8:26** Or *allowable* [F]**9:14** Lit *your heart*

3:16). Pharaoh could not stop Yahweh from filling Egypt with **gnats** (cp. Ps 105:31). This time God did not allow **the magicians** to replicate His miracle, and in their failure they recognized that **This is the finger** [cp. 31:18; Dt 9:10; Lk 11:20] **of God** [Hb *'Elohim*]. Pharaoh responded as predicted (cp. v. 15). There is no record of relief.

8:20-24 Moses was commanded to interrupt Pharaoh **in the morning** as his first order of business and to present him with a choice of yielding to God's demand or else. He had 24 hours to decide. This time God determined that the **sign** would **take place tomorrow**—He did not solicit Pharaoh's input (cp. 8:9-10). Making a distinction between the Egyptians and Hebrews implies that the first three plagues had afflicted everyone in Egypt, including God's people. To send the **swarms of flies** only against the Egyptians proved to Pharaoh that Yahweh was not localized. He was both protecting His people and attacking Egypt (cp. Pss 78:45; 105:31). **The land was ruined** (Hb *shachat*, "mar, injure, destroy, corrupt, spoil"). Two different words are used to express the way God would demonstrate that He had claimed the Hebrews as *His* people: **special treatment** (Hb *palah*, "set apart, separate, distinguish, make a distinction between, put á difference between," cp. 9:4; 11:7; Ps 4:3) and **distinction** (Hb *padut*, "division"; "ransom, redemption," cp. Pss 111:9; 130:7; Is 50:2), a word used only four times in the Old Testament and occurring only once in Exodus.

8:25-32 Pharaoh tried to say "yes" to God's command on his own terms, by allowing the Hebrews to worship their God **within the country**. The sacrifice of sheep would offend religious Egyptians. Moses promised to **appeal** [Hb *'atar*, "entreat, make supplication, pray, plead"; used only in the context of the negotiations between Moses and Pharaoh in Exodus—8:28-30; 9:28; 10:17-18; cp. Gn 25:21; Jdg 13:8; 2 Sm 24:25] **to the LORD** about the flies. Because Moses also warned him against acting **deceptively**, Pharaoh's choice not to keep his end of the bargain took his culpability to another level.

9:1-7 The God of the Israelites reissued His command to Pharaoh and gave him an opportunity to comply. **The LORD** was faithful to His word and struck only **the Egyptian livestock**. Pharaoh's messengers corroborated the miracle announced beforehand and fulfilled precisely. Still, the earthly king was unyielding.

9:13-17 As in the fourth plague, Yahweh commanded Moses to confront Pharaoh **in the morning** with yet another opportunity for Pharaoh to submit to God's terms of peace.

9:22-26 God had demonstrated His control over fertility, disease, water, the lives of animals, time, and weather. The intensity of the **hail** and **lightning** would be unnatural, therefore unmistakably an "act of God." For the sake of his pride, Pharaoh put his own people in danger. To follow God's instructions would be a sign of weakness, and he was determined to withstand anything the God of his slaves could throw at him. None of their deities protected the Egyptians from the terror and devastation wrought by the storm.

9:27-35 Pharaoh finally spoke truth but without the will to submit. Neither admission of sin and guilt nor acknowledgment that **Yahweh is the Righteous One** in itself constitutes genuine repentance or faith. Although Moses agreed to intercede and assured Pharaoh with utter confidence that the storm would cease, he confronted the king with the whole truth. Pharaoh did **not fear Yahweh**. When the immediate danger passed, the Egyptians reverted to hardened hearts.

10:1-2 The Lord provided three reasons why He had put up with the continued resistance of Pharaoh and his court:

- The Egyptians' hardened hearts served as a platform for God to **do these miraculous signs** [Hb *'ot,* "tokens" of the truth of His word, "proofs, witnesses" of His power; cp. 7:3; Dt 4:34; Ps 135:9; Jr 32:20-21] **. . . among them** [cp. Ex 7:5,17; 9:16; 14:4,18].
- The history of God's mighty rescue mission would be passed down from generation to generation in Moses' family and, implicitly, in all Israelite families (cp. Dt 6:20-23; 11:1-3).
- God was ensuring that Moses and the Israelites would **know** that He is **Yahweh** (Ex 10:2; cp. 6:7).

10:3 The message that **Moses and Aaron** delivered **to Pharaoh** no longer began with Yahweh's demand for the release of His people. Rather, He reproached Pharaoh with a question that specified his sin—**how long will you refuse to humble** [Hb *'anah,* "submit oneself to, bow down to"] **yourself before** God? "How long" [Hb *'ad-matay,* "until when?"] — not a request for information but an expression of indignation at the unflinching rebellion against God (v. 3; cp. Nm 14:27; 1Kg 18:21; Ps 74:10; Pr 1:22).

10:7 The response of Pharaoh's officials echoed the Lord's indignation. **How long,** they asked, would he hold out? They admitted that the nation was

and you would have been obliterated
from the earth. [16] However, I have let
you live for this purpose: to show
you My power and to make My name
known in all the earth. [17] You are
still acting arrogantly against[A] My
people by not letting them go. [18] Tomorrow at this time I will rain down
the worst hail that has ever occurred
in Egypt from the day it was founded
until now. [19] Therefore give orders to
bring your livestock and all that you
have in the field into shelters. Every
person and animal that is in the field
and not brought inside will die when
the hail falls on them." [20] Those
among Pharaoh's officials who
•feared the word of the LORD made
their servants and livestock flee to
shelters, [21] but those who didn't take
the LORD's word seriously left their
servants and livestock in the field.

[22] Then the LORD said to Moses,
"Stretch out your hand toward heav-
en and let there be hail throughout
the land of Egypt—on man and
beast and every plant of the field
in the land of Egypt." [23] So Moses
stretched out his staff toward heav-
en, and the LORD sent thunder and
hail. Lightning struck the earth,
and the LORD rained hail on the land
of Egypt. [24] The hail, with lightning
flashing through it, was so severe
that nothing like it had occurred
in the land of Egypt since it had
become a nation. [25] Throughout the
land of Egypt, the hail struck down
everything in the field, both man
and beast. The hail beat down every
plant of the field and shattered every
tree in the field. [26] The only place it
didn't hail was in the land of Goshen
where the Israelites were.

[27] Pharaoh sent for Moses and
Aaron. "I have sinned this time," he
said to them. "Yahweh is the Righteous One, and I and my people are
the •guilty ones. [28] Make an appeal
to Yahweh. There has been enough
of God's thunder and hail. I will let
you go; you don't need to stay any
longer."

[29] Moses said to him, "When I have
left the city, I will extend my hands
to Yahweh. The thunder will cease,
and there will be no more hail, so
that you may know the earth belongs to Yahweh. [30] But as for you
and your officials, I know that you
still do not fear Yahweh our God."

[31] The flax and the barley were destroyed because the barley was ripe[B]
and the flax was budding, [32] but the
wheat and the spelt were not destroyed since they are later crops.[C]

[33] Moses went out from Pharaoh
and the city, and extended his hands
to the LORD. Then the thunder and
hail ceased, and rain no longer
poured down on the land. [34] When
Pharaoh saw that the rain, hail, and
thunder had ceased, he sinned again
and hardened his heart, he and his
officials. [35] So Pharaoh's heart hardened, and he did not let the Israelites go, as the LORD had said through
Moses.

Locusts (10:1-20)

10 Then the LORD said to Moses,
"Go to Pharaoh, for I have
hardened his heart and the hearts of
his officials so that I may do these
miraculous signs of Mine among
them,[D] [2] and so that you may tell[E]
your son and grandson how severely
I dealt with the Egyptians and performed miraculous signs among
them, and you will know that I am
•Yahweh."

[3] So Moses and Aaron went in to
Pharaoh and told him, "This is what
Yahweh, the God of the Hebrews,
says: How long will you refuse to
humble yourself before Me? Let My
people go, that they may worship
Me. [4] But if you refuse to let My people go, then tomorrow I will bring
locusts into your territory. [5] They
will cover the surface of the land so
that no one will be able to see the
land. They will eat the remainder
left to you that escaped the hail;
they will eat every tree you have
growing in the fields. [6] They will fill
your houses, all your officials' houses, and the houses of all the Egyptians—something your fathers and
ancestors never saw since the time
they occupied the land until today."
Then he turned and left Pharaoh's
presence.

[7] Pharaoh's officials asked him,
"How long must this man be a snare

[A]9:17 Or *still obstructing* [B]9:31 Lit *was ears of grain* [C]9:32 Lit *are late* [D]10:1 Lit *Mine in his midst* [E]10:2 Lit *tell in the ears of*

to us? Let the men go, so that they may worship Yahweh their God. Don't you realize yet that Egypt is devastated?"

8 So Moses and Aaron were brought back to Pharaoh. "Go, worship Yahweh your God," Pharaoh said. "But exactly who will be going?"

9 Moses replied, "We will go with our young and our old; we will go with our sons and daughters and with our flocks and herds because we must hold Yahweh's festival."

10 He said to them, "May Yahweh be with you if I ever let you and your families go![A] Look out—you are planning evil. 11 No, only the men may go and worship Yahweh, for that is what you have been asking for." And they were driven from Pharaoh's presence.

12 The LORD then said to Moses, "Stretch out your hand over the land of Egypt and the locusts will come up over it and eat every plant in the land, everything that the hail left." 13 So Moses stretched out his staff over the land of Egypt, and the LORD sent an east wind over the land all that day and through the night. By morning the east wind had brought in the locusts. 14 The locusts went up over the entire land of Egypt and settled on the whole territory of Egypt. Never before had there been such a large number of locusts, and there never will be again. 15 They covered the surface of the whole land so that the land was black, and they consumed all the plants on the ground and all the fruit on the trees that the hail had left. Nothing green was left on the trees or the plants in the field throughout the land of Egypt.

16 Pharaoh urgently sent for Moses and Aaron and said, "I have sinned against Yahweh your God and against you. 17 Please forgive my sin once more and make an appeal to Yahweh your God, so that He will take this death away from me." 18 Moses left Pharaoh's presence and appealed to the LORD. 19 Then the LORD changed the wind to a strong west[B] wind, and it carried off the locusts and blew them into the •Red Sea. Not a single locust was left in all the territory of Egypt. 20 But the LORD hardened Pharaoh's heart, and he did not let the Israelites go.

Darkness (10:21-29)

21 Then the LORD said to Moses, "Stretch out your hand toward heaven, and there will be darkness over the land of Egypt, a darkness that can be felt." 22 So Moses stretched out his hand toward heaven, and there was thick darkness throughout the land of Egypt for three days. 23 One person could not see another, and for three days they did not move from where they were. Yet all the Israelites had light where they lived.

24 Pharaoh summoned Moses and said, "Go, worship Yahweh. Even your families may go with you; only your flocks and herds must stay behind."

25 Moses responded, "You must also let us have[C] sacrifices and •burnt offerings to prepare for Yahweh our God. 26 Even our livestock must go with us; not a hoof will be left behind because we will take some of them to worship Yahweh our God. We will not know what we will use to worship Yahweh until we get there."

27 But the LORD hardened Pharaoh's heart, and he was unwilling to let them go. 28 Pharaoh said to him, "Leave me! Make sure you never see my face again, for on the day you see my face, you will die."

29 "As you have said," Moses replied, "I will never see your face again."

Death of the firstborn (11:1-10)

11 The LORD said[D] to Moses, "I will bring one more plague on Pharaoh and on Egypt. After that, he will let you go from here. When he lets you go,[E] he will drive you out of here. 2 Now announce to the people that both men and women should ask their neighbors for silver and gold jewelry." 3 The LORD gave[F] the people favor in the sight of the Egyptians. And the man Moses was highly regarded[G] in the land of Egypt by[H] Pharaoh's officials and the people.

4 So Moses said, "This is what

[A]10:10 Pharaoh's reply is sarcastic. [B]10:19 Lit *sea* [C]10:25 Lit *also give in our hand* [D]11:1 Or *had said* [E]11:1 Or *go, it will be finished—* [F]11:3 Or *had given* [G]11:3 Lit *was very great* [H]11:3 Or *in the eyes of*

devastated (Hb *ʾavad*, "destroy; perish or be exterminated," used only here in Exodus; cp. Dt 7:10; Pss 2:12; 5:6; Is 60:12); and though they acknowledged the reality of **the LORD**, their counsel still reflected the idea that they were negotiating with mortal men. They regarded Moses as **a snare** (Hb *moqēsh*, lit. a "noose or trap for catching wild animals"; figuratively a "cause of injury"; cp. 23:33; 34:12; Am 3:5) rather than as the mouthpiece of Yahweh, who alone is God. They referred to Yahweh as the Israelites' **God**, not as the One to whom they also owed their allegiance. The counselors may have recognized that God was too powerful for the Egyptians, but they recommended only capitulation to this God's demands, not admission to His universal sovereignty.

10:12-15 Even when acting in judgment, **the LORD** demonstrated mercy toward Egypt. The obedient **east wind** blew long enough to give Pharaoh time to acknowledge that something bad was about to happen again and to change his mind. As predicted, however, **the locusts** arrived as a living, moving, destructive force of horrific proportion, leaving nothing but famine in their wake.

10:16-20 Although **Pharaoh** admitted to having **sinned** and although he asked for his **sin** to be forgiven, he really wanted the removal of the terrible consequences instead of the removal of sin itself. **From me** encompassed Pharaoh and the whole of Egypt under his aegis. Pharaoh exemplifies the recalcitrance of human nature when a person freely but ungratefully accepts God's mercy, when one seeks to be saved from the earthly consequences of sin without true repentance. The author notes that **not a single locust** remained when **the LORD changed** the direction of **the wind**, sending the swarm to their watery grave in **the Red Sea**.

10:21-23 Like the third and sixth plagues, no warning or announcement preceded the ninth plague against Egypt. God abruptly turned out the lights. The **three days** of unnatural, palpable **darkness** must have signaled to many Egyptians the death of Atum-Re, the sun god, and perhaps symbolized Pharaoh's death, or at least the cancellation of his claim to supernatural power.

11:1-3 The LORD announced that when He delivered His last **plague** [Hb *negaʿ*, "stroke, blow, wound," esp. calamity brought by God against men; used only here in Exodus; cp. Gn 12:17; Ps 39:10; Is 53:8] **on Pharaoh and on Egypt**, the Israelites would definitely be sent away—they would be driven out completely. It was time for the Israelites, **both men and women**, to ask their Egyptian neighbors to relinquish any items of precious metal. The Egyptians, unlike their ruler, feared Moses and the Hebrews. Having experienced the judgment of God in every area of life, they were disposed to do anything to be rid of the Israelites and their mighty God.

11:5-6 No **firstborn**, of either human or **livestock** (assuming these had been acquired or stolen during whatever time span had elapsed since Egypt's livestock were destroyed by previous plagues), would be exempt from the deathblow (cp. Pss 78:51; 105:36; 135:8; 136:10). Also, marked by the singular **cry of anguish** (Hb *tse'aqah gadol*, "great cry of distress, a crying aloud in grief," the intense emotional response to the irrevocable loss, e.g., of life or something of great worth, v. 6; cp. Gn 27:34; Ps 9:12), this would be a one-time event.

12:1-28 The Lord's instructions for the institution of **Passover** concerned protection from Yahweh's death blow against Egypt (vv. 11-12,23,27). Clearly the immediate events would be of prime significance to their birth as a nation permanently bound to Yahweh (vv. 14,17,24-27). The Passover was to celebrate God's deliverance of His people from bondage in Egypt.

12:2 A change in the Israelites' calendar marked the nation's birth. The month of the first Passover and the celebration of their exodus henceforth would be the **first month** of the year ("Abib" in 13:4; 23:15; later "Nisan," Neh 2:1; Est 3:7). Similarly, the modern calendar dates all historical events as taking place "Before Christ" or *"Anno Domini,"* "in the year of our Lord," a reference to the advent of the world's Savior who would provide atonement for sin. Jesus' crucifixion coincided with the observance of Passover (Jn 18:28,39; 19:14; 1Co 5:7).

12:5 The **animal** selected for slaughter had to be **unblemished** (Hb *tamim*, "complete, whole, entire, sound, without defect, perfect"; cp. Dt 18:13; 32:4) and **a year-old male** (i.e., in the prime of life; Ex 12:3-6). Christ's life, too, was untainted by sin (cp. Heb 9:14; 1Pt 1:18-19).

12:7 The blood had to be applied **on the two doorposts and the lintel of the houses** in which the families and neighbors ate the roasted meat. A precursor of Christ's death on the cross, the blood was "a distinguishing mark" (v. 13), an external symbol whereby God passed over those homes without destroying the firstborn within their walls (Ex 12:7-14). Obedient faith was required to follow these instructions.

•Yahweh says: 'About midnight I will go throughout Egypt, 5 and every firstborn male in the land of Egypt will die, from the firstborn of Pharaoh who sits on his throne to the firstborn of the servant girl who is behind the millstones, as well as every firstborn of the livestock. 6 Then there will be a great cry of anguish through all the land of Egypt such as never was before, or ever will be again. 7 But against all the Israelites, whether man or beast, not even a dog will snarl,[A] so that you may know that Yahweh makes a distinction between Egypt and Israel. 8 All these officials of yours will come down to me and bow before me, saying: Leave, you and all the people who follow you.[B] After that, I will leave.'" And he left Pharaoh's presence in fierce anger.

9 The LORD said to Moses, "Pharaoh will not listen to you, so that My wonders may be multiplied in the land of Egypt." 10 Moses and Aaron did all these wonders before Pharaoh, but the LORD hardened Pharaoh's heart, and he would not let the Israelites go out of his land.

Passover (12:1–13:16)

Instructions for the First Passover (12:1-28)

12 The LORD said to Moses and Aaron in the land of Egypt: 2 "This month is to be the beginning of months for you; it is the first month of your year. 3 Tell the whole community of Israel that on the tenth day of this month they must each select an animal of the flock according to their fathers' households, one animal per household. 4 If the household is too small for a whole animal, that person and the neighbor nearest his house are to select one based on the combined number of people; you should apportion the animal according to what each person[C] will eat. 5 You must have an unblemished animal, a year-old male; you may take it from either the sheep or the goats. 6 You are to keep it until the fourteenth day of this month; then the whole assembly of the community of Israel will slaughter the animals at twilight. 7 They must take some of the blood and put it on the two doorposts and the lintel of the houses where they eat them. 8 They are to eat the meat that night; they should eat it, roasted over the fire along with unleavened bread and bitter herbs. 9 Do not eat any of it raw or cooked in boiling[D] water, but only roasted over fire—its head as well as its legs and inner organs. 10 Do not let any of it remain until morning; you must burn up any part of it that does remain before morning. 11 Here is how you must eat it: you must be dressed for travel,[E] your sandals on your feet, and your staff in your hand. You are to eat it in a hurry; it is the LORD's •Passover.

12 "I will pass through the land of Egypt on that night and strike every firstborn male in the land of Egypt, both man and beast. I am •Yahweh; I will execute judgments against all the gods of Egypt. 13 The blood on the houses where you are staying will be a distinguishing mark for you; when I see the blood, I will pass over you. No plague will be among you to destroy you when I strike the land of Egypt.

14 "This day is to be a memorial for you, and you must celebrate it as a festival to the LORD. You are to celebrate it throughout your generations as a permanent statute. 15 You must eat unleavened bread for seven days. On the first day you must remove yeast from your houses. Whoever eats what is leavened from the first day through the seventh day must be cut off from Israel. 16 You are to hold a sacred assembly on the first day and another sacred assembly on the seventh day. No work may be done on those days except for preparing what people need to eat—you may do only that.

17 "You are to observe the Festival of •Unleavened Bread because on this very day I brought your divisions out of the land of Egypt. You must observe this day throughout your generations as a permanent statute. 18 You are to eat unleavened

[A]**11:7** Lit *point its tongue* [B]**11:8** Lit *people at your feet* [C]**12:4** Or *household* [D]**12:9** Or *or boiled at all in* [E]**12:11** Lit *it: with your loins girded*

bread in the first month, from the evening of the fourteenth day of the month until the evening of the twenty-first day. 19 Yeast must not be found in your houses for seven days. If anyone eats something leavened, that person, whether a foreign resident or native of the land, must be cut off from the community of Israel. 20 Do not eat anything leavened; eat unleavened bread in all your homes."[A]

21 Then Moses summoned all the elders of Israel and said to them, "Go, select an animal from the flock according to your families, and slaughter the Passover animal. 22 Take a cluster of hyssop, dip it in the blood that is in the basin, and brush the lintel and the two doorposts with some of the blood in the basin. None of you may go out the door of his house until morning. 23 When the LORD passes through to strike Egypt and sees the blood on the lintel and the two doorposts, He will pass over the door and not let the destroyer enter your houses to strike you.

24 "Keep this command permanently as a statute for you and your descendants. 25 When you enter the land that the LORD will give you as He promised, you are to observe this ritual. 26 When your children ask you, 'What does this ritual mean to you?' 27 you are to reply, 'It is the Passover sacrifice to the LORD, for He passed over the houses of the Israelites in Egypt when He struck the Egyptians and spared our homes.'" So the people bowed down and worshiped. 28 Then the Israelites went and did this; they did just as the LORD had commanded Moses and Aaron.

Plunder (12:29-36)

29 Now at midnight the LORD struck every firstborn male in the land of Egypt, from the firstborn of Pharaoh who sat on his throne to the firstborn of the prisoner who was in the dungeon, and every firstborn of the livestock. 30 During the night Pharaoh got up, he along with all his officials and all the Egyptians, and there was a loud wailing throughout Egypt because there wasn't a house without someone dead. 31 He summoned Moses and Aaron during the night and said, "Get up, leave my people, both you and the Israelites, and go, worship Yahweh as you have asked. 32 Take even your flocks and your herds as you asked and leave, and also bless me."

33 Now the Egyptians pressured the people in order to send them quickly out of the country, for they said, "We're all going to die!" 34 So the people took their dough before it was leavened, with their kneading bowls wrapped up in their clothes on their shoulders.

35 The Israelites acted on Moses' word and asked the Egyptians for silver and gold jewelry and for clothing. 36 And the LORD gave the people such favor in the Egyptians' sight that they gave them what they requested. In this way they plundered the Egyptians.

End of Captivity (12:37-42)

37 The Israelites traveled from Rameses to Succoth, about 600,000 soldiers on foot, besides their families. 38 An ethnically diverse crowd also went up with them, along with a huge number of livestock, both flocks and herds. 39 The people baked the dough they had brought out of Egypt into unleavened loaves, since it had no yeast; for when they had been driven out of Egypt they could not delay and had not prepared any provisions for themselves.

40 The time that the Israelites lived in Egypt[B] was 430 years. 41 At the end of 430 years, on that same day, all the LORD's divisions went out from the land of Egypt. 42 It was a night of vigil in honor of the LORD, because He would bring them out of the land of Egypt. This same night is in honor of the LORD, a night vigil for all the Israelites throughout their generations.

Passover Regulations (12:43–13:16)

43 The LORD said to Moses and Aaron, "This is the statute of the Passover: no foreigner may eat it. 44 But any slave a man has purchased may eat it, after you have circumcised him. 45 A temporary resident or hired hand may not eat the Passover. 46 It

Just as the lamb's death, signified by its blood on the door, was regarded as a substitute for the lives of the firstborn, Christ's death on the cross is counted as the substitute for all who entrust their lives to Him in obedient faith (1Co 1:18; Eph 1:7). The words of John the Baptist make explicit Jesus' fulfillment of the role of the Passover (Jn 1:29).

12:8-18 In Scripture, yeast often symbolizes sin. God expects believers to get rid of sin in their lives as illustrated in **the Festival of Unleavened Bread** (cp. 1Co 5:7-8). In Passover celebrations, the **bitter herbs** (usually horseradish) remind partakers of the bitterness of the suffering in Egypt (cp. Ex 1:14; Zch 12:10).

12:24-27 Passover was a testimony of how **the LORD** had **spared** (Hb *natsal*, "rescued; delivered from enemies, trouble, or death"; cp. 2:19; 3:8; 6:6; 18:8-10) Israel. The **ritual**, accompanied by its oral history, would recall the story of deliverance for their **descendants** (Hb *bēn*, "sons, grandsons, children"—both male and female). The crucial link between the Passover instructions and the subsequent narrative of the actual events of the exodus is that the people not only **bowed down** [Hb *qadad*, "bow low" in reverence; cp. 4:31; 34:8] **and worshiped** [Hb *shachah*, "prostrate themselves, honor, submit themselves to"] the Lord but also obeyed Him.

12:29-36 Just as **the LORD** foretold, the death of every firstborn in the land elicited a **loud wailing** [Hb *tse ʾaqah gadol*, "great cry"; see 11:6] **throughout Egypt** and prompted Pharaoh's orders to leave (vv. 29-32). Fearing that the Israelites' God, who had selectively taken the lives of their firstborn, would kill them all, the battered Egyptians gladly surrendered their wealth to the departing slaves, eager to hasten the departure of those who had wreaked such havoc on their land and families.

12:37-39 The departure of the sons of Israel is described in military terms: **600,000 soldiers** [Hb *gever*, "men, strong men, warriors," connoting manly strength or fighting ability] **on foot**. Multiplying this number by four (men, women, and children must be calculated) provides a very conservative estimate of the actual number of individuals who comprised the Israelite company: 2,400,000.

12:40-42 The writer noticeably stressed the timing of the exodus not only by repeating the fact that the Israelites had been in Egypt for 430 years but also by emphasizing that they left at the very end of that

[A] **12:20** Or *settlements* [B] **12:40** LXX, Sam add *and in Canaan*

span—**on that same day**, a phrase that marks other significant events in Israel's history (cp. Gn 7:13; 17:23,26; Dt 32:48). The length of Israel's sojourn should be considered historically accurate and included in attempts to locate the biblical events on the timeline of Egyptian history.

12:43-51 This passage prohibits the participation of any **foreigner** (Hb *ben-nēkar*, "son of a stranger") or the **temporary resident or hired hand** in the Passover. A **slave** could **eat** the Passover **after** being identified with Israel as a son of the covenant by circumcision (cp. Gn 17:9-14; Ex 4:24-26). A resident **foreigner** could eat the Passover when he became **like a native of the land**, meaning that he and **every male in his household must be circumcised**.

13:1-3 Since He had accepted the publicly displayed blood of the Passover lambs as the redemptive substitute for the lives of Israel's firstborn on the night when He struck Egypt's firstborn (12:21-23,29), **the LORD** insisted that **every firstborn male** rightfully belonged to Him and must therefore be consecrated to Him. **Consecrate** (Hb *qadash*), meaning "set apart, honor, or hallow as sacred, dedicate," is the root word for "holy" and "holiness" and appears only once in Scripture before Ex 13:2. In Gn 2:3, "God blessed the seventh day and *declared it holy*." In contrast, the word is used at least 25 times in Exodus. To consecrate the firstborn was an act of humble gratitude—the family was giving back to **the LORD** what He had saved **by the strength of His hand** when He **brought** His people **out of the place of slavery**. To obey God in giving to Him the firstborn, the first reward for one's labor, also challenged the parents' faith—that they would have more children was not guaranteed.

13:8-16 The truth conveyed by the observance of Passover was to **serve as a sign** (Hb *ʾot*, "token of remembrance, reminder") on the **hand** and a **reminder** (Hb *zikron*, "memorial, reminder"; cp. 12:14) or **symbol** on the **forehead** (vv. 9,16). In traditional Judaism, "symbol" (Hb *tophaphah*, "bands, frontlets"; cp. Dt 6:8; 11:18) refers to "phylacteries" (Gk *phulacteria*, Mt 23:5) or *tefillin*, parchment scrolls with portions of the Torah (traditionally Ex 13:1-10,11-16; Dt 6:4-9; 11:13-21) written on them and placed in a square leather box. Jewish men have worn these strapped to the forehead and left wrist.

13:17-18 The text takes for granted that **God**, not Moses on his own, was leading the people. They **left . . . in battle formation** (Hb *chamush*, "arrayed for battle, martial or military

is to be eaten in one house. You may
not take any of the meat outside the
house, and you may not break any of
its bones. 47 The whole community
of Israel must celebrate[A] it. 48 If a foreigner resides with you and wants to
celebrate the LORD's Passover, every
male in his household must be circumcised, and then he may participate;[B] he will become like a native
of the land. But no uncircumcised
person may eat it. 49 The same law
will apply to both the native and the
foreigner who resides among you."
50 Then all the Israelites did this;
they did just as the LORD had commanded Moses and Aaron. 51 On that
same day the LORD brought the Israelites out of the land of Egypt according to their divisions.

13 The LORD spoke to Moses: 2 "Consecrate every firstborn male to
Me, the firstborn from every womb
among the Israelites, both man and
domestic animal; it is Mine."
3 Then Moses said to the people,
"Remember this day when you came
out of Egypt, out of the place of slavery, for the LORD brought you out of
here by the strength of His hand.
Nothing leavened may be eaten.
4 Today, in the month of Abib,[C] you
are leaving. 5 When the LORD brings
you into the land of the Canaanites,
Hittites, Amorites, Hivites, and Jebusites,[D] which He swore to your fathers that He would give you, a land
flowing with milk and honey, you
must carry out this ritual in this
month. 6 For seven days you must
eat unleavened bread, and on the
seventh day there is to be a festival
to the LORD. 7 Unleavened bread is to
be eaten for those seven days. Nothing leavened may be found among
you, and no yeast may be found
among you in all your territory. 8 On
that day explain to your son, 'This is
because of what the LORD did for me
when I came out of Egypt.' 9 Let it
serve as a sign for you on your hand
and as a reminder on your forehead,[E] so that the LORD's instruction
may be in your mouth; for the LORD
brought you out of Egypt with a
strong hand. 10 Keep this statute at
its appointed time from year to year.
11 "When the LORD brings you into
the land of the Canaanites, as He
swore to you and your fathers, and
gives it to you, 12 you are to present
to the LORD every firstborn male of
the womb. All firstborn offspring
of the livestock you own that are
males will be the LORD's. 13 You must
redeem every firstborn of a donkey
with a flock animal, but if you do not
redeem it, break its neck. However,
you must redeem every firstborn
among your sons.
14 "In the future, when your son
asks you, 'What does this mean?' say
to him, 'By the strength of His hand
the LORD brought us out of Egypt,
out of the place of slavery. 15 When
Pharaoh stubbornly refused to let us
go, the LORD killed every firstborn
male in the land of Egypt, from the
firstborn of man to the firstborn
of livestock. That is why I sacrifice
to the LORD all the firstborn of the
womb that are males, but I redeem
all the firstborn of my sons.' 16 So
let it be a sign on your hand and a
symbol[F] on your forehead, for the
LORD brought us out of Egypt by the
strength of His hand."

Route of the Exodus (13:17–14:4)

17 When Pharaoh let the people
go, God did not lead them along the
road to the land of the Philistines,
even though it was nearby; for God
said, "The people will change their
minds and return to Egypt if they
face war." 18 So He led the people
around toward the •Red Sea along
the road of the wilderness. And the
Israelites left the land of Egypt in
battle formation.
19 Moses took the bones of Joseph
with him, because Joseph had made
the Israelites swear a solemn oath,
saying, "God will certainly come to
your aid; then you must take my
bones with you from this place."
20 They set out from Succoth and
camped at Etham on the edge of the
wilderness. 21 The LORD went ahead of
them in a pillar of cloud to lead them

A 12:47 Lit *do* B 12:48 Lit *may come near to do it* C 13:4 March–April; called Nisan in the post-exilic period; Neh 2:1; Est 3:7 D 13:5 DSS, Sam, LXX, Syr add *Girgashites* and *Perizzites*; Jos 3:10 E 13:9 Lit *reminder between your eyes* F 13:16 Or *phylactery*

on their way during the day and in a pillar of fire to give them light at night, so that they could travel day or night. 22 The pillar of cloud by day and the pillar of fire by night never left its place in front of the people.

14 Then the LORD spoke to Moses: 2 "Tell the Israelites to turn back and camp in front of Pi-hahiroth, between Migdol and the sea; you must camp in front of Baal-zephon, facing it by the sea. 3 Pharaoh will say of the Israelites: They are wandering around the land in confusion; the wilderness has boxed them in. 4 I will harden Pharaoh's heart so that he will pursue them. Then I will receive glory by means of Pharaoh and all his army, and the Egyptians will know that I am •Yahweh." So the Israelites did this.

Egyptian Pursuit (14:5-14)

5 When the king of Egypt was told that the people had fled, Pharaoh and his officials changed their minds about the people and said: "What have we done? We have released Israel from serving us." 6 So he got his chariot ready and took his troops[A] with him; 7 he took 600 of the best chariots and all the rest of the chariots of Egypt, with officers in each one. 8 The LORD hardened the heart of Pharaoh king of Egypt, and he pursued the Israelites, who were going out triumphantly.[B] 9 The Egyptians—all Pharaoh's horses and chariots, his horsemen,[C] and his army—chased after them and caught up with them as they camped by the sea beside Pi-hahiroth, in front of Baal-zephon.

10 As Pharaoh approached, the Israelites looked up and saw the Egyptians coming after them. Then the Israelites were terrified and cried out to the LORD for help. 11 They said to Moses: "Is it because there are no graves in Egypt that you took us to die in the wilderness? What have you done to us by bringing us out of Egypt? 12 Isn't this what we told you in Egypt: Leave us alone so that we may serve the Egyptians? It would have been better for us to serve the Egyptians than to die in the wilderness."

13 But Moses said to the people, "Don't be afraid. Stand firm and see the LORD's salvation He will provide for you today; for the Egyptians you see today, you will never see again. 14 The LORD will fight for you; you must be quiet."

Salvation of Yahweh (14:15-31)

15 The LORD said to Moses, "Why are you crying out to Me? Tell the Israelites to break camp. 16 As for you, lift up your staff, stretch out your hand over the sea, and divide it so that the Israelites can go through the sea on dry ground. 17 I am going to harden the hearts of the Egyptians so that they will go in after them, and I will receive glory by means of Pharaoh, all his army, and his chariots and horsemen. 18 The Egyptians will know that I am Yahweh when I receive glory through Pharaoh, his chariots, and his horsemen."

19 Then the Angel of God, who was going in front of the Israelite forces, moved and went behind them. The pillar of cloud moved from in front of them and stood behind them. 20 It came between the Egyptian and Israelite forces. The cloud was there in the darkness, yet it lit up the night.[D] So neither group came near the other all night long.

21 Then Moses stretched out his hand over the sea. The LORD drove the sea back with a powerful east wind all that night and turned the sea into dry land. So the waters were divided, 22 and the Israelites went through the sea on dry ground, with the waters like a wall to them on their right and their left.

23 The Egyptians set out in pursuit—all Pharaoh's horses, his chariots, and his horsemen—and went into the sea after them. 24 Then during the morning watch, the LORD looked down on the Egyptian forces from the pillar of fire and cloud, and threw them into confusion. 25 He caused their chariot wheels to swerve[E,F] and made them drive[G] with difficulty. "Let's get away from

[A]**14:6** Lit *people* [B]**14:8** Lit *with a raised hand* [C]**14:9** Or *chariot drivers* [D]**14:20** Perhaps the cloud brought darkness to the Egyptians but light to the Israelites; Ex 10:22-23; Ps 105:39. [E]**14:25** Sam, LXX, Syr read *He bound their chariot wheels* [F]**14:25** Or *fall off* [G]**14:25** Or *and they drove them*

arrangement" of fighting men, probably in groups of five; in the OT, used only here and Jos 1:14; 4:12; Jdg 7:11). However, the route God chose led them away from Egyptian fortifications. Exodus 13:18, like 12:37, is one clue in a complex assortment of data used to determine the route of the exodus and the locations of the Red Sea crossing and of Mount Sinai. Experts in the fields of archaeology, anthropology, historical geography, and others, continue to offer hypotheses for harmonizing the available evidence to one degree or another. Some scholars have argued that the literal translation of the **Red Sea** (Hb *Yam Suph*, "Sea of Reeds") indicates that the Israelites actually crossed a marshy, reed-filled area in the delta. However, the only body of water having the depth and surrounding topography to fit the biblical description of the sea crossing is one of the two arms of the Red Sea—the western Gulf of Suez or the eastern Gulf of Aqaba. The translators of the Septuagint may have recognized this fact when they identified *Yam Suph* as the "Red [Gk *eruthran*] Sea" (cp. Ac 7:36; Heb 11:29).

13:19 On behalf of the Israelites, **Moses** fulfilled an **oath** sworn long before he was born. Taking Joseph's **bones** out of Egypt also signified God's fulfillment of prophecy through **Joseph** to his brothers, the sons of Jacob (Gn 50:24-25).

14:5-14 Pharaoh and his officials had second thoughts when they realized their work force was gone. They sent forth the choice **troops** and **all . . . the chariots of Egypt** for what Pharaoh must have imagined would be a round-up and reenslavement of the Hebrews. The manner in which **the Israelites** went out discounts some portrayals of them as a cowed, helpless, weak-spirited people. Instead, Scripture has consistently presented a people who maintained health and strength despite the oppression of Egypt. Even through long years of oppression, they had maintained their identity as "the sons of Israel" along with a fairly structured society and an active form of self-government. Having obeyed the God who was redeeming them from slavery, they went **out** exultant (cp. Nm 33:3). Nevertheless, the Israelites were caught off guard and were justifiably **terrified** when they suddenly noticed the Egyptian army fast approaching. Their first response—crying **out to the LORD for help**—was the right response (cp. Neh 9:9), but hurling a barrage of complaints at Moses exemplified the natural tendency to assume the worst and to lash out at the nearest human target, typically a person in leadership. Moses told the people to stop being **afraid** and to **be quiet** because he knew **the LORD** would

fight [Hb *lacham*, "wage war, engage in battle," cp. Ex 14:25] **for** them.

14:16-31 Moses stretched out his hand over the sea (vv. 16,21). His action visibly signaled Yahweh's imminent supernatural intervention. The people had to act in faith without waiting for God to act first. God's flawless battle plan displayed His **power** (Hb *yad*, lit "hand," a figurative expression for a display of "strength," v. 31). The Egyptians' relentless pursuit of the Israelites serves as a vivid picture of the way sin persistently musters all its forces in efforts to reenslave those who have already been rescued from bondage (e.g., Gl 4:8-9). A person's human understanding, will power, or resolve alone are insufficient defenses, but when the believer moves forward in obedience and faith, God makes a way where there seems to be none (e.g., Ps 77:19-20).

15:1-18 Celebration ensued on the other side of the Red Sea. The first verse of this "Song to Yahweh" or "Song of Moses" has the same refrain as Miriam's song in verse 21. First person pronouns dominate the first three verses, making this part of the song an individual or personal expression of praise. Like other extended songs recorded in Scripture (see 1Ch 15:7-36; Ps 18; Lk 1:67-79), this one is rich in its declarations of who God is, what He has done, and how He has revealed Himself to human beings. The depth of its content was born out of the people's profound experience of God's grace and of powerful manifestations of His sovereignty. Reflecting on Israel's history as the people of such a God and prophetically anticipating the grace and sovereign power to be displayed in Christ's redemption, Mary's song of praise in Luke 1:46-55 echoes some of the themes of Exodus 15:1-21. Moses' song declares unchanging truths *about* **the Lord**, truths meant to be recounted to Him in praise, and He is also extolled for what He does for His people. The finale proclaims one of the major themes of Scripture and a fundamental basis for the rest of the song's affirmations: **The Lord will reign** [Hb *malak*, "be king"] **forever and ever!**

15:19-21 Verse 19 succinctly summarizes the historical events constituting indisputable proof of God's mighty power. The refrain **Miriam sang** is the introductory summary of Moses' song (v. 1) and probably represents the whole song. Uniquely identified here as **the prophetess** (Hb *neviʾah*, feminine form of *naviʾ*, "prophet, spokesman"; cp. 7:1), Miriam picked up **a tambourine** and led **all the women** to make music and dance in exuberant celebration of what the Lord had done.

15:22-25 The Israelites did not stay at the site of God's victory but were led into

Israel," the Egyptians said, "because
Yahweh is fighting for them against
Egypt!"
26 Then the LORD said to Moses,
"Stretch out your hand over the
sea so that the waters may come
back on the Egyptians, on their
chariots and horsemen." 27 So Moses
stretched out his hand over the sea,
and at daybreak the sea returned to
its normal depth. While the Egyptians were trying to escape from it,
the LORD threw them into the sea.
28 The waters came back and covered
the chariots and horsemen, the entire army of Pharaoh, that had gone
after them into the sea. None of
them survived.
29 But the Israelites had walked
through the sea on dry ground,
with the waters like a wall to them
on their right and their left. 30 That
day the LORD saved Israel from the
power of the Egyptians, and Israel
saw the Egyptians dead on the seashore. 31 When Israel saw the great
power that the LORD used against
the Egyptians, the people •feared the
LORD and believed in Him and in His
servant Moses.

Song to Yahweh (15:1-21)

15 Then Moses and the Israelites
sang this song to the LORD.
They said:

I will sing to the LORD,
for He is highly exalted;
He has thrown the horse
and its rider into the sea.
2 The LORD is my strength
and my song;[A]
He has become my salvation.
This is my God,
and I will praise Him,
my father's God,
and I will exalt Him.
3 The LORD is a warrior;
•Yahweh is His name.

4 He threw Pharaoh's chariots
and his army into the sea;
the elite of his officers
were drowned in the •Red Sea.
5 The floods covered them;
they sank to the depths
like a stone.
6 LORD, Your right hand
is glorious in power.
LORD, Your right hand
shattered the enemy.
7 You overthrew
Your adversaries
by Your great majesty.
You unleashed
Your burning wrath;
it consumed them
like stubble.
8 The waters heaped up
at the blast of Your nostrils;
the currents stood firm
like a dam.
The watery depths congealed
in the heart of the sea.
9 The enemy said:
"I will pursue, I will overtake,
I will divide the spoil.
My desire will be gratified
at their expense.
I will draw my sword;
my hand will destroy[B] them."
10 But You blew
with Your breath,
and the sea covered them.
They sank like lead
in the mighty waters.
11 LORD, who is like You
among the gods?
Who is like You, glorious
in holiness,
revered with praises,
performing wonders?
12 You stretched out
Your right hand,
and the earth swallowed them.
13 You will lead the people
You have redeemed
with Your faithful love;
You will guide them
to Your holy dwelling
with Your strength.

14 When the peoples hear,
they will shudder;
anguish will seize
the inhabitants of Philistia.
15 Then the chiefs of Edom
will be terrified;
trembling will seize
the leaders of Moab;
the inhabitants of Canaan
will panic;
16 and terror and dread will fall
on them.
They will be as still[C] as a stone
because of Your powerful arm

[A]**15:2** Or *might* [B]**15:9** Or *conquer* [C]**15:16** Or *silent*

CHARACTER PROFILE

Miriam A Gifted but Imperfect Leader

Her Background	• The daughter of Amram and Jochebed (Nm 26:59) • A prophetess and musician (Ex 15:20)
Her Story	• She helped her mother hide baby Moses (Ex 2:3-10). • With Moses and Aaron, she led the people of Israel through the wilderness (Nm 12:1-4). • She challenged Moses for marrying a "Cushite" woman (Nm 12:1). • She was punished by God with leprosy for criticizing Moses (Nm 12:10-14). • She was restored to health (Nm 12:15-16). • She died before reaching the promised land (Nm 20:1).
Life Lessons	• The creation order, prescribed by God Himself, is a pattern for leadership roles. • Those in leadership have a greater accountability to honor God. • Jealousy and pride can cause a leader's downfall.

until Your people pass by,
LORD,
until the people
whom You purchased[A]
pass by.
17 You will bring them in
and plant them
on the mountain
of Your possession;
LORD, You have prepared
the place
for Your dwelling;
Lord,[B] Your hands
have established
the sanctuary.
18 The LORD will reign forever
and ever!

19 When Pharaoh's horses with his
chariots and horsemen went into
the sea, the LORD brought the waters
of the sea back over them. But the
Israelites walked through the sea
on dry ground. 20 Then Miriam the
prophetess, Aaron's sister, took a
tambourine in her hand, and all the
women followed her with their tambourines and danced. 21 Miriam sang
to them:

Sing to the LORD,
for He is
highly exalted;
He has thrown the horse
and its rider into the sea.

Yahweh's Testing of the Israelites at Marah (15:22-27)

22 Then Moses led Israel on from
the Red Sea, and they went out to
the Wilderness of Shur. They journeyed for three days in the wilderness without finding water. 23 They
came to Marah, but they could not
drink the water at Marah because
it was bitter—that is why it was
named Marah.[C] 24 The people grumbled to Moses, "What are we going
to drink?" 25 So he cried out to the
LORD, and the LORD showed him a
tree. When he threw it into the water, the water became drinkable.

He made a statute and ordinance
for them at Marah and He tested
them there. 26 He said, "If you will
carefully obey the LORD your God,
do what is right in His eyes, pay attention to His commands, and keep
all His statutes, I will not inflict any
illnesses on you that I inflicted on
the Egyptians. For I am Yahweh who
heals you."

27 Then they came to Elim, where
there were 12 springs of water and
70 date palms, and they camped
there by the waters.

A 15:16 Or *created* B 15:17 Some Hb mss, DSS, Sam, Tg read *LORD* C 15:23 = bitter or bitterness

a **wilderness** where they initially found only undrinkable **water** and **grumbled** [Hb *lun*, "complained, murmured"] **to Moses**. The region is identified as **the Wilderness of Shur** [Hb "wall"] located in the Sinai peninsula. For at least 2 million people plus livestock, the situation was desperate. By crying **out to the LORD**, Moses expressed his helplessness and put himself in a position to receive guidance from the Lord. God made the water **drinkable** for His people when the need and their utter dependency on Him had been acknowledged and when Moses had obeyed His command to throw the **tree . . . into the water**. Moses' action merely made visible the fact that God was working in ways for which there was no natural explanation.

15:26-27 To demonstrate faithfulness to God, the people were given the responsibility to **carefully obey** (Hb *shamoʿ shamaʿ*, "surely listen, heed, hearken unto") Yahweh their **God**, the mighty Deliverer about whom they had so recently sung; to **do what is right** [Hb *yashar*, "correct, upright, straight, level, pleasing, fitting, proper," the only use of this word in Exodus; cp. Dt 6:18] **in His eyes** rather than their own; and to **pay attention** [Hb *ʾazan*, "hear, listen, give ear, obey," the only use of this word in Exodus] **to His commands** and **keep** [Hb *shamar*, "guard, observe, give heed to"] **all His statutes** [Hb *choq*, "ordinances, laws, decrees; prescribed tasks, limits, or boundaries"]. If they fulfilled their responsibility to submit completely to God's "spiritual health plan," then He guaranteed He would not bring upon them **any** of the sicknesses that He had **inflicted on the Egyptians** (cp. Dt 28:58-61). He also declared to them one of His names: **I am Yahweh who heals you** (Hb *Yahweh-Roph'eka*). On the other side of the Red Sea, the people of Israel could begin life anew, but they rapidly discovered at Marah that they could not make it on their own. If they proved faithful to live "under new management," however, God would continually resolve every difficulty they encountered. After Marah, they were led to an oasis, a place of virtually unlimited supply for both needs and refreshment (cp. Nm 33:9-10).

16:1-12 Traveling through **the wilderness of Sin** was the occasion for another round of grumbling against the community's God-appointed leadership. When living life God's way becomes difficult, memory can portray even the life of slavery as "the good life." The Israelites pined for what they had left behind to follow this seemingly uncertain path marked out by Moses and Aaron. The text does not record either the people or the leaders crying out to Yahweh regarding hunger, but three times it is noted that **the Lord** had **heard** their **complaints** (vv. 7,9,11). Because Moses and Aaron recognized that God was meeting this need Himself, they clarified that the complaints were actually directed at God, as though He was not already aware of their situation and its challenges. The totally unexpected and miraculous way that Yahweh was going to provide food would serve a twofold spiritual purpose (cp. Dt 8:2-3,16; Mt 4:4; Lk 4:4): He would **test** their obedience, **whether or not** the people would **follow** (Hb *halak*, "walk, proceed, live by") His **instructions** (Hb *torah*, "law"); and He would accomplish His goal, repeatedly emphasized, of proving to His people that He, and none other, had **brought** them **out of the land of Egypt**—that He, and none other, was their **God**. The One who has rescued His people from slavery can also meet every need (e.g., 2Co 9:8).

16:13-18 As He had promised, **quail** arrived **at evening**, and **the bread** of heaven was ready to be gathered **in the morning** (vv. 13-15; cp. Gn 1:5; Ps 78:23-31; Jn 6:26-58). The question, **What is it?** (Hb *manhu'*, transliterated as "manna," a substance resembling coriander seed with a sweet, honey-like taste, Ex 16:15,31) was God's provision. Although God provided the food, the people had to gather it. The work involved the efforts of everyone in the community, representing individuals of unequal abilities. There was nevertheless an equal distribution of the provision and enough for each person—**no surplus** and **no shortage**, only what was **needed** for that day (cp. Mt 6:11; Lk 11:3). The daily activities of gathering and measuring and eating the manna served as an ongoing object lesson in day-by-day dependence on God who provided day-to-day proof of His faithfulness.

16:19-20 Disobedience resulted in a putrid, worm-infested mess. This spoiling not only punished the disobedient but also set a pattern for the people of living by faith.

16:31-36 This description of manna as well as the details in verse 14 have led some to see similarities between the **substance** and a variety of tree resins and insect excretions (cp. Nm

Yahweh's Testing of the Israelites in the Wilderness of Sin (16:1-36)

Grumbling and Complaints (16:1-12)

16 The entire Israelite community departed from Elim and came to the Wilderness of Sin, which is between Elim and Sinai, on the fifteenth day of the second month after they had left the land of Egypt. 2 The entire Israelite community grumbled against Moses and Aaron in the wilderness. 3 The Israelites said to them, "If only we had died by the Lord's hand in the land of Egypt, when we sat by pots of meat and ate all the bread we wanted. Instead, you brought us into this wilderness to make this whole assembly die of hunger!"

4 Then the Lord said to Moses, "I am going to rain bread from heaven for you. The people are to go out each day and gather enough for that day. This way I will test them to see whether or not they will follow My instructions. 5 On the sixth day, when they prepare what they bring in, it will be twice as much as they gather on other days."[A]

6 So Moses and Aaron said to all the Israelites: "This evening you will know that it was the Lord who brought you out of the land of Egypt; 7 in the morning you will see the Lord's glory because He has heard your complaints about Him. For who are we that you complain about us?" 8 Moses continued, "The Lord will give you meat to eat this evening and more than enough bread in the morning, for He has heard the complaints that you are raising against Him. Who are we? Your complaints are not against us but against the Lord."

9 Then Moses told Aaron, "Say to the entire Israelite community, 'Come before the Lord, for He has heard your complaints.'" 10 As Aaron was speaking to the entire Israelite community, they turned toward the wilderness, and there in a cloud the Lord's glory appeared.

11 The Lord spoke to Moses, 12 "I have heard the complaints of the Israelites. Tell them: At twilight you will eat meat, and in the morning you will eat bread until you are full. Then you will know that I am •Yahweh your God."

Quail and Manna (16:13-36)

13 So at evening quail came and covered the camp. In the morning there was a layer of dew all around the camp. 14 When the layer of dew evaporated, there were fine flakes on the desert surface, as fine as frost on the ground. 15 When the Israelites saw it, they asked one another, "What is it?" because they didn't know what it was.

Moses told them, "It is the bread the Lord has given you to eat. 16 This is what the Lord has commanded: 'Gather as much of it as each person needs to eat. You may take two quarts[B] per individual, according to the number of people each of you has in his tent.'"

17 So the Israelites did this. Some gathered a lot, some a little. 18 When they measured it by quarts,[C] the person who gathered a lot had no surplus, and the person who gathered a little had no shortage. Each gathered as much as he needed to eat. 19 Moses said to them, "No one is to let any of it remain until morning." 20 But they didn't listen to Moses; some people left part of it until morning, and it bred worms and smelled. Therefore Moses was angry with them.

21 They gathered it every morning. Each gathered as much as he needed to eat, but when the sun grew hot, it melted. 22 On the sixth day they gathered twice as much food, four quarts[D] apiece, and all the leaders of the community came and reported this to Moses. 23 He told them, "This is what the Lord has said: 'Tomorrow is a day of complete rest, a holy Sabbath to the Lord. Bake what you want to bake, and boil what you want to boil, and set aside everything left over to be kept until morning.'"

24 So they set it aside until morning as Moses commanded, and it didn't smell or have any maggots in it. 25 "Eat it today," Moses said, "because today is a Sabbath to the Lord. Today you won't find any in the field.

[A] **16:5** Lit *as gathering day to day* [B] **16:16** Lit *an omer* [C] **16:18** Lit *by an omer* [D] **16:22** Lit *two omers*

26 For six days you may gather it, but on the seventh day, the Sabbath, there will be none."

27 Yet on the seventh day some of the people went out to gather, but they did not find any. 28 Then the LORD said to Moses, "How long will you[A] refuse to keep My commands and instructions? 29 Understand that the LORD has given you the Sabbath; therefore on the sixth day He will give you two days' worth of bread. Each of you stay where you are; no one is to leave his place on the seventh day." 30 So the people rested on the seventh day.

31 The house of Israel named the substance manna.[B] It resembled coriander seed, was white, and tasted like wafers made with honey. 32 Moses said, "This is what the LORD has commanded: 'Two quarts[C] of it are to be preserved throughout your generations, so that they may see the bread I fed you in the wilderness when I brought you out of the land of Egypt.'"

33 Moses told Aaron, "Take a container and put two quarts[D] of manna in it. Then place it before the LORD to be preserved throughout your generations." 34 As the LORD commanded Moses, Aaron placed it before the •testimony to be preserved.

35 The Israelites ate manna for 40 years, until they came to an inhabited land. They ate manna until they reached the border of the land of Canaan. 36 (Two quarts are[E] a tenth of an ephah.)

The Israelites' Testing of Yahweh at Rephidim (17:1-7)

Grumbling and Complaints (17:1-4)

17 The entire Israelite community left the Wilderness of Sin, moving from one place to the next according to the LORD's command. They camped at Rephidim, but there was no water for the people to drink. 2 So the people complained to Moses, "Give us water to drink."

"Why are you complaining to me?" Moses replied to them. "Why are you testing the LORD?"

3 But the people thirsted there for water, and grumbled against Moses. They said, "Why did you ever bring us out of Egypt to kill us and our children and our livestock with thirst?"

4 Then Moses cried out to the LORD, "What should I do with these people? In a little while they will stone me!"

Water from the Rock (17:5-7)

5 The LORD answered Moses, "Go on ahead of the people and take some of the elders of Israel with you. Take the staff you struck the Nile with in your hand and go. 6 I am going to stand there in front of you on the rock at Horeb; when you hit the rock, water will come out of it and the people will drink." Moses did this in the sight of the elders of Israel. 7 He named the place Massah[F] and Meribah[G] because the Israelites complained, and because they tested the LORD, saying, "Is the LORD among us or not?"

Amalek's Attack of Israel at Rephidim (17:8-16)

8 At Rephidim, Amalek[H] came and fought against Israel. 9 Moses said to Joshua, "Select some men for us and go fight against Amalek. Tomorrow I will stand on the hilltop with God's staff in my hand."

10 Joshua did as Moses had told him, and fought against Amalek, while Moses, Aaron, and Hur went up to the top of the hill. 11 While Moses held up his hand,[I] Israel prevailed, but whenever he put his hand[I] down, Amalek prevailed. 12 When Moses' hands grew heavy, they took a stone and put it under him, and he sat down on it. Then Aaron and Hur supported his hands, one on one side and one on the other so that his hands remained steady until the sun went down. 13 So Joshua defeated Amalek and his army[J] with the sword.

14 The LORD then said to Moses, "Write this down on a scroll as a reminder and recite it to Joshua: I will completely blot out the memory of Amalek under heaven."

11:7-9). Of course, God could have used nature with His own adjustments to make this provision. However, even if manna shared every characteristic of any of these, at least three important aspects of God's provision thoroughly magnify the indisputable fact of the Lord's supernatural intervention for His people. First, **two quarts** per person amounted to a huge quantity of manna, greater than any incidental secretions of the tamarisk tree (Ex 16:16,32,36). Second, **manna** appeared steadily in every season of the year. Finally, every week, **for 40 years**, more manna was provided on the sixth day and none on the seventh (v. 35). No plant, even if blossoming year-round, functions on such a precise calendar.

17:1-4 The misdirected complaint of the people **at Rephidim** (Hb "resting places") and their lack of faith were all too familiar to Moses. Fearing for his life, he took his exasperation to **the LORD** (cp. 16:1-3,8). According to **Moses**, they were making a critical error by **testing the LORD** (cp. v. 7). To test the people who belonged to Him was God's prerogative, not the other way around (cp. Dt 6:16; Mt 4:7).

17:5-7 **The LORD** did not chide Moses for his desperate cry for help. Instead, He instructed Moses to involve some of the elders, to take in hand **the staff** that had signaled God's transformation of **the Nile** into blood, and to **go on ahead of the people**. As the site of his encounter with the burning bush, **Horeb** was familiar territory for Moses (cp. 3:1). The Lord promised to be present, standing **on** a particular **rock** from which **water** would flow when Moses **hit** it with the staff. No description is provided to explain how God presented Himself to Moses and **the elders** to indicate His intention for them simply to take Him at His word. The text takes for granted that the water came forth as predicted. Greater emphasis is given to the Israelites' sin of testing **the LORD**, although God asserted His sovereignty in Ps 81:7 as the One who was doing the testing. **Massah** [Hb "testing"] **and Meribah** [Hb "arguing"] became places infamous for the rebellious attitude displayed there by the people's demand for immediate gratification and their choice to complain to the human leaders rather than cry out to God (cp. Dt 6:16; 9:22; 33:8; Nm 20:13,24; 27:14; Pss 95:8; 106:32).

17:8-14 **Joshua** and **Hur** appear in the narrative for the first time here. Joshua was selected to lead the Israelites' military defense against **Amalek**; and Hur, along with Aaron, aided in holding up Moses' hands, one or both of which held **God's staff**. God allowed the battle's success to parallel this signal of triumph. Amalek (Hb, "valley dweller";

[A] **16:28** The Hb word for you is pl, referring to the whole nation. [B] **16:31** = what?; Ex 16:15 [C] **16:32** Lit *A full omer* [D] **16:33** Lit *a full omer* [E] **16:36** Lit *The omer is* [F] **17:7** = testing [G] **17:7** = arguing [H] **17:8** A semi-nomadic people descended from Amalek, a grandson of Esau; Gn 36:12 [I] **17:11** Sam, LXX, Syr, Tg, Vg read *hands* [J] **17:13** Or *people*

cp. Nm 14:25) was Esau's grandson. The aggression of his descendants against Israel incurred God's wrath (Gn 36:12; Dt 25:17-19; 1Sm 15:1-3,6,18). While Moses certainly may have raised his hands in intercessory prayer for the Israelites' army, the text does not clearly explain the meaning of Moses' posture except for the correlation between his holding up the staff and whether or not Israel **prevailed** in battle. God's promise to **blot out** [Hb *machah*, "wipe away, destroy, obliterate"; cp. Dt 9:14; Rv 3:5] **the memory of Amalek** was written down especially for Joshua (Ex 17:14).

17:15-16 Moses built an altar (Hb *mizbēach*, from a verbal root *zavach* meaning "slaughter," a structure on which offerings were made; the first mention of an altar in Exodus) to serve as a public testament of worship and gratitude to the Lord. He had won that day's battle and would always **be at war** with those who opposed His people. The altar's name, "The Lord Is My Banner" (Hb *Yahweh-Nissi*; cp. Ps 60:4) comes from the root *nes*, denoting a "standard, signal pole, banner, or something lifted up" as a rallying point (cp. Nm 21:8-9; Is 5:26; 11:10-12; 18:3; 49:22; 62:10).

18:1-12 News of the happenings in Egypt and at the Red Sea, of an enormous group of people traveling through the wilderness, and of the defeat of the Amalekites reached **Moses' father-in-law** in **Midian**. Having learned that Moses and the Israelites were **camped at the mountain of God**, Jethro brought **Moses' wife** and **sons** to Horeb to reunite the family. What sort of **priest** Jethro was remains a mystery, but after hearing Moses recount the details of God's deliverance and provision, he exclaimed that for him the superiority of Yahweh over **all** other **gods** was indisputable. **The Lord** had stepped in to show **the Egyptians** the folly of acting **arrogantly** (Hb *zud*, "act presumptuously," connoting an attitude of proud insolence and even wickedness; used only here in Exodus and rarely in the OT, v. 11; cp. Dt 1:43; 17:13; Neh 9:10,16,29; Jr 50:29) against His people. As a priest, Jethro led in sacrificial worship. In God's presence—presumably out in the open, in view of the pillar of cloud and of the altar of sacrifice—he and **Aaron** and **all the elders** ate **a meal** together, an event signifying the parties' commitment to peace and mutual friendship and possibly Jethro's desire to identify with the people of Yahweh.

18:13-27 Jethro's visit not only reunited Moses with his family and directed the Israelites' leaders to worship together, he also provided a solution to an overwhelming problem.

15 And Moses built an altar and named it, "The Lord Is My Banner."[A] 16 He said, "Indeed, my hand is lifted up toward[B] the Lord's throne. The Lord will be at war with Amalek from generation to generation."

Jethro's Visit (18:1-27)

Family Reunion (18:1-12)

18 Moses' father-in-law Jethro, the priest of Midian, heard about everything that God had done for Moses and His people Israel, and how the Lord had brought Israel out of Egypt.

2 Now Jethro, Moses' father-in-law, had taken in Zipporah, Moses' wife, after he had sent her back, 3 along with her two sons, one of whom was named Gershom (because Moses had said, "I have been a foreigner in a foreign land")[C] 4 and the other Eliezer (because he had said, "The God of my father was my helper and delivered me from Pharaoh's sword").[D]

5 Moses' father-in-law Jethro, along with Moses' wife and sons, came to him in the wilderness where he was camped at the mountain of God. 6 He sent word to Moses, "I, your father-in-law Jethro, am coming to you with your wife and her two sons."

7 So Moses went out to meet his father-in-law, bowed down, and then kissed him. They asked each other how they had been[E] and went into the tent. 8 Moses recounted to his father-in-law all that the Lord had done to Pharaoh and the Egyptians for Israel's sake, all the hardships that confronted them on the way, and how the Lord delivered them.

9 Jethro rejoiced over all the good things the Lord had done for Israel when He rescued them from the power of the Egyptians. 10 "Praise the Lord," Jethro exclaimed, "who rescued you from Pharaoh and the power of the Egyptians and snatched the people from the power of the Egyptians. 11 Now I know that •Yahweh is greater than all gods, because He did wonders when the Egyptians acted arrogantly against Israel."[F]

12 Then Jethro, Moses' father-in-law, brought a •burnt offering and sacrifices to God, and Aaron came with all the elders of Israel to eat a meal with Moses' father-in-law in God's presence.

Good Advice (18:13-27)

13 The next day Moses sat down to judge the people, and they stood around Moses from morning until evening. 14 When Moses' father-in-law saw everything he was doing for them he asked, "What is this thing you're doing for the people? Why are you alone sitting as judge, while all the people stand around you from morning until evening?"

15 Moses replied to his father-in-law, "Because the people come to me to inquire of God. 16 Whenever they have a dispute, it comes to me, and I make a decision between one man and another. I teach them God's statutes and laws."

17 "What you're doing is not good," Moses' father-in-law said to him. 18 "You will certainly wear out both yourself and these people who are with you, because the task is too heavy for you. You can't do it alone. 19 Now listen to me; I will give you some advice, and God be with you. You be the one to represent the people before God and bring their cases to Him. 20 Instruct them about the statutes and laws, and teach them the way to live and what they must do. 21 But you should select from all the people able men, God-fearing, trustworthy, and hating bribes. Place them over the people as commanders of thousands, hundreds, fifties, and tens. 22 They should judge the people at all times. Then they can bring you every important case but judge every minor case themselves. In this way you will lighten your load,[G] and they will bear it with you. 23 If you do this, and God so directs you, you will be able to endure, and also all these people will be able to go home satisfied."[H]

24 Moses listened to his father-in-law and did everything he said. 25 So Moses chose able men from all Is-

[A]17:15 Or *Yahweh-nissi* [B]17:16 Or *hand was on*, or *hand was against*; Hb obscure [C]18:3 In Hb the name Gershom sounds like the phrase "a stranger there." [D]18:4 = My God Is Help [E]18:7 Lit *other about well-being* [F]18:11 Hb obscure [G]18:22 Lit *lighten from on you* [H]18:23 Lit *go to their place in peace*

rael and made them leaders over the
people as commanders of thousands,
hundreds, fifties, and tens. 26 They
judged the people at all times; they
would bring the hard cases to Moses, but they would judge every minor case themselves.
27 Then Moses said good-bye to his
father-in-law, and he journeyed to
his own land.

Covenant Mediation (19:1-25)

Betrothal (19:1-8)

19 In the third month, on the
same day of the month that the
Israelites had left the land of Egypt,
they entered the Wilderness of Sinai.
2 After they departed from Rephidim,
they entered the Wilderness of Sinai
and camped in the wilderness, and
Israel camped there in front of the
mountain.
3 Moses went up the mountain
to God, and the LORD called to him
from the mountain: "This is what
you must say to the house of Jacob, and explain to the Israelites:
4 'You have seen what I did to the
Egyptians and how I carried you
on eagles' wings and brought you
to Me. 5 Now if you will listen to Me
and carefully keep My covenant, you
will be My own possession out of all
the peoples, although all the earth is
Mine, 6 and you will be My kingdom
of priests and My holy nation.' These
are the words that you are to say to
the Israelites."
7 After Moses came back, he summoned the elders of the people and
set before them all these words that
the LORD had commanded him.
8 Then all the people responded together, "We will do all that the LORD
has spoken." So Moses brought the
people's words back to the LORD.

Preparations (19:9-15)

9 The LORD said to Moses, "I am going to come to you in a dense cloud,
so that the people will hear when I
speak with you and will always believe you." Then Moses reported the
people's words to the LORD. 10 And
the LORD told Moses, "Go to the
people and consecrate them today
and tomorrow. They must wash
their clothes 11 and be prepared by
the third day, for on the third day
the LORD will come down on Mount
Sinai in the sight of all the people.
12 Put boundaries for the people all
around the mountain and say: Be
careful that you don't go up on the
mountain or touch its base. Anyone
who touches the mountain will be
put to death. 13 No hand may touch
him; instead he will be stoned or
shot with arrows. No animal or
man will live. When the ram's horn
sounds a long blast, they may go up
the mountain."
14 Then Moses came down from the
mountain to the people and consecrated them, and they washed their
clothes. 15 He said to the people, "Be
prepared by the third day. Do not
have sexual relations with women."

The Third Day (19:16-25)

16 On the third day, when morning
came, there was thunder and lightning, a thick cloud on the mountain, and a loud trumpet sound,
so that all the people in the camp
shuddered. 17 Then Moses brought
the people out of the camp to meet
God, and they stood at the foot of
the mountain. 18 Mount Sinai was

Doctrine THE CHURCH

The Lord intended the nation of Israel to be noticeably different from all the rest, set apart for God's sacred purposes. This expectation is carried into the New Testament expectation that the church (i.e., the followers of Christ) will reflect God's holiness (Eph 1:4; 5:27; 1Pt 1:15-16). The people of Israel were appointed as God's **kingdom of priests**—a people who, under sovereign rule, would live to worship Yahweh and to intercede for the nations, as the priests within Israel ministered to the Israelites (Ex 19:6; cp. Dt 21:5; Rv 1:6; 5:10). Likewise, the church is addressed as "a holy priesthood" and "a royal priesthood" (1Pt 2:5,9), emphasizing the responsibility of Christ's followers to worship, intercede, and draw people to Christ by their example of complete obedience of the Lord.

Finally, God says the people would be His **holy nation**, a phrase the New Testament also applies to the church. Israel was essentially a theocracy, ruled supremely by Yahweh alone (Ex 19:6). As subjects of their divine King, the Israelites were automatically bound to reflect His holiness (cp. Lv 11:44-45). Likewise, Jesus Christ is the head of the church (Eph 1:22-23), and His followers are commanded to be holy as He is holy (1Pt 1:15-16; cp. Eph 1:4). God's people, both individually and corporately, together form an entire kingdom, a domain to which other nations could come to find reconciliation with the Lord of Israel who is Lord of all (cp. Col 1:13-23,27).

The people's "Yes" was a commitment to **do all** God required (Ex 19:8). Partial or selective obedience was out of the question.

19:3-8 God's message resembled a proposal of marriage, and the people's response was like a bride's pledge to be married. God's proposal poetically rehearsed how He had proven His love and His worthiness to have their love in return (v. 4).

19:16-25 The LORD did not intend to create a comfortable atmosphere but to arrest the people's attention and inspire their awe and fear. His descent **on Mount Sinai** made the site holy. He knows the human propensity to test boundaries, even those **put** up explicitly for their protection. Every "Do not" established a boundary for the spiritual protection of God's people.

completely enveloped in smoke because the LORD came down on it
in fire. Its smoke went up like the
smoke of a furnace, and the whole
mountain shook violently. 19 As the
sound of the trumpet grew louder
and louder, Moses spoke and God
answered him in the thunder.
20 The LORD came down on Mount
Sinai at the top of the mountain.
Then the LORD summoned Moses
to the top of the mountain, and he
went up. 21 The LORD directed Moses,
"Go down and warn the people not
to break through to see the LORD;
otherwise many of them will die.
22 Even the priests who come near
the LORD must purify themselves
or the LORD will break out in anger
against them."
23 But Moses responded to the
LORD, "The people cannot come up
Mount Sinai, since You warned us:
Put a boundary around the mountain and consider it holy." 24 And
the LORD replied to him, "Go down
and come back with Aaron. But the
priests and the people must not
break through to come up to the
LORD, or He will break out in anger
against them." 25 So Moses went
down to the people and told them.

God's Words: The Ten Commandments (20:1-26)

20 Then God spoke all these
words:

2 I am the LORD your God, who
brought you out of the land of
Egypt, out of the place of slavery.
3 Do not have other gods besides Me.
4 Do not make an idol for yourself, whether in the shape of
anything in the heavens above
or on the earth below or in the
waters under the earth. 5 You
must not bow down to them or
worship them; for I, the LORD
your God, am a jealous God,
punishing the children for the
fathers' sin, to the third and
fourth generations of those
who hate Me, 6 but showing
faithful love to a thousand
generations of those who love
Me and keep My commands.
7 Do not misuse the name of
the LORD your God, because
the LORD will not leave anyone
unpunished who misuses His
name.
8 Remember the Sabbath day, to
keep it holy: 9 You are to labor
six days and do all your work,
10 but the seventh day is a Sabbath to the LORD your God. You
must not do any work—you,
your son or daughter, your
male or female slave, your
livestock, or the foreigner who
is within your gates. 11 For the
LORD made the heavens and
the earth, the sea, and everything in them in six days; then
He rested on the seventh day.
Therefore the LORD blessed the
Sabbath day and declared it
holy.
12 Honor your father and your
mother so that you may have
a long life in the land that the
LORD your God is giving you.
13 Do not murder.
14 Do not commit adultery.
15 Do not steal.
16 Do not give false testimony
against your neighbor.
17 Do not covet your neighbor's
house. Do not covet your
neighbor's wife, his male or
female slave, his ox or donkey,
or anything that belongs to
your neighbor.

18 All the people witnessed[A] the

A**20:18** Lit *saw*

>WORD|*study*

20:4-6 Sin (Hb *'awon*, "perversity, depravity; guilt or punishment of iniquity"; cp. 34:7-9; Is 53:6) is a strong word for iniquity. It refers not simply to discrete acts of disobedience but to pervasive corruption and guilt, somewhat like the difference between having a broken nose and terminal cancer. Derived from a verb meaning "to bend, twist, or pervert; to do wrong," sin is taking what is good and making it into something evil or using what is good for evil purposes. Although God is gracious to limit the effects of such a choice, the blessings of choosing to love Him are beyond counting.

20:1-26 These commandments address all Israelites "as one man" or as a corporate body in masculine singular form. The masculine form does not suggest that He was excluding women from the audience. God's covenant was made with a singular people or nation.

20:1-3 The first commandment heads the list as well as in importance. All the rest depend on being in exclusive covenant relationship with the sovereign Lord of all. As a bride who vows to honor her husband above all others, so Israel, in accepting these covenant terms embodied in the Law, was expected to worship Yahweh exclusively. Keeping in place the first boundary binds people to the Lord, separating them from all other contenders.

20:4-6 The second commandment makes the first explicit, closing any conceivable loopholes.

20:7 Misuse pulls together both the verb (Hb *nasa'*, "take, lift up, bear, carry") and the adverb phrase "in vain" or "for vanity" (Hb *shaw*, "emptiness, nothingness, falsehood; emptiness of speech, lying; worthlessness"). This commandment deals with speech. It forbids frivolous use of God's **name**—overtly maligning His name or dishonoring the true God who has revealed His name to reveal Himself. Blasphemy and cursing are intensified expressions of irreverence. Blaming God for the problems or failures of your own making is a more subtle way to "misuse" His name

20:8-11 By observing **the Sabbath**, Israel would dramatize God's creation of the world every week (Gn 2:2-3). The Sabbath is a gift from God to man, but it is also a means of reflecting His image, of living according to the pattern He established. The Sabbath, for believers, has been celebrated on Sunday in honor of Christ's resurrection on the first day of the week. Many have grossly neglected obedience to this commandment. We have become adept at rationalizing our disobedience and stiff-necked in our selfish refusals to make the radical lifestyle changes that would be necessary to put the command into effect.

20:12 To **honor** one's parents is to give them the honor they deserve because of their God-assigned roles, whether they fulfilled those roles honorably or not. Learning to submit to parental authority in the home is the training ground for learning to honor God. The promise is not an automatic reward of **long life** for the individual but a testimony to the overall stability of homes, of extended families, and of a society built on a culture of respect for

thunder and lightning, the sound of
the trumpet, and the mountain surrounded by smoke. When the people
saw it[A] they trembled and stood at
a distance. 19“You speak to us, and
we will listen,” they said to Moses,
“but don’t let God speak to us, or we
will die.”
20Moses responded to the people,
“Don’t be afraid, for God has come
to test you, so that you will *fear
Him and will not[B] sin.” 21And the
people remained standing at a distance as Moses approached the thick
darkness where God was.
22Then the LORD told Moses, “This
is what you are to say to the Israelites: You have seen that I have spoken to you from heaven. 23You must
not make gods of silver to rival Me;
you must not make gods of gold for
yourselves.[C]
24“You must make an earthen altar
for Me and sacrifice on it your *burnt
offerings and *fellowship offerings,
your sheep and goats, as well as your
cattle. I will come to you and bless
you in every place where I cause My
name to be remembered. 25If you
make a stone altar for Me, you must
not build it out of cut stones. If you
use your chisel on it, you will defile
it. 26You must not go up to My altar
on steps, so that your nakedness is
not exposed on it.

Additional Laws (21:1–23:19)

Slaves (21:1-11)

21 “These are the ordinances that
you must set before them:
2“When you buy a Hebrew slave,
he is to serve for six years; then in
the seventh he is to leave as a free
man[D] without paying anything. 3If
he arrives alone, he is to leave alone;
if he arrives with[E] a wife, his wife
is to leave with him. 4If his master
gives him a wife and she bears him
sons or daughters, the wife and her
children belong to her master, and
the man must leave alone.
5“But if the slave declares: ‘I love
my master, my wife, and my children;
I do not want to leave as a free man,’
6his master is to bring him to the
judges[F] and then bring him to the
door or doorpost. His master must
pierce his ear with an awl, and he will
serve his master for life.
7“When a man sells his daughter
as a slave,[G] she is not to leave as the
male slaves do. 8If she is displeasing to her master, who chose her for
himself, then he must let her be redeemed. He has no right to sell her
to foreigners because he has acted
treacherously toward her. 9Or if he
chooses her for his son, he must
deal with her according to the customary treatment of daughters. 10If
he takes an additional wife, he must
not reduce the food, clothing, or
marital rights of the first wife. 11And
if he does not do these three things
for her, she may leave free of charge,
without any exchange of money.[H]

Personal Injury (21:12-36)

12“Whoever strikes a person so that
he dies must be put to death. 13But if
he didn’t intend any harm,[I] and yet
God caused it to happen by his hand,
I will appoint a place for you where
he may flee. 14If a person schemes
and willfully[J] acts against his neighbor to murder him, you must take
him from My altar to be put to death.
15“Whoever strikes his father or
his mother must be put to death.
16“Whoever kidnaps a person must
be put to death, whether he sells
him or the person is found in his
possession.
17“Whoever curses his father or
his mother must be put to death.
18“When men quarrel and one
strikes the other with a stone or
his fist, and the injured man does
not die but is confined to bed, 19if
he can later get up and walk around
outside leaning on his staff, then
the one who struck him will be exempt from punishment. Nevertheless, he must pay for his lost work
time[K] and provide for his complete
recovery.
20“When a man strikes his male
or female slave with a rod, and the
slave dies under his abuse,[L] the

[A]**20:18** Sam, LXX, Syr, Tg, Vg read *smoking; the people* (or *they*) *were afraid* [B]**20:20** Lit *that the fear of Him may be in you, and you do not* [C]**20:23** Hb obscure [D]**21:2** Lit *to go forth* [E]**21:3** Lit *he is the husband of* [F]**21:6** Or *to God*; that is, to His sanctuary or court [G]**21:7** Or *concubine* [H]**21:11** She doesn’t have to pay any redemption price. [I]**21:13** Lit *he was not lying in wait* [J]**21:14** Or *maliciously* [K]**21:19** Lit *his inactivity* [L]**21:20** Lit *hand*

God’s principles, which include how children relate to their parents.

20:13 This command does not prohibit taking human life under absolutely all circumstances but upholds God’s exclusive lordship over life and death. Jesus defined “murder” in a comprehensive manner, indicating that God examines the thoughts, motivations, and intentions of the heart, not just the actions overtly expressing these (Mt 5:21-22).

20:14 This commandment draws a boundary around the sacredness of marriage as designed by the Creator. According to His plan, one man and one woman commit themselves exclusively to the Lord and to each other. Within the “bonds of marriage,” sexual intimacy can be enjoyed fully and freely. All sexual activity outside that marriage relationship is forbidden in order to preserve the purity and passion of the marriage bed within the commitment of one man to one woman for a lifetime (cp. Gn 2:24; Heb 13:4).

20:15 To take for oneself what rightfully belongs to another is to insult God, to act as though He is unable to provide and therefore less than God.

20:16 This commandment protects a person’s name and character just as the third commandment protects the name of God (v. 7). Telling lies is prohibited.

20:17 This commandment strikes at the root of sin—an individual’s thought life. Stealing and adultery may be the most obvious outward manifestations of indulging discontentment (e.g., Jos 7:21; Mc 2:2), but the sinful actions begin as sinful longings of the heart for the very things that are beyond reach because they belong to someone else. Coveting robs God of praise and gratitude and interferes with personal relationships. The Hebrew word translated **covet** (Hb *chamad*, “desire, take pleasure in, delight in”) has a wide range of connotations, not all of which are sinful. The question to identify is the object of one’s desires. This range of meaning can be seen in these translations of the same word: “desirable” (Ps 19:9-10) and “lust” (Pr 6:25).

21:1-5 The law was not defining the perfect society; rather the law was to reveal to the Israelites how God’s character could be reflected in their own society. God provides a contrasting picture of how even slavery, under His guidelines, could reflect the holiness and compassion of God. God never mandates slavery or praises its virtues; He simply provides wisdom for living even in these tragic conditions. Compared with the practices and laws of surrounding nations these rules were distinctive regarding the treatment of women as persons of worth, not as property or chattel. When a servant accepted a wife from his master, he was making a choice to stay or go when the six years were completed. If he did not love his wife enough to commit himself to her on these terms, then she was better off remaining in the master's household than to risk being divorced and left destitute.

21:12-32 In this section, the **death** penalty is prescribed for five different crimes. The first four cases did not offer exceptions based on the guilty person's gender.

21:22-25 A man who **hit a pregnant woman,** even if accidentally, and caused her to give birth **prematurely** would be obligated to **pay** whatever fine her **husband** demanded *and* the judges approved. Specific laws in the Torah were intended to be examples of how the Ten Commandments and foundational principles of justice were to be applied in situations not spelled out in Scripture. Some interpreters argue that this law suggests the inferior status of women because the husband, rather than the mother, was given the say-so in the guilty party's punishment. In a patriarchal society, however, the father and husband did have the obligation to ensure that women and children were treated with equal dignity as moral and spiritual beings and the responsibility to provide for and protect those in his household. One's worth was measured by the treatment required by the law. The worth of a wife and mother was clear by the severe penalty to be assessed for *any* injury incurred.

Nothing should be discounted when exacting punishment involving injury to those most precious to a man—his wife and children, and to those in society needing the highest degree of protection—newborn babies and their mothers. The premature infants described here would be regarded by many as only fetuses not entitled to basic human rights. In contrast, concern for the unborn child and the sanctity of life is evident since the pregnancy is an integral element of the case. When Jesus referred to the *lex talionis* (a Latin legal term for the law of retaliations), He was addressing its misuse among the Pharisees who made it a tool for exacting retribution for personal insults rather than a juridical policy for punishing violent acts that killed or maimed a person (cp. Mt 5:38-42).

owner must be punished.[A] 21 However, if the slave can stand up after a day or two, the owner should not be punished[B] because he is his owner's property.[C]

22 "When men get in a fight and hit a pregnant woman so that her children are born prematurely[D] but there is no injury, the one who hit her must be fined as the woman's husband demands from him, and he must pay according to judicial assessment. 23 If there is an injury, then you must give life for life, 24 eye for eye, tooth for tooth, hand for hand, foot for foot, 25 burn for burn, bruise for bruise, wound for wound.

26 "When a man strikes the eye of his male or female slave and destroys it, he must let the slave go free in compensation for his eye. 27 If he knocks out the tooth of his male or female slave, he must let the slave go free in compensation for his tooth.

28 "When an ox[E] gores a man or a woman to death, the ox must be stoned, and its meat may not be eaten, but the ox's owner is innocent. 29 However, if the ox was in the habit of goring, and its owner has been warned yet does not restrain it, and it kills a man or a woman, the ox must be stoned, and its owner must also be put to death. 30 If instead a ransom is demanded of him, he can pay a redemption price for his life in the full amount demanded from him. 31 If it gores a son or a daughter, he is to be dealt with according to this same law. 32 If the ox gores a male or female slave, he must give 30 •shekels of silver[F] to the slave's master, and the ox must be stoned.

33 "When a man uncovers a pit or digs a pit, and does not cover it, and an ox or a donkey falls into it, 34 the owner of the pit must give compensation; he must pay money to its owner, but the dead animal will become his.

35 "When a man's ox injures his neighbor's ox and it dies, they must sell the live ox and divide its proceeds; they must also divide the dead animal. 36 If, however, it is known that the ox was in the habit of goring, yet its owner has not restrained it, he must compensate fully, ox for ox; the dead animal will become his.

Theft (22:1-4)

22 [G] "When a man steals an ox or a sheep and butchers it or sells it, he must repay five cattle for the ox or four sheep for the sheep. 2 [H]If a thief is caught in the act of breaking in, and he is beaten to death, no one is •guilty of bloodshed. 3 But if this happens after sunrise,[I] there is guilt of bloodshed. A thief must make full restitution. If he is unable, he is to be sold because of his theft. 4 If what was stolen—whether ox, donkey, or sheep—is actually found alive in his possession, he must repay double.

Crop Protection (22:5-6)

5 "When a man lets a field or vineyard be grazed in, and then allows his animals to go and graze in someone else's field, he must repay[J] with the best of his own field or vineyard.

6 "When a fire gets out of control, spreads to thornbushes, and consumes stacks of cut grain, standing grain, or a field, the one who started the fire must make full restitution for what was burned.

Personal Property (22:7-15)

7 "When a man gives his neighbor money or goods to keep, but they are stolen from that person's house, the thief, if caught, must repay double. 8 If the thief is not caught, the owner of the house must present himself to the judges[K] to determine[L] whether or not he has taken his neighbor's property. 9 In any case of wrongdoing involving an ox, a donkey, a sheep, a garment, or anything else lost, and someone claims, 'That's mine,'[M] the case between the two parties is to come before the judges.[N] The one the judges condemn[O] must repay double to his neighbor.

10 "When a man gives his neighbor a donkey, an ox, a sheep, or any

[A] **21:20** Or *must suffer vengeance* [B] **21:21** Or *not suffer vengeance* [C] **21:21** Lit *money* [D] **21:22** Either a live birth or a miscarriage [E] **21:28** Or *a bull*, or *a steer* [F] **21:32** About 1 pound of silver [G] **22:1** Ex 21:37 in Hb [H] **22:2** Ex 22:1 in Hb [I] **22:3** Lit *if the sun has risen over him* [J] **22:5** LXX adds *from his field according to its produce. But if someone lets his animals graze an entire field, he must repay*; DSS, Sam also support this reading. [K] **22:8** Or *to God* [L] **22:8** LXX, Tg, Vg read *swear* [M] **22:9** Lit *That is it* [N] **22:9** Or *before God* [O] **22:9** Or *one whom God condemns*

other animal to care for, but it dies, is injured, or is stolen, while no one is watching, [11] there must be an oath before the LORD between the two of them to determine whether or not he has taken his neighbor's property. Its owner must accept the oath, and the other man does not have to make restitution. [12] But if, in fact, the animal was stolen from his custody, he must make restitution to its owner. [13] If it was actually torn apart by a wild animal, he is to bring it as evidence; he does not have to make restitution for the torn carcass.

[14] "When a man borrows an animal from his neighbor, and it is injured or dies while its owner is not there with it, the man must make full restitution. [15] If its owner is there with it, the man does not have to make restitution. If it was rented, the loss is covered by[A] its rental price.

Seduction (22:16-17)

[16] "If a man seduces a virgin who is not engaged, and he has sexual relations with her, he must certainly pay the bridal price for her to be his wife. [17] If her father absolutely refuses to give her to him, he must pay an amount in silver equal to the bridal price for virgins.

Capital Offenses (22:18-20)

[18] "You must not allow a sorceress to live.

[19] "Whoever has sexual intercourse with an animal must be put to death.

[20] "Whoever sacrifices to any gods, except the LORD alone, is to be •set apart for destruction.

Protection of the Vulnerable (22:21-27)

[21] "You must not exploit a foreign resident or oppress him, since you were foreigners in the land of Egypt.

[22] "You must not mistreat any widow or fatherless child. [23] If you do mistreat them, they will no doubt cry to Me, and I will certainly hear their cry. [24] My anger will burn, and I will kill you with the sword; then your wives will be widows and your children fatherless.

[25] "If you lend money to My people, to the poor person among you, you must not be like a moneylender to him; you must not charge him interest.

[26] "If you ever take your neighbor's cloak as collateral, return it to him before sunset. [27] For it is his only covering; it is the clothing for his body.[B] What will he sleep in? And if he cries out to Me, I will listen because I am compassionate.

Respect for God (22:28-31)

[28] "You must not blaspheme God[C] or curse a leader among your people.

[29] "You must not hold back offerings from your harvest or your vats. Give Me the firstborn of your sons. [30] Do the same with your cattle and your flock. Let them stay with their mothers for seven days, but on the eighth day you are to give them to Me.

[31] "Be My holy people. You must not eat the meat of a mauled animal found in the field; throw it to the dogs.

Honesty and Justice (23:1-9)

23 "You must not spread a false report. Do not join[D] the wicked to be a malicious witness.

[2] "You must not follow a crowd in wrongdoing. Do not testify in a lawsuit and go along with a crowd to pervert justice. [3] Do not show favoritism to a poor person in his lawsuit.

[4] "If you come across your enemy's stray ox or donkey, you must return it to him.

[5] "If you see the donkey of someone who hates you lying helpless under its load, and you want to refrain from helping it, you must help with it.[E]

[6] "You must not deny justice to a poor person among you in his lawsuit. [7] Stay far away from a false accusation. Do not kill the innocent and the just, because I will not justify the •guilty. [8] You must not take a bribe, for a bribe blinds the clear-sighted and corrupts the words[F] of the righteous. [9] You must not oppress a foreign resident; you yourselves know how it feels to be a foreigner because you were foreigners in the land of Egypt.

[A] **22:15** Lit *rented, it comes with* [B] **22:27** Lit *skin* [C] **22:28** Or *judges* [D] **23:1** Lit *join hands with* [E] **23:5** Or *load, you must refrain from leaving it to him; you must set it free with him* [F] **23:8** Or *and subverts the cause*

22:16-17 Seduces (Hb *patah*, "persuade, entice, lure"; cp. Pr 1:10; 16:29) implies that the man took the lead. Virgin (Hb *betulah*) denoted a "maiden who was pure or unspotted." This law specified a "virgin who was not promised in marriage" (Hb *'aras*, "betrothed, engaged"). The man guilty of seduction had to "pay the bridal price" whether or not the girl's father allowed him to marry her. Considering the possible outcomes of throwing away her virginity, a woman foolishly risked everything. If the sin was never discovered *and* the man's marriage proposal was successful, she and her husband would nevertheless have to hide their guilt for life. Keeping the sin hidden from her parents would be almost impossible because they kept the blood-stained sheet from her wedding night as proof of her virginity in case a discontented new husband tried to annul the marriage by accusing her of fornication (Dt 22:13-15).

22:18 Being a **sorceress** was a capital crime (Hb *kashaph, "practicing magic; witchcraft, sorcery, or enchantment"*; cp. 7:11; Dt 18:10). Attempting to exercise power in the spiritual realm, to manipulate objects or people through unseen forces, or to establish illegitimate communication between the physical and spiritual realms are occult practices completely incompatible with the worship of Yahweh. All power and authority belong exclusively to Him. Such practices have always permeated idolatrous religions, but Christians cannot write off such Old Testament laws as outdated and irrelevant in light of contemporary society's vulnerability to the allurements of the occult.

22:22-24 God sternly warned His people not to **mistreat** (Hb *'anah*, "afflict, humiliate"; cp. Jms 1:27) the most needy and vulnerable—widows and orphans. Yahweh assured His people that He would come to their defense and implied that His **anger** would be like that unleashed on Egypt (cp. Ex 4:22-23).

23:10-12 God gave the agricultural system a Sabbath year of **rest**, which not only allowed the land to be revitalized by lying fallow for a year, but also provided a source of food—what would naturally grow without cultivation or pruning—and seed for **the poor among** the Israelites. God reiterated the vital importance of the people's observance of the Sabbath day itself. Everyone—including the work animals, the slave's **son**, and the **foreign resident**—needed to **be refreshed** (Hb *naphash*, "take a breath" when weary; "rest, cease" working) by a regular day off, and the blessing of Sabbath rest must be shared by all.

23:14-17 All Israelite men were required **to appear** [Hb *ra'ah*, "present oneself, be seen"] **before the Lord God** for **three** annual feasts:

- **The Festival of Unleavened Bread** associated with the Passover. **No one** could come **empty-handed** (Hb *rêqam*, "emptily," as though too poor to bring any gift at all; "in vain, with no purpose," cp. 3:21; 34:20; Dt 16:16; 2Ch 8:13).
- **The Festival of Harvest**, also called the "Festival of Weeks" (34:22; Pentecost, Ac 2:1).
- **The Festival of Ingathering,** elsewhere called the "Festival of Booths" (Lv 23:34-36).

These three feasts celebrated God's grace—His redemption from slavery; the provision of abundant sustenance from the fields, vineyards, and trees. The men were to lead their families in obeying the Lord and in gratefully enjoying His goodness.

23:19b Boiling a young goat in milk does not seem to be the issue, but doing so in it own mother's milk (that which had sustained and nourished its life) seems to depict cruel treachery. As a proverb, this command may have prohibited the reversal of nature's design—exemplified here by a mother's milk, normally taken in by her young to sustain life, being used to surround or envelop her dead offspring—in order to satisfy a human craving (for the delicacy of a kid boiled in milk).

23:24-25 No one could take credit for leading the Israelites out of Egypt. God reminded them to worship *their* God *only*. They *must* destroy the gods left behind when God drove the idolaters out of the land. **The Lord** tolerates *no* rivals. The intolerance God demanded from His people in order to set them apart for Himself is a vivid picture of how resolutely He is against sin in a believer's life.

24:1-11 Moses ascended the mountain with his brother **Aaron**, his nephews **Nadab** and **Abihu**, and **70 of Israel's elders** (24:1,9-11; cp. 19:24). Many

Sabbaths and Festivals (23:10-19)

[10] "Sow your land for six years and
gather its produce. [11] But during the
seventh year you are to let it rest
and leave it uncultivated, so that
the poor among your people may
eat from it and the wild animals may
consume what they leave. Do the
same with your vineyard and your
olive grove.

[12] "Do your work for six days but
rest on the seventh day so that your
ox and your donkey may rest, and
the son of your female slave as well
as the foreign resident may be refreshed.

[13] "Pay strict attention to everything I have said to you. You must
not invoke the names of other gods;
they must not be heard on your
lips.[A]

[14] "Celebrate a festival in My honor
three times a year. [15] Observe the
Festival of •Unleavened Bread. As
I commanded you, you are to eat
unleavened bread for seven days at
the appointed time in the month
of Abib,[B] because you came out of
Egypt in that month. No one is to
appear before Me empty-handed.
[16] Also observe the Festival of Harvest[C] with the •firstfruits of your
produce from what you sow in the
field, and observe the Festival of
Ingathering[D] at the end of the year,
when you gather your produce[E]
from the field. [17] Three times a year
all your males are to appear before
the Lord God.

[18] "You must not offer the blood
of My sacrifices with anything leavened. The fat of My festival offering
must not remain until morning.

[19] "Bring the best of the firstfruits
of your land to the house of the Lord
your God.

"You must not boil a young goat in
its mother's milk.

Preview of Conquest (23:20-33)

[20] "I am going to send an angel before you to protect you on the way
and bring you to the place I have
prepared. [21] Be attentive to him and
listen to his voice. Do not defy[F] him,
because he will not forgive your acts
of rebellion, for My name is in him.
[22] But if you will carefully obey him
and do everything I say, then I will be
an enemy to your enemies and a foe
to your foes. [23] For My angel will go
before you and bring you to the land
of the Amorites, Hittites, Perizzites,
Canaanites, Hivites, and Jebusites,
and I will wipe them out. [24] You must
not bow down to their gods or worship them. Do not imitate their practices. Instead, demolish them[G] and
smash their sacred pillars to pieces.
[25] Worship the Lord your God, and
He[H] will bless your bread and your
water. I will remove illnesses from
you. [26] No woman will miscarry or be
childless in your land. I will give you
the full number of your days.

[27] "I will cause the people ahead
of you to feel terror[I] and throw into
confusion all the nations you come
to. I will make all your enemies turn
their backs to you in retreat. [28] I will
send the hornet[J] in front of you, and
it will drive the Hivites, Canaanites,
and Hittites away from you. [29] I will
not drive them out ahead of you in
a single year; otherwise, the land
would become desolate, and wild
animals would multiply against you.
[30] I will drive them out little by little
ahead of you until you have become
numerous[K] and take possession of
the land. [31] I will set your borders
from the •Red Sea to the Mediterranean Sea,[L] and from the wilderness
to the Euphrates River.[M] For I will
place the inhabitants of the land under your control, and you will drive
them out ahead of you. [32] You must
not make a covenant with them or
their gods. [33] They must not remain
in your land, or else they will make
you sin against Me. If you worship
their gods, it will be a snare for you."

Covenant Ceremony (24:1-18)

24 Then He said to Moses, "Go up
to the Lord, you and Aaron,

[A]**23:13** Lit *mouth* [B]**23:15** March–April; called Nisan in the post-exilic period; Neh 2:1; Est 3:7 [C]**23:16** The Festival of Harvest is called Festival of Weeks elsewhere; Ex 34:22. In the NT it is called Pentecost; Ac 2:1. [D]**23:16** The Festival of Ingathering is called Festival of Booths elsewhere; Lv 23:34-36. [E]**23:16** Lit *labors* [F]**23:21** Or *embitter* [G]**23:24** Probably the idols [H]**23:25** LXX, Vg read *I* [I]**23:27** Lit *will send terror of Me ahead of you* [J]**23:28** Or *send panic* [K]**23:30** Lit *fruitful* [L]**23:31** Lit *the Sea of the Philistines* [M]**23:31** Lit *the River*

Nadab, and Abihu, and 70 of Israel's elders, and bow in worship at a distance. 2 Moses alone is to approach the LORD, but the others are not to approach, and the people are not to go up with him."

3 Moses came and told the people all the commands of the LORD and all the ordinances. Then all the people responded with a single voice, "We will do everything that the LORD has commanded." 4 And Moses wrote down all the words of the LORD. He rose early the next morning and set up an altar and 12 pillars for the 12 tribes of Israel at the base of the mountain. 5 Then he sent out young Israelite men, and they offered •burnt offerings and sacrificed bulls as •fellowship offerings to the LORD. 6 Moses took half the blood and set it in basins; the other half of the blood he sprinkled on the altar. 7 He then took the covenant scroll and read it aloud to the people. They responded, "We will do and obey everything that the LORD has commanded."

8 Moses took the blood, sprinkled it on the people, and said, "This is the blood of the covenant that the LORD has made with you concerning all these words."

9 Then Moses went up with Aaron, Nadab, and Abihu, and 70 of Israel's elders, 10 and they saw the God of Israel. Beneath His feet was something like a pavement made of sapphire[A] stone, as clear as the sky itself. 11 God did not harm[B] the Israelite nobles; they saw Him, and they ate and drank.

12 The LORD said to Moses, "Come up to Me on the mountain and stay there so that I may give you the stone tablets with the law and commandments I have written for their instruction."

13 So Moses arose with his assistant Joshua and went up the mountain of God. 14 He told the elders, "Wait here for us until we return to you. Aaron and Hur are here with you. Whoever has a dispute should go to them." 15 When Moses went up the mountain, the cloud covered it. 16 The glory of the LORD settled on Mount Sinai, and the cloud covered it for six days. On the seventh day He called to Moses from the cloud. 17 The appearance of the LORD's glory to the Israelites was like a consuming fire on the mountaintop. 18 Moses entered the cloud as he went up the mountain, and he remained on the mountain 40 days and 40 nights.

An Offering for Yahweh (25:1-9)

25 The LORD spoke to Moses: 2 "Tell the Israelites to take an offering for Me. You are to take My offering from everyone who is willing to give. 3 This is the offering you are to receive from them: gold, silver, and bronze; 4 blue, purple, and scarlet yarn; fine linen and goat hair; 5 ram skins dyed red and manatee skins;[C] acacia wood; 6 oil for the light; spices for the anointing oil and for the fragrant incense; 7 and onyx[D] along with other gemstones for mounting on the •ephod and breastpiece.[E]

8 "They are to make a sanctuary for Me so that I may dwell among them, 9 You must make it according to all that I show you—the pattern of the tabernacle as well as the pattern of all its furnishings.

The Furnishings for the Tabernacle (25:10-40)

The Ark (25:10-22)

10 "They are to make an ark of acacia wood, 45 inches long, 27 inches wide, and 27 inches high.[F] 11 Overlay it with pure gold; overlay it both inside and out. Also make a gold molding all around it. 12 Cast four gold rings for it and place them on its four feet, two rings on one side and two rings on the other side. 13 Make poles of acacia wood and overlay them with gold. 14 Insert the poles into the rings on the sides of the ark in order to carry the ark with them. 15 The poles are to remain in the rings of the ark; they must not be removed from it. 16 Put the tablets of the •testimony that I will give you into the ark. 17 Make a •mercy seat of pure gold, 45 inches

questions remain unanswered about what these men actually **saw** (Hb *ra'ah*, "perceived, looked at, observed, discerned") with their eyes because no one could "see" God "and live" (33:20). The text emphasized that **they saw . . . God** by stating the fact twice and by noting that **God did not harm** them (24:9-11). The only descriptive detail of the vision, however, was what they saw **beneath His feet**, indicating that God made His presence visible and recognizable. The fellowship meal they shared in His presence confirmed peace among the participants, culminating the covenant process; and the breathtaking sight of their God, whose throne is in heaven, should have put to rest any doubts about God's favor toward His people.

25:1-9 The LORD commanded **the Israelites** as a group **to take an offering for** Him, but individuals gave the materials requested for making **a sanctuary** (Hb *miqdash*, "sacred or holy place") for God. A heart that loves always stirs (Hb *nadav*, "incites, impels, makes willing") a person **to give**. In addition to their freedom, the ex-slaves had left Egypt laden with the finest of materials in their possession as plunder from Yahweh's victory over Pharaoh (vv. 3-7; cp. 3:22; 11:2-3; 12:35-36). The people were called to offer to the Lord some of the abundance that He had lavished on them. God made it a priority to dwell **among** His people. The detailed instructions for building **the tabernacle** reflect the significance of the structure and of the worship offered to Him there.

25:10-16 Acacia wood was the required building material throughout the instructions. Among other woods, both native and imported, this hard and durable wood, resistant to decay and insects, was used by Egyptians for shipbuilding and coffins. Archaeologists have recently discovered on the Red Sea coast of Egypt what seems to be a ship breaker's yard, a site where new ships were assembled from lumber, prepared at a Nile shipyard, and where used ships were taken apart for recycling the lumber, which was stored in man-made caves. The products acquired on Egypt's sea expeditions included spices like frankincense and myrrh. The discovery provides another plausible explanation for the availability of wood meeting the description in this account; it could have been picked up during the trek, gathered at a similar site on the other side of the Red Sea, or simply transported directly from Egypt.

The **ark** (Hb *'aron*, "chest," not the word used for Noah's "ark" [Hb *tēvah*, 2:3; Gn 6–9]) identified the holiest place in the tabernacle. It was not an object to be worshiped but God's way of revealing His presence and emphasizing His holiness. The box

A **24:10** Or *lapis lazuli* B **24:11** Lit *not stretch out His hand against* C **25:5** Or *and dolphin skins*, or *and fine leather*; Hb obscure D **25:7** Or *carnelian* E **25:7** Traditionally, *breastplate* F **25:10** Lit *two and a half cubits its length, one and a half cubits its width, and one and a half cubits its height*

itself, resembling an oversized hope chest, was to be completely overlaid with **pure** [Hb *tahor*, "unalloyed," the impurities having been removed] **gold . . . inside and out.** The **poles** for carrying it stayed in place so that it was always read to move. **The testimony** (Hb *ʿēdut*, "witness; the law," esp. the Decalogue) was to be placed in the ark.

25:17-22 The ark's cover, called **a mercy seat** (Hb *kapporet*, "covering," used only of the ark; from *kaphar*, "cover or atone for sin") was designated by the Lord as the place where He would **meet with** (Hb *yaʿad*, "meet by appointment"; cp. Lv 16:2) the people's representative and from which He would speak to **command** His people. **Cherubim** were visual representations of unseen beings serving as guardians of holy places (cp. Gn 3:24).

25:30 The bread of the Presence served as a picture of the King's presence: He was at home, and a meal representing the fellowship He extended to His people was always ready (cp. Lv 24:5-6).

26:1-6 Ten curtains (Hb *yeriʿah*, "drape," from the verb *yaraʿ*, "tremble, quiver") comprised **the tabernacle** [Hb *mishkan*, "dwelling place, tent"] **itself**, forming **a single unit**. Made of the finest fabric these walls of cloth were beautiful, like nothing adorning an ordinary home. **Finely spun** (Hb *shazar*, lit "twisted together of many threads") suggests a difference in quality like that of modern bed linens priced according to "thread count." **Linen** (Hb *shēsh*; cp. Gn 41:42; Rv 19:14) means bleached "white," also symbolic of purity. **Blue** [Hb *tekēlet*, "shellfish" in the Mediterranean Sea from which a cerulean purple or violet dye was derived by crushing thousands of them], **purple** [Hb *ʾargaman*, "purple," a precious reddish-purple dye obtained from another Mediterranean shellfish], **and scarlet** [Hb *shani*, "*coccus*," an insect from which a "crimson" dye was obtained] were expensive, regal colors, and the design included depictions of **cherubim**. God provided precise measurements. **Gold clasps** and **blue yarn** held **the curtains together** as one.

long and 27 inches wide.[A] 18 Make two •cherubim of gold; make them of hammered work at the two ends of the mercy seat. 19 Make one cherub at one end and one cherub at the other end. At its two ends, make the cherubim of one piece with the mercy seat. 20 The cherubim are to have wings spread out above, covering the mercy seat with their wings, and are to face one another. The faces of the cherubim should be toward the mercy seat. 21 Set the mercy seat on top of the ark and put the testimony that I will give you into the ark. 22 I will meet with you there above the mercy seat, between the two cherubim that are over the ark of the testimony; I will speak with you from there about all that I command you regarding the Israelites.

The Table (25:23-30)

23 "You are to construct a table of acacia wood, 36 inches long, 18 inches wide, and 27 inches high.[B] 24 Overlay it with pure gold and make a gold molding all around it. 25 Make a three-inch[C] frame all around it and make a gold molding for it all around its frame. 26 Make four gold rings for it, and attach the rings to the four corners at its four legs. 27 The rings should be next to the frame as holders for the poles to carry the table. 28 Make the poles of acacia wood and overlay them with gold, and the table can be carried by them. 29 You are also to make its plates and cups, as well as its pitchers and bowls for pouring •drink offerings. Make them out of pure gold. 30 Put the •bread of the Presence on the table before Me at all times.

The Lampstand (25:31-40)

31 "You are to make a lampstand out of pure, hammered gold. It is to be made of one piece: its base and shaft, its ornamental cups, and its calyxes[D] and petals. 32 Six branches are to extend from its sides, three branches of the lampstand from one side and three branches of the lampstand from the other side. 33 There are to be three cups shaped like almond blossoms, each with a calyx and petals, on the first branch, and three cups shaped like almond blossoms, each with a calyx and petals, on the next branch. It is to be this way for the six branches that extend from the lampstand. 34 There are to be four cups shaped like almond blossoms on the lampstand shaft along with its calyxes and petals. 35 For the six branches that extend from the lampstand, a calyx must be under the first pair of branches from it, a calyx under the second pair of branches from it, and a calyx under the third pair of branches from it. 36 Their calyxes and branches are to be of one piece.[E] All of it is to be a single hammered piece of pure gold.

37 "Make seven lamps on it. Its lamps are to be set up so they illuminate the area in front of it. 38 Its snuffers and firepans must be of pure gold. 39 The lampstand[F] with all these utensils is to be made from 75 pounds[G] of pure gold. 40 Be careful to make them according to the pattern you have been shown on the mountain.

The Tabernacle Itself (26:1-36)

The Curtains (26:1-14)

26 "You are to construct the tabernacle itself with 10 curtains. You must make them of finely spun linen, and blue, purple, and scarlet yarn, with a design of •cherubim worked into them. 2 The length of each curtain should be 42 feet,[H] and the width of each curtain six feet;[I] all the curtains are to have the same measurements. 3 Five of the curtains should be joined together, and the other five curtains joined together. 4 Make loops of blue yarn on the edge of the last curtain[J] in the first set, and do the same on the edge of the outermost curtain in the second set. 5 Make 50 loops on the one curtain and make 50 loops on the edge of the curtain in the second set, so that the loops line up together. 6 Also make 50 gold clasps and join the curtains together with the clasps, so that the tabernacle may be a single unit.

[A]25:17 Lit *two and a half cubits its length, one and a half cubits its width* [B]25:23 Lit *two cubits its length, one cubit its width, and one and a half cubits its height* [C]25:25 Lit *Make it a handbreadth* [D]25:31 = the outer covering of a flower [E]25:36 Lit *piece with it* [F]25:39 Lit *It* [G]25:39 Lit *a talent* [H]26:2 Lit *28 cubits* [I]26:2 Lit *four cubits* [J]26:4 Lit *the one curtain on the end*

7 "You are to make curtains of goat hair for a tent over the tabernacle; make 11 of these curtains. 8 The length of each curtain should be 45 feet[A] and the width of each curtain six feet.[B] All 11 curtains are to have the same measurements. 9 Join five of the curtains by themselves, and the other six curtains by themselves. Then fold the sixth curtain double at the front of the tent. 10 Make 50 loops on the edge of the one curtain, the outermost in the first set, and make 50 loops on the edge of the corresponding curtain of the second set. 11 Make 50 bronze clasps; put the clasps through the loops and join the tent together so that it is a single unit. 12 As for the flap that is left over from the tent curtains, the leftover half curtain is to hang down over the back of the tabernacle. 13 The half yard[C] on one side and the half yard[D] on the other of what is left over along the length of the tent curtains should be hanging down over the sides of the tabernacle on either side to cover it. 14 Make a covering for the tent from ram skins dyed red and a covering of manatee skins[E] on top of that.

The Planks and Crossbars (26:15-30)

15 "You are to make upright planks[F] of acacia wood for the tabernacle. 16 The length of each plank is to be 15 feet,[G] and the width of each plank 27 inches.[H] 17 Each plank must be connected together with two tenons. Do the same for all the planks of the tabernacle. 18 Make the planks for the tabernacle as follows: 20 planks for the south side, 19 and make 40 silver bases under the 20 planks, two bases under the first plank for its two tenons, and two bases under the next plank for its two tenons; 20 20 planks for the second side of the tabernacle, the north side, 21 along with their 40 silver bases, two bases under the first plank and two bases under each plank; 22 and make six planks for the west side of the tabernacle. 23 Make two additional planks for the two back corners of the tabernacle. 24 They are to be paired at the bottom, and joined together[I] at the top in a single ring. So it should be for both of them; they will serve as the two corners. 25 There are to be eight planks with their silver bases: 16 bases; two bases under the first plank and two bases under each plank.

26 "You are to make five crossbars of acacia wood for the planks on one side of the tabernacle, 27 five crossbars for the planks on the other side of the tabernacle, and five crossbars for the planks of the back side of the tabernacle on the west. 28 The central crossbar is to run through the middle of the planks from one end to the other. 29 Then overlay the planks with gold, and make their rings of gold as the holders for the crossbars. Also overlay the crossbars with gold. 30 You are to set up the tabernacle according to the plan for it that you have been shown on the mountain.

The Veil (26:31-35)

31 "You are to make a veil of blue, purple, and scarlet yarn, and finely spun linen with a design of cherubim worked into it. 32 Hang it on four gold-plated posts of acacia wood that have gold hooks and that stand on four silver bases. 33 Hang the veil under the clasps[J] and bring the ark of the •testimony there behind the veil, so the veil will make a separation for you between the holy place and the most holy place. 34 Put the •mercy seat on the ark of the testimony in the most holy place. 35 Place the table outside the veil and the lampstand on the south side of the tabernacle, opposite the table; put the table on the north side.

The Entrance (26:36-37)

36 "For the entrance to the tent you are to make a screen embroidered with blue, purple, and scarlet yarn, and finely spun linen. 37 Make five posts of acacia wood for the screen and overlay them with gold; their hooks are to be gold, and you are to cast five bronze bases for them.

The Altar (27:1-8)

27 "You are to construct the altar of acacia wood. The altar

26:7-14 Curtains of goat hair would form **a tent** (Hb *'ohel*, "covering, tent" of a nomad, representing portability; "dwelling, home") of protection, a kind of roof for the interior rooms of the tabernacle. More durable but less valuable bronze clasps were required. Another layer of **ram skins** made the tent tougher. These were **dyed red,** however, and would generally not be visible, hidden between the goat hair tent cover inside and the third layer on the outside. Some regard this layer's color as a symbol of the blood of Christ's atonement, but the color may have served the practical purpose of drawing attention to any holes in the other two. It is unclear what animal's skin made up the third layer, but the **manatee** (Hb *tachash*; the English root means "soft-dressed leather, tanned skins") or dugong from the Red Sea is a possibility. The skins of a sea mammal would provide a tough waterproof covering of fine leather.

26:15-30 Again, the Lord reiterated that the structure must be **set up** according to His blueprints.

26:31-35 A veil (Hb *pareket*, used only of this "veil") as beautiful as the curtains and of the same design would divide the tabernacle, marking the space occupied by **the ark of the testimony** as the most holy of all. Outside the veil would be **the table on the north side** and the **lampstand on the south.** This area enclosed by the lovely tabernacle curtains was called **the holy place.**

26:36-37 The entrance to the tent was a **screen** (Hb *masak*, "covering," from the verb *sasak*, "cover, hedge, block, shut off, stop the approach"; cp. 25:20) of the same fine **linen** and beautifully **embroidered . . . yarn** but apparently designed without the cherubim symbolically guarding every length of the tabernacle's perimeter.

[A]26:8 Lit *30 cubits* [B]26:8 Lit *four cubits* [C]26:13 Lit *The cubit* [D]26:13 Lit *the cubit* [E]26:14 Or *of dolphin skins*, or *of fine leather*; Hb obscure [F]26:15 Or *frames*, or *beams* [G]26:16 Lit *10 cubits* [H]26:16 Lit *a cubit and a half* [I]26:24 Lit *and together they are to be complete* [J]26:33 The clasps that join the 10 curtains of the tabernacle; Ex 26:6

27:1-8 A priest entering the courtyard surrounding the tabernacle would first encounter a large **altar** made **of acacia wood** overlaid **with bronze**, a metal alloy capable of withstanding the heat of the burnt offerings. This altar was the structure on which sacrifices were made to satisfy God's provisional requirement for granting access to His presence. The book of Leviticus describes these sacrifices in detail.

27:9-19 The tabernacle was enclosed in a manner that visually established the boundary between God's holiness and man's sin. Nevertheless, the structure also conveyed God's mercy in establishing His presence among His people even in this provisional way.

27:20-21 These verses link the instruction for the tabernacle as God's dwelling place among His people and the instructions for setting apart a high priest. While the people slept, **Aaron and his sons** were responsible to make sure **the light** never went out.

28:1-5 The men appointed to serve **as priests** would wear clothing that reflected their sacred duties. The instructions specified three purposes for the special wardrobe:

- ***For glory***. The clothes would visually represent the weighty, heavily significant role of the priests and associate them with the place God would fill with His "glory."
- ***For beauty*** (Hb *tiph'eret*, "splendor, glory, honor"; cp. Dt 26:19; 1Ch 29:11; Ps 96:6). Just as the servants in a king's palace wore clothes appropriate to their setting, the ministers in Yahweh's royal abode would wear garments compatible with the lavish "beauty" of the tabernacle.
- ***For consecrating*** (Hb *qadash*, "setting apart, honoring, dedicating as sacred"), *the* ***priest*** *for service*. The special clothing would identify the wearer as someone set apart for the duties prescribed by Yahweh. The materials to be used also visually connected the priest with the tabernacle (Ex 28:5-6).

28:6-8 The **ephod** and its **waistband** were of one piece. **Embroidered** (Hb *chashav*, "carefully planned or thought out, valued and esteemed for design") and **artistically woven** (Hb *cheshev*, "ingenious work," used eight times in the Old Testament only of the priest's ephod and breastpiece) are related words, intended together to describe the intricate beauty and artistry of the clothing made especially for the high priest's ministry in the tabernacle.

must be square, $7\frac{1}{2}$ feet long, and $7\frac{1}{2}$ feet wide;[A] it must be $4\frac{1}{2}$ feet high.[B] 2 Make horns for it on its four corners; the horns are to be of one piece.[C] Overlay it with bronze. 3 Make its pots for removing ashes, and its shovels, basins, meat forks, and firepans; make all its utensils of bronze. 4 Construct a grate for it of bronze mesh, and make four bronze rings on the mesh at its four corners. 5 Set it below, under the altar's ledge,[D] so that the mesh comes halfway up[E] the altar. 6 Then make poles for the altar, poles of acacia wood, and overlay them with bronze. 7 The poles are to be inserted into the rings so that the poles are on two sides of the altar when it is carried. 8 Construct the altar with boards so that it is hollow. They are to make it just as it was shown to you on the mountain.

The Courtyard (27:9-19)

9 "You are to make the courtyard for the tabernacle. Make the hangings on the south of the courtyard out of finely spun linen, 150 feet[F] long on that side. 10 There are to be 20 posts and 20 bronze bases. The hooks and bands[G] of the posts must be silver. 11 Then make the hangings on the north side 150 feet[H] long. There are to be 20 posts and 20 bronze bases. The hooks and bands[G] of the posts must be silver. 12 Make the hangings of the courtyard on the west side 75 feet[I] long, including their 10 posts and 10 bases. 13 Make the hangings of the courtyard on the east side toward the sunrise 75 feet.[I] 14 Make the hangings on one side of the gate $22\frac{1}{2}$ feet,[J] including their three posts and their three bases. 15 And make the hangings on the other side $22\frac{1}{2}$ feet,[K] including their three posts and their three bases. 16 The gate of the courtyard is to have a thirty-foot[L] screen embroidered with blue, purple, and scarlet yarn, and finely spun linen. It is to have four posts including their four bases.

17 "All the posts around the courtyard are to be banded with silver and have silver hooks and bronze bases. 18 The length of the courtyard is to be 150 feet, the width 75 feet at each end, and the height $7\frac{1}{2}$ feet,[M] all of it made of finely spun linen. The bases of the posts must be bronze. 19 All the tools of the tabernacle for every use and all its tent pegs as well as all the tent pegs of the courtyard are to be made of bronze.

The Oil for the Lamp (27:20-21)

20 "You are to command the Israelites to bring you pure oil from crushed olives for the light, in order to keep the lamp burning continually. 21 In the tent of meeting outside the veil that is in front of the •testimony, Aaron and his sons are to tend the lamp from evening until morning before the LORD. This is to be a permanent statute for the Israelites throughout their generations.

The Priestly Garments (28:1-43)

The Holy Garments (28:1-5)

28 "Have your brother Aaron, with his sons, come to you from the Israelites to serve Me as priest—Aaron, his sons Nadab and Abihu, Eleazar and Ithamar. 2 Make holy garments for your brother Aaron, for glory and beauty. 3 You are to instruct all the skilled craftsmen,[N] whom I have filled with a spirit of wisdom, to make Aaron's garments for consecrating him to serve Me as priest. 4 These are the garments that they must make: a breastpiece, an •ephod, a robe, a specially woven tunic,[O] a turban, and a sash. They are to make holy garments for your brother Aaron and his sons so that they may serve Me as priests. 5 They should use[P] gold; blue, purple, and scarlet yarn; and fine linen.

The Ephod (28:6-14)

6 "They are to make the ephod of finely spun linen embroidered with gold, and with blue, purple, and scarlet yarn. 7 It must have two shoulder

[A] **27:1** Lit *five cubits in length and five cubits in width* [B] **27:1** Lit *wide; and its height three cubits* [C] **27:2** Lit *piece with it* [D] **27:5** Perhaps a ledge around the altar on which the priests could stand; Lv 9:22 [E] **27:5** Or *altar's rim, so that the grid comes halfway down* [F] **27:9** Lit *100 cubits* [G] **27:10,11** Or *connecting rods* [H] **27:11** Lit *100 cubits* [I] **27:12,13** Lit *50 cubits* [J] **27:14** Lit *15 cubits* [K] **27:15** Lit *15 cubits* [L] **27:16** Lit *twenty-cubit* [M] **27:18** Lit *be 100 by the cubit, and the width 50 by 50, and the height five cubits* [N] **28:3** Lit *all wise of heart* [O] **28:4** Hb obscure [P] **28:5** Lit *receive*

pieces attached to its two edges so
that it can be joined together. 8 The
artistically woven waistband that is
on the ephod[A] must be of one piece,[B]
according to the same workmanship
of gold, of blue, purple, and scarlet
yarn, and of finely spun linen.
9 "Take two onyx stones and engrave
on them the names of Israel's sons:
10 six of their names on the first stone
and the remaining six names on the
second stone, in the order of their
birth. 11 Engrave the two stones with
the names of Israel's sons as a gem
cutter engraves a seal. Mount them,
surrounded with gold filigree settings.
12 Fasten both stones on the shoulder pieces of the ephod as memorial
stones for the Israelites. Aaron will
carry their names on his two shoulders before the LORD as a reminder.
13 Fashion gold filigree settings 14 and
two chains of pure gold; you will make
them of braided cord work, and attach
the cord chains to the settings.

The Breastpiece (28:15-30)

15 "You are to make an embroidered
breastpiece for making decisions.[C]
Make it with the same workmanship as the ephod; make it of gold,
of blue, purple, and scarlet yarn,
and of finely spun linen. 16 It must
be square and folded double, nine
inches long and nine inches wide.[D]
17 Place a setting of gemstones[E] on it,
four rows of stones:

The first row should be
a row of carnelian, topaz,
and emerald;[F]
18 the second row,
a turquoise,[G] a sapphire,[H]
and a diamond;[I]
19 the third row,
a jacinth,[J] an agate,
and an amethyst;
20 and the fourth row,
a beryl, an onyx, and a jasper.

They should be adorned with gold
filigree in their settings. 21 The 12
stones are to correspond to the
names of Israel's sons. Each stone
must be engraved like a seal, with
one of the names of the 12 tribes.
22 "You are to make braided
chains[K] of pure gold cord work for
the breastpiece. 23 Fashion two gold
rings for the breastpiece and attach
them to its two corners. 24 Then attach the two gold cords to the two
gold rings at the corners of the
breastpiece. 25 Attach the other ends
of the two cords to the two filigree
settings, and in this way attach
them to the ephod's shoulder pieces
in the front. 26 Make two other gold
rings and put them at the two other
corners of the breastpiece on the
edge that is next to the inner border of the ephod. 27 Make two more
gold rings and attach them to the
bottom of the ephod's two shoulder pieces on its front, close to its
seam,[L] and above the ephod's woven
waistband. 28 The craftsmen are to
tie the breastpiece from its rings to
the rings of the ephod with a cord
of blue yarn, so that the breastpiece
is above the ephod's waistband
and does not come loose from the
ephod.
29 "Whenever he enters the sanctuary, Aaron is to carry the names
of Israel's sons over his heart on the
breastpiece for decisions, as a continual reminder before the LORD.
30 Place the •Urim and Thummim
in the breastpiece for decisions, so
that they will also be over Aaron's
heart whenever he comes before
the LORD. Aaron will continually
carry the means of decisions for the
Israelites over his heart before the
LORD.

The Robe (28:31-35)

31 "You are to make the robe of the
ephod entirely of blue yarn. 32 There
should be an opening at its top in
the center of it. Around the opening,
there should be a woven collar with
an opening like that of body armor[M]
so that it does not tear. 33 Make
pomegranates of blue, purple, and
scarlet yarn[N] on its lower hem and
all around it. Put gold bells between

[A] **28:8** Lit *waistband of its ephod, which is on it* [B] **28:8** Lit *piece with the ephod* [C] **28:15** Used for determining God's will; Nm 27:21 [D] **28:16** Lit *a span its length and a span its width* [E] **28:17** Many of these stones cannot be identified with certainty. [F] **28:17** Or *beryl* [G] **28:18** Or *malachite*, or *garnet* [H] **28:18** Or *lapis lazuli* [I] **28:18** Hb obscure; LXX, Vg read *jasper* [J] **28:19** Hb obscure [K] **28:22** The same chains mentioned in v. 14 [L] **28:27** The place where the shoulder pieces join the front of the ephod [M] **28:32** Hb obscure [N] **28:33** Sam, LXX add *of finely spun linen*

28:9-14 Two onyx stones, probably black, each engraved with **six** of the **names** of Israel's tribes, set in **gold**, and attached to the ephod's **shoulder pieces** would constantly remind the high priest of the responsibility he bore in representing all the people before the Lord. Two **gold** cords were required for attaching the breastpiece.

28:17-29 Four rows of three **gemstones**, one for each of the 12 tribes, would be set in **gold** to adorn the front of the breastpiece that hung by **gold cords** from the shoulders. The 12 sons of Israel were thus represented by stones—hard, solid material that could, nevertheless, be cut and polished and fashioned into gems of beauty (cp. Rv 21:9-27). The engraved onyx stones were certainly of equal weight and demonstrated the *unity* of the two groups of six. On the breastpiece, however, each stone was different and corresponded *individually* to one of the 12 tribes, according to the names **engraved like a seal** (Hb *chotam*, "signet ring"), one name per stone. Specific instructions were given for fastening **the breastpiece** to the ephod so that it hung **above the . . . waistband** and **over** the priest's **heart**.

28:30 This article of the high priest's garments served as a beautiful, tangible, and perpetual reminder both to the priest and the people that the priest served in the tabernacle on the people's behalf. Called **the breastpiece for decisions** (Hb *mishpat*; cp. vv. 15,29), the pouch held the mysterious **Urim** [Hb "lights, flames"] **and Thummim** [Hb "perfection," pl. of *tom*, "integrity, completeness, innocence"], which the priest used to determine God's judgment on various matters.

28:31-35 The **blue** seamless and sleeveless **robe** was worn under the ephod. Even practical details were included in the tailoring instructions—the **opening** for putting on the garment had to include a military-style **woven collar**, which would prevent it from tearing when pulled over the head. From the **lower hem** would hang a row of **pomegranates** of **yarn**, matching the ephod and breastpiece, alternating with **gold bells**, each of which would ring independently. **Pomegranates** (Hb *rimmon*, also the name of a town) generally symbolized fruitfulness because of the many seeds contained within them, but what God intended this fruit to represent to His people is not clear. **Bells** enabled the priest to be heard when he went alone into the holy of holies—if there was no sound, he could be presumed dead, struck down in the holy presence of God.

28:36-38 The long shirt-like garment worn next to the priest's skin and the turban worn on his head were woven from fine linen representing righteousness. Lest anyone, especially the priest, forget the reason for wearing the particular garments described, he would also wear an engraved **gold** sign on his **forehead**, attached to his **turban**, unmistakably identifying him as the one set apart for carrying the burden of Israel's **guilt** (Hb *'awon*, "iniquity, perversity, punishment for sin") to the place of sacrifice, atonement, and forgiveness. **Always** the gold plate would be worn because he never entered the holy place for his own sake alone but for the Israelites to **find acceptance** [Hb *ratson*, "delight, pleasure, satisfaction; favor, goodwill," the only use of this word in Exodus] **with the LORD.**

28:42-43 Wearing the prescribed **linen undergarments** under the tunic was a prerequisite even for entering the tabernacle or coming near **the altar** and prevented any inappropriate exposure of the body, which was to remain covered (cp. Ezk 44:18).

29:1-9 This passage records instructions that were to be given to Moses and carried out after the tabernacle was established (see Lv 8–9).

29:10-14 As Moses, when Aaron and his sons entered **the tent of meeting**, they would immediately encounter **the altar**. Laying **their hands on the bull's head** would symbolically identify Aaron and his sons as "living sacrifices" for which **the bull** would be slaughtered as their substitute. **Some of the bull's blood** would mark the altar's **horns** to which all future sacrifices would be tied. The rest would surround and soak into the ground under the altar. The best parts of the bull had to be burned on the altar—committed to the fire to be completely consumed. The rest of the bull would also be burned but **outside the camp** because it represented sin.

29:15-18 The first **ram** offering followed a similar procedure at first. This animal's **blood** would be sprinkled **on all sides of the altar**, setting it apart and dedicating it to Yahweh. The ram's head would be separated from the body. The blood was to be completely rinsed from the rest of the body, which was **cut . . . into pieces**, and all—the whole, including the rinsed **entrails**—would be burned. The ram's lifeblood, representing the lives of the priests, made the altar holy as an instrument of worship. The ram's body was given as well—nothing was held back for any other purpose. Once given to the flames, the offering could not be recovered; symbolically it

them all the way around, 34 so that gold bells and pomegranates alternate around the lower hem of the robe. 35 The robe must be worn by Aaron whenever he ministers, and its sound will be heard when he enters the sanctuary before the LORD and when he exits, so that he does not die.

The Turban (28:36-38)

36 "You are to make a pure gold medallion and engrave it, like the engraving of a seal:

HOLY TO THE LORD.

37 Fasten it to a cord of blue yarn so it can be placed on the turban; the medallion is to be on the front of the turban. 38 It will be on Aaron's forehead so that Aaron may bear the •guilt connected with the holy offerings that the Israelites consecrate as all their holy gifts. It is always to be on his forehead, so that they may find acceptance with the LORD.

The Tunics, Sashes, and Headbands (28:39-41)

39 "You are to weave the tunic from fine linen, make a turban of fine linen, and make an embroidered sash. 40 Make tunics, sashes, and headbands for Aaron's sons to give them glory and beauty. 41 Put these on your brother Aaron and his sons; then anoint, ordain,[A] and consecrate them, so that they may serve Me as priests.

The Linen Undergarments (28:42-43)

42 Make them linen undergarments to cover their naked bodies; they must extend from the waist[B] to the thighs. 43 These must be worn by Aaron and his sons whenever they enter the tent of meeting or approach the altar to minister in the sanctuary area, so that they do not incur guilt and die. This is to be a permanent statute for Aaron and for his future descendants.

Consecration (29:1-37)

Aaron and His Sons (29:1-36a)

29 "This is what you are to do for them to consecrate them to serve Me as priests. Take a young bull and two unblemished rams, 2 with unleavened bread, unleavened cakes mixed with oil, and unleavened wafers coated with oil. Make them out of fine wheat flour, 3 put them in a basket, and bring them in the basket, along with the bull and two rams. 4 Bring Aaron and his sons to the entrance to the tent of meeting and wash them with water. 5 Then take the garments and clothe Aaron with the tunic, the robe for the •ephod, the ephod itself, and the breastpiece; fasten the ephod on him with its woven waistband. 6 Put the turban on his head and place the holy diadem on the turban. 7 Take the anointing oil, pour it on his head, and anoint him. 8 You must also bring his sons and clothe them with tunics. 9 Tie the sashes on Aaron and his sons and fasten headbands on them. The priesthood is to be theirs by a permanent statute. This is the way you will ordain Aaron and[C] his sons.

10 "You are to bring the bull to the front of the tent of meeting, and Aaron and his sons must lay their hands on the bull's head. 11 Slaughter the bull before the LORD at the entrance to the tent of meeting. 12 Take some of the bull's blood and apply it to the horns of the altar with your finger; then pour out all the rest of the blood at the base of the altar. 13 Take all the fat that covers the entrails, the fatty lobe of the liver, and the two kidneys with the fat on them, and burn them on the altar. 14 But burn up the bull's flesh, its hide, and its dung outside the camp; it is a •sin offering.

15 "Take one ram, and Aaron and his sons are to lay their hands on the ram's head. 16 You are to slaughter the ram, take its blood, and sprinkle it on all sides of the altar. 17 Cut the ram into pieces. Wash its entrails and shanks, and place them with its head and its pieces on the altar. 18 Then burn the whole ram on the altar; it is a •burnt offering to the LORD. It is a pleasing aroma, a fire offering to the LORD.

19 "You are to take the second

[A]28:41 Lit *anoint them, fill their hand* [B]28:42 Lit *loins* [C]29:9 Lit *you will fill the hand of Aaron and the hand of*; Ex 29:23-24 ram, and Aaron and his sons must lay their hands on the ram's head. 20 Slaughter the ram, take some of its blood, and put it on Aaron's right earlobe, on his sons' right earlobes, on the thumbs of their right hands, and on the big toes of their right feet. Sprinkle the remaining blood on all sides of the altar. 21 Take some of the blood that is on the altar and some of the anointing oil, and sprinkle them on Aaron and his garments, as well as on his sons and their garments. In this way, he and his garments will become holy, as well as his sons and their garments.

22 "Take the fat from the ram, the fat tail, the fat covering the entrails, the fatty lobe of the liver, the two kidneys and the fat on them, and the right thigh (since this is a ram for ordination[A]); 23 take one loaf of bread, one cake of bread made with oil, and one wafer from the basket of unleavened bread that is before the LORD; 24 and put all of them in the hands of Aaron and his[B] sons and wave them as a presentation offering before the LORD. 25 Take them from their hands and burn them on the altar on top of the burnt offering, as a pleasing aroma before the LORD; it is a fire offering to the LORD.

26 "Take the breast from the ram of Aaron's ordination and wave it as a presentation offering before the LORD; it is to be your portion. 27 Consecrate for Aaron and his sons the breast of the presentation offering that is waved and the thigh of the contribution that is lifted up from the ram of ordination. 28 This will belong to Aaron and his sons as a regular portion from the Israelites, for it is a contribution. It will be the Israelites' contribution from their •fellowship sacrifices, their contribution to the LORD.

29 "The holy garments that belong to Aaron are to belong to his sons after him, so that they can be anointed and ordained[C] in them. 30 Any priest who is one of his sons and who succeeds him and enters the tent of meeting to minister in the sanctuary must wear them for seven days.

31 "You are to take the ram of ordination and boil its flesh in a holy place. 32 Aaron and his sons are to eat the meat of the ram and the bread that is in the basket at the entrance to the tent of meeting. 33 They must eat those things by which •atonement was made at the time of their ordination[D] and consecration. An unauthorized person must not eat them, for these things are holy. 34 If any of the meat of ordination or any of the bread is left until morning, burn up what is left over. It must not be eaten because it is holy.

35 "This is what you are to do for Aaron and his sons based on all I have commanded you. Take seven days to ordain them. 36 Sacrifice a bull as a sin offering each day for atonement.

The Altar (29:36b-37)

Purify[E] the altar when you make atonement for it, and anoint it in order to consecrate it. 37 For seven days you must make atonement for the altar and consecrate it. The altar will become especially holy; whatever touches the altar will become holy.

Regular Offerings (29:38-46)

38 "This is what you are to offer regularly on the altar every day: two year-old lambs. 39 In the morning offer one lamb, and at twilight offer the other lamb. 40 With the first lamb offer two quarts[F] of fine flour mixed with one quart[G] of oil from crushed olives, and a •drink offering of one quart[G] of wine. 41 You are to offer the second lamb at twilight. Offer a •grain offering and a drink offering with it, like the one in the morning, as a pleasing aroma, a fire offering to the LORD. 42 This will be a regular burnt offering throughout your generations at the entrance to the tent of meeting before the LORD, where I will meet you[H] to speak with you. 43 I will also meet with the Israelites there, and that place will be consecrated by My glory. 44 I will consecrate the tent of meeting and the altar; I will

A 29:22 The priest would normally receive the right thigh to be eaten, but here it is burned; Lv 7:32-34. B 29:24 Lit *in the hands of his* C 29:29 Lit *him for anointing in them and for filling their hand* D 29:33 Lit *made to fill their hand* E 29:36 Or *Make a sin offering on* F 29:40 Lit *offer a tenth* G 29:40 Lit *a fourth of a hin* H 29:42 = Moses

belonged entirely to the Lord to whom it had been given—a "no turning back" event.

29:19-25 Two sacrifices preceded the offering of **the second ram**. Symbolically, the first dealt with the sin carried by Aaron and his sons. The second represented the priests' complete dedication of their lives (29:18). Finally, another ram upon which they laid their hands would be slaughtered. This time, Moses was instructed to mark parts of the priests' bodies that were not covered by clothing. The text does not explain the significance of this ritual. Perhaps blood specifically dedicated the ears to hear God's word, the priests' hands to perform His work, and their feet to walk in His ways. To mark the tip of each part on the **right** side presumably signified the inclusion of both. Moses would fill their hands with the best parts of **the ram for ordination** (Hb *millu'*, "inauguration to or delivery of an office, installation, consecration"), its **right** thigh, and three different pieces of **unleavened bread**. What was given to them they would actively present to Yahweh before Moses removed the items and burned them on top of the smoldering remains of the burnt offering.

29:26-28 God designated the meatiest piece of the animal as Moses' **portion**, which would serve as Moses' **presentation offering**, consecrated **for Aaron and his sons**. This "portion" also represented the Israelites' **contribution** (Hb *terumah*, "offering," from the verb *rum*, "lift up, raise, exalt").

29:36-37 The entire procedure would be followed **for seven days**, representing completeness, whenever the high priest was installed. After this initial ceremony, **the altar** would **become especially holy** (Hb *qodesh qodesh*). It could not be used, therefore, by one who was not a priest. Furthermore, whatever touched it had to be regarded as completely set apart for the Lord alone; the altar was to be an object treated with the highest respect as it represented the heavy cost borne for covering sin and restoring fellowship with sinful people.

29:38-45 Assuming the establishment of a holy priesthood and a holy altar, instructions regarding daily offerings could be given. Morning and evening followed by morning and evening, day after day without fail, burnt offerings would be made on the altar. Every 12 hours a **year-old lamb** would be offered with **flour . . . oil** and **wine**. Offered at the tabernacle's **entrance**, these **regular** sacrifices continually yet provisionally atoned for sin until Jesus' self-sacrifice as *the* "Lamb of God" (Jn 1:29; Heb 10:11-18).

29:46 When its context is expanded beyond the Pentateuch and even beyond the Old Testament to the entire canon of Scripture, the exodus also succinctly expresses the most basic theme of Scripture. Yahweh, the one and only **God**, has orchestrated all of history to rescue people from self-enslavement to sin so that **they will know** Him intimately, exclusively, and irrevocably as **their God.**

30:1-10 This **altar** was designed specifically and exclusively for the purpose of burning **fragrant incense** in the tabernacle. Like the other furnishings in the tabernacle itself, it was made with **acacia wood** and overlaid with **pure gold**. Like the dimensions of the holy of holies, it was shaped as a **square**. Its holiness would be renewed with the application of **blood** from the annual **offering** of **atonement**. On a twice-daily basis, the priests would keep the incense burning—representing the prayers and intercession of God's people, their communication to Him, just as they kept the lights of the lampstand burning—representing the light of His holy presence (cp. Ps 141:2).

30:11-16 Numbers 1 records the **census** that was conducted to organize Israel's army. The **half shekel** contributed by each man of fighting age would verify the registration count. As **a ransom** (Hb *kopher*, "price of a life, redemption price," cp. Ex 21:30) the payment emphasized equality before God—no individual was deemed to be worth more than another; it reminded the rest of the Israelites of the universal need for each person's life to be ransomed; and it provided **for the service of the** tabernacle, such as the purchase of the costly ingredients of the prescribed incense. The collection of thousands of silver coins, each representing the life of a treasured son of Israel putting his life on the line at the Lord's command, would visually remind the priests of God's perspective on atonement. In most cases, in addition to his own life, each man's half shekel signified that wives and children, mothers and sisters and younger siblings whose lives had been ransomed by the Lord (Is 43:3), were receiving atonement symbolized by the regular sacrifices (Heb 10:1-4).

30:17-21 Washing outwardly represented inward purification, especially in the requirement that priests must wash before approaching **the altar**. The **basin** also served a practical purpose. The priests' **hands and feet** would be dirty and blood-stained after performing the sacrifices on the altar. The **water** placed between the altar and the tabernacle made cleansing convenient as well

also consecrate Aaron and his sons
to serve Me as priests. 45 I will dwell
among the Israelites and be their
God. 46 And they will know that I am
•Yahweh their God, who brought
them out of the land of Egypt, so that
I might dwell among them. I am Yahweh their God.

The Altar for Burning Incense (30:1-10)

30 "You are to make an altar for
the burning of incense; make
it of acacia wood. 2 It must be square,
18 inches long and 18 inches wide;[A]
it must be 36 inches high.[B] Its horns
must be of one piece.[C] 3 Overlay
its top, all around its sides, and its
horns with pure gold; make a gold
molding all around it. 4 Make two
gold rings for it under the molding
on two of its sides; put these on opposite sides of it to be holders for
the poles to carry it with. 5 Make
the poles of acacia wood and overlay
them with gold.

6 "You are to place the altar in front
of the veil by the ark of the •testimo-
ny—in front of the •mercy seat that
is over the testimony—where I will
meet with you. 7 Aaron must burn
fragrant incense on it; he must burn
it every morning when he tends the
lamps. 8 When Aaron sets up the
lamps at twilight, he must burn incense. There is to be an incense offering before the LORD throughout
your generations. 9 You must not offer unauthorized incense on it, or a
•burnt or •grain offering; you are not
to pour a •drink offering on it.

10 "Once a year Aaron is to perform
the purification rite[D] on the horns of
the altar. Throughout your generations he is to perform the purification
rite[D] for[E] it once a year, with the blood
of the •sin offering for •atonement. The
altar is especially holy to the LORD."

The Atonement Money (30:11-16)

11 The LORD spoke to Moses: 12 "When
you take a census of the Israelites to
register them, each of the men must
pay a ransom for himself to the LORD
as they are registered. Then no plague
will come on them as they are registered. 13 Everyone who is registered
must pay half a •shekel[F] according to
the sanctuary shekel (20 *gerahs* to the
shekel). This half shekel is a contribution to the LORD. 14 Each man who is
registered, 20 years old or more, must
give this contribution to the LORD.
15 The wealthy may not give more and
the poor may not give less than half a
shekel when giving the contribution
to the LORD to atone for[G] your lives.
16 Take the atonement money[H] from
the Israelites and use it for the service
of the tent of meeting. It will serve as
a reminder for the Israelites before
the LORD to atone for[G] your lives."

The Bronze Basin (30:17-21)

17 The LORD spoke to Moses: 18 "Make
a bronze basin for washing and a
bronze stand for it. Set it between
the tent of meeting and the altar, and
put water in it. 19 Aaron and his sons
must wash their hands and feet from
the basin. 20 Whenever they enter the
tent of meeting or approach the altar
to minister by burning up an offering to the LORD, they must wash with
water so that they will not die. 21 They
must wash their hands and feet so
that they will not die; this is to be a
permanent statute for them, for Aaron and his descendants throughout
their generations."

The Anointing Oil (30:22-33)

22 The LORD spoke to Moses:
23 "Take for yourself the finest spices:
12½ pounds[I] of liquid myrrh, half
as much (6¼ pounds[J]) of fragrant
cinnamon, 6¼ pounds[J] of fragrant
cane, 24 12½ pounds[I] of cassia (by
the sanctuary shekel), and one gallon[K] of olive oil. 25 Prepare from
these a holy anointing oil, a scented
blend, the work of a perfumer; it will
be holy anointing oil.

26 "With it you are to anoint the tent
of meeting, the ark of the testimony,
27 the table with all its utensils, the
lampstand with its utensils, the altar
of incense, 28 the altar of burnt offering with all its utensils, and the basin

[A]30:2 Lit *one cubit its length and one cubit its width* [B]30:2 Lit *wide; and two cubits its height* [C]30:2 Lit *piece with it* [D]30:10 Or *to make atonement* [E]30:10 Or *on* [F]30:13 About 2/5 of an ounce of silver [G]30:15,16 Or *to ransom* [H]30:16 Lit *the silver of the atonement* [I]30:23,24 Lit *500* (shekels) [J]30:23 Lit *250* (shekels) [K]30:24 Lit *a hin*

>WORD|*study*

30:23 Spices (Hb *besem*, "good smell or fragrance") or sweet "perfumes" were used in the "beauty treatments" required of Esther before she and the other women in the harem of Ahasuerus were presented to the king as candidates from whom he would choose a new wife (Est 2:12). The word is used several times in the Song of Songs referring to the allurement of the bride's perfume and garden (Sg 4:10,14,16), to the pleasing smell of the groom's cheeks and gardens (Sg 5:13), and figuratively to the bride's beckoning her love to hurry to her (Sg 8:14). This term also was an ingredient used in medicine and for preparing anointing oil.

Myrrh (Hb *mor*, sap of a balsam bush), along with "aloes and cassia," perfume all the clothing of the King in His wedding song (Ps 45:8). Six months of "treatments with oil of myrrh" were also included in the "perfumes and cosmetics" of Esther's beautification (Est 2:12), and a seductive woman is described as luring naïve men to her bed perfumed with "myrrh, aloes and cinnamon" (Pr 7:17). In the Song of Songs, the bride describes her "love" as "a sachet of myrrh" (Sg 1:13). Solomon was accompanied by the scent of "myrrh and frankincense" (Sg 3:6), the groom describes his bride as having the same scent (Sg 4:6,14; 5:1), and she describes the groom's lips as "dripping with flowing myrrh." These examples indicate that sweet-smelling fragrances were used to inflame the desire of both a bride and groom and to enhance the pleasure and intimacy of the physical union intended for a husband and wife in covenant relationship. This spice was very commonly used to prepare the body for burial (Lk 23:56; Jn 19:39).

Cinnamon (bark of the cinnamon tree) is also mentioned in Pr 7:17 and Sg 4:14. Perhaps it is best known as a condiment for enhancing foods.

Cane (Hb *qaneh*, "aromatic *calamus*," a pink-colored pith from the root of a reed plant, known as "sweet flag" in North America), an imported spice also mentioned in Sg 4:14, was regarded as an aphrodisiac in ancient Egypt (see Is 43:24; Jr 6:20).

Cassia (Hb *qiddah*, aromatic bark of an evergreen tree, which also produces a fragrance similar to cinnamon) and myrrh were among the aromatics used in the embalming process in ancient Egypt (cp. Jn 19:39). Both cassia and cane are mentioned as merchandise in Ezk 27:19.

with its stand. 29 Consecrate them and they will be especially holy. Whatever touches them will be consecrated. 30 Anoint Aaron and his sons and consecrate them to serve Me as priests.

31 "Tell the Israelites: This will be My holy anointing oil throughout your generations. 32 It must not be used for ordinary anointing on a person's body, and you must not make anything like it using its formula. It is holy, and it must be holy to you. 33 Anyone who blends something like it or puts some of it on an unauthorized person must be cut off from his people."

The Sacred Incense (30:34-38)

34 The LORD said to Moses: "Take fragrant spices: stacte, onycha, and galbanum; the spices and pure frankincense are to be in equal measures. 35 Prepare expertly blended incense from these; it is to be seasoned with salt, pure and holy. 36 Grind some of it into a fine powder and put some in front of the testimony in the tent of meeting, where I will meet with you. It must be especially holy to you. 37 As for the incense you are making, you must not make any for yourselves using its formula. It is to be regarded by you as sacred to the LORD. 38 Anyone who makes something like it to smell its fragrance must be cut off from his people."

The Appointment of Artisans (31:1-11)

31 The LORD also spoke to Moses: 2 "Look, I have appointed by name Bezalel son of Uri, son of Hur, of the tribe of Judah. 3 I have filled him with God's Spirit, with wisdom, understanding, and ability in every craft 4 to design artistic works in gold, silver, and bronze, 5 to cut gemstones for mounting, and to carve wood for work in every craft. 6 I have also selected Oholiab[A] son of Ahisamach, of the tribe of Dan, to be with him. I have placed wisdom within every skilled craftsman[B] in order to make all that I have commanded you: 7 the tent of meeting, the ark of the •testimony, the •mercy seat that is on top of it, and all the other furnishings of the tent— 8 the table with its utensils, the pure gold lampstand with all its

A31:6 LXX, Syr read *Eliab* B31:6 Lit *every person skilled of heart*

as necessary before entering the holy place.

30:22-33 God specified the ingredients for the **oil** to be used in the priests' ordination ceremony (v. 30; 29:7,21,29) and in the consecration of all the tabernacles' furnishings (30:26-29). His words heavily emphasized the holiness of this oil, which is a picture of the Holy Spirit who indwells believers. Made from the **finest** [Hb *ro'sh*, lit. "head, chief," connoting "that which is highest, supreme, choice"] **spices**, the formula was special and was not to be duplicated or imitated. Spices, aromatic and often pungent, were used in preparing food, in mixing oils to be used for sacred tasks such as anointings or incense, as well as in preparing perfumes and ointments for personal hygiene and for burying the dead.

30:34-38 Like the formula for anointing oil, the **incense** prepared for the tabernacle was to be regarded as **sacred** and exclusive to its prescribed purpose. Despite variations in value, the recipe called for **equal measures** of the following ingredients:

- **stacte** (Hb *nataph*, "storax") is an aromatic gum resin that drops from the bush producing it;
- **onycha** (Hb *shechelet*) is derived from burning the shell or membrane of a mollusk found in the Red Sea;
- **galbanum** (Hb *chelbenah*) refers to a gum resin from the perennial plant *Ferula galbaniflua*. The plant exudes a milky liquid resembling teardrops when dried;
- **pure frankincense** (Hb *levonah*, from *lavan*, "white"), a white gum resin derived from the Boswellia tree, in ancient times rivaled gold in terms of economic value. Frankincense is mentioned three times in the Song of Songs—always in conjunction with myrrh (Sg 3:6; 4:6,14)—and in various other contexts (e.g., Neh 13:5-9; Is 60:6; Jr 6:20).

The **LORD** also required the incense to be salted (cp. Lv 2:13) to ensure that it remained **pure** [Hb *tahor*, "clean," esp. in a ceremonial or moral sense] **and holy**.

31:1-11 God singularly honored the tribes **of Judah** and **Dan** with His appointment of two men to lead and oversee the numerous artistic elements of the tabernacle's construction (see 35:30–36:2). They were entrusted with the unique opportunity to fulfill the Lord's detailed specifications with both precision and creativity.

31:18 The "Torah" generally refers to the first five books of the Bible, or Pentateuch, but it specifically refers to the covenant law, or Ten Commandments, written by God on **stone tablets** and given to Israel. A Jewish tradition views the Torah given at Mount Sinai as the marriage contract, or *ketubah* (Hb "that which is written"), between Yahweh and Israel. Throughout the Old Testament, Israel's role is that of the beloved wife of Yahweh; and her pursuit of other gods, therefore, is consistently portrayed as adultery and harlotry.

utensils, the altar of incense, [9] the
altar of •burnt offering with all its
utensils, the basin with its stand—
[10] the specially woven[A] garments,
both the holy garments for Aaron
the priest and the garments for
his sons to serve as priests, [11] the
anointing oil, and the fragrant incense for the sanctuary. They must
make them according to all that I
have commanded you."

Yahweh's Sabbath (31:12-17)

[12] The LORD said to Moses: [13] "Tell
the Israelites: You must observe My
Sabbaths, for it is a sign between
Me and you throughout your generations, so that you will know
that I am •Yahweh who sets you
apart. [14] Observe the Sabbath, for
it is holy to you. Whoever profanes
it must be put to death. If anyone
does work on it, that person must
be cut off from his people. [15] Work
may be done for six days, but on
the seventh day there must be a
Sabbath of complete rest, dedicated to the LORD. Anyone who does
work on the Sabbath day must be
put to death. [16] The Israelites must
observe the Sabbath, celebrating it
throughout their generations as a
perpetual covenant. [17] It is a sign
forever between Me and the Israelites, for in six days the LORD made
the heavens and the earth, but on
the seventh day He rested and was
refreshed."

The Stone Tablets (31:18)

[18] When He finished speaking with
Moses on Mount Sinai, He gave him

[A] **31:10** Hb obscure

BIBLICAL WOMANHOOD A Document of Commitment

For Jewish marriages, the *ketubah* is a unilateral contract required from the groom. At the wedding (Hb *kiddushin*, lit "sanctification"), which officially sanctifies and blesses this contract, the *ketubah* is read aloud. This custom is seen as a reenactment of the giving of the law in Ex 24:7—"He then took the covenant scroll and read it aloud to the people. They responded, 'We will do and obey everything that the LORD has commanded.'" The properly signed and witnessed document is received by the bride, who is entrusted with its safekeeping. The *ketubah* is often written in an aesthetically beautiful way as an illuminated manuscript that many couples display as a work of art in itself.

Because the *ketubah* does not serve as a religious or ceremonial document, it is written in Aramaic, the legal language of Talmudic law, rather than in Hebrew. In the State of Israel, the *ketubah* is upheld as a legally binding and enforceable agreement. The document is signed by the groom and witnessed by two people who, in effect, attest to the groom's promises. The bride is not required to sign because she receives this commitment; it is a unilateral rather than a mutual agreement. The traditionally worded *ketubah* attests to the groom's proposal to the bride with the statement: "You are hereby betrothed unto me according to the law of Moses and Israel." Similarly, in the document the witnesses confirm the bride's willing acceptance of the proposal as she ". . . consented and became his wife" (cp. Ru 4:13).

The responsibilities of the bridegroom are carefully listed in the *ketubah*. This document:

- details the bridegroom's responsibilities to his wife during their wedded life together—food, clothing, a home, and pleasure (i.e., her conjugal rights)—as he promises (in what is called the alimentation clause), ". . . I will work for you, honor, provide for, and support you, in accordance with the practice of Jewish husbands, who work for their wives, honor, provide for and support them in truth";
- designates the wife as the heir to the estate if he predeceases her; and,
- guarantees the man's provision of a financial settlement for his wife if he divorces her.

In the event of the husband's death or his pursuit of divorce, the contract places a lien on all his property to supply her financial support. Since this lien obligates the husband personally, it becomes a mortgage not only on his real estate but also on his personal assets.

These funds are called *mohar*, which once constituted the cash gift the groom gave to his bride's father, later was added to the bride's dowry, ultimately serving as a minimal life insurance. The *ketubah* also records the specific dowry arrangements and the groom's acceptance of them. The dowry, provided by the bride's father, represents her share of her family's inheritance. Additional funds promised voluntarily by the groom are called *mattan*. If the marriage is dissolved, all three—*mohar*, dowry, and *mattan*—are to belong to the wife.

The *ketubah* stands as a monumental example of the protection of the rights of women. God's plan for the woman in marriage is manifested beautifully in this very one-sided document in which the groom makes his commitments to his bride.

the two tablets of the testimony, stone
tablets inscribed by the finger of God.

The Golden Calf (32:1–33:6)

Faithlessness (32:1-6)

32 When the people saw that Moses delayed in coming down
from the mountain, they gathered
around Aaron and said to him,
"Come, make us a god[A] who will go
before us because this Moses, the
man who brought us up from the
land of Egypt—we don't know what
has happened to him!"
2 Then Aaron replied to them,
"Take off the gold rings that are on
the ears of your wives, your sons,
and your daughters and bring them
to me." 3 So all the people took off
the gold rings that were on their
ears and brought them to Aaron.
4 He took the gold from their hands,
fashioned it with an engraving tool,
and made it into an image of a calf.
Then they said, "Israel, this is your
God,[B] who brought you up from the
land of Egypt!"
5 When Aaron saw this, he built
an altar before it; then he made an
announcement: "There will be a festival to the LORD tomorrow." 6 Early
the next morning they arose, offered
•burnt offerings, and presented •fel-
lowship offerings. The people sat
down to eat and drink, then got up
to play.

Yahweh's Wrath (32:7-10)

7 The LORD spoke to Moses: "Go
down at once! For your people you
brought up from the land of Egypt
have acted corruptly. 8 They have
quickly turned from the way I commanded them; they have made for
themselves an image of a calf. They
have bowed down to it, sacrificed to
it, and said, 'Israel, this is your God,[B]
who brought you up from the land
of Egypt.'" 9 The LORD also said to
Moses: "I have seen this people, and
they are indeed a stiff-necked people. 10 Now leave Me alone, so that
My anger can burn against them and
I can destroy them. Then I will make
you into a great nation."

Moses' Intercession (32:11-14)

11 But Moses interceded with the
LORD his God: "LORD, why does Your
anger burn against Your people You
brought out of the land of Egypt
with great power and a strong hand?
12 Why should the Egyptians say, 'He
brought them out with an evil intent to kill them in the mountains
and wipe them off the face of the
earth'? Turn from Your great anger
and relent concerning this disaster
planned for Your people. 13 Remember Your servants Abraham, Isaac,
and Israel—You swore to them by
Your very self and declared, 'I will
make your •offspring as numerous
as the stars of the sky and will give
your offspring all this land that I
have promised, and they will inherit
it forever.'" 14 So the LORD relented
concerning the disaster He said He
would bring on His people.

Moses' Wrath (32:15-19)

15 Then Moses turned and went
down the mountain with the two
tablets of the •testimony in his
hands. They were inscribed on both
sides—inscribed front and back.
16 The tablets were the work of God,
and the writing was God's writing,
engraved on the tablets.
17 When Joshua heard the sound of
the people as they shouted, he said
to Moses, "There is a sound of war
in the camp."
18 But Moses replied:

It's not the sound
  of a victory cry
 and not the sound of a cry
  of defeat;
 I hear the sound of singing!

19 As he approached the camp and
saw the calf and the dancing, Moses became enraged and threw the
tablets out of his hands, smashing
them at the base of the mountain.

Punishment (32:20–33:6)

20 Then he took the calf they had
made, burned it up, and ground it to
powder. He scattered the powder over
the surface of the water and forced
the Israelites to drink the water.
21 Then Moses asked Aaron, "What
did these people do to you that you
have led them into such a grave
sin?"

[A] **32:1** Or *us gods* [B] **32:4,8** Or *Israel, this is your god*, or *Israel, these are your gods*

32:1-5 To understand why Moses' anger against Aaron was justified in verses 19-25, note his role's prominence in verses 1-5. The first two commandments of the Decalogue clearly forbade such an effort.

32:6 When the Lord prescribed in detail the offerings to be made to Him, He included **burnt offerings** and **fellowship offerings** by which the people would express their devotion to and desire for peace with God (Lv 1–3). The worship offered to the gold calf notably lacked a sin or guilt offering (Lv 4–6). **The people** reverted to what they knew, worshiped in a manner that made sense to them, and **got up to play** (Hb *tsachaq*, "play, make sport, jest")—"to party" or celebrate, not with innocent fun but implying sexual immorality as in pagan fertility rituals (cp. Gn 26:8; 39:14,17).

32:7-10 The LORD immediately distanced Himself from *Moses'* **people**; yet He spoke as though only Moses were standing in the way of His annihilating them. Yahweh responded with the jealous wrath of a groom whose bride has been caught in an affair the night before the wedding.

32:11-13 Interceded (Hb *chalah*, used only here in Exodus), more literally "stroke or smooth" a person's face, is as an idiom for seeking favor or making supplication (e.g., 1Sm 13:12; Pr 19:6). Moses' intercession exemplifies not "How to Get God to Relent" but "How to Pray God's Point of View."

32:14 Relented (Hb *nacham*) translates one verb with a range of meaning: "be sorry, have compassion; lamented, grieve; repent, rue, regret." The word suggests the involvement of both decision-making and emotional response (cp. Gn 6:6; Jnh 3:10; Am 7:1-6).

32:19 In a heated rage, Moses **threw** down the stone **tablets** described so carefully as God's "work" and words. **Smashing** (Hb *shavar*, "break in pieces, crush"; cp. 23:24) is a strong form of the verb meaning "break thoroughly or altogether shatter."

32:20 Moses acted swiftly and decisively in reducing the idol to dust.

32:21-24 Moses called **Aaron** to account, and his defense was completely implausible. Aaron implied that the people's inclination to evil was so strong that he could have done nothing to stop their pursuit of **evil**. Then he insisted that the calf image had emerged from the fire on its own, as though he had no direct role in fashioning that image, in stark contrast to the truth reported in verses 2-5.

32:25-29 The verb translated **out of control** (Hb *para'*, "let loose or loosen") denotes "letting go, casting off restraint" in the sense of "being lawless or unbridled." It can also denote "ignore, avoid, neglect; reject counsel" (cp. 2Ch 28:19; Pr 1:25; 8:33; 15:32). The latter definition may illumine the context that serves as the backdrop for the enigmatic order to kill fellow Israelite "men." Moses' order followed his recognition that Aaron had allowed the people to **get out of control, resulting in weakness** [Hb *shimtsah*, "shame; whispering, derision; overthrow"] **before their enemies**. Not only had the people let down their guard, but their behavior also put them, and Yahweh by implication, to shame among any who might be watching.

32:30-35 Presumably the dead were buried, and both mourning for the deceased and a sober reckoning of what they had done continued for the Israelites into **the following day**. Moses verbally impressed upon the people the gravity of their sin. The day before had been only a taste of the potential consequences, should **the LORD** decide to destroy them after all.

33:1-6 God knew that because of His intolerance of sin even after three demonstrations of judgment, the people would continue to be stubborn and would therefore bring judgment upon themselves (vv. 3,5; cp. 32:20,27-29,35). **Destroy** (Hb *kalah*) suggests "completing, finishing, bringing to an end, putting an end to, exterminating, consuming." Obstinate refusal to yield to God's authority warrants His termination of any claim to a relationship with Him. The idea of traveling without God's favor crushed the people's hope, and they **mourned** the **bad news.**

33:7-11 The tent of meeting described here seems to have served as a temporary chapel, a designated place of prayer for **anyone who wanted to consult** [Hb *biqqēsh*, "search, seek," esp. God's face, figuratively speaking] **the LORD**. Joshua was always there to govern their use of the tent. The people's behavior when Moses walked out of the camp **to the tent** demonstrated their dependence on and respect for him as their mediator. Likewise, **when Moses entered the tent,** the visible signs of Yahweh's presence confirmed the reality of Moses' unique role as intercessor on the people's behalf.

33:12-14 Given that **the LORD** had already told Moses that His angel would accompany the people (23:20-23; 32:33-35; 33:1-4), the initial statement in this conversation seems disrespectful. But Moses was pleading for Yahweh's personal presence and insisting that no substitute could

22 "Don't be enraged, my lord," Aaron replied. "You yourself know that the people are intent on evil. 23 They said to me, 'Make us a god[A] who will go before us because this Moses, the man who brought us up from the land of Egypt—we don't know what has happened to him!' 24 So I said to them, 'Whoever has gold, take it off,' and they gave it to me. When I threw it into the fire, out came this calf!"

25 Moses saw that the people were out of control, for Aaron had let them get out of control, resulting in weakness before their enemies.[B] 26 And Moses stood at the camp's entrance and said, "Whoever is for the LORD, come to me." And all the Levites gathered around him. 27 He told them, "This is what the LORD, the God of Israel, says, 'Every man fasten his sword to his side; go back and forth through the camp from entrance to entrance, and each of you kill his brother, his friend, and his neighbor.'" 28 The Levites did as Moses commanded, and about 3,000 men fell dead that day among the people. 29 Afterward Moses said, "Today you have been dedicated[C] to the LORD, since each man went against his son and his brother. Therefore you have brought a blessing on yourselves today."

30 The following day Moses said to the people, "You have committed a grave sin. Now I will go up to the LORD; perhaps I will be able to atone for your sin."

31 So Moses returned to the LORD and said, "Oh, these people have committed a grave sin; they have made a god of gold for themselves. 32 Now if You would only forgive their sin. But if not, please erase me from the book You have written."

33 The LORD replied to Moses: "I will erase whoever has sinned against Me from My book. 34 Now go, lead the people to the place I told you about; see, My angel will go before you. But on the day I settle accounts, I will hold them accountable for their sin." 35 And the LORD inflicted a plague on the people for what they did with the calf Aaron had made.

33 The LORD spoke to Moses: "Go, leave here, you and the people you brought up from the land of Egypt, to the land I promised to Abraham, Isaac, and Jacob, saying: I will give it to your •offspring. 2 I will send an angel ahead of you and will drive out the Canaanites, Amorites, Hittites, Perizzites,[D] Hivites, and Jebusites. 3 Go up to a land flowing with milk and honey. But I will not go with you because you are a stiff-necked people; otherwise, I might destroy you on the way." 4 When the people heard this bad news, they mourned and didn't put on their jewelry.

5 For the LORD said to Moses: "Tell the Israelites: You are a stiff-necked people. If I went with you for a single moment, I would destroy you. Now take off your jewelry, and I will decide what to do with you." 6 So the Israelites remained stripped of their jewelry from Mount Horeb onward.

Outside the Camp: The Tent of Meeting (33:7–34:4)

7 Now Moses took a tent and set it up outside the camp, far away from the camp; he called it the tent of meeting. Anyone who wanted to consult the LORD would go to the tent of meeting that was outside the camp. 8 Whenever Moses went out to the tent, all the people would stand up, each one at the door of his tent, and they would watch Moses until he entered the tent. 9 When Moses entered the tent, the pillar of cloud would come down and remain at the entrance to the tent, and the LORD would speak with Moses. 10 As all the people saw the pillar of cloud remaining at the entrance to the tent, they would stand up, then bow in worship, each one at the door of his tent. 11 The LORD spoke with Moses face to face, just as a man speaks with his friend. Then Moses would return to the camp, but his assistant, the young man Joshua son of Nun, would not leave the inside of the tent.

12 Moses said to the LORD, "Look, You have told me, 'Lead this people

[A]32:23 Or *us gods* [B]32:25 Hb obscure; or *resulting in derision* [C]32:29 Text emended; MT reads *Today dedicate yourselves*; LXX, Vg read *Today you have dedicated yourselves* [D]33:2 Sam, LXX add *Girgashites*

up,' but You have not let me know whom You will send with me. You said, 'I know you by name, and you have also found favor in My sight.' 13 Now if I have indeed found favor in Your sight, please teach me Your ways, and I will know You and find favor in Your sight. Now consider that this nation is Your people."

14 Then He replied, "My presence will go with you, and I will give you rest."

15 "If Your presence does not go," Moses responded to Him, "don't make us go up from here. 16 How will it be known that I and Your people have found favor in Your sight unless You go with us? I and Your people will be distinguished by this from all the other people on the face of the earth."

17 The LORD answered Moses, "I will do this very thing you have asked, for you have found favor in My sight, and I know you by name."

18 Then Moses said, "Please, let me see Your glory."

19 He said, "I will cause all My goodness to pass in front of you, and I will proclaim the name •Yahweh before you. I will be gracious to whom I will be gracious, and I will have compassion on whom I will have compassion." 20 But He answered, "You cannot see My face, for no one can see Me and live." 21 The LORD said, "Here is a place near Me. You are to stand on the rock, 22 and when My glory passes by, I will put you in the crevice of the rock and cover you with My hand until I have passed by. 23 Then I will take My hand away, and you will see My back, but My face will not be seen."

34 The LORD said to Moses, "Cut two stone tablets like the first ones, and I will write on them the words that were on the first tablets, which you broke. 2 Be prepared by morning. Come up Mount Sinai in the morning and stand before Me on the mountaintop. 3 No one may go up with you; in fact, no one must be seen anywhere on the mountain. Even the flocks and herds are not to graze in front of that mountain."

4 Moses cut two stone tablets like the first ones. He got up early in the morning, and taking the two stone tablets in his hand, he climbed Mount Sinai, just as the LORD had commanded him.

Yahweh's Presence in the Crevice of the Rock (34:5-9)

The Revelation of God's Name and Character (34:5-7)

5 The LORD came down in a cloud, stood with him there, and proclaimed His name •Yahweh. 6 Then the LORD passed in front of him and proclaimed:

> Yahweh—Yahweh is a compassionate and gracious God, slow to anger and rich in faithful love and truth, 7 maintaining faithful love to a thousand generations, forgiving wrongdoing, rebellion, and sin. But He will not leave the •guilty unpunished, bringing the consequences of the fathers' wrongdoing on the children and grandchildren to the third and fourth generation.

Moses' Plea (34:8-9)

8 Moses immediately bowed down to the ground and worshiped. 9 Then he said, "My Lord, if I have indeed found favor in Your sight, my Lord, please go with us. Even though this is a stiff-necked people, forgive our wrongdoing and sin, and accept us as Your own possession."

Yahweh's Covenant (34:10-28)

10 And the LORD responded: "Look, I am making a covenant. I will perform wonders in the presence of all your people[A] that have never been done[B] in all the earth or in any nation. All the people you live among will see the LORD's work, for what I am doing with you is awe-inspiring. 11 Observe what I command you today. I am going to drive out before you the Amorites, Canaanites, Hittites, Perizzites, Hivites,[C] and Jebusites. 12 Be careful not to make a treaty with the inhabitants of the land that you are going to enter; otherwise, they will become a snare among you. 13 Instead, you must tear down their altars, smash their

convince the watching nations that he and the people had **found favor** [Hb *chen*, "grace, acceptance"] in His sight. The Lord answered Moses' prayer *and* promised **rest**.

33:15-17 Moses' next request seems to reflect doubt, as though he did not take the Lord's initial reply at face value. Moses' expression of reluctance when the Lord commissioned him from the burning bush followed a similar pattern, and the Lord's gracious affirmations are the reader's reward. Because God did accept Moses—his motives and his devotion to the Lord—God agreed to do what His servant asked. Yahweh repeated to Moses the greatest assurance of all—He knew Moses **by name** (cp. v. 12).

33:18-19 God did not say "no" to Moses' request to **see** His **glory**. Instead He described the measure of His glory that He would reveal to Moses.

33:20-23 For sinful man, seeing God's holy **face** would be like an asteroid getting too close to the sun—disintegration.

34:5-7 On the basis of this combination of "faithful love and truth," Yahweh both forgives and punishes. Associating His twin response to sin with **a thousand** and **generations** emphasized how extensively God's forgiveness exceeds the punishment required by His just character. **The fathers' wrongdoing** (Hb *'awon*, "guilt resulting from iniquity, penalty of sin, calamity, misery"; cp. 28:36-38,43) in ways they could never imagine would pass on to their **children and grandchildren** and great-grandchildren the harmful effects of one generation's sins to succeeding generations just as every member of the human family will reap the rebellious nature of their forefather Adam. Only God's intervention in a person's life can break the power of sinful habits and overcome the negative effects of one person's sins upon his family.

34:10-11 God announced that what He did with Israel would put His unique power on display for all to see. **Wonders** (Hb *pala'*) refers to "what is difficult to do or understand; that which is wonderful, extraordinary, marvelous, or miraculous." In establishing His covenant relationship with Israel, God was doing something **awe-inspiring** (Hb *yarē'*), something "to be feared," something that would "cause astonishment, inspire reverence, or promote godly fear." The Old Testament recites the history of how this covenant between God and His people unfolded, an altogether true story full of God-orchestrated events considered impossible from a human point of view and therefore intended to elicit fear and

[A]**34:10** Lit *in all nations* [B]**34:10** Lit *created* [C]**34:11** DSS, Sam, LXX add *Girgashites*

awe both in the people who already call Him by name and in the people He is drawing to Himself (cp. Lk 4:35-36; 5:20-26; Jn 12:32).

34:12-14 The highlights of Yahweh's covenant are presented in 20:1–23:33 (cp. Dt 5:1–11:32), particularly as the Israelites would be expected to distinguish their daily lives in covenant with God from the lives of the people serving pagan gods in the nations surrounding them as well as describing Israel's role in driving out the idolatrous nations (34:12-26). God would do it, but Israel would be His instrument of judgment by observing what He commanded them. Yahweh specifically warned them to spurn the temptations that would confront them as they entered the land. With the glimpse of the pagan practices of the idolatrous nations, one can see clearly God's rationale for the commandments He gave Israel—they were to protect her from being pulled into idolatry. Each specific command, nonetheless, would be broken, repeatedly bringing guilt and judgment upon Israel.

34:29-35 Moses' face somehow physically reflected the brilliance of God's glory after his second 40-day sojourn with God on Mount Sinai. The effect apparently lasted, because verses 34-35 describe his wearing **a veil** (Hb *masweh*, used only here in the OT) as customary except when he consulted **the Lord**, presumably in the tent of meeting set up outside the camp until the tabernacle was ready. The shining **skin** of Moses' **face** mysteriously radiated a glow of holiness that set him apart from the rest of the people, including **Aaron**, such that others were afraid to approach him. Whenever Moses told **the Israelites what** God had **commanded** about a matter, he would have to wear **the veil** to protect the people from the brilliance of the manifestation of God's holiness.

35:1-3 Again, the observance of the **Sabbath** was brought to the forefront in terms of what the people must do to obey God's commands. God's pattern of work and rest had to be established from the start as the people undertook the task of constructing the tabernacle. The death penalty was still prescribed for violators (cp. 31:14-15), and a specific prohibition was noted. Maintaining a fire in one's home was likely a different activity than lighting one. The latter was undoubtedly somewhat labor intensive, and the need to have a fire going may have been used as an excuse for doing work on the Sabbath. Rest did not simply mean the cessation of all work; rather, it required the forethought for preparing to stop all work.

35:4-29 These verses begin the account

sacred pillars, and chop down their •Asherah poles. 14 You are never to bow down to another god because Yahweh, being jealous by nature,[A] is a jealous God.

15 "Do not make a treaty with the inhabitants of the land, or else when they prostitute themselves with their gods and sacrifice to their gods, they will invite you, and you will eat their sacrifices. 16 Then you will take some of their daughters as brides for your sons. Their daughters will prostitute themselves with their gods and cause your sons to prostitute themselves with their gods.

17 "Do not make cast images of gods for yourselves.

18 "Observe the Festival of •Unleavened Bread. You are to eat unleavened bread for seven days at the appointed time in the month of Abib[B] as I commanded you. For you came out of Egypt in the month of Abib.

19 "The firstborn male from every womb belongs to Me, including all your male[C,D] livestock, the firstborn of cattle or sheep. 20 You must redeem the firstborn of a donkey with a sheep, but if you do not redeem it, break its neck. You must redeem all the firstborn of your sons. No one is to appear before Me empty-handed.

21 "You are to labor six days but you must rest on the seventh day; you must even rest during plowing and harvesting times.

22 "Observe the Festival of Weeks with the •firstfruits of the wheat harvest, and the Festival of Ingathering[E] at the turn of the agricultural year. 23 Three times a year all your males are to appear before the Lord God, the God of Israel. 24 For I will drive out nations before you and enlarge your territory. No one will covet your land when you go up three times a year to appear before the Lord your God.

25 "Do not present[F] the blood for My sacrifice with anything leavened. The sacrifice of the •Passover Festival must not remain until morning.

26 "Bring the best firstfruits of your land to the house of the Lord your God.

"You must not boil a young goat in its mother's milk."

27 The Lord also said to Moses, "Write down these words, for I have made a covenant with you and with Israel based on these words."

28 Moses was there with the Lord 40 days and 40 nights; he did not eat bread or drink water. He wrote the Ten Commandments, the words of the covenant, on the tablets.

The Radiant Face of Moses (34:29-35)

29 As Moses descended from Mount Sinai—with the two tablets of the •testimony in his hands as he descended the mountain—he did not realize that the skin of his face shone as a result of his speaking with the Lord.[G] 30 When Aaron and all the Israelites saw Moses, the skin of his face shone! They were afraid to come near him. 31 But Moses called out to them, so Aaron and all the leaders of the community returned to him, and Moses spoke to them. 32 Afterward all the Israelites came near, and he commanded them to do everything the Lord had told him on Mount Sinai. 33 When Moses had finished speaking with them, he put a veil over his face. 34 But whenever Moses went before the Lord to speak with Him, he would remove the veil until he came out. After he came out, he would tell the Israelites what he had been commanded, 35 and the Israelites would see that Moses' face[H] was radiant. Then Moses would put the veil over his face again until he went to speak with the Lord.

The Sabbath (35:1-3)

35 Moses assembled the entire Israelite community and said to them, "These are the things that the Lord has commanded you to do: 2 For six days work is to be done, but on the seventh day you are to have a holy day, a Sabbath of complete rest to the Lord. Anyone who does

[A] **34:14** Lit *Yahweh—His name is Jealous*, or *Yahweh is jealous for His name, He* [B] **34:18** March–April; called Nisan in the post-exilic period; Neh 2:1; Est 3:7 [C] **34:19** LXX, Theod, Vg, Tg read *males* [D] **34:19** Hb obscure [E] **34:22** The Festival of Ingathering is called Festival of Booths elsewhere; Lv 23:34-36. [F] **34:25** Lit *slaughter* [G] **34:29** Lit *with Him* [H] **34:35** Lit *see Moses' face, that the skin of his face*

work on it must be executed. 3 Do not light a fire in any of your homes on the Sabbath day."

The Construction of the Tabernacle (35:4–38:20)

4 Then Moses said to the entire Israelite community, "This is what the LORD has commanded: 5 Take up an offering among you for the LORD. Let everyone whose heart is willing bring this as the LORD's offering: gold, silver, and bronze; 6 blue, purple, and scarlet yarn; fine linen and goat hair; 7 ram skins dyed red and manatee skins;[A] acacia wood; 8 oil for the light; spices for the anointing oil and for the fragrant incense; 9 and onyx with gemstones to mount on the •ephod and breastpiece.

10 "Let all the skilled craftsmen[B] among you come and make everything that the LORD has commanded: 11 the tabernacle—its tent and covering, its clasps and planks, its crossbars, its posts and bases; 12 the ark with its poles, the •mercy seat, and the veil for the screen; 13 the table with its poles, all its utensils, and the •bread of the Presence; 14 the lampstand for light with its utensils and lamps as well as the oil for the light; 15 the altar of incense with its poles; the anointing oil and the fragrant incense; the entryway screen for the entrance to the tabernacle; 16 the altar of •burnt offering with its bronze grate, its poles, and all its utensils; the basin with its stand; 17 the hangings of the courtyard, its posts and bases, and the screen for the gate of the courtyard; 18 the tent pegs for the tabernacle and the tent pegs for the courtyard, along with their ropes; 19 and the specially woven[C] garments for ministering in the sanctuary—the holy garments for Aaron the priest and the garments for his sons to serve as priests."

20 Then the entire Israelite community left Moses' presence. 21 Everyone whose heart was moved and whose spirit prompted him came and brought an offering to the LORD for the work on the tent of meeting, for all its services, and for the holy garments. 22 Both men and women came; all who had willing hearts brought brooches, earrings, rings, necklaces, and all kinds of gold jewelry—everyone who waved a presentation offering of gold to the LORD. 23 Everyone who had in his possession blue, purple, or scarlet yarn, fine linen or goat hair, ram skins dyed red or manatee skins,[D] brought them. 24 Everyone making an offering of silver or bronze brought it as a contribution to the LORD. Everyone who possessed acacia wood useful for any task in the work brought it. 25 Every skilled[E] woman spun yarn with her hands and brought it: blue, purple, and scarlet yarn, and fine linen. 26 And all the women whose hearts were moved spun the goat hair by virtue of their skill. 27 The leaders brought onyx and gemstones to mount on the ephod and breastpiece, 28 as well as the spice and oil for the light, for the anointing oil, and for the fragrant incense. 29 So the Israelites brought a freewill offering to the LORD, all the men and women whose hearts prompted them to bring something for all the work that the LORD, through Moses, had commanded to be done.

30 Moses then said to the Israelites: "Look, the LORD has appointed by name Bezalel son of Uri, son of Hur, of the tribe of Judah. 31 He has filled him with God's Spirit, with wisdom, understanding, and ability in every kind of craft 32 to design artistic works in gold, silver, and bronze, 33 to cut gemstones for mounting, and to carve wood for work in every kind of artistic craft. 34 He has also given both him and Oholiab son of Ahisamach, of the tribe of Dan, the ability to teach others. 35 He has filled them with skill[F] to do all the work of a gem cutter; a designer; an embroiderer in blue, purple, and scarlet yarn and fine linen; and a weaver. They can do every kind of craft and design artistic designs.

36 1 Bezalel, Oholiab, and all the skilled[E] people are to work based on everything the LORD has commanded. The LORD has given

of how Moses faithfully conveyed to the people what **the LORD . . . commanded** them to do and how they faithfully followed His instructions for establishing His provisional dwelling place among them. The enterprise involved **the entire Israelite community**. With **willing** hearts they offered to **the LORD** the materials He specified for building **the tabernacle**, making its furnishings, blending the **oil** and **incense**, and fashioning the priestly **garments**. The adjective **willing** (Hb *nadiv*, "ready, voluntary, giving spontaneously or liberally, generous," vv. 5,22) described an inner motivation that was evident in the attitude with which the people gave their newly acquired luxuries to God—not under compulsion but in glad obedience. David used the same word in praying for God to restore the joy of his salvation (Ps 51:12) and in describing the men who would be available for Solomon's task of building the temple (1Ch 28:21; cp. 2Ch 29:31). The text emphasizes that **both men and women** brought offerings (Ex 35:22,29), including an array **of gold jewelry** (Hb *keli*, "articles, vessels, utensils, implements").

Also, **skilled** women contributed yarn they had **spun**. The root meaning of skilled (Hb *chakam*, vv. 10,25) is "able to judge" and in other contexts denotes "wise, intelligent, or knowledgeable" and suggests "expertise or mastery" gained from extensive training and experience. In verse 10, *chakam-lev* ("wise-hearted") is translated as "skilled craftsmen." **Skill** (Hb *chokmah*, "wisdom, prudence; dexterity," v. 26) is a related word. Emphasis again was placed on the generosity of women in contributing their skills to the extraordinary preparation of materials for making God's dwelling place beautiful and functional, according to His plans.

35:30–36:2 Such a collaborative effort required not only stringent adherence to God's directions but also creativity, the highest standards of excellence, and an eye for beauty. **The LORD . . . appointed** (Hb *qara'*, "call, call out, summon, commission or endow") two men **by name** and **filled** them with a diversity of gifts (v. 31):

- **God's Spirit**, indicating that their work was supernaturally under the creative supervision of God Himself;
- **wisdom** (Hb *chokmah*, v. 31; 36:1; see "skill" in notes, 35:4-29; **Word Study**, p. 783);
- **understanding** (Hb *tavun*, "intelligence, insight," v. 31; 36:1);
- **ability in every kind of craft** (Hb *da'at*, "knowledge, skill," 35:31);
- **the ability to teach others**, lit "has put in his heart to teach" (Hb *yarah*, "instruct, direct, point out, show," v. 34); and

[A]35:7 Or *and dolphin skins*, or *and fine leather*; Hb obscure [B]35:10 Lit *the skilled of heart* [C]35:19 Hb obscure [D]35:23 Or *or dolphin skins*, or *or fine leather*; Hb obscure [E]35:25; 36:1 Lit *wise of heart* [F]35:35 Lit *with wisdom of heart*

• **skill** [Hb *chokmah-lēv*, lit. "wisdom of heart," v. 35; 36:1-2] **to do all the work.** **Bezalel** (Hb "in the shadow of God, i.e., under His protection") and **Oholiab** (Hb "Father's tent") may have been naturally talented and/ or trained; but God publicly selected them for special service and poured into them such wisdom, leadership ability, and artistic and technical skills that He would garner the praise for their designs. The list of specific tasks entrusted to these men and those under their supervision is a reminder that although God's primary call is to a relationship with Himself, He also calls out individuals to apply both natural abilities and spiritual gifts to His work, including short-term projects. In addition, this passage illustrates the high value God places on artistic abilities and the contribution of visual beauty to worship and to His mission (35:32-35).

36:3-7 Bezalel, Oholiab, and their crew of volunteers became custodians of all the materials that were contributed every **morning** until the giving exceeded what was **needed** to fulfill God's blueprints for the tabernacle and its ministry. Here the Hebrew conveys the abundance of the people's offering with a verb. *Ravah* is a participle that indicated an ongoing activity of "multiplying, increasing, making much" (i.e., the store of materials was accumulating), and the amount was becoming so great that the workers could not use it all.

36:8-38 The description of the tabernacle's construction parallels the instructions God gave to Moses almost word for word (chaps. 25–27).

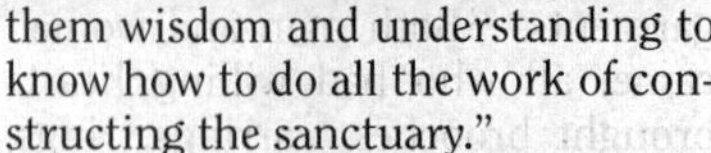

them wisdom and understanding to know how to do all the work of constructing the sanctuary."

2 So Moses summoned Bezalel, Oholiab, and every skilled[A] person in whose heart the LORD had placed wisdom, everyone whose heart moved him, to come to the work and do it. 3 They took from Moses' presence all the contributions that the Israelites had brought for the task of making the sanctuary. Meanwhile, the people continued to bring freewill offerings morning after morning.

4 Then all the craftsmen who were doing all the work for the sanctuary came one by one from the work they were doing 5 and said to Moses, "The people are bringing more than is needed for the construction of the work the LORD commanded to be done."

6 After Moses gave an order, they sent a proclamation throughout the camp: "Let no man or woman make anything else as an offering for the sanctuary." So the people stopped. 7 The materials were sufficient for them to do all the work. There was more than enough.

8 All the skilled craftsmen[B] among those doing the work made the tabernacle with 10 curtains. Bezalel made them of finely spun linen, as well as blue, purple, and scarlet yarn, with a design of •cherubim worked into them. 9 The length of each curtain was 42 feet,[C] and the width of each curtain six feet;[D] all the curtains had the same measurements. 10 He joined five of the curtains to each other, and the other five curtains he joined to each other. 11 He made loops of blue yarn on the edge of the last curtain in the first set and did the same on the edge of the outermost curtain in the second set. 12 He made 50 loops on the one curtain and 50 loops on the edge of the curtain in the second set, so that the loops lined up with each other. 13 He also made 50 gold clasps and joined the curtains to each other, so that the tabernacle became a single unit.

14 He made curtains of goat hair for a tent over the tabernacle; he made 11 of them. 15 The length of each curtain was 45 feet,[E] and the width of each curtain six feet.[D] All 11 curtains had the same measurements. 16 He joined five of the curtains together, and the other six together. 17 He made 50 loops on the edge of the outermost curtain in the first set and 50 loops on the edge of the corresponding curtain in the second set. 18 He made 50 bronze clasps to join the tent together as a single unit. 19 He also made a covering for the tent from ram skins dyed red and a covering of manatee skins[F] on top of it.

20 He made upright planks[G] of acacia wood for the tabernacle. 21 The length of each plank was 15 feet,[H] and the width of each was 27 inches.[I] 22 There were two tenons connected to each other for each plank. He did the same for all the planks of the tabernacle. 23 He made planks for the tabernacle as follows: 20 for the south side, 24 and he made 40 silver bases to put under the 20 planks, two bases under the first plank for its two tenons, and two bases under each of the following planks for their two tenons; 25 for the second side of the tabernacle, the north side, he made 20 planks, 26 with their 40 silver bases, two bases under the first plank and two bases under each of the following ones; 27 and for the west side of the tabernacle he made six planks. 28 He also made two additional planks for the two back corners of the tabernacle. 29 They were paired at the bottom and joined together[J] at the[K] top in a single ring. This is what he did with both of them for the two corners. 30 So there were eight planks with their 16 silver bases, two bases under each one.

31 He made five crossbars of acacia wood for the planks on one side of the tabernacle, 32 five crossbars for the planks on the other side of the tabernacle, and five crossbars for those at the back of the tabernacle on the west. 33 He made the central crossbar run through the middle of the planks from one end to the

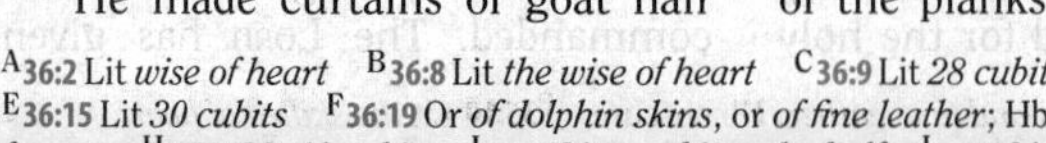

[A] **36:2** Lit *wise of heart* [B] **36:8** Lit *the wise of heart* [C] **36:9** Lit *28 cubits* [D] **36:9,15** Lit *four cubits* [E] **36:15** Lit *30 cubits* [F] **36:19** Or *of dolphin skins*, or *of fine leather*; Hb obscure [G] **36:20** Or *made frames* [H] **36:21** Lit *10 cubits* [I] **36:21** Lit *a cubit and a half* [J] **36:29** Lit *and together they are to be complete* [K] **36:29** Lit *its*

other. 34 He overlaid them with gold and made their rings out of gold as holders for the crossbars. He also overlaid the crossbars with gold.

35 Then he made the veil with blue, purple, and scarlet yarn, and finely spun linen. He made it with a design of cherubim worked into it. 36 He made four posts of acacia wood for it and overlaid them with gold; their hooks were of gold. And he cast four silver bases for the posts.

37 He made a screen embroidered with blue, purple, and scarlet yarn, and finely spun linen for the entrance to the tent, 38 together with its five posts and their hooks. He overlaid the tops of the posts and their bands with gold, but their five bases were bronze.

37 Bezalel made the ark of acacia wood, 45 inches long, 27 inches wide, and 27 inches high.[A] 2 He overlaid it with pure gold inside and out and made a gold molding all around it. 3 He cast four gold rings for it, for its four feet, two rings on one side and two rings on the other side. 4 He made poles of acacia wood and overlaid them with gold. 5 He inserted the poles into the rings on the sides of the ark for carrying the ark.

6 He made a •mercy seat of pure gold, 45 inches long and 27 inches wide.[B] 7 He made two •cherubim of gold; he made them of hammered work at the two ends of the mercy seat, 8 one cherub at one end and one cherub at the other end. At each end, he made a cherub of one piece with the mercy seat. 9 They had wings spread out. They faced each other and covered the mercy seat with their wings. The faces of the cherubim were looking toward the mercy seat.

10 He constructed the table of acacia wood, 36 inches long, 18 inches wide, and 27 inches high.[C] 11 He overlaid it with pure gold and made a gold molding all around it. 12 He made a three-inch[D] frame all around it and made a gold molding all around its frame. 13 He cast four gold rings for it and attached the rings to the four corners at its four legs. 14 The rings were next to the frame as holders for the poles to carry the table. 15 He made the poles for carrying the table from acacia wood and overlaid them with gold. 16 He also made the utensils that would be on the table out of pure gold: its plates and cups, as well as its bowls and pitchers for pouring •drink offerings.

17 Then he made the lampstand out of pure hammered gold. He made it all of one piece: its base and shaft, its ornamental cups, and its calyxes[E] and petals. 18 Six branches extended from its sides, three branches of the lampstand from one side and three branches of the lampstand from the other side. 19 There were three cups shaped like almond blossoms, each with a calyx and petals, on the first branch, and three cups shaped like almond blossoms, each with a calyx and petals, on the next branch. It was this way for the six branches that extended from the lampstand. 20 On the lampstand shaft there were four cups shaped like almond blossoms with its calyxes and petals. 21 For the six branches that extended from it, a calyx was under the first pair of branches from it, a calyx under the second pair of branches from it, and a calyx under the third pair of branches from it. 22 Their calyxes and branches were of one piece.[F] All of it was a single hammered piece of pure gold. 23 He also made its seven lamps, snuffers, and firepans of pure gold. 24 He made it and all its utensils of 75 pounds[G] of pure gold.

25 He made the altar of incense out of acacia wood. It was square, 18 inches long and 18 inches wide; it was 36 inches high.[H] Its horns were of one piece.[F] 26 He overlaid it, its top, all around its sides, and its horns with pure gold. Then he made a gold molding all around it. 27 He made two gold rings for it under the molding on two of its sides; he put these on opposite sides of it to be

37:1-29 Bezalel faithfully constructed **the ark, the table** and **lampstand** and their **utensils**, and **the altar of incense**, all according to the Lord's specifications (cp. 25:10-40; 30:1-10). He also prepared the **holy anointing oil** and **expertly blended** [Hb *raqach*, "one who mixes (spices), a perfumer"; cp. 2Ch 16:14] **incense** [lit "the work of a perfumer"; cp. 30:7-8,22-38].

A **37:1** Lit *two and a half cubits its length, one and a half cubits its width, and one and a half cubits its height* B **37:6** Lit *two and a half cubits its length and one and a half cubits its width* C **37:10** Lit *two cubits its length, one cubit its width, and one and a half cubits its height* D **37:12** Lit *a handbreadth* E **37:17** = the outer covering of a flower F **37:22,25** Lit *piece with it* G **37:24** Lit *a talent* H **37:25** Lit *a cubit its length, a cubit its width, and two cubits its height*

38:1-7 Bezalel was also responsible for constructing **the altar of burnt offering,** which, like the planks and crossbars and all of the furnishings except the lampstand, was made of **acacia wood**. Unlike these articles housed within the tabernacle and the structure of the tabernacle itself, all of which shone with the breathtaking beauty of pure gold, the imposing altar was **overlaid . . . with bronze**, a metal alloy able to withstand the heat of a **burnt offering** (cp. 27:1-8).

38:8 One of the most intriguing details included in this account is its description of the **bronze basin** [Hb *kiyor*, "laver"] **and its stand**, not previously mentioned. The text refers to a particular group of **women who served at the entrance** of the tabernacle. The Hebrew text uses two forms of the same verb (*tsava'*) to denote the active and ongoing service of the women who were faithfully carrying out tasks of service, and the meaning of the word here ("serve") is restricted to the context of sacred duties. These women were memorialized for contributing their **bronze mirrors** of Egyptian design, to be refashioned into the basin. Numerous bronze mirrors used in ancient Egypt have been discovered by archaeologists. The gold-colored, typically round circle of metal with a bronze handle was polished to produce a reflection. A mirror must have been a prized acquisition for these Israelite women who donated this luxury item to be melted down and reshaped into the basin for the priests' daily cleansing.

38:9-20 The courtyard and its **gate** were constructed and assembled according to specifications (cp. 27:9-19). This structure established the perimeter of the sacred space within which the tabernacle would stand and the priests would carry out their duties.

holders for the poles to carry it with. 28 He made the poles of acacia wood and overlaid them with gold.

29 He also made the holy anointing oil and the pure, fragrant, and expertly blended incense.

38 Bezalel constructed the altar of •burnt offering from acacia wood. It was square, 7½ feet long and 7½ feet wide,[A] and was 4½ feet[B] high. 2 He made horns for it on its four corners; the horns were of one piece.[C] Then he overlaid it with bronze.

3 He made all the altar's utensils: the pots, shovels, basins, meat forks, and firepans; he made all its utensils of bronze. 4 He constructed for the altar a grate of bronze mesh under its ledge,[D] halfway up from the bottom. 5 At the four corners of the bronze grate he cast four rings as holders for the poles. 6 Also, he made the poles of acacia wood and overlaid them with bronze. 7 Then he inserted the poles into the rings on the sides of the altar in order to carry it with them. He constructed the altar with boards so that it was hollow.

8 He made the bronze basin and its stand from the bronze mirrors of the women who served at the entrance to the tent of meeting.

9 Then he made the courtyard. The hangings on the south side of the courtyard were of finely spun linen, 150 feet in length,[E] 10 including their 20 posts and 20 bronze bases. The hooks and bands[F] of the posts were silver. 11 The hangings on the north side were also 150 feet in length,[E] including their 20 posts and 20 bronze bases. The hooks and bands[F] of the posts were silver. 12 The hangings on the west side were 75 feet in length,[G] including their 10 posts and 10 bases. The hooks and bands of the posts were silver. 13 The hangings on the east toward the sunrise were also 75 feet in length.[G] 14 The hangings on one side of the gate were 22½ feet,[H] including their three posts and three bases. 15 It was the same for the other side. The hangings were 22½ feet,[H] including their three posts and three bases on both sides of the courtyard gate. 16 All the hangings around the courtyard were of finely spun linen. 17 The bases for the posts were bronze; the hooks and bands[F] of the posts were silver; and the plating for the tops of the posts was silver. All the posts of the courtyard were banded with silver.

18 The screen for the gate of the courtyard was embroidered with blue, purple, and scarlet yarn, and finely spun linen. It was 30 feet[I] long, and like the hangings of the courtyard, 7½ feet[J] high.[K] 19 It had four posts, including their four bronze bases. Their hooks were silver, and the bands[F] as well as the plating of their tops were silver. 20 All the tent pegs for the tabernacle and for the surrounding courtyard were bronze.

The Inventory of the Tabernacle (38:21-31)

21 This is the inventory for the tabernacle, the tabernacle of the •testimony, that was recorded at Moses' command. It was the work of the Levites under the direction of[L] Ithamar son of Aaron the priest. 22 Bezalel son of Uri, son of Hur, of the tribe of Judah, made everything that the LORD commanded Moses. 23 With him was Oholiab son of Ahisamach, of the tribe of Dan, a gem cutter, a designer, and an embroiderer with blue, purple, and scarlet yarn, and fine linen.

24 All the gold of the presentation offering that was used for the project in all the work on the sanctuary, was 2,193 pounds,[M] according to the sanctuary •shekel. 25 The silver from those of the community who were registered was 7,544 pounds,[N] according to the sanctuary shekel— 26 ⅖ of an ounce[O] per man, that is, half a shekel according to the sanctuary shekel, from everyone 20 years old or more who had crossed over to the registered group, 603,550 men. 27 There were 7,500 pounds[P] of silver used to cast the bases of the sanctuary and the bases of the veil—

[A]38:1 Lit *five cubits its length and five cubits its width* [B]38:1 Lit *three cubits* [C]38:2 Lit *piece with it* [D]38:4 Or *rim* [E]38:9,11 Lit *100 cubits* [F]38:10,11,17,19 Or *connecting rods* [G]38:12,13 Lit *50 cubits* [H]38:14,15 Lit *15 cubits* [I]38:18 Lit *20 cubits* [J]38:18 Lit *five cubits* [K]38:18 Lit *high in width* [L]38:21 Lit *Levites by the hand of* [M]38:24 Lit *29 talents and 730 shekels* [N]38:25 Lit *100 talents and 1,775 shekels* [O]38:26 Lit *a beka* [P]38:27 Lit *100 talents*

100 bases from 7,500 pounds,[A] 75 pounds[B] for each base. 28 With the remaining 44 pounds[C] he made the hooks for the posts, overlaid their tops, and supplied bands[D] for them.

29 The bronze of the presentation offering totaled 5,310 pounds.[E] 30 He made with it the bases for the entrance to the tent of meeting, the bronze altar and its bronze grate, all the utensils for the altar, 31 the bases for the surrounding courtyard, the bases for the gate of the courtyard, all the tent pegs for the tabernacle, and all the tent pegs for the surrounding courtyard.

The Construction of the Priestly Garments (39:1-31)

39 They made specially woven[F] garments for ministry in the sanctuary, and the holy garments for Aaron from the blue, purple, and scarlet yarn, just as the LORD had commanded Moses.

2 Bezalel made the •ephod of gold, of blue, purple, and scarlet yarn, and of finely spun linen. 3 They hammered out thin sheets of gold, and he[G] cut threads from them to interweave with the blue, purple, and scarlet yarn, and the fine linen in a skillful design. 4 They made shoulder pieces for attaching it; it was joined together at its two edges. 5 The artistically woven waistband that was on the ephod was of one piece with the ephod, according to the same workmanship of gold, of blue, purple, and scarlet yarn, and of finely spun linen, just as the LORD had commanded Moses.

6 Then they mounted the onyx stones surrounded with gold filigree settings, engraved with the names of Israel's sons as a gem cutter engraves a seal. 7 He fastened them on the shoulder pieces of the ephod as memorial stones for the Israelites, just as the LORD had commanded Moses.

8 He also made the embroidered breastpiece with the same workmanship as the ephod of gold, of blue, purple, and scarlet yarn, and of finely spun linen. 9 They made the breastpiece square and folded double, nine inches long and nine inches wide.[H] 10 They mounted four rows of gemstones[I] on it. The first row was a row of carnelian, topaz, and emerald;[J] 11 the second row, a turquoise,[K] a sapphire,[L] and a diamond;[M] 12 the third row, a jacinth,[F] an agate, and an amethyst; 13 and the fourth row, a beryl, an onyx, and a jasper. They were surrounded with gold filigree in their settings.

14 The 12 stones corresponded to the names of Israel's sons. Each stone was engraved like a seal with one of the names of the 12 tribes.

15 They made braided chains of pure gold cord for the breastpiece. 16 They also fashioned two gold filigree settings and two gold rings and attached the two rings to its two corners. 17 Then they attached the two gold cords to the two gold rings on the corners of the breastpiece. 18 They attached the other ends of the two cords to the two filigree settings and, in this way, attached them to the ephod's shoulder pieces in front. 19 They made two other gold rings and put them at the two other corners of the breastpiece on the edge that is next to the inner border of the ephod. 20 They made two more gold rings and attached them to the bottom of the ephod's two shoulder pieces on its front, close to its seam,[N] above the ephod's woven waistband. 21 Then they tied the breastpiece from its rings to the rings of the ephod with a cord of blue yarn, so that the breastpiece was above the ephod's waistband and did not come loose from the ephod. They did just as the LORD had commanded Moses.

22 They made the woven robe of the ephod entirely of blue yarn. 23 There was an opening in the center of the robe like that of body armor[F] with a collar around the opening so that it would not tear. 24 They made pomegranates of finely spun blue, purple, and scarlet yarn[O] on the lower hem of the robe. 25 They made bells of pure gold and attached the

39:1-31 This passage repeats almost verbatim the details included in God's instructions for making the priestly **garments** (chap. 28). The purpose of giving such a closely paralleled account of the work was to demonstrate the people's complete obedience, repeatedly affirmed by the phrase **just as the LORD had commanded Moses** (39:1,5,7,21,26,29,31).

[A]**38:27** Lit *100 talents* [B]**38:27** Lit *one talent* [C]**38:28** Lit *1,775* (shekels) [D]**38:28** Or *connecting rods* [E]**38:29** Lit *70 talents and 2,400 shekels* [F]**39:1,12,23** Hb obscure [G]**39:3** Sam, Syr, Tg read *they* [H]**39:9** Lit *a span its length and a span its width* [I]**39:10** Many of these stones cannot be identified with certainty. [J]**39:10** Or *beryl* [K]**39:11** Or *malachite*, or *garnet* [L]**39:11** Or *lapis lazuli* [M]**39:11** Hb uncertain; LXX, Vg read *jasper* [N]**39:20** The place where the shoulder pieces join the front of the ephod [O]**39:24** Sam, LXX, Vg add *and linen*

39:32-43 All of the royal-colored curtains, veils, and garments reflected the obedience of God's people in using their skills for His glory. The entire endeavor was a masterpiece befitting the inhabitation of the King because it was made according to His design yet with the minds and willing hearts and skilled hands of people created in His image and set apart for His pleasure.

40:1-15 The Lord designated a particular day for putting together all the elements of **the tabernacle**—the first day of month number one, the first month on the nation's calendar according to their instructions for keeping the Passover (12:1-3). The day probably marked the beginning of the second year after the exodus from Egypt. Moses remained in charge of carrying out Yahweh's instructions. Significantly, the terms "tabernacle" and **tent of meeting** are used as synonyms referring to the same structure (40:1-2, 6). The **ark of the testimony**, where God promised to meet with His people, was the first and central part of the tabernacle to be positioned. **The veil** would **screen off** (Hb *sakak*) the ark, "act as a fence or hedge, cover or hide" it. The veil served as a barrier of protection, not so much for the ark itself as for the people, lest anyone should approach the holiest place of God's presence without His explicit permission and die. The veil in the same position in Herod's temple of New Testament Jerusalem was torn from top to bottom when Jesus died, demonstrating that the Son's death made complete atonement and forgiveness, and therefore God's presence, accessible (Mk 15:38; cp. Heb 6:19; 9:3,8,11-12; 10:19-20).] When the tabernacle was in place, **Moses** consecrated **everything** with **the anointing oil**, including the **priests**.

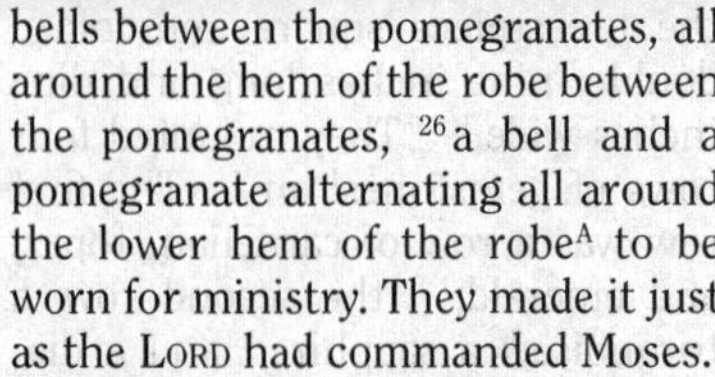

bells between the pomegranates, all around the hem of the robe between the pomegranates, 26 a bell and a pomegranate alternating all around the lower hem of the robe[A] to be worn for ministry. They made it just as the Lord had commanded Moses.

27 They made the tunics of fine woven linen for Aaron and his sons. 28 They also made the turban and the ornate headbands[B] of fine linen, the undergarments, 29 and the sash of finely spun linen of embroidered blue, purple, and scarlet yarn. They did just as the Lord had commanded Moses.

30 They also made a medallion, the holy diadem, out of pure gold and wrote on it an inscription like the engraving on a seal:

HOLY TO THE LORD.

31 Then they attached a cord of blue yarn to it in order to mount it on the turban, just as the Lord had commanded Moses.

The Inspection (39:32-43)

32 So all the work for the tabernacle, the tent of meeting, was finished. The Israelites did everything just as the Lord had commanded Moses. 33 Then they brought the tabernacle to Moses: the tent with all its furnishings, its clasps, its planks, its crossbars, and its posts and bases; 34 the covering of ram skins dyed red and the covering of manatee skins;[C] the veil for the screen; 35 the ark of the •testimony with its poles and the •mercy seat; 36 the table, all its utensils, and the •bread of the Presence; 37 the pure gold lampstand, with its lamps arranged and all its utensils, as well as the oil for the light; 38 the gold altar; the anointing oil; the fragrant incense; the screen for the entrance to the tent; 39 the bronze altar with its bronze grate, its poles, and all its utensils; the basin with its stand; 40 the hangings of the courtyard, its posts and bases, the screen for the gate of the courtyard, its ropes and tent pegs, and all the equipment for the service of the tabernacle, the tent of meeting; 41 and the specially woven[D] garments for ministering in the sanctuary, the holy garments for Aaron the priest and the garments for his sons to serve as priests. 42 The Israelites had done all the work according to everything the Lord had commanded Moses. 43 Moses inspected all the work they had accomplished. They had done just as the Lord commanded. Then Moses blessed them.

The First Day of the First Month (40:1-38)

Yahweh's Instructions (40:1-15)

40 The Lord spoke to Moses: 2 "You are to set up the tabernacle, the tent of meeting, on the first day of the first month.[E] 3 Put the ark of the •testimony there and screen off the ark with the veil. 4 Then bring in the table and lay out its arrangement; also bring in the lampstand and set up its lamps. 5 Place the gold altar for incense in front of the ark of the testimony. Put up the screen for the entrance to the tabernacle. 6 Position the altar of •burnt offering in front of the entrance to the tabernacle, the tent of meeting. 7 Place the basin between the tent of meeting and the altar, and put water in it. 8 Assemble the surrounding courtyard and hang the screen for the gate of the courtyard.

9 "Take the anointing oil and anoint the tabernacle and everything in it; consecrate it along with all its furnishings so that it will be holy. 10 Anoint the altar of burnt offering and all its utensils; consecrate the altar so that it will be especially holy. 11 Anoint the basin and its stand and consecrate it.

12 "Then bring Aaron and his sons to the entrance to the tent of meeting and wash them with water. 13 Clothe Aaron with the holy garments, anoint him, and consecrate him, so that he can serve Me as a priest. 14 Have his sons come forward and clothe them in tunics. 15 Anoint them just as you anointed their father, so that they may also serve Me as priests. Their anointing will serve to inaugurate a permanent priest-

[A] **39:26** Lit *bell and pomegranate, bell and pomegranate, on the hem of the robe around*
[B] **39:28** Lit *and the headdresses of headbands* [C] **39:34** Or *of dolphin skins*, or *of fine leather*; Hb obscure [D] **39:41** Hb obscure [E] **40:2** Lit *on the day of the first month, on the first of the month*

hood for them throughout their generations."

Moses' Faithfulness to Finish the Work (40:16-33)

16 Moses did everything just as the LORD had commanded him.
17 The tabernacle was set up in the first month of the second year, on the first day of the month.[A] 18 Moses set up the tabernacle: he laid its bases, positioned its planks, inserted its crossbars, and set up its posts.
19 Then he spread the tent over the tabernacle and put the covering of the tent on top of it, just as the LORD had commanded Moses.

20 Moses took the testimony and placed it in the ark, and attached the poles to the ark. He set the •mercy seat on top of the ark. 21 He brought the ark into the tabernacle, put up the veil for the screen, and screened off the ark of the testimony, just as the LORD had commanded him.

22 Moses placed the table in the tent of meeting on the north side of the tabernacle, outside the veil.
23 He arranged the bread on it before the LORD, just as the LORD had commanded him. 24 He also put the lampstand in the tent of meeting opposite the table on the south side of the tabernacle 25 and set up the lamps before the LORD, just as the LORD had commanded him.

26 Moses also installed the gold altar in the tent of meeting, in front of the veil, 27 and burned fragrant incense on it, just as the LORD had commanded him. 28 He put up the screen at the entrance to the tabernacle. 29 Then he placed the altar of burnt offering at the entrance to the tabernacle, the tent of meeting, and offered the burnt offering and the •grain offering on it, just as the LORD had commanded him.

30 He set the basin between the tent of meeting and the altar and put water in it for washing. 31 Moses, Aaron, and his sons washed their hands and feet from it. 32 They washed whenever they came to the tent of meeting and approached the altar, just as the LORD had commanded Moses.

33 Next Moses set up the surrounding courtyard for the tabernacle and the altar and hung a screen for the gate of the courtyard. So Moses finished the work.

The Glory of the LORD (40:34-38)

34 The cloud covered the tent of meeting, and the glory of the LORD filled the tabernacle. 35 Moses was unable to enter the tent of meeting because the cloud rested on it, and the glory of the LORD filled the tabernacle.

36 The Israelites set out whenever the cloud was taken up from the tabernacle throughout all the stages of their journey. 37 If the cloud was not taken up, they did not set out until the day it was taken up. 38 For the cloud of the LORD was over the tabernacle by day, and there was a fire inside the cloud by night, visible to the entire house of Israel throughout all the stages of their journey.

[A] **40:17** DSS, Sam, LXX add *of their coming out of Egypt*

40:16-33 Moses is the subject of these verses which summarize again how he completed the project of establishing the tabernacle in thorough compliance with Yahweh's specifications. The passage emphasizes his faithfulness to implement God's instructions.

40:34-38 Not even **Moses** was permitted to enter **the tabernacle** as God **filled** it with **the glory** of His presence made visible by **the cloud** that **rested** [Hb *shakan*; see 29:38-45] **on it**. In the context of the whole, especially of the last five chapters, this text portrays **the LORD** responding immediately and favorably to the obedience of Moses and the people in providing an earthly dwelling place according to His own design. When their work was done, He gloriously took up residence there, provisionally fulfilling His purpose of dwelling in the midst of His people. Verses 36-38 indicate that the cloud remained visible by day and night. Everyone could see it. Whenever it lifted and moved, the people pulled up stakes and followed. Twice the brief passage emphasized that the close connection between the people and God's visible manifestation of His presence remained **throughout all the stages of their journey** to the promised land, the dwelling place *He* was preparing for *them*. Although "the rest of the story" recounted in Scripture reveals Israel's unfaithfulness, comparing the nation's sin to adultery and harlotry, these verses describe the covenant relationship as God meant it to be—a reciprocal relationship in which Yahweh made His home among the people who revered Him for Himself, obeyed Him, and followed Him **whenever** and wherever He went. Yahweh proved His faithful love to Israel by His faithfulness to dwell in and among His people. Significantly, "the sons of Israel" for the first time are called **the entire house of Israel** (cp. 16:31; 19:3), for **the LORD** had made His dwelling among them.

EXODUS... WRITTEN ON MY Heart

The God who rescued the Israelites from bondage in Egypt is the same God who paid the penalty for our sin so we would not be in bondage to sin. We should not be like the Israelites who longed for their old lives in Egypt; God has set us free.

Leviticus

Timeline

- World Events
- Biblical Events

1529 BC	1526 BC	1486 BC	1447 BC
Birth of Aaron	Birth of Moses	Moses' flight to Midian.	God's commission to Moses at the burning bush

"You are to be holy to Me because I, Yahweh, am holy" (20:26a).

Who wrote Leviticus?

Although Leviticus never directly claims Mosaic authorship, the available internal and external evidence supports the conclusion that Moses was the author of Leviticus.

Who were the recipients?

The book of Leviticus was given to the Israelites by God through Moses. The recipients were not only the priesthood but also the nation as a whole. God intended for all His people to know and keep His law. Over and over Moses is told, "Speak to the Israelites" (e.g., 1:2). Leviticus contains the instructions that outlined how Israel was to serve their God.

When was Leviticus written?

Since the book of Leviticus records revelations from Mount Sinai, it was presumably written at some point during the 40 years of wandering in the wilderness, soon after the book of Exodus was written. Moses received this revelation after the tabernacle had been built, which occurred exactly a year after the Israelites left Egypt (ca 1445 B.C.; Ex 40:17).

Where did it happen?

The revelation recorded in the book of Leviticus was given to the Israelites as they were encamped at the foot of Mount Sinai, part of a mountain range at the southern tip of the Sinai Peninsula. This mountain has an adjacent plain that would have been able to accommodate the Israelites. God spoke to the people from the mountain (Lv 25:1) and from the "tent of meeting" (1:1).

What is Leviticus about?

The book of Leviticus is dominated by at least three major themes:

- *Holiness.* The various forms of the word "holy" (Hb *qadash*) occur more than 150 times in Leviticus, indicating its importance. A motto for the book could be, "You must be holy because I am holy" (cp. 11:44-45; 19:2; 20:26). The book of Leviticus covers in some detail how the holy God defines sin, forgives sin, and helps people avoid sin.
- *Sacrifice.* The offering of sacrifice was the principal act of worship for the Israelites and is the first matter presented in the book of Leviticus. The covenant God made with Israel at Mount Sinai (Ex 19) restored the relationship and created harmony between God and man. Sacrifice was given by God as the only way the Israelites could maintain this restored fellowship with Him. God cannot tolerate sin, and the gift of the sacrificial system shows God's mercy and grace in allowing man access to His forgiveness in order to cancel out his sin and thus have fellowship with God.
- *Atonement.* The word most often translated "atonement" (Hb *kaphar*, lit. "cover over") appears more than 40 times in the book of Leviticus, always in the context of sacrifice, the divinely appointed way to obtain pardon for sin (17:11). To make atonement is to give or to do that through which alienation ceases and reconciliation ensues. Individuals need atonement for three reasons: the universality of sin, the seriousness of sin, and the human inability to deal with sin.

Why should women read Leviticus?

Leviticus is central, literally and figuratively, to the Pentateuch. Yet, it has been largely ignored by the church. To many modern readers, Leviticus seems strange and irrelevant. To remove it from the canon, however, would leave as inexplicable whole sections of Scripture. In fact, without the book of Leviticus, the key event of all time, the death of Jesus Christ, is an enigma.

In order to understand God's desire for His people to be set apart and distinct in thought, word, and deed from the pagan world that surrounds them, one must understand how seriously God takes sin. In reading Leviticus, women can gain understanding about the God who made those laws and guidelines for His people in order to keep them from sin. Women will also gain appreciation for the specific protections God put in place for them in Leviticus, effectively debunking the common misconception that the OT portrays God as uncaring towards women.

How do you read Leviticus?

The 613 laws in Leviticus develop, comment on, and expand the Ten Commandments (Ex 20). Jesus summarized all God's law in two commandments on which "all the Law and the Prophets depend" (Mt 22:39-40). Jesus' summary provides a helpful two-part overview of Leviticus. The first 16 chapters reflect and expand the first four commandments of the Decalogue. Chapters 17–27 deal with the second of the two commandments (Lv 19:18).

Outline

I. Love the Lord Your God with All Your Heart (1:1–16:34).
   A. The Laws Concerning Offerings and Sacrifices (1:1–7:38)
   B. The Institution of the Priesthood (8:1–10:20)
   C. The Laws of Purity (11:1–15:33)
   D. The Day of Atonement (16:1-34)

II. Love Your Neighbor as Yourself (17:1–27:34).
   A. The Laws of Personal Holiness (17:1–26:46)
   B. Vows and Tithes (27:1-34)

1446 BC	**1446 BC**	**1445 BC**	**1445 BC**
God's deliverance of Israel from slavery in Egypt.	God's covenant with Israel at Sinai	Dedication of the tabernacle	Events in Leviticus

Love the LORD Your God with All Your Heart (1:1–16:34).

The Laws Concerning Offerings and Sacrifices (1:1–7:38)

The commissioning of the sacrificial system by God (1:1-2)

1 Then the LORD summoned Moses and spoke to him from the
tent of meeting: 2 "Speak to the Israelites and tell them: When any of
you brings an offering to the LORD
from the livestock, you[A] may bring
your offering from the herd or the
flock.

The burnt offering (1:3-17)

3 "If his gift is a •burnt offering
from the herd, he is to bring an unblemished male. He must bring it
to the entrance to the tent of meeting so that he[B] may be accepted by
the LORD. 4 He is to lay his hand on
the head of the burnt offering so
it can be accepted on his behalf to
make •atonement for him. 5 He is to
slaughter the bull before the LORD;
Aaron's sons the priests are to present the blood and sprinkle it on all
sides of the altar that is at the entrance to the tent of meeting. 6 Then
he must skin the burnt offering and
cut it into pieces.[C] 7 The sons of Aaron the priest will prepare a fire on
the altar and arrange wood on the
fire. 8 Aaron's sons the priests are to
arrange the pieces, the head, and the
suet on top of the burning wood on
the altar. 9 The offerer must wash

[A] 1:2 Or *LORD, from the livestock you* [B] 1:3 Or *it* [C] 1:6 Lit *its pieces*

HARD QUESTION

Can we trust the authorship of the Pentateuch?

Scholars have debated for many years whether or not Mosaic authorship is valid for the first five books of the Bible. Complicated theories about different editors and redactors for the books based upon the names used for God have been constructed. Although the book of Leviticus never directly claims Mosaic authorship, the internal testimony (what the book says about itself) is quite conclusive:

- First, the phrase, "The LORD spoke to Moses" or "The LORD said to Moses" occurs 56 times in 27 chapters. The fact that God commanded the content of this book through Moses forms an *inclusio* (repetition at the beginning and end) around the entire text (1:1; 27:34). Since the contents of the book were revealed to or through Moses, he must be the source and very likely the one who also recorded its words.
- Second, Exodus claims Mosaic authorship (Ex 17:14; 24:4,7; 34:27-28). Therefore, Moses can probably be assumed as the author of Leviticus since Leviticus is a continuation of Exodus.
- Last, the New Testament contains many references to the Mosaic authorship of Leviticus. Moses could have used an amanuensis or scribe to assist him as did Paul, but he is obviously the authority and source for the book's message. Jesus affirms this fact when He refers to the Levitical law of cleansing (Mt 8:4; Lv 14:2-32). Paul declares the Mosaic authorship of the words, "The one who does these things will live by them" (Rm 10:5; see Lv 18:5). Also, the New Testament repeatedly refers to the Pentateuch and the prophets as "the Law of Moses and the Prophets" (e.g., Lk 16:29,31; 24:27,44; Ac 28:23).

>WORD|*study*

1:1 Summoned (Hb *qara'*, "called") implies speaking a specific message addressed to a specific recipient intended to elicit a specific response.

Title In the Hebrew Bible, Leviticus is the third book of the Torah or the Law. By Jewish tradition the first word of a book was used as a title. The first word of the Hebrew text of Leviticus is *wayyiqra'* ("and He called"). Leviticus was also commonly described as "the law of the priests" or "the book of the priests," referring to its contents. The translators of the Septuagint, or Greek version of the OT, used the adjective *Leuitikon* (Gk, "levitical, priestly"). The English title comes from the Latinized form of this word—*Leviticum* (in the Latin Vulgate) or *Leviticus*, meaning "that which concerns the priests."

1:1 The LORD summoned Moses so that He could reveal how the Israelites could approach God through sacrifices. Through the revelation of His sacrificial system, God provided understanding of the atonement. Moses was summoned by God **from the tent of meeting**, the movable tabernacle that was constructed at the conclusion of Exodus (Ex 40:17). Here "the tent of meeting," which Moses set up outside the camp (Ex 33:7), seems to have been a temporary tent used for worship during the time at Sinai. Certainly God would not have left Israel without a place of worship for a year's time. This "tent of meeting" had a twofold purpose: (1) the central place of worship for the Israelites, and (2) frequently the location of God's revelation to Israel. It is presented in Scripture as the visible sign of God's presence among His people.

1:1–7:38 In these opening chapters, God uses the description of sacrifices and the instruction on how to offer a sacrifice in an acceptable manner to remind the Israelites of their basic needs as God's chosen people. The five major offerings can be ordered into two categories. The burnt (1:3-17), grain (2:1-16) and fellowship offerings (3:1-17; also identified as peace offerings) were voluntary acts of worship with no stated reason. These offerings always produced a "pleasing aroma to the Lord." The second category included the sin (4:1–5:13) and guilt (5:14–6:7) offerings, which were required upon the violation of a law. These offerings resulted in atonement and forgiveness, which, however, was not the order to be followed by the worshiper in presenting his offerings to the Lord. The normal order of presentation was sin/guilt offering, burnt/grain offering, and then fellowship or peace offering. This order reveals the differing purposes of the offerings: The sin and guilt offerings made it possible to approach God; the burnt and grain offerings showed one's honor of and thanksgiving to God. The fellowship offering recognized the need for peace and reconciliation between the individual and God.

2:1 The **grain offering** (Hb *minchah*) could be offered voluntarily in one of five forms: **fine flour**, oven-baked cakes, cakes baked in a pan, cakes baked in a frying pan (on a griddle), or crushed roasted heads of new grain—each of these reflecting a woman's activity in providing daily bread for her family. The meaning of the word for "grain offering" is broad. The technical use of the word is administrative or political rather than sacred. It was a tribute paid to a king. It was both a form of taxation and an offering of goodwill, and your tribute meant that you would remain faithful. In the sacrificial context of Leviticus, it refers to a gift given by a worshiper to his Lord.

2:2-3 Some of this offering, a **memorial portion** (Hb *ʾazkarah*, the noun form of the verb *zakar*, "remember"), was to be burned on the altar, and the rest was for the use of the priests. In giving this "portion," the worshiper is remembering God's grace and offering praises to God as the Giver of all good things. The **grain offering** represented a product of the worshiper's work and therefore seems to dedicate to God the work of one's hands.

2:11-12 The **grain offering** was to be made without **yeast** or **honey**. There is much debate as to the reason for this. There are two prominent theories. Some argue that nothing subject to fermentation or rapid decay would be **a pleasing aroma** to the Lord and therefore should not be given as an offering to Him. Others take the position that yeast and honey were unacceptable because they were often used to symbolize corruption. In the New Testament, Jesus also uses yeast as symbolic of sin (Lk 12:1; cp. 1Co 5:7-8).

2:13-16 The Israelite was to **season** each of the **grain offerings with salt**. Salt, which is referred to as **the salt of the covenant with your God**, was necessary in every grain offering. Salt was also associated with the Sinaitic covenant (Nm 18:19) and the Davidic covenant (2Ch 13:5). A covenant of salt refers to an eternal covenant. Salt

its entrails and shanks with water. Then the priest will burn all of it on the altar as a burnt offering, a fire offering of a pleasing aroma to the LORD.

10 "But if his gift for a burnt offering is from the flock, from sheep or goats, he is to present an unblemished male. 11 He will slaughter it on the north side of the altar before the LORD. Aaron's sons the priests will sprinkle its blood against the altar on all sides. 12 He will cut the animal into pieces[A] with its head and its suet, and the priest will arrange them on top of the burning wood on the altar. 13 But he is to wash the entrails and shanks with water. The priest will then present all of it and burn it on the altar; it is a burnt offering, a fire offering of a pleasing aroma to the LORD.

14 "If his gift to the LORD is a burnt offering of birds, he is to present his offering from the turtledoves or young pigeons.[B] 15 Then the priest must bring it to the altar, and must twist off its head and burn it on the altar; its blood should be drained at the side of the altar. 16 He will remove its digestive tract,[C] cutting off the tail feathers, and throw it on the east side of the altar at the place for ashes. 17 He will tear it open by its wings without dividing the bird. Then the priest is to burn it on the altar on top of the burning wood. It is a burnt offering, a fire offering of a pleasing aroma to the LORD.

The grain offering (2:1-16)

2 "When anyone presents a •grain offering as a gift to the LORD, his gift must consist of fine flour.[D] He is to pour olive oil on it, put frankincense on it,[E] 2 and bring it to Aaron's sons the priests. The priest will take a handful of fine flour and oil from it, along with all its frankincense, and will burn this memorial portion of it on the altar, a fire offering of a pleasing aroma to the LORD. 3 But the rest of the grain offering will belong to Aaron and his sons; it is the holiest part of the fire offerings to the LORD.

4 "When you present a grain offering baked in an oven, it must be made of fine flour, either unleavened cakes mixed with oil or unleavened wafers coated with oil. 5 If your gift is a grain offering prepared on a griddle, it must be unleavened bread made of fine flour mixed with oil. 6 Break it into pieces and pour oil on it; it is a grain offering. 7 If your gift is a grain offering prepared in a pan, it must be made of fine flour with oil. 8 When you bring[F] to the LORD the grain offering made in any of these ways, it is to be presented to the priest, and he will take it to the altar. 9 The priest will remove the memorial portion[G] from the grain offering and burn it on the altar, a fire offering of a pleasing aroma to the LORD. 10 But the rest of the grain offering will belong to Aaron and his sons; it is the holiest part of the fire offerings to the LORD.

11 "No grain offering that you present to the LORD is to be made with yeast, for you are not to burn[H] any yeast or honey as a fire offering to the LORD. 12 You may present them to the LORD as an offering of •firstfruits, but they are not to be offered on the altar as a pleasing aroma. 13 You are to season each of your grain offerings with salt; you must not omit from your grain offering the salt of the covenant with your God. You are to present salt[I] with each of your offerings.

14 "If you present a grain offering of firstfruits to the LORD, you must present fresh heads of grain, crushed kernels, roasted on the fire, for your grain offering of firstfruits. 15 You are to put oil and frankincense on it; it is a grain offering. 16 The priest will then burn some of its crushed kernels and oil with all its frankincense as a fire offering to the LORD.

The fellowship offering (3:1-17)

3 "If his offering is a •fellowship sacrifice, and he is presenting an animal from the herd, whether male or female, he must present one without blemish before the LORD. 2 He is to lay his hand on the head

[A]**1:12** Lit *its pieces* [B]**1:14** Or *or pigeons* [C]**1:16** Or *its crop*, or *its crissum* [D]**2:1** = wheat flour; Ex 29:2 [E]**2:1** DSS, Sam, LXX add *it is a grain offering* [F]**2:8** DSS, LXX read *When he brings* [G]**2:9** Lit *portion of it* [H]**2:11** Some Hb mss, Sam, LXX, Tg read *present* [I]**2:13** Salt, used as a preservative, is a symbol of the permanence of the covenant.

>WORD|*study*

4:2 The word for **sin** (Hb *chata'*, "miss the mark") occurs more frequently in Leviticus than in any other book of the Old Testament and is heavily concentrated in 4:1–6:7. By sinning, the offender misses his objective of living in obedience to God's commands.

of his offering and slaughter it at the entrance to the tent of meeting. Then Aaron's sons the priests will sprinkle the blood on all sides of the altar. 3 He will present part of the fellowship sacrifice as a fire offering to the LORD: the fat surrounding the entrails, all the fat that is on the entrails, 4 and the two kidneys with the fat on them at the loins; he will also remove the fatty lobe of the liver with the kidneys. 5 Aaron's sons will burn it on the altar along with the •burnt offering that is on the burning wood, a fire offering of a pleasing aroma to the LORD.

6 "If his offering as a fellowship sacrifice to the LORD is from the flock, he must present a male or female without blemish. 7 If he is presenting a lamb for his offering, he is to present it before the LORD. 8 He must lay his hand on the head of his offering, then slaughter it before the tent of meeting. Aaron's sons will sprinkle its blood on all sides of the altar. 9 He will then present part of the fellowship sacrifice as a fire offering to the LORD consisting of its fat and the entire fat tail, which he is to remove close to the backbone. He will also remove the fat surrounding the entrails, all the fat on the entrails, 10 the two kidneys with the fat on them at the loins, and the fatty lobe of the liver above the kidneys. 11 Then the priest will burn the food on the altar, as a fire offering to the LORD.

12 "If his offering is a goat, he is to present it before the LORD. 13 He must lay his hand on its head and slaughter it before the tent of meeting. Aaron's sons will sprinkle[A] its blood on all sides of the altar. 14 He will present part of his offering as a fire offering to the LORD: the fat surrounding the entrails, all the fat that is on the entrails, 15 and the two kidneys with the fat on them at the loins; he will also remove the fatty lobe of the liver with the kidneys. 16 Then the priest will burn the food on the altar, as a fire offering for a pleasing aroma.[B]

"All fat belongs to the LORD. 17 This is a permanent statute throughout your generations, wherever you live: you must not eat any fat or any blood."

The sin offering (4:1–5:13)

4 Then the LORD spoke to Moses: 2 "Tell the Israelites: When someone sins unintentionally against any of the LORD's commands and does anything prohibited by them—

3 "If the anointed priest[C] sins, bringing •guilt on the people, he is to present to the LORD a young, unblemished bull as a •sin[D] offering for the sin he has committed. 4 He must bring the bull to the entrance to the tent of meeting before the LORD, lay his hand on the bull's head, and slaughter it before the LORD. 5 The anointed priest must then take some of the bull's blood and bring it into the tent of meeting. 6 The priest is to dip his finger in the blood and sprinkle some of it seven times before the LORD in front of the veil of the sanctuary. 7 The priest must apply some of the blood to the horns of the altar of fragrant incense that is before the LORD in the tent of meeting. He must pour out the rest of the bull's blood at the base of the altar of burnt offering that is at the entrance to the tent of meeting. 8 He is to remove all the fat from the bull of the sin offering: the fat surrounding the entrails, all the fat that is on the entrails, 9 and the two kidneys with the fat on them at the loins. He will also remove the fatty lobe of the liver with the kidneys, 10 just as the fat is removed from the ox of the •fellowship sacrifice. The priest

cannot be destroyed by fire or decay, and salt preserved food from spoiling. Adding salt to the grain offering reminded the worshiper of his eternal covenant relationship with his God.

3:3-4 The **fat surrounding** the internal organs was to be removed and burned on the altar as **a pleasing aroma to the LORD**. In the ancient Near East, the fat was considered the best part of the meat, and more fat increased the value of the meat. The fat, both literally and metaphorically, signified the best or choicest portion of the offering. That **all fat belongs to the LORD** shows that God requires the best from us, not an inferior portion (v. 16).

4:1-2 The first three offerings could be viewed as voluntary, whereas the sin and restitution offerings were to be made because of a certain offense. The sin offering was for someone who **sins unintentionally against any of the LORD's commands**. Instances of unintentional sins may be found in 5:1-6, and the distinction between unintentional sins and "defiant" sins is noted in Nm 15:22-31. Unintentional sins were a consequence of human frailty. This mandatory offering was required for committing sin (i.e., a violation of the covenant). On many occasions a sin offering was offered not because of an individual sin but because the person had become impure by some unintended means. The sin offering reminded the Israelites that one is a sinner by virtue of his very nature.

4:3-5 The first situation calling for the presentation of a sin offering was the unintentional sin committed by **the anointed priest**—apparently the most serious since it brought **guilt on the people** of Israel. To atone for his sin, the anointed priest had to **present to the LORD a young, unblemished bull**, which may have served as a reminder of Israel's great sin of worshiping a golden calf after the exodus (Ex 32:1-6). By presenting this sacrifice and performing the ritual exactly as prescribed, the priest was acknowledging his own sin. This was an act of repentance.

4:6-7 In performing the ritual of this sacrifice, the priest was **to dip his finger in the blood and sprinkle some of it seven times before the LORD in front of the veil of the sanctuary**. The veil separated the holy of holies, where the ark of the covenant was housed, from the rest of the sanctuary. In the New Testament, a veil serving the same function in the temple was torn in two from top to bottom when Christ was crucified (Mt 27:51; Mk 15:38; Lk 23:45). The priest was also to **apply some of the blood**

[A] **3:13** Or *dash* [B] **3:16** Sam, LXX add *to the LORD* [C] **4:3** Probably the high priest; Lv 6:22 [D] **4:3** Or *purification*

to the horns of the altar of fragrant incense that is before the Lord. These features made the sin offering unique. For the blood to be brought so near to the inner sanctum or holy of holies highlighted just how serious the sin was for Israel's spiritual leader.

4:13-21 The next situation called for the presentation of the sin offering when **the whole community of Israel errs.** Of critical importance in this section is the addition of the statement that **the priest will make atonement on their behalf, and they will be forgiven** (Hb *salach*, "pardon," v. 20; in the OT, God is the only subject for this verb). Ultimately, atonement and forgiveness are the desired results of the sin offering for all. In the entire Bible only God dispenses *salach* since the word does not convey a forgiveness that humans are able to extend.

4:18 The burnt offering was the most common sacrifice in Israelite worship. The process began with the worshiper's bringing an animal without defect to the priest. The worshiper raised the animal himself or paid for it with his earnings, so that the animal represented a "sacrifice" in the modern sense of the word. It cost the worshiper something. King David showed his understanding of this when he refused to offer up to God "burnt offerings that cost me nothing" (2Sm 24:24). The burnt offering was a daily reminder that one must continually confess sins to God. Moreover, the offering was made wholly to God and thus was an expression of total obedience. Sacrifice in the Old Testament is a picture of Christ's sacrifice in the New Testament. Alluding to the whole burnt offering, Paul admonished believers to present themselves to God "as a living sacrifice" (Rm 12:1-2). In the Old Testament, the extent of the sacrifice was seen in the entirety of the burnt offering; in the New Testament, it is seen in Christ's death and His demand for your life in response. Sacrifice is costly. Worship that is pleasing to God must cost the worshiper something.

Offerings Prescribed in Leviticus

Offering

Offering	Hebrew Word	Meaning	Purpose
Sin Offering 4:1–5:13; 6:24-30	*chatta'at*	Sin, wickedness (i.e., an offense to what is the moral standard)	Forgiveness of sin and purification of ceremonial uncleanness
Restitution Offering 5:14–6:7; 7:1-10	*'asham*	Guilt offering (i.e., an atoning sacrifice)	Forgiveness for specific personal sins
Burnt Offering 1:3-17; 6:8-13; cp. Gn 8:20	*'olah*	An offering of the entire part of a sacrifice that was clean and acceptable for sacrifice	Symbol of the voluntary devotion of one's total being to God through the complete consumption of the sacrifice
Grain Offering 2:1-16; 6:14-18	*minchah*	A sacrifice (i.e., a gift offered to God as a religious activity)	Thanking God and offering one's life and work to His service
Fellowship Offering 3:1-17; 7:11-21,28-36	*shelem*	An offering for alliance or friendship in fulfillment of a promise or vow	Participating in the blessings of fellowship with God

is to burn them on the altar of burnt
offering. 11 But the hide of the bull
and all its flesh, with its head and
shanks, and its entrails and dung—
12 all the rest of the bull—he must
bring to a ceremonially •clean place
outside the camp to the ash heap,
and must burn it on a wood fire. It is
to be burned at the ash heap.
13 "Now if the whole community of
Israel errs, and the matter escapes
the notice of the assembly, so that
they violate any of the Lord's commands and incur guilt by doing
what is prohibited, 14 then the assembly must present a young bull
as a sin offering. When the sin they
have committed in regard to the
command becomes known, they are
to bring it before the tent of meeting. 15 The elders of the community
are to lay their hands on the bull's
head before the Lord and it is to be
slaughtered before the Lord. 16 The
anointed priest will bring some
of the bull's blood into the tent of
meeting. 17 The priest is to dip his
finger in the blood and sprinkle it
seven times before the Lord in front
of the veil. 18 He is to apply some of
the blood to the horns of the altar
that is before the Lord in the tent of
meeting. He must pour out the rest
of the blood at the base of the altar

Content			Theological Significance	
God's Portion	**Priest's Portion**	**Worshiper's Portion**	**OT**	**NT**
Fatty portions; fat covering kidneys, liver, and entrails (4:8-9)	Remainder eaten by the officiating priest in a holy place (6:26)	None	Provided atonement for unintentional sins	Prefigured the atoning death of Jesus Christ (Rm 5)
Fatty portions; fat covering kidneys, liver, and entrails (7:3-4)	Remainder eaten by any male among the priests in a holy place (7:6-7)	None	Provided atonement for intentional sins; offering was accompanied by a payment of restitution to the wronged party	Foreshadowed Jesus Christ as our guilt offering (Is 53:10; Col 2:13)
Entire offering (1:9) except skin (7:8)	Skin only (7:8)	None	Demonstrated worshiper's total commitment to God	Signified total surrender of the believer's life to God (Rm 12:1-2)
Memorial portion; a handful (2:2)	Remainder to be eaten in a holy place (6:16)	None	Demonstrated commitment of worshiper's life and work to God	Symbolized the humanity of Jesus Christ with the absence of leaven reflecting His sinlessness (Heb 4:15) and the presence of oil symbolizing the Holy Spirit (Lk 4:18)
Fatty portions; fat covering kidneys, liver, and entrails (3:3-4)	Breast (wave offering) and right thigh (7:30-34)	Remainder eaten by the worshiper and his family on the first or second day (7:15-18)	Worshiper fellowshipped with God through a communal meal	Foreshadowed the peace and rest the believer will have sharing in the sacrifice meal at the table of the Lord (Jn 6:53-58)

of burnt offering that is at the entrance to the tent of meeting. 19 He
is to remove all the fat from it and
burn it on the altar. 20 He is to offer
this bull just as he did with the bull
in the sin offering; he will offer it the
same way. So the priest will make
•atonement on their behalf, and they
will be forgiven. 21 Then he will bring
the bull outside the camp and burn
it just as he burned the first bull. It
is the sin offering for the assembly.
22 "When a leader[A] sins and unintentionally violates any of the commands of the LORD his God by doing
what is prohibited, and incurs guilt,
23 or someone informs him about the
sin he has committed, he is to bring
an unblemished male goat as his offering. 24 He is to lay his hand on the
head of the goat and slaughter it at
the place where the •burnt offering
is slaughtered before the LORD. It is a
sin offering. 25 Then the priest must
take some of the blood from the sin
offering with his finger and apply it
to the horns of the altar of burnt offering. The rest of its blood he must
pour out at the base of the altar of
burnt offering. 26 He must burn all
its fat on the altar, like the fat of the
fellowship sacrifice. In this way the

4:22-28 The last section called for the presentation of the sin offering **when a leader** or **any of the common people sins unintentionally by violating one of the LORD's commands**. This sacrificial ritual differs in two ways from the sacrifice of the high priest:

- The leader **is to bring an unblemished male goat as his offering** instead of a bull (v. 23). A commoner is to bring **an unblemished female goat** for his sin (v. 28).
- The priest applies the blood of the sin offering **to the horns of the altar of burnt offering** instead of upon the altar of incense (v. 25).

[A]**4:22** Or *ruler*

5:1-4 Four specific ways are described in which an individual can sin unintentionally:

- not testifying to an oath (v. 1);
- touching **unclean** animals (v. 2);
- touching unclean people (v. 3);
- making an improper **oath** (v. 4).

5:5-13 If someone incurs guilt in one of these cases, he is to confess [Hb *yadah*, "show oneself as guilty"] **he has committed that sin**. Before atonement could be made, confession, the sign of true repentance, was mandatory. The sin offering always preceded a burnt offering. This sacrificial order is significant. First, atonement must be made for sin. The sin offering had to take place to reconcile the worshiper to God before there could be fellowship with God. After the worshiper received forgiveness through his sin offering, his next act of worship was to devote himself wholly to the Lord by offering a burnt offering.

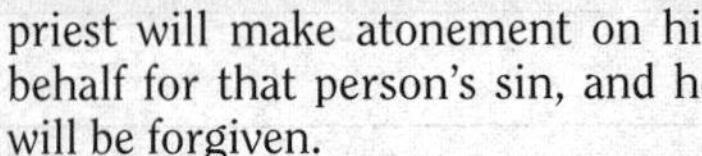

priest will make atonement on his
behalf for that person's sin, and he
will be forgiven.
27 "Now if any of the common
people[A] sins unintentionally by violating one of the LORD's commands,
does what is prohibited, and incurs
guilt, 28 or if someone informs him
about the sin he has committed,
then he is to bring an unblemished
female goat as his offering for the
sin that he has committed. 29 He is
to lay his hand on the head of the
sin offering and slaughter it at the
place of the burnt offering. 30 Then
the priest must take some of its
blood with his finger and apply it to
the horns of the altar of burnt offering. He must pour out the rest
of its blood at the base of the altar.
31 He is to remove all its fat just as
the fat is removed from the fellowship sacrifice. The priest is to burn
it on the altar as a pleasing aroma to
the LORD. In this way the priest will
make atonement on his behalf, and
he will be forgiven.
32 "Or if the offering that he brings
as a sin offering is a lamb, he is to
bring an unblemished female. 33 He
is to lay his hand on the head of the
sin offering and slaughter it as a sin
offering at the place where the burnt
offering is slaughtered. 34 Then the
priest must take some of the blood
of the sin offering with his finger
and apply it to the horns of the altar
of burnt offering. He must pour out
the rest of its blood at the base of
the altar. 35 He is to remove all its fat
just as the fat of the lamb is removed
from the fellowship sacrifice. The
priest will burn it on the altar along
with the fire offerings to the LORD. In
this way the priest will make atonement on his behalf for the sin he has
committed, and he will be forgiven.

5 "When someone sins in any of
these ways:

If he has seen, heard, or known
about something he has witnessed, and did not respond to
a public call to testify, he is responsible for his sin.
2 Or if someone touches anything •unclean—a carcass of
an unclean wild animal, or unclean livestock, or an unclean
swarming creature[B]—without
being aware of it, he is unclean
and •guilty.
3 Or if he touches human uncleanness—any uncleanness
by which one can become defiled—without being aware of
it, but later recognizes it, he is
guilty.
4 Or if someone swears rashly to
do what is good or evil—concerning anything a person may
speak rashly in an oath—without being aware of it, but later
recognizes it, he incurs guilt in
such an instance.[C]

5 If someone incurs guilt in one of
these cases, he is to confess he has
committed that sin. 6 He must bring
his restitution for the sin he has
committed to the LORD: a female
lamb or goat from the flock as a •sin
offering. In this way the priest will
make •atonement on his behalf for
his sin.
7 "But if he cannot afford an animal from the flock, then he may
bring to the LORD two turtledoves or
two young pigeons as restitution for
his sin—one as a sin offering and
the other as a •burnt offering. 8 He
is to bring them to the priest, who
will first present the one for the sin
offering. He must twist its head at
the back of the neck without severing it. 9 Then he will sprinkle some
of the blood of the sin offering on
the side of the altar, while the rest
of the blood is to be drained out at
the base of the altar; it is a sin offering. 10 He must prepare the second
bird as a burnt offering according to
the regulation. In this way the priest
will make atonement on his behalf
for the sin he has committed, and he
will be forgiven.
11 "But if he cannot afford[D] two
turtledoves or two young pigeons,
he may bring two quarts[E] of fine[F]
flour[G] as an offering for his sin. He
must not put olive oil or frankincense on it, for it is a sin offering.
12 He is to bring it to the priest, who

[A]**4:27** Lit *the people of the land* [B]**5:2** Perhaps a fish, insect, rodent, or reptile; Gn 1:20; Lv 11:20-23,29-31 [C]**5:4** Lit *in one of such things* [D]**5:11** Lit *if his hand is not sufficient for* [E]**5:11** Lit *one-tenth of an ephah* [F]**5:11** Or *wheat*; Ex 29:2 [G]**5:11** Lit *flour as a sin offering*

will take a handful from it as its memorial portion and burn it on the altar along with the fire offerings to the LORD; it is a sin offering. 13 In this way the priest will make atonement on his behalf concerning the sin he has committed in any of these cases, and he will be forgiven. The rest will belong to the priest, like the •grain offering."

The restitution offering (5:14–6:7)

14 Then the LORD spoke to Moses: 15 "If someone offends by sinning unintentionally in regard to any of the LORD's holy things,[A] he must bring his •restitution offering to the LORD: an unblemished ram from the flock (based on your assessment of its value in silver •shekels, according to the sanctuary shekel) as a restitution offering. 16 He must make restitution for his sin regarding any holy thing, adding a fifth of its value to it, and give it to the priest. Then the priest will make atonement on his behalf with the ram of the restitution offering, and he will be forgiven.

17 "If someone sins and without knowing it violates any of the LORD's commands concerning anything prohibited, he bears the consequences of his guilt. 18 He must bring an unblemished ram from the flock according to your assessment of its value as a restitution offering to the priest. Then the priest will make atonement on his behalf for the error he has committed unintentionally, and he will be forgiven. 19 It is a restitution offering; he is indeed guilty before the LORD."

6 [B] The LORD spoke to Moses: 2 "When someone sins and offends the LORD by deceiving his neighbor in regard to a deposit, a security,[C] or a robbery; or defrauds his neighbor; 3 or finds something lost and lies about it; or swears falsely about any of the sinful things a person may do— 4 once he has sinned and acknowledged his •guilt—he must return what he stole or defrauded, or the deposit entrusted to him, or the lost item he found, 5 or anything else about which he swore falsely. He must make full restitution for it and add a fifth of its value to it. He is to pay it to its owner on the day he acknowledges his guilt. 6 Then he must bring his •restitution offering to the LORD: an unblemished ram from the flock according to your assessment of its value as a restitution offering to the priest. 7 In this way the priest will make •atonement on his behalf before the LORD, and he will be forgiven for anything he may have done to incur guilt."

The disposal of offerings (6:8–7:38)

8 [D] The LORD spoke to Moses: 9 "Command Aaron and his sons: This is the law of the •burnt offering; the burnt offering itself must remain on the altar's hearth all night until morning, while the fire of the altar is kept burning on it. 10 The priest is to put on his linen robe and linen undergarments.[E] He is to remove the ashes of the burnt offering the fire has consumed on the altar, and place them beside the altar. 11 Then he must take off his garments, put on other clothes, and bring the ashes outside the camp to a ceremonially •clean place. 12 The fire on the altar is to be kept burning; it must not go out. Every morning the priest will burn wood on the fire. He is to arrange the burnt offering on the fire and burn the fat portions from the •fellowship offerings on it. 13 Fire

CHRIST OUR RESTITUTION OFFERING

The restitution offering (5:14–6:7), in contrast with the sin offering (4:1–5:13), was required for the type of offense that created a debt calling for compensation. Sin does enslave a person; it creates an indebtedness. The offering of the Lord's Servant in Isaiah is described as a restitution offering (Is 53:10). Since the New Testament writers interpreted this to be a prophecy of Christ, Jesus' death must be understood as a restitution offering that has removed the debt every sinner owes to God, which is the basis for the proclamation that Jesus "paid" for our sin (1Co 6:20; Rv 5:9). Jesus' death was the perfect sin offering in that He met the demands of the law by dying in your place. But His death was also your perfect restitution offering in that He carried out the will of God completely by an act of voluntary obedience. It is the payment of a debt to render satisfaction for the wrongs committed.

5:14-19 The sin offering and the restitution or guilt offering were usually grouped together and sometimes referenced interchangeably since their meaning and the ritual prescribed were similar. The latter was generally associated with mistreatment of or damage to a neighbor or perhaps improper treatment of the tabernacle or **the LORD's holy things** (v. 15). Therefore, repair of the damage, together with the penalty of **a fifth** [or 20 percent] **of its value** was required (v. 16; 6:5). The priest was appointed to assess the value plus penalty. Clearly, all sins were covered: Christ's atonement covered all when He fulfilled completely the Old Testament requirement for sacrifice (1Jn 1:7). The distinction between the sin offering and **restitution** offering is in the text—the matter of compensation. Both offerings were concerned with compensation, but the restitution offering was required for an offense that created a debt calling for compensation. In other words, the restitution offering was a specialized kind of sin offering that provided restitution for a wrong, together with atonement for the wrong.

6:5 The **restitution** offering demanded the heaviest cost. Sin is personal and costly. Forgiveness was not without cost in any of these five sacrifices, but the restitution offering confirmed that sin places a person in debt. In the case of the restitution offering, the cost was monetary. Restitution was made through payment, adding **a fifth of its value to it**.

6:8-13 These verses give supplemental instructions regarding the five types of offerings. The first section refers to the disposal of the burnt offering. First, **the burnt offering itself must remain on the altar's hearth all night until morning**. Second, the priest's removal of **the ashes** reinforced the idea that the burnt offering was wholly God's.

[A] **5:15** Things dedicated to the LORD such as tabernacle furnishings, priestly portions of the sacrifices, tenths, firstfruits, and firstborn livestock [B] **6:1** Lv 5:20 in Hb [C] **6:2** Or *an investment* [D] **6:8** Lv 6:1 in Hb [E] **6:10** Lit *undergarments on his flesh*

6:14 The word for **law** (Hb *torah*) has the sense of meaning of "instruction" in this verse.

6:15-23 The second section refers to the disposal of the grain offering. **A handful of fine flour**, or memorial portion, is to be burned on the altar. The remainder of the grain offering was to be eaten by the priests **in a holy place**. If, however, the grain offering is presented by a priest, **it must be completely burned as a permanent portion for the Lord. . . . It is not to be eaten**. The priest could not eat from his own offering because it was made on his behalf. The priest could not benefit in any way from his own sacrifice.

6:24–7:10 The third section refers to the disposal of the sin and restitution offerings. **The priest who offers it as a sin offering is to eat it** as long as the offering was not in any way made on behalf of the priest. The restitution offering is like the sin offering; it belongs to the priest who makes atonement with it.

7:11-36 The next section refers to the disposal of the **fellowship offering**. The uniqueness of the fellowship offering is that the offerer was invited to join in eating his **sacrifice**. The sacrifice was divided. The fatty portions were burned **on the altar** (v. 31), a symbolic expression of offering the best to God. **The breast** belonged to the priests and was **to be waved as a presentation offering before the Lord**. The exact meaning of the ritual term "wave" has been debated. Many modern commentators have agreed that this motion was vertical instead of horizontal, not a waving side-to-side but rather simply elevating the offering to the Lord. The sacrifice was completely eaten on the day it was presented (v. 15).

must be kept burning on the altar continually; it must not go out.

14 "Now this is the law of the •grain offering: Aaron's sons will present it before the LORD in front of the altar. 15 The priest is to remove a handful of fine flour and olive oil from the grain offering, with all the frankincense that is on the offering, and burn its memorial portion on the altar as a pleasing aroma to the LORD. 16 Aaron and his sons may eat the rest of it. It is to be eaten in the form of unleavened bread in a holy place; they are to eat it in the courtyard of the tent of meeting. 17 It must not be baked with yeast; I have assigned it as their portion from My fire offerings. It is especially holy, like the •sin offering and the restitution offering. 18 Any male among Aaron's descendants may eat it. It is a permanent portion[A] throughout your generations from the fire offerings to the LORD. Anything that touches the offerings will become holy."

19 The LORD spoke to Moses: 20 "This is the offering that Aaron and his sons must present to the LORD on the day that he is anointed: two quarts[B] of fine flour as a regular[C] grain offering, half of it in the morning and half in the evening. 21 It is to be prepared with oil on a griddle; you are to bring it well-kneaded. You must present it as a grain offering of baked pieces,[D] a pleasing aroma to the LORD. 22 The priest, who is one of Aaron's sons and will be anointed to take his place, is to prepare it. It must be completely burned as a permanent portion for the LORD. 23 Every grain offering for a priest will be a whole burnt offering; it is not to be eaten."

24 The LORD spoke to Moses: 25 "Tell Aaron and his sons: This is the law of the sin offering. The sin offering is most holy and must be slaughtered before the LORD at the place where the burnt offering is slaughtered. 26 The priest who offers it as a sin offering is to eat it. It must be eaten in a holy place, in the courtyard of the tent of meeting. 27 Anything that touches its flesh will become holy, and if any of its blood spatters on a garment, then you must wash that garment[E] in a holy place. 28 A clay pot in which the sin offering is boiled must be broken; if it is boiled in a bronze vessel, it must be scoured and rinsed with water. 29 Any male among the priests may eat it; it is especially holy. 30 But no sin offering may be eaten if its blood has been brought into the tent of meeting to make atonement in the holy place; it must be burned up.

7 "Now this is the law of the •restitution offering; it is especially holy. 2 The restitution offering must be slaughtered at the place where the •burnt offering is slaughtered, and the priest is to sprinkle its blood on all sides of the altar. 3 The offerer must present all the fat from it: the fat tail, the fat surrounding the entrails,[F] 4 and the two kidneys with the fat on them at the loins; he will also remove the fatty lobe of the liver with the kidneys. 5 The priest will burn them on the altar as a fire offering to the LORD; it is a restitution offering. 6 Any male among the priests may eat it. It is to be eaten in a holy place; it is especially holy.

7 "The restitution offering is like the •sin offering; the law is the same for both. It belongs to the priest who makes •atonement with it. 8 As for the priest who presents someone's burnt offering, the hide of the burnt offering he has presented belongs to him; it is the priest's. 9 Any •grain offering that is baked in an oven or prepared in a pan or on a griddle belongs to the priest who presents it; it is his. 10 But any grain offering, whether dry or mixed with oil, belongs equally[G] to all of Aaron's sons.

11 "Now this is the law of the •fellowship sacrifice that someone may present to the LORD: 12 If he presents it for thanksgiving, in addition to the thanksgiving sacrifice,[H] he is to present unleavened cakes mixed with olive oil, unleavened wafers coated with oil, and well-kneaded

[A]**6:18** Or *statute* [B]**6:20** Lit *a tenth of an ephah* [C]**6:20** Daily [D]**6:21** Hb obscure [E]**6:27** Lit *wash what it spattered on* [F]**7:3** LXX, Sam add *and all the fat that is on the entrails*; Lv 3:3,9,14; 4:8 [G]**7:10** Lit *oil, will be a man like his brother* [H]**7:12** The thanksgiving sacrifice is the first of three kinds of fellowship sacrifices. It was given to express gratitude to God (Jr 33:11) in circumstances such as answered prayer (Ps 50:14-15) or safe travel (Ps 107:22-25).

cakes of fine flour mixed with oil.
13 He is to present as his offering
cakes of leavened bread[A] with his
thanksgiving sacrifice of fellowship.
14 From the cakes he must present
one portion of each offering as a
contribution to the LORD. It will belong to the priest who sprinkles the
blood of the fellowship offering; it is
his. 15 The meat of his thanksgiving
sacrifice of fellowship must be eaten
on the day he offers it; he may not
leave any of it until morning.
16 "If the sacrifice he offers is a vow[B]
or a freewill offering,[C] it is to be eaten
on the day he presents his sacrifice,
and what is left over may be eaten on
the next day. 17 But what remains of
the sacrificial meat by the third day
must be burned up. 18 If any of the
meat of his fellowship sacrifice is
eaten on the third day, it will not be
accepted. It will not be credited to the
one who presents it; it is repulsive.
The person who eats any of it will be
responsible for his sin.[D]
19 "Meat that touches anything
•unclean must not be eaten; it is
to be burned up. Everyone who
is •clean may eat any other meat.
20 But the one who eats meat from
the LORD's fellowship sacrifice while
he is unclean,[E] that person must be
cut off from his people. 21 If someone touches anything unclean,
whether human uncleanness, an
unclean animal, or any unclean, detestable[F] creature, and eats meat
from the LORD's fellowship sacrifice,
that person must be cut off from his
people."
22 The LORD spoke to Moses: 23 "Tell
the Israelites: You are not to eat any
fat of an ox, a sheep, or a goat. 24 The
fat of an animal that dies naturally
or is mauled by wild beasts[G] may be
used for any purpose, but you must
not eat it. 25 If anyone eats animal fat
from a fire offering presented to the
LORD, the person who eats it must be
cut off from his people. 26 Wherever
you live, you must not eat the blood
of any bird or animal. 27 Whoever
eats any blood, that person must be
cut off from his people."
28 The LORD spoke to Moses: 29 "Tell
the Israelites: The one who presents
a fellowship sacrifice to the LORD
must bring an offering to the LORD
from his sacrifice. 30 His own hands
will bring the fire offerings to the
LORD. He will bring the fat together
with the breast. The breast is to be
waved as a presentation offering before the LORD. 31 The priest is to burn
the fat on the altar, but the breast
belongs to Aaron and his sons. 32 You
are to give the right thigh to the
priest as a contribution from your
fellowship sacrifices. 33 The son of
Aaron who presents the blood of the
fellowship offering and the fat will
have the right thigh as a portion. 34 I
have taken from the Israelites the
breast of the presentation offering
and the thigh of the contribution
from their fellowship sacrifices, and
have assigned them to Aaron the
priest and his sons as a permanent
portion[H] from the Israelites."
35 This is the portion from the fire
offerings to the LORD for Aaron and
his sons since the day they were presented to serve the LORD as priests.
36 The LORD commanded this to be
given to them by the Israelites on
the day He anointed them. It is a
permanent portion[H] throughout
their generations.
37 This is the law for the burnt offering, the grain offering, the sin
offering, the restitution offering,
the ordination offering, and the fellowship sacrifice, 38 which the LORD
commanded Moses on Mount Sinai
on the day He[I] commanded the Israelites to present their offerings to
the LORD in the Wilderness of Sinai.

The Institution of the Priesthood (8:1–10:20)

The ordination of Aaron and his sons (8:1-36)

8 The LORD spoke to Moses: 2 "Take
Aaron, his sons with him, the

7:37-38 Chapter 7 concludes the instruction on personal offerings by repeating material from the introduction (1:1-2), implying that this passage should be viewed as a unit. This literary technique, called *inclusio*, is used frequently throughout the Old Testament. These two verses also serve as a summary/conclusion by listing the offerings of the sacrificial system.

8:1–10:20 Leviticus 1–7 describes the procedures for the Israelite sacrificial system. In order for these sacrifices to be carried out properly, the priesthood must administer them. In this second division in the book of Leviticus the priesthood is officially established. This section of Leviticus is a continuation and implementation of the priestly instructions given to Moses in Ex 29. The Israelite priests, coming from the tribe of Levi, were divided into three groups: (1) the high priest who was the descendant of Aaron through his son Eleazar; (2) the Levites who were the general descendants of Levi; and (3) the ordinary priests who were the descendants of Levi through Aaron.

8:1-4 In this chapter, Moses was instructed by God to consecrate and appoint **Aaron** and **his sons** to the priesthood. Before he began this process of consecration, Moses gathered together the **whole community** (Hb *'ēdah*, "assembly, appointed meeting"; cp. 4:13; Ex 35:1), i.e., the entire congregation of Israelites including women and children (Lv 8:1-5). The verb for **assemble** (Hb *qahal*, "call together"; here an imperative) and **assembled** (here an obedient action, v. 4) is not common in the Old Testament and is used only here in Leviticus, suggesting the magnitude of this event in Israel's history (cp. Ex 35:1; Dt 31:12; 1Ch 15:3). It was imperative for all the tribes (i.e., the entire nation) to witness the divine appointment of Aaron and his sons, who would be the priests entrusted with the grave responsibility of performing the prescribed sacrifices on the annual Day of Atonement (Lv 16).

A **7:13** Although yeast was prohibited from being burned on the altar (Lv 2:11), leavened bread could still be an offering (Lv 23:17-20) to be eaten by the priests and their families. B **7:16** The vow offering, the second category of fellowship sacrifice, was brought as an expression of gratitude to fulfill a vow; Gn 28:20; 2Sm 15:7-8; Pr 7:14. C **7:16** The freewill offering, the third category of fellowship sacrifice, was a voluntary expression of gratitude toward God for any reason; Dt 16:10; Ps 54:6. D **7:18** Or *will bear his guilt* E **7:20** Lit *while his uncleanness is upon him* F **7:21** Some Hb mss, Sam, Syr, Tg read *swarming* G **7:24** Lit *fat of a carcass or the fat of a mauled beast* H **7:34,36** Or *statute* I **7:38** Or *he*

8:6 Moses then **presented Aaron and his sons and washed them with water**, not only for purifying their physical bodies but also for symbolizing their spiritual purification.

8:7-9 After the cleansing, Moses focused his attention on the high priest, **Aaron**. Moses clothed Aaron in special priestly garments (cp. Ex 28): a linen **tunic** fastened with an embroidered **sash**, the **robe** with its **ephod**, the embroidered **breastpiece**, and the fine linen **turban** with **the holy diadem** (Hb *nēzer*, "crown"). The most notable was the breastpiece, made predominantly of gold. It contained a pouch, nine or ten inches square. After putting the breastpiece on Aaron, Moses placed the **Urim** [Hb "lights, flames"] **and Thummim** [Hb "perfection," pl. of *tom*, "integrity, completeness, innocence"] into the breastpiece. Much study has been devoted to uncovering the meaning and purpose of the Urim and Thummim. According to Ex 28:15-30, they were used to convey the will of God to the people. The breastpiece, symbolizing the unity of Israel and their total dependence on God, was the most important article of clothing in the high priestly garment. The breastpiece also symbolized the role of high priest as mediator, for he carried on it the names of the twelve tribes of Israel. Whenever the high priest officiated, he always had the names of the tribes literally on his chest; He always had immediately before him those on whose behalf he was serving as priest.

8:10-13 Moses continued by using **the anointing oil** to consecrate Aaron. Anointing with oil was a means of conveying divine appointment to a task. Here it also symbolized the sanctification of the new priests. Having been set apart by anointing, the Lord's servant would be held accountable for faithfully carrying out his assigned duties. Then Moses, as God's appointed mediator, performed the priestly duties of offering sacrifices on behalf of Aaron and his sons. The sacrifices were again offered in a significant order: (1) a sin offering to obtain forgiveness, (2) a burnt offering of dedication to God, and (3) a fellowship offering in gratitude for the restoration of communion and fellowship with God.

8:14-36 Finally, after anointing **the altar** with blood, Moses anointed with blood Aaron and his sons. Anointing with blood symbolized consecration. The blood on the priest's ears, hands, and feet indicates the dedication of the whole man to God (v. 24). With his ears the priest was accountable to hear and obey God's word. With the

garments, the anointing oil, the bull of the •sin[A] offering, the two rams, and the basket of unleavened bread, 3 and assemble the whole community at the entrance to the tent of meeting." 4 So Moses did as the LORD commanded him, and the community assembled at the entrance to the tent of meeting. 5 Moses said to them, "This is what the LORD has commanded to be done."

6 Then Moses presented Aaron and his sons and washed them with water. 7 He put the tunic on Aaron, wrapped the sash around him, clothed him with the robe, and put the •ephod on him. He put the woven band of the ephod around him and fastened it to him. 8 Then he put the breastpiece on him and placed the •Urim and Thummim into the breastpiece. 9 He also put the turban on his head and placed the gold medallion, the holy diadem, on the front of the turban, as the LORD had commanded Moses.

10 Then Moses took the anointing oil and anointed the tabernacle and everything in it to consecrate them. 11 He sprinkled some of the oil on the altar seven times, anointing the altar with all its utensils, and the basin with its stand, to consecrate them. 12 He poured some of the anointing oil on Aaron's head and anointed and consecrated him. 13 Then Moses presented Aaron's sons, clothed them with tunics, wrapped sashes around them, and fastened headbands on them, as the LORD had commanded Moses.

14 Then he brought the bull near for the sin offering, and Aaron and his sons laid their hands on the head of the bull for the sin offering. 15 Then Moses slaughtered it,[B] took the blood, and applied it with his finger to the horns of the altar on all sides, purifying the altar. He poured out the blood at the base of the altar and consecrated it so that •atonement can be made on it.[C] 16 Moses took all the fat that was on the entrails, the fatty lobe of the liver, and the two kidneys with their fat, and he burned them on the altar. 17 He burned up the bull with its hide, flesh, and dung outside the camp, as the LORD had commanded Moses.

18 Then he presented the ram for the •burnt offering, and Aaron and his sons laid their hands on the head of the ram. 19 Moses slaughtered it and[D] sprinkled the blood on all sides of the altar. 20 Moses cut the ram into pieces and burned the head, the pieces, and the suet, 21 but he washed the entrails and shanks with water. He then burned the entire ram on the altar. It was a burnt offering for a pleasing aroma, a fire offering to the LORD as He had commanded Moses.

22 Next he presented the second ram, the ram of ordination, and Aaron and his sons laid their hands on the head of the ram. 23 Moses slaughtered it,[E] took some of its blood, and put it on Aaron's right earlobe, on the thumb of his right hand, and on the big toe of his right foot. 24 Moses also presented Aaron's sons and put some of the blood on their right earlobes, on the thumbs of their right hands, and on the big toes of their right feet. Then Moses sprinkled the blood on all sides of the altar. 25 He took the fat—the fat tail, all the fat that was on the entrails, the fatty lobe of the liver, and the two kidneys with their fat—as well as the right thigh. 26 From the basket of unleavened bread that was before the LORD he took one cake of unleavened bread, one cake of bread made with oil, and one wafer, and placed them on the fat portions and the right thigh. 27 He put all these in the hands of Aaron and his sons and waved them before the LORD as a presentation offering. 28 Then Moses took them from their hands and burned them on the altar with the burnt offering. This was an ordination offering for a pleasing aroma, a fire offering to the LORD. 29 He also took the breast and waved it before the LORD as a presentation offering; it was Moses' portion of the ordination ram as the LORD had commanded him.

30 Then Moses took some of the

[A]**8:2** Or *purification* [B]**8:14-15** Or *offering, and he slaughtered it.* [15] *Then Moses* [C]**8:15** Or *it by making •atonement for it* [D]**8:18-19** Or *ram,* [19] *and he slaughtered it. Moses* [E]**8:22-23** Or *ram,* [23] *and he slaughtered it. Moses*

anointing oil and some of the blood that was on the altar and sprinkled them on Aaron and his garments, as well as on his sons and their garments. In this way he consecrated Aaron and his garments, as well as his sons and their garments.

31 Moses said to Aaron and his sons, "Boil the meat at the entrance to the tent of meeting and eat it there with the bread that is in the basket for the ordination offering as I commanded:[A] Aaron and his sons are to eat it. 32 You must burn up what remains of the meat and bread. 33 You must not go outside the entrance to the tent of meeting for seven days, until the time your days of ordination are completed, because it will take seven days to ordain you.[B] 34 The LORD commanded what has been done today in order to make atonement for you. 35 You must remain at the entrance to the tent of meeting day and night for seven days and keep the LORD's charge so that you will not die, for this is what I was commanded." 36 So Aaron and his sons did everything the LORD had commanded through Moses.

The beginning of priestly service (9:1-24)

9 On the eighth day Moses summoned Aaron, his sons, and the elders of Israel. 2 He said to Aaron, "Take a young bull for a •sin[C] offering and a ram for a •burnt offering, both without blemish, and present them before the LORD. 3 And tell the Israelites:[D] Take a male goat for a sin offering; a calf and a lamb, male yearlings without blemish, for a burnt offering; 4 an ox and a ram for a •fellowship offering to sacrifice before the LORD; and a •grain offering mixed with oil. For today the LORD is going to appear to you."

5 They brought what Moses had commanded to the front of the tent of meeting, and the whole community came forward and stood before the LORD. 6 Moses said, "This is what the LORD commanded you to do, that the glory of the LORD may appear to you." 7 Then Moses said to Aaron, "Approach the altar and sacrifice your sin offering and your burnt offering; make •atonement for yourself and the people.[E] Sacrifice the people's offering and make atonement for them, as the LORD commanded."

8 So Aaron approached the altar and slaughtered the calf as a sin offering for himself. 9 Aaron's sons brought the blood to him, and he dipped his finger in the blood and applied it to the horns of the altar. He poured out the blood at the base of the altar. 10 He burned the fat, the kidneys, and the fatty lobe of the liver from the sin offering on the altar, as the LORD had commanded Moses. 11 He burned up the flesh and the hide outside the camp.

12 Then he slaughtered the burnt offering. Aaron's sons brought him the blood, and he sprinkled it on all sides of the altar. 13 They brought him the burnt offering piece by piece, along with the head, and he burned them on the altar. 14 He washed the entrails and the shanks and burned them with the burnt offering on the altar.

15 Aaron presented the people's offering. He took the male goat for the people's sin offering, slaughtered it, and made a sin offering with it as he did before. 16 He presented the burnt offering and sacrificed it according to the regulation. 17 Next he presented the grain offering, took a handful of it, and burned it on the altar in addition to the morning burnt offering.

18 Finally, he slaughtered the ox and the ram as the people's fellowship sacrifice. Aaron's sons brought him the blood, and he sprinkled it on all sides of the altar. 19 They also brought the fat portions from the ox and the ram—the fat tail, the fat surrounding the entrails, the kidneys, and the fatty lobe of the liver—20 and placed these on the breasts. Aaron burned the fat portions on the altar, 21 but he waved the breasts and the right thigh as a presentation offering before the LORD, as Moses had commanded.[F]

22 Aaron lifted up his hands toward the people and blessed them.

right hand representing his strength, he must faithfully do the Lord's work in the Lord's strength. With his feet the priest must carefully walk in the ways of the Lord.

9:1-22 After the ordination of the priesthood, the priests were commanded to offer sacrifices to **the LORD**. All of the sacrifices, except the guilt offering, were presented. The order again was significant. One must deal with sin before he can be completely dedicated to the Lord and have fellowship with Him. These offerings were required because God intended to manifest His presence among His people. Faithfully carrying out God's prescribed means of worship prepares the people for meeting with God; the observance of rituals is not an end in itself.

[A] **8:31** LXX, Syr, Tg read *was commanded*; Ex 29:31-32 [B] **8:33** Lit *because he will fill your hands for seven days* [C] **9:2** Or *purification* [D] **9:3** Sam, LXX read *elders of Israel* [E] **9:7** LXX reads *and your household* [F] **9:21** Some Hb mss, LXX, Sam read *as the LORD commanded Moses*

He came down after sacrificing the
sin offering, the burnt offering, and
the fellowship offering. 23 Moses
and Aaron then entered the tent of
meeting. When they came out, they
blessed the people, and the glory of
the LORD appeared to all the people.
24 Fire came from the LORD and consumed the burnt offering and the fat
portions on the altar. And when all
the people saw it, they shouted and
fell facedown on the ground.

The role of priests in Israel (10:1-20)

10 Aaron's sons Nadab and Abihu
each took his own firepan, put
fire in it, placed incense on it, and
presented unauthorized fire before
the LORD, which He had not commanded them to do. 2 Then fire came
from the LORD and burned them to
death before the LORD. 3 So Moses
said to Aaron, "This is what the LORD
meant when He said:

> I will show My holiness[A]
> to those who are near Me,
> and I will reveal My glory[B]
> before all the people."

But Aaron remained silent.
4 Moses summoned Mishael and
Elzaphan, sons of Aaron's uncle Uzziel, and said to them, "Come here
and carry your relatives away from
the front of the sanctuary to a place
outside the camp." 5 So they came
forward and carried them in their
tunics outside the camp, as Moses
had said.
6 Then Moses said to Aaron and
his sons Eleazar and Ithamar, "Do
not let your hair hang loose and do
not tear your garments, or else you
will die, and the LORD will become
angry with the whole community.
However, your brothers, the whole
house of Israel, may mourn over
that tragedy when the LORD sent the
fire. 7 You must not go outside the
entrance to the tent of meeting or
you will die, for the LORD's anointing
oil is on you." So they did as Moses
said.
8 The LORD spoke to Aaron: 9 "You
and your sons are not to drink wine
or beer when you enter the tent of
meeting, or else you will die; this is a
permanent statute throughout your
generations. 10 You must distinguish
between the holy and the common,
and the •clean and the •unclean,
11 and teach the Israelites all the
statutes that the LORD has given to
them through Moses."
12 Moses spoke to Aaron and his remaining sons, Eleazar and Ithamar:
"Take the •grain offering that is left
over from the fire offerings to the
LORD, and eat it prepared without
yeast beside the altar, because it is
especially holy. 13 You must eat it
in a holy place because it is your
portion[C] and your sons' from the
fire offerings to the LORD, for this is
what I was commanded. 14 But you
and your sons and your daughters
may eat the breast of the presentation offering and the thigh of the
contribution in any ceremonially
clean place, because these portions
have been assigned to you and your
children from the Israelites' •fellow-
ship sacrifices. 15 They are to bring
the thigh of the contribution and
the breast of the presentation offering, together with the offerings
of fat portions made by fire, to wave
as a presentation offering before the
LORD. It will belong permanently to
you and your children, as the LORD
commanded."
16 Later, Moses inquired about the
male goat of the •sin offering, but
it had already been burned up. He

[A] **10:3** Or *will be treated as holy* [B] **10:3** Or *will be glorified* [C] **10:13** Or *statute*

9:23-24 Moses and Aaron then entered the tent of meeting. In the book of Exodus, Moses could not enter the tabernacle because of the glory of the Lord (Ex 40:35). Now Moses and Aaron were free to enter because the sacrifices had been offered as the Lord commanded. When Moses and Aaron came out, **they blessed the people, and the glory of the LORD appeared to all**. God's pattern was established. Only when God's people were obedient to His pattern of worship did He bless them.

10:1 God displayed His pleasure in and approval of the Levitical priesthood by sending down fire from heaven (Lv 9:24). **Fire** could also display God's disapproval and judgment. On the first official day of the sacrificial system, Aaron's sons, **Nadab and Abihu**, failed to obey the Lord's commands regarding proper ritual practice by presenting **unauthorized fire**. The basic meaning of "unauthorized" (Hb *zur*) is "strange," in the sense here of being foreign to what has been prescribed. There was something "unlawful or profane" (i.e., *not* holy) about the fire (cp. 22:12-13; Dt 32:16; Jl 3:17). Offering "unauthorized incense" on the incense altar (Ex 30:9) and putting God's specially blended "holy anointing oil" on "an unauthorized person" (Ex 30:33) were specifically forbidden. For example, Aaron's sons may have used coals from outside the consecrated tabernacle courtyard. Whatever they offered reflected an inexcusable disregard both for God's holiness and for the gravity of their responsibilities of serving as anointed priests before Him. God's commands, however, are absolute—they cannot be tailored to suit one's fancy.

10:2-3 The serious consequence of Nadab and Abihu's disobedience is a reminder of how important worship is to God. The worship of God should never be carried out in a careless fashion, nor should it be based on how you feel or what you find pleasing but rather on what God requires of you. The severity of God's judgment upon these two priests underscores how egregious their offense was. To establish a pattern of obedience for the nation, they had to be vigilant in upholding God's standards of holiness. Israel served the living God,

BIBLICAL WOMANHOOD Priesthood

Consistently, the Levitical priests who performed the required offerings were men. This male role of representing the Israelites before God paralleled the responsibility of the male head of the household to provide spiritual leadership (cp. Jb 1:5). The fact that men were assigned these duties neither precluded a woman's access to God (cp. 1Sm 1:1–2:10) nor implied her inferiority. Rather these role assignments affirmed the creation order.

was angry with Eleazar and Ithamar,
Aaron's surviving sons, and asked,
17 "Why didn't you eat the sin offering in the sanctuary area? For it is
especially holy, and He has assigned
it to you to take away the •guilt of
the community and make •atone-
ment for them before the LORD.
18 Since its blood was not brought
inside the sanctuary, you should
have eaten it in the sanctuary area,
as I commanded."
19 But Aaron replied to Moses,
"See, today they presented their sin
offering and their •burnt offering
before the LORD. Since these things
have happened to me, if I had eaten
the sin offering today, would it have
been acceptable in the LORD's sight?"
20 When Moses heard this, it was acceptable to him.[A]

The Laws of Purity (11:1–15:33)

Clean and unclean animals (11:1-47)

11 The LORD spoke to Moses and
Aaron: 2 "Tell the Israelites: You
may eat all these kinds of land animals. 3 You may eat any animal with
divided hooves and that chews the
cud. 4 But among the ones that chew
the cud or have divided hooves you
are not to eat these:

the camel, though it chews
the cud,
does not have divided
hooves—it is •unclean
for you;
5 the hyrax,[B] though it chews
the cud,
does not have hooves—it is
unclean for you;
6 the hare, though it chews
the cud,
does not have hooves—it is
unclean for you;
7 the pig, though it has
divided hooves,
does not chew the cud—it is
unclean for you.

8 Do not eat any of their meat or
touch their carcasses—they are unclean for you.
9 "This is what you may eat from
all that is in the water: You may
eat everything in the water that
has fins and scales, whether in the
seas or streams. 10 But these are to
be detestable to you: everything in
the seas or streams that does not
have fins and scales among all the
swarming things and other living
creatures in the water. 11 They are to
remain detestable to you; you must
not eat any of their meat, and you
must detest their carcasses. 12 Everything in the water that does not
have fins and scales will be detestable to you.
13 "You are to detest these birds.
They must not be eaten because
they are detestable:

the eagle,[C]
the bearded[D] vulture,
the black vulture,[E] 14 the kite,[F]
any kind of falcon,[G]
15 every kind of raven,
16 the ostrich,[H]
the short-eared owl,[I]
the gull,[J]
any kind of hawk,
17 the little[K] owl, the cormorant,[L]
the long-eared owl,[M]
18 the white[N] owl, the desert owl,[O]
the osprey,[P] 19 the stork,[Q]
any kind of heron,[R]
the hoopoe, and the bat.

20 "All winged insects that walk on
all fours are to be detestable to you.
21 But you may eat these kinds of all
the winged insects that walk on all
fours: those that have jointed legs
above their feet for hopping on the
ground. 22 You may eat these:

any kind of locust, katydid,
cricket, and grasshopper.

23 All other winged insects that have
four feet are to be detestable to you.
24 "These will make you unclean.
Whoever touches their carcasses
will be unclean until evening, 25 and
whoever carries any of their carcasses must wash his clothes and
will be unclean until evening. 26 All
animals that have hooves but do
not have a divided hoof and do not

[A] **10:20** Lit *acceptable in his sight* [B] **11:5** A rabbit-like animal [C] **11:13** Or *griffon-vulture* [D] **11:13** Or *black* [E] **11:13** Or *the osprey*, or *the bearded vulture* [F] **11:14** Or *hawk* [G] **11:14** Or *buzzards*, or *hawks* [H] **11:16** Or *eagle owl* [I] **11:16** Or *the night hawk*, or *the screech owl* [J] **11:16** Or *long-eared owl* [K] **11:17** Or *tawny* [L] **11:17** Or *fisher owl*, or *pelican* [M] **11:17** Or *the ibis* [N] **11:18** Or *little* [O] **11:18** Or *the pelican*, or *the horned owl* [P] **11:18** Or *Egyptian vulture* [Q] **11:19** Or *heron* [R] **11:19** Or *cormorant*, or *hawk*

whose laws were given not merely as a set of religious rituals but as the revelation of the glory of His holiness and of the opportunity for obedience to the mandates of His righteousness (cp. Jos 7; 1Ch 13:8-10; Ac 5:1-11).

11:1–15:33 At the end of the priestly legislation, Aaron was commanded to distinguish between the holy and the common, between the clean and the unclean, and to teach the Israelites all the statutes that the Lord has given to them through Moses. This was to be the major task of the priesthood. In Lv 11–15 Moses received instruction from the Lord about what was to be considered clean and unclean. The Israelites' concern for the clean and the unclean was an essential part of their response to a holy God. Ceremonial cleanness was the tangible picture of holiness. Everything that is clean is not necessarily holy, but without exception what is holy will always be clean.

11:1-47 As far back as the flood narrative (Gn 7:2) a distinction has been made between clean and unclean animals. In fact, even in the creation narrative, the first law God gave to man identified eating something forbidden as sin (Gn 2:16-17). Although the rationale behind the dietary laws is not provided here, the Israelites were to submit and obey because these laws were given by God and reflected His will for Israel. You can be assured that God has His own reasons for whatever He decrees. Hygienic principles may have had a part in these distinctions, through which one is reminded of God's concern and care for the well-being of His children. Some have suggested that the animals identified as unclean may have been used in pagan worship. Although these laws may have had some background in hygiene or nutrition or even in an effort to avoid pagan practices, their primary importance was clearly to teach the Israelites the concept of being holy and distinct, belonging to the Lord and living a life set apart unto Him. Whether or not you understand the reasons for such distinctions makes no difference when it comes to whether or not you are to obey. The distinctions in animals were decreed by God to make Israel a holy nation. There was nothing inherently sinful about the animals designated as unclean.

In the beginning, God acknowledged all of His creation as "very good." (Gn 1:31) However, separating the animals into these two categories was a concrete illustration of God's separation of His people Israel from the surrounding nations, whose idolatrous and immoral practices were in contrast to what God expected of His people. Israel's obedience in maintaining these distinctions between what they would and would not eat was a point of distinction for their culture in contrast to other cultures. The Israelites would also have to be cognizant, on a daily basis, that belonging to God means that He is Lord over all aspects of life.

Since the coming of Christ, all salvific distinctions between the Jews and Gentiles have been abolished (Gl 3:26-28; Eph 2:11-18). Accordingly, the distinctions between clean and unclean animals are no longer a concern (Mk 7:14-23; Ac 10:9-23; Rm 14:14; Col 2:16). Nevertheless, the principle of separation still stands as believers are admonished to be separate and distinct from the world and set apart unto the Lord by obedience to His mandates (1Jn 1:6-7).

chew the cud are unclean for you. Whoever touches them becomes unclean. 27 All the four-footed animals that walk on their paws are unclean for you. Whoever touches their carcasses will be unclean until evening, 28 and anyone who carries their carcasses must wash his clothes and will be unclean until evening. They are unclean for you.

29 "These creatures that swarm on the ground are unclean for you:

the weasel,[A] the mouse,
any kind of large lizard,[B]
30 the gecko, the monitor lizard,[C]
the common lizard,[D]
the skink,[E]
and the chameleon.[F]

31 These are unclean for you among all the swarming creatures. Whoever touches them when they are dead will be unclean until evening. 32 When any one of them dies and falls on anything it becomes unclean—any item of wood, clothing, leather, •sackcloth, or any implement used for work. It is to be rinsed with water and will remain unclean until evening; then it will be •clean. 33 If any of them falls into any clay pot, everything in it will become unclean; you must break it. 34 Any edible food coming into contact with that unclean water will become unclean, and any drinkable liquid in any container will become unclean. 35 Anything one of their carcasses falls on will become unclean. If it is an oven or stove, it must be smashed; it is unclean and will remain unclean for you. 36 A spring or cistern containing water will remain clean, but someone who touches a carcass in it will become unclean. 37 If one of their carcasses falls on any seed that is to be sown, it is clean; 38 but if water has been put on the seed and one of their carcasses falls on it, it is unclean for you.

39 "If one of the animals that you use for food dies,[G] anyone who touches its carcass will be unclean until evening. 40 Anyone who eats some of its carcass must wash his clothes and will be unclean until evening. Anyone who carries its carcass must wash his clothes and will be unclean until evening.

41 "All the creatures that swarm on the earth are detestable; they must not be eaten. 42 Do not eat any of the creatures that swarm on the earth, anything that moves on its belly or walks on all fours or on many feet,[H] for they are detestable. 43 Do not become contaminated by any creature that swarms; do not become unclean or defiled by them. 44 For I am •Yahweh your God, so you must consecrate yourselves and be holy because I am holy. You must not defile yourselves by any swarming creature that crawls on the ground. 45 For I am Yahweh, who brought you up from the land of Egypt to be your God, so you must be holy because I am holy.

46 "This is the law concerning animals, birds, all living creatures that move in the water, and all creatures that swarm on the ground, 47 in order to distinguish between the unclean and the clean, between the animals that may be eaten and those that may not be eaten."

Purification after childbirth (12:1-8)

12 The LORD spoke to Moses: 2 "Tell the Israelites: When a woman becomes pregnant and gives birth to a male child, she will be •unclean seven days, as she is during the days of her menstrual impurity. 3 The flesh of his foreskin must be circumcised on the eighth day. 4 She will continue in purification from her bleeding for 33 days. She must not touch any holy thing or go into the sanctuary until completing her days of purification. 5 But if she gives birth to a female child, she will be unclean for two weeks as she is during her menstrual impurity. She will continue in purification from her bleeding for 66 days.

6 "When her days of purification are complete, whether for a son or daughter, she is to bring to the

[A]**11:29** Or *mole rat*, or *rat* [B]**11:29** Or *of thorn-tailed* or *dabb lizard*, or *of crocodile* [C]**11:30** Or *the spotted lizard*, or *the chameleon* [D]**11:30** Or *the gecko*, or *the newt*, or *the salamander* [E]**11:30** Or *sand lizard*, or *newt*, or *snail* [F]**11:30** Or *salamander*, or *mole* [G]**11:39** Dies of itself or by predators; this does not apply to animals slaughtered for food. [H]**11:42** Lit *fours, to anything multiplying pairs of feet*

priest at the entrance to the tent of meeting a year-old male lamb for a •burnt offering, and a young pigeon or a turtledove for a •sin[A] offering. [7]He will present them before the LORD and make •atonement on her behalf; she will be •clean from her discharge of blood. This is the law for a woman giving birth, whether to a male or female. [8]But if she doesn't have sufficient means[B] for a sheep, she may take two turtledoves or two young pigeons, one for a burnt offering and the other for a sin[A] offering. Then the priest will make atonement on her behalf, and she will be clean."

Skin infections and mildew (13:1–14:57)

13 The LORD spoke to Moses and Aaron: [2]"When a person has a swelling,[C] scab,[D] or spot on the skin of his body, and it becomes a disease on the skin of his body, he is to be brought to Aaron the priest or to one of his sons, the priests. [3]The priest will examine the infection on the skin of his body. If the hair in the infection has turned white and the infection appears to be deeper than the skin of his body, it is a skin disease. After the priest examines him, he must pronounce him •unclean.
[4]But if the spot on the skin of his body is white and does not appear to be deeper than the skin, and the hair in it has not turned white, the priest must quarantine the infected person for seven days. [5]The priest will then reexamine him on the seventh day. If he sees that the infection remains unchanged and has not spread on the skin, the priest must quarantine him for another seven days. [6]The priest will examine him again on the seventh day. If the infection has faded and has not spread on the skin, the priest is to pronounce him •clean; it is a scab. The person is to wash his clothes and will become clean. [7]But if the scab spreads further on his skin after he has presented himself to the priest for his cleansing, he must present himself again to the priest. [8]The priest will examine him, and if the scab has spread on the skin, then the priest must pronounce him unclean; he has a skin disease.
[9]"When a skin disease develops on a person, he is to be brought to the priest. [10]The priest will examine him. If there is a white swelling on the skin that has turned the hair white, and there is a patch of raw flesh in the swelling, [11]it is a chronic disease on the skin of his body, and

A 12:6,8 Or *purification* B 12:8 Lit *if her hand cannot obtain what is sufficient* C 13:2 Or *discoloration* D 13:2 Or *rash*, or *eruption*

12:1-8 In this chapter, the laws regarding a new mother are given, and here only purification after childbirth is discussed. The reason for purification is not stated in the text, but being in a state of uncleanness was not necessarily due to sin. The flow of blood, both from the menstrual cycle and from childbirth, caused ceremonial uncleanness, but not because these processes were sinful or demeaning. Rather, the woman was considered unclean to prevent her from approaching the sanctuary or worshiping with the covenant community (15:19-24). The primary reason for this appears to be God's concern for the separateness of His people. Some have added the possibility of the association of pregnancy with fertility rites found in pagan religious worship. However, a more likely reason is the contact with the blood accompanying childbirth.

BIBLICAL WOMANHOOD Why is There a Difference in Purity Laws?

There has been much debate as to the reason for the difference in the length of time a woman is unclean after the birth of a male child compared with a female child. After a woman **gives birth to a male child, she will be unclean seven days, as she is during the days of her menstrual impurity**. This is the same length of time a woman was unclean after menstruation (15:19-24), implying that the uncleanness resulted from the issue of blood. Since life is in the blood (17:11), any loss of blood called for purification in honoring the sanctity of life.

Perhaps after the birth of a son the period of uncleanness was interrupted by his circumcision **on the eighth day** (12:3-4). After the birth of **a female child, she will be unclean for two weeks**. The length of her uncleanness was also doubled. Some scholars argue that this teaches the inferiority of females, but such an interpretation is not derived from a plain reading of the text. Whether the woman gave birth to a son or a daughter, she was required to bring the same offering for her purification, suggesting that all children were considered equally valuable (vv. 6-7).

After sacrifice, a mother was ceremonially **clean** from the flow of **blood** (v. 7). Note the use of "clean" rather than "forgiven," affirming that the issue prompting the sacrifice was not sinfulness. This longer period of purification may simply have served to work against the ideas of pagan religions, in which case excluding new mothers from the sanctuary for a longer period after the birth of a daughter erected a barrier between fertility and the worship of God. However, much more likely is the fact that the period of purification after the birth of a son was interrupted by the mandated circumcision on the eighth day, a time when the mother's loving care would be especially needed for her infant son.

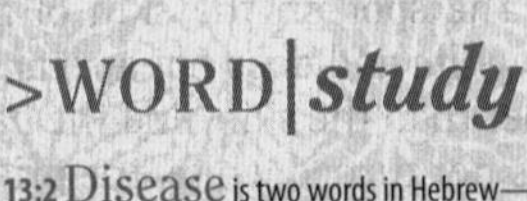

13:2 Disease is two words in Hebrew—*nega*ʿ ("mark or spot," as on the skin) and *tsaraʿat* ("leprosy or malignant skin disease"). **Infection** (Hb *nega*ʿ, v. 3) was often regarded as visible evidence of an eruption of leprosy. Most modern commentators and lexicographers have abandoned the traditional translation of "leprosy," a word which now denotes a particular medical condition also called Hansen's Disease. Both Hebrew words, however, have a much broader range of meaning, including, but not restricted to, "leprosy." Depending on the context, *nega*ʿ can denote "plague or calamity" (e.g., "plague," 1Kg 8:37; Ps 91:10; "afflictions," 1Kg 8:38; Ps 38:11), "stroke or wound" (e.g., "assaults," Dt 17:8; "blows," 2Sm 7:14; Ps 89:32; "torment," Ps 39:10). *Tsaraʿat* can be used for various skin diseases or as a referent to mold and mildew.

An Israelite found to have **an infectious skin disease** (Lv 13:43) was isolated to prevent the disease from spreading. A person pronounced **unclean** by **the priest** had to **live alone** [Hb *badad*, "separately, solitarily, in isolation"] **in a place outside the camp** (v. 46). To be outside the camp was to be cut off from God. When Adam and Eve sinned (Gn 3), they were sent out of the garden, i.e., "outside the camp." To live outside the camp was to be cut off from the blessings of the covenant. When an individual was pronounced unclean, understandably he went into mourning, evidenced by having **his clothes torn and his hair hanging loose** (Lv 13:45). The Israelites had multiple images of the restrictions of holiness built into their everyday living: Just as any sin was an obstacle to communion with God, so any flow of blood for women, or any infectious skin disease for anyone, was an obstacle to participating in community worship. The Israelites were not like other peoples, and the law of God continually reminded them of their set-apartness.

the priest must pronounce him unclean. He need not quarantine him, for he is unclean. 12 But if the skin disease breaks out all over the skin so that it covers all the skin of the infected person from his head to his feet so far as the priest can see, 13 the priest will look, and if the skin disease has covered his entire body, he is to pronounce the infected person clean. Since he has turned totally white, he is clean. 14 But whenever raw flesh appears on him, he will be unclean. 15 When the priest examines the raw flesh, he must pronounce him unclean. Raw flesh is unclean; it is a skin disease. 16 But if the raw flesh changes[A] and[B] turns white, he must go to the priest. 17 The priest will examine him, and if the infection has turned white, the priest must pronounce the infected person clean; he is clean.

18 "When a boil appears on the skin of one's body and it heals, 19 and a white swelling or a reddish-white spot develops where the boil was, the person must present himself to the priest. 20 The priest will make an examination, and if the spot seems to be beneath the skin and the hair in it has turned white, the priest must pronounce him unclean; it is a skin disease that has broken out in the boil. 21 But when the priest examines it, if there is no white hair in it, and it is not beneath the skin but is faded, the priest must quarantine him seven days. 22 If it spreads further on the skin, the priest must pronounce him unclean; it is an infection. 23 But if the spot remains where it is and does not spread, it is only the scar from the boil. The priest is to pronounce him clean.

24 "When there is a burn on the skin of one's body produced by fire, and the patch made raw by the burn becomes reddish-white or white, 25 the priest is to examine it. If the hair in the spot has turned white and the spot appears to be deeper than the skin, it is a skin disease that has broken out in the burn. The priest must pronounce him unclean; it is a skin disease. 26 But when the priest examines it, if there is no white hair in the spot and it is not beneath the skin but is faded, the priest must quarantine him seven days. 27 The priest will reexamine him on the seventh day. If it has spread further on the skin, the priest must pronounce him unclean; it is a skin disease. 28 But if the spot has remained where it was and has not spread on the skin but is faded, it is the swelling from the burn. The priest is to pronounce him clean, for it is only the scar from the burn.

29 "When a man or woman has an infection on the head or chin, 30 the priest must examine the infection. If it appears to be deeper than the skin, and the hair in it is yellow and sparse, the priest must pronounce the person unclean. It is a scaly outbreak,[C] a skin disease of the head or

[A]**13:16** Or *recedes* [B]**13:16** Or *flesh again* [C]**13:30** Or *is scall*; Hb obscure

chin. [31]When the priest examines the scaly infection, if it does not appear to be deeper than the skin, and there is no black hair in it, the priest must quarantine the person with the scaly infection for seven days. [32]The priest will reexamine the infection on the seventh day. If the scaly outbreak has not spread and there is no yellow hair in it and it does not appear to be deeper than the skin, [33]the person must shave himself but not shave the scaly area. Then the priest must quarantine the person who has the scaly outbreak for another seven days. [34]The priest will examine the scaly outbreak on the seventh day, and if it has not spread on the skin and does not appear to be deeper than the skin, the priest is to pronounce the person clean. He is to wash his clothes, and he will be clean. [35]But if the scaly outbreak spreads further on the skin after his cleansing, [36]the priest is to examine the person. If the scaly outbreak has spread on the skin, the priest does not need to look for yellow hair; the person is unclean. [37]But if as far as he can see, the scaly outbreak remains unchanged and black hair has grown in it, then it has healed; he is clean. The priest is to pronounce the person clean.

[38]"When a man or a woman has white spots on the skin of the body, [39]the priest is to make an examination. If the spots on the skin of the body are dull white, it is only a rash[A] that has broken out on the skin; the person is clean.

[40]"If a man loses the hair of his head, he is bald, but he is clean. [41]Or if he loses the hair at his hairline, he is bald on his forehead, but he is clean. [42]But if there is a reddish-white infection on the bald head or forehead, it is a skin disease breaking out on his head or forehead. [43]The priest is to examine him, and if the swelling of the infection on his bald head or forehead is reddish-white, like the appearance of a skin disease on his body, [44]the man is afflicted with a skin disease; he is unclean. The priest must pronounce him unclean; the infection is on his head.

[45]"The person afflicted with an infectious skin disease is to have his clothes torn and his hair hanging loose, and he must cover his mouth and cry out, 'Unclean, unclean!' [46]He will remain unclean as long as he has the infection; he is unclean. He must live alone in a place outside the camp.

[47]"If a fabric is contaminated with mildew—in wool or linen fabric, [48]in the warp or woof of linen or wool, or in leather or anything made of leather— [49]and if the contamination is green or red in the fabric, the leather, the warp, the woof, or any leather article, it is a mildew contamination and is to be shown to the priest. [50]The priest is to examine the contamination and quarantine the contaminated fabric for seven days. [51]The priest is to reexamine the contamination on the seventh day. If it has spread in the fabric, the warp, the woof, or the leather, regardless of how it is used, the contamination is harmful mildew; it is unclean. [52]He is to burn the fabric, the warp or woof in wool or linen, or any leather article, which is contaminated. Since it is harmful mildew it must be burned up.

[53]"When the priest examines it, if the contamination has not spread in the fabric, the warp or woof, or any leather article, [54]the priest is to order whatever is contaminated to be washed and quarantined for another seven days. [55]After it has been washed, the priest is to reexamine the contamination. If the appearance of the contaminated article has not changed, it is unclean. Even though the contamination has not spread, you must burn up the fabric. It is a fungus[B] on the front or back of the fabric.

[56]"If the priest examines it, and the contamination has faded after it has been washed, he must cut the contaminated section out of the fabric, the leather, or the warp or woof. [57]But if it reappears in the fabric, the warp or woof, or any leather article, it has broken out again. You must burn up whatever is contaminated. [58]But if the contamination disappears from the fabric, the warp or

13:47-59 The priest is given instructions here for serving as the expert regarding molded or mildewed fabrics. Whatever he determined upon examination to be **contaminated** with a **harmful** growth of **mildew** or **fungus** had to **be burned up**.

[A]13:39 Hb obscure [B]13:55 Hb obscure

14:1-32 Elaborate instructions are given for restoring a **person** who, though **afflicted with a skin disease,** finally gets well. Just as the priest's duty was to determine whether or not someone must be declared ceremonially unclean, it was also his duty to perform a **restitution offering** on the behalf of one who had been **cleansed**. When Jesus healed a man with leprosy, He instructed the man to fulfill these obligations (Mk 1:40-44).

woof, or any leather article, which have been washed, it is to be washed again, and it will be clean.

59 "This is the law concerning a mildew contamination in wool or linen fabric, warp or woof, or any leather article, in order to pronounce it clean or unclean."

14 The LORD spoke to Moses: 2 "This is the law concerning the person afflicted with a skin disease on the day of his cleansing. He is to be brought to the priest, 3 who will go outside the camp and examine him. If the skin disease has disappeared from the afflicted person,[A] 4 the priest will order that two live •clean birds, cedar wood, scarlet yarn, and hyssop be brought for the one who is to be cleansed. 5 Then the priest will order that one of the birds be slaughtered over fresh water in a clay pot. 6 He is to take the live bird together with the cedar wood, scarlet yarn, and hyssop, and dip them all into the blood of the bird that was slaughtered over the fresh water. 7 He will then sprinkle the blood seven times on the one who is to be cleansed from the skin disease. He is to pronounce him clean and release the live bird over the open countryside. 8 The one who is to be cleansed must wash his clothes, shave off all his hair, and bathe with water; he is clean. Afterward he may enter the camp, but he must remain outside his tent for seven days. 9 He is to shave off all his hair again on the seventh day: his head, his beard, his eyebrows, and the rest of his hair. He is to wash his clothes and bathe himself with water; he is clean.

10 "On the eighth day he must take two unblemished male lambs, an unblemished year-old ewe lamb, a •grain offering of three quarts[B] of fine flour mixed with olive oil, and one-third of a quart[C] of olive oil. 11 The priest who performs the cleansing will place the person who is to be cleansed, together with these offerings, before the LORD at the entrance to the tent of meeting. 12 The priest is to take one male lamb and present it as a •restitution offering, along with the one-third quart[C] of olive oil, and he must wave them as a presentation offering before the LORD. 13 He is to slaughter the male lamb at the place in the sanctuary area where the •sin offering and •burnt offering are slaughtered, for like the sin offering, the restitution offering belongs to the priest; it is especially holy. 14 The priest is to take some of the blood from the restitution offering and put it on the lobe of the right ear of the one to be cleansed, on the thumb of his right hand, and on the big toe of his right foot. 15 Then the priest will take some of the one-third quart[C] of olive oil and pour it into his left palm. 16 The priest will dip his right finger into the oil in his left palm and sprinkle some of the oil with his finger seven times before the LORD. 17 From the oil remaining in his palm the priest will put some on the lobe of the right ear of the one to be cleansed, on the thumb of his right hand, and on the big toe of his right foot, on top of the blood of the restitution offering. 18 What is left of the oil in the priest's palm he is to put on the head of the one to be cleansed. In this way the priest will make •atonement for him before the LORD. 19 The priest must sacrifice the sin offering and make atonement for the one to be cleansed from his uncleanness. Afterward he will slaughter the burnt offering. 20 The priest is to offer the burnt offering and the grain offering on the altar. The priest will make atonement for him, and he will be clean.

21 "But if he is poor and cannot afford these,[D] he is to take one male lamb for a restitution offering to be waved in order to make atonement for him, along with two quarts[E] of fine flour mixed with olive oil for a grain offering, one-third of a quart[C] of olive oil, 22 and two turtledoves or two young pigeons, whatever he can afford,[F] one to be a sin offering and the other a burnt offering. 23 On the eighth day he is to bring these things for his cleansing to the priest at the entrance to the tent of

[A] **14:3** Lit *the person afflicted with skin disease* [B] **14:10** Lit *three-tenths*; probably 3/10 of an ephah [C] **14:10,12,15,21** Lit *one log* [D] **14:21** Lit *and his hand is not* [E] **14:21** Lit *him, and one-tenth*; probably 1/10 of an ephah [F] **14:22** Lit *pigeons, for which his hand is sufficient*

meeting before the LORD. 24 The priest will take the male lamb for the restitution offering and the one-third quart[A] of olive oil, and wave them as a presentation offering before the LORD. 25 After he slaughters the male lamb for the restitution offering, the priest is to take some of the blood of the restitution offering and put it on the right earlobe of the one to be cleansed, on the thumb of his right hand, and on the big toe of his right foot. 26 Then the priest will pour some of the oil into his left palm. 27 With his right finger the priest will sprinkle some of the oil in his left palm seven times before the LORD. 28 The priest will also put some of the oil in his palm on the right earlobe of the one to be cleansed, on the thumb of his right hand, and on the big toe of his right foot, on the same place as the blood of the restitution offering. 29 What is left of the oil in the priest's palm he is to put on the head of the one to be cleansed to make atonement for him before the LORD. 30 He must then sacrifice one type of what he can afford,[B] either the turtledoves or young pigeons, 31 one as a sin offering and the other as a burnt offering, sacrificing what he can afford[C,D] together with the grain offering. In this way the priest will make atonement before the LORD for the one to be cleansed. 32 This is the law for someone who has[E] a skin disease and cannot afford[F] the cost of his cleansing."

33 The LORD spoke to Moses and Aaron: 34 "When you enter the land of Canaan that I am giving you as a possession, and I place a mildew contamination in a house in the land you possess,[G] 35 the owner of the house is to come and tell the priest: Something like mildew contamination has appeared[H] in my house. 36 The priest must order them to clear the house before he enters to examine the contamination, so that nothing in the house becomes •unclean. Afterward the priest will come to examine the house. 37 He will examine it, and if the contamination in the walls of the house consists of green or red indentations[I] that appear to be beneath the surface of the wall, 38 the priest is to go outside the house to its doorway and quarantine the house for seven days. 39 The priest is to return on the seventh day and examine it. If the contamination has spread on the walls of the house, 40 the priest must order that the stones with the contamination be pulled out and thrown into an unclean place outside the city. 41 He is to have the inside of the house completely scraped, and the plaster[J] that is scraped off must be dumped in an unclean place outside the city. 42 Then they must take different stones to replace the former ones and take additional plaster[J] to replaster the house.

43 "If the contamination reappears in the house after the stones have been pulled out, and after the house has been scraped and replastered, 44 the priest must come and examine it. If the contamination has spread in the house, it is harmful mildew; the house is unclean. 45 It must be torn down with its stones, its beams, and all its plaster, and taken outside the city to an unclean place. 46 Whoever enters the house during any of the days the priest quarantines it will be unclean until evening. 47 Whoever lies down in the house is to wash his clothes, and whoever eats in it is to wash his clothes.

48 "But when the priest comes and examines it, if the contamination has not spread in the house after it was replastered, he is to pronounce the house clean because the contamination has disappeared.[K] 49 He is to take two birds, cedar wood, scarlet yarn, and hyssop to purify the house, 50 and he is to slaughter one of the birds over a clay pot containing fresh water. 51 He will take the cedar wood, the hyssop, the scarlet yarn, and the live bird, dip them in the blood of the slaughtered bird and the fresh water, and sprinkle the house seven times. 52 He will purify the house with the blood of the bird,

14:33-56 Extensive measures are also described for dealing with **a house** that **the priest** concluded was contaminated with **mildew**. These instructions were applied to houses in **the land of Canaan**, presumably built by Canaanites but inhabited by the conquering Israelites. **The LORD** does not explain why He would **place** such **contamination** in a house, but God's affliction of such a house would perhaps draw attention to the condemnation deserved by a life not fashioned for Yahweh's glory. Likewise, the thorough and severe measures prescribed for restoring such a structure to make it habitable again would vividly illustrate the radical "clean-up" process necessary to redeem a life under the new ownership of Yahweh.

[A] **14:24** Lit *one log* [B] **14:30** Lit *of that for which his hand is sufficient* [C] **14:31** LXX, Syr, Vg omit *what he can afford* [D] **14:31** Lit *sacrificing that for which his hand is sufficient* [E] **14:32** Lit *someone on whom there is* [F] **14:32** Lit *disease whose hand is not sufficient for* [G] **14:34** Lit *land of your possession* [H] **14:35** Lit *appeared to me* [I] **14:37** Or *eruptions*; Hb obscure [J] **14:41,42** Lit *dust* [K] **14:48** Lit *healed*

14:54-57 These verses serve as a summary and conclusion for both chapters. The same information from the beginning of chapter 13 is repeated as an *inclusio* marking out these two chapters as a unit.

15:1-30 This chapter addresses additional conditions that would make a person ritually **unclean**:

- abnormal discharges of men (vv. 2-15),
- normal discharges of men (vv. 16-18),
- normal discharges of women (vv. 19-24), and
- abnormal discharges of women (vv. 25-30).

15:18 Sexual intercourse rendered **both** the man and the woman **unclean until evening**. This declaration does not indicate that sex was sinful. However, it does illustrate the great distinction between Israel and the religions of the pagan nations around them. In many of the pagan religions of the ancient Near East, sexual activity was a part of worship. This activity was even performed within the shrines and temples of pagan gods. The greatest issue in uncleanness was its prevention of the unclean Israelite from entering the sanctuary area. This standard assured that sexual activity would not occur in the area of the sanctuary.

15:19-23 A woman was declared unclean for seven days during her regular menstruation or **discharge** (Hb *zuv*, "flow or gush). Menstruation was later used as a metaphor for Israel's sins (2Ch 29:5; Ezr 9:11; Ezk 36:17; Zch 13:1). Whatever a woman touched and whoever touched what she touched was unclean until evening. Sexual intercourse was considered **unclean** during this time. Restraint was part of sexual intimacy. Sexual acts were never meant to be an obsession. One rabbi suggested that these laws help strengthen marriage by adding a rhythm and sense of spirituality to sexual intimacy. A period of separation adds to the mystery, romance, and magic of the marital relationship. He even noted that this law calling for interludes of restraint each month could serve to reunite the husband and wife with the freshness and delight of a bride and groom. In any case, the woman's status as unclean was not a punishment but perhaps a form of protection. The woman with menstrual cramps and some ensuing weakness, as the natural result of this law, had a short break from daily cooking, cleaning, caring for family needs, and marital relations.

15:24-30 No sacrifices were required, perhaps because this monthly flow of bodily fluids was natural. Undoubtedly

the fresh water, the live bird, the cedar wood, the hyssop, and the scarlet yarn. 53 Then he is to release the live bird into the open countryside outside the city. In this way he will make atonement for the house, and it will be clean.

54 "This is the law for any skin disease or mildew, for a scaly outbreak,[A] 55 for mildew in clothing or on a house, 56 and for a swelling, scab, or spot, 57 to determine when something is unclean or clean. This is the law regarding skin disease and mildew."

Bodily discharges (15:1-33)

15 The LORD spoke to Moses and Aaron: 2 "Speak to the Israelites and tell them: When any man has a discharge from his body, he is •unclean. 3 This is uncleanness of his discharge: Whether his body secretes the discharge or retains it, he is unclean. All the days that his body secretes or retains anything because of his discharge,[B] he is unclean.[C] 4 Any bed the man with the discharge lies on will be unclean, and any furniture he sits on will be unclean. 5 Anyone who touches his bed is to wash his clothes and bathe with water, and he will remain unclean until evening. 6 Whoever sits on furniture that the man with the discharge was sitting on is to wash his clothes and bathe with water, and he will remain unclean until evening. 7 Whoever touches the body of the man with a discharge is to wash his clothes and bathe with water, and he will remain unclean until evening. 8 If the man with the discharge spits on anyone who is •clean, he is to wash his clothes and bathe with water, and he will remain unclean until evening. 9 Any saddle the man with the discharge rides on will be unclean. 10 Whoever touches anything that was under him will be unclean until evening, and whoever carries such things is to wash his clothes and bathe with water, and he will remain unclean until evening. 11 If the man with the discharge touches anyone without first rinsing his hands in water, the person who was touched is to wash his clothes and bathe with water, and he will remain unclean until evening. 12 Any clay pot that the man with the discharge touches must be broken, while any wooden utensil must be rinsed with water.

13 "When the man with the discharge has been cured of it, he is to count seven days for his cleansing, wash his clothes, and bathe his body in fresh water; he will be clean. 14 He must take two turtledoves or two young pigeons on the eighth day, come before the LORD at the entrance to the tent of meeting, and give them to the priest. 15 The priest is to sacrifice them, one as a •sin offering and the other as a •burnt offering. In this way the priest will make •atonement for him before the LORD because of his discharge.

16 "When a man has an emission of semen, he is to bathe himself completely with water, and he will remain unclean until evening. 17 Any clothing or leather on which there is an emission of semen must be washed with water, and it will remain unclean until evening. 18 If a man sleeps with a woman and has an emission of semen, both of them are to bathe with water, and they will remain unclean until evening.

19 "When a woman has a discharge, and it consists of blood from her body, she will be unclean because of her menstruation for seven days. Everyone who touches her will be unclean until evening. 20 Anything she lies on during her menstruation will become unclean, and anything she sits on will become unclean. 21 Everyone who touches her bed is to wash his clothes and bathe with water, and he will remain unclean until evening. 22 Everyone who touches any furniture she was sitting on is to wash his clothes and bathe with water, and he will remain unclean until evening. 23 If discharge is on the bed or the furniture she was sitting on, when he touches it he will be unclean until evening. 24 If a man sleeps with her, and blood from her menstruation gets on him, he will be unclean for seven days,

[A]**14:54** Or *for a scall* [B]**15:3** DSS, Sam, LXX; MT omits *he is unclean. All the days that his body secretes or retains anything because of his discharge* [C]**15:3** A urinary tract infection

and every bed he lies on will become unclean.

[25] "When a woman has a discharge of her blood for many days, though it is not the time of her menstruation, or if she has a discharge beyond her period, she will be unclean all the days of her unclean discharge, as she is during the days of her menstruation. [26] Any bed she lies on during the days of her discharge will be like her bed during menstrual impurity; any furniture she sits on will be unclean as in her menstrual period. [27] Everyone who touches them will be unclean; he must wash his clothes and bathe with water, and he will remain unclean until evening. [28] When she is cured of her discharge, she is to count seven days, and after that she will be clean. [29] On the eighth day she must take two turtledoves or two young pigeons and bring them to the priest at the entrance to the tent of meeting. [30] The priest is to sacrifice one as a sin offering and the other as a burnt offering. In this way the priest will make atonement for her before the LORD because of her unclean discharge.

[31] "You must keep the Israelites from their uncleanness, so that they do not die by defiling My tabernacle that is among them. [32] This is the law for someone with a discharge: a man who has an emission of semen, becoming unclean by it; [33] a woman who is in her menstrual period; anyone who has a discharge, whether male or female; and a man who sleeps with an unclean woman."

The Day of Atonement (16:1-34)

General instructions (16:1-10)

16 The LORD spoke to Moses after the death of two of Aaron's sons when they approached the presence of[A] the LORD and died. [2] The LORD said to Moses: "Tell your brother Aaron that he may not come whenever he wants into the holy place behind the veil in front of the •mercy seat on the ark or else he will die, because I appear in the cloud above the mercy seat.

[3] "Aaron is to enter the most holy place in this way: with a young bull for a •sin offering and a ram for a •burnt offering. [4] He is to wear a holy linen tunic, and linen undergarments are to be on his body. He must tie a linen sash around him and wrap his head with a linen turban. These are holy garments; he must bathe his body with water before he wears them. [5] He is to take from the Israelite community two male goats for a sin offering and one ram for a burnt offering.

[6] "Aaron will present the bull for his sin offering and make •atonement for himself and his household. [7] Next he will take the two goats and place them before the LORD at the entrance to the tent of meeting. [8] After Aaron casts lots for the two goats, one lot for the LORD and the other for azazel,[B] [9] he is to present the goat chosen by lot for the LORD and sacrifice it as a sin offering. [10] But the goat chosen by lot for azazel[B] is to be presented alive before the LORD to make purification with it by sending it into the wilderness for azazel.

The offerings of the high priest in the holy place (16:11-14)

[11] "When Aaron presents the bull for his sin offering and makes atonement for himself and his household, he will slaughter the bull for his sin offering. [12] Then he must take a firepan full of fiery coals from the altar before the LORD and two handfuls of finely ground fragrant incense, and bring them inside the veil. [13] He is to put the incense on the fire before the LORD, so that the cloud of incense covers the mercy seat that is over the •testimony, or else he will die. [14] He is to take some of the bull's blood and sprinkle it with his finger against the east side of the mercy seat; then he will sprinkle some of the blood with his finger before the mercy seat seven times.

The purification for the tabernacle (16:15-19)

[15] "When he slaughters the male goat for the people's sin offering and brings its blood inside the veil, he must do the same with its blood

[A] **16:1** LXX, Tg, Syr, Vg read *they brought strange fire before*; Nm 3:4 [B] **16:8,10** Perhaps a term that means "for the goat that departs," or "for removal," or "for a rough, difficult place," or "for a goat demon"; Hb obscure

these laws made Israel distinct from other nations and served as a deterrent to intermarriage with pagan people who refused to honor these divine mandates. An abnormal **discharge** left a woman **unclean** as long as it lasted, and an additional seven days was required before she would be ceremonially clean (15:25-28). An **offering** was also required (15:29-30) because the discharges were not normal as in the case of the usual menstruation cycle.

16:1-34 This chapter of the book of Leviticus gives instruction about what is to take place on the Day of Atonement, although this title does not occur until later in the book (Lv 23:27). The forgiveness of the nation is the critical idea throughout this chapter. Chapter 16, which occupies the central position, seemingly is the consummation of the preceding 15 chapters, providing the motivation to live in obedience to the legislation of Lv 17–27.

16:1-3 Moses was first instructed to tell Aaron that **he may not come whenever he wants into the holy place behind the veil**. There was one designated day on which he could enter. The Talmudic document on the Day of Atonement is entitled *Yoma*, "the day," which sufficiently expressed the importance of this ritual observance. "Yom Kippur" was celebrated annually by the people of Israel on the tenth day of the seventh month, probably October (23:27), and remains until now the most important celebration for the Jews. On that day, more than any other, the high priest acted as a mediator between God and man. Only once each year could he enter the holy of holies. The restriction on Aaron's entrance into the holy place demonstrates the limits of the sacrificial system: Access to God was still strictly limited. Full access would not be granted until the atoning work of God's Son was fulfilled.

16:11-14 At this time the high priest enters into the most holy place, the location of God's presence. Three times it is repeated that the offering the high priest was presenting was **for himself**. He was to present a **bull**, which was the designated animal for the sin offering of the high priest (4:3-12). The high priest was to take **some of the bull's blood and sprinkle it with his finger . . . before the mercy seat seven times.** This is the only occasion when blood was brought into the most holy place. The **mercy seat** (Hb *kapporet*, lit a "covering," from the verb *kaphar*, "atone") covered the ark of the **testimony**, suggesting that this ark was the place of **atonement** (Hb *kaphar*, "make atonement, cover or pardon sin"). The ark contained the Ten Commandments, some manna, and Aaron's rod (Heb 9:4-5).

as he did with the bull’s blood: he is to sprinkle it against the mercy seat and in front of it. 16 He will purify the most holy place in this way for all their sins because of the Israelites’ impurities and rebellious acts. He will do the same for the tent of meeting that remains among them, because it is surrounded by their impurities. 17 No one may be in the tent of meeting from the time he enters to make atonement in the most holy place until he leaves after he has made atonement for himself, his household, and the whole assembly of Israel. 18 Then he will go out to the altar that is before the LORD and make atonement for it. He is to take some of the bull’s blood and some of the goat’s blood and put it on the horns on all sides of the altar. 19 He is to sprinkle some of the blood on it with his finger seven times to cleanse and set it apart from the Israelites’ impurities.

The scapegoat (16:20-22)

20 “When he has finished purifying the most holy place, the tent of meeting, and the altar, he is to present the live male goat. 21 Aaron will lay both his hands on the head of the live goat and confess over it all the Israelites’ wrongdoings and rebellious acts—all their sins. He is to put them on the goat’s head and send it away into the wilderness by the man appointed for the task.[A] 22 The goat will carry on it all their wrongdoings into a desolate land, and he will release it there.

The procedures after dispatching the scapegoat (16:23-28)

23 “Then Aaron is to enter the tent of meeting, take off the linen garments he wore when he entered the most holy place, and leave them there. 24 He will bathe his body with water in a holy place and put on his clothes. Then he must go out and sacrifice his burnt offering and the people’s burnt offering; he will make atonement for himself and for the people. 25 He is to burn the fat of the sin offering on the altar. 26 The man who released the goat for azazel[B] is to wash his clothes and bathe his body with water; afterward he may reenter the camp. 27 The bull for the sin offering and the goat for the sin offering, whose blood was brought into the most holy place to make atonement, must be brought outside the camp and their hide, flesh, and dung burned up. 28 The one who burns them is to wash his clothes and bathe himself with water; afterward he may reenter the camp.

The Day of Atonement as a permanent statute (16:29-34)

29 “This is to be a permanent statute for you: In the seventh month, on the tenth day of the month you are to practice self-denial[C] and do no work, both the native and the foreigner who resides among you. 30 Atonement will be made for you on this day to cleanse you, and you will be •clean from all your sins before the LORD. 31 It is a Sabbath of complete rest for you, and you must practice self-denial; it is a permanent statute. 32 The priest who is anointed and ordained[D] to serve as high priest in place of his father will make atonement. He will put on the linen garments, the holy garments, 33 and purify the most holy place. He will purify the tent of meeting and the altar and will make atonement for the priests and all the people of the assembly. 34 This is to be a permanent statute for you, to make atonement for the Israelites once a year because of all their sins.” And all this was done as the LORD commanded Moses.

Love Your Neighbor as Yourself (17:1–27:34)

The Laws of Personal Holiness (17:1–26:46)

The regulations regarding sacrifices and blood (17:1-16)

17 The LORD spoke to Moses: 2 “Speak to Aaron, his sons, and all the Israelites and tell them: This is what the LORD has commanded: 3 Anyone from the house of Israel

[A]16:21 Lit *wilderness in the hand of a ready man* [B]16:26 Perhaps a term that means “for the goat that departs,” or “for removal,” or “for a rough, difficult place,” or “for a goat demon”; Hb obscure [C]16:29 Traditionally, fasting, abstinence from sex, and refraining from personal grooming [D]16:32 Lit *and will fill his hand*

16:15-19 After the sin offering had been presented, purification was made for the tabernacle and its furnishings **because of the Israelites’ impurities and rebellious acts** (Hb *pesha‘*, “trespass, transgression,” the strongest word for “sin” in the OT and an expression for the worst manifestations of sin). The unrestricted nature of forgiveness on this day indicates why the blood was to be carried directly into God’s presence.

16:20-22 The high priest was to “cast lots” for two goats (16:8). One of the goats was offered as a sin offering, but the other was to be presented alive before the Lord. Aaron, the high priest, placed both of his hands on the live goat and was to **confess over it** all of Israel’s **wrongdoings and rebellious acts**. The high priest was the representative to God for the entire nation. On the Day of Atonement, the two animals were one sacrifice. The first **goat** symbolizes the means for atonement, the shedding of blood in death. The scapegoat’s release represents the effect of atonement—the complete removal of guilt.

16:23-28 After bathing and putting on his high priestly garments, Aaron **must go out and sacrifice his burnt offering and the people’s burnt offering**. It was the usual order for burnt offerings of dedication and devotion to follow sin offerings of atonement and forgiveness.

16:29-34 The writer of Hebrews mentioned the significance of the Day of **Atonement** for believers (Heb 10:4). Its Old Testament observance pointed toward Christ who would be the perfect High Priest because He had no need to make atonement for His own sins (Heb 7:26-28). He also became the sin offering, presenting Himself for the sins of all (Heb 9:11-15). As the scapegoat He also carried away those sins (Ps 103:12; Is 53:6). No longer are sacrifices required because Christ offered Himself and shed His own blood to provide redemption and atonement (Heb 7:27; 10:10).

17:1–27:34 Reflecting and expanding on the last six commandments of the Decalogue, the second half of Leviticus (chaps. 17–27) corresponds to Jesus’ words, “Love your neighbor as yourself” (cp. 19:18 and Mt 22:39). These commandments explain the worshiper’s responsibility to his fellow man. This section describes the walk of holiness. In these chapters, God instructs the Israelites on how to live in peace with humanity. This was a part of their worship. Worshiping and obeying God must be concurrent with loving one’s neighbor. Loving God is inseparable from loving others.

who slaughters an ox, sheep, or goat in the camp, or slaughters it outside the camp, 4 instead of bringing it to the entrance to the tent of meeting to present it as an offering to the LORD before His tabernacle—that person will be considered •guilty.[A] He has shed blood and must be cut off from his people. 5 This is so the Israelites will bring to the LORD the sacrifices they have been offering in the open country. They are to bring them to the priest at the entrance to the tent of meeting and offer them as •fellowship sacrifices to the LORD. 6 The priest will then sprinkle the blood on the LORD's altar at the entrance to the tent of meeting and burn the fat as a pleasing aroma to the LORD. 7 They must no longer offer their sacrifices to the goat-demons that they have prostituted themselves with. This will be a permanent statute for them throughout their generations.

8 "Say to them: Anyone from the house of Israel or from the foreigners who live among them who offers a •burnt offering or a sacrifice 9 but does not bring it to the entrance to the tent of meeting to sacrifice it to the LORD, that person must be cut off from his people.

10 "Anyone from the house of Israel or from the foreigners who live among them who eats any blood, I will turn[B] against that person who eats blood and cut him off from his people. 11 For the life of a creature is in the blood, and I have appointed it to you to make •atonement on the altar for[C] your lives, since it is the lifeblood that makes atonement. 12 Therefore I say to the Israelites: None of you and no foreigner who lives among you may eat blood.

13 "Any Israelite or foreigner living among them, who hunts down a wild animal or bird that may be eaten must drain its blood and cover it with dirt. 14 Since the life of every creature is its blood, I have told the Israelites: You must not eat the blood of any creature, because the life of every creature is its blood; whoever eats it must be cut off.

15 "Every person, whether the native or the foreigner, who eats an animal that died a natural death or was mauled by wild beasts is to wash his clothes and bathe with water, and he will remain •unclean until evening; then he will be •clean. 16 But if he does not wash his clothes and bathe himself, he will bear his punishment."

Sexual prohibitions (18:1-30)

18 •Yahweh spoke to Moses: 2 "Speak to the Israelites and tell them: I am Yahweh your God. 3 Do not follow the practices of the land of Egypt, where you used to live, or follow the practices of the land of Canaan, where I am bringing you. You must not follow their customs. 4 You are to practice My ordinances and you are to keep My statutes by following them; I am Yahweh your God. 5 Keep My statutes and ordinances; a person will live if he does them. I am Yahweh.

6 "You are not to come near any close relative[D] for sexual intercourse; I am Yahweh. 7 You are not to shame your father by having sex with your mother. She is your mother; you must not have sexual intercourse with her. 8 You are not to have sex with your father's wife; it will shame your father. 9 You are not to have sexual intercourse with your sister, either your father's daughter or your mother's, whether born at home or born elsewhere. You are not to have sex with her. 10 You are not to have sexual intercourse with your son's daughter or your daughter's daughter, because it will shame your family.[E] 11 You are not to have sexual intercourse with your father's wife's daughter,[F] who is adopted by[G] your father; she is your sister. 12 You are not to have sexual intercourse with your father's sister; she is your father's close relative. 13 You are not to have sexual intercourse with your mother's sister, for she is your mother's close relative. 14 You are not to shame your father's brother by coming near his wife to have sexual intercourse; she is your aunt. 15 You are not to have sexual

[A] **17:4** Lit *tabernacle—blood will be charged against that person* [B] **17:10** Lit *will set My face* [C] **17:11** Or *to ransom* [D] **18:6** Lit *any flesh of his flesh* [E] **18:10** Lit *because they are your nakedness* [F] **18:11** This must refer to a daughter from a previous marriage. [G] **18:11** Lit *daughter, a relative of*

Leviticus 17–26 is identified as the Holiness Code by modern biblical scholars because of its demand for the Israelites to live in holiness. This section addresses the everyday life of the Israelite community, illustrating that holiness affects every area of life. Clear instructions concerning separation are included (17:1–22:33). The dominant concept in Lv 1–16 was atonement; the dominant concept in this section is holiness. Holiness and a desire to obey God, demonstrated in how one relates to people, are evidences of a proper relationship to God.

17:10-16 The Israelites were also not to eat **any blood** (vv. 10,12; cp. Gn 9:4; Dt 12:23). The reason for this law is stated clearly in the text:

- Blood represents a creature's **life**.
- The Lord had commanded His people **to make atonement on the altar**, i.e., sacrifices in which a prescribed animal's blood was shed as a substitute for the life of the human sinner (v. 11).

Blood alone, because it is regarded as the source of life and is representative of life, may atone for life. This passage is foundational for understanding the New Testament references to the atoning blood of Christ (see Rm 3:25; Heb 9:14).

18:1-30 This chapter defines specific boundaries for the family. The family is the foundation of a strong and stable society. A nation cannot exist if the family is not well-defined and protected. Therefore, this instruction is integral to the fulfillment of the promise that Abraham was to be the ancestor of a great nation. Limits are placed on sexual relations. Adultery, incest, homosexuality, and bestiality are forbidden. Adultery and incest are assaults upon the family (vv. 6-18). Marriage was instituted by God, and any assault on this holy union is an attack on Him. Adultery was used as a metaphor in reference to the people's infidelity toward the Lord (Jr 7:9; 23:10). It was to be punished by the death of both guilty parties (Lv 20:10; Dt 22:22).

The Israelites were to be different from their neighbors, especially in the area of their sexual behavior. Sexual activity was buttressed with divine mandates because it was the source of life, the gift of God. These laws were specifically designed to distinguish the Israelites from the inhabitants of the land that they were about to possess. Compared with the worship practices and lifestyles of the Canaanite nations, these boundaries for the sexual practices of the Israelites would clearly set them apart. Incest or **sexual intercourse** (Hb *legallot 'erwah*, lit. "uncovering the nakedness," a euphemism for sexual intercourse) with **any close relative** (Hb *she'ēr*, i.e., mother, father, son, daughter, brother, sister) was forbidden. This law was important to the Israelites since they could not intermarry with foreigners, meaning fewer options for choosing a mate, and because the family land had to remain within the tribe. Families often lived together as clans, so there were reasons for such explicit instructions. The prohibition of sexual relations with a brother's wife (Lv 18:16) did not contradict the law of levirate marriage since in the latter instance the brother would be dead (Dt 25:5-10).

18:22 Homosexuality is clearly characterized as sin. It was not a disease or viable lifestyle. Although lesbianism is not specifically mentioned in the Old Testament, it is condemned in the New Testament (Rm 1:26-27) and in the Talmud. **It is detestable** (Hb *toʿēbah*, "an act that is repugnant, abhorrent, an abomination"). Other such offenses considered "detestable" include human sacrifice (Dt 12:31), eating unclean animals (Dt 14:3-8), sacrificing defective animals (Dt 17:1), practicing occult activities (Dt 18:9-14), dishonesty in business (Dt 25:13-16), and ritual prostitution (1Kg 14:23-24).

18:23 Bestiality is labeled **a perversion** that steps over the boundaries God has established. "Perversion" (Hb *tebel*, "profanation," only v. 23 and 20:12 in the OT) literally means "confusion" in the sense of mixing what does not belong together. "Perversion" is thus a violation of divine order.

19:1-2 This chapter, perhaps better than any other, explains the meaning of being holy, set apart from evil and unto good. The underlying theme is summed up in the self-identifying formula, **I am Yahweh your God**, which appears 16 times in 37 verses.

19:3-37 Various moral laws are outlined. In fact, there is a consensus that all of the Ten Commandments are present in Lv 19; and, as in Ex 20, they are summarized under love for God and love for your neighbor (Ex 20:1-17; Mt 22:35-40). The basis for this appropriate lifestyle is God's covenant with His people (Lv 19:36). The only right response is obedience. Holiness or set-apartness is at the heart of the regulations. The mention of the **mother** first is unusual (v. 3; cp. Ex 20:12; Eph 6:2). There are several possible reasons for this word order:

- deference to the mother;
- a means of making the role of a mother in a polygamous household easier.

Or perhaps there is no reason. Nevertheless, holiness surely must begin at home so that children are able to learn from observing their

intercourse with your daughter-in-law. She is your son's wife; you are not to have sex with her. 16 You are not to have sexual intercourse with your brother's wife; it will shame your brother. 17 You are not to have sexual intercourse with a woman and her daughter. You are not to marry her son's daughter or her daughter's daughter and have sex with her. They are close relatives; it is depraved. 18 You are not to marry a woman as a rival to her sister and have sexual intercourse with her during her sister's lifetime.

19 "You are not to come near a woman during her menstrual impurity to have sexual intercourse with her. 20 You are not to have sexual intercourse with[A] your neighbor's wife, defiling yourself with her.

21 "You are not to make any of your children pass through the fire to •Molech. Do not profane the name of your God; I am Yahweh. 22 You are not to sleep with a man as with a woman; it is detestable. 23 You are not to have sexual intercourse with[B] any animal, defiling yourself with it; a woman is not to present herself to an animal to mate with it; it is a perversion.

24 "Do not defile yourselves by any of these practices, for the nations I am driving out before you have defiled themselves by all these things. 25 The land has become defiled, so I am punishing it for its sin, and the land will vomit out its inhabitants. 26 But you are to keep My statutes and ordinances. You must not commit any of these detestable things—not the native or the foreigner who lives among you. 27 For the men who were in the land prior to you have committed all these detestable things, and the land has become defiled. 28 If you defile the land, it will vomit you out as it has vomited out the nations that were before you. 29 Any person who does any of these detestable practices must be cut off from his people. 30 You must keep My instruction to not do any of the detestable customs that were practiced before you, so that you do not defile yourselves by them; I am Yahweh your God."

A lifestyle of holiness (19:1-37)

19 The LORD spoke to Moses: 2 "Speak to the entire Israelite community and tell them: Be holy because I, •Yahweh your God, am holy.

3 "Each of you is to respect his mother and father. You are to keep My Sabbaths; I am Yahweh your God. 4 Do not turn to idols or make cast images of gods for yourselves; I am Yahweh your God.

5 "When you offer a •fellowship sacrifice to the LORD, sacrifice it so that you may be accepted. 6 It is to be eaten on the day you sacrifice it or on the next day, but what remains on the third day must be burned up. 7 If any is eaten on the third day, it is a repulsive thing; it will not be accepted. 8 Anyone who eats it will bear his punishment, for he has profaned what is holy to the LORD. That person must be cut off from his people.

9 "When you reap the harvest of your land, you are not to reap to the very edge of your field or gather the gleanings of your harvest. 10 You must not strip your vineyard bare or gather its fallen grapes. Leave them for the poor and the foreign resident; I am Yahweh your God.

11 "You must not steal. You must not act deceptively or lie to one another. 12 You must not swear falsely by My name, profaning the name of your God; I am Yahweh.

13 "You must not oppress your neighbor or rob him. The wages due a hired hand must not remain with you until morning. 14 You must not curse the deaf or put a stumbling block in front of the blind, but you are to •fear your God; I am Yahweh.

15 "You must not act unjustly when deciding a case. Do not be partial to the poor or give preference to the rich; judge your neighbor fairly. 16 You must not go about spreading slander among your people; you must not jeopardize[C] your neighbor's life; I am Yahweh.

17 "You must not harbor hatred against your brother.[D] Rebuke your neighbor directly, and you will not

[A]18:20 Lit *to give your emission of semen to stand against* [B]18:23 Lit *to give your emission to* [C]19:16 Lit *not* [D]19:17 Or *your fellow Israelite*

The Ten Commandments

Leviticus 19	Exodus 20
"Do not turn to idols" (v. 4a).	v. 3
Do not "make cast images of gods for yourselves" (vv. 4b).	vv. 4-6
"You must not swear falsely by My name, profaning the name of your God" (v. 12).	v. 7
"You are to keep My Sabbaths" (vv. 3,30).	vv. 8-12
"Each of you is to respect his mother and father" (v. 3).	v. 12
"You must not jeopardize your neighbor's life" (v. 16).	v. 13
"There must be punishment" for adultery between a master and "a woman who is a slave designated for another man" (v. 20). "Do not debase your daughter by making her a prostitute" (v. 29).	v. 14
"You must not steal" (v. 11). "Do not oppress or rob your neighbor"; promptly pay "the wages due a hired hand" (v. 13). Use "honest" weights and measures (vv. 35-36).	v. 15
"You must not act deceptively or lie to one another" (v. 11). "You must not go about spreading slander" (v. 16).	v. 16
"Do not take revenge or bear a grudge" (v. 18).	v. 17

incur •guilt because of him. [18]Do
not take revenge or bear a grudge
against members of your community,
but love your neighbor as yourself;
I am Yahweh.
[19]"You are to keep My statutes.
You must not crossbreed two different
kinds of your livestock, sow your
fields with two kinds of seed, or put
on a garment made of two kinds of
material.
[20]"If a man has sexual intercourse
with a woman who is a slave designated
for another man, but she
has not been redeemed or given
her freedom, there must be punishment.[A]
They are not to be put
to death, because she had not been
freed. [21]However, he must bring a
ram as his •restitution offering to
the LORD at the entrance to the tent
of meeting. [22]The priest will make
•atonement on his behalf before the
LORD with the ram of the restitution
offering for the sin he has committed,
and he will be forgiven for the
sin he committed.
[23]"When you come into the land
and plant any kind of tree for food,
you are to consider the fruit forbidden.[B]
It will be forbidden to you for
three years; it is not to be eaten. [24]In
the fourth year all its fruit must be
consecrated as a praise offering to
the LORD. [25]But in the fifth year you
may eat its fruit. In this way its yield
will increase for you; I am Yahweh
your God.
[26]"You are not to eat anything with
blood in it.[C] You are not to practice
•divination or sorcery. [27]You are not
to cut off the hair at the sides of
your head or mar the edge of your
beard. [28]You are not to make gashes
on your bodies for the dead or put
tattoo marks on yourselves; I am
Yahweh.
[29]"Do not debase[D] your daughter
by making her a prostitute, or the
land will be prostituted and filled
with depravity. [30]You must keep My

[A]**19:20** Or *compensation* [B]**19:23** Lit *uncircumcised* [C]**19:26** Or *anything over its blood*
[D]**19:29** Lit *profane*

own parents who God is and what He requires.

19:9 God presents His own welfare program. The poor and stranger have needs to be met. God prescribes a program whereby **gleanings** are left in the fields to be harvested by those in need, not demeaning them but enabling them to meet their pressing needs by their own efforts.

19:18 This verse, which seems to climax the chapter, goes beyond a summary of Christian principles. The principles undergirding all the laws are effectively epitomized in this one statement. Of the 37 verses in chapter 19, verse 18 is in the exact center. An Israeli scholar has observed that Leviticus is the center of the Torah, with chapter 19 at the center of the book, and finally the commandment in verse 18 in the center of the chapter—perfectly pinpointing what should be considered the heart of the entire Torah. Leviticus 19:18 expresses the core of what the rest of the laws are supposed to accomplish in the lives of God's people. The chapter's contents demonstrate that relationships with people are inseparable from one's relationship with God—holy living and love are mutually dependent. Being identified with the Lord, who is holy, necessitates mirroring His holiness.

20:1-21 The content of this chapter is very similar to that of Lv 18 and continues the emphasis on holiness with exhortations to avoid both pagan religious practices and violations of God's created order. The prohibitions are clearly presented before the punishments are prescribed, affirming that warnings come before the consequences begin. In Lv 20, however, more attention is given to the punishments that will result should the ordinances be broken. Both Leviticus 18 and 20 strongly indicate the connection between pagan religious practices, particularly the sexual activities involved in the fertility cults, and moral degeneracy. The Lord legislated far higher standards of righteousness and holiness for His people.

Another distinction can be made between chapters 18 and 20. Leviticus 18 addresses the possible offender of a God-given law, whereas Leviticus 20 addresses the entire Israelite community regarding its responsibility for seeing that violations receive their proper penalty. The nature of the punishment shows the seriousness of sin. That such a wide range of offenses should be punishable by death seems incredibly harsh to the modern reader. However, the offenses listed either are in deliberate defiance of God's holy law or are offenses against people—not property. In contrast to other ancient Near Eastern civilizations, where violations of law that resulted in economic loss tended to be treated more severely, crimes against family life or those of a spiritual nature received the strongest punishment in Israel. This pattern contrasts with the cuneiform laws of the ancient Near East. God always placed more value on human life than on any material possessions.

20:22-27 This chapter concludes by relating Israel's obedience to the occupation of the promised land. Because God was providing the land for His people, the Israelites were to be different from the surrounding nations. They were to distinguish the clean animal from the unclean one. Only by keeping all God's statutes and ordinances could they expect to survive as holy people. God separated them specifically from all other nations so that they might reflect His intrinsic holiness and glorify Him. By observing God's law, the Israelites would imitate the ways of God and make Him known.

21:1-6 Chaps. 21–22 differ from the rest of what is called the "Holiness Code." In these two chapters the regulations given are directed specifically toward the priests. All the Israelites were called to holiness, but a greater degree of separation had to characterize the life of the priests who modeled the life of holiness for the rest of the nation. The first regulation

Sabbaths and revere My sanctuary; I am Yahweh.

31 "Do not turn to mediums[A] or consult spiritists,[B] or you will be defiled by them; I am Yahweh your God.

32 "You are to rise in the presence of the elderly and honor the old. Fear your God; I am Yahweh.

33 "When a foreigner lives with you in your land, you must not oppress him. 34 You must regard the foreigner who lives with you as the native-born among you. You are to love him as yourself, for you were foreigners in the land of Egypt; I am Yahweh your God.

35 "You must not be unfair in measurements of length, weight, or volume. 36 You are to have honest balances, honest weights, an honest dry measure,[C] and an honest liquid measure;[D] I am Yahweh your God, who brought you out of the land of Egypt. 37 You must keep all My statutes and all My ordinances and do them; I am Yahweh."

The punishment for violations of holiness (20:1-27)

20 The LORD spoke to Moses: 2 "Say to the Israelites: Any Israelite or foreigner living in Israel who gives any of his children to •Molech must be put to death; the people of the country are to stone him. 3 I will turn[E] against that man and cut him off from his people, because he gave his •offspring to Molech, defiling My sanctuary and profaning My holy name. 4 But if the people of the country look the other way when that man[F] gives any of his children to Molech, and do not put him to death, 5 then I will turn[E] against that man and his family, and cut off from their people both him and all who follow[G] him in prostituting themselves with Molech.

6 "Whoever turns to mediums[A] or spiritists[J] and prostitutes himself with them, I will turn[E] against that person and cut him off from his people. 7 Consecrate yourselves and be holy, for I am •Yahweh your God. 8 Keep My statutes and do them; I am Yahweh who sets you apart.

9 "If anyone curses his father or mother, he must be put to death. He has cursed his father or mother; his blood is on his own hands.[H]

10 "If a man commits adultery with a married woman—if he commits adultery with his neighbor's wife—both the adulterer and the adulteress must be put to death. 11 If a man sleeps with his father's wife, he has shamed his father. Both of them must be put to death; their blood is on their own hands.[I] 12 If a man sleeps with his daughter-in-law, both of them must be put to death. They have acted perversely; their blood is on their own hands.[I] 13 If a man sleeps with a man as with a woman, they have both committed a detestable thing. They must be put to death; their blood is on their own hands.[I] 14 If a man marries a woman and her mother, it is depraved. Both he and they must be burned with fire, so that there will be no depravity among you. 15 If a man has sexual intercourse with[J] an animal, he must be put to death; you are also to kill the animal. 16 If a woman comes near any animal and mates with it, you are to kill the woman and the animal. They must be put to death; their own blood is on them. 17 If a man marries his sister, whether his father's daughter or his mother's daughter, and they have sexual relations,[K] it is a disgrace. They must be cut off publicly from their people. He has had sexual intercourse with his sister; he will bear his punishment. 18 If a man sleeps with a menstruating woman and has sexual intercourse with her, he has exposed the source of her flow, and she has uncovered the source of her blood. Both of them must be cut off from their people. 19 You must not have sexual intercourse with your mother's sister or your father's sister, for it is exposing one's own blood relative; both people will bear their pun-

[A]**19:31; 20:6** Or *spirits of the dead* [B]**19:31; 20:6** Or *familiar spirits* [C]**19:36** Lit *honest ephah*; an *ephah* is a dry measure of grain equivalent to about 23 quarts. [D]**19:36** Lit *honest hin*; a *hin* is a liquid measure of about 1 gallon. [E]**20:3,5,6** Lit *will set My face* [F]**20:4** Lit *country ever close their eyes from that man when he* [G]**20:5** Lit *prostitute themselves with* [H]**20:9** Lit *on him* [I]**20:11,12,13** Lit *on them* [J]**20:15** Lit *man gives his emission to* [K]**20:17** Lit *and he sees her nakedness and she sees his nakedness*

ishment. 20 If a man sleeps with his aunt, he has shamed his uncle; they will bear their •guilt and die childless. 21 If a man marries his brother's wife, it is impurity. He has shamed his brother; they will be childless.

22 "You are to keep all My statutes and all My ordinances, and do them, so that the land where I am bringing you to live will not vomit you out. 23 You must not follow the statutes of the nations I am driving out before you, for they did all these things, and I abhorred them. 24 And I promised you: You will inherit their land, since I will give it to you to possess, a land flowing with milk and honey. I am Yahweh your God who set you apart from the peoples. 25 Therefore you must distinguish the •clean animal from the •unclean one, and the unclean bird from the clean one. Do not become contaminated by any land animal, bird, or whatever crawls on the ground; I have set these apart as unclean for you. 26 You are to be holy to Me because I, Yahweh, am holy, and I have set you apart from the nations to be Mine.

27 "A man or a woman who is[A] a medium or a spiritist must be put to death. They are to be stoned; their blood is on their own hands."[B]

The regulations for priests (21:1–22:33)

21 The LORD said to Moses: "Speak to Aaron's sons, the priests, and tell them: A priest is not to make himself ceremonially •unclean for a dead person among his relatives, 2 except for his immediate family: his mother, father, son, daughter, or brother. 3 He may make himself unclean for his young unmarried sister in his immediate family. 4 He is not to make himself unclean for those related to him by marriage[C] and so defile himself.

5 "Priests may not make bald spots on their heads, shave the edge of their beards, or make gashes on their bodies. 6 They are to be holy to their God and not profane the name of their God. For they present the fire offerings to •Yahweh, the food of their God, and they must be holy. 7 They are not to marry a woman defiled by prostitution.[D] They are not to marry one divorced by her husband, for the priest is holy to his God. 8 You are to consider him holy since he presents the food of your God. He will be holy to you because I, Yahweh who sets you apart, am holy. 9 If a priest's daughter defiles herself by promiscuity,[E] she defiles her father; she must be burned up.

10 "The priest who is highest among his brothers, who has had the anointing oil poured on his head and has been ordained[F] to wear the garments, must not dishevel his hair[G] or tear his garments. 11 He must not go near any dead person or make himself unclean even for his father or mother. 12 He must not leave the sanctuary or he will desecrate the sanctuary of his God, for the consecration of the anointing oil of his God is on him; I am Yahweh.

13 "He is to marry a woman who is a virgin. 14 He is not to marry a widow, a divorced woman, or one defiled by prostitution. He is to marry a virgin from his own people, 15 so that he does not corrupt his bloodline[H] among his people, for I am Yahweh who sets him apart."

16 The LORD spoke to Moses: 17 "Tell Aaron: None of your descendants throughout your generations who has a physical defect is to come near to present the food of his God. 18 No man who has any defect is to come near: no man who is blind, lame, facially disfigured, or deformed; 19 no man who has a broken foot or hand, 20 or who is a hunchback or a dwarf,[I] or who has an eye defect, a festering rash, scabs, or a crushed testicle. 21 No descendant of Aaron the priest who has a defect is to come near to present the fire offerings to the LORD. He has a defect and is not to come near to present the food of his God. 22 He may eat the food of his God from what is especially holy as well as from what is holy. 23 But because he has a defect, he must not go near the curtain or approach the altar. He is not to desecrate My sanctuaries, for I am Yahweh who

pertained to physical contact with the dead, which rendered the priest unclean and therefore effectively ruled out any funerary role for the priesthood. It is reasonable to conclude that this prohibition was to avoid sanctioning cults of the dead and as a polemic against the widespread worship of the dead among Israel's neighbors. As with bodily discharges, however, there is an underlying sense that the world and human life are inherently unholy; and therefore that ordinary living, all by itself, would make one unholy. The priests had to abstain from even some ordinary parts of life in order to live out the role of priest and mediator between an unholy people and the holy God.

21:7-15 Priests are also prohibited from marrying **a woman defiled by prostitution** or **divorced by her husband**. The high priest was held to an even higher standard than an ordinary priest. The high priest could only **marry a woman who is a virgin**. Pagan worship often involved cultic prostitution and sexual promiscuity. The priest was not in any way to be associated with these wicked practices because he was considered holy and set apart for the service of God.

21:16–22:33 This section opens with the summary statement that a priest with **a physical defect** is unqualified for priestly service, suggesting that there is an outward expression of inward holiness. In all things God must be glorified, and His holiness is profaned by anything that is obviously less than perfect, whether it is the sacrificial animal or the sacrificing priest. This shared quality between the priest and the sacrificial offering emphasized the close relationship between the two. Only the very best is acceptable to God. The common denominator in all these regulations is that God has sanctified the **priest**. Therefore, he is to be holy. This section is rich with the unique expression, **I am Yahweh who sets them** [or you] **apart** (Hb *qadash*, "regard or declare holy, consecrate," 21:23; 22:9,16,32; also Ex 31:13; Lv 20:8; Ezk 20:12; cp. Lv 20:26; 21:8). Because the Israelite priests alone had the awesome responsibility of presenting offerings to God, they were to be holy, set apart unto God.

God's perfection demanded the highest degree of perfection possible among those who minister and in the selection of offerings that were to be presented to Him. The requirement that the priest and the animal be without defect foreshadowed the sacrifice of Christ. This demand for perfection of both the priest and the offering was ultimately and uniquely fulfilled in the person of Jesus Christ, who as High Priest was not only holy, innocent, undefiled, separate from sinners,

[A]**20:27** Lit *is in them* [B]**20:27** Lit *on them* [C]**21:4** Lit *unclean a husband among his people* [D]**21:7** Or *a prostitute* or *a defiled woman* [E]**21:9** Or *prostitution* [F]**21:10** Lit *and one has filled his hand* [G]**21:10** Or *not uncover his head* [H]**21:15** Lit *not profane his seed* [I]**21:20** Or *or emaciated*

and exalted above the heavens (Heb 7:26), but as the sacrificial lamb was a sacrifice without defect or blemish (1Pt 1:19).

sets them apart." 24 Moses said this
to Aaron and his sons and to all the
Israelites.

22 The LORD spoke to Moses:
2 "Tell Aaron and his sons to
deal respectfully with the holy offerings of the Israelites that they
have consecrated to Me, so they
do not profane My holy name; I
am •Yahweh. 3 Say to them: If any
man from any of your descendants
throughout your generations is in a
state of uncleanness yet approaches
the holy offerings that the Israelites
consecrate to the LORD, that person
will be cut off from My presence; I
am Yahweh. 4 No man of Aaron's descendants who has a skin disease[A] or
a discharge is to eat from the holy
offerings until he is •clean. Whoever
touches anything made •unclean by
a dead person or by a man who has
an emission of semen, 5 or whoever
touches any swarming creature that
makes him unclean or any person
who makes him unclean—whatever his uncleanness— 6 the man
who touches any of these will remain unclean until evening and
is not to eat from the holy offerings unless he has bathed his body
with water. 7 When the sun has set,
he will become clean, and then he
may eat from the holy offerings,
for that is his food. 8 He must not
eat an animal that died naturally or
was mauled by wild beasts,[B] making
himself unclean by it; I am Yahweh.
9 They must keep My instruction, or
they will be •guilty and die because
they profane it; I am Yahweh who
sets them apart.

10 "No one outside a priest's family[C] is to eat the holy offering. A
foreigner staying with a priest or
a hired hand is not to eat the holy
offering. 11 But if a priest purchas-
es someone with his money, that
person may eat it, and those born
in his house may eat his food. 12 If
the priest's daughter is married
to a man outside a priest's family,[D] she is not to eat from the holy
contributions.[E] 13 But if the priest's
daughter becomes widowed or
divorced, has no children, and returns to her father's house as in her
youth, she may share her father's
food. But no outsider may share
it. 14 If anyone eats a holy offering
in error, he must add a fifth to its
value and give the holy offering to
the priest. 15 The priests must not
profane the holy offerings the Israelites give to the LORD 16 by letting
the people eat their holy offerings
and having them bear the penalty
of restitution. For I am Yahweh
who sets them apart."

17 The LORD spoke to Moses:
18 "Speak to Aaron, his sons, and
all the Israelites and tell them: Any
man of the house of Israel or of
the foreign residents in Israel who
presents his offering—whether
they present freewill gifts or payment of vows to the LORD as •burnt
offerings— 19 must offer an unblemished male from the cattle,
sheep, or goats in order for you
to be accepted. 20 You are not to
present anything that has a defect,
because it will not be accepted on
your behalf.

21 "When a man presents a •fellow-
ship sacrifice to the LORD to fulfill a
vow or as a freewill offering from the
herd or flock, it has to be unblemished to be acceptable; there must
be no defect in it. 22 You are not to
present any animal to the LORD that
is blind, injured, maimed, or has
a running sore, festering rash, or
scabs; you may not put any of them
on the altar as a fire offering to the
LORD. 23 You may sacrifice as a freewill offering any animal from the
herd or flock that has an elongated
or stunted limb, but it is not acceptable as a vow offering. 24 You are not
to present to the LORD anything that
has bruised, crushed, torn, or sev-
ered testicles; you must not sacrifice
them in your land. 25 Neither you
nor[F] a foreigner are to present food
to your God from any of these animals. They will not be accepted for
you because they are deformed and
have a defect."

26 The LORD spoke to Moses:
27 "When an ox, sheep, or goat is
born, it must remain with[G] its moth-

[A] 22:4 Or *has leprosy* or *scale disease* [B] 22:8 Lit *eat a carcass or a mauled beast* [C] 22:10 Lit *No stranger* [D] 22:12 Lit *man, a stranger* [E] 22:12 Lit *the contribution of holy offerings* [F] 22:25 Lit *nor from the hand of* [G] 22:27 Lit *under*

er for seven days; from the eighth
day on, it will be acceptable as a gift,
a fire offering to the LORD. [28] But you
are not to slaughter an animal from
the herd or flock on the same day
as its young. [29] When you sacrifice a
thank offering to the LORD, sacrifice
it so that you may be accepted. [30] It is
to be eaten on the same day. Do not
let any of it remain until morning; I
am Yahweh.
[31] "You are to keep My commands
and do them; I am Yahweh. [32] You
must not profane My holy name; I
must be treated as holy among the
Israelites. I am Yahweh who sets you
apart, [33] the One who brought you
out of the land of Egypt to be your
God; I am Yahweh."

The appointed festivals (23:1-44)

23 The LORD spoke to Moses:
[2] "Speak to the Israelites and
tell them: These are My appointed
times, the times of the LORD that you
will proclaim as sacred assemblies.
[3] "Work may be done for six days,
but on the seventh day there must
be a Sabbath of complete rest, a
sacred assembly. You are not to do
any work; it is a Sabbath to the LORD
wherever you live.
[4] "These are the LORD's appointed
times, the sacred assemblies you
are to proclaim at their appointed
times. [5] The •Passover to the LORD
comes in the first month, at twilight
on the fourteenth day of the month.
[6] The Festival of •Unleavened Bread
to the LORD is on the fifteenth day of
the same month. For seven days you
must eat unleavened bread. [7] On the
first day you are to hold a sacred assembly; you are not to do any daily
work. [8] You are to present a fire offering to the LORD for seven days. On
the seventh day there will be a sacred assembly; you must not do any
daily work."
[9] The LORD spoke to Moses:
[10] "Speak to the Israelites and tell

23:1-2 This chapter lists the Lord's **appointed times** (Hb *mo'ēd*, "set, fixed")—occasions on which He would meet with His people throughout the Hebrew year. The people were expected to come, and God promised to meet with them there. It was not the people's prerogative to decide when they would meet God; God set the time and place, and He always keeps His appointments. These appointed times were **sacred assemblies** (Hb *miqra'*, "a calling together, convocation"), and they were to be national celebrations reminding Israel of God's sovereign rule—a time to renew the devotion of the people to God and remember His mighty acts on their behalf. The instruction in this chapter provides a context for many New Testament events. In fact, the Hebrew calendar clearly expressed the continuity between the testaments. The purpose of these appointed times in the framework of holiness was to remind God's people that not only are persons, places, and actions holy, but times are also holy. These days set apart from the calendar of the regular pursuits of life enabled God's people to meditate upon the meaning of their own existence and consider the holy task to which they had been called.

Hebrew Calendar of Festivals

Celebration	Date	Reference	Purpose	OT Significance	NT Significance
Passover & Festival of Unleavened Bread	Abib 14 (April)	Lv 23:5-8; Dt 16:1-8	Remembering	Remembering Israel's deliverance from Egyptian bondage	The death of Christ our sacrificial lamb
Festival of Weeks	Ziv 5 (June)	Lv 23:9-14; Dt 16:9-12	Reaping	According to Jewish tradition, the day Moses received the Ten Commandments	The coming of the Holy Spirit upon the church
Festival of Trumpets	Tishri 1 (Sept–Oct)	Nm 28:11-15; 29:1-6	Reunion	Sounding the trumpets as a triumphant memorial of God's relationship to Israel through the Sinai covenant	The second coming of Christ
The Day of Atonement	Tishri 10 (Sept–Oct)	Ex 30:10-30; Lv 16:1-34; Nm 29:7-11	Redemption	One gracious day a year given by God in order that the community could receive forgiveness	The pardon of God's people
Festival of Booths (Tabernacles)	Tishri 15–22 (Sept–Oct)	Lv 23:34-42; Nm 29:12; Dt 16:13-17	Rejoicing	Remembering the wilderness wandering and rejoicing in the completion of all the harvests	The fellowship of God's people dwelling together in peace.

them: When you enter the land I am
giving you and reap its harvest,[A] you
are to bring the first sheaf of your
harvest to the priest. 11 He will wave
the sheaf before the LORD so that
you may be accepted; the priest is to
wave it on the day after the Sabbath.
12 On the day you wave the sheaf, you
are to offer a year-old male lamb[B]
without blemish as a •burnt offering
to the LORD. 13 Its •grain offering is to
be four quarts[C] of fine flour mixed
with oil as a fire offering to the LORD,
a pleasing aroma, and its •drink offering will be one quart[D] of wine.
14 You must not eat bread, roasted
grain, or any new grain[E] until this
very day, and until you have brought
the offering to your God. This is to
be a permanent statute throughout
your generations wherever you live.
15 "You are to count seven[F] complete weeks[G] starting from the
day after the Sabbath, the day you
brought the sheaf of the presentation offering. 16 You are to count
50 days until the day after the seventh Sabbath and then present an
offering of new grain[H] to the LORD.
17 Bring two loaves of bread from
your settlements as a presentation
offering, each of them made from
four quarts[C] of fine flour, baked
with yeast, as •firstfruits to the LORD.
18 You are to present with the bread
seven unblemished male lambs a
year old, one young bull, and two
rams. They will be a burnt offering
to the LORD, with their grain offerings and drink offerings, a fire offering of a pleasing aroma to the
LORD. 19 You are also to prepare one
male goat as a •sin offering, and
two male lambs a year old as a •fel-
lowship sacrifice. 20 The priest will
wave the lambs with the bread of
firstfruits as a presentation offering
before the LORD; the bread and the
two lambs will be holy to the LORD
for the priest. 21 On that same day
you are to make a proclamation and
hold a sacred assembly. You are not
to do any daily work. This is to be
a permanent statute wherever you
live throughout your generations.
22 When you reap the harvest of your
land, you are not to reap all the way
to the edge of your field or gather
the gleanings of your harvest. Leave
them for the poor and the foreign
resident; I am •Yahweh your God."
23 The LORD spoke to Moses: 24 "Tell
the Israelites: In the seventh month,
on the first day of the month, you
are to have a day of complete rest,
commemoration, and joyful shouting[I]—a sacred assembly. 25 You must
not do any daily work, but you must
present a fire offering to the LORD."
26 The LORD again spoke to Moses:
27 "The tenth day of this seventh
month is the Day of •Atonement.
You are to hold a sacred assembly
and practice self-denial;[J] you are to
present a fire offering to the LORD.
28 On this particular day you are
not to do any work, for it is a Day
of Atonement to make atonement
for yourselves before the LORD your
God. 29 If any person does not practice self-denial on this particular
day, he must be cut off from his
people. 30 I will destroy among his
people anyone who does any work
on this same day. 31 You are not to
do any work. This is a permanent
statute throughout your generations wherever you live. 32 It will be
a Sabbath of complete rest for you,
and you must practice self-denial.
You are to observe your Sabbath
from the evening of the ninth day
of the month until the following
evening."
33 The LORD spoke to Moses:
34 "Tell the Israelites: The Festival of
Booths[K] to the LORD begins on the
fifteenth day of this seventh month
and continues for seven days.
35 There is to be a sacred assembly
on the first day; you are not to do
any daily work. 36 You are to present
a fire offering to the LORD for seven
days. On the eighth day you are to
hold a sacred assembly and present
a fire offering to the LORD. It is a
solemn gathering; you are not to do
any daily work.
37 "These are the LORD's appointed
times that you are to proclaim as

[A] **23:10** = the barley harvest [B] **23:12** Or *a male lamb in its first year* [C] **23:13,17** Lit *two-tenths of an ephah* [D] **23:13** Lit *one-fourth of a hin* [E] **23:14** Grain or bread from the new harvest [F] **23:15** Lit *count; they will be seven* [G] **23:15** Or *Sabbaths* [H] **23:16** = the wheat harvest; Ex 34:22 [I] **23:24** Or *blast*; traditionally trumpet blasts [J] **23:27** Traditionally, fasting, abstinence from sex, and refraining from personal grooming [K] **23:34** Or *Feast of Tabernacles* sacred assemblies for presenting fire offerings to the LORD, burnt offerings and grain offerings, sacrifices and drink offerings, each on its designated day. 38 These are in addition to the offerings for the LORD's Sabbaths, your gifts, all your vow offerings, and all your freewill offerings that you give to the LORD.

39 "You are to celebrate the LORD's festival on the fifteenth day of the seventh month for seven days after you have gathered the produce of the land. There will be complete rest on the first day and complete rest on the eighth day. 40 On the first day you are to take the product of majestic trees—palm fronds, boughs of leafy trees, and willows of the brook—and rejoice before the LORD your God for seven days. 41 You are to celebrate it as a festival to the LORD seven days each year. This is a permanent statute for you throughout your generations; you must celebrate it in the seventh month. 42 You are to live in booths for seven days. All the native-born of Israel must live in booths, 43 so that your generations may know that I made the Israelites live in booths when I brought them out of the land of Egypt; I am Yahweh your God." 44 So Moses declared the LORD's appointed times to the Israelites.

Oil, bread, sanctuary (24:1-9)

24 The LORD spoke to Moses: 2 "Command the Israelites to bring you pure oil from crushed olives for the light, in order to keep the lamp burning continually. 3 Aaron is to tend it continually from evening until morning before the LORD outside the veil of the •testimony in the tent of meeting. This is a permanent statute throughout your generations. 4 He must continually tend the lamps on the pure gold lampstand in the LORD's presence.

5 "Take fine flour and bake it into 12 loaves; each loaf is to be made with four quarts.[A] 6 Arrange them in two rows, six to a row, on the pure gold table before the LORD. 7 Place pure frankincense near each row, so that it may serve as a memorial portion for the bread and a fire offering to the LORD. 8 The bread is to be set out before the LORD every Sabbath day as a perpetual covenant obligation on the part of the Israelites. 9 It belongs to Aaron and his sons, who are to eat it in a holy place, for it is the holiest portion for him from the fire offerings to the LORD; this is a permanent rule."

The stoning of a blasphemer (24:10-23)

10 Now the son of an Israelite mother and an Egyptian father was[B] among the Israelites. A fight broke out in the camp between the Israelite woman's son and an Israelite man. 11 Her son cursed and blasphemed the Name, and they brought him to Moses. (His mother's name was Shelomith, a daughter of Dibri of the tribe of Dan.) 12 They put him in custody until the LORD's decision could be made clear to them.

13 Then the LORD spoke to Moses: 14 "Bring the one who has cursed to the outside of the camp and have all who heard him lay their hands on his head; then have the whole community stone him. 15 And tell the Israelites: If anyone curses his God, he will bear the consequences of his sin. 16 Whoever blasphemes the name of •Yahweh is to be put to death; the whole community must stone him. If he blasphemes the Name, he is to be put to death, whether the foreign resident or the native.

17 "If a man kills anyone, he must be put to death. 18 Whoever kills an animal is to make restitution for it, life for life. 19 If any man inflicts a permanent injury on his neighbor, whatever he has done is to be done to him: 20 fracture for fracture, eye for eye, tooth for tooth. Whatever injury he inflicted on the person, the same is to be inflicted on him. 21 Whoever kills an animal is to make restitution for it, but whoever kills a person is to be put to death. 22 You are to have the same law for the foreign resident and the native, because I am Yahweh your God."

23 After Moses spoke to the Israelites, they brought the one who had cursed to the outside of the camp and stoned him. So the Israelites did as the LORD had commanded Moses.

[A] **24:5** Lit *two-tenths of an ephah* [B] **24:10** Lit *went out*

24:1-4 Chapter 24 turns from a discussion of special feasts to noting two regular duties of the priest. First, **Aaron** was required to **tend** [Hb *'arak*, "arrange or put in order"] **the lamps on the pure gold lampstand** so that **the lamp** will burn **continually** (cp. Ex 27:20-21). The plans for the structure of the lampstand are given in Ex 25:31-40, and the actual construction of the lampstand is described in Ex 37:17-24. Perhaps the Lord repeated this law to emphasize that Aaron was to tend the lamps **continually from evening until morning before the LORD.**

The lighting of the lamps is described as **a permanent statute throughout your generations** (i.e., until these things, of which the candlestick and its lamps were a type, are made manifest). The observance of this law was to continue until its typological fulfillment in Jesus Christ, the true light for revelation to the Gentiles and for the glory to His people Israel (cp. Mt 4:16; Lk 2:32; Jn 1:4-9; 12:46; Rv 21:23). The oil was a higher grade, beaten to produce a higher grade than by pressing. Aaron and the priests tended the lamps, but the people were to provide the oil.

24:5-9 Twelve loaves, representing the 12 tribes of Israel, were to be baked and arranged **in two rows, six to a row, on the pure gold table before the LORD.** The bread and incense were **to be set out before the LORD every Sabbath day as a perpetual covenant obligation on the part of the Israelites**, reminding the people that they were continually under the watchful eye of the Lord. The bread, made from fine flour without impurities, and thus foreshadowing the humanity of the Lord (cp. Jn 6:30-59), was closely associated with the covenant and represented God's sustenance for His people. The bread was separated from the holy of holies only by a curtain and symbolized fellowship between God and His creation. The old bread was eaten only by the priests and then replenished each Sabbath (cp. 1Sm 21:4-6; Mt 12:3-4).

24:10-23 After Moses received the laws regarding tending the lamps and the bread in the sanctuary, an incidence of blasphemy occurred in Israel. A man **cursed and blasphemed** [Hb *naqav*, "curse," lit "pierce"] **the Name** of the Lord (vv. 10-11). Note that his mother is named (v. 11), but the father, an Egyptian, was not named. Even though resident foreigners were required to keep the laws (vv. 10-16), the son's heritage passed through his mother, who was an Israelite. **The name of Yahweh** was to be revered and held in high esteem (v. 16). In the ancient Near East a person's name was intimately bound up with his character so that in the case of God, blasphemy was in effect an act of repudiation against the character of God. The holiness of God is reinforced by the drastic penalty prescribed for blasphemy. **The LORD** gave his judgment (vv. 13-22), and **the Israelites** obeyed by stoning the offender **outside of the camp**. God is as concerned about holiness and justice in the Israelite camp as He was for purity in the tabernacle.

25:1-23 The principle of **Sabbath** rest is applied to **the seventh year** and to that which follows the completion of the seventh seven-year cycle, referred to as the **Year of Jubilee**. The Jewish festal system is readily arranged into groupings of seven. For example, the people rest on the seventh day (the Sabbath). Pentecost, when harvesters rest, comes during the seventh week (after Passover). The nation rests during the seventh month at the Festival of Trumpets. The Year of Jubilee, when everything rests, comes following the seventh seven of years (forty-nine years). Rest for God's creation systematically comes on the seventh day, week, month, year, and even the seventh seven of years.

The basic idea of the Year of Jubilee was to set aside a **holy** year in which land, **property,** and debts were totally restored. During the Jubilee, all property reverted back to its original owner. All the land belonged to the Lord and He could do with it as He wished (v. 23). By allowing the land to rest in the seventh year, its productivity would be enhanced. Also the people would be acknowledging that the land ultimately belonged to the Lord. **The land** was **not to be permanently sold** because it belonged to the Lord; the people of Israel were **only foreigners and temporary residents** (i.e., they were stewards entrusted with God's land).

The Sabbath Year and the Year of Jubilee (25:1-55)

25 The LORD spoke to Moses on
Mount Sinai: 2 "Speak to the
Israelites and tell them: When you
enter the land I am giving you, the
land will observe a Sabbath to the
LORD. 3 You may sow your field for
six years, and you may prune your
vineyard and gather its produce for
six years. 4 But there will be a Sabbath of complete rest for the land in
the seventh year, a Sabbath to the
LORD: you are not to sow your field
or prune your vineyard. 5 You are
not to reap what grows by itself from
your crop, or harvest the grapes of
your untended vines. It must be a
year of complete rest for the land.
6 Whatever the land produces during the Sabbath year can be food
for you—for yourself, your male or
female slave, and the hired hand or
foreigner who stays with you. 7 All
of its growth may serve as food for
your livestock and the wild animals
in your land.

8 "You are to count seven sabbatical years, seven times seven years,
so that the time period of the sev-
en sabbatical years amounts to 49.
9 Then you are to sound a trumpet
loudly in the seventh month, on the
tenth day of the month; you will
sound it throughout your land on
the Day of •Atonement. 10 You are
to consecrate the fiftieth year and
proclaim freedom in the land for all
its inhabitants. It will be your Jubilee, when each of you is to return
to his property and each of you to
his clan. 11 The fiftieth year will be
your Jubilee; you are not to sow,
reap what grows by itself, or harvest
its untended vines. 12 It is to be holy
to you because it is the Jubilee; you
may only eat its produce directly
from the field.

13 "In this Year of Jubilee, each of
you will return to his property. 14 If
you make a sale to your neighbor or
a purchase from him, do not cheat
one another. 15 You are to make the
purchase from your neighbor based
on the number of years since the last
Jubilee. He is to sell to you based on
the number of remaining harvest
years. 16 You are to increase its price
in proportion to a greater amount of
years, and decrease its price in proportion to a lesser amount of years,
because what he is selling to you is
a number of harvests. 17 You are not
to cheat one another, but •fear your
God, for I am •Yahweh your God.

18 "You are to keep My statutes and
ordinances and carefully observe
them, so that you may live securely
in the land. 19 Then the land will
yield its fruit, so that you can eat,
be satisfied, and live securely in the
land. 20 If you wonder: 'What will we
eat in the seventh year if we don't
sow or gather our produce?' 21 I will
appoint My blessing for you in the
sixth year, so that it will produce
a crop sufficient for three years.
22 When you sow in the eighth year,
you will be eating from the previous
harvest. You will be eating this until the ninth year when its harvest
comes in.

23 "The land is not to be permanently sold because it is Mine, and
you are only foreigners and temporary residents on My land.[A] 24 You are
to allow the redemption of any land
you occupy. 25 If your brother becomes destitute and sells part of his
property, his nearest relative may
come and redeem what his brother
has sold. 26 If a man has no •family
redeemer, but he prospers[B] and obtains enough to redeem his land,
27 he may calculate the years since
its sale, repay the balance to the
man he sold it to, and return to his
property. 28 But if he cannot obtain
enough to repay him, what he sold
will remain in the possession of its
purchaser until the Year of Jubilee.
It is to be released at the Jubilee, so
that he may return to his property.

29 "If a man sells a residence in a
walled city, his right of redemption
will last until a year has passed after
its sale; his right of redemption will
last a year. 30 If it is not redeemed
by the end of a full year, then the
house in the walled city is permanently transferred to its purchaser
throughout his generations. It is not
to be released on the Jubilee. 31 But
houses in villages that have no walls
around them are to be classified as
open fields. The right to redeem

[A] 25:23 Lit *residents with Me* [B] 25:26 Lit *but his hand reaches*

Principle of the Sabbath

Name	Reference	Time	Purpose	Prophetic Significance
Sabbath	Ex 20:8-11; 31:12-17; Lv 23:3; Dt 5:12-15	The evening of the sixth day to the evening of the next day	• To rest from work, to honor God, and to reflect on God's covenant with Israel • To commemorate God's completion of creation	Jesus is Lord of the Sabbath and should be at the center of its observance (Mk 2:23-28).
Sabbath Year	Ex 23:10,11; Lv 25:1-7, 20-22; Dt 15:1-18	Every seventh year	• To allow the land to rest or lie fallow • To forgive debts • To release Hebrews bound to servitude because of debt	God through Jesus Christ has systematically and faithfully given rest, forgiven us, and set us free (Mt 11:28; Jn 8:36; Eph 1:7).
Year of Jubilee	Lv 25:8-55; 27:17-24; Ezk 46:17	The fiftieth year following seven Sabbath years	• To proclaim liberty to those who were slaves because of debt • To return land to the former owners • To rejoice and celebrate	This observance pictures the deliverance from the bondage and slavery of sin that comes in Christ (Jn 8:36; Gl 5:1).

such houses stays in effect, and they
are to be released at the Jubilee.
32 "Concerning the Levitical cities,
the Levites always have the right
to redeem houses in the cities they
possess. 33 Whatever property one of
the Levites can redeem[A]—a house
sold in a city they possess—must
be released at the Jubilee, because
the houses in the Levitical cities are
their possession among the Israelites. 34 The open pastureland around
their cities may not be sold, for it is
their permanent possession.
35 "If your brother becomes destitute and cannot sustain himself
among[B] you, you are to support him
as a foreigner or temporary resident, so that he can continue to live
among you. 36 Do not profit or take
interest from him, but fear your God
and let your brother live among you.
37 You are not to lend him your silver
with interest or sell him your food
for profit. 38 I am Yahweh your God,
who brought you out of the land of
Egypt to give you the land of Canaan
and to be your God.
39 "If your brother among you becomes destitute and sells himself
to you, you must not force him to
do slave labor. 40 Let him stay with
you as a hired hand or temporary
resident; he may work for you until
the Year of Jubilee. 41 Then he and
his children are to be released from
you, and he may return to his clan
and his ancestral property. 42 They
are not to be sold as slaves,[C] because
they are My slaves that I brought out
of the land of Egypt. 43 You are not
to rule over them harshly but fear
your God. 44 Your male and female
slaves are to be from the nations
around you; you may purchase male
and female slaves. 45 You may also
purchase them from the foreigners
staying with you, or from their families living among you—those born
in your land. These may become
your property. 46 You may leave them
to your sons after you to inherit as
property; you can make them slaves
for life. But concerning your brothers, the Israelites, you must not rule
over one another harshly.
47 "If a foreigner or temporary
resident living among you prospers,
but your brother living near him
becomes destitute and sells himself
to the foreigner living among you,
or to a member of the foreigner's
clan, 48 he has the right of redemption after he has been sold. One of
his brothers may redeem him. 49 His
uncle or cousin may redeem him,
or any of his close relatives from
his clan may redeem him. If he

25:24-55 Besides reminding the people that the land belongs to God, the Jubilee was also to prevent the wealthy from permanently amassing land at the expense of the common people. Israelites were not to take advantage of fellow needy Israelites; in fact, they were admonished to aid those in need. Much of this chapter will depend on the Israelites remembering their own exodus and deliverance from Egypt, reminding them to be just and gracious with those who may have fallen into difficult times. The practical application of loving a neighbor as oneself is stressed here.

[A] **25:33** Hb obscure [B] **25:35** Lit *and his hand falters with* [C] **25:42** Lit *sold with a sale of a slave*

26:1-46 Chapter 26 serves as a conclusion to the book as a whole and deals with the subject of blessings and curses. The occurrence of these blessings and curses after the laws have been given plays a critical role in the structure of the entire book, since they occur at the end as a promise and a warning. Deuteronomy 28 contains a listing of blessings and curses parallel to Lv 26. The blessings for obedience and curses for disobedience reflect the principle that a person should be justly recompensed for his actions. These are the blessings and curses for the Israelites based on the degree of their loyalty to the Mosaic covenant. One may note the symmetry between the blessings and the curses.

prospers, he may redeem himself.
50 The one who purchased him is to
calculate the time from the year he
sold himself to him until the Year of
Jubilee. The price of his sale will be
determined by the number of years.
It will be set for him like the daily
wages of a hired hand. 51 If many
years are still left, he must pay his
redemption price in proportion to
them based on his purchase price.
52 If only a few years remain until the
Year of Jubilee, he will calculate and
pay the price of his redemption in
proportion to his remaining years.
53 He will stay with him like a man
hired year by year. A foreign owner
is not to rule over him harshly in
your sight. 54 If he is not redeemed
in any of these ways, he and his children are to be released at the Year
of Jubilee. 55 For the Israelites are
My slaves. They are My slaves that I
brought out of the land of Egypt; I
am Yahweh your God.

Blessings and curses (26:1-46)

26 "Do not make idols for yourselves, set up a carved image
or sacred pillar for yourselves, or
place a sculpted stone in your land
to bow down to it, for I am •Yahweh
your God. 2 You must keep My Sabbaths and revere My sanctuary; I am
Yahweh.
3 "If you follow My statutes and
faithfully observe My commands, 4 I
will give you rain at the right time,
and the land will yield its produce,
and the trees of the field will bear
their fruit. 5 Your threshing will
continue until grape harvest, and
the grape harvest will continue until
sowing time; you will have plenty of
food to eat and live securely in your
land. 6 I will give peace to the land,
and you will lie down with nothing
to frighten you. I will remove dangerous animals from the land, and
no sword will pass through your
land. 7 You will pursue your enemies, and they will fall before you
by the sword. 8 Five of you will pursue 100, and 100 of you will pursue
10,000; your enemies will fall before
you by the sword.
9 "I will turn to you, make you
fruitful and multiply you, and confirm My covenant with you. 10 You
will eat the old grain of the previous year and will clear out the old to
make room for the new. 11 I will place
My residence[A] among you, and I will
not reject you. 12 I will walk among
you and be your God, and you will be
My people. 13 I am Yahweh your God,
who brought you out of the land of
Egypt, so that you would no longer
be their slaves. I broke the bars of
your yoke and enabled you to live in
freedom.[B]
14 "But if you do not obey Me and
observe all these commands— 15 if
you reject My statutes and despise
My ordinances, and do not observe
all My commands—and break My
covenant, 16 then I will do this to you:
I will bring terror on you—wasting
disease and fever that will cause
your eyes to fail and your life to ebb
away. You will sow your seed in vain
because your enemies will eat it. 17 I
will turn[C] against you, so that you
will be defeated by your enemies.
Those who hate you will rule over
you, and you will flee even though
no one is pursuing you.
18 "But if after these things you
will not obey Me, I will proceed to
discipline you seven times for your
sins. 19 I will break down your strong

[A] 26:11 Or *tabernacle* [B] 26:13 Lit *to walk uprightly* [C] 26:17 Lit *will set My face*

Blessings	Curses
Fertility in the land (vv. 4-5,10)	Infertility in the land (vv. 16,19-20,26)
Living in safety in the land (v. 5)	Uprooting to foreign nations (v. 33)
Removal of dangerous animals (v. 6)	Danger of wild animals (v. 22)
Removal of the sword (v. 6)	Avenging by the sword (v. 25)
Victory over enemies (v. 7)	Defeat by enemies (vv. 17,25)
God's favor (v. 9)	God's disfavor (v. 17)

pride. I will make your sky like iron
and your land like bronze, 20 and
your strength will be used up for
nothing. Your land will not yield its
produce, and the trees of the land
will not bear their fruit.
21 "If you act with hostility toward
Me and are unwilling to obey Me,
I will multiply your plagues seven
times for your sins. 22 I will send wild
animals against you that will deprive
you of your children, ravage your
livestock, and reduce your numbers
until your roads are deserted.
23 "If in spite of these things you
do not accept My discipline, but act
with hostility toward Me, 24 then I
will act with hostility toward you;
I also will strike you seven times
for your sins. 25 I will bring a sword
against you to execute the vengeance of the covenant. Though
you withdraw into your cities, I will
send a pestilence among you, and
you will be delivered into enemy
hands. 26 When I cut off your supply
of bread, 10 women will bake your
bread in a single oven and ration out
your bread by weight, so that you
will eat but not be satisfied.
27 "And if in spite of this you do
not obey Me but act with hostility toward Me, 28 I will act with furious hostility toward you; I will
also discipline you seven times for
your sins. 29 You will eat the flesh of
your sons; you will eat the flesh of
your daughters. 30 I will destroy your
•high places, cut down your incense
altars, and heap your dead bodies on
the lifeless bodies of your idols; I will
reject you. 31 I will reduce your cities
to ruins and devastate your sanctuaries. I will not smell the pleasing
aroma of your sacrifices. 32 I also
will devastate the land, so that your
enemies who come to live there will
be appalled by it. 33 But I will scatter
you among the nations, and I will
draw a sword to chase after you. So
your land will become desolate, and
your cities will become ruins.
34 "Then the land will make up for
its Sabbath years during the time it
lies desolate, while you are in the
land of your enemies. At that time
the land will rest and make up for its
Sabbaths. 35 As long as it lies desolate, it will have the rest it did not
have during your Sabbaths when
you lived there.
36 "I will put anxiety in the hearts
of those of you who survive in the
lands of their enemies. The sound
of a wind-driven leaf will put them
to flight, and they will flee as one
flees from a sword, and fall though
no one is pursuing them. 37 They will
stumble over one another as if fleeing from a sword though no one is
pursuing them. You will not be able
to stand against your enemies. 38 You
will perish among the nations; the
land of your enemies will devour
you. 39 Those[A] who survive in the
lands of your enemies will waste
away because of their sin; they will
also waste away because of their fathers' sins along with theirs.
40 "But if they will confess their sin
and the sin of their fathers—their
unfaithfulness that they practiced
against Me, and how they acted
with hostility toward Me, 41 and I
acted with hostility toward them
and brought them into the land of
their enemies—and if their uncircumcised hearts will be humbled,
and if they will pay the penalty for
their sin, 42 then I will remember
My covenant with Jacob. I will also
remember My covenant with Isaac
and My covenant with Abraham, and
I will remember the land. 43 For the
land abandoned by them will make
up for its Sabbaths by lying desolate
without the people, while they pay
the penalty for their sin, because
they rejected My ordinances and
abhorred My statutes. 44 Yet in spite
of this, while they are in the land of
their enemies, I will not reject or abhor them so as to destroy them and
break My covenant with them, since
I am Yahweh their God. 45 For their
sake I will remember the covenant
with their fathers, whom I brought
out of the land of Egypt in the sight
of the nations to be their God; I am
Yahweh."
46 These are the statutes, ordinances, and laws the LORD established
between Himself and the Israelites
through Moses on Mount Sinai.

[A] **26:39** Lit *Those of you*

27:1-33 The last chapter of the book of Leviticus deals with vows and dedications made to the Lord. Since these vows and dedications go above and beyond the normal sacrificial offerings, their unveiling comes after the conclusion of the Law. They were not mandated since the decision to make a vow is personal, involving one's own choice.

Ten laws in this chapter seem to correspond to the Ten Commandments, which would mean that in the same way giving of the Law at Sinai began with the Ten Commandments in Exodus, the book of Leviticus now ends with the listing of 10 laws. These 10 laws unveil the process of the payment of vows and tithes to the Lord:

1. persons dedicated to the Lord (27:1-8),
2. animals dedicated to the Lord (27:9-13),
3. houses dedicated to the Lord (27:14-15),
4. inherited land dedicated to the Lord (27:16-21),
5. purchased land dedicated to the Lord (27:22-25),
6. the prohibition of the dedication of firstborn animals (27:26-27),
7. the procedure for total devotion to the Lord (27:28),
8. the procedure for total devotion of a person to the Lord (27:29),
9. the procedure for tithes from the produce of the land (27:30-31), and
10. the procedure for tithes from the livestock (27:32-34).

Vows and Tithes (27:1-34)

The regulation of vows and tithes (27:1-33)

27 The LORD spoke to Moses:
2 "Speak to the Israelites and
tell them: When someone makes a
special vow to the LORD that involves
the assessment of people, 3 if the assessment concerns a male from 20
to 60 years old, your assessment is
50 silver •shekels measured by the
standard sanctuary shekel. 4 If the
person is a female, your assessment
is 30 shekels. 5 If the person is from
five to 20 years old, your assessment
for a male is 20 shekels and for a
female 10 shekels. 6 If the person is
from one month to five years old,
your assessment for a male is five
silver shekels, and for a female your
assessment is three shekels of silver.
7 If the person is 60 years or more,
your assessment is 15 shekels for a
male and 10 shekels for a female.
8 But if one is too poor to pay the assessment, he must present the person before the priest and the priest
will set a value for him. The priest
will set a value for him according to
what the one making the vow can
afford.

9 "If the vow involves one of the
animals that may be brought as an
offering to the LORD, any of these he
gives to the LORD will be holy. 10 He
may not replace it or make a substitution for it, either good for bad,
or bad for good. But if he does substitute one animal for another, both
that animal and its substitute will be
holy.

11 "If the vow involves any of the
•unclean animals that may not be
brought as an offering to the LORD,
the animal must be presented before the priest. 12 The priest will set
its value, whether high or low; the
price will be set as the priest makes
the assessment for you. 13 If the one
who brought it decides to redeem it,
he must add a fifth to the[A] assessed
value.

14 "When a man consecrates his
house as holy to the LORD, the priest
will assess its value, whether high
or low. The price will stand just as
the priest assesses it. 15 But if the one
who consecrated his house redeems
it, he must add a fifth to the[A] assessed value, and it will be his.

16 "If a man consecrates to the
LORD any part of a field that he possesses, your assessment of value will
be proportional to the seed needed
to sow it, at the rate of 50 silver
shekels for every five bushels[B] of
barley seed.[C] 17 If he consecrates his
field during the Year of Jubilee, the
price will stand according to your
assessment. 18 But if he consecrates
his field after the Jubilee, the priest
will calculate the price for him in
proportion to the years left until
the next Year of Jubilee, so that your
assessment will be reduced. 19 If the
one who consecrated the field decides to redeem it, he must add a
fifth to the[A] assessed value, and the
field will transfer back to him. 20 But
if he does not redeem the field or if
he has sold it to another man, it is
no longer redeemable. 21 When the
field is released in the Jubilee, it will
be holy to the LORD like a field permanently set apart; it becomes the
priest's property.

22 "If a person consecrates to the
LORD a field he has purchased that
is not part of his inherited landholding, 23 then the priest will calculate
for him the amount of the[A] assessment up to the Year of Jubilee, and
the person will pay the assessed
value on that day as a holy offering
to the LORD. 24 In the Year of Jubilee
the field will return to the one he
bought it from, the original owner.
25 All your assessed values will be
measured by the standard sanctuary
shekel, 20 *gerahs* to the shekel.

26 "But no one can consecrate a
firstborn of the livestock, whether
an animal from the herd or flock, to
the LORD, because a firstborn already
belongs to the LORD. 27 If it is one of
the unclean livestock, it must be
ransomed according to your assessment by adding a fifth of its value
to it. If it is not redeemed, it can be
sold according to your assessment.

28 "Nothing that a man permanently sets apart to the LORD from all he
owns, whether a person, an animal,
or his inherited landholding, can
be sold or redeemed; everything set
apart is especially holy to the LORD.

A **27:13,15,19,23** Lit *your* B **27:16** Lit *for a homer* C **27:16** Or *grain*

[29]No person who has been set apart
for destruction is to be ransomed;
he must be put to death.
[30]"Every tenth of the land's produce, grain from the soil or fruit
from the trees, belongs to the LORD;
it is holy to the LORD. [31]If a man
decides to redeem any part of this
tenth, he must add a fifth to its
value. [32]Every tenth animal from
the herd or flock, which passes under the shepherd's rod, will be holy
to the LORD. [33]He is not to inspect
whether it is good or bad, and he
is not to make a substitution for it.
But if he does make a substitution,
both the animal and its substitute
will be holy; they cannot be redeemed."

Conclusion (27:34)

[34]These are the commands the
LORD gave Moses for the Israelites on
Mount Sinai.

27:34 The book of Leviticus ends with the statement that **the commands the LORD gave Moses for the Israelites on Mount Sinai** have come to a conclusion. All of the requirements for Israel's covenant relationship with the Lord are now recorded.

LEVITICUS... WRITTEN ON MY *Heart* The God who gave the Israelites the law in order to guide them towards holiness was also aware of their complete inability of maintaining that holiness on their own accord. God knew humanity would need a Savior and sent his Son to die in our place. Leviticus points us to the holy God and to our desperate need for atonement in order to have a relationship with Him.

Numbers

Timeline	1526–1406 BC	1490–1380 BC	1446 BC	1445 BC
World Events Biblical Events	Life of Moses	Life of Joshua	Exodus and parting of the Red Sea	Tabernacle built and dedicated

"The whole earth is filled with the LORD's glory" (14:21b).

Who wrote Numbers?

Traditionally Moses is considered the author of Numbers. There are passages in the Pentateuch and in the whole of Scripture affirming that Moses wrote Numbers and the entire Pentateuch (e.g., Ex 34:27; Dt 31:9,22,24; Jos 23:6; 2Ch 35:12; Ezr 6:18; Mk 10:3; Jn 1:17).

Who were the recipients?

Undoubtedly the message of the book is addressed to two generations of Israelites. Some see the first section (1:1–25:18) as focusing on the first generation and their journey through the wilderness. The second section (26:1–36:13) speaks to the emerging second generation, who were being prepared to enter the promised land.

When was Numbers written?

Sometime during the wilderness wandering ca 1445 to 1405 B.C.

Where did it happen?

Numbers records the Israelites' journey from Mount Sinai where they have felt God's presence, to the wilderness where they grumble against the same God who led them out of the bondage of Egypt, and finally to the plains of Moab near the Jordan River at the edge of the promised land.

What is Numbers about?

The overarching theme in Numbers is *God's faithfulness* to His covenant in contrast with *Israel's faithlessness*. Time and again God proves to be trustworthy and shows loving-kindness to Israel in restoring their relationship. He keeps His promises through provision and deliverance even when the people are rebellious and disobedient. Other themes include:

- *Holiness*, including rites of purification and an emphasis on being set apart unto the Lord and obedient to Him even in an isolated setting;
- The importance of *godly leadership* to accomplish the divine plan efficiently and effectively;
- The vulnerability of even godly leaders and the *consequences of disobedience*.

Christ is found in Numbers in the sacrifices required of the Israelites for sin, but He is especially depicted in the story of the bronze serpent to which the Israelites had to look in faith for life. So too, in coming to salvation you must look to Christ in faith for the forgiveness of sin.

Why should women read Numbers?

The book of Numbers is abundant evidence of the Lord's lovingkindness to an undeserving people. While the Israelites began with characteristic obedience, their turning away from the Lord, as recorded in the middle of the book of Numbers, reveals what would become the cycle of rebellion, repentance, and renewed covenantal love between the Lord and His people Israel. God has not changed since His dealings with the Israelites in the wilderness. People continue to be as sinful, depraved, and undeserving of God's faithful love as the Israelites. Let the lessons be taken to heart, and let all be found faithful to a merciful Lord.

How do you read Numbers?

Like the rest of the books in the Pentateuch, Numbers is set within a narrative frame; it begins one month after the close of Exodus and covers the 39 remaining years of the wilderness wanderings. However, the arrangement of the book is not chronological (chaps. 1–6 take place after 7:1–10:10). Woven among the narrative portions are censuses and legal codes. The only passages that diverge in genre from the rest of the book are those of Balaam's oracles, which contain poetry.

Outline

I. The First Census of Israel (1:1–2:34)
   A. The Descendants (1:1-46)
   B. The Duties of the Levites (1:47-54)
   C. The Organization of the Israelite Camp (2:1-34)

II. The Levites (3:1–4:49)
   A. The Sons of Aaron (3:1-51)
   B. The Kohathites (4:1-20)
   C. The Gershonites (4:21-28)
   D. The Merarites (4:29-49)

III. Instructions and Rituals (5:1–10:36)

IV. Complaints Against the Lord and Moses (11:1–12:16)

V. The Land of Canaan (13:1–14:45)

VI. Further Instructions (15:1-41)

VII. Korah's Rebellion (16:1-50)

VIII. The Priesthood (17:1–19:22)

IX. The Rebellion of Moses and Aaron (20:1-13)

X. The Conquests (20:14–21:35)

XI. Balaam's Oracles (22:1–24:25)

XII. The Incident with Baal of Peor (25:1-18)

XIII. Preparations for Entering the Promised Land (26:1–36:13)

1445 BC	1445 BC	1445–1407 BC	1406 BC
Exploration of Canaan by 12 spies	Events in Leviticus	Events in Numbers	Events in Deuteronomy

The First Census of Israel (1:1–2:34)

The Descendants (1:1-46)

1 The LORD spoke to Moses in the tent of meeting in the Wilderness of Sinai, on the first day of the second month of the second year after Israel's departure from the land of Egypt: [2] "Take a census of the entire Israelite community by their clans and their ancestral houses, counting the names of every male one by one. [3] You and Aaron are to register those who are 20 years old or more by their military divisions—everyone who can serve in Israel's army.[A] [4] A man from each tribe is to be with you, each one the head of his ancestral house. [5] These are the names of the men who are to assist you:

Elizur son of Shedeur
from Reuben;
6 Shelumiel son of Zurishaddai
from Simeon;
7 Nahshon son of Amminadab
from Judah;
8 Nethanel son of Zuar
from Issachar;
9 Eliab son of Helon
from Zebulun;
10 from the sons of Joseph:
Elishama son of Ammihud
from Ephraim,
Gamaliel son of Pedahzur
from Manasseh;
11 Abidan son of Gideoni
from Benjamin;

[A]1:3 Lit *everyone going out to war in Israel*

Title The title "Numbers," so named because of the censuses recorded in the book, is derived from the Latin Vulgate (*Liber Numeri*). However, the Hebrew title for this fourth book in the Pentateuch is "In the Wilderness" (Hb *bemidbar*), which is taken from the first verse of Numbers. In the Greek translation of the Old Testament (the LXX), the title is *Arithmoi* (Gk "numbers"), most certainly because of the prominence given to figures and census statistics.

1:1-15 Verse 1 gives a summary of the who, when, and where of Numbers. **The LORD spoke to Moses in the tent of meeting**, which is also called the tabernacle. The notation of the **first day of the second month of the second year** after the exodus is exactly one month after the tent of meeting had been erected (see Ex 40:1). The date designation also lets the reader know that Numbers is not chronological because the Passover celebration

Biblical Womanhood Patriarchy and God as Father

Although considered by some a quibbling over the unimportant, the language used in this passage is precise and very important in the overall understanding of the God-ordained creation order. The Lord instructed particular men to help Moses and Aaron with the census—**a man from each tribe . . . each one the head of his ancestral house.** The more literal translation of the Hebrew phrase is "head of the household of his father, head of his father's house."

The importance of the father's role is fully developed throughout Scripture as the father rebukes (Gn 37:10), loves (Gn 37:4; 44:20), pities (Ps 103:13), blesses (Gn 27:41), rejoices (Pr 10:1; 15:20), grieves (Gn 37:35). He is also clearly the object of honor as well as of obedience and love (Gn 28:7; Ex 20:12; 21:15,17; Dt 21:18-21; Eph 6:1-3). Since *'av* appears in the lexicon as "father or forefather," to follow the more straightforward translation seems more precise. Every forefather is an ancestor, but every ancestor is not a forefather. The context is quite clear that the reference is to the father as the "begetter or genitor" (Pr 23:22) and thus certainly an ancestor. The word may designate anyone who occupies a position as a father-figure, receiving the recognition and responsibility as would be assigned thereto.

This metaphor becomes more important because God identifies Himself as the "Father" of Israel (Is 63:16), and His fatherhood is very much a part of the covenantal relationship with His people (Ex 4:22; Jr 31:9). He not only redeemed them but also continued to bestow upon them His providence and guidance (Jr 31:9-10). In the passing of His covenant from generation to generation, the language again returns to this carefully selected metaphor, beginning with Abraham who is to be the "father of many nations" (Gn 17:5). God also expresses particular concern for the poor and suffering (Pr 22:22-23) and those who are fatherless (Ps 68:5). The Lord's role toward those who fear Him is that of a father (Ps 103:13; cp. Rm 8:15; Gl 4:6). He describes His guidance and correction of believers in the language of father and children (Pr 3:12; Jr 3:4).

The Census of Israel

Tribe	Head of Ancestral House	Tribal Count	References
Reuben	Elizur	46,500	vv. 5,20-21
Simeon	Shelumiel	59,300	vv. 6,22-23
Judah	Nahshon	74,600	vv. 7,26-27
Issachar	Nethanel	54,400	vv. 8,28-29
Zebulun	Eliab	57,400	vv. 9,30-31
Ephraim (Joseph's son)	Elishama	40,500	vv. 10,32-33
Manasseh (Joseph's son)	Gamaliel	32,200	vv. 10,34-35
Benjamin	Abidan	35,400	vv. 11,36-37
Dan	Ahiezer	62,700	vv. 12,38-39
Asher	Pagiel	41,500	vv. 13,40-41
Gad	Eliasaph	45,650	vv. 14,24-25
Naphtali	Ahira	53,400	vv. 15,42-43
Census Total		**603,550**	**v. 46**

12 Ahiezer son of Ammishaddai
from Dan;
13 Pagiel son of Ochran
from Asher;
14 Eliasaph son of Deuel[A]
from Gad;
15 Ahira son of Enan
from Naphtali.

16 These are the men called from the
community; they are leaders of their
ancestral tribes, the heads of Israel's
clans."
17 So Moses and Aaron took these
men who had been designated by
name, 18 and they assembled the
whole community on the first day
of the second month. They recorded
their ancestry by their clans and
their ancestral houses, counting one
by one the names of those 20 years
old or more, 19 just as the LORD commanded Moses. He registered them
in the Wilderness of Sinai:

20 The descendants of Reuben,
the firstborn of Israel: according to their family records by
their clans and their ancestral
houses, counting one by one
the names of every male 20
years old or more, everyone
who could serve in the army,
21 those registered for the tribe
of Reuben numbered 46,500.

22 The descendants of Simeon:
according to their family records by their clans and their ancestral houses, those registered
counting one by one the names
of every male 20 years old or
more, everyone who could
serve in the army, 23 those registered for the tribe of Simeon
numbered 59,300.

24 The descendants of Gad: according to their family records
by their clans and their ancestral houses, counting the names
of those 20 years old or more,
everyone who could serve in the
army, 25 those registered for the
tribe of Gad numbered 45,650.

26 The descendants of Judah:
according to their family records by their clans and their

[A] 1:14 LXX, Syr read *Reuel*

recorded in Nm 9:1-14 takes place in the first month of the second year. This verse also indicates that the Israelites have not moved from Mount Sinai, located in the **Wilderness of Sinai**, also known as "Horeb" (Hb "waste, desert"; e.g., Dt 1:19), in the south-central part of the Arabian peninsula.

The order of the 12 tribes is given according to the sons of Leah and Rachel, followed by the sons of the concubines of Jacob. The order of tribal patriarchs generally followed this pattern of listing according to birth order of each mother's offspring:

- Leah (Gn 29:31-35; 30:17-21);
- Rachel (Gn 30:22-24; 35:16-18; 41:50-52);
- Zilpah (Gn 30:9-13);
- Bilhah (Gn 30:4-8).

However, in the actual census, the order was different, with Gad's count coming between those of Simeon and Judah because in the military divisions of chapter 2, Gad was placed under the same division as Reuben and Simeon (Nm 2:10-16). Of note is that the tribe of Levi was not counted in this census. The total number of the tribes still came to 12, however, because Joseph was given a double portion through his sons, Ephraim and Manasseh.

ancestral houses, counting the names of those 20 years old or more, everyone who could serve in the army, 27 those registered for the tribe of Judah numbered 74,600.

28 The descendants of Issachar: according to their family records by their clans and their ancestral houses, counting the names of those 20 years old or more, everyone who could serve in the army, 29 those registered for the tribe of Issachar numbered 54,400.

30 The descendants of Zebulun: according to their family records by their clans and their ancestral houses, counting the names of those 20 years old or more, everyone who could serve in the army, 31 those registered for the tribe of Zebulun numbered 57,400.

32 The descendants of Joseph:

The descendants of Ephraim: according to their family records by their clans and their ancestral houses, counting the names of those 20 years old or more, everyone who could serve in the army, 33 those registered for the tribe of Ephraim numbered 40,500.

34 The descendants of Manasseh: according to their family records by their clans and their ancestral houses, counting the names of those 20 years old or more, everyone who could serve in the army, 35 those registered for the tribe of Manasseh numbered 32,200.

36 The descendants of Benjamin: according to their family records by their clans and their ancestral houses, counting the names of those 20 years old or more, everyone who could serve in the army, 37 those registered for the tribe of Benjamin numbered 35,400.

38 The descendants of Dan: according to their family records by their clans and their ancestral houses, counting the names of those 20 years old or more, everyone who could serve in the army, 39 those registered for the tribe of Dan numbered 62,700.

40 The descendants of Asher: according to their family records by their clans and their ancestral houses, counting the names of those 20 years old or more, everyone who could serve in the army, 41 those registered for the tribe of Asher numbered 41,500.

42 The descendants of Naphtali: according to their family records by their clans and their ancestral houses, counting the names of those 20 years old or more, everyone who could serve in the army, 43 those registered for the tribe of Naphtali numbered 53,400.

44 These are the men Moses and Aaron registered, with the assistance of the 12 leaders of Israel; each represented his ancestral house. 45 So all the Israelites 20 years old or more, everyone who could serve in Israel's army, were registered by their ancestral houses. 46 All those registered numbered 603,550.

HARD QUESTION

Numbers in the Book of Numbers—Are There Errors?

In examining the book of Numbers, an accounting of the censuses found therein is of vital importance. Many moderate and liberal theologians claim that the large number of people noted in Numbers could not have left Egypt, concluding that the numbers must be metaphorical or altogether unbelievable. However, this view does not fit with the presupposition that the Bible is without error. You need not fret over perceived "problems" in the text of Scripture. With God, what is unusual is by no means impossible.

In general, there are guidelines to observe when looking at the biblical text. There are times when numbers used are rounded, as in English you may refer to "a dozen" when in fact there are anywhere from a few less or more than 12 items. The key is that God does not lie (see Nm 23:19). His words are true and reliable. The problems lie in the human ability, which is always limited, to explain puzzling phenomena. And Yahweh is affirmed again and again as the God of miracles. To sustain such a multitude required the supernatural intervention of God.

1:46 Moses, Aaron, and the representatives of the households conducted the census as the Lord instructed, the total number of men of fighting age coming to 603,550. If we consider there to be one woman and two children or elderly for each man of fighting age, an approximate total figure for Israel would be well over 2,000,000—not including the Levites. That women, children, and the elderly were not included in the census indicates its purpose as a military tool in preparation for the conquest of the promised land.

1:47-54 Just as God set aside Israel as a holy nation unto Himself, so He set aside **the tribe of Levi** to serve Him alone. Moses did not include **the Levites** in the **census** because God had given him special instructions for them. The main duty of the Levites was the **care** of the tabernacle, both its upkeep and transportation; they were not to engage in battle. In verse 50, the tabernacle is called the **tabernacle of the testimony**. The "testimony" is the Ten Commandments, which were placed in the ark of the covenant (Ex 25:21-22) to represent the whole of the law. The Levites could not take part in military campaigns because they needed to be clean before the Lord. When camping, their concern was the protection of **the tabernacle**; they were told to surround it (Nm 1:53). Not only is the tabernacle a place of worship, but it is also the place where God's glory is seen and where He speaks to Israel. If an **unauthorized person** even goes **near** the tabernacle, he is to be **put to death** (v. 51), underscoring the seriousness of the duty of the Levites.

2:1-34 The taking of a census and the organization of military camps might seem a bit out of the ordinary, but these were no ordinary events. Israel was beginning its journey to the promised land. The preparations for this sacred event were full of ceremonial order. While the tribes were divided into different military groups, rather than reflecting on a notion of their divisions, the divine arrangement of the camp affirmed oneness, community, and purpose. Each head of household is mentioned by name (vv. 5,7,10,12,14, 18,20,22,25,27,29). Clearly the tribal descent is marked through the father.

2:1-2 Each tribe was **to camp under** its respective **banner**, thus reinforcing the distinctions of family and tribe.

2:3-9 Every **division** surrounded the tabernacle, impressing again on the Israelites the central role God was to play in the life of Israel. The ark and the tabernacle are representative of God's revelation of Himself, and they were to be treated as holy by the people. Judah's **military division**, also containing the tribes of **Issachar** and **Zebulun**, was to protect the eastern flank. **The east side** was the most important, and thus shows the priority of Judah over Reuben, who was Jacob's firstborn (also over Simeon and Levi, who were next in birth order). Judah had been identified as the one responsible for leadership, perhaps because of the blessing he received from Jacob (Gn 49:10; cp. Nm 24:17). As the sun rose in the east, Judah's division would be responsible for protecting the tabernacle as the Levites set it up

The Duties of the Levites (1:47-54)

[47] But the Levites were not registered with them by their ancestral tribe. [48] For the LORD had told Moses: [49] "Do not register or take a census of the tribe of Levi with the other Israelites. [50] Appoint the Levites over the tabernacle of the •testimony, all its furnishings, and everything in it. They are to transport the tabernacle and all its articles, take care of it, and camp around it. [51] Whenever the tabernacle is to move, the Levites are to take it down, and whenever it is to stop at a campsite, the Levites are to set it up. Any unauthorized person who comes near it must be put to death.

[52] "The Israelites are to camp by their military divisions, each man with his encampment and under his banner. [53] The Levites are to camp around the tabernacle of the testimony and watch over it, so that no wrath will fall on the Israelite community." [54] The Israelites did everything just as the LORD had commanded Moses.

The Organization of the Israelite Camp (2:1-34)

2 The LORD spoke to Moses and Aaron: [2] "The Israelites are to camp under their respective banners beside the flags of their ancestral houses. They are to camp around the tent of meeting at a distance from it:

[3] Judah's military divisions will camp on the east side toward the sunrise under their banner. The leader of the descendants of Judah is Nahshon son of Amminadab. [4] His military division numbers 74,600. [5] The tribe of Issachar will camp next to it. The leader of the Issacharites is Nethanel son of Zuar. [6] His military division numbers 54,400. [7] The tribe of Zebulun will be next. The leader of the Zebulunites is Eliab son of Helon. [8] His military division numbers 57,400. [9] The total number in their military divisions who belong to Judah's encampment is 186,400; they will move out first.

[10] Reuben's military divisions will camp on the south side under their banner. The leader of the Reubenites is Elizur son of Shedeur. [11] His military division numbers 46,500. [12] The tribe of Simeon will camp next to it. The leader of the Simeonites is Shelumiel son of Zurishaddai. [13] His military division numbers 59,300. [14] The tribe of Gad will be next. The leader of the Gadites is Eliasaph son of Deuel.[A] [15] His military division numbers 45,650. [16] The total number in their military divisions who belong to Reuben's encampment is 151,450; they will move out second.

[17] The tent of meeting is to move out with the Levites' camp, which is in the middle of the camps. They are to move out just as they camp, each in his place,[B] with their banners.

[18] Ephraim's military divisions will camp on the west side under their banner. The leader of the Ephraimites is Elishama son of Ammihud. [19] His military division numbers 40,500. [20] The tribe of Manasseh will be next to it. The leader of the Manassites is Gamaliel son of Pedahzur. [21] His military division numbers 32,200. [22] The tribe of Benjamin will be next. The leader of the Benjaminites is Abidan son of Gideoni. [23] His military division numbers 35,400. [24] The total in their military divisions who belong to Ephraim's encampment number 108,100; they will move out third.

[25] Dan's military divisions will camp on the north side under their banner. The leader of the Danites is Ahiezer son of Ammishaddai. [26] His military division numbers 62,700. [27] The tribe of Asher will camp next to it. The leader of the Asherites is Pagiel son of Ochran. [28] His military division numbers 41,500. [29] The tribe of Naphtali will be next. The leader of the Naphtalites is

[A] **2:14** Some Hb mss, Sam, Vg; other Hb mss read *Reuel* [B] **2:17** Lit *each on his hand*

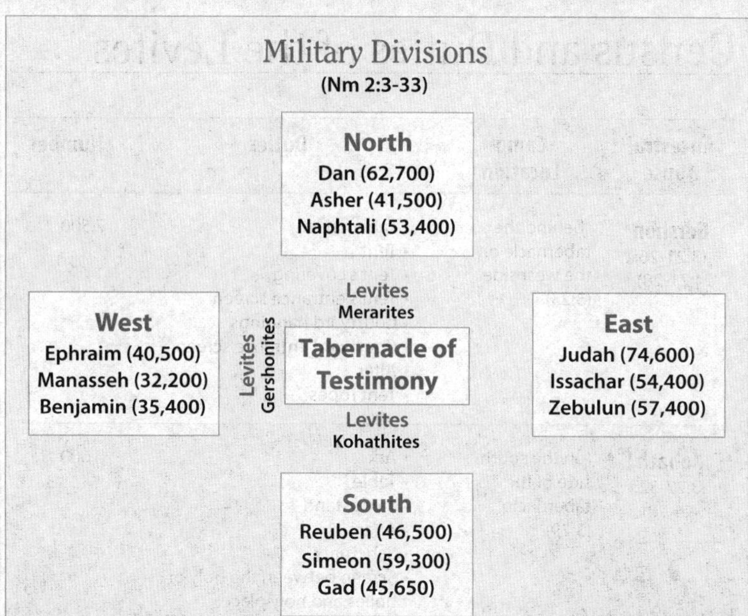

Ahira son of Enan. [30]His military division numbers 53,400.
[31]The total number who belong to Dan's encampment is
157,600; they are to move out
last, with their banners."

[32]These are the Israelites registered by their ancestral houses.
The total number in the camps
by their military divisions is
603,550. [33]But the Levites were
not registered among the Israelites, just as the LORD had
commanded Moses.

[34]The Israelites did everything the
LORD commanded Moses; they
camped by their banners in this way
and moved out the same way, each
man by his clan and by his ancestral
house.

The Levites (3:1–4:49)

The Sons of Aaron (3:1-51)

3 These are the family records of
Aaron and Moses at the time the
LORD spoke with Moses on Mount
Sinai. [2]These are the names of Aaron's sons: Nadab, the firstborn, and
Abihu, Eleazar, and Ithamar. [3]These
are the names of Aaron's sons, the
anointed priests, who were ordained
to serve as priests. [4]But Nadab and
Abihu died in the LORD's presence
when they presented unauthorized
fire before the LORD in the Wilderness of Sinai, and they had no sons.
So Eleazar and Ithamar served as
priests under the direction of Aaron
their father.

[5]The LORD spoke to Moses: [6]"Bring
the tribe of Levi near and present
them to Aaron the priest to assist
him. [7]They are to perform duties
for[A] him and the entire community
before the tent of meeting by attending to the service of the tabernacle.
[8]They are to take care of[A] all the furnishings of the tent of meeting and
perform duties for[B] the Israelites
by attending to the service of the
tabernacle. [9]Assign the Levites to
Aaron and his sons; they have been
assigned exclusively to him[C] from
the Israelites. [10]You are to appoint
Aaron and his sons to carry out their
priestly responsibilities, but any unauthorized person who comes near
the sanctuary must be put to death."

[11]The LORD spoke to Moses: [12]"See,
I have taken the Levites from the
Israelites in place of every firstborn
Israelite from the womb. The Le-
vites belong to Me, [13]because every
firstborn belongs to Me. At the time
I struck down every firstborn in the

[A]3:7,8 Or *to guard* [B]3:8 Or *and guard* [C]3:9 Some Hb mss, LXX, Sam read *Me*; Nm 8:16

and prepared for their journey in the morning.

2:10-34 The rest of the military divisions followed the same basic order as the census given in chapter 1. Reuben was to guard the south, Ephraim the west, and Dan the north, with the Levites in the center, surrounding the tabernacle. The tabernacle, which was symbolic of God's presence, was always to be centrally located whether the Israelites were resident in camp or moving forward on their journey. That **the Israelites did everything the LORD commanded Moses** is recorded three times, each phrase following the carrying out of a command (1:19,54; 2:34). Obedience is essential to maintaining and growing in a right relationship with the Lord as the Israelites will discover. The descent of the Israelites into disobedience, which was recorded in the book of Numbers, is tragic and foreshadows the grumbling, disobedience, and rebellion to come during their stay in the promised land.

3:1-4 A standard genealogical account of Aaron and his family is given. Each genealogy given is important for a number of reasons. Perhaps most important is the connection it provides from the past to the present, preserving family and community structures, affirming the current positions of authority, and giving an individual as well as the family a sense of pride. Aaron and his four sons were **the anointed priests**, with **Aaron** serving as high priest (Lv 16:1-34). Of note is the sin of **Aaron's sons: Nadab, the firstborn, and Abihu**. In Lv 10:1-2 is the story of how the brothers offered **unauthorized fire before the LORD**, and what occurred is briefly recounted here. Even God's anointed priests do not go unpunished for wrongdoing. God left Nadab and Abihu without heirs, which was the ultimate judgment. In fact, their punishment, as spiritual leaders of the community, was swift and more severe because of the solemn responsibility God had given them. With the death of the eldest sons, the younger two were now left to serve as priests under **their father**.

3:5-13 The LORD again spoke **to Moses**, giving instructions concerning the Levites previously excluded from the census. Moses was to **bring the tribe of Levi** before **Aaron**. The entire tribe of Levi was put into place as the **firstborn** in Israel, consecrated to serve the Lord in this special way (vv. 11-13,41). This recognition of "the tribe of Levi" is ceremonial in nature and important to the Lord and His people. **Aaron and his sons**, Eleazar and Ithamar, would now have help performing their **priestly** duties. The tribe of Levi was to attend to **the service of the tabernacle** (vv. 7,9).

God had identified the Levites as a substitute replacing the **firstborn**, which He claimed for Himself at the time of the Israelites' exodus from Egypt (Ex 13:11-15), with **the Levites** (Nm 3:41). Just as all firstborn humans and animals had been designated to be dedicated to God, now the entire tribe of Levi would wholly dedicate their services to God.

3:14-15 The LORD again spoke **to Moses**, commanding him to take a separate census of **the Levites**. Moses was obedient. The census was done by age, gender, and Levitical lineage. Only males **one month old or more** were to be counted. Rather than being military in nature, as the previous census, this counting was to record all those available (or to be available when of age) for priestly duties. Then, three groups, according to the three sons of Levi, were registered and given duties.

3:38-39 All totaled, the tribe of Levi came to 22,000 males. Each ancestral house was not only given maintenance tasks but also the main duty of protection. The ancestral houses were responsible for guarding one of the positions around **the tabernacle**, with Aaron and his sons protecting the eastern side because the doors opened on the east, and they were to guard the entrance. The strategic placing of the houses for protection points to the sacredness and solemnity of the tabernacle and what it represents. The tabernacle was where the holy God would meet with His people. So holy is He that every effort must be made to keep **unauthorized** people away. Israel was thus continually reminded that their God is righteous, and so He has separated them and called them to be holy.

3:40-51 The themes of ransom, substitution, and holiness are clearly seen in these verses. First, Moses is **commanded** by God to **register** all the **firstborn** males **of the Israelites**, and the **Levites** are to be taken in their place (vv. 40-41), again demonstrating that the Levites are set apart for the Lord's work and are holy unto Him. Thus substitution as a way of worship and offering in Israel was established. Moses was again obedient; after counting, there were 273 more **firstborn** male Israelites than Levites (vv. 39,43,46).

Not only were the Levites set apart to God in place of **the firstborn males**, but **the Levites' cattle** were also set apart to the Lord in place of the firstborn cattle of the Israelites (v. 44). Twice the Lord clearly told **Moses** that the Levites were for Him (vv. 41,45). Why? The Lord gave an answer each time—**I am Yahweh**. God is worthy of their worship and service. And, just as He is holy, the Levites would be

Census and Duties of the Levites

Ancestral House	Camp Location	Duties	Number
Gershon (3:21-26; 4:21-28)	"behind the tabernacle on the west side" (3:23)	• Tabernacle • Tent • Tent's covering • Tent's entrance screen • Courtyard hangings • Courtyard entrance screen • Altar • Tent ropes	7,500
Kohath (3:27-32; 4:4-20)	"on the south side of the tabernacle" (3:29)	• Ark • Table • Lampstand • Altars • Sanctuary • Screen between the holy of holies and holy place	8,600
Merari (3:33-37; 4:29-33)	"on the north side of the tabernacle" (3:35)	• Tabernacle's supports, crossbars, posts, bases • Courtyard's posts, bases, tent pegs, and ropes	6,200

land of Egypt, I consecrated every
firstborn in Israel to Myself, both
man and animal. They are Mine; I
am •Yahweh."
14 The LORD spoke to Moses in the
Wilderness of Sinai: 15 "Register the
Levites by their ancestral houses
and their clans. You are to register
every male one month old or more."
16 So Moses registered them in obedience to the LORD as he had been
commanded:

17 These were Levi's sons by
name: Gershon, Kohath, and
Merari. 18 These were the names
of Gershon's sons by their
clans: Libni and Shimei. 19 Kohath's sons by their clans were
Amram, Izhar, Hebron, and
Uzziel. 20 Merari's sons by their
clans were Mahli and Mushi.
These were the Levite clans by
their ancestral houses.

21 The Libnite clan and the
Shimeite clan came from Gershon; these were the Gershonite clans. 22 Those registered,
counting every male one month
old or more, numbered 7,500.
23 The Gershonite clans camped
behind the tabernacle on the
west side, 24 and the leader of the
Gershonite family was Eliasaph
son of Lael. 25 The Gershonites'
duties at the tent of meeting involved the tabernacle, the tent,
its covering, the screen for the
entrance to the tent of meeting,
26 the hangings of the courtyard,
the screen for the entrance
to the courtyard that surrounds
the tabernacle and the altar, and
the tent ropes—all the work relating to these.

27 The Amramite clan, the
Izharite clan, the Hebronite
clan, and the Uzzielite clan
came from Kohath; these were
the Kohathites. 28 Counting
every male one month old or
more, there were 8,600[A] responsible for the duties of[B]

[A] **3:28** LXX reads *8,300* [B] **3:28** Or *for guarding* the sanctuary. [29]The clans of the Kohathites camped on the south side of the tabernacle, [30]and the leader of the family of the Kohathite clans was Elizaphan son of Uzziel. [31]Their duties involved the ark, the table, the lampstand, the altars, the sanctuary utensils that were used with these, and the screen[A]—and all the work relating to them. [32]The chief of the Levite leaders was Eleazar son of Aaron the priest; he had oversight of those responsible for the duties of[B] the sanctuary.

[33]The Mahlite clan and the Mushite clan came from Merari; these were the Merarite clans. [34]Those registered, counting every male one month old or more, numbered 6,200. [35]The leader of the family of the Merarite clans was Zuriel son of Abihail; they camped on the north side of the tabernacle. [36]The assigned duties of Merari's descendants involved the tabernacle's supports, crossbars, posts, bases, all its equipment, and all the work related to these, [37]in addition to the posts of the surrounding courtyard with their bases, tent pegs, and ropes.

[38]Moses, Aaron, and his sons, who performed the duties of[C] the sanctuary as a service on behalf of the Israelites, camped in front of the tabernacle on the east, in front of the tent of meeting toward the sunrise. Any unauthorized person who came near it was to be put to death.

[39]The total number of all the Levite males one month old or more that Moses and Aaron[D] registered by their clans at the LORD's command was 22,000.

[40]The LORD told Moses: "Register every firstborn male of the Israelites one month old or more, and list their names. [41]You are to take the Levites for Me—I am Yahweh—in place of every firstborn among the Israelites, and the Levites' cattle in place of every firstborn among the Israelites' cattle." [42]So Moses registered every firstborn among the Israelites, as the LORD commanded him. [43]The total number of the firstborn males one month old or more listed by name was 22,273.

[44]The LORD spoke to Moses again: [45]"Take the Levites in place of every firstborn among the Israelites, and the Levites' cattle in place of their cattle. The Levites belong to Me; I am Yahweh. [46]As the redemption price for the 273 firstborn Israelites who outnumber the Levites, [47]collect five •shekels for each person, according to the standard sanctuary shekel—20 *gerahs* to the shekel. [48]Give the money to Aaron and his sons as the redemption price for those who are in excess among the Israelites."

Doctrine: REDEMPTION IN THE OLD TESTAMENT

Numbers 3:46-48 and the entire sacrificial system in the Old Testament foreshadow an understanding of the atonement. Jesus Christ, the holy, unblemished, firstborn of all creation, was ransomed, dying in the place of sinful, disobedient, and unholy men and women. Ultimately only Christ can redeem. The seriousness of sin, the condemnation under the law, and the holiness of God are clear in Numbers. Thus, the Old Testament not only points to your sin but also to your need for a Savior.

[49]So Moses collected the redemption money from those in excess of the ones redeemed by the Levites. [50]He collected the money from the firstborn Israelites: 1,365 shekels[E] measured by the standard sanctuary shekel. [51]He gave the redemption money to Aaron and his sons in obedience to the LORD, just as the LORD commanded Moses.

The Kohathites (4:1-20)

4 The LORD spoke to Moses and Aaron: [2]"Among the Levites, take a census of the Kohathites by their clans and their ancestral houses,

a reminder to all of Israel that they are called to a life of purity. Thus, all the censuses, as well as the ordering of Israel, point to the greatness and holiness of their God and the holiness they are to have before Him.

3:46-48 Due to the inequality between the number of Israelite firstborn and Levite firstborn, **five shekels** were to be given to the priests as **the redemption price** (Hb *padah*, "ransom") in order to make up for the greater number of the firstborn Israelites. **The standard sanctuary shekel** (cp. Ex 30:13) was to be used to redeem or buy back each Israelite firstborn. For the average laborer, the **five shekels** probably represented about six months of salary. This special tax was the price of a male slave under the age of five (Lv 27:6). The money was paid to Aaron and his sons. Interestingly, God did not demand the life or the enslavement of these Israelites; but they did have to be redeemed. A shekel (0.4 oz.) was roughly the equivalent of a U.S. dollar today, and the total number of shekels collected—1,365 pieces—would have been around 34 pounds of silver.

4:1-4 The LORD again spoke **to Moses and Aaron**, giving them orders to **take a census of the Kohathites** and orders for the work of the Kohathites. The reason the Kohathites instead of the Gershonites are listed first becomes clear—the Kohathites would be responsible for the most holy things of the tabernacle.

Though the Kohathites' duty concerned **the most holy objects**, they were still not permitted to touch them. These objects included the ark of the covenant, the bronze laver, the seven-tiered menorah, and the other items for the tabernacle.

[A]3:31 The screen between the most holy place and the holy place; Ex 35:12 [B]3:32 Or *for guarding* [C]3:38 Or *who guarded* [D]3:39 Some Hb mss, Sam, Syr omit *and Aaron* [E]3:50 Over 34 pounds of silver

4:5-15 Aaron and his sons were the ones who would wrap and pack "the most holy objects" for travel. Then, once packed, **the Kohathites** were to **carry** the objects. Aaron and his sons were to cover almost everything—including **the ark**, the **table of the Presence** (always having bread, which was never moved from the table until the Sabbath when the service was renewed, Ex 25:30), and **the lampstand**—with **a blue cloth** and then possibly **manatee**, or porpoise **skin**, for transportation. Though translated "blue" in verses 11 and 12, the color of the cloth was actually "purple or violet" (Hb *tekēlet*; see note on Ex 26:1-6). The color purple is usually associated with royalty and riches, and thus the color is very appropriate in the tabernacle of the King of kings.

4:19 Aaron and his sons were to delegate **the transportation** duties to each of the Kohathites. Thus, in the order of the Levitical priesthood, Aaron and his sons were in charge, with the Kohathites, Gershonites, and Merarites following.

4:20 The threat of death for touching or even looking at the holy objects is another reminder of the holiness of God. The objects did not belong to the Israelites to be treated as they pleased; they belonged to God and were to be treated appropriately.

4:21-28 Like the Kohathites, **the Gershonites** were counted according to those who were **qualified to perform service**, those who were 30 to 50 years **old**. The Gershonites were to be concerned with the **transportation** and set-up of the items that cover the tent of meeting and the hangings of the courtyard (see Ex. 26:1-14,36-37 for a detailed description of these items). And, once again, **Aaron and his sons** were to assign these tasks to the Gershonites. While Eleazar was supervising more duties of the Kohathites, **Ithamar** would be in charge of the Gershonites. Even though the Gershonites' task did not concern "the most holy objects," their duty was important. The significance of their task is emphasized in that they were to guard the items for which they were responsible.

3 men from 30 years old to 50 years old—everyone who is qualified[A] to do work at the tent of meeting.

4 "The service of the Kohathites at the tent of meeting concerns the most holy objects. 5 Whenever the camp is about to move on, Aaron and his sons are to go in, take down the screening veil, and cover the ark of the •testimony with it. 6 They are to place over this a covering made of manatee skin,[B] spread a solid blue cloth on top, and insert its poles.

7 "They are to spread a blue cloth over the table of the Presence and place the plates and cups on it, as well as the bowls and pitchers for the •drink offering. The regular bread offering is to be on it. 8 They are to spread a scarlet cloth over them, cover them with a covering made of manatee skin,[B] and insert the poles in the table.

9 "They are to take a blue cloth and cover the lampstand used for light, with its lamps, snuffers, and firepans, as well as its jars of oil by which they service it. 10 Then they must place it with all its utensils inside a covering made of manatee skin[B] and put them on the carrying frame.

11 "They are to spread a blue cloth over the gold altar, cover it with a covering made of manatee skin,[B] and insert its poles. 12 They are to take all the serving utensils they use in the sanctuary, place them in a blue cloth, cover them with a covering made of manatee skin,[B] and put them on a carrying frame.

13 "They are to remove the ashes from the bronze altar, spread a purple cloth over it, 14 and place all the equipment on it that they use in serving: the firepans, meat forks, shovels, and basins—all the equipment of the altar. They are to spread a covering made of manatee skin[B] over it and insert its poles.[C]

15 "Aaron and his sons are to finish covering the holy objects and all their equipment whenever the camp is to move on. The Kohathites will come and carry them, but they are not to touch the holy objects or they will die. These are the transportation duties of the Kohathites regarding the tent of meeting.

16 "Eleazar, son of Aaron the priest, has oversight of the lamp oil, the fragrant incense, the daily •grain offering, and the anointing oil. He has oversight of the entire tabernacle and everything in it, the holy objects and their utensils."[D]

17 Then the LORD spoke to Moses and Aaron: 18 "Do not allow the Kohathite tribal clans to be wiped out from the Levites. 19 Do this for them so that they may live and not die when they come near the most holy objects: Aaron and his sons are to go in and assign each man his task and transportation duty. 20 The Kohathites are not to go in and look at the holy objects, even for a moment,[E] or they will die."

The Gershonites (4:21-28)

21 The LORD spoke to Moses: 22 "Take a census of the Gershonites also, by their ancestral houses and their clans. 23 Register men from 30 years old to 50 years old, everyone who is qualified to perform service, to do work at the tent of meeting. 24 This is the service of the Gershonite clans regarding work and transportation duties: 25 They are to transport the tabernacle curtains, the tent of meeting with its covering and the covering made of manatee skin[B] on top of it, the screen for the entrance to the tent of meeting, 26 the hangings of the courtyard, the screen for the entrance at the gate of the courtyard that surrounds the tabernacle and the altar, along with their ropes and all the equipment for their service. They will carry out everything that needs to be done with these items.

27 "All the service of the Gershonites, all their transportation duties and all their other work, is to be done at the command of Aaron and his sons; you are to assign to them all that they are responsible to carry. 28 This is the service of the Gershon-

[A] **4:3** Lit *everyone entering the service* [B] **4:6,8,10,11,12,14,25** Or *of dolphin skin*, or *of fine leather*; Hb obscure [C] **4:14** Sam, LXX add *They are to take a purple cloth and cover the wash basin and its base. They are to place them in a covering made of manatee skin and put them on the carrying frame.* [D] **4:16** Or *the sanctuary and its furnishings* [E] **4:20** Or *at the covering of the holy objects*

ite clans at the tent of meeting, and
their duties will be under the direction of Ithamar son of Aaron the
priest.

The Merarites (4:29-49)

29 "As for the Merarites, you are
to register them by their clans and
their ancestral houses. 30 Register
men from 30 years old to 50 years
old, everyone who is qualified to
do the work of the tent of meeting.
31 This is what they are responsible
to carry as the whole of their service
at the tent of meeting: the supports
of the tabernacle, with its crossbars,
posts, and bases, 32 the posts of the
surrounding courtyard with their
bases, tent pegs, and ropes, including all their equipment and all the
work related to them. You are to
assign by name the items that they
are responsible to carry. 33 This is
the service of the Merarite clans
regarding all their work at the tent
of meeting, under the direction of
Ithamar son of Aaron the priest."
34 So Moses, Aaron, and the leaders
of the community registered the Kohathites by their clans and their ancestral houses, 35 men from 30 years
old to 50 years old, everyone who
was qualified for work at the tent of
meeting. 36 The men registered by
their clans numbered 2,750. 37 These
were the registered men of the Kohathite clans, everyone who could
serve at the tent of meeting. Moses
and Aaron registered them at the
LORD's command through Moses.
38 The Gershonites were registered
by their clans and their ancestral
houses, 39 men from 30 years old to
50 years old, everyone who was qualified for work at the tent of meeting. 40 The men registered by their
clans and their ancestral houses
numbered 2,630. 41 These were the
registered men of the Gershonite
clans. At the LORD's command Moses
and Aaron registered everyone who
could serve at the tent of meeting.
42 The men of the Merarite clans
were registered by their clans and
their ancestral houses, 43 those from
30 years old to 50 years old, everyone who was qualified for work at
the tent of meeting. 44 The men
registered by their clans numbered
3,200. 45 These were the registered
men of the Merarite clans; Moses
and Aaron registered them at the
LORD's command through Moses.
46 Moses, Aaron, and the leaders
of Israel registered all the Levites
by their clans and their ancestral
houses, 47 from 30 years old to 50
years old, everyone who was qualified to do the work of serving at the
tent of meeting and transporting it.
48 Their registered men numbered
8,580. 49 At the LORD's command they
were registered under the direction
of Moses, each one according to
his work and transportation duty,
and his assignment was as the LORD
commanded Moses.

Instructions and Rituals (5:1–10:36)

Isolation of the Unclean (5:1-4)

5 The LORD instructed Moses:
2 "Command the Israelites to
send away anyone from the camp
who is afflicted with a skin disease,
anyone who has a bodily discharge,
or anyone who is defiled because of
a corpse. 3 You must send away both
male or female; send them outside
the camp, so that they will not defile
their camps where I dwell among
them." 4 The Israelites did this,
sending them outside the camp. The
Israelites did as the LORD instructed
Moses.

Compensation for Wrongdoing (5:5-10)

5 The LORD spoke to Moses: 6 "Tell
the Israelites: When a man or woman commits any sin against another,
that person acts unfaithfully toward
the LORD and is •guilty. 7 The person
is to confess the sin he has committed. He is to pay full compensation,
add a fifth of its value to it, and give
it to the individual he has wronged.
8 But if that individual has no relative to receive compensation,[A] the
compensation goes to the LORD for
the priest, along with the •atone-
ment ram by which the priest will
make atonement for the guilty person. 9 Every holy contribution the Israelites present to the priest will be
his. 10 Each one's holy contribution

[A]5:8 If the individual has died

4:29-33 The duty of **the Merarites** may have required the most physical strength. They were responsible for transporting **the supports of the tabernacle** and **the posts**. Only the men ages 30 to 50 would be able to serve just as with the other clans. The Merarites would be accountable to **Ithamar**.

4:34-49 Moses and Aaron obediently carried out the Lord's commands. They gathered first **the Kohathites**, then **the Gershonites**, and finally **the Merarites**. A census was taken, with the Kohathites registering 2,750 males, the Gershonites 2,630, and the Merarites 3,200. The total came to 8,580 men ages 30 to 50 serving the Lord and the priests by caring for and transporting **the tent of meeting**. Again, Moses and the people were completely obedient in what the Lord had commanded. This was repeated several times. After each registration, the point was made that the registry was carried out at **the LORD's command** (vv. 37,41,45), and then in verse 49 clearly everything was done according to the command of the Lord.

5:1-4 Holiness is again of central importance as chapter 5 sets forth a series of legal codes. **The LORD** affirmed the commands He gave to Moses and the Israelites in Leviticus. Anyone who was unclean, **afflicted with a skin disease**, had **a bodily discharge**, or was **defiled because of a corpse** had to be sent **outside the camp**. All of the above conditions are discussed extensively in Leviticus (see Lv 13:1-46; 14:1-15:33; 21:1-3). Because the Lord who is holy and clean was dwelling among the Israelites, there could be no uncleanness in the camp. Again, **the Israelites** were obedient, establishing a consistent pattern thus far.

5:5-10 The command to make **compensation** for wrongdoing is addressed in several passages in the Pentateuch. The command first appears in Ex 22:7-15, which addresses personal property. Then, the same idea is found in Lv 6:1-7, which deals with defrauding or stealing from one's neighbor. The Numbers passage makes clear that when **any sin** is committed against someone, that sin is also committed against **the LORD**. When one sins, he **is guilty** before the Lord and under the law. He must **confess** and repent. In this case, once the person repents, if there is **no relative** to whom to give the **compensation**, then the compensation will be given to **the priest**, along with an **atonement** offering for the sin committed.

5:11-31 A husband who became suspicious that his **wife** might be **unfaithful** could request that his wife submit to a test to determine her guilt or innocence. God wants the trust restored in a broken relationship. The husband was to bring his suspicions before the judges (the priests), and the wife was forced to drink water mixed with bitter herbs. The **holy** water dedicated to the Lord contained dust from the floor of the tabernacle and scrapings of curses written in the scrolls (v. 23). Through this ritual known as the Law of *Sotah* or *shevu'at ha'alah* ("oath of cursing"), the name of God was dissolved into the waters. As a general rule it was forbidden to erase God's name, which is one reason traditional Jews never write out the name of God. In this one exception, God allowed His name to be dissolved to rebuild the trust between husband and wife. While no reciprocal provision was made for a woman to bring charges against her husband, the procedure is governed by the provision of covenant law (see Ex 20:14). An innocent woman, unjustly accused, had God's protection, and He desired that the woman not be unfairly abused, killed, or divorced by her suspicious husband. Rather than granting the husband free rein to divorce his wife or abuse her at will, very specific restrictions were placed on his rights over his wife. Throughout the text the judgment of the Lord, and not man, is evident. The phrase **before the LORD** occurs four times (Nm 5:16,18,25,30). The actual efficacy of the ritual rested upon psychological suggestion and memory as individuals stood before God; the bitter water was not a magical potion intended as a means of determining guilt. The water mixed with dust from the sanctuary symbolized the presence of God in the test, and drinking it demonstrated the woman's submission of her case to God. Once the trial by ordeal took place, if innocent, the wife's reputation would be restored, and **her husband** could rest at ease and rebuild his trust. The Lord's care and protection of women is clearly evident.

6:1-2 Continuing with the theme of holiness, this passage gives the prescriptions for making **a special** [Hb *yapli'*, "do extraordinarily or exceptionally," from the root *pala'* usually referring to God's "miracles, wonders"—e.g., Ex 3:20; 34:10; Jos 3:5; Ps 71:17] **vow, a Nazirite vow** before the Lord. The "Nazirite" (Hb *nazar*, "dedicate or separate") vow called for the voluntary adoption of the life similar to that of a priest for a specific time. Without the Lord's help, one would not be able to fulfill the vow made. This vow—only to a deity—was one that both men and women could voluntarily make. The term could be limited in time or made

is his to give; what each one gives to the priest will be his."

The Jealousy Ritual (5:11-31)

11 The LORD spoke to Moses: 12 "Speak to the Israelites and tell them: If any man's wife goes astray, is unfaithful to him, 13 and sleeps with another,[A] but it is concealed from her husband, and she is undetected, even though she has defiled herself, since there is no witness against her, and she wasn't caught in the act; 14 and if a feeling of jealousy comes over the husband and he becomes jealous because of his wife who has defiled herself—or if a feeling of jealousy comes over him and he becomes jealous of her though she has not defiled herself— 15 then the man is to bring his wife to the priest. He is also to bring an offering for her of two quarts[B] of barley flour. He is not to pour oil over it or put frankincense on it because it is a •grain offering of jealousy, a grain offering for remembrance that brings sin to mind.

16 "The priest is to bring her forward and have her stand before the LORD. 17 Then the priest is to take holy water in a clay bowl, and take some of the dust from the tabernacle floor and put it in the water. 18 After the priest has the woman stand before the LORD, he is to let down her hair[C] and place in her hands the grain offering for remembrance, which is the grain offering of jealousy. The priest is to hold the bitter water that brings a curse. 19 The priest will require the woman to take an oath and will say to her, 'If no man has slept with you, if you have not gone astray and become defiled while under your husband's authority, be unaffected by this bitter water that brings a curse. 20 But if you have gone astray while under your husband's authority, if you have defiled yourself and a man other than your husband has slept with you'— 21 at this point the priest must make the woman take the oath with the sworn curse, and he is to say to her—'May the LORD make you into an object of your people's cursing and swearing when He makes your thigh[D] shrivel and your belly swell.[E] 22 May this water that brings a curse enter your stomach, causing your belly to swell and your thigh to shrivel.'

"And the woman must reply, "Amen, Amen.'

23 "Then the priest is to write these curses on a scroll and wash them off into the bitter water. 24 He will require the woman to drink the bitter water that brings a curse, and it will enter her and cause bitter suffering. 25 The priest is to take the grain offering of jealousy from the woman's hand, wave the offering before the LORD, and bring it to the altar. 26 The priest is to take a handful of the grain offering as a memorial portion and burn it on the altar. Then he will require the woman to drink the water.

27 "When he makes her drink the water, if she has defiled herself and been unfaithful to her husband, the water that brings a curse will enter her and cause bitter suffering; her belly will swell, and her thigh will shrivel. She will become a curse among her people. 28 But if the woman has not defiled herself and is pure, she will be unaffected and will be able to conceive children.

29 "This is the law regarding jealousy when a wife goes astray and defiles herself while under her husband's authority, 30 or when a feeling of jealousy comes over a husband and he becomes jealous of his wife. He is to have the woman stand before the LORD, and the priest will apply this entire ritual to her. 31 The husband will be free of guilt, but that woman will bear the consequences of her guilt."

The Nazirite Vow (6:1-21)

6 The LORD instructed Moses: 2 "Speak to the Israelites and tell them: When a man or woman makes a special vow, a Nazirite vow, to consecrate himself to[F] the LORD, 3 he is to abstain[G] from wine and beer. He must not drink vinegar made from wine or from beer. He must not

[A] **5:13** Lit *and man lies with her and has an emission of semen* [B] **5:15** Lit *a tenth of an ephah* [C] **5:18** Or *to uncover her head* [D] **5:21-22** Possibly a euphemism for the reproductive organs [E] **5:21** Or *flood* [F] **6:2** Or *vow, to live as a Nazirite for* [G] **6:3** In Hb, the words Nazirite, consecrate, and abstain are related and involve the idea of separation.

drink any grape juice or eat fresh grapes or raisins. 4 He is not to eat anything produced by the grapevine, from seeds to skin,[A] during his vow.

5 "You must not cut his hair[B] throughout the time of his vow of consecration. He must be holy until the time is completed during which he consecrates himself to the LORD; he is to let the hair of his head grow long. 6 He must not go near a dead body during the time he consecrates himself to the LORD. 7 He is not to defile himself for his father or mother, or his brother or sister, when they die, because the hair consecrated to his God is on his head. 8 He is holy to the LORD during the time of consecration.

9 "If someone suddenly dies near him, defiling his consecrated head of hair, he must shave his head on the day of his purification; he is to shave it on the seventh day. 10 On the eighth day he is to bring two turtledoves or two young pigeons to the priest at the entrance to the tent of meeting. 11 The priest is to offer one as a •sin offering and the other as a •burnt offering to make •atonement on behalf of the Nazirite, since he sinned because of the corpse. On that day he must consecrate[C] his head again. 12 He is to rededicate his time of consecration to the LORD and to bring a year-old male lamb as a •restitution offering. But do not count the previous period, because his consecrated hair became defiled.

13 "This is the law of the Nazirite: On the day his time of consecration is completed, he must be brought to the entrance to the tent of meeting. 14 He is to present an offering to the LORD of one unblemished year-old male lamb as a burnt offering, one unblemished year-old female lamb as a sin offering, one unblemished ram as a •fellowship offering, 15 along with their •grain offerings and •drink offerings, and a basket of unleavened cakes made from fine flour mixed with oil, and unleavened wafers coated with oil.

16 "The priest is to present these before the LORD and sacrifice the Nazirite's sin offering and burnt offering. 17 He will also offer the ram as a fellowship sacrifice to the LORD, together with the basket of unleavened bread. Then the priest will offer the accompanying grain offering and drink offering.

18 "The Nazirite is to shave his consecrated head at the entrance to the tent of meeting, take the hair from his head, and put it on the fire under the fellowship sacrifice. 19 The priest is to take the boiled shoulder from the ram, one unleavened cake from the basket, and one unleavened wafer, and put them into the hands of the Nazirite after he has shaved his consecrated head. 20 The priest is to wave them as a presentation offering before the LORD. It is a holy portion for the priest, in addition to the breast of the presentation offering and the thigh of the contribution. After that, the Nazirite may drink wine.

21 "This is the ritual of the Nazirite who vows his offering to the LORD for his consecration, in addition to whatever else he can afford; he must fulfill whatever vow he makes in keeping with the ritual for his consecration."

The Priestly Blessing (6:22-27)

22 The LORD spoke to Moses: 23 "Tell Aaron and his sons how you are to bless the Israelites. Say to them:

24 May •Yahweh bless you
and protect you;
25 may Yahweh make His face
shine on you
and be gracious to you;
26 may Yahweh look with favor
on you[D]
and give you peace.[E]

27 In this way they will pronounce My name over[F] the Israelites, and I will bless them."

Offering from the Leaders (7:1-89)

7 On the day Moses finished setting up the tabernacle, he anointed and consecrated it and all its furnishings, along with the altar and all its utensils. After he anointed and consecrated these things, 2 the leaders of Israel, the heads of their ancestral houses, presented an offering.

for a lifetime. Thus, while women could not serve in the priesthood, they could still serve God in this special way. The Nazirite vow was to separate oneself unto the Lord, pointing to the awesome holiness of the Lord.

6:3-4 The Nazirite had to abide by three prohibitions during the vow. First, he had to **abstain from wine and beer** and was not even to **eat anything produced by the grapevine.** This restriction concerning wine was greater than that observed by the priests, who could not drink wine while in the tent of meeting (Lv 10:9). The Nazirite vow was "a special vow" calling for the person to be completely set apart and holy to the Lord. Any intoxicating drink would not aid the Nazirite in making wise decisions for God but rather cloud his judgment.

6:5-8 The second prohibition was that **his hair** could not be **cut**, which was an outward sign of his consecration. Third, **he must not go near a dead body**. To fail in either of the latter two matters would be public signs of the defilement of his consecration **to the LORD.**

6:22-27 At the conclusion of the section on various legalities, **the LORD** gave **Moses** a command for **Aaron and his sons** concerning how they were **to bless the Israelites.** These three poetic lines are succinct and yet profound as they proclaim God's goodness to His people. Each line of the blessing begins with **the LORD**. Without the Lord, Israel will become desolate. **The LORD** wanted to do five things for Israel, and the evidence is clear that He had already blessed them in these ways. Blessing, protection, **favor**, grace, and **peace** are the things **the LORD** desired to do for Israel. The favor of the Lord is seen in the expression "(May) His face shine on you" (Hb *Yahweh panaw ēleka*, "[may] Yahweh [shine] his face upon you"). The turning of God's face upon His people demonstrates His attention and care for them. The Lord had made Israel a great nation and delivered them from bondage—all of the blessing was already coming to fruition. Thus, the priestly blessing reminded Israel of the greatness of God—who He had been in the past and who He desired to be for them in the present and the future.

7:1-2 The events of chapter 7 occurred the month prior, right after **the tabernacle** was set up, for the Lord spoke to Moses in the tent of meeting in chap. 1 (see 1:1). Thus, the tabernacle must have been put up prior to Moses' being able to meet with the Lord in the tent of meeting. On this day Moses **consecrated** both the tabernacle and **the leaders of Israel** to the Lord,

[A] **6:4** Or *from unripe grapes to hulls* [B] **6:5** Lit *A razor is not to pass over his head* [C] **6:11** Lit *set apart* [D] **6:26** Lit *LORD lift His face to you* [E] **6:26** Or *prosperity* [F] **6:27** Or *put My name on*

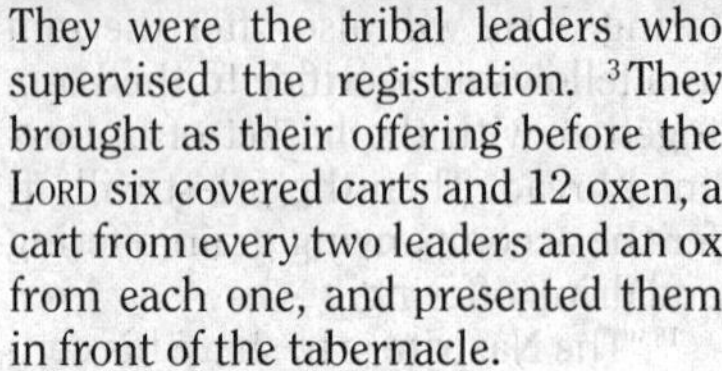

and each of the 12 leaders brought an **offering**.

7:3-83 The Lord commanded **Moses** to **give this offering to the Levites** for their use in **service**. This offering of **carts and oxen** would be especially helpful to the Levites as they transported the tabernacle. Only **the Kohathites** did not receive this offering because they had to carry the most holy objects **on their shoulders**. Each leader of his tribe also presented a **dedication gift for the altar**. This occurred over 12 days, the gift being the same each time. The dedication gift included **one silver dish**, **one silver basin**, **one gold bowl . . . full of incense**, **one young bull**, **one ram**, **one male lamb a year old**, **one male goat**, **two bulls**, **five rams**, **five male breeding goats**, and **five male lambs a year old**. Each gift was specifically for an offering, including **a grain offering**, an incense offering, **a burnt offering**, **a sin offering**, and a **fellowship** offering.

They were the tribal leaders who supervised the registration. 3 They brought as their offering before the Lord six covered carts and 12 oxen, a cart from every two leaders and an ox from each one, and presented them in front of the tabernacle.

4 The Lord said to Moses, 5 "Accept these from them to be used in the work of the tent of meeting, and give this offering to the Levites, to each division according to their service."

6 So Moses took the carts and oxen and gave them to the Levites. 7 He gave the Gershonites two carts and four oxen corresponding to their service, 8 and gave the Merarites four carts and eight oxen corresponding to their service, under the direction of Ithamar son of Aaron the priest. 9 But he did not give any to the Kohathites, since their responsibility was service related to the holy objects carried on their shoulders.

10 The leaders also presented the dedication gift for the altar when it was anointed. The leaders presented their offerings in front of the altar. 11 The Lord told Moses, "Each day have one leader present his offering for the dedication of the altar."

12 The one who presented his offering on the first day was Nahshon son of Amminadab from the tribe of Judah. 13 His offering was one silver dish weighing $3\frac{1}{4}$ pounds[A] and one silver basin weighing $1\frac{3}{4}$ pounds,[B] measured by the standard sanctuary •shekel, both of them full of fine flour mixed with oil for a •grain offering; 14 one gold bowl weighing four ounces,[C] full of incense; 15 one young bull, one ram, and one male lamb a year old, for a •burnt offering; 16 one male goat for a •sin offering; 17 and two bulls, five rams, five male breeding goats, and five male lambs a year old, for the •fellowship sacrifice. This was the offering of Nahshon son of Amminadab.

18 On the second day Nethanel son of Zuar, leader of Issachar, presented an offering. 19 As his offering, he presented one silver dish weighing $3\frac{1}{4}$ pounds[A] and one silver basin weighing $1\frac{3}{4}$ pounds,[B] measured by the standard sanctuary shekel, both of them full of fine flour mixed with oil for a grain offering; 20 one gold bowl weighing four ounces,[C] full of incense; 21 one young bull, one ram, and one male lamb a year old, for a burnt offering; 22 one male goat for a sin offering; 23 and two bulls, five rams, five male breeding goats, and five male lambs a year old, for the fellowship sacrifice. This was the offering of Nethanel son of Zuar.

24 On the third day Eliab son of Helon, leader of the Zebulunites, presented an offering. 25 His offering was one silver dish weighing $3\frac{1}{4}$ pounds[A] and one silver basin weighing $1\frac{3}{4}$ pounds,[B] measured by the standard sanctuary shekel, both of them full of fine flour mixed with oil for a grain offering; 26 one gold bowl weighing four ounces,[C] full of incense; 27 one young bull, one ram, and one male lamb a year old, for a burnt offering; 28 one male goat for a sin offering; 29 and two bulls, five rams, five male breeding goats, and five male lambs a year old, for the fellowship sacrifice. This was the offering of Eliab son of Helon.

30 On the fourth day Elizur son of Shedeur, leader of the Reubenites, presented an offering. 31 His offering was one silver dish weighing $3\frac{1}{4}$ pounds[A] and one silver basin weighing $1\frac{3}{4}$ pounds,[B] measured by the standard sanctuary shekel, both of them full of fine flour mixed with oil for a grain offering; 32 one gold bowl weighing four ounces,[C] full of incense; 33 one young bull, one ram, and one male lamb a year

[A] **7:13,19,25,31** Lit *dish, 130 its shekel-weight* [B] **7:13,19,25,31** Lit *70 shekels* [C] **7:14,20,26,32** Lit *10* (shekels)

old, for a burnt offering; 34 one
male goat for a sin offering;
35 and two bulls, five rams, five
male breeding goats, and five
male lambs a year old, for the
fellowship sacrifice. This was
the offering of Elizur son of
Shedeur.

36 On the fifth day Shelumiel
son of Zurishaddai, leader of
the Simeonites, presented an
offering. 37 His offering was
one silver dish weighing 3¼
pounds[A] and one silver basin
weighing 1¾ pounds,[B] measured by the standard sanctuary shekel, both of them full of
fine flour mixed with oil for a
grain offering; 38 one gold bowl
weighing four ounces,[C] full of
incense; 39 one young bull, one
ram, and one male lamb a year
old, for a burnt offering; 40 one
male goat for a sin offering;
41 and two bulls, five rams, five
male breeding goats, and five
male lambs a year old, for the
fellowship sacrifice. This was
the offering of Shelumiel son
of Zurishaddai.

42 On the sixth day Eliasaph
son of Deuel,[D] leader of the
Gadites, presented an offering.
43 His offering was one silver
dish weighing 3¼ pounds[A]
and one silver basin weighing 1¾ pounds,[B] measured by
the standard sanctuary shekel,
both of them full of fine flour
mixed with oil for a grain offering; 44 one gold bowl weighing
four ounces,[C] full of incense;
45 one young bull, one ram, and
one male lamb a year old, for
a burnt offering; 46 one male
goat for a sin offering; 47 and
two bulls, five rams, five male
breeding goats, and five male
lambs a year old, for the fellowship sacrifice. This was
the offering of Eliasaph son of
Deuel.[D]

48 On the seventh day Elishama
son of Ammihud, leader of
the Ephraimites, presented an
offering. 49 His offering was
one silver dish weighing 3¼
pounds[A] and one silver basin
weighing 1¾ pounds,[B] measured by the standard sanctuary shekel, both of them full of
fine flour mixed with oil for a
grain offering; 50 one gold bowl
weighing four ounces,[C] full of
incense; 51 one young bull, one
ram, and one male lamb a year
old, for a burnt offering; 52 one
male goat for a sin offering;
53 and two bulls, five rams, five
male breeding goats, and five
male lambs a year old, for the
fellowship sacrifice. This was
the offering of Elishama son of
Ammihud.

54 On the eighth day Gamaliel
son of Pedahzur, leader of the
Manassites, presented an offering. 55 His offering was one silver dish weighing 3¼ pounds[A]
and one silver basin weighing 1¾ pounds,[B] measured by
the standard sanctuary shekel,
both of them full of fine flour
mixed with oil for a grain offering; 56 one gold bowl weighing
four ounces,[C] full of incense;
57 one young bull, one ram, and
one male lamb a year old, for
a burnt offering; 58 one male
goat for a sin offering; 59 and
two bulls, five rams, five male
breeding goats, and five male
lambs a year old, for the fellowship sacrifice. This was the
offering of Gamaliel son of Pedahzur.

60 On the ninth day Abidan
son of Gideoni, leader of the
Benjaminites, presented an
offering. 61 His offering was
one silver dish weighing 3¼
pounds[A] and one silver basin
weighing 1¾ pounds,[B] measured by the standard sanctuary shekel, both of them full of
fine flour mixed with oil for a
grain offering; 62 one gold bowl
weighing four ounces,[C] full of
incense; 63 one young bull, one
ram, and one male lamb a year
old, for a burnt offering; 64 one

[A] **7:37,43,49,55,61** Lit *dish, 130 its shekel-weight* [B] **7:37,43,49,55,61** Lit *70 shekels*
[C] **7:38,44,50,56,62** Lit *10* (shekels) [D] **7:42,47** LXX, Syr read *Reuel*

7:84-88 When all totaled, each tribe brought an equal gift for the dedication of the altar.

7:89 Once the setup and dedication of **the tent of meeting** and the leaders occurred, **Moses** could enter to meet **with the Lord**. Just as the Lord promised, saying "I will speak with you from there [the mercy seat] about all that I command you regarding the Israelites" (Ex 25:22b); so He did. The Israelites had followed the instructions given in Ex 25:17-22 regarding **the mercy seat**. Moses entered the tent of meeting expecting to hear God's **voice** and believed God would be faithful to His word. Thus, the way the Lord would communicate to His chosen people was established. This verse helps to explain what occurred in Nm 1 as the Lord spoke to Moses in the tent of meeting and then in the following chapters.

8:1-4 Extensive instructions regarding the making of the **lampstand** are found in Ex 25:31-40. The lampstand consisted of **seven lamps** and was made of pure **gold**. The Lord reiterates in Numbers the way **the lamps** were to be set in order that there be **light in front of the lampstand** (cp. Ex 25:37).

8:5-6 In order for the Levites to carry out the duties assigned to them by the Lord, they had to be clean. If the Levites were unclean, the effects upon the community would be detrimental; for they would not be able to perform their tasks or represent the people before the Lord. Thus, God spoke **to Moses** and had him **ceremonially cleanse** the **Levites**. The ceremonial part of the cleansing not only made this event an act of worship before the Lord, but all the Israelites were also to be gathered to see this event, which again reminded them of the holiness of God and that they had been called to be holy.

8:7 Three steps, similar to the procedure for the cleansing of lepers (cp. Ex 19:10-11; Lv 14:8-9), were prescribed for preparation to worship:

- sprinkling with **purification water**;
- shaving **their entire bodies**;
- washing **their clothes**.

The washing and shaving of the Levites was merely the outward cleansing intended to represent the inward turning of their hearts to God to be made pure and holy.

male goat for a sin offering; 65 and two bulls, five rams, five male breeding goats, and five male lambs a year old, for the fellowship sacrifice. This was the offering of Abidan son of Gideoni.

66 On the tenth day Ahiezer son of Ammishaddai, leader of the Danites, presented an offering. 67 His offering was one silver dish weighing 3¼ pounds[A] and one silver basin weighing 1¾ pounds,[B] measured by the standard sanctuary shekel, both of them full of fine flour mixed with oil for a grain offering; 68 one gold bowl weighing four ounces,[C] full of incense; 69 one young bull, one ram, and one male lamb a year old, for a burnt offering; 70 one male goat for a sin offering; 71 and two bulls, five rams, five male breeding goats, and five male lambs a year old, for the fellowship sacrifice. This was the offering of Ahiezer son of Ammishaddai.

72 On the eleventh day Pagiel son of Ochran, leader of the Asherites, presented an offering. 73 His offering was one silver dish weighing 3¼ pounds[A] and one silver basin weighing 1¾ pounds,[B] measured by the standard sanctuary shekel, both of them full of fine flour mixed with oil for a grain offering; 74 one gold bowl weighing four ounces,[C] full of incense; 75 one young bull, one ram, and one male lamb a year old, for a burnt offering; 76 one male goat for a sin offering; 77 and two bulls, five rams, five male breeding goats, and five male lambs a year old, for the fellowship sacrifice. This was the offering of Pagiel son of Ochran.

78 On the twelfth day Ahira son of Enan, leader of the Naphtalites, presented an offering. 79 His offering was one silver dish weighing 3¼ pounds[A] and one silver basin weighing 1¾ pounds,[B] measured by the standard sanctuary shekel, both of them full of fine flour mixed with oil for a grain offering; 80 one gold bowl weighing four ounces,[C] full of incense; 81 one young bull, one ram, and one male lamb a year old, for a burnt offering; 82 one male goat for a sin offering; 83 and two bulls, five rams, five male breeding goats, and five male lambs a year old, for the fellowship sacrifice. This was the offering of Ahira son of Enan.

84 This was the dedication gift from the leaders of Israel for the altar when it was anointed: 12 silver dishes, 12 silver basins, and 12 gold bowls. 85 Each silver dish weighed 3¼ pounds,[D] and each basin 1¾ pounds.[E] The total weight of the silver articles was 60 pounds[F] measured by the standard sanctuary shekel. 86 The 12 gold bowls full of incense each weighed four ounces[B] measured by the standard sanctuary shekel. The total weight of the gold bowls was three pounds.[G] 87 All the livestock for the burnt offering totaled 12 bulls, 12 rams, and 12 male lambs a year old, with their grain offerings, and 12 male goats for the sin offering. 88 All the livestock for the fellowship sacrifice totaled 24 bulls, 60 rams, 60 male breeding goats, and 60 male lambs a year old. This was the dedication gift for the altar after it was anointed.

89 When Moses entered the tent of meeting to speak with the LORD, he heard the voice speaking to him from above the •mercy seat that was on the ark of the •testimony, from between the two •cherubim. He spoke to him that way.

The Lighting of the Tabernacles (8:1-4)

8 The LORD spoke to Moses: 2 "Speak to Aaron and tell him: When you set up the lamps, the seven lamps are to give light in front of the lampstand." 3 So Aaron did this; he set

[A]7:67,73,79 Lit *dish, 130 its shekel-weight* [B]7:67,73,79 Lit *70 shekels* [C]7:68,74,80,86 Lit *10* (shekels) [D]7:85 Lit *130* (shekels) [E]7:85 Lit *70* (shekels) [F]7:85 Lit *2,400* (shekels) [G]7:86 Lit *120* (shekels)

up its lamps to give light in front of
the lampstand just as the LORD had
commanded Moses. 4 This is the way
the lampstand was made: it was a
hammered work of gold, hammered
from its base to its flower petals.
The lampstand was made according
to the pattern the LORD had shown
Moses.

Consecration of the Levites (8:5-26)

5 The LORD spoke to Moses: 6 "Take
the Levites from among the Israelites and ceremonially cleanse them.
7 This is what you must do to them
for their purification: Sprinkle them
with the purification water. Have
them shave their entire bodies and
wash their clothes, and so purify
themselves.
8 "They are to take a young bull
and its •grain offering of fine flour
mixed with oil, and you are to take a
second young bull for a •sin offering.
9 Bring the Levites before the tent of
meeting and assemble the entire
Israelite community. 10 Then present the Levites before the LORD, and
have the Israelites lay their hands
on them. 11 Aaron is to present the
Levites before the LORD as a presentation offering from the Israelites,
so that they may perform the LORD's
work. 12 Next the Levites are to lay
their hands on the heads of the
bulls. Sacrifice one as a sin offering
and the other as a •burnt offering to
the LORD, to make •atonement for
the Levites.
13 "You are to have the Levites
stand before Aaron and his sons, and
you are to present them before the
LORD as a presentation offering. 14 In
this way you are to separate the Levites from the rest of the Israelites
so that the Levites will belong to Me.
15 After that the Levites may come to
serve at the tent of meeting, once
you have ceremonially cleansed
them and presented them as a presentation offering. 16 For they have
been exclusively assigned to Me from
the Israelites. I have taken them for
Myself in place of all who come first
from the womb, every Israelite firstborn. 17 For every firstborn among
the Israelites is Mine, both man and
animal. I consecrated them to Myself on the day I struck down every
firstborn in the land of Egypt. 18 But
I have taken the Levites in place of
every firstborn among the Israelites.
19 From the Israelites, I have given
the Levites exclusively to Aaron and
his sons to perform the work for the
Israelites at the tent of meeting and
to make atonement on their behalf,
so that no plague will come against
the Israelites when they approach
the sanctuary."
20 Moses, Aaron, and the entire
Israelite community did this to the
Levites. The Israelites did everything to them the LORD commanded
Moses regarding the Levites. 21 The
Levites purified themselves and
washed their clothes; then Aaron
presented[A] them before the LORD as
a presentation offering. Aaron also
made atonement for them to ceremonially cleanse them. 22 After that,
the Levites came to do their work at
the tent of meeting in the presence
of Aaron and his sons. So they did to
them as the LORD had commanded
Moses concerning the Levites.
23 The LORD spoke to Moses: 24 "In
regard to the Levites: From 25 years
old or more, a man enters the service in the work at the tent of meeting. 25 But at 50 years old he is to
retire from his service in the work
and no longer serve. 26 He may assist
his brothers to fulfill responsibilities[B] at the tent of meeting, but he
must not do the work. This is how
you are to deal with the Levites regarding their duties."

The Second Passover (9:1-14)

9 In the first month of the second year after their departure
from the land of Egypt, the LORD
told Moses in the Wilderness of Sinai: 2 "The Israelites are to observe
the •Passover at its appointed time.
3 You must observe it at its appointed time on the fourteenth day of this
month at twilight; you are to observe it according to all its statutes
and ordinances." 4 So Moses told the
Israelites to observe the Passover,
5 and they observed it in the first
month on the fourteenth day at twilight in the Wilderness of Sinai. The

8:8-12 Along with the purification ritual, they were also to take two young bulls, one **for a sin offering** and one for **a burnt offering**. Thus, with the sin offering, **atonement** was made **for the Levites.**

8:13-15 A grain offering and **a presentation offering** were also to be made. The presentation offering demonstrated that **the Levites** were set apart unto the Lord.

8:16-22 The Lord reiterated that the Levites had been **taken . . . in place of** the **firstborn** of Israel. Only after the ceremonial cleansing took place were the Levites to **perform** their duties. This was vital to Israel's standing before God because **Aaron** and **the Levites** were the ones to make **atonement** for **the entire Israelite community**.

8:23-26 Moses, Aaron, the Levites, and the Israelites followed the Lord's instructions. At the conclusion of the carrying out of the consecration instructions, **the LORD** spoke again **to Moses** concerning the working age of the Levites. While the earlier census of the Levites only counted men ages 30 to 50, the Lord said a man **from** 25 years old could enter **the service** until the retirement age of 50. However, even after retirement, a man could **assist** the Levites in fulfilling their **responsibilities**, as long as he was not doing the assigned **work**. In this way, the Lord continued to keep things orderly among **the Levites**.

9:1-5 Now **the second year after** the Israelites fled from **Egypt**, **the LORD** told **Moses** they were to continue keeping **the Passover**. **The Israelites**, as commanded in Exodus 12, would now observe the memorial celebration **on the fourteenth day** of the first month of their year. This observance was only the second Passover for the Israelites, the first having been held before they escaped from Egypt. The **statutes and ordinances** to which the Lord refers are found in Ex 12. They detail the number of days, the unleavened bread that was to be eaten, and how the meat was to be cooked (Ex 12:14-28). This observance was to last seven days, from the fourteenth day until the twenty-first day. Even though the Israelites were **in the Wilderness of Sinai**, the Lord desired them to have a day of remembrance for what He did by bringing them out of their bondage in Egypt. They were a fully constituted nation, and they were to act like one by commemorating their "independence day" from slavery in Egypt.

[A]8:21 Lit *waved* [B]8:26 Or *to keep guard*

9:6-14 Desiring to serve the Lord and **observe the Passover** celebration, some of the Israelites had questions for Moses concerning who might be disqualified to participate in the memorial. Moses took the question before the Lord. Normally, if a person was **unclean**, he could not participate in such a ceremony. Holy ceremonies required cleanliness and purity, and thus after being unclean a ritual of purification had to be finished before one could observe such occasions. However, the Lord made an exception for **Passover**, for He still desired that His people remember His faithfulness. Instead of observing the celebration in the first month, a person who was **unclean** could observe Passover **in the second month** but still **on the fourteenth day**. So important was the Passover that those who were **clean** and yet did not **observe** it were to be **cut off from his people**. This may seem to be severe; but the Lord had freed the Israelites from bondage and had set them apart for Himself. They were not set free to do whatever they wished—they were set apart to serve the Lord. Now, the Lord had given the Israelites, and even foreigners who had been circumcised (Ex 12:48-49), every opportunity to remember Him through the Passover, and to fail to do so was evidence of rebellion against God.

9:15-23 The central themes of this passage are the Lord's presence and guidance and the obedience of the people. Just as God led them during the exodus by **cloud** and **fire**, so He would continue to do so now (cp. Ex 13:21-22; 40:36-38). Surely, the visible presence of the Lord was a comfort to Israel as they prepared to journey out into the wilderness. The Israelites were to respond to the movement of the presence of the Lord—staying if the cloud remained in a set position and departing when the cloud moved. Obedience was a response to what God had revealed—as here, through His cloud.

10:2 In order to assemble the Israelites, the Lord commanded Moses to have **two trumpets of hammered silver** made. The trumpets became a human signal to be coupled with divine signs to guide the Israelites. The instruments would have many uses and were only to be sounded by the priests. The trumpets were to assemble leaders of the congregation, to announce advance and departure or to sound an alarm; they were to be used in battle; over burnt offerings, fellowship sacrifices, and festivals (the trumpets were a part of solemn feast days); and at the beginning of each month (vv. 9-10). By sounding the trumpets when heading into battle, the Israelites would be asking the Lord to remember them and bring them victory. The sounding of the

Israelites did everything as the LORD
had commanded Moses.
6 But there were some men who
were •unclean because of a human
corpse, so they could not observe
the Passover on that day. These men
came before Moses and Aaron the
same day 7 and said to him, "We are
unclean because of a human corpse.
Why should we be excluded from
presenting the LORD's offering at its
appointed time with the other Israelites?"
8 Moses replied to them, "Wait
here until I hear what the LORD commands for you."
9 Then the LORD spoke to Moses:
10 "Tell the Israelites: When any one
of you or your descendants is unclean because of a corpse or is on a
distant journey, he may still observe
the Passover to the LORD. 11 Such
people are to observe it in the second month, on the fourteenth day at
twilight. They are to eat the animal
with unleavened bread and bitter
herbs; 12 they may not leave any of
it until morning or break any of its
bones. They must observe the Passover according to all its statutes.
13 "But the man who is ceremonially •clean, is not on a journey, and
yet fails to observe the Passover is to
be cut off from his people, because
he did not present the LORD's offering at its appointed time. That man
will bear the consequences of his
sin.
14 "If a foreigner resides with you
and wants to observe the Passover
to the LORD, he is to do so according
to the Passover statute and its ordinances. You are to apply the same
statute to both the foreign resident
and the native of the land."

Guidance by Cloud (9:15-23)

15 On the day the tabernacle was set
up, the cloud covered the tabernacle,
the tent of the •testimony, and it appeared like fire above the tabernacle
from evening until morning. 16 It remained that way continuously: the
cloud would cover it,[A] appearing like
fire at night. 17 Whenever the cloud
was lifted up above the tent, the Israelites would set out; at the place
where the cloud stopped, there the
Israelites camped. 18 At the LORD's
command the Israelites set out,
and at the LORD's command they
camped. As long as the cloud stayed
over the tabernacle, they camped.
19 Even when the cloud stayed
over the tabernacle many days, the
Israelites carried out the LORD's
requirement and did not set out.
20 Sometimes the cloud remained
over the tabernacle for only a few
days. They would camp at the LORD's
command and set out at the LORD's
command. 21 Sometimes the cloud
remained only from evening until
morning; when the cloud lifted in
the morning, they set out. Or if it
remained a day and a night, they
moved out when the cloud lifted.
22 Whether it was two days, a month,
or longer,[B] the Israelites camped
and did not set out as long as the
cloud stayed over the tabernacle.
But when it was lifted, they set out.
23 They camped at the LORD's command, and they set out at the LORD's
command. They carried out the
LORD's requirement according to His
command through Moses.

Two Silver Trumpets (10:1-10)

10 The LORD spoke to Moses:
2 "Make two trumpets of hammered silver to summon the community and have the camps set out.
3 When both are sounded in long
blasts, the entire community is to
gather before you at the entrance
to the tent of meeting. 4 However, if
one is sounded, only the leaders, the
heads of Israel's clans, are to gather
before you.
5 "When you sound short blasts,
the camps pitched on the east are
to set out. 6 When you sound short
blasts a second time, the camps
pitched on the south are to set
out. Short blasts are to be sounded
for them to set out. 7 When calling
the assembly together, you are to
sound long blasts, not short ones.
8 The sons of Aaron, the priests,
are to sound the trumpets. Your
use of these is a permanent statute
throughout your generations.
9 "When you enter into battle in
your land against an adversary who
is attacking you, sound short blasts

[A] **9:16** LXX, Vg, Syr, Tg read *it by day* [B] **9:22** Or *a year*

on the trumpets, and you will be remembered before the LORD your God
and be delivered from your enemies.
10 You are to sound the trumpets
over your •burnt offerings and your
•fellowship sacrifices and on your
joyous occasions, your appointed
festivals, and the beginning of each
of your months. They will serve as a
reminder for you before your God: I
am •Yahweh your God."

From Sinai to Paran (10:11-36)

11 During the second year, in the
second month on the twentieth day
of the month, the cloud was lifted
up above the tabernacle of the •tes-
timony. 12 The Israelites traveled on
from the Wilderness of Sinai, moving from one place to the next until
the cloud stopped in the Wilderness
of Paran. 13 They set out for the first
time according to the LORD's command through Moses.
14 The military divisions of the
camp of Judah with their banner set
out first, and Nahshon son of Amminadab was over Judah's divisions.
15 Nethanel son of Zuar was over the
division of the Issachar tribe, 16 and
Eliab son of Helon was over the division of the Zebulun tribe. 17 The tabernacle was then taken down, and
the Gershonites and the Merarites
set out, transporting the tabernacle.
18 The military divisions of the
camp of Reuben with their banner
set out, and Elizur son of Shedeur
was over Reuben's division. 19 Shelumiel son of Zurishaddai was over
the division of Simeon's tribe, 20 and
Eliasaph son of Deuel was over the
division of the tribe of Gad. 21 The
Kohathites then set out, transporting the holy objects; the tabernacle
was to be set up before their arrival.
22 Next the military divisions of the
camp of Ephraim with their banner set out, and Elishama son of
Ammihud was over Ephraim's division. 23 Gamaliel son of Pedahzur
was over the division of the tribe of
Manasseh, 24 and Abidan son of Gideoni was over the division of the tribe
of Benjamin.
25 The military divisions of the
camp of Dan with their banner set
out, serving as rear guard for all
the camps, and Ahiezer son of Ammishaddai was over Dan's division.
26 Pagiel son of Ochran was over the
division of the tribe of Asher, 27 and
Ahira son of Enan was over the division of the tribe of Naphtali. 28 This
was the order of march for the Israelites by their military divisions as
they set out.
29 Moses said to Hobab, son of
Moses' father-in-law[A] Reuel[B] the
Midianite: "We're setting out for
the place the LORD promised: 'I will
give it to you.' Come with us, and we
will treat you well, for the LORD has
promised good things to Israel."
30 But he replied to him, "I don't
want to go. Instead, I will go to my
own land and my relatives."
31 "Please don't leave us," Moses
said, "since you know where we
should camp in the wilderness, and
you can serve as our eyes. 32 If you
come with us, whatever good the
LORD does for us we will do for you."
33 They set out from the mountain
of the LORD on a three-day journey
with the ark of the LORD's covenant
traveling ahead of them for those
three days to seek a resting place
for them. 34 Meanwhile, the cloud of
the LORD was over them by day when
they set out from the camp.
35 Whenever the ark set out, Moses
would say:

Arise, LORD!
Let Your enemies
be scattered,
and those who hate You flee
from Your presence.

36 When it came to rest, he would
say:

Return, LORD,
to the countless thousands
of Israel.

Complaints Against the LORD and Moses (11:1–12:16)

Complaints About Hardship (11:1-3)

11 Now the people began complaining openly before[C] the
LORD about hardship. When the LORD
heard, His anger burned, and fire
from the LORD blazed among them

[A]**10:29** Or *said to Hobab's brother-in-law* [B]**10:29** = Jethro; Ex 2:16-18; 3:1; 4:18 [C]**11:1** Lit *in the ears of*

trumpets in battle would also serve to show that the Israelites were relying on their God and not on themselves to win. Ultimately, each time the trumpets were blown they were to cause the Israelites to remember that Yahweh is their God. Once again, the Israelites would be reminded by the trumpets that they had been set apart by a faithful God, who had been faithful in the past and promised to be faithful in the future.

10:11-28 For the first time, the Israelites moved out according to all of the commands the Lord had given to them through Moses. Their first destination was **the Wilderness of Paran**, an area west of Midian and east of Egypt. As discussed in chapter 2, **the military divisions** moved out according to plan, with the camp of Judah leading the Israelites. **The Gershonites and the Merarites** followed with **the tabernacle**. In the center of the procession were **the Kohathites**, carrying **the holy objects**. This picture of harmony, obedience, and holiness appeared in stark contrast with the complaints and rebellion that had preceded and were soon to follow.

10:29-32 Hobab was the son of **Reuel**, or Jethro, and the brother of Moses' wife Zipporah (see Ex 2:18; 3:1). Moses' desire for Hobab to continue on the journey with him stemmed from two reasons. First, Hobab was a trusted family member; and second, he was a good guide with firsthand knowledge of the best place for the Israelites to **camp**. Each time Moses tried to convince his brother-in-law, he pointed to the promises of **the LORD**. Hobab would have had reason to trust Moses as God had shown Himself to be faithful to the Israelites in their exodus from Egypt thus far. While the text does not say explicitly that Hobab went with the Israelites, a reference in the book of Judges (Jdg 1:16), and even this passage, leave the option open.

10:33-36 These verses portray a triumphant Israel, obediently following God into the wilderness. The repetition of **the LORD** (Hb *Yahweh*) three times in verses 33 and 34 signals the powerful presence of God and the focus of Israel. At this stage in Israel's journey, the people were focused on the Lord. They did not move or stop without His guidance. Even **the ark of the LORD's covenant** was now in front of the Israelites, leading them through the wilderness. The battle cry of **Moses** opened with a cry to **the LORD**. Before moving, Moses and the Israelites sought God's protection for the journey. Of note is that Moses asked for the **enemies** of the Lord, not of Israel, to **be scattered**. They realized that ultimately anyone who did not serve the Lord was not only against them but also against Him. Finally, when Israel was brought to a resting place, Moses requested that the Lord **return** to His people. Moses was again asking the Lord for His presence and protection for **Israel**. The glory ascribed to the Lord in this passage contrasts sharply with what was to follow. Faithful Israel would become faithless Israel.

11:1-3 This first rebellion establishes the pattern for the several provocations of the Lord's anger to follow. First, there was **complaining** and rebellion, then the Lord's wrath and punishment, followed by intercession by the people or Moses for the Lord's anger to end. The Lord's **anger** literally **burned** (Hb *charah*, "kindle") as **fire** that **blazed** [Hb *ba'ar*, "burn up, consume with fire"; cp. Lv 6:12; Dt 4:11; Is 30:27] **among them**. The Israelites turned **to Moses** for aid, and he interceded for them.

11:4 Contemptible people (also translated "the mixed multitude") could be a reference to descendants of mixed religious marriages (i.e., unions between Hebrews and Egyptians who were accompanying them, Ex 12:38).

11:5-6 Israel was so tired of God's daily provision of sustenance (manna) that they wished they were back in Egypt.

11:7 Coriander seed is an aromatic and sweet herb associated with the carrot family. It is common in modern kitchens as well and is found especially in Middle Eastern pastries. **Bdellium**, similar to myrrh, is a gum resin highly valued as an ingredient in perfume and incense.

11:8 A more thorough description of manna is found in Ex 16:14-36. The manna is said to have **tasted like a pastry cooked with the finest oil** or "tasted like wafers made with honey" (Ex 16:31). The Lord provided excellent food that would sustain His people during their travels. If God stopped providing the manna, they would starve; and at this point seemingly the Israelites would rather die of starvation than eat any more manna.

11:10-15 Just as gossip spreads quickly, so, too, does grumbling. A bitter attitude had taken over the Israelite camp. The complaints became so voluminous that they provoked God's anger. The name of Yahweh is used in the text, reminding the reader that Yahweh had shown Himself faithful. **Moses**, too, was **provoked**, but his anger was in the wrong place. Instead of being upset with the ungrateful attitude of the people, Moses was upset with God for assigning him to lead the ungrateful people. He did not believe

and consumed the outskirts of the
camp. 2 Then the people cried out
to Moses, and he prayed to the LORD,
and the fire died down. 3 So that
place was named Taberah,[A] because
the LORD's fire had blazed among
them.

Complaints About Food (11:4-15)

4 Contemptible people[B] among
them had a strong craving for other
food. The Israelites cried again and
said, "Who will feed us meat? 5 We
remember the free fish we ate in
Egypt, along with the cucumbers,
melons, leeks, onions, and garlic.
6 But now our appetite is gone;[C]
there's nothing to look at but this
manna!"

7 The manna resembled coriander seed, and its appearance was
like that of bdellium.[D] 8 The people
walked around and gathered it.
They ground it on a pair of grinding stones or crushed it in a mortar,
then boiled it in a cooking pot and
shaped it into cakes. It tasted like
a pastry cooked with the finest oil.
9 When the dew fell on the camp at
night, the manna would fall with it.

10 Moses heard the people, family
after family, crying at the entrance
of their tents. The LORD was very angry; Moses was also provoked.[E] 11 So
Moses asked the LORD, "Why have
You brought such trouble on Your
servant? Why are You angry with
me, and why do You burden me with
all these people? 12 Did I conceive all
these people? Did I give them birth
so You should tell me, 'Carry them
at your breast, as a nursing woman
carries a baby,' to the land that You[F]
swore to give their fathers? 13 Where
can I get meat to give all these people?
For they are crying to me: 'Give us
meat to eat!' 14 I can't carry all these
people by myself. They are too much
for me. 15 If You are going to treat me
like this, please kill me right now. If
You are pleased with me, don't let me
see my misery[G] anymore."

The Anointing of Seventy Elders (11:16-30)

16 The LORD answered Moses, "Bring
Me 70 men from Israel known to you
as elders and officers of the people.
Take them to the tent of meeting
and have them stand there with you.
17 Then I will come down and speak
with you there. I will take some of
the Spirit who is on you and put
the Spirit on them. They will help
you bear the burden of the people,
so that you do not have to bear it by
yourself.

18 "Tell the people: Purify yourselves in readiness for tomorrow,
and you will eat meat because you
cried before the LORD: 'Who will feed
us meat? We really had it good in
Egypt.' The LORD will give you meat
and you will eat. 19 You will eat, not
for one day, or two days, or five days,
or 10 days, or 20 days, 20 but for a
whole month—until it comes out
of your nostrils and becomes nauseating to you—because you have
rejected the LORD who is among you,
and cried to Him: 'Why did we ever
leave Egypt?'"

21 But Moses replied, "I'm in the
middle of a people with 600,000
foot soldiers, yet You say, 'I will give
them meat, and they will eat for a
month.' 22 If flocks and herds were
slaughtered for them, would they
have enough? Or if all the fish in
the sea were caught for them, would
they have enough?"

23 The LORD answered Moses, "Is

Doctrine THE INDWELLING OF THE HOLY SPIRIT IN THE OLD TESTAMENT

In order to alleviate some of the pressure of leadership on Moses, the Lord set forth a plan. Seventy elders would be chosen by Moses and given **some of the Spirit**, through whom he had been empowered (11:17). The anointing of these men took nothing from Moses but simply equipped and empowered the men to assist him in the great work God had given him. In the Old Testament the Holy Spirit was given to certain people—i.e., the Lord's anointed, including Saul, David, and the prophets—to give them power for certain specific tasks. He would indwell them for a time, and this indwelling was not always permanent (1Sm 16:14; Ps 51:11). However, in the New Testament after Jesus' death and resurrection, those who are believers receive the Holy Spirit at conversion, and He never leaves (Jn 14:16; Ac 5:32; 1Co 6:19).

[A]**11:3** = blaze [B]**11:4** Or *The mixed multitude*; Hb obscure [C]**11:6** Or *our lives are wasting away*, or *our throat is dry* [D]**11:7** A yellowish, transparent gum resin [E]**11:10** Lit *and it was evil in the eyes of Moses* [F]**11:12** One Hb ms, Sam, LXX, Syr, Tg read *I* [G]**11:15** Ancient Jewish tradition reads *Your misery*

the LORD's power limited?[A] You will see whether or not what I have promised will happen to you."

24 Moses went out and told the people the words of the LORD. He brought 70 men from the elders of the people and had them stand around the tent. 25 Then the LORD descended in the cloud and spoke to him. He took some of the Spirit that was on Moses and placed the Spirit on the 70 elders. As the Spirit rested on them, they prophesied, but they never did it again. 26 Two men had remained in the camp, one named Eldad and the other Medad; the Spirit rested on them—they were among those listed, but had not gone out to the tent—and they prophesied in the camp. 27 A young man ran and reported to Moses, "Eldad and Medad are prophesying in the camp."

28 Joshua son of Nun, assistant to Moses since his youth,[B] responded, "Moses, my lord, stop them!"

29 But Moses asked him, "Are you jealous on my account? If only all the LORD's people were prophets and the LORD would place His Spirit on them!" 30 Then Moses returned to the camp along with the elders of Israel.

Quail in the Camp (11:31-35)

31 A wind sent by the LORD came up and blew quail in from the sea; it dropped them at the camp all around, three feet[C] off[D] the ground, about a day's journey in every direction. 32 The people were up all that day and night and all the next day gathering the quail—the one who took the least gathered 50 bushels[E]—and they spread them out all around the camp.[F]

33 While the meat was still between their teeth, before it was chewed, the LORD's anger burned against the people, and the LORD struck them with a very severe plague. 34 So they named that place Kibroth-hattaavah,[G] because there they buried the people who had craved the meat.

35 From Kibroth-hattaavah the people moved on to Hazeroth[H] and remained there.

The Rebellion of Miriam and Aaron (12:1-16)

12 Miriam and Aaron criticized Moses because of the •Cushite[I,J] woman he married (for he had married a Cushite woman). 2 They said, "Does the LORD speak only through Moses? Does He not also speak through us?" And the LORD heard it. 3 Moses was a very humble man, more so than any man on the face of the earth.

4 Suddenly the LORD said to Moses, Aaron, and Miriam, "You three come out to the tent of meeting." So the three of them went out. 5 Then the LORD descended in a pillar of cloud, stood at the entrance to the tent, and summoned Aaron and Miriam. When the two of them came forward, 6 He said:

"Listen to what I say:
If there is a prophet
among you from the LORD,
I make Myself known to him
in a vision;
I speak with him in a dream.
7 Not so with My servant Moses;
he is faithful in[K] all
My household.
8 I speak with him directly,[L]
openly, and not in riddles;
he sees the form of the LORD.

So why were you not afraid to speak against My servant Moses?" 9 The LORD's anger burned against them, and He left.

10 As the cloud moved away from the tent, Miriam's skin suddenly became diseased, as white as snow. When Aaron turned toward her, he saw that she was diseased 11 and said to Moses, "My lord, please don't hold against us this sin we have so foolishly committed. 12 Please don't let her be like a dead baby[M] whose flesh is half eaten away when he comes out of his mother's womb."

13 Then Moses cried out to the LORD, "God, please heal her!"

14 The LORD answered Moses, "If

[A]11:23 Lit *LORD's arm too short* [B]11:28 LXX, some Sam mss read *Moses, from his chosen ones* [C]11:31 Lit *two cubits* [D]11:31 Or *on*, or *above* [E]11:32 Lit *10 homers* [F]11:32 To dry or cure the meat; 2Sm 17:19; Ezk 26:5,14 [G]11:34 = Graves of Craving [H]11:35 = settlements; Nm 12:16; 33:16-17 [I]12:1 LXX reads *Ethiopian* [J]12:1 = Sudan and Ethiopia [K]12:7 Or *is entrusted with* [L]12:8 Lit *mouth to mouth* [M]12:12 Ancient Jewish tradition reads *baby who comes out of our mother's womb and our flesh is half eaten away.*

the Lord was doing anything to help, and he felt that he alone was carrying all the burdens of Israel. He described himself and his discontent with vivid hyperbole as **a nursing woman carries a baby**. Moses lamented that the Israelites had lost their faith in God and needed to be nursed as helpless babies. "Nursing woman" (Hb *'aman*) is a masculine noun better translated "foster father," despite the fact that the "baby" (Hb participle form of *yanaq*, "suckling child") suggests a female foster parent. In essence Moses' complaint was, "You have burdened me with too much. I cannot handle this trial, and I do not trust You to help me." Moses, with whom the Lord spoke face to face, was now relying on himself instead of God.

11:24-30 So powerful was the Lord that **the Spirit rested on** two of the elders, **Eldad and Medad**, who did not come to **the tent** of meeting, **and they prophesied in the camp**. One of the youths felt this to be newsworthy and ran to inform Moses. **Joshua**, Moses' **assistant**, appeared to be **jealous** for Moses, requesting that he make them **stop**. His faith apparently restored, Moses instead was more concerned for God's glory than his own, wishing that all Israelites would have the Spirit of the Lord on them (cp. Lk 9:49-50).

11:31-32 The Lord's provision of meat came in the form of **quail** (cp. Ex 16:13). There were quail piled **three feet off the ground** around the camp, and the person carrying the least amount **gathered** 50 bushels. Three bushels is equivalent to about 10 barrels.

11:33-35 Swiftly, **the LORD's anger burned against** those who craved the meat. Before even a bite was swallowed, they were struck dead by a plague. The Israelites named the place of the Lord's judgment **Kibroth-hattaavah** in Hebrew, meaning "graves of craving," referring to the burial of those who complained and died in the fire of the Lord. Their rejection of God and their turning to the things they lustfully desired had killed them.

12:1-16 The next rebellion of Israel came from the most unlikely place (i.e., Moses' key supporters)—his sister Miriam and his brother Aaron, who was the high priest. The placing of Miriam's name first could well suggest that she was the main critic of Moses. The **Cushite woman** may be a reference to Zipporah (Ex 2:21; 4:25), Moses' wife, who had not been mentioned since Ex 18:1-5. However, the fact that Zipporah was a Midianite and had not been mentioned could mean she had died, which would leave the possibility for

Moses to take a second wife. Cush was a region south of Egypt, possibly modern-day Ethiopia or Sudan.

The reason for the critique of Moses appears to be the cover for the real complaint—Miriam and Aaron's dissatisfaction with their lowlier positions in comparison to their brother Moses. They felt that Moses was hoarding all the power. But, Moses is described as the most **humble man** on earth, which would affirm that he did not flaunt his God-ordained role. Some suggest this statement dismisses Moses' authorship of Numbers, but he could have offered this statement objectively in his own defense (cp. Paul's statements about himself, Ac 20:19; 26:29; 1Co 4:16; 7:7). In addition, anyone writing under inspiration of the Holy Spirit would not hesitate to record his own weaknesses and strengths. The swiftness with which the Lord sought to condemn Miriam and Aaron is striking. He **suddenly** summoned the three siblings to the tent of meeting, and in response they came. The awesome presence of the Lord descended upon the tent in a cloud; and standing at the entrance, the Lord called out Miriam and Aaron. In speaking to the two dissenters, the Lord said that He had made Himself known to others as Miriam and Aaron had said in their complaint. But, there was a difference with Moses. Unlike with Miriam, Aaron, and others, the Lord spoke with Moses directly (Hb *peh ʾel-peh*, lit "mouth to mouth") and openly. The Lord's parting rhetorical question shows the foolishness of Miriam and Aaron's complaint—they did not fear the Lord.

12:10-16 Once the Lord's presence departed, Aaron was able to see God's punishment upon them. Miriam's skin was now white with disease. Moses cried out to the Lord. While God agreed to heal Miriam, she would still be punished for seven days. This penalty would not only humble Miriam but would also be an example to the rest of Israel of what happens when someone goes against the Lord's anointed. The Lord and the Israelites did not move until Miriam was able to join them again. However, God's response to this rebellion also shows the far-reaching consequences of sin. Not only was Miriam unclean for **seven days** (see Lv 14:1-32), but Israel was not able to continue its journey toward the promised land while waiting on her. Israel finally departed Hazeroth with a cleansed Miriam and settled in the **Wilderness of Paran**. Moses described this area (also known as Kadesh or Kadesh-barnea) as a great and terrible wilderness (Dt 1:19). The borders of Kadesh were Canaan to the north, the Valley of Arabah to the east, the desert of Sinai to the south, and the river or brook *Wadi el Arish* to the west.

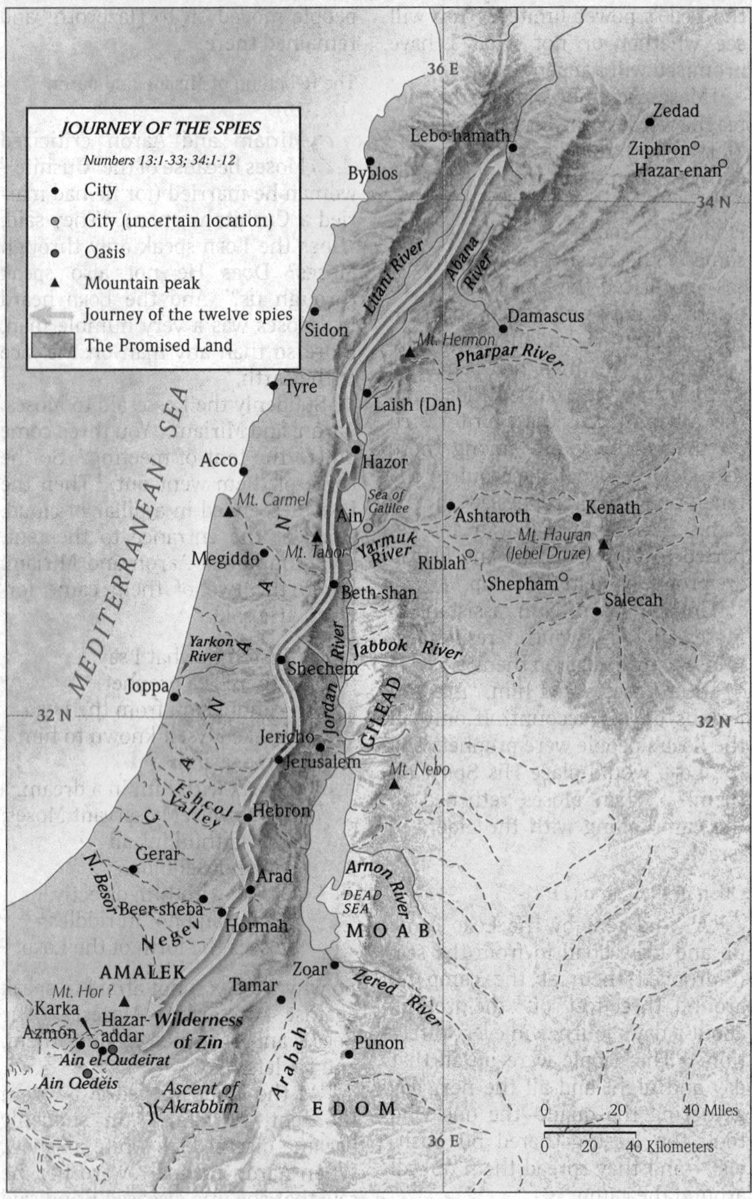

The mission of the twelve scouts was undertaken over a period of 40 days. The distance from their point of origin, the Wilderness of Zin, to Lebo-hamath was approximately 240 miles. The time and distance is consistent with records of Egyptian military campaigns where foot soldiers were said to traverse 12-15 miles per day. Biblical writers typically describe the promised land as being from Dan to Beersheba —from north to south. This description in Numbers naturally moves from south to north. Lebo-Hamath, the northernmost point, is north of Dan and is included in the delineation of the promised land in Numbers 34:7. It was a part of the kingdom of David and Solomon (1Kg 8:45).

her father had merely spit in her
face, wouldn't she remain in disgrace for seven days? Let her be
confined outside the camp for seven
days; after that she may be brought
back in." 15 So Miriam was confined
outside the camp for seven days, and
the people did not move on until
Miriam was brought back in. 16 After
that, the people set out from Hazeroth and camped in the Wilderness of Paran.

The Land of Canaan (13:1–14:45)

Scouting Out Canaan (13:1-25)

13 The LORD spoke to Moses:
2 "Send men to scout out the
land of Canaan I am giving to the
Israelites. Send one man who is a
leader among them from each of
their ancestral tribes." 3 Moses sent
them from the Wilderness of Paran
at the LORD's command. All the men
were leaders in Israel. 4 These were
their names:

Shammua son of Zaccur
from the tribe of Reuben;
5 Shaphat son of Hori
from the tribe of Simeon;
6 Caleb son of Jephunneh
from the tribe of Judah;
7 Igal son of Joseph
from the tribe of Issachar;
8 Hoshea son of Nun
from the tribe of Ephraim;
9 Palti son of Raphu
from the tribe of Benjamin;
10 Gaddiel son of Sodi
from the tribe of Zebulun;
11 Gaddi son of Susi
from the tribe of Manasseh
(from the tribe of Joseph);
12 Ammiel son of Gemalli
from the tribe of Dan;
13 Sethur son of Michael
from the tribe of Asher;
14 Nahbi son of Vophsi
from the tribe of Naphtali;
15 Geuel son of Machi
from the tribe of Gad.

16 These were the names of the men
Moses sent to scout out the land,
and Moses renamed Hoshea son of
Nun, Joshua.
17 When Moses sent them to scout
out the land of Canaan, he told them,
"Go up this way to the •Negev, then
go up into the hill country. 18 See
what the land is like, and whether
the people who live there are strong
or weak, few or many. 19 Is the land
they live in good or bad? Are the
cities they live in encampments or
fortifications? 20 Is the land fertile or
unproductive? Are there trees in it
or not? Be courageous. Bring back
some fruit from the land." It was the
season for the first ripe grapes.
21 So they went up and scouted out
the land from the Wilderness of Zin[A]
as far as Rehob[B] near the entrance to
Hamath.[C] 22 They went up through
the Negev and came to Hebron,
where Ahiman, Sheshai, and Talmai,
the descendants of Anak, were living. Hebron was built seven years
before Zoan in Egypt. 23 When they
came to the Valley of Eshcol, they
cut down a branch with a single
cluster of grapes, which was carried
on a pole by two men. They also took
some pomegranates and figs. 24 That
place was called the Valley of Eshcol[D] because of the cluster of grapes
the Israelites cut there. 25 At the end
of 40 days they returned from scouting out the land.

Report About Canaan (13:26-33)

26 The men went back to Moses,
Aaron, and the entire Israelite community in the Wilderness of Paran at
Kadesh. They brought back a report
for them and the whole community,
and they showed them the fruit of
the land. 27 They reported to Moses:
"We went into the land where you
sent us. Indeed it is flowing with
milk and honey, and here is some of
its fruit. 28 However, the people living in the land are strong, and the
cities are large and fortified. We also
saw the descendants of Anak there.
29 The Amalekites are living in the
land of the Negev; the Hittites, Jebusites, and Amorites live in the hill
country; and the Canaanites live by
the sea and along the Jordan."
30 Then Caleb quieted the people in
the presence of Moses and said, "We
must go up and take possession of

[A]**13:21** Southern border of the promised land [B]**13:21** Northern border of the promised land
[C]**13:21** Or *near Lebo-hamath* [D]**13:24** = cluster

13:8 The travels of the Israelites now brought them close to what the Lord said He would give them, the promised land. As was customary, the Lord spoke to Moses, giving him instructions concerning scouting out the land of Canaan. One scout from each tribe was chosen. Of particular importance was the choosing of **Hoshea**, whom Moses identified as **Joshua** (Hb "Yahweh is salvation"), signaling Joshua's future leadership role.

13:16-20 Moses gave the spies eight instructions each of which would prove the LORD's faithfulness in fulfilling His promise to give them a land flowing with milk and honey:

- See the land from the **Negev** to the **hill country**, south to north.
- Are the people **strong or weak**?
- Are the people **few or many**?
- Is the land **good or bad**?
- Do the people live in **encampments or fortifications**?
- Is the land **fertile or unproductive**?
- Is the land barren or lush?
- **Bring back some fruit from the land.**

13:21-25 The scouts did as Moses commanded, taking them on a 40-day journey. On their mission they found the Anakites—who would become central to the scouting report later—in the land. And the spies also took fruit back to the Israelites, including grapes, pomegranates, and figs. The inclusion of **pomegranates and figs** suggests a date of August or September, when those fruits were ripe, for the scouting mission. Indeed, even from the spies' brief description of the journey, the land was fruitful. What the Lord promised was good.

13:26-27 At first, the debriefing of the spies seemed to be going well. The fruit was presented, and the scouts agreed that the land was flowing with **milk and honey** as the Lord promised. This description became a synonym for a land full of agricultural richness.

13:28-33 However, 10 of the scouts reported an insurmountable obstacle—the people and the fortresses of the promised land. Even mentioning the people currently living in Canaan, including the descendants of Anak and the **Amalekites**, caused distress in the camp of Israel. This was obvious as **Caleb**, the scout from the tribe of Judah, had to quieten the people before speaking. He disagreed with the other spies, believing the Israelites could easily conquer the land. Caleb knew God was with the Israelites and trusted the Lord to provide the land He promised. But, the majority of the spies continued their negative report, stirring more fear in the hearts of the

Israelites by describing the giants that lived in the land, the descendants of the **Nephilim**, (Hb, "the fallen ones, rebels; giants"), noted in Gn 6:4 as the offspring of the "sons of God" and the "daughters of men." All of the Nephilim would have been destroyed in the flood (Gn 6:11-13) so the reference here was probably just a way for the 10 spies to describe their large stature and instill fear in the Israelites.

14:1-4 The pessimistic report given was the last straw for the Israelites. Their faith in God now shaken, they succumbed to weeping and complaining. Not only did the Israelites not trust the Lord, but they also believed that He had been deceiving them and that the promised land was meant for their death and not for their blessing. The Israelites were remembering the bondage of Egypt as better than the true promised land.

14:5-9 Moses and Aaron, still faithful to God, humbled themselves before the Lord and the Israelite community, falling face down before them. The two faithful scouts, Joshua and Caleb, tore their clothes in a display of frustration and mourning, speaking to the community. They reported that the land was good. Thus, there was no just cause for the Israelites' rebellion. To be afraid of a people whom God had given into their hands was to show the utmost doubt and unbelief. This was the chance for the Israelites to turn their hearts back to God and claim the land He had promised.

14:10-12 The hearts of the Israelites were hardened, and they sought to stone the minority; but when all seemed lost, God intervened. The glory of the Lord appeared to all Israel at the **tent of meeting**. As the people were ready to strike down Moses and the faithful, so God was ready to destroy Israel with **a plague** and then build a greater nation. The question of Israel's following of the Lord would continue to be a theme throughout its history.

14:13-19 Moses' love for Israel was on full display as he again became Israel's intercessor before the Lord. Of central importance in Moses' petition was the Lord's reputation. Moses pointed to the Lord's witness to Egypt and the other nations, which would become extinct if He wiped out Israel. They would believe the Lord was not mighty enough to bring Israel to the promised land. Moses then cited Ex 34:6-7, when the Lord passed in front of him, proclaiming His greatness.

14:20-38 The Lord showed His faithful love to Israel, as He had consistently done through the generations. Instead of wiping Israel out instantly and

the land because we can certainly conquer it!"

31 But the men who had gone up with him responded, "We can't go up against the people because they are stronger than we are!" 32 So they gave a negative report to the Israelites about the land they had scouted: "The land we passed through to explore is one that devours its inhabitants, and all the people we saw in it are men of great size. 33 We even saw the Nephilim[A] there—the descendants of Anak come from the Nephilim! To ourselves we seemed like grasshoppers, and we must have seemed the same to them."

Israel's Refusal to Enter Canaan (14:1-10)

14 Then the whole community broke into loud cries, and the people wept that night. 2 All the Israelites complained about Moses and Aaron, and the whole community told them, "If only we had died in the land of Egypt, or if only we had died in this wilderness! 3 Why is the LORD bringing us into this land to die by the sword? Our wives and little children will become plunder. Wouldn't it be better for us to go back to Egypt?" 4 So they said to one another, "Let's appoint a leader and go back to Egypt."

5 Then Moses and Aaron fell down with their faces to the ground in front of the whole assembly of the Israelite community. 6 Joshua son of Nun and Caleb son of Jephunneh, who were among those who scouted out the land, tore their clothes 7 and said to the entire Israelite community: "The land we passed through and explored is an extremely good land. 8 If the LORD is pleased with us, He will bring us into this land, a land flowing with milk and honey, and give it to us. 9 Only don't rebel against the LORD, and don't be afraid of the people of the land, for we will devour them. Their protection has been removed from them, and the LORD is with us. Don't be afraid of them!"

10 While the whole community threatened to stone them, the glory of the LORD appeared to all the Israelites at the tent of meeting.

God's Judgment of Israel's Rebellion (14:11-38)

11 The LORD said to Moses, "How long will these people despise Me? How long will they not trust in Me despite all the signs I have performed among them? 12 I will strike them with a plague and destroy them. Then I will make you into a greater and mightier nation than they are."

13 But Moses replied to the LORD, "The Egyptians will hear about it, for by Your strength You brought up this people from them. 14 They will tell it to the inhabitants of this land. They have heard that You, LORD, are among these people, how You, LORD, are seen face to face, how Your cloud stands over them, and how You go before them in a pillar of cloud by day and in a pillar of fire by night. 15 If You kill this people with a single blow,[B] the nations that have heard of Your fame will declare, 16 'Since the LORD wasn't able to bring this people into the land He swore to give them, He has slaughtered them in the wilderness.'

17 "So now, may my Lord's power be magnified just as You have spoken: 18 The LORD is slow to anger and rich in faithful love, forgiving wrongdoing and rebellion. But He will not leave the •guilty unpunished, bringing the consequences of the fathers' wrongdoing on the children to the third and fourth generation. 19 Please pardon the wrongdoing of this people, in keeping with the greatness of Your faithful love, just as You have forgiven them from Egypt until now."

20 The LORD responded, "I have pardoned them as you requested. 21 Yet as surely as I live and as the whole earth is filled with the LORD's glory, 22 none of the men who have seen My glory and the signs I performed in Egypt and in the wilderness, and have tested Me these 10 times and did not obey Me, 23 will ever see the land I swore to give their fathers. None of those who have despised Me will see it. 24 But since My servant Caleb has a different spirit and has followed Me completely, I will bring him into the land where he

[A] **13:33** Possibly means fallen ones; traditionally, "giants"; Gn 6:4 [B] **14:15** Lit *people as one man*

has gone, and his descendants will
inherit it. 25 Since the Amalekites
and Canaanites are living in the
lowlands,[A] turn back tomorrow and
head for the wilderness in the direction of the •Red Sea."
26 Then the LORD spoke to Moses
and Aaron: 27 "How long must I endure this evil community that keeps
complaining about Me? I have heard
the Israelites' complaints that they
make against Me. 28 Tell them: As
surely as I live," this is the LORD's
declaration, "I will do to you exactly
as I heard you say. 29 Your corpses
will fall in this wilderness—all of
you who were registered in the
census, the entire number of you
20 years old or more—because
you have complained about Me. 30 I
swear that none of you will enter
the land I promised[B] to settle you
in, except Caleb son of Jephunneh and Joshua son of Nun. 31 I will
bring your children whom you said
would become plunder into the land
you rejected, and they will enjoy it.
32 But as for you, your corpses will
fall in this wilderness. 33 Your children will be shepherds in the wilderness for 40 years and bear the
penalty for your acts of unfaithfulness until all your corpses lie scattered in the wilderness. 34 You will
bear the consequences of your sins
40 years based on the number of the
40 days that you scouted the land, a
year for each day.[C] You will know My
displeasure.[D] 35 I, •Yahweh, have spoken. I swear that I will do this to the
entire evil community that has conspired against Me. They will come to
an end in the wilderness, and there
they will die."
36 So the men Moses sent to scout
out the land, and who returned
and incited the entire community
to complain about him by spreading a negative report about the
land— 37 those men who spread the
negative report about the land were
struck down by the LORD. 38 Only
Joshua son of Nun and Caleb son of
Jephunneh remained alive of those
men who went to scout out the land.

Israel Routed (14:39-45)

39 When Moses reported these
words to all the Israelites, the people
were overcome with grief. 40 They
got up early the next morning and
went up the ridge of the hill country, saying, "Let's go to the place the
LORD promised, for we were wrong."
41 But Moses responded, "Why are
you going against the LORD's command? It won't succeed. 42 Don't
go, because the LORD is not among
you and you will be defeated by your
enemies. 43 The Amalekites and Canaanites are right in front of you,
and you will fall by the sword. The
LORD won't be with you, since you
have turned from following Him."
44 But they dared to go up the ridge
of the hill country, even though the
ark of the LORD's covenant and Moses did not leave the camp. 45 Then
the Amalekites and Canaanites who
lived in that part of the hill country came down, attacked them, and
routed them as far as Hormah.

Further Instructions (15:1-41)

Laws About Offerings (15:1-31)

15 The LORD instructed Moses:
2 "Speak to the Israelites and
tell them: When you enter the land I
am giving you to settle in, 3 and you
make a fire offering to the LORD from
the herd or flock—either a •burnt
offering or a sacrifice, to fulfill a
vow, or as a freewill offering, or at
your appointed festivals—to produce a pleasing aroma for the LORD,
4 the one presenting his offering to
the LORD must also present a •grain
offering of two quarts[E] of fine flour
mixed with a quart[F] of oil. 5 Prepare
a quart[F] of wine as a •drink offering
with the burnt offering or sacrifice
of each lamb.
6 "If you prepare a grain offering
with a ram, it must be four quarts[G]
of fine flour mixed with a third of a
gallon[H] of oil. 7 Also present a third
of a gallon[H] of wine for a drink offering as a pleasing aroma to the LORD.
8 "If you prepare a young bull as
a burnt offering or as a sacrifice,
to fulfill a vow, or as a •fellowship

completely, the Israelites who were rebellious despite having been brought out of Egypt and having seen the Lord's mighty hand would not enter the promised land. (Nm 14:22,29,32). The Lord even told Moses to begin heading back toward the wilderness in the direction of the **Red Sea**. Their children, too, would be punished for their actions, wandering 40 years—perhaps representing the 40 days of scouting of the promised land—in the wilderness. The eight scouts who brought the negative report were swiftly struck down by the Lord. Of the Israelites who were 20 years old at the time of the census, only **Joshua** and **Caleb** would be allowed to live and see the promised land (vv. 24,30,38). Caleb was given praise by the Lord for following the Lord **completely**.

14:39-45 Once the Israelites heard the pronounced judgment of the Lord from Moses, they regretted their actions. But the sorrow over their disobedience was too late. Now willing to obey the Lord, some wanted to go and take the land even though Moses warned them that the Lord was not with them. Moses did not go with them, and Aaron and the priests did not let the ark of the covenant make the trip. The battle was lost from the start. Israel was routed by the Amalekites and the Canaanites. The lives of many of the Israelites were likely characterized by regret and what could have been if they had been faithful to the Lord.

15:1-41 This chapter is a reminder that the Lord had not abandoned Israel. Not only was He still speaking to the Israelites through His servant Moses, but He also affirmed that He would give them the promised land. That commitment was so certain that the Lord would continue to give instructions for living in the land.

15:3-21 God gave Moses instructions concerning the **fire offering**. When presenting something before the Lord God, the actions must be taken seriously. Thus, the Lord provided instructions for each offering. Of note is that the statute concerning the fire offering applied both to the foreigner and the Israelite. As with the fire offering, instructions for the contribution offering were given for the time when the Israelites entered the promised land. Again, God demonstrated His commitment to His promise with these words. Similar to the offering of firstfruits, the contribution offering was **a loaf . . . of dough**, an expression of thanks to the Lord for His provision and a successful harvest.

[A]**14:25** Lit *valley* [B]**14:30** Lit *I raised My hand* [C]**14:34** Lit *a day for the year, a day for the year* [D]**14:34** Or *My opposition* [E]**15:4** Lit *a tenth* (of an ephah) [F]**15:4,5** Lit *a fourth hin* [G]**15:6** Lit *two-tenths* (of an ephah) [H]**15:6,7** Lit *a third hin*

offering to the LORD, 9 a grain offering of six quarts[A] of fine flour mixed with two quarts[B] of oil must be presented with the bull. 10 Also present two quarts[B] of wine as a drink offering. It is a fire offering of pleasing aroma to the LORD. 11 This is to be done for each ox, ram, lamb, or goat. 12 This is how you must prepare each of them, no matter how many.

13 "Every Israelite is to prepare these things in this way when he presents a fire offering as a pleasing aroma to the LORD. 14 When a foreigner resides with you or someone else is among you and wants to prepare a fire offering as a pleasing aroma to the LORD, he is to do exactly as you do throughout your generations. 15 The assembly is to have the same statute for[C] both you and the foreign resident as a permanent statute throughout your generations. You and the foreigner will be alike before the LORD. 16 The same law and the same ordinance will apply to both you and the foreigner who resides with you."

17 The LORD instructed Moses: 18 "Speak to the Israelites and tell them: After you enter the land where I am bringing you, 19 you are to offer a contribution to the LORD when you eat from the food of the land. 20 You are to offer a loaf from your first batch of dough as a contribution; offer it just like a contribution from the threshing floor. 21 Throughout your generations, you are to give the LORD a contribution from the first batch of your dough.

22 "When you sin unintentionally and do not obey all these commands that the LORD spoke to Moses— 23 all that the LORD has commanded you through Moses, from the day the LORD issued the commands and onward throughout your generations— 24 and if it was done unintentionally without the community's awareness, the entire community is to prepare one young bull for a burnt offering as a pleasing aroma to the LORD, with its grain offering and drink offering according to the regulation, and one male goat as a •sin offering. 25 The priest must then make •atonement for the entire Israelite community so that they may be forgiven, for the sin was unintentional. They are to bring their offering, one made by fire to the LORD, and their sin offering before the LORD for their unintentional sin. 26 The entire Israelite community and the foreigner who resides among them will be forgiven, since it happened to all the people unintentionally.

27 "If one person sins unintentionally, he is to present a year-old female goat as a sin offering. 28 The priest must then make atonement before the LORD on behalf of the person who acts in error sinning unintentionally, and when he makes atonement for him, he will be forgiven. 29 You are to have the same law for the person who acts in error, whether he is an Israelite or a foreigner who lives among you.

30 "But the person who acts defiantly,[D] whether native or foreign resident, blasphemes the LORD. That person is to be cut off from his people. 31 He will certainly be cut off, because he has despised the LORD's word and broken His command; his •guilt remains on him."

Sabbath Violation (15:32-36)

32 While the Israelites were in the wilderness, they found a man gathering wood on the Sabbath day. 33 Those who found him gathering wood brought him to Moses, Aaron, and the entire community. 34 They placed him in custody because it had not been decided what should be done to him. 35 Then the LORD told Moses, "The man is to be put to death. The entire community is to stone him outside the camp." 36 So the entire community brought him outside the camp and stoned him to death, as the LORD had commanded Moses.

Tassels for Remembrance (15:37-41)

37 The LORD said to Moses, 38 "Speak to the Israelites and tell them that throughout their generations they are to make tassels for the corners

[A]**15:9** Lit *three-tenths* (of an ephah) [B]**15:9,10** Lit *a half hin* [C]**15:14-15** Sam, LXX read [14]. . . *the LORD, the assembly must do exactly as you do.* [15] *The same statute will apply to . . .* [D]**15:30** Lit *with a high hand*

15:22-31 This passage deals with unintentional sin of the whole community and of individuals. This statute applied both to the Israelite and the foreigner. Leviticus 4 also explains in further detail the offerings concerning unintentional sin. Verses 30 and 31 stand in stark contrast to the passage on unintentional sin. These verses depict how seriously the Lord takes sin and rejection, and the sin is described here with the word **defiantly** (Hb *be-yad ramah*, "with a high hand," an idiom for displaying arrogance and rebellion). Sins committed with defiance, in full knowledge of the law, called for punishment, exclusion from the community, and even death (vv. 32-36). While forgiveness was to be found when one sinned unintentionally, there was continued guilt for the one who blasphemed the Lord and His commands (v. 31). This person had rejected the Lord as the true God. This statute also applied both to the Israelites and the foreigners living among them. The punishment of being cut off, though seemingly harsh, is very appropriate. Israel is God's chosen people. To reject the Lord is also to hate the nation and to reject a calling to holy living.

15:32-36 This passage illustrates one who defiantly breaks the law and must be examined in light of Ex 35:2-3.

15:37-41 The **blue cord** of the tassel (Hb *tsitsit*, "fringed edge"; cp. *gadil*, "intertwined threads, tassels," Dt 22:12), or **tassels**, was reminiscent of the colors used in the tabernacle. They served as a reminder of the call to obedience. This command is also the source of the Jewish traditional prayer shawl (Hb *tallit*, "little covering") and concurs with Dt 6:6-9 in which the statutes of the Lord are to be passed from generation to generation. In the New Testament, the woman with an issue of blood simply touched the hem (Gk *kraspedon*, "tassel or edge"; Mt 9:20) of the Savior's garment and received healing. A definition of sin is given—becoming **unfaithful by following your own heart and your own eyes**. When you go your own way, you are sinning against the Lord (e.g. the rebellion of Korah, Nm 16).

16:1-3 Full of jealousy and pride, **Korah**, a Levite, gathered 250 Israelite men who were in agreement that the leadership of Moses and Aaron should come to an end. Korah mistook the leadership roles of Moses and Aaron as self-exaltation, believing them to have **gone too far**, but they did not exalt themselves above the people—God put them in their positions of leadership and the people followed them (see Ex 4:27-31). Korah demonstrated his ignorance of the holiness of God in his claim that all

of their garments, and put a blue cord on the tassel at each corner. [39] These will serve as tassels for you to look at, so that you may remember all the LORD's commands and obey them and not become unfaithful by following your own heart and your own eyes. [40] This way you will remember and obey all My commands and be holy to your God. [41] I am •Yahweh your God who brought you out of the land of Egypt to be your God; I am Yahweh your God."

Korah's Rebellion (16:1-50)

16 Now Korah son of Izhar, son of Kohath, son of Levi, with Dathan and Abiram, sons of Eliab, and On son of Peleth, sons of Reuben, took [2] 250 prominent Israelite men who were leaders of the community and representatives in the assembly, and they rebelled against Moses. [3] They came together against Moses and Aaron and told them, "You have gone too far![A] Everyone in the entire community is holy, and the LORD is among them. Why then do you exalt yourselves above the LORD's assembly?"

[4] When Moses heard this, he fell facedown. [5] Then he said to Korah and all his followers, "Tomorrow morning the LORD will reveal who belongs to Him, who is set apart, and the one He will let come near Him. He will let the one He chooses come near Him. [6] Korah, you and all your followers are to do this: take firepans, and tomorrow [7] place fire in them and put incense on them before the LORD. Then the man the LORD chooses will be the one who is set apart. It is you Levites who have gone too far!"[B]

[8] Moses also told Korah, "Now listen, Levites! [9] Isn't it enough for you that the God of Israel has separated you from the Israelite community to bring you near to Himself, to perform the work at the LORD's tabernacle, and to stand before the community to minister to them? [10] He has brought you near, and all your fellow Levites who are with you, but you are seeking the priesthood as well. [11] Therefore, it is you and all your followers who have conspired against the LORD! As for Aaron, who is he[C] that you should complain about him?"

[12] Moses sent for Dathan and Abiram, the sons of Eliab, but they said, "We will not come! [13] Is it not enough that you brought us up from a land flowing with milk and honey to kill us in the wilderness? Do you also have to appoint yourself as ruler over us? [14] Furthermore, you didn't bring us to a land flowing with milk and honey or give us an inheritance of fields and vineyards. Will you gouge out the eyes of these men? We will not come!"

[15] Then Moses became angry and said to the LORD, "Don't respect their offering. I have not taken one donkey from them or mistreated a single one of them." [16] So Moses told Korah, "You and all your followers are to appear before the LORD tomorrow—you, they, and Aaron. [17] Each of you is to take his firepan, place incense on it, and present his firepan before the LORD—250 firepans. You and Aaron are each to present your firepan also."

[18] Each man took his firepan, placed fire in it, put incense on it, and stood at the entrance to the tent of meeting along with Moses and Aaron. [19] After Korah assembled the whole community against them at the entrance to the tent of meeting, the glory of the LORD appeared to the whole community. [20] The LORD spoke to Moses and Aaron, [21] "Separate yourselves from this community so I may consume them instantly."

[22] But Moses and Aaron fell facedown and said, "God, God of the spirits[D] of all flesh, when one man sins, will You vent Your wrath on the whole community?"

[23] The LORD replied to Moses, [24] "Tell the community: Get away from the dwellings of Korah, Dathan, and Abiram."

[25] Moses got up and went to Dathan and Abiram, and the elders of Israel followed him. [26] He warned the community, "Get away now from the tents of these wicked men. Don't touch anything that belongs

[A] **16:3** Lit *Enough of you* [B] **16:7** Lit *Enough of you, sons of Levi* [C] **16:11** Or *Aaron, what has he done* [D] **16:22** Or *breath*; Nm 27:16

Israelites were holy in the same way and in his belief that the men were to choose the roles they would have in worship.

16:4-11 Moses, true to character, humbled himself before the people and God, falling face down before them. Korah and the dissenting group were not in reality rebelling against Moses and Aaron but against the Lord.

16:12-21 Moses also addressed the sons of Reuben, the second in command after Korah. **Dathan** and **Abiram** had questioned Moses' integrity, which had finally stirred Moses' anger to the surface; for he had never mistreated them. Moses did not answer Dathan and Abiram but rather presented his case before the Lord. He knew that though the sons of Eliab might feel cheated, God knew the truth. The Lord would judge between Korah and Moses and Aaron. Moses told the men to bring their firepans before the Lord, as he and Aaron would. An offering of incense was given, and the Lord would decide whose was acceptable; He would identify His chosen leaders and priests. Korah and his followers immediately did as Moses and the Lord requested; but instead of assembling with only their followers, Korah assembled the entire community against Moses and Aaron at the tent of meeting. Due to Korah's blatant challenge to God's authority and his leading astray of Israel and turning them against Moses and Aaron, the Lord appeared in His glory ready to perform wrathful vengeance on the entire community, with the exception of His faithful followers, Moses and Aaron.

16:22 Showing their character and their love for Israel, Moses and Aaron humbled themselves before the Lord, falling **facedown**, requesting that the community be spared. Their cry to the **God of the spirits of all flesh**, or the God of the breath of all flesh, pointed to God as the life giver.

16:23-27 The Lord in His patience, grace, and forgiveness turned His attention to the ring leaders of the rebellion. Moses and the elders warned the Israelites not to touch anything of **Korah, Dathan**, or **Abiram** lest they, too, become unclean. Korah and his followers had offered unauthorized fire before the Lord, as had Nadab and Abihu (Lv 10:1-7), who were put to death by the Lord for this offense. While the Israelites distanced themselves from the tents of the rebels, the families of Dathan and Abiram actually stood outside their tents. After the Israelites separated themselves, the Lord was ready to pass His judgment upon them.

16:28-30 Moses explained what would happen, being sure God would receive the glory and awe due Him. If something natural happened to the sinners, then the judgment was from Moses; but if something completely new and unexpected occurred, the people would know that the Lord had acted and that these men were unrighteous in what they did.

16:31-40 The earth's opening and swallowing of the rebels let all Israel know the judgment was from God and a reminder of the Lord's holiness and omnipotence. A terrifying scene unfolded, with the disobedient being taken with their homes down to **Sheol** and the Israelites running in fear that they, too, would be **swallowed**. The Lord also punished the followers of Korah, who were unauthorized to offer incense, by consuming them with fire. However, the Lord had Eleazar remove the firepans from the fire and create an altar for them, calling them holy. This altar would now serve as a reminder to the Israelites that God chooses His anointed and appoints whom He selects for service to Him. Rebellion against those chosen by God brings punishment.

16:41-50 The scene that unfolded the following day was unbelievable. Instead of turning their hearts back to the Lord and submitting to the leadership of Moses and Aaron, the people blamed them for the deaths of Korah and his followers. The decisive and awesome judgment, which had so obviously come from the Lord, was now being credited to Moses. While the Israelites were trying to diminish the Lord and His might, the Lord's glory again appeared over the tent of meeting. His wrath was evident. For the second time in two days He was ready to annihilate the Israelite community. The Lord revealed to Moses that He had started a **plague** among the Israelites. In order to stop it, Aaron was sent with his **firepan** and **fire from the altar** among the people. Aaron **made atonement** for the people and stopped the plague. Aaron's actions are a vivid example of what is involved in the role of high priest. Christ, our ultimate High Priest, intercedes for us before the Father.

17:1-11 After so much complaining and quarreling over who the spiritual leaders of Israel were, the Lord was ready to settle the issue before the Israelites once and for all. First, the tribal staffs of each of the 12 tribes were to be gathered, including the tribe of Levi, and the name of the leader of each house was to be written on the representative tribal **staff**, with Aaron's name being placed on the Levitical staff. Moses then took the staffs and placed them not just in the tent of

to them, or you will be swept away because of all their sins." 27 So they got away from the dwellings of Korah, Dathan, and Abiram. Meanwhile, Dathan and Abiram came out and stood at the entrance of their tents with their wives, children, and infants.

28 Then Moses said, "This is how you will know that the LORD sent me to do all these things and that it was not of my own will: 29 If these men die naturally as all people would, and suffer the fate of all, then the LORD has not sent me. 30 But if the LORD brings about something unprecedented, and the ground opens its mouth and swallows them along with all that belongs to them so that they go down alive into •Sheol, then you will know that these men have despised the LORD."

31 Just as he finished speaking all these words, the ground beneath them split open. 32 The earth opened its mouth and swallowed them and their households, all Korah's people, and all their possessions. 33 They went down alive into Sheol with all that belonged to them. The earth closed over them, and they vanished from the assembly. 34 At their cries, all the people of Israel who were around them fled because they thought, "The earth may swallow us too!" 35 Fire also came out from the LORD and consumed the 250 men who were presenting the incense.

36[A] Then the LORD spoke to Moses: 37 "Tell Eleazar son of Aaron the priest to remove the firepans from the burning debris, because they are holy, and scatter the fire far away. 38 As for the firepans of those who sinned at the cost of their own lives, make them into hammered sheets as plating for the altar, for they presented them before the LORD, and the firepans are holy. They will be a sign to the Israelites."

39 So Eleazar the priest took the bronze firepans that those who were burned had presented, and they were hammered into plating for the altar, 40 just as the LORD commanded him through Moses. It was to be a reminder for the Israelites that no unauthorized person outside the lineage of Aaron should approach to offer incense before the LORD and become like Korah and his followers.

41 The next day the entire Israelite community complained about Moses and Aaron, saying, "You have killed the LORD's people!" 42 When the community assembled against them, Moses and Aaron turned toward the tent of meeting, and suddenly the cloud covered it, and the LORD's glory appeared.

43 Moses and Aaron went to the front of the tent of meeting, 44 and the LORD said to Moses, 45 "Get away from this community so that I may consume them instantly." But they fell facedown.

46 Then Moses told Aaron, "Take your firepan, place fire from the altar in it, and add incense. Go quickly to the community and make •atonement for them, because wrath has come from the LORD; the plague has begun." 47 So Aaron took his firepan as Moses had ordered, ran into the middle of the assembly, and saw that the plague had begun among the people. After he added incense, he made atonement for the people. 48 He stood between the dead and the living, and the plague was halted. 49 But those who died from the plague numbered 14,700, in addition to those who died because of the Korah incident. 50 Aaron then returned to Moses at the entrance to the tent of meeting, since the plague had been halted.

The Priesthood (17:1–19:22)

The Selection of Aaron's Staff (17:1-13)

17 [B] The LORD instructed Moses: 2 "Speak to the Israelites and take one staff from them for each ancestral house, 12 staffs from all the leaders of their ancestral houses. Write each man's name on his staff. 3 Write Aaron's name on Levi's staff, because there must be one staff for the head of each ancestral house. 4 Then place them in the tent of meeting in front of the •testimony where I meet with you. 5 The staff of the man I choose will sprout, and I will rid Myself of the Israelites' com-

[A] **16:36** Nm 17:1 in Hb [B] **17:1** Nm 17:16 in Hb

plaints that they have been making
about you."
6 So Moses spoke to the Israelites,
and each of their leaders gave him a
staff, one for each of the leaders of
their ancestral houses, 12 staffs in
all. Aaron's staff was among them.
7 Moses placed the staffs before the
LORD in the tent of the testimony.
8 The next day Moses entered the
tent of the testimony and saw that
Aaron's staff, representing the house
of Levi, had sprouted, formed buds,
blossomed, and produced almonds!
9 Moses then brought out all the
staffs from the LORD's presence to
all the Israelites. They saw them,
and each man took his own staff.
10 The LORD told Moses, "Put Aaron's
staff back in front of the testimony
to be kept as a sign for the rebels,
so that you may put an end to their
complaints before Me, or else they
will die." 11 So Moses did as the LORD
commanded him.
12 Then the Israelites declared
to Moses, "Look, we're perishing!
We're lost; we're all lost! 13 Anyone
who comes near the LORD's tabernacle will die. Will we all perish?"

Provision for the Priesthood (18:1-7)

18 The LORD said to Aaron, "You,
your sons, and your ancestral
house will be responsible for sin
against the sanctuary. You and your
sons will be responsible for sin involving your priesthood. 2 But also
bring your relatives with you from
the tribe of Levi, your ancestral
tribe, so they may join you and assist you and your sons in front of the
tent of the •testimony. 3 They are to
perform duties for you and for the
whole tent. They must not come
near the sanctuary equipment or the
altar; otherwise, both they and you
will die. 4 They are to join you and
guard the tent of meeting, doing all
the work at the tent, but no unauthorized person may come near you.
5 "You are to guard the sanctuary
and the altar so that wrath may not
fall on the Israelites again. 6 Look,
I have selected your fellow Levites
from the Israelites as a gift for you,[A]
assigned by the LORD to work at the
tent of meeting. 7 But you and your
sons will carry out your priestly
responsibilities for everything concerning the altar and for what is
inside the veil, and you will do that
work. I am giving you the work of
the priesthood as a gift,[B] but an unauthorized person who comes near
the sanctuary will be put to death."

Support for the Priests and Levites (18:8-32)

8 Then the LORD spoke to Aaron,
"Look, I have put you in charge of
the contributions brought to Me.
As for all the holy offerings of the
Israelites, I have given them to you
and your sons as a portion and a
permanent statute. 9 A portion of the
holiest offerings kept from the fire
will be yours; every one of their offerings that they give Me, whether
the •grain offering, •sin offering, or
•restitution offering will be most
holy for you and your sons. 10 You
are to eat it as a most holy offering.[C]
Every male may eat it; it is to be holy
to you.
11 "The contribution of their gifts
also belongs to you. I have given all
the Israelites' presentation offerings
to you and to your sons and daughters as a permanent statute. Every
ceremonially •clean person in your
house may eat it. 12 I am giving you
all the best of the fresh olive oil, new
wine, and grain, which the Israelites
give to the LORD as their •firstfruits.
13 The firstfruits of all that is in their
land, which they bring to the LORD,
belong to you. Every clean person in
your house may eat them.
14 "Everything in Israel that is
permanently dedicated to the LORD
belongs to you. 15 The firstborn of
every living thing, man or animal,
presented to the LORD belongs to
you. But you must certainly redeem
the firstborn of man, and redeem
the firstborn of an •unclean animal.
16 You will pay the redemption price
for a month-old male according to
your assessment: five •shekels of silver by the standard sanctuary shekel, which is 20 *gerahs*.
17 "However, you must not redeem
the firstborn of an ox, a sheep, or a

meeting but in the holy of holies before the ark of the covenant, the seat of the Lord's glory. The Lord's chosen would be evidenced by the sprouting of the tribal staff, and in this way the Lord would put an end to the question of leadership among the Israelites. Moses obediently carried out this task, and there were no surprises the next morning as the staff of the tribe of Levi, with Aaron's name, had been chosen and was sprouting—but there was a surprise in that the staff also blossomed and produced almonds. The Lord emphatically showed whom He had chosen to lead His people. Not only the tribal leaders saw what had occurred overnight, but also all Israel observed the phenomenon; thus there could be no dispute. Aaron's rod was kept in front of the ark so that it was a sign to any who would rebel and seek to usurp Aaron's leadership. The punishment for any rebellion, as seen in chapter 16, is death.

18:1-2 With the issue of the leadership of the priesthood settled, the Lord spoke directly to **Aaron** rather than Moses concerning the duties of the priesthood. Aaron and his sons not only were given the heavy responsibility of atoning for sin for the community but now had also added the burden of sin against the sanctuary and sin in the priesthood.

18:3-4 While the Aaronic line bore the brunt of the weight of responsibility, the Lord brought the Levites to serve alongside them. The Levites, the tribal brothers of Aaron, while equally family, would serve in a subordinate role to Aaron and his sons. The function of the Levites would be to guard the tent and perform duties for Aaron and his sons. One prohibition was given to the Levites. They were not to go near the **sanctuary**; and if they did, not only would they die, but also Aaron and his sons would die. Thus, while the Levites were given as a gift to the priesthood, the priests would ultimately be responsible for the sanctuary, the holy of holies. This passage speaks volumes to those serving in leadership positions. They have the responsibility of preparing people lacking in personal holiness for the perfectly holy God. A woman who is leading a women's ministry will have women whom God brings to serve alongside her. But, she must remember that she is called to be a guardian of the holiest things. Her walk with the Lord, together with being a woman of the highest integrity, will give her the spiritual guidance she needs for the women she leads.

[A]**18:6** LXX, Syr, Vg omit *for you* [B]**18:7** Or *veil. So you are to perform the service; a gift of your priesthood I grant* [C]**18:10** Or *it in a most holy place*

goat; they are holy. You are to sprinkle their blood on the altar and burn their fat as a fire offering for a pleasing aroma to the LORD. [18]But their meat belongs to you. It belongs to you like the breast of the presentation offering and the right thigh.

[19]"I give to you and to your sons and daughters all the holy contributions that the Israelites present to the LORD as a permanent statute. It is a permanent covenant of salt before the LORD for you as well as your •offspring."

[20]The LORD told Aaron, "You will not have an inheritance in their land; there will be no portion among them for you. I am your portion and your inheritance among the Israelites.

[21]"Look, I have given the Levites every tenth in Israel as an inheritance in return for the work they do, the work of the tent of meeting. [22]The Israelites must never again come near the tent of meeting, or they will incur •guilt and die. [23]The Levites will do the work of the tent of meeting, and they will bear the consequences of their sin. The Levites will not receive an inheritance among the Israelites; this is a permanent statute throughout your generations. [24]For I have given them the tenth that the Israelites present to the LORD as a contribution for their inheritance. That is why I told them that they would not receive an inheritance among the Israelites."

[25]The LORD instructed Moses, [26]"Speak to the Levites and tell them: When you receive from the Israelites the tenth that I have given you as your inheritance, you must present part of it as an offering to the LORD—a tenth of the tenth. [27]Your offering will be credited to you as if it were your grain from the threshing floor or the full harvest from the winepress. [28]You are to present an offering to the LORD from every tenth you receive from the Israelites. Give some of it to Aaron the priest as an offering to the LORD. [29]You must present the entire offering due the LORD from all your gifts. The best part of the tenth is to be consecrated.

[30]"Tell them further: Once you have presented the best part of the tenth, and it is credited to you Levites as the produce of the threshing floor or the winepress, [31]then you and your household may eat it anywhere. It is your wage in return for your work at the tent of meeting. [32]You will not incur guilt because of it once you have presented the best part of it, but you must not defile the Israelites' holy offerings, so that you will not die."

Purification Ritual (19:1-22)

19 The LORD spoke to Moses and Aaron, [2]"This is the legal statute that the LORD has commanded: Instruct the Israelites to bring you an unblemished red cow that has no defect and has never been yoked. [3]Give it to Eleazar the priest, and he will have it brought outside the camp and slaughtered in his presence. [4]Eleazar the priest is to take some of its blood with his finger and sprinkle it seven times toward the front of the tent of meeting. [5]The cow must be burned in his sight. Its hide, flesh, and blood, are to be burned along with its dung. [6]The priest is to take cedar wood, hyssop, and crimson yarn, and throw them onto the fire where the cow is burning. [7]Then the priest must wash his clothes and bathe his body in water; after that he may enter the camp, but he will remain ceremonially •unclean until evening. [8]The one who burned the cow must also wash his clothes and bathe his body in water, and he will remain unclean until evening.

[9]"A man who is •clean is to gather up the cow's ashes and deposit them outside the camp in a ceremonially clean place. The ashes must be kept by the Israelite community for preparing the water to remove impurity; it is a •sin offering. [10]Then the one who gathers up the cow's ashes must wash his clothes, and he will remain unclean until evening. This is a permanent statute for the Israelites and for the foreigner who resides among them.

[11]"The person who touches any human corpse will be unclean for seven days. [12]He is to purify himself with the water[A] on the third day

18:19-20 This covenant between the Lord and the priests would be a **covenant of salt** (Hb *berit melach ʿolam*, "everlasting covenant of salt"). The terminology is used twice elsewhere. Salt must always be added with grain offerings (Lv 2:13); and in 2Ch 13:5 salt is found in the description of the Davidic covenant. Salt is a preservative, and when combined with the word "everlasting," salt prompts remembrance that God will honor and preserve His covenant with His people. While the priesthood would not have an inheritance in the promised land, they could be content in knowing the Lord is their **portion** and **inheritance**.

18:21-32 This passage deals with the tithe, which can also be seen as a wage, for the Levites.

19:1-22 The whole of chapter 19 discusses the purification ritual and statutes concerning defilement by touching a corpse. The extreme measures taken to maintain cleanness were tedious, but the Lord continually reminded the Israelites of the purity He required because He is a holy God.

20:1 The Israelite community had moved past its rebellious attitude. Their wandering brought them to the Wilderness of Zin and back to Kadesh, where the spies had returned from their scouting of the promised land (13:26). There, on the outskirts of the promised land, Miriam, the prophetess and beloved sister of Moses and Aaron (see Ex 15:20), died and was buried. After Miriam spoke ill of the leadership of Moses, the Lord's anointed leader, she is not mentioned again until her death. Miriam's ministry had been ruined when she sought her own way rather than God's. Prior to this incident, she played a vital role in the saving of Moses' life and was a leader among the women. Thus, marking the death of this great woman served to show that a generation of the Israelites was passing.

20:2-5 The second time in Kadesh was no better than the first in terms of grumbling and distrust in the Lord. Once again, the Israelites were distraught, and instead of turning to God in faith, they blamed Moses and Aaron for the lack of water. Some of the Israelites even wished they had died among those punished for their rebellion. And, most astonishingly, the Israelites believed Kadesh to be the promised land; and they attacked the integrity of Joshua, Caleb, Moses, and Aaron. They complained that there were no **figs, vines, and pomegranates, and there is no water** like the spies upon their return from the promised land in chapter 13. Instead of seeing the land God was giving them as good, the Israelites declared it to be **evil**.

[A]**19:12** Or *ashes*; lit *with it*

and the seventh day; then he will be clean. But if he does not purify himself on the third and seventh days, he will not be clean. 13 Anyone who touches a body of a person who has died, and does not purify himself, defiles the tabernacle of the LORD. That person will be cut off from Israel. He remains unclean because the water for impurity has not been sprinkled on him, and his uncleanness is still on him.

14 "This is the law when a person dies in a tent: everyone who enters the tent and everyone who is already in the tent will be unclean for seven days, 15 and any open container without a lid tied on it is unclean. 16 Anyone in the open field who touches a person who has been killed by the sword or has died, or who even touches a human bone, or a grave, will be unclean for seven days. 17 For the purification of the unclean person, they are to take some of the ashes of the burnt sin offering, put them in a jar, and add fresh water to them. 18 A person who is clean is to take hyssop, dip it in the water, and sprinkle the tent, all the furnishings, and the people who were there. He is also to sprinkle the one who touched a bone, a grave, a corpse, or a person who had been killed.

19 "The one who is clean is to sprinkle the unclean person on the third day and the seventh day. After he purifies the unclean person on the seventh day, the one being purified must wash his clothes and bathe in water, and he will be clean by evening. 20 But a person who is unclean and does not purify himself, that person will be cut off from the assembly because he has defiled the sanctuary of the LORD. The water for impurity has not been sprinkled on him; he is unclean. 21 This is a permanent statute for them. The person who sprinkles the water for impurity is to wash his clothes, and whoever touches the water for impurity will be unclean until evening. 22 Anything the unclean person touches will become unclean, and anyone who touches it will be unclean until evening."

The Rebellion of Moses and Aaron (20:1-13)

20 The entire Israelite community entered the Wilderness of Zin in the first month, and they[A] settled in Kadesh. Miriam died and was buried there.

2 There was no water for the community, so they assembled against Moses and Aaron. 3 The people quarreled with Moses and said, "If only we had perished when our brothers perished before the LORD. 4 Why have you brought the LORD's assembly into this wilderness for us and our livestock to die here? 5 Why have you led us up from Egypt to bring us to this evil place? It's not a place of grain, figs, vines, and pomegranates, and there is no water to drink!"

6 Then Moses and Aaron went from the presence of the assembly to the doorway of the tent of meeting. They fell down with their faces to the ground, and the glory of the LORD appeared to them. 7 The LORD spoke to Moses, 8 "Take the staff and assemble the community. You and your brother Aaron are to speak to the rock while they watch, and it will yield its water. You will bring out water for them from the rock and provide drink for the community and their livestock."

9 So Moses took the staff from the LORD's presence just as He had commanded him. 10 Moses and Aaron summoned the assembly in front of the rock, and Moses said to them, "Listen, you rebels! Must we bring water out of this rock for you?" 11 Then Moses raised his hand and struck the rock twice with his staff, so that a great amount of water gushed out, and the community and their livestock drank.

12 But the LORD said to Moses and Aaron, "Because you did not trust Me to show My holiness in the sight of the Israelites, you will not bring this assembly into the land I have given them." 13 These are the waters of Meribah,[B] where the Israelites quarreled with the LORD, and He showed His holiness to them.

20:6-10 The Lord was longsuffering and merciful in His provision for the Israelites. By having Moses and Aaron use the staff to perform this miracle, the Lord's reminder to the Israelites was twofold. First, the Israelites would be reminded of the might and faithfulness of the Lord; and second, they would be reminded that Moses and Aaron had been called of God to lead Israel. The Lord went above and beyond responding to the issues about which the Israelites were grumbling since He would provide drink not only for the people of Israel but also for their livestock.

20:9-10 Moses and Aaron followed the first two commands of the Lord perfectly, taking the staff of Aaron **from the LORD's presence** and assembling the community around the rock. However, Moses and Aaron failed miserably in the most important part of the assignment God had given them—to demonstrate faith in Him. Instead of saying the power of God was at work on the rock, Moses appeared to give the glory to himself and Aaron by pronouncing, **Must we bring water out of this rock for you?** The one calling Israel rebellious, in this case, was defying God himself. Moses seemed vengeful against the Israelites, and perhaps in his heart he was wishing the Lord would punish them rather than provide for them.

20:11-13 Though much is made of Moses' actions, the only one who truly knew the sin of Israel's leaders was the Lord, and Moses and Aaron's sin, which essentially was a lack of faith, had dire consequences. Moses let the Lord down by his obstinate attitude and rash actions toward the Lord and impatience with his people. Moses and Aaron had led Israel out of Egypt and through the wilderness these many years, yet they would not be allowed to lead the assembly into the promised land. While their mighty leaders had fallen, the Lord did not forsake His people, and He still used Moses and Aaron as human agents to bring forth the water. Both the Lord's provision and His judgment were to be remembered by the Israelites, and the Lord named the site **Meribah** (Hb "quarreling").

[A]20:1 Lit *the people* [B]20:13 = quarreling

The Conquests (20:14–21:35)

Edom's Denial of Passage (20:14-21)

14 Moses sent messengers from Kadesh to the king of Edom, "This is what your brother Israel says, 'You know all the hardships that have overtaken us. 15 Our fathers went down to Egypt, and we lived in Egypt many years, but the Egyptians treated us and our fathers badly. 16 When we cried out to the LORD, He heard our voice, sent an angel,[A] and brought us out of Egypt. Now look, we are in Kadesh, a city on the border of your territory. 17 Please let us travel through your land. We won't travel through any field or vineyard, or drink any well water. We will travel the King's Highway; we won't turn to the right or the left until we have traveled through your territory.'"

18 But Edom answered him, "You must not travel through our land, or we will come out and confront you with the sword."

19 "We will go on the main road," the Israelites replied to them, "and if we or our herds drink your water, we will pay its price. There will be no problem; only let us travel through on foot."

20 Yet Edom insisted, "You must not travel through." And they came out to confront them with a large force of heavily-armed people.[B] 21 Edom refused to allow Israel to travel through their territory, and Israel turned away from them.

Aaron's Death (20:22-29)

22 After they set out from Kadesh, the entire Israelite community came to Mount Hor. 23 The LORD said to Moses and Aaron at Mount Hor on the border of the land of Edom, 24 "Aaron will be gathered to his people; he will not enter the land I have given the Israelites, because you both rebelled against My command at the waters of Meribah. 25 Take Aaron and his son Eleazar and bring them up Mount Hor. 26 Remove Aaron's garments and put them on his son Eleazar. Aaron will be gathered to his people and die there."

27 So Moses did as the LORD commanded, and they climbed Mount Hor in the sight of the whole community. 28 After Moses removed Aaron's garments and put them on his son Eleazar, Aaron died there on top of the mountain. Then Moses and Eleazar came down from the mountain. 29 When the whole community saw that Aaron had passed away, the entire house of Israel mourned for him 30 days.

The Defeat of the Canaanite King (21:1-3)

21 When the Canaanite king of Arad, who lived in the •Negev, heard that Israel was coming on the Atharim road, he fought against Israel and captured some prisoners. 2 Then Israel made a vow to the LORD, "If You will deliver this people into our hands, we will •completely destroy their cities." 3 The LORD listened to Israel's request, the Canaanites were defeated, and Israel completely destroyed them and their cities. So they named the place Hormah.[C]

4 Then they set out from Mount Hor by way of the •Red Sea to bypass the land of Edom, but the people[D] became impatient because of the journey. 5 The people spoke against God and Moses: "Why have you led us up from Egypt to die in the wilderness? There is no bread or water, and we detest this wretched food!"

The Bronze Snake (21:6-9)

6 Then the LORD sent poisonous[E,F] snakes among the people, and they bit them so that many Israelites died.

7 The people then came to Moses and said, "We have sinned by speaking against the LORD and against you. Intercede with the LORD so that He will take the snakes away from us." And Moses interceded for the people.

8 Then the LORD said to Moses, "Make a snake image and mount it on a pole. When anyone who is bitten looks at it, he will recover." 9 So Moses made a bronze snake and mounted it on a pole. Whenever

20:14-17 The Israelites prepared for the last leg of their journey into the promised land. Before departing from Kadesh, the Israelites needed permission to pass through the land of Edom, which was not part of the land God was giving them but on the way to it. Moses' messages to Edom were not those of the leader representing a superior nation to a subordinate nation, but rather an exchange of words between equals. The king of Edom was thus called **brother**, a term evolving from their connection to the lineage of Esau.

20:17 The Israelite army traveled on **the King's Highway**, the famous trade route that connected Damascus with Arabia, Sinai, and Egypt. It was probably known as *Wadi el Ghuweir*, a military road built by a king. With its good pastures and spring wells, the highway is in use even now.

20:18-21 Edom did not want the Israelites to travel through their land and would meet them with **the sword**. Another round of messages occurred, with Israel's insistence that they would travel along the main road and pay Edom for watering their herds, as would be the standard procedure in that day. This time the reply from Edom was clearly understood as confrontational. Not only did the Edomites refuse Israel passage through their land, but armed men were sent out to ward off the Israelites from even attempting to pass through Edom. Israel had to take the much longer route around Edom to the promised land.

20:22 Israel began its journey around Edom from Kadesh and arrived at **Mount Hor**, present-day Harun, traditionally located about 30 miles northeast of Kadesh-barnea.

20:23-26 The Lord spoke to Moses and Aaron in a gesture of comfort for what was about to happen. Aaron would die and **be gathered to his people** on **Mount Hor**. This formula is used throughout the Pentateuch when a man of God dies and especially when describing the deaths of the patriarchs. The Lord reminded Aaron of why his death had to occur before he reached the promised land—because of his rebellion, together with Moses, at Meribah. The Lord allowed Aaron to see his son **Eleazar** succeed him as high priest.

20:27-29 The scene is bittersweet as Moses, Aaron's brother and close friend, removed the garments that marked Aaron's relationship with the Lord and the Israelite community and placed them on Aaron's son Eleazar. The wording of this passage makes Aaron's death appear peaceful. When

[A] **20:16** Or *a messenger* [B] **20:20** Lit *with numerous people and a strong hand* [C] **21:3** = destruction [D] **21:4** Lit *soul of the people* [E] **21:6** LXX reads *deadly*; Syr reads *cruel*; Vg reads *fiery* [F] **21:6** Lit *burning*

someone was bitten, and he looked
at the bronze snake, he recovered.

Journey Around Moab (21:10-20)

10 The Israelites set out and camped
at Oboth. 11 They set out from Oboth
and camped at Iye-abarim in the
wilderness that borders Moab on
the east. 12 From there they went
and camped at Zered Valley. 13 They
set out from there and camped on
the other side of the Arnon River, in
the wilderness that extends from the
Amorite border, because the Arnon
was the Moabite border between
Moab and the Amorites. 14 Therefore
it is stated in the Book of the LORD's
Wars:

Waheb[A] in Suphah
and the ravines of the Arnon,
15 even the slopes of the ravines
that extend to the site of Ar[B]
and lie along the border
of Moab.

16 From there they went to Beer,[C]
the well the LORD told Moses about,
"Gather the people so I may give
them water." 17 Then Israel sang this
song:

Spring up, well—sing to it!
18 The princes dug the well;
the nobles of the people
hollowed it out
with a scepter and with
their staffs.

They went from the wilderness
to Mattanah, 19 from Mattanah to
Nahaliel, from Nahaliel to Bamoth,
20 from Bamoth to the valley in the
territory of Moab near the Pisgah
highlands[D] that overlook the wasteland.[E]

The Defeat of the Amorite King (21:21-35)

21 Israel sent messengers to say to
Sihon king of the Amorites: 22 "Let
us travel through your land. We
won't go into the fields or vineyards.
We won't drink any well water. We
will travel the King's Highway until
we have traveled through your territory." 23 But Sihon would not let
Israel travel through his territory.
Instead, he gathered his whole army
and went out to confront Israel in
the wilderness. When he came to
Jahaz, he fought against Israel. 24 Israel struck him with the sword and
took possession of his land from the
Arnon to the Jabbok, but only up
to the Ammonite border, because it
was fortified.[F,G]

25 Israel took all the cities and lived
in all these Amorite cities, including
Heshbon and all its villages. 26 Heshbon was the city of Sihon king of the
Amorites, who had fought against
the former king of Moab and had
taken control of all his land as far
as the Arnon. 27 Therefore the poets[H]
say:

Come to Heshbon,
let it be rebuilt;
let the city of Sihon
be restored.[I]
28 For fire came out of Heshbon,
a flame from the city
of Sihon.
It consumed Ar of Moab,
the lords of[J] Arnon's heights.
29 Woe to you, Moab!
You have been destroyed,
people of Chemosh!
He gave up his sons
as refugees,
and his daughters
into captivity
to Sihon the Amorite king.
30 We threw them down;
Heshbon has been destroyed
as far as Dibon.[K]
We caused desolation
as far as Nophah,
which reaches
as far as Medeba.[L]

31 So Israel lived in the Amorites'
land. 32 After Moses sent spies to
Jazer, Israel captured its villages and
drove out the Amorites who were
there.
33 Then they turned and went up
the road to Bashan, and Og king of
Bashan came out against them with
his whole army to do battle at Edrei.

only Eleazar and Moses returned from atop the mountain, the impact of Aaron's life and death was evident as the whole community **mourned for 30 days**. Now, two of Moses' siblings had died, and he was aware his own death was nearing. The closer the Israelites got to the promised land, a change in leadership was more and more apparent as the old generation passed and the new one prepared to enter into the land God promised.

21:1-5 Chapter 21 begins the first test of the new generation of Israelites in taking the promised land. Due to the menacing Edomites, Israel had to travel around them by a longer way near the **Red Sea**.

21:6-7 The Lord would not have His goodness questioned, and thus He sent a punishment on the Israelites in the form of **poisonous snakes**. After many died, the Israelites realized their disgraceful and sinful actions. In a show of humility and desperation, they turned to Moses to intercede for them. The Israelites acknowledged their sin against Moses, and the Lord began turning the tide of His judgment.

21:8-9 Instead of merely stopping the plague, the Lord issued a command that would again test the faith and obedience of the Israelites. Looking upon the **bronze snake** made by Moses did not ward off the poisonous snakes, but this act of faith saved those who had been bitten and followed the Lord's instruction. Numbers 21 is perhaps the most pregnant with imagery foreshadowing Christ. In the Gospel of John, Jesus refers to Himself, saying as the snake was lifted up, so the Son of Man must be lifted up so that all who believe in Him will have eternal life (Jn 3:14-15). Thus the passage in John affirms that the issue of looking at the snake was the personal choice to believe God, trusting the Lord to save. Any woman must turn to the Lord and Savior Jesus Christ for salvation, not trusting in her own "good" but in the Savior whose blood was shed on Calvary.

21:10-20 A summary of the Israelites' travel and battles through the land of the Amorites is noted. The list here matches the itinerary of the Israelites' journey found in chapter 33. Extrabiblical material found in **the Book of the LORD's War** has not yet been discovered but apparently was the Israelites' record of their different battles recorded along their journey.

[A] **21:14** = the source of the Arnon River [B] **21:15** A city in Moab; Nm 21:28; Dt 2:9,18,29; Is 15:1 [C] **21:16** = well [D] **21:20** = Moabite mountain plateau; Nm 23:14; Dt 3:17,27; 4:49; 34:1; Jos 12:3; 13:20 [E] **21:20** Or *overlook Jeshimon* [F] **21:24** LXX reads *was Jazer* [G] **21:24** Or *was at Az* [H] **21:27** Lit *ones who speak proverbs* [I] **21:27** Or *firmly founded* [J] **21:28** LXX reads *Moab, and swallowed* [K] **21:30** LXX reads *Their seed will perish from Heshbon*; Vg reads *Their yoke has perished from Heshbon* [L] **21:30** LXX reads *Dibon. And their women have further kindled a fire against Moab*; Hb uncertain

34 But the LORD said to Moses, "Do not fear him, for I have handed him over to you along with his whole army and his land. Do to him as you did to Sihon king of the Amorites, who lived in Heshbon." 35 So they struck him, his sons, and his whole army until no one was left,[A] and they took possession of his land.

Balaam's Oracles (22:1–24:25)

Balak's Hiring of Balaam (22:1-21)

22 The Israelites traveled on and camped in the plains of Moab near the Jordan across from Jericho. 2 Now Balak son of Zippor saw all that Israel had done to the Amorites. 3 Moab was terrified of the people because they were numerous, and Moab dreaded the Israelites. 4 So the Moabites said to the elders of Midian, "This horde will devour everything around us like an ox eats up the green plants in the field."

Since Balak son of Zippor was Moab's king at that time, 5 he sent messengers to Balaam son of Beor at Pethor, which is by the Euphrates in the land of his people.[B,C] Balak said to him: "Look, a people has come out of Egypt; they cover the surface of the land and are living right across from me. 6 Please come and put a curse on these people for me because they are more powerful than I am. I may be able to defeat them and drive them out of the land, for I know that those you bless are blessed and those you curse are cursed."

7 The elders of Moab and Midian departed with fees for •divination in hand. They came to Balaam and reported Balak's words to him. 8 He said to them, "Spend the night here, and I will give you the answer the LORD tells me." So the officials of Moab stayed with Balaam.

9 Then God came to Balaam and asked, "Who are these men with you?"

10 Balaam replied to God, "Balak son of Zippor, king of Moab, sent this message to me: 11 'Look, a people has come out of Egypt, and they cover the surface of the land. Now come and put a curse on them for me. I may be able to fight against them and drive them away.'"

12 Then God said to Balaam, "You are not to go with them. You are not to curse this people, for they are blessed."

13 So Balaam got up the next morning and said to Balak's officials, "Go back to your land, because the LORD has refused to let me go with you."

14 The officials of Moab arose, returned to Balak, and reported, "Balaam refused to come with us."

15 Balak sent officials again who were more numerous and higher in rank than the others. 16 They came to Balaam and said to him, "This is what Balak son of Zippor says: 'Let nothing keep you from coming to me, 17 for I will greatly honor you and do whatever you ask me. So please come and put a curse on these people for me!'"

18 But Balaam responded to the servants of Balak, "If Balak were to give me his house full of silver and gold, I could not go against the command of the LORD my God to do anything small or great. 19 Please stay here overnight as the others did, so that I may find out what else the LORD has to tell me."

20 God came to Balaam at night and said to him, "Since these men have come to summon you, get up and go with them, but you must only do what I tell you." 21 When he got up in the morning, Balaam saddled his donkey and went with the officials of Moab.

Balaam's Donkey and the Angel (22:22-41)

22 But God was incensed that Balaam was going, and the Angel of the LORD took His stand on the path to oppose him. Balaam was riding his donkey, and his two servants were with him. 23 When the donkey saw the Angel of the LORD standing on the path with a drawn sword in His hand, she turned off the path and went into the field. So Balaam hit her to return her to the path. 24 Then the Angel of the LORD stood in a narrow passage between the vineyards, with a stone wall on ei-

22:1-4 The Israelite victories must have made news throughout the region, as **Balak**, the king of Moab, and the Moabites were **terrified** of the Israelites. Midianites had come to live in Moab as well and were thus allies against Israel.

22:5-6 Balak was so concerned that he concluded the only way Moab could defeat Israel was if a curse was put upon them to reverse the blessing of the Lord currently upon them. The man Balak chose for this task was **Balaam** of **Pethor**. Balak was willing to pay Balaam, a diviner who sought to discern the will of God by reading omens. Pethor was about 400 miles from Moab, so each roundtrip for the messengers from the king would have taken close to two months.

22:7-11 Both the Moabite and Midianite elders presented Balaam with the money and the king's request; but Balaam did not respond immediately, wanting to receive an answer from the Lord. Balaam was obviously familiar with Israel's God and His leading the Israelites out of Egypt.

22:12-19 Balak was not pleased that Balaam did not return, and he tried to bribe Balaam by sending officers to him who were higher in rank than the first messengers. Balak wanted Balaam to do as he asked so much that he was willing to give Balaam great honor and do whatever the diviner requested. However, Balaam responded as he did the first time, requesting a night to hear from the Lord. Balaam addressed **the LORD my God**, which seems to point to a knowledge of God that is intimate and personal. However, in light of further examination, Balaam was the one who incited Israel to idolatry (chap. 25; see 31:16). Clearly he thought human will could change God's will (Dt 23:4-5; Jos 24:10). The New Testament confirms Balaam's apostasy (Jd 1:11).

22:22-30 God may appear to have changed His mind since He told Balaam to go with the men (v. 20). Balaam thought God would allow him to curse Israel since he was now allowed to go to Balak. God often stopped men during a journey on which He had directed them in order to demonstrate that He was ultimately in control. For example, Jacob wrestled with God at Peniel (Gn 32:22-32), and Moses was confronted about his sin on his way back to Egypt (Ex 4:24-26). As with Jacob, **the Angel of the LORD** appeared to Balaam, but the **donkey** and not the diviner was aware of this. Three times the angel stood in Balaam's way, but each time Balaam was not sensitive to God and instead beat the donkey. The Lord will use whatever necessary, even a beast of burden, to reveal Himself.

[A]21:35 Lit *left to him* [B]22:5 Sam, Vg, Syr read *of the Ammonites* [C]22:5 Or *of the Amawites*

ther side. 25 The donkey saw the Angel of the LORD and pressed herself against the wall, squeezing Balaam's foot against it. So he hit her once again. 26 The Angel of the LORD went ahead and stood in a narrow place where there was no room to turn to the right or the left. 27 When the donkey saw the Angel of the LORD, she crouched down under Balaam. So he became furious and beat the donkey with his stick.

28 Then the LORD opened the donkey's mouth, and she asked Balaam, "What have I done to you that you have beaten me these three times?"

29 Balaam answered the donkey, "You made me look like a fool. If I had a sword in my hand, I'd kill you now!"

30 But the donkey said, "Am I not the donkey you've ridden all your life until today? Have I ever treated you this way before?"

"No," he replied.

31 Then the LORD opened Balaam's eyes, and he saw the Angel of the LORD standing in the path with a drawn sword in His hand. Balaam knelt and bowed with his face to the ground. 32 The Angel of the LORD asked him, "Why have you beaten your donkey these three times? Look, I came out to oppose you, because what you are doing is evil in My sight. 33 The donkey saw Me and turned away from Me these three times. If she had not turned away from Me, I would have killed you by now and let her live."

34 Balaam said to the Angel of the LORD, "I have sinned, for I did not know that You were standing in the path to confront me. And now, if it is evil in Your sight, I will go back."

35 Then the Angel of the LORD said to Balaam, "Go with the men, but you are to say only what I tell you." So Balaam went with Balak's officials.

36 When Balak heard that Balaam was coming, he went out to meet him at the Moabite city[A] on the Arnon border at the edge of his territory. 37 Balak asked Balaam, "Did I not send you an urgent summons? Why didn't you come to me? Am I really not able to reward you?"

38 Balaam said to him, "Look, I have come to you, but can I say anything I want? I must speak only the message God puts in my mouth."
39 So Balaam went with Balak, and they came to Kiriath-huzoth.[B]
40 Balak sacrificed cattle and sheep, and sent for Balaam and the officials who were with him.

41 In the morning, Balak took Balaam and brought him to Bamoth-baal.[C] From there he saw the outskirts of the people's camp.

Balaam's First Oracle (23:1-12)

23 Then Balaam said to Balak, "Build me seven altars here and prepare seven bulls and seven rams for me." 2 So Balak did as Balaam directed, and they offered a bull and a ram on each altar. 3 Balaam said to Balak, "Stay here by your •burnt offering while I am gone. Maybe the LORD[D] will meet with me. I will tell you whatever He reveals to me." So he went to a barren hill.

4 God[E] met with him and Balaam said to Him, "I have arranged seven altars and offered a bull and a ram on each altar." 5 Then the LORD put a message in Balaam's mouth and said, "Return to Balak and say what I tell you."

6 So he returned to Balak, who was standing there by his burnt offering with all the officials of Moab.
7 Balaam proclaimed his poem:

Balak brought me from Aram;
the king of Moab, from
the eastern mountains:
"Come, put a curse on Jacob
for me;
come, denounce Israel!"
8 How can I curse someone
God has not cursed?
How can I denounce
someone the LORD
has not denounced?
9 I see them from the top
of rocky cliffs,
and I watch them
from the hills.
There is a people living alone;
it does not consider itself
among the nations.

[A]22:36 Or *at Ir-moab*, or *at Ar of Moab* [B]22:39 = The City of Streets [C]22:41 = The High Places of Baal [D]23:3 DSS, LXX, Sam read *Maybe God* [E]23:4 DSS, Sam read *The Angel of God*

22:31-35 Amazingly, the donkey began to make clear to Balaam the reason for its actions, and then the Lord opened Balaam's eyes. His reaction was one of humility, and the angel asked a similar question to that of the donkey. The angel made clear that Balaam was intending evil, and indeed the donkey saved his life. The donkey showed more discernment than he, and Balaam realized this. He acknowledged his sin and was willing to return home. However, Balaam was allowed to continue only after the Angel of the Lord reasserted the command that Balaam was to speak only what he was told. Thus Balaam continued toward Balak with a stern warning.

22:36-40 Balak was obviously anxious for the cursing to commence. For a king to come out and greet someone personally instead of sending his servants to extend welcome in his behalf was a high honor. Thus the importance of Balaam to Balak's desire to defeat Israel is apparent. Although Balaam does not tell Balak that the Lord desired to bless Israel, admittedly he could only speak the message given him by God. Balak offered sacrifices in order to attempt to appease the Lord and in preparation for what he thought would be a change of course for Israel the next day.

22:41 The site for Balaam's first oracle was to be on the outskirts of the Israelite camp at **Bamoth-baal** (Hb "high places of Baal"), which was a center for worship of the deity Baal, the central god of the Canaanite religion.

23:1-3 Balak appeared ready to aid Balaam in the cursing of Israel in whatever way he could in order to get on with the battle. Balaam's instructions concerning the altars and offerings were followed by Balak. In the ancient Near East, the practice of having multiple altars or rituals was common.

23:4-5 Once Balak left, God met with Balaam, who seemed a little uncertain about what would happen. Balaam confirmed that he had performed sacrifices; and then the Lord, as He often does with prophets, put a **message** in Balaam's mouth.

23:6-12 Balaam began his first **poem** or oracle with a standard introduction, and the blessing of Israel ensued. Several things are clear in Balaam's oracle. Israel was blessed, not cursed, and its people were set apart. Unlike other nations, they belonged to the Lord. The evidence of the Lord's blessing was seen in the size of the Israelite nation. Balaam closed by wishing to die as an Israelite who is **upright**. While Balaam spoke these words, his death would be the exact opposite. After inciting Israel to sin by worshiping Baal of Peor, he was killed in vengeance according to the Lord (31:8). Balak was incredulous at the pronouncement of Balaam over Israel. But Balaam continued to say that he could only say exactly what the Lord put in his mouth.

23:13-26 Balak would not settle for the blessing, and he assumed that perhaps the location was wrong for the curse; so he moved Balaam to where he could barely see the Israelite camp. The same scene unfolded at the field of Zophim, or **Lookout Field**, as at Bamoth-baal, with the offering of sacrifices and the Lord again putting His message in Balaam's mouth. Balak was hopeful when Balaam returned, but again an oracle of blessing for Israel spilled from Balaam's mouth. This time the point was grander and clearer. The presence of the Lord was what made the Israelite nation so great. Unlike Balak and Balaam, and everyone on earth, the Lord is full of integrity, never changing; and thus He always fulfills His word. Because the Lord had blessed Israel, He would not reverse that blessing based upon the whims of men. Balak was infuriated, but Balaam again answered that he could only speak what the Lord said.

23:27–24:9 A third time Balak took Balaam to another site, hoping again to turn the heart of the Lord against His people. They moved to **Peor**, and once again the altars and sacrifices were prepared, but there was one thing done differently. Apparently, Balaam first sought **omens,** signs of nature, but now he realized the Lord was pleased when Israel was blessed so on this third attempt Balaam did not seek omens. When Balaam turned toward where the Israelites were encamped, the **Spirit of God** descended on him with another oracle. The first part of Balaam's oracle is a beautiful description of the bounty of the promised land. Then, the oracle turns to the future king of Israel, who will be greater than **Agag**, the king of the Amalekites, a tribal people who lived in the Negev and Sinai Peninsula. "Agag" is a common name for an Amalekite king similar to the use of "Pharaoh" for an Egyptian ruler. The prophecy found in Gn 49:9 in the blessing of Judah is recalled as the words are repeated (Nm 24:9). Thus, the focus of the third oracle is again the faithfulness of Israel's God and the greatness of their coming king.

24:10-14 Balaam had now so defied Balak that he would receive no payment because he did the exact opposite of what was requested. For the final time Balaam repeated that he could not go against what the Lord puts in his mouth and then launched into a

10 Who has counted the dust
of Jacob
or numbered the dust clouds[A]
of Israel?
Let me die the death
of the upright;
let the end of my life
be like theirs.

11 "What have you done to me?" Balak asked Balaam. "I brought you to curse my enemies, but look, you have only blessed them!"

12 He answered, "Shouldn't I say exactly what the LORD puts in my mouth?"

Balaam's Second Oracle (23:13-26)

13 Then Balak said to him, "Please come with me to another place where you can see them. You will only see the outskirts of their camp; you won't see all of them. From there, put a curse on them for me." 14 So Balak took him to Lookout Field[B] on top of Pisgah, built seven altars, and offered a bull and a ram on each altar.

15 Balaam said to Balak, "Stay here by your burnt offering while I seek the LORD over there."

16 The LORD met with Balaam and put a message in his mouth. Then He said, "Return to Balak and say what I tell you."

17 So he returned to Balak, who was standing there by his burnt offering with the officials of Moab. Balak asked him, "What did the LORD say?"

18 Balaam proclaimed his poem:

Balak, get up and listen;
son of Zippor, pay attention
to what I say!
19 God is not a man who lies,
or a son of man who changes
His mind.
Does He speak and not act,
or promise and not fulfill?
20 I have indeed received
a command to bless;
since He has blessed,[C]
I cannot change it.
21 He considers no disaster
for Jacob;
He sees no trouble for Israel.[D]
The LORD their God is
with them,
and there is rejoicing
over the King among them.
22 God brought them
out of Egypt;
He is like the horns
of a wild ox for them.[E]
23 There is no magic curse
against Jacob
and no •divination
against Israel.
It will now be said
about Jacob and Israel,
"What great things
God has done!"
24 A people rise up like a lioness;
They rouse themselves
like a lion.
They will not lie down
until they devour the prey
and drink the blood
of the slain.

25 Then Balak told Balaam, "Don't curse them and don't bless them!"

26 But Balaam answered him, "Didn't I tell you: Whatever the LORD says, I must do?"

Balaam's Third Oracle (23:27–24:14)

27 Again Balak said to Balaam, "Please come. I will take you to another place. Maybe it will be agreeable to God that you can put a curse on them for me there." 28 So Balak took Balaam to the top of Peor, which overlooks the wasteland.[F]

29 Balaam told Balak, "Build me seven altars here and prepare seven bulls and seven rams for me." 30 So Balak did as Balaam said and offered a bull and a ram on each altar.

24 Since Balaam saw that it pleased the LORD to bless Israel, he did not go to seek omens as on previous occasions, but turned[G] toward the wilderness. 2 When Balaam looked up and saw Israel encamped tribe by tribe, the Spirit of God came on him, 3 and he proclaimed his poem:

The •oracle of Balaam
son of Beor,
the oracle of the man
whose eyes are opened,[H]

[A]**23:10** Or *numbered a fourth* [B]**23:14** Or *to the field of Zophim* [C]**23:20** Sam, LXX read *since I will bless* [D]**23:21** Or *not observe sin in Jacob; not see wrongdoing* [E]**23:22** Or *Egypt; they have the horns of a wild ox* [F]**23:28** Or *overlooks Jeshimon* [G]**24:1** Lit *set his face* [H]**24:3** LXX reads *true*; Vg reads *closed*

4 the oracle of one who hears
the sayings of God,
who sees a vision
from the •Almighty,
who falls into a trance
with his eyes uncovered:
5 How beautiful are your tents,
Jacob,
your dwellings, Israel.
6 They stretch out
like river valleys,[A]
like gardens beside a stream,
like aloes the LORD
has planted,
like cedars beside the water.
7 Water will flow
from his buckets,
and his seed will be
by abundant water.
His king will be greater
than Agag,[B]
and his kingdom
will be exalted.
8 God brought him
out of Egypt;
He is like[C] the horns
of a wild ox for them.
He will feed on enemy nations
and gnaw their bones;
he will strike them
with his arrows.
9 He crouches, he lies down
like a lion
or a lioness—who dares
to rouse him?
Those who bless you
will be blessed,
and those who curse you
will be cursed.

10 Then Balak became furious with
Balaam, struck his hands together,
and said to him, "I summoned you
to put a curse on my enemies, but
instead, you have blessed them
these three times. 11 Now go to your
home! I said I would reward you
richly, but look, the LORD has denied
you a reward."
12 Balaam answered Balak, "Didn't
I previously tell the messengers you
sent me: 13 If Balak were to give me
his house full of silver and gold, I
could not go against the LORD's command, to do anything good or bad of
my own will? I will say whatever the
LORD says. 14 Now I am going back to
my people, but first, let me warn you
what these people will do to your
people in the future."

Balaam's Fourth Oracle (24:15-25)

15 Then he proclaimed his poem:

The oracle of Balaam
son of Beor,
the oracle of the man
whose eyes are opened;[D]
16 the oracle of one who hears
the sayings of God
and has knowledge
from the •Most High,
who sees a vision
from the Almighty,
who falls into a trance
with his eyes uncovered:
17 I see him,[E] but not now;
I perceive him,[E] but not near.
A star will come from Jacob,
and a scepter will arise
from Israel.
He will smash the forehead[F]
of Moab
and strike down[G]
all the Shethites.[H]
18 Edom will become
a possession;
Seir will become a possession
of its enemies,
but Israel will be triumphant.
19 One who comes from Jacob
will rule;
he will destroy
the city's survivors.

20 Then Balaam saw Amalek and
proclaimed his poem:

Amalek was first
among the nations,
but his future is destruction.

21 Next he saw the Kenites and proclaimed his poem:

Your dwelling place
is enduring;
your nest is set in the cliffs.
22 Kain will be destroyed
when Asshur
takes you captive.

23 Once more he proclaimed his
poem:

Ah, who can live
when God does this?

prophecy concerning how Israel would deal with Balak and his people.

24:15-10 The vision was obviously given by God, and in what seems amazingly ironic, the pagan prophet gave a messianic oracle, speaking of a king who is a **star . . . from Jacob**, whose **scepter will arise from Israel**. Jesus is referenced as the "Bright Morning Star" (Rv 22:16); and, as previously noted, the scepter would not depart from Judah (Gn 49:10), referring to the king who would come from the tribe of Judah, as did Jesus the Messiah. The nations who had treated Israel ruthlessly—the Moabites and Edomites—would be wiped out by this future Israelite King.

24:20-24 Balaam then turned to three other nations—the Amalekites, Kenites, and Asshurites—all of whom had put their trust in their history or geographical location. But because they were enemies of Israel, they, too, would be destroyed.

24:25 After this condemning oracle, Balaam returned home. Balaam's final oracle expressed Israel's hope that there would be a coming king and announced severe warning and judgment for the nations who opposed Israel and her God. The enemies of Israel would be defeated during the reign of David, and Christ will ultimately be the king of all nations.

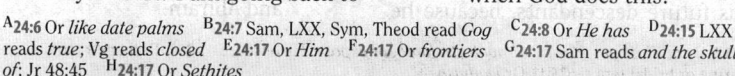

[A]24:6 Or *like date palms* [B]24:7 Sam, LXX, Sym, Theod read *Gog* [C]24:8 Or *He has* [D]24:15 LXX reads *true*; Vg reads *closed* [E]24:17 Or *Him* [F]24:17 Or *frontiers* [G]24:17 Sam reads *and the skulls of*; Jr 48:45 [H]24:17 Or *Sethites*

25:1-3 Chapter 25 contrasts the goodness of God, seen in the oracles of Balaam, with the depravity of humanity evidenced in the sins of Israel. As is clear throughout Scripture, with physical promiscuity comes spiritual promiscuity as well. The Israelites, while in the land of Moab, where both Moabites and Midianites lived (see 22:4), began to commit fornication with the **women of Moab** and joined their worship of **Baal** [the god] **of Peor.** This sin produced estrangement from God. The Israelites committed both physical and spiritual adultery by aligning themselves with and offering sacrifices to an idol. The Lord's wrath ensued.

25:4 Instead of killing the entire community, the Lord told Moses to **execute the leaders of the people**. The leaders represented the people and would thus serve as examples of what happens because of disobedience. Also, the leaders should have better protected and guided the people instead of allowing them to act so treacherously.

25:6-11 This passage focuses specifically on one event that occurred during this time of Israel's idolatry. As punishment for Israel's sin, the Lord sent a plague on the Israelites. While the nation was mourning over its sin and the deaths of its leaders, the ravaging plague spread through the camp. During this time of lamentation, one of the Israelite men blatantly and boldly brought one of the Midianite women to his relatives. Thus, even during supposed repentance, some of the Israelites were still continuing in their sin. **Phinehas**, a priest and grandson of Aaron, did not ignore this arrogant display of wickedness and acted swiftly. The quick succession of verbs (**got up**, **took**, **followed**, **drove**) emphasize the passion with which Phinehas took action. Gruesome as was the death sentence on those committing fornication, Phinehas **turned back** the wrath of God with his actions and the plague was halted. However, the consequences of the Israelites' sin were severe with 24,000 dead. Phinehas's zeal for God was a great example for the Israelites, for he knew the Lord desired holiness from His people.

25:11 The Lord clearly states that Phinehas's **zeal** (Hb *qin'ah*, "ardor, jealousy") was of God and similar to the Lord's jealous zeal as well as like that of a husband protecting his wife. God is a jealous god (Ex 34:14; Dt 4:24; 6:15), and His people had stirred up that jealousy by worshiping other gods. Thus, Phinehas was jealous for the Lord.

25:12-13 His reward was a covenant of peace with the Lord and perpetual priesthood. Because the covenant

24 Ships will come
from the coast of Kittim;
they will afflict Asshur
and Eber,
but they too will come
to destruction.

25 Balaam then arose and went back to his homeland, and Balak also went his way.

The Incident with Baal of Peor (25:1-18)

25 While Israel was staying in the Acacia Grove,[A] the people began to have sexual relations with the women of Moab. 2 The women invited them to the sacrifices for their gods, and the people ate and bowed in worship to their gods. 3 So Israel aligned itself with •Baal of Peor, and the LORD's anger burned against Israel. 4 The LORD said to Moses, "Take all the leaders of the people and execute[B] them in broad daylight before the LORD so that His burning anger may turn away from Israel."

5 So Moses told Israel's judges, "Kill each of the men who aligned themselves with Baal of Peor."

6 An Israelite man came bringing a Midianite woman to his relatives in the sight of Moses and the whole Israelite community while they were weeping at the entrance to the tent of meeting. 7 When Phinehas son of Eleazar, son of Aaron the priest, saw this, he got up from the assembly, took a spear in his hand, 8 followed the Israelite man into the tent,[C] and drove it through both the Israelite man and the woman—through her belly. Then the plague on the Israelites was stopped, 9 but those who died in the plague numbered 24,000.

10 The LORD spoke to Moses, 11 "Phinehas son of Eleazar, son of Aaron the priest, has turned back My wrath from the Israelites because he was zealous among them with My zeal,[D] so that I did not destroy the Israelites in My zeal. 12 Therefore declare: I grant him My covenant of peace. 13 It will be a covenant of perpetual priesthood for him and his future descendants, because he was zealous for his God and made •atonement for the Israelites."

14 The name of the slain Israelite man, who was struck dead with the Midianite woman, was Zimri son of Salu, the leader of a Simeonite ancestral house. 15 The name of the slain Midianite woman was Cozbi, the daughter of Zur, a tribal head of an ancestral house in Midian.

16 The LORD told Moses: 17 "Attack the Midianites and strike them dead. 18 For they attacked you with the treachery that they used against you in the Peor incident. They did the same in the case involving their sister Cozbi, daughter of the Midianite leader who was killed the day the plague came at Peor."

Preparations for Entering the Promised Land (26:1–36:13)

The Second Census (26:1-65)

26 After the plague, the LORD said to Moses and Eleazar son of Aaron the priest, 2 "Take a census of the entire Israelite community by their ancestral houses of those 20 years old or more who can serve in Israel's army." 3 So Moses and Eleazar the priest said to them in the plains of Moab by the Jordan across from Jericho, 4 "Take a census of those 20 years old or more, as the LORD had commanded Moses and the Israelites who came out of the land of Egypt."

5 Reuben was the firstborn
of Israel.
Reuben's descendants:
the Hanochite clan
from Hanoch;
the Palluite clan from Pallu;
6 the Hezronite clan
from Hezron;
the Carmite clan from Carmi.
7 These were
the Reubenite clans,
and their registered men
numbered 43,730.
8 The son of Pallu was Eliab.
9 The sons of Eliab
were Nemuel, Dathan,
and Abiram.

[A]25:1 Or *in Shittim* [B]25:4 Or *impale*, or *hang*, or *expose*; Hb obscure [C]25:8 Perhaps a tent shrine or bridal tent [D]25:11 Or *jealousy*

The Second Census

Tribe	Census One	Census Two	References
Reuben	46,500	43,730	1:20-21; 26:5-11
Simeon	59,300	22,200	1:22-23; 26:12-14
Gad	45,650	40,500	1:24-25; 26:15-18
Judah	74,600	76,500	1:26-27; 26:19-22
Issachar	54,400	64,300	1:28-29; 26:23-25
Zebulun	57,400	60,500	1:30-31; 26:26-27
Manasseh	32,200	52,700	1:34-35; 26:29-34
Ephraim	40,500	32,500	1:32-33; 26:35-37
Benjamin	35,400	45,600	1:36-37; 26:38-41
Dan	62,700	64,400	1:38-39; 26:42-43
Asher	41,500	53,400	1:40-41; 26:44-47
Naphtali	53,400	45,400	1:42-43; 26:48-50
Totals	**603,550**	**601,730**	**1:46; 26:51**

(It was Dathan and Abiram,
chosen by the community,
who fought against Moses
and Aaron; they and Korah's
followers fought against the
LORD. 10 The earth opened
its mouth and swallowed
them with Korah, when his
followers died and the fire
consumed 250 men. They
serve as a warning sign. 11 The
sons of Korah, however, did
not die.)

12 Simeon's descendants
by their clans:
the Nemuelite clan
from Nemuel;[A]
the Jaminite clan from Jamin;
the Jachinite clan
from Jachin;
13 the Zerahite clan from Zerah;
the Shaulite clan from Shaul.
14 These were the
Simeonite clans,
numbering 22,200 men.

15 Gad's descendants
by their clans:
the Zephonite clan
from Zephon;
the Haggite clan from Haggi;
the Shunite clan from Shuni;
16 the Oznite clan from Ozni;
the Erite clan from Eri;
17 the Arodite clan from Arod;
the Arelite clan from Areli.
18 These were the Gadite
clans numbered by their
registered men: 40,500.

19 Judah's sons included Er and
Onan, but they died in the
land of Canaan. 20 Judah's
descendants by their clans:
the Shelanite clan
from Shelah;
the Perezite clan from Perez;
the Zerahite clan from Zerah.
21 The descendants of Perez:
the Hezronite clan
from Hezron;
the Hamulite clan
from Hamul.
22 These were Judah's clans
numbered by their
registered men: 76,500.

is God's, called **My covenant of peace**, Phinehas trusted that God would be faithful and honor this word. With his passion for the Lord and for righteousness, he brought the favor of the Lord upon himself and his entire family. Phinehas was exemplary in his work as a priest, serving as a mediator, acting in behalf of the people before the Lord. Thus, Phinehas's actions also affirmed the words of the Lord, and he and his descendants would be the line of high priests (1Ch 6:4-15).

25:14-15 A brief description of the couple slain by Phinehas is noted; they were both from prominent families. **Zimri** was from the tribe of Simeon; and **Cozbi**, was a daughter of one of the tribal heads in Midian. The swift and just action of Phinehas stopped the plague. By placing these verses last, the deadly effects of sin are emphasized.

25:16-18 This passage foreshadows the conflict that will occur with the Midianites in chapter 31. The Lord's anger against the Midianites arose because of their **treachery,** enticing the Israelites to idolatry. The Lord is a jealous God and will not stand for this; thus, the punishment is severe.

26:1-51 After the plague the Lord ordered a census to be taken. As the first census 38 years before, males 20 years of age and able to serve in the army were counted. The old generation had almost passed away; this census was for the new generation, who would fight to take over the promised land. Moses and Eleazar sent forth the command, and the ancestral tribes each took a count of their descendants. The ordering of the census changed in only one way compared to the first. The tribe of Manasseh is listed first in this census as opposed to its position after Ephraim in the first census. Also, the second census includes the names of the families or clans within the tribes. Twice during the census, Moses stopped to comment on certain people (vv. 9-11,33).

26:9-11 Moses commented on the tribe of Reuben's descendants, **Dathan** and **Abiram**, who rebelled against the Lord and were swallowed by the earth (16:25-33). Their tragedy was to be a reminder, or **warning sign**, to the Israelites.

[A]**26:12** Syr reads *Jemuel* (Gn 46:10; Ex 6:15); 1Ch 4:24 reads *Nemuel*

26:33 Moses also commented on **Zelophehad**, a descendant of the tribe of Manasseh. Zelophehad bore no sons; his daughters are then listed. This statement points to what will occur in the next chapter regarding land inheritance in the promised land. Will daughters be allowed to have their father's inheritance passed to them?

26:52-56 With the second census complete, the Lord gave Moses further instructions. According to the size of each tribe, the portion of land to be inherited after entrance to the promised land is established. The formula was a simple one—smaller tribes would receive a smaller and bigger tribes a larger allotment of land. Thus, the reason for the second census was ordered as part of the preparation for entry into the promised land.

26:57-65 The **Levites** were also counted, even though they would receive no inheritance of land. Thus, the Levites are excluded from the main census but counted nonetheless. The number of Levites had increased by 1,000 from the time of the first census to reach 23,000 (v. 62; 3:39). The rationale behind providing the ancestry of Moses, Aaron, and Miriam is most likely to establish that Moses and Aaron were Kohathite Levites, entitling them to the privileges of the priesthood. The words of the Lord have again proven true as the punishment for the Israelites' unfaithfulness was fulfilled. Numbers 14:26-35 describes the actions of God because of the Israelites' rebellion. The Lord said those 20 and older would fall in the wilderness except Joshua and Caleb, who had remained true. Thus, the Lord's word came to fruition; the sentence was carried out; and faithful **Joshua** and **Caleb** stood firm.

23 Issachar's descendants
by their clans:
the Tolaite clan from Tola;
the Punite clan from Puvah;[A]
24 the Jashubite clan
from Jashub;
the Shimronite clan
from Shimron.
25 These were Issachar's
clans numbered by their
registered men: 64,300.

26 Zebulun's descendants
by their clans:
the Seredite clan from Sered;
the Elonite clan from Elon;
the Jahleelite clan
from Jahleel.
27 These were the Zebulunite
clans numbered by their
registered men: 60,500.

28 Joseph's descendants
by their clans
from Manasseh
and Ephraim:
29 Manasseh's descendants:
the Machirite clan
from Machir.
Machir fathered Gilead;
the Gileadite clan
from Gilead.
30 These were
Gilead's descendants:
the Iezerite clan from Iezer;
the Helekite clan from Helek;
31 the Asrielite clan from Asriel;
the Shechemite clan
from Shechem;
32 the Shemidaite clan
from Shemida;
the Hepherite clan
from Hepher;
33 Zelophehad son of Hepher
had no sons—only daughters.
The names of Zelophehad's
daughters were Mahlah,
Noah, Hoglah, Milcah, and
Tirzah.
34 These were Manasseh's
clans, numbered by their
registered men: 52,700.
35 These were Ephraim's
descendants by their clans:
the Shuthelahite clan
from Shuthelah;
the Becherite clan
from Becher;
the Tahanite clan from Tahan.
36 These were
Shuthelah's descendants:
the Eranite clan from Eran.
37 These were the Ephraimite
clans numbered by their
registered men: 32,500.
These were Joseph's
descendants by their clans.

38 Benjamin's descendants
by their clans:
the Belaite clan from Bela;
the Ashbelite clan
from Ashbel;
the Ahiramite clan
from Ahiram;
39 the Shuphamite clan
from Shupham;[B]
the Huphamite clan
from Hupham.
40 Bela's descendants from Ard
and Naaman:
the Ardite clan from Ard;
the Naamite clan
from Naaman.
41 These were the Benjaminite
clans numbered by their
registered men: 45,600.

42 These were Dan's descendants
by their clans:
the Shuhamite clan
from Shuham.
These were the clans of Dan
by their clans.
43 All the Shuhamite clans
numbered by their
registered men: 64,400.
44 Asher's descendants
by their clans:
the Imnite clan from Imnah;
the Ishvite clan from Ishvi;
the Beriite clan from Beriah.
45 From Beriah's descendants:
the Heberite clan from Heber;
the Malchielite clan
from Malchiel.
46 And the name
of Asher's daughter
was Serah.
47 These were the Asherite
clans numbered by their
registered men: 53,400.
48 Naphtali's descendants
by their clans:

[A]26:23 Sam, LXX, Vg, Syr read *Puite clan from Puah*; 1Ch 7:1 [B]26:39 Some Hb mss, Sam, LXX, Syr, Tg, Vg; other Hb mss read *Shephupham*

CHARACTER PROFILE

Daughters of Zelophehad "Faithful Daughters"

Their Background	• Five sisters: Mahlah, Noah, Hoglah, Milcah, and Tirzah (Nm 26:33; 27:1; 36:11) • The daughters of Zelophehad, the son of Hepher • Residents of Manasseh's tract of land (27:1,7; Jos 17:3-6)
Their Story	• They asked to receive the land inheritance of their father. • God granted their request (27:4-11). • They were given the right to choose their own husbands (36:6).
Life Lessons	• The women claimed their legal right. • They acted in a respectful and appropriate manner.

the Jahzeelite clan
from Jahzeel;
the Gunite clan from Guni;
49 the Jezerite clan from Jezer;
the Shillemite clan
from Shillem.
50 These were the Naphtali
clans numbered by their
registered men: 45,400.
51 These registered Israelite men
numbered 601,730.

52 The LORD spoke to Moses, 53 "The
land is to be divided among them as
an inheritance based on the number
of names. 54 Increase the inheritance
for a large tribe and decrease it for
a small one. Each is to be given its
inheritance according to those who
were registered in it. 55 The land must
be divided by lot; they will receive an
inheritance according to the names
of their ancestral tribes. 56 Each
inheritance will be divided by lot
among the larger and smaller tribes."

57 These were the Levites
registered by their clans:
the Gershonite clan
from Gershon;
the Kohathite clan
from Kohath;
the Merarite clan
from Merari.
58 These were the Levite family
groups:
the Libnite clan,
the Hebronite clan,
the Mahlite clan,
the Mushite clan,
and the Korahite clan.

Kohath was the ancestor of Amram. 59 The name of Amram's wife
was Jochebed, a descendant of Levi,
born to Levi in Egypt. She bore to
Amram: Aaron, Moses, and their sister Miriam. 60 Nadab, Abihu, Eleazar,
and Ithamar were born to Aaron,
61 but Nadab and Abihu died when
they presented unauthorized fire
before the LORD. 62 Those registered
were 23,000, every male one month
old or more; they were not registered among the other Israelites,
because no inheritance was given to
them among the Israelites.

63 These were the ones registered
by Moses and Eleazar the priest
when they registered the Israelites
on the plains of Moab by the Jordan
across from Jericho. 64 But among
them there was not one of those
who had been registered by Moses
and Aaron the priest when they
registered the Israelites in the Wilderness of Sinai. 65 For the LORD had
said to them that they would all die
in the wilderness. None of them was
left except Caleb son of Jephunneh
and Joshua son of Nun.

The Case of Daughters' Inheritance (27:1-11)

27 The daughters of Zelophehad
approached; Zelophehad was
the son of Hepher, son of Gilead,
son of Machir, son of Manasseh from
the clans of Manasseh, the son of Joseph. These were the names of his
daughters: Mahlah, Noah, Hoglah,
Milcah, and Tirzah. 2 They stood before Moses, Eleazar the priest, the
leaders, and the entire community
at the entrance to the tent of meeting and said, 3 "Our father died in the
wilderness, but he was not among

27:1-7 After the registration and instructions concerning distribution of the promised land was given, there was one minor oversight. One of the clans from the tribe of **Manasseh** had not been included in the **inheritance** because **Zelophehad**, the father and leader of the clan, had only **daughters**. In Israel's patriarchal system, only sons would inherit their father's land. The male heirs, however, were mandated to support the women in the family. Women had the responsibility of creating families by bearing and nurturing children, which could best be done in a stable and secure environment provided by the husband and father. Both roles were critically important and thus regulated by law. In some ways daughters were better off than sons since through the dowry they received their interest in the father's estate at the beginning of their married life. The text gives full attention to this case concerning the daughters of Zelophehad and recognizes each of these women by name (cp. 26:33; 36:11).

27:2-4 Concerned about continuing the family **name**, the daughters of Zelophehad rightly subjected their petition to the authority of **Moses, Eleazar the priest, the leaders, and the entire community**. Their case was twofold. One, Zelophehad was not part of the rebellion of Korah but rather died in the wilderness due **to his own sin.** Two, Zelophehad had no sons, and thus his clan would be wiped out by virtue of his untimely death, receiving no inheritance in the promised land. Not only would the clan of Zelophehad be forgotten, but the tribe of Manasseh would be diminished.

27:5-11 Moses took the case of Zelophehad's daughters before the ultimate judge, **the LORD**, and God agreed with Zelophehad's daughters. Thus, the procedure for **inheritance** rights was changed so that the property of a man who dies without having a son is legally transferred to his daughter. Only if he has no daughter would the inheritance be given to the father's brothers and then closest relatives. The provision of inheritance for the daughters was a gracious way the Lord provided for and protected them, while at the same time caring and giving full strength to the Israelite nation, ensuring no tribe would be diminished if only daughters were born to a man (cp. 36:1-13).

27:12-13 Because of Moses' disobedience and selfishness (ch. 20), he would not be permitted to enter the promised land; but the Lord was gracious and would show Moses the land before he died. He would be told to go up to the mountain range of **Abarim** and Mount Nebo in particular (Dt 32:49).

27:14 The Lord reminded Moses of the quarrel at **Meribah** and the consequences of his disobedience. Throughout Scripture often God gives reasons for His actions even when He does not have to do so. When His children are being punished, He wants them to know why.

27:15-17 Moses' love and concern for the Israelites' spiritual well-being was again brought to the forefront as his request to the Lord was not for his life but for a shepherd over the people. The appeal was made to Yahweh as a personal God and as the sovereign, creator God, **the God of the spirits of all flesh**. As the Lord had delivered His people out of Egypt and guided them through the wilderness, so the Israelites would need a human shepherd in the absence of Moses. Thus, the focus of the passage is not on the death of Moses, which does not occur until later (Dt 34:5), but on the need for the future leadership of Israel.

27:18-21 Immediately, the Lord revealed the man whom He had called for this overwhelming task—**Joshua**, Moses' friend and co-laborer. Joshua showed himself capable and faithful throughout the book of Numbers, being one of two spies left to live and enter the promised land. Joshua recognized the holiness of God as well as His faithfulness. The most important matter, however, was that the Spirit of the living God was in Joshua. The Lord says Joshua had **the Spirit in him**; therefore, God's Spirit had been upon Joshua and was not just imparted now. God's call upon Joshua's life was clearly evident, as should the case be

Korah's followers, who gathered together against the LORD. Instead, he died because of his own sin, and he had no sons. 4 Why should the name of our father be taken away from his clan? Since he had no son, give us property among our father's brothers."

5 Moses brought their case before the LORD, 6 and the LORD answered him, 7 "What Zelophehad's daughters say is correct. You are to give them hereditary property among their father's brothers and transfer their father's inheritance to them. 8 Tell the Israelites: When a man dies without having a son, transfer his inheritance to his daughter. 9 If he has no daughter, give his inheritance to his brothers. 10 If he has no brothers, give his inheritance to his father's brothers. 11 If his father has no brothers, give his inheritance to the nearest relative of his clan, and he will take possession of it. This is to be a statutory ordinance for the Israelites as the LORD commanded Moses."

Joshua's Commission to Succeed Moses (27:12-23)

12 Then the LORD said to Moses, "Go up this mountain of the Abarim range[A] and see the land that I have given the Israelites. 13 After you have seen it, you will also be gathered to your people, as Aaron your brother was. 14 When the community quarreled in the Wilderness of Zin, both of you rebelled against My command to show My holiness in their sight at the waters." Those were the waters of Meribah[B] of Kadesh in the Wilderness of Zin.

15 So Moses appealed to the LORD, 16 "May the LORD, the God of the spirits of all flesh, appoint a man over the community 17 who will go out before them and come back in before them, and who will bring them out and bring them in, so that the LORD's community won't be like sheep without a shepherd."

18 The LORD replied to Moses, "Take Joshua son of Nun, a man who has the Spirit in him, and lay your hands on him. 19 Have him stand before Eleazar the priest and the whole community, and commission him in their sight. 20 Confer some of your authority on him so that the entire Israelite community will obey him. 21 He will stand before Eleazar who will consult the LORD for him with the decision of the •Urim. He and all the Israelites with him, even the entire community, will go out and come back in at his command."

22 Moses did as the LORD commanded him. He took Joshua, had him stand before Eleazar the priest and the entire community, 23 laid his hands on him, and commissioned him, as the LORD had spoken through Moses.

Prescribed Offerings (28:1-3a)

28 The LORD spoke to Moses, 2 "Command the Israelites and say to them: Be sure to present to Me at its appointed time My offering and My food as My fire offering, a pleasing aroma to Me. 3 And say to them: This is the fire offering you are to present to the LORD:

Daily Offerings (28:3b-8)

"Each day present two unblemished year-old male lambs as a regular •burnt offering. 4 Offer one lamb in the morning and the other lamb at twilight, 5 along with two quarts[C] of fine flour for a •grain offering mixed with a quart[D] of olive oil from crushed olives. 6 It is a regular burnt offering established at Mount Sinai for a pleasing aroma, a fire offering to the LORD. 7 The •drink offering is to be a quart[D] with each lamb. Pour out the offering of beer to the LORD in the sanctuary area. 8 Offer the second lamb at twilight, along with the same kind of grain offering and drink offering as in the morning. It is a fire offering, a pleasing aroma to the LORD.

Sabbath Offerings (28:9-10)

9 "On the Sabbath day present two unblemished year-old male lambs, four quarts[E] of fine flour mixed with oil as a grain offering, and its drink offering. 10 It is the burnt offering for every Sabbath, in addition to the

[A]**27:12** = Mount Nebo; Nm 33:47-48; Dt 32:49; Jr 22:20 [B]**27:14** = quarreling [C]**28:5** Lit *one-tenth of an ephah* [D]**28:5,7** Lit *a fourth of a hin* [E]**28:9** Lit *two-tenths* (of an ephah)

regular burnt offering and its drink offering.

Monthly Offerings (28:11-15)

11 “At the beginning of each of your months present a burnt offering to the LORD: two young bulls, one ram, seven male lambs a year old—all unblemished— 12 with six quarts[A] of fine flour mixed with oil as a grain offering for each bull, four quarts[B] of fine flour mixed with oil as a grain offering for the ram, 13 and two quarts[C] of fine flour mixed with oil as a grain offering for each lamb. It is a burnt offering, a pleasing aroma, a fire offering to the LORD. 14 Their drink offerings are to be two quarts[D] of wine with each bull, one and a third quarts[E] with the ram, and one quart[F] with each male lamb. This is the monthly burnt offering for all the months of the year. 15 And one male goat is to be offered as a •sin offering to the LORD, in addition to the regular burnt offering with its drink offering.

Offerings for Passover (28:16-25)

16 “The •Passover to the LORD comes in the first month, on the fourteenth day of the month. 17 On the fifteenth day of this month there will be a festival; unleavened bread is to be eaten for seven days. 18 On the first day there is to be a sacred assembly; you are not to do any daily work. 19 Present a fire offering, a burnt offering to the LORD: two young bulls, one ram, and seven male lambs a year old. Your animals are to be unblemished. 20 The grain offering with them is to be of fine flour mixed with oil; offer six quarts[A] with each bull and four quarts[B] with the ram. 21 Offer two quarts[C] with each of the seven lambs 22 and one male goat for a sin offering to make •atonement for yourselves. 23 Offer these with the morning burnt offering that is part of the regular burnt offering. 24 You are to offer the same food each day for seven days as a fire offering, a pleasing aroma to the LORD. It is to be offered with its drink offering and the regular burnt offering. 25 On the seventh day you are to hold a sacred assembly; you are not to do any daily work.

Offerings for the Festival of Weeks (28:26-31)

26 “On the day of •firstfruits, you are to hold a sacred assembly when you present an offering of new grain to the LORD at your Festival of Weeks; you are not to do any daily work. 27 Present a burnt offering for a pleasing aroma to the LORD: two young bulls, one ram, and seven male lambs a year old, 28 with their grain offering of fine flour mixed with oil, six quarts[A] with each bull, four quarts[B] with the ram, 29 and two quarts[C] with each of the seven lambs, 30 and one male goat to make atonement for yourselves. 31 Offer them with their drink offerings in addition to the regular burnt offering and its grain offering. Your animals are to be unblemished.

Offerings for the Festival of Trumpets (29:1-6)

29 “You are to hold a sacred assembly in the seventh month, on the first day of the month, and you are not to do any daily work. This will be a day of joyful shouting[G] for you. 2 Offer a •burnt offering as a pleasing aroma to the LORD: one young bull, one ram, seven male lambs a year old—all unblemished— 3 with their •grain offering of fine flour mixed with oil, six quarts[A] with the bull, four quarts[B] with the ram, 4 and two quarts[C] with each of the seven male lambs. 5 Also offer one male goat as a •sin offering to make •atonement for yourselves. 6 These are in addition to the monthly and regular burnt offerings with their prescribed grain offerings and •drink offerings. They are a pleasing aroma, a fire offering to the LORD.

Offerings for the Day of Atonement (29:7-11)

7 “You are to hold a sacred assembly on the tenth day of this seventh month and practice self-denial;[H] you must not do any work. 8 Present a burnt offering to the LORD, a

[A] **28:12,20,28; 29:3** Lit *three-tenths* (of an ephah) [B] **28:12,20,28; 29:3** Lit *two-tenths* (of an ephah) [C] **28:13,21,29; 29:4** Lit *one-tenth* (of an ephah) [D] **28:14** Lit *a half hin* [E] **28:14** Lit *bull, a third hin* [F] **28:14** Lit *a fourth hin* [G] **29:1** Or *blast*; traditionally, *trumpet blasts* [H] **29:7** Traditionally, fasting, abstinence from sex, and refraining from personal grooming

for all shepherds of the Lord's flock. The Lord then gave Moses directions on how the transfer of leadership was to occur, as this was no small matter and one requiring great ceremony. First, Moses would lay his hands upon Joshua, a sign of blessing and conferral. Second, Moses was to bring Joshua before **Eleazar**, the priest, and **the entire Israelite community**. Moses would grant Joshua his authority, but Eleazar would also consult the **Urim**, which were used to determine the will of God. Both of these actions would be abundant evidence of Joshua's established leadership for the Israelite community.

28:1–29:40 The Lord again gave Moses instructions, this time concerning offerings.

28:16 One difference in the **Passover** as compared to the other celebrations is that most of the Passover was actually celebrated in the households of Israel and not at the tent of meeting. Thus, the celebration of Passover helped the Israelites to remember not only the leadership of the Lord in their exodus from Egypt but also the importance of family. The foods used during the celebration (Ex 12:8) were the Passover lamb, unleavened bread, and bitter herbs. In the New Testament Christ is often referred to as the Passover Lamb or as the Passover (1Co 5:7).

28:26 The **Festival of Weeks**, also known as the Feast of Harvest (lit "Day of Firstfruits"), in which the Israelites offer the firstfruits of their crops, is a thanksgiving offering for God's provision of food and abundance. The Israelites, just as Christians today, are to recognize everything they have as coming from the Lord. This day is also to be a day of rest for the Israelites, which was most likely well-deserved and needed after much hard labor.

29:1 The third, fourth, and fifth major offerings are held in the seventh month. On the first day of the seventh month is the celebration of **joyful shouting** (Hb, lit "blowing of trumpets"). Not only will trumpets be blown, as is customary for all of the days of celebration, but the day of jubilation is set aside specifically for rest and commemoration (Lv 23:23-24).

29:7 The Day of Atonement is a sacred day in the **seventh month** on the **tenth day** and is one that draws attention to the sins of Israel and the forgiveness of God. On that day atonement will be made for the Israelites to cleanse them from their sins before the Lord (Lv 16:30). Unlike the rest of the offering days, this one is different in that the Israelites are to **practice self-denial**, meaning fasting from food and most likely refraining from sexual intimacy as well as work. Christians, too, have a Day of Atonement, on which with repentance they confessed their sins to Jesus Christ, accepting His sacrifice upon the cross to forgive them of their sin, becoming true sons and daughters of God.

29:12 The Festival of Booths, or Festival of Tabernacles, was the longest of the offerings, lasting over seven days. More offerings were made during this time than any other. The festival was held to commemorate the wilderness wandering and to set their thoughts upon the Lord, who brought them out of Egypt (Lv 23:43). During this week the Israelites would live in booths or tents, and on the first day they would begin for the whole week to worship the Lord with tree branches (see Lv 23:39-44). All of the offerings centered around the Lord and what He had done for the Israelites. In addition, the offerings helped the Israelites set their calendar, and they are clearly presented in addition to their regular offerings.

30:1-16 Chapter 30 provides an excellent example of God's protection of women in His laws. The Lord set up a patriarchal society in Gn 1 and continued to affirm His creation order. These laws concerning vows were addressed specifically to **the leaders of the Israelite tribes** (cp. 1Kg 8:1-2; 2Ch 5:2). The exception clauses concerning the vows of women were not meant to belittle or oppress women but rather to encourage fathers and husbands to provide, protect, and lead the women in their respective families and to be careful with their words. The regulations recognized that both men and women took vows. The laws also upheld the serious nature of both a woman's word and a man's acceptance of responsibility for others—his tacit approval of the vow of his wife or daughter obligated him to the fulfillment of that vow as well. The parents of the prophet Samuel exemplify a wife's freedom to make a vow and the husband's responsibility in allowing the vow to stand. Hannah committed to the Lord the son He gave her in answer to prayer, and her husband Elkanah permitted her to entrust Samuel, after he was weaned, to Eli the priest as she had promised the Lord (1Sm 1:17-28).

Because the commitments of a woman living within a family inevitably affected the rest of the family, the one who bore the greatest responsibility for the welfare of the entire family (i.e., the father or husband) not only had to consider carefully his own vows but also had to consent to the vows of those for whom he was responsible. These laws protected households from the effects of a rash vow or a commitment made under duress. For example, the

pleasing aroma: one young bull, one ram, and seven male lambs a year old. All your animals are to be unblemished. 9 Their grain offering is to be of fine flour mixed with oil, six quarts[A] with the bull, four quarts[B] with the ram, 10 and two quarts[C] with each of the seven lambs. 11 Offer one male goat for a sin offering. The regular burnt offering with its grain offering and drink offerings are in addition to the sin offering of atonement.

Offerings for the Festival of Booths (29:12-40)

12 "You are to hold a sacred assembly on the fifteenth day of the seventh month; you must not do any daily work. You are to celebrate a seven-day festival for the LORD. 13 Present a burnt offering, a fire offering as a pleasing aroma to the LORD: 13 young bulls, two rams, and 14 male lambs a year old. They are to be unblemished. 14 Their grain offering is to be of fine flour mixed with oil, six quarts[A] with each of the 13 bulls, four quarts[B] with each of the two rams, 15 and two quarts[C] with each of the 14 lambs. 16 Also offer one male goat as a sin offering. These are in addition to the regular burnt offering with its grain and drink offerings.

17 "On the second day present 12 young bulls, two rams, and 14 male lambs a year old—all unblemished— 18 with their grain and drink offerings for the bulls, rams, and lambs, in proportion to their number. 19 Also offer one male goat as a sin offering. These are in addition to the regular burnt offering with its grain and drink[D] offerings.

20 "On the third day present 11 bulls, two rams, 14 male lambs a year old—all unblemished— 21 with their grain and drink offerings for the bulls, rams, and lambs, in proportion to their number. 22 Also offer one male goat as a sin offering. These are in addition to the regular burnt offering with its grain and drink offerings.

23 "On the fourth day present 10 bulls, two rams, 14 male lambs a year old—all unblemished— 24 with their grain and drink offerings for the bulls, rams, and lambs, in proportion to their number. 25 Also offer one male goat as a sin offering. These are in addition to the regular burnt offering with its grain and drink offerings.

26 "On the fifth day present nine bulls, two rams, 14 male lambs a year old—all unblemished— 27 with their grain and drink offerings for the bulls, rams, and lambs, in proportion to their number. 28 Also offer one male goat as a sin offering. These are in addition to the regular burnt offering with its grain and drink offerings.

29 "On the sixth day present eight bulls, two rams, 14 male lambs a year old—all unblemished— 30 with their grain and drink offerings for the bulls, rams, and lambs, in proportion to their number. 31 Also offer one male goat as a sin offering. These are in addition to the regular burnt offering with its grain and drink[E] offerings.

32 "On the seventh day present seven bulls, two rams, and 14 male lambs a year old—all unblemished— 33 with their grain and drink offerings for the bulls, rams, and lambs, in proportion to their number. 34 Also offer one male goat as a sin offering. These are in addition to the regular burnt offering with its grain and drink offerings.

35 "On the eighth day you are to hold a solemn assembly; you are not to do any daily work. 36 Present a burnt offering, a fire offering as a pleasing aroma to the LORD: one bull, one ram, seven male lambs a year old—all unblemished— 37 with their grain and drink offerings for the bull, rams, and lambs, in proportion to their number. 38 Also offer one male goat as a sin offering. These are in addition to the regular burnt offering with its grain and drink offerings.

39 "You must offer these to the LORD at your appointed times in addition to your vow and freewill offerings, whether burnt, grain, drink, or

[A]**29:9,14** Lit *three-tenths* (of an ephah) [B]**29:9,14** Lit *two-tenths* (of an ephah) [C]**29:10,15** Lit *one-tenth* (of an ephah) [D]**29:19** Some Hb mss, Syr, Vg, Sam; other Hb mss, LXX read *and their drink* [E]**29:31** Some Hb mss, Syr, Tg, Vg; other Hb mss, Sam read *and their drink*

•fellowship offerings." 40[A]So Moses told the Israelites everything the LORD had commanded him.

Regulations About Vows (30:1-16)

30 Moses told the leaders of the Israelite tribes, "This is what the LORD has commanded: 2 When a man makes a vow to the LORD or swears an oath to put himself under an obligation, he must not break his word; he must do whatever he has promised.

3 "When a woman in her father's house during her youth makes a vow to the LORD or puts herself under an obligation, 4 and her father hears about her vow or the obligation she put herself under, and he says nothing to her, all her vows and every obligation she put herself under are binding. 5 But if her father prohibits her on the day he hears about it, none of her vows and none of the obligations she put herself under are binding. The LORD will absolve her because her father has prohibited her.

6 "If a woman marries while her vows or the rash commitment she herself made are binding, 7 and her husband hears about it and says nothing to her when he finds out, her vows are binding, and the obligations she put herself under are binding. 8 But if her husband prohibits her when he hears about it, he will cancel her vow that is binding or the rash commitment she herself made, and the LORD will forgive her.

9 "Every vow a widow or divorced woman puts herself under is binding on her.

10 "If a woman in her husband's house has made a vow or put herself under an obligation with an oath, 11 and her husband hears about it, says nothing to her, and does not prohibit her, all her vows are binding, and every obligation she put herself under is binding. 12 But if her husband cancels them on the day he hears about it, nothing that came from her lips, whether her vows or her obligation, is binding. Her husband has canceled them, and the LORD will absolve her. 13 Her husband may confirm or cancel any vow or any sworn obligation to deny herself. 14 If her husband says nothing at all to her from day to day, he confirms all her vows and obligations, which are binding. He has confirmed them because he said nothing to her when he heard about them. 15 But if he cancels them after he hears about them, he will be responsible for her[B] commitment."[C]

16 These are the statutes that the LORD commanded Moses concerning the relationship between a man and his wife, or between a father and his daughter in his house during her youth.

War with Midian (31:1-54)

31 The LORD spoke to Moses, 2 "Execute vengeance for the Israelites against the Midianites. After that, you will be gathered to your people."

3 So Moses spoke to the people, "Equip some of your men for war. They will go against Midian to inflict the LORD's vengeance on them. 4 Send 1,000 men to war from each Israelite tribe." 5 So 1,000 were recruited from each Israelite tribe out of the thousands[D] in Israel—12,000 equipped for war. 6 Moses sent 1,000 from each tribe to war. They went with Phinehas son of Eleazar the priest, in whose care were the holy objects and signal trumpets.

7 They waged war against Midian, as the LORD had commanded Moses, and killed every male. 8 Along with the others slain by them, they killed the Midianite kings—Evi, Rekem, Zur, Hur, and Reba, the five kings of Midian. They also killed Balaam son of Beor with the sword. 9 The Israelites took the Midianite women and their children captive, and they plundered all their cattle, flocks, and property. 10 Then they burned all the cities where the Midianites lived, as well as all their encampments, 11 and took away all the spoils of war and the captives, both man and beast. 12 They brought the prisoners, animals, and spoils of war to Moses, Eleazar the priest, and the Israelite community at the camp on the

vow of a daughter could obligate her father, or a wife's vow her husband, in a way that would bring harm to the family's livelihood or name. These rules legally allowed the father or husband to cancel such obligations. However, the right of the husband or father to overrule the commitment of a wife or daughter was potentially the woman's glad release from over-commitment or from a promise reflecting the priority of personal relationships over measured words and careful consideration.

Making a **vow** (Hb *neder)* is an act of commitment, a promise or willing self-obligation to a future action. While a man had to keep a vow he had made to the Lord or to another person, the vow of a woman living in a household under male leadership could be rescinded under certain conditions:

- A **father** could prohibit his unmarried daughter's vow while she was still in his house (vv. 3-5).
- If a **husband** who is newly married to his wife **prohibits** (Hb *mu'*, "refuse, forbid, disallow," in a legal sense; cp. 32:7,9; Ps 33:10) her vow that is **binding** (Hb *'asar 'al-nephesh*, lit "bind one's soul," Nm 30:6-8) or her **rash commitment** (Hb *mibta'*, "something uttered rashly" from her *saphah*, "lips," suggesting a commitment made thoughtlessly and possibly incurring guilt; cp. Lv 5:4), then she is released from her obligation. The law in such cases might liberate the marriage from a burdensome obligation made before the man assumed responsibility for his bride.
- A **husband** who has been married to a woman for a while can **cancel** her vow on the day he hears about it; but if he waited, the commitment became his responsibility (Nm 30:10-15).

30:9 The only woman who had to keep her vows was **a widow or divorced woman** because she would not be living under the leadership and protection of a father or husband who could overrule her commitment. Having made the vow independently, she had no recourse other than keeping it. Ultimately, the Lord was reaffirming and upholding His design for the family with these statutes.

31:1-12 Moses' last act before dying was to exact vengeance upon the **Midianites** for the trouble caused at Baal of Peor. The Israelites had greatly sinned against God, committing idolatry and fornication (see chap. 25). Phinehas led the army, as was his priestly duty, though he would not fight, along with 12,000 Israelites—1,000 men from each tribe. Zealous Phinehas was the perfect one to lead the Israelites out in battle as he was the one who helped turn the

[A]**29:40** Nm 30:1 in Hb [B]**30:15** Sam, LXX, some Syr mss read *his* [C]**30:15** Or *will bear her guilt* [D]**31:5** Or *clans*

tide of disobedience and turn back the anger of God. The victory was decisive, with the putting to death of the Midianite kings, along with Balaam, who was responsible for stirring the Israelites to disobedience in the incident. Interestingly, the warriors killed all the men but left alive the Midianite women, who actually seduced the Israelite men.

31:13-18 In what could have been a celebratory scene, the triumphant return of the fighters being met by Moses and Eleazar quickly turned into a confrontation and rebuke. Moses was indignant that the men would let those who had turned the hearts of the Israelites away from God live. To bring the women back was to invite temptation into the heart of the Israelite camp. Thus, the army was told to kill every woman who was not a virgin along with every male child, but the virgins were allowed to live.

31:19-24 Moses further reminded the Israelites that they were to be set apart as he gave directions concerning their purification and the cleanness of the camp. Obviously, in battle the men had touched many corpses and therefore had to go through the purification ritual (cp. 19:1-22). The spoils brought back from Midian were also to be cleaned. Eleazar, the priest, gave these commands to the army. Both fire and water—purifying elements—were to be used as appropriate for the items returned. Only after the men had cleansed themselves and their spoils could they reenter the camp (see 19:11-13). Thus, the Lord first required the Israelites to be clean internally and then externally. The men's hearts were in the wrong place when they let the temptresses live, and thus they had to get their hearts right. Then, physically they needed to be clean as well to rejoin those holy and set apart by God.

31:25-47 This passage details the distribution of the plunder of Midian. The spoils were divided in half, with half going to the troops and the other half to the community. A tribute to the Lord for the priests was then taken from the fighting men, **one out of every** 500 of the spoils, including humans and animals, which came to 0.2 percent. However, the portion taken from the Israelites who did not go to war for the Levites was larger. One out of every 50 men and animals were to go to the Levites, which came to 2 percent. Moses and Eleazar dutifully carry out the Lord's command, and the 675,000 sheep and goats, 72,000 cattle, 61,000 donkeys, and 32,000 people were divided in half and the tributes offered to the Lord, together with the priests and Levites.

plains of Moab by the Jordan across
from Jericho.
13 Moses, Eleazar the priest, and
all the leaders of the community
went to meet them outside the
camp. 14 But Moses became furious
with the officers, the commanders
of thousands and commanders of
hundreds, who were returning from
the military campaign. 15 "Have[A]
you let every female live?" he asked
them. 16 "Yet they are the ones who,
at Balaam's advice, incited the Israelites to unfaithfulness against the
LORD in the Peor incident, so that
the plague came against the LORD's
community. 17 So now, kill all the
male children and kill every woman
who has had sexual relations with a
man, 18 but keep alive for yourselves
all the young females who have not
had sexual relations.
19 "You are to remain outside the
camp for seven days. All of you and
your prisoners who have killed a
person or touched the dead are to
purify yourselves on the third day
and the seventh day. 20 Also purify everything: garments, leather
goods, things made of goat hair, and
every article of wood."
21 Then Eleazar the priest said to
the soldiers who had gone to battle,
"This is the legal statute the LORD
commanded Moses: 22 Only the gold,
silver, bronze, iron, tin, and lead—
23 everything that can withstand
fire—you are to pass through fire,
and it will be •clean. It must still be
purified with the purification water.
Anything that cannot withstand fire,
pass through the water. 24 On the
seventh day wash your clothes, and
you will be clean. After that you may
enter the camp."
25 The LORD told Moses, 26 "You, Eleazar the priest, and the family leaders of the community are to take a
count of what was captured, man
and beast. 27 Then divide the captives
between the troops who went out
to war and the entire community.
28 Set aside a tribute for the LORD
from what belongs to the fighting
men who went out to war: one out
of every 500 humans, cattle, donkeys, sheep, and goats. 29 Take the
tribute from their half and give it to
Eleazar the priest as a contribution
to the LORD. 30 From the Israelites'
half, take one out of every 50 from
the people, cattle, donkeys, sheep,
and goats, all the livestock, and give
them to the Levites who perform the
duties of[B] the LORD's tabernacle."
31 So Moses and Eleazar the priest
did as the LORD commanded Moses.
32 The captives remaining from the
plunder the army had taken totaled:

675,000 sheep and goats,
33 72,000 cattle,
34 61,000 donkeys,
35 and 32,000 people,
all the females
who had not had
sexual relations with a man.

36 The half portion for those who
went out to war numbered:

337,500 sheep and goats,
37 and the tribute to the LORD
was 675
from the sheep and goats;
38 from the 36,000 cattle,
the tribute to the LORD
was 72;
39 from the 30,500 donkeys,
the tribute to the LORD
was 61;
40 and from the 16,000 people,
the tribute to the LORD
was 32 people.

41 Moses gave the tribute to Eleazar
the priest as a contribution for the
LORD, as the LORD had commanded
Moses.
42 From the Israelites' half, which
Moses separated from the men who
fought, 43 the community's half was:

337,500 sheep and goats,
44 36,000 cattle,
45 30,500 donkeys,
46 and 16,000 people.

47 Moses took one out of every 50, selected from the people and the livestock of the Israelites' half. He gave
them to the Levites who perform the
duties of the LORD's tabernacle, as
the LORD had commanded him.
48 The officers who were over the
thousands of the army, the commanders of thousands and of hundreds, approached Moses 49 and told

[A]31:15 Sam, LXX, Syr, Vg read *Why have* [B]31:30 Or *who protect*

him, "Your servants have taken a
census of the fighting men under
our command, and not one of us
is missing. 50 So we have presented
to the LORD an offering of the gold
articles each man found—armlets,
bracelets, rings, earrings, and necklaces—to make •atonement for ourselves before the LORD."
51 Moses and Eleazar the priest
received from them all the articles
made out of gold. 52 All the gold of
the contribution they offered to
the LORD, from the commanders of
thousands and of hundreds, was 420
pounds.[A] 53 Each of the soldiers had
taken plunder for himself. 54 Moses
and Eleazar the priest received the
gold from the commanders of thousands and of hundreds and brought
it into the tent of meeting as a memorial for the Israelites before the
LORD.

Transjordan Settlements (32:1-42)

32 The Reubenites and Gadites
had a very large number of
livestock. When they surveyed the
lands of Jazer and Gilead, they saw
that the region was a good one for
livestock. 2 So the Gadites and Reubenites came to Moses, Eleazar the
priest, and the leaders of the community and said: 3 "The territory
of Ataroth, Dibon, Jazer, Nimrah,
Heshbon, Elealeh, Sebam,[B] Nebo,
and Beon, 4 which the LORD struck
down before the community of Israel, is good land for livestock, and
your servants own livestock." 5 They
said, "If we have found favor in your
sight, let this land be given to your
servants as a possession. Don't make
us cross the Jordan."
6 But Moses asked the Gadites and
Reubenites, "Should your brothers
go to war while you stay here? 7 Why
are you discouraging[C] the Israelites
from crossing into the land the LORD
has given them? 8 That's what your
fathers did when I sent them from
Kadesh-barnea to see the land. 9 After
they went up as far as Eshcol Valley
and saw the land, they discouraged
the Israelites from entering the land
the LORD had given them. 10 So the
LORD's anger burned that day, and
He swore an oath: 11 'Because they
did not follow Me completely, none
of the men 20 years old or more who
came up from Egypt will see the
land I swore to give Abraham, Isaac,
and Jacob— 12 none except Caleb
son of Jephunneh the Kenizzite and
Joshua son of Nun, because they did
follow the LORD completely.' 13 The
LORD's anger burned against Israel,
and He made them wander in the
wilderness 40 years until the whole
generation that had done what was
evil in the LORD's sight was gone.
14 And here you, a brood of sinners,
stand in your fathers' place adding
even more to the LORD's burning
anger against Israel. 15 If you turn
back from following Him, He will
once again leave this people in the
wilderness, and you will destroy all
of them."
16 Then they approached him and
said, "We want to build sheepfolds
here for our livestock and cities for
our dependents. 17 But we will arm
ourselves and be ready to go ahead of
the Israelites until we have brought
them into their place. Meanwhile,
our dependents will remain in the
fortified cities because of the inhabitants of the land. 18 We will not return to our homes until each of the
Israelites has taken possession of his
inheritance. 19 Yet we will not have
an inheritance with them across the
Jordan and beyond, because our inheritance will be across the Jordan
to the east."
20 Moses replied to them, "If you
do this—if you arm yourselves for
battle before the LORD, 21 and every
one of your armed men crosses the
Jordan before the LORD until He has
driven His enemies from His presence, 22 and the land is subdued before the LORD—afterward you may
return and be free from obligation
to the LORD and to Israel. And this
land will belong to you as a possession before the LORD. 23 But if you
don't do this, you will certainly sin
against the LORD; be sure your sin
will catch up with you. 24 Build cities for your dependents and folds for
your flocks, but do what you have
promised."

31:49-54 The officers took a census of the men who returned from the battle and discovered that not one was missing. The Lord had protected His people as they fulfilled His command. An offering, or ransom, was presented to the Lord from the spoils of gold as atonement for their lives. Exodus 30:12 says when a census is taken, each man must pay a ransom for himself to the Lord. This can also be seen as a thanksgiving offering for the life God sustained. The offering was accepted by Moses and Eleazar and thus something that was viewed as good. Moses and Eleazar placed the gold in the tent of meeting as **a memorial for the Israelites** of the Lord's faithfulness.

32:1-5 Again the issue of land came to the forefront as the **Reubenites and Gadites** saw the land just taken as best for their large number of flocks. The two tribes took the matter before Moses, Eleazar, and the leaders, requesting that they be allowed to stay in the land and not cross the Jordan. Moses viewed this request as similar to the return of the scouts who discouraged the Israelites from going into the land of Canaan, causing the wilderness wandering. Their request to stay was seen as sin because the Lord desired the Israelites to enter Canaan. To refuse to enter would be disobedient and a rejection of the Lord's blessing.

32:19 Instead of receiving an inheritance across the Jordan, the Reubenites and Gadites considered the land on the east of the Jordan their inheritance.

32:20-24 The second attempt was much more successful as the Lord and Moses agree to the stipulations. However, Moses made clear that should the Reubenites and Gadites go back on their word, their sin could find them, for they would have sinned gravely against the Lord.

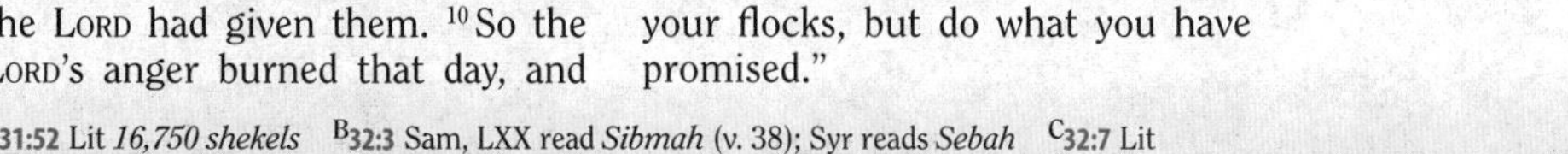
[A] **31:52** Lit *16,750 shekels* [B] **32:3** Sam, LXX read *Sibmah* (v. 38); Syr reads *Sebah* [C] **32:7** Lit *discouraging the hearts of*

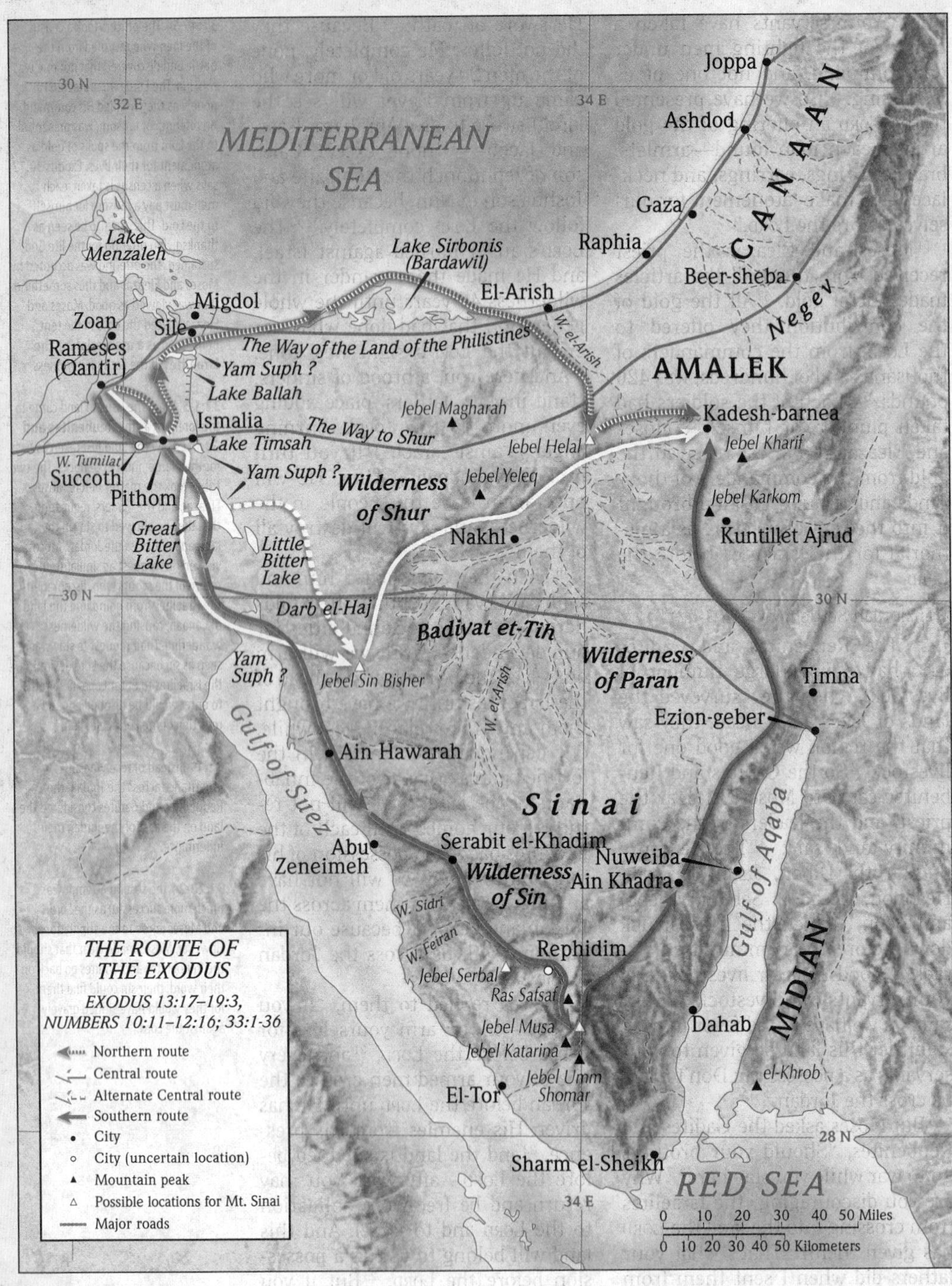
THE ROUTE OF THE EXODUS
EXODUS 13:17–19:3, NUMBERS 10:11–12:16; 33:1-36
Northern route
Central route
Alternate Central route
Southern route
City
City (uncertain location)
Mountain peak
Possible locations for Mt. Sinai
Major roads
MEDITERRANEAN SEA
CANAAN
AMALEK
Negev
Joppa
Ashdod
Gaza
Raphia
Beer-sheba
El-Arish
W. el-Arish
Lake Sirbonis (Bardawil)
Lake Menzaleh
Migdol
Zoan
Sile
Rameses (Qantir)
Yam Suph ?
Lake Ballah
The Way of the Land of the Philistines
Ismalia
Lake Timsah
W. Tumilat
Succoth
Pithom
The Way to Shur
Jebel Magharah
Jebel Helal
Kadesh-barnea
Jebel Kharif
Jebel Yeleq
Wilderness of Shur
Jebel Karkom
Kuntillet Ajrud
Nakhl
Great Bitter Lake
Little Bitter Lake
Darb el-Haj
Badiyat et-Tih
Wilderness of Paran
Yam Suph ?
Jebel Sin Bisher
Timna
Ezion-geber
Gulf of Suez
Ain Hawarah
Sinai
Abu Zeneimeh
Serabit el-Khadim
Wilderness of Sin
Nuweiba
Ain Khadra
Gulf of Aqaba
W. Sidri
W. Feiran
Rephidim
Jebel Serbal
Ras Safsaf
Jebel Musa
Jebel Katarina
Jebel Umm Shomar
El-Tor
Dahab
MIDIAN
el-Khrob
Sharm el-Sheikh
RED SEA
30 N
32 E
34 E
28 N
0 10 20 30 40 50 Miles
0 10 20 30 40 50 Kilometers

25 The Gadites and Reubenites answered Moses, "Your servants will do just as my lord commands. 26 Our little children, wives, livestock, and all our animals will remain here in the cities of Gilead, 27 but your servants are equipped for war before the LORD and will go across to the battle as my lord orders."

28 So Moses gave orders about them to Eleazar the priest, Joshua son of Nun, and the family leaders of the Israelite tribes. 29 Moses told them, "If the Gadites and Reubenites cross the Jordan with you, every man in battle formation before the LORD, and the land is subdued before you, you are to give them the land of Gilead as a possession. 30 But if they don't go across with you in battle formation, they must accept land in Canaan with you."

31 The Gadites and Reubenites replied, "What the LORD has spoken to your servants is what we will do. 32 We will cross over in battle formation before the LORD into the land of Canaan, but we will keep our hereditary possession across the Jordan."

33 So Moses gave them—the Gadites, Reubenites, and half the tribe of Manasseh son of Joseph—the kingdom of Sihon king of the Amorites and the kingdom of Og king of Bashan, the land including its cities with the territories surrounding them. 34 The Gadites rebuilt Dibon, Ataroth, Aroer, 35 Atroth-shophan, Jazer, Jogbehah, 36 Beth-nimrah, and Beth-haran as fortified cities, and built sheepfolds. 37 The Reubenites rebuilt Heshbon, Elealeh, Kiriathaim, 38 as well as Nebo and Baal-meon (whose names were changed), and Sibmah. They gave names to the cities they rebuilt.

39 The descendants of Machir son of Manasseh went to Gilead, captured it, and drove out the Amorites who were there. 40 So Moses gave Gilead to the clan of Machir son of Manasseh, and they settled in it. 41 Jair, a descendant of Manasseh, went and captured their villages, which he renamed Jair's Villages.[A] 42 Nobah went and captured Kenath with its villages and called it Nobah after his own name.

Review of Wilderness Travels (33:1-49)

33 These were the stages of the Israelites' journey when they went out of the land of Egypt by their military divisions under the leadership of Moses and Aaron. 2 At the LORD's command, Moses wrote down the starting points for the stages of their journey; these are the stages listed by their starting points:

3 They departed from Rameses in the first month, on the fifteenth day of the month. On the day after the •Passover the Israelites went out triumphantly[B] in the sight of all the Egyptians.
4 Meanwhile, the Egyptians were burying every firstborn male the LORD had struck down among them, for the LORD had executed judgment against their gods. 5 The Israelites departed from Rameses and camped at Succoth.
6 They departed from Succoth and camped at Etham, which is on the edge of the wilderness.
7 They departed from Etham and turned back to Pi-hahiroth, which faces Baal-zephon, and they camped before Migdol.
8 They departed from Pi-hahiroth[C] and crossed through the middle of the sea into the wilderness. They took a three-day journey into the Wilderness of Etham and camped at Marah.
9 They departed from Marah and came to Elim. There were 12 springs of water and 70 date palms at Elim, so they camped there.
10 They departed from Elim and camped by the •Red Sea.
11 They departed from the Red Sea and camped in the Wilderness of Sin.

32:33-41 Though not mentioned with the tribes of Reuben and Gad, **half the tribe of Manasseh** wanted the same deal, for they had taken Amorite territory. Thus, two and a half tribes would be located east of the Jordan. The major preparations for entry into the promised land had now begun.

33:1-49 This passage provides an extensive itinerary of the Israelite journey through the wilderness. Of particular importance is verse 2, in which Mosaic authorship is affirmed. Moses is given credit for the writing of the list at the Lord's command. That Moses was able to write during the journey lends credibility to his authorship of the Pentateuch. The journey is described from the starting point, and clearly the Israelites were led by Moses and Aaron, going out in military formation on each leg of the journey. Brief notes of description are given with some of the more important points along the journey. There is much debate over the actual location of many of these sites. Archaeology is proving very helpful in pinpointing more precisely many of the places mentioned in the Bible. However, Christians can trust God's word to be true and accurate without physical evidence because God does not lie (23:19).

33:3-4 Leaving Egypt is central in the lives of the Israelites, as is noted in Exodus, when the Israelites left one day after Passover. The Lord was given the glory for leading His people out of that land, and He is the one who judged the **Egyptians** and their gods.

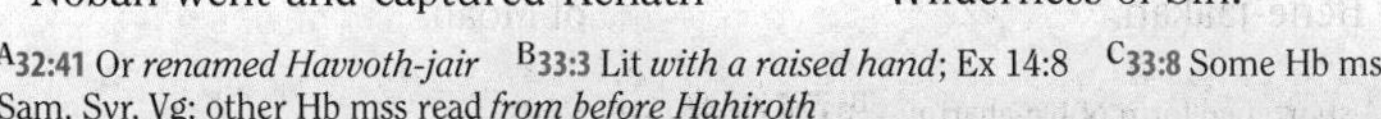
[A]32:41 Or *renamed Havvoth-jair* [B]33:3 Lit *with a raised hand*; Ex 14:8 [C]33:8 Some Hb mss, Sam, Syr, Vg; other Hb mss read *from before Hahiroth*

33:38-40 Aaron's death and the arrival on the outskirts of the promised land are the focus of the rest of the chapter. The death of Aaron marked the passing of a generation. He died on the **first day of the fifth month in the fortieth year** of the journey. Thus, there is recognition that the wandering is over, which is echoed in that the Canaanite king heard of the Israelites' coming. By then, the Israelites were drawing ever closer to their ultimate destination.

33:48-49 The section concludes on the banks of the Jordan **across from Jericho**, and the Lord begins giving instructions to Moses for entering the promised land.

33:52 That Yahweh is a jealous God is evident as His first command to the Israelites concerning their admission to the land of promise was to destroy all of the idols (**stone images and cast images**) and **high places**. The images were representations of pagan gods, and the high places were the centers used to worship those gods. To keep the Canaanites in the land would be to invite temptation to worship their gods and thus not receive the full blessing of God, for the land belonged to the Israelites by promise of God's covenant.

33:53-56 Thus, as the Lord commanded, the Canaanites were to be driven completely out of the promised land. The Lord gave His reason for the seemingly harsh directives to be carried out—**I have given you the land to possess**. Once in the land, the distribution would be given according to lots, the physical means of revealing God's will in those days. The inheritance would also be given according to ancestral tribe and thus the importance of the second census (chap. 26). The Israelites were to be the only people living in the land God had given them. Disobedience to the Lord's command to drive out the Canaanites would result in the driving out of the Israelites instead.

12 They departed from the Wilderness of Sin and camped in Dophkah.
13 They departed from Dophkah and camped at Alush.
14 They departed from Alush and camped at Rephidim, where there was no water for the people to drink.
15 They departed from Rephidim and camped in the Wilderness of Sinai.
16 They departed from the Wilderness of Sinai and camped at Kibroth-hattaavah.
17 They departed from Kibroth-hattaavah and camped at Hazeroth.
18 They departed from Hazeroth and camped at Rithmah.
19 They departed from Rithmah and camped at Rimmon-perez.
20 They departed from Rimmon-perez and camped at Libnah.
21 They departed from Libnah and camped at Rissah.
22 They departed from Rissah and camped at Kehelathah.
23 They departed from Kehelathah and camped at Mount Shepher.
24 They departed from Mount Shepher and camped at Haradah.
25 They departed from Haradah and camped at Makheloth.
26 They departed from Makheloth and camped at Tahath.
27 They departed from Tahath and camped at Terah.
28 They departed from Terah and camped at Mithkah.
29 They departed from Mithkah and camped at Hashmonah.
30 They departed from Hashmonah and camped at Moseroth.
31 They departed from Moseroth and camped at Bene-jaakan.
32 They departed from Bene-jaakan and camped at Hor-haggidgad.
33 They departed from Hor-haggidgad and camped at Jotbathah.
34 They departed from Jotbathah and camped at Abronah.
35 They departed from Abronah and camped at Ezion-geber.
36 They departed from Ezion-geber and camped in the Wilderness of Zin (that is, Kadesh).
37 They departed from Kadesh and camped at Mount Hor on the edge of the land of Edom.
38 At the LORD's command, Aaron the priest climbed Mount Hor and died there on the first day of the fifth month in the fortieth year after the Israelites went out of
the land of Egypt. 39 Aaron was
123 years old when he died
on Mount Hor. 40 At that time
the Canaanite king of Arad, who lived in the •Negev in the land of Canaan, heard the Israelites were coming.
41 They departed from Mount Hor and camped at Zalmonah.
42 They departed from Zalmonah and camped at Punon.
43 They departed from Punon and camped at Oboth.
44 They departed from Oboth and camped at Iye-abarim on the border of Moab.
45 They departed from Iyim[A] and camped at Dibon-gad.
46 They departed from Dibon-gad and camped at Almon-diblathaim.
47 They departed from Almon-diblathaim and camped in the Abarim range facing Nebo.
48 They departed from the Abarim range and camped on the plains of Moab by the Jordan across from Jericho.
49 They camped by the Jordan from Beth-jeshimoth to the Acacia Meadow[B] on the plains of Moab.

[A]**33:45** A shortened form of Iye-abarim [B]**33:49** Or *Abel-shittim*

Instructions for Occupying Canaan (33:50-56)

50 The LORD spoke to Moses in the
plains of Moab by the Jordan across
from Jericho, 51 "Tell the Israelites:
When you cross the Jordan into the
land of Canaan, 52 you must drive out
all the inhabitants of the land before
you, destroy all their stone images
and cast images, and demolish all
their •high places. 53 You are to take
possession of the land and settle in it
because I have given you the land to
possess. 54 You are to receive the land
as an inheritance by lot according to
your clans. Increase the inheritance
for a large clan and decrease it for a
small one. Whatever place the lot indicates for someone will be his. You
will receive an inheritance according to your ancestral tribes. 55 But if
you don't drive out the inhabitants
of the land before you, those you allow to remain will become thorns in
your eyes and in your sides; they will
harass you in the land where you
will live. 56 And what I had planned
to do to them, I will do to you."

Boundaries of the Promised Land (34:1-15)

34 The LORD spoke to Moses,
2 "Command the Israelites and
say to them: When you enter the
land of Canaan, it will be allotted
to you as an inheritance[A] with these
borders:

3 Your southern side will be
from the Wilderness of Zin
along the boundary of Edom.
Your southern border on the
east will begin at the east end
of the Dead Sea. 4 Your border
will turn south of the Ascent of
Akrabbim,[B] proceed to Zin, and
end south of Kadesh-barnea.
It will go to Hazar-addar and
proceed to Azmon. 5 The border
will turn from Azmon to the
Brook of Egypt, where it will
end at the Mediterranean Sea.

6 Your western border will be
the coastline of the Mediterranean Sea; this will be your
western border.

7 This will be your northern
border: From the Mediterranean Sea draw a line to Mount
Hor;[C] 8 from Mount Hor draw
a line to the entrance of Hamath,[D] and the border will
reach Zedad. 9 Then the border
will go to Ziphron and end at
Hazar-enan. This will be your
northern border.

10 For your eastern border,
draw a line from Hazar-enan to
Shepham. 11 The border will go
down from Shepham to Riblah
east of Ain. It will continue down
and reach the eastern slope of
the Sea of Chinnereth.[E] 12 Then
the border will go down to the
Jordan and end at the Dead Sea.
This will be your land defined by
its borders on all sides."

13 So Moses commanded the Israelites, "This is the land you are to receive by lot as an inheritance, which
the LORD commanded to be given
to the nine and a half tribes. 14 For
the tribe of the Reubenites and the
tribe of the Gadites have received
their inheritance according to their
ancestral houses, and half the tribe
of Manasseh has received its inheritance. 15 The two and a half tribes
have received their inheritance
across the Jordan from Jericho,
eastward toward the sunrise."

Leaders for Distributing the Land (34:16-29)

16 The LORD spoke to Moses,
17 "These are the names of the men
who are to distribute the land as
an inheritance for you: Eleazar the
priest and Joshua son of Nun. 18 Take
one leader from each tribe to distribute the land. 19 These are the
names of the men:

Caleb son of Jephunneh from
the tribe of Judah;
20 Shemuel son of Ammihud
from the tribe of Simeon;
21 Elidad son of Chislon from
the tribe of Benjamin;
22 Bukki son of Jogli, a leader
from the tribe of Dan;
23 from the sons of Joseph:

34:1-29 This passage is one of several describing the inheritance of the land of Canaan, which the Israelites received from the Lord. Other passages also outline distribution of the land (1Sm 3:20; Ezk 47:13-20).

34:2 Following the instructions for taking the land of Canaan, the Lord affirmed that the Israelites would enter the land. The borders were drawn from south to west to north to east. Basically, the land runs from the Wilderness of Zin in the south to Zedad in the north, with the Mediterranean Sea marking the western border and the Dead Sea marking the eastern border.

34:14 The Reubenites, Gadites, and half the tribe of Manasseh had already received their inheritance across from Jericho by driving out the Midianites, and thus they were not included in this portion of the inheritance.

34:17-18 The Lord provided an organized way for distribution of the land. **Eleazar** and **Joshua** would ultimately be in charge since they were the new leaders of Israel, but then a leader from each of the 10 tribes receiving land in Canaan was chosen to help distribute the inheritance.

34:19-29 This list did not fit the order of either census but rather was fashioned according to the configuration of land grants to the tribes south to north (see Jos 13–17).

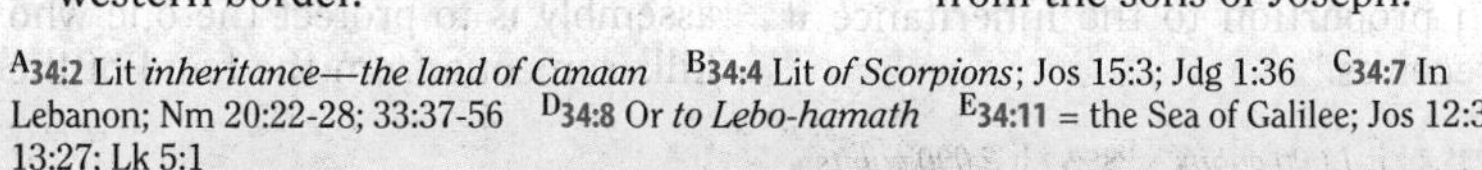

[A]34:2 Lit *inheritance—the land of Canaan* [B]34:4 Lit *of Scorpions*; Jos 15:3; Jdg 1:36 [C]34:7 In Lebanon; Nm 20:22-28; 33:37-56 [D]34:8 Or *to Lebo-hamath* [E]34:11 = the Sea of Galilee; Jos 12:3; 13:27; Lk 5:1

Hanniel son of Ephod, a
leader from the tribe of
Manasseh,
24 Kemuel son of Shiphtan,
a leader from the tribe of
Ephraim;
25 Eli-zaphan son of Parnach,
a leader from the tribe of
Zebulun;
26 Paltiel son of Azzan, a leader
from the tribe of Issachar;
27 Ahihud son of Shelomi, a
leader from the tribe of Asher;
28 Pedahel son of Ammihud,
a leader from the tribe of
Naphtali."

29 These are the ones the LORD commanded to distribute the inheritance to the Israelites in the land of Canaan.

Cities for the Levites (35:1-8)

35 The LORD again spoke to Moses in the plains of Moab by the Jordan across from Jericho: 2 "Command the Israelites to give cities out of their hereditary property for the Levites to live in and pastureland around the cities. 3 The cities will be for them to live in, and their pasturelands will be for their herds, flocks, and all their other animals. 4 The pasturelands of the cities you are to give the Levites will extend from the city wall 500 yards[A] on every side. 5 Measure 1,000 yards[B] outside the city for the east side, 1,000 yards[B] for the south side, 1,000 yards[B] for the west side, and 1,000 yards[B] for the north side, with the city in the center. This will belong to them as pasturelands for the cities.

6 "The cities you give the Levites will include six cities of refuge, which you must provide so that the one who kills someone may flee there; in addition to these, give 42 other cities. 7 The total number of cities you give the Levites will be 48, along with their pasturelands. 8 Of the cities that you give from the Israelites' territory, you should take more from a larger tribe and less from a smaller one. Each tribe is to give some of its cities to the Levites in proportion to the inheritance it receives."

Cities of Refuge (35:9-34)

9 The LORD said to Moses, 10 "Speak to the Israelites and tell them: When you cross the Jordan into the land of Canaan, 11 designate cities to serve as cities of refuge for you, so that a person who kills someone unintentionally may flee there. 12 You will have the cities as a refuge from the avenger, so that the one who kills someone will not die until he stands trial before the assembly. 13 The cities you select will be your six cities of refuge. 14 Select three cities across the Jordan and three cities in the land of Canaan to be cities of refuge. 15 These six cities will serve as a refuge for the Israelites and for the foreigner or temporary resident among them, so that anyone who kills a person unintentionally may flee there.

16 "If anyone strikes a person with an iron object and death results, he is a murderer; the murderer must be put to death. 17 If a man has in his hand a stone capable of causing death and strikes another person and he dies, the murderer must be put to death. 18 If a man has in his hand a wooden object capable of causing death and strikes another person and he dies, the murderer must be put to death. 19 The avenger of blood himself is to kill the murderer; when he finds him, he is to kill him. 20 Likewise, if anyone in hatred pushes a person or throws an object at him with malicious intent and he dies, 21 or if in hostility he strikes him with his hand and he dies, the one who struck him must be put to death; he is a murderer. The avenger of blood is to kill the murderer when he finds him.

22 "But if anyone suddenly pushes a person without hostility or throws any object at him without malicious intent 23 or without looking drops a stone that could kill a person and he dies, but he was not his enemy and wasn't trying to harm him, 24 the assembly is to judge between the slayer and the avenger of blood according to these ordinances. 25 The assembly is to protect the one who kills someone from the hand of the

[A]**35:4** Lit *1,000 cubits* [B]**35:5** Lit *2,000 cubits*

35:1-8 As the Lord was the inheritance of the Levites, they would not receive land as the other tribes. Instead, each tribe was to give to the Levites from its hereditary property cities where they could live. The Lord provided measurements for the cities and the pasturelands for the Levites' flocks. The Lord was fair in His dealings as the smaller tribes were to give less and the larger tribes more. Again the Lord provided for the ones who served Him only.

35:6-7 In total, the Israelites were to receive 48 cities, but 6 would be specifically designated as **cities of refuge** (lit, "city of intaking") for those who had killed someone. Three cities would be located on each side of the Jordan. These cities provided asylum for a person until a trial could be conducted to decide guilt or innocence. If the person was judged to be innocent, the person could live in the city of refuge without fear of reprisal by the dead person's family (Jos 20:2-6). Four passages in the OT address these cities of refuge (Ex 21:12-14; Nm 35:6-34; Dt 19:1-13; Jos 20:1-9).

35:9-34 The Lord gave further instructions regarding the **cities of refuge**. These cities were to be placed in Canaan and across the Jordan River, where the Reubenites and Gadites were located, with three cities in each place. These cities were for the one who had killed unintentionally and for the one waiting to stand trial. The cities could be used by both the Israelites and those temporarily traveling through the land as sojourners.

35:16-29 The one who kills intentionally (vv. 16-21) is contrasted with the one who kills unintentionally (vv. 22-25). The murderer who kills intentionally will be put to death by the victim's **avenger**. However, if the killing was unintentional, the assembly is to judge what happened and the person is to go to a city of refuge. The penalty is close to a life sentence (but in a city of refuge instead of prison) as the slayer must remain in the city of refuge until the death of the high priest; and if he fails to do so, the avenger may kill him. A system of justice is thus set in place.

35:30-34 The Lord also added that no one can be put to death on the **testimony of one witness**. And the punishments, whether death or asylum in the city of refuge, were to be fulfilled, for the accused could not be ransomed. Justice was of paramount importance. The Lord's value of life is evident. There are harsh consequences for taking the life of another. Murder defiles the land, making it unclean. The only way to make atonement is by the one who shed the blood—a strong deterrent.

avenger of blood. Then the assembly
will return him to the city of refuge
he fled to, and he must live there
until the death of the high priest
who was anointed with the holy oil.
26 "If the one who kills someone
ever goes outside the border of the
city of refuge he fled to, 27 and the
avenger of blood finds him outside
the border of his city of refuge and
kills him, the avenger will not be
•guilty of bloodshed, 28 for the one
who killed a person was supposed
to live in his city of refuge until the
death of the high priest. Only after
the death of the high priest may the
one who has killed a person return
to the land he possesses. 29 These
instructions will be a statutory ordinance for you throughout your generations wherever you live.
30 "If anyone kills a person, the
murderer is to be put to death based
on the word of witnesses. But no
one is to be put to death based on
the testimony of one witness. 31 You
are not to accept a ransom for the
life of a murderer who is guilty of
killing someone; he must be put to
death. 32 Neither should you accept
a ransom for the person who flees
to his city of refuge, allowing him
to return and live in the land before
the death of the high priest.[A]
33 "Do not defile the land where you
are,[B] for bloodshed defiles the land,
and there can be no •atonement for
the land because of the blood that is
shed on it, except by the blood of the
person who shed it. 34 Do not make
the land •unclean where you live and
where I reside; for I, •Yahweh, reside
among the Israelites."

The Inheritance of Zelophehad's Daughters (36:1-13)

36 The family leaders from the
clan of the descendants of
Gilead—the son of Machir, son of
Manasseh—who were from the clans
of the sons of Joseph, approached and
addressed Moses and the leaders who
were over the Israelite families. 2 They
said, "•Yahweh commanded my lord
to give the land as an inheritance by
lot to the Israelites. My lord was further commanded by Yahweh to give
our brother Zelophehad's inheritance
to his daughters. 3 If they marry any
of the men from the other Israelite
tribes, their inheritance will be taken
away from our fathers' inheritance
and added to that of the tribe into
which they marry. Therefore, part
of our allotted inheritance would be

God, as the author of life, hates to see those created in His image destroyed.

36:1-13 As the Israelites came closer to entering the promised land, their thoughts dwelt on what would take place there. Some of the family leaders from the clan of **Gilead** within the tribe of **Manasseh** considered the earlier ruling concerning the **daughters of Zelophehad**. They realized that if the daughters of Zelophehad married outside the tribe of Manasseh, the inheritance would move with them during the time of Jubilation. Thus, the reason behind the first issuing of the **inheritance** had a loophole, so to speak, and the land might still be lost to another tribe. Thus, Moses, at the word of the Lord, made a stipulation—the daughters of Zelophehad could **marry** only within the clan of their ancestral tribe, ensuring that the land would not move from the tribe of Manasseh. The daughters of Zelophehad demonstrated their character in that they were obedient and married within their clan. This command is the conclusion of the commands set forth by the Lord through Moses on the plains of Moab. The stage was thus set for the Israelites to enter the promised land flowing with milk and honey, which they had time and again rejected through disobedience.

[A]**35:32** Sam, LXX, Syr read *high priest* [B]**35:33** Sam, LXX, Syr, Vg, Tg read *live*

Biblical Womanhood The Daughters of Zelophehad

The daughters of Zelophehad are important women to set forth as examples (27:1-11; 36:1-13). Not only did these daughters fight against injustice, but they were concerned about family and about being obedient to God. The fear of the Lord is the foundation for biblical womanhood, and these women had it. Having discovered that their family would be left out of the inheritance unjustly because their father only had daughters, they respectfully went to those in authority about this unfairness (see 27:1-11). Women today must fight against injustice as well, but in the midst of the struggle, they must never lose the Christian virtues. Zelophehad's daughters' main concern was the continuation of the family name. Behind the priority of a relationship with Jesus Christ, each woman's main concern should be for family. The paradigm for biblical womanhood is consistent throughout Scripture, and the case of Zelophehad's daughters is no exception. They are models of godly obedience, maternal nurture, and righteous justice.

While life is not always fair, God is always just. The daughters of Zelophehad realized this. Christians should never stand for injustice; and when it occurs, they must go about righting the wrong in a proper way. For example, Zelophehad's daughters did not grumble about their personal sorrow and their family's plight. Rather, with grace and respect, the matter was taken before the leadership of the community and before the Lord. When unfairness strikes in life, a believer must not groan and complain. The Bible continually says that followers of Christ will encounter suffering. In the midst of pain and sorrow and perhaps unjust accusations or a muddied reputation, a Christian woman must remember that God keeps the record book of her life. Though justice may not be served here, the heavenly Father knows and will richly reward the faithful (Heb 6:10). Just as God remembered His faithful servants, Joshua and Caleb, and was gracious to the daughters of Zelophehad and the tribe of Manasseh, so He will be gracious to you.

taken away. [4]When the Jubilee comes
for the Israelites, their inheritance
will be added to that of the tribe into
which they marry, and their inheritance will be taken away from the inheritance of our ancestral tribe."
[5]So Moses commanded the Israelites at the word of the LORD,
"What the tribe of Joseph's descendants says is right. [6]This is what the
LORD has commanded concerning
Zelophehad's daughters: They may
marry anyone they like provided
they marry within a clan of their
ancestral tribe. [7]An inheritance belonging to the Israelites must not
transfer from tribe to tribe, because
each of the Israelites is to retain the
inheritance of his ancestral tribe.
[8]Any daughter who possesses an
inheritance from an Israelite tribe
must marry someone from the
clan of her ancestral tribe, so that
each of the Israelites will possess
the inheritance of his fathers. [9]No
inheritance is to transfer from one
tribe to another, because each of
the Israelite tribes is to retain its
inheritance."
[10]The daughters of Zelophehad
did as the LORD commanded Moses.
[11]Mahlah, Tirzah, Hoglah, Milcah,
and Noah, the daughters of Zelophehad, married cousins on their
father's side. [12]They married men
from the clans of the descendants of
Manasseh son of Joseph, and their
inheritance remained within the
tribe of their father's clan.
[13]These are the commands and
ordinances the LORD commanded
the Israelites through Moses in the
plains of Moab by the Jordan across
from Jericho.

NUMBERS… WRITTEN ON MY *Heart* The Israelite nation was to serve as a beacon to pagan nations to point them to the one, true God. God proves Himself faithful over and over again to this nation who proved to be faithless on many occasions. God's desire for His people to be holy is for His glory and so that the lost world could come to know Him. Today, as you read about the Israelites' journey to the promised land, remember that you serve the same faithful God whose desire is still that you would be a light to the lost world surrounding you. God's desire is for you to impact the world around you and not that you would become indistinguishable from the world.

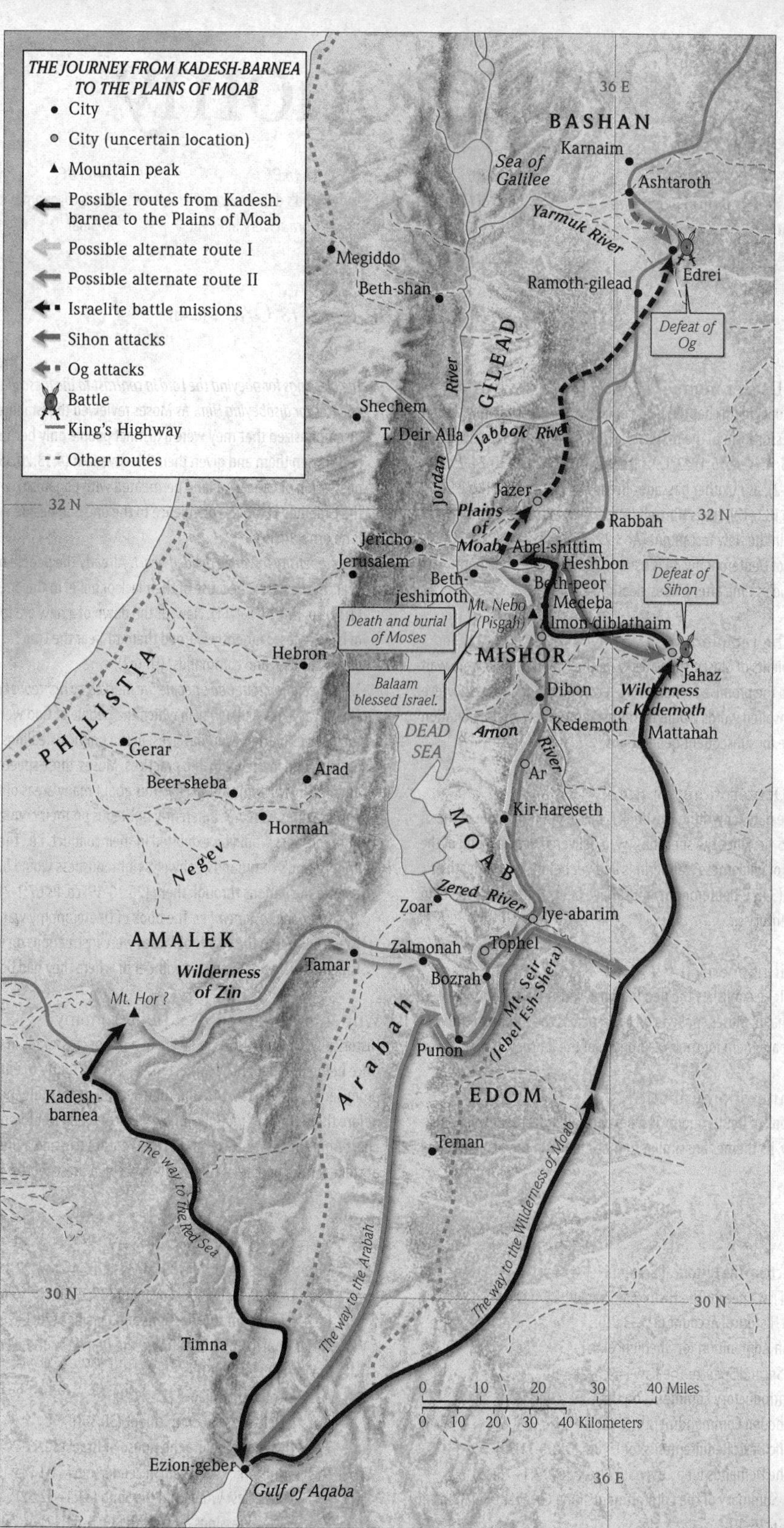
THE JOURNEY FROM KADESH-BARNEA TO THE PLAINS OF MOAB
City
City (uncertain location)
Mountain peak
Possible routes from Kadesh-barnea to the Plains of Moab
Possible alternate route I
Possible alternate route II
Israelite battle missions
Sihon attacks
Og attacks
Battle
King's Highway
Other routes
36 E
BASHAN
Karnaim
Sea of Galilee
Ashtaroth
Yarmuk River
Megiddo
Edrei
Beth-shan
Ramoth-gilead
Defeat of Og
GILEAD
River
Shechem
T. Deir Alla
Jabbok River
Jordan
Jazer
32 N
Plains of Moab
32 N
Rabbah
Jericho
Abel-shittim
Jerusalem
Heshbon
Beth-jeshimoth
Beth-peor
Defeat of Sihon
Mt. Nebo (Pisgah)
Medeba
Death and burial of Moses
Almon-diblathaim
Hebron
MISHOR
Jahaz
Balaam blessed Israel.
Dibon
Wilderness of Kedemoth
PHILISTIA
DEAD SEA
Arnon
Kedemoth
Mattanah
Gerar
River
Arad
Ar
Beer-sheba
Kir-hareseth
Hormah
MOAB
Negev
Zoar
Zered River
Iye-abarim
AMALEK
Tophel
Tamar
Zalmonah
Wilderness of Zin
Bozrah
Mt. Seir (Jebel Esh-Shera)
Mt. Hor ?
Arabah
Punon
Kadesh-barnea
EDOM
Teman
The way to the Red Sea
The way to the Arabah
The way to the Wilderness of Moab
30 N
30 N
Timna
0 10 20 30 40 Miles
0 10 20 30 40 Kilometers
Ezion-geber
Gulf of Aqaba
36 E

Deuteronomy

Timeline World Events Biblical Events	*1529 BC* Birth of Aaron	*1526 BC* Birth of Moses	*1446 BC* God's deliverance of Israel from slavery in Egypt	*1446 BC* God's covenant with Israel at Sinai

"The Lord our God, the Lord is One" (6:4b).

Who wrote Deuteronomy?

Except for the concluding chapter of the book, which was probably written by Moses' successor Joshua, the text itself strongly supports Mosaic authorship (e.g., 1:1-5; 4:44-46; 5:1; 27:1,9,11; 29:1-2; 31:1-2,7,9-10,24-25,30; 32:44-46; 33:1-2), as do other passages in the Old Testament (1Kg 2:3; 8:53; 2Kg 14:6; 18:6,12), Jesus Himself (Mt 19:7-8; Mk 10:3-5; Jn 5:46-47), and references in the New Testament (Ac 3:22; 7:37-38; Rm 10:19; 1Co 9:9). A portion of Deuteronomy 34 is usually ascribed to Joshua because it refers to a period of time after Moses' death (34:5-12).

Who were the recipients?

The initial recipients of Moses' speeches were the Israelites who were waiting to cross into the promised land. Moses recorded the speeches, however, so these God-inspired words would be both a reminder to that generation and a challenge for subsequent generations.

When was Deuteronomy written?

An approximate date for writing the book is based upon the date of the exodus, ca 1445 B.C. Since the speeches were delivered near the end of the 40-year period of wilderness wanderings and yet before Moses' death at the age of 120 (34:7), Deuteronomy must have been written ca 1406 or in the fifteenth century B.C.

Where did it happen?

Deuteronomy 1:1 establishes the geographical setting at the southeastern entrance to Canaan; Moses spoke to all Israel across the Jordan in the wilderness to prepare them for their next phase of the journey.

What is Deuteronomy about?

Because the book of Deuteronomy is an expansion or further explanation of the Law, its themes are similar to those found in the rest of the Pentateuch:

- *The blessings for obeying the Lord in contrast to the inescapable consequences for disobeying Him.* As Moses reviewed the Israelites' history, he emphasized that they were a distinct people only because Yahweh had chosen them and given them His covenant (4:13,20,35-40). Taking possession of Canaan, a land permeated with paganism, would require the Israelites' complete obedience to the one God beside whom there is no other (4:15).
- *The propensity toward a divided heart.* Already the people had spent 40 years in the desert because of their lack of belief in the one true God (1:32; cp. Nm 14:1-4,11). Now, at the dawn of a new era for the people of Israel, Moses urgently warned them to "fear the Lord . . . by keeping all His statutes and commands" (Dt 6:2).
- *The expectation that God's people are marked by righteous conduct.* There was a particular way in which the people of God were to conduct themselves in their everyday lives, in the political dealings with other nations, and in their worship practices. Moses' three speeches all gave detailed instructions to the Israelites about many areas of their lives. The Israelites were not inherently righteous on their own, but their righteousness would be exhibited in their conduct, i.e., their obedience to God's commands; Yahweh's righteousness would be on display among the nations through them (26:16-19; cp. Ps 67:1-2).
- *The command to remember.* The book of Deuteronomy was a history of Israel. Central to the words of Moses were instructions on where the Israelites were going and a reminder of where they had been.

Why should women read Deuteronomy?

Historically, the people of God were at a major crossroads in their journey. Once before the people had rejected their opportunity to enter the promised land (Nm 13–14), and their second opportunity now loomed before them. The instructions for living recorded in Deuteronomy stand apart from the rest of the books of the Pentateuch, and a great deal was at stake for the people of God as they received these words. This book

Outline

I. Introduction: The Historical Setting (1:1-4)

II. Moses' First Speech: The History of Israel (1:5–4:43)
   A. A Historical Account (1:5–3:29)
   B. An Admonition for Obedience (4:1-43)

III. Moses' Second Speech: The Law (4:44–26:19)
   A. Introductory Comments on the Law (4:44-49)
   B. The Ten Commandments (5:1-21)
   C. The Basic Requirements for Living (5:22–11:32)
   D. The Demands for a Covenant Lifestyle (12:1–26:15)
   E. A Summary of the Commitments for a Covenant Relationship (26:16-19)

IV. Moses' Third Speech: The Blessings and Cursings (27:1–29:1)
   A. The Renewal of the Covenant (27:1-26)
   B. A Listing of the Blessings and Cursings (28:1–29:1)

V. Moses' Fourth Speech: Defining the Demands of the Covenant with the Lord (29:2–30:20)
   A. A Call to Obedience (29:2-29)
   B. A Demand for Commitment (30:1-10)
   C. The Choice Before the House of Israel (30:11-20)

VI. The Conclusion: A Transition in Leadership (31:1–34:12)
   A. Moses' Last Words and His Song (31:1–32:52)
   B. Moses' Blessings and Death (33:1–34:12)

1407 BC	1406 BC	1406 BC	1406 BC
Death of Miriam and Aaron	Moses' farewell address in the plains of Moab	Moses' appointment of Joshua as Israel's leader	Moses' death after viewing the promised land from Mount Nebo

outlines the meaning of being a "set-apart" people for God in the midst of a world diametrically opposed to Him. Women today live in a similar type of culture, and the choice faced by the Israelites is the same one women today face: Conform to the worldly culture or transform the culture by living holy lives.

How do you read Deuteronomy?

To understand Deuteronomy, one must understand the purpose for the other four books in the Pentateuch. In Genesis, the author described the creation of the world and the establishment of God's covenant with Abraham. Abraham was the father of the nation of Israel, and God chose Israel to bless the rest of the nations of the earth (Gn 12:1-3). Exodus further describes the history of Israel's birth and constitution as a nation. Leviticus focuses on setting up ceremonial laws for the people of Israel or explaining how the nation of Israel, God's chosen people, should worship Him. The book of Numbers traces the lineage and families of the people of God, emphasizing from generation to generation who was related to whom and how they were related. Deuteronomy, then, concludes the beginning segment of Israel's story as a nation and deals with instructions for the people of Israel as they began their lives in the promised land. The book contains the last words of Moses before his death and consists of a series of speeches in which Moses recounts the Israelites' journeys, reviews their history as God's people, and rehearses the meaning of living in covenant relationship with the Lord.

Introduction: The Historical Setting (1:1-4)

1 These are the words Moses spoke
to all Israel across the Jordan in
the wilderness, in the ·Arabah opposite Suph,[A] between Paran and
Tophel, Laban, Hazeroth, and Di-
zahab. 2 It is an eleven-day journey
from Horeb to Kadesh-barnea by
way of Mount Seir. 3 In the fortieth
year, in the eleventh month, on the
first of the month, Moses told the
Israelites everything the LORD had
commanded him to say to them.
4 This was after he had defeated Sihon king of the Amorites, who lived
in Heshbon, and Og king of Bashan,
who lived in Ashtaroth, at Edrei.

Moses' First Speech: The History of Israel (1:5–4:43)

5 Across the Jordan in the land of
Moab, Moses began to explain this
law, saying:

Departure from Horeb (1:6-8)

6 "The LORD our God spoke to us
at Horeb: 'You have stayed at this
mountain long enough. 7 Resume
your journey and go to the hill
country of the Amorites and their
neighbors in the Arabah, the hill
country, the Judean foothills,[B] the
·Negev and the sea coast—to the
land of the Canaanites and to Lebanon as far as the Euphrates River.[C]
8 See, I have set the land before you.
Enter and take possession of the
land the LORD swore to give to your
fathers Abraham, Isaac, and Jacob
and their future descendants.'

Leaders for the Tribes (1:9-18)

9 "I said to you at that time: I can't
bear the responsibility for you on
my own. 10 The LORD your God has
so multiplied you that today you are
as numerous as the stars of the sky.
11 May ·Yahweh, the God of your fathers, increase you a thousand times
more, and bless you as He promised
you. 12 But how can I bear your troubles, burdens, and disputes by myself? 13 Appoint for yourselves wise,
understanding, and respected men

[A]1:1 LXX, Tg, Vg read *the Red Sea* [B]1:7 Or *the Shephelah* [C]1:7 Lit *the great river, the river Euphrates*

Title The Hebrew title *ʾelleh haddebarim* is derived from the first words of the text, **These are the words** (1:1). Regarding the document as essentially a restatement of the law given in Exodus (see Dt 17:18), the translators of the Septuagint entitled the book *Deuteronomion* (Gk, "second law"), from which came the English title "Deuteronomy." This title aptly reflects the book's purpose of reviewing the law for a new generation of Israelites, who at last were preparing to enter the promised land.

1:2-3 The journey from **Horeb** (or Sinai, where God established His covenant with Israel) to **Kadesh-barnea** (located about 50 miles southwest of Beer-sheba and 150 miles from Horeb), their point of entry into Canaan, should not have taken more than 11 days. However, their unbelief and disobedience extended to 40 years of wandering (Nm 14:7-23). The older generation would die before the people could enter the promised land.

1:5-6 Across the Jordan in the land of Moab, Moses began to explain [Hb *baʾar*, "make absolutely plain or clear," which is the purpose of biblical exposition] **this law, saying: The LORD our God spoke to us at Horeb.** The journey for the Israelites was not without geographical significance. The people would soon cross the Jordan River to take the land the Lord had given them; however, first they had to hear this explanation of the law from Moses. Horeb was also called the Mountain of God and Mount Sinai. There Moses received the Ten Commandments (Ex 19:1–20:17). Later the prophet Elijah, when exhausted and discouraged from battling the false prophets and Jezebel, would run to this place (1Kg 18–19). The Israelites identified certain places with the presence of God, and Horeb was especially associated with the works of the one true God. From the very beginning, Moses reminded the Israelites of this location where God had spoken to them, prompting them to remember that He would continue to speak to them in the future.

1:9-14 From the time the Lord chose Abraham and promised to give him a land for his descendants, God had also promised to make them a great people. He specifically promised Abraham that his descendants would be more numerous than the stars in the sky (Gn 15:4-5). By the time the people left Egypt, God had already fulfilled His promise, which would remind the people of God's ability to fulfill all of His covenant with Abraham (Gn 15:5; 22:17; Ex 1:7). This vast growth, however, provided certain challenges for leadership. Moses discovered that trying to deal with the problems of all the people was too much. Therefore, from each of the tribes he set up **wise, understanding, and respected men** (Dt 1:13), who were charged with listening to the problems and helping the people settle their disputes.

He wanted the leaders to come from the people and be recognized by the people. In choosing contemporary leaders for local church ministries, the biblical precedent is that leaders are recognized or known as being "wise" by the people around them and "respected" among the people.

1:15 Moses realized that the job of leading so many people was more than one man could do effectively. In appointing these judges by **thousands, hundreds, fifties, and tens**, Moses acknowledged his own inadequacy and the giftedness of others.

1:16-18 Moses instructed the judges how they should lead the people. Spiritual and political leaders ought not to show **partiality** in their leadership, a warning issued in the New Testament as well (Jms 2:1-13). Moses realized that the judges might not be able to adjudicate every case. However, he recognized his ultimate responsibility before God, and his willingness to delegate duties was not to relieve himself of all responsibility but rather to administer the task more effectively and efficiently. Contemporary leaders

from each of your tribes, and I will make them your leaders.

14 "You replied to me, 'What you propose to do is good.'

15 "So I took the leaders of your tribes, wise and respected men, and set them over you as leaders: officials for thousands, hundreds, fifties, and tens, and officers for your tribes. 16 I commanded your judges at that time: Hear the cases between your brothers, and judge rightly between a man and his brother or a foreign resident. 17 Do not show partiality when deciding a case; listen to small and great alike. Do not be intimidated by anyone, for judgment belongs to God. Bring me any case too difficult for you, and I will hear it. 18 At that time I commanded you about all the things you were to do.

Israel's Disobedience at Kadesh-barnea (1:19-46)

19 "We then set out from Horeb and went across all the great and terrible wilderness you saw on the way to the hill country of the Amorites, just as the LORD our God had commanded us. When we reached Kadesh-barnea, 20 I said to you: You have reached the hill country of the Amorites, which the LORD our God is giving us. 21 See, the LORD your God has set the land before you. Go up and take possession of it as Yahweh, the God of your fathers, has told you. Do not be afraid or discouraged.

22 "Then all of you approached me and said, 'Let's send men ahead of us, so that they may explore the land for us and bring us back a report about the route we should go up and the cities we will come to.' 23 The plan seemed good to me, so I selected 12 men from among you, one man for each tribe. 24 They left and went up into the hill country and came to the Valley of Eshcol, scouting the land. 25 They took some of the fruit from the land in their hands, carried it down to us, and brought us back a report: 'The land the LORD our God is giving us is good.'

26 "But you were not willing to go up, rebelling against the command of the LORD your God. 27 You grumbled in your tents and said, 'The LORD brought us out of the land of Egypt to deliver us into the hands of the Amorites so they would destroy us, because He hated us. 28 Where can we go? Our brothers have discouraged us, saying: The people are larger and taller than we are; the cities are large, fortified to the heavens. We also saw the descendants of the Anakim there.'

29 "So I said to you: Don't be terrified or afraid of them! 30 The LORD your God who goes before you will fight for you, just as you saw Him do for you in Egypt. 31 And you saw in the wilderness how the LORD your God carried you as a man carries his son all along the way you traveled until you reached this place. 32 But in spite of this you did not trust the LORD your God, 33 who went before you on the journey to seek out a place for you to camp. He went in the fire by night and in the cloud by day to guide you on the road you were to travel.

34 "When the LORD heard your[A] words, He grew angry and swore an oath: 35 'None of these men in this evil generation will see the good land I swore to give your fathers, 36 except Caleb the son of Jephunneh. He will see it, and I will give him and his descendants the land

HARD QUESTION

Does God Get Angry?

Twice in this passage (1:34-37) Moses referred to the Lord's response to His people—**He grew angry** (Hb *qatsaph*, "break forth in anger, be furious") upon hearing the Israelites' grumbling, and He also **was angry** (Hb *ʾanaph*, "show oneself to be angry"; cp. 4:21; 9:8,20) with Moses because of them. While the Bible is clear that God is a loving God, God is also a just God and must punish sin. However, do not confuse the sometimes sinful human response of anger with God's response to His people. God is slow to anger or wrath and does not stay angry for an indeterminate amount of time (Pss 30:5; 78:38; Is 12:1). God's wrath is on account of sin or evil, while human wrath or anger is often a self-centered response that can be irrational and impulsive. God's anger is always a righteous response to sin.

[A] **1:34** Lit *the sound of your*

on which he has set foot, because he followed the LORD completely.’

37 “The LORD was angry with me also because of you and said: ‘You will not enter there either. 38 Joshua son of Nun, who attends you, will enter it. Encourage him, for he will enable Israel to inherit it. 39 Your little children, whom you said would be plunder, your sons who[A] don’t know good from evil, will enter there. I will give them the land, and they will take possession of it. 40 But you are to turn back and head for the wilderness by way of the •Red Sea.’

41 “You answered me, ‘We have sinned against the LORD. We will go up and fight just as the LORD our God commanded us.’ Then each of you put on his weapons of war and thought it would be easy to go up into the hill country.

42 “But the LORD said to me, ‘Tell them: Don’t go up and fight, for I am not with you to keep you from being defeated by your enemies.’ 43 So I spoke to you, but you didn’t listen. You rebelled against the LORD’s command and defiantly went up into the hill country. 44 Then the Amorites who lived there came out against you and chased you like a swarm of bees. They routed you from Seir as far as Hormah. 45 When you returned, you wept before the LORD, but He didn’t listen to your requests or pay attention to you. 46 For this reason you stayed in Kadesh as long as you did.[B]

Journey Past Seir (2:1-7)

2 “Then we turned back and headed for the wilderness by way of the •Red Sea, as the LORD had told me, and we traveled around the hill country of Seir for many days. 2 The LORD then said to me, 3 ‘You’ve been traveling around this hill country long enough; turn north. 4 Command the people: You are about to travel through the territory of your brothers, the descendants of Esau, who live in Seir. They will be afraid of you, so you must be very careful. 5 Don’t fight with them, for I will not give you any of their land, not even an inch of it,[C] because I have given Esau the hill country of Seir as his possession. 6 You may purchase food from them with silver, so that you may eat, and buy water from them to drink. 7 For the LORD your God has blessed you in all the work of your hands. He has watched over your journey through this immense wilderness. The LORD your God has been with you this past 40 years, and you have lacked nothing.’

Journey Past Moab (2:8-15)

8 “So we bypassed our brothers, the descendants of Esau, who live in Seir. We turned away from the •Arabah road and from Elath and Ezion-geber. We traveled along the road to the Wilderness of Moab. 9 The LORD said to me, ‘Show no hostility toward Moab, and do not provoke them to battle, for I will not give you any of their land as a possession, since I have given Ar as a possession to the descendants of Lot.’ ”

10 The Emim, a great and numerous people as tall as the Anakim, had previously lived there. 11 They were also regarded as Rephaim, like the Anakim, though the Moabites called them Emim. 12 The Horites had previously lived in Seir, but the descendants of Esau drove them out, destroying them completely[D] and settling in their place, just as Israel did in the land of its possession the LORD gave them.

13 “The LORD said, ‘Now get up and cross the Zered Valley.’ So we crossed the Zered Valley. 14 The time we spent traveling from Kadesh-barnea until we crossed the Zered Valley was 38 years until the entire generation of fighting men had perished from the camp, as the LORD had sworn to them. 15 Indeed, the LORD’s hand was against them, to eliminate them from the camp until they had all perished.

Journey Past Ammon (2:16-23)

16 “When all the fighting men had died among the people, 17 the LORD spoke to me, 18 ‘Today you are going to cross the border of Moab at Ar. 19 When you get close to the Ammonites, don’t show any hostility to

[A]1:39 Lit *who today* [B]1:46 Lit *Kadesh for many days, according to the days you stayed* [C]2:5 Lit *land as far as the width of a sole of a foot* [D]2:12 Lit *them before them*

must also exhibit to their followers loving concern and reasonable availability practically and spiritually.

1:19-45 Moses reminded the people of their rebellion, which caused the costly detour of 40 years wandering in the desert. God had already told the people of Israel that the land was theirs. The people ignored the command of the Lord; they listened to men rather than God and refused to go into the land. They not only rebelled, but they complained and even questioned the motives of the Lord. The people who had been delivered from the hands of the Egyptians doubted the Lord’s power to deliver the land He had promised.

1:28 The descendants of the Anakim, according to tradition, were a tribe of giants seven to nine feet tall, who were compared to the Nephilim, a race that would have perished in the flood (Nm 13:33; Gn 6:4). The Anakim were named after Anak, the son of Arba. Arba founded Hebron (Jos 21:11).

1:45 God’s refusal to save them from the consequences of rebellion is not a refusal to listen to their cries for help. He did hear their cries for help when they were slaves in Egypt, and He sent a deliverer to lead them out of bondage. The issue was not the Lord’s unwillingness to hear, but the unwillingness of the Israelites to obey. Therefore, the Lord **didn’t listen** to their requests or **pay attention** to them.

2:4-5 When the Israelites left Kadesh-barnea, they traveled through the land of **Seir**, the home of **the descendants of Esau**. The Lord did not allow them to cause trouble for the descendants of Esau, to whom He had promised their own inheritance (Gn 27:39-40).

2:10-12 An explanatory note occurs in these verses: The **Emim** (Hb, “terrors”) were obviously a feared people of large stature as were the **Anakim** and **Rephaim** (Hb, “giants”). These early inhabitants evidently later disappeared.

2:14 The Israelites spent 38 years traveling between **Kadesh-barnea** and the **Zered Valley** until all the **fighting men** of the rebellious generation had died—a somber example of the trustworthiness of God to keep His word. Not all in the group that escaped from Egypt perished in the wilderness; God apparently spared the children who were not yet “fighting” age.

2:19 The **Ammonites**, along with the Moabites, were descendants of Lot’s sons Ammon and Moab (see 2:9), whom Lot fathered after a drunken encounter with his own daughters following the destruction of Sodom and Gomorrah (Gn 19:30-38). Since Lot was the nephew of Abraham, his descendants were treated with favor by the Lord.

2:20-21 Another feared group is mentioned: the **Zamzummim** (Hb, "noisy ones") who were also called **Rephaim** (Hb, "giants"). They were driven out of the land by the Ammonites before the Israelites settled in the land.

2:24-25 The Lord instructed them to take possession of the land of **Sihon the Amorite, king of Heshbon**. Taking the land from Sihon was a military move to motivate the nation of Israel for later victories. Even in his military strategy, the Lord was modeling His faithful love to the Israelites and teaching them how He would lead and guide them in taking possession of the promised land.

2:26-30 As the Israelites obeyed the voice of the Lord to take possession of the land, their actions first seem to counter His order when they made the offer of peace to the king. However, offering peace to the king would have been the accepted practice. Therefore, as King Sihon refused **an offer of peace** from Moses and the Israelites, **the Lord** made **his spirit stubborn and his heart obstinate**. The king's hardening of his heart began with his choice to reject Yahweh God, and the consequence of his choice is an act of divine judgment (Gn 15:14; cp. Ex 4:21; 7:3; 9:12; 10:1-2,20,27; 11:10; Jos 11:20). The Lord was confirming the choice Sihon had already made (Nm 21:21-23).

2:34 The stubbornness of the heart of King Sihon led to the possession of his land by the Israelites according to the will of God. God used the ancient practice of **completely** destroying (Hb *charam*, "devoted to destruction") to remove anyone or anything in opposition to His holiness or a barrier to His keeping of the covenant with His people. This destruction not only manifested God's judgment on the wicked nations who rejected Him (9:4; Gn 15:16) but also provided a protection for His people from the influences of false gods and the evil practices of pagan nations so they could accomplish the task God had given to them to represent Him to the nations (Dt 20:17-18).

2:36-37 At this point the Israelites were obedient and teachable. They went only into the lands that God told them to enter, and they did not attempt to battle the other nations. The people understood that only God had given them victory.

them or fight with them, for I will
not give you any of the Ammonites'
land as a possession; I have given it
as a possession to the descendants of
Lot.'"
20 This too used to be regarded
as the land of the Rephaim. The
Rephaim lived there previously,
though the Ammonites called them
Zamzummim, 21 a great and numerous people, tall as the Anakim. The
Lord destroyed the Rephaim at the
advance of the Ammonites, so that
they drove them out and settled in
their place. 22 This was just as He
had done for the descendants of
Esau who lived in Seir, when He
destroyed the Horites before them;
they drove them out and have lived
in their place until now. 23 The Caphtorim, who came from Caphtor,[A]
destroyed the Avvim, who lived in
villages as far as Gaza, and settled in
their place.

Defeat of Sihon the Amorite (2:24-37)

24 "The Lord also said, 'Get up,
move out, and cross the Arnon Valley. See, I have handed Sihon the
Amorite, king of Heshbon, and his
land over to you. Begin to take possession of it; engage him in battle.
25 Today I will begin to put the fear
and dread of you on the peoples everywhere under heaven. They will
hear the report about you, tremble,
and be in anguish because of you.'
26 "So I sent messengers with
an offer of peace to Sihon king of
Heshbon from the Wilderness of
Kedemoth, saying, 27 'Let us travel
through your land; we will keep
strictly to the highway. We will not
turn to the right or the left. 28 You
can sell us food in exchange for silver so we may eat, and give us water
for silver so we may drink. Only let
us travel through on foot, 29 just as
the descendants of Esau who live
in Seir did for us, and the Moabites
who live in Ar, until we cross the
Jordan into the land the Lord our
God is giving us.' 30 But Sihon king
of Heshbon would not let us travel
through his land, for the Lord your
God had made his spirit stubborn
and his heart obstinate in order to
hand him over to you, as has now
taken place.
31 "Then the Lord said to me, 'See,
I have begun to give Sihon and his
land to you. Begin to take possession
of it.' 32 So Sihon and his whole army
came out against us for battle at Jahaz. 33 The Lord our God handed him
over to us, and we defeated him, his
sons, and his whole army. 34 At that
time we captured all his cities and
•completely destroyed the people
of every city, including the women
and children. We left no survivors.
35 We took only the livestock and the
spoil from the cities we captured as
plunder for ourselves. 36 There was
no city that was inaccessible to[B] us,
from Aroer on the rim of the Arnon
Valley, along with the city in the valley, even as far as Gilead. The Lord
our God gave everything to us. 37 But
you did not go near the Ammonites'
land, all along the bank of the Jabbok River, the cities of the hill country, or any place that the Lord our
God had forbidden.

Defeat of Og of Bashan (3:1-7)

3 "Then we turned and went up
the road to Bashan, and Og king
of Bashan came out against us with
his whole army to do battle at Edrei.
2 But the Lord said to me, 'Do not
fear him, for I have handed him over
to you along with his whole army
and his land. Do to him as you did
to Sihon king of the Amorites, who
lived in Heshbon.' 3 So the Lord our
God also handed over Og king of
Bashan and his whole army to us.
We struck him until there was no
survivor left. 4 We captured all his
cities at that time. There wasn't a
city that we didn't take from them:
60 cities, the entire region of Argob,
the kingdom of Og in Bashan. 5 All
these were fortified with high walls,
gates, and bars, besides a large number of rural villages. 6 We •complete-
ly destroyed them, as we had done to
Sihon king of Heshbon, destroying
the men, women, and children of
every city. 7 But we took all the livestock and the spoil from the cities as
plunder for ourselves.

[A] **2:23** Probably Crete [B] **2:36** Or *was too high for*

The Land of the Transjordan Tribes (3:8-20)

8 “At that time we took the land from the two Amorite kings across the Jordan, from the Arnon Valley as far as Mount Hermon, 9 which the Sidonians call Sirion, but the Amorites call Senir, 10 all the cities of the plateau, Gilead, and Bashan as far as Salecah and Edrei, cities of Og's kingdom in Bashan. 11 (Only Og king of Bashan was left of the remnant of the Rephaim. His bed was made of iron.[A] Isn't it in Rabbah of the Ammonites? It is 13 feet six inches long and six feet wide by a standard measure.[B])

12 “At that time we took possession of this land. I gave to the Reubenites and Gadites the area extending from Aroer by the Arnon Valley, and half the hill country of Gilead along with its cities. 13 I gave to half the tribe of Manasseh the rest of Gilead and all Bashan, the kingdom of Og. The entire region of Argob, the whole territory of Bashan, used to be called the land of the Rephaim. 14 Jair, a descendant of Manasseh, took over the entire region of Argob as far as the border of the Geshurites and Maacathites. He called Bashan by his own name, Jair's Villages,[C] as it is today. 15 I gave Gilead to Machir, 16 and I gave to the Reubenites and Gadites the area extending from Gilead to the Arnon Valley (the middle of the valley was the border) and up to the Jabbok River, the border of the Ammonites. 17 The •Arabah and Jordan are also borders from Chinnereth[D] as far as the Sea of the Arabah, the Dead Sea, under the slopes of Pisgah on the east.

18 “I commanded you at that time: The LORD your God has given you this land to possess. All your fighting men will cross over in battle formation ahead of your brothers the Israelites. 19 But your wives, young children, and livestock—I know that you have a lot of livestock—will remain in the cities I have given you 20 until the LORD gives rest to your brothers as He has to you, and they also take possession of the land the LORD your God is giving them across the Jordan. Then each of you may return to his possession that I have given you.

The Transfer of Israel's Leadership (3:21-29)

21 “I commanded Joshua at that time: Your own eyes have seen everything the LORD your God has done to these two kings. The LORD will do the same to all the kingdoms you are about to enter. 22 Don't be afraid of them, for the LORD your God fights for you.

23 “At that time I begged the LORD: 24 Lord GOD, You have begun to show Your greatness and power to Your servant, for what god is there in heaven or on earth who can perform deeds and mighty acts like Yours? 25 Please let me cross over and see the beautiful land on the other side of the Jordan, that good hill country and Lebanon.

26 “But the LORD was angry with me on account of you and would not listen to me. The LORD said to me, ‘That's enough! Do not speak to Me again about this matter. 27 Go to the top of Pisgah and look to the west, north, south, and east, and see it with your own eyes, for you will not cross this Jordan. 28 But commission Joshua and encourage and strengthen him, for he will cross over ahead of the people and enable them to inherit this land that you will see.’ 29 So we stayed in the valley facing Beth-peor.

The Call to Obedience (4:1-14)

4 “Now, Israel, listen to the statutes and ordinances I am teaching you to follow, so that you may live, enter, and take possession of the land •Yahweh, the God of your fathers, is giving you. 2 You must not add anything to what I command you or take anything away from it, so that you may keep the commands of the LORD your God I am giving you. 3 Your eyes have seen what the LORD did at Baal-peor, for the LORD your God destroyed every one of you who followed •Baal of Peor. 4 But you who have remained faithful[E] to the LORD

[A]**3:11** Or *His sarcophagus was made of basalt* [B]**3:11** Lit *Nine cubits its length and four cubits its width, by a man's cubit* [C]**3:14** Or *Havvoth-jair* [D]**3:17** = the Sea of Galilee; Jos 12:3; 13:27; Lk 5:1 [E]**4:4** Lit *have held on*

3:1 Bashan, a particularly fertile track of land, is the northernmost region of Palestine east of the Jordan River (Dt 32:14). It was apportioned to the tribal land of Manasseh during the time of Moses, after the Israelites defeated Bashan's King **Og** (Dt 3:13; Nm 21:33-35).

3:11 The **bed . . . of iron** of Og could be a reference to his coffin or sarcophagus made of an iron-like mineral known as basalt. The dimensions of it make clear that Og was probably a man large in stature.

3:12-20 When they first attempted to cross the land, the men from the tribes of Reuben, Gad, and the half tribe of Manasseh declared they would like a certain part of the land, which was located just outside the entrance to the promised land (cp. Nm 32). They saw that this land was good for their herds of livestock. However, the Lord required that the **fighting men** help the rest of the nation of Israel take possession of the land that He was giving to them (Dt 3:18-20). Undoubtedly these women and children would not have been left defenseless. Some men would have remained to protect the families and possessions of those who went off to war (cp. 20:5-8). However, also apparent is the fact that women did not participate in the military operation.

3:21-27 God had forbidden Moses to enter the promised land because he struck the rock twice rather than speaking to the rock as he was instructed (Nm 20:1-13). Because of his anger and disobedience, Moses would not be allowed to enter the promised land, and he was instructed not to speak of entering the land. However, the Lord did allow Moses to see the land from **the top of Pisgah** (located in modern-day Jordan).

3:28-29 When Moses charged Joshua with remembering how the Lord gave the lands of Sihon, Og, and the Amorites into the hands of Israel while they were still outside the promised land, he was preparing Joshua for leadership after his departure. Moses continued to strengthen and encourage Joshua, and this same mentoring and teaching has been used throughout the generations of Christendom to equip the younger generations, who need time and preparation to step into their new roles of leadership. Moses' example is a prime model of God's plan for preparing for transitions in leadership.

4:1-3 In the preceding chapters Moses had summarized the history of the people. He went back over their wandering and the failures and victories they experienced after the exodus. Then Moses said, **Now, Israel.**

>WORD|*study*

4:24 As a description of God, jealous (Hb *qanna'*, "tolerating no rivals"; cp. 5:9; 6:15; Ex 20:5; 34:14) conveys the very nature of covenant fidelity. Like a husband whose marriage covenant entitles him to the exclusive devotion of his wife, God will not share His people's devotion with anything or anyone. Jealous does not describe God in human terms as angry or hurt over petty things or as envious of another. Rather, He is the one true God who rightly demands that no other god should be worshiped by His people, whom He rescued from Egyptian slavery. God cannot tolerate losing His people's love for and loyalty to Him. Their breaking the covenant would forfeit the blessing and prosperity He promised to those who would remain faithful to Him. In the Septuagint, the Greek translation of jealous is *zēlōtēs*, "burning with zeal." God's jealousy is part of His love, i.e., His fervent devotion to His people, but He is particularly jealous for righteousness. To assert that God is "a jealous God" clarifies why He is also "a consuming fire." Idolatry is a treasonous violation of the covenant demanding divine judgment, vindicating the Lord in His unfailing commitment to that covenant.

your God are all alive today. 5 Look,
I have taught you statutes and ordinances as the LORD my God has commanded me, so that you may follow
them in the land you are entering
to possess. 6 Carefully follow them,
for this will show your wisdom and
understanding in the eyes of the
peoples. When they hear about all
these statutes, they will say, 'This
great nation is indeed a wise and understanding people.' 7 For what great
nation is there that has a god near
to it as the LORD our God is to us
whenever we call to Him? 8 And what
great nation has righteous statutes
and ordinances like this entire law I
set before you today?

9 "Only be on your guard and diligently watch yourselves, so that you
don't forget the things your eyes
have seen and so that they don't
slip from your mind as long as you
live. Teach them to your children
and your grandchildren. 10 The day
you stood before the LORD your God
at Horeb, the LORD said to me, 'Assemble the people before Me, and I
will let them hear My words, so that
they may learn to •fear Me all the
days they live on the earth and may
instruct their children.' 11 You came
near and stood at the base of the
mountain, a mountain blazing with
fire into the heavens and enveloped
in a dense, black cloud. 12 Then the
LORD spoke to you from the fire. You
kept hearing the sound of the words,
but didn't see a form; there was only
a voice. 13 He declared His covenant
to you. He commanded you to follow the Ten Commandments, which
He wrote on two stone tablets. 14 At
that time the LORD commanded me
to teach you statutes and ordinances
for you to follow in the land you are
about to cross into and possess.

Worshiping the True God (4:15-40)

15 "For your own good, be extremely careful—because you did
not see any form on the day the
LORD spoke to you out of the fire at
Horeb— 16 not to act corruptly and
make an idol for yourselves in the
shape of any figure: a male or female
form, 17 or the form of any beast on
the earth, any winged creature that
flies in the sky, 18 any creature that
crawls on the ground, or any fish in
the waters under the earth. 19 When
you look to the heavens and see the
sun, moon, and stars—all the array
of heaven—do not be led astray to
bow down and worship them. The
LORD your God has provided them
for all people everywhere under
heaven. 20 But the LORD selected you
and brought you out of Egypt's iron
furnace to be a people for His inheritance, as you are today.

21 "The LORD was angry with me on
your account. He swore that I would
not cross the Jordan and enter the
good land the LORD your God is giving you as an inheritance. 22 I won't
be crossing the Jordan because I am
going to die in this land. But you are
about to cross over and take possession of this good land. 23 Be careful
not to forget the covenant of the
LORD your God that He made with
you, and make an idol for yourselves
in the shape of anything He has forbidden you. 24 For the LORD your God
is a consuming fire, a jealous God.

25 "When you have children and
grandchildren and have been in the
land a long time, and if you act corruptly, make an idol in the form of
anything, and do what is evil in the
sight of the LORD your God, provoking Him to anger, 26 I call heaven and
earth as witnesses against you today
that you will quickly perish from

This transition brought the people to the understanding that Moses was now turning to another topic as they were on the eve of a new beginning. Moses was calling the people to consider how they might live in the promised land. **Listen to the statutes and ordinances**—there is a direct correlation to Israel's understanding of how to live in the promised land and their listening to the voice of God. Moses highlighted the relationship the people of God were to have to the voice of God. They were to listen; they would know how to live because they listened.

4:4 Moses refers again to the new generation who were the chosen ones to enter the land. They had seen several instances of rebellion from the older generation of relatives and peers. Moses called the younger generation to obedience not only based on the instruction of the Lord but also on the reminder that to disobey leads to destruction and death (4:1-3).

4:5-7 Moses reminded the people that if they obeyed, the Lord would honor them by demonstrating their **wisdom and understanding in the eyes of the peoples.** The surrounding nations would know that their God was different, and they would ultimately fear and respect Israel.

4:8 The statutes and ordinances, including the Ten Commandments and more, are the way Moses commonly referred to requirements of the Lord for the Israelites with whom He had entered a covenantal relationship. For example, the purity laws outlined in Leviticus would be considered part of these statutes and ordinances.

4:9 Moses drew a connection between their likeliness to obey and their ability to remember all that God had already done for them.

4:15-20 The people were not to worship any image they had seen. God only revealed Himself to them through His voice. They had seen nothing specifically referred to as "God"; therefore, they were to make nothing representative of God to aid their worship. Moses reminded the people that all creation—beasts, birds, fish, plants, **sun, moon, and stars**—were part of God's provision for them. However, they were not to worship the creation or be tempted to incorporate created things into their worship.

4:23 God created Israel and rescued them to be in relationship with Him. Therefore, at the heart of all the Lord's commands and statutes was the character of God.

the land you are about to cross the
Jordan to possess. You will not live
long there, but you will certainly
be destroyed. 27 The LORD will scatter you among the peoples, and you
will be reduced to a few survivors[A]
among the nations where the LORD
your God will drive you. 28 There
you will worship man-made gods of
wood and stone, which cannot see,
hear, eat, or smell. 29 But from there,
you will search for the LORD your
God, and you will find Him when
you seek Him with all your heart
and all your soul. 30 When you are
in distress and all these things have
happened to you, you will return to
the LORD your God in later days and
obey Him. 31 He will not leave you,
destroy you, or forget the covenant
with your fathers that He swore to
them by oath, because the LORD your
God is a compassionate God.

32 "Indeed, ask about the earlier
days that preceded you, from the
day God created man on the earth
and from one end of the heavens
to the other: Has anything like this
great event ever happened, or has
anything like it been heard of? 33 Has
a people heard God's voice speaking from the fire as you have, and
lived? 34 Or has a god attempted to
go and take a nation as his own out
of another nation, by trials, signs,
wonders, and war, by a strong hand
and an outstretched arm, by great
terrors, as the LORD your God did
for you in Egypt before your eyes?
35 You were shown these things so
that you would know that the LORD
is God; there is no other besides
Him. 36 He let you hear His voice
from heaven to instruct you. He
showed you His great fire on earth,
and you heard His words from the
fire. 37 Because He loved your fathers, He chose their descendants
after them and brought you out of
Egypt by His presence and great
power, 38 to drive out before you nations greater and stronger than you
and to bring you in and give you
their land as an inheritance, as is
now taking place. 39 Today, recognize and keep in mind that the LORD
is God in heaven above and on earth
below; there is no other. 40 Keep His
statutes and commands, which I am
giving you today, so that you and
your children after you may prosper
and so that you may live long in the
land the LORD your God is giving
you for all time."

Cities of Refuge (4:41-43)

41 Then Moses set apart three cities across the Jordan to the east.
42 Someone could flee there who
committed manslaughter, killing
his neighbor accidentally without
previously hating him. He could
flee to one of these cities and stay
alive: 43 Bezer in the wilderness on
the plateau land, belonging to the
Reubenites; Ramoth in Gilead, belonging to the Gadites; or Golan in
Bashan, belonging to the Manassites.

Moses' Second Speech: The Law (4:44–26:19)

Introductory Comments on the Law (4:44-49)

44 This is the law Moses gave the
Israelites. 45 These are the decrees,

[A]**4:27** Lit *be left few in number*

4:24 The word picture Moses used to describe God as **a consuming fire** would have reminded the Israelites of the way the Lord appeared to them by night to show them the way to travel while in the desert. Also, when Moses received the Ten Commandments on Mount Sinai, "The appearance of the LORD's glory to the Israelites was like a consuming fire on the mountaintop" (Ex 24:17).

4:25-31 In these verses Moses anticipated the future rebellion of the people with words of correction to them.

4:32-40 God was unquestionably doing a new thing in the history of Israel at this time. Moses did not want them to miss this significant event in their history. He also did not want them to overlook that the covenant was happening just because God chose for it to happen. God's selection of Israel was based solely on His love for their forefathers and the establishment of His covenant with them. There was nothing that the descendants of Abraham had done to deserve His favor or prompt His action on their behalf. God, for some unknown reason, revealed Himself to all people through the nation of Israel. Therefore, Moses strongly admonished them to remember that God chose to bring them into existence. He determined that they would be a people set free from slavery, having food and water in the wilderness. The Israelites' responsibility rested in the fact that they were to remember and obey, to **recognize and keep in mind** and to **keep His statutes and commands** (vv. 39-40). Did they want to live well in the land, which they were preparing to possess? Then they were to listen and obey the voice of the Lord.

4:41-43 These three **cities** of refuge for the nation of Israel were geographically located throughout the nation as places to ensure that if a crime had been committed **accidentally** (i.e., **manslaughter**), the person responsible could flee to one of these cities while the incident

Biblical Womanhood The Responsibility of Parenthood

Over and over again the book of Deuteronomy emphasizes the importance of listening to and obeying the Lord, and Moses linked this to the responsibility of parenting. Not only were the adults to listen to and obey the Lord, but they were to teach their children how to listen to and walk with God. Your actions today affect those who come after you. Do you live in a way that will bless those who come after you? Are you listening and making choices that are in accord with the commandments and statutes of God? Are you allowing your children to see you respond to the Lord in your daily life? Are you teaching your children to know God and obey Him? Moses was not asked to be the primary teacher to all the children; parents were given that responsibility. In the same way today, even though pastors, teachers, and church leaders will play a role in the spiritual development of children, parents have the primary responsibility of passing down spiritual truths to their children.

was investigated. In the meantime, they were to be protected in these cities from family members who might have been blinded by the desire for vengeance (see 19:1-13).

5:2 Before Moses reminded the people of the Ten Commandments, he transitioned by addressing the current generation. He reminded them that the Lord made a covenant with them at **Horeb** (Hb "waste" or "wilderness area"); this name is a general term for the area where Mount Sinai or "the mountain of God" is located where God appeared to Moses in the burning bush and later gave the Israelites the Ten Commandments (Ex 3:1-12; 19:1-20:17; Dt 1:19).

5:2-4 The present **covenant** was not with their **fathers** but with them, the present generation. This fact is significant because here Moses summoned all of Israel to be accountable to the Lord, and He is formally addressing the people who will go into the land. While most of this generation would have been only children when the Lord delivered them from Egypt and protected and provided for them in the wilderness (presumably some of them had been born after the deliverance from Egypt), some of them still had observed His glory. Therefore, Moses reminded the people of Israel that **the Lord spoke to you face to face from the fire on the mountain.** These people, while young, had heard and were ultimately accountable to the commands of the Lord.

5:6-11 Monotheism is the theme of the first four commandments. God was to be worshiped as the one true God of the Israelites. No other god had heard their cries in the land of Egypt. No other god had delivered them from the hands of their enemies. No other god had protected them in the wilderness and appeared to them in the cloud and in the pillar of fire. Therefore, at the dawn of their journey into the promised land, Moses firmly admonished them to remember that the Lord their God is one. He would have no other gods before Him, and the people were to be on their guard to avoid worshiping other gods. This included not making any idols that would be in the image of creatures or beings, even though those objects might be thought to represent the Lord. They were not to make for themselves anything to worship, and they were not to bow down to anyone else's creations.

5:9 The consequences of their not listening and obeying the voice of the Lord on these matters were serious. If they did not listen, their sin would affect their children and grandchildren. Children are not punished for their parents' rebellion but because they

>WORD|*study*

4:44-45 Moses begins his discussion of the Ten Commandments, and three important words are used as descriptors for the law (Hb *torah*, used here as synonymous with the covenant):

- decrees (Hb *'edah*, pl. *'edot*, "testimonies," i.e., the covenant stipulations; cp. 6:17; Ps 99:7);
- statutes (Hb *choq*, pl. *chuqqim*, "decrees, ordinances, laws; prescribed tasks limits, or boundaries"; cp. Ex 18:20);
- ordinances (Hb *mishpat*, pl. *mishpatim*, "laws, judgments, decisions" from the verb *shapat*, "judge, govern"; cp. Dt 5:1).

The phrase "statutes and ordinances" functions as a technical term commonly used in ancient Near Eastern covenants to stipulate the commitments to be kept by the dependent or vassal nation as prescribed by the suzerain or dominant power (cp. Ex 18:20). Yahweh took the initiative both to redeem Israel and to make this covenant. As the sovereign, He alone had the right to determine the terms of their agreement. If Israel would honor this covenant by obeying the Lord's commands, He would live in their midst (Dt 4:6-7).

statutes, and ordinances Moses proclaimed to them after they came out
of Egypt, 46 across the Jordan in the
valley facing Beth-peor in the land
of Sihon king of the Amorites. He
lived in Heshbon, and Moses and the
Israelites defeated him after they
came out of Egypt. 47 They took possession of his land and the land of
Og king of Bashan, the two Amorite
kings who were across the Jordan
to the east, 48 from Aroer on the rim
of the Arnon Valley as far as Mount
Sion (that is, Hermon) 49 and all the
•Arabah on the east side of the Jordan as far as the Dead Sea below the
slopes of Pisgah.

The Ten Commandments (5:1-21)

5 Moses summoned all Israel and
said to them, "Israel, listen to
the statutes and ordinances I am
proclaiming as you hear them today.
Learn and follow them carefully.
2 The LORD our God made a covenant
with us at Horeb. 3 He did not make
this covenant with our fathers, but
with all of us who are alive here today. 4 The LORD spoke to you face to
face from the fire on the mountain.
5 At that time I was standing between
the LORD and you to report the word[A]
of the LORD to you, because you were
afraid of the fire and did not go up
the mountain. And He said:

6 I am the LORD your God, who
brought you out of the land of
Egypt, out of the place of slavery.

7 Do not have other gods besides Me.

8 Do not make an idol for yourself in the shape of anything
in the heavens above or on the
earth below or in the waters
under the earth. 9 You must
not bow down to them or worship them, because I, the LORD
your God, am a jealous God,
punishing the children for the
fathers' sin to the third and
fourth generations of those
who hate Me, 10 but showing
faithful love to a thousand
generations of those who love
Me and keep My commands.

11 Do not misuse the name of
the LORD your God, because
the LORD will not leave anyone
unpunished who misuses His
name.

12 Be careful to remember the
Sabbath day, to keep it holy
as the LORD your God has
commanded you. 13 You are
to labor six days and do all
your work, 14 but the seventh
day is a Sabbath to the LORD
your God. You must not do
any work—you, your son or
daughter, your male or female slave, your ox or donkey, any of your livestock, or
the foreigner who lives within
your gates, so that your male
and female slaves may rest
as you do. 15 Remember that
you were a slave in the land
of Egypt, and the LORD your
God brought you out of there

[A]**5:5** One Hb ms, DSS, Sam, LXX, Syr, Vg read *words*

with a strong hand and an
outstretched arm. That is why
the LORD your God has commanded you to keep the Sabbath day.
16 Honor your father and your
mother, as the LORD your God
has commanded you, so that
you may live long and so that
you may prosper in the land
the LORD your God is giving
you.
17 Do not murder.
18 Do not commit adultery.
19 Do not steal.
20 Do not give dishonest testimony against your neighbor.
21 Do not covet your neighbor's
wife or desire your neighbor's
house, his field, his male or female slave, his ox or donkey,
or anything that belongs to
your neighbor.

The People's Response (5:22-33)

22 "The LORD spoke these commands in a loud voice to your entire
assembly from the fire, cloud, and
thick darkness on the mountain; He
added nothing more. He wrote them
on two stone tablets and gave them
to me. 23 All of you approached me
with your tribal leaders and elders
when you heard the voice from the
darkness and while the mountain
was blazing with fire. 24 You said,
'Look, the LORD our God has shown
us His glory and greatness, and we
have heard His voice from the fire.
Today we have seen that God speaks
with a person, yet he still lives. 25 But
now, why should we die? This great
fire will consume us and we will die
if we hear the voice of the LORD our
God any longer. 26 For who out of all
mankind has heard the voice of the
living God speaking from the fire, as
we have, and lived? 27 Go near and
listen to everything the LORD our
God says. Then you can tell us everything the LORD our God tells you;
we will listen and obey.'
28 "The LORD heard your[A] words
when you spoke to me. He said to
me, 'I have heard the words that
these people have spoken to you.
Everything they have said is right.
29 If only they had such a heart to
•fear Me and keep all My commands
always, so that they and their children will prosper forever. 30 Go and
tell them: Return to your tents.
31 But you stand here with Me, and
I will tell you every command—the
statutes and ordinances—you are to
teach them, so that they may follow
them in the land I am giving them
to possess.'
32 "Be careful to do as the LORD
your God has commanded you; you
are not to turn aside to the right or

Doctrine THE TEN COMMANDMENTS

Scholars are divided as to the exact reason for the giving of Ten Commandments (5:6-21). Some say that to fit into the tradition of oral recitation and memorization of ancient civilization, the number "ten" (brought to mind by 10 fingers and 10 toes) would make recall easier. Whatever the reason, the Lord made His covenant with the people by giving 10 commandments for them to hear and obey for their own good. Scholars also vary as to the basic ordering or structure of the commandments. Jesus, in the New Testament, when asked which commandment was the greatest, answered, "Love the Lord your God with all your heart, with all your soul, and with all your mind. This is the greatest and most important command. The second is like it: Love your neighbor as yourself. All the Law and the Prophets depend on these two commands" (Mt 22:37-40). Here a structure or a simplification is given to provide a framework through which to understand the commandments. Some scholars, Saint Augustine included, believed that Dt 5:6-10 made the first commandment "Love the Lord," and then the rest of the commandments were the second grouping of instructions from the Lord to "love your neighbor." Later theologians believed that the command to **be careful to remember the Sabbath day, . . . as the LORD your God has commanded you** made up the central theme for the people of Israel, along with honoring their parents (vv. 12,16). The first-century Jewish scholars Philo and Josephus believed this because these are the only two commandments given in a positive format. The other commandments form a parallel structure around these two commandments describing for the Israelites how they were to live. Regardless of how the reader views the structure, the instructions of the Lord are clear, waiting to be heard and heeded by His children then and now. The repetition of the Ten Commandments in Deuteronomy is very close to the first instructions given in Exodus (Ex 20:1-17); however, Moses is not repeating them here without reason. He had a very clear purpose in mind for reminding the new generation of Israelites of the covenant the Lord had made with them. Later, the context of his address illustrates that Moses was reminding the people of the commands of the Lord as a way of introduction for his comments to them before they enter the promised land.

choose to rebel in the same manner. Children observe the lives of their parents and often pass their lifestyles on to their own children. Unbelieving parents more often than not produce unbelieving children. However, if the people did listen and obey only the Lord who had delivered them from Egypt, then He would show faithful love to all the generations after them. The implications of this commandment would have weighed heavily upon the original audience—who were entering the promised land without their parents and grandparents—as it should on Christians of every generation.

5:11 The word **misuse** literally means to use the Lord's name in an empty or purposeless way, thereby making light of the very holiness of God's name.

5:12-15 Instructions given regarding the **Sabbath** were extended to the entire households of the Israelites. In this rendering of the Ten Commandments, the rest commanded for the people would have been mandatory for all the people of Israel and their servants. In this account, the Israelites' deliverance from the land of Egypt was given as a reason for the need for the Sabbath rest—not just the act of God in creation when He rested on the seventh day. The truth that God had a particular way for the people of Israel to live and that their blessing and future depended on their obedience to His commandments cannot be overemphasized. Over and over Moses wanted the people to remember that God chose them to live in a particular way because they were His people. God rescued them from the land of Egypt. He was their protector and provider; however, they had to listen in order to experience a good life.

5:16 The commandment to **honor your father and . . . mother** implies the notion of mental obedience and obedience through actions. A child that "goes through the motions" and physically obeys parents yet rebels inwardly is not "honoring" her parents. To honor someone you must regard or think about them in high esteem. If they listened to the voice of the Lord in this matter, the people were promised that they would **live long** and that they would **prosper**. God wanted to bless the people; however, their obedience would determine how well their life in the promised land would go.

5:22-32 Once the people saw how the Lord spoke to them, they were afraid. Therefore, they requested that Moses listen to the voice of the Lord for them and interpret His words to them, and they promised to obey. The Lord heard their request and agreed to communicate with them through Moses. God communicated to them

[A]**5:28** Lit *the sound of your*

the fact that He wanted their hearts to be right before Him. He wanted their hearts to listen and obey so He could prosper them.

6:1 Moses reiterates the divine source of the **command** (Hb *mitswah*, "commandment, precept"). The word is singular, encompassing the Law as a whole or referring to the covenant stipulations—"the statutes and ordinances" (see 4:44-45)—as a unified body of "instruction." In words nearly identical to his report of Yahweh's in 5:31, Moses includes his divine appointment **to teach** the Law to the people. The word translated "teach" (Hb *lamad*, "cause to learn") is used for both "learn" and "instruct" (e.g., 4:10). The verb form used here denotes "training to do what is right" (Pss 119:68,108; 143:10) and is the root word of "Talmud," the collection of ancient rabbinic writings that comprise Jewish traditional and civil law. God had **instructed** (Hb *tsawah*, "command, charge, commission, appoint," the root word of *mitswah*; cp. 4:12) Moses not merely to *tell* the people *what* He said but to *train* the people *how* to **follow** (Hb *ʿasah*, "do, act on, put into effect") His "command" (i.e., to live in obedience to His Word).

6:4-5 In this portion of Scripture the *Shema*, the equivalent of a Jewish call to worship, is first observed. Recited morning and night by Jews during the Second Temple period (520 B.C.–A.D. 70), the prayer officially included both 6:4-9 and 11:13-21. Grammatically, the imperative **Listen** (Hb *shamaʿ*, "hear, heed") addresses a singular "you" (i.e., **Israel** as a single corporate body—"one" people or nation). However, the plural possessive pronoun **our** also conveys that Israel is a community of individuals. The first statement of the *Shema* declares that Yahweh, the God who has entered into covenant relationship with Israel, **is One** (Hb *ʾechad*, "one and only," having no article or other modifiers). In contrast to the plurality of gods worshiped by other nations, Yahweh alone is proclaimed to be the one and only **God**, to whom Israel confesses exclusive devotion. Judaism is, therefore, monotheistic. God warned the Israelites to be on their guard against idolatry (4:15-20), and the prohibition is the first of the Ten Commandments (5:7; Ex 20:3). Furthermore, the word "one" also implies that **the LORD** is an indivisible unity, which is consistent with the Christian doctrine of the Trinity. To keep the command to **love** (Hb *ʾahav*), Yahweh requires commitment rather than emotion. Nevertheless, the command is to "love" Him with all one's being—**with all your heart, with all your soul, and with all your strength** (cp. 5:10).

the left. 33 Follow the whole instruction the LORD your God has commanded you, so that you may live,
prosper, and have a long life in the
land you will possess.

The Greatest Command (6:1-9)

6 "This is the command—the statutes and ordinances—the LORD
your God has instructed me to teach
you, so that you may follow them
in the land you are about to enter
and possess. 2 Do this so that you
may •fear the LORD your God all the
days of your life by keeping all His
statutes and commands I am giving
you, your son, and your grandson,
and so that you may have a long life.
3 Listen, Israel, and be careful to follow them, so that you may prosper
and multiply greatly, because •Yah-
weh, the God of your fathers, has
promised you a land flowing with
milk and honey.
4 "Listen, Israel: The LORD our
God, the LORD is One.[A] 5 Love the
LORD your God with all your heart,
with all your soul, and with all your
strength. 6 These words that I am
giving you today are to be in your
heart. 7 Repeat them to your children. Talk about them when you sit
in your house and when you walk
along the road, when you lie down
and when you get up. 8 Bind them as
a sign on your hand and let them be
a symbol[B] on your forehead.[C] 9 Write
them on the doorposts of your house
and on your gates.

Remembering God through Obedience (6:10-25)

10 "When the LORD your God brings
you into the land He swore to your
fathers Abraham, Isaac, and Jacob
that He would give you—a land with
large and beautiful cities that you
did not build, 11 houses full of every
good thing that you did not fill them
with, wells dug that you did not dig,
and vineyards and olive groves that
you did not plant—and when you
eat and are satisfied, 12 be careful not
to forget the LORD who brought you
out of the land of Egypt, out of the
place of slavery. 13 Fear Yahweh your
God, worship Him, and take your
oaths in His name. 14 Do not follow

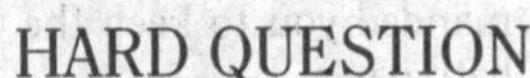

HARD QUESTION

How do you teach children to obey?

Formal educational theory suggests that certain teaching methodologies aid different types of learning. In Dt 6:4-9 several of these learning methodologies are observed. First, the Lord told the people to **listen** and to **repeat** the words of the Law to their children (vv. 4,7). In this instruction the value of learning facts and memorization is seen. God knew that some information needs to be learned and accepted. Basic facts about the character of God are included in this. God is loving. He is kind. He is the Provider. He is one. This type of factual information about God needs to be taught to younger generations.

Moses also told the people to **talk** about these truths with their children (v. 7). When they sat down and when they rose up, the Israelites were to dialogue with their children how the basic truths of God's law applied to their lives. God was concerned that the people and their children would listen to His voice and obey Him all the days of their lives. Therefore, He gave responsibility to the younger generation to teach it to their children in practical ways.

Moses also told them that they were to **bind** up the words of the Law and tie them around their hands and their foreheads as visible symbols to remember and learn God's law (v. 8). Here, a final learning method is observed. Sometimes people, especially children, need to see what they are being told. They need visual representations to help information or ideas connect inside their minds. Therefore, Moses instructed the people to make visible markers to represent the Law and its teachings to their children. By having a visual reminder, listening to and learning God's law would be integrated even more readily into the lives of the Israelites.

So, how does this apply to learning styles and pedagogy today? Parents and teachers are to learn the lessons that God wanted the younger Israelites to learn. Teaching children the truths of God's Word is more complex than memorizing several Bible verses. God's Word must be applied to the heart as part of your daily routine. You must talk about these words and repeat them and create visible signs in your homes and workplaces, reminding you of the goodness of God and the truth of His Word. Listening to the voice of the Lord for the Israelites included learning to know and apply His commands. They were to learn to do this by using several different methods, which should serve subsequent generations as well.

other gods, the gods of the peoples
around you, 15 for the LORD your God,
who is among you, is a jealous God.
Otherwise, the LORD your God will
become angry with you and wipe
you off the face of the earth. 16 Do
not test the LORD your God as you

[A]**6:4** Or *Yahweh is our God; Yahweh is One*, or *The LORD is our God, the LORD alone*, or *The LORD our God is one LORD* [B]**6:8** Or *phylactery*; Mt 23:5 [C]**6:8** Lit *symbol between your eyes*

Teaching as You Go

Opportunity	Mode	Role	Goal
Morning Time	Encouraging words to give vision for the day	Coach who encourages and gives vision	Cast a vision for the day and its opportunities
Travel Time	Informal conversation as you make your way through the daily schedule	Friend who influences as you talk about real life decisions	Apply biblical truths to real life issues
Family Time	Discussion of purpose with family altogether	Teacher who trains with planned conversation	Establish God's truth in the hearts of your family
Bedtime	Intimate sharing with each child at the end of the day	Counselor who guides through wisdom	Build rapport and knit your hearts together

tested Him at Massah. 17 Carefully
observe the commands of the LORD
your God, the decrees and statutes
He has commanded you. 18 Do what
is right and good in the LORD's sight,
so that you may prosper and so that
you may enter and possess the good
land the LORD your God swore to
give your fathers, 19 by driving out
all your enemies before you, as the
LORD has said.
20 "When your son asks you in the
future, 'What is the meaning of the
decrees, statutes, and ordinances,
which the LORD our God has commanded you?' 21 tell him, 'We were
slaves of Pharaoh in Egypt, but the
LORD brought us out of Egypt with
a strong hand. 22 Before our eyes the
LORD inflicted great and devastating signs and wonders on Egypt, on
Pharaoh, and on all his household,
23 but He brought us from there in
order to lead us in and give us the
land that He swore to our fathers.
24 The LORD commanded us to follow all these statutes and to fear
the LORD our God for our prosperity
always and for our preservation, as
it is today. 25 Righteousness will be
ours if we are careful to follow every one of these commands before
the LORD our God, as He has commanded us.'

Israel's Destruction of Idolatrous Nations (7:1-26)

7 "When the LORD your God brings
you into the land you are entering
to possess, and He drives out many
nations before you—the Hittites,
Girgashites, Amorites, Canaanites,
Perizzites, Hivites and Jebusites,
seven nations more numerous and
powerful than you— 2 and when the
LORD your God delivers them over to
you and you defeat them, you must
•completely destroy them. Make no
treaty with them and show them
no mercy. 3 Do not intermarry with
them. Do not give your daughters
to their sons or take their daughters for your sons, 4 because they
will turn your sons away from Me to
worship other gods. Then the LORD's
anger will burn against you, and He
will swiftly destroy you. 5 Instead,
this is what you are to do to them:
tear down their altars, smash their
sacred pillars, cut down their •Ashe-
rah poles, and burn up their carved
images. 6 For you are a holy people
belonging to the LORD your God. The
LORD your God has chosen you to
be His own possession out of all the
peoples on the face of the earth.
7 "The LORD was devoted to you and
chose you, not because you were
more numerous than all peoples, for
you were the fewest of all peoples.
8 But because the LORD loved you
and kept the oath He swore to your
fathers, He brought you out with a
strong hand and redeemed you from
the place of slavery, from the power
of Pharaoh king of Egypt. 9 Know
that •Yahweh your God is God, the
faithful God who keeps His gracious
covenant loyalty for a thousand generations with those who love Him
and keep His commands. 10 But He
directly pays back[A] and destroys

[A]7:10 Lit *He pays back to their faces*

6:6 Moses reminded the Israelites that **these words** God was giving them were **to be in** their **heart** in order not to stray from Him. The Lord wants to circumcise the hearts of His people so they will love Him wholeheartedly and not have hearts that turn away to worship other gods (10:16; 29:18; 30:6,17). The Hebrew word for "heart" (Hb *lēvav*) appears only a total of eight times in the other four books of the Pentateuch but over 40 times in Deuteronomy, underscoring this book's message that belonging to the Lord is demonstrated not *merely* in legalistic obedience of doing certain things but in whole-hearted devotion to Him (cp. 15:9-10; 28:47-48; 30:14). There was no room for the Israelites to listen to the words of Moses only with their heads but not with their hearts. He wanted them to listen and apply the words of the Law, which include the command to pass on these instructions to later generations.

6:7-9 Parents are responsible for the spiritual training of their children, a process that involves both verbal instruction and modeling obedience. Four commands are given to parents for making God's words integral to daily life:

- **Repeat** [Hb *shanan*, "inculcate, teach persistently and earnestly, implant or impress upon the mind by frequent and repeated instruction, instill"] **them to your children.**
- **Talk about them** all the time.
- **Bind them as a sign** [Hb *'ot*, "memory aid"] **on your hand and let them be a symbol on your forehead.** In traditional Judaism, "symbol" (Hb *tophaphah*, "bands, frontlets"; cp. 11:18) refers to "phylacteries" (Gk *phulacteria*, Mt 23:5) or *tefillin*, parchment scrolls with portions of the Torah (traditionally Ex 13:1-10,11-16; Dt 6:4-9; 11:13-21) written on them and placed in a square leather box. Jewish men have worn these

strapped to the forehead and left arm.

- **Write them on the doorposts of your house and on your gates.** The same verses as those placed in phylacteries are also traditionally put in a *mezuzah*, a small cylinder attached to the doorpost of a Jewish home and entry gate.

Keeping God's Word in your heart does not mean keeping faith private but rather is an impetus to making it the standard for daily public life. The ideas of this command are further explained by telling the people how to teach their children. First, they were to repeat these words to their children. They were to talk about them when they went about their daily routines—when they sat in their houses and when they traveled. These words were to be the first things on their lips in the morning and the last thing to discuss at night. The words of the Law were literally to pervade every area of their lives. The people were to love and cherish the commandments so strongly that they thought about them and knew how to apply them to every area of their lives. Not only that, but they were also to be able to explain the Law and its application to their children while doing ordinary life chores.

8:2 Moses reminded the people of all that the Lord had already done for them. He had a purpose in mind. These particular people were getting ready to cross the Jordan River to enter the promised land. Moses was calling them back to remember the nature of the God who chose them. He had rescued them from the Egyptians and taken them through their 40 years in the wilderness. Therefore, as they crossed over the Jordan to inhabit the land, Moses, with fresh intensity, called the people to remember anew what the Lord had done for them.

8:3 Manna (Hb *manhu'*, transliterated as "manna," a substance resembling coriander seed with a sweet, honey-like taste) was God's food provision to the Israelites during the wilderness wanderings (see note on Ex 16:13-18).

8:11 Moses repeats his command for them to keep **the ordinances and statutes**, which the Israelites agreed was part of their covenant with God (see 4:44-45). Surely the Israelites would not forget that the Lord actually exists, but failing to keep His commands would be living as if God does not exist or forgetting Him.

those who hate Him. He will not
hesitate to directly pay back[A] the
one who hates Him. 11 So keep the
command—the statutes and ordinances—that I am giving you to follow today.
12 "If you listen to and are careful
to keep these ordinances, the LORD
your God will keep His covenant loyalty with you, as He swore to your
fathers. 13 He will love you, bless you,
and multiply you. He will bless your
descendants,[B] and the produce of
your land—your grain, new wine,
and oil—the young of your herds,
and the newborn of your flocks, in
the land He swore to your fathers
that He would give you. 14 You will
be blessed above all peoples; there
will be no infertile male or female
among you or your livestock. 15 The
LORD will remove all sickness from
you; He will not put on you all the
terrible diseases of Egypt that you
know about, but He will inflict them
on all who hate you. 16 You must destroy all the peoples the LORD your
God is delivering over to you and
not look on them with pity. Do not
worship their gods, for that will be a
snare to you.
17 "If you say to yourself, 'These nations are greater than I; how can I
drive them out?' 18 do not be afraid
of them. Be sure to remember what
the LORD your God did to Pharaoh
and all Egypt: 19 the great trials that
you saw, the signs and wonders, the
strong hand and outstretched arm,
by which the LORD your God brought
you out. The LORD your God will do
the same to all the peoples you fear.
20 The LORD your God will also send
the hornet against them until all the
survivors and those hiding from you
perish. 21 Don't be terrified of them,
for the LORD your God, a great and
awesome God, is among you. 22 The
LORD your God will drive out these
nations before you little by little.
You will not be able to destroy them
all at once; otherwise, the wild animals will become too numerous for
you. 23 The LORD your God will give
them over to you and throw them
into great confusion until they
are destroyed. 24 He will hand their
kings over to you, and you will wipe
out their names under heaven. No
one will be able to stand against
you; you will annihilate them. 25 You
must burn up the carved images of
their gods. Don't covet the silver
and gold on the images and take it
for yourself, or else you will be ensnared by it, for it is abhorrent to
the LORD your God. 26 You must not
bring any abhorrent thing into your
house, or you will be •set apart for
destruction like it. You are to utterly
detest and abhor it, because it is set
apart for destruction.

Remember the LORD (8:1-20)

8 "You must carefully follow every
command I am giving you today,
so that you may live and increase,
and may enter and take possession
of the land the LORD swore to your
fathers. 2 Remember that the LORD
your God led you on the entire
journey these 40 years in the wilderness, so that He might humble
you and test you to know what was
in your heart, whether or not you
would keep His commands. 3 He
humbled you by letting you go hungry; then He gave you manna to eat,
which you and your fathers had not
known, so that you might learn that
man does not live on bread alone
but on every word that comes from
the mouth of the LORD. 4 Your clothing did not wear out, and your feet
did not swell these 40 years. 5 Keep
in mind that the LORD your God has
been disciplining you just as a man
disciplines his son. 6 So keep the
commands of the LORD your God
by walking in His ways and •fear-
ing Him. 7 For the LORD your God is
bringing you into a good land, a land
with streams of water, springs, and
deep water sources, flowing in both
valleys and hills; 8 a land of wheat,
barley, vines, figs, and pomegranates; a land of olive oil and honey; 9 a
land where you will eat food without
shortage, where you will lack nothing; a land whose rocks are iron and
from whose hills you will mine copper. 10 When you eat and are full, you
will praise the LORD your God for the
good land He has given you.
11 "Be careful that you don't forget the LORD your God by failing

[A] **7:10** Lit *to pay back to their faces* [B] **7:13** Lit *bless the fruit of your womb*

to keep His command—the ordinances and statutes—I am giving you today. 12 When you eat and are full, and build beautiful houses to live in, 13 and your herds and flocks grow large, and your silver and gold multiply, and everything else you have increases, 14 be careful that your heart doesn't become proud and you forget the Lord your God who brought you out of the land of Egypt, out of the place of slavery. 15 He led you through the great and terrible wilderness with its poisonous[A] snakes and scorpions, a thirsty land where there was no water. He brought water out of the flint-like rock for you. 16 He fed you in the wilderness with manna that your fathers had not known, in order to humble and test you, so that in the end He might cause you to prosper. 17 You may say to yourself, 'My power and my own ability have gained this wealth for me,' 18 but remember that the Lord your God gives you the power to gain wealth, in order to confirm His covenant He swore to your fathers, as it is today. 19 If you ever forget the Lord your God and go after other gods to worship and bow down to them, I testify against you today that you will perish. 20 Like the nations the Lord is about to destroy before you, you will perish if you do not obey the Lord your God.

Warning Against Self-Righteousness (9:1-6)

9 "Listen, Israel: Today you are about to cross the Jordan to go and drive out nations greater and stronger than you, with large cities fortified to the heavens. 2 The people are strong and tall, the descendants of the Anakim. You know about them and you have heard it said about them, 'Who can stand up to the sons of Anak?' 3 But understand that today the Lord your God will cross over ahead of you as a consuming fire; He will devastate and subdue them before you. You will drive them out and destroy them swiftly, as the Lord has told you. 4 When the Lord your God drives them out before you, do not say to yourself, 'The Lord brought me in to take possession of this land because of my righteousness.' Instead, the Lord will drive out these nations before you because of their wickedness. 5 You are not going to take possession of their land because of your righteousness or your integrity. Instead, the Lord your God will drive out these nations before you because of their wickedness, in order to keep the promise He swore to your fathers, Abraham, Isaac, and Jacob. 6 Understand that the Lord your God is not giving you this good land to possess because of your righteousness, for you are a stiff-necked people.

Israel's Rebellion and Moses' Intercession (9:7-29)

7 "Remember and do not forget how you provoked the Lord your God in the wilderness. You have been rebelling against the Lord from the day you left the land of Egypt until you reached this place. 8 You provoked the Lord at Horeb, and He was angry enough with you to destroy you. 9 When I went up the mountain to receive the stone tablets, the tablets of the covenant the Lord made with you, I stayed on the mountain 40 days and 40 nights. I did not eat bread or drink water. 10 On the day of the assembly the Lord gave me the two stone tablets, inscribed by God's finger. The exact words were on them, which the Lord spoke to you from the fire on the mountain. 11 The Lord gave me the two stone tablets, the tablets of the covenant, at the end of the 40 days and 40 nights.

12 "The Lord said to me, 'Get up and go down immediately from here. For your people whom you brought out of Egypt have acted corruptly. They have quickly turned from the way that I commanded them; they have made a cast image for themselves.' 13 The Lord also said to me, 'I have seen this people, and indeed, they are a stiff-necked people. 14 Leave Me alone, and I will destroy them and blot out their name under heaven. Then I will make you into a nation stronger and more numerous than they.'

9:2 Moses confirmed that when the people crossed the Jordan they would encounter **the descendants of the Anakim**, giants who descended from the Nephilim (Nm 13:33).

9:5-6 Moses assured the Israelites that the Lord was going ahead of them to subdue these enemies before them, but he also warned them not to take pride in this victory. The Lord would drive out the nations of Canaan, but not because of Israel's inherent superiority; they were not righteous, as they might suppose, but **stiff-necked**, demonstrated in their rebellion while Moses was receiving **the covenant of the Lord** on Mount Sinai (vv. 7-29). God was replacing these nations with Israel to bring due judgment on them **because of their wickedness** and to keep His **promise** to the patriarchs.

9:7-29 The purpose of recounting these events was to help the people remember and not forget the Lord's mercy in renewing His covenant with them despite their tendency to rebel against Him. The Israelites' history underscored why they should remain humbly dependent on the Lord (cp. Ex 34 and 37).

[A] **8:15** Lit *burning*

10:2 Moses himself did not build **the ark** in which the stone tablets were placed, but he had received from the Lord the instructions for building it and had given these to the craftsman, Bezalel (Ex 25:10-22; 37:1-9).

10:8-9 Israel was distinguished by her covenant with the Lord, which included the establishment of the priesthood. **The tribe of Levi** had been **set apart** by the Lord Himself for this purpose. This tribe of priests, unlike the other tribes, would not receive an allotment of land. Instead, their needs would be met by the people's offerings (vv. 6-9; 18:1-8).

10:16 Having reviewed their history as a people in covenant with the Lord, Moses returned to what God asks of His people and urged the Israelites to **circumcise your hearts and don't be stiff-necked any longer**. The metaphor of circumcision stresses the deliberate and irrevocable cutting away of any affections or priorities that would compete for a person's whole-hearted devotion to someone or something other than the Lord (cp. Rm 2:28-29). Therefore, the people were required to be faithful to the God who had been faithful to them (cp. Gn 15:5; 22:17; 26:4).

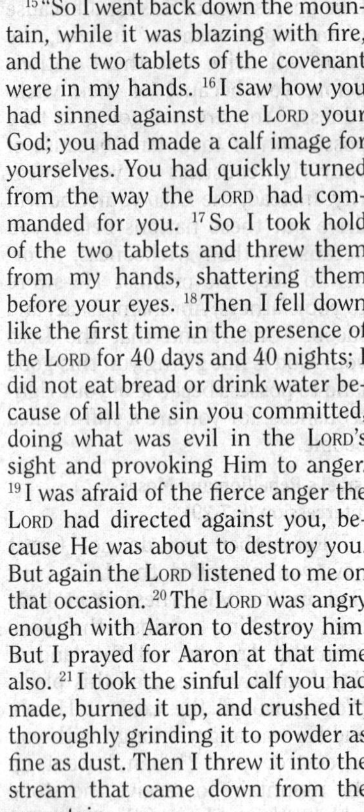

15 "So I went back down the mountain, while it was blazing with fire, and the two tablets of the covenant were in my hands. 16 I saw how you had sinned against the LORD your God; you had made a calf image for yourselves. You had quickly turned from the way the LORD had commanded for you. 17 So I took hold of the two tablets and threw them from my hands, shattering them before your eyes. 18 Then I fell down like the first time in the presence of the LORD for 40 days and 40 nights; I did not eat bread or drink water because of all the sin you committed, doing what was evil in the LORD's sight and provoking Him to anger. 19 I was afraid of the fierce anger the LORD had directed against you, because He was about to destroy you. But again the LORD listened to me on that occasion. 20 The LORD was angry enough with Aaron to destroy him. But I prayed for Aaron at that time also. 21 I took the sinful calf you had made, burned it up, and crushed it, thoroughly grinding it to powder as fine as dust. Then I threw it into the stream that came down from the mountain.

22 "You continued to provoke the LORD at Taberah, Massah, and Kibroth-hattaavah. 23 When the LORD sent you from Kadesh-barnea, He said, 'Go up and possess the land I have given you'; you rebelled against the command of the LORD your God. You did not believe or obey Him. 24 You have been rebelling against the LORD ever since I have[A] known you.

25 "I fell down in the presence of the LORD 40 days and 40 nights because the LORD had threatened to destroy you. 26 I prayed to the LORD:

> Lord GOD, do not annihilate Your people, Your inheritance, whom You redeemed through Your greatness and brought out of Egypt with a strong hand. 27 Remember Your servants Abraham, Isaac, and Jacob. Disregard this people's stubbornness, and their wickedness and sin. 28 Otherwise, those in the land you brought us from will say, 'Because the LORD wasn't able to bring them into the land He had promised them, and because He hated them, He brought them out to kill them in the wilderness.' 29 But they are Your people, Your inheritance, whom You brought out by Your great power and outstretched arm.

Renewal of the Covenant (10:1-11)

10 "The LORD said to me at that time, 'Cut two stone tablets like the first ones and come to Me on the mountain and make a wooden ark. 2 I will write on the tablets the words that were on the first tablets you broke, and you are to place them in the ark.' 3 So I made an ark of acacia wood, cut two stone tablets like the first ones, and climbed the mountain with the two tablets in my hand. 4 Then on the day of the assembly, the LORD wrote on the tablets what had been written previously, the Ten Commandments that He had spoken to you on the mountain from the fire. The LORD gave them to me, 5 and I went back down the mountain and placed the tablets in the ark I had made. And they have remained there, as the LORD commanded me."

6 The Israelites traveled from Beeroth Bene-jaakan[B] to Moserah. Aaron died and was buried there, and Eleazar his son became priest in his place. 7 They traveled from there to Gudgodah, and from Gudgodah to Jotbathah, a land with streams of water.

8 "At that time the LORD set apart the tribe of Levi to carry the ark of the LORD's covenant, to stand before •Yahweh to serve Him, and to pronounce blessings in His name, as it is today. 9 For this reason, Levi does not have a portion or inheritance like his brothers; the LORD is his inheritance, as the LORD your God told him.

10 "I stayed on the mountain 40 days and 40 nights like the first time. The LORD also listened to me on this occasion; He agreed not to annihilate you. 11 Then the LORD

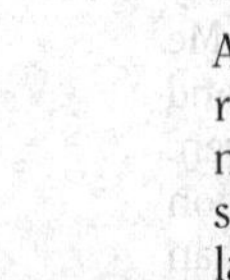

[A] **9:24** Sam, LXX read *since He has* [B] **10:6** Or *from the wells of Bene-jaakan*, or *from the wells of the Jaakanites*

said to me, ‘Get up. Continue your journey ahead of the people, so that they may enter and possess the land I swore to give their fathers.’

What God Requires (10:12-22)

12 “And now, Israel, what does the LORD your God ask of you except to •fear the LORD your God by walking in all His ways, to love Him, and to worship the LORD your God with all your heart and all your soul? 13 Keep the LORD’s commands and statutes I am giving you today, for your own good. 14 The heavens, indeed the highest heavens, belong to the LORD your God, as does the earth and everything in it. 15 Yet the LORD was devoted to your fathers and loved them. He chose their descendants after them—He chose you out of all the peoples, as it is today. 16 Therefore, circumcise your hearts and don’t be stiff-necked any longer. 17 For the LORD your God is the God of gods and Lord of lords, the great, mighty, and awesome God, showing no partiality and taking no bribe. 18 He executes justice for the fatherless and the widow, and loves the foreigner, giving him food and clothing. 19 You also must love the foreigner, since you were foreigners in the land of Egypt. 20 You are to fear Yahweh your God and worship Him. Remain faithful[A] to Him and take oaths in His name. 21 He is your praise and He is your God, who has done for you these great and awesome works your eyes have seen. 22 Your fathers went down to Egypt, 70 people in all, and now the LORD your God has made you as numerous as the stars of the sky.

Remember and Obey (11:1-25)

11 “Therefore, love the LORD your God and always keep His mandate and His statutes, ordinances, and commands. 2 You must understand today that it is not your children who experienced or saw the discipline of the LORD your God:

His greatness, strong hand, and outstretched arm; 3 His signs and the works He did in Egypt to Pharaoh king of Egypt and all his land; 4 what He did to Egypt’s army, its horses and chariots, when He made the waters of the •Red Sea flow over them as they pursued you, and He destroyed them completely;[B] 5 what He did to you in the wilderness until you reached this place; 6 and what He did to Dathan and Abiram, the sons of Eliab the Reubenite, when in the middle of the whole Israelite camp the earth opened its mouth and swallowed them, their households, their tents, and every living thing with them.

7 Your own eyes have seen every great work the LORD has done.

8 “Keep every command I am giving you today, so that you may have the strength to cross into and possess the land you are to inherit, 9 and so that you may live long in the land the LORD swore to your fathers to give them and their descendants, a land flowing with milk and honey. 10 For the land you are entering to possess is not like the land of Egypt, from which you have come, where you sowed your seed and irrigated by hand[C] as in a vegetable garden. 11 But the land you are entering to possess is a land of mountains and valleys, watered by rain from the sky. 12 It is a land the LORD your God cares for. He is always watching over it from the beginning to the end of the year.

13 “If you carefully obey my commands I am giving you today, to love the LORD your God and worship Him with all your heart and all your soul, 14 I[D] will provide rain for your land in the proper time, the autumn and spring rains,[E] and you will harvest your grain, new wine, and oil. 15 I[D] will provide grass in your fields for your livestock. You will eat and be satisfied. 16 Be careful that you are not enticed to turn aside, worship, and bow down to other gods. 17 Then the LORD’s anger will burn against you. He will close the sky, and there will be no rain; the land will not

11:1-2 Although the Lord’s goodness could never be repaid, the people who received His generous provision should have such grateful hearts from which obedience and commitment flowed. They were at the beginning of an entirely new era in the nation of Israel. They could now listen to the Lord and obey Him. Although their parents had failed and they as children had not had the opportunity to see the greatness of God in the ways experienced by their parents, still an opportunity was now before them. **Love the LORD** and obey Him—that was all they were required to do.

God’s **discipline** was never administered frivolously but with the purpose of educating the people. Both His grace and His punishment were poured out to teach them about His holiness and His demands on their lives in preparation for the future.

11:6-12 Dathan and Abiram had thought **Egypt** was “a land flowing with milk and honey” (Nm 16:12-13), and they led a rebellion against Moses in the wilderness. Here Moses brings the focus of the people to the promised land, which was described as genuinely **flowing with milk and honey** because of its great potential for productivity.

11:14 The autumn and spring rains refer to the rainy season, which occurred in Canaan between October and April. These torrents of rain were needed for productivity of the land, and they would come in measure according to Israel’s obedience.

[A]**10:20** Lit *Hold on* [B]**11:4** Lit *to this day* [C]**11:10** Lit *foot* [D]**11:14,15** DSS, Sam, LXX read *He*
[E]**11:14** Following the Hb calendar, the early rain came in September/October and the late rain in March/April.

11:18-20 In order to ensure the continued blessing of the Lord, it was imperative for His people to **teach** (Hb *lamad*) His Word to their children (cp. 6:6-9).

11:22 Every generation would be held responsible to **remain faithful** [Hb *davaq*, "cleave, adhere to firmly as with glue"; cp. 10:20; Gn 2:24] **to Him.**

11:26-28 Moses reemphasized the heart of the message in the most basic way he could put it. If you want blessing, then obey. If you want curses, then disobey. God instructed the Israelites to destroy all the idols and all evidence of their existence to remove the temptation to worship false gods in years to come. God wanted to bless His people, but the choice was ultimately up to them.

11:29 The people are commanded **to proclaim the blessing at Mount Gerizim and the curse at Mount Ebal** (cp. 27:11–28:14). These mountains overlooked the valley where ancient Shechem was located. Jacob dug a well here, where later Jesus encountered the Samaritan woman (Gn 33:19-20; Jn 4:6).

12:1-7 Moses began with worship. Although the Canaanites built worship centers on every high hill in lush arbors, according to personal whim, the Israelites would have one central sanctuary of worship chosen by God Himself. Although there would be altars at Shiloh and Mount Ebal as well as in Jerusalem, the main impetus of this caution concerned a warning against the use of unauthorized places of worship.

12:8 Specifically, Moses admonished the Israelites not to live according to what was **right in** their **own eyes**; yet one generation later, that would be the exact phrase describing the people of Israel during the era of Israelite history under the judges (Jdg 21:25).

yield its produce, and you will perish
quickly from the good land the LORD
is giving you.
18 "Imprint these words of mine
on your hearts and minds, bind
them as a sign on your hands, and
let them be a symbol[A] on your foreheads.[B] 19 Teach them to your children, talking about them when you
sit in your house and when you walk
along the road, when you lie down
and when you get up. 20 Write them
on the doorposts of your house and
on your gates, 21 so that as long as
the heavens are above the earth,
your days and those of your children
may be many in the land the LORD
swore to give your fathers. 22 For if
you carefully observe every one of
these commands I am giving you to
follow—to love the LORD your God,
walk in all His ways, and remain
faithful[C] to Him— 23 the LORD will
drive out all these nations before
you, and you will drive out nations
greater and stronger than you are.
24 Every place the sole of your foot
treads will be yours. Your territory
will extend from the wilderness to
Lebanon and from the Euphrates River[D] to the Mediterranean
Sea. 25 No one will be able to stand
against you; the LORD your God will
put fear and dread of you in all the
land where you set foot, as He has
promised you.

A Blessing and a Curse (11:26-32)

26 "Look, today I set before you a
blessing and a curse: 27 there will be a
blessing, if you obey the commands
of the LORD your God I am giving
you today, 28 and a curse, if you do
not obey the commands of the LORD
your God and you turn aside from
the path I command you today by
following other gods you have not
known. 29 When the LORD your God
brings you into the land you are
entering to possess, you are to proclaim the blessing at Mount Gerizim and the curse at Mount Ebal.
30 Aren't these mountains across the
Jordan, beyond the western road in
the land of the Canaanites, who live
in the •Arabah, opposite Gilgal, near
the oaks[E] of Moreh? 31 For you are
about to cross the Jordan to enter
and take possession of the land the
LORD your God is giving you. When
you possess it and settle in it, 32 be
careful to follow all the statutes and
ordinances I set before you today.

The Chosen Place to Worship (12:1-14)

12 "Be careful to follow these
statutes and ordinances in the
land that •Yahweh, the God of your
fathers, has given you to possess
all the days you live on the earth.
2 Destroy completely all the places
where the nations that you are driving out worship their gods—on the
high mountains, on the hills, and
under every green tree. 3 Tear down
their altars, smash their sacred pillars, burn up their •Asherah poles,
cut down the carved images of their
gods, and wipe out their names from
every[F] place. 4 Don't worship the
LORD your God this way. 5 Instead,
you must turn to the place Yahweh
your God chooses from all your
tribes to put His name for His dwelling and go there. 6 You are to bring
there your •burnt offerings and sacrifices, your tenths and personal
contributions,[G] your vow offerings
and freewill offerings, and the firstborn of your herds and flocks. 7 You
will eat there in the presence of
the LORD your God and rejoice with
your household in everything you
do,[H] because the LORD your God has
blessed you.
8 "You are not to do as we are doing
here today; everyone is doing whatever seems right in his own eyes.
9 Indeed, you have not yet come into
the resting place and the inheritance the LORD your God is giving
you. 10 When you cross the Jordan
and live in the land the LORD your
God is giving you to inherit, and He
gives you rest from all the enemies
around you and you live in security,
11 then Yahweh your God will choose
the place to have His name dwell.
Bring there everything I command
you: your burnt offerings, sacrifices,
offerings of the tenth, personal contributions,[I] and all your choice of-

[A] **11:18** Or *phylactery*; Mt 23:5 [B] **11:18** Lit *symbol between your eyes*; Ex 13:16; Dt 6:8 [C] **11:22** Lit *and hold on* [D] **11:24** Some Hb mss, LXX, Tg, Vg read *the great river, the river Euphrates* [E] **11:30** Sam, LXX, Syr, Aq, Sym read *oak*; Gn 12:6 [F] **12:3** Lit *that* [G] **12:6** Lit *and the contributions from your hands* [H] **12:7** Lit *you put your hand to* [I] **12:11** Lit *tenth, the contributions from your hands*

ferings you vow to the LORD. 12 You will rejoice before the LORD your God—you, your sons and daughters, your male and female slaves, and the Levite who is within your gates, since he has no portion or inheritance among you. 13 Be careful not to offer your burnt offerings in all the sacred places you see. 14 You must offer your burnt offerings only in the place the LORD chooses in one of your tribes, and there you must do everything I command you.

Slaughtering Animals to Eat (12:15-32)

15 "But whenever you want, you may slaughter and eat meat within any of your gates, according to the blessing the LORD your God has given you. Those who are •clean or •unclean may eat it, as they would a gazelle or deer, 16 but you must not eat the blood; pour it on the ground like water. 17 Within your gates you may not eat: the tenth of your grain, new wine, or oil; the firstborn of your herd or flock; any of your vow offerings that you pledge; your freewill offerings; or your personal contributions.[A] 18 You must eat them in the presence of the LORD your God at the place the LORD your God chooses—you, your son and daughter, your male and female slave, and the Levite who is within your gates. Rejoice before the LORD your God in everything you do,[B] 19 and be careful not to neglect the Levite, as long as you live in your land.

20 "When the LORD your God enlarges your territory as He has promised you, and you say, 'I want to eat meat' because you have a strong desire to eat meat, you may eat it whenever you want. 21 If the place where Yahweh your God chooses to put His name is too far from you, you may slaughter any of your herd or flock He has given you, as I have commanded you, and you may eat it within your gates whenever you want. 22 Indeed, you may eat it as the gazelle and deer are eaten; both the clean and the unclean may eat it. 23 But don't eat the blood, since the blood is the life, and you must not eat the life with the meat. 24 Do not eat blood; pour it on the ground like water. 25 Do not eat it, so that you and your children after you will prosper, because you will be doing what is right in the LORD's sight.

26 "But you are to take the holy offerings you have and your vow offerings and go to the place the LORD chooses. 27 Present the meat and blood of your burnt offerings on the altar of the LORD your God. The blood of your other sacrifices is to be poured out beside the altar of the LORD your God, but you may eat the meat. 28 Be careful to obey all these things I command you, so that you and your children after you may prosper forever, because you will be doing what is good and right in the sight of the LORD your God.

29 "When the LORD your God annihilates the nations before you, which you are entering to take possession of, and you drive them out and live in their land, 30 be careful not to be ensnared by their ways after they have been destroyed before you. Do not inquire about their gods, asking, 'How did these nations worship their gods? I'll also do the same.' 31 You must not do the same to the LORD your God, because they practice every detestable thing, which the LORD hates, for their gods. They even burn their sons and daughters in the fire to their gods. 32[C] You must be careful to do everything I command you; do not add anything to it or take anything away from it.

The False Prophet (13:1-5)

13 "If a prophet or someone who has dreams arises among you and proclaims a sign or wonder to you, 2 and that sign or wonder he has promised you comes about, but he says, 'Let us follow other gods,' which you have not known, 'and let us worship them,' 3 do not listen to that prophet's words or to that dreamer. For the LORD your God is testing you to know whether you love the LORD your God with all your heart and all your soul. 4 You must follow the LORD your God and •fear Him. You must keep His commands and listen to His voice; you must worship Him and remain faithful[D] to Him. 5 That prophet or dreamer

[A] 12:17 Lit *or the contributions from your hands* in Hb [B] 12:18 Lit *you put your hand to* [C] 12:32 Dt 13:1 [D] 13:4 Lit *and hold on*

12:16 A particular restriction regarding the Israelites' diet was not eating **the blood** of any meat. Blood symbolized life and, therefore, was to be treated with respect. Pouring it on the ground showed the Israelite's acknowledgment of the sacredness of life created and given only by God.

13:1-5 The first verse in chapter 13 in the Hebrew text (12:32) serves as an introduction to the section on false prophets. Anyone could claim divine revelation and usurp prophecy or dreams—both of which were used by Yahweh—to pull the people away from the Lord. Here God told the people how to recognize whether a man or woman spoke as His true representative. In other words, for someone to arise in their midst and predict what was going to happen could be a good thing; however, if someone urged the people to worship anyone other than the Lord God, they were to ignore his message, and the false prophet must be put to death, demonstrating the seriousness of an offense for one to urge **rebellion against the LORD**.

13:6-11 Evil and especially idolatry were not light matters to the Lord. They were to be dealt with expeditiously and carefully. Stoning seems harsh, but punishment was severe as a deterrent against such evil, which would have a tendency to spread among the people. Action was to be taken first by persons reporting the violation of God's command, but then that action was to be supported by **the hands of all the people.** From the very beginning the Lord told the Israelites that He loved them, but He was also clear in expressing His expectation that they live holy lives.

14:1-21 Because the Israelites were **a holy people belonging to the Lord,** certain practices and characteristics were necessary. Moses first listed the foods that were acceptable (**clean**) and those that were not (**unclean**). As a nation set apart unto the Lord, the Israelites were not to identify themselves with pagan practices—not by disfiguring their bodies or by defiling themselves with unclean food.

must be put to death, because he has urged rebellion against the LORD your God who brought you out of the land of Egypt and redeemed you from the place of slavery, to turn you from the way the LORD your God has commanded you to walk. You must purge the evil from you.

Intolerance for Idolatry (13:6-18)

6 "If your brother, the son of your mother,[A] or your son or daughter, or the wife you embrace, or your closest friend secretly entices you, saying, 'Let us go and worship other gods'—which neither you nor your fathers have known, 7 any of the gods of the peoples around you, near you or far from you, from one end of the earth to the other— 8 you must not yield to him or listen to him. Show him no pity,[B] and do not spare him or shield him. 9 Instead, you must kill him. Your hand is to be the first against him to put him to death, and then the hands of all the people. 10 Stone him to death for trying to turn you away from the LORD your God who brought you out of the land of Egypt, out of the place of slavery. 11 All Israel will hear and be afraid, and they will no longer do anything evil like this among you.

12 "If you hear it said about one of your cities the LORD your God is giving you to live in, 13 that •wicked men have sprung up among you, led the inhabitants of their city astray, and said, 'Let us go and worship other gods,' which you have not known, 14 you are to inquire, investigate, and interrogate thoroughly. If the report turns out to be true that this detestable thing has happened among you, 15 you must strike down the inhabitants of that city with the sword. •Completely destroy everyone in it as well as its livestock with the sword. 16 You are to gather all its spoil in the middle of the city square and completely burn up the city and all its spoil for the LORD your God. The city must remain a mound of ruins forever; it is not to be rebuilt. 17 Nothing •set apart for destruction is to remain in your hand, so that the LORD will turn from His burning anger and grant you mercy, show you compassion, and multiply you as He swore to your fathers. 18 This will occur if you obey the LORD your God, keeping all His commands I am giving you today, doing what is right in the sight of the LORD your God.

Forbidden Practices (14:1-2)

14 "You are sons of the LORD your God; do not cut yourselves or make a bald spot on your head[C] on behalf of the dead, 2 for you are a holy people belonging to the LORD your God. The LORD has chosen you to be His own possession out of all the peoples on the face of the earth.

Clean and Unclean Foods (14:3-21)

3 "You must not eat any detestable thing. 4 These are the animals you may eat:

the ox, the sheep, the goat,
5 the deer, the gazelle,
the roe deer,
the wild goat, the ibex,
the antelope,
and the mountain sheep.

6 You may eat any animal that has hooves divided in two and chews the cud. 7 But among the ones that chew the cud or have divided hooves, you are not to eat these:

the camel, the hare,
and the hyrax,
though they chew the cud,
they do not have hooves—
they are •unclean for you;
8 and the pig, though it
has hooves, it does not
chew the cud—
it is unclean for you.

You must not eat their meat or touch their carcasses.

9 "You may eat everything from the water that has fins and scales, 10 but you may not eat anything that does not have fins and scales—it is unclean for you.

11 "You may eat every •clean bird, 12 but these are the ones you may not eat:

the eagle, the bearded vulture,
the black vulture, 13 the kite,
any kind of falcon,[D]

[A]**13:6** DSS, Sam, LXX read *If the son of your father or the son of your mother* [B]**13:8** Lit *Your eye must not pity him* [C]**14:1** Or *forehead* [D]**14:13** Some Hb mss, Sam, LXX; other Hb mss, Vg read *the falcon, the various kinds of kite*

14 every kind of raven,
15 the ostrich,
the short-eared owl, the gull,
any kind of hawk,
16 the little owl,
the long-eared owl,
the white owl,
17 the desert owl,
the osprey, the cormorant,
18 the stork,
any kind of heron,
the hoopoe, and the bat.[A]

19 All winged insects are unclean for
you; they may not be eaten. 20 But
you may eat every clean flying creature.

21 "You are not to eat any carcass;
you may give it to a temporary resident living within your gates, and
he may eat it, or you may sell it to a
foreigner. For you are a holy people
belonging to the LORD your God.
You must not boil a young goat in
its mother's milk.

A Tenth for the LORD (14:22-29)

22 "Each year you are to set aside
a tenth of all the produce grown in
your fields. 23 You are to eat a tenth
of your grain, new wine, and oil, and
the firstborn of your herd and flock,
in the presence of •Yahweh your
God at the place where He chooses
to have His name dwell, so that you
will always learn to •fear the LORD
your God. 24 But if the distance is
too great for you to carry it, since
the place where Yahweh your God
chooses to put His name is too far
away from you and since the LORD
your God has blessed you, 25 then exchange it for money, take the money
in your hand, and go to the place
the LORD your God chooses. 26 You
may spend the money on anything
you want: cattle, sheep, wine, beer,
or anything you desire. You are to
feast there in the presence of the
LORD your God and rejoice with your
family. 27 Do not neglect the Levite
within your gates, since he has no
portion or inheritance among you.

28 "At the end of every three years,
bring a tenth of all your produce for
that year and store it within your
gates. 29 Then the Levite, who has no
portion or inheritance among you,
the foreigner, the fatherless, and the
widow within your gates may come,
eat, and be satisfied. And the LORD
your God will bless you in all the
work of your hands that you do.

Cancellation of Debts (15:1-6)

15 "At the end of every seven years
you must cancel debts. 2 This
is how to cancel debt: Every creditor[B] is to cancel what he has lent his
neighbor. He is not to collect anything from his neighbor or brother,
because the LORD's release of debts
has been proclaimed. 3 You may collect something from a foreigner,
but you must forgive whatever your
brother owes you.

4 "There will be no poor among
you, however, because the LORD is
certain to bless you in the land the
LORD your God is giving you to possess as an inheritance— 5 if only you
obey the LORD your God and are careful to follow every one of these commands I am giving you today. 6 When
the LORD your God blesses you as He
has promised you, you will lend to
many nations but not borrow; you
will rule over many nations, but
they will not rule over you.

Lending to the Poor (15:7-11)

7 "If there is a poor person among
you, one of your brothers within any
of your gates in the land the LORD
your God is giving you, you must
not be hardhearted or tightfisted
toward your poor brother. 8 Instead,
you are to open your hand to him
and freely loan him enough for
whatever need he has. 9 Be careful
that there isn't this wicked thought
in your heart, 'The seventh year,
the year of canceling debts, is near,'
and you are stingy toward your poor
brother and give him nothing. He
will cry out to the LORD against you,
and you will be •guilty. 10 Give to
him, and don't have a stingy heart[C]
when you give, and because of this
the LORD your God will bless you in
all your work and in everything you
do.[D] 11 For there will never cease to
be poor people in the land; that is
why I am commanding you, 'You
must willingly open your hand to

14:21 There is no consensus of interpretation regarding the command against boiling **a young goat in its mother's milk**, which seems to depict cruel treachery (cp. Ex 23:19b; 34:26). As a proverb, this command may have prohibited the reversal of nature's design in order to satisfy a human craving—for the delicacy of a kid boiled in milk (i.e., a mother's milk)—normally taken *in* by her young to sustain life, to be used to *surround* or *envelop* her dead offspring.

14:22 The giving of a tithe or one-**tenth** of one's produce—whether grain, fruit, oil, cattle, or sheep—is closely associated with the giving of the "first born of your sons" (Ex 22:29). It has always been an act of worship and a way of acknowledging the Lord as Creator and owner of all (Lv 27:30-33; Mal 3:10). In addition, the law establishes a systematic approach to meeting the needs of those who could not provide for themselves. By accepting the Lord's requirement for the tithe, the Israelites were recognizing the Lord's provision and care for them.

15:1-11 This chapter deals with practices concerning money and property. The Lord built into Israel's calendar a provision by which debts were to be cancelled every **seven years**. In establishing a nation and a society, God desired that His people be just and merciful. The systematic release of debt in this seventh year actually helped free the nation from poverty and created a spirit of loving concern within the community. Moses told the people, **There will be no poor among you**. However, some took advantage of this cycle to withhold generosity because of approaching cancellation of debt. Moses warned against this attitude, reminding the people that God's blessing upon them was dependent upon their own hearts of generous sharing.

15:7-11 God also set up regulations on the proper procedure for lending money. If the Israelites were going to lend to other people, they would do so in a way that was fitting to the Lord. God instructed the people to guard against having stingy hearts. They were to be merciful in their dealings with poor people. If they saw a need, they were to be willing to meet it.

[A] **14:5-18** The identification of some of these animals is uncertain. [B] **15:2** Lit *owner of a loan of his hand* [C] **15:10** Lit *and let not your heart be grudging* [D] **15:10** Lit *you put your hand to*

16:1 Moses turned his attention to the different festivals to be acknowledged and celebrated by the covenant people of God. Each feast was built into the year as a reminder to the people of the Lord's goodness to them. The first was the Festival of **Passover**. The Lord instructed the people to remember always what He did in delivering them from the slavery of Egypt. He had heard their cries, and He was the one who could and did rescue them through His servant Moses. This redemption from Egypt was to be forever remembered by the people of Israel. This remembrance consisted of a celebration wherein they literally experienced again the Passover ritual, which the Lord had required of them the night the angel of the Lord killed all the firstborn Egyptians. The Passover was observed on the fourteenth of **Abib**, a month in spring corresponding to March and April. Then, the Festival of Unleavened Bread began on the fifteenth of the same month and lasted seven days (Ex 23:15).

16:9-12 During the **Festival of Weeks** or Harvest (Christians celebrate this as Pentecost), the Lord was again reminding the people of their dependence on Him for everything. This feast celebrated the blessing of God through the harvest and began the day following the Sabbath of the Festival of Passover (Ex 23:16; 34:22; Lv 23:15-16). They were to express their gratitude to the Lord by giving Him a freewill offering **seven weeks** after the first fruits of grain were gathered. Moses reminded them that they had been **slaves**; however, now the Lord had given freedom to them. Therefore, they were to give freely back to Him. The Lord did not specify how much was to be given back to Him but only that they were to determine what to give in proportion to how the Lord had blessed them (see 1Co 16:2; 2Co 9:7). This freewill gift was beyond the tithe.

16:13-17 Next, the Lord required that they celebrate a **Festival of Booths** or Tabernacles or Ingathering in remembrance of all the Lord had done for the people in the bounty from their crops. As they finished the ingathering of their crops, the Lord required that they celebrate together all He had done for them. The Lord was good to Israel in their harvest;,therefore, they should celebrate. The people were to live in booths, which are constructed in connection even with its modern observance, as they rejoiced in the goodness of God (Lv 23:34-39,42; Nm 29:12). In addition to the observance of this feast, in every seventh year a public reading of the law was included (Dt 31:10). This festival was one of the three in which participation by **all** Israelite **males** as the representatives of their respective homes was required (16:16-17). Women did participate in

your afflicted and poor brother in
your land.'

Release of Slaves (15:12-18)

12 "If your fellow Hebrew, a man
or woman, is sold to you and serves
you six years, you must set him
free in the seventh year. 13 When
you set him free, do not send him
away empty-handed. 14 Give generously to him from your flock, your
threshing floor, and your winepress. You are to give him whatever
the LORD your God has blessed you
with. 15 Remember that you were a
slave in the land of Egypt and the
LORD your God redeemed you; that
is why I am giving you this command today. 16 But if your slave says
to you, 'I don't want to leave you,'
because he loves you and your family, and is well off with you, 17 take an
awl and pierce through his ear into
the door, and he will become your
slave for life. Also treat your female
slave the same way. 18 Do not regard
it as a hardship[A] when you set him
free, because he worked for you six
years—worth twice the wages of
a hired hand. Then the LORD your
God will bless you in everything
you do.

Consecration of Firstborn Animals (15:19-23)

19 "You must consecrate to the
LORD your God every firstborn male
produced by your herd and flock.
You are not to put the firstborn of
your oxen to work or shear the firstborn of your flock. 20 Each year you
and your family are to eat it before
the LORD your God in the place the
LORD chooses. 21 But if there is a defect in the animal, if it is lame or
blind or has any serious defect, you
must not sacrifice it to the LORD
your God. 22 Eat it within your gates;
both the •unclean person and the
•clean may eat it, as though it were
a gazelle or deer. 23 But you must not
eat its blood; pour it on the ground
like water.

The Festival of Passover (16:1-8)

16 "Observe the month of Abib[B]
and celebrate the •Passover
to the LORD your God, because the
LORD your God brought you out
of Egypt by night in the month of
Abib. 2 Sacrifice to •Yahweh your
God a Passover animal from the
herd or flock in the place where
the LORD chooses to have His name
dwell. 3 You must not eat leavened
bread with it. For seven days you
are to eat unleavened bread with it,
the bread of hardship—because you
left the land of Egypt in a hurry—so
that you may remember for the rest
of your life the day you left the land
of Egypt. 4 No yeast is to be found
anywhere in your territory for seven
days, and none of the meat you sacrifice in the evening of the first day
is to remain until morning. 5 You
are not to sacrifice the Passover
animal in any of the towns the LORD
your God is giving you. 6 You must
only sacrifice the Passover animal
at the place where Yahweh your God
chooses to have His name dwell. Do
this in the evening as the sun sets at
the same time of day you departed
from Egypt. 7 You are to cook and
eat it in the place the LORD your

HARD QUESTION

Is slavery condoned in the Bible?

Slavery in the time of the OT was very different than the practice of slavery in early colonial America. In the Bible a slave was usually someone who owed a particular debt to another but could not pay the debt. Therefore, he agreed to work to pay his debt to his debtor (cp. Lv 25:39). This guideline was established: The debtor would work for **six years**, at the end of which time he should be released and given his freedom as well as enough provision to set up his household and not end up in the same situation again (Dt 15:12-23). However, if the slave did not want to leave—whether because of fear for the future or the development of a deep affection for his master—the master was instructed to push a piercing tool through the ear lobe of the slave and into the door of the home. The mark on the slave's ear was a public testimony of his desire to commit himself permanently to his master—it was a voluntary act on the part of the slave to submit himself in this way. In this case, the slave became part of his master's household for life (Ex 21:5-6). The slavery described here is different from what the Israelites experienced in Egypt, and Moses refers to the Israelites' treatment in Egypt to remind them to treat someone in debt kindly.

[A] **15:18** Lit *Let it not be hard in your sight* [B] **16:1** March–April; called Nisan in the post-exilic period; Neh 2:1; Est 3:7

God chooses, and you are to return
to your tents in the morning. [8]You
must eat unleavened bread for six
days. On the seventh day there is to
be a solemn assembly to the LORD
your God, and you must not do any
work.

The Festival of Weeks (16:9-12)

[9]“You are to count seven weeks,
counting the weeks from the time
the sickle is first put to the standing grain. [10]You are to celebrate the
Festival of Weeks to the LORD your
God with a freewill offering that you
give in proportion to how the LORD
your God has blessed you. [11]Rejoice
before Yahweh your God in the place
where He chooses to have His name
dwell—you, your son and daughter, your male and female slave, the
Levite within your gates, as well as
the foreigner, the fatherless, and
the widow among you. [12]Remember
that you were slaves in Egypt; carefully follow these statutes.

The Festival of Booths (16:13-17)

[13]“You are to celebrate the Festival
of Booths for seven days when you
have gathered in everything from
your threshing floor and winepress.
[14]Rejoice during your festival—you,
your son and daughter, your male
and female slave, as well as the Levite, the foreigner, the fatherless,
and the widow within your gates.
[15]You are to hold a seven-day festival for the LORD your God in the
place He chooses, because the LORD
your God will bless you in all your
produce and in all the work of your
hands, and you will have abundant
joy.
[16]“All your males are to appear
three times a year before the LORD
your God in the place He chooses:
at the Festival of •Unleavened Bread,
the Festival of Weeks, and the Festival of Booths. No one is to appear
before the LORD empty-handed.
[17]Everyone must appear with a gift
suited to his means, according to
the blessing the LORD your God has
given you.

Appointment of Judges and Officials (16:18-20)

[18]“Appoint judges and officials for
your tribes in all your towns the
LORD your God is giving you. They
are to judge the people with righteous judgment. [19]Do not deny justice or show partiality to anyone. Do
not accept a bribe, for it blinds the
eyes of the wise and twists the words
of the righteous. [20]Pursue justice
and justice alone, so that you will
live and possess the land the LORD
your God is giving you.

Forbidden Worship (16:21-17:1)

[21]“Do not set up an •Asherah of
any kind of wood next to the altar
you will build for the LORD your God,
[22]and do not set up a sacred pillar;
the LORD your God hates them.

17 “You must not sacrifice to the
LORD your God an ox or sheep
with a defect or any serious flaw, for
that is detestable to the LORD your
God.

The Judicial Procedure of Idolatry (17:2-7)

[2]“If a man or woman among you
in one of your towns that the LORD
your God will give you is discovered
doing evil in the sight of the LORD
your God and violating His covenant
[3]and has gone to worship other gods
by bowing down to the sun, moon,
or all the stars in the sky—which
I have forbidden— [4]and if you are
told or hear about it, you must investigate it thoroughly. If the report
turns out to be true that this detestable thing has happened in Israel,
[5]you must bring out to your •gates
that man or woman who has done
this evil thing and stone them to
death. [6]The one condemned to die
is to be executed on the testimony
of two or three witnesses. No one
is to be executed on the testimony
of a single witness. [7]The witnesses’
hands are to be the first in putting
him to death, and after that, the
hands of all the people. You must
purge the evil from you.

Difficult Cases (17:8-13)

[8]“If a case is too difficult for
you—concerning bloodshed, lawsuits, or assaults—cases disputed
at your gates, you must go up to
the place the LORD your God chooses. [9]You are to go to the Levitical
priests and to the judge who pre-
sides at that time. Ask, and they will

these annual pilgrimages (vv. 11,14), but they were not required to do so. For example, during a woman’s menstrual cycle she was considered unclean and therefore not allowed to participate (Lv 15:19-33). Domestic duties may also have made one or more of these annual pilgrimages more burdensome than necessary for a wife and mother as well as for young children.

16:21-22 Moses again mentions **Asherah**, a Canaanite goddess who was worshiped through fertility rituals, and a **sacred pillar**, a cult object often used in the worship of Baal. The fact that these objects were not to be set up **next to the altar** may suggest that the Israelites were blending worship of the Lord God with worship of pagan deities. Syncretism is the practice of blending different, and in some cases contradictory, beliefs, traditions, or practices into one belief system. The Lord was clear that He **hates** this; He is the one true God.

17:2-13 Moses laid out for the people official judiciary procedures. Those who did not obey the Lord and who worshiped other gods were to be put to death. However, first a careful investigation was to take place, and no one could **be executed** based **on the testimony of a single witness** (v. 6). The Lord was setting up careful parameters for the people. He was adamant that they were not to worship other gods; however, He also emphasized that they were to be a people of mercy and justice. Moses dealt with the issues of cases being heard by judges and by the future kings of Israel. God required that the people who had issues with their neighbors be heard by Levitical priests, who would judge according to the respective cases. Whatever the priests decided was to be obeyed carefully; and if someone ignored the words of the priests, he was to be punished. Arrogance was to be shunned and avoided at all costs.

17:5 The **gates** of a town or city were the place where the judges met to hear the people and where leaders of the city met to do business. In Ru 4:1-12, Boaz meets with his kinsman and ten elders of the city to discuss who the kinsman redeemer would be for Ruth.

17:14-20 Moses closed this portion of his monologue with instructions for choosing a **king** to reign over Israel. God told the Israelites that He would choose someone from the nation of Israel who would be different than they expected. Their king would not be one who sought to acquire servants and wealth. Rather, the king God selected was to be concerned with the law of God; and while on His throne, he was to write a personal copy of the law of God, from which he would read and which he would obey all the days of his life. The connection between reading God's instruction and learning to live it out faithfully is made in this text (v. 18). These were to be the characteristics of the king whom God would choose for the nation of Israel. Nevertheless, as is evident in the book of 1 Samuel, Saul, the first king, did not fulfill these qualifications. He did not maintain his integrity and commitment to the Lord.

18:1 Moses addressed the special provisions for the **Levitical priests** because they were the descendants of Levi, and their **inheritance** would be different than that of the rest of the people. They were to be visible symbols of the entire nation's dependence on the Lord for leadership and life in general.

18:9-22 The people were to avoid the idolatry and occult practices of the neighboring nations. The Israelites were given a tangible way to tell the difference between someone who spoke for the Lord and a person who did not. In today's world such discernment is still important to know whether or not messages are from the Lord. God's Word is to be the measuring rod to discern good from evil.

give you a verdict in the case. 10 You must abide by the verdict they give you at the place the LORD chooses. Be careful to do exactly as they instruct you. 11 You must abide by the instruction they give you and the verdict they announce to you. Do not turn to the right or the left from the decision they declare to you. 12 The person who acts arrogantly, refusing to listen either to the priest who stands there serving the LORD your God or to the judge, must die. You must purge the evil from Israel. 13 Then all the people will hear about it, be afraid, and no longer behave arrogantly.

The Appointment of a King (17:14-20)

14 "When you enter the land the LORD your God is giving you, take possession of it, live in it, and say, 'I will set a king over me like all the nations around me,' 15 you are to appoint over you the king the LORD your God chooses. Appoint a king from your brothers. You are not to set a foreigner over you, or one who is not of your people. 16 However, he must not acquire many horses for himself or send the people back to Egypt to acquire many horses, for the LORD has told you, 'You are never to go back that way again.' 17 He must not acquire many wives for himself so that his heart won't go astray. He must not acquire very large amounts of silver and gold for himself. 18 When he is seated on his royal throne, he is to write a copy of this instruction for himself on a scroll in the presence of the Levitical priests. 19 It is to remain with him, and he is to read from it all the days of his life, so that he may learn to •fear the LORD his God, to observe all the words of this instruction, and to do these statutes. 20 Then his heart will not be exalted above his countrymen, he will not turn from this command to the right or the left, and he and his sons will continue ruling many years[A] over Israel.

Provisions for the Levites (18:1-8)

18 "The Levitical priests, the whole tribe of Levi, will have no portion or inheritance with Israel. They will eat the LORD's fire offerings; that is their[B,C] inheritance. 2 Although Levi has no inheritance among his brothers, the LORD is his inheritance, as He promised him. 3 This is the priests' share from the people who offer a sacrifice, whether it is an ox, a sheep, or a goat; the priests are to be given the shoulder, jaws, and stomach. 4 You are to give him the •firstfruits of your grain, new wine, and oil, and the first sheared wool of your flock. 5 For •Yahweh your God has chosen him and his sons from all your tribes to stand and minister in His name from now on.[D] 6 When a Levite leaves one of your towns where he lives in Israel and wants to go to the place the LORD chooses, 7 he may serve in the name of Yahweh his God like all his fellow Levites who minister there in the presence of the LORD. 8 They will eat equal portions besides what he has received from the sale of the family estate.[E]

Occult Practice Versus Prophetic Revelation (18:9-22)

9 "When you enter the land the LORD your God is giving you, do not imitate the detestable customs of those nations. 10 No one among you is to make his son or daughter pass through the fire,[F] practice •divination, tell fortunes, interpret omens, practice sorcery, 11 cast spells, consult a medium or a familiar spirit, or inquire of the dead. 12 Everyone who does these things is detestable to the LORD, and the LORD your God is driving out the nations before you because of these detestable things. 13 You must be blameless before the LORD your God. 14 Though these nations you are about to drive out listen to fortune-tellers and diviners, the LORD your God has not permitted you to do this.

15 "The LORD your God will raise up for you a prophet like me from among your own brothers. You must listen to him. 16 This is what you requested from the LORD your God at Horeb on the day of the assembly when you said, 'Let us not continue to hear the voice of the LORD our

[A] **17:20** Lit *will lengthen days on his kingdom* [B] **18:1** LXX; MT reads *his* [C] **18:1** Or *His* [D] **18:5** Lit *name all the days* [E] **18:8** Hb obscure [F] **18:10** Either a Canaanite cult practice or child sacrifice

God or see this great fire any longer, so that we will not die!' 17 Then the LORD said to me, 'They have spoken well. 18 I will raise up for them a prophet like you from among their brothers. I will put My words in his mouth, and he will tell them everything I command him. 19 I will hold accountable whoever does not listen to My words that he speaks in My name. 20 But the prophet who dares to speak a message in My name that I have not commanded him to speak, or who speaks in the name of other gods—that prophet must die.' 21 You may say to yourself, 'How can we recognize a message the LORD has not spoken?' 22 When a prophet speaks in the LORD's name, and the message does not come true or is not fulfilled, that is a message the LORD has not spoken. The prophet has spoken it presumptuously. Do not be afraid of him.

Cities of Refuge (19:1-13)

19 "When the LORD your God annihilates the nations whose land He is giving you, so that you drive them out and live in their cities and houses, 2 you are to set apart three cities for yourselves within the land the LORD your God is giving you to possess. 3 You are to determine the distances[A] and divide the land the LORD your God is granting you as an inheritance into three regions, so that anyone who commits manslaughter can flee to these cities.[B]

4 "Here is the law concerning a case of someone who kills a person and flees there to save his life, having killed his neighbor accidentally without previously hating him: 5 If he goes into the forest with his neighbor to cut timber, and his hand swings the ax to chop down a tree, but the blade flies off the handle and strikes his neighbor so that he dies, that person may flee to one of these cities and live. 6 Otherwise, the avenger of blood in the heat of his anger[C] might pursue the one who committed manslaughter, overtake him because the distance is great, and strike him dead. Yet he did not deserve to die,[D] since he did not previously hate his neighbor. 7 This is why I am commanding you to set apart three cities for yourselves. 8 If the LORD your God enlarges your territory as He swore to your fathers, and gives you all the land He promised to give them— 9 provided you keep every one of these commands I am giving you today and follow them, loving the LORD your God and walking in His ways at all times—you are to add three more cities to these three. 10 In this way, innocent blood will not be shed, and you will not become •guilty of bloodshed in the land the LORD your God is giving you as an inheritance. 11 But if someone hates his neighbor, lies in ambush for him, attacks him, and strikes him fatally, and flees to one of these cities, 12 the elders of his city must send for him, take him from there, and hand him over to the avenger of blood and he will die. 13 You must not look on him with pity but purge from Israel the guilt of shedding innocent blood, and you will prosper.

Boundary Markers (19:14)

14 "You must not move your neighbor's boundary marker, established at the start in the inheritance you will receive in the land the LORD your God is giving you to possess.

Witnesses in Court (19:15-21)

15 "One witness cannot establish any wrongdoing or sin against a person, whatever that person has done. A fact must be established by the testimony of two or three witnesses.

16 "If a malicious witness testifies against someone accusing him of a crime, 17 the two people in the dispute must stand in the presence of the LORD before the priests and judges in authority at that time. 18 The judges are to make a careful investigation, and if the witness turns out to be a liar who has falsely accused his brother, 19 you must do to him as he intended to do to his brother. You must purge the evil from you. 20 Then everyone else will hear and be afraid, and they will never again do anything evil like this among you. 21 You must not show pity: life

[A]19:3 Or *to prepare the roads* [B]19:3 Lit *flee there* [C]19:6 Lit *heart* [D]19:6 Lit *did not have a judgment of death*

19:1-3 The Israelites, upon entering the promised land and taking it from the people who currently lived there, were to set up **three cities** of refuge. These were to be geographically located at specific points in the land. Therefore, if there was an accident and someone was killed, the person responsible could run to one of these sites while a fair investigation was conducted. Justice and mercy were to mark their lives. When unfortunate events happened, knowing the fallen nature of mankind, God provided a safety net through the cities of refuge to curb their propensity to seek revenge. These cities were primarily from the allotment of land given to the Levites within the tribal boundaries (Jos 20:7-8; 21:1-42). This arrangement tied the cities of refuge closely to these servants of the Lord. The cities of refuge were for people who committed **manslaughter**, killing someone without malicious intent. Criteria with supporting illustrations were set up for the Israelites to determine the difference between murder and manslaughter and the punishment appropriate for each. As the Israelites expanded their conquest of land, they were to set up more cities of this type.

19:14 Continuing the theme of establishing an orderly and fair society, Moses expanded on his previous instructions about living together as a people. The boundary markers of their land must be respected. Moses instructed them not to move a **boundary marker** for the land that the Lord gave their neighbors. The Lord had given to each according to what was best. The land was an important part of God's covenant, and the people were not allowed to change the boundaries God had set among themselves. The land ultimately belonged to God, and the people occupied it according to His will, not their own whims. Thus the people were acknowledging the inheritances distributed among them as coming from God.

19:15-20 Next, Moses elaborated on instructions for witnesses in disputes. Realizing that there would be some disagreements among the people, the Lord gave guidelines for judging disputes that arose. First, at least **two or three witnesses** were required even to consider conviction of a person. Then, there was to be a careful investigation of the matter. If a person accused someone and the accusation was found to be unsupported, then that person was to receive the punishment he had attempted to have inflicted on his **brother**. This practice would cause people to be careful with their accusations against their neighbors.

20:1 War was common during the time of Moses. God had directed the people to "take possession," meaning to conquer the land (17:14). He was giving the land to them, but He gave His people specific instructions on how He wanted them to conquer the land. The Israelites were to remember that **the Lord** was with them, just as He was when they left Egypt.

20:5-9 There were no standing armies of specially trained soldiers; these were everyday Israelites who were called up to battle, and the regulations reflect that reality.

20:10-16 Next, specific battle instructions were given to the Israelites. When the people approached a city, their course of action depended on whether the city was or was not among those the Lord was giving them as an inheritance. If it was a **far away** city, they were first to **make an offer of peace** to the people of that land. If the people accepted their offer, then they were not to attack that particular city. Instead, its residents would serve the Israelites as **forced laborers**. However, if the city engaged the Israelites in battle, then they were to lay siege to the city, kill **all its males**, and keep everything else, including **the women** and **children**.

20:17-18 The principle of *cherem* (Hb, "the ban," a policy that called for the Lord's enemies to be killed by His people and all their possessions destroyed or declared to belong to God for His use; cp. 2:34-35; 7:2-6) comes into play here. In the Lord's eyes, these pagan peoples were not rightfully in the land because He had already promised the land to Abraham and his descendants (Gn 12:1,7; 13:17; 15:18).

20:19-20 The Israelites are instructed to spare the **trees**, which would have nutritional value for the Israelites and be useful in warfare as well.

21:1-9 The instruction regarding unsolved **murder** is not elsewhere present in the giving of the law.

21:10-14 Instructions for the treatment of female captives are given. If a **beautiful woman** was taken prisoner, then the Lord required that she was not to be sold into slavery if she had been taken as a wife. Although prisoners of war were *de facto* slaves, one taken as a wife became an exception and was removed from the rank of slave and protected from future slavery. These regulations are given to protect women. If an Israelite man wanted to marry her, then he could. At first glance, these instructions seem to contradict earlier warnings not to marry women from other nations (7:3-4). A

for life, eye for eye, tooth for tooth,
hand for hand, and foot for foot.

Rules for War (20:1-20)

20 "When you go out to war
against your enemies and see
horses, chariots, and an army larger
than yours, do not be afraid of them,
for the LORD your God, who brought
you out of the land of Egypt, is with
you. 2 When you are about to engage
in battle, the priest is to come forward and address the army. 3 He is
to say to them: 'Listen, Israel: Today
you are about to engage in battle
with your enemies. Do not be cowardly. Do not be afraid, alarmed, or
terrified because of them. 4 For the
LORD your God is the One who goes
with you to fight for you against
your enemies to give you victory.'
5 "The officers are to address the
army, 'Has any man built a new
house and not dedicated it? Let him
leave and return home. Otherwise,
he may die in battle and another
man dedicate it. 6 Has any man
planted a vineyard and not begun to
enjoy its fruit?[A] Let him leave and
return home. Otherwise he may die
in battle and another man enjoy its
fruit.[B] 7 Has any man become •en-
gaged to a woman and not married
her? Let him leave and return home.
Otherwise he may die in battle and
another man marry her.' 8 The officers will continue to address the
army and say, 'Is there any man who
is afraid or cowardly? Let him leave
and return home, so that his brothers' hearts won't melt like his own.'
9 When the officers have finished addressing the army, they will appoint
military commanders to lead it.
10 "When you approach a city to
fight against it, you must make an
offer of peace. 11 If it accepts your
offer of peace and opens its gates
to you, all the people found in it
will become forced laborers for
you and serve you. 12 However, if it
does not make peace with you but
wages war against you, lay siege to
it. 13 When the LORD your God hands
it over to you, you must strike down
all its males with the sword. 14 But
you may take the women, children,
animals, and whatever else is in the
city—all its spoil—as plunder. You
may enjoy the spoil of your enemies
that the LORD your God has given
you. 15 This is how you are to treat
all the cities that are far away from
you and are not among the cities
of these nations. 16 However, you
must not let any living thing survive among the cities of these people
the LORD your God is giving you as
an inheritance. 17 You must •com-
pletely destroy them—the Hittite,
Amorite, Canaanite, Perizzite, Hivite, and Jebusite—as the LORD your
God has commanded you, 18 so that
they won't teach you to do all the
detestable things they do for their
gods, and you sin against the LORD
your God.
19 "When you lay siege to a city
for a long time, fighting against it
in order to capture it, you must not
destroy its trees by putting an ax
to them, because you can get food
from them. You must not cut them
down. Are trees of the field human,

HARD QUESTION

What is a Christian response to war?

War is a reality that reflects the fallen nature of the world, and in the Old Testament there are times when God allows war or even encourages it. For Christians today, the question must be asked, what is the Christian response to war? To be fair, Christians do not agree on how to answer this question, and a summary of several approaches is below.

- *Pacifism*—belief that there is never any justification for war. Jesus commends the "peacemakers" in Mt 5:9 and advocates loving your enemies and turning the other cheek.
- *Holy War or Crusade*—belief that war is initiated and led by God and carried out by His servants. The conquest of the promised land is often pointed out as an example of a just war.
- *Just War*—belief that due to the fallen nature of the world, war is sometimes a tragic necessity. Daniel 9:26 alludes to the fact that war will continue until the end, and Is 2:2-4 tells of the day when wars will cease after Christ returns. Until that time, war will be present. For the Christian, war should be a last resort, and there must be a just cause. Augustine taught the idea of a "mournful warrior"—an attitude that regards war not with zeal but with an attitude of regret that a resolution cannot be found any other way.

[A]**20:6** Lit *not put it to use* [B]**20:6** Lit *man put it to use*

to come under siege by you? 20 But you may destroy the trees that you know do not produce food. You may cut them down to build siege works against the city that is waging war against you, until it falls.

Unsolved Murders (21:1-9)

21 "If a murder victim is found lying in a field in the land the LORD your God is giving you to possess, and it is not known who killed him, 2 your elders and judges must come out and measure the distance from the victim to the nearby cities. 3 The elders of the city nearest to the victim are to get a young cow that has not been yoked or used for work. 4 The elders of that city will bring the cow down to a continually flowing stream, to a place not tilled or sown, and they will break its neck there by the stream. 5 Then the priests, the sons of Levi, will come forward, for •Yahweh your God has chosen them to serve Him and pronounce blessings in His name, and they are to give a ruling in[A] every dispute and case of assault. 6 All the elders of the city nearest to the victim will wash their hands by the stream over the young cow whose neck has been broken. 7 They will declare, 'Our hands did not shed this blood; our eyes did not see it. 8 LORD, forgive Your people Israel You redeemed, and do not hold the shedding of innocent blood against them.' Then they will be absolved of responsibility for bloodshed. 9 You must purge from yourselves the •guilt of shedding innocent blood, for you will be doing what is right in the LORD's sight.

Fair Treatment of Captured Women (21:10-14)

10 "When you go to war against your enemies and the LORD your God hands them over to you and you take some of them prisoner, and 11 if you see a beautiful woman among the captives, desire her, and want to take her as your wife, 12 you are to bring her into your house. She must shave her head, trim her nails, 13 remove the clothes she was wearing when she was taken prisoner, live in your house, and mourn for her father and mother a full month. After that, you may have sexual relations with her and be her husband, and she will be your wife. 14 Then if you are not satisfied with her, you are to let her go where she wants, but you must not sell her for money or treat her as merchandise,[B] because you have humiliated her.

The Right of the Firstborn (21:15-17)

15 "If a man has two wives, one loved and the other unloved, and both the loved and the unloved bear him sons, and if the unloved wife has the firstborn son, 16 when that man gives what he has to his sons as an inheritance, he is not to show favoritism to the son of the loved wife as his firstborn over the firstborn of the unloved wife. 17 He must acknowledge the firstborn, the son of the unloved wife, by giving him two shares[C,D] of his estate, for he is the firstfruits of his virility; he has the rights of the firstborn.

A Rebellious Son (21:18-21)

18 "If a man has a stubborn and rebellious son who does not obey his father or mother and doesn't listen to them even after they discipline him, 19 his father and mother must take hold of him and bring him to the elders of his city, to the •gate of his hometown. 20 They will say to the elders of his city, 'This son of ours is stubborn and rebellious; he doesn't obey us. He's a glutton and a drunkard.' 21 Then all the men of his city will stone him to death. You must purge the evil from you, and all Israel will hear and be afraid.

Display of Executed People (21:22-23)

22 "If anyone is found guilty of an offense deserving the death penalty and is executed, and you hang his body on a tree, 23 you are not to leave his corpse on the tree overnight but are to bury him that day, for anyone hung on a tree is under God's curse. You must not defile the land the LORD your God is giving you as an inheritance.

prisoner of war, however, would be required to take on the culture and religion of the conquering people. In this case, she would become an Israelite and thus separate herself from idolatry. This principle may have been a reference to women who were willing to embrace the God of Israel, citing the prostitute Rahab as a possible example of a woman who did just that.

21:15-17 This passage is not necessarily a reference to polygamy since the **two wives** could have been successive rather than concurrent. In any case, if it does refer to polygamy the practice is not encouraged or mandated. The concern here is for fairness and justice toward one's children and especially protection of **the rights of the firstborn** son of the legitimate marriage relationship. Regardless of whether or not the son's mother was the wife the father **loved**, that son was due **two shares** of all the man possessed. The need for this law indicates that a father's favoritism rather than primogeniture was being practiced by some or would be tempting when the inheritance of land was involved. While diverse effects would come from their practice of polygamy, God required that the firstborn in the nation of Israel be blessed because he would have been innocent of the choices of his parents.

21:18-21 As He promised, the Lord rewarded the people according to their obedience. Rebellion, from the very beginning, was a serious matter to the Lord. The values of obedience and listening were to be taught and practiced from early childhood. Surely basic listening and obedience to earthly parents were reflections of the relationship that each Israelite would have with his heavenly Father. Therefore, strict instructions were given for the **son** who chose to be utterly resistant to correction. Such a son is without excuse. His parents have done their job, yet their son is consistently choosing a life of unbridled self-indulgence and is forcefully going his own way—in opposition to what his parents taught him.

While stoning such a son may seem overly harsh, laws such as this one were to prevent the influence of such ungodliness on all Israel. Here again is an example of how seriously God takes a sinful influence that could lead to corruption of His people.

21:22-23 Further developing the sin/consequence theme, Moses allowed for the public display of an executed man's body. However, the body was not to be displayed **overnight**, or it would **defile the land the LORD** their God was giving to them. The land belonged to the Lord and must not be defiled.

[A]21:5 Lit *and according to their mouth will be* [B]21:14 Hb obscure [C]21:17 Lit *mouth of two*, or *two mouthfuls* [D]21:17 Or *two-thirds*; the two-thirds interpretation holds that the firstborn son receives two-thirds of the total estate no matter how many sons are in the family.

22:1-4 Caring for a brother's property was the next concern about which Moses spoke to the people. Moses challenged them with the fact that if they saw a need, they could not ignore it.

22:5 In this verse Moses wrote that **everyone** who does not dress according to his gender is **detestable to the Lord**. Several times in the New Testament, the importance of what is appropriate for godliness in the outward appearance of women is discussed (1Co 11:2-12; 1Tm 2:9-10; 1Pt 3:3-4).

22:6-7 To take the **mother** bird along with her **chicks or eggs** would curtail reproduction of the birds. To include the contents of her nest in the food supply was permitted but not the mother so as not to inhibit this supply.

22:13-21 If a man took a wife and for some reason decided that she did not please him any longer, he was expected to love her anyway. However, these specific verses deal with the man who decided that his wife was not a virgin when they married or that she had been unfaithful to her vows in marriage. Her parents were to bring her to the elders at the city gate and present their evidence that she was a virgin at the time of marriage. **The evidence of her virginity** was the bed sheet or other cloth bearing the bloodstains of the woman's first intercourse and kept by her parents as proof of her fidelity. Once the elders observed this proof of her innocence, the husband was to be punished and fined because he **gave an Israelite virgin a bad name** by falsely accusing her. However, he was not allowed to **divorce her** because no wrong was found with the woman. On the other hand, if the **accusation** of the woman was true and no proof can be found of her virginity, then she was required to be punished. Of utmost importance to the Lord was the purity of His people, especially with regard to sexuality. Therefore, the Lord gave them these guidelines by which to live, with the bottom line being that the people of God's covenant must be pure. The role played by the woman's family is also important. Because a woman was to be protected and treasured by her family, under the leadership of her father or husband, responsibility was given to men to protect their daughters and wives. However, because of the human sinful nature, the Lord set up this part of the law to protect women who were not being protected by the men in their lives.

22:22-30 Moses continued giving the people instructions for living in sexual purity. He did so by giving examples of acts that would be unacceptable

Caring for Your Brother's Property (22:1-4)

22 "If you see your brother's ox or sheep straying, you must not ignore it; make sure you return it to your brother. [2] If your brother does not live near you or you don't know him, you are to bring the animal to your home to remain with you until your brother comes looking for it; then you can return it to him. [3] Do the same for his donkey, his garment, or anything your brother has lost and you have found. You must not ignore it. [4] If you see your brother's donkey or ox fallen down on the road, you must not ignore it; you must help him lift it up.

Preserving Natural Distinctions (22:5-12)

[5] "A woman is not to wear male clothing, and a man is not to put on a woman's garment, for everyone who does these things is detestable to the Lord your God.

[6] "If you come across a bird's nest with chicks or eggs, either in a tree or on the ground along the road, and the mother is sitting on the chicks or eggs, you must not take the mother along with the young. [7] You may take the young for yourself, but be sure to let the mother go free, so that you may prosper and live long. [8] If you build a new house, make a railing around your roof, so that you don't bring bloodguilt on your house if someone falls from it. [9] Do not plant your vineyard with two types of seed; otherwise, the entire harvest, both the crop you plant and the produce of the vineyard, will be defiled. [10] Do not plow with an ox and a donkey together. [11] Do not wear clothes made of both wool and linen. [12] Make tassels on the four corners of the outer garment you wear.

Violations of Proper Sexual Conduct (22:13-30)

[13] "If a man marries a woman, has sexual relations with her, and comes to hate her, [14] and accuses her of shameful conduct, and gives her a bad name, saying, 'I married this woman and was intimate with her, but I didn't find any evidence of her virginity,' [15] the young woman's father and mother will take the evidence of her virginity and bring it to the city elders at the •gate. [16] The young woman's father will say to the elders, 'I gave my daughter to this man as a wife, but he hates her. [17] He has accused her of shameful conduct, saying: "I didn't find any evidence of your daughter's virginity," but here is the evidence of my daughter's virginity.' They will spread out the cloth before the city elders. [18] Then the elders of that city will take the man and punish him. [19] They will also fine him 100 silver shekels and give them to the young woman's father, because that man gave an Israelite virgin a bad name. She will remain his wife; he cannot divorce her as long as he lives. [20] But if this accusation is true and no evidence of the young woman's virginity is found, [21] they will bring the woman to the door of her father's house, and the men of her city will stone her to death. For she has committed an outrage in Israel by being promiscuous in her father's house. You must purge the evil from you.

[22] "If a man is discovered having sexual relations with another man's wife, both the man who had sex with the woman and the woman must die. You must purge the evil from Israel. [23] If there is a young woman who is a virgin •engaged to a man, and another man encounters her in the city and has sex with her, [24] you must take the two of them out to the gate of that city and stone them to death—the young woman because she did not cry out in the city and the man because he has violated his neighbor's fiancée. You must purge the evil from you. [25] But if the man encounters an engaged woman in the open country, and he seizes and rapes her, only the man who raped her must die. [26] Do nothing to the young woman, because she is not •guilty of an offense deserving death. This case is just like one in which a man attacks his neighbor and murders him. [27] When he found her in the field, the engaged woman cried out, but there was no one to rescue her. [28] If a man encounters a young woman, a virgin who is not engaged, takes hold of her and rapes her, and

they are discovered, 29 the man who raped her must give the young woman's father 50 silver shekels, and she must become his wife because he violated her. He cannot divorce her as long as he lives.

30 "A man is not to marry his father's wife; he must not violate his father's marriage bed.[A,B]

Exclusion and Inclusion (23:1-8)

23 "No man whose testicles have been crushed[C] or whose penis has been cut off may enter the LORD's assembly. 2 No one of illegitimate birth may enter the LORD's assembly; none of his descendants, even to the tenth generation, may enter the LORD's assembly. 3 No Ammonite or Moabite may enter the LORD's assembly; none of their descendants, even to the tenth generation, may ever enter the LORD's assembly. 4 This is because they did not meet you with food and water on the journey after you came out of Egypt, and because Balaam son of Beor from Pethor in Aram-naharaim was hired to curse you. 5 Yet the LORD your God would not listen to Balaam, but He turned the curse into a blessing for you because the LORD your God loves you. 6 Never seek their peace or prosperity as long as you live. 7 Do not despise an Edomite, because he is your brother. Do not despise an Egyptian, because you were a foreign resident in his land. 8 The children born to them in the third generation may enter the LORD's assembly.

Cleanliness of the Camp (23:9-14)

9 "When you are encamped against your enemies, be careful to avoid anything offensive. 10 If there is a man among you who is •unclean because of a bodily emission during the night, he must go outside the camp; he may not come anywhere inside the camp. 11 When evening approaches, he must wash with water, and when the sun sets he may come inside the camp. 12 You must have a place outside the camp and go there to relieve yourself. 13 You must have a digging tool in your equipment; when you relieve yourself, dig a hole with it and cover up your excrement. 14 For the LORD your God walks throughout your camp to protect you and deliver your enemies to you; so your encampments must be holy. He must not see anything improper among you or He will turn away from you.

Fugitive Slaves (23:15-16)

15 "Do not return a slave to his master when he has escaped from his master to you. 16 Let him live among you wherever he wants within your gates. Do not mistreat him.

The Forbidding of Cult Prostitution (23:17-18)

17 "No Israelite woman is to be a cult prostitute, and no Israelite man is to be a cult prostitute. 18 Do not bring a female prostitute's wages or a male prostitute's[D] earnings into the house of the LORD your God to fulfill any vow, because both are detestable to the LORD your God.

Interest on Loans (23:19-20)

19 "Do not charge your brother interest on money, food, or anything that can earn interest. 20 You may charge a foreigner interest, but you must not charge your brother interest, so that the LORD your God may bless you in everything you do[E] in the land you are entering to possess.

Keeping Vows (23:21-23)

21 "If you make a vow to the LORD your God, do not be slow to keep it, because He will require it of you, and it will be counted against you as sin. 22 But if you refrain from making a vow, it will not be counted against you as sin. 23 Be careful to do whatever comes from your lips, because you have freely vowed what you promised[F] to the LORD your God.

Neighbor's Crops (23:24-25)

24 "When you enter your neighbor's vineyard, you may eat as many grapes as you want until you are full, but you must not put any in your container. 25 When you enter your neighbor's standing grain, you may pluck heads of grain with your hand, but you must not put a sickle to your neighbor's grain.

[A] **22:30** Dt 23:1 in Hb [B] **22:30** Lit *not uncover the edge of his father's garment*; Ru 3:9; Ezk 16:8 [C] **23:1** Lit *man bruised by crushing* [D] **23:18** Lit *a dog's* [E] **23:20** Lit *you put your hand to* [F] **23:23** Lit *promised with your mouth*

and by denoting for the people what the consequences would be for those who did not obey. Ultimately, he stated over and over the point that **you must purge the evil from you**. A distinction is made for a woman who was raped in the city versus the open country. A woman who was raped in the city was to be stoned along with her assailant because she **did not cry out.** However, a woman who was raped in the open country would not be stoned to death like her assailant because presumably there would be no one around to hear her if she cried out **to be rescued.**

23:1-8 People from other nations were allowed to be a part of Israel's religion, as is obvious from other biblical texts; therefore, this portion of the law must pertain to those people who were disqualified from participating in public worship in Israel.

23:9-18 In these verses, Moses emphasized the importance of purity with regard to the people's religious practices during wartime (vv. 9-14), situations arising in everyday living (vv. 15-17), and finally forbidden acts in worship (vv. 17-18).

23:17-18 A **cult prostitute** was a person (man or woman) who in the temple engaged in ceremonies or fertility rites that involved sexual acts. Temple prostitution was common in Canaanite worship but absolutely not acceptable for the people of Israel. The practice was not only forbidden as a part of worship, but also any earnings from such detestable deeds would not be accepted as an offering. For the covenant people of God, no sexual immorality was acceptable, and certainly none would be integrated with their worship.

23:21-23 The people were responsible for any **vow** or promise they made to the Lord. "Do not be hasty to speak, and do not be impulsive to make a speech before God. God is in heaven and you are on earth, so let your words be few" (Ec 5:2). In the New Testament, the Apostle Peter urged those with the responsibility of speaking in the early church: "Based on the gift each one has received, use it to serve others, as good managers of the varied grace of God. If anyone speaks, it should be as one who speaks God's words" (1Pt 4:10-11). The importance of speaking words is emphasized throughout Scripture by warnings to be careful in speech because words bring life or death to those who speak them and to those to whom they are spoken.

23:24-25 Hospitality is encouraged among the Israelites, and in that spirit, allowance is made for a passerby or traveler who enters a field or **vineyard**. The owner of the **grapes** or **grain** must allow a visitor to take enough to make a meal for himself, but no one helping himself to his neighbor's produce could gather more than this allowance. This ensured a spirit of hospitality in the owner of the grapes or grain, but also disallowed the traveler from taking advantage of the hospitality and stealing from the owner.

24:5 The integrity of marriage is further protected in prescribing that a man must be exempt from military duty during his first year of marriage, during which he would be able to establish a home for him and his wife, and she would likely become pregnant with their first child. An important reason given in the text is to **bring joy** [Hb *samach*, "gladden, give happiness to, cause to rejoice"] **to the wife he has married**. The fact that the joy of the wife was considered important for the husband underscores the fact that God cares for and loves women. Some erroneously say that God seems to hate women in the Old Testament. However, when you read the Old Testament, clearly in many ways God is trying to protect women and care for them in the midst of the fallen world in which they live.

Marriage and Divorce Laws (24:1-5)

24 "If a man marries a woman, but she becomes displeasing to him because he finds something improper about her, he may write her a divorce certificate, hand it to her, and send her away from his house. 2 If after leaving his house she goes and becomes another man's wife, 3 and the second man hates her, writes her a divorce certificate, hands it to her, and sends her away from his house or if he[A] dies, 4 the first husband who sent her away may not marry her again after she has been defiled, because that would be detestable to the LORD. You must not bring •guilt on the land the LORD your God is giving you as an inheritance.

5 "When a man takes a bride, he must not go out with the army or be liable for any duty. He is free to stay at home for one year, so that he can bring joy to the wife he has married.

Safeguarding Life (24:6-9)

6 "Do not take a pair of millstones or an upper millstone as security for a debt, because that is like taking a life as security.

7 "If a man is discovered kidnapping one of his Israelite brothers, whether he treats him as a slave or sells him, the kidnapper must die. You must purge the evil from you.

8 "Be careful in a case of infectious skin disease, following carefully everything the Levitical priests instruct you to do. Be careful to do as I have commanded them. 9 Remember what the LORD your God did to Miriam on the journey after you left Egypt.

Consideration for People in Need (24:10-22)

10 "When you make a loan of any kind to your neighbor, do not enter his house to collect what he offers as security. 11 You must stand outside while the man you are making the loan to brings the security out to you. 12 If he is a poor man, you must not sleep in the garment he has given as security. 13 Be sure to return it[B] to him at sunset. Then he will sleep in it and bless you, and this will be counted as righteousness to you before the LORD your God.

14 "Do not oppress a hired hand who is poor and needy, whether one of your brothers or one of the foreigners residing within a town[C] in your land. 15 You are to pay him his wages each day before the sun sets, because he is poor and depends on them. Otherwise he will cry out to

Doctrine DIVORCE

According to 24:1-4, divorce was allowed in Israel but not for just any reason. A husband could send away his wife with **a divorce certificate** (i.e., a written document officially severing the relationship), but this stipulation implies that she could not simply be thrown out whenever the husband was unhappy with her. First, he had to have a compelling reason—**he finds something improper** [Hb *'erwah*, "shameful exposure or nakedness"; cp. Lm 1:8; Ezk 16:8,36-37; "indecent conduct," cp. Lv 18:6-19; 20:17-21] **about her**. Although the precise meaning is not clear, this offense is probably not synonymous with adultery because such an offense incurred the death penalty (Lv 20:10). Second, he had to give her the divorce document when he dismissed her. The law neither forbids nor condones the wife's second marriage. However, if another man marries her and either dies or, like the first husband, **writes her a divorce certificate**, the law forbids **the first husband** from remarrying her because she has now been joined to someone else. Strong language underscores God's opposition toward treating marriage as something less than a sacred union (see Gn 2:24; Mt 19:6):

- Having been married to a second man means that the woman **has been defiled** (Hb *tame'*, "be unclean or impure,").
- The forbidden practice described here **would be detestable** [Hb *to'evah*, "an abomination, a disgusting thing"; in the same category as idolatry—cp. 12:31] **to the LORD**.
- It would also **bring guilt** [Hb *chata'*, "lead into sin, thereby incurring condemnation"] **on the land** (i.e., the ramifications of disobedience in this matter reach beyond the individual persons involved).

As was clear from Genesis, allowing divorce was not the intention of God. Jesus said that God allowed divorce because of the hardness of the Israelites' hearts (Mt 5:31; 19:1-9). Because a primary tool for interpreting Scripture is to do so in light of other Scripture, Jesus' comments on this text should be considered carefully. Jesus referred back to the creation order and the divine purpose in creating the man and the woman. Regaining a biblical understanding of what God intended for men and women from the beginning is especially important. Considering what Moses was telling the Israelites in light of the Matthew text sheds light on the reasons for only giving permission in the matter of divorce in this text. There is absolutely no mandate to dissolve the marital union.

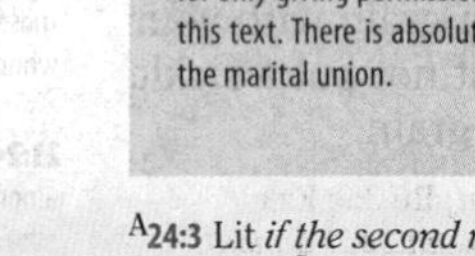

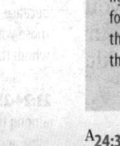

[A]**24:3** Lit *if the second man who has taken her as his wife* [B]**24:13** Lit *return what he has given as security* [C]**24:14** Lit *within the gates*

the Lord against you, and you will be
held guilty.
[16]"Fathers are not to be put to
death for their children or children
for their fathers; each person will be
put to death for his own sin. [17]Do
not deny justice to a foreigner or
fatherless child, and do not take a
widow's garment as security. [18]Re-
member that you were a slave in
Egypt, and the Lord your God redeemed you from there. Therefore I
am commanding you to do this.
[19]"When you reap the harvest in
your field, and you forget a sheaf in
the field, do not go back to get it. It
is to be left for the foreigner, the fatherless, and the widow, so that the
Lord your God may bless you in all
the work of your hands. [20]When you
knock down the fruit from your olive tree, you must not go over the
branches again. What remains will
be for the foreigner, the fatherless,
and the widow. [21]When you gather
the grapes of your vineyard, you
must not glean what is left. What
remains will be for the foreigner,
the fatherless, and the widow. [22]Re-
member that you were a slave in the
land of Egypt. Therefore I am commanding you to do this.

Fairness and Mercy (25:1-4)

25 "If there is a dispute between
men, they are to go to court,

24:19 The admonition to leave **a sheaf in the field** that may have been forgotten shows God's care for the disadvantaged—**the foreigner, the fatherless, and the widow**. He was building into the practices of His people the responsibility to care for the poor and needy. This exact principle is illustrated in the story of Ruth who went to glean in the field of Boaz (Ru 2:15-18).

Biblical Womanhood A Lesson from the Life of Miriam

In 24:8-9 Moses refers to his sister **Miriam** and an incident that occurred on the journey after they left Egypt in order to warn the people about the danger of **infectious skin disease**. Earlier in the Pentateuch, Moses identified Miriam as his older sister (Ex 2:4-8). When Pharaoh ordered all the firstborn sons of the Hebrew slaves to be executed, Miriam watched as the baby Moses was hidden "among the reeds by the bank of the Nile" in order to save him from being killed (Ex 2:3), carefully observing him until Pharaoh's daughter found him and then offering to find a nurse for Moses. Miriam, more than any other human agent, was responsible for returning Moses to the bosom of his mother Jochebed to be nurtured until Moses was old enough to move into the household of Pharaoh's daughter. The next time Miriam is mentioned, she is identified as a prophetess and leader of the women of Israel (Ex 15:20-21). After the Hebrew slaves were rescued from the Egyptians, Moses led the people in a song of praise, and then Miriam led the women in their own song. Miriam had been a woman of influence among the women of Israel. Though the text does not say that she told the women to follow her, she picked up her tambourine and they followed. Miriam was a natural leader among the women.

The next time Miriam is mentioned her attitudes and actions are not so laudatory (Nm 12:1). At some point in their lives, Miriam and her older brother Aaron lost their focus. They had gotten distracted with petty concerns and forgotten that the Lord called Moses to be the leader of Israel. They were privileged to be a part of his family, but God chose Moses to be the leader. In their pettiness, they criticized the wife of Moses and exhibited their jealousy because of Moses' influence with the people. The Lord took this insolence and rebellion very seriously. In fact, He called Moses, Aaron, and Miriam to the tent of meeting to rebuke Aaron and Miriam publicly and to defend Moses. He specifically charged Miriam and Aaron with not respecting Moses and not fearing the consequences of speaking against God's servant. Then, Miriam was struck with leprosy (see Nm 12). The leprosy, or skin disease, not only was a condition separating her from the people by law but also was a visible sign of her guilt as well as Aaron's. Moses, however, exhibiting his humility, cried out to the Lord on her behalf. He asked God to heal her. God did, but she was still required to remain outside the camp for seven days and the people had to wait to continue their journey. Miriam died after the Israelites entered the Wilderness of Zin when they settled in Kadesh (Nm 20:1).

Underlying this account is the theme of obedience and blessings versus rebellion and curses. Miriam, who started out wonderfully with her brothers as a leader of the Hebrews, chose not to listen to the Lord and to respect His servant Moses, and consequently she was struck with leprosy. Moses used the example of Miriam as a reminder that the people were responsible to listen to the Lord and obey Him in every respect. If and when someone did become infected with a disease, then he should be careful to obey and listen carefully to the Lord's instructions in every area of his life.

So, in Miriam, modern women have an example of a woman who once faithfully followed the Lord and then faltered in her obedience. Like Miriam, women in this generation also have the responsibility for obedience with its rewards and the capacity for failure to obey with its consequences. The choice is up to you. Miriam should also be remembered as a woman who at different points in her life walked with God and used her influence to encourage other women to do the same.

and the judges will hear their case. They will clear the innocent and condemn the •guilty. 2 If the guilty party deserves to be flogged, the judge will make him lie down and be flogged in his presence with the number of lashes appropriate for his crime. 3 He may be flogged with 40 lashes, but no more. Otherwise, if he is flogged with more lashes than these, your brother will be degraded in your sight.

4 "Do not muzzle an ox while it treads out grain.

Preserving the Family Line (25:5-12)

5 "When brothers live on the same property[A] and one of them dies without a son, the wife of the dead man may not marry a stranger outside the family. Her brother-in-law is to take her as his wife, have sexual relations with her, and perform the duty of a brother-in-law for her. 6 The first son she bears will carry on the name of the dead brother, so his name will not be blotted out from Israel. 7 But if the man doesn't want to marry his sister-in-law, she must go to the elders at the city •gate and say, 'My brother-in-law refuses to preserve his brother's name in Israel. He isn't willing to perform the duty of a brother-in-law for me.' 8 The elders of his city will summon him and speak with him. If he persists and says, 'I don't want to marry her,' 9 then his sister-in-law will go up to him in the sight of the elders, remove his sandal from his foot, and spit in his face. Then she will declare, 'This is what is done to a man who will not build up his brother's house.' 10 And his family name in Israel will be called 'The house of the man whose sandal was removed.'

11 "If two men are fighting with each other, and the wife of one steps in to rescue her husband from the one striking him, and she puts out her hand and grabs his genitals, 12 you are to cut off her hand. You must not show pity.

Honest Weights and Measures (25:13-16)

13 "You must not have two different weights[B] in your bag, one heavy and one light. 14 You must not have two differing dry measures in your house, a larger and a smaller. 15 You must have a full and honest weight, a full and honest dry measure, so that you may live long in the land the LORD your God is giving you. 16 For everyone who does such things and acts unfairly is detestable to the LORD your God.

Revenge on the Amalekites (25:17-19)

17 "Remember what the Amalekites did to you on the journey after you left Egypt. 18 They met you along the way and attacked all your stragglers from behind when you were tired and weary. They did not •fear God. 19 When the LORD your God gives you rest from all the enemies around you in the land the LORD your God is giving you to possess as an inheritance, blot out the memory of Amalek under heaven. Do not forget.

Giving the Firstfruits (26:1-11)

26 "When you enter the land the LORD your God is giving you as an inheritance, and you take possession of it and live in it, 2 you must take some of the first of all the land's produce that you harvest from the land •Yahweh your God is giving you and put it in a container. Then go to the place where the LORD your God chooses to have His name dwell. 3 When you come before the priest who is serving at that time, you must say to him, 'Today I acknowledge to the LORD your[C] God that I have entered the land the LORD swore to our fathers to give us.'

4 "Then the priest will take the container from your hand and place it before the altar of the LORD your God. 5 You are to respond by saying in the presence of the LORD your God:

> My father was a wandering Aramean. He went down to Egypt with a few people and lived there. There he became a great, powerful, and populous nation. 6 But the Egyptians mistreated and afflicted us, and forced us to do hard labor. 7 So we called out to Yahweh, the God of our fathers, and the LORD heard our

25:1-3 Moses told the Israelites that each person was to be treated fairly. If a disagreement arose, then it should be handled in accordance to the law. If there was a need for punishment, then it should be carried out faithfully. The **guilty party** may be **flogged**, but the maximum number of **lashes** is set at 40 (cp. 2Co 11:24).

25:4 The regulation regarding **an ox** at work allows the animal to eat while pulling the threshing sledge over the grain. In the New Testament, this principle is cited to defend a worker's right to what is earned (1Co 9:9; 1Tm 5:18).

25:5-10 The law of levirate marriage has an important influence in the book of Ruth (Ru 3:3-9). Both the continuity of the family and the rightful inheritance and distribution of land are secured by this regulation. Here, both brothers (i.e., the husband who dies and the brother who takes the widow as his wife) **live on the same property**, sharing responsibility for the family unit's provision. In addition, since no son had been born to the deceased man, he is left with no heir. In this case, his wife should marry his brother to produce heirs. However, if the man did not want to marry her, then she went to the elders at the city gate and requested help from them. They were to help her by urging the man to fulfill his responsibilities. Persistence in refusing to assume this duty would bring public humiliation on the man, indicated by the sister-in-law's removing the man's sandal and spitting in his face in front of the elders. The significance of these commands lies in the protection of a widow. An unmarried woman lived as a dependent within her father's household, and married women depended upon their husbands and sons. A widowed woman without sons would be helpless and without hope for mere sustenance. These commands ensure provision for her livelihood through her husband's brother and his heir. These verses also underscore the importance of the family name. Blessing centered around the family and its generations, which continued through sons.

25:11-12 This passage regarding the punishment for a woman who grabs her husband's opponent by the **genitals** in order to rescue him has been debated by scholars. One option could be that the woman was so severely punished because the act could threaten the possibility for the man to have children in the future. However, the text does not give an explicit reason for this severe punishment.

25:13-16 Having different **weights** and **measures** could lead to dishonesty

[A] 25:5 Lit *live together* [B] 25:13 Lit *have a stone and a stone* [C] 26:3 LXX reads *my*

cry and saw our misery, hardship, and oppression. 8 Then the LORD brought us out of Egypt with a strong hand and an outstretched arm, with terrifying power, and with signs and wonders. 9 He led us to this place and gave us this land, a land flowing with milk and honey. 10 I have now brought the first of the land's produce that You, LORD, have given me.

You will then place the container before the LORD your God and bow down to Him. 11 You, the Levite, and the foreign resident among you will rejoice in all the good things the LORD your God has given you and your household.

The Tenth in the Third Year (26:12-15)

12 "When you have finished paying all the tenth of your produce in the third year, the year of the tenth, you are to give it to the Levite, the foreigner, the fatherless, and the widow, so that they may eat in your towns and be satisfied. 13 Then you will say in the presence of the LORD your God:

> I have taken the consecrated portion out of my house; I have also given it to the Levite, the foreigner, the fatherless, and the widow, according to all the commands You gave me. I have not violated or forgotten Your commands. 14 I have not eaten any of it while in mourning, or removed any of it while •unclean, or offered any of it for the dead. I have obeyed the LORD my God; I have done all You commanded me. 15 Look down from Your holy dwelling, from heaven, and bless Your people Israel and the land You have given us as You swore to our fathers, a land flowing with milk and honey.

Covenant Summary (26:16-19)

16 "The LORD your God is commanding you this day to follow these statutes and ordinances. You must be careful to follow them with all your heart and all your soul. 17 Today you have affirmed that the LORD is your God and that you will walk in His ways, keep His statutes, commands, and ordinances, and obey Him. 18 And today the LORD has affirmed that you are His special people as He promised you, that you are to keep all His commands, 19 that He will elevate you to praise, fame, and glory above all the nations He has made, and that you will be a holy people to the LORD your God as He promised."

Moses' Third Speech: The Blessings and Cursings (27:1–29:1)

The Renewal of the Covenant (27:1-26)

27 Moses and the elders of Israel commanded the people, "Keep every command I am giving you today. 2 At the time you cross the Jordan into the land the LORD your God is giving you, you must set up large stones and cover them with plaster. 3 Write all the words of this law on the stones after you cross to enter the land the LORD your God is giving you, a land flowing with milk and honey, as •Yahweh, the God of your fathers, has promised you. 4 When you have crossed the Jordan, you are to set up these stones on Mount Ebal, as I am commanding you today, and you are to cover them with plaster. 5 Build an altar of stones there to the LORD your God—you must not use any iron tool on them. 6 Use uncut stones to build the altar of the LORD your God and offer •burnt offerings to the LORD your God on it. 7 There you are to sacrifice •fellowship offerings, eat, and rejoice in the presence of the LORD your God. 8 Write clearly all the words of this law on the plastered stones."

9 Moses and the Levitical priests spoke to all Israel, "Be silent, Israel, and listen! This day you have become the people of the LORD your God. 10 Obey the LORD your God and follow His commands and statutes I am giving you today."

11 On that day Moses commanded the people, 12 "When you have crossed the Jordan, these tribes will stand on Mount Gerizim to bless the people: Simeon, Levi, Judah, Issachar, Joseph, and Benjamin. 13 And these tribes will stand on Mount Ebal

and theft, and God called such actions **detestable**.

26:5-10 These verses give a brief history of the Israelites. The requirement for the Israelites to recite it when offering the first fruits of the first harvest in the land ensured that they would not forgot the mighty deeds the Lord had done on their behalf.

26:16-19 Moses summarized the contents of the covenant in these verses. He reminded the people that the Lord was commanding them to be obedient to His law and statutes. Moses repeated the word **today** several times in this discourse. This word could have been used to draw the attention of the younger generation to the magnitude of the promise now being fulfilled. They had wandered for 40 years in the wilderness; however, they were going to cross the Jordan River shortly. Moses highlighted the fact that today the Lord was calling them to listen and obey His commands, and today He was promising them abundant blessing if they obeyed those commands. The time for waiting was over; the time for action had come.

27:1-8 To reiterate the earlier commands, visible symbols of the law were to be worn on their bodies as a tool for teaching the younger generation to listen and learn from the Lord (Dt 6:6-9). Moses gave instructions for more tangible reminders of the goodness of the Lord. The people were to set up **large stones and cover them with plaster** and then **write all the words of this law**. This was to be the first official site of worship in the promised land. To write laws upon large gypsum stones, which were readily available in the Dead Sea valley, was a common practice in the ancient Near East. These stones were heated to produce lime. The effect would be a whitewashed stone, which could easily display words or laws. Moses commanded the Israelites to set up these stones on **Mount Ebal**, which was located about 35 miles north of Jerusalem. The city of Shechem, where God appeared to Abraham and gave him the promise of the land (see Gn 12:1-7), was situated at the base of Mount Ebal. The stones would serve as a continual reminder of God's covenant with His people.

27:15 Moses gave the people directions for how they would celebrate on the day they crossed the Jordan River. Some of the tribes would stand on Mount Gerizim and bless the people. Some of them would stand on Mount Ebal and remind the people of their horrible fate if they did not listen to the Lord. At the end of each proclamation of the Levites, the people were to reply **Amen** (Hb, "so be it," signifying something that is certain or valid). This Hebrew word signified the Israelites' agreement with each point. Christians often end prayers with Amen, and it has devolved to mean little more than "over and out." However, this word should be used as an affirmation of the truth of a statement or prayer and as an acceptance of a good word. Jesus is called "the Amen" (Rv 3:14) noting that he is a true witness of God.

28:2 This final part of Moses' speech vividly described the difference between the life of blessing and the life of curses the people would experience based on their choices in the promised land. Moses said that the blessings of God would literally **overtake you**. There would be no way for them to escape God's blessing if they were faithful to listen to and obey Him. God promised that He would place the Israelites over the surrounding nations. They would have an existence far better than anything they could imagine—if they obeyed.

to deliver the curse: Reuben, Gad, Asher, Zebulun, Dan, and Naphtali.
14 The Levites will proclaim in a loud voice to every Israelite:

15 'The person who makes a carved idol or cast image, which is detestable to the LORD, the work of a craftsman, and sets it up in secret is cursed.'
And all the people will reply, '•Amen!'
16 'The one who dishonors his father or mother is cursed.'
And all the people will say, 'Amen!'
17 'The one who moves his neighbor's boundary marker is cursed.'
And all the people will say, 'Amen!'
18 'The one who leads a blind person astray on the road is cursed.'
And all the people will say, 'Amen!'
19 'The one who denies justice to a foreigner, a fatherless child, or a widow is cursed.'
And all the people will say, 'Amen!'
20 'The one who sleeps with his father's wife is cursed, for he has violated his father's marriage bed.'[A]
And all the people will say, 'Amen!'
21 'The one who has sexual intercourse with any animal is cursed.'
And all the people will say, 'Amen!'
22 'The one who sleeps with his sister, whether his father's daughter or his mother's daughter is cursed.'
And all the people will say, 'Amen!'
23 'The one who sleeps with his mother-in-law is cursed.'
And all the people will say, 'Amen!'
24 'The one who secretly kills his neighbor is cursed.'
And all the people will say, 'Amen!'
25 'The one who accepts a bribe to kill an innocent person is cursed.'
And all the people will say, 'Amen!'
26 'Anyone who does not put the words of this law into practice is cursed.'
And all the people will say, 'Amen!'

A Listing of the Blessings and Cursings (28:1–29:1)

28 "Now if you faithfully obey the LORD your God and are careful to follow all His commands I am giving you today, the LORD your God will put you far above all the nations of the earth. 2 All these blessings will come and overtake you, because you obey the LORD your God:

3 You will be blessed
in the city
and blessed in the country.
4 Your descendants[B]
will be blessed,
and your land's produce,
and the offspring
of your livestock,
including the young
of your herds
and the newborn
of your flocks.
5 Your basket and kneading bowl
will be blessed.
6 You will be blessed
when you come in
and blessed when you go out.

7 "The LORD will cause the enemies who rise up against you to be defeated before you. They will march out against you from one direction but flee from you in seven directions. 8 The LORD will grant you a blessing on your storehouses and on everything you do;[C] He will bless you in the land the LORD your God is giving you. 9 The LORD will establish you as His holy people, as He swore to you, if you obey the commands of the LORD your God and walk in His ways. 10 Then all the peoples of the earth will see that you are called by •Yahweh's name, and they will stand in awe of you. 11 The LORD

[A] **27:20** Lit *has uncovered the edge of his father's garment*; Ru 3:9; Ezk 16:8 [B] **28:4** Lit *The fruit of your womb* [C] **28:8** Lit *you put your hand to*

will make you prosper abundantly with children,[A] the offspring of your livestock, and your land's produce in the land the LORD swore to your fathers to give you. 12 The LORD will open for you His abundant storehouse, the sky, to give your land rain in its season and to bless all the work of your hands. You will lend to many nations, but you will not borrow. 13 The LORD will make you the head and not the tail; you will only move upward and never downward if you listen to the LORD your God's commands I am giving you today and are careful to follow them. 14 Do not turn aside to the right or the left from all the things I am commanding you today, and do not go after other gods to worship them.

15 "But if you do not obey the LORD your God by carefully following all His commands and statutes I am giving you today, all these curses will come and overtake you:

16 You will be cursed in the city
and cursed in the country.
17 Your basket
and kneading bowl
will be cursed.
18 Your descendants[B]
will be cursed,
and your land's produce,
the young of your herds,
and the newborn
of your flocks.
19 You will be cursed
when you come in
and cursed when you go out.

20 The LORD will send against you curses, confusion, and rebuke in everything you do[C] until you are destroyed and quickly perish, because of the wickedness of your actions in abandoning Me. 21 The LORD will make pestilence cling to you until He has exterminated you from the land you are entering to possess. 22 The LORD will afflict you with wasting disease, fever, inflammation, burning heat, drought,[D] blight, and mildew; these will pursue you until you perish. 23 The sky above you will be bronze, and the earth beneath you iron. 24 The LORD will turn the rain of your land into falling[E] dust; it will descend on you from the sky until you are destroyed. 25 The LORD will cause you to be defeated before your enemies. You will march out against them from one direction but flee from them in seven directions. You will be an object of horror to all the kingdoms of the earth. 26 Your corpses will be food for all the birds of the sky and the wild animals of the land, with no one to scare them away.

27 "The LORD will afflict you with the boils of Egypt, tumors, a festering rash, and scabies, from which you cannot be cured. 28 The LORD will afflict you with madness, blindness, and mental confusion, 29 so that at noon you will grope as a blind man gropes in the dark. You will not be successful in anything you do. You will only be oppressed and robbed continually, and no one will help you. 30 You will become •engaged to a woman, but another man will rape her. You will build a house but not live in it. You will plant a vineyard but not enjoy its fruit. 31 Your ox will be slaughtered before your eyes, but you will not eat any of it. Your donkey will be taken away from you and not returned to you. Your flock will be given to your enemies, and no one will help you. 32 Your sons and daughters will be given to another people, while your eyes grow weary looking for them every day. But you will be powerless to do anything.[F] 33 A people you don't know will eat your land's produce and everything you have labored for. You will only be oppressed and crushed continually. 34 You will be driven mad by what you see. 35 The LORD will afflict you with painful and incurable boils on your knees and thighs—from the sole of your foot to the top of your head.

36 "The LORD will bring you and your king that you have appointed to a nation neither you nor your fathers have known, and there you will worship other gods, of wood and stone. 37 You will become an object of horror, scorn, and ridicule among

28:15-68 If the Israelites forgot the Lord and His commandments in the promised land, their fate would be much worse than anything they could imagine. They would be miserable in the city and the country. Literally, none would escape the judgment of God. Their children, also, would suffer for the parents who did not listen to the Lord. Everyone in the house of Israel would suffer if they forgot the commands of God. Moses wanted the people to have a vivid picture of both the blessings and the curses involved in a relationship with the Lord. Being His people meant something. He had chosen His people to bless them and have a relationship with them. However, if they chose not to listen to and obey Him, then sad consequences would result. God faithfully loved His people and would not allow them to act in a manner contradictory to who they are or who He is. Therefore, He took their obedience, or lack of obedience, seriously. The same is true in subsequent generations (Heb 12:5-8). By coming to the Israelites on Mount Sinai, God was changing the course of their lives. Their choices in light of their relationship with the Lord had consequences, either for blessings if they obeyed or curses if they chose not to obey. That was the nature of their relationship with Him.

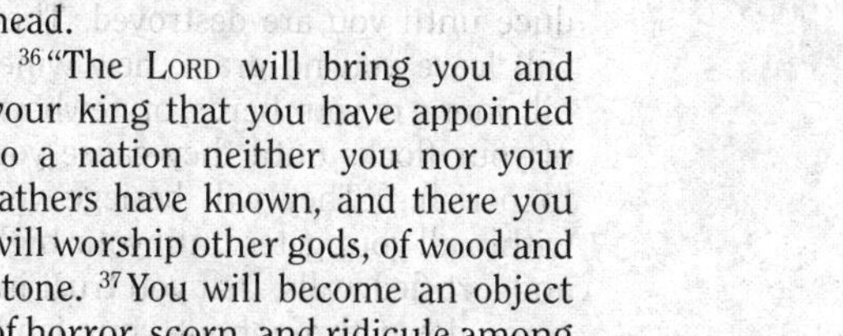

[A] **28:11** Lit *abundantly in the fruit of your womb* [B] **28:18** Lit *The fruit of your womb* [C] **28:20** Lit *you put your hand to* [D] **28:22** Or *sword* [E] **28:24** Lit *powder and* [F] **28:32** Lit *day, and not for power your hand*

all the peoples where the Lord will
drive you.
38 “You will sow much seed in the
field but harvest little, because locusts will devour it. 39 You will plant
and cultivate vineyards but not
drink the wine or gather the grapes,
because worms will eat them. 40 You
will have olive trees throughout
your territory but not anoint yourself with oil, because your olives will
drop off. 41 You will father sons and
daughters, but they will not remain
yours, because they will be taken
prisoner. 42 Whirring insects will
take possession of all your trees and
your land's produce. 43 The foreign
resident among you will rise higher
and higher above you, while you
sink lower and lower. 44 He will lend
to you, but you won't lend to him.
He will be the head, and you will be
the tail.
45 “All these curses will come,
pursue, and overtake you until you
are destroyed, since you did not
obey the Lord your God and keep
the commands and statutes He
gave you. 46 These curses will be a
sign and a wonder against you and
your descendants forever. 47 Because
you didn't serve the Lord your God
with joy and a cheerful heart, even
though you had an abundance of everything, 48 you will serve your enemies the Lord will send against you,
in famine, thirst, nakedness, and a
lack of everything. He will place an
iron yoke on your neck until He
has destroyed you. 49 The Lord will
bring a nation from far away, from
the ends of the earth, to swoop down
on you like an eagle, a nation whose
language you don't understand, 50 a
ruthless nation,[A] showing no respect for the old and not sparing the
young. 51 They will eat the offspring
of your livestock and your land's produce until you are destroyed. They
will leave you no grain, new wine,
oil, young of your herds, or newborn
of your flocks until they cause you
to perish. 52 They will besiege you
within all your gates until your high
and fortified walls, that you trust in,
come down throughout your land.
They will besiege you within all your
gates throughout the land the Lord
your God has given you.
53 “You will eat your children,[B] the
flesh of your sons and daughters the
Lord your God has given you during
the siege and hardship your enemy
imposes on you. 54 The most sensitive and refined man among you
will look grudgingly[C] at his brother,
the wife he embraces,[D] and the rest
of his children, 55 refusing to share
with any of them his children's flesh
that he will eat because he has nothing left during the siege and hardship your enemy imposes on you in
all your towns. 56 The most sensitive
and refined woman among you, who
would not venture to set the sole
of her foot on the ground because
of her refinement and sensitivity,
will begrudge the husband she embraces, her son, and her daughter,
57 the afterbirth that comes out from
between her legs and the children
she bears, because she will secretly
eat them for lack of anything else
during the siege and hardship your
enemy imposes on you within your
gates.
58 “If you are not careful to obey
all the words of this law, which
are written in this scroll, by •fear-
ing this glorious and awesome
name—Yahweh, your God— 59 He
will bring extraordinary plagues on
you and your descendants, severe
and lasting plagues, and terrible and
chronic sicknesses. 60 He will afflict
you again with all the diseases of
Egypt, which you dreaded, and they
will cling to you. 61 The Lord will
also afflict you with every sickness
and plague not recorded in the book
of this law, until you are destroyed.
62 Though you were as numerous
as the stars of the sky, you will be
left with only a few people, because
you did not obey the Lord your God.
63 Just as the Lord was glad to cause
you to prosper and to multiply you,
so He will also be glad to cause
you to perish and to destroy you.
You will be deported from the land
you are entering to possess. 64 Then
the Lord will scatter you among all
peoples from one end of the earth
to the other, and there you will

[A] **28:50** Lit *a nation strong of face* [B] **28:53** Lit *eat the fruit of your womb* [C] **28:54** Lit *you his eye will be evil* [D] **28:54** Lit *wife of his bosom*

worship other gods, of wood and stone, which neither you nor your fathers have known. 65 You will find no peace among those nations, and there will be no resting place for the sole of your foot. There the Lord will give you a trembling heart, failing eyes, and a despondent spirit. 66 Your life will hang in doubt before you. You will be in dread night and day, never certain of survival. 67 In the morning you will say, 'If only it were evening!' and in the evening you will say, 'If only it were morning!'—because of the dread you will have in your heart and because of what you will see. 68 The Lord will take you back in ships to Egypt by a route that I said you would never see again. There you will sell yourselves to your enemies as male and female slaves, but no one will buy you."

29 [A]These are the words of the covenant the Lord commanded Moses to make with the Israelites in the land of Moab, in addition to the covenant He had made with them at Horeb.

Moses' Fourth Speech: Defining the Demands of the Covenant with the Lord (29:2–30:20)

A Call to Obedience (29:2-29)

2[B]Moses summoned all Israel and said to them, "You have seen with your own eyes everything the Lord did in Egypt to Pharaoh, to all his officials, and to his entire land. 3 You saw with your own eyes the great trials and those great signs and wonders. 4 Yet to this day the Lord has not given you a mind to understand, eyes to see, or ears to hear. 5 I led you 40 years in the wilderness; your clothes and the sandals on your feet did not wear out; 6 you did not eat bread or drink wine or beer—so that you might know that I am •Yahweh your God. 7 When you reached this place, Sihon king of Heshbon and Og king of Bashan came out against us in battle, but we defeated them. 8 We took their land and gave it as an inheritance to the Reubenites, the Gadites, and half the tribe of Manasseh. 9 Therefore, observe the words of this covenant and follow them, so that you will succeed in everything you do.

10 "All of you are standing today before the Lord your God—your leaders, tribes, elders, officials, all the men of Israel, 11 your children, your wives, and the foreigners in your camps who cut your wood and draw your water— 12 so that you may enter into the covenant of the Lord your God, which He is making with you today, so that you may enter into His oath 13 and so that He may establish you today as His people and He may be your God as He promised you and as He swore to your fathers Abraham, Isaac, and Jacob. 14 I am making this covenant and this oath not only with you, 15 but also with those who are standing here with us today in the presence of the Lord our God and with those who are not here today.

16 "Indeed, you know how we lived in the land of Egypt and passed through the nations where you traveled. 17 You saw their detestable images and idols made of wood, stone, silver, and gold, which were among them. 18 Be sure there is no man, woman, clan, or tribe among you today whose heart turns away from the Lord our God to go and worship the gods of those nations. Be sure there is no root among you bearing poisonous and bitter fruit. 19 When someone hears the words of this oath, he may consider himself exempt,[C] thinking, 'I will have peace even though I follow my own stubborn heart.' This will lead to the destruction of the well-watered land as well as the dry land. 20 The Lord will not be willing to forgive him. Instead, His anger and jealousy will burn against that person, and every curse written in this scroll will descend on him. The Lord will blot out his name under heaven, 21 and single him out for harm from all the tribes of Israel, according to all the curses of the covenant written in this book of the law.

22 "Future generations of your children who follow you and the foreigner who comes from a distant

29:10-11 Moses called the people to be accountable for their choices. **All of you are standing today before the Lord your God.** All—not just the men or the leaders—but all the people were accountable for their choices. God established His covenant with all the people, calling all to remember what the Lord had done and consider all that He was promising them.

29:18 There would be many temptations for the Israelites in the promised land, especially idolatry, and God warned them of even allowing a **root** or hint of idolatrous practice in their midst. Even the smallest compromise or concession could lead to a poisonous fruit in their hearts and lives. God knows well human frailty. The problem is that humans overestimate their own strength. Sin can take root in your life starting with a small compromise or concession in your thoughts or actions. Temptation that is fed gives birth to sin (Jms 1:14-15). By allowing in your life those things that may tempt you, you are inviting your own misery and ruin. God knew this and warned the Israelites against allowing in their midst even a root that could bear fruit.

29:22-29 Moses warned the Israelites that their choices would have consequences. He drew attention not just to the present generation but to future generations as well. If the people chose not to obey the Lord, their land would be severely judged, affecting not only the Israelites and their future generations but also the surrounding nations. Rather than the people looking to the nation of Israel in awe of the goodness of the Lord their God, the people would look to them and ask, **Why has the Lord done this to this land? Why this great outburst of anger?** The role of the land is still central as a silent witness to the relationship between Yahweh and His people. When the people obeyed, the land would be fruitful and provide for them an abundant life. But when they disobeyed, the land would lie waste and desolate, revealing the enmity between Israel and her God.

[A]**29:1** Dt 28:69 in Hb [B]**29:2** Dt 29:1 in Hb [C]**29:19** Lit *may bless himself in his heart*

30:2 The people were to **return to the Lord your God and obey Him with all your heart and all your soul by doing everything I am giving you today**. Then the Lord would restore their fortunes and pour out His compassion on them. The return to the land not only is literal but also is symbolic of the restored relationship between Yahweh and His people.

30:6 When the people entered the land, Moses wanted them to know all the possibilities for blessing and cursing and speaks of the circumcision of the **heart**. At that time Moses could not have fully known all that this phrase would mean in the future. But the term does foreshadow another covenant, which God would make with His people through Jesus. Before giving the Law, Abraham, Isaac, and Jacob, the forefathers of the Israelites, followed God solely by faith; and they were made righteous. While faith was still central to the lives of the Israelites, the Law brought a new understanding of how to walk with God. The Lord's statutes and commands, which the people were to obey for their own good, were not sufficient. This is why the curses were given—because God knew the people would disobey. Something more was required to enable the people to follow God's word. Therefore, the circumcision of the heart was necessary. The image is one of complete vulnerability to God so that nothing is hidden from Him. A person with a circumcised heart is a fully devoted follower of God.

30:11-20 Moses charged the Israelites to listen to the Lord and obey. No matter what the Israelites encountered in the promised land, they were to keep in mind that they were to choose to obey. The final responsibility always rests with the people. They not only had to choose, but the only right choice was obedience. There were no options. They were commanded to choose obedience and life.

31:1-5 Moses moves into more formal closing remarks, reminding the people of his age and of the fact that he cannot enter the land. The Lord would go before the Israelites into the land, but He also appointed Joshua to be the next leader of the Israelites. Moses reminded the people again that the Lord would give them the surrounding lands as He had given them the lands of **Og** and **Sihon**.

country will see the plagues of the
land and the sicknesses the LORD
has inflicted on it. 23 All its soil will
be a burning waste of sulfur and
salt, unsown, producing nothing,
with no plant growing on it, just
like the fall of Sodom and Gomorrah, Admah and Zeboiim, which the
LORD demolished in His fierce anger. 24 All the nations will ask, 'Why
has the LORD done this to this land?
Why this great outburst of anger?'
25 Then people will answer, 'It is because they abandoned the covenant
of Yahweh, the God of their fathers,
which He had made with them when
He brought them out of the land of
Egypt. 26 They began to worship other gods, bowing down to gods they
had not known—gods that the LORD
had not permitted them to worship.
27 Therefore the LORD's anger burned
against this land, and He brought
every curse written in this book on
it. 28 The LORD uprooted them from
their land in His anger, rage, and
great wrath, and threw them into
another land where they are today.' 29 The hidden things belong to
the LORD our God, but the revealed
things belong to us and our children
forever, so that we may follow all the
words of this law.

A Demand for Commitment (30:1-10)

30 "When all these things happen to you—the blessings and
curses I have set before you—and
you come to your senses while you
are in all the nations where the LORD
your God has driven you, 2 and you
and your children return to the
LORD your God and obey Him with
all your heart and all your soul by
doing[A] everything I am giving you
today, 3 then He will restore your
fortunes,[B] have compassion on you,
and gather you again from all the
peoples where the LORD your God
has scattered you. 4 Even if your exiles are at the ends of the earth,[C] He
will gather you and bring you back
from there. 5 The LORD your God
will bring you into the land your
fathers possessed, and you will take
possession of it. He will cause you
to prosper and multiply you more
than He did your fathers. 6 The LORD
your God will circumcise your heart
and the hearts of your descendants,
and you will love Him with all your
heart and all your soul so that you
will live. 7 The LORD your God will
put all these curses on your enemies who hate and persecute you.
8 Then you will again obey Him and
follow all His commands I am giving you today. 9 The LORD your God
will make you prosper abundantly
in all the work of your hands with
children,[D] the offspring of your
livestock, and your land's produce.
Indeed, the LORD will again delight
in your prosperity, as He delighted
in that of your fathers, 10 when you
obey the LORD your God by keeping
His commands and statutes that are
written in this book of the law and
return to Him with all your heart
and all your soul.

The Choice Before the House of Israel (30:11-20)

11 "This command that I give you
today is certainly not too difficult
or beyond your reach. 12 It is not
in heaven so that you have to ask,
'Who will go up to heaven, get it for
us, and proclaim it to us so that we
may follow it?' 13 And it is not across
the sea so that you have to ask, 'Who
will cross the sea, get it for us, and
proclaim it to us so that we may follow it?' 14 But the message is very
near you, in your mouth and in your
heart, so that you may follow it.
15 See, today I have set before you life
and prosperity, death and adversity.
16 For[E] I am commanding you today
to love the LORD your God, to walk
in His ways, and to keep His commands, statutes, and ordinances,
so that you may live[F] and multiply,
and the LORD your God may bless
you in the land you are entering to
possess. 17 But if your heart turns
away and you do not listen and you
are led astray to bow down to other
gods and worship them, 18 I tell you
today that you will certainly perish
and will not live long in the land
you are entering to possess across
the Jordan. 19 I call heaven and earth
as witnesses against you today that

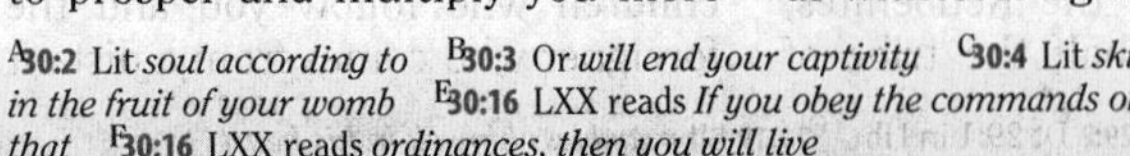

[A]**30:2** Lit *soul according to* [B]**30:3** Or *will end your captivity* [C]**30:4** Lit *skies* [D]**30:9** Lit *hands in the fruit of your womb* [E]**30:16** LXX reads *If you obey the commands of the LORD your God that* [F]**30:16** LXX reads *ordinances, then you will live*

I have set before you life and death, blessing and curse. Choose life so that you and your descendants may live, 20 love the LORD your God, obey Him, and remain faithful[A] to Him. For He is your life, and He will prolong your life in the land the LORD swore to give to your fathers Abraham, Isaac, and Jacob."

The Conclusion: A Transition in Leadership (31:1–34:12)

Moses' Last Words and His Song (31:1–32:52)

31 Then Moses continued to speak these[B] words to all Israel, 2 saying, "I am now 120 years old; I can no longer act as your leader.[C] The LORD has told me, 'You will not cross this Jordan.' 3 The LORD your God is the One who will cross ahead of you. He will destroy these nations before you, and you will drive them out. Joshua is the one who will cross ahead of you, as the LORD has said. 4 The LORD will deal with them as He did Sihon and Og, the kings of the Amorites, and their land when He destroyed them. 5 The LORD will deliver them over to you, and you must do to them exactly as I have commanded you. 6 Be strong and courageous; don't be terrified or afraid of them. For it is the LORD your God who goes with you; He will not leave you or forsake you."

7 Moses then summoned Joshua and said to him in the sight of all Israel, "Be strong and courageous, for you will go with[D] this people into the land the LORD swore to give to their fathers. You will enable them to take possession of it. 8 The LORD is the One who will go before you. He will be with you; He will not leave you or forsake you. Do not be afraid or discouraged."

9 Moses wrote down this law and gave it to the priests, the sons of Levi, who carried the ark of the LORD's covenant, and to all the elders of Israel. 10 Moses commanded them, "At the end of every seven years, at the appointed time in the year of debt cancellation, during the Festival of Booths, 11 when all Israel assembles[E] in the presence of the LORD your God at the place He chooses, you are to read this law aloud before all Israel. 12 Gather the people—men, women, children, and foreigners living within your gates—so that they may listen and learn to •fear the LORD your God and be careful to follow all the words of this law. 13 Then their children who do not know the law will listen and learn to fear the LORD your God as long as you live in the land you are crossing the Jordan to possess."

14 The LORD said to Moses, "The time of your death is now approaching. Call Joshua and present yourselves at the tent of meeting so that I may commission him." When Moses and Joshua went and presented themselves at the tent of meeting, 15 the LORD appeared at the tent in a pillar of cloud, and the cloud stood at the entrance to the tent.

16 The LORD said to Moses, "You are about to rest with your fathers, and these people will soon commit adultery with the foreign gods of the land they are entering. They will abandon Me and break the covenant I have made with them. 17 My anger will burn against them on that day; I will abandon them and hide My face from them so that they will become easy prey.[F] Many troubles and afflictions will come to them. On that day they will say, 'Haven't these troubles come to us because our God is no longer with us?' 18 I will certainly hide My face on that day because of all the evil they have done by turning to other gods. 19 Therefore write down this song for yourselves and teach it to the Israelites; have them recite it,[G] so that this song may be a witness for Me against the Israelites. 20 When I bring them into the land I swore to give their fathers, a land flowing with milk and honey, they will eat their fill and prosper.[H] They will turn to other gods and worship them, despising Me and breaking My covenant. 21 And when many troubles and afflictions come to them, this song will testify against them,

31:6 Be strong and courageous—This statement is the first time the Lord would speak this command to the younger Israelites. The task ahead of the people would require courage and steadfastness on their part. They had to depend totally on the Lord for their deliverance from the people who already inhabited their promised land.

31:7-8 These verses are directed specifically to Joshua as the new leader of Israel. The people would need to know that the Lord spoke the same message to Joshua as He did to Moses. This transfer of leadership from Moses to Joshua was crucial for Israel. Each party would need to know that he had completed that for which he was responsible in this transitional part of the history of Israel.

31:9-13 Moses wrote down the law and gave it to the priests. He instructed that **this law** was to be read aloud before all the nation of Israel **every seven years** so that the people would hear from the Lord. The law referenced here was most likely the book of Deuteronomy. The people were to **gather**—every man, woman, child, and even **foreigners**—so that they could **learn** about the Lord as they listened to the reading of the law. In this way the foreigners, as well as each new generation, learned about the Lord.

31:19 Moses' address to the Israelites was not in the least bit optimistic. He had experienced their rebellious nature for 40 years. When he finished writing down all the words the Lord gave him, he commanded that they take the book of the law and place it in the ark of the covenant as a witness against the wrong choices they would make in the promised land. Moses was a seasoned leader who knew his people. The Lord was clear that they would fail in the future. He had Moses recite the **song** as a **witness** to instruct them about what they should do when that failure occurred. The rebellious nature of the people would not be left behind in the wilderness. Even though Moses commanded them over and over again to remember the Lord's commands and listen to Him, they would fail eventually and live their lives according to what seemed right to them.

[A] **30:20** Lit *and hold on* [B] **31:1** Some Hb mss, DSS, LXX, Syr, Vg read *all these* [C] **31:2** Lit *no longer go out or come in* [D] **31:7** Some Hb mss, Sam, Syr, Vg read *you will bring* [E] **31:11** Lit *comes to appear* [F] **31:17** Lit *will be for devouring* [G] **31:19** Lit *Israelites; put it in their mouths* [H] **31:20** Lit *be fat*

32:1 Because the Lord God was the Lord of all the heavens and the earth, Moses reminded the people of His sovereignty in creation. If the people of Israel were to choose to serve lesser false gods, the **heavens** and the **earth** would be witnesses to the power and strength of the character of the one true God. The central theme of the song is the apostasy of Israel and the nation's propensity toward idolatry. The Lord wanted the people to remember that He was their God and He was for them.

because[A] their descendants will not
have forgotten it. For I know what
they are prone to do,[B] even before I
bring them into the land I swore to
give them." 22 So Moses wrote down
this song on that day and taught it
to the Israelites.

23 The LORD commissioned Joshua
son of Nun, "Be strong and courageous, for you will bring the Israelites into the land I swore to them,
and I will be with you."

24 When Moses had finished writing down on a scroll every single
word[C] of this law, 25 he commanded
the Levites who carried the ark of
the LORD's covenant, 26 "Take this
book of the law and place it beside
the ark of the covenant of the LORD
your God so that it may remain
there as a witness against you. 27 For
I know how rebellious and stiff-
necked you are. If you are rebelling
against the LORD now, while I am
still alive, how much more will you
rebel after I am dead! 28 Assemble all
your tribal elders and officers before
me so that I may speak these words
directly to them and call heaven and
earth as witnesses against them.
29 For I know that after my death
you will become completely corrupt
and turn from the path I have commanded you. Disaster will come to
you in the future, because you will
do what is evil in the LORD's sight,
infuriating Him with what your
hands have made." 30 Then Moses
recited aloud every single word[D] of
this song to the entire assembly of
Israel:

32 Pay attention, heavens, and I
will speak;
listen, earth, to the words
of my mouth.
2 Let my teaching fall like rain
and my word settle like dew,
like gentle rain on new grass
and showers on tender plants.
3 For I will proclaim
•Yahweh's name.
Declare the greatness
of our God!
4 The Rock—His work is perfect;
all His ways are entirely just.
A faithful God,
without prejudice,
He is righteous and true.
5 His people have acted
corruptly toward Him;
this is their
defect[E]—they are not
His children
but a devious
and crooked generation.
6 Is this how you repay the LORD,
you foolish
and senseless people?
Isn't He your Father
and Creator?
Didn't He make you
and sustain you?
7 Remember the days of old;
consider the years long past.
Ask your father,
and he will tell you,
your elders,
and they will teach you.
8 When the •Most High
gave the nations
their inheritance[F]
and divided the •human race,
He set the boundaries
of the peoples
according to the number
of the people of Israel.[G]
9 But the LORD's portion is
His people,
Jacob, His own inheritance.

10 He found him
in a desolate land,
in a barren,
howling wilderness;
He surrounded him,
cared for him,
and protected him as the pupil
of His eye.
11 He watches over[H] His nest
like an eagle
and hovers over His young;
He spreads His wings,
catches him,
and lifts him up
on His pinions.
12 The LORD alone led him,
with no help from
a foreign god.[I]

[A]**31:21** Lit *because the mouths of the words to their completion* [B]**31:21** Or *know the plans they are devising* [C]**31:24** Lit *scroll* [D]**31:30** Lit *recited the words to their completion* [E]**32:5** Or *Him; through their fault*; Hb obscure [F]**32:8** Or *Most High divided the nations* [G]**32:8** One DSS reads *number of the sons of God*; LXX reads *number of the angels of God* [H]**32:11** Or *He stirs up* [I]**32:12** Lit *him, and no foreign god with Him*

13 He made him ride
on the heights of the land
and eat the produce of the field.
He nourished him with honey
from the rock
and oil from flint-like rock,
14 cream from the herd and milk
from the flock,
with the fat of lambs,
rams from Bashan, and goats,
with the choicest grains
of wheat;
you drank wine
from the finest grapes.[A]
15 Then[B] Jeshurun[C] became fat
and rebelled—
you became fat, bloated,
and gorged.
He abandoned the God
who made him
and scorned the Rock
of his salvation.
16 They provoked His jealousy
with foreign gods;
they enraged Him
with detestable practices.
17 They sacrificed to demons,
not God,
to gods they had not known,
new gods that had
just arrived,
which your fathers
did not fear.
18 You ignored the Rock
who gave you birth;
you forgot the God
who gave birth to you.

19 When the LORD saw this,
He despised them,
provoked to anger by His sons
and daughters.
20 He said: "I will hide My face
from them;
I will see what will become
of them,
for they are
a perverse generation—
unfaithful children.
21 They have provoked
My jealousy
with their so-called gods;[D]
they have enraged Me
with their worthless idols.
So I will provoke
their jealousy
with an inferior people;[E]
I will enrage them
with a foolish nation.
22 For fire has been kindled
because of My anger
and burns to the depths
of •Sheol;
it devours the land
and its produce,
and scorches the foundations
of the mountains.

23 "I will pile disasters on them;
I will use up My arrows
against them.
24 They will be weak
from hunger,
ravaged by pestilence
and bitter plague;
I will unleash on them
wild beasts with fangs,
as well as venomous snakes
that slither in the dust.
25 Outside, the sword will take
their children,
and inside, there will be terror;
the young man and the young
woman will be killed,
the infant
and the gray-haired man.

26 "I would have said:
I will cut them to pieces[F]
and blot out the memory
of them from mankind,
27 if I had not feared insult
from the enemy,
or feared that these foes
might misunderstand
and say: 'Our own hand
has prevailed;
it wasn't the LORD who did
all this.'"

28 Israel is a nation
lacking sense
with no understanding at all.[G]
29 If only they were wise,
they would figure it out;
they would understand
their fate.
30 How could one man pursue
a thousand,
or two put ten thousand
to flight,
unless their Rock had sold
them,

32:15-18 No matter how much the Lord did for Israel, they responded with rebellion. **Jeshurun**, another name for Israel, meant "upright" or "straight" so there is a play on words that the "upright" ones turned to rebellion. Their pursuit of other gods was the nature of the transgressions the Lord predicted Israel would commit. They **ignored the Rock** who gave them **birth**; they **forgot the God** who brought them forth. Throughout the book of Deuteronomy, Moses had warned the Israelites to listen to the Lord and to remember all that the Lord had done for them and the consequences to their parents who had rebelled and died in the wilderness.

32:28 Israel had forgotten all that the Lord had done for His people. Moses accused them of not only **lacking sense** but also of being unwise. He predicted that the people would leave the Lord because of their attraction to false gods. However, the one true God was the one who brings death and gives life. The power to wound and to heal belongs to the hand of the Lord. He is the one who chose Israel; however, they would choose to leave Him.

[A]32:14 Lit *the blood of grapes* [B]32:15 DSS, Sam, LXX add *Jacob ate his fill;* [C]32:15 = Upright One, referring to Israel [D]32:21 Lit *with no gods* [E]32:21 Lit *with no people* [F]32:26 LXX reads *will scatter them* [G]32:28 Lit *understanding in them*

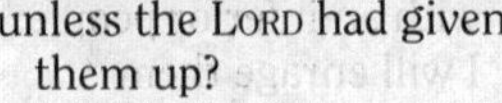

32:49 The Lord commanded Moses to **go up Mount Nebo** to **view the land of Canaan**, the promised land, which the Lord was giving to the Israelites. However, Moses could not enter the land but would die there on the mountain. Here the intimacy of the relationship between God and Moses is noted again. God knew that Moses earnestly wanted to enter the promised land, but he was not allowed to do so because of his disobedience. Even with Moses, the man who enjoyed intimate fellowship with God, the holiness of God was paramount. There is no sense of a scale with good outweighing bad. Any disobedience is an offense against God's holiness and requires a response.

unless the LORD had given
them up?
31 But their "rock" is not
like our Rock;
even our enemies concede.
32 For their vine is from the vine
of Sodom
and from the fields
of Gomorrah.
Their grapes are poisonous;
their clusters are bitter.
33 Their wine is serpents' venom,
the deadly poison of cobras.
34 "Is it not stored up with Me,
sealed up in My vaults?
35 Vengeance[A] belongs to Me;
I will repay.[B]
In time their foot will slip,
for their day of disaster is near,
and their doom
is coming quickly."
36 The LORD will indeed vindicate
His people
and have compassion
on His servants
when He sees that
their strength is gone
and no one is
left—slave or free.
37 He will say:
"Where are their gods,
the 'rock'
they found refuge in?
38 Who ate the fat
of their sacrifices
and drank the wine
of their •drink offerings?
Let them rise up and help you;
let it[C] be a shelter for you.
39 See now that I alone am He;
there is no God but Me.
I bring death and I give life;
I wound and I heal.
No one can rescue anyone
from My hand.
40 I raise My hand to heaven
and declare:
As surely as I live forever,
41 when I sharpen
My flashing sword,
and My hand takes hold
of judgment,
I will take vengeance
on My adversaries
and repay those who hate Me.
42 I will make My arrows drunk
with blood
while My sword devours
flesh—
the blood of the slain
and the captives,
the heads
of the enemy leaders."[D]

43 Rejoice, you nations,
concerning His people,[E]
for He will avenge the blood
of His servants.[F]
He will take vengeance
on His adversaries;[G]
He will purify His land
and His people.[H]

44 Moses came with Joshua[I] son of
Nun and recited all the words of this
song in the presence of the people.
45 After Moses finished reciting all
these words to all Israel, 46 he said to
them, "Take to heart all these words
I am giving as a warning to you today, so that you may command your
children to carefully follow all the
words of this law. 47 For they are not
meaningless words to you but they
are your life, and by them you will
live long in the land you are crossing the Jordan to possess."

48 On that same day the LORD spoke
to Moses, 49 "Go up Mount Nebo
in the Abarim range in the land of
Moab, across from Jericho, and view
the land of Canaan I am giving the
Israelites as a possession. 50 Then
you will die on the mountain that
you go up, and you will be gathered
to your people, just as your brother
Aaron died on Mount Hor and was
gathered to his people. 51 For both of
you broke faith with Me among the
Israelites at the waters of Meribath-kadesh in the Wilderness of Zin by
failing to treat Me as holy in their
presence. 52 Although from a distance you will view the land that I

[A] **32:35** Sam, LXX read *On a day of vengeance* [B] **32:35** LXX, Tg, Vg read *Me; and recompense I will recompense* [C] **32:38** Sam, LXX, Tg, Vg read *them* [D] **32:42** Or *the long-haired heads of the enemy* [E] **32:43** LXX reads *Rejoice, you heavens, along with Him, and let all the sons of God worship Him; rejoice, you nations, with His people, and let all the angels of God strengthen themselves in Him*; DSS read *Rejoice, you heavens, along with Him, and let all the angels worship Him*; Heb 1:6 [F] **32:43** DSS, LXX read *sons* [G] **32:43** DSS, LXX add *and He will recompense those who hate Him*; v. 41 [H] **32:43** Syr, Tg; DSS, Sam, LXX, Vg read *His people's land* [I] **32:44** LXX, Syr, Vg; MT reads *Hoshea*; Nm 13:8,16

am giving the Israelites, you will not go there."

Moses' Blessings and Death (33:1–34:12)

33 This is the blessing that Moses, the man of God, gave the Israelites before his death. [2] He said:

The LORD came from Sinai
and appeared to them
from Seir;
He shone on them
from Mount Paran
and came with ten thousand
holy ones,[A]
with lightning[B]
from His right hand[C]
for them.
3 Indeed He loves the people.[D]
All Your[E] holy ones[F] are
in Your hand,
and they assemble[G]
at Your feet.
Each receives Your words.
4 Moses gave us instruction,
a possession for the assembly
of Jacob.
5 So He became King
in Jeshurun[H]
when the leaders of the people
gathered
with the tribes of Israel.

6 Let Reuben live and not die
though his people
become few.

7 He said this about Judah:

LORD, hear Judah's cry
and bring him to his people.
He fights for his cause[I]
with his own hands,
but may You be a help
against his foes.

8 He said about Levi:

Your Thummim and •Urim
belong to Your faithful one;[J]
You tested him at Massah
and contended with him
at the waters of Meribah.
9 He said about his father
and mother,
"I do not regard them."
He disregarded his brothers
and didn't acknowledge
his sons,
for they kept Your word
and maintained
Your covenant.
10 They will teach
Your ordinances to Jacob
and Your instruction to Israel;
they will set incense
before You
and whole •burnt offerings
on Your altar.
11 LORD, bless his possessions,[K]
and accept the work
of his hands.
Smash the loins
of his adversaries
and enemies,
so that they cannot rise again.

12 He said about Benjamin:

The LORD's beloved rests[L]
securely on Him.
He[M] shields him all day long,
and he rests
on His shoulders.[N]

13 He said about Joseph:

May his land be blessed
by the LORD
with the dew
of heaven's bounty
and the watery depths
that lie beneath;
14 with the bountiful harvest
from the sun
and the abundant yield
of the seasons;
15 with the best products
of the ancient mountains
and the bounty
of the eternal hills;
16 with the choice gifts
of the land
and everything in it;
and with the favor of Him
who appeared[O]
in the burning bush.
May these rest on the head
of Joseph,
on the crown of the prince
of his brothers.

[A] **33:2** LXX reads *Mount Paran with ten thousands from Kadesh* [B] **33:2** Or *fiery law*; Hb obscure [C] **33:2** Or *ones, from His southland to the mountain slopes* [D] **33:3** Or *peoples* [E] **33:3** Lit *His*, or *its* [F] **33:3** Either the saints of Israel or angels [G] **33:3** Hb obscure [H] **33:5** = Upright One, referring to Israel [I] **33:7** Or *He contends for them* [J] **33:8** DSS, LXX read *Give to Levi Your Thummim, Your Urim to Your favored one* [K] **33:11** Or *abilities* [L] **33:12** Or *Let the LORD's beloved rest* [M] **33:12** LXX reads *The Most High* [N] **33:12** Or *and He dwells among his mountain slopes* [O] **33:16** Lit *dwelt*

33:1-5 Moses was fully aware of the possibility of future rebellion of the Israelites, as indicated in his song. But as a leader he still blessed them before his death. Surely Moses felt many things for the people. He had led them through innumerable experiences in the last forty years. He probably felt everything from anger to fear to joy. Moses knew, as did the Lord, of the propensity of the people to grumble and to stray from the Lord. However, the last recorded words that Moses spoke to the people were words of blessing rather than cursing. He spoke specifically to each tribe a word of affirmation and support. In a similar way, the Lord deals with His children today. He still knows the nature of His children. He knows that they are prone to wander and to demand their own way. However, He chooses to love them and extend mercy to them. This does not mean that there are not consequences for poor choices you make or sins you commit, but the nature of the Lord is to be patient. He, like Moses, wants to bless His children. He waits patiently to bless. For parents and those in other leadership positions, this principle is important. Moses had plenty of frustrating experiences with the people of Israel. He knew them as well as he knew his own children. They were stiff-necked and stubborn most of the time; however, when the time came to say the most important words to them, Moses blessed them. He spoke directly to each tribe a word of blessing and promise. His example is instructive for godly leaders in every generation. The entire book of Deuteronomy is a lesson in how to speak to people the last words of peace, instruction, and warning. However, Moses' last words are especially insightful in learning to bring closure to a time of leadership.

33:6-25 In these verses, Moses spoke specific blessings to each of the tribes. The blessings he spoke are similar to the blessings Jacob gave his sons in Genesis 49. However, the role of the tribe of **Judah** is less emphasized in Moses' blessing. Moses paid more attention to the blessing of the Levites and the tribe of **Joseph**. The tribe of **Levi** was given the role of teaching the Torah. The tribes of Joseph (**Ephraim** and **Manasseh**), on the other hand, are described as being the tribes that would enjoy the most abundant portion of the promised land. Kingship was not a major focus of Moses, but the role of the Levites (priests) and the life of Joseph (alluding to time in Egypt) were. The entire nation was blessed in Moses' last words to them.

17 His firstborn bull
has[A] splendor,
and horns like[B] those
of a wild ox;
he gores all the peoples
with them
to the ends of the earth.
Such are the ten thousands
of Ephraim,
and such are the thousands
of Manasseh.

18 He said about Zebulun:

Rejoice, Zebulun,
in your journeys,
and Issachar, in your tents.
19 They summon the peoples
to a mountain;
there they offer
acceptable sacrifices.
For they draw
from the wealth of the seas
and the hidden treasures
of the sand.

20 He said about Gad:

The one who enlarges
Gad's territory
will be blessed.
He lies down like a lion
and tears off an arm or even
a head.
21 He chose the best part
for himself,
because a ruler's portion
was assigned there
for him.
He came with the leaders
of the people;
he carried out
the LORD's justice
and His ordinances
for Israel.

22 He said about Dan:

Dan is a young lion,
leaping out of Bashan.

23 He said about Naphtali:

Naphtali, enjoying approval,
full of the LORD's blessing,
take[C] possession to the west
and the south.

24 He said about Asher:

May Asher[D] be
the most blessed
of the sons;
may he be the most favored
among his brothers
and dip his foot in olive oil.[E]
25 May the bolts of your gate
be iron and bronze,
and your strength last
as long as you live.

26 There is none like the God
of Jeshurun,[F]
who rides the heavens
to your aid,
the clouds in His majesty.
27 The God of old is
your dwelling place,
and underneath are
the everlasting arms.
He drives out the enemy
before you
and commands, "Destroy!"
28 So Israel dwells securely;
Jacob lives untroubled[G]
in a land of grain
and new wine;
even his skies drip with dew.
29 How happy you are, Israel!
Who is like you,
a people saved by the LORD?
He is the shield
that protects you,
the sword you boast in.
Your enemies will cringe
before you,
and you will tread
on their backs.[H]

34 Then Moses went up from the
plains of Moab to Mount Nebo,
to the top of Pisgah, which faces
Jericho, and the LORD showed him
all the land: Gilead as far as Dan, 2 all
of Naphtali, the land of Ephraim and
Manasseh, all the land of Judah as
far as the Mediterranean[I] Sea, 3 the
•Negev, and the region from the Valley of Jericho, the City of Palms, as
far as Zoar. 4 The LORD then said to
him, "This is the land I promised
Abraham, Isaac, and Jacob, 'I will
give it to your descendants.' I have
let you see it with your own eyes,
but you will not cross into it."
5 So Moses the servant of the LORD

A33:17 Some DSS, Sam, LXX, Syr, Vg read *A firstborn bull—he has* B33:17 Lit *and his horns are* C33:23 Sam, LXX, Syr, Vg, Tg read *he will take* D33:24 = Happy or Blessed; Gn 30:13 E33:24 A symbol for prosperity F33:26 = Upright One, referring to Israel G33:28 Text emended; MT reads *Jacob's fountain is alone* H33:29 Or *high places* I34:2 Lit *Western*

33:26-27 Moses ended his address to the Israelites by ascribing praise and honor to the Lord. As was emphasized throughout Deuteronomy, the Lord of Israel is a great God. There is none like Him in all the earth. Therefore, Moses concluded his words to the Israelites with praise and honor addressed to the Lord. Moses reminded the people that the Lord would drive out their enemies before them and would issue commands to **destroy**. The people of Israel came into covenant with the Lord because He rescued them from the hands of the Egyptians. Their future blessing rested on the Lord's faithfulness to deliver their enemies into their hands. The promised land was the possession of the Israelites; however, they had to take the land, which, at the time of Moses' last speech to the Israelites, was inhabited by other nations. The Lord promised to give the land to them, but the Israelites had to be willing to fight for it. Therefore, their belief and trust were required for them to attack the nations according to the Lord's command.

33:28-29 Only because the Lord gives security do people experience rest and confidence. Moses reminded the Israelites that even if they had to fight the people in the promised land the Lord was on their side. He would be faithful to do all that He had told them He would do. He was the source of their strength and security. There is no other lasting source of rest and peace. Therefore, Moses admonished the people to acknowledge and obey the Lord in order to experience His security.

34:1-4 After the words of blessing, Moses went up to Mount Nebo, and the Lord showed him the land. Many years had passed since the Lord first appeared to him at Horeb, the mountain of God. Moses lived an unusual life, and the end of it was no different. While the Lord refused to let Moses enter the land, He was faithful to let him see the land. The Lord's address to Moses is interesting because He reminded Moses that **this is the land I promised Abraham, Isaac, and Jacob**. The beginning of this story is not with the life of Moses but earlier with the lives of the patriarchs. God's plan is far greater than any human lifetime. The gift of the land began with the promise made to Abraham, and the life of Moses was just one more chapter.

Repeatedly in the book of Deuteronomy, the promise of blessing was directly related to the land. The Lord promised to give His people the land. The land often symbolized the entire blessing promised to them. Therefore, when the Lord allowed Moses to view the land, the emphasis again was on the land itself. Each boundary was detailed and Moses could observe it. The land was what

died there in the land of Moab, as
the Lord had said. 6 He buried him[A]
in the valley in the land of Moab facing Beth-peor, and no one to this
day knows where his grave is. 7 Moses was 120 years old when he died;
his eyes were not weak, and his vitality had not left him. 8 The Israelites
wept for Moses in the plains of Moab
30 days. Then the days of weeping
and mourning for Moses came to an
end.
9 Joshua son of Nun was filled with
the spirit of wisdom because Moses
had laid his hands on him. So the
Israelites obeyed him and did as the
Lord had commanded Moses. 10 No
prophet has arisen again in Israel
like Moses, whom the Lord knew
face to face. 11 He was unparalleled
for all the signs and wonders the
Lord sent him to do against the land
of Egypt—to Pharaoh, to all his officials, and to all his land, 12 and for
all the mighty acts of power and terrifying deeds that Moses performed
in the sight of all Israel.

[A]**34:6** Or *He was buried*

DEUTERONOMY . . . WRITTEN ON MY *Heart* The central message of the book is clear: God has provided everything you need and has proven Himself faithful time and time again. Choose to follow His ways and listen to His commands. Choose obedience. Refuse the paths that lead away from Him to disobedience.

the people had refused to take 40 years earlier, and the land was what they now were on the brink of possessing. The younger generation of Israelites stood at the edge of crossing the Jordan River to take possession of the promised land.

34:5-8 Likely Joshua recorded this portion of the text concerning the death of Moses. The people wept for Moses because, though the people had times when they were not happy with him, Moses had faithfully led them. The people wept for Moses because he was an unusual man who had risen in a unique way to become the greatest leader they had known. Moses did not die from old age or ailment. The text says Moses' age was 120 years old and **his vitality** had not left him, suggesting that his death was not from physical causes. Moses had completed the task God had for him, and the Lord took him home.

34:9 Joshua, Moses' successor, **was filled with the spirit of wisdom, because Moses had laid hands on him.** Moses expressed his approval of the leadership of Joshua. On a human level, the people followed Joshua because Moses had laid his hands on him. The people followed Joshua because the Lord had commanded them to do so through Moses. There are many leadership lessons to be learned from Moses. First, Moses was sensitive enough to walk with God and to identify the successor whom the Lord had chosen. Once identified, Moses included Joshua in many leadership tasks, thereby giving the younger man experience. Finally, Moses publicly acknowledged Joshua's coming leadership. Moses admonished the people to follow Joshua. While the bulk of the book was given to the commands of the Lord and the necessity of the Israelites' obedience to His commands, Moses also required the people to follow Joshua. Recognizing this leader from the Lord was a part of the people's obedience and their following the Lord into the promised land.

34:10-12 No other man of God was like Moses. He had walked with God since his earliest years in unique ways. The text says that **he was unparalleled for all the signs and wonders the Lord sent him to do** through such difficult circumstances as living in the wilderness for forty years.

Joshua

Timeline	1446 BC	1445 BC	1406 BC	1406–1380 BC
■ World Events ■ Biblical Events	Exodus and defeat of Pharaoh at the Red Sea	Exploration of Canaan by the 12 spies	Events in Deuteronomy	Events in Joshua

"Haven't I commanded you: be strong and courageous? Do not be afraid or discouraged, for the LORD your God is with you wherever you go" (1:9).

Who wrote Joshua?

Joshua is believed to have recorded the events in this book that carries his name.

Who were the recipients?

The book was written initially to the nation of Israel, especially the new generation who were taking possession of the promised land.

When was Joshua written?

During the latter years of Joshua's life in the late Bronze Age around 1385 B.C.

Where did it happen?

The promised land, located in a strategic place connecting the continents of Asia and Africa

What is Joshua about?

- God's covenant faithfulness to His people
- Israel's entrance into the promised land and inheritance of God's promises
- The Lord's provision and protection, no matter how discouraging the circumstances
- The necessity of a believer's obedience

Why should women read Joshua?

While the initial message was written with the nation of Israel in mind, the book directly applies to your life today. The God who led Israel into Canaan and drove out their enemies is the same God who, through His Son Jesus, conquered the enemies of sin and death by the new covenant in His blood (1Co 11:25; 15:26,56-57; Heb 9:15). God fights for His children as we follow Him in faith. A beautiful example of faith-filled obedience is Rahab (chap. 2), whose life is a promise of the grace and mercy to come in the salvation offered to all people through Jesus.

How do you read Joshua?

The book of Joshua is the first of what are commonly known as the historical books of the Bible. These books build on the foundation established in the Pentateuch, the first five books of the Bible. These books contain the Torah or God's law, instruction to His people for establishing the nation of Israel. One of God's promises to Abraham was to give His covenant people a land. The book of Joshua shows the fulfillment of that promise to Abraham.

Outline

I. The Preparations for Conquest (1:1–5:15)
   - A. Preparing the People (1:1–2:24)
   - B. Preparing the Strategy (3:1–5:15)

II. The Actual Conquest (6:1–12:24)
   - A. The First Cities (6:1–8:35)
   - B. The Gibeonites and the Rest of the Land (9:1–12:24)

III. The Division of the Land (13:1–22:34)
   - A. A Portion of the Land for Each Tribe (13:1–19:51)
   - B. Special Instructions for the Cities of Refuge, the Levites, and the Eastern Tribes (20:1–22:34)

IV. The Final Message of Joshua (23:1–24:33)
   - A. Joshua's Final Words (23:1–24:13)
   - B. A Renewal of the Covenant (24:14-33)

>WORD|*study*

1:9 Be Strong (Hb *chazaq*, "be firm") conveys a strength that grows. The verb's main meaning is "tie or bind fast, gird," as in "girding the loins." The idea is that one secures a garment in order to free the legs for action (Eph 6:14; 1Pt 1:13—lit "gird the loins of your minds").

1:9 Courageous (Hb *ʾamats*, "be alert, firm, brave, strong, undaunted"). Though often used in reference to one's feet ("being swift-footed"), the verb figuratively means having an alert or vigorous mind.

1:9 Joshua was commanded not to be **discouraged** (Hb *chatat*, "be broken down with fear, be dismayed or confounded"; cp. Dt 31:8).

1406 BC	1406 BC	1406–1400 BC	1380 BC
Crossing of the Jordan River	Destruction of Jericho	Joshua's campaigns of conquest	Death of Joshua

Preparing the People (1:1–2:24)

Encouragement of Joshua (1:1-9)

1 After the death of Moses the LORD's servant, the LORD spoke to Joshua[A] son of Nun, who had served Moses: 2 "Moses My servant is dead. Now you and all the people prepare to cross over the Jordan to the land I am giving the Israelites. 3 I have given you every place where the sole of your foot treads, just as I promised Moses. 4 Your territory will be from the wilderness and Lebanon to the great Euphrates River—all the land of the Hittites—and west to the Mediterranean Sea.[B] 5 No one will be able to stand against you as long as you live. I will be with you, just as I was with Moses. I will not leave you or forsake you.

6 "Be strong and courageous, for you will distribute the land I swore to their fathers to give them as an inheritance. 7 Above all, be strong and very courageous to carefully observe the whole instruction My servant Moses commanded you. Do not turn from it to the right or the left, so that you will have success wherever you go. 8 This book of instruction must not depart from your mouth; you are to recite[C] it day and night so that you may carefully observe everything written in it. For then you will prosper and succeed in whatever you do. 9 Haven't I commanded you: be strong and courageous? Do not be afraid or discouraged, for the LORD your God is with you wherever you go."

Joshua's Preparation of the People (1:10-18)

10 Then Joshua commanded the officers of the people: 11 "Go through the camp and tell the people, 'Get provisions ready for yourselves, for within three days you will be crossing the Jordan to go in and take possession of the land the LORD your God is giving you to inherit.'"

12 Joshua said to the Reubenites, the Gadites, and half the tribe of Manasseh: 13 "Remember what Moses the LORD's servant commanded you when he said, 'The LORD your God will give you rest, and He will give you this land.' 14 Your wives, young children, and livestock may remain in the land Moses gave you on this side of the Jordan.[D] But your fighting men must cross over in battle formation[E] ahead of your brothers[F] and help them 15 until the LORD gives your brothers rest, as He has given you, and they too possess the land the LORD your God is giving them. You may then return to the land of your inheritance and take possession of what Moses the LORD's servant gave you on the east side of the Jordan."

16 They answered Joshua, "Everything you have commanded us we will do, and everywhere you send us we will go. 17 We will obey you, just as we obeyed Moses in everything. And may the LORD your God be with you, as He was with Moses. 18 Anyone who rebels against your order and does not obey your words in all that you command him, will be put to death. Above all, be strong and courageous!"

Sending of Spies to Jericho (2:1-7)

2 Joshua son of Nun secretly sent two men as spies from the Acacia

[A]1:1 = The LORD Will Save, or The LORD Is Salvation; Joshua is related to the name Jesus. [B]1:4 Lit *and to the Great Sea, the going down of the sun* [C]1:8 Or *meditate on* [D]1:14 = east of the Jordan River [E]1:14 Or *over armed* [F]1:14 = fellow Israelites

Title: This book is named for the man through whom the Lord conquered the idolatrous nations of Canaan.

1:1 Having served Moses during the nation's 40 years of wandering, Joshua was poised to lead Israel after Moses' death. He demonstrated that one's leadership potential is often identified in the faithfulness with which he serves others in authority over him.

1:2-3 Crossing **the Jordan** was the first step in possessing the land. Treading upon the soil symbolized the nation's claim to ownership of the property. Since the time of Abraham, inheriting the promised land was inextricably tied to God's faithfulness to His people, Israel.

1:4 Despite skepticism, archaeological excavation has verified the existence of the Hittites from ancient Egyptian and Assyrian texts. The Hittites' greatest period of influence was between 1650–1500 B.C. and 1380–1200 B.C.

1:5-9 Having repeatedly assured Joshua of His unfailing presence, God commanded him three times to **be strong and courageous**. Joshua's success was tied to his devotion to and continuous study of God's **whole instruction**, the book of the law. Joshua was told to **recite** (Hb *hagah*, "meditate"; cp Ps 1:2) its words just as a student would repeat a text in order to memorize it. Since God told Joshua not to let His words **depart from** [his] **mouth**, Joshua was literally to speak His Word aloud.

1:10-18 Joshua assumed leadership over the people, instructing the officers to prepare to cross the Jordan and reminding **the Reubenites, the Gadites, and half the tribe of Manasseh** of their commitment to help the other tribes inherit the land (v. 12; cp. Nm 34:14-15). The people acknowledged and submitted themselves to Joshua's authority, recognizing that the Lord was with him as He had been with Moses.

2:1 Perhaps recalling the dissenting report of the ten spies sent out by Moses (Nm 13), Joshua **secretly sent two men** to investigate the land.

2:1-7 Rahab was an innkeeper and a **prostitute**. Her house was likely built over the gap between the two walls surrounding the city, which probably allowed the spies to come and go undetected. To protect the spies from being captured, she denied knowledge of the spies' whereabouts and intentions. Her lie may be compared to the falsehood told by the Israelite midwives, under extreme circumstances involving the protection of innocent life (Ex 3).

2:8-11 Rahab acknowledged that the Canaanites were panicking over the Israelites' arrival. These were people of whom the Israelites were afraid just a generation before (Nm 13:31–14:10). The Canaanites' fear was not due to Israel's strength in numbers or military might but because Israel's God was **the Lord**. They heard how He had delivered Israel from Egypt and had recently dealt with **two Amorite kings**. Their fear demonstrated that God was already bringing His promise to fruition.

2:12-13 Most scholars identify this passage to be Rahab's confession of faith. She asked for the protection of her family and her. The phrase **show kindness** is also used when Abraham's servant asked God for direction in finding a wife for Isaac (Gn 24:12,14).

CHARACTER PROFILE

Rahab A Courageous Canaanite

Her Background	• a Canaanite woman • a prostitute who lived in Jericho (2:1)
Her Story	• She hid the Israelite spies (2:4). • She made an agreement with the spies to save her family (2:12). • Her name is in the genealogy of the Messiah (Mt 1:5-6). • She is remembered as one of God's faithful servants (Heb 11:31).
Life Lessons	• Rahab's quick thinking and courageous response saved her life and that of her family (Jos 2:2-14). • Despite her sinful past, she was obedient to the God of Israel (Heb 11:31). • She found a new identity with God's people through her marriage to Salmon of the tribe of Judah (Mt 1:5).

Grove,[A] saying, "Go and scout the land, especially Jericho." So they left, and they came to the house of a woman, a prostitute named Rahab, and stayed there.
2 The king of Jericho was told, "Look, some of the Israelite men have come here tonight to investigate the land." 3 Then the king of Jericho sent word to Rahab and said, "Bring out the men who came to you and entered your house, for they came to investigate the entire land."
4 But the woman had taken the two men and hidden them. So she said, "Yes, the men did come to me, but I didn't know where they were from. 5 At nightfall, when the gate was about to close, the men went out, and I don't know where they were going. Chase after them quickly, and you can catch up with them!" 6 But she had taken them up to the roof and hidden them among the stalks of flax that she had arranged on the roof. 7 The men pursued them along the road to the fords of the Jordan, and as soon as they left to pursue them, the gate was shut.

The Promise to Rahab (2:8-24)

8 Before the men fell asleep, she went up on the roof 9 and said to them, "I know that the Lord has given you this land and that the terror of you has fallen on us, and everyone who lives in the land is panicking because of you.[B] 10 For we have heard how the Lord dried up the waters of the •Red Sea before you when you came out of Egypt, and what you did to Sihon and Og, the two Amorite kings you •completely destroyed across the Jordan. 11 When we heard this, we lost heart, and everyone's courage failed[C] because of you, for the Lord your God is God in heaven above and on earth below. 12 Now please swear to me by the Lord that you will also show kindness to my family, because I showed kindness to you.[D] Give me a sure sign[E] 13 that you will spare the lives of my father, mother, brothers, sisters, and all who belong to them, and save us from death."
14 The men answered her, "We will give our lives for yours. If you don't report our mission, we will show kindness and faithfulness to you when the Lord gives us the land."
15 Then she let them down by a rope through the window, since she lived in a house that was built into the wall of the city. 16 "Go to the hill country so that the men pursu-

[A]2:1 Or *from Shittim* [B]2:9 Or *land panics at your approach* [C]2:11 Lit *and spirit no longer remained in anyone* [D]2:12 Lit *to your father's house* [E]2:12 Or *a sign of truth*

ing you won't find you," she said to them. "Hide yourselves there for three days until they return; afterward, go on your way."
[17] The men said to her, "We will be free from this oath you made us swear, [18] unless, when we enter the land, you tie this scarlet cord to the window through which you let us down. Bring your father, mother, brothers, and all your father's family into your house. [19] If anyone goes out the doors of your house, his blood will be on his own head, and we will be innocent. But if anyone with you in the house should be harmed,[A] his blood will be on our heads. [20] And if you report our mission, we are free from the oath you made us swear."
[21] "Let it be as you say," she replied, and she sent them away. After they had gone, she tied the scarlet cord to the window.
[22] So the two men went into the hill country and stayed there three days until the pursuers had returned. They searched all along the way, but did not find them. [23] Then the men returned, came down from the hill country, and crossed the Jordan. They went to Joshua son of Nun and reported everything that had happened to them. [24] They told Joshua, "The LORD has handed over the entire land to us. Everyone who lives in the land is also panicking because of us."[B]

Preparing the Strategy (3:1–5:15)

Crossing the Jordan (3:1-17)

3 Joshua started early the next morning and left the Acacia Grove[C] with all the Israelites. They went as far as the Jordan and stayed there before crossing. [2] After three days the officers went through the camp [3] and commanded the people: "When you see the ark of the covenant of the LORD your God carried by the Levitical priests, you must break camp and follow it. [4] But keep a distance of about 1,000 yards[D] between yourselves and the ark. Don't go near it, so that you can see the way to go, for you haven't traveled this way before."[E]
[5] Joshua told the people, "Consecrate yourselves, because the LORD will do wonders among you tomorrow." [6] Then he said to the priests, "Take the ark of the covenant and go on ahead of the people." So they carried the ark of the covenant and went ahead of them.
[7] The LORD spoke to Joshua: "Today I will begin to exalt you in the sight of all Israel, so they will know that I will be with you just as I was with Moses. [8] Command the priests carrying the ark of the covenant: When you reach the edge of the waters,[F] stand in the Jordan."
[9] Then Joshua told the Israelites, "Come closer and listen to the words of the LORD your God." [10] He said: "You will know that the living God is among you and that He will certainly dispossess before you the Canaanites, Hittites, Hivites, Perizzites, Girgashites, Amorites, and Jebusites [11] when the ark of the covenant of the Lord of all the earth goes ahead of you into the Jordan. [12] Now choose 12 men from the tribes of Israel, one man for each tribe. [13] When the feet[G] of the priests who carry the ark of the LORD, the Lord of all the earth, come to rest in the Jordan's waters, its waters will be cut off. The water flowing downstream will stand up in a mass."
[14] When the people broke camp to cross the Jordan, the priests carried the ark of the covenant ahead of the

2:17-20 The spies told Rahab to tie a **scarlet cord** to her window as an indication that her house was to be spared by the Israelites. Just as the scarlet cord was a mark of protection for Rahab and her family, the blood on the doorframes of the households of God's people in Egypt was a sign to the angel of death to spare those within from death.

2:24 Their report was a fulfillment of the prophecy and power of God on behalf of Israel (Ex 15:13-17). Unlike the previous generation's spies, whose unbelief caused them to perish in the wilderness, these men returned full of faith in God's work and courage to conquer the land.

3:1-17 The people's preparation demonstrates that God is not concerned only with life in the promised land but also with the way His people get there.

3:6 The **ark of the covenant** symbolized God's presence with His people. With the ark going before the people into battle, Israel's strength did not come from their military might but from the Lord's presence with and defense of His people.

[A] **2:19** Lit *if a hand should be on him* [B] **2:24** Or *also panics at our approach* [C] **3:1** Or *left Shittim* [D] **3:4** Lit *2,000 cubits* [E] **3:4** Lit *yesterday and the day before* [F] **3:8** Lit *waters of the Jordan* [G] **3:13** Lit *soles of the feet*

>WORD|*study*

3:5 To consecrate (Hb *qadash*, "make yourself holy") has the sense of setting yourself apart. This term of worship commands a person to prepare herself to be purified, knowing that she will meet with God. That the Israelites were told, **"Consecrate yourselves,"** shows that their conquest was more than a military operation; it was also a spiritual journey.

people. 15 Now the Jordan overflows its banks throughout the harvest season. But as soon as the priests carrying the ark reached the Jordan, their feet touched the water at its edge 16 and the water flowing downstream stood still, rising up in a mass that extended as far as[A] Adam, a city next to Zarethan. The water flowing downstream into the Sea of the •Arabah (the Dead Sea) was completely cut off, and the people crossed opposite Jericho. 17 The priests carrying the ark of the LORD's covenant stood firmly on dry ground in the middle of the Jordan, while all Israel crossed on dry ground until the entire nation had finished crossing the Jordan.

The Memorial Stones (4:1-24)

4 After the entire nation had finished crossing the Jordan, the LORD spoke to Joshua: 2 "Choose 12 men from the people, one man for each tribe, 3 and command them: Take 12 stones from this place in the middle of the Jordan where the priests[B] are standing, carry them with you, and set them down at the place where you spend the night."

4 So Joshua summoned the 12 men he had selected from the Israelites, one man for each tribe, 5 and said to them, "Go across to the ark of the LORD your God in the middle of the Jordan. Each of you lift a stone onto his shoulder, one for each[C] of the Israelite tribes, 6 so that this will be a sign among you. In the future, when your children ask you, 'What do these stones mean to you?' 7 you should tell them, 'The waters of the Jordan were cut off in front of the ark of the LORD's covenant. When it crossed the Jordan, the Jordan's waters were cut off.' Therefore these stones will always be a memorial for the Israelites."

8 The Israelites did just as Joshua had commanded them. The 12 men took stones from the middle of the Jordan, one for each[D] of the Israelite tribes, just as the LORD had told Joshua. They carried them to the camp and set them down there. 9 Joshua also set up 12 stones in the middle[E] of the Jordan where the priests[B] who carried the ark of the covenant were standing. The stones are there to this day.

10 The priests carrying the ark continued standing in the middle of the Jordan until everything was completed that the LORD had commanded Joshua to tell the people, in keeping with all that Moses had commanded Joshua. The people hurried across, 11 and after everyone had finished crossing, the priests with the ark of the LORD crossed in the sight of the people. 12 The Reubenites, Gadites, and half the tribe of Manasseh went in battle formation in front of the Israelites, as Moses had instructed them. 13 About 40,000 equipped for war crossed to the plains of Jericho in the LORD's presence.

14 On that day the LORD exalted Joshua in the sight of all Israel, and they revered him throughout his life, as they had revered Moses. 15 The LORD told Joshua, 16 "Command the priests who carry the ark of the •testimony[G] to come up from the Jordan."

17 So Joshua commanded the priests, "Come up from the Jordan." 18 When the priests carrying the ark of the LORD's covenant came up from the middle of the Jordan, and their feet[H] stepped out on solid ground, the waters of the Jordan resumed their course, flowing over all the banks as before.

19 The people came up from the Jordan on the tenth day of the first month,[H] and camped at Gilgal on the eastern limits of Jericho. 20 Then Joshua set up in Gilgal the 12 stones they had taken from the Jordan, 21 and he said to the Israelites, "In the future, when your children ask their fathers, 'What is the meaning of these stones?' 22 you should tell your children, 'Israel crossed the Jordan on dry ground.' 23 For the LORD your God dried up the waters of the Jordan before you until you had crossed over, just as the LORD your God did to the •Red Sea, which He dried up before us until we had

3:15 As the people's spiritual leaders, the priests were the first to step out into the Jordan River. Their stepping into the Jordan's swift current demonstrated faith that God would intervene as He had promised.

3:15-16 Even at the river's flood stage, God demonstrated His power by leading His people across the river on dry ground. He did this so no one could doubt the hand of God.

3:17 Just as crossing the Red Sea led by Moses marked their exodus from slavery and Egypt, crossing the Jordan River marked the Israelites' entry into the promised land.

4:2 These are the **12 men** selected in 3:12.

4:3-7 The **12 stones**—representing the 12 tribes of Israel—were a visible reminder of God's actions for His people. Future generations were to remember with thanksgiving how the Lord led them to cross on dry ground. The memorial's focus is that **the ark of the Lord's covenant**, God's presence, enabled their crossing of the river.

4:8-9 Joshua set up another memorial of **12 stones** where **the priests who carried the ark of the covenant** had stood. Joshua gave honor to Israel's spiritual leaders, who were the only ones to get their feet wet.

4:14 The Lord fulfilled His promise to Joshua when He exalted him (3:7-8). The people revered Joshua as they did Moses, another fulfillment of God's promise to Joshua (1:5).

4:20-23 God's actions for His people were not hidden. He intended that future generations learn about His works from their parents.

A3:16 Alt Hb tradition reads *mass at* B4:3,9 Lit *feet of the priests* C4:5 Lit *shoulder according to the number* D4:8 Lit *Jordan according to the number* E4:9 Or *Now Joshua set up the 12 stones that had been in the middle* F4:16 = the ark of the covenant G4:18 Lit *and the soles of the feet of the priests* H4:19 = Nisan (March–April)

crossed over. 24 This is so that all the
people of the earth may know that
the LORD's hand is mighty, and so
that you may always •fear the LORD
your God."

Circumcision of the Israelites (5:1-9)

5 When all the Amorite kings
across the Jordan to the west and
all the Canaanite kings near the sea
heard how the LORD had dried up the
waters of the Jordan before the Israelites until they had crossed over,
they lost heart and their courage
failed[A] because of the Israelites.
2 At that time the LORD said to
Joshua, "Make flint knives and circumcise the Israelite men again."
3 So Joshua made flint knives and
circumcised the Israelite men at
Gibeath-haaraloth.[B] 4 This is the reason Joshua circumcised them: All
the people who came out of Egypt
who were males—all the men of
war—had died in the wilderness
along the way after they had come
out of Egypt. 5 Though all the people
who came out were circumcised,
none of the people born in the wilderness along the way were circumcised after they had come out of
Egypt. 6 For the Israelites wandered
in the wilderness 40 years until all
the nation's men of war who came
out of Egypt had died off because
they did not obey the LORD. So the
LORD vowed never to let them see the
land He had sworn to their fathers
to give us, a land flowing with milk
and honey. 7 Joshua raised up their
sons in their place; it was these he
circumcised. They were still uncircumcised, since they had not been
circumcised along the way. 8 After
the entire nation had been circumcised, they stayed where they were
in the camp until they recovered.
9 The LORD then said to Joshua, "Today I have rolled away the disgrace
of Egypt from you." Therefore, that
place is called Gilgal[C] to this day.

Food from the Land (5:10-12)

10 While the Israelites camped at
Gilgal on the plains of Jericho, they
kept the •Passover on the evening of
the fourteenth day of the month.[D]
11 The day after Passover they ate
unleavened bread and roasted grain
from the produce of the land. 12 And
the day after they ate from the produce of the land, the manna ceased.
Since there was no more manna
for the Israelites, they ate from the
crops of the land of Canaan that
year.

Commander of the LORD's Army (5:13-15)

13 When Joshua was near Jericho,
he looked up and saw a man standing in front of him with a drawn
sword in His hand. Joshua approached Him and asked, "Are You
for us or for our enemies?"
14 "Neither," He replied. "I have
now come as commander of the
LORD's army."
Then Joshua bowed with his face
to the ground in worship and asked
Him, "What does my Lord want to
say to His servant?"
15 The commander of the LORD's
army said to Joshua, "Remove the
sandals from your feet, for the place
where you are standing is holy." And
Joshua did so.

The First Cities (6:1–8:35)

The Conquest of Jericho (6:1-21)

6 Now Jericho was strongly fortified because of the Israelites—no
one leaving or entering. 2 The LORD
said to Joshua, "Look, I have handed
Jericho, its king, and its fighting
men over to you. 3 March around
the city with all the men of war, circling the city one time. Do this for
six days. 4 Have seven priests carry
seven ram's-horn trumpets in front
of the ark. But on the seventh day,
march around the city seven times,
while the priests blow the trumpets.
5 When there is a prolonged blast of
the horn and you hear its sound,
have all the people give a mighty
shout. Then the city wall will collapse, and the people will advance,
each man straight ahead."
6 So Joshua son of Nun summoned
the priests and said to them, "Take
up the ark of the covenant and have
seven priests carry seven trumpets
in front of the ark of the LORD." 7 He
said to the people, "Move forward,
march around the city, and have the

[A]5:1 Lit *and they did not have spirit in them any more* [B]5:3 Or *The Hill of Foreskins* [C]5:9 = to roll [D]5:10 = Nisan (March–April)

4:24 The purpose of the memorial is that the people would know God's might and fear Him.

5:1 The descendants of the very people who seemed like giants to the earlier generation of Israelites **lost heart and their courage** had **failed** upon hearing how the Lord dried up the river for His people.

5:2 The command to **circumcise** the men implies that the nation had not kept the covenant of circumcision among the new generation. Their adherence to it demonstrated a renewal of the covenant between Yahweh and His people.

5:9 The disgrace of Egypt was the previous generation's rebellion. With a new leader, the death of the older generation, and the reinstatement of circumcision, Israel was entering a new phase of its history.

5:14 The **commander of the LORD's army** was regarded as worthy of worship. This "commander" was likely a visible appearance of the pre-incarnate Christ (called a *theophany*) and would have been another affirmation of Joshua's leadership.

5:15 The command harkens back to God's appearance to Moses at the burning bush (Ex 3:5). God would help Joshua conquer the land because it was indeed holy.

6:1 In being **strongly fortified,** the city was literally "very much shut." Their defense was not only physical but was also a resistance to God's plans.

6:3-7 Such strategy in the modern day would suggest intense psychological warfare. To watch Israel's **men of war** circle the city **for six days** undoubtedly heightened the fears of the inhabitants of Jericho. God intended to build trust and faith in the His people's hearts through this strange military strategy. In following and obeying Him, they would experience His faithfulness toward and care for them. Further, His method demonstrated that Yahweh God was different from the pagan gods of the land.

6:5 In addition to the ark, **the horn** refers to the *shophar*, which was sounded every fiftieth year on the Day of Atonement to announce the Year of Jubilee (Lv 25:9). The symbols of God's redemption once again preceded the people's victory.

6:20 The wording shows that the people went directly into the city as the Lord promised, full of faith that He had given them victory.

6:22-24 The text reports no defectors or offers of surrender. Only Rahab and her family were to be spared because of Rahab's belief in the Lord God of Israel.

6:23 The settling of Rahab and her family **outside the camp** was a temporary measure (v. 25; cp. Eph 2:13), and she eventually married Salmon of the tribe of Judah. Rahab is included in Jesus' genealogy (Mt 1:5).

7:1-4 Unfaithfulness on the part of the younger generation of the Israelites occurred. One man took from the things **set apart** to the Lord, but the entire nation of Israel suffered. When **Achan** (Hb, "troubler") took for himself some of the things dedicated to the Lord, the Israelites met defeat at the next city they attacked (vv. 2-5).

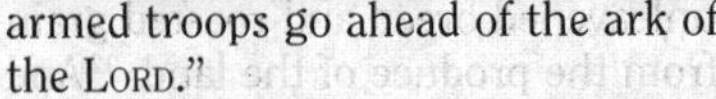

armed troops go ahead of the ark of the LORD."

8 After Joshua had spoken to the people, seven priests carrying seven trumpets before the LORD moved forward and blew the trumpets; the ark of the LORD's covenant followed them. 9 While the trumpets were blowing, the armed troops went in front of the priests who blew the trumpets, and the rear guard went behind the ark. 10 But Joshua had commanded the people: "Do not shout or let your voice be heard. Don't let one word come out of your mouth until the time I say, 'Shout!' Then you are to shout." 11 So the ark of the LORD was carried around the city, circling it once. They returned to the camp and spent the night there.[A]

12 Joshua got up early the next morning. The priests took the ark of the LORD, 13 and the seven priests carrying seven trumpets marched in front of the ark of the LORD. While the trumpets were blowing, the armed troops went in front of them, and the rear guard went behind the ark of the LORD. 14 On the second day they marched around the city once and returned to the camp. They did this for six days.

15 Early on the seventh day, they started at dawn and marched around the city seven times in the same way. That was the only day they marched around the city seven times. 16 After the seventh time, the priests blew the trumpets, and Joshua said to the people, "Shout! For the LORD has given you the city. 17 But the city and everything in it are •set apart to the LORD for destruction. Only Rahab the prostitute and everyone with her in the house will live, because she hid the men[B] we sent. 18 But keep yourselves from the things set apart, or you will be set apart for destruction. If you[C] take any of those things, you will set apart the camp of Israel for destruction and bring disaster on it. 19 For all the silver and gold, and the articles of bronze and iron, are dedicated to the LORD and must go into the LORD's treasury."

20 So the people shouted, and the trumpets sounded. When they heard the blast of the trumpet, the people gave a great shout, and the wall collapsed. The people advanced into the city, each man straight ahead, and they captured the city. 21 They •completely destroyed everything in the city with the sword—every man and woman, both young and old, and every ox, sheep, and donkey.

The Sparing of Rahab and Her Family (6:22-27)

22 Joshua said to the two men who had scouted the land, "Go to the prostitute's house and bring the woman out of there, and all who are with her, just as you promised her." 23 So the young men who had scouted went in and brought out Rahab and her father, mother, brothers, and all who belonged to her. They brought out her whole family and settled them outside the camp of Israel.

24 They burned up the city and everything in it, but they put the silver and gold and the articles of bronze and iron into the treasury of the LORD's house. 25 However, Joshua spared Rahab the prostitute, her father's household, and all who belonged to her, because she hid the men Joshua had sent to spy on Jericho, and she lives in Israel to this day.

26 At that time Joshua imposed this curse:

> The man who undertakes
> the rebuilding of this city,
> Jericho,
> is cursed before the LORD.
> He will lay its foundation
> at the cost of his firstborn;
> he will set up its gates
> at the cost of his youngest.

27 And the LORD was with Joshua, and his fame spread throughout the land.

Defeat at Ai (7:1-15)

7 The Israelites, however, were unfaithful regarding the things •set apart for destruction. Achan son of Carmi, son of Zabdi, son of Zerah, of the tribe of Judah, took some of what was set apart, and the LORD's anger burned against the Israelites.

2 Joshua sent men from Jericho to Ai, which is near Beth-aven, east of

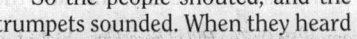

[A] **6:11** Lit *at the camp* [B] **6:17** Lit *messengers* [C] **6:18** LXX reads *you covet and*; Jos 7:21

>WORD|*study*

7:1 Things set apart (Hb *chērem*, "devoted, accursed") is derived from the verb *charam* (Hb "prohibit," as in the common use of something; "utterly destroy because cursed or devoted to God"; e.g., 6:21). The English word "anathema," which has a religious meaning of "excommunication or ban" from church membership, comes from the word used in the LXX translation of this term (Gk *anathematos*, "person or thing doomed to destruction because cursed or devoted to God without hope of being redeemed"; cp. Rm 9:3; Gl 1:8-9).

Bethel, and told them, "Go up and
scout the land." So the men went up
and scouted Ai.
3 After returning to Joshua they
reported to him, "Don't send all
the people, but send about 2,000 or
3,000[A] men to attack Ai. Since the
people of Ai are so few, don't wear
out all our people there." 4 So about
3,000 men[B] went up there, but they
fled from the men of Ai. 5 The men
of Ai struck down about 36 of them
and chased them from outside the
gate to the quarries,[C] striking them
down on the descent. As a result, the
people's hearts melted and became
like water.
6 Then Joshua tore his clothes and
fell before the ark of the LORD with
his face to the ground until evening,
as did the elders of Israel; they all
put dust on their heads. 7 "Oh, Lord
GOD," Joshua said, "why did You ever
bring these people across the Jordan
to hand us over to the Amorites for
our destruction? If only we had been
content to remain on the other side
of the Jordan! 8 What can I say, Lord,
now that Israel has turned its back
and run from its enemies? 9 When
the Canaanites and all who live in
the land hear about this, they will
surround us and wipe out our name
from the earth. Then what will You
do about Your great name?"
10 The LORD then said to Joshua,
"Stand up! Why are you on the
ground?[D] 11 Israel has sinned. They
have violated My covenant that I appointed for them. They have taken
some of what was set apart. They
have stolen, deceived, and put the
things with their own belongings.
12 This is why the Israelites cannot
stand against their enemies. They
will turn their backs and run from
their enemies, because they have
been set apart for destruction. I will
no longer be with you unless you
remove from you what is set apart.
13 "Go and consecrate the people.
Tell them to consecrate themselves
for tomorrow, for this is what the
LORD, the God of Israel, says: There
are things that are set apart among
you, Israel. You will not be able to
stand against your enemies until
you remove what is set apart. 14 In
the morning you must present
yourselves tribe by tribe. The tribe
the LORD selects is to come forward
clan by clan. The clan the LORD selects is to come forward family by
family. The family the LORD selects is
to come forward man by man. 15 The
one who is caught with the things
set apart must be burned,[E] along
with everything he has, because he

Doctrine GOD'S PROVISION

God cares and provides for each of His children. However, the loving Father is also the Master and Lord who is worthy of our obedience. Every Christian woman must trust Him to be faithful to provide for her exactly as He has promised. God told the Israelites that He was giving them the promised land. The land would be theirs! However, **Achan** allowed his own selfishness to rule his desires and actions by taking for himself from the things that were **set apart** unto the Lord (7:1, 10-26).

God was not withholding any goodness or benefit from His people. In fact, in Israel's next conquest, at the city of Ai, God commanded the people to plunder the city's livestock and spoil. Ironically, had Achan waited on God's timing, he would have received a portion of the plunder. As with all idolatry, Achan failed to trust God's goodness and sufficiency and pursued what he wanted.

Every daughter of God must trust her heavenly Father with her future and the provision of her needs. God had already given the people a land flowing with milk and honey, and He delights in providing for His children (Mt 7:7-11). But Achan chose to take on his own self-serving terms that which only God had the right to give. You can learn from the example of Achan. You can trust the heart of your Father, choose obedience, and accept God's way and timing. The difference is between life and death, blessings and curses (Dt 30:19-20).

7:5-14 Following Israel's defeat at Ai, the people's **hearts melted and became like water** when 36 of their men were **struck down** (v. 5). Joshua humbly sought the Lord, knowing the people's propensity for whining and concerned that the people's confidence would be destroyed (vv. 6-9). God answered Joshua by telling him, **Stand up!** (v. 10). There is a time for contrition and desperation before the Lord. However, in this instance, the Lord commanded Joshua to be aware that sin had occurred and something must be done about it.

7:15 God reminded the people of the gravity of the mission they had been given by requiring that the guilty person, along with all he owned, be burned. This extreme punishment came because the covenant between the Lord and His people had been violated. God wanted Israel to know that He would do what He promised.

[A]7:3 Or *send two or three military units of* [B]7:4 Lit *men from the people* [C]7:5 Or *to Shebarim*
[D]7:10 Lit *Why have you fallen on your face?* [E]7:15 Lit *burned with fire*

7:16-24 While Achan's sin would require his life, the exposure and judgment of sin would restore purity to the people. Achan's acknowledgement demonstrates the marks of a true confession: He agreed with the Lord; admitted that his sin was an offense **against the LORD, the God of Israel**; explained his actions honestly and specifically; confessed to the sin that was first in his heart (**I coveted them** [cp. Ex. 20:17]); and released what had captured his heart, allowing them to be seen and removed from his presence (vv. 20-23). Achan's confession followed the pattern of true repentance, a changing of the mind and heart through the contrition of the soul. Yet sadly, it came too late—after he was caught (v. 15).

7:25-26 God takes sin very seriously. Sin brings death. The severe and comprehensive punishment of Achan reminded God's people of the nature of His covenant with them and the consequences for their unfaithfulness and disobedience (Jos 7:24-26; cp. Ac 5:1-11).

8:1 With the nation's sin purged from among them, the people of Israel returned to their original task—possessing the land.

has violated the LORD's covenant and committed an outrage in Israel."

The Judgment of Achan (7:16-26)

16 Joshua got up early the next morning. He had Israel come forward tribe by tribe, and the tribe of Judah was selected. 17 He had the clans of Judah come forward, and the Zerahite clan was selected. He had the Zerahite clan come forward by heads of families,[A] and Zabdi was selected. 18 He then had Zabdi's family come forward man by man, and Achan son of Carmi, son of Zabdi, son of Zerah, of the tribe of Judah, was selected.

19 So Joshua said to Achan, "My son, give glory to the LORD, the God of Israel, and make a confession to Him.[B] I urge you, tell me what you have done. Don't hide anything from me."

20 Achan replied to Joshua, "It is true. I have sinned against the LORD, the God of Israel. This is what I did: 21 When I saw among the spoils a beautiful cloak from Babylon,[C] 200 silver *shekels,[D] and a bar of gold weighing 50 shekels,[E] I coveted them and took them. You can see for yourself. They are concealed in the ground inside my tent, with the money under the cloak." 22 So Joshua sent messengers who ran to the tent, and there was the cloak, concealed in his tent, with the money underneath. 23 They took the things from inside the tent, brought them to Joshua and all the Israelites, and spread them out in the LORD's presence.

24 Then Joshua and all Israel with him took Achan son of Zerah, the silver, the cloak, and the bar of gold, his sons and daughters, his ox, donkey, and sheep, his tent, and all that he had, and brought them up to the Valley of Achor. 25 Joshua said, "Why have you troubled us? Today the LORD will trouble you!" So all Israel stoned them[F] to death. They burned their bodies,[G] threw stones on them, 26 and raised over him a large pile of rocks that remains to this day. Then the LORD turned from His burning anger. Therefore that place is called the Valley of Achor[H] to this day.

The Conquest of Ai (8:1-29)

8 The LORD said to Joshua, "Do not be afraid or discouraged. Take the whole military force with you and go attack Ai. Look, I have handed over to you the king of Ai, his people, city, and land. 2 Treat Ai and its king as you did Jericho and its king; you may plunder its spoil and livestock for yourselves. Set an ambush behind the city."

3 So Joshua and the whole military force set out to attack Ai. Joshua selected 30,000 fighting men and sent them out at night. 4 He commanded them: "Pay attention. Lie in ambush behind the city, not too far from it, and all of you be ready. 5 Then I and all the people who are with me will approach the city. When they come out against us as they did the first time, we will flee from them. 6 They

HARD QUESTION

How could a just God command His people to destroy a nation?

How could a just God command His people to destroy a nation? (e.g. 6:17; 8:1-2) In light of Israel's war tactics, some people call God's character into question, believing Him to be unjust. However, God's purpose in establishing His people was to communicate His nature to the entire world. He required that Israel wipe out the Canaanites for two reasons: Because God is holy, He will not allow sin to go unpunished and appoints a judgment day (2Pt 3:2-10); and because the Canaanites' religious practices, if they were at all accommodated, would lure Israel away from Yahweh to worship other gods (Ex 34:12-16; Dt 7:3-6; Ps 106:34-39). God's directive to destroy completely the inhabitants of Canaan underscores His righteousness in bringing wickedness to judgment. Modern readers who protest that the Israelites ruthlessly killed innocent people in order to take their land must understand that, before God, no one is innocent or righteous (Gn 18:23-33; Pss 14:1-3; 53:3; Is 53:6; Rm 3:10-18), that all are subject to His judgment since no sin can go unpunished (Pr 11:21; Ec 12:14; Jr 30:11; Mt 12:36; Jn 5:22-30; Rm 2:1-16; Heb 9:27), and that, in His overriding love and mercy, God always provides a way to escape judgment on His terms (Jn 3:16; 1Co 10:13). He chose the nation of Israel not because of its merit but because of His own nature and purposes (Dt 9:1-6). God was reinforcing to the people that He was the one true God and that He alone was worthy of worship.

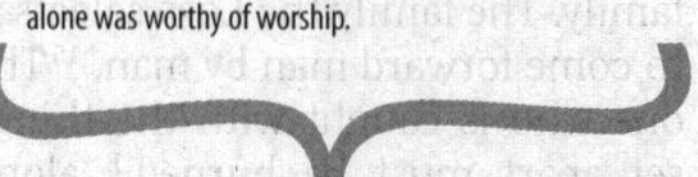

[A] **7:17** Lit *forward man by man* [B] **7:19** Or *and praise Him* [C] **7:21** Lit *Shinar* [D] **7:21** About 5 pounds of silver [E] **7:21** About 1 pound of gold [F] **7:25** Lit *him* [G] **7:25** Lit *burned them with fire* [H] **7:26** Or *of Trouble*

will come after us until we have drawn them away from the city, for they will say, 'They are fleeing from us as before.' While we are fleeing from them,
7 you are to come out of your ambush and seize the city, for the LORD your God has handed it over to you.
8 After taking the city, set it on fire. Follow the LORD's command—see that you do as I have ordered you."
9 So Joshua sent them out, and they went to the ambush site and waited between Bethel and Ai, to the west of Ai. But he spent that night with the troops.

10 Joshua started early the next morning and mobilized them. Then he and the elders of Israel led the troops up to Ai.
11 All those[A] who were with him went up and approached the city, arriving opposite Ai, and camped to the north of it, with a valley between them and the city.
12 Now Joshua had taken about 5,000 men and set them in ambush between Bethel and Ai, to the west of the city.
13 The military force was stationed in this way: the main[B] camp to the north of the city and its rear guard to the west of the city. And that night Joshua went into the valley.

14 When the king of Ai saw the Israelites, the men of the city hurried and went out early in the morning so that he and all his people could engage Israel in battle at a suitable place facing the •Arabah. But he did not know there was an ambush waiting for him behind the city.
15 Joshua and all Israel pretended to be beaten back by them and fled toward the wilderness.
16 Then all the troops of Ai were summoned to pursue them, and they pursued Joshua and were drawn away from the city.
17 Not a man was left in Ai or Bethel who did not go out after Israel, leaving the city exposed while they pursued Israel.

18 Then the LORD said to Joshua, "Hold out the sword in your hand toward Ai, for I will hand the city over to you." So Joshua held out his sword toward it.
19 When he held out his hand, the men in ambush rose quickly from their position. They ran, entered the city, captured it, and immediately set it on fire.

20 The men of Ai turned and looked back, and smoke from the city was rising to the sky! They could not escape in any direction, and the troops who had fled to the wilderness now became the pursuers.
21 When Joshua and all Israel saw that the men in ambush had captured the city and that smoke was rising from it, they turned back and struck down the men of Ai.
22 Then men in ambush came out of the city against them, and the men of Ai were trapped between the Israelite forces, some on one side and some on the other. They struck them down until no survivor or fugitive remained,
23 but they captured the king of Ai alive and brought him to Joshua.

24 When Israel had finished killing everyone living in Ai who had pursued them into the open country, and when every last one of them had fallen by the sword, all Israel returned to Ai and struck it down with the sword.
25 The total of those who fell that day, both men and women, was 12,000—all the people of Ai.
26 Joshua did not draw back his hand that was holding the sword until all the inhabitants of Ai were •completely destroyed.
27 Israel plundered only the cattle and spoil of that city for themselves, according to the LORD's command that He had given Joshua.

28 Joshua burned Ai and left it a permanent ruin, desolate to this day.
29 He hung[C] the body of the king of Ai on a tree[D] until evening, and at sunset Joshua commanded that they take his body down from the tree. They threw it down at the entrance of the city gate and put a large pile of rocks over it, which remains to this day.

Renewed Commitment to the Law (8:30-35)

30 At that time Joshua built an altar on Mount Ebal to the LORD, the God of Israel,
31 just as Moses the LORD's servant had commanded the Israelites. He built it according to what is written in the book of the law of Moses: an altar of uncut stones on

8:30-33 Before his death, **Moses** instructed the people to set up **an altar** on **Mount Ebal** and worship the Lord there. The altar was a reminder to the people that if they sinned they could return to the Lord through repentance and confession, by abandoning the way of sin and returning to God.

A 8:11 Lit *the people of war* B 8:13 Lit *way: all the* C 8:29 Or *impaled* D 8:29 Or *wooden stake*

8:34 Meditating on and understanding the words of the Lord were directly related to the people's ability to obey and stay in fellowship with God.

9:1-15 Joshua was fooled by the deceptive Gibeonites because he **did not seek the LORD's counsel** before making an alliance with them (v. 14), causing the Israelites to fall prey to their plot. The clear lesson here is for God's people to be careful to seek His will about relationships and decisions.

which no iron tool has been used. Then they offered •burnt offerings to the LORD and sacrificed •fellowship offerings on it. 32 There on the stones, Joshua copied the law of Moses, which he had written in the presence of the Israelites. 33 All Israel, foreigner and citizen alike, with their elders, officers, and judges, stood on either side of the ark of the LORD's covenant facing the Levitical priests who carried it. As Moses the LORD's servant had commanded earlier, half of them were in front of Mount Gerizim and half in front of Mount Ebal, to bless the people of Israel. 34 Afterward, Joshua read aloud all the words of the law—the blessings as well as the curses—according to all that is written in the book of the law. 35 There was not a word of all that Moses had commanded that Joshua did not read before the entire assembly of Israel, including the women, the little children, and the foreigners who were with them.

The Gibeonites and the Rest of the Land (9:1–12:24)

Deception by Gibeon (9:1-15)

9 When all the kings heard about Jericho and Ai, those who were west of the Jordan in the hill country, in the Judean foothills,[A] and all along the coast of the Mediterranean Sea toward Lebanon—the Hittites, Amorites, Canaanites, Perizzites, Hivites, and Jebusites— 2 they formed a unified alliance to fight against Joshua and Israel.

3 When the inhabitants of Gibeon heard what Joshua had done to Jericho and Ai, 4 they acted deceptively. They gathered provisions[B] and took worn-out sacks on their donkeys and old wineskins, cracked and mended. 5 They wore old, patched sandals on their feet and threadbare clothing on their bodies. Their entire provision of bread was dry and crumbly. 6 They went to Joshua in the camp at Gilgal and said to him and the men of Israel, "We have come from a distant land. Please make a treaty with us."

7 The men of Israel replied to the Hivites,[C] "Perhaps you live among us. How can we make a treaty with you?"

8 They said to Joshua, "We are your servants."

Then Joshua asked them, "Who are you and where do you come from?"

9 They replied to him, "Your servants have come from a far away land because of the reputation of the LORD your God. For we have heard of His fame, and all that He did in Egypt, 10 and all that He did to the two Amorite kings beyond the Jordan—Sihon king of Heshbon and Og king of Bashan, who was in Ashtaroth. 11 So our elders and all the inhabitants of our land told us, 'Take provisions with you for the journey; go and meet them and say, "We are your servants. Please make a treaty with us."' 12 This bread of ours was warm when we took it from our houses as food on the day we left to come to you. But take a look, it is now dry and crumbly. 13 These wineskins were new when we filled them, but look, they are cracked. And these clothes and sandals of ours are worn out from the extremely long journey." 14 Then the men of Israel took some of their provisions, but did not seek the LORD's counsel. 15 So Joshua established peace with them and made a treaty to let them live, and the leaders of the community swore an oath to them.

Gibeon's Deception Discovered (9:16-27)

16 Three days after making the treaty with them, they heard that the Gibeonites were their neighbors, living among them. 17 So the Israelites set out and reached the Gibeonite cities on the third day. Now their cities were Gibeon, Chephirah, Beeroth, and Kiriath-jearim. 18 But the Israelites did not attack them, because the leaders of the community had sworn an oath to them by the LORD, the God of Israel. Then the whole community grumbled against the leaders.

19 All the leaders answered them, "We have sworn an oath to them by the LORD, the God of Israel, and now we cannot touch them. 20 This is how

[A]**9:1** Or *the Shephelah* [B]**9:4** Some Hb mss, LXX, Syr, Vg; other Hb mss read *They went disguised as ambassadors* [C]**9:7** = the men of Gibeon

we will treat them: we will let them
live, so that no wrath will fall on
us because of the oath we swore to
them." 21 They also said, "Let them
live." So the Gibeonites became
woodcutters and water carriers for
the whole community, as the leaders had promised them.
22 Joshua summoned the Gibeonites and said to them, "Why did
you deceive us by telling us you
live far away from us, when in fact
you live among us? 23 Therefore
you are cursed and will always be
slaves—woodcutters and water carriers for the house of my God."
24 The Gibeonites answered him,
"It was clearly communicated to
your servants that the LORD your
God had commanded His servant
Moses to give you all the land and
to destroy all the inhabitants of the
land before you. We greatly feared
for our lives because of you, and that
is why we did this. 25 Now we are in
your hands. Do to us whatever you
think is right."[A] 26 This is what Joshua did to them: he delivered them
from the hands of the Israelites, and
they did not kill them. 27 On that day
he made them woodcutters and water carriers—as they are today—for
the community and for the LORD's
altar at the place He would choose.

The Day the Sun Stood Still (10:1-15)

10 Now Adoni-zedek king of Jerusalem heard that Joshua
had captured Ai and •completely destroyed it, treating Ai and its king as
he had Jericho and its king, and that
the inhabitants of Gibeon had made
peace with Israel and were living
among them. 2 So Adoni-zedek and
his people were[B] greatly alarmed because Gibeon was a large city like one
of the royal cities; it was larger than
Ai, and all its men were warriors.
3 Therefore Adoni-zedek king of Jerusalem sent word to Hoham king
of Hebron, Piram king of Jarmuth,
Japhia king of Lachish, and Debir
king of Eglon, saying, 4 "Come up
and help me. We will attack Gibeon,
because they have made peace with
Joshua and the Israelites." 5 So the
five Amorite kings—the kings of Jerusalem, Hebron, Jarmuth, Lachish,
and Eglon—joined forces, advanced
with all their armies, besieged
Gibeon, and fought against it.
6 Then the men of Gibeon sent
word to Joshua in the camp at Gilgal: "Don't abandon[C] your servants.
Come quickly and save us! Help us,
for all the Amorite kings living in
the hill country have joined forces
against us." 7 So Joshua and his
whole military force, including all
the fighting men, came from Gilgal.
8 The LORD said to Joshua, "Do not
be afraid of them, for I have handed
them over to you. Not one of them
will be able to stand against you."
9 So Joshua caught them by surprise, after marching all night from
Gilgal. 10 The LORD threw them into
confusion before Israel. He defeated
them in a great slaughter at Gibeon,
chased them through the ascent of
Beth-horon, and struck them down
as far as Azekah and Makkedah. 11 As
they fled before Israel, the LORD
threw large hailstones on them from
the sky along the descent of Beth-
horon all the way to Azekah, and
they died. More of them died from
the hail than the Israelites killed
with the sword.
12 On the day the LORD gave the
Amorites over to the Israelites, Joshua spoke to the LORD in the presence
of Israel:

"Sun, stand still over Gibeon,
and moon, over the Valley
of Aijalon."
13 And the sun stood still
and the moon stopped
until the nation
took vengeance
on its enemies.

Isn't this written in the Book of
Jashar?[D]

So the sun stopped
in the middle of the sky
and delayed its setting
almost a full day.

14 There has been no day like it before
or since, when the LORD listened to
the voice of a man, because the LORD
fought for Israel. 15 Then Joshua and

9:20-21 By keeping their word, even though it had been given rashly and without consulting God, Israel's leaders revealed their character.

9:27 This type of servanthood is unlike the contemporary idea of servitude or slavery. In ancient cultures, a conquered people often served their conquerors and were treated humanely.

10:1-27 Joshua publicly executed the five Amorite kings in a manner that demonstrated his confidence in God's commands and promises. For the **military commanders** to put their **feet on the necks of these kings** (vv. 22-24), symbolizing Israel's defeat of and complete sovereignty over them and their kingdoms as well as a reminder that God was giving them the land—everywhere they set their foot (Dt 1:36; 11:25; Jos 14:9).

A **9:25** Lit *us as is good and as is right in your eyes do* B **10:2** One Hb ms, Syr, Vg read *So he was*
C **10:6** Lit *Don't let your hand go from* D **10:13** Or *of the Upright*

10:30-42 The text makes clear that their victory was from **the Lord,** who **handed** the kings and their cities **over to Israel** (vv. 30,32) and **fought for** His people (v. 42).

all Israel with him returned to the
camp at Gilgal.

Execution of Five Kings (10:16-27)

16 Now the five defeated kings had
fled and hidden themselves in the
cave at Makkedah. 17 It was reported
to Joshua: "The five kings have been
found; they are hiding in the cave at
Makkedah."

18 Joshua said, "Roll large stones
against the mouth of the cave, and
station men by it to guard the kings.
19 But as for the rest of you, don't
stay there. Pursue your enemies and
attack them from behind. Don't let
them enter their cities, for the Lord
your God has handed them over
to you." 20 So Joshua and the Israelites finished inflicting a terrible
slaughter on them until they were
destroyed, although a few survivors
ran away to the fortified cities. 21 The
people returned safely to Joshua in
the camp at Makkedah. And no one
dared to threaten[A] the Israelites.

22 Then Joshua said, "Open the
mouth of the cave, and bring those
five kings to me out of there." 23 That
is what they did. They brought the
five kings of Jerusalem, Hebron, Jarmuth, Lachish, and Eglon to Joshua
out of the cave. 24 When they had
brought the kings to him, Joshua
summoned all the men of Israel and
said to the military commanders
who had accompanied him, "Come
here and put your feet on the necks
of these kings." So the commanders
came forward and put their feet on
their necks. 25 Joshua said to them,
"Do not be afraid or discouraged. Be
strong and courageous, for the Lord
will do this to all the enemies you
fight."

26 After this, Joshua struck them
down and executed them. He hung[B]
their bodies on five trees[C] and they
were there until evening. 27 At sunset Joshua commanded that they
be taken down from the trees[C] and
thrown into the cave where they
had hidden. Then large stones were
placed against the mouth of the
cave, and the stones are there to this
day.

Conquest of Southern Cities (10:28-43)

28 On that day Joshua captured
Makkedah and struck it down with
the sword, including its king. He
completely destroyed it[D] and everyone in it, leaving no survivors. So he
treated the king of Makkedah as he
had the king of Jericho.

29 Joshua and all Israel with him
crossed from Makkedah to Libnah
and fought against Libnah. 30 The
Lord also handed it and its king
over to Israel. He struck it down,
putting everyone in it to the sword,
and left no survivors in it. He treated
Libnah's king as he had the king of
Jericho.

31 From Libnah, Joshua and all
Israel with him crossed to Lachish.
They laid siege to it and attacked it.
32 The Lord handed Lachish over to
Israel, and Joshua captured it on the
second day. He struck it down, putting everyone in it to the sword, just
as he had done to Libnah. 33 At that
time Horam king of Gezer went to
help Lachish, but Joshua struck him
down along with his people, leaving
no survivors in it.

34 Then Joshua crossed from Lachish to Eglon and all Israel with
him. They laid siege to it and attacked it. 35 On that day they captured it and struck it down, putting
everyone in it to the sword. He completely destroyed it that day, just as
he had done to Lachish.

36 Next, Joshua and all Israel with
him went up from Eglon to Hebron
and attacked it. 37 They captured it
and struck down its king, all its villages, and everyone in it with the
sword. He left no survivors, just as
he had done at Eglon. He completely destroyed Hebron and everyone
in it.

38 Finally, Joshua turned toward
Debir and attacked it. And all Israel
was with him. 39 He captured it—its
king and all its villages. They struck
them down with the sword and
completely destroyed everyone in
it, leaving no survivors. He treated
Debir and its king as he had treated
Hebron and as he had treated Libnah and its king.

[A]**10:21** Lit *No one sharpened his tongue against* [B]**10:26** Or *impaled* [C]**10:26,27** Or *wooden stakes*
[D]**10:28** Some Hb mss read *them*

40 So Joshua conquered the whole
region—the hill country, the •Ne-
gev, the Judean foothills,[A] and the
slopes—with all their kings, leaving no survivors. He completely
destroyed every living being, as the
LORD, the God of Israel, had commanded. 41 Joshua conquered everyone from Kadesh-barnea to Gaza,
and all the land of Goshen as far as
Gibeon. 42 Joshua captured all these
kings and their land in one campaign,[B] because the LORD, the God
of Israel, fought for Israel. 43 Then
Joshua returned with all Israel to
the camp at Gilgal.

Conquest of Northern Cities (11:1-15)

11 When Jabin king of Hazor
heard this news, he sent a message to:

Jobab king of Madon,
the kings of Shimron
and Achshaph,
2 and the kings of the north
in the hill country,
the •Arabah south
of Chinnereth,
the Judean foothills,[A]
and the Slopes of Dor[C]
to the west,
3 the Canaanites in the east
and west,
the Amorites, Hittites,
Perizzites,
and Jebusites
in the hill country,
and the Hivites at the foot
of Hermon
in the land of Mizpah.

4 They went out with all their
armies—a multitude as numerous
as the sand on the seashore—along
with a vast number of horses and
chariots. 5 All these kings joined
forces; they came together and
camped at the waters of Merom to
attack Israel.

6 The LORD said to Joshua, "Do not
be afraid of them, for at this time
tomorrow I will cause all of them
to be killed before Israel. You are
to hamstring their horses and burn
up their chariots." 7 So Joshua and
his whole military force surprised
them at the waters of Merom and
attacked them. 8 The LORD handed
them over to Israel, and they struck
them down, pursuing them as far as
Great Sidon and Misrephoth-maim,
and to the east as far as the Valley
of Mizpeh.[D] They struck them down,
leaving no survivors. 9 Joshua treated them as the LORD had told him; he
hamstrung their horses and burned
up their chariots.

10 At that time Joshua turned back,
captured Hazor, and struck down
its king with the sword, because
Hazor had formerly been the leader
of all these kingdoms. 11 They struck
down everyone in it with the sword,
•completely destroying them; he left
no one alive. Then he burned down
Hazor.

12 Joshua captured all these kings
and their cities and struck them
down with the sword. He completely
destroyed them, as Moses the LORD's
servant had commanded. 13 However, Israel did not burn any of the
cities that stood on their mounds
except Hazor, which Joshua burned.
14 The Israelites plundered all the
spoils and cattle of these cities for
themselves. But they struck down
every person with the sword until
they had annihilated them, leaving no one alive. 15 Just as the LORD
had commanded His servant Moses,
Moses commanded Joshua. That is
what Joshua did, leaving nothing
undone of all that the LORD had commanded Moses.

Summary of Conquests (11:16-23)

16 So Joshua took all this land—the
hill country, all the •Negev, all the
land of Goshen, the foothills,[A] the
Arabah, and the hill country of Israel with its foothills[E]— 17 from Mount
Halak, which ascends to Seir, as far
as Baal-gad in the Valley of Lebanon
at the foot of Mount Hermon. He
captured all their kings and struck
them down, putting them to death.
18 Joshua waged war with all these
kings for a long time. 19 No city made
peace with the Israelites except the
Hivites who inhabited Gibeon; all of
them were taken in battle. 20 For it
was the LORD's intention to harden
their hearts, so that they would

11:1-15 Armed with God's assurance of victory, Joshua **attacked** instead of allowing the Canaanite hosts to put Israel in a defensive position (vv. 7-8; cp. v. 5).

11:15 Israel's conquests were not the same as other wars for the sake of the pride of the leaders. God had chosen to give this land to His people and to execute judgment on the idolatrous nations inhabiting the land (Gn 15:16; Dt 9:4-5).

11:16-21 Because the Canaanite kings opposed the Israelites, they were **completely destroyed without mercy** (v. 20). Their wickedness had reached a stage demanding God's justice against such iniquity (Gn 15:16; cp. Gn 18:20-32; 19:12-14,27-29). Yahweh hardened **their hearts** as part of His plan for planting in their place a people who would reflect His goodness and righteousness.

[A] **10:40; 11:2,16** Or *the Shephelah* [B] **10:42** Lit *land at one time* [C] **11:2** Or *and in Naphoth-dor*
[D] **11:8** = Mizpah; Jos 11:3; 18:26 [E] **11:16** Or *its Shephelah*

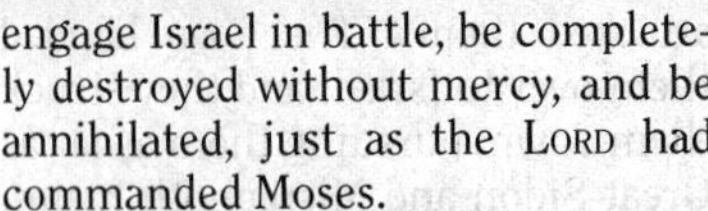

11:21-23 As God had promised, Joshua eliminated the **Anakim**, the "giants" who had seemed invincible to Israel's first scouting party (cp. Nm 13:33; Dt 9:1-3).

12:1-24 This chapter recounts the Israelites' conquests as a matter of record.

engage Israel in battle, be completely destroyed without mercy, and be annihilated, just as the LORD had commanded Moses.

21 At that time Joshua proceeded to exterminate the Anakim from the hill country—Hebron, Debir, Anab—all the hill country of Judah and of Israel. Joshua completely destroyed them with their cities. 22 No Anakim were left in the land of the Israelites, except for some remaining in Gaza, Gath, and Ashdod.

23 So Joshua took the entire land, in keeping with all that the LORD had told Moses. Joshua then gave it as an inheritance to Israel according to their tribal allotments. After this, the land had rest from war.

Territory East of the Jordan (12:1-24)

12 The Israelites struck down the following kings of the land and took possession of their land beyond the Jordan to the east and from the Arnon Valley to Mount Hermon, including all the •Arabah eastward:

2 Sihon king of the Amorites lived in Heshbon. He ruled over the territory from Aroer on the rim of the Arnon Valley, along the middle of the valley, and half of Gilead up to the Jabbok River (the border of the Ammonites), 3 the Arabah east of the Sea of Chinnereth[A] to the Sea of the Arabah (that is, the Dead Sea), eastward through Beth-jeshimoth and southward[B] below the slopes of Pisgah.

4 Og[C] king of Bashan, of the remnant of the Rephaim, lived in Ashtaroth and Edrei. 5 He ruled over Mount Hermon, Salecah, all Bashan up to the Geshurite and Maacathite border, and half of Gilead to the border of Sihon, king of Heshbon.

6 Moses the LORD's servant and the Israelites struck them down. And Moses the LORD's servant gave their land as an inheritance to the Reubenites, Gadites, and half the tribe of Manasseh.

7 Joshua and the Israelites struck down the following kings of the land beyond the Jordan to the west, from Baal-gad in the Valley of Lebanon to Mount Halak, which ascends toward Seir (Joshua gave their land as an inheritance to the tribes of Israel according to their allotments: 8 the hill country, the Judean foothills,[D] the Arabah, the slopes, the desert, and the •Negev of the Hittites, Amorites, Canaanites, Perizzites, Hivites, and Jebusites):

9 the king of Jericho one
the king of Ai, which is next to Bethel one
10 the king of Jerusalem one
the king of Hebron one
11 the king of Jarmuth one
the king of Lachish one
12 the king of Eglon one
the king of Gezer one
13 the king of Debir one
the king of Geder one
14 the king of Hormah one
the king of Arad one
15 the king of Libnah one
the king of Adullam one
16 the king of Makkedah one
the king of Bethel one
17 the king of Tappuah one
the king of Hepher one
18 the king of Aphek one
the king of Lasharon one
19 the king of Madon one
the king of Hazor one
20 the king of Shimron-meron one
the king of Achshaph one
21 the king of Taanach one
the king of Megiddo one
22 the king of Kedesh one
the king of Jokneam in Carmel one
23 the king of Dor in Naphath-dor[E] one
the king of Goiim in Gilgal[F] one
24 the king of Tirzah one
the total number of all kings: 31.

A Portion of the Land for Each Tribe (13:1–19:51)

Unconquered Lands (13:1-14)

13 Joshua was now old, getting on in years, and the LORD said to

[A] **12:3** = the Sea of Galilee [B] **12:3** Or *and from Teman* [C] **12:4** LXX; MT reads *The territory of Og* [D] **12:8** Or *the Shephelah* [E] **12:23** Or *in the Slopes of Dor* [F] **12:23** LXX reads *Galilee*

him, "You have become old, getting on in years, but a great deal of the land remains to be possessed. [2]This is the land that remains:

All the districts of the Philistines and the Geshurites: [3]from the Shihor east of Egypt to the border of Ekron on the north (considered to be Canaanite territory)—the five Philistine rulers of Gaza, Ashdod, Ashkelon, Gath, and Ekron, as well as the Avvites [4]in the south; all the land of the Canaanites: from Arah of the Sidonians to Aphek and as far as the border of the Amorites; [5]the land of the Gebalites; and all Lebanon east from Baal-gad below Mount Hermon to the entrance of Hamath[A]— [6]all the inhabitants of the hill country from Lebanon to Misrephoth-maim, all the Sidonians.

I will drive them out before the Israelites, only distribute the land as an inheritance for Israel, as I have commanded you. [7]Therefore, divide this land as an inheritance to the nine tribes and half the tribe of Manasseh."

[8]With the other half of the tribe, the Reubenites and Gadites had received the inheritance Moses gave them beyond the Jordan to the east, just as Moses the LORD's servant had given them:

[9]From Aroer on the rim of the Arnon Valley, along with the city in the middle of the valley, all the Medeba plateau as far as Dibon, [10]and all the cities of Sihon king of the Amorites, who reigned in Heshbon, to the border of the Ammonites; [11]also Gilead and the territory of the Geshurites and Maacathites, all Mount Hermon, and all Bashan to Salecah— [12]the whole kingdom of Og in Bashan, who reigned in Ashtaroth and Edrei; he was one of the remaining Rephaim.

Moses struck them down and drove them out, [13]but the Israelites did not drive out the Geshurites and Maacathites. So Geshur and Maacath live in Israel to this day.

[14]He did not give any inheritance to the tribe of Levi. This was its inheritance, just as He had promised: the offerings made by fire to the LORD, the God of Israel.

Reuben's Inheritance (13:15-23)

[15]To the tribe of the Reubenites by their clans, Moses gave [16]this as their territory:

From Aroer on the rim of the Arnon Valley, along with the city in the middle of the valley, to the whole plateau as far as[B] Medeba, [17]with Heshbon and all its cities on the plateau—Dibon, Bamoth-baal, Beth-baal-meon, [18]Jahaz, Kedemoth, Mephaath, [19]Kiriathaim, Sibmah, Zereth-shahar on the hill in the valley, [20]Beth-peor, the slopes of Pisgah, and Beth-jeshimoth— [21]all the cities of the plateau, and all the kingdom of Sihon king of the Amorites, who reigned in Heshbon. Moses had killed him and the chiefs of Midian—Evi, Rekem, Zur, Hur, and Reba—the princes of Sihon who lived in the land. [22]Along with those the Israelites put to death, they also killed the diviner, Balaam son of Beor, with the sword.

[23]The border of the Reubenites was the Jordan and its plain. This was the inheritance of the Reubenites by their clans, with the cities and their villages.

Gad's Inheritance (13:24-28)

[24]To the tribe of the Gadites by their clans, Moses gave [25]this as their territory:

Jazer and all the cities of Gilead, and half the land of the Ammonites to Aroer, near Rabbah; [26]from Heshbon to Ramath-mizpeh and Betonim, and from Mahanaim to the border of Debir;[C] [27]in the valley:[D] Beth-haram, Beth-nimrah, Succoth, and Zaphon—the rest of the

13:1-14 God told Joshua that He would be their leader in driving out the remaining inhabitants. Joshua's only responsibility was to be faithful to distribute the land as God instructed.

13:14 The Levites did not receive any land because they were to be the priests. Their inheritance as God's representatives of the people of Israel was to be **the offerings made by fire**.

13:15-33 The land was the physical manifestation of the blessing of God and the fulfillment of His specific promises to give the land to them.

[A]**13:5** Or *to Lebo-hamath* [B]**13:16** Some Hb mss read *plateau near* [C]**13:26** Or *Lidbir*, or *Lo-debar*
[D]**13:27** = the Jordan River Valley

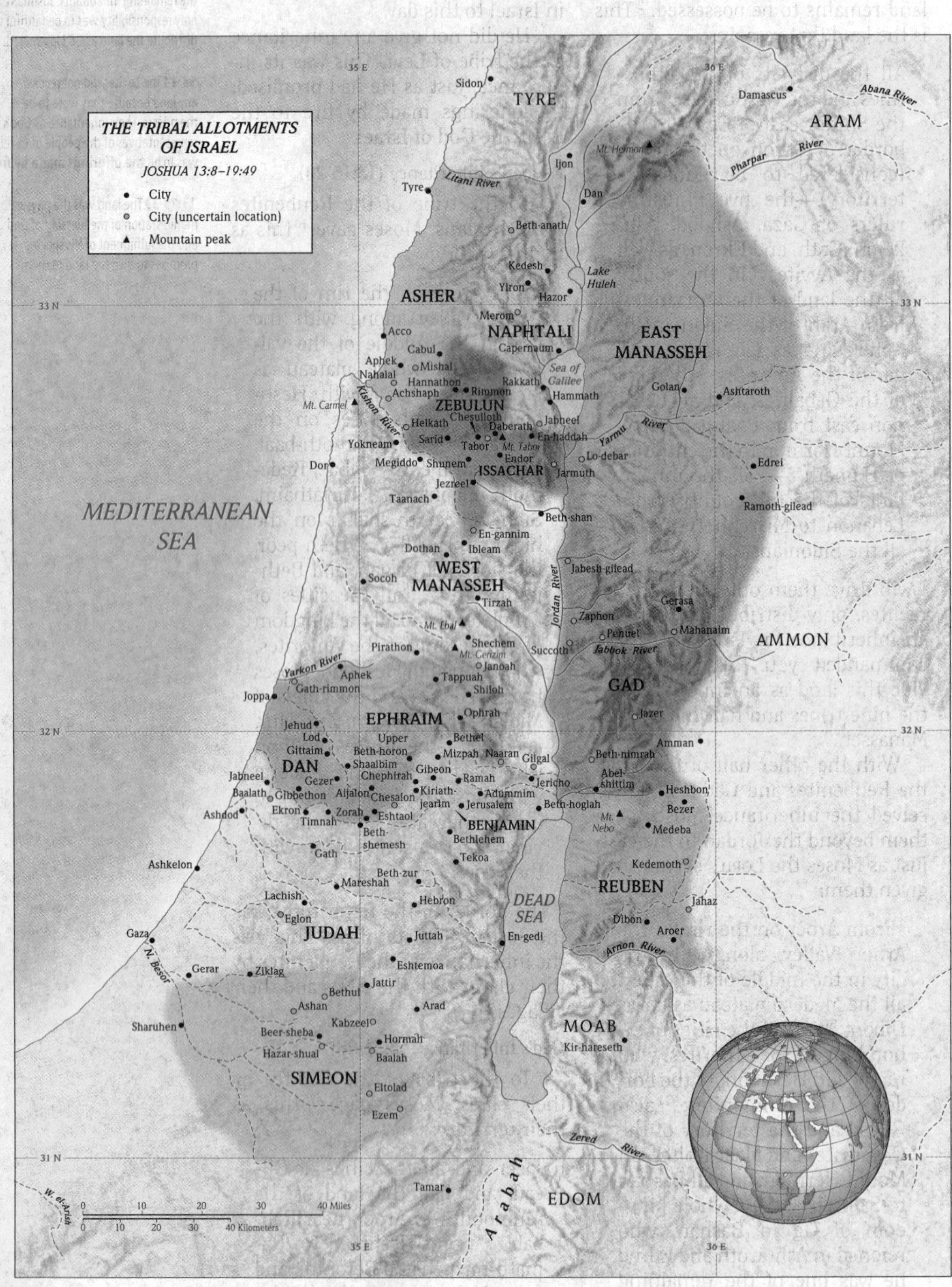
THE TRIBAL ALLOTMENTS OF ISRAEL
JOSHUA 13:8–19:49
City
City (uncertain location)
Mountain peak
35 E
36 E
33 N
32 N
31 N
MEDITERRANEAN SEA
Sidon
TYRE
Damascus
Abana River
ARAM
Mt. Hermon
Pharpar
River
Ijon
Tyre
Litani River
Dan
Beth-anath
Kedesh
Yiron
Lake Huleh
Hazor
ASHER
Merom
NAPHTALI
EAST MANASSEH
Acco
Cabul
Capernaum
Aphek
Mishal
Nahalal
Hannathon
Sea of Galilee
Achshaph
Rimmon
Rakkath
Hammath
Golan
Ashtaroth
Mt. Carmel
Kishon River
ZEBULUN
Chesulloth
Jabneel
Helkath
Daberath
En-haddah
Yarmuk
River
Sarid
Tabor
Mt. Tabor
Yokneam
Endor
Lo-debar
Dor
Megiddo
Shunem
ISSACHAR
Jarmuth
Edrei
Jezreel
Taanach
Ramoth-gilead
Beth-shan
En-gannim
Dothan
Ibleam
WEST MANASSEH
Jabesh-gilead
Socoh
Jordan River
Tirzah
Gerasa
Zaphon
Mt. Ebal
Penuel
Mahanaim
Shechem
Pirathon
Mt. Gerizim
Succoth
Jabbok River
AMMON
Yarkon River
Janoah
Aphek
Tappuah
GAD
Gath-rimmon
Shiloh
Joppa
EPHRAIM
Ophrah
Jazer
Jehud
Lod
Upper Beth-horon
Bethel
Amman
Gittaim
Mizpah
Naaran
Gilgal
Beth-nimrah
DAN
Shaalbim
Gibeon
Chephirah
Ramah
Jabneel
Gezer
Jericho
Abel-shittim
Heshbon
Baalath
Gibbethon
Aijalon
Chesalon
Kiriath-jearim
Adummim
Ashdod
Ekron
Zorah
Eshtaol
Jerusalem
Beth-hoglah
Bezer
Timnah
BENJAMIN
Mt. Nebo
Medeba
Beth-shemesh
Bethlehem
Gath
Tekoa
Ashkelon
Kedemoth
Beth-zur
Mareshah
Lachish
Hebron
DEAD SEA
REUBEN
Jahaz
Eglon
Dibon
Aroer
Gaza
JUDAH
Juttah
En-gedi
Arnon River
N. Besor
Eshtemoa
Gerar
Ziklag
Jattir
Bethul
Arad
Ashan
Kabzeel
MOAB
Sharuhen
Beer-sheba
Hormah
Kir-hareseth
Hazar-shual
Baalah
SIMEON
Eltolad
Ezem
Zered
River
Arabah
Tamar
EDOM
W. el-Arish
0 10 20 30 40 Miles
0 10 20 30 40 Kilometers

14:1-5 The other **nine and a half tribes** were to receive their land portions **by lot**, an ancient practice commonly used for this type of decision (v. 2). The Israelites respected the outcome as having been directed by God.

14:6-15 Caleb, Joshua's old friend and companion, wanted to take possession of the exact land he had spied out and to conquer **the Anakim** living there. Certain that he would receive what God had promised him, Caleb was obedient to the Lord's commands. God honored Caleb with the land of **Hebron**, which he wanted for his inheritance (vv. 13-15).

CHARACTER PROFILE

Achsah A Clever Daughter

Her Background
- The daughter of Caleb (15:16)
- The wife of Caleb's nephew Othniel (15:16-17)

Her Story
- She persuaded Othniel to ask her father for land (15:18).
- She asked her father for additional land that contained springs of water, which were necessary for the land to be productive (15:19).

Life Lessons
- Achsah was assertive but not disrespectful or greedy in her request.
- She sought to provide land for the future of her family.

kingdom of Sihon king of Heshbon. Their land also included the Jordan and its territory as far as the edge of the Sea of Chinnereth[A] on the east side of the Jordan.[B]

28 This was the inheritance of the Gadites by their clans, with the cities and their villages.

East Manasseh's Inheritance (13:29-33)

29 And to half the tribe of Manasseh, that is, to half the tribe of Manasseh's descendants by their clans, Moses gave 30 this as their territory:

From Mahanaim through all Bashan—all the kingdom of Og king of Bashan, including all of Jair's Villages[C] that are in Bashan—60 cities. 31 But half of Gilead, and Og's royal cities in Bashan—Ashtaroth and Edrei—are for the descendants of Machir son of Manasseh, that is, half the descendants of Machir by their clans.

32 These were the portions Moses gave them on the plains of Moab beyond the Jordan east of Jericho.
33 But Moses did not give a portion to the tribe of Levi. The LORD, the God of Israel, was their inheritance, just as He had promised them.

Israel's Inheritance in Canaan (14:1-5)

14 The Israelites received these portions that Eleazar the priest, Joshua son of Nun, and the heads of the families of the Israelite tribes gave them in the land of Canaan. 2 Their inheritance was by lot as the LORD commanded through Moses for the nine and a half tribes,
3 because Moses had given the inheritance to the two and a half tribes beyond the Jordan.[D] But he gave no inheritance among them to the Levites. 4 The descendants of Joseph became two tribes, Manasseh and Ephraim. No portion of the land was given to the Levites except cities to live in, along with pasturelands for their cattle and livestock. 5 So the Israelites did as the LORD commanded Moses, and they divided the land.

Caleb's Inheritance (14:6-15)

6 The descendants of Judah approached Joshua at Gilgal, and Caleb son of Jephunneh the Kenizzite said to him, "You know what the LORD promised Moses the man of God at Kadesh-barnea about you and me.
7 I was 40 years old when Moses the LORD's servant sent me from Kadesh-barnea to scout the land, and I brought back an honest report. 8 My brothers who went with me caused the people's hearts to melt with fear, but I remained loyal to the LORD my God. 9 On that day Moses promised me: 'The land where you have set foot will be an inheritance for you and your descendants forever, because you have remained loyal to the LORD my God.'

A 13:27 = the Sea of Galilee B 13:27 Lit *Chinnereth beyond the Jordan to the east* C 13:30 Or *all of Havvoth-jair* D 14:3 = east of the Jordan River

10 “As you see, the LORD has kept me alive these 45 years as He promised, since the LORD spoke this word to Moses while Israel was journeying in the wilderness. Here I am today, 85 years old. 11 I am still as strong today as I was the day Moses sent me out. My strength for battle and for daily tasks[A] is now as it was then. 12 Now give me this hill country the LORD promised me on that day, because you heard then that the Anakim are there, as well as large fortified cities. Perhaps the LORD will be with me and I will drive them out as the LORD promised.”

13 Then Joshua blessed Caleb son of Jephunneh and gave him Hebron as an inheritance. 14 Therefore, Hebron belongs to Caleb son of Jephunneh the Kenizzite as an inheritance to this day, because he remained loyal to the LORD, the God of Israel. 15 Hebron's name used to be Kiriath-arba; Arba was the greatest man among the Anakim. After this, the land had rest from war.

Judah's Inheritance (15:1-12)

15 Now the allotment for the tribe of the descendants of Judah by their clans was in the southernmost region, south to the Wilderness of Zin and over to the border of Edom.

2 Their southern border began at the tip of the Dead Sea on the south bay[B] 3 and went south of the Ascent of Akrabbim,[C] proceeded to Zin, ascended to the south of Kadesh-barnea, passed Hezron, ascended to Addar, and turned to Karka. 4 It proceeded to Azmon and to the Brook of Egypt and so the border ended at the Mediterranean Sea. This is your[D] southern border.

5 Now the eastern border was along the Dead Sea to the mouth of the Jordan.[E]

The border on the north side was from the bay of the sea at the mouth of the Jordan. 6 It ascended to Beth-hoglah, proceeded north of Beth-arabah, and ascended to the Stone of Bohan son of Reuben. 7 Then the border ascended to Debir from the Valley of Achor, turning north to the Gilgal that is opposite the Ascent of Adummim, which is south of the ravine. The border proceeded to the waters of En-shemesh and ended at En-rogel. 8 From there the border ascended the Valley of Hinnom to the southern Jebusite slope (that is, Jerusalem) and ascended to the top of the hill that faces the Valley of Hinnom on the west, at the northern end of the Valley of Rephaim. 9 From the top of the hill the border curved to the spring of the Waters of Nephtoah, went to the cities of Mount Ephron, and then curved to Baalah (that is, Kiriath-jearim). 10 The border turned westward from Baalah to Mount Seir, went to the northern slope of Mount Jearim (that is, Chesalon), descended to Beth-shemesh, and proceeded to Timnah. 11 Then the border reached to the slope north of Ekron, curved to Shikkeron, proceeded to Mount Baalah, went to Jabneel, and ended at the Mediterranean Sea.

12 Now the western border was the coastline of the Mediterranean Sea.

This was the boundary of the descendants of Judah around their clans.

Caleb and Othniel (15:13-19)

13 He gave Caleb son of Jephunneh the following portion among the descendants of Judah based on the LORD's instruction to Joshua: Kiriath-arba (that is, Hebron; Arba was the father of Anak). 14 Caleb drove out from there the three sons of Anak: Sheshai, Ahiman, and Talmai, descendants of Anak. 15 From there he marched against the inhabitants of Debir whose name used to be Kiriath-sepher, 16 and Caleb said, “I will give my daughter Achsah as a wife to the one who strikes down

[A] 14:11 Lit *for going out and coming in* [B] 15:2 Lit *Sea at the tongue that turns southward* [C] 15:3 Lit *of scorpions* [D] 15:4 LXX reads *their* [E] 15:5 = the southern end of the Jordan River at the Dead Sea

and captures Kiriath-sepher." [17]So
Othniel son of Caleb's brother, Kenaz, captured it, and Caleb gave his
daughter Achsah to him as a wife.
[18]When she arrived, she persuaded
Othniel to ask her father for a field.
As she got off her donkey, Caleb
asked her, "What do you want?"
[19]She replied, "Give me a blessing.
Since you have given me land in the
•Negev, give me the springs of water
also." So he gave her the upper and
lower springs.

Judah's Cities (15:20-63)

[20]This was the inheritance of the
tribe of the descendants of Judah by
their clans.

[21]These were the outer-
most cities of the tribe of
the descendants of Judah toward the border of Edom in
the Negev: Kabzeel, Eder,
Jagur, [22]Kinah, Dimonah,
Adadah, [23]Kedesh, Hazor, Ith-
nan, [24]Ziph, Telem, Bealoth,
[25]Hazor-hadattah, Kerioth-hez-
ron (that is, Hazor), [26]Amam,
Shema, Moladah, [27]Hazar-
gaddah, Heshmon, Beth-pelet,
[28]Hazar-shual, Beer-sheba, Biz-
iothiah, [29]Baalah, Iim, Ezem,
[30]Eltolad, Chesil, Hormah,
[31]Ziklag, Madmannah, Sansan-
nah, [32]Lebaoth, Shilhim, Ain,
and Rimmon—29 cities in all,
with their villages.

[33]In the Judean foothills:[A]
Eshtaol, Zorah, Ashnah, [34]Za-
noah, En-gannim, Tappuah,[B]
Enam, [35]Jarmuth, Adullam,
Socoh,[C] Azekah, [36]Shaaraim,
Adithaim, Gederah, and Gede-
rothaim—14 cities, with their
villages; [37]Zenan, Hadashah,
Migdal-gad, [38]Dilan, Mizpeh,
Jokthe-el, [39]Lachish, Bozkath,
Eglon, [40]Cabbon, Lahmam, Chit-
lish, [41]Gederoth, Beth-dagon,
Naamah, and Makkedah—16
cities, with their villages; [42]Lib-
nah, Ether, Ashan, [43]Iphtah,
Ashnah, Nezib, [44]Keilah, Achzib,
and Mareshah—nine cities, with
their villages; [45]Ekron, with
its towns and villages; [46]from
Ekron to the sea, all the cities
near Ashdod, with their villages;
[47]Ashdod, with its towns and villages; Gaza, with its towns and
villages, to the Brook of Egypt
and the coastline of the Mediterranean Sea.

[48]In the hill country: Shamir,
Jattir, Socoh, [49]Dannah, Kiriath-
sannah (that is, Debir), [50]Anab,
Eshtemoh, Anim, [51]Goshen,
Holon, and Giloh—11 cities,
with their villages; [52]Arab,
Dumah,[D] Eshan, [53]Janim, Beth-
tappuah, Aphekah, [54]Humtah,
Kiriath-arba (that is, Hebron),
and Zior—nine cities, with
their villages; [55]Maon, Carmel,
Ziph, Juttah, [56]Jezreel, Jok-
deam, Zanoah, [57]Kain, Gibeah,
and Timnah—10 cities, with
their villages; [58]Halhul, Beth-
zur, Gedor, [59]Maarath, Beth-
anoth, and Eltekon—six cities,
with their villages;[E] [60]Kiriath-
baal (that is, Kiriath-jearim),
and Rabbah—two cities, with
their villages.

[61]In the wilderness: Beth-arabah, Middin, Secacah, [62]Nib-
shan, the City of Salt,[F] and
En-gedi—six cities, with their
villages.

[63]But the descendants of Judah
could not drive out the Jebusites
who lived in Jerusalem. So the
Jebusites live in Jerusalem among
the descendants of Judah to this
day.

Joseph's Inheritance (16:1-4)

16 The allotment for the descendants of Joseph[G] went
from the Jordan at Jericho to
the waters of Jericho on the
east, through the wilderness
ascending from Jericho into
the hill country of Bethel.
[2]From Bethel it went to Luz
and proceeded to the border
of the Archites by Ataroth. [3]It
then descended westward to

15:63 This indicates Israel's unfaithfulness. Future troubles would often be related to the Canaanites who remained in the land—in this case, some of **the Jebusites.**

[A]**15:33** Or *the Shephelah* [B]**15:34** Or *En-gannim-tappuah* [C]**15:35** Or *Adullam-socoh*
[D]**15:52** Some Hb mss read *Rumah* [E]**15:59** LXX adds *Tekoa, Ephrathah (that is, Bethlehem), Peor, Etam, Culom, Tatam, Sores, Carem, Gallim, Baither, and Manach—11 cities, with their villages* [F]**15:62** Or *Ir-hamelach* [G]**16:1** = the tribes of Ephraim and Manasseh

17:1-6 Traditionally, a man's inheritance was given to the family's sons. Zelophehad had no sons, but he did have five **daughters**, who had requested permission to be given **an inheritance** among their father's brothers (vv. 3-4; cp. Nm 27:1-11; 36:1-12). The daughters were familiar with the words of the Lord, and they were willing to remind their leaders of the Lord's words on their behalf. The text gives no indication that they were rude or defensive in their encounter with Eleazar and Joshua but simply that they were bold in their appeal. They went humbly before the leaders to request their inheritance, leaving the details of how it would be dispensed in the hands of those in authority. The record of allotments confirms that **Eleazar**, **Joshua**, and **the leaders** honored the Lord's decision and gave the women their promised inheritance.

the border of the Japhletites as
far as the border of lower Beth-
horon, then to Gezer, and ended at the Mediterranean Sea.
4 So Ephraim and Manasseh,
the sons of Joseph, received
their inheritance.

Ephraim's Inheritance (16:5-10)

5 This was the territory of the descendants of Ephraim by their clans:

The border of their inheritance
went from Ataroth-addar on
the east of Upper Beth-horon.
6 In the north the border went
westward from Michmethath;
it turned eastward from Ta-
anath-shiloh and passed it east
of Janoah. 7 From Janoah it descended to Ataroth and Naarah,
and then reached Jericho and
went to the Jordan. 8 From Tappuah the border[A] went westward along the Brook of Kanah
and ended at the Mediterranean Sea.

This was the inheritance of the
tribe of the descendants of Ephraim
by their clans, together with 9 the
cities set apart for the descendants
of Ephraim within the inheritance
of the descendants of Manasseh—all
these cities with their villages.
10 But, they did not drive out the Canaanites who lived in Gezer. So the
Canaanites live in Ephraim to this
day, but they are forced laborers.

West Manasseh's Inheritance (17:1-13)

17 This was the allotment for the
tribe of Manasseh as Joseph's
firstborn. Gilead and Bashan came
to Machir, the firstborn of Manasseh
and the father of Gilead, who was a
man of war. 2 So the allotment was
for the rest of Manasseh's descendants by their clans, for the sons
of Abiezer, Helek, Asriel, Shechem,
Hepher, and Shemida. These are the
male descendants of Manasseh son
of Joseph, by their clans.
3 Now Zelophehad son of Hepher,
son of Gilead, son of Machir, son of
Manasseh, had no sons, only daughters. These are the names of his
daughters: Mahlah, Noah, Hoglah,
Milcah, and Tirzah. 4 They came
before Eleazar the priest, Joshua
son of Nun, and the leaders, saying, "The LORD commanded Moses
to give us an inheritance among
our male relatives."[B] So they gave
them an inheritance among their father's brothers, in keeping with the
LORD's instruction. 5 As a result, 10
tracts fell to Manasseh, besides the
land of Gilead and Bashan, which
are beyond the Jordan,[C] 6 because
Manasseh's daughters received an
inheritance among his sons. The
land of Gilead belonged to the rest
of Manasseh's sons.

7 The border of Manasseh went
from Asher to Michmethath
near Shechem. It then went
southward toward the inhabitants of En-tappuah. 8 The
region of Tappuah belonged
to Manasseh, but Tappuah itself on Manasseh's border belonged to the descendants of
Ephraim. 9 From there the border descended to the Brook of
Kanah; south of the brook, cities belonged to Ephraim among
Manasseh's cities. Manasseh's
border was on the north side
of the brook and ended at the
Mediterranean Sea. 10 Ephraim's

[A] **16:8** Ephraim's northern border [B] **17:4** Lit *our brothers* [C] **17:5** = east of the Jordan River

Biblical Womanhood A Woman's Boldness

Today's Christian woman can learn from Zelophehad's daughters how to approach those in authority in a diplomatic way and how to present her case in a godly manner. The women could have responded as having been victimized since they did not fit into the apportioning rationale for the land. They also could have approached the leaders demanding their own solutions for how they wanted their case to be resolved. However, all they did was remind those in authority of the law of the Lord, leaving the resolution of the problem in the hands of God-assigned leaders and trusting God for the outcome. By waiting patiently for their answer, the daughters' example echoes the wisdom of Esther, who also went boldly before her authority with an attitude of humility (Est 5:1-8; 7:1-6).

territory was to the south and Manasseh's to the north, with the Sea as its border. They[A] reached Asher on the north and Issachar on the east. [11] Within Issachar and Asher, Manasseh had Beth-shean with its towns, Ibleam with its towns, and the inhabitants of Dor with its towns; the inhabitants of Endor with its towns, the inhabitants of Taanach with its towns, and the inhabitants of Megiddo with its towns—the three cities of[B] Naphath.

[12] The descendants of Manasseh could not possess these cities, because the Canaanites were determined to stay in this land. [13] However, when the Israelites grew stronger, they imposed forced labor on the Canaanites but did not drive them out completely.

Joseph's Additional Inheritance (17:14-18)

[14] Joseph's descendants said to Joshua, "Why did you give us only one tribal allotment[C] as an inheritance? We have many people, because the LORD has been blessing us greatly."

[15] "If you have so many people," Joshua replied to them, "go to the forest and clear an area for yourselves there in the land of the Perizzites and the Rephaim, because Ephraim's hill country is too small for you."

[16] But the descendants of Joseph said, "The hill country is not enough for us, and all the Canaanites who inhabit the valley area have iron chariots, both at Beth-shean with its towns and in the Jezreel Valley."

[17] So Joshua replied to Joseph's family (that is, Ephraim and Manasseh), "You have many people and great strength. You will not have just one allotment, [18] because the hill country will be yours also. It is a forest; clear it and its outlying areas will be yours. You can also drive out the Canaanites, even though they have iron chariots and are strong."

Land Distribution at Shiloh (18:1-10)

18 The entire Israelite community assembled at Shiloh where it set up the tent of meeting there; the land had been subdued by them. [2] Seven tribes among the Israelites were left who had not divided up their inheritance. [3] So Joshua said to the Israelites, "How long will you delay going out to take possession of the land that the LORD, the God of your fathers, gave you? [4] Appoint for yourselves three men from each tribe, and I will send them out. They are to go and survey the land, write a description of it for the purpose of their inheritance, and return to me. [5] Then they are to divide it into seven portions. Judah is to remain in its territory in the south and Joseph's family in their[D] territory in the north. [6] When you have written a description of the seven portions of land and brought it to me, I will cast lots for you here in the presence of the LORD our God. [7] But the Levites among you do not get a portion, because their inheritance is the priesthood of the LORD. Gad, Reuben, and half the tribe of Manasseh have taken their inheritance beyond the Jordan to the east, which Moses the LORD's servant gave them."

[8] As the men prepared to go, Joshua commanded them[E] to write down a description of the land, saying, "Go and survey the land, write a description of it, and return to me. I will then cast lots for you here in Shiloh in the presence of the LORD." [9] So the men left, went through the land, and described it by towns in a document of seven sections. They returned to Joshua at the camp in Shiloh. [10] Joshua cast lots for them at Shiloh in the presence of the LORD where he distributed the land to the Israelites according to their divisions.

Benjamin's Inheritance (18:11-20)

[11] The lot came up for the tribe of Benjamin's descendants by their clans, and their allotted territory lay

18:1-10 To move the **tent of meeting** and the ark of the covenant from Gilgal, on the edge of the promised land, to **Shiloh**, which was more centrally located (on a hill between Bethel and Shechem), symbolized the Israelites' assertion of permanent residence in and control of the land.

[A] **17:10** The people of Manasseh, or Manasseh's borders [B] **17:11** LXX, Vg read *the third is* [C] **17:14-17** Lit *one lot and one territory* [D] **18:5** = the tribes of Ephraim and Manasseh [E] **18:8** Lit *the ones going around*

between Judah's descendants and Joseph's descendants.

12 Their border on the north side began at the Jordan, ascended to the slope of Jericho on the north, through the hill country westward, and ended at the wilderness of Beth-aven. 13 From there the border went toward Luz, to the southern slope of Luz (that is, Bethel); it then went down by Ataroth-addar, over the hill south of Lower Beth-horon.

14 On the west side, from the hill facing Beth-horon on the south, the border curved, turning southward, and ended at Kiriath-baal (that is, Kiriath-jearim), a city of the descendants of Judah. This was the west side of their border.

15 The south side began at the edge of Kiriath-jearim, and the border extended westward; it went to the spring at the Waters of Nephtoah. 16 The border descended to the foot of the hill that faces the Valley of Hinnom at the northern end of the Valley of Rephaim. It ran down the Valley of Hinnom toward the south Jebusite slope and downward to En-rogel. 17 It curved northward and went to En-shemesh and on to Geliloth, which is opposite the Ascent of Adummim, and continued down to the Stone of Bohan son of Reuben. 18 Then it went north to the slope opposite the Jordan Valley[A,B] and proceeded into the valley.[B] 19 The border continued to the north slope of Beth-hoglah and ended at the northern bay of the Dead Sea, at the southern end of the Jordan. This was the southern border.

20 The Jordan formed the border on the east side.

This was the inheritance of Benjamin's descendants, by their clans, according to its surrounding borders.

Benjamin's Cities (18:21-28)

21 These were the cities of the tribe of Benjamin's descendants by their clans:

Jericho, Beth-hoglah, Emek-keziz, 22 Beth-arabah, Zemaraim, Bethel, 23 Avvim, Parah, Ophrah, 24 Chephar-ammoni, Ophni, and Geba—12 cities, with their villages; 25 Gibeon, Ramah, Beeroth, 26 Mizpeh,[C] Chephirah, Mozah, 27 Rekem, Irpeel, Taralah, 28 Zela, Haeleph, Jebus[D] (that is, Jerusalem), Gibeah, and Kiriath[E]—14 cities, with their villages.

This was the inheritance for Benjamin's descendants by their clans.

Simeon's Inheritance (19:1-9)

19 The second lot came out for Simeon, for the tribe of his descendants by their clans, but their inheritance was within the portion of Judah's descendants. 2 Their inheritance included:

Beer-sheba (or Sheba), Moladah, 3 Hazar-shual, Balah, Ezem, 4 Eltolad, Bethul, Hormah, 5 Ziklag, Beth-marcaboth, Hazar-susah, 6 Beth-lebaoth, and Sharuhen—13 cities, with their villages; 7 Ain, Rimmon, Ether, and Ashan—four cities, with their villages; 8 and all the villages surrounding these cities as far as Baalath-beer (Ramah of the south[F]).

This was the inheritance of the tribe of Simeon's descendants by their clans. 9 The inheritance of Simeon's descendants was within the territory of Judah's descendants, because the share for Judah's descendants was too large for them. So Simeon's descendants received an inheritance within Judah's portion.

Zebulun's Inheritance (19:10-16)

10 The third lot came up for Zebulun's descendants by their clans.

The territory of their inheri-

[A] **18:18** LXX reads *went northward to Beth-arabah* [B] **18:18** Or *the Arabah* [C] **18:26** = Mizpah; Jos 11:3,8 [D] **18:28** Lit *Jebusite* [E] **18:28** LXX, Syr read *Kiriath-jearim* [F] **19:8** Or *the Negev*

tance stretched as far as Sarid;
[11] their border went up westward to Maralah, reached Dabbesheth, and met the brook east of Jokneam.
[12] From Sarid, it turned east toward the sunrise along the border of Chisloth-tabor, went to Daberath, and went up to Japhia.
[13] From there, it went east toward the sunrise to Gath-hepher and to Eth-kazin; it extended to Rimmon, curving around to Neah.
[14] The border then circled around Neah on the north to Hannathon and ended at the Valley of Iphtah-el,
[15] along with Kattath, Nahalal, Shimron, Idalah, and Bethlehem—12 cities, with their villages.

[16] This was the inheritance of Zebulun's descendants by their clans, these cities, with their villages.

Issachar's Inheritance (19:17-23)

[17] The fourth lot came out for the tribe of Issachar's descendants by their clans.

[18] Their territory went to Jezreel, and included Chesulloth, Shunem,
[19] Hapharaim, Shion, Anaharath,
[20] Rabbith, Kishion, Ebez,
[21] Remeth, En-gannim, En-haddah, Beth-pazzez.
[22] The border reached Tabor, Shahazumah, and Beth-shemesh, and ended at the Jordan—16 cities, with their villages.

[23] This was the inheritance of the tribe of Issachar's descendants by their clans, the cities, with their villages.

Asher's Inheritance (19:24-31)

[24] The fifth lot came out for the tribe of Asher's descendants by their clans.

[25] Their boundary included Helkath, Hali, Beten, Achshaph,
[26] Allammelech, Amad, and Mishal and reached westward to Carmel and Shihor-libnath.
[27] It turned eastward to Beth-dagon, passed Zebulun and the Valley of Iphtah-el, north toward Beth-emek and Neiel, and went north to Cabul,
[28] Ebron, Rehob, Hammon, and Kanah, as far as Great Sidon.
[29] The boundary then turned to Ramah as far as the fortified city of Tyre; it turned back to Hosah and ended at the sea, including Mahalab, Achzib,[A]
[30] Ummah, Aphek, and Rehob—22 cities, with their villages.

[31] This was the inheritance of the tribe of Asher's descendants by their clans, these cities with their villages.

Naphtali's Inheritance (19:32-39)

[32] The sixth lot came out for Naphtali's descendants by their clans.

[33] Their boundary went from Heleph and from the oak in Zaanannim, including Adami-nekeb and Jabneel, as far as Lakkum, and ended at the Jordan.
[34] To the west, the boundary turned to Aznoth-tabor and went from there to Hukkok, reaching Zebulun on the south, Asher on the west, and Judah[B] at the Jordan on the east.
[35] The fortified cities were Ziddim, Zer, Hammath, Rakkath, Chinnereth,[C]
[36] Adamah, Ramah, Hazor,
[37] Kedesh, Edrei, En-hazor,
[38] Iron, Migdal-el, Horem, Beth-anath, and Beth-shemesh—19 cities, with their villages.

[39] This was the inheritance of the tribe of Naphtali's descendants by their clans, the cities with their villages.

Dan's Inheritance (19:40-48)

[40] The seventh lot came out for the Danite tribe by its clans.

[41] The territory of their inheritance included Zorah, Eshtaol, Ir-shemesh,
[42] Shaalabbin, Aijalon, Ithlah,
[43] Elon, Timnah, Ekron,
[44] Eltekeh, Gibbethon, Baalath,
[45] Jehud, Bene-berak, Gath-rimmon,
[46] Me-jarkon, and Rakkon, with the territory facing Joppa.

[47] When the territory of the Danites

19:40-48 The Danites had to fight to take **possession** of the land, which at some point **slipped out of their control** (v. 47). Judges 18 records the story behind Dan's taking, rebuilding, and renaming of the city.

[A]19:29 Or *sea, in the region of Achzib* [B]19:34 LXX omits *Judah* [C]19:35 A town near the Sea of Galilee

20:1-9 The Lord was aware that Israel's existence in the land would not be without death or misfortune. The cities of refuge were a way of constructing a just society. People could run to these cities for protection if someone were killed accidentally.

21:1-42 The Levites were comprised of family groups, three of which had been assigned specific duties in the maintenance and transport of the tabernacle. These three groups bore the names of Levi's three sons—Gershon, Kohath, and Merari (Nm 3:17; 26:47-62).

slipped out of their control,[A] they
went up and fought against Leshem,
captured it, and struck it down with
the sword. So they took possession
of it, lived there, and renamed Leshem after[B] their ancestor Dan.
48 This was the inheritance of the
Danite tribe by its clans, these cities
with their villages.

Joshua's Inheritance (19:49-51)

49 When they had finished distributing the land into its territories,
the Israelites gave Joshua son of
Nun an inheritance among them.
50 By the LORD's command, they gave
him the city Timnath-serah in the
hill country of Ephraim, which he
requested. He rebuilt the city and
lived in it.

51 These were the portions that
Eleazar the priest, Joshua son of
Nun, and the heads of the families
distributed to the Israelite tribes by
lot at Shiloh in the LORD's presence
at the entrance to the tent of meeting. So they finished dividing up the
land.

Special Instructions for the Cities of Refuge, the Levites, and the Eastern Tribes (20:1–22:34)

Cities of Refuge (20:1-9)

20 Then the LORD spoke to Joshua, 2 "Tell the Israelites: Select
your cities of refuge, as I instructed
you through Moses, 3 so that a person who kills someone unintentionally or accidentally may flee there.
These will be your refuge from the
avenger of blood. 4 When someone
flees to one of these cities, stands at
the entrance of the city •gate, and
states his case before[C] the elders of
that city, they are to bring him into
the city and give him a place to live
among them. 5 And if the avenger of
blood pursues him, they must not
hand the one who committed manslaughter over to him, for he killed
his neighbor accidentally and did
not hate him beforehand. 6 He is to
stay in that city until he stands trial
before the assembly and until the
death of the high priest serving at
that time. Then the one who committed manslaughter may return
home to his own city from which he
fled."

7 So they designated Kedesh in
the hill country of Naphtali in Galilee, Shechem in the hill country of
Ephraim, and Kiriath-arba (that
is, Hebron) in the hill country of
Judah. 8 Across the Jordan east of
Jericho, they selected Bezer on the
wilderness plateau from Reuben's
tribe, Ramoth in Gilead from Gad's
tribe, and Golan in Bashan from
Manasseh's tribe.

9 These are the cities appointed
for all the Israelites and foreigners
among them, so that anyone who
kills a person unintentionally may
flee there and not die at the hand of
the avenger of blood until he stands
before the assembly.

Cities of the Levites (21:1-8)

21 The heads of the Levite families approached Eleazar the
priest, Joshua son of Nun, and the
heads of the families of the Israelite tribes. 2 At Shiloh, in the land of
Canaan, they told them, "The LORD
commanded through Moses that we
be given cities to live in, with their
pasturelands for our livestock." 3 So
the Israelites, by the LORD's command, gave the Levites these cities
with their pasturelands from their
inheritance.

4 The lot came out for the Kohathite clans: The Levites who
were the descendants of Aaron
the priest received 13 cities by
lot from the tribes of Judah,
Simeon, and Benjamin. 5 The
remaining descendants of Kohath[D] received 10 cities by lot
from the clans of the tribes of
Ephraim, Dan, and half the
tribe of Manasseh.

6 Gershon's descendants received 13 cities by lot from the
clans of the tribes of Issachar,
Asher, Naphtali, and half the
tribe of Manasseh in Bashan.

7 Merari's descendants received
12 cities for their clans from

[A] **19:47** Lit *territory of the sons of Dan went out from them* [B] **19:47** Lit *and called Leshem, Dan, after the name of* [C] **20:4** Lit *in the ears of* [D] **21:5** Descendants not in Aaron's priestly line

the tribes of Reuben, Gad, and
Zebulun.

[8] The Israelites gave these cities with
their pasturelands around them to
the Levites by lot, as the LORD had
commanded through Moses.

Cities of Aaron's Descendants (21:9-19)

[9] The Israelites gave these cities by
name from the tribes of the descendants of Judah and Simeon [10] to the
descendants of Aaron from the Kohathite clans of the Levites, because
they received the first lot. [11] They
gave them Kiriath-arba (that is, Hebron) with its surrounding pasturelands in the hill country of Judah.
Arba was the father of Anak. [12] But
they gave the fields and villages of
the city to Caleb son of Jephunneh
as his possession.
[13] They gave to the descendants of
Aaron the priest:

Hebron, the city of refuge
for the one who commits
manslaughter, with its pasturelands, Libnah with its
pasturelands, [14] Jattir with its
pasturelands, Eshtemoa with
its pasturelands, [15] Holon with
its pasturelands, Debir with its
pasturelands, [16] Ain with its pasturelands, Juttah with its pasturelands, and Beth-shemesh
with its pasturelands—nine
cities from these two tribes.

[17] From the tribe of Benjamin they
gave:

Gibeon with its pasturelands,
Geba with its pasturelands,
[18] Anathoth with its pasturelands, and Almon with its pasturelands—four cities. [19] All 13
cities with their pasturelands
were for the priests, the descendants of Aaron.

Cities of Kohath's Other Descendants (21:20-26)

[20] The allotted cities to the remaining clans of Kohath's descendants,
who were Levites, came from the
tribe of Ephraim. [21] The Israelites
gave them:

Shechem, the city of refuge for
the one who commits man-
slaughter, with its pasturelands
in the hill country of Ephraim,
Gezer with its pasturelands,
[22] Kibzaim with its pasturelands, and Beth-horon with its
pasturelands—four cities.

[23] From the tribe of Dan they gave:

Elteke with its pasturelands,
Gibbethon with its pasturelands, [24] Aijalon with its pasturelands, and Gath-rimmon with
its pasturelands—four cities.

[25] From half the tribe of Manasseh
they gave:

Taanach with its pasturelands
and Gath-rimmon[A] with its
pasturelands—two cities.

[26] All 10 cities with their pasturelands were for the clans of Kohath's
other descendants.

Cities of Gershon's Descendants (21:27-33)

[27] From half the tribe of Manasseh,
they gave to the descendants of Gershon, who were one of the Levite
clans:

Golan, the city of refuge for the
one who commits manslaughter, with its pasturelands in
Bashan, and Beeshterah with
its pasturelands—two cities.

[28] From the tribe of Issachar they
gave:

Kishion with its pasturelands,
Daberath with its pasturelands,
[29] Jarmuth with its pasturelands, and En-gannim with its
pasturelands—four cities.

[30] From the tribe of Asher they gave:

Mishal with its pasturelands,
Abdon with its pasturelands,
[31] Helkath with its pasturelands, and Rehob with its pasturelands—four cities.

[32] From the tribe of Naphtali they
gave:

Kedesh in Galilee, the city of
refuge for the one who commits
manslaughter, with its pasturelands, Hammoth-dor with its

[A] **21:25** Or *Ibleam*

21:43-45 Everything the Lord promised them came to fruition. Not one thing that He promised was overlooked. Just as He had been with Moses, so He was with Joshua and the entire nation of Israel.

22:1-9 The theme of faithfulness is evident even in this treatment of the tribes. The men of Gad, Manasseh, and Reuben were faithful to the Lord and their brothers; the Lord was faithful to them by giving them the land; therefore, Joshua granted them permission not only to return home but also to go with great reward (v. 8).

22:10-34 When the rest of the nation thought this altar was erected against the instructions of the Lord, they prepared for battle. The text does not say that the eastern tribes planned to worship the false gods, which was assumed by their Israelite brothers. The Gadites, Reubenites, and the half-tribe of Manasseh did not plan to worship on their own terms but wanted a reminder for their descendants of their origins with the entire nation. Evidently, the three eastern tribes were keenly aware of the fact that the rest of Israel was capable of forgetting the Lord's commands.

pasturelands, and Kartan with its pasturelands—three cities.

33 All 13 cities with their pasturelands were for the Gershonites by their clans.

Cities of Merari's Descendants (21:34-42)

34 From the tribe of Zebulun, they gave to the clans of the descendants of Merari, who were the remaining Levites:

Jokneam with its pasturelands,
Kartah with its pasturelands,
35 Dimnah with its pasturelands, and Nahalal with its pasturelands—four cities.

36 From the tribe of Reuben they gave:

Bezer with its pasturelands,
Jahzah[A] with its pasturelands,
37 Kedemoth with its pasturelands, and Mephaath with its pasturelands—four cities.[B]

38 From the tribe of Gad they gave:

Ramoth in Gilead, the city of refuge for the one who commits manslaughter, with its pasturelands, Mahanaim with its pasturelands, 39 Heshbon with its pasturelands, and Jazer with its pasturelands—four cities in all. 40 All 12 cities were allotted to the clans of Merari's descendants, the remaining Levite clans.

41 Within the Israelite possession there were 48 cities in all with their pasturelands for the Levites. 42 Each of these cities had its own surrounding pasturelands; this was true for all the cities.

Fulfillment of the LORD's Promises (21:43-45)

43 So the LORD gave Israel all the land He had sworn to give their fathers, and they took possession of it and settled there. 44 The LORD gave them rest on every side according to all He had sworn to their fathers. None of their enemies were able to stand against them, for the LORD handed over all their enemies to them. 45 None of the good promises the LORD had made to the house of Israel failed. Everything was fulfilled.

Return Home of the Eastern Tribes (22:1-8)

22 Joshua summoned the Reubenites, Gadites, and half the tribe of Manasseh 2 and told them, "You have done everything Moses the LORD's servant commanded you and have obeyed me in everything I commanded you. 3 You have not deserted your brothers even once this whole time but have carried out the requirement of the command of the LORD your God. 4 Now that He has given your brothers rest, just as He promised them, return to your homes in your own land that Moses the LORD's servant gave you across the Jordan. 5 Only carefully obey the command and instruction that Moses the LORD's servant gave you: to love the LORD your God, walk in all His ways, keep His commands, remain faithful[C] to Him, and serve Him with all your heart and all your soul."

6 Joshua blessed them and sent them on their way, and they went to their homes. 7 Moses had given territory to half the tribe of Manasseh in Bashan, but Joshua had given territory to the other half,[D] with their brothers, on the west side of the Jordan. When Joshua sent them to their homes and blessed them, 8 he said, "Return to your homes with great wealth: a huge number of cattle, and silver, gold, bronze, iron, and a large quantity of clothing. Share the spoil of your enemies with your brothers."

Building of an Altar by the Eastern Tribes (22:9-12)

9 The Reubenites, Gadites, and half the tribe of Manasseh left the Israelites at Shiloh in the land of Canaan to return to their own land of Gilead, which they took possession of according to the LORD's command through Moses. 10 When they came to the region of[E] the Jordan in the land of Canaan, the Reubenites, Gadites, and half the tribe of Manasseh built a large, impressive altar there by the Jordan.

11 Then the Israelites heard it said, "Look, the Reubenites, Gadites, and

[A] **21:36** Or *Jahaz* [B] **21:36-37** Some Hb mss omit these vv. [C] **22:5** Lit *commands, hold on* [D] **22:7** Lit *to his half* [E] **22:10** Or *to Geliloth by*

half the tribe of Manasseh have built an altar on the frontier of the land of Canaan at the region of[A] the Jordan, on the Israelite side." 12 When the Israelites heard this, the entire Israelite community assembled at Shiloh to go to war against them.

Explanation of the Altar (22:13-29)

13 The Israelites sent Phinehas son of Eleazar the priest to the Reubenites, Gadites, and half the tribe of Manasseh, in the land of Gilead. 14 They sent 10 leaders with him—one family leader for each tribe of Israel. All of them were heads of their families among the clans of Israel. 15 They went to the Reubenites, Gadites, and half the tribe of Manasseh, in the land of Gilead, and told them, 16 "This is what the LORD's entire community says: 'What is this treachery you have committed today against the God of Israel by turning away from the LORD and building an altar for yourselves, so that you are in rebellion against the LORD today? 17 Wasn't the sin of Peor, which brought a plague on the LORD's community, enough for us, so that we have not cleansed ourselves from it even to this day, 18 and now, you would turn away from the LORD? If you rebel against the LORD today, tomorrow He will be angry with the entire community of Israel. 19 But if the land you possess is defiled, cross over to the land the LORD possesses where the LORD's tabernacle stands, and take possession of it among us. But don't rebel against the LORD or against us by building for yourselves an altar other than the altar of the LORD our God. 20 Wasn't Achan son of Zerah unfaithful regarding what was •set apart for destruction, bringing wrath on the entire community of Israel? He was not the only one who perished because of his sin.'"

21 The Reubenites, Gadites, and half the tribe of Manasseh answered the leaders of the Israelite clans, 22 "•Yahweh is the God of gods! Yahweh is the God of gods![B] He knows, and may Israel also know. Do not spare us today, if it was in rebellion or treachery against the LORD 23 that we have built for ourselves an altar to turn away from Him. May the LORD Himself hold us accountable if we intended to offer •burnt offerings and •grain offerings on it, or to sacrifice •fellowship offerings on it. 24 We actually did this from a specific concern that in the future your descendants might say to our descendants, 'What relationship do you have with the LORD, the God of Israel? 25 For the LORD has made the Jordan a border between us and you descendants of Reuben and Gad. You have no share in the LORD!' So your descendants may cause our descendants to stop fearing the LORD.

26 "Therefore we said: Let us take action and build an altar for ourselves, but not for burnt offering or sacrifice. 27 Instead, it is to be a witness between us and you, and between the generations after us, so that we may carry out the worship of the LORD in His presence with our burnt offerings, sacrifices, and fellowship offerings. Then in the future, your descendants will not be able to say to our descendants, 'You have no share in the LORD!' 28 We thought that if they said this to us or to our generations in the future, we would reply: Look at the replica of the LORD's altar that our fathers made, not for burnt offering or sacrifice, but as a witness between us and you. 29 We would never rebel against the LORD or turn away from Him today by building an altar for burnt offering, grain offering, or sacrifice, other than the altar of the LORD our God, which is in front of His tabernacle."

Conflict Resolution (22:30-34)

30 When Phinehas the priest and the community leaders, the heads of Israel's clans who were with him, heard what the descendants of Reuben, Gad, and Manasseh had to say, they were pleased. 31 Phinehas son of Eleazar the priest said to the descendants of Reuben, Gad, and Manasseh, "Today we know that the LORD is among us, because you have not committed this treachery against Him. As a result, you have

22:27-29 The altar was built out of fear that future descendants would not include the eastern tribes as a part of the Israelites. This kind of concern by the eastern tribes hints at the coming period of the judges, in which everyone did whatever he wanted (Jdg 21:25).

[A]**22:11** Or *at Geliloth by* [B]**22:22** Or *The Mighty One, God, the LORD! The Mighty One, God, the LORD!*, or *God, the LORD God! God, the LORD God!*

23:1-11 Just as the last words of Moses were central at the end of Deuteronomy (Dt 32:1-43; 33:1-29), Joshua's final instructions mark a key turning point in Israel's history. Joshua did not appoint a successor. After his death, Israel was to function as a theocracy with Yahweh as their Supreme Ruler and Defender. Joshua repeatedly called Israel's attention to who God is and what He had done, for Israel's existence and identity existed in the Lord.

23:12-16 The covenant between Yahweh and Israel clearly demanded that the Israelites must have no god but Him (Ex 20:3-5; Dt 5:7-9). To intermingle and intermarry with these people, whom God intended to remove because of their degrading worship practices and pluralism, was intolerable since God's people would thereby be led away from Him and into sin.

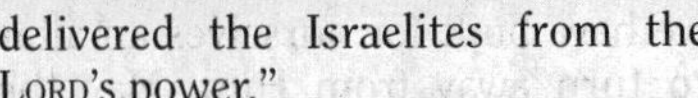

delivered the Israelites from the
LORD's power."
[32]Then Phinehas son of Eleazar
the priest and the leaders returned
from the Reubenites and Gadites in
the land of Gilead to the Israelites
in the land of Canaan and brought
back a report to them. [33]The Israelites were pleased with the report,
and they praised God. They spoke
no more about going to war against
them to ravage the land where the
Reubenites and Gadites lived. [34]So
the Reubenites and Gadites named
the altar: It[A] is a witness between us
that the LORD is God.

Joshua's Final Words (23:1–24:13)

Joshua's Farewell Address (23:1-16)

23 A long time after the LORD had
given Israel rest from all the
enemies around them, Joshua was
old, getting on in years. [2]So Joshua
summoned all Israel, including its
elders, leaders, judges, and officers,
and said to them, "I am old, getting
on in years, [3]and you have seen for
yourselves everything the LORD your
God did to all these nations on your
account, because it was the LORD
your God who was fighting for you.
[4]See, I have allotted these remaining nations to you as an inheritance
for your tribes, including all the
nations I have destroyed, from the
Jordan westward to the Mediterranean Sea. [5]The LORD your God will
force them back on your account
and drive them out before you so
that you can take possession of their
land, as the LORD your God promised
you.
[6]"Be very strong and continue
obeying all that is written in the
book of the law of Moses, so that
you do not turn from it to the right
or left [7]and so that you do not associate with these nations remaining among you. Do not call on the
names of their gods or make an oath
to them; do not worship them or
bow down to them. [8]Instead, remain
faithful to the LORD your God, as you
have done to this day.
[9]"The LORD has driven out great
and powerful nations before you, and
no one is able to stand against you to
this day. [10]One of you routed a thousand because the LORD your God was
fighting for you, as He promised.[B]
[11]So be very diligent to love the LORD
your God for your own well-being.
[12]For if you turn away and cling to
the rest of these nations remaining
among you, and if you intermarry or
associate with them and they with
you, [13]know for certain that the LORD
your God will not continue to drive
these nations out before you. They
will become a snare and a trap for
you, a scourge for your sides and
thorns in your eyes, until you disappear from this good land the LORD
your God has given you.
[14]"I am now going the way of all
the earth,[C] and you know with all
your heart and all your soul that
none of the good promises the LORD
your God made to you has failed.
Everything was fulfilled for you;
not one promise has failed. [15]Since
every good thing the LORD your
God promised you has come about,
so He will bring on you every bad
thing until He has annihilated you
from this good land the LORD your
God has given you. [16]If you break
the covenant of the LORD your God,
which He commanded you, and go
and worship other gods, and bow
down to them, the LORD's anger

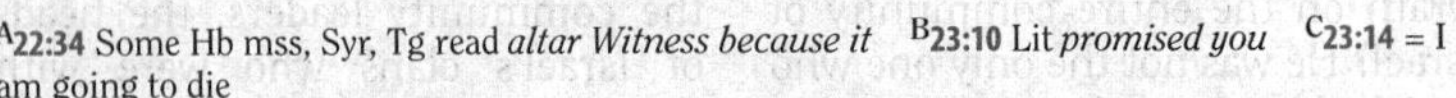

[A]**22:34** Some Hb mss, Syr, Tg read *altar Witness because it* [B]**23:10** Lit *promised you* [C]**23:14** = I am going to die

>WORD|*study*

23:13 Joshua cautioned that for the Israelites, **these nations** would **become**:

- A snare (Hb *pach*), literally a "net" spread out to trap birds. Metaphorically, as "a snare" an idolatrous nation might appear harmless, but blindly incorporating these cultures would cost Israel her life with Yahweh (Pr 7:23).
- A trap (Hb *moqēsh*), literally a "noose or snare" for capturing wild animals or birds. Metaphorically, it refers not only to a means of subjecting to control what is otherwise free (Pss 140:5; 141:9) but also to that which causes injury or death (2Sm 22:6; Ps 18:5).
- A scourge [Hb *shotēt*, "whip"] **for your sides** figuratively indicates punishment.
- Thorns [Hb *tsanin*, "prick"; cp. Nm 33:55] **in your eyes**, which is more literally "puncture or cause pain," or figuratively, "obstacles" (cp. Hb *tsēn*, "barb").

Doctrine MESSIANIC PROPHECY

That the judgment for turning away from the Lord and failing to love Him would be **a scourge for** [their] **sides and thorns in** [their] **eyes** is no random statement (23:13; cp. Nm 33:55). Among the many agonies endured by the Son of God was a brutal Roman scourging and a crown of thorns (Mk 15:15,17). Within the prophecy of Israel's failure is also a prophecy of hope: "Christ has redeemed us from the curse of the law by becoming a curse for us" (Gl 3:13). At His crucifixion, the Messiah received all that we deserved for our failure to love God as He deserves.

will burn against you, and you will quickly disappear from this good land He has given you."

Review of Israel's History (24:1-13)

24 Joshua assembled all the tribes of Israel at Shechem and summoned Israel's elders, leaders, judges, and officers, and they presented themselves before God. 2 Joshua said to all the people, "This is what the LORD, the God of Israel, says: 'Long ago your ancestors, including Terah, the father of Abraham and Nahor, lived beyond the Euphrates River and worshiped other gods. 3 But I took your father Abraham from the region beyond the Euphrates River, led him throughout the land of Canaan, and multiplied his descendants. I gave him Isaac, 4 and to Isaac I gave Jacob and Esau. I gave the hill country of Seir to Esau as a possession, but Jacob and his sons went down to Egypt.

5 "'Then I sent Moses and Aaron; I plagued Egypt by what I did there and afterward I brought you out. 6 When I brought your fathers out of Egypt and you reached the •Red Sea, the Egyptians pursued your fathers with chariots and horsemen as far as the sea. 7 Your fathers cried out to the LORD, so He put darkness between you and the Egyptians, and brought the sea over them, engulfing them. Your own eyes saw what I did to Egypt. After that, you lived in the wilderness a long time.

8 "'Later, I brought you to the land of the Amorites who lived beyond the Jordan. They fought against you, but I handed them over to you. You possessed their land, and I annihilated them before you. 9 Balak son of Zippor, king of Moab, set out to fight against Israel. He sent for Balaam son of Beor to curse you, 10 but I would not listen to Balaam. Instead, he repeatedly blessed you, and I delivered you from his hand.

11 "'You then crossed the Jordan and came to Jericho. The people of Jericho—as well as the Amorites, Perizzites, Canaanites, Hittites, Girgashites, Hivites, and Jebusites—fought against you, but I handed them over to you. 12 I sent the hornet[A] ahead of you, and it drove out the two Amorite kings before you. It was not by your sword or bow. 13 I gave you a land you did not labor for, and cities you did not build, though you live in them; you are eating from vineyards and olive groves you did not plant.'

A Renewal of the Covenant (24:14-33)

The Covenant Renewal (24:14-28)

14 "Therefore, •fear the LORD and worship Him in sincerity and truth. Get rid of the gods your fathers worshiped beyond the Euphrates River and in Egypt, and worship •Yahweh. 15 But if it doesn't please you to worship Yahweh, choose for yourselves today the one you will worship: the gods your fathers worshiped beyond the Euphrates River or the gods of the Amorites in whose land you are living. As for me and my family, we will worship Yahweh."

16 The people replied, "We will certainly not abandon the LORD to worship other gods! 17 For the LORD our God brought us and our fathers out of the land of Egypt, out of the place of slavery, and performed these great signs before our eyes. He also protected us all along the way we went and among all the peoples whose lands we traveled through. 18 The LORD drove out before us all the peoples, including the Amorites who lived in the land. We too will worship the LORD, because He is our God."

19 But Joshua told the people, "You will not be able to worship Yahweh, because He is a holy God. He is a

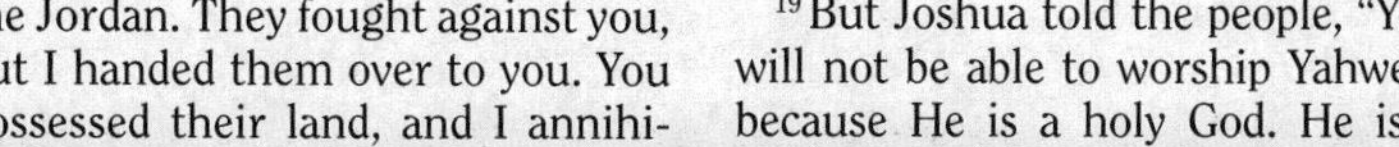

[A]**24:12** Or *sent terror*

24:1-13 Shechem had historic significance for Israel. God had first promised Abraham to give his "offspring" the land then occupied by the Canaanites (Gn 12:6-7), and Jacob had purchased a piece of land and set up an altar there (Jos 24:32; cp. Gn 33:18-20).

24:2-13 The Lord reminded His people of their history—how He had established and pursued them to be His own. Ultimately, they had no history apart from Him. Without Him, they were nothing. Therefore, their ability to live in the promised land was dependent on remembering this truth.

24:14-18 To serve Yahweh necessitates the rejection and removal of all other competing loyalties. The choice laid before Israel at this juncture was to **worship** *either* **Yahweh**, Who had demonstrated His faithfulness to Israel throughout her history, *or* the idols of the nations (v. 15). There is no middle ground (Jn 3:18; Rv 3:15-16). Life in the promised land was to be an intentional choice of worship, in full recognition of what the Lord had done.

24:19-28 Despite their verbal commitment to worship Yahweh exclusively, Joshua, who knew people's tendencies toward evil and deception, warned them that they were incapable of keeping their promises. The warning that God would not forgive the Israelites' **transgressions and sins** does not contradict His eternal commitment to bring about redemption and to offer forgiveness of all sin through Jesus Christ. Repentance is the prerequisite for receiving God's forgiveness. To reject a relationship with God on His terms is to forfeit His forgiveness. Because God is holy and just, He cannot leave rebellion unpunished (Heb 10:26-27).

24:29-33 With the passing of these leaders, the Israelites began functioning solely under the leadership of the Lord through the priests. The next phase for the nation of Israel is the period of the judges, which was very unlike the first days in the promised land.

>WORD|*study*

24:19-20 Two aspects of God's character warranted Joshua's foreboding statement (24:19-20): First, God is holy (Hb *qadosh*, "set apart, sacred; pure, clean, free from defilement"). Sinful human beings cannot approach the perfection of God's holiness (Rm 3:9-31; 5:18; 8:1-17). Only the sinless Christ is worthy to be called "holy" (1Sm 2:2; Pss 71:22; 78:41; Is 6:3-5; 30:15; Jn 6:69; Ac 3:14; 4:27-30; Heb 7:26-28; Rv 3:7; 4:8; 15:4). Second, God is jealous (Hb *qanno'*, "intolerant of rivalry or unfaithfulness"). This form of the word is found only here and in Nahum 1:2.

jealous God; He will not remove
your transgressions and sins. 20 If you
abandon the LORD and worship foreign gods, He will turn against you,
harm you, and completely destroy
you, after He has been good to you."
21 "No!" the people answered Joshua. "We will worship the LORD."
22 Joshua then told the people,
"You are witnesses against yourselves that you yourselves have chosen to worship Yahweh."
"We are witnesses," they said.
23 "Then get rid of the foreign gods
that are among you and offer your
hearts to the LORD, the God of Israel."
24 So the people said to Joshua,
"We will worship the LORD our God
and obey Him."
25 On that day Joshua made a covenant for the people at Shechem and
established a statute and ordinance
for them. 26 Joshua recorded these
things in the book of the law of God;
he also took a large stone and set it
up there under the oak next to the
sanctuary of the LORD. 27 And Joshua
said to all the people, "You see this
stone—it will be a witness against
us, for it has heard all the words the
LORD said to us, and it will be a witness against you, so that you will not
deny your God." 28 Then Joshua sent
the people away, each to his own inheritance.

Burial of Three Leaders (24:29-33)

29 After these things, the LORD's
servant, Joshua son of Nun, died at
the age of 110. 30 They buried him in
his allotted territory at Timnath-serah, in the hill country of Ephraim
north of Mount Gaash. 31 Israel worshiped Yahweh throughout Joshua's
lifetime and during the lifetimes of
the elders who outlived Joshua and
who had experienced all the works
Yahweh had done for Israel.
32 Joseph's bones, which the Israelites had brought up from Egypt,
were buried at Shechem in the parcel
of land Jacob had purchased from the
sons of Hamor, Shechem's father, for
100 *qesitahs*.[A] It was an inheritance
for Joseph's descendants.
33 And Eleazar son of Aaron died,
and they buried him at Gibeah,[B]
which had been given to his son
Phinehas in the hill country of
Ephraim.

[A]24:32 The value of this currency is unknown. [B]24:33 = the Hill

JOSHUA... WRITTEN ON MY *Heart*

Just as God promised to be with Joshua, He has promised to be with us (Jos 1:5; Mt 28:20). Like Israel, our enemies are defeated foes. The Lord Jesus not only nailed our record of debt to the cross, He also disarmed and publicly disgraced our enemies when He triumphed over them (Col 2:14-15). Like Israel, we have been given an inheritance, His "very great and precious promises" (2Pt 1:4). And, like Israel, we must "walk worthy of the Lord, fully pleasing to Him, bearing fruit in every good work and growing in the knowledge of God" (Col 1:10).

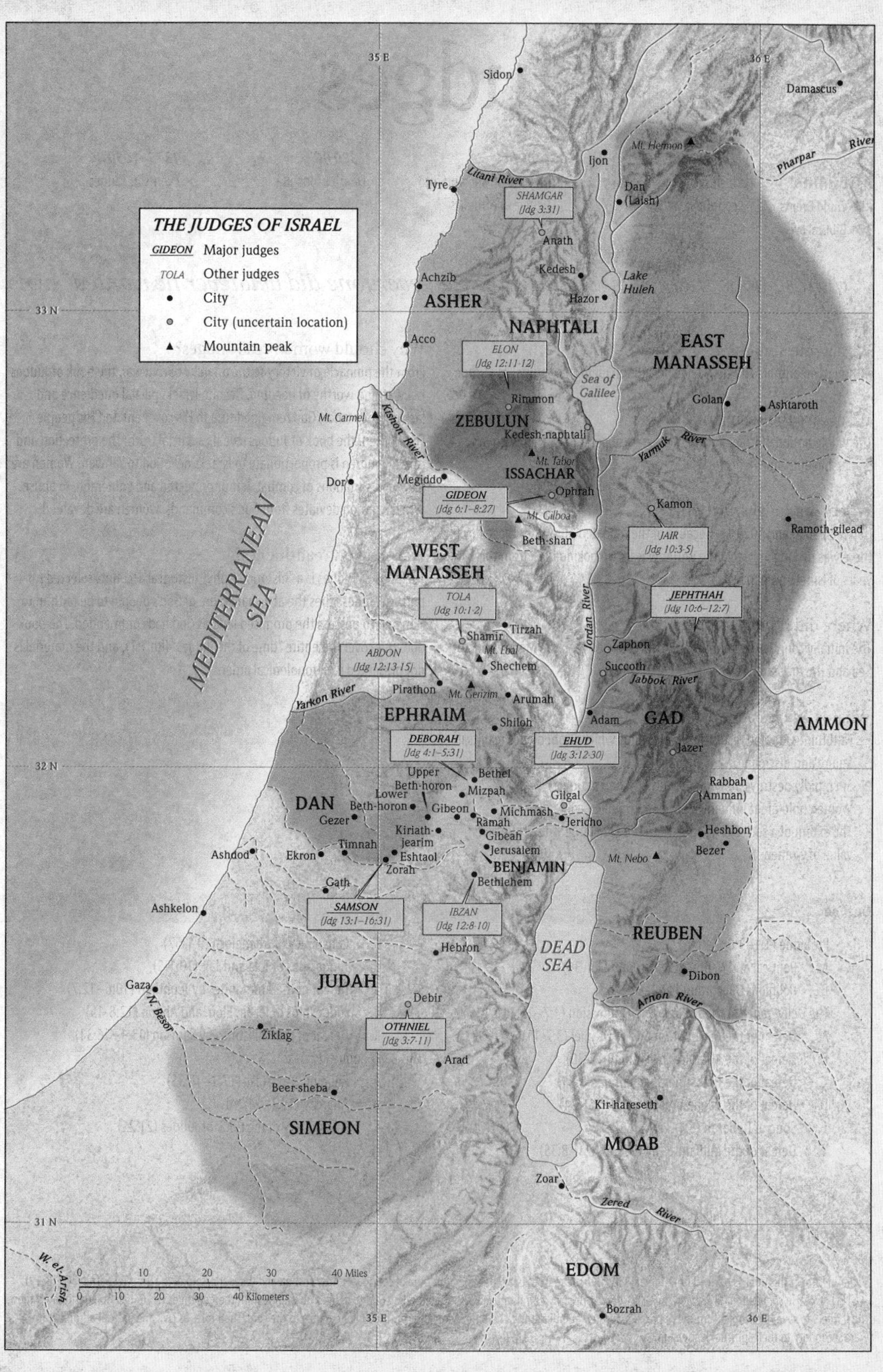
THE JUDGES OF ISRAEL
GIDEON Major judges
TOLA Other judges
City
City (uncertain location)
Mountain peak
MEDITERRANEAN SEA
SHAMGAR (Jdg 3:31)
ELON (Jdg 12:11-12)
GIDEON (Jdg 6:1–8:27)
JAIR (Jdg 10:3-5)
TOLA (Jdg 10:1-2)
JEPHTHAH (Jdg 10:6–12:7)
ABDON (Jdg 12:13-15)
DEBORAH (Jdg 4:1–5:31)
EHUD (Jdg 3:12-30)
SAMSON (Jdg 13:1–16:31)
IBZAN (Jdg 12:8-10)
OTHNIEL (Jdg 3:7-11)
ASHER
NAPHTALI
ZEBULUN
ISSACHAR
WEST MANASSEH
EAST MANASSEH
EPHRAIM
DAN
BENJAMIN
JUDAH
SIMEON
GAD
REUBEN
AMMON
MOAB
EDOM
Sidon
Damascus
Tyre
Litani River
Mt. Hermon
Pharpar River
Ijon
Dan (Laish)
Anath
Kedesh
Lake Huleh
Hazor
Achzib
Acco
Sea of Galilee
Rimmon
Golan
Ashtaroth
Mt. Carmel
Kishon River
Kedesh-naphtali
Yarmuk River
Mt. Tabor
Dor
Megiddo
Ophrah
Kamon
Mt. Gilboa
Beth-shan
Ramoth-gilead
Jordan River
Shamir
Tirzah
Mt. Ebal
Zaphon
Shechem
Succoth
Jabbok River
Pirathon
Mt. Gerizim
Arumah
Yarkon River
Adam
Shiloh
Jazer
Upper Beth-horon
Bethel
Lower Beth-horon
Mizpah
Gilgal
Rabbah (Amman)
Gezer
Gibeon
Michmash
Ramah
Jericho
Kiriath-jearim
Gibeah
Heshbon
Timnah
Ashdod
Ekron
Eshtaol
Jerusalem
Bezer
Zorah
Mt. Nebo
Gath
Bethlehem
Ashkelon
Hebron
DEAD SEA
Dibon
Gaza
N. Besor
Debir
Arnon River
Ziklag
Arad
Beer-sheba
Kir-hareseth
Zoar
Zered River
Bozrah
W. el-Arish
33 N
32 N
31 N
35 E
36 E
0 10 20 30 40 Miles
0 10 20 30 40 Kilometers

Judges

Timeline	1406–1400 BC	1385 BC	1380 BC	1375–1050 BC
World Events Biblical Events	Joshua's campaigns of conquest	Division of the land into twelve allotments	Death of Joshua	Events in Judges

"In those days there was no king in Israel; everyone did whatever he wanted" (21:25).

Who wrote Judges?

Although no author is named, Jewish tradition identifies Samuel as author.

Who were the recipients?

The whole nation of Israel during the historical period between Joshua's leadership and Saul's kingship

When was Judges written?

Between 1040 and 1020 B.C. Because of the repeated phrase "in those days there was no king in Israel," the writer was likely looking back from the years of Israel's monarchy.

Where did it happen?

The initially conquered promised land, located between the Mediterranean Sea and the Arabian Desert

What is Judges about?

- Faithfulness to God results in His blessings while disobedience results in failure and discipline.
- Sin rapidly destroys individuals, families, and nations.
- Women hold great influence, either for good or evil.
- The extent of a society's obedience to the Lord largely determines its value of women.

Why should women read Judges?

From the pinnacle of victory to the anarchy of civil war, the book of Judges is a warning worthy of heeding. Despite Israel's partial obedience and lack of repentance, God remained true to His covenant and His people. For women, the book of Judges reveals a crucial truth: The protection and care of women is proportionate to Israel's devotion to Yahweh. Women are placed in situations of combat, left unprotected and vulnerable to abuse. When a nation deviates from God's commands, women are devalued.

How do you read Judges?

The book of Judges is a "historiography," historical accounts selected for a purpose. It describes the abysmal failure of God's people to be faithful to Him and to possess the promised land as God had commanded. The book does not cover the entire "time of the judges" (Ru 1:1), and the material is not presented in chronological order.

Outline

I. Prologue (1:1–3:6)
   - A. Political and Military Background (1:1-36)
   - B. Religious Background (2:1–3:6)

II. The Deliverance of the Judges from Oppression (3:7–16:31)
   - A. Defeat of the Mesopotamians by Othniel (3:7-11)
   - B. Defeat of the Moabites by Ehud (3:12-30)
   - C. Defeat of the Philistines by Shamgar (3:31)
   - D. Defeat of the Canaanites by Barak (4:1-24)
   - E. Song of Deborah (5:1-31)
   - F. Defeat of the Midianites by Gideon (6:1–8:35)
   - G. Conspiracy of Abimelech (9:1-57)
   - H. Judgeships of Tola and Jair (10:1-5)
   - I. Defeat of the Ammonites by Jephthah (10:6–12:7)
   - J. Judgeships of Ibzan, Elon, and Abdon (12:8-15)
   - K. Defeat of the Philistines by Samson (13:1–16:31)

III. Epilogue (17:1–21:25)
   - A. Religious Apostasy (17:1–18:35)
   - B. Anarchy (19:1–21:24)
   - C. A Summary of the Book of Judges (21:25)

>WORD|*study*

Title The title of this book is derived from the activity of the leaders of Israel between the time of conquest under Joshua and the leadership of the prophet Samuel (2:16-19). Judges (Hb *shophetim*; Gk *kritai* in the LXX) served primarily as military leaders appointed by God to deliver His people from their enemies (2:16-17). God designated these tribal rulers to save His people from the oppression of their enemies and to lead the people to continue in obedience to the Lord. Their roles as civil and judicial administrators were secondary to their spiritual leadership.

1320 BC	1170 BC	1175–1125 BC	1120–1060 BC
Deborah and Barak defeat the Canaanites.	Jephthah defeats the Ammonites and Philistines.	Life of Ruth	Life of Samson

Prologue (1:1–3:6)

Political and Military Background (1:1-36)

1 After the death of Joshua, the
Israelites inquired of the LORD,
"Who will be the first to fight for us
against the Canaanites?"
2 The LORD answered, "Judah is to
go. I have handed the land over to
him."
3 Judah said to his brother Simeon,
"Come with me to my territory, and
let us fight against the Canaanites.
I will also go with you to your territory." So Simeon went with him.
4 When Judah attacked, the LORD
handed the Canaanites and Perizzites over to them. They struck
down 10,000 men in Bezek. 5 They
found Adoni-bezek in Bezek, fought
against him, and struck down the
Canaanites and Perizzites.
6 When Adoni-bezek fled, they pursued him, seized him, and cut off his
thumbs and big toes. 7 Adoni-bezek
said, "Seventy kings with their
thumbs and big toes cut off used to
pick up scraps[A] under my table. God
has repaid me for what I have done."
They brought him to Jerusalem, and
he died there.
8 The men of Judah fought against
Jerusalem and captured it. They
put the city to the sword and set it
on fire. 9 Afterward, the men of Judah marched down to fight against
the Canaanites who were living
in the hill country, the •Negev, and
the Judean foothills.[B] 10 Judah also
marched against the Canaanites
who were living in Hebron (Hebron was formerly named Kiriath-
arba). They struck down Sheshai,
Ahiman, and Talmai. 11 From there
they marched against the residents
of Debir (Debir was formerly named
Kiriath-sepher).
12 Caleb said, "Whoever strikes
down and captures Kiriath-sepher,
I will give my daughter Achsah to
him as a wife." 13 So Othniel son of
Kenaz, Caleb's youngest brother,
captured it, and Caleb gave his
daughter Achsah to him as his wife.
14 When she arrived, she persuaded Othniel[C] to ask her father for a
field. As she got off her donkey, Caleb asked her,[D] "What do you want?"
15 She answered him, "Give me a
blessing. Since you have given me
land in the Negev, give me springs of
water also." So Caleb gave her both
the upper and lower springs.[E]
16 The descendants of the Kenite,
Moses' father-in-law, had gone up
with the men of Judah from the City
of Palms[F] to the Wilderness of Judah, which was in the Negev of Arad.
They went to live among the people.
17 Judah went with his brother
Simeon, struck the Canaanites
who were living in Zephath, and
•completely destroyed the town.
So they named the town Hormah.
18 Judah captured Gaza and its territory, Ashkelon and its territory,
and Ekron and its territory.[G] 19 The
LORD was with Judah and enabled
them to take possession of the hill
country, but they could not drive
out the people who were living in

1:1-2 At the beginning of Israel's time in the land, the nation rightly **inquired of the LORD** for direction.

1:6-7 This common ancient Near Eastern practice humiliated the prisoner and prevented him from running away. Although God handed the Canaanites over to the Israelites to be conquered, Israel demonstrated the surrounding pagan culture's influence by treating their enemies according to Canaanite custom rather than God's commands (Dt 7:1-2; 20:16-17).

1:12-13 A woman's parents often arranged her marriage to a suitable man. While women had little voice in these matters, there is no evidence that they inherently felt devalued because of their father's decisions. As is clear elsewhere in Judges, father-rule ("patriarchy") is not the inherent culprit for the plight of women. Rather, the misuse of this family and social structure leads to such mistreatment.

1:14-15 Achsah was honored when a man paid her bride price with military conquest. She initiated the request for a property with a water source to her father Caleb, and he honored her with **both the upper and the lower springs**. Achsah's honorable treatment during the time of Israel's initial obedience sharply contrasts the barbaric treatment of women in Jdg 19–20 during Israel's disobedience.

A 1:7 Lit *toes are gathering* B 1:9 Or *the Shephelah* C 1:14 LXX reads *arrived, he pressured her* D 1:14 LXX reads . . . *field. She grumbled while on the donkey, and she cried out from the donkey, "Into the southland you sent me out," and Caleb said* E 1:15 LXX reads *give me redemption of water, and Caleb gave her according to her heart the redemption of the upper and the redemption of the lower* F 1:16 = Jericho; Dt 34:3; Jdg 3:13; 2Ch 28:15 G 1:18 LXX reads *Judah did not inherit Gaza and its borders nor Ashkelon and its borders nor Ekron and its borders nor Azotus and its surrounding lands*

1:27-36 Israel not only failed to take the land, but they also allowed the Canaanites to live among them, directly disobeying God's commands. This abbreviated account is the backdrop of the entire book. Because the nation failed to obey God completely, the tribes that employed the Canaanites as forced labor were eventually controlled by the very enemy they believed they had subdued.

2:1-3 The Angel of the Lord is likely the preincarnate Christ, since He speaks in the first person of God's deliverance. He reminded Israel of God's mighty works on their behalf and His covenant faithfulness. He then confronted them with their dual sin—making a covenant with the Canaanites and not tearing down their pagan altars.

the valley because those people had iron chariots.[A]

20 Judah gave Hebron to Caleb, just as Moses had promised. Then Caleb drove out the three sons of Anak who lived there.[B]

21 At the same time the Benjaminites did not drive out the Jebusites who were living in Jerusalem. The Jebusites have lived among the Benjaminites in Jerusalem to this day.

22 The house of Joseph also attacked Bethel, and the Lord was with them. 23 They sent spies to Bethel (the town was formerly named Luz). 24 The spies saw a man coming out of the town and said to him, "Please show us how to get into town, and we will treat you well." 25 When he showed them the way into the town, they put the town to the sword but released the man and his entire family. 26 Then the man went to the land of the Hittites, built a town, and named it Luz. That is its name to this day.

27 At that time Manasseh failed to take possession of Beth-shean[C] and its villages,[D] or Taanach and its villages, or the residents of Dor and its villages, or the residents of Ibleam[E] and its villages, or the residents of Megiddo and its villages; the Canaanites refused to leave[F] this land. 28 When Israel became stronger, they made the Canaanites serve as forced labor but never drove them out completely.

29 At that time Ephraim failed to drive out the Canaanites who were living in Gezer, so the Canaanites have lived among them in Gezer.[G]

30 Zebulun failed to drive out the residents of Kitron or the residents of Nahalol, so the Canaanites lived among them and served as forced labor.

31 Asher failed to drive out the residents of Acco[H] or of Sidon, or Ahlab, Achzib, Helbah, Aphik, or Rehob. 32 The Asherites lived among the Canaanites who were living in the land, because they failed to drive them out.

33 Naphtali did not drive out the residents of Beth-shemesh or the residents of Beth-anath. They lived among the Canaanites who were living in the land, but the residents of Beth-shemesh and Beth-anath served as their forced labor.

34 The Amorites forced the Danites into the hill country and did not allow them to go down into the valley. 35 The Amorites refused to leave[I] Har-heres, Aijalon, and Shaalbim. When the house of Joseph got the upper hand,[J] the Amorites[K] were made to serve as forced labor. 36 The territory of the Amorites extended from the Ascent of Akrabbim, that is from Sela upward.

Religious Background (2:1–3:6)

2 The Angel of the Lord went up from Gilgal to Bochim[L] and said, "I brought you out of Egypt and led

[A]1:19 LXX reads *hill country, for they were not able to drive out the residents of the valley because Rechab separated it* [B]1:20 LXX reads *And he inherited from there the three cities of the sons of Anak.* [C]1:27 LXX reads *Beth-shean, which is a Scythian city* [D]1:27 LXX reads *its villages or the fields around it* [E]1:27 LXX reads *Balaam* [F]1:27 LXX reads *Canaanites began to live in* [G]1:29 LXX reads *Gezer, and became forced labor* [H]1:31 LXX reads *Acco, and they became for him forced labor and the residents of Dor* [I]1:35 Or *Amorites determined to live in* [J]1:35 Lit *When the hand of the house of Joseph was heavy* [K]1:35 LXX reads *Joseph became strong on the Amorites, they* [L]2:1 LXX reads *to the weeping place and to Bethel and to the house of Israel*

Biblical Womanhood Teaching the Next Generation

The new generation of Israelites did not know the Lord or obey His Word (2:10). How tragic that the generation led by Joshua saw such miracles at the hand of God yet failed to instill in their children a living faith. Every generation must develop a personal faith. Parents are responsible for teaching their children spiritual truths and encouraging them in spiritual growth. The neglect of parental responsibility carries heavy consequences, as seen in the weak and superstitious faith of the Israelites. Instructions to parents were clear: The words of the Law were to be taught every day at every moment and lived before the children by their parents (Dt 6:4-9). While Christian schools can be an enrichment to a child's faith, teaching and modeling the Christian faith remains the primary responsibility of parents and family.

>WORD|*study*

2:11-13 Baal, meaning, "lord, master, owner or husband," is the Canaanite name for Hadad, a Syrian god of storms and war. That diverse forms of this god were worshiped is implied by its plural. Astoreth, a fertility goddess, was Baal's consort. Pagan worship consisted of orgies conducted in elevated areas in order to be closer to the gods. God commanded Israel to tear down "the high places," destroying these abominable practices (Nm 33:52). Since God continually compared His covenant with Israel to a marriage, worshiping Baal was compared to spiritual adultery.

you into the land I had promised to
your fathers. I also said: I will never
break My covenant with you. 2 You
are not to make a covenant with the
people who are living in this land,
and you are to tear down their altars.[A] But you have not obeyed Me.
What is this you have done? 3 Therefore, I now say: I will not drive out
these people before you. They will
be thorns[B,C] in your sides, and their
gods will be a trap for you." 4 When
the Angel of the LORD had spoken
these words to all the Israelites, the
people wept loudly. 5 So they named
that place Bochim[D] and offered sacrifices there to the LORD.
6 Joshua sent the people away, and
the Israelites went to take possession of the land, each to his own
inheritance. 7 The people worshiped
the LORD throughout Joshua's lifetime and during the lifetimes of the
elders who outlived[E] Joshua. They
had seen all the LORD's great works
He had done for Israel.
8 Joshua son of Nun, the servant
of the LORD, died at the age of 110.
9 They buried him in the territory of
his inheritance, in Timnath-heres,
in the hill country of Ephraim,
north of Mount Gaash. 10 That
whole generation was also gathered
to their ancestors. After them another generation rose up who did
not know the LORD or the works He
had done for Israel.
11 The Israelites did what was evil
in the LORD's sight. They worshiped
the •Baals 12 and abandoned the
LORD, the God of their fathers, who
had brought them out of Egypt.
They went after other gods from
the surrounding peoples and bowed
down to them. They infuriated the
LORD, 13 for they abandoned Him
and worshiped Baal and the •Ash-
toreths.
14 The LORD's anger burned against
Israel, and He handed them over to
marauders who raided them. He
sold them to[F] the enemies around
them, and they could no longer resist their enemies. 15 Whenever the
Israelites went out, the LORD[G] was
against them and brought disaster
on them, just as He had promised
and sworn to them. So they suffered greatly.
16 The LORD raised up judges, who
saved them from the power of their
marauders, 17 but they did not listen to their judges. Instead, they
prostituted themselves with other
gods, bowing down to them. They
quickly turned from the way of
their fathers, who had walked in
obedience to the LORD's commands.
They did not do as their fathers

Doctrine THE BELIEVER'S OBEDIENCE

God commanded the Israelites to drive the Canaanites from the land and to possess it for themselves according to His promise to Abraham. However, they did not follow the word of the Lord and thus failed their first test after the death of Joshua. Israel failed to obey the Lord completely, primarily due to spiritual apathy (2:1-3). The people had little spiritual hunger or motivation for the things of God, which translated into disobedience. As the prophet Samuel said to the disobedient King Saul, "To obey is better than sacrifice," (1Sm 15:22). According to Scripture, partial obedience is disobedience. Failure to follow through in obedience to God's commands results in spiritual failure. The Holy Spirit residing within believers empowers them to follow Christ fully. His Spirit is at work in you "enabling you both to desire and to work out His good purpose" (Php 2:13). If you have been crucified with Christ, Jesus' record of perfect obedience has been credited to your account; sin's power has been broken in your life; and you are freed to obey out of love for and devotion to God (Rm 5:16-19; 6:1-2,6,11-14; Col 1:13-22).

2:3-4 Because of the people's rebellion, God withdrew His protection. While God would not break His eternal covenant, He would punish His children to draw them back to Him. The people found that disobedience to God brought destruction and sorrow. Although the people responded with great emotion and even sacrifices, they did not repent. The evidence of true repentance is turning from sin and embracing a changed life.

2:6-7 This flashback connects Joshua's generation to the new generation who were to possess the land. The new generation did not know the Lord in a personal, experiential sense. While they were aware of His past works, they did not have personal faith and trust in Yahweh God.

2:11-19 This passage summarizes the cycle of sin and deliverance within the book of Judges.

[A]**2:2** LXX reads *with those lying in wait in this land; neither are you to fall down in worship to their gods, but their carved images you must break to pieces and their altars you must destroy* [B]**2:3** LXX reads *affliction* [C]**2:3** Lit *traps* [D]**2:5** Or *Weeping* [E]**2:7** Lit *extended their days after* [F]**2:14** Lit *into the hand of* [G]**2:15** Lit *the hand of the LORD*

The Period of the Judges 1375–1050 B.C.

Judge	Scripture References	Oppressor	Length of Oppression	Period of Rest/ Judgeship
Othniel from Judah	Jos 15:16-19; Jdg 1:11-15; 3:7-11 1Ch 4:13	Mesopotamians (Jdg 3:8)	8 yrs. (Jdg 3:8)	40 yrs. (Jdg 3:11)
Ehud from Benjamin	Jdg 3:12-30; 4:1	Moabites Ammonites Amalekites (Jdg 3:12-13)	18 yrs. (Jdg 3:14)	80 yrs. (Jdg 3:30)
Shamgar (perhaps a foreigner)	Jdg 3:31; 5:6	Philistines (Jdg 3:31)		
Deborah from Ephraim	Jdg 4:1–5:31	Canaanites (Jdg 4:2)	20 yrs. (Jdg 4:3)	40 yrs. (Jdg 5:31)
Gideon (Jerubbaal or Jerubbesheth) from Manasseh	Jdg 6:1–8:32; Heb 11:32	Midianites Amalekites (Jdg 6:1,3,33; 7:12)	7 yrs. (Jdg 6:1)	40 yrs. (Jdg 8:28)
Abimelech from Manasseh ("ruled," but not identified as a judge)	Jdg 8:33–9:57; 2Sm 11:21	Civil war (Jdg 9)		3 yrs. (Jdg 9:22)
Tola from Issachar	Jdg 10:1-2			23 yrs. (Jdg 10:2)
Jair from Manasseh	Jdg 10:3-5		18 yrs. (Jdg 10:8)	22 yrs. (Jdg 10:3)
Jephthah from Manasseh	Jdg 10:6–12:7; Heb 11:32	Philistines Ammonites Civil war with Ephraimites (Jdg 10:7; 12:4)		6 yrs. (Jdg 12:7)
Ibzan from Judah or Zebulun	Jdg 12:8-10			7 yrs. (Jdg 12:9)
Elon from Zebulun	Jdg 12:11-12			10 yrs. (Jdg 12:11)
Abdon from Ephraim	Jdg 12:13-15			8 yrs. (Jdg 12:14)
Samson from Dan	Jdg 13:1–16:31; Heb 11:32	Philistines (Jdg 13:1)	40 yrs. (Jdg 13:1)	20 yrs. (Jdg 15:20; 16:31)

Adapted from *The Woman's Study Bible*, ed. Dorothy Kelley Patterson and Rhonda Harrington Kelley (Nashville: Thomas Nelson, 1995).

did. [18]Whenever the LORD raised up a judge for the Israelites, the LORD was with him and saved the people from the power of their enemies while the judge was still alive.[A] The LORD was moved to pity whenever they groaned because of those who were oppressing and afflicting them. [19]Whenever the judge died, the Israelites would act even more corruptly than their fathers, going after other gods to worship and bow down to them. They did not turn from their evil practices or their obstinate ways.

[20]The LORD's anger burned against Israel, and He declared, "Because this nation has violated My covenant that I made with their fathers and disobeyed Me, [21]I will no longer drive out before them any of the nations Joshua left when he died. [22]I did this to test Israel and to see whether they would keep the LORD's way by walking in it, as their fathers had." [23]The LORD left these nations and did not drive them out immediately. He did not hand them over to Joshua.

3 These are the nations the LORD left in order to test Israel, since the Israelites had fought none of these in[B] any of the wars with Canaan. [2]This was to teach the future generations of the Israelites how to fight in battle, especially those who had not fought before.[C] [3]These nations included: the five rulers of the Philistines and all of the Canaanites, the Sidonians, and the Hivites who lived in the Lebanese mountains[D] from Mount Baal-hermon as far as the entrance to Hamath.[E] [4]The LORD left them to test Israel, to determine if they would keep the LORD's commands He had given their fathers through[F] Moses. [5]But they settled among the Canaanites, Hittites, Amorites, Perizzites, Hivites, and Jebusites. [6]The Israelites took their daughters as wives for themselves, gave their own daughters to their sons, and worshiped their gods.

The Deliverance of the Judges from Oppression (3:7–16:31)

Defeat of the Mesopotamians by Othniel (3:7-11)

[7]The Israelites did what was evil in the LORD's sight; they forgot the LORD their God and worshiped the •Baals and the •Asherahs. [8]The LORD's anger burned against Israel, and He sold them to[G] Cushan-rishathaim[H] king of Aram-naharaim,[I] and the Israelites served him eight years.

[9]The Israelites cried out to the LORD. So the LORD raised up Othniel son of Kenaz, Caleb's youngest brother, as a deliverer to save the Israelites. [10]The Spirit of the LORD came on him, and he judged Israel. Othniel went out to battle, and the LORD handed over Cushan-rishathaim king of Aram to him, so that Othniel overpowered him. [11]Then the land was peaceful 40 years, and Othniel son of Kenaz died.

Defeat of the Moabites by Ehud (3:12-30)

[12]The Israelites again did what was evil in the LORD's sight. He gave Eglon king of Moab power over Israel, because they had done what was evil in the LORD's sight. [13]After Eglon convinced the Ammonites and the Amalekites to join forces with him, he attacked and defeated Israel and took possession of the City of Palms.[J] [14]The Israelites served Eglon king of Moab 18 years.

[15]Then the Israelites cried out to the LORD, and He raised up Ehud son of Gera, a left-handed Benjaminite,[K] as a deliverer for them. The Israelites sent him to Eglon king of Moab with tribute money.

[16]Ehud made himself a double-edged sword 18 inches long.[L] He strapped it to his right thigh under his clothes [17]and brought the tribute to Eglon king of Moab, who was an extremely fat man. [18]When Ehud had finished presenting the tribute, he dismissed the people who had carried it. [19]At the carved images near Gilgal he returned and

2:20–3:2 God permitted the Canaanites to overpower His people in order to judge Israel's apostasy, to test whether Israel would follow Him as their fathers had, and to train the new generation in warfare and trusting in God for victory.

3:6 Because the Canaanites settled among the people, Israel gave their children to the Canaanites in marriage, a direct violation of their covenant (Dt 7:3-4). Israel's intermarriage with pagan peoples resulted in their worship of pagan gods.

3:7-8 The writer repeatedly introduces another cycle of sin → judgment → cry for help → deliverance → by stating what led to Israel's distress: **The Israelites did what was evil in the LORD's sight.** Israel's unfaithfulness infuriated Yahweh, and He **sold them** to an enemy. In this context, the word "sold" suggests that He gave them to an enemy's control.

3:12-14 The Moabites were the result of the incest between Lot and his daughters (Gn 19:30-38). They worshiped Baal along with Chemosh and Astarte.

3:15-17 Ehud's left-handedness may have meant that he was ambidextrous, a great value in warfare. He was likely an Israelite leader, since he was designated to take tribute or a tax to **Eglon**. Since men typically tied their swords onto their left thighs, Ehud's right-thighed weapon went unnoticed.

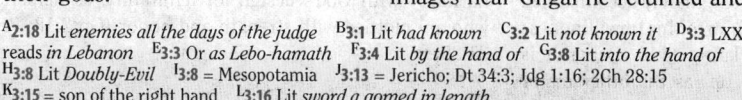

[A]2:18 Lit *enemies all the days of the judge* [B]3:1 Lit *had known* [C]3:2 Lit *not known it* [D]3:3 LXX reads *in Lebanon* [E]3:3 Or *as Lebo-hamath* [F]3:4 Lit *by the hand of* [G]3:8 Lit *into the hand of* [H]3:8 Lit *Doubly-Evil* [I]3:8 = Mesopotamia [J]3:13 = Jericho; Dt 34:3; Jdg 1:16; 2Ch 28:15 [K]3:15 = son of the right hand [L]3:16 Lit *sword a gomed in length*

>WORD|*study*

4:4 A **prophetess** (Hb *nevi'ah*) was called upon to speak for God. Other Old Testament prophetesses include Miriam (Ex 15:20), Huldah (2 Kg 22:14), Isaiah's wife (Is 8:3), and Noadiah, a false prophetess (Neh 6:14). New Testament prophetesses include Anna (Lk 2:36) and Phillip's "four virgin daughters" (Ac 21:9).

said, "King Eglon, I have a secret
message for you." The king called
for silence, and all his attendants
left him. [20] Then Ehud approached
him while he was sitting alone in
his room upstairs where it was cool.
Ehud said, "I have a word from God
for you," and the king stood up
from his throne.[A] [21] Ehud[B] reached
with his left hand, took the sword
from his right thigh, and plunged it
into Eglon's belly. [22] Even the handle
went in after the blade, and Eglon's
fat closed in over it, so that Ehud
did not withdraw the sword from his
belly. And Eglon's insides came out.
[23] Ehud escaped by way of the porch,
closing and locking the doors of the
upstairs room behind him.
[24] Ehud was gone when Eglon's
servants came in. They looked and
found the doors of the upstairs room
locked and thought he was relieving
himself[C] in the cool room. [25] The
servants waited until they became
worried and saw that he had still
not opened the doors of the upstairs
room. So they took the key and
opened the doors—and there was
their lord lying dead on the floor!
[26] Ehud escaped while the servants
waited. He crossed over the Jordan
near the carved images and reached
Seirah. [27] After he arrived, he sounded the ram's horn throughout the
hill country of Ephraim. The Israelites came down with him from the
hill country, and he became their
leader. [28] He told them, "Follow
me, because the LORD has handed
over your enemies, the Moabites,
to you." So they followed him, captured the fords of the Jordan leading
to Moab, and did not allow anyone
to cross over. [29] At that time they
struck down about 10,000 Moabites,
all strong and able-bodied men. Not
one of them escaped. [30] Moab became subject to Israel that day, and
the land was peaceful 80 years.

Defeat of the Philistines by Shamgar (3:31)

[31] After Ehud, Shamgar son of
Anath became judge. He delivered
Israel by striking down 600 Philis-
tines with an oxgoad.

Defeat of the Canaanites by Barak (4:1-24)

4 The Israelites again did what was
evil in the sight of the LORD after
Ehud had died. [2] So the LORD sold

[A] **3:20** LXX reads *"A word of my God for you, O king," and Eglon rose up from the throne near him.* [B] **3:21** LXX reads *It happened that when he rose up, Ehud immediately* [C] **3:24** Lit *was covering his feet*

BIBLICAL WOMANHOOD Feminine Leadership

Deborah models distinct feminine leadership. Unlike the public ministries of male prophets (e.g., Isaiah and Jeremiah), she spoke privately to individuals who came to her. In her exhortation to Barak, Deborah confronted the military leader with the question, **"Hasn't the LORD . . . commanded you . . ."** (4:6)? Her purpose was to inspire Barak toward obedient action, supporting and affirming his leadership. Feminist interpretations of this passage claim that Deborah was a military leader. However, the text reveals that she merely accompanied Barak at his request, rebuking him for his unwillingness to act in faith in God's revelation (4:8). Deborah is not said to have been "raised up" as the other major judges. This nuance in no way discredits or downplays Deborah's extraordinary leadership and strength but rather demonstrates that God's employment of feminine leadership is distinct from masculine leadership and in harmony with His original design for womanhood. As with other godly women in the Bible, Deborah demonstrates that feminine leadership is conducted in a manner that supports the creation order. Like Deborah, you, too, can express your gifts and personality in harmony with God's design for femininity, as helpers who are clothed with strength and honor (Gn 2:18; Pr 31:25).

CHARACTER PROFILE

Deborah A Woman with Discernment

Her Background	• A name meaning "bee" • The wife of Lappidoth (4:4) • A judge of Israel during the oppression by Jabin (4:3-5) • A "mother in Israel" (5:7)
Her Story	• She summoned Barak to go up against Sisera and the Canaanites (4:6-7). • She accompanied Barak and exhorted him to fight (4:8-10,14). • She commemorated the victory in song (5:1-31).
Life Lessons	• Deborah's wisdom and courage were beneficial not only to her own family but also to her nation. • The opportunity to do something great for God is often preceded by everyday responsibilities faithfully performed.

them into the hand of Jabin king of
Canaan, who reigned in Hazor. The
commander of his forces was Sisera
who lived in Harosheth of the Nations.[A] 3 Then the Israelites cried out
to the LORD, because Jabin had 900
iron chariots, and he harshly oppressed them 20 years.
4 Deborah, a woman who was a
prophetess and the wife of Lappidoth, was judging Israel at that time.
5 It was her custom to sit under the
palm tree of Deborah between Ramah and Bethel in the hill country
of Ephraim, and the Israelites went
up to her for judgment.
6 She summoned Barak son of
Abinoam from Kedesh in Naphtali
and said to him, "Hasn't the LORD,
the God of Israel, commanded you:
'Go, deploy the troops on Mount
Tabor, and take with you 10,000
men from the Naphtalites and Zebulunites? 7 Then I will lure Sisera
commander of Jabin's forces, his
chariots, and his army at the •Wadi
Kishon to fight against you, and I
will hand him over to you.'"
8 Barak said to her, "If you will go
with me, I will go. But if you will not
go with me, I will not go."
9 "I will go with you," she said, "but
you will receive no honor on the
road you are about to take, because
the LORD will sell Sisera into a woman's hand." So Deborah got up and
went with Barak to Kedesh. 10 Barak
summoned Zebulun and Naphtali to
Kedesh; 10,000 men followed him,
and Deborah also went with him.
11 Now Heber the Kenite had
moved away from the Kenites, the
sons of Hobab, Moses' father-in-law,
and pitched his tent beside the oak
tree of Zaanannim, which was near
Kedesh.
12 It was reported to Sisera that
Barak son of Abinoam had gone up
Mount Tabor. 13 Sisera summoned
all his 900 iron chariots and all the
people who were with him from
Harosheth of the Nations[A] to the
Wadi Kishon. 14 Then Deborah said
to Barak, "Move on, for this is the
day the LORD has handed Sisera over
to you. Hasn't the LORD gone before
you?" So Barak came down from
Mount Tabor with 10,000 men following him.
15 The LORD threw Sisera, all his
charioteers, and all his army into
confusion with the sword before
Barak. Sisera left his chariot and
fled on foot. 16 Barak pursued the
chariots and the army as far as Harosheth of the Nations,[A] and the whole
army of Sisera fell by the sword; not
a single man was left.
17 Meanwhile, Sisera had fled on
foot to the tent of Jael, the wife of
Heber the Kenite, because there was
peace between Jabin king of Hazor
and the family of Heber the Kenite.
18 Jael went out to greet Sisera and

4:4-5 Deborah (Hb "honeybee") was identified as a **prophetess...judging Israel**, as **the wife of Lappidoth** and as "a mother in Israel" (5:7). She administered her judgments under a **palm tree**.

4:8 Barak hesitated to follow God's specific instruction and refused to go to battle without Deborah. Although he was a man of faith (Heb 11:32-33), here he was not confident in God's power.

4:14 Deborah exhorted Barak to begin the battle, reminding him that the Lord had gone before them and delivered their enemy, **Sisera**. Deborah's leadership and motivational skills are evident as she influenced Barak to action. Deborah did not go into battle herself but rather encouraged those who fought.

4:17-18 Sisera fled to Heber's tent where he assumed he would find safety. **Jael**, Heber's wife, took initiative to meet him and welcomed him to her home.

[A]**4:2,13,16** Or *Harosheth-ha-goiim*

4:19-21 After the battle-weary Sisera fell into a deep sleep, Jael drove a tent peg into Sisera's temple. Jael may have been an Israelite since intermarriage was so common, explaining her loyalty to Israel despite her husband's loyalty to Jabin.

4:22-24 By the time Barak arrived at Heber's tent, Sisera was already dead. Deborah's prophecy that God would give the honor for delivering Sisera to a woman was fulfilled in Jael.

5:2 When godly leaders lead and the people **volunteer** (Hb *nadav*, "offer oneself willingly"), then God's purposes are accomplished—a sure formula for success.

5:7 As **a mother in Israel** Deborah may have been identifying herself as a mother to her children or affirming her nurturing maternal skills in judging the nation.

5:8 Deborah's humility is evident in her first-person song. She marked her era not as "the days of Deborah," but as **the days of Shamgar son of Anath** (v. 6), the previous judge (3:31), and **the days of Jael** (5:6; cp. 4:17-22).

CHARACTER PROFILE

Jael An Artful Assassin

Her Background	• The wife of Heber, an ally of Jabin (4:17) • A Kenite living near Hazor (4:17)
Her Story	• She lured Sisera into her tent after the battle with Barak, pretending to hide him (4:18). • She lulled him into sleep (4:19-20). • She killed him by driving a tent peg into his head (4:21). • She reported to Barak, the leader of God's army (4:22). • She received the promise given to Barak for victory by the hand of a woman (4:7,9).
Life Lessons	• God will work out His purposes through whom He chooses. • Every woman can choose to make herself available to Him.

said to him, "Come in, my lord.
Come in with me. Don't be afraid."
So he went into her tent, and she
covered him with a rug. 19 He said
to her, "Please give me a little water to drink for I am thirsty." She
opened a container of milk, gave
him a drink, and covered him again.
20 Then he said to her, "Stand at the
entrance to the tent. If a man comes
and asks you, 'Is there a man here?'
say, 'No.'" 21 While he was sleeping
from exhaustion, Heber's wife Jael
took a tent peg, grabbed a hammer, and went silently to Sisera. She
hammered the peg into his temple
and drove it into the ground, and he
died.
22 When Barak arrived in pursuit
of Sisera, Jael went out to greet him
and said to him, "Come and I will
show you the man you are looking
for." So he went in with her, and
there was Sisera lying dead with a
tent peg through his temple!
23 That day God subdued Jabin
king of Canaan before the Israelites.
24 The power of the Israelites continued to increase against Jabin king of
Canaan until they destroyed him.

Song of Deborah (5:1-31)

5 On that day Deborah and Barak son of Abinoam sang:

2 When the leaders lead[A] in Israel,
when the people volunteer,
praise the LORD.
3 Listen, kings! Pay attention,
princes!
I will sing to the LORD;
I will sing praise
to the LORD God of Israel.
4 LORD, when You came from Seir,
when You marched
from the fields of Edom,
the earth trembled,
the heavens poured rain,
and the clouds poured water.
5 The mountains melted
before the LORD,
even Sinai[B] before the LORD,
the God of Israel.

6 In the days of Shamgar
son of Anath,
in the days of Jael,
the main ways were deserted
because travelers kept
to the side roads.
7 Villages were deserted,[C]
they were deserted in Israel,
until I, Deborah,[D] arose,
a mother in Israel.
8 Israel chose new gods,
then war was in the gates.
Not a shield or spear was seen
among 40,000 in Israel.
9 My heart is with the leaders
of Israel,
with the volunteers
of the people.
Praise the LORD!
10 You who ride
on white[E] donkeys,
who sit on saddle blankets,

A5:2 Or *the locks of hair are loose* B5:5 Or LORD, *this One of Sinai* C5:7,10 Hb obscure
D5:7 Or *you*

and who travel on the road,
give praise!
11 Let them tell the righteous acts
of the LORD,
the righteous deeds
of His warriors in Israel,
with the voices of the singers
at the watering places.[A]

Then the LORD's people went
down to the gates.
12 "Awake! Awake, Deborah!
Awake! Awake, sing a song!
Arise, Barak,
and take hold of your captives,
son of Abinoam!"
13 The survivors came down
to the nobles;
the LORD's people came down
to me[B] with the warriors.
14 Those with their roots
in Amalek[C] came
from Ephraim;
Benjamin came with
your people after you.
The leaders came down
from Machir,
and those who carry
a marshal's staff came
from Zebulun.
15 The princes of Issachar were
with Deborah;
Issachar was with Barak.
They set out at his heels
in the valley.
There was great searching[D]
of heart
among the clans of Reuben.
16 Why did you sit
among the sheepfolds
listening to the playing
of pipes for the flocks?
There was great searching
of heart
among the clans of Reuben.
17 Gilead remained
beyond the Jordan.
Dan, why did you linger
at the ships?
Asher remained
at the seashore
and stayed in his harbors.
18 Zebulun was a people risking
their lives,
Naphtali also, on the heights
of the battlefield.

19 Kings came and fought.
Then the kings of Canaan
fought
at Taanach by the waters
of Megiddo,
but they took no spoil
of silver.
20 The stars fought
from the heavens;
the stars fought with Sisera
from their courses.
21 The river Kishon swept them
away,
the ancient river,
the river Kishon.
March on, my soul,
in strength!
22 The horses' hooves then
hammered—
the galloping, galloping
of his[E] stallions.
23 "Curse Meroz," says the Angel
of the LORD,
"Bitterly curse
her inhabitants,
for they did not come to help
the LORD,
to help the LORD against
the mighty warriors."
24 Jael is most blessed of women,
the wife of Heber the Kenite;
she is most blessed among
tent-dwelling women.
25 He asked for water; she gave
him milk.
She brought him
curdled milk
in a majestic bowl.
26 She reached for a tent peg,
her right hand,
for a workman's mallet.
Then she hammered Sisera—
she crushed his head;
she shattered and pierced
his temple.
27 He collapsed, he fell,
he lay down at[F] her feet;
he collapsed, he fell
at her feet;
where he collapsed,
there he fell—dead.

28 Sisera's mother looked
through the window;
she peered through
the lattice, crying out:
"Why is his chariot so long
in coming?

[A]**5:11** Hb obscure [B]**5:13** LXX reads *down for him* [C]**5:14** LXX reads *in the valley* [D]**5:15** Some Hb mss, Syr read *There were great resolves* [E]**5:22** = Sisera's [F]**5:27** Lit *between*

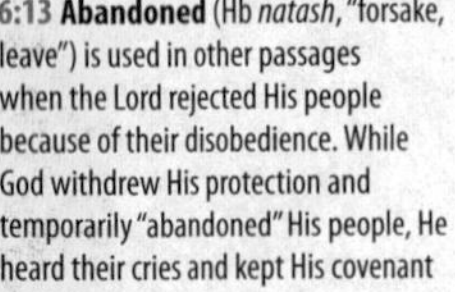
6:13 Abandoned (Hb *natash*, "forsake, leave") is used in other passages when the Lord rejected His people because of their disobedience. While God withdrew His protection and temporarily "abandoned" His people, He heard their cries and kept His covenant with them.

Why don't I hear
  the hoofbeats
  of his horses?"[A]
29 Her wisest princesses
  answer her;
she even answers herself:[B]
30 "Are they not finding
  and dividing the spoil—
a girl or two for each warrior,
the spoil of colored garments
  for Sisera,
the spoil of
  an embroidered garment
  or two for my neck?"[C]

31 LORD, may all your enemies
  perish as Sisera did.[D]
But may those who love Him
be like the rising of the sun
  in its strength.

And the land was peaceful 40 years.

Defeat of the Midianites by Gideon (6:1–8:35)

6 The Israelites did what was evil in the sight of the LORD. So the LORD handed them over to Midian seven years, 2 and they oppressed Israel. Because of Midian, the Israelites made hiding places for themselves in the mountains, caves, and strongholds. 3 Whenever the Israelites planted crops, the Midianites, Amalekites, and the Qedemites came and attacked them. 4 They encamped against them and destroyed the produce of the land, even as far as Gaza. They left nothing for Israel to eat, as well as no sheep, ox or donkey. 5 For the Midianites came with their cattle and their tents like a great swarm of locusts. They and their camels were without number, and they entered the land to waste it. 6 So Israel became poverty-stricken because of Midian, and the Israelites cried out to the LORD.

7 When the Israelites cried out to Him because of Midian, 8 the LORD sent a prophet to them. He said to them, "This is what the LORD God of Israel says: 'I brought you out of Egypt and out of the place of slavery. 9 I delivered you from the power of Egypt and the power of all who oppressed you. I drove them out before you and gave you their land. 10 I said to you: I am •Yahweh your God. Do not fear the gods of the Amorites whose land you live in. But you did not obey Me.'"

11 The Angel[E] of the LORD came, and He[F] sat under the oak that was in Ophrah, which belonged to Joash, the Abiezrite. His son Gideon was threshing wheat in the wine vat in order to hide it from the Midianites. 12 Then the Angel of the LORD appeared to him and said: "The LORD is with you, mighty warrior."

13 Gideon said to Him, "Please Sir,[G] if the LORD is with us, why has all this happened?[H] And where are all His wonders that our fathers told us about? They said, 'Hasn't the LORD brought us out of Egypt?' But now the LORD has abandoned us and handed us over to Midian."

14 The LORD[I] turned to him and said, "Go in the strength you have and deliver Israel from the power of Midian. Am I not sending you?"

15 He said to Him, "Please, Lord, how can I deliver Israel? Look, my family is the weakest in Manasseh, and I am the youngest in my father's house."

16 "But I will be with you," the LORD said to him. "You will strike Midian down as if it were one man."

17 Then he said to Him, "If I have found favor in Your sight, give me a sign that You are speaking with me. 18 Please do not leave this place until I return to You. Let me bring my gift and set it before You."

And He said, "I will stay until you return."

19 So Gideon went and prepared a young goat and unleavened bread from a half bushel[J] of flour. He placed the meat in a basket and the broth in a pot. He brought them out and offered them to Him under the oak.

20 The Angel of God said to him, "Take the meat with the unleavened bread, put it on this stone, and pour the broth on it." And he did so.

21 The Angel of the LORD extended the tip of the staff that was in His

[A]5:28 Lit *Why have the hoofbeats of his chariots delayed* [B]5:29 Lit *answers her words* [C]5:30 Hb obscure [D]5:31 Lit *perish in this way* [E]6:11 Or *angel* [F]6:11 Or *he* [G]6:13 Lit *Please, my Lord,* or *Please, my lord* [H]6:13 Lit *this found us out* [I]6:14 LXX reads *The Angel of the LORD* [J]6:19 Lit *an ephah*

hand and touched the meat and the
unleavened bread. Fire came up
from the rock and consumed the
meat and the unleavened bread.
Then the Angel of the LORD vanished
from his sight.
22 When Gideon realized that He
was the Angel of the LORD, he said,
"Oh no, Lord GOD! I have seen the
Angel of the LORD face to face!"
23 But the LORD said to him, "Peace
to you. Don't be afraid, for you will
not die." 24 So Gideon built an altar
to the LORD there and called it Yahweh Shalom.[A] It is in Ophrah of the
Abiezrites until today.
25 On that very night the LORD said
to him, "Take your father's young
bull and a second bull seven years
old. Then tear down the altar of
•Baal that belongs to your father and
cut down the •Asherah pole beside
it. 26 Build a well-constructed altar
to the LORD your God on the top of
this rock. Take the second bull and
offer it as a •burnt offering with the
wood of the Asherah pole you cut
down." 27 So Gideon took 10 of his
male servants and did as the LORD
had told him. But because he was
too afraid of his father's household
and the men of the city to do it in
the daytime, he did it at night.
28 When the men of the city got up
in the morning, they found Baal's
altar torn down, the Asherah pole
beside it cut down, and the second
bull offered up on the altar that had
been built. 29 They said to each other, "Who did this?" After they made
a thorough investigation, they said,
"Gideon son of Joash did it."
30 Then the men of the city said to
Joash, "Bring out your son. He must
die, because he tore down Baal's altar and cut down the Asherah pole
beside it."
31 But Joash said to all who stood
against him, "Would you plead
Baal's case for him? Would you save

HARD QUESTION

Should you ask God for signs in decision-making?

Many Christians have used Gideon's example to "put out a **fleece**" as a way of seeking guidance from God (6:36-40). The Lord had clearly told Gideon that He was sending him, would be with him, and would give him victory over the Midianites (vv. 14-16). Gideon proved himself a mighty warrior, but he struggled with fear and unbelief. His doubt caused him to seek additional signs, an evidence of his weak faith. God's direction can be found in His Word, His revelation to mankind. If you need God's guidance, do not seek additional signs but study Scripture (2Tm 3:16-17) and rely on the leading of the Holy Spirit. God promised that His Spirit will guide you into all the truth (Jn 16:13; Ps 32:8).

him? Whoever pleads his case will be
put to death by morning! If he is a
god, let him plead his own case because someone tore down his altar."
32 That day, Gideon's father called
him Jerubbaal, saying, "Let Baal
plead his case with him," because he
tore down his altar.
33 All the Midianites, Amalekites,
and Qedemites gathered together,
crossed over the Jordan, and camped
in the Valley of Jezreel.
34 The Spirit of the LORD took control of[B] Gideon, and he blew the
ram's horn and the Abiezrites rallied behind him. 35 He sent messengers throughout all of Manasseh,
who rallied behind him. He also
sent messengers throughout Asher,
Zebulun, and Naphtali, who also
came to meet him.
36 Then Gideon said to God, "If You
will deliver Israel by my hand, as You
said, 37 I will put a fleece of wool here
on the threshing floor. If dew is only
on the fleece, and all the ground is
dry, I will know that You will deliver
Israel by my strength, as You said."
38 And that is what happened. When

[A] **6:24** = The LORD Is Peace [B] **6:34** Lit *LORD clothed Himself with*; 1Ch 12:18; 2Ch 24:20

6:25-32 Before Gideon could begin his military endeavor he had to **tear down the altar of Baal** in his father's backyard. This principle occurs often in Scripture—you must deal with your own sins before attempting to correct others (Mt 7:1-5).

6:33-39 Gideon was not asking for a revelation of God's will. He was looking for reassurance of God's presence. God answered Gideon's requests. He wants to build the faith of His children.

>WORD|*study*

6:34 The Spirit of the Lord took control of [Hb *lavash*, lit "put on as clothing or a garment"] **Gideon.** The Spirit of God "filled"—empowered and acted through—Gideon. Similarly, "the Spirit of God took control of Zechariah," enabling the priest's son to confront the people with their sin (2Ch 24:20). Before His ascension, Jesus instructed the disciples to stay in Jerusalem until they were "empowered (Gk *endusēsthe*, 'clothed' with power, Lk 24:49) from on high."

7:16-25 The Midianites' confusion was doubtless caused by what appeared to be a much larger army. The offensive attack occurred at the beginning of the middle watch (v. 19), approximately midnight. Some of them were asleep, others were just finishing their watch and wanting to sleep, and others were just waking up for their turn to watch. Likely no one was entirely alert.

he got up early in the morning, he
squeezed the fleece and wrung dew
out of it, filling a bowl with water.
39 Gideon then said to God, "Don't
be angry with me; let me speak one
more time. Please allow me to make
one more test with the fleece. Let it
remain dry, and the dew be all over
the ground." 40 That night God did
as Gideon requested: only the fleece
was dry, and dew was all over the
ground.

7 Jerubbaal (that is, Gideon) and
everyone who was with him, got
up early and camped beside the
spring of Harod. The camp of Midian was north of them, below the
hill of Moreh, in the valley. 2 The
LORD said to Gideon, "You have too
many people for Me to hand the
Midianites over to you,[A] or else Israel might brag:[B] 'I did it myself.'
3 Now announce in the presence of
the people: 'Whoever is fearful and
trembling may turn back and leave
Mount Gilead.'" So 22,000 of the
people turned back, but 10,000 remained.
4 Then the LORD said to Gideon,
"There are still too many people.
Take them down to the water, and I
will test them for you there. If I say
to you, 'This one can go with you,'
he can go. But if I say about anyone,
'This one cannot go with you,' he
cannot go." 5 So he brought the people down to the water, and the LORD
said to Gideon, "Separate everyone
who laps water with his tongue like
a dog. Do the same with everyone
who kneels to drink." 6 The number of those who lapped with their
hands to their mouths was 300 men,
and all the rest of the people knelt
to drink water. 7 The LORD said to
Gideon, "I will deliver you with the
300 men who lapped and hand the
Midianites over to you. But everyone
else is to go home." 8 So Gideon sent
all the Israelites to their tents but
kept the 300, who took[C] the people's
provisions and their trumpets. The
camp of Midian was below him in
the valley.
9 That night the LORD said to him,
"Get up and go into the camp, for I
have given it into your hand. 10 But if
you are afraid to go to the camp, go
with Purah your servant. 11 Listen to
what they say, and then you will be
strengthened to go to the camp." So
he went with Purah his servant to
the outpost of the troops[D] who were
in the camp.
12 Now the Midianites, Amalekites,
and all the Qedemites had settled
down in the valley like a swarm of
locusts, and their camels were as innumerable as the sand on the seashore. 13 When Gideon arrived, there
was a man telling his friend about
a dream. He said, "Listen, I had a
dream: a loaf of barley bread came
tumbling into the Midianite camp,
struck a tent, and it fell. The loaf
turned the tent upside down so that
it collapsed."
14 His friend answered: "This is
nothing less than the sword of
Gideon son of Joash, the Israelite.
God has handed the entire Midianite
camp over to him."
15 When Gideon heard the account
of the dream and its interpretation,
he bowed in worship. He returned
to Israel's camp and said, "Get up,
for the LORD has handed the Midianite camp over to you." 16 Then he
divided the 300 men into three companies and gave each of the men a
trumpet in one hand and an empty
pitcher with a torch inside it in the
other.
17 "Watch me," he said,[E] "and do
the same. When I come to the outpost of the camp, do as I do. 18 When
I and everyone with me blow our
trumpets, you are also to blow your
trumpets all around the camp. Then
you will say, 'For •Yahweh and for
Gideon!'"
19 Gideon and the 100 men who
were with him went to the outpost
of the camp at the beginning of
the middle watch after the sentries
had been stationed. They blew their
trumpets and broke the pitchers
that were in their hands. 20 The three
companies blew their trumpets and
shattered their pitchers. They held
their torches in their left hands,
their trumpets[F] in their right hands,
and shouted, "A sword for Yahweh

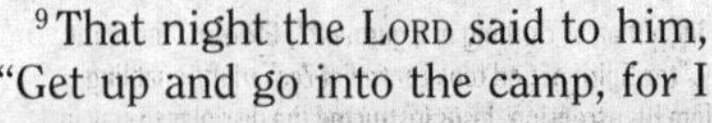

A 7:2 Lit *them* B 7:2 Lit *brag against Me* C 7:8 Lit *took in their hands* D 7:11 Lit *of those who were arranged in companies of 50* E 7:17 Lit *said to them* F 7:20 Lit *trumpets to blow*

and for Gideon!" 21 Each Israelite took his position around the camp, and the entire Midianite army fled, and cried out as they ran. 22 When Gideon's men blew their 300 trumpets, the LORD set the swords of each man in the army against each other. They fled to Beth-shittah in the direction of Zererah as far as the border of Abel-meholah near Tabbath. 23 Then the men of Israel were called from Naphtali, Asher, and Manasseh, and they pursued the Midianites.

24 Gideon sent messengers throughout the hill country of Ephraim with this message: "Come down to intercept the Midianites and take control of the watercourses ahead of them as far as Beth-barah and the Jordan." So all the men of Ephraim were called out, and they took control of the watercourses as far as Beth-barah and the Jordan. 25 They captured Oreb and Zeeb, the two princes of Midian; they killed Oreb at the rock of Oreb and Zeeb at the winepress of Zeeb, while they were pursuing the Midianites. They brought the heads of Oreb and Zeeb to Gideon across the Jordan.

8 The men of Ephraim said to him, "Why have you done this to us, not calling us when you went to fight against the Midianites?" And they argued with him violently.

2 So he said to them, "What have I done now compared to you? Is not the gleaning of Ephraim better than the vintage of Abiezer? 3 God handed over to you Oreb and Zeeb, the two princes of Midian. What was I able to do compared to you?" When he said this, their anger against him subsided.

4 Gideon and the 300 men came to the Jordan and crossed it. They were exhausted but still in pursuit. 5 He said to the men of Succoth, "Please give some loaves of bread to the people who are following me,[A] because they are exhausted, for I am pursuing Zebah and Zalmunna, the kings of Midian."

6 But the princes of Succoth asked, "Are[B] Zebah and Zalmunna now in your hands that we should give bread to your army?"

7 Gideon replied, "Very well, when the LORD has handed Zebah and Zalmunna over to me, I will trample[C] your flesh on thorns and briers from the wilderness!" 8 He went from there to Penuel and asked the same thing from them. The men of Penuel answered just as the men of Succoth had answered. 9 He also told the men of Penuel, "When I return in peace, I will tear down this tower!"

10 Now Zebah and Zalmunna were in Karkor, and with them was their army of about 15,000 men, who were all those left of the entire army of the Qedemites. Those who had been killed were 120,000 warriors.[D] 11 Gideon traveled on the caravan route[E] east of Nobah and Jogbehah and attacked their army while the army was unsuspecting. 12 Zebah and Zalmunna fled, and he pursued them. He captured these two kings of Midian and routed the entire army.

13 Gideon son of Joash returned from the battle by the Ascent of Heres. 14 He captured a youth from the men of Succoth and interrogated him. The youth wrote down for him the names of the 77 princes and elders of Succoth. 15 Then he went to the men of Succoth and said, "Here are Zebah and Zalmunna. You taunted me about them, saying, 'Are[B] Zebah and Zalmunna now in your power that we should give bread to your exhausted men?'" 16 So he took the elders of the city, and he took some thorns and briers from the wilderness, and he disciplined the men of Succoth with them. 17 He also tore down the tower of Penuel and killed the men of the city.

18 He asked Zebah and Zalmunna, "What kind of men did you kill at Tabor?"

"They were like you," they said. "Each resembled the son of a king."

19 So he said, "They were my brothers, the sons of my mother! As the LORD lives, if you had let them live, I would not kill you." 20 Then he said to Jether, his firstborn, "Get up and kill them." The youth did not draw

8:1-3 Gideon's word picture described **the vintage of Abiezer** as compared to **the gleaning of Ephraim**. Both terms refer to the grape harvest, with which all the men would instantly identify.

8-4-17 Gideon's initial fearfulness and cowardice seem to have disappeared, only to be replaced by anger and vindictiveness. Although his actions are not justified, God was not only delivering His people but also protecting the reputation of His deliverer. God's chosen deliverer was not to be mocked without consequences.

A **8:5** Lit *are at my feet* B **8:6,15** Lit *Are the hands of* C **8:7** Or *tear* D **8:10** Lit *men who drew the sword* E **8:11** Lit *on the route of those who live in tents*

8:22-28 Gideon refused to assume the status of a king or to allow his son to rule over Israel, stating that Yahweh was their king. Nevertheless, other aspects of Gideon's legacy are troubling. What God accomplishes through His deliverers did not guarantee their invulnerability to the forms of idolatry in their culture. Unfortunately, Gideon did not finish well (2Tm 4:7).

9:1-6 Abimelech was the son of Gideon (or **Jerubbaal**, 8:33-35) and his concubine.

his sword, for he was afraid because
he was still a youth.
21 Zebah and Zalmunna said, "Get
up and kill us yourself, for a man is
judged by his strength." So Gideon
got up, killed Zebah and Zalmunna,
and took the crescent ornaments
that were on the necks of their camels.
22 Then the Israelites said to Gideon, "Rule over us, you as well as
your sons and your grandsons, for
you delivered us from the power of
Midian."
23 But Gideon said to them, "I will
not rule over you, and my son will
not rule over you; the LORD will rule
over you." 24 Then he said to them,
"Let me make a request of you: Everyone give me an earring from his
plunder." Now the enemy had gold
earrings because they were Ishmaelites.
25 They said, "We agree to give
them." So they spread out a mantle,
and everyone threw an earring from
his plunder on it. 26 The weight of
the gold earrings he requested was
about 43 pounds[A] of gold, in addition to the crescent ornaments and
ear pendants, the purple garments
on the kings of Midian, and the
chains on the necks of their camels. 27 Gideon made an ephod from
all this and put it in Ophrah, his
hometown. Then all Israel prostituted themselves with it there, and
it became a snare to Gideon and his
household.
28 So Midian was subdued before
the Israelites, and they were no longer a threat.[B] The land was peaceful
40 years during the days of Gideon.
29 Jerubbaal (that is, Gideon) son of
Joash went back to live at his house.
30 Gideon had 70 sons, his own
offspring, since he had many
wives. 31 His concubine who was in
Shechem also bore him a son, and

HARD QUESTION

Is Christianity like other world religions?

The truth of Christianity hinges upon the reality of Jesus Christ. Attempts to blend Christianity with other belief systems and to explain the history of Judaism and/or Christianity in the same category as other world religions distort the singular truth that Jesus alone is Lord and Messiah (Mt 24:4-5,23-27; Jn 14:6, Ac 4:12; Php 2:9-11). The tenets of Buddhism could exist without Buddha, and Islam could exist without Muhammad. However, Christianity cannot exist apart from Jesus Christ.

he named him Abimelech. 32 Then
Gideon son of Joash died at a ripe
old age and was buried in the tomb
of his father Joash in Ophrah of the
Abiezrites.
33 When Gideon died, the Israelites
turned and prostituted themselves
with the •Baals and made Baal-berith[C] their god. 34 The Israelites
did not remember the LORD their
God who had delivered them from
the power of the enemies around
them. 35 They did not show kindness
to the house of Jerubbaal (that is,
Gideon) for all the good he had done
for Israel.

Conspiracy of Abimelech (9:1-57)

9 Abimelech son of Jerubbaal
went to his mother's brothers at
Shechem and spoke to them and to
all his maternal grandfather's clan,
saying, 2 "Please speak in the presence of all the lords of Shechem,
'Is it better for you that 70 men,
all the sons of Jerubbaal, rule over
you or that one man rule over you?'
Remember that I am your own flesh
and blood."[D]
3 His mother's relatives spoke all
these words about him in the pres-

[A]**8:26** Lit *1,700 shekels* [B]**8:28** Lit *they no longer raised their head* [C]**8:33** Lit *Baal of the Covenant*, or *Lord of the Covenant* [D]**9:2** Lit *your bone and your flesh*

>WORD|*study*

9:1-6 Baal-berith (Hb, "Baal or lord of the covenant") reflects Israel's tendency toward syncretism—blending aspects of the covenant relationship with Yahweh and the local Canaanite religions. That the temple of Baal-berith was at **Shechem**, the site of covenant renewal between Yahweh and Israel (cp. Jos 8:30-35; 24:25-27), is also evidence of Israel's accommodation to Canaanite worldviews.

ence of all the lords of Shechem, and
they were favorable to Abimelech,
for they said, "He is our brother."
4 So they gave him 70 pieces of silver from the temple of Baal-berith.[A]
Abimelech hired worthless and
reckless men with this money, and
they followed him. 5 He went to his
father's house in Ophrah and killed
his 70 brothers, the sons of Jerubbaal, on top of a large stone. But Jotham, the youngest son of Jerubbaal,
survived, because he hid himself.
6 Then all the lords of Shechem and
of Beth-millo gathered together and
proceeded to make Abimelech king
at the oak of the pillar in Shechem.
7 When they told Jotham, he
climbed to the top of Mount Gerizim,
raised his voice, and called to them:

Listen to me,
lords of Shechem,
and may God listen to you:

8 The trees set out
to anoint a king
over themselves.
They said to the olive tree,
"Reign over us."
9 But the olive tree said to them,
"Should I stop giving my oil
that honors both God
and man,
and rule[B] over the trees?"
10 Then the trees said
to the fig tree,
"Come and reign over us."
11 But the fig tree said to them,
"Should I stop giving
my sweetness
and my good fruit,
and rule[B] over trees?"

12 Later, the trees said
to the grapevine,
"Come and reign over us."
13 But the grapevine said to them,
"Should I stop giving my wine
that cheers both God
and man,
and rule[B] over trees?"
14 Finally, all the trees said
to the bramble,
"Come and reign over us."
15 The bramble said to the trees,
"If you really are
anointing me
as king over you,
come and find refuge
in my shade.
But if not,
may fire come out
from the bramble
and consume the cedars
of Lebanon."

16 "Now if you have acted faithfully
and honestly in making Abimelech
king, if you have done well by Jerubbaal and his family, and if you have
rewarded him appropriately for what
he did— 17 for my father fought for
you, risked his life, and delivered
you from the hand of Midian, 18 and
now you have attacked my father's
house today, killed his 70 sons on
top of a large stone, and made Abimelech, the son of his slave, king over
the lords of Shechem 'because he is
your brother'— 19 if then you have
acted faithfully and honestly with
Jerubbaal and his house this day, rejoice in Abimelech and may he also
rejoice in you. 20 But if not, may fire
come from Abimelech and consume
the lords of Shechem and Beth-
millo, and may fire come from the
lords of Shechem and Beth-millo
and consume Abimelech." 21 Then
Jotham fled, escaping to Beer, and
lived there because of his brother
Abimelech.
22 When Abimelech had ruled over
Israel three years, 23 God sent an
evil spirit between Abimelech and
the lords of Shechem. They treated
Abimelech deceitfully, 24 so that the
crime against the 70 sons of Jerubbaal might come to justice and
their blood would be avenged on
their brother Abimelech, who killed
them, and on the lords of Shechem,
who had helped him kill his brothers. 25 The lords of Shechem rebelled
against him by putting people on
the tops of the mountains to ambush and rob everyone who passed
by them on the road. So this was reported to Abimelech.
26 Gaal son of Ebed came with his
brothers and crossed into Shechem,
and the lords of Shechem trusted
him. 27 So they went out to the
countryside and harvested grapes
from their vineyards. They trampled

9:6 How ironic that the very place where Abimelech was crowned king—**at the oak of the pillar in Shechem**—is likely the same location where Jacob buried his foreign gods (Gn 35:4) and where Joshua memorialized the covenant with God (Jos 24:25-26).

9:7-21 In Jotham's story, **the trees** of the forest represented the Shechemites and their foolish choice of a king, who would bring them nothing but suffering.

[A]**9:4** Lit *Baal of the Covenant*, or *Lord of the Covenant* [B]**9:9,11,13** Lit *and go to sway*

CHARACTER PROFILE

Abimelech's Killer **A Patriot**

Her Background	• A resident of Thebez, 10 miles from Shechem (9:50-53) • A brave woman, whose name is not recorded
Her Story	• She, along with other inhabitants of Thebez, was hiding from Abimelech in the tower in the city (9:50-55). • She dropped a millstone on Abimelech's head and fractured his skull as he approached the tower to burn it (9:52-53).
Life Lessons	• This woman's resourcefulness saved her people from death (9:51-53). • She did not let fear deter her from doing what she could (9:51-53).

the grapes and held a celebration.
Then they went to the house of their
god, and as they ate and drank, they
cursed Abimelech. 28 Gaal son of
Ebed said, "Who is Abimelech and
who is Shechem that we should
serve him? Isn't he the son of Jerubbaal, and isn't Zebul his officer?
You are to serve the men of Hamor,
the father of Shechem. Why should
we serve Abimelech? 29 If only these
people were in my power, I would
remove Abimelech." So he said[A] to
Abimelech, "Gather your army and
come out."

30 When Zebul, the ruler of the
city, heard the words of Gaal son
of Ebed, he was angry. 31 So he sent
messengers secretly to Abimelech,
saying, "Look, Gaal son of Ebed,
with his brothers, have come to
Shechem and are turning the city
against you.[B] 32 Now tonight, you
and the people with you are to come
wait in ambush in the countryside.
33 Then get up early, and at sunrise
charge the city. When he and the
people who are with him come out
against you, do to him whatever you
can."[C] 34 So Abimelech and all the
people with him got up at night and
waited in ambush for Shechem in
four units.

35 Gaal son of Ebed went out and
stood at the entrance of the city
gate. Then Abimelech and the people who were with him got up from
their ambush. 36 When Gaal saw
the people, he said to Zebul, "Look,
people are coming down from the
mountaintops!" But Zebul said to
him, "The shadows of the mountains look like men to you."

37 Then Gaal spoke again, "Look,
people are coming down from the
central part of the land, and one
unit is coming from the direction of
the Diviners' Oak." 38 Zebul replied,[D]
"Where is your mouthing off now?
You said, 'Who is Abimelech that we
should serve him?' Aren't these the
people you despised? Now go and
fight them!"

39 So Gaal went out leading the
lords of Shechem and fought
against Abimelech, 40 but Abimelech
pursued him, and Gaal fled before
him. Many wounded died as far as
the entrance of the gate. 41 Abimelech stayed in Arumah, and Zebul
drove Gaal and his brothers from
Shechem.

42 The next day when the people
went into the countryside, this was
reported to Abimelech. 43 He took
the people, divided them into three
companies, and waited in ambush in
the countryside. He looked, and the
people were coming out of the city,
so he arose against them and struck
them down. 44 Then Abimelech and
the units that were with him rushed
forward and took their stand at the
entrance of the city gate. The other

[A]9:29 DSS read *They said*; LXX reads *I would say* [B]9:31 Hb obscure [C]9:33 Lit *him as your hand will find* [D]9:38 Lit *replied to him*

two units rushed against all who were in the countryside and struck them down. [45] So Abimelech fought against the city that entire day, captured it, and killed the people who were in it. Then he tore down the city and sowed it with salt.

[46] When all the lords of the Tower of Shechem heard, they entered the inner chamber[A] of the temple of El-berith.[B] [47] Then it was reported to Abimelech that all the lords of the Tower of Shechem had gathered together. [48] So Abimelech and all the people who were with him went up to Mount Zalmon. Abimelech took his ax in his hand and cut a branch from the trees. He picked up the branch, put it on his shoulder, and said to the people who were with him, "Hurry and do what you have seen me do." [49] Each person also cut his own branch and followed Abimelech. They put the branches against the inner chamber and set it on fire around the people, and all the people in the Tower of Shechem died—about 1,000 men and women.

[50] Abimelech went to Thebez, camped against it, and captured it. [51] There was a strong tower inside the city, and all the men, women, and lords of the city fled there. They locked themselves in and went up to the roof of the tower. [52] When Abimelech came to attack the tower, he approached its entrance to set it on fire. [53] But a woman threw the upper portion of a millstone on Abimelech's head and fractured his skull. [54] He quickly called his armor-bearer and said to him, "Draw your sword and kill me, or they'll say about me, 'A woman killed him.'" So his armor-bearer thrust him through, and he died. [55] When the Israelites saw that Abimelech was dead, they all went home.

[56] In this way, God turned back on Abimelech the evil that he had done against his father, by killing his 70 brothers. [57] And God also returned all the evil of the men of Shechem on their heads. So the curse of Jotham son of Jerubbaal came on them.

Judgeships of Tola and Jair (10:1-5)

10 After Abimelech, Tola son of Puah, son of Dodo became judge and began to deliver Israel. He was from Issachar and lived in Shamir in the hill country of Ephraim. [2] Tola judged Israel 23 years and when he died, was buried in Shamir.

[3] After him came Jair the Gileadite, who judged Israel 22 years. [4] He had 30 sons who rode on 30 donkeys. They had 30 towns[C] in Gilead, which are called Jair's Villages[D] to this day. [5] When Jair died, he was buried in Kamon.

Defeat of the Ammonites by Jephthah (10:6–12:7)

[6] Then the Israelites again did what was evil in the sight of the LORD. They worshiped the •Baals and the •Ashtoreths, the gods of Aram, Sidon, and Moab, and the gods of the Ammonites and the Philistines. They abandoned •Yahweh and did not worship Him. [7] So the LORD's anger burned against Israel, and He sold them to[E] the Philistines and the Ammonites. [8] They shattered and crushed the Israelites that year, and for 18 years they did the same to all the Israelites who were on the other side of the Jordan in the land of the Amorites in Gilead. [9] The Ammonites also crossed the Jordan to fight against Judah, Benjamin, and the house of Ephraim. Israel was greatly oppressed, [10] so they cried out to the LORD, saying, "We have sinned against You. We have abandoned our God and worshiped the Baals."

[11] The LORD said to the Israelites, "When the Egyptians, Amorites, Ammonites, Philistines, [12] Sidonians, Amalekites, and Maonites[F] oppressed you, and you cried out to Me, did I not deliver you from their power? [13] But you have abandoned Me and worshiped other gods. Therefore, I will not deliver you again. [14] Go and cry out to the gods you have chosen. Let them deliver you in the time of your oppression."

[15] But the Israelites said, "We have sinned. Deal with us as You see fit;[G]

9:45 Archaeology has confirmed this destruction of Shechem, which was not rebuilt until the time of Jeroboam I (1Kg 12:25).

9:56-57 Retribution is the job of God, not man; but God most often uses people to accomplish His purpose:—sometimes using their wickedness and sometimes using them as His righteous agents of judgment (Dt 32:35).

10:10 This verse records the Israelites' first confession of sin in this book and acknowledgment of worshiping Baal.

[A] **9:46** Or *the crypt*, or *the vault* [B] **9:46** = God of the Covenant [C] **10:4** LXX; MT reads *donkeys* [D] **10:4** Or *called Havvoth-jair* [E] **10:7** Lit *into the hand of* [F] **10:12** LXX reads *Midianites* [G] **10:15** Lit *Do to us what is good in Your eyes*

11:10-11 While Scripture does not indicate that **Jephthah** was chosen by the Lord, it does record that God was a witness to Jephthah's commissioning ceremonies.

only deliver us today!" [16] So they got
rid of the foreign gods among them
and worshiped the LORD, and He became weary of Israel's misery.
[17] The Ammonites were called together, and they camped in Gilead.
So the Israelites assembled and
camped at Mizpah. [18] The rulers[A] of
Gilead said to one another, "Which
man will lead the fight against the
Ammonites? He will be the leader of
all the inhabitants of Gilead."

11 Jephthah the Gileadite was a
great warrior, but he was the
son of a prostitute, and Gilead was
his father. [2] Gilead's wife bore him
sons, and when they grew up, they
drove Jephthah out and said to him,
"You will have no inheritance in our
father's house, because you are the
son of another woman." [3] So Jephthah fled from his brothers and lived
in the land of Tob. Then some lawless men joined Jephthah and traveled with him.
[4] Some time later, the Ammonites
fought against Israel. [5] When the
Ammonites made war with Israel,
the elders of Gilead went to get Jephthah from the land of Tob. [6] They
said to him, "Come, be our commander, and let's fight against the
Ammonites."
[7] Jephthah replied to the elders
of Gilead, "Didn't you hate me and
drive me from my father's house?
Why then have you come to me now
when you're in trouble?"
[8] They answered Jephthah, "Since
that's true, we now turn to you.
Come with us, fight the Ammonites,
and you will become leader of all the
inhabitants of Gilead."
[9] So Jephthah said to them, "If you
are bringing me back to fight the
Ammonites and the LORD gives them
to me, I will be your leader."
[10] The elders of Gilead said to Jephthah, "The LORD is our witness if we
don't do as you say." [11] So Jephthah
went with the elders of Gilead. The
people put him over themselves as
leader and commander, and Jephthah repeated all his terms in the
presence of the LORD at Mizpah.
[12] Jephthah sent messengers to
the king of the Ammonites, saying,
"What do you have against me that
you have come to fight against me
in my land?"
[13] The king of the Ammonites said
to Jephthah's messengers, "When
Israel came from Egypt, they seized
my land from the Arnon to the Jabbok and the Jordan. Now restore it
peaceably."
[14] Jephthah again sent messengers
to the king of the Ammonites [15] to
tell him, "This is what Jephthah says:

[A] **10:18** Lit *The people, rulers*

CHARACTER PROFILE

Jephthah's Daughter

An Honorable Daughter

Her Background	The only child of Jephthah, the eighth judge of Israel (11:34)
Her Story	• Jephthah offered a vow to the Lord before going into battle (11:30). • He vowed that upon his return home whatever came out first to greet him would be sacrificed to the Lord (11:30-31). • To his great sorrow, his daughter was the first to greet him (11:34-35). • She asked permission to mourn her virginity with her friends for two months (11:37).
Life Lessons	• Children often bear the consequences of a parent's poor decision. • Despite her grief, Jephthah's daughter was obedient to her father.

>WORD|*study*

11:30 A VOW (Hb *neder*, "promise,") in the Old Testament was usually an expression of devotion made as a promise to the Lord in exchange for something. Jephthah did not need to make a vow about the upcoming battle. His cause was just (vv. 27-28), and he was empowered by the Spirit.

The announcement of Jephthah's vow is sandwiched between verse 29—noting that he **crossed over to the Ammonites**—and verse 32, which picks up the same wording to carry the story forward—he **crossed over to the Ammonites to fight . . . them**. Consequently, the report of the battle's outcome—**the Lord handed them** [Ammonites] **over to him** [Jephthah]—not only recognizes what God did for Israel but also prompts the reader to anticipate how Jephthah will or will not keep his vow since the Lord had done exactly what the man asked.

11:34 The text *does* note that this daughter was his only child (Hb *yechidah*, "only one," implying that which is most dear and cannot be replaced) and even reiterates that he had no other children at all. This detail underscores the tragic nature of the situation in which Jephthah had entrapped himself.

Israel did not take away the land of
Moab or the land of the Ammonites.
16 But when they came from Egypt,
Israel traveled through the wilderness to the •Red Sea and came to
Kadesh. 17 Israel sent messengers to
the king of Edom, saying, 'Please let
us travel through your land,' but the
king of Edom would not listen. They
also sent messengers to the king
of Moab, but he refused. So Israel
stayed in Kadesh.
18 "Then they traveled through the
wilderness and around the lands of
Edom and Moab. They came to the
east side of the land of Moab and
camped on the other side of the Arnon but did not enter into the territory of Moab, for the Arnon was the
boundary of Moab.
19 "Then Israel sent messengers to
Sihon king of the Amorites, king of
Heshbon. Israel said to him, 'Please
let us travel through your land to
our country,' 20 but Sihon would not
trust Israel to pass through his territory. Instead, Sihon gathered all his
people, camped at Jahaz, and fought
with Israel. 21 Then the LORD God of
Israel handed over Sihon and all his
people to Israel, and they defeated
them. So Israel took possession of
the entire land of the Amorites who
lived in that country. 22 They took
possession of all the territory of the
Amorites from the Arnon to the Jabbok and from the wilderness to the
Jordan.
23 "The LORD God of Israel has now
driven out the Amorites before His
people Israel, and will you now force
us out? 24 Isn't it true that you may
possess whatever your god Chemosh
drives out for you, and we may possess everything the LORD our God
drives out before us? 25 Now are you
any better than Balak son of Zippor,
king of Moab? Did he ever contend
with Israel or fight against them?
26 While Israel lived 300 years in
Heshbon and its villages, in Aroer
and its villages, and in all the cities that are on the banks of the Arnon, why didn't you take them back
at that time? 27 I have not sinned
against you, but you have wronged
me by fighting against me. Let the
LORD who is the Judge decide today between the Israelites and the
Ammonites." 28 But the king of the
Ammonites would not listen to Jephthah's message that he sent him.
29 The Spirit of the LORD came on
Jephthah, who traveled through Gilead and Manasseh, and then through
Mizpah of Gilead. He crossed over
to the Ammonites from Mizpah of
Gilead. 30 Jephthah made this vow
to the LORD: "If You will hand over
the Ammonites to me, 31 whatever
comes out of the doors of my house
to greet me when I return in peace
from the Ammonites will belong
to the LORD, and I will offer it as a
•burnt offering."
32 Jephthah crossed over to the
Ammonites to fight against them,
and the LORD handed them over to
him. 33 He defeated 20 of their cities
with a great slaughter from Aroer all
the way to the entrance of Minnith
and to Abel-keramim. So the Ammonites were subdued before the
Israelites.
34 When Jephthah went to his
home in Mizpah, there was his
daughter, coming out to meet him
with tambourines and dancing! She

11:34-35 The text does not reveal what Jephthah expected to come, specifically, "out of the doors of [his] house" (v. 31) to meet him when he returned, nor does it provide any clues with which to make a reasonable guess. Clearly, however, he did *not* expect to see his daughter. He reacted to her celebration of his return with signs of grief and dismay. Particularly in Jewish culture, to tear one's clothes was an expression of intense emotion, whether heart-wrenching sadness or outrage. The text does not explain Jephthah's apparent assumption that his daughter would be somewhere other than in his house.

11:34-40 In a culture that regarded seriously the spoken word, especially vows made to the Lord, Jephthah knew (and the original audience recognized) that he faced a horrifying dilemma—*either* to keep the vow by sacrificing his precious daughter *or* to subject himself to the judgment of God (cp. Lv 19:12; Nm 30:2; Dt 23:21-23), who had already done what the man asked. The option of literally fulfilling the vow is now so unthinkable that readers are tempted to search for an explanation of how the vow might have been fulfilled in some other way. For example, some scholars argue that Jephthah must have known of God's abhorrence and strict prohibition of human sacrifice (Lv 18:21; 20:1-5; Dt 12:29-32; 18:9-12) and therefore may have given his daughter to lifelong, celibate service to the tabernacle (cp. Ex 38:8; 1 Sm 2:22). This idea also addresses the daughter's request to mourn her **virginity**. In this case, Jephthah mourned having no descendants, and the daughter mourned never being allowed to marry and bear children.

Others suggest that Jephthah kept his vow by paying the "valuation" price for a person as described in Leviticus 27. Alternatively, since there was little knowledge of God's Word in the days of the judges, perhaps Jephthah did not know about the provision and therefore literally fulfilled the vow, further illustrating the extent to which Israel was influenced by the surrounding pagan cultures, which practiced human sacrifice.

Neither interpretation reflects the plain sense of the text—that **he kept the vow he had made** (without suggestion of an alternative or substitute), which, in light of that specific vow, showcases the honorable response of his daughter (v. 36) and, in context, makes sense both of her request and the description of how her sacrifice was commemorated (vv. 39-40). Tragically, rather than simply being an instrument used by "the Spirit of the LORD" to achieve victory over the Ammonites, Jephthah had attempted to bargain with the Lord, potentially for his own glory, as He had done with the elders (who agreed to his terms, vv. 5-11) and the king of the Ammonites (who "would not listen to" him, vv. 12-28). The text records no response from the Lord regarding the vow and no commentary from the writer; the reader is expected to recognize Jephthah's tragic mistake and lament with **the young women of Israel** (v. 40) the senseless sacrifice of his only child and his future.

12:5-6 The word **Shibboleth** was chosen as a test, since the Ephraimites pronounced the initial letter of the word with an "s" instead of a "sh" sound.

13:1-2 Some of the most prominent leaders and spokesmen for God came from seemingly barren wombs. The reproach of childlessness became a God-glorifying testimony with the birth of a son who would become prominent in God's plan.

11:35 In Hebrew, the exclamation that Jephthah's daughter had devastated (Hb *kara'*, "caused to bow down or kneel"; cp. 5:27) him suggests a picture of this great warrior sinking to his knees, emotionally undone.

was his only child; he had no other son or daughter besides her. 35 When he saw her, he tore his clothes and said, "No! Not my daughter! You have devastated me! You have brought great misery on me.[A] I have given my word to the LORD and cannot take it back."

36 Then she said to him, "My father, you have given your word to the LORD. Do to me as you have said, for the LORD brought vengeance on your enemies, the Ammonites." 37 She also said to her father, "Let me do this one thing: Let me wander two months through the mountains with my friends and mourn my virginity."

38 "Go," he said. And he sent her away two months. So she left with her friends and mourned her virginity as she wandered through the mountains. 39 At the end of two months, she returned to her father, and he kept the vow he had made about her. And she had never been intimate with a man. Now it became a custom in Israel 40 that four days each year the young women of Israel would commemorate the daughter of Jephthah the Gileadite.

12 The men of Ephraim were called together and crossed the Jordan to Zaphon. They said to Jephthah, "Why have you crossed over to fight against the Ammonites but didn't call us to go with you? We will burn your house down with you in it!"

2 Then Jephthah said to them, "My people and I had a serious conflict with the Ammonites. So I called for you, but you didn't deliver me from their power. 3 When I saw that you weren't going to deliver me, I took my life in my own hands and crossed over to the Ammonites, and the LORD handed them over to me. Why then have you come[B] today to fight against me?"

4 Then Jephthah gathered all of the men of Gilead. They fought and defeated Ephraim, because Ephraim had said, "You Gileadites are Ephraimite fugitives in the territories of Ephraim and Manasseh." 5 The Gileadites captured the fords of the Jordan leading to Ephraim. Whenever a fugitive from Ephraim said, "Let me cross over," the Gileadites asked him, "Are you an Ephraimite?" If he answered, "No," 6 they told him, "Please say Shibboleth." If he said, "Sibboleth," because he could not pronounce it correctly, they seized him and killed him at the fords of the Jordan. At that time 42,000 from Ephraim died.

7 Jephthah judged Israel six years, and when he died, he was buried in one of the cities of Gilead.[C]

Judgeships of Ibzan, Elon, and Abdon (12:8-15)

8 Ibzan, who was from Bethlehem, judged Israel after Jephthah 9 and had 30 sons. He gave his 30 daughters in marriage to men outside the tribe and brought back 30 wives for his sons from outside the tribe. Ibzan judged Israel seven years, 10 and when he died, he was buried in Bethlehem.

11 Elon, who was from Zebulun, judged Israel after Ibzan. He judged Israel 10 years, 12 and when he died, he was buried in Aijalon in the land of Zebulun.

13 After Elon, Abdon son of Hillel, who was from Pirathon, judged Israel. 14 He had 40 sons and 30 grandsons, who rode on 70 donkeys. Abdon judged Israel eight years, 15 and when he died, he was buried in Pirathon in the land of Ephraim, in the hill country of the Amalekites.

Defeat of the Philistines by Samson (13:1-16:31)

13 The Israelites again did what was evil in the LORD's sight, so

[A]11:35 Lit *have been among those who trouble me* [B]12:3 Lit *come to me* [C]12:7 LXX reads *in his city in Gilead*

The Nazirite Vow Judges 13:3-8

The vow was taken voluntarily.	• The one making the vow consecrated himself—devoted and separated himself "to the LORD" (Nm 6:2,5-6). • The vow involved specific *personal* restrictions indicated by the repetition of personal pronouns (Nm 6:7).
The vow had a sacred purpose.	• The person consecrated himself "to the LORD" (Nm 6:2,5-6,12). • During the time of consecration, the person was "holy to the LORD" (Nm 6:8). • Upon completion of the vow, an offering and sacrifice were presented "to the LORD" (Nm 6:14,17,21).
The vow was symbolic.	• The vow demanded abstinence from the fruit of the vine (Nm 6:3-4). • The vow prohibited cutting one's hair unless defiled (Nm 6:5,7,9,12,18). • The vow demanded staying away from dead bodies (Nm 6:6-12).
The vow was temporary.	• The vow was in effect for a set length of time (Nm 6:5). • Offerings and sacrifices were prescribed to mark the completion of the time of consecration (Nm 6:13-21). • After the vow's completion, its personal restrictions were lifted (Nm 6:18-20).

NOTE: Included in Scripture are the accounts of the following men whose Nazirite vows constituted a lifelong commitment to the Lord: Samson (Jdg 13:2-7,13-14), Samuel (1Sm 1:11,27-28), and possibly John the Baptist (Lk 1:15). Paul (Ac 18:18) and four unnamed Christians (Ac 21;23-24) took a Nazirite vow. Jesus was *not* a Nazirite (Mt 11:18-19).

the LORD handed them over to the Philistines 40 years. 2 There was a certain man from Zorah, from the family of Dan, whose name was Manoah; his wife was unable to conceive and had no children. 3 The Angel of the LORD appeared to the woman and said to her, "It is true that you are unable to conceive and have no children, but you will conceive and give birth to a son. 4 Now please be careful not to drink wine or beer, or to eat anything •unclean; 5 for indeed, you will conceive and give birth to a son. You must never cut his hair,[A] because the boy will be a Nazirite to God from birth, and he will begin to save Israel from the power of the Philistines."

6 Then the woman went and told her husband, "A man of God came to me. He looked like the awe-inspiring Angel of God. I didn't ask Him where He came from, and He didn't tell me His name. 7 He said to me, 'You will conceive and give birth to a son. Therefore, do not drink wine or beer, and do not eat anything unclean, because the boy will be a Nazirite to God from birth until the day of his death.'"

8 Manoah prayed to the LORD and said, "Please Lord, let the man of God you sent come again to us and teach us what we should do for the boy who will be born."

9 God listened to[B] Manoah, and the Angel of God came again to the woman. She was sitting in the field, and her husband Manoah was not with her. 10 The woman ran quickly to her husband and told him, "The man who came to me today has just come back!"

11 So Manoah got up and followed his wife. When he came to the man, he asked, "Are You the man who spoke to my wife?"

"I am," He said.

12 Then Manoah asked, "When Your words come true, what will the boy's responsibilities and mission[C] be?"

13 The Angel of the LORD answered Manoah, "Your wife needs to do

[A] **13:5** Lit *And a razor is not to go up on his head* [B] **13:9** Lit *to the voice of* [C] **13:12** Lit *work*

13:3-8 The **Nazirite** vow set one apart for service to the Lord and was usually temporary. Samson's vow, however, was to be permanent. This vow required the avoidance of three things: wine, the razor, and contact with dead bodies (Nm 6:2-13).

13:24-25 Samson's work was not done in the manner typical of previous judges who raised armies and went into battle. His deliverance was enacted more with individual intervention.

14:1-4 Samson proved to be a headstrong young man intent on having his own way, leading to poor choices about women and to decisions that violated his Nazirite vow. Despite the Mosaic law's specific forbidding of intermarriage, Samson demanded that his parents get a **young Philistine woman** as a bride (Ex 34:15-16; Dt 7:1-3). God did not condone breaking His law, but His purposes overrule the foolish decisions of sinful people.

Samson's Mother A Godly Mother

Her Background	• The wife of Manoah of the tribe of Dan (13:2) • The mother of Samson (13:24)
Her Story	• She was barren (13:2). • An angel appeared to her and told her she would give birth to a son (13:3). • Her son would be a Nazirite and a deliverer of Israel (13:5). • At her husband's request, an angel appeared again (13:8,10). • She and Manoah were grieved when Samson sought a Philistine wife (14:3).
Life Lessons	• Samson's mother made godly choices. • Tragically, her spiritual discernment did not ensure that her adult son would follow her example.

everything I told her. 14 She must not eat anything that comes from the grapevine or drink wine or beer. And she must not eat anything unclean. Your wife must do everything I have commanded her."

15 "Please stay here," Manoah told Him, "and we will prepare a young goat for You."

16 The Angel of the LORD said to him, "If I stay, I won't eat your food. But if you want to prepare a •burnt offering, offer it to the LORD." For Manoah did not know He was the Angel of the LORD.

17 Then Manoah said to Him, "What is Your name, so that we may honor You when Your words come true?"

18 "Why do you ask My name," the Angel of the LORD asked him, "since it is wonderful."

19 Manoah took a young goat and a •grain offering and offered them on a rock to the LORD, and He did a wonderful thing[A] while Manoah and his wife were watching. 20 When the flame went up from the altar to the sky, the Angel of the LORD went up in its flame. When Manoah and his wife saw this, they fell facedown on the ground. 21 The Angel of the LORD did not appear again to Manoah and his wife. Then Manoah realized that it was the Angel of the LORD.

22 "We're going to die," he said to his wife, "because we have seen God!"

23 But his wife said to him, "If the LORD had intended to kill us, He wouldn't have accepted the burnt offering and the grain offering from us, and He would not have shown us all these things or spoken to us now like this."

24 So the woman gave birth to a son and named him Samson. The boy grew, and the LORD blessed him. 25 Then the Spirit of the LORD began to direct him in the Camp of Dan,[B] between Zorah and Eshtaol.

14 Samson went down to Timnah and saw a young Philistine woman there. 2 He went back and told his father and his mother: "I have seen a young Philistine woman in Timnah. Now get her for me as a wife."

3 But his father and mother said to him, "Can't you find[C] a young woman among your relatives or among any of our people? Must you go to the uncircumcised Philistines for a wife?"

But Samson told his father, "Get her for me, because I want her."[D] 4 Now his father and mother did not know this was from the LORD, who was seeking an occasion against the Philistines. At that time, the Philistines were ruling over Israel.

5 Samson went down to Timnah

[A]**13:19** LXX reads *to the LORD, to the One who works wonders* [B]**13:25** Or *in Mahaneh-dan*
[C]**14:3** Lit *Is there not* [D]**14:3** Lit *because she is right in my eyes*

14:5-9 By touching the carcass, Samson knowingly made himself unclean and violated one of the key tenets of his Nazirite vow. Further, he dishonored and defiled his parents by giving them the honey without telling them of the ceremonially unclean manner by which he obtained it.

CHARACTER PROFILE

Samson's Bride **A Treacherous Wife**

Her Background	A Philistine woman from Timnah (14:1-2)
Her Story	• Through tears and nagging she manipulated Samson to tell her the answer to his riddle (14:16-17). • She was more loyal to her Philistine people than to her husband (14:14-17). • She was eventually given in marriage to another man (14:20).
Life Lessons	• This marriage was doomed because of the divided loyalties of both husband and wife. • Samson and his wife were both self-centered.

with his father and mother and
came to the vineyards of Timnah.
Suddenly a young lion came roaring at him, 6 the Spirit of the LORD
took control of[A] him, and he tore the
lion apart with his bare hands as he
might have torn a young goat. But
he did not tell his father or mother
what he had done. 7 Then he went
and spoke to the woman, because
Samson wanted her.[B]
8 After some time, when he returned to get her, he left the road to
see the lion's carcass, and there was
a swarm of bees with honey in the
carcass. 9 He scooped some honey
into his hands and ate it as he went
along. When he returned to his father and mother, he gave some to
them and they ate it. But he did not
tell them that he had scooped the
honey from the lion's carcass.
10 His father went to visit the
woman, and Samson prepared a
feast there, as young men were accustomed to do. 11 When the Philistines saw him, they brought 30 men
to accompany him.
12 "Let me tell you a riddle," Samson said to them. "If you can explain it to me during the seven days
of the feast and figure it out, I will
give you 30 linen garments and 30
changes of clothes. 13 But if you can't
explain it to me, you must give me
30 linen garments and 30 changes
of clothes."
"Tell us your riddle," they replied.[C]
"Let's hear it."
14 So he said to them:

Out of the eater came
something to eat,
and out of the strong came
something sweet.

After three days, they were unable to explain the riddle. 15 On the
fourth[D] day they said to Samson's
wife, "Persuade your husband to
explain the riddle to us, or we will

[A]14:6 Lit *LORD rushed on* [B]14:7 Lit *because she was right in the eyes of Samson* [C]14:13 Lit *replied to him* [D]14:15 LXX, Syr; MT reads *seventh*

Biblical Womanhood Parenting a Strong-Willed Child

Samson was a selfish, self-centered and self-absorbed adult. Although this characteristic may not have been a result of his upbringing, mothers of strong-willed children should be warned. In one sense all children have strong wills—they all want their own way! Wise parenting techniques protect the vulnerable spirit of a child, shaping rather than crushing his will and directing the development of his spiritual disciplines. Often parents of strong-willed children find themselves reacting in anger and frustration. Anger is not a right motivation for discipline and can often lead to serious resentment and rebellion on the child's part. Wise parents need to heed admonitions of Scripture (Eph 6:1-4; Pr 22:6) and understand that working with a strong-willed child requires much prayer, wisdom, and energy.

CHARACTER PROFILE

The Women in Samson's Life Judges 13–16

	His Mother	His Wife	The Prostitute	Delilah
Her Situation	She was the wife of Manoah the Danite and was barren.	Samson saw her in Timnah and demanded her as his wife.	Samson saw her in Gaza and went to bed with her.	Samson fell in love with this woman who lived in the Sorek Valley.
Her Story	The Angel of the Lord told her she would have a son. She was to observe the Nazirite vow while she was pregnant.	The men of Timnah used her to persuade Samson to explain a riddle.	The men of Gaza used her in an attempt to ambush Samson.	The Philistine leaders used her to discover the source of Samson's great strength so they could overpower him.
Her Significance	She is a godly example of practical sensibility and encouragement—she responded to her husband's fears and her son's demands with wisdom.	She is an example of nagging petulance—she used tears and manipulation to get what she wanted from her husband.	Although Scripture does not mention her role in the attempt to ambush Samson, she played a part in his downfall.	She is an example of greedy sensuality—she used deceit and lust to destroy Samson.

burn you and your father's household to death. Did you invite us here
to rob us?"
[16] So Samson's wife came to him,
weeping, and said, "You hate me and
don't love me! You told my people
the riddle, but haven't explained it
to me."
"Look," he said,[A] "I haven't even
explained it to my father or mother,
so why should I explain it to you?"
[17] She wept the whole seven days
of the feast, and at last, on the seventh day, he explained it to her, because she had nagged him so much.
Then she explained it to her people.
[18] On the seventh day, before sunset,
the men of the city said to him:

> What is sweeter than honey?
> What is stronger than a lion?

So he said to them:

> If you hadn't plowed with
> my young cow,
> you wouldn't know
> my riddle now!

[19] The Spirit of the LORD took control of him, and he went down to
Ashkelon and killed 30 of their men.
He stripped them and gave their
clothes to those who had explained
the riddle. In a rage, Samson returned to his father's house, [20] and
his wife was given to one of the men
who had accompanied him.

15 Later on, during the wheat
harvest, Samson took a young
goat as a gift and visited his wife. "I
want to go to my wife in her room,"
he said. But her father would not let
him enter.
[2] "I was sure you hated her," her
father said, "so I gave her to one
of the men who accompanied you.
Isn't her younger sister more beautiful than she is? Why not take her
instead?"
[3] Samson said to them, "This time
I won't be responsible when I harm
the Philistines." [4] So he went out and
caught 300 foxes. He took torches,
turned the foxes tail-to-tail, and put
a torch between each pair of tails.
[5] Then he ignited the torches and
released the foxes into the standing
grain of the Philistines. He burned
up the piles of grain and the stand-

[A] 14:16 Lit *said to her*

>WORD|*study*

16:4 Love (Hb *'ahav*) is equal to its English counterpart with a wide variance of meaning. When it is used of a man's love for a woman, as it is here, it means a physical and emotional attraction.

ing grain as well as the vineyards and olive groves.

6 Then the Philistines asked, "Who did this?"

They were told, "It was Samson, the Timnite's son-in-law, because he has taken Samson's wife and given her to another man." So the Philistines went to her and her father and burned them to death.

7 Then Samson told them, "Because you did this, I swear that I won't rest until I have taken vengeance on you." 8 He tore them limb from limb[A] with a great slaughter, and he went down and stayed in the cave at the rock of Etam.

9 The Philistines went up, camped in Judah, and raided Lehi. 10 So the men of Judah said, "Why have you attacked us?"

They replied, "We have come to arrest Samson and pay him back for what he did to us."

11 Then 3,000 men of Judah went to the cave at the rock of Etam, and they asked Samson, "Don't you realize that the Philistines rule over us? What have you done to us?"

"I have done to them what they did to me," he answered.[B]

12 They said to him, "We've come to arrest you and hand you over to the Philistines."

Then Samson told them, "Swear to me that you yourselves won't kill me."

13 "No," they said,[C] "we won't kill you, but we will tie you up securely and hand you over to them." So they tied him up with two new ropes and led him away from the rock.

14 When he came to Lehi, the Philistines came to meet him shouting. The Spirit of the LORD took control of[D] him, and the ropes that were on his arms became like burnt flax and his bonds fell off his wrists. 15 He found a fresh jawbone of a donkey, reached out his hand, took it, and killed 1,000 men with it. 16 Then Samson said:

> With the jawbone of a donkey
> I have piled them in a heap.
> With the jawbone of a donkey
> I have killed 1,000 men.

17 When he finished speaking, he threw away the jawbone and named that place Ramath-lehi.[E] 18 He became very thirsty and called out to the LORD: "You have accomplished this great victory through[F] Your servant. Must I now die of thirst and fall into the hands of the uncircumcised?" 19 So God split a hollow place in the ground at Lehi, and water came out of it. After Samson drank, his strength returned, and he revived. That is why he named it En-hakkore,[G] which is in Lehi to this day. 20 And he judged Israel 20 years in the days of the Philistines.

16 Samson went to Gaza, where he saw a prostitute and went to bed with her. 2 When the Gazites heard that Samson was there, they surrounded the place and waited in ambush for him all that night at the city gate. While they were waiting quietly,[H] they said, "Let us wait until dawn; then we will kill him." 3 But Samson stayed in bed until midnight when he got up, took hold of the doors of the city gate along with the two gateposts, and pulled them out, bar and all. He put them on his shoulders and took them to the top of the mountain overlooking Hebron.

4 Some time later, he fell in love with a woman named Delilah, who lived in the Sorek Valley. 5 The Philistine leaders went to her and said, "Persuade him to tell you[I] where his great strength comes from, so we can overpower him, tie him up, and make him helpless. Each of us will then give you 1,100 pieces of silver."

15:14-20 Despite Samson's self-serving and reactionary approach to life, God repeatedly used him for His glory. For the first time Samson, in his need, is recorded here as calling out for **the Lord**, and God provided water for him.

16:4-20 Learning little from his past mistakes, Samson became a victim of his own lack of self-control, lust, and foolish impulses when he fell in love with **Delilah** (Hb, "feeble, weak, delicate; pining with desire"). Ironically, the one time Samson appeared to love and trust someone, she proved to be as callous and uncaring to him as he had been to others.

[A]15:8 Lit *He struck them hip on thigh* [B]15:11 Lit *answered them* [C]15:13 Lit *said to him* [D]15:14 Lit *LORD rushed on* [E]15:17 = High Place of the Jawbone [F]15:18 Lit *through the hand of* [G]15:19 = Spring of the One Who Cried Out [H]16:2 Lit *quietly all night* [I]16:5 Lit *him and see*

CHARACTER PROFILE

Delilah A Scheming Seductress

Her Background	• A Philistine woman • A resident of the Sorek Valley (16:4)
Her Story	• She was approached by the Philistines to find the source of Samson's strength in return for a large sum of money (16:5). • She manipulated Samson into telling her the truth by constant pouting, weeping, and nagging (16:16). • While Samson slept, she allowed his hair to be cut, causing him to lose his strength (16:19).
Life Lessons	• Samson's weak character destroyed his life. • His lack of spiritual sensitivity caused God's people to be exploited by his enemies.

6 So Delilah said to Samson, "Please
tell me, where does your great
strength come from? How could
someone tie you up and make you
helpless?"
7 Samson told her, "If they tie me
up with seven fresh bowstrings that
have not been dried, I will become
weak and be like any other man."
8 The Philistine leaders brought
her seven fresh bowstrings that had
not been dried, and she tied him
up with them. 9 While the men in
ambush were waiting in her room,
she called out to him, "Samson,
the Philistines are here!"[A] But he
snapped the bowstrings as a strand
of yarn snaps when it touches fire.
The secret of his strength remained
unknown.
10 Then Delilah said to Samson,
"You have mocked me and told me
lies! Won't you please tell me how
you can be tied up?"
11 He told her, "If they tie me up
with new ropes that have never been
used, I will become weak and be like
any other man."
12 Delilah took new ropes, tied him
up with them, and shouted, "Samson, the Philistines are here!"[A] But
while the men in ambush were waiting in her room, he snapped the
ropes off his arms like a thread.
13 Then Delilah said to Samson,
"You have mocked me all along and
told me lies! Tell me how you can be
tied up."
He told her, "If you weave the seven braids on my head with the web
of a loom—"[B]
14 She fastened the braids with a
pin and called to him, "Samson,
the Philistines are here!"[A] He awoke

[A] 16:9,12,14 Lit *are on you* [B] 16:13-14 LXX reads *loom and fasten them with a pin into the wall and I will become weak and be like any other man."* [14] *And while he was sleeping, Delilah wove the seven braids on his head into the loom.*

BIBLICAL WOMANHOOD The Manipulative Woman

Samson was a man of incredible physical strength, but he was weak in spirit. He seemed especially vulnerable to nagging, manipulative women, first his wife and later Delilah. Delilah slowly and cleverly wore Samson down with her manipulative words, both by nagging (vv. 14-16) and by accusing Samson of not loving her. Job's wife was another nagging woman, yet her manipulative words failed to wear down Job, a man of faith and character (Jb 2:9-10). Proverbs 19:13 describes a wife's nagging as an "endless dripping" that can wear down a husband (or anyone) and drive him to distraction. Nagging may accomplish a goal, but it never produces intimacy or deep love. Similar word pictures of an argumentative woman are found in 21:9,19; 25:24; 27:15.

from his sleep and pulled out the pin, with the loom and the web.

15 "How can you say, 'I love you,'" she told him, "when your heart is not with me? This is the third time you have mocked me and not told me what makes your strength so great!"

16 Because she nagged him day after day and pleaded with him until she wore him out,[A] 17 he told her the whole truth and said to her, "My hair has never been cut,[B] because I am a Nazirite to God from birth. If I am shaved, my strength will leave me, and I will become weak and be like any other man."

18 When Delilah realized that he had told her the whole truth, she sent this message to the Philistine leaders: "Come one more time, for he has told me the whole truth." The Philistine leaders came to her and brought the money with them.

19 Then she let him fall asleep on her lap and called a man to shave off the seven braids on his head. In this way, she made him helpless,[C] and his strength left him. 20 Then she cried, "Samson, the Philistines are here!"[D] When he awoke from his sleep, he said, "I will escape as I did before and shake myself free." But he did not know that the LORD had left him.

21 The Philistines seized him and gouged out his eyes. They brought him down to Gaza and bound him with bronze shackles, and he was forced to grind grain in the prison. 22 But his hair began to grow back after it had been shaved.

23 Now the Philistine leaders gathered together to offer a great sacrifice to their god Dagon. They rejoiced and said:

> Our god has handed over
> our enemy Samson to us.

24 When the people saw him, they praised their god and said:

> Our god has handed over
> to us
> our enemy who destroyed
> our land
> and who multiplied our dead.

25 When they were drunk,[E] they said, "Bring Samson here to entertain us." So they brought Samson from prison, and he entertained them. They had him stand between the pillars.

26 Samson said to the young man who was leading him by the hand, "Lead me where I can feel the pillars supporting the temple, so I can lean against them." 27 The temple was full of men and women; all the leaders of the Philistines were there, and about 3,000 men and women were on the roof watching Samson entertain them. 28 He called out to the LORD: "Lord GOD, please remember me. Strengthen me, God, just once more. With one act of vengeance, let me pay back the Philistines for my two eyes." 29 Samson took hold of the two middle pillars supporting the temple and leaned against them, one on his right hand and the other on his left. 30 Samson said, "Let me die with the Philistines." He pushed with all his might, and the temple fell on the leaders and all the people in it. And the dead he killed at his death were more than those he had killed in his life.

31 Then his brothers and his father's family came down, carried him back, and buried him between Zorah and Eshtaol in the tomb of his father Manoah. So he judged Israel 20 years.

Epilogue (17:1–21:25)

Religious Apostasy (17:1–18:35)

Micah's idolatry (17:1-13)

17 There was a man from the hill country of Ephraim named Micah. 2 He said to his mother, "The 1,100 pieces of silver taken from you, and that I heard you utter a curse about—here, I have the silver with me. I took it. So now I return it to you."[F]

Then his mother said, "My son, you are blessed by the LORD!"

3 He returned the 1,100 pieces of silver to his mother, and his mother said, "I personally consecrate the silver to the LORD for my son's benefit to make a carved image overlaid

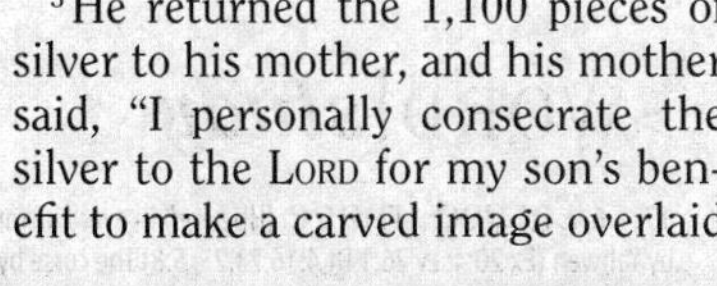

16:20 What followed Samson's foolish decisions is one of the most tragic statements in the Bible—**But he did not know that the LORD had left him**. Samson's physical strength had not actually been in his hair but in the vow that bound him to the strength of the Lord. The seven braids were to represent public devotion to Yahweh (vv. 13,19); when these were cut, Samson yielded any claim on the Spirit's power. He had lived in such selfishness and disobedience that, when God left him, he did not even know it.

16:31 Samson's life illustrates the tragedy of a person's determination to live on his own terms rather than surrender himself to God's purposes. Nevertheless, God's overriding determination to empower and use Samson ultimately brought glory to the name of Yahweh.

17:1-6 The final chapters of Judges (17–21) do not follow the previous chapter chronologically but rather serve to illustrate Israel's spiritual depravity during this period. Ironically, Micah's name means, "Who is like Yahweh?" to which the implied answer is, "No one is like Him." His name may reflect the writer's intention to underscore Micah's apostasy in turning from worship of the God of Israel and to self-styled idolatry.

[A] **16:16** Lit *him and he became short to death* [B] **16:17** Lit *A razor has not gone up on my head* [C] **16:19** LXX reads *way he began to weaken* [D] **16:20** Lit *are on you* [E] **16:25** Or *When they were feeling good* [F] **17:2** MT places this sentence at the end of v. 3.

17:5 Micah's mother may have meant well, but she was spiritually ignorant. Rather than worshiping the true God, she resorted to common pagan practices. She and her son typify the generation of Israel who knew neither the Lord nor His works.

17:7-13 The Levites had not been given a land inheritance since they were to live and minister in 48 designated cities throughout the promised land (Nm 35:1-18). The tithes of the Israelites were used to provide for the needs of the Levites (Nm 18:21-24). In hiring a Levite, Micah employed a man who most likely was unqualified to serve and superstitiously believed he would have better fortune because of it.

with silver."[A] 4 So he returned the silver to his mother, and she took five pounds of silver and gave it to a silversmith. He made it into a carved image overlaid with silver,[A] and it was in Micah's house.

5 This man Micah had a shrine, and he made an •ephod and household idols, and installed one of his sons to be his priest. 6 In those days there was no king in Israel; everyone did whatever he wanted.[B]

7 There was a young man, a Levite from Bethlehem in Judah, who resided within the clan of Judah. 8 The man left the town of Bethlehem in Judah to settle wherever he could find a place. On his way he came to Micah's home in the hill country of Ephraim.

9 "Where do you come from?" Micah asked him.

He answered him, "I am a Levite from Bethlehem in Judah, and I'm going to settle wherever I can find a place."

10 Micah replied,[C] "Stay with me and be my father and priest, and I will give you four ounces of silver a year, along with your clothing and provisions." So the Levite went in 11 and agreed to stay with the man, and the young man became like one of his sons. 12 Micah consecrated the Levite, and the young man became his priest and lived in Micah's house. 13 Then Micah said, "Now I know that the LORD will be good to me, because a Levite has become my priest."

The Danites' migration (18:1-31)

18 In those days, there was no king in Israel, and the Danite tribe was looking for territory to occupy. Up to that time no territory had been captured by them among the tribes of Israel. 2 So the Danites sent out five brave men from all their clans, from Zorah and Eshtaol, to scout out the land and explore it. They told them, "Go and explore the land."

They came to the hill country of Ephraim as far as the home of Micah and spent the night there. 3 While they were near Micah's home, they recognized the speech of the young Levite. So they went over to him and asked, "Who brought you here? What are you doing in this place? What is keeping you here?" 4 He told them what Micah had done for him and that he had hired him as his priest.

5 Then they said to him, "Please inquire of God so we will know if we will have a successful journey."

6 The priest told them, "Go in peace. The LORD is watching over the journey you are going on."

7 The five men left and came to Laish. They saw that the people who were there were living securely, in the same way as the Sidonians, quiet and unsuspecting. There was nothing lacking[D] in the land and no oppressive ruler. They were far from the Sidonians, having no alliance with anyone.[E]

8 When the men went back to their clans at Zorah and Eshtaol, their people asked them, "What did you find out?"

9 They answered, "Come on, let's go up against them, for we have seen the land, and it is very good. Why wait? Don't hesitate to go and invade and take possession of the land! 10 When you get there, you will come to an unsuspecting people and a spacious land, for God has handed it over to you. It is a place where nothing on earth is lacking." 11 Six hundred Danites departed from Zorah and Eshtaol armed with weapons of war. 12 They went up and camped at Kiriath-jearim in Judah. This is why the place is called the Camp of

[A] **17:3,4** Or *image and a cast image* [B] **17:6** Lit *did what was right in his eyes* [C] **17:10** Lit *replied to him* [D] **18:7** Hb obscure [E] **18:7** MT; some LXX mss, Sym, Old Lat, Syr read *Aram*

>WORD|*study*

17:1-6 Carved image (Hb *pesel*) in every instance refers to man-made "idols," which were expressly forbidden by Yahweh (Ex 20:4; Lv 26:1 Dt 4:16,23,25; 5:8) The curse by Micah's mother seems ironic. Before entering Canaan, Israel was told, "The person who makes a carved idol [Hb *pesel*] or cast image . . . is cursed" (Dt 27:15). The human curse upon Micah for stealing money may have been revoked, but God's curse upon idolaters among His people would not fail.

CHARACTER PROFILE

Micah's Mother A Unfaithful Mother

Her Background	• A resident of Ephraim (17:1-2) • A mother with no evidence of spiritual discernment
Her Story	• 1,100 pieces of silver had been stolen from her (17:1-4). • She pronounced a curse on the thief (17:2). • The thief, who was her son, returned the money to avoid the curse (17:2-4). • She dedicated part of the silver to the Lord but then gave it to a silversmith to make an idol (17:4).
Life Lessons	• Without understanding and knowledge of God's Word, superstition can often be mistaken for spiritual truth. • Mothers have much influence on their children—for good or evil.

Dan[A] to this day; it is west of Kiriath-
jearim. 13 From there they traveled
to the hill country of Ephraim and
arrived at Micah's house.
14 The five men who had gone to
scout out the land of Laish told their
brothers, "Did you know that there
are an •ephod, household gods, and
a carved image overlaid with silver[B]
in these houses? Now think about
what you should do." 15 So they de-
toured there and went to the house
of the young Levite at the home of
Micah and greeted him. 16 The 600
Danite men were standing by the
entrance of the gate, armed with
their weapons of war. 17 Then the five
men who had gone to scout out the
land went in and took the carved image overlaid with silver,[B] the ephod,
and the household idols, while the
priest was standing by the entrance
of the gate with the 600 men armed
with weapons of war.
18 When they entered Micah's
house and took the carved image
overlaid with silver,[B] the ephod, and
the household idols, the priest said
to them, "What are you doing?"
19 They told him, "Be quiet. Keep
your mouth shut.[C] Come with us
and be a father and a priest to us.
Is it better for you to be a priest for
the house of one person or for you to
be a priest for a tribe and family in
Israel?" 20 So the priest was pleased
and took his ephod, household
idols, and carved image, and went
with the people. 21 They prepared to
leave, putting their small children,
livestock, and possessions in front
of them.
22 After they were some distance
from Micah's house, the men who
were in the houses near it mobilized
and caught up with the Danites.
23 They called to the Danites, who
turned to face them, and said to
Micah, "What's the matter with you
that you mobilized the men?"
24 He said, "You took the gods I had
made and the priest, and went away.
What do I have left? How can you say
to me, 'What's the matter with you?'"
25 The Danites said to him, "Don't
raise your voice against us, or angry
men will attack you, and you and
your family will lose your lives."
26 The Danites went on their way,
and Micah turned to go back home,
because he saw that they were stronger than he was.
27 After they had taken the gods
Micah had made and the priest that
belonged to him, they went to Laish,
to a quiet and unsuspecting people.
They killed them with their swords
and burned down the city. 28 There
was no one to rescue them because
it was far from Sidon and they had
no alliance with anyone. It was in a
valley that belonged to Beth-rehob.
They rebuilt the city and lived in it.
29 They named the city Dan, after the

18:22-26 Micah, who stole from his own mother, became the victim of theft. Possession of an idol that he perceived as an advantage turned into his demise. When the idol was stolen, he was bereft of a false security. Micah's anguish reveals that, whatever his original intent to worship Yahweh, he was attached to the physical image. Micah was not worshiping the invisible Lord God of Israel through his idol; he was worshiping an idol—a lesson that Israel would finally learn through exile from the land.

18:27-31 The first-time reader familiar with Israel's history would be stunned to learn the identity of the Levite first referenced in 17:7—**Jonathan son of Gershom, son of Moses** (Ex 2:21-22). The grandson of the one though whom God gave the Law was guilty of setting up a center for idol worship. Faith is not automatically passed from generation to generation.

A **18:12** Or *called Mahaneh-dan* B **18:14,17,18** Or *image, the cast image* C **18:19** Lit *Put your hand on your mouth*

19:1-10 For the third time, the writer notes that **there was no king in Israel** (cp. 17:6; 18:1), a statement assessing both the nation's spiritual vacuum and political situation, which would be remedied in the near future. That a Levite took a woman to be his concubine is symptomatic of the social chaos developing in this setting. The custom of establishing a marital relationship with a woman without granting her the full status of a wife was socially acceptable but displeasing to God, though He had established boundaries for this practice among His people to prevent the unjust treatment of such women (Ex 21:7-11; Dt 21:10-14).

19:11-26 Parallels abound between this narrative and the story of Lot's angelic visitors in Sodom and Gomorrah in Gn 19:1-3. By using a similar language and structure, the inspired writer of Judges was indicating the depth of depravity to which Israel had sunk and that the immorality of the times was similar to that of Sodom and Gomorrah.

name of their ancestor Dan, who
was born to Israel. The city was formerly named Laish.
30 The Danites set up the carved
image for themselves. Jonathan
son of Gershom, son of Moses,[A] and
his sons were priests for the Danite
tribe until the time of the exile from
the land. 31 So they set up for themselves Micah's carved image that he
had made, and it was there as long
as the house of God was in Shiloh.

Anarchy (19:1–21:24)

Crime at Gibeah (19:1-30)

19 In those days, when there was
no king in Israel, a Levite living in a remote part of the hill country of Ephraim acquired a woman
from Bethlehem in Judah as his
concubine. 2 But she was unfaithful to[B] him and left him for her father's house in Bethlehem in Judah.
She was there for a period of four
months. 3 Then her husband got up
and went after her to speak kindly
to her[C] and bring her back. He had
his servant with him and a pair of
donkeys. So she brought him to her
father's house, and when the girl's
father saw him, he gladly welcomed
him. 4 His father-in-law, the girl's
father, detained him, and he stayed
with him for three days. They ate,
drank, and spent the nights there.
5 On the fourth day, they got up early in the morning and prepared to go,
but the girl's father said to his son-
in-law, "Have something to eat to
keep up your strength and then you
can go." 6 So they sat down and the
two of them ate and drank together.
Then the girl's father said to the man,
"Please agree to stay overnight and
enjoy yourself." 7 The man got up to
go, but his father-in-law persuaded
him, so he stayed and spent the night
there again. 8 He got up early in the
morning of the fifth day to leave, but
the girl's father said to him, "Please
keep up your strength." So they waited until late afternoon and the two of
them ate. 9 The man got up to go with
his concubine and his servant, when
his father-in-law, the girl's father,
said to him, "Look, night is coming.
Please spend the night. See, the day
is almost over. Spend the night here,
enjoy yourself, then you can get up
early tomorrow for your journey and
go home."
10 But the man was unwilling to
spend the night. He got up, departed, and arrived opposite Jebus (that
is, Jerusalem). The man had his two
saddled donkeys and his concubine
with him. 11 When they were near Jebus and the day was almost gone, the
servant said to his master, "Please,
why not[D] let us stop at this Jebusite
city and spend the night here?"
12 But his master replied to him,
"We will not stop at a foreign city
where there are no Israelites. Let's
move on to Gibeah." 13 "Come on,"
he said,[E] "let's try to reach one of
these places and spend the night in
Gibeah or Ramah." 14 So they continued on their journey, and the sun
set as they neared Gibeah in Benjamin. 15 They stopped[F] to go in and
spend the night in Gibeah. The Levite went in and sat down in the city
square, but no one took them into
their home to spend the night.
16 In the evening, an old man came
in from his work in the field. He was
from the hill country of Ephraim but
was residing in Gibeah, and the men
of that place were Benjaminites.
17 When he looked up and saw the
traveler in the city square, the old
man asked, "Where are you going,
and where do you come from?"
18 He answered him, "We're traveling from Bethlehem in Judah to
the remote hill country of Ephraim,
where I am from. I went to Bethlehem in Judah, and now I'm going to
the house of the LORD.[G] No one has
taken me into his home, 19 although
we have both straw and feed for our
donkeys, and bread and wine for me,
your female servant, and the young
man with your servant.[H] There is
nothing we lack."
20 "Peace to you," said the old man.
"I'll take care of everything you
need. Only don't spend the night in
the square." 21 So he brought him to

[A] **18:30** Some Hb mss, LXX, Vg; other Hb mss read *Manasseh* [B] **19:2** LXX, Vg read *was angry with* [C] **19:3** Lit *speak to her heart* [D] **19:11** Lit *Come, please* [E] **19:13** Lit *said to his servant* [F] **19:15** Lit *stopped there* [G] **19:18** LXX reads *to my house* [H] **19:19** Some Hb mss, Syr, Tg, Vg; other Hb mss read *servants*

his house and fed the donkeys. Then
they washed their feet and ate and
drank. 22 While they were enjoying
themselves, all of a sudden, •per-
verted men of the city surrounded
the house and beat on the door.
They said to the old man who was
the owner of the house, "Bring out
the man who came to your house so
we can have sex with him!"
23 The owner of the house went out
and said to them, "No, don't do this
evil, my brothers. After all, this man
has come into my house. Don't do
this horrible thing. 24 Here, let me
bring out my virgin daughter and
the man's concubine now. Use them
and do whatever you want[A] to them.
But don't do this horrible thing to
this man."
25 But the men would not listen to
him, so the man seized his concubine and took her outside to them.
They raped[B] her and abused her all
night until morning. At daybreak
they let her go. 26 Early that morning, the woman made her way
back, and as it was getting light,
she collapsed at the doorway of the
man's house where her master was.
27 When her master got up in the
morning, opened the doors of the
house, and went out to leave on his
journey, there was the woman, his
concubine, collapsed near the doorway of the house with her hands on
the threshold. 28 "Get up," he told her.
"Let's go." But there was no response.

A 19:24 Lit *do what is good in your eyes* B 19:25 Lit *knew*

HARD QUESTION

Does male leadership lead to women's abuse?

The harrowing account of the unnamed concubine bears witness to the chaos that occurs when a nation turns its back on Yahweh. The unnamed concubine's abuse was so repugnant to the Lord that He included in His Word an account of this abuse as a measure of how depraved Israel had become. Many feminist interpretations claim that biblical narratives such as Jdg 19–21 prove that the Bible's patriarchal (father-ruled) culture is the source of women's mistreatment, claiming that it leads to their devaluation and oppression. However, the narrator included these horrific accounts precisely *because* God values women. The degree to which a nation regards its women is a direct indication of that nation's degree of obedience to the Lord. A panoramic view of Judges reveals that when godly male leadership is lacking, women are pushed toward more socially and spiritually dominant roles as well as left unprotected and vulnerable to abuse. The atrocity of the discarded woman of Judges 19 is a charge against a nation that turns its back on God and distorts and exploits His design for male leadership and protection in the home and culture.

19:22-25 During their meal, the house was surrounded by wicked, **perverted men** (Hb *benē-beliya'al,* "sons of worthlessness, wickedness, or vileness, i.e., men devoid of worth or honor," 20:13; cp. Dt 13:13; 1Sam 2:12; 2Co 6:15). The man offered his own virgin daughter and the Levite's concubine to the men, knowing the helpless women would be repeatedly raped and abused during the night. He even specifies they were to use them and do whatever they wanted with them. The concubine was **raped** throughout the night until she was at the point of death.

19:27-30 The account of this event is surely one of the most sickening in Scripture. The fact that the woman's hands were stretched toward the doorway after being raped and tortured—reaching for safety—is a heart-wrenching scene. The injustice toward the concubine and the virgin daughter is appalling. The sexual sin committed against the women is obviously in direct violation of God's law. But the men's total disregard for the women's welfare is scandalous. The Israelites were acting like the wicked people whom God had utterly destroyed. It was a dark time in Israel.

CHARACTER PROFILE

The Levite's Concubine A Powerless Woman

Her Background	• A resident of Bethlehem (19:1) • The concubine of a Levite (19:1)
Her Story	• She left the Levite for her father's house (19:2). • He came for her, and on their return trip they stayed in Gibeah (19:9-21). • There she was given to the "perverted men" who clamored for the visiting Levite to be turned over to their sexual appetites (19:22-25). • She was raped repeatedly through the night and collapsed on the doorstep the next morning (19:27). • The Levite cut her body into 12 pieces and sent them throughout the territory (19:28-29).
Life Lessons	• A culture that does not understand the intrinsic value of life will tolerate abuse, violence, and victimization of the most defenseless among them. • Those set apart unto God, as the Levites, do not always follow the Lord's ways.

19:29-30 The Levite's intent in dismembering the woman's corpse is not clearly stated but may have been readily understood by the original audience. Perhaps he was calling for a national judicial hearing on the murder. He could have been charging the nation with her death as a result of their hard-heartedness. Whatever the Levite's intent, the consciences of the Israelites were stricken.

20:4-7 The crime at Gibeah stirred up the nation, resulting in civil war between the Benjaminites and the other tribes. True to his self-serving pattern, the Levite told his story, omitting important details such as his participation in the crime (Jdg 19:20-30).

20:12-18 Within God's command that Judah be the first tribe to go up against the Benjaminites' injustice is the reminder that He had future plans for the leadership of Judah. One day, kings would come from that tribe. And, one glorious day, the eternal King would be born from that tribe.

20:6 Horrible shame translates two Hebrew words paired with a conjunction. The first, *zimmah*, denotes "a wicked deed," especially "lewdness" or a heinous sexually immoral act such a rape and incest, and is translated elsewhere as "depraved" (Lv 18:17), "disgrace" (Jb 31:11), "indecency" (Ezk 16:58), "immoral acts" (Ezk 22:9), and with its verbal force as "wickedly defiles" (Ezk 22:11). The second word, *nevalah*, "shameful act of wickedness, senseless folly," intensifies the repulsive nature of the act. Used together, the words convey what happened as an atrocity so shameful that the call for swift execution of justice could not go unheeded by a nation that had any sense of honor.

20:13 Eradicate (Hb *ba'ar*, "remove, eliminate, exterminate,") frequently follows a command to impose the death penalty for certain transgressions of God's law. The Israelites' demand echoes this sense of necessity not only to punish the evildoers but, in doing so, to remove the guilt and shame their sin cast upon the whole nation.

So the man put her on his donkey
and set out for home.
29 When he entered his house, he
picked up a knife, took hold of his
concubine, cut her into 12 pieces,
limb by limb, and then sent her
throughout the territory of Israel.
30 Everyone who saw it said, "Nothing like this has ever happened or
has been seen since the day the Israelites came out of the land of Egypt
to this day.[A] Think it over, discuss it,
and speak up!"

The Benjaminite war (20:1-48)

20 All the Israelites from Dan to
Beer-sheba and from the land
of Gilead came out, and the community assembled as one body before
the LORD at Mizpah. 2 The leaders of
all the people and of all the tribes of
Israel presented themselves in the
assembly of God's people: 400,000
armed foot soldiers. 3 The Benjaminites heard that the Israelites had
gone up to Mizpah.
The Israelites asked, "Tell us, how
did this outrage occur?"
4 The Levite, the husband of the
murdered woman, answered: "I
went to Gibeah in Benjamin with my
concubine to spend the night. 5 Citizens of Gibeah ganged up on me and
surrounded the house at night. They
intended to kill me, but they raped
my concubine, and she died. 6 Then
I took my concubine and cut her
in pieces, and sent her throughout
Israel's territory, because they committed a horrible shame in Israel.
7 Look, all of you are Israelites. Give
your judgment and verdict here and
now."
8 Then all the people stood united
and said, "None of us will go to his
tent or return to his house. 9 Now
this is what we will do to Gibeah:
we will go against it by lot. 10 We will
take 10 men out of every 100 from
all the tribes of Israel, and 100 out
of every 1,000, and 1,000 out of every 10,000 to get provisions for the
people when they go to Gibeah in
Benjamin to punish them for all the
horror they did in Israel."
11 So all the men of Israel gathered
united against the city. 12 Then the
tribes of Israel sent men throughout the tribe of Benjamin, saying,
"What is this outrage that has occurred among you? 13 Hand over the
•perverted men in Gibeah so we can
put them to death and eradicate evil
from Israel." But the Benjaminites
would not obey their fellow Israelites. 14 Instead, the Benjaminites
gathered together from their cities
to Gibeah to go out and fight against
the Israelites. 15 On that day the Benjaminites rallied 26,000 armed men
from their cities, besides 700 choice
men rallied by the inhabitants of
Gibeah. 16 There were 700 choice
men who were left-handed among
all these people; all could sling a
stone at a hair and not miss.
17 The Israelites, apart from Benjamin, rallied 400,000 armed men,
every one an experienced warrior.
18 They set out, went to Bethel,
and inquired of God. The Israelites

[A] **19:30** LXX reads *day." He commanded the men he sent out, saying, "You will say this to all the men of Israel: Has anything like this happened since the day the Israelites came out of Egypt until this day?*

asked, "Who is to go first to fight for us against the Benjaminites?"

And the LORD answered, "Judah will be first."

19 In the morning, the Israelites set out and camped near Gibeah. 20 The men of Israel went out to fight against Benjamin and took their battle positions against Gibeah. 21 The Benjaminites came out of Gibeah and slaughtered 22,000 men of Israel on the field that day. 22 But the Israelite army rallied and again took their battle positions in the same place where they positioned themselves on the first day. 23 They went up, wept before the LORD until evening, and inquired of Him: "Should we again fight against our brothers the Benjaminites?"

And the LORD answered: "Fight against them."

24 On the second day the Israelites advanced against the Benjaminites. 25 That same day the Benjaminites came out from Gibeah to meet them and slaughtered an additional 18,000 Israelites on the field; all were armed men.

26 The whole Israelite army went to Bethel where they wept and sat before the LORD. They fasted that day until evening and offered •burnt offerings and •fellowship offerings to the LORD. 27 Then the Israelites inquired of the LORD. In those days, the ark of the covenant of God was there, 28 and Phinehas son of Eleazar, son of Aaron, was serving before it. The Israelites asked: "Should we again fight against our brothers the Benjaminites or should we stop?"

The LORD answered: "Fight, because I will hand them over to you tomorrow." 29 So Israel set up an ambush around Gibeah. 30 On the third day the Israelites fought against the Benjaminites and took their battle positions against Gibeah as before. 31 Then the Benjaminites came out against the people and were drawn away from the city. They began to attack the people as before, killing about 30 men of Israel on the highways, one of which goes up to Bethel and the other to Gibeah through the open country. 32 The Benjaminites said, "We are defeating them as before."

But the Israelites said, "Let's flee and draw them away from the city to the highways." 33 So all the men of Israel got up from their places and took their battle positions at Baal-tamar, while the Israelites in ambush charged out of their places west of[A] Geba. 34 Then 10,000 choice men from all Israel made a frontal assault against Gibeah, and the battle was fierce, but the Benjaminites did not know that disaster was about to strike them. 35 The LORD defeated Benjamin in the presence of Israel, and on that day the Israelites slaughtered 25,100 men of Benjamin; all were armed men. 36 Then the Benjaminites realized they had been defeated.

The men of Israel had retreated before Benjamin, because they were confident in the ambush they had set against Gibeah. 37 The men in ambush had rushed quickly against Gibeah; they advanced and put the whole city to the sword. 38 The men of Israel had a prearranged signal with the men in ambush: when they sent up a great cloud of smoke from the city, 39 the men of Israel would return to the battle. When Benjamin had begun to strike them down, killing about 30 men of Israel, they said, "They're defeated before us, just as they were in the first battle." 40 But when the column of smoke began to go up from the city, Benjamin looked behind them, and the whole city was going up in smoke.[B] 41 Then the men of Israel returned, and the men of Benjamin were terrified when they realized that disaster had struck them. 42 They retreated before the men of Israel toward the wilderness, but the battle overtook them, and those who came out of the cities[C] slaughtered those between them. 43 They surrounded the Benjaminites, pursued them, and easily overtook them near Gibeah toward the east. 44 There were 18,000 men who died from Benjamin; all were warriors. 45 Then Benjamin turned and fled toward the wilderness to the rock of Rimmon, and

20:19-28 The **ark of the covenant** is only mentioned in Judges here (v. 27). The inclusion of **Phinehas son of Eleazar** and grandson of Aaron indicates that these events took place earlier—probably within just decades after Joshua's death (Jos 22:13).

[A] **20:33** LXX, Syr, Vg; MT reads *places in the plain of*, or *places in the cave of* [B] **20:40** Lit *up to the sky* [C] **20:42** LXX, Vg read *city*

21:1-7 Although **the men of Israel** vowed that none of their daughters would be given **to a Benjaminite in marriage,** the potential cessation of even one family line was regarded as a tragedy. The loss of an entire tribe would have been catastrophic.

21:8-12 That **no one from Jabesh-gilead had come** to the **assembly** at **Mizpah** became the justification for punishing Jabesh-gilead for not sending warriors to fight for Israel. After killing the city's inhabitants, they brought **400** young virgins to Shiloh for the remaining Benjaminites to marry.

CHARACTER PROFILE

The Wives of Benjamin **Innocent Victims**

Their Background	• From Jabesh-gilead, 400 young women who were virgins (21:12) • From Shiloh, young women dancing at the annual festival (21:19-23)
Their Story	• Due to civil war, the tribes vowed to forbid their daughters to marry Benjaminites (20:1–21:1,17-18). • They soon recognized that without wives, the tribe of Benjamin would die (21:3). • Consequently, they murdered all the inhabitants of Jabesh-gilead but abducted the young women who were virgins (21:10-13). • To complete the number of wives needed, the unmarried Benjaminites kidnapped young women from Shiloh as they were dancing in a festival celebration (21:19-23).
Life Lessons	• The book of Judges concludes with this tragic story, again illustrating the downward spiral of morality in Israel (21:25). • Those who pursue what is right in their own eyes are doomed to spiritual failure.

Israel killed 5,000 men on the highways. They overtook them at Gidom
and struck 2,000 more dead.
46 All the Benjaminites who died
that day were 25,000 armed men;
all were warriors. 47 But 600 men
escaped into the wilderness to the
rock of Rimmon and stayed there
four months. 48 The men of Israel
turned back against the other Benjaminites and killed them with their
swords—the entire city, the animals, and everything that remained.
They also burned down all the cities
that remained.

The Benjaminite preservation (21:1-24)

21 The men of Israel had sworn
an oath at Mizpah: "None
of us will give his daughter to a
Benjaminite in marriage." 2 So the
people went to Bethel and sat there
before God until evening. They wept
loudly and bitterly, 3 and cried out,
"Why, LORD God of Israel, has it occurred[A] that one tribe is missing
in Israel today?" 4 The next day the
people got up early, built an altar
there, and offered •burnt offerings
and •fellowship offerings. 5 The Israelites asked, "Who of all the tribes of
Israel didn't come to the LORD with
the assembly?" For a great oath had
been taken that anyone who had not
come to the LORD at Mizpah would
certainly be put to death.
6 But the Israelites had compassion
on their brothers, the Benjaminites,
and said, "Today a tribe has been cut
off from Israel. 7 What should we do
about wives for the survivors? We've
sworn to the LORD not to give them
any of our daughters as wives."
8 They asked, "Which city among the
tribes of Israel didn't come to the
LORD at Mizpah?" It turned out that
no one from Jabesh-gilead had come
to the camp and the assembly. 9 For
when the people were counted, no
one was there from the inhabitants
of Jabesh-gilead.
10 The congregation sent 12,000
brave warriors[B] there and commanded them: "Go and kill the inhabitants of Jabesh-gilead with the
sword, including women and children. 11 This is what you should do:
•Completely destroy every male, as
well as every female who has slept
with a man." 12 They found among
the inhabitants of Jabesh-gilead 400
young women, who had not had sexual relations with a man, and they

[A]**21:3** Lit *has this occurred in Israel* [B]**21:10** Lit *12,000 of their sons of valor*

brought them to the camp at Shiloh in the land of Canaan.

[13] The whole congregation sent a message of peace to the Benjaminites who were at the rock of Rimmon. [14] Benjamin returned at that time, and Israel gave them the women they had kept alive from Jabesh-gilead. But there were not enough for them.

[15] The people had compassion on Benjamin, because the LORD had made this gap in the tribes of Israel. [16] The elders of the congregation said, "What should we do about wives for those who are left, since the women of Benjamin have been destroyed?" [17] They said, "There must be heirs for the survivors of Benjamin, so that a tribe of Israel will not be wiped out. [18] But we can't give them our daughters as wives." For the Israelites had sworn, "Anyone who gives a wife to a Benjaminite is cursed." [19] They also said, "Look, there's an annual festival to the LORD in Shiloh, which is north of Bethel, east of the highway that goes up from Bethel to Shechem, and south of Lebonah."

[20] Then they commanded the Benjaminites: "Go and hide in the vineyards. [21] Watch, and when you see the young women of Shiloh come out to perform the dances, each of you leave the vineyards and catch a wife for yourself from the young women of Shiloh, and go to the land of Benjamin. [22] When their fathers or brothers come to us and protest, we will tell them, 'Show favor to them, since we did not get enough wives for each of them in the battle. You didn't actually give the women to them, so[A] you are not •guilty of breaking your oath.'"

[23] The Benjaminites did this and took the number of women they needed from the dancers they caught. They went back to their own inheritance, rebuilt their cities, and lived in them. [24] At that time, each of the Israelites returned from there to his own tribe and family. Each returned from there to his own inheritance.

A Summary of the Book of Judges (21:25)

[25] In those days there was no king in Israel; everyone did whatever he wanted.[B]

[A]**21:22** Lit *at this time* [B]**21:25** Lit *did what was right in his eyes*

21:13-24 With 200 Benjaminite men still needing wives, the Israelites devised an additional plan. According to their vow, the men of Israel could not **give** their **daughters** to a Benjaminite. But a Benjaminite could "take" a wife. The young women danced before the Lord at the **annual festival** in **Shiloh** (v. 19). The unmarried Benjaminites planned to hide **in the vineyards** and at the right time seize one of **the young women** (vv. 20-21). **Their fathers**, when protesting, were to be told that the Benjaminites were innocent of violating the vow because their daughters were taken and not given.

21:25 This verse serves as a succinct conclusion to the book—a reminder that when people are left to the schemes and desires of their own hearts, the devastating effects of sin follow.

JUDGES... WRITTEN ON MY Heart – Israel's downward spiral within the book of Judges manifests the sober admonition from the Puritan pastor, John Owen: "Be killing sin or sin will be killing you." The nation disobeyed God's commands, perhaps believing that they themselves were in control of the outcome. Yet what they chose to accommodate led to their destruction. May you and I heed and learn from their failures, which "were written as a warning to us, on whom the ends of the ages have come" (1Co 10:11).

Ruth

Timeline	1406–1400 BC	1375–1050 BC	1170 BC	1175–1125 BC
■ World Events ■ Biblical Events	Joshua's campaigns of conquest	Events in Judges	Jephthah defeats the Ammonites and Philistines.	Life of Ruth

"For wherever you go, I will go, and wherever you live, I will live" (1:16b).

Who wrote Ruth?
Likely someone with duties in King David's royal household or perhaps a scribe during his reign.

Who were the recipients?
Not identified in the text

When was Ruth written?
The events occurred within the period of the judges (ca 1375–1050 B.C.), but the book was likely written during David's reign (1010–970 B.C.).

Where did it happen?
The village of Bethlehem, located near Jerusalem

What is Ruth about?
- The providence of God in the midst of tragedy
- The redemption that is later fully provided through Jesus Christ
- The sanctity of marriage and the importance of family
- The concern God has for individual women

Why should women read Ruth?
When it seemed that their circumstances could not be more devastating, two impoverished and desolate women found themselves to be the objects of God's sovereign care. The book highlights sacrificial love within human relationships, between a mother-in-law and a daughter-in-law and between an honorable man and a virtuous woman in courtship. But the greatest display of selfless love in the book of Ruth is the foreshadowing of the coming Kinsman-Redeemer, Jesus Christ, who would give up Himself to rescue His Bride.

How do you read Ruth?
The book of Ruth is a historical "short story," reminding all who hear its message of God's providence. The book uses an ancient literary device called a *chiasm* (repeating a series of elements in reverse order from the form in which they were first presented) and providing organization to the narrative. The chiasm had special significance for ancient people, who were accustomed to being guided by the story structure.

1:1-5 The Family of Elimelech
  1:6-22 The Faithfulness of Ruth
    2:1-23 The Kinsman-Redeemer (Family Redeemer) in the Barley Field
    3:1-18 The Kinsman-Redeemer (Family Redeemer) at the Threshing Floor
  4:1-17 The Faithfulness of Boaz
4:18-22 The Family of David

>WORD|*study*

1:8 Faithful love (Hb *chesed*, "unfailing love"), often translated "lovingkindness," is a description of God's covenant love, emphasizing the absolute fidelity and unwavering constancy of His love. Bound up in this "faithful love" are His compassion, forgiveness, and blessings.

Outline

I. Naomi's Challenge: Despair, Death, Depression (1:1-22)
   A. The Famine in Bethlehem: Leaving Land and Friends (1:1-5)
   B. The Return to Judah: Emptiness (1:6-22)
II. Ruth's Work of Gleaning (2:1-23)
   A. The Provision of Boaz (2:1-17)
   B. The Response of Ruth (2:18-23)
III. Ruth's Appeal for Redemption (3:1-18)
   A. Naomi's Plan for Ruth: Husband and House (3:1-4)
   B. Ruth's Response to Naomi's Counsel: Obedience (3:5-9)
   C. The Response of Others (3:10-18)
IV. The Reward for Ruth and Naomi: Redemption (4:1-22)
   A. Boaz as Redeemer (4:1-12)
   B. Ruth's Marriage to Boaz (4:13)
   C. The Restoration of Naomi (4:14-16)
   D. The Epilogue: The Legacy of Obedience (4:17-22)

1120–1060 BC	1105–1025 BC	1080–1010 BC	1050–970 BC
Life of Samson	Life of Samuel	Life of Saul	Life of David

Naomi's Challenge: Despair, Death, Depression (1:1-22)

The Famine in Bethlehem: Leaving Land and Friends (1:1-5)

1 During the time[A] of the judges,
there was a famine in the land. A
man left Bethlehem[B] in Judah with
his wife and two sons to live in the
land of Moab for a while. 2 The man's
name was Elimelech,[C] and his wife's
name was Naomi.[D] The names of his
two sons were Mahlon[E] and Chilion.[F] They were Ephrathites from
Bethlehem in Judah. They entered
the land of Moab and settled there.
3 Naomi's husband Elimelech died,
and she was left with her two sons.
4 Her sons took Moabite women as
their wives: one was named Orpah
and the second was named Ruth.
After they lived in Moab about 10
years, 5 both Mahlon and Chilion also
died, and Naomi was left without
her two children and without her
husband.

The Return to Judah: Emptiness (1:6-22)

6 She and her daughters-in-law
prepared to leave the land of Moab,
because she had heard in Moab that
the LORD had paid attention to His
people's need by providing them
food. 7 She left the place where she
had been living, accompanied by her
two daughters-in-law, and traveled
along the road leading back to the
land of Judah.
8 She said to them, "Each of you
go back to your mother's home. May
the LORD show faithful love to you
as you have shown to the dead and
to me. 9 May the LORD enable each
of you to find security in the house

[A]1:1 Lit *In the days of the judging* [B]1:1 = House of Bread [C]1:2 = My God Is King [D]1:2 = Pleasant [E]1:2 = Sickly [F]1:2 = Weak or failing

CHARACTER PROFILE

Naomi A Woman of Persevering Faith

Her Background	• The wife of Elimelech • The mother of Mahlon and Chilion
Her Story	• Due to a famine, her family had relocated to Moab (1:1). • While in Moab, her husband and sons died (1:3,5). • Naomi returned to Bethlehem with Ruth (1:16-17). • Ruth gleaned in the fields of Boaz, a distant relative, to provide support (2:1-2). • Naomi sought security for Ruth, encouraging her to approach Boaz, their kinsman-redeemer ("family redeemer," 3:1-5). • She cared for her grandchild, the son of Ruth and Boaz and grandfather of King David (4:13-17).
Life Lessons	• Despite her bitter disappointments, Naomi persevered in her faith. • The journey of faith brings rewards, whether on earth or in eternity.

Title Since Ruth was from Moab, a nation hated by Israel, the fact that the Hebrew canon contains a book bearing her name as the title is astounding.

1:1 The story of Ruth occurred during one of the darkest times of the nation's history. Not only were the people in an era of disobedience and anarchy, but the land was overtaken by famine.

1:1-5 The text does not indicate that **Elimelech** sought God's direction before acting. Instead he seemed to react to his circumstances with a drastic self-determined solution. He chose to leave the promised land for the pagan land of **Moab**, which he thought would be more secure than the land that God had provided for His people. Removing yourself from where God has placed you without His direction jeopardizes the privileged position found in the center of His will.

1:4 The sons of Elimelech and Naomi married Moabite women, though the Lord had forbidden His people to intermarry with people from pagan nations (Ex 34:15-16; Dt 7:1-4).

1:4-6 Naomi was left without property, possessions, extended family support, and with two dependent daughters-in-law. She seemed even more destitute than she was when the family lived in Bethlehem. Widowhood has never been easy; but Naomi, as a foreigner without sons or extended family, faced an almost impossible situation.

1:11-15 Naomi was likely releasing Ruth and Orpah from the demands of the Israelite household into which they married. The Hebrew custom of levirate (Lat *levir*, "brother-in-law or husband's brother"; see Gn 38:8; Dt 25:5-9; Mt 22:24-28) marriage stipulated that when a brother died without leaving descendants, his unmarried brother was to marry his widowed sister-in-law to produce offspring for his deceased brother. This insured the continuity of the family and the rightful land distribution through a legal heir within the tribe. The action was voluntary; the brother-in-law could refuse to marry the widow (Dt 25:7). When the brother-in-law took the widow of his brother as his wife, their firstborn son would be considered the son of the deceased brother. Naomi was telling her daughters-in-law not to return with her to Bethlehem since she could not provide them with sons to be their future husbands.

1:13 These words are readily understood by any who have experienced the tragedies and suffering of life. Naomi, in a sense, was shaking her fist at God, who, according to His promised faithfulness, seemed in her finite understanding to have abandoned her.

1:16-17 Ruth's words of commitment have been immortalized over the centuries. They are used most often in wedding ceremonies by a bride pledging her commitment to her husband, but in the text Ruth expressed her affection for and commitment to Naomi. Ruth's decision to bind herself to Naomi was ultimately based on her new faith in the God of Naomi—Yahweh of Israel. She was even willing to accept the uncertainties of lifelong widowhood rather than give up her commitment to the true God.

1:20 Call me Mara (Hb, "bitter") expressed Naomi's bitterness. The changing of her name from "Naomi" (Hb, "sweetness, the pleasant one") to "Mara" used wordplay to express her own despair over the changes in her life. She clearly saw herself as a bitter old woman without hope.

CHARACTER PROFILE

Ruth **Loyal Daughter-In-Law**

Her Background	• A native of Moab, east of the Jordan River (1:4-5) • The wife of Mahlon (4:10) • The daughter-in-law of Naomi and Elimelech (1:4)
Her Story	• Her husband died before they had a child (1:4-13). • She loved her mother-in-law Naomi and left her homeland to go with Naomi to Bethlehem (1:16-18). • She listened to Naomi's advice (3:1-5). • Her spirit and character attracted Boaz, the kinsman-redeemer ("family redeemer," 2:11; 3:11). • Boaz agreed to buy Naomi's estate and take Ruth as his wife (3:10-13). • Through their family line came King David and ultimately Jesus, the Messiah (4:17,21-22; Mt 1:5-6).
Life Lessons	• Ruth's vow to Naomi is one of the most beautiful statements of commitment in Scripture (Ru 1:16-17). • Her obedience to Yahweh God brought rich rewards (4:10-17).

of your new husband." She kissed them, and they wept loudly.

10 "No," they said to her. "We will go with you to your people."

11 But Naomi replied, "Return home, my daughters. Why do you want to go with me? Am I able to have any more sons[A] who could become your husbands? 12 Return home, my daughters. Go on, for I am too old to have another husband. Even if I thought there was still hope for me to have a husband tonight and to bear sons, 13 would you be willing to wait for them to grow up? Would you restrain yourselves from remarrying?[B] No, my daughters, my life is much too bitter for you to share,[C] because the LORD's hand has turned against me." 14 Again they wept loudly, and Orpah kissed her mother-in-law, but Ruth clung to her. 15 Naomi said, "Look, your sister-in-law has gone back to her people and to her god.[D] Follow your sister-in-law."

16 But Ruth replied:

Do not persuade me
  to leave you
or go back and not follow you.
For wherever you go,
  I will go,
and wherever you live,
  I will live;
your people will be my people,
and your God will be my God.
17 Where you die, I will die,
and there I will be buried.
May •Yahweh punish me,[E]
and do so severely,
if anything but death
  separates you and me.

18 When Naomi saw that Ruth was determined to go with her, she stopped trying to persuade her.

19 The two of them traveled until they came to Bethlehem. When they entered Bethlehem, the whole town was excited about their arrival[F] and the local women exclaimed, "Can this be Naomi?"

20 "Don't call me Naomi. Call me Mara,"[G] she answered,[H] "for the •Almighty has made me very bitter. 21 I went away full, but the LORD has brought me back empty. Why do you call me Naomi, since the LORD has pronounced judgment on[I] me, and the Almighty has afflicted me?"

22 So Naomi came back from the land of Moab with her daughter-in-law Ruth the Moabitess. They arrived in Bethlehem at the beginning of the barley harvest.

[A]1:11 Lit *More to me sons in my womb* [B]1:13 Lit *marrying a man* [C]1:13 Lit *daughters, for more bitter to me than you* [D]1:15 Or *gods* [E]1:17 A solemn oath formula; 1Sm 3:17; 2Sm 3:9,35; 1Kg 2:23; 2Kg 6:31 [F]1:19 Lit *excited because of them* [G]1:20 = Bitter [H]1:20 Lit *answered them* [I]1:21 LXX, Syr, Vg read *has humiliated*

Ruth's Work of Gleaning (2:1-23)

The Provision of Boaz (2:1-17)

2 Now Naomi had a relative on her husband's side named Boaz. He was a prominent man of noble character from Elimelech's family.

[2] Ruth the Moabitess asked Naomi, "Will you let me go into the fields and gather fallen grain behind someone who allows me to?"

Naomi answered her, "Go ahead, my daughter." [3] So Ruth left and entered the field to gather grain behind the harvesters. She happened to be in the portion of land belonging to Boaz, who was from Elimelech's family.

[4] Later, when Boaz arrived from Bethlehem, he said to the harvesters, "The LORD be with you."

"The LORD bless you," they replied.

[5] Boaz asked his servant who was in charge of the harvesters, "Whose young woman is this?"

[6] The servant answered, "She is the young Moabite woman who returned with Naomi from the land of Moab. [7] She asked, 'Will you let me gather fallen grain among the bundles behind the harvesters?' She came and has remained from early morning until now, except that she rested a little in the shelter."[A]

[8] Then Boaz said to Ruth, "Listen, my daughter.[B] Don't go and gather grain in another field, and don't leave this one, but stay here close to my female servants. [9] See which field they are harvesting, and follow them. Haven't I ordered the young men not to touch you?[C] When you are thirsty, go and drink from the jars the young men have filled."

[10] She bowed with her face to the ground and said to him, "Why are you so kind to notice me, although I am a foreigner?"

[11] Boaz answered her, "Everything you have done for your mother-in-law since your husband's death has been fully reported to me: how you left your father and mother and the land of your birth, and how you came to a people you didn't previously know. [12] May the LORD reward you for what you have done, and may you receive a full reward from the LORD God of Israel, under whose wings you have come for refuge."

[13] "My lord," she said, "you have been so kind to me, for you have comforted and encouraged[D] your slave, although I am not like one of your female servants."

[14] At mealtime Boaz told her, "Come over here and have some bread and dip it in the vinegar sauce." So she sat beside the harvesters, and he offered her roasted grain. She ate and was satisfied and had some left over.

[15] When she got up to gather grain, Boaz ordered his young men, "Let her even gather grain among the bundles, and don't humiliate her. [16] Pull out some stalks from the bundles for her and leave them for her to gather. Don't rebuke her." [17] So Ruth gathered grain in the field until evening. She beat out what she had gathered, and it was about 26 quarts[E] of barley.

The Response of Ruth (2:18-23)

[18] She picked up the grain and went into the town, where her mother-in-law saw what she had gleaned. Then she brought out what she had left over from her meal and gave it to her.

[19] Then her mother-in-law said to her, "Where did you gather barley today, and where did you work? May the LORD bless the man who noticed you."

Ruth told her mother-in-law about the men she had worked with

Doctrine PROVIDENCE

God's hand is apparent throughout the book of Ruth. No one can understand the ways of the Lord, "who works out everything in agreement with the decision of His will" (Eph 1:11). Providence is the umbrella of God's activity among His people throughout history and in the present world. Believers are not subject to fate but remain always under the providential care of God, who even in the midst of tragedy is working His purposes for the ultimate good of His children (see Rm 8:28).

2:1 Boaz (Hb, "in him is strength") was an honorable man of wealth and influence. He was respected by his employees and the community (vv. 3-4) and was a gentleman, even in dealing with women who were not from his ethnic or economic background (vv. 8-9,13,15-16).

2:2 The **fallen grain** was God's provision for the poor and the homeless (Lv 19:9-10; 23:22). The ancient custom of gleaning was codified in the law so that the widow, or an alien woman like Ruth, had the right to gather fallen grain from any field she chose (Lv 19:9; 23:22; Dt 24:19).

2:3 When Ruth chose the field in which to glean, she had no idea of the circumstances surrounding Boaz and his connection to her deceased husband's family. The entire book of Ruth clearly presents the providence of God working behind the scenes and preparing the way for His plan (see Gn 24:12; 27:20; Nm 11:23; Is 41:21-24; 46:8-11).

2:18 In saving her leftover food from Boaz's meal, Ruth may have risked embarrassment in order to provide for her mother-in-law's needs.

[A]**2:7** LXX reads *until evening she has not stopped in the field*; Vg reads *now and she did not return to the house*; Hb uncertain [B]**2:8** Lit *Haven't you heard, my daughter?* [C]**2:9** Either sexual or physical harassment [D]**2:13** Lit *and spoken to the heart of* [E]**2:17** Lit *about an ephah*

2:19-23 The Hebrew custom of the kinsman-redeemer is uniquely portrayed in the book of Ruth. The **close relative** (Hb *qarov*), who was one of Naomi's kinsman-redeemers (Hb *go'ēl*), functioned on behalf of another person to redeem in a time of crisis in three ways: by purchasing lost property and returning it to the family member who had been forced to sell the family's land (Lv 25:25-28), by buying back a relative who was forced to sell himself into slavery (Lv 25:47-55), or by avenging the blood of a relative who had been murdered (Nm 35:16-21, 31). Boaz was eligible to be the kinsman-redeemer for Naomi and Ruth since he was related to Elimelech. This concept, which would keep the property of the dead man within his family usually included care for the widow (in this case, Ruth), according to the law of levirate marriage (Dt 25:5-10; see Ru 3). Since Naomi was beyond child-bearing years, Ruth could act as her substitute to produce an heir and redeem the family's land. Together these practices—levirate marriage and the relative—would provide the deliverer or "redeemer" for the family.

3:2 The threshing floor would have been an outdoor area and provided an open area in which the grain would be separated from the chaff. This public place was accessible and open to view. While the text does not give a reason for Boaz's presence in such a working area, he may have been guarding his grain.

3:3-4 Any suggestion of moral impropriety here is not only beyond the text but also completely counter to the characterization of Ruth and Boaz, who are both described as virtuous—"of noble character" (Hb *chayil*, "strength, integrity, virtue, ability"; Boaz in 2:1; Ruth in 3:11). An honorable man like Boaz would not have considered destroying Ruth's reputation, not to mention his own. The term **feet** is sometimes used as a euphemism for the sexual organs (3:7; see Ex 4:25;

and said, "The name of the man I
worked with today is Boaz."
20 Then Naomi said to her daughter-in-law, "May he be blessed by
the LORD, who has not forsaken his[A]
kindness to the living or the dead."
Naomi continued, "The man is a
close relative. He is one of our •fam-
ily redeemers."
21 Ruth the Moabitess said, "He
also told me, 'Stay with my young
men until they have finished all of
my harvest.'"
22 So Naomi said to her daughter-
in-law Ruth, "My daughter, it is good
for you to work[B] with his female servants, so that nothing will happen to
you in another field." 23 Ruth stayed
close to Boaz's female servants and
gathered grain until the barley and
the wheat harvests were finished.
And she lived with[C] her mother-in-
law.

Ruth's Appeal for Redemption (3:1-18)

Naomi's Plan for Ruth: Husband and House (3:1-4)

3 Ruth's mother-in-law Naomi said
to her, "My daughter, shouldn't
I find security for you, so that you
will be taken care of? 2 Now isn't
Boaz our relative? Haven't you been
working with his female servants?
This evening he will be winnowing
barley on the threshing floor. 3 Wash,
put on perfumed oil, and wear your
best clothes. Go down to the threshing floor, but don't let the man know
you are there until he has finished

REDEMPTION

Boaz pre-figured the ultimate Kinsman-Redeemer, Jesus Christ. Jesus faithfully fulfills this responsibility for every believer. He was related by blood (Php 2:5-8), able to pay the price (1Pt 1:18-19), and willing to redeem (Mt 20:28). The book of Ruth beautifully portrays that the relative in redemption without hesitation paid the cost required for the one he loved, just as Christ later redeemed mankind. The *go'ēl* protects property and people in the family. The levirate duty illustrated an act of pure love—the one who responded did not gain. Both inspire selfless, sacrificial love.

eating and drinking. 4 When he lies
down, notice the place where he's lying, go in and uncover his feet, and
lie down. Then he will explain to you
what you should do."

Ruth's Response to Naomi's Counsel: Obedience (3:5-9)

5 So Ruth said to her, "I will do everything you say."[D] 6 She went down
to the threshing floor and did everything her mother-in-law had instructed her. 7 After Boaz ate, drank,
and was in good spirits,[E] he went to
lie down at the end of the pile of barley. Then she went in secretly, uncovered his feet, and lay down.
8 At midnight, Boaz was startled,
turned over, and there lying at his
feet was a woman! 9 So he asked,
"Who are you?"
"I am Ruth, your slave," she replied. "Spread your cloak[F] over me,
for you are a •family redeemer."

[A]2:20 Or *His* [B]2:22 Lit *go out* [C]2:23 Some Hb mss, Vg read *she returned to* [D]3:5 Alt Hb tradition reads *say to me* [E]3:7 Lit *and his heart was glad* [F]3:9 Or *Spread the edge of your garment*; lit *Spread the wing of your garment*; Ru 2:12

BIBLICAL WOMANHOOD Dating

While we may not find cultural terms such as *dating* or *courtship* in the Bible, God has given us "everything required for life and godliness" (2Pt 1:3), including timeless principles for God-honoring dating relationships. Boaz and Ruth beautifully depict the dynamic of pre-marital romance between a man and a woman. Boaz was an honorable man (2:1) who acted with integrity and respected authority (3:11-13; 4:1-10). He protected Ruth's reputation from potential harm (2:9), guarded her honor (3:14) and provided for her overall well-being (2:8,14-16). Boaz respectfully pursued Ruth for the purpose of marriage and was capable of providing for a wife. Ruth was a virtuous woman who was concerned for the needs of others (2:2-3), hard-working and submissive (2:23; 3:5), and committed to her family (1:16-17). While Ruth made herself available to Boaz, she did not initiate their romantic relationship (3:1-11). Further, she received and followed the counsel of an older, godly woman (3:5). Both Ruth and Boaz were known for their noble character and devotion to God (2:1; 3:11), the ideal prerequisite for a potential spouse.

Comparison Between Ruth and the Virtuous Woman

Description	Reference in Ruth	Reference in Proverbs
Her family commitment is noted by others.	2:11-12	31:11-12
She provided sustenance for her household.	2:14,18	31:15
She gave attention to her appearance.	3:3,5	31:22
Her selfless lifestyle drew praise from others.	2:11; 3:10; 4:15	31:28
She committed herself to Yahweh as God.	1:16	31:30

The Response of Others (3:10-18)

From Boaz (3:10-14)

10 Then he said, "May the LORD bless
you, my daughter. You have shown
more kindness now than before,[A] because you have not pursued younger
men, whether rich or poor. 11 Now
don't be afraid, my daughter. I will
do for you whatever you say,[B] since
all the people in my town[C] know that
you are a woman of noble character.
12 Yes, it is true that I am a family
redeemer, but there is a redeemer
closer than I am. 13 Stay here tonight,
and in the morning, if he wants to
redeem you, that's good. Let him redeem you. But if he doesn't want to
redeem you, as the LORD lives, I will.
Now lie down until morning."
14 So she lay down at his feet until
morning but got up while it was still
dark.[D] Then Boaz said, "Don't let it
be known that a[E] woman came to
the threshing floor."

From Naomi (3:15-18)

15 And he told Ruth, "Bring the
shawl you're wearing and hold it
out." When she held it out, he shov-
eled six measures of barley into her
shawl, and she[F] went into the town.
16 She went to her mother-in-law,
Naomi, who asked her, "How did it
go,[G] my daughter?"
Then Ruth told her everything the
man had done for her. 17 She said,
"He gave me these six measures of
barley, because he said,[H] 'Don't go
back to your mother-in-law empty-
handed.'"
18 Naomi said, "My daughter, wait
until you find out how things go, for
he won't rest unless he resolves this
today."

The Reward for Ruth and Naomi: Redemption (4:1-22)

Boaz as Redeemer (4:1-12)

4 Boaz went to the •gate of the
town and sat down there. Soon
the •family redeemer Boaz had spoken about came by. Boaz called him
by name and said, "Come[I] over here
and sit down." So he went over and
sat down. 2 Then Boaz took 10 men
of the town's elders and said, "Sit
here." And they sat down. 3 He said
to the redeemer, "Naomi, who has
returned from the land of Moab,
is selling a piece of land that belonged to our brother Elimelech. 4 I
thought I should inform you:[J] Buy it
back in the presence of those seated
here and in the presence of the elders of my people. If you want to
redeem it, do so. But if you do[K] not
want to redeem it, tell me so that I
will know, because there isn't anyone other than you to redeem it, and
I am next after you."
"I want to redeem it," he answered.
5 Then Boaz said, "On the day you
buy the land from Naomi, you will
also acquire[L] Ruth the Moabitess,

Jdg 3:24), but there is no hint of such in this passage, nor would the context allow for Naomi to direct Ruth to such blatant immorality. **Lie down** (Hb *shakav*) does sometimes refer to sexual intercourse, but again the context does not point to such an interpretation here. In keeping with their character, Ruth and Boaz acted honorably and with chaste decorum.

3:5-9 Spread your cloak over me reveals clearly Ruth's petition. The phrase is a metaphor suggesting Ruth's need for protection and in other Old Testament passages indicates a request for marriage (Dt 22:30).

3:10-14 Boaz understood Ruth's request and reaffirmed her moral character, again making clear that there was no immorality that night (v. 11). However, he knew there was a nearer kinsman-redeemer. This interjection is also evidence of Boaz's honorable character, who, despite his attraction to Ruth, acted with determination and integrity to obey the law.

3:15-18 Naomi believed that Boaz would move forward. Even more she had regained her faith in the providence of Yahweh God to provide whatever was needed—but in His timing. After you fulfill your responsibility, you must wait in expectant hopefulness for God to carry out His plan.

4:1-7 The kinsman-redeemer was prepared to redeem Elimelech's land until Boaz told him this would entail marrying Ruth the Moabitess (v. 5). Boaz was personally prepared to accept the moral obligation of marrying Ruth and fathering a child through her in behalf of Elimelech and Mahlon. Boaz was not the genuine *levir* or brother of the deceased Elimelech, which underscores that he had no legal obligation to marry Naomi or Ruth. The text does not state why **the redeemer** refused his responsibility except to say **I will ruin my own inheritance.** Perhaps the cost of acquiring the property as well as maintaining the widow Naomi could drain his own personal resources. Furthermore, if Ruth did bear a son, the child she bore would then inherit the land he had redeemed.

A **3:10** Lit *kindness at the last than at the first* B **3:11** Some Hb mss, Orig, Syr, Tg, Vg read *say to me* C **3:11** Lit *all the gate of my people* D **3:14** Lit *up before a man could recognize his companion* E **3:14** LXX; MT reads *the* F **3:15** Some Hb mss, Aram, Syr, Vg; other Hb mss read *he* G **3:16** Lit *Who are you* H **3:17** Alt Hb tradition, LXX, Syr, Tg read *said to me* I **4:1** Lit *Boaz said so-and-so come* J **4:4** Lit *should uncover your ear, saying* K **4:4** Some Hb mss, LXX, Syr, Vg; other Hb mss read *if he does* L **4:5** Vg; MT reads *Naomi and from*

4:8-10 So the redeemer removed his sandal . . ., a symbolic act by which he abdicated his own right and allowed that right to be transferred to the next in line. With the completion of the legal proceeding, the right to the estate of Elimelech and the responsibility for the two widows were officially transferred to Boaz, who became the kinsman-redeemer.

4:14-16 The relationship between a woman and her mother-in-law has been described as the most difficult in the family. Yet the commitment between these two women is presented as a pattern for reciprocal care and a conduit for spiritual blessing.

4:17-22 In giving birth to a son, Ruth found herself in the ancestry of Israel's King David and the Messiah. Just as Ruth, outside the people of God, forbidden to enter the congregation of the Lord (Dt 23:3), without hope and alienated from God, humbled herself at the feet of the kinsman-redeemer Boaz asking for his acceptance and help, every woman must humble herself at the feet of the Lord Jesus and seek His saving redemption (see Eph 2:12-13). Just as Ruth found earthly security, any woman who humbles herself before the Lord Jesus will find spiritual rest.

the wife of the deceased man, to perpetuate the man's name on his property."

6 The redeemer replied, "I can't redeem it myself, or I will ruin my own inheritance. Take my right of redemption, because I can't redeem it."

7 At an earlier period in Israel, a man removed his sandal and gave it to the other party in order to make any matter legally binding concerning the right of redemption or the exchange of property. This was the method of legally binding a transaction in Israel.

8 So the redeemer removed his sandal and said to Boaz, "Buy back the property yourself."

9 Boaz said to the elders and all the people, "You are witnesses today that I am buying from Naomi everything that belonged to Elimelech, Chilion, and Mahlon. 10 I will also acquire Ruth the Moabitess, Mahlon's widow, as my wife, to perpetuate the deceased man's name on his property, so that his name will not disappear among his relatives or from the gate of his home. You are witnesses today."

11 The elders and all the people who were at the gate said, "We are witnesses. May the LORD make the woman who is entering your house like Rachel and Leah, who together built the house of Israel. May you be powerful in Ephrathah and famous in Bethlehem. 12 May your house become like the house of Perez, the son Tamar bore to Judah, because of the offspring the LORD will give you by this young woman."

Ruth's Marriage to Boaz (4:13)

13 Boaz took Ruth and she became his wife. When he was intimate with her, the LORD enabled her to conceive, and she gave birth to a son.

The Restoration of Naomi (4:14-16)

14 Then the women said to Naomi, "Praise the LORD, who has not left you without a family redeemer today. May his name become well known in Israel. 15 He will renew your life and sustain you in your old age. Indeed, your daughter-in-law, who loves you and is better to you than seven sons, has given birth to him." 16 Naomi took the child, placed him on her lap, and took care of him.

The Epilogue: The Legacy of Obedience (4:17-22)

17 The neighbor women said, "A son has been born to Naomi," and they named him Obed.[A] He was the father of Jesse, the father of David.

18 Now this is the genealogy of Perez:

Perez fathered Hezron.
19 Hezron fathered Ram,[B]
who fathered Amminadab.
20 Amminadab
fathered Nahshon,
who fathered Salmon.
21 Salmon fathered Boaz,
who fathered Obed.
22 And Obed fathered Jesse,
who fathered David.

[A] **4:17** = Servant [B] **4:19** LXX reads *Aram*; Mt 1:3-4

RUTH . . . WRITTEN ON MY *Heart*

The significance of Ruth's story could not be fully appreciated until decades after her death. Like Ruth, your faithfulness and devotion to God will affect generations to come in ways you may never live to see. You, too, must trust in God's sovereign provision and rest in the truth that He causes all things, even the bleakest of circumstances, to work together "for the good of those who love God: those who are called according to His purpose" (Rm 8:28).

From Law to Love

Mother-in-Law	Daughter-in-Law
Commits (1:7-8)	Commits (1:16-17)
Expresses gratitude (1:8-9)	Expresses loyalty (1:10)
Acts unselfishly (1:11-13)	Responds unselfishly (2:14-18)
Becomes bitter (1:20-21)	Exercises creativity (2:1-3)
Shows interest (2:19)	Answers respectfully (2:19,21,23)
Offers counsel (3:2-4,18)	Accepts counsel (3:5-6)

- There must be a mutuality of commitment between the two women to move from legal codes to loving hearts.
- The gratitude in the heart of one awakens loyalty in the heart of the other.
- The selflessness on the part of one demands unselfishness from the other.
- The bitterness in one gives opportunity for creativity in the other.
- The interest from one is rewarded by a warm response from the other.
- The counsel from one bears fruit when accepted and honored by the other.

1 Samuel

Timeline	1157–1059 BC	1105–1025 BC	1080–1010 BC	1050 BC
World Events Biblical Events	Life of Eli	Life of Samuel	Life of Saul	Anointing of Saul as Israel's first king

"To obey is better than sacrifice" (15:22a).

Who wrote 1 Samuel?
Though unidentified, the author likely compiled this book from writings by Samuel and the prophets Nathan and Gad.

Who were the recipients?
The people of Israel and Judah between the end of Solomon's reign and the northern kingdom's fall to Assyria in 722 B.C.

When was 1 Samuel written?
Between 930 and 722 B.C.

Where did it happen?
The nation of Israel, inhabited by the twelve tribes

What is 1 Samuel about?
- The sovereignty of God in both nations and individuals
- The devotion-filled obedience that God desires of every believer
- The Lord's care for the hearts of women

Why should women read 1 Samuel?
Juxtaposing the lives of David and Saul provides a clear picture of the difference between love for God and love for self. Whereas David was a man after God's own heart (13:14), Saul was a man after his own heart, choosing to obey according to his convenience. Along with the lives of these two kings, women can also glean practical and poignant principles from the lives of two biblical heroines, Hannah and Abigail (chaps. 1–2; 25).

How do you read 1 Samuel?
With the exception of the poetic hymn in chapter 2, 1 Samuel is a narrative account of events in Israel's history, specifically the beginning of the monarchy.

>WORD|*study*

1:3 Shiloh (Hb, "place of rest, tranquility," 1:3,9,24; 2:14; 3:21; 4:3-4,12; 14:3; cp. Jdg 21) was the name of the town—about 30 miles north of Jerusalem and 12 miles south of Shechem—in which Israel's tabernacle rested in a semi-permanent structure after the conquest for over three centuries (see Jos 18:1,8-10; 19:51). Archaeologists digging in this location announced in 2013 the discovery of ashes and a broken clay pitcher dating to 1050 B.C., strongly suggesting that the site was burned to the ground (cp. Ps 78:60-61; Jr 7:12-20, God's warning that Jerusalem would be destroyed as Shiloh was). "Shiloh" also appears in Gn 49:10, where it is translated "He whose right it is," designating the coming Messiah (see note, Gn 49:8-12; cp. 1Ch 22:9; Is 9:5).

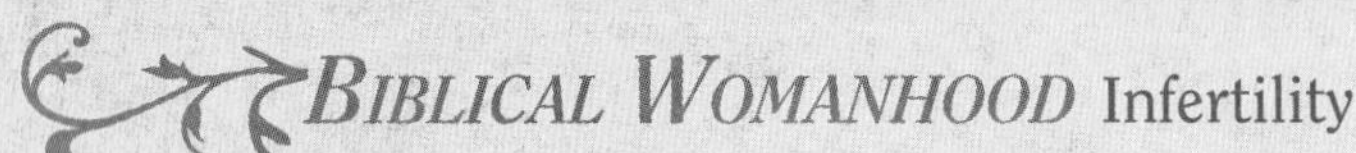

BIBLICAL WOMANHOOD Infertility

The desire for children is one that runs deep within a woman's heart, since she was created to bear and nurture children. Couples often struggle for months and years to conceive a child, enduring frustration, confusion, and strain to both their marriage and walk with the Lord. Infertile couples, however, must always be reminded that God has not abandoned them. While there are no easy answers, God is still sovereign and His plans and purposes always ultimately work for the good of those who love Him and are called according to His purpose (Rm 8:28). God does not always give every couple their own biological offspring. He may choose to bless them in other ways.

In the midst of the pain associated with infertility, women must be reminded that their source of life comes from God. Nothing is as important as a woman's walk with the Lord. Children, who are a blessing from God (Ps 127:3), can become idols in a woman's life if she allows their presence or absence to consume her, just as can seeking a husband or a career for the wrong reasons.

Hannah's heartache is felt in the first chapter of 1 Samuel as she was constantly reminded of her childlessness and, furthermore, provoked by the cruelty of Peninnah. Yet, at the point of her despair, Hannah poured her heart out before the Lord (1Sm 1:10). Within Hannah's request for a son is the vow that she would give him back to the Lord's service. Even in her grief, Hannah gave priority to God's glory over her desires. Verse 18 describes the physical evidence of her quietened spirit following her time with the Lord. Hannah left the tabernacle and returned to her husband **no longer . . . despondent** (v. 18). Women struggling with the matter of infertility can gain enormous encouragement from the example of Hannah as a woman of faith who unashamedly poured out her grief and anguish to the Lord and trusted Him to hear her prayer.

1050–970 BC	***1029 BC***	***1010 BC***	***1010–970 BC***
Life of David	David anointed king	Death of Saul and his sons	David's reign as king of Judah and Israel

Outline

- I. The Preparation for Israel's Monarchy (1:1–7:17)
  - A. The Birth and Childhood of Samuel (1:1–2:11)
    - 1. Samuel's Family (1:1-3)
    - 2. Hannah's Barrenness and Prayer for Deliverance (1:4-18)
    - 3. Hannah's Obedience Through Dedication (1:19-28)
    - 4. Hannah's Hymn of Praise (2:1-11)
  - B. The Corruption of the Priesthood (2:12-36)
  - C. Samuel's Encounter with God (3:1-21)
    - 1. God's Call of Samuel (3:1-14)
    - 2. Samuel's Response in Obedience (3:15-18)
    - 3. Samuel's Role as God's Prophet (3:19-21)
  - D. The Ark of the Covenant (4:1–7:17)
    - 1. The Capture of the Ark (4:1–5:12)
    - 2. The Return of the Ark (6:1–7:17)
- II. The Establishment of Israel's Monarchy (8:1–15:35)
  - A. The Rise of Saul to Kingship (8:1–12:25)
  - B. The Fall of Saul from the Throne (13:1–14:52)
  - C. Saul Rejected as King (15:1-35)
- III. The Continuation of Israel's Monarchy (16:1–31:13)
  - A. David Anointed by God (16:1-23)
  - B. David Taunted by Goliath (17:1-58)
  - C. David Hunted by Saul (18:1–31:13)

The Birth and Childhood of Samuel (1:1–2:11)

Samuel's Family (1:1-3)

1 There was a man from Ramathaim-
zophim in[A] the hill country of
Ephraim. His name was Elkanah
son of Jeroham, son of Elihu, son of
Tohu, son of Zuph, an Ephraimite.
2 He had two wives, the first named
Hannah and the second Peninnah.
Peninnah had children, but Hannah was childless. 3 This man would
go up from his town every year to
worship and to sacrifice to the LORD
of •Hosts at Shiloh, where Eli's two
sons, Hophni and Phinehas, were
the LORD's priests.

Hannah's Barrenness and Prayer for Deliverance (1:4-18)

4 Whenever Elkanah offered a sacrifice, he always gave portions of the
meat to his wife Peninnah and to
each of her sons and daughters. 5 But
he gave a double[B] portion to Hannah,
for he loved her even though the
LORD had kept her from conceiving.
6 Her rival would taunt her severely
just to provoke her, because the LORD
had kept Hannah from conceiving.
7 Whenever she went up to the LORD's
house, her rival taunted her in this
way every year. Hannah wept and
would not eat. 8 "Hannah, why are
you crying?" her husband Elkanah
asked. "Why won't you eat? Why are
you troubled? Am I not better to you
than 10 sons?"

9 Hannah got up after they ate and
drank at Shiloh.[C] Eli the priest was
sitting on a chair by the doorpost of
the LORD's tabernacle. 10 Deeply hurt,
Hannah prayed to the LORD and wept
with many tears. 11 Making a vow,
she pleaded, "LORD of Hosts, if You
will take notice of Your servant's affliction, remember and not forget
me, and give Your servant a son,[D] I
will give him to the LORD all the days
of his life, and his hair will never be
cut."[E]

12 While she continued praying in
the LORD's presence, Eli watched her
lips. 13 Hannah was praying silently,[F]
and though her lips were moving,
her voice could not be heard. Eli
thought she was drunk 14 and scolded her, "How long are you going to
be drunk? Get rid of your wine!"

15 "No, my lord," Hannah replied.

A **1:1** Or *from Ramathaim, a Zuphite from* B **1:5** Or *gave only one*; Hb obscure C **1:9** LXX adds *and presented herself before the LORD* D **1:11** Lit *a seed of men* E **1:11** Lit *and no razor will go up on his head* F **1:13** Lit *praying to her heart*

Title: First Samuel is named for Samuel, the last of Israel's judges, a prophet (3:20) and central figure of the book. Also see **Title** for 2 Samuel.

1:2 Although polygamy was a culturally acceptable practice, it was not God's original intention for marriage (Gn 2:24) and often caused serious family upheaval. Elkanah **had two wives**, probably because his beloved wife, Hannah, was barren.

1:4-8 Elkanah **loved** Hannah despite her inability to bear children. His response to Hannah suggests that her infertility was not a problem within their marital relationship. Rather, Hannah's sadness seemed linked to her relationship with the Lord, who had closed her womb — **the LORD had kept her from conceiving**; (Hb *sagar be'ad*, "closed up, shut up," with the object *rechem*, "womb," cp. Gn 16:2; 20:18; 30:2). A woman's inability to produce children was considered a disgrace.

1:9-18 Hannah was **deeply hurt** (Hb *mar*, "bitter, sad," modifying *nephesh*, "soul," v. 10; cp. "discontented," 22:2) and openly **wept** before the Lord. She was so heartbroken over her infertility that Eli, the priest, mistook her emotional outburst as drunkenness. Hannah vowed that if the Lord gave her a son, she would **give him** back to **the LORD** as long as he lived (v. 11). That **his hair will never be cut** refers to the Nazirite vow (Jdg 13:4-5), which served as a sign to others that he would be wholly devoted to the Lord's service.

1:19 The writer states that Hannah conceived because **the Lord remembered** [Hb *zakar*, "bring to mind or be mindful of, call back to memory"] **her**. Rather than implying that the Lord had previously forgotten Hannah, this verb idiomatically expresses His action on behalf of one to whom He is committed, the decisive action of one who has power and uses it to directly benefit another (e.g., Gn 40:14,23; Nm 10:9; Ps 136:23-24).

1:21-25 The **vow** that Samuel would be dedicated to the Lord's service is also referenced as Elkanah's vow. While Hannah made this vow initially, Elkanah took responsibility as the head of their home to fulfill it. Hannah's delay was not a lack of faith or commitment, but rather the reflection of a mother's wisdom in caring for her child's well-being. Samuel was approximately three years old when he was delivered to the Lord's service.

1:26-27 In an attitude of reverence and obedience, which was uncommon in Israel at that time, Hannah fulfilled her vow. As a Levite (1Ch 6:33-38), Samuel was qualified for service as a priest in the tabernacle (1Sm 7:9; 9:13; 10:8; 11:15; 16:5). Hannah was not giving up Samuel, but rather she was returning him to God. Although not promised any future children, she still surrendered her only child to the Lord.

CHARACTER PROFILE

Hannah A Devoted Mother

Her Background	• She was an Israelite (1:1-3,15-16). • Her name means "grace."
Her Story	• She married Elkanah, who truly loved her but had taken a second wife, Peninnah (1:2,5). • Hannah was barren, but Peninnah had produced children (1:4-6). • She asked God for a son and promised to devote the child to Him (1:11). • She fulfilled her promise (1:27- 28). • Her son Samuel served the Lord as one of Israel's greatest prophets (3:20; 2Ch 35:18; Ps 99:6).
Life Lessons	• Hannah sought the Lord alone for her heart's desire (1:11). • Hannah kept her promise to the Lord, relinquishing her son to Eli with thanksgiving and joy (2:1).

"I am a woman with a broken heart. I haven't had any wine or beer; I've been pouring out my heart before the LORD. 16 Don't think of me as a wicked woman; I've been praying from the depth of my anguish and resentment."

17 Eli responded, "Go in peace, and may the God of Israel grant the petition you've requested from Him."

18 "May your servant find favor with you," she replied. Then Hannah went on her way; she ate and no longer looked despondent.[A]

Hannah's Obedience Through Dedication (1:19-28)

19 The next morning Elkanah and Hannah got up early to bow in worship before the LORD. Afterward, they returned home to Ramah. Then Elkanah was intimate with his wife Hannah, and the LORD remembered her. 20 After some time,[B] Hannah conceived and gave birth to a son. She named him Samuel,[C] because she said, "I requested him from the LORD."

21 When Elkanah and all his household went up to make the annual sacrifice and his vow offering to the LORD, 22 Hannah did not go and explained to her husband, "After the child is weaned, I'll take him to appear in the LORD's presence and to stay there permanently."

23 Her husband Elkanah replied, "Do what you think is best,[D] and stay here until you've weaned him. May the LORD confirm your[E] word." So Hannah stayed there and nursed her son until she weaned him. 24 When she had weaned him, she took him with her to Shiloh, as well as a three-year-old bull,[F] half a bushel[G] of flour, and a jar of wine. Though the boy was still young,[H] she took him to the LORD's house at Shiloh. 25 Then they slaughtered the bull and brought the boy to Eli.

26 "Please, my lord," she said, "as sure as you live, my lord, I am the woman who stood here beside you praying to the LORD. 27 I prayed for this boy, and since the LORD gave me what I asked Him for, 28 I now give the boy to the LORD. For as long as he lives, he is given to the LORD." Then he[I] bowed in worship to the LORD there.[J]

Hannah's Hymn of Praise (2:1-11)

2 Hannah prayed:

My heart rejoices in the LORD;

[A]1:18 Lit *and her face was not to her again* [B]1:20 Lit *In the turning of the days* [C]1:20 In Hb, the name Samuel sounds like the phrase "requested from God." [D]1:23 Lit *what is good in your eyes* [E]1:23 DSS, LXX, Syr; MT reads *His* [F]1:24 DSS, LXX, Syr; MT reads *Shiloh with three bulls* [G]1:24 Lit *bull and an ephah* [H]1:24 Lit *And the youth was a youth* [I]1:28 DSS read *she*; some Hb mss, Syr, Vg read *they* [J]1:28 LXX reads *Then she left him there before the LORD*

my ·horn is lifted up
by the LORD.
My mouth boasts
over my enemies,
because I rejoice
in Your salvation.
2 There is no one holy
like the LORD.
There is no one besides You!
And there is no rock
like our God.
3 Do not boast so proudly,
or let arrogant words come
out of your mouth,
for the LORD is a God
of knowledge,
and actions are weighed
by Him.
4 The bows of the warriors
are broken,
but the feeble are clothed
with strength.
5 Those who are full hire
themselves out for food,
but those who are starving
hunger no more.
The woman who is childless
gives birth to seven,
but the woman
with many sons pines away.
6 The LORD brings death
and gives life;
He sends some to ·Sheol,
and He raises others up.
7 The LORD brings poverty
and gives wealth;
He humbles and He exalts.
8 He raises the poor
from the dust
and lifts the needy
from the garbage pile.
He seats them with noblemen
and gives them a throne
of honor.[A]
For the foundations
of the earth are the LORD's;
He has set the world on them.
9 He guards the steps[B]
of His faithful ones,
but the wicked perish
in darkness,
for a man does not prevail by
his own strength.
10 Those who oppose the LORD
will be shattered;[C]
He will thunder
in the heavens
against them.
The LORD will judge the ends
of the earth.
He will give power to His king;
He will lift up the horn
of His anointed.

11 Elkanah went home to Ramah,
but the boy served the LORD in the
presence of Eli the priest.

The Corruption of the Priesthood (2:12-36)

12 Eli's sons were ·wicked men;
they had no regard for the LORD 13 or
for the priests' share of the sacrifices
from the people. When any man offered a sacrifice, the priest's servant
would come with a three-pronged
meat fork while the meat was boiling
14 and plunge it into the container or
kettle or cauldron or cooking pot.
The priest would claim for himself
whatever the meat fork brought up.
This is the way they treated all the
Israelites who came there to Shiloh.
15 Even before the fat was burned,
the priest's servant would come and
say to the man who was sacrificing,
"Give the priest some meat to roast,
because he won't accept boiled meat
from you—only raw." 16 If that man
said to him, "The fat must be burned
first; then you can take whatever you
want for yourself," the servant would
reply, "No, I insist that you hand it
over right now. If you don't, I'll take
it by force!" 17 So the servants' sin
was very severe in the presence of
the LORD, because they treated the
LORD's offering with contempt.

18 The boy Samuel served in the
LORD's presence and wore a linen
ephod. 19 Each year his mother made
him a little robe and took it to him
when she went with her husband
to offer the annual sacrifice. 20 Eli
would bless Elkanah and his wife:
"May the LORD give you children by
this woman in place of the one she[D]
has given to the LORD." Then they
would go home.

21 The LORD paid attention to
Hannah's need, and she conceived
and gave birth to three sons and
two daughters. Meanwhile, the boy

2:1-11 Hannah's praise is recorded in the form of Hebrew poetry. Her hymn is often compared to Mary's song, the *Magnificat* (Lk 1:46-55), because of its praise to God for His blessing. The song functions not only as Hannah's own expression of joy but also as Israel's triumphant expression of hope in being governed by the God who is the judge of all the earth (1Sm 2:10). Her prayer declares the omnipotence, holiness, omniscience, and sovereignty of God—all key themes emphasized throughout this book.

2:12-17 The piety and reverence of Elkanah and Hannah starkly contrasts the corruption of Israel's priesthood. Eli's sons, Hophni and Phinehas, **had no regard for** [Hb *lo'-yada*, "did not know or acknowledge,"] **the LORD.** They greedily took unlawful portions from animal sacrifices before the Lord received what was due Him. Not only did they treat this act of worship with contempt, but they also caused the Lord's people to sin (v. 24).

2:18-21 Though Hannah had given Samuel to the Lord, she continued to nurture him as a loving mother. **The LORD** later provided Hannah and Elkanah with more children.

[A]**2:8** DSS, LXX add *He gives the vow of the one who makes a vow and He blesses the years of the just* [B]**2:9** Lit *feet* [C]**2:10** DSS, LXX read *The LORD shatters those who dispute with Him*
[D]**2:20** DSS; MT reads *he*

2:22-26 The promiscuity of Eli's sons probably mimicked the ritual prostitution practiced in Canaanite fertility religions. Eli confronted his sons with a striking question: **If a man sins against the Lord, who can intercede for him?** (v. 25). No one was suitable to stand as a mediator between a sinful priest and God. Jesus the Messiah is the only mediator who, being without sin, can intercede on our behalf (Heb 7:22-28). Eli's sons did not respond to their father's rebuke and had succumbed to the judgment of hardened hearts. Samuel's submission to Eli and to the Lord is in contrast to the rebellion of Eli's sons.

2:27-36 The crux of Eli's failure was that he **honored** his sons more than he honored the Lord (v. 29). That Eli's **descendants** would **die violently** probably describes Saul's slaughter of the priests at Nob (22:13-20; 1Kg 2:26-27). **Distress in the place of worship** likely refers to the Philistines' capture of the ark (1Sm 2:32; 4:1-22). When God promised to **raise up a faithful** [Hb *'aman*, "upright, trustworthy"] **priest** who would serve as His **anointed one** forever (v. 35), He referred ultimately to Jesus, who is both Priest and King (Heb 5:6-9).

3:1 The spiritual condition of the nation, including the priesthood, was so corrupt that the Lord rarely visited His people with revelation during this time.

Samuel grew up in the presence of the LORD.

22 Now Eli was very old. He heard about everything his sons were doing to all Israel and how they were sleeping with the women who served at the entrance to the tent of meeting. 23 He said to them, "Why are you doing these things? I have heard about your evil actions from all these people. 24 No, my sons, the report I hear from the LORD's people is not good. 25 If a man sins against another man, God can intercede for him, but if a man sins against the LORD, who can intercede for him?" But they would not listen to their father, since the LORD intended to kill them. 26 By contrast, the boy Samuel grew in stature and in favor with the LORD and with men.

27 A man of God came to Eli and said to him, "This is what the LORD says: 'Didn't I reveal Myself to your ancestral house when it was in Egypt and belonged to Pharaoh's palace? 28 Out of all the tribes of Israel, I selected your house[A] to be priests, to offer sacrifices on My altar, to burn incense, and to wear an •ephod in My presence. I also gave your house all the Israelite fire offerings. 29 Why, then, do all of you despise My sacrifices and offerings that I require at the place of worship? You have honored your sons more than Me, by making yourselves fat with the best part of all of the offerings of My people Israel.'

30 "Therefore, this is the declaration of the LORD, the God of Israel:

'Although I said
your family and
  your ancestral house
would walk before Me forever,
the LORD now says,
  "No longer!"
I will honor those
  who honor Me,
but those who despise Me
  will be disgraced.

31 "'Look, the days are coming when I will cut off your strength and the strength of your ancestral family, so that none in your family will reach old age. 32 You will see distress in the place of worship, in spite of all that is good in Israel, and no one in your family will ever again reach old age. 33 Any man from your family I do not cut off from My altar will bring grief[B] and sadness to you. All your descendants will die violently.[C,D] 34 This will be the sign that will come to you concerning your two sons Hophni and Phinehas: both of them will die on the same day.

35 "'Then I will raise up a faithful priest for Myself. He will do whatever is in My heart and mind. I will establish a lasting dynasty for him, and he will walk before My anointed one for all time. 36 Anyone who is left in your family will come and bow down to him for a piece of silver or a loaf of bread. He will say: Please appoint me to some priestly office so I can have a piece of bread to eat.'"

Samuel's Encounter with God (3:1-21)

God's Call of Samuel (3:1-14)

3 The boy Samuel served the LORD in Eli's presence. In those days the word of the LORD was rare and prophetic visions were not widespread.

2 One day Eli, whose eyesight was failing, was lying in his room. 3 Before the lamp of God had gone out, Samuel was lying down in the tabernacle of the LORD, where the ark of God was located.

4 Then the LORD called Samuel,[E] and he answered, "Here I am." 5 He

[A]2:28 Lit *selected him* [B]2:33 Lit *grief to your eyes* [C]2:33 DSS, LXX read *die by the sword of men* [D]2:33 Lit *die men* [E]3:4 DSS, LXX read *called, "Samuel! Samuel!"*

>WORD|*study*

3:4 Here I am (Hb *hinnêni*) is a simple reply confirming that one hears and is listening to the speaker. Abraham, Jacob, Moses, Isaiah, and other great men of faith also responded to the Lord by replying, *"Hinnêni"* (Gn 22:1; 46:2; Ex 3:4; Is 6:8) when they were called. This common response should be characteristic of believers, demonstrating not only that they are ready to listen to the Lord but also that they are surrendered to obeying His command.

ran to Eli and said, "Here I am; you called me."

"I didn't call," Eli replied. "Go back and lie down." So he went and lay down.

6 Once again the LORD called, "Samuel!"

Samuel got up, went to Eli, and said, "Here I am; you called me."

"I didn't call, my son," he replied. "Go back and lie down."

7 Now Samuel had not yet experienced the LORD, because the word of the LORD had not yet been revealed to him. 8 Once again, for the third time, the LORD called Samuel. He got up, went to Eli, and said, "Here I am; you called me."

Then Eli understood that the LORD was calling the boy. 9 He told Samuel, "Go and lie down. If He calls you, say, 'Speak, LORD, for Your servant is listening.'" So Samuel went and lay down in his place.

10 The LORD came, stood there, and called as before, "Samuel, Samuel!"

Samuel responded, "Speak, for Your servant is listening."

11 The LORD said to Samuel, "I am about to do something in Israel that everyone who hears about it will shudder. 12 On that day I will carry out against Eli everything I said about his family, from beginning to end. 13 I told him that I am going to judge his family forever because of the iniquity he knows about: his sons are defiling the sanctuary,[A] and he has not stopped them. 14 Therefore, I have sworn to Eli's family: The iniquity of Eli's family will never be wiped out by either sacrifice or offering."

Samuel's Response in obedience (3:15-18)

15 Samuel lay down until the morning; then he opened the doors of the LORD's house. He was afraid to tell Eli the vision, 16 but Eli called him and said, "Samuel, my son."

"Here I am," answered Samuel.

17 "What was the message He gave you?" Eli asked. "Don't hide it from me. May God punish you and do so severely if you hide anything from me that He told you." 18 So Samuel told him everything and did not hide anything from him. Eli responded, "He is the LORD. He will do what He thinks is good."[B]

Samuel's Role as God's Prophet (3:19-21)

19 Samuel grew, and the LORD was with him, and He fulfilled everything Samuel prophesied.[C] 20 All Israel from Dan to Beer-sheba knew that Samuel was a confirmed prophet of the LORD. 21 The LORD continued to appear in Shiloh, because there He revealed Himself to Samuel by His word.

The Ark of the Covenant (4:1–7:17)

The Capture of the Ark (4:1–5:12)

4 1 And Samuel's words came to all Israel.

Israel went out to meet the Philistines in battle and[D] camped at Ebenezer while the Philistines camped at Aphek. 2 The Philistines lined up in battle formation against Israel, and as the battle intensified, Israel was defeated by the Philistines, who struck down about 4,000 men on the battlefield.

3 When the troops returned to the camp, the elders of Israel asked, "Why did the LORD let us be defeated today by the Philistines? Let's bring the ark of the LORD's covenant from Shiloh. Then it[E] will go with us and save us from the hand of our enemies." 4 So the people sent men to Shiloh to bring back the ark of the covenant of the LORD of •Hosts,

3:4-14 Although he knew much about God as a young priest-in-training, Samuel had not personally encountered the living God until now. Upon realizing the voice came from God, not Eli, Samuel referenced Himself as **Your servant**, reflecting his willing spirit (vv. 9-10).

3:15-18 Despite being **afraid**, Samuel displayed the courage and power needed to proclaim the word of the Lord to the people of Israel.

3:19–4:1 The phrase **from Dan to Beer-sheba** (v. 20) is commonly used in Scripture referring to all of Israel. Because Samuel's predictions were fulfilled, the people recognized that his prophetic role was genuine (see Dt 18:21-22).

4:1-11 The Israelites responded to the ark's abduction by attempting to handle the situation in their own way, doing what seemed reasonable according to a pagan worldview. Their actions indicate a superstitious confusion of the ark with God's actual presence. They trusted in the holy representation of God, but not in God Himself (v. 3). The Israelites were either treating **the ark of the covenant of the LORD of Hosts** as a magical object, or they were trying to manipulate God into doing their will (v. 4). Eli and his sons are mentioned here rather than Samuel. Israel's elders asked why the Lord allowed their defeat; yet they failed to seek the wisdom of Samuel, whom they recognized as God's true spokesman.

[A] **3:13** Ancient Jewish tradition, LXX, Old Lat read *are cursing God* [B] **3:18** Lit *what is good in His eyes* [C] **3:19** Lit *He let no words fall to the ground* [D] **4:1** LXX reads *In those days the Philistines gathered together to fight against Israel, and Israel went out to engage them in battle. They* [E] **4:3** Or *He*

>WORD|*study*

3:20 Confirmed (Hb *'aman*, "upright, trustworthy") is the same word the Lord used to describe the "faithful priest," whom He promised to "raise up" for Himself (2:35). Jesus is described both as our "faithful (Gk *pistos*, the same word used in the LXX to translate the Hebrew *'aman*) high priest in service to God" (Heb 2:17) and as the "high priest" whose faithfulness as the Son is compared with, but deemed superior to, that of the prophet Moses (Heb 3:1-6). Samuel's leadership foreshadows the three roles that the Messiah later fulfilled. Samuel served as Israel's last judge, anointed the nation's first kings, interceded as a priest, and is called "a confirmed prophet of the Lord" (cp. 1Sm 7:15; 10:1; 16:12–13; 7:3-9).

4:12-22 Phinehas' wife appropriately named her son **Ichabod** (Hb, "Where is the glory?"), correctly interpreting the departure of God's glory as a sign of judgment (vv. 21-22; cp. Ezk 1:9-11).

5:1-12 The Philistine god **Dagon** lay prostrate before the ark, symbolizing that there is no other god than the God of Israel.

who dwells between the •cherubim. Eli's two sons, Hophni and Phinehas, were there with the ark of the covenant of God. [5]When the ark of the covenant of the LORD entered the camp, all the Israelites raised such a loud shout that the ground shook.

[6]The Philistines heard the sound of the war cry and asked, "What's this loud shout in the Hebrews' camp?" When the Philistines discovered that the ark of the LORD had entered the camp, [7]they panicked. "The gods have entered their camp!" they said. "Woe to us, nothing like this has happened before.[A] [8]Woe to us, who will rescue us from the hand of these magnificent gods? These are the gods that slaughtered the Egyptians with all kinds of plagues in the wilderness. [9]Show some courage and be men, Philistines! Otherwise, you'll serve the Hebrews just as they served you. Now be men and fight!"

[10]So the Philistines fought, and Israel was defeated, and each man fled to his tent. The slaughter was severe—30,000 of the Israelite foot soldiers fell. [11]The ark of God was captured, and Eli's two sons, Hophni and Phinehas, died.

[12]That same day, a Benjaminite man ran from the battle and came to Shiloh. His clothes were torn, and there was dirt on his head. [13]When he arrived, there was Eli sitting on his chair beside the road watching, because he was anxious about the ark of God. When the man entered the city to give a report, the entire city cried out.

[14]Eli heard the outcry and asked, "Why this commotion?" The man quickly came and reported to Eli. [15]At that time Eli was 98 years old, and his gaze was fixed[B] because he couldn't see.

[16]The man said to Eli, "I'm the one who came from the battle.[C] I fled from there today."

"What happened, my son?" Eli asked.

[17]The messenger answered, "Israel has fled from the Philistines, and also there was a great slaughter among the people. Your two sons, Hophni and Phinehas, are both dead, and the ark of God has been captured." [18]When he mentioned the ark of God, Eli fell backward off the chair by the city gate, and since he was old and heavy, his neck broke and he died. Eli had judged Israel 40 years.

[19]Eli's daughter-in-law, the wife of Phinehas, was pregnant and about to give birth. When she heard the news about the capture of God's ark and the deaths of her father-in-law and her husband, she collapsed and gave birth because her labor pains came on her. [20]As she was dying,[D] the women taking care of her said, "Don't be afraid. You've given birth to a son!" But she did not respond or pay attention. [21]She named the boy Ichabod,[E] saying, "The glory has departed from Israel," referring to the capture of the ark of God and to the deaths of her father-in-law and her husband. [22]"The glory has departed from Israel," she said, "because the ark of God has been captured."

5 After the Philistines had captured the ark of God, they took it from Ebenezer to Ashdod, [2]brought it into the temple of Dagon[F] and placed it next to his statue.[G] [3]When the people of Ashdod got up early the next morning, there was Dagon, fallen with his face to the ground before the ark of the LORD. So they took Dagon and returned him to his place. [4]But when they got up early the next morning, there was Dagon, fallen with his face to the ground before the ark of the LORD. This time, both Dagon's head and the palms of his hands were broken off and lying on the threshold. Only Dagon's torso remained.[H] [5]That is why, to this day, the priests of Dagon and everyone who enters the temple of Dagon in Ashdod do not step on Dagon's threshold.

[6]The LORD's hand was heavy on the people of Ashdod, terrorizing and afflicting the people of Ashdod and its territory with tumors.[I,J] [7]When

[A]**4:7** Lit *yesterday or the day before* [B]**4:15** Lit *his eyes stood*; 1Kg 14:4 [C]**4:16** LXX reads *camp* [D]**4:20** LXX reads *And in her time of delivery, she was about to die* [E]**4:21** = Where is Glory? [F]**5:2** A Philistine god of the sea, grain, or storm [G]**5:2** Lit *to Dagon* [H]**5:4** LXX; Hb reads *Only Dagon remained on it* [I]**5:6** LXX adds *He brought up mice against them, and they swarmed in their ships. Then mice went up into the land and there was a mortal panic in the city.* [J]**5:6** Perhaps bubonic plague

the men of Ashdod saw what was happening, they said, "The ark of Israel's God must not stay here with us, because His hand is strongly against us and our god Dagon." [8]So they called all the Philistine rulers together and asked, "What should we do with the ark of Israel's God?"

"The ark of Israel's God should be moved to Gath," they replied. So the men of Ashdod moved the ark. [9]After they had moved it, the LORD's hand was against the city of Gath, causing a great panic. He afflicted the men of the city, from the youngest to the oldest, with an outbreak of tumors.

[10]The Gittites then sent the ark of God to Ekron, but when it got there, the Ekronites cried out, "They've moved the ark of Israel's God to us to kill us and our people!"[A]

[11]The Ekronites called all the Philistine rulers together. They said, "Send the ark of Israel's God away. It must return to its place so it won't kill us and our people!"[B] For the fear of death pervaded the city; God's hand was oppressing them. [12]The men who did not die were afflicted with tumors, and the outcry of the city went up to heaven.

The Return of the Ark (6:1–7:17)

6 When the ark of the LORD had been in the land of the Philistines for seven months, [2]the Philistines summoned the priests and the diviners and pleaded, "What should we do with the ark of the LORD? Tell us how we can send it back to its place."

[3]They replied, "If you send the ark of Israel's God away, you must not send it without an offering. You must send back a restitution offering to Him, and you will be healed. Then the reason His hand hasn't been removed from you will be revealed."[C]

[4]They asked, "What restitution offering should we send back to Him?"

And they answered, "Five gold tumors and five gold mice corresponding to the number of Philistine rulers, since there was one plague for both you[D] and your rulers. [5]Make images of your tumors and of your mice that are destroying the land. Give glory to Israel's God, and perhaps He will stop oppressing you,[E] your gods, and your land. [6]Why harden your hearts as the Egyptians and Pharaoh hardened theirs? When He afflicted them, didn't they send Israel away, and Israel left?

[7]"Now then, prepare one new cart and two milk cows that have never been yoked. Hitch the cows to the cart, but take their calves away and pen them up. [8]Take the ark of the LORD, place it on the cart, and put the gold objects that you're sending Him as a restitution offering in a box beside the ark. Send it off and let it go its way. [9]Then watch: If it goes up the road to its homeland toward Beth-shemesh, it is the LORD who has made this terrible trouble for us. However, if it doesn't, we will know that it was not His hand that punished us—it was just something that happened to us by chance."

[10]The men did this: They took two milk cows, hitched them to the cart, and confined their calves in the pen. [11]Then they put the ark of the LORD on the cart, along with the box containing the gold mice and the images of their tumors. [12]The cows went straight up the road to Beth-shemesh. They stayed on that one highway, lowing as they went; they never strayed to the right or to the left. The Philistine rulers were walking behind them to the territory of Beth-shemesh.

[13]The people of Beth-shemesh were harvesting wheat in the valley, and when they looked up and saw the ark, they were overjoyed to see it. [14]The cart came to the field of Joshua of Beth-shemesh and stopped there near a large rock. The people of the city chopped up the cart and offered the cows as a •burnt offering to the LORD. [15]The Levites removed the ark of the LORD, along with the box containing the gold objects, and placed them on the large rock. That day the men of Beth-shemesh offered burnt offerings and made sacrifices to the LORD. [16]When

6:1-12 Requiring two untrained cows to leave their calves behind and pull together in the same direction was designed to circumstantially fail without Yahweh's intervention. However, the God of Israel did what these priests thought impossible and demonstrated His power and glory before the Philistines.

6:13–7:1 In their celebration the Israelites disobeyed God's law by looking inside **the ark.** The Lord struck the men at **Beth-shemesh** due to their lack of respect and honor in approaching His presence.

[A]**5:10** DSS, LXX read *Why have you moved . . . people?* [B]**5:11** DSS, LXX read *Why don't you return it to . . . people?* [C]**6:3** DSS, LXX read *healed, and an atonement shall be made for you. Shouldn't His hand be removed from you?* [D]**6:4** Some Hb mss, LXX; other Hb mss read *them* [E]**6:5** Lit *will lighten the heaviness of His hand from you*

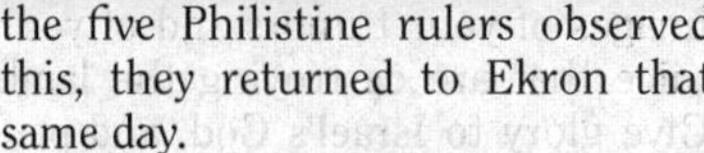

7:2-6 Twenty years after the return of the ark of the covenant, **the whole house of Israel** finally **began to seek the Lord.** Samuel challenged the Israelites to put away their idols, consecrate themselves to the Lord, and serve Him alone. Awareness of their sin led to repentance as they prayed, **fasted**, and **poured** out water before the Lord , a symbolic practice that reflected their confession before God and, as a nation, marked their corporate repentance in failing to obey God's commands (Lm 2:19).

7:7-12 Israel's assembly of corporate repentance at **Mizpah** (Hb, "watchtower") was interpreted as a military maneuver by the **Philistines,** who launched an attack on Israel. When the Lord defeated the Philistines in a mighty demonstration of His power, Samuel consecrated the place and built a monument which he named **Ebenezer** (Hb *ʾeven*, "stone," and *ʿēzer*, "help"—"stone of help").

7:13-17 The Lord blessed Israel for their obedience to Him in repenting and seeking Him first before going to battle. The people learned that victory is preceded by a return to God and His ways. The account underscores the basis for Samuel's opposition to Israel's demand for a king—Yahweh's mighty deliverance of Israel from the Philistines demonstrated His power to rule and defend Israel (8:6-7).

the five Philistine rulers observed
this, they returned to Ekron that
same day.
17 As a restitution offering to the
LORD, the Philistines had sent back
one gold tumor for each city: Ashdod, Gaza, Ashkelon, Gath, and
Ekron. 18 The number of gold mice
also corresponded to the number of
Philistine cities of the five rulers,
the fortified cities and the outlying
villages. The large rock[A] on which
the ark of the LORD was placed is in
the field of Joshua of Beth-shemesh
to this day.
19 God struck down the men of
Beth-shemesh because they looked
inside the ark of the LORD.[B] He
struck down 70 men out of 50,000
men.[C] The people mourned because
the LORD struck them with a great
slaughter. 20 The men of Beth-shemesh asked, "Who is able to stand
in the presence of this holy LORD
God? Who should the ark go to from
here?"
21 They sent messengers to the
residents of Kiriath-jearim, saying,
"The Philistines have returned the
ark of the LORD. Come down and get
it."[D]

7 So the men of Kiriath-jearim
came for the ark of the LORD and
took it to Abinadab's house on the
hill. They consecrated his son Eleazar to take care of it.
2 Time went by until 20 years had
passed since the ark had been taken
to Kiriath-jearim. Then the whole
house of Israel began to seek the
LORD. 3 Samuel told them, "If you are
returning to the LORD with all your
heart, get rid of the foreign gods and
the •Ashtoreths that are among you,
dedicate yourselves to[E] the LORD,
and worship only Him. Then He will
rescue you from the hand of the Philistines." 4 So the Israelites removed
the •Baals and the Ashtoreths and
only worshiped the LORD.
5 Samuel said, "Gather all Israel at
Mizpah, and I will pray to the LORD
on your behalf." 6 When they gathered at Mizpah, they drew water and
poured it out in the LORD's presence.
They fasted that day, and there they
confessed, "We have sinned against
the LORD." And Samuel judged the
Israelites at Mizpah.
7 When the Philistines heard that
the Israelites had gathered at Mizpah, their rulers marched up toward
Israel. When the Israelites heard
about it, they were afraid because of
the Philistines. 8 The Israelites said
to Samuel, "Don't stop crying out
to the LORD our God for us, so that
He will save us from the hand of the
Philistines."
9 Then Samuel took a young lamb
and offered it as a whole •burnt offering to the LORD. He cried out to
the LORD on behalf of Israel, and
the LORD answered him. 10 Samuel
was offering the burnt offering as
the Philistines drew near to fight
against Israel. The LORD thundered
loudly against the Philistines that
day and threw them into such confusion that they fled before Israel.
11 Then the men of Israel charged
out of Mizpah and pursued the Philistines striking them down all the
way to a place below Beth-car.
12 Afterward, Samuel took a stone
and set it upright between Mizpah
and Shen. He named it Ebenezer,[F]
explaining, "The LORD has helped us
to this point." 13 So the Philistines
were subdued and[G] did not invade
Israel's territory again. The LORD's
hand was against the Philistines all
of Samuel's life. 14 The cities from
Ekron to Gath, which they had
taken from Israel, were restored; Israel even rescued their surrounding
territories from Philistine control.
There was also peace between Israel
and the Amorites.
15 Samuel judged Israel throughout
his life. 16 Every year he would go on a
circuit to Bethel, Gilgal, and Mizpah
and would judge Israel at all these
locations. 17 Then he would return to
Ramah because his home was there,
he judged Israel there, and he built
an altar to the LORD there.

[A] **6:18** Some Hb mss, DSS, LXX, Tg; other Hb mss read *meadow* [B] **6:19** LXX reads *But the sons of Jeconiah did not rejoice with the men of Beth-shemesh when they saw the ark of the LORD.* [C] **6:19** Some Hb mss, Josephus read *70 men*; other Hb mss read *50,070 men* [D] **6:21** Lit *and bring it up to you* [E] **7:3** Lit *you and set your hearts on* [F] **7:12** = Stone of Help [G] **7:13** LXX reads *The LORD humbled the Philistines and they*

The Rise of Saul to Kingship (8:1–12:25)

Israel's Demand for a King (8:1-22)

8 When Samuel grew old, he appointed his sons as judges over Israel. [2] His firstborn son's name was Joel and his second was Abijah. They were judges in Beer-sheba. [3] However, his sons did not walk in his ways—they turned toward dishonest gain, took bribes, and perverted justice.

[4] So all the elders of Israel gathered together and went to Samuel at Ramah. [5] They said to him, "Look, you are old, and your sons do not follow your example. Therefore, appoint a king to judge us the same as all the other nations have."

[6] When they said, "Give us a king to judge us," Samuel considered their demand sinful, so he prayed to the LORD. [7] But the LORD told him, "Listen to the people and everything they say to you. They have not rejected you; they have rejected Me as their king. [8] They are doing the same thing to you that they have done to Me,[A] since the day I brought them out of Egypt until this day, abandoning Me and worshiping other gods. [9] Listen to them, but you must solemnly warn them and tell them about the rights of the king who will rule over them."

[10] Samuel told all the LORD's words to the people who were asking him for a king. [11] He said, "These are the rights of the king who will rule over you: He will take your sons and put them to his use in his chariots, on his horses, or running in front of his chariots. [12] He can appoint them for his use as commanders of thousands or commanders of fifties, to plow his ground or reap his harvest, or to make his weapons of war or the equipment for his chariots. [13] He can take your daughters to become perfumers, cooks, and bakers. [14] He can take your best fields, vineyards, and olive orchards and give them to his servants. [15] He can take a tenth of your grain and your vineyards and give them to his officials and servants. [16] He can take your male servants, your female servants, your best young men,[B] and your donkeys and use them for his work. [17] He can take a tenth of your flocks, and you yourselves can become his servants. [18] When that day comes, you will cry out because of the king you've chosen for yourselves, but the LORD won't answer you on that day."

[19] The people refused to listen to Samuel. "No!" they said. "We must have a king over us. [20] Then we'll be like all the other nations: our king will judge us, go out before us, and fight our battles."

[21] Samuel listened to all the people's words and then repeated them to the LORD.[C] [22] "Listen to them," the LORD told Samuel. "Appoint a king for them."

Then Samuel told the men of Israel, "Each of you, go back to your city."

The Anointing of Saul as King (9:1–10:16)

9 There was an influential man of Benjamin named Kish son of Abiel, son of Zeror, son of Becorath, son of Aphiah, son of a Benjaminite. [2] He had a son named Saul, an impressive young man. There was no one more impressive among the Israelites than he. He stood a head taller than anyone else.[D]

[3] One day the donkeys of Saul's father Kish wandered off. Kish said to his son Saul, "Take one of the attendants with you and go look for the donkeys." [4] Saul and his attendant went through the hill country of Ephraim and then through the region of Shalishah, but they didn't find them. They went through the region of Shaalim—nothing. Then they went through the Benjaminite region but still didn't find them.

[5] When they came to the land of Zuph, Saul said to the attendant who was with him, "Come on, let's go back, or my father will stop worrying about the donkeys and start worrying about us."

[6] "Look," the attendant said, "there's a man of God in this city who is highly respected; everything he says is sure to come true. Let's go there now. Maybe he'll tell us which way we should go."

[7] "Suppose we do go," Saul said

8:1-6 Samuel's sons, **Joel** (Hb, "Yahweh is God") and **Abijah** (Hb, "Yahweh is my father"), served **as judges** but did not follow in their father's spiritual footsteps (v. 3). Concerned about the future leadership of the nation, **the elders of Israel** approached Samuel with the demand for **a king** (v. 5). The prophet's response demonstrated a key quality of leadership—prayer (v. 6). Even the prophet Jeremiah recounted the powerful intercession of Samuel (Jr 15:1). The people knew Samuel was a man of prayer (1Sm 7:8-9) and that God heard and answered his supplications (7:8; 12:19). The people's request for a king was not wrong, since this was promised to them in Genesis 49:10. Rather, the people's motivation troubled Samuel and the Lord (1Sm 8:6). They desired a king in order to be like **all the other nations** (v. 5).

8:7-22 The Lord assured Samuel that the people's request was not a rejection of Samuel but rather of Him (vv. 7-9). This book demonstrates that punishment follows disobedience, while blessing follows the obedient heart.

[A] **8:8** LXX; MT omits *to Me* [B] **8:16** LXX reads *best cattle* [C] **8:21** Lit *them in the LORD's ears*
[D] **9:2** Lit *From his shoulder and up higher than any of the people*

9:17-27 Saul (Hb, "the one who was asked for") is a fitting name for one who was requested by the people in contrast to the one who would succeed Saul as the king chosen by God (i.e., David). God's sovereignty is demonstrated in the manner in which God chose a king for His people, led him to Samuel, and confirmed in Samuel's heart that Saul was the one He had ordained as leader over Israel.

>WORD|*study*

9:9 Seer (Hb *ro'eh*, "one who sees") was likely used to describe Samuel's function of receiving divine revelation about present circumstances. A "prophet" (Hb *navi'*, "spokesman of God") served as one who proclaimed divine revelation. Both terms are interchangeably used to describe Samuel.

to his attendant, "what do we take
the man? The food from our packs
is gone, and there's no gift to take to
the man of God. What do we have?"
8 The attendant answered Saul:
"Here, I have a piece[A] of silver. I'll
give it to the man of God, and he will
tell us our way."
9 Formerly in Israel, a man who
was going to inquire of God would
say, "Come, let's go to the seer," for
the prophet of today was formerly
called the seer.
10 "Good," Saul replied to his attendant. "Come on, let's go." So
they went to the city where the man
of God was. 11 As they were climbing
the hill to the city, they found some
young women coming out to draw
water and asked, "Is the seer here?"
12 The women answered, "Yes, he
is ahead of you. Hurry, he just now
came to the city, because there's a
sacrifice for the people at the •high
place today. 13 If you go quickly, you
can catch up with him before he goes
to the high place to eat. The people
won't eat until he comes because he
must bless the sacrifice; after that,
the guests can eat. Go up immediately—you can find him now." 14 So
they went up toward the city.
Saul and his attendant were entering the city when they saw Samuel
coming toward them on his way to
the high place. 15 Now the day before
Saul's arrival, the LORD had informed
Samuel,[B] 16 "At this time tomorrow I
will send you a man from the land
of Benjamin. Anoint him ruler over
My people Israel. He will save them
from the hand of the Philistines because I have seen the affliction of
My people, for their cry has come to
Me." 17 When Samuel saw Saul, the
LORD told him, "Here is the man I
told you about; he will rule over My
people."
18 Saul approached Samuel in the
gate area and asked, "Would you
please tell me where the seer's house
is?"
19 "I am the seer," Samuel answered.[C] "Go up ahead of me to the
high place and eat with me today.
When I send you off in the morning,
I'll tell you everything that's in your
heart. 20 As for the donkeys that wandered away from you three days ago,
don't worry about them because
they've been found. And who does
all Israel desire but you and all your
father's family?"
21 Saul responded, "Am I not a
Benjaminite from the smallest of
Israel's tribes and isn't my clan the
least important of all the clans of the
Benjaminite tribe? So why have you
said something like this to me?"
22 Samuel took Saul and his attendant, brought them to the banquet
hall, and gave them a place at the head
of the 30[D] or so men who had been invited. 23 Then Samuel said to the cook,
"Get the portion of meat that I gave
you and told you to set aside."
24 The cook picked up the thigh
and what was attached to it and set it
before Saul. Then Samuel said, "Notice that the reserved piece is set before you. Eat it because it was saved
for you for this solemn event at the
time I said, 'I've invited the people.'"
So Saul ate with Samuel that day.
25 Afterward, they went down from
the high place to the city, and Samuel spoke with Saul on the roof.[E]
26 They got up early, and just before dawn, Samuel called to Saul on
the roof, "Get up, and I'll send you
on your way!" Saul got up, and both
he and Samuel went outside. 27 As
they were going down to the edge of
the city, Samuel said to Saul, "Tell
the attendant to go on ahead of us,
but you stay for a while, and I'll reveal the word of God to you." So the
attendant went on.

[A]**9:8** Lit *a quarter of a shekel* [B]**9:15** Lit *had uncovered Samuel's ear, saying* [C]**9:19** Lit *answered Saul* [D]**9:22** LXX reads *70* [E]**9:25** LXX reads *city. They prepared a bed for Saul on the roof, and he slept.*

10 Samuel took the flask of oil,
poured it out on Saul's head,
kissed him, and said, "Hasn't the LORD
anointed you ruler over His inheritance?[A] 2 Today when you leave me,
you'll find two men at Rachel's Grave
at Zelzah in the land of Benjamin.
They will say to you, 'The donkeys you
went looking for have been found,
and now your father has stopped being concerned about the donkeys and
is worried about you, asking: What
should I do about my son?'
3 "You will proceed from there
until you come to the oak of Tabor.
Three men going up to God at Bethel will meet you there, one bringing three goats, one bringing three
loaves of bread, and one bringing
a skin of wine. 4 They will ask how
you are and give you two loaves[B] of
bread, which you will accept from
them.
5 "After that you will come to the
Hill of God[C] where there are Philistine garrisons.[D] When you arrive
at the city, you will meet a group
of prophets coming down from the
•high place prophesying. They will
be preceded by harps, tambourines,
flutes, and lyres. 6 The Spirit of
the LORD will control you, you will
prophesy with them, and you will be
transformed into a different person.
7 When these signs have happened
to you, do whatever your circumstances require[E] because God is with
you. 8 Afterward, go ahead of me to
Gilgal. I will come to you to offer
•burnt offerings and to sacrifice •fel-
lowship offerings. Wait seven days
until I come to you and show you
what to do."
9 When Saul turned around[F] to
leave Samuel, God changed his
heart,[G] and all the signs came about
that day. 10 When Saul and his attendant arrived at Gibeah, a group of
prophets met him. Then the Spirit
of God took control of him, and he
prophesied along with them.
11 Everyone who knew him previously and saw him prophesy with the
prophets asked each other, "What
has happened to the son of Kish? Is
Saul also among the prophets?"
12 Then a man who was from there
asked, "And who is their father?"
As a result, "Is Saul also among
the prophets?" became a popular
saying. 13 Then Saul finished prophesying and went to the high place.
14 Saul's uncle asked him and his
attendant, "Where did you go?"
"To look for the donkeys," Saul answered. "When we saw they weren't
there, we went to Samuel."
15 "Tell me," Saul's uncle asked,
"what did Samuel say to you?"
16 Saul told him, "He assured us
the donkeys had been found." However, Saul did not tell him what
Samuel had said about the matter of
kingship.

The Reception of Saul as King (10:17-27)

17 Samuel summoned the people
to the LORD at Mizpah 18 and said to
the Israelites, "This is what the LORD,
the God of Israel, says: 'I brought Israel out of Egypt, and I rescued you
from the power of the Egyptians and
all the kingdoms that were oppressing you.' 19 But today you have rejected your God, who saves you from
all your troubles and afflictions. You
said to Him, 'You[H] must set a king
over us.' Now therefore present

10:1-8 The anointing with oil signified Saul's inauguration and consecration to office and symbolized the endowment of the Holy Spirit for his divinely appointed task of leadership (vv. 1,6; 9:16; cp. Ex 28:41; 30:30; 40:13-15; 2Co 1:21; 1Jn 2:20,27).

10:10 While Saul exhibited a prophetic gift, he did not assume a prophetic ministry.

[A] **10:1** LXX adds *And you will reign over the LORD's people, and you will save them from the hand of their enemies all around. And this is the sign to you that the LORD has anointed you ruler over his inheritance.* [B] **10:4** DSS, LXX read *wave offerings* [C] **10:5** Or *to Gibeath-elohim* [D] **10:5** Or *governors* [E] **10:7** Lit *do for yourself whatever your hand finds* [F] **10:9** Lit *turned his shoulder* [G] **10:9** Lit *God turned to him another heart* [H] **10:19** Some Hb mss, LXX, Syr, Vg read *You said, 'No, you . . .*

>WORD|*study*

10:6,10 When used of God's Spirit, will control/took control (Hb *tsalach*, cp. 11:6) figuratively means "fall upon, attack." The sense is not that the Spirit intends to destroy the person but that His movement is sudden and overwhelming so that the person's actions or abilities are not self-generated but must be attributed to God.

10:9 The change (Hb *haphak*, "turn, convert, transform," from the primary meaning, "overturn") in Saul's heart occurred as a result of God's work within him.

11:1-15 Still humble, Saul gave God the glory for Israel's victory for defeating the Ammonites (vv. 12-13). As the place where the children of Israel first set foot on the promised land and erected a memorial to God's deliverance from Egypt (Jos 4:19-20), Gilgal was a fitting location for their victory celebration.

yourselves before the LORD by your tribes and clans."

20 Samuel had all the tribes of Israel come forward, and the tribe of Benjamin was selected. 21 Then he had the tribe of Benjamin come forward by its clans, and the Matrite clan was selected.[A] Finally, Saul son of Kish was selected. But when they searched for him, they could not find him. 22 They again inquired of the LORD, "Has the man come here yet?"

The LORD replied, "There he is, hidden among the supplies."

23 They ran and got him from there. When he stood among the people, he stood a head taller than anyone else.[B] 24 Samuel said to all the people, "Do you see the one the LORD has chosen? There is no one like him among the entire population."

And all the people shouted,[C] "Long live the king!"

25 Samuel proclaimed to the people the rights of kingship. He wrote them on a scroll, which he placed in the presence of the LORD. Then Samuel sent all the people away, each to his home.

26 Saul also went to his home in Gibeah, and brave men whose hearts God had touched went with him. 27 But some •wicked men said, "How can this guy save us?" They despised him and did not bring him a gift, but Saul said nothing.[D,E]

Saul's Deliverance of Jabesh-gilead (11:1-11)

11 Nahash[F] the Ammonite came up and laid siege to Jabesh-gilead. All the men of Jabesh said to him, "Make a treaty with us, and we will serve you."

2 Nahash the Ammonite replied, "I'll make one with you on this condition: that I gouge out everyone's right eye and humiliate all Israel."

3 "Don't do anything to us for seven days," the elders of Jabesh said to him, "and let us send messengers throughout the territory of Israel. If no one saves us, we will surrender to you."

4 When the messengers came to Gibeah, Saul's hometown, and told the terms to[G] the people, all wept aloud. 5 Just then Saul was coming in from the field behind his oxen. "What's the matter with the people? Why are they weeping?" Saul inquired, and they repeated to him the words of the men from Jabesh.

6 When Saul heard these words, the Spirit of God suddenly took control of him, and his anger burned furiously. 7 He took a team of oxen, cut them in pieces, and sent them throughout the land of Israel by messengers who said, "This is what will be done to the ox of anyone who doesn't march behind Saul and Samuel." As a result, the terror of the LORD fell on the people, and they went out united.

8 Saul counted them at Bezek. There were 300,000[H] Israelites and 30,000[I] men from Judah. 9 He told the messengers who had come, "Tell this to the men of Jabesh-gilead: 'Deliverance will be yours tomorrow by the time the sun is hot.'" So the messengers told the men of Jabesh, and they rejoiced.

10 Then the men of Jabesh said to Nahash, "Tomorrow we will come out, and you can do whatever you want[J] to us."

11 The next day Saul organized the troops into three divisions. During the morning watch, they invaded the Ammonite camp and slaughtered them until the heat of the day. There were survivors, but they were so scattered that no two of them were left together.

Saul's Confirmation as King (11:12-15)

12 Afterward, the people said to Samuel, "Who said that Saul should not[K] reign over us? Give us those men so we can kill them!"

[A]**10:21** LXX adds *And he had the Matrite clan come forward, man by man.* [B]**10:23** Lit *people, and he was higher than any of the people from his shoulder and up* [C]**10:24** LXX reads *acknowledged and said* [D]**10:27** DSS add *Nahash king of the Ammonites had been severely oppressing the Gadites and Reubenites. He gouged out the right eye of each of them and brought fear and trembling on Israel. Of the Israelites beyond the Jordan none remained whose right eye Nahash, king of the Ammonites, had not gouged out. But there were 7,000 men who had escaped from the Ammonites and entered Jabesh-gilead.* [E]**10:27** Lit *gift, and he was like a mute person* [F]**11:1** DSS, LXX read *About a month later, Nahash* [G]**11:4** Lit *in the ears of* [H]**11:8** LXX reads *600,000* [I]**11:8** DSS, LXX read *70,000* [J]**11:10** Lit *do what is good in your eyes* [K]**11:12** Some Hb mss, LXX; other Hb mss omit *not*

>WORD|*study*

12:9 With Yahweh as the object, **forgot** (Hb *shakach*, "cease to care, ignore"), like "remember" (see 1:19), does not mean a mere lapse of memory but a willful turning away from God, i.e., turning a deaf ear to His Word. The Lord had warned His people specifically against forgetting Him (Dt 6:10-15; 8:11-20) and had punished them for the evil and idolatry they pursued when **they forgot the Lord their God** (cp. Dt 32:15-27; Jdg 3:7; cp. Heb 12:5-11; 2Pt 1:9).

13 But Saul ordered, "No one will be
executed this day, for today the LORD
has provided deliverance in Israel."
14 Then Samuel said to the people,
"Come, let's go to Gilgal, so we can
renew the kingship there." 15 So all
the people went to Gilgal, and there
in the LORD's presence they made
Saul king. There they sacrificed •fel-
lowship offerings in the LORD's presence, and Saul and all the men of
Israel greatly rejoiced.

Samuel's Final Public Speech (12:1-25)

12 Then Samuel said to all Israel,
"I have carefully listened to everything you said to me and placed
a king over you. 2 Now you can see
that the king is leading you. As for
me, I'm old and gray, and my sons
are here with you. I have led you
from my youth until today. 3 Here I
am. Bring charges against me before
the LORD and His anointed: Whose
ox or donkey have I taken? Whom
have I wronged or mistreated? From
whose hand have I taken a bribe to
overlook something?[A,B] I will return
it to you."
4 "You haven't wronged us, you
haven't mistreated us, and you
haven't taken anything from anyone's hand," they responded.
5 He said to them, "The LORD is a
witness against you, and His anointed is a witness today that you haven't
found anything in my hand."
"He is a witness," they said.
6 Then Samuel said to the people,
"The LORD, who appointed Moses
and Aaron and who brought your
ancestors up from the land of Egypt,
is a witness.[C] 7 Now present yourselves, so I may confront you before
the LORD about all the righteous acts
He has done for you and your ancestors.
8 "When Jacob went to Egypt,[D]
your ancestors cried out to the LORD,
and He sent them Moses and Aaron,
who led your ancestors out of Egypt
and settled them in this place. 9 But
they forgot the LORD their God, so
He handed them over to Sisera commander of the army of Hazor, to the
Philistines, and to the king of Moab.
These enemies fought against them.
10 Then they cried out to the LORD
and said, 'We have sinned, for we
abandoned the LORD and worshiped
the •Baals and the •Ashtoreths. Now
deliver us from the power of our enemies, and we will serve You.' 11 So
the LORD sent Jerubbaal, Barak,[E]
Jephthah, and Samuel. He rescued
you from the power of the enemies
around you, and you lived securely.
12 But when you saw that Nahash
king of the Ammonites was coming against you, you said to me,
'No, we must have a king rule over
us'—even though the LORD your
God is your king.
13 "Now here is the king you've chosen, the one you requested. Look,
this is the king the LORD has placed
over you. 14 If you •fear the LORD, worship and obey Him, and if you don't
rebel against the LORD's command,
then both you and the king who
rules over you will follow the LORD
your God. 15 However, if you disobey
the LORD and rebel against His command, the LORD's hand will be against
you and against your ancestors.[F]
16 "Now, therefore, present yourselves and see this great thing that
the LORD will do before your eyes.
17 Isn't the wheat harvest today? I
will call on the LORD and He will
send thunder and rain, so that you
will know and see what a great evil
you committed in the LORD's sight
by requesting a king for yourselves."

[A]**12:3** LXX reads *bribe or a pair of shoes? Testify against me.* [B]**12:3** Lit *bribe and will hide my eyes with it?* [C]**12:6** LXX; MT omits *is a witness* [D]**12:8** LXX reads *When Jacob and his sons went to Egypt and Egypt humbled them* [E]**12:11** LXX, Syr; MT reads *Bedan*; Jdg 4:6; Heb 11:32 [F]**12:15** LXX reads *your king*

12:1-13 While Saul reigned as king, Samuel still performed the ministries of priest, prophet, and judge, providing spiritual counsel and guidance. Samuel's exhortation focused on three major points. First, Yahweh would decide who should lead His people. Second, Samuel reminded the people of their waywardness in forgetting God and His goodness toward them (vv. 9,12). Third, Yahweh would be faithful to help His people (vv. 8,11). Despite Israel's string of broken promises, necessitating God's judgment, **the LORD** never failed to answer their repentant cries for help with His deliverance.

12:14-19 Samuel's request for the Lord to **send thunder and rain** was bold, considering that it was during **the wheat harvest**, a season when rain was rare. Confirming the words of His servant, the Lord poured rain from heaven, bringing the people to repentance.

12:20-25 Samuel's example in praying for this hardened people serves as a reminder to those in ministry never to cease praying for the people in their care, regardless of how hardened their hearts have become. This great prophet of God concluded his challenge and farewell address by underscoring three things: Fear the Lord, serve Him alone, and remember His faithfulness.

13:1 Ancient manuscripts differ on the length of Saul's reign. Based on Paul's summary of Israel's history, Saul reigned 40 years (Ac 13:21).

13:8-9 Rather than wait for Samuel's return as he had promised (10:8), Saul took on a role that was not his and offered sacrifices to God as a means of securing their victory.

13:10-18 Because of Saul's disobedience, his dynasty would end and another would be raised up in his place. The next king would be **a man loyal to Him** (i.e., a man after God's own heart v. 14). Saul's foolishness in acting impulsively and not trusting in the Lord led to his demise as the royal leader of Israel. He failed to submit to the Lord and to the divine leadership of Samuel, a pattern of disobedience that continued throughout his life.

18 Samuel called on the LORD, and on that day the LORD sent thunder and rain. As a result, all the people greatly feared the LORD and Samuel.

19 They pleaded with Samuel, "Pray to the LORD your God for your servants, so we won't die! For we have added to all our sins the evil of requesting a king for ourselves."

20 Samuel replied, "Don't be afraid. Even though you have committed all this evil, don't turn away from following the LORD. Instead, worship the LORD with all your heart. 21 Don't turn away to follow worthless[A] things that can't profit or deliver you; they are worthless. 22 The LORD will not abandon His people, because of His great name and because He has determined to make you His own people.

23 "As for me, I vow that I will not sin against the LORD by ceasing to pray for you. I will teach you the good and right way. 24 Above all, fear the LORD and worship Him faithfully with all your heart; consider the great things He has done for you. 25 However, if you continue to do what is evil, both you and your king will be swept away."

The Fall of Saul from the Throne (13:1–15:35)

Saul's Failure (13:1-22)

13 Saul was 30 years[B] old when he became king, and he reigned 42 years[C] over Israel.[D] 2 He chose 3,000 men from Israel for himself: 2,000 were with Saul at Michmash and in Bethel's hill country, and 1,000 were with Jonathan in Gibeah of Benjamin. He sent the rest of the troops away, each to his own tent.

3 Jonathan attacked the Philistine garrison[E] that was in Geba, and the Philistines heard about it. So Saul blew the ram's horn throughout the land saying, "Let the Hebrews hear!"[F] 4 And all Israel heard the news, "Saul has attacked the Philistine garrison,[E] and Israel is now repulsive to the Philistines." Then the troops were summoned to join Saul at Gilgal.

5 The Philistines also gathered to fight against Israel: 3,000[G] chariots, 6,000 horsemen, and troops as numerous as the sand on the seashore. They went up and camped at Michmash, east of Beth-aven.[H]

6 The men of Israel saw that they were in trouble because the troops were in a difficult situation. They hid in caves, thickets, among rocks, and in holes and cisterns. 7 Some Hebrews even crossed the Jordan to the land of Gad and Gilead.

Saul, however, was still at Gilgal, and all his troops were gripped with fear. 8 He waited seven days for the appointed time that Samuel had set, but Samuel didn't come to Gilgal, and the troops were deserting him. 9 So Saul said, "Bring me the •burnt offering and the •fellowship offerings." Then he offered the burnt offering.

10 Just as he finished offering the burnt offering, Samuel arrived. So Saul went out to greet him, 11 and Samuel asked, "What have you done?"

Saul answered, "When I saw that the troops were deserting me and you didn't come within the appointed days and the Philistines were gathering at Michmash, 12 I thought: The Philistines will now descend on me at Gilgal, and I haven't sought the LORD's favor. So I forced myself to offer the burnt offering."

13 Samuel said to Saul, "You have been foolish. You have not kept the command which the LORD your God gave you. It was at this time that the LORD would have permanently established your reign over Israel, 14 but now your reign will not endure. The LORD has found a man loyal to Him,[I] and the LORD has appointed him as ruler over His people, because you have not done what the LORD commanded." 15 Then Samuel went[J] from Gilgal to Gibeah in Benjamin. Saul registered the troops who were with him, about 600 men.

[A]**12:21** LXX reads *away after empty* [B]**13:1** Some LXX mss; MT reads *was one year* [C]**13:1** Text emended; MT reads *two years* [D]**13:1** Some LXX mss omit v. 1 [E]**13:3,4** Or *governor* [F]**13:3** LXX reads *The slaves have revolted* [G]**13:5** One LXX ms, Syr; MT reads *30,000* [H]**13:5** LXX reads *Michmash, opposite Beth-horon to the south* [I]**13:14** Lit *man according to His heart* [J]**13:15** LXX reads *Samuel left Gilgal and went on his way, and the rest of the people followed Saul to join the people in his army. They went*

16 Saul, his son Jonathan, and the
troops who were with them were
staying in Geba of Benjamin, and
the Philistines were camped at Michmash. 17 Raiding parties went out
from the Philistine camp in three divisions. One division headed toward
the Ophrah road leading to the land
of Shual. 18 The next division headed
toward the Beth-horon road, and the
last division headed down the border
road that looks out over the Valley of
Zeboim toward the wilderness.

19 No blacksmith could be found
in all the land of Israel, because the
Philistines had said, "Otherwise,
the Hebrews will make swords or
spears." 20 So all the Israelites went
to the Philistines to sharpen their
plows, mattocks, axes, and sick-
les.[A] 21 The price was two-thirds of a
•shekel[B] for plows and mattocks, and
one-third of a shekel for pitchforks
and axes, and for putting a point on
an oxgoad. 22 So on the day of battle
not a sword or spear could be found
in the hand of any of the troops
who were with Saul and Jonathan;
only Saul and his son Jonathan had
weapons.

23 Now a Philistine garrison took
control of the pass at Michmash.

Jonathan's Victory over the Philistines (14:1-23a)

14 1 That same day Saul's son
Jonathan said to the attendant
who carried his weapons, "Come on,
let's cross over to the Philistine garrison on the other side." However,
he did not tell his father.

2 Saul was staying under the pomegranate tree in Migron on the outskirts of Gibeah.[C] The troops with
him numbered about 600. 3 Ahijah,
who was wearing an •ephod, was
also there. He was the son of Ahitub,
the brother of Ichabod son of Phinehas, son of Eli the LORD's priest at
Shiloh. But the troops did not know
that Jonathan had left.

4 There were sharp columns[D] of
rock on both sides of the pass that
Jonathan intended to cross to reach
the Philistine garrison. One was
named Bozez and the other Seneh;
5 one stood to the north in front of
Michmash and the other to the south
in front of Geba. 6 Jonathan said to
the attendant who carried his weapons, "Come on, let's cross over to
the garrison of these uncircumcised
men. Perhaps the LORD will help us.
Nothing can keep the LORD from saving, whether by many or by few."

7 His armor-bearer responded, "Do
what is in your heart. You choose.
I'm right here with you whatever
you decide."

8 "All right," Jonathan replied,
"we'll cross over to the men and
then let them see us. 9 If they say,
'Wait until we reach you,' then we
will stay where we are and not go
up to them. 10 But if they say, 'Come
on up,' then we'll go up, because
the LORD has handed them over to
us—that will be our sign."

11 They let themselves be seen by
the Philistine garrison, and the Philistines said, "Look, the Hebrews
are coming out of the holes where
they've been hiding!" 12 The men of
the garrison called to Jonathan and
his armor-bearer. "Come on up, and
we'll teach you a lesson!" they said.

"Follow me," Jonathan told his armor-bearer, "for the LORD has handed them over to Israel." 13 Jonathan
climbed up using his hands and feet,
with his armor-bearer behind him.
Jonathan cut them down, and his
armor-bearer followed and finished
them off. 14 In that first assault Jonathan and his armor-bearer struck
down about 20 men in a half-acre
field.

15 Terror spread through the Philistine camp and the open fields to
all the troops. Even the garrison and
the raiding parties were terrified.
The earth shook, and terror spread
from God.[E] 16 When Saul's watchmen
in Gibeah of Benjamin looked, they
saw the panicking troops scattering
in every direction. 17 So Saul said to
the troops with him, "Call the roll
and determine who has left us." They
called the roll and saw that Jonathan
and his armor-bearer were gone.

18 Saul told Ahijah, "Bring the ark
of God," for it was with the Israelites[F] at that time. 19 While Saul spoke

14:1-18 Saul requested **the ark** or, as the Septuagint records, "the ephod" (Gk *to ephoud*, v. 18), perhaps referring to the Urim and Thummim, which Saul may have used to inquire of the Lord about pursuing the Philistines (vv. 37-41; cp. Ex 28:30). The **ephod** was a priestly garment worn by all priests (1Sm 14:3). The high priest's ephod, however, included a pouch on the ephod that contained the Urim and Thummim, two small objects used to determine God's will (cp. Lv 8:8).

[A]**13:20** LXX; MT reads *plowshares* [B]**13:21** Lit *of a pim*; about 1/4 ounce of silver [C]**14:2** LXX reads *on top of the hill* [D]**14:4** Lit *There was a tooth* [E]**14:15** Or *and a great terror spread* [F]**14:18** LXX reads *"Bring the ephod." For he wore the ephod before Israel*

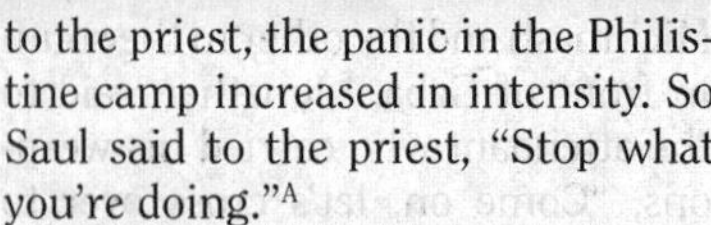

14:19-46 Consistent with previous events in his life, Saul began to allow his circumstances to dictate the degree of his faithfulness to the Lord. Responding to the Philistine panic, Saul asked the priest to remove his hand from the ephod, showing his lack of concern for God's will. While the priest exhorted, **We must consult God here**, (v. 36), Saul appears to be out of touch with God (vv. 20-30). Saul's rashness caused him and the people to sin (v. 32; cp. Lv 17) and resulted in a lack of confidence in his leadership as well as in the Lord. **Do whatever you want** is repeated throughout this account (1Sm 14:36,40), as though to reflect the people's hearts. While this may be an indication of their submission to their king, it harkens back to the period of the judges, when "everyone did whatever he wanted" (Jdg 21:25).

to the priest, the panic in the Philistine camp increased in intensity. So Saul said to the priest, "Stop what you're doing."[A]

20 Saul and all the troops with him assembled and marched to the battle, and there, the Philistines were fighting against each other in great confusion! 21 There were Hebrews from the area who had gone earlier into the camp to join the Philistines, but even they joined the Israelites who were with Saul and Jonathan. 22 When all the Israelite men who had been hiding in the hill country of Ephraim heard that the Philistines were fleeing, they also joined Saul and Jonathan in the battle. 23 So the LORD saved Israel that day.

Saul's Rash Oath (14:23b-46)

The battle extended beyond Beth-aven, 24 and the men of Israel were worn out that day, for Saul had[B] placed the troops under an oath: "The man who eats food before evening, before I have taken vengeance on my enemies is cursed." So none of the troops tasted any food.

25 Everyone[C] went into the forest, and there was honey on the ground. 26 When the troops entered the forest, they saw the flow of honey, but none of them ate any of it[D] because they feared the oath. 27 However, Jonathan had not heard his father make the troops swear the oath. He reached out with the end of the staff he was carrying and dipped it into the honeycomb. When he ate the honey,[E] he had renewed energy. 28 Then, one of the troops said, "Your father made the troops solemnly swear, 'The man who eats food today is cursed,' and the troops are exhausted."

29 Jonathan replied, "My father has brought trouble to the land. Just look at how I have renewed energy because I tasted a little honey. 30 How much better if the troops had eaten freely today from the plunder they took from their enemies! Then the slaughter of the Philistines would have been much greater."

31 The Israelites struck down the Philistines that day from Michmash all the way to Aijalon. Since the Israelites were completely exhausted, 32 they rushed to the plunder, took sheep, cattle, and calves, slaughtered them on the ground, and ate meat with the blood still in it. 33 Some reported to Saul: "Look, the troops are sinning against the LORD by eating meat with the blood still in it."

Saul said, "You have been unfaithful. Roll a large stone over here at once." 34 He then said, "Go among the troops and say to them, 'Each man must bring me his ox or his sheep. Do the slaughtering here and then you can eat. Don't sin against the LORD by eating meat with the blood in it.'" So every one of the troops brought his ox that night and slaughtered it there. 35 Then Saul built an altar to the LORD; it was the first time he had built an altar to the LORD.

36 Saul said, "Let's go down after the Philistines tonight and plunder them until morning. Don't let even one remain!"

"Do whatever you want,"[F] the troops replied.

But the priest said, "We must consult God here."

37 So Saul inquired of God, "Should I go after the Philistines? Will You hand them over to Israel?" But God did not answer him that day.

38 Saul said, "All you leaders of the troops, come here. Let us investigate how this sin has occurred today. 39 As surely as the LORD lives who saves Israel, even if it is because of my son Jonathan, he must die!" Not one of the troops answered him.

40 So he said to all Israel, "You will be on one side, and I and my son Jonathan will be on the other side."

And the troops replied, "Do whatever you want."[F]

41 So Saul said to the LORD, "God of Israel, give us the right decision."[G]

[A] **14:19** Lit *Withdraw your hand* [B] **14:24** LXX adds *committed a great act of ignorance and* [C] **14:25** Lit *All the land* [D] **14:26** Lit *but there was none who raised his hand to his mouth* [E] **14:27** Lit *he returned his hand to his mouth* [F] **14:36,40** Lit *Do what is good in your eyes* [G] **14:41** LXX reads *Israel, why have You not answered Your servant today? If the unrighteousness is in me or in my son Jonathan, LORD God of Israel, give Urim; but if the guilt is in Your people Israel, give Thummim.*"

Jonathan and Saul were selected, and the troops were cleared of the charge.

42 Then Saul said, "Cast the lot between me and my son Jonathan," and Jonathan was selected. 43 Saul commanded him, "Tell me what you did."

Jonathan told him, "I tasted a little honey with the end of the staff I was carrying. I am ready to die!"

44 Saul declared to him, "May God punish me and do so severely if you do not die, Jonathan!"

45 But the people said to Saul, "Must Jonathan die, who accomplished such a great deliverance for Israel? No, as the LORD lives, not a hair of his head will fall to the ground, for he worked with God's help today." So the people redeemed Jonathan, and he did not die. 46 Then Saul gave up the pursuit of the Philistines, and the Philistines returned to their own territory.

Summary of Saul's Kingship (14:47-52)

47 When Saul assumed the kingship over Israel, he fought against all his enemies in every direction: against Moab, the Ammonites, Edom, the kings of Zobah, and the Philistines. Wherever he turned, he caused havoc.[A] 48 He fought bravely, defeated the Amalekites, and delivered Israel from the hand of those who plundered them.

49 Saul's sons were Jonathan, Ishvi, and Malchishua. The names of his two daughters were: Merab, his firstborn, and Michal, the younger. 50 The name of Saul's wife was Ahinoam daughter of Ahimaaz. The name of the commander of his army was Abner son of Saul's uncle Ner. 51 Saul's father was Kish. Abner's father was Ner son of Abiel.

52 The conflict with the Philistines was fierce all of Saul's days, so whenever Saul noticed any strong or brave man, he enlisted him.

The Rejection of Saul as King (15:1-35)

15 Samuel told Saul, "The LORD sent me to anoint you as king over His people Israel. Now, listen to the words of the LORD. 2 This is what the LORD of •Hosts says: 'I witnessed[B] what the Amalekites did to the Israelites when they opposed them along the way as they were coming out of Egypt. 3 Now go and attack the Amalekites and •completely destroy everything they have. Do not spare them. Kill men and women, children and infants, oxen and sheep, camels and donkeys.'"

4 Then Saul summoned the troops and counted them at Telaim: 200,000 foot soldiers and 10,000 men from Judah. 5 Saul came to the city of Amalek and set up an ambush in the •wadi. 6 He warned the Kenites, "Since you showed kindness to all the Israelites when they came out of Egypt, go on and leave! Get away from the Amalekites, or I'll sweep you away with them." So the Kenites withdrew from the Amalekites.

7 Then Saul struck down the Amalekites from Havilah all the way to Shur, which is next to Egypt. 8 He captured Agag king of Amalek alive, but he completely destroyed all the rest of the people with the sword. 9 Saul and the troops spared Agag, and the best of the sheep, cattle, and choice animals,[C] as well as the young rams and the best of everything else. They were not willing to destroy them, but they did destroy all the worthless and unwanted things.

10 Then the word of the LORD came to Samuel, 11 "I regret that I made Saul king, for he has turned away from following Me and has not carried out My instructions." So Samuel became angry and cried out to the LORD all night.

12 Early in the morning Samuel got up to confront Saul, but it was reported to Samuel, "Saul went to Carmel where he set up a monument for himself. Then he turned around and went down to Gilgal." 13 When Samuel came to him, Saul said, "May the LORD bless you. I have carried out the LORD's instructions."

14 Samuel replied, "Then what is this sound of sheep[D] and cattle I hear?"

15 Saul answered, "The troops brought them from the Amalekites

15:1-9 Saul continued to disobey the direct orders from the Lord when he failed to **completely destroy** (Hb *charan*) **the Amalekites** and their livestock. Everything belonging to the Amalekites, like the city of Jericho (Jos 6:17-21), was "devoted only to God" (Hb *chērem*; see **Word Study**, p. 261).

15:10-23 When confronted by Samuel, Saul attempted to justify his actions by claiming that the stolen livestock were for sacrifice. In this entire account, Saul referred to God as **your God,** not "*our* God" (vv. 15,21,30). Samuel's response encapsulates the book's theme, a timeless principle for believers: **To obey is better than sacrifice** (v. 22).

15:11-29 Some question how God can **regret** (Hb *nacham*, "be moved to pity; lament or grieve over one's actions; rue"; cp. Gn 6:6-7) something, calling into question His omniscience. God foreknew that Saul would fall into disobedience and rebellion and that He would raise up another to take His place, but He still purposed to use Saul in delivering Israel from her enemies. God "regretted" this matter to the extent that He was deeply troubled about Saul and His disobedience, but the verb is also used to affirm that God "does not . . . change His mind" (v. 29). **The Eternal One** (Hb *netsach*, "splendor, glory, eternity, perfection, completeness"; cp. 1Ch 29:11) is immutable, and His purposes will stand forever.

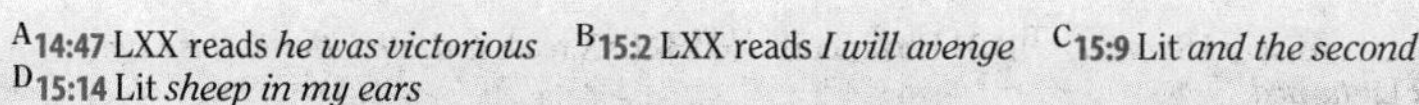

A 14:47 LXX reads *he was victorious* B 15:2 LXX reads *I will avenge* C 15:9 Lit *and the second*
D 15:14 Lit *sheep in my ears*

15:24-35 There is a penalty for direct disobedience to God's word (Nm 15:31). Saul's rebellion cost him his regal position, his life, and the lives of his family, not to mention the cost to the nation. The blessing of God was completely removed from Saul (1Sm 15:35), and Samuel never visited Saul again. Saul's life teaches that partial obedience, from God's perspective, is total disobedience.

>WORD|*study*

15:22 Although the word **obey** (Hb *shama'*) literally means "hear or listen," it usually implies that the hearer will follow hearing with obedience. Numerous Old Testament passages demonstrate this usage (e.g., Dt 28:15; Jos 5:6; Ps 18:44; Pr 8:33; Mc 5:15). *Shama'* can also be translated "discern or heed," emphasizing the response one should have when confronted with the truth of God (cp. Jms 1:19-25). Obedience of those who love the Lord and seek to follow Him is required. Your obedience to God reflects an inner reality of your commitment to and love for Him.

and spared the best sheep and cattle in order to offer a sacrifice to the LORD your God, but the rest we destroyed."

16 "Stop!" exclaimed Samuel. "Let me tell you what the LORD said to me last night."

"Tell me," he replied.

17 Samuel continued, "Although you once considered yourself unimportant, have you not become the leader of the tribes of Israel? The LORD anointed you king over Israel
18 and then sent you on a mission and said: 'Go and completely destroy the sinful Amalekites. Fight against them until you have annihilated them.'
19 So why didn't you obey the LORD? Why did you rush on the plunder and do what was evil in the LORD's sight?"

20 "But I did obey the LORD!" Saul answered.[A] "I went on the mission the LORD gave me: I brought back Agag, king of Amalek, and I completely destroyed the Amalekites.
21 The troops took sheep and cattle from the plunder—the best of what was •set apart for destruction—to sacrifice to the LORD your God at Gilgal."

22 Then Samuel said:

> Does the LORD take pleasure
> in •burnt offerings
> and sacrifices
> as much as in obeying
> the LORD?
>
> Look: to obey is better
> than sacrifice,
> to pay attention is better
> than the fat of rams.
> 23 For rebellion is like the sin
> of •divination,
> and defiance is
> like wickedness
> and idolatry.
> Because you have rejected
> the word of the LORD,
> He has rejected you
> as king.

24 Saul answered Samuel, "I have sinned. I have transgressed the LORD's command and your words. Because I was afraid of the people, I obeyed them.
25 Now therefore, please forgive my sin and return with me so I can worship the LORD."

26 Samuel replied to Saul, "I will not return with you. Because you rejected the word of the LORD, the LORD has rejected you from being king over Israel."
27 When Samuel turned to go, Saul grabbed the hem of his robe, and it tore.
28 Samuel said to him, "The LORD has torn the kingship of Israel away from you today and has given it to your neighbor who is better than you.
29 Furthermore, the Eternal One of Israel does not lie or change His mind, for He is not man who changes his mind."

30 Saul said, "I have sinned. Please honor me now before the elders of my people and before Israel. Come back with me so I can bow in worship to the LORD your God."
31 Then Samuel went back, following Saul, and Saul bowed down to the LORD.

32 Samuel said, "Bring me Agag king of Amalek."

Agag came to him trembling,[B] for he thought, "Certainly the bitterness of death has come."[C,D]

33 Samuel declared:

> As your sword has made
> women childless,
> so your mother will be
> childless among women.

[A]15:20 Lit *answered Samuel* [B]15:32 Hb obscure [C]15:32 LXX reads *Is death bitter in this way?* [D]15:32 Lit *turned*

Then he hacked Agag to pieces before the LORD at Gilgal.

34 Samuel went to Ramah, and Saul went up to his home in Gibeah of Saul. 35 Even to the day of his death, Samuel never again visited Saul. Samuel mourned for Saul, and the LORD regretted He had made Saul king over Israel.

The Anointing of David by God (16:1-23)

Samuel's Anointing of David (16:1-13)

16 The LORD said to Samuel, "How long are you going to mourn for Saul, since I have rejected him as king over Israel? Fill your horn with oil and go. I am sending you to Jesse of Bethlehem because I have selected a king from his sons."

2 Samuel asked, "How can I go? Saul will hear about it and kill me!"

The LORD answered, "Take a young cow with you and say, 'I have come to sacrifice to the LORD.' 3 Then invite Jesse to the sacrifice, and I will let you know what you are to do. You are to anoint for Me the one I indicate to you."

4 Samuel did what the LORD directed and went to Bethlehem. When the elders of the town met him, they trembled[A] and asked, "Do[B] you come in peace?"

5 "In peace," he replied. "I've come to sacrifice to the LORD. Consecrate yourselves and come with me to the sacrifice."[C] Then he consecrated Jesse and his sons and invited them to the sacrifice. 6 When they arrived, Samuel saw Eliab and said, "Certainly the LORD's anointed one is here before Him."

7 But the LORD said to Samuel, "Do not look at his appearance or his stature, because I have rejected him. Man does not see what the LORD sees,[D] for man sees what is visible,[E] but the LORD sees the heart."

8 Jesse called Abinadab and presented him to Samuel. "The LORD hasn't chosen this one either," Samuel said. 9 Then Jesse presented Shammah, but Samuel said, "The LORD hasn't chosen this one either." 10 After Jesse presented seven of his sons to him, Samuel told Jesse, "The LORD hasn't chosen any of these." 11 Samuel asked him, "Are these all the sons you have?"

"There is still the youngest," he answered, "but right now he's tending the sheep." Samuel told Jesse, "Send for him. We won't sit down to eat until he gets here." 12 So Jesse sent for him. He had beautiful eyes and a healthy,[F] handsome appearance.

Then the LORD said, "Anoint him, for he is the one." 13 So Samuel took the horn of oil, anointed him in the presence of his brothers, and the Spirit of the LORD took control of David from that day forward. Then Samuel set out and went to Ramah.

David's Presence in Saul's Court (16:14-23)

14 Now the Spirit of the LORD had left Saul, and an evil spirit sent from the LORD began to torment him, 15 so Saul's servants said to him, "You see that an evil spirit from God is tormenting you. 16 Let our lord command your servants here in your presence to look for someone who knows how to play the lyre. Whenever the evil spirit from God troubles you, that person can play the lyre, and you will feel better."

16:1 Samuel was so broken over Saul's disobedience and so gripped over the future of the nation that he needed the Lord's encouragement to press on with his ministry in anointing the future king of Israel.

16:7-13 Contrary to Saul's pleasing physical appearance as a ruler, which caught the attention of men, David had the inner qualities that attracted the attention of God.

16:11-13 Samuel **anointed** David with oil, symbolizing that he had been set apart for service to God as the future king over Israel (v. 13). Unlike Saul, from whom the Spirit of the Lord had departed (v. 14), God's **Spirit** came upon David **from that day forward**.

16:14-23 Despite his initial humility, Saul found himself troubled and depressed because of his rebellion against God.

Doctrine THE HOLY SPIRIT IN THE OLD TESTAMENT

Many readers may find 16:14 troubling, especially in light of Saul's evidence of being filled with the Holy Spirit in an earlier reference (10:10). In the Old Testament, the Holy Spirit came upon individuals temporarily and could leave them. The presence or absence of God's Spirit in the Old Testament did not exclusively pertain to salvation but rather to God's work in those whom He had selected for service (Jdg 3:10; 1Sm 10:10; 16:13). New Testament believers, however, live during the time of the New Covenant, a better covenant (Heb 7:22-24), in which God's Spirit dwells within us, will never leave us, and is a guarantee of the coming inheritance that God has given His children (Jr 31:33; Jn 14:17; 1Co 3:16; Eph 1:13-14).

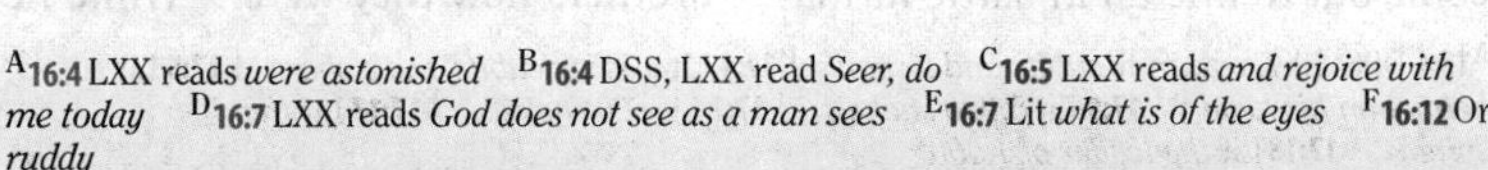

[A] **16:4** LXX reads *were astonished* [B] **16:4** DSS, LXX read *Seer, do* [C] **16:5** LXX reads *and rejoice with me today* [D] **16:7** LXX reads *God does not see as a man sees* [E] **16:7** Lit *what is of the eyes* [F] **16:12** Or *ruddy*

17 Then Saul commanded his servants, "Find me someone who plays well and bring him to me."

18 One of the young men answered, "I have seen a son of Jesse of Bethlehem who knows how to play the lyre. He is also a valiant man, a warrior, eloquent, handsome, and the LORD is with him."

19 Then Saul dispatched messengers to Jesse and said, "Send me your son David, who is with the sheep." 20 So Jesse took a donkey loaded with bread, a skin of wine, and one young goat and sent them by his son David to Saul. 21 When David came to Saul and entered his service, Saul admired him greatly, and David became his armor-bearer. 22 Then Saul sent word to Jesse: "Let David remain in my service, for I am pleased with him." 23 Whenever the spirit from God troubled Saul, David would pick up his lyre and play, and Saul would then be relieved, feel better, and the evil spirit would leave him.

Taunting of David by Goliath (17:1-58)

17 The Philistines gathered their forces for war at Socoh in Judah and camped between Socoh and Azekah in Ephes-dammim. 2 Saul and the men of Israel gathered and camped in the Valley of Elah; then they lined up in battle formation to face the Philistines.

3 The Philistines were standing on one hill, and the Israelites were standing on another hill with a ravine between them. 4 Then a champion named Goliath, from Gath, came out from the Philistine camp. He was nine feet, nine inches tall[A,B] 5 and wore a bronze helmet[C] and bronze scale armor that weighed 125 pounds.[D] 6 There was bronze armor on his shins, and a bronze sword was slung between his shoulders. 7 His spear shaft was like a weaver's beam, and the iron point of his spear weighed 15 pounds.[E] In addition, a shield-bearer was walking in front of him.

8 He stood and shouted to the Israelite battle formations: "Why do you come out to line up in battle formation?" He asked them, "Am I not a Philistine and are you not servants of Saul? Choose one of your men and have him come down against me. 9 If he wins in a fight against me and kills me, we will be your servants. But if I win against him and kill him, then you will be our servants and serve us." 10 Then the Philistine said, "I defy the ranks of Israel today. Send me a man so we can fight each other!" 11 When Saul and all Israel heard these words from the Philistine, they lost their courage and were terrified.

12 Now David was the son of the Ephrathite from Bethlehem of Judah named Jesse. Jesse had eight sons and during Saul's reign was already an old man. 13 Jesse's three oldest sons had followed Saul to the war, and their names were Eliab, the firstborn, Abinadab, the next, and Shammah, the third, 14 and David was the youngest. The three oldest had followed Saul, 15 but David kept going back and forth from Saul to tend his father's flock in Bethlehem.

16 Every morning and evening for 40 days the Philistine came forward and took his stand. 17 One day Jesse had told his son David: "Take this half-bushel[F] of roasted grain along with these 10 loaves of bread for your brothers and hurry to their camp. 18 Also take these 10 portions of cheese to the field commander.[G] Check on the welfare of your brothers and bring a confirmation from them. 19 They are with Saul and all the men of Israel in the Valley of Elah fighting with the Philistines."

20 So David got up early in the morning, left the flock with someone to keep it, loaded up, and set out as Jesse had instructed him.

He arrived at the perimeter of the camp as the army was marching out to its battle formation shouting their battle cry. 21 Israel and the Philistines lined up in battle formation facing each other. 22 David left his supplies in the care of the quartermaster and ran to the battle line. When he arrived, he asked his brothers how they were. 23 While he

[A] **17:4** DSS, LXX read *four cubits and a span* [B] **17:4** Lit *was six cubits and a span* [C] **17:5** Lit *helmet on his head* [D] **17:5** Lit *5,000 shekels* [E] **17:7** Lit *600 shekels* [F] **17:17** Lit *this ephah* [G] **17:18** Lit *the leader of 1,000*

was speaking with them, suddenly
the champion named Goliath, the
Philistine from Gath, came forward
from the Philistine battle line and
shouted his usual words, which
David heard. 24 When all the Israelite men saw Goliath, they retreated
from him terrified.

25 Previously, an Israelite man had
declared: "Do you see this man who
keeps coming out? He comes to defy
Israel. The king will make the man
who kills him very rich and will give
him his daughter. The king will also
make the household of that man's
father exempt from paying taxes in
Israel."

26 David spoke to the men who
were standing with him: "What will
be done for the man who kills that
Philistine and removes this disgrace from Israel? Just who is this
uncircumcised Philistine that he
should defy the armies of the living
God?"

27 The people told him about the
offer, concluding, "That is what will
be done for the man who kills him."

28 David's oldest brother Eliab listened as he spoke to the men, and
became angry with him. "Why did
you come down here?" he asked.
"Who did you leave those few sheep
with in the wilderness? I know your
arrogance and your evil heart—you
came down to see the battle!"

29 "What have I done now?" protested David. "It was just a question." 30 Then he turned from those
beside him to others in front of
him and asked about the offer. The
people gave him the same answer as
before.

31 What David said was overheard
and reported to Saul, so he had David brought to him. 32 David said to
Saul, "Don't let anyone be discouraged by[A] him; your servant will go
and fight this Philistine!"

33 But Saul replied, "You can't go
fight this Philistine. You're just a
youth, and he's been a warrior since
he was young."

34 David answered Saul: "Your servant has been tending his father's
sheep. Whenever a lion or a bear
came and carried off a lamb from
the flock, 35 I went after it, struck it
down, and rescued the lamb from
its mouth. If it reared up against
me, I would grab it by its fur,[B] strike
it down, and kill it. 36 Your servant
has killed lions and bears; this uncircumcised Philistine will be like
one of them, for he has defied the
armies of the living God." 37 Then
David said, "The LORD who rescued
me from the paw of the lion and the
paw of the bear will rescue me from
the hand of this Philistine."

Saul said to David, "Go, and may
the LORD be with you."

38 Then Saul had his own military clothes put on David. He put
a bronze helmet on David's head
and had him put on armor. 39 David
strapped his sword on over the military clothes and tried to walk, but he
was not used to them. "I can't walk
in these," David said to Saul, "I'm
not used to them." So David took
them off. 40 Instead, he took his staff
in his hand and chose five smooth
stones from the •wadi and put them
in the pouch, in his shepherd's bag.
Then, with his sling in his hand, he
approached the Philistine.

41 The Philistine came closer and
closer to David, with the shield-
bearer in front of him. 42 When the
Philistine looked and saw David, he
despised him because he was just
a youth, healthy[C] and handsome.
43 He said to David, "Am I a dog that
you come against me with sticks?"[D]
Then he cursed David by his gods.
44 "Come here," the Philistine called
to David, "and I'll give your flesh
to the birds of the sky and the wild
beasts!"

45 David said to the Philistine:
"You come against me with a dag-
ger, spear, and sword, but I come
against you in the name of •Yah-
weh of •Hosts, the God of Israel's
armies—you have defied Him.
46 Today, the LORD will hand you
over to me. Today, I'll strike you
down, cut your head off, and give
the corpses[E] of the Philistine camp
to the birds of the sky and the creatures of the earth. Then all the

17:26-47 Rather than relying on his own strength, David depended on the Lord for victory (v. 37). He was more concerned about the reproach upon the Lord's name and Israel brought by Goliath than about his own safety (v. 26). He did not allow his circumstances, particularly his lack of equipment and small stature, to trump his faith (vv. 45-47). David called upon God as the Lord of Hosts, a fitting reminder to Goliath that he was not fighting against David but rather against the Warrior God who defends those who trust in Him (vv. 45-46).

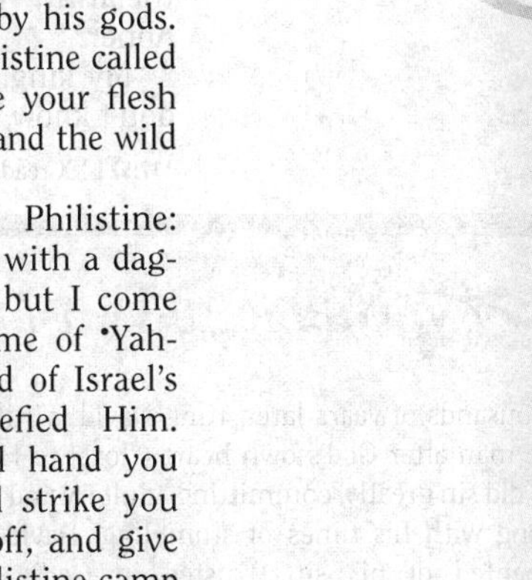

[A] **17:32** Lit *let a man's heart fall over* [B] **17:35** LXX reads *throat*; lit *beard* [C] **17:42** Or *ruddy*
[D] **17:43** Some LXX mss add *and stones?" And David said, "No! Worse than a dog!"* [E] **17:46** LXX reads *give your limbs and the limbs*

18:1-6 Jonathan's gift of his own royal regalia demonstrated his acknowledgment of David as the heir to his father Saul's throne. The covenant they made to each other bound them in loyalty and was characterized by self-sacrifice, love, and complete devotion to their friendship, even though it was tested greatly during their lifetimes.

world will know that Israel has a
God, 47 and this whole assembly will
know that it is not by sword or by
spear that the LORD saves, for the
battle is the LORD's. He will hand
you over to us."
48 When the Philistine started forward to attack him, David ran quickly
to the battle line to meet the Philistine. 49 David put his hand in the bag,
took out a stone, slung it, and hit the
Philistine on his forehead. The stone
sank into his forehead, and he fell
on his face to the ground. 50 David
defeated the Philistine with a sling
and a stone. Even though David had
no sword, he struck down the Philistine and killed him. 51 David ran
and stood over him. He grabbed the
Philistine's sword, pulled it from its
sheath, and used it to kill him. Then
he cut off his head. When the Philistines saw that their hero was dead,
they ran. 52 The men of Israel and Judah rallied, shouting their battle cry,
and chased the Philistines to the entrance of the valley and to the gates
of Ekron.[A] Philistine bodies were
strewn all along the Shaaraim road
to Gath and Ekron.
53 When the Israelites returned
from the pursuit of the Philistines,
they plundered their camps. 54 David
took Goliath's[B] head and brought it
to Jerusalem, but he put Goliath's
weapons in his own tent.
55 [C] When Saul had seen David going out to confront the Philistine,
he asked Abner the commander of
the army, "Whose son is this youth,
Abner?"

"My king, as surely as you live, I
don't know," Abner replied.
56 The king said, "Find out whose
son this young man is!"
57 When David returned from killing the Philistine, Abner took him
and brought him before Saul with
the Philistine's head still in his
hand. 58 Saul said to him, "Whose
son are you, young man?"

"The son of your servant Jesse of
Bethlehem," David answered.

The Hunting of David by Saul (18:1–31:13)

David's Success (18:1-9)

18 When David had finished
speaking with Saul, Jonathan
committed himself to David, and
loved him as much as he loved himself. 2 Saul kept David with him from
that day on and did not let him return to his father's house.
3 Jonathan made a covenant with
David because he loved him as much
as himself. 4 Then Jonathan removed
the robe he was wearing and gave it
to David, along with his military tunic, his sword, his bow, and his belt.
5 David marched out with the army
and was successful in everything
Saul sent him to do. Saul put him
in command of the soldiers, which
pleased all the people and Saul's servants as well.
6 As the troops were coming back,
when David was returning from killing the Philistine, the women came
out from all the cities of Israel to
meet King Saul, singing and dancing with tambourines, with shouts
of joy, and with three-stringed instruments. 7 As they celebrated, the
women sang:

[A] **17:52** LXX reads *Ashkelon* [B] **17:54** Lit *the Philistine's* [C] **17:55** LXX omits 1Sm 17:55–18:5

Biblical Womanhood A Woman After God's Own Heart

Thousands of years later, King David is still revered as the man after God's own heart ("loyal to Him," 13:14). He did sin greatly, committing adultery and murder. But along with his times of stumbling, David continually repented of his sin, trusted in God's mercy, and delighted himself in the Lord's instruction (Ps 40:8). When a woman truly understands the truth of grace, she is motivated to love others as Christ commands, to serve those around her, to pray, to study and read God's Word, and continually to surrender her will to the will of God. This spirit will demonstrate outwardly and inwardly that God is transforming her into a woman after His own heart. As you run the race of faith, stumbling along the way and wondering how you can ever be used by God, be encouraged as you study the life of David. His desire was to know and love the Lord. Like this remarkable king, you, too, can be motivated to obedience and service by love for God. As you strive to follow and submit to God, you are able to experience the deeper spiritual joys of knowing Him.

Saul has killed his thousands,
but David his tens
of thousands.

8 Saul was furious and resented this
song.[A] "They credited tens of thousands to David," he complained, "but
they only credited me with thousands. What more can he have but
the kingdom?" 9 So Saul watched David jealously from that day forward.

Saul's Attempts to Kill David (18:10-19)

10 The next day an evil spirit sent
from God took control of Saul, and
he began to rave[B] inside the palace.
David was playing the lyre as usual,
but Saul was holding a spear, 11 and
he threw it, thinking, "I'll pin David to the wall." But David got away
from him twice.
12 Saul was afraid of David, because
the LORD was with David but had left
Saul. 13 Therefore, Saul reassigned
David and made him commander
over 1,000 men. David led the troops
14 and continued to be successful in
all his activities because the LORD
was with him. 15 When Saul observed that David was very successful, he dreaded him. 16 But all Israel
and Judah loved David because he
was leading their troops. 17 Saul told
David, "Here is my oldest daughter
Merab. I'll give her to you as a wife,
if you will be a warrior for me and
fight the LORD's battles." But Saul
was thinking, "My hand doesn't
need to be against him; let the hand
of the Philistines be against him."
18 Then David responded, "Who am
I, and what is my family or my father's clan in Israel that I should become the king's son-in-law?" 19 When
it was time to give Saul's daughter
Merab to David, she was given to
Adriel the Meholathite as a wife.

David's Marriage to Michal (18:20-30)

20 Now Saul's daughter Michal
loved David, and when it was reported to Saul, it pleased him.[C] 21 "I'll give
her to him," Saul thought. "She'll be
a trap for him, and the hand of the
Philistines will be against him." So
Saul said to David a second time,
"You can now be my son-in-law."
22 Saul then ordered his servants,
"Speak to David in private and tell
him, 'Look, the king is pleased with
you, and all his servants love you.
Therefore, you should become the
king's son-in-law.'"
23 Saul's servants reported these
words directly to David,[D] but he replied, "Is it trivial in your sight to
become the king's son-in-law? I am
a poor man who is common."
24 The servants reported back to
Saul, "These are the words David
spoke."
25 Then Saul replied, "Say this to
David: 'The king desires no other
bride-price except 100 Philistine
foreskins, to take revenge on his enemies.'" Actually, Saul intended to
cause David's death at the hands of
the Philistines.
26 When the servants reported
these terms to David, he was pleased[E]
to become the king's son-in-law.
Before the wedding day arrived,[F]
27 David and his men went out and
killed 200[G] Philistines. He brought

[A] **18:8** Lit *furious; this saying was evil in his eyes* [B] **18:10** Or *prophesy* [C] **18:20** Lit *Saul, the thing was right in his eyes* [D] **18:23** Lit *words in David's ears* [E] **18:26** Lit *David, it was right in David's eyes* [F] **18:26** Lit *And the days were not full* [G] **18:27** LXX reads *100*

18:7-30 In his anger and jealousy, Saul attempted to kill David. Yet, rather than frightening David, Saul grew fearful of him **because the LORD was with David** (v. 12). Saul's pride is a direct contrast to David's humility. Saul continued to exalt himself, deceived into thinking that he could manipulate God's will and destroy David. But David remained humble in the sight of God and men and trusted God to accomplish His purpose (Ps 138:8). God resists the proud and exalts the humble (Jms 4:6); and His hand was clearly on David, lifting Him up and preparing Him to be an exalted king among His people.

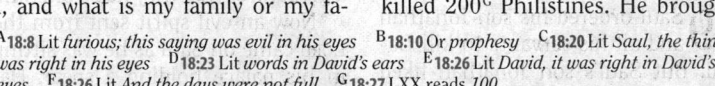

BIBLICAL WOMANHOOD The Danger of Comparison

At its heart, the sin of comparison with which women struggle on many different levels—material, emotional, physical, and even spiritual—takes a dangerous turn from focusing on God to relying on another or even on oneself. Soon, statements such as "If only I could be like . . ." begin to occupy your mind, as greed, jealousy, and feelings of inadequacy seep into the heart. The Christian life, however, is not about competing with others but about completing the will of God. Being spurred on to good works by another's conduct (Heb 10:24) is certainly healthy to our walk of faith, but allowing ourselves to become consumed with being like someone else as opposed to like Christ is harmful. Ultimately, such comparisons shift the focus of our lives from God's glory to our own. As women, we must choose to believe that God has given us all that we need to live according to His perfect plan for our lives.

CHARACTER PROFILE

Michal **A Scornful Wife**

Her Background	• The daughter of King Saul (14:49; 18:20) • The wife of King David (18:27)
Her Story	• She loved David and was given to him in marriage by her father (18:27). • She helped David escape from Saul's murderous plot (19:11-17). • She was given to Paltiel as his wife after David became a fugitive (25:44). • She was forced to return to David years later to establish his legitimacy to the throne (2Sm 3:13). • She scornfully rebuked David publicly for his worship (2Sm 6:20). • She had no children (2Sm 6:23).
Life Lessons	• A woman who refuses to forgive and harbors resentment toward her husband will reveal a heart of bitterness. • Bitterness destroys relationships and brings overwhelming sorrow and grief.

their foreskins and presented them as full payment to the king to become his son-in-law. Then Saul gave his daughter Michal to David as his wife. 28 Saul realized that the Lord was with David and that his daughter Michal loved him, 29 and he became even more afraid of David. As a result, Saul was David's enemy from then on.

30 Every time the Philistine commanders came out to fight, David was more successful than all of Saul's officers. So his name became well known.

David's Deliverance from Saul (19:1-24)

19 Saul ordered his son Jonathan and all his servants to kill David. But Saul's son Jonathan liked David very much, 2 so he told him: "My father Saul intends to kill you. Be on your guard in the morning and hide in a secret place and stay there. 3 I'll go out and stand beside my father in the field where you are and talk to him about you. When I see what he says, I'll tell you."

4 Jonathan spoke well of David to his father Saul. He said to him: "The king should not sin against his servant David. He hasn't sinned against you; in fact, his actions have been a great advantage to you. 5 He took his life in his hands when he struck down the Philistine, and the Lord brought about a great victory for all Israel. You saw it and rejoiced, so why would you sin against innocent blood by killing David for no reason?"

6 Saul listened to Jonathan's advice and swore an oath: "As surely as the Lord lives, David will not be killed." 7 So Jonathan summoned David and told him all these words. Then Jonathan brought David to Saul, and he served him as he did before.

8 When war broke out again, David went out and fought against the Philistines. He defeated them with such a great force that they fled from him.

9 Now an evil spirit sent from the Lord came on Saul as he was sitting in his palace holding a spear. David was playing the lyre, 10 and Saul tried to pin David to the wall with the spear. As the spear struck the wall, David eluded Saul, ran away, and escaped that night. 11 Saul sent agents to David's house to watch for him and kill him in the morning. But his wife Michal warned David, "If you don't escape tonight, you will be dead tomorrow!" 12 So she lowered David from the window, and he fled and escaped. 13 Then Michal took the household idol and put it on the bed, placed some goat hair on its head, and covered it with a gar-

ment. 14 When Saul sent agents to seize David, Michal said, "He's sick."

15 Saul sent the agents back to see David and said, "Bring him on his bed so I can kill him." 16 When the messengers arrived, to their surprise, the household idol was on the bed with some goat hair on its head.

17 Saul asked Michal, "Why did you deceive me like this? You sent my enemy away, and he has escaped!"

She answered him, "He said to me, 'Let me go! Why should I kill you?'"

18 So David fled and escaped and went to Samuel at Ramah and told him everything Saul had done to him. Then he and Samuel left and stayed at Naioth.

19 When it was reported to Saul that David was at Naioth in Ramah, 20 he sent agents to seize David. However, when they saw the group of prophets prophesying with Samuel leading them, the Spirit of God came on Saul's agents, and they also started prophesying. 21 When they reported to Saul, he sent other agents, and they also began prophesying. So Saul tried again and sent a third group of agents, and even they began prophesying. 22 Then Saul himself went to Ramah. He came to the large cistern at Secu, looked around, and asked, "Where are Samuel and David?"

"At Naioth in Ramah," someone said.

23 So he went to Naioth in Ramah. The Spirit of God also came on him, and as he walked along, he prophesied until he entered Naioth in Ramah. 24 Saul then removed his clothes and also prophesied before Samuel; he collapsed and lay naked all that day and all that night. That is why they say, "Is Saul also among the prophets?"

Jonathan's Protection of David (20:1-42)

20 David fled from Naioth in Ramah and came to Jonathan and asked, "What have I done? What did I do wrong? How have I sinned against your father so that he wants to take my life?"

2 Jonathan said to him, "No, you won't die. Listen, my father doesn't do anything, great or small, without telling me.[A] So why would he hide this matter from me? This can't be true."

3 But David said, "Your father certainly knows that you have come to look favorably on me. He has said, 'Jonathan must not know of this, or else he will be grieved.'" David also swore, "As surely as the LORD lives and as you yourself live, there is but a step between me and death."

4 Jonathan said to David, "Whatever you say, I will do for you."

5 So David told him, "Look, tomorrow is the New Moon, and I'm supposed to sit down and eat with the king. Instead, let me go, and I'll hide in the field until the third night. 6 If your father misses me at all, say, 'David urgently requested my permission to quickly go to his town Bethlehem for an annual sacrifice there involving the whole clan.' 7 If he says, 'Good,' then your servant is safe, but if he becomes angry, you will know he has evil intentions. 8 Deal faithfully with your servant, for you have brought me into a covenant with you before the LORD. If I have done anything wrong, then kill me yourself; why take me to your father?"

9 "No!" Jonathan responded. "If I ever find out my father has evil intentions against you, wouldn't I tell you about it?"

10 So David asked Jonathan, "Who will tell me if your father answers you harshly?"

11 He answered David, "Come on, let's go out to the field." So both of them went out to the field. 12 "By the LORD, the God of Israel, I will sound out my father by this time tomorrow or the next day. If I find out that he is favorable toward you, will I not send for you and tell you?[B] 13 If my father intends to bring evil on you, may God punish Jonathan and do so severely if I do not tell you[C] and send you away so you may go in peace. May the LORD be with you, just as He was with my father. 14 If I continue to live, treat me with the LORD's faithful love, but if I die, 15 don't ever withdraw your faithful

19:18 Interestingly, Saul first met Samuel and was anointed at **Ramah**. Now Samuel was protecting David, Israel's next king, in the same town. Ramah may have been the location of the so-called "School of the Prophets," whose members followed Samuel's leadership and whose legacy continued until the days of Elijah and Elisha (1Kg 20:35; 2Kg 6:1-7).

19:19-24 With Saul's evil purpose thwarted once again, the sovereignty of God and the power of His Spirit in changing and directing hearts is displayed.

20:1-17 Jonathan clung to Saul's oath to him that he would spare David's life (19:6); thus for David to demonstrate Saul's real intentions to Jonathan was important. Saul expressed these in a conversation with Michal (19:17).

[A] **20:2** Lit *without uncovering my ear* [B] **20:12** Lit *and uncover your ear* [C] **20:13** Lit *will uncover your ears*

20:18-42 Saul's reaction to David's absence from the festivities indicated the motive and desire of his heart. The events in chapter 19 should have impressed upon Saul the impossibility of fighting against the Lord and His purposes. But Saul hardened his heart against the Lord and sought to kill David. Jonathan warned David of Saul's intent to kill him (vv. 30-40). Jonathan and David had made a covenant with each other before the Lord (v. 42). It was expressed by their unfailing commitment and mutual love (vv. 17,41) and extended to their descendants, exhibited by mercy to them for as long as they lived (vv. 15). David kept this vow by treating Mephibosheth, Jonathan's son, with unusual kindness (2Sm 9:3-7; 21:7). Jonathan recognized the hand of God on David's life and repeatedly promised his loyalty to David even in the face of his father's jealous rage.

>WORD|*study*

20:14-15 Faithful love (Hb *chesed*, lit "graciousness, kindness, mercy, lovingkindness") not only describes the type of love existing within the human family but, more importantly, originating in the love God has for those who are in a covenant relationship with Him (Dt 7:9). It describes God's character as one who abundantly loves and is great in mercy (Nm 14:18-19; Neh 13:22; Ps 103:8-11).

love from my household—not even when the LORD cuts off every one of David's enemies from the face of the earth." [16]Then Jonathan made a covenant with the house of David, saying, "May the LORD hold David's enemies accountable."[A] [17]Jonathan once again swore to David[B] in his love for him, because he loved him as he loved himself.

[18]Then Jonathan said to him, "Tomorrow is the New Moon; you'll be missed because your seat will be empty. [19]The following day hurry down and go to the place where you hid on the day this incident began and stay beside the rock Ezel. [20]I will shoot three arrows beside it as if I'm aiming at a target. [21]Then I will send the young man and say, 'Go and find the arrows!' Now, if I expressly say to the young man, 'Look, the arrows are on this side of you—get them,' then come, because as the LORD lives, it is safe for you and there is no problem. [22]But if I say this to the youth: 'Look, the arrows are beyond you!' then go, for the LORD is sending you away. [23]As for the matter you and I have spoken about, the LORD will be a witness[C] between you and me forever." [24]So David hid in the field.

At the New Moon, the king sat down to eat the meal. [25]He sat at his usual place on the seat by the wall. Jonathan sat facing him[D] and Abner took his place beside Saul, but David's place was empty. [26]Saul did not say anything that day because he thought, "Something unexpected has happened; he must be ceremonially •unclean—yes, that's it, he is unclean."

[27]However, the day after the New Moon, the second day, David's place was still empty, and Saul asked his son Jonathan, "Why didn't Jesse's son come to the meal either yesterday or today?"

[28]Jonathan answered, "David asked for my permission to go to Bethlehem. [29]He said, 'Please let me go because our clan is holding a sacrifice in the town, and my brother has told me to be there. So now, if you are pleased with me, let me go so I can see my brothers.' That's why he didn't come to the king's table."

[30]Then Saul became angry with Jonathan and shouted, "You son of a perverse and rebellious woman! Don't I know that you are siding with Jesse's son to your own shame and to the disgrace of your mother?[E] [31]Every day Jesse's son lives on earth you and your kingship are not secure. Now send for him and bring him to me—he deserves to die."

[32]Jonathan answered his father back: "Why is he to be killed? What has he done?"

[33]Then Saul threw his spear at Jonathan to kill him, so he knew that his father was determined to kill David. [34]He got up from the table in fierce anger and did not eat any food that second day of the New Moon, for he was grieved because of his father's shameful behavior toward David.

[35]In the morning Jonathan went out to the field for the appointed meeting with David. A small young man was with him. [36]He said to the young man, "Run and find the arrows I'm shooting." As the young man ran, Jonathan shot an arrow beyond him. [37]He came to the location of the arrow that Jonathan had shot, but Jonathan called to him and said, "The arrow is beyond you, isn't it?" [38]Then Jonathan called to him, "Hurry up and don't stop!" Jonathan's young man picked up the arrow and returned to his master. [39]He

[A]**20:16** Lit *LORD require it from the hand of David's enemies* [B]**20:17** LXX; MT reads *Jonathan once again made David swear* [C]**20:23** LXX; MT omits *a witness* [D]**20:25** Text emended; MT reads *Jonathan got up* [E]**20:30** Lit *your mother's genitals*

did not know anything; only Jonathan and David knew the arrangement. 40 Then Jonathan gave his
equipment to the young man who
was with him and said, "Go, take it
back to the city."
41 When the young man had gone,
David got up from the south side of
the stone Ezel, fell with his face to
the ground, and bowed three times.
Then he and Jonathan kissed each
other and wept with each other,
though David wept more.
42 Jonathan then said to David,
"Go in the assurance the two of us
pledged in the name of the LORD
when we said: The LORD will be a
witness between you and me and
between my offspring and your offspring forever."[A] Then David left,
and Jonathan went into the city.

David's Escape to Nob (21:1-9)

21 David went to Ahimelech the
priest at Nob. Ahimelech was
afraid to meet David, so he said to
him, "Why are you alone and no one
is with you?"
2 David answered Ahimelech the
priest, "The king gave me a mission,
but he told me, 'Don't let anyone
know anything about the mission
I'm sending you on or what I have
ordered you to do.' I have stationed
my young men at a certain place.
3 Now what do you have on hand?
Give me five loaves of bread or whatever can be found."
4 The priest told him, "There is no
ordinary bread on hand. However,
there is consecrated bread, but the
young men may eat it[B] only if they
have kept themselves from women."
5 David answered him, "I swear
that women are being kept from us,
as always when I go out to battle.
The young men's bodies[C] are consecrated even on an ordinary mission, so of course their bodies are
consecrated today." 6 So the priest
gave him the consecrated bread, for
there was no bread there except the
•bread of the Presence that had been
removed from the presence of the
LORD. When the bread was removed,
it had been replaced with warm
bread.
7 One of Saul's servants, detained
before the LORD, was there that day.
His name was Doeg the Edomite,
chief of Saul's shepherds.
8 David said to Ahimelech, "Do
you have a spear or sword on hand?
I didn't even bring my sword or my
weapons since the king's mission
was urgent."
9 The priest replied, "The sword
of Goliath the Philistine, whom
you killed in the Valley of Elah, is
here, wrapped in a cloth behind the
•ephod. If you want to take it for
yourself, then take it, for there isn't
another one here."
"There's none like it!" David said.
"Give it to me."

David's Flight to Gath (21:10-15)

10 David fled that day from Saul's
presence and went to King Achish
of Gath. 11 But Achish's servants said
to him, "Isn't this David, the king of
the land? Don't they sing about him
during their dances:

> Saul has killed his thousands,
> but David his tens
> of thousands?"

12 David took this to heart[D] and became very afraid of King Achish of
Gath, 13 so he pretended to be insane
in their presence. He acted like a
madman around them,[E] scribbling[F]
on the doors of the gate and letting
saliva run down his beard.
14 "Look! You can see the man is
crazy," Achish said to his servants.
"Why did you bring him to me? 15 Do
I have such a shortage of crazy people that you brought this one to act
crazy around me? Is this one going
to come into my house?"

Saul's Increasing Paranoia (22:1-10)

22 So David left Gath and took
refuge in the cave of Adullam. When David's brothers and his
father's whole family heard, they
went down and joined him there.
2 In addition, every man who was
desperate, in debt, or discontented
rallied around him, and he became
their leader. About 400 men were
with him.
3 From there David went to Mizpeh

21:1-6 In order to receive help from **Ahimelech the priest**, David found it necessary to fabricate the story that he was on a secret mission for Saul (vv. 1-3). Since there was no ordinary bread available, David requested the holy showbread or **bread of the Presence**. This bread was only for the priests and only for those who were ceremonially clean (Lv 15:18). In Mt 12:3-4, Jesus referred to this account when teaching the Pharisees that mercy exists in the law; and thus David did not sin by eating this special bread. Life was more holy than the bread itself.

21:7-15 Sensing danger at being discovered by Saul's servant, David chose to flee into Philistine territory, Goliath's hometown no less. David underestimated his reputation among the Philistines and was recognized by **Achish**, the lord of **Gath**. Hoping to escape the Philistines' revenge, he pretended and succeeded in convincing the Philistine lord that he was an **insane** man. During this time David penned the words of Ps 34:6, "This poor man cried, and the LORD heard him and saved him from all his troubles." Even in the midst of suffering, David declared the Lord's goodness and faithfulness.

22:1-5 These men are described as **desperate, in debt, or discontented**—reminiscent of Gideon's untrained army (Jdg 7:7). But God uses the seemingly weak people to bring great glory and victory in His name. Concerned about his family's safety, David pleaded for the king of Moab to protect them and to allow them to dwell with those who might have been related to his great-grandmother, the Moabitess Ruth (1Sm 22:3-4).

[A] **20:42** The last sentence of v. 42 is 1Sm 21:1 in Hb. [B] **21:4** DSS; MT omits *may eat it* [C] **21:5** Lit *vessels* [D] **21:12** Lit *David placed these words in his heart* [E] **21:13** Lit *madman in their hand* [F] **21:13** LXX reads *drumming*

22:6-23 David demonstrates his character and leadership by his immediate claim to be **responsible for the lives** lost because he failed to deter **the Edomite** from reporting to Saul (v. 22).

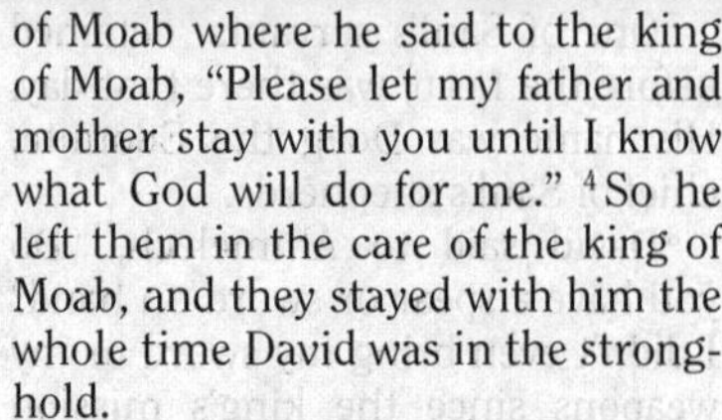

of Moab where he said to the king of Moab, "Please let my father and mother stay with you until I know what God will do for me." 4 So he left them in the care of the king of Moab, and they stayed with him the whole time David was in the stronghold.

5 Then the prophet Gad said to David, "Don't stay in the stronghold. Leave and return to the land of Judah." So David left and went to the forest of Hereth.

6 Saul heard that David and his men had been discovered. At that time Saul was in Gibeah, sitting under the tamarisk tree at the •high place. His spear was in his hand, and all his servants were standing around him. 7 Saul said to his servants, "Listen, men of Benjamin: Is Jesse's son going to give all of you fields and vineyards? Do you think he'll make all of you commanders of thousands and commanders of hundreds? 8 That's why all of you have conspired against me! Nobody tells me[A] when my own son makes a covenant with Jesse's son. None of you cares about me or tells me[B] that my son has stirred up my own servant to wait in ambush for me, as is the case today."

9 Then Doeg the Edomite, who was in charge of Saul's servants, answered: "I saw Jesse's son come to Ahimelech son of Ahitub at Nob. 10 Ahimelech inquired of the LORD for him and gave him provisions. He also gave him the sword of Goliath the Philistine."

Slaughter of the Priests (22:11-23)

11 The king sent messengers to summon Ahimelech the priest, son of Ahitub, and his father's whole family, who were priests in Nob. All of them came to the king. 12 Then Saul said, "Listen, son of Ahitub!"

"I'm at your service, my lord," he said.

13 Saul asked him, "Why did you and Jesse's son conspire against me? You gave him bread and a sword and inquired of God for him, so he could rise up against me and wait in ambush, as is the case today."

14 Ahimelech replied to the king: "Who among all your servants is as faithful as David? He is the king's son-in-law, captain of your bodyguard, and honored in your house. 15 Was today the first time I inquired of God for him? Of course not! Please don't let the king make an accusation against your servant or any of my father's household, for your servant didn't have any idea[C] about all this."

16 But the king said, "You will die, Ahimelech—you and your father's whole family!"

17 Then the king ordered the guards standing by him, "Turn and kill the priests of the LORD because they sided with David. For they knew he was fleeing, but they didn't tell me."[D] But the king's servants would not lift a hand to execute the priests of the LORD.

18 So the king said to Doeg, "Go and execute the priests!" So Doeg the Edomite went and executed the priests himself. On that day, he killed 85 men who wore linen •ephods. 19 He also struck down Nob, the city of the priests, with the sword—both men and women, children and infants, oxen, donkeys, and sheep.

20 However, one of the sons of Ahimelech son of Ahitub escaped. His name was Abiathar, and he fled to David. 21 Abiathar told David that Saul had killed the priests of the LORD. 22 Then David said to Abiathar, "I knew that Doeg the Edomite was there that day and that he was sure to report to Saul. I myself am responsible for[E] the lives of everyone in your father's family. 23 Stay with me. Don't be afraid, for the one who wants to take my life wants to take your life. You will be safe with me."

Deliverance at Keilah (23:1-14)

23 It was reported to David: "Look, the Philistines are fighting against Keilah and raiding the threshing floors."

2 So David inquired of the LORD: "Should I launch an attack against these Philistines?"

The LORD answered David, "Launch an attack against the Philistines and rescue Keilah."

3 But David's men said to him,

[A] **22:8** Lit *No one uncovers my ear* [B] **22:8** Lit *or uncovers my ear* [C] **22:15** Lit *didn't know a thing, small or large* [D] **22:17** Lit *didn't uncover my ear* [E] **22:22** LXX, Syr, Vg; MT reads *I myself turn in*

"Look, we're afraid here in Judah; how much more if we go to Keilah against the Philistine forces!"

4 Once again, David inquired of the LORD, and the LORD answered him: "Go at once to Keilah, for I will hand the Philistines over to you." 5 Then David and his men went to Keilah, fought against the Philistines, drove their livestock away, and inflicted heavy losses on them. So David rescued the inhabitants of Keilah. 6 Abiathar son of Ahimelech fled to David at Keilah, and he brought an •ephod with him.

7 When it was reported to Saul that David had gone to Keilah, he said, "God has handed him over to me, for he has trapped himself by entering a town with barred gates." 8 Then Saul summoned all the troops to go to war at Keilah and besiege David and his men.

9 When David learned that Saul was plotting evil against him, he said to Abiathar the priest, "Bring the ephod."

10 Then David said, "LORD God of Israel, Your servant has heard that Saul intends to come to Keilah and destroy the town because of me. 11 Will the citizens of Keilah hand me over to him? Will Saul come down as Your servant has heard? LORD God of Israel, please tell Your servant."

The LORD answered, "He will come down."

12 Then David asked, "Will the citizens of Keilah hand me and my men over to Saul?"

"They will," the LORD responded.

13 So David and his men, numbering about 600, left Keilah at once and moved from place to place. When it was reported to Saul that David had escaped from Keilah, he called off the expedition. 14 David then stayed in the wilderness strongholds and in the hill country of the Wilderness of Ziph. Saul searched for him every day, but God did not hand David over to him.

A Renewed Covenant (23:15-18)

15 David was in the Wilderness of Ziph in Horesh when he saw that Saul had come out to take his life. 16 Then Saul's son Jonathan came to David in Horesh and encouraged him in his faith in God, 17 saying, "Don't be afraid, for my father Saul will never lay a hand on you. You yourself will be king over Israel, and I'll be your second-in-command. Even my father Saul knows it is true." 18 Then the two of them made a covenant in the LORD's presence. Afterward, David remained in Horesh, while Jonathan went home.

David's Narrow Escape (23:19-29)

19 Some Ziphites came up to Saul at Gibeah and said, "David is[A] hiding among us in the strongholds in Horesh on the hill of Hachilah south of Jeshimon. 20 Now, whenever the king wants to come down, let him come down. Our part will be to hand him over to the king."

21 "May you be blessed by the LORD," replied Saul, "for you have taken pity on me. 22 Go and check again. Investigate and watch carefully where he goes[B] and who has seen him there; they tell me he is extremely cunning. 23 Look and find out all the places where he hides. Then come back to me with accurate information, and I'll go with you. If it turns out he really is in the region, I'll search for him among all the clans[C] of Judah." 24 So they went to Ziph ahead of Saul.

Now David and his men were in the wilderness near Maon in the •Arabah south of Jeshimon, 25 and Saul and his men went to look for him. When David was told about it, he went down to the rock and stayed in the Wilderness of Maon. Saul heard of this and pursued David there.

26 Saul went along one side of the mountain and David and his men went along the other side. Even though David was hurrying to get away from Saul, Saul and his men were closing in on David and his men to capture them. 27 Then a messenger came to Saul saying, "Come quickly, because the Philistines have raided the land!" 28 So Saul broke off his pursuit of David and went to engage the Philistines. Therefore, that place was named

23:1-5 In addition to fleeing from his enemy, David also **rescued** others from danger.

23:6-13 David, in contrast to Saul, while taking into consideration what he heard from men, ultimately consulted God and followed His instruction. God knows all the alternatives and the intent of human hearts (vv. 11-12).

23:14-18 Jonathan came to David and **encouraged him in his faith in God**, reminding him of the promises of God. This encounter was the last recorded meeting between David and Jonathan.

23:19-29 In the midst of betrayal, the Lord continually protected David. God is always faithful to His promises and fulfills what He has purposed, even when it looks as though the circumstances could not be worse.

[A] **23:19** Lit *Is David not . . . Jeshimon?* [B] **23:22** Lit *watch his place where his foot will be*
[C] **23:23** Or *thousands*

24:1-16 Despite the counsel of his men, David restrained them from harming Saul and instead cut a **corner** from his **robe**. He reminded his men that Saul was **the Lord's anointed** and his master (vv. 5-7). He not only respected Saul's position as the anointed king over Israel, but he also respected the Lord and trusted Him to bring justice (Rm 12:17-21). David's address to Saul cuts to the heart of Saul's problem—he listened to men and trusted his own heart rather than listening to God and trusting His plans (1Sm 24:9). David urged Saul to let the Lord decide, judge, avenge, and deliver.

24:17-22 Saul's reply contains the most truthful and observant remarks recorded by this fallen king. David's position as the future king of Israel was affirmed by the people, Jonathan, the prophet Gad, Abiathar, and now King Saul.

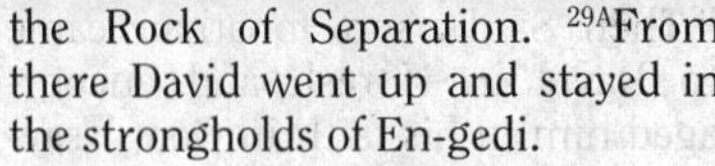

the Rock of Separation. 29[A]From there David went up and stayed in the strongholds of En-gedi.

David's Sparing of Saul (24:1-22)

24 When Saul returned from pursuing the Philistines, he was told, "David is in the wilderness near En-gedi." 2 So Saul took 3,000 of Israel's choice men and went to look for David and his men in front of the Rocks of the Wild Goats. 3 When Saul came to the sheep pens along the road, a cave was there, and he went in to relieve himself.[B] David and his men were staying in the back of the cave, 4 so they said to him, "Look, this is the day the LORD told you about: 'I will hand your enemy over to you so you can do to him whatever you desire.'" Then David got up and secretly cut off the corner of Saul's robe.

5 Afterward, David's conscience bothered[C] him because he had cut off the corner of Saul's robe.[D] 6 He said to his men, "I swear before the LORD: I would never do such a thing to my lord, the LORD's anointed. I will never lift my hand against him, since he is the LORD's anointed." 7 With these words David persuaded[E] his men, and he did not let them rise up against Saul.

Then Saul left the cave and went on his way. 8 After that, David got up, went out of the cave, and called to Saul, "My lord the king!" When Saul looked behind him, David bowed to the ground in homage. 9 David said to Saul, "Why do you listen to the words of people who say, 'Look, David intends to harm you'? 10 You can see with your own eyes that the LORD handed you over to me today in the cave. Someone advised me to kill you, but I[FG] took pity on you and said: I won't lift my hand against my lord, since he is the LORD's anointed. 11 See, my father! Look at the corner of your robe in my hand, for I cut it off, but I didn't kill you. Look and recognize that there is no evil or rebellion in me. I haven't sinned against you even though you are hunting me down to take my life.

HARD QUESTION

Is it ever right to take revenge?

Undoubtedly, there are times when we are called to right a wrong, particularly when the action is for the benefit of another or when a sin must be confronted. But personal payback for a wrong committed against us is not ours to give. Judgment belongs only to the Lord: "Vengeance belongs to Me, I will repay" (Heb 10:30). King David so trusted God's faithfulness that he refused to take wrongfully what only God could rightfully give. For David, the result of retribution was not as valuable as honoring the Lord (1Sm 24:1-15). When you trust that your just God will right every wrong in perfect measure and entrust the results to Him, you place yourself under His sovereign protection, knowing that "He is a shield to all who take refuge in Him," (Ps 18:30).

12 "May the LORD judge between you and me, and may the LORD take vengeance on you for me, but my hand will never be against you. 13 As the old proverb says, 'Wickedness comes from wicked people.' My hand will never be against you. 14 Who has the king of Israel come after? What are you chasing after? A dead dog? A flea? 15 May the LORD be judge and decide between you and me. May He take notice and plead my case and deliver[H] me from you."

16 When David finished saying these things to him, Saul replied, "Is that your voice, David my son?" Then Saul wept aloud 17 and said to David, "You are more righteous than I, for you have done what is good to me though I have done what is evil to you. 18 You yourself have told me today what good you did for me: when the LORD handed me over to you, you didn't kill me. 19 When a man finds his enemy, does he let him go unharmed?[I] May the LORD repay you with good for what you've done for me today.

20 "Now I know for certain you will be king, and the kingdom of Israel will be established[J] in your hand. 21 Therefore swear to me by the LORD that you will not cut off my descendants or wipe out my name from my father's family." 22 So David swore to

[A] **23:29** 1Sm 24:1 in Hb [B] **24:3** Lit *to cover his feet* [C] **24:5** Lit *David's heart struck* [D] **24:5** Some Hb mss, LXX, Syr, Vg; other Hb mss omit *robe* [E] **24:7** Or *restrained* [F] **24:10** LXX, Syr, Tg; MT reads *she* or *it* [G] **24:10** Or *my eye* [H] **24:15** Lit *render a verdict for* [I] **24:19** Lit *go on a good way* [J] **24:20** Or *will flourish*

CHARACTER PROFILE

Abigail An Intelligent Beauty

Her Background	• The wife of Nabal, a wealthy rancher (1Sm 25:2-3) • Her husband's foolish behavior put her and her household in a dangerous situation (25:1-17).
Her Story	• She quickly gathered food supplies for David's men and intercepted him before he could carry out his threats to the household (25:18-19). • Her gracious speech and gifts softened David's heart (25:33). • She appealed to him on the basis of his kingship, and he recognized her wise counsel (25:35). • After Nabal's death, she accepted David's proposal to become his wife (25:39).
Life Lessons	• Abigail's actions revealed her wise and godly heart. • Crises do not make character; they reveal it.

Saul. Then Saul went back home,
and David and his men went up to
the stronghold.

David, Nabal, and Abigail (25:1-44)

25 Samuel died, and all Israel assembled to mourn for him,
and they buried him by his home
in Ramah. David then went down to
the Wilderness of Paran.[A]
2 A man in Maon had a business in
Carmel; he was a very rich man with
3,000 sheep and 1,000 goats and
was shearing his sheep in Carmel.
3 The man's name was Nabal, and
his wife's name, Abigail. The woman
was intelligent and beautiful, but
the man, a Calebite, was harsh and
evil in his dealings.
4 While David was in the wilderness, he heard that Nabal was
shearing sheep, 5 so David sent 10
young men instructing them, "Go
up to Carmel, and when you come
to Nabal, greet him in my name.[B]
6 Then say this: 'Long life to you,[C]
and peace to you, to your family,
and to all that is yours. 7 I hear that
you are shearing.[D] When your shepherds were with us, we did not harass them, and nothing of theirs was
missing the whole time they were in
Carmel. 8 Ask your young men, and
they will tell you. So let my young
men find favor with you, for we have
come on a feast[E] day. Please give
whatever you can afford to your servants and to your son David.'"
9 David's young men went and said
all these things to Nabal on David's
behalf,[F] and they waited.[G] 10 Nabal
asked them, "Who is David? Who is
Jesse's son? Many slaves these days
are running away from their masters. 11 Am I supposed to take my
bread, my water, and my meat that
I butchered for my shearers and give
them to these men? I don't know
where they are from."
12 David's men retraced their steps.
When they returned to him, they
reported all these words. 13 He said
to his men, "All of you, put on your
swords!" So David and all his men
put on their swords. About 400 men
followed David while 200 stayed
with the supplies.
14 One of Nabal's young men informed Abigail, Nabal's wife: "Look,
David sent messengers from the wilderness to greet our master, but he
yelled at them. 15 The men treated us
well. When we were in the field, we
weren't harassed and nothing of ours
was missing the whole time we were
living among them. 16 They were a
wall around us, both day and night,
the entire time we were herding the
sheep. 17 Now consider carefully what
you must do, because there is certain

[A]25:1 LXX reads *to Maon* [B]25:5 Or *Nabal, and ask him for peace* [C]25:6 Lit *To life* [D]25:7 Lit *you have shearers* [E]25:8 Lit *good* [F]25:9 Lit *name* [G]25:9 LXX reads *and he became arrogant*

25:1 The fact that all of Israel gathered to mourn Samuel's death points to the great impact this prophet made on the entire nation. He encouraged spiritual reformation for the nation and was instrumental in the establishment of Israel's monarchy.

25:2-4 Nabal's name (Hb, "fool") is fitting, given his behavior toward David and his men. By contrast, Abigail, Nabal's wife, was an **intelligent** and **beautiful** woman of admirable character.

25:4-13 Nabal's lack of generosity and, in fact, unashamed selfishness incited David to the point of ordering his men to arm themselves and take vengeance on Nabal and his family (vv. 12-13). David's impassioned desire to remedy the situation could have been catastrophic; yet God protected him from making such a terrible mistake through the intervention of Abigail.

25:18-31 Abigail's quick response demonstrated her wisdom. She took responsibility for her husband's selfishness, suggesting that she should have been alert to David's men when they first arrived (v. 25). More importantly, she reminded David that the Lord alone is the avenger of the wicked (v. 28), and that a fool will eventually reap the consequences of his own foolishness (v. 26). In speaking of David's life as being **tucked safely in the place where the LORD your God protects the living** (v. 29), Abigail acknowledged that David would be bundled and securely protected from any harm by God. This word picture suggests a valuable item being bundled in order to protect it from injury. The second image she used is fitting, considering how the Lord had already protected David from his enemies through the use of a sling (v. 29; cp. 17:50).

25:32-42 Contrary to the opinion of some scholars that David initiated a quarrel with Nabal in order to obtain Abigail as his wife, the text speaks otherwise. His concern for the safety of his men led him to make the request for food from Nabal. Yet, in the end, he was rewarded with much more than food; he was given Abigail, the wise woman, as his wife. This episode demonstrates the great impact a woman who submits to the Lord and cooperates with His plan can make in a precarious situation.

to be trouble for our master and his
entire family. He is such a worthless
fool nobody can talk to him!"
18 Abigail hurried, taking 200 loaves
of bread, two skins of wine, five
butchered sheep, a bushel[A] of roasted
grain, 100 clusters of raisins, and
200 cakes of pressed figs, and loaded
them on donkeys. 19 Then she said to
her male servants, "Go ahead of me. I
will be right behind you." But she did
not tell her husband Nabal.
20 As she rode the donkey down a
mountain pass hidden from view,
she saw David and his men coming
toward her and met them. 21 David
had just said, "I guarded everything
that belonged to this man in the
wilderness for nothing. He was not
missing anything, yet he paid me
back evil for good. 22 May God punish me[B] and do so severely if I let any
of his men[C] survive until morning."
23 When Abigail saw David, she
quickly got off the donkey and fell
with her face to the ground in front
of David. 24 She fell at his feet and
said, "The •guilt is mine, my lord,
but please let your servant speak to
you directly. Listen to the words of
your servant. 25 My lord should pay
no attention to this worthless man
Nabal, for he lives up to his name:[D]
His name is Nabal,[E] and stupidity is
all he knows.[F] I, your servant, didn't
see my lord's young men whom you
sent. 26 Now my lord, as surely as the
LORD lives and as you yourself live, it
is the LORD who kept you from participating in bloodshed and avenging yourself by your own hand. May
your enemies and those who want
trouble for my lord be like Nabal.
27 Accept this gift your servant has
brought to my lord, and let it be giv-
en to the young men who follow my
lord. 28 Please forgive your servant's
offense, for the LORD is certain to
make a lasting dynasty for my lord
because he fights the LORD's battles.
Throughout your life, may evil[G] not
be found in you.
29 "When someone pursues you
and attempts to take your life, my
lord's life will be tucked safely in
the place[H] where the LORD your God
protects the living. However, He
will fling away your enemies' lives
like stones from a sling. 30 When the
LORD does for my lord all the good
He promised and appoints you ruler
over Israel, 31 there will not be remorse or a troubled conscience for
my lord because of needless bloodshed or my lord's revenge. And when
the LORD does good things for my
lord, may you remember me your
servant."
32 Then David said to Abigail,
"Praise to the LORD God of Israel,
who sent you to meet me today!
33 Your discernment is blessed, and
you are blessed. Today you kept me
from participating in bloodshed and
avenging myself by my own hand.
34 Otherwise, as surely as the LORD
God of Israel lives, who prevented
me from harming you, if you had
not come quickly to meet me, Nabal
wouldn't have had any men[I] left by
morning light." 35 Then David accepted what she had brought him
and said, "Go home in peace. See, I
have heard what you said and have
granted your request."
36 Then Abigail went to Nabal, and

[A] **25:18** Lit *sheep, five seahs* [B] **25:22** LXX; MT reads *David's enemies* [C] **25:22** Lit *of those of his who are urinating against the wall* [D] **25:25** Lit *for as is his name is, so he is* [E] **25:25** = Fool [F] **25:25** Lit *and foolishness is with him* [G] **25:28** Or *trouble* [H] **25:29** Lit *bundle* [I] **25:34** Lit *had anyone urinating against a wall*

Biblical Womanhood A Woman's Influence

Abigail's story demonstrates the great impact a woman who speaks with restraint and wisdom can make in a precarious situation (25:1-42). Abigail resourcefully preempted David's rash plan of revenge by confronting with discretion. Her language, demeanor, and actions communicated a humble servanthood. She appealed to his status as the future king, persuading David to reconsider his response and to take into account the dire consequences of his intended actions. Her submission in this passage is evident and demonstrates in particular the beauty and influence of a woman who respects those in authority over her. Abigail remains a model of the effectiveness of gracious words in the midst of tumultuous circumstances.

>WORD|*study*

25:24 Servant (Hb *ʾamah,* "maidservant, bondwoman, handmaiden") is applied both to literal slaves and those who figuratively call themselves a servant as an expression of humility and submission. Hannah used this term for herself when confronted by Eli's accusations of drunkenness (1:13-16) and when referring to her relationship with the Lord (1:11). Paul used the word similarly in the New Testament (e.g., "slave," Rm 1:1; Col 4:7; Ti 1:1). Abigail used the term to demonstrate her humility and submission to David's authority.

25:43-44 Michal, David's wife, was given by Saul to another man seemingly to spite David.

26:1-25 David's encounter with Saul here is very similar to the events in chapter 24. David's address to Saul in verses 18-20 is strikingly similar to 24:9-15, as is Saul's confession (26:21). Saul's promises and confession were empty, however, compared to David's confession that the Lord would deliver him out of his tribulation (v. 24). This seems to be the last time Saul chased after David; yet he continued to pursue trouble.

there he was in his house, holding a feast fit for a king. Nabal was in a good mood[A] and very drunk, so she didn't say anything[B] to him until morning light.

37 In the morning when Nabal sobered up,[C] his wife told him about these events. Then he had a seizure[D] and became paralyzed.[E] 38 About 10 days later, the LORD struck Nabal dead.

39 When David heard that Nabal was dead, he said, "Praise the LORD who championed my cause against Nabal's insults and restrained His servant from doing evil. The LORD brought Nabal's evil deeds back on his own head."

Then David sent messengers to speak to Abigail about marrying him. 40 When David's servants came to Abigail at Carmel, they said to her, "David sent us to bring you to him as a wife."

41 She stood up, then bowed her face to the ground and said, "Here I am, your servant, to wash the feet of my lord's servants." 42 Then Abigail got up quickly, and with her five female servants accompanying her, rode on the donkey following David's messengers. And so she became his wife.

43 David also married Ahinoam of Jezreel, and the two of them became his wives. 44 But Saul gave his daughter Michal, David's wife, to Palti son of Laish, who was from Gallim.

David's Sparing of Saul (26:1-25)

26 Then the Ziphites came to Saul at Gibeah saying, "David is hiding on the hill of Hachilah opposite Jeshimon." 2 So Saul, accompanied by 3,000 of the choice men of Israel, went to the Wilderness of Ziph to search for David there. 3 Saul camped beside the road at the hill of Hachilah opposite Jeshimon. David was living in the wilderness and discovered Saul had come there after him. 4 So David sent out spies and knew for certain that Saul had come. 5 Immediately, David went to the place where Saul had camped. He saw the place where Saul and Abner son of Ner, the general of his army, were lying down. Saul was lying inside the inner circle of the camp with the troops camped around him. 6 Then David asked Ahimelech the Hittite and Joab's brother Abishai son of Zeruiah, "Who will go with me into the camp to Saul?"

"I'll go with you," answered Abishai.

7 That night, David and Abishai came to the troops, and Saul was lying there asleep in the inner circle of the camp with his spear stuck in the ground by his head. Abner and the troops were lying around him. 8 Then Abishai said to David, "Today God has handed your enemy over to you. Let me thrust the spear through him into the ground just once. I won't have to strike him twice!"

9 But David said to Abishai, "Don't destroy him, for who can lift a hand against the LORD's anointed and be blameless?" 10 David added, "As the LORD lives, the LORD will certainly strike him down: either his day will come and he will die, or he will go into battle and perish. 11 However, because of the LORD, I will never lift my hand against the LORD's anointed. Instead, take the spear and the water jug by his head, and let's go."

12 So David took the spear and the water jug by Saul's head, and they went their way. No one saw them, no one knew, and no one woke up; they all remained asleep because

[A] **25:36** Lit *Nabal's heart was good on him* [B] **25:36** Lit *anything small or great* [C] **25:37** Lit *when the wine had gone out of Nabal* [D] **25:37** Lit *Then his heart died within him* [E] **25:37** Lit *became a stone*

27:1-12 David had fled to **Gath** once before, pretending to be insane (21:10-15). **Achish**, aware of the hostility between Saul and David, presumed David would be loyal to him and thus would assist the Philistines in their struggle with Israel. Contrary to what David reported to Achish, however, he and his men raided Israel's enemies, completely annihilating the men, women, and their livestock so that no one would be able to report to Achish on his activities.

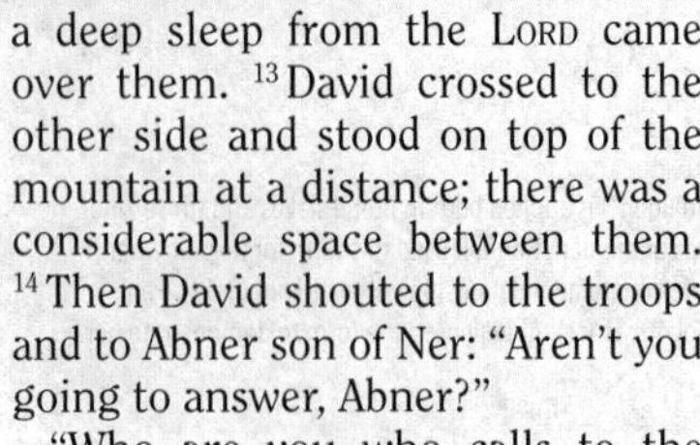

a deep sleep from the LORD came
over them. 13 David crossed to the
other side and stood on top of the
mountain at a distance; there was a
considerable space between them.
14 Then David shouted to the troops
and to Abner son of Ner: "Aren't you
going to answer, Abner?"

"Who are you who calls to the
king?" Abner asked.

15 David called to Abner, "You're
a man, aren't you? Who in Israel is
your equal? So why didn't you protect
your lord the king when one
of the people came to destroy him?
16 What you have done is not good.
As the LORD lives, all of you deserve
to die since you didn't protect your
lord, the LORD's anointed. Now look
around; where are the king's spear
and water jug that were by his head?"

17 Saul recognized David's voice
and asked, "Is that your voice, my
son David?"

"It is my voice, my lord and king,"
David said. 18 Then he continued,
"Why is my lord pursuing his servant?
What have I done? What evil
is in my hand? 19 Now, may my lord
the king please hear the words of his
servant: If it is the LORD who has incited
you against me, then may He
accept an offering. But if it is people,
may they be cursed in the presence
of the LORD, for today they have
driven me away from sharing in the
inheritance of the LORD saying, 'Go
and worship other gods.' 20 So don't
let my blood fall to the ground far
from the LORD's presence, for the
king of Israel has come out to search
for a flea, like one who pursues a
partridge in the mountains."

21 Saul responded, "I have sinned.
Come back, my son David, I will
never harm you again because today
you considered my life precious. I
have been a fool! I've committed a
grave error."

22 David answered, "Here is the
king's spear; have one of the young
men come over and get it. 23 May the
LORD repay every man for his righteousness
and his loyalty. I wasn't
willing to lift my hand against the
LORD's anointed, even though the
LORD handed you over to me today.
24 Just as I considered your life valuable
today, so may the LORD consider
my life valuable and rescue me from
all trouble."

25 Saul said to him, "You are
blessed, my son David. You will certainly
do great things and will also
prevail." Then David went on his
way, and Saul returned home.

David's Escape to Ziklag (27:1-12)

27 David said to himself, "One of
these days I'll be swept away
by Saul. There is nothing better
for me than to escape immediately
to the land of the Philistines. Then
Saul will stop searching for me everywhere
in Israel, and I'll escape
from him." 2 So David set out with
his 600 men and went to Achish son
of Maoch, the king of Gath. 3 David
and his men stayed with Achish in
Gath. Each man had his family with
him, and David had his two wives:
Ahinoam of Jezreel and Abigail of
Carmel, Nabal's widow. 4 When it
was reported to Saul that David had
fled to Gath, he no longer searched
for him.

5 Now David said to Achish, "If I
have found favor with you, let me
be given a place in one of the outlying
towns, so I can live there. Why
should your servant live in the royal
city with you?" 6 That day Achish
gave Ziklag to him, and it still belongs
to the kings of Judah today.
7 The time that David stayed in the
Philistine territory amounted to a
year and four months.

8 David and his men went up and
raided the Geshurites, the Girzites,[A]
and the Amalekites. From ancient
times they had been the inhabitants
of the region through Shur as far as
the land of Egypt. 9 Whenever David
attacked the land, he did not leave
a single person alive, either man or
woman, but he took flocks, herds,
donkeys, camels, and clothing. Then
he came back to Achish, 10 who inquired,
"Where did you raid today?"[B]

David replied, "The south country
of Judah," "The south country of
the Jerahmeelites," or "Against the
south country of the Kenites."

11 David did not let a man or woman
live to be brought to Gath, for

[A]27:8 Alt Hb tradition reads *Gezerites* [B]27:10 Some Hb mss, Syr, Tg; LXX, Vg, DSS read *Against whom did you raid today?*

CHARACTER PROFILE

The Medium of En-dor An Accomplice to Disobedience

Her Background	• She was a "medium" in the city of En-dor in Israel (28:7). • Saul had banned all spiritists from the land, but she remained (28:3).
Her Story	• She was sought out by Saul, who was desperate to hear a word from the Lord (28:6,15). • Saul came to her in disguise and asked her to call up Samuel, which she did after being assured of her personal safety (28:8). • She was frightened at Samuel's appearance and recognized Saul (28:12). • She offered food to Saul and his men (28:22).
Life Lessons	• Witchcraft is forbidden by God. • Spiritual needs are met fully through Christ.

he said, "Or they will inform on us
and say, 'This is what David did.'"
This was David's custom during the
whole time he stayed in the Philistine territory. 12 So Achish trusted
David, thinking, "Since he has made
himself detestable to his people Israel, he will be my servant forever."

Saul and the Medium (28:1-25)

28 At that time, the Philistines
brought their military units
together into one army to fight
against Israel. So Achish said to David, "You know, of course, that you
and your men must march out in
the army[A] with me."
2 David replied to Achish, "Good,
you will find out what your servant
can do."
So Achish said to David, "Very
well, I will appoint you as my permanent bodyguard."
3 By this time Samuel had died,
and all Israel had mourned for
him and buried him in Ramah, his
city, and Saul had removed the mediums and spiritists from the land.
4 The Philistines came together and
camped at Shunem. So Saul gathered
all Israel, and they camped at Gilboa.
5 When Saul saw the Philistine camp,
he was afraid and trembled violently.
6 He inquired of the LORD, but the
LORD did not answer him in dreams
or by the •Urim or by the prophets.
7 Saul then said to his servants, "Find
me a woman who is a medium, so I
can go and consult her."
His servants replied, "There is a
woman at En-dor who is a medium."
8 Saul disguised himself by putting on different clothes and set out
with two of his men. They came to
the woman at night, and Saul said,
"Consult a spirit for me. Bring up
for me the one I tell you."
9 But the woman said to him, "You
surely know what Saul has done,
how he has killed the mediums
and spiritists in the land. Why are
you setting a trap for me to get me
killed?"
10 Then Saul swore to her by the

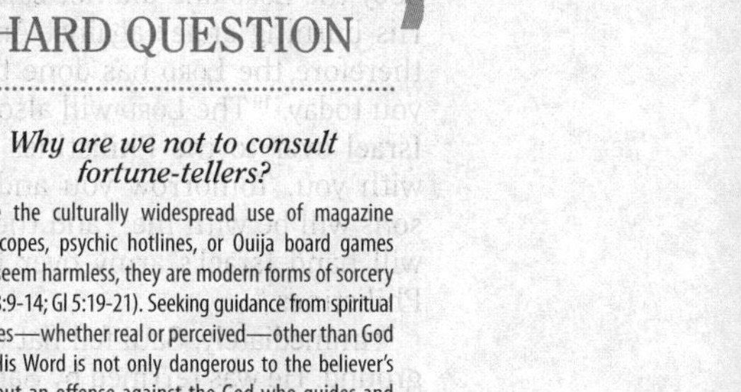

HARD QUESTION

Why are we not to consult fortune-tellers?

While the culturally widespread use of magazine horoscopes, psychic hotlines, or Ouija board games may seem harmless, they are modern forms of sorcery (Dt 18:9-14; Gl 5:19-21). Seeking guidance from spiritual sources—whether real or perceived—other than God and His Word is not only dangerous to the believer's soul but an offense against the God who guides and provides for His children (1Sm 28:3, 7-20; Ps 31:3; 32:8; Jn 16:13). The Father wants you to rely on His leading for direction in life-decisions and to trust in His goodness and sovereign care over all aspects of your future.

28:1-2 David, an exile in Philistine territory, remained faithful to the Lord and fought those who stood against Israel, while Saul—living within Israel—continued to demonstrate his disloyalty to the nation and to the Lord.

28:3-11 Saul reached his spiritual low. His attention turned from seeking advice on matters from the Lord to taking the counsel of men, and finally, even from a **medium**. Overcome with his circumstances and disregarding the reason for the Lord's silence (i.e., his own rebellious and disobedient heart), Saul did not wait for an answer from the Lord. He was conscious of his wrongdoing, disguising himself and traveling at night to find a medium who could help him consult the late prophet Samuel for advice (v. 8). This medium lived in the Canaanite city **En-dor**, located in the northwest portion of Israel. She practiced divination, a ritual strictly prohibited (Dt 18:9-13) and consulted the dead on behalf of the living.

[A] **28:1** DSS, LXX read *battle*

28:12-25 The text states that Saul asked the medium to **bring up Samuel** (v. 11), but it is careful never to say that *she* brought up Samuel. Quite the contrary seems to be true, based on her reaction of actually seeing an apparition. Apparently, God allowed Samuel's spirit to be seen in some form for the purpose of delivering a final word to the evil king who had once served Him. The message Saul received from Samuel only confirmed what he had been told previously about the punishment that would befall him because of his disobedience. Rather than receiving a word of exhortation, Saul received a word of judgment from the prophet (vv. 16-19). Samuel identified the source of Saul's problem and the reason for his inability to hear God's voice—his failure to obey the commands of the Lord.

LORD: "As surely as the LORD lives,
nothing bad will happen to you because of this."
11 "Who is it that you want me to
bring up for you?" the woman asked.
"Bring up Samuel for me," he answered.
12 When the woman saw Samuel,
she screamed, and then she asked
Saul, "Why did you deceive me? You
are Saul!"
13 But the king said to her, "Don't
be afraid. What do you see?"
"I see a spirit form[A] coming up out
of the earth," the woman answered.
14 Then Saul asked her, "What does
he look like?"
"An old man is coming up," she
replied. "He's wearing a robe." Then
Saul knew that it was Samuel, and
he bowed his face to the ground and
paid homage.
15 "Why have you disturbed me
by bringing me up?" Samuel asked
Saul.
"I'm in serious trouble," replied
Saul. "The Philistines are fighting
against me and God has turned away
from me. He doesn't answer me anymore, either through the prophets
or in dreams. So I've called on you
to tell me what I should do."
16 Samuel answered, "Since the
LORD has turned away from you
and has become your enemy, why
are you asking me? 17 The LORD has
done[B] exactly what He said through
me: The LORD has torn the kingship
out of your hand and given it to
your neighbor David. 18 You did not
obey the LORD and did not carry out
His burning anger against Amalek;
therefore the LORD has done this to
you today. 19 The LORD will also hand
Israel over to the Philistines along
with you. Tomorrow you and your
sons will be with me,[C] and the LORD
will hand Israel's army over to the
Philistines."
20 Immediately, Saul fell flat on the
ground. He was terrified by Samuel's
words and was also weak because he
hadn't had any food all day and all
night. 21 The woman came over to
Saul, and she saw that he was terrified and said to him, "Look, your servant has obeyed you. I took my life in
my hands and did what you told me
to do. 22 Now please listen to your servant. Let me set some food in front of
you. Eat and it will give you strength
so you can go on your way."
23 He refused, saying, "I won't eat,"
but when his servants and the woman urged him, he listened to them.
He got up off the ground and sat on
the bed.
24 The woman had a fattened calf at
her house, and she quickly slaughtered it. She also took flour, kneaded
it, and baked unleavened bread.
25 She served it to Saul and his servants, and they ate. Afterward, they
got up and left that night.

David's Rejection by the Philistines (29:1-11)

29 The Philistines brought all
their military units together
at Aphek while Israel was camped
by the spring in Jezreel. 2 As the
Philistine leaders were passing in
review with their units of hundreds
and thousands, David and his men
were passing in review behind them
with Achish. 3 Then the Philistine
commanders asked, "What are these
Hebrews doing here?"
Achish answered the Philistine
commanders, "That is David, servant
of King Saul of Israel. He has been
with me a considerable period of
time.[D] From the day he defected until
today, I've found no fault with him."
4 The Philistine commanders, however, were enraged with Achish and
told him, "Send that man back and
let him return to the place you assigned him. He must not go down
with us into battle only to become
our adversary during the battle.
What better way could he regain his
master's favor than with the heads of
our men? 5 Isn't this the David they
sing about during their dances:

> Saul has killed his thousands,
> but David his tens
> of thousands?"

6 So Achish summoned David and
told him, "As the LORD lives, you are
an honorable man. I think it is good[E]
to have you working[F] with me in the

[A]**28:13** Or *a god*, or *a divine being* [B]**28:17** Some Hb, some LXX mss, Vg read *done to you* [C]**28:19** LXX reads *sons will fall* [D]**29:3** Hb obscure [E]**29:6** Lit *It was good in my eyes* [F]**29:6** Lit *you going out and coming in*

camp, because I have found no fault
in you from the day you came to me
until today. But the leaders don't
think you are reliable. [7] Now go back
quietly and you won't be doing anything the Philistine leaders think is
wrong."
[8] "But what have I done?" David
replied to Achish. "From the first
day I was with you until today, what
have you found against your servant
to keep me from going along to fight
against the enemies of my lord the
king?"
[9] Achish answered David, "I'm convinced that you are as reliable as
the Angel of God. But the Philistine
commanders have said, 'He must
not go into battle with us.' [10] So get
up early in the morning, you and
your masters' servants who came
with you.[A] When you've all gotten
up early, go as soon as it's light."
[11] So David and his men got up early
in the morning to return to the land
of the Philistines. And the Philistines went up to Jezreel.

David's Defeat of the Amalekites (30:1-31)

30 David and his men arrived in
Ziklag on the third day. The
Amalekites had raided the •Negev
and attacked and burned down
Ziklag. [2] They also had kidnapped
the women and everyone[B] in it from
the youngest to the oldest. They had
killed no one but had carried them
off as they went on their way.
[3] When David and his men arrived at the town, they found it
burned down. Their wives, sons,
and daughters had been kidnapped.
[4] David and the troops with him
wept loudly until they had no
strength left to weep. [5] David's two
wives, Ahinoam the Jezreelite and
Abigail the widow of Nabal the Carmelite, had also been kidnapped.
[6] David was in a difficult position
because the troops talked about
stoning him, for they were all very
bitter over the loss of their sons
and daughters. But David found
strength in the LORD his God.
[7] David said to Abiathar the priest,
son of Ahimelech, "Bring me the
•ephod." So Abiathar brought it to
him, [8] and David asked the LORD:
"Should I pursue these raiders? Will
I overtake them?"
The LORD replied to him, "Pursue
them, for you will certainly overtake
them and rescue the people."
[9] David and the 600 men with
him went as far as the •Wadi Besor,
where 200 men who were to remain
behind would stop. [10] They stopped
because they were too exhausted to
cross the Wadi Besor. David and 400
of the men continued in pursuit.
[11] They found an Egyptian in the
open country and brought him to
David. They gave him some bread to
eat and water to drink. [12] Then they
gave him some pressed figs and two
clusters of raisins. After he ate he
revived, for he hadn't eaten food or
drunk water for three days and three
nights.
[13] Then David said to him, "Who
do you belong to? Where are you
from?"
"I'm an Egyptian, the slave of an
Amalekite man," he said. "My master abandoned me when I got sick
three days ago. [14] We raided the
south country of the Cherethites,
the territory of Judah, and the south
country of Caleb, and we burned
down Ziklag."
[15] David then asked him, "Will you
lead me to these raiders?"
He said, "Swear to me by God that
you won't kill me or turn me over
to my master, and I will lead you to
them."
[16] So he led him, and there were
the Amalekites, spread out over the
entire area, eating, drinking, and
celebrating because of the great
amount of plunder they had taken
from the land of the Philistines and
the land of Judah. [17] David slaughtered them from twilight until the
evening of the next day. None of
them escaped, except 400 young
men who got on camels and fled.
[18] David recovered everything the
Amalekites had taken; he also rescued
his two wives. [19] Nothing of theirs was
missing from the youngest to the oldest, including the sons and daughters, of all the plunder the Amalekites
had taken. David got everything back.

29:6-10 Achish referred to the God of Israel twice in his conversation with David, apparently out of respect for David rather than an indication that he rejected the Philistine gods.

[A] **29:10** LXX adds *and go to the place I appointed you to. Don't take this evil matter to heart, for you are good before me.* [B] **30:2** LXX; MT omits *and everyone*

30:23-25 David, in the midst of his success, remained compassionate, humble, and wise and rebuked his warriors for their selfishness, reminding them that it was the Lord who gave them victory and preserved their belongings. David's experience of the Lord's mercy informed the sense of justice God had established in him as a leader over His people. He led by modeling dependence on the Lord and a heart of gratitude.

31:1-13 Saul's final demonstration of his lack of trust and confidence in the Lord is evidenced in his death. The result was tragic for not only Saul and his family but also for the Israelites, who suffered defeat that day (vv. 7-13). Saul's disobedience cost him, his family, and the nation of Israel a great deal. The book ends with the reminder that punishment follows disobedience.

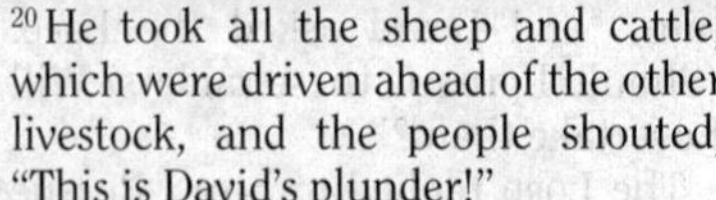

20 He took all the sheep and cattle,
which were driven ahead of the other
livestock, and the people shouted,
"This is David's plunder!"
21 When David came to the 200
men who had been too exhausted to
go with him and had been left at the
Wadi Besor, they came out to meet
him and to meet the troops with
him. When David approached the
men, he greeted them, 22 but all the
corrupt and •worthless men among
those who had gone with David argued, "Because they didn't go with
us, we will not give any of the plunder we recovered to them except for
each man's wife and children. They
may take them and go."
23 But David said, "My brothers,
you must not do this with what the
LORD has given us. He protected us
and handed over to us the raiders
who came against us. 24 Who can
agree to your proposal? The share
of the one who goes into battle is to
be the same as the share of the one
who remains with the supplies. They
will share equally." 25 And it has been
so from that day forward. David established this policy as a law and an
ordinance for Israel and it continues
to this very day.
26 When David came to Ziklag,
he sent some of the plunder to his
friends, the elders of Judah, saying, "Here is a gift for you from the
plunder of the LORD's enemies." 27 He
sent gifts to those in Bethel, in Ramoth of the Negev, and in Jattir; 28 to
those in Aroer, in Siphmoth, and in
Eshtemoa; 29 to those in Racal, in the
towns of the Jerahmeelites, and in
the towns of the Kenites; 30 to those
in Hormah, in Bor-ashan, and in
Athach; 31 to those in Hebron, and to
those in all the places where David
and his men had roamed.

The Death of Saul and His Sons (31:1-13)

31 The Philistines fought against
Israel, and Israel's men fled from
them. Many were killed on Mount
Gilboa. 2 The Philistines overtook
Saul and his sons and killed his sons,
Jonathan, Abinadab, and Malchishua.
3 When the battle intensified against
Saul, the archers caught up with him
and severely wounded him.[A] 4 Then
Saul said to his armor-bearer, "Draw
your sword and run me through
with it, or these uncircumcised men
will come and run me through and
torture me." But his armor-bearer
would not do it because he was terrified. Then Saul took his sword and
fell on it. 5 When his armor-bearer
saw that Saul was dead, he also fell
on his own sword and died with him.
6 So on that day, Saul died together
with his three sons, his armor-bearer,
and all his men.
7 When the men of Israel on the
other side of the valley and on the
other side of the Jordan saw that
Israel's men had run away and that
Saul and his sons were dead, they
abandoned the cities and fled. So the
Philistines came and settled in them.
8 The next day when the Philistines
came to strip the dead, they found
Saul and his three sons dead on
Mount Gilboa. 9 They cut off Saul's
head, stripped off his armor, and
sent messengers throughout the
land of the Philistines to spread the
good news in the temples of their
idols and among the people. 10 Then
they put his armor in the temple of
the •Ashtoreths and hung his body
on the wall of Beth-shan.
11 When the residents of Jabesh-
gilead heard what the Philistines
had done to Saul, 12 all their brave
men set out, journeyed all night,
and retrieved the body of Saul and
the bodies of his sons from the wall
of Beth-shan. When they arrived at
Jabesh, they burned the bodies there.
13 Afterward, they took their bones
and buried them under the tamarisk
tree in Jabesh and fasted seven days.

A **31:3** LXX reads *and he was wounded under the ribs*

---

1 SAMUEL… WRITTEN ON MY *Heart*

As you strive to live a life of eternal significance, may you rest in God's sovereignty over all of your days (Ps 139:16). May you acquire the surrendered worship of Hannah and the skillful wisdom of Abigail. And above all, may you be a woman after God's own heart—zealous for God's glory (1Sm 17:46-47), trusting that He will fulfill His purpose for you (Ps 138:8) and believing that obedience is indeed better than sacrifice (1Sm 15:22).

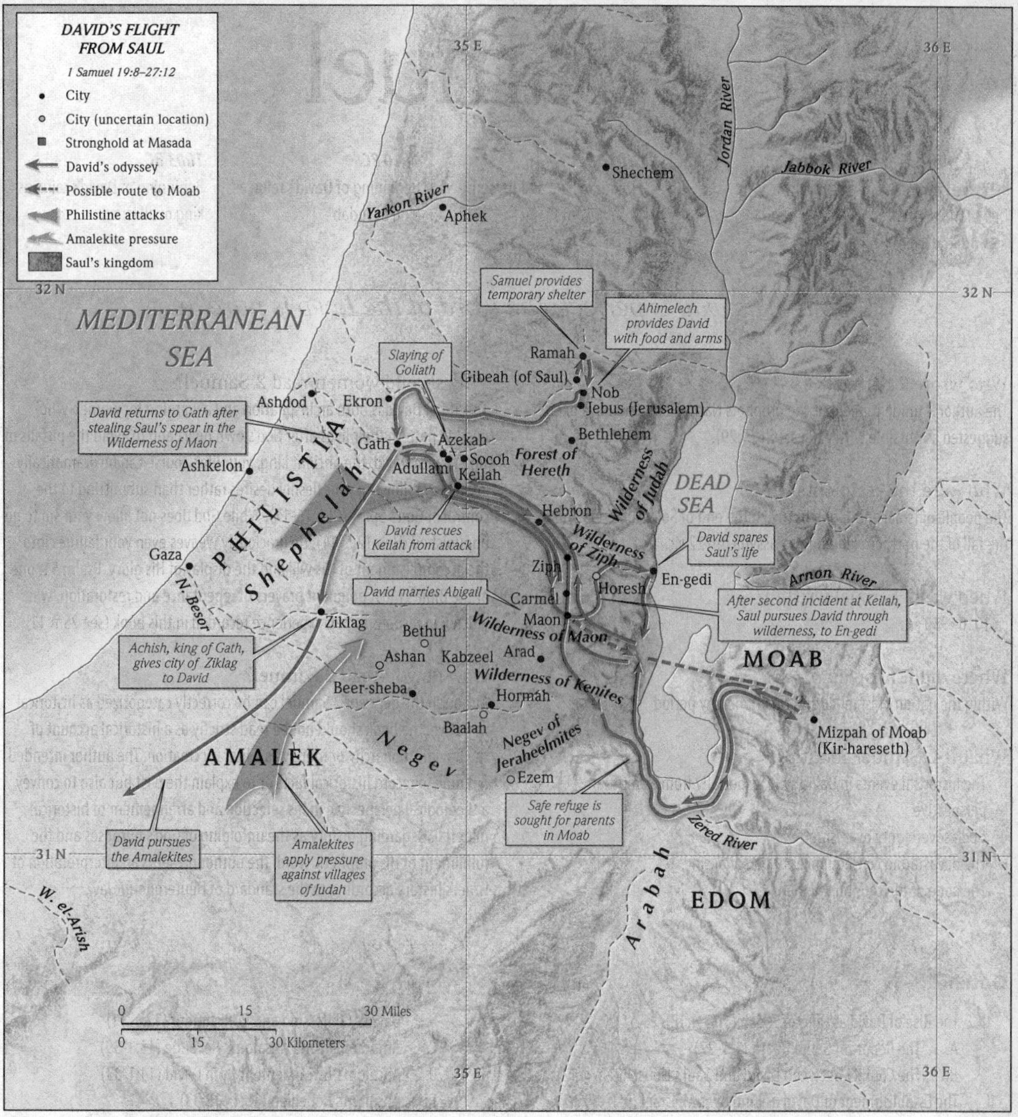

DAVID'S FLIGHT FROM SAUL

1 Samuel 19:8–27:12

- City
- City (uncertain location)
- Stronghold at Masada
- David's odyssey
- Possible route to Moab
- Philistine attacks
- Amalekite pressure
- Saul's kingdom

35 E
36 E
32 N
31 N
MEDITERRANEAN SEA
DEAD SEA
PHILISTIA
Shephelah
AMALEK
Negev
MOAB
EDOM
Arabah
Jordan River
Jabbok River
Yarkon River
Arnon River
Zered River
N. Besor
W. el-Arish
Shechem
Aphek
Ramah
Gibeah (of Saul)
Nob
Jebus (Jerusalem)
Bethlehem
Ashdod
Ekron
Gath
Azekah
Socoh
Adullam
Keilah
Ashkelon
Gaza
Forest of Hereth
Wilderness of Judah
Hebron
Wilderness of Ziph
Ziph
Horesh
En-gedi
Carmel
Maon
Wilderness of Maon
Ziklag
Bethul
Ashan
Kabzeel
Arad
Wilderness of Kenites
Beer-sheba
Hormah
Baalah
Negev of Jeraheelmites
Ezem
Mizpah of Moab (Kir-hareseth)

Samuel provides temporary shelter

Ahimelech provides David with food and arms

Slaying of Goliath

David returns to Gath after stealing Saul's spear in the Wilderness of Maon

David rescues Keilah from attack

David spares Saul's life

David marries Abigail

After second incident at Keilah, Saul pursues David through wilderness, to En-gedi

Achish, king of Gath, gives city of Ziklag to David

Safe refuge is sought for parents in Moab

David pursues the Amalekites

Amalekites apply pressure against villages of Judah

0 15 30 Miles
0 15 30 Kilometers

2 Samuel

Timeline World Events Biblical Events	*1050–970 BC* Life of David	*1010 BC* Death of Saul and his sons	*1010 BC* Beginning of David's reign as king of Judah	*1003 BC* Beginning of David's reign as king of all Israel

"God—His way is perfect; the word of the LORD is pure" (22:31).

Who wrote 2 Samuel?

The author is unidentified, but the prophets Nathan and Gad have been suggested as possible writers (see 1Ch 29:29).

Who were the recipients?

The people of Israel and Judah between the end of Solomon's reign and the fall of the northern kingdom to Assyria in 722 B.C.

When was 2 Samuel written?

ca 1010–930 B.C.

Where did it happen?

Within the nation of Israel during the monarchy period

What is 2 Samuel about?

- The historical events in David's life, especially from a spiritual perspective
- God's sovereignty over Israel
- The devastating consequences of personal sin
- The hope of the coming Messiah

Why should women read 2 Samuel?

The life of David is both an inspiration and a warning for women who need to pattern their lives after God's own heart and to avoid the pitfalls of sin. As with David, the ancient king, your life's course can be dramatically altered by following your fleshly desires rather than submitting to the control of God's Spirit (Gl 5:16-17). While God does not allow your sin to go unpunished (Heb 12:5-11), He graciously weaves even your failures into the accomplishment of His will and the display of His glory. Psalm 51, one of the Bible's most poignant prayers of repentance and restoration, was written in response to an experience recorded in this book (see 2Sm 11).

How do you read 2 Samuel?

Although the genre of 2 Samuel can be correctly categorized as historical narrative, the book should not be read strictly as a historical account of the Davidic monarchy or merely as a literary creation. The author intended not only to record historical facts or to explain the past but also to convey a theological perspective in his selection and arrangement of historical material. Regarding history as the unfolding of God's purposes and the fulfillment of His prophetic word, the author presents an interpretation of Israel's history according to the standard of Deuteronomic law.

Outline

I. The Rise of David as King of Judah (1:1–4:12)
  A. The Report of Saul's Death (1:1-27)
  B. The Conflict Between David and Saul's House (2:1–4:12)
II. The Establishment of David as King over All Israel (5:1–10:19)
  A. The Capital at Jerusalem (5:1-25)
  B. The Return of the Ark of the Covenant to Jerusalem (6:1-23)
  C. The Davidic Covenant (7:1-29)
  D. The Conquests of David (8:1-18)
  E. The Kindness of David to Mephibosheth (9:1-13)
  F. The Victory over Ammon and Syria (10:1-19)
III. The Decline of David's House (11:1–20:26)
  A. David's Sin Against Uriah and Bathsheba (11:1-27)
  B. David's Confession and Punishment (12:1-31)
  C. Amnon's Sin and Absalom's Revenge (13:1-39)
  D. Absalom's Estrangement from David (14:1-33)
  E. Absalom's Rebellion (15:1–18:33)
  F. David's Restoration of Power (19:1-43)
  G. Sheba's Revolt (20:1-26)
IV. The Final Years of David's Reign (21:1–24:25)
  A. The Execution of Saul's Sons (21:1-22)
  B. The Song of David (22:1-51)
  C. The Elite Warriors of David (23:1-39)
  D. The Census of the People and Plague (24:1-25)

1002 BC	1025–960 BC	975BC	970 BC
David's capture of Jerusalem	Life of Bathsheba	Absalom's revolt	Death of David. Solomon becomes king

The Rise of David as King of Judah (1:1–4:12)

The Report of Saul's Death (1:1-27)

1 After the death of Saul, David returned from defeating the Amalekites and stayed at Ziklag two days.
2 On the third day a man with torn
clothes and dust on his head came
from Saul's camp. When he came to
David, he fell to the ground and paid
homage. 3 David asked him, "Where
have you come from?"

He replied to him, "I've escaped
from the Israelite camp."

4 "What was the outcome? Tell
me," David asked him.

"The troops fled from the battle,"
he answered. "Many of the troops
have fallen and are dead. Also, Saul
and his son Jonathan are dead."

5 David asked the young man who
had brought him the report, "How
do you know Saul and his son Jonathan are dead?"

6 "I happened to be on Mount
Gilboa," he replied, "and there was
Saul, leaning on his spear. At that
very moment the chariots and the
cavalry were closing in on him.
7 When he turned around and saw
me, he called out to me, so I answered: I'm at your service. 8 He
asked me, 'Who are you?' I told him:
I'm an Amalekite. 9 Then he begged
me, 'Stand over me and kill me, for
I'm mortally wounded,[A] but my life
still lingers.' 10 So I stood over him
and killed him because I knew that
after he had fallen he couldn't survive. I took the crown that was on
his head and the armband that was
on his arm, and I've brought them
here to my lord."

11 Then David took hold of his
clothes and tore them, and all the
men with him did the same. 12 They
mourned, wept, and fasted until the
evening for those who died by the
sword—for Saul, his son Jonathan,
the LORD's people, and the house of
Israel.

13 David inquired of the young
man who had brought him the report, "Where are you from?"

"I'm the son of a foreigner," he
said. "I'm an Amalekite."

14 David questioned him, "How is it
that you were not afraid to lift your
hand to destroy the LORD's anointed?" 15 Then David summoned one
of his servants and said, "Come here
and kill him!" The servant struck
him, and he died. 16 For David had
said to the Amalekite, "Your blood is
on your own head because your own
mouth testified against you by saying, 'I killed the LORD's anointed.'"

17 David sang the following lament
for Saul and his son Jonathan, 18 and
he ordered that the Judahites be
taught The Song of the Bow. It is
written in the Book of Jashar:[B]

19 The splendor of Israel
lies slain on your heights.
How the mighty have fallen!
20 Do not tell it in Gath,
don't announce it
in the marketplaces
of Ashkelon,
or the daughters
of the Philistines
will rejoice,
and the daughters
of the uncircumcised
will gloat.
21 Mountains of Gilboa,
let no dew or rain be on you,
or fields of offerings,[C]

Title The title "2 Samuel" provides little direct information about the book's contents. The death of the prophet Samuel is recorded in 1Sm 25:1, and the narrative from 1Sm 25:2 to the end of 2 Samuel focuses on David's rise to power and his reign over Israel. Originally, the books known as 1 and 2 Samuel, along with 1 and 2 Kings, were regarded as one undivided literary unit. In the Jewish Bible, these books, along with Joshua and Judges, comprise the "Former Prophets," a subdivision of the "The Prophets" (Hb *Nevi'im*), the second main section in the Hebrew Bible. When the Hebrew Bible was translated into Greek (i.e., the Septuagint or LXX), the Samuel-Kings material was divided into four books called "1–4 Kingdoms," reflecting the unity of these books. The Latin Vulgate followed this tradition, calling the books "1–4 Kings." Several LXX manuscripts even extended 2 Samuel through what is now 1Kg 2:11. The division in modern Bibles between 1 and 2 Samuel was not introduced until the sixteenth-century printing of a standard Hebrew text.

1:1-12 Compared to the account of Saul's death in 1Sm 31, various aspects of the Amalekite's story suggest that he was an opportunist hoping that David would reward him for obeying Saul's command and sparing Israel's king from dishonor at the hand of the Philistines.

1:13-16 David did not question the man's account of the events surrounding Saul's death but rather rebuked his foolishness in destroying **the LORD's anointed**, for which he was judged according to his own account and executed.

[A] **1:9** LXX reads *for terrible darkness has taken hold of me* [B] **1:18** Or *of the Upright* [C] **1:21** LXX reads *firstfruits*

1:26 David regarded Jonathan as a brother and praised him for his love that **was more wonderful** [Hb *pala'*, "distinguished, remarkable, extraordinary, marvelous"] **than the love of women** (v. 26). This does not describe an inappropriate, immoral relationship between David and Jonathan. Rather, its testimony is to the love between two friends who became as close as brothers in their loyalty to and friendship with one another. The selfless love between these two men serves as a model of sacrificial giving between committed friends.

2:1-15 After being anointed by Samuel as the future king, David waited more than 15 years before assuming the responsibilities as ruler. His first recorded action as king was to reward **the men of Jabesh-gilead** who honored Saul by burying him. David ruled over the house of Judah for seven and one-half years before making Jerusalem his capital (vv. 10-11).

for there the shield
of the mighty was defiled—
the shield of Saul, no longer
anointed with oil.
22 Jonathan's bow
never retreated,
Saul's sword never returned
unstained,[A]
from the blood of the slain,
from the bodies of the mighty.
23 Saul and Jonathan,
loved and delightful,
they were not parted in life
or in death.
They were swifter than eagles,
stronger than lions.
24 Daughters of Israel,
weep for Saul,
who clothed you in scarlet,
with luxurious things,
who decked your garments
with gold ornaments.
25 How the mighty have fallen
in the thick of battle!
Jonathan lies slain
on your heights.
26 I grieve for you, Jonathan,
my brother.
You were such a friend to me.
Your love for me was
more wonderful
than the love of women.
27 How the mighty have fallen
and the weapons of war
have perished!

The Conflict Between David and Saul's House (2:1–4:12)

2 Some time later, David inquired
of the LORD: "Should I go to one
of the towns of Judah?"
The LORD answered him, "Go."
Then David asked, "Where should
I go?"
"To Hebron," the LORD replied.
2 So David went there with his two
wives, Ahinoam the Jezreelite and
Abigail, the widow of Nabal the Carmelite. 3 In addition, David brought
the men who were with him, each
one with his household, and they
settled in the towns near Hebron.
4 Then the men of Judah came, and
there they anointed David king over
the house of Judah. They told David:
"It was the men of Jabesh-gilead
who buried Saul."
5 David sent messengers to the
men of Jabesh-gilead and said to
them, "The LORD bless you, because
you have shown this kindness to
Saul your lord when you buried
him. 6 Now, may the LORD show
kindness and faithfulness to you,
and I will also show the same goodness to you because you have done
this deed. 7 Therefore, be strong and
courageous, for though Saul your
lord is dead, the house of Judah has
anointed me king over them."
8 Abner son of Ner, commander
of Saul's army, took Saul's son Ish-
bosheth[B,C] and moved him to Mahanaim. 9 He made him king over
Gilead, Asher, Jezreel, Ephraim,
Benjamin—over all Israel. 10 Saul's
son Ish-bosheth was 40 years old
when he began his reign over Israel;
he ruled for two years. The house
of Judah, however, followed David.
11 The length of time that David was
king in Hebron over the house of Judah was seven years and six months.
12 Abner son of Ner and soldiers
of Ish-bosheth son of Saul marched
out from Mahanaim to Gibeon. 13 So
Joab son of Zeruiah and David's soldiers marched out and met them by
the pool of Gibeon. The two groups
took up positions on opposite sides
of the pool.
14 Then Abner said to Joab, "Let's
have the young men get up and
compete in front of us."
"Let them get up," Joab replied.
15 So they got up and were counted off—12 for Benjamin and Ish-
bosheth son of Saul, and 12 from
David's soldiers. 16 Then each man
grabbed his opponent by the head
and thrust his sword into his opponent's side so that they all died
together. So this place, which is in
Gibeon, is named Field of Blades.[D]
17 The battle that day was extremely fierce, and Abner and the men of
Israel were defeated by David's soldiers. 18 The three sons of Zeruiah
were there: Joab, Abishai, and Asahel. Asahel was a fast runner, like
one of the wild gazelles. 19 He chased
Abner and did not turn to the right
or the left in his pursuit of him.

[A]**1:22** Lit *empty* [B]**2:8** Some LXX mss read *Ishbaal*; 1Ch 8:33; 9:39 [C]**2:8** = Man of Shame
[D]**2:16** Or *Helkath-hazzurim*

20 Abner glanced back and said, "Is
that you, Asahel?"
"Yes it is," Asahel replied.
21 Abner said to him, "Turn to your
right or left, seize one of the young
soldiers, and take whatever you can
get from him." But Asahel would
not stop chasing him. 22 Once again,
Abner warned Asahel, "Stop chasing
me. Why should I strike you to the
ground? How could I ever look your
brother Joab in the face?"
23 But Asahel refused to turn away,
so Abner hit him in the stomach
with the end of his spear. The spear
went through his body, and he fell
and died right there. When all who
came to the place where Asahel had
fallen and died, they stopped, 24 but
Joab and Abishai pursued Abner. By
sunset, they had gone as far as the
hill of Ammah, which is opposite
Giah on the way to the wilderness of
Gibeon.
25 The Benjaminites rallied to Abner; they formed a single unit and
took their stand on top of a hill.
26 Then Abner called out to Joab:
"Must the sword devour forever?
Don't you realize this will only end
in bitterness? How long before you
tell the troops to stop pursuing their
brothers?"
27 "As God lives," Joab replied, "if
you had not spoken up, the troops
wouldn't have stopped pursuing their
brothers until morning." 28 Then
Joab blew the ram's horn, and all
the troops stopped; they no longer
pursued Israel or continued to fight.
29 So Abner and his men marched
through the •Arabah all that night.
They crossed the Jordan, marched all
morning,[A] and arrived at Mahanaim.
30 When Joab had turned back
from pursuing Abner, he gathered
all the troops. In addition to Asahel,
19 of David's soldiers were missing, 31 but they had killed 360 of
the Benjaminites and Abner's men.
32 Afterward, they carried Asahel
to his father's tomb in Bethlehem
and buried him. Then Joab and his
men marched all night and reached
Hebron at dawn.

3 The war between the house of
Saul and the house of David was
long and drawn out, with David
growing stronger and the house of
Saul becoming weaker.
2 Sons were born to David in Hebron:

his firstborn was Amnon,
by Ahinoam the Jezreelite;
3 his second was Chileab,
by Abigail, the widow of Nabal
the Carmelite;
the third was Absalom,
son of Maacah the daughter
of King Talmai of Geshur;
4 the fourth was Adonijah,
son of Haggith;
the fifth was Shephatiah,
son of Abital;
5 the sixth was Ithream,
by David's wife Eglah.

These were born to David in Hebron.
6 During the war between the
house of Saul and the house of
David, Abner kept acquiring more
power in the house of Saul. 7 Now
Saul had a concubine whose name
was Rizpah daughter of Aiah, and
Ish-bosheth questioned Abner, "Why
did you sleep with my father's concubine?"
8 Abner was very angry about Ish-
bosheth's accusation. "Am I a dog's
head[B] who belongs to Judah?" he
asked. "All this time I've been loyal
to the house of your father Saul, to
his brothers, and to his friends and
haven't handed you over to David,
but now you accuse me of wrongdoing with this woman! 9 May God
punish Abner and do so severely if
I don't do for David what the LORD
swore to him: 10 to transfer the kingdom from the house of Saul and
establish the throne of David over
Israel and Judah from Dan to Beer-
sheba." 11 Ish-bosheth could not answer Abner because he was afraid of
him.
12 Abner sent messengers as his
representatives to say to David,
"Whose land is it? Make your covenant with me, and you can be certain I am on your side to hand all
Israel over to you."
13 David replied, "Good, I will
make a covenant with you. However,
there's one thing I require of you:
Do not appear before me unless you

3:1 In the power struggle between the houses of David and Saul, David's house grew in strength while Saul's house became weaker.

3:2-5 While a common cultural practice, polygamy was never God's intent for families (Gn 2:24). God explicitly commanded that kings should not multiply wives for themselves so that their hearts would be turned away from God (Dt 17:17).

3:6-10 In ancient times, a king's harem was passed on to his successor as part of his property and served as a concrete symbol of his power and position. **Ish-bosheth** confronted **Abner** with an accusation of sleeping with **Rizpah**, Saul's **concubine**. This would have been an act of treason on the part of Abner. Abner's response strongly suggests that Ish-bosheth's accusation was false. The Bible nowhere contradicts Abner's response to Ish-bosheth.

3:11-16 David had been involuntarily separated from his first wife **Michal** and now sought to restore her to his family. Some suggest that David's request was motivated purely out of political gain, yet this cannot be clearly known from the text. Whether Michal rejoiced at her reunion with David or grew bitter toward him is unclear.

[A] **2:29** Or *marched through the Bithron* [B] **3:8** = a despised person

3:28-29 David called upon the justice of God on **Joab** and his house for killing Abner. He cursed them both with leprosy, disability, death, and poverty. To curse someone with disease was a serious matter, since such a person would be prohibited from entering the tabernacle to worship (Lv 13:1-46). Early in Solomon's reign, punishment was delivered on Joab (1Kg 2:28-35).

bring Saul's daughter Michal here when you come to see me."
[14] Then David sent messengers to say to Ish-bosheth son of Saul, "Give me back my wife, Michal. I was •engaged to her for the price of 100 Philistine foreskins."
[15] So Ish-bosheth sent someone to take her away from her husband, Paltiel son of Laish. [16] Her husband followed her, weeping all the way to Bahurim. Abner said to him, "Go back." So he went back.
[17] Abner conferred with the elders of Israel: "In the past you wanted David to be king over you. [18] Now take action, because the LORD has spoken concerning David: 'Through My servant David I will save My people Israel from the power of the Philistines and the power of all Israel's enemies.'"
[19] Abner also informed the Benjaminites and went to Hebron to inform David about all that was agreed on by Israel and the whole house of Benjamin. [20] When Abner and 20 men came to David at Hebron, David held a banquet for him and his men.
[21] Abner said to David, "Let me now go and I will gather all Israel to my lord the king. They will make a covenant with you, and you will rule over all you desire." So David dismissed Abner, and he went in peace.
[22] Just then David's soldiers and Joab returned from a raid and brought a large amount of plundered goods with them. Abner was not with David in Hebron because David had dismissed him, and he had gone in peace. [23] When Joab and all his army arrived, Joab was informed, "Abner son of Ner came to see the king, the king dismissed him, and he went in peace."
[24] Joab went to the king and said, "What have you done? Look here, Abner came to you. Why did you dismiss him? Now he's getting away. [25] You know that Abner son of Ner came to deceive you and to find out about your activities and everything you're doing." [26] Then Joab left David and sent messengers after Abner. They brought him back from the well[A] of Sirah, but David was unaware of it. [27] When Abner returned to Hebron, Joab pulled him aside to the middle of the gateway, as if to speak to him privately, and there Joab stabbed him in the stomach. So Abner died in revenge for the death of Asahel,[B] Joab's brother.
[28] David heard about it later and said: "I and my kingdom are forever innocent before the LORD concerning the blood of Abner son of Ner. [29] May it hang over Joab's head and his father's whole house, and may the house of Joab never be without someone who has a discharge or a skin disease, or a man who can only work a spindle,[C] or someone who falls by the sword or starves." [30] Joab and his brother Abishai killed Abner because he had put their brother Asahel to death in the battle at Gibeon.
[31] David then ordered Joab and all the people who were with him, "Tear your clothes, put on •sackcloth, and mourn over Abner." And King David walked behind the funeral procession.[D]
[32] When they buried Abner in Hebron, the king wept aloud at Abner's tomb. All the people wept, [33] and the king sang a lament for Abner:

Should Abner die as a fool
dies?
[34] Your hands were not bound,
your feet not placed
in bronze shackles.
You fell like one who falls
victim to criminals.

And all the people wept over him even more.
[35] Then they came to urge David to eat bread while it was still day, but David took an oath: "May God punish me and do so severely if I taste bread or anything else before sunset!" [36] All the people took note of this, and it pleased them. In fact, everything the king did pleased them. [37] On that day all the troops and all Israel were convinced that the king had no part in the killing of Abner son of Ner.
[38] Then the king said to his soldiers, "You must know that a great

[A]**3:26** Or *cistern* [B]**3:27** Lit *And he died for the blood of Asahel* [C]**3:29** LXX reads *who uses a crutch* [D]**3:31** Or *the bier*; lit *the bed*

leader has fallen in Israel today.
39 As for me, even though I am the
anointed king, I have little power today. These men, the sons of Zeruiah,
are too fierce for me. May the LORD
repay the evildoer according to his
evil!"

4 When Saul's son Ish-bosheth
heard that Abner had died in Hebron, his courage failed, and all Israel was dismayed. 2 Saul's son had
two men who were leaders of raiding parties: one named Baanah and
the other Rechab, sons of Rimmon
the Beerothite of the Benjaminites.
Beeroth is also considered part of
Benjamin, 3 and the Beerothites fled
to Gittaim and still live there as foreigners to this very day.
4 Saul's son Jonathan had a son
whose feet were crippled. He was
five years old when the report about
Saul and Jonathan came from Jezreel. The one who had nursed him[A]
picked him up and fled, but as she
was hurrying to flee, he fell and
became lame. His name was Mephibosheth.
5 Rechab and Baanah, the sons of
Rimmon the Beerothite, set out and
arrived at Ish-bosheth's house during the heat of the day while the
king was taking his midday nap.
6 They entered the interior of the
house as if to get wheat and stabbed
him in the stomach. Then Rechab
and his brother Baanah escaped.
7 They had entered the house while
Ish-bosheth was lying on his bed in
his bedroom and stabbed and killed
him. Then they beheaded him, took
his head, and traveled by way of the
•Arabah all night. 8 They brought
Ish-bosheth's head to David at Hebron and said to the king, "Here's
the head of Ish-bosheth son of Saul,
your enemy who intended to take
your life. Today the LORD has granted vengeance to my lord the king
against Saul and his offspring."
9 But David answered Rechab and
his brother Baanah, sons of Rimmon the Beerothite, "As the LORD
lives, the One who has redeemed
my life from every distress, 10 when
the person told me, 'Look, Saul is
dead,' he thought he was a bearer of
good news, but I seized him and put
him to death at Ziklag. That was my
reward to him for his news! 11 How
much more when wicked men kill a
righteous man in his own house on
his own bed! So now, should I not
require his blood from your hands
and wipe you off the earth?"
12 So David gave orders to the
young men, and they killed Rechab and Baanah. They cut off their
hands and feet and hung their bodies by the pool in Hebron, but they
took Ish-bosheth's head and buried
it in Abner's tomb in Hebron.

The Establishment of David as King over All Israel (5:1–10:19)

The Capital at Jerusalem (5:1-25)

5 All the tribes of Israel came to
David at Hebron and said, "Here
we are, your own flesh and blood.[B]
2 Even while Saul was king over us,
you were the one who led us out
to battle and brought us back. The
LORD also said to you, 'You will shepherd My people Israel and be ruler
over Israel.'"
3 So all the elders of Israel came
to the king at Hebron. King David
made a covenant with them at Hebron in the LORD's presence, and
they anointed David king over Israel.
4 David was 30 years old when he
began his reign; he reigned 40 years.
5 In Hebron he reigned over Judah
seven years and six months, and in
Jerusalem he reigned 33 years over
all Israel and Judah.
6 The king and his men marched to
Jerusalem against the Jebusites who
inhabited the land. The Jebusites
had said to David: "You will never
get in here. Even the blind and lame
can repel you"; thinking, "David
can't get in here."
7 Yet David did capture the stronghold of •Zion, that is, the city of
David. 8 He said that day, "Whoever attacks the Jebusites must go
through the water shaft to reach the
lame and the blind who are despised
by David."[C] For this reason it is said,
"The blind and the lame will never
enter the house."[D]

4:1-12 The narrator demonstrates yet again that David did not take the throne of Israel by force or tolerate brutality that was allegedly done in the Lord's name. David recognized that the Lord protected him from danger and that He alone would establish David's throne (v. 9).

5:6-10 Jerusalem was a strategic capital since it was located on the border between the northern tribes and Judah. Jerusalem still serves as the capital of the nation of Israel even to this day. David took the stronghold at Zion, the southern mountain of Jerusalem. Later, it became known as **the city of David**, a designation still recognized in modern-day Israel.

[A]4:4 Lit *His nurse* [B]5:1 Lit *your bone and flesh* [C]5:8 Alt Hb tradition, LXX, Tg, Syr read *who despise David* [D]5:8 Or *temple*, or *palace*

5:11-16 David recognized that his strength came from the Lord and that his success went beyond his own accomplishments and pointed instead to the Lord's purposes for His people (v. 12). However, he continued to acquire a large harem, taking **more concubines and wives** while he resided in Jerusalem (vv. 13-16).

5:17-25 The defeat of **the Philistines** was so great that they ceased to be a serious threat to Israel.

6:1-2 With Jerusalem the political capital, David moved to retrieve the **ark** of the covenant, establishing the city as the nation's spiritual center.

6:3-13 The **ark** represented the holiness of God and was to be treated with special care in reverence for His presence. In the midst of their jubilation, David and the people did not carry out these requirements as instructed (vv. 3-8). Rather than carrying the ark on poles as the law commanded (Ex 25:12-14), they placed it on a **cart** pulled by **oxen** and guided by **Uzzah and Ahio** (2Sm 6:4). When Uzzah attempted to steady the ark **because the oxen had stumbled**, he was killed immediately by the Lord (v. 7). He seemed sincere in his desire to protect the ark, but tragically he was sincerely wrong in disobeying God's command, which showed his disregard for the holiness of God.

9 David took up residence in the
stronghold, which he named the city
of David. He built it up all the way
around from the supporting terraces inward. 10 David became more
and more powerful, and the LORD
God of •Hosts was with him. 11 King
Hiram of Tyre sent envoys to David;
he also sent cedar logs, carpenters,
and stonemasons, and they built a
palace for David. 12 Then David knew
that the LORD had established him as
king over Israel and had exalted his
kingdom for the sake of His people
Israel.

13 After he arrived from Hebron, David took more concubines and wives
from Jerusalem, and more sons and
daughters were born to him. 14 These
are the names of those born to him
in Jerusalem: Shammua, Shobab,
Nathan, Solomon, 15 Ibhar, Elishua,
Nepheg, Japhia, 16 Elishama, Eliada,
and Eliphelet.

17 When the Philistines heard that
David had been anointed king over
Israel, they all went in search of David, but he heard about it and went
down to the stronghold. 18 So the
Philistines came and spread out in
the Valley of Rephaim.

19 Then David inquired of the LORD:
"Should I go to war against the Philistines? Will you hand them over to
me?"

The LORD replied to David, "Go, for
I will certainly hand the Philistines
over to you."

20 So David went to Baal-perazim
and defeated them there and said,
"Like a bursting flood, the LORD has
burst out against my enemies before
me." Therefore, he named that place
the Lord Bursts Out.[A] 21 The Philistines abandoned their idols there,
and David and his men carried them
off.

22 The Philistines came up again
and spread out in the Valley of
Rephaim. 23 So David inquired of the
LORD, and He answered, "Do not
make a frontal assault. Circle around
behind them and attack them opposite the balsam trees. 24 When you
hear the sound of marching in the
tops of the balsam trees, act decisively, for then the LORD will have
marched out ahead of you to attack
the camp of the Philistines." 25 So
David did exactly as the LORD commanded him, and he struck down
the Philistines all the way from Geba
to Gezer.

The Return of the Ark of the Covenant to Jerusalem (6:1-23)

6 David again assembled all the
choice men in Israel, 30,000. 2 He
and all his troops set out to bring the
ark of God from Baale-judah.[B] The
ark is called by the Name, the name
of •Yahweh of •Hosts who dwells between the •cherubim. 3 They set the
ark of God on a new cart and transported it from Abinadab's house,
which was on the hill. Uzzah and
Ahio,[C] sons of Abinadab, were guiding the cart 4 and brought it with the
ark of God from Abinadab's house
on the hill. Ahio walked in front of
the ark. 5 David and the whole house
of Israel were celebrating before
the LORD with all kinds of fir wood
instruments,[D] lyres, harps, tambourines, sistrums,[E] and cymbals.

6 When they came to Nacon's
threshing floor, Uzzah reached out
to the ark of God and took hold of
it because the oxen had stumbled.
7 Then the LORD's anger burned
against Uzzah, and God struck him
dead on the spot for his irreverence,
and he died there next to the ark of
God. 8 David was angry because of
the LORD's outburst against Uzzah,
so he named that place an Outburst
Against Uzzah,[F] as it is today. 9 David
feared the LORD that day and said,
"How can the ark of the LORD ever
come to me?" 10 So he was not willing to move the ark of the LORD to
the city of David; instead, he took it
to the house of Obed-edom the Gittite. 11 The ark of the LORD remained
in his house three months, and the
LORD blessed Obed-edom and his
whole family.

12 It was reported to King David:
"The LORD has blessed Obed-edom's
family and all that belongs to him
because of the ark of God." So David
went and had the ark of God brought
up from Obed-edom's house to the

[A] **5:20** Or *Baal-perazim*; 2Sm 6:8; 1Ch 13:11 [B] **6:2** = Kiriath-jearim in 1Sm 7:1; 1Ch 13:6; 2Ch 1:4 [C] **6:3** Or *and his brothers* [D] **6:5** DSS, LXX read *with tuned instruments with strength, with songs*; 1Ch 13:8 [E] **6:5** = an Egyptian percussion instrument [F] **6:8** Or *Perez-uzzah*; 2Sm 5:20

>WORD|*study*

The content of chapter 7 is built on the meaning of the word house (Hb *bayit*), which is used 15 times in the chapter. The word palace (Hb *bayit*, vv. 1-2; cp. 5:11) is determined by context, i.e., the particular "house" in which a king dwells (cp. "house," Jdg 11:31). The same word can also refer to:

- a "household" in the sense of a single family unit (including servants)—everyone under the leadership and protection of a family head or patriarch (e.g., 2Sm 6:20; Gn 17:23);
- a larger family grouping such as a clan or tribe (e.g., 2Sm 2:10-11; Ex 1:1-5);
- a royal dynasty (e.g., 2Sm 7:11; 1Kg 12:26; 21:22);
- everyone descended from a named ancestor (e.g., 2Sm 6:5; Ex 40:38); and
- a temple, figuratively God's "house" (e.g., 2Sm 7:5).

city of David with rejoicing. 13 When
those carrying the ark of the LORD
advanced six steps, he sacrificed an
ox and a fattened calf. 14 David was
dancing[A] with all his might before
the LORD wearing a linen •ephod.
15 He and the whole house of Israel
were bringing up the ark of the LORD
with shouts and the sound of the
ram's horn. 16 As the ark of the LORD
was entering the city of David, Saul's
daughter Michal looked down from
the window and saw King David
leaping and dancing before the LORD,
and she despised him in her heart.
17 They brought the ark of the LORD
and set it in its place inside the tent
David had set up for it. Then David
offered •burnt offerings and •fellow-
ship offerings in the LORD's presence. 18 When David had finished
offering the burnt offering and the
fellowship offerings, he blessed the
people in the name of Yahweh of
Hosts. 19 Then he distributed a loaf of
bread, a date cake, and a raisin cake
to each one in the entire Israelite
community, both men and women.
Then all the people left, each to his
own home.
20 When David returned home to
bless his household, Saul's daughter
Michal came out to meet him. "How
the king of Israel honored himself
today!" she said. "He exposed himself today in the sight of the slave
girls of his subjects like a vulgar
person would expose himself."
21 David replied to Michal, "I was
dancing[B] before the LORD who chose
me over your father and his whole
family to appoint me ruler over the
LORD's people Israel. I will celebrate
before the LORD, 22 and I will humble
myself even more and humiliate myself.[C,D] I will be honored by the slave
girls you spoke about." 23 And Saul's
daughter Michal had no child to the
day of her death.

The Davidic Covenant (7:1-29)

7 When the king had settled into
his palace and the LORD had given
him rest on every side from all his
enemies, 2 the king said to Nathan
the prophet, "Look, I am living in a
cedar house while the ark of God sits
inside tent curtains."
3 So Nathan told the king, "Go and
do all that is on your heart, for the
LORD is with you."
4 But that night the word of the
LORD came to Nathan: 5 "Go to My
servant David and say, 'This is what
the LORD says: Are you to build a
house for Me to live in? 6 From the
time I brought the Israelites out of
Egypt until today I have not lived in
a house; instead, I have been moving around with a tent as My dwelling. 7 In all My journeys with all the
Israelites, have I ever asked anyone
among the tribes of Israel, whom I
commanded to shepherd My people
Israel: Why haven't you built Me a
house of cedar?'
8 "Now this is what you are to say
to My servant David: 'This is what
the LORD of •Hosts says: I took you
from the pasture and from following the sheep to be ruler over My
people Israel. 9 I have been with you
wherever you have gone, and I have
destroyed all your enemies before
you. I will make a name for you like
that of the greatest in the land. 10 I
will establish a place for My people
Israel and plant them, so that they

6:16-23 Michal was more concerned with royal dignity than with spiritual authenticity and was embarrassed by David's behavior. Perhaps because her reaction reflected more the heart of her father, Saul, than of her husband, the narrator refers to her in this passage as **Saul's daughter.** She accused David of improperly displaying himself in front of the crowds, even suggesting he had exhibited lewd behavior. Michal's words of hatred, jealousy, and preoccupation with others' opinions echoed Saul's attitudes. Michal, in turn, was humbled by the Lord, for she **had no child to the day of her death,** which for women at this time was considered a curse (v. 23). David's heart, however, is revealed in his motivation for worshiping and glorifying the Lord (v. 21).

7:1-17 The extremely important Davidic covenant is established with David's descendants and ultimately fulfilled in the person and kingdom of Jesus the Messiah (Mt 11:28-29; Heb 4:8-11).

[A] **6:14** Or *whirling* [B] **6:21** LXX; MT omits *I was dancing* [C] **6:22** LXX reads *more and I will be humble in your eyes* [D] **6:22** Lit *more and I will be humble in my own eyes*

7:12-13 David wanted to build for God a temple worthy of housing the ark. But while David played a key role in preparing for the temple's construction, God had not given David the task of building it.

7:18-23 David's recognition of his unworthiness to receive the grace that God lavished upon him typifies the humility and thanksgiving believers should continually express. David perceived and concluded that God's promise to him was ultimately for the glory of God and His eternal kingdom (v. 21).

THE DAVIDIC COVENANT

The passage 7:1-17 is a significant section binding the prophetic material in the Torah (Dt 12:10-11), the Davidic covenant established here, and the fulfillment of God's promise to David in the reign of his son Solomon (1Kg 5:4; 1Ch 22:9), and ultimately in the person and kingdom of Jesus the Messiah. God promised that by His own will and power, He would:

- **raise up** (Hb *qum*, "cause to stand or come forth") David's own **descendant** (Hb *zera'*, "seed, offspring") to assume the throne;
- **establish** (Hb *kun*, "firmly set up, constitute, confirm") both **his kingdom** (Hb *mamlakah*, "dominion," v. 12) and **the throne of his kingdom**—i.e., both a nation to rule and the power to exercise uncontested sovereignty in his realm; and
- **be a father to him**, including a commitment to **discipline** [Hb *yakach*, "correct, reprove, chasten," v. 14] **him** as a father trains his son to live according to the father's standards and uphold the family name, but foreshadowing Solomon's unfaithfulness;

In addition, the Lord assured David that his successor would not end up like Saul (v. 15; 1Sm 16:14-23) and promised to **establish** (Hb *kun*, "set upright, erect," as on a throne, vv. 13,16) eternally David's **throne** (vv. 13,16), **house**, and **kingdom** (v. 16).

This covenant was a central pillar in the hope of the Israelites throughout the rest of their history. When all seemed lost—the failure of the monarchy and the loss of the land—they clung to this promise of God that a son of David would again ascend the throne and reign forever. Jesus Christ, "the Son of David, Son of Abraham" (Mt 1:1) indeed fulfilled all of these promises (cp. Ps 89:3-4,26-37; Is 9:6-7; 11:1-10; Jr 33:15; Ezk 34:23-24; Mt 1:1-17; Lk 3:31). When Jesus took the form of a man, God made humanity His dwelling place (Php 2:5-8). Since Jesus removed the barrier of sin on our behalf, God is our Father (Rm 8:14-17; 1Jn 3:1). And because Jesus is the rightful and resurrected Lord, His kingdom and His throne are forever and ever (Lk 1:31-33; Jn 1:1-2; Heb 1:8; Rv 11:15).

may live there and not be disturbed again. Evildoers will not afflict them as they have done [11] ever since the day I ordered judges to be over My people Israel. I will give you rest from all your enemies.

"'The LORD declares to you: The LORD Himself will make a house for you. [12] When your time comes and you rest with your fathers, I will raise up after you your descendant, who will come from your body, and I will establish his kingdom. [13] He will build a house for My name, and I will establish the throne of his kingdom forever. [14] I will be a father to him, and he will be a son to Me. When he does wrong, I will discipline him with a human rod and with blows from others. [15] But My faithful love will never leave him as I removed it from Saul; I removed him from your way. [16] Your house and kingdom will endure before Me[A] forever, and your throne will be established forever.'"

[17] Nathan spoke all these words and this entire vision to David.

[18] Then King David went in, sat in the LORD's presence, and said,

Who am I, Lord GOD, and what is my house that You have brought me this far? [19] What You have done so far[B] was a little thing to You, Lord GOD, for You have also spoken about Your servant's house in the distant future. And this is a revelation[C] for mankind, Lord GOD. [20] What more can David say to You? You know Your servant, Lord GOD. [21] Because of Your word and according to Your will, You have revealed all these great things to Your servant.

[22] This is why You are great, Lord GOD. There is no one like You, and there is no God besides You, as all we have heard confirms. [23] And who is like Your people Israel? God came to one nation on earth in order to redeem a people for Himself, to make a name for Himself, and to perform for them[D] great and awesome acts, driving out nations and their gods before Your people You redeemed for Yourself from Egypt. [24] You established Your people Israel to be Your own people forever, and You, LORD, have become their God.

[25] Now, LORD God, fulfill the promise forever that You have made to Your servant and his house. Do as You have promised, [26] so that Your name will be exalted forever, when it is said, "The LORD of Hosts is

[A] **7:16** Some Hb mss, LXX, Syr; other Hb mss read *you* [B] **7:19** Lit *Yet this* [C] **7:19** Or *custom*, or *instruction* [D] **7:23** Some Hb mss, Tg, Vg, Syr; other Hb mss read *you*

God over Israel." The house of Your servant David will be established before You 27 since You, LORD of Hosts, God of Israel, have revealed this to Your servant when You said, "I will build a house for you." Therefore, Your servant has found the courage to pray this prayer to You. 28 Lord GOD, You are God; Your words are true, and You have promised this grace to Your servant. 29 Now, please bless Your servant's house so that it will continue before You forever. For You, Lord GOD, have spoken, and with Your blessing Your servant's house will be blessed forever.

The Conquests of David (8:1-18)

8 After this, David defeated the Philistines, subdued them, and took Metheg-ammah[A] from Philistine control.[B] 2 He also defeated the Moabites, and after making them lie down on the ground, he measured them off with a cord. He measured every two cord lengths of those to be put to death and one length of those to be kept alive. So the Moabites became David's subjects and brought tribute.

3 David also defeated Hadadezer son of Rehob, king of Zobah, who went to restore his control at the Euphrates River. 4 David captured 1,700 horsemen[C] and 20,000 foot soldiers from him, and he hamstrung all the horses and kept 100 chariots.[D]

5 When the Arameans of Damascus came to assist King Hadadezer of Zobah, David struck down 22,000 Aramean men. 6 Then he placed garrisons in Aram of Damascus, and the Arameans became David's subjects and brought tribute. The LORD made David victorious wherever he went.

7 David took the gold shields of Hadadezer's officers and brought them to Jerusalem. 8 King David also took huge quantities of bronze from Betah[E] and Berothai, Hadadezer's cities.

9 When King Toi of Hamath heard that David had defeated the entire army of Hadadezer, 10 he sent his son Joram to King David to greet him and to congratulate him because David had fought against Hadadezer and defeated him, for Toi and Hadadezer had fought many wars. Joram had items of silver, gold, and bronze with him. 11 King David also dedicated these to the LORD, along with the silver and gold he had dedicated from all the nations he had subdued— 12 from Edom,[F] Moab, the Ammonites, the Philistines, the Amalekites, and the spoil of Hadadezer son of Rehob, king of Zobah.

13 David made a reputation for himself when he returned from striking down 18,000 Edomites[G] in the Valley of Salt.[H] 14 He placed garrisons throughout Edom, and all the Edomites were subject to David. The LORD made David victorious wherever he went.

15 So David reigned over all Israel, administering justice and righteousness for all his people.

16 Joab son of Zeruiah was
over the army;
Jehoshaphat son of Ahilud
was court historian;
17 Zadok son of Ahitub
and Ahimelech
son of Abiathar were priests;
Seraiah was court secretary;
18 Benaiah son of Jehoiada
was over
the Cherethites
and the Pelethites;
and David's sons were
chief officials.[I]

The Kindness of David to Mephibosheth (9:1-13)

9 David asked, "Is there anyone remaining from Saul's family I can show kindness to because of Jonathan?" 2 There was a servant of Saul's family named Ziba. They summoned him to David, and the king said to him, "Are you Ziba?"

"I am your servant," he replied.

3 So the king asked, "Is there

8:6 The writer does not let his readers forget that Yahweh deserved the glory for David's military victories.

8:14 Repeating the statement that David was **victorious** only because of **the LORD** points to the theological significance of these accomplishments The wars described in this chapter likely occurred before the establishment of the Davidic covenant, when "the LORD had given him rest on every side" (7:1).

[A]**8:1** Or *took control of the mother city*; Hb obscure [B]**8:1** LXX reads *them, and David took tribute out of the hand of the Philistines* [C]**8:4** LXX, DSS read *1,000 chariots and 7,000 horsemen* [D]**8:4** Or *chariot horses* [E]**8:8** Some LXX mss, Syr read *Tebah* [F]**8:12** Some Hb mss, LXX, Syr; other Hb mss read *Aram*; 1Ch 18:11 [G]**8:13** Some Hb mss, LXX, Syr; other Hb mss read *Arameans*; 1Ch 18:12 [H]**8:13** = the Dead Sea region [I]**8:18** LXX; MT reads *were priests*; 1Ch 18:17

9:6-13 Customarily, kings would kill the members of a previous dynasty as a means of eliminating the threat of rivalry for the throne. After calming Mephibosheth's fears, David went beyond his promise to Jonathan (1Sm 20:14-17) and made a permanent place for **Mephibosheth** at the king's **table**. David restored Mephibosheth's honor, provided for his needs (9:9-10), and bestowed dignity on him because of his love for Jonathan. What a beautiful picture of what the Father does for those who accept His invitation to accept the mercy and grace He offers through Jesus.

10:4 When **Hanun . . . shaved off half their beards** and **cut their clothes in half at the hips,** he grossly insulted David's **emissaries.**

9:3 Kindness (Hb *chesed*, "constant or abiding favor, grace, or mercy; goodness; lovingkindness, devotion, zeal, ardor; covenant loyalty or faithfulness") is rich in meaning. Yahweh proclaimed *chesed* as an integral aspect of His character (Ex 34:5-7; Dt 5:10; 7:9,12). Although *chesed* may be translated in English with such words as "love" or "mercy," it never conveys a fleeting emotion but always expresses an abiding devotion manifested in such acts of "kindness" (9:1) and loving "discipline" (7:14). David had promised Jonathan never to withdraw his "faithful love" (Hb *chesed*, 1Sm 20:14-16) from Jonathan's household. Here, David's determination to fulfill this promise demonstrates in human terms the Lord's commitment never to remove His "faithful love" (Hb *chesed*, 2Sm 7:15) from David's heir (Solomon). When asked directly to Ziba, David's question indicates more specifically his desire to bestow "the kindness [Hb *chesed*] of God" on someone from "Saul's family" (9:3).

anyone left of Saul's family that I can show the kindness of God to?"
Ziba said to the king, "There is still Jonathan's son who was injured in both feet."
4 The king asked him, "Where is he?"
Ziba answered the king, "You'll find him in Lo-debar at the house of Machir son of Ammiel."
5 So King David had him brought from the house of Machir son of Ammiel in Lo-debar.
6 Mephibosheth son of Jonathan son of Saul came to David, bowed down to the ground and paid homage. David said, "Mephibosheth!"
"I am your servant," he replied.
7 "Don't be afraid," David said to him, "since I intend to show you kindness because of your father Jonathan. I will restore to you all your grandfather Saul's fields, and you will always eat meals at my table."
8 Mephibosheth bowed down and said, "What is your servant that you take an interest in a dead dog like me?"
9 Then the king summoned Saul's attendant Ziba and said to him, "I have given to your master's grandson all that belonged to Saul and his family.
10 You, your sons, and your servants are to work the ground for him, and you are to bring in the crops so your master's grandson will have food to eat. But Mephibosheth, your master's grandson, is always to eat at my table." Now Ziba had 15 sons and 20 servants.
11 Ziba said to the king, "Your servant will do all my lord the king commands."
So Mephibosheth ate at David's[A] table just like one of the king's sons.

12 Mephibosheth had a young son whose name was Mica. All those living in Ziba's house were Mephibosheth's servants.
13 However, Mephibosheth lived in Jerusalem because he always ate at the king's table. His feet had been injured.

The Victory over Ammon and Syria (10:1-19)

10 Some time later the king of the Ammonites died, and his son Hanun became king in his place.
2 Then David said, "I'll show kindness to Hanun son of Nahash, just as his father showed kindness to me."
So David sent his emissaries to console Hanun concerning his father. However, when they arrived in the land of the Ammonites,
3 the Ammonite leaders said to Hanun their lord, "Just because David has sent men with condolences for you, do you really believe he's showing respect for your father? Instead, hasn't David sent his emissaries in order to scout out the city, spy on it, and demolish it?"
4 So Hanun took David's emissaries, shaved off half their beards, cut their clothes in half at the hips, and sent them away.
5 When this was reported to David, he sent someone to meet them, since they were deeply humiliated. The king said, "Stay in Jericho until your beards grow back; then return."
6 When the Ammonites realized they had become repulsive to David, they hired 20,000 foot soldiers from the Arameans of Beth-rehob and Zobah, 1,000 men from the king of Maacah, and 12,000 men from Tob.

[A] 9:11 LXX; Syr reads *the king's*; Vg reads *your*; MT reads *my*

[7]David heard about it and sent Joab and all the fighting men. [8]The Ammonites marched out and lined up in battle formation at the entrance to the city gate while the Arameans of Zobah and Rehob and the men of Tob and Maacah were in the field by themselves. [9]When Joab saw that there was a battle line in front of him and another behind him, he chose some men out of all the elite troops of Israel and lined up in battle formation to engage the Arameans. [10]He placed the rest of the forces under the command of his brother Abishai who lined up in battle formation to engage the Ammonites.

[11]"If the Arameans are too strong for me," Joab said, "then you will be my help. However, if the Ammonites are too strong for you, I'll come to help you. [12]Be strong! We must prove ourselves strong for our people and for the cities of our God. May the LORD's will be done."[A]

[13]Joab and his troops advanced to fight against the Arameans, and they fled before him. [14]When the Ammonites saw that the Arameans had fled, they too fled before Abishai and entered the city. So Joab withdrew from the attack against the Ammonites and went to Jerusalem.

[15]When the Arameans saw that they had been defeated by Israel, they regrouped. [16]Hadadezer sent messengers to bring the Arameans who were across the Euphrates River, and they came to Helam with Shobach, commander of Hadadezer's army, leading them.

[17]When this was reported to David, he gathered all Israel, crossed the Jordan, and went to Helam. Then the Arameans lined up in formation to engage David in battle and fought against him. [18]But the Arameans fled before Israel, and David killed 700 of their charioteers and 40,000 foot soldiers.[B] He also struck down Shobach commander of their army, who died there. [19]When all the kings who were Hadadezer's subjects saw that they had been defeated by Israel, they made peace with Israel and became their subjects. After this, the Arameans were afraid to ever help the Ammonites again.

The Decline of David's House (11:1–20:26)

David's Sin Against Uriah and Bathsheba (11:1-27)

11 In the spring when kings march out to war, David sent Joab with his officers and all Israel. They destroyed the Ammonites and besieged Rabbah, but David remained in Jerusalem.

[2]One evening David got up from his bed and strolled around on the roof of the palace. From the roof he saw a woman bathing—a very beautiful woman. [3]So David sent someone to inquire about her, and he reported, "This is Bathsheba, daughter of Eliam and wife of Uriah the Hittite."[C]

[4]David sent messengers to get her, and when she came to him, he slept with her. Now she had just been purifying herself from her uncleanness. Afterward, she returned home. [5]The woman conceived and sent

[A]10:12 Lit *the LORD do what is good in His eyes* [B]10:18 Some LXX mss; MT reads *horsemen*; 1Ch 19:18 [C]11:3 DSS add *Joab's armor-bearer*

10:15-19 First and 2 Samuel remind readers of the cost of listening to men rather than to God. Wise counsel does provide safety (Pr 15:22), as was the case with the prophetic words of Samuel and Nathan given respectively to Saul and David. But unwise counsel founded on human perceptions always leads to destruction. By listening to the foolish counsel of his men, Hanun turned a blessing into a curse, and unnecessary death and destruction came upon him and his country.

11:1 From this high point in his rule, David began his downfall. David's experience should be a reminder to believers that following great victory they can be susceptible to temptation and stumbling. That David stayed in Jerusalem **when kings march out to war** sets the stage for David's affair with Bathsheba and implies that the absence of Israel's king from this battle was unusual.

11:2-3 Bathsheba is often blamed for seducing David. Yet this assumption is highly speculative since the text does not reveal Bathsheba's intent or response, nor does it describe her location. She may have been unaware that she was seen. Further, the writer draws attention to David's guilt (11:26–12:10).

11:4 The detail that Bathsheba **had just been purifying herself from her uncleanness** likely means that she had been cleansing herself at the end of her seven days of being ritually unclean due to her menstrual cycle (Lv 15:19-24). Thus, at the time of her adultery with David, she was not pregnant by Uriah. When another monthly cycle did not occur, the child in her womb was unquestionably his.

BIBLICAL WOMANHOOD Sexual Integrity

Bathsheba is certainly not to blame for David's sin, and the text does not state whether she resisted the king's advances or submitted willingly. Given the king's prerogative to obtain what he wanted and the text's silence about her response, there is no foundation for assuming any questionable intent on her part. However, the fact that she withheld the affair from her husband Uriah suggests that she was at least complicit, if not, culpable for attempting to deceive him about her pregnancy. Even if she had been able to give the appearance of marital faithfulness to others, she still would have been accountable to God for her sexual unfaithfulness. As Numbers 32:23 warns, "Be sure your sin will catch up with you." God offers forgiveness and cleansing for all sexual sin. But unlike Bathsheba, you must not attempt to cover up your sin but rather confess it and turn away from it. The pain of revealing past choices is not worth the greater shame of waiting for your sin to find you out.

11:6-8 David attempted to cover up his sin, for which the law prescribed the death penalty (Dt 22:22). He called for Bathsheba's husband **Uriah** from the battle and encouraged him to return home and enjoy the intimacies of marriage (2Sm 11:5-13), as implied by the idiom **wash your feet** (v. 8).

11:9-13 During ancient times soldiers were expected to refrain from sexual activity during military service as a matter of honor. Uriah remained loyal to David when he refused to go home to his wife.

11:14-16 David's scheming only grew more serious—lust when conceived brings forth sin and death (Jms 1:15).

CHARACTER PROFILE

Bathsheba The Wife of the King

Her Background	• The daughter of Eliam and the wife of Uriah the Hittite—both elite soldiers (23:34,39) • The wife of David and mother of Solomon—both kings (11:26-27; 12:24; 1Kg 1:11-40; Mt 1:6)
Her Story	• David noticed her as she bathed on her rooftop (2Sm 11:2). • He called for her to come to the palace, where they had sexual relations (11:3-4). • She soon informed David that she was pregnant (11:5). • In order to cover his sinful actions, David arranged for Uriah's death (11:14-25). • God held David accountable for this sin (11:27–12:19). • The baby of David and Bathsheba died at birth, as Nathan prophesied he would (12:15-19). • They had another son, Solomon (12:24).
Life Lessons	• Bathsheba ultimately found grace and redemption. She served honorably as the wife of King David and the mother King Solomon. • By following wise counsel, she played a key role in securing the throne for her son and the Davidic lineage ultimately of Jesus the Messiah (1Kg 1:11-40; Mt 1:6).

word to inform David: "I am pregnant."
6 David sent orders to Joab: "Send me Uriah the Hittite." So Joab sent Uriah to David. 7 When Uriah came to him, David asked how Joab and the troops were doing and how the war was going. 8 Then he said to Uriah, "Go down to your house and wash your feet." So Uriah left the palace, and a gift from the king followed him. 9 But Uriah slept at the door of the palace with all his master's servants; he did not go down to his house.
10 When it was reported to David, "Uriah didn't go home," David questioned Uriah, "Haven't you just come from a journey? Why didn't you go home?"
11 Uriah answered David, "The ark, Israel, and Judah are dwelling in tents, and my master Joab and his soldiers[A] are camping in the open field. How can I enter my house to eat and drink and sleep with my wife? As surely as you live and by your life, I will not do this!"
12 "Stay here today also," David said to Uriah, "and tomorrow I will send you back." So Uriah stayed in Jerusalem that day and the next.
13 Then David invited Uriah to eat and drink with him, and David got him drunk. He went out in the evening to lie down on his cot with his master's servants, but he did not go home.
14 The next morning David wrote a letter to Joab and sent it with Uriah.
15 In the letter he wrote:

> Put Uriah at the front of the fiercest fighting, then withdraw from him so that he is struck down and dies.

16 When Joab was besieging the city, he put Uriah in the place where he knew the best enemy soldiers were.
17 Then the men of the city came out and attacked Joab, and some of the men from David's soldiers fell in battle; Uriah the Hittite also died.
18 Joab sent someone to report to David all the details of the battle.
19 He commanded the messenger, "When you've finished telling the king all the details of the battle—
20 if the king's anger gets stirred up

[A] **11:11** Lit *servants*

and he asks you, 'Why did you get so close to the city to fight? Didn't you realize they would shoot from the top of the wall? 21 At Thebez, who struck Abimelech son of Jerubbesheth?[A,B] Didn't a woman drop an upper millstone on him from the top of the wall so that he died? Why did you get so close to the wall?'—then say, 'Your servant Uriah the Hittite is dead also.'" 22 Then the messenger left.

When he arrived, he reported to David all that Joab had sent him to tell. 23 The messenger reported to David, "The men gained the advantage over us and came out against us in the field, but we counterattacked right up to the entrance of the gate. 24 However, the archers shot down on your soldiers from the top of the wall, and some of the king's soldiers died. Your servant Uriah the Hittite is also dead."

25 David told the messenger, "Say this to Joab: 'Don't let this matter upset you because the sword devours all alike. Intensify your fight against the city and demolish it.' Encourage him."

26 When Uriah's wife heard that her husband Uriah had died, she mourned for him.[C] 27 When the time of mourning ended, David had her brought to his house. She became his wife and bore him a son. However, the LORD considered what David had done to be evil.

David's Confession and Punishment (12:1-31)

12 So the LORD sent Nathan to David. When he arrived, he said to him:

> There were two men in a certain city, one rich and the other poor. 2 The rich man had a large number of sheep and cattle, 3 but the poor man had nothing except one small ewe lamb that he had bought. He raised it, and it grew up, living with him and his children. It shared his meager food and drank from his cup; it slept in his arms, and it was like a daughter to him. 4 Now a traveler came to the rich man, but the rich man could not bring himself to take one of his own sheep or cattle to prepare for the traveler who had come to him. Instead, he took the poor man's lamb and prepared it for his guest.[D]

5 David was infuriated with the man and said to Nathan: "As the LORD lives, the man who did this deserves to die! 6 Because he has done this thing and shown no pity, he must pay four lambs for that lamb."

7 Nathan replied to David, "You are the man! This is what the LORD God of Israel says: 'I anointed you king over Israel, and I delivered you from the hand of Saul. 8 I gave your master's house to you and your master's wives into your arms,[E] and I gave you the house of Israel and Judah, and if that was not enough, I would have given you even more. 9 Why then have you despised the command of the LORD by doing what I consider[F] evil? You struck down Uriah the Hittite with the sword and took his wife as your own wife—you murdered him with the Ammonite's sword. 10 Now therefore, the sword will never leave your house because you despised Me and took the wife of Uriah the Hittite to be your own wife.'

11 "This is what the LORD says, 'I am going to bring disaster on you from your own family: I will take your wives and give them to another[G] before your very eyes, and he will sleep

[A]**11:21** LXX reads *Jerubbaal* [B]**11:21** = Gideon [C]**11:26** Lit *her husband* [D]**12:4** Lit *for the man who had come to him* [E]**12:8** Lit *bosom* [F]**12:9** Alt Hb tradition reads *what He considers* [G]**12:11** Or *to your neighbor*

11:17-27 David's responses showed his lack of brokenness over his sin. His words to Joab, **Don't let this matter upset** [Hb *yara'*, "displease, grieve," v. 25] **you**, more literally read, "Don't let this matter be evil in your eyes." The last sentence of the chapter, which transitions between this account and the prophet's message from the Lord, uses the same wording to highlight God's view of David's sin. **The LORD considered** David's actions **to be evil** or more literally, "What David had done was evil in the LORD's eyes" (v. 27; cp. 12:9; Gn 38:10).

12:1-9 Secret sin is always exposed before God and often before men, even when a person tries to cover his guilt. Appealing to David as the judge of the land, Nathan described a scenario that would have been brought before the king. David did not suspect that he had condemned himself until Nathan responded, **You are the man** and proceeded to deliver the LORD's verdict on David's sin (v. 7). In return for the outpouring of God's blessing, David had **despised the command of the LORD** and the Lord Himself by committing adultery and murder, doing **evil** in the Lord's sight (vv. 9-10; cp. 11:25,27).

12:8 Receiving his **master's wives** may refer to David's inheritance of Saul's harem, symbolizing his acquisition of the exclusive privileges of the king, when he finally assumed the throne of Israel.

>WORD|*study*

12:9 To despise (Hb *bazah*, "treat with disdain, scorn or contempt; take lightly") **the command of the Lord** is a general term encompassing the more specific offenses of acting "defiantly" and blaspheming (Nm 15:30-31). In most cases, the object of disdain is someone or something either expecting (e.g., 2Kg 19:21; Neh 2:19) or deserving of the opposite treatment (e.g., Gn 25:34; 1Sm 2:30; 10:27).

12:13 He made no excuse for his behavior but simply acknowledged his own guilt. In response to David's genuine confession, Nathan announced God's forgiveness of the king. This serves as a powerful testimony to God's grace and the restoration available to those who repent of sin.

12:14-23 God still used David despite his sin, but his sin cost him greatly and affected his role as king. While his relationship with the Lord was renewed, the consequences of his actions remained.

12:24-25 Solomon was also endowed with the name **Jedidiah** (Hb, "Beloved of the Lord"). Nathan delivered the message about the child's second name, given to David by the Lord as a sign that he was loved by Him.

with them publicly.[A] 12 You acted in secret, but I will do this before all Israel and in broad daylight.'"[B]

13 David responded to Nathan, "I have sinned against the LORD."

Then Nathan replied to David, "The LORD has taken away your sin; you will not die. 14 However, because you treated[C] the LORD with such contempt in this matter, the son born to you will die." 15 Then Nathan went home.

The LORD struck the baby that Uriah's wife had borne to David, and he became ill. 16 David pleaded with God for the boy. He fasted, went home, and spent the night lying on the ground. 17 The elders of his house stood beside him to get him up from the ground, but he was unwilling and would not eat anything with them.

18 On the seventh day the baby died. But David's servants were afraid to tell him the baby was dead. They said, "Look, while the baby was alive, we spoke to him, and he wouldn't listen to us. So how can we tell him the baby is dead? He may do something desperate."

19 When David saw that his servants were whispering to each other, he guessed that the baby was dead. So he asked his servants, "Is the baby dead?"

"He is dead," they replied.

20 Then David got up from the ground. He washed, anointed himself, changed his clothes, went to the LORD's house, and worshiped. Then he went home and requested something to eat. So they served him food, and he ate.

21 His servants asked him, "What did you just do? While the baby was alive, you fasted and wept, but when he died, you got up and ate food."

22 He answered, "While the baby was alive, I fasted and wept because I thought, 'Who knows? The LORD may be gracious to me and let him live.' 23 But now that he is dead, why should I fast? Can I bring him back again? I'll go to him, but he will never return to me."

24 Then David comforted his wife Bathsheba; he went and slept with her. She gave birth to a son and named[D] him Solomon.[E] The LORD loved him, 25 and He sent a message through Nathan the prophet, who named[F] him Jedidiah,[G] because of the LORD.

26 Joab fought against Rabbah of the Ammonites and captured the royal fortress. 27 Then Joab sent messengers to David to say, "I have fought against Rabbah and have also captured the water supply. 28 Now therefore, assemble the rest of the troops, lay siege to the city, and capture it. Otherwise I will be the one to capture the city, and it will be named after me." 29 So David assembled all the troops and went to Rabbah; he fought against it and captured it. 30 He took the crown from the head of their king,[H] and it was placed on David's head. The crown weighed 75 pounds[I] of gold, and it had a precious stone in it. In addition, David took away a large quantity of plunder from the city. 31 He removed the people who were in the city and put them to work with saws, iron picks, and iron axes, and to labor at brickmaking. He did the same to all the Ammonite cities. Then he and all his troops returned to Jerusalem.

HARD QUESTION

Do infants go to heaven?

Second Samuel 12:23 gives hope to mothers who experienced a miscarriage or have tragically lost an infant. Upon hearing that his child had died, David declared in faith, "I'll go to him, but he will never return to me."

Amnon's Sin and Absalom's Revenge (13:1-39)

13 Some time passed. David's son Absalom had a beautiful sister named Tamar, and David's son Amnon was infatuated with her. 2 Am-

[A] **12:11** Lit *in the eyes of this sun* [B] **12:12** Lit *and before the sun* [C] **12:14** Ancient Jewish tradition, one LXX ms; MT reads *treated the enemies of*; DSS read *treated the word of* [D] **12:24** Alt Hb tradition reads *he named* [E] **12:24** In Hb, the name Solomon sounds like "peace." [F] **12:25** Or *prophet to name* [G] **12:25** = Beloved of the LORD [H] **12:30** LXX reads *of Milcom*; some emend to *Molech*; 1Kg 11:5,33 [I] **12:30** Lit *a talent*

>WORD|*study*

13:12 Tamar's appeal recalls the holiness that was expected of those **in Israel**, calling his intention a horrible thing (Hb *nevalah*, v. 13). While this phrase includes the idea of "senselessness or folly," in this context it denotes something more serious, even "vile or profane"—a "shameful act of wickedness, outrage" (cp. Jdg 19:23-24; 20:6,10; Jr 29:23). Furthermore, Tamar reminded Amnon that she would be shamed everywhere because of this sin, and he would acquire the reputation of "immoral men" (Hb *naval*, v. 13), more literally translated "fools" but here referring to "wicked or ungodly" men (cp. Ps 74:18; Pr 17:21; Is 32:5-6).

13:15 Amnon's change in behavior demonstrated his lack of care and concern for his sister, indicating that he had only desired to gratify his lustful passions rather than to express true love for Tamar. Tamar's innocence was protected under the law—only Amnon was guilty of a capital crime (Dt 22:25-29). However, her virginity and, therefore, her eligibility for an honorable marriage were lost.

13:15-19 Referring to Tamar only as **this woman**, Amnon commanded his servant to throw her out as though she were a piece of trash and bolting **the door behind her** as though to seal her fate. Tamar left Amnon's house, tearing her beautiful regal robe and putting **ashes on her head**, expressions of inconsolable grief. She wept over the humiliation and disgrace she now bore (v. 19).

non was frustrated to the point of
making himself sick over his sister
Tamar because she was a virgin, but
it seemed impossible to do anything
to her. 3 Amnon had a friend named
Jonadab, a son of David's brother
Shimeah. Jonadab was a very shrewd
man, 4 and he asked Amnon, "Why
are you, the king's son, so miserable
every morning? Won't you tell me?"
Amnon replied, "I'm in love with
Tamar, my brother Absalom's sister."
5 Jonadab said to him, "Lie down
on your bed and pretend you're
sick. When your father comes to see
you, say to him, 'Please let my sister Tamar come and give me something to eat. Let her prepare food in
my presence so I can watch and eat
from her hand.'"
6 So Amnon lay down and pretended to be sick. When the king came to
see him, Amnon said to him, "Please
let my sister Tamar come and make
a couple of cakes in my presence so I
can eat from her hand."
7 David sent word to Tamar at the
palace: "Please go to your brother
Amnon's house and prepare a meal
for him."
8 Then Tamar went to his house
while Amnon was lying down. She
took dough, kneaded it, made cakes
in his presence, and baked them.
9 She brought the pan and set it
down in front of him, but he refused to eat. Amnon said, "Everyone
leave me!" And everyone left him.
10 "Bring the meal to the bedroom,"
Amnon told Tamar, "so I can eat
from your hand." Tamar took the
cakes she had made and went to her
brother Amnon's bedroom. 11 When
she brought them to him to eat, he
grabbed her and said,[A] "Come sleep
with me, my sister!"
12 "Don't, my brother!" she cried.
"Don't humiliate me, for such a
thing should never be done in Israel. Don't do this horrible thing!
13 Where could I ever go with my
disgrace? And you—you would be
like one of the immoral men in Israel! Please, speak to the king, for he
won't keep me from you." 14 But he
refused to listen to her, and because
he was stronger than she was, he
raped her.
15 After this, Amnon hated Tamar
with such intensity that the hatred
he hated her with was greater than
the love he had loved her with. "Get
out of here!" he said.
16 "No," she cried,[B] "sending me
away is much worse than the great
wrong you've already done to me!"
But he refused to listen to her. 17 Instead, he called to the servant who
waited on him: "Throw this woman
out and bolt the door behind her!"
18 Amnon's servant threw her out and

HARD QUESTION

Does God care about victims of rape?

Tamar's tragedy is compounded by the fact that culturally her virginity was necessary for marriage (13:11-15). Thus, Tamar suffered not only the physical and psychological trauma of rape but also the cultural shame of being still unmarried and bereft of her biological virginity. This story does not mandate that if a woman is raped she is no longer eligible for marriage or deserves shame. The Lord considers rape to be a sin worthy of the perpetrator's death and the victim of rape to be faultless in the crime committed against her (Dt 22:25). God knows the hurting and broken hearts of every woman who has ever been forced to suffer sexual violence. No woman should feel shame for losing that which was stolen from her against her will. In God's eyes, the victim of rape is still pure. He has promised to restore all that was broken and to repay every wrong in perfect measure (Pss 23:3; 147:3; Rm 12:19; Rv 21:5).

[A] **13:11** Lit *said to her* [B] **13:16** Lit *she said to him*

13:21-22 Although **King David . . . was furious**, he failed to confront Amnon, who was likely regarded as the crown prince, about his crime. By doing little, if anything, to punish Amnon for the atrocity, David allowed the anger and hurt to build within his family. By saying nothing to Amnon, Absalom allowed his half brother to become secure in the assumption that his sin incurred no public repercussions.

13:20 Tamar remained at her brother's house as a desolate [Hb *shamem*, lit "as one laid waste"] woman. The word's primary meaning is "silence," as would be encountered in an empty wasteland. That she was "desolate" may be a way of conveying her hopeless situation and also the fact that she never married. The tragic summary of Tamar's life implies that she was bereft of what normally brought joy and hope to a woman's life—being a wife and mother.

bolted the door behind her. Now
Tamar was wearing a long-sleeved[A]
garment, because this is what
the king's virgin daughters wore.
19 Tamar put ashes on her head and
tore the long-sleeved garment she
was wearing. She put her hand on
her head and went away crying out.
20 Her brother Absalom said to her:
"Has your brother Amnon been with
you? Be quiet for now, my sister.
He is your brother. Don't take this
thing to heart." So Tamar lived as a
desolate woman in the house of her
brother Absalom.

HARD QUESTION

Why didn't David confront Amnon for raping Tamar?

We ought to be outraged by the injustice done to Tamar, not only by her half-brother Amnon's violence but also by what appears to be her father's moral failure (13:1-22). While David responded with the appropriate emotions (**he was furious**, v. 21), he did not take the appropriate action. With no rebuke or confrontation mentioned, the king seemed to have valued harmony rather than justice. In failing to confront and punish Amnon, he not only permitted unrepentant sin to remain in his household, but he also set into motion the undermining of his entire family and kingdom. David's passivity may have communicated that Amnon would not be held accountable for violating his half-sister Tamar, a false representation of the justice that God would execute (Pss 103:6; 140:12). Perhaps David valued quiet more than he valued justice? Perhaps David felt that, because of his own sexual sin, he was disqualified to rebuke his son (2Sm 11). However, while you must confess and repent of your own sin before addressing another's (Mt 7:3-5), no past personal failing ought to keep you from confronting an individual with God's Word and ultimately with the Lord Himself. Absalom took his righteous desire for justice and misdirected it into an unrighteous response of revenge. Perhaps Amnon's murder, Absalom's rebellion, and the near-civil war within David's kingdom could have been avoided if David had chosen to confront sin rather than to dismiss it.

21 When King David heard about
all these things, he was furious.[B]
22 Absalom didn't say anything to
Amnon, either good or bad, because
he hated Amnon since he disgraced
his sister Tamar.
23 Two years later, Absalom's
sheepshearers were at Baal-hazor
near Ephraim, and Absalom invited
all the king's sons. 24 Then he went
to the king and said, "Your servant
has just hired sheepshearers. Will
the king and his servants please
come with your servant?"
25 The king replied to Absalom,
"No, my son, we should not all go,
or we would be a burden to you."
Although Absalom urged him, he
wasn't willing to go, though he did
bless him.
26 "If not," Absalom said, "please
let my brother Amnon go with us."
The king asked him, "Why should
he go with you?" 27 But Absalom
urged him, so he sent Amnon and
all the king's sons.[C]
28 Now Absalom commanded his
young men, "Watch Amnon until
he is in a good mood from the wine.
When I order you to strike Amnon,
then kill him. Don't be afraid. Am
I not the one who has commanded
you? Be strong and courageous!"
29 So Absalom's young men did to
Amnon just as Absalom had commanded. Then all the rest of the
king's sons got up, and each fled on
his mule.
30 While they were on the way, a report reached David: "Absalom struck
down all the king's sons; not even
one of them survived!" 31 In response
the king stood up, tore his clothes,
and lay down on the ground, and
all his servants stood by with their
clothes torn.
32 But Jonadab, son of David's
brother Shimeah, spoke up: "My

[A]**13:18** Or *an ornamented*; Gn 37:3 [B]**13:21** LXX, DSS add *but he did not grieve the spirit of Amnon his son, for he loved him because he was his firstborn*; 1Kg 1:6 [C]**13:27** LXX adds *And Absalom prepared a feast like a royal feast.*

CHARACTER PROFILE

Tamar A Violated Beauty

Her Background	• The daughter of King David (3:3) • The sister of Absalom and half-sister of Amnon, who desired her (3:2-4)
Her Story	• She desperately rejected Amnon's advances, while caring for him during his feigned illness (13:7-14). • Yet he raped her and left her in humiliation (13:17). • Absalom had Amnon killed in retribution (13:32). • Tamar was cared for by Absalom in his home but lived as a "desolate woman" (13:20).
Life Lessons	• Tamar, as other women, was a victim of rape by someone whom she trusted. • Spiritual and emotional support was not available to her even within her family, adding to this tragic story.

lord must not think they have killed
all the young men, the king's sons,
because only Amnon is dead. In
fact, Absalom has planned this[A] ever
since the day Amnon disgraced his
sister Tamar. 33 So now, my lord the
king, don't take seriously the report
that says all the king's sons are dead.
Only Amnon is dead."

34 Meanwhile, Absalom had fled.
When the young man who was
standing watch looked up, there
were many people coming from
the road west of him from the side
of the mountain.[B] 35 Jonadab said to
the king, "Look, the king's sons have
come! It's exactly like your servant
said." 36 Just as he finished speaking,
the king's sons entered and wept
loudly. Then the king and all his servants also wept bitterly.

37 Now Absalom fled and went to
Talmai son of Ammihud, king of
Geshur. And David mourned for his
son[C] every day. 38 Absalom had fled
and gone to Geshur where he stayed
three years. 39 Then King David[D]
longed to go to Absalom, for David
had finished grieving over Amnon's
death.

Absalom's Estrangement from David
(14:1-33)

14 Joab son of Zeruiah observed
that the king's mind was on
Absalom. 2 So Joab sent someone
to Tekoa to bring a clever woman
from there. He told her, "Pretend to
be in mourning: dress in mourning
clothes and don't put on any oil. Act
like a woman who has been mourning for the dead for a long time. 3 Go
to the king and speak these words
to him." Then Joab told her exactly
what to say.

4 When the woman from Tekoa
came[E] to the king, she fell with her
face to the ground in homage and
said, "Help me, my king!"

5 "What's the matter?" the king
asked her.

"To tell the truth, I am a widow;
my husband died," she said. 6 "Your
servant had two sons. They were
fighting in the field with no one
to separate them, and one struck
the other and killed him. 7 Now the
whole clan has risen up against your
servant and said, 'Hand over the one
who killed his brother so we may
put him to death for the life of the
brother he murdered. We will destroy the heir!' They would extinguish my one remaining ember by
not preserving my husband's name
or posterity on earth."

8 The king told the woman, "Go
home. I will issue a command on
your behalf."

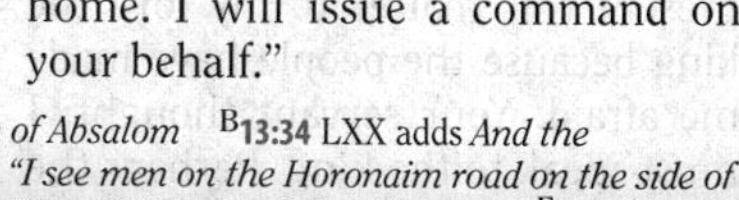

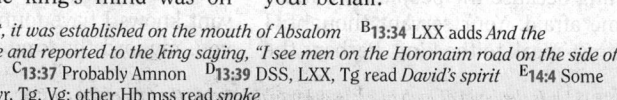

[A] **13:32** Lit *In fact, it was established on the mouth of Absalom* [B] **13:34** LXX adds *And the watchman came and reported to the king saying, "I see men on the Horonaim road on the side of the mountain."* [C] **13:37** Probably Amnon [D] **13:39** DSS, LXX, Tg read *David's spirit* [E] **14:4** Some Hb mss, LXX, Syr, Tg, Vg; other Hb mss read *spoke*

13:37-39 David was already seeing the fulfillment of Nathan's prophecy that the sword would never depart from his house (12:10).

14:1 While **Absalom** should have been next in line to be king, the murder of his brother disqualified him to inherit David's throne.

14:1-7 The **clever** [Hb *chakam*, "skillful," cp. Ex 35:25; "wise, intelligent," v. 2] **woman** from **Tekoa** employed wit and perception before the king. A key similarity between her story and David's situation was the need for punishment of the murderer. Joab intended to convey to the king that just as he pronounced mercy on the woman, so, too, he might grant mercy to Absalom.

14:9-14 The woman of Tekoa spoke respectfully and wisely and appealed to the king's sense of compassion. She reminded him of the brevity of life, comparing it to **water poured out on the ground, which can't be recovered** (cp. 23:13-17). She also reminded David of the mercy of God in restoring sinners who deserved to be banished. Certainly, this resonated with David's own experience of being forgiven by God even though he deserved to die for his sin.

14:19 The saying **turn to the right or left** underscored that her answer to the king did not deviate from the truth in the slightest way.

CHARACTER PROFILE

Wise Woman of Tekoa **A Gifted Orator**

Her Background	• She lived in Tekoa (14:2). • Joab perceived that David wished to be reconciled with Absalom and enlisted her help to convince him to do so (14:1).
Her Story	• She presented the fictional story about her sons (devised by Joab) to the king and asked for his protection (14:1-20). • Her story was obviously analogous to David's situation. • David discerned that Joab was the mastermind of this drama and consented to bringing Absalom home (14:18-19).
Life Lessons	• This woman agreed to be used for Joab's purposes. • As stewards of God's gifts, women must be responsible to use those gifts in an honorable way.

9 Then the woman of Tekoa said to the king, "My lord the king, may any blame be on me and my father's house, and may the king and his throne be innocent."

10 "Whoever speaks to you," the king said, "bring him to me. He will not trouble you again!"

11 She replied, "Please, may the king invoke the LORD your God, so that the avenger of blood will not increase the loss, and they will not eliminate my son!"

"As the LORD lives," he vowed, "not a hair of your son will fall to the ground."

12 Then the woman said, "Please, may your servant speak a word to my lord the king?"

"Speak," he replied.

13 The woman asked, "Why have you devised something similar against the people of God? When the king spoke as he did about this matter, he has pronounced his own •guilt. The king has not brought back his own banished one. 14 We will certainly die and be like water poured out on the ground, which can't be recovered. But God would not take away a life; He would devise plans so that the one banished from Him does not remain banished.

15 "Now therefore, I've come to present this matter to my lord the king because the people have made me afraid. Your servant thought: I must speak to the king. Perhaps the king will grant his servant's request. 16 The king will surely listen in order to rescue his servant from the hand of this man who would eliminate both me and my son from God's inheritance. 17 Your servant thought: May the word of my lord the king bring relief, for my lord the king is able to discern the good and the bad like the Angel of God. May the LORD your God be with you."

18 Then the king answered the woman, "I'm going to ask you something; don't conceal it from me!"

"Let my lord the king speak," the woman replied.

19 The king asked, "Did Joab put you up to[A] all this?"

The woman answered. "As you live, my lord the king, no one can turn to the right or left from all my lord the king says. Yes, your servant Joab is the one who gave orders to me; he told your servant exactly what to say. 20 Joab your servant has done this to address the issue indirectly,[B] but my lord has wisdom like the wisdom of the Angel of God, knowing everything on earth."

21 Then the king said to Joab, "I hereby grant this request. Go, bring back the young man Absalom."

22 Joab fell with his face to the ground in homage and praised the king. "Today," Joab said, "your servant knows I have found favor with you, my lord the king, because the

[A]14:19 Lit *Is the hand of Joab in* [B]14:20 Lit *to go around the face of the matter*

king has granted the request of your
servant."
23 So Joab got up, went to Geshur,
and brought Absalom to Jerusalem.
24 However, the king added, "He may
return to his house, but he may not
see my face." So Absalom returned
to his house, but he did not see the
king.[A]
25 No man in all Israel was as handsome and highly praised as Absalom.
From the sole of his foot to the top
of his head, he did not have a single
flaw. 26 When he shaved his head—he
shaved it every year because his hair
got so heavy for him that he had to
shave it off—he would weigh the
hair from his head and it would be
five pounds[B] according to the royal
standard.
27 Three sons were born to Absalom, and a daughter named Tamar,
who was a beautiful woman. 28 Absalom resided in Jerusalem two years
but never saw the king. 29 Then Absalom sent for Joab in order to send
him to the king, but Joab was unwilling to come. So he sent again,
a second time, but he still wouldn't
come. 30 Then Absalom said to his
servants, "See, Joab has a field right
next to mine, and he has barley
there. Go and set fire to it!" So Absalom's servants set the field on fire.[C]
31 Then Joab came to Absalom's
house and demanded, "Why did your
servants set my field on fire?"
32 "Look," Absalom explained to
Joab, "I sent for you and said, 'Come
here. I want to send you to the king
to ask: Why have I come back from
Geshur? I'd be better off if I were
still there.' So now, let me see the
king. If I am guilty, let him kill me."
33 Joab went to the king and told
him. So David summoned Absalom,
who came to the king and bowed
down with his face to the ground
before him. Then the king kissed
Absalom.

Absalom's Rebellion (15:1–18:33)

15 After this, Absalom got himself
a chariot, horses, and 50 men
to run before him. 2 He would get
up early and stand beside the road
leading to the city •gate. Whenever
anyone had a grievance to bring
before the king for settlement, Absalom called out to him and asked,
"What city are you from?" If he replied, "Your servant is from one of
the tribes of Israel," 3 Absalom said
to him, "Look, your claims are good
and right, but the king does not have
anyone to listen to you." 4 He added,
"If only someone would appoint me
judge in the land. Then anyone who
had a grievance or dispute could
come to me, and I would make sure
he received justice." 5 When a person
approached to bow down to him,
Absalom reached out his hand, took
hold of him, and kissed him. 6 Absalom did this to all the Israelites who
came to the king for a settlement.
So Absalom stole the hearts of the
men of Israel.
7 When four[D] years had passed,
Absalom said to the king, "Please let
me go to Hebron to fulfill a vow I
made to the LORD. 8 For your servant
made a vow when I lived in Geshur
of Aram, saying: If the LORD really
brings me back to Jerusalem, I will
worship the LORD in Hebron."[E]
9 "Go in peace," the king said to
him. So he went to Hebron.
10 Then Absalom sent messengers
throughout the tribes of Israel with
this message: "When you hear the
sound of the ram's horn, you are to
say, 'Absalom has become king in
Hebron!'"
11 Two hundred men from Jerusalem went with Absalom. They had
been invited and were going inno-
cently, for they knew nothing about
the whole matter. 12 While he was
offering the sacrifices, Absalom sent
for David's adviser Ahithophel the
Gilonite, from his city of Giloh. So
the conspiracy grew strong, and the
people supporting Absalom continued to increase.
13 Then an informer came to David and reported, "The hearts of the
men of Israel are with Absalom."
14 David said to all the servants
with him in Jerusalem, "Get up. We
have to flee, or we will not escape
from Absalom! Leave quickly, or he
will soon overtake us, heap disaster

14:23-25 Absalom apparently counted on being pardoned by the king. An acquittal would eliminate the barrier to his pursuit of the popular appeal needed to supplant David.

14:26 The detail about Absalom's remarkably thick **hair** foreshadows the way he died (cp. 18:9-15). Certainly, he seemed the ideal heir to David's throne.

14:27 Absalom's only daughter was **named Tamar** in honor of the girl's aunt.

15:1-16 Being reconciled with his father, **Absalom** turned his attention to winning the people's favor and taking David's throne. The unfolding account of his revolt and its consequences demonstrated the folly of attempting to circumvent God's plan and timetable.

15:2-5 Absalom launched his campaign for favorable public opinion in several ways. He deceived the people by telling them that David had no one to hear their cases, baiting the people into believing that if only *he* were made **judge in the land**, the people's rights would be upheld. Further, when someone began to greet him as royalty, Absalom stopped him and feigned humility in greeting him as an equal.

15:7-12 Absalom apparently sustained the pretense of worship while his **messengers** (Hb *ragal*, "one who goes about slandering or making false and malicious reports," cp. 19:27) spread the word that he was about to become **king in Hebron**, the place where David was anointed as king over Judah and where Absalom was born (2:3-4; 3:2-3).

[A]**14:24** Lit *king's face* [B]**14:26** Lit *200 shekels* [C]**14:30** DSS, LXX add *So Joab's servants came to him with their clothes torn and said, "Absalom's servants have set the field on fire!"* [D]**15:7** Some LXX mss, Syr, Vg; other LXX mss, MT read *40* [E]**15:8** Some LXX mss; MT omits *in Hebron*

15:22-24 Leaving the nation's capital marks a tragic time in Israel's history as the people fled along with David. Despite his circumstances, David still demonstrated the heart of a king and the heart of a man committed to trusting God. He clearly refused to use **the ark of the covenant** as a "good luck charm" for victory against Absalom and sent it back to Jerusalem where it belonged (see 11:11). David's utmost concern was the safety and well-being of the ark of the covenant and the priests.

15:25-26 In his instructions to **Zadok**, David acknowledged his dependence on God's favor and on God's authority over the throne. The king also accepted God's judgment on him and his house.

15:30 David's appearance as he and his supporters ascended **the Mount of Olives** publicly displayed his sense of shame over departing Jerusalem by **walking barefoot.**

15:12 Conspiracy (Hb *qesher*, "treason, unlawful alliance or confederacy") is derived from the verb *qashar*, the root meaning of which is "bind together." "Conspiring" involves joining forces or working together to accomplish an illicit goal. Here, the noun calls attention to a growing league of people banding together to install a new king without God's authorization.

on us, and strike the city with the edge of the sword."

15 The king's servants said to him, "Whatever my lord the king decides, we are your servants." 16 Then the king set out, and his entire household followed him. But he left behind 10 concubines to take care of the palace. 17 So the king set out, and all the people followed him. They stopped at the last house 18 while all his servants marched past him. Then all the Cherethites, the Pelethites, and the Gittites—600 men who came with him from Gath—marched past the king.

19 The king said to Ittai the Gittite, "Why are you also going with us? Go back and stay with the new king since you're both a foreigner and an exile from your homeland. 20 Besides, you only arrived yesterday; should I make you wander around with us today while I go wherever I can? Go back and take your brothers with you. May the LORD show you kindness and faithfulness."

21 But in response, Ittai vowed to the king, "As the LORD lives and as my lord the king lives, wherever my lord the king is, whether it means life or death, your servant will be there!"

22 "March on," David replied to Ittai. So Ittai the Gittite marched past with all his men and the children who were with him. 23 Everyone in the countryside was weeping loudly while all the people were marching past. As the king was crossing the Kidron Valley, all the people were marching past on the road that leads to the desert.

24 Zadok was also there, and all the Levites with him were carrying the ark of the covenant of God. They set the ark of God down, and Abiathar offered sacrifices[A] until the people had finished marching past. 25 Then the king instructed Zadok, "Return the ark of God to the city. If I find favor in the LORD's eyes, He will bring me back and allow me to see both it and its dwelling place. 26 However, if He should say, 'I do not delight in you,' then here I am—He can do with me whatever pleases Him."[B]

27 The king also said to Zadok the priest, "Look,[C] return to the city in peace and your two sons with you: your son Ahimaaz and Abiathar's son Jonathan. 28 Remember, I'll wait at the fords of the wilderness until word comes from you to inform me." 29 So Zadok and Abiathar returned the ark of God to Jerusalem and stayed there.

30 David was climbing the slope of the Mount of Olives, weeping as he ascended. His head was covered, and he was walking barefoot. Each of the people with him covered their heads and went up, weeping as they ascended.

31 Then someone reported to David: "Ahithophel is among the conspirators with Absalom."

"LORD," David pleaded, "please turn the counsel of Ahithophel into foolishness!"

32 When David came to the summit where he used to worship God, Hushai the Archite was there to meet him with his robe torn and dust on his head. 33 David said to him, "If you go away with me, you'll be a burden to me, 34 but if you return to the city and tell Absalom, 'I will be your servant, my king! Previously, I was your father's servant, but now I will be your servant,' then you can counteract Ahithophel's counsel for me. 35 Won't Zadok and Abiathar the priests be there with you? Report everything you hear from the king's palace to Zadok and Abiathar the priests. 36 Take note: their two sons, Zadok's son Ahimaaz and

[A] **15:24** Or *Abiathar went up* [B] **15:26** Lit *me what is good in His eyes* [C] **15:27** LXX; MT reads *Are you a seer?*

Abiathar's son Jonathan, are there
with them. Send me everything you
hear through them." 37 So Hushai,
David's personal adviser, entered Jerusalem just as Absalom was entering the city.

Ziba's Help to David (16:1-4)

16 When David had gone a little
beyond the summit,[A] Ziba,
Mephibosheth's servant, was right
there to meet him. He had a pair
of saddled donkeys loaded with 200
loaves of bread, 100 clusters of raisins, 100 bunches of summer fruit,
and a skin of wine. 2 The king said to
Ziba, "Why do you have these?"
Ziba answered, "The donkeys are
for the king's household to ride, the
bread and summer fruit are for the
young men to eat, and the wine is
for those to drink who become exhausted in the desert."
3 "Where is your master's grandson?" the king asked.
"Why, he's staying in Jerusalem,"
Ziba replied to the king, "for he said,
'Today, the house of Israel will restore my grandfather's kingdom to
me.'"
4 The king said to Ziba, "All that
belongs to Mephibosheth is now
yours!"
"I bow before you," Ziba said. "May
you look favorably on me, my lord
the king!"

Shimei's Cursing of David (16:5-14)

5 When King David got to Bahurim,
a man belonging to the family of the
house of Saul was just coming out.
His name was Shimei son of Gera,
and he was yelling curses as he approached. 6 He threw stones at David and at all the royal[B] servants,
the people and the warriors on David's right and left. 7 Shimei said as
he cursed: "Get out, get out, you
worthless murderer! 8 The LORD has
paid you back for all the blood of the
house of Saul in whose place you became king, and the LORD has handed
the kingdom over to your son Absalom. Look, you are in trouble because you're a murderer!"
9 Then Abishai son of Zeruiah said
to the king, "Why should this dead
dog curse my lord the king? Let me
go over and cut his head off!"
10 The king replied, "Sons of Zeruiah, do we agree on anything? He
curses me this way because the LORD[C]
told him, 'Curse David!' Therefore,
who can say, 'Why did you do that?'"
11 Then David said to Abishai and all
his servants, "Look, my own son,
my own flesh and blood,[D] intends to
take my life—how much more now
this Benjaminite! Leave him alone
and let him curse me; the LORD has
told him to. 12 Perhaps the LORD will
see my affliction[E] and restore goodness to me instead of Shimei's curses today." 13 So David and his men
proceeded along the road as Shimei
was going along the ridge of the hill
opposite him. As Shimei went, he
cursed David, and threw stones and
dirt at him. 14 Finally, the king and
all the people with him arrived[F] exhausted, so they rested there.

Absalom's Advisors (16:15–17:14)

15 Now Absalom and all the Israelites came to Jerusalem. Ahithophel
was also with him. 16 When David's
friend Hushai the Archite came to
Absalom, Hushai said to Absalom,
"Long live the king! Long live the
king!"
17 "Is this your loyalty to your
friend?" Absalom asked Hushai.
"Why didn't you go with your
friend?"
18 "Not at all," Hushai answered
Absalom. "I am on the side of the
one that the LORD, the people, and
all the men of Israel have chosen. I
will stay with him. 19 Furthermore,
whom will I serve if not his son? As
I served in your father's presence, I
will also serve in yours."
20 Then Absalom said to Ahithophel, "Give me your advice. What
should we do?"
21 Ahithophel replied to Absalom,
"Sleep with your father's concubines
he left to take care of the palace.
When all Israel hears that you have
become repulsive to your father,
everyone with you will be encouraged." 22 So they pitched a tent for

16:1-4 When David inquired about Mephibosheth, **Ziba** capitalized on what he correctly regarded as an opportunity to discredit his master for his own gain. Despite the unlikelihood of Ziba's explanation, David yielded to a heightened level of suspicion and responded rashly (cp. 19:24-30).

16:5-14 Shimei's curses amounted to a public assault on David's integrity, interpreting his situation as the Lord's punishment for all the bloodshed inflicted against the house of Saul (v. 12). The writer, however, has clearly vindicated David for the deaths of Saul and Jonathan (1Sm 24; 26; 31; 2Sm 1), Abner (2Sm 3:12-39), and Ish-bosheth (2Sm 4). Believing that the Lord had ordained the barrage of curses because he deserved the rebuke, David insisted that his men leave Shimei **alone** and wait on the Lord to **restore goodness** to him (16:11-12). David submitted himself to the Lord's correction and hoped in God's mercy even while Shimei followed alongside him cursing David and pelting him with **stones and dirt** (vv. 13-14).

16:15-19 Hushai carefully crafted his words—e.g., avoiding the use of names—to be honest expressions of his loyalty to David as the rightful king while playing on Absalom's arrogance in setting himself up as king (vv. 16-19). Hushai successfully promoted himself to Absalom's inner circle and thereby effectively **served** David's cause in the usurper's **presence** (16:19).

16:20-23 Ahithophel advised Absalom to make himself **repulsive** (Hb *ba'ash*, "become odious, fetid"; cp. 10:6; 1Sm 13:4; Ec 10:1) to David by sleeping with the 10 **concubines** left behind to care for the palace (2Sm 16:21; 15:16). Among other results, this act would sever Absalom's relationship with his father, making reconciliation with David impossible, signal the end of David's rule (cp. Gn 49:4), fulfill God's judgment upon David's adultery with Bathsheba and murder of Uriah (2Sm 12:11-12), and ironically make Absalom 10 times an adulterer like his father (2Sm 11:2-4) and rapist like his brother Amnon (13:10-18). Absalom sadly followed Ahithophel's foolish advice and even did so publicly (16:22-23).

[A] **16:1** = Mount of Olives [B] **16:6** Lit *all King David's* [C] **16:10** Alt Hb tradition reads *If he curses, and if the LORD* [D] **16:11** Lit *son who came from my belly* [E] **16:12** Some Hb mss, LXX, Syr, Vg; one Hb tradition reads *iniquity*; alt Hb tradition reads *eyes*; ancient Jewish tradition reads *will look with His eye* [F] **16:14** LXX adds *at the Jordan*

17:1-14 Absalom's anger and jealousy toward his father had obviously turned to intense hatred, since he agreed to have him killed. Yet, in the providence of God, Absalom called for a second opinion from **Hushai**, who seized the chance to keep his promise to David to undermine Ahithophel's advice (17:5,14). His advice appealed to Absalom's ego. Under Hushai's plan, not only would Absalom himself gain the glory of victory in securing the throne but also his power would be consolidated as men from **all Israel** joined forces under his leadership and eradicated David's supporters (vv. 12-13). The writer bluntly attributes Absalom's rejection of his counsel to the sovereignty of God. Yahweh's plan—to undermine that advice and **to bring about Absalom's ruin**—was invincible (v. 14; Pr 21:1).

17:15-21 Hushai's advice was intended to provide David with enough time to organize his defense. The intelligence network, set in motion when Hushai left Absalom's presence, worked almost flawlessly. The Lord used two unnamed women to discretely deliver information to David and protect his other messengers (vv. 17-19).

Absalom on the roof, and he slept with his father's concubines in the sight of all Israel.

23 Now the advice Ahithophel gave in those days was like someone asking about a word from God—such was the regard that both David and Absalom had for Ahithophel's advice.

17 1 Ahithophel said to Absalom, "Let me choose 12,000 men, and I will set out in pursuit of David tonight. 2 I will attack him while he is weak and weary, throw him into a panic, and all the people with him will scatter. I will strike down only the king 3 and bring all the people back to you. When everyone returns except the man you're seeking, all[A] the people will be at peace." 4 This proposal seemed good to Absalom and all the elders of Israel.

5 Then Absalom said, "Summon Hushai the Archite also. Let's hear what he has to say as well."

6 So Hushai came to Absalom, and Absalom told him: "Ahithophel offered this proposal. Should we carry out his proposal? If not, what do you say?"

7 Hushai replied to Absalom, "The advice Ahithophel has given this time is not good." 8 Hushai continued, "You know your father and his men. They are warriors and are desperate like a wild bear robbed of her cubs. Your father is an experienced soldier who won't spend the night with the people. 9 He's probably already hiding in one of the caves[B] or some other place. If some of our troops fall[C] first, someone is sure to hear and say, 'There's been a slaughter among the people who follow Absalom.' 10 Then, even a brave man with the heart of a lion will melt because all Israel knows that your father and the valiant men with him are warriors. 11 Instead, I advise that all Israel from Dan to Beersheba—as numerous as the sand by the sea—be gathered to you and that you personally go into battle. 12 Then we will attack David wherever we find him, and we will descend on him like dew on the ground. Not even one will be left of all the men with him. 13 If he retreats to some city, all Israel will bring ropes to that city, and we will drag its stones into the valley until not even a pebble can be found there." 14 Since the LORD had decreed that Ahithophel's good advice be undermined in order to bring about Absalom's ruin, Absalom and all the men of Israel said, "The advice of Hushai the Archite is better than Ahithophel's advice."

David's Report on Absalom's Plans (17:15-29)

15 Hushai then told the priests Zadok and Abiathar, "This is what[D] Ahithophel advised Absalom and the elders of Israel, and this is what[E] I advised. 16 Now send someone quickly and tell David, 'Don't spend the night at the wilderness ford of the Jordan, but be sure to cross over, or the king and all the people with him will be destroyed.'"

17 Jonathan and Ahimaaz were staying at En-rogel, where a servant girl would come and pass along information to them. They in turn would go and inform King David, because they dared not be seen entering the city. 18 However, a young man did see them and informed Absalom. So the two left quickly and came to the house of a man in Bahurim. He had a well in his courtyard, and they climbed down into it. 19 Then his wife took the cover, placed it over the mouth of the well, and scattered grain on it so nobody would know anything.

20 Absalom's servants came to the woman at the house and asked, "Where are Ahimaaz and Jonathan?"

"They passed by toward the water,"[F] the woman replied to them. The men searched but did not find them, so they returned to Jerusalem.

21 After they had gone, Ahimaaz and Jonathan climbed out of the well and went and informed King David. They told him, "Get up and immediately ford the river, for Ahithophel has given this advice against you." 22 So David and all the people with him got up and crossed the Jordan. By daybreak, there was no one who

[A]**17:3** LXX reads *to you as a bride returns to her husband. You seek the life of only one man, and all* [B]**17:9** Or *pits*, or *ravines* [C]**17:9** Lit *And it will be when a falling on them at* [D]**17:15** Lit *Like this and like this* [E]**17:15** Lit *and like this and like this* [F]**17:20** Or *brook*; Hb obscure

had not crossed the Jordan. 23 When Ahithophel realized that his advice had not been followed, he saddled his donkey and set out for his house in his hometown. He set his affairs in order[A] and hanged himself. So he died and was buried in his father's tomb.

24 David had arrived at Mahanaim by the time Absalom crossed the Jordan with all the men of Israel. 25 Now Absalom had appointed Amasa over the army in Joab's place. Amasa was the son of a man named Ithra[B] the Israelite;[C] Ithra had married Abigail daughter of Nahash.[D] Abigail was a sister to Zeruiah, Joab's mother. 26 And Israel and Absalom camped in the land of Gilead. 27 When David came to Mahanaim, Shobi son of Nahash from Rabbah of the Ammonites, Machir son of Ammiel from Lodebar, and Barzillai the Gileadite from Rogelim 28 brought beds, basins,[E] and pottery items. They also brought wheat, barley, flour, roasted grain, beans, lentils,[F] 29 honey, curds, sheep, and cheese[G] from the herd for David and the people with him to eat. They had reasoned, "The people must be hungry, exhausted, and thirsty in the desert."

Absalom's Defeat (18:1-8)

18 David reviewed his troops and appointed commanders of hundreds and of thousands over them. 2 He then sent out the troops, a third under Joab, a third under Joab's brother Abishai son of Zeruiah, and a third under Ittai the Gittite. The king said to the troops, "I will also march out with you."

3 "You must not go!" the people pleaded. "If we have to flee, they will not pay any attention to us. Even if half of us die, they will not pay any attention to us because you are worth[H] 10,000 of us. Therefore, it is better if you support us from the city."

4 "I will do whatever you think is best," the king replied to them. So he stood beside the gate while all the troops marched out by hundreds and thousands. 5 The king commanded Joab, Abishai, and Ittai, "Treat the young man Absalom gently for my sake." All the people heard the king's orders to all the commanders about Absalom.

6 Then David's forces marched into the field to engage Israel in battle, which took place in the forest of Ephraim. 7 The people of Israel were defeated by David's soldiers, and the slaughter there was vast that day—20,000 casualties. 8 The battle spread over the entire region, and that day the forest claimed more people than the sword.

Absalom's Death (18:9-33)

9 Absalom was riding on his mule when he happened to meet David's soldiers. When the mule went under the tangled branches of a large oak tree, Absalom's head was caught fast in the tree. The mule under him kept going, so he was suspended in midair.[I] 10 One of the men saw him and informed Joab. He said, "I just saw Absalom hanging in an oak tree!"

11 "You just saw him!" Joab exclaimed.[J] "Why didn't you strike him to the ground right there? I would have given you 10 silver pieces[K] and a belt!"

12 The man replied to Joab, "Even if I had the weight of 1,000 pieces of silver[L] in my hand, I would not raise my hand against the king's son. For we heard the king command you, Abishai, and Ittai, 'Protect the young man Absalom for me.'[M] 13 If I had jeopardized my own[N] life—and nothing is hidden from the king—you would have abandoned me."

14 Joab said, "I'm not going to waste time with you!" He then took three spears in his hand and thrust them into Absalom's heart while he was still alive in the oak tree, 15 and 10 young men who were Joab's

17:23 Knowing that Absalom's course of action would fail and that he would undoubtedly be executed for his betrayal when David returned, Ahithophel took his own life.

18:1-5 David expressed his concern over how his son would be treated and spoke as a father who still loved his son despite the young man's rebellious spirit.

18:9 The combination of the tree's **tangled branches** and the earlier description of the great length and weight of Absalom's hair (14:26) suggest the common interpretation that Absalom was stripped from his mule and left hanging by his hair in the tree.

18:10-18 David's men neither rescued Absalom nor harmed him but left him hanging in the tree. The prince was denied any glory in death, and his father was denied sight of his son's body (vv. 16-17). Such was the end of Absalom's revolt.

[A] **17:23** Lit *He commanded his house* [B] **17:25** Or *Jether* [C] **17:25** Some LXX mss read *Ishmaelite* [D] **17:25** Some LXX mss read *Jesse* [E] **17:28** LXX reads *brought 10 embroidered beds with double coverings, 10 vessels* [F] **17:28** LXX, Syr; MT adds *roasted grain* [G] **17:29** Hb obscure [H] **18:3** Some Hb mss, LXX, Vg; other Hb mss read *because there would now be about* [I] **18:9** Lit *was between heaven and earth* [J] **18:11** Lit *Joab said to the man who told him* [K] **18:11** About 4 ounces of silver [L] **18:12** About 25 pounds of silver [M] **18:12** Some Hb mss, LXX, Tg, Vg; other Hb mss read *Protect, whoever, the young man Absalom*; Hb obscure [N] **18:13** Alt Hb tradition reads *jeopardized his*

18:19-33 Ahimaaz was eager to **tell** David **the good news** (Hb *basar*, "bear glad tidings, make cheerful by bringing a happy report," vv. 19-20; cp. 1Sm 31:9; Ps 68:1) of God's deliverance, but Joab knew that David would not regard his son's death as good news—twice he had executed the messengers who delivered such information (2Sm 1:14-16; 4:9-12). Joab wisely sent a non-Israelite servant instead and undoubtedly did not expect Ahimaaz to outrun him when allowed to run behind (18:23). The Cushite confirmed David's worst fear—not that he would lose the fight for the kingdom but that his son would be killed in the process (vv. 28-29).

19:1-4 David was so overcome with grief that the people shrank back into the city in shame. What should have been a day of celebration turned into a day of **mourning** in respect for the king's personal sorrow over Absalom's death. Although natural expressions of love for a son, David's display communicated to the people that he was so preoccupied with his own grief that he did not care about those who had risked their lives to deliver him from the son who had openly shamed him and attempted his assassination.

armor-bearers surrounded Absalom,
struck him, and killed him.
16 Afterward, Joab blew the ram's
horn, and the troops broke off their
pursuit of Israel because Joab restrained them. 17 They took Absalom, threw him into a large pit in
the forest, and piled a huge mound
of stones over him. And all Israel
fled, each to his tent.
18 When he was alive, Absalom
had set up a pillar for himself in
the King's Valley, for he had said, "I
have no son to preserve the memory
of my name." So he gave the pillar
his name. It is still called Absalom's
Monument today.
19 Ahimaaz son of Zadok said,
"Please let me run and tell the king
the good news that the LORD has delivered him from his enemies."
20 Joab replied to him, "You are not
the man to take good news today.
You may do it another day, but today you aren't taking good news, because the king's son is dead." 21 Joab
then said to the •Cushite, "Go tell
the king what you have seen." The
Cushite bowed to Joab and took off
running.
22 However, Ahimaaz son of Zadok
persisted and said to Joab, "No matter what, please let me also run behind the Cushite!"
Joab replied, "My son, why do you
want to run since you won't get a
reward?"
23 "No matter what, I want to run!"
"Then run!" Joab said to him. So
Ahimaaz ran by way of the plain and
outran the Cushite.
24 David was sitting between the
two gates when the watchman went
up to the roof of the gate and over to
the wall. The watchman looked out
and saw a man running alone. 25 He
called out and told the king.
The king said, "If he's alone, he
bears good news."
As the first runner came closer,
26 the watchman saw another man
running. He called out to the gatekeeper, "Look! Another man is running alone!"
"This one is also bringing good
news," said the king.
27 The watchman said, "The way
the first man runs looks to me like
the way Ahimaaz son of Zadok runs."
"This is a good man; he comes
with good news," the king commented.
28 Ahimaaz called out to the king,
"All is well," and then bowed down to
the king with his face to the ground.
He continued, "May the LORD your
God be praised! He delivered up the
men who rebelled against my lord
the king."
29 The king asked, "Is the young
man Absalom all right?"
Ahimaaz replied, "When Joab sent
the king's servant and your servant,
I saw a big disturbance, but I don't
know what it was."
30 The king said, "Move aside and
stand here." So he stood to one side.
31 Just then the Cushite came and
said, "May my lord the king hear the
good news: today the LORD has delivered you from all those rising up
against you!"
32 The king asked the Cushite, "Is
the young man Absalom all right?"
The Cushite replied, "May what
has become of the young man happen to the enemies of my lord the
king and to all who rise up against
you with evil intent."
33A The king was deeply moved and
went up to the gate chamber and
wept. As he walked, he cried, "My
son Absalom! My son, my son Absalom! If only I had died instead of
you, Absalom, my son, my son!"

David's Restoration of Power (19:1-43)

19 It was reported to Joab, "The
king is weeping. He's mourning over Absalom." 2 That day's victory was turned into mourning for
all the troops because on that day
the troops heard, "The king is grieving over his son." 3 So they returned
to the city quietly that day like people come in when they are humiliated after fleeing in battle. 4 But the
king hid his face and cried out at the
top of his voice, "My son Absalom!
Absalom, my son, my son!"
5 Then Joab went into the house to
the king and said, "Today you have
shamed all your soldiers—those
who rescued your life and the lives
of your sons and daughters, your

A **18:33** 2Sm 19:1 in Hb

>WORD|*study*

18:33 Deeply moved (Hb *ragaz*) literally means to "tremble or shake," usually expressing a deeply rooted emotion. David was physically overcome with grief and shook or heaved with profound weeping.

wives, and your concubines. [6]You
love your enemies and hate those
who love you! Today you have made
it clear that the commanders and
soldiers mean nothing to you. In
fact, today I know that if Absalom
were alive and all of us were dead, it
would be fine with you![A]

[7]"Now get up! Go out and encourage[B] your soldiers, for I swear by the
LORD that if you don't go out, not a
man will remain with you tonight.
This will be worse for you than all
the trouble that has come to you
from your youth until now!"

[8]So the king got up and sat in the
•gate, and all the people were told:
"Look, the king is sitting in the
gate." Then they all came into the
king's presence.

Meanwhile, each Israelite had fled
to his tent. [9]All the people among
all the tribes of Israel were arguing: "The king delivered us from the
grasp of our enemies, and he rescued us from the grasp of the Philistines, but now he has fled from the
land because of Absalom. [10]But Absalom, the man we anointed over us,
has died in battle. So why do you say
nothing about restoring the king?"

[11]King David sent word to the
priests, Zadok and Abiathar: "Say
to the elders of Judah, 'Why should
you be the last to restore the king to
his palace? The talk of all Israel has
reached the king at his house. [12]You
are my brothers, my flesh and blood.
So why should you be the last to
restore the king?' [13]And tell Amasa,
'Aren't you my flesh and blood? May
God punish me and do so severely
if you don't become commander
of the army from now on instead of
Joab!'"

[14]So he won over[C] all the men of
Judah, and they sent word to the
king: "Come back, you and all your
servants." [15]Then the king returned.
When he arrived at the Jordan, Judah came to Gilgal to meet the king
and escort him across the Jordan.

[16]Shimei son of Gera, a Benjaminite from Bahurim, hurried down
with the men of Judah to meet King
David. [17]There were 1,000 men from
Benjamin with him. Ziba, an attendant from the house of Saul, with
his 15 sons and 20 servants also
rushed down to the Jordan ahead of
the king. [18]They forded the Jordan
to bring the king's household across
and do whatever the king desired.[D]

When Shimei son of Gera crossed
the Jordan, he fell down before the
king [19]and said to him, "My lord,
don't hold me •guilty, and don't
remember your servant's wrongdoing on the day my lord the king left
Jerusalem. May the king not take it
to heart. [20]For your servant knows
that I have sinned. But look! Today I
am the first one of the entire house
of Joseph to come down to meet my
lord the king."

[21]Abishai son of Zeruiah asked,
"Shouldn't Shimei be put to death
for this, because he cursed the
LORD's anointed?"

[22]David answered, "Sons of Zeruiah, do we agree on anything? Have
you become my adversary today?
Should any man be killed in Israel
today? Am I not aware that today I'm
king over Israel?" [23]So the king said
to Shimei, "You will not die." Then
the king gave him his oath.

[24]Mephibosheth, Saul's grandson,
also went down to meet the king.
He had not taken care of his feet,
trimmed his mustache, or washed
his clothes from the day the king
left until the day he returned safely.
[25]When he came from Jerusalem to
meet the king, the king asked him,
"Mephibosheth, why didn't you
come with me?"

[26]"My lord the king," he replied,
"my servant Ziba betrayed me. Actually your servant said: 'I'll saddle

19:5-8a Joab confronted and rebuked David. Perceiving that he was about to lose his army's loyalty, if he did not start acting like a commander-in-chief who loved and appreciated his **commanders and soldiers** for rescuing him and his household, David followed Joab's advice and sat in the gate to **encourage** and comfort his people.

19:8b-23 With the nation still divided and confused over David's authority (vv. 8b-10), the king needed to tie up the loose ends that were quickly unraveling. By addressing Judah separately, even though all the people of Israel seemed supportive of David's authority, the king drove a wedge between Judah and the rest of the kingdom. This would later result in a divided kingdom. David recognized his need to win back the support of Absalom's men, especially those in the tribe of Judah, and he determined that Amasa's new role would help stabilize and solidify Judah's support. Despite Abishai's proposal to execute **Shimei** for cursing the Lord's anointed, David pardoned Shimei, swearing to him that he would not die (vv. 21-23). David himself would not mete out the punishment Shimei deserved. However, obviously he never fully trusted Shimei's pledge of loyalty (1Kg 2:8).

19:24-30 The question David posed to Mephibosheth, **why didn't you come with me** was justified, considering the report David had received from **Ziba**. David could not understand how Jonathan's son, the one to whom he had shown such grace and kindness, failed to demonstrate his loyalty to the king at such a critical time. Mephibosheth's response points to Ziba's deception and maliciousness in taking advantage of his handicapped master. He successfully convinced David and was rewarded with his master's land and possessions. Mephibosheth appealed to David to recognize his loyalty to the king, understanding that his servant had slandered him. David partially retracted his hasty decree (16:4)—yet he restored Mephibosheth's property without completely withdrawing Ziba's reward for his loyalty. Clearly, Mephibosheth's commitment to the king is evident from his response to David's decree. He expressed gratitude for the king's peaceful return to the city (v. 30).

[A]**19:6** Lit *be right in your eyes* [B]**19:7** Lit *speak to the heart of* [C]**19:14** Lit *he turned the heart of*
[D]**19:18** Lit *do what is good in his eyes*

19:40-43 Samuel's fear because of the people's desire for a king was justifiable as the men of **Israel** and **Judah** argued over who had the greater claim on David.

20:1-2 Sheba failed to understand what he possessed through David's reign as king over Israel, the inheritance ultimately found in the Messiah. The men of Israel responded to his call and abandoned David to return home, while **the men of Judah . . . remained loyal** to their king, i.e., more literally, "clave to their king."

the donkey for myself[A] so that I may ride it and go with the king'—for your servant is lame. 27 Ziba slandered your servant to my lord the king. But my lord the king is like the Angel of God, so do whatever you think best.[B] 28 For my grandfather's entire family deserves death from my lord the king, but you set your servant among those who eat at your table. So what further right do I have to keep on making appeals to the king?"

29 The king said to him, "Why keep on speaking about these matters of yours? I hereby declare: you and Ziba are to divide the land."

30 Mephibosheth said to the king, "Instead, since my lord the king has come to his palace safely, let Ziba take it all!"

31 Barzillai the Gileadite had come down from Rogelim and accompanied the king to the Jordan River to see him off at the Jordan. 32 Barzillai was a very old man—80 years old—and since he was a very wealthy man, he had provided for the needs of the king while he stayed in Mahanaim.

33 The king said to Barzillai, "Cross over with me, and I'll provide for you[C] at my side in Jerusalem."

34 Barzillai replied to the king, "How many years of my life are left that I should go up to Jerusalem with the king? 35 I'm now 80 years old. Can I discern what is pleasant and what is not? Can your servant taste what he eats or drinks? Can I still hear the voice of male and female singers? Why should your servant be an added burden to my lord the king? 36 Since your servant is only going with the king a little way across the Jordan, why should the king repay me with such a reward? 37 Please let your servant return so that I may die in my own city near the tomb of my father and mother. But here is your servant Chimham: let him cross over with my lord the king. Do for him what seems good to you."[D]

38 The king replied, "Chimham will cross over with me, and I will do for him what seems good to you,[D] and whatever you desire from me I will do for you." 39 So all the people crossed the Jordan, and then the king crossed. The king kissed Barzillai and blessed him, and Barzillai returned to his home.

40 The king went on to Gilgal, and Chimham went with him. All the troops of Judah and half of Israel's escorted the king. 41 Suddenly, all the men of Israel came to the king. They asked him, "Why did our brothers, the men of Judah, take you away secretly and transport the king and his household across the Jordan, along with all of David's men?"

42 All the men of Judah responded to the men of Israel, "Because the king is our relative. Why does this make you angry? Have we ever eaten anything of the king's or been honored at all?"[E]

43 The men of Israel answered the men of Judah: "We have 10 shares in the king, so we have a greater claim to David than you. Why then do you despise us? Weren't we the first to speak of restoring our king?" But the words of the men of Judah were harsher than those of the men of Israel.

Sheba's Revolt (20:1-26)

20 Now a •wicked man, a Benjaminite named Sheba son of Bichri, happened to be there. He blew the ram's horn and shouted:

> We have no portion in David,
> no inheritance in Jesse's son.
> Each man to his tent, Israel!

2 So all the men of Israel deserted David and followed Sheba son of Bichri, but the men of Judah from the Jordan all the way to Jerusalem remained loyal to their king.

3 When David came to his palace in Jerusalem, he took the 10 concubines he had left to take care of the palace and placed them under guard. He provided for them, but he was not intimate with them. They were confined until the day of their death, living as widows.

4 The king said to Amasa, "Sum-

[A] 19:26 LXX, Syr, Vg read *said to him, 'Saddle the donkey for me* [B] 19:27 Lit *do what is good in your eyes* [C] 19:33 LXX reads *for your old age*; Ru 4:15 [D] 19:37,38 Lit *what is good in your eyes* [E] 19:42 LXX reads *king's or has he given us a gift or granted us a portion*

mon the men of Judah to me within three days and be here yourself."
[5]Amasa went to summon Judah, but he took longer than the time allotted him. [6]So David said to Abishai, "Sheba son of Bichri will do more harm to us than Absalom. Take your lord's soldiers and pursue him, or he will find fortified cities and elude us."[A]

[7]So Joab's men, the Cherethites, the Pelethites, and all the warriors marched out under Abishai's command;[B] they left Jerusalem to pursue Sheba son of Bichri. [8]They were at the great stone in Gibeon when Amasa joined them. Joab was wearing his uniform and over it was a belt around his waist with a sword in its sheath. As he approached, the sword fell out. [9]Joab asked Amasa, "Are you well, my brother?" Then with his right hand Joab grabbed Amasa by the beard to kiss him.
[10]Amasa was not on guard against the sword in Joab's hand, and Joab stabbed him in the stomach with it and spilled his intestines out on the ground. Joab did not stab him again for Amasa was dead. Joab and his brother Abishai pursued Sheba son of Bichri.

[11]One of Joab's young men had stood over Amasa saying, "Whoever favors Joab and whoever is for David, follow Joab!" [12]Now Amasa was writhing in his blood in the middle of the highway, and the man had seen that all the people stopped. So he moved Amasa from the highway to the field and threw a garment over him because he realized that all those who encountered Amasa were stopping. [13]When he was removed from the highway, all the men passed by and followed Joab to pursue Sheba son of Bichri.

[14]Sheba passed through all the tribes of Israel to Abel of Beth-maacah. All the Berites[C] came together and followed him. [15]Joab's troops came and besieged Sheba in Abel of Beth-maacah. They built an assault ramp against the outer wall of the city. While all the troops with Joab were battering the wall to make it collapse, [16]a wise woman called out from the city, "Listen! Listen! Please tell Joab to come here and let me speak with him."

[17]When he had come near her, the woman asked, "Are you Joab?"

"I am," he replied.

"Listen to the words of your servant," she said to him.

He answered, "I'm listening."

[18]She said, "In the past they used to say, 'Seek counsel in Abel,' and that's how they settled disputes. [19]I am a peaceful person, one of the faithful in Israel, but you're trying to destroy a city that is like a mother in Israel. Why would you devour the LORD's inheritance?"

[20]Joab protested: "Never! I do not want to destroy! [21]That is not my intention. There is a man named Sheba son of Bichri, from the hill country of Ephraim, who has rebelled against King David. Deliver this one man, and I will withdraw from the city."

The woman replied to Joab, "All right. His head will be thrown over the wall to you." [22]The woman went to all the people with her wise counsel, and they cut off the head of Sheba son of Bichri and threw it to Joab. So he blew the ram's horn, and they dispersed from the city, each to his own tent. Joab returned to the king in Jerusalem.

[23]Joab commanded the whole army of Israel; Benaiah son of Jehoiada was over the Cherethites and Pelethites; [24]Adoram[D] was in charge of forced labor; Jehoshaphat son of Ahilud was court historian; [25]Sheva was court secretary; Zadok and Abiathar were priests; [26]and in addition, Ira the Jairite was David's priest.

The Final Years of David's Reign (21:1–24:25)

The Execution of Saul's Sons (21:1-22)

21 During David's reign there was a famine for three successive years, so David inquired of the LORD. The LORD answered, "It is because of the blood shed by Saul and his family when he killed the Gibeonites."

[2]The Gibeonites were not Israelites but rather a remnant of the

[A]20:6 Lit *and snatch away our eyes* [B]20:7 Lit *out following him* [C]20:14 LXX, Vg read *Bichrites* [D]20:24 Some Hb mss, LXX, Syr read *Adoniram*; 1Kg 4:6; 5:14

20:3-13 Although David's 10 concubines were not responsible for Absalom's actions, they still were considered unclean and, therefore, could not serve in David's household any longer. Yet, David showed kindness toward them by caring for them, since they were unable to marry, having been a part of the king's harem (v. 3). Such was the unfortunate result of polygamy as well as the rebellious spirit of David's son.

20:14-22 The **wise woman** of **Abel** displayed courage by intervening in the attack, appealing directly to the commander of the army. She spoke to Joab respectfully and convincingly, recognizing her need to intervene in order to save the city. She identified herself as **peaceful** and **faithful**, whereas she described Joab as the one who sought **to destroy a city** that was **like a mother in Israel** (vv. 18-19). Joab assured her that he only meant to destroy **Sheba**, David's enemy (vv. 20-21). After making her appeal to Joab and hearing his intent, she persuaded her people to sacrifice Sheba and throw his **head** over the city wall, thus ending the war (vv. 21-22). Many of the women in 1 and 2 Samuel displayed wisdom, courage, and a commitment to justice. And they demonstrated respect and submission to the authorities placed over them.

20:23-26 David remained a man loyal to the LORD (1Sm 13:14); yet he faced enormous challenges and heartache because of his disobedience. God's grace enabled him to continue in his reign and to receive the blessing of God so that his throne endured throughout the ages; yet David also faced the reality of the consequences of his sin.

21:1-2 The Lord answered David and explained that the famine was due to Saul's sin and his killing of the Gibeonites. The **Gibeonites** were foreigners who Joshua allowed to live in Israel (Jos 9:3-27). In his zeal to demonstrate his power and authority over the nation, Saul killed many of the Gibeonites and sought to destroy them. This situation demonstrates God's concern and care that justice be extended to all people.

21:3-9 David agreed to the Gibeonites' request and gave them seven men from Saul's household, but he spared **Mephibosheth** because of his covenant with **Jonathan**.

21:10-14 Rizpah's care for her sons and the manner in which she honored their deaths affected David to the point that he, too, decided to honor the memory of Saul and Jonathan. David continued to demonstrate honor for the Lord's anointed, even though Saul's sin had brought a curse upon the nation.

>WORD|*study*

21:3 The word atone (Hb *kaphar*, "cover, atone by offering a substitute") is extremely significant in both the Old and New Testaments. This word is the root for many other forms that may be translated "atonement," "purge," "cover," and "ransom." The verb is almost always used in connection with the removal of sin or defilement. The practice of sacrificing animals in the Old Testament was a symbolic expression of the exchange of innocent life on behalf of the guilty. This word forms the foundation for understanding the ultimate sacrifice of atonement made on behalf of all through the death of the Messiah, Jesus.

Amorites. The Israelites had taken an oath concerning them, but Saul had tried to kill them in his zeal for the Israelites and Judah. So David summoned the Gibeonites
and spoke to them. 3 He asked the Gibeonites, "What should I do for you? How can I make atonement so that you will bring a blessing on[A] the LORD's inheritance?"

4 The Gibeonites said to him, "We are not asking for money from[B] Saul or his family, and we cannot put anyone to death in Israel."

"Whatever you say, I will do for you," he said.

5 They replied to the king, "As for the man who annihilated us and plotted to destroy us so we would not exist within the whole territory
of Israel, 6 let seven of his male descendants be handed over to us so we may hang[C] them in the presence of the LORD at Gibeah of Saul, the LORD's chosen."

The king answered, "I will hand them over."

7 David spared Mephibosheth, the son of Saul's son Jonathan, because of the oath of the LORD that was between David and Jonathan, Saul's
son. 8 But the king took Armoni and Mephibosheth, who were the two sons whom Rizpah daughter of Aiah had borne to Saul, and the five sons whom Merab[D] daughter of Saul had borne to Adriel son of Barzillai the
Meholathite 9 and handed them over to the Gibeonites. They hanged[E] them on the hill in the presence of the LORD; the seven of them died together. They were executed in the first days of the harvest at the beginning of the barley harvest.[F]

10 Rizpah, Aiah's daughter, took •sackcloth and spread it out for herself on the rock from the beginning of the harvest[G] until the rain poured down from heaven on the bodies. She kept the birds of the sky from them by day and the wild animals by night.

11 When it was reported to David what Saul's concubine Rizpah, daughter of Aiah, had done, 12 he
went and got the bones of Saul and his son Jonathan from the leaders of Jabesh-gilead. They had stolen them from the public square of Beth-shan where the Philistines had hung the bodies the day the Philistines killed Saul at Gilboa. 13 David had
the bones brought from there. They gathered up the bones of Saul's family who had been hung[E] 14 and buried
the bones of Saul and his son Jonathan at Zela in the land of Benjamin in the tomb of Saul's father Kish. They did everything the king commanded. After this, God answered prayer for the land.

15 The Philistines again waged war against Israel. David went down with his soldiers, and they fought the Philistines, but David became exhausted. 16 Then Ishbi-benob, one
of the descendants of the giant,[H] whose bronze spear weighed about eight pounds[I] and who wore new armor, intended to kill David. 17 But
Abishai son of Zeruiah came to his aid, struck the Philistine, and killed him. Then David's men swore to him: "You must never again go out with us to battle. You must not extinguish the lamp of Israel."

18 After this, there was another battle with the Philistines at Gob. At that time Sibbecai the Hushathite killed Saph, who was one of the descendants of the giant.[H]

19 Once again there was a battle with the Philistines at Gob, and Elhanan son of Jaare-oregim the Beth-

[A] 21:3 Lit *will bless* [B] 21:4 Lit *"Not for us silver and gold with* [C] 21:6 Or *impale*, or *expose*
[D] 21:8 Some Hb mss, LXX, Syr, Tg; other Hb mss read *Michal* [E] 21:9,13 Or *impaled*, or *exposed*
[F] 21:9 = March–April [G] 21:10 = April to October [H] 21:16,18 Or *Raphah* [I] 21:16 Lit *300* (shekels)

22:1 David's song of deliverance is nearly identical to Ps 18. It summarized his confidence in the Lord and showed his delight that peace would rest on his house forever. David's words serve as a reminder of God's promise to David, describing his relationship with the Lord and reflecting upon the blessings he found in obedience to God and His ways—themes found in 1 and 2 Samuel.

CHARACTER PROFILE

Rizpah A Protective Mother

Her Background	One of Saul's concubines, who bore him two sons (3:7)
Her Story	• The famine was God's punishment for Saul's murder of the Gibeonites (21:1). • To make restitution, David agreed to hand over seven of Saul's sons to be killed. Two of them were Rizpah's sons (21:5-8). • Rizpah stationed herself near her sons' bodies, protecting them from being consumed by animals (21:10). • Her fierce actions moved David to arrange for an honorable burial for all Saul's descendents (21: 11-13).
Life Lessons	• Rizpah could not save the lives of her sons. • However, she did all she possibly could to protect their bodies from disgrace.

lehemite killed[A] Goliath the Gittite.
The shaft of his spear was like a
weaver's beam.
20 At Gath there was still another
battle. A huge man was there with
six fingers on each hand and six toes
on each foot—24 in all. He, too, was
descended from the giant.[B] 21 When
he taunted Israel, Jonathan, son of
David's brother Shimei, killed him.
22 These four were descended from
the giant[B] in Gath and were killed by
David and his soldiers.

The Song of David (22:1-51)

22 David spoke the words of this
song to the LORD on the day the
LORD rescued him from the hand of
all his enemies and from the hand of
Saul. 2 He said:

The LORD is my rock,
my fortress,
and my deliverer,
3 my God, my mountain[C] where
I seek refuge.
My shield, the •horn
of my salvation,
my stronghold, my refuge,
and my Savior, You save me
from violence.
4 I called to the LORD,
who is worthy of praise,
and I was saved
from my enemies.
5 For the waves of death
engulfed me;
the torrents of destruction
terrified me.
6 The ropes of •Sheol
entangled me;
the snares of death
confronted me.

7 I called to the LORD
in my distress;
I called to my God.
From His temple He heard
my voice,
and my cry for help reached
His ears.
8 Then the earth shook
and quaked;
the foundations
of the heavens[D] trembled;
they shook because
He burned with anger.
9 Smoke rose from His nostrils,
and consuming fire came
from His mouth;
coals were set ablaze by it.[E]
10 He parted the heavens
and came down,
a dark cloud
beneath His feet.
11 He rode on a cherub
and flew,
soaring[F] on the wings
of the wind.
12 He made darkness a canopy
around Him,

[A]21:19 1Ch 20:5 adds *the brother of* [B]21:20,22 Or *Raphah* [C]22:3 LXX; MT reads *God of my mountain*; Ps 18:2 [D]22:8 Some Hb mss, Syr, Vg read *mountains*; Ps 18:7 [E]22:9 Or *ablaze from Him* [F]22:11 Some Hb mss; other Hb mss, Syr, Tg read *He was seen*

22:21-46 David was blessed as a result of his sincere devotion to the law of God, desiring to walk in the ways of God. That David referred to himself as **blameless** and **pure** does not mean that he denied his sinfulness. However, having confessed his sins in repentance to the Lord, David was forgiven and stood blameless and pure before Him (v. 25). His life was characterized by his desire to follow the Lord, remaining obedient to His commands and reflecting humility before Almighty God. David emphasized that the Lord provided sure footing like that of **a deer** (vv. 32-34), depicting the swiftness and sureness with which he was able to climb to the high, difficult-to-reach places, enabled by the Lord's strength (cp. Hab 3:19). God's grace was demonstrated in David's deliverance from his enemies and his uncleanness as a sinful man.

>WORD|*study*

22:17 The psalmist used the verb pulled (Hb *mashah*, "draw,") to speak of David being drawn from the mighty waters. This verb is used only two other times in the Old Testament—in Ps 18:16 and, most notably, in Ex 2:10 with the name "Moses." His name is explained with reference to this Hebrew verb, as he was "drawn out" of the waters of the Nile. So, too, David was drawn out of the great waters by the Lord's mighty hand.

a gathering[A] of water
and thick clouds.
13 From the radiance
of His presence,
flaming coals were ignited.
14 The LORD thundered
from heaven;
the •Most High projected
His voice.
15 He shot arrows
and scattered them;
He hurled lightning bolts
and routed them.
16 The depths of the sea
became visible,
the foundations of the world
were exposed
at the rebuke of the LORD,
at the blast of the breath
of His nostrils.

17 He reached down
from heaven
and took hold of me;
He pulled me
out of deep waters.
18 He rescued me
from my powerful enemy
and from those
who hated me,
for they were too strong
for me.
19 They confronted me
in the day of my distress,
but the LORD was my support.
20 He brought me out
to a spacious place;
He rescued me because
He delighted in me.

21 The LORD rewarded me
according to
my righteousness;
He repaid me
according to the cleanness
of my hands.
22 For I have kept the ways
of the LORD
and have not turned
from my God to wickedness.
23 Indeed, I have kept
all His ordinances in mind[B]
and have not disregarded
His statutes.
24 I was blameless before Him
and kept myself
from sinning.
25 So the LORD repaid me
according to
my righteousness,
according to my cleanness[C]
in His sight.

26 With the faithful
You prove Yourself faithful;
with the blameless man
You prove Yourself blameless;
27 with the pure
You prove Yourself pure,
but with the crooked
You prove Yourself shrewd.
28 You rescue
an afflicted people,
but Your eyes are set
against the proud—
You humble them.
29 LORD, You are my lamp;
the LORD illuminates
my darkness.
30 With You I can attack
a barrier,[D]
and with my God I can leap
over a wall.
31 God—His way is perfect;
the word of the LORD is pure.
He is a shield to all
who take refuge in Him.

32 For who is God
besides the LORD?
And who is a rock?
Only our God.
33 God is my strong refuge;[E]
He makes my way perfect.[F]
34 He makes my feet like
the feet of a deer

[A]**22:12** Or *sieve*, or *mass*; Hb obscure [B]**22:23** Lit *Indeed, all His ordinances have been in front of me* [C]**22:25** LXX, Syr, Vg read *to the cleanness of my hands*; Ps 18:24 [D]**22:30** Or *ridge* [E]**22:33** DSS, some LXX mss, Syr, Vg read *God clothes me with strength*; Ps 18:32 [F]**22:33** Some LXX mss, Syr; MT reads *He sets free the blameless His way*; Hb obscure

and sets me securely
on the[A] heights.[B]
35 He trains my hands for war;
my arms can bend a bow
of bronze.
36 You have given me the shield
of Your salvation;
Your help[C] exalts me.
37 You widen a place beneath me
for my steps,
and my ankles do not
give way.
38 I pursue my enemies
and destroy them;
I do not turn back
until they are wiped out.
39 I wipe them out
and crush them,
and they do not rise;
they fall beneath my feet.
40 You have clothed me
with strength for battle;
You subdue my adversaries
beneath me.
41 You have made my enemies
retreat before me;[D]
I annihilate those
who hate me.
42 They look, but there is no one
to save them—
they look to the LORD,
but He does not
answer them.
43 I pulverize them like dust
of the earth;
I crush them
and trample them like mud
in the streets.
44 You have freed me
from the feuds
among my people;
You have appointed me
the head of nations;
a people I had not known
serve me.
45 Foreigners submit to me
grudgingly;
as soon as they hear,
they obey me.
46 Foreigners lose heart
and come trembling
from their fortifications.
47 The LORD lives—may my rock
be praised!
God, the rock of my salvation,
is exalted.
48 God—He gives me vengeance
and casts down peoples
under me.
49 He frees me from my enemies.
You exalt me
above my adversaries;
You rescue me
from violent men.
50 Therefore I will praise You,
LORD, among the nations;
I will sing about Your name.
51 He is a tower of salvation
for[E] His king;
He shows loyalty
to His anointed,
to David and his descendants
forever.

The Elite Warriors of David (23:1-39)

23 These are the last words of David:

The declaration of David
son of Jesse,
the declaration of the man
raised on high,[F]
the one anointed by the God
of Jacob,
the favorite singer of Israel:
2 The Spirit of the LORD spoke
through me,
His word was on my tongue.
3 The God of Israel spoke;
the Rock of Israel said to me,
"The one who rules the people
with justice,
who rules in the •fear of God,
4 is like the morning light
when the sun rises
on a cloudless morning,
the glisten of rain
on sprouting grass."
5 Is it not true my house is
with God?
For He has established
an everlasting covenant
with me,
ordered and secured
in every detail.
Will He not bring about
my whole salvation
and my every desire?
6 But all the wicked are
like thorns raked aside;
they can never be picked up
by hand.

22:47-51 The Lord was so great that David felt compelled to praise Him among the Gentiles, not just among his own people. As in Hannah's song of praise (1Sm 2), David's words proved to be prophetic in speaking of the Anointed One—the Messiah—who would come from David's royal line.

23:1-7 David evaluated God's promise to him in chapter 7, along with its significance in light of his failure as a father. He described a coming ruler who would be just. He would rule over **the people** (Hb *ʾadam*, "man"), i.e., the entire human race, and would exercise his authority **in the fear of God**. David's hopes were ultimately realized in the person of Jesus, whose name means "salvation."

[A] **22:34** LXX; some Hb mss read *my*; other Hb mss read *His* [B] **22:34** Or *on my high places*
[C] **22:36** LXX reads *humility*; Ps 18:35 [D] **22:41** Lit *You gave me the neck of my enemies* [E] **22:51** DSS read *He gives great victory to* [F] **23:1** Or *raised up by the high God*

7 The man who touches them
must be armed with iron
and the shaft of a spear.
They will be completely
burned up on the spot.

8 These are the names of David's
warriors:

Josheb-basshebeth the Tahchemo-
nite was chief of the officers.[A] He
wielded his spear[B] against 800 men
that he killed at one time.

9 After him, Eleazar son of Dodo
son of an Ahohite was among the
three warriors with David when they
defied the Philistines. The men of Israel retreated in the place they had
gathered for battle, 10 but Eleazar
stood his ground and attacked the
Philistines until his hand was tired
and stuck to his sword. The LORD
brought about a great victory that
day. Then the troops came back to
him, but only to plunder the dead.

11 After him was Shammah son of
Agee the Hararite. The Philistines
had assembled in formation where
there was a field full of lentils. The
troops fled from the Philistines,
12 but Shammah took his stand in
the middle of the field, defended it,
and struck down the Philistines. So
the LORD brought about a great victory.

13 Three of the 30 leading warriors went down at harvest time
and came to David at the cave of
Adullam, while a company of Philistines was camping in the Valley
of Rephaim. 14 At that time David
was in the stronghold, and a Philistine garrison was at Bethlehem.
15 David was extremely thirsty[C] and
said, "If only someone would bring
me water to drink from the well at
the city gate of Bethlehem!" 16 So
three of the warriors broke through
the Philistine camp and drew water
from the well at the gate of Bethlehem. They brought it back to David,
but he refused to drink it. Instead,
he poured it out to the LORD. 17 David said, "LORD, I would never do
such a thing! Is this not the blood
of men who risked their lives?" So
he refused to drink it. Such were the
exploits of the three warriors.

18 Abishai, Joab's brother and son
of Zeruiah, was leader of the Three.[D]
He raised his spear against 300 men
and killed them, gaining a reputation among the Three. 19 Was he
not more honored than the Three?
He became their commander even
though he did not become one of
the Three.

20 Benaiah son of Jehoiada was the
son of a brave man from Kabzeel,
a man of many exploits. Benaiah
killed two sons[E] of Ariel[F] of Moab,
and he went down into a pit on a
snowy day and killed a lion. 21 He
also killed an Egyptian, a huge man.
Even though the Egyptian had a
spear in his hand, Benaiah went
down to him with a club, snatched
the spear out of the Egyptian's hand,
and then killed him with his own
spear. 22 These were the exploits of
Benaiah son of Jehoiada, who had
a reputation among the three warriors. 23 He was the most honored of
the Thirty, but he did not become
one of the Three. David put him in
charge of his bodyguard.

24 Among the Thirty were:

Joab's brother Asahel,
Elhanan son of Dodo
of Bethlehem,
25 Shammah the Harodite,
Elika the Harodite,
26 Helez the Paltite,
Ira son of Ikkesh the Tekoite,
27 Abiezer the Anathothite,
Mebunnai the Hushathite,
28 Zalmon the Ahohite,
Maharai the Netophathite,
29 Heleb son of Baanah
the Netophahite,
Ittai son of Ribai from Gibeah
of the Benjaminites,
30 Benaiah the Pirathonite,
Hiddai from the •wadis
of Gaash,[G]
31 Abi-albon the Arbathite,
Azmaveth the Barhumite,
32 Eliahba the Shaalbonite,
the sons of Jashen,
Jonathan son of[H] 33 Shammah
the Hararite,

[A]23:8 Some Hb mss, LXX read *Three* [B]23:8 Some Hb mss; other Hb mss, LXX read *He was Adino the Eznite* [C]23:15 Lit *And David craved* [D]23:18 Some Hb mss, Syr read *the Thirty* [E]23:20 LXX; MT omits *sons* [F]23:20 Or *two warriors* [G]23:30 Or *from Nahale-gaash* [H]23:32 Some LXX mss; MT omits *son of*; 1Ch 11:34

Ahiam son of Sharar
the Hararite,
34 Eliphelet son of Ahasbai
son of the Maacathite,
Eliam son of Ahithophel
the Gilonite,
35 Hezro the Carmelite,
Paarai the Arbite,
36 Igal son of Nathan
from Zobah,
Bani the Gadite,
37 Zelek the Ammonite,
Naharai the Beerothite,
the armor-bearer for Joab
son of Zeruiah,
38 Ira the Ithrite,
Gareb the Ithrite,
39 and Uriah the Hittite.

There were 37 in all.

HARD QUESTION

Does God tempt us to sin?

There is a difference between what God allows to happen and what He causes to happen. The situation in 24:1 is similar to that of Job when the Lord permitted Satan to torment Job's family (Jb 1:12). The Lord did not incite David to sin, for "God is not tempted by evil, and He Himself doesn't tempt anyone" (Jms 1:13). God's purposes are always pure. He desired to teach David and the people in a way that would humble them once again. Similarly, 1 Peter records that while Satan wishes to devour the saints by persecuting believers, God uses these hardships to strengthen their faith and to enable them to share in the sufferings of Christ (1Pt 4–5). Because God will not allow you to be tempted beyond what you can bear, the only attack against our faith that the enemy has permission to launch is that for which God has given you the grace and power to overcome. What Satan uses to destroy your faith God uses to reveal your faith. And if any believer does sin, she has an "advocate . . . Jesus Christ the Righteous One." "If we confess our sins He is faithful and righteous to forgive us our sin and to cleanse us from all unrighteousness" (1Jn 2:1).

The Census of the People and the Plague (24:1-25)

24 The Lord's anger burned
against Israel again, and He
stirred up David against them to
say: "Go, count the people of Israel
and Judah."
2 So the king said to Joab, the commander of his army, "Go through
all the tribes of Israel from Dan to
Beer-sheba and register the troops
so I can know their number."
3 Joab replied to the king, "May
the Lord your God multiply the
troops 100 times more than they
are—while my lord the king looks
on! But why does my lord the king
want to do this?"
4 Yet the king's order prevailed
over Joab and the commanders of
the army. So Joab and the commanders of the army left the king's
presence to register the troops of
Israel.
5 They crossed the Jordan and
camped in Aroer, south of the town
in the middle of the valley, and then
proceeded toward Gad and Jazer.
6 They went to Gilead and to the land
of the Hittites[A] and continued on
to Dan-jaan and around to Sidon.
7 They went to the fortress of Tyre
and all the cities of the Hivites and
Canaanites. Afterward, they went to
the •Negev of Judah at Beer-sheba.
8 When they had gone through the
whole land, they returned to Jerusalem at the end of nine months and
20 days. 9 Joab gave the king the total of the registration of the troops.
There were 800,000 fighting men
from Israel and 500,000 men from
Judah.
10 David's conscience troubled him
after he had taken a census of the
troops. He said to the Lord, "I have
sinned greatly in what I've done.
Now, Lord, because I've been very
foolish, please take away Your servant's •guilt."
11 When David got up in the morning, a revelation from the Lord had
come to the prophet Gad, David's
seer: 12 "Go and say to David, 'This
is what the Lord says: I am offering
you three choices. Choose one of
them, and I will do it to you.' "
13 So Gad went to David, told him
the choices, and asked him, "Do you
want three[B] years of famine to come
on your land, to flee from your foes
three months while they pursue
you, or to have a plague in your land
three days? Now, think it over and
decide what answer I should take
back to the One who sent me."

[A] **24:6** LXX; MT reads *of Tahtim-hodshi*; Hb obscure [B] **24:13** LXX; MT reads *seven*; 1Ch 21:12

23:39 Uriah the Hittite is mentioned at the conclusion of this list as though to remind the reader not only of Uriah's faithful service to the king but also of the king's failure in disobeying God's law. This sets the stage for chapter 24, which describes David's final failure as king.

24:1-4 David lost confidence in God's help and relied on his own strength. He had apparently grown proud in his military achievements, and he began to attribute his greatness more to the power and strength of his army instead of the faithfulness of God. The story's parallel account in 1 Chronicles states that Satan was the "immediate cause," provoking David to sin by numbering the people. In 2 Samuel, God was the "ultimate cause," who punished David (by using Satan). The texts are not contradictory but give two views of the same event.

24:10-14 Instead of trying to justify his actions, David sensed his own sinfulness and immediately repented. Rather than choosing to **fall into human hands**, David chose to entrust himself to the **mercies** of Yahweh (v. 14).

24:19-25 David refused to accept Araunah's offer, not desiring to offer to God something that cost him nothing. Instead, he purchased the site and the oxen and built an altar to the Lord where he offered a burnt offering. First Chronicles 21 and 22 identify this place as the future site for the temple of the Lord. At this place the Lord made known His gracious presence to David and answered his prayers, and here the Lord would continue to abide with His people. Now that the future place for the temple was identified, the next question was, "Who will build it?" This question is addressed in the book of 1 Kings. Whereas 1 Samuel ended with the tragic deaths of Saul and his sons, 2 Samuel ends on a note of hope as God delivered the people from tragedy and extended grace to David and his house.

14 David answered Gad, "I have
great anxiety. Please, let us fall into
the LORD's hands because His mercies are great, but don't let me fall
into human hands."
15 So the LORD sent a plague on
Israel from that morning until the
appointed time, and from Dan to
Beer-sheba 70,000 men died. 16 Then
the angel extended his hand toward
Jerusalem to destroy it, but the LORD
relented concerning the destruction
and said to the angel who was destroying the people, "Enough, withdraw your hand now!" The angel of
the LORD was then at the threshing
floor of Araunah[A] the Jebusite.
17 When David saw the angel
striking the people, he said to the
LORD, "Look, I am the one who has
sinned; I am the one[B] who has done
wrong. But these sheep, what have
they done? Please, let Your hand be
against me and my father's family."
18 Gad came to David that day and
said to him, "Go up and set up an
altar to the LORD on the threshing floor of Araunah the Jebusite."
19 David went up in obedience to
Gad's command, just as the LORD
had commanded. 20 Araunah looked
down and saw the king and his servants coming toward him, so he
went out and bowed to the king with
his face to the ground.
21 Araunah said, "Why has my lord
the king come to his servant?"
David replied, "To buy the threshing floor from you in order to build
an altar to the LORD, so the plague on
the people may be halted."
22 Araunah said to David, "My
lord the king may take whatever
he wants[C] and offer it. Here are the
oxen for a •burnt offering and the
threshing sledges and ox yokes for
the wood. 23 My king, Araunah gives
everything here to the king." Then
he said to the king, "May the LORD
your God accept you."
24 The king answered Araunah,
"No, I insist on buying it from you
for a price, for I will not offer to the
LORD my God burnt offerings that
cost me nothing." David bought the
threshing floor and the oxen for 20
ounces[D] of silver. 25 He built an altar
to the LORD there and offered burnt
offerings and •fellowship offerings.
Then the LORD answered prayer on
behalf of the land, and the plague on
Israel ended.

[A]**24:16** = Ornan in 1Ch 21:15-28; 2Ch 3:1 [B]**24:17** LXX reads *shepherd* [C]**24:22** Lit *take what is good in his eyes* [D]**24:24** Lit *50 shekels*

---

2 SAMUEL… WRITTEN ON MY *Heart*

What peace to know that God has covenanted with you and me, individually and irreversibly (Jr 31:31-34)! As with King David, God's faithful love for us does not depend on our following religious rigors or maintaining perfect performances but rather on trusting in Him (Eph 2:8-9). By faith in Jesus Christ, we as sinners can declare with the Psalmist, "How joyful is the one whose transgression is forgiven, whose sin is covered! How joyful is the man the LORD does not charge with sin and in whose spirit is no deceit!" (Ps 32:1).

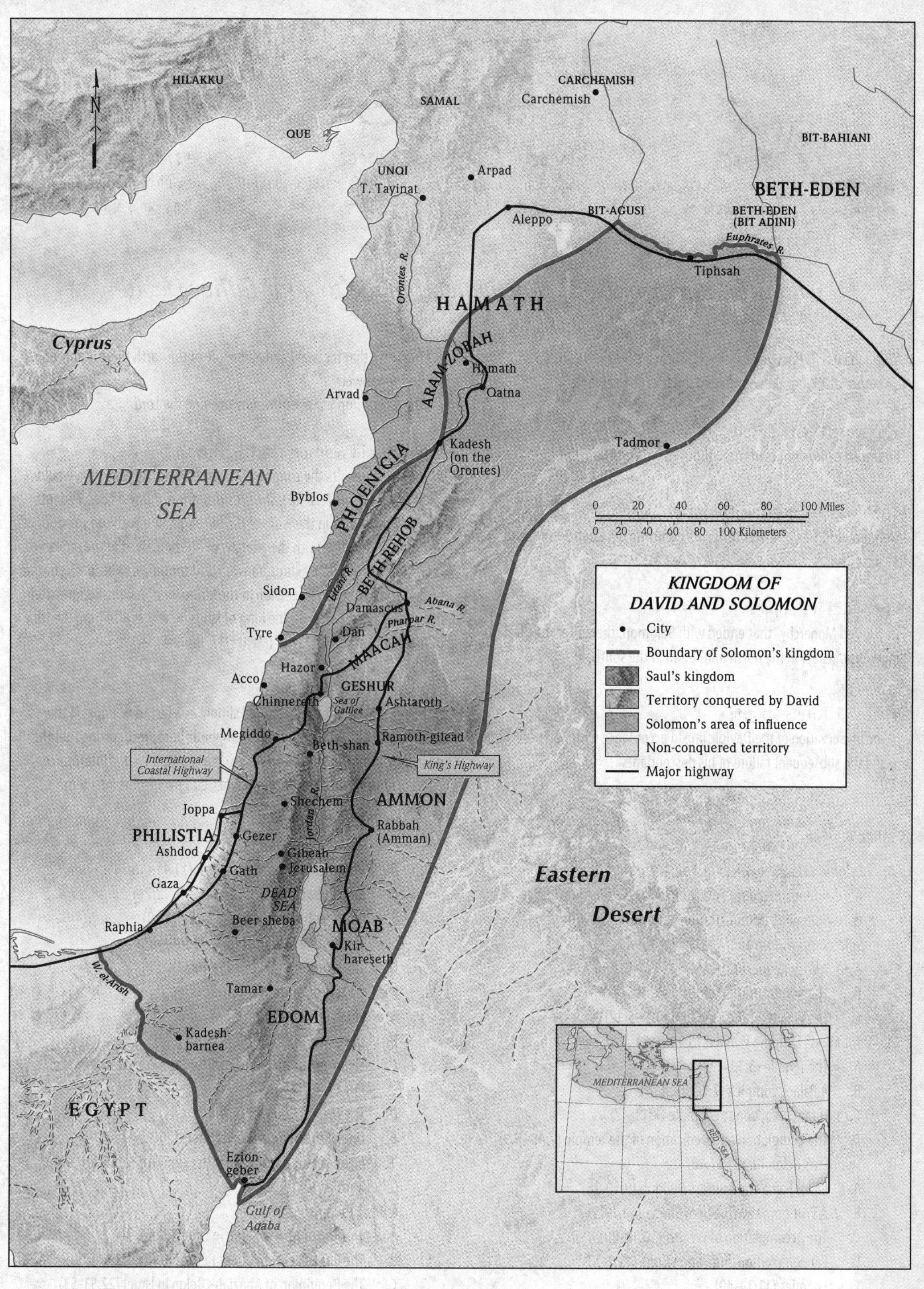

KINGDOM OF DAVID AND SOLOMON
City
Boundary of Solomon's kingdom
Saul's kingdom
Territory conquered by David
Solomon's area of influence
Non-conquered territory
Major highway
0 20 40 60 80 100 Miles
0 20 40 60 80 100 Kilometers
HILAKKU
QUE
SAMAL
CARCHEMISH
Carchemish
BIT-BAHIANI
UNQI
T. Tayinat
Arpad
Aleppo
BIT-AGUSI
BETH-EDEN
BETH-EDEN (BIT ADINI)
Euphrates R.
Tiphsah
Orontes R.
HAMATH
ARAM-ZOBAH
Hamath
Qatna
Cyprus
Arvad
Kadesh (on the Orontes)
Tadmor
MEDITERRANEAN SEA
PHOENICIA
Byblos
BETH-REHOB
Litani R.
Sidon
Damascus
Abana R.
Pharpar R.
Tyre
Dan
MAACAH
Hazor
Acco
GESHUR
Chinnereth
Sea of Galilee
Ashtaroth
Megiddo
Ramoth-gilead
Beth-shan
International Coastal Highway
King's Highway
Jordan R.
Shechem
AMMON
Joppa
PHILISTIA
Gezer
Rabbah (Amman)
Ashdod
Gibeah
Jerusalem
Gath
Gaza
DEAD SEA
Eastern Desert
Raphia
Beer-sheba
MOAB
Kir-hareseth
W. el-Arish
Tamar
EDOM
Kadesh-barnea
EGYPT
Ezion-geber
Gulf of Aqaba
MEDITERRANEAN SEA
RED SEA

1 Kings

Timeline	970 BC	959 BC	940 BC	931 BC
World Events / Biblical Events	Death of David. Solomon becomes king.	Solomon's temple is dedicated.	The Queen of Sheba visits Solomon.	Death of Solomon. The kingdom is divided.

"I will fulfill My promise to you, which I made to your father David" (6:12).

Who wrote 1 Kings?

The author of 1 Kings unidentified in the text or elsewhere

Who were the recipients?

The Jewish exiles dispersed throughout Assyria and Babylon

When was 1 Kings written?

Likely around 550 B.C., with the events occurring between 970 B.C. and 853 B.C.

Where did it happen?

The "United Monarchy" that ended with Solomon, thereafter the divided kingdoms of Israel in the north and Judah in the south

What is 1 Kings about?

- The preservation of the Davidic line in accordance with God's covenant and the subsequent failure of his descendants
- The truth that for Israel and all people of the earth there is only one God—Yahweh
- The crucial importance of wholly obeying the Lord

Why should women read 1 Kings?

As the reader awaits the coming of the true David, the One who would reign forever (2Sm 7:12-16), she sees the string of David's descendants who failed to "walk in the ways of David," beginning with the splendor of Solomon and ending with the anarchy of Ahaziah. Despite the repeated moral failures of earthly kings, Yahweh God continues to keep His covenant by preserving Davidic succession in the kingdom of Judah and ultimately by coming as the Messiah, the King of kings, who was also from the tribe of Judah and a "son of David" (Mt 1:1-17; Rm 9:4–5).

How do you read 1 Kings?

Although 1 Kings is often regarded simply as a historical book, in the Jewish canon it is categorized as a prophetic book, recognizing that the divinely inspired writer intentionally concentrated on *and* interpreted particular events in order to illuminate God's perspective on them.

Outline

- I. Solomon's Enthronement (1:1–2:46)
  - A. Adonijah's Bid for Power (1:1–2:22)
  - B. Solomon's Demonstration of Power (2:23-46)
- II. Solomon's Wisdom and Wealth (3:1–5:12)
  - A. A Wise Request (3:1-15)
  - B. The Administration of Justice (3:16-28)
  - C. The Wealth of the Kingdom (4:1–5:12)
- III. Solomon's Building Projects (5:13–9:9)
  - A. The Temple (5:13–6:38)
  - B. A Palace Complex (7:1-12)
  - C. Hiram's Work on the Temple (7:13-47)
  - D. The Completion and Dedication of the Temple (7:48–9:9)
- IV. Solomon's Reign (9:10–11:40)
  - A. Labor Force and Military Buildup (9:10-28)
  - B. A Visit from the Queen of Sheba (10:1-13)
  - C. The Accumulation of Wealth (10:14-29)
  - D. Foreign Women and Pagan Gods (11:1-13)
  - E. Enemies (11:14-40)
- V. The Division of Solomon's Kingdom (11:41–16:34)
  - A. King Rehoboam in Judah (11:41–12:24)
  - B. King Jeroboam in Israel (12:25–14:20)
  - C. The Kings of Judah (14:21–15:24)
  - D. The Kings of Israel (15:25–16:34)
- VI. The Prophets of Yahweh (17:1–22:38)
  - A. Elijah (17:1-24)
  - B. Obadiah (18:1-16)
  - C. Elijah versus Ahab, Jezebel, and the Prophets of Baal (18:17–19:21)
  - D. The Man of God (20:1-34)
  - E. One of the Sons of the Prophets (20:35-43)
  - F. Elijah versus Ahab in Naboth's Vineyard (21:1-29)
  - G. Micaiah (22:1-38)
- VII. A Bleak Picture (22:39-53)
  - A. The End of Ahab's Reign in Israel (22:39-40)
  - B. The End of Jehoshaphat's Reign in Judah (22:41-50)
  - C. The Beginning of Ahaziah's Reign in Israel (22:51-53)

>WORD|*study*

1:1 Now translates a special usage of the Hebrew conjunction *waw*, which here closely links what follows with preceding material (i.e., 2 Samuel; cp. Ex 1:1; Ezra 1:1). Chapters 1–2 provide the conclusion to 2Sm 9–20 regarding David's reign and recount the battle for succession.

925 BC	880 BC	857 BC	874–853 BC	962–852 BC
Pharaoh Shoshenq I (Shishak) of Egypt invades Jerusalem and takes treasures from the temple and royal palaces.	Omri makes Samaria the capital of the northern kingdom.	Ben-hadad of Aram attacks Samaria.	Ahab and Jezebel reign in the northern kingdom.	Elijah the prophet ministers in a time of apostasy.

Adonijah's Bid for Power (1:1–2:22)

Introduction of Abishag (1:1-4)

1 Now King David was old and getting on in years. Although they covered him with bedclothes, he could not get warm. 2 So his servants said to him: "Let us[A] search for a young virgin for my lord the king. She is to attend the king and be his caregiver. She is to lie by your side so that my lord the king will get warm." 3 They searched for a beautiful girl throughout the territory of Israel; they found Abishag the Shunammite[B] and brought her to the king. 4 The girl was of unsurpassed beauty, and she became the king's caregiver. She served him, but he was not intimate with[C] her.

Conspiracy (1:5-27)

5 Adonijah son of Haggith kept exalting himself, saying, "I will be king!" He prepared chariots, cavalry, and 50 men to run ahead of him.[D] 6 But his father had never once reprimanded[E] him by saying, "Why do you act this way?" In addition, he was quite handsome and was born after Absalom. 7 He conspired[F] with Joab son of Zeruiah and with Abiathar the priest. They supported Adonijah, 8 but Zadok the priest, Benaiah son of Jehoiada, Nathan the prophet, Shimei, Rei, and David's warriors did not side with Adonijah.

9 Adonijah sacrificed sheep, oxen, and fattened cattle near the stone of Zoheleth, which is next to En-rogel. He invited all his royal brothers and all the men of Judah, the servants of the king, 10 but he did not invite Nathan the prophet, Benaiah, the warriors, or his brother Solomon.

11 Then Nathan said to Bathsheba, Solomon's mother, "Have you not heard that Adonijah son of Haggith has become king and our lord David does not know it? 12 Now please come and let me advise you. Save your life and the life of your son Solomon. 13 Go, approach King David and say to him, 'My lord the king, did you not swear to your servant: Your son Solomon is to become king after me, and he is the one who is to sit on my throne? So why has Adonijah become king?' 14 At that moment, while you are still there speaking with the king, I'll come in after you and confirm your words."

15 So Bathsheba went to the king in his bedroom. Since the king was very old, Abishag the Shunammite was serving him. 16 Bathsheba bowed down and paid homage to the king, and he asked, "What do you want?"

17 She replied, "My lord, you swore to your servant by the LORD your God, 'Your son Solomon is to become king after me, and he is the one who is to sit on my throne.' 18 Now look, Adonijah has become king. And,[G] my lord the king, you didn't know it. 19 He has lavishly sacrificed oxen, fattened cattle, and sheep. He invited all the king's sons, Abiathar the priest, and Joab the commander of the army, but he did not invite your servant Solomon. 20 Now, my lord the king, the eyes of all Israel are on you to tell them who will sit on the throne of my lord the king after him. 21 Otherwise, when my lord the king rests with his

[A]1:2 Lit *them* [B]1:3 Shunem was a town in the hill country of Issachar at the foot of Mt. Moreh; Jos 19:17-18. [C]1:4 Lit *he did not know* [D]1:5 Heralds announcing his procession [E]1:6 Or *grieved* [F]1:7 Lit *His words were* [G]1:18 Some Hb mss, LXX, Vg, Syr; other Hb mss read *And now*

Title The title "Kings" originated in the fourth-century Latin Vulgate translation, in which Jerome entitled the first half "The Book of the Kings."

1:1-4 A symptom of David's aging was his inability to **get warm**. With all of David's wives and concubines who could have kept him warm, the solution seems strange. Based on the given details and ancient beliefs linking political power with virility, some scholars think the woman may have been a sort of virility test. The lack of intimacy would have been seen as proof of the king's physical impotence, confirming his inability to reign and underscoring the need to identify his successor. **A young virgin** (Hb *na'arah betulah*) combines two Hebrew words. The first specifies the woman's age—she would be "a young woman," and the second ("a virgin or maiden") emphasizes her purity and suitability for marriage if so desired. The text clearly emphasizes that David **was not intimate with** [Hb *lo' yeda'ah*, "he did not know," a euphemism for sexual relations] **her**.

1:5-21 As the eldest of David's surviving sons, **Adonijah**, (Hb, "my Lord is Yahweh") **son of Haggith** (Hb, "festive") naturally considered himself as the heir to the throne, and the people probably expected him to become **king** (cp. 2Sm 3:4). However, David had already sworn that **Solomon** would inherit the throne (1Kg 1:13,17,24; cp. 1Ch 28:4-8; 29:1). Adonijah's overt bid for the throne progressed without reverence for the dying king, but David is indicted as having **never once reprimanded** his son for his presumption (1Kg 1:6; cp. Eli, 1Sm 3:13; Samuel, 1Sm 8:1-3). Some of Adonijah's actions mirrored Absalom's (cp. 1Kg 1:5; 2Sm 15:1,6) and were an affront to his father, whose oath he surely knew. They were also tantamount to conspiracy against God and against the son divinely appointed to be the next king (cp. Dt. 17:14-15)

Adonijah strategically did not invite key people who did not support him in David's kingdom(1Kg 1:8-10). Also, he astutely selected **En-rogel** as the place of sacrifice (v. 9). Located near Jerusalem where the Kidron and Hinnom Valleys meet and lying on the border between the territories of Judah and Benjamin (Jos 15:7; 18:16), En-rogel was appealing to both sides.

Although Nathan had coached **Bathsheba** how to approach David in a manner that would call into question the king's failure to restrain Adonijah, she simply declared the facts and pressed the issue (cp. 1Kg 1:13-14 and 17-21). She was likely David's favorite wife and certainly had influence as a queen, but she approached David as a petitioning suppliant.

1:22-27 Nathan acted appropriately in his role as a **prophet** in communicating God's will to the king and the people. His account of the guests' saying, **Long live King Adonijah!** prevented David from dismissing the gravity of the situation.

1:35-53 David's proclamation extended to Solomon the reign **over Israel and Judah**, both of which had anointed David king over all Israel in Hebron (2Sm 5:1-5; 1Kg 2:11; 1Ch 11:1-3; 12:38). During Absalom's revolt a schism between Judah and the rest of Israel had become apparent. The explicit mention of both would also remind the readers of 1 Kings who were in exile that God's promises were for the whole nation, not just one tribe. David's decisive plan and its speedy execution effectively established the kingdom in Solomon's hands, as **Adonijah** and his party instantly recognized. Fearing execution, Adonijah secured protection from Solomon by taking **hold of the horns of the altar** (vv. 50-53). Only when Adonijah had been assured that he would not be killed did he release his grip on the altar and go before Solomon to pay him **homage** as king (v. 53).

1:39-40 Solomon's coronation procession would have been heard by Adonijah's party—only about 2,000 feet south at En-rogel—but not visible to them because of an intervening hill.

fathers, I and my son Solomon will be regarded as criminals."

[22] At that moment, while she was still speaking with the king, Nathan the prophet arrived, [23] and it was announced to the king, "Nathan the prophet is here." He came into the king's presence and bowed to him with his face to the ground.

[24] "My lord the king," Nathan said, "did you say, 'Adonijah is to become king after me, and he is the one who is to sit on my throne'? [25] For today he went down and lavishly sacrificed oxen, fattened cattle, and sheep. He invited all the sons of the king, the commanders of the army, and Abiathar the priest. And look! They're eating and drinking in his presence, and they're saying, 'Long live King Adonijah!' [26] But he did not invite me—me, your servant—or Zadok the priest or Benaiah son of Jehoiada or your servant Solomon. [27] I'm certain my lord the king would not have let this happen without letting your servant[A] know who will sit on my lord the king's throne after him."

Solomon's Anointing as King (1:28–2:12)

[28] King David responded by saying, "Call in Bathsheba for me." So she came into the king's presence and stood before him. [29] The king swore an oath and said, "As the LORD lives, who has redeemed my life from every difficulty, [30] just as I swore to you by the LORD God of Israel: Your son Solomon is to become king after me, and he is the one who is to sit on my throne in my place, that is exactly what I will do this very day."

[31] Bathsheba bowed with her face to the ground, paying homage to the king, and said, "May my lord King David live forever!"

[32] King David then said, "Call in Zadok the priest, Nathan the prophet, and Benaiah son of Jehoiada for me." So they came into the king's presence. [33] The king said to them, "Take my servants with you, have my son Solomon ride on my own mule, and take him down to Gihon. [34] There, Zadok the priest and Nathan the prophet are to anoint him as king over Israel. You are to blow the ram's horn and say, 'Long live King Solomon!' [35] You are to come up after him, and he is to come in and sit on my throne. He is the one who is to become king in my place; he is the one I have commanded to be ruler over Israel and Judah."

[36] "Amen," Benaiah son of Jehoiada replied to the king. "May the LORD, the God of my lord the king, so affirm it. [37] Just as the LORD was with my lord the king, so may He[B] be with Solomon and make his throne greater than the throne of my lord King David."

[38] Then Zadok the priest, Nathan the prophet, Benaiah son of Jehoiada, the Cherethites, and the Pelethites went down, had Solomon ride on King David's mule, and took him to Gihon. [39] Zadok the priest took the horn of oil from the tabernacle and anointed Solomon. Then they blew the ram's horn, and all the people proclaimed, "Long live King Solomon!" [40] All the people followed him, playing flutes and rejoicing with such a great joy that the earth split open from the sound.[C]

[41] Adonijah and all the invited guests who were with him heard the noise as they finished eating. Joab heard the sound of the ram's horn and said, "Why is the town in such an uproar?" [42] He was still speaking when Jonathan son of Abiathar the priest, suddenly arrived. Adonijah said, "Come in, for you are an excellent man, and you must be bringing good news."

[43] "Unfortunately not," Jonathan answered him. "Our lord King David has made Solomon king. [44] And with Solomon, the king has sent Zadok the priest, Nathan the prophet, Benaiah son of Jehoiada, the Cherethites, and the Pelethites, and they have had him ride on the king's mule. [45] Zadok the priest and Nathan the prophet have anointed him king in Gihon. They have gone from there rejoicing. The town has been in an uproar; that's the noise you heard. [46] Solomon has even taken his seat on the royal throne.

[47] "The king's servants have also gone to congratulate our lord King David, saying, 'May your God make

[A] **1:27** Some Hb mss, LXX; alt Hb tradition reads *servants* [B] **1:37** Alt Hb tradition reads *so He will* [C] **1:40** LXX reads *the land resounded with their noise*

the name of Solomon more well
known than your name, and may
He make his throne greater than
your throne.' Then the king bowed
in worship on his bed. 48 And the
king went on to say this: 'May the
LORD God of Israel be praised! Today
He has provided one to sit on my
throne, and I am a witness.'"[A]
49 Then all of Adonijah's guests got
up trembling and went their separate ways. 50 Adonijah was afraid of
Solomon, so he got up and went to
take hold of the horns of the altar.
51 It was reported to Solomon:
"Look, Adonijah fears King Solomon, and he has taken hold of the
horns of the altar, saying, 'Let King
Solomon first[B] swear to me that he
will not kill his servant with the
sword.'"
52 Then Solomon said, "If he is a
man of character, not a single hair
of his will fall to the ground, but if
evil is found in him, he dies." 53 So
King Solomon sent for him, and
they took him down from the altar.
He came and paid homage to King
Solomon, and Solomon said to him,
"Go to your home."

2 As the time approached for David to die, he instructed his son
Solomon, 2 "As for me, I am going
the way of all of the earth. Be strong
and be courageous like a man, 3 and
keep your obligation to the LORD
your God to walk in His ways and to
keep His statutes, commands, ordinances, and decrees. This is written
in the law of Moses, so that you will
have success in everything you do
and wherever you turn, 4 and so that
the LORD will carry out His promise
that He made to me: 'If your sons
are careful to walk faithfully before
Me with their whole mind and heart,
you will never fail to have a man on
the throne of Israel.'
5 "You also know what Joab son of
Zeruiah did to me and what he did
to the two commanders of Israel's
army, Abner son of Ner and Amasa
son of Jether. He murdered them in
a time of peace to avenge blood shed
in war. He spilled that blood on his
own waistband and on the sandals
of his feet.[C] 6 Act according to your
wisdom, and do not let his gray head
descend to •Sheol in peace.
7 "Show loyalty to the sons of Barzillai the Gileadite and let them be
among those who eat at your table
because they supported me when I
fled from your brother Absalom.
8 "Keep an eye on Shimei son of
Gera, the Benjaminite from Bahurim who is with you. He uttered
malicious curses against me the day
I went to Mahanaim. But he came
down to meet me at the Jordan River, and I swore to him by the LORD:
'I will never kill you with the sword.'
9 So don't let him go unpunished, for
you are a wise man. You know how
to deal with him to bring his gray
head down to Sheol with blood."
10 Then David rested with his fathers and was buried in the city of
David. 11 The length of time David
reigned over Israel was 40 years: he
reigned seven years in Hebron and
33 years in Jerusalem. 12 Solomon
sat on the throne of his father David, and his kingship was firmly established.

Adonijah's Request for Abishag (2:13-22)

13 Now Adonijah son of Haggith
came to Bathsheba, Solomon's
mother. She asked, "Do you come
peacefully?"
"Peacefully," he replied, 14 and
then asked, "May I talk with you?"[D]
"Go ahead," she answered.
15 "You know the kingship was
mine," he said. "All Israel expected
me to be king, but then the kingship
was turned over to my brother, for
the LORD gave it to him. 16 So now I
have just one request of you; don't
turn me down."[E]

2:1-12 Solomon ruled with David as co-regent during the short span that David remained alive (1 Ch 29:22). Note that spiritual counsel (1 Kg 2:1-4) preceded political directives (vv. 5-9) in David's final instructions to his son.

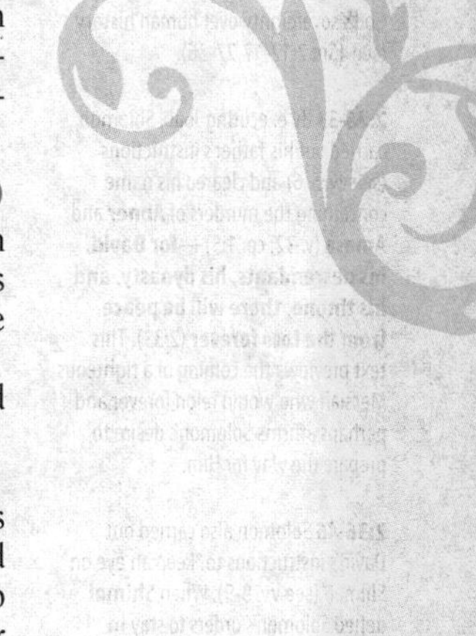

[A]**1:48** Lit *and my eyes are seeing* [B]**1:51** Some Hb mss, LXX, Syr, Vg read *today* [C]**2:5** LXX, Old Lat read *on my waistband and . . . my feet*; v. 31 [D]**2:14** Lit *then said, "I have a word for you."* [E]**2:16** Lit *don't make me turn my face*

>WORD|*study*

2:2 David instructed Solomon to be brave (Hb *wehayita le'ish*, v. 2), more literally "be a man, show yourself a man." In one instance in the New Testament, Paul similarly commanded believers to be brave (Gk *andrizesthe*, "Be alert, stand firm in the faith, act like a man, be strong." see 1Co 16:13).

2:13-22 Surely Adonijah was aware of the political implications and risk of petitioning Solomon for **the Shunammite** to **be given to** him **as a wife** (vv. 17,21; cp. Ahithophel's advice to Absalom, 2Sm 16:21-22), a request that subtly signaled his claim on his father's entire estate, including the throne. Whether motivated by lust for the beautiful Abishag, a desire for the accoutrements of the royal office, or a fixation for the throne itself, Adonijah's request displayed poor judgment.

2:19-20 Given how astutely Bathsheba earlier presented Adonijah's threat to David, she likely understood the folly of Adonijah's request and expected Solomon's response to provide greater security in having the throne pass to him.

2:23-46 Solomon immediately interpreted Adonijah's request as evidence of his brother's intent to acquire the throne, and in response he sent **Benaiah** to execute Adonijah (vv. 20,22,25). King Solomon treated with utter seriousness the responsibility of his office to both the legacy of his father David and the Lord's sovereign decision to place him on the throne (vv. 15,24-25).

2:27 By interpreting Abiathar's loss of priestly status as the fulfillment of **the Lord's prophecy . . . spoken at Shiloh against Eli's family**, the narrator demonstrates his attention to God's sovereignty over human history (see 1Sm 2:12-17,27-36).

2:28-33 By executing Joab, Solomon carried out his father's instructions (see vv. 5-6) and cleared his name concerning the murders of **Abner** and **Amasa** (v. 32; cp. 1:5)—**for David, his descendants, his dynasty, and his throne, there will be peace from the Lord forever** (2:33). This text previews the coming of a righteous Messiah who would reign forever and perhaps affirms Solomon's desire to prepare the way for Him.

2:36-46 Solomon also carried out David's instructions to "keep an eye on Shimei" (see vv. 8-9). When **Shimei** defied Solomon's orders to stay **in Jerusalem**, Solomon had him executed (vv. 38,44,46).

She said to him, "Go on."
17 He replied, "Please speak to King
Solomon since he won't turn you
down. Let him give me Abishag the
Shunammite as a wife."
18 "Very well," Bathsheba replied.
"I will speak to the king for you."
19 So Bathsheba went to King
Solomon to speak to him about
Adonijah. The king stood up to greet
her, bowed to her, sat down on his
throne, and had a throne placed for
the king's mother. So she sat down
at his right hand.
20 Then she said, "I have just one
small request of you. Don't turn me
down."
"Go ahead and ask, mother," the
king replied, "for I won't turn you
down."
21 So she said, "Let Abishag the
Shunammite be given to your
brother Adonijah as a wife."
22 King Solomon answered his
mother, "Why are you requesting
Abishag the Shunammite for Adonijah? Since he is my elder brother,
you might as well ask the kingship
for him, for Abiathar the priest, and
for Joab son of Zeruiah."[A]

Solomon's Demonstration of Power (2:23-46)

23 Then Solomon took an oath by
the Lord: "May God punish me and
do so severely if Adonijah has not
made this request at the cost of his
life. 24 And now, as the Lord lives,
the One who established me, seated
me on the throne of my father David, and made me a dynasty as He
promised—I swear Adonijah will
be put to death today!" 25 Then King
Solomon gave the order to Benaiah
son of Jehoiada, who struck down
Adonijah, and he died.
26 The king said to Abiathar the
priest, "Go to your fields in Anathoth. Even though you deserve to
die, I will not put you to death today,
since you carried the ark of the Lord
God in the presence of my father
David and you suffered through all
that my father suffered." 27 So Solomon banished Abiathar from being
the Lord's priest, and it fulfilled the
Lord's prophecy He had spoken at
Shiloh against Eli's family.
28 The news reached Joab. Since
he had supported Adonijah but not
Absalom, Joab fled to the Lord's tabernacle and took hold of the horns
of the altar.
29 It was reported to King Solomon: "Joab has fled to the Lord's
tabernacle and is now beside the
altar." Then Solomon sent[B] Benaiah
son of Jehoiada and told him, "Go
and strike him down!"
30 So Benaiah went to the tabernacle and said to Joab, "This is what
the king says: 'Come out!'"
But Joab said, "No, for I will die
here."
So Benaiah took a message back
to the king, "This is what Joab said,
and this is how he answered me."
31 The king said to him, "Do just as
he says. Strike him down and bury
him in order to remove from me and
from my father's house the blood
that Joab shed without just cause.
32 The Lord will bring back his own
blood on his head because he struck
down two men more righteous and
better than he, without my father
David's knowledge. With his sword,
Joab murdered Abner son of Ner,
commander of Israel's army, and
Amasa son of Jether, commander
of Judah's army. 33 Their blood will
come back on Joab's head and on
the head of his descendants forever,
but for David, his descendants, his
dynasty, and his throne, there will
be peace from the Lord forever."
34 Benaiah son of Jehoiada went
up, struck down Joab, and put him
to death. He was buried at his house
in the wilderness. 35 Then the king
appointed Benaiah son of Jehoiada
in Joab's place over the army, and he
appointed Zadok the priest in Abiathar's place.
36 Then the king summoned Shimei
and said to him, "Build a house for
yourself in Jerusalem and live there,
but don't leave there and go anywhere else. 37 On the day you do leave
and cross the Kidron Valley, know for
sure that you will certainly die. Your
blood will be on your own head."

[A] **2:22** LXX, Vg, Syr read *kingship for him, and on his side are Abiathar the priest and Joab son of Zeruiah* [B] **2:29** LXX adds *Joab a message: "What is the matter with you, that you have fled to the altar?" And Joab replied, "Because I feared you, I have fled to the Lord." And Solomon the king sent*

>WORD|*study*

3:3 High places (Hb *bamah*) referred to open-air "shrines or cultic platforms" typically located on hills or ridges—sites of higher elevation. The Israelites, like their pagan neighbors, had adopted the practice of offering sacrifices at "high places" both to Yahweh and to idols. After the temple was built, the term referred specifically to idolatrous practices (14:22-24). The writer of 1 and 2 Kings also used the rulers' disposition toward "high places" as a criterion for evaluating their respective reigns:

- A good king destroyed the high places (e.g., Hezekiah, 2Kg 18:3-6).
- A second-rate king did nothing about them (e.g., Joash, 2Kg 12:2-3).
- A wicked king actually participated in or promoted worship at the high places (e.g., Jeroboam, 1Kg 12:25-33).

38 Shimei said to the king, "The
sentence is fair; your servant will
do as my lord the king has spoken."
And Shimei lived in Jerusalem for a
long time.
39 But then, at the end of three
years, two of Shimei's slaves ran
away to Achish son of Maacah,
king of Gath. Shimei was informed,
"Look, your slaves are in Gath." 40 So
Shimei saddled his donkey and set
out to Achish at Gath to search for
his slaves. He went and brought
them back from Gath.
41 It was reported to Solomon that
Shimei had gone from Jerusalem
to Gath and had returned. 42 So the
king summoned Shimei and said to
him, "Didn't I make you swear by
the LORD and warn you, saying, 'On
the day you leave and go anywhere
else, know for sure that you will certainly die'? And you said to me, 'The
sentence is fair; I will obey.' 43 So why
have you not kept the LORD's oath
and the command that I gave you?"
44 The king also said, "You yourself
know all the evil that you did to my
father David. Therefore, the LORD has
brought back your evil on your head,
45 but King Solomon will be blessed,
and David's throne will remain established before the LORD forever."
46 Then the king commanded Benaiah son of Jehoiada, and he went
out and struck Shimei down, and
he died. So the kingdom was established in Solomon's hand.

A Wise Request (3:1-15)

3 Solomon made an alliance[A] with
Pharaoh king of Egypt by marrying Pharaoh's daughter. Solomon
brought her to live in the city of
David until he finished building his
palace, the LORD's temple, and the
wall surrounding Jerusalem. 2 However, the people were sacrificing on
the •high places, because until that
time a temple for the LORD's name
had not been built. 3 Solomon loved
the LORD by walking in the statutes
of his father David, but he also sacrificed and burned incense on the
high places.
4 The king went to Gibeon to sacrifice there because it was the most
famous high place. He offered 1,000
•burnt offerings on that altar. 5 At
Gibeon the LORD appeared to Solomon in a dream at night. God said,
"Ask. What should I give you?"
6 And Solomon replied, "You have
shown great and faithful love to Your
servant, my father David, because he
walked before You in faithfulness,
righteousness, and[B] integrity. You
have continued this great and faithful love for him by giving him a son
to sit on his throne, as it is today.
7 "LORD my God, You have now
made Your servant king in my father
David's place. Yet I am just a youth
with no experience in leadership.[C]
8 Your servant is among Your people
You have chosen, a[D] people too numerous to be numbered or counted.
9 So give Your servant an obedient
heart to judge Your people and to
discern between good and evil. For
who is able to judge this great people of Yours?"
10 Now it pleased the Lord that
Solomon had requested this. 11 So
God said to him, "Because you have
requested this and did not ask for
long life[E] or riches for yourself, or
the death[F] of your enemies, but you

[A]**3:1** Lit *Solomon made himself a son-in-law* [B]**3:6** Lit *and with You* [C]**3:7** Lit *am a little youth and do not know to go out or come in* [D]**3:8** Lit *chosen many* [E]**3:11** Lit *for many days* [F]**3:11** Lit *life*

3:1-3 The narrator introduces three aspects of Solomon's reign, none of which are entirely positive. First, **by marrying** the **daughter** of **Pharaoh king of Egypt** (possibly Pharaoh Siamun of the weak 21st dynasty), he forged a political **alliance** that ensured peace on Israel's southwest border (v. 1; cp. 4:21). However, the Lord had explicitly forbidden the Israelites to intermarry or make a treaty with the various peoples living in Canaan (Dt 7:1-4; cp. 1Kg 11:2). While marrying an Egyptian did not explicitly break this command since Egypt is not included in the list of nations (Dt 7:1), the effect of Solomon's marriage proved to be just as harmful in turning his heart away from the Lord and toward other gods (see 1Kg 11:1-2).

Second, Solomon's most important building projects included **his palace** [Hb *bayit*, "house"], **the LORD's temple, and the wall surrounding Jerusalem.** The size of the palace complex may have warranted the greater time investment (1Kg 6:38–7:1; cp. 9:1,10,15).

Third, Solomon is described in positive terms as one who **loved the LORD.** However, both he and the people **were sacrificing on the high places** until the temple was built. In addition, the text notes that Solomon walked **in the statutes of his father David**, one of only three references in the Old Testament to "the statutes" of a man rather than of God, the other two being negative references to idolatrous behavior (1Kg 3:3; Ezk 20:18; Mc 6:16). The narrator may be implicating Solomon for his later failure as the spiritual leader of Israel (1Kg 11:4-10).

3:4 The tabernacle was in **Gibeon** (2Ch 1:3), but it had also been the site of a large pagan shrine. Second Chronicles explains that David had "put the bronze altar . . . in front of the LORD's tabernacle" or "tent of meeting," which was at "the high place . . . in Gibeon" (2Ch 1:3-5).

3:4-15 Solomon was keenly aware that he could not lead God's **chosen** people without wisdom, so the only request that he placed before the Lord was for the courage and **discernment** to rule justly and with integrity (vv. 8-9,11; cp. 2Ch 1:10). **The Lord** was **pleased** with Solomon's request, not because such blessings as wealth and fame would have been poor choices, for these rewards were considered to be evidences of God's blessing and favor (3:10). Having chosen a better gift than these good gifts, however, Solomon received not only **a wise and understanding heart** but also what he **did not ask for: both riches and honor** (Hb *kavod*, "glory, fame" usually ascribed only to deity, 1Kg 3:10-12; cp. 2Ch 1:11-12).

3:16-28 Although this story portrays the essence of a mother's love, it primarily functions to verify and illustrate that God had indeed endowed Solomon with His **wisdom** (Hb *chokmah 'elohim*, "wisdom of or from God, divine wisdom," a phrase not found elsewhere in the Old Testament, v. 28; cp. 3:11-12). The **two women who were prostitutes** by occupation **came to the king** as the highest authority for the administration of justice but also because they had no one else to adjudicate the matter for them. They believed that the king would actually follow through on his threat to **cut** [Hb *gazar*, "divide, cut in two"; cp. Ps 136:13] **the living boy in two**, but neither the text nor the religious context in which they lived suggests that Solomon would actually have done so. The child's real mother **felt** [Hb *kamar*, "yearn, be or become hot, grow warm"; figuratively, "become emotionally agitated"] **great compassion** [Hb *rachamim*, "bowels" in this plural form, understood to be the seat of human emotions—cp. Pr 12:10, "merciful acts"; from the singular, *rechem*, "womb"—cp. Gn 49:25; Is 46:3] **for her son** and begged Solomon to **give** the other woman the child rather than killing him. Not only had Solomon employed unusual discernment in a difficult case, but he had also administered **justice** (Hb *mishpat*) on behalf of citizens of the lowest social status (cp. Pr 29:14).

4:1-28 Solomon's wisdom is illustrated in his portrayal as a master organizer over all the detailed affairs of his kingdom. The specificity of the lists here confirms for the reader the historicity of the kingdom described.

4:4-5 The banished **Abiathar** may have been mentioned out of respect for the permanent status of priests (see 2:26-27,35). **Zabud** (Hb, "given"), a name appropriate for a **son of Nathan** (Hb, "giver") the prophet, also served as **a priest** [Hb *kohēn*, "chief ruler, principal officer"; cp. 2Sm 8:18] **and adviser** [Hb *rē'eh*, "friend"] **to the king.**

>WORD|*study*

3:19-27 Significantly, the mother referred to her child with the uncommon term baby (Hb *yalud*, "the one born," vv. 26-27; 1Ch 14:4; Jb 14:1; 15:14; 25:4). Also in the narrative, two other words have been used: son (Hb *bēn*, 1Kg 3:19-23,26) and boy (Hb *yeled*, the ordinary Hebrew word for "child," v. 25). The true mother used a word more closely connected to the experience of childbirth. Her use of the word *yalud* seems to authenticate her claim that she had actually given birth to the boy. The king discerned the self-sacrificial love of the real "mother" and, picking up her word for the child, awarded "the living baby" (Hb *yalud*, v. 27) to her.

asked discernment for yourself to understand justice, [12] I will therefore do what you have asked. I will give you a wise and understanding heart, so that there has never been anyone like you before and never will be again. [13] In addition, I will give you what you did not ask for: both riches and honor, so that no man in any kingdom will be your equal during your entire life. [14] If you walk in My ways and keep My statutes and commands just as your father David did, I will give you a long life."

[15] Then Solomon woke up and realized it had been a dream. He went to Jerusalem, stood before the ark of the Lord's covenant, and offered burnt offerings and •fellowship offerings. Then he held a feast for all his servants.

The Administration of Justice (3:16-28)

[16] Then two women who were prostitutes came to the king and stood before him. [17] One woman said, "Please my lord, this woman and I live in the same house, and I had a baby while she was in the house. [18] On the third day after I gave birth, she also had a baby and we were alone. No one else[A] was with us in the house; just the two of us were there. [19] During the night this woman's son died because she lay on him. [20] She got up in the middle of the night and took my son from my side while your servant was asleep. She laid him at her breast, and she put her dead son in my arms. [21] When I got up in the morning to nurse my son, I discovered he was dead. That morning, when I looked closely at him I realized that he was not the son I gave birth to."

[22] "No," the other woman said. "My son is the living one; your son is the dead one."

The first woman said, "No, your son is the dead one; my son is the living one." So they argued before the king.

[23] The king replied, "This woman says, 'This is my son who is alive, and your son is dead,' but that woman says, 'No, your son is dead, and my son is alive.'" [24] The king continued, "Bring me a sword." So they brought the sword to the king. [25] Solomon said, "Cut the living boy in two and give half to one and half to the other."

[26] The woman whose son was alive spoke to the king because she felt great compassion[B] for her son. "My lord, give her the living baby," she said, "but please don't have him killed!"

But the other one said, "He will not be mine or yours. Cut him in two!"

[27] The king responded, "Give the living baby to the first woman, and don't kill him. She is his mother." [28] All Israel heard about the judgment the king had given, and they stood in awe of the king because they saw that God's wisdom was in him to carry out justice.

The Wealth of the Kingdom (4:1–5:12)

Peace and Provision (4:1-28)

4 King Solomon ruled over Israel, [2] and these were his officials:

> Azariah son of Zadok, priest;
> [3] Elihoreph and Ahijah the sons of Shisha, secretaries;
> Jehoshaphat son of Ahilud, court historian;
> [4] Benaiah son of Jehoiada, in charge of the army;
> Zadok and Abiathar, priests;

[A]3:18 Lit *No stranger* [B]3:26 Lit *because her compassion grew hot*

> 5 Azariah son of Nathan, in charge of the deputies;
> Zabud son of Nathan, a priest and adviser to the king;
> 6 Ahishar, in charge of the palace;
> and Adoniram son of Abda, in charge of forced labor.

7 Solomon had 12 deputies for all Israel. They provided food for the king and his household; each one made provision for one month out of the year. 8 These were their names:

> Ben-hur, in the hill country of Ephraim;
> 9 Ben-deker, in Makaz, Shaalbim, Beth-shemesh, and Elon-beth-hanan;
> 10 Ben-hesed, in Arubboth (he had Socoh and the whole land of Hepher);
> 11 Ben-abinadab, in all Naphath-dor (Taphath daughter of Solomon was his wife);
> 12 Baana son of Ahilud, in Taanach, Megiddo, and all Beth-shean which is beside Zarethan below Jezreel, from Beth-shean to Abel-meholah, as far as the other side of Jokmeam;
> 13 Ben-geber, in Ramoth-gilead (he had the villages of Jair son of Manasseh, which are in Gilead, and he had the region of Argob, which is in Bashan, 60 great cities with walls and bronze bars);
> 14 Ahinadab son of Iddo, in Mahanaim;
> 15 Ahimaaz, in Naphtali (he also had married a daughter of Solomon—Basemath);
> 16 Baana son of Hushai, in Asher and Bealoth;
> 17 Jehoshaphat son of Paruah, in Issachar;
> 18 Shimei son of Ela, in Benjamin;
> 19 Geber son of Uri, in the land of Gilead, the country of Sihon king of the Amorites and of Og king of Bashan.

There was one deputy in the land of Judah.[A]

20 Judah and Israel were as numerous as the sand by the sea; they were eating, drinking, and rejoicing. 21[B] Solomon ruled over all the kingdoms from the Euphrates River to the land of the Philistines and as far as the border of Egypt. They offered tribute and served Solomon all the days of his life.

22 Solomon's provisions for one day were 150 bushels[C] of fine flour and 300 bushels[D] of meal, 23 10 fattened oxen, 20 range oxen, and 100 sheep, besides deer, gazelles, roebucks, and pen-fed poultry,[E] 24 for he had dominion over everything west of the Euphrates from Tiphsah to Gaza and over all the kings west of the Euphrates. He had peace on all his surrounding borders. 25 Throughout Solomon's reign, Judah and Israel lived in safety from Dan to Beersheba, each man under his own vine and his own fig tree. 26 Solomon had 40,000[F] stalls of horses for his chariots, and 12,000 horsemen. 27 Each of those deputies for a month in turn provided food for King Solomon and for everyone who came to King Solomon's table. They neglected nothing. 28 Each man brought the barley and the straw for the chariot teams and the other horses to the required place according to his assignment.[G]

HARD QUESTION

Are women today eligible to receive wisdom like Solomon?

While King Solomon's gift (3:12; 4:29-31) was certainly an extraordinary one, we who love the Lord Jesus Christ and belong to God are daughters of the King of kings. In Christ you are invited to come into the King's presence and to ask for what you need. James 1:5-6 affirms God's desire to answer requests for wisdom: "Now if any of you lacks wisdom, he should ask God, who gives to all generously and without criticizing, and it will be given to him. But let him ask in faith without doubting." Christ encouraged His disciples to "keep asking . . . searching . . . knocking" (Mt 7:7) and revealed the extravagant promise that "the heavenly Father [will] give the Holy Spirit to those who ask Him" (Lk 11:9-13). Elsewhere Christ promised that the Holy Spirit "will guide you into all the truth" (Jn 16:13). Wisdom is a birthright for every daughter of God and is hers for the asking.

4:7-15 The list of the **12 deputies** and their districts included two sons-in-law of King Solomon: **Ben-abinadab,** whose **wife** was **Taphath** [Hb, "ornament," v. 11] **daughter of Solomon**, and **Ahimaaz**, whose wife was another **daughter of Solomon—Basemath** (Hb "spice," v. 15). Appointment of these men suggests that Solomon hand-picked people he could trust and who would be loyal to the throne.

4:25 That **each man** lived safely **under his own vine and his own fig tree**, expressed the nation's prosperity and security, particularly as signs of God's covenant blessing or the restoration of His favor (cp. Dt 8:7-8; 2Kg 18:31; Sg 2:13; Is 36:16; Jl 2:22; Mc 4:4; Zch 3:10; Hg 2:19). Conversely, withered vines and fig trees or their production of bad fruit signifies God's judgment or the withdrawal of His blessing (cp. Is 34:4; Jr 5:17; 8:13; Hs 2:12; Jl 1:6-7,12; Am 4:9; Mt 21:19; Mk 11:13,20-21; Lk 13:6-7). **From Dan to Beersheba** is the customary reference to all the land occupied by Israel. As the Lord had promised David, He gave Solomon "rest from all his surrounding enemies" and "peace and quiet to Israel during his reign" (1Ch 22:9; 2Sm 7:10-11).

[A] **4:19** LXX; MT omits *of Judah* [B] **4:21** 1Kg 5:1 in Hb [C] **4:22** Lit *30 cors* [D] **4:22** Lit *60 cors*
[E] **4:23** Hb obscure [F] **4:26** 2Ch 9:25 reads *4,000 stalls* [G] **4:28** Lit *judgment*

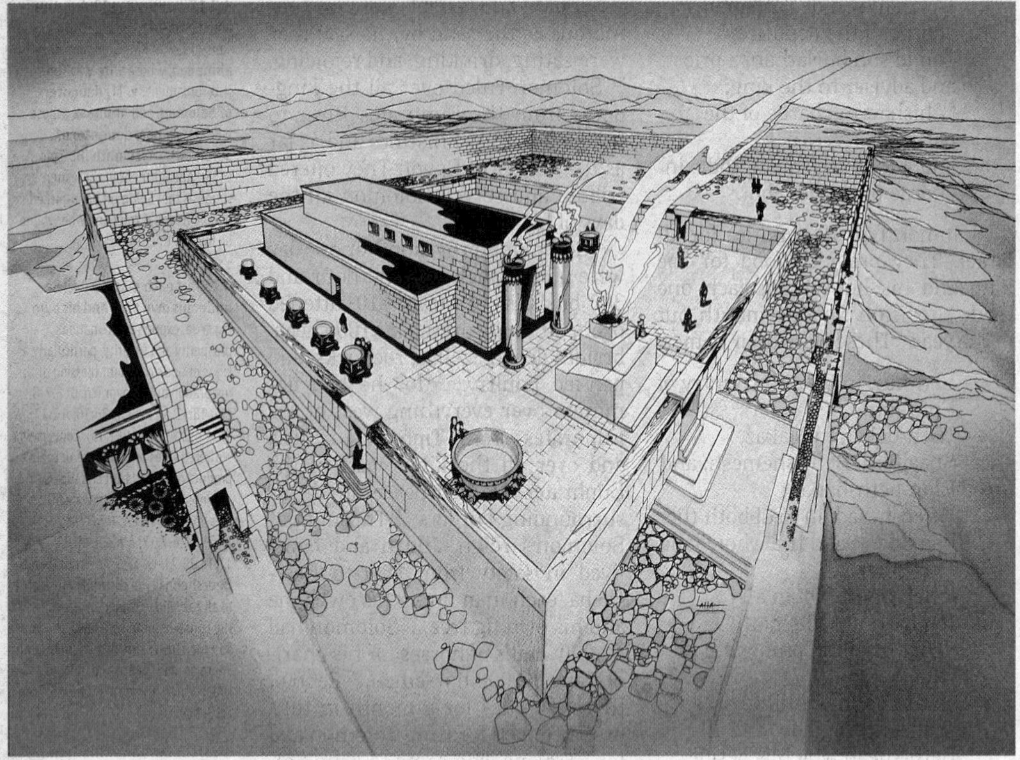

Reconstruction of Solomon's Temple (957–586 B.C.). Shown are the 10 lavers (five on each side of the temple), the Molten Sea (lower, center), and the Altar of Burnt Offerings (center).

Fame and Friendship (4:29–5:12)

[29]God gave Solomon wisdom,
very great insight, and understanding as vast as the sand on the seashore. [30]Solomon's wisdom was
greater than the wisdom of all the
people of the East, greater than all
the wisdom of Egypt. [31]He was wiser
than anyone—wiser than Ethan the
Ezrahite, and Heman, Calcol, and
Darda, sons of Mahol. His reputation extended to all the surrounding
nations.
[32]Solomon composed 3,000 proverbs, and his songs numbered 1,005.
[33]He described trees, from the cedar
in Lebanon to the hyssop growing
out of the wall. He also taught about
animals, birds, reptiles, and fish.
[34]People came from everywhere,
sent by every king on earth who had
heard of his wisdom, to listen to
Solomon's wisdom.

5 [A]Hiram king of Tyre sent his servants to Solomon when he heard
that he had been anointed king in
his father's place, for Hiram had always been friends with David.
[2]Solomon sent this message to
Hiram: [3]"You know my father David was not able to build a temple
for the name of •Yahweh his God.
This was because of the warfare all
around him until the LORD put his
enemies under his feet. [4]The LORD
my God has now given me rest all
around; there is no enemy or crisis.
[5]So I plan to build a temple for the
name of Yahweh my God, according to what the LORD promised my
father David: 'I will put your son on
your throne in your place, and he
will build the temple for My name.'
[6]"Therefore, command that cedars from Lebanon be cut down for
me. My servants will be with your
servants, and I will pay your servants' wages according to whatever

[A]5:1 1Kg 5:15 in Hb

you say, for you know that not a man among us knows how to cut timber like the Sidonians."

[7]When Hiram heard Solomon's words, he greatly rejoiced and said, "May the LORD be praised today! He has given David a wise son to be over this great people!" [8]Then Hiram sent a reply to Solomon, saying, "I have heard your message; I will do everything you want regarding the cedar and cypress timber. [9]My servants will bring the logs down from Lebanon to the sea, and I will make them into rafts to go by sea to the place you indicate. I will break them apart there, and you can take them away. You then can meet my needs by providing my household with food."

[10]So Hiram provided Solomon with all the cedar and cypress timber he wanted, [11]and Solomon provided Hiram with 100,000 bushels[A] of wheat as food for his household and 110,000 gallons[B] of oil from crushed olives. Solomon did this for Hiram year after year.

[12]The LORD gave Solomon wisdom, as He had promised him. There was peace between Hiram and Solomon, and the two of them made a treaty.

The Temple (5:13–6:38)

[13]Then King Solomon drafted forced laborers from all Israel; the labor force numbered 30,000 men. [14]He sent 10,000 to Lebanon each month in shifts; one month they were in Lebanon, two months they were at home. Adoniram was in charge of the forced labor. [15]Solomon had 70,000 porters and 80,000 stonecutters in the mountains, [16]not including his 3,300[C] deputies in charge of the work. They ruled over the people doing the work. [17]The king commanded them to quarry large, costly stones to lay the foundation of the temple with dressed stones. [18]So Solomon's builders and Hiram's builders, along with the Gebalites, quarried the stone and prepared the timber and stone for the temple's construction.

6 Solomon began to build the temple for the LORD in the four hundred eightieth year after the Israelites came out of the land of Egypt, in the fourth year of his reign over Israel, in the second month, in the month of Ziv.[D] [2]The temple that King Solomon built for the LORD was 90 feet[E] long, 30 feet[F] wide, and 45 feet[G] high. [3]The portico in front of the temple sanctuary was 30 feet[F] long extending across the temple's width, and 15 feet deep[H] in front of the temple. [4]He also made windows with beveled frames[I] for the temple.

[5]He then built a chambered structure[J] along the temple wall, encircling the walls of the temple, that is, the sanctuary and the inner sanctuary. And he made side chambers[K] all around. [6]The lowest chamber was 7½ feet[L] wide, the middle was nine feet[M] wide, and the third was 10½ feet[N] wide. He also provided offset ledges for the temple all around the outside so that nothing would be inserted into the temple walls. [7]The temple's construction used finished stones cut at the quarry so that no hammer, chisel, or any iron tool was heard in the temple while it was being built.

[8]The door for the lowest[O] side chamber was on the right side of the temple. They[P] went up a stairway[I] to the middle chamber, and from the middle to the third. [9]When he finished building the temple, he paneled it with boards and planks of cedar. [10]He built the chambers along the entire temple, joined to the temple with cedar beams; each story was 7½ feet[L] high.

[11]The word of the LORD came to Solomon: [12]"As for this temple you are building—if you walk in My statutes, observe My ordinances, and keep all My commands by walking in them, I will fulfill My promise to you, which I made to your father David. [13]I will live among the Israelites and not abandon My people Israel."

[14]When Solomon finished building the temple,[Q] [15]he paneled the

5:12 That Solomon and Hiram **made a treaty** (Hb *berit*, "alliance, covenant, agreement") was likely not cited in praise of Solomon's wisdom since God had forbidden the Israelites to make treaties with the surrounding nations (cp. 11:1-2,5; Gn 10:19; Ex 34:12-15).

6:1 The building of the temple was the most significant achievement of Solomon's reign. The writer carefully marked when construction began—480 years after the Israelites' exodus from **Egypt**, in the spring of **the fourth year of his reign**. Establishment of a permanent place of worship affirmed the fulfillment of God's promises to give the land to Israel and to dwell among them.

6:11-13 The description of the temple construction strategically came to an abrupt halt in the middle, between depictions of the exterior and interior of the temple, when **the word of the LORD came to Solomon**. If Solomon would be faithful to obey God's laws and would make sure His commandments were carried out in Israel, then God would **fulfill** (Hb *qum*, "build, constitute, establish, confirm, make binding, effect, carry out") His **promise** (Hb *davar*, "spoken word, utterance").

[A]5:11 Lit *20,000 cors* [B]5:11 LXX reads *20,000 baths*; MT reads *20 cors* [C]5:16 Some LXX mss read *3,600*; 2Ch 2:2,18 [D]6:1 April–May [E]6:2 Lit *60 cubits* [F]6:2,3 Lit *20 cubits* [G]6:2 Lit *30 cubits* [H]6:3 Lit *10 cubits wide* [I]6:4,8 Hb obscure [J]6:5 Lit *built the house of chamber* [K]6:5 Lit *made ribs* or *sides* [L]6:6,10 Lit *five cubits* [M]6:6 Lit *six cubits* [N]6:6 Lit *seven cubits* [O]6:8 LXX, Tg; MT reads *middle* [P]6:8 = people [Q]6:11-14 LXX omits these vv.

6:16-38 Though similar to the tabernacle in many ways, **the temple** was twice its size—90 feet long and 30 feet wide. Like the tabernacle, the temple entrance faced the east, and similar furnishings were provided, though on a grander scale. Solomon used only the best materials for the temple, namely the durable **cedar** wood and weather-resistant **cypress**. The gold **cherubim** represented the angels who stand in God's presence and reflect His glory (cp. Ezk 9:3; 10:1-22). While many attribute the temple's extravagance to Solomon's desire to display his wealth, use of the best materials reflects the tabernacle's construction "according to the pattern" that Moses had "been shown on the mountain" (Ex 25:40; see Ex 25–30 and 36–39 for details of the extensive use of gold in the tabernacle and the priestly garments). **Completed in every detail and according to every specification** (probably in 959 B.C.), the grandeur of Solomon's temple was a reflection of the majesty of God and a testimony of His greatness to all the surrounding nations (1Kg 6:38).

7:1-8 Solomon took seven years to build the temple (6:38) and **13 years** for the **palace complex**. The section's placement in the middle of the account of the temple hints that the temple itself was not at the center of Solomon's affections and loyalty.

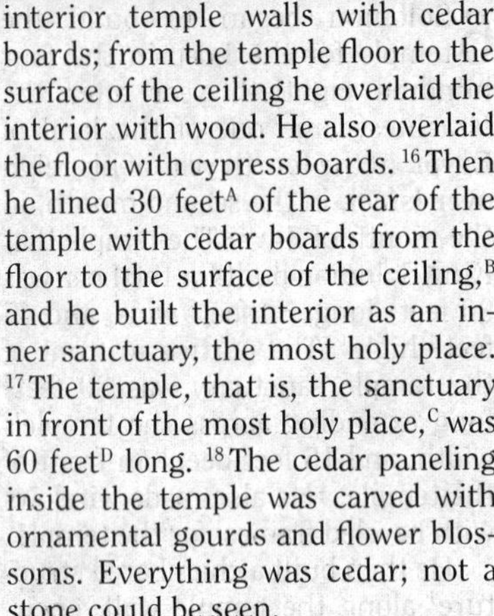

interior temple walls with cedar
boards; from the temple floor to the
surface of the ceiling he overlaid the
interior with wood. He also overlaid
the floor with cypress boards. 16 Then
he lined 30 feet[A] of the rear of the
temple with cedar boards from the
floor to the surface of the ceiling,[B]
and he built the interior as an inner sanctuary, the most holy place.
17 The temple, that is, the sanctuary
in front of the most holy place,[C] was
60 feet[D] long. 18 The cedar paneling
inside the temple was carved with
ornamental gourds and flower blossoms. Everything was cedar; not a
stone could be seen.
19 He prepared the inner sanctuary inside the temple to put the
ark of the LORD's covenant there.
20 The interior of the sanctuary was
30 feet[A] long, 30 feet[A] wide, and 30
feet[G] high; he overlaid it with pure
gold. He also overlaid the cedar altar. 21 Next, Solomon overlaid the interior of the temple with pure gold,
and he hung[E] gold chains across
the front of the inner sanctuary and
overlaid it with gold. 22 So he added
the gold overlay to the entire temple
until everything was completely finished, including the entire altar that
belongs to the inner sanctuary.
23 In the inner sanctuary he made
two •cherubim 15 feet[F] high out of
olive wood. 24 One wing of the first
cherub was 7½ feet long,[G] and the
other wing was 7½ feet long. The
wingspan was 15 feet[F] from tip to
tip. 25 The second cherub also was 15
feet;[F] both cherubim had the same
size and shape. 26 The first cherub's
height was 15 feet[F] and so was the
second cherub's. 27 Then he put the
cherubim inside the inner temple.
Since their wings were spread out,
the first one's wing touched one
wall while the second cherub's wing
touched the other[H] wall, and in the
middle of the temple their wings
were touching wing to wing. 28 He
also overlaid the cherubim with
gold.
29 He carved all the surrounding
temple walls with carved engrav-
ings—cherubim, palm trees and
flower blossoms—in both the inner
and outer sanctuaries. 30 He overlaid
the temple floor with gold in both
the inner and outer sanctuaries.
31 For the entrance of the inner sanctuary, he made olive wood
doors. The pillars of the doorposts
were five-sided.[I] 32 The two doors
were made of olive wood. He carved
cherubim, palm trees, and flower
blossoms on them and overlaid
them with gold, hammering gold
over the cherubim and palm trees.
33 In the same way, he made four-
sided[I] olive wood doorposts for the
sanctuary entrance. 34 The two doors
were made of cypress wood; the first
door had two folding sides, and the
second door had two folding panels. 35 He carved cherubim, palm
trees, and flower blossoms on them
and overlaid them with gold applied evenly over the carving. 36 He
built the inner courtyard with three
rows of dressed stone and a row of
trimmed cedar beams.
37 The foundation of the LORD's
temple was laid in Solomon's fourth
year in the month of Ziv. 38 In his
eleventh year in the eighth month,
in the month of Bul,[J] the temple was
completed in every detail and according to every specification. So he
built it in seven years.

A Palace Complex (7:1-12)

7 Solomon completed his entire
palace complex after 13 years of
construction. 2 He built the House
of the Forest of Lebanon. It was
150 feet[K] long, 75 feet[L] wide, and
45 feet[M] high on four rows of cedar
pillars, with cedar beams on top of
the pillars. 3 It was paneled above
with cedar at the top of the chambers that rested on 45 pillars, 15
per row. 4 There were three rows of
window frames, facing each other[N]
in three tiers.[O] 5 All the doors and
doorposts had rectangular frames,
the openings facing each other[P] in
three tiers.[O] 6 He made the hall of

[A] **6:16,20** Lit *20 cubits* [B] **6:16** LXX; MT omits *of the ceiling*; 1Kg 6:15 [C] **6:17** Lit *front of me*; Hb obscure [D] **6:17** Lit *40 cubits* [E] **6:21** Lit *he caused to pass across* [F] **6:23,24,25,26** Lit *10 cubits* [G] **6:24** Lit *five cubits* [H] **6:27** Lit *the second* [I] **6:31,33** Hb obscure [J] **6:38** = October–November [K] **7:2** Lit *100 cubits* [L] **7:2** Lit *50 cubits* [M] **7:2** Lit *30 cubits* [N] **7:4** Lit *frames, window to window* [O] **7:4,5** Lit *three times*; = at 3 different places [P] **7:5** Lit *frames, opposing window to window*

pillars 75 feet[A] long and 45 feet[B]
wide. A portico was in front of the
pillars, and a canopy with pillars[C]
was in front of them. 7 He made the
Hall of the Throne where he would
judge—the Hall of Judgment. It was
paneled with cedar from the floor to
the rafters.[D] 8 Solomon's own palace
where he would live, in the other
courtyard behind the hall, was of
similar construction. And he made
a house like this hall for Pharaoh's
daughter, his wife.[E]

9 All of these buildings were of
costly stones, cut to size and sawed
with saws on the inner and outer
surfaces, from foundation to coping
and from the outside to the great
courtyard. 10 The foundation was
made of large, costly stones 12 and
15 feet[F] long. 11 Above were also costly stones, cut to size, as well as cedar
wood. 12 Around the great courtyard,
as well as the inner courtyard of the
LORD's temple and the portico of the
temple, were three rows of dressed
stone and a row of trimmed cedar
beams.

Hiram's Work on the Temple (7:13-47)

13 King Solomon had Hiram[G]
brought from Tyre. 14 He was a widow's son from the tribe of Naphtali,
and his father was a man of Tyre, a
bronze craftsman. Hiram had great
skill, understanding, and knowledge
to do every kind of bronze work. So
he came to King Solomon and carried out all his work.

15 He cast two hollow bronze pillars: each 27 feet[H] high and 18 feet[I]
in circumference.[J] 16 He also made
two capitals of cast bronze to set
on top of the pillars; 7½ feet[K] was
the height of the first capital, and
7½ feet[K] was also the height of the
second capital. 17 The capitals on top
of the pillars had gratings of latticework, wreaths[L] made of chainwork—seven for the first capital and
seven for the second.

18 He made the pillars with two
encircling rows of pomegranates on
the one grating to cover the capital on top; he did the same for the
second capital. 19 And the capitals
on top of the pillars in the portico
were shaped like lilies, six feet[M] high.
20 The capitals on the two pillars
were also immediately above the
rounded surface next to the grating,
and 200 pomegranates were in rows
encircling each[N] capital. 21 He set up
the pillars at the portico of the sanctuary: he set up the right pillar and
named it Jachin;[O] then he set up the
left pillar and named it Boaz.[P] 22 The
tops of the pillars were shaped like
lilies. Then the work of the pillars
was completed.

23 He made the cast metal reservoir,[Q] 15 feet[R] from brim to brim,
perfectly round. It was 7½ feet[K] high
and 45 feet[B] in circumference. 24 Ornamental gourds encircled it below
the brim, 10 every half yard,[S] completely encircling the reservoir. The
gourds were cast in two rows when
the reservoir was cast. 25 It stood on
12 oxen, three facing north, three
facing west, three facing south, and
three facing east. The reservoir was
on top of them and all their hindquarters were toward the center.
26 The reservoir was three inches[T]
thick, and its rim was fashioned like
the brim of a cup or of a lily blossom. It held 11,000 gallons.[U]

27 Then he made 10 bronze water
carts.[V] Each water cart was six feet[M]
long, six feet[M] wide, and 4½ feet[W]
high. 28 This was the design of the
carts: They had frames; the frames
were between the cross-pieces,
29 and on the frames between the
cross-pieces were lions, oxen, and
•cherubim. On the cross-pieces
there was a pedestal above, and below the lions and oxen were wreaths
of hanging[X] work. 30 Each cart had
four bronze wheels with bronze axles. Underneath the four corners of
the basin were cast supports, each

7:13-47 For the author, the temple was the main emphasis, and he continued to describe its furnishings in great detail. **Two hollow bronze pillars,** apparently freestanding, were **set up at the portico of the sanctuary** (vv. 15-22; cp. 2 Ch 3:15-17) and given the names **Jachin** (Hb, "He will establish") and **Boaz** (Hb, "in Him is strength," the name of David's great-grandfather, 1Ch 2:12-13). The pillars were 27 feet high with a circumference of 18 feet. In addition, each was topped with an ornamental capital over seven feet, bringing the total height to nearly 35 feet. The seeming discrepancy in the measurement of the capitals as reported here (7.5 feet) and in 2Kg 25:17 (5 feet) could easily reflect a scribe's confusion between the Hebrew letters representing "five" and "three" respectively (in reference to cubits; cp. Jr 52:22).

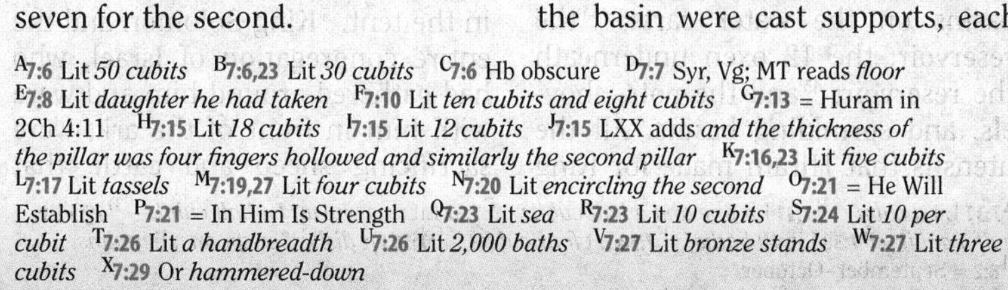

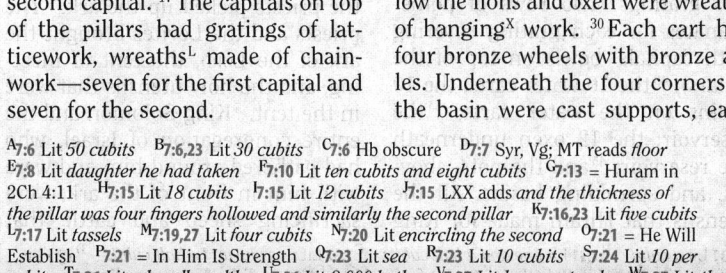

A 7:6 Lit *50 cubits* B 7:6,23 Lit *30 cubits* C 7:6 Hb obscure D 7:7 Syr, Vg; MT reads *floor* E 7:8 Lit *daughter he had taken* F 7:10 Lit *ten cubits and eight cubits* G 7:13 = Huram in 2Ch 4:11 H 7:15 Lit *18 cubits* I 7:15 Lit *12 cubits* J 7:15 LXX adds *and the thickness of the pillar was four fingers hollowed and similarly the second pillar* K 7:16,23 Lit *five cubits* L 7:17 Lit *tassels* M 7:19,27 Lit *four cubits* N 7:20 Lit *encircling the second* O 7:21 = He Will Establish P 7:21 = In Him Is Strength Q 7:23 Lit *sea* R 7:23 Lit *10 cubits* S 7:24 Lit *10 per cubit* T 7:26 Lit *a handbreadth* U 7:26 Lit *2,000 baths* V 7:27 Lit *bronze stands* W 7:27 Lit *three cubits* X 7:29 Or *hammered-down*

7:51 Notably, both here and in the next chapter, references to the temple frequently specify it as **the Lord's temple**, belonging to Yahweh rather than to Solomon. The temple's significance was not that Solomon had built such a lavish edifice for his God but that God chose to dwell there among His people.

8:1-13 **Solomon** chose **to bring** to the temple **the ark of the Lord's covenant** at the celebration of a key annual holiday in the religious life of the nation—the Festival of Booths (v. 1). The ark did not contain God's presence, but God made His presence discernible in **the cloud** and **the glory of the Lord**, which **filled the Lord's temple** just as His glory had filled the tabernacle in the wilderness (cp. Ex 19:9,16; 40:34-38).

next to a wreath. 31 And the water cart's opening inside the crown on top was 18 inches[A] wide. The opening was round, made as a pedestal 27 inches[B] wide. On it were carvings, but their frames were square, not round. 32 There were four wheels under the frames, and the wheel axles were part of the water cart; each wheel was 27 inches[C] tall. 33 The wheels' design was similar to that of chariot wheels: their axles, rims, spokes, and hubs were all of cast metal. 34 Four supports were at the four corners of each water cart; each support was one piece with the water cart. 35 At the top of the cart was a band nine inches[D] high encircling it; also, at the top of the cart, its braces and its frames were one piece with it. 36 He engraved cherubim, lions, and palm trees on the plates of its braces and on its frames, wherever each had space, with encircling wreaths. 37 In this way he made the 10 water carts using the same casting, dimensions, and shape for all of them.

38 Then he made 10 bronze basins—each basin holding 220 gallons[E] and each was six feet[F] wide—one basin for each of the 10 water carts. 39 He set five water carts on the right side of the temple and five on the left side. He put the reservoir near the right side of the temple toward the southeast. 40 Then Hiram made the basins, the shovels, and the sprinkling basins.

So Hiram finished all the work that he was doing for King Solomon on the Lord's temple: 41 two pillars; bowls for the capitals that were on top of the two pillars; the two gratings for covering both bowls of the capitals that were on top of the pillars; 42 the 400 pomegranates for the two gratings (two rows of pomegranates for each grating covering both capitals' bowls on top of the pillars); 43 the 10 water carts; the 10 basins on the water carts; 44 the reservoir; the 12 oxen underneath the reservoir; 45 and the pots, shovels, and sprinkling basins. All the utensils that Hiram made for King Solomon at the Lord's temple were made of burnished bronze. 46 The king had them cast in clay molds in the Jordan Valley between Succoth and Zarethan. 47 Solomon left all the utensils unweighed because there were so many; the weight of the bronze was not determined.

The Completion and Dedication of the Temple (7:48–9:9)

Gold Furnishings (7:48-51)

48 Solomon also made all the equipment in the Lord's temple: the gold altar; the gold table that the •bread of the Presence was placed on; 49 the pure gold lampstands in front of the inner sanctuary, five on the right and five on the left; the gold flowers, lamps, and tongs; 50 the pure gold ceremonial bowls, wick trimmers, sprinkling basins, ladles,[G] and firepans; and the gold hinges for the doors of the inner temple (that is, the most holy place) and for the doors of the temple sanctuary.

51 So all the work King Solomon did in the Lord's temple was completed. Then Solomon brought in the consecrated things of his father David—the silver, the gold, and the utensils—and put them in the treasuries of the Lord's temple.

God's Glory (8:1-13)

8 At that time Solomon assembled the elders of Israel, all the tribal heads and the ancestral leaders of the Israelites before him at Jerusalem in order to bring the ark of the Lord's covenant from the city of David, that is •Zion. 2 So all the men of Israel were assembled in the presence of King Solomon in the seventh month, the month of Ethanim,[H] at the festival.

3 All the elders of Israel came, and the priests picked up the ark. 4 The priests and the Levites brought the ark of the Lord, the tent of meeting, and the holy utensils that were in the tent. 5 King Solomon and the entire congregation of Israel, who had gathered around him and were with him in front of the ark, were sacrificing sheep and cattle that

[A] **7:31** Lit *a cubit* [B] **7:31** Lit *one and a half cubits* [C] **7:32** Lit *was one and a half cubits* [D] **7:35** Lit *half a cubit* [E] **7:38** Lit *40 baths* [F] **7:38** Lit *four cubits* [G] **7:50** Or *dishes*, or *spoons*; lit *palms* [H] **8:2** = September–October

could not be counted or numbered,
because there were so many. [6]The
priests brought the ark of the LORD's
covenant to its place, into the inner
sanctuary of the temple, to the most
holy place beneath the wings of the
•cherubim. [7]For the cherubim were
spreading their wings over[A] the place
of the ark, so that the cherubim
covered the ark and its poles from
above. [8]The poles were so long that
their ends were seen from the holy
place in front of the inner sanctuary,
but they were not seen from outside
the sanctuary; they are there to this
day. [9]Nothing was in the ark except
the two stone tablets that Moses had
put there at Horeb,[B] where the LORD
made a covenant with the Israelites
when they came out of the land of
Egypt.

[10]When the priests came out of
the holy place, the cloud filled the
LORD's temple, [11]and because of the
cloud, the priests were not able to
continue ministering, for the glory
of the LORD filled the temple.

[12]Then Solomon said:

The LORD said that
He would dwell
in thick darkness.
13 I have indeed built
an exalted temple for You,
a place
for Your dwelling forever.

The King's Blessing of Israel (8:14-21)

[14]The king turned around and
blessed the entire congregation of
Israel while they were standing.
[15]He said:

May the LORD God of Israel
be praised!
He spoke directly
to my father David,
and He has fulfilled
the promise by His power.
He said,
16 "Since the day I brought
My people Israel
out of Egypt,
I have not chosen a city
to build a temple in
among any of the tribes
of Israel,
so that My name
would be there.
But I have chosen David
to rule My people Israel."
17 It was in the desire
of my father David
to build a temple
for the name of •Yahweh,
the God of Israel.
18 But the LORD said
to my father David,
"Since it was your desire
to build a temple
for My name,
you have done well to have
this desire.
19 Yet you are not the one
to build it;
instead, your son,
your own offspring,
will build it for My name."
20 The LORD has fulfilled
what He promised.
I have taken the place
of my father David,
and I sit on
the throne of Israel,
as the LORD promised.
I have built the temple
for the name of Yahweh, the
God of Israel.
21 I have provided a place there
for the ark,
where the LORD's covenant is
that He made
with our ancestors
when He brought them out
of the land of Egypt.

The King's Prayer Before the Altar (8:22-53)

[22]Then Solomon stood before the
altar of the LORD in front of the
entire congregation of Israel and
spread out his hands toward heaven.
[23]He said:

LORD God of Israel,
there is no God like You
in heaven above or on earth
below,
keeping
the gracious covenant
with Your servants who walk
before You
with their whole heart.
24 You have kept
what You promised

8:14-21 Solomon's blessing defined the occasion as the fulfillment of the Lord's promise to his **father David**, whom he mentioned by name five times in these verses. Solomon quoted the Lord's acknowledgment of David's **desire . . . to build a temple** and His approval of that **desire** (Hb *'im lēvav*, it was "in [his] heart"). Nevertheless, God had declared that David's **son** would **build it** (cp. 2Sm 7:13). Solomon's words of blessing emphasized that he had not built the temple on his own initiative but had fulfilled the Lord's promise to Israel's beloved King David and his father's desire. In addition, each of the five times that **the temple** is mentioned, its purpose is reiterated—**the temple for the name of Yahweh, the God of Israel** (see 1Kg 8:16-20), clearly *not* for the aggrandizement of Solomon's name or even of David's.

8:16 The event fulfilled the Lord's promise to "choose the place to have His name dwell" after His people were settled in the promised land (Dt 12:10-11). This prophecy included a command to worship Him nowhere else: "You must offer your burnt offerings only in the place the LORD chooses in one of your tribes" (Dt 12:14). God claimed Jerusalem as the dwelling place of His name (2Ch 33:4; Ps 135:21). Often, in both the Psalms and the prophets, "Jerusalem" represents not only the geographical location but also:

- its inhabitants, particularly God's people (e.g., Pss 125:2; 147:2; Is 65:19);
- the wisdom and authority of God (e.g., Is 2:3);
- the entire people of Israel (e.g., Jr 2:2-4);
- the Messianic kingdom of God (e.g., Jr. 3:14-17; 33:14-18; Zch 14:8-9,11); or
- the people whom God has chosen and redeemed, personified as His bride and therefore the object of His tender love and jealous protection (e.g., Is 31:5; 40:2; 52:1; 52:9; 62; Jr 2:2; Zch 1:14,17; 2:12; 3:2; 8:1-8; 9:9 [cp. Mt 21:1-5]).

God's choice of Jerusalem was, therefore, a historical event fulfilling past prophecy and carrying forward His plan of redemption (cp. Is 65:17-19 and Rv 21:1-3; 22:3).

8:23-48 Solomon's request was on the basis of what the Lord had been faithful to accomplish. The language of Solomon's prayer quickly counteracted any doubt that God's presence was restricted to the temple—the Lord dwelled there through the presence of His Name: **May You hear in Your dwelling place in heaven** that transcends any physical building (v. 30). While the God of Israel is no local deity confined to a region or building, His presence in the temple

[A]8:7 LXX; MT reads *toward* [B]8:9 = Sinai

was a fulfillment of His promise to choose "the place to have His name dwell" and thereby serve as *the* center of worship for all Israel (cp. v. 29; Dt 12:5,10-11,14,18; 14:23; 16:2,6,11; 26:2). Anticipating Israel's failure to keep the covenant, Solomon asked God to **forgive** (1Kg 8:30), perhaps with keen awareness of the blessings for obedience and curses for disobedience cited by Moses as part of "the words of the covenant" (vv. 53,58; Dt 28–30; specifically, Dt 29:1). The prerequisite attitude of prayer for forgiveness, restoration, or intervention in each case was obedience and repentance, knowing that they had offended a holy God and needed to return to the Lord "with their whole mind and heart" (1Kg 8:48).

to Your servant,
my father David.
You spoke directly to him
and You fulfilled
Your promise
by Your power
as it is today.
25 Therefore, LORD God of Israel,
keep what You promised
to Your servant,
my father David:
You will never fail to have
a man
to sit before Me on the throne
of Israel,
if only your sons guard
their walk before Me
as you have walked before Me.
26 Now LORD[A] God of Israel,
please confirm
what You promised
to Your servant,
my father David.

27 But will God indeed live
on earth?
Even heaven,
the highest heaven,
cannot contain You,
much less this temple
I have built.
28 Listen[B] to Your servant's
prayer and his petition,
LORD my God,
so that You may hear the cry
and the prayer
that Your servant prays
before You today,
29 so that Your eyes
may watch over this temple
night and day,
toward the place
where You said:
My name will be there,
and so that You may hear
the prayer
that Your servant prays
toward this place.
30 Hear the petition
of Your servant
and Your people Israel,
which they pray
toward this place.
May You hear
in Your dwelling place
in heaven.
May You hear and forgive.

31 When a man sins
against his neighbor
and is forced to take an oath,[C]
and he comes to take an oath
before Your altar
in this temple,
32 may You hear in heaven
and act.
May You judge Your servants,
condemning the wicked man
by bringing
what he has done
on his own head
and providing justice
for the righteous
by rewarding him
according to
his righteousness.

33 When Your people
Israel are defeated
before an enemy,
because they have sinned
against You,
and they return to You
and praise Your name,
and they pray and plead
with You
for mercy in this temple,
34 may You hear in heaven
and forgive the sin
of Your people Israel.
May You restore them
to the land
You gave their ancestors.

35 When the skies are shut
and there is no rain,
because they have sinned
against You,
and they pray
toward this place
and praise Your name,
and they turn from their sins
because You
are afflicting them,
36 may You hear in heaven
and forgive the sin
of Your servants
and Your people Israel,
so that You may teach them
the good way
they should walk in.
May You send rain
on Your land
that You gave Your people
for an inheritance.

[A] 8:26 Some Hb mss, LXX, Syr, Tg, Vg, 2Ch 6:16; other Hb mss omit LORD [B] 8:28 Lit *Turn*
[C] 8:31 Lit *and he lifts a curse against him to curse him*

37 When there is famine
on the earth,
when there is pestilence,
when there is blight, mildew,
locust, or grasshopper,
when their enemy
besieges them
in the region
of their fortified cities,[A]
when there is any plague
or illness,
38 whatever prayer or petition
anyone
from Your people Israel
might have—
each man knowing
his own afflictions[B]
and spreading out his hands
toward this temple—
39 may You hear in heaven,
Your dwelling place,
and may You forgive, act,
and repay the man,
according to all his ways,
since You know his heart,
for You alone know
every human heart,
40 so that they may •fear You
all the days they live
on the land
You gave our ancestors.

41 Even for the foreigner
who is not
of Your people Israel
but has come
from a distant land
because of Your name—
42 for they will hear
of Your great name,
mighty hand,
and outstretched arm,
and will come and pray
toward this temple—
43 may You hear in heaven,
Your dwelling place,
and do according to
all the foreigner
asks You for.
Then all the people on earth
will know Your name,
to fear You
as Your people Israel do
and know that this temple
I have built
is called by Your name.

44 When Your people
go out to fight
against their enemies,[C]
wherever You send them,
and they pray to Yahweh
in the direction of the city
You have chosen
and the temple I have built
for Your name,
45 may You hear their prayer
and petition in heaven
and uphold their cause.

46 When they sin against You—
for there is no one
who does not sin—
and You are angry with them
and hand them over
to the enemy,
and their captors deport them
to the enemy's country—
whether distant or nearby—
47 and when they come
to their senses[D]
in the land where
they were deported
and repent and petition You
in their captors' land:
"We have sinned
and done wrong;
we have been wicked,"
48 and when they return to You
with their whole mind
and heart
in the land of their enemies
who took them captive,
and when they pray
to You in the direction
of their land
that You gave their ancestors,
the city You have chosen,
and the temple I have built
for Your name,
49 may You hear in heaven,
Your dwelling place,
their prayer and petition
and uphold their cause.
50 May You forgive Your people
who sinned against You
and all their rebellions[E]
against You,
and may You give
them compassion
in the eyes of their captors,
so that they may be
compassionate to them.

[A]8:37 Lit *besieges him in the land of his gates* [B]8:38 Lit *knowing in his heart of a plague* [C]8:44 Some Hb mss, some ancient versions, 2Ch 6:34; other Hb mss read *enemy* [D]8:47 Lit *they return to their heart* [E]8:50 Lit *rebellions that they have rebelled*

8:56 Solomon **praised** the Lord for His faithfulness, specifically citing His giving **rest to His people** since the consecration of a permanent place of worship marked an end to their wilderness wanderings (cp. Dt 12:9).

8:57-66 The king also highlighted the ultimate purpose of His covenant with Israel: "All the peoples of the earth" would **know** that **there is no other** God except the Lord as they witnessed how the Lord upheld His servants' **cause** (vv. 58-60).

8:62-66 The offerings that Solomon gave were the same that were given at the initial covenant ceremony (Ex 24:5), at the dedication of the altar of the tabernacle (Nm 7:88), and when David moved the ark to a tent in Jerusalem (2Sm 6:17-18; 24:24-25). Also, **Solomon and all Israel with him** expressed their devotion by celebrating the Festival of Booths (Feast of Tabernacles), mandatory for all Israelite males (Dt 16:16), for the required **seven days** and also for an extra **seven more days** (cp. 2Ch 7:10).

9:1-9 God confirmed to Solomon His part of the covenant. He **heard** Solomon's **prayer and petition**; He observed Solomon's consecration of the **temple** by His presence; and He cared for His people at all times. God's inclusion of the king's sons in His warning implies Solomon's responsibility as a father to teach his sons to follow the Lord.

>WORD|*study*

8:58 The word devoted (Hb *natah*; "turn away, influence,") also describes the way Solomon's heart was turned away from the Lord to foreign gods (1Kg 11:2-4,9).

51 For they are Your people
and Your inheritance;
You brought them
out of Egypt,
out of the middle
of an iron furnace.
52 May Your eyes be open
to Your servant's petition
and to the petition
of Your people Israel,
listening to them whenever
they call to You.
53 For You, Lord God,
have set them apart
as Your inheritance
from all the people on earth,
as You spoke
through Your servant Moses
when You brought
their ancestors
out of Egypt.

Blessing, Consecration, and Rejoicing (8:54-66)

54 When Solomon finished praying this entire prayer and petition
to the Lord, he got up from kneeling before the altar of the Lord, with
his hands spread out toward heaven,
55 and he stood and blessed the whole
congregation of Israel with a loud
voice: 56 "May the Lord be praised!
He has given rest to His people Israel according to all He has said.
Not one of all the good promises He
made through His servant Moses
has failed. 57 May the Lord our God
be with us as He was with our ancestors. May He not abandon us or
leave us 58 so that He causes us to be
devoted[A] to Him, to walk in all His
ways, and to keep His commands,
statutes, and ordinances, which He
commanded our ancestors. 59 May
my words I have made my petition
with before the Lord be near the
Lord our God day and night, so that
He may uphold His servant's cause
and the cause of His people Israel, as
each day requires, 60 and so that all
the peoples of the earth may know
that Yahweh is God. There is no other! 61 Let your heart be completely
devoted to the Lord our God to walk
in His statutes and to keep His commands, as it is today."

62 The king and all Israel with
him were offering sacrifices in the
Lord's presence. 63 Solomon offered
a sacrifice of •fellowship offerings to
the Lord: 22,000 cattle and 120,000
sheep. In this manner the king and
all the Israelites dedicated the Lord's
temple.

64 On the same day, the king consecrated the middle of the courtyard
that was in front of the Lord's temple because that was where he offered the •burnt offering, the •grain
offering, and the fat of the fellowship offerings since the bronze altar
before the Lord was too small to accommodate the burnt offerings, the
grain offerings, and the fat of the fellowship offerings.

65 Solomon and all Israel with
him—a great assembly, from the
entrance of Hamath[B] to the Brook of
Egypt—observed the festival at that
time in the presence of the Lord our
God, seven days, and seven more
days—14 days.[C] 66 On the fifteenth
day[D] he sent the people away. So they
blessed the king and went home to
their tents rejoicing and with joyful
hearts for all the goodness that the
Lord had done for His servant David
and for His people Israel.

God's Promises (9:1-9)

9 When Solomon finished building the temple of the Lord, the
royal palace, and all that Solomon
desired to do, 2 the Lord appeared to
Solomon a second time just as He
had appeared to him at Gibeon. 3 The
Lord said to him:

I have heard your prayer and
petition you have made before
Me. I have consecrated this

[A]8:58 Lit *causes our hearts to be inclined* [B]8:65 Or *from Lebo-hamath* [C]8:65 Temple dedication lasted seven days, and the Festival of Tabernacles lasted seven days. [D]8:66 Lit *the eighth day*

temple you have built, to put My name there forever; My eyes and My heart will be there at all times.

4 As for you, if you walk before Me as your father David walked, with a heart of integrity and in what is right, doing everything I have commanded you, and if you keep My statutes and ordinances, 5 I will establish your royal throne over Israel forever, as I promised your father David: You will never fail to have a man on the throne of Israel.

6 If you or your sons turn away from following Me and do not keep My commands—My statutes that I have set before you—and if you go and serve other gods and worship them, 7 I will cut off Israel from the land I gave them, and I will reject[A] the temple I have sanctified for My name. Israel will become an object of scorn and ridicule among all the peoples. 8 Though this temple is now exalted,[B] everyone who passes by will be appalled and will mock.[C] They will say: Why did the LORD do this to this land and this temple? 9 Then they will say: Because they abandoned the LORD their God who brought their ancestors out of the land of Egypt. They clung to other gods and worshiped and served them. Because of this, the LORD brought all this ruin on them.

Labor Force and Military Buildup (9:10-28)

10 At the end of 20 years during which Solomon had built the two houses, the LORD's temple and the royal palace— 11 Hiram king of Tyre having supplied him with cedar and cypress logs and gold for his every wish—King Solomon gave Hiram 20 towns in the land of Galilee. 12 So Hiram went out from Tyre to look over the towns that Solomon had given him, but he was not pleased with them. 13 So he said, "What are these towns you've given me, my brother?" So he called them the Land of Cabul,[D] as they are still called today. 14 Now Hiram had sent the king 9,000 pounds[E] of gold.

15 This is the account of the forced labor that King Solomon had imposed to build the LORD's temple, his own palace, the supporting terraces, the wall of Jerusalem, and Hazor, Megiddo, and Gezer. 16 Pharaoh king of Egypt had attacked and captured Gezer. He then burned it down, killed the Canaanites who lived in the city, and gave it as a dowry to his daughter, Solomon's wife. 17 Then Solomon rebuilt Gezer, Lower Beth-horon, 18 Baalath, Tamar[F,G] in the Wilderness of Judah, 19 all the storage cities that belonged to Solomon, the chariot cities, the cavalry cities, and whatever Solomon desired to build in Jerusalem, Lebanon, or anywhere else in the land of his dominion.

20 As for all the peoples who remained of the Amorites, Hittites, Perizzites, Hivites, and Jebusites, who were not Israelites— 21 their descendants who remained in the land after them, those whom the Israelites were unable to •completely destroy—Solomon imposed forced labor on them; it is this way until today. 22 But Solomon did not consign the Israelites to slavery; they were soldiers, his servants, his

9:10-28 Despite the help that **Hiram king of Tyre** gave to **Solomon** in his building projects, Solomon apparently dishonored him by giving him a gift of **20 towns,** which upon inspection, were deemed worthless. To voice his displeasure, Hiram named the area **Land of Cabul**, which may have meant "good-for-nothing" (vv. 10-14). Whatever Solomon's reason for ceding this territory, the fact that he gave up any of the land God had given Israel (not to mention the people who lived in these towns) makes the exchange a blemish on Solomon's career.

[A]**9:7** Lit *send from My presence* [B]**9:8** Some ancient versions read *temple will become a ruin* [C]**9:8** Lit *hiss* [D]**9:13** = Like Nothing [E]**9:14** Lit *120 talents* [F]**9:18** Alt Hb traditions, LXX, Syr, Tg, Vg read *Tadmor*; 2Ch 8:4 [G]**9:18** Tamar was a city in southern Judah; Ezk 47:19; 48:28.

>WORD|*study*

9:4 What is right (Hb *yosher*, "quality of conforming to a standard; godliness") is the standard of perfection, which is bestowed ultimately only by God's grace (vv. 4-5; cp. Lv 11:45; 1Pt 1:16). Although adherence to God's Word, which was expected of any king of Israel (Dt 17:18-20), would result in a measure of "uprightness," all people—except Jesus Christ—fall short of perfection (Ps 143:2; Rm 3:10,20-26).

9:7 The word translated reject (Hb *shalach*, "cast or throw out, send away, expel, put away, let go") is a strong form of the verb. In Genesis 3:23, God "sent . . . away" Adam "from the garden," but in five other instances the verb is used as a term for "divorce" (Dt 21:14; 22:19,29; Is 50:1; Jr 3:8). This word is translated "let go" in the famous command of Yahweh to Pharaoh: "Let My people go!" (Ex 5:1; 7:16; 8:1,20; 9:1,13; 10:3).

10:1-13 The account of the Queen of Sheba's coming **to Jerusalem** verified **Solomon's fame** (Hb *shēma'*, "report, hearing") among the nations of his day. In this case, rather than "an object of scorn and ridicule" (9:7), Israel was the object of adulation, and Israel's God received praise and recognition from the leader of another nation (10:9). As an eyewitness of Solomon's wealth and wisdom, her appraisal of his kingdom provided an outsider's view of Israel at the height of national splendor. She also attributed the abundance to **the Lord's eternal love for Israel** and emphasized God's purpose in making Solomon **king to carry out justice and righteousness** (cp. Lk 11:31). This evaluation is a stark contrast with the later description of Israel's demise due to Solomon's idolatry (1Kg 11).

commanders, his captains, and commanders of his chariots and his cavalry. 23 These were the deputies who
were over Solomon's work: 550 who
ruled over the people doing the work.
24 Pharaoh's daughter moved from
the city of David to the house that
Solomon had built for her; he then
built the terraces.
25 Three times a year Solomon offered •burnt offerings and •fellow-
ship offerings on the altar he had
built for the Lord, and he burned incense with them in the Lord's presence. So he completed the temple.
26 King Solomon put together a
fleet of ships at Ezion-geber, which
is near Eloth on the shore of the
•Red Sea in the land of Edom. 27 With
the fleet, Hiram sent his servants,
experienced seamen, along with
Solomon's servants. 28 They went to
Ophir and acquired gold there—16
tons[A]—and delivered it to Solomon.

A Visit from the Queen of Sheba (10:1-13)

10 The queen of Sheba heard
about Solomon's fame con-
nected with the name of •Yahweh
and came to test him with difficult
questions. 2 She came to Jerusalem
with a very large entourage, with
camels bearing spices, gold in great
abundance, and precious stones.
She came to Solomon and spoke to
him about everything that was on
her mind. 3 So Solomon answered
all her questions; nothing was too
difficult for the king to explain to
her. 4 When the queen of Sheba observed all of Solomon's wisdom, the
palace he had built, 5 the food at his
table, his servants' residence, his attendants' service and their attire, his
cupbearers, and the •burnt offerings
he offered at the Lord's temple, it
took her breath away.
6 She said to the king, "The report
I heard in my own country about
your words and about your wisdom
is true. 7 But I didn't believe the reports until I came and saw with my
own eyes. Indeed, I was not even told
half. Your wisdom and prosperity
far exceed the report I heard. 8 How
happy are your men.[B] How happy are
these servants of yours, who always
stand in your presence hearing your
wisdom. 9 May Yahweh your God be
praised! He delighted in you and put
you on the throne of Israel, because
of the Lord's eternal love for Israel.
He has made you king to carry out
justice and righteousness."
10 Then she gave the king four and
a half tons[C] of gold, a great quantity
of spices, and precious stones. Never
again did such a quantity of spices

[A] **9:28** Lit *420 talents* [B] **10:8** LXX, Syr read *your wives* [C] **10:10** Lit *120 talents*

Queen of Sheba An Admirer of Wisdom

Her Background	• She was ruler of Sheba, part of the Arabian Peninsula (10:1). • She had heard of Solomon's fame and was inquisitive (10:1).
Her Story	• She traveled to Jerusalem and presented Solomon with elaborate gifts (10:10). • She was stunned at the magnitude of Solomon's riches and possessions (10:4-8). • She praised God for giving Solomon the throne and carrying out justice and righteousness (10:9). • Solomon gave her whatever gifts she desired, and she returned home (10:13).
Life Lessons	• The queen's testimony to God's greatness stands as an example. • Even pagans can recognize the glory and blessing of God.

arrive as those the queen of Sheba gave to King Solomon.

[11] In addition, Hiram's fleet that carried gold from Ophir brought from Ophir a large quantity of almug[A] wood and precious stones. [12] The king made the almug wood into steps for the LORD's temple and the king's palace and into lyres and harps for the singers. Never before had such almug wood come, and the like has not been seen again even to this very day.

[13] King Solomon gave the queen of Sheba her every desire—whatever she asked—besides what he had given her out of his royal bounty. Then she, along with her servants, returned to her own country.

The Accumulation of Wealth (10:14-29)

[14] The weight of gold that came to Solomon annually was 25 tons,[B] [15] besides what came from merchants, traders' merchandise, and all the Arabian kings and governors of the land.

[16] King Solomon made 200 large shields of hammered gold; 15 pounds[C] of gold went into each shield. [17] He made 300 small shields of hammered gold; about four pounds[D] of gold went into each shield. The king put them in the House of the Forest of Lebanon.

[18] The king also made a large ivory throne and overlaid it with fine gold. [19] The throne had six steps; there was a rounded top at the back of the throne, armrests on either side of the seat, and two lions standing beside the armrests. [20] Twelve lions were standing there on the six steps, one at each end. Nothing like it had ever been made in any other kingdom.

[21] All of King Solomon's drinking cups were gold, and all the utensils of the House of the Forest of Lebanon were pure gold. There was no silver, since it was considered as nothing in Solomon's time, [22] for the king had ships of Tarshish at sea with Hiram's fleet, and once every three years the ships of Tarshish would arrive bearing gold, silver, ivory, apes, and peacocks.[E]

[23] King Solomon surpassed all the kings of the world in riches and in wisdom. [24] The whole world wanted an audience with Solomon to hear the wisdom that God had put in his heart. [25] Every man would bring his annual tribute: items[F] of silver and gold, clothing, weapons,[G] spices, and horses and mules.

[26] Solomon accumulated 1,400 chariots and 12,000 horsemen and stationed them in the chariot cities and with the king in Jerusalem. [27] The king made silver as common in Jerusalem as stones, and he made cedar as abundant as sycamore in the Judean foothills. [28] Solomon's horses were imported from Egypt and Kue.[H] The king's traders bought them from Kue at the going price. [29] A chariot was imported from Egypt for 15 pounds[I] of silver, and a horse for about four pounds.[J] In the same way, they exported them to all the kings of the Hittites and to the kings of Aram through their agents.

Foreign Women and Pagan Gods (11:1-13)

11 King Solomon loved many foreign women in addition to Pharaoh's daughter: Moabite, Ammonite, Edomite, Sidonian, and Hittite women [2] from the nations that the LORD had told the Israelites about, "Do not intermarry with them, and they must not intermarry with you, because they will turn you away from Me to their gods." Solomon was deeply attached to these women and loved them. [3] He had 700 wives who were princesses and 300 concubines, and they turned his heart away from the LORD.

[4] When Solomon was old, his wives seduced him to follow other gods. He was not completely devoted to •Yahweh his God, as his father David had been. [5] Solomon followed •Ashtoreth, the goddess of the Sidonians, and •Milcom, the detestable idol of the Ammonites. [6] Solomon did what was evil in the LORD's sight, and

10:14-29 The writer carefully selected details that cumulatively paint two conflicting portraits of King Solomon. On the one hand, he must be lauded for establishing and maintaining an empire unparalleled both in wealth and **wisdom** (vv. 20,23-24; cp. 3:11-13; Ec 5:10). On the other hand, Solomon's extravagant accumulation of wealth, particularly of **horses** and **chariots**—especially those **imported from Egypt**—violated the Lord's command regarding Israel's kings (see Dt 17:14-17). The commerce between Israel and **all the kings of the Hittites and . . . the kings of Aram** is further evidence of careless disregard for Israel's spiritual identity among the nations (1Kg 10:29; see Ex 23:31-33; 34:12-16; Dt 7:1-11; 20:17-18; cp. Ezr 9:1-4; Is 31:1).

11:1-13 While Solomon initially led the nation in devotion to the Lord, over time he neglected his primary responsibility to love the Lord, and his love for **many foreign women** ultimately **turned his heart away from the LORD** (vv. 1-4). The Lord had explicitly forbidden intermarriage between the Israelites and the sons and daughters of the Canaanites (Dt 7:1-4). Regarding God's warning that Canaanite wives would "turn you away from Me to their gods" (1Kg 11:2), Solomon may have made the common mistake of thinking that he was the exception. Yet Solomon's **wives seduced him** [Hb *natah* with the object *lēv*, "turn away the heart; incline, influence, stretch, thrust aside the heart," vv. 2-4,9] **to follow other gods.** When Solomon was led astray, he forfeited the integrity of his leadership roles both as a Hebrew father (Dt 6) and as Israel's king (2Sm 7:13-16). Ironically, Solomon's **old** age did not ensure wise decisions (1 Kg 11:4).

[A] **10:11** = algum in 2Ch 2:8; 9:10-11 [B] **10:14** Lit *666 talents* [C] **10:16** Lit *600* (shekels) [D] **10:17** Lit *three minas* [E] **10:22** Or *baboons* [F] **10:25** Or *vessels*, or *weapons* [G] **10:25** Or *fragrant balsam* [H] **10:28** = Cilicia [I] **10:29** Lit *600 shekels* [J] **10:29** Lit *150 shekels*

11:9-10 These verses convey a sense of exasperation with Solomon's failure. The king had willfully provoked God's wrath by rejecting **Yahweh, the God of Israel**, the true God whose reality had been personally manifested **to him twice**.

11:11-13 Although God told Solomon that He would tear the kingdom away from him, He would spare Solomon's reign from experiencing this division of the kingdom for David's sake. And for the sake of **David** and **of Jerusalem** God would **give one tribe** (Hb *shēvet*, "rod, staff, branch, scepter," figuratively representing the leader of a family or tribe) to Solomon's son, ensuring that a descendant of David would remain on the throne in Jerusalem.

11:14-25 As the locations of these enemies demonstrate, **Egypt** could not be trusted as an ally, despite the high-profile marriage between Solomon and the Egyptian princess. Hadad's antagonism and Rezon's loathing had been smoldering in the background, held in check as God prospered Solomon during the years of his obedience (vv. 21,25). The text makes clear not only that Solomon's destiny depended on his keeping the covenant but also that the rise and fall of enemy nations lay in the hands of God (vv. 11,14,23).

HARD QUESTION

In a culture that does not worship physical idols, how do God's warnings against idolatry apply to you today?

Anything or anyone who becomes your *supreme* love, surpassing your allegiance to God, quickly compromises your loyalty toward God. Solomon elevated his liaisons with foreign women as being most important in his life, which led directly to his disobedience of God and thus apostasy (11:7-13, cp. Dt 4:15-20). Idolatry is not expressed primarily in what your speech affirms or what you bow down to worship but in the source of your affection and highest loyalty. Anything in your life, good or evil, that you love, cherish, and serve with honor and devotion worthy of God alone is an idol. Ultimately, everyone follows what she truly loves. Thus, Jesus ascribed as the greatest and most important commandment, "Love the Lord your God with all your heart, with all your soul, and with all your mind" (Mt 22:37).

unlike his father David, he did not completely follow Yahweh.

7 At that time, Solomon built a •high place for Chemosh, the detestable idol of Moab, and for Milcom,[A] the detestable idol of the Ammonites, on the hill across from Jerusalem. 8 He did the same for all his foreign wives, who were burning incense and offering sacrifices to their gods.

9 The LORD was angry with Solomon, because his heart had turned away from Yahweh, the God of Israel, who had appeared to him twice. 10 He had commanded him about this, so that he would not follow other gods, but Solomon did not do what the LORD had commanded.

11 Then the LORD said to Solomon, "Since you have done this[B] and did not keep My covenant and My statutes, which I commanded you, I will tear the kingdom away from you and give it to your servant. 12 However, I will not do it during your lifetime because of your father David; I will tear it out of your son's hand. 13 Yet I will not tear the entire kingdom away from him. I will give one tribe to your son because of my servant David and because of Jerusalem that I chose."

Enemies (11:14-40)

14 So the LORD raised up Hadad the Edomite as an enemy against Solomon. He was of the royal family in Edom. 15 Earlier, when David was in Edom, Joab, the commander of the army, had gone to bury the dead and had struck down every male in Edom. 16 For Joab and all Israel had remained there six months, until he had killed every male in Edom. 17 Hadad fled to Egypt, along with some Edomites from his father's servants. At the time Hadad was a small boy. 18 Hadad and his men set out from Midian and went to Paran. They took men with them from Paran and went to Egypt, to Pharaoh king of Egypt, who gave Hadad a house, ordered that he be given food, and gave him land. 19 Pharaoh liked Hadad so much that he gave him a wife, the sister of his own wife, Queen Tahpenes. 20 Tahpenes' sister gave birth to Hadad's son Genubath. Tahpenes herself weaned him in Pharaoh's palace, and Genubath lived there along with Pharaoh's sons.

21 When Hadad heard in Egypt that David rested with his fathers and that Joab, the commander of the army, was dead, Hadad said to Pharaoh, "Let me leave, so I can go to my own country."

22 But Pharaoh asked him, "What do you lack here with me for you to want to go back to your own country?"

"Nothing," he replied, "but please let me leave."

23 God raised up Rezon son of Eliada as an enemy against Solomon. Rezon had fled from his master Hadadezer king of Zobah 24 and gathered men to himself. He became captain of a raiding party when David killed the Zobaites. He[C] went to Damascus, lived there, and became king in Damascus. 25 Rezon was Israel's enemy throughout Solomon's reign, adding to the trouble Hadad had caused. He ruled over Aram,[D] but he loathed Israel.

26 Now Solomon's servant, Jeroboam

[A]**11:7** Lit *Molech* [B]**11:11** Lit *Since this was with you* [C]**11:24** LXX; Hb reads *They* [D]**11:25** Some Hb mss, LXX, Syr read *Edom*

CHARACTER PROFILE

Solomon's Pagan Wives **A Snare to the King**

Their Background	• Solomon married 700 women who were princesses and added 300 concubines (11:1-2). • Some of these marriages were likely for political purposes (11:1-2). • These women were not believers in Yahweh but followed after pagan deities (11:4-8).
Their Story	• God had clearly told His people not to intermarry with foreigners (Dt 7:1-4). • They influenced Solomon from following after God (11:3). • Solomon not only tolerated their worship of idols but participated in it (11:2,5).
Life Lessons	• Solomon disobeyed the Lord by following other gods, which was the beginning of his downfall (11:9-11). • However, his wives stood responsible for their own respective relationships to God.

son of Nebat, was an Ephraimite
from Zeredah. His widowed mother's name was Zeruah. Jeroboam
rebelled against Solomon, 27 and
this is the reason he rebelled against
the king: Solomon had built the
supporting terraces and repaired
the opening in the wall of the city
of his father David. 28 Now the man
Jeroboam was capable, and Solomon
noticed the young man because he
was getting things done. So he appointed him over the entire labor
force of the house of Joseph.
29 During that time, the prophet
Ahijah the Shilonite met Jeroboam
on the road as Jeroboam came out of
Jerusalem. Now Ahijah had wrapped
himself with a new cloak, and the
two of them were alone in the open
field. 30 Then Ahijah took hold of the
new cloak he had on, tore it into
12 pieces, 31 and said to Jeroboam,
"Take 10 pieces for yourself, for this
is what the Lord God of Israel says:
'I am about to tear the kingdom out
of Solomon's hand. I will give you 10
tribes, 32 but one tribe will remain
his because of my servant David
and because of Jerusalem, the city I
chose out of all the tribes of Israel.
33 For they have abandoned Me; they
have bowed the knee to Ashtoreth,
the goddess of the Sidonians, to
Chemosh, the god of Moab, and to
Milcom, the god of the Ammonites.
They have not walked in My ways to
do what is right in My eyes and to
carry out My statutes and My judgments as his father David did.
34 "'However, I will not take the
whole kingdom from his hand but
will let him be ruler all the days of
his life because of My servant David, whom I chose and who kept My
commands and My statutes. 35 I will
take 10 tribes of the kingdom from
his son's hand and give them to you.
36 I will give one tribe to his son, so
that My servant David will always
have a lamp before Me in Jerusalem,
the city I chose for Myself to put My
name there. 37 I will appoint you,
and you will reign as king over all
you want, and you will be king over
Israel.
38 "'After that, if you obey all I
command you, walk in My ways,
and do what is right in My sight in
order to keep My statutes and My
commands as My servant David did,
I will be with you. I will build you
a lasting dynasty just as I built for
David, and I will give you Israel. 39 I
will humble David's descendants,
because of their unfaithfulness, but
not forever.'"[A]
40 Therefore, Solomon tried to kill
Jeroboam, but he fled to Egypt, to

[A] **11:38-39** LXX omits *and I will give . . . but not forever*

11:26-40 Jeroboam posed an internal threat. He **rebelled against Solomon** when **the Lord God of Israel** revealed through **the prophet Ahijah** that He would take **10 tribes of the kingdom from** the **hand** of Solomon's son and give them to Jeroboam (vv. 26-31). Solomon's reaction recalls the experience of Saul, when God **tore** from him "the kingship of Israel" and gave it to David (vv. 30-31; 1Sm 15–16). The narrative also echoes God's selection of David revealed through Samuel and Saul's efforts to kill David out of jealousy (1Sm 18:1-16).

Because Israel **abandoned** (Hb *'azav*, "forsake, depart from, leave") the Lord (1Kg 11:33, cp. 6:13), God allowed the united kingdom of Israel to be split after Solomon's death.

11:31-39 What Solomon had led Israel to do, God appointed Jeroboam to undo as **king over Israel**. The Lord extended to Jeroboam the covenant relationship broken by Solomon. Jeroboam's rise to power was orchestrated by the Lord. Unlike accounts of how God singled out Saul, David, and Solomon, the text does not record that Jeroboam was anointed. That Ahijah **tore** [Hb *qara'*; vv. 30-31; see vv. 11-13] a **new cloak**, representing the one nation of Israel, into **12 pieces**, which represented her 12 tribes, symbolically emphasized that no one would do such a thing to a "new" garment without good reason. Like a new garment, which would not rip easily on its own, Israel would be divided only when and how God decided. The physical separation of the 10 pieces from the other two (also regarded together as **one tribe** to be called Judah after the larger geographical area; vv. 32,36) also illustrated the stark reality of the action God was about to take—the damage was irreparable; only another new garment could replace the one torn apart by God's hand.

11:35-36 From Solomon's **son's hand**, God Himself would **take** and **give** to Jeroboam all but David's **tribe** and **Jerusalem**, **the city** where God had chosen **to put** His **name** (vv. 31-39). Of all the kings of Israel, David remained the paradigm, and for David's sake God pledged not only to maintain **a lamp . . . in Jerusalem** but also to limit His judgment of Israel.

Kings of the Divided Monarchy (All dates are B.C.)

JUDAH	Bright[1]	Miller/Hays[2]
Rehoboam	922–915	924–907
Abijam	915–913	907–906
Asa	913–873	905–874
Jehoshaphat	873–849	874–850
Jehoram	849–843	850–843
Ahaziah	843–842	843
Athaliah (usurper)	842–837	843–837
Joash	837–800	837–?
Amaziah	800–783	?-?
Uzziah (Azariah)	783–742	?-?
Jotham	742–735	? –742
Ahaz	735–715	742–727
Hezekiah	715–687/6	727–698
Manasseh	687/6–642	697–942
Amon	642–640	
Josiah	640–609	639–609
Jehoahaz	609	609
Jehoiakim	609–598	609–598
Jehoichin	598/7	598/7
Zedekiah	597–587	597–586
Destruction of Jerusalem and the temple: 586		

ISRAEL	Bright[1]	Miller/Hays[2]
Jeroboam I	922–901	924–903
Nadab*	901–900	903–902
Baasha	900–877	902–886
Elah*	877–876	886–885
Zimri (suicide)	876	
Omri	876–869	885–873
Ahab	869–850	873–851
Ahaziah	850–849	851–849
Jehoram*	849–842	849–843
Jehu	843/2–815	843–816
Jehoahaz	815–802	816–800
Jehoash (Joash)	802–786	800–785
Jeroboam II	786–746	785–745
Zechariah*	746–745	745
Shallum*	745	745
Menahem	745–737	745–736
Pekahiah*	737–736	736–735
Pekah*	736–732	735–732
Hoshea	732–724	732–723
Fall of Samaria	722	

*Assassinated

The two sets of dates reflect the differing views of:

[1] John Bright, *A History of Israel*, 3rd. ed.

[2] J. Maxwell Miller and John H. Hayes, *A History of Ancient Israel and Judah*

Shishak king of Egypt, where he remained until Solomon's death.

King Rehoboam in Judah (11:41–12:24)

[41] The rest of the events of Solomon's reign, along with all his accomplishments and his wisdom, are written in the Book of Solomon's Events. [42] The length of Solomon's reign in Jerusalem over all Israel totaled 40 years. [43] Solomon rested with his fathers and was buried in the city of his father David. His son Rehoboam became king in his place.

12 Then Rehoboam went to Shechem, for all Israel had gone to Shechem to make him king. [2] When Jeroboam son of Nebat heard about it, for he was still in Egypt where he had fled from King Solomon's presence, Jeroboam stayed in Egypt.[A] [3] They summoned him, and Jeroboam and the whole assembly of Israel came and spoke to Rehoboam: [4] "Your father made our yoke difficult. You, therefore, lighten your father's harsh service and the heavy yoke he put on us, and we will serve you."

[5] Rehoboam replied, "Go home for three days and then return to me." So the people left. [6] Then King Rehoboam consulted with the elders who had served his father Solomon when he was alive, asking, "How do you advise me to respond to these people?"

[7] They replied, "Today if you will be a servant to these people and serve them, and if you respond to them by speaking kind words to them, they will be your servants forever."

[8] But he rejected the advice of the elders who had advised him and consulted with the young men who had grown up with him and served him. [9] He asked them, "What message do you advise that we send back to these people who said to me, 'Lighten the yoke your father put on us'?"

[10] Then the young men who had grown up with him told him, "This is what you should say to these people who said to you, 'Your father made our yoke heavy, but you, make it lighter on us!' This is what you should tell them: 'My little finger is thicker than my father's loins! [11] Although my father burdened you with a heavy yoke, I will add to your yoke; my father disciplined you with whips, but I will discipline you with barbed whips.'"[B]

[12] So Jeroboam and all the people came to Rehoboam on the third day, as the king had ordered: "Return to me on the third day." [13] Then the king answered the people harshly. He rejected the advice the elders had given him [14] and spoke to them according to the young men's advice: "My father made your yoke heavy, but I will add to your yoke; my father disciplined you with whips, but I will discipline you with barbed whips."[B]

[15] The king did not listen to the people, because this turn of events came from the LORD to carry out His word, which the LORD had spoken through Ahijah the Shilonite to Jeroboam son of Nebat. [16] When all Israel saw that the king had not listened to them, the people answered him:

What portion do we have
in David?
We have no inheritance
in the son of Jesse.
Israel, return to your tents;
David, now look
after your own house!

So Israel went to their tents, [17] but Rehoboam reigned over the Israelites living in the cities of Judah.

[18] Then King Rehoboam sent Adoram,[C] who was in charge of forced labor, but all Israel stoned him to death. King Rehoboam managed to get into the chariot and flee to Jerusalem. [19] Israel is in rebellion against the house of David until today.

[20] When all Israel heard that Jeroboam had come back, they summoned him to the assembly and made him king over all Israel. No one followed the house of David except the tribe of Judah alone. [21] When Rehoboam arrived in Jerusalem, he mobilized 180,000 choice warriors

11:41–12:24 This account of Rehoboam's decision-making process emphasizes his lack of wisdom in contrast to his father Solomon and draws a clear contrast between the diplomacy counseled by the voices of experience and authority and the harsh answer recommended by Rehoboam's peers. The **turn of events** (i.e., the resulting rift between Rehoboam and **the people**, 12:15) fulfilled the words of the prophet **Ahijah**, through whom **the LORD** had promised **to Jeroboam** 10 tribes of the kingdom (11:29-35). Note the tension between human responsibility and the sovereignty of God. One poor decision changed the course of history for the nation of Israel; nevertheless, God clearly was in control (v. 24). God works through human instruments without excusing sinful arrogance and foolishness.

12:18-20 The people's violent response prompted Rehoboam's flight to **Jerusalem** while **all Israel** proceeded to make **Jeroboam** king. **Judah**, as God had promised, remained faithful to **the house of David** (cp. 11:13,36).

[A] **12:2** LXX, Vg read *Jeroboam returned from Egypt*; 2Ch 10:2 [B] **12:11,14** Lit *with scorpions*
[C] **12:18** LXX reads *Adoniram*; 1Kg 4:6; 5:14

from the entire house of Judah
and the tribe of Benjamin to fight
against the house of Israel to restore
the kingdom to Rehoboam son of
Solomon. 22 But a revelation from
God came to Shemaiah, the man of
God: 23 "Say to Rehoboam son of Solomon, king of Judah, to the whole
house of Judah and Benjamin, and
to the rest of the people, 24 'This is
what the LORD says: You are not to
march up and fight against your
brothers, the Israelites. Each of you
must return home, for I have done
this.'"

So they listened to what the LORD
said and went back as He had told
them.

King Jeroboam in Israel (12:25–14:20)

25 Jeroboam built Shechem in the
hill country of Ephraim and lived
there. From there he went out and
built Penuel. 26 Jeroboam said to
himself, "The way things are going
now, the kingdom might return to
the house of David. 27 If these people
regularly go to offer sacrifices in
the LORD's temple in Jerusalem, the
heart of these people will return to
their lord, Rehoboam king of Judah.
They will murder me and go back
to the king of Judah." 28 So the king
sought advice.

Then he made two golden calves,
and he said to the people, "Going to
Jerusalem is too difficult for you. Israel, here is your God[A] who brought
you out of the land of Egypt." 29 He
set up one in Bethel, and put the
other in Dan. 30 This led to sin; the
people walked in procession before
one of the calves all the way to Dan.[B]

31 Jeroboam also built shrines on
the •high places and set up priests
from every class of people who were
not Levites. 32 Jeroboam made a festival in the eighth month on the
fifteenth day of the month, like the
festival in Judah. He offered sacrifices on the altar; he made this offering
in Bethel to sacrifice to the calves he
had set up. He also stationed the
priests in Bethel for the high places
he had set up. 33 He offered sacrifices
on[C] the altar he had set up in Bethel
on the fifteenth day of the eighth
month. He chose this month on his
own. He made a festival for the Israelites, offered sacrifices on the altar,
and burned incense.

13 A man of God came from Judah to Bethel by a revelation
from the LORD while Jeroboam was
standing beside the altar to burn
incense. 2 The man of God cried
out against the altar by a revelation
from the LORD: "Altar, altar, this is
what the LORD says, 'A son will be
born to the house of David, named
Josiah, and he will sacrifice on you
the priests of the •high places who
are burning incense on you. Human
bones will be burned on you.'" 3 He
gave a sign that day. He said, "This
is the sign that the LORD has spoken:
'The altar will now be ripped apart,
and the ashes that are on it will be
poured out.'"

4 When the king heard the word
that the man of God had cried out
against the altar at Bethel, Jeroboam stretched out his hand from
the altar and said, "Arrest him!" But
the hand he stretched out against
him withered, and he could not pull
it back to himself. 5 The altar was
ripped apart, and the ashes poured
from the altar, according to the sign
that the man of God had given by
the word of the LORD.

6 Then the king responded to the
man of God, "Plead for the favor of
the LORD your God and pray for me
so that my hand may be restored to
me." So the man of God pleaded for
the favor of the LORD, and the king's
hand was restored to him and became as it had been at first.

7 Then the king declared to the
man of God, "Come home with me,
refresh yourself, and I'll give you a
reward."

8 But the man of God replied,
"If you were to give me half your
house, I still wouldn't go with you,
and I wouldn't eat bread or drink
water in this place, 9 for this is what
I was commanded by the word of
the LORD: 'You must not eat bread or
drink water or go back the way you
came.'" 10 So he went another way;

12:22 As Solomon turned away from the Lord and from his role as Israel's spiritual leader, prophetic activity increased.

12:25 **Jeroboam** established **Shechem** as his capital city. Shechem lay at the foot of Mount Gerizim, 34 miles north of Jerusalem, and had been an important site both in Israel's history (a city of refuge—Jos 20:7; 21:21; the burial place of Joseph's bones—Jos 24:32; the site where Joshua led Israel to renew their covenant with the Lord—Jos 24); and as a center of Canaanite idolatry (Jdg 9:3-4,46).

12:28 Relying on reason rather than God, Jeroboam concluded that geography posed a threat to the establishment of his kingdom. But Jeroboam's subsequent actions indicate either that he followed ungodly advice or that he simply secured support for the plan he already had in mind.

12:28-30 Although some try to justify Jeroboam's innovation by arguing that the "calves" merely functioned as the seat of the invisible Yahweh, Scripture's verdict on his revision of Israelite religion is clearly negative:

- The **golden calves** and Jeroboam's presentation of them as the God who delivered the people from Egypt echoes the apostasy Israel committed at the foot of Mount Sinai when Aaron facilitated their worship of a gold calf presented with the same words (cp. Ex 32:4,8).
- The narrator explicitly states: **This led to sin**. He also notes that **the people** apparently embraced idol worship without objection.
- The reason for Israel's later destruction by Assyria is traced back to the people's sin of idolatry, including specific mention of the "two calves" (2Kg 17:7,16).

12:31-33 Jeroboam compounded this sin by replacing God's instructions for worship with his own:

- He provided the people with multiple shrines for Canaanite-style idolatry.
- He appointed illegitimate priests **who were not Levites** and **stationed** them **in Bethel** for service at the high places (Ex 40:12-15; Nm 3:1-13; Dt 10:8-9).
- He initiated his own religious feast to be celebrated in the eighth month in substitution for **the festival in Judah** in the seventh month (see 8:1-13).
- Twice the narrator points out that Jeroboam himself **offered sacrifices on the altar** and included in his summary of the king's sins that he also **burned incense**.

[A] **12:28** Or *here are your gods* [B] **12:30** Some LXX mss read *calves to Bethel and the other to Dan*
[C] **12:33** Or *He went up to*

he did not go back by the way he had come to Bethel.

11 Now a certain old prophet was living in Bethel. His son[A] came and told him all the deeds that the man of God had done that day in Bethel. His sons also told their father the words that he had spoken to the king. 12 Then their father said to them, "Which way did he go?" His sons had seen[B] the way taken by the man of God who had come from Judah. 13 Then he said to his sons, "Saddle the donkey for me." So they saddled the donkey for him, and he got on it. 14 He followed the man of God and found him sitting under an oak tree. He asked him, "Are you the man of God who came from Judah?"

"I am," he said.

15 Then he said to him, "Come home with me and eat bread."

16 But he answered, "I cannot go back with you, eat bread, or drink water with you in this place, 17 for a message came to me by the word of the LORD: 'You must not eat bread or drink water there or go back by the way you came.'"

18 He said to him, "I am also a prophet like you. An angel spoke to me by the word of the LORD: 'Bring him back with you to your house so that he may eat bread and drink water.'" The old prophet deceived him, 19 and the man of God went back with him, ate bread in his house, and drank water.

20 While they were sitting at the table, the word of the LORD came to the prophet who had brought him back, 21 and the prophet cried out to the man of God who had come from Judah, "This is what the LORD says: 'Because you rebelled against the command of the LORD and did not keep the command that the LORD your God commanded you— 22 but you went back and ate bread and drank water in the place that He said to you, "Do not eat bread and do not drink water"—your corpse will never reach the grave of your fathers.'"

23 So after he had eaten bread and after he had drunk, the old prophet saddled the donkey for the prophet he had brought back. 24 When he left,[C] a lion attacked[D] him along the way and killed him. His corpse was thrown on the road, and the donkey was standing beside it; the lion was standing beside the corpse too.

25 There were men passing by who saw the corpse thrown on the road and the lion standing beside it, and they went and spoke about it in the city where the old prophet lived. 26 When the prophet who had brought him back from his way heard about it, he said, "He is the man of God who disobeyed the command of the LORD. The LORD has given him to the lion, and it has mauled and killed him, according to the word of the LORD that He spoke to him."

27 Then the old prophet instructed his sons, "Saddle the donkey for me." They saddled it, 28 and he went and found the corpse of the man of God thrown on the road with the donkey and the lion standing beside the corpse. The lion had not eaten the corpse or mauled the donkey. 29 So the prophet lifted the corpse of the man of God and laid it on the donkey and brought it back. The old prophet came into the city to mourn and bury him. 30 Then he laid the corpse in his own grave, and they mourned over him: "Oh, my brother!"

31 After he had buried him, he said to his sons, "When I die, you must bury me in the grave where the man of God is buried; lay my bones beside his bones, 32 for the word that he cried out by a revelation from the LORD against the altar in Bethel and against all the shrines of the high places in the cities of Samaria is certain to happen."

33 After all this Jeroboam did not repent of his evil way but again set up priests for the high places from every class of people. He ordained whoever so desired it, and they became priests of the high places. 34 This was the sin that caused the house of Jeroboam to be wiped out and annihilated from the face of the earth.

14 At that time Abijah son of Jeroboam became sick. 2 Jeroboam said to his wife, "Go disguise yourself, so they won't know that you're

"Jeroboam's sins" and walking "in the way of Jeroboam" became persistent indictments against Israel's kings (14:16; 15:30; 16:2,19.26.31: 2Kg 3:3; 10:29-31; 13:2,6,11; 14:24; 15:9, 18,24,28; 17:22).

13:1 Jeroboam had been given the same promise and warning as Solomon (11:38), but he ignored God's agency in placing the 10 tribes of the kingdom into his hands. He chose to go his own way rather than exercise faith in God's promises.

13:2-6 Mercy abounded for Jeroboam—the prophecy was directed **against the altar**, not at him, and God heeded the prophet's intercessory prayer and **restored** his hand.

13:7-10 The prophet adamantly refused Jeroboam's offer of refreshment and **a reward** (Hb *mattat*, "gift"; cp. Ec 5:19) because of God's clear command not to **eat bread or drink water or go back the way you came**.

13:11-34 The man of God failed to discern the difference between what he had been **commanded** *directly* **by the word of the Lord** (v. 17) and what was said by a man from Bethel whom he did not know, who **deceived him** (v. 18), reportedly hearing from **an angel** who had spoken to him **by the word of the Lord**. Not only did the second message contradict the first, but it also came from a suspicious source. Divine communication flowing from God to an angel to the "prophet" to "the man of God" should not have been trusted more than that flowing from God to "the man of God" (vv. 8,17-19).

[A] **13:11** Some Hb mss, LXX, Syr, Vg read *sons* [B] **13:12** LXX, Syr, Tg, Vg read *sons showed him*
[C] **13:23-24** LXX reads *donkey, and he turned* [24] *and left, and* [D] **13:24** Lit *met*

14:4-6 Neither Ahijah's apparent physical blindness nor the woman's disguise prevented the Lord from revealing to the prophet all he needed to know. The prophet's perceptive greeting and immediate announcement of **bad news** probably stunned **Jeroboam's wife** and confirmed the truth of his message to her husband.

14:17-18 Although the death of the child, Abijah (v. 1), was inevitable, the timing was critical, since it was connected to the prophet's announcement and thus ensured the credibility of the rest of the message.

14:21-31 Although divided into two separate kingdoms, Israel still constituted one people. Thus the narrator records the history of both. Naamah's maternal influence, in addition to Solomon's syncretism (the mixture of different belief systems, i.e., incorporating pagan practices into covenant-prescribed worship of Yahweh), may have undermined any godly influence of Solomon during the first 20 years of Rehoboam's life while the temple and palace were being built (11:1,5). Rehoboam's syncretism is indicated by the fact that he continued to enter **the Lord's temple** while allowing the people to follow Canaanite deities (14:28).

Jeroboam's wife, and go to Shiloh. Ahijah the prophet is there; it was he who told about me becoming king over this people. 3 Take with you 10 loaves of bread, some cakes, and a jar of honey, and go to him. He will tell you what will happen to the boy."

4 Jeroboam's wife did that: she went to Shiloh and arrived at Ahijah's house. Ahijah could not see; his gaze was fixed[A] due to his age. 5 But the Lord had said to Ahijah, "Jeroboam's wife is coming soon to ask you about her son, for he is sick. You are to say such and such to her. When she arrives, she will be disguised."

6 When Ahijah heard the sound of her feet entering the door, he said, "Come in, wife of Jeroboam! Why are you disguised? I have bad news for you. 7 Go tell Jeroboam, 'This is what the Lord God of Israel says: I raised you up from among the people, appointed you ruler over My people Israel, 8 tore the kingdom away from the house of David, and gave it to you. But you were not like My servant David, who kept My commands and followed Me with all of his heart, doing only what is right in My eyes. 9 You behaved more wickedly than all who were before you. In order to provoke Me, you have proceeded to make for yourself other gods and cast images, but you have flung Me behind your back. 10 Because of all this, I am about to bring disaster on the house of Jeroboam:

I will eliminate all of
  Jeroboam's males,[B]
both slave and free,[C] in Israel;
I will sweep away the house
  of Jeroboam
as one sweeps away dung
  until it is all gone!
11 Anyone who belongs
  to Jeroboam and dies
  in the city,
the dogs will eat,
and anyone who dies
  in the field,
the birds of the sky will eat,
  for the Lord has said it!'

12 "As for you, get up and go to your house. When your feet enter the city, the boy will die. 13 All Israel will mourn for him and bury him. He alone out of Jeroboam's house will be put in the family tomb, because out of the house of Jeroboam the Lord God of Israel found something good only in him. 14 The Lord will raise up for Himself a king over Israel, who will eliminate the house of Jeroboam. This is the day, yes,[C] even today! 15 For the Lord will strike Israel and the people will shake as a reed shakes in water. He will uproot Israel from this good soil that He gave to their ancestors. He will scatter them beyond the Euphrates because they made their •Asherah poles, provoking the Lord. 16 He will give up Israel because of Jeroboam's sins that he committed and caused Israel to commit."

17 Then Jeroboam's wife got up and left and went to Tirzah. As she was crossing the threshold of the house, the boy died. 18 He was buried, and all Israel mourned for him, according to the word of the Lord He had spoken through His servant Ahijah the prophet.

19 As for the rest of the events of Jeroboam's reign, how he waged war and how he reigned, note that they are written in the Historical Record of Israel's Kings. 20 The length of Jeroboam's reign was 22 years. He rested with his fathers, and his son Nadab became king in his place.

The Kings of Judah (14:21–15:24)

Rehoboam (14:21-31)

21 Now Rehoboam, Solomon's son, reigned in Judah. Rehoboam was 41 years old when he became king; he reigned 17 years in Jerusalem, the city where •Yahweh had chosen from all the tribes of Israel to put His name. Rehoboam's mother's name was Naamah the Ammonite.

22 Judah did what was evil in the Lord's eyes. They provoked Him to jealous anger more than all that their ancestors had done with the sins they committed. 23 They also built for themselves •high places, sacred pillars, and Asherah poles on every high hill and under every

[A] **14:4** Lit *see, for his eyes stood*; 1Sm 4:15 [B] **14:10** Lit *eliminate Jeroboam's one who urinates against the wall* [C] **14:10,14** Hb obscure

green tree; 24 there were even male cult prostitutes in the land. They imitated all the detestable practices of the nations the LORD had dispossessed before the Israelites.

25 In the fifth year of King Rehoboam, Shishak king of Egypt went to war against Jerusalem. 26 He seized the treasuries of the LORD's temple and the treasuries of the royal palace. He took everything. He took all the gold shields that Solomon had made. 27 King Rehoboam made bronze shields in their place and committed them into the care of the captains of the royal escorts[A] who guarded the entrance to the king's palace. 28 Whenever the king entered the LORD's temple, the royal escorts would carry the shields, then they would take them back to the royal escorts' armory.

29 The rest of the events of Rehoboam's reign, along with all his accomplishments, are written about in the Historical Record of Judah's Kings. 30 There was war between Rehoboam and Jeroboam throughout their reigns. 31 Rehoboam rested with his fathers and was buried with his fathers in the city of David. His mother's name was Naamah the Ammonite. His son Abijam[B] became king in his place.

Abijam (15:1-8)

15 In the eighteenth year of Israel's King Jeroboam son of Nebat, Abijam became king over Judah 2 and reigned three years in Jerusalem. His mother's name was Maacah daughter[C] of Abishalom.

3 Abijam walked in all the sins his father before him had committed, and he was not completely devoted to the LORD his God as his ancestor David had been. 4 But because of David, the LORD his God gave him a lamp in Jerusalem to raise up his son after him and to establish Jerusalem. 5 For David did what was right in the LORD's eyes, and he did not turn aside from anything He had commanded him all the days of his life, except in the matter of Uriah the Hittite.

6 There had been war between Rehoboam and Jeroboam all the days of Rehoboam's life. 7 The rest of the events of Abijam's reign, along with all his accomplishments, are written in the Historical Record of Judah's Kings. There was also war between Abijam and Jeroboam. 8 Abijam rested with his fathers and was buried in the city of David. His son Asa became king in his place.

Asa (15:9-24)

9 In the twentieth year of Israel's King Jeroboam, Asa became king of Judah 10 and reigned 41 years in Jerusalem. His grandmother's[D] name was Maacah daughter[C] of Abishalom.

11 Asa did what was right in the LORD's eyes, as his ancestor David had done. 12 He banished the male cult prostitutes from the land and removed all of the idols that his fathers had made. 13 He also removed his grandmother[E] Maacah from being queen mother because she had made an obscene image of •Asherah. Asa chopped down her obscene image and burned it in the Kidron Valley. 14 The •high places were not taken away; but Asa's heart was completely devoted to the LORD his entire life. 15 He brought his father's consecrated gifts and his own consecrated gifts into the LORD's temple: silver, gold, and utensils.

16 There was war between Asa and Baasha king of Israel throughout their reigns. 17 Israel's King Baasha went to war against Judah. He built Ramah in order to deny anyone access to Judah's King Asa. 18 So Asa withdrew all the silver and gold that remained in the treasuries of the LORD's temple and the treasuries of the royal palace and put it into the hands of his servants. Then King Asa sent them to Ben-hadad son of Tabrimmon son of Hezion king of Aram who lived in Damascus, saying, 19 "There is a treaty between me and you, between my father and your father. Look, I have sent you a gift of silver and gold. Go and break your treaty with Baasha king of Israel so that he will withdraw from me."

20 Ben-hadad listened to King Asa and sent the commanders of his armies against the cities of Israel. He attacked Ijon, Dan,

15:1-8 Despite failing to walk in the ways of **his ancestor David** like his father Rehoboam, God blessed **Abijam** on David's account with a son to succeed him after his brief three-year reign. Abijam's mother, **Maacah**, was an influential source of paganism in Judah.

15:9-15 Jeroboam still ruled in Israel when Abijam's son **Asa** inherited the throne of Judah. He was the third king after Solomon and the first in either Israel or Judah to be described in a positive light—like **his ancestor David**. The key to his success was doing what was right in the LORD's eyes rather than his own. Asa banished the leaders and removed the objects of pagan worship, including:

- the **male cult prostitutes** (Hb *qadēsh*, "consecrated" " v. 12;) which were explicitly forbidden—see Dt 23:17; cp. 1Kg 14:22-24; 22:46; 2Kg 23:7;
- **all of the idols** [Hb *gillul*, "trunks, logs, blocks" that could be rolled; cp. Lv 26:30; 2Kg 17:12; Ezk 6:1-14] **that his fathers had made** (1Kg 15:12);
- **his grandmother Maacah from being queen mother**; and
- her **obscene image** [Hb *miphletset*, "horrid or horrible thing," from a verbal root meaning "shudder or tremble" as at something fearful; used only here and 2Ch 15:16] **of Asherah**, which he **burned in . . . the Kidron Valley** (location of the garden of Gethsemane, 1Kg 15:13; cp. 2Kg 23:4-6,12; 2Ch 29:16; 30:14; Jr 31:40; Jn 18:1).

Asa's dramatic course correction stopped short of removing **the high places**, however. The narrator did not ignore this failure but made a concession for it since Asa's **heart was completely devoted to** [Hb *shalēm*, "whole, full, perfect" in keeping the covenant, v. 14] **the LORD** (see 3:1-3).

15:16-22 Known as el-Ram today, **Ramah** was located in Benjamin, about five miles north of Jerusalem. **Baasha king of Israel** fortified the city as his frontier stronghold against Judah until **Asa** persuaded **Ben-hadad** to withdraw from Judah and direct his forces against Israel instead.

15:25–16:34 These six kings, following Jeroboam's reign of 22 years in Israel, all came to power during the 41-year reign of Asa in Judah, and all led Israel further away from the Lord. In contrast to Judah where the Lord kept His promise to sustain David's royal lineage, Israel witnessed a violent series of power plays as unworthy men seized the throne.

[A] **14:27** Lit *the runners* [B] **14:31** = Abijah in 2Ch 13 [C] **15:2,10** Possibly granddaughter; 2Ch 13:2
[D] **15:10** Lit *mother's* [E] **15:13** Lit *mother*

15:25-32 The text clearly states that God had appointed Baasha to execute His judgment on Jeroboam because of the former king who **had caused Israel to commit** sin and had grievously **provoked** [Hb *ka'as*; see 14:9] **the LORD God of Israel.**

15:33–16:7 Having taken the throne of Israel by force, **Baasha** also proved strong enough to maintain power for 24 years. However, he squandered his God-given opportunity to give Israel a fresh start by foolishly following **the example of Jeroboam**, the same pattern of sin that had incurred the demise that Baasha himself had executed against Jeroboam's household.

>WORD|*study*

15:26 Commit (Hb *chata'*, lit "sin"), here, is the verb expressing an archer's failure to hit the mark—his arrow "sinned" when it "missed or erred from the mark" (cp. Jdg 20:16). Used in a spiritual sense, "sin" likewise means "to miss or wander from" God's ways. Romans 3:23 identifies "the glory of God" as the target or mark toward which every person's life is aimed, but "all have sinned and fall short" of that aim. Figuratively, the picture is not of missing the bull's-eye but of missing or falling short of the target altogether.

Abel-beth-maacah, all Chinnereth,
and the whole land of Naphtali.
21 When Baasha heard about it, he
quit building Ramah and stayed in
Tirzah. 22 Then King Asa gave a command to everyone without exception
in Judah, and they carried away the
stones of Ramah and the timbers
Baasha had built it with. Then King
Asa built Geba of Benjamin and Mizpah with them.
23 The rest of all the events of Asa's
reign, along with all his might, all
his accomplishments, and the cities
he built, are written in the Historical Record of Judah's Kings. But in
his old age he developed a disease
in his feet. 24 Then Asa rested with
his fathers and was buried in the
city of his ancestor David. His son
Jehoshaphat became king in his
place.

The Kings of Israel (15:25–16:34)

Nadab (15:25-32)

25 Nadab son of Jeroboam became
king over Israel in the second year of
Judah's King Asa; he reigned over Israel two years. 26 Nadab did what was
evil in the LORD's sight and followed
the example of his father and the sin
he had caused Israel to commit.
27 Then Baasha son of Ahijah of the
house of Issachar conspired against
Nadab, and Baasha struck him down
at Gibbethon of the Philistines while
Nadab and all Israel were besieging
Gibbethon. 28 In the third year of Judah's King Asa, Baasha killed Nadab
and reigned in his place.
29 When Baasha became king, he
struck down the entire house of Jeroboam. He did not leave Jeroboam
any survivors but[A] destroyed his
family according to the word of
the LORD He had spoken through
His servant Ahijah the Shilonite.
30 This was because Jeroboam had
provoked[B] the LORD God of Israel by
the sins he had committed and had
caused Israel to commit.
31 The rest of the events of Nadab's reign, along with all his accomplishments, are written in the
Historical Record of Israel's Kings.
32 There was war between Asa and
Baasha king of Israel throughout
their reigns.

Baasha (15:33–16:7)

33 In the third year of Judah's King
Asa, Baasha son of Ahijah became
king over all Israel and reigned in
Tirzah 24 years. 34 He did what was
evil in the LORD's sight and followed
the example of Jeroboam and the sin
he had caused Israel to commit.

16 Now the word of the LORD came
to Jehu son of Hanani against
Baasha: 2 "Because I raised you up
from the dust and made you ruler
over My people Israel, but you have
walked in the way of Jeroboam and
have caused My people Israel to sin,
provoking Me with their sins, 3 take
note: I will sweep away Baasha and
his house, and I will make your
house like the house of Jeroboam
son of Nebat:

4 Anyone who belongs
to Baasha and dies
in the city,
the dogs will eat,
and anyone who is his
and dies in the field,
the birds of the sky
will eat."

5 The rest of the events of Baasha's
reign, along with all his accomplishments and might, are written in the
Historical Record of Israel's Kings.
6 Baasha rested with his fathers and
was buried in Tirzah. His son Elah
became king in his place. 7 Through
the prophet Jehu son of Hanani the
word of the LORD also came against

[A]15:29 Lit *Jeroboam anyone breathing until* [B]15:30 Lit *provoked in the provocation of*

Baasha and against his house because of all the evil he had done in the LORD's sight, provoking Him with the work of his hands and being like the house of Jeroboam, and because Baasha had struck down the house of Jeroboam.

Elah (16:8-14)

8 In the twenty-sixth year of Judah's King Asa, Elah son of Baasha became king over Israel and reigned in Tirzah two years.

9 His servant Zimri, commander of half his chariots, conspired against him while Elah was in Tirzah getting drunk in the house of Arza, who was in charge of the household at Tirzah. 10 In the twenty-seventh year of Judah's King Asa, Zimri went in, struck Elah down, killing him. Then Zimri became king in his place.

11 When he became king, as soon as he was seated on his throne, Zimri struck down the entire house of Baasha. He did not leave a single male,[A] including his kinsmen and his friends. 12 So Zimri destroyed the entire house of Baasha, according to the word of the LORD He had spoken against Baasha through Jehu the prophet. 13 This happened because of all the sins of Baasha and those of his son Elah, which they committed and caused Israel to commit, provoking the LORD God of Israel with their worthless idols.

14 The rest of the events of Elah's reign, along with all his accomplishments, are written in the Historical Record of Israel's Kings.

Zimri (16:15-20)

15 In the twenty-seventh year of Judah's King Asa, Zimri became king for seven days in Tirzah. Now the troops were encamped against Gibbethon of the Philistines. 16 When these troops heard that Zimri had not only conspired but had also struck down the king, then all Israel made Omri, the army commander, king over Israel that very day in the camp. 17 Omri along with all Israel marched up from Gibbethon and besieged Tirzah. 18 When Zimri saw that the city was captured, he entered the citadel of the royal palace and burned it down over himself. He died 19 because of the sin he committed by doing what was evil in the LORD's sight and by following the example of Jeroboam and the sin he caused Israel to commit.

20 The rest of the events of Zimri's reign, along with the conspiracy that he instigated, are written in the Historical Record of Israel's Kings.

Omri (16:21-28)

21 At that time the people of Israel were divided: half the people followed Tibni son of Ginath, to make him king, and half followed Omri. 22 However, the people who followed Omri proved stronger than those who followed Tibni son of Ginath. So Tibni died and Omri became king.

23 In the thirty-first year of Judah's King Asa, Omri became king over Israel and reigned 12 years. He reigned six years in Tirzah, 24 then he bought the hill of Samaria from Shemer for 150 pounds[B] of silver, and he built up the hill. He named the city he built Samaria[C] based on the name Shemer, the owner of the hill.

25 Omri did what was evil in the LORD's sight; he did more evil than all who were before him. 26 He followed the example of Jeroboam son of Nebat and in his sins that he caused Israel to commit, provoking the LORD God of Israel with their worthless idols. 27 The rest of the events of Omri's reign, along with his accomplishments and the might he exercised, are written in the Historical Record of Israel's Kings. 28 Omri rested with his fathers and was buried in Samaria. His son Ahab became king in his place.

Ahab (16:29-34)

29 Ahab son of Omri became king over Israel in the thirty-eighth year of Judah's King Asa; Ahab son of Omri reigned over Israel in Samaria 22 years. 30 But Ahab son of Omri did what was evil in the LORD's sight more than all who were before him. 31 Then, as if following the sin

16:15-20 The people—**all Israel**—demonstrated their outrage at **Zimri's** acts of treason and murder by making **Omri** their **king** and following him to besiege the capital (v. 17). As with the deaths of his predecessors, the text explained Zimri's death in spiritual terms. Even though he committed suicide, his cause of death was **sin** (vv. 18-19).

16:21-28 His purchase and establishment of **Samaria** as Israel's capital city was the one important accomplishment of Omri's reign for the narrator's purposes of recounting the nation's spiritual history. Extrabiblical evidence indicates that from a secular perspective Omri was a prominent ruler and was respected by surrounding rulers. For example, an Assyrian document dated ca 733 B.C. refers to Israel as the "land of Omri."

16:29-34 The account of Israel's history under the rule of **Ahab** extends to 22:50, but the summary of his wickedness established the context for the greater prominence of prophetic activity in the following narrative (v. 29). What Ahab did was so egregious that **following the sin of Jeroboam** looked like child's play by comparison (vv. 30-31,33). Among his many moral failures, **He married Jezebel** [Hb, "Baal exalts, unchaste"]**, the daughter of Ethbaal king of the Sidonians** (i.e., Phoenicians; see v. 31; cp. Jos 13:4-6; Jdg 3:1-6). He sinned by marrying a Canaanite woman, and readers are already alerted here to Jezebel's role in propagating worship of Baal (or Melqart, the idol's Tyrian or Phoenician name). Jezebel's legacy of wickedness extended into the New Testament era, as she is referenced in the letter to "the church in Thyatira" in Rv 2:20-23.

[A] **16:11** Lit *leave him one who urinates against the wall* [B] **16:24** Lit *for two talents*
[C] **16:24** = Belonging to Shemer's Clan

16:34 For readers familiar with Joshua's prophetic curse following the destruction of **Jericho**, that the city was rebuilt indicates Israel's shocking disregard for their identity as the people of Yahweh (see Jos 6:26).

17:1 **Elijah** (Hb, "Yahweh is my God") is introduced without ceremony, immediately proclaiming to Ahab that a drought would befall the land as certainly as **the Lord God of**

of Jeroboam son of Nebat were a trivial matter, he married Jezebel, the daughter of Ethbaal king of the Sidonians, and then proceeded to serve •Baal and worship him.
32 He set up an altar for Baal in the temple of Baal that he had built in Samaria.
33 Ahab also made an •Asherah pole. Ahab did more to provoke the Lord God of Israel than all the kings of Israel who were before him.
34 During his reign, Hiel the Bethelite built Jericho. At the cost of Abiram his firstborn, he laid its foundation, and at the cost of Segub his youngest, he set up its gates, according to the word of the Lord He had spoken through Joshua son of Nun.

Queens of the Old Testament (Listed alphabetically)

Abigail	• Widow of Nabal the Carmelite (1Sm 25:2,14-38) • Wife of King David (1Sm 25:39-42; 27:3; 30:5; 2Sm 2:2) • Mother of Chileab (Daniel), the second son born to David in Hebron (2Sm 3:2; 1Ch 3:1)
Abi (Abijah)	• Daughter of Zechariah (2Kg 18:1-2; 2Ch 29:1) • Wife of King Ahaz of Judah (2Kg 16:20; 2Kg 18:1-2) • Mother of King Hezekiah of Judah (2Kg 18:1-2; 2Ch 29:1)
Ahinoam	The name of two different women: • Wife of King Saul (1Sm 14:50) • "The Jezreelite"—wife of King David and mother of his firstborn son Amnon (1Sm 25:43; 27:3; 30:5; 2Sm 2:2; 3:2; 1Ch 3:1)
Athaliah	• Granddaughter of King Omri of Israel (2Kg 8:26; 2Ch 22:2-3) • Daughter of Jezebel and Ahab of Israel (2Kg 8:18; 2Ch 22:3) • Wife of King Jehoram of Judah (2Kg 8:18) • Mother of King Ahaziah of Judah (2Kg 11:1; 2Ch 22:2,10) • Usurper of the throne of Judah (2Kg 11:1-16; 2Ch 22:10-23:15,21; 24:7)
Azubah	• Daughter of Shilhi (1Kg 22:42; 2Ch 20:31) • Wife of King Asa of Judah (1Kg 15:24; 22:41-42) • Mother of King Jehoshaphat of Judah (1Kg 22:42; 2Ch 20:31)
Bathsheba	• Daughter of Eliam (Ammiel) (2Sm 11:3; 1Ch 3:5) • Wife of Uriah the Hittite (2Sm 11:3-26; 12:15; Mt 1:6) • Wife of King David (2Sm 11:27; 12:9; Mt 1:6) • Mother of King Solomon (2Sm 12:24; 1Kg 1:11-31; 2:13-19; Mt 1:6)
Esther	• Daughter of Abihail (Est 2:15; 9:29) • Cousin and adopted daughter of Mordecai, a distant relative of King Saul (Est 2:5-7,15) • Jewish wife of King Ahasuerus of Persia (Est 2:16-17)
Haggith	• Wife of King David (2Sm 3:4) • Mother of David's fourth son, Adonijah (1Kg 1:5,11; 2:13; 1Ch 3:2)
Hamutal	• Daughter of Jeremiah of Libnah (2Kg 23:31; 24:18; Jr 52:1) • Wife of King Josiah of Judah (2 Kg 23:31; 24:18; Jr 1:3; 22:11,18) • Mother of King Jehoahaz (Shallum) and King Zedekiah (Mattaniah) of Judah (2 Kg 23:31; 24:18; Jr 52:1)
Hephzibah	• Wife of King Hezekiah of Judah (2Kg 20:21; 21:1; 1Ch 3:13; 2Ch 32:33) • Mother of King Manasseh of Judah (2Kg 21:1)
Jecoliah	• Wife of King Amaziah of Judah (2Kg 14:21; 15:1-2) • Mother of King Azariah (Uzziah) of Judah (2Kg 15:1-2; 2Ch 26:3)
Jedidah	• Daughter of Adaiah of Bozkath (2Kg 22:1) • Wife of King Amon of Judah (2Kg 21:25–22:1) • Mother of King Josiah of Judah (2Kg 22:1)
Jehoaddan	• Wife of King Joash of Judah (2Kg 12:19,21; 14:1-2) • Mother of King Amaziah of Judah (2Kg 14:2; 2 Ch 25:1)

Elijah (17:1-24)

The Announcement of Famine (17:1-7)

17 Now Elijah the Tishbite, from
the Gilead settlers,[A] said to
Ahab, "As the LORD God of Israel
lives, I stand before Him, and there
will be no dew or rain during these
years except by my command!"

[A]17:1 LXX reads *from Tishbe of Gilead*

2 Then a revelation from the LORD
came to him: 3 "Leave here, turn eastward, and hide yourself at the •Wadi
Cherith where it enters the Jordan.
4 You are to drink from the wadi. I
have commanded the ravens to provide for you there."
5 So he did what the LORD commanded. Elijah left and lived by the

Israel lives (v. 1). Worshipers of Baal believed that this fertility god could produce rain. God's withdrawal of rain, therefore, directly challenged and served as a clear sign of God's judgment (Lv 26:18-20; Dt 11:13-17; 28:15,23). This first prophetic proclamation and its immediate fulfillment clearly marked Elijah as a true prophet (cp. Dt 18:22).

17:2-7 In doing **what the LORD commanded**, Elijah experienced

Queens of the Old Testament (continued)

Name	Description
Jerusha	• Daughter of Zadok (2Kg 15:33) • Wife of King Uzziah of Judah (2Kg 15:32-34) • Mother of King Jotham of Judah (2Kg 15:32-34)
Jezebel	• Daughter of King Ethbaal of Sidon (1Kg 16:31) • Wife of King Ahab of Israel (1Kg 18:13,19; 19:1-2; 21:1-25; 2Kg 9:30-37) • Mother of Queen Athaliah (2Kg 8:18,26)
Maacah	• Daughter of King Talmai of Geshur (2Sm 3:3; 13:1) • Wife of King David (2Sm 3:3) • Mother of Absalom and Tamar (2Sm 3:3; 13:1)
Maacah (Micaiah)	• Granddaughter of Abishalom (Absalom) (1Kg 15:1-2,10; 2Ch 11:20) • Daughter of Uriel from Gibeah (2Ch 13:2) • Wife of King Rehoboam of Judah (2Ch 11:20-22) • Mother of King Abijam (Abijah) of Judah (1Kg 15:1-2; 2Ch 13:1-2) • Grandmother of King Asa of Judah (1Kg 15:9-10; 2Ch 15:16)
Mahalath	• Daughter of Jerimoth (King David's son) and Abihail (daughter of David's brother Eliab) (2Ch 11:18) • Wife of King Rehoboam of Judah (2Ch 11:18) • Mother of three sons (2Ch 11:19)
Meshullemeth	• Daughter of Haruz of Jotbah (2Kg 21:19) • Wife of King Manasseh of Judah (2Kg 21:18-19) • Mother of King Amon of Judah (2Kg 21:19)
Michal	• Daughter of King Saul (1Sm 14:49) • First wife of King David (1Sm 18:20-28; 19:11-14; 2Sm 3:13-16; 6:20-23) • Temporarily, wife of Paltiel (Palti), son of Laish from Gallim (1Sm 25:44; 2Sm 3:13-16)
Naamah	• An Ammonitess (1Kg 14:21,31; 2Ch 12:13) • Wife of King Solomon (1Kg 11:43; 14:21,31) • Mother of King Rehoboam of Judah (1Kg 14:21,31; 2Ch 12:13)
Nehushta	• Daughter of Elnathan of Jerusalem (2Kg 24:8) • Wife of King Jehoiakim of Judah (2Kg 24:6,8) • Mother of King Jehoachin (Jeconiah/Coniah) of Judah (2Kg 24:8,12)
Queen of Sheba	• Visitor to the court of King Solomon (1Kg 10:1-13; 2 Ch 9:1-12; Mt 12:42) • Identified as Nikauli by the Jewish historian Josephus
Tahpenes	• Wife of a weak pharaoh (21st dynasty) who ruled at the end of David's reign and the beginning of Solomon's reign (1Kg 11:19-20) • Sister-in-law to Hadad, a son of the king of Edom (1Kg 11:17-19) • Aunt and foster mother to Hadad's son Genubath (1Kg 11:20)
Vashti	• Wife of King Ahasuerus of Persia (Est 1:9,16,19)
Zebidah	• Daughter of Pedaiah of Rumah (2Kg 23:36) • Wife of King Josiah of Judah (2Kg 23:34,36) • Mother of King Jehoiakim of Judah (2Kg 23:36)

God's faithfulness **to provide** (Hb *kul*, "sustain, support, nourish"; cp. 4:27; Gn 45:11; 47:12; 50:21) him with water and food—both **bread and meat**—even in the midst of famine (1Kg 17:3-7; cp. Mt 6:11). Elijah's name retained a prominent role in Scripture, linking his ministry during the reign of Ahab to the prophetic announcement of the coming "Day of the Lord" (Mal 4:5), to John the Baptist's heralding of Jesus as the Messiah (Mt 11:13-14; Lk 1:17), and to Jesus' transfiguration (Mt 17:3-12).

17:8-16 When "the wadi dried up" (v. 7), **the word of the Lord** sent Elijah to Zarephath, and he made the 80 to 90-mile journey without question. In **Sidon**, Jezebel's country of origin, Elijah was a safe distance from Ahab in perhaps the least likely place the king would search for him. More importantly, God continued to meet Elijah's needs through another unlikely source—a poverty-stricken Gentile **woman** whose role indicated God's inclusion of Gentiles in His eternal scheme of salvation (cp. 2Kg 5:17; Jnh 1:2; Lk 4:25-27) and the scarcity of God-fearing people in Israel. Although Elijah's request for water may have been a test to identify her as one whom God had chosen (cp. Gn 24:14-27,42-48), the difference between her responses to the prophet's requests—first for water, which **she** immediately **went to get**, and then for **a piece of bread** (Hb *lechem*, "food, grain," 1Kg 17:11) she didn't have—may also indicate that her food shortage resulted more from her status as a young widow than from the economic repercussions of Israel's drought, which apparently extended to Sidon.

CHARACTER PROFILE

Widow of Zarephath A Woman of Faith

Her Background	• She was a widow from Zarephath (17: 8-9). • She had a young son (17:12). • She had only a small amount of oil and flour for food and expected to starve (17:12).
Her Story	• She met Elijah while gathering kindling and recognized him as a follower of the Lord God (17:12-16). • She agreed to bring him bread despite her desperate circumstances (17:13-15). • Elijah promised her God's provision (17:14-16). • Her son became sick and died (17:17-21). • Elijah healed the child, causing the widow to recognize God's power (17:22-24).
Life Lessons	• Her generosity toward Elijah brought provision for her and her son. • Service to others is pleasing to God.

Wadi Cherith where it enters the
Jordan. [6]The ravens kept bringing
him bread and meat in the morning
and in the evening, and he drank
from the wadi. [7]After a while, the
wadi dried up because there had
been no rain in the land.

The Ministry to the Widow of Zarephath (17:8-24)

[8]Then the word of the Lord came
to him: [9]"Get up, go to Zarephath
that belongs to Sidon and stay
there. Look, I have commanded a
woman who is a widow to provide
for you there." [10]So Elijah got up
and went to Zarephath. When he
arrived at the city gate, there was
a widow woman gathering wood.
Elijah called to her and said, "Please
bring me a little water in a cup and
let me drink." [11]As she went to get
it, he called to her and said, "Please
bring me a piece of bread in your
hand."

[12]But she said, "As the Lord your
God lives, I don't have anything
baked—only a handful of flour in
the jar and a bit of oil in the jug.
Just now, I am gathering a couple of
sticks in order to go prepare it for
myself and my son so we can eat it
and die."

[13]Then Elijah said to her, "Don't
be afraid; go and do as you have said.
But first make me a small loaf from it
and bring it out to me. Afterward, you
may make some for yourself and your
son, [14]for this is what the Lord God
of Israel says, 'The flour jar will not
become empty and the oil jug will not
run dry until the day the Lord sends
rain on the surface of the land.'"

[15]So she proceeded to do according to the word of Elijah. Then the
woman, Elijah, and her household
ate for many days. [16]The flour jar
did not become empty, and the oil
jug did not run dry, according to
the word of the Lord He had spoken
through[A] Elijah.

[17]After this, the son of the woman
who owned the house became ill.
His illness became very severe until
no breath remained in him. [18]She
said to Elijah, "Man of God, what
do we have in common? Have you
come to remind me of my •guilt and
to kill my son?"

[19]But Elijah said to her, "Give me
your son." So he took him from her
arms, brought him up to the upper
room where he was staying, and
laid him on his own bed. [20]Then he
cried out to the Lord and said, "My
Lord God, have You also brought
tragedy on the widow I am staying
with by killing her son?" [21]Then he
stretched himself out over the boy

[A]**17:16** Lit *by the hand of*

three times. He cried out to the LORD
and said, "My LORD God, please let
this boy's life return to him!"
22 So the LORD listened to Elijah's
voice, and the boy's life returned to
him, and he lived. 23 Then Elijah took
the boy, brought him down from
the upper room into the house, and
gave him to his mother. Elijah said,
"Look, your son is alive."
24 Then the woman said to Elijah, "Now I know you are a man of
God and the LORD's word from your
mouth is true."

Obadiah (18:1-16)

18 After a long time, the word of
the LORD came to Elijah in the
third year: "Go and present yourself
to Ahab. I will send rain on the surface of the land." 2 So Elijah went to
present himself to Ahab.
The famine was severe in Samaria.
3 Ahab called for Obadiah, who was
in charge of the palace. Obadiah
was a man who greatly •feared the
LORD 4 and took 100 prophets and
hid them, 50 men to a cave, and
provided them with food and water
when Jezebel slaughtered the LORD's
prophets. 5 Ahab said to Obadiah, "Go
throughout the land to every spring
of water and to every •wadi. Perhaps
we'll find grass so we can keep the
horses and mules alive and not have
to destroy any cattle." 6 They divided
the land between them in order to
cover it. Ahab went one way by himself, and Obadiah went the other
way by himself.
7 While Obadiah was walking along
the road, Elijah suddenly met him.
When Obadiah recognized him, he
fell with his face to the ground and
said, "Is it you, my lord Elijah?"
8 "It is I," he replied. "Go tell your
lord, 'Elijah is here!'"
9 But Obadiah said, "What sin have
I committed, that you are handing
your servant over to Ahab to put me
to death? 10 As the LORD your God
lives, there is no nation or kingdom
where my lord has not sent someone
to search for you. When they said,
'He is not here,' he made that kingdom or nation swear they had not
found you.
11 "Now you say, 'Go tell your lord,
"Elijah is here!"' 12 But when I leave
you, the Spirit of the LORD may carry
you off to some place I don't know.
Then when I go report to Ahab and
he doesn't find you, he will kill me.
But I, your servant, have feared
the LORD from my youth. 13 Wasn't
it reported to my lord what I did
when Jezebel slaughtered the LORD's
prophets? I hid 100 of the prophets
of the LORD, 50 men to a cave, and I
provided them with food and water.
14 Now you say, 'Go tell your lord,
"Elijah is here!"' He will kill me!"
15 Then Elijah said, "As the LORD of
•Hosts lives, before whom I stand,
today I will present myself to Ahab."
16 Obadiah went to meet Ahab and

17:17-23 That **no breath** [Hb *neshamah*, "spirit, soul," referring to a person's life] **remained in him** is an expression for death and cannot be used to argue for some explanation of the boy's condition other than that he died. With a mother's anguish she blamed Elijah for killing her son as punishment for her own **guilt** (Hb *'awon*, "iniquity," often expressing the "punishment or consequences" thereof). Elijah's prayer reflected genuine grief and compassion for this single mother. He gave her orders once again to hand him her son. The significance of Elijah's particular actions accompanying his prayer is uncertain. However, the text does state that:

- He was not magically transferring his life to the boy or the boy's sickness to himself.
- He did plead specifically with Yahweh as the only God who could **return** the **boy's life . . . to him.**
- When he presented **the boy** to **his mother**, he did not take credit for the miracle but merely announced, **"Look, your son is alive."**

The woman's next words reveal that the miracle validated Elijah's ministry as a spokesman for God (cp. Jn 3:2; Ac 2:22; Heb 2:4).

18:1-16 Despite his high-ranking position of service to Ahab, **Obadiah** was devoted to Yahweh and saved **100** of the Lord's **prophets** from the murderous hands of **Jezebel**. Obadiah's reaction to Elijah's orders echoed the widow's reaction to her son's death (vv. 9-14; cp. 17:18). Those whose faith has been proven in mighty ways in the past can expect to face more tests of faith—opportunities to demonstrate complete trust in the Lord and thereby to glorify Him in His faithfulness (cp. Gn 12:4; 22:1-19; 2Co 1:9-10; Heb 11:8,17-19; Jms 1:2-4,12-13; 1Pt 1:6-7).

CHARACTER PROFILE

Jezebel A Vicious Queen

Her Background	• The daughter of the king of Sidon (16:31) • The wife of King Ahab (16:31) • An avid worshiper of Baal and an antagonist toward the true God (18:4,13,19; 19:1-2)
Her Story	• She ordered that the prophets of God be murdered (18:4,13). • She threatened to kill Elijah (19:2). • She plotted to steal Naboth's vineyard (21:7-10). • She goaded her husband into evil acts (21:25). • She was cursed by Elijah, who prophesied that dogs would eat her body (2Kg 9:30-37).
Life Lesson	• Jezebel's hatred of Israel's God led to her disgraceful and gruesome death (21:23). • There are always consequences to the rejection of Yahweh God.

18:17-18 Ahab blamed the prophet for causing the drought, greeting Elijah as the **destroyer** [Hb *ʿakar*, one who was "troubling or disturbing" the peace] **of Israel.** Elijah quickly corrected him. Ahab and Omri's **house** had **destroyed Israel** by their sin.

18:19-29 The purpose of the "contest" was to prove **to the people** that **Yahweh** alone **is God**, not **Baal**—the people could not follow both. Although politically the people were under the authority of a king who had sold out to paganism, Elijah confronted them with the truth that no middle ground existed regarding spiritual authority. To choose any other god was to reject Yahweh; to choose to follow Yahweh *required* the rejection of all rivals or opponents. God's claim upon His people was exclusive. The people, not the pagan prophets or even the king, had to agree to proceed with the "contest."

18:30-39 Elijah told the people to come close to him so they could observe everything he did. **He built an altar** with **12 stones** representing **the tribes** of Israel **in the name of Yahweh**, since God still had one people even though the tribes had been divided into two nations. This people was distinguished from all others in that **the word of the Lord had come** to them and had given them the **name** of **Israel** (cp. Gn 32:28; 35:9-10). By soaking the sacrifice and the altar with water and filling a trench around it, only the one true God would be able to set fire to **the offering**.

>WORD|*study*

18:21 The verb hesitate (Hb *pasach*, "fluctuate" between) more literally suggests "skip, limp or halt," conveying either the ambivalence of "skipping" back and forth between divided commitments or the halting steps of one who is lame because of a wrenched or dislocated joint (v. 21). The narrator later uses a wordplay to make fun of the Baal prophets' lame dance [Hb *pasach*] "around the altar they had made" to Baal (v. 26).

18:26-29 The narrator used no (Hb *ʾayin*, "nothing, nought") five times to emphasize the total lack of response. The word's repetition in the Hebrew text would sound emphatic in the reader's ear: "*No* sound; *no*" answer (v. 26); "*no* sound, *no*" answer, "*no*" response (v. 29).

18:37 This form of the verb turned . . . back (Hb *savav*, "cause to turn, reverse, bring back") often indicates the transfer of something *to* its rightful place or possession *from* a place or owner where it did not belong (cp. 1Ch 10:14; 12:23; 13:3). Elijah recognized that Yahweh's public victory over and discrediting of Baal declared His power to reclaim Israel's heart. "Back" (Hb *ʾachorannit*, "backward," indicating direction, or "again") reinforces the sense of God causing Israel's heart to change spiritual direction.

told him. Then Ahab went to meet Elijah.

Elijah Versus Ahab, Jezebel, and the Prophets of Baal (18:17–19:21)

The Victory at Mount Carmel (18:17-46)

17 When Ahab saw Elijah, Ahab said
to him, "Is that you, you destroyer
of Israel?"
18 He replied, "I have not destroyed
Israel, but you and your father's
house have, because you have abandoned the LORD's commands and
followed the •Baals. 19 Now summon
all Israel to meet me at Mount Carmel, along with the 450 prophets of
Baal and the 400 prophets of •Asherah who eat at Jezebel's table."
20 So Ahab summoned all the Israelites and gathered the prophets
at Mount Carmel. 21 Then Elijah approached all the people and said,
"How long will you hesitate between two opinions? If •Yahweh is God, follow Him. But if Baal, follow him."
But the people didn't answer him a word.
22 Then Elijah said to the people,
"I am the only remaining prophet of the LORD, but Baal's prophets are
450 men. 23 Let two bulls be given
to us. They are to choose one bull for themselves, cut it in pieces, and place it on the wood but not light the fire. I will prepare the other bull and place it on the wood but not light the
fire. 24 Then you call on the name of
your god, and I will call on the name of Yahweh. The God who answers with fire, He is God."

All the people answered, "That sounds good."
25 Then Elijah said to the prophets
of Baal, "Since you are so numerous, choose for yourselves one bull and prepare it first. Then call on the name of your god but don't light the fire."
26 So they took the bull that he
gave them, prepared it, and called on the name of Baal from morning until noon, saying, "Baal, answer us!" But there was no sound; no one answered. Then they danced, hobbling around the altar they had made.
27 At noon Elijah mocked them.
He said, "Shout loudly, for he's a god! Maybe he's thinking it over; maybe he has wandered away;[A] or maybe he's on the road. Perhaps he's
sleeping and will wake up!" 28 They
shouted loudly, and cut themselves with knives and spears, according to their custom, until blood gushed
over them. 29 All afternoon they kept
on raving until the offering of the evening sacrifice, but there was no sound; no one answered, no one paid attention.
30 Then Elijah said to all the people, "Come near me." So all the people approached him. Then he repaired the LORD's altar that had
been torn down: 31 Elijah took 12
stones—according to the number of the tribes of the sons of Jacob, to whom the word of the LORD had come, saying, "Israel will be your
name"— 32 and he built an altar
with the stones in the name of Yahweh. Then he made a trench around the altar large enough to

[A]18:27 Or *has turned aside*; possibly to relieve himself

hold about four gallons.[A,B] 33 Next,
he arranged the wood, cut up the
bull, and placed it on the wood. He
said, "Fill four water pots with water and pour it on the offering to be
burned and on the wood." 34 Then
he said, "A second time!" and they
did it a second time. And then he
said, "A third time!" and they did it
a third time. 35 So the water ran all
around the altar; he even filled the
trench with water.
36 At the time for offering the evening sacrifice, Elijah the prophet
approached the altar and said, "Yahweh, God of Abraham, Isaac, and Israel, today let it be known that You
are God in Israel and I am Your servant, and that at Your word I have
done all these things. 37 Answer me,
LORD! Answer me so that this people
will know that You, Yahweh, are
God and that You have turned their
hearts back."
38 Then Yahweh's fire fell and
consumed the •burnt offering, the
wood, the stones, and the dust, and
it licked up the water that was in the
trench. 39 When all the people saw it,
they fell facedown and said, "Yahweh, He is God! Yahweh, He is God!"
40 Then Elijah ordered them,
"Seize the prophets of Baal! Do not
let even one of them escape." So
they seized them, and Elijah brought
them down to the Wadi Kishon and
slaughtered them there. 41 Elijah said
to Ahab, "Go up, eat and drink, for
there is the sound of a rainstorm."
42 So Ahab went to eat and drink,
but Elijah went up to the summit
of Carmel. He bowed down on the
ground and put his face between his
knees. 43 Then he said to his servant,
"Go up and look toward the sea."
So he went up, looked, and said,
"There's nothing."
Seven times Elijah said, "Go back."
44 On the seventh time, he reported, "There's a cloud as small as
a man's hand coming from the sea."
Then Elijah said, "Go and tell
Ahab, 'Get your chariot ready and go
down so the rain doesn't stop you.'"
45 In a little while, the sky grew
dark with clouds and wind, and
there was a downpour. So Ahab got

HARD QUESTION

How do we overcome spiritual depression?

Seasons of spiritual depression seem to be a universal challenge for nearly every woman. Oftentimes, in your response to difficult circumstances or spiritual struggles, spiritual depression sets in when you doubt God's goodness and trustworthiness just as Elijah did here. Elijah succumbed to self-pitying despair when his eyes were fixed on him and his situation more than on the Lord and His promises (19:3-8). You will often be tempted to despair as Elijah did, believing that you are the "only one" in your circumstances. These times require you to do as the Psalmist did in his depression and proclaim to your own soul the hope that you will praise God again. When facing seasons of debilitating spiritual depression, you must tune yourself to hear God's voice (vv. 11-13), cling to His truth (v. 18; cp. 18:3,13), and heed His instruction (19:11,15-17).

in his chariot and went to Jezreel.
46 The power of the LORD was on Elijah, and he tucked his mantle under
his belt and ran ahead of Ahab to the
entrance of Jezreel.

The Flight from Jezebel (19:1-18)

19 Ahab told Jezebel everything
that Elijah had done and how
he had killed all the prophets with
the sword. 2 So Jezebel sent a messenger to Elijah, saying, "May the
gods punish me and do so severely if
I don't make your life like the life of
one of them by this time tomorrow!"
3 Then Elijah became afraid[C] and
immediately ran for his life. When
he came to Beer-sheba that belonged
to Judah, he left his servant there,
4 but he went on a day's journey into
the wilderness. He sat down under a
broom tree and prayed that he might
die. He said, "I have had enough!
LORD, take my life, for I'm no better
than my fathers." 5 Then he lay down
and slept under the broom tree.
Suddenly, an angel touched him.
The angel told him, "Get up and eat."
6 Then he looked, and there at his
head was a loaf of bread baked over
hot stones, and a jug of water. So he
ate and drank and lay down again.
7 Then the angel of the LORD returned
for a second time and touched him.
He said, "Get up and eat, or the journey will be too much for you." 8 So he

18:40-46 Elijah's subsequent words and actions demonstrated his faith in God's promise to "send rain" (v. 1) and God's affirmation of his prophetic ministry. Elijah's role as the Lord's prophet was indelibly written in Israel's spiritual history (see Mal 4:4-6 and Lk 1:17; 9:18-20; 17:1-13; Jn 1:19-27).

9:3-8 Despite being powerfully used of God, Elijah was human and subject to the despair and depression that often follow a period of intense activity, a traumatic experience, or a crushing disappointment. Most remarkable in this passage is how tenderly **the LORD** met Elijah's needs and restored his **strength** for another 40 days and nights of travel further south to **Horeb**, where God had spoken to Moses, provided water from a rock, and later established His covenant with Israel (cp. 8:9; Ex 3:1; 17:6; Dt 4:10-13; 5:2-4).

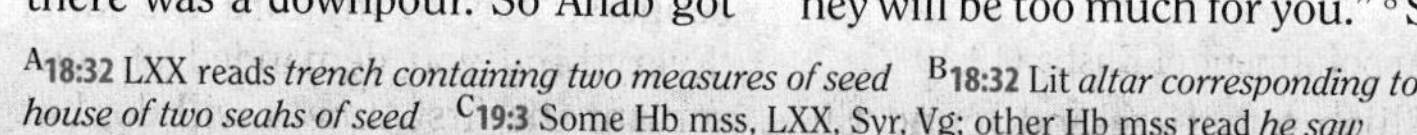
[A] **18:32** LXX reads *trench containing two measures of seed* [B] **18:32** Lit *altar corresponding to a house of two seahs of seed* [C] **19:3** Some Hb mss, LXX, Syr, Vg; other Hb mss read *he saw*

19:9-10 The word of the Lord commanded Elijah's attention with a question about his purpose. Elijah's response conveyed another dimension of the depression that set in about six weeks before. His isolation magnified the distorted feeling that he was standing completely alone against the powers of evil.

19:10-18 Instead of responding to Elijah's complaint, the Lord sent him on a three-part mission requiring him to **go and return by the way** he had come. The instructions assured Elijah of God's continuing sovereignty over and active involvement in Israel's affairs and pushed the prophet back into active duty (vv. 15-18).

19:19-21 Elisha seemed to understand what it meant for **Elijah** to throw **his mantle over him**—the action suggested his being anointed for service in a divinely appointed role (cp. Jesus' teaching on the cost of discipleship in Lk 9:61-62).

got up, ate, and drank. Then on the strength from that food, he walked 40 days and 40 nights to Horeb, the mountain of God. 9 He entered a cave there and spent the night.

Then the word of the LORD came to him, and He said to him, "What are you doing here, Elijah?"

10 He replied, "I have been very zealous for the LORD God of •Hosts, but the Israelites have abandoned Your covenant, torn down Your altars, and killed Your prophets with the sword. I alone am left, and they are looking for me to take my life."

11 Then He said, "Go out and stand on the mountain in the LORD's presence."

At that moment, the LORD passed by. A great and mighty wind was tearing at the mountains and was shattering cliffs before the LORD, but the LORD was not in the wind. After the wind there was an earthquake, but the LORD was not in the earthquake. 12 After the earthquake there was a fire, but the LORD was not in the fire. And after the fire there was a voice, a soft whisper. 13 When Elijah heard it, he wrapped his face in his mantle and went out and stood at the entrance of the cave.

Suddenly, a voice came to him and said, "What are you doing here, Elijah?"

14 "I have been very zealous for the LORD God of Hosts," he replied, "but the Israelites have abandoned Your covenant, torn down Your altars, and killed Your prophets with the sword. I alone am left, and they're looking for me to take my life."

15 Then the LORD said to him, "Go and return by the way you came to the Wilderness of Damascus. When you arrive, you are to anoint Hazael as king over Aram. 16 You are to anoint Jehu son of Nimshi as king over Israel and Elisha son of Shaphat from Abel-meholah as prophet in your place. 17 Then Jehu will put to death whoever escapes the sword of Hazael, and Elisha will put to death whoever escapes the sword of Jehu. 18 But I will leave 7,000 in Israel—every knee that has not bowed to •Baal and every mouth that has not kissed him."

The Appointment of Elisha (19:19-21)

19 Elijah left there and found Elisha son of Shaphat as he was plowing. Twelve teams of oxen were in front of him, and he was with the twelfth team. Elijah walked by him and threw his mantle over him. 20 Elisha left the oxen, ran to follow Elijah, and said, "Please let me kiss my father and mother, and then I will follow you."

"Go on back," he replied, "for what have I done to you?"

21 So he turned back from following him, took the team of oxen, and slaughtered them. With the oxen's wooden yoke and plow, he cooked the meat and gave it to the people, and they ate. Then he left, followed Elijah, and served him.

The Man of God (20:1-34)

20 Now Ben-hadad king of Aram assembled his entire army. Thirty-two kings, along with horses and chariots, were with him. He marched up, besieged Samaria, and fought against it. 2 He sent messengers into the city to Ahab king of Israel and said to him, "This is what Ben-hadad says: 3 'Your silver and your gold are mine! And your best wives and children are mine as well!'"

4 Then the king of Israel answered, "Just as you say, my lord the king: I am yours, along with all that I have."

5 The messengers then returned and said, "This is what Ben-hadad says: 'I have sent messengers to you, saying: You are to give me your silver, your gold, your wives, and your children. 6 But at this time tomorrow I will send my servants to you, and they will search your palace and your servants' houses. They will lay their hands on and take away whatever is precious to you.'"

7 Then the king of Israel called for all the elders of the land and said, "Think it over and you will see that this one is only looking for trouble, for he demanded my wives, my children, my silver, and my gold, and I didn't turn him down."

8 All the elders and all the people said to him, "Don't listen or agree."

9 So he said to Ben-hadad's messengers, "Say to my lord the king, 'Everything you demanded of your servant the first time, I will do, but

this thing I cannot do.'" So the messengers left and took word back to him.

10 Then Ben-hadad sent messengers to him and said, "May the gods punish me and do so severely if Samaria's dust amounts to a handful for each of the people who follow me."

11 The king of Israel answered, "Say this: 'Don't let the one who puts on his armor boast like the one who takes it off.'"

12 When Ben-hadad heard this response, while he and the kings were drinking in the tents, he said to his servants, "Take your positions." So they took their positions against the city.

13 A prophet came to Ahab king of Israel and said, "This is what the LORD says: 'Do you see this entire great army? Watch, I am handing it over to you today so that you may know that I am •Yahweh.'"

14 Ahab asked, "By whom?"

And the prophet said, "This is what the LORD says: 'By the young men of the provincial leaders.'"

Then he asked, "Who is to start the battle?"

He said, "You."

15 So Ahab counted the young men of the provincial leaders, and there were 232. After them he counted all the Israelite troops: 7,000. 16 They marched out at noon while Ben-hadad and the 32 kings who were helping him were getting drunk in the tents. 17 The young men of the provincial leaders marched out first. Then Ben-hadad sent out scouts, and they reported to him, saying, "Men are marching out of Samaria."

18 So he said, "If they have marched out in peace, take them alive, and if they have marched out for battle, take them alive."

19 The young men of the provincial leaders and the army behind them marched out from the city, 20 and each one struck down his opponent. So the Arameans fled and Israel pursued them, but Ben-hadad king of Aram escaped on a horse with the cavalry. 21 Then the king of Israel marched out and attacked the cavalry and the chariots. He inflicted a great slaughter on Aram.

22 The prophet approached the king of Israel and said to him, "Go and strengthen yourself, then consider what you should do, for in the spring the king of Aram will march against you."

23 Now the king of Aram's servants said to him, "Their gods are gods of the hill country. That's why they were stronger than we were. Instead, we should fight with them on the plain; then we will certainly be stronger than they will be. 24 Also do this: remove each king from his position and appoint captains in their place. 25 Raise another army for yourself like the army you lost—horse for horse, chariot for chariot—and let's fight with them on the plain; and we will certainly be stronger than they will be." The king listened to them and did so.

26 In the spring, Ben-hadad mobilized the Arameans and went up to Aphek to battle Israel. 27 The Israelites mobilized, gathered supplies, and went to fight them. The Israelites camped in front of them like two little flocks of goats, while the Arameans filled the landscape.

28 Then the man of God approached and said to the king of Israel, "This is what the LORD says: 'Because the Arameans have said: Yahweh is a god of the mountains and not a god of the valleys, I will hand over all this great army to you. Then you will know that I am the LORD.'"

29 They camped opposite each other for seven days. On the seventh day, the battle took place, and the Israelites struck down the Arameans—100,000 foot soldiers in one day. 30 The ones who remained fled into the city of Aphek, and the wall fell on those 27,000 remaining men.

Ben-hadad also fled and went into an inner room in the city. 31 His servants said to him, "Consider this: we have heard that the kings of the house of Israel are merciful kings. So let's put •sackcloth around our waists and ropes around our heads, and let's go out to the king of Israel. Perhaps he will spare your life."

32 So they dressed with sackcloth around their waists and ropes around their heads, went to the king of Israel, and said, "Your servant Ben-hadad says, 'Please spare my life.'"

20:1-34 Details of the battles emphasize that Israel was outnumbered and militarily under-equipped in comparison with its foes, but the seemingly impossible circumstances served to magnify the superiority and sovereignty of the God of Israel (vv. 1,13,15,20-21,27-30). In both cases, the **man of God** reported to Ahab God's promise to **hand over** the whole Aramean army to him for a particular purpose: **Then you will know that I am the LORD** (vv. 13,28; cp. Ezk 20:44).

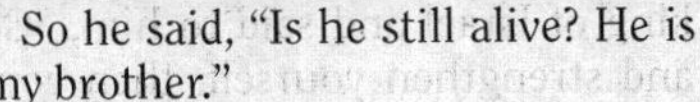

20:35-36 Reminiscent of the fate of "the man of God" who deviated from God's instructions in chapter 13, another **man** who **did not listen to the voice of the Lord**, however absurd the command seemed, was **killed** by **a lion**, as predicted by **one of the sons of the prophets**.

21:1-6 Naboth's response to Ahab's requesting his land was decisive but not disrespectful. Selling one's family **inheritance** was unthinkable (see Lv 25:23-28). Ahab's moping gained Jezebel's attention; then he misrepresented why the bargain had failed (1Kg 21:3,6).

21:7-10 **Jezebel**'s plot demonstrated that she knew enough Jewish law to manipulate it as a cloak for her sin. **Two wicked** [Hb *beliya'al*, "worthless, good for nothing, scoundrels," cp. Pr 6:12; 16:27; 19:28] **men** played the role of the two witnesses required to secure the death penalty for a capital offense (Dt 17:6-7). **Naboth** was falsely accused of cursing **God** and was stoned to death (1Kg 21:8-14; cp. Ex 22:28).

So he said, "Is he still alive? He is my brother."

33 Now the men were looking for a sign of hope, so they quickly picked up on this[A] and responded, "Yes, it is your brother Ben-hadad."

Then he said, "Go and bring him."

So Ben-hadad came out to him, and Ahab had him come up into the chariot. 34 Then Ben-hadad said to him, "I restore to you the cities that my father took from your father, and you may set up marketplaces for yourself in Damascus, like my father set up in Samaria."

Ahab responded, "On the basis of this treaty, I release you." So he made a treaty with him and released him.

One of the Sons of the Prophets (20:35-43)

35 One of the sons of the prophets said to his fellow prophet by the word of the Lord, "Strike me!" But the man refused to strike him.

36 He told him, "Because you did not listen to the voice of the Lord, mark my words: When you leave me, a lion will kill you." When he left him, a lion attacked and killed him.

37 The prophet found another man and said to him, "Strike me!" So the man struck him, inflicting a wound. 38 Then the prophet went and waited for the king on the road. He disguised himself with a bandage over his eyes. 39 As the king was passing by, he cried out to the king and said, "Your servant marched out into the middle of the battle. Suddenly, a man turned aside and brought someone to me and said, 'Guard this man! If he is ever missing, it will be your life in place of his life, or you will weigh out 75 pounds[B] of silver.' 40 But while your servant was busy here and there, he disappeared."

The king of Israel said to him, "That will be your sentence; you yourself have decided it."

41 He quickly removed the bandage from his eyes. The king of Israel recognized that he was one of the prophets. 42 The prophet said to him, "This is what the Lord says: 'Because you released from your hand the man I had •set apart for destruction, it will be your life in place of his life and your people in place of his people.'" 43 The king of Israel left for home resentful and angry, and he entered Samaria.

Elijah Versus Ahab in Naboth's Vineyard (21:1-29)

21 Some time passed after these events. Naboth the Jezreelite had a vineyard; it was in Jezreel next to the palace of Ahab king of Samaria. 2 So Ahab spoke to Naboth, saying, "Give me your vineyard so I can have it for a vegetable garden, since it is right next to my palace. I will give you a better vineyard in its place, or if you prefer, I will give you its value in silver."

3 But Naboth said to Ahab, "I will never give my fathers' inheritance to you."

4 So Ahab went to his palace resentful and angry because of what Naboth the Jezreelite had told him. He had said, "I will not give you my fathers' inheritance." He lay down on his bed, turned his face away, and didn't eat any food.

5 Then his wife Jezebel came to him and said to him, "Why are you so upset that you refuse to eat?"

6 "Because I spoke to Naboth the Jezreelite," he replied. "I told him: Give me your vineyard for silver, or if you wish, I will give you a vineyard in its place. But he said, 'I won't give you my vineyard!'"

7 Then his wife Jezebel said to him, "Now, exercise your royal power over Israel. Get up, eat some food, and be happy. For I will give you the vineyard of Naboth the Jezreelite." 8 So she wrote letters in Ahab's name and sealed them with his seal. She sent the letters to the elders and nobles who lived with Naboth in his city. 9 In the letters, she wrote:

> Proclaim a fast and seat Naboth at the head of the people.
> 10 Then seat two •wicked men opposite him and have them testify against him, saying, "You have cursed God and the king!" Then take him out and stone him to death.

[A] **20:33** Some Hb mss, alt Hb tradition, LXX; other Hb mss read *they hastened and caught hold; "Is this it?"* [B] **20:39** Lit *a talent*

11 The men of his city, the elders
and nobles who lived in his city, did
as Jezebel had commanded them, as
was written in the letters she had
sent them. 12 They proclaimed a fast
and seated Naboth at the head of
the people. 13 The two wicked men
came in and sat opposite him. Then
the wicked men testified against Naboth in the presence of the people,
saying, "Naboth has cursed God and
the king!" So they took him outside
the city and stoned him to death
with stones. 14 Then they sent word
to Jezebel, "Naboth has been stoned
to death."

15 When Jezebel heard that Naboth
had been stoned to death, she said to
Ahab, "Get up and take possession of
the vineyard of Naboth the Jezreelite who refused to give it to you for
silver, since Naboth isn't alive, but
dead." 16 When Ahab heard that Naboth was dead, he got up to go down
to the vineyard of Naboth the Jezreelite to take possession of it.

17 Then the word of the LORD came
to Elijah the Tishbite: 18 "Get up and
go to meet Ahab king of Israel, who
is in Samaria. You'll find him in Naboth's vineyard, where he has gone
to take possession of it. 19 Tell him,
'This is what the LORD says: Have you
murdered and also taken possession?' Then tell him, 'This is what
the LORD says: In the place where the
dogs licked Naboth's blood, the dogs
will also lick your blood!'"

20 Ahab said to Elijah, "So, you
have caught me, my enemy."

He replied, "I have caught you
because you devoted yourself to
do what is evil in the LORD's sight.
21 This is what the LORD says:[A] 'I am
about to bring disaster on you and
will sweep away your descendants:

> I will eliminate all of
> Ahab's males,[B]
> both slave and free, in Israel;

22 I will make your house like the
house of Jeroboam son of Nebat and
like the house of Baasha son of Ahijah, because you have provoked My
anger and caused Israel to sin. 23 The
LORD also speaks of Jezebel: The dogs
will eat Jezebel in the plot of land[C]
at Jezreel:

> 24 He who belongs to Ahab
> and dies in the city,
> the dogs will eat,
> and he who dies in the field,
> the birds of the sky
> will eat.'"

25 Still, there was no one like Ahab,
who devoted himself to do what was
evil in the LORD's sight, because his
wife Jezebel incited him. 26 He committed the most detestable acts by
going after idols as the Amorites
had, whom the LORD had dispossessed before the Israelites.

27 When Ahab heard these words, he
tore his clothes, put •sackcloth over
his body, and fasted. He lay down in
sackcloth and walked around subdued. 28 Then the word of the LORD
came to Elijah the Tishbite: 29 "Have
you seen how Ahab has humbled
himself before Me? I will not bring
the disaster during his lifetime, because he has humbled himself before
Me. I will bring the disaster on his
house during his son's lifetime."

Micaiah (22:1-38)

22 There was a lull of three years
without war between Aram
and Israel. 2 However, in the third
year, Jehoshaphat king of Judah
went to visit the king of Israel.
3 The king of Israel had said to his
servants, "Don't you know that
Ramoth-gilead is ours, but we have
failed to take it from the hand of
the king of Aram?" 4 So he asked Jehoshaphat, "Will you go with me to
fight Ramoth-gilead?"

Jehoshaphat replied to the king of
Israel, "I am as you are, my people
as your people, my horses as your
horses." 5 But Jehoshaphat said to the
king of Israel, "First, please ask what
the LORD's will is."

6 So the king of Israel gathered the
prophets, about 400 men, and asked
them, "Should I go against Ramoth-
gilead for war or should I refrain?"

They replied, "March up, and the
Lord will hand it over to the king."

7 But Jehoshaphat asked, "Isn't

21:17-29 Through **Elijah**, God accused **Ahab** of murder. What his wife, the men of Naboth's city, and two false witnesses had done did not remove Ahab's personal guilt in the matter. God invoked the *lex talionis*, the law requiring that the punishment be proportionate to the crime—"an eye for an eye and a tooth for a tooth" (see Gn 9:6; cp. Ex 21:22-25; Lv 24:17; Dt 19:16-21; Mt 5:38). Ahab's end, therefore, would be like that of his victim (1Kg 21:17-19,23-24; 22:37-38; cp. 2Kg 9:36). The role reversal in this couple's marriage—Jezebel's taking on the divinely-given leadership role that Ahab refused to exercise—exhibited a root problem in the king's home. God's response to Ahab's grief over the disclosure of his sin exemplifies His eagerness to dispense mercy rather than judgment (1Kg 21:27-29). Because Ahab **humbled himself** (Hb *kana'*, "submit oneself, behave submissively, be brought low as a vanquished enemy," v. 29), the Lord delayed bringing **disaster** on his house.

22:1-38 Ahab's choices demonstrated his unyielding resistance to God's word. Jehoshaphat's choices to leave his realm for uncertain gain and to follow Ahab's lead demonstrated a lack of discernment. Even if Ahab's apparent turn-around had convinced Jehoshaphat to pursue a peaceful and mutually beneficial alliance with Israel, the narrative indicates that **Jehoshaphat** had more than enough evidence before the battle to realize his folly. By God's grace, Jehoshaphat did seem to learn his lesson. When Ahab's son later requested to send his servants on one of Judah's ships, "Jehoshaphat was not willing" (22:49).

[A] **21:21** LXX; MT omits *This is what the LORD says* [B] **21:21** Lit *eliminate Ahab's one who urinates against the wall* [C] **21:23** Some Hb mss, Syr, Tg, Vg, 2Kg 9:36; other Hb mss, LXX read *the rampart*

22:23-38 Ahab was unsuccessful in thwarting the **disaster** prophesied against him (vv. 8,18; cp. vv. 21-28). The prophecy that Ahab's life would be forfeited because he had allowed Ben-hadad **king of Aram** to live was also fulfilled, ironically, by the army of Aram (22:31). God protected the king of Judah from Ahab's attempt to jeopardize Jehoshaphat's life, and He appointed a stray arrow to execute judgment on Ahab.

there a prophet of •Yahweh here anymore? Let's ask him."

8 The king of Israel said to Jehoshaphat, "There is still one man who can ask Yahweh, but I hate him because he never prophesies good about me, but only disaster. He is Micaiah son of Imlah."

"The king shouldn't say that!" Jehoshaphat replied.

9 So the king of Israel called an officer and said, "Hurry and get Micaiah son of Imlah!"

10 Now the king of Israel and Jehoshaphat king of Judah, clothed in royal attire, were each sitting on his own throne. They were on the threshing floor at the entrance to Samaria's •gate, and all the prophets were prophesying in front of them. 11 Then Zedekiah son of Chenaanah made iron horns and said, "This is what the LORD says: 'You will gore the Arameans with these until they are finished off.'" 12 And all the prophets were prophesying the same: "March up to Ramoth-gilead and succeed, for the LORD will hand it over to the king."

13 The messenger who went to call Micaiah instructed him, "Look, the words of the prophets are unanimously favorable for the king. So let your words be like theirs, and speak favorably."

14 But Micaiah said, "As the LORD lives, I will say whatever the LORD says to me."

15 So he went to the king, and the king asked him, "Micaiah, should we go to Ramoth-gilead for war, or should we refrain?"

Micaiah told him, "March up and succeed. Yahweh will hand it over to the king."

16 But the king said to him, "How many times must I make you swear not to tell me anything but the truth in the name of Yahweh?"

17 So Micaiah said:

I saw all Israel scattered
on the hills
like sheep without a shepherd.
And the LORD said,
"They have no master;
let everyone return home
in peace."

18 So the king of Israel said to Jehoshaphat, "Didn't I tell you he never prophesies good about me, but only disaster?"

19 Then Micaiah said, "Therefore, hear the word of the LORD: I saw the LORD sitting on His throne, and the whole heavenly •host was standing by Him at His right hand and at His left hand. 20 And the LORD said, 'Who will entice Ahab to march up and fall at Ramoth-gilead?' So one was saying this and another was saying that.

21 "Then a spirit came forward, stood before the LORD, and said, 'I will entice him.'

22 "The LORD asked him, 'How?'

"He said, 'I will go and become a lying spirit in the mouth of all his prophets.'

"Then He said, 'You will certainly entice him and prevail. Go and do that.'

23 "You see, the LORD has put a lying spirit into the mouth of all these prophets of yours, and the LORD has pronounced disaster against you."

24 Then Zedekiah son of Chenaanah came up, hit Micaiah in the face, and demanded, "Did[A] the Spirit of the LORD leave me to speak to you?"

25 Micaiah replied, "You will soon see when you go to hide yourself in an inner chamber on that day."

26 Then the king of Israel ordered, "Take Micaiah and return him to Amon, the governor of the city, and to Joash, the king's son, 27 and say, 'This is what the king says: Put this guy in prison and feed him only bread and water[B] until I come back safely.'"

28 But Micaiah said, "If you ever return safely, the LORD has not spoken through me." Then he said, "Listen, all you people!"[C]

29 Then the king of Israel and Judah's King Jehoshaphat went up to Ramoth-gilead. 30 But the king of Israel said to Jehoshaphat, "I will disguise myself and go into battle, but you wear your royal attire." So the king of Israel disguised himself and went into battle.

31 Now the king of Aram had ordered his 32 chariot commanders,

[A] **22:24** Lit *Which way did* [B] **22:27** Lit *him on bread of oppression and water of oppression*
[C] **22:28** LXX omits *Then he said, "Listen, all you people!"*

"Do not fight with anyone at all except the king of Israel."

32 When the chariot commanders saw Jehoshaphat, they shouted, "He must be the king of Israel!" So they turned to fight against him, but Jehoshaphat cried out. 33 When the chariot commanders saw that he was not the king of Israel, they turned back from pursuing him.

34 But a man drew his bow without taking special aim and struck the king of Israel through the joints of his armor. So he said to his charioteer, "Turn around and take me out of the battle,[A] for I am badly wounded!" 35 The battle raged throughout that day, and the king was propped up in his chariot facing the Arameans. He died that evening, and blood from his wound flowed into the bottom of the chariot. 36 Then the cry rang out in the army as the sun set, declaring:

> Each man to his own city,
> and each man to his own land!

37 So the king died and was brought to Samaria. They buried the king in Samaria. 38 Then someone washed the chariot at the pool of Samaria. The dogs licked up his blood, and the prostitutes bathed in it, according to the word of the LORD that He had spoken.

The End of Ahab's Reign in Israel (22:39-40)

39 The rest of the events of Ahab's reign, along with all his accomplishments, including the ivory palace he built, and all the cities he built, are written in the Historical Record of Israel's Kings. 40 Ahab rested with his fathers, and his son Ahaziah became king in his place.

The End of Jehoshaphat's Reign in Judah (22:41-50)

41 Jehoshaphat son of Asa became king over Judah in the fourth year of Israel's King Ahab. 42 Jehoshaphat was 35 years old when he became king; he reigned 25 years in Jerusalem. His mother's name was Azubah daughter of Shilhi. 43 He walked in all the ways of his father Asa; he did not turn away from them but did what was right in the LORD's sight. However, the •high places were not taken away;[B] the people still sacrificed and burned incense on the high places. 44 Jehoshaphat also made peace with the king of Israel.

45 The rest of the events of Jehoshaphat's reign, along with the might he exercised and how he waged war, are written in the Historical Record of Judah's Kings. 46 He removed from the land the rest of the male cult prostitutes who were left from the days of his father Asa. 47 There was no king in Edom; a deputy served as king. 48 Jehoshaphat made ships of Tarshish to go to Ophir for gold, but they did not go because the ships were wrecked at Ezion-geber. 49 At that time, Ahaziah son of Ahab said to Jehoshaphat, "Let my servants go with your servants in the ships," but Jehoshaphat was not willing. 50 Jehoshaphat rested with his fathers and was buried with them in the city of his ancestor David. His son Jehoram became king in his place.

The Beginning of Ahaziah's Reign in Israel (22:51-53)

51 Ahaziah son of Ahab became king over Israel in Samaria in the seventeenth year of Judah's King Jehoshaphat and reigned over Israel two years. 52 He did what was evil in the LORD's sight. He walked in the way of his father, in the way of his mother, and in the way of Jeroboam son of Nebat, who had caused Israel to sin. 53 He served •Baal and worshiped him. He provoked the LORD God of Israel just as his father had done.

22:41-42 Unlike most of Israel's kings, the mothers of Judah's kings are typically named, perhaps to emphasize God's faithfulness in maintaining David's descendants on the throne. Traditionally, having a Jewish mother has constituted proof of Jewish ethnicity. A pure lineage in any sense could not be claimed by those who ruled in the northern kingdom of Israel.

22:43-50 Despite following **ways of his father Asa** (cp. 15:11) and doing **what was right in the LORD's sight**, Jehoshaphat also failed to remove the high places. As long as these pagan altars were left standing, **the people** continued using them.

22:51-53 The error of Ahaziah's ways was threefold: **He walked in the way of his father** Ahab, he walked **in the way of his mother**, a unique phrase describing this son of an exceptionally wicked woman, and he walked **in the way of Jeroboam son of Nebat**, the notorious forefather of idolatry in the northern kingdom of **Israel.**

22:53 First Kings ends with this abysmal characterization of Ahaziah's reign. The account of judgment God had promised to bring on Ahab's house during this son's reign is told in 2Kg 8. Second Kings continues the history of the kings and prophets of both Israel and Judah.

[A]**22:34** LXX; MT reads *camp* [B]**22:43** LXX, Syr, Vg read *he did not remove the high places*

1 KINGS... WRITTEN ON MY *Heart*

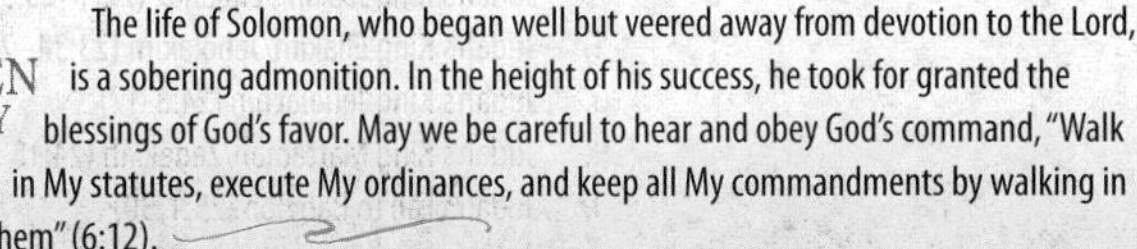

The life of Solomon, who began well but veered away from devotion to the Lord, is a sobering admonition. In the height of his success, he took for granted the blessings of God's favor. May we be careful to hear and obey God's command, "Walk in My statutes, execute My ordinances, and keep all My commandments by walking in them" (6:12).

2 Kings

Timeline	850–798 BC	812 BC	745–732 BC	742–700 BC
World Events / Biblical Events	Ministry of Elisha	Second temple reform under Joash	Tiglath-pileser's invasion of Israel	Ministry of Isaiah

"Because they have done what is evil in My sight and have provoked Me from the day their ancestors came out of Egypt until today" (21:15).

Who wrote 2 Kings?

The author is not identified in the text or elsewhere.

Who were the recipients?

The Jewish exiles dispersed throughout Assyria and Babylon

When was 2 Kings written?

Likely before the return of the Jews to Jerusalem from Babylonian exile around 536 B.C.

Where did it happen?

The divided kingdom—Israel in the north and Judah in the south—both of which were invaded and captured by the Assyrians and the Babylonians, respectively

What is 2 Kings about?

- The record of Israel's continued covenant failure, leading to their national demise
- The enduring faithfulness of God in contrast to the fleeting faithlessness of His people
- The ultimate kingship of Yahweh not only over His own people but also over all other nations

Why should women read 2 Kings?

As during the period of the Judges, when Israel is most spiritually unstable and politically volatile, God's care for and value of women is most evident. Many named and unnamed women, each of whom exercised both prominent and subtle influence in the lives of men—whether good or evil—played seemingly minor roles in the various stories selected by the writer. The women of 2 Kings demonstrate that God's sovereignty encompasses their needs and that His faithfulness to judge sin does not exclude them.

How do you read 2 Kings?

Second Kings is historical narrative—history written in story form. In the Hebrew Bible, the book is categorized as prophetic, indicating that Israel's spiritual history is given priority over her national or political history. Further, 2 Kings was originally written to the Jewish exiles dispersed throughout Assyria and Babylon, setting forth the legacies of their unfaithfulness to their faithful God. Thus, you must keep in mind the writer's spiritual purpose for these historical records when you read them today.

Outline

I. Elijah the Prophet (1:1–2:12)
- A. Ahaziah's Sickness and Death (1:1-18)
- B. A Chariot of Fire and the Whirlwind (2:1-12)

II. Elisha the Prophet (2:13–8:15)
- A. Elijah's Mantle (2:13-25)
- B. Israel's King Joram and Moab's Rebellion (3:1-27)
- C. The Widow's Oil (4:1-7)
- D. The Shunammite Woman (4:8-37)
- E. Food During Famine (4:38-44)
- F. Naaman's Healing and Gehazi's Leprosy (5:1-27)
- G. The Floating Ax Head (6:1-7)
- H. War with Aram (6:8–7:20)
- I. Restoration of the Shunammite's Land (8:1-6)
- J. Hazael, King of Aram (8:7-15)

III. The Kings of Judah and Israel (8:16–12:21)
- A. Kings of Judah (8:16-29)
- B. Jehu of Israel (9:1–10:36)
- C. Kings of Judah (11:1–12:21)
- D. Kings of Israel (13:1-25)
- E. Kings of Judah (14:1-22)
- F. King Jeroboam of Israel (14:23-29)
- G. King Azariah of Judah (15:1-7)
- H. Kings of Israel (15:8-31)
- I. Kings of Judah (15:32–16:20)
- J. King Hoshea of Israel (17:1-2)

IV. Israel's Fall to Assyria (17:3-41)
- A. Invasion and Deportation (17:3-6)
- B. Why Israel Fell (17:7-23)
- C. The Return of a Priest to Bethel (17:24-28)
- D. The Fear of the LORD Mixed with Idolatry (17:29-41)

V. Judah's Kings and the Fall to Babylon (18:1–25:30)
- A. Judah's King Hezekiah (18:1–19:37)
- B. Isaiah the prophet (20:1-21)
- C. Judah's King Manasseh (21:1-18)
- D. Judah's King Amon (21:19-26)
- E. Judah's King Josiah/Jehoahaz (22:1–23:33)
- F. Judah's King Eliakim/Jehoiakim (23:34–24:7)
- G. Judah's King Jehoiachin (24:8-17)
- H. Judah's King Mattaniah/Zedekiah (24:18-20)
- I. Judah's Fall to Babylon (25:1-30)

715 BC	*640–609 BC*	*622 BC*	*586 BC*
Third temple reform under Hezekiah	Life of Josiah	Fourth temple reform under Josiah	Destruction of the temple of Solomon

Ahaziah's Sickness and Death (1:1-18)

1 After the death of Ahab, Moab
rebelled against Israel. 2 Ahaziah
had fallen through the latticed window of his upper room in Samaria
and was injured. So he sent messengers instructing them: "Go inquire
of Baal-zebub,[A] the god of Ekron, if I
will recover from this injury."
3 But the angel of the LORD said to
Elijah the Tishbite, "Go and meet
the messengers of the king of Samaria and ask them, 'Is it because
there is no God in Israel that you
are going to inquire of Baal-zebub,
the god of Ekron?' 4 Therefore, this
is what the LORD says: 'You will not
get up from your sickbed—you will
certainly die.'" Then Elijah left.
5 The messengers returned to the
king, who asked them, "Why have
you come back?"
6 They replied, "A man came to
meet us and said, 'Go back to the
king who sent you and declare to
him: This is what the LORD says: Is
it because there is no God in Israel
that you're sending these men to
inquire of Baal-zebub, the god of
Ekron? Therefore, you will not get
up from your sickbed—you will certainly die.'"
7 The king asked them, "What sort
of man came up to meet you and
spoke those words to you?"
8 They replied, "A hairy man with a
leather belt around his waist."
He said, "It's Elijah the Tishbite."
9 So King Ahaziah sent a captain
of 50 with his 50 men to Elijah.
When the captain went up to him,
he was sitting on top of the hill. He
announced, "Man of God, the king
declares, 'Come down!'"
10 Elijah responded to the captain
of the 50, "If I am a man of God,
may fire come down from heaven
and consume you and your 50
men." Then fire came down from
heaven and consumed him and his
50 men.
11 So the king sent another captain of 50 with his 50 men to Elijah.
He took in the situation[B] and announced, "Man of God, this is what
the king says: 'Come down immediately!'"
12 Elijah responded, "If I am a man
of God, may fire come down from
heaven and consume you and your
50 men." So a divine fire[C] came
down from heaven and consumed
him and his 50 men.
13 Then the king sent a third captain of 50 with his 50 men. The third
captain of 50 went up and fell on his
knees in front of Elijah and begged
him, "Man of God, please let my life
and the lives of these 50 servants
of yours be precious in your sight.
14 Already fire has come down from
heaven and consumed the first two

[A] 1:2 = Lord of the Flies [B] 1:11 Lit *He answered* [C] 1:12 Lit *a fire of God*

Title: Second Kings is a continuation of 1 Kings, originally constituting one document. In the fourth-century Latin Vulgate translation, Jerome titled the combined work "The Book of the Kings."

1:1-4 When Israel's King **Ahab** died, his son **Ahaziah** became king and reigned only two years. The king's **upper room** was on the palace roof or on a balcony typical of Syrian *bit-hilani* architecture—featuring a long wooden-pillared porch or portico with an adjoining staircase to the upper level. **Ekron**, one of the five principal cities of the Philistines, located on Judah's southwestern border, had been conquered by Israel under David's rule.

1:5-15 As Ahab's son, Ahaziah was familiar with the Elijah's prophetic ministry. From the messengers' description of Elijah's distinct clothing, Ahaziah knew that he had delivered the bad news (cp. description of John the Baptist, Mt 3:1-4,8-15; Mt 17:11-13; Lk 1:17). The king responded not with repentance but with persistent attempts to assert his own royal authority. He dispatched **a captain** with **50 men to Elijah**, presumably to arrest or kill him.

1:13-15 God's merciful response to the humble and fearful approach of the last group, however, illustrates that the 102 men previously consumed by fire were responsible for their choice to obey the foolish king.

>WORD|*study*

1:3 Baal-zebub (Hb "Lord of the Flies," likely a parody of the princely name *Baal-zebul* [Aram, "Lord of the House"]), was a Philistine god of evil. "Beelzebul" appears in the New Testament as a name for Satan, "the ruler of the demons" (Mt 10:25; 12:24-27; Mk 3:22; Lk 11:15-19).

1:14 The third captain asked that his life and those of his men be regarded as precious (Hb *yaqar*, "be esteemed, prized, dear, valuable"). Saul used the same word to describe David's choice to spare his life (1 Sm 26:21), and the Lord declared a costly devotion to His people: "Because you are precious in My sight and honored, and I love you" (Is 43:4).

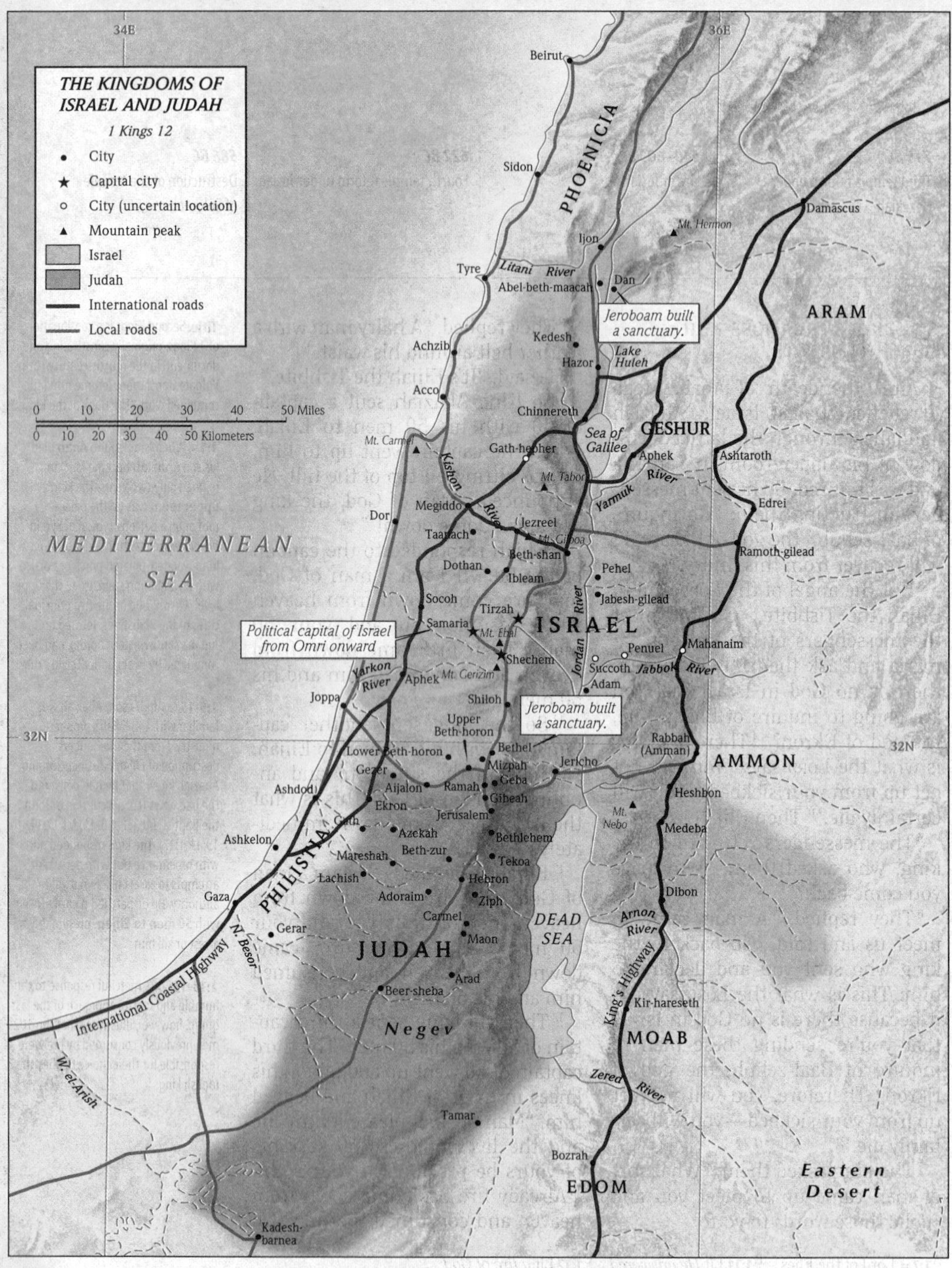

Upon the death of Saul and his son Jonathan, David moved to Hebron where the citizens crowned him king of Judah. Seven years later, the northern tribes acknowledged David as their king. He captured the city of Jerusalem and made it his capital. David gained control of the land God had promised to Israel's forefathers. The united kingdom continued and flourished under David's son, Solomon. At Solomon's death, this united kingdom became two political states—Israel, the northern kingdom, and Judah, the southern kingdom. The two states existed as separate countries from 924 B.C. until 722 B.C. when the northern kingdom fell to Assyria. Judah continued to exist until 586 B.C. when Babylon's King Nebuchadnezzar destroyed most of the city, including the temple, and took large numbers of Judah's citizens to Babylon.

captains of 50 with their fifties, but this time let my life be precious in your sight."

15 The angel of the LORD said to Elijah, "Go down with him. Don't be afraid of him." So he got up and went down with him to the king.

16 Then Elijah said to King Ahaziah, "This is what the LORD says: 'Because you have sent messengers to inquire of Baal-zebub, the god of Ekron—is it because there is no God in Israel for you to inquire of His will?—you will not get up from your sickbed; you will certainly die.'"

17 Ahaziah died according to the word of the LORD that Elijah had spoken. Since he had no son, Joram[A] became king in his place. This happened in the second year of Judah's King Jehoram son of Jehoshaphat.[B] 18 The rest of the events of Ahaziah's reign, along with his accomplishments, are written in the Historical Record of Israel's Kings.[C]

A Chariot of Fire and the Whirlwind (2:1-12)

2 The time had come for the LORD to take Elijah up to heaven in a whirlwind. Elijah and Elisha were traveling from Gilgal, 2 and Elijah said to Elisha, "Stay here; the LORD is sending me on to Bethel."

But Elisha replied, "As the LORD lives and as you yourself live, I will not leave you." So they went down to Bethel.

3 Then the sons of the prophets who were at Bethel came out to Elisha and said, "Do you know that the LORD will take your master away from you today?"

He said, "Yes, I know. Be quiet."

4 Elijah said to him, "Elisha, stay here; the LORD is sending me to Jericho."

But Elisha said, "As the LORD lives and as you yourself live, I will not leave you." So they went to Jericho.

5 Then the sons of the prophets who were in Jericho came up to Elisha and said, "Do you know that the LORD will take your master away from you today?"

He said, "Yes, I know. Be quiet."

6 Elijah said to him, "Stay here; the LORD is sending me to the Jordan."

But Elisha said, "As the LORD lives and as you yourself live, I will not leave you." So the two of them went on.

7 Fifty men from the sons of the prophets came and stood facing them from a distance while the two of them stood by the Jordan. 8 Elijah took his mantle, rolled it up, and struck the waters, which parted to the right and left. Then the two of them crossed over on dry ground. 9 After they had crossed over, Elijah said to Elisha, "Tell me what I can do for you before I am taken from you."

So Elisha answered, "Please, let me inherit two shares[D] of your spirit."

10 Elijah replied, "You have asked for something difficult. If you see me being taken from you, you will have it. If not, you won't."

11 As they continued walking and talking, a chariot of fire with horses of fire suddenly appeared and separated the two of them. Then Elijah went up into heaven in the whirlwind. 12 As Elisha watched, he kept crying out, "My father, my father, the chariots and horsemen of Israel!" Then he never saw Elijah again. He took hold of his own clothes and tore them into two pieces.

Elijah's Mantle (2:13-25)

13 Elisha picked up the mantle that had fallen off Elijah and went back and stood on the bank of the Jordan. 14 Then he took the mantle Elijah had dropped and struck the waters. "Where is the LORD God of Elijah?" he asked. He struck the waters himself, and they parted to the right and the left, and Elisha crossed over.

15 When the sons of the prophets from Jericho who were facing him saw him, they said, "The spirit of Elijah rests on Elisha." They came to meet him and bowed down to the ground in front of him.

16 Then the sons of the prophets

1:16-18 With **no son** to succeed Ahaziah, Joram, another "son of Ahab," **became king** of Israel (vv. 17-18; see 3:1). Joram's sister Athaliah became the wife of King Jehoram of Judah (8:25-26).

2:1-12 The text does not explain why the prophets were in Gilgal, and the only explanation Elijah gave for the trips to Bethel, Jericho, and the Jordan was: **The LORD is sending me.** Because all three cities were of great significance in Israel's history, journeying to each may have served to rehearse God's faithfulness to the covenant being broken by Israel and her kings. **Gilgal** was the place of Joshua's memorial after the people crossed the Jordan River (Jos 3:7–4:24) as well as the location where Israel's monarchy began with Saul (1Sm 11:15). **Bethel** was the place where Jacob built an altar as instructed by the Lord and set a stone marker where God had spoken to him (Gn 35:1-15). **Jericho** (2Kg 2:4-5) was the first city the Lord conquered for Israel (Jos 6). Finally, at **the Jordan** River Elijah's use of his mantle to part the waters demonstrated to him and the sons of the prophets the link between God's appointment to the prophetic office and His provision of spiritual power to fulfill it (2Kg 2:5-9).

When offered a parting gift, Elisha requested **two shares** of Elijah's spirit. Elisha was evoking the rights of the firstborn son to receive a double portion of his father's inheritance or of "everything that belongs to him" (Dt 21:17). He was asking to be recognized as the rightful heir to Elijah's special status among the prophets.

2:12 Elijah, like Enoch (Gn 5:24), did not experience death.

2:13-22 Elisha's public ministry as Israel's prophet—which lasted 50 years covering the reigns of Joram, Jehu, and Jehoahaz—was signaled by two incidents illustrating God's miraculous power: parting the Jordan River and restoring Jericho's water supply. Because the **water** of **the city** was **bad,** their **land was unfruitful** (Hb *shakol*, "causing or showing barrenness or bereavement, making childless, causing miscarriage or abortion," v. 19; cp. Ex 23:26). Although Jericho had been rebuilt during the reign of Ahab (1Kg 16:34), the city remained without productivity and with its waters evidently still affected by the curse of Joshua (Jos 6:26). However, Elisha used the people of Jericho to bring healing and restoration (2Kg 2:20-22). The contrast between the spiritual pollution of Baal worship and the physical health of the cleansed water is obvious.

[A]**1:17** Lit *Jehoram*; 2Kg 8:16 [B]**1:17** LXX omits *in the second year . . . Jehoshaphat* [C]**1:18** LXX adds 4 more vv. here similar to 2Kg 3:1-3. [D]**2:9** Two shares is the inheritance of blessing for the firstborn son; Dt 21:17. Here Elisha is asking for the leadership role among the prophets.

2:15-18 When the **50 strong men** reported that Elijah was nowhere to be found, Elisha's credibility among **the sons of the prophets** was confirmed.

2:20 Salt was a symbol of purity also associated with covenant (cp. Lv 2:13; Nm 18:19; 2Ch 13:5; Ezk 43:24).

2:23 Bethel was where one of the two golden calves in Israel was worshiped in place of Yahweh, whose temple was in Jerusalem in the southern kingdom of Judah (1Kg 12:25-30).

2:23-25 The serious nature of what took place implies that the boys were old enough to be held responsible for their behavior and that their aggressive disrespect was more than child's play. Elisha was not expressing his own ill temper or revenge; rather, God issued judgment (1Kg 20:36). If God so punished those who merely derided His servant, what would He do to those who derided God Himself? A scoffing attitude toward "God's messengers" incited His wrath against Israel and contributed to the nation's downfall (see 2Ch 36:15-16).

3:1-3 Joram (Hb *Yehoram*, "Yahweh is exalted") reigned in Israel until Jehu carried out Elijah's prophecy (2Kg 9).

3:8-19 In the middle of the water crisis, the two kings responded quite differently: Joram blamed **the Lord** (v. 10), while **Jehoshaphat** wanted to seek direction from **a prophet of the Lord** and expressed confidence in Elisha (vv. 11-12; cp. 1Kg 22:5,7-8). Elisha the prophet also responded differently to each of them: He addressed Joram with, **We have nothing in common** (Hb *halak*, "go, walk, depart, go away," an imperative verb having the sense here of "Take a hike!" or "Get out of here!"). Elisha was emphatic about his allegiance to **the Lord of hosts** and told Joram that he would cooperate only because he respected **Jehoshaphat** (2Kg 3:14).

>WORD|*study*

2:23-24 The words translated small boys (Hb *na'ar*, "boy, lad,") and "youths" (Hb *yeled*, "child, boy,") can refer to young men ages 12 to 30 or to younger children.

2:23 Harassed (Hb *qalas*, "mock, deride, make fun of,") suggests that Elisha, though clearly identified at least by his "mantle" as a prophet of God, was treated with contempt, which may have reflected the youths' disdain for authority in general (cp. Hab 1:10).

said to Elisha, "Since there are 50
strong men here with your servants,
please let them go and search for
your master. Maybe the Spirit of the
Lord has carried him away and put
him on one of the mountains or into
one of the valleys."

He answered, "Don't send them."
17 However, they urged him to the
point of embarrassment, so he said,
"Send them." They sent 50 men,
who looked for three days but did
not find him. 18 When they returned
to him in Jericho where he was staying, he said to them, "Didn't I tell
you not to go?"

19 Then the men of the city said to
Elisha, "Even though our lord can
see that the city's location is good,
the water is bad and the land unfruitful."

20 He replied, "Bring me a new
bowl and put salt in it."

After they had brought him one,
21 Elisha went out to the spring
of water, threw salt in it, and said,
"This is what the Lord says: 'I have
healed this water. No longer will
death or unfruitfulness result from
it.'" 22 Therefore, the water remains
healthy to this very day according to
the word that Elisha spoke.

23 From there Elisha went up to
Bethel. As he was walking up the
path, some small boys came out of
the city and harassed him, chanting, "Go up, baldy! Go up, baldy!"
24 He turned around, looked at them,
and cursed them in the name of the
Lord. Then two female bears came
out of the woods and mauled 42 of
the children. 25 From there Elisha
went to Mount Carmel, and then he
returned to Samaria.

Israel's King Joram and Moab's Rebellion (3:1-27)

3 Joram son of Ahab became king
over Israel in Samaria during
the eighteenth year of Judah's King
Jehoshaphat and reigned 12 years.
2 He did what was evil in the Lord's
sight, but not like his father and
mother, for he removed the sacred
pillar of •Baal his father had made.
3 Nevertheless, Joram clung to the
sins that Jeroboam son of Nebat had
caused Israel to commit. He did not
turn away from them.

4 King Mesha of Moab was a sheep
breeder. He used to pay the king of
Israel 100,000 lambs and the wool
of 100,000 rams, 5 but when Ahab
died, the king of Moab rebelled
against the king of Israel. 6 So King
Joram marched out from Samaria
at that time and mobilized all Israel.
7 Then he sent a message to King
Jehoshaphat of Judah: "The king
of Moab has rebelled against me.
Will you go with me to fight against
Moab?"

Jehoshaphat said, "I will go. I am
as you are, my people as your people,
my horses as your horses." 8 Then he
asked, "Which route should we take?"

Joram replied, "The route of the
Wilderness of Edom."

9 So the king of Israel, the king of
Judah, and the king of Edom set out.
After they had traveled their indirect
route for seven days, they had no water for the army or their animals.

10 Then the king of Israel said, "Oh
no, the Lord has summoned three
kings, only to hand them over to
Moab."

11 But Jehoshaphat said, "Isn't there
a prophet of the Lord here? Let's inquire of •Yahweh through him."

One of the servants of the king
of Israel answered, "Elisha son of
Shaphat, who used to pour water on
Elijah's hands, is here."

12 Jehoshaphat affirmed, "The Lord's
words are with him." So the king of
Israel and Jehoshaphat and the king
of Edom went to him.

13 However, Elisha said to King Joram of Israel, "We have nothing in
common. Go to the prophets of your
father and your mother!"
But the king of Israel replied, "No,
because it is the LORD who has summoned these three kings to hand
them over to Moab."
14 Elisha responded, "As the LORD
of •Hosts lives, I stand before Him.
If I did not have respect for King Jehoshaphat of Judah, I would not look
at you; I wouldn't take notice of you.
15 Now, bring me a musician."
While the musician played, the
LORD's hand came on Elisha. 16 Then
he said, "This is what the LORD says:
'Dig ditch after ditch in this •wadi.'
17 For the LORD says, 'You will not
see wind or rain, but the wadi will
be filled with water, and you will
drink—you and your cattle and your
animals.' 18 This is easy in the LORD's
sight. He will also hand Moab over
to you. 19 Then you must attack every
fortified city and every choice city.
You must cut down every good tree
and stop up every spring of water. You
must ruin every good piece of land
with stones."
20 About the time for the •grain offering the next morning, water suddenly came from the direction of
Edom and filled the land.
21 All Moab had heard that the kings
had come up to fight against them.
So all who could bear arms, from the
youngest to the oldest, were summoned and took their stand at the
border. 22 When they got up early in
the morning, the sun was shining
on the water, and the Moabites saw
that the water across from them was
red like blood. 23 "This is blood!" they
exclaimed. "The kings have clashed
swords and killed each other. So, to
the spoil, Moab!"
24 However, when the Moabites came
to Israel's camp, the Israelites attacked them, and they fled from
them. So Israel went into the land
and struck down the Moabites. 25 They
destroyed the cities, and each of them
threw stones to cover every good
piece of land. They stopped up every
spring of water and cut down every
good tree. In the end, only the buildings of Kir-hareseth were left. Then
men with slings surrounded the city
and attacked it.
26 When the king of Moab saw that
the battle was too fierce for him, he
took 700 swordsmen with him to try
to break through to the king of Edom,
but they could not do it. 27 So he took
his firstborn son, who was to become
king in his place, and offered him as a
•burnt offering on the city wall. Great
wrath was on the Israelites, and they
withdrew from him and returned to
their land.

The Widow's Oil (4:1-7)

4 One of the wives of the sons of
the prophets cried out to Elisha,
"Your servant, my husband, has

3:15 The request for **a musician** required obedience and the demonstration of a willingness to wait for and rely on the Lord's answer to their dilemma (cp. 1Sm 10:5; 1Ch 25:1-3).

3:19-27 The text does not make clear whether God or the Israelites exhibited **great wrath** as an apparent reaction to Mesha's offering, which would have been made to the Moabite god Chemosh; but the Israelites, whether repulsed by Mesha's action or afraid of his god, withdrew without fully carrying out the Lord's command through Elisha.

4:1-7 If the widow's sons were taken away, she would soon have been without provision and destitute. No explanation was given for the debt, but many Israelites suffered poverty and, consequently, slavery. The Mosaic law allowed an Israelite who was "destitute" to sell himself as "a hired hand," but he and his children must be fully released from this obligation in the Year of Jubilee (Lv 25:39-41), an unenforced restriction. The Lord began with the little she had and demonstrated His concern for her plight and His readiness to meet the needs of those who cry out to Him.

CHARACTER PROFILE

The Prophet's Widow A Desperate Woman

Her Background	A poor widow of one of Elisha's prophets (4:1-7)
Her Story	• She was in great danger of losing her sons to be sold as slaves to repay her debts (4:1). • Her only possession was a jar of oil (4:2). • She desperately approached Elisha for help (4:1). • He instructed her to borrow containers from neighbors and pour the oil into them (4:3-4). • The oil miraculously filled every container she had (4:5-6). • Elisha instructed her to sell the oil and thus pay her debt (4:7).
Life Lessons	• Faith in the promises of God does bear fruit. • The widow's faith in God's prophet brought her the means to meet the needs of her household.

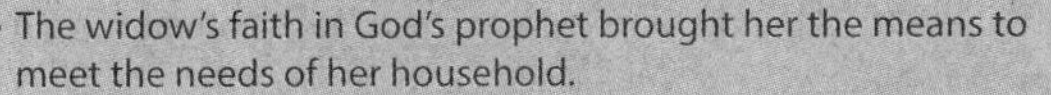

4:8-10 The text does not describe what made the **woman** in **Shunem prominent** (Hb *gadol*, "great, important, distinguished"), but she demonstrated faith in and reverence for the **God** of Israel by extending her hospitality and home to His prophet. In a nation led by pagan kings, those who remained faithful to Yahweh probably regarded Elisha's presence as a blessing.

4:11-17 Because the woman's **husband** was **old** and she had **no son**, hardship would likely befall her upon her husband's death. By God's word spoken through Elisha, the woman was blessed with the unsolicited promise of a son, a prophetic and gracious word that was fulfilled as predicted.

died. You know that your servant
•feared the LORD. Now the creditor is
coming to take my two children as
his slaves."
[2] Elisha asked her, "What can I do
for you? Tell me, what do you have
in the house?"
She said, "Your servant has nothing in the house except a jar of oil."
[3] Then he said, "Go and borrow empty containers from everyone—from all your neighbors. Do
not get just a few. [4] Then go in and
shut the door behind you and your
sons, and pour oil into all these
containers. Set the full ones to one
side." [5] So she left.
After she had shut the door behind her and her sons, they kept bringing her containers, and she kept pouring. [6] When they were full, she said
to her son, "Bring me another container."
But he replied, "There aren't any more." Then the oil stopped.
[7] She went and told the man of God, and he said, "Go sell the oil and pay your debt; you and your sons can live on the rest."

The Shunammite Woman (4:8-37)

Her Hospitality (4:8-10)

[8] One day Elisha went to Shunem.
A prominent woman who lived there persuaded him to eat some food. So whenever he passed by, he stopped
there to eat. [9] Then she said to her
husband, "I know that the one who often passes by here is a holy man
of God, [10] so let's make a small room upstairs and put a bed, a table, a chair, and a lamp there for him. Whenever he comes, he can stay there."

The Gift of a Son (4:11-17)

[11] One day he came there and stopped and went to the room upstairs to lie down. [12] He ordered his
attendant Gehazi, "Call this Shunammite woman." So he called her and she stood before him.
[13] Then he said to Gehazi, "Say to her, 'Look, you've gone to all this trouble for us. What can we do for you? Can we speak on your behalf to the king or to the commander of the army?'"
She answered, "I am living among my own people."
[14] So he asked, "Then what should be done for her?"
Gehazi answered, "Well, she has no son, and her husband is old."
[15] "Call her," Elisha said. So Gehazi called her, and she stood in the
doorway. [16] Elisha said, "At this time
next year you will have a son in your arms."

CHARACTER PROFILE

The Shunammite Woman A Generous Hostess

Her Background	• A prominent woman in Shunem (4:8) • The wife of an elderly man (4:14)
Her Story	• She built a guest room for Elisha's use (4:9-10). • Elisha prophesied that she would have a son (4:11-17). • Her son became ill and died (4:18-21). • Elisha raised him from the dead (4:22-37). • Elisha urged her family to leave the land because famine was approaching (8:1). • She returned home after seven years (8:2-3). • The king restored her ownership of her land and her income (8:3-6).
Life Lessons	• The Shunammite's hospitality to Elisha brought her great blessings. • Sensitivity to the needs of others is a gift as unto the Lord (Mt 25:40).

Then she said, "No, my lord. Man of God, do not deceive your servant."
[17] The woman conceived and gave birth to a son at the same time the following year, as Elisha had promised her.

The Raising of Her Son to Life (4:18-37)

[18] The child grew and one day went out to his father and the harvesters.
[19] Suddenly he complained to his father, "My head! My head!"

His father told his servant, "Carry him to his mother."
[20] So he picked him up and took him to his mother. The child sat on her lap until noon and then died.
[21] Then she went up and laid him on the bed of the man of God, shut him in, and left.
[22] She summoned her husband and said, "Please send me one of the servants and one of the donkeys, so I can hurry to the man of God and then come back."
[23] But he said, "Why go to him today? It's not a New Moon or a Sabbath."

She replied, "Everything is all right."
[24] Then she saddled the donkey and said to her servant, "Hurry, don't slow the pace for me unless I tell you."
[25] So she set out and went to the man of God at Mount Carmel.

When the man of God saw her at a distance, he said to his attendant Gehazi, "Look, there's the Shunammite woman.
[26] Run out to meet her and ask, 'Are you all right? Is your husband all right? Is your son all right?'"

And she answered, "Everything's all right."
[27] When she came up to the man of God at the mountain, she clung to his feet. Gehazi came to push her away, but the man of God said, "Leave her alone—she is in severe anguish, and the LORD has hidden it from me. He hasn't told me."
[28] Then she said, "Did I ask my lord for a son? Didn't I say, 'Do not deceive me?'"
[29] So Elisha said to Gehazi, "Tuck your mantle under your belt, take my staff with you, and go. If you meet anyone, don't stop to greet him, and if a man greets you, don't answer him. Then place my staff on the boy's face."
[30] The boy's mother said to Elisha, "As the LORD lives and as you yourself live, I will not leave you." So he got up and followed her.
[31] Gehazi went ahead of them and placed the staff on the boy's face, but there was no sound or sign of life, so he went back to meet Elisha and told him, "The boy didn't wake up."
[32] When Elisha got to the house, he discovered the boy lying dead on his bed.
[33] So he went in, closed the door behind the two of them, and prayed to the LORD.
[34] Then he went up and lay on the boy: he put mouth to mouth, eye to eye, hand to hand. While he bent down over him, the boy's flesh became warm.
[35] Elisha got up, went into the house, and paced back and forth. Then he went up and bent down over him again. The boy sneezed seven times and opened his eyes.
[36] Elisha called Gehazi and said, "Call the Shunammite woman." He called her and she came. Then Elisha said, "Pick up your son."
[37] She came, fell at his feet, and bowed to the ground; she picked up her son and left.

Food During Famine (4:38-44)

[38] When Elisha returned to Gilgal, there was a famine in the land. The sons of the prophets were sitting at his feet.[A] He said to his attendant, "Put on the large pot and make stew for the sons of the prophets."
[39] One went out to the field to gather herbs and found a wild vine from which he gathered as many wild gourds as his garment would hold. Then he came back and cut them up into the pot of stew, but they were unaware of what they were.
[40] They served some for the men to eat, but when they ate the stew they cried out, "There's death in the pot, man of God!" And they were unable to eat it.
[41] Then Elisha said, "Get some meal." He threw it into the pot and said, "Serve it for the people to eat." And there was nothing bad in the pot.
[42] A man from Baal-shalishah came

4:18-31 The Shunammite woman demonstrated exemplary faith while **in severe anguish** (Hb *nephesh marar*, lit, "[her] soul is bitter," v. 27). She **laid him on** Elisha's **bed**, an act of hope that the prophet would be able to restore the boy's life (vv. 18-21). Elijah had done so for the widow at Zarephath during Ahab's reign (1Kg 17:17-24). Without threatening her husband's health with the news of the boy's death, she requested a servant and a donkey in order to **hurry** [Hb *ruts*, "run"] **to the man of God** (2Kg 4:22-24). By insisting on staying with Elisha, perhaps she sensed what Elisha did not—Gehazi's lack of faith and spiritual power, evident in his lack of effectiveness in placing Elisha's **staff on the boy's face**, though at the prophet's command (vv. 29-31).

4:32-37 Elisha **prayed** [Hb *palal*, "intercede"] **to the LORD** and **lay** parallel to **the boy** in the same fashion that Elijah is described (1Kg 17:21). God's care for the two women in chapter 4 emphasized His commitment to the needy through Elisha as He had expressed through Elijah.

4:38-44 The next two miracles in this series of Elisha's prophetic deeds have to do with food. In the first event described, deadly food was made edible; in the second, bread was multiplied to feed **100 men**. They served to validate the prophet's ministry and to certify that God spoke through him (2:14,20,24; 3:16; 4:3,13,32,41,43; cp. Jesus' miracles, Mt 14:13-21; 15:32-39). The man who brought loaves **from the first bread of the harvest** to the prophets was delivering an offering properly belonging to the priests and Levites (Lv 23:10-14; Dt 18:1-6). But His gift indicates that God-fearing people remained in Israel and that they esteemed **the sons of the prophets** as religious leaders.

[A]4:38 Lit *sitting before him*

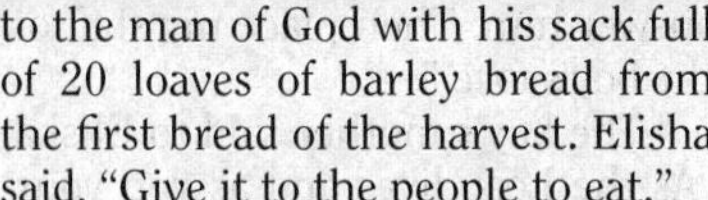

5:1-5 The account of Naaman's healing emphasized the Lord's sovereignty over *all* nations and exemplified His missionary purpose for Israel. The **young** [Hb *qatan*, "small, insignificant, unimportant"] **girl** serving **Naaman's wife** expressed uncommon faith in her God, for she had no doubt that God would extend healing even to a pagan Gentile (cp. Mt 5:44).

5:6-8 Instead of sending for Elisha, Joram misinterpreted his enemy's concern for Naaman as a ploy for inciting war between the nations of Israel and Aram. After hearing of King Joram's public outrage, Elisha boldly rebuked the king and intervened so that Naaman, and Joram as well, would have convincing proof that God was actively speaking and working through **Israel**.

5:9-14 God was interested in testing the condition of Naaman's heart. Having to **wash seven times** prevented anyone from crediting the river with magic powers and thoroughly tested Naaman's faith. To wash *seven* times signified doing so completely, seeing the assigned task through to the end.

5:15-19 Naaman received both physical and spiritual healing that day. His confession that there is **no God** other than **Israel**'s sharply contrasted with the spiritual state of Israel and her kings. According to the New Testament, of all the lepers of Naaman's day, only he received God's healing (Lk 4:27).

5:17-19 The mule-loads of dirt would represent for Naaman not only the place where God had wrought the miracle but also the place where ceremonial worship of the true God was conducted.

to the man of God with his sack full of 20 loaves of barley bread from the first bread of the harvest. Elisha said, "Give it to the people to eat."

43 But Elisha's attendant asked, "What? Am I to set 20 loaves before 100 men?"

"Give it to the people to eat," Elisha said, "for this is what the LORD says: 'They will eat, and they will have some left over.'" 44 So he gave it to them, and as the LORD had promised, they ate and had some left over.

Naaman's Healing and Gehazi's Leprosy (5:1-27)

5 Naaman, commander of the army for the king of Aram, was a great man in his master's sight[A] and highly regarded because through him, the LORD had given victory to Aram. The man was a brave warrior, but he had a skin disease.

2 Aram had gone on raids and brought back from the land of Israel a young girl who served Naaman's wife. 3 She said to her mistress, "If only my master would go to[B] the prophet who is in Samaria, he would cure him of his skin disease."

4 So Naaman went and told his master what the girl from the land of Israel had said. 5 Therefore, the king of Aram said, "Go and I will send a letter with you to the king of Israel."

So he went and took with him 750 pounds[C] of silver, 150 pounds[D] of gold, and 10 changes of clothes. 6 He brought the letter to the king of Israel, and it read:

> When this letter comes to you, note that I have sent you my servant Naaman for you to cure him of his skin disease.

7 When the king of Israel read the letter, he tore his clothes and asked, "Am I God, killing and giving life that this man expects me to cure a man of his skin disease? Think it over and you will see that he is only picking a fight with[E] me."

8 When Elisha the man of God heard that the king of Israel tore his clothes, he sent a message to the king, "Why have you torn your clothes? Have him come to me, and he will know there is a prophet in Israel." 9 So Naaman came with his horses and chariots and stood at the door of Elisha's house.

10 Then Elisha sent him a messenger, who said, "Go wash seven times in the Jordan and your flesh will be restored and you will be •clean."

11 But Naaman got angry and left, saying, "I was telling myself: He will surely come out, stand and call on the name of •Yahweh his God, and will wave his hand over the spot and cure the skin disease. 12 Aren't Abana and Pharpar, the rivers of Damascus, better than all the waters of Israel? Could I not wash in them and be clean?" So he turned and left in a rage.

13 But his servants approached and said to him, "My father, if the prophet had told you to do some great thing, would you not have done it? How much more should you do it when he tells you, 'Wash and be clean'?" 14 So Naaman went down and dipped himself in the Jordan seven times, according to the command of the man of God. Then his skin was restored and became like the skin of a small boy, and he was clean.

15 Then Naaman and his whole company went back to the man of God, stood before him, and declared, "I know there's no God in the whole world except in Israel. Therefore, please accept a gift from your servant."

16 But Elisha said, "As the LORD lives, I stand before Him. I will not accept it." Naaman urged him to accept it, but he refused.

17 Naaman responded, "If not, please let your servant be given as much soil as a pair of mules can carry, for your servant will no longer offer a •burnt offering or a sacrifice to any other god but Yahweh. 18 However, in a particular matter may the LORD pardon your servant: When my master, the king of Aram, goes into the temple of Rimmon to worship and I, as his right-hand man,[F] bow in the temple of Rimmon—when I

[A] **5:1** Lit *man before his master* [B] **5:3** Lit *master was before* [C] **5:5** Lit *10 talents* [D] **5:5** Lit *6,000 shekels* [E] **5:7** Lit *only seeking an occasion against* [F] **5:18** Lit *worship, and he leans on my hand, and I*

CHARACTER PROFILE

Naaman's Maidservant **A Faithful Witness**

Her Background	• A young Hebrew girl who had been captured and brought to Syria (5:1-2) • Servant to the wife of Naaman, commander of Syrian army (5:1-2)
Her Story	• She urged her mistress to persuade her husband to go see Elisha, who could heal him from his skin disease (5:3). • She testified to the power of Yahweh to heal through His prophet (5:3). • Her bold proposal resulted in Naaman's healing and in his declaration of Yahweh's supremacy (5:11-15).
Life Lessons	• This child's simple faith, her confidence in God's prophet, and her desire for her master's welfare led to Naaman's miraculous healing. • Being an instrument of God even in difficult circumstances brings satisfaction.

bow[A] in the temple of Rimmon, may the LORD pardon your servant in this matter."
19 So he said to him, "Go in peace."
After Naaman had traveled a short distance from Elisha, 20 Gehazi, the attendant of Elisha the man of God, thought: My master has let this Aramean Naaman off lightly by not accepting from him what he brought. As the LORD lives, I will run after him and get something from him.
21 So Gehazi pursued Naaman. When Naaman saw someone running after him, he got down from the chariot to meet him and asked, "Is everything all right?"
22 Gehazi said, "It's all right. My master has sent me to say, 'I have just now discovered that two young men from the sons of the prophets have come to me from the hill country of Ephraim. Please give them 75 pounds[B] of silver and two changes of clothes.'"
23 But Naaman insisted, "Please, accept 150 pounds."[C] He urged Gehazi and then packed 150 pounds[C] of silver in two bags with two changes of clothes. Naaman gave them to two of his young men who carried them ahead of Gehazi. 24 When Gehazi came to the hill,[D] he took the gifts from them and stored them in the house. Then he dismissed the men, and they left.
25 Gehazi came and stood by his master. "Where did you go, Gehazi?" Elisha asked him.
"Your servant didn't go anywhere," he replied.
26 But Elisha questioned him, "Wasn't my spirit there[E] when the man got down from his chariot to meet you? Is it a time to accept money and clothes, olive orchards and vineyards, sheep and oxen, and male and female slaves? 27 Therefore, Naaman's skin disease will cling to you and your descendants forever." So Gehazi went out from his presence diseased—white as snow.

The Floating Ax Head (6:1-7)

6 The sons of the prophets said to Elisha, "Please notice that the place where we live under your supervision[F] is too small for us.
2 Please let us go to the Jordan where we can each get a log and can build ourselves a place to live there."
"Go," he said.
3 Then one said, "Please come with your servants."
"I'll come," he answered.
4 So he went with them, and when they came to the Jordan, they cut down trees. 5 As one of them was

5:20-27 Elisha's **attendant** became a tragic example of how susceptible human nature is to "the lust of the eyes" (1Jn 2:16). **Gehazi**, because of his greed, missed the whole point of the miracle—bringing Naaman and other observers to believe in Israel's God. Notice the rapid progression of sin involved in Gehazi's illicit pursuit: He tried to justify himself in his own mind and misused God's name in doing so (cp. Dt 5:11), acted on the wrong thoughts, lied to and deceived Naaman by pretending to speak for Elisha, **took the gifts** and hid **them,** then tried to fool **his master** and lied when asked **where** he had gone. Elisha's question reflected his role of being God's spokesman—no sin escapes God's notice (cp. Pr 5:21-22; 15:3; Jr 16:17). The nature of Gehazi's punishment reinforces the implicit contrast between him and Naaman. In their respective countries, each served the man who exercised the most power—Naaman served the king of Aram, and Gehazi served Elisha. However, Naaman laid down his pride, received healing, and left "in peace" (2Kg 5:19). Gehazi, on the other hand, attempted to bolster his pride, received punishment, and **went out from** Elisha's **presence diseased** (vv. 14,19,26-27).

6:1-7 Restoring the tool to its owner was probably critical for maintaining the prophet's reputation and possibly his resources. Elisha's actions drew attention to God's power in action on behalf of His prophets. For the Jews in exile, this account may have been a source of hope. God's doing what was humanly impossible demonstrated His power to restore the nation both physically and spiritually and to meet the needs of its people.

[A]5:18 LXX, Vg read *when he bows himself* [B]5:22 Lit *a talent* [C]5:23 Lit *two talents* [D]5:24 Or *citadel* [E]5:26 Lit *"Did not my heart go* [F]6:1 Lit *we are living before you*

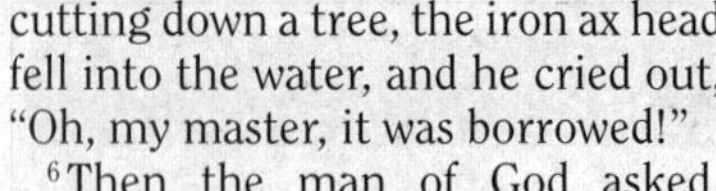

6:8-23 This conflict between **Aram** and **Israel** is not dated, nor are the kings identified. The writer was more concerned about emphasizing the absolute sovereignty of God as He worked through His prophet Elisha (6:12,17; 7:1). Even though the location of **the man of God** apparently was common knowledge (6:13; cp. 3:11-13; 4:25; 5:3), the king of Aram overlooked the folly of trying to interfere with God's obvious intent to protect Israel at that time.

6:24-33 The siege at **Samaria** caused such a scarcity of food that exorbitant prices were being paid for **a donkey's head,** the worst part of an unclean animal (v. 25). King Joram's wearing **sackcloth under his clothes** indicated that he was already mourning the results of the famine when confronted with the utter degradation of the people exemplified in the women's cannibalism (vv. 26-30). For the writer of Kings and for any readers who knew God's law, this dire situation in Israel would be understood as clear evidence that the judgment God had promised would result from the nation's disobedience (cp. Lv 26:27-29; Dt 28:15,52-53).

cutting down a tree, the iron ax head
fell into the water, and he cried out,
"Oh, my master, it was borrowed!"
6 Then the man of God asked,
"Where did it fall?"

When he showed him the place,
the man of God cut a stick, threw
it there, and made the iron float.
7 Then he said, "Pick it up." So he
reached out and took it.

War with Aram (6:8–7:20)

Prayers for Open Eyes and Blindness (6:8-23)

8 When the king of Aram was waging war against Israel, he conferred
with his servants, "My camp will be
at such and such a place."
9 But the man of God sent word to
the king of Israel: "Be careful passing by this place, for the Arameans
are going down there." 10 Consequently, the king of Israel sent word
to the place the man of God had told
him about. The man of God repeatedly[A] warned the king, so the king
would be on his guard.
11 The king of Aram was enraged
because of this matter, and he called
his servants and demanded of them,
"Tell me, which one of us is for the
king of Israel?"
12 One of his servants said, "No
one, my lord the king. Elisha, the
prophet in Israel, tells the king of
Israel even the words you speak in
your bedroom."
13 So the king said, "Go and see
where he is, so I can send men to
capture him."

When he was told, "Elisha is in
Dothan," 14 he sent horses, chariots, and a massive army there. They
went by night and surrounded the
city.
15 When the servant of the man of
God got up early and went out, he
discovered an army with horses and
chariots surrounding the city. So he
asked Elisha, "Oh, my master, what
are we to do?"
16 Elisha said, "Don't be afraid, for
those who are with us outnumber
those who are with them."
17 Then Elisha prayed, "LORD,
please open his eyes and let him
see." So the LORD opened the servant's eyes. He looked and saw that
the mountain was covered with
horses and chariots of fire all around
Elisha.
18 When the Arameans came
against him, Elisha prayed to the
LORD, "Please strike this nation with
blindness." So He struck them with
blindness, according to Elisha's
word. 19 Then Elisha said to them,
"This is not the way, and this is not
the city. Follow me, and I will take
you to the man you're looking for."
And he led them to Samaria. 20 When
they entered Samaria, Elisha said,
"LORD, open these men's eyes and let
them see." So the LORD opened their
eyes. They looked and discovered
they were in Samaria.
21 When the king of Israel saw
them, he said to Elisha, "My father,
should I kill them? I will kill them."
22 Elisha replied, "Don't kill them.
Do you kill those you have captured
with your sword or your bow? Set
food and water in front of them so
they can eat and drink and go to
their master."
23 So he prepared a great feast for
them. When they had eaten and
drunk, he sent them away, and they
went to their master. The Aramean
raiders did not come into Israel's
land again.

Siege of Samaria (6:24–7:2)

24 Some time later, King Ben-hadad of Aram brought all his military
units together and marched up to
besiege Samaria. 25 So there was a
great famine in Samaria, and they
continued the siege against it until
a donkey's head sold for 80 silver
•shekels,[B] and a cup[C] of dove's dung[D]
sold for five silver shekels.[E]
26 As the king of Israel was passing
by on the wall, a woman cried out to
him, "My lord the king, help!"
27 He answered, "If the LORD
doesn't help you, where can I get
help for you? From the threshing
floor or the winepress?" 28 Then the
king asked her, "What's the matter?"

She said, "This woman said to me,
'Give up your son, and we will eat
him today. Then we will eat my son
tomorrow.' 29 So we boiled my son

[A]**6:10** Lit *not once and not twice* [B]**6:25** About 2 pounds of silver [C]**6:25** Lit *a fourth of a kab* [D]**6:25** Or *seedpods*, or *wild onions* [E]**6:25** About 2 ounces of silver

and ate him, and I said to her the
next day, 'Give up your son, and we
will eat him,' but she has hidden her
son."
30 When the king heard the woman's words, he tore his clothes.
Then, as he was passing by on the
wall, the people saw that there was
•sackcloth under his clothes next
to his skin. 31 He announced, "May
God punish me and do so severely
if the head of Elisha son of Shaphat
remains on his shoulders today."
32 Elisha was sitting in his house,
and the elders were sitting with
him. The king sent a man ahead of
him, but before the messenger got
to him, Elisha said to the elders, "Do
you see how this murderer has sent
someone to cut off my head? Look,
when the messenger comes, shut
the door to keep him out. Isn't the
sound of his master's feet behind
him?"
33 While Elisha was still speaking
with them, the messenger[A] came
down to him. Then he said, "This disaster is from the LORD. Why should
I wait for the LORD any longer?"

7 Elisha replied, "Hear the word of
the LORD! This is what the LORD
says: 'About this time tomorrow at
the gate of Samaria, six quarts[B] of
fine meal will sell for a •shekel[C] and
12 quarts[D] of barley will sell for a
shekel.'"[c]
2 Then the captain, the king's
right-hand man, responded to the
man of God, "Look, even if the LORD
were to make windows in heaven,
could this really happen?"
Elisha announced, "You will in
fact see it with your own eyes, but
you won't eat any of it."

Plunder of the Aramean Camp (7:3-20)

3 Four men with a skin disease
were at the entrance to the gate.
They said to each other, "Why just
sit here until we die? 4 If we say, 'Let's
go into the city,' we will die there because the famine is in the city, but if
we sit here, we will also die. So now,
come on. Let's go to the Arameans'
camp. If they let us live, we will live;
if they kill us, we will die."
5 So the diseased men got up at twilight to go to the Arameans' camp.
When they came to the camp's edge,
they discovered that there was not
a single man there, 6 for the LORD[E]
had caused the Aramean camp to
hear the sound of chariots, horses,
and a great army. The Arameans
had said to each other, "The king of
Israel must have hired the kings of
the Hittites and the kings of Egypt
to attack us." 7 So they had gotten
up and fled at twilight, abandoning
their tents, horses, and donkeys.
The camp was intact, and they had
fled for their lives.
8 When these men came to the
edge of the camp, they went into
a tent to eat and drink. Then they
picked up the silver, gold, and clothing and went off and hid them.
They came back and entered another tent, picked things up, and hid
them. 9 Then they said to each other,
"We're not doing what is right. Today is a day of good news. If we are
silent and wait until morning light,
our sin will catch up with us. Let's
go tell the king's household."
10 The diseased men went and
called to the city's gatekeepers and
told them, "We went to the Aramean
camp and no one was there—no human sounds. There was nothing but
tethered horses and donkeys, and
the tents were intact." 11 The gatekeepers called out, and the news was
reported to the king's household.
12 So the king got up in the night
and said to his servants, "Let me tell
you what the Arameans have done
to us. They know we are starving, so
they have left the camp to hide in the
open country, thinking, 'When they
come out of the city, we will take
them alive and go into the city.'"
13 But one of his servants responded, "Please, let messengers take five
of the horses that are left in the city.
Their fate is like the entire Israelite
community who will die,[F] so let's
send them and see."
14 The messengers took two chariots with horses, and the king sent

7:1-2 God's perfect timing, not the king's threat, brought an end to the famine the next day.

[A]6:33 Some emend to *king* [B]7:1 Lit *a seah* [C]7:1 About 1/2 ounce of silver [D]7:1 Lit *two seahs*
[E]7:6 Some Hb mss read *LORD* [F]7:13 Some Hb mss, LXX, Syr, Vg; other Hb mss read *left in it. Indeed, they are like the whole multitude of Israel that are left in it; indeed, they are like the whole multitude of Israel who will die.*

8:1-6 Ben-hadad's siege of Samaria (6:24–7:7) may have taken place sometime *after* the "seven-year famine," and the narrator may have backtracked to include details about this particular individual for whom the Lord provided (cp. 6:8-24). That the account is not in chronological order highlights its significance. This story demonstrates God's faithfulness to save and restore those who honor Him in contrast to those whom the Lord afflicted with famine. The remnant in exile may have been encouraged by the account of the Shunammite woman. The Lord had sent her and her household out of Israel to preserve their lives. Here God not only brought her back to her homeland but also restored her inheritance (cp. Dt 28:1-10; Is 10:22-23; 1Pt 1:3-7).

them after the Aramean army, saying, "Go and see." 15 So they followed them as far as the Jordan. They saw that the whole way was littered with clothes and equipment the Arameans had thrown off in their haste. The messengers returned and told the king. 16 Then the people went out and plundered the Aramean camp.

It was then that six quarts[A] of fine meal sold for a shekel[B] and 12 quarts[C] of barley sold for a shekel,[B] according to the word of the LORD. 17 The king had appointed the captain, his right-hand man, to be in charge of the gate, but the people trampled him in the gateway. He died, just as the man of God had predicted when the king came to him. 18 When the man of God had said to the king, "About this time tomorrow 12 quarts[C] of barley will sell for a shekel[B] and six quarts[A] of fine meal will sell for a shekel[B] at the gate of Samaria," 19 this captain had answered the man of God, "Look, even if the LORD were to make windows in heaven, could this really happen?" Elisha had said, "You will in fact see it with your own eyes, but you won't eat any of it." 20 This is what happened to him: the people trampled him in the gateway, and he died.

Restoration of the Shunammite's Land (8:1-6)

8 Elisha said to the woman whose son he had restored to life, "Get ready, you and your household, and go and live as a foreigner wherever you can. For the LORD has announced a seven-year famine, and it has already come to the land."

2 So the woman got ready and did what the man of God said. She and her household lived as foreigners in the land of the Philistines for seven years. 3 When the woman returned from the land of the Philistines at the end of seven years, she went to appeal to the king for her house and field.

4 The king had been speaking to Gehazi, the attendant of the man of God, saying, "Tell me all the great things Elisha has done."

5 While he was telling the king how Elisha restored the dead son to life, the woman whose son he had restored to life came to appeal to the king for her house and field. So Gehazi said, "My lord the king, this is the woman and this is the son Elisha restored to life."

6 When the king asked the woman, she told him the story. So the king appointed a court official for her, saying, "Restore all that was hers, along with all the income from the field from the day she left the country until now."

Hazael, King of Aram (8:7-15)

7 Elisha came to Damascus while Ben-hadad king of Aram was sick, and the king was told, "The man of God has come here." 8 So the king said to Hazael, "Take a gift with you and go meet the man of God. Inquire of the LORD through him, 'Will I recover from this sickness?'"

9 Hazael went to meet Elisha, taking with him a gift: 40 camel-loads of all kinds of goods from Damascus. When he came and stood before him, he said, "Your son, Ben-hadad king of Aram, has sent me to ask you, 'Will I recover from this sickness?'"

10 Elisha told him, "Go say to him, 'You are sure to[D] recover.' But the LORD has shown me that he is sure to die." 11 Then Elisha stared steadily at him until Hazael was ashamed.

The man of God wept, 12 and Hazael asked, "Why is my lord weeping?"

He replied, "Because I know the evil you will do to the people of Israel. You will set their fortresses on fire. You will kill their young men with the sword. You will dash their little ones to pieces. You will rip open their pregnant women."

13 Hazael said, "How could your servant, a mere dog, do this monstrous thing?"

Elisha answered, "The LORD has shown me that you will be king over Aram."

14 Hazael left Elisha and went to his master, who asked him, "What did Elisha say to you?"

He responded, "He told me you are sure to recover." 15 The next day Hazael took a heavy cloth, dipped

[A]7:16,18 Lit *a seah* [B]7:16,18 About 1/2 ounce of silver [C]7:16,18 Lit *two seahs* [D]8:10 Alt Hb tradition reads *You will not*

it in water, and spread it over the
king's face. Ben-hadad died, and
Hazael reigned instead of him.

Kings of Judah (8:16-29)

Jehoram (8:16-24)

16 In the fifth year of Israel's King
Joram son of Ahab, Jehoram[A] son
of Jehoshaphat became king of Judah, replacing his father.[B] 17 He was
32 years old when he became king
and reigned eight years in Jerusalem. 18 He walked in the way of the
kings of Israel, as the house of Ahab
had done, for Ahab's daughter was
his wife. He did what was evil in the
LORD's sight. 19 The LORD was unwilling to destroy Judah because of His
servant David, since He had promised to give a lamp to David and his
sons forever.

20 During Jehoram's reign, Edom
rebelled against Judah's control and
appointed their own king. 21 So Jehoram crossed over to Zair with all
his chariots. Then at night he set out
to attack the Edomites who had surrounded him and the chariot commanders, but his troops fled to their
tents. 22 So Edom is still in rebellion
against Judah's control today. Libnah also rebelled at that time.

23 The rest of the events of Jehoram's reign, along with all his
accomplishments, are written in the
Historical Record of Judah's Kings.
24 Jehoram rested with his fathers
and was buried with his fathers in
the city of David, and his son Ahaziah became king in his place.

Ahaziah (8:25-29)

25 In the twelfth year of Israel's
King Joram son of Ahab, Ahaziah
son of Jehoram became king of
Judah. 26 Ahaziah was 22 years old
when he became king and reigned
one year in Jerusalem. His mother's
name was Athaliah, granddaughter
of Israel's King Omri. 27 He walked
in the way of the house of Ahab and
did what was evil in the LORD's sight
like the house of Ahab, for he was a
son-in-law to Ahab's family.

28 Ahaziah went with Joram son of
Ahab to fight against Hazael king of
Aram in Ramoth-gilead, and the Arameans wounded Joram. 29 So King
Joram returned to Jezreel to recover
from the wounds that the Arameans
had inflicted on him in Ramoth-gilead[C] when he fought against Aram's
King Hazael. Then Judah's King
Ahaziah son of Jehoram went down
to Jezreel to visit Joram son of Ahab
since Joram was ill.

King Jehu of Israel (9:1–10:36)

Jehu's Anointing as King (9:1-13)

9 The prophet Elisha called one of
the sons of the prophets and said,
"Tuck your mantle under your belt,
take this flask of oil with you, and
go to Ramoth-gilead. 2 When you
get there, look for Jehu son of Jehoshaphat, son of Nimshi. Go in, get
him away from his colleagues, and
take him to an inner room. 3 Then,
take the flask of oil, pour it on his
head, and say, 'This is what the
LORD says: "I anoint you king over
Israel."' Open the door and escape.
Don't wait." 4 So the young prophet
went to Ramoth-gilead.

5 When he arrived, the army commanders were sitting there, so he
said, "I have a message for you, commander."

Jehu asked, "For which one of us?"

He answered, "For you, commander."

6 So Jehu got up and went into the
house. The young prophet poured
the oil on his head and said, "This
is what the LORD God of Israel says:
'I anoint you king over the LORD's
people, Israel. 7 You are to strike
down the house of your master Ahab
so that I may avenge the blood shed
by the hand of Jezebel—the blood of
My servants the prophets and of all
the servants of the LORD. 8 The whole
house of Ahab will perish, and I will
eliminate all of Ahab's males,[D] both
slave and free, in Israel. 9 I will make
the house of Ahab like the house
of Jeroboam son of Nebat and like
the house of Baasha son of Ahijah.
10 The dogs will eat Jezebel in the
plot of land at Jezreel—no one will
bury her.'" Then the young prophet
opened the door and escaped.

8:16 From this point on the narrative focuses more on the kings of Israel and Judah and less on the role of the prophet Elisha.

8:18 This detail of Jehoram's wife, Athaliah, implicitly underscores the powerful influence of a wife on the moral and spiritual patterns of her husband's life—in this case, for evil (cp. 1Kg 11:4; 16:31). Athaliah was married to Jehoram as part of an alliance between Jehoshaphat and Ahab. She was the daughter of the wicked Jezebel and, "like mother, like daughter," she undoubtedly worshiped Baal.

8:25-29 Jehoram's youngest son **Ahaziah** followed the pagan practices of Ahab's house. The pattern had been set by his mother **Athaliah**, Ahab's daughter, and by his own wife, who was also from **Ahab's family** (cp. v. 18). Together they led the nation down a dangerous path that would eventually lead to Judah's exile in Babylon.

9:1-13 The Lord had instructed Elijah to anoint **Jehu**, Joram's army commander, as king over Israel (1Kg 19:16-17); but the task fell to Elisha, who gave **one of the sons of the prophets** specific instructions for carrying out the assignment. Not only was Jehu supposed to succeed Joram, but he was also commissioned to carry out the judgment that God had issued against the house of Ahab (1Kg 21:21-24). The introduction to the prophet's message—**This is what the LORD God of Israel says**—especially following the many incidents proving that Israel's prophets were speaking from God, was important in setting the stage for the bloodbath the writer was about to describe.

God Himself chose Jehu to be king over the LORD's people, indicating that He remained faithful to Israel despite her kings' evil ways. Also, Jehu was obeying God's commands as an appointed instrument of judgment against the house of Ahab and against Jezebel (cp. 1Kg 14:6-12; 15:29-30; 15:34–16:13). Jehu was welcomed to the throne by Israel's army.

[A] **8:16** = The LORD is Exalted [B] **8:16** Lit *Judah; Jehoshaphat had been king of Judah* [C] **8:29** Lit *Ramah* [D] **9:8** Lit *eliminate Ahab's one who urinates against a wall*

9:14-15 Despite the military's enthusiastic reception of the newly anointed king, Jehu began a pattern of demanding proof of loyalty. **If** the **commanders** were for him, they would prevent the news from reaching King Joram in **Jezreel**, his father Ahab's old capital (vv. 14-15; cp. 3:1; 8:16).

9:23-26 Jehu's words to **Bidkar** emphasized that they were fulfilling **the Lord's declaration** by leaving Joram's body on the land of **Naboth the Jezreelite** (cp. 1Kg 21:19).

11 When Jehu came out to his master's servants, they asked, "Is everything all right? Why did this crazy person come to you?"

Then he said to them, "You know the sort and their ranting."

12 But they replied, "That's a lie! Tell us!"

So Jehu said, "He talked to me about this and that and said, 'This is what the LORD says: I anoint you king over Israel.'"

13 Each man quickly took his garment and put it under Jehu on the bare steps.[A] They blew the ram's horn and proclaimed, "Jehu is king!"

Jehu's Killing of Joram and Ahaziah (9:14-29)

14 Then Jehu son of Jehoshaphat, son of Nimshi, conspired against Joram. Joram and all Israel had been at Ramoth-gilead on guard against Hazael king of Aram. 15 But King Joram had returned to Jezreel to recover from the wounds that the Arameans had inflicted on him when he fought against Aram's King Hazael. Jehu said, "If you commanders wish to make me king, then don't let anyone escape from the city to go tell about it in Jezreel."

16 Jehu got into his chariot and went to Jezreel since Joram was laid up there and Ahaziah king of Judah had gone down to visit Joram. 17 Now the watchman was standing on the tower in Jezreel. He saw Jehu's troops approaching and shouted, "I see troops!"

Joram responded, "Choose a rider and send him to meet them and have him ask, 'Do you come in peace?'"

18 So a horseman went to meet Jehu and said, "This is what the king asks: 'Do you come in peace?'"

Jehu replied, "What do you have to do with peace?[B] Fall in behind me."

The watchman reported, "The messenger reached them but hasn't started back."

19 So he sent out a second horseman, who went to them and said, "This is what the king asks: 'Do you come in peace?'"

Jehu answered, "What do you have to do with peace?[B] Fall in behind me."

20 Again the watchman reported, "He reached them but hasn't started back. Also, the driving is like that of Jehu son of Nimshi—he drives like a madman."

21 "Harness!" Joram shouted, and they harnessed his chariot. Then Joram king of Israel and Ahaziah king of Judah set out, each in his own chariot, and met Jehu at the plot of land of Naboth the Jezreelite. 22 When Joram saw Jehu he asked, "Do you come in peace, Jehu?"

He answered, "What peace can there be as long as there is so much prostitution and witchcraft from your mother Jezebel?"

23 Joram turned around and fled, shouting to Ahaziah, "It's treachery, Ahaziah!"

24 Then Jehu drew his bow and shot Joram between the shoulders. The arrow went through his heart, and he slumped down in his chariot. 25 Jehu said to Bidkar his aide, "Pick him up and throw him on the plot of ground belonging to Naboth the Jezreelite. For remember when you and I were riding side by side behind his father Ahab, and the LORD uttered this •oracle against him: 26 'As surely as I saw the blood of Naboth and the blood of his sons yesterday'—this is the LORD's declaration—'so will I repay you on this plot of land'—this is the LORD's declaration. So now, according to the word of the LORD, pick him up and throw him on the plot of land."

27 When King Ahaziah of Judah saw what was happening, he fled up the road toward Beth-haggan. Jehu pursued him, shouting, "Shoot him too!" So they shot him in his chariot[C] at Gur Pass near Ibleam, but he fled to Megiddo and died there. 28 Then his servants carried him to Jerusalem in a chariot and buried him in his fathers' tomb in the city of David. 29 It was in the eleventh year of Joram son of Ahab that Ahaziah had become king over Judah.

[A] **9:13** Lit *on the bones of the steps* [B] **9:18,19** Lit *What to you and to peace* [C] **9:27** LXX, Syr, Vg; MT omits *So they shot him*

Jehu's Killing of Jezebel and the House of Ahab (9:30–10:17)

30 When Jehu came to Jezreel, Jezebel heard about it, so she painted her eyes, adorned her head, and looked down from the window. 31 As Jehu entered the gate, she said, "Do you come in peace, Zimri,[A] killer of your master?"

32 He looked up toward the window and said, "Who is on my side? Who?" Two or three eunuchs looked down at him, 33 and he said, "Throw her down!" So they threw her down, and some of her blood splattered on the wall and on the horses, and Jehu rode over her.

34 Then he went in, ate and drank, and said, "Take care of this cursed woman and bury her, since she's a king's daughter." 35 But when they went out to bury her, they did not find anything but her skull, her feet, and the palms of her hands. 36 So they went back and told him, and he said, "This fulfills the LORD's word that He spoke through His servant Elijah the Tishbite: 'In the plot of land at Jezreel, the dogs will eat Jezebel's flesh. 37 Jezebel's corpse will be like manure on the surface of the field in the plot of land at Jezreel so that no one will be able to say: This is Jezebel.'"

10 Since Ahab had 70 sons in Samaria, Jehu wrote letters and sent them to Samaria to the rulers of Jezreel, to the elders, and to the guardians of Ahab's sons,[B] saying:

> 2 When this letter arrives, since your master's sons are with you and you have chariots, horses, a fortified city, and weaponry, 3 select the most qualified[C] of your master's sons, set him on his father's throne, and fight for your master's house.

4 However, they were terrified and reasoned, "Look, two kings couldn't stand against him; how can we?"

5 So the overseer of the palace, the overseer of the city, the elders, and the guardians sent a message to Jehu: "We are your servants, and we will do whatever you tell us. We will not make anyone king. Do whatever you think is right."[D]

6 Then Jehu wrote them a second letter, saying:

> If you are on my side, and if you will obey me, bring me the heads of your master's sons at this time tomorrow at Jezreel.

All 70 of the king's sons were being cared for by the city's prominent men. 7 When the letter came to them, they took the king's sons and slaughtered all 70, put their heads in baskets, and sent them to Jehu at Jezreel. 8 When the messenger came and told him, "They have brought the heads of the king's sons," the king said, "Pile them in two heaps at the entrance of the gate until morning."

9 The next morning when he went out and stood at the gate, he said to all the people, "You are innocent. It was I who conspired against my master and killed him. But who struck down all these? 10 Know, then, that not a word the LORD spoke against the house of Ahab will fail, for the LORD has done what He promised through His servant Elijah." 11 So Jehu killed all who remained of the house of Ahab in Jezreel—all his great men, close friends, and priests—leaving him no survivors.

12 Then he set out and went on his way to Samaria. On the way, while he was at Beth-eked of the Shepherds, 13 Jehu met the relatives of Ahaziah king of Judah and asked, "Who are you?"

They answered, "We're Ahaziah's relatives. We've come down to greet the king's sons and the queen mother's sons."

14 Then Jehu ordered, "Take them alive." So they took them alive and then slaughtered them at the pit of Beth-eked—42 men. He didn't spare any of them.

15 When he left there, he found Jehonadab son of Rechab coming to meet him. He greeted him and then asked, "Is your heart one with mine?"[E]

9:30-37 Having learned of the military coup in progress and knowing she was a target, **Jezebel** prepared to confront Jehu by beautifying herself. Some interpret her actions as a desperate attempt to seduce Jehu, but the taunting attitude with which she addressed him does not support this idea. She was a powerful woman who probably expected that the people, when they saw her regal appearance and heard her comparison of Jehu with **Zimri**—whose treacherous seizure of the throne had lasted just a week—would rally to do her bidding (cp 1Kg 16:9-20). The gruesome details of Jezebel's death fulfilled **the LORD's word** spoken by **Elijah** (cp. 1Kg 21:23-24).

10:12-14 Some claim that Jehu's slaughter of Ahaziah's relatives falls outside the boundaries of what he was commissioned to do. That the Lord's promise to "bring the bloodshed of Jezreel on the house of Jehu" (Hs 1:4) seems to support this view. Still, the text simply reports the event without comment, taking for granted that these men were considered to be Ahab's descendants (cp. 2Ch 22:2-9). While some object to the violence with which Jehu purged Israel from Ahab's household, it is important to recognize that the focus here was not on the method and manner of execution but on the overriding theological issue of judgment executed by a holy God. Extending the purge to Judah helped preserve the Davidic line from being thoroughly corrupted by intermarriage with Ahab's family (2Kg 11:1-3).

[A]**9:31** A sarcastic reference to Zimri who usurped the throne; 1Kg 16:8-20 [B]**10:1** LXX; MT reads *of Ahab* [C]**10:3** Lit *the good and the upright* [D]**10:5** Lit *Do what is good in your eyes* [E]**10:15** Lit *heart upright like my heart is with your heart*

10:18-27 The destruction of Ahab and his household effectively swept away one political dynasty to make way for government under a new king, the first to be anointed as God's choice for Israel's king since the kingdom divided. Making the place of **Baal** worship **a latrine** (Hb *machara'ah*, "sewer, cesspool,") was a lasting, concrete reminder of God's opinion of Baalism and its heinous practices.

10:28-36 The writer seems to make a connection between Jehu's failure to **turn** (Hb *sur*, "turn aside from, depart from, come to an end"; cp. 3:2) from worshiping the golden calves and the Lord's allowing Israel's enemies to dominate them (10:31-33).

"It is," Jehonadab replied.
Jehu said, "If it is,[A] give me your hand."
So he gave him his hand, and Jehu pulled him up into the chariot with
him. 16 Then he said, "Come with me and see my zeal for the LORD!" So he let him ride with him in his chariot.
17 When Jehu came to Samaria, he struck down all who remained from the house of Ahab in Samaria until he had annihilated his house, according to the word of the LORD spoken to Elijah.

Jehu's Killing of the Baal Worshipers (10:18-27)

18 Then Jehu brought all the people together and said to them, "Ahab served •Baal a little, but Jehu will
serve him a lot. 19 Now, therefore, summon to me all the prophets of Baal, all his servants, and all his priests. None must be missing, for I have a great sacrifice for Baal. Whoever is missing will not live." However, Jehu was acting deceptively in order to destroy the servants of Baal.
20 Jehu commanded, "Consecrate a solemn assembly for Baal." So they called one.
21 Then Jehu sent messengers throughout all Israel, and all the servants of Baal[B] came; there was not a man left who did not come. They entered the temple of Baal, and it was filled from one end to the other.
22 Then he said to the custodian of the wardrobe, "Bring out the garments for all the servants of Baal." So he brought out their garments.
23 Then Jehu and Jehonadab son of Rechab entered the temple of Baal, and Jehu said to the servants of Baal, "Look carefully to see that there are no servants of the LORD here among you—only servants of Baal."
24 Then they went in to offer sacrifices and •burnt offerings.
Now Jehu had stationed 80 men outside, and he warned them, "Whoever allows any of the men I am delivering into your hands to escape will forfeit his life for theirs."
25 When he finished offering the burnt offering, Jehu said to the guards and officers, "Go in and kill them. Don't let anyone out." So they struck them down with the sword. Then the guards and officers threw the bodies out and went into the inner room of the temple of Baal.
26 They brought out the pillars of the temple of Baal and burned them
27 and tore down the pillar of Baal. Then they tore down the temple of Baal and made it a latrine—which it is to this day.

Jehu's Defeat by Hazael (10:28-36)

28 Jehu eliminated Baal worship from Israel,
29 but he did not turn away from the sins that Jeroboam son of Nebat had caused Israel to commit—worshiping the gold calves that were in Bethel and Dan.
30 Nevertheless, the LORD said to Jehu, "Because you have done well in carrying out what is right in My sight and have done to the house of Ahab all that was in My heart, four generations of your sons will sit on the throne of Israel."
31 Yet Jehu was not careful to follow the instruction of the LORD God of Israel with all his heart. He did not turn from the sins that Jeroboam had caused Israel to commit.
32 In those days the LORD began to reduce the size of Israel. Hazael defeated the Israelites throughout their territory:
33 from the Jordan eastward, all the land of Gilead—the Gadites, the Reubenites, and the Manassites—from Aroer which is by the Arnon Valley through Gilead to Bashan.[C]
34 Now the rest of the events of Jehu's reign, along with all his accomplishments and all his might, are written in the Historical Record of Israel's Kings.
35 Jehu rested with his fathers and was buried in Samaria. His son Jehoahaz became king in his place.
36 The length of Jehu's reign over Israel in Samaria was 28 years.

Kings of Judah (11:1–12:21)

Overthrowing of Athaliah by Jehoiada the Priest (11:1-16)

11 When Athaliah, Ahaziah's mother, saw that her son was dead, she proceeded to annihilate all the royal heirs.
2 Jehosheba, who was

[A]**10:15** LXX, Syr, Vg; MT reads *mine?" Jehonadab said, "It is and it is* [B]**10:21** LXX adds *—all his priests and all his prophets—* [C]**10:33** Lit *Arnon Valley and Gilead and Bashan*

CHARACTER PROFILE

Athaliah A Murdering Queen

Her Background	• The daughter of Ahab and Jezebel, who followed in their ways (8:18,26) • The wife of Jehoram, the son of godly King Jehoshaphat of Judah (2Ch 22:5) • A follower of Baal and enemy of Israel's God (2Kg 8:26-27; 11:18-20)
Her Story	• After Jehoram's premature death, his son Ahaziah succeeded him (2Ch 22:3). • Ahaziah died and Athaliah seized the opportunity to murder all the royal heirs in order to ascend to the throne illegitimately (2Kg 11:1). • She ruled for six years and was killed due to a coup (11:4-16).
Life Lessons	• Athaliah's ambition was evil and unlawful. • Her rule brought great suffering to God's people.

King Jehoram's daughter and Ahaziah's sister, secretly rescued Joash
son of Ahaziah from the king's sons
who were being killed and put him
and the one who nursed him in a
bedroom. So he was hidden from
Athaliah and was not killed. 3 Joash
was in hiding with Jehosheba in the
LORD's temple six years while Athaliah ruled over the land.
4 Then in the seventh year, Jehoiada sent messengers and brought in
the commanders of hundreds, the
Carites, and the guards. He had
them come to him in the LORD's
temple, where he made a covenant
with them and put them under oath.
He showed them the king's son 5 and
commanded them, "This is what you
are to do: a third of you who come
on duty on the Sabbath are to provide protection for the king's palace.
6 A third are to be at the Sur gate
and a third at the gate behind the
guards. You are to take turns providing protection for the palace.[A]
7 "Your two divisions that go off
duty on the Sabbath are to provide
protection for the LORD's temple.
8 You must completely surround the
king with weapons in hand. Anyone
who approaches the ranks is to be
put to death. You must be with the
king in all his daily tasks."[B]
9 So the commanders of hundreds
did everything Jehoiada the priest
commanded. They each brought
their men—those coming on duty
on the Sabbath and those going off
duty—and went to Jehoiada the
priest. 10 The priest gave to the commanders of hundreds King David's
spears and shields that were in the
LORD's temple. 11 Then the guards
stood with their weapons in hand
surrounding the king—from the
right side of the temple to the left
side, by the altar and by the temple.
12 He brought out the king's son,
put the crown on him, gave him the
•testimony,[C] and made him king.
They anointed him and clapped
their hands and cried, "Long live the
king!"
13 When Athaliah heard the noise
from the guard and the crowd, she
went out to the people at the LORD's
temple. 14 As she looked, there was
the king standing by the pillar according to the custom. The commanders and the trumpeters were
by the king, and all the people of
the land were rejoicing and blowing
trumpets. Athaliah tore her clothes
and screamed "Treason! Treason!"
15 Then Jehoiada the priest ordered the commanders of hundreds
in charge of the army, "Take her out
between the ranks, and put to death
by the sword anyone who follows

11:1-16 The narrative shifts from growing gloom in Israel to a time of revival in Judah. Two women take center stage in this section and present the continuing biblical contrast between good and evil. When Jehu of Israel killed Athaliah's son Ahaziah (9:27), she saw her opportunity to gain control of the kingdom and attempted to kill all the royal heirs, including her own grandsons. Had she succeeded in killing **Joash**, God's promise to preserve the Davidic lineage would have failed. But the Lord used **Jehosheba** (Hb, "Yahweh has sworn"; Jehoshabeath in 2Ch 22:11) to intervene. As **Jehoram's daughter,** Jehosheba was either the daughter or stepdaughter of Athaliah, and she was the wife of Jehoiada the priest (2Ch 22:11). This marriage between a woman in the royal line and an Aaronic priest is the only such union recorded in Scripture. Jehosheba's daring and cunning rescue of the infant Joash kept hope alive. The successful coronation of Joash demanded the execution of the apostate queen **Athaliah** and thereby constituted a stunning victory over evil (2Kg 11:13-16).

[A] **11:6** Hb obscure [B] **11:8** Lit *king when he goes out and when he comes in* [C] **11:12** Or *him the copy of the covenant*, or *him a diadem*, or *him jewels*

12:1-2 Although their personal stories are not told in Scripture, the importance of the role of mothers is noted by the record of the names of the mothers of every king of Judah. The text does not record what happened to **Zibiah** (Hb, "roe," v. 1), the mother of **Joash**, if she were alive when Athaliah usurped the throne. The only detail provided—that she **was from Beer-sheba** at Judah's southernmost border—indicates that she was probably a Jewish woman rather than a wife taken to forge a political alliance.

12:4-16 From a 40-year reign, the writer selected the events of greatest theological importance in the story of God's people. The highlight of Joash's royal career was his effort to have **the LORD's temple** repaired, which, under Athaliah's rule, had been looted and desecrated (2Ch 24:7).

her," for the priest had said, "She is not to be put to death in the LORD's temple." 16 So they arrested her, and she went through the horse entrance to the king's palace, where she was put to death.

Joash's Restoration and Guidance by Jehoiada (11:17–12:3)

17 Then Jehoiada made a covenant between the LORD, the king, and the people that they would be the LORD's people and another covenant between the king and the people.[A] 18 So all the people of the land went to the temple of •Baal and tore it down. They broke its altars and images into pieces, and they killed Mattan, the priest of Baal, at the altars.

Then Jehoiada the priest appointed guards for the LORD's temple. 19 He took the commanders of hundreds, the Carites, the guards, and all the people of the land, and they brought the king from the LORD's temple. They entered the king's palace by way of the guards' gate. Then Joash sat on the throne of the kings. 20 All the people of the land rejoiced, and the city was quiet, for they had put Athaliah to death by the sword in the king's palace.

12 21[B] Joash[C] was seven years old when he became king. 1 In the seventh year of Jehu, Joash became king and reigned 40 years in Jerusalem. His mother's name was Zibiah, who was from Beer-sheba. 2 Throughout the time Jehoiada the priest instructed him, Joash did what was right in the LORD's sight. 3 Yet the •high places were not taken away; the people continued sacrificing and burning incense on the high places.

Joash and the Temple (12:4-18)

4 Then Joash said to the priests, "All the dedicated money brought to the LORD's temple, census money, money from vows, and all money voluntarily given for the LORD's temple, 5 each priest is to take from his assessor[D] and repair whatever damage to the temple is found."[E]

6 But by the twenty-third year of the reign of King Joash, the priests had not repaired the damage[F] to the temple. 7 So King Joash called Jehoiada the priest and the other priests and said, "Why haven't you repaired the temple's damage? Since you haven't, don't take any money from your assessors; instead, hand it over for the repair of the temple." 8 So the priests agreed they would not take money from the people and they would not repair the temple's damage.

9 Then Jehoiada the priest took a chest, bored a hole in its lid, and set it beside the altar on the right side as one enters the LORD's temple; in it the priests who guarded the threshold put all the money brought into the LORD's temple. 10 Whenever they saw there was a large amount of money in the chest, the king's secretary and the high priest would go to the LORD's temple and count the money found there and tie it up in bags. 11 Then they would put the counted money into the hands of those doing the work—those who oversaw the LORD's temple. They in turn would pay it out to those working on the LORD's temple—the carpenters, the builders, 12 the masons, and the stonecutters—and would use it to buy timber and quarried stone to repair the damage to the LORD's temple and for all spending for temple repairs.

13 However, no silver bowls, wick trimmers, sprinkling basins, trumpets, or any articles of gold or silver were made for the LORD's temple from the money brought into the temple. 14 Instead, it was given to those doing the work, and they repaired the LORD's temple with it. 15 No accounting was required from the men who received the money to pay those doing the work, since they worked with integrity. 16 The money from the •restitution offering and the •sin offering was not brought to the LORD's temple since it belonged to the priests.

17 At that time Hazael king of Aram marched up and fought against Gath and captured it. Then he planned to attack Jerusalem. 18 So King Joash of

[A] **11:17** Some Gk versions, 2Ch 23:16 omit *and another covenant between the king and the people* [B] **11:21** 2Kg 12:1 in Hb [C] **11:21** = The LORD Has Bestowed [D] **12:5** Hb obscure [E] **12:5** Lit *repair the breach of the house wherever there is found a breach* [F] **12:6** Lit *breach* in 2Kg 12:5-12

Judah took all the consecrated items
that his ancestors—Judah's kings
Jehoshaphat, Jehoram, and Ahaziah—had consecrated, along with
his own consecrated items and all
the gold found in the treasuries of
the LORD's temple and in the king's
palace, and he sent them to Hazael
king of Aram. Then Hazael withdrew
from Jerusalem.

The Assassination of Joash (12:19-21)

19 The rest of the events of Joash's
reign, along with all his accomplishments, are written in the Historical
Record of Judah's Kings. 20 Joash's
servants conspired against him and
killed him at Beth-millo on the road
that goes down to Silla. 21 His servants Jozabad[A] son of Shimeath and
Jehozabad son of Shomer struck
him down, and he died. Then they
buried him with his fathers in the
city of David, and his son Amaziah
became king in his place.

Kings of Israel (13:1-25)

Jehoahaz (13:1-9)

13 In the twenty-third year of Judah's King Joash son of Ahaziah, Jehoahaz son of Jehu became
king over Israel in Samaria and
reigned 17 years. 2 He did what was
evil in the LORD's sight and followed
the sins that Jeroboam son of Nebat
had caused Israel to commit; he did
not turn away from them. 3 So the
LORD's anger burned against Israel,
and He surrendered them to the
power of Hazael king of Aram and
his son Ben-hadad during their
reigns.

4 Then Jehoahaz sought the LORD's
favor, and the LORD heard him, for
He saw the oppression the king of
Aram inflicted on Israel. 5 Therefore,
the LORD gave Israel a deliverer, and
they escaped from the power of the
Arameans. Then the people of Israel
dwelt in their tents as before, 6 but
they didn't turn away from the sins
that the house of Jeroboam had
caused Israel to commit. Jehoahaz
walked in them, and the •Asherah
pole also remained standing in Samaria. 7 Jehoahaz did not have an
army left, except for 50 horsemen,
10 chariots, and 10,000 foot soldiers, because the king of Aram had
destroyed them, making them like
dust at threshing.

8 The rest of the events of Jehoahaz's reign, along with all his accomplishments and his might, are
written in the Historical Record of
Israel's Kings. 9 Jehoahaz rested with
his fathers, and he was buried in
Samaria. His son Jehoash[B] became
king in his place.

Jehoash (13:10-19)

10 In the thirty-seventh year of
Judah's King Joash, Jehoash son of
Jehoahaz became king over Israel
in Samaria and reigned 16 years.
11 He did what was evil in the LORD's
sight. He did not turn away from all
the sins that Jeroboam son of Nebat
had caused Israel to commit, but he
walked in them.

12 The rest of the events of Jehoash's reign, along with all his
accomplishments and the power
he had to wage war against Judah's
King Amaziah, are written in the
Historical Record of Israel's Kings.
13 Jehoash rested with his fathers,
and Jeroboam sat on his throne. Jehoash was buried in Samaria with
the kings of Israel.

14 When Elisha became sick with
the illness that he died from, Jehoash king of Israel went down and
wept over him and said, "My father,
my father, the chariots and horsemen of Israel!"

15 Elisha responded, "Take a bow
and arrows." So he got a bow and
arrows. 16 Then Elisha said to the
king of Israel, "Put your hand on the
bow." So the king put his hand on
it, and Elisha put his hands on the
king's hands. 17 Elisha said, "Open
the east window." So he opened it.

[A]**12:21** Some Hb mss, LXX read *Jozacar*; 2Ch 24:26 reads *Zabad* [B]**13:9** Lit *Joash*

12:19-21 Like Solomon, Joash began well but did not finish well. The account of his apostasy (cp. v. 2; 2Ch 24:15-25; cp. 2Kg 12:2) accounts for the abrupt end to the record of his life.

13:1-7 God's **anger** regarding Israel's persistence in sin prompted Him to give the kings **of Aram** success against the northern kingdom. However, the same God who had surrendered Israel to a foreign power readily **gave Israel** an unidentified **deliverer** when her king turned to Him in need. Historians note that the Assyrian king Adad-nirari III attacked Damascus about 805 B.C., making Hazael a vassal by 802 B.C. Thereafter, Hazael's son Ben-hadad III lacked the strength to dominate Israel (see vv. 24-25).

13:8-9 The narrator did not specify Jehoahaz's **accomplishments and . . . might,** but the attentive reader can recognize that God was fulfilling His promise to Jehu to allow four generations of sons to rule Israel as king (v. 10:30).

13:14-19 Like his father, **Jehoash** missed an opportunity to turn the nation around when he visited the prophet **Elisha** on his deathbed. Placement of Elisha's **hands** on **the king's hands** possibly represented the unseen hands of Yahweh, who would act powerfully on behalf of His people as they went into battle. **The arrow of victory** (Hb *teshu'ah*, "salvation or deliverance" usually won by God through human agency, v. 17) **over Aram** was shot through **the east window** in the direction of that enemy nation. Striking the remaining **arrows** on **the ground** apparently symbolized the number of occasions on which Israel would defeat Aram, but the interpretation was not revealed until the level of Jehoash's faith and zeal were proved by the extent of his obedience in doing something he did not understand.

>WORD|*study*

13:4 Both the noun oppression ("distress, pressure") and the verb inflicted ("oppress, squeeze, press") are from the same Hebrew root (*lachats*; cp. Ex 3:9; Jdg 10:12).

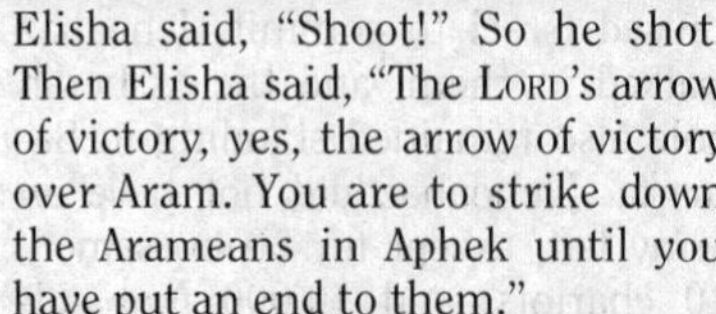

13:20-21 The unprecedented revival of the unnamed dead **man**, upon touching **Elisha's bones**, indicated the continuing presence of God's power in Israel to restore life even when the nation *seemed* to have been conquered by death and *seemed* to have been discarded in the effort to escape from their enemies.

13:22-23 The language referring to Hazael's oppression of Israel echoes that of Exodus as **the Lord** powerfully demonstrated His deliverance and character (Ex 2:24). Even now **He has not banished** (Hb *shalak*, "cast off or down, hurl, fling, throw away") Israel **from His presence**.

14:9-14 Israel's **King Jehoash** replied to Amaziah's challenge with a parable illustrating the extent to which Judah's king was overestimating his reach and also suggesting that engagement in war would be unwise for both parties while **a wild animal**, probably Aram or Assyria, remained a serious threat. The rhetorical question of his reply cleverly turned Amaziah's boasting into a charge of royal irresponsibility.

Elisha said, "Shoot!" So he shot.
Then Elisha said, "The Lord's arrow
of victory, yes, the arrow of victory
over Aram. You are to strike down
the Arameans in Aphek until you
have put an end to them."
[18]Then Elisha said, "Take the arrows!" So he took them. Then Elisha
said to the king of Israel, "Strike the
ground!" So he struck the ground
three times and stopped. [19]The man
of God was angry with him and
said, "You should have struck the
ground five or six times. Then you
would have struck down Aram until you had put an end to them, but
now you will only strike down Aram
three times."

God's Grace and Compassion (13:20-25)

[20]Then Elisha died and was buried.
Now Moabite raiders used to come
into the land in the spring of the
year. [21]Once, as the Israelites were
burying a man, suddenly they saw
a raiding party, so they threw the
man into Elisha's tomb. When he
touched Elisha's bones, the man revived and stood up!
[22]Hazael king of Aram oppressed
Israel throughout the reign of Jehoahaz, [23]but the Lord was gracious to
them, had compassion on them, and
turned toward them because of His
covenant with Abraham, Isaac, and
Jacob. He was not willing to destroy
them. Even now He has not banished them from His presence.
[24]King Hazael of Aram died, and
his son Ben-hadad became king in
his place. [25]Then Jehoash son of Jehoahaz took back from Ben-hadad
son of Hazael the cities that Hazael
had taken in war from Jehoash's
father Jehoahaz. Jehoash defeated
Ben-hadad three times and recovered the cities of Israel.

Kings of Judah (14:1-22)

Amaziah (14:1-20)

14 In the second year of Israel's
King Jehoash[A] son of Jehoahaz,[B] Amaziah son of Joash became
king of Judah. [2]He was 25 years old
when he became king and reigned
29 years in Jerusalem. His mother's
name was Jehoaddan[C] and was from
Jerusalem. [3]He did what was right
in the Lord's sight, but not like his
ancestor David. He did everything
his father Joash had done. [4]Yet the
•high places were not taken away,
and the people continued sacrificing
and burning incense on the high
places.
[5]As soon as the kingdom was
firmly in his grasp, Amaziah killed
his servants who had murdered his
father the king. [6]However, he did
not put the children of the murderers to death, as it is written in the
book of the law of Moses where the
Lord commanded, "Fathers must
not be put to death because of children, and children must not be put
to death because of fathers; instead,
each one will be put to death for his
own sin."
[7]Amaziah killed 10,000 Edomites
in the Valley of Salt. He took Sela in
battle and called it Joktheel, which
is its name to this very day. [8]Amazi-
ah then sent messengers to Jehoash
son of Jehoahaz, son of Jehu, king
of Israel, saying, "Come, let us meet
face to face."
[9]King Jehoash of Israel sent word
to Amaziah king of Judah, saying,
"The thistle that was in Lebanon
once sent a message to the cedar
that was in Lebanon, saying, 'Give
your daughter to my son as a wife.'
Then a wild animal that was in Lebanon passed by and trampled the
thistle. [10]You have indeed defeated
Edom, and you have become overconfident. Enjoy your glory and stay
at home. Why should you stir up
such trouble that you fall—you and
Judah with you?"
[11]But Amaziah would not listen,
so King Jehoash of Israel advanced.
He and King Amaziah of Judah faced
off at Beth-shemesh that belongs to
Judah. [12]Judah was routed before
Israel, and everyone fled to his own
tent. [13]King Jehoash of Israel captured Judah's King Amaziah son of
Joash,[D] son of Ahaziah, at Beth-shemesh. Then Jehoash went to Jerusalem and broke down 200 yards[E] of
Jerusalem's wall from the Ephraim
Gate to the Corner Gate. [14]He took
all the gold and silver, all the articles

[A]14:1 Lit *Joash* [B]14:1 Lit *Joahaz* [C]14:2 Alt Hb tradition, some Hb mss, Syr, Tg, Vg, 2Ch 25:1; other Hb mss, LXX read *Jehoaddin* [D]14:13 Lit *Jehoash* [E]14:13 Lit *400 cubits*

found in the LORD's temple and in the treasuries of the king's palace, and some hostages. Then he returned to Samaria.

15 The rest of the events of Jehoash's reign, along with his accomplishments, his might, and how he waged war against Amaziah king of Judah, are written in the Historical Record of Israel's Kings. 16 Jehoash rested with his fathers, and he was buried in Samaria with the kings of Israel. His son Jeroboam became king in his place.

17 Judah's King Amaziah son of Joash lived 15 years after the death of Israel's King Jehoash son of Jehoahaz. 18 The rest of the events of Amaziah's reign are written in the Historical Record of Judah's Kings. 19 A conspiracy was formed against him in Jerusalem, and he fled to Lachish. However, men were sent after him to Lachish, and they put him to death there. 20 They carried him back on horses, and he was buried in Jerusalem with his fathers in the city of David.

Azariah (14:21-22)

21 Then all the people of Judah took Azariah,[A] who was 16 years old, and made him king in place of his father Amaziah. 22 He rebuilt Elath[B] and restored it to Judah after Amaziah the king rested with his fathers.

King Jeroboam of Israel (14:23-29)

23 In the fifteenth year of Judah's King Amaziah son of Joash, Jeroboam son of Jehoash[C] became king of Israel in Samaria and reigned 41 years. 24 He did what was evil in the LORD's sight. He did not turn away from all the sins Jeroboam son of Nebat had caused Israel to commit.

25 He restored Israel's border from Lebo-hamath as far as the Sea of the •Arabah, according to the word the LORD, the God of Israel, had spoken through His servant, the prophet Jonah son of Amittai from Gath-hepher. 26 For the LORD saw that the affliction of Israel was very bitter. There was no one to help Israel, neither bond nor free. 27 However, the LORD had not said He would blot out the name of Israel under heaven, so He delivered them by the hand of Jeroboam son of Jehoash.[C]

28 The rest of the events of Jeroboam's reign—along with all his accomplishments, the power he had to wage war, and how he recovered for Israel Damascus and Hamath, which had belonged to Judah[D]—are written in the Historical Record of Israel's Kings. 29 Jeroboam rested with his fathers, the kings of Israel. His son Zechariah became king in his place.

King Azariah of Judah (15:1-7)

15 In the twenty-seventh year of Israel's King Jeroboam, Azariah[E] son of Amaziah became king of Judah. 2 He was 16 years old when he became king and reigned 52 years in Jerusalem. His mother's name was Jecoliah, who was from Jerusalem. 3 Azariah did what was right in the LORD's sight just as his father Amaziah had done. 4 Yet the •high places were not taken away; the people continued sacrificing and burning incense on the high places.

5 The LORD afflicted the king, and he had a serious skin disease until the day of his death. He lived in a separate house,[F] while Jotham, the king's son, was over the household governing the people of the land.

6 The rest of the events of Azariah's reign, along with all his accomplishments, are written in the Historical Record of Judah's Kings. 7 Azariah rested with his fathers and was buried with his fathers in the city of David. His son Jotham became king in his place.

Kings of Israel (15:8-31)

Zechariah (15:8-12)

8 In the thirty-eighth year of Judah's King Azariah, Zechariah son of Jeroboam became king over Israel in Samaria for six months. 9 He did what was evil in the LORD's sight as his fathers had done. He did not turn away from the sins Jeroboam

14:15-20 The narrator reminds his readers that **the Historical Record of Israel's Kings** contained the rest of the facts about Jehoash's reign. These two documents possibly served the writer as the historical backbone of the material in Kings. He selected only the details considered to be theologically significant in Israel's history and referred the reader to these court records for more thorough accounts of the kings' political and military accomplishments.

15:1-7 The name **Azariah** designates 25 different individuals in the Old Testament, so it is helpful to remember that Scripture also refers to this king as Uzziah (e.g., 2Ch 26:1; Is 6:1). Like his father and grandfather, Azariah started out well but finished poorly. The only hope for those in exile, as they reflected on the history of their earthly kings, was to look ahead by faith to a king who would both begin and finish his reign perfectly. This king would be the "anointed one," the Christ (Gk, "anointed").

15:8-12 **Zechariah** (Hb, "Yahweh remembers") made no improvements in the spiritual life of Israel (cp. description of the social situation he inherited—Hs 4:1-3; 7:1-7); and he was the last of the **four generations** of Jehu's **sons**, whom God had promised would sit on Israel's **throne**.

[A]**14:21** = Uzziah in 2Ch 26:1 [B]**14:22** = Eloth in 2Ch 26:2 [C]**14:23,27** Lit *Joash* [D]**14:28** Lit *recovered Damascus and for Judah in Israel*; Hb obscure [E]**15:1** = Uzziah in 2Ch 26:3 [F]**15:5** Lit *house of freedom*, or *house of exemption*

15:13-22 Menahem (Hb, "comforter"), who **struck down Shallum**, not only took the throne of Israel by violence but also exercised in **Tiphsah** the sort of brutal and merciless tactics that characterized Hazael's military exploits against Israel and brought tears of sorrow to Elisha's eyes when he foresaw the Aramean king's future (8:11-12; cp. 1Kg 4:24). For **10 years** another evil king reigned, and Israel's demise approached swiftly (2Kg 15:17-18). Paying off **Pul** (the Babylonian throne name of Tiglath-pileser III) only delayed the inevitable. For **20 ounces of silver** (50 shekels) each, the price of an Assyrian slave, **the wealthy men** of Israel temporarily ransomed themselves.

15:27-31 Pekah ruled when **Tiglath-pileser king of Assyria** took the cities of the tribal land of **Naphtali** and carried that region's people into exile.

son of Nebat had caused Israel to
commit.
10 Shallum son of Jabesh conspired
against Zechariah. He struck him
down publicly,[A] killed him, and became king in his place. 11 As for the
rest of the events of Zechariah's
reign, they are written in the Historical Record of Israel's Kings. 12 The
word of the LORD that He spoke to
Jehu was, "Four generations of your
sons will sit on the throne of Israel,"
and it was so.

Shallum (15:13-15)

13 In the thirty-ninth year of Judah's King Uzziah, Shallum son of
Jabesh became king; he reigned in
Samaria a full month. 14 Then Menahem son of Gadi came up from
Tirzah to Samaria and struck down
Shallum son of Jabesh there. He
killed him and became king in his
place. 15 As for the rest of the events
of Shallum's reign, along with the
conspiracy that he formed, they are
written in the Historical Record of
Israel's Kings.

Menahem (15:16-22)

16 At that time, starting from
Tirzah, Menahem attacked Tiphsah,
all who were in it, and its territory.
Because they wouldn't surrender, he
attacked it and ripped open all the
pregnant women.
17 In the thirty-ninth year of Judah's King Azariah, Menahem son
of Gadi became king over Israel and
reigned 10 years in Samaria. 18 He
did what was evil in the LORD's sight.
Throughout his reign, he did not
turn away from the sins Jeroboam
son of Nebat had caused Israel to
commit.
19 Pul[B] king of Assyria invaded the
land, so Menahem gave Pul 75,000
pounds[C] of silver so that Pul would
support him to strengthen his grip
on the kingdom. 20 Then Menahem
exacted 20 ounces[D] of silver from
each of the wealthy men of Israel to
give to the king of Assyria. So the
king of Assyria withdrew and did not
stay there in the land.
21 The rest of the events of Menahem's reign, along with all his accomplishments, are written in the
Historical Record of Israel's Kings.
22 Menahem rested with his fathers,
and his son Pekahiah became king
in his place.

Pekahiah (15:23-26)

23 In the fiftieth year of Judah's
King Azariah, Pekahiah son of Menahem became king over Israel in
Samaria and reigned two years. 24 He
did what was evil in the LORD's sight
and did not turn away from the sins
Jeroboam son of Nebat had caused
Israel to commit.
25 Then his officer, Pekah son of
Remaliah, conspired against him
and struck him down in Samaria at
the citadel of the king's palace —as
well as Argob and Arieh.[E] There were
50 Gileadite men with Pekah. He
killed Pekahiah and became king in
his place.
26 As for the rest of the events of
Pekahiah's reign, along with all his
accomplishments, they are written
in the Historical Record of Israel's
Kings.

Pekah (15:27-31)

27 In the fifty-second year of Judah's King Azariah, Pekah son of
Remaliah became king over Israel in
Samaria and reigned 20 years. 28 He
did what was evil in the LORD's sight.
He did not turn away from the sins
Jeroboam son of Nebat had caused
Israel to commit.
29 In the days of Pekah king of Israel, Tiglath-pileser king of Assyria
came and captured Ijon, Abel-beth-
maacah, Janoah, Kedesh, Hazor,
Gilead, and Galilee—all the land of
Naphtali—and deported the people
to Assyria.
30 Then Hoshea son of Elah organized a conspiracy against Pekah
son of Remaliah. He attacked him,
killed him, and became king in his
place in the twentieth year of Jotham son of Uzziah.
31 As for the rest of the events of
Pekah's reign, along with all his
accomplishments, they are written
in the Historical Record of Israel's
Kings.

[A]**15:10** Some LXX mss read *at Ibleam*; Hb uncertain [B]**15:19** = Tiglath-pileser [C]**15:19** Lit *1,000 talents* [D]**15:20** Lit *50 shekels* [E]**15:25** Hb obscure

Kings of Judah (15:32–16:20)

Jotham (15:32-38)

32 In the second year of Israel's
King Pekah son of Remaliah, Jotham
son of Uzziah became king of Judah.
33 He was 25 years old when he became king and reigned 16 years in
Jerusalem. His mother's name was
Jerusha daughter of Zadok. 34 He did
what was right in the LORD's sight
just as his father Uzziah had done.
35 Yet the high places were not taken
away; the people continued sacrificing and burning incense on the high
places.
Jotham built the Upper Gate of
the LORD's temple. 36 The rest of the
events of Jotham's reign, along with
all his accomplishments, they are
written in the Historical Record of
Judah's Kings. 37 In those days the
LORD began sending Rezin king of
Aram and Pekah son of Remaliah
against Judah. 38 Jotham rested with
his fathers and was buried with his
fathers in the city of his ancestor
David. His son Ahaz became king in
his place.

Ahaz (16:1-20)

16 In the seventeenth year of Pekah son of Remaliah, Ahaz son
of Jotham became king of Judah.
2 Ahaz was 20 years old when he became king and reigned 16 years in
Jerusalem. He did not do what was
right in the sight of the LORD his God
like his ancestor David 3 but walked
in the way of the kings of Israel. He
even made his son pass through the
fire,[A] imitating the detestable practices of the nations the LORD had dispossessed before the Israelites. 4 He
sacrificed and burned incense on the
•high places, on the hills, and under
every green tree.
5 Then Aram's King Rezin and Israel's King Pekah son of Remaliah
came to wage war against Jerusalem. They besieged Ahaz but were
not able to conquer him. 6 At that
time Rezin king of Aram recovered
Elath for Aram and expelled the
Judahites from Elath. Then the Arameans came to Elath, and they live
there until today.
7 So Ahaz sent messengers to
Tiglath-pileser king of Assyria, saying, "I am your servant and your
son. March up and save me from
the power of the king of Aram and
of the king of Israel, who are rising
up against me." 8 Ahaz also took the
silver and gold found in the LORD's
temple and in the treasuries of
the king's palace and sent them to
the king of Assyria as a gift. 9 So the
king of Assyria listened to him and
marched up to Damascus and captured it. He deported its people to
Kir but put Rezin to death.
10 King Ahaz went to Damascus to
meet Tiglath-pileser king of Assyria.
When he saw the altar that was in
Damascus, King Ahaz sent a model
of the altar and complete plans for

[A] 16:3 Either a Canaanite cult practice or child sacrifice

15:32-38 Jotham reigned with his father about four years because of Uzziah's leprosy. During his reign, **Rezin king of Aram** and Israel's king **Pekah** began to antagonize Judah. The writer consistently provided a theological interpretation of historical events. These enemies served as God's instruments of judgment against Judah for her apostasy.

16:1-4 The writer leveled severe indictments against Ahaz. He **made his son pass through** [Hb *'avar*, "dedicate, devote, consecrate," in the sense of offering a child to be burned in dedication to the Canaanite deities Molech or Baal; cp. Lv 18:21; Dt 18:9-10; 2Ch 28:3; Jr 7:30-31; 19:5; 32:35; Ezk 16:21; 20:31] **the fire.** The phrase locating his worship practices **on the hills, and under every green tree** (cp. Dt 12:2; 1Kg 14:23; 2Kg 17:10) indicated the extent to which Israel was explicitly violating God's prohibitions against **imitating** Canaanite religions (16:3-4; cp. Dt 12:29-32).

16:5-20 Ahaz was privileged to be the recipient of some of the most astounding words ever uttered by a prophet—the promise of Immanuel to be born of a virgin (Is 7:14). Isaiah's message offered hope for the exiles and promised salvation for all humanity, but Ahaz spurned the prophecies. Ahaz's evil reign marked a turning point in Judah's history. Still, God was faithful to preserve the Davidic line.

Biblical Womanhood A Mother's Influence

Surveying the various queen-mothers of 2 Kings sparks a crucial question: Did a righteous mother have a definitive influence on the future kings who would later attempt to uphold the worship of Yahweh and do "what was right in the LORD's sight"? Although Joash eventually turned away from the Lord, his overall reign was regarded as good. More notable, however, is the possible heritage of positive spiritual influence begun with Jehoaddan, probably the first of the two wives Jehoiada handpicked for King Joash. Like Jehoaddan, her son's wife Jecoliah was from Jerusalem, strongly suggesting that her parents worshiped Yahweh. Her grandson's wife, Jerusha, was noted not for her city of origin but for her father Zadock, whose name suggests that he may have been from a line of priests or that he served as a priest himself. Each of the three kings following Joash was described as doing right. Ahaz's wife, Abijah, was "the daughter of Zechariah," likely a man of priestly descent. As the mother of the only king credited with being like "his ancestor David," perhaps she was instrumental in shielding the heart of her son Hezekiah from the evil propagated by his father and nurturing in him a zeal for serving the Lord. Furthermore, the influence of these mothers played a pivotal role in the spiritual lives of their respective sons and also had an untold impact on the religious life of the kingdom of Judah. Whether or not recognition is ever given for your influence as a mother, the Lord knows how He will use your faithful training of a son or daughter for the blessing and expansion of His kingdom.

Did a Righteous Mother Make the Difference?

King of Judah	Age at ascent to throne	King's mother	Overall evaluation	References
Joash	7	**Zibiah**, from Beer-sheba; rescued as an infant from assassination and cared for by his aunt **Jehosheba**, wife of Jehoiada the priest	good	2Kg 12:1-3; 2Ch 24:1-2,17-22
Amaziah	25	**Jehoaddan**, from Jerusalem	good	2Kg 14:1-4; 2Ch 25:1,27-28
Azariah (Uzziah)	16	**Jecoliah**, from Jerusalem	good	2Kg 15:1-4; 2Ch 26:1-5,16-21
Jotham	25	**Jerusha**, daughter of Zadok	good	2Kg 15:32-35; 2Ch 27:1-2,6
Ahaz	20	not mentioned	very bad	2Kg 16:1-4; 2Ch 28:1-4,19-25
Hezekiah	25	**Abi** (Abijah), daughter of Zechariah	very good, like David	2Kg 18:1-7 2Ch 24:20-22; 26:5; 29:1-2

its construction to Uriah the priest.
11 Uriah built the altar according
to all the instructions King Ahaz
sent from Damascus. Therefore,
by the time King Ahaz came back
from Damascus, Uriah the priest
had completed it. 12 When the king
came back from Damascus, he saw
the altar. Then he approached the
altar and ascended it. 13 He offered
his •burnt offering and his •grain
offering, poured out his drink offering, and sprinkled the blood of his
•fellowship offerings on the altar.
14 He took the bronze altar that was
before the LORD in front of the temple between his altar and the LORD's
temple, and put it on the north side
of his altar.
15 Then King Ahaz commanded
Uriah the priest, "Offer on the great
altar the morning burnt offering,
the evening grain offering, and the
king's burnt offering and his grain
offering. Also offer the burnt offering of all the people of the land,
their grain offering, and their drink
offerings. Sprinkle on the altar all
the blood of the burnt offering and
all the blood of sacrifice. The bronze
altar will be for me to seek guidance."[A] 16 Uriah the priest did everything King Ahaz commanded.
17 Then King Ahaz cut off the
frames of the water carts[B] and removed the bronze basin from each
of them. He took the reservoir[C] from
the bronze oxen that were under it
and put it on a stone pavement.
18 To satisfy the king of Assyria, he
removed from the LORD's temple the
Sabbath canopy they had built in the
palace, and he closed the outer entrance for the king.
19 The rest of the events of Ahaz's
reign, along with his accomplishments, are written in the Historical Record of Judah's Kings. 20 Ahaz
rested with his fathers and was buried with his fathers in the city of
David, and his son Hezekiah became
king in his place.

King Hoshea of Israel (17:1-2)

17 In the twelfth year of Judah's
King Ahaz, Hoshea son of Elah
became king over Israel in Samaria
and reigned nine years. 2 He did
what was evil in the LORD's sight, but

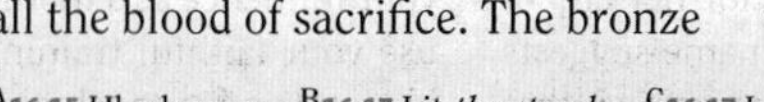
A 16:15 Hb obscure B 16:17 Lit *the stands* C 16:17 Lit *sea*

not like the kings of Israel who preceded him.

Invasion and Deportation at the Hands of Assyria (17:3-6)

3 Shalmaneser king of Assyria attacked him, and Hoshea became his vassal and paid him tribute money. 4 But the king of Assyria discovered Hoshea's conspiracy. He had sent envoys to So king of Egypt and had not paid tribute money to the king of Assyria as in previous years.[A] Therefore the king of Assyria arrested him and put him in prison. 5 Then the king of Assyria invaded the whole land, marched up to Samaria, and besieged it for three years.

6 In the ninth year of Hoshea, the king of Assyria captured Samaria. He deported the Israelites to Assyria and settled them in Halah and by the Habor, Gozan's river, and in the cities of the Medes.

The Fall of Israel (17:7-23)

7 This disaster happened because the people of Israel had sinned against the LORD their God who had brought them out of the land of Egypt from the power of Pharaoh king of Egypt and because they had worshiped[B] other gods. 8 They had lived according to the customs of the nations that the LORD had dispossessed before the Israelites and the customs the kings of Israel had introduced. 9 The Israelites secretly did what was not right[C] against the LORD their God. They built •high places in all their towns from watchtower to fortified city. 10 They set up for themselves sacred pillars and •Asherah poles on every high hill and under every green tree. 11 They burned incense on all the high places just like those nations that the LORD had driven out before them. They did evil things, provoking the LORD. 12 They served idols, although the LORD had told them, "You must not do this." 13 Still, the LORD warned Israel and Judah through every prophet and every seer, saying, "Turn from your evil ways and keep My commands and statutes according to all the law I commanded your ancestors and sent to you through My servants the prophets."

14 But they would not listen. Instead they became obstinate like[D] their ancestors who did not believe the LORD their God. 15 They rejected His statutes and His covenant He had made with their ancestors and the decrees He had given them. They pursued worthless idols and became worthless themselves, following the surrounding nations the LORD had commanded them not to imitate.

16 They abandoned all the commands of the LORD their God. They made cast images for themselves, two calves, and an Asherah pole. They worshiped the whole heavenly •host and served •Baal. 17 They made their sons and daughters pass through the fire and practiced •divination and interpreted omens. They devoted themselves to do what was evil in the LORD's sight and provoked Him.

18 Therefore, the LORD was very angry with Israel, and He removed them from His presence. Only the tribe of Judah remained. 19 Even Judah did not keep the commands of the LORD their God but lived according to the customs Israel had introduced. 20 So the LORD rejected all the descendants of Israel, afflicted them, and handed them over to plunderers until He had banished them from His presence.

21 When the LORD tore Israel from the house of David, Israel made Jeroboam son of Nebat king. Then Jeroboam led Israel away from following the LORD and caused them to commit great sin. 22 The Israelites persisted in all the sins that Jeroboam committed and did not turn away from them. 23 Finally, the LORD removed Israel from His presence just as He had declared through all His servants the prophets. So Israel has been exiled to Assyria from their homeland until today.

The Return of a Priest to Bethel (17:24-28)

24 Then the king of Assyria brought

[A] **17:4** Lit *as year by year* [B] **17:7** Lit *feared* [C] **17:9** Or *Israelites spoke untrue words* [D] **17:14** Lit *they stiffened their neck like the neck of*

17:3-6 Hoshea's conspiring with **Egypt**, the land from which Yahweh had delivered His people, was the last straw—not only for Assyria but also for the Lord (cp. Is 30:1-7; Hs 11:5). The northern kingdom fell to Assyria in 722 B.C., the same year **Shalmaneser** died and was succeeded by Sargon II, who, according to an inscription, claimed to have taken captive nearly 27,290 of the city's inhabitants. Hoshea was among this group, probably the last of those already deported by Shalmaneser and Tiglath-pileser.

17:7-23 The writer's theological purpose was magnified in his blunt explanation for Israel's demise. He laid the guilt at the feet of Israel's people who had **sinned against the LORD**. The writer published Israel's list of offenses to demonstrate why God **removed them from his presence** (v. 18). If you are a parent and can imagine what similar offenses might be committed by your children in contradiction to your authority and despite every effort to teach and direct them in God's ways, you may have a taste of God's righteous anger against Israel's crimes. They had defiantly:

- **rejected** [Hb *ma'as*, "despised, refused," v. 15; cp. 1Sm 15:23; Am 2:4] **His statutes** (Hb *choq*, "appointed law, ordinance or decree; defined limit or boundary"] and scorned the boundaries God had set in place to protect them from evil and to proclaim the goodness of His name;
- rejected **His covenant**, much like a wife who not only violates her wedding vows but also repudiates her husband's unwavering commitment to her;
- rejected **the decrees** [Hb *'edut*, "admonition"] **He had given** (Hb *'ud*, "warned or exhorted solmenly") **them**, like driving into head-on traffic even after seeing the "Wrong Way" signs.

17:24-28 Assyria's policy of deportation both moved the Israelites out of their land and **settled** other conquered peoples in Israel, in **the cities of Samaria. The Lord** manifested His continuing sovereignty over the land by maintaining His expectation that the people living there must **fear** Him. The wording of their message **to the king of Assyria** indicated that they were convinced of the need to worship Yahweh.

17:29-41 Overall, syncretism prevailed. **The people** failed to learn that worship of Yahweh requires the exclusion of all other **gods.** The continued practice of idol worship proved the point that they really did not **fear the Lord** at all.

18:1-8 Hezekiah (Hb, "Yahweh is my strength") was the first king after Solomon to be compared favorably with **his ancestor David** (vv. 1-3). While other kings had instituted religious reforms, Hezekiah was the only king to do something about **the high places**, which had been such a persistent snare to the Israelites. Hezekiah's efforts to restore worship of Yahweh were thorough and uncompromising. He was able to effect such sweeping reforms because his devotion to **the Lord** freed his heart and mind to make clear distinctions between what honored the Lord and what violated His commands.

18:4-8 The **bronze snake** had served its specific purpose during Israel's wilderness wanderings (Nm 21:4-9). Hezekiah contemptuously **called it Nehushtan** (Hb, "brass thing") because the people had been treating it as an object of worship.

18:9-12 The narrator closely correlated the chronological intersections between the kings of Judah and Israel. Reviewing Israel's fall reemphasized the depth of Judah's guilt. Judah had the best possible opportunity to repent. Not only did the nation have a virtuous leader unparalleled since David's reign, but also the consequences of Israel's apostasy were in full view, practically at Judah's doorstep.

>WORD|*study*

17:29 The people of Samaria, used only here in the Old Testament, referred to Israelites who had been loyal to apostate Samaria rather than to Yahweh, whose name dwelt in Jerusalem. Later use of the term in the New Testament referred to a particular religious group also distinguished by geography and mixed ethnicity.

people from Babylon, Cuthah, Avva,
Hamath, and Sepharvaim and settled them in place of the Israelites
in the cities of Samaria. The settlers
took possession of Samaria and lived
in its cities. 25 When they first lived
there, they did not •fear •Yahweh.
So the Lord sent lions among them,
which killed some of them. 26 The
settlers spoke to the king of Assyria,
saying, "The nations that you have
deported and placed in the cities of
Samaria do not know the requirements of the God of the land. Therefore He has sent lions among them
that are killing them because the
people don't know the requirements
of the God of the land."
27 Then the king of Assyria issued
a command: "Send back one of the
priests you deported. Have him go
and live there so he can teach them
the requirements of the God of the
land." 28 So one of the priests they
had deported came and lived in
Bethel, and he began to teach them
how they should fear Yahweh.

The Fear of the Lord Mixed with Idolatry (17:29-41)

29 But the people of each nation
were still making their own gods in
the cities where they lived and putting them in the shrines of the high
places that the people of Samaria
had made. 30 The men of Babylon
made Succoth-benoth, the men of
Cuth made Nergal, the men of Hamath made Ashima, 31 the Avvites
made Nibhaz and Tartak, and the
Sepharvites burned their children in
the fire to Adrammelech and Anam-
melech, the gods of the Sepharvaim.
32 They feared the Lord, but they
also appointed from their number
priests to serve them in the shrines
of the high places. 33 They feared the
Lord, but they also worshiped their
own gods according to the custom
of the nations where they had been
deported from.
34 They are still practicing the former customs to this day. None of
them fear the Lord or observe their
statutes and ordinances, the law
and commandments the Lord commanded the descendants of Jacob.
He had renamed him Israel. 35 The
Lord made a covenant with them
and commanded them, "Do not
fear other gods; do not bow down
to them; do not serve them; do not
sacrifice to them. 36 Instead fear the
Lord, who brought you from the
land of Egypt with great power and
an outstretched arm. You are to bow
down to Him, and you are to sacrifice to Him. 37 You are to be careful
always to observe the statutes, the
ordinances, the law, and the commandments He wrote for you; do
not fear other gods. 38 Do not forget
the covenant that I have made with
you. Do not fear other gods, 39 but
fear the Lord your God, and He will
deliver you from the hand of all your
enemies."
40 However, they would not listen
but continued practicing their former customs. 41 These nations feared
the Lord but also served their idols.
Their children and grandchildren
continue doing as their fathers did
until today.

Judah's King Hezekiah (18:1–19:37)

Obedience (18:1-8)

18 In the third year of Israel's
King Hoshea son of Elah, Hezekiah son of Ahaz became king of
Judah. 2 He was 25 years old when
he became king and reigned 29
years in Jerusalem. His mother's
name was Abi[A] daughter of Zechariah. 3 He did what was right in the

[A] **18:2** = Abijah in 2Ch 29:1

>WORD|*study*

18:7 Hezekiah also prospered (Hb *sakal*, a verb with a wider range of meaning than "prosper,"), which in English tends to connote material success. Hezekiah probably "prospered" materially, but this verb also suggests that he "had insight and comprehension, was prudent, acted wisely or uprightly" in every situation. From a biblical perspective, the two definitions are related, and this detail echoes both the cause-effect promises of Dt 29:9 (cp. Jos 1:7-8; 1Kg 2:3) and the example of King David (1Sm 18:5,14-15,30). Two political examples of how Hezekiah "prospered" politically as the result of his faith are mentioned.

LORD's sight just as his ancestor David had done. [4] He removed the •high places, shattered the sacred pillars, and cut down the •Asherah poles. He broke into pieces the bronze snake that Moses made, for the Israelites burned incense to it up to that time. He called it Nehushtan.[A]

[5] Hezekiah trusted in the LORD God of Israel; not one of the kings of Judah was like him, either before him or after him. [6] He remained faithful to •Yahweh and did not turn from following Him but kept the commands the LORD had commanded Moses.

[7] The LORD was with him, and wherever he went he prospered. He rebelled against the king of Assyria and did not serve him. [8] He defeated the Philistines as far as Gaza and its borders, from watchtower to fortified city.

Review of Israel's Fall (18:9-12)

[9] In the fourth year of King Hezekiah, which was the seventh year of Israel's King Hoshea son of Elah, Shalmaneser king of Assyria marched against Samaria and besieged it. [10] The Assyrians captured it at the end of three years. In the sixth year of Hezekiah, which was the ninth year of Israel's King Hoshea, Samaria was captured. [11] The king of Assyria deported the Israelites to Assyria and put them in Halah and by the Habor, Gozan's river, and in the cities of the Medes, [12] because they did not listen to the voice of the LORD their God but violated His covenant—all He had commanded Moses the servant of the LORD. They did not listen, and they did not obey.

Deliverance from Sennacherib of Assyria (18:13–19:37)

[13] In the fourteenth year of King Hezekiah, Sennacherib king of Assyria attacked all the fortified cities of Judah and captured them. [14] So Hezekiah king of Judah sent word to the king of Assyria at Lachish, saying, "I have done wrong; withdraw from me. Whatever you demand from me, I will pay." The king of Assyria demanded 11 tons[B] of silver and one ton[C] of gold from King Hezekiah of Judah. [15] So Hezekiah gave him all the silver found in the LORD's temple and in the treasuries of the king's palace.

[16] At that time Hezekiah stripped the gold from the doors of the LORD's sanctuary and from the doorposts he had overlaid and gave it to the king of Assyria.

[17] Then the king of Assyria sent the Tartan, the Rab-saris, and the •Rabshakeh, along with a massive army, from Lachish to King Hezekiah at Jerusalem. They advanced and came to Jerusalem, and[D] they took their position by the aqueduct of the upper pool, which is by the highway to the Fuller's Field. [18] Then they called for the king, but Eliakim son of Hilkiah, who was in charge of the palace, Shebnah the court secretary, and Joah son of Asaph, the court historian, came out to them.

[19] Then the Rabshakeh said to them, "Tell Hezekiah this is what the great king, the king of Assyria, says: 'What are you relying on?[E] [20] You think mere words are strategy and strength for war. What are you now relying on so that you have rebelled against me? [21] Look, you are now trusting in Egypt, that splintered reed of a staff that will enter and pierce the hand of anyone who leans on it. This is how Pharaoh king of Egypt is to all who trust in him. [22] Suppose you say to me: We trust in

18:13-37 Although Hezekiah met Assyria's costly price for backing off, the king of Assyria continued threatening Jerusalem and accused Judah of conspiracy with Egypt (vv. 20-21,24). Sennacherib sent three high-ranking military and administrative officials to Jerusalem: **the Tartan**, or "commander-in-chief" (cp. Is 20:1); **the Rab-saris** (lit "chief eunuch"); and **the Rabshakeh** (lit "chief cupbearer"). **The Rabshakeh** spoke for **the king of Assyria**, but his question is one every person must consider: **What** [Hb *mah bittachon*, "what hope, confidence"] **are you relying** [Hb *batach*, "trust"; see v. 5] **on?** Reporting the official words of **the king of Assyria** in the same manner that God announced His message when speaking through the prophets (vv. 19,28-29; cp. Is 7:7; 37:33; Jr 6:22), the Rabshakeh did more than deliver a political threat. His speech foolishly pitted the king of one place and time against the King of the universe and eternity. The diplomat's question launched a verbal assault on Judah's government, illustrating some of the tactics frequently used by God's enemies against those who claim to **trust** Him.

- The Assyrian official *began with a fairly true statement*—to **trust in** Egypt would backfire (2Kg 18:21; cp. 24:7; Ezk 29:6-7).
- Then he *cast doubt* on Judah's worship practices and suggested that Hezekiah himself had restricted worship of **the LORD** (2Kg 18:22). To the pluralistic way of thinking, removing the high places did not make sense because it limited access to the gods.
- The Assyrian *scoffed* at Hezekiah's religious position, which, by reinstituting the exclusivity of worship at the temple in Jerusalem, actually affirmed Yahweh's prescriptions for fearing Him as the holy and omnipotent God rather than as a territorial deity. Therefore, "the Rabshakeh" also *scoffed* at Judah as a powerless nation, which was in no position to resist Assyrian might, and mockingly offered them **a bargain** they could not accept (vv. 23-24).
- He even claimed to be acting under the Lord's authority (v. 25).

Hezekiah's officials requested to negotiate in Aramaic to prevent the people of Jerusalem from understanding their enemy's derisive words spoken in their heart language to divide and conquer by "diplomacy." But the Assyrian official wanted his master's words of terror to be heard by all since, in his view, all would be driven to desperation when Assyria besieged the city (vv. 26-27).

[A]**18:4** = A bronze thing [B]**18:14** Lit *300 talents* [C]**18:14** Lit *30 talents* [D]**18:17** LXX, Syr, Vg; MT reads *and came and* [E]**18:19** Lit *What is this trust which you trust*

19:1-13 The Rabshakeh heard of Sennacherib's change in position to counterattack the **Tirhakah king of Cush** and went to fight with him (v. 8; Is 37:9). When Tirhakah—an important pharaoh of Cushite (Ethiopian) lineage in the 25th Dynasty of Egypt—assumed the throne around 690 B.C., he set out to fight Assyria and later was soundly defeated by Sennacherib's son Esarhaddon.

the LORD our God. Isn't He the One whose high places and altars Hezekiah has removed, saying to Judah and to Jerusalem: You must worship at this altar in Jerusalem?'

23 "So now make a bargain with my master the king of Assyria. I'll give you 2,000 horses if you're able to supply riders for them! 24 How then can you drive back a single officer among the least of my master's servants and trust in Egypt for chariots and for horsemen? 25 Have I attacked this place to destroy it without the LORD's approval? The LORD said to me, 'Attack this land and destroy it.'"

26 Then Eliakim son of Hilkiah, Shebnah, and Joah said to the Rabshakeh, "Please speak to your servants in Aramaic, since we understand it. Don't speak with us in Hebrew[A] within earshot of the people on the wall."

27 But the Rabshakeh said to them, "Has my master sent me only to your master and to you to speak these words? Hasn't he also sent me to the men who sit on the wall, destined with you to eat their own excrement and drink their own urine?"

28 The Rabshakeh stood and called out loudly in Hebrew.[A] Then he spoke: "Hear the word of the great king, the king of Assyria. 29 This is what the king says: 'Don't let Hezekiah deceive you; he can't deliver you from my hand. 30 Don't let Hezekiah persuade you to trust in the LORD by saying: Certainly the LORD will deliver us! This city will not be handed over to the king of Assyria.'

31 "Don't listen to Hezekiah, for this is what the king of Assyria says: 'Make peace[B] with me and surrender to me. Then every one of you may eat from his own vine and his own fig tree, and every one may drink water from his own cistern 32 until I come and take you away to a land like your own land—a land of grain and new wine, a land of bread and vineyards, a land of olive trees and honey—so that you may live and not die. But don't listen to Hezekiah when he misleads you, saying: The LORD will deliver us. 33 Has any of the gods of the nations ever delivered his land from the power of the king of Assyria? 34 Where are the gods of Hamath and Arpad? Where are the gods of Sepharvaim, Hena, and Ivvah?[C] Have they delivered Samaria from my hand? 35 Who among all the gods of the lands has delivered his land from my power? So will the LORD deliver Jerusalem?'"

36 But the people kept silent; they didn't say anything, for the king's command was, "Don't answer him." 37 Then Eliakim son of Hilkiah, who was in charge of the palace, Shebna the court secretary, and Joah son of Asaph, the court historian, came to Hezekiah with their clothes torn and reported to him the words of the Rabshakeh.

19 When King Hezekiah heard their report, he tore his clothes, covered himself with •sackcloth, and went into the LORD's temple. 2 Then he sent Eliakim, who was in charge of the palace, Shebna the court secretary, and the leading priests, who were wearing sackcloth, to the prophet Isaiah son of Amoz. 3 They said to him, "This is what Hezekiah says: 'Today is a day of distress, rebuke, and disgrace, for children have come to the point of birth, but there is no strength to deliver them. 4 Perhaps •Yahweh your God will hear all the words of the •Rabshakeh, whom his master the king of Assyria sent to mock the living God, and will rebuke him for the words that Yahweh your God has heard. Therefore, offer a prayer for the surviving remnant.'"

5 So the servants of King Hezekiah went to Isaiah, 6 who said to them, "Tell your master this, 'The LORD says: Don't be afraid because of the words you have heard, that the king of Assyria's attendants have blasphemed Me with. 7 I am about to put a spirit in him, and he will hear a rumor and return to his own land where I will cause him to fall by the sword.'"

8 When the Rabshakeh heard that the king of Assyria had left Lachish, he returned and found him fighting against Libnah. 9 The king had heard

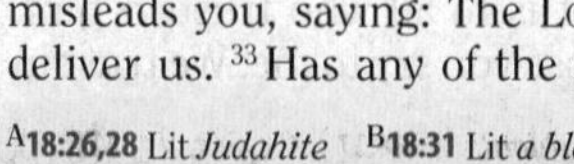

A 18:26,28 Lit *Judahite* B 18:31 Lit *a blessing* C 18:34 Some LXX mss, Old Lat read *Sepharvaim? Where are the gods of the land of Samaria?*

this about Tirhakah king of •Cush:
"Look, he has set out to fight against
you." So he again sent messengers to
Hezekiah, saying, 10 "Say this to Hezekiah king of Judah: 'Don't let your
God, whom you trust, deceive you by
promising that Jerusalem will not be
handed over to the king of Assyria.
11 Look, you have heard what the
kings of Assyria have done to all the
countries: they •completely destroyed
them. Will you be rescued? 12 Did the
gods of the nations that my predecessors destroyed rescue them—nations
such as Gozan, Haran, Rezeph, and
the Edenites in Telassar? 13 Where is
the king of Hamath, the king of Arpad, the king of the city of Sepharvaim, Hena, or Ivvah?'"

14 Hezekiah took the letter from
the hand of the messengers, read it,
then went up to the LORD's temple,
and spread it out before the LORD.
15 Then Hezekiah prayed before the
LORD:

LORD God of Israel who is enthroned above the •cherubim,
You are God—You alone—of
all the kingdoms of the earth.
You made the heavens and the
earth. 16 Listen closely, LORD,
and hear; open Your eyes, LORD,
and see. Hear the words that
Sennacherib has sent to mock
the living God. 17 LORD, it is true
that the kings of Assyria have
devastated the nations and
their lands. 18 They have thrown
their gods into the fire, for they
were not gods but made by human hands—wood and stone.
So they have destroyed them.
19 Now, LORD our God, please
save us from his hand so that
all the kingdoms of the earth
may know that You are the
LORD God—You alone.

20 Then Isaiah son of Amoz sent a
message to Hezekiah: "The LORD, the
God of Israel says: 'I have heard your
prayer to Me about Sennacherib
king of Assyria.' 21 This is the word
the LORD has spoken against him:

Virgin Daughter •Zion
despises you and scorns you:
Daughter Jerusalem
shakes her head
behind your back.[A]
22 Who is it you mocked
and blasphemed?
Against whom have you raised
your voice
and lifted your eyes in pride?
Against the Holy One of Israel!
23 You have mocked the Lord[B]
through[C] your messengers.
You have said:

With my many chariots
I have gone up to the heights
of the mountains,
to the far recesses of Lebanon.
I cut down its tallest cedars,
its choice cypress trees.
I came to its farthest outpost,
its densest forest.
24 I dug wells,
and I drank foreign waters.
I dried up all the streams
of Egypt
with the soles of my feet.

25 Have you not heard?
I designed it long ago;
I planned it in days gone by.
I have now brought it to pass,
and you have crushed
fortified cities
into piles of rubble.
26 Their inhabitants have
become powerless,
dismayed, and ashamed.
They are plants of the field,
tender grass,
grass on the rooftops,
blasted by the east wind.[D]

27 But I know
your sitting down,[E]
your going out
and your coming in,
and your raging against Me.
28 Because your raging
against Me
and your arrogance
have reached My ears,
I will put My hook
in your nose
and My bit in your mouth;
I will make you go back
the way you came.

19:14-19 Well-known for their brutality against those who resisted, the Assyrians intended to make Hezekiah look utterly foolish in refusing to negotiate the surrender of Jerusalem. Hezekiah demonstrated courage rather than cowardice, however, by taking the matter straight to **the LORD**.

19:20-37 In poetic form (i.e., a level of communication more elevated than Assyria's diplomacy of terror), Yahweh's **word** confronted Judah's enemy as a powerful father mocking a criminal who demanded that His daughter be given to him in marriage in order to prevent her being taken forcibly in a devastating war. God's message to Sennacherib was that the Assyrian was out of his league. His **Daughter** (Hb *betulah*, "virgin"), called both **Zion** and **Jerusalem**, would not have him—she held him in contempt and ridiculed him (v. 21). After all, how could she possibly give herself to someone with the audacity to taunt, blaspheme, and foolishly act so high and mighty toward her Father? The Father dismissed Assyria's braggadocio (vv. 23-24). Sennacherib had done nothing except what God Himself had planned (vv. 25-26). The sense of verse 27 is, "I know where you live. I know every move you make, including your angry attacks **against Me**."

[A]**19:21** Lit *behind you* [B]**19:23** Many mss read *LORD* [C]**19:23** Lit *by the hand of* [D]**19:26** DSS; MT reads *blasted before standing grain*; Is 37:27 [E]**19:27** LXX, DSS read *your rising up and your sitting down*; Is 37:28

>WORD|*study*

19:28 The Assyrians often **put** a **hook** through the **nose** or a metal ring through the lips or cheeks of persons taken captive and marched to slavery or another locale, so God used that imagery to assert His sovereign power over Assyria (v. 28; cp. 2Ch 33:11). Use of a bit (Hb *meteg*, "bridle"; cp. Ps 32:9) also represented Yahweh's control over Assyria—like that of a man over his horse—and His authority to **make** Sennacherib go back (Hb *shuv*, "turn, cause to return, reverse") home.

20:12-21 Allowing pride to cloud his judgment, Hezekiah displayed to the pagan dignitary all that would later **be carried off** (Hb *nasa'*, "take away, sweep away") to his guest's **distant** [Hb *rachoq*, "remote, far"] **country** (vv. 13-15). Scripture does not conceal the flaws even of faith's champions. Hezekiah was like his ancestor David both in his zeal for worship of Yahweh alone and in his capitulation to pride's deceit (cp. 1Ch 21; 2Ch 32:24-26).

29 "This will be the sign for you: This year you will eat what grows on its own, and in the second year what grows from that. But in the third year sow and reap, plant vineyards and eat their fruit. 30 The surviving remnant of the house of Israel will again take root downward and bear fruit upward. 31 For a remnant will go out from Jerusalem and survivors, from Mount Zion. The zeal of the LORD of •Hosts will accomplish this.

32 Therefore, this is
what the LORD says
about the king of Assyria:
He will not enter this city
or shoot an arrow there
or come before it with a shield
or build up an assault ramp
against it.
33 He will go back
on the road that he came
and he will not enter this city.
This is
the LORD's declaration.
34 I will defend this city
and rescue it
for My sake and for the sake
of My servant David."

35 That night the angel of the LORD went out and struck down 185,000 in the camp of the Assyrians. When the people got up the next morning—there were all the dead bodies! 36 So Sennacherib king of Assyria broke camp and left. He returned home and lived in Nineveh.

37 One day, while he was worshiping in the temple of his god Nisroch, his sons Adrammelech and Sharezer struck him down with the sword and escaped to the land of Ararat. Then his son Esar-haddon became king in his place.

Isaiah the Prophet (20:1-21)

20 In those days Hezekiah became terminally ill. The prophet Isaiah son of Amoz came and said to him, "This is what the LORD says: 'Put your affairs in order,[A] for you are about to die; you will not recover.'"

2 Then Hezekiah turned his face to the wall and prayed to the LORD, 3 "Please LORD, remember how I have walked before You faithfully and wholeheartedly and have done what pleases You."[B] And Hezekiah wept bitterly.

4 Isaiah had not yet gone out of the inner courtyard when the word of the LORD came to him: 5 "Go back and tell Hezekiah, the leader of My people, 'This is what the LORD God of your ancestor David says: I have heard your prayer; I have seen your tears. Look, I will heal you. On the third day from now you will go up to the LORD's temple. 6 I will add 15 years to your life. I will deliver you and this city from the hand of the king of Assyria. I will defend this city for My sake and for the sake of My servant David.'"

7 Then Isaiah said, "Bring a lump of pressed figs." So they brought it and applied it to his infected skin, and he recovered.

8 Hezekiah had asked Isaiah, "What is the sign that the LORD will heal me and that I will go up to the LORD's temple on the third day?"

9 Isaiah said, "This is the sign to you from the LORD that He will do what He has promised: Should the shadow go ahead 10 steps or go back 10 steps?"

10 Then Hezekiah answered, "It's easy for the shadow to lengthen 10 steps. No, let the shadow go back 10 steps." 11 So Isaiah the prophet called out to the LORD, and He brought the shadow[C] back the 10 steps it had descended on Ahaz's stairway.[D]

12 At that time Merodach-baladan[E] son of Baladan, king of Babylon, sent letters and a gift to Hezekiah since he heard that he had been sick. 13 Hezekiah gave them a hearing and

[A]**20:1** Lit *Command your house* [B]**20:3** Lit *what is good in Your eyes* [C]**20:11** Lit *shadow on the steps* [D]**20:11** Tg, Vg; DSS read *on the steps of Ahaz's roof chamber*; Is 38:8 [E]**20:12** Some Hb mss, LXX, Syr, Tg, some Vg mss, Is 39:1; other Hb mss read *Berodach-baladan*

>WORD|*study*

20:16 The verb will come in **The time will certainly come** (Hb *bo'*, "come in, come upon, come to pass," vv. 16-17)—lit "Behold, the days are coming" or "are to come"—is an active participle used to announce an impending action and assure its certainty. God's decision was final, and His spoken word had already set the events in motion that would culminate in Jerusalem's fall to Babylon under Nebuchadnezzar II (see Jr 27:21-22; 52:17).

showed them his whole treasure house—the silver, the gold, the spices, and the precious oil—and his armory, and everything that was found in his treasuries. There was nothing in his palace and in all his realm that Hezekiah did not show them.

14 Then the prophet Isaiah came to King Hezekiah and asked him, "Where did these men come from and what did they say to you?"

Hezekiah replied, "They came from a distant country, from Babylon."

15 Isaiah asked, "What have they seen in your palace?"

Hezekiah answered, "They have seen everything in my palace. There isn't anything in my treasuries that I didn't show them."

16 Then Isaiah said to Hezekiah, "Hear the word of the LORD: 17 'The time will certainly come when everything in your palace and all that your fathers have stored up until this day will be carried off to Babylon; nothing will be left,' says the LORD. 18 'Some of your descendants who come from you will be taken away, and they will become eunuchs[A] in the palace of the king of Babylon.'"

19 Then Hezekiah said to Isaiah, "The word of the LORD that you have spoken is good," for he thought: Why not, if there will be peace and security during my lifetime?

20 The rest of the events of Hezekiah's reign, along with all his might and how he made the pool and the tunnel and brought water into the city, are written in the Historical Record of Judah's Kings. 21 Hezekiah rested with his fathers, and his son Manasseh became king in his place.

Judah's King Manasseh (21:1-18)

21 Manasseh was 12 years old when he became king and reigned 55 years in Jerusalem. His mother's name was Hephzibah. 2 He did what was evil in the LORD's sight, imitating the detestable practices of the nations that the LORD had dispossessed before the Israelites. 3 He rebuilt the •high places that his father Hezekiah had destroyed and reestablished the altars for •Baal. He made an •Asherah, as King Ahab of Israel had done; he also worshiped the whole heavenly •host and served them. 4 He built altars in the LORD's temple, where the LORD had said, "Jerusalem is where I will put My name." 5 He built altars to the whole heavenly host in both courtyards of the LORD's temple. 6 He made his son pass through the fire, practiced witchcraft and •divination, and consulted mediums and spiritists. He did a great amount of evil in the LORD's sight, provoking Him.

7 Manasseh set up the carved image of Asherah, which he made, in the temple that the LORD had spoken about to David and his son Solomon, "I will establish My name forever in this temple and in Jerusalem, which I have chosen out of all the tribes of Israel. 8 I will never again cause the feet of the Israelites to wander from the land I gave to their ancestors if only they will be careful to do all I have commanded them—the whole law that My servant Moses commanded them." 9 But they did not listen; Manasseh caused them to stray so that they did greater evil than the nations the LORD had destroyed before the Israelites.

10 The LORD spoke through His servants the prophets, saying, 11 "Since Manasseh king of Judah has committed all these detestable

[A]20:18 Or *court officials*

21:1-18 Although Manasseh reigned longer than any other king of Judah, he abandoned his father's "restrictive" monotheism for "religious diversity" (vv. 1-2). A human analogy for his profaning of **the LORD's temple** (vv. 5,7-8) would be for a wife's adulterous lovers to move in while her husband still lived in the house. With each mention of this sin is included what **the LORD** had said **about** placing His **name** in or dwelling in that **temple and in Jerusalem**. Verse 16 portrays **Manasseh** as a murderer of many and suggests that he used violence and terror to assert his power. **The prophets** may have been silenced by such bloodshed (vv. 10,16). Jewish tradition holds that Manasseh had Isaiah sawn in two. God would measure Judah by the same perfect standard He had used on Israel and would find her deficiency to be so grave that He would blot her out. Like the entire structure of a house, the religious system from top to bottom throughout Judah was deemed unsound. God declared that he would **abandon** [Hb *natash*, "forsake, leave, desert" used only here in 2 Kings; cp. Is 2:6; Jr 12:7] **the remnant of** His **inheritance**, i.e., the people whom He chose to be His treasured possession (2Kg 21:14-15; see Dt 32:9).

CHARACTER PROFILE

Huldah A Prophetess of Integrity

Her Background	• The wife of Shallum (22:14) • A prophetess in Jerusalem (22:14)
Her Story	• When King Josiah's anguish over his nation's corporate sin led him immediately to seek God's will, Hilkiah the high priest and others from the royal court consulted Huldah (22:11-14). • She prophesied that God would judge the nation's sin; yet because of Josiah's devout love for God, it would not happen during his reign (22:15-20).
Life Lessons	• Huldah's timely prophetic gifts served God, King Josiah, and her people very well. • Being ready often opens the door for extraordinary service.

things—greater evil than the
Amorites who preceded him had
done—and by means of his idols
has also caused Judah to sin, 12 this
is what the LORD God of Israel says: 'I
am about to bring such disaster on
Jerusalem and Judah that everyone
who hears about it will shudder. 13 I
will stretch over Jerusalem the measuring line used on Samaria and
the mason's level used on the house
of Ahab, and I will wipe Jerusalem
•clean as one wipes a bowl—wiping
it and turning it upside down. 14 I will
abandon the remnant of My inheritance and hand them over to their
enemies. They will become plunder
and spoil to all their enemies, 15 because they have done what is evil
in My sight and have provoked Me
from the day their ancestors came
out of Egypt until today.'"

16 Manasseh also shed so much innocent blood that he filled Jerusalem with it from one end to another.
This was in addition to his sin that
he caused Judah to commit. Consequently, they did what was evil in
the LORD's sight.
17 The rest of the events of Manasseh's reign, along with all his
accomplishments and the sin that
he committed, are written in the
Historical Record of Judah's Kings.
18 Manasseh rested with his fathers
and was buried in the garden of his
own house, the garden of Uzza. His
son Amon became king in his place.

Judah's King Amon (21:19-26)

19 Amon was 22 years old when he
became king and reigned two years
in Jerusalem. His mother's name
was Meshullemeth daughter of Ha-

BIBLICAL WOMANHOOD Feminism and Interpreting Scripture

Interpreting 2 Kings 22:8-20 from a feminist perspective tends to distort the text's purpose. For example, Josiah has been noted for his tender heart, humility, and weeping. To attempt to demonstrate a sort of role reversal by regarding Josiah as a man exhibiting feminine qualities and Huldah, in contrast, as a woman exhibiting masculinity in asserting her authority, is faulty. Josiah's spiritual sensitivity should characterize both men and women. Huldah was clearly God's spokesperson for this occasion, but she neither acted nor spoke independently. She did not assert her own authority but was faithful to proclaim what God spoke through her, delivering a prophetic message that came from "the LORD God of Israel." Both Josiah and Huldah are pictures of responding appropriately to the Lord by seeking, acknowledging, and speaking God's word as authoritative truth to be honored, believed, and obeyed. Scripture does not make an issue of Huldah's gender but has, instead, faithfully recorded this woman's role in the history of Israel. God chose to speak through her to affirm that what Josiah had read was indeed a proclamation of judgment.

ruz; she was from Jotbah. 20 He did what was evil in the LORD's sight as his father Manasseh had done. 21 He walked in all the ways his father had walked; he served the idols his father had served, and he worshiped them. 22 He abandoned the LORD God of his ancestors and did not walk in the way of the LORD.

23 Amon's servants conspired against the king and killed him in his own house. 24 Then the common people[A] executed all those who had conspired against King Amon and made his son Josiah king in his place.

25 The rest of the events of Amon's reign, along with his accomplishments, are written in the Historical Record of Judah's Kings. 26 He was buried in his tomb in the garden of Uzza, and his son Josiah became king in his place.

Judah's King Josiah (22:1–23:30)

Repair of the Temple (22:1-13)

22 Josiah was eight years old when he became king and reigned 31 years in Jerusalem. His mother's name was Jedidah the daughter of Adaiah; she was from Bozkath. 2 He did what was right in the LORD's sight and walked in all the ways of his ancestor David; he did not turn to the right or the left.

3 In the eighteenth year of King Josiah, the king sent the court secretary Shaphan son of Azaliah, son of Meshullam, to the LORD's temple, saying, 4 "Go up to Hilkiah the high priest so that he may total up the money brought into the LORD's temple—the money the doorkeepers have collected from the people. 5 It is to be put into the hands of those doing the work—those who oversee the LORD's temple. They in turn are to give it to the workmen in the LORD's temple to repair the damage. 6 They are to give it to the carpenters, builders, and masons to buy timber and quarried stone to repair the temple. 7 But no accounting is to be required from them for the money put into their hands since they work with integrity."

8 Hilkiah the high priest told Shaphan the court secretary, "I have found the book of the law in the LORD's temple," and he gave the book to Shaphan, who read it.

9 Then Shaphan the court secretary went to the king and reported,[B] "Your servants have emptied out the money that was found in the temple and have put it into the hand of those doing the work—those who oversee the LORD's temple." 10 Then Shaphan the court secretary told the king, "Hilkiah the priest has given me a book," and Shaphan read it in the presence of the king.

11 When the king heard the words of the book of the law, he tore his clothes. 12 Then he commanded Hilkiah the priest, Ahikam son of Shaphan, Achbor son of Micaiah, Shaphan the court secretary, and the king's servant Asaiah: 13 "Go and inquire of the LORD for me, the people, and all Judah about the instruction in this book that has been found. For great is the LORD's wrath that is kindled against us because our ancestors have not obeyed the words of this book in order to do everything written about us."

Huldah's Prophecy (22:14-20)

14 So Hilkiah the priest, Ahikam, Achbor, Shaphan, and Asaiah went to the prophetess Huldah, wife of Shallum son of Tikvah, son of Harhas,[C] keeper of the wardrobe. She lived in Jerusalem in the Second District. They spoke with her.

15 She said to them, "This is what the LORD God of Israel says, 'Say to the man who sent you to Me: 16 This is what the LORD says: I am about to bring disaster on this place and on its inhabitants, fulfilling all the words of the book that the king of Judah has read, 17 because they have abandoned Me and burned incense to other gods in order to provoke Me with all the work of their hands. My wrath will be kindled against this place, and it will not be quenched. 18 Say this to the king of Judah who sent you to inquire of the LORD: This is what the LORD God of Israel says: As for the words that you heard,

22:1-7 Josiah, the last good king of Judah, received the greatest commendation of all the faithful kings in Israel's history (23:25; Jr 22:15-16). His reforms, including rejection of the official Assyrian cult promoted by Manasseh, far exceeded those of any king before him. "The common people" who made him king may have recognized the boy's name as the fulfillment of the prophecy against Jeroboam and the pagan altar where he burned incense to idols (21:24; 1Kg 13:1-3). Since Josiah was forcibly brought to power by the people of Judah who supported the Davidic monarchy and because **he became king** at such a young age, conceivably the 180-degree turn from unbridled idolatry to worship of Yahweh may have begun with the influence of the priest (v. 1).

22:8-13 The scroll in the temple containing **the book of the law** had either been discarded or hidden for safekeeping; in either case, it had been forgotten. Most scholars believe that **Shaphan** read the book of Deuteronomy, if not the entire Pentateuch, to the king.

22:14-20 Although Jeremiah and Zephaniah also prophesied during Josiah's reign, **the prophetess Huldah** as the **wife of Shallum** was a resident of Jerusalem and may have been, therefore, immediately accessible.

[A] **21:24** Lit *the people of the land* [B] **22:9** Lit *and returned a word to the king and said*
[C] **22:14** = Hasrah in 2Ch 34:22

23:1-20 Without a public commitment to reinstitute the covenant, a formal declaration of allegiance to Yahweh alone, any attempt at reform would have been superficial. Although other men under his direction may have done some of the work, the text repeatedly makes Josiah the subject of the actions taken to purge from Judah and even "greater Israel" every vestige of paganism and polytheism. Josiah's uncompromising and aggressive stand against sin models the attitude Christians should have toward sin in their personal lives and in the life of the church. The Holy Spirit residing in those whom Christ has redeemed from sin is the presence of the same Lord who would tolerate no "alternative" religious affections in Israel. Sin does not make a peaceful exit. Note Josiah's deliberate and intentional war against idolatry and its resemblance to the Christian's call to war in Rm 6:1-4.

>WORD|*study*

22:19 The Lord described Josiah's heart as tender (Hb *rakak*, "be contrite, weakened, delicate, soft," v. 19), implying that he was sensitive and responsive to spiritual truth, that his heart was easily broken over sin. The inner response of his heart was manifested in the outward expression of humbling himself **before the Lord**, placing himself in a position to demonstrate submission to the God of Israel.

[19]because your heart was tender
and you humbled yourself before
the LORD when you heard what I
spoke against this place and against
its inhabitants, that they would become a desolation and a curse, and
because you have torn your clothes
and wept before Me, I Myself have
heard you—this is the LORD's declaration— [20]therefore, I will indeed
gather you to your fathers, and you
will be gathered to your grave in
peace. Your eyes will not see all the
disaster that I am bringing on this
place.'"

Then they reported[A] to the king.

Covenant Renewal (23:1-27)

23 So the king sent messengers,
and they gathered all the elders of Jerusalem and Judah to him.
[2]Then the king went to the LORD's
temple with all the men of Judah
and all the inhabitants of Jerusalem,
as well as the priests and the prophets—all the people from the youngest to the oldest. As they listened,
he read all the words of the book of
the covenant that had been found in
the LORD's temple. [3]Next, the king
stood by the pillar[B] and made a covenant in the presence of the LORD
to follow the LORD and to keep His
commands, His decrees, and His
statutes with all his mind and with
all his heart, and to carry out the
words of this covenant that were
written in this book; all the people
agreed to[C] the covenant.

[4]Then the king commanded Hilkiah the high priest and the priests of
the second rank and the doorkeepers to bring out of the LORD's temple
all the articles made for •Baal, •Ashe-
rah, and the whole heavenly •host.
He burned them outside Jerusalem
in the fields of the Kidron and carried their ashes to Bethel. [5]Then he
did away with the idolatrous priests
the kings of Judah had appointed to
burn incense at the •high places in
the cities of Judah and in the areas
surrounding Jerusalem. They had
burned incense to Baal, and to the
sun, moon, constellations, and the
whole heavenly host. [6]He brought
out the Asherah pole from the
LORD's temple to the Kidron Valley
outside Jerusalem. He burned it at
the Kidron Valley, beat it to dust,
and threw its dust on the graves of
the common people.[D] [7]He also tore
down the houses of the male cult
prostitutes that were in the LORD's
temple, in which the women were
weaving tapestries[E] for Asherah.

[8]Then Josiah brought all the
priests from the cities of Judah, and
he defiled the high places from Geba
to Beer-sheba, where the priests
had burned incense. He tore down
the high places of the gates at the
entrance of the •gate of Joshua the
governor of the city (on the left at
the city gate). [9]The priests of the
high places, however, did not come
up to the altar of the LORD in Jerusalem; instead, they ate unleavened
bread with their fellow priests.

[10]He defiled •Topheth, which is in
the Valley of Hinnom, so that no one
could make his son or daughter pass
through the fire to •Molech. [11]He
did away with the horses that the
kings of Judah had dedicated to the
sun. They had been at the entrance
of the LORD's temple in the precincts
by the chamber of Nathan-melech
the court official, and he burned up
the chariots of the sun.

[12]The king tore down the altars
that were on the roof—Ahaz's upper
chamber that the kings of Judah had
made—and the altars that Manasseh
had made in the two courtyards of
the LORD's temple. Then he smashed
them[F] there and threw their dust
into the Kidron Valley. [13]The king

[A]**22:20** Lit *returned a word* [B]**23:3** 2Ch 34:31 reads *platform* [C]**23:3** Lit *people took a stand in*
[D]**23:6** Lit *the sons of the people* [E]**23:7** Or *clothing* [F]**23:12** Text emended; MT reads *he ran from*

also defiled the high places that were
across from Jerusalem, to the south
of the Mount of Destruction, which
King Solomon of Israel had built for
•Ashtoreth, the detestable idol of the
Sidonians; for Chemosh, the detestable idol of Moab; and for •Milcom,
the abomination of the Ammonites.
14 He broke the sacred pillars into
pieces, cut down the Asherah poles,
then filled their places with human
bones.

15 He even tore down the altar at
Bethel and the high place that Jeroboam son of Nebat, who caused
Israel to sin, had made. Then he
burned the high place, crushed it to
dust, and burned the Asherah. 16 As
Josiah turned, he saw the tombs
there on the mountain. He sent
someone to take the bones out of
the tombs, and he burned them on
the altar. He defiled it according
to the word of the LORD proclaimed
by the man of God[A] who proclaimed
these things. 17 Then he said, "What
is this monument I see?"

The men of the city told him, "It
is the tomb of the man of God who
came from Judah and proclaimed
these things that you have done to
the altar at Bethel."

18 So he said, "Let him rest. Don't
let anyone disturb his bones." So
they left his bones undisturbed with
the bones of the prophet who came
from Samaria.

19 Josiah also removed all the
shrines of the high places that were
in the cities of Samaria, which the
kings of Israel had made to provoke
the LORD. Josiah did the same things
to them that he had done at Bethel.
20 He slaughtered on the altars all the
priests of the high places who were
there, and he burned human bones
on the altars. Then he returned to
Jerusalem.

21 The king commanded all the
people, "Keep the •Passover of
the LORD your God as written in the
book of the covenant." 22 No such
Passover had ever been kept from
the time of the judges who judged
Israel through the entire time of the
kings of Israel and Judah. 23 But in
the eighteenth year of King Josiah,
this Passover was observed to the
LORD in Jerusalem.

24 In addition, Josiah removed the
mediums, the spiritists, household
idols, images, and all the detestable
things that were seen in the land
of Judah and in Jerusalem. He did
this in order to carry out the words
of the law that were written in the
book that Hilkiah the priest found
in the LORD's temple. 25 Before him
there was no king like him who
turned to the LORD with all his mind
and with all his heart and with all
his strength according to all the law
of Moses, and no one like him arose
after him.

26 In spite of all that, the LORD
did not turn from the fury of His
great burning anger, which burned
against Judah because of all that
Manasseh had provoked Him with.
27 For the LORD had said, "I will also
remove Judah from My sight just as
I have removed Israel. I will reject
this city Jerusalem, that I have chosen, and the temple about which I
said, 'My name will be there.'"

Confrontation with Pharaoh Neco (23:28-30a)

28 The rest of the events of Josiah's
reign, along with all his accomplishments, are written in the Historical
Record of Judah's Kings. 29 During
his reign, Pharaoh Neco king of

[A] **23:16** LXX adds *when Jeroboam stood by the altar of the feast. And he turned and raised his eyes to the tomb of the man of God*

23:21-23 Sweeping Judah clean of all rival deities paralleled meeting the **Passover** requirement of ridding the territory of all yeast, a symbol of sin (Dt 16:4). The writer lauded this event as unlike any Passover ever kept. Although 2Ch 30 describes at length a similar Passover observance under King Hezekiah, the celebration under Josiah was unique because Josiah apparently removed the idols *before* commanding the Passover celebration whereas *after* Hezekiah's Passover, "all Israel who had attended" proceeded to rid the nation of idols (2Ch 31:1).

23:25-27 In contrast to every king before and after him, Josiah exemplified man's best effort to fulfill **the law**. Nevertheless, even Josiah's righteous reign could not save Judah from God's judgment. However, what God had already determined could not be undone (21:12-15). The contrast between Josiah wholly turning to the Lord and the Lord not turning from His burning anger against Judah's provocative sins illustrates, on a national level, the central truth that man cannot be righteous enough to make up for his sin. God's perfect righteousness demands justice and judgment, which only He can supply. Through the prophets, God sketched portraits of the Redeemer of Israel—His Son Jesus, who alone embodied God's perfect righteousness and fulfilled in His death God's just demand that man's sin be judged (Rm 3:10-12,20-26; 8:1).

23:28-30a Josiah's violent death at the hands of **Pharaoh Neco** may seem inconsistent with the prophetic word given in 22:20 and with Josiah's zeal for Yahweh (23:29). The timing rather than the circumstances of Josiah's death, however, may have fulfilled God's promise to spare him from seeing "all the disaster" to be brought upon Judah (22:20).

>WORD|*study*

23:24-27 Household idols (Hb *teraphim*, "domestic gods, family idols used in household shrines"; cp. 1Sm 15:23; Ezk 21:21; Zch 10:2) is derived from the verbal root *rapha'*, "heal or make healthful," indicating that a family relied on such objects as sources of health, well-being, or blessing, like "good luck charms." Such articles believed to have influence or powers of protection to ward off demons or disease are idolatrous because they usurp God's rightful place as "the LORD who heals" (Hb *YHWH rapha'*, Ex 15:26).

23:34–24:7 Pharaoh Neco placed Josiah's second son **Eliakim** (Hb, "God raises or sets up") on Judah's throne and renamed him **Jehoiakim** (Hb, "Yahweh raises up") to signify his power over the vassal king and perhaps in mockery of Yahweh. During the third year of Jehoiakim's reign, Nebuchadnezzar II besieged Jerusalem and ordered that the city's choice young men—including Daniel—be brought to the Babylonian palace (ca 605 B.C.; Dn 1:1-7). The return of the Jews to Judah around 535 B.C. under Zerubbabel's leadership marked the end of the prophesied 70 years of Babylonian captivity (Ezr 1:1; 3:8; Jr 25:11).

24:8-17 Nebuchadnezzar's eighth year—calculated since he became the army's commander-in-chief—coincides with Jehoiakim's fourth year (v. 12; cp. Jr 25:1).

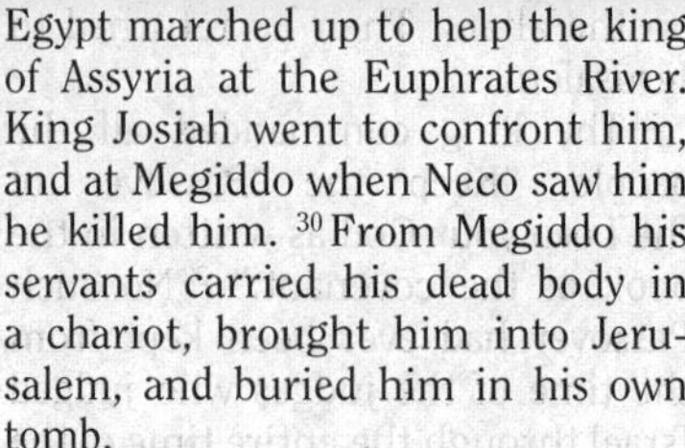

Egypt marched up to help the king
of Assyria at the Euphrates River.
King Josiah went to confront him,
and at Megiddo when Neco saw him
he killed him. [30] From Megiddo his
servants carried his dead body in
a chariot, brought him into Jerusalem, and buried him in his own
tomb.

Judah's King Jehoahaz (23:30b-33)

Then the common people[A] took Jehoahaz son of Josiah, anointed him,
and made him king in place of his
father.
[31] Jehoahaz was 23 years old when
he became king and reigned three
months in Jerusalem. His mother's
name was Hamutal daughter of Jeremiah, from Libnah. [32] He did what
was evil in the LORD's sight just as
his ancestors had done. [33] Pharaoh
Neco imprisoned him at Riblah in
the land of Hamath to keep him
from reigning in Jerusalem, and he
imposed on the land a fine of 7,500
pounds[B] of silver and 75 pounds[C] of
gold.

Judah's King Eliakim/ Jehoiakim (23:34–24:7)

[34] Then Pharaoh Neco made Eliakim son of Josiah king in place of his
father Josiah and changed Eliakim's
name to Jehoiakim. But Neco took
Jehoahaz and went to Egypt, and he
died there. [35] So Jehoiakim gave the
silver and the gold to Pharaoh, but
at Pharaoh's command he taxed the
land to give the money. He exacted
the silver and the gold from the
common people,[A] each man according to his assessment, to give it to
Pharaoh Neco.
[36] Jehoiakim was 25 years old
when he became king and reigned
11 years in Jerusalem. His mother's
name was Zebidah daughter of Pedaiah, from Rumah. [37] He did what
was evil in the LORD's sight just as
his ancestors had done.

24 During Jehoiakim's reign, Nebuchadnezzar king of Babylon
attacked. Jehoiakim became his
vassal for three years, and then he
turned and rebelled against him.
[2] The LORD sent Chaldean, Aramean,
Moabite, and Ammonite raiders
against Jehoiakim. He sent them
against Judah to destroy it, according to the word of the LORD He had
spoken through His servants the
prophets. [3] Indeed, this happened
to Judah at the LORD's command to
remove them from His sight. It was
because of the sins of Manasseh, according to all he had done, [4] and also
because of all the innocent blood he
had shed. He had filled Jerusalem
with innocent blood, and the LORD
would not forgive.
[5] The rest of the events of Jehoiakim's reign, along with all his accomplishments, are written in the
Historical Record of Judah's Kings.
[6] Jehoiakim rested with his fathers,
and his son Jehoiachin became king
in his place.
[7] Now the king of Egypt did not
march out of his land again, for the
king of Babylon took everything that
belonged to the king of Egypt, from
the Brook of Egypt to the Euphrates
River.

Judah's King Jehoiachin (24:8-17)

[8] Jehoiachin was 18 years old when
he became king and reigned three
months in Jerusalem. His mother's
name was Nehushta daughter of
Elnathan, from Jerusalem. [9] He did
what was evil in the LORD's sight as
his father had done.
[10] At that time the servants of
Nebuchadnezzar king of Babylon
marched up to Jerusalem, and the
city came under siege. [11] Then King
Nebuchadnezzar of Babylon came
to the city while his servants were
besieging it. [12] Jehoiachin king of
Judah, along with his mother, his
servants, his commanders, and his
officials, surrendered to the king of
Babylon.
So the king of Babylon took him
captive in the eighth year of his
reign. [13] He also carried off from
there all the treasures of the LORD's
temple and the treasures of the
king's palace, and he cut into pieces
all the gold articles that Solomon
king of Israel had made for the

[A] **23:30,35** Lit *the people of the land* [B] **23:33** Lit *100 talents* [C] **23:33** Lit *one talent*

>WORD|*study*

24:4 Forgive (Hb *salach*, "pardon, be merciful") in the Old Testament is generally used in one of two ways—someone prays for God to **forgive** sin (e.g., Dt 21:8) or God prescribes the basis upon which He will **forgive** sin (e.g., Lv 19:22). Psalm 86:5 declares that God is "ready to forgive," those who call on Him because they recognize that He alone is God. The Lord longed to find anyone in Jerusalem who acted "justly" or sought "to be faithful" so He could "forgive her" (Jr 5:1). Nevertheless, His law required and He provided atonement for sin (e.g., Lv 6:7). Only when the Lord had placed His law "within them" and had written it "on their hearts" could He promise to "forgive" completely and "purify them" (Jr 31:33-34; 33:8; cp. 1Jn 1:9). True repentance is a prerequisite for receiving God's forgiveness (Is 55:7; Jr 36:3).

LORD's sanctuary, just as God had
predicted. 14 Then he deported all
Jerusalem and all the commanders
and all the fighting men, 10,000
captives, and all the craftsmen and
metalsmiths. Except for the poorest
people of the land, no one remained.
15 Nebuchadnezzar deported Jehoiachin to Babylon. Also, he took
the king's mother, the king's wives,
his officials, and the leading men of
the land into exile from Jerusalem
to Babylon. 16 The king of Babylon
also brought captive into Babylon
all 7,000 fighting men and 1,000
craftsmen and metalsmiths—all
strong and fit for war. 17 Then the
king of Babylon made Mattaniah, Jehoiachin's[A] uncle,[B] king in his place
and changed his name to Zedekiah.

Judah's King Mattaniah/ Zedekiah (24:18-20)

18 Zedekiah was 21 years old when
he became king and reigned 11
years in Jerusalem. His mother's
name was Hamutal daughter of Jeremiah, from Libnah. 19 Zedekiah did
what was evil in the LORD's sight just
as Jehoiakim had done. 20 Because
of the LORD's anger, it came to the
point in Jerusalem and Judah that
He finally banished them from His
presence. Then, Zedekiah rebelled
against the king of Babylon.

Judah's Fall to Babylon (25:1-30)

Nebuchadnezzar's Siege of Jerusalem (25:1-7)

25 In the ninth year of Zedekiah's
reign, on the tenth day of the
tenth month, King Nebuchadnezzar
of Babylon advanced against Jerusalem with his entire army. They laid
siege to the city and built a siege
wall against it all around. 2 The city
was under siege until King Zedekiah's eleventh year.
3 By the ninth day of the fourth
month the famine was so severe
in the city that the people of the
land had no food. 4 Then the city
was broken into, and all the warriors fled by night by way of the
gate between the two walls near
the king's garden, even though the
Chaldeans surrounded the city. As
the king made his way along the
route to the •Arabah, 5 the Chaldean
army pursued him and overtook
him in the plains of Jericho. Zedekiah's entire army was scattered
from him. 6 The Chaldeans seized
the king and brought him up to
the king of Babylon at Riblah, and
they passed sentence on him. 7 They
slaughtered Zedekiah's sons before
his eyes. Finally, the king of Babylon blinded Zedekiah, bound him
in bronze chains, and took him to
Babylon.

Destruction of Jerusalem (25:8-21)

8 On the seventh day of the fifth
month, which was the nineteenth
year of Nebuchadnezzar king of
Babylon, Nebuzaradan, the commander of the guards, a servant
of the king of Babylon, entered
Jerusalem. 9 He burned the LORD's
temple, the king's palace, and
all the houses of Jerusalem; he
burned down all the great houses.
10 The whole Chaldean army with
the commander of the guards tore
down the walls surrounding Jerusalem. 11 Nebuzaradan, the commander of the guards, deported the
rest of the people who were left in
the city, the deserters who had defected to the king of Babylon, and
the rest of the population. 12 But
the commander of the guards left

24:17-20 Mattaniah (Hb, "gift of Yahweh"), known primarily as **Zedekiah** (Hb, "Yahweh is righteous," perhaps suggesting, even from Babylon's point of view, that Judah had gotten what she deserved), was Josiah's third son and the brother of Jehoahaz who initially assumed Judah's throne upon the death of their father.

25:1-7 Babylon had intended to allow Judah to retain her geographical identity. The basic furnishings of the temple were left intact, and enough people were left behind to occupy the land. Nevertheless, the empire would not tolerate insurrection, so with Zedekiah's revolt King Nebuchadnezzar determined to make an example of him and **Jerusalem**.

[A]24:17 Lit *his* [B]24:17 = brother in 2Ch 36:10; Jr 37:1

25:22-24 Nebuchadnezzar **appointed Gedaliah** to govern Judah. Gedaliah was the **son of Ahikam**, who had saved the prophet Jeremiah from death (see Jr 26:24), and the grandson of **Shaphan**, who probably served as King Josiah's scribe (cp. 2Kg 22:3; Jr 39:11-14; 40:5,9). A seal bearing the inscription "Gedaliah, who is over the house," has been found at Lachish, 24 miles southwest of Jerusalem. **Mizpah** (Hb, "watchtower"), located on an imposing hill about four miles northwest of Jerusalem, had been the site of past assemblies during national crises (e.g., 1Sm 7:5-16) and the place where Saul was proclaimed king (1Sm 10:17-19). Since Jerusalem was uninhabitable, Mizpah became the seat of government.

25:25-26 Chaldean was synonymous with "Babylonian" since the new dynasty's rulers were from this originally Aramean tribe that became dominant in Mesopotamia during Assyrian rule.

some of the poorest of the land to be vinedressers and farmers.
13 Now the Chaldeans broke into pieces the bronze pillars of the LORD's temple, the water carts, and the bronze reservoir, which were in the LORD's temple, and carried the bronze to Babylon.
14 They also took the pots, the shovels, the wick trimmers, the dishes, and all the bronze articles used in temple service.
15 The commander of the guards took away the firepans and the sprinkling basins—whatever was gold or silver.
16 As for the two pillars, the one reservoir, and the water carts that Solomon had made for the LORD's temple, the weight of the bronze of all these articles was beyond measure.
17 One pillar was 27 feet[A] tall and had a bronze capital on top of it. The capital, encircled by a grating and pomegranates of bronze, stood five feet[B] high. The second pillar was the same, with its own grating.
18 The commander of the guards also took away Seraiah the chief priest, Zephaniah the priest of the second rank, and the three doorkeepers.
19 He took a court official who had been appointed over the warriors from the city; five trusted royal aides[C] found in the city; the secretary of the commander of the army, who enlisted the people of the land for military duty; and 60 men from the common people[D] who were found within the city.
20 Nebuzaradan, the commander of the guards, took them and brought them to the king of Babylon at Riblah.
21 The king of Babylon put them to death at Riblah in the land of Hamath. So Judah went into exile from its land.

Appointment of Gedaliah as Governor (25:22-24)

22 Nebuchadnezzar king of Babylon appointed Gedaliah son of Ahikam, son of Shaphan, over the rest of the people he left in the land of Judah.
23 When all the commanders of the armies—they and their men—heard that the king of Babylon had appointed Gedaliah, they came to Gedaliah at Mizpah. The commanders included Ishmael son of Nethaniah, Johanan son of Kareah, Seraiah son of Tanhumeth the Netophathite, and Jaazaniah son of the Maacathite—they and their men.
24 Gedaliah swore an oath to them and their men, assuring them, "Don't be afraid of the servants of the Chaldeans. Live in the land and serve the king of Babylon, and it will go well for you."

Emigration to Egypt (25:25-26)

25 In the seventh month, however, Ishmael son of Nethaniah, son of Elishama, of the royal family, came with 10 men and struck down Gedaliah, and he died. Also, they killed the Judeans and the Chaldeans who were with him at Mizpah.
26 Then all the people, from the youngest to the oldest, and the commanders of the army, left and went to Egypt, for they were afraid of the Chaldeans.

Jehoiachin's Leadership in Babylon (25:27-30)

27 On the twenty-seventh day of the twelfth month of the thirty-

HARD QUESTION

What is God's purpose for times of exile?

Are you in the midst of an extended trial—a situation that feels like God has placed you in "exile?" Do you long to be free, to laugh again? Have you wondered what God's purpose is through it all? Could it be that God desires intimacy with you and over time has been drawing you closer to Him? Romans 8:28-39 reveals God's purpose for His children—to bring you into a living union with Him and to make you a trophy of His grace for others to see. If you are in Christ, God is for you (Rm 8:31). You will never meet a trial that He has not already purposed to work together for your good (Rm 8:28-30). This was God's redemptive purpose for those in the Babylonian exile (2Kg 25:27-30). God had to strip them of everything in order to cause them to depend on and acknowledge Him alone. Even the harshest circumstances are redemptive for the people of God. Be encouraged that God is sovereign. His providential purposes are being accomplished—for your good and His glory.

[A]25:17 Lit *18 cubits* [B]25:17 Lit *three cubits* [C]25:19 Lit *five men who look on the king's face* [D]25:19 Lit *the people of the land*

seventh year of the exile of Judah's King Jehoiachin, in the year Evil-merodach became king of Babylon, he pardoned King Jehoiachin of Judah and released him from prison.
28 He spoke kindly to him and set his throne over the thrones of the kings who were with him in Babylon.
29 So Jehoiachin changed his prison clothes, and he dined regularly in the presence of the king of Babylon for the rest of his life.
30 As for his allowance, a regular allowance was given to him by the king, a portion for each day, for the rest of his life.

25:27-30 After 37 years in captivity, **Jehoiachin** was released from prison, having been pardoned by Nebuchadnezzar's successor, **Evil-merodach** (Bab *Awil-Marduk*, "Man of Marduk," the chief god of the Babylonian pantheon). The kind treatment and favor shown to the former king of Judah was a sign of God's mercy. Thus, a ray of hope brings the book of 2 Kings to its conclusion.

---

2 KINGS... WRITTEN ON MY *Heart*

While you and I may never be political rulers or authoritative monarchs, like the Israelite kings of old, we are faced with the same choice. Will you be a woman who walks in the ways of your spiritual forefather, David, ridding your life of all idolatry and tearing down the high places that vie for the Lord's devotion, affection, and worship? Or, will you succumb to the deceptive self-destruction of attempting to worship God your way, comfortably accommodating the infiltration of the culture? May we as modern "Josiahs" humble our hearts, grieve over our sins, and do what is "right in the LORD's sight."

1 Chronicles

Timeline	1010 BC	1003 BC	1002 BC	1000 BC
World Events Biblical Events	With the death of Saul, David becomes king of Judah.	David becomes king of Israel, and rules over a united kingdom.	David captures Jerusalem from the Jebusites.	David moves the ark of the covenant to Jerusalem.

"The task is great, because the temple will not be for man but for the Lord God" (29:1b).

Who wrote 1 Chronicles?

The authorship of Chronicles traditionally, and with persuasive evidence, is attributed to Ezra the scribe. Because the writer's identity is uncertain, most scholars refer to the author as "the Chronicler."

Who were the recipients?

The Jews returning from exile were the immediate audience, the writer had "all Israel" in view, including not only the remnant but also those who had escaped exile and those who were still scattered abroad.

When was 1 Chronicles written?

Likely near the end of the fifth century B.C.

Where did it happen?

While the events recorded in Chronicles occurred during the nation's monarchy period, the books were written for the Jews returning from exile. For a Jew born and raised in Babylon, far away from Israel, returning home meant facing some dramatic changes. Not only did the postexilic community struggle to reestablish order and revitalize their culture, but they also faced primitive living conditions (Neh 2:17) and a food shortage (Hg 1:11). Spiritual renewal was a high priority, especially for those in positions of leadership. The need was great for the people of Israel both to reclaim their national identity and to renew their spiritual identity as stewards of God's promises.

What is 1 Chronicles about?

- Restoring the identity and unity of "all Israel" as God's chosen people through the Passover and temple worship
- Affirming God's covenant with David and his descendants
- Depicting the correlation between the hearts of the king and the people and the manner in which they treated the temple.

Why should women read 1 Chronicles?

Surveying the genealogies from Adam to David leads to an awe-filled acknowledgement of God's faithfulness. The very One who created the first man in His image (1:1), preserved Noah through the flood (1:4), called out Abraham to be the father of a chosen race (1:27), and raised up a king after His own heart (2:15) is the same One who would later descend into His own story as a man, the Messiah Jesus Christ (Mt 1:1). Despite the systemic unfaithfulness of Israel generation after generation, God was true to His Word and purchased the redemption of mankind at the cross. Far from merely re-telling the historical events recorded in 1 and 2 Kings, the book of 1 Chronicles highlights the enduring faithfulness of the covenant-keeping Yahweh God.

How do you read 1 Chronicles?

Chronicles was written primarily as a historical narrative—history in story form. However, the reader first encounters nine chapters of genealogical records, effectively tracing Israel's history back to Adam and forward to the remnant of "all Israel" who had returned from exile—the writer's contemporary audience.

Outline

I. Genealogies (1:1–10:14)
   A. Adam to the Nation of Israel (1:1–2:2)
   B. Judah's Descendants (2:3-55)
   C. David's Descendants (3:1-24)
   D. More Descendants of Judah (4:1-23)
   E. Simeon's Descendants (4:24-43)
   F. The Tribes Taken into Exile by Assyria (5:1-26)
   G. The Levites (6:1-81)
   H. Issachar's Descendants (7:1-5)
   I. Benjamin's Descendants (7:6-12)
   J. The Descendants of Naphtali, Manasseh, Ephraim, and Asher (7:13-40)
   K. More Descendants of Benjamin (8:1-40)
   L. Judah After the Babylonian Exile (9:1-34)
   M. Saul (9:35–10:14)

II. The Reign of King David (11:1–22:1)
   A. The Establishment of David's Reign (11:1-9)
   B. David's Military Might (11:10–12:40)
   C. The Ark of God (13:1–16:43)
   D. The Lord's Covenant with David (17:1-27)
   E. Military Campaigns (18:1–20:8)
   F. A Military Census (21:1–22:1)

III. The Preparations for the Temple (22:2–29:30)
   A. Building Materials and Charge to Solomon (22:2–23:1)
   B. The Levites and Aaron's Sons (23:2–26:32)
   C. Military Divisions and Counselors (27:1-34)
   D. The Commissioning of Solomon (28:1-21)
   E. Contributions from the People (29:1-9)
   F. Worship (29:10-30)

995 BC	972 BC	972 BC	970 BC	970 BC
God makes a covenant with David.	David begins gathering materials for building the temple.	David and Solomon rule as co-regents.	David dies after reigning 40 years as king of Judah and Israel.	Solomon is anointed king of the united kingdom.

Adam to the Nation of Israel (1:1–2:2)

Adam to Isaac (1:1-34a)

1 Adam, Seth, Enosh,
2 Kenan, Mahalalel, Jared,
3 Enoch, Methuselah, Lamech,
4 Noah, Noah's sons:[A]
Shem, Ham, and Japheth.

5 Japheth's sons: Gomer,
Magog, Madai, Javan, Tubal,
Meshech, and Tiras.
6 Gomer's sons: Ashkenaz,
Riphath,[B] and Togarmah.
7 Javan's sons: Elishah,
Tarshish, Kittim, and
Rodanim.[C]

8 Ham's sons: Cush,
Mizraim,[D] Put, and Canaan.
9 Cush's sons: Seba, Havilah,
Sabta, Raama, and Sabteca.
Raama's sons: Sheba and
Dedan.
10 Cush fathered Nimrod, who
was the first to become a
great warrior on earth.
11 Mizraim fathered Ludim,
Anamim, Lehabim,
Naphtuhim, 12 Pathrusim,
Casluhim (the Philistines
came from them), and
Caphtorim.
13 Canaan fathered Sidon
as his firstborn, then Heth,
14 the Jebusites, Amorites,
Girgashites, 15 Hivites,
Arkites, Sinites, 16 Arvadites,
Zemarites, and Hamathites.

17 Shem's sons: Elam, Asshur,
Arpachshad, Lud, Aram, Uz,
Hul, Gether, and Meshech.
18 Arpachshad fathered
Shelah, and Shelah fathered
Eber. 19 Two sons were born
to Eber. One of them was
named Peleg[E] because the
earth was divided during his
lifetime, and the name of his
brother was Joktan. 20 Joktan
fathered Almodad, Sheleph,
Hazarmaveth, Jerah,
21 Hadoram, Uzal, Diklah,
22 Ebal, Abimael, Sheba,
23 Ophir, Havilah, and Jobab.
All of these were Joktan's
sons.

24 Shem, Arpachshad, Shelah,
25 Eber, Peleg, Reu,
26 Serug, Nahor, Terah,
27 and Abram (that is,
Abraham).

28 Abraham's sons: Isaac
and Ishmael.

29 These are their family
records: Nebaioth, Ishmael's
firstborn, Kedar, Adbeel,
Mibsam, 30 Mishma, Dumah,
Massa, Hadad, Tema, 31 Jetur,
Naphish, and Kedemah.
These were Ishmael's sons.

32 The sons born to Keturah,
Abraham's concubine:
Zimran, Jokshan, Medan,
Midian, Ishbak, and Shuah.
Jokshan's sons: Sheba and
Dedan.
33 Midian's sons: Ephah,
Epher, Hanoch, Abida, and
Eldaah.
All of these were Keturah's
sons.

34 Abraham fathered Isaac.

Esau's Descendants, the Edomites (1:34b-54)

Isaac's sons: Esau and Israel.

A1:4 LXX; MT omits *Noah's sons* B1:6 Some Hb mss, LXX, Vg; other Hb mss read *Diphath*; Gn 10:3 C1:7 Some Hb mss, Syr read *Dodanim*; Gn 10:4 D1:8 = Egypt E1:19 = Division

Title: The postexilic remnant of Israel needed confirmation that they had remaining roots grounded in God's covenantal promises to King David. The Chronicler provided this affirmation by taking them back to the garden of Eden and reminding them of God's creative purpose. The genealogy—beginning with mankind and narrowing to focus only on the unfolding of God's redemptive purpose—would provide proof that the Davidic line remained unbroken and, therefore, that God's promised Messiah was still coming.

1:1 The author assumed the historicity of the book of Genesis, from which he borrowed genealogical material (Gn 5; 10-11; 25; 36). Duplication of the Genesis records emphasized that God had a plan from the very beginning.

1:1 Seth (Hb, "compensation") is listed as Adam's son, but Cain is mentioned nowhere. Although Cain was Adam's firstborn son, he forfeited God's blessing when he murdered his brother Abel (Gn 4:1-24). Similar shifts in birthrights run throughout the genealogy and highlight the principle of divine intervention.

1:5-16 Japheth's sons were progenitors of the Indo-Europeans (1Ch 1:5-7; cp. Gn 10:2-5), and **Ham's sons** (1Ch 1:8-16; cp. Gn 10:6-20) were ancestors of the peoples of **Cush** (Ethiopia and Arabia), **Mizraim** (Egypt), **Put** (Libya), **Canaan**, and, through **Nimrod** (1Ch 1:10; cp. Gn 10:8-10), the Assyrian and Babylonian civilizations.

1:1-34a That all people can trace their ancestry back to **Adam** emphasizes that no nation is essentially superior to another (cp. Dt 7:7; 9:4-6). Through Adam all have sinned and all are in need of atonement before they are able to stand before God (Rm 5:12; cp. 3:9-12,23,29-30; 1Co 15:22). Because all peoples are traced back to Adam and Eve, all thus have a responsibility to the one God, despite their worship of anything else. While Israel claimed a unique relationship with Yahweh as their God, all other nations were, and are still, accountable to Him as their rightful Lord.

1:35 Reuel may have been the forefather of Moses' father-in-law, a priest of Midian who is also called Reuel (Ex 2:18; Nm 10:29).

1:38-54 The exiles working to reestablish the nation of Israel in keeping with the Law would be guided in part by an injunction to prohibit anyone "of illegitimate birth" from entering "the Lord's assembly" (Dt 23:2) and by the prophetic judgments against Edom for their hostility toward Israel (e.g., Ezk 25:12-14; 35:1-15). However, the prohibition was mitigated by a command not to "despise an Edomite, because he is your brother" and a provision that their third generation should be allowed in the "assembly" (Dt 23:7-8). **Seir's sons** are probably listed because of the intermarriage between his and Esau's families, whose descendants are noted as the **kings** and **chiefs** of **Edom** (Gn 36:9,43), the Horite clans living in Edom before Israel was ruled by a monarchy (cp. Gn 36:20-30). The "land of Seir" was synonymous with "Edom," another name for Esau (Gn 25:30; 32:3; 36:8-9,43; Dt 2:4-6,12; Ezk 35).

1:43 Another son or descendant of **Beor** was Balaam, from whom the elders of Moab and Midian tried to procure a curse against Israel (Nm 22–24; Dt 23:4-5). Balaam also prophesied against Amalek (Nm 24:20-24).

2:1-2 The writer's inclusion of all 12 sons supports the book's view that "all Israel" was comprised of all people related genealogically to these 12 forefathers, regardless of the tribal unit to which they had belonged—whether the northern kingdom of Israel dispersed by the Assyrians or the southern kingdom of Judah exiled by the Babylonians and released by the Persians.

2:3-55 The Chronicler demonstrates that God's plan was working preeminently in and through Judah. Although some exiles returning to Jerusalem were from other tribes, for them to recognize and identify with the lineage of David, the king to whom God had promised an enduring kingdom (2Sm 7:16), was essential. Judah was placed first in the order of discussion, which conveyed Judah's exalted position among the 12 tribes (1Ch 2:3). This was a departure from the order of names announced in 2:1.

2:3-8 The Chronicler had a specific message for the restoration community: The 12 tribes were still central to God's plan (2:1-2), and Judah had been elected as the tribe through whom David would be chosen as king (cp. 2:13). Scripture does not gloss over the negative aspects of Israel's history. When the exiles confronted their sin

>WORD|*study*

2:1 Sons (Hb *bēn*) does not always refer to parents' immediate descendants. The obvious gaps in these genealogical records reflect the writer's frequent use of the broader definition "descendant."

35 Esau's sons: Eliphaz, Reuel,
Jeush, Jalam, and Korah.
36 Eliphaz's sons: Teman,
Omar, Zephi, Gatam, and
Kenaz; and by Timna,
Amalek.[A]
37 Reuel's sons: Nahath,
Zerah, Shammah, and
Mizzah.

38 Seir's sons: Lotan, Shobal,
Zibeon, Anah, Dishon, Ezer,
and Dishan.
39 Lotan's sons: Hori and
Homam. Timna was Lotan's
sister.
40 Shobal's sons: Alian,
Manahath, Ebal, Shephi, and
Onam.
Zibeon's sons: Aiah and Anah.
41 Anah's son: Dishon.
Dishon's sons: Hamran,
Eshban, Ithran, and Cheran.
42 Ezer's sons: Bilhan, Zaavan,
and Jaakan.
Dishan's sons: Uz and Aran.

43 These were the kings who ruled
in the land of Edom before any king
ruled over the Israelites: Bela son
of Beor. Bela's town was named
Dinhabah. 44 When Bela died, Jobab
son of Zerah from Bozrah ruled
in his place. 45 When Jobab died,
Husham from the land of the Temanites ruled in his place. 46 When
Husham died, Hadad son of Bedad,
who defeated Midian in the country
of Moab, ruled in his place. Hadad's
town was named Avith. 47 When Hadad died, Samlah from Masrekah
ruled in his place. 48 When Samlah
died, Shaul from Rehoboth on the
Euphrates River ruled in his place.
49 When Shaul died, Baal-hanan son
of Achbor ruled in his place. 50 When
Baal-hanan died, Hadad ruled in his
place. Hadad's city was named Pai,
and his wife's name was Mehetabel
daughter of Matred, daughter of
Me-zahab. 51 Then Hadad died.

Edom's chiefs: Timna, Alvah,[B]
Jetheth, 52 Oholibamah, Elah,
Pinon, 53 Kenaz, Teman,
Mibzar, 54 Magdiel, and Iram.
These were Edom's chiefs.

Jacob's Descendants, the Israelites (2:1-2)

2 These were Israel's sons:
Reuben, Simeon, Levi,
Judah, Issachar, Zebulun,
2 Dan, Joseph, Benjamin,
Naphtali, Gad, and Asher.

Judah's Descendants (2:3-55)

3 Judah's sons: Er, Onan, and
Shelah. These three were born
to him by Bath-shua the Canaanite woman. Er, Judah's
firstborn, was evil in the Lord's
sight, so He put him to death.
4 Judah's daughter-in-law Tamar bore Perez and Zerah to
him. Judah had five sons in all.

5 Perez's sons: Hezron and
Hamul.
6 Zerah's sons: Zimri,
Ethan, Heman, Calcol, and
Dara[C]—five in all.
7 Carmi's son: Achar,[D] who
brought trouble on Israel
when he was unfaithful by
taking the things •set apart
for destruction.
8 Ethan's son: Azariah.
9 Hezron's sons, who were
born to him: Jerahmeel,
Ram, and Chelubai.[E]

10 Ram fathered Amminadab,
and Amminadab fathered
Nahshon, a leader of Judah's
descendants.
11 Nahshon fathered Salma,
and Salma fathered Boaz.
12 Boaz fathered Obed, and
Obed fathered Jesse.

[A]**1:36** LXX; MT reads *and Timna and Amalek*; Gn 36:12 [B]**1:51** Alt Hb tradition reads *Aliah* [C]**2:6** Some Hb mss, LXX, Syr, Tg, Vg read *Darda*; 1Kg 4:31 [D]**2:7** = Trouble; Achan in Jos 7:1,16-26 [E]**2:9** = Caleb

13 Jesse fathered Eliab, his
firstborn; Abinadab was
born second, Shimea third,
14 Nethanel fourth, Raddai
fifth, 15 Ozem sixth, and
David seventh. 16 Their sisters
were Zeruiah and Abigail.
Zeruiah's three sons: Abishai,
Joab, and Asahel. 17 Amasa's
mother was Abigail, and
his father was Jether the
Ishmaelite.

18 Caleb son of Hezron had children by his wife Azubah and by
Jerioth. These were Azubah's
sons: Jesher, Shobab, and Ar-
don. 19 When Azubah died,
Caleb married Ephrath, and
she bore Hur to him. 20 Hur
fathered Uri, and Uri fathered
Bezalel. 21 After this, Hezron
slept with the daughter of
Machir the father of Gilead.
Hezron had married her when
he was 60 years old, and she
bore Segub to him. 22 Segub
fathered Jair, who possessed
23 towns in the land of Gilead. 23 But Geshur and Aram
captured[A] Jair's Villages[B] along
with Kenath and its villag-
es—60 towns. All these were
the sons of Machir father of
Gilead. 24 After Hezron's death
in Caleb-ephrathah, his wife
Abijah bore Ashhur to him. He
was the father of Tekoa.

25 The sons of Jerahmeel,
Hezron's firstborn: Ram,
his firstborn, Bunah,
Oren, Ozem, and Ahijah.
26 Jerahmeel had another wife
named Atarah, who was the
mother of Onam.
27 The sons of Ram,
Jerahmeel's firstborn: Maaz,
Jamin, and Eker.
28 Onam's sons: Shammai and
Jada.
Shammai's sons: Nadab and
Abishur. 29 Abishur's wife was
named Abihail, who bore
Ahban and Molid to him.
30 Nadab's sons: Seled and
Appaim. Seled died without
children.
31 Appaim's son: Ishi.
Ishi's son: Sheshan.
Sheshan's descendant: Ahlai.
32 The sons of Jada, brother
of Shammai: Jether and
Jonathan. Jether died without
children.
33 Jonathan's sons: Peleth
and Zaza. These were the
descendants of Jerahmeel.
34 Sheshan had no sons, only
daughters, but he did have an
Egyptian servant whose name
was Jarha. 35 Sheshan gave his
daughter in marriage to his
servant Jarha, and she bore
Attai to him.

36 Attai fathered Nathan, and
Nathan fathered Zabad.
37 Zabad fathered Ephlal, and
Ephlal fathered Obed.
38 Obed fathered Jehu, and
Jehu fathered Azariah.
39 Azariah fathered Helez, and
Helez fathered Elasah.
40 Elasah fathered Sismai, and
Sismai fathered Shallum.
41 Shallum fathered Jekamiah,
and Jekamiah fathered
Elishama.

42 The sons of Caleb brother
of Jerahmeel: Mesha, his
firstborn, fathered Ziph, and
Mareshah, his second son,[C]
fathered Hebron.
43 Hebron's sons: Korah,
Tappuah, Rekem, and Shema.

A **2:23** Lit *took from them* B **2:23** Or *captured Havvoth-jair* C **2:42** Lit *and the sons of Mareshah*

>WORD|*study*

2:10 In this section, the use of the verb fathered (Hb *yalad*, "beget, become the father of") does not necessarily signify the direct relationship of father and son but that of founder or head to the cities or regions named after them. For example, **Ziph**, **Mareshah**, and **Tappuah** (vv. 42-43; Jos 15:44,53,55) were all cities allocated in the time of Joshua. This section must have been clearly understood and valued by the readers of the Chronicler's day, for the information covered geographical and societal detail, as well as family history that would have helped them reclaim land that was rightfully theirs.

of intermarrying with Canaanites and other pagan peoples (Ezr 9–10), they could hope in God's sovereignty and His faithfulness to the covenant demonstrated by the fact that Judah's sin could not derail His plan.

2:10-24 Even though **Ram** apparently was not Hezron's firstborn (see v. 9), the writer lists Ram's descendants before those of his brothers because of the significance of this segment of the genealogy—it provides the lineage of King David (cp. Mt 1:1-6, in which "Aram" = "Ram" of 1 Chronicles). Mentioned here for the first time in 1 Chronicles, **David** is listed among his brothers as Jesse's **seventh** son (v. 13). Though David was regarded as the youngest of Jesse's eight sons in 1Sm 16:10 and 17:12-14, the Chronicler probably selected the number seven to mark him as the anointed. As today "the seventh heaven" is used to reference the utmost or highest level of heaven, so "the seventh son" was likely a means of expressing "the most important son."

2:16-17 Apart from their own military prowess and exploits, **Abishai, Joab, and Asahel** figured prominently in the Davidic kingdom because they were also the king's nephews, the sons of David's sister **Zeruiah**. Similarly, David's son Absalom, when attempting to usurp the throne, appointed his cousin Amasa—the son of David's sister **Abigail**—as commander of his army.

2:18-25 This **Caleb** (1Ch 2:18-20; "Chelubai," v. 9; "brother of Jerahmeel," v. 42) should not be confused with the man who later entered the promised land (see 4:15; cp. Nm 14:30; Jos 14:6-13)); rather, Caleb son of Jephunneh and his daughter Achsah may have been descendants of Hezron's son (cp. 1Ch 2:49; Jos 15:16-17; Jdg 3:9; see note on 1Ch 4:11-20).

Before continuing to outline the descendants of **Jerahmeel**, (1Ch 2:25-35) and Caleb (vv. 42-50), the writer inserted significant data resulting from the late-in-life marriage of their father to Abijah, **the daughter of Machir**—the eldest son of Manasseh and **the father of Gilead**, after whom an entire region was named (1Ch 2:21; 7:14-17; cp. Nm 26:29; Dt 3:15; Jos 17:1). Tracing Jair's descent through his paternal grandmother (Manasseh's daughter Machir, the mother of Jair's father Segub) rather than his father **Hezron** demonstrated the marital link between Manasseh and Judah.

2:26 The writer's pointed inclusion of information about **another wife** suggests that the cultural norm was a man's having one wife.

3:1-9 David is the key figure among all the descendants of Judah. First Chronicles 2:3-17 traced his lineage back to Judah; this genealogy charts his descendants. Significantly, each son is identified by the name of his mother.

3:10-24 All of **Solomon's** descendants who ascended the throne of Judah after the kingdom divided are listed chronologically (vv. 10-16). The Chronicler's omission of Athaliah, the queen who reigned between Ahaziah and his son Joash, is no surprise since she was not of Davidic lineage (2Kg 8:26; 11:1-16). Once again this confirms the message that only descendants of David can legitimately hold the throne, hinting at the importance of the use of "Son of David" in the New Testament (Mt 1:1; 9:27; Lk 18:38).

3:19-20 Pedaiah may have been Zerubbabel's biological father in order to provide a legal heir for his brother Shealtiel. Both New Testament genealogies tracing the lineage of Jesus list Shealtiel as the father of **Zerubbabel** (Mt 1:12; Lk 3:27). One theory for harmonizing the genealogies of Jesus found in Matthew (who traced the Messiah's lineage through Solomon) with the one in Luke (who traced the lineage through David's son Nathan) notes that Lk 3:27 identifies Shealtiel as the "son of Neri" and suggests that Shealtiel's mother may have been a daughter of Jeconiah and his father a man whose name or whose father's name was Neri (Hb *Neriah*, "lamp of Yahweh").

44 Shema fathered Raham,
who fathered Jorkeam, and
Rekem fathered Shammai.
45 Shammai's son was Maon,
and Maon fathered Beth-zur.
46 Caleb's concubine Ephah
was the mother of Haran,
Moza, and Gazez. Haran
fathered Gazez.
47 Jahdai's sons: Regem,
Jotham, Geshan, Pelet,
Ephah, and Shaaph.
48 Caleb's concubine Maacah
was the mother of Sheber
and Tirhanah. 49 She was
also the mother of Shaaph,
Madmannah's father, and
of Sheva, the father of
Machbenah and Gibea. Caleb's
daughter was Achsah.
50 These were Caleb's
descendants.

The sons of Hur, Ephrathah's
firstborn:
Shobal fathered Kiriath-
jearim;
51 Salma fathered Bethlehem,
and Hareph fathered Beth-
gader.

52 These were the descendants
of Shobal the father of Kiriath-
jearim: Haroeh, half of the Ma-
nahathites,[A] 53 and the families
of Kiriath-jearim—the Ithrites,
Puthites, Shumathites, and
Mishraites. The Zorathites and
Eshtaolites descended from
these.

54 Salma's sons: Bethlehem,
the Netophathites, Atroth-beth-
joab, and half of the Manahath-
ites, the Zorites, 55 and the
families of scribes who lived in
Jabez—the Tirathites, Shime-
athites, and Sucathites. These
are the Kenites who came
from Hammath, the father of
Rechab's family.

David's Descendants (3:1-24)

3 These were David's sons who
were born to him in Hebron:
Amnon was the firstborn, by
Ahinoam of Jezreel;
Daniel was born second, by
Abigail of Carmel;
2 Absalom son of Maacah,
daughter of King Talmai of
Geshur, was third;
Adonijah son of Haggith was
fourth;
3 Shephatiah, by Abital, was
fifth;
and Ithream, by David's wife
Eglah, was sixth.
4 Six sons were born to David
in Hebron, where he ruled
seven years and six months,
and he ruled in Jerusalem 33
years.
5 These sons were born to him
in Jerusalem:
Shimea, Shobab, Nathan, and
Solomon. These four were
born to him by Bath-shua
daughter of Ammiel.
6 David's other sons: Ibhar,
Elishua,[B] Eliphelet, 7 Nogah,
Nepheg, Japhia, 8 Elishama,
Eliada, and Eliphelet—nine
sons.
9 These were all David's sons,
with their sister Tamar, in
addition to the sons by his
concubines.

10 Solomon's son was Rehoboam;
his son was Abijah, his son
Asa,
his son Jehoshaphat, 11 his son
Jehoram,[C,D]
his son Ahaziah, his son Joash,
12 his son Amaziah, his son
Azariah,
his son Jotham, 13 his son Ahaz,
his son Hezekiah, his son
Manasseh,
14 his son Amon, and his son
Josiah.
15 Josiah's sons:
Johanan was the firstborn,
Jehoiakim second,
Zedekiah third, and Shallum
fourth.
16 Jehoiakim's sons:
his sons Jeconiah
and Zedekiah.

17 The sons of Jeconiah the
captive:
his sons Shealtiel,
18 Malchiram, Pedaiah,

[A] **2:52** Lit *Manuhoth* [B] **3:6** Lit *Elishama*; 2Sm 5:15; 1Ch 14:5 [C] **3:11** Lit *Joram* [D] **3:11** = The LORD is Exalted

>WORD|*study*

3:19 Biblical names deserve special study. For example, the names in this family line reflect the shifting hopes from one generation to the next. **Zerubbabel** (Hb, "scattered, sown, or born in Babylon") lived through the exile. His children's names, however, look forward in great hope and with expectation of the restoration: **Meshullam** (Hb, "friend"), **Hananiah** (Hb, "given by God" or "God has favored"), his daughter **Shelomith** (Hb, "peaceful"), **Hashubah** (Hb, "Yahweh has considered or estimated"), **Ohel** (Hb, "tent of Yahweh"), **Berechiah** (Hb, "Yahweh has blessed"), **Hasadiah** (Hb, "whom Yahweh loves" or "Yahweh has been faithful") and **Jushab-hesed** (Hb, "whose covenant love is returned").

4:10 In other contexts, the word translated **cause any pain** (Hb *'atsav*) conveys a sense of heart-wrenching grief over sin, inflicting irreparable damage or circumstances and resulting in painful disappointment and dismay (cp. Gn 6:6; 34:7; 45:5; 1Sm 20:3,34; Neh 8:10-11; Ps 78:40; Is 63:10). **Jabez** may already have suffered such pain as reflected by his name.

Shenazzar, Jekamiah,
Hoshama, and Nedabiah.
19 Pedaiah's sons: Zerubbabel
and Shimei.
Zerubbabel's sons: Meshullam
and Hananiah, with their
sister Shelomith; 20 and five
others—Hashubah, Ohel,
Berechiah, Hasadiah, and
Jushab-hesed.
21 Hananiah's descendants:
Pelatiah, Jeshaiah, and the
sons of Rephaiah, Arnan,
Obadiah, and Shecaniah.[A]
22 The son[B] of Shecaniah:
Shemaiah.
Shemaiah's sons: Hattush,
Igal, Bariah, Neariah, and
Shaphat—six.
23 Neariah's sons: Elioenai,
Hizkiah, and Azrikam—three.
24 Elioenai's sons: Hodaviah,
Eliashib, Pelaiah, Akkub,
Johanan, Delaiah, and
Anani—seven.

More Descendants of Judah (4:1-23)

4 Judah's sons: Perez, Hezron,
Carmi, Hur, and Shobal.
2 Reaiah son of Shobal
fathered Jahath, and Jahath
fathered Ahumai and Lahad.
These were the families of the
Zorathites.
3 These were Etam's sons:[C]
Jezreel, Ishma, and Idbash,
and their sister was named
Hazzelelponi.
4 Penuel fathered Gedor, and
Ezer fathered Hushah.
These were the sons of Hur,
Ephrathah's firstborn and the
father of Bethlehem:
5 Ashhur fathered Tekoa and
had two wives, Helah and
Naarah.
6 Naarah bore Ahuzzam,
Hepher, Temeni, and
Haahashtari to him. These
were Naarah's sons.
7 Helah's sons: Zereth, Zohar,[D]
and Ethnan. 8 Koz fathered
Anub, Zobebah,[E] and the
families of Aharhel son of
Harum.

9 Jabez[F] was more honorable than
his brothers. His mother named
him Jabez and said, "I gave birth to
him in pain."
10 Jabez called out to the God of
Israel: "If only You would bless me,
extend my border, let Your hand be
with me, and keep me from harm,
so that I will not cause any pain."[G,H]
And God granted his request.

11 Chelub brother of Shuhah
fathered Mehir, who was the
father of Eshton. 12 Eshton
fathered Beth-rapha, Paseah,
and Tehinnah the father of
Irnahash. These were the men
of Recah.
13 Kenaz's sons: Othniel and
Seraiah.
Othniel's sons: Hathath and
Meonothai.[I]
14 Meonothai fathered Ophrah,

[A] **3:21** LXX reads *Jeshaiah, his son Rephaiah, his son Arnan, his son Obadiah, and his son Shecaniah* [B] **3:22** LXX; MT reads *sons* [C] **4:3** LXX; MT reads *father* [D] **4:7** Alt Hb tradition reads *Izhar* [E] **4:8** Or *Hazzobebah* [F] **4:9** In Hb, the name Jabez sounds like "he causes pain." [G] **4:10** LXX reads *and act in knowledge which doesn't hurt me* [H] **4:10** Or *so that I will not experience pain* [I] **4:13** LXX, Vg; MT omits *and Meonothai*

4:1-8 The return to **Judah's** descendants reflected the priority of David's tribe in the writer's perspective. These verses list groups of descendants rather than tracing lines of direct descent.

4:9-10 Jabez is one of the few people in the genealogies with a specific comment attached to his name. When he **called out to the God of Israel . . . God granted his request**, placing him in contrast to Saul who had "consulted a medium" (1Ch 10:13) but in comparison with David who "inquired of God" (14:10,14). In the context of 1 Chronicles and of Scripture as a whole, the identity of the God to whom Jabez prayed is more significant than his particular petition. Nevertheless, Jabez's requests demonstrate his faith in God's promises.

- The Old Testament records only one other instance of the personal request, **Bless me**—that of Jacob (Hb, "schemer, supplanter") in Gn 32:26-29. The Lord responded by changing Jacob's name to Israel (Hb, "Yahweh prevails"). In calling on "the God of Israel," Jabez undoubtedly prayed with confidence that God would keep His promises to bless those who were faithful to obey Him (Ex 23:25; Dt 7:12-16; 15:4-6; 28:1-14; 30:19-20).
- Given that he also did not want to **cause any pain**, Jabez may also have hoped that the Lord would respond to his plea as He had responded to Jacob (i.e., with a name reflecting his heart rather than the circumstances of his birth). By asking that God's **hand be with** him, Jabez acknowledged his need for the power of God's presence and protection (cp. Gn 28:20; Jos 14:12; cp. Ex 13:9).
- **Keep** [Hb *'asah*, "do, accomplish, make"] **me from harm** (Hb *ra'*, "evil, displeasing to God; that which is bad, hurtful, malignant"; cp. Gn 48:15-16) expressed Jabez's desire not merely for protection from personal injury or distress but for the Lord to do for him what he could not do for himself, i.e., to prevent him from doing anything that he would regret.

4:11-20 This section continues to feature groups of Judah's descendants without always connecting them clearly to any particular branch of the family tree. First Chronicles 4:14-15 simply lists **the sons of Caleb**, who, with Joshua, believed God could give the Israelites victory over any opponents to their settlement in the promised land. His immediate descendants included a grandson named **Kenaz**, bearing the same name as Caleb's "brother," whose son Othniel married Caleb's daughter Achsah (Jos 15:15-19).

4:24-43 Underscoring the close association of the two tribes, the Chronicler described the descendants of Simeon immediately after those of Judah. Joshua 19:1-9 explained that Simeon's "inheritance was within" Judah's. Here, the writer explained why the tribe was smaller than Judah and listed Simeon's cities. Presumably, when **David became king** (1Ch 4:31) these cities were irretrievably incorporated into Judah. **Beer-sheba**, **Moladah**, **Hazar-shual**, and **Ziklag** were all named in the list of "farming settlements" inhabited by "some of Judah's descendants" after the exile (Neh 11:25-29). Despite being absorbed by the larger and more prominent tribe of Judah, both politically and geographically, Simeon's descendants **kept a genealogical record for themselves** (1Ch 4:33). The Chronicler's provision of separate information about the tribe of Judah served his purpose of emphasizing God's inclusion of "all Israel" (9:1) among His people (cp. Gn 46:10; Ex 6:15; Nm 26:12-14).

and Seraiah fathered Joab, the ancestor of those in the Valley of Craftsmen,[A] for they were craftsmen.

15 The sons of Caleb son of Jephunneh: Iru, Elah, and Naam.
Elah's son: Kenaz.
16 Jehallelel's sons: Ziph, Ziphah, Tiria, and Asarel.
17 Ezrah's sons: Jether, Mered, Epher, and Jalon. Mered's wife Bithiah gave birth to Miriam, Shammai, and Ishbah the
father of Eshtemoa. 18 These
were the sons of Pharaoh's daughter Bithiah; Mered had married her. His Judean wife gave birth to Jered the father of Gedor, Heber the father of Soco, and Jekuthiel the
father of Zanoah. 19 The sons
of Hodiah's wife, the sister of Naham: the father of Keilah the Garmite and the father of Eshtemoa the Maacathite.
20 Shimon's sons: Amnon, Rinnah, Ben-hanan, and Tilon.
Ishi's sons: Zoheth and Ben-zoheth.

21 The sons of Shelah son of Judah: Er the father of Lecah, Laadah the father of Mareshah, the families of the guild[B] of linen
workers at Beth-ashbea, 22 Jo-
kim, the men of Cozeba; and Joash and Saraph, who married Moabites[C] and returned to Lehem. These names are from
ancient records. 23 They were
the potters and residents of Netaim and Gederah. They lived there in the service of the king.

Simeon's Descendants (4:24-43)

24 Simeon's sons: Nemuel, Jamin, Jarib, Zerah, and Shaul;
25 Shaul's sons: his son Shallum, his son Mibsam, and his son Mishma.
26 Mishma's sons: his son Hammuel, his son Zaccur, and his son Shimei.

27 Shimei had 16 sons and six daughters, but his brothers did not have many children, so their whole family did not become as numerous as the Judeans.
28 They lived in Beer-sheba,
Moladah, Hazar-shual, 29 Bilhah, Ezem, Tolad, 30 Bethuel,
Hormah, Ziklag, 31 Beth-mar-
caboth, Hazar-susim, Beth-biri, and Shaaraim. These were their cities until David became king.
32 Their villages were Etam,
Ain, Rimmon, Tochen, and
Ashan—five cities, 33 and all
their surrounding villages as far as Baal. These were their settlements, and they kept a genealogical record for themselves.

34 Meshobab, Jamlech, Joshah son of Amaziah,
35 Joel, Jehu son of Joshibiah, son of Seraiah, son of Asiel,
36 Elioenai, Jaakobah, Jeshohaiah, Asaiah, Adiel,
Jesimiel, Benaiah, 37 and Ziza
son of Shiphi, son of Allon, son of Jedaiah, son of Shimri, son of Shemaiah—

38 these mentioned by name were leaders in their families. Their ancestral houses increased greatly. 39 They went to
the entrance of Gedor, to the east side of the valley to seek
pasture for their flocks. 40 They
found rich, good pasture, and the land was broad, peaceful, and quiet, for some Hamites had lived there previously.

41 These who were recorded by name came in the days of King Hezekiah of Judah, attacked the Hamites' tents and the Meunites who were found there, and •set them apart for destruction, as they are today. Then they settled in their place because there was pasture for their flocks.
42 Now 500 men from these sons of
Simeon went with Pelatiah, Neariah, Rephaiah, and Uzziel, the sons of Ishi, as their leaders to Mount Seir.
43 They struck down the remnant of
the Amalekites who had escaped, and they still live there today.

[A] 4:14 Or *the Ge-harashim* [B] 4:21 Lit *house* [C] 4:22 Or *who ruled over Moab*

The Tribes Taken into Exile by Assyria (5:1-26)

The Tribe of Reuben (5:1-10)

5 These were the sons of Reuben the firstborn of Israel. He was the firstborn, but his birthright was given to the sons of Joseph son of Israel, because Reuben defiled his father's bed. He is not listed in the genealogy according to birthright. 2 Although Judah became strong among his brothers and a ruler came from him, the birthright was given to Joseph.

3 The sons of Reuben, Israel's firstborn:
Hanoch, Pallu, Hezron, and Carmi.
4 Joel's sons: his son Shemaiah, his son Gog, his son Shimei,
5 his son Micah, his son Reaiah,
his son Baal, 6 and his son Beerah.

Beerah was a leader of the Reubenites, and Tiglath-pileser[A] king of Assyria took him into exile. 7 His relatives by their families as they are recorded in their genealogy:

Jeiel the chief, Zechariah,
8 and Bela son of Azaz,
son of Shema, son of Joel.

They settled in Aroer as far as Nebo and Baal-meon. 9 They also settled in the east as far as the edge of the desert that extends to the Euphrates River, because their herds had increased in the land of Gilead. 10 During Saul's reign they waged war against the Hagrites, who were defeated by their power. And they lived in their tents throughout the region east of Gilead.

The Tribe of Gad (5:11-22)

11 The sons of Gad lived next to them in the land of Bashan as far as Salecah:
12 Joel the chief, Shapham the second in command, Janai, and Shaphat in Bashan.
13 Their relatives according to their ancestral houses:
Michael, Meshullam, Sheba, Jorai, Jacan, Zia, and Eber—seven.
14 These were the sons of Abihail son of Huri,
son of Jaroah, son of Gilead,
son of Michael, son of Jeshishai,
son of Jahdo, son of Buz.
15 Ahi son of Abdiel, son of Guni, was head of their ancestral houses. 16 They lived in Gilead, in Bashan and its towns, and throughout the pasturelands of Sharon. 17 All of them were registered in the genealogies during the reigns of Judah's King Jotham and Israel's King Jeroboam.

18 The sons of Reuben and Gad
and half the tribe of Manasseh had
44,760 warriors who could serve in
the army—men who carried shield
and sword, drew the bow, and were
trained for war. 19 They waged war
against the Hagrites, Jetur, Naphish,
and Nodab. 20 They received help
against these enemies because they
cried out to God in battle, and the
Hagrites and all their allies were
handed over to them. He granted
their request because they trusted
in Him. 21 They captured the Hagrites' livestock—50,000 of their
camels, 250,000 sheep, and 2,000
donkeys—as well as 100,000 people.
22 Many of the Hagrites were killed
because it was God's battle. And they
lived there in the Hagrites' place until the exile.

The Tribe of Manasseh (5:23-26)

23 The sons of half the tribe of
Manasseh settled in the land from
Bashan to Baal-hermon (that is, Senir or Mount Hermon); they were
numerous. 24 These were the heads
of their ancestral houses: Epher,
Ishi, Eliel, Azriel, Jeremiah, Hodaviah, and Jahdiel. They were brave
warriors, famous men, and heads of
their ancestral houses. 25 But they
were unfaithful to the God of their
ancestors. They prostituted themselves with the gods of the nations[B]
God had destroyed before them. 26 So
the God of Israel put it into the mind
of Pul (that is, Tiglath-pileser[A]) king

[A]**5:6,26** LXX; MT reads *Tilgath-pilneser* [B]**5:25** Lit *the peoples of the land*

5:1 Chapter 5 chronicles the three Transjordanian tribes, those located on the east side of the Jordan River. The Gadites lived next to the Reubenites (v. 11), and these combined military forces with the half-tribe of Manasseh (v. 18; cp. Nm 32).

5:1-2 Here, the writer explained why Reuben's lineage had not been featured first in the record even though he was Israel's **firstborn** (cp. Gn 35:22; 49:3-4). The firstborn son typically received a "double portion" of the father's inheritance, but Reuben's sin gave Israel cause to deny Reuben and transfer this right to the firstborn son of Rachel, the wife he loved (cp. Dt 21:15-17; Ezk 47:13). Jacob consequently claimed Joseph's two sons as his own and gave his blessing to Joseph through them. Although Manasseh was Joseph's firstborn, Jacob deliberately extended the firstborn's rights to the younger brother, Ephraim (see Gn 48:5-15; 49:22-28). This background undergirded the Chronicler's understanding of why Judah, despite the tribe's honor and strength, did not occupy the favored position of the son receiving **the birthright**, even though this tribe clearly gained ascendancy over the others through David and, ultimately, through the Son of David, the Messiah (cp. Gn 49:8-12; Ps 108:8; Mt 1:1; Rm 1:3-4; 9:5; Heb 1:8; 7:14-16,27-28).

5:18-22 The term **Hagrites** generally referred to descendants of Ishmael, the son of Abraham by his concubine Hagar. The writer observed that **it was God's battle**—not merely because the Israelites prayed and not primarily because they relied on Him.

5:23-26 A series of imperfect verbs in this passage suggested ongoing apostasy as the basis for God's arrangement of the exile of the three Transjordanian tribes who must have suffered the first waves of Assyrian assaults on Israel. Like a beloved wife who spurned her husband's devotion, defied his protection, and adulterously pursued the dangerous men he had driven from the neighborhood, they **were unfaithful** [Hb *ma'al*, "act treacherously, transgress, offend"; cp. 2Ch 29:6; Neh 1:8] and **prostituted themselves** (Hb *zanah*, "play the harlot, go whoring after," a verb used chiefly of adultery or fornication committed by a woman, cp. Dt 31:16; Jr 5:7; Ezk 23:30) with Canaanite gods. Sadly, these members of Israel's family remained in exile when others were returning from Babylonian captivity (cp. 2Kg 17:7-18).

6:1-15 In Chronicles, the genealogies of the priests, like those of Judah and Benjamin, were central to the writer's purpose. Such a comprehensive list of the **sons** or descendants of Levi appears nowhere else in Scripture (cp. 9:1-34; cp. Ex 6:16-27; Neh 11:1–12:26). Notably, all three children of Amram are listed—**Aaron, Moses, and Miriam**—each name recalling the person's role in Israel's history (cp. Nm 26:59; Mc 6:4; for Miriam's role, see Ex 2:1-8; 15:20-21; Nm 12:1-15).

6:16-30 The next section was introduced in the same way as the first (cp. 6:1,16) to offer a parallel list having a different focus—**the Levites' families** grouped **according to** the three clans headed by **Levi's** three **sons** (vv. 16-19).

6:31-47 Although singing had always been an important aspect of Hebrew worship, David formalized the extensive use of **music** which served as an integral part of worship for Israel and later for the church as well. **Ethan** the Merarite (v. 44) should not be confused with Ethan the Ezrahite, whose renowned wisdom was surpassed by Solomon (cp. 2:6-7; 1Kg 4:29-31; superscription of Ps 89).

>WORD|*study*

5:26 Because the verb took (Hb *bo'*, "bring away, carry with oneself") is singular, **Pul** and **Tiglath-pileser III** (Tilgath-pilneser in the Hebrew text) are correctly identified as the same person, as indicated by the phrase **that is**. This conclusion counters an argument that 1Ch 5:26 proves the Bible to be historically inaccurate because it treats the two names as two different kings.

of Assyria to take the Reubenites, Gadites, and half the tribe of Manasseh into exile. He took them to Halah, Habor, Hara, and Gozan's river, where they are until today.

The Levites (6:1-81)

Priests (6:1-30)

6[A] Levi's sons: Gershom,[B]
Kohath, and Merari.
2 Kohath's sons: Amram, Izhar,
Hebron, and Uzziel.
3 Amram's children: Aaron,
Moses, and Miriam.
Aaron's sons: Nadab, Abihu,
Eleazar, and Ithamar.
4 Eleazar fathered Phinehas;
Phinehas fathered Abishua;
5 Abishua fathered Bukki;
Bukki fathered Uzzi;
6 Uzzi fathered Zerahiah;
Zerahiah fathered Meraioth;
7 Meraioth fathered Amariah;
Amariah fathered Ahitub;
8 Ahitub fathered Zadok;
Zadok fathered Ahimaaz;
9 Ahimaaz fathered Azariah;
Azariah fathered Johanan;
10 Johanan fathered Azariah,
who served as priest in the
temple that Solomon built
in Jerusalem;
11 Azariah fathered Amariah;
Amariah fathered Ahitub;
12 Ahitub fathered Zadok;
Zadok fathered Shallum;
13 Shallum fathered Hilkiah;
Hilkiah fathered Azariah;
14 Azariah fathered Seraiah;
and Seraiah fathered
Jehozadak.
15 Jehozadak went into exile
when the LORD sent
Judah and Jerusalem
into exile at the hands of
Nebuchadnezzar.

16[C] Levi's sons: Gershom,
Kohath, and Merari.
17 These are the names
of Gershom's sons: Libni
and Shimei.
18 Kohath's sons: Amram, Izhar,
Hebron and Uzziel.
19 Merari's sons: Mahli
and Mushi.
These are the Levites' families
according to their fathers:
20 Of Gershom: his son Libni,
his son Jahath, his son
Zimmah,
21 his son Joah, his son Iddo,
his son Zerah, and his son
Jeatherai.
22 Kohath's sons: his son
Amminadab,
his son Korah, his son Assir,
23 his son Elkanah, his son
Ebiasaph,
his son Assir, 24 his son
Tahath,
his son Uriel, his son Uzziah,
and his son Shaul.
25 Elkanah's sons: Amasai
and Ahimoth,
26 his son Elkanah, his son
Zophai,
his son Nahath, 27 his son
Eliab,
his son Jeroham, and his son
Elkanah.
28 Samuel's sons: his firstborn
Joel,[D]
and his second son Abijah.
29 Merari's sons: Mahli, his son
Libni,
his son Shimei, his son
Uzzah,
30 his son Shimea, his son
Haggiah,
and his son Asaiah.

Musicians (6:31-47)

31 These are the men David put in
charge of the music in the LORD's
temple after the ark came to rest
there. 32 They ministered with song
in front of the tabernacle, the tent

[A] **6:1** 1Ch 5:27 in Hb [B] **6:1** Levi's son's name is spelled Gershon in Ex. [C] **6:16** 1Ch 6:1 in Hb
[D] **6:28** Some LXX mss, Syr, Arabic; other Hb mss omit *Joel*; 1Sm 8:2

of meeting, until Solomon built
the LORD's temple in Jerusalem, and
they performed their task according
to the regulations given to them.
33 These are the men who served
with their sons.

From the Kohathites:
Heman the singer,
son of Joel, son of Samuel,
34 son of Elkanah, son of Jeroham,
son of Eliel, son of Toah,
35 son of Zuph, son of Elkanah,
son of Mahath, son of Amasai,
36 son of Elkanah, son of Joel,
son of Azariah,
son of Zephaniah,
37 son of Tahath, son of Assir,
son of Ebiasaph,
son of Korah,
38 son of Izhar, son of Kohath,
son of Levi, son of Israel.
39 Heman's relative was •Asaph,
who stood at his right hand:
Asaph son of Berechiah,
son of Shimea,
40 son of Michael, son of Baaseiah,
son of Malchijah,
41 son of Ethni,
son of Zerah, son of Adaiah,
42 son of Ethan, son of Zimmah,
son of Shimei, 43 son of Jahath,
son of Gershom, son of Levi.

44 On the left, their relatives
were Merari's sons:
Ethan son of Kishi,
son of Abdi,
son of Malluch,
45 son of Hashabiah,
son of Amaziah, son of Hilkiah,
46 son of Amzi, son of Bani,
son of Shemer, 47 son of Mahli,
son of Mushi, son of Merari,
son of Levi.

Aaron's Descendants (6:48-81)

48 Their relatives, the Levites, were
assigned to all the service of the tabernacle, God's temple. 49 But Aaron
and his sons did all the work of the
most holy place. They presented the
offerings on the altar of •burnt offerings and on the altar of incense to
make atonement for Israel according to all that Moses the servant of
God had commanded.

50 These are Aaron's sons:
his son Eleazar,
his son Phinehas, his son
Abishua,
51 his son Bukki, his son Uzzi,
his son Zerahiah, 52 his son
Meraioth,
his son Amariah, his son
Ahitub,
53 his son Zadok, and his son
Ahimaaz.

54 These were the places assigned
to Aaron's sons from the Kohathite
family for their settlements in their
territory, because the first lot was
for them. 55 They were given Hebron
in the land of Judah and its surrounding pasturelands, 56 but the
fields and villages around the city
were given to Caleb son of Jephunneh. 57 Aaron's sons were given:

Hebron (a city of refuge),
Libnah and its pasturelands,
Jattir, Eshtemoa and its
pasturelands, 58 Hilen[A] and
its pasturelands, Debir and its
pasturelands, 59 Ashan and its
pasturelands, and Beth-shemesh
and its pasturelands. 60 From
the tribe of Benjamin they were
given Geba and its pasturelands,
Alemeth and its pasturelands,
and Anathoth and its pasturelands. They had 13 towns in all
among their families.

61 To the rest of the Kohathites,
10 towns from half the tribe of
Manasseh were assigned by lot.
62 The Gershomites were assigned
13 towns from the tribes of Issachar,
Asher, Naphtali, and Manasseh in
Bashan according to their families.
63 The Merarites were assigned by
lot 12 towns from the tribes of Reuben, Gad, and Zebulun according
to their families. 64 So the Israelites
gave these towns and their pasturelands to the Levites. 65 They assigned
by lot the towns named above from
the tribes of the Judahites, Simeonites, and Benjaminites.

66 Some of the families of the Kohathites were given towns from the
tribe of Ephraim for their territory:

6:49 Just as **Aaron** and his descendants performed their priestly responsibilities during David's reign as he prepared for the building of the temple, so their descendants returning from exile would be expected to fulfill their God-given roles when the second temple was built.

6:54-81 Having established the cities that belonged to **Aaron's** descendants, the writer later was able to summarize that "priests, Levites, and temple servants" were among "the first" to resettle in the places historically belonging to them (9:2).

[A] **6:58** Some Hb mss, LXX; other Hb mss read *Hilez*

7:1-5 With the descendants of Jacob's first four sons by his first wife Leah—Reuben, Simeon, Levi, and Judah—already represented, the writer turns to the descendants of Issachar, who was Leah's next son, born after the four sons of the two handmaids. **Tola**, a descendant of **Issachar's** firstborn son by the same name, became one of Israel's judges (Jdg 10:1). Emphasis on the number of fighting men in Tola's clan may indicate that the Chronicler used a military census as the source material for this section (1Ch 7:1-2; cp. 5:18).

7:6-12 The writer focused here on only **three of Benjamin's sons** (cp. Gn 46:21; Nm 26:38-41); an expanded genealogical record is provided in chapter 8 to provide the lineage of King Saul (1Ch 8:33). Zebulun seems to be the only tribe omitted, and some suggest that the genealogy for this tribe is included with the records for Benjamin.

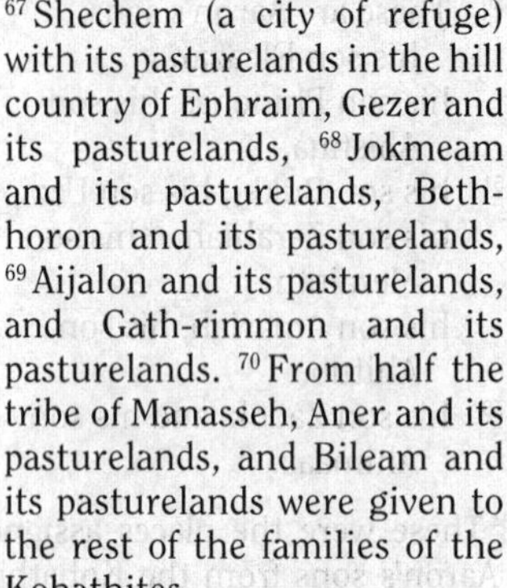

67 Shechem (a city of refuge) with its pasturelands in the hill country of Ephraim, Gezer and its pasturelands, 68 Jokmeam and its pasturelands, Beth-horon and its pasturelands, 69 Aijalon and its pasturelands, and Gath-rimmon and its pasturelands. 70 From half the tribe of Manasseh, Aner and its pasturelands, and Bileam and its pasturelands were given to the rest of the families of the Kohathites.

71 The Gershomites received:

Golan in Bashan and its pasturelands, and Ashtaroth and its pasturelands from the families of half the tribe of Manasseh. 72 From the tribe of Issachar they received Kedesh and its pasturelands, Daberath and its pasturelands, 73 Ramoth and its pasturelands, and Anem and its pasturelands. 74 From the tribe of Asher they received Mashal and its pasturelands, Abdon and its pasturelands, 75 Hukok and its pasturelands, and Rehob and its pasturelands. 76 From the tribe of Naphtali they received Kedesh in Galilee and its pasturelands, Hammon and its pasturelands, and Kiriathaim and its pasturelands.

77 The rest of the Merarites received:

From the tribe of Zebulun they received Rimmono and its pasturelands and Tabor and its pasturelands. 78 From the tribe of Reuben across the Jordan at Jericho, to the east of the Jordan, they received Bezer in the desert and its pasturelands, Jahzah and its pasturelands, 79 Kedemoth and its pasturelands, and Mephaath and its pasturelands. 80 From the tribe of Gad they received Ramoth in Gilead and its pasturelands, Mahanaim and its pasturelands, 81 Heshbon and its pasturelands, and Jazer and its pasturelands.

Issachar's Descendants (7:1-5)

7 Issachar's sons: Tola, Puah, Jashub, and Shimron—four.
2 Tola's sons: Uzzi, Rephaiah, Jeriel, Jahmai, Ibsam, and Shemuel, the heads of their ancestral houses. During David's reign, 22,600 descendants of Tola were recorded as warriors in their genealogies.
3 Uzzi's son: Izrahiah.
Izrahiah's sons: Michael, Obadiah, Joel, Isshiah. All five of them were chiefs. 4 Along with them, they had 36,000 troops for battle according to the genealogical records of their ancestral houses, for they had many wives and children. 5 Their tribesmen who were warriors belonging to all the families of Issachar totaled 87,000 in their genealogies.

Benjamin's Descendants (7:6-12)

6 Three of Benjamin's sons: Bela, Becher, and Jediael.
7 Bela's sons: Ezbon, Uzzi, Uzziel, Jerimoth, and Iri—five. They were warriors and heads of their ancestral houses; 22,034 were listed in their genealogies.
8 Becher's sons: Zemirah, Joash, Eliezer, Elioenai, Omri, Jeremoth, Abijah, Anathoth, and Alemeth; all these were Becher's sons. 9 Their genealogies were recorded according to the heads of their ancestral houses—20,200 warriors.
10 Jediael's son: Bilhan.
Bilhan's sons: Jeush, Benjamin, Ehud, Chenaanah, Zethan, Tarshish, and Ahishahar. 11 All these sons of Jediael listed by heads of families were warriors; there were 17,200 who could serve in the army. 12 Shuppim and Huppim were sons of Ir, and the Hushim were the sons of Aher.

The Descendants of Naphtali, Manasseh, Ephraim, and Asher (7:13-40)

13 Naphtali's sons:
Jahziel, Guni, Jezer, and
Shallum—Bilhah's sons.

14 Manasseh's sons through
his Aramean concubine:
Asriel and Machir the father
of Gilead. 15 Machir took wives
from Huppim and Shuppim.
The name of his sister was
Maacah. Another descendant
was named Zelophehad, but
he had only daughters.
16 Machir's wife Maacah gave
birth to a son, and she named
him Peresh. His brother was
named Sheresh, and his sons
were Ulam and Rekem.
17 Ulam's son: Bedan. These
were the sons of Gilead son
of Machir, son of Manasseh.
18 His sister Hammolecheth
gave birth to Ishhod, Abiezer,
and Mahlah.
19 Shemida's sons: Ahian,
Shechem, Likhi, and Aniam.

20 Ephraim's sons: Shuthelah,
and his son Bered,
his son Tahath,
his son Eleadah,
his son Tahath,
21 his son Zabad,
his son Shuthelah, also Ezer,
and Elead.

The men of Gath, born in
the land, killed them because
they went down to raid their
cattle. 22 Their father Ephraim
mourned a long time, and his
relatives[A] came to comfort
him. 23 He slept with his wife,
and she conceived and gave
birth to a son. So he named
him Beriah, because there
had been misfortune in his
home.[B] 24 His daughter was
Sheerah, who built Lower and
Upper Beth-horon and Uzzen-sheerah,

25 his son Rephah,[C]
his son Resheph,
his son Telah, his son Tahan,
26 his son Ladan,
his son Ammihud,
his son Elishama,
27 his son Nun,
and his son Joshua.

28 Their holdings and settlements were Bethel and its villages; Naaran to the east, Gezer
and its villages to the west, and
Shechem and its villages as far
as Ayyah and its villages, 29 and
along the borders of the sons
of Manasseh, Beth-shean and
its villages, Taanach and its
villages, Megiddo and its villages, and Dor and its villages.
The sons of Joseph son of Israel
lived in these towns.

30 Asher's sons: Imnah, Ishvah,
Ishvi, and Beriah, with their
sister Serah.
31 Beriah's sons: Heber, and
Malchiel, who fathered
Birzaith.
32 Heber fathered Japhlet,
Shomer, and Hotham, with
their sister Shua.
33 Japhlet's sons: Pasach,
Bimhal, and Ashvath. These
were Japhlet's sons.
34 Shemer's sons: Ahi, Rohgah,
Hubbah, and Aram.
35 His brother Helem's sons:
Zophah, Imna, Shelesh, and
Amal.
36 Zophah's sons: Suah,
Harnepher, Shual, Beri,
Imrah, 37 Bezer, Hod,
Shamma, Shilshah, Ithran,
and Beera.
38 Jether's sons: Jephunneh,
Pispa, and Ara.
39 Ulla's sons: Arah, Hanniel,
and Rizia.
40 All these were Asher's
sons. They were the heads
of their ancestral houses,
chosen men, warriors, and
chiefs among the leaders.
The number of men listed in
their genealogies for military
service was 26,000.

7:13 For reasons unknown to us, no record of Dan's descendants was included in Chronicles, perhaps indicating that the remnant of this formerly numerous tribe included few who could claim to be Danites (cp. Nm 1:39).

7:14-19 The writer seems to have selected several loosely connected pieces of **Manasseh's** heritage, which demonstrated the inclusion in "all Israel" of people whose bloodlines were not entirely Jewish.

7:15 **Zelophehad** was a prominent **descendant** of Manasseh through **Machir**. Since their father had no sons, his five **daughters** requested and received an inheritance (cp. Nm 26:33; 36:1-12; Jos 17:3-6).

7:20-23 The account of the murder of **Ephraim's sons** does not appear elsewhere in Scripture, but here it serves as background for the naming of **Beriah** (Hb "calamity, tragedy," based on the root *ra'*, "evil," vv. 23,30), Joshua's ancestor (v. 27).

7:28-29 Geographically, the **towns** inhabited by **the sons of Joseph**—the descendants of Ephraim and Manasseh—were central to the land of **Israel**. Ephraim was the dominant tribe (see Gn 48:11-20), and the name was used synonymously with Israel and the northern kingdom (e.g., Is 7:9; 9:21; Jr 31:9).

7:30-40 Many of the names included here do not appear elsewhere in Scripture, perhaps because the tribe of Asher had simply not played a prominent role in Israel's history. For example, the tribe is not mentioned in the list of those "in charge of the tribes of Israel" (27:16-22; cp. Jdg 5:17). In contrast, the New Testament prophetess Anna from the tribe of Asher played a significant role in identifying the infant Jesus as the one through whom God would bring about "the redemption of Jerusalem" (Lk 2:36-38). The Chronicler emphasized the positive roles demonstrated by the past men of Asher to support the tribe's full inclusion in "all Israel" (1Ch 9:1). Yet no comment was made regarding their spiritual condition. The early failure of the tribe of Asher to drive the Canaanites out of their land should remind readers that the most exemplary human leaders cannot bring God's plans to fruition without fully obeying Him (Jdg 1:31-32).

[A]**7:22** Or *his brothers* [B]**7:23** In Hb, the name Beriah sounds like "in misfortune." [C]**7:25** Probably Ephraim's son

8:1-40 An expanded account of Benjamin's descendants finished the genealogical framework. Verses 1-28 outlined the descendants who lived in Jerusalem. Then the writer identified another line from **Gibeon** (v. 29) and traced in detail the lineage of Israel's first king, **Saul**, and his descendants (vv. 33-40).

9:1-16 Verses 1-2 provide a hinge between the writer's review of the genealogical heritage of **all Israel** and his attention to the restoration of temple worship as the central institution by which Israel's national identity and spiritual purity would be reestablished and preserved. The names of God's people were recorded in the historical records of **the Book of the Kings of Israel**, but the genealogical records would have little meaning unless the remnant from **Judah** not only returned to their land but also reversed their history of **unfaithfulness** to the Lord. Therefore, the Chronicler focused on those who had served in the temple and who would resume their assigned duties when the temple was rebuilt.

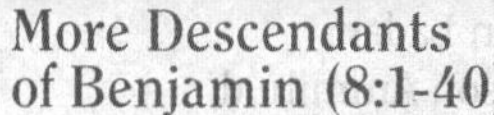

More Descendants of Benjamin (8:1-40)

8 Benjamin fathered Bela, his
firstborn; Ashbel was born
second, Aharah third, 2 Nohah
fourth, and Rapha fifth.
3 Bela's sons: Addar, Gera,
Abihud, 4 Abishua, Naaman,
Ahoah, 5 Gera, Shephuphan,
and Huram.
6 These were Ehud's sons, who
were the heads of the families
living in Geba and who
were deported to Manahath:
7 Naaman, Ahijah, and Gera.
Gera deported them and
was the father of Uzza and
Ahihud.
8 Shaharaim had sons in
the country of Moab after
he had divorced his wives
Hushim and Baara. 9 His
sons by his wife Hodesh:
Jobab, Zibia, Mesha, Malcam,
10 Jeuz, Sachia, and Mirmah.
These were his sons, heads
of families. 11 He also had
sons by Hushim: Abitub and
Elpaal.
12 Elpaal's sons: Eber, Misham,
and Shemed who built Ono
and Lod and its villages,
13 Beriah and Shema, who
were the heads of families of
Aijalon's residents and who
drove out the residents of
Gath, 14 Ahio,[A] Shashak, and
Jeremoth.
15 Zebadiah, Arad, Eder,
16 Michael, Ishpah, and Joha
were Beriah's sons.
17 Zebadiah, Meshullam, Hizki,
Heber, 18 Ishmerai, Izliah, and
Jobab were Elpaal's sons.
19 Jakim, Zichri, Zabdi,
20 Elienai, Zillethai, Eliel,
21 Adaiah, Beraiah, and
Shimrath were Shimei's sons.
22 Ishpan, Eber, Eliel, 23 Abdon,
Zichri, Hanan, 24 Hananiah,
Elam, Anthothijah,
25 Iphdeiah, and Penuel were
Shashak's sons.
26 Shamsherai, Shehariah,
Athaliah, 27 Jaareshiah, Elijah,
and Zichri were Jeroham's
sons.
28 These were heads of
families, chiefs according to
their genealogies, and lived in
Jerusalem.
29 Jeiel[B] fathered Gibeon
and lived in Gibeon. His
wife's name was Maacah.
30 Abdon was his firstborn
son, then Zur, Kish, Baal,
Nadab, 31 Gedor, Ahio, Zecher,
32 and Mikloth who fathered
Shimeah. These also lived
opposite their relatives in
Jerusalem, with their other
relatives.
33 Ner fathered Kish,
Kish fathered Saul, and
Saul fathered Jonathan,
Malchishua, Abinadab, and
Esh-baal.[C]
34 Jonathan's son was Merib-
baal,[D] and Merib-baal fathered
Micah.
35 Micah's sons: Pithon,
Melech, Tarea, and Ahaz.
36 Ahaz fathered Jehoaddah,
Jehoaddah fathered Alemeth,
Azmaveth, and Zimri, and
Zimri fathered Moza.
37 Moza fathered Binea. His
son was Raphah, his son
Elasah, and his son Azel.
38 Azel had six sons, and these
were their names: Azrikam,
Bocheru, Ishmael, Sheariah,
Obadiah, and Hanan. All these
were Azel's sons.
39 His brother Eshek's sons:
Ulam was his firstborn, Jeush
second, and Eliphelet third.
40 Ulam's sons were warriors
and archers.[E] They had many
sons and grandsons—150 of
them.
All these were among
Benjamin's sons.

Judah After the Babylonian Exile (9:1-34)

9 All Israel was registered in the
genealogies that are written in
the Book of the Kings of Israel. But
Judah was exiled to Babylon because of their unfaithfulness. 2 The
first to live in their towns on their

[A] **8:13-14** LXX reads *Gath* 14 *and their brother* [B] **8:29** LXX; MT omits *Jeiel*; 1Ch 9:35 [C] **8:33** = Man of Baal [D] **8:34** = Baal Contends [E] **8:40** Lit *valiant ones who string the bow*

>WORD|*study*

9:22 Appointed (Hb *yasad;* the only use of this word in 1 Chronicles) had the primary definition of "laying a foundation or establishing," but this form of the verb could also mean "ordain." **Trusted positions** (Hb *ʾemunah,* "faithfulness, fidelity, security," vv. 22,26,31) conveyed the weighty responsibility of those charged with guarding the entrance to the tabernacle or temple in Israel and of those "entrusted with" the interior of the temple.

own property again were Israelites, priests, Levites, and temple servants.

3 These people from the
descendants of Judah,
Benjamin, Ephraim,
and Manasseh settled in
Jerusalem:
4 Uthai son of Ammihud, son
of Omri, son of Imri, son of
Bani, a descendant[A] of Perez
son of Judah;
5 from the Shilonites:
Asaiah the firstborn and his
sons;
6 and from the sons of Zerah:
Jeuel and 690 of their
relatives.

7 The Benjaminites: Sallu
son of Meshullam, son of
Hodaviah, son of Hassenuah;
8 Ibneiah son of Jeroham;
Elah son of Uzzi, son of
Michri;
Meshullam son of Shephatiah,
son of Reuel, son of Ibnijah;
9 and 956 of their relatives
according to their
genealogical records. All
these men were heads of their
ancestral houses.

10 The priests: Jedaiah;
Jehoiarib; Jachin;
11 Azariah son of Hilkiah,
son of Meshullam, son of
Zadok, son of Meraioth, son
of Ahitub, the chief official of
God's temple;
12 Adaiah son of Jeroham, son
of Pashhur, son of Malchijah;
Maasai son of Adiel, son of
Jahzerah, son of Meshullam,
son of Meshillemith, son of
Immer;
13 and 1,760 of their relatives,
the heads of households. They
were capable men employed
in the ministry of God's
temple.

14 The Levites: Shemaiah son
of Hasshub, son of Azrikam,
son of Hashabiah of the
Merarites;
15 Bakbakkar, Heresh, Galal,
and Mattaniah, son of Mica,
son of Zichri, son of •Asaph;
16 Obadiah son of Shemaiah,
son of Galal, son of Jeduthun;
and Berechiah son of Asa, son
of Elkanah who lived in the
villages of the Netophathites.

17 The gatekeepers: Shallum,
Akkub, Talmon, Ahiman, and
their relatives.
Shallum was their chief;
18 he was previously stationed
at the King's Gate on the
east side. These were the
gatekeepers from the camp of
the Levites.
19 Shallum son of Kore, son
of Ebiasaph, son of Korah
and his relatives from his
ancestral household, the
Korahites, were assigned
to guard the thresholds of
the tent.[B] Their ancestors
had been assigned to the
LORD's camp as guardians
of the entrance. 20 In earlier
times Phinehas son of
Eleazar had been their
leader, and the LORD was
with him. 21 Zechariah son
of Meshelemiah was the
gatekeeper at the entrance to
the tent of meeting.

22 The total number of those chosen to be gatekeepers at the thresholds was 212. They were registered
by genealogy in their villages. David
and Samuel the seer had appointed
them to their trusted positions. 23 So
they and their sons were assigned to

9:17-27 Next, the Chronicler gave particular attention to **the gatekeepers** and their responsibilities. He emphasized that the various Levitical families had inherited these roles from their **ancestors** and spotlighted **Phinehas**, for **the LORD was with him**, a phrase used to describe Yahweh's presence, blessing, and empowerment of the most prominent of Israel's leaders (vv. 19-20; cp. Nm 25:6-13). The gatekeepers served by royal and prophetic appointment, since **David and Samuel . . . had appointed them** (1Ch 9:22).

[A]9:4 Lit *Bani, from the sons* [B]9:19 = the temple

9:33-34 The writer reiterated that the **Levite** men serving the temple **lived in Jerusalem** and that they were **the heads** or **chiefs** of their **families.** From this one can infer that they had already demonstrated their capability and integrity in the context of their homes and relationships with extended family members and that these priests were not expected to remain celibate or give up their roles as family leaders.

9:35-44 To finish setting the stage for King David's enthronement, the writer repeated a portion of Saul's genealogy. In 1 Chronicles, the brief narrative recounting the tragic end of Saul's reign served as an interlude between the genealogical background of the exiles resettling Israel and an account of David's reign, which, for the human author, exhibited the ideal that Israel hoped to recover.

10:1-14 This account of Saul's death is nearly identical to the account recorded in 1Sm 31, but the Chronicler added interpretive commentary echoing his explanation of Judah's exile (1Ch 10:13-14; cp. 9:1): **The Lord** executed Saul because of **his unfaithfulness** and replaced him with **David** (10:13-14; cp. 1Sm 13:13-14).

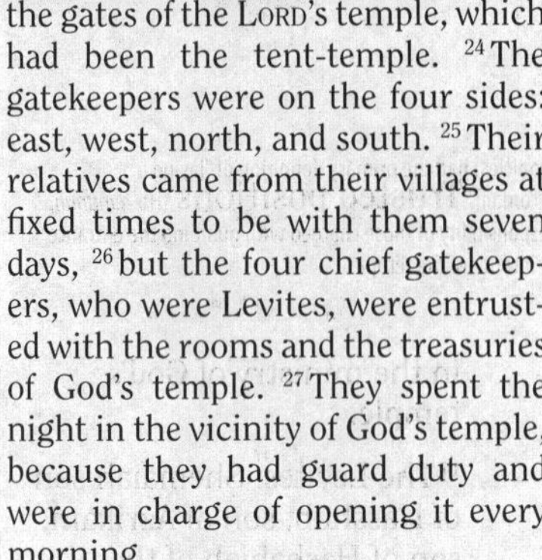

the gates of the LORD's temple, which had been the tent-temple. 24 The gatekeepers were on the four sides: east, west, north, and south. 25 Their relatives came from their villages at fixed times to be with them seven days, 26 but the four chief gatekeepers, who were Levites, were entrusted with the rooms and the treasuries of God's temple. 27 They spent the night in the vicinity of God's temple, because they had guard duty and were in charge of opening it every morning.

28 Some of them were in charge of the utensils used in worship. They would count them when they brought them in and when they took them out. 29 Others were put in charge of the furnishings and all the utensils of the sanctuary, as well as the fine flour, wine, oil, incense, and spices. 30 Some of the priests' sons mixed the spices. 31 A Levite called Mattithiah, the firstborn of Shallum the Korahite, was entrusted with baking the bread.[A] 32 Some of the Kohathites' relatives were responsible for preparing the rows of the •bread of the Presence every Sabbath.

33 The singers, the heads of the Levite families, stayed in the temple chambers and were exempt from other tasks because they were on duty day and night. 34 These were the heads of the Levite families, chiefs according to their genealogies, and lived in Jerusalem.

Saul (9:35–10:14)

35 Jeiel fathered Gibeon and
lived in Gibeon. His wife's
name was Maacah. 36 Abdon
was his firstborn son, then
Zur, Kish, Baal, Ner, Nadab,
37 Gedor, Ahio, Zechariah, and
Mikloth. 38 Mikloth fathered
Shimeam. These also lived
opposite their relatives in
Jerusalem with their other
relatives.
39 Ner fathered Kish,
Kish fathered Saul, and
Saul fathered Jonathan,
Malchishua, Abinadab, and
Esh-baal.
40 Jonathan's son was Merib-
baal, and Merib-baal fathered
Micah.
41 Micah's sons: Pithon,
Melech, Tahrea, and Ahaz.[B]
42 Ahaz fathered Jarah;
Jarah fathered Alemeth,
Azmaveth, and Zimri;
Zimri fathered Moza.
43 Moza fathered Binea.
His son was Rephaiah, his son
Elasah, and his son Azel.
44 Azel had six sons, and these
were their names: Azrikam,
Bocheru, Ishmael, Sheariah,
Obadiah, and Hanan. These
were Azel's sons.

10 The Philistines fought against Israel, and Israel's men fled from them and were killed on Mount Gilboa. 2 The Philistines pursued Saul and his sons and killed Saul's sons Jonathan, Abinadab, and Malchishua. 3 When the battle intensified against Saul, the archers found him and severely wounded him. 4 Then Saul said to his armor-bearer, "Draw your sword and run me through with it, or these uncircumcised men will come and torture me!" But his armor-bearer wouldn't do it because he was terrified. Then Saul took his sword and fell on it. 5 When his armor-bearer saw that Saul was dead, he also fell on his own sword and died. 6 So Saul and his three sons died—his whole house died together.

7 When all the men of Israel in the valley saw that the army had fled and that Saul and his sons were dead, they abandoned their cities and fled.

[A] **9:31** Lit *with things prepared in pans* [B] **9:41** LXX, Syr, Tg, Vg, Arabic; MT omits *and Ahaz*; 1Ch 8:35

>WORD|*study*

10:13 Unfaithfulness (Hb *ma'al*) occurs twice in the Hebrew text—as a noun meaning "treachery, sin, transgression, trespass" and as a verb expressing this idea in the form of an action ("act unfaithfully or treacherously against, commit a trespass against"; cp. 1Ch 2:7; 5:25) directed at "the Lord."

So the Philistines came and settled in them.

[8]The next day when the Philistines came to strip the slain, they found Saul and his sons dead on Mount Gilboa. [9]They stripped Saul, cut off his head, took his armor, and sent messengers throughout the land of the Philistines to spread the good news to their idols and their people. [10]Then they put his armor in the temple of their gods and hung his skull in the temple of Dagon.

[11]When all Jabesh-gilead heard of everything the Philistines had done to Saul, [12]all their brave men set out and retrieved the body of Saul and the bodies of his sons and brought them to Jabesh. They buried their bones under the oak[A] in Jabesh and fasted seven days.

[13]Saul died for his unfaithfulness to the LORD because he did not keep the LORD's word. He even consulted a medium for guidance, [14]but he did not inquire of the LORD. So the LORD put him to death and turned the kingdom over to David son of Jesse.

The Establishment of David's Reign (11:1-9)

11 All Israel came together to David at Hebron and said, "Here we are, your own flesh and blood.[B] [2]Even when Saul was king, you led us out to battle and brought us back. The LORD your God also said to you, 'You will shepherd My people Israel and be ruler over My people Israel.'"

[3]So all the elders of Israel came to the king at Hebron. David made a covenant with them at Hebron in the LORD's presence, and they anointed David king over Israel, in keeping with the LORD's word through Samuel.

[4]David and all Israel marched to Jerusalem (that is, Jebus); the Jebusites who inhabited the land were there. [5]The inhabitants of Jebus said to David, "You will never get in here." Yet David did capture the stronghold of •Zion, that is, the city of David.

[6]David said, "Whoever is the first to kill a Jebusite will become chief commander." Joab son of Zeruiah went up first, so he became the chief.

[7]Then David took up residence in the stronghold; therefore, it was called the city of David. [8]He built up the city all the way around, from the supporting terraces to the surrounding parts, and Joab restored the rest of the city. [9]David steadily grew more powerful, and the LORD of •Hosts was with him.

David's Military Might (11:10–12:40)

David's Warriors (11:10-25)

[10]The following were the chiefs of David's warriors who, together with all Israel, strongly supported him in his reign to make him king according to the LORD's word about Israel. [11]This is the list of David's warriors:

Jashobeam son of Hachmoni was chief of the Thirty;[C] he wielded his spear against 300 and killed them at one time.

[12]After him, Eleazar son of Dodo the Ahohite was one of the three warriors. [13]He was with David at Pas-dammim when the Philistines had gathered there for battle. There was a portion of a field full of barley, where the troops had fled from the Philistines. [14]But Eleazar and David[D] took their stand in the middle of the field and defended it. They killed the Philistines, and the LORD gave them a great victory.

[15]Three of the 30 chief men went down to David, to the rock at the cave of Adullam, while the Philistine army was encamped in the Valley of Rephaim. [16]At that time David was in the stronghold, and a Philistine garrison was at Bethlehem. [17]David was extremely thirsty[E] and said, "If only someone would bring me water to drink from the well at the city gate of Bethlehem!" [18]So the Three broke through the Philistine camp and drew water from the well at the gate of Bethlehem. They brought it back to David, but he refused to drink it. Instead, he poured it out to the LORD. [19]David said, "I would never do such a thing in the presence of God! How can I drink the blood of these men who risked their lives?"

11:1-9 Certain differences in wording in comparison to 2Sm 5:1-10 illuminate the Chronicler's purpose. The repeated phrase, **all Israel** (1Ch 11:1,4), emphasizes the nation's unity, a perspective vital to the physical survival and spiritual revival of the remnant dispersed during the exile. His observation that David's kingship was accomplished by **the LORD's word** reveals his theological understanding of God's faithfulness to complete what He has begun (v. 3). Just as God had fulfilled His "word" by bringing David to power, so He would fulfill His word to the preexilic prophets through whom He had promised to redeem and restore His people (e.g., Is 11:1-10). The Israelites knew that David's God, Yahweh, had told David he would **shepherd** the Lord's **people Israel** (1Ch 11:2). Inserting this phrase in his account of the momentous event in Israel's history underscored what made Israel distinctive—not her national identity but the fact that Yahweh called her His own "people" (cp. Is 51:16; 65:10).

11:11 Jashobeam (Hb, "the people will return") is a variant of the name used by the writer of 2Sm 23:8—"Josheb-basshebeth" (Hb, "dwelling in rest")—and may reflect the fulfillment of God's promise unfolding in the Israelites' return from exile. The number of men killed by Jashobeam (**300**) differs from the parallel account ("800," 2Sm 23:8). A scribe may have misread the number in Samuel. The few examples like this found in Scripture point to the challenge for scribes who had the arduous task of copying numbers but in no way is the accuracy of the text discredited.

[A]**10:12** Or *terebinth*, or *large tree* [B]**11:1** Lit *your bone and flesh* [C]**11:11** Alt Hb tradition reads *Three* [D]**11:14** Lit *But they* [E]**11:17** Lit *And David craved*

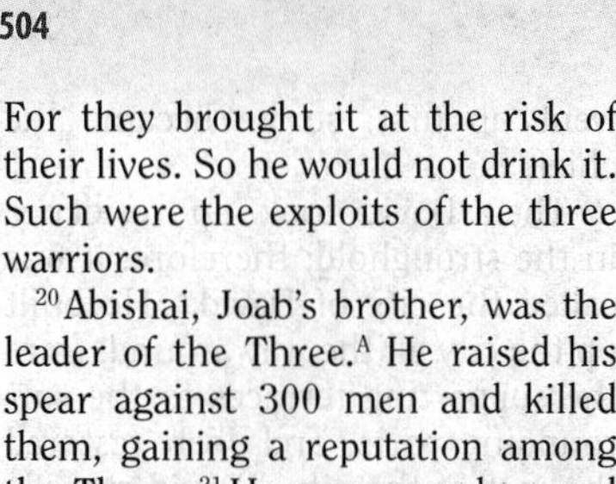

For they brought it at the risk of
their lives. So he would not drink it.
Such were the exploits of the three
warriors.
20 Abishai, Joab's brother, was the
leader of the Three.[A] He raised his
spear against 300 men and killed
them, gaining a reputation among
the Three. 21 He was more honored
than the Three and became their
commander even though he did not
become one of the Three.
22 Benaiah son of Jehoiada was the
son of a brave man[B] from Kabzeel,
a man of many exploits. Benaiah
killed two sons of Ariel of Moab,[C]
and he went down into a pit on a
snowy day and killed a lion. 23 He
also killed an Egyptian who was sev-
en and a half feet tall.[D] Even though
the Egyptian had a spear in his hand
like a weaver's beam, Benaiah went
down to him with a club, snatched
the spear out of the Egyptian's hand,
and then killed him with his own
spear. 24 These were the exploits of
Benaiah son of Jehoiada, who had
a reputation among the three warriors. 25 He was the most honored of
the Thirty, but he did not become
one of the Three. David put him in
charge of his bodyguard.

The Fighting Men, Warriors, and Soldiers (11:26–12:40)

26 The fighting men were:

Joab's brother Asahel,
Elhanan son of Dodo
of Bethlehem,
27 Shammoth the Harorite,
Helez the Pelonite,
28 Ira son of Ikkesh the Tekoite,
Abiezer the Anathothite,
29 Sibbecai the Hushathite,
Ilai the Ahohite,
30 Maharai the Netophathite,
Heled son of Baanah
the Netophathite,
31 Ithai son of Ribai from Gibeah
of the Benjaminites,
Benaiah the Pirathonite,
32 Hurai from the •wadis
of Gaash,
Abiel the Arbathite,
33 Azmaveth the Baharumite,
Eliahba the Shaalbonite,
34 the sons of[E] Hashem
the Gizonite,
Jonathan son of Shagee
the Hararite,
35 Ahiam son of Sachar
the Hararite,
Eliphal son of Ur,
36 Hepher the Mecherathite,
Ahijah the Pelonite,
37 Hezro the Carmelite,
Naarai son of Ezbai,
38 Joel the brother of Nathan,
Mibhar son of Hagri,
39 Zelek the Ammonite,
Naharai the Beerothite,
the armor-bearer for Joab
son of Zeruiah,
40 Ira the Ithrite,
Gareb the Ithrite,
41 Uriah the Hittite,
Zabad son of Ahlai,
42 Adina son of Shiza
the Reubenite, chief
of the Reubenites, and 30
with him,
43 Hanan son of Maacah,
Joshaphat the Mithnite,
44 Uzzia the Ashterathite,
Shama and Jeiel the sons
of Hotham the Aroerite,
45 Jediael son of Shimri
and his brother Joha
the Tizite,
46 Eliel the Mahavite,
Jeribai and Joshaviah,
the sons of Elnaam,
Ithmah the Moabite,
47 Eliel, Obed, and Jaasiel
the Mezobaite.

12 The following were the men
who came to David at Ziklag
while he was still banned from the
presence of Saul son of Kish. They
were among the warriors who
helped him in battle. 2 They were archers who could use either the right
or left hand, both to sling stones and
shoot arrows from a bow. They were
Saul's relatives from Benjamin:

3 Their chief was Ahiezer son
of Shemaah the Gibeathite.
Then there was his brother
Joash;
Jeziel and Pelet sons of
Azmaveth;
Beracah, Jehu the Anathothite;

[A] **11:20** Syr reads *Thirty* [B] **11:22** Or *was a valiant man* [C] **11:22** Or *He killed two Moabite warriors* [D] **11:23** Lit *who measured five cubits* [E] **11:34** LXX omits *the sons of*; 2Sm 23:32

[4] Ishmaiah the Gibeonite, a
warrior among the Thirty and
a leader over the Thirty;
[A]Jeremiah, Jahaziel, Johanan,
Jozabad the Gederathite;
[5] Eluzai, Jerimoth, Bealiah,
Shemariah, Shephatiah the
Haruphite;
[6] Elkanah, Isshiah, Azarel,
Joezer, and Jashobeam, the
Korahites;
[7] and Joelah and Zebadiah, the
sons of Jeroham from Gedor.

[8] Some Gadites defected to David
at his stronghold in the desert. They
were fighting men, trained for battle, expert with shield and spear.
Their faces were like the faces of
lions, and they were as swift as gazelles on the mountains.

9 Ezer was the chief,
Obadiah second, Eliab third,
10 Mishmannah fourth,
Jeremiah fifth,
11 Attai sixth, Eliel seventh,
12 Johanan eighth, Elzabad ninth,
13 Jeremiah tenth, and
Machbannai eleventh.

[14] These Gadites were army commanders; the least of them was a
match for a hundred, and the greatest of them for a thousand. [15] These
are the men who crossed the Jordan in the first month[B] when it was
overflowing all its banks, and put to
flight all those in the valleys to the
east and to the west.
[16] Other Benjaminites and men
from Judah also went to David at
the stronghold. [17] David went out to
meet them and said to them, "If you
have come in peace to help me, my
heart will be united with you, but if
you have come to betray me to my
enemies even though my hands
have done no wrong, may the God of
our ancestors look on it and judge."
[18] Then the Spirit took control of[C]
Amasai, chief of the Thirty, and he
said:

We are yours, David,
we are with you, son of Jesse!
Peace, peace to you,
and peace to him
who helps you,
for your God helps you.

So David received them and made
them leaders of his troops.
[19] Some Manassites defected to
David when he went with the Philistines to fight against Saul. However,
they did not help the Philistines
because the Philistine rulers sent
David away after a discussion. They
said, "It will be our heads if he de-
fects to his master Saul." [20] When
David went to Ziklag, some men
from Manasseh defected to him:
Adnah, Jozabad, Jediael, Michael,
Jozabad, Elihu, and Zillethai, chiefs
of thousands in Manasseh. [21] They
helped David against the raiders,
for they were all brave warriors and
commanders in the army. [22] At that
time, men came day after day to help
David until there was a great army,
like an army of God.[D]
[23] The numbers of the armed
troops who came to David at Hebron
to turn Saul's kingdom over to him,
according to the LORD's word, were
as follows:

24 From the Judahites: 6,800
armed troops bearing
shields and spears.
25 From the Simeonites:
7,100 brave warriors
ready for war.
26 From the Levites: 4,600 [27] in
addition to Jehoiada, leader
of the house of Aaron, with
3,700 men; [28] and Zadok,
a young brave warrior,
with 22 commanders from
his own ancestral house.
29 From the Benjaminites, the
relatives of Saul: 3,000 (up
to that time the majority
of the Benjaminites
maintained their
allegiance to the house
of Saul).
30 From the Ephraimites:
20,800 brave warriors who
were famous men in their
ancestral houses.
31 From half the tribe of
Manasseh: 18,000
designated by name to come
and make David king.
32 From the Issacharites, who
understood the times

12:1-22 This record demonstrated broad support for the new king, and its portrayal of the sort of men who voluntarily followed David sheds light on the king's character. That such disparate groups of powerful men united behind him testified to David's strength, integrity, wisdom, and courage.

[A] **12:4** 1Ch 12:5 in Hb [B] **12:15** = Nisan (March–April) [C] **12:18** Lit *Spirit clothed Himself with*; Jdg 6:34; 2Ch 24:20 [D] **12:22** Or *like the ultimate army*

12:23-37 All 12 tribes were represented in the census of **armed troops** (Hb *chalats*, the ones "being equipped or prepared for war") who were on hand to put **the Lord's word** into effect, including **the Levites** (vv. 26-28). The representatives of each tribe in his audience could vicariously take pride in their ancestors' participation in such a glorious event (vv. 24-37).

and knew what Israel
should do: 200 chiefs
with all their relatives
under their command.
33 From Zebulun: 50,000 who
could serve in the army,
trained for battle with
all kinds of weapons of
war, with one purpose
to help David.[A]
34 From Naphtali: 1,000
commanders accompanied
by 37,000 men with
shield and spear.
35 From the Danites: 28,600
trained for battle.
36 From Asher: 40,000 who
could serve in the army,
trained for battle.
37 From across the Jordan—
from the Reubenites,
Gadites, and half the tribe
of Manasseh: 120,000
men equipped with all the
military weapons of war.

38 All these warriors, lined up in
battle formation, came to Hebron
fully determined to make David king
over all Israel. All the rest of Israel
was also of one mind to make David
king. 39 They spent three days there
eating and drinking with David,
for their relatives had provided for
them. 40 In addition, their neighbors
from as far away as Issachar, Zebulun, and Naphtali came and brought
food on donkeys, camels, mules, and
oxen—abundant provisions of flour,
fig cakes, raisins, wine and oil, oxen,
and sheep. Indeed, there was joy in
Israel.

The Ark of God (13:1–16:43)

Outburst Against Uzzah (13:1-14)

13 David consulted with all his leaders, the commanders of
hundreds and of thousands. 2 Then
he said to the whole assembly of Israel, "If it seems good to you, and if
this is from the LORD our God, let us
spread out and send the message to
the rest of our relatives in all the districts of Israel, including the priests
and Levites in their cities with pasturelands, that they should gather
together with us. 3 Then let us bring
back the ark of our God, for we did
not inquire of Him in Saul's days."
4 Since the proposal seemed right to
all the people, the whole assembly
agreed to do it.
5 So David assembled all Israel,
from the Shihor of Egypt to the entrance of Hamath,[B] to bring the ark
of God from Kiriath-jearim. 6 David
and all Israel went to Baalah (that
is, Kiriath-jearim that belongs to
Judah) to take the ark of God from
there, which is called by the name
of the LORD who dwells between the
•cherubim. 7 At Abinadab's house
they set the ark of God on a new
cart. Uzzah and Ahio[C] were guiding
the cart.
8 David and all Israel were celebrating with all their might before God with songs and with lyres,
harps, tambourines, cymbals, and
trumpets. 9 When they came to Chidon's threshing floor, Uzzah reached
out to hold the ark because the oxen
had stumbled. 10 Then the LORD's
anger burned against Uzzah, and
He struck him dead because he had
reached out to the ark. So he died
there in the presence of God.
11 David was angry because of the
LORD's outburst against Uzzah, so he
named that place Outburst Against
Uzzah,[D] as it is still named today.
12 David feared God that day and
said, "How can I ever bring the ark
of God to me?" 13 So David did not
move the ark of God home[E] to the
city of David; instead, he took it to
the house of Obed-edom the Gittite. 14 The ark of God remained with
Obed-edom's family in his house for
three months, and the LORD blessed
his family and all that he had.

David's Fame (14:1-17)

14 King Hiram of Tyre sent envoys to David, along with
cedar logs, stonemasons, and carpenters to build a palace for him.
2 Then David knew that the LORD
had established him as king over Israel and that his kingdom had been
exalted for the sake of His people
Israel.
3 David took more wives in Jerusalem, and he became the father of

[A]**12:33** LXX; MT omits *David* [B]**13:5** Or *to Lebo-hamath* [C]**13:7** Or *and his brothers* [D]**13:11** Or *Perez-uzzah* [E]**13:13** Lit *to himself*

more sons and daughters. [4]These
are the names of the children born
to him in Jerusalem: Shammua,
Shobab, Nathan, Solomon, [5]Ibhar,
Elishua, Elpelet, [6]Nogah, Nepheg,
Japhia, [7]Elishama, Beeliada, and
Eliphelet.
[8]When the Philistines heard that
David had been anointed king over
all Israel, they all went in search
of David; when David heard of this,
he went out to face them. [9]Now the
Philistines had come and raided in
the Valley of Rephaim, [10]so David inquired of God, "Should I go to war
against the Philistines? Will You
hand them over to me?"
The LORD replied, "Go, and I will
hand them over to you."
[11]So the Israelites went up to
Baal-perazim, and David defeated
the Philistines there. Then David
said, "Like a bursting flood, God has
used me to burst out against my enemies." Therefore, they named that
place the Lord Bursts Out.[A] [12]The
Philistines abandoned their idols
there, and David ordered that they
be burned in the fire.
[13]Once again the Philistines raided in the valley. [14]So David again
inquired of God, and God answered
him, "Do not pursue them directly.
Circle around them and attack them
opposite the balsam trees. [15]When
you hear the sound of marching in
the tops of the balsam trees, then
march out to battle, for God will
have marched out ahead of you to
attack the camp of the Philistines."
[16]So David did exactly as God commanded him, and they struck down
the Philistine army from Gibeon to
Gezer. [17]Then David's fame spread
throughout the lands, and the LORD
caused all the nations to be terrified
of him.

The Celebration in Jerusalem (15:1–16:6)

15 David built houses for himself
in the city of David, and he prepared a place for the ark of God and
pitched a tent for it. [2]Then David
said, "No one but the Levites may
carry the ark of God, because the
LORD has chosen them to carry the
ark of the LORD and to minister before Him forever."
[3]David assembled all Israel at Jerusalem to bring the ark of the LORD
to the place he had prepared for it.
[4]Then he gathered together the descendants of Aaron and the Levites:
[5]From the Kohathites, Uriel the
leader and 120 of his relatives; [6]from
the Merarites, Asaiah the leader and
220 of his relatives; [7]from the Gershomites,[B] Joel the leader and 130
of his relatives; [8]from the Elizaphanites, Shemaiah the leader and
200 of his relatives; [9]from the Hebronites, Eliel the leader and 80 of
his relatives; [10]from the Uzzielites,
Amminadab the leader and 112 of
his relatives.
[11]David summoned the priests
Zadok and Abiathar and the Levites
Uriel, Asaiah, Joel, Shemaiah, Eliel,
and Amminadab. [12]He said to them,
"You are the heads of the Levite families. You and your relatives must
consecrate yourselves so that you
may bring the ark of the LORD God
of Israel to the place I have prepared
for it. [13]For the LORD our God burst
out in anger against us because you
Levites were not with us the first
time, for we didn't inquire of Him
about the proper procedures." [14]So
the priests and the Levites consecrated themselves to bring up the
ark of the LORD God of Israel. [15]Then
the Levites carried the ark of God
the way Moses had commanded according to the word of the LORD: on
their shoulders with the poles.
[16]Then David told the leaders of the
Levites to appoint their relatives as
singers and to have them raise their
voices with joy accompanied by musical instruments—harps, lyres, and
cymbals. [17]So the Levites appointed
Heman son of Joel; from his relatives, Asaph son of Berechiah; and
from their relatives the Merarites,
Ethan son of Kushaiah. [18]With them
were their relatives second in rank:
Zechariah, Jaaziel,[C] Shemiramoth,
Jehiel, Unni, Eliab, Benaiah, Maaseiah, Mattithiah, Eliphelehu, Mikneiah, and the gatekeepers Obed-edom
and Jeiel. [19]The singers Heman,
Asaph, and Ethan were to sound the

12:38-40 This section should be read in tandem with 11:1-3 for a more complete picture of this celebration at which David made a covenant with Israel and was anointed their king.

13:1-14 The narrative of these events in 2Sm 6 does not include the Chronicler's emphasis on the breadth of support David garnered for the idea of bringing the ark to Jerusalem (1Ch 13:1-4). From the historical vantage point of postexilic Israel, the writer recognized the theological significance of David's priority for directly associating his reign and his city with the presence of his God, **the LORD who dwells between the cherubim** of **the ark of God** (vv. 6-7; cp. Ex 25:22).

13:9-14 Although David apparently acted according to God's will (1Ch 13:2), Uzzah's tragic death magnified the dangers of failing to do God's will in His way (cp. 15:12-15; Ex 25:14). God demonstrated that His **presence**, uniquely revealed in the ark of the covenant, was undeniably real, holy, and powerful—not to be treated casually (1Ch 13:10). God's anger, David learned, was overshadowed by His mercy as He **blessed** the **family** of **Obed-edom** while the ark **remained** at **his house** (cp. Ps 2:10-12; 30:5).

14:1-17 With minor variations in wording, the content of chapter 14 parallels the account in 2Sm 5:11-25, except for the Chronicler's interpretation of these events in 1Ch 14:17. Despite his political prowess **David** was not justified in expanding his harem. Taking **more wives** was typical of a powerful ruler in the ancient Near East, but polygamy represented a deviation from God's standard (Dt 17:17; cp. the New Testament command for church leaders, 1Tm 3:2). Two sons—Elpelet and Nogah (1Ch 14:5-6), who are listed among the children born to David **in Jerusalem,** are not mentioned in the parallel account in 2Sm 5:13-16.

[A]**14:11** Or *Baal-perazim* [B]**15:7** = Gershonites [C]**15:18** Some Hb mss, LXX; other Hb mss read *Zechariah son and Jaaziel*

15:1-15 The narrative core of this chapter is also recorded in 2Sm 6:12-23. This expanded account details the involvement of those appointed by God to conduct worship for Israel—**the descendants of Aaron and the Levites**. These families remained responsible for carrying out the prescriptions of the sacrificial system when the temple was built by Solomon and rebuilt under Ezra's direction after the exile. By referring to **the ark** as that **of the LORD God of Israel**, David specified by the name *Yahweh* the one God of the people he served as king (vv. 12,14). David's unwavering devotion to and upholding of Yahweh as Israel's one and only God marked his reign and set the standard for every subsequent king of Israel and Judah.

15:16-24 David applied his personal interest in music to the organization of worship leaders specifically responsible for incorporating music in the corporate expression of joyful worship (cp. 6:31-46). The musicians' roles included singing—raising **their voices with joy**—and playing various **musical instruments** (15:16; cp. 13:8).

bronze cymbals; 20 Zechariah, Aziel,
Shemiramoth, Jehiel, Unni, Eliab,
Maaseiah, and Benaiah were to play
harps according to *Alamoth*;[A] 21 and
Mattithiah, Eliphelehu, Mikneiah,
Obed-edom, Jeiel, and Azaziah were
to lead the music with lyres according to the •*Sheminith*. 22 Chenaniah,
the leader of the Levites in music,
was to direct the music because he
was skillful. 23 Berechiah and Elkanah were to be gatekeepers for
the ark. 24 The priests, Shebaniah,
Joshaphat, Nethanel, Amasai, Zechariah, Benaiah, and Eliezer, were to
blow trumpets before the ark of God.
Obed-edom and Jehiah were also to
be gatekeepers for the ark.

25 David, the elders of Israel, and
the commanders of thousands went
with rejoicing to bring the ark of the
covenant of the LORD from the house
of Obed-edom. 26 While the Levites
were carrying the ark of the covenant of the LORD, with God's help,
they sacrificed seven bulls and seven
rams.

27 Now David was dressed in a robe
of fine linen, as were all the Levites
who were carrying the ark, as well as
the singers and Chenaniah, the music leader of the singers. David also
wore a linen •ephod. 28 So all Israel
brought up the ark of the covenant
of the LORD with shouts, the sound
of the ram's horn, trumpets, and
cymbals, and the playing of harps
and lyres. 29 As the ark of the covenant of the LORD was entering the
city of David, Saul's daughter Michal
looked down from the window and
saw King David dancing[B] and celebrating, and she despised him in
her heart.

16 They brought the ark of God and placed it inside the tent
David had pitched for it. Then they
offered •burnt offerings and •fellowship offerings in God's presence.
2 When David had finished offering
the burnt offerings and the fellowship offerings, he blessed the people
in the name of •Yahweh. 3 Then he
distributed to each and every Israelite, both men and women, a loaf of
bread, a date cake, and a raisin cake.
4 David appointed some of the Levites to be ministers before the ark
of the LORD, to celebrate the LORD
God of Israel, and to give thanks and
praise to Him. 5 •Asaph was the chief
and Zechariah was second to him.
Jeiel, Shemiramoth, Jehiel, Mattithiah, Eliab, Benaiah, Obed-edom,
and Jeiel played the harps and lyres,
while Asaph sounded the cymbals
6 and the priests Benaiah and Jahaziel blew the trumpets regularly
before the ark of the covenant of
God.

David's Psalm of Praise (16:7-43)

7 On that day David decreed for the
first time that thanks be given to the
LORD by Asaph and his relatives:

8 Give thanks to Yahweh;
call on His name;
proclaim His deeds among
the peoples.
9 Sing to Him; sing praise
to Him;
tell about all
His wonderful works!
10 Honor His holy name;
let the hearts of those
who seek Yahweh rejoice.
11 Search for the LORD and for
His strength;
seek His face always.
12 Remember the wonderful works
He has done,
His wonders,
and the judgments
He has pronounced,[C]
13 you offspring of Israel
His servant,
Jacob's descendants—
His chosen ones.

14 He is the LORD our God;
His judgments govern
the whole earth.
15 Remember His covenant
forever—
the promise He ordained
for a thousand generations,
16 the covenant He made
with Abraham,
swore[D] to Isaac,
17 and confirmed to Jacob
as a decree,
and to Israel
as an everlasting covenant:

[A] **15:20** This may refer to a high pitch, perhaps a tune sung by soprano voices; the Hb word means "young women"; Ps 46 title [B] **15:29** Or *whirling* [C] **16:12** Lit *judgments of His mouth* [D] **16:16** Lit *and His oath*

>WORD|*study*

16:8 The psalm begins with two imperatives:

- Give thanks (Hb *yadah*, "laud, praise, celebrate"), which follows from the primary meaning "to throw or cast," requiring the extension of one's hand. Its alternate meaning, "to profess or confess," draws from this picture of extending one's hand "to show or point out."
- Proclaim (Hb *yada'*, "make known, show something to someone, teach, acquaint") connects giving thanks with talking about what God has done—not just among themselves but publicly, "among the peoples."

18 "I will give the land of Canaan
to you
as your inherited portion."
19 When they[A] were few
in number,
very few indeed,
and temporary residents
in Canaan
20 wandering from nation
to nation
and from one kingdom
to another,
21 He allowed no one to oppress
them;
He rebuked kings
on their behalf:
22 "Do not touch My anointed ones
or harm My prophets."
23 Sing to the LORD, all the earth.
Proclaim His salvation
from day to day.
24 Declare His glory
among the nations,
His wonderful works
among all peoples.
25 For the LORD is great
and highly praised;
He is feared above all gods.
26 For all the gods of the peoples
are idols,
but the LORD made
the heavens.
27 Splendor and majesty are
before Him;
strength and joy are
in His place.
28 Ascribe to the LORD, families
of the peoples,
ascribe to the LORD glory
and strength.
29 Ascribe to Yahweh the glory
of His name;
bring an offering and come
before Him.
Worship the LORD
in the splendor
of His holiness;
30 tremble before Him,
all the earth.
The world is
firmly established;
it cannot be shaken.
31 Let the heavens be glad
and the earth rejoice,
and let them say
among the nations,
"The LORD is King!"
32 Let the sea and everything
in it resound;
let the fields and all that is
in them exult.
33 Then the trees of the forest
will shout for joy
before the LORD,
for He is coming to judge
the earth.
34 Give thanks to the LORD,
for He is good;
His faithful love
endures forever.
35 And say: "Save us,
God of our salvation;
gather us and rescue us from
the nations
so that we may give thanks to
Your holy name
and rejoice in Your praise.
36 May Yahweh, the God
of Israel, be praised
from everlasting
to everlasting."

Then all the people said, "Amen"
and "Praise the LORD."
37 So David left Asaph and his
relatives there before the ark of the
LORD's covenant to minister regularly before the ark according to the
daily requirements. 38 He assigned

15:25-29 David's clothing not only displayed his spiritual preparation and reverence but also signaled his leadership here as chief among the divine King's servants rather than as a regal head of state. The Chronicler again emphasized that **all Israel** participated in the triumphant procession of bringing **the ark of the covenant** to the city of David.

16:1-6 By sharing both bread and sweet cakes with the people, David acted as a joyful and generous host, enlisting them to exult with him in the joy of experiencing God's favor (v. 3).

16:7-36 Whether or not David himself composed the psalm, portions of which also comprise Ps 105:1-15 (1Ch 16:8-22); Ps 96:1b,2b-9,10b,11-13a (1Ch 16:23-33); and Ps 106:1,47-48 (1Ch 16:34-36) is not clear. It does not appear in its entirety in the book of Psalms, and some differences in wording reflect the Chronicler's historical perspective and context (e.g., v. 27b—"strength and *joy* are in His *place*"; Ps 96:6—strength and *beauty* are in His *sanctuary*"), but neither of these facts rules out the possibility that the parallel portions of Ps 96; 105; and 106 were borrowed from this one to suit subsequent occasions for worship.

16:37 David followed through in his mission of restoring the ark of the covenant to its central position in the nation of Israel (cp. "tent of meeting," Nm 2:1,17).

[A] **16:19** One Hb ms, LXX, Vg; other Hb mss read *you*

16:39-43 The return of both **the people** and the king to their respective **homes** illustrated the people's security, the priority of the **household** as the fundamental unit of society, and David's modeling of this priority in his intention to share his joy with those at the palace awaiting his return. Although he undoubtedly verbalized a blessing, his *presence* at home surely blessed his household as well, in much the same way that the presence of the divine King blessed Jerusalem and all Israel with His favor, protection, and **faithful love** (vv. 34,41; cp. 15:29; 2Sm 6:19-22).

17:1-27 Chapter 17 closely parallels 2Sm 7, thus repeating the Davidic covenant (cp. 1Ch 17:11-14 and 2Sm 7:12-17) and David's psalm of thanksgiving (cp. 1Ch 17:16-27 and 2Sm 7:18-29). Appreciating God's word to David given through Nathan the prophet is crucial not only for understanding the theological significance of David's reign over Israel but also for recognizing Christ's ongoing fulfillment of the divine promise. God answered David's desire to build Him a **house** (Hb *bayit*, "dwelling, home, tent, palace, temple," 1Ch 17:4) with a declaration that He would **build a house for** David (i.e., a "dynasty or heritage"; cp. 1Sm 2:35). A messianic interpretation of God's promise to David would not have been missed by the Chronicler's original audience attuned to the Scripture's use of the words "seed" (**descendant**, 1Ch 17:11) and **forever** (cp. Gn 3:15; 13:15; 17:19; 48:4; Ex 15:18; 32:13). The earliest witnesses and followers of Jesus likewise recognized Him to be both "the Son of David"—the Christ (Jn 7:42; Ac 13:22-23; Rm 1:3; 9:7-8; Gl 3:14-29; 2Tm 2:8) and the one true King of all (Zch 9:9; Mt 2:1-2; 21:5; Jn 1:49; 12:15; Rv 15:3; 17:14; 19:16).

Obed-edom and his[A] 68 relatives.
Obed-edom son of Jeduthun and
Hosah were to be gatekeepers. 39 David left Zadok the priest and his fellow priests before the tabernacle of
the LORD at the •high place in Gibeon
40 to offer burnt offerings regularly,
morning and evening, to the LORD
on the altar of burnt offerings and
to do everything that was written in
the law of the LORD, which He had
commanded Israel to keep. 41 With
them were Heman, Jeduthun, and
the rest who were chosen and designated by name to give thanks to the
LORD—for His faithful love endures
forever. 42 Heman and Jeduthun had
with them trumpets and cymbals
to play and musical instruments of
God. Jeduthun's sons were at the
gate.
43 Then all the people left for their
homes, and David returned home to
bless his household.

The LORD's Covenant with David (17:1-27)

17 When David had settled into
his palace, he said to Nathan
the prophet, "Look! I am living in
a cedar house while the ark of the
LORD's covenant is under tent curtains."
2 So Nathan told David, "Do all
that is on your heart, for God is with
you."
3 But that night the word of God
came to Nathan: 4 "Go to David My
servant and say, 'This is what the
LORD says: You are not the one to
build Me a house to dwell in. 5 From
the time I brought Israel out of
Egypt until today I have not lived
in a house; instead, I have moved
from tent to tent and from tabernacle to tabernacle. 6 In all My travels
throughout Israel, have I ever spoken a word to even one of the judges
of Israel, whom I commanded to
shepherd My people, asking: Why
haven't you built Me a house of cedar?'
7 "Now this is what you will say
to My servant David: 'This is what
the LORD of •Hosts says: I took you
from the pasture and from following the sheep to be ruler over My
people Israel. 8 I have been with you
wherever you have gone, and I have
destroyed all your enemies before
you. I will make a name for you like
that of the greatest in the land. 9 I
will establish a place for My people
Israel and plant them, so that they
may live there and not be disturbed
again. Evildoers will not continue to
oppress them as they formerly have
10 ever since the day I ordered judges
to be over My people Israel. I will
also subdue all your enemies.
"'Furthermore, I declare to you
that the LORD Himself will build a
house for you. 11 When your time
comes to be with your fathers, I will
raise up after you your descendant,
who is one of your own sons, and I
will establish his kingdom. 12 He will
build a house for Me, and I will establish his throne forever. 13 I will be
a father to him, and he will be a son
to Me. I will not take away My faithful love from him as I took it from
the one who was before you. 14 I will
appoint him over My house and My
kingdom forever, and his throne will
be established forever.'"
15 Nathan reported all these words
and this entire vision to David.
16 Then King David went in, sat in
the LORD's presence, and said,

Who am I, LORD God, and what
is my house that You have
brought me this far? 17 This was
a little thing to You,[B] God, for
You have spoken about Your
servant's house in the distant
future. You regard me as a
man of distinction,[C] LORD God.
18 What more can David say to
You for honoring Your servant?
You know Your servant. 19 LORD,
You have done all this greatness, making known all these
great promises because of Your
servant and according to Your
will. 20 LORD, there is no one like
You, and there is no God besides
You, as all we have heard confirms. 21 And who is like Your
people Israel? God, You came to
one nation on earth to redeem
a people for Yourself, to make
a name for Yourself through
great and awesome works by

[A]16:38 LXX, Syr, Vg; Hb reads *their* [B]17:17 Lit *thing in Your eyes* [C]17:17 Hb obscure

18:1 In keeping with the building of the temple as an integral theme of 1 Chronicles, chapter 17 unveils David's hopes for building the temple and the Lord's promise that it would be built by David's son. Chapters 18–20 establish the historical and political contexts for the enterprise. Chapter 18 varies little from its parallel in 2Sm 8.

>WORD|*study*

17:1 Tent curtains (Hb *yeri'ah*, "drapes,") were the fabric walls that formed the structure of the tabernacle according to its original design (Ex 26:1-14; 36:8-17). Many of the former exiles would have recalled the symbolic significance of the tabernacle's curtains in both (1) God's prior descriptions of judgment proclaimed in Jerusalem by Jeremiah the prophet—"Suddenly my tents are destroyed, my tent curtains, in a moment" (Jr 4:20;10:20)—and (2) God's promise of restoration, including the command, "Enlarge the site of your tent, and let your tent curtains be stretched out" (Is 54:2).

driving out nations before Your
people You redeemed from
Egypt. 22 You made Your people
Israel Your own people forever,
and You, LORD, have become
their God.

23 Now, LORD, let the word that
You have spoken concerning
Your servant and his house be
confirmed forever, and do as
You have promised. 24 Let Your
name be confirmed and magnified forever in the saying, "Yahweh of Hosts, the God of Israel,
is God over Israel." May the
house of Your servant David be
established before You. 25 Since
You, my God, have revealed
to[A] Your servant that You will
build him a house, Your servant has found courage to pray
in Your presence. 26 Yahweh,
You indeed are God, and You
have promised this good thing
to Your servant. 27 So now, You
have been pleased to bless Your
servant's house that it may
continue before You forever.
For You, LORD, have blessed it,
and it is blessed forever.

Military Campaigns (18:1–20:8)

Philistines, Moabites, Arameans, and Edomites (18:1-17)

18 After this, David defeated the
Philistines, subdued them, and
took Gath and its villages from Philistine control. 2 He also defeated the
Moabites, and they became David's
subjects and brought tribute.
3 David also defeated King Hadadezer of Zobah at Hamath when he
went to establish his control at the
Euphrates River. 4 David captured
1,000 chariots, 7,000 horsemen, and
20,000 foot soldiers from him, hamstrung all the horses, and kept 100
chariots.[B]
5 When the Arameans of Damascus came to assist King Hadadezer
of Zobah, David struck down 22,000
Aramean men. 6 Then he placed garrisons[C] in Aram of Damascus, and
the Arameans became David's subjects and brought tribute. The LORD
made David victorious wherever he
went.
7 David took the gold shields carried by Hadadezer's officers and
brought them to Jerusalem. 8 From
Tibhath and Cun, Hadadezer's cities,
David also took huge quantities of
bronze, from which Solomon made
the bronze reservoir, the pillars, and
the bronze articles.
9 When King Tou of Hamath heard
that David had defeated the entire
army of King Hadadezer of Zobah,
10 he sent his son Hadoram to King
David to greet him and to congratulate him because David had fought
against Hadadezer and defeated him,
for Tou and Hadadezer had fought
many wars. Hadoram brought all
kinds of gold, silver, and bronze
items. 11 King David also dedicated
these to the LORD, along with the silver and gold he had carried off from
all the nations—from Edom, Moab,
the Ammonites, the Philistines, and
the Amalekites.
12 Abishai son of Zeruiah struck
down 18,000 Edomites in the Valley
of Salt. 13 He put garrisons in Edom,
and all the Edomites were subject to
David. The LORD made David victorious wherever he went.
14 So David reigned over all Israel,

[A] 17:25 Lit *have uncovered the ear of* [B] 18:4 Or *chariot horses* [C] 18:6 Some Hb mss, LXX, Vg; other Hb mss omit *garrisons*; 2Sm 8:6

19:1-19 Except for differences in a few details and in wording, chapter 19 parallels 2Sm 10 and 12:26-31. Chronicles does not mention the unsavory events described in 2Sm 11 and 13:1–21:14, including the king's adultery with Bathsheba, a daughter's rape by one of his sons and the attempt of her avenging brother to usurp the throne. These events did not suit the Chronicler's purpose of focusing the attention of Israel's remnant on what had made David's kingdom glorious as a paradigm for God's promised restoration and ultimately for the coming Messiah's kingdom.

>WORD|*study*

18:14 David's reign was characterized by justice [Hb *mishpat*, "the act of judging or upholding the law, right judgment, fairness"] and righteousness (Hb *tsedaqah*, "justice, integrity, virtue"), twin characteristics attributed to "the Almighty" (Jb 37:23), exalted as what the Lord "loves" and that in which He takes "delight" (Pss 33:5; 99:4; Jr 9:24), and repeatedly descriptive of the Lord's reign and His expectations, therefore, of His people (Ps 71:1-2; Is 5:7,16; 28:17; 33:5; 51:5; 56:1; Hs 2:19; Am 5:24). Especially from the Chronicler's perspective of hindsight, David was unmistakably linked with messianic prophecy (1Ch 18:14; cp. Is 9:2-7; Jr 23:5; 33:15).

administering justice and righteousness for all his people.

15 Joab son of Zeruiah was
over the army;
Jehoshaphat son of Ahilud
was court historian;
16 Zadok son of Ahitub
and Ahimelech[A]
son of Abiathar were priests;
Shavsha was court secretary;
17 Benaiah son of Jehoiada
was over
the Cherethites
and the Pelethites;
and David's sons were
the chief officials
at the king's side.

Ammonites and Arameans (19:1–20:3)

19 Some time later, King Nahash
of the Ammonites died, and his
son became king in his place. 2 Then
David said, "I'll show kindness to
Hanun son of Nahash, because his
father showed kindness to me."
So David sent messengers to console him concerning his father. However, when David's emissaries arrived
in the land of the Ammonites to console him, 3 the Ammonite leaders said
to Hanun, "Just because David has sent men with condolences for you, do you really believe he's showing respect for your father? Instead, hasn't David sent his emissaries in order to scout out, overthrow, and spy on
the land?" 4 So Hanun took David's
emissaries, shaved them, cut their clothes in half at the hips, and sent them away.
5 It was reported to David about his
men, so he sent messengers to meet them, since the men were deeply humiliated. The king said, "Stay in Jericho until your beards grow back; then return."
6 When the Ammonites realized
they had made themselves repulsive to David, Hanun and the Ammonites sent 38 tons[B] of silver to hire chariots and horsemen from Aram-naharaim, Aram-maacah, and Zobah.
7 They hired 32,000 chariots and the
king of Maacah with his army, who came and camped near Medeba. The Ammonites also came together from their cities for the battle.
8 David heard about this and sent
Joab and the entire army of warriors.
9 The Ammonites marched out and
lined up in battle formation at the entrance of the city while the kings who had come were in the field by
themselves. 10 When Joab saw that
there was a battle line in front of him and another behind him, he chose some men out of all the elite troops[C] of Israel and lined up in battle formation to engage the Arameans. 11 He
placed the rest of the forces under the command of his brother Abishai, and they lined up in battle formation to engage the Ammonites.
12 "If the Arameans are too strong
for me," Joab said, "then you'll be my help. However, if the Ammonites are too strong for you, I'll help you.
13 Be strong! We must prove ourselves strong for our people and for the cities of our God. May the LORD's will be done."[D]
14 Joab and the people with him approached the Arameans for battle, and
they fled before him. 15 When the Ammonites saw that the Arameans had fled, they likewise fled before Joab's brother Abishai and entered the city. Then Joab went to Jerusalem.
16 When the Arameans realized
that they had been defeated by Israel, they sent messengers to summon the Arameans who were across the Euphrates. They were led by Sho-

[A] **18:16** Some Hb mss, LXX, Syr, Vg; other Hb mss read *Abimelech*; 2Sm 8:17 [B] **19:6** Lit *1,000 talents* [C] **19:10** Lit *the choice ones*; 2Sm 6:1 [D] **19:13** Lit *the LORD do what is good in His eyes*

>WORD|*study*

21:1 The Chronicler identified Satan (Hb "adversary, accuser, enemy"), rather than "the LORD's anger . . . against Israel," as the personal instigator of David's sin (cp. 2Sm 24:1). This is the first time "Satan" appears in Scripture without an article and, therefore, as a name (cp. Jb 1:6 and Zch 3:1-2, the only other uses of the name in the Old Testament).

21:3 Prior to Joab's comment reported by the Chronicler, the word guilt (Hb *'ashmah*, "fault, sin, trespass,") appeared only in Leviticus and denoted "wrongdoing or offense" against God (Lv 4:3; 6:5-7; 22:16). The word appears infrequently in the Old Testament despite Scripture's extensive treatment of sin but typically designates the comprehensive "guilt" ascribed to all those under the authority of the one who actually committed the sin. David's own use of the word in Ps 69:5 demonstrated his recognition of the corporate consequences of his personal "guilty acts" (Ps 69:6). Unfortunately for the lives of "70,000 Israelite men," David asserted his own will against the wise advice of his top-ranking general and incurred God's punishment on "the whole territory of Israel" (1Ch 21:5-6,12,14).

phach, the commander of Hadadezer's army.
17 When this was reported to David,
he gathered all Israel and crossed
the Jordan. He came up to the Arameans and lined up in battle formation against them. When David
lined up to engage them in battle,
they fought against him. 18 But the
Arameans fled before Israel, and David killed 7,000 of their charioteers
and 40,000 foot soldiers. He also
killed Shophach, commander of the
army. 19 When Hadadezer's subjects
saw that they had been defeated by
Israel, they made peace with David
and became his subjects. After this,
the Arameans were never willing to
help the Ammonites again.

20 In the spring[A] when kings
march out to war, Joab led the
army and destroyed the Ammonites'
land. He came to Rabbah and besieged it, but David remained in Jerusalem. Joab attacked Rabbah and
demolished it. 2 Then David took the
crown from the head of their king,[B,C]
and it was placed on David's head.
He found that the crown weighed 75
pounds[D] of gold, and there was a precious stone in it. In addition, David
took away a large quantity of plunder
from the city. 3 He brought out the
people who were in it and put them
to work with saws,[E] iron picks, and
axes.[F] David did the same to all the
Ammonite cities. Then he and all his
troops returned to Jerusalem.

Philistines (20:4-8)

4 After this, a war broke out with
the Philistines at Gezer. At that time
Sibbecai the Hushathite killed Sip-
pai, a descendant of the giants,[G] and
the Philistines were subdued.
5 Once again there was a battle
with the Philistines, and Elhanan
son of Jair killed Lahmi the brother
of Goliath the Gittite. The shaft of
his spear was like a weaver's beam.
6 There was still another battle at
Gath where there was a man of extraordinary stature with six fingers
on each hand and six toes on each
foot—24 in all. He, too, was descended from the giant.[H] 7 When he
taunted Israel, Jonathan son of David's brother Shimei killed him.
8 These were the descendants of
the giant[H] in Gath killed by David
and his soldiers.

A Military Census (21:1–22:1)

Sin (21:1-8)

21 Satan[I] stood up against Israel
and incited David to count
the people of Israel. 2 So David said
to Joab and the commanders of the
troops, "Go and count Israel from
Beer-sheba to Dan and bring a report to me so I can know their number."
3 Joab replied, "May the LORD
multiply the number of His people
a hundred times over! My lord the
king, aren't they all my lord's servants? Why does my lord want to do
this? Why should he bring •guilt on
Israel?"
4 Yet the king's order prevailed
over Joab. So Joab left and traveled throughout Israel and then

20:1-3 Readers familiar with the monarchy's history recounted in 2 Samuel would easily recognize the setting established in verse 1 as that of David's pursuit of Bathsheba (2Sm 11:1–12:25)—the writer assumed that the account of David's sin did not need to be repeated. The narrative here wraps up the account of David's subjection of the Ammonites, including his placement of the offending king's stunning crown upon his own head, visually asserting his rule over his enemies.

20:4-8 Second Samuel reported that **Elhanan** (Hb, "God has been gracious") killed Goliath himself (v. 5; 2Sm 21:19). Although the two accounts present textual difficulties, which scholars have not fully resolved, a possible solution to the discrepancy is that more than one **Gittite** boasted the name "Goliath"—perhaps even the son of the man slain by David—just as David's soldiers apparently included two different men by the name "Elhanan"—the **son of Jair** (1Ch 20:5; cp. 2Sm 21:9) and the "son of Dodo," one of "the Thirty" (2Sm 23:24; 1Ch 11:26).

21:1-30 An account of the events described in chapter 21 can be found in 2Sm 24, but the Chronicler's narrative reflects a different perspective and purpose.

21:1-8 To attribute to Satan the idea for taking an unauthorized census would immediately alert readers to the spiritual nature of the narrative. The text makes clear that David gave the orders **to count** all Israel only to satisfy his desire **to know their number**, contrary to the two occasions that God Himself commanded that a census be taken (Ex 30:11-16; 38:25, Nm 26). Joab, protesting David's decision, used potent language to warn the king about the spiritual danger involved. Pursuing the census amounted to bringing **guilt** not merely on David's head but **on Israel**. The Chronicler added an important detail beyond the account in 2 Samuel. Because Joab regarded the king's orders to be **detestable** (Hb *ta'av*, "abhorrent, abominable, or revolting"), he intervened to spare **Levi and Benjamin**, tribes of particular importance to the writer (1Ch 21:6; cp. 1Ch 6–8). In 2Sm 24:9, the numbers of **swordsmen** were reported differently—"800,000 fighting men from Israel and 500,000 men from Judah." The figure for Judah was probably rounded up.

A **20:1** Lit *At the time of the return of the year* B **20:2** LXX, Vg read *of Milcom* C **20:2** = Molech; 1Kg 11:5,7 D **20:2** Lit *a talent* E **20:3** Text emended; MT reads *and sawed them with the saw*; 2Sm 12:31 F **20:3** Text emended; MT reads *saws*; 2Sm 12:31 G **20:4** Or *the Rephaites* H **20:6,8** Or *Raphah* I **21:1** Or *An adversary*; Jb 1:6; Zch 3:1-2

21:9-15 The prophet **Gad** was instructed by God to give **David** a choice of punishment, one of the agonizing consequences for David (v. 13). The king who had decided to do as he pleased about the census was confronted with a God-sized dilemma, which confirmed his lack of discernment and wisdom. David's preference for the affliction of the Lord demonstrated his hope in God's mercy. David should have trusted God to maintain a sufficient number of men eligible for military service throughout Israel, and He should have recognized that the people were God's to count, not his. Note that God was setting the conditions for the consequences of sin.

21:17–22:1 The Chronicler's commentary explains how Ornan's **threshing floor** came to be designated as the site for **the house of the Lord God**. As the former exiles embraced the task of rebuilding the temple, to remember why its location was considered sacred was fundamental. The **fire from heaven** (v. 25) dramatically signified God's acceptance of the sacrifice, the appeasing of His wrath, and the selection of the altar and threshing floor as the place where a temple would be built for His Name (2Ch 6:5-6).

returned to Jerusalem. 5 Joab gave the total troop registration to David. In all Israel there were 1,100,000 swordsmen and in Judah itself 470,000 swordsmen. 6 But he did not include Levi and Benjamin in the count because the king's command was detestable to him. 7 This command was also evil in God's sight, so He afflicted Israel.

8 David said to God, "I have sinned greatly because I have done this thing. Now, please take away Your servant's guilt, for I've been very foolish."

Punishment (21:9-15)

9 Then the LORD instructed Gad, David's seer, 10 "Go and say to David, 'This is what the LORD says: I am offering you three choices. Choose one of them for yourself, and I will do it to you.'"

11 So Gad went to David and said to him, "This is what the LORD says: 'Take your choice: 12 three years of famine, or three months of devastation by your foes with the sword of your enemy overtaking you, or three days of the sword of the LORD—a plague on the land, the angel of the LORD bringing destruction to the whole territory of Israel.' Now decide what answer I should take back to the One who sent me."

13 David answered Gad, "I'm in anguish. Please, let me fall into the LORD's hands because His mercies are very great, but don't let me fall into human hands."

14 So the LORD sent a plague on Israel, and 70,000 Israelite men died. 15 Then God sent an angel to Jerusalem to destroy it, but when the angel was about to destroy the city,[A] the LORD looked, relented concerning the destruction, and said to the angel who was destroying the people, "Enough, withdraw your hand now!" The angel of the LORD was then standing at the threshing floor of Ornan[B] the Jebusite.

Repentance, Obedience, and Answered Prayer (21:16–22:1)

16 When David looked up and saw the angel of the LORD standing between earth and heaven, with his drawn sword in his hand stretched out over Jerusalem, David and the elders, clothed in •sackcloth, fell down with their faces to the ground. 17 David said to God, "Wasn't I the one who gave the order to count the people? I am the one who has sinned and acted very wickedly. But these sheep, what have they done? My LORD God, please let Your hand be against me and against my father's family, but don't let the plague be against Your people."

18 So the angel of the LORD ordered Gad to tell David to go and set up an altar to the LORD on the threshing floor of Ornan the Jebusite. 19 David went up at Gad's command spoken in the name of the LORD.

20 Ornan was threshing wheat when he turned and saw the angel. His four sons, who were with him, hid themselves. 21 David came to Ornan, and when Ornan looked and saw David, he left the threshing floor and bowed to David with his face to the ground.

22 Then David said to Ornan, "Give me this threshing-floor plot so that I may build an altar to the LORD on it. Give it to me for the full price, so the plague on the people may be stopped."

23 Ornan said to David, "Take it! My lord the king may do whatever

HARD QUESTION

How should we respond to God's discipline?

Have you ever wrestled over how God's providence (His sovereign purposes working through history) fits with your failures? Have you had a genuine heart of repentance while still facing the consequences of your foolish sin (Heb 12:5-11)? Be encouraged as you remembers that God works "all things" together "for the good of those who love God: those who are called according to His purpose" (Rm 8:28). God often prepares you for particular tasks in His kingdom in unexpected ways, including the painful process of exposing your sin and developing humility. David's repentance and renewed obedience did not undo the terrible effects of his sin on the people for whom he was responsible, but God mercifully spared many lives on account of David's honest confession and costly sacrifice. (1Ch 21:17–22:1)

[A] **21:15** Lit *but as he was destroying* [B] **21:15-28** = Araunah in 2Sm 24:16-24

>WORD|*study*

22:5 David may have described Solomon as inexperienced (Hb *rak*, "tender, weak, immature"; cp. 29:1) because of his son's age. However, Solomon had grown up without the responsibilities of the shepherd's life David had and without the faith-building challenges of being a fugitive leading a growing army of outcasts. The word suggests that David, sensing the magnitude of the task, recognized that without all the help he could muster, Solomon would be like a young boy trying to run in his daddy's shoes.

22:9 Rest is used as both verb and noun in this passage. The word's core meaning is "respiration or drawing a breath." God promised, **I will give him rest** (Hb *nuach*, a verb), emphasizing that deliverance and protection of Israel from her "surrounding enemies" was His doing—the result neither of the strength of David's army nor of Solomon's wisdom (cp. Ex 33:14). The New Testament writer of Hebrews recognized a parallel between God's giving rest to Israel from her enemies and the believer's having "rested" (Gk *katepausen*, "caused to be at rest") from the fruitless efforts to achieve peace with God through one's "own works" (Heb 4:8-10).

Regarding David's son, God promised:

- He would be a man of rest (Hb *menuchah*, "quietness, resting place"; cp. 1Ch 28:2-3; Ps 132:8,14; Is 32:17-18; 66:1);
- He would be named Solomon (Hb "Peace," from the noun *shalom*);
- He would be given peace (Hb *shalom*, "peace, quiet, safety" in the sense of being "whole and complete" rather than involved in conflict or division);
- He would be given quiet (Hb *sheqet*, "tranquility"), a word that appears only here in the Old Testament but is derived from the verb *shaqat*, and has the sense of "freedom from being harassed, being undisturbed, or given relief," and therefore being "at peace" rather than at war (cp. 1Ch 4:40; Jos 11:23; 14:15; Ps 94:13).

Such "rest," furnished by God's power and presence, had been forfeited when Israel spurned the Lord and was exiled as a result (Dt 28:64-65). Those who have entered into a covenant relationship with Jesus Christ have been given an eternal rest (Heb 4:10-11).

22:6-16 The king's speech presented Solomon with the weighty commission born in the heart of his earthly father but ordained and assigned by **the Lord**, his heavenly **father** (vv. 10-11). Rehearsing David's speech to Solomon—with its emphasis on this son's responsibility to build the temple, on Solomon's reign being one of unprecedented unity and peace, and on his inheritance of an eternal throne—undoubtedly stoked the fires of hope among those rebuilding the temple for complete restoration of Israel as the people of the eternal, promise-keeping God.

he wants.[A] See, I give the oxen for
the •burnt offerings, the threshing
sledges for the wood, and the wheat
for the •grain offering—I give it all."
24 King David answered Ornan,
"No, I insist on paying the full price,
for I will not take for the LORD what
belongs to you or offer burnt offerings that cost me nothing."
25 So David gave Ornan 15 pounds
of gold[B] for the plot. 26 He built an
altar to the LORD there and offered
burnt offerings and •fellowship offerings. He called on the LORD, and
He answered him with fire from
heaven on the altar of burnt offering.
27 Then the LORD spoke to the
angel, and he put his sword back
into its sheath. 28 At that time, David offered sacrifices there when
he saw that the LORD answered
him at the threshing floor of Ornan the Jebusite. 29 The tabernacle
of the LORD, which Moses made in
the desert, and the altar of burnt
offering were at the •high place in
Gibeon, 30 but David could not go
before it to inquire of God, because
he was terrified of the sword of the
22 LORD's angel. 1 Then David said,
"This is the house of the LORD
God, and this is the altar of •burnt
offering for Israel."

Building Materials and Charge to Solomon (22:2–23:1)

2 So David gave orders to gather
the foreigners that were in the land
of Israel, and he appointed stonecutters to cut finished stones for building God's house. 3 David supplied a
great deal of iron to make the nails
for the doors of the gateways and for
the fittings, together with an immeasurable quantity of bronze, 4 and
innumerable cedar logs because the
Sidonians and Tyrians had brought
a large quantity of cedar logs to David. 5 David said, "My son Solomon
is young and inexperienced, and the
house that is to be built for the LORD
must be exceedingly great and famous and glorious in all the lands.
Therefore, I must make provision
for it." So David made lavish preparations for it before his death.
6 Then he summoned his son Solomon and instructed him to build a
house for the LORD God of Israel.
7 "My son," David said to Solomon,
"It was in my heart to build a house
for the name of •Yahweh my God,
8 but the word of the LORD came to
me: 'You have shed much blood and
waged great wars. You are not to
build a house for My name because
you have shed so much blood on the

[A]21:23 Lit *do what is good in his eyes* [B]21:25 Lit *600 shekels of gold by weight*

22:9 See **Word Study**, p. 515.

23:1 Not only did **David** personally commission **Solomon** and Israel's leaders to build the Lord's temple, but David also personally transferred the office of king to **his son**. First Kings 1–2 demonstrates that the Lord effected this transition of power through the words and actions of a variety of people.

23:2-32 Before his death, David himself summoned and organized the companies of **Levites** who would carry out the duties of worship when the temple was complete. The 24 **divisions** of 1,000 members each illustrate the importance of continuity between the structure of tabernacle service and service of the temple to be built by Solomon (vv. 4-6). These details would also have been of keen interest to the former exiles engaged in building or maintaining a second temple (cp. 1Ch 9:2,10-33; Ezr 1:5; 2:36-54,70).

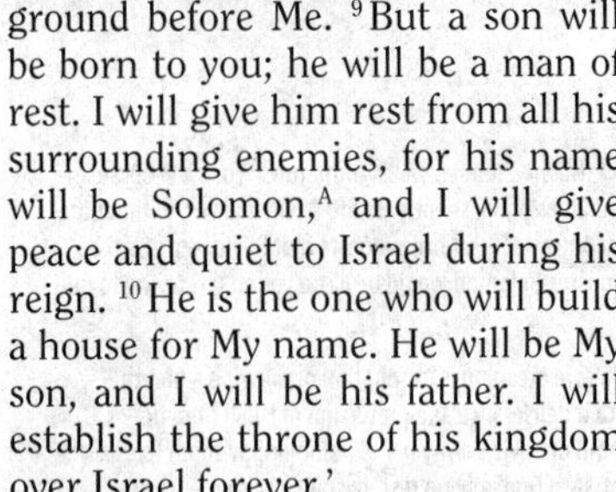

ground before Me. 9 But a son will
be born to you; he will be a man of
rest. I will give him rest from all his
surrounding enemies, for his name
will be Solomon,[A] and I will give
peace and quiet to Israel during his
reign. 10 He is the one who will build
a house for My name. He will be My
son, and I will be his father. I will
establish the throne of his kingdom
over Israel forever.'

11 "Now, my son, may the LORD be
with you, and may you succeed in
building the house of the LORD your
God, as He said about you. 12 Above
all, may the LORD give you insight and
understanding when He puts you in
charge of Israel so that you may keep
the law of the LORD your God. 13 Then
you will succeed if you carefully follow the statutes and ordinances the
LORD commanded Moses for Israel.
Be strong and courageous. Don't be
afraid or discouraged.

14 "Notice I have taken great pains
to provide for the house of the
LORD—3,775 tons of gold, 37,750
tons of silver,[B] and bronze and iron
that can't be weighed because there
is so much of it. I have also provided
timber and stone, but you will need
to add more to them. 15 You also
have many workers: stonecutters,
masons, carpenters, and people
skilled in every kind of work 16 in
gold, silver, bronze, and iron—beyond number. Now begin the work,
and may the LORD be with you."

17 Then David ordered all the leaders of Israel to help his son Solomon: 18 "The LORD your God is with
you, isn't He? And hasn't He given
you rest on every side? For He has
handed the land's inhabitants over
to me, and the land has been subdued before the LORD and His people.
19 Now determine in your mind and
heart to seek the LORD your God. Get
started building the LORD God's sanctuary so that you may bring the ark
of the LORD's covenant and the holy
articles of God to the temple that is
to be built for the name of Yahweh."

23 When David was old and full
of days, he installed his son
Solomon as king over Israel.

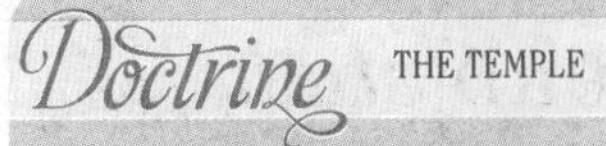

THE TEMPLE

The temple, commissioned and being staffed by David in chapters 23–26, was destroyed when Judah was taken into exile. The second temple, built by the remnant who returned from exile and rebuilt centuries later by Herod, was likewise destroyed in A.D. 70. Jesus claimed the temple building as His "Father's house" and demonstrated His authority over it in driving out "the money changers" (Jn 2:13-22). Jesus also associated the temple with His own physical body, speaking of His death and resurrection in terms of destroying and raising "the sanctuary of His body" (Jn 2:21). The New Testament letters extend the temple metaphor to the believer's body indwelt by the Holy Spirit (1Co 3:16-17) and to the church "body" (2Co 6:16; Eph 2:21-22). In Christ, the ultimate king and high priest (Heb 3:1-6; 4:14–5:10; 6:19–8:6; Rv 19:11-16; cp. Ps 24:9-10), God's presence with His people is secure forever (Mt 11:28-29; 28:20; Heb 4:1-11; Rv 3:11-12; 21:1-7).

The Levites and Aaron's Sons (23:2–26:32)

Divisions and Duties of the Levites (23:2-32)

2 Then he gathered all the leaders of
Israel, the priests, and the Levites.
3 The Levites 30 years old or more
were counted; the total number of
men was 38,000 by headcount. 4 "Of
these," David said, "24,000 are to be
in charge of the work on the LORD's
temple, 6,000 are to be officers and
judges, 5 4,000 are to be gatekeepers,
and 4,000 are to praise the LORD with
the instruments that I have made
for worship."

6 Then David divided them into
divisions according to Levi's sons:
Gershom,[C] Kohath, and Merari.

7 The Gershonites: Ladan and
Shimei.
8 Ladan's sons: Jehiel was
the first, then Zetham, and
Joel—three.
9 Shimei's sons: Shelomoth,
Haziel, and Haran—three.
Those were the heads of the
families of Ladan.
10 Shimei's sons: Jahath,
Zizah,[D] Jeush, and Beriah.
Those were Shimei's
sons—four. 11 Jahath was
the first and Zizah was the
second; however, Jeush and
Beriah did not have many
sons, so they became an

[A]**22:9** In Hb, the name Solomon sounds like "peace." [B]**22:14** Lit *100,000 talents of gold and 1,000,000 talents of silver* [C]**23:6** Lit *Gershon* [D]**23:10** LXX, Vg; MT reads *Zina*

ancestral house and received
a single assignment.
[12] Kohath's sons: Amram,
Izhar, Hebron, and
Uzziel—four.
[13] Amram's sons: Aaron and
Moses.

Aaron, along with his descendants,
was set apart forever to consecrate
the most holy things, to burn incense in the presence of •Yahweh, to
minister to Him, and to pronounce
blessings in His name forever. [14] As
for Moses the man of God, his sons
were named among the tribe of Levi.
[15] Moses' sons: Gershom and
Eliezer.
[16] Gershom's sons: Shebuel
was first.
[17] Eliezer's sons were
Rehabiah, first; Eliezer did
not have any other sons, but
Rehabiah's sons were very
numerous.
[18] Izhar's sons: Shelomith was
first.
[19] Hebron's sons: Jeriah
was first, Amariah second,
Jahaziel third, and Jekameam
fourth.
[20] Uzziel's sons: Micah was
first, and Isshiah second.
[21] Merari's sons: Mahli and
Mushi.
Mahli's sons: Eleazar and
Kish.
[22] Eleazar died having no
sons, only daughters. Their
cousins, the sons of Kish,
married them.
[23] Mushi's sons: Mahli, Eder,
and Jeremoth—three.

[24] These were the sons of Levi by
their ancestral houses—the heads of
families, according to their registration by name in the headcount—20
years old or more, who worked in
the service of the LORD's temple.
[25] For David said, "The LORD God of
Israel has given rest to His people,
and He has come to stay in Jerusalem forever. [26] Also, the Levites no
longer need to carry the tabernacle
or any of the equipment for its service"— [27] for according to the last
words of David, the Levites 20 years
old or more were to be counted—
[28] "but their duty will be to assist the
sons of Aaron with the service of the
LORD's temple, being responsible for
the courts and the chambers, the
purification of all the holy things,
and the work of the service of God's
temple— [29] as well as the rows of the
•bread of the Presence, the fine flour
for the •grain offering, the wafers
of unleavened bread, the baking,[A]
the mixing, and all measurements
of volume and length. [30] They are
also to stand every morning to give
thanks and praise to the LORD, and
likewise in the evening. [31] Whenever
•burnt offerings are offered to the
LORD on the Sabbaths, New Moons,
and appointed festivals, they are to
do so regularly in the LORD's presence according to the number prescribed for them. [32] They are to carry
out their responsibilities for the tent
of meeting, for the holy place, and
for their relatives, the sons of Aaron,
in the service of the LORD's temple."

Divisions and Duties of Aaron's Sons (24:1-31)

24 The divisions of the descendants of Aaron were as follows:
Aaron's sons were Nadab, Abihu,
Eleazar, and Ithamar. [2] But Nadab
and Abihu died before their father,
and they had no sons, so Eleazar and
Ithamar served as priests. [3] Together
with Zadok from the sons of Eleazar and Ahimelech from the sons of
Ithamar, David divided them according to the assigned duties of their
service. [4] Since more leaders were
found among Eleazar's descendants
than Ithamar's, they were divided
accordingly: 16 heads of ancestral
houses were from Eleazar's descendants, and eight heads of ancestral
houses were from Ithamar's. [5] They
were assigned by lot, for there were
officers of the sanctuary and officers
of God among both Eleazar's and
Ithamar's descendants.

[6] The secretary, Shemaiah son of
Nethanel, a Levite, recorded them
in the presence of the king and the
officers, Zadok the priest, Ahimelech son of Abiathar, and the heads
of families of the priests and the
Levites. One ancestral house was

A 23:29 Lit *the griddle*

24:10 The New Testament notes that the father of John the Baptist, Zechariah, served in the priestly division of **Abijah** (Lk 1:5).

24:20-31 The casting of **lots** (v. 31; cp. 24:5; 25:8) was personally witnessed by the highest authorities in Israel and is described as one that left no room for favoritism.

25:1-31 **David and** his military commanders **set apart** three prominent men **to prophesy** in the temple (vv. 1-2). These men, were not only authorized by King David to prophesy but were also held accountable by the king for their **service** (v. 1).

taken for Eleazar, and then one for Ithamar.

7 The first lot fell to Jehoiarib,
the second to Jedaiah,
8 the third to Harim, the fourth
to Seorim,
9 the fifth to Malchijah,
the sixth to Mijamin,
10 the seventh to Hakkoz,
the eighth to Abijah,
11 the ninth to Jeshua, the tenth
to Shecaniah,
12 the eleventh to Eliashib,
the twelfth to Jakim,
13 the thirteenth to Huppah,
the fourteenth to Jeshebeab,
14 the fifteenth to Bilgah,
the sixteenth to Immer,
15 the seventeenth to Hezir,
the eighteenth
to Happizzez,
16 the nineteenth to Pethahiah,
the twentieth to Jehezkel,
17 the twenty-first to Jachin,
the twenty-second
to Gamul,
18 the twenty-third to Delaiah,
and the twenty-fourth
to Maaziah.

19 These had their assigned duties for service when they entered the LORD's temple, according to their regulations, which they received from their ancestor Aaron, as the LORD God of Israel had commanded him.

20 As for the rest of Levi's sons:
from Amram's sons: Shubael;
from Shubael's sons:
Jehdeiah.
21 From Rehabiah:
from Rehabiah's sons: Isshiah
was the first.
22 From the Izharites:
Shelomoth;
from Shelomoth's sons:
Jahath.
23 Hebron's[A] sons:
Jeriah the first, Amariah the
second,
Jahaziel the third, and
Jekameam the fourth.
24 From Uzziel's sons: Micah;
from Micah's sons: Shamir.
25 Micah's brother: Isshiah;
from Isshiah's sons:
Zechariah.
26 Merari's sons: Mahli and
Mushi,
and from his sons, Jaaziah his
son.[B]
27 Merari's sons, by his son
Jaaziah:[C]
Shoham, Zaccur, and Ibri.
28 From Mahli: Eleazar, who
had no sons.
29 From Kish, from Kish's
sons: Jerahmeel.
30 Mushi's sons: Mahli, Eder,
and Jerimoth.

Those were the sons of the Levites according to their ancestral houses.
31 They also cast lots the same way as their relatives the sons of Aaron did in the presence of King David, Zadok, Ahimelech, and the heads of the families of the priests and Levites—the family heads and their younger brothers alike.

Levitical Musicians (25:1-31)

25 David and the officers of the army also set apart some of the sons of ˚Asaph, Heman, and Jeduthun, who were to prophesy accompanied by lyres, harps, and cymbals. This is the list of the men who performed their service:

2 From Asaph's sons:
Zaccur, Joseph, Nethaniah,
and Asarelah, sons of Asaph,
under Asaph's authority,
who prophesied under the
authority of the king.
3 From Jeduthun: Jeduthun's
sons:
Gedaliah, Zeri, Jeshaiah,
Shimei,[D] Hashabiah, and
Mattithiah—six—under
the authority of their father
Jeduthun, prophesying to
the accompaniment of lyres,
giving thanks and praise to
the LORD.
4 From Heman: Heman's sons:
Bukkiah, Mattaniah, Uzziel,
Shebuel, Jerimoth, Hananiah,
Hanani, Eliathah, Giddalti,
Romamti-ezer, Joshbekashah,
Mallothi, Hothir, and
Mahazioth. 5 All these sons of

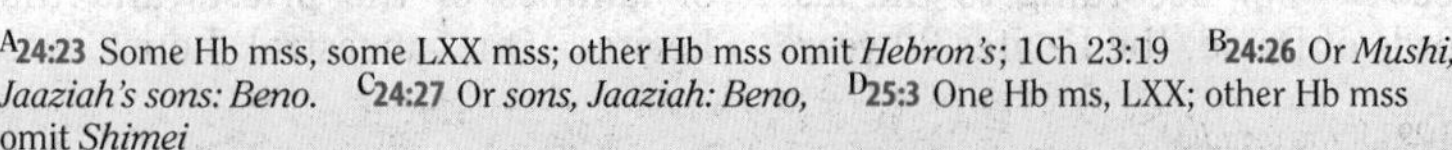
[A]**24:23** Some Hb mss, some LXX mss; other Hb mss omit *Hebron's*; 1Ch 23:19 [B]**24:26** Or *Mushi; Jaaziah's sons: Beno.* [C]**24:27** Or *sons, Jaaziah: Beno,* [D]**25:3** One Hb ms, LXX; other Hb mss omit *Shimei*

>WORD|*study*

25:1 Prophesy (Hb *nava'*, "speak by divine power"; cp. 1Sm 10:5-6) is a passive verb, reflecting the nature and source of prophetic utterance. The one "prophesying" neither initiated the activity nor determined entirely on his own what would be said; rather, the prophet was moved by God's power.

25:6 Authority (Hb *yad*, lit "hand") was an idiom for "strength or power" similar to the English description of someone in charge as "having the upper hand." To be under "authority" was to be under the "guidance or superintendence" of another having the power or authority to appoint or commission someone to a task. Such a person is able to make and enforce the rules, both to shape and enact policies for promoting effective operations and to maintain orderly conduct.

Heman, the king's seer, were
given by the promises of God
to exalt him,[A] for God had
given Heman fourteen sons
and three daughters.

6 All these men were under their
own fathers' authority for the music in the LORD's temple, with cymbals, harps, and lyres for the service
of God's temple. Asaph, Jeduthun,
and Heman were under the king's
authority. 7 They numbered 288 together with their relatives who were
all trained and skillful in music for
the LORD. 8 They cast lots for their
duties, young and old alike, teacher
as well as pupil.

9 The first lot for Asaph
fell to Joseph, his sons,
and his brothers— 12
to Gedaliah the second:
him, his brothers,
and his sons— 12
10 the third to Zaccur,
his sons,
and his brothers— 12
11 the fourth to Izri,[B]
his sons,
and his brothers— 12
12 the fifth to Nethaniah,
his sons,
and his brothers— 12
13 the sixth to Bukkiah,
his sons,
and his brothers— 12
14 the seventh to Jesarelah,
his sons,
and his brothers— 12
15 the eighth to Jeshaiah,
his sons,
and his brothers— 12
16 the ninth to Mattaniah,
his sons,
and his brothers— 12
17 the tenth to Shimei,
his sons,
and his brothers— 12
18 the eleventh to Azarel,[C]
his sons,
and his brothers— 12
19 the twelfth to Hashabiah,
his sons,
and his brothers— 12
20 the thirteenth to Shubael,
his sons,
and his brothers— 12
21 the fourteenth
to Mattithiah, his sons,
and his brothers— 12
22 the fifteenth to Jeremoth,
his sons,
and his brothers— 12
23 the sixteenth to Hananiah,
his sons,
and his brothers— 12
24 the seventeenth
to Joshbekashah,
his sons,
and his brothers— 12
25 the eighteenth to Hanani,
his sons,
and his brothers— 12
26 the nineteenth to Mallothi,
his sons,
and his brothers— 12
27 the twentieth to Eliathah,
his sons,
and his brothers— 12
28 the twenty-first to Hothir,
his sons,
and his brothers— 12
29 the twenty-second
to Giddalti, his sons,
and his brothers— 12
30 the twenty-third
to Mahazioth, his sons,
and his brothers— 12
31 and the twenty-fourth
to Romamti-ezer,

A 25:5 Or *Him*; lit *by the words of God to lift a horn* B 25:11 Variant of Zeri C 25:18 Variant of Uzziel

26:1-19 The gatekeepers, together with **their brothers**, the Levitical prophets and musicians of chapter 25, ministered in the **temple** (v. 12). For the former exiles who had served as gatekeepers, this list, along with the record in 9:17-27, would have established in writing the heritage of this branch of Levitical guardians of the temple.

26:20-28 The Chronicler's choice of details may have particularly encouraged the Levites who first returned from exile. The names of both Gershon (Levi's firstborn) and Gershom (Moses' firstborn) mean "exile, a stranger there" (cp. Ex 2:22; 18:3), yet the descendants of both were called to protect and administer the resources for God's temple (cp. Nm 3:21-26; 4:21-28; 10:17). Similarly, including **Shelomith** (Hb, "peaceful," 1Ch 26:28) by name may have been regarded as evidence of God's redemptive character since this was the name of "an Israelite mother," whose son had been executed for blasphemy in Moses' day (Lv 24:10-23).

his sons,
and his brothers— 12.

Levitical Gatekeepers (26:1-19)

26 The following were the divisions of the gatekeepers:

From the Korahites:
Meshelemiah son of Kore, one of the sons of •Asaph.
2 Meshelemiah had sons:
Zechariah the firstborn,
Jediael the second,
Zebadiah the third, Jathniel the fourth,
3 Elam the fifth, Jehohanan the sixth,
and Eliehoenai the seventh.
4 Obed-edom also had sons:
Shemaiah the firstborn,
Jehozabad the second,
Joah the third, Sachar the fourth,
Nethanel the fifth, 5 Ammiel the sixth,
Issachar the seventh, and Peullethai the eighth,
for God blessed him.
6 Also, to his son Shemaiah were born sons who ruled over their ancestral houses because they were strong, capable men.
7 Shemaiah's sons: Othni, Rephael, Obed, and Elzabad; his brothers Elihu and Semachiah were also capable men. 8 All of these were among the sons of Obed-edom with their sons and brothers; they were capable men with strength for the work—62 from Obed-edom.
9 Meshelemiah also had sons and brothers who were capable men—18.
10 Hosah, from the Merarites, also had sons: Shimri the first (although he was not the firstborn, his father had appointed him as the first),
11 Hilkiah the second, Tebaliah the third, and Zechariah the fourth. The sons and brothers of Hosah were 13 in all.

12 These divisions of the gatekeepers, under their leading men, had duties for ministering in the LORD's temple, just as their brothers did.
13 They cast lots for each gate according to their ancestral houses, young and old alike.
14 The lot for the east gate fell to Shelemiah.[A] They also cast lots for his son Zechariah, an insightful counselor, and his lot came out for
the north gate. 15 Obed-edom's was the south gate, and his sons' lot was for the storehouses;
16 it was the west gate and the gate of Shallecheth on the ascending highway for Shuppim and Hosah.

There were guards stationed at every watch.
17 There were six Levites each day[B] on the east, four each day on the north, four each day on the south, and two pair at the storehouses.
18 As for the court on the west, there were four at the highway and two at the court.
19 Those were the divisions of the gatekeepers from the sons of the Korahites and Merarites.

Levitical Treasurers and Other Officials (26:20-32)

20 From the Levites, Ahijah was in charge of the treasuries of God's temple and the treasuries of what had been dedicated.
21 From the sons of Ladan, who were the sons of the Gershonites through Ladan and were the heads of families belonging to Ladan the Gershonite: Jehieli.
22 The sons of Jehieli, Zetham and his brother Joel, were in charge of the treasuries of the LORD's temple.
23 From the Amramites, the Izharites, the Hebronites, and the Uzzielites:
24 Shebuel, a descendant of Moses' son Gershom, was the officer in charge of the treasuries.
25 His relative through Eliezer: his son Rehabiah, his son Jeshaiah, his son Joram, his son Zichri, and his son Shelomith.[C]
26 This Shelomith[C] and his brothers were in charge of all the treasuries of what had been dedicated by King David, by the heads of families who were the commanders of thousands and of hundreds, and by the army commanders.
27 They dedicated part of the plunder from their battles for the repair of the LORD's temple.
28 All that Samuel the seer, Saul son of Kish, Abner son of

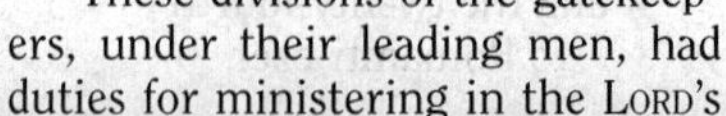

A 26:14 Variant of Meshelemiah B 26:17 LXX; MT omits *each day* C 26:25,26 Or *Shelomoth*

Ner, and Joab son of Zeruiah had dedicated, along with everything else that had been dedicated, were in the care of Shelomith[A] and his brothers.
29 From the Izrahites: Chenaniah and his sons had the outside duties as officers and judges over Israel.
30 From the Hebronites: Hashabiah and his relatives, 1,700 capable men, had assigned duties in Israel west of the Jordan for all the work of the LORD and for the service of the king.
31 From the Hebronites: Jerijah was the head of the Hebronites, according to the genealogical records of his ancestors. A search was made in the fortieth year of David's reign and strong, capable men were found among them at Jazer in Gilead.
32 There were among Jerijah's relatives, 2,700 capable men who were heads of families. King David appointed them over the Reubenites, the Gadites, and half the tribe of Manasseh as overseers in every matter relating to God and the king.

Military Divisions and Counselors (27:1-34)

27 This is the list of the Israelites, the heads of families, the commanders of thousands and the commanders of hundreds, and their officers who served the king in every matter to do with the divisions that were on rotated military duty each month throughout[B] the year. There were 24,000 in each division:

2 Jashobeam son of Zabdiel was in charge of the first division, for the first month; 24,000 were in his division.
3 He was a descendant of Perez and chief of all the army commanders for the first month.
4 Dodai the Ahohite was in charge of the division for the second month, and Mikloth was the leader; 24,000 were in his division.
5 The third army commander, as chief for the third month, was Benaiah son of Jehoiada the priest; 24,000 were in his division.
6 This Benaiah was a mighty man among the Thirty and over the Thirty, and his son Ammizabad was in charge[C] of his division.
7 The fourth commander, for the fourth month, was Joab's brother Asahel, and his son Zebadiah was commander after him; 24,000 were in his division.
8 The fifth, for the fifth month, was the commander Shamhuth the Izrahite; 24,000 were in his division.
9 The sixth, for the sixth month, was Ira son of Ikkesh the Tekoite; 24,000 were in his division.
10 The seventh, for the seventh month, was Helez the Pelonite from the sons of Ephraim; 24,000 were in his division.
11 The eighth, for the eighth month, was Sibbecai the Hushathite, a Zerahite; 24,000 were in his division.
12 The ninth, for the ninth month, was Abiezer the Anathothite, a Benjaminite; 24,000 were in his division.
13 The tenth, for the tenth month, was Maharai the Netophathite, a Zerahite; 24,000 were in his division.
14 The eleventh, for the eleventh month, was Benaiah the Pirathonite from the sons of Ephraim; 24,000 were in his division.
15 The twelfth, for the twelfth month, was Heldai the Netophathite, of Othniel's family;[D] 24,000 were in his division.

16 The following were in charge of the tribes of Israel:
For the Reubenites, Eliezer son of Zichri was the chief official;
for the Simeonites, Shephatiah son of Maacah;
17 for the Levites, Hashabiah son of Kemuel; for Aaron, Zadok;

27:1-22 In keeping with the Chronicler's priorities, an account of the administrative affairs is given *after* the description of how Israel's religious life was structured.

[A] **26,28** Or *Shelomoth* [B] **27:1** Lit *that came in and went out month by month for all months of* [C] **27:6** LXX; MT omits *in charge* [D] **27:15** Lit *belonging to Othniel*

27:23-24 The Chronicler's comments recalled the tragic episode of chapter 21 but implied that David had made widely known what he learned from experiencing God's **wrath against Israel** on account of his sin.

28:1-21 As the executive head over all the leaders in Israel, David employed a powerful strategy for ensuring that his vision for building the temple would be carried out even after he was no longer present to direct the project himself.

18 for Judah, Elihu, one of
David's brothers; for Issachar,
Omri son of Michael;
19 for Zebulun, Ishmaiah son
of Obadiah;
for Naphtali, Jerimoth son of
Azriel;
20 for the Ephraimites, Hoshea
son of Azaziah;
for half the tribe of Manasseh,
Joel son of Pedaiah;
21 for half the tribe of
Manasseh in Gilead, Iddo son
of Zechariah;
for Benjamin, Jaasiel son of
Abner;
22 for Dan, Azarel son of
Jeroham.
Those were the leaders of the
tribes of Israel.

23 David didn't count the men aged
20 or under, for the LORD had said
He would make Israel as numerous
as the stars of heaven. 24 Joab son of
Zeruiah began to count them, but
he didn't complete it. There was
wrath against Israel because of this
census, and the number was not
entered in the Historical Record[A] of
King David.

25 Azmaveth son of Adiel
was in charge of the king's
storehouses.
Jonathan son of Uzziah was
in charge of the storehouses
in the country, in the cities,
in the villages, and in the
fortresses.
26 Ezri son of Chelub was in
charge of those who worked
in the fields tilling the soil.
27 Shimei the Ramathite was
in charge of the vineyards.
Zabdi the Shiphmite was in
charge of the produce of the
vineyards for the wine cellars.
28 Baal-hanan the Gederite
was in charge of the olive and
sycamore trees in the Judean
foothills.[B]
Joash was in charge of the
stores of olive oil.
29 Shitrai the Sharonite was
in charge of the herds that
grazed in Sharon, while
Shaphat son of Adlai was in
charge of the herds in the
valleys.
30 Obil the Ishmaelite was in
charge of the camels.
Jehdeiah the Meronothite was
in charge of the donkeys.
31 Jaziz the Hagrite was in
charge of the flocks.
All these were officials in
charge of King David's
property.

32 David's uncle Jonathan was a
counselor; he was a man of understanding and a scribe. Jehiel son
of Hachmoni attended[C] the king's
sons. 33 Ahithophel was the king's
counselor. Hushai the Archite was
the king's friend. 34 After Ahithophel
came Jehoiada son of Benaiah, then
Abiathar. Joab was the commander
of the king's army.

The Commissioning of Solomon (28:1-21)

28 David assembled all the leaders of Israel in Jerusalem: the
leaders of the tribes, the leaders
of the divisions in the king's service, the commanders of thousands
and the commanders of hundreds,
and the officials in charge of all the
property and cattle of the king and
his sons, along with the court officials, the fighting men, and all the
brave warriors. 2 Then King David
rose to his feet and said, "Listen to
me, my brothers and my people. It
was in my heart to build a house
as a resting place for the ark of the
LORD's covenant and as a footstool
for our God. I had made preparations to build, 3 but God said to me,
'You are not to build a house for My
name because you are a man of war
and have shed blood.'

4 "Yet the LORD God of Israel chose
me out of all my father's household
to be king over Israel forever. For He
chose Judah as leader, and from the
house of Judah, my father's household, and from my father's sons,
He was pleased to make me king
over all Israel. 5 And out of all my
sons—for the LORD has given me
many sons—He has chosen my son
Solomon to sit on the throne of the

[A]27:24 LXX; MT reads *Number* [B]27:28 Or *the Shephelah* [C]27:32 Lit *was with*

LORD's kingdom over Israel. 6 He said to me, 'Your son Solomon is the one who is to build My house and My courts, for I have chosen him to be My son, and I will be his father. 7 I will establish his kingdom forever if he perseveres in keeping My commands and My ordinances as he is today.'

8 "So now in the sight of all Israel, the assembly of the LORD, and in the hearing of our God, observe and follow all the commands of the LORD your God so that you may possess this good land and leave it as an inheritance to your descendants forever.

9 "As for you, Solomon my son, know the God of your father, and serve Him with a whole heart and a willing mind, for the LORD searches every heart and understands the intention of every thought. If you seek Him, He will be found by you, but if you forsake Him, He will reject you forever. 10 Realize now that the LORD has chosen you to build a house for the sanctuary. Be strong, and do it."

11 Then David gave his son Solomon the plans for the portico of the temple and its buildings, treasuries, upper rooms, inner rooms, and a room for the •mercy seat. 12 The plans contained everything he had in mind[A] for the courts of the LORD's house, all the surrounding chambers, the treasuries of God's house, and the treasuries for what is dedicated. 13 Also included were plans for the divisions of the priests and the Levites; all the work of service in the LORD's house; all the articles of service of the LORD's house; 14 the weight of gold for all the articles for every kind of service; the weight of all the silver articles for every kind of service; 15 the weight of the gold lampstands and their gold lamps, including the weight of each lampstand and its lamps; the weight of each silver lampstand and its lamps, according to the service of each lampstand; 16 the weight of gold for each table for the rows of the •bread of the Presence and the silver for the silver tables; 17 the pure gold for the forks, sprinkling basins, and pitchers; the weight of each gold dish; the weight of each silver bowl; 18 the weight of refined gold for the altar of incense; and the plans for the chariot of[B] the gold •cherubim that spread out their wings and cover the ark of the LORD's covenant.

19 David concluded, "By the LORD's hand on me, He enabled me to understand everything in writing, all the details of the plan."[C]

20 Then David said to his son Solomon, "Be strong and courageous, and do the work. Don't be afraid or discouraged, for the LORD God, my God, is with you. He won't leave you or forsake you until all the work for the service of the LORD's house is finished. 21 Here are the divisions of the priests and the Levites for all the service of God's house. Every willing man of any skill will be at your disposal for the work, and the leaders and all the people are at your every command."

Contributions from the People (29:1-9)

29 Then King David said to all the assembly, "My son Solomon—God has chosen him alone—is young and inexperienced. The task is great because the temple will not be for man but for the LORD God. 2 So to the best of my ability I've made provision for the house of my God: gold for the gold articles, silver for the silver, bronze for the bronze, iron for the iron, and wood for the wood, as well as onyx, stones for mounting,[D] antimony,[E] stones of various colors, all kinds of precious stones, and a great quantity of marble. 3 Moreover, because of my delight in the house of my God, I now give my personal treasures of gold and silver for the house of my God over and above all that I've provided for the holy house: 4 100 tons[F] of gold (gold of Ophir) and 250 tons[G] of refined silver for overlaying the walls of the buildings, 5 the gold for the gold work and the silver for the silver, for all the work to be done by the craftsmen. Now who will

[A] **28:12** Or *he received from the Spirit* [B] **28:18** Or *chariot, that is*; Ps 18:10; Ezk 1:5,15 [C] **28:19** Hb obscure [D] **29:2** Or *mosaic* [E] **29:2** In Hb, the word antimony is similar to "turquoise"; Ex 28:18. [F] **29:4** Lit *3,000 talents* [G] **29:4** Lit *7,000 talents*

29:10-22a Before directing the leaders to **praise the Lord**, David modeled "praise" in fervent public prayer that focused on exalting and thanking **the Lord** for who He is (vv. 10-13). Having run out of words to express the incomparability of the Lord of the universe, David contrasted himself and the people as transient human beings merely returning to God what He had provided.

29:22b-25 The writer heavily emphasized the sacred nature of the office and the occasion. The **anointed** king Solomon was designated as **the Lord's ruler**. The Lord is credited with making Solomon great **in the sight of all Israel** and giving him unprecedented **royal majesty** (Hb *hod*, "honor, glory, splendor," cp. 16:27; 29:11; Zch 6:12-15).

29:26-30 These closing verses provide a satisfying summary to the chapter of Israel's history that the Chronicler regarded as the standard Israel hoped to recover. The book's earliest readers, who wanted to explore the events in detail beyond the high points noted and theologically interpreted in 1 Chronicles, are referred to three sources—the writings of the three prophets through whom God spoke to David. One of these—**The Events of Samuel the Seer**—may refer to the canonical books of 1 and 2 Samuel or to portions of these books. The Chronicler's final comments also emphasized the fact that David's reign was concretely situated, both historically and geographically. Like Christians who are citizens of God's kingdom ruled by Jesus Christ, the perfect Son of David, Israel was not called to be an insular people unto itself but a nation testifying in obedient worship to the glory of God in **all the kingdoms** of the earth (cp. Ps 68:32-35; Php 3:20).

volunteer to consecrate himself to
the Lord today?"
6 Then the leaders of the households, the leaders of the tribes of Israel, the commanders of thousands
and of hundreds, and the officials
in charge of the king's work gave
willingly. 7 For the service of God's
house they gave 185 tons[A] of gold
and 10,000 gold coins,[B] 375 tons[C]
of silver, 675 tons[D] of bronze, and
4,000 tons[E] of iron. 8 Whoever had
precious stones gave them to the
treasury of the Lord's house under
the care of Jehiel the Gershonite.
9 Then the people rejoiced because
of their leaders' willingness to give,
for they had given to the Lord with
a whole heart. King David also rejoiced greatly.

Worship (29:10-30)

10 Then David praised the Lord in
the sight of all the assembly. David
said,

May You be praised, Lord God
of our father Israel, from eternity to eternity. 11 Yours, Lord,
is the greatness and the power
and the glory and the splendor
and the majesty, for everything
in the heavens and on earth
belongs to You. Yours, Lord, is
the kingdom, and You are exalted as head over all. 12 Riches
and honor come from You, and
You are the ruler of everything.
Power and might are in Your
hand, and it is in Your hand to
make great and to give strength
to all. 13 Now therefore, our
God, we give You thanks and
praise Your glorious name.

14 But who am I, and who are
my people, that we should be
able to give as generously as
this? For everything comes
from You, and we have given
You only what comes from
Your own hand.[F] 15 For we live
before You as foreigners and
temporary residents in Your
presence as were all our ancestors. Our days on earth are
like a shadow, without hope.
16 •Yahweh our God, all this
wealth that we've provided for
building You a house for Your
holy name comes from Your
hand; everything belongs to
You. 17 I know, my God, that
You test the heart and that You
are pleased with what is right.
I have willingly given all these
things with an upright heart,
and now I have seen Your people who are present[G] here giving joyfully and[H] willingly to
You. 18 Lord God of Abraham,
Isaac, and Israel, our ancestors, keep this desire forever
in the thoughts of the hearts of
Your people, and confirm their
hearts toward You. 19 Give my
son Solomon a whole heart to
keep and to carry out all Your
commands, Your decrees, and
Your statutes, and to build the
temple for which I have made
provision.

20 Then David said to the whole assembly, "Praise the Lord your God."
So the whole assembly praised the
Lord God of their ancestors. They
bowed down and paid homage to the
Lord and the king.
21 The following day they offered
sacrifices to the Lord and •burnt
offerings to the Lord: 1,000 bulls,
1,000 rams, and 1,000 lambs, along
with their •drink offerings, and sacrifices in abundance for all Israel.
22 They ate and drank with great joy
in the Lord's presence that day.
Then, for a second time, they
made David's son Solomon king;
they anointed him[I] as the Lord's
ruler, and Zadok as the priest. 23 Solomon sat on the Lord's throne as
king in place of his father David. He
prospered, and all Israel obeyed him.
24 All the leaders and the mighty
men, and all of King David's sons
as well, pledged their allegiance to
King Solomon. 25 The Lord highly
exalted Solomon in the sight of all
Israel and bestowed on him such
royal majesty as had not been be-

[A]29:7 Lit *5,000 talents* [B]29:7 Or *drachmas*, or *darics* [C]29:7 Lit *10,000 talents* [D]29:7 Lit *18,000 talents* [E]29:7 Lit *100,000 talents* [F]29:14 Lit *and from Your hand we have given to You* [G]29:17 Lit *found* [H]29:17 Or *now with joy I've seen Your people who are present here giving* [I]29:22 LXX, Tg, Vg; MT omits *him*

stowed on any king over Israel before him.
[26]David son of Jesse was king
over all Israel. [27]The length of his
reign over Israel was 40 years; he
reigned in Hebron for seven years
and in Jerusalem for 33. [28]He died
at a ripe old age, full of days, riches,
and honor, and his son Solomon
became king in his place. [29]As for
the events of King David's reign,
from beginning to end, note that
they are written in the Events of
Samuel the Seer, the Events of Nathan the Prophet, and the Events of
Gad the Seer, [30]along with all his
reign, his might, and the incidents
that affected him and Israel and all
the kingdoms of the surrounding
lands.

---

1 CHRONICLES … WRITTEN ON MY *Heart* All who are the Body of Christ are a part of the house that God built for His name, temples inhabited by the Holy Spirit (1Co 3:16). He has made His home within you and me, and He will never depart (Jn 14:23). Daughter of God, you were redeemed at the highest price and are indwelled by the God who gave Himself for your ransom. You are not your own. You are a living temple for the Lord's name.

2 Chronicles

Timeline

- World Events
- Biblical Events

970 BC	966 BC	959 BC	940 BC
Solomon succeeds David as king of a united kingdom.	Solomon begins construction of the temple in Jerusalem.	Solomon dedicates the temple.	Queen of Sheba visits Solomon in Jerusalem.

"If . . . My people . . . humble themselves, pray and seek My face, and turn from their evil ways, then I will hear from heaven, forgive their sin, and heal their land" (7:13-14).

Who wrote 2 Chronicles?

The authorship of Chronicles traditionally, and with persuasive evidence, is attributed to Ezra the scribe. Because the writer's identity is uncertain, most scholars refer to the author as "the Chronicler."

Who were the recipients?

Often called the restoration community, the Jews returning to Israel from exile included the descendants of exiled Jews who had not forfeited their heritage through intermarriage.

When was 2 Chronicles written?

Likely sometime after Cyrus's decree was issued in 538 B.C.

Where did it happen?

The events of 2 Chronicles occurred during the unstable monarchies of Israel and Judah and end with the people's exile to Babylon.

What is 2 Chronicles about?

- Restoring the identity and unity of "all Israel" as God's chosen people
- Affirming God's covenant with David and his descendants
- Depicting the correlation between the hearts of the king and of the people and especially how they responded to the temple

Why should women read 2 Chronicles?

Seasons of God's discipline can cause you to remember the past blessings of living in obedience. In such times, you are often tempted to despair because of the consequences of your sin, to remain in defeating shame and estrangement from the Savior. But the message of Chronicles provides a new hope: Before God ever chastens His children, He has already planned to restore them to Himself. His discipline is never without hope and is always for the ultimate good of His children.

How do you read 2 Chronicles?

Second Chronicles is primarily historical narrative—history in story form. The writer of 2 Chronicles composed this account of God's people from a perspective different than the writer of 1 and 2 Kings. For the sake of the Jews whose families had lived in captivity for 70 years in Babylon and had returned to Israel where Jerusalem and the temple were being rebuilt, the Chronicler provided a theological interpretation, demonstrating God's unshakable faithfulness to His people both in times of obedience and during periods of outright rebellion.

Outline

I. Solomon's Reign (1:1–9:30)
   - A. Solomon's Wisdom and Wealth (1:1-17)
   - B. The Construction and Dedication of the Temple (2:1–6:2)
   - C. The King's Blessing of the Congregation of Israel (6:3-11)
   - D. The King's Prayer (6:12–7:3)
   - E. The Consecration of the Temple (7:4-11)
   - F. God's Covenant with Solomon (7:12-22)
   - G. Building Projects (8:1-11)
   - H. Worship and Wealth (8:12–9:30)

II. The Kingdom of Judah (9:31–35:27)

III. The Fall of Judah to Babylon (36:1-23)
   - A. The Last Kings of Judah (36:1-13)
   - B. Sinful Deeds and Practices (36:14-16)
   - C. The Destruction of Jerusalem (36:17-21)
   - D. The Proclamation of King Cyrus of Persia (36:22-23)

932 BC	715 BC	622 BC	586 BC	538 BC
Solomon dies and the kingdom is divided.	Hezekiah leads a third reform of the temple.	Josiah leads a fourth reform of the temple.	Babylonians destroy Jerusalem and the temple.	Cyrus, king of Persia, encourages the Jews to return to Judah and rebuild the temple.

Solomon's Wisdom and Wealth (1:1-17)

1 Solomon son of David strengthened his hold on his kingdom.
The LORD his God was with him and
highly exalted him. 2 Then Solomon
spoke to all Israel, to the commanders of thousands and of hundreds,
to the judges, and to every leader in
all Israel—the heads of the families.
3 Solomon and the whole assembly
with him went to the •high place
that was in Gibeon because God's
tent of meeting, which the LORD's
servant Moses had made in the
wilderness, was there. 4 Now David
had brought the ark of God from
Kiriath-jearim to the place[A] he had
set up for it, because he had pitched
a tent for it in Jerusalem, 5 but he
put[B] the bronze altar, which Bezalel
son of Uri, son of Hur, had made, in
front of the LORD's tabernacle. Solomon and the assembly inquired of
Him[C] there. 6 Solomon offered sacrifices there in the LORD's presence
on the bronze altar at the tent of
meeting; he offered 1,000 •burnt offerings on it.

7 That night God appeared to Solomon and said to him: "Ask. What
should I give you?"

8 And Solomon said to God: "You
have shown great and faithful love to
my father David, and You have made
me king in his place. 9 LORD God, let
Your promise to my father David
now come true. For You have made
me king over a people as numerous
as the dust of the earth. 10 Now grant
me wisdom and knowledge so that I
may lead these people, for who can
judge this great people of Yours?"

11 God said to Solomon, "Since this
was in your heart, and you have not
requested riches, wealth, or glory,
or for the life of those who hate you,
and you have not even requested
long life, but you have requested
for yourself wisdom and knowledge that you may judge My people
over whom I have made you king,
12 wisdom and knowledge are given
to you. I will also give you riches,
wealth, and glory, unlike what was
given to the kings who were before
you, or will be given to those after
you." 13 So Solomon went to Jerusalem from[D] the high place that was in
Gibeon in front of the tent of meeting, and he reigned over Israel.

14 Solomon accumulated 1,400
chariots and 12,000 horsemen,
which he stationed in the chariot
cities and with the king in Jerusalem. 15 The king made silver and gold
as common in Jerusalem as stones,
and he made cedar as abundant as
sycamore in the Judean foothills.
16 Solomon's horses came from
Egypt and Kue.[E] The king's traders
would get them from Kue at the going price. 17 A chariot could be imported from Egypt for 15 pounds[F]
of silver and a horse for about four
pounds.[G] In the same way, they exported them to all the kings of the
Hittites and to the kings of Aram
through their agents.

The Construction and Dedication of the Temple (2:1–6:2)

Help from King Hiram of Tyre (2:1-16)

2 [H] Solomon decided to build a
temple for the name of •Yahweh

[A]1:4 Vg; MT omits *the place* [B]1:5 Some Hb mss, Tg, Syr; other Hb mss, LXX, Vg read *but there was* [C]1:5 Or *it* [D]1:13 LXX, Vg; MT reads *to* [E]1:16 = Cilicia [F]1:17 Lit *600 shekels* [G]1:17 Lit *150 shekels* [H]2:1 2Ch 1:18 in Hb

Title: Second Chronicles continues the story of the Davidic kingdom, beginning with Solomon. The Chronicler's purpose was to present the king and kingdom in the fullness of their glory and majesty. This testimony was a source of great encouragement to postexilic Israel because of the memory of ungodly leadership and the harshness of their current life. Knowing that God had judged and forgiven them, they upheld in Israel the ideal of unity, which characterized the reign of Solomon.

1:2 The phrase **all Israel**, used throughout 1 Chronicles to convey Israel's unity under David's reign, reappears in the narrative that focuses on **Solomon** as his successor.

1:3 The term **high place** (Hb *bamah*, v. 3) reflects a general recognition of Gibeon as a worship site, utilized as such because of its elevation. Although Israel had been commanded to destroy the high places of pagan gods, worship at such sites, nevertheless, was common throughout Israel (Dt 12:1-14; 2Ch 14:3-5).

1:7-13 The Chronicler's wording in this account indicates his priorities. As Solomon humbly acknowledged his royal, God-given responsibility for **a people as numerous as the dust of the earth**, he was also acknowledging the fulfillment of God's promise to Abraham and Jacob (Gn 13:16; 28:14; 2Ch 1:9). In his report of God's response, the Chronicler emphasized that God had **made** Solomon **king** over His people (2Ch 1:11; in contrast to the emphasis in Kings) and thus required that Solomon remain obedient like his father David (1Kg 3:14). The difference reflects the Chronicler's intention to review the continuity of the Davidic covenant, demonstrating God's sovereignty in keeping His promises despite the failures and disobedience of the men He appointed to lead.

1:14-17 The original audience would recognize implicit criticism in the details of **Solomon's** accumulation of **horses** and chariots **from Egypt** (cp. Dt 17:14-17; 1Kg 10:26-29).

2:17-18 Solomon's **census** was carefully distinguished from the illicit one **David had conducted** (cp. 1Ch 21).

>WORD|*study*

2:6 The primary sense of able (Hb *ʿatsar*) is to "shut in, surround or enclose so as to hold back or detain." The concrete meaning of contain (Hb *kul*, "take in, hold") was used to describe a vessel "holding" water (e.g., 1Kg 7:26,38; Is 40:12). Although here it denotes "having ability," the sentence sets the two verbs in apposition, suggesting that they convey a picture of contrasts, making this supreme expression of God's being especially vivid. No one can fence God in, hold Him back, impose a boundary upon Him, or set limits for where He can be. Even **heaven** [Hb *shamayim*, "the visible universe; heaven, as God's dwelling place"] **and the highest heaven** (Hb *shemē hashshamayim*, more lit, "the heaven of the heavens") cannot do that.

and a royal palace for himself, 2[A]so he assigned 70,000 men as porters, 80,000 men as stonecutters in the mountains, and 3,600 as supervisors over them.

3 Then Solomon sent word to King Hiram[B] of Tyre:

> Do for me what you did for my father David. You sent him cedars to build him a house to live in. 4 Now I am building a temple for the name of Yahweh my God in order to dedicate it to Him for burning fragrant incense before Him, for displaying the rows of the •bread of the Presence continuously, and for sacrificing •burnt offerings for the morning and the evening, the Sabbaths and the New Moons, and the appointed festivals of the LORD our God. This is ordained for Israel forever. 5 The temple that I am building will be great, for our God is greater than any of the gods. 6 But who is able to build a temple for Him, since even heaven and the highest heaven cannot contain Him? Who am I then that I should build a temple for Him except as a place to burn incense before Him? 7 Therefore, send me a craftsman who is skilled in engraving to work with gold, silver, bronze, and iron, and with purple, crimson, and blue yarn. He will work with the craftsmen who are with me in Judah and Jerusalem, appointed by my father David. 8 Also, send me cedar, cypress, and algum[C] logs from Lebanon, for I know that your servants know how to cut the trees of Lebanon. Note that my servants will be with your servants 9 to prepare logs for me in abundance because the temple I am building will be great and wonderful. 10 I will give your servants, the woodcutters who cut the trees, 100,000 bushels[D] of wheat flour, 100,000 bushels[D] of barley, 110,000 gallons[E] of wine, and 110,000 gallons[E] of oil.

11 Then King Hiram of Tyre wrote a letter[F] and sent it to Solomon:

> Because the LORD loves His people, He set you over them as king.

12 Hiram also said:

> May the LORD God of Israel, who made the heavens and the earth, be praised! He gave King David a wise son with insight and understanding, who will build a temple for the LORD and a royal palace for himself. 13 I have now sent Huram-abi,[G] a skillful man who has understanding. 14 He is the son of a woman from the daughters of Dan. His father is a man of Tyre. He knows how to work with gold, silver, bronze, iron, stone, and wood, with purple, blue, crimson yarn, and fine linen. He knows how to do all kinds of engraving and to execute any design that may be given him. I have sent him to be with your craftsmen and the craftsmen of my lord, your father David. 15 Now, let my lord send the wheat, barley, oil, and wine to his servants as promised. 16 We will cut logs from Lebanon, as many as you need,

[A]2:2 2Ch 2:1 in Hb [B]2:3 Some Hb mss, LXX, Syr, Vg; other Hb mss read *Huram*; 2Sm 5:11; 1Kg 5:1-2 [C]2:8 = almug in 1Kg 10:11-12 [D]2:10 Lit *20,000 cors* [E]2:10 Lit *20,000 baths* [F]2:11 Lit *Tyre said in writing* [G]2:13 Lit *Huram my father*

and bring them to you as rafts
by sea to Joppa. You can then
take them up to Jerusalem.

Solomon's Work (2:17–5:1)

17 Solomon took a census of all the
foreign men in the land of Israel, after the census that his father David
had conducted, and the total was
153,600. 18 Solomon made 70,000 of
them porters, 80,000 stonecutters
in the mountains, and 3,600 supervisors to make the people work.

3 Then Solomon began to build
the LORD's temple in Jerusalem
on Mount Moriah where the LORD[A]
had appeared to his father David, at
the site David had prepared on the
threshing floor of Ornan[B] the Jebusite. 2 He began to build on the
second day of the second month in
the fourth year of his reign. 3 These
are Solomon's foundations[C] for
building God's temple: the length[D]
was 90 feet,[E] and the width 30 feet.[F]
4 The portico, which was across the
front extending across the width of
the temple, was 30 feet[F] wide; its
height was 30 feet;[F,G] he overlaid its
inner surface with pure gold. 5 The
larger room[H] he paneled with cypress wood, overlaid with fine gold,
and decorated with palm trees and
chains. 6 He adorned the temple
with precious stones for beauty,
and the gold was the gold of Par-
vaim. 7 He overlaid the temple—the
beams, the thresholds, its walls and
doors—with gold, and he carved
•cherubim on the walls.

8 Then he made the most holy
place; its length corresponded to the
width of the temple, 30 feet,[F] and
its width was 30 feet.[F] He overlaid
it with 45,000 pounds[I] of fine gold.
9 The weight of the nails was 20
ounces[J] of gold, and he overlaid the
ceiling with gold.

10 He made two cherubim of sculp-
tured work, for the most holy place,
and he overlaid them with gold.
11 The overall length of the wings of
the cherubim was 30 feet:[F] the wing
of one was 7½ feet,[K] touching the
wall of the room; its other wing was
7½ feet,[K] touching the wing of the
other cherub. 12 The wing of the other[L] cherub was 7½ feet,[K] touching
the wall of the room; its other wing
was 7½ feet,[K] reaching the wing of
the other cherub. 13 The wingspan of
these cherubim was 30 feet.[F] They
stood on their feet and faced the
larger room.[M]

14 He made the veil of blue, purple,
and crimson yarn and fine linen,
and he wove cherubim into it.

15 In front of the temple he made
two pillars, each 27 feet[N,O] high. The
capital on top of each was 7½ feet[K]
high. 16 He had made chainwork in
the inner sanctuary and also put it
on top of the pillars. He made 100
pomegranates and fastened them
into the chainwork. 17 Then he set
up the pillars in front of the sanctuary, one on the right and one on
the left. He named the one on the
right Jachin[P] and the one on the left
Boaz.[Q]

4 He made a bronze altar 30 feet[F]
long, 30 feet[F] wide, and 15 feet[R]
high.

2 Then he made the cast metal reservoir, 15 feet[R] from brim to brim,
perfectly round. It was 7½ feet[K]
high and 45 feet[S] in circumference.
3 The likeness of oxen[T] was below it,
completely encircling it, 10 every
half yard,[U] completely surrounding
the reservoir. The oxen were cast
in two rows when the reservoir was
cast. 4 It stood on 12 oxen, three facing north, three facing west, three
facing south, and three facing east.
The reservoir was on top of them
and all their hindquarters were toward the center. 5 The reservoir was
three inches[V] thick, and its rim was
fashioned like the brim of a cup or
a lily blossom. It could hold 11,000
gallons.[W]

6 He made 10 basins for washing
and he put five on the right and five

3:1 This verse provides a piece of information that illuminates God's orchestration of history for the purpose of redemption—**the LORD's temple** was built **on Mount Moriah** (Hb, "chosen by Yahweh"; cp. Dt 12:5,11; 1Kg 8:16). Three key events are tied to this place:

- In Gn 22:1-19, God commanded Abraham to "go to the land of Moriah and offer" his "only son Isaac" there. Because God spared Isaac and provided a ram for the burnt offering, Abraham "named that place The LORD Will Provide" (Hb *YHWH-yireh*, "Yahweh sees").
- **The LORD** had led **David** to purchase **the site** and build there an altar for sacrifice in the midst of the plague by which God judged David's disobedience. (2Sm 24:16-18; 1Ch 21:15; 21:28–22:1).
- The northernmost part of Mount Moriah was later called Golgotha, the place where Jesus Christ was crucified as the spotless Lamb of God for the sins of his people (Jn 19:17-22). Figuratively referring to His own body as a temple, Jesus had claimed while in Jerusalem, "Destroy this sanctuary, and I will raise it up in three days" (Jn 2:19).

In the place of Abraham's son of promise, in the place of the people of Israel, in place of all people subject to God's sword of destruction because of sin, the death of Jesus Christ the chosen One was the "once and for all" sacrifice for sin (Lk 9:35; Heb 10:5-22).

3:14 Although not mentioned in 1 Kings, a **veil** woven as prescribed in Ex 26:31-34 was **made** to separate the most holy place from the holy place. Jesus' sacrifice provides direct access to the most holy place of God's presence. In contrast to the veil that is over the hearts of those with only the Law but not Christ, "whenever a person turns to the Lord the veil is removed" (2Co 3:16).

3:15-17 The tall, pomegranate-encircled pillars named **Jachin** (Hb, "he will establish") and **Boaz** (Hb, "swiftness or strength is in him"), possibly symbolized the power of Yahweh to build His temple and preserve it forever (cp. 1Kg 7:15-22).

4:1-22 As in 1Kg 7:13-51, **Solomon** was the subject of most verbs describing the other temple furnishings that were **made** (2Ch 4:1-2,6-10). This does not suggest that he physically completed the work but that he took personal responsibility for delegating the instructions entrusted to him by his father and for ensuring that they were carried out precisely and faithfully (cp. 1Ch 28:19-21). The temple's furnishings met the requirements of the tabernacle's design but on a much grander scale. Similarly, the "new Jerusalem" as John saw it in Rv 21–22

[A]**3:1** LXX; Tg reads *the Angel of the LORD*; MT reads *He* [B]**3:1** = Araunah in 2Sm 24:16-24 [C]**3:3** Tg reads *The measurements which Solomon decreed* [D]**3:3** Lit *length—cubits in the former measure—* [E]**3:3** Lit *60 cubits* [F]**3:3,4,8,11,13; 4:1** Lit *20 cubits* [G]**3:4** LXX, Syr; MT reads *120 cubits* [H]**3:5** Lit *The house* [I]**3:8** Lit *600 talents* [J]**3:9** Lit *50 shekels* [K]**3:11,12,15; 4:2** Lit *five cubits* [L]**3:12** Syr, Vg; MT reads *the one* [M]**3:13** Lit *the house* [N]**3:15** Hb uncertain [O]**3:15** Lit *35 cubits* [P]**3:17** = He Will Establish [Q]**3:17** = Strength Is in Him [R]**4:1,2** Lit *10 cubits* [S]**4:2** Lit *30 cubits* [T]**4:3** = gourds in 1Kg 7:24 [U]**4:3** Lit *10 per cubit* [V]**4:5** Lit *a handbreadth* [W]**4:5** Text emended; MT reads *3,000 baths* in 1Kg 7:26

corresponded in some respects to the earthly temple representing God's presence in the midst of His people, but the dimensions of the city "coming down out of heaven from God" were multiplied to a heavenly degree (Rv 21:2, cp. 2Ch 3:8 and Rv 21:18,21; cp. 2Ch 3:9 and Rv 22:1; cp. Ezk 47:1-12).

5:2–6:2 Addressing their **praise** [Hb *halal*, "sing, celebrate," 5:13; part of the exclamation *hallelujah*, "praise Yahweh"] **to the Lord**, the Levitical musicians acknowledged two aspects of His character that together form a confession of His unmatched worth:

- **He is good** (Hb *tov*, "excellent, benevolent"). Yahweh, the only true God, alone possesses perfection of moral character and action. Because He is "good" He does good—He acts in perfect consistency with His nature. Holy, pure, just, and righteous, God alone is worthy of complete trust and unrestrained love. Jesus implicitly affirmed His divine nature when He asked a man who called Him "Good Teacher," "Why do you call Me good? No one is good but One—God" (Mk 10:17-18). Jesus did not deny that He should rightly be called "good" but pointed out the meaning of doing so.
- **His faithful love** [Hb *chesed*, "mercy, kindness"] **endures forever**. The relational chasm between the God who "is good" and man who is not cannot be bridged unless God chooses to extend His goodness to undeserving man. This statement ties God's mercy to His eternal being. His "faithful love" extends beyond time and ultimately deals with the eternal offense of man's sin in the eternally effective, "once for all" self-sacrifice of the Son on the cross (Heb 1:1-3; 7:23-28; 1Pt 1:3-5).

This two-part statement of praise, which occurs only eight more times in Scripture, first appeared within David's psalm of thanksgiving for celebrating the arrival of the ark of the covenant in Jerusalem (1Ch 16:34). It is uniquely associated with the salvation and restoration brought by Yahweh's presence (cp. 1Ch 16:35; Pss 106:1,4-5,8,10,43-47; 107:1-3,6-8,13-16,19-22,28-32; 118:1,14,21,25,29; Jr 33:10-11). The former exiles would recognize in 1 Chronicles the same pattern of praise they themselves had followed when they celebrated the foundation of the second temple (Ezr 3:10-11).

on the left. The parts of the •burnt offering were rinsed in them, but the reservoir was used by the priests for washing.

7 He made the 10 gold lampstands according to their specifications and put them in the sanctuary, five on the right and five on the left. 8 He made 10 tables and placed them in the sanctuary, five on the right and five on the left. He also made 100 gold bowls.

9 He made the courtyard of the priests and the large court, and doors for the court. He overlaid the doors with bronze. 10 He put the reservoir on the right side, toward the southeast. 11 Then Huram[A] made the pots, the shovels, and the bowls.

So Huram finished doing the work that he was doing for King Solomon in God's temple: 12 two pillars; the bowls and the capitals on top of the two pillars; the two gratings for covering both bowls of the capitals that were on top of the pillars; 13 the 400 pomegranates for the two gratings (two rows of pomegranates for each grating covering both capitals' bowls on top of the pillars). 14 He also made the water carts[B] and the basins on the water carts. 15 The one reservoir and the 12 oxen underneath it, 16 the pots, the shovels, the forks, and all their utensils—Huram-abi[C] made them for King Solomon for the Lord's temple. All these were made of polished bronze. 17 The king had them cast in clay molds in the Jordan Valley between Succoth and Zeredah. 18 Solomon made all these utensils in such great abundance that the weight of the bronze was not determined.

19 Solomon also made all the equipment in God's temple: the gold altar; the tables on which to put the •bread of the Presence; 20 the lampstands and their lamps of pure gold to burn in front of the inner sanctuary according to specifications; 21 the flowers, lamps, and gold tongs—of purest gold; 22 the wick trimmers, sprinkling basins, ladles,[D] and firepans—of purest gold; and the entryway to the temple, its inner doors to the most holy place, and the doors of the temple sanctuary—of gold.

5 So all the work Solomon did for the Lord's temple was completed. Then Solomon brought the consecrated things of his father David—the silver, the gold, and all the utensils—and put them in the treasuries of God's temple.

The Glory of the Lord (5:2–6:2)

2 At that time Solomon assembled at Jerusalem the elders of Israel—all the tribal heads, the ancestral chiefs of the Israelites—in order to bring the ark of the covenant of the Lord up from the city of David, that is, •Zion. 3 So all the men of Israel were assembled in the king's presence at the festival; this was in the seventh month.[E]

4 All the elders of Israel came, and the Levites picked up the ark. 5 They brought up the ark, the tent of meeting, and the holy utensils that were in the tent. The priests and the Levites brought them up. 6 King Solomon and the entire congregation of Israel who had gathered around him were in front of the ark sacrificing sheep and cattle that could not be counted or numbered because there were so many. 7 The priests brought the ark of the Lord's covenant to its place, into the inner sanctuary of the temple, to the most holy place, beneath the wings of the •cherubim. 8 And the cherubim spread their wings over the place of the ark so that the cherubim formed a cover above the ark and its poles. 9 The poles were so long that their ends were seen from the holy place[F] in front of the inner sanctuary, but they were not seen from outside; they are there to this very day. 10 Nothing was in the ark except the two tablets that Moses had put in it at Horeb,[G] where the Lord had made a covenant with the Israelites when they came out of Egypt.

11 Now all the priests who were present had consecrated themselves regardless of their divisions. When the priests came out of the holy place, 12 the Levitical singers dressed in fine linen and carrying cymbals,

[A] 4:11 = Hiram in 1Kg 7:13,40,45 [B] 4:14 Lit *the stands* [C] 4:16 Lit *Huram my father* [D] 4:22 Or *dishes*, or *spoons*; lit *palms* [E] 5:3 = Tishri (September–October) [F] 5:9 Some Hb mss, LXX; other Hb mss read *the ark*; 1Kg 8:8 [G] 5:10 = Sinai

harps, and lyres were standing east of the altar, and with them were 120 priests blowing trumpets. The Levitical singers were descendants of •Asaph, Heman, and Jeduthun and their sons and relatives. 13 The trumpeters and singers joined together to praise and thank the LORD with one voice. They raised their voices, accompanied by trumpets, cymbals, and musical instruments, in praise to the LORD:

For He is good;
His faithful love
endures forever.

The temple, the LORD's temple, was filled with a cloud. 14 And because of the cloud, the priests were not able to continue ministering, for the glory of the LORD filled God's temple.

6 Then Solomon said:

The LORD said He would dwell
in thick darkness,
2 but I have built
an exalted temple for You,
a place
for Your residence forever.

The King's Blessing of the Congregation of Israel (6:3-11)

3 Then the king turned and blessed the entire congregation of Israel while they were standing. 4 He said:

May the LORD God of Israel
be praised!
He spoke directly
to my father David,
and He has fulfilled
the promise
by His power.
He said,
5 "Since the day I brought
My people Israel
out of the land of Egypt,
I have not chosen a city
to build a temple in
among any of the tribes
of Israel,
so that My name
would be there,
and I have not chosen a man
to be ruler
over My people Israel.
6 But I have chosen Jerusalem
so that My name will be there,
and I have chosen David
to be over My people Israel."
7 Now it was in the heart
of my father David
to build a temple
for the name of •Yahweh,
the God of Israel.
8 However, Yahweh said
to my father David,
"Since it was your desire
to build a temple
for My name,
you have done well to have
this desire.
9 Yet, you are not the one
to build the temple,
but your son,
your own offspring,
will build the temple
for My name."
10 So Yahweh has fulfilled
what He promised.
I have taken the place
of my father David
and I sit on the throne
of Israel,
as Yahweh promised.
I have built the temple
for the name of Yahweh,
the God of Israel.
11 I have put the ark there,
where Yahweh's covenant is
that He made
with the Israelites.

The King's Prayer (6:12–7:3)

Confirmation of That Promised (6:12-17)

12 Then Solomon stood before the altar of the LORD in front of the entire congregation of Israel and spread out his hands. 13 For Solomon had made a bronze platform 7½ feet[A] long, 7½ feet[A] wide, and 4½ feet[B] high and put it in the court. He stood on it, knelt down in front of the entire congregation of Israel, and spread out his hands toward heaven. 14 He said:

LORD God of Israel,
there is no God like You
in heaven or on earth,
keeping
His gracious covenant
with Your servants who walk
before You

5:13-14 Signaling Yahweh's approval and acceptance of the temple, **the glory of the LORD** appeared as **a cloud** that **filled** the **temple**, the same way He had made His presence known in the tabernacle constructed by Moses (cp. 7:1-3; Ex 20:21; 40:34-35; Dt 4:11; 5:22).

6:12-17 The Chronicler's description of Solomon's position and posture is more detailed than that found in 1 Kings 8:22. His humble posture was unlike other ancient Near Eastern monarchs, who were not noted for bowing publicly before anyone.

A 6:13 Lit *five cubits* B 6:13 Lit *three cubits*

6:18 Verse 18 clarifies the rhetorical question that also appears in 1Kg 8:27. Both verses express wonder that **God** would **live on earth**. With amazement 2Ch 6:18 augments the fact that God would live **with man**.

6:19-38 To Pray (Hb *palal*, "make petition or supplication, intercede") involves heartfelt intercession often accompanied by tears (cp. 20:1-5). One must pray on the basis of faith in God's promises and the truth revealed in His word (Ps 145:18), believing that God is both willing and able to act (Mk 11:23). Sacrifice in the Old Testament was the basic expression of penitent prayer, of thanksgiving, and of petition. In the New Testament, prayer is possible on the basis of Christ's sacrifice and mediation rather than on animal sacrifices. Christ Himself "lives to intercede" for "those who come to God through Him" (Heb 7:25).

with their whole heart.
15 You have kept
what You promised
to Your servant,
my father David.
You spoke directly to him,
and You fulfilled Your promise
by Your power,
as it is today.
16 Therefore, LORD God of Israel,
keep what You promised
to Your servant,
my father David:
"You will never fail to have
a man
to sit before Me on the throne
of Israel,
if only your sons guard
their way to walk in My Law
as you have walked
before Me."
17 Now, LORD God of Israel,
please confirm
what You promised
to Your servant David.

Solomon's Petition (6:18-40)

18 But will God indeed live
on earth with man?
Even heaven,
the highest heaven,
cannot contain You,
much less this temple
I have built.
19 Listen[A] to Your servant's
prayer and his petition,
LORD my God,
so that You may hear the cry
and the prayer
that Your servant prays
before You,
20 so that Your eyes watch over
this temple
day and night,
toward the place
where You said
You would put Your name;
and so that You may hear
the prayer
Your servant prays
toward this place.
21 Hear the petitions
of Your servant
and Your people Israel,
which they pray
toward this place.
May You hear
in Your dwelling place
in heaven.
May You hear and forgive.

22 If a man sins
against his neighbor
and is forced to take an oath[B]
and he comes to take an oath
before Your altar
in this temple,
23 may You hear in heaven
and act.
May You judge Your servants,
condemning the wicked man
by bringing
what he has done
on his own head
and providing justice
for the righteous
by rewarding him
according to
his righteousness.

24 If Your people
Israel are defeated
before an enemy,
because they have sinned
against You,
and they return to You
and praise Your name,
and they pray and plead
for mercy
before You in this temple,
25 may You hear in heaven
and forgive the sin
of Your people Israel.
May You restore them
to the land
You gave them
and their ancestors.

A 6:19 Lit *Turn* B 6:22 Lit *and he lifts a curse against him to curse him*

26 When the skies are shut
and there is no rain
because they have sinned
against You,
and they pray
toward this place
and praise Your name,
and they turn from their sins
because You are
afflicting[A] them,
27 may You hear in heaven
and forgive the sin
of Your servants
and Your people Israel,
so that You may teach them
the good way
they should walk in.
May You send rain
on Your land
that You gave Your people
for an inheritance.

28 When there is famine
on the earth,
when there is pestilence,
when there is blight, mildew,
locust, or grasshopper,
when their enemies
besiege them
in the region
of their fortified cities,[B]
when there is any plague
or illness,
29 whatever prayer or petition
anyone
from your people Israel
might have—
each man knowing
his own affliction[C]
and suffering,
and spreading out his hands
toward this temple—
30 may You hear in heaven,
Your dwelling place,
and may You forgive
and repay the man
according to all his ways,
since You know his heart,
for You alone know
the human heart,
31 so that they may •fear You
and walk in Your ways
all the days they live
on the land
You gave our ancestors.
32 Even for the foreigner who is
not of Your people Israel
but has come from
a distant land
because of Your great name
and Your mighty hand
and outstretched arm:
when he comes and prays
toward this temple,
33 may You hear in heaven
in Your dwelling place,
and do all the foreigner
asks You.
Then all the peoples
of the earth will know
Your name,
to fear You as Your people
Israel do
and know that this temple
I have built
is called by Your name.

34 When Your people go
out to fight against
their enemies,
wherever You send them,
and they pray to You
in the direction of this city
You have chosen
and the temple that
I have built for Your name,
35 may You hear their prayer
and petition in heaven
and uphold their cause.

36 When they sin against You—
for there is no one
who does not sin—
and You are angry with them
and hand them over
to the enemy,
and their captors deport them
to a distant or nearby country,
37 and when they come
to their senses
in the land where they
were deported
and repent and petition You
in their captors' land,
saying: "We have sinned
and done wrong;
we have been wicked,"
38 and when they return to
You with their whole mind
and heart
in the land of their captivity
where they were
taken captive,
and when they pray

[A]**6:26** LXX, Vg; MT reads *answering*; 1Kg 8:35 [B]**6:28** Lit *if his* (Israel's) *enemies besiege him in the land of his gates*; Jos 2:7; Jdg 16:2-3 [C]**6:29** Lit *plague*

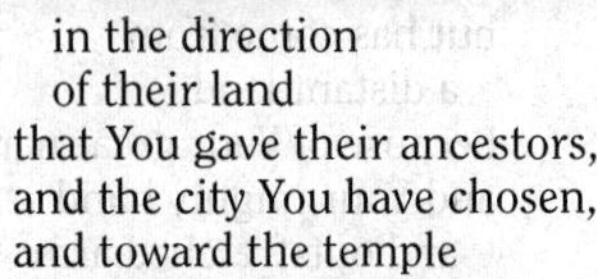

7:12-16 The context of verses 13-15 was not included in the parallel 1 Kings account. In addition to the conditions laid down for Solomon as the king (vv. 17-22; cp. 1Kg 9:4-9), **the LORD** set the conditions for answering the corporate prayer of His people in the midst of God's destruction of their self-sufficiency (2Ch 7:12). The setting described here is Yahweh's judgment on *His* **people who are called by** His **name**—those who belong to *Him* and publicly represent His "name" yet disobey Him; present-day application of this text (or any other) should carefully consider its biblical context (v. 14). All three concrete actions—withholding **rain**, commanding **the grasshopper to consume the land**, and sending **pestilence** (Hb *dever*, "destruction, death, plague") on the **people**—would directly undermine their dependence on **the land** and their physical health, with the purpose of steering them away from trusting anyone or anything other than Him (v. 13). The exiles who returned to Israel undoubtedly recognized not only that God had judged them by these means but also that He was keeping His promise to **hear** them, **forgive their sin, and heal their land** (v. 14).

in the direction
of their land
that You gave their ancestors,
and the city You have chosen,
and toward the temple
I have built for Your name,
39 may You hear their prayer
and petitions in heaven,
Your dwelling place,
and uphold their cause.[A]
May You forgive Your people
who sinned against You.

40 Now, my God,
please let Your eyes be open
and Your ears attentive
to the prayer of this place.

The Endurance of His Faithful Love (6:41–7:3)

41 Now therefore:

Arise, LORD God, come
to Your resting place,
You and Your powerful ark.
May Your priests, LORD God,
be clothed with salvation,
and may Your godly people
rejoice in goodness.
42 LORD God, do not reject
Your anointed one;[B]
remember the loyalty
of Your servant David.

7 When Solomon finished praying, fire descended from heaven and consumed the •burnt offering and the sacrifices, and the glory of the LORD filled the temple. 2 The priests were not able to enter the LORD's temple because the glory of the LORD filled the temple of the LORD. 3 All the Israelites were watching when the fire descended and the glory of the LORD came on the temple. They bowed down on the pavement with their faces to the ground. They worshiped and praised the LORD:

For He is good,
for His faithful love
endures forever.

The Consecration of the Temple (7:4-11)

4 The king and all the people were offering sacrifices in the LORD's presence. 5 King Solomon offered a sacrifice of 22,000 cattle and 120,000 sheep. In this manner the king and all the people dedicated God's temple. 6 The priests and the Levites were standing at their stations. The Levites had the musical instruments of the LORD, which King David had made to praise the LORD—"for His faithful love endures forever"—when he offered praise with them. Across from the Levites, the priests were blowing trumpets, and all the people were standing. 7 Since the bronze altar that Solomon had made could not accommodate the burnt offering, the •grain offering, and the fat of the •fellowship offerings, Solomon first consecrated the middle of the courtyard that was in front of the LORD's temple and then offered the burnt offerings and the fat of the fellowship offerings there.

8 So Solomon and all Israel with him—a very great assembly, from the entrance to Hamath[C] to the Brook of Egypt—observed the festival at that time for seven days. 9 On the eighth day[D] they held a sacred assembly, for the dedication of the altar lasted seven days and the festival seven days. 10 On the twenty-third day of the seventh month he sent the people away to their tents, rejoicing and with happy hearts for the goodness the LORD had done for David, for Solomon, and for His people Israel.

11 So Solomon finished the LORD's temple and the royal palace. Everything that had entered Solomon's heart to do for the LORD's temple and for his own palace succeeded.

God's Covenant with Solomon (7:12-22)

12 Then the LORD appeared to Solomon at night and said to him:

I have heard your prayer and have chosen this place for Myself as a temple of sacrifice. 13 If I close the sky so there is no rain, or if I command the grasshopper to consume the land, or if I send pestilence on My people, 14 and My people who are called by My name humble themselves, pray and

[A] **6:39** Lit *and do their judgment* or *justice* [B] **6:42** Some Hb mss, LXX; other Hb mss read *ones*; Ps 132:10 [C] **7:8** Or *from Lebo-hamath* [D] **7:9** = the day after the festival, or the 15th day

>WORD|*study*

7:14 To humble (Hb *kana'*, "behave submissively, bend the knee") is to place oneself voluntarily under another's power rather than being forcefully subdued or unwillingly brought under subjection. In relating to authority, it is the opposite of pride (cp. 12:7,12; 32:26; 34:26-28).

7:14 Seek (Hb *baqash*, "seek the king's face") means "desiring, asking for, or requesting" the privilege of being heard by the king—having a face-to-face audience with the highest authority. In Isaiah 51:1, seeking the Lord's "face" is coupled with pursuing "righteousness." To "seek" also involves an inner determination not to give up until the desired object is found (cp. Jr 29:13). Repentance involves going to the One against whom the sin was committed and seeking both His forgiveness and favor. Like prayer, seeking requires faith and genuine desire (cp. Is 26:9; Heb 11:6).

7:14 Turn (Hb *shuv*, "return, turn back") relates to an act of the will—one who stops, does an about-face, and resolutely follows a path back to the starting point. In order to change direction, people must first acknowledge and confess that they are headed the wrong way (Pr 28:13). For the Lord's people not to turn from sin would convey their desire merely to be released from unpleasant consequences. God wants to see a complete turnaround, a genuine rejection of "evil ways" in order to embrace God's righteous ways.

7:15 Attentive (Hb *qashshav*) is used twice in 2 Chronicles (6:40; 7:15). Elsewhere in the Old Testament, it appears only three times—twice in Nehemiah's prayer (Neh 1:6,11) and once in a prayer of David (Ps 130:2). Both prayers focused on sin and forgiveness.

7:17-21 The rest of the Lord's message, addressed to Solomon, directly linked the king's obedience to the nation's stability and warned that idolatry on his part would set a national pattern resulting in tragedy for the **exalted** temple over which they had so recently rejoiced (v. 21).

seek My face, and turn from
their evil ways, then I will hear
from heaven, forgive their sin,
and heal their land. [15] My eyes
will now be open and My ears
attentive to prayer from this
place. [16] And I have now chosen
and consecrated this temple so
that My name may be there forever; My eyes and My heart will
be there at all times.

[17] As for you, if you walk before
Me as your father David walked,
doing everything I have commanded you, and if you keep
My statutes and ordinances,
[18] I will establish your royal
throne, as I promised your father David: You will never fail
to have a man ruling in Israel.

[19] However, if you turn away and
abandon My statutes and My
commands that I have set before you and if you go and serve
other gods and worship them,
[20] then I will uproot Israel from
the soil that I gave them, and
this temple that I have sanctified for My name I will banish from My presence; I will
make it an object of scorn and
ridicule among all the peoples.
[21] As for this temple, which was
exalted, everyone who passes
by will be appalled and will
say: Why did the LORD do this
to this land and this temple?
[22] Then they will say: Because
they abandoned the LORD God
of their ancestors who brought
them out of the land of Egypt.
They clung to other gods and
worshiped and served them.
Because of this, He brought all
this ruin on them.

Building Projects (8:1-11)

8 At the end of 20 years during
which Solomon had built the
LORD's temple and his own palace—
[2] Solomon had rebuilt the cities Hiram[A] gave him and settled Israelites
there— [3] Solomon went to Hamath-
zobah and seized it. [4] He built Tadmor in the wilderness along with all
the storage cities that he built in Hamath. [5] He built Upper Beth-horon
and Lower Beth-horon—fortified
cities with walls, gates, and bars—
[6] Baalath, all the storage cities that
belonged to Solomon, all the chariot
cities, the cavalry cities, and everything Solomon desired to build in
Jerusalem, Lebanon, or anywhere
else in the land of his dominion.

[7] As for all the peoples who remained of the Hittites, Amorites,
Perizzites, Hivites, and Jebusites,
who were not from Israel— [8] their
descendants who remained in
the land after them, those the Israelites had not completely destroyed—Solomon imposed forced

[A] **8:2** = the king of Tyre

8:11 First Kings 3:1 explains why **Solomon** married Pharaoh's **daughter**, but the Chronicler supplied the reason for the location of her palace outside Jerusalem (cp. 1Kg 3:1). For the Chronicler's audience, this detail may have been particularly important in that it demonstrated Solomon's sensitivity to the problem his marriage to this woman precipitated. The **ark of the LORD** had been located close to David's palace during many years of his reign, and numerous wives lived in the palace. More likely Solomon's decision reflected the improper and dangerous proximity of his *non-Jewish* **wife** to God's holy presence marked by the ark's presence in the temple. The concern would be particularly acute if Pharaoh's daughter, like his many other foreign wives, did not exchange her native worship of other gods for the one God of Israel (cp. 1Kg 11:1).

8:12-16 Although Solomon **carried out** the **work** (v. 16), the reader is never allowed to forget that **David** was both Solomon's **father** and the king (v. 14). At *David's* **command**, both **the priests** and the new king made the **temple** truly **the LORD's**.

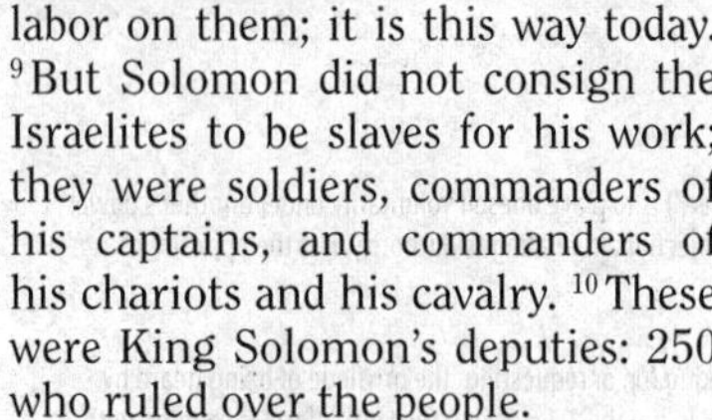

labor on them; it is this way today. 9 But Solomon did not consign the Israelites to be slaves for his work; they were soldiers, commanders of his captains, and commanders of his chariots and his cavalry. 10 These were King Solomon's deputies: 250 who ruled over the people.

11 Solomon brought the daughter of Pharaoh from the city of David to the house he had built for her, for he said, "My wife must not live in the house[A] of David king of Israel because the places the ark of the LORD has come into are holy."

Worship and Wealth (8:12–9:30)

The Completion of the Temple (8:12-16)

12 At that time Solomon offered •burnt offerings to the LORD on the LORD's altar he had made in front of the portico. 13 He followed the daily requirement for offerings according to the commandment of Moses for Sabbaths, New Moons, and the three annual appointed festivals: the Festival of •Unleavened Bread, the Festival of Weeks, and the Festival of Booths. 14 According to the ordinances of his father David, he appointed the divisions of the priests over their service, of the Levites over their responsibilities to offer praise and to minister before the priests following the daily requirement, and of the gatekeepers by their divisions with respect to each gate, for this had been the command of David, the man of God. 15 They did not turn aside from the king's command regarding the priests and the Levites concerning any matter or concerning the treasuries. 16 All of Solomon's work was carried out from the day the foundation was laid for the LORD's temple until it was finished. So the LORD's temple was completed.

The Acquisition of Gold (8:17-18)

17 At that time Solomon went to Ezion-geber and to Eloth on the seashore in the land of Edom. 18 So Hiram[B] sent ships to him by his servants along with crews of experienced seamen. They went with Solomon's servants to Ophir, took from there 17 tons[C] of gold, and delivered it to King Solomon.

The Queen of Sheba's Visit (9:1-12)

9 The queen of Sheba heard of Solomon's fame, so she came to test Solomon with difficult questions at Jerusalem with a very large entourage, with camels bearing spices, gold in abundance, and precious stones. She came to Solomon and spoke with him about everything that was on her mind. 2 So Solomon answered all her questions; nothing was too difficult for Solomon to explain to her. 3 When the queen of Sheba observed Solomon's wisdom, the palace he had built, 4 the food at his table, his servants' residence, his attendants' service and their attire, his cupbearers and their attire, and the •burnt offerings he offered at the LORD's temple, it took her breath away.

5 She said to the king, "The report I heard in my own country about your words and about your wisdom is true. 6 But I didn't believe their reports until I came and saw with my own eyes. Indeed, I was not even told half of your great wisdom! You far exceed the report I heard. 7 How happy are your men.[D] How happy are these servants of yours, who always stand in your presence hearing your wisdom. 8 May the LORD your God be praised! He delighted in you and put you on His throne as king for the LORD your God. Because Your God loved Israel enough to establish them forever, He has set you over them as king to carry out justice and righteousness."

9 Then she gave the king four and a half tons[E] of gold, a great quantity of spices, and precious stones. There never were such spices as those the queen of Sheba gave to King Solomon. 10 In addition, Hiram's servants and Solomon's servants who brought gold from Ophir also brought algum wood and precious stones. 11 The king made the algum wood into walkways for the LORD's temple and for the king's palace and into lyres and harps for the singers.

[A] 8:11 LXX reads *city* [B] 8:18 Lit *Huram* [C] 8:18 Lit *450 talents* [D] 9:7 LXX, Old Lat read *wives*; 1Kg 10:8 [E] 9:9 Lit *120 talents*

Never before had anything like them
been seen in the land of Judah.
12 King Solomon gave the queen
of Sheba her every desire, whatever
she asked—far more than she had
brought the king. Then she, along
with her servants, returned to her
own country.

Fame and Fortune (9:13-30)

13 The weight of gold that came
to Solomon annually was 25 tons,[A]
14 besides what was brought by the
merchants and traders. All the Arabian kings and governors of the land
also brought gold and silver to Solomon.
15 King Solomon made 200 large
shields of hammered gold; 15
pounds[B] of hammered gold went
into each shield. 16 He made 300
small shields of hammered gold;
about eight pounds[C] of gold went
into each shield. The king put them
in the House of the Forest of Lebanon.
17 The king also made a large ivory
throne and overlaid it with pure
gold. 18 The throne had six steps;
there was a footstool covered in gold
for the throne, armrests on either
side of the seat, and two lions standing beside the armrests. 19 Twelve
lions were standing there on the six
steps, one at each end. Nothing like
it had ever been made in any other
kingdom.
20 All of King Solomon's drinking
cups were gold, and all the utensils
of the House of the Forest of Lebanon were pure gold. There was no
silver, since it was considered as
nothing in Solomon's time, 21 for the
king's ships kept going to Tarshish
with Hiram's servants, and once every three years the ships of Tarshish
would arrive bearing gold, silver,
ivory, apes, and peacocks.[D]
22 King Solomon surpassed all the
kings of the world in riches and wisdom. 23 All the kings of the world
wanted an audience with Solomon
to hear the wisdom God had put
in his heart. 24 Each of them would
bring his own gift—items[E] of silver
and gold, clothing, weapons,[FG] spices, and horses and mules—as an annual tribute.
25 Solomon had 4,000 stalls for
horses and chariots, and 12,000
horsemen. He stationed them in the
chariot cities and with the king in
Jerusalem. 26 He ruled over all the
kings from the Euphrates River to
the land of the Philistines and as far
as the border of Egypt. 27 The king
made silver as common in Jerusalem as stones, and he made cedar
as abundant as sycamore in the Judean foothills. 28 They were bringing
horses for Solomon from Egypt and
from all the countries.
29 The remaining events of Solomon's reign, from beginning to end,
are written in the Events of Nathan
the Prophet, the Prophecy of Ahijah the Shilonite, and the Visions of
Iddo the Seer concerning Jeroboam
son of Nebat. 30 Solomon reigned in
Jerusalem over all Israel for 40 years.

King Rehoboam (9:31–12:16)

Rejection of the Elders' Advice (9:31–10:19)

31 Solomon rested with his fathers
and was buried in the city of his father David. His son Rehoboam became king in his place.

10 Then Rehoboam went to
Shechem, for all Israel had
gone to Shechem to make him king.
2 When Jeroboam son of Nebat heard
about it—for he was in Egypt where
he had fled from King Solomon's
presence—Jeroboam returned from
Egypt. 3 So they summoned him.
Then Jeroboam and all Israel came
and spoke to Rehoboam: 4 "Your father made our yoke difficult. Therefore, lighten your father's harsh
service and the heavy yoke he put on
us, and we will serve you."
5 Rehoboam replied, "Return to
me in three days." So the people left.
6 Then King Rehoboam consulted
with the elders who had served his
father Solomon when he was alive,
asking, "How do you advise me to
respond to these people?"
7 They replied, "If you will be kind
to these people and please them by

9:13-28 Verses 13-25 and 27-28 of this passage follow the description in 1Kg 10:14-27. The Chronicler completely left out the account of Solomon's unfaithfulness and of the enemies "the Lord raised up" against him (2Ch 9:26; 1Kg 11:1-40). He could safely assume that his audience was painfully aware of Solomon's role in accommodating the worship of false gods in his realm. The former exiles had less need to be reminded of the genesis of the kingdom's downward spiral than to receive restoration of hope in the unchanging promises of God.

9:29-30 Portions of this section also parallel 1Kg 11:41-43. The most significant difference between these two brief concluding statements about Solomon's reign are the sources to which the reader is referred for more information.

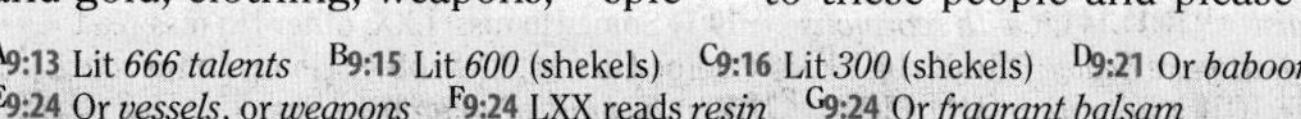
A 9:13 Lit *666 talents* B 9:15 Lit *600* (shekels) C 9:16 Lit *300* (shekels) D 9:21 Or *baboons*
E 9:24 Or *vessels*, or *weapons* F 9:24 LXX reads *resin* G 9:24 Or *fragrant balsam*

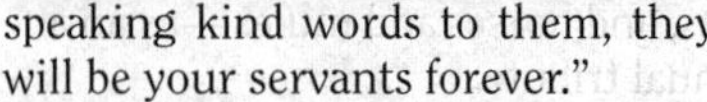

11:1-4 As the historical narrative proceeds from Rehoboam's reign forward, the writer's emphasis, in contrast to Kings, is clearly on the southern kingdom of Judah and the continuation of David's succession. The kings of the northern kingdom of Israel are mentioned only when doing so contributes to the story of Judah's history.

11:5-17 When the kingdom divided (between the 10 tribes of **Israel** on the one hand and Judah and Benjamin, or **David** on the other—vv. 16-17), the temple in Jerusalem remained the exclusive place for the worship of Israel's one God. Therefore, **the priests and Levites** abandoned the towns and cities set aside for them in the north when the northern king Jeroboam created a rival form of worship in Bethel and Dan, which included the appointment of non-Levitical **priests** (vv. 14-15; see notes on 1Kg 12:25-33). As the religious leaders **went to Judah and Jerusalem**, an untold number of Israelites followed them because their allegiance lay with **Yahweh their God** (2Ch 11:16).

speaking kind words to them, they will be your servants forever."

8 But he rejected the advice of the elders who had advised him, and he consulted with the young men who had grown up with him, the ones serving him. 9 He asked them, "What message do you advise we send back to these people who said to me, 'Lighten the yoke your father put on us'?"

10 Then the young men who had grown up with him told him, "This is what you should say to the people who said to you, 'Your father made our yoke heavy, but you, make it lighter on us!' This is what you should say to them: 'My little finger is thicker than my father's loins.[A] 11 Now therefore, my father burdened you with a heavy yoke, but I will add to your yoke; my father disciplined you with whips, but I, with barbed whips.'"[B]

12 So Jeroboam and all the people came to Rehoboam on the third day, just as the king had ordered, saying, "Return to me on the third day." 13 Then the king answered them harshly. King Rehoboam rejected the elders' advice 14 and spoke to them according to the young men's advice, saying, "My father made your yoke heavy,[C] but I will add to it; my father disciplined you with whips, but I, with barbed whips."[B]

15 The king did not listen to the people because the turn of events came from God, in order that the LORD might carry out His word that He had spoken through Ahijah the Shilonite to Jeroboam son of Nebat.

16 When all Israel saw[D] that the king had not listened to them, the people answered the king:

> What portion do we have
> in David?
> We have no inheritance
> in the son of Jesse.
> Israel, each man to your tent;
> David, look after
> your own house now!

So all Israel went to their tents. 17 But as for the Israelites living in the cities of Judah, Rehoboam reigned over them.

18 Then King Rehoboam sent Hadoram,[E] who was in charge of the forced labor, but the Israelites stoned him to death. However, King Rehoboam managed to get into his chariot to flee to Jerusalem. 19 Israel is in rebellion against the house of David until today.

The Kingdom of Judah (11:1-23)

11 When Rehoboam arrived in Jerusalem, he mobilized the house of Judah and Benjamin—180,000 choice warriors—to fight against Israel to restore the reign to Rehoboam. 2 But the word of the LORD came to Shemaiah, the man of God: 3 "Say to Rehoboam son of Solomon, king of Judah, to all Israel in Judah and Benjamin, and to the rest of the people: 4 'This is what the LORD says: You are not to march up and fight against your brothers. Each of you must return home, for this incident has come from Me.'"

So they listened to what the LORD said and turned back from going against Jeroboam.

5 Rehoboam stayed in Jerusalem, and he fortified cities[F] in Judah. 6 He built up Bethlehem, Etam, Tekoa, 7 Beth-zur, Soco, Adullam, 8 Gath, Mareshah, Ziph, 9 Adoraim, Lachish, Azekah, 10 Zorah, Aijalon, and Hebron, which are fortified cities in Judah and in Benjamin. 11 He strengthened their fortifications and put leaders in them with supplies of food, oil, and wine. 12 He also put large shields and spears in each and every city to make them very strong. So Judah and Benjamin were his.

13 The priests and Levites from all their regions throughout Israel took their stand with Rehoboam, 14 for the Levites left their pasturelands and their possessions and went to Judah and Jerusalem, because Jeroboam and his sons refused to let them serve as priests of •Yahweh. 15 Jeroboam appointed his own priests for the •high places, the goat-demons, and the golden calves he had made. 16 Those from

[A] 10:10 Or *waist* [B] 10:11,14 Lit *with scorpions* [C] 10:14 Some Hb mss, LXX; other Hb mss read *I will make your yoke heavy*; 1Kg 12:14 [D] 10:16 Some Hb mss, LXX; other Hb mss omit *saw*; 1Kg 12:16 [E] 10:18 = Adoram in 1Kg 12:18 [F] 11:5 Lit *he built cities for a fortress*

>WORD|*study*

12:2 The charge against Israel, Jerusalem, and the king of being **unfaithful** (Hb *ma'al*, "act treacherously, break faith with"; cp. Dt 32:51) was comparable to charging an entire corporation, including its CEO and stockholders, with corruption that blatantly and defiantly contradicted everything the owner and founder intended the business to be. Because being "unfaithful" essentially applies to relationships mutually and legally bound by an agreement, contract, or covenant, the word can also mean "transgressing or committing a trespass against"—intentionally violating the terms of the agreement. The sin of being "unfaithful" to the Lord was especially egregious since He was completely faithful, perfectly keeping His covenant commitments to Israel. In the human relationship of marriage, for a wife with a loving, blameless husband to commit adultery against him would be blatant unfaithfulness.

every tribe of Israel who had determined in their hearts to seek Yahweh their God followed the Levites
to Jerusalem to sacrifice to Yahweh,
the God of their ancestors. 17 So they
strengthened the kingdom of Judah
and supported Rehoboam son of
Solomon for three years, because
they walked in the way of David and
Solomon for three years.
18 Rehoboam married Mahalath,
daughter of David's son Jerimoth
and of Abihail daughter of Jesse's son
Eliab. 19 She bore sons to him: Jeush,
Shemariah, and Zaham. 20 After her,
he married Maacah daughter[A] of Absalom. She bore Abijah, Attai, Ziza,
and Shelomith to him. 21 Rehoboam
loved Maacah daughter[A] of Absalom
more than all his wives and concubines. He acquired 18 wives and 60
concubines and was the father of 28
sons and 60 daughters.
22 Rehoboam appointed Abijah son
of Maacah as chief, leader among
his brothers, intending to make
him king. 23 Rehoboam also showed
discernment by dispersing some of
his sons to all the regions of Judah
and Benjamin and to all the fortified
cities. He gave them plenty of provisions and sought many wives for
them.

Shishak's Invasion (12:1-12)

12 When Rehoboam had established his sovereignty and
royal power, he abandoned the law
of the LORD—he and all Israel with
him. 2 Because they were unfaithful
to the LORD, in the fifth year of King
Rehoboam, Shishak king of Egypt
went to war against Jerusalem 3 with
1,200 chariots, 60,000 cavalrymen,
and countless people who came with
him from Egypt—Libyans, Sukki-
im, and Cushites. 4 He captured the
fortified cities of Judah and came as
far as Jerusalem.
5 Then Shemaiah the prophet went
to Rehoboam and the leaders of Judah who were gathered at Jerusalem because of Shishak. He said to
them: "This is what the LORD says:
'You have abandoned Me; therefore,
I have abandoned you into the hand
of Shishak.'"
6 So the leaders of Israel and the
king humbled themselves and said,
"Yahweh is righteous."
7 When the LORD saw that they
had humbled themselves, the LORD's
message came to Shemaiah: "They
have humbled themselves; I will not
destroy them but will grant them
a little deliverance. My wrath will
not be poured out on Jerusalem
through Shishak. 8 However, they
will become his servants so that
they may recognize the difference
between serving Me and serving the
kingdoms of other lands."
9 So King Shishak of Egypt went
to war against Jerusalem. He seized
the treasuries of the LORD's temple
and the treasuries of the royal palace. He took everything. He took
the gold shields that Solomon had
made. 10 King Rehoboam made
bronze shields in their place and
committed them into the care of the
captains of the royal escorts[B] who
guarded the entrance to the king's
palace. 11 Whenever the king entered
the LORD's temple, the royal escorts
would carry the shields and take
them back to the royal escorts' armory. 12 When Rehoboam humbled
himself, the LORD's anger turned
away from him, and He did not destroy him completely. Besides that,
conditions were good in Judah.

11:18-26 The details about Rehoboam's family are unique to Chronicles and demonstrate that he married within the Davidic line. **Mahalath** and **Maacah** were his cousins (cp. "Maacah," 1Ch 3:2). Maacah was probably Absalom's granddaughter born to his daughter Tamar and Uriel (2Sm 14:27; 2Ch 13:2).

12:1-6 During the first three years of his reign, Rehoboam and Judah remained obedient. Chapter 12, however, starkly illustrates the tragedy of a leader's becoming complacent in the midst of God's blessings. **Rehoboam** did not merely forget that **the LORD** had enabled him to establish his **royal power**—he neglected to remember that he had no claim to self-sufficiency (v. 1). Given the weight of the spoken word in Israel's culture, **the leaders**' declaration that **Yahweh is righteous** not only constituted a significant theological statement but also an open acknowledgment that they accepted Yahweh's verdict on their guilt and the punishment incurred (v. 6).

[A]**11:20,21** Possibly *granddaughter*; 2Ch 13:2 [B]**12:10** Lit *the runners*

13:1-2 Micaiah is an alternate spelling for Maacah, the beloved wife of Rehoboam described in 11:20-22 (see also 15:16).

13:5-10 Abijah's speech confirmed that he understood the privilege of being a direct descendant of David, but his interpretation of Israel's history was only half right (cp. 1Kg 15:4-5). The kingdom was divided not because of Jeroboam's rebellion against Solomon but because of Solomon's sin (see 1Kg 11:7-13,29-39). Abijah's characterization of Jeroboam's apostasy was accurate (2Ch 13:8-9; see 1Kg 12:26-13:6), but his boasting that Judah was completely obedient contradicts the judgment that "he was not completely devoted to the LORD" (2Ch 13:10-12; 1Kg 15:3). Whatever success Abijah enjoyed was attributed to the Lord's commitment to His covenant with David.

>WORD|*study*

13:5 The term covenant of salt, found only here and in Nm 18:19, emphasizes the "perpetual" character of the Lord's covenant with Aaron. As a preservative and purifying agent, salt was likely a vivid symbol of an unchanging nature and therefore an apt qualifier to describe this covenant, which could not be broken (cp. Lv 2:13; 2Sm 7:13,15-16; 1Ch 17:12-14; Ezk 43:24).

An Overview of Rehoboam's Reign (12:13-16)

13 King Rehoboam established his royal power in Jerusalem. Rehoboam was 41 years old when he became king and reigned 17 years in Jerusalem, the city the LORD had chosen from all the tribes of Israel to put His name. Rehoboam's mother's name was Naamah the Ammonite. 14 Rehoboam did what was evil, because he did not determine in his heart to seek the LORD.

15 The events of Rehoboam's reign, from beginning to end, are written in the Events of Shemaiah the Prophet and of Iddo the Seer concerning genealogies. There was war between Rehoboam and Jeroboam throughout their reigns. 16 Rehoboam rested with his fathers and was buried in the city of David. His son Abijah[A] became king in his place.

Abijah (13:1–14:1)

13 In the eighteenth year of Israel's King Jeroboam, Abijah[A] became king over Judah 2 and reigned three years in Jerusalem. His mother's name was Micaiah[B] daughter of Uriel; she was from Gibeah.

There was war between Abijah and Jeroboam. 3 Abijah set his army of warriors in order with 400,000 choice men. Jeroboam arranged his mighty army of 800,000 choice men in battle formation against him. 4 Then Abijah stood on Mount Zemaraim, which is in the hill country of Ephraim, and said, "Jeroboam and all Israel, hear me. 5 Don't you know that the LORD God of Israel gave the kingship over Israel to David and his descendants forever by a covenant of salt? 6 But Jeroboam son of Nebat, a servant of Solomon son of David, rose up and rebelled against his lord. 7 Then worthless and •wicked men gathered around him to resist Rehoboam son of Solomon when Rehoboam was young, inexperienced, and unable to assert himself against them.

8 "And now you are saying you can assert yourselves against the LORD's kingdom, which is in the hand of one of David's sons. You are a vast number and have with you the golden calves that Jeroboam made for you as gods.[C] 9 Didn't you banish the priests of •Yahweh, the descendants of Aaron and the Levites, and make your own priests like the peoples of other lands do? Whoever comes to ordain himself with a young bull and seven rams may become a priest of what are not gods.

10 "But as for us, Yahweh is our God. We have not abandoned Him; the priests ministering to the LORD are descendants of Aaron, and the Levites serve at their tasks. 11 They offer a •burnt offering and fragrant incense to the LORD every morning and every evening, and they set the rows of the •bread of the Presence on the ceremonially •clean table. They light the lamps of the gold lampstand every evening. We are carrying out the requirements of Yahweh our God, while you have abandoned Him. 12 Look, God and His priests are with us at our head. The trumpets are ready to sound the charge against you. Israelites, don't fight against the LORD God of your ancestors, for you will not succeed."

13 Now Jeroboam had sent an ambush around to advance from behind them. So they were in front of Judah, and the ambush was behind them. 14 Judah turned and discovered that the battle was in front of them and behind them, so they cried out to the LORD. Then the priests blew the trumpets, 15 and the men of Ju-

[A] **12:16; 13:1** = Abijam in 1Kg 14:31–15:8 [B] **13:2** LXX, Syr, Arabic read *Maacah*; 1Kg 15:2; 2Ch 11:22 [C] **13:8** Or *God*; 1Kg 12:28

dah raised the battle cry. When the
men of Judah raised the battle cry,
God routed Jeroboam and all Israel
before Abijah and Judah. 16 So the
Israelites fled before Judah, and God
handed them over to them. 17 Then
Abijah and his people struck them
with a mighty blow, and 500,000
choice men of Israel were killed.
18 The Israelites were subdued at
that time. The Judahites succeeded
because they depended on the LORD,
the God of their ancestors.
19 Abijah pursued Jeroboam and
captured some cities from him:
Bethel and its villages, Jeshanah
and its villages, and Ephron[A] and
its villages. 20 Jeroboam no longer
retained his power[B] during Abijah's
reign; ultimately, the LORD struck
him and he died.
21 However, Abijah grew strong, acquired 14 wives, and fathered 22 sons
and 16 daughters. 22 The rest of the
events of Abijah's reign, along with
his ways and his sayings, are written
in the Writing of the Prophet Iddo.

14 1[C]Abijah rested with his fathers
and was buried in the city of
David. His son Asa became king in
his place. During his reign the land
experienced peace for 10 years.

Asa (14:2–16:14)

His Opposition to Idolatry (14:2-7)

2[D]Asa did what was good and right
in the sight of the LORD his God. 3 He
removed the pagan altars and the
•high places. He shattered their sacred pillars and chopped down their
•Asherah poles. 4 He told the people
of Judah to seek the LORD God of
their ancestors and to carry out the
instruction and the commands. 5 He
also removed the high places and
the incense altars from all the cities
of Judah, and the kingdom experienced peace under him.
6 Because the land experienced
peace, Asa built fortified cities in
Judah. No one made war with him
in those days because the LORD gave
him rest. 7 So he said to the people of
Judah, "Let's build these cities and
surround them with walls and towers, with doors and bars. The land
is still ours because we sought the
LORD our God. We sought Him and
He gave us rest on every side." So
they built and succeeded.

God's Victory over the Cushites (14:8-15)

8 Asa had an army of 300,000 from
Judah bearing large shields and
spears, and 280,000 from Benjamin
bearing regular shields and drawing the bow. All these were brave
warriors. 9 Then Zerah the •Cushite
came against them with an army of
one million men and 300[E] chariots.
They came as far as Mareshah. 10 So
Asa marched out against him and
lined up in battle formation in the
Valley of Zephathah at Mareshah.
11 Then Asa cried out to the LORD
his God: "LORD, there is no one besides You to help the mighty and
those without strength. Help us,
LORD our God, for we depend on You,
and in Your name we have come
against this large army. •Yahweh,
You are our God. Do not let a mere
mortal hinder You."
12 So the LORD routed the Cushites
before Asa and before Judah, and the
Cushites fled. 13 Then Asa and the
people who were with him pursued
them as far as Gerar. The Cushites
fell until they had no survivors, for
they were crushed before Yahweh
and His army. So the people of Judah carried off a great supply of loot.
14 Then they attacked all the cities
around Gerar because the terror of
the LORD was on them. They also
plundered all the cities, since there
was a great deal of plunder in them.
15 They also attacked the tents of the
herdsmen and captured many sheep
and camels. Then they returned to
Jerusalem.

Covenant and Rest (15:1-19)

15 The Spirit of God came on
Azariah son of Oded. 2 So he
went out to meet Asa and said to
him, "Asa and all Judah and Benjamin, hear me. The LORD is with you
when you are with Him. If you seek
Him, He will be found by you, but
if you abandon Him, He will abandon you. 3 For many years Israel has
been without the true God, without a teaching priest, and without

14:2-7 While Israel plummeted into idolatry, Asa became God's instrument to revive His people in Judah and turn their hearts back to Him (vv. 2-4). The writer credited **the LORD** with giving Asa **rest**, and the king led his people to recognize the connection between their seeking **the LORD** and God's blessing them with relief from war and with the opportunity, therefore, to prepare various **cities in Judah** to defend the nation from future attacks (vv. 6-7).

14:12 By narrating the Lord's utter defeat of the enemy immediately after reporting Asa's prayer for help, the writer implied that God acted in direct response to the king's expression of dependence on Him.

15:1-19 **Azariah** (Hb, "Yahweh has helped"), **son of Oded** [Hb, "restorer"] **the prophet**, delivered God's **words** to King **Asa**, who **took courage** from them to lead Judah in religious reform (vv. 1-2,8). Through Azariah, **the Spirit of God** reminded His people that **the LORD** would always remain faithful to the covenant He made with His people. If ever He were not present with them, the reason would be that *they* were not **with Him**, that *they* had abandoned **Him** (v. 2). The gravity of the people's **covenant** (vv. 10-15; cp. Dt 17:2-7) reflected their understanding of their covenant responsibility. Revival took place among the people primarily because of their leader's obedience to the Lord. Before the actions marking renewal, however, both the king and the people had to listen to the word of the Lord and have a change of heart (vv. 2,8). Then they had to deal radically with any remaining sin in their midst. Next, they restored what had been damaged as a consequence of sin (v. 8). Finally, they united in worship and public commitment to the Lord (vv. 9-10).

[A]**13:19** Alt Hb tradition reads *Ephrain* [B]**13:20** Lit *He did not restrain the power of Jeroboam*
[C]**14:1** 2Ch 13:23 in Hb [D]**14:2** 2Ch 14:1 in Hb [E]**14:9** Syr, Arabic read *30,000*

16:7-10 For the first time, an Israelite king imprisoned one of the Lord's spokesmen and was said to have **mistreated** (Hb *ratsats*, "break in pieces, crush, grievously oppress," suggesting the use of torture; cp. 1Sm 12:3-4) others. The direct result of his "foolish" reliance on earthly powers rather than on the Lord was the loss of peace. In the resulting **wars**, the people paid the price for their ruler's faithless choices.

instruction, 4 but when they turned to the LORD God of Israel in their distress and sought Him, He was found by them. 5 In those times there was no peace for those who went about their daily activities because the residents of the lands had many conflicts. 6 Nation was crushed by nation and city by city, for God troubled them with every possible distress. 7 But as for you, be strong; don't be discouraged,[A] for your work has a reward."

8 When Asa heard these words and the prophecy of Azariah son of Oded the prophet, he took courage and removed the detestable idols from the whole land of Judah and Benjamin and from the cities he had captured in the hill country of Ephraim. He renovated the altar of the LORD that was in front of the portico of the LORD's temple. 9 Then he gathered all Judah and Benjamin, as well as those from the tribes of Ephraim, Manasseh, and Simeon who had settled among them, for they had defected to him from Israel in great numbers when they saw that •Yahweh his God was with him.

10 They were gathered in Jerusalem in the third month of the fifteenth year of Asa's reign. 11 At that time they sacrificed to the LORD 700 cattle and 7,000 sheep from all the plunder they had brought. 12 Then they entered into a covenant to seek the LORD God of their ancestors with all their mind and all their heart. 13 Whoever would not seek the LORD God of Israel would be put to death, young or old,[B] man or woman. 14 They took an oath to the LORD in a loud voice, with shouting, with trumpets, and with rams' horns. 15 All Judah rejoiced over the oath, for they had sworn it with all their mind. They had sought Him with all their heart, and He was found by them. So the LORD gave them rest on every side.

16 King Asa also removed Maacah, his grandmother,[C] from being queen mother because she had made an obscene image of •Asherah. Asa chopped down her obscene image, then crushed it and burned it in the Kidron Valley. 17 The •high places were not taken away from Israel; nevertheless, Asa was wholehearted his entire life.[D] 18 He brought his father's consecrated gifts and his own consecrated gifts into God's temple: silver, gold, and utensils.

19 There was no war until the thirty-fifth year of Asa's reign.

Failure to Depend on the LORD (16:1-14)

16 In the thirty-sixth year of Asa, Israel's King Baasha went to war against Judah. He built Ramah in order to deny access to anyone—going or coming—to Judah's King Asa. 2 So Asa brought out the silver and gold from the treasuries of the LORD's temple and the royal palace and sent it to Aram's King Ben-hadad, who lived in Damascus, saying, 3 "There's a treaty between me and you, between my father and your father. Look, I have sent you silver and gold. Go break your treaty with Israel's King Baasha so that he will withdraw from me."

4 Ben-hadad listened to King Asa and sent the commanders of his armies to the cities of Israel. They attacked Ijon, Dan, Abel-maim,[E] and all the storage cities[F] of Naphtali. 5 When Baasha heard about it, he quit building Ramah and stopped his work. 6 Then King Asa brought all Judah, and they carried away the stones of Ramah and the timbers Baasha had built it with. Then he built Geba and Mizpah with them.

7 At that time, Hanani the seer came to King Asa of Judah and said to him, "Because you depended on the king of Aram and have not depended on the LORD your God, the army of the king of Aram has escaped from your hand. 8 Were not the •Cushites and Libyans a vast army with many chariots and horsemen? When you depended on •Yahweh, He handed them over to you. 9 For the eyes of Yahweh roam throughout the earth to show Himself strong for those whose hearts are completely His. You have been foolish in this matter.

[A] **15:7** Lit *don't let your hands fail* [B] **15:13** Or *insignificant or great* [C] **15:16** Lit *mother*; 1Kg 15:2; 2Ch 11:22 [D] **15:17** Lit *wholehearted all his days* [E] **16:4** *Abel-beth-maacah* in 1Kg 15:20 [F] **16:4** = all Chinnereth in 1Kg 15:20

Therefore, you will have wars from
now on.” 10 Asa was angry with the
seer and put him in prison[A] because
of his anger over this. And Asa mistreated some of the people at that
time.
11 Note that the events of Asa’s
reign, from beginning to end, are
written in the Book of the Kings
of Judah and Israel. 12 In the thirty-
ninth year of his reign, Asa developed a disease in his feet, and his
disease became increasingly severe.
Yet even in his disease he didn’t seek
the LORD but only the physicians.
13 Asa died in the forty-first year of
his reign and rested with his fathers.
14 He was buried in his own tomb
that he had made for himself in the
city of David. They laid him out in
a coffin that was full of spices and
various mixtures of prepared ointments; then they made a great fire
in his honor.

Jehoshaphat (17:1–20:37)

The Establishment of His Kingdom (17:1-19)

17 His son Jehoshaphat became
king in his place and strengthened himself against Israel. 2 He
stationed troops in every fortified
city of Judah and set garrisons in
the land of Judah and in the cities
of Ephraim that his father Asa had
captured.
3 Now the LORD was with Jehoshaphat because he walked in the
former ways of his father David.[B] He
did not seek the •Baals 4 but sought
the God of his father and walked by
His commands, not according to the
practices of Israel. 5 So the LORD established the kingdom in his hand.
Then all Judah brought him tribute, and he had riches and honor
in abundance. 6 His mind rejoiced
in the LORD’s ways, and he again removed the •high places and •Ashe-
rah poles from Judah.
7 In the third year of his
reign, Jehoshaphat sent his officials—Ben-hail,[C] Obadiah, Zechariah, Nethanel, and Micaiah—to
teach in the cities of Judah. 8 The
Levites with them were Shemaiah,
Nethaniah, Zebadiah,[D] Asahel, Shemiramoth, Jehonathan, Adonijah,
Tobijah, and Tob-adonijah; the
priests, Elishama and Jehoram,
were with these Levites. 9 They
taught throughout Judah, having
the book of the LORD’s instruction
with them. They went throughout
the towns of Judah and taught the
people.
10 The terror of the LORD was on all
the kingdoms of the lands that surrounded Judah, so they didn’t fight
against Jehoshaphat. 11 Some of the
Philistines also brought gifts and
silver as tribute to Jehoshaphat, and

[A]16:10 Lit *the house of stocks* [B]17:3 Some Hb mss, LXX omit *David* [C]17:7 = Son of Power
[D]17:8 Some Hb mss, Syr, Tg, Arabic read *Zechariah*

HARD QUESTION

How should you respond to rebuke from the Word of God?

The unmasking of your sin, especially by those who love and care for you, is not an easy thing to accept, but there are only two options for response—repent or “dig in your heels.” Awareness of sin does not automatically bring about positive and lasting change. If you are a new creation in Christ, you may choose not to sin or to respond biblically when you do sin. Let Asa’s spiritual decline (chap. 16) serve as a warning against this subtle thinking: “I have confidence that after coming through such an impossible battle, I will never turn to worldly things.” Your victory in one “test of faith” is no guarantee that you are not vulnerable to fail other “tests.” Unlike Asa, however, believers have hope for continuing victory because of Christ (see Rm 8:1-9). May it be your aim never to ignore the loving rebuke of fellow believers but to repent, receive forgiveness in Christ, and renew daily dependence on His care (1Jn 1:6-9).

16:11-14 The descriptive report of this sickness and its severity shows the depth of Asa’s stubborn resistance to self-reform. The text does not suggest that he sinned by consulting the **physicians** but clearly implies that he was following a pattern of foolish reliance on human strength and wisdom rather than on **the LORD**.

17:1-19 Asa’s **son Jehoshaphat** (Hb, “Yahweh has judged,”) assumed the throne of Judah at age 35, during the fourth year of King Ahab’s reign in Israel (1Kg 22:41-42).

>WORD|*study*

17:6 When describing a person’s mind (Hb *lēv*, “heart”) or character, the word translated rejoiced (Hb *gavahh*, “be lifted up, take courage”) usually has the negative connotation of “being haughty or proud, exalting oneself” (2Ch 26:16; 32:25; Ps 131:1; Pr 18:12; Ezk 28:2,5,17). Here, however, the sense is that Jehoshaphat’s confidence to rule was not dependent on his position or abilities but was derived from doing everything God’s way.

18:1-34 Jehoshaphat was headed in the right direction until he made himself Ahab's son-in-law (v. 1). War ceased between Judah and Israel, but the price of friendship with a wicked king like **Ahab** was steep (19:1-2). The account here, including the role of **Micaiah** the prophet, closely follows that in the books of Kings. Micaiah's vision provides a glimpse of God's sovereignty in action in the court of heaven. Even demonic spirits must submit their plans to Him and ultimately remain under His power. In this case, God used the lying false prophets to execute judgment on Ahab (cp. 1Sm 16:14; Jb 1:12; 2:6).

the Arabs brought him flocks: 7,700 rams and 7,700 male goats.

12 Jehoshaphat grew stronger and stronger. He built fortresses and storage cities in Judah 13 and carried out great works in the towns of Judah. He had fighting men, brave warriors, in Jerusalem. 14 These are their numbers according to their ancestral families. For Judah, the commanders of thousands:

> Adnah the commander and 300,000 brave warriors with him;
> 15 next to him, Jehohanan the commander and 280,000 with him;
> 16 next to him, Amasiah son of Zichri, the volunteer of the LORD, and 200,000 brave warriors with him;
> 17 from Benjamin, Eliada, a brave warrior, and 200,000 with him armed with bow and shield;
> 18 next to him, Jehozabad and 180,000 with him equipped for war.

19 These were the ones who served the king, besides those he stationed in the fortified cities throughout all Judah.

Micaiah's Prophecy and Jehu's Rebuke (18:1–19:3)

18 Now Jehoshaphat had riches and honor in abundance, and he made an alliance with Ahab through marriage.[A] 2 Then after some years, he went down to visit Ahab in Samaria. Ahab sacrificed many sheep and cattle for him and for the people who were with him. Then he persuaded him to march up to Ramoth-gilead, 3 for Israel's King Ahab asked Judah's King Jehoshaphat, "Will you go with me to Ramoth-gilead?"

He replied to him, "I am as you are, my people as your people; we will be with you in the battle." 4 But Jehoshaphat said to the king of Israel, "First, please ask what the LORD's will is."

5 So the king of Israel gathered the prophets, 400 men, and asked them, "Should we go to Ramoth-gilead for war or should I refrain?"

They replied, "March up, and God will hand it over to the king."

6 But Jehoshaphat asked, "Isn't there a prophet of •Yahweh here anymore? Let's ask him."

7 The king of Israel said to Jehoshaphat, "There is still one man who can ask Yahweh, but I hate him because he never prophesies good about me, but only disaster. He is Micaiah son of Imlah."

"The king shouldn't say that," Jehoshaphat replied.

8 So the king of Israel called an officer and said, "Hurry and get Micaiah son of Imlah!"

9 Now the king of Israel and King Jehoshaphat of Judah, clothed in royal attire, were each sitting on his own throne. They were sitting on the threshing floor at the entrance to Samaria's •gate, and all the prophets were prophesying in front of them. 10 Then Zedekiah son of Chenaanah made iron horns and said, "This is what the LORD says: 'You will gore the Arameans with these until they are finished off.'" 11 And all the prophets were prophesying the same, saying, "March up to Ramoth-gilead and succeed, for the LORD will hand it over to the king."

12 The messenger who went to call Micaiah instructed him, "Look, the words of the prophets are unanimously favorable for the king. So let your words be like theirs, and speak favorably."

13 But Micaiah said, "As the LORD lives, I will say whatever my God says."[B]

14 So he went to the king, and the king asked him, "Micaiah, should we go to Ramoth-gilead for war, or should I[C] refrain?"

Micaiah said, "March up and succeed, for they will be handed over to you."

15 But the king said to him, "How many times must I make you swear not to tell me anything but the truth in the name of Yahweh?"

16 So Micaiah said:

> I saw all Israel scattered
> on the hills

[A] **18:1** Lit *made himself a son-in-law to Ahab*; 1Kg 3:1; Ezr 9:14 [B] **18:13** LXX, Vg add *to me*; 1Kg 22:14 [C] **18:14** LXX reads *we*; 1Kg 22:15

like sheep
without a shepherd.
And the LORD said,
"They have no master;
let each return home
in peace."

17 So the king of Israel said to Jehoshaphat, "Didn't I tell you he never prophesies good about me, but only disaster?"

18 Then Micaiah said, "Therefore, hear the word of the LORD. I saw the LORD sitting on His throne, and the whole heavenly •host was standing at His right hand and at His left hand. 19 And the LORD said, 'Who will entice Ahab king of Israel to march up and fall at Ramoth-gilead?' So one was saying this and another was saying that.

20 "Then a spirit came forward, stood before the LORD, and said, 'I will entice him.'

"The LORD asked him, 'How?'

21 "So he said, 'I will go and become a lying spirit in the mouth of all his prophets.'

"Then He said, 'You will entice him and also prevail. Go and do that.'

22 "Now, you see, the LORD has put a lying spirit into the mouth of[A] these prophets of yours, and the LORD has pronounced disaster against you."

23 Then Zedekiah son of Chenaanah came up, hit Micaiah in the face, and demanded, "Which way did the spirit from the LORD leave me to speak to you?"

24 Micaiah replied, "You will soon see when you go to hide yourself in an inner chamber on that day."

25 Then the king of Israel ordered, "Take Micaiah and return him to Amon, the governor of the city, and to Joash, the king's son, 26 and say, 'This is what the king says: Put this guy in prison and feed him only bread and water[B] until I come back safely.'"

27 But Micaiah said, "If you ever return safely, the LORD has not spoken through me." Then he said, "Listen, all you people!"

28 Then the king of Israel and Judah's King Jehoshaphat went up to Ramoth-gilead. 29 But the king of Israel said to Jehoshaphat, "I will disguise myself and go into battle, but you wear your royal attire." So the king of Israel disguised himself, and they went into battle.

30 Now the king of Aram had ordered his chariot commanders, "Do not fight with anyone, small or great, except the king of Israel."

31 When the chariot commanders saw Jehoshaphat, they shouted, "He must be the king of Israel!" So they turned to attack him, but Jehoshaphat cried out and the LORD helped him. God drew them away from him. 32 When the chariot commanders saw that he was not the king of Israel, they turned back from pursuing him.

33 But a man drew his bow without taking special aim and struck the king of Israel through the joints of his armor. So he said to the charioteer, "Turn around and take me out of the battle,[C] for I am badly wounded!" 34 The battle raged throughout that day, and the king of Israel propped himself up in his chariot facing the Arameans until evening. Then he died at sunset.

19 Jehoshaphat king of Judah returned to his home in Jerusalem in peace. 2 Then Jehu son of Hanani the seer went out to confront him[D] and said to King Jehoshaphat, "Do you help the wicked and love those who hate the LORD? Because of this, the LORD's wrath is on you. 3 However, some good is found in you, for you have removed the •Asherah poles from the land and have decided to seek God."

The Appointment of Judges (19:4-11)

4 Jehoshaphat lived in Jerusalem, and once again he went out among the people from Beer-sheba to the hill country of Ephraim and brought them back to •Yahweh, the God of their ancestors. 5 He appointed judges in all the fortified cities of the land of Judah, city by city. 6 Then he said to the judges, "Consider what you are doing, for you do not judge for man, but for the LORD, who is with you in the matter of judgment. 7 And now, may the terror

19:4-10 Jehoshaphat resumed his grassroots effort to turn the hearts of the people to Yahweh their God. "Phase 1" of his strategy for reform involved teaching the people the law. "Phase 2" held them accountable for keeping it. Already "stationed in the fortified cities" were military "commanders" (2Ch 17:19). Now the king **appointed judges** to govern **for the LORD** (19:5-7; cp. Dt 16:18–17:13) in these cities. Given the spiritual darkness of idolatry, which was choking their brothers in Israel to the north, the leaders of Judah could not afford to be weak in their roles if they were to nurture and maintain the southern kingdom's loyalty to **the LORD**.

[A] **18:22** Some Hb mss, LXX, Syr, Vg add *all*; 1Kg 22:23 [B] **18:26** Lit *him on bread of oppression and water of oppression* [C] **18:33** LXX, Vg; MT reads *camp* [D] **19:2** Lit *to his face*

20:1-12 Here the Chronicler reported on a battle not described in the books of Kings. Although Jehoshaphat admitted to being **afraid**, his fear of **the Lord** prevailed because he turned to Him for help (v. 3; cp. Pss 27:3; 46:2; 56:3; 118:6). In the midst of leading his people to become a God-fearing nation, Jehoshaphat must have been tempted to interpret his circumstances as a sign of God's abandonment or of the futility of serving a God who could not keep His promises. Instead, he chose to regard the appearance of this very real threat as proof of their need for Yahweh to "show Himself strong for those whose hearts are completely His" (2Ch 16:9). The content of his exemplary prayer should be read in the context of Solomon's prayer of dedication of the temple (chap. 6; 1Kg 8). The prayer's climax was the king's admission that apart from the Lord Judah could do nothing to save herself (v. 12). When people admit they are utterly helpless before God, they are most ready to receive His help. How often people admit, even in anguish, "We do not know what to do" without actually throwing themselves on God's mercy with faith and humble resolve. Yet the Lord often waits to help until He hears a cry of desperation sincerely expressing complete dependence on Him.

>WORD | *study*

19:10 The command to warn (Hb *zahar*, "admonish") the people was a command to "teach" them how to live righteously (cp. Ex 18:20; Dt 12:3 ; Ezk 3:17-21; 33:3-9). The verb literally means to "shine or send out light." Instead of fostering dependence upon themselves as though only they could discern right from wrong, the leaders were charged with entrusting knowledge of the law to the people to become for them "a lamp" for their "feet" and a "light" on their "path" (Ps 119:105).

of the Lord be on you. Watch what you do, for there is no injustice or partiality or taking bribes with the Lord our God."

8 Jehoshaphat also appointed in Jerusalem some of the Levites and priests and some of the heads of the Israelite families for deciding the Lord's will and for settling disputes of the residents of[A] Jerusalem. 9 He commanded them, saying, "In the •fear of the Lord, with integrity, and with a whole heart, you are to do the following: 10 for every dispute that comes to you from your brothers who dwell in their cities—whether it regards differences of bloodguilt, law, commandment, statutes, or judgments—you are to warn them, so they will not incur •guilt before the Lord and wrath will not come on you and your brothers. Do this, and you will not incur guilt.

11 "Note that Amariah, the chief priest, is over you in all matters related to the Lord, and Zebadiah son of Ishmael, the ruler of the house of Judah, in all matters related to the king, and the Levites are officers in your presence. Be strong; may the Lord be with those who do what is good."

God's Answer to the King's Prayer (20:1-30)

20 After this, the Moabites and Ammonites, together with some of the Meunites,[B] came to fight against Jehoshaphat. 2 People came and told Jehoshaphat, "A vast number from beyond the Dead Sea and from Edom[C] has come to fight against you; they are already in Hazazon-tamar" (that is, En-gedi). 3 Jehoshaphat was afraid, and he resolved to seek the Lord. Then he proclaimed a fast for all Judah, 4 who gathered to seek the Lord. They even came from all the cities of Judah to seek Him.

5 Then Jehoshaphat stood in the assembly of Judah and Jerusalem in the Lord's temple before the new courtyard. 6 He said:

•Yahweh, the God of our ancestors, are You not the God who is in heaven, and do You not rule over all the kingdoms of the nations? Power and might are in Your hand, and no one can stand against You. 7 Are You not our God who drove out the inhabitants of this land before Your people Israel and who gave it forever to the descendants of Abraham Your friend? 8 They have lived in the land and have built You a sanctuary in it for Your name and have said, 9 "If disaster comes on us—sword or judgment, pestilence or famine—we will stand before this temple and before You, for Your name is in this temple. We will cry out to You because of our distress, and You will hear and deliver."

HARD QUESTION

How do you win your spiritual battles?

What "impossible" battle are you facing right now? For the believer, no battle is hers to fight alone. Are you abandoning yourself to God in prayer as did **Jehoshaphat** and **all Judah** (20:1-12)? Perhaps He wants you to stop, stand still, know that He is God, and watch Him work. The people's right response to the Lord's instructions ensured their victory the following day. Likewise, victory in even the small battles of life depends on your bringing them to the Lord. You must heed His commands and then, in glad and resolute obedience, position yourself accordingly. As the psalmist proclaimed, "With God we will perform valiantly; He will trample our foes" (Ps 60:12).

[A] **19:8** LXX, Vg; MT reads *disputes and they returned to* [B] **20:1** LXX; MT reads *Ammonites*; 2Ch 26:7 [C] **20:2** Some Hb mss, Old Lat; other Hb mss read *Aram*

>WORD|*study*

20:6 Here, the verb translated rule (Hb *mashal*, "have dominion, reign") is an active participle, indicating an action of unbroken continuity (i.e., Yahweh's reign is present and ongoing). See also Pss 22:28; 59:13; 66:7; 89:9.

20:13 With (Hb *gam*, "also, even, indeed") gave emphasis to what followed, as though with the addition of these details the reader would not necessarily assume that the families were included among those "standing before the LORD." Infants (Hb *taph*, "children, little ones, little children") comes from the verb *taphaph* (Hb, "skip, take quick little steps," characterizing the gait of a child). Some regard the word's use here as a collective term for "families," which is followed by the subsets of "wives" and **children** (Hb *bēn*, "sons"). However, the writer may have been especially emphasizing on this occasion that **all** (Hb *kol*) truly included everyone, not just the men.

10 Now here are the Ammonites,
Moabites, and the inhabitants
of Mount Seir. You did not let
Israel invade them when Israel
came out of the land of Egypt,
but Israel turned away from
them and did not destroy them.
11 Look how they repay us by
coming to drive us out of Your
possession that You gave us as
an inheritance. 12 Our God, will
You not judge them? For we are
powerless before this vast number that comes to fight against
us. We do not know what to do,
but we look to You.[A]

13 All Judah was standing before
the LORD with their infants, their
wives, and their children. 14 In the
middle of the congregation, the
Spirit of the LORD came on Jahaziel
(son of Zechariah, son of Benaiah,
son of Jeiel, son of Mattaniah, a
Levite from •Asaph's descendants),
15 and he said, "Listen carefully, all
Judah and you inhabitants of Jerusalem, and King Jehoshaphat.
This is what the LORD says: 'Do not
be afraid or discouraged because of
this vast number, for the battle is
not yours, but God's. 16 Tomorrow,
go down against them. You will
see them coming up the Ascent of
Ziz, and you will find them at the
end of the valley facing the Wilderness of Jeruel. 17 You do not have to
fight this battle. Position yourselves,
stand still, and see the salvation of
the LORD. He is with you, Judah and
Jerusalem. Do not be afraid or discouraged. Tomorrow, go out to face
them, for Yahweh is with you.'"
18 Then Jehoshaphat bowed with
his face to the ground, and all Judah
and the inhabitants of Jerusalem fell
down before the LORD to worship
Him. 19 Then the Levites from the
sons of the Kohathites and the Korahites stood up to praise the LORD God of
Israel shouting with a loud voice.
20 In the morning they got up early
and went out to the wilderness of
Tekoa. As they were about to go out,
Jehoshaphat stood and said, "Hear
me, Judah and you inhabitants of
Jerusalem. Believe in Yahweh your
God, and you will be established; believe in His prophets, and you will
succeed." 21 Then he consulted with
the people and appointed some to
sing for the LORD and some to praise
the splendor of His holiness. When
they went out in front of the armed
forces, they kept singing:[B]

> Give thanks to the LORD,
> for His faithful love
> endures forever.

22 The moment they began their
shouts and praises, the LORD set an
ambush against the Ammonites,
Moabites, and the inhabitants of
Mount Seir who came to fight
against Judah, and they were defeated. 23 The Ammonites and Moabites
turned against the inhabitants of
Mount Seir and •completely annihilated them. When they had finished
with the inhabitants of Seir, they
helped destroy each other.
24 When Judah came to a place
overlooking the wilderness, they
looked for the large army, but
there were only corpses lying on
the ground; nobody had escaped.
25 Then Jehoshaphat and his people
went to gather the plunder. They
found among them[C] an abundance
of goods on the bodies[D] and valuable

20:13-19 The structure of verse 13 indicates, at least in this passage, that **all Judah** refers to the men of Judah. This phrase is distinguished from the list of other family members. Verse 27 affirms that although entire families had assembled and heard God's prophetic word regarding **the battle**, only the men of Judah had gone out to the battlefield.

20:20-30 Because of Judah's praise the place of victory was called **the Valley of Beracah** (Hb, "blessing," v. 26). Worship thus took place before, during, and after battle (cp. Php 4:4). The temple, where they pleaded for victory, now became the place where they applauded God with honor.

[A]20:12 Lit *but on You our eyes* [B]20:21 Lit *saying* [C]20:25 LXX reads *found cattle* [D]20:25 Some Hb mss, Old Lat, Vg read *goods, garments*

20:31-37 This section closely follows 1Kg 22:41-49. However, the Chronicler's emphases are different. The Chronicler assumed that his audience would connect the specific practice noted in Kings with his more general diagnosis. Despite Jehoshaphat's efforts to turn their hearts back to exclusive worship of Yahweh, the people's commitment to Him was not as firm as the king's. Second Chronicles 20:35-37 gives a slightly different account of the **alliance** (Hb *chavar*, "join together with, bring into fellowship," a verb indicating a cooperative or joint effort, not merely a treaty) between Judah and Israel, which resulted in disaster for Judah's commercial fleet. The Chronicles account provides the theological explanation for this blot on Jehoshaphat's otherwise commendable record by revealing the word of judgment delivered by **Eliezer** (Hb, "God is help," 2Ch 20:37). Judah's joining with any king known for wickedness constituted a failure to trust God fully.

items. So they stripped them until nobody could carry any more. They were gathering the plunder for three days because there was so much.
[26] They assembled in the Valley of Beracah[A] on the fourth day, for there they praised the LORD. Therefore, that place is still called the Valley of Beracah today.

[27] Then all the men of Judah and Jerusalem turned back with Jehoshaphat their leader, returning joyfully to Jerusalem, for the LORD enabled them to rejoice over their enemies. [28] So they came into Jerusalem to the LORD's temple with harps, lyres, and trumpets.

[29] The terror of God was on all the kingdoms of the lands when they heard that Yahweh had fought against the enemies of Israel. [30] Then Jehoshaphat's kingdom was quiet, for his God gave him rest on every side.

God's Response to the King's Alliance (20:31-37)

[31] Jehoshaphat became king over Judah. He was 35 years old when he became king and reigned 25 years in Jerusalem. His mother's name was Azubah daughter of Shilhi. [32] He walked in the way of Asa his father; he did not turn away from it but did what was right in the LORD's sight. [33] However, the •high places were not taken away; the people had not yet set their hearts on the God of their ancestors.

[34] The rest of the events of Jehoshaphat's reign from beginning to end are written in the Events of Jehu son of Hanani, which is recorded in the Book of Israel's Kings.

[35] After this, Judah's King Jehoshaphat made an alliance with Israel's King Ahaziah, who was •guilty of wrongdoing. [36] Jehoshaphat formed an alliance with him to make ships to go to Tarshish, and they made the ships in Ezion-geber. [37] Then Eliezer son of Dodavahu of Mareshah prophesied against Jehoshaphat, saying, "Because you formed an alliance with Ahaziah, the LORD has broken up what you have made." So the ships were wrecked and were not able to go to Tarshish.

HARD QUESTION

Does the Bible contradict itself in these historical records?

The best approach to harmonizing different historical accounts in Scripture is first to recognize that the separate accounts are generally written from different perspectives and with different goals in mind, so accordingly they will record different aspects of an event. Texts such as 20:31-37 often can be appropriately harmonized. When information is unavailable for doing so, the reader nevertheless should not be deterred from focusing on what these passages reveal about God and man's response to Him.

Jehoram (21:1-20)

21 Jehoshaphat rested with his fathers and was buried with his fathers in the city of David. His son Jehoram[B] became king in his place. [2] He had brothers, sons of Jehoshaphat: Azariah, Jehiel, Zechariah, Azariah, Michael, and Shephatiah; all these were the sons of Jehoshaphat, king of Judah.[C] [3] Their father had given them many gifts of silver, gold, and valuable things, along with fortified cities in Judah, but he gave the kingdom to Jehoram because he was the firstborn. [4] When Jehoram had established himself over his father's kingdom, he strengthened his position by killing with the sword all his brothers as well as some of the princes of Israel.

[5] Jehoram was 32 years old when he became king and reigned eight years in Jerusalem. [6] He walked in the way of the kings of Israel, as the house of Ahab had done, for Ahab's daughter was his wife. He did what was evil in the LORD's sight, [7] but because of the covenant the LORD had made with David, He was unwilling to destroy the house of David since

[A] 20:26 = Blessing [B] 21:1 = Joram [C] 21:2 Some Hb mss, LXX, Syr, Vg, Arabic; other Hb mss read *Israel*

>WORD|*study*

21:11 Led . . . astray (Hb *nadach*) suggests that the king "impelled, moved, or thrust" his people toward adopting idolatrous practices or that he "seduced or drew [them] away" from the Lord (cp. "drove away," Jr 23:2; 50:17).

the LORD had promised to give a lamp to David and to his sons forever.
[8] During Jehoram's reign, Edom rebelled against Judah's domination and appointed their own king. [9] So
Jehoram crossed into Edom with his commanders and all his chariots. Then at night he set out to attack the Edomites who had surrounded him and the chariot commanders.
[10] And now Edom is still in rebellion against Judah's domination today. Libnah also rebelled at that time against his domination because he had abandoned •Yahweh, the God of his ancestors. [11] Jehoram also built
•high places in the hills[A] of Judah, and he caused the inhabitants of Jerusalem to prostitute themselves, and he led Judah astray.
[12] Then a letter came to Jehoram from Elijah the prophet, saying:

> This is what Yahweh, the God of your ancestor David says: "Because you have not walked in the ways of your father Jehoshaphat or in the ways of Asa king of Judah [13] but have
> walked in the way of the kings of Israel, have caused Judah and the inhabitants of Jerusalem to prostitute themselves like the house of Ahab prostituted itself, and also have killed your brothers, your father's family, who were better than
> you, [14] Yahweh is now about to
> strike your people, your sons, your wives, and all your possessions with a horrible affliction.
> [15] You yourself will be struck with many illnesses, including a disease of the intestines, until your intestines come out day after day because of the disease."

[16] The LORD put it into the mind
of the Philistines and the Arabs who live near the •Cushites to attack Jehoram. [17] So they went to war
against Judah and invaded it. They carried off all the possessions found in the king's palace and also his sons and wives; not a son was left to him except Jehoahaz,[B] his youngest son.
[18] After all these things, the LORD
afflicted him in his intestines with an incurable disease. [19] This contin-
ued day after day until two full years passed. Then his intestines came out because of his disease, and he died from severe[C] illnesses. But his people did not hold a fire in his honor like the fire in honor of his fathers.
[20] Jehoram was 32 years old when he became king; he reigned eight years in Jerusalem. He died to no one's regret[D] and was buried in the city of David but not in the tombs of the kings.

Ahaziah (22:1-9)

22 Then the inhabitants of Jerusalem made Ahaziah, his youngest son, king in his place, because the troops that had come with the Arabs to the camp had killed all the older sons.[E] So Ahaziah son of Jehoram became king of Judah.
[2] Ahaziah was 22[F] years old when he became king and reigned one year in Jerusalem. His mother's name was Athaliah, granddaughter[G] of Omri.
[3] He walked in the ways of the house of Ahab, for his mother gave him evil advice. [4] So he did what was
evil in the LORD's sight like the house of Ahab, for they were his advisers after the death of his father, to his destruction. [5] He also followed their
advice and went with Joram[H] son of Israel's King Ahab to fight against Hazael, king of Aram, in Ramoth-gilead. The Arameans[I] wounded Joram, [6] so he returned to Jezreel
to recover from the wounds they

21:8-20 In contrast to the surrounding nations' fear of attacking Judah because God was clearly fighting for them (20:29), Jehoram's abandonment of **Yahweh** set the conditions for **Edom** and **Libnah**, foreign provinces captured by David, to rebel against Judah's control (21:8-10). Turning away from the Lord also automatically opens the door to some form of idolatry. The consequences were severe, and the description of Jehoram's burial starkly contrasts with that of his grandfather Asa (16:14; 21:14-20).

22:1-9 Only because of God's faithfulness to His covenant with David was **Ahaziah,** a descendant of the Davidic lineage left to continue the Davidic dynasty in Judah.

[A] **21:11** Some Hb mss, LXX, Vg read *cities* [B] **21:17** LXX, Syr, Tg read *Ahaziah* [C] **21:19** Lit *evil* [D] **21:20** Lit *He walked in no desirability* [E] **22:1** Lit *the former ones* [F] **22:2** Some LXX mss, Syr; MT reads *42*; 2Kg 8:26 [G] **22:2** Lit *daughter* [H] **22:5** = Jehoram [I] **22:5** Lit *Rammites*

22:10-12 Three women played key roles in the dramatic events precipitated by Israel's new king Jehu and his purge of Ahab's descendants, including Judah's king Ahaziah, whose **mother** was Ahab's daughter **Athaliah** (cp. 24:7; 2Kg 11:1-3). Her scheme of eliminating all legitimate heirs was thwarted by two courageous women. **Jehoshabeath** (Hb, "whose oath is Yahweh") and her husband, **Jehoiada** [Hb, "Yahweh knows"] **the priest**, hid the child for **six years** in the **temple**. The second woman, the baby's nurse (Hb *yanaq*, one who "gives suck, breastfeeds"), apparently trusted the princess enough to do her bidding at a moment's notice. By going into **hiding** with the child, she may have saved his life from Athaliah's killing spree.

CHARACTER PROFILE

Jehoshabeath A Courageous Wife

Her Background	• The sister of King Ahaziah (22:11) • The daughter of King Jehoram and Athaliah (22:11; 2Kg 11:2) • The wife of Jehoiada the priest (2Ch 22:11)
Her Story	• She rescued Joash from being murdered by his grandmother (22:11). • She hid Joash for six years (22:12).
Life Lessons	• Jehoshabeath's courage protected the Davidic line of rulers, through whom the Messiah would come. • One never knows the extent of blessing and influence that will come through simple obedience to the Lord.

inflicted on him in Ramoth-gilead[A] when he fought against Aram's King Hazael. Then Judah's King Ahaziah[B] son of Jehoram went down to Jezreel to visit Joram son of Ahab since Joram was ill.

7 Ahaziah's downfall came from God when he went to Joram. When Ahaziah arrived, he went out with Joram to meet Jehu son of Nimshi, whom the LORD had anointed to destroy the house of Ahab. 8 So when Jehu executed judgment on the house of Ahab, he found the rulers of Judah and the sons of Ahaziah's brothers who were serving Ahaziah, and he killed them. 9 Then Jehu looked for Ahaziah, and Jehu's soldiers captured him (he was hiding in Samaria). So they brought Ahaziah to Jehu, and they killed him. The soldiers buried him, for they said, "He is the grandson of Jehoshaphat who sought the LORD with all his heart." So no one from the house of Ahaziah had the strength to rule the kingdom.

Athaliah (22:10–23:15)

10 When Athaliah, Ahaziah's mother, saw that her son was dead, she proceeded to annihilate all the royal heirs[C] of the house of Judah. 11 Jehoshabeath,[D] the king's daughter, rescued Joash son of Ahaziah from the king's sons who were being killed and put him and the one who nursed him in a bedroom. Now Jehoshabeath was the daughter of King Jehoram and the wife of Jehoiada the priest. Since she was Ahaziah's sister, she hid Joash from Athaliah so that she did not kill him. 12 While Athaliah ruled over the land, he was hiding with them in God's temple six years.

23 Then, in the seventh year, Jehoiada summoned his courage and took the commanders of hundreds into a covenant with him: Azariah son of Jeroham, Ishmael son of Jehohanan, Azariah son of Obed, Maaseiah son of Adaiah, and Elishaphat son of Zichri. 2 They made a circuit throughout Judah. They gathered the Levites from all the cities of Judah and the heads of the families of Israel, and they came to Jerusalem.

3 Then the whole assembly made a covenant with the king in God's temple. Jehoiada said to them, "Here is the king's son! He must reign, just as the LORD promised concerning David's sons. 4 This is what you are to do: a third of you, priests and Levites who are coming on duty on the Sabbath, are to be gatekeepers. 5 A third are to be at the king's palace, and a third are to be at the Foundation Gate, and all the troops will be in the courtyards of the LORD's temple. 6 No one is to enter the LORD's temple but the priests and those Levites who serve; they may enter because they

[A]22:6 Lit *in Ramah* [B]22:6 Some Hb mss, LXX, Syr, Vg; other Hb mss read *Azariah* [C]22:10 Lit *seed* [D]22:11 = Jehosheba; 2Kg 11:2

are holy, but all the people are to obey the requirement of the LORD. 7 You must completely surround the king with weapons in hand. Anyone who enters the temple is to be put to death. You must be with the king in all his daily tasks."[A]

8 So the commanders of hundreds did everything Jehoiada the priest commanded. They each brought their men—those coming on duty on the Sabbath and those going off duty on the Sabbath—for Jehoiada the priest did not release the divisions. 9 Jehoiada the priest gave to the commanders of hundreds King David's spears, shields, and quivers[B] that were in God's temple. 10 Then he stationed all the troops with their weapons in hand surrounding the king—from the right side of the temple to the left side, by the altar and by the temple.

11 They brought out the king's son, put the crown on him, gave him the •testimony, and made him king. Jehoiada and his sons anointed him and cried, "Long live the king!"

12 When Athaliah heard the noise from the troops, the guards, and those praising the king, she went to the troops in the LORD's temple. 13 As she looked, there was the king standing by his pillar[C] at the entrance. The commanders and the trumpeters were by the king, and all the people of the land were rejoicing and blowing trumpets while the singers with musical instruments were leading the praise. Athaliah tore her clothes and screamed, "Treason, treason!"

14 Then Jehoiada the priest sent out the commanders of hundreds, those in charge of the army, saying, "Take her out between the ranks, and put anyone who follows her to death by the sword," for the priest had said, "Don't put her to death in the LORD's temple." 15 So they arrested her, and she went by the entrance of the Horses' Gate to the king's palace, where they put her to death.

Joash (23:16–24:27)

16 Then Jehoiada made a covenant between himself, the king, and the people that they would be the LORD's people. 17 So all the people went to the temple of •Baal and tore it down. They broke its altars and images into pieces and killed Mattan, the priest of Baal, at the altars.

18 Then Jehoiada put the oversight of the LORD's temple into the hands of the Levitical priests, whom David had appointed over the LORD's temple, to offer •burnt offerings to the LORD as it is written in the law of Moses, with rejoicing and song ordained by[D] David. 19 He stationed gatekeepers at the gates of the LORD's temple so that nothing •unclean could enter for any reason. 20 Then he took with him the commanders of hundreds, the nobles, the governors of the people, and all the people of the land and brought the king down from the LORD's temple. They entered the king's palace through the Upper Gate and seated the king on the throne of the kingdom. 21 All the people of the land rejoiced, and the city was quiet, for they had put Athaliah to death by the sword.

24 Joash was seven years old when he became king and reigned 40 years in Jerusalem. His mother's name was Zibiah; she was from Beer-sheba. 2 Throughout the time of Jehoiada the priest, Joash did what was right in the LORD's sight. 3 Jehoiada acquired two wives for him, and he was the father of sons and daughters.

4 Afterward, Joash took it to heart to renovate the LORD's temple. 5 So he gathered the priests and Levites and said, "Go out to the cities of Judah and collect money from all Israel to repair the temple of your God as needed year by year, and do it quickly."

However, the Levites did not hurry. 6 So the king called Jehoiada the high priest and said, "Why haven't you required the Levites to bring from Judah and Jerusalem the tax imposed by the LORD's servant Moses and the assembly of Israel for the tent of the testimony? 7 For the sons of that wicked Athaliah broke into the LORD's temple and even used the

24:3 No explanation is given either here or in 2 Kings about why the priest **Jehoiada** selected **two wives for** Joash rather than one (2Ch 24:3). Although a first wife may have died without producing a son, the text does not rule out the possibility that Joash was married to both at the same time. Both texts foreshadow a retreat from doing what was right after Jehoiada the priest died. Given that Jehoiada was 130 years old **at his death**, he was between 90 and 100 years old when he orchestrated the overthrow of Athaliah, in his mid-70s under Jehoram's reign, in his early 50s under Jehoshaphat, and probably most impressionable as a young man growing up under Asa's rule (v. 15).

24:4-15 Second Chronicles contrasts Joash's instructions to collect the money **quickly** (Hb *mahar*, "hasten, be prompt") with the observation that **the Levites did not hurry** (Hb *mahar*, v. 5). Despite the strong and positive influence of Jehoiada's tutelage, the king was clearly the one in charge and here called the **high priest** to account for not doing his will (v. 6).

[A]**23:7** Lit *king when he comes in and when he goes out* [B]**23:9** Or *spears and large and small shields* [C]**23:13** LXX reads *post* [D]**23:18** Lit *song on the hands of*

24:16-27 Jehoram's honorable burial **in the city of David with the kings** (v. 16) sharply contrasts with the ignominious death and burial of Joash **in the city of David, but . . . not . . . in the tombs of the kings** (v. 25). Despite their honor for the priest, the people quickly traded worship of Yahweh for **Asherah poles and idols** (vv. 16-18).

24:18-22 Some scholars give great weight to the role of the human author of Chronicles in selecting and shaping its message. For example, based on comparisons of how the same historical material is treated in Kings and Chronicles, they conclude that the Chronicler aimed to highlight the positive side of the kings' reigns and to minimize their shortcomings. However, verses 18-22 indicate that although understanding of the human author's historical context and probable intention has interpretive value, what God has revealed about Himself and His relationship to man are more important questions to ask of the biblical text. In this passage, the Spirit portrayed the ugly realities of Joash's reign, following Jehoiada's death, which were merely summarized in Kings (cp. 2Kg 12:3).

24:22-24 The dying priest's prophetic words were fulfilled when an **Aramean army** rose up against Judah. The Chronicler made it impossible for the reader to miss God's execution of **judgment** [Hb *shephet*, "punishment"; cp. Ex 12:12; Pr 19:29] **on Joash**, not only by reporting the facts but also by underscoring the correct interpretation of those facts. **Because** they **had abandoned** [Hb *'azav*, "forsake, leave, depart from"; cp. 2Kg 17:16] **Yahweh**, He abandoned them to their enemies.

sacred things of the LORD's temple for the •Baals."

8 At the king's command a chest was made and placed outside the gate of the LORD's temple. 9 Then a proclamation was issued in Judah and Jerusalem that the tax God's servant Moses imposed on Israel in the wilderness be brought to the LORD. 10 All the leaders and all the people rejoiced, brought the tax, and put it in the chest until it was full. 11 Whenever the chest was brought by the Levites to the king's overseers, and when they saw that there was a large amount of money, the king's secretary and the high priest's deputy came and emptied the chest, picked it up, and returned it to its place. They did this daily and gathered the money in abundance. 12 Then the king and Jehoiada gave it to those in charge of the labor on the LORD's temple, who were hiring stonecutters and carpenters to renovate the LORD's temple, also blacksmiths and coppersmiths to repair the LORD's temple.

13 The workmen did their work, and through them the repairs progressed. They restored God's temple to its specifications and reinforced it. 14 When they finished, they presented the rest of the money to the king and Jehoiada, who made articles for the LORD's temple with it—articles for ministry and for making •burnt offerings, and ladles[A] and articles of gold and silver. They regularly offered burnt offerings in the LORD's temple throughout Jehoiada's life.

15 Jehoiada died when he was old and full of days; he was 130 years old at his death. 16 He was buried in the city of David with the kings because he had done what was good in Israel with respect to God and His temple.

17 However, after Jehoiada died, the rulers of Judah came and paid homage to the king. Then the king listened to them, 18 and they abandoned the temple of •Yahweh, the God of their ancestors and served the •Asherah poles and the idols. So there was wrath against Judah and Jerusalem for this •guilt of theirs. 19 Nevertheless, He sent them prophets to bring them back to the LORD; they admonished them, but the people would not listen.

20 The Spirit of God took control of[B] Zechariah son of Jehoiada the priest. He stood above the people and said to them, "This is what God says, 'Why are you transgressing the LORD's commands and you do not prosper? Because you have abandoned the LORD, He has abandoned you.'" 21 But they conspired against him and stoned him at the king's command in the courtyard of the LORD's temple. 22 King Joash didn't remember the kindness that Zechariah's father Jehoiada had extended to him, but killed his son. While he was dying, he said, "May the LORD see and demand an account."

23 At the turn of the year, an Aramean army went to war against Joash. They entered Judah and Jerusalem and destroyed all the leaders of the people among them and sent all the plunder to the king of Damascus. 24 Although the Aramean army came with only a few men, the LORD handed over a vast army to them because the people of Judah had abandoned Yahweh, the God of their ancestors. So they executed judgment on Joash.

25 When the Arameans saw that Joash had many wounds, they left him. His servants conspired against him, and killed him on his bed, because he had shed the blood of the sons of Jehoiada the priest. So he died, and they buried him in the city of David, but they did not bury him in the tombs of the kings.

26 Those who conspired against him were Zabad, son of the Ammonite woman Shimeath, and Jehozabad, son of the Moabite woman Shimrith.[C] 27 Concerning his sons, the many •oracles about him, and the restoration of the LORD's temple, they are recorded in the Writing of the Book of the Kings. His son Amaziah became king in his place.

Amaziah (25:1-28)

25 Amaziah became king when he was 25 years old and reigned

[A]**24:14** Or *dishes*, or *spoons*; lit *palms* [B]**24:20** Lit *God clothed Himself with*; Jdg 6:34; 1Ch 12:18 [C]**24:26** = Shomer in 2Kg 12:21

29 years in Jerusalem. His mother's
name was Jehoaddan; she was from
Jerusalem. 2 He did what was right
in the LORD's sight but not wholeheartedly.
3 As soon as the kingdom was firmly in his grasp,[A] he executed his servants who had murdered his father
the king. 4 However, he did not put
their children to death, because—as
it is written in the Law, in the book
of Moses, where the LORD commanded—"Fathers must not die because
of children, and children must not
die because of fathers, but each one
will die for his own sin."
5 Then Amaziah gathered Judah
and assembled them according to
ancestral house, according to commanders of thousands, and according to commanders of hundreds.
He numbered those 20 years old or
more for all Judah and Benjamin.
He found there to be 300,000 choice
men who could serve in the army,
bearing spear and shield. 6 Then
for 7,500 pounds[B] of silver he hired
100,000 brave warriors from Israel.
7 However, a man of God came to
him and said, "King, do not let Israel's army go with you, for the LORD
is not with Israel—all the Ephraimites. 8 But if you go with them, do it!
Be strong for battle! But God will
make you stumble before the enemy, for God has the power to help
or to make one stumble."
9 Then Amaziah said to the man
of God, "What should I do about the
7,500 pounds[B] of silver I gave to Israel's division?"
The man of God replied, "The LORD
is able to give you much more than
this."
10 So Amaziah released the division
that came to him from Ephraim to
go home. But they got very angry
with Judah and returned home in a
fierce rage.
11 Amaziah strengthened his position and led his people to the Valley
of Salt. He struck down 10,000 Seirites,[C] 12 and the Judahites captured
10,000 alive. They took them to the
top of a cliff where they threw them
off, and all of them were dashed to
pieces.
13 As for the men of the division
that Amaziah sent back so they
would not go with him into battle,
they raided the cities of Judah from
Samaria to Beth-horon, struck
down 3,000 of their people, and took
a great deal of plunder.
14 After Amaziah came from the
attack on the Edomites, he brought
the gods of the Seirites[C] and set
them up as his gods. He worshiped
before them and burned incense
to them. 15 So the LORD's anger was
against Amaziah, and He sent a
prophet to him, who said, "Why
have you sought a people's gods that
could not deliver their own people
from your hand?"
16 While he was still speaking to
him, the king asked, "Have we made
you the king's counselor? Stop, why
should you lose your life?"
So the prophet stopped, but he
said, "I know that God intends to
destroy you, because you have done
this and have not listened to my advice."
17 King Amaziah of Judah took
counsel and sent word to Jehoash[D]
son of Jehoahaz, son of Jehu, king
of Israel, saying, "Come, let us meet
face to face."
18 King Jehoash of Israel sent word
to King Amaziah of Judah, saying,
"The thistle that was in Lebanon
sent a message to the cedar that
was in Lebanon, saying, 'Give your
daughter to my son as a wife.' Then
a wild animal that was in Lebanon
passed by and trampled the thistle.
19 You have said, 'Look, I[E] have defeated Edom,' and you have become
overconfident that you will get glory. Now stay at home. Why stir up
such trouble so that you fall and Judah with you?"
20 But Amaziah would not listen,
for this turn of events was from God
in order to hand them over to their
enemies because they went after the
gods of Edom. 21 So King Jehoash of
Israel advanced. He and King Amaziah of Judah faced off at Beth-shemesh in Judah. 22 Judah was routed
before Israel, and each fled to his
own tent. 23 King Jehoash of Israel
captured Judah's King Amaziah son

25:1-4 Amaziah (Hb, "Yahweh is mighty") immediately avenged his father's murder but spared the assassins' sons, according to **the Law** (cp. Dt 24:16; cp. 2Kg 14:1-6; Jr 31:30), which, in this regard, precluded family feuding by treating individuals as personally responsible for their own sins.

25:17-28 The Chronicler included theological explanations for Amaziah's demise (2Ch 25:20,27). **God** allowed Judah and her king to experience defeat to punish them for their idolatry. The writer also revealed a direct correlation between Amaziah's sin and the formation of the **conspiracy** (Hb *qesher*, "treason, unlawful alliance," v. 27) against him as additional evidence for the Lord's sovereignty over history.

[A] 25:3 LXX, Syr; MT reads *was strong on him*; 1Kg 14:4 [B] 25:6,9 Lit *100 talents*
[C] 25:11,14 = Edomites [D] 25:17 Lit *Joash* [E] 25:19 Some LXX mss, Old Lat, Tg, Vg; MT reads *you*

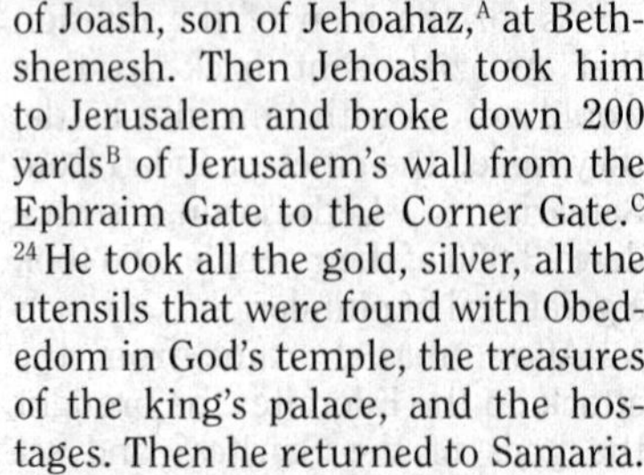

26:1-15 The explanation of how **Uzziah** became king suggests that **the people** responded to a critical situation, probably King Amaziah's being taken captive by Israel (see 25:23). Having summarized Uzziah's achievements in detail, the Chronicler directed the reader's attention to God as the source of Uzziah's military might and prosperity in order to show that the king's presumptuous actions described in the remaining part of this chapter were ridiculous.

26:16-23 Uzziah's pride crowded out his sense of reverence for the holiness of God to the point that he believed he was above the law. Exalting himself and perhaps believing that he had been so richly blessed because he deserved God's favor, Uzziah made the grave mistake of attempting to worship God his way rather than God's way. When he refused the correction of God's Word (v. 18; cp. Ex 30:7-8; Nm 16:40), **the Lord** forced Uzziah from His **temple** by afflicting him with **a serious skin disease** (Hb *tsara'at*, "leprosy or malignant skin disease"; cp. Lv 13–14; Dt 24:8), which not only made him ceremonially unclean but also excluded him from the people (2Ch 26:18-21). Isaiah, who served as court historian during the last years of Uzziah's life, was commissioned to serve the Lord as a prophet in the year of this king's death (Is 6).

of Joash, son of Jehoahaz,[A] at Beth-shemesh. Then Jehoash took him to Jerusalem and broke down 200 yards[B] of Jerusalem's wall from the Ephraim Gate to the Corner Gate.[C] 24 He took all the gold, silver, all the utensils that were found with Obed-edom in God's temple, the treasures of the king's palace, and the hostages. Then he returned to Samaria.

25 Judah's King Amaziah son of Joash lived 15 years after the death of Israel's King Jehoash son of Jehoahaz. 26 The rest of the events of Amaziah's reign, from beginning to end, are written in the Book of the Kings of Judah and Israel.

27 From the time Amaziah turned from following the LORD, a conspiracy was formed against him in Jerusalem, and he fled to Lachish. However, men were sent after him to Lachish, and they put him to death there. 28 They carried him back on horses and buried him with his fathers in the city of Judah.[D]

Uzziah (26:1-23)

26 All the people of Judah took Uzziah,[E] who was 16 years old, and made him king in place of his father Amaziah. 2 He rebuilt Eloth[F] and restored it to Judah after Amaziah the king rested with his fathers.

3 Uzziah was 16 years old when he became king and reigned 52 years in Jerusalem. His mother's name was Jecoliah from Jerusalem. 4 He did what was right in the LORD's sight as his father Amaziah had done. 5 He sought God throughout the lifetime of Zechariah, the teacher of the •fear[G] of God. During the time that he sought the LORD, God gave him success.

6 Uzziah went out to wage war against the Philistines, and he tore down the wall of Gath, the wall of Jabneh, and the wall of Ashdod. Then he built cities in the vicinity of Ashdod and among the Philistines. 7 God helped him against the Philistines, the Arabs that live in Gur-baal, and the Meunites. 8 The Ammonites[H] gave Uzziah tribute money, and his fame spread as far as the entrance of Egypt, for God made him very powerful. 9 Uzziah built towers in Jerusalem at the Corner Gate, the Valley Gate, and the corner buttress, and he fortified them. 10 Since he had many cattle both in the Judean foothills[I] and the plain, he built towers in the desert and dug many wells. And since he was a lover of the soil, he had farmers and vinedressers in the hills and in the fertile lands.[J]

11 Uzziah had an army equipped for combat that went out to war by division according to their assignments, as recorded by Jeiel the court secretary and Maaseiah the officer under the authority of Hananiah, one of the king's commanders. 12 The total number of heads of families was 2,600 brave warriors. 13 Under their authority was an army of 307,500 equipped for combat, a powerful force to help the king against the enemy. 14 Uzziah provided the entire army with shields, spears, helmets, armor, bows and slingstones. 15 He made skillfully designed devices in Jerusalem to shoot arrows and catapult large stones for use on the towers and on the corners. So his fame spread even to distant places, for he was marvelously helped until he became strong.

16 But when he became strong, he grew arrogant and it led to his own destruction. He acted unfaithfully against the LORD his God by going into the LORD's sanctuary to burn incense on the incense altar. 17 Azariah the priest, along with 80 brave priests of the LORD, went in after him. 18 They took their stand against King Uzziah and said, "Uzziah, you have no right to offer incense to the LORD—only the consecrated priests, the descendants of Aaron, have the right to offer incense. Leave the sanctuary, for you have acted unfaithfully! You will not receive honor from the LORD God."

19 Uzziah, with a firepan in his hand to offer incense, was enraged. But when he became enraged with the priests, in the presence of the priests in the LORD's temple beside

[A] **25:23** = Ahaziah in 2Kg 14:13 [B] **25:23** Lit *400 cubits* [C] **25:23** Some Hb mss; other Hb mss read *to Happoneh* [D] **25:28** Some Hb mss read *city of David* [E] **26:1** = Azariah in 2Kg 14:21 [F] **26:2** LXX, Syr, Vg read *Elath* [G] **26:5** Some Hb mss, LXX, Syr, Tg, Arabic; other Hb mss, Vg read *visions* [H] **26:8** LXX reads *Meunites* [I] **26:10** Or *the Shephelah* [J] **26:10** Or *in Carmel*

the altar of incense, a skin disease broke out on his forehead. [20] Then Azariah the chief priest and all the priests turned to him and saw that he was diseased on his forehead. They rushed him out of there. He himself also hurried to get out because the LORD had afflicted him. [21] So King Uzziah was diseased to the time of his death. He lived in quarantine[A] with a serious skin disease and was excluded from access to the LORD's temple, while his son Jotham was over the king's household governing the people of the land.

[22] Now the prophet Isaiah son of Amoz wrote about the rest of the events of Uzziah's reign, from beginning to end. [23] Uzziah rested with his fathers, and he was buried with his fathers in the burial ground of the kings' cemetery, for they said, "He has a skin disease." His son Jotham became king in his place.

Jotham (27:1-9)

27 Jotham was 25 years old when he became king and reigned 16 years in Jerusalem. His mother's name was Jerushah daughter of Zadok. [2] He did what was right in the LORD's sight as his father Uzziah had done. In addition, he didn't enter the LORD's sanctuary, but the people still behaved corruptly.

[3] Jotham built the Upper Gate of the LORD's temple, and he built extensively on the wall of Ophel. [4] He also built cities in the hill country of Judah and fortresses and towers in the forests. [5] He waged war against the king of the Ammonites. He overpowered the Ammonites, and that year they gave him 7,500 pounds[B] of silver, 50,000 bushels[C] of wheat, and 50,000 bushels[C] of barley. They paid him the same in the second and third years. [6] So Jotham strengthened himself because he did not waver in obeying[D] the LORD his God.

[7] As for the rest of the events of Jotham's reign, along with all his wars and his ways, note that they are written in the Book of the Kings of Israel and Judah. [8] He was 25 years old when he became king and reigned 16 years in Jerusalem. [9] Jotham rested with his fathers and was buried in the city of David. His son Ahaz became king in his place.

Ahaz (28:1-27)

28 Ahaz was 20 years old when he became king and reigned 16 years in Jerusalem. He did not do what was right in the LORD's sight like his ancestor David, [2] for he walked in the ways of the kings of Israel and made cast images of the •Baals. [3] He burned incense in the Valley of Hinnom and burned his children in[E] the fire, imitating the detestable practices of the nations the LORD had dispossessed before the Israelites. [4] He sacrificed and burned incense on the •high places, on the hills, and under every green tree.

[5] So the LORD his God handed Ahaz over to the king of Aram. He attacked him and took many captives to Damascus.

Ahaz was also handed over to the king of Israel, who struck him with great force: [6] Pekah son of Remaliah killed 120,000 in Judah in one day—all brave men—because they had abandoned the LORD God of their ancestors. [7] An Ephraimite warrior named Zichri killed the king's son Maaseiah, Azrikam governor of the palace, and Elkanah who was second to the king. [8] Then the Israelites took 200,000 captives from their brothers—women, sons, and daughters. They also took a great deal of plunder from them and brought it to Samaria.

[9] A prophet of the LORD named Oded was there. He went out to meet the army that came to Samaria and said to them, "Look, the LORD God of your ancestors handed them over to you because of His wrath against Judah, but you slaughtered them in a rage that has reached heaven. [10] Now you plan to reduce the people of Judah and Jerusalem, male and female, to slavery. Are you not also •guilty before •Yahweh your God? [11] Listen to me and return the captives you took from your brothers, for the LORD's burning anger is on you."

[12] So some men who were leaders

27:1-9 Among the facts of Jotham's reign, however, the Chronicler did not mention what his immediate audience would have known—that the Lord did not leave the people's idolatry unpunished but "began sending" foreign powers "against Judah" (2Kg 15:36-38). Jotham's 16-year reign could neither undo the damage done by his father nor effectively prepare his son to walk in God's ways (2Ch 27:1,7-9).

28:1-27 Ahaz's 16-year reign, unlike his father's, brought Judah to an all-time spiritual low (vv. 1-4; see notes on 2Kg 16:1-4). Having entrusted himself, his family, and his kingdom to the forces of darkness rather than to the only true God, Ahaz was defenseless against his surrounding enemies.

28:8-15 **The LORD** sent **Oded** the **prophet** to Israel's army to condemn their ruthless slaughter of Judah's men and to denounce the plan to subjugate their **brothers** (v. 8). The text makes clear *both* that God intentionally allowed Judah's suffering *and* that His **burning anger** was on those who inflicted the suffering (vv. 11,13). In both ways God acted consistently with His character. Judah clearly invited her own defeat when she abandoned her Redeemer. Israel also clearly incurred **much guilt** and God's wrath (v. 13). Neither did so in ignorance (cp. v. 2 and Dt 27:14-15; 31:16-17; Is 1:29-31; 42:17; also cp. Lv 25:46,55 and 2Ch 28:10). Heeding God's merciful warning about their sin, Israel released the captives and treated them with kindness befitting brothers, thereby averting God's wrath. In this instance Israel's obedience demonstrated a fear of the Lord that Ahaz lacked.

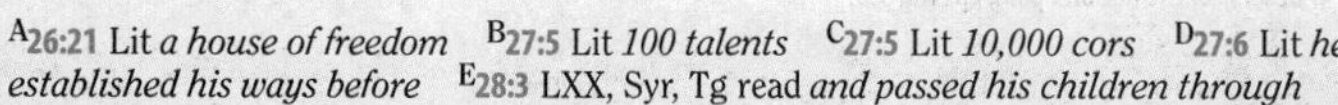

[A]26:21 Lit *a house of freedom* [B]27:5 Lit *100 talents* [C]27:5 Lit *10,000 cors* [D]27:6 Lit *he established his ways before* [E]28:3 LXX, Syr, Tg read *and passed his children through*

28:23-25 When Ahaz attributed his enemies' success to their gods and **sacrificed to** them, he was insulting the one true God who is sovereign over all earthly powers, as well as causing his own **downfall** (Hb *kashal*, "cause to stumble, totter, stagger, or fail," cp. Is 3:8). Not only did Ahaz defy God's chastening, but he also recklessly defiled the **temple** and proceeded to fill the nation with idolatry (cp. 2Kg 16:10-18).

29:1-11 Since the kingdom divided, **Hezekiah** (Hb, "Yahweh is my strength") was only the second of 12 kings to be commended for doing **right** according to the standard set by **David**. While other kings before him like Uzziah (26:4) and Jotham (27:2) had been pleasing to the Lord, they were only noted for exemplifying their immediate father. Jehoshaphat was the first king commended for walking "in the former ways of his father David" (17:3). Even though his father had left him a nation lacking stability and vulnerable to attack, his primary focus was to restore Judah's spiritual health rather than to rebuild her political strength. Hezekiah knew where his real defenses were to be found—in his devotion to and obedience of Yahweh.

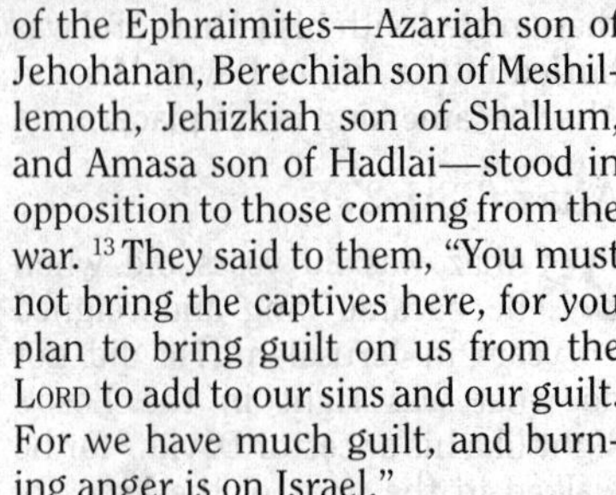

of the Ephraimites—Azariah son of Jehohanan, Berechiah son of Meshillemoth, Jehizkiah son of Shallum, and Amasa son of Hadlai—stood in opposition to those coming from the war. 13 They said to them, "You must not bring the captives here, for you plan to bring guilt on us from the LORD to add to our sins and our guilt. For we have much guilt, and burning anger is on Israel."

14 The army left the captives and the plunder in the presence of the officers and the congregation. 15 Then the men who were designated by name took charge of the captives and provided clothes for their naked ones from the plunder. They clothed them, gave them sandals, food and drink, dressed their wounds, and provided donkeys for all the feeble. The Israelites brought them to Jericho, the City of Palms, among their brothers. Then they returned to Samaria.

16 At that time King Ahaz asked the king of Assyria for help. 17 The Edomites came again, attacked Judah, and took captives. 18 The Philistines also raided the cities of the Judean foothills[A] and the •Negev of Judah and captured Beth-shemesh, Aijalon, Gederoth, Soco and its villages, Timnah and its villages, Gimzo and its villages, and they lived there. 19 For the LORD humbled Judah because of King Ahaz of Judah,[B] who threw off restraint in Judah and was unfaithful to the LORD. 20 Then Tiglath-pileser[C] king of Assyria came against Ahaz; he oppressed him and did not give him support. 21 Although Ahaz plundered the LORD's temple and the palace of the king and of the rulers and gave the plunder to the king of Assyria, it did not help him.

22 At the time of his distress, King Ahaz himself became more unfaithful to the LORD. 23 He sacrificed to the gods of Damascus which had defeated him; he said, "Since the gods of the kings of Aram are helping them, I will sacrifice to them so that they will help me." But they were the downfall of him and of all Israel.

24 Then Ahaz gathered up the utensils of God's temple, cut them into pieces, shut the doors of the LORD's temple, and made himself altars on every street corner in Jerusalem. 25 He made high places in every city of Judah to offer incense to other gods, and he provoked the LORD, the God of his ancestors.

26 As for the rest of his deeds and all his ways, from beginning to end, they are written in the Book of the Kings of Judah and Israel. 27 Ahaz rested with his fathers and was buried in the city, in Jerusalem, but they did not bring him into the tombs of the kings of Israel. His son Hezekiah became king in his place.

Hezekiah (29:1–32:33)

The Repair and Cleansing of the Temple (29:1-19)

29 Hezekiah was 25 years old when he became king and reigned 29 years in Jerusalem. His mother's name was Abijah[D] daughter of Zechariah. 2 He did what was right in the LORD's sight just as his ancestor David had done.

3 In the first year of his reign, in the first month, he opened the doors of the LORD's temple and repaired them. 4 Then he brought in the priests and Levites and gathered

[A]28:18 Or *the Shephelah* [B]28:19 Some Hb mss; other Hb mss read *Israel* [C]28:20 Text emended; MT reads *Tilgath-pilneser*; 1Ch 5:6,26 [D]29:1 = Abi in 2Kg 18:2

>WORD|*study*

29:8 Because of sin, God had **made** Judah **an object of**:

- terror (Hb *za'awah*, "a horror, agitation, trouble"; cp. Dt 28:25)—to hear what befell Judah would send chills up your spine;
- horror (Hb *shammah*, "wasting, desolation"; cp. Dt 28:37)—one would be unnerved or dismayed to see the devastation and misery left in the wake of God's hand of judgment; and
- mockery (Hb *sherēqah*, "hissing, whistling," as an expression of incredulity over the calamity experienced and in "mockery" of the nation's pain; cp. 1Kg 9:8).

them in the eastern public square.
[5]He said to them, "Hear me, Levites.
Consecrate yourselves now and
consecrate the temple of •Yahweh,
the God of your ancestors. Remove
everything impure from the holy
place. [6]For our fathers were unfaithful and did what is evil in the sight of
the LORD our God. They abandoned
Him, turned their faces away from
the LORD's tabernacle, and turned
their backs on Him.[A] [7]They also
closed the doors of the portico, extinguished the lamps, did not burn
incense, and did not offer •burnt offerings in the holy place of the God
of Israel. [8]Therefore, the wrath of
the LORD was on Judah and Jerusalem, and He made them an object of
terror, horror, and mockery,[B] as you
see with your own eyes. [9]Our fathers
fell by the sword, and our sons, our
daughters, and our wives are in captivity because of this. [10]It is in my
heart now to make a covenant with
Yahweh, the God of Israel so that His
burning anger may turn away from
us. [11]My sons, don't be negligent
now, for the LORD has chosen you to
stand in His presence, to serve Him,
and to be His ministers and burners
of incense."

[12]Then the Levites stood up:

Mahath son of Amasai and
Joel son of Azariah from the
Kohathites;
Kish son of Abdi and Azariah
son of Jehallelel from the
Merarites;
Joah son of Zimmah and
Eden son of Joah from the
Gershonites;
[13]Shimri and Jeuel from the
Elizaphanites;
Zechariah and Mattaniah
from the Asaphites;
[14]Jehiel[C] and Shimei from the
Hemanites;
Shemaiah and Uzziel from the
Jeduthunites.

[15]They gathered their brothers together, consecrated themselves, and
went according to the king's command by the words of the LORD to
cleanse the LORD's temple.

[16]The priests went to the entrance
of the LORD's temple to cleanse it.
They took all the unclean things
they found in the LORD's sanctuary to the courtyard of the LORD's
temple. Then the Levites received
them and took them outside to the
Kidron Valley. [17]They began the consecration on the first day of the first
month, and on the eighth day of the
month they came to the portico of
the LORD's temple. They consecrated
the LORD's temple for eight days,
and on the sixteenth day of the first
month they finished.

[18]Then they went inside to King
Hezekiah and said, "We have
cleansed the whole temple of the
LORD, the altar of burnt offering and
all its utensils, and the table for the
rows of the •bread of the Presence
and all its utensils. [19]We have set up
and consecrated all the utensils that
King Ahaz rejected during his reign
when he became unfaithful. They
are in front of the altar of the LORD."

Sacrifices and Offerings at the Temple (29:20-36)

[20]King Hezekiah got up early,
gathered the city officials, and went
to the LORD's temple. [21]They brought
seven bulls, seven rams, seven
lambs, and seven male goats as a
•sin offering for the kingdom, for
the sanctuary, and for Judah. Then
he told the descendants of Aaron,
the priests, to offer them on the
altar of the LORD. [22]So they slaughtered the bulls, and the priests received the blood and sprinkled it
on the altar. They slaughtered the
rams and sprinkled the blood on the
altar. They slaughtered the lambs
and sprinkled the blood on the altar.
[23]Then they brought the goats for
the sin offering right into the presence of the king and the congregation, who laid their hands on them.
[24]The priests slaughtered the goats
and put their blood on the altar for a
sin offering, to make •atonement for
all Israel, for the king said that the
burnt offering and sin offering were
for all Israel.

[25]Hezekiah stationed the Levites
in the LORD's temple with cymbals,
harps, and lyres according to the

29:20-25 By Hezekiah's command, the offerings **were for all Israel**, reflecting the king's resolve to extend reform beyond the bounds of his own kingdom (cp. 30:1; 31:1-3). Scripture records the sacrifice of **seven bulls** and **seven rams** on only three other occasions:

- by God's command to Job's friends on account of their folly (Jb 42:8);
- during David's reign, when the ark of the covenant was brought to Jerusalem (1Ch 15:25-26); and
- in the prophet Ezekiel's vision of a restored temple and Passover celebration (Ezk 45:23).

The offering of seven of each kind of animal under Hezekiah's direction may reflect a deliberate effort to obey the Law, follow David's example, demonstrate a desire for ongoing and complete cleansing from sin—by offering **seven goats,** not just one (v. 21).

[A]**29:6** Lit *and they gave the back of the neck* [B]**29:8** Lit *hissing* [C]**29:14** Alt Hb tradition reads *Jehuel*

30:1-5 The Chronicler magnified Hezekiah's historical significance as the first king since David and Solomon to rule over both Judah and Israel as a unified nation. By observing **the Passover** in **all Israel**, the people would be required to review the history of God's deliverance of Israel from Egypt but also to identify themselves as God's people redeemed by the lamb's blood (cp. Ex 12:47; 2Ch 29:20-36; see Ex 12:1–13:16). Therefore, Hezekiah's invitation was a call for **all Israel, from Beer-sheba to Dan**, to repent.

>WORD|*study*

29:24 Put (Hb *chata'*) **their blood on the altar for a sin offering** has more force than the English translation conveys. The verb *chata'* does mean "offer for sin or expiate," but its particular sense is that of "purging or cleansing" by a sacred ceremony (cp. Lv 8:15).

29:36 Suddenly (Hb *pit'om*, "surprisingly") indicates that the spiritual turnaround happened fast enough to catch "the people" by surprise. Within weeks of Hezekiah's ascension to the throne, the nation had been recentered on worship of Yahweh. Given the depth of wickedness to which Ahaz had led them, **how God had prepared** [Hb *kun*, "establish, strengthen, constitute, make ready"] **the people** in such a short time was amazing.

command of David, Gad the king's seer, and Nathan the prophet. For the command was from the LORD
through His prophets. 26 The Levites
stood with the instruments of David, and the priests with the trumpets.

27 Then Hezekiah ordered that the burnt offering be offered on the altar. When the burnt offerings began, the song of the LORD and the trumpets began, accompanied by the instruments of David king of Israel. 28 The
whole assembly was worshiping, singing the song, and blowing the trumpets—all of this continued until the burnt offering was completed.
29 When the burnt offerings were completed, the king and all those present with him bowed down and
worshiped. 30 Then King Hezekiah
and the officials told the Levites to sing praise to the LORD in the words of David and of •Asaph the seer. So they sang praises with rejoicing and bowed down and worshiped.

31 Hezekiah concluded, "Now you are consecrated[A] to the LORD. Come near and bring sacrifices and thank offerings to the LORD's temple." So the congregation brought sacrifices and thank offerings, and all those with willing hearts brought burnt
offerings. 32 The number of burnt
offerings the congregation brought was 70 bulls, 100 rams, and 200 lambs; all these were for a burnt
offering to the LORD. 33 Six hundred
bulls and 3,000 sheep were consecrated.

34 However, since there were not enough priests, they weren't able to skin all the burnt offerings, so their Levite brothers helped them until the work was finished and until the priests consecrated themselves. For the Levites were more conscientious[B] to consecrate themselves than
the priests were. 35 Furthermore,
the burnt offerings were abundant, along with the fat of the •fellowship offerings and with the •drink offerings for the burnt offering.

So the service of the LORD's temple
was established. 36 Then Hezekiah
and all the people rejoiced over how God had prepared the people, for it had come about suddenly.

The Celebration of Passover (30:1–31:1)

30 Then Hezekiah sent word throughout all Israel and Judah, and he also wrote letters to Ephraim and Manasseh to come to the LORD's temple in Jerusalem to observe the •Passover of •Yahweh,
the God of Israel. 2 For the king and
his officials and the entire congregation in Jerusalem decided to observe the Passover of the LORD in the second month, 3 because they were not
able to observe it at the appropriate time. Not enough of the priests had consecrated themselves and the people hadn't been gathered together in Jerusalem. 4 The proposal
pleased the king and the congregation, 5 so they affirmed the proposal
and spread the message throughout all Israel, from Beer-sheba to Dan, to come to observe the Passover of Yahweh, the God of Israel in Jerusalem, for they hadn't observed it often,[C] as prescribed.[D]

6 So the couriers went throughout Israel and Judah with letters from the hand of the king and his officials, and according to the king's command, saying, "Israelites, return to Yahweh, the God of Abraham, Isaac, and Israel so that He may return to those of you who

[A]**29:31** Lit *Now you have filled your hands* [B]**29:34** Lit *upright of heart*; Ps 32:11; 64:10 [C]**30:5** Or *in great numbers* [D]**30:5** Lit *often, according to what is written*

remain, who have escaped from the grasp of the kings of Assyria. 7 Don't be like your fathers and your brothers who were unfaithful to Yahweh, the God of their ancestors so that He made them an object of horror as you yourselves see. 8 Don't become obstinate[A] now like your fathers did. Give your allegiance[B] to Yahweh, and come to His sanctuary that He has consecrated forever. Serve the LORD your God so that He may turn His burning anger away from you, 9 for when you return to Yahweh, your brothers and your sons will receive mercy in the presence of their captors and will return to this land. For Yahweh your God is gracious and merciful; He will not turn His face away from you if you return to Him."

10 The couriers traveled from city to city in the land of Ephraim and Manasseh as far as Zebulun, but the inhabitants[C] laughed at them and mocked them. 11 But some from Asher, Manasseh, and Zebulun humbled themselves and came to Jerusalem. 12 Also, the power of God was at work in Judah to unite them[D] to carry out the command of the king and his officials by the word of the LORD.

13 A very large assembly of people was gathered in Jerusalem to observe the Festival of •Unleavened Bread in the second month. 14 They proceeded to take away the altars that were in Jerusalem, and they took away the incense altars and threw them into the Kidron Valley. 15 They slaughtered the Passover lamb on the fourteenth day of the second month. The priests and Levites were ashamed, and they consecrated themselves and brought •burnt offerings to the LORD's temple. 16 They stood at their prescribed posts, according to the law of Moses, the man of God. The priests sprinkled the blood received from the hand of the Levites, 17 for there were many in the assembly who had not consecrated themselves, and so the Levites were in charge of slaughtering the Passover lambs for every •unclean person to consecrate the lambs to the LORD. 18 A large number of the people—many from Ephraim, Manasseh, Issachar, and Zebulun—were ritually unclean, yet they had eaten the Passover contrary to what was written. But Hezekiah had interceded for them, saying, "May the good LORD provide •atonement on behalf of 19 whoever sets his whole heart on seeking God, Yahweh, the God of his ancestors, even though not according to the purification rules of the sanctuary." 20 So the LORD heard Hezekiah and healed the people. 21 The Israelites who were present in Jerusalem observed the Festival of Unleavened Bread seven days with great joy, and the Levites and the priests praised the LORD day after day with loud instruments. 22 Then Hezekiah encouraged[E] all the Levites who performed skillfully before the LORD. They ate at the appointed festival for seven days, sacrificing •fellowship offerings and giving thanks to Yahweh, the God of their ancestors.

23 The whole congregation decided to observe seven more days, so they observed seven days with joy, 24 for Hezekiah king of Judah contributed 1,000 bulls and 7,000 sheep for the congregation. Also, the officials contributed 1,000 bulls and 10,000 sheep for the congregation, and many priests consecrated themselves. 25 Then the whole assembly of Judah with the priests and Levites, the whole assembly that came from Israel, the foreigners who came from the land of Israel, and those who were living in Judah, rejoiced. 26 There was great rejoicing in Jerusalem, for nothing like this was known since the days of Solomon son of David, the king of Israel.

27 Then the priests and the Levites stood to bless the people, and God heard their voice, and their prayer came into His holy dwelling place in heaven.

31 When all this was completed, all Israel who had attended went out to the cities of Judah and broke up the sacred pillars, chopped down the •Asherah poles, and tore down the •high places and altars

30:13–31:1 Throwing any altars competing with that of the temple into **the Kidron Valley** signified the intent to get rid of them permanently (cp. 29:16; 1Kg 15:13; 2Kg 23:4,6,12). Seeing the vivid picture of God's deliverance enacted in the slaughter of the Passover lamb apparently penetrated the hearts of the priests and Levites who were bucking the new wave of religious reform (2Ch 30:15-16). The fact that so many people **had eaten the Passover** despite being **unclean** posed a serious problem but also served as the occasion for an exemplary prayer of intercession to be recorded in Scripture (v. 18). **Hezekiah** did not ask for a blanket pardon but for **the LORD** Himself to **provide atonement** (Hb *kaphar*, "cover or pardon sin, free an offender from the charge against him") according to the motives of their hearts (v. 18).

[A] **30:8** Lit *Don't stiffen your neck* [B] **30:8** Lit *hand one heart* [E] **30:22** Lit *spoke to the heart of* [C] **30:10** Lit *but they* [D] **30:12** Lit *to give them*

31:2-21 Hezekiah knew that a long-lasting reestablishment of right worship was desperately needed. He continued demonstrating exceptional spiritual leadership by modeling for **the people** the generosity he asked of them in order to meet a specific need (vv. 1-4).

32:1-8 Hezekiah ascended the throne of Judah as Israel was in spiritual and political decline. In the fourth year of Hezekiah's reign, Samaria, Israel's capital, was besieged and fell three years later (see 2Kg 17:3–18:12 regarding events occurring between the periods of time covered by 2Ch 31 and 32). Although God blessed and rewarded Hezekiah's godly leadership (2Ch 31:21), his reign was not trouble-free. Only when faced with unprovoked opposition does a leader's character become most evident (32:1).

throughout Judah and Benjamin, as well as in Ephraim and Manasseh, to the last one.[A] Then all the Israelites returned to their cities, each to his own possession.

The Reestablishment of the Priestly Ministries (31:2-21)

[2] Hezekiah reestablished the divisions of the priests and Levites for the •burnt offerings and •fellowship offerings, for ministry, for giving thanks, and for praise in the gates of the camp of the LORD, each division corresponding to his service among the priests and Levites. [3] The king contributed[B] from his own possessions for the regular morning and evening burnt offerings, the burnt offerings of the Sabbaths, of the New Moons, and of the appointed feasts, as written in the law of the LORD. [4] He told the people who lived in Jerusalem to give a contribution for the priests and Levites so that they could devote their energy to the law of the LORD. [5] When the word spread, the Israelites gave liberally of the best of the grain, new wine, oil, honey, and of all the produce of the field, and they brought in an abundance, a tenth of everything. [6] As for the Israelites and Judahites who lived in the cities of Judah, they also brought a tenth of the cattle and sheep, and a tenth of the dedicated things that were consecrated to the LORD their God. They gathered them into large piles. [7] In the third month they began building up the piles, and they finished in the seventh month. [8] When Hezekiah and his officials came and viewed the piles, they praised the LORD and His people Israel.

[9] Hezekiah asked the priests and Levites about the piles. [10] Azariah, the chief priest of the household of Zadok, answered him, "Since they began bringing the offering to the LORD's temple, we eat and are satisfied and there is plenty left over because the LORD has blessed His people; this abundance is what is left over."

[11] Hezekiah told them to prepare chambers in the LORD's temple, and they prepared them. [12] The offering, the tenth, and the dedicated things were brought faithfully. Conaniah the Levite was the officer in charge of them, and his brother Shimei was second. [13] Jehiel, Azaziah, Nahath, Asahel, Jerimoth, Jozabad, Eliel, Ismachiah, Mahath, and Benaiah were deputies under the authority of Conaniah and his brother Shimei by appointment of King Hezekiah and of Azariah the chief official of God's temple.

[14] Kore son of Imnah the Levite, the keeper of the East Gate, was over the freewill offerings to God to distribute the contribution to the LORD and the consecrated things. [15] Eden, Miniamin, Jeshua, Shemaiah, Amariah, and Shecaniah in the cities of the priests were to faithfully distribute it under his authority to their brothers by divisions, whether large or small. [16] In addition, they distributed it to males registered by genealogy three[C] years old and above; to all who would enter the LORD's temple for their daily duty, for their service in their responsibilities according to their divisions. [17] They distributed also to those recorded by genealogy of the priests by their ancestral families and the Levites 20 years old and above, by their responsibilities in their divisions; [18] to those registered by genealogy—with all their infants, wives, sons, and daughters—of the whole assembly (for they had faithfully consecrated themselves as holy); [19] and to the descendants of Aaron, the priests, in the common fields of their cities, in each and every city. There were men who were registered by name to distribute a portion to every male among the priests and to every Levite recorded by genealogy.

[20] Hezekiah did this throughout all Judah. He did what was good and upright and true before the LORD his God. [21] He was diligent in every deed that he began in the service of God's temple, in the instruction and the commands, in order to seek his God, and he prospered.

The Invasion of Sennacherib, the King of Assyria (32:1-23)

32 After these faithful deeds, Sennacherib king of Assyria came and entered Judah. He laid siege to

[A]31:1 Lit *Manasseh, until finishing* [B]31:3 Lit *The king's portion* [C]31:16 Or *30*; 1Ch 23:3

the fortified cities and intended[A]
to break into them. 2 Hezekiah saw
that Sennacherib had come and that
he planned[B] war on Jerusalem, 3 so
he consulted with his officials and
his warriors about stopping up the
waters of the springs that were outside the city, and they helped him.
4 Many people gathered and stopped
up all the springs and the stream
that flowed through the land; they
said, "Why should the kings of Assyria come and find plenty of water?"
5 Then Hezekiah strengthened his
position by rebuilding the entire bro-
ken-down wall and heightening the
towers and the other outside wall. He
repaired the supporting terraces of
the city of David, and made an abundance of weapons and shields.
6 He set military commanders over
the people and gathered the people
in the square of the city gate. Then
he encouraged them,[C] saying, 7 "Be
strong and courageous! Don't be
afraid or discouraged before the
king of Assyria or before the large
army that is with him, for there
are more with us than with him.
8 He has only human strength,[D] but
we have •Yahweh our God to help
us and to fight our battles." So the
people relied on the words of King
Hezekiah of Judah.
9 After this, while Sennacherib
king of Assyria with all his armed
forces besieged[E] Lachish, he sent his
servants to Jerusalem against King
Hezekiah of Judah and against all
those of Judah who were in Jerusalem, saying, 10 "This is what King
Sennacherib of Assyria says: 'What
are you relying on that you remain
in Jerusalem under siege? 11 Isn't
Hezekiah misleading you to give you
over to death by famine and thirst
when he says, "Yahweh our God will
deliver us from the power of the
king of Assyria"? 12 Didn't Hezekiah
himself remove His •high places and
His altars and say to Judah and Jerusalem, "You must worship before
one altar, and you must burn incense on it"?
13 "'Don't you know what I and my
fathers have done to all the peoples
of the lands? Have any of the national gods of the lands been able to
deliver their land from my power?
14 Who among all the gods of these
nations that my predecessors •com-
pletely destroyed was able to deliver
his people from my power, that your
God should be able to do the same
for you? 15 So now, don't let Hezekiah deceive you, and don't let him
mislead you like this. Don't believe
him, for no god of any nation or
kingdom has been able to deliver
his people from my power or the
power of my fathers. How much less
will your God deliver you from my
power!'"
16 His servants said more against
the LORD God and against His servant Hezekiah. 17 He also wrote letters to mock Yahweh, the God of
Israel, saying against Him:

> Just like the national gods of
> the lands that did not deliver
> their people from my power, so
> Hezekiah's God will not deliver
> His people from my power.

18 Then they called out loudly in
Hebrew[F] to the people of Jerusalem,
who were on the wall, to frighten
and discourage them in order that
he might capture the city. 19 They
spoke against the God of Jerusalem like they had spoken against
the gods of the peoples of the earth,
which were made by human hands.
20 King Hezekiah and the prophet
Isaiah son of Amoz prayed about
this and cried out to heaven, 21 and
the LORD sent an angel who annihilated every brave warrior, leader, and
commander in the camp of the king
of Assyria. So the king of Assyria
returned in disgrace to his land.
He went to the temple of his god,
and there some of his own children
struck him down with the sword.
22 So the LORD saved Hezekiah and
the inhabitants of Jerusalem from
the power of King Sennacherib of
Assyria and from the power of all
others. He gave them rest[G] on every
side. 23 Many were bringing an offering to the LORD to Jerusalem and
valuable gifts to King Hezekiah of

32:9-23 The crisis was simply a great test of the nation's faith in God. Not only were Judah's enemies put on notice by Yahweh's annihilation of the dreaded Assyrian army, but they also looked up to **King Hezekiah** (v. 23).

[A]32:1 Lit *said to himself* [B]32:2 Lit *that his face was for* [C]32:6 Lit *he spoke to their hearts*
[D]32:8 Lit *With him an arm of flesh* [E]32:9 Lit *with his dominion was against* [F]32:18 Lit *Judahite*
[G]32:22 Lit *He led them*; Ps 23:2

32:24-26 In 2 Kings, written for the Jews living in exile, the author gave more attention to the prophet Isaiah's role, Hezekiah's prayer, and to God's lengthy reply to that prayer. The Kings account also elaborated at length on Hezekiah's illness, recovery, and his pride—a topic covered by Chronicles in only these three verses (cp. 2Kg 20). However, the Chronicler concentrated on the temple's reform, the aspect of Hezekiah's reign most relevant and instructive for the postexilic Jews who were facing the challenge of rebuilding the temple and renewing its celebrations and worship. This account of revival is the most extensive in Scripture, with the exception of Pentecost in Acts 2.

32:24-33 The Chronicler's account of Hezekiah's illness briefly summarized the theological lessons rather than repeat the details found in 2Kg 20:1-11, which was likely based on Isaiah 36–39:

- Even good kings get **sick**. The text gives no indication that God had afflicted him as punishment (2Ch 32:24).
- **The Lord** hears and answers prayer, yet God does not always answer with healing (v. 24).
- The Chronicler emphasized that God met Hezekiah's **pride** (Hb *govah*, "arrogance," from the more literal meaning of "height, exaltation"; Ps 10:4; Pr 16:18) with **wrath** but delayed judgment because of Hezekiah's repentant humility (2Ch 32:25-26).
- True to the pattern of Israel and Judah's history, the entire kingdom was affected by the state of the king's **heart** toward **the Lord** (vv. 25-26).
- Verses 27-30 give the reader a snapshot of Hezekiah's Solomon-like wealth and success, which would tempt any man to be proud. Verse 31 provides a different view—a glimpse of how God tests those who trust in Him to **discover** (Hb *yada'*, "know, especially by experience") what is really in one's **heart**.

Hezekiah's friendly reception of the Babylonian delegates indicates that he regarded Babylon as an ally against Assyria (cp. 2Kg 20:12-19).

33:1-10 Although the description of Manasseh's apostasy echoes that of Ahaz (cp. 2Ch 33:2-3,6 and 28:1-4), Manasseh's wickedness was even worse (33:3-5,7-9).

>WORD|*study*

32:31 Test (Hb *nasah*, "try, prove, put to the test") does not suggest that God does not already know what is in a person's heart. Especially in this passage, with the detail that "God left him to test him," the sense is that God purposefully uses circumstances to manifest our weakness, to show His children and a watching world how utterly dependent they are upon Him. "Passing the test" typically requires faith expressed in obedient action (cp. Gn 22:1; Ex 16:4; Dt 8:2,16; 13:4; Jdg 2:22).

Judah, and he was exalted in the
eyes of all the nations after that.

A Successful Reign (32:24-33)

24 In those days Hezekiah became
sick to the point of death, so he
prayed to the Lord, and He spoke
to him and gave him a miraculous
sign. 25 However, because his heart
was proud, Hezekiah didn't respond
according to the benefit that had
come to him. So there was wrath on
him, Judah, and Jerusalem. 26 Then
Hezekiah humbled himself for the
pride of his heart—he and the inhabitants of Jerusalem—so the
Lord's wrath didn't come on them
during Hezekiah's lifetime.

27 Hezekiah had abundant riches
and glory, and he made himself treasuries for silver, gold, precious stones,
spices, shields, and every desirable
item. 28 He made warehouses for the
harvest of grain, new wine, and oil,
and stalls for all kinds of cattle, and
pens for flocks. 29 He made cities for
himself, and he acquired herds of
sheep and cattle in abundance, for
God gave him abundant possessions.

30 This same Hezekiah blocked
the outlet of the water of the Upper
Gihon and channeled it smoothly
downward and westward to the city
of David. Hezekiah succeeded in everything he did. 31 When the ambassadors of Babylon's rulers were sent[A]
to him to inquire about the miraculous sign that happened in the land,
God left him to test him and discover what was in his heart.

32 As for the rest of the events of
Hezekiah's reign and his deeds of
faithful love, note that they are written in the Visions of the Prophet
Isaiah son of Amoz, and in the Book
of the Kings of Judah and Israel.
33 Hezekiah rested with his fathers
and was buried on the ascent to the
tombs of David's descendants. All Judah and the inhabitants of Jerusalem
paid him honor at his death. His son
Manasseh became king in his place.

Manasseh (33:1-20)

33 Manasseh was 12 years old
when he became king and
reigned 55 years in Jerusalem. 2 He
did what was evil in the Lord's sight,
imitating the detestable practices of
the nations that the Lord had dispossessed before the Israelites. 3 He rebuilt the •high places that his father
Hezekiah had torn down and reestablished the altars for the •Baals. He
made •Asherah poles, and he worshiped the whole heavenly •host and
served them. 4 He built altars in the
Lord's temple, where •Yahweh had
said, "Jerusalem is where My name
will remain forever." 5 He built altars
to the whole heavenly host in both
courtyards of the Lord's temple. 6 He
passed his sons through the fire in
the Valley of Hinnom. He practiced
witchcraft, •divination, and sorcery,
and consulted mediums and spiritists. He did a great deal of evil in the
Lord's sight, provoking Him.

7 Manasseh set up a carved image
of the idol he had made, in God's
temple, about which God had said to
David and his son Solomon, "I will
establish My name forever[B] in this
temple and in Jerusalem, which I
have chosen out of all the tribes of
Israel. 8 I will never again remove
the feet of the Israelites from the
land where I stationed your[C] ancestors, if only they will be careful to
do all that I have commanded them
through Moses—all the law, statutes, and judgments." 9 So Manasseh
caused Judah and the inhabitants of
Jerusalem to stray so that they did
worse evil than the nations the Lord
had destroyed before the Israelites.

10 The Lord spoke to Manasseh and
his people, but they didn't listen. 11 So

[A] **32:31** LXX, Tg, Vg; MT reads *of Babylon sent* [B] **33:7** LXX, Syr, Tg, Vg; 2Kg 21:7; MT reads *name for Elom* [C] **33:8** LXX, Syr, Vg read *land I gave to their*; 2Kg 21:8

He brought against them the military
commanders of the king of Assyria.
They captured Manasseh with hooks,
bound him with bronze shackles, and
took him to Babylon. 12 When he was
in distress, he sought the favor of
Yahweh his God and earnestly humbled himself before the God of his
ancestors. 13 He prayed to Him, so He
heard his petition and granted his request, and brought him back to Jerusalem, to his kingdom. So Manasseh
came to know that Yahweh is God.

14 After this, he built the outer wall
of the city of David from west of Gihon in the valley to the entrance of
the Fish Gate; he brought it around
the Ophel, and he heightened it considerably. He also placed military
commanders in all the fortified cities of Judah.

15 He removed the foreign gods and
the idol from the LORD's temple, along
with all the altars that he had built
on the mountain of the LORD's temple
and in Jerusalem, and he threw them
outside the city. 16 He built[A] the altar
of the LORD and offered •fellowship
and thank offerings on it. Then he
told Judah to serve Yahweh, the God
of Israel. 17 However, the people still
sacrificed at the high places, but only
to Yahweh their God.

18 The rest of the events of Manasseh's reign, along with his prayer
to his God and the words of the seers
who spoke to him in the name of
Yahweh, the God of Israel, are written in the Records of Israel's Kings.
19 His prayer and how God granted his
request, and all his sin and unfaithfulness and the sites where he built
high places and set up Asherah poles
and carved images before he humbled himself, they are written in the
Records of Hozai. 20 Manasseh rested
with his fathers, and he was buried
in his own house. His son Amon became king in his place.

Amon (33:21-25)

21 Amon was 22 years old when he
became king and reigned two years
in Jerusalem. 22 He did what was evil
in the LORD's sight just as his father
Manasseh had done. Amon sacrificed
to all the carved images that his father Manasseh had made, and he
served them. 23 But he did not humble himself before the LORD like his
father Manasseh humbled himself;
instead, Amon increased his •guilt.

24 So his servants conspired
against him and put him to death in
his own house. 25 Then the common
people[B] executed all those who conspired against King Amon and made
his son Josiah king in his place.

Josiah (34:1–35:27)

The Removal of Idols and Repair of the Temple (34:1-13)

34 Josiah was eight years old
when he became king and
reigned 31 years in Jerusalem. 2 He
did what was right in the LORD's
sight and walked in the ways of his
ancestor David; he did not turn
aside to the right or the left.

3 In the eighth year of his reign,
while he was still a youth, Josiah
began to seek the God of his ancestor David, and in the twelfth year he
began to cleanse Judah and Jerusalem of the •high places, the •Asherah
poles, the carved images, and the
cast images. 4 Then in his presence
the altars of the •Baals were torn
down, and he chopped down the incense altars that were above them.
He shattered the Asherah poles, the
carved images, and the cast images,
crushed them to dust, and scattered
them over the graves of those who
had sacrificed to them. 5 He burned
the bones of the priests on their altars. So he cleansed Judah and Jerusalem. 6 He did the same in the
cities of Manasseh, Ephraim, and
Simeon, and as far as Naphtali and
on their surrounding mountain
shrines.[C] 7 He tore down the altars,
and he smashed the Asherah poles
and the carved images to powder. He
chopped down all the incense altars
throughout the land of Israel and returned to Jerusalem.

8 In the eighteenth year of his
reign, in order to cleanse the land
and the temple, Josiah sent Shaphan
son of Azaliah, along with Maaseiah
the governor of the city and the court

33:11-20 In Nineveh, Manasseh learned firsthand that **Yahweh** alone **is God** (vv. 12-13). Only He could hear Manasseh's prayer in a foreign land and take him from such humiliating and dire circumstances back to Jerusalem. The Chronicler not only observed that Manasseh **earnestly** [Hb *me'od*, "greatly, exceedingly"] **humbled himself** but also listed his many actions demonstrating a genuine change of heart (vv. 15-17). The immediate audience of postexilic Jews probably identified with and drew encouragement from this account of Manasseh's life. Despite the depth of sin to which Manasseh had plunged Israel, in his brokenness he had **sought** God's **favor** with true repentance, and God had restored his throne (v. 12). Perhaps because the positive outcome of Manasseh's life was not recorded in 2 Kings, the Chronicler insisted that both the good and the bad were included in the historical **Records** (v. 19).

34:1-13 Josiah's actions exemplify what should take place in the heart of a new believer. Repentance and submission to Christ's lordship involves deliberate "clean-up" efforts to rid one's life of sin (i.e., anything that rivals God for top priority in your life; cp. Ti 2:14; Heb 9:14; Jms 4:8; 1Jn 1:9). A more detailed description of Josiah's comprehensive attack on the nation's idolatry—*after* the discovery of the law—appears in 2Kg 23:4-20.

[A] **33:16** Some Hb mss, Syr, Tg, Arabic; other Hb mss, LXX, Vg read *restored* [B] **33:25** Lit *the people of the land* [C] **34:6** One Hb tradition reads *Naphtali with their swords*; alt Hb tradition, Syr, Vg read *Naphtali, the ruins all around*; Hb obscure

34:22-28 See additional notes on this passage in 2Kg 22:14-20.

historian Joah son of Joahaz, to repair the temple of the LORD his God.

9 So they went to Hilkiah the high priest, and gave him the money brought into God's temple. The Levites and the doorkeepers had collected money from Manasseh, Ephraim, and from the entire remnant of Israel, and from all Judah, Benjamin, and the inhabitants of Jerusalem. 10 They put it into the hands of those doing the work—those who oversaw the LORD's temple. They gave it to the workmen who were working in the LORD's temple, to repair and restore the temple; 11 they gave it to the carpenters and builders and also used it to buy quarried stone and timbers—for joining and making beams—for the buildings that Judah's kings had destroyed.

12 The men were doing the work with integrity. Their overseers were Jahath and Obadiah, Levites from the Merarites, and Zechariah and Meshullam from the Kohathites as supervisors. The Levites were all skilled with musical instruments. 13 They were also over the porters and were supervising all those doing the work task by task. Some of the Levites were secretaries, officers, and gatekeepers.

Hilkiah's Discovery (34:14-21)

14 When they brought out the money that had been deposited in the LORD's temple, Hilkiah the priest found the book of the law of the LORD written by the hand of Moses. 15 Consequently, Hilkiah told Shaphan the court secretary, "I have found the book of the law in the LORD's temple," and he gave the book to Shaphan.

16 Shaphan took the book to the king, and also reported, "Your servants are doing all that was placed in their hands. 17 They have emptied out the money that was found in the LORD's temple and have put it into the hand of the overseers and the hand of those doing the work." 18 Then Shaphan the court secretary told the king, "Hilkiah the priest gave me a book," and Shaphan read from it in the presence of the king.

19 When the king heard the words of the law, he tore his clothes. 20 Then he commanded Hilkiah, Ahikam son of Shaphan, Abdon son of Micah, Shaphan the court secretary, and the king's servant Asaiah, 21 "Go. Ask •Yahweh for me and for those remaining in Israel and Judah, concerning the words of the book that was found. For great is the LORD's wrath that is poured out on us because our fathers have not kept the word of the LORD in order to do everything written in this book."

Huldah's Prophecy (34:22-33)

22 So Hilkiah and those the king had designated[A] went to the prophetess Huldah, the wife of Shallum son of Tokhath, son of Hasrah, keeper of the wardrobe. She lived in Jerusalem in the Second District. They spoke with her about this.

23 She said to them, "This is what Yahweh, the God of Israel says: Say to the man who sent you to Me, 24 'This is what Yahweh says: I am about to bring disaster on this place and on its inhabitants, fulfilling all the curses written in the book that they read in the presence of the king of Judah, 25 because they have abandoned Me and burned incense to other gods in order to provoke Me with all the works of their hands. My wrath will be poured out on this place, and it will not be quenched.' 26 Say this to the king of Judah who sent you to ask Yahweh, 'This is what Yahweh, the God of Israel says: As for the words that you heard, 27 because your heart was tender and you humbled yourself before God when you heard His words against this place and against its inhabitants, and because you humbled yourself before Me, and you tore your clothes and wept before Me, I Myself have heard'—this is the LORD's declaration. 28 'I will indeed gather you to your fathers, and you will be gathered to your grave in peace. Your eyes will not see all the disaster that I am bringing on this place and on its inhabitants.'"

Then they reported to the king.

29 So the king sent messengers and gathered all the elders of Judah and Jerusalem. 30 The king went up to the LORD's temple with all the men of Judah and the inhabitants of Jerusalem, as well as the priests and

[A]**34:22** LXX; MT omits *designated*

the Levites—all the people from
great to small. He read in their hearing all the words of the book of the
covenant that had been found in the
LORD's temple. 31 Then the king stood
at his post and made a covenant in
the LORD's presence to follow the
LORD and to keep His commands,
His decrees, and His statutes with
all his heart and with all his soul in
order to carry out the words of the
covenant written in this book.

32 He had all those present in Jerusalem and Benjamin agree[A] to it.
So all the inhabitants of Jerusalem
carried out the covenant of God, the
God of their ancestors.

33 So Josiah removed everything
that was detestable from all the
lands belonging to the Israelites,
and he required all who were present in Israel to serve the LORD their
God. Throughout his reign they did
not turn aside from following Yahweh, the God of their ancestors.

The Celebration of Passover (35:1-19)

35 Josiah observed the LORD's
•Passover and slaughtered the
Passover lambs on the fourteenth
day of the first month. 2 He appointed the priests to their responsibilities and encouraged them to
serve in the LORD's temple. 3 He said
to the Levites who taught all Israel
the holy things of the LORD, "Put
the holy ark in the temple built by
Solomon son of David king of Israel.
Since you do not have to carry it on
your shoulders, now serve •Yahweh
your God and His people Israel.

4 "Organize your ancestral houses
by your divisions according to the
written instruction of David king of
Israel and that of his son Solomon.
5 Serve in the holy place by the divisions of the ancestral houses for
your brothers, the lay people,[B] and
the distribution of the tribal household of the Levites. 6 Slaughter the
Passover lambs, consecrate yourselves, and make preparations for
your brothers to carry out the word
of the LORD through Moses."

7 Then Josiah donated 30,000
sheep, lambs, and young goats, plus
3,000 bulls from his own possessions, for the Passover sacrifices for
all the lay people[B] who were present.

8 His officials also donated willingly for the people, the priests, and
the Levites. Hilkiah, Zechariah, and
Jehiel, chief officials of God's temple, gave 2,600 Passover sacrifices
and 300 bulls for the priests. 9 Conaniah and his brothers Shemaiah
and Nethanel, and Hashabiah, Jeiel,
and Jozabad, officers of the Levites,
donated 5,000 Passover sacrifices for
the Levites, plus 500 bulls.

10 So the service was established;
the priests stood at their posts and
the Levites in their divisions according to the king's command. 11 Then
they slaughtered the Passover
lambs, and while the Levites were
skinning the animals, the priests
sprinkled the blood[C] they had been
given.[D] 12 They removed the •burnt
offerings so that they might be giv-
en to the divisions of the ancestral
houses of the lay people[B] to offer
to the LORD, according to what is
written in the book of Moses; they
did the same with the bulls. 13 They
roasted the Passover lambs with
fire according to regulation. They
boiled the holy sacrifices in pots,
kettles, and bowls; and they quickly
brought them to the lay people.[B]
14 Afterward, they made preparations
for themselves and for the priests,
since the priests, the descendants of
Aaron, were busy offering up burnt
offerings and fat until night. So
the Levites made preparations for
themselves and for the priests, the
descendants of Aaron.

15 The singers, the descendants of
•Asaph, were at their stations according to the command of David, Asaph,
Heman, and Jeduthun the king's
seer. Also, the gatekeepers were at
each gate. None of them left their
tasks because their Levite brothers
had made preparations for them.

16 So all the service of the LORD
was established that day for observing the Passover and for offering
burnt offerings on the altar of the
LORD, according to the command
of King Josiah. 17 The Israelites who
were present in Judah also observed
the Passover at that time and the

35:1-19 The declaration that this **Passover** observance was unlike any other **since the days of Samuel** suggests that it was greater than the Passover kept by Hezekiah (v. 18; cp. 2Kg 23:22). The Passover led by Josiah more closely adhered to the law because everyone participated at the prescribed time (cp. 30:1-3,15-20).

35:3 Why **the holy ark** was being carried about instead of occupying its prescribed position in the holiest place of the temple is not explained. Perhaps it was removed to protect it from being defiled by the idols placed in the temple under Ahaz, Manasseh, and likely Amon (cp. 29:16-17; 33:4-5,15,22-23).

[A] 34:32 Lit *take a stand.* [B] 35:5,7,12,13 Lit *the sons of the people* [C] 35:11 LXX, Vg, Tg; MT omits *blood* [D] 35:11 Lit *sprinkled from their hand*

35:25-26 The prophet Jeremiah is mentioned for the first time in Chronicles as one who **chanted a dirge** (Hb *qonēn*, "lament in song," cp. 2Sm 1:17; 3:33) over Josiah. The king was mourned in such a way as to prompt a decree to include him **in the Dirges,** a book of laments regularly used in times of mourning and sung by both **men** and **women**. This outpouring of grief was appropriate since Josiah's reign was the last to have recalled the joyful obedience known under David and Solomon. Furthermore, the Chronicler ascribed to Josiah **deeds of faithful love** (Hb *chesed*, "goodness, kindness, mercy" usually reserved for God's character and works; see **Word Study**, p. 322), a rare commendation (cp. 24:22; 32:32; 1Ch 19:2).

36:1-3 The people's loss of power and the nation's loss of its sovereignty are evident in the king's removal by the pharaoh.

36:4-8 Neco renamed **Jehoahaz's brother Eliakim** as a sign of control.

36:9-10 Most of the deportation of people and valuables to Babylon was conducted during Jehoiachin's brief reign. When Nebuchadnezzar finally brought him to Babylon, the temple's **valuable** [Hb *chemdah*, "precious"] **utensils** went with him.

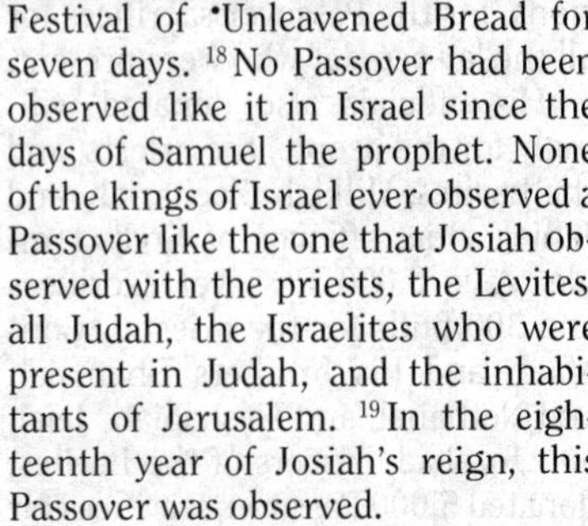

Festival of •Unleavened Bread for
seven days. 18 No Passover had been
observed like it in Israel since the
days of Samuel the prophet. None
of the kings of Israel ever observed a
Passover like the one that Josiah observed with the priests, the Levites,
all Judah, the Israelites who were
present in Judah, and the inhabitants of Jerusalem. 19 In the eighteenth year of Josiah's reign, this
Passover was observed.

Josiah's Death (35:20-27)

20 After all this that Josiah had
prepared for the temple, Neco king
of Egypt marched up to fight at
Carchemish by the Euphrates, and
Josiah went out to confront him.
21 But Neco sent messengers to him,
saying, "What is the issue between
you and me, king of Judah? I have
not come against you today[A] but I
am fighting another dynasty.[B] God
told me to hurry. Stop opposing God
who is with me; don't make Him destroy you!"
22 But Josiah did not turn away
from him; instead, in order to fight
with him he disguised himself.[C] He
did not listen to Neco's words from
the mouth of God, but went to the
Valley of Megiddo to fight. 23 The archers shot King Josiah, and he said
to his servants, "Take me away, for
I am severely wounded!" 24 So his
servants took him out of the war
chariot, carried him in his second
chariot, and brought him to Jerusalem. Then he died, and they buried
him in the tomb of his fathers. All
Judah and Jerusalem mourned for
Josiah. 25 Jeremiah chanted a dirge
over Josiah, and all the singing men
and singing women still speak of Josiah in their dirges to this very day.
They established them as a statute
for Israel, and indeed they are written in the Dirges.
26 The rest of the events of Josiah's
reign, along with his deeds of faithful love according to what is written in the law of the LORD, 27 and his
words, from beginning to end, are
written in the Book of the Kings of
Israel and Judah.

The Last Kings of Judah (36:1-13)

Jehoahaz (36:1-3)

36 Then the common people[D]
took Jehoahaz son of Josiah
and made him king in Jerusalem in
place of his father.
2 Jehoahaz[E] was 23 years old when
he became king and reigned three
months in Jerusalem. 3 The king of
Egypt deposed him in Jerusalem and
fined the land 7,500 pounds[F] of silver and 75 pounds[G] of gold.

Eliakim/Jehoiakim (36:4-8)

4 Then Neco king of Egypt made
Jehoahaz's brother Eliakim king
over Judah and Jerusalem and
changed Eliakim's name to Jehoiakim. But Neco took his brother Jehoahaz[E] and brought him to Egypt.
5 Jehoiakim was 25 years old when
he became king and reigned 11
years in Jerusalem. He did what was
evil in the sight of the LORD his God.
6 Now Nebuchadnezzar king of Babylon attacked him and bound him in
bronze shackles to take him to Babylon. 7 Also Nebuchadnezzar took
some of the utensils of the LORD's
temple to Babylon and put them in
his temple in Babylon.
8 The rest of the deeds of Jehoiakim, the detestable things he did,
and what was found against him, are
written in the Book of Israel's Kings.
His son Jehoiachin became king in
his place.

Jehoiachin (36:9-10)

9 Jehoiachin was 18[H] years old when
he became king and reigned three
months and 10 days in Jerusalem. He
did what was evil in the LORD's sight.
10 In the spring[I] Nebuchadnezzar sent
for him and brought him to Babylon
along with the valuable utensils of
the LORD's temple. Then he made
Jehoiachin's brother Zedekiah king
over Judah and Jerusalem.

Zedekiah (36:11-13)

11 Zedekiah was 21 years old when
he became king and reigned 11
years in Jerusalem. 12 He did what
was evil in the sight of the LORD his

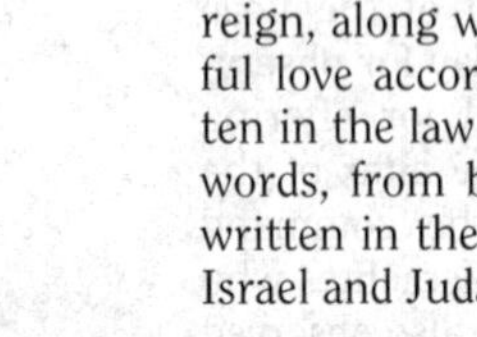

[A] **35:21** LXX, Syr, Tg, Vg; MT reads *Not against you, you today* [B] **35:21** Lit *house* [C] **35:22** LXX reads *he was determined* [D] **36:1** Lit *the people of the land* [E] **36:2,4** = Joahaz [F] **36:3** Lit *100 talents* [G] **36:3** Lit *one talent* [H] **36:9** Some Hb mss, LXX; 2Kg 24:8; other Hb mss read *eight* [I] **36:10** Lit *At the return of the year*

>WORD|*study*

36:19 In the Old Testament, burned (Hb *saraph*, "consumed"; see 2Kg 23:6) usually denotes the intentional and complete destruction by fire of idols (Dt 7:5,25; 12:3; 13:16; 1Ch 14:12; 2Ch 15:16) or of the bones of the idols' priests (34:15). The verb choice is fitting, therefore, to describe the devastation of the physical dwelling place God had abandoned because of the people's sin and their scorn for His covenant.

God and did not humble himself before Jeremiah the prophet at the LORD's command. 13 He also rebelled against King Nebuchadnezzar who had made him swear allegiance by God. He became obstinate[A] and hardened his heart against returning to •Yahweh, the God of Israel.

Sinful Deeds and Practices (36:14-16)

14 All the leaders of the priests and the people multiplied their unfaithful deeds, imitating all the detestable practices of the nations, and they defiled the LORD's temple that He had consecrated in Jerusalem.

15 But Yahweh, the God of their ancestors sent word against them by the hand of His messengers, sending them time and time again, for He had compassion on His people and on His dwelling place. 16 But they kept ridiculing God's messengers, despising His words, and scoffing at His prophets, until the LORD's wrath was so stirred up against His people that there was no remedy.

The Destruction of Jerusalem (36:17-21)

17 So He brought up against them the king of the Chaldeans, who killed their choice young men with the sword in the house of their sanctuary. He had no pity on young men or young women, elderly or aged; He handed them all over to him. 18 He took everything to Babylon—all the articles of God's temple, large and small, the treasures of the LORD's temple, and the treasures of the king and his officials. 19 Then the Chaldeans burned God's temple. They tore down Jerusalem's wall, burned down all its palaces, and destroyed all its valuable articles.

20 He deported those who escaped from the sword to Babylon, and they became servants to him and his sons until the rise of the Persian[B] kingdom. 21 This fulfilled the word of the LORD through Jeremiah and the land enjoyed its Sabbath rest all the days of the desolation until 70 years were fulfilled.

The Proclamation of King Cyrus of Persia (36:22-23)

22 In the first year of Cyrus king of Persia, the word of the LORD spoken through[C] Jeremiah was fulfilled. The LORD put it into the mind of King Cyrus of Persia to issue a proclamation throughout his entire kingdom and also to put it in writing:

> 23 This is what King Cyrus of Persia says: The LORD, the God of heaven, has given me all the kingdoms of the earth and has appointed me to build Him a temple at Jerusalem in Judah. Whoever among you of His people may go up, and may the LORD his God be with him.

[A] **36:13** Lit *He stiffened his neck* [B] **36:20** LXX reads *Median* [C] **36:22** Lit *LORD by the mouth of*

36:14-16 The Lord's compassion was shown most clearly, perhaps, in His persistent efforts to draw His people back to Himself. Over and over **again**, God took the initiative to reveal to them the widening gap between the life they were choosing and who He had ordained them to be. Nevertheless, they continued in disobedience.

36:17-21 Judah's repeated and continual demonstrations of contempt for God's love, truth, and chastisement reached the point where His only recourse was to destroy **everything** they had defiled and refused to cleanse, including **His dwelling place** (v. 15), the **temple** (vv. 16-19). The writer asserts that the Lord remained in control (v. 17). The book of Lamentations expresses the disillusionment and crushing sorrow of those whose lives were spared. However, although the city of Jerusalem was totally destroyed, there was still hope for succeeding generations. **Jeremiah** had prophesied of a day when the exiles would return (vv. 20-21; cp. Jr 29:10; Lm 3:19-33). The Chronicler ended the narrative on a positive note. Once the people had been in exile with time to repent, the Lord would bring them back to the promised land. Their hope was that a remnant would recover the Davidic dynasty, and that the city of Jerusalem and the temple would be rebuilt.

36:22-23 Consistent with his perspective throughout Chronicles, the Chronicler pointed out that all events affecting His people, whether prompting joy or sorrow, were directed by **the LORD**, who always remained faithful to His covenant, though sometimes in surprising ways (cp. Jr 29:10). These verses also serve as the introduction to the book of Ezra, thus forming a literary, historical, and theological link to the postexilic history of Israel and contributing to the unity of the Old Testament canon.

2 CHRONICLES... WRITTEN ON MY *Heart*

As the Chronicler communicates, disobedience brings devastating consequences. In times of enduring the Lord's discipline, recall His words and humbly turn your heart to seek Him (2Ch 7:14). And also remember that Yahweh is a God of restoration, who "will make a way in the wilderness, rivers in the desert" (Is 43:19). His redemptive purpose in chastening is "for our benefit, so that we can share His holiness" (Hb 12:10). He is making all things new, including broken lives (Rv. 21:5).

Ezra

Timeline	605 BC	605–530 BC	597 BC	586 BC
World Events / Biblical Events	First of Nebuchadnezzar's three invasions of Judah	Events in Daniel	Nebuchadnezzar's second invasion of Judah	Nebuchadnezzar's destruction of Jerusalem, including the temple of Solomon

"Though we are slaves, our God has not abandoned us in our slavery. He has extended grace to us" (9:9a).

Who wrote Ezra?

While the author does not identify himself, Jewish tradition attributes the book to Ezra.

Who were the recipients?

The Israelites in Jerusalem after they returned from exile

When was Ezra written?

While the book's events occurred between 537 B.C. and 458 B.C., Ezra was written in 425 B.C.

Where did it happen?

Ezra begins in the city of Babylon and concludes in the ruins of post-exilic Jerusalem.

What is Ezra about?

- God's restoration of His people to the promised land
- God's sovereignty over pagan rulers
- The vital importance of God's Word to His people

Why should women read Ezra?

Ezra testifies to the truth that God keeps His promises. As the Lord vowed through the prophet Ezekiel, "Now I will restore the fortunes of Jacob and have compassion on the whole house of Israel, and I will be jealous for My holy name. . . . They will know that I am Yahweh their God when I regather them to their own land after having exiled them among the nations. I will leave none of them behind" (Ezk 39:25,28). Your Father chastises in order to restore you to Himself—He will not leave you behind. As He enabled the temple to be rebuilt, He will restore the people to His presence and to worship. You can trust that upon genuine confession and repentance, He will restore the temple of His Spirit—your heart (Jn 14:23; Rm 8:9; 1Co 6:19).

How do you read Ezra?

The book of Ezra is written in thematic rather than chronological order and includes court orders, lists, letters, and narratives. Chapters 1–6 outline the return of the first exiles and the rebuilding of the temple, and chapters 7–10 recount the return of Ezra to his ministry in Jerusalem. One unique feature of this book is the preservation of seven official documents and letters comparable to other Persian documents from the period (see 1:2-4; 4:8-16; 4:17-22; 5:6-17; 6:1-5; 6:6-12; 7:11-26).

Outline

- I. The Return of the Exiles Led by Zerubbabel (1:1–6:22)
  - A. The Decree of Cyrus (1:1-4)
  - B. The First Return of the Exiles (1:5–2:70)
  - C. The Restoration of Temple Worship (3:1-7)
  - D. The Rebuilding of the Temple (3:8–6:22)
- II. The Return of the Exiles Led by Ezra (7:1–10:44)
  - A. The Second Return of the Exiles (7:1–8:36)
  - B. The Reforms of Ezra (9:1–10:44)

Persian Kings in the Book of Ezra

KING	REIGN	SIGNIFICANCE	REFERENCES
Cyrus	538–530 B.C.	Issued "a proclamation" allowing the return of Yahweh's people to Judah	Ezr 1:1-4; 2Ch 36:22-23; see also Is 44:24-28
Darius (married to Cyrus's daughter Atossa)	521–486 B.C.	Located King Cyrus's decree and issued his own decree ordering the unhindered reconstruction of the temple, government funding for the project, and severe punishment for "any man who interferes with this directive"	Ezr 4:24; 6:1-13
Ahasuerus (son of Darius), elsewhere known as Xerxes	486–465 B.C.	Received "an accusation against the residents of Judah and Jerusalem"	Ezr 4:6; the book of Esther
Artaxerxes (son of Xerxes	465–425 B.C.	Ordered a stop to the rebuilding of "God's house in Jerusalem"	Ezr 4:7-24; 7:1–8:1; see also Neh 2:1-8; 5:14; 13:6

538 BC	537–458 BC	515 BC	486–465 BC	458 BC	445–430 BC
Cyrus's decree allowing return of Jews from exile	Events in Ezra	Dedication of second temple	Events in Esther	Ezra's journey to Jerusalem	Events in Nehemiah

The Return of the Exiles Led by Zerubbabel (1:1–6:22)

The Decree of Cyrus (1:1-4)

1 In the first year of Cyrus king of
Persia,[A] the word of the LORD spoken through Jeremiah was fulfilled.
The LORD put it into the mind of
King Cyrus to issue a proclamation
throughout his entire kingdom and
to put it in writing:

> 2 This is what King Cyrus of
> Persia says: "The LORD, the God
> of heaven, has given me all the
> kingdoms of the earth and has
> appointed me to build Him a
> house at Jerusalem in Judah.
> 3 Whoever is among His people,
> may his God be with him, and
> may he go to Jerusalem in Ju-
> dah and build the house of the
> LORD, the God of Israel, the God
> who is in Jerusalem. 4 Let every
> survivor, wherever he lives, be
> assisted by the men of that re-
> gion with silver, gold, goods,
> and livestock, along with a
> freewill offering for the house
> of God in Jerusalem."

The First Return of the Exiles (1:5-11)

5 So the family leaders of Judah and
Benjamin, along with the priests and
Levites—everyone God had motivated[B]—prepared to go up and rebuild
the LORD's house in Jerusalem. 6 All
their neighbors supported them[C]
with silver articles, gold, goods,
livestock, and valuables, in addition
to all that was given as a freewill offering. 7 King Cyrus also brought out
the articles of the LORD's house that
Nebuchadnezzar had taken from
Jerusalem and had placed in the
house of his gods. 8 King Cyrus of
Persia had them brought out under
the supervision of Mithredath the
treasurer, who counted them out
to Sheshbazzar the prince of Judah.
9 This was the inventory:

> 30 gold basins,
> 1,000 silver basins,
> 29 silver knives,
> 10 30 gold bowls,
> 410 various[D] silver bowls,
> and 1,000 other articles.

11 The gold and silver articles totaled
5,400. Sheshbazzar brought all of
them when the exiles went up from
Babylon to Jerusalem.

The Exiles Who Returned (2:1-70)

2 These now are the people of the
province who came from those
captive exiles King Nebuchadnezzar
of Babylon[E] had deported to Babylon. They returned to Jerusalem
and Judah, each to his own town.
2 They came with Zerubbabel, Jeshua, Nehemiah, Seraiah, Reelaiah,
Mordecai, Bilshan, Mispar, Bigvai,
Rehum, and Baanah.

The number of the Israelite men
included:[F]

[A]1:1 Cyrus reigned 559–530 B.C. [B]1:5 Lit *everyone whose spirit God had stirred* [C]1:6 Lit *supported their hands* [D]1:10 Or *similar* [E]2:1 Nebuchadnezzar reigned 605–562 B.C. [F]2:2 Lit *the men of the people of Israel*

>WORD|*study*

1:5 God motivated (Hb *ruach*, "spirit"; *'ur*, "stir up, awake, incite") or "stirred the spirit" of those exiles who would return to Jerusalem—about 50,000 people. The same verb is used in 1:1 to describe how God used King Cyrus.

Title The book is named for its main character, Ezra, who played an instrumental role in leading God's people back to Judea after their captivity in Babylon.

1:1-4 Cyrus, also known as Cyrus II or Cyrus the Great, became **king of Persia** around 559 B.C. After defeating the city of Babylon, where many deported Jews lived, he encouraged the Jewish exiles to return to their homeland. This event was prophesied over 200 years before by Isaiah and later by Jeremiah (Is 44:28–45:6; Jr 25:11-12; 29:10). Cyrus's decree was not issued because of his personal commitment to Yahweh but as a reflection of his polytheism, which the Lord used to fulfill His purpose for His people. Cyrus was king at that time not by coincidence; God had orchestrated everything. Cyrus's role in the book of Ezra is a testimony of the sovereignty of God, who delights in using pagan kings to accomplish His will (see Pr 21:1; Rm 13:1).

1:5 The journey back to Jerusalem could have taken up to four months since Jerusalem was approximately 900 miles away. Scripture does not criticize the exiles who did not wish to return. A few years later God used exiles like Mordecai and Esther, who remained in Babylon or Persia, to make His name known (see the book of Esther, p. 604).

1:8-11 Scholars have questioned the identity of Sheshbazzar. Zerubbabel is listed in chapter 3 as overseeing the laying of the foundation of the temple, whereas **Sheshbazzar** is said to have this same role in chapter 5. Whether these men were the same person or two men working alongside each other in similar roles is not clear in the text.

2:1-70 This list is almost identical to the one found in Neh 7:6-72.

2:2 Nehemiah is not the man for whom the book of the Bible is named because that Nehemiah did not return with the first group of exiles. Also, **Mordecai** is not the same Mordecai mentioned in the book of Esther.

KINGS OF PERSIA

PERSIAN KING	DATES (B.C.)	BIBLICAL CONNECTIONS	EVENTS AND ACCOMPLISHMENTS
Cyrus II (the Great)	559-530	Permitted return of the Jews from exile Facilitated rebuilding of the temple at Jerusalem (Ezr 1:1-4; 6:3-5) The "Anointed One" of Isaiah 45:1	King of Anshan, 559 B.C. Conquered kingdom of Media (550 B.C.) and Lydian kingdom (546 B.C.) Conquered Babylon, 539 B.C.
Cambyses II	530-521	Not mentioned in the Bible	Son of Cyrus the Great Conquered Egypt, 525 B.C. His death (suicide?) in 522 B.C. led to two years of fighting between rival claimants to the throne.
Darius I Hystaspes	521-486	Haggai and Zechariah preached during the 2nd year of Darius I (520 B.C.). Temple rebuilt and dedicated 517/516 B.C. (cp. Ezr 6:12–15)	Member of a collateral royal line Secured the throne ending the unrest following the death of Cambyses Reorganized the Persian Empire into satrapies Established royal postal system Began building Persepolis Invaded Greece and was defeated at Marathon, 490 B.C. Revolt in Egypt
Xerxes I	486–465	Possibly Ahasuerus of the Book of Esther	Son of Darius I Continued building Persepolis Encountered numerous rebellions at the beginning of his reign (Egypt, Babylon) Invaded Greece, sacked Athens (480 B.C.), but was defeated by the Greeks in a naval engagement (Salamis, 480 B.C.) and on land (Plataea and Mycale, 479 B.C.) Killed in a palace coup in 465 B.C.
Artaxerxes I Longimanus	465–425	Nehemiah, cup bearer of Artaxerxes came to Judah (445 B.C., cp. Neh 2:1; 13:6) traditional date of Ezra's mission in the 7th year of his reign (458 B.C., cp. Ezr 7:7)	Faced revolt in Egypt Completed major buildings at Persepolis; made peace with Greeks (Peace of Callais, 449 B.C.); died of natural causes
Xerxes II	423	Not mentioned in the Bible	Ruled less than two months
Darius II Nothus	423–404	Not mentioned in the Bible Jews in Egypt (Elephantine) appealed to Samaria and Jerusalem for help in rebuilding their temple about 407 B.C.	Peloponnesian War, 431–404 B.C. Persia recovered several Greek cities in Asia Minor
Artaxerxes II Mnemon	405–359/8	Some scholars place Ezra's mission in the 7th year of Artaxerxes II, about 398 B.C.	Egypt regained freedom from Persia for a time Revolt of the satraps, 366–360 B.C.
Artaxerxes III Ochus	359/8–338/7	Not mentioned in the Bible	Philip II of Macedon Rises to power about 359 B.C. Alexander the Great born, 356 B.C. Persia reclaims Egypt, 342 B.C.
Arses	338/7–336	Not mentioned in the Bible	Unknown
Darius III Codomannus	336–330	Alexander subdues the Levant Tyre and Gaza besieged, 332 B.C. Conquest of Egypt by Alexander, 332 B.C.	Philip assassinated, 336 B.C.; Alexander the Great invades the Persian Empire, 334 B.C. Darius III defeated by Alexander at Issus, 333 B.C., and Guagamela, 331 B.C.; death of Darius, 330 B.C.

3 Parosh's descendants 2,172
4 Shephatiah's descendants 372
5 Arah's descendants 775
6 Pahath-moab's descendants:
Jeshua's and
Joab's descendants 2,812
7 Elam's descendants 1,254
8 Zattu's descendants 945
9 Zaccai's descendants 760
10 Bani's descendants 642
11 Bebai's descendants 623
12 Azgad's descendants 1,222
13 Adonikam's descendants 666
14 Bigvai's descendants 2,056
15 Adin's descendants 454
16 Ater's descendants:
of Hezekiah 98
17 Bezai's descendants 323
18 Jorah's descendants 112
19 Hashum's descendants 223
20 Gibbar's descendants 95
21 Bethlehem's people 123
22 Netophah's men 56
23 Anathoth's men 128
24 Azmaveth's people 42
25 Kiriatharim's,
Chephirah's,
and Beeroth's people 743
26 Ramah's and Geba's
people 621
27 Michmas's men 122
28 Bethel's and Ai's men 223
29 Nebo's people 52
30 Magbish's people 156
31 the other
Elam's people 1,254
32 Harim's people 320
33 Lod's, Hadid's,
and Ono's people 725
34 Jericho's people 345
35 Senaah's people 3,630

36 The priests included:

Jedaiah's descendants of
the house of Jeshua 973
37 Immer's descendants 1,052
38 Pashhur's descendants 1,247
39 and Harim's
descendants 1,017

40 The Levites included:

Jeshua's and Kadmiel's
descendants
from Hodaviah's
descendants 74

41 The singers included:

•Asaph's descendants 128

42 The gatekeepers' descendants included:

Shallum's descendants,
Ater's descendants,
Talmon's descendants,
Akkub's descendants,
Hatita's descendants,
Shobai's descendants,
in all 139

43 The temple servants included:

Ziha's descendants,
Hasupha's descendants,
Tabbaoth's descendants,
44 Keros's descendants,
Siaha's descendants,
Padon's descendants,
45 Lebanah's descendants,
Hagabah's descendants,
Akkub's descendants,
46 Hagab's descendants,
Shalmai's[A] descendants,
Hanan's descendants,
47 Giddel's descendants,
Gahar's descendants,
Reaiah's descendants,
48 Rezin's descendants,
Nekoda's descendants,
Gazzam's descendants,
49 Uzza's descendants,
Paseah's descendants,
Besai's descendants,
50 Asnah's descendants,
Meunim's[B] descendants,
Nephusim's[C] descendants,
51 Bakbuk's descendants,
Hakupha's descendants,
Harhur's descendants,
52 Bazluth's descendants,
Mehida's descendants,
Harsha's descendants,
53 Barkos's descendants,
Sisera's descendants,
Temah's descendants,
54 Neziah's descendants,
and Hatipha's descendants.

2:36-70 Serving as a temple priest was a hereditary duty for the descendants of Aaron. Had this group not returned, there would be no reason to rebuild the temple since there would be no one qualified to minister on behalf of the people. Zerubbabel forbade any priest who could not prove his ancestry from serving in the temple until he could be tested by the **Urim and Thummim**, objects kept by the high priest in his breastplate for consulting God's will in different matters (v. 63; cp. Ex 28:15).

[A]2:46 Alt Hb tradition reads *Shamlai's* [B]2:50 Alt Hb tradition reads *Meinim's* [C]2:50 Alt Hb tradition reads *Nephisim's*

3:1-7 Though the temple was not completed, the people did not refrain from resuming their worship of God. When **Jeshua** and **Zerubbabel** built the altar, the people came together in Jerusalem from their neighboring towns, despite their fear of attack from **surrounding peoples**. They feared and honored God more than they feared what men could do to them.

55 The descendants of Solomon's servants included:

Sotai's descendants,
Hassophereth's descendants,
Peruda's descendants,
56 Jaalah's descendants,
Darkon's descendants,
Giddel's descendants,
57 Shephatiah's descendants,
Hattil's descendants,
Pochereth-hazzebaim's descendants,
and Ami's descendants.
58 All the temple servants
and the descendants
of Solomon's servants 392.

59 The following are those who came from Tel-melah, Tel-harsha, Cherub, Addan, and Immer but were unable to prove that their families and ancestry were Israelite:

60 Delaiah's descendants,
Tobiah's descendants,
Nekoda's descendants 652

61 and from the descendants of the
priests: the descendants of Hobaiah,
the descendants of Hakkoz, the descendants of Barzillai—who had
taken a wife from the daughters of
Barzillai the Gileadite and was called
by their name. 62 These searched for
their entries in the genealogical records, but they could not be found,
so they were disqualified from the
priesthood. 63 The governor ordered
them not to eat the most holy things
until there was a priest who could
consult the •Urim and Thummim.

64 The whole combined
assembly numbered 42,360
65 not including
their 7,337 male
and female slaves,
and their 200 male
and female singers.
66 They had 736 horses,
245 mules,
67 435 camels,
and 6,720 donkeys.

68 After they arrived at the LORD's
house in Jerusalem, some of the
family leaders gave freewill offerings
for the house of God in order to have
it rebuilt on its original site. 69 Based
on what they could give, they gave
61,000 gold coins,[A] 6,250 pounds[B]
of silver, and 100 priestly garments
to the treasury for the project. 70 The
priests, Levites, singers, gatekeepers, temple servants, and some of
the people settled in their towns,
and the rest of Israel settled in their
towns.

The Restoration of Temple Worship (3:1-7)

3 By the seventh month, the Israelites had settled in their towns,
and the people gathered together in
Jerusalem. 2 Jeshua son of Jozadak
and his brothers the priests along
with Zerubbabel son of Shealtiel
and his brothers began to build the
altar of Israel's God in order to offer
•burnt offerings on it, as it is written
in the law of Moses, the man of God.
3 They set up the altar on its foundation and offered burnt offerings
for the morning and evening on it
to the LORD even though they feared

[A]2:69 Or *drachmas*, or *darics* [B]2:69 Lit *5,000 minas*

Biblical Womanhood Redeeming the Time

Israel did not wait until conditions were comfortable before serving and worshiping the Lord. Unfortunately, many women say they will make time for God someday—once their children are grown, once they finish school, once their careers are on track, or once their lives are moving smoothly. James warns against living as though you are guaranteed tomorrow: "You don't even know what tomorrow will bring—what your life will be! For you are like smoke that appears for a little while, then vanishes" (Jms 4:14). Instead, your focus must be to do The Lord's will and to worship Him (Jms 4:15; Jn 4:23-24). As the psalmist prayed, "Teach us to number our days that we may gain a heart of wisdom" (Ps 90:12). What changes are needed in your daily life in order to serve and worship God right now? Do not fall into the trap of believing you will be faithful to serve, worship, follow and know God more "someday." Someday is today!

>WORD|*study*

4:4 Discouraged (Hb *raphah*, "let down," and *yad*, "hand") captures the meaning of the Hebrew expression more literally rendered, "weaken, relax, or let down one's hands." This phrase has the sense of destroying one's courage or causing despair. The same word is used in Jr 38:4 to describe an ongoing process of discouragement.

the surrounding peoples. 4 They celebrated the Festival of Booths as prescribed, and offered burnt offerings each day, based on the number specified by ordinance for each festival day. 5 After that, they offered the regular burnt offering and the offerings for the beginning of each month[A] and for all the LORD's appointed holy occasions, as well as the freewill offerings brought to[B] the LORD.

6 On the first day of the seventh month they began to offer burnt offerings to the LORD, even though the foundation of the LORD's temple had not yet been laid. 7 They gave money to the stonecutters and artisans, and gave food, drink, and oil to the people of Sidon and Tyre, so they could bring cedar wood from Lebanon to Joppa by sea, according to the authorization given them by King Cyrus of Persia.

The Rebuilding of the Temple (3:8-9)

8 In the second month of the second year after they arrived at God's house in Jerusalem, Zerubbabel son of Shealtiel, Jeshua son of Jozadak, and the rest of their brothers, including the priests, the Levites, and all who had returned to Jerusalem from the captivity, began to build. They appointed the Levites who were 20 years old or more to supervise the work on the LORD's house. 9 Jeshua with his sons and brothers, Kadmiel with his sons, and the sons of Judah[C] and of Henadad, with their sons and brothers, the Levites, joined together to supervise those working on the house of God.

The Temple Foundation Completed (3:10-13)

10 When the builders had laid the foundation of the LORD's temple, the priests, dressed in their robes and holding trumpets, and the Levites descended from •Asaph, holding cymbals, took their positions to praise the LORD, as King David of Israel had instructed. 11 They sang with praise and thanksgiving to the LORD: "For He is good; His faithful love to Israel endures forever." Then all the people gave a great shout of praise to the LORD because the foundation of the LORD's house had been laid.

12 But many of the older priests, Levites, and family leaders, who had seen the first temple, wept loudly when they saw the foundation of this house, but many others shouted joyfully. 13 The people could not distinguish the sound of the joyful shouting from that of the[D] weeping, because the people were shouting so loudly. And the sound was heard far away.

Opposition to Rebuilding the Temple (4:1-5)

4 When the enemies of Judah and Benjamin heard that the returned exiles[E] were building a temple for •Yahweh, the God of Israel, 2 they approached Zerubbabel and the leaders of the families and said to them, "Let us build with you, for we also worship your God and have been sacrificing to Him[F] since the time King Esar-haddon of Assyria[G] brought us here."

3 But Zerubbabel, Jeshua, and the other leaders of Israel's families answered them, "You may have no part with us in building a house for our God, since we alone must build it for Yahweh, the God of Israel, as King Cyrus, the king of Persia has commanded us." 4 Then the people who were already in the land[H] discouraged[I] the people of Judah and made them afraid to build. 5 They also

3:8-9 A little over 13 months after the exiles returned to Jerusalem the temple began to be rebuilt; gathering materials took time before the work could be started.

3:10-13 The older generation was lamenting the lost glory of Solomon's temple, falling into the trap of comparison and imagining how things used to be. By holding onto the past they were unable to perceive that God was "about to do something new" (Is 43:19). Those who had not seen Solomon's temple had nothing with which to compare the newly-laid foundation. They simply praised God because they were seeing the beginning of the temple, which they had desired for such a long time.

4:1-5 Although the enemies who offered to help had been offering sacrifices to the God of Israel, they created a syncretistic religion that involved the worship of many gods. Allowing pagans to be involved with the project could have meant that these unbelievers would expect to have some say in the worship. The Israelites had been exiled from their land because of their idolatry, and they would not risk any association with idolaters now that they had returned to the land. Cooperation can sometimes lead to compromise. The people of God must stand for truth. Does that mean that you can never interact with unbelievers? Absolutely not! You are called to be salt and light, but you must be wise in the influence you allow unbelievers to have on your life.

[A] **3:5** Lit *for the new moons* [B] **3:5** Lit *well as those of everyone making a freewill offering to* [C] **3:9** Or *Hodaviah*; Neh 7:43; 1 Esdras 5:58 [D] **3:13** Lit *the people* [E] **4:1** Lit *the sons of the exile* [F] **4:2** Alt Hb tradition reads *have not been sacrificing* [G] **4:2** Esar-haddon reigned 681–669 B.C. [H] **4:4** Lit *people of the land* [I] **4:4** Lit *relaxed the hands of*

4:6-23 This section interrupts the chronological sequence of the text, possibly to illustrate the opposition that Israel faced in trying to rebuild not only the temple but also the city. King **Ahasuerus** ruled Persia from 486 to 465 B.C. This king was also known as Xerxes, the king mentioned in the book of Esther. Later in a letter to King Artaxerxes, son of Ahasuerus, the opponents claimed that the Israelites were preparing to revolt against the king once the city had been rebuilt. The king investigated their claims and then ordered the building to be stopped **until a further decree has been pronounced** by him (v. 21). The opponents went to the Jews and **forcibly stopped them** (v. 23), indicating that they may have torn down what had already been built. When Nehemiah, Artaxerxes' cupbearer, asked for permission to start the building again, the king obviously was persuaded to overturn any order he had previously given since the project was completed under Nehemiah's supervision (Neh 6:15).

bribed officials to act against them to frustrate their plans throughout the reign of King Cyrus of Persia and until the reign of King Darius of Persia.[A]

Opposition to Rebuilding the City (4:6-16)

6 At the beginning of the reign of Ahasuerus,[B] the people who were already in the land[C] wrote an accusation against the residents of Judah and Jerusalem. 7 During the time of King Artaxerxes of Persia,[D] Bishlam, Mithredath, Tabeel and the rest of his colleagues wrote to King Artaxerxes. The letter was written in Aramaic and translated.[E,F]

8 Rehum the chief deputy and Shimshai the scribe wrote a letter to King Artaxerxes concerning Jerusalem as follows:

> 9 From Rehum[G] the chief deputy, Shimshai the scribe, and the rest of their colleagues—the judges and magistrates[H] from Tripolis, Persia, Erech, Babylon, Susa (that is, the people of Elam),[I] 10 and the rest of the peoples whom the great and illustrious Ashurbanipal[J] deported and settled in the cities of Samaria and the region west of the Euphrates River.

11 This is the text of the letter they sent to him:

> To King Artaxerxes from your servants, the men from the region west of the Euphrates River:
>
> 12 Let it be known to the king that the Jews who came from you have returned to us at Jerusalem. They are rebuilding that rebellious and evil city, finishing its walls, and repairing its foundations. 13 Let it now be known to the king that if that city is rebuilt and its walls are finished, they will not pay tribute, duty, or land tax, and the royal revenue[I] will suffer. 14 Since we have taken an oath of loyalty to the king,[K] and it is not right for us to witness his dishonor, we have sent to inform the king 15 that a search should be made in your fathers' record books. In these record books you will discover and verify that the city is a rebellious city, harmful to kings and provinces. There have been revolts in it since ancient times. That is why this city was destroyed. 16 We advise the king that if this city is rebuilt and its walls are finished, you will not have any possession west of the Euphrates.

Artaxerxes' Reply (4:17-23)

17 The king sent a reply to his chief deputy Rehum, Shimshai the scribe, and the rest of their colleagues living in Samaria and elsewhere in the region west of the Euphrates River:

> Greetings.
>
> 18 The letter you sent us has been translated and read[L] in my presence. 19 I issued a decree and a search was conducted. It was discovered that this city has had uprisings against kings since ancient times, and there have been rebellions and revolts in it. 20 Powerful kings have also ruled over Jerusalem and exercised authority over the whole region, and tribute, duty, and land tax were paid to them. 21 Therefore, issue an order for these men to stop, so that this city will not be rebuilt until a further decree has been pronounced by me. 22 See that you not neglect this matter. Otherwise, the damage will increase and the royal interests[M] will suffer.

23 As soon as the text of King Artaxerxes' letter was read to Rehum, Shimshai the scribe, and their colleagues, they immediately went to the Jews in Jerusalem and forcibly stopped them.

[A] **4:5** Darius reigned 521–486 B.C. [B] **4:6** = Xerxes; he reigned 486–465 B.C. [C] **4:6** Lit *people of the land* [D] **4:7** Artaxerxes reigned 465–425 B.C. [E] **4:7** Lit *translated. Aramaic:* [F] **4:7** Ezr 4:8–6:18 is written in Aram. [G] **4:9** Lit *Then Rehum* [H] **4:9** Or *ambassadors* [I] **4:9,13** Aram obscure [J] **4:10** Lit *Osnappar* [K] **4:14** Lit *have eaten the salt of the palace* [L] **4:18** Or *been read clearly* [M] **4:22** Lit *the kings*

Resuming the Rebuilding of the Temple (4:24–5:5)

24 Now the construction of God's
house in Jerusalem had stopped and
remained at a standstill until the second year of the reign of King Darius
5 of Persia. 1 But when the prophets
Haggai and Zechariah son of Iddo
prophesied to the Jews who were in
Judah and Jerusalem, in the name
of the God of Israel who was over
them, 2 Zerubbabel son of Shealtiel
and Jeshua son of Jozadak began
to rebuild God's house in Jerusalem. The prophets of God were with
them, helping them.
3 At that time Tattenai the governor of the region west of the Euphrates River, Shethar-bozenai, and
their colleagues came to the Jews
and asked, "Who gave you the order to rebuild this temple and finish
this structure?"[A] 4 They also asked
them, "What are the names of the
workers[B] who are constructing this
building?" 5 But God was watching[C]
over the Jewish elders. These men
wouldn't stop them until a report
was sent to Darius, so that they
could receive written instructions
about this matter.

The Letter to Darius (5:6-17)

6 This is the text of the letter that
Tattenai the governor of the region
west of the Euphrates River, Shethar-bozenai, and their colleagues,
the officials in the region, sent to
King Darius. 7 They sent him a report, written as follows:

To King Darius:

All greetings.

8 Let it be known to the king
that we went to the house of
the great God in the province
of Judah. It is being built with
cut[D] stones, and its beams are
being set in the walls. This
work is being done diligently
and succeeding through the
people's efforts. 9 So we questioned the elders and asked,
"Who gave you the order to
rebuild this temple and finish this structure?"[A] 10 We also
asked them for their names, so
that we could write down the
names of their leaders for your
information.

11 This is the reply they gave us:

We are the servants of the God
of heaven and earth and are
rebuilding the temple that was
built many years ago, which
a great king of Israel built
and finished. 12 But since our
fathers angered the God of
heaven, He handed them over
to King Nebuchadnezzar of
Babylon, the Chaldean, who
destroyed this temple and deported the people to Babylon.
13 However, in the first year of
Cyrus king of Babylon, he issued a decree to rebuild the
house of God. 14 He also took
from the temple in Babylon
the gold and silver articles of
God's house that Nebuchadnezzar had taken from the
temple in Jerusalem and carried them to the temple in
Babylon. He released them
from the temple in Babylon to
a man named Sheshbazzar, the
governor by the appointment
of King Cyrus. 15 Cyrus told
him, "Take these articles, put
them in the temple in Jerusalem, and let the house of God
be rebuilt on its original site."
16 Then this same Sheshbazzar
came and laid the foundation
of God's house in Jerusalem. It
has been under construction
from that time until now, yet
it has not been completed.

17 So if it pleases the king, let a
search of the royal archives[E] in
Babylon be conducted to see if
it is true that a decree was issued by King Cyrus to rebuild
the house of God in Jerusalem.
Let the king's decision regarding this matter be sent to us.

4:24–5:5 This section picks up where Ezra 4:5 ends. God sent the prophets **Haggai and Zechariah** (5:1) to prophesy that the Jews were to resume rebuilding the city, to encourage them, and to bring focus to their work.

5:2 Zerubbabel and **Jeshua** are the same two leaders mentioned in the earlier chapters of Ezra. God used spiritual leaders and those with organizational and administrative abilities to work in harmony with one another. He works this way within the body of Christ—His church, and you should be encouraged to use whatever gift God has given you to build up the body of Christ.

5:3-5 Throughout the book of Ezra, when Israel's work begins, their opposition also arises. But **God was watching over** them (more literally, God's "eyes were on them"). He would not leave or forsake His people—a key theme in Ezra and Nehemiah. No matter what the opposition, God has His eyes on you.

5:6-17 By observing the civil authorities' place over them and treating **Tattenai** with respect, the Israelites were given the opportunity to be a light. God uses adversity and opposition to strengthen the faith of His people and to proclaim His glory to the lost world.

[A]5:3,9 Or *finish its furnishings* [B]5:4 One Aram ms, LXX, Syr; MT reads *Then we told them exactly what the names of the men were* [C]5:5 Lit *But the eye of their God was* [D]5:8 Or *huge* [E]5:17 Lit *treasure house*

6:1-15 That Darius would have his servants search so thoroughly for the document that proved Israel's right to rebuild is another indication of God's watching over His people. Because of Darius's assistance, the Israelites were able to complete the temple about four years later and 70 years after it had first been destroyed—around 515 B.C.

6:16-22 The temple was dedicated just five weeks before Passover began. **Twelve male goats** were offered as a **sin offering** (Aram *chatta'ah*, "sin offering, expiation"), representing each of the 12 tribes and thus emphasizing the continuity of the remnant (most of whom were from the tribes of Judah, Benjamin, and Levi) with the entire people of God (vv. 16-17). God not only directed the pagan nation to bring His people into captivity as punishment for their sin 70 years earlier, but He also brought His people full circle by directing Cyrus to free them and Darius to allow Yahweh's temple to be completed. God's sovereignty is once again demonstrated in His use of pagan kings for His purposes. Nothing is out of the control of God (Pr 21:1).

Darius's Search (6:1-5)

6 King Darius gave the order, and
they searched in the library of
Babylon in the archives.[A] 2 But it was
in the fortress of Ecbatana in the
province of Media that a scroll was
found with this record written on it:

3 In the first year of King Cyrus,
he issued a decree concerning
the house of God in Jerusalem:
Let the house be rebuilt as a
place for offering sacrifices,
and let its original foundations be retained.[B] Its height
is to be 90 feet[C] and its width
90 feet,[C,D] 4 with three layers of
cut[E] stones and one of timber.
The cost is to be paid from the
royal treasury. 5 The gold and
silver articles of God's house
that Nebuchadnezzar took
from the temple in Jerusalem
and carried to Babylon must
also be returned. They are to be
brought to the temple in Jerusalem where they belong[F] and
put into the house of God.

Darius's Decree (6:6-15)

6 Therefore, you must stay away
from that place, Tattenai governor of the region west of the
Euphrates River, Shethar-bozenai, and your[G] colleagues, the
officials in the region. 7 Leave
the construction of the house of
God alone. Let the governor and
elders of the Jews rebuild this
house of God on its original site.

8 I hereby issue a decree concerning what you must do, so
that the elders of the Jews can
rebuild the house of God:
The cost is to be paid in full
to these men out of the royal
revenues from the taxes of the
region west of the Euphrates
River, so that the work will
not stop. 9 Whatever is needed—young bulls, rams, and
lambs for •burnt offerings to
the God of heaven, or wheat,
salt, wine, and oil, as requested by the priests in Jerusalem—let it be given to them
every day without fail, 10 so
that they can offer sacrifices
of pleasing aroma to the God of
heaven and pray for the life of
the king and his sons.

11 I also issue a decree concerning any man who interferes
with this directive:
Let a beam be torn from his
house and raised up; he will be
impaled on it, and his house
will be made into a garbage
dump because of this offense.
12 May the God who caused
His name to dwell there overthrow any king or people who
dares[H] to harm or interfere
with this house of God in Jerusalem. I, Darius, have issued
the decree. Let it be carried
out diligently.

13 Then Tattenai governor of the
region west of the Euphrates River,
Shethar-bozenai, and their colleagues diligently carried out what
King Darius had decreed. 14 So the
Jewish elders continued successfully with the building under the
prophesying of Haggai the prophet
and Zechariah son of Iddo. They
finished the building according
to the command of the God of Israel and the decrees of Cyrus, Darius, and King Artaxerxes of Persia.
15 This house was completed on the
third day of the month of Adar[I] in
the sixth year of the reign of King
Darius.

The Temple Dedication and the Passover (6:16-22)

16 Then the Israelites, including
the priests, the Levites, and the rest
of the exiles, celebrated the dedication of the house of God with joy.
17 For the dedication of God's house
they offered 100 bulls, 200 rams, and
400 lambs, as well as 12 male goats
as a •sin offering for all Israel—one
for each Israelite tribe. 18 They also

[A]**6:1** Lit *Babylon where the treasures were stored* [B]**6:3** Lit *be brought forth* [C]**6:3** Lit *60 cubits* [D]**6:3** A copyist seemingly overlooked the term for length and inadvertently read the 60 cubits for height and width. Like Solomon's temple, this temple was probably 90 feet long, 30 feet wide, and 45 feet high. [E]**6:4** Or *huge* [F]**6:5** Lit *Jerusalem, to its place,* [G]**6:6** Lit *their* [H]**6:12** Lit *who stretches out its hand* [I]**6:15** = February–March

appointed the priests by their divisions and the Levites by their groups
to the service of God in Jerusalem,
according to what is written in the
book of Moses.
19 The exiles observed the •Pass-
over on the fourteenth day of the
first month. 20 All of the priests and
Levites were ceremonially •clean,
because they had purified themselves. They killed the Passover
lamb for themselves, their priestly
brothers, and all the exiles. 21 The
Israelites who had returned from
exile ate it, together with all who
had separated themselves from the
uncleanness of the Gentiles of the
land[A] in order to worship •Yahweh,
the God of Israel. 22 They observed
the Festival of •Unleavened Bread
for seven days with joy, because the
LORD had made them joyful, having
changed the Assyrian king's attitude
toward them, so that he supported
them[B] in the work on the house of
the God of Israel.

The Return of the Exiles Led by Ezra (7:1–10:44)

Ezra's Arrival (7:1-10)

7 After these events, during the
reign of King Artaxerxes of Persia, Ezra—

Seraiah's son, Azariah's son,
Hilkiah's son, 2 Shallum's son,
Zadok's son, Ahitub's son,
3 Amariah's son, Azariah's son,
Meraioth's son,
4 Zerahiah's son,
Uzzi's son, Bukki's son,
5 Abishua's son, Phinehas's son,
Eleazar's son, Aaron
the chief priest's son

6—came up from Babylon. He was
a scribe skilled in the law of Moses,
which •Yahweh, the God of Israel,
had given. The king had granted him
everything he requested because
the hand of Yahweh his God was on
him. 7 Some of the Israelites, priests,
Levites, singers, gatekeepers, and
temple servants accompanied him
to Jerusalem in the seventh year of
King Artaxerxes.
8 Ezra[C] came to Jerusalem in the
fifth month, during the seventh year
of the king. 9 He began the journey
from Babylon on the first day of the
first month and arrived in Jerusalem
on the first day of the fifth month
since the gracious hand of his God
was on him. 10 Now Ezra had determined in his heart to study the law
of the LORD, obey it, and teach its
statutes and ordinances in Israel.

Letter from Artaxerxes (7:11-28)

11 This is the text of the letter King
Artaxerxes gave to Ezra the priest
and scribe, an expert in matters of
the LORD's commands and statutes
for Israel:[D]

12 Artaxerxes, king of kings, to
Ezra the priest, an expert in the
law of the God of heaven:
Greetings.

13 I issue a decree that any of
the Israelites in my kingdom,
including their priests and Levites, who want to go to Jerusalem, may go with you. 14 You
are sent by the king and his
seven counselors to evaluate
Judah and Jerusalem according
to the law of your God, which
is in your possession. 15 You are
also to bring the silver and gold
the king and his counselors
have willingly given to the God
of Israel, whose dwelling is in
Jerusalem, 16 and all the silver
and gold you receive throughout the province of Babylon,
together with the freewill offerings given by the people and
the priests to the house of their
God in Jerusalem. 17 Then you
are to buy with this money as
many bulls, rams, and lambs as
needed, along with their •grain
and •drink offerings, and offer
them on the altar at the house
of your God in Jerusalem. 18 You
may do whatever seems best to
you and your brothers with the
rest of the silver and gold, according to the will of your God.
19 You must deliver to the God
of Jerusalem all the articles giv-
en to you for the service of the
house of your God. 20 You may
use the royal treasury to pay

6:22 God not only directed the pagan nation to bring His people into captivity as punishment for their sin 70 years earlier, but He also brought His people full circle by directing Cyrus to free them and Darius to allow Yahweh's temple to be completed. God's sovereignty is once again demonstrated in His use of pagan kings for His purposes. Nothing is out of the control of God (Pr 21:1).

7:1-10 This chapter begins in 458 B.C., about 50 or 60 years after the events at the end of chapter 6. During that interval, the events recorded in the book of Esther took place (between 483 and 471 B.C.). Israel was at a spiritually low point when Ezra brought the second group of exiles to Jerusalem at this time. Also, this section changes from third to first person, supporting the idea that Ezra authored this book.

Ezra (Hb, possibly a shortened form of "Yahweh is my help," v. 1) was chosen by God to lead His people. He was **a scribe skilled in the law of Moses** (v. 6). This training might not seem too remarkable except that Ezra had been born in Babylon. He devoted himself to the study of God's Word, even while living in a foreign land, rather than being assimilated into the foreign culture. The Bible notes that the **gracious hand of His God was on him** (v. 9; see also 7:28; 8:18,22,31; Neh 2:8,18) because **Ezra had determined in his heart to study the law of the LORD**, to **obey** [Hb *'asah*, "do"] **it**, and to **teach its statues and ordinances in Israel** (Ezr 7:10).

[A] **6:21** Lit *land to them* [B] **6:22** Lit *their hands* [C] **7:8** LXX, Syr, Vg read *They* [D] **7:11** Ezr 7:12-26 is written in Aram.

7:27 God used a pagan king to accomplish His purpose because He **put it into the king's mind to glorify the house of the Lord in Jerusalem.**

8:1-20 Only about 2,000 people returned with Ezra. This generation of exiles had never seen Jerusalem.

for anything else needed for the
house of your God.

21 I, King Artaxerxes, issue a decree to all the treasurers in the
region west of the Euphrates
River:

Whatever Ezra the priest, an
expert in the law of the God
of heaven, asks of you must
be provided promptly, 22 up to
7,500 pounds[A] of silver, 500
bushels[B] of wheat, 550 gallons[C]
of wine, 550 gallons[C] of oil, and
salt without limit.[D] 23 Whatever
is commanded by the God of
heaven must be done diligently for the house of the God of
heaven, so that wrath will not
fall on the realm of the king
and his sons. 24 Be advised that
tribute, duty, and land tax must
not be imposed on any priests,
Levites, singers, doorkeepers,
temple servants, or other servants of this house of God.

25 And you, Ezra, according to[E]
God's wisdom that you possess,
appoint magistrates and judges
to judge all the people in the
region west of the Euphrates
who know the laws of your God
and to teach anyone who does
not know them. 26 Anyone who
does not keep the law of your
God and the law of the king,
let a fair judgment be executed
against him, whether death,
banishment, confiscation of
property, or imprisonment.

27 Praise Yahweh the God of our fathers, who has put it into the king's
mind to glorify the house of the
Lord in Jerusalem, 28 and who has
shown favor to me before the king,
his counselors, and all his powerful
officers. So I took courage because
I was strengthened by Yahweh my
God,[F] and I gathered Israelite leaders to return with me.

Those Returning with Ezra (8:1-20)

8 These are the family leaders and
the genealogical records of those
who returned with me from Babylon
during the reign of King Artaxerxes:

2 Gershom, from Phinehas's
descendants;
Daniel, from
Ithamar's descendants;
Hattush,
from David's descendants,
3 who was of
Shecaniah's descendants;
Zechariah,
from Parosh's descendants,
and 150 men[G] with him
who were registered
by genealogy;
4 Eliehoenai son of Zerahiah
from Pahath-moab's
descendants,
and 200 men with him;
5 Shecaniah[H] son of Jahaziel
from Zattu's descendants,
and 300 men with him;
6 Ebed son of Jonathan
from Adin's descendants,
and 50 men with him;
7 Jeshaiah son of Athaliah
from Elam's descendants,
and 70 men with him;
8 Zebadiah son of Michael
from Shephatiah's
descendants,
and 80 men with him;
9 Obadiah son of Jehiel
from Joab's descendants,
and 218 men with him;
10 Shelomith[I] son of Josiphiah
from Bani's descendants,
and 160 men with him;
11 Zechariah son of Bebai
from Bebai's descendants,
and 28 men with him;
12 Johanan son of Hakkatan
from Azgad's descendants,
and 110 men with him;
13 these are the last ones,
from Adonikam's
descendants,
and their names are:
Eliphelet, Jeuel,
and Shemaiah,
and 60 men with them;
14 Uthai and Zaccur[J]
from Bigvai's descendants,
and 70 men with them.

[A] 7:22 Lit *100 talents* [B] 7:22 Lit *100 cors* [C] 7:22 Lit *100 baths* [D] 7:22 Lit *without instruction* [E] 7:25 Lit *to your* [F] 7:28 Lit *because the hand of the Lord my God was on me* [G] 8:3 Or *males*; also in vv. 4-14 [H] 8:5 LXX, 1 Esdras 8:32; MT reads *the descendants of Shecaniah* [I] 8:10 Some LXX mss, 1 Esdras 8:36; MT reads *the descendants of Shelomith* [J] 8:14 Alt Hb tradition, some LXX mss read *Zabud*

15 I gathered them at the river[A]
that flows to Ahava, and we camped
there for three days. I searched
among the people and priests, but
found no Levites there. 16 Then I
summoned the leaders: Eliezer,
Ariel, Shemaiah, Elnathan, Jarib,
Elnathan, Nathan, Zechariah, and
Meshullam, as well as the teachers
Joiarib and Elnathan. 17 I sent them
to Iddo, the leader at Casiphia, with
a message for[B] him and his brothers,
the temple servants at Casiphia, that
they should bring us ministers for
the house of our God. 18 Since the
gracious hand of our God was on
us, they brought us Sherebiah—a
man of insight from the descendants of Mahli, a descendant of Levi
son of Israel—along with his sons
and brothers, 18 men, 19 plus Hashabiah, along with Jeshaiah, from
the descendants of Merari, and his
brothers and their sons, 20 men.
20 There were also 220 of the temple
servants, who had been appointed by
David and the leaders for the work
of the Levites. All were identified by
name.

Preparation to Return (8:21-30)

21 I proclaimed a fast by the Ahava
River,[C] so that we might humble
ourselves before our God and ask
Him for a safe journey for us, our
children, and all our possessions. 22 I
did this because I was ashamed to
ask the king for infantry and cavalry
to protect us from enemies during
the journey, since we had told him,
"The hand of our God is gracious to
all who seek Him, but His great anger is against all who abandon Him."
23 So we fasted and pleaded with our
God about this, and He granted our
request.

24 I selected 12 of the leading
priests, along with Sherebiah, Hashabiah, and 10 of their brothers. 25 I
weighed out to them the silver, the
gold, and the articles—the contribution for the house of our God that
the king, his counselors, his leaders, and all the Israelites who were
present had offered. 26 I weighed out
to them 24 tons[D] of silver, silver
articles weighing 7,500 pounds,[E]
7,500 pounds[E] of gold, 27 20 gold
bowls worth 1,000 gold coins,[F]
and two articles of fine gleaming
bronze, as valuable as gold. 28 Then
I said to them, "You are holy to the
LORD, and the articles are holy. The
silver and gold are a freewill offering to the LORD God of your fathers.
29 Guard them carefully until you
weigh them out in the chambers of
the LORD's house before the leading
priests, Levites, and heads of the Israelite families in Jerusalem." 30 So
the priests and Levites took charge
of the silver, the gold, and the articles that had been weighed out, to
bring them to the house of our God
in Jerusalem.

Arrival in Jerusalem (8:31-36)

31 We set out from the Ahava River[C] on the twelfth day of the first
month to go to Jerusalem. We were
strengthened by our God,[G] and He
protected us from the power of the
enemy and from ambush along the
way. 32 So we arrived at Jerusalem
and rested there for three days. 33 On
the fourth day the silver, the gold,
and the articles were weighed out
in the house of our God into the
care of Meremoth the priest, son of
Uriah. Eleazar son of Phinehas was
with him. The Levites Jozabad son
of Jeshua and Noadiah son of Binnui
were also with them. 34 Everything
was verified by number and weight,
and the total weight was recorded at
that time.

35 The exiles who had returned
from the captivity offered •burnt offerings to the God of Israel: 12 bulls
for all Israel, 96 rams, and 77 lambs,
along with 12 male goats as a •sin offering. All this was a burnt offering
for the LORD. 36 They also delivered
the king's edicts to the royal satraps
and governors of the region west of
the Euphrates, so that they would
support the people and the house of
God.

Israel's Intermarriage with Pagans (9:1-15)

9 After these things had been
done, the leaders approached
me and said: "The people of Israel,

8:21-30 Because Ezra had boasted of God's goodness **to all who seek Him** and **anger . . . against all who abandon Him**, to ask for military protection would signal fear or a lack of confidence in God's power to protect them (v. 22). Ezra desired that God would be glorified in all that he did, and he trusted God to protect him. The writer notes that God **granted** their **request** for protection (v. 23). Later, Nehemiah did ask the king for a military escort, which gave evidence of God's provision for them, showing that God can work differently in similar situations in order to glorify Himself and to provide for His people. One situation brought glory to God for His protection, the other for His provision.

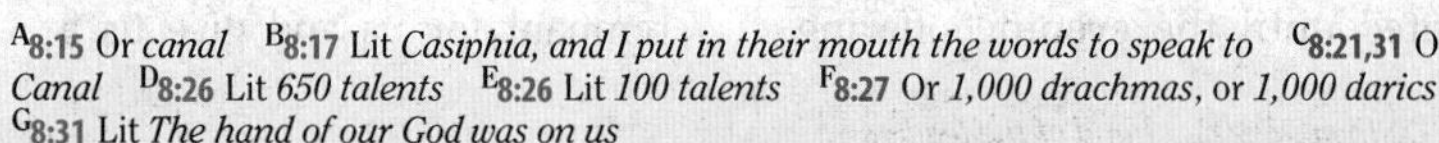
[A]**8:15** Or *canal* [B]**8:17** Lit *Casiphia, and I put in their mouth the words to speak to* [C]**8:21,31** Or *Canal* [D]**8:26** Lit *650 talents* [E]**8:26** Lit *100 talents* [F]**8:27** Or *1,000 drachmas*, or *1,000 darics* [G]**8:31** Lit *The hand of our God was on us*

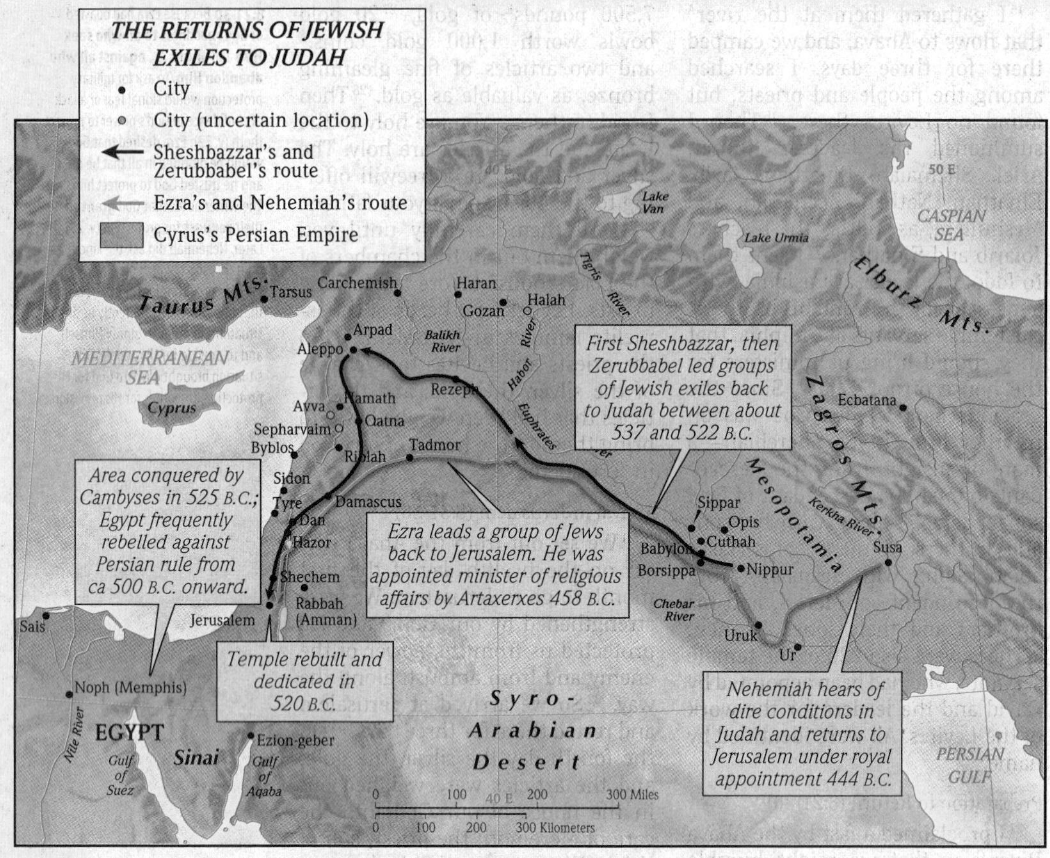

the priests, and the Levites have not separated themselves from the surrounding peoples whose detestable practices are like those of the Canaanites, Hittites, Perizzites, Jebusites, Ammonites, Moabites, Egyptians, and Amorites.
[2]Indeed, the Israelite men[A] have taken some of their daughters as wives for themselves and their sons, so that the holy •seed has become mixed with the surrounding peoples. The leaders[B] and officials have taken the lead in this unfaithfulness!"
[3]When I heard this report, I tore my tunic and robe, pulled out some of the hair from my head and beard, and sat down devastated.

[4]Everyone who trembled at the words of the God of Israel gathered around me, because of the unfaithfulness of the exiles, while I sat devastated until the evening offering.
[5]At the evening offering, I got up from my humiliation, with my tunic and robe torn. Then I fell on my knees and spread out my hands to •Yahweh my God.
[6]And I said:

My God, I am ashamed and embarrassed to lift my face toward You, my God, because our iniquities are higher than our heads and our •guilt is as high as the heavens.
[7]Our guilt has been terrible from the days of our fathers until the present. Because of our iniquities we have been handed over, along with our kings and priests, to the surrounding kings, and to the sword, captivity, plundering, and open shame, as it is today.
[8]But now, for a brief moment, grace has come from Yahweh our God to preserve a remnant for us and give us a

9:1-3 The **leaders** who had come with Ezra discovered **unfaithfulness** (Hb *ma'al*, literally, "an act of unfaithfulness," which was understood as a sin against God) among the Israelites in Jerusalem. The leaders who were already there were leading the people into sin. The people were adopting the **detestable practices** of the pagans who surrounded them and were even intermarrying with them (cp Dt 7:1-4). The first exiles knew how seriously God took sin since they had been taken into exile because of their unfaithfulness. Now, just 80 years after God had brought them back to Israel, the priests, Levites, and other leaders were moving in the same direction. These tragic verses illustrate how quickly sin can take hold in people. True followers of God will always be grieved for sin.

9:4–10:1 Ezra's actions in these verses are a model for any leader on how to deal with sin. Note that he did not give up or cast the sinners aside. He prayed for them and then confessed their sins to God. Ezra did exactly what God had instructed His people to do in 2Ch 7:14 by humbling himself and praying and seeking God's face.

[A]**9:2** Lit *they* [B]**9:2** Lit *hand of the leaders*

stake in His holy place. Even in
our slavery, God has given us
new life and light to our eyes.
9 Though we are slaves, our God
has not abandoned us in our
slavery. He has extended grace
to us in the presence of the
Persian kings, giving us new
life, so that we can rebuild the
house of our God and repair its
ruins, to give us a wall in Judah
and Jerusalem.

10 Now, our God, what can we
say in light of[A] this? For we
have abandoned the commands
11 You gave through Your servants the prophets, saying:
"The land you are entering to
possess is an impure land. The
surrounding peoples have filled
it from end to end with their
uncleanness by their impurity
and detestable practices. 12 So
do not give your daughters
to their sons in marriage or
take their daughters for your
sons. Never seek their peace or
prosperity, so that you will be
strong, eat the good things of
the land, and leave it as an inheritance to your sons forever."
13 After all that has happened
to us because of our evil deeds
and terrible guilt—though
You, our God, have punished us
less than our sins deserve and
have allowed us to survive[B]—
14 should we break Your commands again and intermarry
with the peoples who commit
these detestable practices?
Wouldn't You become so angry
with us that You would destroy
us, leaving no survivors? 15 LORD
God of Israel, You are righteous, for we survive as a remnant today. Here we are before
You with our guilt, though no
one can stand in Your presence
because of this.

Sending Away of Foreign Wives (10:1-17)

10 While Ezra prayed and confessed, weeping and falling
facedown before the house of God,
an extremely large assembly of Is-

HARD QUESTION

Are we responsible for confessing another's sin?

Although Ezra himself had not committed any of the sins he was confessing, he took responsibility for the people as their leader. Today, many have become numb to sin. They are no longer shocked by sin or willing to do something about it. However, Ezra was humiliated and devastated, trembling before the Lord when he heard what the Israelites were doing (9:4-15). He represented the people to the Lord and appealed to God's mercy: **Even in our slavery, God has given us new life and light to our eyes. Though we are slaves, our God has not abandoned us in our slavery. He has extended grace to us in the presence of the Persian kings, giving us new life, so that we can rebuild the house of our God and repair its ruins, to give us a wall in Judah and Jerusalem** (9:8-9). When people saw Ezra praying, they themselves were moved to repentance (10:1). As Ezra was driven to pray for his people, so, too, should believers be driven to pray over their sins and the sins of others. When was the last time you were so moved by sin towards God that you went to your knees in prayer? Unfortunately, women sometimes are guilty of gossiping instead of praying for a Christian sister or brother who is caught in sin. May we be women of God who react like Ezra for the sins of our nation!

raelite men, women, and children
gathered around him. The people
also wept bitterly. 2 Then Shecaniah
son of Jehiel, an Elamite, responded
to Ezra: "We have been unfaithful to
our God by marrying foreign wom-
en from the surrounding peoples,
but there is still hope for Israel in
spite of this. 3 Let us therefore make
a covenant before our God to send
away all the foreign wives and their
children, according to the counsel
of my lord and of those who tremble
at the command of our God. Let it
be done according to the law. 4 Get
up, for this matter is your responsibility, and we support you. Be strong
and take action!"

5 Then Ezra got up and made the
leading priests, Levites, and all Israel take an oath to do what had
been said; so they took the oath.
6 Ezra then went from the house of
God and walked to the chamber of
Jehohanan son of Eliashib, where
he spent the night.[C] He did not eat
food or drink water, because he was

10:2 The sin of **marrying foreign women** (cp. v. 10; Lv 26:40) precipitated the division of the kingdom after the reign of King Solomon, whose love of "many foreign women" also marked the spiritual decline of Judah under the following Davidic kings of Judah (1Kg 11:1-13). Intermarrying with **the surrounding peoples** not only threatened to adulterate the Israelite remnant's identity as the people whose God was Yahweh but also would have led to the replacement of this distinct people with an indistinct and syncretistic people (cp. Gn 12:1-3; Dt 7:6-7; Ps 106:34-47). Israel's separation from the pagan nations was intended to testify to their purity as God's holy nation.

10:3 The men in leadership carried out the plan thoroughly, in an orderly manner and **according to the law**, presumably Dt 24:1 (Ezr 10:16-18). In the concluding verses of this chapter, Ezra listed all those who had taken pagan wives; the number was more than 100. The mood was hopeful; yet only 13 years later Nehemiah would be faced with the same problem of mixed marriages (Neh 13:23-31).

A 9:10 Lit *say after* B 9:13 Lit *and gave us a remnant like this* C 10:6 1 Esdras 9:2, Syr; MT, Vg read *he went*

mourning over the unfaithfulness of
the exiles.
⁷They circulated a proclamation
throughout Judah and Jerusalem
that all the exiles should gather at
Jerusalem. ⁸Whoever did not come
within three days would forfeit all
his possessions,[A] according to the
decision of the leaders and elders,
and would be excluded from the assembly of the exiles.
⁹So all the men of Judah and Benjamin gathered in Jerusalem within
the three days. On the twentieth day
of the ninth month, all the people
sat in the square at the house of
God, trembling because of this matter and because of the heavy rain.
¹⁰Then Ezra the priest stood up and
said to them, "You have been unfaithful by marrying foreign women,
adding to Israel's •guilt. ¹¹Therefore,
make a confession to •Yahweh the
God of your fathers and do His will.
Separate yourselves from the surrounding peoples and your foreign
wives."
¹²Then all the assembly responded
with a loud voice: "Yes, we will do
as you say! ¹³But there are many
people, and it is the rainy season. We
don't have the stamina to stay out in
the open. This isn't something that
can be done in a day or two, for we
have rebelled terribly in this matter.
¹⁴Let our leaders represent the entire assembly. Then let all those in
our towns who have married foreign
women come at appointed times,
together with the elders and judges
of each town, in order to avert the
fierce anger of our God concerning[B]
this matter." ¹⁵Only Jonathan son of
Asahel and Jahzeiah son of Tikvah
opposed this, with Meshullam and
Shabbethai the Levite supporting
them.
¹⁶The exiles did what had been proposed. Ezra the priest selected men[C]
who were family leaders, all identified by name, to represent[D] their
ancestral houses. They convened on
the first day of the tenth month to
investigate the matter, ¹⁷and by the
first day of the first month they had
dealt with all the men who had married foreign women.

Those Married to Foreign Wives (10:18-44)

¹⁸The following were found to
have married foreign women from
the descendants of the priests:

from the descendants of
Jeshua son of Jozadak and his
brothers: Maaseiah, Eliezer,
Jarib, and Gedaliah. ¹⁹They
pledged[E] to send their wives
away, and being guilty, they
offered a ram from the flock
for their guilt;

HARD QUESTION

Did God condone divorce in Ezra 10?

Because God clearly says in His Word that He hates divorce (Mal 2:16), Ezra 10 is a difficult passage. From the beginning, marriage was designed to display the nature of God's covenant relationship with His people (Gn 2:24; Mt 19:6). Thus, for Israel to take pagan wives constituted adultery—treachery and injustice against God and His covenant—and was legitimate grounds for God to divorce His people (Ezr 10:2,10; cp. Is 50:1; Jr 3:8; Hs 2:2-13; 5:1-7). Israel realized that unless they took drastic measures, they were only one generation away from losing their distinctive identity as God's "holy people" (Hb *zeraʿ*, "seed," Ezr 9:2). Intermarriage within the nation of Israel would prevent Israel from maintaining unadulterated devotion to Yahweh, making God's preservation and restoration of the remnant to the promised land all for naught. Though sending away the pagan wives was a painful and tragic measure, Israel's leaders felt this action would show God their repentant hearts and, above all, preserve the remnant.

This drastic solution to Israel's sin in Ezra 10 is not meant to illustrate God's perspective on divorce; rather, it demonstrates the radical change expected in the lives of those entering a covenant relationship with God through Christ. Ezra 10 is not a didactic passage regarding marriage. Jesus clarified that Mosaic law merely *permitted* divorce "because of the hardness of your hearts" (Mt 19:3-9; cp. Dt 24:1). The New Testament clearly teaches Christians not to leave unbelieving spouses but to live in such a manner as to win them to Christ (1Co 7:12-16; 1Pt 3:1-7). Further, God commands believers not to marry unbelievers or be unequally yoked ("mismatched," 2Co 6:14) in the first place. As a marriage covenant establishes an exclusive relationship between a wife and her husband (Gn 2:24), so the new covenant in Christ's blood establishes between a believer and the Lord an exclusive relationship, which cannot allow compromise with sin (Lk 14:25-27; cp. Mt 5:29-30; Rm 6:2-7; 1Co 6:14-18; 2Co 5:17; Col 1:22; Heb 10:26).

[A]**10:8** Lit *would •set apart all his possessions for destruction* [B]**10:14** Some Hb mss, LXX, Vg; other Hb mss read *until* [C]**10:16** 1 Esdras 9:16, Syr; MT, Vg read *priest and men were selected* [D]**10:16** Lit *name, for* [E]**10:19** Lit *gave their hand*

>WORD|*study*

10:11 The command to separate (Hb *badal*) meant to "distinguish oneself" from what was unclean or unholy (Lv 10:10; 11:47; 20:25; Ezk 22:26). When applied to God's people, separation required imposing a concrete difference between those who belonged exclusively to the Lord and all other nations (Lv 20:24,26; cp. Gn 17:9-14). The purpose was not simply to create a "pure" racial or ethnic identity for Israel but to protect Israel's spiritual identity as the people of promise. For believers today, the "distinction between Jew and Greek" has been dissolved in Christ. For those who follow Christ, the command to "be holy" has a new dimension (see Eph 1:4,13; 1Pt 1:14-23; cp. Jr 31:31-34).

20 Hanani and Zebadiah from
Immer's descendants;
21 Maaseiah, Elijah, Shemaiah,
Jehiel, and Uzziah
from Harim's descendants;
22 Elioenai, Maaseiah, Ishmael,
Nethanel, Jozabad,
and Elasah from Pashhur's
descendants.

23 The Levites:

Jozabad, Shimei, Kelaiah
(that is Kelita), Pethahiah,
Judah, and Eliezer.

24 The singers:

Eliashib.

The gatekeepers:

Shallum, Telem, and Uri.

25 The Israelites:

Parosh's descendants:
Ramiah, Izziah, Malchijah,
Mijamin, Eleazar,
Malchijah,[A] and Benaiah;
26 Elam's descendants:
Mattaniah, Zechariah,
Jehiel, Abdi, Jeremoth,
and Elijah;
27 Zattu's descendants: Elioenai,
Eliashib, Mattaniah,
Jeremoth, Zabad, and Aziza;
28 Bebai's descendants:
Jehohanan, Hananiah,
Zabbai, and Athlai;
29 Bani's descendants:
Meshullam, Malluch,
Adaiah, Jashub, Sheal,
and Jeremoth;
30 Pahath-moab's descendants:
Adna, Chelal, Benaiah,
Maaseiah, Mattaniah,
Bezalel, Binnui,
and Manasseh;
31 Harim's descendants: Eliezer,
Isshijah, Malchijah,
Shemaiah, Shimeon,
32 Benjamin, Malluch, and
Shemariah;
33 Hashum's descendants:
Mattenai, Mattattah,
Zabad, Eliphelet, Jeremai,
Manasseh, and Shimei;

34 Bani's descendants: Maadai,
Amram, Uel, 35 Benaiah,
Bedeiah, Cheluhi, 36 Vaniah,
Meremoth, Eliashib,
37 Mattaniah, Mattenai, Jaasu,
38 Bani, Binnui, Shimei,
39 Shelemiah, Nathan, Adaiah,
40 Machnadebai, Shashai,
Sharai, 41 Azarel, Shelemiah,
Shemariah, 42 Shallum,
Amariah, and Joseph;
43 Nebo's descendants: Jeiel,
Mattithiah, Zabad, Zebina,
Jaddai, Joel, and Benaiah.

44 All of these had married foreign
women, and some of the wives had
given birth to children.

[A]**10:25** Some LXX mss, 1 Esdras 9:26 read *Hashabiah*

EZRA ... WRITTEN ON MY *Heart* Women—and men—who once could not stand before God because of their guilt have been restored to peace with Him through faith in Jesus Christ (Ezr 9:15; Rm 5:1). Like the restored remnant of Israel, may every believer demonstrate her thankfulness to God by zealously removing any unfaithfulness from her heart in honor of the One who reconciled her to Himself with His own blood (Rm 5:10).

Nehemiah

Timeline
- World Events
- Biblical Events

538 BC	538–457 BC	515 BC	486–465 BC
Cyrus's decree, allowing return of Jews from exile	Events in Ezra	Dedication of second temple	Events in Esther

"Come, let's rebuild Jerusalem's wall, so that we will no longer be a disgrace" (2:17).

Who wrote Nehemiah?

The first-person wording throughout the book suggests the scribe Nehemiah.

Who were the recipients?

The Israelites who had returned from exile to Jerusalem

When was Nehemiah written?

Between 430 and 424 B.C.

Where did it happen?

The main setting is the ruined city of Jerusalem, where Nehemiah leads a remnant of the Jewish people in rebuilding the city's walls.

What is Nehemiah about?

- The rebuilding of Jerusalem's walls as the last group of exiles returned
- The protection and empowerment God gives to those doing His will
- The leadership qualities required to endure hardship
- The power of personal prayer

Why should women read Nehemiah?

Thousands of insecure exiles were returning to the promised land. Extensive repairs were done on Jerusalem's demolished walls. During 52 days of constant labor, dozens of enemies were spreading insults, rumors, and death threats. A few men were attempting to cause dissension among God's people. In the midst of these challenging conditions, Nehemiah was one leader with a single vision and one great God, leading the nation of Israel to rebuild the city walls. This lone leader is a picture of the character and faith that every woman of God must have if she is to make an effective and enduring impact in His kingdom.

How do you read Nehemiah?

This book is in narrative form and contains the longest first-person account found in Scripture. The book of Nehemiah is part of the Writings (*Kethuvim*) in the Hebrew Bible where it was originally grouped with Ezra as one book. Some sources identified Ezra and Nehemiah as 1 Ezra and 2 Ezra. The books of Ezra and Nehemiah should be read together, as each provides an important historical and theological account of postexilic Israel.

Outline

I. The Rebuilding of the Wall (1:1–6:19)
   - A. Nehemiah's Concern over Jerusalem (1:1–2:10)
   - B. Nehemiah's Inspection of the Walls (2:11-20)
   - C. The Efforts to Rebuild the Walls (3:1-32)
   - D. The Opposition to Rebuilding the Walls (4:1–6:14)
   - E. The Completion of the Walls (6:15-19)

II. The Restoration of the People (7:1–12:47)
   - A. The First Exiles Return (7:1-73)
   - B. The Revival Among the People (8:1–9:38)
   - C. The Sealing of the Covenant (10:1-39)
   - D. The Repopulation of Jerusalem (11:1–12:26)
   - E. The Dedication of the Walls (12:27-47)

III. The Reforms of Nehemiah (13:1-31)

>WORD|*study*

Title Nehemiah (Hb, "Yahweh has compassion"), the book's main character, played an instrumental role in leading God's people after their return from captivity in Babylon. As **the king's cupbearer** (1:11), Nehemiah tested the drink of the king to ensure it had not been poisoned. Because this position provided constant access to the king, it often included great influence. Nehemiah's compassion for the remnant of Jews in Jerusalem marks him as a great leader, as does his prayer for God to **have compassion** [Hb *racham*, "love, pity, be merciful, show favor"] **on him** in the king's **presence** (1:11). The Hebrew words for "bowels" (rachamim) and "womb" (rechem) come from the same root as "compassion," indicating the word's origin in the physical experience of feeling with and for others. One of the Greek words translated as "compassion" in the New Testament—*splagchnizomai* ("have the bowels yearn," i.e., "feel sympathy or pity, be moved with compassion," Mt 9:36; 14:14)—is used specifically to describe Jesus' emotions when He saw people in need (e.g., Mt 15:32).

458 BC	446 BC	445 BC	445 BC	445 BC
Ezra's journey from Babylon to Jerusalem	Hanani's report to Nehemiah about the deplorable conditions in Jerusalem	Nehemiah's request of Artaxerxes to return to Jerusalem	Rebuilding of Jerusalem's walls under Nehemiah's leadership in six weeks	Ezra's leadership of a study of the law of Moses in Jerusalem

The Rebuilding of the Wall (1:1–6:19)

Nehemiah's Concern over Jerusalem (1:1–2:10)

1 The words of Nehemiah son of
Hacaliah:
During the month of Chislev[A] in
the twentieth year,[B] when I was in
the fortress city of Susa, 2 Hanani,
one of my brothers, arrived with
men from Judah, and I questioned
them about Jerusalem and the Jewish remnant that had survived the
exile. 3 They said to me, "The remnant in the province, who survived
the exile, are in great trouble and
disgrace. Jerusalem's wall has been
broken down, and its gates have
been burned down."
4 When I heard these words, I sat
down and wept. I mourned for a
number of days, fasting and praying
before the God of heaven. 5 I said,

•Yahweh, the God of heaven,
the great and awe-inspiring
God who keeps His gracious
covenant with those who love
Him and keep His commands,
6 let Your eyes be open and Your
ears be attentive to hear Your
servant's prayer that I now
pray to You day and night for
Your servants, the Israelites. I
confess the sins[C] we have committed against You. Both I and
my father's house have sinned.
7 We have acted corruptly toward You and have not kept the
commands, statutes, and ordinances You gave Your servant
Moses. 8 Please remember what
You commanded Your servant
Moses: "If you are unfaithful, I
will scatter you among the peoples. 9 But if you return to Me
and carefully observe My commands, even though your exiles were banished to the ends
of the earth,[D] I will gather them
from there and bring them to
the place where I chose to have
My name dwell." 10 They are
Your servants and Your people.
You redeemed them by Your
great power and strong hand.
11 Please, Lord, let Your ear be
attentive to the prayer of Your
servant and to that of Your
servants who delight to revere
Your name. Give Your servant
success today, and have compassion on him in the presence
of this man.[E]

At the time, I was the king's cupbearer.

2 During the month of Nisan[F] in
the twentieth year of King Artaxerxes, when wine was set before
him, I took the wine and gave it to
the king. I had never been sad in his
presence, 2 so the king said to me,
"Why are you[G] sad, when you aren't
sick? This is nothing but depression."[H]
I was overwhelmed with fear 3 and
replied to the king, "May the king
live forever! Why should I[I] not be
sad when the city where my ancestors are buried lies in ruins and its
gates have been destroyed by fire?"
4 Then the king asked me, "What is
your request?"
So I prayed to the God of heav-
en 5 and answered the king, "If it
pleases the king, and if your servant
has found favor with you, send me

1:1-3 The book opens around 445 B.C., approximately 13 years after Ezra's return (Ezr 7:7) and **the twentieth year** in the reign of King Artaxerxes I, the son of King Ahasuerus (Xerxes 1), who made Esther his queen (Est 1:1-2; 2:15-17). The month of **Chislev** was between November and December. Although an estimated 50,000 Jews returned to Judea, many remained behind in the Persian Empire. At this point, the number of Israelites had dwindled, and they had become scattered among the nations.

1:2-3 Since the strength of a city's walls symbolized the strength of that people's god, people around the city of **Jerusalem** would see its **broken down** walls as a sign that the God of Israel had abandoned them. A city without walls was defenseless and too dangerous for occupation. Even more disappointing, this news meant that the expected time of restoration had not yet come, and the Lord had not yet fulfilled His promise given through the prophets.

1:4 Upon hearing of his people's distress, Nehemiah **wept**, prayed, and fasted. Nehemiah's practice of prayer provides many lessons. He considered God to be his most trusted advisor and turned directly to Him. Not only did Nehemiah attribute the current condition of his people and his homeland to his own sin, but he took responsibility for the sins of the entire Israelite nation. Nehemiah understood that he could not separate himself from his nation and yearned for the restoration and holiness of all God's people. Amidst mounting frustrations, he turned away from reacting in anger and toward trusting God in prayer. Nehemiah realized his place before God, the power that comes from God, and the peace that flows from an intimate prayer life.

2:1 Nehemiah prayed for four months before he approached the king to seek his help.

2:2 Nehemiah violated the rules of the Susa court by appearing **sad** in the king's presence. Had his sadness been interpreted as displeasure with the

[A]1:1 = November–December [B]1:1 Artaxerxes reigned 465–425 B.C. [C]1:6 Lit *sins of the Israelites* [D]1:9 Lit *skies* [E]1:11 = the king [F]2:1 = March–April; called Abib in the pre-exilic period; Ex 13:4; Dt 16:1 [G]2:2 Lit *Why is your face* [H]2:2 Lit *sadness of heart* [I]2:3 Lit *my face*

king, Nehemiah could have been put to death immediately. By asking the king for help, Nehemiah was asking Artaxerxes to overturn his own edict, which had stopped the work in the first place (see Ezr 4:19-22).

2:8 With no idea how extensive the damage would be when he got to Jerusalem, Nehemiah prepared by asking the king for materials for building. City walls were invariably massive, averaging 15 feet thick and 25 feet high. Others had attempted **to rebuild** the walls of Jerusalem but failed. However, Nehemiah had a vision for the run-down city. God enabled him to see possibilities in a task that seemed impossible.

2:10 Under subsequent Babylonian rule, Jerusalem and parts of Judah were assigned to Samaria's governance. **Sanballat**, a **Horonite** of mixed ancestry, governed parts of Judah from Samaria (i.e., the land belonging to the northern kingdom of Israel until the Assyrian conquest). **Tobiah** (Hb, "Yahweh is gracious") was the governor of the Persian-controlled Transjordan. Both Sanballat and Tobiah followed syncretistic religions of the area and no doubt saw Nehemiah's arrival as a threat to their authority over the region.

2:11-16 Before he called a meeting to share his vision, Nehemiah investigated the damage, evaluating the work that needed to be done. When Nehemiah decided to share his vision, he shared it with people who could accomplish it—the **priests, nobles, and officials**. Nehemiah realized if he could get the leaders to support him, then others would follow.

to Judah and to the city where my
ancestors are buried,[A] so that I may
rebuild it."
[6] The king, with the queen seated
beside him, asked me, "How long
will your journey take, and when
will you return?" So I gave him a
definite time, and it pleased the king
to send me.
[7] I also said to the king: "If it pleases the king, let me have letters written to the governors of the region
west of the Euphrates River, so that
they will grant me safe passage until I reach Judah. [8] And let me have
a letter written to Asaph, keeper of
the king's forest, so that he will give
me timber to rebuild the gates of
the temple's fortress, the city wall,
and the home where I will live."[B]
The king granted my requests, for I
was graciously strengthened by my
God.[C]
[9] I went to the governors of the region west of the Euphrates and gave
them the king's letters. The king
had also sent officers of the infantry
and cavalry with me. [10] When Sanballat the Horonite and Tobiah the
Ammonite official heard that someone had come to seek the well-being
of the Israelites, they were greatly
displeased.

Nehemiah's Inspection of the Walls (2:11-20)

[11] After I arrived in Jerusalem and
had been there three days, [12] I got
up at night and took a few men
with me. I didn't tell anyone what
my God had laid on my heart to do
for Jerusalem. The only animal I
took[D] was the one I was riding. [13] I
went out at night through the Valley Gate toward the Serpent's[E] Well
and the Dung Gate, and I inspected
the walls of Jerusalem that had been
broken down and its gates that had
been destroyed by fire. [14] I went on
to the Fountain Gate and the King's
Pool, but farther down it became
too narrow for my animal to go
through. [15] So I went up at night by
way of the valley and inspected the
wall. Then heading back, I entered
through the Valley Gate and returned. [16] The officials did not know
where I had gone or what I was doing, for I had not yet told the Jews,
priests, nobles, officials, or the rest
of those who would be doing the
work. [17] So I said to them, "You see
the trouble we are in. Jerusalem
lies in ruins and its gates have been
burned down. Come, let's rebuild
Jerusalem's wall, so that we will no
longer be a disgrace." [18] I told them
how the gracious hand of my God
had been on me, and what the king
had said to me.

They said, "Let's start rebuilding," and they were encouraged[F] to do this good work.

[A] **2:5** Lit *city, the house of the graves of my fathers,* [B] **2:8** Lit *enter* [C] **2:8** Lit *for the gracious hand of my God was on me* [D] **2:12** Lit *animal with me* [E] **2:13** Or *Dragon's* [F] **2:18** Lit *they put their hands*

Biblical Womanhood A Woman's Attitude

Nehemiah discovered three important truths about one's attitude in managing opposition. First, he must have known that attitude is a choice. He determined that no matter what the circumstances were, he had control over his own attitude. Second, his attitude determined his actions. When his intentions were questioned by Sanballat (chap. 2) and various intimidation tactics were used (chap. 6), Nehemiah responded by reaffirming his faith in God rather than become defensive. Despite his struggles with disappointment and even despair, Nehemiah remained devoted to the task and refused to allow the opposition to distract him from the work God had given him to do, often not even answering his critics. Finally, Nehemiah demonstrates that people will mirror the attitude of their leader. The way Nehemiah reacted to the threats and insults of his enemies had a huge impact on the people whom he was leading in the rebuilding of the wall. He could either inspire confidence or elicit cowardice from the people. He could show them compassion or cruelty. Nehemiah utilized the tool of a positive and resourceful attitude to inspire the people of Jerusalem and quieten their enemies.

19 When Sanballat the Horonite, Tobiah the Ammonite official, and Geshem the Arab heard about this, they mocked and despised us, and said, "What is this you're doing? Are you rebelling against the king?"

20 I gave them this reply, "The God of heaven is the One who will grant us success. We, His servants, will start building, but you have no share, right, or historic claim in Jerusalem."

The Efforts to Rebuild the Walls (3:1-32)

3 Eliashib the high priest and his fellow priests began rebuilding the Sheep Gate. They dedicated it and installed its doors. After building the wall to the Tower of the Hundred and the Tower of Hananel, they dedicated it. 2 The men of Jericho built next to Eliashib, and next to them Zaccur son of Imri built.

3 The sons of Hassenaah built the Fish Gate. They built it with beams and installed its doors, bolts, and bars. 4 Next to them Meremoth son of Uriah, son of Hakkoz, made repairs. Beside them Meshullam son of Berechiah, son of Meshezabel, made repairs. Next to them Zadok son of Baana made repairs. 5 Beside them the Tekoites made repairs, but their nobles did not lift a finger to help[A] their supervisors.

6 Joiada son of Paseah and Meshullam son of Besodeiah repaired the Old[B] Gate. They built it with beams and installed its doors, bolts, and bars. 7 Next to them the repairs were done by Melatiah the Gibeonite, Jadon the Meronothite, and the men of Gibeon and Mizpah, who were under the authority[C] of the governor of the region west of the Euphrates River. 8 After him Uzziel son of Harhaiah, the goldsmith, made repairs, and next to him Hananiah son of the perfumer made repairs. They restored Jerusalem as far as the Broad Wall.

9 Next to them Rephaiah son of Hur, ruler over half the district of Jerusalem, made repairs. 10 After them Jedaiah son of Harumaph made repairs across from his house. Next to him Hattush the son of Hashabneiah made repairs. 11 Malchijah son of Harim and Hasshub son of Pahath-moab made repairs to another section, as well as to the Tower of the Ovens. 12 Beside him Shallum son of Hallohesh, ruler over half the district of Jerusalem, made repairs—he and his daughters.

13 Hanun and the inhabitants of Zanoah repaired the Valley Gate. They rebuilt it and installed its doors, bolts, and bars, and repaired 500 yards[D] of the wall to the Dung Gate. 14 Malchijah son of Rechab, ruler over the district of Beth-haccherem, repaired the Dung Gate. He rebuilt it and installed its doors, bolts, and bars.

15 Shallun[E] son of Col-hozeh, ruler over the district of Mizpah, repaired the Fountain Gate. He rebuilt it and roofed it. Then he installed its doors, bolts, and bars. He also made repairs to the wall of the Pool of Shelah near the king's garden, as far as the stairs that descend from the city of David.

16 After him Nehemiah son of Azbuk, ruler over half the district of Beth-zur, made repairs up to a point opposite the tombs of David, as far as the artificial pool and the House of the Warriors. 17 Next to him the Levites made repairs under Rehum son of Bani. Beside him Hashabiah, ruler over half the district of Keilah, made repairs for his district. 18 After him their fellow Levites made repairs under Binnui[F] son of Henadad, ruler over half the district of Keilah. 19 Next to him Ezer son of Jeshua, ruler over Mizpah, made repairs to another section opposite the ascent to the armory at the Angle.

20 After him Baruch son of Zabbai[G] diligently repaired another section, from the Angle to the door of the house of Eliashib the high priest. 21 Beside him Meremoth son of Uriah, son of Hakkoz, made repairs to another section, from the door of Eliashib's house to the end of his house. 22 And next to him the priests

2:18-19 Regardless of Nehemiah's preparation, unexpected problems were bound to occur, but the way Nehemiah handled those problems displayed his faith in God. Throughout the story, those who opposed Nehemiah ridiculed him, plotted to kill him, and challenged his character. He was mocked, accused of sedition, and his motives for rebuilding the wall were questioned. Yet, Nehemiah refused to participate in the slander or to become sidetracked by fear and hesitation. He responded by declaring that God would give them success in their endeavor to build the wall.

3:1-32 Nehemiah was able to motivate a diverse group by assigning them to sections close to their homes if they lived in or near Jerusalem or by giving them responsibility over specific sections. This decision demonstrates careful planning and great organizational ability.

3:1 Over 40 sections of **the wall** are specifically mentioned. The first section was attended to by **Eliashib** the high priest, the son of Joiakim and grandson of Jeshua (12:10-11), who traveled with Zerubbabel and the first group of exiles to Jerusalem. He led a group of priests to rebuild the **Sheep Gate,** the area where sheep were brought to be sacrificed, and the wall up to the **Tower of the Hundred** and the **Tower of Hananel.** This northern section of the wall was nearest to the temple, and the towers were especially important for defensive purposes.

3:3-12 The Fish Gate was located on the western corner of the north wall and was so named because fish were brought in from the Mediterranean Sea and the Jordan River to this area. The western section included the **Old Gate** (v. 6), the **Broad Wall** (v. 8), and the **Tower of the Ovens** (v. 11). The Old (Hb *Yeshanah*) Gate was also known as the Jeshanah Gate, the village near Bethel toward which the Gate pointed. The Broad Wall was located on the northwest corner near the Gate of Ephraim (see also 12:38).

3:13-32 The southern and eastern sections of the wall were addressed with the same care and attention to detail as the other sections. The eastern section, measuring about 1,400 yards, was longer than the western section. It contained five gates; however, only the Fountain Gate is specifically mentioned as needing repair, perhaps because this section of the wall incurred less damage. Its location on the top of a hill may have shielded it from invaders.

[A]**3:5** Lit *not bring their neck to the work of* [B]**3:6** Or *Jeshanah* [C]**3:7** Or *Mizpah, the seat* [D]**3:13** Lit *1,000 cubits* [E]**3:15** Some Hb mss, Syr read *Shallum* [F]**3:18** Some Hb mss, Syr, LXX; Neh 3:24; other Hb mss, Vg read *Bavvai* [G]**3:20** Alt Hb tradition, Vg read *Zaccai*; Ezr 2:9

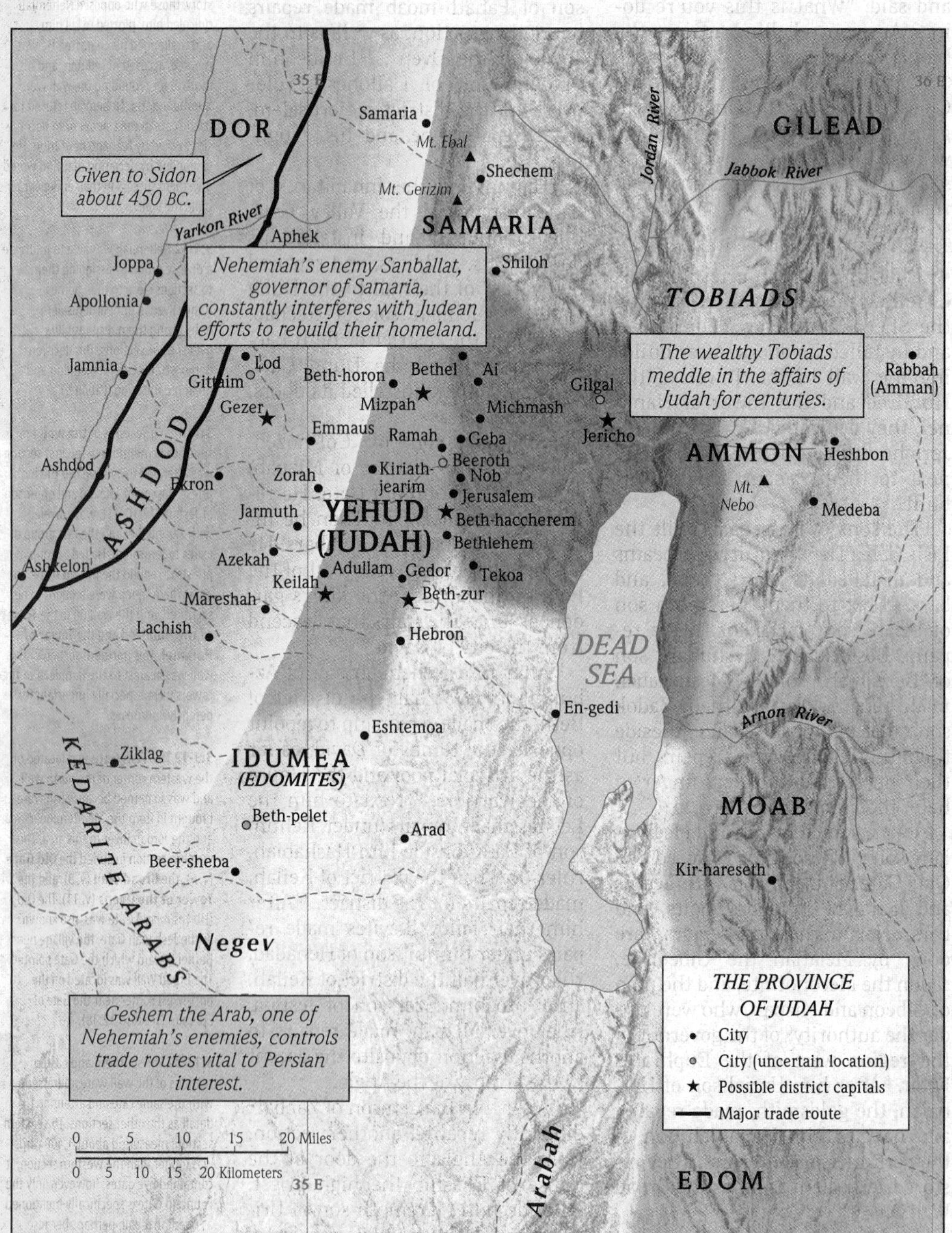

The Province of Judah and Nehemiah's Enemies in the Fifth Century

from the surrounding area made repairs.

23 After them Benjamin and Hasshub made repairs opposite their house. Beside them Azariah son of Maaseiah, son of Ananiah, made repairs beside his house. 24 After him Binnui son of Henadad made repairs to another section, from the house of Azariah to the Angle and the corner. 25 Palal son of Uzai made repairs opposite the Angle and tower that juts out from the upper palace[A] of the king, by the courtyard of the guard. Beside him Pedaiah son of Parosh, 26 and the temple servants living on Ophel[B] made repairs opposite the Water Gate toward the east and the tower that juts out. 27 Next to him the Tekoites made repairs to another section from a point opposite the great tower that juts out, as far as the wall of Ophel.

28 Each of the priests made repairs above the Horse Gate, each opposite his own house. 29 After them Zadok son of Immer made repairs opposite his house. And beside him Shemaiah son of Shecaniah, guard of the East Gate, made repairs. 30 Next to him Hananiah son of Shelemiah and Hanun the sixth son of Zalaph made repairs to another section.

After them Meshullam son of Berechiah made repairs opposite his room. 31 Next to him Malchijah, one of the goldsmiths, made repairs to the house of the temple servants and the merchants, opposite the Inspection[C] Gate, and as far as the upper room of the corner. 32 The goldsmiths and merchants made repairs between the upper room of the corner and the Sheep Gate.

Progress Despite of Opposition (4:1-14)

4 [D] When Sanballat heard that we were rebuilding the wall, he became furious. He mocked the Jews 2 before his colleagues and the powerful men[E] of Samaria, and said, "What are these pathetic Jews doing? Can they restore it by themselves? Will they offer sacrifices? Will they ever finish it? Can they bring these burnt stones back to life from the mounds of rubble?" 3 Then Tobiah the Ammonite, who was beside him, said, "Indeed, even if a fox climbed up what they are building, he would break down their stone wall!"

4 Listen, our God, for we are despised. Make their insults return on their own heads and let them be taken as plunder to a land of captivity. 5 Do not cover their •guilt or let their sin be erased from Your sight, because they have provoked[F] the builders.

6 So we rebuilt the wall until the entire wall was joined together up to half its height, for the people had the will to keep working.

7 [G]When Sanballat, Tobiah, and the Arabs, Ammonites, and Ashdodites heard that the repair to the walls of Jerusalem was progressing and that the gaps were being closed, they became furious. 8 They all plotted together to come and fight against Jerusalem and throw it into confusion. 9 So we prayed to our God and stationed a guard because of them day and night.

10 In Judah, it was said:[H]

> The strength of the laborer
> fails,
> since there is so much rubble.
> We will never be able
> to rebuild the wall.

11 And our enemies said, "They won't know or see anything until we're among them and can kill them and stop the work." 12 When the Jews who lived nearby arrived, they said to us time and again,[I] "Everywhere you turn, they attack[J] us." 13 So I stationed people behind the lowest sections of the wall, at the vulnerable areas. I stationed them by families with their swords, spears, and bows. 14 After I made an inspection, I stood up and said to the nobles, the officials, and the rest of the people, "Don't be afraid of them. Remember the great and awe-inspiring Lord, and fight for your countrymen, your sons and daughters, your wives and homes."

3:26-27 Ophel (Hb, "fat; bulge or mound," cp. 2Ch 27:3), the hill just south of Mount Moriah, served as the living quarters for some of the workers rebuilding the wall. It was located just outside the city wall between the City of David and the temple area.

The Water Gate was used to bring water into the city

3:28 Among the city gates listed, **The Horse Gate** was one Jeremiah had promised would be rebuilt (cp. Jr 31:40).

3:31 The Inspection Gate (Hb *miphkad*, "review or registry") was the gate through which strangers to Jerusalem gained entry to the city.

4:1-14 With the people's progress came their rivals' resistance. Sanballat, along with the **Ashdodites**, residents of a former Philistine town (v. 7), attacked the workers by mocking the Israelites who worked on the task, calling them **pathetic** (Hb, "withering or fading," v. 2), plotting to attack the Israelites and create confusion (v. 8), spreading rumors (v. 10), and even planning to kill them (v. 11). Nehemiah knew that if his people were focused on their enemies instead of the project God had given them to do, nothing would be accomplished. With each new attack, Nehemiah prayed to the Lord for help (vv. 4-5,9). As Nehemiah did, you can persevere through troubling times when you refuse to take your focus off God.

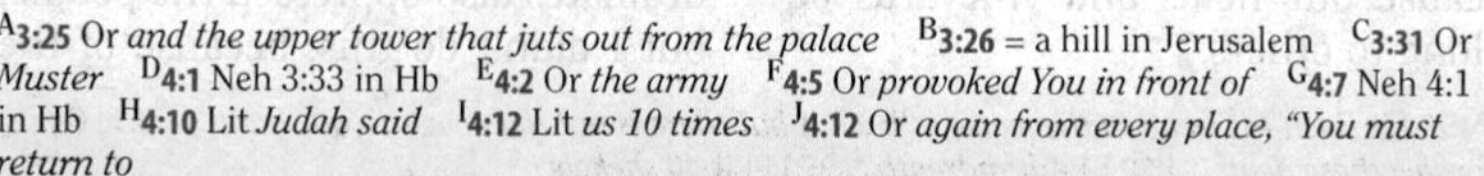

[A]**3:25** Or *and the upper tower that juts out from the palace* [B]**3:26** = a hill in Jerusalem [C]**3:31** Or *Muster* [D]**4:1** Neh 3:33 in Hb [E]**4:2** Or *the army* [F]**4:5** Or *provoked You in front of* [G]**4:7** Neh 4:1 in Hb [H]**4:10** Lit *Judah said* [I]**4:12** Lit *us 10 times* [J]**4:12** Or *again from every place, "You must return to*

4:15 God indeed was fighting for the Israelites, whose courage was a testimony to their enemies about their faith in Him.

4:16-23 The people's faithful perseverance in the face of opposition is an encouragement for all the people of God not to grow weary in doing good (Gl 6:9). Perseverance, along with the discernment to know when to persevere, are key attributes for the believer.

5:1-5 The Jewish people faced economic challenges as food became scarce and Jewish rulers were exacting a heavy **tax** upon them. Evidently, the Jews who were not able to pay the tax were forced into **slavery** or forced to put members of their family into slavery to cover their debts. The plight of the children, especially their **daughters**, is noted as being difficult.

5:6-10 The people participating in usury and **lending** brought reproach on the Israelite people because Gentiles would see the hypocrisy in their actions. Nehemiah confessed his own part in this situation, admitting to lending money and **charging . . . interest**, and he called for immediate repentance. Deuteronomy 23:19-20 indicated that God would bless those Jews who did not charge their fellow Jews interest when lending food, money, or anything else. The people agreed to do as Nehemiah asked, even returning **the percentage of the money, grain**, etc. that had been charged to the people. This would have been "the hundredth part" or about 12 percent, which would have been the annual interest rate charged.

5:14-19 Nehemiah was focused on supporting the community and not his own personal gain. As the appointed governor over Judah, he chose not to take advantage of his food allotment and never once required the people to pay an additional tax to support him in his governmental office. He even bore some of his position's necessary expenses himself rather than burden the people (vv. 17-19).

Sword and Trowel (4:15-23)

[15] When our enemies heard that we knew their scheme and that God had frustrated it, every one of us returned to his own work on the wall. [16] From that day on, half of my men did the work while the other half held spears, shields, bows, and armor. The officers supported all the people of Judah, [17] who were rebuilding the wall. The laborers who carried the loads worked with one hand and held a weapon with the other. [18] Each of the builders had his sword strapped around his waist while he was building, and the trumpeter was beside me. [19] Then I said to the nobles, the officials, and the rest of the people: "The work is enormous and spread out, and we are separated far from one another along the wall. [20] Wherever you hear the trumpet sound, rally to us there. Our God will fight for us!" [21] So we continued the work, while half of the men were holding spears from daybreak until the stars came out. [22] At that time, I also said to the people, "Let everyone and his servant spend the night inside Jerusalem, so that they can stand guard by night and work by day." [23] And I, my brothers, my men, and the guards with me never took off our clothes. Each carried his weapon, even when washing.[A]

Social Injustice (5:1-13)

5 There was a widespread outcry from the people and their wives against their Jewish countrymen. [2] Some were saying, "We, our sons, and our daughters are numerous. Let us get grain so that we can eat and live." [3] Others were saying, "We are mortgaging our fields, vineyards, and homes to get grain during the famine." [4] Still others were saying, "We have borrowed money to pay the king's tax on our fields and vineyards. [5] We and our children are just like our countrymen and their children, yet we are subjecting our sons and daughters to slavery. Some of our daughters are already enslaved, but we are powerless[B] because our fields and vineyards belong to others."

[6] I became extremely angry when I heard their outcry and these complaints. [7] After seriously considering the matter, I accused the nobles and officials, saying to them, "Each of you is charging his countrymen interest." So I called a large assembly against them [8] and said, "We have done our best to buy back our Jewish countrymen who were sold to foreigners, but now you sell your own countrymen, and we have to buy them back." They remained silent and could not say a word. [9] Then I said, "What you are doing isn't right. Shouldn't you walk in the •fear of our God and not invite the reproach of our foreign enemies? [10] Even I, as well as my brothers and my servants, have been lending them money and grain. Please, let us stop charging this interest.[C] [11] Return their fields, vineyards, olive groves, and houses to them immediately, along with the percentage[D] of the money, grain, new wine, and olive oil that you have been assessing them."

[12] They responded: "We will return these things and require nothing more from them. We will do as you say."

So I summoned the priests and made everyone take an oath to do this. [13] I also shook the folds of my robe and said, "May God likewise shake from his house and property everyone who doesn't keep this promise. May he be shaken out and have nothing!"

The whole assembly said, "•Amen," and they praised the LORD. Then the people did as they had promised.

Good and Bad Governors (5:14-19)

[14] Furthermore, from the day King Artaxerxes appointed me to be their governor in the land of Judah—from the twentieth year until his thirty-second year, 12 years—I and my associates never ate from the food allotted to the governor. [15] The governors who preceded me had heavily burdened the people, taking food and wine from them, as well as a pound[E] of silver. Their subordinates also oppressed the people, but I didn't do this, because of the

[A] 4:23 Lit *Each his weapon the water* [B] 5:5 Lit *but there is not the power in our hand* [C] 5:10 Or *us forgive these debts* [D] 5:11 Lit *hundredth* [E] 5:15 Lit *40 shekels*

fear of God. 16 Instead, I devoted myself to the construction of the wall,
and all my subordinates were gathered there for the work. We didn't
buy any land.
17 There were 150 Jews and officials, as well as guests from the
surrounding nations at my table.
18 Each[A] day, one ox, six choice
sheep, and some fowl were prepared
for me. An abundance of all kinds
of wine was provided every 10 days.
But I didn't demand the food allotted to the governor, because the
burden on the people was so heavy.
19 Remember me favorably, my
God, for all that I have done for this
people.

Attempts to Discourage the Builders (6:1-9)

6 When Sanballat, Tobiah, Geshem
the Arab, and the rest of our enemies heard that I had rebuilt the
wall and that no gap was left in
it—though at that time I had not
installed the doors in the gates—
2 Sanballat and Geshem sent me a
message: "Come, let's meet together
in the villages of[B] the Ono Valley."
But they were planning to harm me.
3 So I sent messengers to them,
saying, "I am doing a great work
and cannot come down. Why should
the work cease while I leave it and
go down to you?" 4 Four times they
sent me the same proposal, and I
gave them the same reply.
5 Sanballat sent me this same message a fifth time by his aide, who had
an open letter in his hand. 6 In it was
written:

> It is reported among the na-
> tions—and Geshem[C] agrees—
> that you and the Jews plan to
> rebel. This is the reason you are
> building the wall. According to
> these reports, you are to be-
> come their king 7 and have even
> set up the prophets in Jerusa-
> lem to proclaim on your be-
> half: "There is a king in Judah."
> These rumors will be heard by
> the king. So come, let's confer
> together.

8 Then I replied to him, "There is
nothing to these rumors you are
spreading; you are inventing them
in your own mind." 9 For they were
all trying to intimidate us, saying,
"They will become discouraged[D] in
the work, and it will never be finished."
But now, my God, strengthen me.[E]

Attempts to Intimidate Nehemiah (6:10-14)

10 I went to the house of Shemaiah
son of Delaiah, son of Mehetabel,
who was restricted to his house. He
said:

> Let us meet at the house
> of God
> inside the temple.
> Let us shut the temple doors
> because they are coming
> to kill you.
> They are coming to kill you
> tonight![F]

11 But I said, "Should a man like
me run away? How can I enter the
temple and live? I will not go." 12 I
realized that God had not sent him,
because of the prophecy he spoke
against me. Tobiah and Sanballat had hired him. 13 He was hired,
so that I would be intimidated, do
as he suggested, sin, and get a bad
reputation, in order that they could
discredit me.
14 My God, remember Tobiah and
Sanballat for what they have done,
and also Noadiah the prophetess and
the other prophets who wanted to
intimidate me.

The Completion of the Walls (6:15-19)

15 The wall was completed in 52
days, on the twenty-fifth day of the
month Elul. 16 When all our enemies
heard this, all the surrounding nations were intimidated and lost their
confidence,[G] for they realized that
this task had been accomplished by
our God.
17 During those days, the nobles of
Judah sent many letters to Tobiah,
and Tobiah's letters came to them.
18 For many in Judah were bound
by oath to him, since he was a son-
in-law of Shecaniah son of Arah,

6:1-13 As the project neared completion, Nehemiah's enemies continued their attempts to thwart the work. They attempted to distract Nehemiah (vv. 3-4), to discredit him with lies, slander, and **rumors** through **an open letter** (vv. 5-8), and to deceive him by setting traps with trusted countrymen (vv. 10-13).

6:3 Nehemiah refused to allow his critics to distract him from his calling. He did not even come down off the wall and leave the work but instead communicated that he would be undeterred.

6:10-11 When Sanballat tried to use one of his countrymen to trick Nehemiah to sin, Nehemiah refused to fall into temptation. He knew that by going **inside the temple**, he would be committing a sin since it was against Levitical law for anyone except the priests to go into the holy place. He refused to tarnish his integrity (6:13-14). Instead of getting frustrated and angry, Nehemiah answered accusations simply and went back to his work. Although Sanballat's lies attacked Nehemiah personally, Nehemiah chose to persist even in the face of the false accusations questioning his character.

6:14 The false **prophetess Noadiah** is not mentioned elsewhere in the Bible. She was one of the false prophets who tried to intimidate Nehemiah and deceive him into abandoning the work.

6:15-19 Israel's enemies recognized that finishing the wall only **52 days** after the work had begun was evidence that God had helped the workers (v. 16). Yet Nehemiah continued to face opposition. Tobiah, who had worked his way into the Jewish nation through intermarriage, had powerful influence within the Jewish community and continued to threaten and try to intimidate Nehemiah (v. 19).

[A] **5:18** Lit *And that which was prepared each* [B] **6:2** Or *together at Kephirim in* [C] **6:6** Lit *Gashmu* [D] **6:9** Lit *saying, "Their hands will fail* [E] **6:9** Lit *my hands* [F] **6:10** Or *by night* [G] **6:16** Lit *and fell greatly in their eyes*

7:1-73 Nehemiah's command to open **the gates of Jerusalem** only during the busiest hours of the day helped to minimize the threat to the city. Their adversaries would be less likely to invade when the city was full of people. In order to begin bringing residents into the city, Nehemiah initiated a census to determine which families could verify their lineage as full-blooded Jews. Nehemiah made use of the census list that Ezra utilized on the return of the first exiles with Sheshbazzar, Zerubbabel, and Jeshua around 537 B.C. (see Ezr 2). The list reproduced in Nehemiah 7 has only minor differences with Ezra's list.

and his son Jehohanan had married the daughter of Meshullam son
of Berechiah. 19 These nobles kept
mentioning Tobiah's good deeds to
me, and they reported my words to
him. And Tobiah sent letters to intimidate me.

The Restoration of the People (7:1–12:47)

The First Exiles Return (7:1-73)

7 When the wall had been rebuilt
and I had the doors installed, the
gatekeepers, singers, and Levites
were appointed. 2 Then I put my
brother Hanani in charge of Jerusalem, along with Hananiah, commander of the fortress, because he
was a faithful man who •feared God
more than most. 3 I said to them,
"Do not open the gates of Jerusalem until the sun is hot, and let
the doors be shut and securely fastened while the guards are on duty.
Station the citizens of Jerusalem
as guards, some at their posts and
some at their homes."
4 The city was large and spacious,
but there were few people in it, and
no houses had been built yet. 5 Then
my God put it into my mind to assemble the nobles, the officials, and
the people to be registered by genealogy. I found the genealogical record of those who came back first,
and I found the following written
in it:
6 These are the people of the province who went up among the captive
exiles deported by King Nebuchadnezzar of Babylon. Each of them
returned to Jerusalem and Judah,
to his own town. 7 They came with
Zerubbabel, Jeshua, Nehemiah,
Azariah, Raamiah, Nahamani, Mordecai, Bilshan, Mispereth, Bigvai,
Nehum, and Baanah.
The number of the Israelite men
included:

8 Parosh's descendants 2,172
9 Shephatiah's descendants 372
10 Arah's descendants 652
11 Pahath-moab's descendants: Jeshua's and Joab's descendants 2,818
12 Elam's descendants 1,254
13 Zattu's descendants 845
14 Zaccai's descendants 760
15 Binnui's descendants 648
16 Bebai's descendants 628
17 Azgad's descendants 2,322
18 Adonikam's descendants 667
19 Bigvai's descendants 2,067
20 Adin's descendants 655
21 Ater's descendants: of Hezekiah 98
22 Hashum's descendants 328
23 Bezai's descendants 324
24 Hariph's descendants 112
25 Gibeon's[A] descendants 95
26 Bethlehem's and Netophah's men 188
27 Anathoth's men 128
28 Beth-azmaveth's men 42
29 Kiriath-jearim's, Chephirah's, and Beeroth's men 743
30 Ramah's and Geba's men 621
31 Michmas's men 122
32 Bethel's and Ai's men 123
33 the other Nebo's men 52
34 the other Elam's people 1,254
35 Harim's people 320
36 Jericho's people 345
37 Lod's, Hadid's, and Ono's people 721
38 Senaah's people 3,930.

39 The priests included:

Jedaiah's descendants of the house of Jeshua 973
40 Immer's descendants 1,052
41 Pashhur's descendants 1,247
42 Harim's descendants 1,017.

43 The Levites included:

Jeshua's descendants: of Kadmiel
Hodevah's descendants 74.

44 The singers included:

•Asaph's descendants 148.

45 The gatekeepers included:

Shallum's descendants, Ater's descendants,
Talmon's descendants, Akkub's descendants,
Hatita's descendants, Shobai's descendants 138.

46 The temple servants included:

[A] 7:25 = Gibbar's in Ezr 2:20

Ziha's descendants,
Hasupha's descendants,
Tabbaoth's descendants,
47 Keros's descendants,
Sia's descendants,
Padon's descendants,
48 Lebanah's descendants,
Hagabah's descendants,
Shalmai's descendants,
49 Hanan's descendants,
Giddel's descendants,
Gahar's descendants,
50 Reaiah's descendants,
Rezin's descendants,
Nekoda's descendants,
51 Gazzam's descendants,
Uzza's descendants,
Paseah's descendants,
52 Besai's descendants,
Meunim's descendants,
Nephishesim's[A] descendants,
53 Bakbuk's descendants,
Hakupha's descendants,
Harhur's descendants,
54 Bazlith's descendants,
Mehida's descendants,
Harsha's descendants,
55 Barkos's descendants,
Sisera's descendants,
Temah's descendants,
56 Neziah's descendants,
Hatipha's descendants.

57 The descendants of Solomon's
servants included:

Sotai's descendants,
Sophereth's descendants,
Perida's descendants,
58 Jaala's descendants,
Darkon's descendants,
Giddel's descendants,
59 Shephatiah's descendants,
Hattil's descendants,
Pochereth-hazzebaim's
descendants,
Amon's descendants.

60 All the temple servants
and the descendants of
Solomon's servants 392.

61 The following are those who
came from Tel-melah, Tel-harsha,
Cherub, Addon, and Immer, but
were unable to prove that their families and ancestors were Israelite:

62 Delaiah's descendants,
Tobiah's descendants,
and Nekoda's
descendants 642

63 and from the priests: the descendants of Hobaiah, the descendants of
Hakkoz, and the descendants of Barzillai—who had taken a wife from
the daughters of Barzillai the Gileadite and was called by their name.
64 These searched for their entries in
the genealogical records, but they
could not be found, so they were
disqualified from the priesthood.
65 The governor ordered them not to
eat the most holy things until there
was a priest who could consult the
•Urim and Thummim.

66 The whole combined
assembly numbered 42,360
67 not including their 7,337
male and female slaves,
as well as their 245 male
and female singers.
68 They had 736 horses,
245 mules,[B]
69 435 camels,
and 6,720 donkeys.

70 Some of the family leaders gave
to the project. The governor gave
1,000 gold coins,[C] 50 bowls, and
530 priestly garments to the treasury. 71 Some of the family leaders
gave 20,000 gold coins and 2,200
silver minas[D] to the treasury for
the project. 72 The rest of the people
gave 20,000 gold coins, 2,000 silver
minas, and 67 priestly garments.
73 So the priests, Levites, gatekeepers, temple singers, some of the people, temple servants, and all Israel
settled in their towns.[E]

Public Reading of the Law (8:1-12)

When the seventh month came
and the Israelites had settled in their
8 towns,[1] all the people gathered
together at the square in front
of the Water Gate. They asked Ezra
the scribe to bring the book of the
law of Moses that the LORD had given
Israel. 2 On the first day of the seventh month, Ezra the priest brought
the law before the assembly of men,
women, and all who could listen

8:1-12 The first day of the seventh month was the traditional day that the Israelites celebrated the Feast of Trumpets (v. 2; cp. Lv 23:24). The modern-day celebration of *Rosh Hashanah* is traced back to this celebration.

8:1-5 When **Ezra** (see Ezra 7:1-10) gathered the people together for a public reading of the **book of the law of Moses**, he read for about five hours (**daybreak until noon**). As a sign of respect for God's Word, everyone **stood** up when Ezra opened the scroll upon which the law of Moses was written.

[A]**7:52** Alt Hb tradition reads *Nephushesim's* [B]**7:68** Some Hb mss, LXX; Ezr 2:66; other Hb mss omit v. 68 [C]**7:70** Or *drachmas*, or *darics*; also in vv. 71-72 [D]**7:71** A Babylonian coin worth 50 shekels [E]**7:73** The second half of v. 73 is better understood when placed with 8:1.

8:8-10 Since some of the Jews grew up in Babylon, they did not know Hebrew and may have been hearing it for the first time (see 13:24). The leaders not only translated the Scripture but also expounded on it. Their reaction was to mourn and weep, yet Nehemiah and the other leaders instructed the people not to mourn or weep because the Feast of Trumpets was a time of celebration. They were to receive strength from rejoicing in the Lord.

8:13-18 These days in Israel's history marked a great revival among the people. As often happens when people turn to God's Word, they became eager to follow the Lord.

8:17-18 Nehemiah notes that this feast had not been celebrated in quite the same way since the days of **Joshua son of Nun**. The people were not just going through the motions as some people do in modern Sunday worship services. God's Word was changing them. During this week-long celebration, Ezra continued to read and teach God's Word to the people.

9:1-2 Wearing **sackcloth** and putting **dust on their heads** signified deep distress. Sackcloth was a course garment of dark goat or camel hair. It had a rough texture that served as a means of physical discomfort, outwardly calling attention to the person's inner turmoil or grief. Additionally, the people broke off any alliances they had with **foreigners** or non-Jews as a sign of how seriously they were taking God's Word (see also Dt 23:3-8).

with understanding. 3 While he was facing the square in front of the Water Gate, he read out of it from daybreak until noon before the men, the women, and those who could understand. All the people listened attentively[A] to the book of the law. 4 Ezra the scribe stood on a high wooden platform made for this purpose. Mattithiah, Shema, Anaiah, Uriah, Hilkiah, and Maaseiah stood beside him on his right; to his left were Pedaiah, Mishael, Malchijah, Hashum, Hash-baddanah, Zechariah, and Meshullam. 5 Ezra opened the book in full view of all the people, since he was elevated above everyone. As he opened it, all the people stood up. 6 Ezra praised the LORD, the great God, and with their hands uplifted all the people said, "•Amen, Amen!" Then they bowed down and worshiped the LORD with their faces to the ground.

7 Jeshua, Bani, Sherebiah, Jamin, Akkub, Shabbethai, Hodiah, Maaseiah, Kelita, Azariah, Jozabad, Hanan, and Pelaiah, who were Levites,[B] explained the law to the people as they stood in their places. 8 They read out of the book of the law of God, translating and giving the meaning so that the people could understand what was read. 9 Nehemiah the governor, Ezra the priest and scribe, and the Levites who were instructing the people said to all of them, "This day is holy to the LORD your God. Do not mourn or weep." For all the people were weeping as they heard the words of the law. 10 Then he said to them, "Go and eat what is rich, drink what is sweet, and send portions to those who have nothing prepared, since today is holy to our Lord. Do not grieve, because the joy of the LORD is your stronghold." 11 And the Levites quieted all the people, saying, "Be still, since today is holy. Do not grieve." 12 Then all the people began to eat and drink, send portions, and have a great celebration, because they had understood the words that were explained to them.

Festival of Booths Observed (8:13-18)

13 On the second day, the family leaders of all the people, along with the priests and Levites, assembled before Ezra the scribe to study the words of the law. 14 They found written in the law how the LORD had commanded through Moses that the Israelites should dwell in booths during the festival of the seventh month. 15 So they proclaimed and spread this news throughout their towns and in Jerusalem, saying, "Go out to the hill country and bring back branches of olive, wild olive, myrtle, palm, and other leafy trees to make booths, just as it is written." 16 The people went out, brought back branches, and made booths for themselves on each of their rooftops, and courtyards, the court of the house of God, the square by the Water Gate, and the square by the Gate of Ephraim. 17 The whole community that had returned from exile made booths and lived in them. They had not celebrated like this from the days of Joshua son of Nun until that day. And there was tremendous joy. 18 Ezra[C] read out of the book of the law of God every day, from the first day to the last. The Israelites celebrated the festival for seven days, and on the eighth day there was an assembly, according to the ordinance.

National Confession of Sin (9:1-38)

9 On the twenty-fourth day of this month the Israelites assembled; they were fasting, wearing •sackcloth, and had put dust on their heads. 2 Those of Israelite descent separated themselves from all foreigners, and they stood and confessed their sins and the •guilt of their fathers. 3 While they stood in their places, they read from the book of the law of the LORD their God for a fourth of the day and spent another fourth of the day in confession and worship of the LORD their God. 4 Jeshua, Bani, Kadmiel, Shebaniah, Bunni, Sherebiah, Bani, and Chenani stood on the raised platform built for the Levites and cried out loudly to the LORD their God. 5 Then

[A] 8:3 Lit *The ears of all the people listened* [B] 8:7 Vg, 1 Esdras 9:48; MT reads *Pelaiah and the Levites* [C] 8:18 Some Hb mss, Syr read *They*

the Levites—Jeshua, Kadmiel, Bani,
Hashabneiah, Sherebiah, Hodiah,
Shebaniah, and Pethahiah—said,
"Stand up. Praise •Yahweh your God
from everlasting to everlasting."

Praise Your glorious name,
and may it be exalted above
all blessing and praise.
6 You[A] alone are Yahweh.
You created the heavens,
the highest heavens with all
their host,
the earth and all that is on it,
the seas and all that is in
them.
You give life to all of them,
and the heavenly host
worships You.
7 You are Yahweh,
the God who chose Abram
and brought him out of Ur
of the Chaldeans,
and changed his name
to Abraham.
8 You found his heart faithful
in Your sight,
and made a covenant
with him
to give the land
of the Canaanites,
Hittites, Amorites, Perizzites,
Jebusites, and Girgashites—
to give it to his descendants.
You have kept Your promise,
for You are righteous.

9 You saw the oppression
of our ancestors in Egypt
and heard their cry
at the •Red Sea.
10 You performed
signs and wonders
against Pharaoh,
all his officials, and all
the people of his land,
for You knew how arrogantly
they treated our ancestors.
You made a name for Yourself
that endures to this day.
11 You divided the sea
before them,
and they crossed through it
on dry ground.
You hurled their pursuers
into the depths
like a stone
into churning waters.
12 You led them with a pillar
of cloud by day,
and with a pillar of fire
by night,
to illuminate the way
they should go.
13 You came down
on Mount Sinai,
and spoke to them
from heaven.
You gave them
impartial ordinances,
reliable instructions,
and good statutes
and commands.
14 You revealed
Your holy Sabbath to them,
and gave them commands,
statutes, and instruction
through Your servant Moses.
15 You provided bread
from heaven
for their hunger;
You brought them
water from the rock
for their thirst.
You told them to go in
and possess the land
You had sworn[B] to give them.

16 But our ancestors
acted arrogantly;
they became stiff-necked
and did not listen
to Your commands.
17 They refused to listen
and did not remember
Your wonders
You performed among them.
They became stiff-necked
and appointed a leader
to return to their slavery
in Egypt.[C]
But You are a forgiving God,
gracious and compassionate,
slow to anger and rich
in faithful love,
and You did not abandon
them.
18 Even after they had cast
an image of a calf
for themselves and said,
"This is your God
who brought you
out of Egypt,"
and they had committed
terrible blasphemies,

9:6-31 Ezra's prayer is one of the greatest in the Old Testament. Verses 6-15 discuss God's supernatural guidance and the deliverance of Israel's forefathers, including events from the Pentateuch. Verses 16-25 describe God's faithfulness despite Israel's disobedience, including events from Israel's history. Verses 26-31 outline the times of the judges, the monarchy of the Israelites, and the days of the prophets, during which God continued to shower mercy upon His people despite their continued unfaithfulness.

[A]**9:6** LXX reads *And Ezra said: You* [B]**9:15** Lit *lifted Your hand* [C]**9:17** Some Hb mss, LXX; other Hb mss read *in their rebellion*

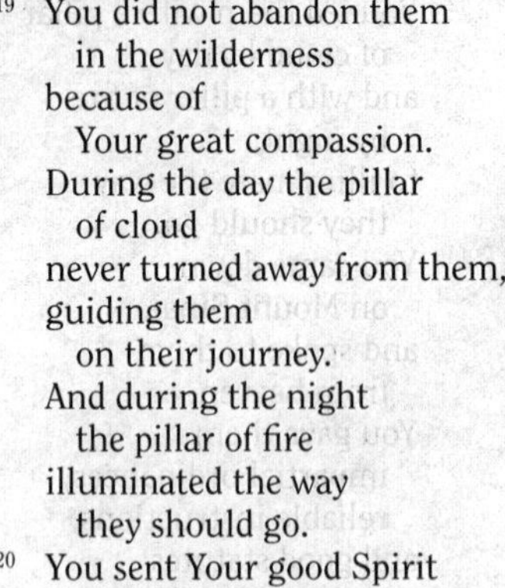

19 You did not abandon them
in the wilderness
because of
Your great compassion.
During the day the pillar
of cloud
never turned away from them,
guiding them
on their journey.
And during the night
the pillar of fire
illuminated the way
they should go.
20 You sent Your good Spirit
to instruct them.
You did not withhold
Your manna
from their mouths,
and You gave them water
for their thirst.
21 You provided for them
in the wilderness 40 years
and they lacked nothing.
Their clothes did not
wear out,
and their feet did not swell.
22 You gave them kingdoms
and peoples
and assigned them to be
a boundary.
They took possession
of the land of Sihon[A]
king of Heshbon
and of the land of Og
king of Bashan.
23 You multiplied
their descendants
like the stars of heaven
and brought them to the land
You told their ancestors
to go in and take possession
of it.
24 So their descendants went in
and possessed the land:
You subdued the Canaanites
who inhabited the land
before them
and handed their kings
and the surrounding
peoples over to them,
to do as they pleased
with them.
25 They captured fortified cities
and fertile land
and took possession of well-
supplied houses,
cisterns cut out of rock,
vineyards,
olive groves, and fruit trees
in abundance.
They ate, were filled,
became prosperous,
and delighted
in Your great goodness.

26 But they were disobedient
and rebelled against You.
They flung Your law
behind their backs
and killed Your prophets
who warned them
in order to turn them back
to You.
They committed
terrible blasphemies.
27 So You handed them over
to their enemies,
who oppressed them.
In their time of distress,
they cried out to You,
and You heard from heaven.
In Your abundant compassion
You gave them deliverers,
who rescued them
from the power
of their enemies.
28 But as soon as they had relief,
they again did what was evil
in Your sight.
So You abandoned
them to the power
of their enemies,
who dominated them.
When they cried out to You
again,
You heard from heaven
and rescued them
many times
in Your compassion.
29 You warned them
to turn back to Your law,
but they acted arrogantly
and would not obey Your
commands.
They sinned against
Your ordinances,
which a person will live by
if he does them.
They stubbornly resisted,[B]

[A] **9:22** One Hb ms, LXX; other Hb mss, Vg read *Sihon, even the land of the* [B] **9:29** Lit *They gave a stubborn shoulder*

>WORD|*study*

9:38 In response to Ezra's prayer, the people made a **binding agreement** (Hb *ʾamanah*, "confirmation, surety, covenant") with God to signify their formal commitment to follow the Lord. In the Old Testament, this word for "agreement" appears only in Nehemiah—here and in 11:23 where it is rendered "ordinance regulating." It is related to the more familiar word *ʾamēn* (Hb, "verily, truly, so be it"; see 5:13; 8:6). Both words come from the root *ʾaman* (Hb, "support, confirm, be or find faithful," 9:8; 13:13; "establish," Ps 89:29).

10:1-29 The people formalized their agreement by signing a written form of the covenant. Nehemiah as governor was the first to sign his name. The elders signed the agreement as representatives of all the people.

stiffened their necks,
and would not obey.
30 You were patient with them
for many years,
and Your Spirit warned them
through Your prophets,
but they would not listen.
Therefore,
You handed them over
to the surrounding peoples.
31 However, in Your abundant
compassion,
You did not destroy them
or abandon them,
for You are a gracious
and compassionate God.
32 So now, our God—the great,
mighty,
and awe-inspiring
God who keeps
His gracious covenant—
do not view lightly
all the hardships
that have afflicted us,
our kings and leaders,
our priests and prophets,
our ancestors and all
Your people,
from the days
of the Assyrian kings
until today.
33 You are righteous concerning
all that has come on us,
because You have acted
faithfully,
while we have acted wickedly.
34 Our kings, leaders, priests,
and ancestors
did not obey Your law
or listen to Your commands
and warnings
You gave them.
35 When they were
in their kingdom,
with Your abundant goodness
that You gave them,
and in the spacious
and fertile land You set
before them,
they would not
serve You or turn
from their wicked ways.
36 Here we are today,
slaves in the land You gave
our ancestors
so that they could enjoy
its fruit and its goodness.
Here we are—slaves in it!
37 Its abundant harvest goes
to the kings
You have set over us,
because of our sins.
They rule over our bodies
and our livestock
as they please.
We are in great distress.

38[A]In view of all this, we are making a binding agreement in writing
on a sealed document containing
the names of our leaders, Levites,
and priests.

The Sealing of the Covenant (10:1-39)

10 Those whose seals were on the
document were:

Nehemiah the governor,
son of Hacaliah,
and Zedekiah,
2 Seraiah, Azariah, Jeremiah,
3 Pashhur, Amariah, Malchijah,
4 Hattush, Shebaniah, Malluch,
5 Harim, Meremoth, Obadiah,
6 Daniel, Ginnethon, Baruch,
7 Meshullam, Abijah, Mijamin,
8 Maaziah, Bilgai, and
Shemaiah.
These were the priests.

9 The Levites were:
Jeshua son of Azaniah,
Binnui of the sons
of Henadad, Kadmiel,
10 and their brothers

[A]**9:38** Neh 10:1 in Hb

10:30-39 The reading of God's Word brought a revival that resulted in changed lives. The Israelites' vow addressed four specific areas:

- Intermarriage (cp. 13:23-28; see also Ex 34:15-16; Dt 7:1-4). Interfaith marriages often led to the worship of other gods and thus to a compromise of God's standards for His people (cp. Solomon, 1Kg 11:1-10; Neh 13:26). Marriage is an institution designed to be a witness for God, and the Israelites had a long history of ignoring this standard.
- **The Sabbath** (Neh 10:31; see also Ex 20:10; Lv 23:3; Dt 5:14) and the sabbatical year regulations (Neh 10:31; see also Ex 23:10-11; Lv 25:4-5; Dt 15:1-2). Not to work one day out of seven demonstrated their trust that God would provide for their needs, an immense test of faith for an agricultural people.
- Temple taxes (Neh 10:32-33). In Ex 30:13 the temple tax was half a shekel, but the requirement here for only **an eighth of an ounce of silver**—one-third of a shekel—may reflect the people's poverty or the changing value of this unit of money from Moses' day or that the people were committing to give one-third of the shekel on top of the regular one-half.
- Offerings (Neh 10:34-39). This showed that they would **not neglect the house** of their God, something that even those within that generation of exiles had done when they worked on their own houses instead of the temple (see Hg 1:4). That the people specifically listed these aspects of temple service indicates their commitment to keep all the worship requirements of the law (Neh 10:32-34).

Shebaniah, Hodiah, Kelita,
Pelaiah, Hanan,
11 Mica, Rehob, Hashabiah,
12 Zaccur, Sherebiah,
Shebaniah,
13 Hodiah, Bani, and Beninu.
14 The leaders of the people
were:
Parosh, Pahath-moab, Elam,
Zattu, Bani,
15 Bunni, Azgad, Bebai,
16 Adonijah, Bigvai, Adin,
17 Ater, Hezekiah, Azzur,
18 Hodiah, Hashum, Bezai,
19 Hariph, Anathoth, Nebai,
20 Magpiash, Meshullam, Hezir,
21 Meshezabel, Zadok, Jaddua,
22 Pelatiah, Hanan, Anaiah,
23 Hoshea, Hananiah, Hasshub,
24 Hallohesh, Pilha, Shobek,
25 Rehum, Hashabnah,
Maaseiah,
26 Ahijah, Hanan, Anan,
27 Malluch, Harim, Baanah.

28 The rest of the people—the
priests, Levites, gatekeepers, singers, and temple servants, along with
their wives, sons, and daughters,
everyone who is able to understand
and who has separated themselves
from the surrounding peoples to
obey the law of God— 29 join with
their noble brothers and commit
themselves with a sworn oath[A] to
follow the law of God given through
God's servant Moses and to carefully
obey all the commands, ordinances,
and statutes of •Yahweh our Lord.

30 We will not give our daughters in marriage to the surrounding peoples and will not
take their daughters as wives
for our sons.

31 When the surrounding peoples bring merchandise or any
kind of grain to sell on the Sabbath day, we will not buy from
them on the Sabbath or a holy
day. We will also leave the land
uncultivated in the seventh
year and will cancel every debt.

32 We will impose the following
commands on ourselves:

To give an eighth of an ounce
of silver[B] yearly for the service
of the house of our God: 33 the
bread displayed before the
LORD,[C] the daily •grain offering,
the regular •burnt offering, the
Sabbath and New Moon offerings, the appointed festivals,
the holy things, the •sin offerings to •atone for Israel, and for
all the work of the house of our
God.

34 We have cast lots among the
priests, Levites, and people for
the donation of wood by our
ancestral houses at the appointed times each year. They
are to bring the wood to our
God's house to burn on the altar of the LORD our God, as it is
written in the law.

35 We will bring the •firstfruits
of our land and of every fruit
tree to the LORD's house year
by year. 36 We will also bring
the firstborn of our sons and
our livestock, as prescribed by
the law, and will bring the firstborn of our herds and flocks to
the house of our God, to the
priests who serve in our God's
house. 37 We will bring a loaf
from our first batch of dough
to the priests at the storerooms
of the house of our God. We
will also bring the firstfruits
of our grain offerings, of every
fruit tree, and of the new wine
and oil. A tenth of our land's
produce belongs to the Levites, for the Levites are to collect the one-tenth offering in
all our agricultural towns. 38 A
priest of Aaronic descent must
accompany the Levites when
they collect the tenth, and the
Levites must take a tenth of
this offering to the storerooms
of the treasury in the house of
our God. 39 For the Israelites
and the Levites are to bring
the contributions of grain, new
wine, and oil to the storerooms
where the articles of the sanctuary are kept and where the
priests who minister are, along
with the gatekeepers and sing-

[A] **10:29** Lit *and enter in a curse and in an oath* [B] **10:32** Lit *give one-third of a shekel* [C] **10:33** Lit *rows of bread*

ers. We will not neglect the house of our God.

The Repopulation of Jerusalem (11:1–12:26)

11 Now the leaders of the people stayed in Jerusalem, and the rest of the people cast lots for one out of ten to come and live in Jerusalem, the holy city, while the other nine-tenths remained in their towns. 2 The people praised all the men who volunteered to live in Jerusalem.

3 These are the heads of the province who stayed in Jerusalem (but in the villages of Judah each lived on his own property in their towns—the Israelites, priests, Levites, temple servants, and descendants of Solomon's servants— 4 while some of the descendants of Judah and Benjamin settled in Jerusalem):

Judah's descendants:

Athaiah son of Uzziah, son of Zechariah, son of Amariah, son of Shephatiah, son of Mahalalel, of Perez's descendants; 5 and Maaseiah son of Baruch, son of Col-hozeh, son of Hazaiah, son of Adaiah, son of Joiarib, son of Zechariah, a descendant of the Shilonite. 6 The total number of Perez's descendants, who settled in Jerusalem, was 468 capable men.

7 These were Benjamin's descendants:

Sallu son of Meshullam, son of Joed, son of Pedaiah, son of Kolaiah, son of Maaseiah, son of Ithiel, son of Jeshaiah, 8 and after him Gabbai and Sallai: 928. 9 Joel son of Zichri was the officer over them, and Judah son of Hassenuah was second in command over the city.

10 The priests:

Jedaiah son of Joiarib, Jachin, and 11 Seraiah son of Hilkiah, son of Meshullam, son of Zadok, son of Meraioth, son of Ahitub, the chief official of God's temple, 12 and their relatives who did the work at the temple: 822. Adaiah son of Jeroham, son of Pelaliah, son of Amzi, son of Zechariah, son of Pashhur, son of Malchijah 13 and his relatives, the leaders of families: 242. Amashsai son of Azarel, son of Ahzai, son of Meshillemoth, son of Immer, 14 and their relatives, capable men: 128. Zabdiel son of Haggedolim, was their chief.

15 The Levites:

Shemaiah son of Hasshub, son of Azrikam, son of Hashabiah, son of Bunni; 16 and Shabbethai and Jozabad, from the leaders of the Levites, who supervised the work outside the house of God; 17 Mattaniah son of Mica, son of Zabdi, son of •Asaph, the leader who began the thanksgiving in prayer; Bakbukiah, second among his relatives; and Abda son of Shammua, son of Galal, son of Jeduthun. 18 All the Levites in the holy city: 284.

19 The gatekeepers:

Akkub, Talmon, and their relatives, who guarded the gates: 172.

20 The rest of Israel, the priests, and the Levites were in all the villages of Judah, each on his own inherited property. 21 The temple servants lived on Ophel;[A] Ziha and Gishpa supervised the temple servants.

22 The leader of the Levites in Jerusalem was Uzzi son of Bani, son of Hashabiah, son of Mattaniah, son of Mica, of the descendants of Asaph, who were singers for the service of God's house. 23 There was, in fact, a command of the king regarding them, and an ordinance regulating[B] the singers' daily tasks. 24 Pethahiah son of Meshezabel, of the descendants of Zerah son of Judah, was the king's agent[C] in every matter concerning the people.

25 As for the farming settlements with their fields:

Some of Judah's descendants
lived in Kiriath-arba
and its villages,

11:1-19 The people realized that Jerusalem needed to be repopulated, yet with the city still needing extensive repair and vulnerable to attack, living inside the city would not have been a very attractive assignment.

The people believed that God would work through the casting of **lots**, an exercise of chance, to designate who should live in the city. Nehemiah required representatives from each of the leading religious families from Judah, Benjamin's descendants, as well as the priests (vv. 10-14) and the Levities (vv. 15-18). These were the same tribes who had populated the city during David's time.

11:1 This list is similar but not identical to the list in 1Ch 9:2-21, which is more detailed. Scholars are not sure why these two lists are different, but the census may simply have been taken at different times and with more people having moved into the city when the census in 1 Chronicles was recorded.

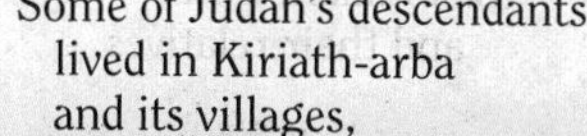

[A] **11:21** = a hill in Jerusalem [B] **11:23** Lit *for* [C] **11:24** Lit *was at the king's hand*

12:1-26 The **priests** and the **Levites** were among the most important people who returned from the exile because they reestablished worship among the people. Of note is Joiada's son **Jonathan**, who married Sanballat's daughter, making the grandson of the high priest **Eliashib** the son-in-law of Sanballat (vv. 10-11,22; see 13:28). This marriage took place before the commitment was made in chapter 11 and may explain why Sanballat was able to gain access to the people and spread rumors during the construction of the wall.

Dibon and its villages,
and Jekabzeel
and its villages;
26 in Jeshua, Moladah,
Beth-pelet,
27 Hazar-shual, and Beer-sheba
and its villages;
28 in Ziklag and Meconah
and its villages;
29 in En-rimmon, Zorah,
Jarmuth, and
30 Zanoah and Adullam
with their villages;
in Lachish with its fields
and Azekah and its villages.
So they settled from
Beer-sheba to the Valley
of Hinnom.

31 Benjamin's descendants:
from Geba,[A] Michmash, Aija,
and Bethel—and its villages,
32 Anathoth, Nob, Ananiah,
33 Hazor, Ramah, Gittaim,
34 Hadid, Zeboim, Neballat,
35 Lod, and Ono, the Valley
of Craftsmen.
36 Some of the Judean
divisions of Levites were
in Benjamin.

12 These are the priests and Levites who went up with Zerubbabel son of Shealtiel and with Jeshua:

Seraiah, Jeremiah, Ezra,
2 Amariah, Malluch, Hattush,
3 Shecaniah, Rehum,
Meremoth,
4 Iddo, Ginnethoi, Abijah,
5 Mijamin, Maadiah, Bilgah,
6 Shemaiah, Joiarib, Jedaiah,
7 Sallu, Amok, Hilkiah, Jedaiah.

These were the leaders of the priests and their relatives in the days of Jeshua.
8 The Levites:

Jeshua, Binnui, Kadmiel,
Sherebiah, Judah,
and Mattaniah—
he and his relatives
were in charge
of the praise songs.
9 Bakbukiah, Unni,[B]
and their relatives
stood opposite them
in the services.
10 Jeshua fathered Joiakim,
Joiakim fathered Eliashib,
Eliashib fathered Joiada,
11 Joiada fathered Jonathan,
and Jonathan fathered
Jaddua.[C]

12 In the days of Joiakim, the leaders of the priestly families were:

	Meraiah	of Seraiah,
	Hananiah	of Jeremiah,
13	Meshullam	of Ezra,
	Jehohanan	of Amariah,
14	Jonathan	of Malluchi,
	Joseph	of Shebaniah,
15	Adna	of Harim,
	Helkai	of Meraioth,
16	Zechariah	of Iddo,
	Meshullam	of Ginnethon,
17	Zichri	of Abijah,
	Piltai	of Moadiah,
		of Miniamin,
18	Shammua	of Bilgah,
	Jehonathan	of Shemaiah,
19	Mattenai	of Joiarib,
	Uzzi	of Jedaiah,
20	Kallai	of Sallai,
	Eber	of Amok,
21	Hashabiah	of Hilkiah,
	and Nethanel	of Jedaiah.

22 In the days of Eliashib, Joiada, Johanan, and Jaddua, the leaders of the families of the Levites and priests were recorded while Darius the Persian ruled. 23 Levi's descendants, the leaders of families, were recorded in the Book of the Historical Records during the days of Johanan son of Eliashib. 24 The leaders of the Levites—Hashabiah, Sherebiah, and Jeshua son of Kadmiel, along with their relatives opposite them—gave praise and thanks, division by division, as David the man of God had prescribed. 25 This included Mattaniah, Bakbukiah, and Obadiah. Meshullam, Talmon, and Akkub were gatekeepers who guarded the storerooms at the gates. 26 These served in the days of Joiakim son of Jeshua, son of Jozadak, and in the days of Nehemiah the governor and Ezra the priest and scribe.

[A] **11:31** Or *descendants from Geba lived in* [B] **12:9** Alt Hb tradition reads *Unno* [C] **12:10-11** These men were high priests.

The Dedication of the Walls (12:27-47)

27 At the dedication of the wall of Jerusalem, they sent for the Levites wherever they lived and brought them to Jerusalem to celebrate the joyous dedication with thanksgiving and singing accompanied by cymbals, harps, and lyres. 28 The singers gathered from the region around Jerusalem, from the villages of the Netophathites, 29 from Beth-gilgal, and from the fields of Geba and Azmaveth, for they had built villages for themselves around Jerusalem. 30 After the priests and Levites had purified themselves, they purified the people, the gates, and the wall.

31 Then I brought the leaders of Judah up on top of the wall, and I appointed two large processions that gave thanks. One went to the right on the wall, toward the Dung Gate. 32 Hoshaiah and half the leaders of Judah followed, 33 along with Azariah, Ezra, Meshullam, 34 Judah, Benjamin, Shemaiah, Jeremiah, 35 and some of the priests' sons with trumpets, and Zechariah son of Jonathan, son of Shemaiah, son of Mattaniah, son of Micaiah, son of Zaccur, son of •Asaph followed 36 as well as his relatives—Shemaiah, Azarel, Milalai, Gilalai, Maai, Nethanel, Judah, and Hanani, with the musical instruments of David, the man of God. Ezra the scribe went in front of them. 37 At the Fountain Gate they climbed the steps of the city of David on the ascent of the wall and went above the house of David to the Water Gate on the east.

38 The second thanksgiving procession went to the left, and I followed it with half the people along the top of the wall, past the Tower of the Ovens to the Broad Wall, 39 above the Gate of Ephraim, and by the Old Gate, the Fish Gate, the Tower of Hananel, and the Tower of the Hundred, to the Sheep Gate. They stopped at the Gate of the Guard. 40 The two thanksgiving processions stood in the house of God. So did I and half of the officials accompanying me, 41 as well as the priests:

Eliakim, Maaseiah, Miniamin,
Micaiah, Elioenai, Zechariah,
and Hananiah, with trumpets;
42 and Maaseiah, Shemaiah,
Eleazar,
Uzzi, Jehohanan, Malchijah,
Elam, and Ezer.

Then the singers sang, with Jezrahiah as the leader. 43 On that day they offered great sacrifices and rejoiced because God had given them great joy. The women and children also celebrated, and Jerusalem's rejoicing was heard far away.

44 On that same day men were placed in charge of the rooms that housed the supplies, contributions, •firstfruits, and tenths. The legally required portions for the priests and Levites were gathered from the village fields, because Judah was grateful to the priests and Levites who were serving. 45 They performed the service of their God and the service of purification, along with the singers and gatekeepers, as David and his son Solomon had prescribed. 46 For long ago, in the days of David and Asaph, there were leaders[A] of the singers and songs of praise and thanksgiving to God. 47 So in the days of Zerubbabel and Nehemiah, all Israel contributed the daily portions for the singers and gatekeepers. They also set aside daily portions for the Levites, and the Levites set aside daily portions for the descendants of Aaron.

The Reforms of Nehemiah (13:1-31)

13 At that time the book of Moses was read publicly to[B] the people. The command was found written in it that no Ammonite or Moabite should ever enter the assembly of God, 2 because they did not meet the Israelites with food and water. Instead, they hired Balaam against them to curse them, but our God turned the curse into a blessing. 3 When they heard the law, they separated all those of mixed descent from Israel.

4 Now before this, Eliashib the priest had been put in charge of the storerooms of the house of our God. He was a relative[C] of Tobiah 5 and had prepared a large room for him

12:44-47 Nehemiah also reestablished the temple service in the manner organized by **David and Solomon** for the first temple. This represents the crescendo in the restoration of Israel; the temple and wall had been secured, God's Word stood once again as Israel's authority, and the temple worship was reinstituted. The people demonstrated their commitment to their vow by bringing their tithes (**tenths**) to the storehouses for the Levites (10:35-39).

13:1-31 This final chapter is a summary of the reforms instituted under Nehemiah's leadership, including how to deal with violations of the covenant that the people had made with God (see 10:29-32). They included:

- The exclusion of foreigners (13:1-3). By excluding all non-Jews from their assembly, they were demonstrating their commitment to God to be a people set apart for His purposes.
- The expulsion of **Tobiah** and the cleansing of the temple (Neh 13:4-9). Nehemiah returned to Persia to visit Artaxerxes as he had promised. Upon his return, he found Tobiah living on the grounds of the temple. Nehemiah's righteous rage and cleansing of the temple brings to mind the similar action of Jesus (Jn 2:19).
- The revival of tithing (Neh 13:10-14). Malachi also addressed this violation (Mal 3:8-10).
- The observance of the Sabbath (Neh 13:15-22).
- The rebuke against mixed marriages (vv. 23-29). The pulling **out of hair** referred to plucking out hair from the men's beards, which was a sign of punishment and public disgrace (v. 25). Nehemiah was particularly harsh on **one of the sons of Jehoiada**, son of the high priest, who married Sanballat's daughter, because he had corrupted the high priestly line (v. 28; see Lv 21:14).

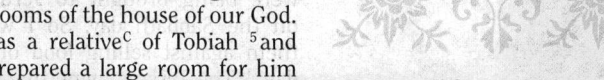

[A]**12:46** Alt Hb tradition reads *there was a leader* [B]**13:1** Lit *read in the ears of* [C]**13:4** Or *an associate*

where they had previously stored the •grain offerings, the frankincense, the articles, and the tenths of grain, new wine, and oil prescribed for the Levites, singers, and gatekeepers, along with the contributions for the priests.

6 While all this was happening, I was not in Jerusalem, because I had returned to King Artaxerxes of Babylon in the thirty-second year of his reign. It was only later that I asked the king for a leave of absence 7 so I could return to Jerusalem. Then I discovered the evil that Eliashib had done on behalf of Tobiah by providing him a room in the courts of God's house. 8 I was greatly displeased and threw all of Tobiah's household possessions out of the room. 9 I ordered that the rooms be purified, and I had the articles of the house of God restored there, along with the grain offering and frankincense. 10 I also found out that because the portions for the Levites had not been given, each of the Levites and the singers performing the service had gone back to his own field. 11 Therefore, I rebuked the officials, saying, "Why has the house of God been neglected?" I gathered the Levites and singers together and stationed them at their posts. 12 Then all Judah brought a tenth of the grain, new wine, and oil into the storehouses. 13 I appointed as treasurers over the storehouses Shelemiah the priest, Zadok the scribe, and Pedaiah of the Levites, with Hanan son of Zaccur, son of Mattaniah to assist them, because they were considered trustworthy. They were responsible for the distribution to their colleagues.

14 Remember me for this, my God, and don't erase the deeds of faithful love I have done for the house of my God and for its services.

15 At that time I saw people in Judah treading wine presses on the Sabbath. They were also bringing in stores of grain and loading them on donkeys, along with wine, grapes, and figs. All kinds of goods were being brought to Jerusalem on the Sabbath day. So I warned them against selling food on that day. 16 The Tyrians living there were importing fish and all kinds of merchandise and selling them on the Sabbath to the people of Judah in Jerusalem.

17 I rebuked the nobles of Judah and said to them: "What is this evil you are doing—profaning the Sabbath day? 18 Didn't your ancestors do the same, so that our God brought all this disaster on us and on this city? And now you are rekindling His anger against Israel by profaning the Sabbath!"

19 When shadows began to fall on the gates of Jerusalem just before the Sabbath, I gave orders that the gates be closed and not opened until after the Sabbath. I posted some of my men at the gates, so that no goods could enter during the Sabbath day. 20 Once or twice the merchants and those who sell all kinds of goods camped outside Jerusalem, 21 but I warned them, "Why are you camping in front of the wall? If you do it again, I'll use force[A] against you." After that they did not come again on the Sabbath. 22 Then I instructed the Levites to purify themselves and guard the gates in order to keep the Sabbath day holy.

Remember me for this also, my God, and look on me with compassion in keeping with Your abundant, faithful love.

23 In those days I also saw Jews who had married women from Ashdod, Ammon, and Moab. 24 Half of their children spoke the language of Ashdod or the language of one of the other peoples but could not speak Hebrew.[B] 25 I rebuked them, cursed them, beat some of their men, and pulled out their hair. I forced them to take an oath before God and said: "You must not give your daughters in marriage to their sons or take their daughters as wives for your sons or yourselves! 26 Didn't King Solomon of Israel sin in matters like this? There was not a king like him among many nations. He was loved by his God and God made him king over all Israel, yet foreign women drew him into sin. 27 Why then should we hear about you doing all this terrible evil and acting unfaith-

[A] **13:21** Lit *again, I will send a hand* [B] **13:24** Lit *Judahite*

fully against our God by marrying
foreign women?"
28 Even one of the sons of Jehoiada,
son of Eliashib the high priest, had
become a son-in-law to Sanballat
the Horonite. So I drove him away
from me.
29 Remember them, my God, for
defiling the priesthood as well as the
covenant of the priesthood and the
Levites.
30 So I purified them from everything foreign and assigned specific
duties to each of the priests and Levites. 31 I also arranged for the donation of wood at the appointed times
and for the •firstfruits.
Remember me, my God, with favor.

13:31 Nehemiah concluded his account with a personal prayer, asking the Lord to **remember** (Hb *zakar*, "meditate upon, pay attention to") his faithfulness. This personal request reflects a man who deeply desired to please the Lord.

In the day of your most daunting of endeavors, your most painful discouragement, and your greatest opposition, may you be a woman who leads like Nehemiah—undeterred from your purpose, unyielding in your integrity, and unceasing in prayer.

Esther

Timeline	538 BC	515 BC	492–449 BC	486–465 BC
➡ World Events ➡ Biblical Events	Cyrus II (reigned 559–530) issued decree permitting Jews' return from exile	Second temple dedicated during reign of Darius I (521–486)	Persian Wars fought as Greeks revolt against Persian rule	Xerxes I (possibly Ahasuerus) rules Persia.

"Who knows, perhaps you have come to your royal position for such a time as this" (4:14b).

Who wrote Esther?

Likely a Persian Jew well acquainted with court life as well as with the history and culture of the period

Who were the recipients?

The Jewish community living during the Diaspora since the events recorded center around the lives of Jews dwelling in exile in Persia. However, God uses the experiences of a few to speak to all future generations who face similar dangers and difficulties.

When was Esther written?

465–331 B.C.

Where did it happen?

Susa (Hb *Shushan*, lit "lily," 1:2) was the royal city and one of the capitals of the ancient Persian Empire. Its ruins are in Iran near the Iraqi border.

What is Esther about?

- The unending providence of God in His loving care for His people
- The sovereignty of God in effecting His purposes
- The free will of man to act on his own choices

Why should women read Esther?

The book of Esther bears the name of a heroine who was beautiful, brave, and brilliant. God used Esther as the primary agent to save His people, the Jews, from destruction. As a Jewess in a cruel despot's court, she risked her life while working a daring plan to deliver her people from certain death. Women are inspired by such an ordinary woman who is used of God in an extraordinary way. Women are also instructed and mentored in virtues and character traits of a woman who is not only used by God to accomplish His purposes but is also a heroine admired by her peers and future generations.

How do you read Esther?

The events recorded in Esther likely occurred during the reign of the Persian king Ahasuerus, the son of Darius I, who ruled from 486–465/64 B.C., a time within the Achaemenid period of biblical history (559–330 B.C.). The geographical setting is the royal city of Susa (Hb *Shushan*, 1:2) within a vast Persian empire described as stretching "from India [Hb *Hodu*] to Cush" (Hb), the latter being another name for Ethiopia, which is located in the region around the Nile River including Nubia and northern Sudan. Thousands of the exiles had remained in Persia despite the opportunity to return to their homeland. They retained a distinctive Jewishness instead of being completely assimilated into the Persian Empire.

The narrative in Esther is historical, as suggested from the opening words: "These events took place . . . ." The introduction of the Festival of Purim adds to the historical credibility of the book as does the fact that the book was readily admitted to the Jewish canon. Some of its statements are further confirmed by extrabiblical historical sources. The plot is woven skillfully with words carefully chosen; characters and their roles are well-developed; and a direct path leads to the denouement and memorable styling of its climactic summary. Irony, drama, suspense, intrigue, humor, and numerous literary devices are also employed in this example of redemptive history, which offers encouragement and hope for Jews and Christians from the time of these historical events until now.

The book of Esther has stirred up controversy over the years. The Jews embrace the book and accord it great honor—seeing its story as a celebration of their miraculous victory over enemies who were seeking their destruction. Others reject the book because of the absence of God's name or any specific reference to Him and His work. The book was not quoted in the New Testament and was rarely mentioned by the Church Fathers. Some find the book lacking in its moral tone and in the character of those who are identified as being God's chosen people. Yet the book is a powerful testimony to the fact that God's people do not always act in godly ways, and consequently they experience His displeasure, which may be exhibited by a veil of silence or even a temporary absence of divine activity. Nevertheless, the behavior of God's people has never changed the fact that God chose them and they are His. The free will of man on one hand and the sovereignty of God on the other effect His extraordinary purposes. Still, without explicitly mentioning God, the temple, the Torah or laws, or even prayer, the book powerfully exemplifies the providence of God, who will forever remain faithful to rescue and deliver His people.

Esther's World

King Ahasuerus and Queen Esther ruled the Persian Empire from Susa, the winter capital of the Empire. The territory is now in Iran. Cyrus made Susa a capital city along with Babylon, Ecbatana, and Persepolis. When Alexander the Great captured Susa, he found a large treasure that he confiscated. Archaeologists have excavated Susa largely around four areas: the royal palace, the acropolis, the royal city, and an artisan tell.

483 BC	480 BC	478 BC	474 BC	473 BC
Vashti is deposed.	Persians defeat Greeks at Battle of Thermopylae then lose their navy at Battle of Salamis.	Esther becomes queen.	Haman solicits royal decree for genocide of Jewish population in the Persian Empire. Esther intercedes for her people.	Festival of Purim is celebrated.

Outline

The Setting for God's Deliverance (1:1–2:23)

The Transition from Vashti to Esther (1:1–2:20)

The feast of Ahasuerus (1:1-9)

1 These events took place during the
days of Ahasuerus,[A] who ruled 127
provinces from India[B] to •Cush. 2 In
those days King Ahasuerus reigned
from his royal throne in the fortress
at Susa. 3 He held a feast in the third
year of his reign for all his officials
and staff, the army of Persia and Media, the nobles, and the officials from
the provinces. 4 He displayed the glorious wealth of his kingdom and the
magnificent splendor of his greatness
for a total of 180 days.
5 At the end of this time, the king
held a week-long banquet in the
garden courtyard of the royal palace
for all the people, from the greatest
to the least, who were present in the
fortress of Susa. 6 White and violet
linen hangings were fastened with
fine white and purple linen cords
to silver rods on marble[C] columns.
Gold and silver couches were arranged on a mosaic pavement of red
feldspar,[D] marble,[C] mother-of-pearl,
and precious stones.
7 Beverages were served in an array
of gold goblets, each with a different
design. Royal wine flowed freely, according to the king's bounty 8 and
no restraint was placed on the drinking. The king had ordered every wine
steward in his household to serve as
much as each person wanted. 9 Queen
Vashti also gave a feast for the women
of King Ahasuerus's palace.

The disobedience of Vashti and her removal from the royal court (1:10-22)

10 On the seventh day, when the
king was feeling good from the wine,
Ahasuerus commanded Mehuman,
Biztha, Harbona, Bigtha, Abagtha,
Zethar, and Carkas, the seven eunuchs who personally served him,
11 to bring Queen Vashti before him
with her royal crown. He wanted to
show off her beauty to the people
and the officials, because she was
very beautiful. 12 But Queen Vashti
refused to come at the king's command that was delivered by his eunuchs. The king became furious and
his anger burned within him.
13 The king consulted the wise men
who understood the times,[E] for it
was his normal procedure to confer
with experts in law and justice. 14 The

A 1:1 = Xerxes; he reigned 486–465 B.C. B 1:1 = modern Pakistan C 1:6 Or *alabaster* D 1:6 Or *of porphyry* E 1:13 Or *understood propitious times*

Title: In the *Mishna*, an important Jewish collection of oral tradition, this book is called "the Roll [Hb *Megillah*, "scroll"] of Esther," since its words were written on a scroll.

1:1 Ahasuerus (Hb of Persian *Khshayarsha*, identified more commonly by the Greek name Xerxes I), reigned as king over Persia 486–465 B.C. (cp. Ezr 4:6). **Cush**, or Ethiopia, in Southern Egypt, includes Nubia, closely identified with the Nile River.

1:3-5 The author states the chronological setting for these events, **in the third year of his** [Ahasuerus's] **reign**. The Greek historian Herodotus described a war council to plan Xerxes' invasion of Greece (480–479 B.C.) during the third year of his reign. Some commentators believe this **feast** (Hb *mishteh*, "banquet," more lit, "a drinking"; cp. 1:9; 2:18; 8:17; 9:17-19,22), lasting six months, occurred in connection with this event.

1:10-12 Only **eunuchs** (castrated males) were permitted contact with the harem because of proving the legitimacy of any offspring coming from the king's wife or concubine. The detail in naming these men points to the historicity of the account.

The king's request for **Queen Vashti** to come **with her royal crown** would most naturally mean that he wanted her to appear at her best and fitting her station as queen. For **the king** to become **furious** (Hb *qatsaph*, "be full of wrath, indignant; break out into anger") is not surprising, not only

CHARACTER PROFILE

Vashti A Deposed Queen

Her Background	The wife of King Ahasuerus, ruler of Persia (1:9-12)
Her Story	• During a period of celebration, Vashti hosted a royal banquet for the women in the palace (1:9). • Her husband simultaneously hosted a banquet for the men, providing as much wine and food as desired (1:3-8). • On the seventh day of the feast, Ahasuerus summoned Vashti in order to show off her beauty (1:10-11). • Vashti refused to appear, was eventually deposed, and then was replaced by Esther (1:12–2:17). • The text does not indicate why Vashti refused to obey the king's command.
Life Lessons	• This dramatic story illustrates the miraculous juxtaposition between man's will and God's sovereignty. • Beauty of appearance is not the key to a happy life.

most trusted ones[A] were Carshena,
Shethar, Admatha, Tarshish, Meres,
Marsena, and Memucan. They were
the seven officials of Persia and Media who had personal access to the
king and occupied the highest positions in the kingdom. 15 The king
asked, "According to the law, what
should be done with Queen Vashti,
since she refused to obey King Ahasuerus's command that was delivered
by the eunuchs?"
16 Memucan said in the presence
of the king and his officials, "Queen
Vashti has wronged not only the
king, but all the officials and the
peoples who are in every one of King
Ahasuerus's provinces. 17 For the
queen's action will become public
knowledge to all the women and
cause them to despise their husbands and say, 'King Ahasuerus ordered Queen Vashti brought before
him, but she did not come.' 18 Before
this day is over, the noble women of
Persia and Media who hear about
the queen's act will say the same
thing to all the king's officials, resulting in more contempt and fury.
19 "If it meets the king's approval,
he should personally issue a royal decree. Let it be recorded in the laws of
Persia and Media, so that it cannot be
revoked: Vashti is not to enter King
Ahasuerus's presence, and her royal
position is to be given to another
woman who is more worthy than she.
20 The decree the king issues will be
heard throughout his vast kingdom,
so all women will honor their husbands, from the least to the greatest."
21 The king and his counselors
approved the proposal, and he followed Memucan's advice. 22 He sent
letters to all the royal provinces,
to each province in its own script
and to each ethnic group in its own
language, that every man should be
master of his own house and speak
in the language of his own people.

The plan to choose a new queen (2:1-11)

2 Some time later, when King Ahasuerus's rage had cooled down, he
remembered Vashti, what she had
done, and what was decided against
her. 2 The king's personal attendants[B]
suggested, "Let a search be made for
beautiful young women for the king.
3 Let the king appoint commissioners
in each province of his kingdom, so
that they may assemble all the beautiful young women to the harem at the
fortress of Susa. Put them under the
care of Hegai, the king's eunuch, who
is in charge of the women, and give
them the required beauty treatments.
4 Then the young woman who pleases
the king will become queen instead of
Vashti." This suggestion pleased the
king, and he did accordingly.

because of public embarrassment, which would have angered any husband or monarch, but also because of his reputation for volatile responses. Vashti **refused** [Hb *maʾēn*, "refuse with resolved mind, which cannot be prevailed on by the means that have been used," figuratively used to refer to a wound that has no cure; cp Jr 15:18] **to come at the king's command**.

1:20 Interestingly, the conclusion of the pagan advisers of the king coincides with God's creation order: **All women will honor** [Hb *yeqar*, "precious, heavy" in the sense of having weighty and thus high responsibility] **their husbands**. The plan of God from creation is expressed as calling for the husband's loving headship and the wife's responding gracious submission, firmly established as the divine mandate long before the time of Ahasuerus and the wise men of Persia (Gn 2:15-18; cp. 1Co 11:3; Eph 5:21-33; Col 3:18; 1Pt 3:1-7).

2:4 Esther became **the young woman who pleases** [Hb *yatav*, "be good"] **the king** (cp. v. 9).

2:8 The words **Esther was also taken** seem to point more to the possibility that Esther was taken forcibly from her foster parent's home.

[A] 1:14 Lit *Those near him* [B] 2:2 Lit *The young men of the king who served him*

5 In the fortress of Susa, there was
a Jewish man named Mordecai son
of Jair, son of Shimei, son of Kish,
a Benjaminite. 6 He had been taken
into exile from Jerusalem with the
other captives when King Nebuchadnezzar of Babylon took King
Jeconiah[A] of Judah into exile. 7 Mordecai was the legal guardian of his
cousin[B] Hadassah (that is, Esther),
because she didn't have a father or
mother. The young woman had a
beautiful figure and was extremely
good-looking. When her father and
mother died, Mordecai had adopted
her as his own daughter.
8 When the king's command and
edict became public knowledge, many
young women gathered at the fortress of Susa under Hegai's care. Esther was also taken to the palace and
placed under the care of Hegai, who
was in charge of the women. 9 The
young woman pleased him and gained
his favor[C] so that he accelerated the
process of the beauty treatments and
the special diet that she received. He
assigned seven hand-picked female
servants to her from the palace and
transferred her and her servants to
the harem's best quarters.
10 Esther did not reveal her ethnic
background or her birthplace, because Mordecai had ordered her not
to. 11 Every day Mordecai took a walk
in front of the harem's courtyard to
learn how Esther was doing and to
see what was happening to her.

The selection of Esther as queen (2:12-20)

12 During the year before each
young woman's turn to go to King
Ahasuerus, the harem regulation
required her to receive beauty treatments with oil of myrrh for six

HARD QUESTION

How could Esther hide her Jewish heritage and faith?

To be godly seed does not guarantee godly actions and attitudes. For Esther or Mordecai to fall short morally or spiritually does not undercut the truthfulness and reliability of Scripture. Through the generations God's people have repeatedly failed to obey Him or even consult Him and His Word. Yet ultimately human sin cannot thwart God's plans.

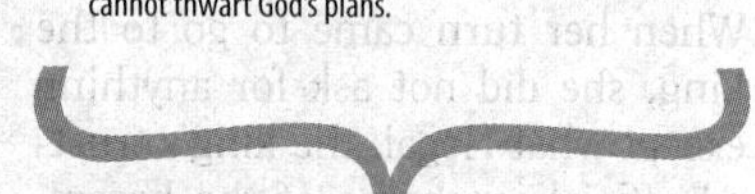

[A]2:6 = Jehoiachin in 2Kg 24; 25:27; 1Ch 3:16-17 [B]2:7 Lit *uncle's daughter* [C]2:9 Lit *and carried faithful love before him*

2:12 The **beauty treatments** (Hb *meruqim*, "cleansing and anointing, treating cosmetically, scraping, rubbing") surely arouse interest, and archaeological discoveries during recent decades have shed light on this process (cp. vv. 3,9). Cosmetic burners dating to this period have helped to explain the ancient beautification process. These burners had four stumpy legs on which rested a carved-out bowl. One such burner had four respective spices mentioned in the Bible inscribed on each of the sides much as apothecary labels. These perfumed spices included oil of roses, sandalwood, the essence of the mimosa tree, musk, and oil of cloves. The spices seem to be chosen not only for scent but also to act as repellant to insects and to serve therapeutic purposes. Even after centuries, the burners had evidence of fragrant resinous substances clinging to their shallow basins. The process itself seems to have taken place in the floor of a tent over a small hole with a fire of charcoal into which these various spices were thrown. A woman would shed her inner garments and allow a large robe to fall as a mantle from her shoulders as she crouched over the fumes under her "tent." Her natural perspiration flowed freely so that the oil from perfumes was absorbed by her skin—a very effective process.

>WORD|*study*

1:16 Wronged (Hb *'awah*, "act perversely," with a sense of bending or making crooked or troubling society, i.e., acting perversely or sinning; cp. Jb 33:27; Is 24:1; Dn 9:5) is a strong word and used sparingly. The queen's action was interpreted not only as insulting to her husband but also as disrespectful to her king. The word choice indicates that Vashti's response was interpreted by the king's advisers as subversive, not simply discourteous. They also expressed dismay over what they perceived to be the resulting influence such action would have over how the women in the kingdom would relate to their respective husbands. Again the language is very precise.

1:18 Hear (Hb *shama'*, "listen, give heed, obey") goes beyond receiving sound advice to the idea of integrating and acting upon what is heard.

1:18 Contempt (Hb *bizzayon* from the verb *bazah*, "despise through pride") seems to express the feelings of the women, who having observed the queen, might in their own hearts have echoed the spirit of her blatant refusal to appear before the king.

1:18 Fury (Hb *qetseph*, from the root *qatsaph*, meaning "break out in anger, express great displeasure"; see note 1:12) would seem to express the response of their husbands, who, like the king, might erupt in anger in light of such defiance.

2:5 Mordecai (Persian, "little man," derived from the name of the Babylonian god Marduk) bore a pagan name, which is not surprising for one born in captivity. Apparently his Jewish name did not survive. His descent from **Kish** of the tribe of Benjamin, the lineage of Israel's first king, is clearly noted (cp. 1Sm 9:1; 14:51), but he did choose to remain in exile instead of returning to the promised land.

2:7 Hadassah Mordecai was a cousin to Hadassah (Hb "myrtle"; used metaphorically in the OT for the Lord's forgiveness and reconciliation with His people). Her Hebrew name reflects the custom of naming daughters after plants or flowers to emphasize attractiveness and beauty (cp. Is 41:19; 55:13; Zch 1:8,10-11).

2:9 Favor (Hb *chesed*, "steadfast love, kindness," also a reference to God's covenant love or His unique lovingkindness; see Ru 1:8) here is used with **pleased** to provide an idiom that suggests winning or earning favor rather than merely passively catching someone's attention (cp. Est 2:9; 5:8; 7:3; 8:5). Hegai **accelerated the process of the beauty treatments** (2:9) because of the potential he saw in Esther. Ultimately Esther became the queen not merely by pleasing the king in a moment's encounter but by winning his "favor" as the best and most beautiful of all the women who had come into his presence.

2:15 Abihail (Hb, "my father is might"), Esther's father, is mentioned twice (2:15; 9:29). This name is also a woman's name in the Old Testament (1Ch 2:29; 2Ch 11:18).

2:16 The tenth month . . . Tebeth, the Babylonian month corresponding to the period December–January in the modern calendar, would have been during **the seventh year of his** [Ahasuerus's] **reign** and thus four years after the removal of Vashti.

2:17 Esther seems to have earned unanimous **approval** (Hb *chên*, "favor, grace, acceptance," cp. v. 15; 5:8; 7:3; 8:5; Ex 12:36; Ru 2:10,13; Ps 84:11) because of her physical beauty and personal charm, which combined poise, elegance, and interpersonal skills befitting a queen and undoubtedly endeared her to the king. Ahasuerus was not merely impressed with her but **loved** [Hb *ʾahav*, "desire, take delight in"—often an inclination leading to preferred treatment or the active choosing of the one "loved" over other possible recipients of such favor; cp. Gn 25:28; 29:18; Ex 21:5; Dt 4:37; Pr 3:12] **Esther**.

2:21-23 The listing of names of the **two eunuchs who** tried **to assassinate King Ahasuerus** underscores the historical accuracy of the events since such information would have been available through the court records of the nation. Although Mordecai's discovery and bringing to light of this treasonous event affirmed his loyalty and were important to King Ahasuerus, Mordecai did not initially receive any recognition. The plot continues, leaving the reward and exaltation for a later time.

3:1 Haman is identified as the **son of Hammedatha the Agagite** and as holding a position above the other nobles in the kingdom. According to Jewish tradition, he was a descendant of Agag, who was an enemy of Israel during the reign of King Saul (8:3,5; 9:24; cp. 1Sm 15:7-33). The Amalekites, a nomadic people living in the southern desert region, frequently raided and killed the Israelites. They were the first nation to go to war with Israel after the exodus (Ex 17:8-16; Dt 25:17-19) and had long been enemies of the Jews—so much so that Saul lost the kingdom when he disobeyed God's command and failed to destroy the Amalekites (1Sm 15:1-9,23). The term "Amalekite" became a synonym for any enemy of Israel not designated in some other distinct way.

3:2 Why Mordecai refused to bow and pay **homage to Haman** in defiance of the king's command is not clear. He may have considered bowing to any man

>WORD|*study*

2:15 Esther (probably Persian in origin, "star"), the name used throughout the book and as its official name, is derived from the same root as the principal goddess of the ancient Near East, Ishtar, associated with eroticism and sexuality. Mordecai assumed the role of "legal guardian" or foster parent to his orphaned relative and continually demonstrated his concern for her even after she entered the king's harem (Est 2:10-11).

months and then with perfumes and
cosmetics for another six months.
13 When the young woman would
go to the king, she was given whatever she requested to take with her
from the harem to the palace. 14 She
would go in the evening, and in the
morning she would return to a second harem under the supervision
of Shaashgaz, the king's eunuch in
charge of the concubines. She never
went to the king again, unless he
desired her and summoned her by
name.

15 Esther was the daughter of Abihail, the uncle of Mordecai who had
adopted her as his own daughter.
When her turn came to go to the
king, she did not ask for anything
except what Hegai, the king's trusted official in charge of the harem,
suggested. Esther won approval in
the sight of everyone who saw her.

16 She was taken to King Ahasuerus in the royal palace in the tenth
month, the month Tebeth, in the
seventh year of his reign. 17 The king
loved Esther more than all the other
women. She won more favor and approval from him than did any of the
other young women. He placed the
royal crown on her head and made
her queen in place of Vashti. 18 The
king held a great banquet for all his
officials and staff. It was Esther's
banquet. He freed his provinces
from tax payments and gave gifts
worthy of the king's bounty.

19 When the young women were
assembled together for a second
time, Mordecai was sitting at the
King's Gate. 20 Esther still had not
revealed her birthplace or her ethnic
background, as Mordecai had directed. She obeyed Mordecai's orders, as
she always had while he raised her.

Mordecai's Action to Save the King's Life (2:21-23)

21 During those days while Mordecai was sitting at the King's Gate,
Bigthan and Teresh, two eunuchs
who guarded the king's entrance,
became infuriated and planned to assassinate[A] King Ahasuerus. 22 When
Mordecai learned of the plot, he reported it to Queen Esther, and she
told the king on Mordecai's behalf.
23 When the report was investigated
and verified, both men were hanged
on the gallows. This event was recorded in the Historical Record in
the king's presence.

The Plot Against the Jews (3:1–4:17)

Haman's Pride and Treachery (3:1-6)

3 After all this took place, King
Ahasuerus honored Haman, son
of Hammedatha the Agagite. He
promoted him in rank and gave him
a higher position than all the other
officials. 2 The entire royal staff at
the King's Gate bowed down and
paid homage to Haman, because
the king had commanded this to be
done for him. But Mordecai would
not bow down or pay homage. 3 The
members of the royal staff at the
King's Gate asked Mordecai, "Why
are you disobeying the king's command?" 4 When they had warned
him day after day and he still would
not listen to them, they told Haman
to see if Mordecai's actions would be
tolerated, since he had told them he
was a Jew.

5 When Haman saw that Mordecai
was not bowing down or paying him
homage, he was filled with rage.
6 And when he learned of Mordecai's
ethnic identity, Haman decided not
to do away with[B] Mordecai alone. He
planned to destroy all of Mordecai's

[A]2:21 Lit *and they sought to stretch out a hand against* [B]3:6 Lit *to stretch out a hand against*

people, the Jews, throughout Ahasuerus's kingdom.

Haman's Decree for the Destruction of the Jews (3:7-15)

[7]In the first month, the month of Nisan,[A] in King Ahasuerus's twelfth year,[B] Pur (that is, the lot) was cast before Haman for each day in each month, and it fell on the twelfth month, the month Adar.[C] [8]Then Haman informed King Ahasuerus, "There is one ethnic group, scattered throughout the peoples in every province of your kingdom, yet living in isolation. Their laws are different from everyone else's and they do not obey the king's laws. It is not in the king's best interest to tolerate them.
[9]If the king approves, let an order be drawn up authorizing their destruction, and I will pay 375 tons of silver to[D] the accountants for deposit in the royal treasury."
[10]The king removed his signet ring from his finger and gave it to Haman son of Hammedatha the Agagite, the enemy of the Jewish people. [11]Then the king told Haman, "The money and people are given to you to do with as you see fit."
[12]The royal scribes were summoned on the thirteenth day of the first month, and the order was written exactly as Haman commanded. It was intended for the royal satraps,

idolatry. However, the custom of such deference to members of the court was quite widespread (cp. 1Sm 24:8; 2Sm 14:4; 1Kg 1:16). On the other hand, his refusal could have been based upon his own pride and the long-standing hostility between the Israelites and the Amalekites.

3:6 Haman's announcement that he would **destroy all of Mordecai's people, the Jews**, brings to the forefront the principal plot of the book—another attempt to destroy the Jews.

3:7 **King Ahasuerus's twelfth year** would be the fifth year of Esther's queenship (cp. 2:16). For more information about **Pur (that is, the lot)**, see **Word Study**, p. 616.

[A]3:7 = March–April; called Abib in the pre-exilic period; Ex 13:4; Dt 16:1 [B]3:7 474 B.C. [C]3:7 = February–March [D]3:9 Lit *will weigh 10,000 silver talents on the hands of*

BIBLICAL WOMANHOOD Submission in the Old Testament

The biblical principle of the husband's headship and the wife's submission is embedded in the creation order and consistently woven throughout both Old and New Testaments (Gn 2:15-18; cp. 1Co 11:3; Eph 5:21-33; Col 3:18; 1Pt 3:1-7), including the pagan court of King Ahasuerus. The foundations laid by the Creator are not time-bound. These timeless principles are not superseded by what appear to be timely manifestations based upon cultural trends; God's principles should not be circumvented or ignored in any generation. Believers in every generation are responsible for understanding biblical principles and determining how they can be obedient in an appropriate outworking of God's plan.

Biblical submission is defined as putting all of yourself—your intellectual understandings, your acquired knowledge from every sphere of life, your personal opinions, your feelings and emotions, your energies and creativity—at the disposal of the divinely assigned authority over you. Nothing in this definition or in the text of Scripture suggests that you subject yourself to tyranny or abuse or to mindless acquiescence to the whims of another person. There is no hint of inferiority or unworthiness. Both man and woman are created in the image of God. Jesus is the New Testament example of submission. When He submits to the Father, He loses neither His deity nor His worth.

In relating to her husband, a wife is submitting to God and His plan for marriage. Thus, a wife's response in submission to her husband's leadership is a duty owed to the Lord and becomes an attitude of beauty to her husband. All relationships in life are designed to be the divine classroom for ultimately teaching submission to the will of God.

In the Old Testament, the book of Esther has references to the principle of submission. Vashti was unwise to refuse her husband's invitation to the feast. Whether she attempted to cover this refusal of her husband (the king) with a hint of modesty or even a sense of propriety, the text indicates that Ahasuerus did nothing more than to issue what may have been a tasteless and inappropriate demand to his wife. Choosing to obey only "reasonable" requests is unwise and selfish and not genuine obedience. On the other hand, Esther seemed to exhibit an inner beauty of the gentle and quiet spirit as she was obedient to Mordecai, her foster father (Est 2:20); responsive to the authorities over her (Est 2:8-9,15), and then respectfully submissive to her husband (Est 2:17; 5:2-4; 8:3).

In the modern era, submission remains at the heart of a woman's responsibility in marriage. The balance between headship on the part of the husband and submission on the part of the wife provides a beautiful plan and results in manifold blessings even if it is wrought with the inevitable challenges coming from two imperfect people living in a sinful world. Above all, every wife must remember:

- Submission is a choice; any coercion is not biblical submission.
- Submission is void of stubbornness, an attitude of joyful support of your husband.
- Submission has limits: It is to your own husband, not to every man, in all things. However, a wife's submission to her husband is not mandated when he demands that she break the law of God (Ac 5:29).
- Submission ultimately is your trust in the providence of God, not merely your confidence in the decisions of your husband.

the governors of each of the provinces, and the officials of each ethnic group and written for each province in its own script and to each ethnic group in its own language. It was written in the name of King Ahasuerus and sealed with the royal signet ring. 13 Letters were sent by couriers to each of the royal provinces telling the officials to destroy, kill, and annihilate all the Jewish people—young and old, women and children—and plunder their possessions on a single day, the thirteenth day of Adar, the twelfth month.[A]

14 A copy of the text, issued as law throughout every province, was distributed to all the peoples so that they might get ready for that day. 15 The couriers left, spurred on by royal command, and the law was issued in the fortress of Susa. The king and Haman sat down to drink, while the city of Susa was in confusion.

Mordecai's Search for an Intercessor to the King (4:1-11)

4 When Mordecai learned all that had occurred, he tore his clothes, put on •sackcloth and ashes, went into the middle of the city, and cried loudly and bitterly. 2 He only went as far as the King's Gate, since the law prohibited anyone wearing sackcloth from entering the King's Gate. 3 There was great mourning among the Jewish people in every province where the king's command and edict came. They fasted, wept, and lamented, and many lay on sackcloth and ashes.

4 Esther's female servants and her eunuchs came and reported the news to her, and the queen was overcome with fear. She sent clothes for Mordecai to wear so he could take off his sackcloth, but he did not accept them. 5 Esther summoned Hathach, one of the king's eunuchs assigned to her, and dispatched him to Mordecai to learn what he was doing and why.[B] 6 So Hathach went out to Mordecai in the city square in front of the King's Gate. 7 Mordecai told him everything that had happened as well as the exact amount of money Haman had promised to pay the royal treasury for the slaughter of the Jews.

8 Mordecai also gave him a copy of the written decree issued in Susa ordering their destruction, so that Hathach might show it to Esther, explain it to her, and command her to approach the king, implore his favor, and plead with him personally for her people. 9 Hathach came and repeated Mordecai's response to Esther.

10 Esther spoke to Hathach and commanded him to tell Mordecai, 11 "All the royal officials and the people of the royal provinces know that one law applies to every man or woman who approaches the king in the inner courtyard and who has not been summoned—the death penalty. Only if the king extends the gold scepter will that person live. I have not been summoned to appear before the king for the last[C] 30 days."

Esther's Acceptance of the Challenge (4:12-17)

12 Esther's response was reported to Mordecai.

13 Mordecai told the messenger to reply to Esther, "Don't think that you will escape the fate of all the Jews because you are in the king's palace. 14 If you keep silent at this

[A]3:13 LXX adds the text of Ahasuerus's letter here. [B]4:5 Lit *what is this and why is this* [C]4:11 Lit *king these*

>WORD|*study*

4:1 Sackcloth In the ancient Near East, people tended to show their grief and pain in visible ways. **Sackcloth** [Hb *saq*, "piece of clothing worn by people in times of sorrow or mourning"] **and ashes** [Hb *'ēpher*, "loose soil crumbling into dust or the remains of any substance burned in the fire"] were almost universally a sign of personal suffering or sorrow over the death of a loved one, of lament and anguish over a calamity, of frustration over bad news, or of military defeat (cp. Gn 37:29; 1Sm 4:12; 1Kg 21:27; 2Kg 18:37; Dn 9:3; Jnh 3:6; Mt 11:21). Typically, one's garments were torn; then a coarse and rough garment of goat or camel hair, a material also used as sieves and strainers or for sacks of grain, was added; and finally ashes were sprinkled over the head. Such a garment was sometimes the clothing of ascetics and prophets (Is 20:2). Some Jewish interpreters suggest that the "ashes" were a covering or bandage for the head used to disguise oneself.

4:1-2 There is no evidence of any regret on Mordecai's part that he had not shown obeisance to Haman, but rather his sorrow was over the seemingly imminent destruction of his people. He **cried** [Hb *za 'aq*, with the nuance of a plaintive "call for help," hoping to produce action] **loudly and bitterly**. He not only expressed his anguish publicly but also, though clothed in this way, moved as close as he could to the palace compound.

4:10-11 A person approaching the king uninvited would be put to death immediately if the king did not pardon him by extending the golden scepter. Esther assumed any approach would imperil her own life. Vashti was banished because she refused the king's summons to his presence; Esther now faced death if she entered the king's presence without invitation—typical of the ironies in the book.

Esther's very logical objection may not have been as much cowardice as the assumption that she would not survive to make an appeal or achieve the needed results, especially if her favor were at as low an ebb as the circumstances suggest.

4:13-14 Mordecai responded with a straightforward and even blunt observation, a prophetic warning and a reminder of the power of divine providence (i.e., that God might have brought her to the position of queen of Persia for this time of action). Surely Mordecai was juxtaposing the vanity of putting trust in kings or any earthly power with the mighty deliverance already demonstrated by divine intervention. He must have been well aware of the prophecies concerning the restoration of the captive Jews and their ultimate victory (Jr 29:10-14; 33:10-11). Mordecai was confident that even if Esther failed the challenge before her, God would not be taken by surprise. He would bring **liberation** [Hb *rewach*, "respite, relief"] **and deliverance . . . from another place** (cp. Jr 29:1-14). If you have position or gifts or opportunity not granted to others, you are then responsible to be the channel through whom that providence works. God never wastes His equipping or timing; rather, He expects His servants to do what He requires.

Many consider **from another place** to be a reference to divine deliverance just as **who knows** may suggest a guarded hope that divine wisdom is superintending every event. Both phrases suggest a veiled reference to the Lord's providential care in making life's circumstances work together to accomplish His purposes.

The reader finds far too many coincidences—natural occurrences—to dismiss without careful consideration. For example, the accession of a Jewess to the Persian throne, the timely

time, liberation and deliverance will come to the Jewish people from another place, but you and your father's house will be destroyed. Who knows, perhaps you have come to your royal position for such a time as this."

15 Esther sent this reply to Mordecai: 16 "Go and assemble all the Jews who can be found in Susa and fast for me. Don't eat or drink for three days, day or night. I and my female servants will also fast in the same way. After that, I will go to the king even if it is against the law. If I perish, I perish." 17 So Mordecai went and did everything Esther had ordered him.

Divine appointment is never about you, but in the biblical schema you are appointed for service to God. In Esther's situation, her placement on the throne of Persia was not to make her a queen but rather to give her the opportunity to intercede for God's people.

The Plan for Deliverance (5:1–7:10)

Esther's Approach to the King (5:1-14)

5 On the third day, Esther dressed
up in her royal clothing and stood
in the inner courtyard of the palace
facing it. The king was sitting on his
royal throne in the royal courtroom,
facing its entrance. 2 As soon as the
king saw Queen Esther standing in
the courtyard, she won his approval.[A] The king extended the gold scepter in his hand toward Esther, and she approached and touched the tip of the scepter.
3 "What is it, Queen Esther?" the king asked her. "Whatever you want, even to half the kingdom, will be given to you."
4 "If it pleases the king," Esther replied, "may the king and Haman come today to the banquet I have prepared for them."
5 The king commanded, "Hurry, and get Haman so we can do as Esther has requested." So the king and Haman went to the banquet Esther had prepared.
6 While drinking the[B] wine, the king asked Esther, "Whatever you

[A]5:2 Lit *she obtained favor in his eyes*; Est 2:15,17 [B]5:6 Lit *During the banquet of*

uncovering of a genuine plot against the king by Mordecai, the delay in rewarding Mordecai for this meritorious act, the king's extending of the scepter to receive Queen Esther, the king's insomnia and the precise entry about Mordecai coming to light belatedly from a reading of the court record, Haman's arrival to carry out the honoring of his enemy Mordecai—all these become testimony to God's working out His purposes so that human coincidences become divine appointments. God's presence and work are declared, not hidden!

4:15-16 Esther's call to **fast** suggests prayer, which is almost always mentioned concurrently with fasting (1Sm 1:7-10; 2Sm 12:16-17; Ezr 8:23; Is 58:2-5; Jr 14:12; Dn 9:3; Zch 7:3-5).

Although fasting was usually observed during the day and broken with a meal in the evening, Esther specified that this **fast** would be **night and day**. Genuine fasting was not merely a ritual but the denying of personal needs and comfort in order to focus on God—hearing from Him and obeying His word. God had brought Esther to the place in history where she could make a difference, but then the choice of whether or not to obey Him became hers.

5:1-2 Esther dressed up in her royal clothing (Hb *malekut*, "power, dominion, dignity, honor")– i.e., the accoutrements of royal office, the same root used in the Hebrew title of **Queen** (Hb *malekah*). Surely these garments

BIBLICAL WOMANHOOD How Is Fasting a Spiritual Discipline?

Fasting (Hb *tsum*, "abstain from food" or more lit "cover over" as preventing food from entering the mouth) was a means for depriving the body of nourishment. A fast most often lasted from sunrise to sunset (2Sm 1:12) and could mean partial or total abstinence or selective abstinence from certain food for a longer period (Ps 35:13; Dn 10:3). For some, fasting is considered a means of attaining spiritual rewards. The ascetics often starved themselves in an effort to demonstrate, through personal pain and deprivation, their devotion to God. Others make fasting a mockery by pursuing a façade of food deprivation as a ritual to be observed by onlookers, while there is no sign of personal devotion to and focus on the Lord.

Fasting in biblical times was done . . .

- to gain God's attention in behalf of someone's suffering (see 2Sm 12:16-23);
- to aid in making critical decisions or following an ominous course of action (see 2Ch 20:3; Est 4:16);
- to mourn the sin of blasphemy and then after participation in the required execution by stoning (1Kg 21:9,12);
- to respond to being confronted with sin in one's life (1Sm 7:6; Dn 9:13-19);
- to accompany intercession for another or for the entire nation in a time of its disobedience to God (Ezr 8:23; Neh 1:4; Dn 9:3);
- to respond in times of extreme crisis (2Ch 20:1-29) or as a national celebration, especially the Day of Atonement (Lv 16:29,31; 23:26-32; Est 9:31).

Jesus fasted for 40 days to prepare for His ministry and for the confrontation with Satan (Mt 4:1-2). He considered fasting a discipline linked with prayer (Mt 17:21) and expected His disciples to fast. First-century believers fasted to prepare for major events (Ac 13:2-3; 14:23).

Fasting in itself, just as any simple abstinence from pleasure, did not move Yahweh God. However, to devote yourself to prayer and reading God's Word is to put a pure and uninhibited focus on the Lord, and to fast is to involve your entire body in seeking God. When the people were truly seeking righteousness and became obedient, God was moved (Is 58:5-7; Ac 10:30-33). Fasting was another tool to draw the believer closer to God (Jl 2:12-15). Without sincere repentance and fruits appropriate for believers, fasting may impress others but will bring no spiritual gain.

added to her natural beauty and set her apart as one worthy to approach the king without an appointment. Esther approached the **royal courtroom**, but in a respectful manner, waiting on the king to acknowledge her presence since she had already violated the law and placed her life in jeopardy (cp. 4:11). **She won his approval** (Hb *chēn,* "favor, pity, compassion," 5:8; see 2:15) and escaped death.

5:7-8 Esther's delay in making her **request** was not without purpose. Because of the delicate nature of implicating the king's highest official, she doubtless wanted a more private setting than the open court. She also knew the centrality of feasts to Persian culture. The guest of a feast would be naturally inclined to acquiesce to the wishes of his hostess—exactly what Esther needed. Although there was some risk in putting off her mission and requesting an investment of the king's time yet again, one cannot dismiss the divine providence guiding every step. There were other details—unknown to Esther but guided by God Himself—still to go into play.

5:14 Zeresh (Persian name, "golden" or "one with disheveled hair"), the wife of Haman, together with his friends, listened to Haman's boasting about his wealth and prestige as well as his lack of satisfaction and happiness because of his hatred for the Jew, Mordecai. Then they offered him some ungodly counsel—a plan to remove the source of his unhappiness. Haman **had the gallows constructed**, more often used in the Persian culture to impale the victim for public display, which may explain the height of **75 feet**.

6:1 The book recording daily events (Hb *zikkaron*, "protocol, memorial, reminder, chronicles"; lit "book of remembrances"; cp. 2:23; 10:2; Ezr 4:15; 6:1-4; Mal 3:16) contained officially authorized accounts written by court historians on scrolls of papyrus or leather—the royal archive of the king's personal history.

6:4-5 Persian kings, as royal protocol, rewarded everyone to whom they were indebted for loyalty and beneficence. The king's bouts with insomnia may have been common, but the timing of this one had to be of God. Equally providential was the timing of Haman's appearance in the court, **just entering . . . standing in the court**, surely not the usual time for even a highly positioned officer of the court to expect to see the king.

All the happenings of this evening worked together to accomplish the divine purposes, illustrating how God places His servants in the right place at the right time. Mordecai was performing his civic duty when he reported a planned assassination of

CHARACTER PROFILE

Esther For Such a Time as This

Her Background	• A beautiful, orphaned Jewish girl (2:2) • The adopted daughter of her cousin Mordecai (2:7,15) • A God-fearing woman living in a pagan court (2:16-20)
Her Story	• She was chosen by King Ahasuerus to be queen (2:17). • She learned that the Jews were to be executed by Haman (2:22). • She risked death by approaching the king (4:10-11, 5:1-2). • She prepared a banquet for the king and Haman (5:4). • She asked the king for a new edict (8:5). • Her delivery of God's people is still celebrated by Jews today during Purim (9:32).
Life Lessons	• Esther's courage and wisdom were used by God to save His people from extinction. • Beauty and creativity are also useful tools for a God-fearing woman.

ask will be given to you. Whatever
you want, even to half the kingdom,
will be done."
7 Esther answered, "This is my petition and my request: 8 If the king
approves of me[A] and if it pleases the
king to grant my petition and perform my request, may the king and
Haman come to the banquet I will
prepare for them. Tomorrow I will
do what the king has asked."
9 That day Haman left full of joy
and in good spirits.[B] But when Haman saw Mordecai at the King's
Gate, and Mordecai didn't rise or
tremble in fear at his presence, Haman was filled with rage toward
Mordecai. 10 Yet Haman controlled
himself and went home. He sent for
his friends and his wife Zeresh to
join him. 11 Then Haman described
for them his glorious wealth and his
many sons. He told them all how the
king had honored him and promoted
him in rank over the other officials
and the royal staff. 12 "What's more,"
Haman added, "Queen Esther invited no one but me to join the king at
the banquet she had prepared. I am
invited again tomorrow to join her
with the king. 13 Still, none of this
satisfies me since I see Mordecai the
Jew sitting at the King's Gate all the
time."
14 His wife Zeresh and all his friends
told him, "Have them build a gallows 75 feet[C] high. Ask the king in
the morning to hang Mordecai on
it. Then go to the banquet with the

HARD QUESTION

What can you do to get through the difficulties of life?

- **Refuse to believe that God is unjust;** He is the essence of justice, which can be achieved even when every outward sign seems to suggest the opposite.
- **Seek the face of the Lord** before you try to fix life's challenging problems (Mt 6:33).
- When dealing with difficult people, **ask the Lord to open their hearts to you.** Even believers are working from different degrees of spiritual maturity. God works through the faithful and obedient as well as the unfaithful and disobedient (Pr 16:7).
- **Wait on the Lord** even when all seems to be lost; give Him time to work (Ps 27:14; Pr 20:22). God is sometimes quiet, and you must wait for Him to speak. Meantime, you never give up working toward whatever assignment God has given you.
- **Do not despair** when no one seems to notice your service to Christ. God's turning points often come through seemingly insignificant events in your life (Est 6:3; cp. Heb 6:10).

[A] **5:8** Lit *If I have found favor in the eyes of the king* [B] **5:9** Lit *left rejoicing and good of heart*
[C] **5:14** Lit *50 cubits*

king and enjoy yourself." The advice pleased Haman, so he had the gallows constructed.

The Honoring of Mordecai by the Adversary Haman (6:1-13)

6 That night sleep escaped the king, so he ordered the book recording daily events to be brought and read to the king. 2 They found the written report of how Mordecai had informed on Bigthana and Teresh, two eunuchs who guarded the king's entrance, when they planned to assassinate King Ahasuerus. 3 The king inquired, "What honor and special recognition have been given to Mordecai for this act?"

The king's personal attendants replied, "Nothing has been done for him."

4 The king asked, "Who is in the court?" Now Haman was just entering the outer court of the palace to ask the king to hang Mordecai on the gallows he had prepared for him.

5 The king's attendants answered him, "Haman is there, standing in the court."

"Have him enter," the king ordered.

6 Haman entered, and the king asked him, "What should be done for the man the king wants to honor?"

Haman thought to himself, "Who is it the king would want to honor more than me?" 7 Haman told the king, "For the man the king wants to honor: 8 Have them bring a royal garment that the king himself has worn and a horse the king himself has ridden, which has a royal diadem on its head. 9 Put the garment and the horse under the charge of one of the king's most noble officials. Have them clothe the man the king wants to honor, parade him on the horse through the city square, and proclaim before him, 'This is what is done for the man the king wants to honor.'"

10 The king told Haman, "Hurry, and do just as you proposed. Take a garment and a horse for Mordecai the Jew, who is sitting at the King's Gate. Do not leave out anything you have suggested." 11 So Haman took the garment and the horse. He clothed Mordecai and paraded him through the city square, crying out before him, "This is what is done for the man the king wants to honor."

12 Then Mordecai returned to the King's Gate, but Haman, overwhelmed,[A] hurried off for home with his head covered. 13 Haman told his wife Zeresh and all his friends everything that had happened. His advisers and his wife Zeresh said to him, "Since Mordecai is Jewish, and you have begun to fall before him, you won't overcome him, because your downfall is certain."

Esther's Unveiling of Haman's Wicked Plan (6:14–7:10)

14 While they were still speaking with him, the eunuchs of the king arrived and rushed Haman to the banquet Esther had prepared.

7 The king and Haman came to feast[B] with Esther the queen. 2 Once again, on the second day while drinking wine, the king asked Esther, "Queen Esther, whatever you ask will be given to you. Whatever you seek, even to half the kingdom, will be done."

3 Queen Esther answered, "If I have obtained your approval,[C] my king, and if the king is pleased, spare my life—this is my request; and spare my people—this is my desire. 4 For my people and I have been sold out to destruction, death, and extermination. If we had merely been sold as male and female slaves, I would have kept silent. Indeed, the trouble wouldn't be worth burdening the king."

5 King Ahasuerus spoke up and asked Queen Esther, "Who is this, and where is the one who would devise such a scheme?"[D]

6 Esther answered, "The adversary and enemy is this evil Haman."

Haman stood terrified before the king and queen. 7 Angered by this, the king arose from where they were drinking wine and went to the palace garden. Haman remained to beg Queen Esther for his life because

the king. The deed was recorded but went unrewarded for as much as five years until this time when God not only inspired the events leading to a reward far beyond anything Mordecai could have imagined but also used that reward as part of His plan for delivering the Jews (cp. 2:21-23).

6:12 Now Haman adopted the dress of mourning **with his head covered,** showing his depression and internal turmoil in a public way. Unfortunately, his wife Zeresh and his friends were discerning in predicting what was to come and crediting the fall of Haman to the invincibility of the Jews, despite their earlier encouragement to Haman to pursue Mordecai's demise relentlessly (5:14). Even pagan unbelievers and enemies of the Jews eventually see the power of the one true God and realize that He keeps His promises to His people (Gn 12:3).

6:13 Their prophetic announcement is clear concerning the defeat of Haman—**you have begun to fall** [Hb *napal*, as falling before or in the sense of falling into ruin; Jos 6:5,20; Is 31:8; 37:7]**. . . you won't overcome** [Hb *yakol*, "be able," in the sense that the outcome was beyond his ability to control]**. . . your downfall** [Hb *napal*] **is certain.**

7:1 To **feast** (Hb *shatah*; cp. 4:16), which suggests victory and joy and security, is in contrast to Esther's earlier fasting, which was done under the pressure of crisis and uncertainty. Another twist in this narrative is that Esther was hosting a feast before her deliverance was assured. Whether or not her personal confidence was inspired by anticipated victory is not stated in the text, but certainly she was showing trust in divine providence by moving forward with her plan to host the second banquet for her husband, the king, and her adversary Haman.

[A]6:12 Lit *mourning* [B]7:1 Lit *drink* [C]7:3 Lit *If I have found favor in your eyes* [D]7:5 Lit *who would fill his heart to do this*

7:9 The reversals and irony continue as **one of the royal eunuchs** informed the king about the gallows Haman **made for Mordecai**, which must have intensified the king's anger since **Harbona** also included the connection of Mordecai as the one **who gave the report that saved the king**. A timely reminder that Haman knowingly planned the execution of the man who had saved the king's life sealed the fate of the Agagite, another example of poetic justice (cp. Pr 11:6; 29:16).

8:1-2 Since Persian law allowed the state to take the property and possessions of condemned criminals, Ahasuerus had control over Haman's vast estate. He immediately gave it to Esther. Ahasuerus further honored Mordecai by giving him the **signet ring**, elevating him officially to the position Haman had held with the right to act in the name of the king (cp. 3:10). Esther also **put him** [Mordecai] **in charge of Haman's estate**.

8:5-12 Though the timing of this transition is not specified other than the immediate execution of Haman, the time elapsing between the edict of Haman (April 17, 474 B.C.) and the new edict issued by Mordecai **on the twenty-third day of the third month** (June 25, 474 B.C.) was two months and 10 days. **Sivan**, during which Pentecost or the Festival of Weeks is observed as a harvest celebration to honor the giving of the Law at Sinai, corresponds with mid-May to mid-June on the modern calendar. Esther moved forward to circumvent Haman's deadly assault on the Jews. Knowing that Persian laws could not be repealed or changed, she suggested the issuing of another edict. She did not blame the king for the earlier edict but placed all the blame on Haman.

8:11-12 The new edict would allow the Jews to initiate the destruction of their enemies rather than remain defenseless against their attackers. **The thirteenth day of the twelfth month** or **Adar** is the period corresponding with mid-February to mid-March on the modern calendar (June 25, 474 B.C.). The phrase **including women and children**, detailing the extent of destruction of their enemies within the second edict, has offended some. One interpretation is supported by the reference to restraint exercised by the Jews when viewing their enemies' spoil, which had been promised to them (cp. 9:10,15-16). Mordecai's words may not be a paraphrase of Haman's edict (3:13), taking the form of instruction to the Jews, but rather a rendering of the original edict, since it would be important for the Jews to know the details of that against which they must defend themselves.

HARD QUESTION

Why do bad things happen to good people?

Tragedy will strike, suffering will come, crisis will intervene at the most inopportune moment. However, in the midst of whatever evil or hurtful scenario you face, a child of God need only wait for her hour of redemption because God has promised that He will be the ultimate Mover in life (Rm 8:28). Nothing can keep you from God's unfailing presence, His perfect knowledge, His matchless wisdom, and His unconditional love (Rm 8:38-39). God is ever working on your behalf for what is ultimately best for you. God never works against you; He is always for you (Rm 8:31-32). Adversities will come as surely as the blessings, but in all you are dependent upon Him; and nothing happens without His permission since He is sovereign over your decisions and actions, guiding all according to His purposes. *Many things happen that are labeled "co-incidence" or human happenstance, but in reality they are "God-incidence" or an expression of divine providence.* In the lives of Esther and the Jewish people, God's providence overruled tragedy and poor judgment to bring good from evil, arranging even the smallest details in order to preserve His people and reward those who were obedient to Him.

he realized the king was planning
something terrible for him. 8 Just as
the king returned from the palace
garden to the house of wine drinking, Haman was falling on the couch
where Esther was reclining. The
king exclaimed, "Would he actually
violate the queen while I am in the
palace?" As soon as the statement
left the king's mouth, Haman's face
was covered.
9 Harbona, one of the royal eunuchs, said: "There is a gallows 75
feet[A] tall at Haman's house that he
made for Mordecai, who gave the report that saved[B] the king."
The king commanded, "Hang him
on it."
10 They hanged Haman on the gallows he had prepared for Mordecai.
Then the king's anger subsided.

The Reward of Divine Deliverance (8:1–9:32)

The Jews' Freedom to Defend Themselves (8:1-14)

8 That same day King Ahasuerus
awarded Queen Esther the estate
of Haman, the enemy of the Jews.
Mordecai entered the king's presence because Esther had revealed
her relationship to Mordecai. 2 The
king removed his signet ring he had
recovered from Haman and gave it
to Mordecai, and Esther put him in
charge of Haman's estate.
3 Then Esther addressed the king
again. She fell at his feet, wept, and
begged him to revoke the evil of Haman the Agagite, and his plot he had
devised against the Jews. 4 The king
extended the gold scepter toward
Esther, so she got up and stood before the king.
5 She said, "If it pleases the king,
and I have found approval before
him, if the matter seems right to the
king and I am pleasing in his sight,
let a royal edict be written. Let it
revoke the documents the scheming Haman son of Hammedatha
the Agagite, wrote to destroy the
Jews who are in all the king's provinces. 6 For how could I bear to see
the disaster that would come on my
people? How could I bear to see the
destruction of my relatives?"
7 King Ahasuerus said to Esther
the Queen and to Mordecai the Jew,
"Look, I have given Haman's estate
to Esther, and he was hanged on
the gallows because he attacked[C] the
Jews. 8 You may write in the king's
name whatever pleases you concerning the Jews, and seal it with the royal signet ring. A document written in
the king's name and sealed with the
royal signet ring cannot be revoked."
9 On the twenty-third day of the
third month (that is, the month

Doctrine — PROVIDENCE

God's providential care for His creation is part of His signature as He sustains and directs the world and all in it. God Himself continually orders the events of your life to fulfill the original purpose for which He created the world in general and you specifically; and He is compassionate, gracious, longsuffering, and ever faithful (Ps 16:9-11). There is no realm into which God cannot enter—no blind fate or inviolable law of cause and effect that can trump God (Pr 16:33). Creation describes the existence of all God made; preservation explains the overall working of His plan; providence—the seen and unseen, the good and the evil—is the umbrella under which life's journey is made.

[A] **7:9** Lit *50 cubits* [B] **7:9** Lit *who spoke good for* [C] **8:7** Lit *stretched out his hand against*

Sivan),[A] the royal scribes were summoned. Everything was written exactly as Mordecai ordered for the Jews, to the satraps, the governors, and the officials of the 127 provinces from India[B] to •Cush. The edict was written for each province in its own script, for each ethnic group in its own language, and to the Jews in their own script and language.

10 Mordecai wrote in King Ahasuerus's name and sealed the edicts with the royal signet ring. He sent the documents by mounted couriers, who rode fast horses bred from the royal racing mares.

11 The king's edict gave the Jews in each and every city the right to assemble and defend themselves, to destroy, kill, and annihilate every ethnic and provincial army hostile to them, including women and children, and to take their possessions as spoils of war. 12 This would take place on a single day throughout all the provinces of King Ahasuerus, on the thirteenth day of the twelfth month, the month Adar.[C]

13 A copy of the text, issued as law throughout every province, was distributed to all the peoples so the Jews could be ready to avenge themselves against their enemies on that day. 14 The couriers rode out in haste on their royal horses at the king's urgent command. The law was also issued in the fortress of Susa.

The Honoring of Mordecai and Esther (8:15–9:19)

15 Mordecai went from the king's presence clothed in royal purple and white, with a great gold crown and a purple robe of fine linen. The city of Susa shouted and rejoiced, 16 and the Jews celebrated[D] with gladness, joy, and honor. 17 In every province and every city, wherever the king's command and his law reached, joy and rejoicing took place among the Jews. There was a celebration and a holiday.[E] And many of the ethnic groups of the land professed themselves to be Jews because fear of the Jews had overcome them.

9 The king's command and law went into effect on the thirteenth day of the twelfth month, the month Adar.[F] On the day when the Jews' enemies had hoped to overpower them, just the opposite happened. The Jews overpowered those who hated them. 2 In each of King Ahasuerus's provinces the Jews assembled in their cities to attack those who intended to harm them.[G] Not a single person could withstand them; terror of them fell on every nationality.

3 All the officials of the provinces, the satraps, the governors, and the royal civil administrators[H] aided the Jews because they were afraid of Mordecai. 4 For Mordecai exercised great power in the palace, and his fame spread throughout the provinces as he became more and more powerful.

5 The Jews put all their enemies to the sword, killing and destroying them. They did what they pleased to those who hated them. 6 In the fortress of Susa the Jews killed and destroyed 500 men, 7 including Parshandatha, Dalphon, Aspatha, 8 Poratha, Adalia, Aridatha, 9 Parmashta, Arisai, Aridai, and Vaizatha. 10 They killed these 10 sons of Haman son of Hammedatha, the enemy of the Jews. However, they did not seize[I] any plunder.

11 On that day the number of people killed in the fortress of Susa was reported to the king. 12 The king said to Queen Esther, "In the fortress of Susa the Jews have killed and destroyed 500 men, including Haman's 10 sons. What have they done in the rest of the royal provinces? Whatever you ask will be given to you. Whatever you seek will also be done."

13 Esther answered, "If it pleases the king, may the Jews who are in Susa also have tomorrow to carry out today's law, and may the bodies of Haman's 10 sons be hung on the gallows." 14 The king gave the orders for this to be done, so a law was announced in Susa, and they hung the bodies of Haman's 10 sons. 15 The Jews in Susa assembled again on the fourteenth day of the month of Adar

8:15-17 The **great gold crown** (Hb *'atarah*, "garland, diadem") worn by Mordecai is not the "crown" or royal turban cited elsewhere in the book (1:11; 2:17; 6:8) and is distinctive from that worn by the king and queen, but the royal headdress did set Mordecai apart as a royal favorite. **Many of the ethnic groups of the land professed themselves to be Jews** (Hb *yahad*, "pose as a Jew, become a Jew, declare oneself to be a Jew"), which may have meant that they pretended to be Jews for security reasons or that they were sympathetic with the Jews and identified with them because of their compassion for them, or perhaps the people even felt not being a Jew was dangerous. The reason given in the text is their **fear** [Hb *pachad*, "dread, terror"] **of the Jews**. This is another reversal or irony: It was once dangerous and life-threatening to be a Jew; now it was dangerous not to be a Jew!

9:1 The thirteenth day of the twelfth month (March 7, 473 B.C., the last month of the sacred year) was the fateful day, and another ironic reversal occurred—**just the opposite happened** (Hb *hapak*, "happen the other way around, be reversed"). Instead of being destroyed by their enemies, the Jews **overpowered** [Hb *shalat*, "gain power, become master"] **those who hated them** (cp. Pr 16:33).

9:5-14 In defending themselves, the Jews sought to remove the threat of those who wished to harm them. They were dealing with an enemy who had been given the license to exterminate them, making their actions not only necessary but justified. Yet, despite their permission to do so, **they did not seize any plunder** (cp. vv. 15-16), underscoring their motivation as self-preservation and not looting. Esther's request for the hanging of **the bodies of Haman's 10 sons**, who were already dead, probably would have been made so that their public impalement, a common practice in the ancient Near East (cp. 1Sm 31:8-13), might provide a deterrent to future aggression against the Jews.

A 8:9 = May–June B 8:9 = modern Pakistan C 8:12 = February–March D 8:16 Lit *had light* E 8:17 Lit *good day* F 9:1 = February–March G 9:2 Lit *cities to send out a hand against the seekers of their evil* H 9:3 Lit *and those who do the king's work*; Est 3:9 I 9:10 Lit *not put their hands on*

>WORD|*study*

9:26 Pur (Hb, "lot") is a Hebrew form of *puru*, an Akkadian word meaning "lot or fate" and referring to a small clay or glass cube with dots or an inscription on each side of the cube. Magicians and astrologers were not the only ones using broken stones or dice to solicit decisions from the gods. The Bible notes different uses for casting lots, e.g., in Joshua's division of the promised land among the 12 tribes (Jos 18:6-10) and the identification of Jonah as the reason for the life-threatening storm (Jnh 1:7). The Israelites practiced this casting of "lots" (Hb *goral*, "stone pebble," ultimately taking the sense of "fate or destiny"; cp. Lv 16:8; Nm 26:55-56; Jos 14:2; 1Sm 14:41-42; 1Ch 26:14; Neh 10:34; Ps 22:18; Pr 16:33; 18:18; Jl 3:3; Gk *klēros* in Ac 1:26). Of course, rolling dice could not determine the destiny of God's people; but the celebration of Purim for Israel did commemorate their confidence in God's sovereignty over their enemies and oppressors. These lots were cast during "the first month" of the year to determine the best days for important events (3:7). The Babylonian style of calendar was adopted by the Jews after the exile. Nisan, formerly Abib, was the month during which the children of Israel were delivered out of Egypt and the month during which Jews throughout the generations have celebrated Passover (cp. Dt 16:1). Now as the Jews celebrated that deliverance in their most important religious holiday, Haman was casting lots to determine the day of their destruction at his hand. The lot fell "on the twelfth month, the month Adar" (i.e., March or April 474 B.C), only a month before the next celebration of Passover (Est 3:7).

and killed 300 men in Susa, but they did not seize[A] any plunder.

16 The rest of the Jews in the royal provinces assembled, defended themselves, and got rid of[B] their enemies. They killed 75,000[C] of those who hated them, but they did not seize[A] any plunder. 17 They fought on the thirteenth day of the month of Adar and rested on the fourteenth, and it became a day of feasting and rejoicing.

18 But the Jews in Susa had assembled on the thirteenth and the fourteenth days of the month. They rested on the fifteenth day of the month, and it became a day of feasting and rejoicing. 19 This explains why the rural Jews who live in villages observe the fourteenth day of the month of Adar as a time of rejoicing and feasting. It is a holiday when they send gifts to one another.

The Institution of the Festival of Purim (9:20-32)

20 Mordecai recorded these events and sent letters to all the Jews in all of King Ahasuerus's provinces, both near and far. 21 He ordered them to celebrate the fourteenth and fifteenth days of the month Adar every year 22 because during those days the Jews got rid of[D] their enemies. That was the month when their sorrow was turned into rejoicing and their mourning into a holiday. They were to be days of feasting, rejoicing, and of sending gifts to one another and the poor.

23 So the Jews agreed to continue the practice they had begun, as Mordecai had written them to do. 24 For Haman son of Hammedatha the Agagite, the enemy of all the Jews, had plotted against the Jews to destroy them. He cast the Pur (that is, the lot) to crush and destroy them. 25 But when the matter was brought before the king, he commanded by letter that the evil plan Haman had devised against the Jews return on his own head and that he should be hanged with his sons on the gallows. 26 For this reason these days are called Purim, from the word Pur.

Because of all the instructions in this letter as well as what they had witnessed and what had happened to them, 27 the Jews bound themselves, their descendants, and all who joined with them to a commitment that they would not fail to celebrate these two days each and every year according to the written instructions and according to the time appointed. 28 These days are remembered and celebrated by every generation, family, province, and city, so that these days of Purim will not lose their significance in Jewish life[E] and their memory will not fade from their descendants.

29 Queen Esther daughter of Abihail, along with Mordecai the

[A]9:15,16 Lit *not put their hands on* [B]9:16 Lit *and gained relief from* [C]9:16 Some LXX mss read *10,107*; other LXX mss read *15,000* [D]9:22 Lit *Jews gained relief from* [E]9:28 LXX reads *will be celebrated into all times*

9:17-32 A day of feasting and rejoicing inaugurated the celebration Jewish Festival of **Purim** (Hb, "lots"), a celebration of deliverance and affirmation. "Feasting and rejoicing" is a hendiadys, a figure of speech that expresses one idea by two independent words—each amplifying the other so the final idea is larger than both—rather than a single word with modifier (cp. vv. 17-19,24,28). The naming of the feast (Purim, or the Festival of Lots), one of two festivals not established in the Pentateuch (cp. Ex 34:18-27; Lv 23:1-44; 25:1-17) but considered by the Jews just as binding as their other celebrations, underscores the importance of the casting of lots as an early indication of God's providential care of His people and control over their enemies (Est 9:24-26).

The first observance of Purim is unveiled in the book of Esther, as well as the only biblical description for its celebration and regulation of its observance (9:28-32; see also 3:7; 9:24). Central to the celebration, the *Megillat Esther* (Hb, "scroll of Esther") has been read in its entirety in assemblies of Jews from the Second Temple period until the present era.

Two days were appointed for celebration (v. 27): **The Jews in Susa** were given two days for killing their enemies, and **they rested on the fifteenth** of **Adar** (late February or early March), and thus their celebration was assigned for that day. Jews in outlying provinces had only **the thirteenth day** of Adar to respond to their enemies, and they celebrated on **the fourteenth** of Adar. The thirteenth day of Adar is also celebrated as the Fast of Esther by some Jews because of the mention of commemorating **the practices of fasting and lamentation** (v. 31).

The emphasis of the feast was not meant to be the destruction of the enemies of the Jews but rather the "resting" of the Jews—their deliverance from the oppression of their enemies. Among modern Jews, the holiday meal is usually on the evening of the fourteenth, which is a month before Passover. The celebration includes sending **gifts to one another**, and **the poor** receive help (vv. 19,22). All men, women, and children are expected to be present because they all had a part in this deliverance. The reading of the Esther scroll in the synagogue is accompanied by the background of noisemakers; and when Haman's name is mentioned, there is booing and hissing. Games and masquerading occur in a carnival-like atmosphere.

Esther's reason for writing **this second letter** seems to have been the endorsement of Mordecai's letter with her authority, emphasizing that the memory of this deliverance is to be celebrated by the Jews in the generations to come (v. 29).

The Festival of Purim

Name	• Purim (Hb *pur*, "part, lot", 3:7) from the word *Pur* (Persian, "lot, portion," 9:26)
Time	• The fourteenth day of Adar (Feb.–Mar.) by those in the villages and unwalled towns; the fifteenth day by those in fortified cities
Purpose	• To celebrate the deliverance of the Jews from genocide—the reversal of "the evil plan Haman had devised" through Esther's influence (9:25) • To remember and preserve the historical significance of this event (9:28)
Practices	• "Feasting and rejoicing" (9:17-18,22) • "Sending gifts to one another" (9:19,22) • Sending gifts (especially of food) to "the poor" (9:22) • In modern practice, preceded by a "minor fast" commemorating Esther's three-day fast in preparation for approaching the king

Jew, wrote this second letter with
full authority to confirm the letter about Purim. 30 He sent letters
with messages of peace and faithfulness to all the Jews who were in
the 127 provinces of the kingdom
of Ahasuerus, 31 in order to confirm
these days of Purim at their proper
time just as Mordecai the Jew and
Queen Esther had established them
and just as they had committed
themselves and their descendants
to the practices of fasting and lamentation. 32 So Esther's command
confirmed these customs of Purim,
which were then written into the
record.

An Epilogue on Mordecai (10:1-3)

10 King Ahasuerus imposed a tax
throughout the land even to the
farthest shores.[A] 2 All of his powerful
and magnificent accomplishments
and the detailed account of Mordecai's great rank to which the king
had honored him, have they not been
written in the Historical Record of
the Kings of Media and Persia? 3 Mordecai the Jew was second only to
King Ahasuerus, famous among the
Jews, and highly popular with many
of his relatives. He continued to seek
good for his people and to speak for
the welfare of all his descendants.

[A] **10:1** Or *imposed forced labor on the land and the coasts of the sea*

The prophet Zechariah prophesied a time of peace and prosperity for God's people, and this reversal culminating in their deliverance is another sign of the still-to-come ultimate fulfillment of that prophecy (Zch 8:19; cp. Est 9:19; 8:16-17), making the book of Esther not only historical, theological, and inspirational but also prophetic.

10:1-3 Ahasuerus had fought a war with Greece costly in resources and lives, and he lost (479 B.C.). Mordecai, as **second only to King Ahasuerus**, probably had a role to play in implementing this policy, giving him a unique place in Jewish history (cp. Daniel in Babylon [Dn 2:48; 5:29] and Joseph in Egypt (Gn 41:43]) and making him an example of how God raised up heroic leaders to the highest positions even in pagan courts in order to deliver His people.

Mordecai achieved great honor because he sought **good** for his people, and he also spoke out courageously **for the welfare** [Hb *shalom*, "peace, absence of war or completeness, wholeness, health, harmony, prosperity, security, fulfillment"] **of all his descendants**. The latter characteristic was far more rare than the former. The author seems to emphasize that well-being and good relationships are most important in a peaceful and safe existence.

>WORD|*study*

10:1 The tax (Hb *mas*, "particularly heavy burden, serfdom tribute, forced payment"; cp. Ex 1:11; 1Kg 5:13; 9:21), which may have included forced labor and elsewhere in the Old Testament may have been used collectively for a group of people in servitude, was a way to replenish his royal treasury.

Someone has noted that a veil does not necessarily cover to keep out but rather may invite the viewer to look through and see what is behind. The book of Esther, if likened to a veil, invites its readers to peer through and see the faithful providence that God has assigned to the care of His people throughout the generations.

THE JEWISH CALENDAR At a Glance

- The Jewish day begins at sunset (6:00 p.m.) of the previous day.
- A month begins at the new moon (when the moon comes closest to being between earth and sun) and averages 29.5 days.
- The names of the months are in Babylonian tradition.
- The Jewish year is lunar (totaling 354 days rather than the 365 of the solar calendar) and follows a 19-year cycle, during which the leap year month (Veadar or Adar II) is added in the 3rd, 6th, 8th, 11th, 14th, 17th, and 19th years of the cycle.
- The Jewish sacred year begins with the new moon of spring—approximately between March 22 and April 25 in cycles of 19 years.
- The civil calendar, differing somewhat from the sacred calendar, was the official calendar for kings, childbirth, and contracts.

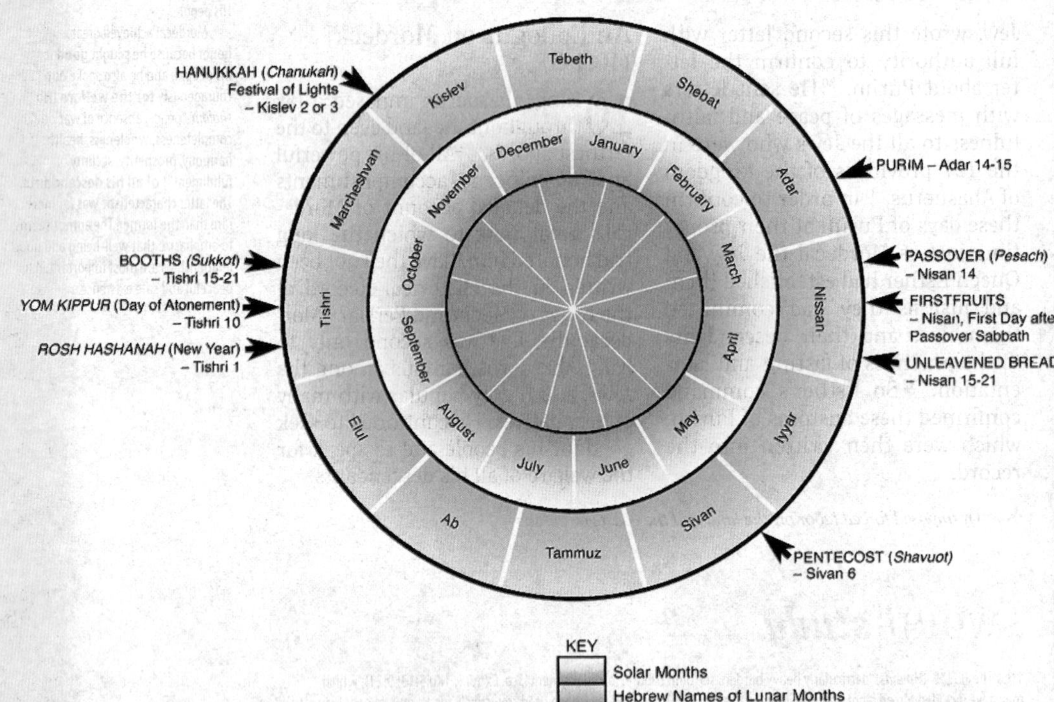

HEBREW MONTH* Sacred/Civil Year	GREGORIAN CALENDAR	DAY	FEATURES	FESTIVALS (Day) of the month in parentheses
1/7 Nisan (Abib)	March–April	**30**	Spring rains [Dt 11:14] Floods [Jos 3:15] Ripening of barley	(1) New Moon (14) Passover, *Pesach* [Ex 12:1-16,21-27; Lv 23:5; Nm 28:16] Firstfruits (First Day after Passover Sabbath) (15-21) Unleavened Bread [Ex 12:17-20; Lv 23:6-8; Nm 28:17-25]
2/8 Iyyar (Ziv)	April–May	**29**	Beginning of summer without rain from April to September Barley harvest [Ru 1:22] Wheat harvest [1Sm 12:17]	(1) New Moon (14) Second Passover, for those unable to keep the first
3/9 Sivan	May–June	**30**	Increased heat Ripening of spring fruits Blossoming of fruit-bearing trees Tending of vines and continued harvesting of wheat	(1) New Moon; regarded as "the same day" of Ex 19:1 (6) Pentecost, *Shavuot* [Nm 28:26-31]; traditionally, "The Day of the Giving of the Torah"
4/10 Tammuz	June–July	**29**	Hot season	(1) New Moon (17) Fast for the first breach of the walls of Jerusalem during Babylonian siege [Zch 8:19]
5/11 Ab	July–August	**30**	Intense heat Drying up of streams Ripening and harvest of grapes, figs, olives [Lv 26:5]	(1) New Moon (9) Fast for the destruction of the temple [Zch 8:19]
6/12 Elul	August–September	**29**	Hottest month of the year Grape harvest	(1) New Moon
7/1 Tishri (Ethanim)	September–October	**30**	Beginning of former or early rains [Jl 2:23] Beginning of plowing and sowing	(1) New Year, *Rosh Hashanah*—Day of Blowing the Trumpet [Lv 23:23-25; Nm 29:1-6]; Day of Judgment and Memorial (3) Fast of Gedaliah [2Kg 25:25-26; Zch 8:19] (10) Day of Atonement, *Yom Kippur* [Lv 16; 23:26-32; Nm 29:7-11] (15-21) Booths, *Sukkot* [Lv 23:33-36,39-43; Nm 29:12-32] (22) Solemn Assembly [Lv 23:35-36,39]
8/2 Marcheshvan (Bul)	October–November	**29 or 30**	Continuing of rain Sowing of wheat and barley	(1) New Moon
9/3 Kislev	November–December	**29 or 30**	Beginning of winter Heavy rain; snow on the mountains	(1) New Moon (25) Dedication [Jn 10:22,29] (3 or 2) Hanukkah [*Chanukah*]—"Festival of Lights" for the rededication of the Second Temple in Jerusalem, 2nd century B.C.
10/4 Tebeth	December–January	**29**	Coldest month Hail and snow [Jos 10:11]	(1) New Moon (10) Fast for the Babylonian siege of Jerusalem [Zch 8:19]
11/5 Shebat	January–February	**30**	Gradually warmer weather	(1) New Moon
12/6 Adar	February–March	**29 or 30**	Frequent thunderstorms Blossoming of almond trees	(1) New Moon (13) Fast of Esther (14-15) Purim
Leap Year: Veadar (Adar II)	March–April	**29**	Intercalary month inserted to make the calendar year correspond with the actual passage of time	(1) New Moon (13) Fast of Esther (14-15) Purim

*Hebrew month names are Babylonian in origin. Names in parentheses—e.g. (Abib)—are Canaanite in origin.

Job

Timeline ■ World Events ■ Biblical Events	*2700 BC*	*2334–2279 BC*	*2285–2250 BC*	*2200–1900 BC*
	Rule of Gilgamesh in city of Uruk (modern-day Warka in Iraq)	Reign of Sargon of Akkad in Mesopotamia	Life of Enheduanna, daughter of Sargon of Akkad and possibly earliest author known by name	Events in Job

"The Lord gives, and the Lord takes away. Praise the name of Yahweh" (Jb 1:21b).

Who wrote Job?
Unknown

Who were the recipients?
The original readers of the book may have been Job's contemporaries. The story of Job's trials continues to have universal appeal since all people experience suffering in life.

When was Job written?
Among the Dead Sea Scrolls discovered at Qumran, only Job and the books of the Pentateuch were written in the ancient Paleo-Hebrew script, distinguishing them as the oldest compositions in the biblical canon. How long ago the book was written is uncertain, but Job probably lived ca 2200–1900 B.C., sometime after Abraham's journey from Ur of the Chaldeans to Canaan (Gn 11:31) and well before the Israelites' exodus from Egypt (ca 1446 B.C.).

Where did it happen?
"The land of Uz" (1:1) was located in the area of Edom, east of northern Arabia (cp. Jr 25:20; Lm 4:21). Job may have lived near the Wadi Sirhan, which extended approximately 200 miles along the eastern part of the region in a northwest-to-southeast direction.

In addition to the physical setting for the lives of Job and his family, decisive conversations between the Lord and Satan take place "before the Lord" (Jb 1:6), in "the Lord's presence" (2:7). In Job's understanding, God is "as high as the heavens" (22:12; cp. 16:19; 28:4-28). The unique glimpse of God's perspective on earthly events places Job's life in a setting that is cosmic in scope. Although Satan claims to be "roaming through the earth . . . and walking around on it" (1:7; 2:2), Yahweh declares that He exercises absolute sovereignty over all the earth (38:1-41; 41:11; cp. 26:6-14; 28:24-28).

What is Job about?
Job addresses the question, Why do the righteous suffer? The Bible teaches that suffering is a result of living in a fallen world. In the book of Job, however, this is the question: Why do those who live godly lives suffer? And, when they do, why does God seem so distant and unavailable?

The book also addresses attitudes toward suffering. The speeches of Job and his friends illustrate opposing ideas about suffering and correct responses to it. On one hand, Job's friends persistently confronted him with variations on the theme of retribution as a black-and-white issue—God punishes only the evildoer, so Job must have done something to merit his suffering. On the other hand, Job is a model of one who questioned God in frustration and anger without renouncing or denying Him.

Why should women read Job?
Women who suffer often long for an explanation and ask, "Why me? What did I do to deserve this?" To ask "why" is not wrong (Jb 3:11-12,16-26); but as Job learned, God is not obligated to answer—He alone is sovereign and free to do as He chooses (23:13). The speeches of Job and his friends reveal the limitations of human understanding of God and His ways (40:1-5; 42:1-6; cp. Is 55:9; Rm 9:20-23). However, the book of Job also affirms that even when life's afflictions are overwhelming, women can count on God always to act in accordance with the perfect goodness, love, mercy, and justice of His own character. The New Testament commends both "Job's endurance" and the Lord's compassion and mercy toward him (Jms 5:11). There will never be a satisfactory answer to the "why" question (chaps. 38–41), but the book of Job proves that a woman who has entrusted her life to the Lord can choose to trust God and His goodness, even in the most heart-rending and debilitating circumstances.

How do you read Job?
To become familiar with the overall structure of the book is critical for making sense of its parts. The headings placed within the biblical text will be especially helpful for navigating your reading. The book begins and ends with a basic storyline—what happens to Job and how his story turns out. This narrative framework—a prologue (1:1–2:13) and epilogue (42:1-17)—establishes several levels of conflict, which are then developed in the material in between through cycles of dramatic monologues and dialogues written in poetry (see "How do you read Psalms," pp. 666-667 for a description of how Hebrew poetry works). Paying careful attention to who is speaking is especially important as you read because you are following a sustained argument among five human beings, none of whom articulates a perfectly reliable understanding of God, as God's speech (chaps. 38–41) demonstrates.

The primary conflict in this account is between God and Satan over Job's motives for fearing and serving God. Satan challenges God regarding Job's righteousness, God agrees to the test, and Job's world is turned upside down. Another ongoing conflict occurs between Job and his friends, with whom the theological disagreements become intense. However, perhaps the most interesting conflict takes place within Job himself as he wrestles with how his suffering is related to God's justice. Each of these conflicts is eventually resolved in chapter 42 as Job repents for speaking about God in ignorance (Jb 42:1-6), as God restores Job's health and blessings (42:10-17), and as He rebukes Job's friends (42:7-9).

Also, as part of the wisdom literature of the Bible, the book of Job addresses both knowing God's truth and applying it to life. The book upholds knowing God by faith to the extent that He reveals Himself and commends perseverance in faith (Jms 5:11); it contends against substituting knowledge *about* God for personal knowledge *of* God. Read Job prayerfully, continually asking God to correct and deepen your understanding of Him in ways that will transform your life and testimony to His faithfulness.

2166-1991 BC	2113–2004 BC	1792–1750 BC	1446 BC	1259 BC
Life of Abraham	Third Dynasty of Ur	Reign of Hammurabi in Babylon as 6th king of Amorite dynasty	The Exodus from Egypt	Peace treaty between Egyptian pharaoh Rameses II and Hittite king Hattusili II

Outline

I. Prologue (1:1–2:13)
   A. The Introduction of Job (1:1-5)
   B. Satan's First Test (1:6-12)
   C. Job's Disaster (1:13-19)
   D. Job's Response (1:20-22)
   E. Satan's Second Test (2:1-8)
   F. The Response of Job's Wife (2:9-10)
   G. The Response of Job's Friends (2:11-13)

II. The First Series of Speeches (3:1–14:22)
   A. Job's Speech (3:1-26)
   B. Eliphaz's Speech (4:1–5:27)
   C. Job's Reply to Eliphaz (6:1–7:21)
   D. Bildad's Speech (8:1-22)
   E. Job's Reply to Bildad (9:1–10:22)
   F. Zophar's Speech (11:1-20)
   G. Job's Reply to Zophar (12:1–14:22)

III. The Second Series of Speeches (15:1–21:34)
   A. Eliphaz's Speech (15:1-35)
   B. Job's Reply to Eliphaz (16:1–17:16)
   C. Bildad's Speech (18:1-21)
   D. Job's Reply to Bildad (19:1-29)
   E. Zophar's Speech (20:1-29)
   F. Job's Reply to Zophar (21:1-34)

IV. The Third Series of Speeches (22:1–28:28)
   A. Eliphaz's Speech (22:1-30)
   B. Job's Reply to Eliphaz (23:1–24:25)
   C. Bildad's Speech (25:1-6)
   D. Job's Reply to Bildad (26:1–27:23)
   E. Job's Hymn to Wisdom (28:1-28)

V. Job's Final Discourse (29:1–31:40)

VI. Elihu's Response (32:1–37:24)

VII. God's Concluding Words (38:1–42:9)
   A. God's First Message (38:1–40:9)
   B. Job's Response to God (40:3-5)
   C. God's Second Message (40:6–41:34)
   D. Job's Response to God (42:1-6)
   E. God Speaks to Job's Friends (42:7-9)

VIII. Epilogue: Job's Restoration and Vindication (42:10-17)

Prologue (1:1–2:13)

The Introduction of Job (1:1-5)

1 There was a man in the country
of Uz named Job. He was a man
of perfect integrity, who •feared God
and turned away from evil. 2 He had
seven sons and three daughters.
3 His estate included 7,000 sheep,
3,000 camels, 500 yoke of oxen, 500
female donkeys, and a very large
number of servants. Job was the
greatest man among all the people
of the east.
4 His sons used to take turns having banquets at their homes. They
would send an invitation to their
three sisters to eat and drink with
them. 5 Whenever a round of ban-
queting was over, Job would send
for his children and purify them,
rising early in the morning to offer
burnt offerings for[A] all of them. For
Job thought: Perhaps my children
have sinned, having cursed God in
their hearts. This was Job's regular
practice.

Satan's First Test (1:6-12)

6 One day the sons of God came to
present themselves before the LORD,
and Satan[B] also came with them.
7 The LORD asked Satan, "Where have
you come from?"
"From roaming through the earth,"
Satan answered Him, "and walking
around on it."
8 Then the LORD said to Satan,
"Have you considered My servant

Title: As in the books of Ruth and Esther, the title "Job" (Hb *ʾIyyov*; Gk *ʾIōb*) identifies the person around whom the narrative is centered. Textual evidence indicates that the Semitic name "Job" was common among ancient Near Eastern cultures but not in Israel. Its meaning remains uncertain despite efforts to connect its origin to Job's experience.

1:1-5 Job's character is one of the primary elements of this story. In Hebrew both the words **perfect** (*tam*, "blameless, upright, innocent"—always in a moral sense; from a root meaning "whole, complete"; cp. 8:20; 9:20-22; Ps 37:37) and **integrity** (*yashar*, "upright, just"; cp. "right," Pr 3:6) are adjectives and are complementary (cp. Jb 1:8 and 2:3 with parallel use of the same Hebrew words in Ps 37:37—"the blameless and . . .

A 1:5 Lit *for the number of* B 1:6 Or *the adversary*

the upright"). "Perfect" does not mean "sinless." Rather, Job was recognized as an honest man who was faithful to his wife, generous to the poor, fair in the treatment of his servants, and one who did not worship idols. The more common word, "integrity" (lit "straight"), characterizes someone who does not deviate from standards of right behavior in how he relates to others. Combined, the two words indicate that Job was a man of sterling character, demonstrating unusual integrity in his dealings with God and man. This description mirrors an early rabbinic view that a true student of the Torah is one whose "inside" (inner character) matches his "outside" (outward behavior).

Job also **feared** [Hb *yarē'*, "revere, worship"; cp. 28:28] **God and turned away from evil**—another paired description (cp. 1:8; 2:3; 28:28; Pr 3:7; 14:16; 16:6). Job was a righteous man who honored and obeyed God while rejecting the wickedness of the day. This assessment of Job was not just the author's but God's as well (Jb 1:8), proving from the outset that his friends' accusations of sin in his life were unfounded.

Not only was Job personally devoted to God and a man of impeccable moral character without a trace of hypocrisy, but he also faithfully exercised exemplary spiritual leadership as the head of his home in a manner appropriate to his context. He openly set his children apart unto the Lord and assumed an intercessory role for them, regularly offering **burnt offerings** for his sons and daughters in case they had **sinned** outwardly or inwardly.

1:8 My servant was one of the most honorable titles anyone could be given by the Lord God (cp. Jb 42:7-8). Job was in good company with Abraham (Gn 26:24), Moses (Ex 14:31), and David (Ps 89:3,20). God's description of Job's character was apparently the source of the narrator's introductory portrayal (Jb 1:1). Satan could not deny Job's righteousness—whatever **the Lord** says is undeniably true.

1:9-11 Satan questioned Job's motives and accused God of placing **a hedge** (Hb *suk*, "protective fence"; cp. Hos 2:6) around Job and **his household.** Suggesting that Job turns away from evil (Jb 1:8) only to keep receiving God's blessings, Satan challenged the Lord to let him prove that Job, like any other man, was subject to his own self-interest. The accuser's attack struck at the nature of God, suggesting that the only way He could get people to worship Him was by giving them wealth.

1:12-19 The Lord demonstrated confidence in Job's faithfulness by permitting **Satan** to have control over

HARD QUESTION

I am a Christian. Can Satan harm me?

The word "satan" is transliterated from the verb *satan* (Hb, "attack, accuse"). With the definite article, the word becomes a proper noun translated "adversary," identifying the enemy called Satan. Originally created as an angel (Jd 9), Satan fell from God's graces because of his pride (see 2Pt 2:4; 1Tm 3:6; Jd 6). His rebellion resulted in one-third of the angelic host rebelling against God (Rv 12:4), and his hatred of God is seen in his role in the fall of man (Gn 3:15; Rm 16:20). Since then, he has been God's enemy and man's adversary, attempting to thwart God's purposes and antagonizing mankind. Nevertheless, he is answerable to God and limited by Him (Jb 1:6), again demonstrating God's sovereignty.

Several verses in Job clarify Satan's role in relation to the believer. He can only be in one place at a time (1:7); therefore, his fallen angels assist him in his work. He cannot read your mind (1:9-11), and he can only act with God's permission (1:12; 2:6). These facts are important for the believer to understand. Satan cannot cause affliction without God's permission, and He cannot force a person to commit sin. Satan's final destruction is described in Rv 20:10.

Job? No one else on earth is like
him, a man of perfect integrity, who
fears God and turns away from evil."
9 Satan answered the LORD, "Does
Job fear God for nothing? 10 Haven't
You placed a hedge around him,
his household, and everything he
owns? You have blessed the work of
his hands, and his possessions have
increased in the land. 11 But stretch
out Your hand and strike everything
he owns, and he will surely curse
You to Your face."
12 "Very well," the LORD told Satan, "everything he owns is in your
power. However, you must not lay a
hand on Job himself." So Satan left
the LORD's presence.

Job's Disaster (1:13-19)

13 One day when Job's sons and
daughters were eating and drinking
wine in their oldest brother's house,
14 a messenger came to Job and reported: "While the oxen were plowing and the donkeys grazing nearby,
15 the Sabeans swooped down and
took them away. They struck down
the servants with the sword, and I
alone have escaped to tell you!"
16 He was still speaking when another messenger came and reported:
"A lightning storm[A] struck from
heaven. It burned up the sheep and
the servants and devoured them,
and I alone have escaped to tell you!"
17 That messenger was still speaking when yet another came and
reported: "The Chaldeans formed
three bands, made a raid on the
camels, and took them away. They
struck down the servants with the
sword, and I alone have escaped to
tell you!"
18 He was still speaking when another messenger came and reported: "Your sons and daughters were
eating and drinking wine in their
oldest brother's house. 19 Suddenly
a powerful wind swept in from the
desert and struck the four corners of
the house. It collapsed on the young
people so that they died, and I alone
have escaped to tell you!"

A 1:16 Lit *The fire of God*

>WORD|*study*

1:7 God's question does not mean that He did not know of Satan's activities. In Old Testament narratives the question **Where . . . from?** (Hb *min'ayin*, "from where") is usually asked with the purpose of identifying a person's native country and therefore his cultural background or intentions (e.g., Gn 29:4; 42:7). For example, the sailors on Jonah's ship desperately asked the derelict prophet, "Where are you from? What is your country and what people are you from?" (Jnh 1:8). A vague answer to this question signifies deceit in Jos 9:8 and awareness of guilt in 2Kg 20:14 (cp. Is 39:3).

1:7 His **roaming through** [Hb *shut*, "walk around, range or go through"; cp. Nm 11:8; 2 Sm 24:2,8; Jr 5:1] **the earth and walking around** [Hb *halak*, "walk up and down, walk about"] **on it** indicate not aimlessness but vigilant supervision and perhaps even defiant enjoyment of his territory (cp. the purposeful activity of Satan in 1Pt 5:8—"Your adversary the Devil is prowling around [Gk *peripateō*, "walk about; make due use of opportunities"] like a roaring lion, looking for anyone he can devour"). This form of the verb *halak* is also used in Gn 3:8 ("the LORD God *walking in* the garden") and in Zch 1:10-11; 6:7 (describing the horses "the LORD has sent to *patrol* the earth"). Satan's power, nevertheless, is always limited under God's sovereign rule. Twice in the Old Testament the verb *shut* is used to assert the Lord's comprehensive oversight of the earth (2Ch 16:9; Zch 4:10).]

Job expressed exemplary faith in the Lord as . . .

"the Almighty," the God before whom Job preferred to argue his case	6:4,14; 13:3; 31:35
one who is "wise and all-powerful," impossible to oppose	9:4,12; 12:13-16
the sovereign Creator over the earth	9:7-10
the source of life	10:8-12,18; 12:10; 14:5; 27:3; 31:15
"the Mighty One"	9:19
"the Holy One"	6:10
the only righteous One and source of justice, "Judge"	9:3,14-15,19,24; 12:17-25; 13:9-10,16; 21:22; 23:7; 24:22-24; 31:5-6,14
the only one who has the right to condemn a man for sin	7:18; 9:32-35; 10:13-17; 31:35
"witness" and "advocate"	16:19
"living Redeemer"	19:25
hope of resurrection and eternal life	13:15; 19:26-27
one who was worthy of unrelenting commitment to righteousness, even when God seemed unfair	6:8-10; 27:1-6

Job's Response (1:20-22)

20 Then Job stood up, tore his robe,
and shaved his head.[A] He fell to the
ground and worshiped, 21 saying:

Naked I came
  from my mother's womb,
and naked I will leave
  this life.[B]
The LORD gives, and the LORD
  takes away.
Praise the name of •Yahweh.

22 Throughout all this Job did not
sin or blame God for anything.[C]

Satan's Second Test (2:1-8)

2 One day the sons of God came
again to present themselves before the LORD, and Satan also came
with them to present himself before
the LORD. 2 The LORD asked Satan,
"Where have you come from?"
"From roaming through the
earth," Satan answered Him, "and
walking around on it."
3 Then the LORD said to Satan,
"Have you considered My servant
Job? No one else on earth is like
him, a man of perfect integrity,
who •fears God and turns away
from evil. He still retains his integrity, even though you incited Me
against him, to destroy him without just cause."
4 "Skin for skin!" Satan answered
the LORD. "A man will give up everything he owns in exchange for his
life. 5 But stretch out Your hand and
strike his flesh and bones, and he
will surely curse You to Your face."
6 "Very well," the LORD told Satan,
"he is in your power; only spare
his life." 7 So Satan left the LORD's
presence and infected Job with terrible boils from the sole of his foot
to the top of his head. 8 Then Job

[A] **1:20** This custom demonstrated mourning. [B] **1:21** Lit *will return there*; Ps 139:13,15 [C] **1:22** Lit *or ascribe blame to God*

everything Job possessed. God limited the scope of Satan's access to Job. Yet without God's specific permission, the adversary could not inflict evil upon Job.

In **one day** Job lost all of his children and his possessions. Four catastrophes occurred in rapid succession—two were caused by forces of nature, and two were human attacks. All four events are linked with the dramatic repetition of the messengers' arrivals, one right after the other, and with their testimonies to being the sole survivor of each calamity. Before Job could process one report, he was assailed with news of a greater loss.

The **Sabeans** were a group of nomadic raiders from Sheba in southwestern Arabia. Their attack was a blow to Job's wealth, but an untold number of **servants** were killed as well, undoubtedly inflicting grief and hardship on their families.

Job might easily have blamed his Sabean enemies for the violent raid on his animals, but apart from divine revelation of the conversation between the Lord and Satan, Job and the surviving servants could only conclude that God Himself had destroyed the flocks and their shepherds with the **lightning storm** (Hb *ʾēsh ʾElohim*, "fire of God"; cp. Nm 11:1-3; 1Kg 18:38).

The **Chaldeans** from Mesopotamia were nomadic marauders who later migrated to Babylon.

Again, Job was left with no one to blame for the most devastating news of all—that all Job's children were dead. That the **powerful wind** had struck **the house** from every direction suggests it was a tornado or whirlwind.

1:20 Tearing one's clothing publicly expressed great mourning (cp. Gn 37:29,34; 44:13). Shaving his head symbolized Job's loss of glory (Is 15:2; Ezk 7:18). In falling to the ground before God, Job acknowledged divine sovereignty and worshiped God despite these catastrophes.

1:21-22 In his poetic response, Job conceded that he came into the world **naked** (Hb *ʿarom*, "bare"; cp. Ec 5:15)—with nothing—and that he would leave with nothing (cp. 1Tm 6:7). Job seems to have passed this first test. His reaction to catastrophic loss proved his faithfulness to God.

2:4 Skin for skin was a proverbial saying that some believe originated from bartering animal skins. It seems to have a similar meaning as "an eye for an eye" (Ex 21:23-25).

2:5 Satan challenged God to **strike** Job with deadly force, to wound His "servant" so deeply that Job's devotion would be unveiled as a sham. Satan always aims to defy the truth of what

God says; in this case he wanted to prove that God had misjudged this "man of perfect integrity" (v. 3; cp. Lk 22:31-32). Again, God set a limit for Satan's activity, and Satan clearly had no power to go beyond that limit—there was no hint whatsoever that Satan would actually be able to take Job's life. Therefore, the narrator and reader know what Job and his friends did not know—that his character must, in the end, pass the test and that its outcome will not be death.

2:8 Ashes (Hb *ʾēpher*, "powdery remains signifying the destruction of physical matter by fire") are associated with expressions of extreme grief and consequent feelings of worthlessness (e.g., 2Sm 13:19; Est 4:1-3; Ps 102:9-10; Jr 6:26; Ezk 27:30-31; Jnh 3:6). Job may have been sitting at the ash heap or dunghill typically located outside a town's entrance. Sitting "among the ashes" was a way of coming to terms with the irrevocable losses, which now included Job's health.

2:9-10 For the first and only time, Job's **wife** speaks. Job mentions her only three times (19:17; 31:9-10). In each case, "wife" is singular. No indication is given that Job had any other wives or concubines, even when the text notes that after his ordeal the Lord blessed him with another seven sons and three daughters (42:13). Job's integrity seems to include monogamy.

Job's wife was urging Job to do what Satan desired (cp. 1:11; 2:5). Though the Hebrew word (*barak*) normally would be translated as "bless," especially with **God** as the object, in this context Job's wife was using the word as a euphemism, avoiding actually saying what she meant—**"Curse . . ."** which in her culture would have been understood as never to be spoken from anyone's lips. The sense is that Job should renounce God, not actually blaspheme Him (cp. 2:5; 1:11). To do either would mean to concede victory to suffering and death in this contest of resignation versus retaliation. Although Job's wife must have been as devastated by the loss of their children and livelihood as he was, her words underscore the contrast between her apparent resentment toward God and her husband's resignation to God's sovereignty.

Job seemed surprised. Her words, which sounded more like those of a **foolish** [Hb *naval*, "impious, ungodly, irreverent"] **woman** than of his wife, betrayed a lack of faith and discernment. "Foolish" also describes unbelievers who deny God's existence and revile Him (Pss 14:1; 53:1; 74:18,22), To her credit, Job's wife recognized that her husband's additional suffering was a test of his **integrity** (Hb *tummah*, "innocence"—from *tom*, "wholeness"; cp. Gn 20:5-6;

CHARACTER PROFILE

Job's Wife A Foolish Woman

Her Background	• The wife of Job, a righteous and prosperous man (1:1-3) • A wife grieving because of her husband's suffering (2:9-10) • A mother doubly blessed by children (42:12-16)
Her Story	• She lost all of her children in one day (1:18-19). • She encouraged her husband to curse God and die (2:9). • She was rebuked by Job for speaking as a "foolish woman" (2:10). • She eventually had 10 more children (42:13).
Life Lessons	• In observing the suffering of her husband, Job's wife urged him to do exactly what Satan desired—curse God. • Natural feelings of grief may tempt us to reject God or become angry at Him.

took a piece of broken pottery to
scrape himself while he sat among
the ashes.[A]

The Response of Job's Wife (2:9-10)

9 His wife said to him, "Do you still
retain your integrity? Curse God and
die!"

10 "You speak as a foolish woman
speaks," he told her. "Should we accept only good from God and not adversity?" Throughout all this Job did
not sin in what he said.[B]

The Response of Job's Friends (2:11-13)

11 Now when Job's three friends—
Eliphaz the Temanite, Bildad the
Shuhite, and Zophar the Naamathite—heard about all this adversity
that had happened to him, each of
them came from his home. They
met together to go and sympathize
with him and comfort him. 12 When
they looked from a distance, they
could barely recognize him. They
wept aloud, and each man tore his
robe and threw dust into the air and
on his head. 13 Then they sat on the
ground with him seven days and
nights, but no one spoke a word to
him because they saw that his suffering was very intense.

HARD QUESTION

How can I trust a God who has allowed such terrible things to happen to people?

Job's rhetorical question articulates one of the primary messages of this book (2:10). The implied answer is that both "good" and "adversity" should be accepted from God. Being able to trust God completely—in times of grief and celebration—depends on right thinking about Him. Job's theology here is consistent with God's revelation of Himself in Scripture:

- As the Creator, the one God—apart from whom "there is no other," Yahweh declares His absolute sovereignty both to "make success and create disaster" at His discretion (Is 45:5-7; cp. Rm 9:20-21). He is Lord of all.
- Not only is God sovereign and omnipotent, He is also completely just (Gn 18:25; Ps 119:75), holy (Lv 11:44-45; Jb 6:10; Ps 99; 1Pt 1:15-16), righteous (Dt 32:4; Pss 7:11; 11:7; 116:5; 145:17; 1Pt 3:18), and good (Ex 33:19; 2Pt 1:3). The apostle John declared, "God is love" (1Jn 4:8; cp. Ex 34:6; Ps 136:2,26).
- In the Sermon on the Mount, Jesus affirmed that the Father "causes His sun to rise on the evil and the good, and sends rain on the righteous and the unrighteous" (Mt 5:45). Ability to endure tragedy depends not on the circumstances but on the foundation of a person's life. A "sensible man" hears God's words "and acts on them"; "a foolish man" hears His words but "doesn't act on them," (Mt 7:24-27; cp. Pr 10:25).

[A]2:8 This custom demonstrated mourning. [B]2:10 Lit *sin with his lips*

The First Series of Speeches (3:1–14:22)

Job's Speech (3:1-26)

3 After this, Job began to speak and cursed the day he was born. [2] He said:

3 May the day I was born perish,
and the night when they said,
"A boy is conceived."
4 If only that day had turned
to darkness!
May God above not care
about it,
or light shine on it.
5 May darkness and gloom
reclaim it,
and a cloud settle over it.
May an eclipse of the sun[A]
terrify it.
6 If only darkness had taken
that night away!
May it not appear[B]
among the days of the year
or be listed in the calendar.[C]
7 Yes, may that night be barren;
may no joyful shout be heard
in it.
8 Let those who curse
certain days
cast a spell on it,
those who are skilled
in rousing •Leviathan.
9 May its morning stars
grow dark.
May it wait for daylight
but have none;
may it not see the breaking[D]
of dawn.
10 For that night did not shut
the doors
of my mother's womb,
and hide sorrow
from my eyes.

11 Why was I not stillborn;
why didn't I die as I came
from the womb?
12 Why did the knees receive me,
and why were there breasts
for me to nurse?
13 Now I would certainly
be lying down in peace;
I would be asleep.
Then I would be at rest
14 with the kings and counselors
of the earth,

HARD QUESTION

Can I actually depend on God to bless my life, if I remain obedient to Him?

The arguments of each of Job's friends began with the premise that good comes to those who are righteous and evil to those who are sinful (3:1–14:22). Therefore, they concluded, if someone is suffering, he must have sinned. This system of thinking is reflected in the concept of "karma" (the idea that your destiny is determined by your actions) taught by eastern religions such as Hinduism and Buddhism. According to these worldviews, suffering, even that of an innocent child, is attributed to sins committed in a previous life. Therefore, the suffering is what that person deserves and must endure. Jesus denounced such reasoning (see Lk 13:1-5). When Jesus' disciples questioned Him about a man blind from birth, they were expressing a perspective similar to that of Job's friends: "Rabbi, who sinned, this man or his parents, that he was born blind?" (Jn 9:1-3).

Although wisdom sayings like Pr 22:8 ("The one who sows injustice will reap disaster") provide a legitimate basis for the belief, proverbs typically articulate *general* rather than *universal* truths. That the person who lives a godly lifestyle will enjoy a life of blessing is generally true, but clearly there are exceptions. In fact, Jesus' promise to His followers that they "will have suffering in this world" (Jn 16:33) is consistent with the testimony of God's people in the Old Testament as well (e.g., Joseph, Gn 50:20).

who rebuilt ruined cities
for themselves,
15 or with princes who had gold,
who filled their houses
with silver.
16 Or why was I not hidden
like a miscarried child,
like infants who never
see daylight?
17 There the wicked cease
to make trouble,
and there the weary find rest.
18 The captives are completely
at ease;
they do not hear the voice
of their oppressor.
19 Both small and
great are there,
and the slave is set free
from his master.
20 Why is light given
to one burdened with grief,
and life to those
whose existence is bitter,

[A]3:5 Lit *May a darkening of daylight* [B]3:6 LXX, Syr, Tg, Vg; MT reads *rejoice* [C]3:6 Lit *or enter the number of months* [D]3:9 Lit *the eyelids*

Pr 11:4). What she said was logical, but her theology did not reflect accurately God's character. She reasoned that if her husband was truly innocent as he maintained, then God was being unjust to reward faithfulness with such suffering. In that case, his "integrity" was worthless.

2:11 Eliphaz was from Teman, located in Edom southeast of the Dead Sea. Some suggest that he was a near descendant of Esau's firstborn son Eliphaz, whose sons included Teman (Gn 36:10-11,15,34,42). However, this possibility depends on the dating of Job's life, for which Scripture offers no solid evidence (see "When was Job written?," p. 620). **Bildad** was from Shuha, possibly indicating a connection with Shuah, Abraham's youngest son by Keturah (Gn 25:2; cp. Gn 38:2). **Zophar** was from Naamath, an undetermined location. Offer sympathy (Hb *nud*, lit, "move to and fro, shake," i.e., "comfort" someone by physically demonstrating grief) likely included shaking one's head and rocking one's body as indications of intense emotions.

2:12 The effects of disease made Job virtually unrecognizable. His friends were horrified at the sight and reacted according to the custom of the day. First, they **wept aloud**, demonstrating intense sorrow. Then they **tore** their robes as Job had done (1:20) and **threw dust** on their heads (1Sm 4:12; 2Sm 1:2; Neh 9:1). The time of sitting with Job in silence was a tradition preserved in the Talmud—a comforter does not speak to a mourner until the comforter is addressed. Here at least, Job's friends beautifully illustrate the ministry of presence, which is often the best gift a friend can give to someone confronted with inexplicable tragedy.

3:1-14:22 This first series of speeches begins with Job's soliloquy lamenting the day of his birth. Despite his anger, frustration, and sorrow regarding his losses, Job still did not curse God. The speeches of Job's three friends display their belief that the righteous are rewarded by God and the guilty are punished (4:7-8). This theological perspective is consistent with Scripture but is misapplied in Job's case. The conclusion that since Job was suffering, he must have sinned is logical but in this case, as Job recognized, is off the mark, a contradiction of God's opinion of Job as expressed in 1:1,8; 2:3.

3:8 Leviathan, a sea monster, according to ancient mythology, would swallow the sun or moon—a poetic expression for reversing creation and thereby preventing Job's life and consequent misery (cp. Gn 1:14-18).

3:1-23 Job refused to curse God, but

he **cursed** [Hb *qalal*, "execrate; treat lightly, i.e., with contempt"] **the day he was born** and **the night** he was **conceived**, indicating belief that his life had begun at conception not merely at birth (cp. 10:10-11). Job's cry of desperation is repeated in various phrases that build or elaborate one upon the other with imagery of a reversal of creation (cp. Gn 1:5), of death's darkness overcoming life's light. Several words convey this theme:

- **Darkness** (Hb *choshek*, "absence of or separation from light, obscurity," Jb 3:4-5) is used at least 25 times in Job, often as a metaphor for death (10:21-22), destruction (20:26), or ignorance of God's ways (12:24-25; 37:19; cp. Ps 18:28).
- Job wanted **darkness and gloom** (Hb *tsalmawet*, "shadow of death, deep or deepest darkness," Jb 3:5; cp. Jb 12:22; 16:16) to **reclaim** (Hb *ga'al*, "redeem, buy back") the day of his birth. If death had overshadowed that day, then Job would not have lived to experience such misery.
- Because ancient peoples regarded **an eclipse of the sun** (Hb *kimrir*, "blackness, gloominess," lit "darkening or obscuring of daylight," 3:5; its only use in the OT) as a sign of doom or impending calamity, it would **terrify** (Hb *ba'at*, "startle with fear, dismay"; cp. 7:4) them.
- **Darkness** (Hb *'ophel*, "thick darkness," 3:6; cp. 23:17) is personified as seizing and taking away **that night** of Job's conception.
- Job hoped for the **stars** shining in the early **morning** hours of his conception to **grow dark** (Hb *chashak*, "be darkened or dimmed," 3:9)—that these "lights would be put out" (cp. 18:6). He wished **that night** had been **barren** (Hb *galmud*, "sterile," lit "hard, desolate," as of stony ground in which nothing will grow or an unsown field, 3:7; cp. Is 49:21), with no **joyful shout** announcing his birth.

Job's wish to erase his beginning from the flow of time turned to an outpouring of the question inevitably spawned by suffering (3:11-23):

- **Why didn't I die** (Hb *gawa'*, "expire, breathe out one's life," 3:11; cp. 10:18; Gn 6:17; Ps 104:29) at birth and bypass this suffering? Job imagined death as relief—being laid **down in peace**, being **asleep** or **at rest**, being remembered in the company of the rich and famous.
- Why could he not have been **a miscarried child** (Hb *nephel*, "untimely birth," Jb 3:16; cp. Ps 58:8; Ec 6:3-5)? Job imagined death as release—from **trouble**

21 who wait for death,
but it does not come,
and search for it more than
for hidden treasure,
22 who are filled with much joy
and are glad when they reach
the grave?
23 Why is life given to a man
whose path is hidden,
whom God has hedged in?
24 I sigh when food
is put before me,
and my groans pour out
like water.[A]
25 For the thing I feared
has overtaken me,
and what I dreaded
has happened to me.
26 I cannot relax or be still;
I have no rest,
for trouble comes.

Eliphaz's Speech (4:1–5:27)

4 Then Eliphaz the Temanite replied:

2 Should anyone try to speak
with you
when you are exhausted?
Yet who can keep
from speaking?
3 Indeed, you have
instructed many
and have strengthened
weak hands.
4 Your words have steadied
the one who was stumbling
and braced the knees
that were buckling.
5 But now that this
has happened to you,
you have become exhausted.
It strikes you, and you
are dismayed.
6 Isn't your piety your confidence,
and the integrity of your life[B]
your hope?
7 Consider: who has perished
when he was innocent?
Where have the honest
been destroyed?
8 In my experience,
those who plow injustice
and those who sow trouble
reap the same.
9 They perish at a single blast
from God
and come to an end
by the breath
of His nostrils.
10 The lion may roar and
the fierce lion growl,
but the fangs of young lions
are broken.
11 The strong lion dies
if it catches no prey,
and the cubs of the lioness
are scattered.

12 A word was brought to me
in secret;
my ears caught a whisper
of it.
13 Among unsettling thoughts
from visions in the night,
when deep sleep descends
on men,
14 fear and trembling came
over me
and made all my bones shake.
15 A wind[C] passed by me,
and I shuddered with fear.[D]
16 A figure stood there,
but I could not recognize
its appearance;
a form loomed
before my eyes.
I heard a quiet voice:
17 "Can a person be
more righteous than God,
or a man more pure
than his Maker?"
18 If God puts no trust
in His servants
and He charges His angels
with foolishness,[E]
19 how much more
those who dwell
in clay houses,
whose foundation is
in the dust,
who are crushed like a moth!
20 They are smashed to pieces
from dawn to dusk;
they perish forever
while no one notices.
21 Are their tent cords not
pulled up?
They die without wisdom.

5 Call out if you please.
Will anyone answer you?
Which of the holy ones
will you turn to?
2 For anger kills a fool,
and jealousy slays the gullible.

[A]3:24 Or *My sighing serves as my food* [B]4:6 Lit *ways* [C]4:15 Or *A spirit* [D]4:15 Or *and the hair on my body stood up* [E]4:18 Or *error*; Hb obscure

>WORD|*study*

4:21 The word translated **tent cords** (Hb *yeter*) can also denote "remnant, that which remains" or "excellence, that which exceeds measure," but the metaphor of death as the collapsing of a tent depends on the literal rendering. When pitching a tent, these "ropes" fastened the tent curtains to the stakes driven into the ground. When the tent pegs were **pulled up** (Hb *nasa'*, "be plucked out"; cp. Is 33:20; 38:12), the otherwise taut cords were loosened so the tent could be moved to another place. A person's death is compared to this process. In the New Testament, the "tent" is a metaphor for the believer's earthly life (2Co 5:1,4; 2Pt 1:13-14).

3 I have seen a fool taking root,
but I immediately
pronounced a curse
on his home.
4 His children are far from safety.
They are crushed
at the city •gate,
with no one to rescue them.
5 The hungry consume
his harvest,
even taking it
out of the thorns.[A]
The thirsty[B] pant
for his children's wealth.
6 For distress does not grow
out of the soil,
and trouble does not sprout
from the ground.
7 But mankind is born for trouble
as surely as sparks fly upward.

8 However, if I were you,
I would appeal to God
and would present my case
to Him.
9 He does great
and unsearchable things,
wonders without number.
10 He gives rain to the earth
and sends water to the fields.
11 He sets the lowly on high,
and mourners are lifted
to safety.
12 He frustrates the schemes
of the crafty
so that they[C] achieve
no success.
13 He traps the wise
in their craftiness
so that the plans
of the deceptive
are quickly brought to an end.
14 They encounter darkness
by day,
and they grope at noon
as if it were night.
15 He saves the needy
from their sharp words[D]
and from the clutches
of the powerful.
16 So the poor have hope,
and injustice shuts its mouth.
17 See how happy the man is
God corrects;
so do not reject the discipline
of the •Almighty.
18 For He crushes but also
binds up;
He strikes, but His hands
also heal.
19 He will rescue you
from six calamities;
no harm will touch you
in seven.
20 In famine He will redeem you
from death,
and in battle, from the power
of the sword.
21 You will be safe from slander[E]
and not fear destruction
when it comes.
22 You will laugh at destruction
and hunger
and not fear the animals
of the earth.
23 For you will have a covenant
with the stones of the field,

[A]5:5 Hb obscure [B]5:5 Aq, Sym, Syr, Vg; MT reads *snares* [C]5:12 Lit *their hands* [D]5:15 Lit *from the sword of their mouth*; Ps 55:21; 59:7 [E]5:21 Lit *be hidden from the whip of the tongue*

>WORD|*study*

5:17 **The Almighty** (Hb *Shadday*, "most powerful") as a name for God appears 31 times in Job—much more frequently than in any other book in the Bible. *Shadday* is often combined with *'ēl* (Hb, "God") and serves as an epithet for Yahweh, generally referring to His power or majesty (e.g., 37:23). This name was first revealed when God identified Himself to Abraham (Gn 17:1). *'Ēl Shadday* was God's covenant name for the patriarchs until the time of Moses. Most rabbis took it to mean "the self-sufficient One."

caused by **the wicked**, from weariness, and from captivity and oppression. He did not acknowledge the grief his mother would have suffered if he had died at birth.

- Why is the person who wishes for death unable to find it (Jb 3:20-22)? Job referred to himself as one **whom God has hedged in** (Hb *sakak*, "enclosed, fenced round, shut in," v. 23; cp. 38:8). A related word was used in Satan's charge that God's blessings were a "hedge" of protection around Job (1:10). In both cases, God had established a boundary beyond which Satan could not reach and which prevented the person so encompassed (like Job) from "going over the edge."

4:6 The rhetorical question implied that if Job's **hope** were truly in God, he would not be in such despair.

4:10-11 These proverbial sayings convey that even the **strong lion** gets his due eventually. Thus, even if Job were a strong lion, mighty and intimidating, he would still ultimately receive his due.

4:12-21 In ancient times and in some non-Western cultures, people put great faith in dreams and visions, expecting to discern through them a message from God. Eliphaz claimed that in this vision a voice spoke to him, asking if a person could be **more righteous than God**. Of course, the implied answer was "No." Eliphaz said that the message **was brought** especially to him—in the Hebrew text, the sentence begins emphatically with, "To me. . ."—and **in secret** (Hb *ganav*, "by stealth"), making suspect the way he applied it directly to Job instead of to himself.

5:1-8 Eliphaz counseled Job to appeal to God and repent of his sin, bluntly stating that Job could not depend on an angel or any other holy being to intervene for him.

5:9-26 Eliphaz eloquently and accurately described God's character but inappropriately suggested that Job needed to recognize and accept divine **discipline** (Hb *musar*, "correction, admonition, chastening," especially that given by parents to children, v. 17; cp. Heb 12:5-10; see **Word Study**, p. 783). To his credit, Eliphaz spoke from a strongly theistic worldview, recognizing God's ultimate control over all that happens—He both **crushes** and **binds up** (Jb 5:18). However, Eliphaz misrepresented God's ways as being neatly categorized and predictable. Unlike the reader, who has been informed about the reason for Job's calamities, Eliphaz had no knowledge of the conversation between Yahweh and Satan (chaps. 1–2) and had no room in his theology for God's freedom to supersede "the law of retribution"—systematically rewarding and protecting the obedient while shutting the mouth of **injustice** (v. 16). There was much truth in Eliphaz's description of the benefits of being under God's care and tutelage (vv. 17-26). Verse 26, for example, was fulfilled in Job's life when God restored his wealth and children after this test (42:17); but this exhortation to Job was misapplied. In Job's case, God had not kept a righteous man **safe** and **secure** from all harm but had permitted Satan to bring incomprehensible disaster and suffering upon him, not as punishment for wrongdoing but to prove Satan wrong (2:3-6).

6:1-5 With vivid poetic imagery, Job contended that his suffering could not be measured, much less understood by his friends. Like Eliphaz, Job attributed his suffering to God's intentional actions against him. The rhetorical question immediately following Job's description further implies that he would have nothing to complain about if God had not withdrawn His provision.

6:5 The word **bray** (Hb *nahaq*, "loud, harsh cry of a donkey") is used only here and in Job 30:7, in which the desperate cries of starving men are likened to the braying of a hungry donkey in the wild (cp. Jr 14:6). Similarly, an ox would **low** (Hb *ga'ah*, "bellow, cry out as cattle") when hungry or in distress (cp. Jl 1:18-20). Naturally, both wild and domestic animals loudly "complained" when their need for daily food was not met; likewise, Job's friends should not be surprised by his cries of despair when his basic need for comfort was not being met.

6:6 **Bland** (Hb *taphēl*, "insipid, tasteless, unseasoned") figuratively describes "foolish" or "deceptive" speech. **Flavor** (Hb *ta'am*, "taste") can also have the figurative sense of "judgment, discernment, or reason" (12:20; cp. "sensibly," Pr 26:16). Imagery inviting comparison of the taste of food (or here, lack thereof) and the wisdom or discernment of one's speech appears more explicitly when Job asks, "Doesn't the ear test words as the palate tastes food?" (Jb 12:11; 34:3). The translators of the LXX understood the second question of 6:6 in this vein: "Is there taste in empty words?" Speaking metaphorically—perhaps of his friend's tasteless, undiscerning speech—Job refused what was set before him as unfit for consumption.

6:14 Job spoke of himself as **a despairing man** (Hb *mas*, "one who is consumed or is pining away"; used

and the wild animals will be
at peace with you.
24 You will know that your tent
is secure,
and nothing will be missing
when you inspect
your home.
25 You will also know
that your offspring
will be many
and your descendants
like the grass of the earth.
26 You will approach the grave
in full vigor,
as a stack of sheaves
is gathered in its season.

27 We have investigated this,
and it is true!
Hear it and understand it
for yourself.

Job's Reply to Eliphaz (6:1–7:21)

6 Then Job answered:

2 If only my grief
could be weighed
and my devastation placed
with it in the scales.
3 For then it would outweigh
the sand of the seas!
That is why my words
are rash.
4 Surely the arrows
of the •Almighty
have pierced[A] me;
my spirit drinks their poison.
God's terrors are arrayed
against me.
5 Does a wild donkey bray
over fresh grass
or an ox low over its fodder?
6 Is bland food eaten without salt?
Is there flavor
in an egg white?[B]
7 I refuse to touch them;
they are like
contaminated food.

HARD QUESTION

Given how much he was suffering with no hope in sight, would it have been okay for Job to have exercised his "right to die"?

Job's words authentically portray a common human response to debilitating and inexplicable suffering. Job was hoping for death to end his misery (6:8-11). His afflictions and grief were, indeed, overwhelming, and he had no hope that his lot would improve. The writer did not sugarcoat his struggle to understand his plight. However, Job desired to remain faithful to God despite what had happened to him. He assumed that only God could rightfully snuff out his life. Consequently, his words model a biblical response to personal suffering when confronted by proponents of euthanasia.

Without hope, Job's **future** (Hb *qēts*, "end, extremity," a contracted form of the verb *qatsats*, "cut off,") seemed so dismal that he questioned why he **should be patient** (Hb *'arak*, figuratively "prolong, live long" with the object *nephesh*, "life, soul"). The English translation captures Job's sense of helplessness and utter depletion of inner resources. The experience of intense suffering prompts people to question whether the pain will ever end and often makes welcome the prospect of death. In contrast to the faithless advice of his wife (2:9), however, Job recognized that God alone rightfully gives and takes away life (cp. 1:20).

8 If only my request
would be granted
and God would provide what
I hope for:
9 that He would decide
to crush me,
to unleash His power
and cut me off!
10 It would still bring me comfort,
and I would leap for joy
in unrelenting pain
that I have not denied[C]
the words of the Holy One.

11 What strength do I have
that I should continue
to hope?

[A]6:4 Lit *Almighty are in* [B]6:6 Hb obscure [C]6:10 Lit *hidden*

>WORD|*study*

6:1 The word translated here as answered (Hb *'anah* "respond, speak up"; lit "sing," Ex 15:21) appears at least 60 times in the book of Job, far more than in any other Old Testament book, predominantly with the forensic sense—reflecting that the narrative is built on dialogue and structured much like court proceedings in which Job's faith and God's justice are put on trial and cross-examined. Context determines this verb's translation. For example, in Ex 32:18, *'anah* is used three times with three different shades of meaning—"victory cry," as of soldiers in battle (Jr 51:14); "a cry of defeat" (Is 13:22); and "singing." Given Job's distress, the verb here may suggest not only that he "replied" to Eliphaz, "solemnly testifying" in his own defense, but also that he cried out loudly in response to his friend's speech.

>WORD|*study*

6:10 Most Old Testament references to the Lord as **the Holy One** (Hb *qadosh*) include the modifier "of Israel" (e.g., Is 1:4; 49:7). References to God simply as "the Holy One" are few in number (only two others in the OT—Is 40:25; Hab 3:3), but they underscore His holiness not only as the God of Israel but also as the one Lord, Creator, and Redeemer of all. The New Testament identifies Jesus Christ as "the Holy One of God" (Mk 1:24; Lk 4:34; Jn 6:69), as "the Holy and Righteous One" (Ac 3:14), and "the Holy One" (1Jn 2:20; Rv 3:7; 16:5). The plural form of *qadosh*—"the holy ones"—is used in Jb 5:1 and 15:15, likely in reference to God's angels (cp. Ps 89:5,7). Calling God "the Holy One"—singular—affirmed Job's faith in the one God already identified as "the LORD" (Hb *Yahweh*, the covenant God of Israel, Jb 1:8-9).

What is my future,
that I should be patient?
12 Is my strength that of stone,
or my flesh made of bronze?
13 Since I cannot help myself,
the hope for success
has been banished from me.

14 A despairing man
should receive loyalty
from his friends,[A]
even if he abandons the •fear
of the Almighty.
15 My brothers are
as treacherous as a •wadi,
as seasonal streams
that overflow
16 and become darkened[B]
because of ice,
and the snow melts
into them.
17 The wadis evaporate
in warm weather;
they disappear
from their channels
in hot weather.
18 Caravans turn away
from their routes,
go up into the desert,
and perish.
19 The caravans of Tema look
for these streams.
The traveling merchants
of Sheba hope for them.
20 They are ashamed because
they had been confident
of finding water.
When they arrive there,
they are frustrated.
21 So this is what you have
now become to me.[C]
When you see something
dreadful, you are afraid.
22 Have I ever said:
"Give me something"
or "Pay a bribe for me
from your wealth"
23 or "Deliver me
from the enemy's power"
or "Redeem me
from the grasp
of the ruthless"?

24 Teach me, and I will be silent.
Help me understand
what I did wrong.
25 How painful honest words
can be!
But what does your rebuke
prove?
26 Do you think that you
can disprove my words
or that a despairing
man's words are mere wind?
27 No doubt you would cast lots
for a fatherless child
and negotiate a price to sell
your friend.

28 But now, please look at me;
would I lie to your face?
29 Reconsider; don't be unjust.
Reconsider; my righteousness
is still the issue.
30 Is there injustice on my tongue
or can my palate
not taste disaster?

7 Isn't mankind consigned
to forced labor on earth?
Are not his days like those
of a hired hand?
2 Like a slave he longs for shade;
like a hired man he waits
for his pay.
3 So I have been made
to inherit months of futility,
and troubled nights
have been assigned to me.
4 When I lie down I think:
When will I get up?
But the evening drags
on endlessly,
and I toss and turn
until dawn.

[A]6:14 Lit *To the despairing his friend loyalty* [B]6:16 Or *turbid* [C]6:21 Alt Hb tradition reads *So you have now become nothing*

only here in the OT). The word is derived from *masas*, meaning "dissolve, melt, or waste away" (cp. Is 10:18; Ps 22:14). Job also expressed disappointment in **his friends**, from whom he did not receive **loyalty** (Hb *chesed*, "faithful love, kindness," a fundamental characteristic of God; cp. Is 54:8; see **Word Study**, p. 322)—unconditional acceptance.

6:15-21 Job compared his "fair-weather friends" to a **wadi**, a riverbed that flowed with water in the rainy season but dried up in the heat of the summer. As a man whose life was melting away (v. 16), Job described them as **treacherous** (Hb *bagad*, "act fraudulently, deliberately forsake or betray"; cp. Pr 13:15; "unreliable person," Pr 25:19). One who is suffering may say things that she ordinarily would not. The most agonizing questions of a desperate heart are often voiced in the hearing of the closest, most trusted friends and family members—people who will be there no matter what. Job cried out in the hearing of three such friends on whom he thought he could count. Initially, their ministry of presence was exemplary. When they ventured to speak, however, they offered neither comfort nor help but the suggestion that Job was at fault.

6:18-20 Tema (modern Tayma), a city and oasis located in the northwest Arabian Peninsula, about 250 miles southeast of Aqaba, was located on the major trade route extending from **Sheba** (Yemen) to Damascus. Job felt like those traveling across the Arabian desert who, having confidently expected to find previously reliable water sources upon which their journeys depended, were **ashamed** (Hb *bush*, "fail in hope and expectation"; cp. Jr 14:3) and **frustrated** (Hb *chapher*, "shame resulting from disappointed hope"; cp. Ps 83:17, Mc 3:7), knowing they would die without water.

6:27 Job compared his friends, who failed to pinpoint what he had done wrong, to creditors bartering over the orphaned son of their debtor (cp. 2Kg 4:1); they were more concerned about providing a rational explanation for Job's situation than in ministering to their friend as a person.

7:1-4 Before he was afflicted, Job led a busy, purposeful life managing both his estate and his family (1:1-5). A man's identity is closely tied to his work, and to live **on earth** automatically entails daily **labor**. Job, however, was deprived of the basic benefits of work enjoyed even by a **slave** or **hired hand**—rest from the sun's heat and wages. Instead, he was **made to inherit** (Hb *nachal*, "acquire unwillingly or by compulsion") **futility** and lonely **nights** of weary tossing and turning in extreme discomfort. Every new day only brought more pain and grief.

7:6-9 The image of a **weaver's shuttle** was common in the ancient world. Life is compared to a thread being woven until, at some unknown point, it was suddenly cut off. Thread moving so quickly that the eye cannot follow it through the shuttle accurately depicted Job's sense that his life was rapidly coming to **an end** (Hb *kalah*, "be completed or fulfilled, be consumed or spent, go by"; "fades away"; cp. 4:9; 21:13).

7:17-21 Job could not understand why human beings were worth God's constant **attention**. Job's complaint directly opposed the attitude of wonder and praise expressed in the parallel wording of Ps 8:4-5. **Inspect** (Hb *paqad*, "visit; search, explore") has the positive meaning in Ps 8:4 of "look after, care for" (cp. Jb 10:12). However, Job used the more negative sense of "visit for the purpose of executing judgment" (cp. Ex 20:5; Ps 89:32).

Before calamity struck, Job regularly offered sacrifices early in the morning out of concern that his children might have sinned (Jb 1:5), but here he longed to escape God's unceasing scrutiny as irritating and unnecessary. The idiom **long enough to swallow** (still used in Arabic) meant that God would not leave Job alone for even one instant.

8:2 Bildad compared Job's **words** (Hb *ʾēmer*, "discourse") to **a blast** [Hb *kabbir*, "great; strong, mighty"] **of wind**. Job had asked if Eliphaz thought "that a despairing man's words (Hb *ʾēmer*, "discourse") are mere wind" (6:26). Here, Bildad showed that he regarded Job's speech not as a senseless stream of words—"mere wind"—but as something powerful and dangerous (cp. *kabbir* describing "waters" in Is 17:12; 28:2), perhaps like the "powerful (Hb *gadol*, "great in magnitude") wind" that caused the deaths of Job's children (Jb 1:19).

8:8-13 Bildad relied confidently on the accumulated wisdom of the previous generations, the most respected source of practical knowledge in ancient times. To reject the traditional wisdom of **the previous generation** and **their fathers** would be unthinkable. Furthermore, the cause-and-effect pattern of the moral universe, according to Bildad's view, was mirrored in nature. Figuratively, to **forget God** or to be **godless** (Hb *chanēph*, "hypocritical, profane"; cp. 27:8) is to **dry up** like marsh plants **without water**.

8:11 Both verbs in the analogy—**grow** (Hb *gaʾah*, "lift up, increase; be lofty, exalted, magnificent"; cp. Ex 15:1,21) and **flourish** (Hb *sagah*) convey a picture of abundant life, not

5 My flesh is clothed
with maggots and encrusted
with dirt.[A]
My skin forms scabs[B]
and then oozes.
6 My days pass more swiftly
than a weaver's shuttle;
they come to an end
without hope.
7 Remember that my life is
but a breath.
My eye will never again see
anything good.
8 The eye of anyone who looks
on me
will no longer see me.
Your eyes will look for me,
but I will be gone.
9 As a cloud fades away
and vanishes,
so the one who goes down
to •Sheol will never
rise again.
10 He will never return
to his house;
his hometown will no longer
remember[C] him.
11 Therefore I will not restrain
my mouth.
I will speak in the anguish
of my spirit;
I will complain
in the bitterness of my soul.
12 Am I the sea[D] or a sea monster,
that You keep me
under guard?
13 When I say: My bed
will comfort me,
and my couch will ease
my complaint,
14 then You frighten me
with dreams,
and terrify me with visions,
15 so that I prefer strangling[E]—
death rather than life
in this body.[F]
16 I give up! I will not
live forever.
Leave me alone, for my days
are a breath.[G]
17 What is man, that You think
so highly of him
and pay so much attention
to him?
18 You inspect him every morning,
and put him to the test
every moment.
19 Will You ever look away
from me,
or leave me alone
long enough to swallow?[H]
20 If I have sinned, what have
I done to You,
Watcher of mankind?
Why have You made me
Your target,
so that I have become
a burden to You?[I]
21 Why not forgive my sin
and pardon my transgression?
For soon I will lie down
in the grave.
You will eagerly seek me,
but I will be gone.

Bildad's Speech (8:1-22)

8 Then Bildad the Shuhite replied:
2 How long will you
go on saying these things?
Your words are a blast
of wind.
3 Does God pervert justice?
Does the •Almighty pervert
what is right?
4 Since your children sinned
against Him,
He gave them over
to their rebellion.
5 But if you earnestly seek God
and ask the Almighty
for mercy,
6 if you are pure and upright,
then He will move even now
on your behalf
and restore the home where
your righteousness dwells.
7 Then, even if your beginnings
were modest,
your final days will be
full of prosperity.
8 For ask the previous generation,
and pay attention to what
their fathers discovered,
9 since we were born only
yesterday and know
nothing.
Our days on earth are
but a shadow.
10 Will they not teach you
and tell you

[A]7:5 Or *and dirty scabs* [B]7:5 Lit *skin hardens* [C]7:10 Lit *know* [D]7:12 Or *the sea god* [E]7:15 Or *suffocation* [F]7:15 Lit *than my bones* [G]7:16 Or *are futile* [H]7:19 Lit *swallow my saliva?* [I]7:20 Ancient Jewish tradition, LXX; MT, Vg read *myself*

and speak from
their understanding?
11 Does papyrus grow where
there is no marsh?
Do reeds flourish
without water?
12 While still uncut shoots,
they would dry up quicker
than any other plant.
13 Such is the destiny[A] of all
who forget God;
the hope of the godless
will perish.
14 His source of confidence
is fragile;[B]
what he trusts in is
a spider's web.
15 He leans on his web,
but it doesn't stand firm.
He grabs it, but it does not
hold up.
16 He is a well-watered plant
in the sunshine;
his shoots spread out
over his garden.
17 His roots are intertwined
around a pile of rocks.
He looks for a home
among the stones.
18 If he is uprooted[C]
from his place,
it will deny knowing him,
saying, "I never saw you."
19 Surely this is the joy
of his way of life;
yet others will sprout
from the dust.
20 Look, God does not reject
a person of integrity,
and He will not support
evildoers.
21 He will yet fill your mouth
with laughter
and your lips with a shout
of joy.
22 Your enemies will be clothed
with shame;
the tent of the wicked
will exist no longer.

Job's Reply to Bildad (9:1–10:22)

9 Then Job answered:
2 Yes, I know what you've said
is true,
but how can a person
be justified before God?
3 If one wanted to take Him
to court,
he could not answer God[D]
once in a thousand times.
4 God is wise and all-powerful
Who has opposed Him
and come out unharmed?
5 He removes mountains
without their knowledge,
overturning them
in His anger.
6 He shakes the earth
from its place
so that its pillars tremble.
7 He commands the sun
not to shine
and seals off the stars.
8 He alone stretches out
the heavens
and treads on the waves
of the sea.[E]
9 He makes the stars: the Bear,[F]
Orion,
the Pleiades,
and the constellations[G]
of the southern sky.
10 He does great
and unsearchable things,
wonders without number.
11 If He passes by me,
I wouldn't see Him;
if He goes right by,
I wouldn't recognize Him.
12 If He snatches something,
who can stop[H] Him?
Who can ask Him, "What are
You doing?"
13 God does not hold back
His anger;
•Rahab's assistants cringe
in fear beneath Him!
14 How then can I answer Him
or choose my arguments
against Him?
15 Even if I were in the right,
I could not answer.
I could only beg my Judge
for mercy.
16 If I summoned Him
and He answered me,
I do not believe He would
pay attention to what I said.
17 He batters me
with a whirlwind
and multiplies my wounds
without cause.

[A]8:13 Lit *Such are the ways* [B]8:14 Or *cut off*; Hb obscure [C]8:18 Lit *swallowed* [D]9:3 Or *court, God would not answer him* [E]9:8 Or *and walks on the back of the sea god* [F]9:9 Or *Aldebaran* [G]9:9 Or *chambers* [H]9:12 Or *dissuade*

merely existence or survival. A thriving **papyrus** plant would grow to a height of 10 to 15 feet.

8:14-15 The **spider's web** served as an equally vivid picture of the deceptively unstable way of life pursued by the godless, the one who **leans on** (Hb *sha'an*, "rest upon, place one's confidence in") that which cannot possibly sustain his weight.

9:1-2 Although he agreed that Bildad's words in themselves were true, Job still questioned why God had singled him out for suffering. Job picked up the theme Eliphaz introduced in 4:17—**how can a person be justified** [Hb *tsadaq*, "have a just cause, be right"] **before God?**—and carried forward the pattern of the book's content in the form of legal disputations. Of the 3 times the verb "be justified" is used in the Old Testament, 2 are in the book of Job. At issue in Job's case was how he could possibly be vindicated before God and therefore treated by Him as just. The last use of *tsadaq* in the book is found in the Lord's speech calling Job to account: "Would you declare Me guilty to *justify* yourself?" (40:8).

9:3-4 Here, Job recognized that **to take Him** [the Lord] **to court** (Hb *riv*, "plead a cause, contend forensically"; cp. 13:8; 33:13; "prosecute," 10:2; 23:6; "indict," 13:19; "contends," 40:2) would be futile. Once the **wise and all-powerful** God began asking the questions, Job would have no defense and would certainly not **come out unharmed** (Hb *shalam*, "be or remain safe"). Bildad had argued that *if* Job were "pure and upright," *then* God could be expected to "restore" (Hb *shalam*) him (8:6). Believing that he was indeed "upright" (cp. the Lord's assessment of Job's character, 1:1,8; 2:3), Job questioned this view.

9:13 Rahab's assistants poetically alluded to Canaanite mythology, in which Rahab (Hb, a different name than that of the woman *Rachav*, Jos 2:1) was a powerful sea monster embodying the primordial powers of chaos (cp. Jb 26:12; Ps 89:9-10; Is 51:9-10). In some cases, Rahab symbolically referred to Egypt or any cosmic force daring to challenge God (Ps 87:4; Is 30:7).

9:15-19 The word **Judge** (Hb *shaphat*) here denotes a "legal opponent" rather than the person who "judges or decides whether to condemn or defend" in a courtroom setting (cp. 23:7, where a different form of the participle is used). Job argued that God was relentlessly punishing him **without cause** (Hb *chinnam*, "undeservedly, for nothing"; cp. 1:9; 2:3). With **strength** and **justice** indisputably on God's side, Job's case was utterly hopeless (9:19-20).

9:20 The verb **condemn** (Hb *rasha'*, "declare guilty or unrighteous") is later used by Eliphaz to accuse Job of implicating himself (15:6). **Declare me guilty** (Hb *'aqash*, "pervert or twist") is a forensic term for "distorting, misconstruing, or misinterpreting" a person's statement or testimony. Countering Bildad's suggestion that if Job were "a person of integrity" (Hb *tam*), God would "fill [his] mouth with laughter" (8:20-21), Job argued that even if he "were blameless" his words of self-defense would be twisted into a false admission of guilt.

9:21-24 To be punished unjustly typically provokes vigorous self-defense, but Job concluded that he would adopt an attitude of resignation in order to maintain his innocence. His particular experience of **despair** (Hb *massah*, "calamity by which God tries or tests" someone) did not match his understanding of God and seemed to contradict Eliphaz's argument that God does not destroy "innocent" people (4:7-9). Human reason would naturally conclude that if God is "all-powerful" (9:4) yet afflicts **the blameless and the wicked** without distinction, then He is cruel and unjust. Having been given the explanation of Job's trial in chapters 1 and 2, the reader is equipped to resist Job's rationalization here.

10:1-2 Job's declaration that he was **disgusted** (Hb *naqat*, "loathe"; used only here in the OT) with his life echoes the sense of meaninglessness expressed earlier (chap. 3; 6:8-10; 7:6-10,16,21). Job's persistent declarations that his life was forfeited may have served as mounting evidence against Satan's claim that when personally afflicted, Job would become like any other man, regarding his life as the one possession to preserve at all costs, even if that meant cursing God (2:4). Job boldly expressed his **complaint** but still never denied or cursed God. Without a mediator, Job rehearsed the case he determined to present **to God**.

10:3-6 Job began this speech with three rhetorical questions confronting God with the apparent impossibility of reconciling Job's conception of Him with his desperate circumstances. The implicit answers pointed out that:

- God could not possibly benefit from turning the moral universe inside out—reversing the law of retribution to which Job's friends unanimously appealed (v. 3).
- God was able to discern the motives of the heart, which are inaccessible to human perception (v. 4; cp. Pr 16:2; 21:2).
- Because God is eternal and omniscient, it did not make sense for Him to search relentlessly for Job's **sin** when He already knew the search would be in vain and

18 He doesn't let me catch
my breath
but soaks me
with bitter experiences.
19 If it is a matter of strength,
look, He is the Mighty One!
If it is a matter of justice,
who can summon Him?[A]
20 Even if I were in the right,
my own mouth would
condemn me;
if I were blameless, my mouth
would declare me •guilty.

21 Though I am blameless,
I no longer care about myself;
I renounce my life.
22 It is all the same. Therefore
I say,
"He destroys both
the blameless
and the wicked."
23 When disaster brings
sudden death,
He mocks the despair
of the innocent.
24 The earth[B] is handed over
to the wicked;
He blindfolds[C] its judges.
If it isn't He, then who is it?

25 My days fly by faster
than a runner;[D]
they flee without seeing
any good.
26 They sweep by like boats
made of papyrus,
like an eagle swooping down
on its prey.
27 If I said, "I will forget
my complaint,
change my expression,
and smile,"
28 I would still live in terror
of all my pains.
I know You will not
acquit me.
29 Since I will be found guilty,
why should I labor in vain?
30 If I wash myself with snow,
and cleanse my hands
with lye,
31 then You dip me in a pit
of mud,
and my own clothes
despise me!

SALVATION

Job lamented the rapidly passing days of his life (9:25-33). Feeling that God would continue to punish him no matter what he did, Job ruled out other possible responses as futile (vv. 27-31). He recognized the vast gap between God's holiness and man's sin. He longed for someone to mediate his case impartially, one of the themes of the book of Job. The book's treatment of this theme reveals the need (and anticipates the solution) for a perfect Mediator between God and man, the Lord Jesus (cp. 16:19 and 1Tm 2:5).

32 For He is not a man like me,
that I can answer Him,
that we can take each other
to court.
33 There is no one to judge
between us,
to lay his hand on both of us.
34 Let Him take His rod away
from me
so His terror will no longer
frighten me.
35 Then I would speak and not
fear Him.
But that is not the case; I am
on my own.

10 I am disgusted with my life.
I will express my complaint
and speak in the bitterness
of my soul.
2 I will say to God:
"Do not declare me •guilty!
Let me know why
You prosecute me.
3 Is it good for You to oppress,
to reject the work
of Your hands,
and favor[E] the plans
of the wicked?
4 Do You have eyes of flesh,
or do You see
as a human sees?
5 Are Your days like those
of a human,
or Your years like those
of a man,
6 that You look for
my wrongdoing
and search for my sin,
7 even though You know that
I am not wicked
and that there is no one
who can deliver
from Your hand?

[A]9:19 LXX; MT reads *me* [B]9:24 Or *land* [C]9:24 Lit *covers the faces of* [D]9:25 = a royal messenger
[E]10:3 Lit *shine on*

8 "Your hands shaped me
and formed me.
Will You now
turn and destroy me?
9 Please remember that You
formed me like clay.
Will You now return me
to dust?
10 Did You not pour me out
like milk
and curdle me like cheese?
11 You clothed me with skin
and flesh,
and wove me together
with bones and tendons.
12 You gave me life
and faithful love,
and Your care has guarded
my life.
13 "Yet You concealed
these thoughts
in Your heart;
I know that this was
Your hidden plan:[A]
14 if I sin, You would notice,[B]
and would not acquit me
of my wrongdoing.
15 If I am wicked, woe to me!
And even if I am righteous,
I cannot lift up my head.
I am filled with shame
and aware of my affliction.
16 If I am proud,[C] You hunt me
like a lion
and again display
Your miraculous power
against me.
17 You produce new witnesses[D]
against me
and multiply Your anger
toward me.
Hardships assault me,
wave after wave.[E]
18 "Why did You bring me out of
the womb?
I should have died and never
been seen.
19 I wish[F] I had never existed
but had been carried
from the womb
to the grave.
20 Are my days not few? Stop it![G]
Leave me alone, so that
I can smile a little
21 before I go to a land
of darkness and gloom,
never to return.
22 It is a land of blackness
like the deepest darkness,
gloomy and chaotic,
where even the light is
like[H] the darkness."

Zophar's Speech (11:1-20)

11 Then Zophar the Naamathite
replied:
2 Should this stream of words
go unanswered
and such a talker[I]
be acquitted?
3 Should your babbling
put others to silence,
so that you can keep on
ridiculing
with no one to humiliate you?
4 You have said, "My teaching
is sound,
and I am pure in Your sight."
5 But if only God would speak
and declare His case[J]
against you,
6 He would show you
the secrets of wisdom,
for true wisdom has two sides.
Know then that God
has chosen to overlook
some of your sin.

7 Can you fathom the depths
of God
or discover the limits
of the •Almighty?
8 They are higher than
the heavens—what can
you do?
They are deeper
than •Sheol—what can
you know?
9 Their measure is longer
than the earth
and wider than the sea.

10 If He passes by and throws
someone in prison
or convenes a court, who can
stop Him?
11 Surely He knows
which people are worthless.
If He sees iniquity, will He not
take note of it?

[A]10:13 Lit *was with You* [B]10:14 Lit *notice me* [C]10:16 Lit *If he lifts up* [D]10:17 Or *You bring fresh troops* [E]10:17 Lit *Changes and a host are with me* [F]10:19 Lit *As if* [G]10:20 Alt Hb tradition reads *Will He not leave my few days alone?* [H]10:22 Lit *chaotic, and shines as* [I]11:2 Lit *a man of lips* [J]11:5 Lit *and open His lips*

that, in any case, Job could not escape (Jb 10:5-6).

10:8-22 Job questioned how God, who had **formed** him in the womb, could turn against and continue to afflict him (cp. Ps 139:13,15). Job demonstrated a correct understanding of God as a personal Creator, the source of **life and faithful love**; but, contrasting David's perspective in Ps 139, Job drew some erroneous conclusions:

- While God, who acts with purpose, was carefully fashioning Job and guarding his life, He secretly planned Job's demise (Jb 10:11-13; contrast Ps 139:13-16).
- Since God sees all and cannot allow sin to go unpunished, Job's actions, whether wicked or righteous, were relentlessly scrutinized by God *in order to* prosecute him (contrast Ps 139:1-12,23-24).

Guarded (Hb *shamar*, Jb 10:12) has the positive sense of "protect or preserve" (cp. "watched over," 29:2). An ironic contrast is established with the same verb—translated **notice** (10:14)—given the sense that God "watches or observes" closely in order to find fault (cp. "take note of," 14:16; "stands watch over" a prisoner, 13:27; 33:11). Job questioned why God had allowed him to live and begged to be released momentarily from God's constant gaze before he died.

10:19-22 Job used five words depicting the **grave**:

- **darkness** (Hb *choshek*; cp. 3:4-5; Gn 1:2; Ps 88:12, in which the psalmist's cry echoes Job's desperation);
- **gloom** and **deepest darkness** (Hb *tsalmawet*, "shadow of death, thick darkness"; cp. 3:5; Ps 23:4);
- **blackness** (Hb *'ephah*, "darkness, utter gloom"; used only here and Am 4:13);
- **gloomy** and **darkness** (Hb *'ophel*, "darkness"; cp. 3:6);
- **chaotic** (Hb *lo'-seder*, "without arrangement or order"; used only here in the OT).

This poetic piling up of synonymous descriptions emphasizes a view of Sheol as a place of miserable isolation. In contrast, David noted that the deepest darkness is penetrated by the light of God's presence (Pss 107:10-14; 139:11-12).

11:1-11 Zophar began with a stinging attack on Job. He rudely rebuked Job for proclaiming his innocence and accusing God of injustice. Strongly objecting to Job's protests of innocence and appeal for justice, Zophar approached his friend as someone attempting to talk his way out of pleading guilty. He sarcastically wished God *would* answer Job and show him the **true wisdom** that **has two sides** (v.

6; Hb *kiphlayim*, "double-folded"; figuratively, "complicated, impenetrable by human reason"). Zophar implied that God's punishment of Job was still not giving him what he really deserved. With a series of rhetorical questions, Zophar emphasized Job's lack of knowledge and power in light of God's immeasurable and limitless being. However, he merely confirmed Job's complaint—no one can **stop** God, and He sees all (vv. 10-11; cp. 9:12; 10:14-17).

11:13-20 Since Job was no match for the Almighty, Zophar advised him to deal squarely with his sin—to **remove** (Hb *rachaq*, "put far away") any **iniquity** (Hb *ʾawen*, "wickedness, emptiness, vanity, falsehood," vv. 11,14) to which he was clinging and pray to the Lord. Then he could **hold** his **head high** rather than being unable to lift it—free from rather than filled with shame (v. 15; cp. 10:15). The days of his **suffering** would be only a memory (11:16), and the future would look bright (vv. 17-19). However, the speech concluded with a warning for Job not to refuse this advice and become one of **the wicked**, who could look forward only to death (v. 20).

12:1–14:22 Although the subject matter did not change significantly, this discourse is longer than the previous ones, and Job addressed all three friends collectively. It marked the end of the first cycle of speeches and precipitated the next round.

12:5-6 By citing the proverb, Job not only indicted his friends for misjudging him but also reiterated his complaint that God was not acting predictably. If the theology of retribution could explain God's actions, then the homes of the righteous rather than those of thieves would be **safe** (Hb *shalah*, "have rest, be at ease, prosper").

12:7-12 Job contrasted God's sovereignty with the limited understanding of his friends, who had neglected to see the obvious—that life is not so simple when it comes to understanding why God does what He does. Job particularly rejected the faulty "wisdom" offered by Zophar. Since the verbs and pronouns in verses 7-8 are second person singular, some argue that Job began summarizing what his friends had been telling *him* (the summary extending to 12:25). A more likely reading is to hear Job sarcastically suggesting *to Zophar* that he needed a refresher course in elementary wisdom. Zophar claimed that God would "show" (Hb *nagad*, "bring to light, inform, make known") Job "the secrets of wisdom" (11:6), but Job noted that even the **animals** could **instruct** (Hb *nagad*, 12:7) Zophar that

12 But a stupid man
will gain understanding
as soon as a wild donkey
is born a man!
13 As for you, if you redirect
your heart
and lift up your hands to Him
in prayer—
14 if there is iniquity
in your hand, remove it,
and don't allow injustice
to dwell in your tents—
15 then you will hold
your head high,
free from fault.
You will be firmly established
and unafraid.
16 For you will forget
your suffering,
recalling it only as waters
that have flowed by.
17 Your life will be brighter
than noonday;
its darkness[A] will be
like the morning.
18 You will be confident, because
there is hope.
You will look carefully about
and lie down in safety.
19 You will lie down without fear,
and many will seek your favor.
20 But the sight of the wicked
will fail.
Their way of escape will be
cut off,
and their only hope
is their last breath.

Job's Reply to Zophar (12:1–14:22)

12 Then Job answered:

2 No doubt you are the people,
and wisdom will die with you!
3 But I also have a mind;
I am not inferior to you.
Who doesn't know the things
you are talking about?[B]
4 I am a laughingstock
to my[C] friends,
by calling on God,
who answers me.[D]
The righteous
and upright man is
a laughingstock.
5 The one who is at ease
holds calamity in contempt
and thinks it is prepared
for those whose feet
are slipping.
6 The tents of robbers are safe,
and those who provoke God
are secure;
God's power provides this.[E]
7 But ask the animals,
and they will instruct you;
ask the birds of the sky,
and they will tell you.
8 Or speak to the earth,
and it will instruct you;
let the fish of the sea
inform you.
9 Which of all these
does not know
that the hand of the LORD
has done this?
10 The life of every living thing
is in His hand,
as well as the breath
of all mankind.
11 Doesn't the ear test words
as the palate tastes food?
12 Wisdom is found
with the elderly,

[A]11:17 Text emended; MT reads *noonday; you are dark, you* [B]12:3 Lit *With whom are not such things as these* [C]12:4 Lit *his* [D]12:4 Lit *him* [E]12:6 Or *secure; to those who bring their god in their hands*

>WORD|*study*

12:5 In this context, **those whose feet are** slipping (Hb *maʿad*, "waver, totter"; used only here and in Psalms) figuratively refers to those who are disobedient and therefore no longer walk securely under God's protection. In three psalms, the word links obedience with security and favor:

- As a "faithful" and "blameless man" (Ps 18:25), David praised God for widening the way for his "steps" so that his "ankles" did not "give way" (Hb *maʿad*, Ps 18:36).
- David prayed for the Lord to "vindicate" him because he had "trusted in the LORD without wavering" (Hb *maʿad*, Ps 26:1).
- In the form of a proverb, David noted that the "steps" of those who hold to God's "instruction . . . do not falter" (Hb *maʿad*, Ps 37:31).

>WORD|*study*

13:4 Coat (Hb *taphal*, literally "patch, sew together; plaster"; figuratively, "frame lies") is used only two other times in the Old Testament. More explicitly contrasting the Lord's goodness with the "hard and insensitive" hearts of his opponents, David complained, "The arrogant have smeared me with lies" (Ps 119:69,70). Both Job and David spoke of making something (or someone) good look bad. Later in this speech (Jb 12–14), Job wildly imagined a scenario in which God "would cover over" (Hb *taphal*) his "iniquity" (14:17)—i.e., overlay something bad with something good (God's grace).

and understanding comes
with long life.
13 Wisdom and strength belong
to God;
counsel and understanding
are His.
14 Whatever He tears down
cannot be rebuilt;
whoever He imprisons cannot
be released.
15 When He withholds
the waters, everything
dries up,
and when He releases them,
they destroy the land.
16 True wisdom and power
belong to Him.
The deceived and the deceiver
are His.
17 He leads counselors away
barefoot
and makes judges go mad.
18 He releases the bonds[A] put on
by kings
and fastens a belt
around their waists.
19 He leads priests away barefoot
and overthrows
established leaders.
20 He deprives trusted advisers
of speech
and takes away the elders'
good judgment.
21 He pours out contempt
on nobles
and disarms[B] the strong.
22 He reveals mysteries
from the darkness
and brings
the deepest darkness
into the light.
23 He makes nations great,
then destroys them;
He enlarges nations,
then leads them away.
24 He deprives
the world's leaders
of reason,
and makes them wander
in a trackless wasteland.
25 They grope around
in darkness without light;
He makes them stagger
like drunken men.

13 Look, my eyes have seen
all this;
my ears have heard
and understood it.
2 Everything you know,
I also know;
I am not inferior to you.
3 Yet I prefer to speak
to the •Almighty
and argue my case
before God.
4 But you coat the truth
with lies;
you are all worthless doctors.
5 If only you would shut up
and let that be your wisdom!
6 Hear now my argument,
and listen to my defense.[C]
7 Would you testify unjustly
on God's behalf
or speak deceitfully for Him?
8 Would you show partiality
to Him
or argue the case
in His defense?
9 Would it go well
if He examined you?
Could you deceive Him
as you would deceive
a man?
10 Surely He would rebuke you
if you secretly
showed partiality.
11 Would God's majesty
not terrify you?
Would His dread not fall
on you?
12 Your memorable sayings
are proverbs of ash;

[A]12:18 Text emended; MT reads *discipline* [B]12:21 Lit *and loosens the belt of* [C]13:6 Lit *to the claims of my lips*

the Lord was apparently responsible for Job's suffering.

Job added to this "review lesson" another basic proverb (v. 10) followed by an idiomatic way of saying, "Am I not right?" (v. 11). Another elementary proverb was then recited (v. 12), likely with a sarcastic tone implying either that Zophar still lacked the wisdom to be expected of the elderly or that he had not lived long enough to be counted among the wise.

12:13-25 In this section, Job demonstrated at length what he had already figured out regarding **wisdom**. It belonged solely to God (v. 13). Zophar had declared that **true wisdom** (Hb *tushiyah*, "counsel, sound knowledge that results in abiding success," v. 16) is beyond human comprehension (11:6); Job insisted that it belongs to God. In Job's view, God's **power** is evident in His absolute control of all nature, people, leaders, and nations (cp. 5:10-16). Whatever God does is irreversible apart from His will, and Job's four examples portrayed His power to destroy (12:14-15). According to Job's litany of evidence, God's wisdom and power are so great that the wisest and most powerful men cannot withstand Him—one after another, all are put to shame, stripped of whatever knowledge or authority they imagined was theirs (cp. Ps 107:40).

13:1-4 Job asserted that he was **not inferior** to his friends—a figure of speech actually implying his superiority. As though the three men represented a court unqualified to hear his case, Job appealed directly to the highest authority—he would **argue** his case before God, the true source of wisdom. Two verses begin with the same strong adversative—**Yet** (Hb *ʾulam*, "but indeed," v. 3) and **But** (Hb *ʾulam*, v. 4)—indicating Job's emphatic choice to pursue a course other than what his friends recommended. Perhaps pressed by the directness of Zophar's speech to think through his rejection of the friends' accusations, Job reconsidered the possibility of confronting God in terms of a courtroom setting. In his reply to Bildad, Job had regarded the notion as impossible (9:3-4), but here he has determined that only before God can the justice of his complaint be made plain.

Job also dismissed Zophar's criticism of his arguments (11:2-4) as "babbling [that] put others to silence" (Hb *charash*, "hold your peace," 11:3); both Eliphaz (4:2; 5:1) and Bildad (8:1) had rebuked Job's rhetoric as well. Responding to Eliphaz, Job agreed to "be silent" (Hb *charash*) so his friends could help him "understand what I did wrong" (6:24). They failed to do so. **But** instead, Job accused, they **coat the truth with lies** (13:4; see **Word Study**, p. 635).

13:13-19 According to Job, his friends had spoken in vain if they intended to soothe his spiritual distress. A better expression of "wisdom" would be for *them* to "shut up" (Hb *charash*, 13:5; cp. Pr 17:28), **be quiet** (Hb *charash*, Jb 13:13), and simply listen to him formally present his "defense" (Hb *riv*, "pleading of one's case," as in the private arguments made between legal opponents before their case is tried publicly, v. 6; cp. Ex 23:2) or **declaration** to God (v. 17).

Preferring God's judgment over his friends' empty and unsatisfying counsel, Job urged his friends not to interfere with his seemingly reckless attempt to grapple with God (vv. 13-14). Despite everything, Job persevered in believing that one day God would vindicate him, which is exactly what would happen. Job knew that his hope, in any circumstance, could only be in his God. Echoing previous expressions of unwavering faith (1:21; 2:10), Job boldly declared that he would **hope** (Hb *yachal*, "trust, expect, wait"; cp. 14:14) in God (13:15-16).

13:20-27 Job did not argue that he had not sinned but decried being treated like a prisoner without warrant. Essentially, Job was asking God if his friends were correct; he wanted to be able to see it for himself.

13:28–14:22 Job turned to a meditation on the futility of life and the certainty of death, a common theme of wisdom literature (cp. Moses, Ps 90:10; David, 1Ch 29:15; "the Teacher," Ec 6:12; Solomon, Pr 10:27; Isaiah, Is 40:7; James, Jms 4:14). The compact series of images links the point Job made in 13:25 with his next question of God, which expressed Job's inability to understand why God would bother to **take notice of** him—a mere man whose life, unlike that of the eternal God, **does not last** (Jb 14:2-3; cp. Ps 103:15). Job suggested that even God could not **produce something pure** [Hb *tahor*, morally "clean, unpolluted"] **from what is impure** (Hb *tame'*, morally "unclean, polluted," Jb 14:4, the only use of this word in the book of Job).

14:7-17 Jesus has answered Job's question—**When a man dies, will he come back to life?**—with a resounding "Yes" (Jn 11:23-26; cp. 1Co 15:3-57).

your defenses are made
of clay.

13 Be quiet,[A] and I will speak.
Let whatever comes happen
to me.
14 Why do I put myself at risk[B]
and take my life
in my own hands?
15 Even if He kills me,
I will hope in Him.[C]
I will still defend my ways
before Him.
16 Yes, this will result
in my deliverance,
for no godless person
can appear before Him.
17 Pay close attention
to my words;
let my declaration ring
in your ears.
18 Now then, I have prepared
my case;
I know that I am right.
19 Can anyone indict me?
If so, I will be silent and die.

20 Only grant these two things
to me, God,
so that I will not have to hide
from Your presence:
21 remove Your hand from me,
and do not let Your terror
frighten me.
22 Then call, and I will answer,
or I will speak, and You
can respond to me.
23 How many iniquities and sins
have I committed?[D]
Reveal to me
my transgression and sin.
24 Why do You hide Your face
and consider me Your enemy?
25 Will You frighten
a wind-driven leaf?
Will You chase after
dry straw?
26 For You record
bitter accusations
against me
and make me inherit
the iniquities of my youth.
27 You put my feet in the stocks
and stand watch over all
my paths,
setting a limit for the soles[E]
of my feet.
28 Man wears out
like something rotten,
like a moth-eaten garment.

14

Man born of woman
is short of days and full
of trouble.
2 He blossoms like a flower,
then withers;
he flees like a shadow
and does not last.
3 Do You really take notice
of one like this?
Will You bring me
into judgment against You?[F]
4 Who can produce
something pure from what
is impure?
No one!
5 Since man's days
are determined
and the number
of his months depends
on You,
and since You have set[G] limits
he cannot pass,
6 look away from him
and let him rest
so that he can enjoy his day
like a hired hand.

7 There is hope for a tree:
If it is cut down, it will
sprout again,
and its shoots will not die.
8 If its roots grow old
in the ground
and its stump starts to die
in the soil,
9 the smell of water
makes it thrive
and produce twigs
like a sapling.
10 But a man dies
and fades away;
he breathes his last—
where is he?
11 As water disappears
from the sea
and a river becomes parched
and dry,
12 so man lies down never
to rise again.
They will not wake up
until the heavens are
no more;

[A]**13:13** Lit *quiet before me* [B]**13:14** Lit *I take my flesh in my teeth* [C]**13:15** Some Hb mss read *I will be without hope* [D]**13:23** Lit *sins are to me* [E]**13:27** Lit *paths. You mark a line around the roots* [F]**14:3** LXX, Syr, Vg read *him* [G]**14:5** Lit *set his*

they will not stir
from their sleep.
13 If only You would hide me
in •Sheol
and conceal me
until Your anger passes.
If only You would appoint
a time for me
and then remember me.
14 When a man dies, will he
come back to life?
If so, I would wait all the days
of my struggle
until my relief comes.
15 You would call, and I would
answer You.
You would long for the work
of Your hands.
16 For then You would count
my steps
but would not take note of
my sin.
17 My rebellion would be
sealed up in a bag,
and You would cover over
my iniquity.

18 But as a mountain collapses
and crumbles
and a rock is dislodged
from its place,
19 as water wears away stones
and torrents wash away
the soil from the land,
so You destroy a man's hope.
20 You completely overpower
him, and he passes on;
You change his appearance
and send him away.
21 If his sons receive honor,
he does not know it;
if they become insignificant,
he is unaware of it.
22 He feels only the pain
of his own body
and mourns only for himself.

The Second Series of Speeches (15:1–21:34)

Eliphaz's Speech (15:1-35)

15 Then Eliphaz the Temanite replied:

2 Does a wise man answer
with empty[A] counsel
or fill himself[B]
with the hot east wind?
3 Should he argue
with useless talk
or with words that serve
no good purpose?
4 But you even undermine
the •fear of God
and hinder meditation
before Him.
5 Your iniquity teaches you
what to say,
and you choose the language
of the crafty.
6 Your own mouth
condemns you, not I;
your own lips testify
against you.
7 Were you the first person
ever born,
or were you brought forth
before the hills?
8 Do you listen in
on the council of God,
or have a monopoly
on wisdom?
9 What do you know that
we don't?
What do you understand that
is not clear to us?
10 Both the gray-haired
and the elderly are with us,
men older than your father.
11 Are God's consolations
not enough for you,
even the words
that deal gently with you?
12 Why has your heart
misled you,
and why do your eyes flash
13 as you turn your anger[C]
against God
and allow such words to leave
your mouth?

14 What is man, that he
should be pure,
or one born of woman, that he
should be righteous?
15 If God puts no trust
in His holy ones
and the heavens are not pure
in His sight,
16 how much less one
who is revolting
and corrupt,
who drinks injustice
like water?

[A]**15:2** Lit *windy*; Jb 16:3 [B]**15:2** Lit *his belly* [C]**15:13** Or *spirit*

14:18-22 The word **But** (Hb *ʾulam*, "but indeed") clearly marks a shift in Job's discourse from hope (vv. 13-17) to the destruction of hope (vv. 18-19). Both extremes depend on or reflect God's control.

15:1–21:34 The second cycle of speeches became more heated as Job's friends realized that their arguments had not convinced Job of his alleged guilt. They continued to rebuke Job, becoming more and more incensed with his declaration of innocence.

15:1-6 Eliphaz compared Job's words to the destructive **east wind** (Hb *qadim*, "hot oppressive wind; violent windstorm that stirs up clouds of dust or sand"; cp. 1:19) of the desert. The words of **a wise man** like Job should be different.

15:4-6 Whether or not Job exhibited the **fear** (Hb *yirʾah*, "terror, reverence") of the Lord also appeared in Eliphaz's first speech, in which he argued that Job's "piety" (Hb *yirʾah*) was his "hope" (Hb *tiqwah*, 4:6; cp. 14:19). Here, he was alarmed that Job would **undermine** [Hb *parar*, "take away, break off, make void"; cp. "challenge," 40:8] **the fear of God**. In the third speech, he argued that Job's "piety" (Hb *yirʾah*) could not possibly be the reason for his trials (22:4). In other passages, *yirʾah* denotes the "fear" of God as a deterrent to sin as well as the respect deserved by the Almighty (cp. Gn 20:11; Ex 20:20; Ps 90:11).

According to Eliphaz, Job's reckless speech also took away from his **meditation** [Hb *sichah*, "pious reflection, prayer"; used only here and in Ps 119:97,99] **before** God. Apparently having abandoned the disciplines that nurtured a life of wisdom, Job spoke like a criminal. Eliphaz charged, therefore, that Job's **own mouth** condemned him, ironically agreeing with Job (9:20).

15:8 Only the narrator and readers were allowed to **listen in on the council of God** when God permitted Satan to inflict suffering on Job (see 1:6-12; 2:1-7; cp. Jr 23:18,22).

15:10-16 For Eliphaz, **the elderly** were irrefutably the source of wisdom (cp. 12:12), and he clearly believed that his own speeches represented God's **words** meant to console Job. When Job asked God, "What is man, that You . . . pay so much attention to him?" (7:17, in his first reply to Eliphaz), he was objecting to the sense that God was watching his every move in order to punish him for the slightest deviation from perfection. Eliphaz picked up this question to attack Job's idea that any man, including Job, could be **pure** (Hb *zakah*, "clean, morally blameless or justified"). In the parallel question, Eliphaz referred to man as **one born of woman** (cp. 14:1). Job had lamented the brevity of man's life; Eliphaz emphasized the impossibility of man's being **righteous** (Hb *tsadaq*, "blameless, justified, vindicated"; cp. 9:1-2) in God's sight—protesting one's innocence does not prove anything.

15:17-35 Eliphaz based his argument on experiential and traditional wisdom (vv. 17-19; cp. 4:8; 8:8), according to which **pain**, fear, despair, **trouble and distress**, loss, ruin and failure befall the **wicked man** (Hb *rasha'*, "unrighteous, criminal," 15:20) who actively opposes God (vv. 20-26).

16:1-5 Job denied that Eliphaz conveyed "God's consolations" (15:11). He called all three friends **miserable comforters** offering only an endless stream of **empty words** (cp. 8:2; 11:2). Job claimed that he would have demonstrated a deeper level of friendship, speaking only to console Eliphaz if he were suffering.

16:6–17:16 In the rest of his lengthy reply to Eliphaz, Job switched abruptly from addressing one audience to another, as though desperate to be heard. Job claimed God had **exhausted** him. He charged God directly with devastating his **entire family** (16:7).

16:8 Job may have used the word **shriveled** (Hb *qamat*, lit "seize firmly, hold fast with the hands"; used in the OT only here and in 22:16) to depict the helplessness of being held tightly in God's grip. The sense of being bodily "shriveled" is both consistent with previous imagery (see 13:25; 14:10-12) and fitting as the basis for Job's complaint that his **frailty** (Hb *kachash*, "leanness") or gaunt appearance made him look defenseless if not guilty.

16:18-22 As though his death were imminent, Job pleaded for the earth not to close his case before it was resolved. After all, Job knew that his key **witness** (Hb *'ēd*, "testimony, one who or that which bears witness") or **advocate** (Hb *sahēd*, "witness, record," occurs only here in the OT) could, at that moment, be pleading his case before God. Although his **friends** apparently made fun of him for his seemingly ridiculous pursuit of acquittal, Job still longed for **someone** [who] **might arbitrate** [Hb *yakach*, "argue, judge, be spokesman for," cp. 9:33] **between a man and God** [i.e., an intercessor who would come to Job's defense] **just as a man** speaks up **for his friend**. Contemporary readers have the advantage of New Testament revelation, which identifies Jesus Christ as the One who fulfills the role of "mediator between God and humanity" (1Tm 2:5; cp. Heb 7:25), for whom Job hoped.

17 Listen to me and I will
inform you.
I will describe what
I have seen,
18 what was declared
by wise men
and was not suppressed
by their ancestors,
19 the land was given
to them alone
when no foreigner passed
among them.
20 A wicked man writhes in pain
all his days;
only a few[A] years are reserved
for the ruthless.
21 Dreadful sounds fill his ears;
when he is at peace, a robber
attacks him.
22 He doesn't believe
he will return
from darkness;
he is destined for the sword.
23 He wanders about for food,
saying, "Where is it?"
He knows the day of darkness
is at hand.
24 Trouble and distress
terrify him,
overwhelming him like a king
prepared for battle.
25 For he has stretched out
his hand against God
and has arrogantly opposed
the •Almighty.
26 He rushes headlong at Him
with his thick,
studded shields.
27 Though his face is covered
with fat[B]
and his waistline bulges
with it,
28 he will dwell in ruined cities,
in abandoned houses destined
to become piles of rubble.
29 He will no longer be rich;
his wealth will not endure.
His possessions[C]
will not increase
in the land.
30 He will not escape
from the darkness;
flames will wither his shoots,
and by the breath
of God's mouth,
he will depart.
31 Let him not put trust
in worthless things, being
led astray,
for what he gets in exchange
will prove worthless.
32 It will be accomplished
before his time,
and his branch
will not flourish.
33 He will be like a vine
that drops its unripe grapes
and like an olive tree
that sheds its blossoms.
34 For the company
of the godless will have
no children,
and fire will consume
the tents of those
who offer bribes.
35 They conceive trouble
and give birth to evil;
their womb
prepares deception.

Job's Reply to Eliphaz (16:1–17:16)

16 Then Job answered:

2 I have heard many things
like these.
You are all
miserable comforters.
3 Is there no end
to your empty[D] words?
What provokes you that you
continue testifying?
4 If you were in my place
I could also talk like you.
I could string words together
against you
and shake my head at you.
5 Instead, I would encourage
you with my mouth,
and the consolation
from my lips
would bring relief.

6 Even if I speak, my suffering
is not relieved,
and if I hold back, what have
I lost?
7 Surely He[E] has now
exhausted me.
You have devastated
my entire family.
8 You have shriveled me up[F]—
it has become a witness;
My frailty rises up against me
and testifies to my face.

[A]15:20 Lit *the number of* [B]15:27 Lit *with his fat* [C]15:29 Text emended; MT reads *their gain* [D]16:3 Lit *windy*; Jb 15:2 [E]16:7 Or *it* [F]16:8 Or *have seized me*; Hb obscure

9 His anger tears at me,
and He harasses me.
He gnashes His teeth at me.
My enemy pierces me
with His eyes.
10 They open their mouths
against me
and strike my cheeks
with contempt;
they join themselves together
against me.
11 God hands me over
to unjust men;[A]
He throws me into the hands
of the wicked.
12 I was at ease,
but He shattered me;
He seized me by the scruff
of the neck
and smashed me to pieces.
He set me up as His target;
13 His archers[B] surround me.
He pierces my kidneys
without mercy
and pours my bile
on the ground.
14 He breaks through
my defenses again
and again;[C]
He charges at me
like a warrior.

15 I have sewn •sackcloth
over my skin;
I have buried my strength[D]
in the dust.
16 My face has grown red
with weeping,
and darkness covers my eyes,
17 although my hands are free
from violence
and my prayer is pure.

18 Earth, do not cover my blood;
may my cry for help find
no resting place.
19 Even now my witness is
in heaven,
and my advocate is
in the heights!
20 My friends scoff at me
as I weep before God.
21 I wish that someone
might arbitrate
between a man and God
just as a •man pleads
for his friend.
22 For only a few years will pass
before I go the way
of no return.

17 My spirit is broken.
My days are extinguished.
A graveyard awaits me.
2 Surely mockers surround[E] me
and my eyes must gaze
at their rebellion.

3 Make arrangements! Put up
security for me.[F]
Who else will be my sponsor?[G]
4 You have closed their minds
to understanding,
therefore You will not
honor them.
5 If a man informs
on his friends for a price,
the eyes of his children
will fail.

6 He has made me an object
of scorn to the people;
I have become a man people
spit at.[H]
7 My eyes have grown dim
from grief,
and my whole body
has become but a shadow.
8 The upright are appalled
at this,
and the innocent are roused
against the godless.
9 Yet the righteous person
will hold to his way,
and the one
whose hands are •clean
will grow stronger.
10 But come back and try again,
all of you.[I]
I will not find a wise man
among you.
11 My days have slipped by;
my plans have been ruined,
even the things dear
to my heart.
12 They turned night into day
and made light seem near
in the face of darkness.
13 If I await •Sheol as my home,
spread out my bed
in darkness,

[A]**16:11** LXX, Vg; MT reads *to a boy* [B]**16:13** Or *arrows* [C]**16:14** Lit *through me, breach on breach* [D]**16:15** Lit *horn* [E]**17:2** Lit *are with* [F]**17:3** Lit *me with You* [G]**17:3** Lit *Who is there that will strike himself into my hand* [H]**17:6** Lit *become a spitting to the faces* [I]**17:10** Some Hb mss, LXX, Vg; other Hb mss read *them*

17:3 Fully expecting to die, Job challenged God to **put up security** (Hb *ʿarav*, "become surety for, pledge"; cp. "guarantee," Ps 119:122) for him, possibly referring to an action like posting bail. Clearly Job wanted God to demonstrate His belief in Job's innocence. The rhetorical question conveys the related idea of Job having no one to be his **sponsor** (Hb *taqaʿ*, "strike" with *yad*, "hand") or, more literally, to "strike himself into my [Job's] hand" (see textual note 17:3). Judah, the fourth son of Israel's patriarch Jacob, embodied the concept when he pledged that he would personally be responsible for (Hb *ʿarav*) the safe return of Jacob's youngest son Benjamin (Gn 43:9; 44:32). Job was saying that none of his friends was willing to stand by him. That Job would ask God to do for him what his friends would not suggest again the possibility of his personal hope for God's direct intervention.

17:4 Job blamed God for the apparent betrayal of his friends by preventing them from having the necessary **understanding** (Hb *sēkel*, "insight, prudence, sense") of his situation. Perhaps they believed they were acting prudently (see Pr 6:1-2; 17:18), but **honor** was only due for someone who did have *sēkel* (Pr 12:8; 13:15).

17:5 This verse, difficult to translate, is best understood as an ancient proverb whose meaning must somehow connect with verse 4. Alone, it suggests that judgment for a man's sins (here, a man's betraying his friends) often falls on his children. Several scholars recognize in the Hebrew a common saying about **a man** who, merely pretending to be wealthy, invites **his friends** to a feast at the expense of his impoverished **children**, whose **eyes . . . fail** with hunger. If this is the intended meaning, then Job viewed his friends, metaphorically, as men who pretended to have "understanding," which actually they lacked.

17:6-10 Job complained that his situation prompted two extreme reactions. For many, he was **an object of scorn** (Hb *meshol*, "byword, song of derision," an OT *hapax* or one-time usage) deserving only contempt as a sinner who was suffering divine retribution (cp. Dt 27–28; Ps 1:3-5). People expressing the same theological mindset mocked Jesus while He hung on the cross (Ps 22:7-8; Mt 27:39-44). **The upright** and **the innocent**—categories, suggested by Job, that did not apply to his friends—were **appalled**, however, at his afflictions and **roused against**, presumably, those who **spit at** him. Probably speaking indirectly of himself, Job declared that someone who is truly **righteous** (Hb *tsaddiq*, "just, lawful" in conduct and character) will not be fazed by what other people think; rather, he will become bolder in the face of opposition.

18:1-4 Bildad launched this speech in the same manner as his first (cp. 8:2). He resented Job's rejection of counsel, exaggerating the effect of Job's claims to have superior wisdom and understanding (cp. 12:2-13; 13:1-12; 16:2-5; 17:10). Bildad then turned Job's words against him.

18:5-21 Bildad spoke of the futility and terrifying, comprehensive destruction of **the wicked**, summarizing again the "theology *du jour*" (vv. 5,21). Implying that Job was **one who does not know God** (v. 21), Bildad constructed a vivid montage of men hounded and harassed, trapped and terrorized, reckoned unworthy to be remembered—all pictures of what results from this "wicked" man's **own schemes** (v. 7). Bildad believed there was evidence enough to prove that Job was guilty as charged.

19:1-12 Although the plural verbs indicate that Job addressed the friends as a group, he borrowed from Bildad's rhetoric and imagery to refute the notion that his suffering must somehow be commensurate with unconfessed sin. Bildad began his first two speeches with an exasperated "How long . . . ?" (cp. 8:2; 18:2). Job's retort likewise began with **How long . . . ?** He had not been "tuning out" his friends' words of counsel. However, Job was deeply wounded rather than encouraged by the words of his supposed friends.

19:4 Have sinned (Hb *shagah*, "wander away, stray, err," and the related noun **mistake** (Hb *meshugah*) usually refer to inadvertent transgressions or errors (cp. Lv 4:13; Ps 119:21,118). In a similar response to Eliphaz, Job had invited his friends to show him what he did wrong (Hb *shagah*, Jb 6:24).

19:7-12 Job mistakenly interpreted God's silence as **no response** and God's *apparent* lack of response as being deprived of **justice** (Hb *mishpat*, "judgment, that which is right or just"; cp. 8:3). The reader has privileged information to the contrary (1:1–2:7). However, Job did not perceive that God was distant or passive; rather, God seemed to be actively opposing and destroying him like a general methodically conquering enemy territory.

19:13-20 Overwhelming loss combined with physical suffering drastically disrupted Job's family and social life, introducing profound loneliness as those closest to him

>WORD|*study*

17:13 People both good (Gn 37:35) and evil (Nm 16:30) were believed to go to **Sheol** (Hb, "grave, the realm of the dead") when they died. It is described poetically as a conscious existence after death (Ps 16:10). To go to Sheol was dreaded because it meant encountering the unknown as well as coming to the end of physical life (Jb 10:21-22). This conception of a shadowy "afterlife" does not support the view of "soul-sleep" or of annihilation of the wicked. Apart from hints at belief in resurrection, the Old Testament reveals very little about the destiny of men's souls. With the advent and resurrection of Christ, the issue of where men and women will spend eternity became a central concern of the New Testament.

14 and say to corruption: You are
my father,
and to the maggot:
My mother or my sister,
15 where then is my hope?
Who can see any hope for me?
16 Will it go down to the gates
of Sheol,
or will we descend together
to the dust?

Bildad's Speech (18:1-21)

18 Then Bildad the Shuhite replied:
2 How long until you
stop talking?
Show some sense, and then
we can talk.
3 Why are we regarded as cattle,
as stupid in your sight?
4 You who tear yourself
in anger[A]—
should the earth
be abandoned
on your account,
or a rock be removed
from its place?

5 Yes, the light of the wicked
is extinguished;
the flame of his fire does
not glow.
6 The light in his tent
grows dark,
and the lamp beside him
is put out.
7 His powerful stride
is shortened,
and his own schemes
trip him up.
8 For his own feet lead him
into a net,
and he strays into its mesh.
9 A trap catches him
by the heel;
a noose seizes him.
10 A rope lies hidden for him
on the ground,
and a snare waits for him
along the path.
11 Terrors frighten him
on every side
and harass him at every step.
12 His strength is depleted;
disaster lies ready for him
to stumble.[B]
13 Parts of his skin
are eaten away;
death's firstborn consumes
his limbs.
14 He is ripped from the security
of his tent
and marched away to the king
of terrors.
15 Nothing he owned remains
in his tent.
Burning sulfur is scattered
over his home.
16 His roots below dry up,
and his branches above
wither away.
17 All memory of him perishes
from the earth;
he has no name anywhere.[C]
18 He is driven from light
to darkness
and chased
from the inhabited world.
19 He has no children
or descendants
among his people,
no survivor where he
used to live.
20 Those in the west are appalled
at his fate,
while those in the east
tremble in horror.
21 Indeed, such is the dwelling
of the unjust man,
and this is the place
of the one who does not
know God.

[A]**18:4** Lit *He who tears himself in his anger* [B]**18:12** Or *disaster hungers for him* [C]**18:17** Or *name in the streets*

Job's Reply to Bildad (19:1-29)

19 Then Job answered:

2 How long will you
torment me
and crush me with words?
3 You have humiliated me
ten times now,
and you mistreat[A] me
without shame.
4 Even if it is true that
I have sinned,
my mistake concerns
only[B] me.
5 If you really want to appear
superior to me
and would use my disgrace
as evidence against me,
6 then understand that it is God
who has wronged me
and caught me in His net.

7 I cry out: "Violence!"
but get no response;
I call for help, but there is
no justice.
8 He has blocked my way so that
I cannot pass through;
He has veiled my paths
with darkness.
9 He has stripped me
of my honor
and removed the crown
from my head.
10 He tears me down
on every side so that
I am ruined.[C]
He uproots my hope
like a tree.
11 His anger burns against me,
and He regards me as one of
His enemies.
12 His troops advance together;
they construct a ramp[D]
against me
and camp around my tent.

13 He has removed my brothers
from me;
my acquaintances
have abandoned me.
14 My relatives stop coming by,
and my close friends
have forgotten me.
15 My house guests[E]
and female servants
regard me as a stranger;
I am a foreigner in their sight.
16 I call for my servant, but he
does not answer,
even if I beg him
with my own mouth.
17 My breath is offensive
to my wife,
and my own family[F]
finds me repulsive.
18 Even young boys scorn me.
When I stand up,
they mock me.
19 All of my best friends[G]
despise me,
and those I love have turned
against me.
20 My skin and my flesh cling
to my bones;
I have escaped by the skin
of my teeth.

21 Have mercy on me,
my friends, have mercy,
for God's hand has struck me.
22 Why do you persecute me
as God does?
Will you never get enough
of my flesh?

23 I wish that my words
were written down,
that they were recorded
on a scroll
24 or were inscribed
in stone forever
by an iron stylus and lead!
25 But I know
my living Redeemer,[H]
and He will stand on the dust[I]
at last.[J]
26 Even after my skin
has been destroyed,[K]
yet I will see God in[L] my flesh.
27 I will see Him myself;
my eyes will look at Him,
and not as a stranger.[M]
My heart longs[N] within me.

28 If you say, "How will
we pursue him,
since the root of the problem
lies with him?"[O]

[A]19:3 Hb obscure [B]19:4 Lit *mistake lives with* [C]19:10 Lit *gone* [D]19:12 Lit *they raise up their way* [E]19:15 Or *The resident aliens in my household* [F]19:17 Lit *and the sons of my belly* [G]19:19 Lit *of the men of my council* [H]19:25 Or *know that my Redeemer is living* [I]19:25 Or *earth* [J]19:25 Or *dust at the last*, or *dust as the Last One* [K]19:26 Lit *skin which they destroyed*, or *skin they destroyed in this way* [L]19:26 Or *apart from* [M]19:27 Or *not a stranger* [N]19:27 Lit *My kidneys grow faint* [O]19:28 Some Hb mss, LXX, Vg; other Hb mss read *me*

were repulsed by his condition and perhaps feared being considered guilty by association with him. Family and friends both neglected to comfort him and seemed to **have forgotten** him (v. 14). The one introduced as "the greatest man among all the people of the east" (1:3) was enduring the loss of his **honor** (v. 9); the love and admiration of his family, friends, and employees; and the respect of the community. Physically, he was barely alive.

19:21-22 Job begged his **friends** to **have mercy** (Hb *chanan*, "be gracious to, deal graciously with") on him because he had been **struck** (Hb *naga*ʿ, "smite, afflict") by God. The reader knows, however, that God permitted *Satan* to afflict Job to any extent except taking his life (2:6). When Satan told God that Job would curse Him if He would "strike [Hb *naga*ʿ] everything he [Job] owns," the Lord placed "everything he owns" in Satan's power (1:11-12). Similarly, when Satan told God that Job would curse Him if He would "strike [Hb *naga*ʿ] his flesh and bones," the Lord placed Job's health in Satan's power (2:4-6). God remained sovereign and omnipotent, but He had not directly "struck" Job. Job reiterated his plea for mercy in the form of two desperate questions to the men who had *not* avoided his presence. Faced with these friends' relentless attacks on his claim to innocence, Job indirectly compared their tenacity to predators gnawing the bones of their prey to get every last shred of meat. The imagery of pursuit is resumed in verse 28.

19:23-27 Job wished that his words could be recorded for posterity so that he could be vindicated, at least posthumously. Ironically, however, Job's longing for his **words** to be **written down** has been fulfilled in the composition and canonization of the book of Job as Scripture. In this account the Holy Spirit has preserved revelation of God's perspective on man's suffering.

The first words of Job 19:25—**But I** (Hb *wa-ʾani*)—establish an emphatic contrast between verses 23-24 and what follows. Although Job expected to die in his wretched condition without vindication in this life, he still believed that one day he would appear before God, who would attest to his innocence and righteousness.

19:25-27 See **Doctrine**, p. 642

19:28-29 Job's warning to his friends against falsely accusing him resumes the imagery of pursuit (see 19:22). **Root of the problem** refers to the ground of the dispute or controversy. Job expected persistent rebuttal from his fellow sages because they were convinced that Job, rather than God, was the source of contention. Job, however, warned his friends that they also would face punishment and judgment someday (cp. 42:7).

20:1-3 Zophar felt threatened and personally insulted by Job's accusations and lack of appreciation for his friends' counsel. He believed that the end of the wicked is very clear, and he was angry at Job's refusal to admit that his suffering was proof of the sin he harbored within his own heart (cp. 20:12).

20:4-19 Zophar began with sarcasm: **Don't you know. . . ?** He seemed to be answering Job's previous declaration of confidence (19:25). Zophar asked, since Job knew so much, did he not know that the **joy** [Hb *renanah*, "a shouting for joy, triumphant cry"; cp. 3:7] **of the wicked** and **happiness** [Hb *simchah*, "gladness; joyful voices or cries"] **of the godless** are brief and temporal? This question expressed an important point of disagreement between Job and his friends. They believed that although the wicked may have a few moments of pleasure, their punishment was sure and swift. Job argued against this common perception, at least in cases like his own.

Zophar crudely compared the fleeting life of the arrogant to **dung** and elaborated that his household and children would be left begging and destitute (vv. 6-10). Since Job's children were dead, this detail and that of a wicked man's ill treatment of **the poor** (Hb *dal*, literally, "something hanging," i.e., dependent; "weak or powerless ones," v. 19) indicate that Zophar was offering a typified portrait of "the wicked" intended to deter Job from that path.

Zophar portrayed **evil** and its consequences in terms of wealth and possessions (v. 12). The wicked man would experience a radical reversal of fortunes. Because he crushed and deserted **the poor** (Hb *dal*, v. 19), his heirs would become so destitute that they would **beg** (Hb *ratsah*, "seek favor, conciliate," i.e., restore goods, v. 10) from his victims. The Old Testament commanded that believers care for the poor and the widows and show hospitality to strangers (Lv 19:10; Dt 15:4; Ps 72:4,12-14; Is 10:1-2). This was a codification of what the people already knew—hospitality was part of the natural law. While the **wealth** (Hb *ʾon*, "substance, goods," Jb 20:10; *chayil*, "riches," v. 15) obtained by a sinner may be **sweet** for a season, Zophar argued that it is short-lived. He also graphically described the destructive consequences of concealing "evil" (v. 12).

TRINITY

In 19:25-27, Job may have been referring to God as **Redeemer** (Hb *goʾēl*, the active participle of *gaʾal*, "one who defends or avenges the cause of another"; cp. Is 49:7)—God's Son Jesus Christ (see Jn 11:23-26). In the Mosaic covenant, the "kinsman-redeemer" was the nearest of kin who would come to the aid of a relative in need, as illustrated in the story of Ruth (Ru 2:20; 3:9). The nearest kinsman assumed responsibility for paying off debts, defending the family, avenging a wrong, or marrying the widow of the deceased (see note on Ru 2:19-23).

Perhaps, though, Job was hoping for another mediator (Jb 9:33) who would plead his case before God (16:19-21). Some scholars argue that Job sought a mediator to obtain justice from God, who is portrayed as Job's adversary (31:35) rather than his advocate. Consequently, they discount the validity of identifying God as the "Redeemer" because doing so logically seems to require that the two be distinct.

Although the doctrine of God as triune is not explicit in the Old Testament, recognizing that God has revealed Himself in Scripture to be three-in-one (i.e., the one God *is* Father, Son, and Holy Spirit) sheds light on the difficulty in this passage. In truth, Job's adversary or accuser was Satan, not God (1:7; 2:2; cp. 1Pt 5:8). Sin confines every man under God's holy wrath (Is 59:2-15a; cp. Jn 8:34; Gl 3:22; Rv 6:16-17), but God Himself is man's advocate (Is 59:1,15b-21; cp. Jn 3:36; 5:24; Rm 5:6; 6:6-7; 1Jn 3:5,8; 2:1).

Job's testimony captures the response of faith demanded ultimately by the incarnation of the "living Redeemer." In this speech, Job confidently announced a different cluster of convictions, the significance of which is clarified only in light of the New Testament and the doctrine of the Trinity:

- Ultimately, vindication before God is secured only by the eternal, **living** One (Jb 19:25; Jn 3:16; 6:40; Heb 9:11-15,28; 1Jn 2:1; 5:11);
- Job's "Redeemer" **will stand** [Hb *qum*, "rise, stand fast"] **. . . at last**, possibly continuing the legal courtroom imagery and so referring to the mediator rising from his seat to deliver the final, vindicating word on Job's behalf (Jb 19:25; cp. Jr 50:34).
- "Last" (Hb *ʾacharon*) is an adjective describing "Redeemer," not an adverb indicating time. This Redeemer is the "last" (i.e., "final, consummate, only") One. Significantly, the prophet Isaiah identifies "the Holy One of Israel" (cp. 2Kg 19:22; Pss 71:22; 78:41; 89:18; Is 1:4; 31:1) as the "Redeemer" (Is 41:14; 43:14; 47:4; 48:17; 49:7; 54:5) and God as "the Lord, the King of Israel and its Redeemer, the Lord of Hosts," who declares that He alone is God—"the first and . . . the last" (Hb *ʾacharon*, Is 44:6; cp. 41:4; 44:24; 49:26; 60:16; 63:16). The risen Christ intentionally identified Himself as this same God, Holy One, and Redeemer when He declared, "I am the First and the Last, and the Living One" (Rv 1:17-18; cp. Rv 2:8; 22:13).
- This "living Redeemer" will stand victoriously "on the dust," representing death (Jb 7:21; Ps 30:9; Is 26:19; Dn 12:2), lowliness or humility (Jb 42:6; Ps 113:7; Is 26:5), or man in his mortality (Jb 4:19; Pss 103:14; 104:29; 119:25). God created man from "dust" (Gn 2:7) and explained death (the consequence of man's sin) to Adam in terms of "dust": "For you [Adam] are dust, and you will return to dust" (Gn 3:19). Job's words hint at the victory over death achieved by Jesus Christ, "the last Adam": "The first man was . . . made of dust; the second man is from heaven" (1Co 15:45-49). Paul portrays a similar picture of the consummation of Christ's work: "The last enemy to be abolished is death. For 'God has put everything under His feet'" (1Co 15:26-27; cp. Ps 8:6).
- Despite his death, Job would see God with his physical **eyes. Skin** refers to Job's physical life (cp. 2:4; 18:13; 19:20). The verb **has been destroyed** (Hb *naqaph*, "cut down") underscores the finality of death and therefore makes Job's statement of faith so remarkable: **I will see God in** [Hb *min*, "from," indicating the vantage point or position from which one looks] **my flesh**. Job fully expected to have this experience as a man, whether in his current condition or in a resurrected one. Job also did not consider his flesh or body to be the problem—he was not seeking to escape from his material body into a purely spiritual world.

29 then be afraid of the sword,
because wrath
brings punishment
by the sword,
so that you may know there is
a judgment.

Zophar's Speech (20:1-29)

20 Then Zophar the Naamathite replied:

2 This is why
my unsettling thoughts
compel me to answer,
because I am upset![A]

3 I have heard a rebuke
that insults me,
and my understanding[B]
makes me reply.

4 Don't you know that
ever since antiquity,
from the time man was placed
on earth,

5 the joy of the wicked
has been brief
and the happiness
of the godless has lasted
only a moment?

6 Though his arrogance
reaches heaven,

[A]**20:2** Lit *because of my feeling within me* [B]**20:3** Lit *and a spirit from my understanding*

and his head touches
the clouds,
7 he will vanish forever
like his own dung.
Those who know[A] him
will ask, "Where is he?"
8 He will fly away like a dream
and never be found;
he will be chased away
like a vision in the night.
9 The eye that saw him
will see him no more,
and his household
will no longer see him.
10 His children will beg
from[B] the poor,
for his own hands
must give back his wealth.
11 His bones may be full of
youthful vigor,
but will lie down with him
in the grave.
12 Though evil tastes sweet
in his mouth
and he conceals it
under his tongue,
13 though he cherishes it
and will not let it go
but keeps it in his mouth,
14 yet the food in his stomach
turns
into cobras' venom
inside him.
15 He swallows wealth but must
vomit it up;
God will force it
from his stomach.
16 He will suck the poison
of cobras;
a viper's fangs[C] will kill him.
17 He will not enjoy the streams,
the rivers flowing with honey
and cream.
18 He must return
the fruit of his labor
without consuming it;
he doesn't enjoy the profits
from his trading.
19 For he oppressed
and abandoned the poor;
he seized a house
he did not build.
20 Because his appetite
is never satisfied,[D]
he does not let anything
he desires escape.
21 Nothing is left for him
to consume;
therefore, his prosperity
will not last.
22 At the height of his success[E]
distress will come to him;
the full weight of misery[F]
will crush him.
23 When he fills his stomach,
God will send
His burning anger
against him,
raining it down on him
while he is eating.[G]
24 If he flees
from an iron weapon,
an arrow from a bronze bow
will pierce him.
25 He pulls it out of his back,
the flashing tip out of
his liver.[H]
Terrors come over him.
26 Total darkness is reserved
for his treasures.
A fire unfanned
by human hands
will consume him;
it will feed on what is left
in his tent.
27 The heavens will expose
his iniquity,
and the earth will rise up
against him.
28 The possessions in his house
will be removed,
flowing away on the day
of God's anger.
29 This is the wicked man's lot
from God,
the inheritance God ordained
for him.

Job's Reply to Zophar (21:1-34)

21 Then Job answered:

2 Pay close attention
to my words;
let this be the consolation
you offer.
3 Bear with me while I speak;
then after I have spoken,
you may continue mocking.

20:20-29 Zophar insisted that **God** (20:15,23,28) would **expose** (Hb *galah*, "reveal what is hidden, uncover one's nakedness") the wicked man's **iniquity** and take away his **possessions** (Hb *yebul*, "produce of the earth, riches laid up in one's house", vv. 27-28). **Distress will come** to the wicked, for they are **never satisfied** (v. 20). Zophar seemed to be warning Job that this fate would befall him if he did not repent. On the other hand, how much more could happen to Job, except that his life be taken? Zophar's theology had no room for God's kindness or mercy; and faced with Job's increasing resistance to it, he apparently was only able to repeat his fundamental belief in God's judgment of "the wicked." Essentially, then, his argument was almost identical to that of Eliphaz and Bildad: Job was guilty, and God was judging him.

21:1-5 Often, those who suffer only want a sympathetic ear, not theological discourses on the reason for their pain. Although Job's friends were trying to help by getting him to repent so his suffering would end, Job asked them to express their pity instead by listening carefully to his words. Job sarcastically added that after he spoke Zophar could **continue mocking** him.

Job's pair of rhetorical questions highlight the dividing line between his approach to understanding what had happened to him and that of his friends. The assumed answer to the first question was that his **complaint** (Hb *siach*, "quarrel"; cp. 7:13; 9:27; 10:1; 23:2) was not **against a man** but against God. With the second question Job implied that since he was contending directly with God, he had every reason to be frustrated with the divine silence. Job was horrified by his condition and invited his friends to cover their mouths and **shudder** (i.e., to respond with stunned disbelief rather than judgment).

[A]**20:7** Lit *have seen* [B]**20:10** Or *children must compensate* [C]**20:16** Lit *tongue* [D]**20:20** Lit *Because he does not know ease in his stomach* [E]**20:22** Lit *In the fullness of his excess* [F]**20:22** Some Hb mss, LXX, Vg; other Hb mss read *the hand of everyone in misery* [G]**20:23** Text emended; MT reads *him, against his flesh* [H]**20:25** Or *gallbladder*

21:6-16 Job explained why his own fear and trembling exemplified the only justifiable response. The strict theology of retribution espoused by his friends was inadequate to explain both the suffering of the righteous and the prosperity of the wicked (cp. Ps 73; Jr 12:1-4). Job argued against Zophar's thesis that suffering is, without exception, God's punishment for one's sins. Job pointed out that the godless seem to prosper despite their rebellion against God. What **they say to God** makes sense, but Job emphatically rejected their attitude toward God and His ways (v. 14; cp. Ex 5:2; Ps 1:1). Why would one worship God in order to have His blessings if one could have them, reject God, and live life his own way?

21:17-34 Job intensified his argument, taking it from the theoretical realm to the personal realm by asking four rhetorical questions summarized this way: "How often have you seen this?" The implied answer is "Hardly ever." These questions appear to be directed particularly toward Bildad, who claimed exactly the opposite (18:5-21), and Zophar (20:23-29). Job questioned their belief that children suffer for their parents' sins, objecting that one should suffer for his own sins. When he is dead, he will not even know about the suffering of his children. And what good would such suffering do the wicked then? Suggesting that no one could **teach God knowledge**, Job pointed out an ironic truth of life: Although some die in peace while others suffer pain and poverty (vv. 22-26), both are buried and **lie in the dust** (Hb *'aphar*, v. 26; cp. 19:25). This is reality, is it not?

However, this recognition undergirds an innate sense of what is fair and just, but it directly conflicts with experience. Job defied his friends, anticipating their response. He expected them to question him regarding the identity of these prosperous wicked. He asked them if they had ever looked outside of their own community or acquaintances to see if this were true. Had they spoken with travelers, those who have seen the world could testify to how **the evil man is spared from the day of disaster** (vv. 27-33). Job declared his friends' counsel as **futile** (i.e., it brought no comfort or understanding to him, v. 34).

22:1–28:28 In the first round of speeches, Job's friends made clear that they believed he was a sinner and needed to repent. In the second series, the rhetoric intensified, and they emphasized the fate of the wicked. By this third series, there seemed to be little love lost between Job and his friends due to the vitriolic nature of the diatribes they directed toward Job. All the while, Job denied their charges by vehemently defending his

4 As for me, is my complaint
against a man?
Then why shouldn't I
be impatient?
5 Look at me and shudder;
put your hand
over your mouth.
6 When I think about it,
I am terrified
and my body trembles
in horror.
7 Why do the wicked continue
to live,
growing old and becoming
powerful?
8 Their children are established
while they are still alive,[A]
and their descendants,
before their eyes.
9 Their homes are secure
and free of fear;
no rod from God strikes
them.
10 Their bulls breed without fail;
their cows calve
and do not miscarry.
11 They let their little ones run
around like lambs;
their children skip about,
12 singing to the tambourine
and lyre
and rejoicing at the sound
of the flute.
13 They spend[B] their days
in prosperity
and go down to ·Sheol
in peace.
14 Yet they say to God:
"Leave us alone!
We don't want to know
Your ways.
15 Who is the ·Almighty, that we
should serve Him,
and what will we gain
by pleading with Him?"
16 But their prosperity is not
of their own doing.
The counsel of the wicked is
far from me!

17 How often is the lamp
of the wicked put out?
Does disaster[C] come on them?
Does He apportion
destruction in His anger?
18 Are they like straw
before the wind,
like chaff a storm
sweeps away?
19 God reserves
a person's punishment
for his children.
Let God repay
the person himself, so that
he may know it.
20 Let his own eyes see
his demise;
let him drink from
the Almighty's wrath!
21 For what does he care
about his family once
he is dead,
when the number
of his months has run out?

22 Can anyone teach God
knowledge,
since He judges
the exalted ones?[D]
23 One person dies
in excellent health,[E]
completely secure[F]
and at ease.
24 His body is[G] well fed,[H]
and his bones are full
of marrow.[I]
25 Yet another person dies
with a bitter soul,
having never
tasted prosperity.
26 But they both lie in the dust,
and worms cover them.

27 I know your thoughts
very well,
the schemes you would
wrong me with.
28 For you say, "Where now is
the nobleman's house?"
and "Where are the tents
the wicked lived in?"
29 Have you never consulted
those who travel the roads?
Don't you accept
their reports?[J]
30 Indeed, the evil man is spared
from the day of disaster,
rescued from the day
of wrath.
31 Who would denounce
his behavior to his face?

[A]**21:8** Lit *established before them with them* [B]**21:13** Alt Hb tradition reads *fully enjoy* [C]**21:17** Lit *their disaster* [D]**21:22** Probably angels [E]**21:23** Lit *in bone of his perfection* [F]**21:23** Text emended; MT reads *health, all at ease* [G]**21:24** Or *His sides are*; Hb obscure [H]**21:24** Lit *is full of milk* [I]**21:24** Lit *and the marrow of his bones is watered* [J]**21:29** Lit *signs*

Who would repay him
for what he has done?
32 He is carried to the grave,
and someone
keeps watch over his tomb.
33 The dirt on his grave is[A] sweet
to him.
Everyone follows behind him,
and those who go before him
are without number.
34 So how can you offer me
such futile comfort?
Your answers are deceptive.

The Third Series of Speeches (22:1–28:28)

Eliphaz's Speech (22:1-30)

22 Then Eliphaz the Temanite replied:

2 Can a man be of any use
to God?
Can even a wise man be of use
to Him?
3 Does it delight the •Almighty
if you are righteous?
Does He profit if you perfect
your behavior?
4 Does He correct you
and take you to court
because of your piety?
5 Isn't your wickedness
abundant
and aren't your iniquities
endless?
6 For you took collateral
from your brothers
without cause,
stripping off their clothes
and leaving them naked.
7 You gave no water
to the thirsty
and withheld food
from the famished,
8 while the land belonged
to a powerful man
and an influential man lived
on it.
9 You sent widows away
empty-handed,
and the strength
of the fatherless
was[B] crushed.
10 Therefore snares
surround you,
and sudden dread
terrifies you,
11 or darkness,
so you cannot see,
and a flood of water
covers you.

12 Isn't God as high
as the heavens?
And look at the
highest stars—
how lofty they are!
13 Yet you say: "What does
God know?
Can He judge
through thick darkness?
14 Clouds veil Him so that
He cannot see,
as He walks on the circle
of the sky."
15 Will you continue
on the ancient path
that wicked men have walked?
16 They were snatched away
before their time,
and their foundations
were washed away
by a river.
17 They were the ones who said
to God, "Leave us alone!"
and "What can the Almighty
do to us?"[C]
18 But it was He who filled
their houses
with good things.
The counsel of the wicked is
far from me!
19 The righteous see this
and rejoice;
the innocent mock them,
saying,
20 "Surely our opponents
are destroyed,
and fire has consumed
what they left behind."

21 Come to terms with God
and be at peace;
in this way[D] good will come
to you.
22 Receive instruction
from His mouth,
and place His sayings
in your heart.
23 If you return to the Almighty,
you will be renewed.
If you banish injustice
from your tent

[A]21:33 Lit *The clods of the wadi are* [B]22:9 LXX, Syr, Vg, Tg read *you have* [C]22:17 LXX, Syr; MT reads *him* [D]22:21 Lit *peace; by them*

righteousness and his view that the wicked often prosper, despite the claim of his friends to the contrary.

22:1-5 Eliphaz asked three paired rhetorical questions to establish the following points:

- In general, God gains nothing from **a man**, even one who is **wise**.
- More personally, in the view of Eliphaz, God did not **profit** from Job's being **righteous**. Job's righteousness, or claims of such, had no effect on God whatsoever.
- God was prosecuting Job because of Job's **wickedness**—there was no other explanation.

The reader, of course, knows that Eliphaz incorrectly assumed God was punishing Job for his sins when God actually was testing Job's devotion to Him and desire to serve Him, whether blessed or not.

22:6-11 Eliphaz listed stereotypical sins, and he believed that Job must be guilty of one or more.

22:12-20 Eliphaz correctly understood that God is transcendent and all-knowing, but he used this truth to portray God in terms of his own predictable theological system. Contrary to Job's description of their prosperity and success (Jb 21:7-13), Eliphaz contended that "wicked men . . . . were snatched away" (Hb *qamat*, "be carried off," 22:16). If, as Job claimed, God had "shriveled" him up (see 16:8), then he belonged with the sinners who died prematurely in the Flood. Repeating a segment of Job's argument, Eliphaz agreed that although God was the source of the prosperity of the wicked, **the righteous** could **rejoice** in seeing the destruction of God's **opponents** (vv. 19-20; cp. 21:14-16). Again, contrary to Job's observation (cp. 21:17-21), the wicked *would* receive what they deserve.

22:21-30 Eliphaz called on Job to **come to terms with** [Hb *sakan*, "become acquainted with, become familiar with again, be reconciled with"] **God**. By getting reacquainted with God and being **at peace** with Him, **good** (Hb *tov*, "gain, profit, prosperity"; cp. 2:10) would **come** to Job—not to the wicked, as Job claimed (21:13). Eliphaz assumed that God always responds to man according to a predictable pattern. **If** Job would follow the prescription given in 22:22-24, **then** he could expect to enjoy restored fellowship with **the Almighty** and effective intercession—it was all up to Job (vv. 25-26).

Ironically, Job's experience exemplifies God's complete sovereignty and freedom to restrain or permit evil according to His purposes (cp. Is 55:8-9; Jn 16:33). God is not obligated to act according to man's understanding; in fact, faithfulness to the Lord often subjects the man or woman of integrity to increased opposition from the world (cp. Mt 5:10-12; 24:9; Mk 13:9-13; Jn 15:18-21; 16:2-3; Eph 6:12).

23:1-9 Verse 1 succinctly reset the focus of discussion on Job's definition of his problem—God had imposed unrelenting pain and grief on Job's life with no sign of attention to his **complaint** or his **groaning**. Clearly rejecting Eliphaz's perspective (22:21-24), yet still believing that God is just, Job longed to be able to **find** God. If only he had the opportunity to confront Him face-to-face, this whole matter would be cleared up.

23:10 Despite his dismay, Job made a brilliant statement of faith. Even though he did not know where God was, he believed that God knew where he was. **Tested** (Hb *bachan*, "try, prove, examine, search out, watch") implies an investigation to find the qualities of its object and usually has a spiritual connotation (cp. Zch 13:9). **Pure gold** refers to the metal when it has been refined by fire. In its natural state, gold is mixed with impurities, and a refining process of extremely high heat is necessary to remove the impurities and produce "pure" or "refined" gold. This contrasted with Eliphaz's accusation that Job trusted in his gold (Jb 22:24-25; cp. Jms 1:2-4).

23:11-12 The metaphor of "walking in the way of the Lord" was commonly used in wisdom literature for obedience to God.

23:13-17 Job tenaciously hung onto his belief in God's sovereignty, aware of his own weakness and God's immense power and glory. God **is unchangeable** (Hb *be-'echad*, lit "as one"—"unique, only one of its kind, sole, incomparable"; cp. Sg 6:9). Therefore, no one **can oppose** [Hb *shuv*, "repulse, drive back," as against an assailant; cp. "who can stop Him?" 9:12; 11:10] **Him**. Knowing that God **does what He desires**, Job was **afraid** of Him but testified that he was **not destroyed** [Hb *tsamat*, "be cut off, be extinguished"; cp. "evaporate," 6:17] **by** [Hb *min*, "because of, on account of"] **the darkness** (Hb *choshek*; see 3:1-10). "Destroyed" as an idiom means to "be silent." In a forensic context, being reduced to silence marks the loss of one's case or argument. The phrase translated "by the darkness" recurs in a similar context in Elihu's speech: "We cannot prepare our case because of our darkness" (37:19).

In contrast to the wicked, who defiantly ask, "What can the Almighty do to us?" (22:17; cp. 21:14-15), Job had a healthy fear of **what** God had **decreed** (Hb *choq*, "that which is

24 and consign your gold
to the dust,
the gold of Ophir
to the stones in the •wadis,
25 the Almighty will be your gold
and your finest silver.
26 Then you will delight in
the Almighty
and lift up your face to God.
27 You will pray to Him,
and He will hear you,
and you will fulfill your vows.
28 When you make a decision,
it will be carried out,[A]
and light will shine
on your ways.
29 When others are humiliated
and you say, "Lift them up,"
God will save the humble.[B]
30 He will even rescue
the •guilty one,
who will be rescued
by the purity of your hands.

Job's Reply to Eliphaz (23:1–24:25)

23 Then Job answered:

2 Today also my complaint
is bitter.[C]
His[D] hand is heavy
despite my groaning.
3 If only I knew how to
find Him,
so that I could go
to His throne.
4 I would plead my case
before Him
and fill my mouth
with arguments.
5 I would learn how[E] He would
answer me;
and understand what
He would say to me.
6 Would He prosecute
me forcefully?
No, He will certainly
pay attention to me.
7 Then an upright man
could reason with Him,
and I would escape
from my Judge forever.

8 If I go east, He is not there,
and if I go west, I cannot
perceive Him.
9 When He is at work
to the north, I cannot
see Him;
when He turns south,
I cannot find Him.
10 Yet He knows the way
I have taken;[F]
when He has tested me,
I will emerge as pure gold.
11 My feet have followed
in His tracks;
I have kept to His way and not
turned aside.
12 I have not departed
from the commands
of His lips;
I have treasured[G] the words
of His mouth
more than my daily food.

13 But He is unchangeable;
who can oppose Him?
He does what He desires.
14 He will certainly accomplish
what He has decreed for me,
and He has many more things
like these in mind.[H]
15 Therefore I am terrified
in His presence;
when I consider this,
I am afraid of Him.
16 God has made my heart faint;
the •Almighty
has terrified me.
17 Yet I am not destroyed[I]
by the darkness,
by the thick darkness
that covers my face.

24 Why does the •Almighty
not reserve times
for judgment?
Why do those who know Him
never see His days?
2 The wicked displace
boundary markers.
They steal a flock and provide
pasture for it.
3 They drive away the donkeys
owned by the fatherless
and take the widow's ox
as collateral.
4 They push the needy off
the road;
the poor of the land are forced
into hiding.
5 Like wild donkeys
in the desert,

[A]22:28 Lit *out for you* [B]22:29 Lit *bowed of eyes* [C]23:2 Syr, Tg, Vg; MT reads *rebellion* [D]23:2 LXX, Syr; MT reads *My* [E]23:5 Lit *the words* [F]23:10 Lit *way with me* [G]23:12 LXX, Vg read *treasured in my bosom* [H]23:14 Lit *these with Him* [I]23:17 Or *silenced*

the poor go out to their task
of foraging for food;
the wilderness provides
nourishment
for their children.
6 They gather their fodder
in the field
and glean the vineyards
of the wicked.
7 Without clothing, they spend
the night naked,
having no covering
against the cold.
8 Drenched by mountain rains,
they huddle
against[A] the rocks,
shelterless.
9 The fatherless infant
is snatched from the breast;
the nursing child of the poor
is seized as collateral.[B]
10 Without clothing,
they wander about naked.
They carry sheaves
but go hungry.
11 They crush olives
in their presses;[C]
they tread the winepresses,
but go thirsty.
12 From the city, men[D] groan;
the mortally wounded cry
for help,
yet God pays no attention
to this crime.
13 The wicked are those
who rebel against the light.
They do not recognize
its ways
or stay on its paths.
14 The murderer rises at dawn
to kill the poor and needy,
and by night he becomes
a thief.
15 The adulterer's eye watches
for twilight,
thinking: No eye will see me;
he covers his face.
16 In the dark they break[E]
into houses;
by day they lock
themselves in,[F]
never experiencing the light.
17 For the morning is
like darkness to them.
Surely they are familiar
with the terrors of darkness!
18 They float[G] on the surface
of the water.
Their section of the land
is cursed,
so that they never go
to their vineyards.
19 As dry ground
and heat snatch away
the melted snow,
so •Sheol steals those
who have sinned.
20 The womb forgets them;
worms feed on them;
they are remembered
no more.
So injustice is broken
like a tree.
21 They prey on[H]
the childless woman
who is unable to conceive,
and do not deal kindly
with the widow.
22 Yet God drags away[I]
the mighty by His power;
when He rises up, they have
no assurance of life.
23 He gives them a sense
of security, so they can rely
on it,
but His eyes watch
over their ways.
24 They are exalted
for a moment, then they
are gone;
they are brought
low and shrivel up
like everything else.[J]
They wither like heads
of grain.
25 If this is not true, then who
can prove me a liar
and show that my speech
is worthless?

Bildad's Speech (25:1-6)

25 Then Bildad the Shuhite replied:

2 Dominion and dread belong
to Him,
the One who establishes
harmony in the heavens.[K]

[A]24:8 Lit *they embrace* [B]24:9 Text emended; MT reads *breast; they seize collateral against the poor* [C]24:11 Lit *olives between their rows* [D]24:12 One Hb ms, Syr read *the dying* [E]24:16 Lit *dig* [F]24:16 Lit *they seal for themselves* [G]24:18 Lit *are insignificant* [H]24:21 LXX, Tg read *They harm* [I]24:22 Or *God prolongs the life of* [J]24:24 LXX reads *like a mallow plant in the heat* [K]25:2 Lit *in His heights*

established or definite, appointed; defined limit or boundary") for him (23:13-16). However, because he counted himself among "those who know Him" (24:1) and regarded himself as "an upright man" (23:7), Job was not deterred in his pursuit of an audience with God (cp. Heb 4:15-16).

24:1-13 Job lamented God's timing—why does God not keep a calendar of when His court is in session? The righteous struggle to make sense of His seeming indifference. Meanwhile, God was allowing the wicked to flourish despite their sinful condition (vv. 2-12a). As if all these abuses themselves were not enough, God seemed to refuse to do anything about it (v. 12b). This conclusion directly contradicted Eliphaz's assurance that God *always* "saves the needy" and that sinful men like Job will, for example, "approach the grave in full vigor" (5:15,26). From Job's point of view, not only **those who know Him** (24:1) but also **those who rebel against the light** (v. 13) proceed unheeded and unchecked by God.

24:18-25 These verses are especially difficult to translate, and Job's assertion that God would ultimately punish the wicked seemed to contradict his argument.

The most logical view is that Job believed that eventually the wicked would pay for their sins. Job never claimed that God would not punish the wicked but that His justice is often not seen by men and may be meted out at another time. This section illustrated Job's argument that God *does* consign the wicked to death (vv. 19-20,22,24) and breaks the power of **injustice** (Hb *'ewel*, "wickedness, iniquity, depravity"). On this point he and his friends could agree (cp. 4:8-11; 5:11; 8:20; 11:11; 15:20-35). The problem, from Job's perspective, was that God treated "the blameless and the wicked" without distinction (9:21-23). Consequently, Job strongly challenged his friends to prove his claim false (24:25; cp. 6:26-30). Job knew that he was right and that the issues of wickedness, righteousness, and judgment were not as cut-and-dried as his friends believed.

25:1-3 Bildad's final speech is short and to the point. He and his friends seemed to have run out of things to say to Job. This speech was the shortest of all and the last offered by the three friends. Zophar did not speak again. That this exceedingly brief speech was followed by Job's exceedingly lengthy discourse (26:1–31:40) indicates that Job outlasted his friends' arguments. Either they reached a stalemate, or Job virtually "won" the debate with them.

26:2–31:40 While Bildad's previous speech (25:2-6) is the shortest in the book, this is the longest. Job began speaking directly to Bildad, using the singular "you" (vv. 1-4); but later he spoke to all three, using the plural "you" (27:12). Overall, however, his speech was directed at all three of his "friends." Job sarcastically mocked Bildad's inability to help or deliver, to counsel or explain.

26:5-14 In stark contrast to Bildad's incapacity to do what only God can do (vv. 2-3), Job described the all-encompassing **power** of God, illustrating His control in three domains that remain a mystery to man:

- the place inhabited by the dead—**Sheol**, also called **Abaddon** (Hb, land of "destruction,"; v. 6; cp. Pr 15:11; Is 14:18; Ezk 32:17-32);
- the **sky** or **heavens**, i.e., the limitless space above or cosmos;
- the **waters** or **sea**.

God **hangs** [Hb *talah*, an active participle indicating unbroken continuity] **the earth**, where man resides, **on nothing** (Hb *belimah*, "not anything, nothingness," v. 7; an OT *hapax* or one-time usage). Although Job was speaking poetically rather than scientifically, this detail demonstrates not only that the earth is entirely dependent on God's providence but also the scientific understanding that the earth is suspended in space. The **pillars that hold up the sky** figuratively refer to mountains reaching to the heavens. Like the earth's "pillars" (v. 11; 9:6), they respond appropriately to God (cp. 2Sm 22:16; Pss 18:15; 104:7; Is 50:2).

God has also triumphed over both **Rahab** (vv. 12-13; 9:13) and **the fleeing** [Hb *bariach*, "fugitive"; used only here and in Is 27:1; 43:14] **serpent** (cp. Is 51:9), or Leviathan (see Is 27:1). Job acknowledged that he had described only a fraction of God's glory—merely **the fringes** [Hb *qatsah*, "end, extremity, edge"] **of His ways** (v. 14).

27:1-6 The subject of **his discourse** (Hb *mashal*, "didactic poem; wise sayings"; cp. 29:1) shifted, but Job was still speaking. The phrase **as God lives** is the form of an ancient oath, ensuring that what Job was saying was as certain as the fact that God lives. Again he complained that **the Almighty**, whose power he so eloquently described in chapter 26, had withheld justice from him and caused his bitterness (cp. 6:4; 7:20; 10:2-3; 16:12-13; 23:14). Job vowed that as long as he lived he would testify to his own integrity and claim of righteousness, refusing to acquiesce to his friends' accusations.

MAN

Bildad's rhetorical questions emphasized that no mere man can stand before this holy God and claim to be righteous, which is true (cp. Rm 3:10-18). Bildad's response to Job's question, "How can a person be justified before God?" (9:2), suggested that to assume that such justification was even remotely possible was ridiculous. Bildad regarded man as nothing more than **a maggot** or **worm** when compared with God. However, Bildad's theology was wrong, especially in regard to man. Man was created by God in His image and remains His special creation. Although sinful man cannot stand before God on his own merits, God has chosen to extend grace to him through the death and resurrection of His incarnate Son. Job was absolutely correct to hold fast to God's character as gracious and merciful.

3 Can His troops be numbered?
Does His light not shine
on everyone?
4 How can a person be justified
before God?
How can one born of woman
be pure?
5 If even the moon
does not shine
and the stars are not pure
in His sight,
6 how much less man, who is
a maggot,
and the son of man, who is
a worm!

Job's Reply to Bildad (26:1–27:23)

26 Then Job answered:

2 How you have helped
the powerless
and delivered the arm
that is weak!
3 How you have counseled
the unwise
and thoroughly explained
the path to success!
4 Who did you speak
these words to?
Whose breath came out of
your mouth?

5 The departed spirits tremble
beneath the waters and all
that inhabit them.
6 •Sheol is naked before God,
and •Abaddon has
no covering.
7 He stretches
the northern skies
over empty space;
He hangs the earth
on nothing.
8 He wraps up the waters
in His clouds,
yet the clouds do not burst
beneath their weight.
9 He obscures the view
of His throne,
spreading His cloud over it.
10 He laid out the horizon
on the surface of the waters
at the boundary between light
and darkness.
11 The pillars that hold up
the sky tremble,
astounded at His rebuke.
12 By His power He stirred
the sea,
and by His understanding
He crushed •Rahab.
13 By His breath
the heavens gained
their beauty;
His hand pierced
the fleeing serpent.[A]
14 These are but the fringes
of His ways;
how faint is the word we hear
of Him!
Who can understand
His mighty thunder?

27 Job continued his discourse, saying:

2 As God lives, who has
deprived me of justice,
and the •Almighty who has
made me bitter,
3 as long as my breath is still
in me
and the breath from God
remains in my nostrils,
4 my lips will not
speak unjustly,
and my tongue will not
utter deceit.
5 I will never affirm that you
are right.
I will maintain my integrity[B]
until I die.
6 I will cling to
my righteousness and never
let it go.
My conscience will not
accuse me as long as I live!

[A] **26:13** = Leviathan [B] **27:5** Lit *will not remove my integrity from me*

[7] May my enemy be
like the wicked
and my opponent
like the unjust.
[8] For what hope does
the godless man have when
he is cut off,
when God takes away his life?
[9] Will God hear his cry
when distress comes on him?
[10] Will he delight
in the Almighty?
Will he call on God
at all times?
[11] I will teach you
about God's power.
I will not conceal
what the Almighty
has planned.[A]
[12] All of you have seen this
for yourselves,
why do you keep up
this empty talk?

[13] This is a wicked man's lot
from God,
the inheritance the ruthless
receive from the Almighty.
[14] Even if his children
increase, they are destined
for the sword;
his descendants will never
have enough food.
[15] Those who survive him
will be buried by the plague,
yet their widows will not weep
for them.
[16] Though he piles up silver
like dust
and heaps up a wardrobe
like clay—
[17] he may heap it up,
but the righteous
will wear it,
and the innocent
will divide up his silver.
[18] The house he built is
like a moth's cocoon
or a booth set up
by a watchman.
[19] He lies down wealthy, but will
do so no more;
when he opens his eyes,
it is gone.
[20] Terrors overtake him
like a flood;
a storm wind sweeps him
away at night.
[21] An east wind picks him up,
and he is gone;
it carries him away
from his place.
[22] It blasts at him
without mercy,
while he flees desperately
from its grasp.
[23] It claps its hands at him
and scorns him from its place.

Job's Hymn to Wisdom (28:1-28)

28 Surely there is a mine for silver
and a place where gold
is refined.
[2] Iron is taken
from the ground,
and copper is smelted
from ore.
[3] A miner puts an end
to the darkness;
he probes[B]
the deepest recesses
for ore
in the gloomy darkness.
[4] He cuts a shaft far
from human habitation,
in places unknown to those
who walk above ground.[C]
Suspended far away
from people,
the miners swing back
and forth.
[5] Food may come
from the earth,
but below the surface
the earth is transformed
as by fire.
[6] Its rocks are a source
of sapphire,[D]
containing flecks of gold.
[7] No bird of prey knows
that path;
no falcon's eye has seen it.
[8] Proud beasts
have never walked on it;
no lion has ever prowled
over it.
[9] The miner strikes the flint
and transforms
the mountains
at their foundations.
[10] He cuts out channels
in the rocks,

27:7-12 Earlier, Job felt that God was unfairly treating him like an enemy (13:24; cp. 33:10), and he vehemently objected to his friends' opinion that his sufferings placed him among **the wicked** or **the unjust** (cp. 18:5,21). Instead, Job saw himself as a man of integrity; therefore, any **enemy** or **opponent** of his deserved to face the same judgment of God as the "wicked" or "unjust" (i.e., those who are His enemies and opponents, 27:7). The rhetorical questions suggest that when **the godless man** is dead, all opportunities for redemption are lost—**God** will not **hear his cry**, and he will not **delight in** or **call on** God. By implication, Job should not be regarded as a "godless man" who has been **cut off**. Job has expressed confidence that God answers him (12:4). Rather than being corrected by his friends, Job would teach *them* **about God's power** (cp. 6:24; 8:10; 12:7-8). Job mocked his friends' boasting that they had **seen** and knew how God worked—their arguments amounted to **empty talk** (cp. 5:27; 15:17; 20:3; 21:34).

27:13-23 Some scholars believe these words were spoken by Zophar as a third speech, but the section lacks the expected introduction that marks the other speeches throughout the book. Others recommend reading this section as Job's quotation or rehearsal of the friends' "empty talk." In this case, Job was probably recalling their views on the **wicked man's lot from God** to warn them that the same fate, ironically, could befall them if they were counted as enemies of Job and of God (cp. 20:29). However, Job did believe in retribution, the punishment of the wicked. The difference was that he believed punishment would not always be immediate as his friends claimed.

28:1-28 This chapter functions as an interlude—a rest-stop for the reader—between the cycles of debate and Job's closing arguments (chaps. 29–31). The poem also directs the reader's attention to central issues underlying both the debates preceding it and the lengthy discourses following it: Where can the answers to life's most profound questions be found? Job's friends assumed that sufficient wisdom from tradition and experience could be deployed to make sense of God's ways. In contrast, Job protested that the extent of his grief and personal afflictions defied the purported wisdom of their explanations. Wisdom and understanding, he argued in this "hymn," cannot be acquired by human effort or ingenuity. Mankind has access to this treasure only through God.

[A] **27:11** Lit *what is with the Almighty* [B] **28:3** Lit *probes all things forgotten by foot* [C] **28:4** Lit *far from with inhabitant,* [D] **28:6** Or *lapis lazuli*

28:11-23 Men can find **silver, gold**, and other valuable metals and jewels buried beneath **the surface of the earth** (vv. 1-5). However, these can be brought out of the darkness and into the light only through the difficult and tedious tasks of mining. Job described the labor involved in mining, of probing into the deepest and darkest parts of the earth. Building a shaft and descending into it is dangerous work, and the precious stones there are otherwise undetected by any living thing on earth. The miner works to unearth treasures **hidden** from view at ground level (v. 11), but **the way to wisdom** is not self-evident (v. 23). Although digging and searching *can* lead men to the discovery of "**treasure**" (vv. 9-11), **wisdom** and **understanding** *cannot* be **located** by human effort (v. 12).

In fact, because **it cannot be found in the land of the living** (i.e., among mortal creatures), man cannot even discover **its value** from experience (v. 13). If not found on land or in the sea, can it be procured through trade or purchase? No, not for any **price** (vv. 14-19). The costliest treasures **do not compare with it** (vv. 17-19). The wisdom of God is the greatest treasure of all. If man cannot find, buy, or trade for wisdom, or even ascertain its value, can he at least know its source (v. 20)? No. Wisdom can in no way be materially discerned (v. 21). To **Abaddon and Death**, wisdom is no more than a rumor (v. 22). Clearly, wisdom is not to be sought from the dead or the place of the dead—for example, séances or other attempts to contact the dead will *not* yield the wisdom of God.

28:28 Job's friends had a limited conception of **wisdom** as knowledge gained by experience. In their context, wisdom was acquired with age and was attributed to ancient traditions and ideas (cp. Jb 8:8-10). However, only God can show men where to find wisdom (cp. Pr 8:22-31), and only God can legitimately define "wisdom." The cycles of debate between Job and his three friends have brought into question the idea that wisdom means being able to explain man's experience categorically in terms of divine punishment and reward. Rather, God defines wisdom in personal terms—wisdom is responding properly to Him with **fear** (Hb *yir'ah*, "terror, reverence, piety"; see 15:4; cp. Ps 111:10; Pr 1:7; 9:10), so it includes turning **from evil** (cp. Pr 8:13; 16:6). Such life-changing reverence and respect result from recognizing the rightful authority of **the Lord** (Hb *Adonai*; the only use of this title in the book of Job) over your life.

Job could quote God's definition of wisdom with the confidence of a man whose life had modeled a proper response to God. Verse 28 should remind the reader of the assessment of

and his eyes spot
every treasure.
11 He dams up the streams
from flowing[A]
so that he may bring to light
what is hidden.

12 But where can wisdom
be found,
and where is understanding
located?
13 No man can know its value,[B]
since it cannot be found
in the land of the living.
14 The ocean depths say, "It's not
in me,"
while the sea declares,
"I don't have it."
15 Gold cannot be exchanged
for it,
and silver
cannot be weighed out
for its price.
16 Wisdom cannot be valued
in the gold of Ophir,
in precious onyx or sapphire.[C]
17 Gold and glass
do not compare with it,
and articles of fine gold
cannot be exchanged for it.
18 Coral and quartz are not
worth mentioning.
The price of wisdom
is beyond pearls.
19 Topaz from •Cush
cannot compare with it,
and it cannot be valued
in pure gold.

20 Where then does wisdom
come from,
and where is understanding
located?
21 It is hidden from the eyes
of every living thing
and concealed from the birds
of the sky.
22 •Abaddon and Death say,
"We have heard news of it
with our ears."
23 But God understands the way
to wisdom,
and He knows its location.
24 For He looks to the ends
of the earth
and sees everything
under the heavens.
25 When God fixed the weight
of the wind
and limited the water
by measure,
26 when He established a limit[D]
for the rain
and a path for the lightning,
27 He considered wisdom
and evaluated it;
He established it
and examined it.
28 He said to mankind,
"The •fear of the Lord is this:
wisdom.
And to turn from evil
is understanding."

Job's Final Discourse (29:1–31:40)

29 Job continued his discourse, saying:

2 If only I could be
as in months gone by,
in the days when God
watched over me,
3 when His lamp shone
above my head,
and I walked
through darkness
by His light!
4 I would be as I was in the days
of my youth
when God's friendship rested
on my tent,
5 when the •Almighty was still
with me
and my children were
around me,
6 when my feet were bathed
in cream
and the rock poured out
streams of oil for me!

7 When I went out
to the city •gate
and took my seat
in the town square,
8 the young men saw me
and withdrew,
while older men stood
to their feet.
9 City officials stopped talking
and covered their mouths
with their hands.
10 The noblemen's voices
were hushed,

[A]28:11 LXX, Vg read *He explores the sources of the streams* [B]28:13 LXX reads *way* [C]28:16 Or *lapis lazuli* [D]28:26 Or *decree*

and their tongues stuck
to the roof of their mouths.
11 When they heard me,
they blessed me,
and when they saw me,
they spoke well of me.[A]
12 For I rescued the poor man
who cried out for help,
and the fatherless child
who had no one
to support him.
13 The dying man blessed me,
and I made the widow's heart
rejoice.
14 I clothed myself
in righteousness,
and it enveloped me;
my just decisions were
like a robe and a turban.
15 I was eyes to the blind
and feet to the lame.
16 I was a father to the needy,
and I examined the case
of the stranger.
17 I shattered the fangs
of the unjust
and snatched the prey
from his teeth.

18 So I thought: I will die
in my own nest
and multiply my days
as the sand.[B]
19 My roots will have access
to water,
and the dew will rest
on my branches all night.
20 My strength will be refreshed
within me,
and my bow will be renewed
in my hand.

21 Men listened to me
with expectation,
waiting silently for my advice.
22 After a word from me
they did not speak again;
my speech settled on them
like dew.
23 They waited for me as for
the rain
and opened their mouths
as for spring showers.
24 If I smiled at them,
they couldn't believe it;
they were thrilled at[C] the light
of my countenance.
25 I directed their course
and presided as chief.
I lived as a king
among his troops,
like one who comforts
those who mourn.

30 But now they mock me,
men younger than I am,
whose fathers I would have
refused to put
with my sheep dogs.
2 What use to me was
the strength of their hands?
Their vigor had left them.
3 Emaciated from poverty
and hunger,
they gnawed the dry land,
the desolate wasteland
by night.
4 They plucked mallow[D]
among the shrubs,
and the roots
of the broom tree were
their food.
5 They were expelled
from human society;
people shouted at them
as if they were thieves.
6 They are living on the slopes
of the •wadis,
among the rocks and in holes
in the ground.
7 They bray among the shrubs;
they huddle
beneath the thistles.
8 Foolish men,
without even a name.
They were forced to leave
the land.

9 Now I am mocked
by their songs;
I have become an object
of scorn to them.
10 They despise me and keep
their distance from me;
they do not hesitate to spit
in my face.
11 Because God has loosened
my[E] bowstring
and oppressed me,
they have cast off restraint
in my presence.
12 The rabble[F] rise up
at my right;
they trap[G] my feet

[A]**29:11** Lit *When an ear heard, it called me blessed, and when an eye saw, it testified for me* [B]**29:18** Or *as the phoenix* [C]**29:24** Lit *they did not cast down* [D]**30:4** Or *saltwort* [E]**30:11** Alt Hb tradition, LXX, Vg read *His* [F]**30:12** Hb obscure [G]**30:12** Lit *stretch out*

Job's character in the prologue—"He was a man . . . who feared God and turned away from evil" (see 1:1) and it effectively introduces the last portion of Job's speech in which he defends his integrity at length.

29:1-6 Job longed for the former **days** when he felt God's presence and guidance, a time when **God's friendship rested on** [his] **tent**. This phrase indicated the intimacy he felt with God and the security he had in God's protection and provision. He missed his **children**, the visible evidence of God's abundant blessings. The references to **cream** and **oil**—symbols of wealth—indicated Job's prosperity.

29:7-17 Job had been a well respected and honorable man known for his integrity and fairness. He had a place in the government of the city, likely functioning as a judge who was revered for his wisdom and eloquence—quite a contrast to the way his friends had treated him. Job was also active in helping the needy (despite Eliphaz's charges, 22:6-7,9). He came to the rescue of the fatherless, the poor, the widows, and the dying. He administered justice and aid, and protected the oppressed and the weak. Undoubtedly, this earned him the respect of his peers.

29:18-25 Job clearly expected to live out his days blessed by God with a long life. He used the metaphor of a tree with **roots** going down deep into the soil, drawing life from the underground waters. He would continually be **refreshed** and strengthened, as symbolized by the **bow** (cp. 30:11). Job yearned wistfully for the time when he was regarded as a statesman with whom men desired an audience, when he exercised authority that men recognized and appreciated.

30:1-11 Three times the word **now** (Hb *we-'attah*, lit "but now," vv. 1,9,16) draws attention to the contrast between life before (chap. 29) and after (chap. 30) the onslaught of Job's calamities (1:13–2:10). Job began this passage with a humiliating charge—that men **younger** than he mocked him, a shocking discourtesy in ancient times. If that were not enough, these were worthless and dishonorable men. They were unproductive—so poor they had to eat off the land—and outcasts. Job's shame was unbearable. These men **mocked** him and even **spit** in his presence, which implied that they considered him as cursed by God. Job attributed the unbridled derision of **foolish men** to God (vv. 8,11). The phrase **God has loosened my bowstring** meant that God had afflicted him, taking away every strength he had.

30:15 As in Bildad's description of the suffering the wicked bring upon themselves (18:9-12), Job experienced **terrors** (cp. 18:11; 24:17; 27:20) as unrelenting assailants. That a righteous man should suffer like the wicked has been Job's complaint.

30:16-23 In contrast to the **days** when he knew the presence of God in his life (29:2-5), **now** Job's days are filled with **suffering**—anguish that never left him and constant **pains**. Obviously from the context, the person referenced in this passage is God. In Job's view, God treated him as badly as his neighbors and friends. **Mud**, **dust**, and **ashes** symbolize his humiliation and are mentioned again in 42:6. Job's deepest hurt was that God seemed to be dispassionately opposed to him. With his lament, Job implicitly raised again one of the central questions of this book: Why does God sometimes seem to be silent in times of suffering?

30:24-29 Job could not understand why God would inflict such suffering on him because, in part, he himself had been active in helping those "who cried out for help" (29:12-17; 30:24-25). Although Job had shown mercy to those who had suffered misfortune, no one was doing the same for him (v. 26). In addition to the physical suffering, Job experienced the isolation of having become an outcast despite his appeal for **help** from **the assembly** (vv. 28-29).

30:31 Finally, the use of Job's instruments of praise and celebration for **mourning** and **weeping** captures the stark contrast between the long, prosperous life expected as the reward for his faithful obedience (29:18-20) and the prolonged agony he was enduring instead (30:31).

31:1-34 Chapter 31 functions as an "oath of innocence," in which Job boldly challenged God either to acquit him or to condemn him as charged. If God then did not appropriately chastise him, Job could interpret His silence or restraint as an official acknowledgment of his innocence. Three times in the chapter he refers to his **heart** (Hb *lēv*), the seat or center of the mind, will, and emotions (i.e., of one's deepest and innermost feelings, vv. 7,9,27). Job argued that his outward actions reflected the integrity of his innermost thoughts and feelings.

At this point Job began a confession of sins that he had *not* committed.

- *Lust* (31:1-2). Job declared, **I have made a covenant with my eyes.** A covenant was regarded as a treaty, an alliance, or a friendship that was sealed by signs and solemn oaths with promises of blessings if the covenant was

and construct
their siege ramp[A]
against me.
13 They tear up my path;
they contribute
to my destruction,
without anyone to help them.
14 They advance as through
a gaping breach;
they keep rolling in through
the ruins.
15 Terrors are turned loose
against me;
they chase my dignity away
like the wind,
and my prosperity
has passed by like a cloud.
16 Now my life is poured out
before my eyes,
and days of suffering
have seized me.
17 Night pierces my bones,
but my gnawing pains
never rest.
18 My clothing is distorted
with great force;
He chokes me by the neck
of my garment.[B]
19 He throws me into the mud,
and I have become like dust
and ashes.

20 I cry out to You for help,
but You do not answer me;
when I stand up,
You merely look at me.
21 You have turned against me
with cruelty;
You harass me
with Your strong hand.
22 You lift me up on the wind
and make me ride it;
You scatter me in the storm.
23 Yes, I know that
You will lead me to death—
the place appointed for all
who live.

24 Yet no one would stretch out
his hand
against a ruined man[C]
when he cries out to him
for help
because of his distress.
25 Have I not wept for those
who have fallen
on hard times?
Has my soul not grieved
for the needy?
26 But when I hoped for good,
evil came;
when I looked for light,
darkness came.
27 I am churning within[D]
and cannot rest;
days of suffering confront me.
28 I walk about blackened,
but not by the sun.[E]
I stood in the assembly
and cried out for help.
29 I have become a brother
to jackals
and a companion of ostriches.
30 My skin blackens
and flakes off,[F]
and my bones burn with fever.
31 My lyre is used for mourning
and my flute for the sound
of weeping.

31 I have made a covenant
with my eyes.
How then could I look
at a young woman?[G]
2 For what portion would I have
from God above,
or what inheritance
from the •Almighty
on high?
3 Doesn't disaster come
to the unjust
and misfortune to evildoers?
4 Does He not see my ways
and number all my steps?
5 If I have walked in falsehood
or my foot has rushed
to deceit,
6 let God weigh me in
accurate scales,
and He will recognize
my integrity.

7 If my step has turned
from the way,
my heart has followed
my eyes,
or impurity has stained
my hands,
8 let someone else eat
what I have sown,
and let my crops be uprooted.
9 If my heart has been

[A] **30:12** Lit *and raise up their destructive paths* [B] **30:18** Hb obscure [C] **30:24** Lit *a heap of ruins* [D] **30:27** Lit *My bowels boil* [E] **30:28** Or *walk in sunless gloom* [F] **30:30** Lit *blackens away from me* [G] **31:1** Or *a virgin*

seduced by
my neighbor's wife
or I have lurked at his door,
10 let my own wife grind grain
for another man,
and let other men
sleep with[A] her.
11 For that would be a disgrace;
it would be a crime
deserving punishment.[B]
12 For it is a fire that consumes
down to •Abaddon;
it would destroy
my entire harvest.
13 If I have dismissed
the case of my male
or female servants
when they made a complaint
against me,
14 what could I do when God
stands up to judge?
How should I answer
Him when He calls me
to account?
15 Did not the One
who made me in the womb
also make them?
Did not the same God
form us both in the womb?
16 If I have refused the wishes
of the poor
or let the widow's eyes
go blind,
17 if I have eaten
my few crumbs alone
without letting the fatherless
eat any of it—
18 for from my youth,
I raised him as his father,
and since the day I was born[C]
I guided the widow—
19 if I have seen anyone dying
for lack of clothing
or a needy person
without a cloak,
20 if he[D] did not bless me
while warming himself
with the fleece
from my sheep,
21 if I ever cast my vote[E]
against a fatherless child
when I saw that I had support
in the city •gate,
22 then let my shoulder blade
fall from my back,
and my arm be pulled
from its socket.
23 For disaster from God
terrifies me,
and because of His majesty
I could not do these things.

24 If I placed my confidence
in gold
or called fine gold my trust,
25 if I have rejoiced because
my wealth is great
or because my own hand
has acquired so much,
26 if I have gazed at the sun
when it was shining
or at the moon moving
in splendor,
27 so that my heart
was secretly enticed
and I threw them a kiss,[F]
28 this would also be a crime
deserving punishment,
for I would have denied
God above.

29 Have I rejoiced over
my enemy's distress,
or become excited
when trouble came his way?
30 I have not allowed my mouth
to sin
by asking for his life
with a curse.
31 Haven't the members
of my household said,
"Who is there who has not
had enough to eat
at Job's table?"
32 No stranger had to spend
the night on the street,
for I opened my door
to the traveler.
33 Have I covered
my transgressions
as others do[G]
by hiding my •guilt
in my heart,
34 because I greatly feared
the crowds,
and the contempt of the clans
terrified me,
so I grew silent and would not
go outside?
35 If only I had someone to hear
my case!

[A]31:10 Lit *men kneel down over* [B]31:11 Lit *crime judges* [C]31:18 Lit *and from my mother's womb* [D]31:20 Lit *his loins* [E]31:21 Lit *I raise my hand* [F]31:27 Lit *and my hand kissed my mouth* [G]31:33 Or *as Adam*

honored (cp. Gn 21:27; Jos 9:6). There is no stronger way to express Job's resolution to keep his eyes and heart pure toward other women.

- *Dishonesty* (31:5-8; cp. Lv 19:35-36; Dt 25:13-16). Job denied any **deceit** (Hb *mirmah*, "fraud, guile"; cp. Pss 10:7; 24:3-4; 34:13; 36:3) in his dealings with others.
- *Adultery* (Jb 31:9-12). Job denied ever being **seduced** (Hb *pathah*, "let oneself be enticed") by the **wife** of another man or of having **lurked** (Hb *ʾarav*, "lie in wait"; cp. Pr 7:12) at a neighbor's door.
- *Unfair treatment of personnel* (31:13-15). Job declared that he had not abused his **male or female servants** but had treated them fairly. He understood the fundamental truth that they were made in the image of God just as he was.
- *Oppression of the poor* (31:16-23; Ezk 16:49). Job denied ever oppressing the needy (cp. Jb 22:7). In the ancient culture of the Old Testament, families and affluent community members were expected to provide for and protect the most vulnerable in society. Job claimed to have demonstrated exemplary charity—sharing his food with **the poor**, giving counsel to **the widow**, clothing and protecting the **needy**. Like the self-imprecation (curse) of verses 9-10, Job strengthened his avowal of never being guilty of abusing his position of privilege by calling for a horrific penalty if ever he **cast** his **vote** [Hb *nuph yad*, "shake or brandish one's hand against, threaten"; cp. Is 19:16] **against a fatherless child** (Hb *yatom*, "orphan"; cp. 22:9; 24:9; Dt 10:17-18; 14:28-29; 24:17; 27:19; Ps 10:18; Is 1:23; 10:1-2). Fear of God restrained him from acting unjustly.
- *Idolatry* (Jb 31:24-28). Job firmly rejected idolatry—from materialism to worship of the sun or moon—as direct denial of God (cp. v. 9).
- *Contempt for enemies* (31:29-30). Job had never **rejoiced** over the trouble of an enemy or acted out of spite or resentment (cp. Pr 17:5).
- *Refusal of hospitality* (Jb 31:31-32). Neither had he denied food and shelter to strangers; rather, he showed generous hospitality to travelers.
- *Hypocrisy* (31:33-34). Finally, he denied being a hypocrite. Job was clearly regarded as an honorable man. Here he claimed that he wasn't **hiding** sin in his heart and pretending to be something outwardly that he was not inwardly. The phrase **as others do**

captures the general point of the contrast—Job claimed that unlike other "men" his good deeds were not a guise for a guilty **heart**. However, the verse may also be an unusual reference to the "cover-up" of Adam in the garden of Eden (see Gn 3:7,11-12).

31:35 Signature (Hb *tav*, v. 35; cp. Ezk 9:4,6; Rv 7:3) captures the intended meaning of the Hebrew expression for the writing of *tav* (ת)—the last letter in the alphabet—as the mark, used typically by illiterate persons, to sign a document. The handwritten *tav* looked like a cross and was comparable to "signing" with an "X" in lieu of one's name. In this context, the expression does not mean that Job was illiterate but may, perhaps, figuratively underscore either the finality of this last plea or his claim to be ignorant of any evidence supporting charges that would warrant such intense suffering.

31:35-40 Job returned to his plea for God to hear him. He concluded his defense and left it to **the Almighty** to respond. He challenged God, perceived as his **Opponent** (Hb *ʾish*, "man" [who is my] *riv*, "legal adversary," i.e., "hostile party" in a lawsuit; cp. "those who contend with you," Is 41:11), to prepare an **indictment**; and he—sure of his innocence—would give him a detailed answer to every charge. Job's rebuttal would convey his conviction that such an indictment was an unwarranted impeachment of his integrity.

Job ended his speeches with one last addition to his oath of innocence, essentially declaring that he enforced godly ethical standards not only in interpersonal relationships but in his gratitude for and respectful treatment of the **land** (Hb *ʾadamah*, "ground, earth"; the source of the word "man" [Hb *ʾadam*], and the name Adam, Gn 2:7,19) itself, **its produce**, and **its tenants**. The penalty he invited for such offenses (Jb 31:40) echoes the punishment God applied to Adam for direct disobedience (Gn 3:18) and to Cain for murder (Gn 4:12). At this point, Job rested his case.

32:1–37:24 Neither Job nor his friends had budged from their opposing theological views. Out of nowhere, a fifth person entered the picture, the younger man **Elihu** (Hb, "He is my God"), a silent onlooker so far. His theology differed significantly from that of the other friends. The three friends had argued that Job had sinned, thereby causing God's wrath to be poured out upon him. Elihu also stated that Job needed to repent—but from spiritual pride exhibited during his suffering. According to Elihu, Job's righteous pride led to his questioning of God's ways. That Elihu was not condemned by God as the others were

Here is my signature;
let the Almighty answer me.
Let my Opponent compose
His indictment.
36 I would surely carry it
on my shoulder
and wear it like a crown.
37 I would give Him an account
of all my steps;
I would approach Him
like a prince.

38 If my land cries out
against me
and its furrows join
in weeping,
39 if I have consumed
its produce
without payment
or shown contempt
for its tenants,[A]
40 then let thorns grow
instead of wheat
and stinkweed
instead of barley.

The words of Job are concluded.

Elihu's Response (32:1–37:24)

32 So these three men quit answering Job, because he was
righteous in his own eyes. 2 Then Eli-
hu son of Barachel the Buzite from
the family of Ram became angry. He
was angry at Job because he had justified himself rather than God. 3 He
was also angry at Job's three friends
because they had failed to refute
him and yet had condemned him.[B]
4 Now Elihu had waited to speak
to Job because they were all older
than he. 5 But when he saw that the
three men could not answer Job, he
became angry.
6 So Elihu son of Barachel the
Buzite replied:

I am young in years,
while you are old;
therefore I was timid
and afraid
to tell you what I know.
7 I thought that age
should speak
and maturity should teach
wisdom.
8 But it is a spirit in man[C]
and the breath
of the •Almighty
that give him understanding.
9 It is not only the old
who are wise
or the elderly who understand
how to judge.
10 Therefore I say, "Listen to me.
I too will declare
what I know."
11 Look, I waited
for your conclusions;
I listened to your insights
as you sought for words.
12 I paid close attention to you.
Yet no one proved Job wrong;
not one of you refuted
his arguments.
13 So do not claim,
"We have found wisdom;
let God deal with him,
not man."
14 But Job has not directed
his argument to me,
and I will not respond to him
with your arguments.

15 Job's friends are dismayed
and can no longer answer;
words have left them.
16 Should I continue to wait
now that they are silent,
now that they stand there
and no longer answer?
17 I too will answer;[D]
yes, I will tell what I know.
18 For I am full of words,
and my spirit[E] compels me
to speak.
19 My heart[F] is
like unvented wine;
it is about to burst
like new wineskins.
20 I must speak so that
I can find relief;
I must open my lips
and respond.
21 I will be partial to no one,
and I will not give anyone
an undeserved title.
22 For I do not know how to give
such titles;
otherwise, my Maker
would remove me
in an instant.

[A] **31:39** Lit *or caused the breath of its tenants to breathe out* [B] **32:3** Ancient Jewish tradition reads *condemned God* [C] **32:8** Or *is the Spirit in a person* [D] **32:17** Lit *answer my part* [E] **32:18** Lit *and the spirit of my belly* [F] **32:19** Lit *belly*

33 But now, Job, pay attention
to my speech,
and listen to all my words.
2 I am going to open
my mouth;
my tongue will form words
on my palate.
3 My words come from
my upright heart,
and my lips speak
with sincerity
what they know.
4 The Spirit of God
has made me,
and the breath
of the •Almighty
gives me life.
5 Refute me if you can.
Prepare your case against me;
take your stand.
6 I am just like you before God;
I was also pinched off
from a piece of clay.
7 Fear of me should not
terrify you;
the pressure I exert[A]
against you will be light.
8 Surely you have spoken
in my hearing,
and I have heard
these very[B] words:
9 "I am pure,
without transgression;
I am •clean and have
no •guilt.
10 But He finds reasons
to oppose me;
He regards me as His enemy.
11 He puts my feet in the stocks;
He stands watch over
all my paths."
12 But I tell you that you
are wrong in this matter,
since God is greater
than man.
13 Why do you take Him to court
for not answering anything
a person asks?[C]
14 For God speaks time
and again,
but a person may not
notice it.
15 In a dream, a vision
in the night,
when deep sleep falls
on people
as they slumber on their beds,
16 He uncovers their ears
at that time
and terrifies them[D]
with warnings,
17 in order to turn a person
from his actions
and suppress his pride.[E]
18 God spares his soul
from the •Pit,
his life from crossing
the river of death.[F]
19 A person may be disciplined
on his bed with pain
and constant distress
in his bones,
20 so that he detests bread,
and his soul despises his
favorite food.
21 His flesh wastes away
to nothing,[G]
and his unseen bones
stick out.
22 He draws near to the Pit,
and his life
to the executioners.
23 If there is an angel
on his side,
one mediator out of
a thousand,
to tell a person what is right
for him[H]

[A]**33:7** Lit *you; my pressure* [B]**33:8** Lit *heard a sound of* [C]**33:13** Lit *court, for He does not answer all his words* [D]**33:16** LXX; MT reads *and seals* [E]**33:17** Lit *and cover pride within a man* [F]**33:18** Or *from perishing by the sword* [G]**33:21** Lit *away from sight* [H]**33:23** Or *to vouch for a person's uprightness*

>WORD|*study*

33:19 The word pain (Hb *mak'ov*) appears only here in the book of Job and only 15 times elsewhere in the Old Testament, usually with the connotation of "pain, sorrow, or suffering" as punishment for sin (Ps 32:10; Jr 30:15; Lm 1:12,18). The root (Hb *ka'av*, "cause pain, afflict") is only used eight times in the Old Testament, two of these in Job—"crushes" (Jb 5:18); "pain" (14:22). Significantly, the noun (*mak'ov*) is used in a prophetic description of the Messiah as "a man of *suffering* . . . [who] carried our *pains*" (Is 53:3-4). Christ fulfilled this prophecy by bearing the punishment for man's sin (Rm 8:3; Heb 9:26-28; 1Pt 4:1).

(42:7-8) suggests that he may have been closer to the truth than they were.

The older men, based on their collective wisdom, could not agree with Job's diagnosis of his fundamental problem—that God was punishing him for nothing. Eliphaz, Bildad, and Zophar were convinced, instead, that Job *must* be guilty of great sin to warrant such great suffering. The younger man's perspective finally exhausts the resources of human understanding in the attempt to make sense of Job's experience. His speech also adds suspense, preparing the reader for God's response.

32:1-5 The narrator identifies Elihu's father as **Barachel** [Hb, "God blesses"; a name not found elsewhere in Scripture] **the Buzite.** He may have been a descendant of Abraham's nephew Buz (Gn 22:20-21; cp. Jr 25:23). The other **three men**—Eliphaz, Bildad, and Zophar—had given up trying to convince Job that his afflictions proved that he could not possibly be **righteous**. Elihu unleashed a righteous indignation against Job because of his pride, contending that Job **had justified** [Hb *tsadaq*; cp. 9:1-2; 40:8] **himself rather than God**. Elihu was also frustrated with Job's friends because they **had condemned** (Hb *rasha'*, "declare guilty or unrighteous") Job without successfully refuting him.

32:6-13 Elihu's words confirm the narrator's description—he had waited to speak out of deference to his elders, as was the custom of the day (v. 6; cp. v. 4). He appealed to a more intuitive **understanding**, which comes directly from God (v. 8; cp. v. 18). Elihu claimed that he had listened closely to the arguments and had a different angle to bring to the discussion (vv. 11-12,14). He brashly denied the patriarchs' claim to **have found wisdom** and rebuked their resolution merely to **let God deal with** (Hb *nadaph*, "drive away"; figuratively, "conquer," v. 13) Job.

32:19 Elihu felt compelled to speak, comparing his **heart** to **new wineskins**. When wine was poured into a fresh animal skin, room was left for expansion of the gasses during fermentation. Filling the skin too full or using an old wineskin (which would not have been pliable) would cause the skin to burst (see Mt 9:17).

33:12-33 Elihu believed Job was **wrong** (Hb *lo'-tsadaq*, "not just," v. 12; cp. 9:1-2) in his assessment. He believed that God does speak, although Job may not have noticed it. Elihu illustrated his point that God still speaks in two ways—through dreams (e.g., those of Eliphaz, 4:12-21; of Elihu, 33:14-17) and through suffering (vv. 18-30). God's purpose in speaking was to turn man from his sin and **suppress**

his pride (v. 17). God's discipline came in the form of physical suffering like Job's (vv. 19-22; cp. 5:17).

33:23-33 Elihu indirectly described his desire to **justify** (v. 32) Job, acting as an intercessor—an **angel** (Hb *mal'ak*, "one sent, messenger") or **mediator** (Hb *luts*, "interpreter, ambassador"; v. 23; cp. Gn 42:23)—speaking to God on Job's behalf. He would offer a **ransom** (Hb *kopher*, "price of redemption or appeasement of God's wrath"; v. 24; cp. Ex 21:30; 30:12; Nm 35:31-32; Is 43:3)—a reason for the sufferer to be relieved of his misery or something given in exchange for the restoration of Job's life, health, and **righteousness** (v. 26). Elihu expected that in response Job would testify that despite his sin, he had been brought back from the brink of death. **God . . . does all these things**, Elihu argued, in order that man may be turned from his destructive ways and enjoy the blessings of God (v. 29).

34:5-9 Elihu rehearsed Job's statements of innocence and accusations against God (cp. 12:4; 13:8; 27:6). However, he condemned Job, just as the three friends had done, for associating with the wicked and for being thoroughly comfortable with an attitude of **derision** (Hb *la'ag*, "mockery, scorning"; cp. 15:16b). Furthermore, Job had claimed that a man finds no profit in worshiping God.

34:10-11 When examined together, the only two instances in Job of the strong Hebrew expression, **it is impossible** (Hb *chalilah*, "far be it, let it not be"), illustrate the opposing theological positions of Job and Elihu. Job had insisted, "I will never [Hb *chalilah*] affirm that you are right" (27:5); his suffering defied the simplistic explanation offered by his friends, so he adamantly refused to plead guilty to crimes he did not commit—"far be it" from Job to do so. Elihu countered with a defense of God's justice; he insisted, "Far be it" from Elihu to support Job's accusation that "God [could] do wrong" (34:10; cp. 27:2; Jos 22:29). Rather, God gives man what man deserves, a clear statement of the doctrine of retribution espoused by Eliphaz, Bildad, and Zophar. Although retribution is taught in the Bible, Job's case illustrated that there can be suffering that has nothing to do with retribution.

34:12-15 Elihu affirmed some important truths about God:

- **The Almighty does not pervert justice**, a point also made by Bildad (cp. 8:3).
- God's sovereignty is original; it is not derived from another source.
- God is the source and sustainer of all that lives.

24 and to be gracious to him
and say,
"Spare him from going down
to the Pit;
I have found a ransom,"
25 then his flesh
will be healthier[A] than
in his youth,
and he will return to the days
of his youthful vigor.
26 He will pray to God, and God
will delight in him.
That man will see His face
with a shout of joy,
and God will restore
his righteousness to him.
27 He will look at men and say,
"I have sinned and perverted
what was right;
yet I did not get
what I deserved.[B]
28 He redeemed my soul
from going down to the Pit,
and I will continue to see
the light."
29 God certainly does all
these things
two or three times to a man
30 in order to turn him back
from the Pit,
so he may shine with the light
of life.
31 Pay attention, Job, and listen
to me.
Be quiet, and I will speak.
32 But if you have something
to say,[C] answer me;
speak, for I would like
to justify you.
33 If not, then listen to me;
be quiet, and I will teach
you wisdom.

34 Then Elihu continued,[D] saying:

2 Hear my words,
you wise men,
and listen to me,
you knowledgeable ones.
3 Doesn't the ear test words
as the palate tastes food?
4 Let us judge for ourselves
what is right;
let us decide together
what is good.
5 For Job has declared,
"I am righteous,
yet God has deprived me
of justice.
6 Would I lie about my case?
My wound[E] is incurable,
though I am
without transgression."
7 What man is like Job?
He drinks derision like water.
8 He keeps company
with evildoers
and walks with wicked men.
9 For he has said,
"A man gains nothing
when he becomes
God's friend."
10 Therefore listen to me,
you men of understanding.
It is impossible for God
to do wrong,
and for the •Almighty
to act unjustly.
11 For He repays a person
according to his deeds,
and He brings his ways
on him.
12 Indeed, it is true that God
does not act wickedly
and the Almighty does not
pervert justice.
13 Who gave Him authority
over the earth?
Who put Him in charge of
the entire world?
14 If He put His mind to it
and withdrew the spirit
and breath He gave,
15 every living thing
would perish together
and mankind would return
to the dust.

16 If you have understanding,
hear this;
listen to what I have to say.
17 Could one who hates justice
govern the world?
Will you condemn the mighty
Righteous One,
18 who says to a king,
"Worthless man!"
and to nobles,
"Wicked men!"?
19 God is not partial to princes
and does not favor the rich
over the poor,
for they are all the work
of His hands.

[A]33:25 Hb obscure [B]33:27 Lit *and the same was not to me* [C]33:32 Lit *If there are words* [D]34:1 Lit *answered* [E]34:6 Lit *arrow*

20 They die suddenly
in the middle of the night;
people shudder,
then pass away.
Even the mighty are removed
without effort.
21 For His eyes watch over
a man's ways,
and He observes all his steps.
22 There is no darkness,
no deep darkness,
where evildoers
can hide themselves.
23 God does not need to examine
a person further,
that one should[A]
approach Him in court.
24 He shatters the mighty
without an investigation
and sets others in their place.
25 Therefore, He recognizes
their deeds
and overthrows them
by night, and they
are crushed.
26 In full view of the public,[B]
He strikes them
for their wickedness,
27 because they turned aside
from following Him
and did not understand any
of His ways
28 but caused the poor to cry out
to Him,
and He heard the outcry
of the afflicted.
29 But when God is silent,
who can declare
Him •guilty?
When He hides His face,
who can see Him?
Yet He watches over both
individuals and nations,
30 so that godless men
should not rule
or ensnare the people.
31 Suppose someone says
to God,
"I have endured
my punishment;
I will no longer act wickedly.
32 Teach me what I cannot see;
if I have done wrong, I won't
do it again."
33 Should God repay you
on your terms
when you have rejected His?
You must choose, not I!
So declare what you know.
34 Reasonable men will say
to me,
along with the wise men
who hear me,
35 "Job speaks
without knowledge;
his words are
without insight."
36 If only Job were tested
to the limit,
because his answers are
like those of wicked men.
37 For he adds rebellion
to his sin;
he scornfully claps
in our presence,
while multiplying his words
against God.

35 Then Elihu continued, saying:

2 Do you think it is just
when you say,
"I am righteous before God"?
3 For you ask, "What does
it profit You,[C]
and what benefit comes
to me, if I do not sin?"
4 I will answer you
and your friends with you.
5 Look at the heavens and see;
gaze at the clouds high
above you.
6 If you sin, how does it
affect God?
If you multiply
your transgressions,
what does it do to Him?
7 If you are righteous,
what do you give Him,
or what does He receive
from your hand?
8 Your wickedness affects
a person like yourself,
and your righteousness
another human being.
9 People cry out because of
severe oppression;
they shout for help because of
the arm of the mighty.
10 But no one asks,
"Where is God my Maker,
who provides us with songs
in the night,
11 who gives us

By emphasizing God's transcendence and His unimpeachable righteousness, Elihu laid a foundation for condemning Job's attempts to put God on trial.

34:21-29 Elihu reminded Job that God is the all-seeing Judge, whose eyes see every step of man (cp. 31:4). Because of His omniscience God **does not need to examine a person**, as would a human judge. Contrary to Job's earlier contention that God was not applying, universally, the rules of his friends' theology of retribution (v. 23; e.g., 21:4-18), Elihu described God's punishment of the wicked, especially of those who abused **the poor** and **afflicted**. However, even **when God is silent** or **hides His face**, man still has no right to condemn Him (vv. 28-29).

34:31-37 The hypothetical situation depicted Elihu's view of Job's challenge in response to Eliphaz: "Teach me . . . . Help me understand what I did wrong" (6:24). Elihu couched this response in terms of speaking to God like a child who promises never again to break the rule for which he has just been punished but who never admits doing wrong. Instead, he demands an explanation of what he has done, as though he **cannot see**. Elihu felt that such an approach was highly inappropriate and told Job to confess, implying by the rhetorical question that Job had **rejected** God's discipline (cp. 5:17). Counting himself an ally of other **wise men**, Elihu presented to Job the purported consensus opinion, a barbed criticism against "the greatest man among all the people of the east" (1:3) whose leadership and counsel used to be widely respected (29:7-11, 21-25; cp. 35:16). The reader, who has knowledge of Job's suffering inaccessible to both Elihu and Job, recognizes the irony in Elihu's wish for Job to be **tested to the limit**, as though that were not what had already prompted the debates about the extent of Job's suffering (34:36; see 1:12; 2:6).

35:1-8 Elihu attempted to summarize Job's position (vv. 2-3) and then refuted him (vv. 4-16). From Elihu's perspective, Job claimed to be **righteous** [Hb *tsedeq*, "moral rectitude; straightness or rightness in an ethical sense"] **before God** (v. 2; cp. 6:29; 29:14) and to question why "living right" was worth it—either to God or to himself (cp. 21:15; 34:9). In the manner of a teacher of wisdom (cp. Mt 6:26), Elihu drew attention to God's sovereignty and the distance between God and man but falsely characterized God as being absolutely unaffected by the sinfulness or righteousness of human beings (Jb 35:5-8).

35:9-16 In Elihu's view, people are motivated to pray only for help or because of **pride**, rather than seeking a relationship with God as the Creator and source of wisdom, so God **does**

[A]**34:23** Some emend to *God has not appointed a time for man to* [B]**34:26** Lit *In a place of spectators* [C]**35:3** Some emend to *me*

not answer. Verse 15 addressed Job's complaint that the wicked escaped God's punishment. Elihu concluded that Job did not know what he was talking about.

36:1-4 Elihu confidently claimed that he had acquired **knowledge from a distant place** and presented himself as **one who has perfect knowledge** (vv. 3-4). Three times Elihu has referred already to his superior insight as "what I know" (32:6,10,17). Here, his swaggering claim is probably linked to his self-appointed task of speaking "on God's behalf" (36:2) because he explicitly ascribes "perfect knowledge" to God (37:16).

36:5-7 Without denying that God **is mighty**, Elihu declares that He **despises** [Hb *ma'as*, "reject, refuse"; cp. "renounce," 9:21] **no one** but treats both the **wicked** and the **afflicted** (Hb *'ani*, "poor"; cp. 24:4,9,14; 34:28) with **justice** (Hb *mishpat*, "judgment, that which is right or just," 36:6; cp. 8:3; 19:7). Elihu countered Job's claim that God unfairly "destroys both the blameless and the wicked" (9:22). His description of the way God honors **the righteous** without interruption implied his belief that the sudden descent from a position of greatness (1:3; 29:7-25) signified Job's move from blamelessness to wickedness (36:7).

36:8-12 According to Elihu, when the righteous go through trials, God attempts to teach them to **repent** and correct their ways (vv. 8-10). Reflecting the theology of retribution argued by the other three friends, Elihu described two options:

- To **serve** God **obediently** would result in **prosperity** and **happiness**.
- To refuse to **obey** God would result in death **without knowledge** (i.e., foolishly or in ignorance).

Job's argument, however, was that God apparently did not always mete out justice before death because the wicked did not always suffer and the righteous were not always rewarded with health and prosperity.

36:14 Elihu further characterized the disobedient in extremes, asserting that they **die . . . among male cult prostitutes** (Hb *qadēsh*, "sodomites"). These men prostituted themselves as part of worship rituals honoring the fertility goddess Astarte, for example. In some pagan cultures of the ancient Near East, people believed that having sexual relations with the temple prostitutes would arouse the gods to cause their fields and flocks to become more fertile.

36:15 Those who reject God stand in contrast to the **afflicted**, whom God

more understanding
than the animals
of the earth
and makes us wiser
than the birds of the sky?"
12 There they cry out,
but He does not answer,
because of the pride
of evil men.
13 Indeed, God does not listen
to empty cries,
and the •Almighty does not
take note of it—
14 how much less
when[A] you complain[B]
that you do not see Him,
that your case is
before Him
and you are waiting for Him.
15 But now, because God's anger
does not punish
and He does not pay attention
to transgression,[C]
16 Job opens his mouth in vain
and multiplies words
without knowledge.

36 Then Elihu continued, saying:

2 Be patient with me
a little longer, and I will
inform you,
for there is still more
to be said on God's behalf.
3 I will get my knowledge from
a distant place
and ascribe justice
to my Maker.
4 For my arguments are
without flaw;[D]
one who has perfect
knowledge is with you.
5 Yes, God is mighty,
but He despises no one;
He understands all things.[E]
6 He does not keep
the wicked alive,
but He gives justice
to the afflicted.
7 He does not remove His gaze
from the righteous,
but He seats them forever
with enthroned kings,
and they are exalted.
8 If people are bound
with chains
and trapped by the cords
of affliction,
9 God tells them
what they have done
and how arrogantly
they have transgressed.
10 He opens their ears
to correction
and insists they repent
from iniquity.
11 If they serve Him obediently,
they will end their days
in prosperity
and their years in happiness.
12 But if they do not obey,
they will cross the river
of death[F]
and die without knowledge.

13 Those who have
a godless heart
harbor anger;
even when God binds them,
they do not cry for help.
14 They die in their youth;
their life ends among
male cult prostitutes.
15 God rescues the afflicted by
their affliction;
He instructs them
by their torment.
16 Indeed, He lured you
from the jaws[G] of distress
to a spacious
and unconfined place.
Your table was spread
with choice food.
17 Yet now you are obsessed
with the judgment due
the wicked;
judgment and justice
have seized you.
18 Be careful that
no one lures you
with riches;[H]
do not let a large ransom[I]
lead you astray.
19 Can your wealth[J] or all
your physical exertion
keep you from distress?
20 Do not long for the night
when nations will disappear
from their places.

[A]**35:14** Or *How then can* [B]**35:14** Lit *say* [C]**35:15** LXX, Vg; MT reads *folly*, or *arrogance*; Hb obscure [D]**36:4** Lit *my words are not false* [E]**36:5** Lit *He is mighty in strength of heart* [F]**36:12** Or *will perish by the sword* [G]**36:16** Lit *from a mouth of narrowness* [H]**36:18** Or *you into mockery* [I]**36:18** Or *bribe* [J]**36:19** Or *cry for help*

21 Be careful that
you do not turn to iniquity,
for that is why you
have been tested
by[A] affliction.
22 Look, God shows Himself
exalted by His power.
Who is a teacher like Him?
23 Who has appointed His way
for Him,
and who has declared,
"You have done wrong"?
24 Remember that you
should praise His work,
which people
have sung about.
25 All mankind has seen it;
people have looked at it
from a distance.
26 Yes, God is exalted
beyond our knowledge;
the number of His years
cannot be counted.
27 For He makes waterdrops
evaporate;[B]
they distill the rain
into its[C] mist,
28 which the clouds pour out
and shower abundantly
on mankind.
29 Can anyone understand
how the clouds spread out
or how the thunder roars
from God's pavilion?
30 See how He spreads
His lightning around Him
and covers the depths
of the sea.
31 For He judges the nations
with these;
He gives food in abundance.
32 He covers His hands
with lightning
and commands it to hit
its mark.
33 The[D] thunder declares
His presence;[E]
the cattle also,
the approaching storm.

37 My heart pounds at this
and leaps from my chest.[F]
2 Just listen to
His thunderous voice
and the rumbling that comes
from His mouth.
3 He lets it loose beneath
the entire sky;
His lightning to the ends
of the earth.
4 Then there comes
a roaring sound;
God thunders
with His majestic voice.
He does not restrain
the lightning
when His rumbling voice
is heard.
5 God thunders marvelously
with His voice;
He does great things that
we cannot comprehend.
6 For He says to the snow,
"Fall to the earth,"
and the torrential rains,
His mighty torrential rains,
7 serve as His sign
to all mankind,
so that all men may know
His work.
8 The wild animals enter
their lairs
and stay in their dens.
9 The windstorm comes
from its chamber,
and the cold from the
driving north winds.
10 Ice is formed by the breath
of God,
and watery expanses
are frozen.
11 He saturates clouds
with moisture;
He scatters His lightning
through them.
12 They swirl about,
turning round and round
at His direction,
accomplishing everything
He commands them
over the surface
of the inhabited world.
13 He causes this to happen
for punishment,
for His land,
or for His faithful love.

14 Listen to this, Job.
Stop and consider
God's wonders.
15 Do you know how God directs
His clouds

[A]**36:21** Or *for you have preferred this to* [B]**36:27** Lit *He draws in waterdrops* [C]**36:27** Or *His* [D]**36:33** Lit *His*, or *Its* [E]**36:33** Lit *thunder announces concerning Him* or *it* [F]**37:1** Lit *from its place*

rescues (Hb *chalats*, "set free, deliver"; cp. Pr 11:8-9) and **instructs . . . by means of their torment** (Hb *lachats*, "oppression, calamity, distress"; cp. Dt 26:7).

36:16-21 God was seeking to bring Job from distress to **a spacious and unconfined place**, figurative language for prosperity and comfort. Elihu then began to counsel Job to be patient and learn what God was saying to him in his affliction. He warned Job:

- not to continue obsession over **the judgment due the wicked**;
- not to trust in his former **riches** or future **wealth** to deliver him;
- not to long for death as an escape;
- not to choose **iniquity** over the **affliction** by which he was being **tested**.
- Job needed to learn the purpose of these trials in his life.

36:22–37:24 In the rest of the speech, Elihu emphasized the incalculable difference between God and man. Given God's greatness and power, Job's proper response should be to **praise** God's **work** and, ultimately, to **fear Him** (36:24; 37:24).

Elihu challenged Job's pursuit of a hearing with God (see 13:18; 23:4). He launched his arguments against Job's complaints that God was afflicting him without cause. Here, Elihu indirectly claimed a superior position for himself and those in agreement with him. Unlike Job, they would not dare to prepare such a case because they recognized that their understanding was like being in the dark compared with God's knowledge, power, and righteousness.

According to Elihu, Job's pursuit of vindication was out of order; God's justice should never be questioned simply because His ways are beyond human grasp. Job had openly declared, "The fear of the Lord is this: wisdom, and to turn from evil is understanding" (28:28). But Elihu, incorrectly presuming to know the purpose of Job's suffering (36:21; cp. 1:6–2:10), concluded that Job did not properly fear God, who has no need even of those **who are wise in heart** (37:23-24).

Although Elihu said much about God that is true and although his proposed explanation of Job's suffering was more satisfying than that of the three friends, his arguments still betray inadequate understanding of the purpose of Job's suffering and of God's character. Job, at least, knew that he was neither being unjustly punished for sin he did not commit nor being afflicted to deter him from sin that had not first taken root in his heart. Elihu's lengthy speech exhausted the resources of human reason to answer Job's complaint; yet his rhetorical questions (36:22-23,29; 37:15-20) and descriptions of God's power prepare the reader for the upcoming barrage of questions with which "the LORD answered Job" (38:1).

38:1-3 God is introduced by His covenant name—**the LORD** (Hb, *Yahweh*, cp. 40:1,6), the One who reveals Himself to His people—rather than the more generic God (Hb *ʾĒl*, e.g., 9:2; *ʾEloah*, e.g., 11:5), which was used more frequently in the book. God **answered** [Hb *ʿanah*; see **Word Study**, p. 628] **Job from the whirlwind** (Hb *saʿar*, "storm, tempest," 38:1; 40:6; cp. 2Kg 2:1,11). His first words immediately settled any issue Job wanted to raise. The question forced Job to recognize that he was the one **who obscures** [God's] **counsel** [Hb *ʿētsah*, "purpose, plan," by which God created and sustains the world; cp. Jb 12:13] **with ignorant words** (Hb *beli-daʿat*, "without knowledge," 38:2; cp. 34:35; 35:16; 36:12). The command is qualified by **like a man** (38:3). God was demanding that Job stand before Him with the dignity of one created in His image but also as one who was not God's equal. Carrying forward the courtroom motif, God's command clarified who was on trial. God holds man accountable—He has the authority to ask the questions, not the other way around.

38:3 Get ready (Hb *ʾazar*, "gird" with *chalats*, "loins,"; 40:7) captures the meaning of the Hebrew idiom "gird up your loins," the action of securing one's garments around the waist to be ready for action, often in the context of preparing for battle.

38:4-38 God illustrates His divine sovereignty by focusing on creation, generally following the order of the Genesis 1 account. The first series of rhetorical questions clearly was intended to humble Job by forcing him to face his ignorance in contrast to the incomprehensible ways of God.

One question particularly captures the force of the whole series. The Lord asked Job, **"Don't you know?"** (Hb *yadaʿ*, v. 21). "Know" refers primarily to knowledge gained through the senses and carries the idea of familiarity, of understanding and thorough knowledge of someone or something. The questions brought to Job's attention are examples of what only the the Creator (and no man) can possibly know.

38:7 The **sons of God** refers to the angels (cp. 1:6; 2:1). These creatures rejoiced at the creation of man's dwelling place.

38:8-11 God described the creation of the oceans (cp. Gn 1:9) with the language and imagery of childbirth. The sea had **burst** [Hb *giach*, "break out

or makes their lightning
flash?
16 Do you understand
how the clouds float,
those wonderful works of Him
who has perfect knowledge?
17 You whose clothes get hot
when the south wind
brings calm to the land,
18 can you help God spread out
the skies
as hard as
a cast metal mirror?
19 Teach us what we should say
to Him;
we cannot prepare our case
because of our darkness.
20 Should He be told that I want
to speak?
Can a man speak
when he is confused?
21 Now men cannot even look
at the sun
when it is in the skies,
after a wind
has swept through
and cleared them away.
22 Yet out of the north
He comes, shrouded
in a golden glow;
awesome majesty
surrounds Him.
23 The •Almighty—we cannot
reach Him—
He is exalted in power!
He will not oppress
justice and
abundant righteousness,
24 Therefore, men •fear Him.
He does not look favorably
on any who are wise
in heart.

God's Concluding Words (38:1–42:6)

God's First Message (38:1–40:2)

38 Then the LORD answered Job
from the whirlwind. He said:

2 Who is this who obscures
My counsel
with ignorant words?
3 Get ready to answer Me
like a man;
when I question you,
you will inform Me.
4 Where were you
when I established
the earth?
Tell Me, if you have[A]
understanding.
5 Who fixed its dimensions?
Certainly you know!
Who stretched
a measuring line across it?
6 What supports
its foundations?
Or who laid its cornerstone
7 while the morning stars
sang together
and all the sons of God
shouted for joy?
8 Who enclosed the sea
behind doors
when it burst from the womb,
9 when I made the clouds
its garment
and thick darkness its blanket,[B]
10 when I determined
its boundaries[C]
and put its bars and doors
in place,
11 when I declared:
"You may come this far,
but no farther;
your proud waves stop here"?
12 Have you ever in your life
commanded the morning
or assigned the dawn
its place,
13 so it may seize the edges
of the earth
and shake the wicked
out of it?
14 The earth is changed as clay
is by a seal;
its hills stand out
like the folds of a garment.
15 Light[D] is withheld
from the wicked,
and the arm raised in violence
is broken.
16 Have you traveled
to the sources of the sea
or walked in the depths
of the oceans?
17 Have the gates of death
been revealed to you?
Have you seen the gates
of deep darkness?
18 Have you comprehended
the extent of the earth?
Tell Me, if you know all this.

[A]38:4 Lit *know* [B]38:9 Lit *swaddling clothes* [C]38:10 Lit *I broke My statute on it* [D]38:15 Lit *Their light*

19 Where is the road
to the home of light?
Do you know
where darkness lives,
20 so you can lead it back
to its border?
Are you familiar
with the paths to its home?
21 Don't you know? You were
already born;
you have lived so long![A]
22 Have you entered the place
where the snow is stored?
Or have you seen
the storehouses of hail,
23 which I hold in reserve
for times of trouble,
for the day of warfare
and battle?
24 What road leads to the place
where light is dispersed?[B]
Where is the source of
the east wind that spreads
across the earth?
25 Who cuts a channel
for the flooding rain
or clears the way
for lightning,
26 to bring rain
on an uninhabited land,
on a desert
with no human life,[C]
27 to satisfy
the parched wasteland
and cause the grass to sprout?
28 Does the rain have a father?
Who fathered the drops
of dew?
29 Whose womb did the ice
come from?
Who gave birth to the frost
of heaven
30 when water becomes as hard
as stone,[D]
and the surface
of the watery depths
is frozen?

31 Can you fasten the chains
of the Pleiades
or loosen the belt of Orion?
32 Can you bring out
the constellations[E]
in their season
and lead the Bear[F]
and her cubs?
33 Do you know the laws
of heaven?
Can you impose its[G] authority
on earth?
34 Can you command[H]
the clouds
so that a flood of water
covers you?
35 Can you send out
lightning bolts,
and they go?
Do they report to you:
"Here we are"?

36 Who put wisdom in the heart[I]
or gave
the mind understanding?
37 Who has the wisdom
to number the clouds?
Or who can tilt the water jars
of heaven
38 when the dust hardens
like cast metal
and the clods of dirt
stick together?

39 Can you hunt prey
for a lioness
or satisfy the appetite
of young lions
40 when they crouch
in their dens
and lie in wait
within their lairs?
41 Who provides the raven's food
when its young cry out to God
and wander about for lack
of food?

39 Do you know when
mountain goats give birth?
Have you watched the deer
in labor?
2 Can you count the months
they are pregnant[J]
so you can know the time
they give birth?
3 They crouch down
to give birth to their young;
they deliver their newborn.[K]
4 Their offspring
are healthy and grow up
in the open field.
They leave and do not return.[L]

or break forth"; cp. Ps 22:9; Mc 4:10] **from the womb**; the **clouds** were **its garment**; **thick darkness** (Hb *'araphel*, "darkness of thick clouds"; cp. 22:13; Ex 20:21; Dt 5:22; 1 Kg 8:12; Ps 97:2; Is 60:2) was **its blanket** (Hb *chathullah*, "swaddling band," with which a newborn would be bundled). Again reminding Job of his limitations, God noted that Job was absent when, by His word, He set the ocean's boundaries.

38:19-21 As though **light** and **darkness** lived in houses with addresses unknown to Job, God figuratively pointed out that Job had no idea where darkness and light begin and end and certainly no authority to escort darkness **back to its border**. God highlighted Job's silence and pressed the issue—Job did *not* **know**, for he had not yet been born when the eternal God separated light from darkness (Gn 1:4).

38:22-30 God has exclusive control over the weather (cp. vv. 34-35; Ex 9:18-34; Ps 148:7-8; Is 30:30). He alone commands the lightning and the **rain**—whether destructive or beneficial. The imagery with which God asserted His indisputable sovereignty over every drop of water—even the **dew** and the **frost**—includes both masculine and feminine metaphors. If rain or dew were said to **have a father**, it would be God; if ice were said to come from a **womb**, it would be God who **gave birth**—i.e., He is the Creator (vv. 28-30).

38:33 Laws of heaven refers to the order of the planets' rotations, the stars, the sun and the moon, and the manner in which they cause the seasons to change.

38:39-41 God turned from the environment of the earth to its creaturely inhabitants over which man was given dominion (Gn 1:28). From the fiercest and most dangerous predators like **lions** to the birds—all creatures depend on God, not man, for **food** (cp. Mt 10:29).

A38:21 Lit *born; the number of your days is great* B38:24 Or *where lightning is distributed* C38:26 Lit *life in it* D38:30 Lit *water hides itself as the stone* E38:32 Or *Mazzaroth*; Hb obscure F38:32 Or *lead Aldebaran* G38:33 Or *God's* H38:34 Lit *lift up your voice to* I38:36 Or *the inner self*; Ps 51:6 J39:2 Lit *months they fulfill* K39:3 Or *they send away their labor pains* L39:4 Lit *return to them*

39:19-25 In contrast to the other animals noted, horses have been tamed by humans. The descriptive language in these verses matches the energy and power of the animal, of which God—not man—is the source. This creature **laughs** [Hb *sachaq*, "deride, laugh at in contempt, mock"] **at fear** (Hb *pachad*, "terror, dread"; v. 22; cp. 13:11; 21:9; 22:10; 25:2), just as "the wild donkey. . . . scoffs" (Hb *sachaq*) at man's preference for civilization (39:5-7) and the ostrich "laughs" (Hb *sachaq*) at man's dependence on the horse for speed (v. 18).

40:1-2 God closed His cross-examination of Job with a devastating question: **Will the one who contends** [Hb *riv*, "strive, fight"; forensically, "plead a cause"; cp. 9:3; Pr 25:8; Is 45:9] **with the Almighty correct** [Hb *yissor*, "instruct, reprove, admonish"] **Him?** He called for Job, who dared to argue with God, to come up with an answer.

Job's arguing with God was not like an angry shouting match. Job, in his attempts to make sense of his suffering, had challenged God's justice. **Argues** (Hb *yakach*, "dispute, discuss") expresses the idea here, and frequently in the book, of reproving, rebuking, or correcting (cp. 5:17; 6:25-26; 13:3,15; 23:7). Yahweh confronted him like a parent strategically responding to a teenage son who is arguing against a decision he does not understand, which has made his life miserable.

Instead of refusing to hear or respond to Job's complaint, God presented an array of matters about which Job knew nothing because he did not even exist when God was creating the world; nor did he have the power to sustain life. In His sovereign freedom, God sets the standards of right and wrong, and He establishes the parameters of human experience and knowledge. He allowed Job the freedom to contend or argue with Him but ultimately demonstrated that no man legitimately has room to indict **the Almighty** God.

40:3-5 Job wisely responded by confessing his ignorance and unworthiness. In the Hebrew text, the first word in Job's response is "Behold" (Hb *hēn*), which could also be rendered "although, since, or if." The declarative statement, **I am so insignificant** (Hb *qalal*, "be diminished; be light, i.e., not heavy"), incorporates the idea that "since" Job could not compare with God, the best way to respond would be to stop talking and listen receptively (cp. 21:5).

40:6-8 God commanded Job not only to listen but also to prepare a response. The leading question directly confronted Job's central concern with the relationship between God's **justice** (Hb *mishpat*; cp. 8:3; 19:7) and his own

5 Who set the wild donkey free?
Who released the swift donkey
from its harness?
6 I made the wilderness
its home,
and the salty wasteland
its dwelling.
7 It scoffs at the noise
of the village
and never hears the shouts
of a driver.
8 It roams the mountains
for its pastureland,
searching for anything green.
9 Would the wild ox be willing
to serve you?
Would it spend the night
by your feeding trough?
10 Can you hold the wild ox
to a furrow by its harness?
Will it plow the valleys
behind you?
11 Can you depend on it because
its strength is great?
Would you leave it to do
your hard work?
12 Can you trust the wild ox
to harvest your grain
and bring it
to your threshing floor?

13 The wings of the ostrich
flap joyfully,
but are her feathers
and plumage
like the stork's?[A]
14 She abandons her eggs
on the ground
and lets them be warmed
in the sand.
15 She forgets that a foot
may crush them
or that some wild animal
may trample them.
16 She treats her young harshly,
as if they were not her own,
with no fear that her labor
may have been in vain.
17 For God has deprived her
of wisdom;
He has not endowed her
with understanding.
18 When she proudly[A] spreads
her wings,
she laughs at the horse
and its rider.

19 Do you give strength
to the horse?
Do you adorn his neck
with a mane?[A]
20 Do you make him leap
like a locust?
His proud snorting
fills one with terror.
21 He paws[B] in the valley
and rejoices in his strength;
He charges into battle.[C]
22 He laughs at fear,
since he is afraid of nothing;
he does not run
from the sword.
23 A quiver rattles at his side,
along with a flashing spear
and a lance.[D]
24 He charges ahead[E]
with trembling rage;
he cannot stand still
at the trumpet's sound.
25 When the trumpet blasts,
he snorts defiantly.[F]
He smells the battle
from a distance;
he hears the officers' shouts
and the battle cry.

26 Does the hawk take flight
by your understanding
and spread its wings
to the south?
27 Does the eagle soar
at your command
and make its nest on high?
28 It lives on a cliff
where it spends the night;
its stronghold is
on a rocky crag.
29 From there it searches
for prey;
its eyes penetrate the distance.
30 Its brood gulps down blood,
and where the slain are,
it is there.

40 The LORD answered Job:

2 Will the one who contends
with the ·Almighty
correct Him?
Let him who argues with God
give an answer.[G]

Job's Response to God (40:3-5)

3 Then Job answered the LORD:

[A]39:13,18,19 Hb obscure [B]39:21 LXX, Syr; MT reads *digs* [C]39:21 Lit *He goes out to meet the weapon* [D]39:23 Or *scimitar* [E]39:24 Lit *He swallows the ground* [F]39:25 Lit *he says, "Aha!"* [G]40:2 Lit *God respond to it*

4 I am so insignificant.
How can I answer You?
I place my hand
over my mouth.
5 I have spoken once,
and I will not reply;
twice, but now
I can add nothing.

God's Second Message (40:6–41:34)

6 Then the LORD answered Job from the whirlwind:

7 Get ready to answer Me
like a man;
When I question you, you will
inform Me.
8 Would you really challenge
My justice?
Would you declare Me •guilty
to justify yourself?
9 Do you have an arm
like God's?
Can you thunder with a voice
like His?
10 Adorn yourself with majesty
and splendor,
and clothe yourself
with honor and glory.
11 Unleash your raging anger;
look on every proud person
and humiliate him.
12 Look on every proud person
and humble him;
trample the wicked
where they stand.[A]
13 Hide them together
in the dust;
imprison them in the grave.[B]
14 Then I will confess to you
that your own right hand
can deliver you.
15 Look at Behemoth,
which I made along with you.
He eats grass like an ox.
16 Look at the strength
of his loins
and the power in the muscles
of his belly.
17 He stiffens his tail
like a cedar tree;
the tendons of his thighs
are woven firmly together.
18 His bones are bronze tubes;
his limbs are like iron rods.
19 He is the foremost
of God's works;
only his Maker can draw
the sword against him.
20 The hills yield food for him,
while all sorts of wild animals
play there.
21 He lies under the lotus plants,
hiding in the protection[C]
of marshy reeds.
22 Lotus plants cover him
with their shade;
the willows by the brook
surround him.
23 Though the river rages,
Behemoth is unafraid;
he remains confident, even if
the Jordan surges up
to his mouth.
24 Can anyone capture him
while he looks on,[D]
or pierce his nose
with snares?

41 [E] Can you pull in •Leviathan
with a hook
or tie his tongue down
with a rope?
2 Can you put a cord[F]
through his nose
or pierce his jaw with a hook?
3 Will he beg you for mercy
or speak softly to you?
4 Will he make a covenant
with you
so that you can take him
as a slave forever?
5 Can you play with him
like a bird
or put him on a leash[G]
for your girls?
6 Will traders bargain for him
or divide him
among the merchants?
7 Can you fill his hide
with harpoons
or his head
with fishing spears?
8 Lay a[H] hand on him.
You will remember the battle
and never repeat it!
9 [I] Any hope of capturing him
proves false.
Does a person not collapse
at the very sight of him?
10 No one is ferocious enough
to rouse Leviathan;

[A]40:12 Lit *wicked in their place* [B]40:13 Lit *together; bind their faces in the hidden place*
[C]40:21 Lit *plants, in the hiding place* [D]40:24 Lit *capture it in its eyes* [E]41:1 Jb 40:25 in Hb
[F]41:2 Lit *reed* [G]41:5 Lit *or bind him* [H]41:8 Lit *your* [I]41:9 Jb 41:1 in Hb

righteousness. In the next question, two more thematically significant words appear: **declare . . . guilty** (Hb *rasha'*; cp. 9:20; 32:3) and **justify** (Hb *tsadaq*; see 9:1-2; cp. 9:13,21; 13:18; 15:14; 32:2). Perhaps the central application question for the reader, as well as for Job, is this: When confronted with personal tragedy and suffering, can any man **really** blame the One who is holy and good in order to make himself appear more righteous and wiser than God?

40:9-14 Job was confronted with the vast difference between God's **arm**—His strength, power, and authority—and Job's personal weakness. God challenged Job to do what he would have to admit was impossible for him—to don the robes of the Judge of the universe and administer perfect justice. In the list of actions to be involved, God spoke only of what He would do to the **proud** and the **wicked** when He finally unleashed His **raging** [Hb *'evrah*, "outpouring"; cp. 21:30; Pr 11:4] **anger**. If Job could demonstrate that he had the power to render moral judgment, then God would consider him fit to save himself, too. Not only did Job lack the power of God as Creator and Sustainer of all, but he was also incapable of exercising moral supremacy, which belongs to God alone.

40:15-24 God turned Job's attention to two creatures—one on the land and one in the sea—that were monstrous in size and terrifying in strength. These animals served as analogies by which God's sovereignty could be acknowledged and appreciated. Some scholars have noted similarities between this imagery and the portrayal of certain creatures in Canaanite mythology, but more likely they were real beasts Job had seen or about which he had heard reliable accounts. In the ancient Near East, both animals were stock symbols of evil and chaos. Since Job could not possibly subdue **Behemoth** (Hb, "large beast"; cp. 12:7) a fellow creature, how could he expect to demand that the Almighty God explain Himself to Job's satisfaction?

41:1-34 Leviathan is a transliteration of the Hebrew word for a "wreathed or coiled" sea creature, generally understood to be an enormous sea serpent (v. 1; 3:8; cp. Pss 74:14; 104:26; Is 27:1). Some speculate that "Leviathan" designated the crocodile or a multiheaded sea monster of pagan mythology. For the modern reader, the description may recall stories of fire-breathing dragons. Similar imagery is used to describe Satan (Rv 12:9). Leviathan had scales (vv. 13-14) and thick skin (vv. 16,23); the traditional weapons of man would not even faze him (v. 26). Even **the mighty** were

terrified of his power and unbelievable strength as he thrashed about in the water (v. 25). This creature feared nothing, indicating that he had **no equal** in the animal kingdom (v. 33).

God challenged Job to subdue these creatures, something he obviously could not do. Job was not qualified to control anything and had no right to challenge God in regard to the way He managed the universe or the earth's chaotic, dangerous creatures. In all God's speeches, He never mentioned Job's former blessings or position in life, for knowing God Himself is the greatest blessing of all.

42:1-6 Job recognized his inadequacy to control evil or make sense of this world; only God could govern all that He had made. Sufficiently humbled, Job repented, abandoning his accusations and complaints (v. 6).

Although Job finally did repent—the response his friends had demanded, he did not repent of sins he had not committed but rather of speaking about **things too wonderful** (Hb *pala'*, "marvelous, hard to understand or comprehend," v. 3; cp. 5:9; 9:10; 37:14) for man **to know**. Scripture commends the proclamation of God's "wonderful works" (Hb *pala'*, e.g., 1Ch 16:9,24; Ps 9:1). Job, however, had ventured to challenge God's justice—questioning why he was ever given life (Jb 3:3-19; 10:18-19) and attributing his suffering to God's unfair treatment of a righteous man (6:4,29; 7:20; 9:2-3,17-24; 10:1-17; 12:6; 13:3,23-27; 14:18-19; 16:6-17; 19:7-22; 21:4-21; 27:1-6). Job confessed, therefore, that his knowledge of God was far more limited than he realized. Before, the level of Job's understanding of God could be described as merely secondhand or hearsay, but now he had been addressed by God and had, therefore, **seen** Him on a more personal level (v. 5). Job finally understood that this great suffering had not come to him because God was unjust.

42:6 The reference to **dust and ashes** was the traditional manner of expressing grief and sorrow in the ancient world.

42:7-9 In an interesting twist, God's anger was directed at Job's three friends. Although they were quite confident in their orthodoxy, God accused them of lying. They believed that all suffering was the result of a person's own sin. This theology misrepresented God, and they were commanded to make extensive sacrifices. Now they were to repent. Unlike the other three men, Elihu was not mentioned by name. Four times, however, God refers to Job with a title of honor, **My servant** (cp. 1:8; 2:3; cp. Gn 26:24; Nm 12:7-8). The man they had excoriated would **pray for** them—

who then can stand
against Me?
11 Who confronted Me, that I
should repay him?
Everything under heaven
belongs to Me.

12 I cannot be silent
about his limbs,
his power,
and his graceful proportions.
13 Who can strip off
his outer covering?
Who can penetrate
his double layer of armor?[A]
14 Who can open his jaws,[B]
surrounded by
those terrifying teeth?
15 His pride is in his rows
of scales,
closely sealed together.
16 One scale is so close
to another[C]
that no air can pass
between them.
17 They are joined
to one another,
so closely connected[D]
they cannot be separated.
18 His snorting[E] flashes
with light,
while his eyes are like the rays[F]
of dawn.
19 Flaming torches shoot
from his mouth;
fiery sparks fly out!
20 Smoke billows
from his nostrils
as from a boiling pot
or burning reeds.
21 His breath sets coals ablaze,
and flames pour out
of his mouth.
22 Strength resides in his neck,
and dismay dances before him.
23 The folds of his flesh
are joined together,
solid as metal[G]
and immovable.
24 His heart is as hard as a rock,
as hard as a lower millstone!
25 When Leviathan rises,
the mighty[H] are terrified;
they withdraw because of
his thrashing.
26 The sword that reaches him
will have no effect,
nor will a spear, dart, or arrow.
27 He regards iron as straw,
and bronze as rotten wood.
28 No arrow can make him flee;
slingstones become
like stubble to him.
29 A club is regarded as stubble,
and he laughs at the sound
of a javelin.
30 His undersides are
jagged potsherds,
spreading the mud
like a threshing sledge.
31 He makes the depths seethe
like a cauldron;
he makes the sea
like an ointment jar.
32 He leaves a shining wake
behind him;[I]
one would think the deep had
gray hair!
33 He has no equal on earth—
a creature devoid of fear!
34 He surveys everything
that is haughty;
he is king over all
the proud beasts.[J]

Job's Response to God (42:1-6)

42 Then Job replied to the LORD:
2 I[K] know that You can do
anything
and no plan of Yours
can be thwarted.
3 You asked, "Who is this
who conceals My counsel
with ignorance?"
Surely I spoke about things
I did not understand,
things too wonderful for me
to[L] know.
4 You said, "Listen now,
and I will speak.
When I question you, you will
inform Me."
5 I had heard rumors about You,
but now my eyes
have seen You.
6 Therefore I take back
my words
and repent in dust and ashes.[M]

[A] **41:13** LXX; MT reads *double bridle* [B] **41:14** Lit *open the doors of his face* [C] **41:16** Lit *One by one they approach* [D] **41:17** Lit *another; they cling together and* [E] **41:18** Or *sneezing* [F] **41:18** Lit *eyelids* [G] **41:23** Lit *together, hard on him* [H] **41:25** Or *the divine beings* [I] **41:32** Lit *a path* [J] **41:34** Lit *the children of pride* [K] **42:2** Alt Hb tradition reads *You* [L] **42:3** Lit *me, and I did not* [M] **42:6** LXX reads *I despise myself and melt; I consider myself dust and ashes*

CHARACTER PROFILE

Job's Daughters Three Unparalleled Beauties (42:14-15)

NAME	MEANING	SIGNIFICANCE
Jemimah	"dove"	a name often used of a bride, describing her fine form and lovely voice
Keziah	"cassia"	a fragrant plant yielding a prized variety of cinnamon; incense (cp. Ps 45:9)
Keren-happuch	"horn of paint"	possibly a cosmetic box (Hb *qeren*, "horn, vessel made of horn," often a figurative reference to "strength"; with *puk*, "pigment, dye," possibly referring to antimony, a black eye paint women used as a form of eyeliner; cp. 2Kg 9:30)

God Speaks to Job's Friends (42:7-9)

7 After the LORD had finished
speaking[A] to Job, He said to Eliphaz
the Temanite: "I am angry with you
and your two friends, for you have
not spoken the truth about Me, as
My servant Job has. 8 Now take seven
bulls and seven rams, go to My servant Job, and offer a burnt offering
for yourselves. Then My servant Job
will pray for you. I will surely accept
his prayer and not deal with you as
your folly deserves. For you have not
spoken the truth about Me, as My
servant Job has." 9 Then Eliphaz the
Temanite, Bildad the Shuhite, and
Zophar the Naamathite went and did
as the LORD had told them, and the
LORD accepted Job's prayer.

Epilogue: Job's Restoration and Vindication (42:10-17)

10 After Job had prayed for his
friends, the LORD restored his prosperity and doubled his previous possessions. 11 All his brothers, sisters,
and former acquaintances came to
his house and dined with him in his
house. They sympathized with him
and comforted him concerning all
the adversity the LORD had brought
on him. Each one gave him a *qesi-
tah*[B] and a gold earring.
12 So the LORD blessed the last part
of Job's life more than the first. He
owned 14,000 sheep, 6,000 camels,
1,000 yoke of oxen, and 1,000 female
donkeys. 13 He also had seven sons
and three daughters. 14 He named his
first daughter Jemimah, his second
Keziah, and his third Keren-hap-
puch. 15 No women as beautiful as
Job's daughters could be found in
all the land, and their father granted them an inheritance with their
brothers.
16 Job lived 140 years after this and
saw his children and their children
to the fourth generation. 17 Then Job
died, old and full of days.

[A]**42:7** Lit *speaking these words* [B]**42:11** The value of the currency is unknown.

surely an indication of God's justice (Jb 42:8). They obeyed God and He heard Job's prayer.

Job began this experience with the same theological bent as his friends—that evil befalls the wicked, never the righteous. However, he questioned this deeply entrenched theology, which, while generally true, was not universally true.

42:10-17 God then, in an outpouring of His grace, restored to Job twice the number of livestock and possessions he had before this calamity. He had 10 more children, including exceptionally **beautiful** daughters, for whom Job reserved an impressive inheritance. **Job lived 140 years** longer, meaning he was likely around 200 years old when he **died** (42:16).

The restoration of Job's physical blessings did not indicate that his friends were right after all but did display to surrounding communities God's pleasure with Job. God does blesses the righteous, but in His sovereignty He works out His own purposes in His own time.

JOB... WRITTEN ON MY Heart

As Job's testimony demonstrates, God does bless those who worship Him and live according to His righteous standards, but prosperity and comfort are false measures of God's favor. In fact, if your faith in Jesus Christ as your living Redeemer is genuine, then Satan will clamor to distract, weaken, and undermine your relationship with God. The book of Job affirms that God remains sovereign and loving even when a woman who truly knows the Lord cannot see or feel the evidence of His presence or providence. God permits the believer's faith to be proved genuine (Jms 1:2-18); in the midst of tragedy He permits His children to express with fierce honesty their dismay and grief; and He establishes the limits for both the testing and the wrestling with Him before He commands your attention to look at your circumstances, yourselves, and others from His perspective.

Psalms

Timeline	1526–1406 BC	1446–1406 BC	1035 BC	1015–1013 BC
World Events / Biblical Events	Composition of Ps 90, a psalm of Moses	The exodus from Egypt and 40 years in the wilderness (Pss 66,78,95,106,114,135)	Composition of Ps 23 by David the shepherd	David's flight from his early enemies (Pss 18,34,41,52,54,55,56,57,59,63,142)

"Let everything that breathes praise the LORD. Hallelujah!" (150:6).

Who wrote Psalms?

Israel's King David and various other authors—including Asaph, Solomon, Ethan, Moses, and the sons of Korah—are often identified by superscriptions, titles, or headings.

Who were the recipients?

The psalms were written primarily for the people who worship the one true God. Initially, many of them were received by the temple's choir director for use in temple worship. The compilation and arrangement of the psalms was finalized during the time of Ezra. The exiles returning to Israel needed the book's guidance and instruction for rediscovering God's standards for worship. However, the wisdom and truths the psalms teach and the perspectives they model are intended to draw all peoples to acknowledge the Lord as King of the universe and to worship Him. In another sense, though God is the supreme author, He is also the primary recipient of these prayers and hymns. As they were written and as they are read and sung, the psalms are primarily, though not exclusively, addressed to the Lord.

When was Psalms written?

Individual psalms and certain groups of them were written at various times throughout Israel's history. For example, Moses wrote Psalm 90 sometime near the end of Israel's wilderness wanderings, ca 1410 B.C. Psalm 126 was probably composed ca 500 B.C. during the exiles' return to Israel or, if written later by Ezra, ca 430 B.C. Most psalms, however, were written during the reigns of David (ca 1010–970 B.C.) and Solomon (ca 970–930 B.C.). Some have superscriptions connecting the psalm with a particular historical setting (e.g., Ps 51 is identified as David's prayer for forgiveness after committing adultery with Bathsheba during his tenth-century B.C. reign).

Where did it happen?

The time-and-place settings reflected in the content of the psalms vary widely, but Israel is usually the geographical reference point for both events and the psalmists' personal experiences and reflections.

What is Psalms about?

- God's presence with His people
- God's Word as the fountain of worship

Why should women read Psalms?

The book of Psalms invites and challenges women to merge head and heart in encountering God and truths about Him. The psalmists speak to and about the Lord, revealing that He is purposefully involved in the world He created and particularly in the lives of His people. Women discover in reading and worshiping with the psalmists' prayers that they, too, can call on the Lord with the certainty that He will hear and answer. When you fear He is absent, you will find company in voicing your complaints. When you sense a need to reexamine and renew your commitment to love and obey the Lord, the rich language of worship can provide the template. When you are devastated by your own sin or by the betrayal of your trust, in the psalms you can discover that you are not alone, that God is listening to your heart's cry and leading you to His way of looking at both your problems and those of the world. In the psalms the Lord meets you as your Creator, Protector, Provider, Sustainer, and Deliverer. Read, memorize, and sing the psalms in order to be equipped to glorify and praise God both for who He is and what He has done, is doing, and will do. The poetry will provide words for speaking about Him, praying to Him, encouraging others in their walk with Him, and in demonstrating that Jesus is the anticipated Messiah. The imagery will engage your senses in celebrating His creation, kingship, deliverance, sovereignty, and love. An inexhaustible treasure of authentic worship, the book of Psalms should be part of every woman's daily diet and adornment—nourishment for her soul, irrepressible joy in the security of God's love and care, strength to persevere, hope for the most depressing circumstances, and rest in the unchanging character of God when the world seems to be falling apart. At the beginning and end and in every moment of each day, women who read with minds and hearts engaged will be glad to see the transformation God's Word is making in their lives, homes, and relationships when they consistently immerse themselves in the book of Psalms.

How do you read Psalms?

Psalms are essentially song lyrics. Most of the biblical psalms could be described as prayers that were set to music. Like contemporary hymns and worship songs, psalms share certain universal features of poetry, but they also have their own characteristics. Poetry in general tends to be more personal than prose, expressing the poet's thoughts and feelings. Like poetry in other languages and contexts, the biblical psalms are marked by elevated discourse, compact language (i.e., word precision, conciseness, terseness), and imagery that intensifies the meaning and effect of the poem. In translation much of the rhythm and musical effect of a poem "heard" in its original language cannot be fully communicated; but word choice, arrangement, and structure offer important clues to the poet's intended meaning. Recognizing basic features of Hebrew poetry (see p. 667) will help you decipher what God is revealing about Himself and what response He desires from you as you read the psalms. Above all, the book of Psalms is permeated with praise. A reading of the 150 psalms will shift your focus to the majesty of the one God truly worthy of your trust and adoration.

998 BC David's conquest of Edom (Ps 60)	*995 BC* David's adultery (Ps 32, 51)	*974 BC* David's flight from his son Absalom (Ps 3)	*586 BC* Babylonians' destruction of Jerusalem (Ps 79)	*605–538 BC* Babylonian exile (Ps 137)

Features of Hebrew Poetry

Two main characteristics of Hebrew poetry are the division of the poem into strophes and the frequent use of parallelism. *Strophe*, a term used originally to describe the structure of Greek and Latin poetry, is comparable to a stanza, though many scholars distinguish between strophes and stanzas. Parallelism is the foundation and hallmark of Hebrew poetry. At one end of the spectrum is *synonymous* parallelism, in which the two lines express the same basic thought:

Wash away my guilt
and cleanse me from my sin (51:2).

At the other end is *antithetical* parallelism, in which the thought of the second line stands in contrast to the first:

For the LORD watches over the way of the righteous,
but the way of the wicked leads to ruin (1:6).

Between these two extremes are countless, though more or less differently nuanced, forms of the technique. The two lines may have the same grammatical structure as in:

The LORD is my light and my salvation—
whom should I fear?
The LORD is the stronghold of my life—
of whom should I be afraid? (27:1).

In other cases, the second line extends, advances, echoes, clarifies, intensifies, exemplifies, or completes the thought of the first line, a form sometimes identified as *synthetic*:

Give thanks to the LORD,
for He is good;
His faithful love endures forever (107:1).

Although the psalms are notoriously unique, making categorization of them difficult and somewhat artificial, noting the shared features of various types of psalms can also be helpful in the effort to understand the psalms individually or as a whole. However, recognizing similar patterns of thought and structure can be helpful. The types of psalms included in the chart on page 668 represent only some of the major categories upon which many scholars have agreed, and not all of the psalms have been placed in one of these categories. For example, debate continues as to whether or not "wisdom psalm" is appropriate as a category.

Outline

I. Book I (1:1–41:13)
II. Book II (42:1–72:20)
III. Book III (73:1–89:52)
IV. Book IV (90:1–106:48)
V. Book V (107:1–150:6)

BOOK I
(Psalms 1:1–41:13)

Psalm 1
The Two Ways

1 How happy is the man
who does not follow[A]
the advice of the wicked
or take[B] the path of sinners
or join a group[C] of mockers!
2 Instead, his delight is
in the LORD's instruction,
and he meditates on it day
and night.
3 He is like a tree planted
beside streams of water[D]
that bears its fruit in season[E]
and whose leaf
does not wither.
Whatever he does prospers.

[A]1:1 Lit *not walk in* [B]1:1 Lit *stand in* [C]1:1 Or *or sit in the seat* [D]1:3 Or *beside irrigation canals* [E]1:3 Lit *in its season*

Title The Hebrew title is *Tehillim* (Hb, plural of *tehillah*, "doxology, song of praise"). The English title evolved from the Greek word *psalmos* (plural, *psalmoi*), which was used in the Septuagint. The title *Psalter*, also frequently applied to the book, was derived from the book's name found in an ancient Greek manuscript known as Codex Alexandrinus.

1:1–2:12 Psalms 1 and 2, the only psalms in Books I–III without an explanatory heading or superscription, may *together* function as an introduction to the psalter. The

>WORD|*study*

1:2 Meditates (Hb *hagah*, "mutter, make a low sound") suggests reading aloud but softly, as only for personal edification. It may also include reciting memorized passages. Such meditation does not emphasize primarily mental knowledge but rather awakens the desire for a constant yielding to the Word and will of God. The word *hagah* is used figuratively in Ps 2:1 of God's enemies in the sense of whispering or speaking in low tones to prevent their evil plans from being heard. In distinct contrast to the man who lives by the *Torah (the law of the LORD)*, **the peoples** who oppose the Lord **plot** [Hb *hagah*, "plan, devise"] **in vain** against Him (see Ac 4:25).

Types of Psalms

Genre/ Classification	Characteristics	Representative Psalms
Praise (Hb *tehillah*)	• a declaration of and/or call to praise God—i.e., to glorify and honor God by proclaiming who He is • the recounting of what God has done in creation and/or redemption • descriptions of God's acts of deliverance or of His greatness and compassion	8 19 33 66 67 95 100 103 104 111 113 114 117 145 147 148 149 150
Thanksgiving (Hb *todah*)	• an expression of gratitude to God for deliverance • a joyful tone • a description of God's acts of deliverance or of His greatness and compassion	8 11 16 18 21 23 27 30 32 34 40 62 63 65 66 67 75 91 92 105 106 107 108 116 118 121 124 125 131 135 136 138
Enthronement (i.e., recognition of royal position)	• an emphasis on divine kingship and sovereignty • the celebration of significant events in the life of a king (e.g., his enthronement, a military victory, or a wedding) • the overall praise of Yahweh as King	2 18 20 21 29 45 47 72 93 95 96 97 98 99 101 110 144
Laments	• cries for deliverance in the face of danger • the expression of need and a sense of helplessness • the transition from issuing complaints to giving expressions of confidence and praise • the exhibition of faith in the midst of real-life experiences	3 4 5 7 9 10 12 13 14 17 22 25 26 27 28 31 36 39 40 41 42 43 44 52 53 54 55 56 57 58 59 60 61 67 70 71 74 77 79 80 83 85 86 89 90 94 120 123 126 129 139 141 142
Penitence (in the early church, traditionally sung on the liturgical holiday Ash Wednesday)	• the admission of moral failure, of having broken the covenant • a prayer for forgiveness of sin	6 32 38 51 102 130 143
Imprecatory requests	• a plea for God's righteous judgment to be executed against evildoers • the pronouncement of curses upon enemies by God and/or the psalmist	11 17 35 55 59 69 83 88 109 137 140
Wisdom	• advice for successful living • a contrast between the righteous and the wicked • a reflection on the brevity of life • the presentation of instructions or lessons	1 8 32 34 37 49 73 112 127 128

4 The wicked are not like this;
instead, they are like chaff
that the wind blows away.
5 Therefore the wicked
will not survive[A]
the judgment,
and sinners will not be
in the community
of the righteous.

6 For the LORD watches over
the way of the righteous,
but the way of the wicked
leads to ruin.

Psalm 2

Coronation of the Son

1 Why do the nations rebel[B]
and the peoples plot in vain?
2 The kings of the earth take
their stand,
and the rulers conspire
together
against the LORD
and His Anointed One:[C]
3 "Let us tear off their chains
and free ourselves
from their restraints."[D]

4 The One enthroned[E]
in heaven laughs;
the Lord ridicules them.
5 Then He speaks to them
in His anger
and terrifies them
in His wrath:
6 "I have consecrated My King[F]
on •Zion, My holy mountain."

7 I will declare
the LORD's decree:
He said to Me, "You are
My Son;[G]
today I have become
Your[H] Father.
8 Ask of Me,
and I will make the nations
Your[H] inheritance
and the ends of the earth
Your[H] possession.
9 You will break[I] them
with a rod of iron;
You[J] will shatter them
like pottery."[K]

10 So now, kings, be wise;
receive instruction,
you judges of the earth.
11 Serve the LORD
with reverential awe
and rejoice with trembling.
12 Pay homage to[L] the Son
or He[M] will be angry
and you will perish
in your rebellion,[N]
for His[O] anger may ignite
at any moment.
All those who take refuge
in Him[P] are happy.

Psalm 3

Confidence in Troubled Times

A psalm of David when he fled from his son Absalom.

1 LORD, how my foes increase!
There are many
who attack me.
2 Many say about me,
"There is no help for him
in God." *•Selah*

3 But You, LORD, are a shield
around me,
my glory, and the One
who lifts up my head.

A1:5 Lit *stand in* B2:1 Or *conspire*, or *rage* C2:2 Or *anointed one* D2:3 Lit *and throw their ropes from us* E2:4 Lit *who sits* F2:6 Or *king* G2:7 Or *me, "You are My son* H2:7,8 Or *your* I2:9 LXX, Syr, Tg read *shepherd* J2:9 Or *you* K2:9 Lit *a potter's vessel* L2:12 Lit *Kiss* M2:12 Or *son, otherwise he* N2:12 Lit *perish way* O2:12 Or *his* P2:12 Or *him*

>WORD|*study*

3:1-4 *Selah* (Hb) appears three times in this psalm—at the end of verses 2 and 4 and as its last word. "Selah" never occurs more than three times, possibly reflecting a practice of singing a psalm in three parts. While the meaning of this term is unknown, it probably has musical significance, especially in the psalm's performance within a worship setting, perhaps indicating:

- a pause either for silence or a musical interlude;
- a signal for cymbals to crash;
- a cue for the choir to sing at a higher pitch; or
- a break during which the worshipers would fall prostrate on the ground.

Selah occurs 71 times in the Psalms and elsewhere only in Hab 3:3,9,13.

thematic statement that begins Ps 1 (**How happy is the man**) is recast at the end of Ps 2 (**All those who take refuge in Him are happy**), thus positioning the two statements like bookends at the beginning and end of a literary unit that "includes" everything in between. If these two psalms are supposed to be read together, then the description of the righteous man in Ps 1 applies to Yahweh's **Anointed One** and **Son** of Ps 2. Likewise, the **group of mockers** and **the wicked** throughout Ps 1 are depicted in corporate rebellion against the **King**, who is established by the Lord in Ps 2.

The book of Psalms begins appropriately with a wisdom psalm that contrasts two ways of life—the way of blessing (vv. 1-3) and the way of destruction (vv. 4-6; cp. Pr 4:10-27)—and suggests that one's source of joy and satisfaction makes the difference by underscoring the fundamental role of God's written revelation in His covenant relationship with man (cp. Jos 1:7-8; 2 Kg 17:13; 21:8; 2 Ch 17:9).

1:1-2 Happy (Hb *'esher*, a noun meaning "blessedness") is plural in the Hebrew text, perhaps denoting fullness of blessing but also functioning as an interjection—"How happy is he . . . !" (cp. 32:1-2; 33:12). Use of the word is linked predominantly to the experience of being in covenant relationship with Yahweh. The LXX translates "happy" with "blessed" (Gk *makarios*, "happy"), the same word used in the New Testament (e.g., Mt 5:3-11; Jms 1:12; Rv 22:14). Genuine happiness is found in willingly living under the authority of God's revelation in His Word.

2:1-12 Psalm 2, often categorized as a royal psalm, deals with the king of Israel. Initially, the poem may have been connected with the ceremony of enthroning a new king of Israel. However, as a messianic psalm, it points prophetically to Jesus' identity as the divine King and Messiah. The New Testament explicitly attributes this psalm to the authorship of God speaking "through the Holy Spirit, by the mouth of . . . David." It is quoted in reference to Christ at least four times (Ac 4:25-28; 13:33; Heb 1:5; 5:5).

3:1-4 Psalm 3, the first psalm with a heading or superscription, invites the reader to recall or consult the historical narrative recounting David's flight from his son Absalom (2Sm 15:1–19:43). As a consequence of his adultery with Bathsheba and the subsequent murder of her husband, David's life was torn apart by family problems (2Sm 12:9-12). When his son Absalom boldly attempted to usurp the throne, David fled from Jerusalem. David expresses in the psalm what the writer of 2 Samuel reported.

In Ps 2, the enemies confronting the Lord's Anointed—the Messiah—were other nations and their kings. In Ps 3, David—the Lord's anointed king on earth—faced opposition from his own people and even his own son. The opposition was so severe that if God had not intervened, David would have been defeated and killed (see 2Sm 15:31-37; 16:15–17:24). Although **many** voiced the conclusion that David had no hope of being delivered by God (Ps 3:2), from beginning to end the psalmist presents the circumstances for what they are but continually places confidence in the Lord.

3:5-8 To be able to have personal rest proved David's complete dependence on the Lord, who continually **sustains** (Hb *samak*, "uphold, help, support"; cp. 37:17,24; 145:14) men and women of faith. The rhythm of this poem intensifies in verses 7-8 as David urgently calls on the Lord to act. In contrast to the **thousands** [Hb *revavah*, "a large number, myriad, multitude"] **of people** who had risen up against David, he called on Yahweh to **rise up** (Hb *qum*, "arise, stand up," here in the sense of "take action, show Yourself to be strong and ready to fight"; cp. Nm 10:35; Ps 7:6; 9:19; 17:13) on his behalf. Furthermore, David beseeched Yahweh, his **God**, for **salvation** (Hb *yeshu'ah*, "deliverance, victory"; cp. Ex 14:13; 2Sm 22:51; see **Word Study**, p. 878), defying the multitudes who were saying that God would not "help" (Hb *yeshu'ah*, 3:2) the king. In Hebrew, the verb forms of **strike** (Hb *nakah*, "smite") and **break** (Hb *shavar*, "thoroughly break in pieces, shatter") suggest actions that have already been completed, expressing a confident assurance of decisive divine intervention. This description uses *anthropomorphic* language, which attributes human characteristics to that which is not human. Such imagery is often used to depict God's actions or character.

4:1–6:10 Thirty-nine Davidic psalms, as well as psalms associated with other groups and individuals, bear a superscription indicating performance under the leadership of the **choir director** (Hb *natsach*, "one who leads in music, chief musician"). Some Bible scholars have suggested that these psalms originally existed as a smaller collection identified as that of "the choir director." Also, these three psalms begin with imperative verbs (4:1; 5:1; 6:1-2) that demonstrate confidence in approaching God in prayer.

5:3-7 Daybreak signifies the renewal of hope that comes with the morning light. Verses 4-6 affirm the Lord's rejection of and judgment on those who act wickedly.

4 I cry aloud to the LORD,
and He answers me
from His holy mountain.
Selah

5 I lie down and sleep;
I wake again because the LORD
sustains me.
6 I am not afraid
of the thousands of people
who have taken their stand
against me on every side.

7 Rise up, LORD!
Save me, my God!
You strike all my enemies
on the cheek;
You break the teeth
of the wicked.
8 Salvation belongs to the LORD;
may Your blessing be
on Your people. *Selah*

Psalm 4
A Night Prayer

*For the choir director:
with stringed instruments.
A Davidic psalm.*

1 Answer me when I call,
God, who vindicates me.[A]
You freed me from affliction;
be gracious to me and hear
my prayer.

2 How long, exalted men,
will my honor be insulted?
How long will you love
what is worthless
and pursue a lie? •*Selah*
3 Know that the LORD
has set apart
the faithful for Himself;
the LORD will hear when I call
to Him.

4 Be angry[B] and do not sin;
on your bed, reflect
in your heart and be still.
Selah

5 Offer sacrifices
in righteousness[C]
and trust in the LORD.

6 Many are saying,
"Who can show us
anything good?"
Look on us with favor, LORD.

7 You have put more joy
in my heart
than they have
when their grain
and new wine abound.
8 I will both lie down and sleep
in peace,
for You alone, LORD, make me
live in safety.

Psalm 5
The Refuge of the Righteous

*For the choir director:
with the flutes. A Davidic psalm.*

1 Listen to my words, LORD;
consider my sighing.
2 Pay attention to the sound
of my cry,
my King and my God,
for I pray to You.

3 At daybreak, LORD, You hear
my voice;
at daybreak I plead my case
to You and watch expectantly.

4 For You are not a God
who delights in wickedness;
evil cannot dwell with You.
5 The boastful cannot stand
in Your presence;
You hate all evildoers.

[A]**4:1** Or *God of my righteousness* [B]**4:4** Or *Tremble* [C]**4:5** Or *Offer right sacrifices*; lit *Sacrifice sacrifices of righteousness*

>WORD|*study*

Ps 6: Superscription Among the singers and musicians appointed by the Levitical leaders (according to David's command when he brought the ark of the covenant to Jerusalem), six men were chosen to play a key role in directing Israel's worship by leading "the music with lyres according to the" *Sheminith* (Hb, "eighth," 1Ch 15:21; cp. superscriptions for Pss 6 and 12). This transliterated word may signify:

- an "octave," indicating that the piece was intended for lower-octave instruments (such as the modern cello);
- an eight-stringed musical instrument;
- the eighth string of an instrument;
- the tuning of a particular musical instrument;
- the scale of the psalm's melody; or
- the eighth and concluding ceremony of the New Year celebration.

HARD QUESTION

As a follower of Jesus, who taught His disciples to love their enemies and to do good to those who mistreat them, how can I apply the imprecatory psalms that invoke a curse or call on God to bring misfortune and disaster on one's enemies; as divinely inspired Scripture? (Pss 5, 11, 17, 35, 55, 59, 69, 109, 137, and 140; Mt 5:43-48)

One must keep several truths in mind in studying statements like those found in this psalm. *Imprecatory* psalms:

- express human emotions, revealing that to express your feelings—even feelings that are not noble or godly—honestly to God in prayer is acceptable;
- teach that vengeance belongs to the Lord—the psalmist did not take matters into his own hands but rather called on the Lord to act;
- remind you that because God is righteous, the wicked—those in opposition to God—ultimately will be judged;
- emphasize that because the Lord loves His people, He is concerned for their welfare and ultimately will act in their best interests.

6 You destroy those who tell lies;
the LORD abhors a man
of bloodshed and treachery.
7 But I enter Your house
by the abundance
of Your faithful love;
I bow down toward
Your holy temple
in reverential awe of You.
8 LORD, lead me
in Your righteousness
because of my adversaries;[A]
make Your way straight
before me.
9 For there is nothing reliable
in what they say;[B]
destruction is within them;
their throat is an open grave;
they flatter with their tongues.
10 Punish them, God;
let them fall
by their own schemes.
Drive them out because of
their many crimes,
for they rebel against You.
11 But let all who take refuge
in You rejoice;
let them shout for joy forever.
May You shelter them,
and may those who love
Your name boast about You.
12 For You, LORD, bless
the righteous one;
You surround him with favor
like a shield.

Psalm 6

A Prayer for Mercy

For the choir director:
with stringed instruments,
according to •Sheminith.
A Davidic psalm.

1 LORD, do not rebuke me
in Your anger;
do not discipline me
in Your wrath.
2 Be gracious to me, LORD,
for I am weak;[C]
heal me, LORD, for my bones
are shaking;
3 my whole being is shaken
with terror.
And You, LORD—how long?
4 Turn, LORD! Rescue me;
save me because of
Your faithful love.
5 For there is no remembrance
of You in death;
who can thank You in •Sheol?
6 I am weary from my groaning;
with my tears I dampen
my pillow[D]
and drench my bed
every night.
7 My eyes are swollen from grief;
they[E] grow old because of all
my enemies.
8 Depart from me, all evildoers,
for the LORD has heard
the sound of my weeping.
9 The LORD has heard my plea
for help;
the LORD accepts my prayer.
10 All my enemies will be
ashamed and shake
with terror;
they will turn back
and suddenly be disgraced.

A 5:8 Or *of those who lie in wait for me* B 5:9 Lit *in his mouth* C 6:2 Or *sick* D 6:6 Lit *bed*
E 6:7 LXX, Aq, Sym, Jer read *I*

Faithful love (Hb *chesed*, "grace, mercy, lovingkindness"; see **Word Study**, p. 322) refers to God's steadfast love or His covenant loyalty. David's assurance of fellowship with the Lord was based on God's unwavering commitment to him, not on his righteousness. In a world filled with **evildoers**, the psalmist clung to his assurance of God's unchanging love, the primary benefit of faith in Him. Such faith leads the believer to respond to the Lord **in reverential awe** (Hb *yir'ah*, "fear"; cp. 2:11). Although the **temple** in Jerusalem was not built during David's lifetime, the word can also refer to the tabernacle or to heaven as God's dwelling place (cp. 11:4).

5:8-11 Knowing he was incapable of fighting his **adversaries** alone, David besought the Lord for leadership. Those who opposed him were also enemies of the Lord. Therefore, he called on the Lord to **punish** or judge them as they deserved. He did not need to be the instrument of judgment. His desire was for God's ways to triumph, which meant the ways of the wicked led to their own ruin. The recognition of God's justice on evildoers would lead the Lord's people to **rejoice**.

5:11-12 Joy, protection, and blessing surround those who put their faith in the Lord. The **righteous one** (i.e., the one in right relationship with the Lord) is blessed with God's **favor**, which surrounds him **like a shield** (Hb *tsinnah*, "large shield designed to protect the entire body"; cp. 1Sm 17:41). Such protection is one of the benefits of faith in the Lord.

6:1 Psalm 6 is the first of seven psalms recognized by the ancient church as *penitential*, dealing particularly with the nature of sin and forgiveness. Although the psalm contains no explicit confession of sin or petition for forgiveness, the vocabulary of the opening parallel lines constituting verse 1 imply an admission of guilt. The psalmist does not beg the Lord to withhold correction and punishment but pleads with God **not to rebuke** [Hb *yakach*, "correct by punishment, chastise, upbraid"] **. . . in Your anger** or **discipline . . . in Your wrath** (Hb *chēmah*, "burning anger, hot displeasure, fury, rage"; cp. Dt 9:19; Ps 89:46; 90:7; 106:23). In the context of the whole canon of Scripture, this request does not suggest that God is simply hot-tempered or prone to overreact, inflicting unwarranted harm rather than effective discipline like human parents often do when anger flares over the discovery of a child's disobedience (cp. Ex 34:6; Nm 14:18; Ps 86:15; 94:12; 103:8; 145:8; Jl 2:13; Nah 1:3).

6:8-10 Desperation gives way to confidence that the situation has been reversed. God has indeed been attentive to the psalmist's **weeping** and **prayer**. Now the **enemies** whose menacing presence had prompted such intense soul-searching would **shake with terror** (Hb *bahal*; cp. vv. 2-3).

7:1-2 Elsewhere the Scripture makes no mention of a **Benjaminite** named **Cush**, who, according to the superscription, provoked David's composition or performance of this psalm. Some scholars have connected this psalm with instances in David's life when he was pursued by the Benjaminite Saul. In any case, the psalm conveys a plea for protection from the false accusations of one's enemies.

The psalm begins with an appeal for rescue and for **refuge** (Hb *chasah*, "flee to a place or person for protection; find, seek, or take refuge") in the Lord. Two verbs—**save** and **rescue**—appear in synonymous parallelism to identify what David desired the Lord to do for him as he sought refuge in the Lord.

7:3-5 David's appeal took into account the ferocity that his opponents displayed. He requested deliverance from his enemies based on his own integrity. Were he indeed in the wrong, he asked that his enemies overcome him. He invited the Lord to search him for any wrong actions or motives on his part and to judge him accordingly.

7:8 David not only called on God to judge his enemies but also appealed to the Lord to judge him, for he was confident of his own **righteousness** and **integrity** (Hb *tom*, "wholeness"; cp. 25:21; 26:1,11; 1Kg 9:4).

7:9-11 David prayed that the end result of the two diverse ways of living—also depicted in Ps 1—would become evident to all observers. **The righteous** would be established in stability while **the evil of the wicked** would come to an end. Such is true because the Lord is a **righteous judge**, and people ultimately reap what they have sown (see vv. 15-16).

>WORD|*study*

7:1 Save (Hb *yasha'*, "set free, preserve, deliver"; cp. 3:7; 6:4) combines military and physical meaning with a strong religious or theological connotation in the Old Testament because typically the Lord is the One to whom His people looked for deliverance. The verb is related to the Hebrew name Joshua and *Yeshua*, or Jesus.

7:1-2 Rescue (Hb *natsal*, "pull away") suggests the graphic imagery of tearing or snatching the object away from danger. David's experience as a shepherd—having "rescued" (Hb *natsal*) lambs from the mouths of "lions and bears" (1Sm 17:34-35) and having witnessed the **ripping . . . apart** (Hb *paraq*, "break or crush," especially in the sense of a wild beast's tearing apart of its prey; cp. "tear off," Zch 11:16) of a lamb **with no one to rescue** (Hb *natsal*)—likely supplied the imagery for describing his situation.

Psalm 7

Prayer for Justice

A Shiggaion[A] of David, which he sang to the Lord concerning the words of •Cush,[B] a Benjaminite.

1 •Yahweh my God, I seek
refuge in You;
save me from all my pursuers
and rescue me
2 or they[C] will tear me
like a lion,
ripping me apart with no one
to rescue me.[D]
3 Yahweh my God,
if I have done this,
if there is injustice
on my hands,
4 if I have done harm to one
at peace with me
or have plundered[E]
my adversary without cause,
5 may an enemy pursue
and overtake me;
may he trample me
to the ground
and leave my honor
in the dust. *•Selah*
6 Rise up, Lord, in Your anger;
lift Yourself up
against the fury
of my adversaries;
awake for me;[F]
You have ordained[G]
a judgment.
7 Let the assembly of peoples
gather around You;
take Your seat[H] on high
over it.
8 The Lord judges the peoples;
vindicate me, Lord,
according to
my righteousness
and my integrity.[I]
9 Let the evil of the wicked
come to an end,
but establish the righteous.
The One who examines
the thoughts and emotions[J]
is a righteous God.
10 My shield is with[K] God,
who saves the upright
in heart.
11 God is a righteous judge
and a God who shows His
wrath every day.

12 If anyone does not repent,
God[L] will sharpen His sword;
He has strung[M] His bow
and made it ready.
13 He has prepared
His deadly weapons;
He tips His arrows with fire.

14 See, the wicked one is
pregnant with evil,
conceives trouble,
and gives birth to deceit.
15 He dug a pit and
hollowed it out
but fell into the hole
he had made.
16 His trouble comes back
on his own head,
and his violence falls
on the top of his head.

17 I will thank the Lord
for His righteousness;
I will sing about the name
of Yahweh the •Most High.

[A] **7:title** Perhaps a passionate song with rapid changes of rhythm, or a dirge [B] **7:title** LXX, Aq, Sym, Theod, Jer read *of the Cushite* [C] **7:2** Lit *he* [D] **7:2** Lit *ripping, and without a rescuer* [E] **7:4** Or *me and have spared* [F] **7:6** LXX reads *awake, Lord my God* [G] **7:6** Or *me; ordain* [H] **7:7** MT reads *and return* [I] **7:8** Lit *integrity on me* [J] **7:9** Lit *examines hearts and kidneys* [K] **7:10** Lit *on* [L] **7:12** Lit *He* [M] **7:12** Lit *bent*; that is, bent the bow to string it

>WORD|*study*

Ps 8:Superscription This first hymn of praise in the Psalter is identified as **on the** *Gittith* (Hb; cp. Pss 81 and 84). The precise meaning of this transliterated word is unknown. It likely refers to a musical instrument—possibly a zither—and may be associated with the Philistine city of Gath as the place where the instrument was produced, as the location of a special singing style, or as a musical setting. The LXX translates the word as "winepress, wine vat" (Gk *lēnōn*), associating the psalm with the vintage Festival of Booths.

8:3 David uses an uncommon expression to describe the **heavens** as **the work of Your** fingers (Hb *ʾetsbaʿ*), figuratively referring to skill (cp. 144:1; Ex 31:18) or to only a small part of the hand (Ex 8:19; Is 59:3), which is often used as a symbol of power, strength, and control (see Jb 12:9-10; Ps 10:12; 74:11; 89:13). With the same vocabulary, Scripture describes idolatry as people bowing "down to the work of their hands, to what their fingers have made" (Is 2:8-9), rather than worshiping the One who created them, as David does in this psalm.

Psalm 8
God's Glory, Man's Dignity

For the choir director:
on the •Gittith. *A Davidic psalm.*

1 •Yahweh, our Lord,
how magnificent
is Your name
throughout the earth!

You have covered the heavens
with Your majesty.[A]
2 Because of Your adversaries,
You have established
a stronghold[B]
from the mouths of children
and nursing infants
to silence the enemy
and the avenger.

3 When I observe Your heavens,
the work of Your fingers,
the moon and the stars,
which You set in place,
4 what is man
that You remember him,
the son of man that You look
after him?
5 You made him little less
than God[C,D]
and crowned him with glory
and honor.
6 You made him lord
over the works
of Your hands;
You put everything
under his feet:[E]
7 all the sheep and oxen,
as well as the animals
in the wild,
8 the birds of the sky,
and the fish of the sea
that pass through
the currents of the seas.

9 Yahweh, our Lord,
how magnificent
is Your name
throughout the earth!

MAN

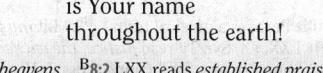

When David turns to consider man's place in creation (8:3-8), he also recalls the account of God's declaration that man "will rule the fish of the sea, the birds of the sky, the livestock, all the earth . . ." (Gn 1:26b): **You made him lord** (Hb *mashal*, "cause to rule or have dominion" v. 6). Having been granted dominion over the earth and its creatures, man has an exalted place in creation; but the honor and responsibility are gifts, not rights that man has acquired or taken for himself. The Lord had **made him little less than God** (Hb *ʾElohim*, v. 5), an expression that alludes to God's creating man in His image (see Gn 1:27-28). In a New Testament application of this passage to Jesus Christ in His humanity, the writer of Hebrews quotes Ps 8:4-6 from the Septuagint, which understands *ʾElohim* in the sense of "heavenly beings, members of the divine court" (cp. Ps 138:1): "You made him lower than the angels for a short time" (Heb 2:7; cp. Ps 97:7 and Heb 1:6). The Lord also **crowned** man **with glory** [Hb *kavod*; see **Word Study**, p. 688] **and honor** (Hb *hadar*, "adornment, majesty"; v. 5; cp. "splendor," 104:1). These two royal qualities are often ascribed to Yahweh as the divine King and appear together elsewhere only in Ps 145:12 ("glorious splendor"). Again, however, the psalm lauds the name of Yahweh as the one who has conferred such assets upon those created in His image (8:1,9).

There is an undeniable gap between the intended role of man in creation (v. 6b) and the reality of human experience after the Fall (Gn 3:17-19). However, the New Testament's use of this psalm points to the fulfillment of this role by the incarnate Christ in His suffering and death. God has indeed "put everything under His [Christ's] feet" (see 1Co 15:27; Eph 1:20-23; Heb 2:5-9). Therefore, this psalm is messianic in the sense that Jesus, as fully man and fully God, has realized God's expectation of human beings by perfect obedience and holiness.

8:2 In the Hebrew text, verse 2 has the unique phrase **from the mouths of children and nursing infants** (i.e., the youngest and most vulnerable human beings, who are completely dependent on those who care for them; cp. 1Sm 22:19; Lm 2:11). In these weakest of human vessels, God has **established** [Hb *yasad*, "found or lay foundation, appoint, ordain"; Gk (LXX) *katertisō*, "prepare; fit or frame for oneself"; cp. Heb 10:5] **a stronghold** [Hb *ʿoz*, "strength, might"; Gk (LXX) *ainon*, "praise"] **. . . to silence** (Hb *shavat*, "cause to cease, still, restrain"; cp. Ps 46:9) the one who threatens or actively opposes His purposes. Jesus quoted part of this verse from the Septuagint (LXX) in response to the religious leaders' indignation over His acceptance of praise from "the children shouting in the temple complex, '*Hosanna* to the Son of David!'" (Mt 21:15).

8:3-7 While the psalm's primary emphasis is on the excellence of God, secondary emphasis falls on the worth and dignity of men and women created in God's image. Considering God's **heavens** (cp. 19:1) and recognizing the Creator for setting **the moon and the stars . . . in place** (cp. Gn 1:16-17), David marvels at the contrast between the vast wonders of creation beyond man's control and the fact that God attends to man (cp. 144:3; Jb 7:17; Heb 2:6).

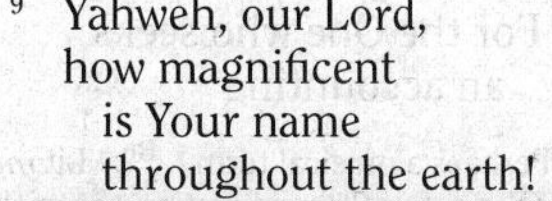

[A]**8:1** Lit *earth, which has set Your splendor upon the heavens* [B]**8:2** LXX reads *established praise*
[C]**8:5** LXX reads *angels* [D]**8:5** Or *gods*, or *a god*, or *heavenly beings*; lit *Elohim* [E]**8:6** Or *authority*

9:1–10:18 Psalms 9 and 10 are closely related in form, language, and subject matter. Psalm 9 bears a heading or superscription that evidently applies also to Psalm 10, and the two psalms appear as a single unit in the LXX. Furthermore, Ps 10 continues the acrostic device begun in Ps 9. Both psalms express confidence in God's victory over evil.

9:1-12 Celebrating the Lord's righteous judgments, the superscription of this psalm of thankful praise specifies that it should be sung or played **according to *Muth-labben*** (Hb, with sense of "death belonging to the son" or "death for the son"). Many scholars believe the designation refers to the tune to which the psalm was to be sung. Some view it as perhaps referring to female (soprano or treble) voices.

Yahweh is called **Most High** (Hb *'Elyon*, "Supreme"; cp. 7:17). Previously Abram called the Lord God "Most High" after receiving a blessing from Melchizedek (Gn 14:17-24). To **know** in Hebrew thought is a term of relationship, referring to personal, intimate knowledge (Ps 9:2,10). Those who have such knowledge of God's **name** (i.e., His character, the essence of who He is) can **trust** (Hb *batach*, "set hope and confidence upon; be secure, fearing nothing") Him **because** they have personally experienced His faithful presence **in times of trouble** (Hb *tsarah*, "distress, adversity, tribulation"; cp. 10:1; 20:1; Gn 35:3).

9:13-14 David prays to be rescued from **the gates** [Hb *sha'ar*, "entrance"; cp. 87:2; 100:4] **of death** in order to celebrate the Lord's victory **within the gates** [Hb *sha'ar*] **of Daughter Zion**, affectionately referring to Jerusalem, the city David had captured and made the capital of Israel (2Sm 5:6-9).

9:15-16 Declaring that **the Lord . . . has executed justice** on his enemies, David perceives the Lord's victory as an accomplished fact. The foolishness of inflicting harm on God's people is evident in the ways God turns the strategies of **the wicked** against them (cp. 10:2).

9:16-18 ***Higgaion*** (Hb, "meditation, striking of harp strings,") is a musical notation. Combined with ***Selah*** it may indicate that verses 17-18 should be sung in a meditative mood or with soft voices or accompaniment.

Psalm 9

Celebration of God's Justice

For the choir director:
according to Muth-labben.[A]
A Davidic psalm.

1 I will thank •Yahweh with all
my heart;
I will declare all
Your wonderful works.
2 I will rejoice and boast
about You;
I will sing about Your name,
•Most High.

3 When my enemies retreat,
they stumble and perish
before You.
4 For You have upheld
my just cause;[B]
You are seated on Your throne
as a righteous judge.
5 You have rebuked the nations:
You have destroyed
the wicked;
You have erased their name
forever and ever.
6 The enemy has come
to eternal ruin;
You have uprooted the cities,
and the very memory of them
has perished.

7 But the LORD sits enthroned
forever;
He has established His throne
for judgment.
8 He judges the world
with righteousness;
He executes judgment
on the nations
with fairness.
9 The LORD is a refuge
for the oppressed,
a refuge in times of trouble.
10 Those who know Your name
trust in You
because You have not
abandoned
those who seek You, Yahweh.

11 Sing to the LORD, who dwells
in •Zion;
proclaim His deeds
among the nations.
12 For the One who seeks
an accounting
for bloodshed
remembers them;
He does not forget the cry
of the afflicted.

13 Be gracious to me, LORD;
consider my affliction
at the hands of those
who hate me.
Lift me up from the gates
of death,
14 so that I may declare
all Your praises.
I will rejoice in Your salvation
within the gates
of Daughter Zion.

15 The nations have fallen
into the pit they made;
their foot is caught in the net
they have concealed.
16 The LORD has revealed
Himself;
He has executed justice,
striking down[C] the wicked[D]
by the work of their hands.
•Higgaion. •Selah

17 The wicked will return
to •Sheol—
all the nations that
forget God.
18 For the oppressed
will not always be forgotten;
the hope of the afflicted[E]
will not perish forever.

19 Rise up, LORD! Do not
let man prevail;
let the nations be judged
in Your presence.
20 Put terror in them, LORD;
let the nations know they are
only men. *Selah*

Psalm 10

1 LORD,[F,G] why do You stand
so far away?
Why do You hide in times
of trouble?
2 In arrogance the wicked
relentlessly pursue
the afflicted;
let them be caught
in the schemes
they have devised.

A**9:title** Perhaps a musical term B**9:4** Lit *my justice and my cause* C**9:16** Or *justice, snaring* D**9:16** LXX, Aq, Syr, Tg read *justice, the wicked is trapped* E**9:18** Alt Hb tradition reads *humble* F**10:1** Some Hb mss, LXX connect Pss 9–10. G**10:1** Together these 2 psalms form a partial •acrostic.

3 For the wicked one boasts
about his own cravings;
the one who is greedy curses[A]
and despises the LORD.
4 In all his scheming,
the wicked arrogantly thinks:[B]
"There is no accountability,
since God does not exist."
5 His ways are always secure;[C]
Your lofty judgments
are beyond his sight;
he scoffs at all his adversaries.
6 He says to himself, "I will
never be moved—
from generation to generation
without calamity."
7 Cursing, deceit, and violence
fill his mouth;
trouble and malice are
under his tongue.
8 He waits in ambush
near the villages;
he kills the innocent
in secret places.
His eyes are on the lookout
for the helpless;
9 he lurks in secret like a lion
in a thicket.
He lurks in order to seize
the afflicted;
he seizes the afflicted
and drags him in his net.
10 So he is oppressed
and beaten down;
the helpless fall because of
his strength.
11 He says to himself,
"God has forgotten;
He hides His face and will
never see."

12 Rise up, LORD God! Lift up
Your hand.
Do not forget the afflicted.
13 Why has the wicked person
despised God?
He says to himself,
"You will not demand
an account."
14 But You Yourself have seen
trouble and grief,
observing it in order to take
the matter into Your hands.
The helpless entrusts himself
to You;
You are a helper
of the fatherless.
15 Break the arm of the wicked
and evil person;
call his wickedness
into account
until nothing remains of it.[D]
16 The LORD is King forever
and ever;
the nations will perish
from His land.
17 LORD, You have heard
the desire of the humble;[E]
You will strengthen
their hearts.
You will listen carefully,
18 doing justice for the fatherless
and the oppressed
so that men of the earth
may terrify them no more.

Psalm 11

Refuge in the LORD

For the choir director. Davidic.

1 I have taken refuge
in the LORD.
How can you say to me,
"Escape to the mountain
like a bird![F]
2 For look, the wicked string
the bow;
they put the[G] arrow
on the bowstring
to shoot from the shadows
at the upright in heart.
3 When the foundations
are destroyed,
what can the righteous do?"

4 The LORD is in
His holy temple;
the LORD's throne is
in heaven.
His eyes watch;
He examines[H] •everyone.
5 The LORD examines
the righteous
and the wicked.
He hates the lover of violence.
6 He will rain burning coals[I]
and sulfur on the wicked;
a scorching wind will be
their portion.[J]

10:1-18 This psalm begins by questioning the Lord's absence in **times of trouble** (Hb *tsarah*, "distress"; cp. 9:9) but ends on a positive note of assurance in recognition that the LORD is King and always will be. He uses His power and authority on behalf of those who know they need Him. In contrast, those who are **wicked** foolishly act as though they can do whatever they want without having to answer to God (vv. 4,11,13,15).

11:1-7 David was facing serious danger and had received counsel to flee from the destructive power of his enemies, but he rejected that advice. Instead, he found **refuge** in the righteous Lord whom he trusted. Interestingly, David has already answered for himself (v. 1) the question he raises (v. 3). When the very **foundations** of life **are destroyed** (Hb *haras*, "are broken down," v. 3), those in right relationship with God can find refuge in Him. David believed in the ultimate defeat of his enemies because of the **righteous** nature of the Lord, who loves those who practice righteousness (i.e., those who make the right choices and display the right attitudes in life).

[A] **10:3** Or *he blesses the greedy* [B] **10:4** Lit *wicked according to the height of his nose* [C] **10:5** Or *prosperous* [D] **10:15** Lit *account You do not find* [E] **10:17** Some Hb mss, LXX, Syr read *afflicted* [F] **11:1** Lit *to your mountain, bird* [G] **11:2** Lit *their* [H] **11:4** Lit *His eyelids examine* [I] **11:6** Sym; MT reads *rain snares, fire* [J] **11:6** Lit *be the portion of their cup*

12:Superscription Regarding the term ***Sheminith***, see **Word Study**, p. 670.

12:1-8 The poet's cry for **help** (Hb *yasha'*, "cause to deliver" from the verb root for "salvation"; see **Word Study**, p. 672) is a cry for salvation or deliverance when he feels all alone in his combat against evil, when all **faithful** or **loyal** people seem to have **disappeared** [Hb *pasas*, "cease, fail, leave off"] **from the human race** (Hb *bēn 'adam*, lit "sons of men"). A central issue in the psalm is the contrast between the speech of **the wicked** (Hb *rasha'*, "unrighteous") and the **pure** [Hb *tahor*, "clean" as opposed to filthy or immoral; "unmixed, unalloyed" like purified gold] **words** of the Lord (cp. Jr 5:1-5; Mc 7:2).

13:1-6 The question **How long . . . ?** (Hb *'ad-'anah*, "until when")—repeated four times in the first two verses—echoes throughout the book of Psalms (e.g., 4:2; 6:3; 35:17; 79:5; 89:46). It implies the speaker's belief that the Lord can and will bring change, eventually, in the circumstances or conditions being endured with difficulty. Here, David complained of mental **agony** (Hb *yagon*, "sorrow, anguish"), fearing that his **foes** were gaining strength and, if not cut short, soon would be flaunting their victory over him. As long as his adversaries were growing more powerful, the Lord seemed to be withholding His favor. David longed for Yahweh to cease hiding His face or His presence from him. To experience the Lord's presence would be to experience wholeness and **deliverance** (Hb *yeshu'ah*, "help, salvation"; see **Word Study**, p. 878); not to experience the Lord's presence would be to **sleep in death**.

Having voiced his prayer, David confidently asserted his trust in the Lord's **faithful love**—choosing the perspective of faith and depending on God's unshakable commitment to His people (cp. 1Pt 2:10), and delighting in the certainty of His salvation. The resolve to **sing to the Lord** did not

7 For the LORD is righteous;
He loves righteous deeds.
The upright will see His face.

Psalm 12
Oppression by the Wicked

For the choir director:
according to •Sheminith.
A Davidic psalm.

1 Help, LORD, for no
faithful one remains;
the loyal have disappeared
from the •human race.
2 They lie to one another;
they speak with flattering lips
and deceptive hearts.
3 May the LORD cut off
all flattering lips
and the tongue
that speaks boastfully.
4 They say, "Through
our tongues
we have power;[A]
our lips are our own—
who can be our master?"

5 "Because of the oppression
of the afflicted
and the groaning of the poor,
I will now rise up,"
says the LORD.
"I will put the one
who longs for it
in a safe place."

6 The words of the LORD
are pure words,
like silver refined
in an earthen furnace,
purified seven times.
7 You, LORD, will guard us;[B]
You will protect us[C]
from this generation
forever.
8 The wicked wander[D]
everywhere,
and what is
worthless is exalted
by the human race.

Psalm 13
A Plea for Deliverance

For the choir director. A Davidic psalm.

1 LORD, how long will You
forget me?
Forever?
How long will You hide
Your face from me?
2 How long will I store up
anxious concerns[E]
within me,
agony in my mind every day?
How long will my enemy
dominate me?

3 Consider me and answer,
LORD my God.
Restore brightness
to my eyes;
otherwise, I will sleep
in death.
4 My enemy will say,
"I have triumphed
over him,"
and my foes will rejoice
because I am shaken.

5 But I have trusted in
Your faithful love;
my heart will rejoice in
Your deliverance.
6 I will sing to the LORD

[A]**12:4** Lit *That say, "By our tongues we are strengthened* [B]**12:7** Some Hb mss, LXX, Jer; other Hb mss read *them* [C]**12:7** Some Hb mss, LXX; other Hb mss read *him* [D]**12:8** Lit *walk about* [E]**13:2** Or *up counsels*

>WORD | *study*

12:5 Groaning (Hb *'anaqah*, "audible crying, moaning, or nonverbal expression of suffering") appears only here and three other times in the Old Testament. In Ps 79:11 and 102:20, God hears the "groans" of "prisoners." Here, the poor (Hb *'evyon*, "those who are needy or undergoing undeserved suffering; the oppressed"; cp. 9:18; 35:10; 40:17; Dt 15:7,9; 24:14) are the ones to whose "groaning" Yahweh responds (cp. Is 33:10).

14:1 Fool (Hb *naval*, "senseless, stupid; wicked"; cp. 1Sm 25:3,25) is better understood as lacking spiritual discernment rather than being bereft of intelligence. In Scripture, a "fool" is one who appears unable to make what should be the obvious best choices. To be foolish is the opposite of being wise (cp. Ps 111:10). The opposite of folly or foolishness in the Old Testament is not intelligence but rather steadfast devotion to the Lord. Paul's use of Ps 14 in Rm 3:10-18 emphasizes that all are foolish who choose to separate themselves from the wisdom of God found in the gospel of Christ.

15:5 The last line of the psalm affirms that the one who **can dwell in** [Yahweh's] **tent** (v. 1) is a person who will never be moved (Hb *mot*, "be shaken, totter, topple, fall over"). Only the "righteous will never be shaken" (Hb *mot*, Pr 10:30; cp. Ps 55:22; 112:6), so the wicked deceive themselves when they claim that they "will never be moved" (10:6). The stability and confidence conveyed by this expression are clearly dependent on "trust in the LORD" (see 125:1). Elsewhere, the psalmist declares that he "will not be shaken" because:

- Yahweh is "at [His] right hand" (16:8);
- Yahweh "will never allow" it (55:22);
- Yahweh "alone is [His] rock, salvation, [and] stronghold" (62:2,6).

because He has treated
me generously.

Psalm 14
A Portrait of Sinners

For the choir director. Davidic.

1 The fool says in his heart,
"God does not exist."
They are corrupt; they do
vile deeds.
There is no one
who does good.
2 The LORD looks
down from heaven
on the •human race
to see if there is one
who is wise,
one who seeks God.
3 All have turned away;
all alike have become corrupt.
There is no
one who does good,
not even one.[A]
4 Will evildoers never
understand?
They consume My people
as they consume bread;
they do not call on the LORD.

5 Then[B] they will be filled
with terror,
for God is with those
who are[C] righteous.
6 You sinners frustrate
the plans of the afflicted,
but the LORD is his refuge.
7 Oh, that Israel's deliverance
would come from •Zion!
When the LORD restores the
fortunes of His people,[D]
Jacob will rejoice;
Israel will be glad.[E]

Psalm 15
A Description of the Godly

A Davidic psalm.

1 LORD, who can dwell
in Your tent?
Who can live on
Your holy mountain?
2 The one who lives honestly,
practices righteousness,
and acknowledges the truth
in his heart—
3 who does not slander
with his tongue,
who does not harm his friend
or discredit his neighbor,
4 who despises the one rejected
by the LORD[F]
but honors those who •fear
the LORD,
who keeps his word
whatever the cost,
5 who does not lend his money
at interest
or take a bribe
against the innocent—
the one who does these things
will never be moved.

Psalm 16
Confidence in the LORD

A Davidic •Miktam.

1 Protect me, God, for I take
refuge in You.
2 I[G] said to •Yahweh, "You are
my Lord;
I have nothing good besides
You."[H]
3 As for the holy people who are
in the land,
they are the noble ones.
All my delight is in them.
4 The sorrows of those who
take another god
for themselves will multiply;
I will not pour out
their •drink offerings
of blood,
and I will not speak
their names with my lips.

5 LORD, You are my portion[I]
and my cup of blessing;
You hold my future.
6 The boundary lines
have fallen for me
in pleasant places;
indeed, I have
a beautiful inheritance.

constitute a denial of the obstacles and dangers David faced but reflected his focus on the unchanging character of God, who had already been good to him.

14:1-7 Psalms 14 and 53 appear substantially the same.

14:1 The fool denies the existence of God. Some persons who never verbally deny the existence of God are nevertheless practical atheists. These individuals conduct their lives as though God did not exist. Fools ignore the reality of their accountability to God and the inevitability of divine judgment. See **Word Study**, p. 676

15:1-5 This psalm deals with requirements or preparation for true worship, for experiencing fellowship with God. The Lord's **tent** (Hb *ʾohel*, "tabernacle, dwelling place, house") and **holy mountain** refer to the designated place of worship in Jerusalem or Mount Zion (cp. 2:6; 99:9; Is 56:7). Those given permission to **dwell** (Hb *gur*, "tarry, sojourn, be a house guest, lodge with," i.e., have the protection and care of the master of the household; cp. Jb 19:15; Ps 61:4) "under God's roof" or **live** (Hb *shakan*, "settle down, encamp, abide, dwell"; cp. 65:4) in His holy presence must avoid evil and seek good (cp. 5:4). Therefore, David answers his question with both positive and negative statements.

16:1-6 This psalm is designated as a ***Miktam*** (see **Word Study**, p. 679). This prayer for preservation reflects David's faith as he asks God to **protect** (Hb *shamar*, "keep safe, watch over, guard"; cp. 1Sm 26:15-16) him (i.e., to do what is naturally expected of one's source of **refuge**). David contrasts his singular devotion to Yahweh with the multiplied **sorrows of those who take another** or, as he implies, who worship a plurality of other gods.

[A] **14:3** Some Hb mss, some LXX mss add the material found in Rm 3:13-18. [B] **14:5** Or *There* [C] **14:5** Lit *with the generation of the* [D] **14:7** Or *restores His captive people* [E] **14:7** Or *let Jacob rejoice; let Israel be glad.* [F] **15:4** Lit *in his eyes the rejected is despised* [G] **16:2** Some Hb mss, LXX, Syr, Jer; other Hb mss read *You* [H] **16:2** Or *"Lord, my good; there is none besides You."* [I] **16:5** Or *allotted portion*

>WORD|*study*

16:5-6 A cluster of images seem to intensify the picture of David's devotion to exclusive worship of Yahweh. Two Hebrew words are translated as portion (Hb *manah-chêleq*, "part of my inheritance, allotted portion, lot"). By itself, *manah* (Hb, "part, lot") usually denotes a worshiper's "portion" of meat (Ex 29:26; Lv 7:33; 8:29; 1Sm 1:4-5; cp. 1Sm 9:23) or the gift of "portions" of food (Neh 8:10-12; Est 9;19,22). Sometimes *chêleq* (Hb, "portion, part, lot") also designates part of an offering to be eaten by the priest (Lv 6:17) but is used more frequently as a synonym for inheritance (Hb *nachalah*, "lot, possession"; see Gn 31:14; Jos 18:7). The Levites were distinguished from the other tribes of Israel in that their priesthood and the Lord Himself, rather than an allotment of land, would be their "portion" and "inheritance" (Nm 18:20; Dt 18:1; 32:9).

Having declared his refusal to participate in pagan rituals with "drink offerings of blood" (Ps 16:4; cp. Dt 32:37-39), David claims Yahweh as his **portion** and **cup** (Hb, *kos*, figuratively here, one's "lot"; cp. 23:5; 116:13). He also declares of the Lord, "**You hold** (Hb *tamak*, "uphold, hold on to, support, sustain, maintain"—an active participle signifying continuous action; cp. 41:12; Is 41:10) my future (Hb *goral*, "what falls to one by lot," especially part of an "inheritance"; cp. Nm 33:54). Boundary lines (Hb *chêvel*, "cord, rope, measuring line," Ps 16:6) marked off a field given by "lot"—an "inheritance" (e.g., Jos 17:5,14; cp. Dt 32:9). Having entrusted himself fully to the Lord, David gladly accepted God's parameters for enjoying His benefits, some of which are recounted in the rest of the psalm.

16:7-11 Because David continually focused on the Lord, David knew he could not be **shaken** (Hb *mot*, see **Word Study**, p. 676) and would not be left in **Sheol,** the dwelling place of the dead. The New Testament apostles realized even more was being said: Jesus, God's **Faithful One** *par excellence*, would be raised miraculously from the grave (v. 10; cp. Ac 2:27; 13:35; cp. Jb 33:18-30).

17:1-15 This psalm is the first in the book to be identified as a **prayer** (Hb *tephillah*; see **Word Study**, p. 679.) David petitioned God in language echoing that of the songs of Moses celebrating Israel's deliverance from Egypt and preparing for their entrance into the promised land (cp. Ex 15:11-13; Dt 32:1-43):

- David appealed to the Lord for **vindication** (Hb *mishpat*, "judgment, the sentence given by a judge," Ps 17:2) and for divine intervention—to **save** him **from the wicked** with His **sword** (Hb *cherev*, v. 13) and His **hand** (Hb *yad*, v. 14), signifying His power. The vocabulary echoes Dt 32:41—"When I sharpen My flashing sword (Hb *cherev*), and My hand (Hb *yad*) takes hold of judgment (Hb *mishpat*), I will . . . repay those who hate Me."
- Moses extolled God for "performing wonders" (Hb *pele'*, "something wonderful or distinguished," Ex 15:11) on Israel's behalf and noted that God would lead them with His "faithful love" (Hb *chesed*, Ex 15:13). In Ps 17:7, David invites the same God to **display the wonders** (Hb *palah*, "be distinguished or wonderful") of His **faithful love.** See **Word Study**, p. 322.
- David calls God **Savior** (Hb *yasha'*, "one who saves", v. 7), linking the song in Ex 15 to its narrative context: "That day the Lord saved [Hb *yasha'*, "save, deliver, give victory to, set free, liberate"; cp. Ex 2:17] Israel . . ." (Ex 14:30).
- The psalm recognizes God as the One who saves **all who seek refuge** [Hb *chasah*, "flee to a place or person for protection"; cp. 2:12; 5:11; 7:1; 11:1; 16:1; 18:2,30] **from those who rebel against**

7 I will praise the Lord
who counsels me—
even at night my conscience
instructs me.
8 I keep the Lord
in mind[A] always.
Because He is
at my right hand,
I will not be shaken.

9 Therefore my heart is glad
and my spirit rejoices;
my body also rests securely.
10 For You will not abandon me
to •Sheol;
You will not allow
Your Faithful One
to see decay.
11 You reveal the path of life
to me;
in Your presence is
abundant joy;
in Your right hand are
eternal pleasures.

Psalm 17

A Prayer for Protection

A Davidic prayer.

1 Lord, hear a just cause;
pay attention to my cry;
listen to my prayer—
from lips free of deceit.
2 Let my vindication come
from You,
for You see what is right.
3 You have tested my heart;
You have examined me
at night.
You have tried me and found
nothing evil;
I have determined that
my mouth will not sin.[B]

4 Concerning what people do:
by the word of Your lips[C]
I have avoided the ways
of the violent.
5 My steps are on Your paths;
my feet have not slipped.

6 I call on You, God,
because You will answer me;
listen closely to me;
hear what I say.
7 Display the wonders
of Your faithful love,
Savior of all who seek refuge
from those who rebel
against Your right hand.[D]
8 Protect me as the pupil
of Your eye;
hide me in the shadow
of Your wings
9 from[E] the wicked
who treat me violently,[F]
my deadly enemies
who surround me.

10 They have become hardened;[G]
their mouths speak arrogantly.
11 They advance against me;[H]
now they surround me.
They are determined[I]
to throw me to the ground.
12 They are[J] like a lion
eager to tear,
like a young lion lurking
in ambush.

13 Rise up, Lord!
Confront him;
bring him down.
With Your sword, save me
from the wicked.
14 With Your hand, Lord,
save me from men,
from men of the world

[A]16:8 Lit *front of me* [B]17:3 Or *evil; my mouth will not sin* [C]17:4 God's instruction [D]17:7 Or *love, You who save with Your right hand those seeking refuge from adversaries* [E]17:9 Lit *from the presence of* [F]17:9 Or *who plunder me* [G]17:10 Lit *have closed up their fat* [H]17:11 Vg; one Hb ms, LXX read *They cast me out*; MT reads *Our steps* [I]17:11 Lit *They set their eyes* [J]17:12 Lit *He is*

whose portion is in this life:
You fill their bellies with what
You have in store;
their sons are satisfied,
and they leave their surplus
to their children.
15 But I will see Your face
in righteousness;
when I awake,
I will be satisfied
with Your presence.[A]

Psalm 18

Praise for Deliverance

For the choir director. Of the servant of the LORD, David, who spoke the words of this song to the LORD on the day the LORD rescued him from the hand of all his enemies and from the hand of Saul. He said:

1 I love You, LORD, my strength.
2 The LORD is my rock,
my fortress, and my deliverer,
my God, my mountain
where I seek refuge,
my shield and the •horn
of my salvation,
my stronghold.
3 I called to the LORD, who is
worthy of praise,
and I was saved
from my enemies.
4 The ropes of death
were wrapped around me;
the torrents of destruction
terrified me.
5 The ropes of •Sheol
entangled me;
the snares of death
confronted me.
6 I called to the LORD
in my distress,
and I cried to my God
for help.
From His temple He heard
my voice,
and my cry to Him
reached His ears.
7 Then the earth shook
and quaked;
the foundations
of the mountains trembled;
they shook
because He burned
with anger.
8 Smoke rose from His nostrils,

[A]**17:15** Lit *form*

Your right hand (Hb *yamin*, 17:7; cp. 16:8,11; 18:35; 20:6; 21:8). Three times the Exodus song attributes Yahweh's deliverance to His "right hand" (Hb *yamin*, Ex 15:6,12), a metaphor signifying God's matchless power, especially when used to rescue His people. In Moses' song "refuge" (Hb *chasah*) is found only in Yahweh and "no one can rescue anyone from . . . [His] hand" (Dt 32:37-39). To "rebel against" God's "right hand," therefore, is futile (Ps 17:7).

- David prays, **Protect** [Hb *shamar*; see 16:1] **me as the pupil** [Hb *ʾishon bat*, "pupil"; lit "little daughter"] **of Your eye; hide me in the shadow of Your wings** (Ps 17:8; cp. 36:7; 57:1; 61:4; 63:7). In Moses' song the Lord had "guarded" (Hb *natsar*, "watch over, keep") His people "as the pupil [Hb *ʾishon*] of His eye" and as an eagle hiding eaglets in the shadow of its wings (Ex 19:4). The imagery also recalls the way the ark of the covenant—with the wings of the cherubim spread over the mercy seat (Ex 25:20)—served as a symbol of God's presence and protection. Just as the Lord showed His power against Egypt, so David confidently expected deliverance from his tormentors.

18:1-2 This hymn of gratitude to God for deliverance appears in a similar form

>WORD|*study*

Ps 18:title Biblical terms for the psalms underscore the fact that most are sacred songs or hymns. The word **song** (Hb *shir*, "vocal music"; e.g. 33:3; 40:3) usually suggests that the poetic text was sung (i.e., set to music)—see also the titles for Pss 30, 46, 65, 66, 67, and 68. Sometimes a particular genre or occasion determines its identification:

- "a dedication song" (Hb *shir-chanukkah*, superscription for Ps 30);
- "a love song" (Hb *shir-yedidot*, superscription for Ps 45);
- "a song of ascents" (Hb *shir-ha-maʿalot*, superscriptions for Pss 120–134);
- "a song for the Sabbath day" (Hb *shir le-yom ha-shavvat*, Ps 92);
- "the songs of Zion" (Hb *shir sion*, Ps 137:3).

Other words for this genre include:

- "Psalm" (Hb *mizmor*, "song, poem, or melody," suggesting accompaniment by a stringed instrument), which frequently appears in the superscriptions (e.g., Pss 3, 30, 49). Some psalms are designated as both "song" (Hb *shir*) and "psalm" (Pss 30, 48, 65, 66, 67, 68, 75, 76, 83, 87, 88, 92, 108), indicating the possibility that these terms prompted a technical or specialized understanding.
- "Prayer" (Hb *tephillah*; "entreaty, supplication," superscriptions for Pss 17, 86, 90, 102, and 142; also see 55:1; 61:1; 72:20; 143:1; cp. 4:1; 6:9; 2 Sm 7:27; 1 Kg 9:3-4).
- "Song" (Hb *zamir*, "hymn, song of praise or triumph," Ps 95:2; 119:54).
- "*Maskil*" (Hb, "contemplative song or poem," probably the participle form of *sakal*, "be or become prudent or understanding; attend to"; cp. "song of instruction" [Hb *maskil*, see textual note for Ps 47:7] appears in the superscriptions of 13 psalms: Pss 32, 42, 44, 45, 52, 53, 54, 55, 74, 78, 88, 89, 142).
- "*Miktam*" (Hb) appears only in the superscriptions for Pss 16, 56, 57, 58, 59, and 60 to introduce a song or "poem" written by Hezekiah. Suggested interpretations include a musical notation or a psalm dealing with the expiation of sin.
- "*Shiggaion*" (Hb, a transliterated word of uncertain meaning; superscription for Ps 7)—if the verbal root is *shagah* (Hb, "go astray, wander, reel"), the term may suggest that the music should have a wandering melody. Some connect it with a thought pattern reflective of laments (cp. Hab 3:1). Others conclude that the word is derived from *shagah* (Hb "joy, sweetness").

18:1 David declares his **love** (Hb *racham*, "cherish, dearly love") for the Lord with a word indicating intimate relationship. *Racham* is associated closely with the Hebrew word for "womb" (*rechem*) and suggests the tender compassion of a mother toward her child or the close relationship enjoyed by siblings born from the same womb. The term expresses the psalmist's close fellowship with God.

18:18 Support (Hb *mishʿen*, "provision, supply, security") is derived from the verb *shaʿan*, meaning "depend, rely, or lean on; trust in." The noun is used only in this psalm (18:18; 2Sm 22:19) and three times in Is 3:1. In contrast to David's recognition that the Lord was his "support," Isaiah prophesied that the Lord would remove from Judah "every kind of security" (Is 3:1)—including "the entire supply" of basic necessities—i.e., everything on which the people relied when they were defying Him (Is 3:8-9).

in 2Sm 22 (also the historical setting indicated by the superscription).

David speaks from a personal point of view, exalting the Lord with a series of direct comparisons and presenting God as the **strength** (Hb *chēzeq*, occurs in Scripture only here in this noun form; from the verb *chazaq*, "hold fast, be firm or strong"; "be courageous," 27:14) and the **stronghold** (Hb *misgav*, "height; lofty place of shelter and security"; cp. 46:7,11; 48:3; 59:9,17; "refuge," 9:9; 94:22) upon which he fully relies. All but one noun in the series is marked by the personal possessive pronoun **my**. David's central affirmation that Yahweh is *his* **God** (Hb *ʾēl*) is preceded and followed by a group of three metaphors illustrating what David means by calling the Lord his "strength" and "stronghold." David piles image upon image to describe God as his protector:

- **rock** (Hb *selaʿ*, also "cliff, crag"), affording both protection from enemies (1Sm 13:6; Ob 1:3) and shade from the desert sun (Is 32:2);
- **fortress** (Hb *matsud*, "stronghold"; cp. 1Sm 22:4; 2Sm 5:7,9,17; Ps 31:3; 71:3; 91:2; Is 33:16);
- **deliverer** (Hb *palat*, "one who causes to escape from danger or rescues," cp. 40:17; 70:5);
- **mountain** (Hb *tsur*, "rock"; cp. 18:31,46; 19:14; 28:1; 31:2; 62:6-7; 78:35; 89:26; 94:22; 95:1; 144:1; Dt 32:4,15,18,30-31,37), a symbol of strength and protection—often a place of **refuge** (see 7:1) in a location high above and inaccessible to one's enemies;
- **shield** (Hb *magēn*, a defensive weapon; cp. 18:30; from the verb root *magan*, "cover, protect"; cp. 3:3; 144:2; see Gn 15:1)—a round shield or buckler smaller than the shield covering the body;
- **horn of my salvation**, a phrase used only in this psalm, 2Sm 22:3, and Lk 1:69.

18:4-19 David then portrays his experience of the Lord's deliverance with vivid storm imagery. Yahweh **heard** David's anguished cry, which was issued from the depths of **Sheol**, and dramatically rescued His servant. David also uses anthropomorphisms that depict God's advancing like a warrior more terrible than any human military commander.

- **He parted** [Hb *natah*, "bow, bend, turn aside"; cp. 144:5; cp. "leave," Is 30:11] **the heavens**—nothing could impede His coming (Ps 18:9).
- **He rode on a cherub** (transliteration of the Hb word for a supernatural being usually associated with God's throne, v. 10)—swiftly through the air and out of reach—rather than on a horse on the ground.

and consuming fire came
from His mouth;
coals were set ablaze by it.[A]
9 He parted the heavens
and came down,
a dark cloud beneath His feet.
10 He rode on a cherub and flew,
soaring on the wings
of the wind.
11 He made darkness
His hiding place,
dark storm clouds His canopy
around Him.
12 From the radiance
of His presence,
His clouds swept onward
with hail and blazing coals.
13 The LORD thundered
from[B] heaven;
the •Most High projected
His voice.[C]
14 He shot His arrows
and scattered them;
He hurled[D] lightning bolts
and routed them.
15 The depths of the sea
became visible,
the foundations of the world
were exposed,
at Your rebuke, LORD,
at the blast of the breath
of Your nostrils.

16 He reached down from heaven
and took hold of me;
He pulled me out of
deep waters.
17 He rescued me
from my powerful enemy
and from those who hated me,
for they were too strong
for me.
18 They confronted me in the day
of my distress,
but the LORD was my support.
19 He brought me out
to a spacious place;
He rescued me
because He delighted in me.

20 The LORD rewarded me
according to
my righteousness;
He repaid me
according to the cleanness
of my hands.
21 For I have kept the ways
of the LORD
and have not turned
from my God to wickedness.
22 Indeed, I have kept all
His ordinances in mind[E]
and have not disregarded
His statutes.
23 I was blameless toward Him
and kept myself from sinning.
24 So the LORD repaid me
according to
my righteousness,
according to the cleanness
of my hands in His sight.

25 With the faithful
You prove Yourself faithful;
with the blameless man
You prove Yourself blameless;
26 with the pure
You prove Yourself pure,
but with the crooked
You prove Yourself shrewd.
27 For You rescue
an afflicted people,
but You humble those
with haughty eyes.
28 LORD, You light my lamp;
my God illuminates
my darkness.
29 With You I can attack
a barrier,[F]
and with my God
I can leap over a wall.
30 God—His way is perfect;
the word of the LORD is pure.
He is a shield to all
who take refuge in Him.
31 For who is God
besides •Yahweh?
And who is a rock?
Only our God.
32 God—He clothes me
with strength
and makes my way perfect.
33 He makes my feet like the feet
of a deer
and sets me securely
on the heights.[G]
34 He trains my hands for war;
my arms can bend a bow
of bronze.
35 You have given me the shield
of Your salvation;

A**18:8** Or *ablaze from Him* B**18:13** Some Hb mss, LXX, Tg, Jer; other Hb mss read *in* C**18:13** Some Hb mss read *voice, with hail and fiery coals* D**18:14** Or *multiplied* E**18:22** Lit *Indeed, all His ordinances have been in front of me* F**18:29** Or *ridge* G**18:33** Or *on my high places*

Your right hand upholds me,
and Your humility exalts me.
36 You widen a place beneath me
for my steps,
and my ankles do not give way.

37 I pursue my enemies
and overtake them;
I do not turn back
until they are wiped out.
38 I crush them, and they cannot
get up;
they fall beneath my feet.
39 You have clothed me
with strength for battle;
You subdue my adversaries
beneath me.
40 You have made my enemies
retreat before me;[A]
I annihilate those
who hate me.
41 They cry for help, but there is
no one to save them—
they cry to the LORD,
but He does not
answer them.
42 I pulverize them like dust
before the wind;
I trample them[B] like mud
in the streets.

43 You have freed me
from the feuds
among the people;
You have appointed me
the head of nations;
a people I had not known
serve me.
44 Foreigners submit to me
grudgingly;
as soon as they hear,[C]
they obey me.
45 Foreigners lose heart
and come trembling
from their fortifications.

46 The LORD lives—may my rock
be praised!
The God of my salvation
is exalted.
47 God—He gives me vengeance
and subdues peoples
under me.
48 He frees me from my enemies.
You exalt me
above my adversaries;
You rescue me
from violent men.
49 Therefore I will praise You,
Yahweh, among the nations;
I will sing about Your name.
50 He gives great victories
to His king;
He shows loyalty
to His anointed,
to David
and his descendants forever.

Doctrine REVELATION

Psalm 19 celebrates the Lord's revelation of Himself through His works and His Word. The heavens **declare** (Hb *saphar*, "recount, speak or tell") God's **glory**—His majesty, revealed in the beauty of His creation for all to see. The wonders of creation should lead one to worship the Creator, not the creation itself (cp. Rm 1:19-20). Because this evidence of God's existence and sovereignty is universally available (cp. Rm 1:18-21) while Scripture is not, theologians typically distinguish between the created order as "general revelation" and the written Word of God as "special revelation," which this psalm also praises in verses 7-11.

Psalm 19

The Witness of Creation and Scripture

For the choir director. A Davidic psalm.

1 The heavens declare the glory
of God,
and the sky[D] proclaims
the work of His hands.
2 Day after day
they pour out speech;
night after night they
communicate knowledge.[E]
3 There is no speech; there are
no words;
their voice is not heard.
4 Their message[F] has gone out
to all the earth,
and their words to the ends
of the world.

In the heavens[G]
He has pitched a tent
for the sun.
5 It is like a groom
coming from
the[H] bridal chamber;

- The position of God's tent on the "battlefield"—and **the radiance of His presence**—are hidden from view by **dark storm clouds** (vv. 11-12).
- **Clouds . . . with hail and blazing coals** constitute the initial wave of "troops," followed by the Lord's thunderous warnings **from heaven** (v. 13).
- God attacks, putting His enemies to flight and destroying them like a mighty army of archers overwhelming opponents with a barrage of flaming **arrows** (v. 14).
- Everything gives way to Yahweh's **rebuke** (Hb *ge'arah*, "reproof," v. 15; cp. 76:6; 104:7; Is 50:2; 66:15) as He pulls His child out of danger and leads him to **a spacious place** (Hb *merchav*, "broad place," Ps 18:19; cp. 31:8; 118:5)—a picture of freedom and release.

18:20-24 David's affirmation that the Lord **rewarded** him because of his **righteousness** (Hb *tsedeq*, "moral rectitude; straightness or rightness in an ethical sense," v. 20) reflects an understanding that his confrontation with death (vv. 4-5) was not evidence of divine judgment but was an occasion on which God proved His commitment to deliver those who obey Him (vv. 20-24).

18:25-50 God's way is blameless or complete—the way of integrity, of soundness, of wholeness. God is utterly reliable. The psalmist has found the Lord trustworthy. God functions as a shield of protection for those who take refuge in Him (see 3:3; cp. Pr 30:5.) The psalm ends on a note of resounding praise to the Lord, who gives His faithful servant victory.

19:1-4 See **Doctrine**: "Revelation," this page.

[A]**18:40** Or *You gave me the necks of my enemies* [B]**18:42** Some Hb mss, LXX, Syr, Tg; other Hb mss read *I poured them out* [C]**18:44** Lit *At the hearing of the ear* [D]**19:1** Or *expanse* [E]**19:2** Or *Day to day pours out speech, and night to night communicates knowledge* [F]**19:4** LXX, Sym, Syr, Vg; MT reads *line* [G]**19:4** Lit *In them* [H]**19:5** Lit *his*

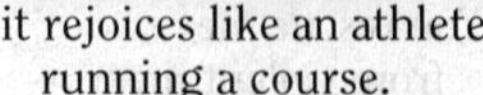

19:6-13 As the beauty and majesty of creation proclaim God's glory, so do God's people when they are doing and being that for which they were created. The psalm not only lauds the Lord's **instruction** [Hb *torah*, "doctrine or teaching, law"], **testimony, precepts, command**, and **ordinances** but also presents the benefits of living God's way—renewed life, growth in wisdom, gladness of heart, understanding, warning, and **great reward**. Having noted that **nothing is hidden** from the sun's heat, the psalmist recognizes the need for cleansing from **hidden** [Hb *satar*, "secret, concealed"] **faults** as well as **sins** both **unintentional** and **willful** (Hb *zēd*, "proud, arrogant").

20:1-9 The theme of this psalm is the need of **the king** for the assurance of God's presence (v. 9). The prayer—which includes a plea for safety, power, and victory—may have been voiced at a time when the king was preparing for battle. The Lord's **anointed** refers to the king (v. 6). Israel's kings were to rely on the Lord rather than on military might. The Lord is faithful to help the one He designates (anoints) for a task.

it rejoices like an athlete
running a course.
6 It rises from one end
of the heavens
and circles[A]
to their other end;
nothing is hidden
from its heat.

7 The instruction of the LORD
is perfect,
renewing one's life;
the •testimony of the LORD
is trustworthy,
making the inexperienced
wise.
8 The precepts of the LORD
are right,
making the heart glad;
the command of the LORD
is radiant,
making the eyes light up.
9 The •fear of the LORD is pure,
enduring forever;
the ordinances of the LORD
are reliable
and altogether righteous.
10 They are more desirable
than gold—
than an abundance
of pure gold;
and sweeter than honey,
which comes
from the honeycomb.
11 In addition, Your servant
is warned by them;
there is great reward
in keeping them.

12 Who perceives
his unintentional sins?
Cleanse me
from my hidden faults.
13 Moreover, keep Your servant
from willful sins;
do not let them rule over me.
Then I will be innocent
and cleansed
from blatant rebellion.
14 May the words of my mouth
and the meditation
of my heart
be acceptable to You,
LORD, my rock
and my Redeemer.

Psalm 20

Deliverance in Battle

For the choir director. A Davidic psalm.

1 May •Yahweh answer you
in a day of trouble;
may the name of Jacob's God
protect you.
2 May He send you help
from the sanctuary
and sustain you from •Zion.
3 May He remember
all your offerings
and accept
your •burnt offering. •*Selah*
4 May He give you what
your heart desires
and fulfill
your whole purpose.
5 Let us shout for joy
at your victory
and lift the banner
in the name of our God.
May Yahweh fulfill
all your requests.

6 Now I know that
the LORD gives victory
to His anointed;
He will answer him
from His holy heaven
with mighty victories
from[B] His right hand.
7 Some take pride in chariots,
and others in horses,

[A]19:6 Lit *its circuit is* [B]20:6 Some Hb mss, Aq, Sym, Jer, Syr read *with the victorious might of*

>WORD|*study*

19:14 Redeemer (Hb *goʾēl*) identified the nearest of kin who was to assume certain duties when a man died (see Ru 2:18-23). He was responsible to purchase land that was in danger of being lost or sold outside the family. When a man died without a son, the kinsman-redeemer also had the duty to marry the widow of the deceased kinsman and raise up a male heir to carry on the family name (Ru 4). Finally, he functioned as the blood avenger. In the case of a murder committed, the kinsman was obligated to seek vengeance. "Redeemer" as a reference to the Lord emphasizes that He will stand with and protect His people (cp. Jb 19:25). By making them "His" people, He has voluntarily taken on Himself the responsibility and obligation for their care.

but we take pride in the name
of Yahweh our God.
8 They collapse and fall,
but we rise and stand firm.
9 LORD, give victory to the king!
May He[A] answer us on the day
that we call.

Psalm 21
The King's Victory

For the choir director. A Davidic psalm.

1 LORD, the king finds joy
in Your strength.
How greatly he rejoices
in Your victory!
2 You have given him
his heart's desire
and have not denied
the request of his lips.
•Selah
3 For You meet him
with rich blessings;
You place a crown
of pure gold on his head.
4 He asked You for life,
and You gave it to him—
length of days forever
and ever.
5 His glory is great
through Your victory;
You confer majesty
and splendor on him.
6 You give him blessings
forever;
You cheer him with joy
in Your presence.
7 For the king relies
on the LORD;
through the faithful love
of the •Most High
he is not shaken.
8 Your hand will capture
all your enemies;
your right hand will seize
those who hate you.
9 You will make them burn
like a fiery furnace
when you appear;
the LORD will engulf them
in His wrath,
and fire will devour them.
10 You will wipe
their descendants
from the earth
and their offspring
from the •human race.
11 Though they intend
to harm[B] you
and devise a wicked plan,
they will not prevail.
12 Instead, you will put them
to flight
when you aim your bow[C]
at their faces.
13 Be exalted, LORD,
in Your strength;
we will sing and praise
Your might.

Psalm 22
From Suffering to Praise

For the choir director: according to "The Deer of the Dawn."[D] *A Davidic psalm.*

1 My God, my God,
why have You forsaken me?
Why are You so far
from my deliverance
and from my words
of groaning?[E]
2 My God, I cry by day, but You
do not answer,
by night, yet I have no rest.

[A]**20:9** Or *LORD, save. May the king* [B]**21:11** Lit *they stretch out evil against* [C]**21:12** Lit *aim with your bowstrings* [D]**22:title** Perhaps a musical term [E]**22:1** Or *My words of groaning are so far from delivering me*

21:1-13 This hymn of thanksgiving for God's blessings on the king ends on a strong note of praise. The Lord who has brought victories to His people in the past could be trusted to grant future victories. The strength and power of the Lord merit His people's praise. The psalmist again affirms that Israel's victories lay in the Lord's power, not in military strength (see Ps 9:1-12 for note on **Most High**).

22:1-31 This psalm may have been intended to be sung to the tune of **"The Deer of the Dawn."** Structurally, it consists of an individual prayer of lament (vv. 1-21) followed by praise (vv. 22-31). Although it may poetically reflect a composite of David's experiences of difficulty, including Saul's pursuit of his life, Jesus' use of the psalm during His suffering on the cross (Mt 27:46; Mk 15:34) magnifies its messianic significance and compels the reader to consider what it reveals about Christ. By crying out to the Father, Jesus, in the psalm's first words, invoked the entire psalm, one of the most quoted in the New Testament, as a prophetic testimony to His suffering.

The wording of the speaker's appeal—**My God, my God, why . . . ?**—emphasizes the enigmatic character of the suffering upon which the psalm elaborates (vv. 1-21). The psalmist clings to his identity as one who has remained faithful to the God of Israel, but God does not seem to be keeping *His* promise not to forsake those who trust in Him and cry out to Him (vv. 1-5).

>WORD|*study*

22:1 The agonizing question of verse 1 centers on the word forsaken (Hb *'azav*, "leave, abandon, desert"). This word is frequently used in the Old Testament to express both God's faithfulness to the covenants He made with His people—i.e., promising *not* to forsake or abandon them (see Gn 17:1-8; 28:10-22; Dt 31:6,8; Jos 1:5; Heb 13:5)—and the people's unfaithfulness to God (Dt 31:16; cp. Jdg 2:13; 10:6; 1Sm 8:8). Because Israel abandoned God, He said, "I will abandon (Hb *'azav*) them and hide my face from them" (Dt 31:17; cp. Jos 24:20; Jdg 10:7; 2Ch 15:2; Neh 9:28,31; Jr 12:7-17). Nevertheless, God honors His promise for those who remain obedient and for those who respond to His discipline (1Kg 6:13; Pss 9:10; 94:14; Is 62:4,12). As a prophetic and poetic account of Christ's suffering, Ps 22 structurally affirms the hope conveyed in Ps 16:10 ("You will not abandon [Hb *'azav*] me to Sheol"), which is fulfilled in Christ's resurrection (Ac 2:27,31). Psalm 22:1-21 reveals the sinless Son's experience of becoming sin on behalf of sinners (2Co 5:21; Heb 4:15); Ps 22:22-31 further notes the triumphant results of the Messiah's death and resurrection.

23:1 David's early career as a shepherd undoubtedly personalized the imagery of being one of the Lord's sheep (cp. 100:3b). However, God also described David's assignment as king of Israel in terms of shepherding His people (78:70-72; cp. 2Sm 5:2; 7:7; 1Ch 11:2; 17:6; Ps 28:9). David understood both the characteristics of sheep and the responsibilities of a shepherd. The declaration, **The Lord is my shepherd**, expresses the psalmist's complete dependence on Him and trust in God to meet every need (cp. Php 4:19). Elsewhere in Scripture, God refers to Himself as the people's shepherd and describes the coming Messiah as such (see Is 13:14; 40:11; Jr 31:10; Ezk 34:7-31; 37:24; cp. Mt 2:6). Jesus pointed to His own identity as Messiah and Lord when He identified Himself as "the good shepherd" (Jn 10:7-18).

23:2 Sheep **lie down** only when the shepherd has met their needs for food and security, and led them to an area with room for each one to rest. Sheep also need to be led to sources of clean, still water where they can drink safely. When a sheep falls over on its back, the shepherd **renews** (Hb *shuv*, "refresh, restore") its life by helping the animal stand again; without help, the sheep will die because it cannot get up by itself. In addition, to avoid harming a pasture, the shepherd must keep the flock moving.

23:3 **Right paths** (Hb *ma'gal*, "way") figuratively refers to a "course or pattern of living" (cp. 17:5; Pr 4:11). As a shepherd, the Lord **leads** His people to act in accordance with His righteousness **for His name's sake** because His reputation and character are reflected in the way He cares for His flock.

23:4-5 David could **go through** the most difficult experiences of life without **fear** because He completely relied on the Lord's presence and active protection. The shepherd's **rod** (Hb *shēvet*; see note on Pr 13:24 and **staff** were tools for keeping the flock together, preventing the sheep from wandering into danger, and defending them from **enemies** (cp. 86:17; 2Tm 3:16). If the imagery is extended to verse 5, **table** may refer to a large leather blanket on which a shepherd might spread fodder when grass was scarce. Also, shepherds soothed the scratched faces of their sheep with **oil**. However, David may be describing God's hospitality, provision, and protection, as well as His establishment of the king of His choosing while rendering powerless any opposition to His will. That the psalmist's **cup overflows** (Hb *rewayah*, "abundance"; cp. 66:12) expands the idea of lacking nothing (23:1) to having more than enough.

3 But You are holy,
enthroned on the praises
of Israel.
4 Our fathers trusted in You;
they trusted,
and You rescued them.
5 They cried to You and were
set free;
they trusted in You
and were not disgraced.

6 But I am a worm and not
a man,
scorned by men and despised
by people.
7 Everyone who sees me
mocks me;
they sneer[A] and shake
their heads:
8 "He relies on[B] the Lord;
let Him rescue him;
let the Lord[C] deliver him,
since He takes pleasure
in him."

9 You took me from the womb,
making me secure while
at my mother's breast.
10 I was given over to You
at birth;[D]
You have been my God
from my mother's womb.

11 Do not be far from me,
because distress is near
and there is no one to help.

12 Many bulls surround me;
strong ones of Bashan
encircle me.
13 They open their mouths
against me—
lions, mauling and roaring.
14 I am poured out like water,
and all my bones
are disjointed;
my heart is like wax,
melting within me.
15 My strength is dried up
like baked clay;
my tongue sticks to the roof
of my mouth.
You put me into the dust
of death.
16 For dogs have
surrounded me;
a gang of evildoers
has closed in on me;
they pierced[E] my hands
and my feet.
17 I can count all my bones;
people[F] look and stare at me.
18 They divided my garments
among themselves,
and they cast lots
for my clothing.

19 But You, Lord, don't be
far away.
My strength, come quickly
to help me.
20 Deliver my life
from the sword,
my only life[G] from the power
of these dogs.
21 Save me from the mouth
of the lion!
You have rescued[H] me
from the horns
of the wild oxen.

22 I will proclaim Your name
to my brothers;
I will praise You
in the congregation.
23 You who •fear •Yahweh,
praise Him!
All you descendants of Jacob,
honor Him!
All you descendants of Israel,
revere Him!
24 For He has not despised
or detested
the torment of the afflicted.
He did not hide His face
from him
but listened when he cried
to Him for help.

25 I will give praise[I]
in the great congregation
because of You;
I will fulfill my vows
before those who fear You.[J]
26 The humble[K] will eat
and be satisfied;
those who seek the Lord
will praise Him.
May your hearts live forever!
27 All the ends of the earth
will remember
and turn to the Lord.

[A]22:7 Lit *separate with the lip* [B]22:8 Or *Rely on* [C]22:8 Lit *let Him* [D]22:10 Lit *was cast on You from the womb* [E]22:16 Some Hb mss, LXX, Syr; other Hb mss read *me; like a lion* [F]22:17 Lit *they* [G]22:20 Lit *my only one* [H]22:21 Lit *answered* [I]22:25 Lit *my praise* [J]22:25 Lit *Him* [K]22:26 Or *poor*, or *afflicted*

All the families of the nations
will bow down before You,
28 for kingship
belongs to the LORD;
He rules over the nations.
29 All who prosper on earth
will eat and bow down;
all those who go down
to the dust
will kneel before Him—
even the one who cannot
preserve his life.
30 Their descendants
will serve Him;
the next generation
will be told about the Lord.
31 They will come and tell
a people yet to be born
about His righteousness—
what He has done.

Psalm 23
The Good Shepherd

A Davidic psalm.

1 The LORD is my shepherd;
there is nothing I lack.
2 He lets me lie down
in green pastures;
He leads me beside
quiet waters.
3 He renews my life;
He leads me
along the right paths[A]
for His name's sake.
4 Even when I go
through the darkest valley,[B]
I fear no danger,
for You are with me;
Your rod and Your staff[C]—
they comfort me.
5 You prepare a table before me
in the presence
of my enemies;
You anoint my head with oil;
my cup overflows.
6 Only goodness
and faithful love
will pursue me
all the days of my life,
and I will dwell in[D] the house
of the LORD
as long as I live.[E]

Psalm 24
The King of Glory

A Davidic psalm.

1 The earth and everything
in it,
the world and its inhabitants,
belong to the LORD;
2 for He laid its foundation
on the seas
and established it
on the rivers.
3 Who may ascend
the mountain of the LORD?
Who may stand
in His holy place?
4 The one who has •clean hands
and a pure heart,
who has not set his mind[F] on
what is false,
and who has not
sworn deceitfully.
5 He will receive blessing
from the LORD,
and righteousness
from the God
of his salvation.
6 Such is the generation
of those who seek Him,
who seek the face of the God
of Jacob.[G] •*Selah*
7 Lift up your heads, you gates!
Rise up, ancient doors!
Then the King of glory
will come in.
8 Who is this King of glory?
The LORD, strong and mighty,
the LORD, mighty in battle.
9 Lift up your heads, you gates!
Rise up, ancient doors!
Then the King of glory
will come in.
10 Who is He, this King of glory?
The LORD of •Hosts,
He is the King of glory.
Selah

Psalm 25
Dependence on the LORD

Davidic.

1 LORD,[H] I turn to You.[I]
2 My God, I trust in You.

23:6 The psalmist expresses hope for a lifetime of security and blessing in Yahweh's presence (cp. 26:8). The image of being followed **only** by God's **goodness and faithful love** (Hb *chesed*, "the steadfast loyalty" of the Lord; see **Word Study**, p. 322) seems especially comforting for a man like David, who had spent years being pursued by Saul.

24:1 This **Davidic** psalm begins by asserting the Lord's dominion over the whole earth and all who dwell in it. The Lord is the sovereign Creator (vv. 1-2), **holy** (vv. 3-6), and the glorious King (vv. 7-10). Who can approach such a great God? The worship of the Lord is both a great privilege and a deep necessity. Such worship also is demanding. Only those who are **clean** and **pure** may fellowship with the Lord (v. 4; cp. Ps 15). The person who would worship God must display sincerity and not **set** [Hb *nasa'*, "lift up"] **his mind** [Hb *nephesh*, "soul, life"] **on what is false** (Hb *shaw'*, "vanity, emptiness; wickedness," v. 4; cp. Ex 23:1). The phrase may convey a warning against practicing hypocrisy, pretending to be something you are not. God is not pleased with those who display such an attitude. He requires that His followers practice honesty and integrity in relationships with Him and with others. Inner purity and integrity is required of those who worship God (see Jn 4:24). The reference to God as **the LORD of Hosts** may describe Him as commander of armies or of the heavenly hosts (Ps 24:10).

25:1-3 The main emphasis of this **Davidic** psalm is confident faith in the Lord. The poet trusted in God's faithfulness as the keeper of His promises. Distressed by the presence of **enemies**, David turned to the Lord in prayer.

A **23:3** Or *me in paths of righteousness* B **23:4** Or *the valley of the shadow of death* C **23:4** A shepherd's equipment D **23:6** LXX, Sym, Syr, Tg, Vg, Jer; MT reads *will return to* E **23:6** Lit *LORD for length of days*; traditionally *LORD forever* F **24:4** Or *not lifted up his soul* G **24:6** LXX; some Hb mss, Syr read *seek Your face, God of Jacob*; other Hb mss read *seek Your face, Jacob* H **25:1** The lines of this poem form an •acrostic. I **25:1** Or *To You, LORD, I lift up my soul*

25:4-6 Moreover, the psalmist's trust in God motivated him to pray for God's guidance and instruction (vv. 4-5). He desired not only to know God's ways; but he also needed the strength to walk in those ways. The psalmist trusted the God of his salvation or deliverance to provide the strength and guidance he needed. David's plea for the Lord to **remember** him by showing him **compassion** (Hb *racham*; see **Word Study**, p. 679) and **faithful love** does not imply that the Lord had forgotten the psalmist or that He had failed to show loving compassion. Rather, David calls on God to act according to the covenant already made in order to provide deliverance.

25:7-11 The psalmist based his plea for forgiveness on God's character, not on his own. A **name** in Hebrew thought represented one's character or reputation.

25:12-22 The psalmist focused on blessings that belong to those who fear or revere the Lord (cp. Pr 1:7) and further appealed to the Lord for deliverance from sins, sufferings, and enemies. This period of affliction had provided him with abundant opportunity for self-examination, and he recognized himself as a sinner. Nevertheless, David waited expectantly and patiently for the Lord to act on his behalf.

26:1-12 David protests that he was innocent and prays for vindication. He affirms his lifestyle as one of **integrity** (Hb *tom*, "wholeness," vv. 1,11; cp. 1Kg 9:4), in which he had followed the way of blessing delineated in Ps 1 (cp. 26:4-5 with 1:1). Therefore, he entreated the Lord to **vindicate** (Hb *shaphat*, "judge," 26:1) and **redeem** (Hb *padah*, "transfer ownership by payment of a price or a substitute of equivalent value," v. 11; cp. Ex 13:13) him. Finally, the psalmist compares reliance on the Lord's justice and favor to standing **on level ground** (Ps 26:12). He promised to testify to the Lord's faithfulness before the assembled congregation of God's people.

Do not let me be disgraced;
do not let my enemies gloat
over me.
3 No one who waits for You
will be disgraced;
those who act treacherously
without cause
will be disgraced.

4 Make Your ways known to me,
LORD;
teach me Your paths.
5 Guide me in Your truth
and teach me,
for You are the God
of my salvation;
I wait for You all day long.
6 Remember, LORD,
Your compassion
and Your faithful love,
for they have existed
from antiquity.[A]
7 Do not remember the sins
of my youth
or my acts of rebellion;
in keeping with
Your faithful love,
remember me
because of Your goodness,
LORD.

8 The LORD is good and upright;
therefore He shows sinners
the way.
9 He leads the humble in what
is right
and teaches them His way.
10 All the LORD's ways show
faithful love and truth
to those who keep
His covenant and decrees.
11 Because of Your name,
•Yahweh,
forgive my sin, for it is great.
12 Who is the man who •fears
the LORD?
He will show him the way
he should choose.
13 He will live a good life,
and his descendants
will inherit the land.[B]
14 The secret counsel of the LORD
is for those who fear Him,
and He reveals His covenant
to them.
15 My eyes are always
on the LORD,
for He will pull my feet
out of the net.

16 Turn to me and be gracious
to me,
for I am alone and afflicted.
17 The distresses of my heart
increase;[C]
bring me out of my sufferings.
18 Consider my affliction
and trouble,
and take away all my sins.
19 Consider my enemies;
they are numerous,
and they hate me violently.
20 Guard me and deliver me;
do not let me be put to shame,
for I take refuge in You.
21 May integrity and what is right
watch over me,
for I wait for You.

22 God, redeem Israel, from all
its distresses.

Psalm 26

Prayer for Vindication

Davidic.

1 Vindicate me, LORD,
because I have lived
with integrity
and have trusted in the LORD
without wavering.
2 Test me, LORD, and try me;
examine my heart and mind.
3 For Your faithful love is
before my eyes,
and I live by Your truth.

4 I do not sit with the worthless
or associate with hypocrites.
5 I hate a crowd of evildoers,
and I do not sit
with the wicked.
6 I wash my hands[D]
in innocence
and go around Your altar,
LORD,
7 raising my voice
in thanksgiving
and telling about
Your wonderful works.

8 LORD, I love the house
where You dwell,
the place where
Your glory resides.

[A]25:6 Or *everlasting* [B]25:13 Or *earth* [C]25:17 Or *Relieve the distresses of my heart* [D]26:6 A ritual or ceremonial washing to express innocence

9 Do not destroy me
along with sinners,
or my life along with men
of bloodshed
10 in whose hands are
evil schemes
and whose right hands
are filled with bribes.
11 But I live with integrity;
redeem me and be gracious
to me.
12 My foot stands
on level ground;
I will praise the LORD
in the assemblies.

Psalm 27
My Stronghold

Davidic.

1 The LORD is my light
and my salvation—
whom should I fear?
The LORD is the stronghold
of my life—
of whom should I be afraid?
2 When evildoers came
against me to devour
my flesh,
my foes and my enemies
stumbled and fell.
3 Though an army deploys
against me,
my heart is not afraid;
though a war breaks out
against me,
still I am confident.
4 I have asked one thing
from the LORD;
it is what I desire:
to dwell in the house
of the LORD
all the days of my life,
gazing on the beauty
of the LORD
and seeking Him
in His temple.
5 For He will conceal me
in His shelter
in the day of adversity;
He will hide me
under the cover of His tent;
He will set me high on a rock.
6 Then my head will be high
above my enemies around me;
I will offer sacrifices
in His tent with shouts
of joy.
I will sing and make music
to the LORD.
7 LORD, hear my voice
when I call;
be gracious to me
and answer me.
8 My heart says this about You,
"You[A] are to seek My face."
LORD, I will seek Your face.
9 Do not hide Your face
from me;
do not turn Your servant away
in anger.
You have been my helper;
do not leave me
or abandon me,
God of my salvation.
10 Even if my father and mother
abandon me,
the LORD cares for me.
11 Because of my adversaries,
show me Your way, LORD,
and lead me on a level path.
12 Do not give me over
to the will of my foes,
for false witnesses rise up
against me,
breathing violence.
13 I am certain that I will see
the LORD's goodness
in the land of the living.
14 Wait for the LORD;
be strong[B] and courageous.
Wait for the LORD.

Psalm 28
My Strength

Davidic.

1 LORD, I call to You;
my rock, do not be deaf
to me.
If You remain silent to me,
I will be like
those going down
to the *Pit.
2 Listen to the sound
of my pleading
when I cry to You for help,
when I lift up my hands
toward Your holy sanctuary.
3 Do not drag me away
with the wicked,
with the evildoers,

27:1-14 David declares his confident faith in the Lord and affirms the Lord as his **light** and **salvation**. Therefore he need not **fear**. God's presence provides the inner resources to overcome fear (Heb 13:5-6). Furthermore, David described the Lord as his **stronghold** to depict Him as the strength of His people, as the One providing a safe refuge for them. David knew real strongholds as well as the fear that sent him to find safety; he spent years hiding in different strongholds in the desert when Saul was seeking his life.

27:10 The refuge of the Lord is more secure than even the love of **father and mother** (v. 10)

28:1 David cried for God's response to him in a time of need, perhaps facing some life-threatening danger at this time as he did on many occasions in his life. The **Pit** (Hb *bor*, "sepulcher, prison"; cp. 30:3; 88:4; Is 24:22) refers to death.

[A]**27:8** You is plural in Hb [B]**27:14** Lit *LORD; let your heart be strong*

28:4-5 David's prayer for God's judgment on the wicked (v. 3)—those who evidently have been oppressing him—does not arise out of some twisted sense of joy in the punishment of others. Rather, he identified his enemies with the Lord's enemies and left their judgment in the Lord's hands.

28:6-7 Verse 6 marks a dramatic shift in the poem's tone to one of confident assurance that the Lord has responded. David **praised** the Lord for hearing his cry. He glorified the Lord as his **strength** and **shield**—his protection. He expressed his faith and gratitude for the Lord's answer to his appeal.

29:1-11 The psalmist commands the **heavenly beings** (Hb *benē ʾēlim*, "sons of the mighty; sons of [the] gods") to **ascribe** [Hb *yahav*, "give"; cp. 96:7-8; 1Ch 16:28-29; Rm 11:36] **the Lord glory . . . the glory due His name** and then proceeds to depict **the God of glory** (v. 3; cp. Ac 7:2) poetically in terms of the power of His **voice** (vv. 3-9a; cp. Rv 19:1) and His eternal enthronement (29:10; cp. Mt 25:31; 1Tm 1:17). Because of who He is, God's name and presence demand honor; worship and praise are due Him. Verse 9b succinctly captures this theme (cp. Lk 2:14).

29:10-11 These verses emphasize two central truths about **the Lord**. First, the same covenant God of Israel who presided over **the flood** still reigns as **King** and will reign **forever**. In both the Old and New Testaments, this word for "flood" (Hb *mabbul*, "inundation of water, deluge"; Gk *kataklusmos*, also the LXX translation of *mabbul*) is used only for the universal flood in which Noah and his family were preserved (see Gn 10:32; cp. Mt 24:38-39; Lk 17:27; 2Pt 2:5). He is the rightful Judge of all who reject His rule. Second, this same God and King shows favor toward those who are **His**, giving them **strength** (Hb *ʿoz*, "might, power," Ps 28:7; cp. 1Sm 2:10; 1Pt 4:11) and blessing them with **peace** (Hb *shalom*; cp. Is 57:19,21; Lk 2:14; Jn 14:27).

30:1-5 In the superscription **the house** refers to the tabernacle or temple (i.e., the house of the Lord). Because of the close association of sin and illness in Hebrew thought, God's healing may have involved His forgiveness as well. David's familiarity with Scripture as well as his personal experience with the Lord undergird the recognition that God's **anger lasts only a moment** (Hb *regaʿ*, "a wink"; cp. Is 54:7-8). In other contexts, *regaʿ* expresses the sudden and swift execution of God's judgment (e.g., Ex 33:5; Nm 16:21,45; Lm 4:6) or quick snatching away of life (e.g., Jb 21:13; 34:20; Ps 73:19; Is 47:9).

who speak in friendly ways
with their neighbors
while malice is in their hearts.
4 Repay them according to what
they have done—
according to the evil
of their deeds.
Repay them according to
the work of their hands;
give them back
what they deserve.
5 Because they do not consider
what the LORD has done
or the work of His hands,
He will tear them down
and not rebuild them.

6 May the LORD be praised,
for He has heard the sound
of my pleading.
7 The LORD is my strength
and my shield;
my heart trusts in Him,
and I am helped.
Therefore my heart rejoices,
and I praise Him
with my song.

8 The LORD is the strength
of His people;[A]
He is a stronghold of salvation
for His anointed.
9 Save Your people,
bless Your possession,
shepherd them, and carry
them forever.

Psalm 29
The Voice of the LORD

A Davidic psalm.

1 Ascribe to •Yahweh,
you heavenly beings,[B]
ascribe to the LORD glory
and strength.
2 Ascribe to Yahweh the glory
due His name;
worship Yahweh
in the splendor of His
holiness.[C]

3 The voice of the LORD is
above the waters.
The God of glory thunders—
the LORD, above vast waters,
4 the voice of the LORD in power,
the voice of the LORD
in splendor.
5 The voice of the LORD
breaks the cedars;
the LORD shatters the cedars
of Lebanon.
6 He makes Lebanon skip
like a calf,
and Sirion,[D]
like a young wild ox.
7 The voice of the LORD flashes
flames of fire.
8 The voice of the LORD shakes
the wilderness;
the LORD shakes the wilderness
of Kadesh.
9 The voice of the LORD
makes the deer give birth[E]
and strips the woodlands bare.

In His temple all cry, "Glory!"
10 The LORD sat enthroned
at the flood;
the LORD sits enthroned,
King forever.
11 The LORD gives
His people strength;
the LORD blesses His people
with peace.

Psalm 30
Joy in the Morning

*A psalm; a dedication song
for the house. Davidic.*

1 I will exalt You, LORD,
because You have lifted me up
and have not allowed
my enemies

[A]**28:8** Some Hb mss, LXX, Syr; other Hb mss read *strength for them* [B]**29:1** Or *you angels*, or *you sons of the mighty*; lit *LORD sons of the gods* [C]**29:2** Or *in holy attire*, or *in holy appearance* [D]**29:6** = Mount Hermon [E]**29:9** Or *the oaks shake*

>WORD|*study*

29:1-2 The Lord's majesty is portrayed in His glory (Hb *kavod*, lit "heaviness, weightiness," cp. 19:1, though the root and its derivatives are used throughout the psalms). The literal meaning is rarely used in Scripture, but in English, the words "heavy" and "weighty" can describe someone who is very important and should be taken seriously or treated with great honor. Generally, people are "weighty" in position or influence because they are honorable, worthy of respect, and thus impressive and noteworthy. Particularly in creation—the signature of God's "glory"—the Lord reveals His own majesty, splendor, and preeminence (cp. Rv 4:9-11).

to triumph over me.
2 Lord my God,
I cried to You for help,
and You healed me.
3 Lord, You brought me up
from •Sheol;
You spared me
from among those
going down[A] to the •Pit.

4 Sing to •Yahweh,
you His faithful ones,
and praise His holy name.
5 For His anger lasts
only a moment,
but His favor, a lifetime.
Weeping may spend the night,
but there is joy
in the morning.

6 When I was secure, I said,
"I will never be shaken."
7 Lord, when You showed
Your favor,
You made me stand
like a strong mountain;
when You hid Your face,
I was terrified.
8 Lord, I called to You;
I sought favor from my Lord:
9 "What gain is there
in my death,
if I go down to the Pit?
Will the dust praise You?
Will it proclaim Your truth?
10 Lord, listen and be gracious
to me;
Lord, be my helper."
11 You turned my lament
into dancing;
You removed my •sackcloth
and clothed me with gladness,
12 so that I can sing to You
and not be silent.
Lord my God, I will praise
You forever.

Psalm 31
A Plea for Protection

For the choir director. A Davidic psalm.

1 Lord, I seek refuge in You;
let me never be disgraced.
Save me
by Your righteousness.
2 Listen closely to me;
rescue me quickly.
Be a rock of refuge for me,
a mountain fortress
to save me.
3 For You are my rock
and my fortress;
You lead and guide me
because of Your name.
4 You will free me from the net
that is secretly set for me,
for You are my refuge.
5 Into Your hand I entrust
my spirit;
You redeem[B] me, Lord,
God of truth.

6 I[C] hate those who are devoted
to worthless idols,
but I trust in the Lord.
7 I will rejoice and be glad
in Your faithful love
because You have seen
my affliction.
You have known the troubles
of my life
8 and have not handed me over
to the enemy.
You have set my feet
in a spacious place.

9 Be gracious to me, Lord,
because I am in distress;
my eyes are worn out
from angry sorrow—
my whole being[D] as well.
10 Indeed, my life is consumed
with grief
and my years with groaning;
my strength has failed
because of my sinfulness,[E]
and my bones waste away.
11 I am ridiculed by all
my adversaries
and even by my neighbors.
I am dreaded by
my acquaintances;
those who see me
in the street run from me.
12 I am forgotten:
gone from memory
like a dead person—
like broken pottery.
13 I have heard the gossip
of many;
terror is on every side.

30:6-10 This psalmist felt **secure** when he enjoyed prosperity and everything was going well. In his self-sufficiency he failed to depend on God. When calamity struck, he turned to God for help and wisely thanked God for His deliverance, having learned a lesson through his painful ordeal.

31:1-24 This **Davidic** psalm alternates between a cry for God's help and thanksgiving for God's faithfulness. David praised the Lord's power by use of such words as **rock, fortress,** and **refuge** as he pleaded for the Lord's protection (vv. 2-4). A keynote of the psalm is David's faith and commitment to the Lord. **Entrust** (Hb *paqad,* "commit, charge" to another's care, v. 5) carries the idea of making someone an overseer. This poet's faith has led him to make the Lord the overseer of his spirit or his life. Jesus' last words from the cross included this prayer of faith (Lk 23:46).

[A] **30:3** Some Hb mss, LXX, Theod, Orig, Syr; other Hb mss, Aq, Sym, Tg, Jer read *from going down* [B] **31:5** Or *You have redeemed,* or *You will redeem,* or *spirit. Redeem* [C] **31:6** One Hb ms, LXX, Syr, Vg, Jer read *You* [D] **31:9** Lit *my soul and my belly* [E] **31:10** LXX, Syr, Sym read *affliction*

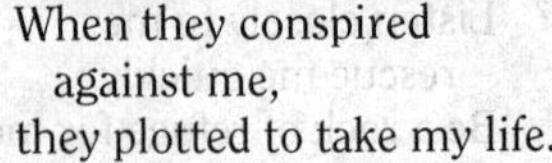

32:1-11 This psalm of thanksgiving is one of the seven penitential psalms. It has been closely related to Ps 51, David's plea for forgiveness after he had committed adultery with Bathsheba. Both psalms have been connected with David's experiences recorded in 2Sm 11–12. Psalm 32 is regarded as David's expression of gratitude after receiving the forgiveness for which he prayed in Ps 51 or as the fulfillment of the resolution David made in Ps 51:13. As a ***Maskil***, Ps 32 may be understood as a psalm that teaches or gives insight into practical living. Certainly the poem contains valuable insight about how to deal with sin.

When they conspired
  against me,
they plotted to take my life.

14 But I trust in You, Lord;
I say, "You are my God."
15 The course of my life is
  in Your power;
deliver me from the power
  of my enemies
and from my persecutors.
16 Show Your favor
  to Your servant;
save me by Your faithful love.
17 Lord, do not let me
  be disgraced when I call
  on You.
Let the wicked be disgraced;
let them be silent[A,B] in •Sheol.
18 Let lying lips be quieted;
they speak arrogantly
  against the righteous
with pride and contempt.

19 How great is Your goodness
that You have stored up
  for those who •fear You
and accomplished in the sight
  of •everyone
for those who take refuge
  in You.
20 You hide them
  in the protection
  of Your presence;
You conceal them
  in a shelter[C]
from the schemes of men,
from quarrelsome tongues.
21 May the Lord be praised,
for He has wonderfully shown
  His faithful love to me
in a city under siege.[D]
22 In my alarm I had said,
"I am cut off
  from Your sight."
But You heard the sound
  of my pleading
when I cried to You for help.

23 Love the Lord,
  all His faithful ones.
The Lord protects the loyal,
but fully repays the arrogant.
24 Be strong[E] and courageous,
all you who put your hope
  in the Lord.

Doctrine SIN AND FORGIVENESS

Psalm 32 constitutes a beatitude celebrating the blessedness of forgiveness, which comes by confessing, not denying, sin. Three Hebrew words for sin appear in these verses:

- **transgression** (Hb *peshaʿ*, "rebellion, revolt")—asserting your will in direct opposition to God's will;
- **sin** (Hb *chattaʾah*, "missing the mark; misstep");
- **sin** (Hb *ʿawon*, "iniquity, moral crookedness, perversity; wrongdoing").

The complete identification with sin suggested by this threefold terminology is matched by the complete forgiveness expressed three ways:

- **Forgiven** (Hb *nasaʾ*, "pardon") pictures sin as a burden that is lifted up and carried away.
- **Covered** (Hb *kasa*, "conceal, pardon") signifies the covering over or atonement of sin so that it will never be seen again.
- **Does not charge** (Hb *chashav*, "reckon, account"; cp. Gn 15:6) emphasizes the offended party's decision to release the offender from any indebtedness. A deliberate choice is made to forfeit any right to hold the sin (i.e., unpaid debt) against the sinner. Such forgiveness comes to the individual who refuses to justify sin but instead honestly confesses it to God.

"Forgiven" and "covered" are passive participles, indicating unbroken continuity of being acted upon—sin is continually being forgiven, continually being covered. Similarly, "does not charge" is an imperfect verb, also indicating an action that is ongoing.

Verses 3-5 describe the effects of unconfessed sin. Rather than symptoms of an illness, the effects are likely physical and psychological, the results of an inner battle occurring when the guilty person refuses to acknowledge his sin to the Lord. When David kept silent, his **bones**—a reference to his entire being—suffered the effects of his refusal to confess his sin. However, when he completely confessed his sin, iniquity, and transgressions (the three words for sin noted in verses 1-2; cp. 1Jn 1:8-9), the Lord **took away the guilt of** his **sin** (v. 5).

Psalm 32

The Joy of Forgiveness

Davidic. A •Maskil.

1 How joyful is the one
whose transgression
  is forgiven,
whose sin is covered!
2 How joyful is the man
the Lord does not charge
  with sin
and in whose spirit is
  no deceit!

[A]**31:17** LXX reads *brought down* [B]**31:17** Or *them perish*, or *them wail* [C]**31:20** Lit *canopy* [D]**31:21** Or *a fortified city* [E]**31:24** Lit *Let your heart be strong*

3 When I kept silent, my bones
became brittle
from my groaning
all day long.
4 For day and night Your hand
was heavy on me;
my strength was drained[A]
as in the summer's heat.
•*Selah*
5 Then I acknowledged my sin
to You
and did not conceal
my iniquity.
I said,
"I will confess
my transgressions
to the LORD,"
and You took away the •guilt
of my sin. *Selah*
6 Therefore let everyone
who is faithful pray to You
at a time
that You may be found.[B]
When great floodwaters come,
they will not reach him.
7 You are my hiding place;
You protect me
from trouble.
You surround me
with joyful shouts
of deliverance. *Selah*
8 I will instruct you
and show you
the way to go;
with My eye on you,
I will give counsel.
9 Do not be like a horse
or mule,
without understanding,
that must be controlled
with bit and bridle
or else it will not come
near you.

10 Many pains come
to the wicked,
but the one who trusts
in the LORD
will have faithful love
surrounding him.
11 Be glad in the LORD
and rejoice,
you righteous ones;
shout for joy,
all you upright
in heart.

Psalm 33

Praise to the Creator

1 Rejoice in the LORD,
you righteous ones;
praise from the upright
is beautiful.
2 Praise the LORD with the lyre;
make music to Him
with a ten-stringed harp.
3 Sing a new song to Him;
play skillfully on the strings,
with a joyful shout.

4 For the word of the LORD
is right,
and all His work
is trustworthy.
5 He loves righteousness
and justice;
the earth is full of the LORD's
unfailing love.

6 The heavens were made
by the word of the LORD,
and all the stars, by the breath
of His mouth.
7 He gathers the waters
of the sea into a heap;[C]
He puts the depths
into storehouses.
8 Let the whole earth tremble
before the LORD;
let all the inhabitants
of the world stand in awe
of Him.
9 For He spoke, and it came
into being;
He commanded, and it came
into existence.

10 The LORD frustrates
the counsel of the nations;
He thwarts the plans
of the peoples.
11 The counsel of the LORD
stands forever,
the plans of His heart
from generation
to generation.
12 Happy is the nation
whose God is •Yahweh—
the people He has chosen
to be His own possession!

13 The LORD looks down
from heaven;
He observes everyone.
14 He gazes on all
the inhabitants of the earth

32:8-11 Here David counsels others on the basis of what he has learned from his painful ordeal. He warned his hearers not to behave as a foolish **horse or mule** that must be compelled by force. Such obstinacy will result in painful consequences. Persons who do not freely respond to God will experience His disciplining judgment. The use of a parable in verse 9 and a proverb in verse 10 are characteristic of wisdom literature and reflect the influence of wisdom teaching.

The proverb presents two ways to deal with sin. The way of sorrow comes to those who persist in their sin. The way of blessedness comes to those who confess their sin and trust in the Lord (cp. Ps 1). Three commands—**be glad, rejoice,** and **shout for joy**—suggest completeness of the joy experienced by those who are honest with God. **Righteous ones** are persons who faithfully fulfill the obligations of their relationships. Psalm 32 is an impressive testimony to the truth about confession of sin.

33:1-3 This hymn of praise celebrates the greatness of the Lord as Creator and Ruler and reveals that Israel's worship of the Lord was a joyful celebration. The expression **new song** may designate the fresh newness that should always characterize our worship (see Rv 5:9).

33:5-9 These verses provide reasons for joyful worship of the Lord. **The earth is full of** His **unfailing love** (Hb *chesed*, the Lord's "covenant loyalty or faithful devotion" to His people; see **Word Study**, p. 322). The covenant, in this context, is made with all of creation (cp. Gn 9). Verses 6-7 and 9 call to mind the account of creation in Gn 1. Because all that is belongs ultimately to the Lord, all the earth's **inhabitants** should **tremble before** (Hb *yarē'*, "fear, **stand in awe** of, respect") Him.

33:10-22 Verses 10-22 celebrate the Lord's rule over all nations and all peoples. He alone is in control. He shows favor toward those who revere Him (v. 18), **depend on** Him (v. 18), **wait for** Him (v. 20), and place their **hope** in Him (v. 22).

[A]32:4 Hb obscure [B]32:6 Lit *time of finding* [C]33:7 LXX, Tg, Syr, Vg, Jer read *sea as in a bottle*

34:1-3 This psalm is an acrostic poem in the Hebrew text. Each of its 22 lines begins with a successive letter of the Hebrew alphabet. Its superscription identifies the historical setting as the time when David feigned insanity before Abimelech. Although the king mentioned in 1Sm 21:10-15 is identified as Achish, "Abimelech" may have been a general title for Philistine kings, just as "Pharaoh" was applied to Egyptian kings.

Like David, you can continually **praise** Yahweh **at all times**, in every kind of circumstance. Such a commitment to praise enables God's people continually to experience His blessings. David calls on the rest of the congregation to join him in praise. Declaring the **greatness** of the Lord in public proclamation makes others aware of His majesty.

34:4-7 David gives thanks because the Lord has **delivered** (Hb *natsal*, "snatch, deliver from danger"; see **Word Study** for "rescue," p.672) him from **all . . .** [his] **fears** (Hb *megurah*, "what one dreads"; cp. Is 66:4). This verb suggests the necessity of God's intervention to experience freedom—both from imminent, life-threatening dangers and from terrors produced by the imagination when all one's senses must be kept on constant alert to dangers lurking around every corner (cp. 1Sm 17:35,37). David also describes the continuous security provided by **the Angel** [Hb *malʾak*, "messenger, one sent"] **of the LORD**—sometimes identified as a "theophany," a visible manifestation of God (cp. Gn 22:11,15-16; 48:16; Ex 23:20-21; Jdg 6:11-23)—with the military imagery of an army that has formed a defensive circle of protection **around those who fear** the Lord.

34:8-10 Perhaps speaking of himself as the paradigmatic example of one who has tasted and seen God's character firsthand, David exclaims, **How happy is the man who takes refuge in Him!** (contrast 52:7).

from His dwelling place.
15 He alone shapes their hearts;
He considers all their works.
16 A king is not saved by
a large army;
a warrior will not be delivered
by great strength.
17 The horse is a false hope
for safety;
it provides no escape by
its great power.

18 Now the eye of the LORD is
on those who •fear Him—
those who depend on
His faithful love
19 to deliver them from death
and to keep them alive
in famine.

20 We wait for Yahweh;
He is our help and shield.
21 For our hearts rejoice in Him
because we trust in
His holy name.
22 May Your faithful love rest
on us, Yahweh,
for we put our hope in You.

Psalm 34

The LORD Delivers the Righteous

Concerning David, when he pretended to be insane in the presence of Abimelech,[A] who drove him out, and he departed.

1 I[B] will praise the LORD
at all times;
His praise will always be
on my lips.
2 I will boast in the LORD;
the humble will hear
and be glad.
3 Proclaim •Yahweh's greatness
with me;
let us exalt
His name together.

4 I sought the LORD,
and He answered me
and delivered me from all
my fears.
5 Those who look to Him
are[C] radiant with joy;
their faces will never
be ashamed.
6 This poor man cried,
and the LORD heard him
and saved him from all
his troubles.
7 The Angel of the LORD
encamps
around those who •fear Him,
and rescues them.

8 Taste and see that the LORD
is good.
How happy is the man
who takes refuge in Him!
9 You who are His holy ones,
fear Yahweh,
for those who fear Him
lack nothing.
10 Young lions[D] lack food
and go hungry,
but those who seek the LORD
will not lack any good thing.

11 Come, children, listen to me;
I will teach you the fear
of the LORD.
12 Who is the man who delights
in life,
loving a long life to enjoy
what is good?
13 Keep your tongue from evil

[A] **34:title** Probably Achish, king of Gath [B] **34:1** The lines of this poem form an •acrostic. [C] **34:5** Some Hb mss, LXX, Aq, Syr, Jer read *Look to Him and be* [D] **34:10** LXX, Syr, Vg read *The rich*

>WORD|*study*

34:8 The word translated man (Hb *gever*) is different than the word used in 1:1 (Hb *ʾish*, "man," frequently generic in use; cp. 34:12) and 32:2 (Hb *ʾadam*, "man, human being"; e.g., 36:6). *Gever* usually denotes "man" as opposed to "woman" (Ex 10:11; Dt 22:5; Jr 30:6), a "husband" (Pr 6:34) or a "warrior" (Jdg 5:30); it conveys the picture of a "strong, powerful man." The specifically masculine definition of this word is not intended to rule out the application of the truth to women. More generic designations of audience appear throughout Ps 34 ("Those who look to Him," v. 5; **those who fear Him**, vv. 7,9; **those who seek the LORD**, v. 10; "the righteous," vv. 15,17; "the brokenhearted . . . those crushed in spirit," v. 18; "the one who is righteous," v. 19; "His servants," v. 22; "all who take refuge in Him," v. 22). The extended description of the many benefits for those belonging to the Lord is also addressed more generally to **you His saints** (Hb *qadosh* [plural], "holy ones, holy people," v. 9; cp. 16:3; Dt 33:3). However, use of *gever* here enhances David's appeal to men in the audience to recognize in him—a celebrated warrior and king—living proof that seeking **refuge** (Hb *chasah*, "flee to a place or person for protection," Ps 34:8; cp. 7:1) in the Lord does not reflect weakness or cowardice but strength. By translating *gever* as "those" or "the person," some modern translations obscure the persuasive structure of this text, in which the invitation "taste and see" is immediately followed by David's testimony to the good results of doing so. In the Psalms, *gever* has the predominant sense of one who fears, trusts in, and obeys God, with whom he has a personal relationship.

34:8-10 To lack nothing (Hb *ʾên*, "there is no," with the object *machesor*, "need"; from the root *chasēr*, "be devoid of, without") means that God meets your needs. The expression is clarified by the promise that they **will not lack** [Hb *chasēr*] **any good thing**, which is implicitly contrasted to the young lions' lack (Hb *rush*, "be needy, suffer want") of physical sustenance.

and your lips
from deceitful speech.
14 Turn away from evil and do
what is good;
seek peace and pursue it.

15 The eyes of the LORD are
on the righteous,
and His ears are open
to their cry for help.
16 The face of the LORD is set
against those who do
what is evil,
to erase[A] all memory of them
from the earth.
17 The righteous[B] cry out,
and the LORD hears,
and delivers them from all
their troubles.
18 The LORD is near
the brokenhearted;
He saves those crushed
in spirit.
19 Many adversities come
to the one who is righteous,
but the LORD delivers him
from them all.
20 He protects all his bones;
not one of them is broken.
21 Evil brings death
to the wicked,
and those who hate
the righteous
will be punished.
22 The LORD redeems the life
of His servants,
and all who take refuge
in Him will not
be punished.

Psalm 35

Prayer for Victory

Davidic.

1 Oppose my opponents, LORD;
fight those who fight me.
2 Take Your shields—
large and small—
and come to my aid.
3 Draw the spear and javelin
against my pursuers,
and assure me: "I am
your deliverance."

4 Let those who seek to kill me
be disgraced and humiliated;
let those who plan
to harm me
be turned back and ashamed.
5 Let them be like chaff
in the wind,
with the angel of the LORD
driving them away.
6 Let their way be dark
and slippery,
with the angel of the LORD
pursuing them.
7 They hid their net for me
without cause;
they dug a pit for me
without cause.
8 Let ruin come
on him unexpectedly,
and let the net that he hid
ensnare him;
let him fall
into it—to his ruin.
9 Then I will rejoice
in the LORD;
I will delight
in His deliverance.
10 My very bones will say,
"LORD, who is like You,
rescuing the poor from one
too strong for him,
the poor or the needy
from one who robs him?"
11 Malicious witnesses
come forward;
they question me
about things I do not know.
12 They repay me evil for good,
making me desolate.
13 Yet when they were sick,
my clothing was •sackcloth;
I humbled myself
with fasting,
and my prayer was genuine.[C]
14 I went about grieving as if
for my friend or brother;
I was bowed down with grief,
like one mourning a mother.
15 But when I stumbled,
they gathered in glee;
they gathered against me.
Assailants I did not know
tore at me and did not stop.
16 With godless mockery[D]
they gnashed their teeth
at me.

17 Lord, how long will You
look on?
Rescue my life
from their ravages,

34:11-14 To beckon the audience as **children** represents a typical pattern used by wisdom teachers (cp. Pr 2:1; 3:1; 4:1; 5:1). David announces that he **will teach . . . the fear of the LORD**, which is the essence of wisdom (cp. 3:7; 9:10; see **Word Study**, p. 784). Wise living involves both your **speech** (cp. Ps 17:1; 24:4; 36:3; Jms 3:2) and what you **do** (cp. Jms 3:13).

34:15-22 David knew firsthand that faith in the Lord does not offer immunity from adversity. **The righteous** often suffer much affliction, but ultimate victory belongs to those who follow the Lord and, therefore, are continually acquiring and exhibiting His character (v. 19; cp. 1Pt 4:12-16). None of those who trust in Him will be condemned. The way of the righteous leads to life; the way of the wicked leads to death (see Ps 1).

35:1-28 David desperately pleaded with the Lord to deal with those who opposed him, seeking to take his physical life and to destroy his confidence in God. Some enemies evoked a deep sense of dismay because they were betraying the kindness he had displayed toward them. Jesus quoted verse 19, warning His disciples that when they experienced the world's hatred, they should remember that the world hated Him first **without cause** (Jn 15:25; cp. Ps 69:4). Knowing that God sees all often makes waiting for Him to act—both to save and to judge—difficult. The psalm ends with David's determination to **praise** the Lord continually, exemplifying the resolution found in many psalms that beg the Lord not to love but to destroy one's enemies (see **Hard Question**, p. 671).

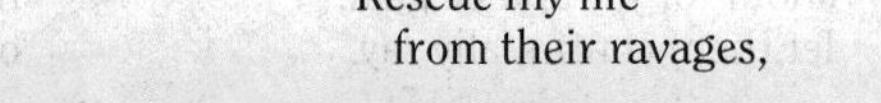

[A]**34:16** Or *cut off* [B]**34:17** Lit *They* [C]**35:13** Lit *prayer returned to my chest* [D]**35:16** Hb obscure

36:1-4 David extols the great love of the Lord against the background of the **transgression** [Hb *pesha*ʿ, "rebellion," deliberate "revolt" against the Lord] **of the wicked** or unrighteous person characterized here:

- He is devoid of fear before God.
- He builds his own self-esteem to the point that he no longer recognizes his sinful nature.
- His speech is **malicious** (Hb *ʾawen*, "iniquity, fraud"; cp. Pr 17:4) and **deceptive** (Hb *mirmah*, "treachery, fraud"; cp. 24:4; 34:13; 50:19; 109:2; Pr 12:17; 14:25).
- **He has stopped acting wisely** [Hb *sakal*, "be or become prudent"; cp. Dt 32:28-29; 1 Sm 18:14-15] **and doing good** (Hb *yatav*, "do well, do what is right or do things the right way"; cp. Gn 4:7; Is 1:17; Jr 4:22).
- While others are sleeping, he is restlessly plotting evil.
- He chooses an ungodly lifestyle, failing to **reject** what is harmful.

36:5-11 In contrast to this portrait of those who defy God is the subsequent rehearsal of the Lord's limitless:

- **faithful love** (Hb *chesed*; cp. 5:7; 17:7-8; see **Word Study**, p. 322),
- **faithfulness** (Hb *ʾemunah*, "reliability in keeping promises"; cp. Dt 32:4),
- **righteousness** (Hb *tsedaqah*, "justice"),
- **judgments** (Hb *mishpat*, "act of deciding a case, judge's sentence"; see **Word Study**, p. 218; see chart, p. 758),
- preservation or protection, and
- provision and refreshment.

God is the source of life and **light**. **Those who know** (Hb *yada*ʿ, "have knowledge from personal experience"; an active participle here, implying an ongoing relationship; see note on Ex 2:24-25, and **Word Study**, p. 725) the Lord, therefore, are characterized by His righteousness from the inside out. Implicitly counting himself among them, David prays for the Lord to prevent pride from gaining a foothold in his life and to keep **the wicked** from causing him to wander (cp. 2Kg 21:8).

36:12 The location or circumstance indicated by **there** is not clearly specified in the psalm. Perhaps it refers to any point of confrontation between **evildoers** and the Lord's "faithful love" and "righteousness" protecting the people who find refuge in Him. In any case, all three verbs describing what happens to the "evildoers" are, grammatically, in the perfect mood (i.e., expressing completed actions):

- **fall** (Hb *naphal*, figuratively "suffer defeat, die"; cp. 82:7);
- **have been thrown down** (Hb *dachah*, "be pushed down or cast out"; cp. 118:13; Jr 23:12)—i.e.,

>WORD|*study*

36:3 The verb stopped (Hb *chadal*, "forbear"; cp. "fails," Nm 9:13; "refrain from," Dt 23:22) does not suggest that the wicked were "acting wisely and doing good" but eventually ceased. In this context the verb means that they have "abstained from, renounced, given no heed to, or given up on" doing what is right.

my only one
from the young lions.
18 I will praise You
in the great congregation;
I will exalt You
among many people.
19 Do not let
my deceitful enemies
rejoice over me;
do not let those who hate me
without cause
look at me maliciously.
20 For they do not speak
in friendly ways,
but contrive
deceitful schemes[A]
against those who live
peacefully in the land.
21 They open their mouths wide
against me and say,
"Aha, aha! We saw it!"[B]
22 You saw it, LORD; do not
be silent.
Lord, do not be far from me.
23 Wake up and rise
to my defense,
to my cause, my God
and my LORD!
24 Vindicate me, LORD my God,
in keeping with
Your righteousness,
and do not let them rejoice
over me.
25 Do not let them say
in their hearts,
"Aha! Just what we wanted."
Do not let them say,
"We have swallowed him up!"
26 Let those who rejoice
at my misfortune
be disgraced and humiliated;
let those who exalt
themselves over me
be clothed with shame
and reproach.
27 Let those who want
my vindication
shout for joy and be glad;
let them continually say,
"The LORD be exalted.
He takes pleasure in
His servant's well-being."
28 And my tongue will proclaim
Your righteousness,
Your praise all day long.

Psalm 36

Human Wickedness and God's Love

For the choir director. A psalm of David, the LORD's servant.

1 An •oracle within my heart
concerning the transgression
of the wicked person:
There is no dread of God
before his eyes,
2 for in his own eyes
he flatters himself too much
to discover and hate his sin.
3 The words of his mouth
are malicious and deceptive;
he has stopped acting wisely
and doing good.
4 Even on his bed he makes
malicious plans.
He sets himself on a path
that is not good
and does not reject evil.
5 LORD, Your faithful love
reaches to heaven,
Your faithfulness
to the clouds.
6 Your righteousness is
like the highest mountains;
Your judgments,
like the deepest sea.
LORD, You preserve man
and beast.
7 God, Your faithful love
is so valuable
that •people take refuge
in the shadow
of Your wings.
8 They are filled
from the abundance
of Your house;

[A]35:20 Lit *but devise deceitful words* [B]35:21 Lit *Our eyes saw!*

You let them drink from
Your refreshing stream,
9 for with You is life's fountain.
In Your light we will see light.

10 Spread Your faithful love
over those who know You,
and Your righteousness
over the upright in heart.
11 Do not let the foot of
the arrogant man
come near me
or the hand of the wicked one
drive me away.
12 There the evildoers fall;
they have been thrown down
and cannot rise.

Psalm 37

Instruction in Wisdom

Davidic.

1 Do[A] not be agitated
by evildoers;
do not envy those
who do wrong.
2 For they wither quickly
like grass
and wilt like tender
green plants.

3 Trust in the LORD and do
what is good;
dwell in the land
and live securely.[B]
4 Take delight in the LORD,
and He will give you
your heart's desires.

5 Commit your way
to the LORD;
trust in Him, and He will act,
6 making your righteousness
shine like the dawn,
your justice like the noonday.

7 Be silent before the LORD
and wait expectantly
for Him;
do not be agitated by one
who prospers in his way,
by the man who carries out
evil plans.

8 Refrain from anger
and give up your rage;
do not be agitated—
it can only bring harm.
9 For evildoers
will be destroyed,
but those who put their hope
in the LORD
will inherit the land.[C]

10 A little while, and
the wicked person will be
no more;
though you look for him,
he will not be there.
11 But the humble will inherit
the land[C]
and will enjoy
abundant prosperity.

12 The wicked person schemes
against the righteous
and gnashes his teeth at him.
13 The Lord laughs at him
because He sees that his day
is coming.

14 The wicked have drawn
the sword and strung
the[D] bow
to bring down the afflicted
and needy
and to slaughter those
whose way is upright.
15 Their swords will enter
their own hearts,
and their bows will be broken.

16 The little that
the righteous man has
is better
than the abundance
of many wicked people.
17 For the arms[E] of the wicked
will be broken,
but the LORD supports
the righteous.

18 The LORD watches over
the blameless all their days,
and their inheritance
will last forever.
19 They will not be disgraced
in times of adversity;
they will be satisfied in days
of hunger.

20 But the wicked will perish;
the LORD's enemies,
like the glory
of the pastures,
will fade away—
they will fade away
like smoke.

[A]**37:1** The lines of this poem form an °acrostic. [B]**37:3** Or *and cultivate faithfulness* [C]**37:9,11** Or *earth* [D]**37:14** Lit *their* [E]**37:17** Or *power*

someone (God) has, figuratively, knocked off his feet;
- **cannot** (Hb *yakol*, not "able") get up again.

37:1-40 This psalm is a collection of wisdom teachings regarding the mindset to be adopted by the righteous toward **evildoers** (v. 1). Three times the psalm instructs, **Do not be agitated** (Hb *charah*, "fret, worry, be angry or vexed," vv. 1,7,8; cp. Pr 24:19) by people who sin willfully and egregiously, yet who profit from their wicked plans. To **envy** (Hb *qana'*, "feel discontented on account of the advantages enjoyed by another; to desire to possess what another has achieved," Ps 37:1) such people is especially tempting when doing wrong seems to be more rewarding than doing **what is good** (vv. 3,27; cp. Ps 73:2-3; Pr 3:31; 23:17; 24:1,19); but the psalm counsels against this response, too. When God seems to be dealing unfairly with the wicked, God's people are encouraged to adopt His perspective:
- Recognize that the wicked and their apparent prosperity are short-lived (Ps 37:2,9-15,17,20,28,35-36,38).
- **Trust** (Hb *batach*, "set one's hope and confidence upon," vv. 3,5) the Lord to render justice on His timetable.
- **Wait** (Hb *chul*, "wait longingly," with the sense of agonizing over the duration of inactivity or over what must be suffered in order to wait obediently (v. 7; *qawah*, "expect," v. 34; cp. "put [one's] hope in," v. 9; 27:14) for the Lord to fulfill His promises. Stay focused on loving and pleasing the Lord (37: 3-5,34) without succumbing to **anger** and **rage** (v. 8).
- Live in a manner consistent with faith in the Lord's faithfulness to His people.

A recurring theme in the psalm is the certainty regarding who may live in and who will **inherit** [Hb *yarash*, "occupy, possess," vv. 9,11,22,29,34] **the land** (Hb *'erets*, "earth," vv. 3,9,11,22,29,34):
- **those who put their hope in the LORD** (v. 9);
- **the humble** (Hb *'anaw*, "meek, gentle, modest; one who prefers to suffer abuse rather than seek retribution," v. 11; cp. Mt 5:5);
- **those who are blessed by Him** (Ps 37:22);
- **the righteous** (v. 29);
- those who **wait for the LORD and keep His way** (v. 34).
- The earth belongs to the Lord (24:1), and He has designated those who humbly submit to His rule to inherit it. In contrast to the temporary material gains of evildoers, the **inheritance** of **the blameless . . . will last forever** (37:18; cp. vv. 3,27,37-38).

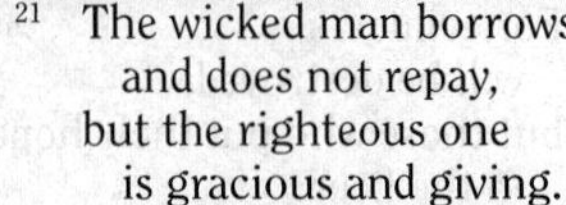

Verses 25 and 35 remind the reader that the wise counsel offered in the psalm comes from a voice of experience. David attests to the Lord's just character (vv. 28,34-38) and faithful care for and salvation of **the righteous** (vv. 25,32-33,39).

38:1-12 This is one of the seven *penitential* psalms of the ancient church, also identified as an individual lament. The word **remembrance** (Hb *zakar*, "cause to remember, bring to remembrance, celebrate," superscription; sometimes associated with the memorial offering, Lv 2:2; 24:7) may imply that the psalm was to be used by a sufferer in order to bring his situation to God's remembrance. The title does not suggest that God forgets or is insensitive to the plight of His suffering children. Rather the cry for God to remember in the Old Testament is a cry for Him to act.

21 The wicked man borrows
and does not repay,
but the righteous one
is gracious and giving.
22 Those who are blessed
by Him will inherit
the land,[A]
but those cursed by Him
will be destroyed.
23 A man's steps are established
by the LORD,
and He takes pleasure
in his way.
24 Though he falls, he will not
be overwhelmed,
because the LORD holds
his hand.[B]
25 I have been young and now
I am old,
yet I have not seen
the righteous abandoned
or his children begging
for bread.
26 He is always generous,
always lending,
and his children are
a blessing.
27 Turn away from evil and do
what is good,
and dwell there[C] forever.
28 For the LORD loves justice
and will not abandon
His faithful ones.
They are kept safe forever,
but the children of the wicked
will be destroyed.
29 The righteous will inherit
the land[A]
and dwell in it permanently.
30 The mouth of the righteous
utters wisdom;
his tongue speaks
what is just.
31 The instruction of his God is
in his heart;
his steps do not falter.
32 The wicked one lies in wait
for the righteous
and seeks to kill him;
33 the LORD will not leave him
in the power of
the wicked one
or allow him to be condemned
when he is judged.
34 Wait for the LORD and keep
His way,
and He will exalt you
to inherit the land.
You will watch
when the wicked
are destroyed.
35 I have seen
a wicked, violent man
well-rooted[D] like
a flourishing native tree.
36 Then I passed by and[E] noticed
he was gone;
I searched for him,
but he could not be found.
37 Watch the blameless
and observe the upright,
for the man of peace will have
a future.[F]
38 But transgressors will all
be eliminated;
the future[F] of the wicked
will be destroyed.
39 The salvation of the righteous
is from the LORD,
their refuge in a time
of distress.
40 The LORD helps
and delivers them;
He will deliver them
from the wicked
and will save them
because they take refuge
in Him.

Psalm 38

Prayer of a Suffering Sinner

A Davidic psalm for remembrance.

1 LORD, do not punish me
in Your anger
or discipline me
in Your wrath.
2 For Your arrows have sunk
into me,
and Your hand has
pressed down on me.
3 There is no health in my body
because of Your indignation;
there is no strength[G]
in my bones
because of my sin.
4 For my sins have flooded
over my head;

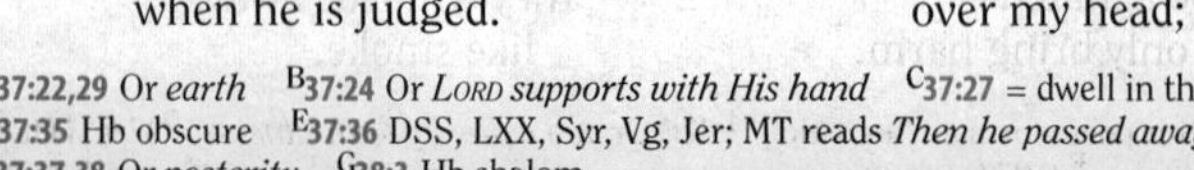

[A]**37:22,29** Or *earth* [B]**37:24** Or *LORD supports with His hand* [C]**37:27** = dwell in the land
[D]**37:35** Hb obscure [E]**37:36** DSS, LXX, Syr, Vg, Jer; MT reads *Then he passed away, and I*
[F]**37:37,38** Or *posterity* [G]**38:3** Hb shalom

HARD QUESTION

Does being sick or disabled or suffering injury mean that God is punishing you?

On one hand, although sickness in general is a result of sin in the world, all illness or infirmity is not due to the afflicted person's sin (see Jn 9:1-3). On the other hand, some suffering is the direct result of specific sins in your life. You cannot judge others when they are suffering; you can only seek to discern for yourself the reasons for your own sufferings. In this psalm, David saw a direct connection between his suffering—affecting him both psychologically and physically—and his sin, which had overwhelmed him (Ps 38:4). In his suffering he felt isolated from God as well as from family and friends (v. 11). He attributed his illness to divine displeasure with his sins and viewed his sufferings as God's chastening (vv. 3,5). Nevertheless, he affirmed that his **hope** was in the Lord (v. 15). David's sense of alienation from God was probably compounded by the presence of strong **enemies** (vv. 19-20). Having confessed his **guilt**, David prayed that God would not **abandon** him (vv. 18,21), believing that God's nearness would bring him healing and forgiveness. His example should encourage believers to call on God in times of suffering and loneliness and to remember that His forgiveness is available when they fail. The Lord is still the **Savior** (v. 22).

they are a burden too heavy
for me to bear.
5 My wounds are foul
and festering
because of my foolishness.
6 I am bent over
and brought low;
all day long I go around
in mourning.
7 For my loins are full of
burning pain,
and there is no health
in my body.
8 I am faint and severely
crushed;
I groan because of
the anguish of my heart.
9 Lord, my every desire
is known to[A] You;
my sighing is not hidden
from You.
10 My heart races, my strength
leaves me,
and even the light of my eyes
has faded.[B]
11 My loved ones
and friends stand back
from my affliction,
and my relatives stand
at a distance.
12 Those who seek my life
set traps,
and those who want
to harm me threaten
to destroy me;
they plot treachery
all day long.
13 I am like a deaf person;
I do not hear.
I am like a speechless person
who does not open his mouth.
14 I am like a man
who does not hear
and has no arguments
in his mouth.
15 I put my hope in You, LORD;
You will answer,
Lord my God.
16 For I said,
"Don't let them rejoice
over me—
those who are arrogant
toward me when I stumble."
17 For I am about to fall,
and my pain is constantly
with me.
18 So I confess my •guilt;
I am anxious because of
my sin.
19 But my enemies are vigorous
and powerful;[C]
many hate me for no reason.
20 Those who repay evil for good
attack me for pursuing good.
21 LORD, do not abandon me;
my God, do not be far
from me.
22 Hurry to help me,
Lord, my Savior.

Psalm 39
The Fleeting Nature of Life

For the choir director,
for Jeduthun. A Davidic psalm.

1 I said, "I will guard my ways
so that I may not sin
with my tongue;
I will guard my mouth
with a muzzle
as long as the wicked are
in my presence."

39:1-13 Jeduthun was one of Israel's chief musicians, "chosen and designated by name to give thanks to the LORD" (1Ch 16:38-42; cp. 1Ch 25:1,3,6; 2Ch 5:12; 35:15; superscriptions of Pss 62; 77).

In a tone similar to that of the book of Ecclesiastes, this psalm addresses the brevity of life, comparing its **short-lived,** (Hb *chadēl*, "frail; ceasing to be," Ps 39:4; cp. "rejected," Is 53:3) nature to a **vapor** (Hb *hevel*, "breath, vanity," Ps 39:5,11; see **Word Study**, p. 831) and a **shadow** (Hb *tselem*, "image," Ps 39:6). The days of life are indeed **short in length** (Hb *tephach*, literally "hand breadth," v. 5), a reference to the width of four fingers or about three inches.

The latter part of verse 6 provides an accurate commentary on the nature of modern society. You **rush around** [Hb *hamah*, literally "hum," the sound made by bees, or "growl, snarl, coo"—make other animal noises, 59:6; "roar" as ocean waves; figuratively describing people as "agitated, distressed, even riotous"; cp. 46:6; 83:2; Is 17:12] **in vain, gathering possessions** (Hb *tsavar*, "heap, store, or pile up"; cp. Jb 27:16; Zch 9:3), forgetting that all too soon you will leave them behind (Ps 39:6). In contrast to thinking of one's future only in materialistic terms, David affirms that his future is governed by the Lord (v. 7), to whom he prays for deliverance from his **transgressions** (Hb *pesha*ʿ, "sin or rebellion against God," v. 8). Acknowledging the Lord's discipline, he makes a desperate appeal for Yahweh to hear and respond to him soon because of the brevity of life (vv. 9-13).

A **38:9** Lit *is in front of* B **38:10** Or *and the light of my eyes—even that is not with me* C **38:19** Or *numerous*

40:1-12 As in Ps 34:8, David exclaims, **How happy** [Hb *ʾesher*; see note on 1:1-2] **is the man** (Hb *gever*; see **Word Study**, p. 692) who follows his example of putting his **trust** [Hb *mivtach*, "confidence, security"] **in the Lord** (40:3-4) instead of two unworthy alternatives:

- **the proud** (Hb *rahav*, "defiant"; from the verb *rahav*, "act fiercely or arrogantly," Is 3:5);
- **those who run after** [Hb *sut*, "swerve, turn aside to"] **lies** (Hb *kazav*, "falsehood, anything that deceives or gives false hope," Ps 40:4).

Verse 6 does not represent a rejection of the sacrificial system. Rather, **sacrifice and offering** were worthless if not presented to God with the right attitude. Ritual acts of worship are meaningless if not accompanied by obedience to the will of God (1Sm 15:22). The primary sacrifice that God desires is the sacrifice of your self-will and self-importance (Ps 51:16-17).

40:13 Overwhelmed by his own weakness and helplessness, David prayed with a sense of urgency. **Hurry** (Hb *chush*; cp. 22:19; 38:22; 70:1,5; 71:12; 141:1) is onomatopoetic—i.e., the sound of the word imitates the referenced sound, here the noise of someone moving hastily. Use of the word **help** (Hb *ʿezrah*, "aid, assistance," 40:13,17) in the book of Psalms is distinctive, always referring to Yahweh as the source. The word is used only 11 times in the rest of the Old Testament, usually referring to human "help."

>WORD|*study*

40:6-8 is quoted in Heb 10:5-7 with a variation reflecting the writer's use of the Greek translation (LXX), which expresses the Hebrew idiom You open my ears to listen with "You prepared a body for Me." Perhaps because the verb also contributes to the messianic interpretation of Ps 22:16, "open (Hb *karah*, lit "dig, excavate") my ears" may have been taken as an allusion to the law regarding a slave who chose to remain with his master rather than "leave as a free man" (Ex 21:5-6). The piercing of the slave's ear with an awl marked the man's permanent commitment to his master, not unlike the Son's acceptance of a human body in obedience to His Father's will (Heb 10:8-10).

2 I was speechless and quiet;
I kept silent, even from
speaking good,
and my pain intensified.
3 My heart grew hot within me;
as I mused, a fire burned.
I spoke with my tongue:
4 "Lord, reveal to me the end
of my life
and the number of my days.
Let me know how short-lived
I am.
5 You, indeed, have made
my days short in length,
and my life span as nothing
in Your sight.
Yes, every mortal man is
only a vapor. *Selah*
6 "Certainly, man walks about
like a mere shadow.
Indeed, they frantically
rush around in vain,
gathering possessions
without knowing
who will get them.
7 Now, Lord, what do I wait for?
My hope is in You.
8 Deliver me from all
my transgressions;
do not make me the taunt
of fools.
9 I am speechless; I do not open
my mouth
because of what You have done.
10 Remove Your torment
from me;
I fade away because of
the force of Your hand.
11 You discipline a man
with punishment for sin,
consuming like a moth
what is precious to him;
every man is only a vapor.
Selah
12 "Hear my prayer, Lord,
and listen to my cry for help;
do not be silent at my tears.
For I am a foreigner residing
with You,
a temporary resident like all
my fathers.
13 Turn Your angry gaze from me
so that I may be cheered up
before I die and am gone."

Psalm 40

Thanksgiving and a Cry for Help

For the choir director. A Davidic psalm.

1 I waited patiently for the Lord,
and He turned to me
and heard my cry for help.
2 He brought me up
from a desolate[A] pit,
out of the muddy clay,
and set my feet on a rock,
making my steps secure.
3 He put a new song
in my mouth,
a hymn of praise to our God.
Many will see and fear
and put their trust in the Lord.
4 How happy is the man
who has put his trust
in the Lord
and has not turned
to the proud
or to those who run after lies!
5 Lord my God, You have done
many things—
Your wonderful works
and Your plans for us;
none can compare with You.
If I were to report and speak
of them,
they are more than can
be told.
6 You do not delight in sacrifice
and offering;
You open my ears to listen.[B]
You do not ask for

[A]40:2 Or *watery* [B]40:6 Lit *You hollow out ears for me*

a whole •burnt offering
or a •sin offering.
7 Then I said, "See, I have come;
it is written about me
in the volume of the scroll.
8 I delight to do Your will,
my God;
Your instruction lives
within me."[A]
9 I proclaim righteousness
in the great assembly;
see, I do not keep
my mouth closed[B]—
as You know, LORD.
10 I did not hide
Your righteousness
in my heart;
I spoke about Your faithfulness
and salvation;
I did not conceal
Your constant love
and truth
from the great assembly.
11 LORD, do not withhold
Your compassion from me;
Your constant love and truth
will always guard me.
12 For troubles without number
have surrounded me;
my sins have overtaken me;
I am unable to see.
They are more than the hairs
of my head,
and my courage leaves me.
13 LORD, be pleased to deliver me;
hurry to help me, LORD.
14 Let those who seek to take
my life
be disgraced and confounded.
Let those who wish
me harm
be driven back
and humiliated.
15 Let those who say to me,
"Aha, aha!"
be horrified because of
their shame.
16 Let all who seek You rejoice
and be glad in You;
let those who love
Your salvation
continually say,
"The LORD is great!"
17 I am afflicted and needy;
the Lord thinks of me.
You are my helper
and my deliverer;
my God, do not delay.

Psalm 41

Victory in Spite of Betrayal

For the choir director. A Davidic psalm.

1 Happy is one who cares
for the poor;
the LORD will save him
in a day of adversity.
2 The LORD will keep him
and preserve him;
he will be blessed in the land.
You will not give him over
to the desire of his enemies.

[A]**40:8** Lit *instruction within my inner being* [B]**40:9** Lit *not restrain my lips*

41:1-13 The psalm begins with a beatitude for the **one who cares for** [Hb *sakal*, "consider, give attention to"; a participle, indicating one who is known for or characterized by "behaving wisely toward" another; cp. Mt 25:31-46; Jms 1:27] **the poor** (Hb *dal*, "helpless, feeble, weak, powerless,"). Shifting back and forth between third person testimony and prayer directly addressed to Yahweh, David elaborates on what is meant by proclaiming the benevolent person to be **happy** (Hb *ʾesher*; see note on 1:1-2.) The one who demonstrates the character of God by meeting people's needs is not immune to experiencing . . .

- **adversity** (41:1);
- being threatened, attacked, and slandered by **enemies** (vv. 2,5-9,11); or
- getting sick (vv. 3,8).

This psalm is often interpreted as the prayer of a person afflicted with sickness; but like many of the psalms, its structure and poetic language resist attempts to confine the song's message to one simple theme. Verses 3,4,8, and 10 allow readers to identify with various possible experiences of this "one who cares for the poor" (v. 1), who counts on the Lord in every negative situation for deliverance, support, and His presence (vv. 2,10-13). See **Word Study** below (vv. 3-4).

That this psalm is the last in Book I of the Psalter is marked by a doxology that is repeated with variations at the end of Book II (72:18-19), Book III (89:52), and Book IV (106:48). The verse functions as a blessing to **Yahweh, the God of Israel** (v. 13).

>WORD|*study*

41:3 To say that the Lord will sustain (Hb *saʿad*, "support, uphold, prop," v. 3) someone on his sickbed (Hb *ʿeres*, "bed" of *deway*, "languishing disease, uncleanness," a noun used in the OT only here and in Jb 6:7 for "contaminated" food) draws on the actions of caregivers whose friend or loved one is too sick to lift his head or whose body must be held up to function. Such ministry requires personal involvement and the humility to help the sick person do what he cannot do without help. However, *deway* is derived from the adjective *daweh* (Hb, "languid, sick, faint"), which is used only five times in the Old Testament—three times referring to a woman's menstruation (Lv 15:33; 20:18; Is 30:22) and twice to being emotionally "sick" (Lm 1:13; 5:17)—and suggests a wider range of reasons for staying in bed than the most obvious one of being physically sick.

41:3-4 Two different words are translated as heal: (1) David affirms that Yahweh **will heal** [Hb *haphak*, "turn, change"] **him** (v. 3). The location where this occurs—**on the bed** [Hb *mishkav*, "couch, a place of lying down"] **where he lies** (Hb *choli*, "illness, sickness, affliction, suffering"; cp. 1Kg 17:17; 2Ch 16:12; Is 53:3-4)—implies that Yahweh meets the sick or grieving person where he is and that He brings about either a "turnaround" in the prognosis of someone with a physical illness or a "change" in perspective of someone suffering debilitating grief (cp. Jr 10:19). David prays for and claims both physical and spiritual restoration (Ps 41:4,10). (2) David also prays, **LORD, . . .** heal [Hb *rapha*ʾ, "sew together, mend"; figuratively, "pardon, comfort"] **me** as a request for forgiveness of sin against God (v. 4).

41:9 Verse 9 notes the betrayal of a **trusted** [Hb *batach*, "confide, place confidence in; be secure, without fear"] **friend** (Hb *ʾish shalom*, "man of peace"). David possibly thought of his advisor Ahithophel, who joined Absalom in a conspiracy to steal the throne (2Sm 15:12–17:23). However, Jesus directly referred to Ps 41:9 as "Scripture [that] must be fulfilled" (Jn 13:18) foreseeing the betrayal of Judas Iscariot (see Jn 13:1-30).

42:1–43:5 Psalms 42 and 43 are so intricately related to one another—especially with the refrain that recurs in 42:5,11 and in 43:5—that they were probably written as one piece. Also, Ps 42 bears a superscription, that seems to apply to both as one psalm of lament.

As a ***Maskil*** this psalm may be understood as one that teaches or gives insight into practical living. It voices the experience of one who belongs to God yet longs for reassurance of His presence when God seems to be absent. The concrete imagery of verse 1 captures the depth of emotion and sets the tone for the entire literary unit (Pss 42–43). The psalmist compares his longing for God to the intensity of a deer's thirst for flowing **streams of water** (42:1), perhaps during a severe drought or upon fleeing from danger.

As the psalmist unfolds an unvarnished account of his experience, both inner and outer sources of distress become apparent: He is anxious to **appear before God** (42:2) for vindication and the defense of his **cause** (43:1), but he is continually confronted by human self-appointed judges, who criticize him for his faith and, in effect, disparage **the living God** Himself (Ps

3 The LORD will sustain him
on his sickbed;
You will heal him on the bed
where he lies.
4 I said, "LORD, be gracious
to me;
heal me, for I have sinned
against You."
5 My enemies speak maliciously
about me:
"When will he die
and be forgotten?"
6 When one of them
comes to visit,
he speaks deceitfully;
he stores up evil in his heart;
he goes out and talks.
7 All who hate me
whisper together about me;
they plan to harm me.
8 "Lethal poison
has been poured into him,
and he won't rise again
from where he lies!"
9 Even my friend[A] in whom
I trusted,
one who ate my bread,
has raised his heel
against me.
10 But You, LORD, be gracious
to me and raise me up;
then I will repay them.
11 By this I know
that You delight in me:
my enemy does not shout
in triumph over me.
12 You supported me because of
my integrity
and set me
in Your presence forever.
13 May •Yahweh, the God
of Israel, be praised
from everlasting
to everlasting.
•Amen and amen.

BOOK II
(Psalms 42:1–72:20)

Psalm 42
Longing for God

For the choir director. A •Maskil of the sons of Korah.

1 As a deer longs for streams
of water,
so I long for You, God.
2 I thirst for God,
the living God.
When can I come and appear
before God?
3 My tears have been my food
day and night,
while all day long people say
to me,

A41:9 Lit *Even a man of my peace*

>WORD|*study*

41:13 Amen (Hb, "truly, verily") comes from the verb *ʾaman* ("confirm, verify, be sure or true") with the basic idea of firmness or certainty. The twofold "amen" may represent the worshiping congregation's emphatic response to the benediction.

42:Superscription The sons of Korah were Levites, descended from Moses' grandfather, Kohath (Ex 6:16,18-21,24; 1Ch 6:22). The Korahites served as gatekeepers for the temple (1Ch 9:19) and may have been among the Levitical musicians and singers as well (2Ch 20:19). As a phrase, "the sons of Korah" appears only here, in the genealogical records of Ex 6:24, and in Nm 26:11—alluding to God's judgment of Korah and "his followers" when they "fought against Moses and Aaron [and] against the LORD" (see Nm 16:1-40; 26:9). The prominent link between "the sons of Korah" who "did not die" (Nm 26:11) and this group of psalms (Pss 42–49; 84–85; 87–88) attributed to their descendants draws attention to a prevailing theme of these 12 psalms—"redemption from Sheol."

42:1 The verb long (Hb *ʿarag*, "desire") is used only here and in a context of God's judgment when "fire has consumed" all means of sustenance so that "even the wild animals cry out" (Hb *ʿarag*) to Yahweh (Jl 1:20). In both verses, the Hebrew verb implies that the subject pursues the Lord with a sense of urgency born of desperation and the knowledge that hope lies in no other.

42:5 The Hebrew wording of the phrase my Savior and my God (Hb *yeshuʿah*, "deliverance, help, salvation" of *panim*, "face, countenance, presence," cp. v. 11; 43:5)—lit "the help of His presence"—shows that the psalmist's faith fits the New Testament definition as "the reality of what is hoped for, the proof of what is not seen" (Heb 11:1). Having asked when he could **appear before God** (42:2), the psalmist praises God for the salvation of His presence (43:3-5)—what he knows to be real, though his feelings and his critics persist in saying otherwise.

42:6 The word depressed (Hb *shachach*, "be cast down") appears once in the psalmist's flat statement of his condition (42:6) and three times in the refrain's first "why" question (42:5,11; 43:5). It provides a snapshot of one who is "downcast," whose head hangs down. In this posture, one can see only the ground. Metaphorically, attention is focused on the seemingly impossible earthly situation.

42:11 The refrain's second question uses the word turmoil (Hb *hamah*, "unsettled emotions"), an onomatopoetic word—i.e., the word itself sounds like what it means. Here the Hebrew word "turmoil" sounds like the humming of bees or other animal sounds (Is 59:11) or the **roar** of water (Pss 42:7; 46:3). It usually has a negative connotation, describing people or situations as tumultuous; noisy from disorderly commotion; or even uncontrollably angry. The word suits the sense of being overwhelmed with grief or anxiety that will not submit to reason and that continually resists peace and rest.

"Where is your God?"
4 I remember this as I pour out
my heart:
how I walked with many,
leading the festive procession
to the house of God,
with joyful
and thankful shouts.

5 Why am I so depressed?
Why this turmoil within me?
Put your hope in God,
for I will still praise Him,
my Savior and my God.
6 I[A] am deeply depressed;
therefore I remember You
from the land of Jordan
and the peaks of Hermon,
from Mount Mizar.
7 Deep calls to deep in the roar
of Your waterfalls;
all Your breakers
and Your billows have swept
over me.
8 The LORD will send
His faithful love by day;
His song will be with me
in the night—
a prayer to the God of my life.

9 I will say to God, my rock,
"Why have You forgotten me?
Why must I go about
in sorrow
because of
the enemy's oppression?"
10 My adversaries taunt me,
as if crushing my bones,
while all day long they say
to me,
"Where is your God?"
11 Why am I so depressed?
Why this turmoil within me?
Put your hope in God,
for I will still praise Him,
my Savior and my God.

Psalm 43[B]

1 Vindicate me, God,
and defend my cause
against an ungodly nation;
rescue me from the deceitful
and unjust man.
2 For You are the God
of my refuge.
Why have You rejected me?
Why must I go about
in sorrow
because of
the enemy's oppression?
3 Send Your light
and Your truth; let them
lead me.
Let them bring me
to Your holy mountain,
to Your dwelling place.
4 Then I will come to the altar
of God,
to God, my greatest joy.
I will praise You with the lyre,
God, my God.

5 Why am I so depressed?
Why this turmoil within me?
Put your hope in God,
for I will still praise Him,
my Savior and my God.

Psalm 44
Israel's Complaint

For the choir director. A •Maskil of the sons of Korah.

1 God, we have heard
with our ears—
our ancestors have told us—
the work You accomplished
in their days,
in days long ago:
2 to plant them,
You drove out the nations
with Your hand;
to settle them,
You crushed the peoples.
3 For they did not take the land
by their sword—
their arm did not
bring them victory—
but by Your right hand,
Your arm,
and the light of Your face,
for You were pleased
with them.
4 You are my King, my God,
who ordains[C] victories
for Jacob.
5 Through You we drive back
our foes;
through Your name
we trample our enemies.
6 For I do not trust in my bow,

42:2). The psalmist cites **the enemy's oppression** (42:9) and the taunting of his **adversaries** (42:10) as the reason he **must . . . go about in sorrow** (Hb *qadar*, an active participle denoting continual "mourning, being darkened," 42:9 and 43:2; cp. 34:14; 38:6). He endures opposition both from those who reject God and from treacherous individuals (43:1).

The psalmist faces not only distressing circumstances and antagonistic people but also an inward battle between despair and hope. The sharp contrast between memories of past joys and current circumstances can intensify one's anguish. Instead of denying the truth that God *is* sovereign and faithful and worthy of praise, the psalmist chooses to entrust the present circumstances and future outcomes to the Lord. Such **hope** (Hb *yachal*, "expect, wait," 42:15) is nourished by remembering one's personal history with God (42:4). Attention shifts away from the present distress to the future refreshment of returning to His **dwelling place** (43:3-4).

The **Hermon** mountain range delineated Israel's northern border and marks the headwaters of the **Jordan** (Hb, "descender; a flowing down," 42:6) River. From the Banias springs at the foot of Mount Hermon, water from melting snow and winter rains thunders through a channel and descends over 600 feet in approximately two miles to form the Banias waterfall. **Mount Mizar** (Hb, "little mountain") probably designated one of the smaller peaks or hills of the Hermon range. In the thunderous, surging flow of water, the psalmist finds an analogy to remembering the God to whom he prays (42:6-7). Some interpret the phrase **deep calls** [Hb *qara'*, "cry out, call upon, summon"—an active participle indicating continuous action] **to deep** (42:7; Hb *tehom*, "wave; water in commotion, making noise"; cp. Hab 3:10) as referring to wave after wave of trouble, chaos, or judgment engulfing the psalmist. However, the water images are ascribed to God—God's **waterfalls . . .** [God's] **breakers and . . .** [God's] **billows**, and the psalm consistently identifies God as the source of **life** (42:1,8), **joy** (42:4; 43:4), stability ("God, my rock," 42:9), and security ("the God of my refuge," 43:2). Furthermore, the psalmist says nothing about God's wrath or judgment, about a need to repent, or about seeking restoration. Instead, 42:6-7 provides a picture of the profound, all-encompassing presence of Yahweh that the psalmist has known in the past and trusts he will experience again (v. 8).

44:1-16 The setting of this psalm must have been a time of national calamity for Israel. The psalmist reflects on what God accomplished for His people in the past, particularly when they entered

[A] **42:5-6** Some Hb mss, LXX, Syr; other Hb mss read *Him, the salvation of His presence.* [6] *My God, I*
[B] **Ps 43** Many Hb mss connect Pss 42–43 [C] **44:4** LXX, Syr, Aq; MT reads *King, God; ordain*

the promised land under Joshua's leadership (vv. 1-3; cp. Dt 9:4-6). He attributes both **victory** and humiliation to **God**, his **King** (Ps 44:4-9). The psalmist expected God to bring military victory for His people in the present, just as He had done in the past. Instead, God's people experienced defeat and the ridicule of their enemies (vv. 9-16), knowing that He promised such adversity as discipline and punishment for the people's disobedience and idolatry (cp. Lv 26:14-33).

44:17-22 The psalm, therefore, turns to protest that they are suffering despite their faithfulness to the Lord. Not only does this experience seem to contradict the pattern of receiving blessings for faithful obedience and afflictions for disobedience (Dt 28), but the psalmist also contends that **because of** God—i.e., for His sake and because they have remained loyal to Him—the people **are counted as sheep to be slaughtered** (Hb *tibchah*, "a slaying of stock animals, slaughterhouse," Ps 44:22; a noun used only here and 1Sm 25:11 [butchered "meat"]; Jr 12:3). In the New Testament, Paul quoted Ps 44:22 in a context affirming that God is always with His children even in the midst of suffering, making them more than conquerors (Rm 8:36).

44:23-26 The challenge to the Lord to quit **sleeping** and **wake up** does not mean the people believed that God was literally asleep. Rather, their plea expressed the urgency for Him to give immediate attention to their situation. The psalmist urged the Lord to act on the basis of His **faithful love** (Hb *chesed*, "unfailing love"; see **Word Study**, p. 322).

and my sword does not
bring me victory.
7 But You give us victory
over our foes
and let those who hate us
be disgraced.
8 We boast in God all day long;
we will praise
Your name forever. *Selah*
9 But You have rejected
and humiliated us;
You do not march out
with our armies.
10 You make us retreat
from the foe,
and those who hate us
have taken plunder
for themselves.
11 You hand us over to be eaten
like sheep
and scatter us
among the nations.
12 You sell Your people
for nothing;
You make no profit
from selling them.
13 You make us an object
of reproach
to our neighbors,
a source of mockery
and ridicule to those
around us.
14 You make us a joke
among the nations,
a laughingstock[A]
among the peoples.
15 My disgrace is before me
all day long,
and shame has covered
my face,
16 because of the voice
of the scorner and reviler,
because of the enemy
and avenger.
17 All this has happened to us,
but we have not forgotten You
or betrayed Your covenant.
18 Our hearts have not
turned back;
our steps have not strayed
from Your path.
19 But You have crushed us
in a haunt of jackals
and have covered us
with deepest darkness.
20 If we had forgotten the name
of our God
and spread out our hands
to a foreign god,
21 wouldn't God have found
this out,
since He knows the secrets
of the heart?

[A]44:14 Lit *shaking of the head*

>WORD|*study*

44:26 Redeem (Hb *padah*, "loose, set free") often means to transfer ownership from one to another by payment of a price or a substitute of equivalent value. The same verb is used of redeeming the firstborn in Ex 13:13.

45:7 The verb anointed (Hb *mashach*, "pour oil" on the head, usually for one being consecrated to the office of priest king, or prophet; ([cp. Heb 7:26–8:2], cp. Gk *chriō*, Lk 4:18 [cp. Is 61:1; Heb 1:9]) appears in only three other New Testament verses—Ac 4:27 and 10:38 speak of God's anointing of Jesus; 2Co 1:21 refers to God's anointing of believers (who are "in Christ").

45:7 In the Old Testament, such joy (Hb *sason*, "gladness, rejoicing, jubilation") is most often associated with the exultant celebration of what Yahweh does or has done (Jr 33:9):

- He rescued the Jews from genocide (Est 8:16-17).
- He heals and restores, removing sorrow and mourning (Ps 51:8,12; Is 35:10; 51:3,11; 61:3; Jr 31:13; 33:11; Zch 8:19).
- He brought His people out of Egyptian bondage (Ps 105:43).
- His "words" (Jr 15:16) and "decrees" (Ps 119:111) bring deep and abiding joy.

Four times the desolation to be experienced by Judah and Jerusalem when God punished their sin is described poignantly as the removal of "the sound of joy . . . and the voices of the bridegroom and the bride," identifying weddings as occasions epitomizing joy (Jr 7:34; 16:9; 25:10; 33:11).

45:7 Because he supremely loves **righteousness** and hates **wickedness** (cp. 11:4-7; 33:5; 89:14; Is 61:8), the king by his anointing is set above his companions (Hb *chavēr*, "associate, fellow")—possibly other princes of the royal family, fellow Israelites, or members of the wedding party—indicating his exalted status. In the LXX the word is *metochos* (Gk, "partner, partaker, one who shares in," a word used only in Lk 5:7; Heb 1:9; 3:1,14; 6:4; 12:8). In Heb 1:9, the immediate context suggests that the word may refer to the angels over whom Christ is clearly superior (Heb 1:4-5). However, in the New Testament both the noun and the verb form, *metechō*, usually refer to followers of Christ (e.g., Heb 3:14; 1Co 9:17,21; cp. Heb 2:14).

22 Because of You we are slain
all day long;
we are counted as sheep
to be slaughtered.
23 Wake up, LORD!
Why are You sleeping?
Get up!
Don't reject us forever!
24 Why do You hide Yourself
and forget our affliction
and oppression?
25 For we have sunk down
to the dust;
our bodies cling
to the ground.
26 Rise up! Help us!
Redeem us because of
Your faithful love.

Psalm 45
A Royal Wedding Song

For the choir director: according to "The Lilies."[A] *A* •Maskil *of the sons of Korah. A love song.*

1 My heart is moved
by a noble theme
as I recite my verses
to the king;
my tongue is the pen
of a skillful writer.
2 You are the most handsome
of •men;
grace flows from your lips.
Therefore God
has blessed you forever.

3 Mighty warrior,
strap your sword
at your side.
In your majesty
and splendor—
4 in your splendor
ride triumphantly
in the cause of truth,
humility, and justice.
May your right hand show
your awe-inspiring acts.
5 Your arrows pierce the hearts
of the king's enemies;
the peoples fall under you.
6 Your throne, God, is[B] forever
and ever;
the scepter of Your[C] kingdom
is a scepter of justice.
7 You love righteousness
and hate wickedness;
therefore God, your God,
has anointed you
with the oil of joy
more than
your companions.
8 Myrrh, aloes, and cassia
perfume all your garments;
from ivory palaces harps
bring you joy.
9 Kings' daughters are among
your honored women;
the queen, adorned with gold
from Ophir,
stands at your right hand.

10 Listen, daughter,
pay attention and consider:
forget your people
and your father's house,
11 and the king will desire
your beauty.
Bow down to him,
for he is your lord.
12 The daughter of Tyre,
the wealthy people,
will seek your favor
with gifts.

13 In her chamber,
the royal daughter
is all glorious,
her clothing embroidered
with gold.
14 In colorful garments
she is led to the king;
after her, the virgins,
her companions,
are brought to you.
15 They are led in with gladness
and rejoicing;
they enter the king's palace.

16 Your sons will succeed
your ancestors;
you will make
them princes
throughout the land.
17 I will cause your name
to be remembered
for all generations;
therefore the peoples
will praise you forever
and ever.

[A] **45:title** Possibly a tune; Pss 60; 69; 80 [B] **45:6** Or *Your divine throne is*, or *Your throne is God's* [C] **45:6** Or *your*

45:1 The superscription's reference to **"The Lilies"** probably indicates the melody for this **love song** (Hb *shir*, "song" of *yedidot*—plural of *yadid*, "beloved, darling"; cp. Is 5:1), which celebrates a royal wedding, about which the psalmist's **heart is moved** (Hb *rachash*, "boil or bubble up" like a fountain). The lyrics do not provide enough information to identify the particular king to whom the **verses** (Hb *ma'aseh*, "product, work, what one has made") were recited.

45:2-6 Some scholars believe that details in the psalm point to the wedding of Ahab and Jezebel (cp. vv. 8-9,12; 1Kg 16:31; 22:39). Others regard Solomon as the bridegroom. More likely the song was written for the wedding of a later Davidic king, especially in light of the New Testament's interpretation of Ps 45:6-7 as referring to "the Son" (i.e., to Jesus the Messiah), who fulfills God's promise to establish a descendant of David on the throne forever (Heb 1:8-9; 2Sm 7:8-16; 1Kg 5:5; 1Ch 17:11-14; Mt 1:1; 12:23; 21:9; Lk 1:32; Rm 1:3; Rv 22:16).

45:9 The king's **honored women** (Hb *yaqar*, "dear or precious, magnificent or splendid, of rare value," v. 9) included other **kings' daughters**—princesses who may have been potential brides—but the psalmist fast-forwards his description of the wedding events to place **the queen** (Hb *shēgal*, "king's wife," only v. 9 and Neh 2:6) by his side. Some regard "the queen" as the king's mother standing to address the bride, but a different word is used elsewhere to designate the "queen mother" (Hb *gevirah*; 1Kg 15:13; 2Kg 10:13; Jr 13:18; 29:2).

45:10-12 The bride is addressed as **daughter**—probably a term of endearment rather than an indication of a familial relationship. She is urged to embrace her new role as the king's wife. To do so, she is advised to let go of the ties to her culture and former relationships—the customs with which she is familiar and the people with whom she is most comfortable.

46:1 The phrase **according to *Alamoth*** (Hb plural of *ʿalmah*, "virgin, girl of marriageable age, maiden") perhaps designates female or soprano voices. The background of this psalm may be the crisis of 701 B.C. when God miraculously delivered the city of Jerusalem from the armies of Sennacherib, king of Assyria (2Kg 18–19).

Speaking for himself and God's people, the psalmist confidently declares, without qualification, that **in times of trouble** God is the one in whom safety, protection, and help are **always found** (Hb *matsaʾ*, "be found, be present or here," modified by *meʾod*, "greatly, exceedingly"; cp. 22:19; 60:11; 108:12). A **refuge** (Hb *machaseh*; from the verb *chasah*; see 7:1; 17:7; and the **Word Study**, p. 692) is a place of "shelter" furnishing protection from the dangers of a storm or a person to whom one runs for "safety" (cp. 61:3; 62:7-8; 71:7; 91:2,9; 142:5).

46:2-6 On the basis of who God is for His people, the psalmist boldly announces **we will not be afraid**. Frequently in Scripture the Lord urges His people not to fear or be afraid; rarely are direct statements like this one recorded (cp. 3:6; 27:3; 78:53; 118:6; Is 41:10). To express his utterly unshakable confidence in God, the psalmist describes devastating circumstances too big for anyone but God to handle—from natural disasters like earthquakes and volcanic eruptions to the rise and fall of **nations** and **kingdoms**.

46:7 The reference to **the God of Jacob** reminds us that He is the God of Israel or Jacob and that He has chosen to link Himself even with those who aren't particularly noble in their attitudes and actions (cp. v. 11).

46:8-9 Whereas verse 1 calls attention to God's omnipresence—"He is a helper who is always found"— these verses focus on God's omnipotence. He is all-powerful.

46:10 The psalmist encouraged his listeners to **stop** (Hb *raphah*, "leave off, let up, relax"; cp. 1Sm 15:16) struggling and experience peace. The hearers are instructed to relax and know the greatness of God. Serenity or peace comes only in the acknowledgement of God's lordship in your life and your surrender to His will.

47:1-9 Because of elements reflecting a coronation ceremony, this psalm is often classified as an enthronement psalm—one that praises the Lord's reign or kingship (see also Pss 93; 96–99). Repeated imperatives call for active worship:

- **Clap your hands** (v. 1).
- **Shout to God** (v. 1).
- **Sing praise** (four times in v. 6).

Psalm 46
God Our Refuge

For the choir director. A song of the sons of Korah. According to Alamoth.[A]

1 God is our refuge
and strength,
a helper who is always found
in times of trouble.
2 Therefore we
will not be afraid,
though the earth trembles
and the mountains topple
into the depths of the seas,
3 though its waters roar
and foam
and the mountains quake
with its turmoil. •*Selah*

4 There is a river—
its streams delight the city
of God,
the holy dwelling place
of the •Most High.
5 God is within her;
she will not be toppled.
God will help her
when the morning dawns.
6 Nations rage,
kingdoms topple;
the earth melts when He lifts
His voice.
7 The LORD of •Hosts is with us;
the God of Jacob is
our stronghold. *Selah*

8 Come, see the works
of the LORD,
who brings devastation
on the earth.
9 He makes wars cease
throughout the earth.
He shatters bows
and cuts spears to pieces;
He burns up the chariots.[B]
10 "Stop your fighting—
and know
that I am God,
exalted among the nations,
exalted on the earth."
11 •Yahweh of Hosts is with us;
the God of Jacob is
our stronghold. *Selah*

Psalm 47
God Our King

For the choir director. A psalm of the sons of Korah.

1 Clap your hands,
all you peoples;
shout to God
with a jubilant cry.
2 For •Yahweh, the •Most High,
is awe-inspiring,
a great King over
all the earth.
3 He subdues peoples under us
and nations under our feet.
4 He chooses for us
our inheritance—
the pride of Jacob,
whom He loves. •*Selah*

5 God ascends among
shouts of joy,
the LORD, among the sound
of trumpets.
6 Sing praise to God,
sing praise;
sing praise to our King,
sing praise!
7 Sing a song of wisdom,[C]
for God is King of all
the earth.

8 God reigns over the nations;
God is seated
on His holy throne.
9 The nobles of the peoples
have assembled
with the people of the God
of Abraham.
For the leaders[D] of the earth
belong to God;
He is greatly exalted.

Psalm 48
Exaltation of Zion

A song. A psalm of the sons of Korah.

1 The LORD is great and
highly praised
in the city of our God.
His holy mountain,
2 rising splendidly,
is the joy of the whole earth.
Mount •Zion on the slopes
of the north
is the city of the great King.
3 God is known as a stronghold
in its citadels.

[A]**46:title** This may refer to a high pitch, perhaps a tune sung by soprano voices; the Hb word means "young women." [B]**46:9** Lit *chariots with fire* [C]**47:7** Hb *a Maskil* [D]**47:9** Lit *shields*

4 Look! The kings assembled;
they advanced together.
5 They looked and froze
with fear;
they fled in terror.
6 Trembling seized them there,
agony like that of a woman
in labor,
7 as You wrecked the ships
of Tarshish
with the east wind.

8 Just as we heard,
so we have seen
in the city of •Yahweh
of •Hosts,
in the city of our God;
God will establish it forever.
•*Selah*

9 God, within Your temple,
we contemplate
Your faithful love.
10 Your name, God,
like Your praise,
reaches to the ends
of the earth;
Your right hand is filled
with justice.
11 Mount Zion is glad.
The towns[A] of Judah rejoice
because of Your judgments.

12 Go around Zion, encircle it;
count its towers,
13 note its ramparts;
tour its citadels
so that you can tell
a future generation:
14 "This God, our God
forever and ever—
He will always lead us."[B]

Psalm 49
Misplaced Trust in Wealth

For the choir director. A psalm of the sons of Korah.

1 Hear this, all you peoples;
listen, all who inhabit
the world,
2 both low and high,[C]
rich and poor together.
3 My mouth speaks wisdom;
my heart's meditation
brings understanding.
4 I turn my ear to a proverb;
I explain my riddle
with a lyre.

5 Why should I fear in times
of trouble?
The iniquity of my foes
surrounds me.
6 They trust in their wealth
and boast of
their abundant riches.
7 Yet these cannot redeem
a person[D]
or pay his ransom to God—
8 since the price
of redeeming him is
too costly,
one should forever
stop trying[E]—
9 so that he may live forever
and not see the •Pit.

10 For one can see
that wise men die;
foolish and stupid men also
pass away.
Then they leave their wealth
to others.
11 Their graves are
their eternal homes,[F]
their homes from generation
to generation,
though they have named
estates after themselves.
12 But despite his assets,[G]
man will not last;
he is like the animals
that perish.

13 This is the way of those
who are arrogant,
and of their followers,
who approve of their words.[H]
•*Selah*
14 Like sheep they are headed
for •Sheol;
Death will shepherd them.
The upright
will rule over them
in the morning,
and their form
will waste away in Sheol,[I]
far from their lofty abode.
15 But God will redeem my life
from the power of Sheol,
for He will take me. *Selah*

[A]**48:11** Lit *daughters* [B]**48:14** Some Hb mss, LXX; other Hb mss read *over death* [C]**49:2** Lit *both sons of Adam and sons of man* [D]**49:7** Or *Certainly he cannot redeem himself*, or *Yet he cannot redeem a brother* [E]**49:8** Or *costly, it will cease forever* [F]**49:11** LXX, Syr, Tg; MT reads *Their inner thought is that their houses are eternal* [G]**49:12** Or *honor* [H]**49:13** Lit *and after them with their mouth they were pleased* [I]**49:14** Hb obscure

• **Sing a song of wisdom** (v. 7). Except for these and part of verse 9, God is the grammatical subject of every sentence, and especially do the verbs depict His activities and role as **King over all the earth** (v. 2; cp. Rv 11:15). Yahweh **is awe-inspiring** (Hb *yare'*, "is dreadful, venerable, illustrious," v. 2) as the one who rules over all places, **peoples**, **nations**, **nobles**, and **leaders of the earth** (vv. 3,8-9). The Lord, the only great **King**, desires to reign supreme in individual hearts as well. One day the reality of the Lord's universal reign will be acknowledged by all (Php 2:10-11).

48:1-14 Like Ps 46, Ps 48 celebrates the security enjoyed by those who place their faith in the Lord. **The city of our God** and **Mount Zion** refer to Jerusalem (vv. 1,8,11). Though the psalm begins and ends with images of the physical elements of military defense, God Himself provided security for the city and the nation of Israel. Verses 4-8 poetically describe His defeat of Israel's enemies when they dared to attack the city. God's people believed that Jerusalem could never be conquered because God would always protect it. When Jerusalem fell to the Babylonians in 586 B.C., God's people learned through bitter experience that authentic faith in Him must reflect itself in moral and ethical living.

49:1-4 Like Ps 1, this is a **wisdom** psalm. The opening verses of invitation to attend the message of wisdom leave room for no one to exclude himself from the intended audience.

49:5-20 Verse 5, which poses the key question of the psalm, suggests that the speaker was concerned about being in a situation—whether referring to personal circumstances or an entire culture—made dangerous by the wickedness of the people who had the most influence, power, or control. In verse 16 the psalmist answers his own question with counsel that reflects the wisdom noted already in verses 6-15 and summarized in verses 17-20.

The antidote for fear of the increasing earthly resources of sinful and self-promoting people is an eternal perspective grounded in the reality of God's sovereignty. Money cannot prevent death and merely passes into the hands of others (cp. Lk 12:15). The psalm does not condemn people who have abundant material possessions, but argues that people who pursue wealth as though it could give real meaning to their lives are mistaken. To have confidence in being redeemed from the grave by the eternal God is far more valuable.

50:1-23 Asaph (Hb, "he collected") was the father of the clan of temple musicians who served throughout the temple's history. David began the tradition of giving psalms to Asaph for the temple musicians to sing (1Ch 16:7). The title may refer to authorship, the singers who sang the psalms in worship, or to a particular collection of psalms (cp. titles of Pss 73–83).

51:3-6 David confessed that he was **conscious** (Hb *yada*ʿ, "know, acknowledge, be personally acquainted with"; see note on Ex 2:24-25 and **Word Study**, p. 725) of his **rebellion**. These words are not a casual admission of wrongdoing, for he lamented that his **sin** confronted him all the time. Once David's keen sense of righteous indignation had been turned on himself and he admitted his guilt (2Sm 12:5-7,13), he recognized that he had, above all, sinned against the Lord. Instead of argument or denial, David also acknowledged that he deserved whatever punishment God gave him. In the New Testament, Paul used verse 4 in the context of arguing that God is right to punish sinners, even though "our unrighteousness highlights God's righteousness" (see Rm 3:1-5).

Verses 5 and 6 both begin with the Hebrew word *hēn* (**Indeed**, v. 5; **surely**, v. 6), often translated "Behold!" arresting the attention of the audience and linking the two verses. In verse 5 David acknowledged man's total depravity; in verse 6 he recognized that God wants something different—He takes delight in a person's **integrity** [Hb ʾ*emet*, "truth, faithfulness, fidelity, uprightness"] **in the inner self** (Hb *tuchah*, "hidden recesses, inner regions"; cp. the only other occurrence, "in the heart," Jb 38:36). Verse 5 emphasizes the universality of sin (cp. Gn 6:5; 8:21; Rm 3:23)—not in the sense that sin is passed along through the genes or that the sexual relationship within marriage is sinful. Psalm 51:5 does not promote celibacy or imply that David was born out of wedlock. Rather, David recognized the hopelessness of his sinful condition and sought divine intervention by pleading with God to **purify** and **wash** him (v. 7). All are sinners and know sin from personal experience. Because Adam and Eve transgressed God's command (Gn 3:6-7), every human being is born with an inherently sinful nature and lives in an environment inclined toward sin.

Verse 6, however, focuses on what pleases God—God wants you to be honest with Him in acknowledging your sin. For sin separates you from God, and only your confession of that sin and your asking for forgiveness of that sin brings your reconciliation to God. Outward obedience—following "the letter" of the law (Rm 2:29)—does not remove the root of sin in the heart (cp.

16 Do not be afraid when a man
gets rich,
when the wealth[A]
of his house increases.
17 For when he dies, he will take
nothing at all;
his wealth[A] will not follow
him down.
18 Though he praises himself
during his lifetime—
and people praise you
when you do well
for yourself—
19 he will go to the generation
of his fathers;
they will never see the light.
20 A man
with valuable possessions[B]
but without understanding
is like the animals that perish.

Psalm 50
God as Judge

A psalm of •Asaph.

1 •Yahweh, the God of gods[C]
speaks;
He summons the earth
from east to west.[D]
2 From •Zion, the perfection
of beauty,
God appears in radiance.[E]
3 Our God is coming;
He will not be silent!
Devouring fire precedes Him,
and a storm rages
around Him.
4 On high, He summons
heaven and earth
in order to judge His people.
5 "Gather My faithful ones
to Me,
those who made a covenant
with Me by sacrifice."
6 The heavens proclaim
His righteousness,
for God is the Judge. *•Selah*
7 "Listen, My people,
and I will speak;
I will testify
against you, Israel.
I am God, your God.
8 I do not rebuke you
for your sacrifices
or for your •burnt offerings,
which are continually
before Me.
9 I will not accept a bull
from your household
or male goats from your pens,
10 for every animal of the forest
is Mine,
the cattle on a thousand hills.
11 I know every bird
of the mountains,[F]
and the creatures of the field
are Mine.
12 If I were hungry, I would not
tell you,
for the world and everything
in it is Mine.
13 Do I eat the flesh of bulls
or drink the blood of goats?
14 Sacrifice a thank offering
to God,
and pay your vows
to the •Most High.
15 Call on Me in a day of trouble;
I will rescue you,
and you will honor Me."
16 But God says to the wicked:
"What right do you have
to recite My statutes
and to take My covenant
on your lips?
17 You hate instruction
and turn your back
on My words.[G]
18 When you see a thief,
you make friends with him,
and you associate
with adulterers.
19 You unleash your mouth
for evil
and harness your tongue
for deceit.
20 You sit,
maligning your brother,
slandering your mother's son.
21 You have done these things,
and I kept silent;
you thought I was just
like you.
But I will rebuke you
and lay out the case
before you.[H]
22 "Understand this,
you who forget God,
or I will tear you apart,

[A]**49:16,17** Or *glory* [B]**49:20** Or *with honor* [C]**50:1** Or *The Mighty One, God, the LORD,* or *The God of gods, the LORD* [D]**50:1** Lit *from the rising of the sun to its setting* [E]**50:2** Or *God shines forth* [F]**50:11** LXX, Syr, Tg read *heavens* [G]**50:17** Or *and cast My words behind you* [H]**50:21** Lit *out before your eyes*

and there will be no one to
rescue you.
23 Whoever sacrifices
a thank offering honors Me,
and whoever orders
his conduct,
I will show him the salvation
of God."

Psalm 51

A Prayer for Restoration

For the choir director. A Davidic psalm, when Nathan the prophet came to him after he had gone to Bathsheba.

1 Be gracious to me, God,
according to
Your faithful love;
according to Your abundant
compassion,
blot out my rebellion.
2 Wash away my •guilt
and cleanse me from my sin.
3 For I am conscious
of my rebellion,
and my sin is always
before me.
4 Against You—You alone—
I have sinned
and done this evil
in Your sight.
So You are right
when You pass sentence;
You are blameless
when You judge.
5 Indeed, I was guilty
when I was born;
I was sinful when my mother
conceived me.
6 Surely You desire integrity
in the inner self,
and You teach me wisdom
deep within.
7 Purify me with hyssop,
and I will be •clean;
wash me, and I will be
whiter than snow.
8 Let me hear joy and gladness;
let the bones
You have crushed rejoice.

HARD QUESTION

Can God forgive me for having an abortion? Or for having an affair? Or for . . . ?

Yes (Jn 3:16-17; Rm 6:23). The separation that sin has caused between you and God (Is 59:2) has already been overcome in the death and resurrection of His Son, Jesus Christ (see Ac 10:43; Rm 3:22-25; 8:1-39; cp. Ps 103:10-14). His blood covers any and all sin (Heb 10:19). The forgiveness and cleansing He offers to you are free because of the great cost He paid (Rm 5:8; 2Co 5:21; Heb 2:17-18). If you are asking this question instead of trying to justify the sin or explain it away, then at least your heart is not hardened against the conviction of the Holy Spirit, who wants to use the guilt to help you recognize that you need Him (Jn 16:8; 1Co 11:32). To experience His peace and healing of the damage done by your sin and cover-up of it, you must confess the sin, genuinely repent, and obey Him in taking whatever specific steps are necessary for you to stay on a path of healing not only your relationship with Him but also the human relationships affected by your sin (Ps 32:1-11; Mt 11:28-30; Jms 4:7-10). In Ps 51, David's prayer of confession and repentance offers a general model for seeking forgiveness (cp. 1Jn 1:7-9). He does not name his specific sins in this poem, perhaps because the Lord wanted every reader to be able to apply this pattern of prayer to her sin, whatever that sin is.

Also, the Lord provided someone—the prophet Nathan—to speak truth to David in a straightforward but loving way. The Lord has provided wise and godly people who can walk with you through the healing process (e.g., a mature Christian woman, your pastoral staff, a Christian ministry or counseling service), which can be difficult not only for you but those who have been hurt by your sin (Is 30:18; Heb 10:23-25).

Pr 26:23; Jr 17:9; Mt 15:19). Instead, as Paul emphasized, "a person is a Jew who is one inwardly" (Rm 2:29). Therefore, the Lord offers a repentant person **wisdom deep within** (Hb *satham*, "secret, what is being hidden")—i.e., God personally applies the truth of His Word to David's will and motives. Your thoughts, desires, plans, and feelings may be concealed from other people, but not from God (Pr 15:11).

51:7 The petition, **Purify** [Hb *chata'*, "expiate or cleanse" from sin] **me with hyssop** (Hb *'ezov*, a plant that grew on the walls, 1Kg 4:33; probably the Syrian marjoram plant), seems to allude to the ritual prescribed for readmitting into the covenant community a person "afflicted with a skin disease" (Lv 14:1-32; cp. Lv 14:33-57, a similar ritual for making "atonement" for a mildewed house; Nm 19:17-19 for the use of hyssop in cleansing someone who has touched a corpse). Hyssop, "two live clean birds, cedar wood, [and] scarlet yarn" were all elements of the initial ritual, in which a bundle of hyssop cuttings were used to sprinkle the blood of one bird on "the one who is to be cleansed"; the other bird was released (Lv 14:4-7).

The entire process of being restored to full participation among God's people involved sacrifices and offerings as well as the process of being marked by the priest with both blood and oil (Lv 14:10-32). The Lord affirmed that in this way, "the priest will make atonement for him [the afflicted one], and he will be clean" (Hb *tāher*, Lv 14:9,20; "cleanse," Ps 51:2). Likewise, David expected this result if the Lord answered his prayer—**I will be clean** (Hb *tāher*).

51:8 The plea to **hear joy** [Hb *sason*; see **Word Study**, p. 702] **and gladness** probably expresses David's desire to hear that he has been pronounced forgiven.

>WORD|*study*

51:7 Wash [Hb *kavas*, "wash"—usually one's clothes; cp. v. 2; Lv 14:8,9,47; Nm 19:19] **me** parallels **purify me**. When the Lord confronted Israel's apostasy through the prophet Jeremiah, He made clear that no amount of washing, even with "a great amount of soap," could remove their guilt (Jr 2:22). The repentant sinner, however, can confidently expect that when the Lord does the washing he **will be whiter than snow** (Hb *lavan*, literally "make white"; metaphorically "purge, cleanse"; cp. Is 1:18; Rv 7:14). Only God can perform the inward cleansing necessary for restored fellowship with Him and His people.

51:8 In the parallel request, bones (Hb *'etsem*) is an idiom for one's entire being, life or self (cp. "life in this body," Jb 7:15). The bones are the framework for the body in which life is lived. David may refer to **the bones You have** crushed (Hb *dakah*, "break to pieces") as a metaphor comparing the severity of God's rebuke and its effect on his spiritually sensitive heart to the debilitating effects of such severe physical injuries. Undoubtedly David himself had inflicted such blows on enemy soldiers in battle and was intimately acquainted with men who had lost the use of one or more limbs as the result of bone-crushing injuries. He is not speaking of a clean break—a bone that can be set and restored in a straightforward manner. Rather, he describes the kind of injury from which one never fully recovers. Recognizing that God has broken him to pieces by confronting him with the truth and ongoing punishment (2Sm 12:7-14), David prays to be allowed to **rejoice** (Hb *gil*, "leap for joy, tremble with joy"; cp. 2:11; 14:7) rather than to resent, the God who loves him enough to address his sin.

51:10 David extends his prayer for full restoration by asking God to **create** (Hb *bara'*, "form by cutting or carving out; produce") for him a **clean** [Hb *tahor*, "undivided, morally pure"] **heart** (i.e., the place of the will or decision-making). In the Old Testament, the verb *bara'*, when denoting an act of creation, appears only with God as its subject (cp. Gn 1:1) as a way of indicating what only God can perform.

In other contexts the word **renew** (Hb *chadash*, "make new") denotes the repair or renovation of a structure or city. That which was ruined is restored (see 2Ch 15:8; 24:4; Is 61:4). In the past David had a **steadfast** [Hb *kun*, "be firm, constant, true, sincere, right; confident, fixed, faithful"] **spirit** (e.g., Ps 57:7), so he prayed that God will rebuild his character from the inside out so that he might again become fixed and resolute in his allegiance to the Lord.

51:11 The Hebrew phrase translated **Your Holy Spirit** (*ruach qadsheka*) occurs rarely in the Old Testament. The intensity of David's plea likely reflects his experience of having witnessed the tragic results of God's Spirit departing from King Saul, who repeatedly disobeyed the Lord (1Sm 16:14-23).

51:12 Salvation brings with it a **joy** (Hb *sason*, "gladness, abounding delight") that can sustain you through many dark experiences, but sin robs you of that delight.

51:13 Not only are you dependent on the Lord for deliverance or salvation, you also must depend on Him to make you willing to walk in His ways. Upon experiencing forgiveness, David vowed to teach others God's ways. Psalm 32 has been viewed as the fulfillment of David's promise. The experience of forgiveness led David to demonstrate concern for others. He wanted to be instrumental in bringing other rebellious individuals back to the Lord.

51:14 The guilt of bloodshed is likely a reference to the murder of Uriah (2Sm 11:14-27).

51:16-17 For murder, adultery, and other serious offenses—often referred to as sins of the high hand—no sacrifices were prescribed by the law. The sinner in such instances could only cast himself on the mercy of God (see 2Sm 12:13-14). The **sacrifice** of your selfish will and self-importance is the ultimate sacrifice God desires. He accepts and forgives those who are honest with Him, humble before Him, and dependent on His grace. Without a right spirit, no sacrifice you offer is **pleasing** to the Lord.

52:1–55:23 Each of these psalms is identified in its superscription as a

>WORD|*study*

51:9 David begs God, Turn [Hb *satar*, "hide, cover"] **Your face away from my sins**. In the Old Testament, this verb is commonly used of God's hiding His face as a way of speaking about the withdrawal of His presence or approval (e.g., Dt 31:17-18; Ps 10:11; Ps 22:24; Is 59:2]. Here, David asks God to forget about his sins (cp. Ps 10:11; 13:1) and **blot** [them] **out** (Hb *machah*; 51:1-2)

51:11 Presence (Hb *panim*) is the same word as "face" in verse 9. Just as David prayed that God would turn His face away from *his sin*, so he prays here that God will not banish (Hb *shalak*, "cast or throw out"; cp. 2Kg 24:20; 2Ch 7:20) *him* from His "presence." The divine Judge and King had every right to have David thrown out and refuse to hear his confession.

51:13 The Hebrew word translated the rebellious (Hb *pasha'*, "transgressor, covenant-breaker"; cp. 1Kg 8:50; Is 1:2) is in synonymous parallelism with the term sinners (Hb *chatta'* "one who bears the blame or is counted as guilty," an emphatic or intensive form of the verb; see 1:1). In this context both words probably convey the idea of deliberate revolt against God.

9 Turn Your face away[A]
from my sins
and blot out all my guilt.

10 God, create a clean heart
for me
and renew a steadfast[B] spirit
within me.
11 Do not banish me
from Your presence
or take Your Holy Spirit
from me.
12 Restore the joy
of Your salvation to me,
and give me a willing spirit.[C]
13 Then I will teach
the rebellious Your ways,
and sinners will return to You.

14 Save me from the guilt
of bloodshed, God,
the God of my salvation,
and my tongue will sing
of Your righteousness.
15 Lord, open my lips,
and my mouth will declare
Your praise.
16 You do not want a sacrifice,
or I would give it;
You are not pleased
with a •burnt offering.
17 The sacrifice pleasing to God
is[D] a broken spirit.
God, You will not despise
a broken and humbled heart.

18 In Your good pleasure,
cause •Zion to prosper;
build[E] the walls of Jerusalem.
19 Then You will delight
in righteous sacrifices,
whole burnt offerings;
then bulls will be offered
on Your altar.

Psalm 52

God Judges the Proud

For the choir director. A Davidic •Maskil. When Doeg the Edomite went and reported to Saul, telling him, "David went to Ahimelech's house."

1 Why brag about evil,
you hero!
God's faithful love is constant.
2 Like a sharpened razor,
your tongue
devises destruction,
working treachery.
3 You love evil instead of good,
lying instead of
speaking truthfully. *•Selah*
4 You love any words
that destroy,
you treacherous tongue!

5 This is why God will bring
you down forever.
He will take you, ripping you
out of your tent;
He will uproot you
from the land of the living.
Selah
6 The righteous will look on
with awe
and will ridicule him:
7 "Here is the man
who would not make God
his refuge,
but trusted in the abundance
of his riches,
taking refuge in
his destructive behavior."[F]

[A]51:9 Lit *Hide Your face* [B]51:10 Or *right* [C]51:12 Or *and sustain me with a noble spirit* [D]51:17 Lit *The sacrifices of God are* [E]51:18 Or *rebuild* [F]52:7 Or *riches, and grew strong in his evil desire*; lit *his destruction*

8 But I am like
a flourishing olive tree
in the house of God;
I trust in God's faithful love
forever and ever.
9 I will praise You forever
for what You have done.
In the presence
of Your faithful people,
I will put my hope
in Your name, for it is good.

Psalm 53

A Portrait of Sinners

For the choir director: on Mahalath.[A]
A Davidic •Maskil.

1 The fool says in his heart,
"God does not exist."
They are corrupt, and they do
vile deeds.
There is no one who does good.
2 God looks down from heaven
on the •human race
to see if there is one
who is wise,
one who seeks God.
3 All have turned away;
all alike have become corrupt.
There is no one who does good,
not even one.

4 Will evildoers
never understand?
They consume My people
as they consume bread;
they do not call on God.
5 Then they will be filled
with terror—
terror like no other—
because God will scatter
the bones of those
who besiege you.
You will put them to shame,
for God has rejected them.

6 Oh, that Israel's deliverance
would come from •Zion!
When God restores the
fortunes of His people,[B]
Jacob will rejoice;
Israel will be glad.

Psalm 54

Prayer for Deliverance

For the choir director:
with stringed instruments.
A Davidic •Maskil. *When the*
Ziphites went and said to Saul, "Is
David not hiding among us?"

1 God, save me by Your name,
and vindicate me
by Your might!
2 God, hear my prayer;
listen to the words
of my mouth.
3 For strangers rise up
against me,
and violent men seek my life.
They have no regard for God.[C]
•Selah

4 God is my helper;
the Lord is the sustainer
of my life.[D]
5 He will repay my adversaries
for their evil.
Because of Your faithfulness,
annihilate them.

6 I will sacrifice
a freewill offering to You.
I will praise Your name,
•Yahweh,
because it is good.
7 For He has delivered me
from every trouble,
and my eye
has looked down on
my enemies.

Psalm 55

Betrayal by a Friend

For the choir director:
with stringed instruments.
A Davidic •Maskil.

1 God, listen to my prayer
and do not ignore[E] my plea
for help.
2 Pay attention to me
and answer me.
I am restless and in turmoil
with my complaint,
3 because of the enemy's voice,
because of the pressure[F]
of the wicked.

[A] **53:title** Perhaps a tune, a musical instrument, or a dance; this may be related to Hb word for "sickness." [B] **53:6** Or *restores His captive people* [C] **54:3** Lit *They do not set God before them* [D] **54:4** Or *is with those who sustain my life* [E] **55:1** Lit *hide Yourself from* [F] **55:3** Or *threat*, or *oppression*

Maskil, understood as a psalm that teaches practical living. See "How do you read Psalms," p. 666.

52:1-7 The superscription identifies the setting as **when Doeg the Edomite** betrayed David to Saul (1Sm 21–22).

Hero (Hb *gibbor*, "strong or mighty one") is a term of derision. The evildoer **brags** about his own power and resources (v. 7), but ultimately God will bring about his downfall and protect His people. The wicked individual's tongue is **razor** sharp, deceitful, and destructive; his speech reflects his heart (cp. Mt 12:34). God will destroy and **uproot** the wicked boaster (cp. 1:4-6). **Destructive behavior** (Hb *havvah*, "ruin, calamity, destruction") refers to actions that injure or harm others. The person depicted by combining these two Hebrew words constantly hurts other people and seems to work at getting better at doing so.

53:1-6 The meaning of ***Mahalath*** (also in the superscription of Ps 88) is uncertain but it is related to the Hebrew word for sickness; therefore, the psalm has been viewed as the prayer of a sick individual. "On *Mahalath*" may indicate the tune to which the psalm was to be sung, a musical instrument (possibly the flute), or a type of dance.

This poem is almost identical to Psalm 14 (see note on 14:1).

54:1-3 The superscription connects this psalm with the Ziphites' betrayal of David's hideout to Saul (see 1Sm 23:15-21). David prays for deliverance from his enemies, who do not look to or obey the one true God as David does).

54:4-7 The psalmist viewed his enemies as God's enemies. David affirms his faith in God as his **helper** (Hb *'azar*, "one who aids or supports," a verb often denoting military assistance), a term encompassing both spiritual and material assistance. The righteous are those who can anticipate God's aid.

David also affirms that God would defeat and repay his **adversaries** for their evil deeds. The Lord's deliverance would provide David an occasion for grateful celebration. Because of the salvation that came by the Lord's name, David would praise the goodness of that **name** (cp. v. 1). The **freewill offering** was a communal offering presented to the Lord but enjoyed in the presence of family and friends. Verse 7 resonates with a triumphant note of victory because of the Lord's deliverance.

55:1-8 David piles synonyms for fear one on top of another to convey how deeply terrified he felt. The wish to be able to **fly away and find rest** as the birds are free to do captures his sense of desperation—he longs to escape the situation and the intense emotions oppressing him (v. 6).

55:9-11 Having poured out before the Lord an honest account of how he was being affected personally by the circumstances (vv. 1-8), David described the situation more objectively, asking the Lord to intervene. In reality, escape was not an option, but prayer was.

55:12-14 Worse than the moral darkness and ongoing corruption and deceit with which David was confronted (vv. 3,9-11) was the betrayal by his **good friend**. David realized that he could have remained hidden from a **foe** or **enemy**, even though doing so would require great effort and much prayer (vv. 1-11). However, not only was it impossible to avoid completely the close friend who had publicly accompanied him to weekly worship, the pain of this person turning against him was almost unbearable.

55:15-19 In calling on the Lord to let his enemies **go down to Sheol alive** (i.e., to death or the grave while fully aware of what is happening—cp. the earth's swallowing of Korah, Dathan, and Abiram, Nm 16:23-40), David expressed righteous indignation on account of their complete association with **evil** and left revenge in God's hands.

55:20-23 David remained grief-stricken over discovering in his friend a cruel enemy, but here he was able to see through the traitor's behavior and to recognize that the **covenant**—probably referring to the man's promise of loyalty to David and others who trusted him—was irreparably broken. **Violates** (Hb *chalal*, "wound, dissolve or break [a covenant], profane, destroy") is in perfect tense, indicating a completed action.

The Lord can be trusted to **sustain** (Hb *kul*, "hold up, nourish, provide for"; cp. 1 Tm 1:12) the one who leaves such matters in His hands. Ultimately, wrong will fail and right will prevail (Ps 55:22-23). The Lord will rescue those who belong to Him and defeat all who oppose Him and His people. The wise individual, therefore, is one who trusts in the Lord.

56:1–60:12 Each of these five psalms is identified as a *Miktam* (see p. 679).

56:title The phrase, **according to "A Silent Dove Far Away,"** probably refers to a tune to which the psalm was intended to be sung. The superscription connects it to the capture of David by the Philistines in Gath. The account in 1Sm 21:10–22:1 indicates only that David feared the Philistines might seize him. He feigned madness before the king of Gath in an attempt to prevent capture.

56:1-7 The statements of faith and

For they bring down disaster
on me[A]
and harass me in anger.

4 My heart shudders
within me;
terrors of death sweep
over me.
5 Fear and trembling grip me;
horror has overwhelmed me.
6 I said, "If only I had[B] wings
like a dove!
I would fly away and find rest.
7 How far away I would flee;
I would stay
in the wilderness. •*Selah*
8 I would hurry to my shelter
from the raging wind
and the storm."

9 Lord, confuse[C] and confound
their speech,[D]
for I see violence and strife
in the city;
10 day and night they make
the rounds on its walls.
Crime and trouble are
within it;
11 destruction is inside it;
oppression and deceit
never leave
its marketplace.

12 Now it is not an enemy
who insults me—
otherwise I could bear it;
it is not a foe who rises up
against me—
otherwise I could hide
from him.
13 But it is you, a man who is
my peer,
my companion
and good friend!
14 We used to have
close fellowship;
we walked with the crowd
into the house of God.

15 Let death take them
by surprise;
let them go down
to •Sheol alive,
because evil is in their homes
and within them.
16 But I call to God,
and the Lord will save me.
17 I complain and groan
morning, noon, and night,
and He hears my voice.
18 Though many are against me,
He will redeem me
from my battle unharmed.
19 God, the One enthroned
from long ago,
will hear and
will humiliate them *Selah*
because they do not change
and do not •fear God.

20 My friend acts violently
against those at peace
with him;
he violates his covenant.
21 His buttery words are smooth,[E]
but war is in his heart.
His words are softer than oil,
but they are drawn swords.

22 Cast your burden on the Lord,
and He will sustain you;
He will never allow
the righteous to be shaken.

23 God, You will
bring them down
to the •Pit of destruction;
men of bloodshed
and treachery
will not live out
half their days.
But I will trust in You.

Psalm 56
A Call for God's Protection

For the choir director:
according to "A Silent Dove
Far Away."[F] *A Davidic* •Miktam.
When the Philistines seized him in Gath.

1 Be gracious to me, God,
for man tramples me;
he fights and oppresses me
all day long.
2 My adversaries trample me
all day,
for many arrogantly fight
against me.[G]
3 When I am afraid,
I will trust in You.
4 In God, whose word I praise,
in God I trust; I will not fear.
What can man do to me?

[A]55:3 LXX, Syr, Sym; MT reads *they cause me to totter* [B]55:6 Lit *"Who will give to me . . . dove?* [C]55:9 Or *destroy* [D]55:9 Lit *and divide their tongue* [E]55:21 Some Hb mss, Sym, Syr, Tg, Jer read *His speech is smoother than butter* [F]56:title Possibly a tune [G]56:2 Or *many fight against me, O exalted One,* or *many fight against me from the heights*

>WORD|*study*

56:8 The Hebrew word translated here as God's **records** (*sēpher*, "book, something written") appears only four times in Psalms. In the context of the whole canon, "the scroll" in Ps 40:7 refers to messianic prophecies written in the Old Testament (see Hb 10:6-8). Psalm 69:28 speaks of God's "book of life" as a record of those counted as "the righteous" (cp. Rv 3:5). While Ps 40:7 directs the worshiper's attention to the future (the coming of the Messiah), Ps 56:11 and 69:28 link present allegiances to an eternal day of reckoning by God as the Judge of all. Psalm 139:16 refers to God's "book," however, as His written plan for the psalmist's life. Rather than a record in the process of being written to make note of what happens in man's present experience or even providing a glimpse of the future, God's "book" in Ps 139:16 demonstrates His knowledge and control over man's life prior to his being brought into existence.

5 They twist my words
all day long;
all their thoughts against me
are evil.
6 They stir up strife,[A] they lurk;
they watch my steps
while they wait to take
my life.
7 Will they escape in spite of
such sin?
God, bring down the nations
in wrath.

8 You Yourself have recorded
my wanderings.[B]
Put my tears in Your bottle.
Are they not in Your records?
9 Then my enemies will retreat
on the day when I call.
This I know: God is for me.
10 In God, whose word I praise,
in the LORD,
whose word I praise,
11 in God I trust; I will not fear.
What can man do to me?

12 I am obligated by vows[C]
to You, God;
I will make
my thank offerings to You.
13 For You delivered me
from death,
even my feet from stumbling,
to walk before God
in the light of life.

Psalm 57
Praise for God's Protection

For the choir director:
"Do Not Destroy."[D] *A Davidic* •Miktam.
When he fled before Saul into the cave.

1 Be gracious to me, God,
be gracious to me,
for I take refuge in You.
I will seek refuge
in the shadow of Your wings
until danger passes.
2 I call to God •Most High,
to God who fulfills
His purpose for me.[E]
3 He reaches down from heaven
and saves me,
challenging the one
who tramples me. •*Selah*
God sends His faithful love
and truth.
4 I am surrounded by lions;
I lie down with those
who devour •men.
Their teeth are spears
and arrows;
their tongues
are sharp swords.
5 God, be exalted
above the heavens;
let Your glory be over
the whole earth.
6 They prepared a net
for my steps;
I was despondent.
They dug a pit ahead of me,
but they fell into it! *Selah*

7 My heart is confident, God,
my heart is confident.
I will sing; I will sing praises.
8 Wake up, my soul![F]
Wake up, harp and lyre!
I will wake up the dawn.
9 I will praise You, Lord,
among the peoples;
I will sing praises to You
among the nations.
10 For Your faithful love is
as high as the heavens;
Your faithfulness reaches
the clouds.
11 God, be exalted
above the heavens;

[A]56:6 Or *They attack* [B]56:8 Or *misery* [C]56:12 Lit *On me the vows* [D]57:title Possibly a tune [E]57:2 Or *who avenges me* [F]57:8 Lit *glory*

praise provide assurance that human beings cannot overcome the individual who trusts in God (cp. Rm 8:37). This sure hope is rooted in God's justice (Ps 56:7) as well as in His mercy (v. 1).

56:8-11 These verses repeat verse 4 as a refrain that expresses the psalm's central expression of faith in God, who tenderly assumes ownership of His followers' sorrows and thoroughly judges those who oppose Him and His people.

56:12-13 David understood that the Lord had **delivered** [him] **from death** not to abandon him thereafter to his own sinful ways but to enable him to live **in the light of life** (cp. Jn 8:12; Eph 2:8-9; Tit 2:11-14).

57:Title "Do Not Destroy" perhaps designates to the tune to which this psalm was to be sung. The heading or superscription probably refers either to David's escape from Saul to **the cave** of Adullam (1Sm 22:1-2) or to David's refusal to take Saul's life in a cave in the wilderness of En-gedi (1Sm 24:1-7).

57:1-4 God is ever the **refuge** to whom David turns in distress (cp. 17:8; 63:7). He addresses his petition to **God Most High** (Hb *'Elohim 'elyon*; cp. Gn 14:17-24). Yahweh is *the* great God, exalted above the idols or false gods worshiped by the heathen nations.

57:5-11 Verse 5 constitutes a refrain repeated in verse 11. Verses 6-11 note the poet's thanksgiving or praise for deliverance. David rejoiced that his enemies reaped what they had sown. He voiced his steadfast faith. The reference to the **heart** is a poetic way of referring to his entire being. So great was the poet's gratitude that he wanted all **peoples** and **nations** to know the Lord. God's mercy and truth are worthy of praise.

58:1-11 As in Ps 57, **"Do Not Destroy"** possibly designates the tune to which this psalm was intended to be sung.

This is considered an *imprecatory* psalm because David calls for God to bring disaster and misfortune on his enemies. Such expressions of a desire for God to take vengeance are not included in Scripture to teach God's people to harbor anger or look for opportunities to avenge themselves in God's name. Instead, these psalms illustrate that God hears the honest prayers of His people, who bring their anger and indignation before Him and, in the process of pouring out their complaints, finally recognize His sovereignty and power to judge righteously. His justice ultimately will prevail, the wicked will receive punishment, and the righteous will receive their reward (cp. Ps 1).

59:1-17 The superscription ties this prayer to the season in David's life when King Saul sent men to kill him. David prays for deliverance from the **enemies** who sought his life for no good reason (v. 3). He compared their insolent and vicious threats to the **snarling** of **dogs** (vv. 6,14). The designation of God as **Lord God of Hosts . . . God of Israel** may be an allusion to God as commander of armies or of the heavenly hosts (v. 5). Additionally, David prayed for the Lord to act on behalf of His people (v. 13). Those acts would witness to others of His sovereignty and His loyal love for His people. This poem, having begun as a lament, ends on a note of confidence in God's faithful protection of His own. David ends his song on a confident note, praising God as his defense and **refuge** (v. 16). **Stronghold** (Hb *misgav*, "lofty place or rock affording shelter and protection; refuge"; from the verb *sagav*, "be inaccessibly high," v. 9) is an image portraying the security and protection David found in God, his source of power and strength.

60:1-4 The Lily of Testimony likely refers to the song's melody. **Aram-naharaim** (Hb "Aram of the two rivers") refers to Mesopotamia, the region between the Euphrates and Tigris Rivers. **Aram-zobah** was a Syrian state that formed its own kingdom during the reigns of Saul, David, and Solomon (see 1Sm 14:47; 2Sm 8:3; 10:6). This psalm, like Ps 108, is regarded as a national lament. Psalm 60 expresses dismay and grief over Edom's successful attack on the southern part of Judah while David and most of his army were fighting in the north. The poem's initial mood is one of defeat rather than victory. Military defeat was viewed as a sign of God's rejection or displeasure. Such defeat seemed as devastating as an earthquake, affecting the people so that they experienced confusion and staggered like drunken

let Your glory be
over the whole earth.

Psalm 58
A Cry Against Injustice

For the choir director:
"Do Not Destroy."[A] *A Davidic* •Miktam.

1 Do you really
speak righteously,
you mighty ones?[B]
Do you judge •people fairly?
2 No, you practice injustice
in your hearts;
with your hands
you weigh out violence
in the land.

3 The wicked go astray
from the womb;
liars err from birth.
4 They have venom
like the venom of a snake,
like the deaf cobra
that stops up its ears,
5 that does not listen
to the sound of the charmers
who skillfully weave spells.

6 God, knock the teeth
out of their mouths;
Lord, tear out
the young lions' fangs.
7 They will vanish like water
that flows by;
they will aim
their useless arrows.[C,D]
8 Like a slug that moves along
in slime,
like a woman's miscarried
child,
they will not see the sun.

9 Before your pots can feel
the heat of the thorns—
whether green or burning—
He will sweep them away.[E]
10 The righteous one will rejoice
when he sees the retribution;
he will wash his feet
in the blood of the wicked.
11 Then people will say,
"Yes, there is a reward
for the righteous!
There is a God who judges
on earth!"

Psalm 59
God Our Stronghold

For the choir director:
"Do Not Destroy."[A] *A Davidic* •Miktam.
When Saul sent agents to watch
the house and kill him.

1 Deliver me from my enemies,
my God;
protect me from those
who rise up against me.
2 Deliver me from those
who practice sin,
and save me from men
of bloodshed.
3 Lord, look! They set
an ambush for me.
Powerful men attack me,
but not because of any sin
or rebellion of mine.
4 For no fault of mine,
they run and take up
a position.
Awake to help me,
and take notice.
5 Lord God of •Hosts, You are
the God of Israel,
rise up to punish
all the nations;
do not show grace
to any wicked traitors.
•*Selah*

6 They return at evening,
snarling like dogs
and prowling around the city.
7 Look, they spew
from their mouths—
sharp words from[F] their lips.
"For who," they say,
"will hear?"
8 But You laugh at them, Lord;
You ridicule all the nations.
9 I will keep watch for You,
my[G] strength,
because God is
my stronghold.
10 My faithful God[H] will come
to meet me;
God will let me look down on
my adversaries.

11 Do not kill them; otherwise,
my people will forget.
By Your power, make them
homeless wanderers

[A]**58:title; 59:title** Possibly a tune [B]**58:1** Or *Can you really speak righteousness in silence?* [C]**58:7** Or *their arrows as if they were circumcised*; Hb obscure [D]**58:7** Or *they wither like trampled grass* [E]**58:9** Or *thorns, He will sweep it away, whether raw or cooking*, or *thorns, He will sweep him away alive in fury* [F]**59:7** Lit *swords are on* [G]**59:9** Some Hb mss, LXX, Vg, Tg; other Hb mss read *his* [H]**59:10** Alt Hb tradition reads *My God in His faithful love*

and bring them down,
Lord, our shield.
12 For the sin of their mouths
and the words of their lips,
let them be caught
in their pride.
They utter curses and lies.
13 Consume them in rage;
consume them until
they are gone.
Then people will know
throughout[A] the earth
that God rules over Jacob.
Selah

14 And they return at evening,
snarling like dogs
and prowling around the city.
15 They scavenge for food;
they growl if they are not
satisfied.

16 But I will sing
of Your strength
and will joyfully proclaim
Your faithful love
in the morning.
For You have been
a stronghold for me,
a refuge in my day of trouble.
17 To You, my strength,
I sing praises,
because God is
my stronghold—
my faithful God.

Psalm 60

Prayer in Difficult Times

For the choir director: according to "The Lily of Testimony."[B] A Davidic •Miktam for teaching. When he fought with Aram-naharaim and Aram-zobah, and Joab returned and struck Edom in the Valley of Salt, killing 12,000.

1 God, You have rejected us;
You have broken out[C]
against us;
You have been angry.
Restore us![D]
2 You have shaken the land
and split it open.
Heal its fissures,
for it shudders.
3 You have made Your people
suffer hardship;
You have given us wine
to drink
that made us stagger.
4 You have given a signal flag
to those who •fear You,
so that they can flee
before the archers.[E] •*Selah*
5 Save with Your right hand,
and answer me,
so that those You love
may be rescued.

6 God has spoken
in His sanctuary:[F]
"I will triumph!
I will divide up Shechem.
I will apportion the Valley
of Succoth.
7 Gilead is Mine,
Manasseh is Mine,
and Ephraim is My helmet;
Judah is My scepter.
8 Moab is My washbasin.
I throw My sandal on Edom;
I shout in triumph
over Philistia."

9 Who will bring me
to the fortified city?
Who will lead me to Edom?
10 God, haven't You rejected us?
God, You do not march out
with our armies.
11 Give us aid against the foe,
for human help is worthless.
12 With God
we will perform valiantly;
He will trample our foes.

Psalm 61

Security in God

For the choir director: on stringed instruments. Davidic.

1 God, hear my cry;
pay attention to my prayer.
2 I call to You from the ends
of the earth
when my heart is
without strength.
Lead me to a rock that is
high above me,
3 for You have been a refuge
for me,
a strong tower in the face
of the enemy.
4 I will live in Your tent forever

[A] **59:13** Lit *know to the ends of* [B] **60:title** Possibly a tune; Pss 45; 69; 80 [C] **60:1** Lit *have burst through* [D] **60:1** Or *Turn back to us* [E] **60:4** Or *can rally before the archers*, or *can rally because of the truth* [F] **60:6** Or *has promised by His holy nature*

men, wondering why God had failed to come to their rescue. Those who **fear** the Lord, however, have confidence in the Lord's power.

60:5-12 **Human help** was **worthless** or useless in the difficult circumstances in which David and his men found themselves (v. 11). However, David clung to hope in God and ultimately defeated the Edomites or Syrians (2Sm 8; 1Ch 18:3,12). This psalm ends with the triumphant note of victory, an expression of confidence that God would defeat the enemies of His people.

61:1-2 As is true in many of the Psalms, notably the psalms of lament, the poet sought the safety of God's presence in difficult times. **From the ends of the earth** has been interpreted as indicating David's experiencing exile from his home (e.g., 2Sm 15:13-23) or his being near death. The phrase also depicts David's despondence, alienation, and spiritual distance from the Lord. In any case, he continued to pray, earnestly petitioning God to hear and answer his cry. The assumption is that God's hearing of David's prayer would be equivalent to God's delivering him from difficulty.

61:3-4 A marked change in tone occurs as the psalmist recognizes the safety and security that he had enjoyed in God's presence. God had sheltered him from his enemies, and God would remain his **refuge** and **strong tower** (cp. Pr 18:10). The reference to abiding in God's **tent** or tabernacle **forever** is reminiscent of Ps 23:6. David knew he would be secure forever in the **shelter** of God's **wings**, a reference to God's care and protection (cp. Ps 27:5; 31:20; 32:7; 91:1; 119:114).

61:5 Those who **fear** or reverence God's **name** or reputation enjoy His **heritage** (Hb *yerushshah*, "possession, inheritance") a term identifying both the promised land and the benefits of life in covenant with the Lord.

61:6-8 The kingship in ancient Israel was established and maintained by the promise of the Lord's **faithful love** and **truth**. The Lord had promised that David's dynasty would last **forever**, a promise fulfilled in Jesus Christ (Lk 1:32).

62:1-8 Only Pss 39,62 and Ps 77 have the notation **according to Jeduthun** (see note on Ps 39:1-13).

In Hebrew the psalm begins with the adverb **alone** (Hb *ʾak*, "only"; in other contexts "yea, truly, surely, certainly, indeed"), which is repeated five more times—also at the beginning of verses 2,4,5,6, and 9—contributing to its unified theme of trusting solely in God. Immediately following this word is the phrase **in God** (Hb *ʾel-ʾelohim*)—"only in God" matches the Hebrew word order. As the first words of the sentence and of the psalm itself, the entire phrase both introduces and emphasizes this theme. Particularly in this context, the word **rest** (Hb *dumiyah*, "silence"; from the verb *damam*, "be quiet or still, cease," v. 5; cp. 37:7; 131:2; used only here and Ps 22:2; 39:2; 65:1) suggests the peace and composure experienced when worries and fears have been relinquished to God (cp. Php 4:7). The LXX translation is *hupotagē* (Gk, "act of subjection, obedience, submission"; cp. 2Co 9:13; Gl 2:5), which suggests a necessary connection between the acknowledgment of God's power and authority and the ability to "cease" restless independent activity.

62:9 This verse (like vv. 1, 2, and 4-6) begins with the word **only** (Hb *ʾak*), emphasizing that sinful, mortal **men** (Hb *bēn-ʾadam*, "sons of Adam, sons of man") are nothing more than **a vapor** (Hb *hevel*, "breath, vanity," i.e., "lacking substance, transitory"; see **Word Study** for "futile", p. 831) when considered in contrast to God. These people are like **an illusion** (Hb *kazav*, "a lie or falsehood, something that deceives"). This verse's vivid illustration of balance **scales** implies a contrast between the unchanging faithfulness of God and, despite any human boasting to the contrary, the *relative* worthlessness of men.

62:10 The three prohibitions are parallel—in Hebrew each begins with **no** (Hb *ʾal*, "not"), followed by the verb, with the force of "you must not . . ."

- Do not **trust** (Hb *batach*, "set one's hope and confidence in") in the ability to acquire security that will not last by taking advantages of others or at their expense.

and take refuge
under the shelter
of Your wings. •*Selah*

5 God, You have heard my vows;
You have given a heritage
to those who •fear Your name.
6 Add days to the king's life;
may his years span
many generations.
7 May he sit enthroned
before God forever;
appoint faithful love and truth
to guard him.
8 Then I will continually sing
of Your name,
fulfilling my vows day by day.

Psalm 62
Trusting in God Alone

For the choir director:
according to Jeduthun.
A Davidic psalm.

1 I am at rest in God alone;
my salvation comes
from Him.
2 He alone is my rock
and my salvation,
my stronghold;
I will never be shaken.

3 How long will you
threaten a man?
Will all of you attack[A]
as if he were a leaning wall
or a tottering stone fence?
4 They only plan to bring him
down
from his high position.
They take pleasure in lying;
they bless with their mouths,
but they curse inwardly.
•*Selah*

5 Rest in God alone, my soul,
for my hope comes from Him.
6 He alone is my rock
and my salvation,
my stronghold; I will not
be shaken.
7 My salvation and glory
depend on God,
my strong rock.
My refuge is in God.
8 Trust in Him at all times,
you people;
pour out your hearts
before Him.
God is our refuge. *Selah*

9 •Men are only a vapor;
exalted men, an illusion.
Weighed in the scales,
they go up;
together they are less than
a vapor.
10 Place no trust in oppression,
or false hope in robbery.
If wealth increases,
pay no attention to it.[B]

11 God has spoken once;
I have heard this twice:
strength belongs to God,
12 and faithful love belongs
to You, LORD.
For You repay each
according to his works.

Psalm 63
Praising God Who Satisfies

A Davidic psalm. When he was
in the Wilderness of Judah.

1 God, You are my God;
I eagerly seek You.
I thirst for You;
my body faints for You
in a land that is dry, desolate,
and without water.
2 So I gaze on You
in the sanctuary
to see Your strength
and Your glory.

3 My lips will glorify You
because Your faithful love
is better than life.
4 So I will praise You as long as
I live;
at Your name, I will lift up
my hands.
5 You satisfy me as with
rich food;[C]
my mouth will praise You
with joyful lips.

6 When I think of You as I lie
on my bed,
I meditate on You
during the night watches
7 because You are my helper;
I will rejoice in the shadow
of Your wings.
8 I follow close to You;

[A]62:3 Some Hb mss read *you be struck down* [B]62:10 Lit *increases, do not set heart* [C]63:5 Lit *with fat and fatness*

Your right hand holds on
to me.
9 But those who seek to destroy
my life
will go into the depths
of the earth.
10 They will be given over
to the power of the sword;
they will become
the jackals' prey.
11 But the king will rejoice
in God;
all who swear by Him[A]
will boast,
for the mouths of liars
will be shut.

Psalm 64
Protection from Evildoers

For the choir director. A Davidic psalm.

1 God, hear my voice
when I complain.
Protect my life
from the terror
of the enemy.
2 Hide me from the scheming
of wicked people,
from the mob of evildoers,
3 who sharpen their tongues
like swords
and aim bitter words
like arrows,
4 shooting
from concealed places
at the innocent.
They shoot at him suddenly
and are not afraid.
5 They encourage each other
in an evil plan;[B,C]
they talk about hiding traps
and say,
"Who will see them?"[D]
6 They devise crimes and say,
"We have perfected
a secret plan."
The inner man and the heart
are mysterious.
7 But God will shoot them
with arrows;
suddenly, they will be
wounded.
8 They will be made to stumble;
their own tongues work
against them.
All who see them will shake
their heads.
9 Then everyone will fear
and will tell about God's work,
for they will understand
what He has done.
10 The righteous one rejoices
in the LORD
and takes refuge in Him;
all those who are upright
in heart
will offer praise.

Psalm 65
God's Care for the Earth

For the choir director.
A Davidic psalm. A song.

1 Praise is rightfully Yours,[E]
God, in •Zion;
vows to You will be fulfilled.
2 All humanity will come
to You,
the One who hears prayer.
3 Iniquities overwhelm me;
only You can •atone for[F]
our rebellions.
4 How happy is the one
You choose
and bring near to live
in Your courts!
We will be satisfied
with the goodness
of Your house,
the holiness of Your temple.[G]
5 You answer us
in righteousness,
with awe-inspiring works,
God of our salvation,
the hope of all the ends
of the earth
and of the distant seas.
6 You establish the mountains
by Your[H] power,
robed with strength.
7 You silence the roar
of the seas,
the roar of their waves,
and the tumult of the nations.
8 Those who live far away
are awed by Your signs;

[A] **63:11** Or *him* [B] **64:5** Or *thing*; lit *word* [C] **64:5** Or *They hold fast to an evil purpose*, or *They establish for themselves an evil purpose* [D] **64:5** Or *us*, or *it* [E] **65:1** Or *Praise is silence to You*, or *Praise awaits You* [F] **65:3** Or *can forgive*, or *can wipe out* [G] **65:4** Or *house, Your holy temple* [H] **65:6** Some LXX mss, Vg; MT reads *His*

- Do not **place . . . false hope** [Hb *haval*, "become vain or worthless, act or speak vainly"] **in robbery** (Hb *gazēl*, "goods obtained by force or theft"; cp. Lv 6:2), which Yahweh hates (Is 61:8).
- Do not **pay . . . attention** (Hb *shit lēv*, "set one's heart on") to increasing **wealth** (Hb *chayil*, "riches, power, strength") even when acquired legitimately.

62:11 This verse introduces the psalm's conclusion with an idiomatic expression verifying and emphasizing what follows as having been **spoken** (Hb *davar*, "speak"—an intensive form here meaning to speak emphatically, to "promise" or "command") by God Himself. David simply reports that **strength** [Hb *ʿoz*, "power, might"; cp. 28:8] **belongs to God**.

62:12 In Hebrew, this verse begins with, "And to You," **LORD** (Hb *ʾAdonay*), reflecting David's commitment to God, the One who possesses both the power and **faithful love** to render perfect justice.

63:1-3 The superscription may refer to incidents in 1Sm 23 or 2Sm 15–18. David acknowledges a personal, intimate relationship with God, for whom he longs as would a man desperate with thirst for life-preserving water in the arid heat of a desert. To live in the presence of God is to experience His power and glory. Through his disciplined practice of worship in **the sanctuary**, the psalmist has experienced God's presence as wonderfully real to him, concluding that God's **faithful love** is more precious to him than life itself.

64:1-4 The plea for God to **hear** was a plea for God to act. David compares the slander from his enemies to sharpened **swords** and **arrows** (i.e., deadly weapons) intended to destroy their target. The Hebrews viewed words as living forces carrying the power to fulfill their purposes. Like an arrow shot from a bow, the spoken word could not be recalled.

65:1-9 The tone of this hymn of thanksgiving is one of joy. Anyone can come to God and experience His forgiveness. God is to be praised because He forgives your sins. **Atone for** (Hb *saphar*) literally means "cover, forgive, wipe out, purge."

God also merits praise because He is the great Creator and Provider. He establishes the **mountains**, controls **the seas**, and sends rain to water the crops. God's control over the seas was particularly significant to people in the ancient world. The sea often was connected with chaotic and life-threatening powers.

66:1-4 All peoples of **the earth** are called upon to praise **God** (cp. 100:1). Whether they do so willingly or unwillingly, every knee ultimately will bow and every tongue will confess that He is Lord (Php 2:10-11).

66:6 God **turned the sea into dry land** when He parted the Red Sea to deliver His people from the Egyptian army (Ex 14). Later the Lord stopped the flow of the Jordan River so the Israelites could cross into the land of Canaan on dry ground (Jos 3).

66:10-12 The Lord's sovereignty had also been evident in His testing of His people. Through trials the Lord had **refined** (Hb *tsaraph*, "prove, purge"; cp. 12:6; 17:3; Pr 25:4; Is 1:25) His people like **silver**, purifying them for His glory as they enjoyed His **abundance** (Hb *rewayah*; cp. "overflows," 23:5) with gratitude and faithfulness.

66:13-15 David expressed gratitude by promising to pay his **vows** and to bring **burnt offerings** (see Lv 1 regarding the burnt offering as personal and voluntary) and sacrifices to the Lord. Such vows were often made during seasons of adversity. This psalmist had experienced personal deliverance from God during a time of trouble.

You make east and west
shout for joy.
9 You visit the earth
and water it abundantly,
enriching it greatly.
God's stream is filled
with water,
for You prepare the earth[A]
in this way,
providing people with grain.
10 You soften it with showers
and bless its growth,
soaking its furrows
and leveling its ridges.
11 You crown the year
with Your goodness;
Your ways overflow
with plenty.[B]
12 The wilderness pastures
overflow,
and the hills are robed
with joy.
13 The pastures are clothed
with flocks
and the valleys covered
with grain.
They shout in triumph;
indeed, they sing.

Psalm 66

Praise for God's Mighty Acts

For the choir director. A song. A psalm.

1 Shout joyfully to God,
all the earth!
2 Sing about the glory
of His name;
make His praise glorious.
3 Say to God,
"How awe-inspiring
are Your works!
Your enemies will cringe
before You
because of Your great strength.
4 All the earth will worship You
and sing praise to You.
They will sing praise
to Your name." •*Selah*

5 Come and see the wonders
of God;
His acts for •humanity
are awe-inspiring.
6 He turned the sea
into dry land,
and they crossed the river
on foot.
There we rejoiced in Him.
7 He rules forever by His might;
He keeps His eye
on the nations.
The rebellious should not
exalt themselves. *Selah*
8 Praise our God, you peoples;
let the sound of His praise
be heard.
9 He keeps us alive[C]
and does not allow our feet
to slip.

10 For You, God, tested us;
You refined us as silver
is refined.
11 You lured us into a trap;
You placed burdens
on our backs.
12 You let men ride
over our heads;
we went through fire
and water,
but You brought us out
to abundance.[D]

13 I will enter Your house
with •burnt offerings;
I will pay You my vows
14 that my lips promised
and my mouth spoke
during my distress.
15 I will offer You fattened sheep
as burnt offerings,
with the fragrant smoke
of rams;
I will sacrifice oxen
with goats. *Selah*

16 Come and listen,
all who •fear God,
and I will tell what
He has done for me.
17 I cried out to Him
with my mouth,
and praise was on my tongue.
18 If I had been aware of malice
in my heart,
the Lord would not
have listened.
19 However, God has listened;
He has paid attention
to the sound of my prayer.
20 May God be praised!
He has not turned away
my prayer
or turned His faithful love
from me.

[A]**65:9** Lit *prepare it* [B]**65:11** Lit *ways drip with fat* [C]**66:9** Lit *He sets our soul in life* [D]**66:12** Or *a place of satisfaction*

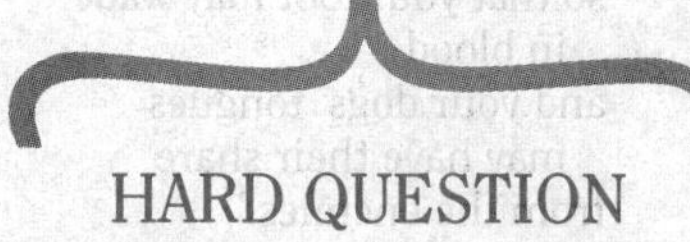

HARD QUESTION

Why does God not answer every prayer as Christ seems to promise in Mt 21:22?

This verse provides one answer. The psalmist knows *both* that God answers prayer *and* that God is holy. The one praying cannot logically expect God to grant the request of a traitor who has not rid his **heart** of **malice**. The presence of sin undercuts the pretense of approaching a holy God (Is 59:2). Parents understand this principle. A child who willfully and continually disobeys will find the parents unwilling to listen to what the child wants.

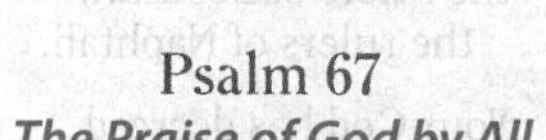

Psalm 67
The Praise of God by All

For the choir director: with stringed instruments. A psalm. A song.

1 May God be gracious to us
and bless us;
look on us with favor •*Selah*
2 so that Your way
may be known on earth,
Your salvation
among all nations.

3 Let the peoples praise You,
God;
let all the peoples praise You.
4 Let the nations rejoice
and shout for joy,
for You judge the peoples
with fairness
and lead the nations
on earth. *Selah*
5 Let the peoples praise
You, God,
let all the peoples praise You.

6 The earth has produced
its harvest;
God, our God, blesses us.
7 God will bless us,
and all the ends of the earth
will •fear Him.

Psalm 68
God's Majestic Power

For the choir director. A Davidic psalm. A song.

1 God arises.
His enemies scatter,
and those who hate Him flee
from His presence.
2 As smoke is blown away,
so You blow them away.
As wax melts before the fire,
so the wicked are destroyed
before God.
3 But the righteous are glad;
they rejoice before God
and celebrate with joy.

4 Sing to God! Sing praises
to His name.
Exalt Him who rides
on the clouds[A] —
His name
is •Yahweh[B]—and rejoice
before Him.
5 God in His holy dwelling is
a father of the fatherless
and a champion of widows.
6 God provides homes for those
who are deserted.
He leads out the prisoners
to prosperity,[C]
but the rebellious live
in a scorched land.

7 God, when You went out
before Your people,
when You marched
through the desert, •*Selah*
8 the earth trembled
and the skies
poured down rain
before God, the God of Sinai,[D]
before God, the God of Israel.
9 You, God, showered
abundant rain;
You revived Your inheritance
when it languished.
10 Your people settled in it;
God, You provided for
the poor by Your goodness.

11 The Lord gave the command;
a great company of women
brought the good news:
12 "The kings of the armies
flee—they flee!"

67:1-2 Verse 1 recalls the blessing or benediction of Aaron in Nm 6:24-26. The stated purpose of requesting God's **favor** reiterates the covenant God made with Abraham (see Gn 12:1-3; 18:18; 22:18). God has always intended for His people to be His instrument for making His **way . . . known on the earth**, His **salvation** [known] **among all nations** (cp. Is 42:6-7; 52:10; Mt 28:28-30).

67:2-7 The psalm repeatedly calls on **the peoples** and **the nations** to praise God to whom praise is due. God is to be praised for His righteous judgment and government; He is the God not only of Israel but also of all people on earth. Verse 7 celebrates an assurance of God's blessing that will result in His worship to **the ends of the earth**.

68:1-6 The blessings of **the righteous**—those in right relationship with God—are contrasted with the destruction of **the wicked**—those who rebel against Him (cp. Ps 1). God is praised for what He does for poor and helpless individuals, represented by **the fatherless** and **widows** as well as **prisoners** and **those who are deserted**. Those who rebel against God forfeit His bountiful care.

68:7-14 These verses celebrate God's triumphant leading of His people out of Egypt to Mount Sinai. God revealed His presence with His people by performing great and mighty acts in their behalf and by the visible assurance of the pillar of cloud by day and of fire by night.

[A]68:4 Or *rides through the desert* [B]68:4 Lit *Yah* [C]68:6 Or *prisoners with joyous music*; Hb uncertain [D]68:8 Lit *God, this Sinai*

68:15-31 These verses celebrate the Lord as One who utterly defeats His enemies and saves His people. In Eph 4:8 the first half of verse 18 is quoted as a reference to the ascended Christ, who as victor gave spiritual gifts to His disciples. The imagery is that of a king coming home from battle leading a triumphant procession as he returns with the defeated captives.

68:32-35 The psalm concludes with a triumphal hymn calling all the peoples of the earth to acknowledge God's sovereignty.

She who stays at home
divides the spoil.
13 While[A] you lie
among the sheepfolds,[B]
the wings of a dove
are covered with silver,
and its feathers
with glistening gold.
14 When the •Almighty scattered
kings in the land,
it snowed on Zalmon.[C]

15 Mount Bashan is
God's towering mountain;
Mount Bashan is a mountain
of many peaks.
16 Why gaze with envy,
you mountain peaks,
at the mountain[D] God desired
for His dwelling?
The LORD will
live there forever!
17 God's chariots are tens
of thousands,
thousands and thousands;
the Lord is among them
in the sanctuary[E]
as He was at Sinai.
18 You ascended to the heights,
taking away captives;
You received gifts
from[F] people,
even from the rebellious,
so that the LORD God
might live there.[G]

19 May the Lord be praised!
Day after day He bears
our burdens;
God is our salvation. *Selah*
20 Our God is a God of salvation,
and escape from death
belongs to the Lord GOD.
21 Surely God crushes the heads
of His enemies,
the hairy head of
one who goes on
in his •guilty acts.
22 The Lord said,
"I will bring them back
from Bashan;
I will bring them back
from the depths of the sea
23 so that your foot may wade[H]
in blood
and your dogs' tongues
may have their share
from the enemies."
24 People have seen
Your procession, God,
the procession of my God,
my King, in the sanctuary.[E]
25 Singers[I] lead the way,
with musicians following;
among them are
young women
playing tambourines.
26 Praise God in the assemblies;
praise the LORD
from the fountain of Israel.
27 There is Benjamin,
the youngest, leading them,
the rulers of Judah
in their assembly,[J]
the rulers of Zebulun,
the rulers of Naphtali.

28 Your God has decreed
your strength.
Show Your strength, God,
You who have acted
on our behalf.
29 Because of Your temple
at Jerusalem,
kings will bring tribute
to You.
30 Rebuke the beast[K]
in the reeds,
the herd of bulls
with the calves
of the peoples.
Trample underfoot those
with bars of silver.[L]
Scatter the peoples
who take pleasure in war.
31 Ambassadors will come[M]
from Egypt;
•Cush will stretch out
its hands[N] to God.

32 Sing to God, you kingdoms
of the earth;
sing praise to the Lord, *Selah*
33 to Him who rides
in the ancient,
highest heavens.

[A]**68:13** Or *If* [B]**68:13** Or *campfires*, or *saddlebags*; Hb obscure [C]**68:14** Or *Black Mountain* [D]**68:16** = Mount Zion [E]**68:17,24** Or *in holiness* [F]**68:18** Lit *among* [G]**68:18** Or *even those rebelling against the LORD God's living there*, or *even rebels are living with the LORD God*; Hb obscure [H]**68:23** LXX, Syr read *dip* [I]**68:25** Some Hb mss, LXX, Syr read *Officials* [J]**68:27** Hb obscure [K]**68:30** Probably Egypt [L]**68:30** Or *peoples, trampling on those who take pleasure in silver*, or *peoples, trampling on the bars of silver*, or *peoples, who trample each other for bars of silver* [M]**68:31** Or *They bring red cloth*, or *They bring bronze* [N]**68:31** Probably with tribute or in submission

Look, He thunders
with His powerful voice!
34 Ascribe power to God.
His majesty is over Israel,
His power among the clouds.
35 God, You are awe-inspiring
in Your sanctuaries.
The God of Israel gives power
and strength to His people.
May God be praised!

Psalm 69

A Plea for Rescue

For the choir director: according to "The Lilies."[A] *Davidic.*

1 Save me, God,
for the water has risen
to my neck.
2 I have sunk in deep mud,
and there is no footing;
I have come into deep waters,
and a flood sweeps over me.
3 I am weary from my crying;
my throat is parched.
My eyes fail,
looking for my God.
4 Those who hate me
without cause
are more numerous
than the hairs of my head;
my deceitful enemies,
who would destroy me,
are powerful.
Though I did not steal,
I must repay.
5 God, You know
my foolishness,
and my •guilty acts are
not hidden from You.
6 Do not let those who put
their hope in You
be disgraced because of me,
Lord God of •Hosts;
do not let those who seek You
be humiliated because of me,
God of Israel.
7 For I have endured insults
because of You,
and shame has covered
my face.
8 I have become a stranger
to my brothers
and a foreigner
to my mother's sons
9 because zeal for Your house
has consumed me,
and the insults of those
who insult You
have fallen on me.
10 I mourned and fasted,
but it brought me insults.
11 I wore •sackcloth
as my clothing,
and I was a joke to them.
12 Those who sit at the city •gate
talk about me,
and drunkards make up songs
about me.
13 But as for me, Lord,
my prayer to You is for a time
of favor.
In Your abundant,
faithful love, God,
answer me with
Your sure salvation.
14 Rescue me
from the miry mud;
don't let me sink.
Let me be rescued from those
who hate me
and from the deep waters.
15 Don't let the floodwaters
sweep over me
or the deep swallow me up;
don't let the •Pit close
its mouth over me.
16 Answer me, Lord,
for Your faithful love is good;
in keeping with
Your great compassion,
turn to me.
17 Don't hide Your face
from Your servant,
for I am in distress.
Answer me quickly!
18 Draw near to me
and redeem me;
ransom me because of
my enemies.

19 You know the insults
I endure—
my shame and disgrace.
You are aware of
all my adversaries.
20 Insults have broken my heart,
and I am in despair.
I waited for sympathy,
but there was none;
for comforters, but found
no one.
21 Instead, they gave me gall[B]
for my food,
and for my thirst

69:1-6 "The Lilies" in the superscription likely designates the tune to which the psalm was to be sung. The poet felt an urgent need for God to rescue him, as would a drowning man in deep waters or someone sinking in quicksand. He was about to go under. His opponents seemed too numerous to count. In humility he feared that his own failures and imperfections would bring shame on those who seek and hope in the Lord or that he would bring disgrace to God's name.

69:7-18 This poet suffered ridicule and estrangement from his loved ones because of his commitment to the Lord. The New Testament quotes from the psalm in reference to Jesus—e.g., when Christ cleansed the temple (v. 9; see Jn 2:17) and experienced alienation from His family (Ps 69:8; see Jn 7:3-5).

69:19-21 This psalmist received no sympathy or comfort from others. His heart was broken. His only comfort lay in the assurance that God knew the shame and suffering he was enduring. Verse 21 anticipates the fact that Christ on the cross was given wine mixed with **gall** to drink (Mt 27:34).

[A] **69:title** Possibly a tune; Pss 45; 60; 80 [B] **69:21** A bitter substance

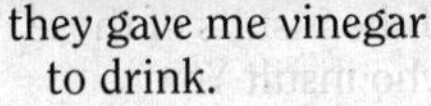

69:29-36 After denouncing his enemies, the psalmist returned to his plea for God's help or deliverance; the psalm itself moves from personal lament to a hymn of thanksgiving enjoining the heavens and the earth to praise the Lord and rehearsing what God will do for His people. This psalm exemplifies praying that works through the gamut of emotion and reflection prompted by painful and unfair experiences. In prayer, those who belong to the Lord can voice their desperation and fear, their complaints about people who have harmed them, as well as their desire to see such people reap what they have sown. However, the prayer does not end in bitterness and despair but reflects a God-centered perspective and attitude of praise that transcends temporal circumstances.

70:1-5 This psalm is essentially identical to Psalm 40:13-17 (see note on 40:13).

71:1-9 Although experiencing distress and longing for deliverance, this elderly person trusted God as his **rock**, **fortress**, **refuge**, and hope (vv. 1-3). He affirmed his trust in God **from** [his] **youth** (v. 5). The God who has sustained him from the **womb** is worthy of his continual praise (v. 6; cp. Is 46:3-4). This psalmist prays that the Lord will continue to value him even in his **old age**; he also prays for continued awareness of God's presence with him (Ps 71:9).

they gave me vinegar
to drink.
22 Let their table set before them
be a snare,
and let it be a trap
for their allies.
23 Let their eyes grow too dim
to see,
and let their loins
continually shake.
24 Pour out Your rage on them,
and let Your burning anger
overtake them.
25 Make their fortification
desolate;
may no one live in their tents.
26 For they persecute the one
You struck
and talk about the pain
of those You wounded.
27 Add guilt to their guilt;
do not let them share
in Your righteousness.
28 Let them be erased
from the book of life
and not be recorded
with the righteous.
29 But as for me—
poor and in pain—
let Your salvation
protect me, God.
30 I will praise God's name
with song
and exalt Him
with thanksgiving.
31 That will please •Yahweh
more than an ox,
more than a bull with horns
and hooves.
32 The humble will see it
and rejoice.
You who seek God, take heart!
33 For the LORD listens
to the needy
and does not despise
His own who are prisoners.
34 Let heaven and earth
praise Him,
the seas and everything
that moves in them,
35 for God will save •Zion
and build up[A] the cities
of Judah.
They will live there
and possess it.
36 The descendants
of His servants
will inherit it,
and those who love His name
will live in it.

Psalm 70

A Call for Deliverance

For the choir director. Davidic. To bring remembrance.

1 God, deliver me.
Hurry to help me, LORD!
2 Let those who seek my life
be disgraced and confounded;
let those who wish me harm
be driven back
and humiliated.
3 Let those who say, "Aha, aha!"
retreat because of
their shame.
4 Let all who seek You rejoice
and be glad in You;
let those who love
Your salvation
continually say,
"God is great!"
5 I am afflicted and needy;
hurry to me, God.
You are my help
and my deliverer;
LORD, do not delay.

Psalm 71

God's Help in Old Age

1 LORD, I seek refuge in You;
let me never be disgraced.
2 In Your justice, rescue
and deliver me;
listen closely to me
and save me.
3 Be a rock of refuge for me,
where I can always go.
Give the command
to save me,
for You are my rock
and fortress.
4 Deliver me, my God, from
the power of the wicked,
from the grasp of the unjust
and oppressive.
5 For You are my hope,
Lord GOD,
my confidence
from my youth.
6 I have leaned on You
from birth;

[A] **69:35** Or *and rebuild*

You took me from
my mother's womb.
My praise is always about You.
7 I have become
an ominous sign to many,
but You are my strong refuge.
8 My mouth is full of praise
and honor to You all day long.

9 Don't discard me in my
old age;
as my strength fails,
do not abandon me.
10 For my enemies talk
about me,
and those who spy on me
plot together,
11 saying, "God
has abandoned him;
chase him and catch him,
for there is no one
to rescue him."
12 God, do not be far from me;
my God, hurry to help me.
13 May my adversaries
be disgraced and destroyed;
may those who seek my harm
be covered with disgrace
and humiliation.
14 But I will hope continually
and will praise You more
and more.
15 My mouth will tell
about Your righteousness
and Your salvation
all day long,
though I cannot
sum them up.
16 I come because of
the mighty acts
of the Lord GOD;
I will proclaim
Your righteousness,
Yours alone.

17 God, You have taught me
from my youth,
and I still proclaim
Your wonderful works.
18 Even when I am old and gray,
God, do not abandon me.
Then I will[A] proclaim
Your power
to another generation,
Your strength to all who are
to come.
19 Your righteousness
reaches heaven, God,
You who have done
great things;
God, who is like You?
20 You caused me to experience
many troubles
and misfortunes,
but You will revive me again.
You will bring me up again,
even from the depths
of the earth.
21 You will increase my honor
and comfort me once again.
22 Therefore, I will praise You
with a harp
for Your faithfulness, my God;
I will sing to You with a lyre,
Holy One of Israel.
23 My lips will shout for joy
when I sing praise to You
because You have
redeemed me.
24 Therefore, my tongue
will proclaim
Your righteousness
all day long,
for those who seek my harm
will be disgraced
and confounded.

Psalm 72

A Prayer for the King

Solomonic.

1 God, give Your justice
to the king
and Your righteousness
to the king's son.
2 He will judge Your people
with righteousness
and Your afflicted ones
with justice.
3 May the mountains
bring prosperity[B]
to the people
and the hills, righteousness.
4 May he vindicate the afflicted
among the people,
help the poor,
and crush the oppressor.
5 May he continue[C] while the
sun endures
and as long as the moon,
throughout all generations.
6 May he be like rain that falls
on the cut grass,
like spring showers that water
the earth.

71:18 The psalmist pledges to proclaim God's **power** to future generations (v. 18) and throughout the psalm models approaching the end of life with a positive outlook of joy in the Lord. Even though the psalmist's troubles have been great, his faith has triumphed.

72:1-4 This royal psalm is the first of two mentioning Solomon in the superscription. The other is found among the songs of ascent (Ps 127). Verses 1-4 remind the reader of Solomon's request for understanding or wisdom with which to judge God's people (1Kg 3:5-10). A righteous king demonstrates a right relationship with God by showing the same concern that God shows for helpless people.

72:5-11 Within a prayer for the king's longevity and universal rule, the analogies in verse 5 probably apply to the length of the king's dynasty rather than to the length of his individual rule.

[A]71:18 Lit *me until I* [B]72:3 Or *peace* [C]72:5 LXX; MT reads *May they fear you*

72:12-14 These verses reveal the marks of a godly ruler. A king known for such benevolence would indeed be unusual in a world in which the values of strong and powerful leaders tend to be the opposite. Readers who follow Jesus the Messiah and are familiar with the biblical revelation of God's character may recognize how well the description fits the Lord.

72:18-20 This doxology marks the end of Book II of the Psalms (cp. Ps 41:13). The end of Book II includes the same twofold **amen** that closed Book I, possibly representing the worshiping congregation's emphatic response to the benediction.

73:1–83:18 Each of these psalms is attributed to **Asaph** (see Ps 50). The name may refer to the clan itself, especially since some or all of these psalms were probably composed after the destruction of Jerusalem and the temple in 587 B.C. The name may also have designated the singers of the psalms in worship or a particular collection of psalms (Pss 50; 73–83).

73:1-14 The psalmist begins by expressing his human weakness and failure in being envious of **the prosperity of the wicked** almost—but not quite—losing his foothold in the faith. The **pure in heart** are not perfect people but those whose lives are characterized by loyalty to the Lord (v. 1; cp. v. 13). They live without hypocrisy.

The psalmist's reflection on the seemingly carefree and successful lives of wicked people coupled with his own experience of suffering prompts him to question the value of serving the Lord. He experiences inner turmoil as he observes the seeming lack of justice in the world. He wonders if his struggle to live in right relationship with God is all **for nothing** (v. 13).

73:15-28 The psalmist voices his concern in prayer, recognizing that the question with which he was struggling would potentially damage the faith of others (v. 15; cp. 1Co 8). Attuning his heart to worship apparently drew the psalmist to see the **destiny** (Hb *'acharit*, "end"; cp. Ps 37:7-8) of the wicked from God's perspective (73:17) and in contrast to his own as one who belongs to the Lord (vv. 24,27-28). To become **embittered** was foolish because the psalmist was the one injured by his envy and anger (vv. 21-22).

74:1-12 A possible setting for this psalm is the period immediately following the destruction of Jerusalem in 587–586 B.C. when the Babylonians conquered Judah. For the first time in the Old Testament, God's people are

7 May the righteous[A] flourish
in his days
and prosperity[B] abound
until the moon is no more.

8 May he rule from sea to sea
and from the Euphrates
to the ends of the earth.
9 May desert tribes kneel
before him
and his enemies lick the dust.
10 May the kings of Tarshish
and the coasts and islands
bring tribute,
the kings of Sheba and Seba
offer gifts.
11 Let all kings bow down to him,
all nations serve him.

12 For he will rescue the poor
who cry out
and the afflicted who have
no helper.
13 He will have pity on the poor
and helpless
and save the lives of the poor.
14 He will redeem them
from oppression
and violence,
for their lives are[C] precious[D]
in his sight.

15 May he live long!
May gold from Sheba be given
to him.
May prayer be offered
for him continually,
and may he be blessed
all day long.
16 May there be plenty of grain
in the land;
may it wave on the tops
of the mountains.
May its crops be like Lebanon.
May people flourish
in the cities
like the grass of the field.
17 May his name endure forever;
as long as the sun shines,
may his fame increase.
May all nations be blessed
by him
and call him blessed.

18 May the LORD God, the God
of Israel,
who alone does wonders,
be praised.
19 May His glorious name
be praised forever;
the whole earth is filled
with His glory.
•Amen and amen.
20 The prayers of David
son of Jesse are concluded.

BOOK III
(Psalms 73:1–89:52)

Psalm 73
Vindication of God's Ways

A psalm of •Asaph.

1 God is indeed good to Israel,
to the pure in heart.
2 But as for me, my feet
almost slipped;
my steps nearly went astray.
3 For I envied the arrogant;
I saw the prosperity
of the wicked.

4 They have an easy time
until they die,[E]
and their bodies are well fed.[F]
5 They are not in trouble
like others;
they are not afflicted
like most people.
6 Therefore, pride is
their necklace,
and violence covers them
like a garment.
7 Their eyes bulge out
from fatness;
the imaginations
of their hearts run wild.
8 They mock,
and they speak maliciously;
they arrogantly
threaten oppression.
9 They set their mouths
against heaven,
and their tongues strut
across the earth.
10 Therefore His people turn
to them[G]
and drink in their
overflowing words.[H]
11 The wicked say,
"How can God know?
Does the •Most High
know everything?"
12 Look at them—the wicked!

[A]**72:7** Some Hb mss, LXX, Syr, Jer read *May righteousness* [B]**72:7** Or *peace* [C]**72:14** Lit *their blood is* [D]**72:14** Or *valuable* [E]**73:4** Lit *For there are no pangs to their death* [F]**73:4** Lit *fat* [G]**73:10** Lit *turn here* [H]**73:10** Lit *and waters of fullness are drained by them*

They are always at ease,
and they increase
their wealth.
13 Did I purify my heart
and wash my hands
in innocence for nothing?
14 For I am afflicted all day long
and punished every morning.
15 If I had decided to say
these things aloud,
I would have betrayed
Your people.[A]
16 When I tried to understand
all this,
it seemed hopeless[B]
17 until I entered
God's sanctuary.
Then I understood
their destiny.
18 Indeed, You put them
in slippery places;
You make them fall into ruin.
19 How suddenly they become
a desolation!
They come to an end,
swept away by terrors.
20 Like one waking
from a dream,
Lord, when arising,
You will despise
their image.
21 When I became embittered
and my innermost being[C]
was wounded,
22 I was stupid
and didn't understand;
I was an unthinking animal
toward You.
23 Yet I am always with You;
You hold my right hand.
24 You guide me
with Your counsel,
and afterward You will
take me up in glory.[D]
25 Who do I have in heaven
but You?
And I desire nothing on earth
but You.
26 My flesh and my heart
may fail,
but God is the strength[E]
of my heart,
my portion forever.
27 Those far from You
will certainly perish;
You destroy all who are
unfaithful to You.
28 But as for me, God's presence
is my good.
I have made the Lord God
my refuge,
so I can tell about all You do.

Psalm 74

Prayer for Israel

A •Maskil of •Asaph.

1 Why have You
rejected us forever, God?
Why does Your anger burn
against the sheep
of Your pasture?
2 Remember
Your congregation,
which You purchased
long ago
and redeemed as the tribe
for Your own possession.
Remember Mount •Zion
where You dwell.
3 Make Your way[F]
to the everlasting ruins,
to all that the enemy
has destroyed
in the sanctuary.
4 Your adversaries roared
in the meeting place
where You met with us.[G]
They set up their emblems
as signs.
5 It was like men in a thicket
of trees,
wielding axes,
6 then smashing
all the carvings
with hatchets and picks.
7 They set Your sanctuary
on fire;
they utterly[H] desecrated
the dwelling place
of Your name.
8 They said in their hearts,
"Let us
oppress them relentlessly."
They burned down every place
throughout the land
where God met with us.[I]

[A]73:15 Lit *betrayed the generation of Your sons* [B]73:16 Lit *it was trouble in my eyes* [C]73:21 Lit *my kidneys* [D]73:24 Or *will receive me with honor* [E]73:26 Lit *rock* [F]74:3 Lit *Lift up Your steps* [G]74:4 Lit *in Your meeting place* [H]74:7 Lit *they to the ground* [I]74:8 Lit *every meeting place of God in the land*

identified by the metaphor **the sheep of Your pasture** (cp. 79:13; 95:7; 100:3; Jr 23:1; Ezk 34:31). This imagery makes the opening "Why" question more poignant, implying the psalmist's sense of betrayal by God. Crying out for God to **remember** His people, the psalmist in effect calls for God to act on behalf of His people, who are (Ps 74:2):

- *God's* **congregation** (cp. 82:1);
- the people *He* **purchased** [Hb *qanah*, "buy, acquire, obtain," implying payment or exchange; cp. Dt 28:68] **long ago**;
- the people *He* **redeemed** (Hb *ga'al*, "ransom, buy back, regain possession of"; cp. Ex 6:6; 15:13);
- **the tribe** of *His* **own possession** (Hb *nachalah*, "portion, inheritance, heritage"; cp. Ex 15:17; Dt 4:20; 9:26; 32:9)—a phrase found only here, and in Is 63:17; Jr 10:16; 51:19.

The people of God had believed that He would never allow Jerusalem and the temple to be destroyed. They claimed that the presence of the temple itself assured their protection from enemies. The prophet Jeremiah had tried to warn the people that Jerusalem would be destroyed if the people did not repent of their evil ways and turn to God (Jr 7). The temple did not lie in **ruins** (Hb *mashshu'ot*, "destruction, desolation," Ps 74:3; cp. 73:18) because God was powerless but because God's people had failed to repent.

The psalmist, however, composed a lament from the perspective of those who cherished the privilege of belonging to Yahweh and of worshiping Him. The extent and horror of the devastation (74:3-8), particularly in contrast to the speaker's unshaken conviction that God can do whatever He pleases at any time (vv. 2,11-23), prompts both the initial questions (vv. 1-2) and the concern for **how long** He would permit the enemy to **mock** and **insult** His name (vv. 9-11,18,22-23).

The first section of the psalm describes the people's state of crisis—every tangible evidence of God's presence has been removed, and the violent and blasphemous acts against God's **dwelling place** are seared into the memories of the people who witnessed these events (v. 7).

74:8 The people were bereft of every place of worship. If multiple places of Yahweh-worship are literally indicated, then **every place . . . where God met with us** may refer to a prototype of the synagogue—i.e., places designated for prayer and instruction in the Torah. The Septuagint (LXX), however, includes the statement in the enemies' plan to destroy the temple and thereby "cause all of God's festivals [Gk *heortēs*, "feast days, holy days"; cp. Col 2:16] to cease from the earth." Similarly, to emphasize that when the temple was destroyed, the one and only legitimate place on earth for meeting with God had been **burned down** may reflect the use of hyperbole.

74:9 No longer was there **a prophet** through whom God spoke. The people saw none of their **signs** (Hb *'ot*, "banner, standard"; cp. Nm 2:2). Instead, the enemies had "set up their emblems" (Hb *'ot*) "as signs" (Hb *'ot*), probably referring to military banners representing the conquering nation, king, or deities (Ps 74:4). Such "emblems" would signify the conqueror's claim to have taken possession of the city marked with such banners, a picture intensifying the psalmist's plea for God to remember the people whom He had "redeemed" (see v. 2).

74:12-17 In the second section the psalmist boldly announces his allegiance to **God** as his **king** (cp. 44:4; 68:24; 84:3) and recounts God's performance of **saving acts** (Hb *yeshu'ah*, "salvation" or "deliverance"; cp. Ex 14:13; 15:2; see **Word Study**, p. 878). In the Hebrew text, verses 13-15 and 17 all begin with an emphatic **You** (Hb *'attah*). Because the verbs are inflected—i.e., their form already indicates that the subject is "you"—the addition of the pronoun emphasizes that, in this case, God alone, or God in contrast to anyone else contending for His place, did these things. The same construction appears in the second line of verse 16 with the verb **established**.

The events described with such intense verbs and symbolic imagery in verses 13-15 recall God's dividing of the Red Sea to deliver His people from the Egyptians (cp. Ex 14:21-30) and of the Jordan River to usher His people into the promised land (Jos 3–4). In these events, God **opened up** [Hb *baqa'*, "divide, cleave asunder"; cp. Ps 78:13,15; Is 63:12] **springs** (Hb *ma'yan*, "fountain"), and **dried up** [Hb *yabēsh*] **ever-flowing** [Hb *'ētan*, "perennial, constantly flowing"; cp. "normal depth," Ex 14:27] **rivers** (see Jos 2:10; 4:23).

God also **smashed** [Hb *shavar*, "break to pieces, shatter"; cp. Ps 48:7] **the heads of the sea monsters** (Hb *tannin*, "great serpent, crocodile, dragon") and **crushed the heads of Leviathan** (Hb, "wreathed or coiled sea creature"; see note on Jb 41:1-34), figuratively portraying the destruction of the Egyptian forces during the exodus (cp. Ex 7:9-12; 15:3-10) with imagery also used by God in disclosing the impending destruction of both Egypt and Babylon. In Jr 51:33-37, the head of Babylon (Nebuchadnezzar) is compared to "a sea monster" (Hb *tannin*) that "has swallowed" the people living in Jerusalem. The Lord promises to avenge His people by making Babylon's "fountain run dry" (Hb *yabēsh*, Jr 51:36; cp. Ps 74:15).

9 There are no signs for us
to see.
There is no longer a prophet.
And none of us knows
how long this will last.
10 God, how long will the
enemy mock?
Will the foe insult
Your name forever?
11 Why do You hold back
Your hand?
Stretch out[A] Your right hand
and destroy them!

12 God my King is
from ancient times,
performing saving acts
on the earth.
13 You divided the sea
with Your strength;
You smashed the heads
of the sea monsters
in the waters;
14 You crushed the heads
of •Leviathan;
You fed him to the creatures
of the desert.
15 You opened up springs
and streams;
You dried up
ever-flowing rivers.
16 The day is Yours,
also the night;
You established the moon
and the sun.
17 You set all the boundaries
of the earth;
You made summer
and winter.

18 Remember this: the enemy
has mocked •Yahweh,
and a foolish people
has insulted Your name.
19 Do not give the life
of Your dove to beasts;[B]
do not forget the lives
of Your poor people forever.
20 Consider the covenant,
for the dark places of the land
are full of violence.
21 Do not let the oppressed
turn away in shame;
let the poor and needy
praise Your name.
22 Rise up, God,
defend Your cause!
Remember the insults
that fools bring against You
all day long.
23 Do not forget the clamor
of Your adversaries,
the tumult of Your opponents
that goes up constantly.

Psalm 75

God Judges the Wicked

For the choir director:
"Do Not Destroy."[C] *A psalm*
of •Asaph. A song.

1 We give thanks to You, God;
we give thanks to You,
for Your name is near.
People tell about
Your wonderful works.

2 "When I choose a time,
I will judge fairly.
3 When the earth and all
its inhabitants shake,
I am the One who steadies
its pillars. •*Selah*
4 I say to the boastful,
'Do not boast,'
and to the wicked, 'Do not
lift up your •horn.
5 Do not lift up your horn
against heaven
or speak arrogantly.'"

[A] **74:11** Lit *From Your bosom* [B] **74:19** One Hb ms, LXX, Syr read *Do not hand over to beasts a soul that praises You* [C] **75:title** Possibly a tune

>WORD|*study*

75:4-10 Horn represents power or strength, particularly in military contexts. The parallelism makes plain the meaning of the idiom, **Do not lift up your horn**—do not boast or speak arrogantly (v. 4-5). Whether the imagery is a picture of a horned animal (e.g., a bull, goat, or stag) pointing its horns in the direction of an opponent or of a warrior raising high in defiance the horn he would blow to signal an offensive attack, the message conveyed is clear—"I'm ready to do battle with you." God declares that He **will cut off** [Hb *gada'*, "break, smash"] **all the horns of the wicked**, signifying that He will break into pieces whatever they believe empowers them to stand on their own in defiance of God's commands (v. 10). In contrast, however, God promises to lift up **the horns of the righteous**—i.e., He will victoriously reward and acclaim His name for the righteous trust in Him to be their strength (v. 10).

6 Exaltation does not come
from the east, the west,
or the desert,
7 for God is the Judge:
He brings down one
and exalts another.
8 For there is a cup
in the LORD's hand,
full of wine blended
with spices, and He pours
from it.
All the wicked of the earth
will drink,
draining it to the dregs.
9 As for me, I will tell
about Him forever;
I will sing praise to the God
of Jacob.
10 "I will cut off all the horns
of the wicked,
but the horns of the righteous
will be lifted up."

Psalm 76

God, the Powerful Judge

For the choir director:
with stringed instruments.
A psalm of •Asaph. A song.

1 God is known in Judah;
His name is great in Israel.
2 His tent is in Salem,[A]
His dwelling place in •Zion.
3 There He shatters the bow's
flaming arrows,
the shield, the sword,
and the weapons of war.
•Selah
4 You are resplendent
and majestic
coming down
from the mountains of prey.
5 The brave-hearted
have been plundered;
they have slipped
into their final sleep.
None of the warriors was able
to lift a hand.
6 At Your rebuke, God of Jacob,
both chariot and horse
lay still.
7 And You—You are
to be •feared.[B]
When You are angry,
who can stand before You?
8 From heaven
You pronounced judgment.
The earth feared
and grew quiet
9 when God rose up to judge
and to save all the lowly
of the earth. *Selah*
10 Even human wrath
will praise You;
You will clothe Yourself
with their remaining wrath.[C]
11 Make and keep your vows
to the LORD your God;
let all who are around Him
bring tribute
to the awe-inspiring One.[D]
12 He humbles the spirit
of leaders;
He is feared by the kings
of the earth.

Psalm 77

Confidence in a Time of Crisis

For the choir director: according to
Jeduthun. Of •Asaph. A psalm.

1 I cry aloud to God,
aloud to God, and He
will hear me.
2 I sought the Lord in my day
of trouble.
My hands were continually
lifted up
all night long;
I refused to be comforted.
3 I think of God; I groan;
I meditate; my spirit
becomes weak. *•Selah*

[A]76:2 = Jerusalem [B]76:7 Or *are awe-inspiring* [C]76:10 Hb obscure [D]76:11 Or *tribute with awe*

>WORD|*study*

76:1 Is known (Hb *yada'*) conveys the concept of knowing by personal experience or by entering into personal relationship. The parallel statement elaborates: God's **name** [i.e., His character or reputation] **is great in Israel**. God's people know Him by personal experience as the God who repeatedly has brought victory into their lives. They can know Him only because He has graciously taken the initiative to establish a relationship with them.

Similarly, the Egyptian head is compared to "the great monster (Hb *tannin*) lying in the middle of his Nile" (Ezk 29:3-5). The Lord promises to haul the crocodile-like Pharaoh out of the Nile River, leave him in the desert, and feed him to the birds and the beasts (Ezk 29:4-5; cp. Ps 74:14).

74:18-23 The psalmist rehearses God's acts of deliverance in the past to express continuing faith in God's unfailing power to **defend** [His] **cause**. Not only has He demonstrated His power to rescue and defend His people, He is the sovereign King over all people everywhere for all time, for He is the one who created "the moon and the sun" worshiped as idols both in Egypt and Babylon (vv. 16-17; cp. 104:19; Dt 4:19; Jos 10:12-13; 2Kg 23:5). Surely God's people had not experienced defeat because God lacked power. Therefore, the psalmist returns to pleading for the Lord to act for the sake of His **name** and **the covenant**.

75:1-10 The designation **"Do Not Destroy"** in the superscription is best understood as the tune to which the psalm was intended to be sung. The theme of this psalm is the judgment of God on wicked people. God alone can judge rightly and fairly because He alone knows the human heart. God's judgments at times may appear surprising, yet He alone knows all the circumstances and thus He alone can judge correctly. For this reason He is worthy of praise (v. 9). This psalm warns against judging others.

76:2 Salem (Hb, "peace") refers to Jerusalem, also identified as **Zion** (Gn 14:18).

76:3-7 This psalm celebrates God's victory over Israel's enemies and His deliverance of His people (see Pss 46 and 48). The implied answer to the rhetorical question in verse 7 is that no one **can stand before** God when He is **angry**.

76:8-12 If we refuse to know God as Savior, we will ultimately know Him as sovereign Judge. In view of God's sovereign judgment, those who are wise respond reverently and obediently to Him.

77:1-20 Jeduthun probably identifies one of David's chief musicians (see note on Ps 39:1-13). Facing difficult circumstances, the psalmist cries out to God for relief from his difficulties. Remembering God's gracious actions in the past gives him hope for the future. The psalmist determines to **reflect** (Hb *hagah*, "meditate," v. 12; see **Word Study**, p. 667) and **meditate** (Hb *siyach*, "talk alone with oneself," vv. 6,12) on all God has done. Focusing on

God's greatness leads to the realization that God is the only true God (v. 13). Then the psalmist turns his attention to God's powerful redemption, deliverance, and leadership of His people under Moses and Aaron (vv. 14-20). Remembering God's goodness in the past enables the psalmist to face a current crisis with hope. Faith in God enables His people to take the long view of life, to see things in proper perspective.

78:1-3 The superscription categorizes this psalm as a ***Maskil***, one that teaches or gives insight into practical living. The introduction (vv. 1-8) also calls attention to the psalm's didactic purpose. The psalmist calls for his **people** (i.e., his generation) to **hear** his **instruction** (Hb *torah*;) and to learn a lesson from Israel's history. The psalm will consist of **wise sayings** (Hb *mashal*, "parable"; see **Word Study**, p. 783; cp. 1Kg 5:12) and **mysteries** [Hb *chidah*, "enigma, parable"; cp. Ps 49:4; Pr 1:6] **from the past**—valuable insights about learning from past failures and passing on God's Word from generation to generation.

78:4-72 The disobedience of God's people despite all the mighty acts He performed on their behalf is the theme. The people responded to God's goodness with ingratitude instead of faith. The present generation should learn from the sins of their forefathers. The psalmist recalled God's actions on behalf of His people at the exodus from Egypt, during the wilderness wanderings, and at the time of the conquest of Canaan. Despite God's goodness, the people repeatedly rebelled against Him (Ps 106). The rebellion of people against God, despite His abundant mercy, remains as great a mystery now as it was in the time of the psalmist.

4 You have kept me
from closing my eyes;
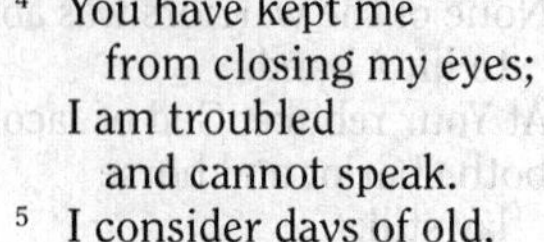
I am troubled
and cannot speak.
5 I consider days of old,
years long past.
6 At night I remember
my music;
I meditate in my heart,
and my spirit ponders.

7 "Will the Lord reject forever
and never again show favor?
8 Has His faithful love
ceased forever?
Is His promise at an end
for all generations?
9 Has God forgotten
to be gracious?
Has He in anger
withheld His compassion?"
Selah

10 So I say, "I am grieved[A]
that the right hand
of the •Most High
has changed."
11 I will remember
the LORD's works;
yes, I will remember
Your ancient wonders.
12 I will reflect on
all You have done
and meditate on Your actions.

13 God, Your way is holy.
What god is great like God?
14 You are the God
who works wonders;
You revealed Your strength
among the peoples.
15 With power You redeemed
Your people,
the descendants of Jacob
and Joseph. *Selah*

16 The waters saw You, God.
The waters saw You;
they trembled.
Even the depths shook.
17 The clouds poured
down water.
The storm clouds thundered;
Your arrows flashed
back and forth.
18 The sound of Your thunder
was in the whirlwind;
lightning lit up the world.
The earth shook and quaked.

19 Your way went through
the sea
and Your path through
the great waters,
but Your footprints
were unseen.
20 You led Your people
like a flock
by the hand of Moses
and Aaron.

Psalm 78

Lessons from Israel's Past

A •Maskil of •Asaph.

1 My people,
hear my instruction;
listen to what I say.
2 I will declare wise sayings;
I will speak mysteries
from the past—
3 things we have heard
and known
and that our fathers
have passed down to us.
4 We must not hide them
from their children,
but must tell
a future generation
the praises of the LORD,
His might,
and the wonderful works
He has performed.
5 He established a •testimony
in Jacob
and set up a law in Israel,
which He commanded
our fathers
to teach to their children
6 so that a future generation—
children yet to be born—
might know.
They were to rise and tell
their children
7 so that they might
put their confidence in God
and not forget God's works,
but keep His commands.
8 Then they would not be
like their fathers,
a stubborn and rebellious
generation,
a generation whose heart
was not loyal
and whose spirit
was not faithful to God.

[A] **77:10** Lit *"My piercing*

9 The Ephraimite archers
turned back
on the day of battle.
10 They did not keep
God's covenant
and refused to live by His law.
11 They forgot what
He had done,
the wonderful works
He had shown them.
12 He worked wonders in
the sight of their fathers
in the land of Egypt,
the region of Zoan.
13 He split the sea
and brought them across;
the water stood firm
like a wall.
14 He led them with a cloud
by day
and with a fiery light
throughout the night.
15 He split rocks
in the wilderness
and gave them drink
as abundant as the depths.
16 He brought streams out of
the stone
and made water flow down
like rivers.

17 But they continued to sin
against Him,
rebelling in the desert
against the •Most High.
18 They deliberately[A] tested God,
demanding the food
they craved.
19 They spoke
against God, saying,
"Is God able to provide food
in the wilderness?
20 Look! He struck the rock
and water gushed out;
torrents overflowed.
But can He also provide bread
or furnish meat
for His people?"
21 Therefore, the LORD heard
and became furious;
then fire broke out
against Jacob,
and anger flared up
against Israel
22 because they did not
believe God
or rely on His salvation.
23 He gave a command
to the clouds above
and opened the doors
of heaven.
24 He rained manna for them
to eat;
He gave them grain
from heaven.
25 People[B] ate the bread
of angels.[C]
He sent them
an abundant supply of food.
26 He made the east wind blow
in the skies
and drove the south wind
by His might.
27 He rained meat on them
like dust,
and winged birds like the sand
of the seas.
28 He made them fall
in His camp,
all around His tent.[D,E]
29 They ate and were
completely satisfied,
for He gave them
what they craved.
30 Before they had satisfied
their desire,
while the food was still
in their mouths,
31 God's anger flared up
against them,
and He killed
some of their best men.
He struck down Israel's
choice young men.

32 Despite all this,
they kept sinning
and did not believe
His wonderful works.
33 He made their days end
in futility,
their years in sudden disaster.
34 When He killed some of them,
the rest began to seek Him;
they repented
and searched for God.
35 They remembered that God
was their rock,
the Most High God,
their Redeemer.
36 But they deceived Him
with their mouths,
they lied to Him
with their tongues,

[A]78:18 Lit *in their heart* [B]78:25 Lit *Man* [C]78:25 Lit *mighty ones* [D]78:28 LXX, Syr read *in their camp, all around their tents* [E]78:28 Or *in its camp, all around its tents*

37 their hearts were insincere
toward Him,
and they were unfaithful
to His covenant.
38 Yet He was compassionate;
He •atoned for[A] their •guilt
and did not destroy them.
He often turned
His anger aside
and did not unleash[B]
all His wrath.
39 He remembered that
they were only flesh,
a wind that passes
and does not return.

40 How often they rebelled
against Him
in the wilderness
and grieved Him
in the desert.
41 They constantly tested God
and provoked the Holy One
of Israel.
42 They did not remember
His power shown
on the day He redeemed them
from the foe,
43 when He performed
His miraculous signs
in Egypt
and His wonders in the region
of Zoan.
44 He turned their rivers
into blood,
and they could not drink
from their streams.
45 He sent among them swarms
of flies,
which fed on them,
and frogs,
which devastated them.
46 He gave their crops
to the caterpillar
and the fruit of their labor
to the locust.
47 He killed their vines with hail
and their sycamore fig trees
with a flood.
48 He handed over
their livestock to hail
and their cattle
to lightning bolts.
49 He sent His burning anger
against them:
fury, indignation,
and calamity—
a band of deadly messengers.[C]
50 He cleared a path
for His anger.
He did not spare them
from death
but delivered their lives
to the plague.
51 He struck all the firstborn
in Egypt,
the first progeny of the tents
of Ham.[D]
52 He led His people out
like sheep
and guided them like a flock
in the wilderness.
53 He led them safely,
and they were not afraid;
but the sea covered
their enemies.
54 He brought them
to His holy land,
to the mountain
His right hand acquired.
55 He drove out nations
before them.
He apportioned
their inheritance by lot
and settled the tribes of Israel
in their tents.

56 But they rebelliously tested
the Most High God,
for they did not keep
His decrees.
57 They treacherously
turned away
like their fathers;
they became warped
like a faulty bow.
58 They enraged Him
with their •high places
and provoked His jealousy
with their carved images.
59 God heard
and became furious;
He completely rejected Israel.
60 He abandoned the tabernacle
at Shiloh,
the tent where He resided
among men.[E]
61 He gave up His strength[F]
to captivity
and His splendor to the hand
of a foe.
62 He surrendered His people
to the sword
because He was enraged
with His heritage.

[A]**78:38** Or *He wiped out*, or *He forgave* [B]**78:38** Or *stir up* [C]**78:49** Or *angels* [D]**78:51** Ham's descendants who settled in Egypt [E]**78:60** Hb adam [F]**78:61** = the ark of the covenant

63 Fire consumed
His chosen young men,
and His young women
had no wedding songs.[A]
64 His priests fell by the sword,
but the[B] widows
could not lament.[C]

65 Then the Lord awoke as if
from sleep,
like a warrior from the effects
of wine.
66 He beat back His foes;
He gave them lasting shame.
67 He rejected the tent of Joseph
and did not choose the tribe
of Ephraim.
68 He chose instead the tribe
of Judah,
Mount •Zion, which He loved.
69 He built His sanctuary
like the heights,[D]
like the earth that
He established forever.
70 He chose David His servant
and took him
from the sheepfolds;
71 He brought him
from tending ewes
to be shepherd
over His people Jacob—
over Israel, His inheritance.
72 He shepherded them
with a pure heart
and guided them
with his skillful hands.

Psalm 79

Faith amid Confusion

A psalm of •Asaph.

1 God, the nations have invaded
Your inheritance,
desecrated Your holy temple,
and turned Jerusalem
into ruins.
2 They gave the corpses
of Your servants
to the birds of the sky
for food,
the flesh of Your godly ones
to the beasts of the earth.
3 They poured out their blood
like water
all around Jerusalem,
and there was no one
to bury them.
4 We have become an object
of reproach
to our neighbors,
a source of mockery
and ridicule
to those around us.
5 How long, •Yahweh? Will You
be angry forever?
Will Your jealousy
keep burning like fire?
6 Pour out Your wrath
on the nations
that don't acknowledge You,
on the kingdoms that don't
call on Your name,
7 for they have devoured Jacob
and devastated his homeland.
8 Do not hold past sins[E]
against us;
let Your compassion come
to us quickly,
for we have become weak.
9 God of our salvation,
help us—
for the glory of Your name.
Deliver us and •atone for[F]
our sins,
because of Your name.
10 Why should the nations ask,
"Where is their God?"
Before our eyes,
let vengeance
for the shed blood
of Your servants
be known among the nations.
11 Let the groans
of the prisoners reach You;
according to
Your great power,
preserve those condemned
to die.

12 Pay back sevenfold
to our neighbors
the reproach they have hurled
at You, Lord.
13 Then we, Your people,
the sheep of Your pasture,
will thank You forever;
we will declare Your praise
to generation
after generation.

79:1-13 The historical background of this psalm is the conquest of Jerusalem when the southern kingdom of Judah fell to the Babylonians (587–586 B.C.; cp. Ps 74). Because the people believed Jerusalem would never be destroyed, the poet must have experienced difficulty comprehending the present destruction of the city. He wonders **how long** God will continue to reject His people and calls on Him to turn His anger toward the enemies of His people (vv. 5-6). If God would only completely destroy their enemies, His people would praise Him forever (v. 13).

The poet's attitude seems harshly vindictive on this side of the cross in light of Jesus' teachings about loving your enemies. However, in the poet's mind, the enemies of God's people were perceived as being God's enemies as well (v. 12). Thus the psalmist's prayer was not a totally selfish prayer. Verse 9 reveals his concern for God's **name** (i.e., His character or reputation). To his credit, the poet also acknowledges guilt personally and on the part of the people, thus recognizing that the nation's fall resulted from their sins, for which the poet seeks forgiveness.

[A]**78:63** Lit *virgins were not praised* [B]**78:64** Lit *His* [C]**78:64** War probably prevented customary funerals. [D]**78:69** Either the heights of heaven or the mountain heights [E]**79:8** Or *hold the sins of past generations* [F]**79:9** Or *and wipe out*, or *and forgive*

80:1 The Lilies may refer to the tune to which the psalm was intended to be sung. This psalm originated in a time of crisis. God's people were suffering at the hands of their enemies. The psalmist calls upon God as the **Shepherd of Israel**, who cares for and restores His people, for they were dependent on Him (cp. Ps 23:1). **Joseph** is a reference to Israel or the northern kingdom. As the one who sits **enthroned on the cherubim**, God was viewed as invisibly dwelling above the ark of the covenant or the ark of the testimony (Ex 25:10-22).

80:3-19 Verses 3,7,19 allude to the blessing or benediction of Aaron (Nm 6:24-26). **Look . . . with favor** more literally suggests "make Your face shine" (v. 7). Whereas the psalmist questions **why** the Lord had allowed His vineyard—i.e., His people—to be destroyed (vv. 8-16), the Lord had revealed in the eighth century B.C. that, although He had tenderly cared for His vineyard, His people had failed to yield the **fruit** of righteousness, making destruction inevitable (Is 5:1-7).

81:1-2 The superscription **on the *Gittith*** also identifies this poem (cp. Ps 8:1; 84:1), which begins with a call to praise God by singing, shouting, and playing musical instruments.

81:3-7 The sound of the ram's **horn** reminded the people of God's presence (Nm 10:10). The people celebrated the harvest festival at the command of God. The Lord reminds His people of His care for them in the past. He had freed the people from the oppressive burden of slavery in Egypt (Ex 1:11). He had revealed Himself and spoken to them in thunder at Mount Sinai (Ex 19:18-19). The Lord also reminds His people of their rebellion at **Meribah** (cp. Ex 17:1-7; Nm 20:1-13).

81:8-10 Hearing or listening to God is understood to include obeying Him. Like a parent distraught over a child in grave danger, God urgently pleads for the people to **listen** to Him. Again, like parents who assert their authority by reference to their identity (e.g., "I am your mother!") and cite the good things they have done for the child to remind him that they have his best interests at heart, the Lord declared, **I am Yahweh**, who had delivered them from bondage Egypt (see Ex 20:1-3). Only by turning to Him to meet their needs would His people experience true fulfillment.

81:11-16 Instead, Israel rebelled against the Lord. God judged His people's disobedience by allowing them to go their own stubborn way and reap the consequences of that rebellion, pleading with them all the while to return to Him. The reference

Psalm 80

A Prayer for Restoration

For the choir director: according to "The Lilies."[A] A testimony of •Asaph. A psalm.

1 Listen, Shepherd of Israel,
who leads Joseph like a flock;
You who sit enthroned
on the •cherubim,
rise up
2 before Ephraim,
Benjamin, and Manasseh.[B]
Rally Your power and come
to save us.
3 Restore us, God;
look on us with favor,
and we will be saved.

4 LORD God of •Hosts,
how long will You be angry
with Your people's prayers?
5 You fed them the bread
of tears
and gave them a full measure[C]
of tears to drink.
6 You make us quarrel
with our neighbors;
our enemies make fun of us.
7 Restore us, God of Hosts;
look on us with favor, and we
will be saved.

8 You uprooted a vine
from Egypt;
You drove out the nations
and planted it.
9 You cleared a place for it;
it took root and filled
the land.
10 The mountains were covered
by its shade,
and the mighty cedars[D]
with its branches.
11 It sent out sprouts
toward the Sea[E]
and shoots toward the River.[F]

12 Why have You broken down
its walls
so that all who pass by
pick its fruit?
13 The boar from the forest
tears it
and creatures of the field
feed on it.
14 Return, God of Hosts.
Look down from heaven
and see;
take care of this vine,
15 the root[G] Your right hand
has planted,
the shoot[H] that
You made strong
for Yourself.
16 It was cut down
and burned up;[I]
they[J] perish at the rebuke
of Your countenance.
17 Let Your hand be
with the man
at Your right hand,
with the son of man
You have made strong
for Yourself.
18 Then we will not turn away
from You;
revive us, and we will call
on Your name.
19 Restore us, •Yahweh,
the God of Hosts;
look on us with favor,
and we will be saved.

Psalm 81

A Call to Obedience

*For the choir director:
on the •Gittith. Of •Asaph.*

1 Sing for joy to God
our strength;
shout in triumph to the God
of Jacob.
2 Lift up a song—
play the tambourine,
the melodious lyre,
and the harp.
3 Blow the horn on the day of
our feasts[K,L]
during the new moon
and during the full moon.
4 For this is a statute for Israel,
a judgment of the God
of Jacob.
5 He set it up as an ordinance
for Joseph
when He went throughout[M]
the land of Egypt.

[A] **80:title** Possibly a tune; Pss 45; 60; 69 [B] **80:2** This is the marching order for the camp of Israel. [C] **80:5** Lit *a one-third measure* [D] **80:10** Lit *the cedars of God* [E] **80:11** = the Mediterranean [F] **80:11** = the Euphrates [G] **80:15** Hb obscure [H] **80:15** Or *son* [I] **80:16** Lit *burned with fire* [J] **80:16** Or *may they* [K] **81:3** Lit *feast* [L] **81:3** Either Passover or Tabernacles [M] **81:5** LXX, Syr, Jer read *out of*

I heard
an unfamiliar language:
6 "I relieved his shoulder
from the burden;
his hands were freed
from carrying the basket.
7 You called out in distress,
and I rescued you;
I answered you
from the thundercloud.
I tested you at the waters
of Meribah. •*Selah*
8 Listen, My people, and I will
admonish you.
Israel, if you would only listen
to Me!
9 There must not be
a strange god among you;
you must not bow down
to a foreign god.
10 I am •Yahweh your God,
who brought you up
from the land of Egypt.
Open your mouth wide,
and I will fill it.
11 "But My people did not listen
to Me;
Israel did not obey Me.
12 So I gave them over
to their stubborn hearts
to follow their own plans.
13 If only My people would listen
to Me
and Israel would follow
My ways,
14 I would quickly subdue
their enemies
and turn My hand
against their foes."
15 Those who hate the LORD
would pretend submission
to Him;
their doom would last forever.
16 But He would feed Israel[A]
with the best wheat.
"I would satisfy you
with honey from the rock."

Psalm 82
A Plea for Righteous Judgment

A psalm of •Asaph.

1 God has taken His place
in the divine assembly;
He judges among the gods:[B]
2 "How long will you
judge unjustly
and show partiality
to the wicked? •*Selah*
3 Provide justice for the needy
and the fatherless;
uphold the rights
of the oppressed
and the destitute.
4 Rescue the poor and needy;
save them from the power of
the wicked."
5 They do not know
or understand;
they wander in darkness.
All the foundations
of the earth are shaken.
6 I said, "You are gods;
you are all sons
of the •Most High.
7 However, you will die
like men
and fall like any other ruler."
8 Rise up, God, judge the earth,
for all the nations
belong to You.

Psalm 83
Prayer Against Enemies

A song. A psalm of •Asaph.

1 God, do not keep silent.
Do not be deaf, God; do not
be idle.
2 See how Your enemies
make an uproar;
those who hate You
have acted arrogantly.[C]
3 They devise clever schemes
against Your people;
they conspire against
Your treasured ones.
4 They say, "Come, let us
wipe them out as a nation
so that Israel's name
will no longer
be remembered."
5 For they have conspired
with one mind;
they form an alliance[D]
against You—
6 the tents of Edom
and the Ishmaelites,
Moab and the Hagrites,
7 Gebal, Ammon, and Amalek,

to **stubborn** [Hb *sherirut*, "hardness, lust"] **hearts**, is a key emphasis of Jeremiah, a prophet whose ministry spanned the time period when Jerusalem and Judah fell to the Babylonians or Chaldeans (see Jr 3:17; 7:24; 9:14; 11:8; 13:10; 16:12; 18:12; 23:17). As a result of their disobedience, God's people missed His greatest blessings.

82:1-8 This psalm immediately sets a dramatic scene: **God** [Hb *ʾElohim*, with a singular verb] **has taken His place in the divine assembly** (Hb *ʿēdah-ʾēl*, "congregation of the mighty" or ". . . of God," v. 1; cp. 74:2; Nm 27:17). **The gods** (Hb *ʾelohim*; Ps 82:1,6) being judged likely refer to unjust rulers who have showed **partiality to the wicked** rather than extending **justice** to the helpless members of society (vv. 2-4). The Old Testament repeatedly emphasizes God's concern for the weaker or more vulnerable members of society (vv. 3-4; cp. Ex 22:21-27; Dt 10:17-19; Jr 7:5-7). In the Gospel of John, Jesus interpreted "gods" (Ps 82:6) to be "those whom the word of God came to" (Jn 10:35), referring to the people of Israel. The psalmist calls on the God of justice to **judge the earth** (Ps 82:8).

83:1-8 The psalmist prays for God to take action against Israel's **enemies**, who were viewed as the enemies of God (v. 2). Israel's existence as a nation was threatened. A list of Israel's enemies follows: **Edom**, **Moab**, **Philistia**, and **Assyria**, the nation that conquered the northern kingdom of Israel in 722/721 B.C. (vv. 6-8).

[A]**81:16** Lit *him* [B]**82:1** Or *the heavenly beings*, or *the earthly rulers*; lit *elohim* [C]**83:2** Lit *have lifted their head* [D]**83:5** Lit *they cut a covenant*

83:9-18 The psalmist requests that God **deal with** Israel's enemies and destroy them (v. 10), making them like **manure** (v. 10), **tumbleweed**, and **straw before the wind** (v. 13; cp. Ps 1:4-6). However, the psalmist's fundamental concern is that all the nations will **know** that Yahweh is **the Most High over all the earth** (Ps 83:18).

84:1–85:13 The **sons of Korah**, descendants of Kohath, were Levites (1Ch 6:22) involved in the music for the temple.

84:1-12 On the *Gittith* also appears in the superscriptions of Ps 8 and Ps 81. The psalmist exults in the joy of being in God's presence and spending time where he is most at home:

- in the **dwelling place** (Hb *mishkan*, "tent," Ps 84:1) of the **Lord of Hosts**, a reference to God as the commander of the armies of heaven (also vv. 8,12);
- in **the courts of the Lord** (vv. 2,10);
- **near** the **altars** of the **Lord of Hosts** (v. 3);
- **in** God's **house** (v. 4);
- **in Zion** (v. 7);
- **at the door of the house of my God** (v. 10);

Three times the psalmist declares the superlative happiness of those who live for the Lord, implicitly counting himself among them (vv. 4-5,12; cp. 65:4; see note on 1:1-2). The psalmist himself expresses passionate appreciation for the beauty of the temple where God's people appeared before their King to worship Him (84:1-4; cp. 44:4; 74:12; 145:1). The poet's **heart** and **flesh** (i.e., his entire being) longs to bask in the blessing of God's presence (84:2). Even the **sparrow** and the **swallow** were privileged to dwell in God's glorious presence (v. 3). How much more blessed then was this psalmist who deems **a day** spent enjoying God's presence to be **better . . . than a thousand** days spent in any other way (v. 10).

84:5-7 Those who make the **pilgrimage** (Hb *mesillah*, "highway, elevated public road"; cp. Pr 16:17; Is 40:3) to the temple in Jerusalem are described as people who depend on God for **strength** (Hb *ʿoz*, "might, power"; cp. Ex 15:2). When passing through **the Valley of Baca** (Hb, "weeping, lamentation"), they turn experiences of sorrow and adversity into sources of life and blessing for others. Unwavering trust in God opens the way for these pilgrims to **go from strength to strength**, to emerge from periods of grief or soul-searching repentance with renewed faith.

84:8-12 The king is identified as God's **anointed one**. The **shield** identifies the king in his role as the protector of the people and is a metaphor for God's protection of His people. God's care for

Philistia with the inhabitants
of Tyre.
8 Even Assyria has joined them;
they lend support[A] to the sons
of Lot.[B] •*Selah*
9 Deal with them as You did
with Midian,
as You did with Sisera
and Jabin at the Kishon River.
10 They were destroyed
at En-dor;
they became manure
for the ground.
11 Make their nobles like Oreb
and Zeeb,
and all their tribal leaders
like Zebah and Zalmunna,
12 who said, "Let us
seize God's pastures
for ourselves."
13 Make them like tumbleweed,
my God,
like straw before the wind.
14 As fire burns a forest,
as a flame blazes
through mountains,
15 so pursue them
with Your tempest
and terrify them
with Your storm.
16 Cover their faces with shame
so that they will seek
Your name •Yahweh.
17 Let them be put to shame
and terrified forever;
let them perish in disgrace.
18 May they know
that You alone—
whose name is Yahweh—
are the •Most High
over all the earth.

Psalm 84

Longing for God's House

For the choir director: on the •*Gittith.*
A psalm of the sons of Korah.

1 How lovely is
Your dwelling place,
Lord of •Hosts.
2 I long and yearn
for the courts of the Lord;
my heart and flesh cry out
for[C] the living God.

3 Even a sparrow
finds a home,
and a swallow, a nest
for herself
where she places her young—
near Your altars,
Lord of Hosts,
my King and my God.
4 How happy are those
who reside
in Your house,
who praise You continually.
•*Selah*

5 Happy are the people
whose strength is in You,
whose hearts are set
on pilgrimage.
6 As they pass
through the Valley
of Baca,[D]
they make it a source
of springwater;
even the autumn rain
will cover it with blessings.[E]
7 They go from strength
to strength;
each appears before God
in •Zion.

8 Lord God of Hosts,
hear my prayer;
listen, God of Jacob. *Selah*
9 Consider our shield,[F]
God;
look on the face
of Your anointed one.

10 Better a day in Your courts
than a thousand
anywhere else.
I would rather be at the door
of the house of my God
than to live in the tents
of wicked people.
11 For the Lord God is a sun
and shield.
The Lord gives grace
and glory;
He does not withhold
the good
from those who live
with integrity.
12 Happy is the person
who trusts in You,
Lord of Hosts!

[A]83:8 Lit *they are an arm* [B]83:8 = Moab and Edom [C]84:2 Or *flesh shout for joy to* [D]84:6 Or *Valley of Tears* [E]84:6 Or *pools* [F]84:9 = the king

Psalm 85

Restoration of Favor

For the choir director. A psalm of the sons of Korah.

1 LORD, You showed favor
to Your land;
You restored
Jacob's prosperity.[A]
2 You took away
Your people's •guilt;
You covered all their sin.
•*Selah*
3 You withdrew all Your fury;
You turned from
Your burning anger.

4 Return to us,
God of our salvation,
and abandon Your displeasure
with us.
5 Will You be angry
with us forever?
Will You prolong Your anger
for all generations?
6 Will You not revive us again
so that Your people
may rejoice in You?
7 Show us
Your faithful love, LORD,
and give us Your salvation.

8 I will listen to what
God will say;
surely the LORD will declare
peace
to His people, His godly ones,
and not let them go back
to foolish ways.
9 His salvation is very near
those who •fear Him,
so that glory may dwell
in our land.

10 Faithful love and truth
will join together;
righteousness and peace
will embrace.
11 Truth will spring up
from the earth,
and righteousness will look
down from heaven.
12 Also, the LORD will provide
what is good,
and our land will yield
its crops.
13 Righteousness will go
before Him
to prepare the way
for His steps.

Psalm 86

Lament and Petition

A Davidic prayer.

1 Listen, LORD, and answer me,
for I am poor and needy.
2 Protect my life,
for I am faithful.
You are my God;
save Your servant
who trusts in You.
3 Be gracious to me, Lord,
for I call to You all day long.
4 Bring joy
to Your servant's life,
because I turn to You, Lord.

5 For You, Lord, are kind
and ready to forgive,
rich in faithful love to all
who call on You.
6 LORD, hear my prayer;
listen to my plea for mercy.
7 I call on You in the day
of my distress,
for You will answer me.

8 Lord, there is no one like You
among the gods,
and there are no works
like Yours.
9 All the nations You have made
will come and bow down
before You, Lord,
and will honor Your name.
10 For You are great
and perform wonders;
You alone are God.
11 Teach me Your way, •Yahweh,
and I will live by Your truth.
Give me an undivided mind
to •fear Your name.
12 I will praise You
with all my heart,
Lord my God,
and will honor
Your name forever.
13 For Your faithful love for me
is great,
and You deliver my life
from the depths of •Sheol.

14 God, arrogant people
have attacked me;
a gang of ruthless men seeks
my life.

[A]**85:1** Or *restored Jacob from captivity*

His children is also compared to the warmth and light provided by **a sun**. The Lord **does not withhold** anything that is best **from those who live with integrity** (Hb *tamim*, "upright, blameless"; cp. 2Sm 22:24; Pr 2:21) and trust or find security in the Lord.

85:1-3 This psalm appeals immediately and directly to Yahweh with a series of statements expressing how He had dealt with Israel's sins in the past:

- He **showed favor** (Hb *ratsah*, "be delighted or pleased with"; cp. 44:3).
- He **restored** their **prosperity**.
- He **took away** [Hb *nasa'*, "lift up, bear"] **. . . guilt**, which can also be translated "iniquity," referring to moral crookedness.
- He **covered all their sin**.
- He **withdrew** and **turned from** His **anger**.

85:4-13 Calamities Israel had experienced were viewed as a sign of God's anger because of the sin of the people, who still need the revival that comes from a fresh encounter with the living Lord and who still need to experience afresh His **faithful love** (Hb *chesed*, "covenant loyalty," vv. 7,10; see **Word Study**, p. 322). Those who **fear** or reverence the Lord will enjoy the blessings of His rule, including complete restoration (Ps 85:9-13).

86:1-10 The psalmist, needing an answer from God in his **distress**, pleads for the Lord to **listen** (Hb *qashav*, "attend to," lit "bend one's ear," v. 6). He identifies himself as both needy and godly. He confesses his faith, identifying the Lord as **my God** and himself as **Your servant who trusts in You** (v. 2). The psalmist recognizes God's nature as kind, forgiving, and **rich in faithful love** (Hb *chesed*; v. 5; see **Word Study**, p. 322) and expresses his faith that God would answer his cry in the day of trouble.

86:11-13 The poet requested that the Lord **teach** him His way. God's law is His instruction regarding how to live the best life possible. To **live by** the Lord's truth, literally to "walk in Your truth," refers to a lifestyle of commitment to Him. To **fear** God's name indicates reverent obedience to Him. God's name represents His character. The psalmist vowed to praise God with his whole being (**all my heart**) and to **honor** His name forever. This psalmist has experienced the Lord as One who is great in **faithful love** (Hb *chesed*, "covenant loyalty"; see **Word Study**, p. 322) and as One who has delivered him from **Sheol**.

86:14-17 The goodness of the Lord is contrasted with the wickedness of the poet's enemies. The poet renews his plea for deliverance based on the Lord's character.

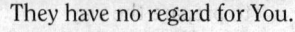

87:1-2 This psalm praises Jerusalem as the city of God and sets forth **Zion** as the spiritual center of the world (see Ps 137:5-6). Jerusalem also may symbolize the poet's longing for God. **Jacob** is an alternate name for Israel.

87:4-7 God is the God of all nations, not just Israel. His purposes include all peoples who respond to Him in faithfulness and worship, regardless of their nationalities. **Rahab** refers to Egypt (cp. Is 30:7). In the latter part of this poem the emphasis shifts from the earthly city of Jerusalem to the heavenly Zion where God's people will dwell forever secure.

88:1-18 The phrase ***according to Mahalath Leannoth*** may refer to a choreographic instruction or an antiphonal performance by two groups who respond to one another. As **a *Maskil***, this psalm is probably intended to teach or give insight into practical living (see **Word Study**, p. 679). **Heman** was one of the temple singers in the time of David and Solomon (1Ch 6:33).

This psalm of lament consists of a long agonized cry to the Lord, reflecting intense sadness and gloom with no echoes of deliverance despite the psalmist's constant prayer. He felt that death was near and that he was cut off from the Lord's care (vv. 3-5). He expressed feelings of alienation from all human and divine contact (vv. 7-8). The psalmist repeatedly referred to the realm of the dead, using such terms as **Sheol** (v. 3), **the Pit** (v. 4), and **Abaddon** (v. 11). Faith is evident, nevertheless, in the continued appeal to the Lord.

They have no regard for You.
15 But You, Lord, are
a compassionate
and gracious God,
slow to anger and rich
in faithful love and truth.
16 Turn to me and be gracious
to me.
Give Your strength
to Your servant;
save the son
of Your female servant.
17 Show me a sign
of Your goodness;
my enemies will see
and be put to shame
because You, LORD,
have helped
and comforted me.

Psalm 87
Zion, the City of God

A psalm of the sons of Korah. A song.

1 His foundation is
on the holy mountains.
2 The LORD loves the gates
of •Zion
more than all the dwellings
of Jacob.
3 Glorious things are said
about you,
city of God.
•Selah
4 "I will mention those
who know Me:
•Rahab, Babylon, Philistia,
Tyre, and •Cush—
each one was born there."
5 And it will be said of Zion,
"This one and that one
were born in her."
The •Most High Himself
will establish her.
6 When He registers
the peoples,
the LORD will record,
"This one was born there."
Selah
7 Singers and dancers alike
will say,
"My whole source of joy is[A]
in you."

Psalm 88
A Cry of Desperation

A song. A psalm of the sons of Korah. For the choir director: according to Mahalath Leannoth. *A •*Maskil *of Heman the Ezrahite.*

1 LORD, God of my salvation,
I cry out before You
day and night.
2 May my prayer reach
Your presence;
listen to my cry.
3 For I have had enough
troubles,
and my life is near •Sheol.
4 I am counted among those
going down to the •Pit.
I am like a man
without strength,
5 abandoned[B] among the dead.
I am like the slain lying
in the grave,
whom You
no longer remember,
and who are cut off
from Your care.[C]
6 You have put me
in the lowest part of the Pit,
in the darkest places,
in the depths.
7 Your wrath weighs heavily
on me;
You have overwhelmed me
with all Your waves. *•Selah*
8 You have distanced my friends
from me;
You have made me repulsive
to them.
I am shut in and cannot
go out.
9 My eyes are worn out
from crying.
LORD, I cry out to You
all day long;
I spread out my hands to You.
10 Do You work wonders
for the dead?
Do departed spirits rise up
to praise You? *Selah*
11 Will Your faithful love
be declared in the grave,
Your faithfulness
in •Abaddon?
12 Will Your wonders be known
in the darkness

[A]**87:7** Lit *"All my springs, are* [B]**88:5** Or *set free* [C]**88:5** Or *hand*

or Your righteousness
in the land of oblivion?
13 But I call to You
for help, LORD;
in the morning my prayer
meets You.
14 LORD, why do You reject me?
Why do You hide Your face
from me?
15 From my youth,
I have been afflicted and near
death.
I suffer Your horrors;
I am desperate.
16 Your wrath sweeps over me;
Your terrors destroy me.
17 They surround me like water
all day long;
they close in on me
from every side.
18 You have distanced loved one
and neighbor from me;
darkness is my only friend.[A]

Psalm 89

Perplexity About God's Promises

A •Maskil *of Ethan the Ezrahite.*

1 I will sing about the LORD's
faithful love forever;
I will proclaim
Your faithfulness to all
generations
with my mouth.
2 For I will declare,
"Faithful love
is built up forever;
You establish
Your faithfulness
in the heavens."
3 The LORD said,
"I have made a covenant
with My chosen one;
I have sworn an oath to David
My servant:
4 'I will establish
your offspring forever
and build up your throne
for all generations.'" •*Selah*
5 LORD, the heavens praise
Your wonders—
Your faithfulness also—
in the assembly
of the holy ones.
6 For who in the skies
can compare with the LORD?
Who among
the heavenly beings[B] is
like the LORD?
7 God is greatly •feared
in the council
of the holy ones,
more awe-inspiring than[C]
all who surround Him.
8 LORD God of •Hosts,
who is strong like You, LORD?
Your faithfulness
surrounds You.
9 You rule the raging sea;
when its waves surge,
You still them.
10 You crushed •Rahab like one
who is slain;
You scattered Your enemies
with Your powerful arm.
11 The heavens are Yours;
the earth also is Yours.
The world and everything
in it—You founded them.
12 North and south—
You created them.
Tabor and Hermon shout
for joy at Your name.
13 You have a mighty arm;
Your hand is powerful;
Your right hand is lifted high.
14 Righteousness and justice are
the foundation
of Your throne;
faithful love and truth
go before You.
15 Happy are the people
who know the joyful shout;
•Yahweh, they
walk in the light
of Your presence.
16 They rejoice in Your name
all day long,
and they are exalted
by Your righteousness.
17 For You are
their magnificent strength;
by Your favor our •horn
is exalted.
18 Surely our shield[D]
belongs to the LORD,
our king to the Holy One
of Israel.

89:1-52 This psalm is identified as **a *Maskil*** [see **Word Study**, p. 679] **of Ethan the Ezrahite**, a Levite and temple singer (1Ch 6:42,44; 15:17). This royal psalm relates to a time of national crisis. A major theme of the psalm is the Lord's covenant with David, which involved God's promise to establish David's descendants on the throne. The psalmist appeals to God's **faithful love** (Hb *chesed*, "covenant loyalty, loyal love"; see **Word Study**, p. 322) and **faithfulness** (Hb *ʾemunah*, "fidelity in keeping promises," v. 1; cp. v. 49). Verses 1-37 celebrate God's nature with repeated emphasis on the Lord's complete dependability—both the evidence of His faithful love as revealed in the establishment of the Davidic covenant and the perceived absence of His faithfulness (vv. 38-51).

The psalmist interpreted whatever calamity had befallen the nation as indicating that the Lord had forsaken His covenant loyalty to David. Remembering the unconditional nature of the covenant (vv. 29-37) only served to sharpen his pain to the point that he charged God with rejecting His people. He prayed to see again evidence of God's loyal love for His people despite the people's unfaithfulness.

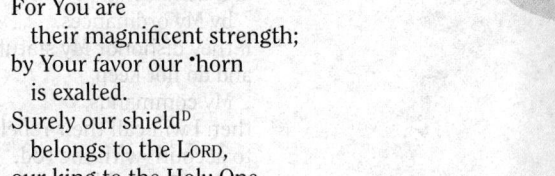

[A] **88:18** Or *from me, my friends. Oh darkness!* [B] **89:6** Or *the angels*, or *the sons of the mighty* [C] **89:7** Or *ones, revered by* [D] **89:18** = the king

19 You once spoke in a vision
to Your loyal ones
and said: "I have granted help
to a warrior;
I have exalted one chosen[A]
from the people.
20 I have found David
My servant;
I have anointed him
with My sacred oil.
21 My hand will always be
with him,
and My arm will
strengthen him.
22 The enemy will not
afflict[B] him;
no wicked man will
oppress him.
23 I will crush his foes
before him
and strike those
who hate him.
24 My faithfulness and love
will be with him,
and through My name
his horn will be exalted.
25 I will extend his power
to the sea
and his right hand
to the rivers.
26 He will call to Me, 'You are
my Father,
my God, the rock
of my salvation.'
27 I will also make him
My firstborn,
greatest of the kings
of the earth.
28 I will always preserve
My faithful love for him,
and My covenant with him
will endure.
29 I will establish
his line forever,
his throne as long as
heaven lasts.[C]
30 If his sons forsake
My instruction
and do not live
by My ordinances,
31 if they dishonor My statutes
and do not keep
My commands,
32 then I will call their rebellion
to account with the rod,
their sin with blows.
33 But I will not withdraw
My faithful love from him
or betray My faithfulness.
34 I will not violate My covenant
or change what My lips
have said.
35 Once and for all
I have sworn an oath
by My holiness;
I will not lie to David.
36 His offspring
will continue forever,
his throne like the sun
before Me,
37 like the moon,
established forever,
a faithful witness in the sky."
Selah
38 But You have spurned
and rejected him;
You have become enraged
with Your anointed.
39 You have repudiated
the covenant
with Your servant;
You have completely
dishonored his crown.[D]
40 You have broken down
all his walls;
You have reduced
his fortified cities to ruins.
41 All who pass by plunder him;
he has become an object of
ridicule
to his neighbors.
42 You have lifted high
the right hand of his foes;
You have made all
his enemies rejoice.
43 You have also turned back
his sharp sword
and have not let him stand
in battle.
44 You have made
his splendor[E] cease
and have overturned
his throne.
45 You have shortened the days
of his youth;
You have covered him
with shame. *Selah*
46 How long, LORD? Will You hide
Yourself forever?
Will Your anger keep burning
like fire?
47 Remember how short
my life is.

[A]**89:19** Or *exalted a young man* [B]**89:22** Or *not exact tribute from* [C]**89:29** Lit *as days of heaven* [D]**89:39** Lit *have dishonored his crown to the ground* [E]**89:44** Hb obscure

Have You created •everyone
for nothing?
48 What man can live
and never see death?
Who can save himself
from the power of •Sheol?
Selah
49 Lord, where are
the former acts
of Your faithful love
that You swore to David
in Your faithfulness?
50 Remember, Lord, the ridicule
against Your servants—
in my heart I carry abuse
from all the peoples—
51 how Your enemies
have ridiculed, LORD,
how they have ridiculed
every step of Your anointed.
52 May the LORD
be praised forever.
•Amen and amen.

BOOK IV
(Psalms 90:1–106:48)

Psalm 90
Eternal God and Mortal Man

A prayer of Moses, the man of God.

1 Lord, You have been
our refuge[A]
in every generation.
2 Before the mountains
were born,
before You gave birth
to the earth and the world,
from eternity to eternity,
You are God.

3 You return mankind
to the dust,
saying, "Return,
descendants of Adam."
4 For in Your sight
a thousand years
are like yesterday that
passes by,
like a few hours of the night.
5 You end their lives;[B]
they sleep.
They are like grass that grows
in the morning—
6 in the morning it sprouts
and grows;
by evening it withers
and dries up.
7 For we are consumed
by Your anger;
we are terrified
by Your wrath.
8 You have set our unjust ways
before You,
our secret sins in the light
of Your presence.
9 For all our days ebb away
under Your wrath;
we end our years like a sigh.
10 Our lives last[C] seventy years
or, if we are strong,
eighty years.
Even the best of them
are[D] struggle and sorrow;
indeed, they pass quickly
and we fly away.
11 Who understands the power
of Your anger?
Your wrath matches the fear
that is due You.
12 Teach us to number
our days carefully
so that we may
develop wisdom
in our hearts.[E]

13 LORD—how long?
Turn and have compassion
on Your servants.
14 Satisfy us in the morning
with Your faithful love
so that we may shout with joy
and be glad all our days.
15 Make us rejoice
for as many days
as You have humbled us,
for as many years as
we have seen adversity.
16 Let Your work be seen
by Your servants,
and Your splendor
by their children.
17 Let the favor of the Lord
our God be on us;
establish for us the work
of our hands—
establish the work
of our hands!

[A]**90:1** Some Hb mss, LXX; other Hb mss read *dwelling place* [B]**90:5** Or *You overwhelm them*; Hb obscure [C]**90:10** Lit *The days of our years in them* [D]**90:10** LXX, Tg, Syr, Vg read *Even their span is*; Hb obscure [E]**90:12** Or *develop a heart of wisdom*

89:52 The doxology of verse 52 marks the end of Book III of the Psalms (cp. Ps 41:13; 72:19).

90:1-6 This psalm, which marks the beginning of Book IV of the Psalter, is the only one associated with Moses. The psalmist contrasts the eternal nature of God with the frail nature of humanity. As God **from eternity to eternity**, He existed before the creation of the earth. The brevity of human life is compared with the short-lived **grass** that flourishes and dies within a single day. Only faith in the eternal God can make life meaningful (cp. 2Pt 3:8).

90:7-12 This heart-rending prayer repeatedly acknowledges how utterly helpless is every man to stand before God whose anger is burning against his sins. The psalmist's response models humility and reflects an accurate picture of God's view of sin. **Wisdom in our hearts** does not refer to skill, technique, or knowledge. It does not refer to the power to control but rather to the grace to submit. A wise heart is one that discerns the Lord's purposes and submits to His will.

90:13-17 The psalmist appealed to the Lord's **compassion** for those who serve Him and expressed full confidence that the Lord can work out His purposes despite the frailty of human beings. Hope lies in the Lord's **faithful love** (Hb *chesed*, "covenant faithfulness," v. 14; see **Word Study**, p. 322).

91:1-5 The psalmist builds image upon image to express the ultimate security found in relationship with the Lord. The Lord is described as the poet's **protection** and **shadow**, suggesting the picture of baby birds finding protection under their mother's **wings** (cp. Mt 23:37). The second pair of terms—**refuge** and **fortress**—indicate military strength or protection. God delivers His people from the **hunter's net** (Hb *yaqush*, "fowler, one who sets a trap to catch prey, bait-layer"). God's faithfulness protects His own like a **shield**.

91:11-12 Satan misused these verses to tempt Jesus (cp. Mt 4:6; Lk 4:10-11). While the Lord may permit some terrible things to happen to His children, they have the security of knowing that He is ultimately in control and that He cares for those who make Him their refuge.

92:1-5 The unidentified psalmist proclaims that **it is good to praise Yahweh**. He praises God for His **faithful love** (Hb *chesed*; see **Word Study**, p. 322) as well as for His **faithfulness** (Hb *'emunah*, "firmness, dependability, trustworthiness"; cp. 33:4). He may not always do what His people want Him to do, but He can be counted on always to act in their best interests. The psalmist praises God continually—**morning and . . . night**. He celebrates the wonderful **works** of the Lord. A note of joy and gladness pervades this hymn of thanksgiving.

92:6-7 The **stupid** [Hb *ba 'ar*, "brutish, like cattle"; used also in 49:10; 73:22, Pr 12:1; 30:2] **person** or fool does not acknowledge the Lord's magnificent works. Fool refers to an obstinate individual who has a pattern of making wrong choices in life. Such a path leads to destruction. The poet realizes that ultimately he will be victorious over his enemies. The psalmist equates his enemies with the Lord's enemies, who would eventually be **eternally destroyed**.

Psalm 91

The Protection of the Most High

1 The one who lives
under the protection
of the •Most High
dwells in the shadow
of the •Almighty.

2 I will say[A] to the LORD,
"My refuge and my fortress,
my God, in whom I trust."

3 He Himself will deliver you
from the hunter's net,
from the destructive plague.
4 He will cover you
with His feathers;
you will take refuge
under His wings.
His faithfulness will be
a protective shield.
5 You will not fear the terror
of the night,
the arrow that flies by day,
6 the plague that stalks
in darkness,
or the pestilence that ravages
at noon.
7 Though a thousand fall
at your side
and ten thousand
at your right hand,
the pestilence will not
reach you.
8 You will only see it
with your eyes
and witness the punishment
of the wicked.

9 Because you have made
the LORD—my refuge,
the Most High—
your dwelling place,
10 no harm will come to you;
no plague will come near
your tent.
11 For He will give His angels
orders concerning you,
to protect you in all
your ways.
12 They will support you
with their hands
so that you will not strike
your foot against a stone.
13 You will tread on the lion
and the cobra;
you will trample
the young lion
and the serpent.
14 Because he is lovingly devoted
to Me,
I will deliver him;
I will protect him
because he knows My name.
15 When he calls out to Me,
I will answer him;
I will be with him in trouble.
I will rescue him
and give him honor.
16 I will satisfy him
with a long life
and show him My salvation.

Psalm 92

God's Love and Faithfulness

A psalm. A song for the Sabbath day.

1 It is good to praise •Yahweh,
to sing praise to Your name,
•Most High,
2 to declare Your faithful love
in the morning
and Your faithfulness
at night,
3 with a ten-stringed harp
and the music of a lyre.

4 For You have made me
rejoice, LORD,
by what You have done;
I will shout for joy
because of the works
of Your hands.
5 How magnificent are
Your works, LORD,
how profound Your thoughts!
6 A stupid person
does not know,
a fool does not
understand this:
7 though the wicked sprout
like grass
and all evildoers flourish,
they will be
eternally destroyed.
8 But You, LORD,
are exalted forever.
9 For indeed, LORD,
Your enemies—
indeed, Your enemies
will perish;
all evildoers will be scattered.
10 You have lifted up my •horn
like that of a wild ox;

[A]91:1-2 LXX, Syr, Jer read [2]*Almighty, saying*, or [2]*Almighty, he will say*

I have been anointed[A]
with oil.
11 My eyes look down on
my enemies;
my ears hear evildoers
when they attack me.

12 The righteous thrive
like a palm tree
and grow like a cedar tree
in Lebanon.
13 Planted in the house
of the LORD,
they thrive in the courts of
our God.
14 They will still bear fruit
in old age,
healthy and green,
15 to declare: "The LORD is just;
He is my rock,
and there is
no unrighteousness
in Him."

Psalm 93
God's Eternal Reign

1 The LORD reigns! He is robed
in majesty;
The LORD is robed,
enveloped in strength.
The world is
firmly established;
it cannot be shaken.
2 Your throne
has been established
from the beginning;[B]
You are from eternity.
3 The floods have
lifted up, LORD,
the floods have lifted up
their voice;
the floods lift up
their pounding waves.
4 Greater than the roar
of many waters—
the mighty breakers
of the sea—
the LORD on high is majestic.

5 LORD, Your testimonies
are completely reliable;
holiness is the beauty
of[C] Your house
for all the days to come.

Psalm 94
The Just Judge

1 LORD, God of vengeance—
God of vengeance, appear.
2 Rise up, Judge of the earth;
repay the proud
what they deserve.
3 LORD, how long will
the wicked—
how long will
the wicked gloat?
4 They pour out arrogant
words;
all the evildoers boast.
5 LORD, they crush Your people;
they afflict Your heritage.
6 They kill the widow
and the foreigner
and murder the fatherless.
7 They say, "The LORD
doesn't see it.
The God of Jacob
doesn't pay attention."

8 Pay attention,
you stupid people!
Fools, when will you be wise?
9 Can the One who shaped
the ear not hear,
the One who formed the eye
not see?
10 The One
who instructs nations,
the One who teaches
man knowledge—
does He not discipline?
11 The LORD knows
man's thoughts;
they are meaningless.

12 LORD, happy is the man
You discipline
and teach from Your law
13 to give him relief
from troubled times
until a pit is dug
for the wicked.
14 The LORD will not forsake
His people
or abandon His heritage,
15 for justice will again
be righteous,
and all the upright in heart
will follow[D] it.

92:12-15 God's people experience stability in Him (cp. 1:3). The righteous are pictured as healthy and fruitful trees, flourishing like the **palm tree** and becoming strong like **a cedar tree in Lebanon**. Both trees portray strength and stability. **The righteous**—those in right relationship with the Lord—continue to be fruitful and vigorous even **in old age**, resulting from God's blessing.

93:1-5 This psalm is one celebrating the eternal kingship of the Lord (cp. Pss 47; 96–99). Such poems focus on the majestic Lord as sovereign over all His creation. His kingship exists forever. The powerful **waters** of the sea were feared by pagan peoples in ancient times. Yet the poet affirms that the Lord is greater than these mighty waters. The Old Testament emphasis on God the Creator stands in stark contrast to the pagan teachings of chaotic and random happenings.

Such psalms, which are often characterized by the phrase **the LORD reigns**, are classified as enthronement psalms and played a significant role in Israel's worship. They affirm the truth that the sovereign Lord is in control of His universe. Not only God's creation but also His **testimonies** or statutes are **firmly established** and are **completely reliable** (Hb *'aman*, "be faithful, trustworthy, sure"), representative of His covenant relationship with His people. Thus believers are eternally secure in their relationship with the Lord.

94:1-3 The psalmist calls on God, to whom **vengeance** belongs, to bring judgment on wicked people. How long would the just **Judge** wait before He takes action against **the wicked**?

94:6 The **widow**, the **foreigner**, and the **fatherless** signify the helpless members of society. The Lord had especially pointed out these as receiving right treatment because they lacked power to defend themselves (cp. Ex 22:21-24).

94:7-8 The poet expressed faith that justice would eventually be done. God remains the defense and rock of refuge for His people. He will judge the wicked in His own time. Only **stupid people** and **fools** fail to discern that one day they will have to give an account for their attitudes and actions.

[A]92:10 Syr reads *You have anointed me* [B]93:2 Lit *from then* [C]93:5 Or *holiness characterizes* [D]94:15 Or *heart will support*; lit *heart after*

95:1-11 The psalmist called believers to worship the Lord. God is worthy of worship because He is **the rock of our salvation** (v. 1). He deserves our worship because He is **a great King above all gods** (v. 3) and Creator of the world and of all persons (vv. 5-6). The images of God as a shepherd and His people as His flock appear here (v. 7; cp. 100:3). God the Creator is worthy of worship, and the proof of genuine worship is obedience.

The remainder of this psalm recalls the years of Israel's rebellious wanderings in the wilderness. The poet urged his generation not to **harden** their hearts as their fathers did at **Meribah** and **Massah** (Ex 17:7; Nm 20:13,24). Faithful obedience is essential to pleasing God (cp. Heb 3:7-11,15; 4:3,5,7). Just as the Hebrew people failed to enter the promised land because of their lack of faithful obedience (Ps 95:11), so God's people still fail to enter into the joyful rest of fellowship with Him because of their lack of trust. That **rest** is still being offered through Jesus Christ.

96:1-5 The appearance of this psalm in a slightly altered form in 1Ch 16:23-33 is the setting for David's movement of the ark of the covenant to Jerusalem. This psalm is often classified as an enthronement psalm, celebrating God's kingship (cp. Pss 47; 93; 97–99). These psalms are characterized by the phrase "the LORD reigns" (96:10). Worshipers are called to sing to the Lord a **new song** based on the universal nature of God's rule (see Rv 5:9; 14:3). God is exalted above all gods. Other gods are merely idols, but the Lord is the Creator.

96:7-9 The psalm calls on all people everywhere to worship the Lord, to give to Him the honor due His name and to bring their offerings. The audience is also instructed to **tremble** before Him in recognition of His awesome majesty, an aspect of worship that is often neglected today. You are to recognize His **holiness**, His set-apartness, His perfect moral purity—all calling for a response of awe and respect.

16 Who stands up for me
against the wicked?
Who takes a stand for me
against evildoers?
17 If the LORD had not been
my helper,
I would soon rest
in the silence of death.
18 If I say, "My foot is slipping,"
Your faithful love
will support me, LORD.
19 When I am filled with cares,
Your comfort brings me joy.

20 Can a corrupt throne—
one that creates trouble
by law—
become Your ally?
21 They band together
against the life
of the righteous
and condemn the innocent
to death.
22 But the LORD is my refuge;
my God is the rock
of my protection.
23 He will pay them back
for their sins
and destroy them
for their evil.
The LORD our God
will destroy them.

Psalm 95

Worship and Warning

1 Come, let us shout joyfully
to the LORD,
shout triumphantly
to the rock of our salvation!
2 Let us enter His presence
with thanksgiving;
let us shout triumphantly
to Him in song.

3 For the LORD is a great God,
a great King above all gods.
4 The depths of the earth
are in His hand,
and the mountain peaks
are His.
5 The sea is His; He made it.
His hands formed
the dry land.

6 Come, let us worship
and bow down;
let us kneel before the LORD
our Maker.
7 For He is our God,
and we are the people
of His pasture,
the sheep under His care.[A]

Today, if you hear His voice:
8 Do not harden your hearts
as at Meribah,
as on that day at Massah
in the wilderness
9 where your fathers tested Me;
they tried Me, though
they had seen what I did.
10 For 40 years I was disgusted
with that generation;
I said, "They are a people
whose hearts go astray;
they do not know My ways."
11 So I swore in My anger,
"They will not enter My rest."

Psalm 96

King of the Earth

1 Sing a new song to the LORD;
sing to the LORD, all the earth.
2 Sing to •Yahweh,
praise His name;
proclaim His salvation
from day to day.
3 Declare His glory
among the nations,
His wonderful works
among all peoples.

4 For the LORD is great and is
highly praised;
He is feared above all gods.
5 For all the gods of the peoples
are idols,
but the LORD made
the heavens.
6 Splendor and majesty are
before Him;
strength and beauty are
in His sanctuary.

7 Ascribe to the LORD, you
families of the peoples,
ascribe to the LORD glory
and strength.
8 Ascribe to Yahweh the glory
of His name;
bring an offering and enter
His courts.
9 Worship the LORD
in the splendor
of His holiness;
tremble before Him,
all the earth.

[A]95:7 Lit *sheep of His hand*

10 Say among the nations:
"The LORD reigns.
The world is firmly
established; it cannot
be shaken.
He judges the peoples fairly."
11 Let the heavens be glad
and the earth rejoice;
let the sea and all
that fills it resound.
12 Let the fields and everything
in them exult.
Then all the trees of the forest
will shout for joy
13 before the LORD,
for He is coming—
for He is coming to judge
the earth.
He will judge the world
with righteousness
and the peoples
with His faithfulness.

Psalm 97
The Majestic King

1 The LORD reigns! Let
the earth rejoice;
let the many coasts and
islands be glad.
2 Clouds and thick darkness
surround Him;
righteousness and justice
are the foundation
of His throne.
3 Fire goes before Him
and burns up His foes
on every side.
4 His lightning lights up
the world;
the earth sees and trembles.
5 The mountains melt like wax
at the presence of the LORD—
at the presence of the Lord
of all the earth.
6 The heavens proclaim
His righteousness;
all the peoples see His glory.
7 All who serve carved images,
those who boast in idols,
will be put to shame.
All the gods[A]
must worship Him.
8 •Zion hears and is glad,
and the towns[B]
of Judah rejoice
because of
Your judgments, LORD.
9 For You, LORD,
are the •Most High over
all the earth;
You are exalted above all
the gods.
10 You who love the LORD,
hate evil!
He protects the lives
of His godly ones;
He rescues them
from the power of
the wicked.
11 Light dawns[C,D]
for the righteous,
gladness for the upright
in heart.
12 Be glad in •Yahweh,
you righteous ones,
and praise His holy name.[E]

Psalm 98
Praise for the King

A psalm.

1 Sing a new song to the LORD,
for He has
performed wonders;
His right hand and holy arm
have won Him victory.
2 The LORD has made
His victory known;
He has revealed
His righteousness
in the sight of the nations.
3 He has remembered His love
and faithfulness to the house
of Israel;
all the ends of the earth
have seen our God's victory.
4 Shout to the LORD, all
the earth;
be jubilant, shout for joy,
and sing.
5 Sing to the LORD with the lyre,
with the lyre
and melodious song.
6 With trumpets and the blast
of the ram's horn
shout triumphantly

96:10-13 God's people were to proclaim the universal rule of God **among the nations**. God is the righteous judge of all peoples. He rules with equity. All nature receives the call to rejoice in the righteous reign of God. God will judge all **peoples** with righteousness and truth. His judgment includes both the punishment of the wicked and the deliverance of the faithful. The Lord is both King and Judge of His universe.

97:1-6 This psalm is another enthronement psalm celebrating God's rule as King (Pss 47; 93; 96; 98–99). Such psalms are often characterized by the phrase **the LORD reigns**. The Lord's rule provides reason for great rejoicing. God reveals Himself in majesty. **Clouds and thick darkness surround** His appearance. **Fire, lightning**, and earth tremors accompany His **presence**. This description of God's revelation of Himself appears similar to His advent on Mount Sinai (Ex 19:16-18). **Righteousness and justice** form the basis of the Lord's reign. The Lord's reign is universal. He is **the Lord of all the earth**. All people see His **glory** (cp. 19:1). The nature of this God of mystery was revealed more fully in the coming of Christ, His Son.

97:7-12 God's awesome advent affects persons in different ways. Those who worship **idols** (Hb *'elil*, "worthless, of nought, empty") or false gods will be put to shame by God's revelation. God alone is King. God's presence brings joy to His people. God's people rejoice in His **judgments** because righteousness and justice form the basis of His rule (cp. v. 2). The title **Most High** designates God as omnipotent, majestic, and exalted (cp. 9:1-12). Those who love the Lord must reject evil. He safely keeps those who belong to Him (97:10). The poet concluded by instructing all those in right relationship with the Lord to rejoice and praise their great King.

98:1-6 This enthronement psalm celebrating God's rule as King begins on the same note as Psalm 96: **Sing a new song to the LORD** (cp. Pss 47; 93; 96-97; 99). The basis for this new song is God's reign as King. The Lord is worthy of praise for His mighty acts. He has brought deliverance to His people. Reminiscent in the references to God's **right hand and holy arm** representing His power (cp. 78:54; 89:13) is the deliverance He brought about for His people in their exodus from Egypt (Ex 15:6,12,16). He alone has brought **victory** to His people. He is the victorious **King**. All the earth is called to participate in the joy of worshiping the Lord as King.

[A]**97:7** LXX, Syr read *All His angels*; Heb 1:6 [B]**97:8** Lit *daughters* [C]**97:11** One Hb ms, LXX, some ancient versions read *rises to shine*; Ps 112:4 [D]**97:11** Lit *Light is sown* [E]**97:12** Or *memory, of His holiness*; lit *praise the mention*

98:7-9 Even nature itself participates in this joyful celebration. The reign of the Lord ultimately will bring justice in the world (cp. 96:11-13.)

99:1-9 This enthronement psalm begins with the phrase **The LORD reigns** (cp. Pss 93; 97). This psalm likewise celebrates God's eternal rule as King. This poet emphasizes God's reign as marked by holiness (vv. 3,5,9), which refers to His otherness, His separateness from His creation. His holiness involves both judgment of sin and forgiveness of sinners (v. 8). The Lord's people exalt Him because He is holy. The place of the Lord's dwelling—**above the cherubim**—is a reference to the ark of the covenant where the Hebrews viewed the Lord as invisibly enthroned (Ex 25:22; 1 Sm 4:4; Ps 80:1). The Lord's **footstool** probably refers to Zion or Jerusalem, the location of His temple (v. 5).

The reminders of what God has done in and through His people (v. 4) leads to a recitation of the Lord's acts and revelation through such Old Testament heroes as Moses, Aaron, and Samuel (vv. 6-7). The eternal reign of God, the primary focus of this psalm, is not only an objective fact to be mentally acknowledged but also demands a lifestyle of personal submission to His rule (cp. Php 2:9-11).

100:1-5 This psalm of thanksgiving emphasizes the joy experienced in praising the Lord. All people are invited to praise the Lord because He alone is God. To **acknowledge** (Hb *yada'*, "know"; see note on Ex 2:24-25 and **Word Study**, p. 725; cp. Ps 76:1) is to know experientially. God is the Creator, and His people are dependent on Him as the good shepherd who cares for **the sheep of His pasture** (cp. 95:7). The imagery of God as a shepherd and His people as sheep, reminiscent of Ps 23, also highlights sinful humanity's weakness and proneness to go astray. Yet **the LORD** is so good. His **love** (Hb *chesed*, "covenant loyalty, steadfast love"; see **Word Study**, p. 322) and His **faithfulness** (Hb *'emunah*, "dependability, trustworthiness") are extended to **all generations**. This simple yet profound psalm moves God's people to express gratitude to Him because of who He is.

101:1-5 The psalmist begins by singing **praise** to Yahweh. The majority of the psalm, however, deals with the Davidic king's promise of faithfulness to the Lord. The king pledges **to live with a heart of integrity**. The Davidic king promises to reject wickedness in himself and in others.

101:6-8 The king also acknowledges his responsibility to his subjects, **the faithful of the land**. Those who practice deceit will not be a part of

in the presence of the LORD,
our King.
7 Let the sea and all that fills it,
the world and those who live
in it, resound.
8 Let the rivers clap
their hands;
let the mountains
shout together for joy
9 before the LORD,
for He is coming to judge
the earth.
He will judge
the world righteously
and the peoples fairly.

Psalm 99
The Holy King

1 The LORD reigns! Let
the peoples tremble.
He is enthroned
above the •cherubim.
Let the earth quake.
2 •Yahweh is great in •Zion;
He is exalted above
all the peoples.
3 Let them praise Your great
and awe-inspiring name.
He is holy.

4 The mighty King
loves justice.
You have established fairness;
You have administered justice
and righteousness in Jacob.
5 Exalt the LORD our God;
bow in worship
at His footstool.
He is holy.
6 Moses and Aaron were
among His priests;
Samuel also was among
those calling on His name.
They called to Yahweh
and He answered them.
7 He spoke to them in a pillar
of cloud;
they kept His decrees
and the statutes
He gave them.
8 LORD our God,
You answered them.
You were a forgiving God
to them,
an avenger of their
sinful actions.
9 Exalt the LORD our God;
bow in worship
at His holy mountain,
for the LORD our God is holy.

Psalm 100
Thankfulness

A psalm of thanksgiving.

1 Shout triumphantly
to the LORD, all the earth.
2 Serve the LORD with gladness;
come before Him
with joyful songs.
3 Acknowledge that •Yahweh
is God.
He made us,
and we are His[A] —
His people, the sheep
of His pasture.
4 Enter His gates
with thanksgiving
and His courts with praise.
Give thanks to Him and praise
His name.
5 For Yahweh is good,
and His love is eternal;
His faithfulness endures
through all generations.

Psalm 101
A Vow of Integrity

A Davidic psalm.

1 I will sing of faithful love
and justice;
I will sing praise to You, LORD.
2 I will pay attention to the way
of integrity.
When will You come to me?
I will live with a heart
of integrity in my house.
3 I will not set
anything worthless
before my eyes.
I hate the practice
of transgression;
it will not cling to me.
4 A devious heart will be far
from me;
I will not be involved
with[B] evil.
5 I will destroy anyone
who secretly slanders
his neighbor;
I cannot tolerate anyone

[A] **100:3** Alt Hb tradition, some Hb mss, LXX, Syr, Vg read *and not we ourselves* [B] **101:4** Lit *not know*

with haughty eyes
or an arrogant heart.
6 My eyes favor the faithful
of the land
so that they may sit down
with me.
The one who follows the way
of integrity
may serve me.
7 No one who acts deceitfully
will live in my palace;
no one who tells lies
will remain in my presence.[A]
8 Every morning I will destroy
all the wicked of the land,
eliminating all evildoers
from the LORD's city.

Psalm 102

Affliction in Light of Eternity

A prayer of an afflicted person who is weak and pours out his lament before the LORD.

1 LORD, hear my prayer;
let my cry for help come
before You.
2 Do not hide Your face
from me in my day
of trouble.
Listen closely to me;
answer me quickly
when I call.
3 For my days vanish
like smoke,
and my bones burn
like a furnace.
4 My heart is afflicted,
withered like grass;
I even forget to eat my food.
5 Because of the sound
of my groaning,
my flesh sticks to my bones.
6 I am like a desert owl,[B]
like an owl among the ruins.
7 I stay awake;
I am like a solitary bird
on a roof.
8 My enemies taunt me
all day long;
they ridicule and curse me.
9 I eat ashes like bread
and mingle my drinks
with tears
10 because of Your indignation
and wrath;
for You have picked me up
and thrown me aside.
11 My days are like
a lengthening shadow,
and I wither away like grass.

12 But You, LORD,
are enthroned forever;
Your fame endures
to all generations.
13 You will rise up
and have compassion
on •Zion,
for it is time to show favor
to her—
the appointed time has come.
14 For Your servants take delight
in its stones
and favor its dust.

15 Then the nations will fear
the name of •Yahweh,
and all the kings of the earth
Your glory,
16 for the LORD will rebuild Zion;
He will appear in His glory.
17 He will pay attention
to the prayer
of the destitute
and will not despise
their prayer.

18 This will be written
for a later generation,
and a newly created people
will praise the LORD:
19 He looked down from
His holy heights—
the LORD gazed out
from heaven to earth—
20 to hear a prisoner's groaning,
to set free those condemned
to die,[C]
21 so that they might declare
the name of Yahweh in Zion
and His praise in Jerusalem,
22 when peoples and kingdoms
are assembled
to serve the LORD.

23 He has broken my[D] strength
in midcourse;
He has shortened my days.
24 I say: "My God, do not
take me
in the middle of my life![E]
Your years continue
through all generations.

his administration. The Davidic king promises to live by high standards. He commits himself to reject evil and to love God's faithful people. He vows to uphold justice in the land. Modern politicians make promises to voters; the Davidic king made promises to the Lord.

102:1-2 The penitential psalms deal with the nature of sin and forgiveness (cp. Pss 6; 32; 38; 51; 130; 143). This psalm constitutes the prayer of one who is **afflicted** (see superscription and v. 4). Though the symptoms are described with vivid imagery, the specific malady is impossible to identify (vv. 3-7). Feeling isolated from God and from others (vv. 6-7), the psalmist cries out to God to no longer **hide** Himself.

102:8-11 This psalmist felt tormented constantly by his **enemies**. The psalmist reflects the general view of suffering as an expression of God's **wrath** against sins the tormented person had committed. The book of Job refutes the theology that all suffering is the direct result of particular sins in the suffering person's life. While all suffering is the result of the entrance of sin into the world with Adam, not all suffering can be directly linked with sins in the sufferer's life. Sometimes God permits suffering in the lives of His children to instruct them and to discipline them. He also may allow suffering in your life to help you realize your insufficiency and lead you to greater faith in Him. Suffering is a reminder that He is in control and you are not. As Job learned, because you can trust God to run the universe, you can trust Him to know what is best for your life.

In the midst of his lament, the psalmist expresses faith. Even though the poet recognizes that life is short, the Lord will endure forever. The older you get the more you realize the truth that your life is like **a lengthening shadow** and withering **grass**. God's eternity stands in stark contrast to humanity's brief life span. God's power is totally opposite to human frailty. The poet's confidence lays in the Lord's eternal sovereignty. Even in his own agony, the poet could look beyond himself to see God's plan, which transcended his own lifetime. God would show favor on His people.

102:12-22 In saying to the Lord that He **will rise up and have compassion** [Hb *racham* "behold with tender affection"; see **Word Study**, p. 679] **on Zion**, the psalmist expresses faith in the certainty that God will take action to demonstrate His power as the King who is **enthroned forever** (102:12-13). The references to Zion throughout this passage signify the covenant relationship and the privileges that accompany it. Other nations would come to stand in awe of the Lord. This

[A]**101:7** Lit *in front of my eyes* [B]**102:6** Or *a pelican of the desert* [C]**102:20** Lit *free sons of death* [D]**102:23** Some Hb mss, LXX read *His* [E]**102:24** Lit *my days*

psalmist had faith that God would bless His people even if the poet did not live to see that blessing in his lifetime. All people and kingdoms would serve the Lord (v. 22). This testimony of faith in a difficult situation reflects the poet's certainty of God's sovereignty.

102:23-28 The psalmist views his agony in terms of God's eternity. God, who laid the foundations of the earth, would endure even after those foundations were destroyed. The earth changes, but God remains eternally the **same** (cp. Heb 1:10-12). Recognizing God's eternal presence gives a new perspective on life. It brings life into proper focus.

103:1-5 The reasons for praising the Lord joyfully overflow from the poet's lips. The Lord forgives all **sin** (Hb *'awon*, "crookedness, twistedness"). The verb **forgives** (Hb *salach*, "pardon") is used solely of God in the Old Testament. The word refers only to God's offer of pardon; never is it applied in the context of one person's forgiving another.

The Lord also brings healing to life. God ultimately **heals all . . . diseases** (Hb *tachalu'im*, "sickness, grief"), a word used in the prophetic description of the Messiah as the Suffering Servant (Is 53:10). In Isaiah 53, sin and sickness are closely related. In the vicarious death of Jesus, God has provided forgiveness. **God** also **redeems** (Hb *ga'al*, "buy back"; cp. **Word Study** on "redeemer," p. 682; Ru 4) from destruction. God does for you what you cannot do for yourself. He further pours out on you His **faithful love** (Hb *chesed*, see **Word Study**, p. 322) and **compassion** (Hb *racham*, "womb; pity, grace, favor"; see **Word Study** on verb root, p. 679). Nothing else provides the kind of fulfillment or satisfaction that comes from a right relationship with the Lord, which brings renewal to your life (see Is 40:31). **The eagle** symbolized vigor and freedom.

103:6-12 The Lord is particularly attentive to the helpless members of society, those who are powerless to defend themselves. **He revealed** Himself to **Moses** and the people of Israel through His mighty acts on their behalf and by giving the law, an expression of His character (cp. 8 and Ex 34:6-7). He does not hold a grudge against His people. God does not treat His people the way they deserve to be treated. He does not mete out the punishment your sins merit; instead He forgives. God's mercy is pictured in geographical dimensions. His mercy is as great as the distance separating the heavens from the earth. He removes **our transgressions . . . as far as the east is from the west**, the distance separating sunrise and sunset, a distance not bound by poles (v. 12).

25 Long ago You established
the earth,
and the heavens are the work
of Your hands.
26 They will perish, but You
will endure;
all of them will wear out
like clothing.
You will change them
like a garment,
and they will pass away.
27 But You are the same,
and Your years will never end.
28 Your servants' children
will dwell securely,
and their offspring will be
established before You."

Psalm 103
The Forgiving God

Davidic.

1 My soul, praise •Yahweh,
and all that is within me,
praise His holy name.
2 My soul, praise the LORD,
and do not forget
all His benefits.

3 He forgives all your sin;
He heals all your diseases.
4 He redeems your life
from the •Pit;
He crowns you
with faithful love
and compassion.
5 He satisfies you[A]
with goodness;
your youth is renewed
like the eagle.

6 The LORD executes acts
of righteousness
and justice for all
the oppressed.
7 He revealed His ways
to Moses,
His deeds to the people
of Israel.
8 The LORD is compassionate
and gracious,
slow to anger and rich
in faithful love.
9 He will not always accuse us
or be angry forever.
10 He has not dealt with us as
our sins deserve
or repaid us according to
our offenses.

11 For as high as the heavens
are above the earth,
so great is His faithful love
toward those who •fear Him.
12 As far as the east is
from the west,
so far has He removed
our transgressions from us.
13 As a father has compassion
on his children,
so the LORD has compassion
on those who fear Him.
14 For He knows what we are
made of,
remembering
that we are dust.

15 As for man, his days are
like grass—
he blooms like a flower
of the field;
16 when the wind passes over it,
it vanishes,
and its place is no longer
known.[B]
17 But from eternity to eternity
the LORD's faithful love is
toward those who fear Him,
and His righteousness
toward the grandchildren
18 of those who keep
His covenant,
who remember to observe
His precepts.
19 The LORD has established
His throne in heaven,
and His kingdom rules
over all.

[A]**103:5** Lit *satisfies your ornament*; Hb obscure [B]**103:16** Lit *place no longer knows it*

>WORD|*study*

103:1-2 The psalmist instructs his **soul**, representative of his whole being, to praise (Hb *barak*, "bless") the Lord. To "bless" someone in the Old Testament generally meant to endue with power for such things as prosperity, success, and long life. In general the blessing was conferred by the superior or more powerful person to the inferior or more vulnerable individual. Thus fathers blessed their sons and kings blessed their subjects. However, the verbal blessing could also be descriptive—an acknowledgment that the person addressed already possessed power for abundant living. Thus blessing someone became a means of expressing thanksgiving and praise. The term is used in verses 1-2 in the latter sense.

20 Praise the LORD,
all His angels
of great strength,
who do His word,
obedient to His command.
21 Praise the LORD, all
His armies,
His servants who do His will.
22 Praise the LORD, all His works
in all the places
where He rules.
My soul, praise Yahweh!

Psalm 104

God the Creator

1 My soul, praise •Yahweh!
LORD my God, You are
very great;
You are clothed with majesty
and splendor.
2 He wraps Himself in light as if
it were a robe,
spreading out the sky
like a canopy,
3 laying the beams of His palace
on the waters above,
making the clouds
His chariot,
walking on the wings
of the wind,
4 and making the winds
His messengers,[A]
flames of fire His servants.

5 He established the earth
on its foundations;
it will never be shaken.
6 You covered it with the deep
as if it were a garment;
the waters stood
above the mountains.
7 At Your rebuke
the waters fled;
at the sound of Your thunder
they hurried away—
8 mountains rose
and valleys sank[B]—
to the place You established
for them.
9 You set a boundary
they cannot cross;
they will never cover
the earth again.
10 He causes the springs to gush
into the valleys;
they flow
between the mountains.
11 They supply water
for every wild beast;
the wild donkeys quench
their thirst.
12 The birds of the sky live
beside the springs;
they sing among the foliage.
13 He waters the mountains
from His palace;
the earth is satisfied
by the fruit of Your labor.

14 He causes grass to grow
for the livestock
and provides crops for man
to cultivate,
producing food
from the earth,
15 wine that makes
man's heart glad—
making his face shine
with oil—
and bread that sustains
man's heart.

16 The trees of the LORD
flourish,[C]
the cedars of Lebanon
that He planted.
17 There the birds make
their nests;
the stork makes its home
in the pine trees.
18 The high mountains are
for the wild goats;
the cliffs are a refuge
for hyraxes.

19 He made the moon to mark
the[D] festivals;[E]
the sun knows when to set.
20 You bring darkness,
and it becomes night,
when all
the forest animals stir.
21 The young lions roar
for their prey
and seek their food from God.
22 The sun rises; they go back
and lie down in their dens.
23 Man goes out to his work
and to his labor until evening.

103:13-18 God is a compassionate and tender Father toward His **children**. He knows that He created you from the dust of the earth (Gn 2:7). **The LORD has compassion** upon human frailty. In contrast to your weakness and the brevity of your life, God's love is everlasting and unchanging. All those who take His covenant seriously and live by faith in obedience to His instructions experience the wonderful reality of His unchanging love. The fear of the Lord described in this passage does not refer to a cringing mistrust of His goodness but rather to the reverent obedience that grows out of a recognition of His awesome nature and faithful love.

103:19-22 The Lord's kingdom is universal. He reigns over all. The psalmist calls on God's **angels** or messengers, **His armies**, and **His servants** to bless or praise the Lord. The poet ended this psalm on the same note on which he began by calling on his entire being to praise God: **My soul, praise Yahweh!** Simply and majestically this Davidic psalm extols the blessing of God's eternal, unchanging love.

104:1-5 This psalm begins with the same marvelous phrase that both introduces and concludes Psalm 103: **My soul, praise Yahweh!** The theme of the poem is the greatness of God as Creator. The Hebrew concept of a three-storied universe with **waters above** and below the earth is reflected in the descriptive imagery (vv. 3-13; cp. Gn 1:7). Moving from the heavens, the poet next extols the Lord as the One who established the **foundations** of **the earth**.

104:6-15 Creation is under God's control. He harnesses the waters for the benefit of His creation. God **provides** for the needs of His creatures. He provides **grass** and vegetation for **food**.

104:16-19 The Lord provides homes for all His creatures. God has established an orderly pattern for His world. He created time and seasons marked by the **sun** and the **moon**. Furthermore the poet notes that the sun and the moon are created objects, not objects to be worshiped (see Gn 1:14-18).

104:23 God gives people a reason for existence. He provides meaning and purpose for their lives. He also provides a time for them to rest.

[A] **104:4** Or *angels* [B] **104:7-8** Or *away. They flowed over the mountains and went down valleys* [C] **104:16** Lit *are satisfied* [D] **104:19** Lit *moon for* [E] **104:19** Or *the appointed times*

104:24-30 God is the source of life. He made the seas and all forms of sea life. **Leviathan** refers to a great sea monster—perhaps a whale (see note on Jb 41:1-34). All creatures depend on God for their food. They are dependent on Him for their breath. God renews the entire earth, both plant and animal life. Life is the gift of the Lord.

104:31-35 The psalmist prays that God might continue to enjoy His creation. He vows to sing praise to God as long as he lives. He expresses his joy in the Lord. He prays that wicked people, those who spoil the beauty and purpose of God's creation, may exist no more. The poet concludes his praise song in the same manner in which he began by calling on his entire being to offer thanksgiving: **My soul, praise Yahweh!** Praise the Lord for the wonders of His creation and His gift of life!

104:35 Hallelujah, the final word of this psalm, is actually a Hebrew word transliterated into English and meaning "praise the Lord."

105:1-15 These verses appear in 1Ch 16 as a psalm of thanksgiving to the Lord when David brought the ark to Jerusalem. The Lord is to be praised for His **wonderful works** on behalf of His chosen people. These acts demonstrate His faithfulness to them. God's people are instructed to **search for the Lord**, to **seek** [Hb *baqash*, "earnest seeking; petition"] **His face** or presence **always** (Hb *tamid*, "continually," referring both to uninterrupted continuity and regular repetition of an action, v. 4).

The poet next recites the acts of God in the history of His chosen people. God made and renewed His covenant of promise with Abraham, Isaac, and Jacob, whose name was changed to Israel (vv. 8-10). The Lord promised to give the land of Canaan to His people as their inheritance (v. 11; see Gn 12:1-3). God made these promises to the patriarchs as wandering nomads (Ps 105:12-13). God protected **Abraham**, **Isaac**, and **Jacob** from the kings of other nations (cp. Gn 12:10-20; 20:1-18). God's **covenant** with the patriarchs, who are identified as prophets (Ps 105:15; see Gn 20:7), was unconditional.

24 How countless are
Your works, LORD!
In wisdom
You have made them all;
the earth is full of
Your creatures.[A]
25 Here is the sea, vast and wide,
teeming with creatures
beyond number—
living things both large
and small.
26 There the ships move about,
and •Leviathan,
which You formed
to play there.

27 All of them wait for You
to give them their food
at the right time.
28 When You give it to them,
they gather it;
when You open Your hand,
they are satisfied
with good things.
29 When You hide Your face,
they are terrified;
when You take away
their breath,
they die and return
to the dust.
30 When You send Your breath,[B]
they are created,
and You renew the face
of the earth.

31 May the glory of the LORD
endure forever;
may the LORD rejoice
in His works.
32 He looks at the earth,
and it trembles;
He touches the mountains,
and they pour out smoke.
33 I will sing to the LORD
all my life;
I will sing praise to my God
while I live.
34 May my meditation
be pleasing to Him;
I will rejoice in the LORD.
35 May sinners vanish
from the earth
and wicked people be
no more.
My soul, praise Yahweh!
•Hallelujah!

Psalm 105

God's Faithfulness to His People

1 Give thanks to •Yahweh,
call on His name;
proclaim His deeds
among the peoples.
2 Sing to Him, sing praise
to Him;
tell about all
His wonderful works!
3 Honor His holy name;
let the hearts of those
who seek Yahweh rejoice.
4 Search for the LORD and for
His strength;
seek His face always.
5 Remember
the wonderful works
He has done,
His wonders,
and the judgments
He has pronounced,[C]
6 you offspring of Abraham
His servant,
Jacob's descendants—
His chosen ones.

7 He is the LORD our God;
His judgments govern
the whole earth.
8 He remembers His covenant
forever,
the promise He ordained
for a thousand generations—
9 the covenant He made
with Abraham,
swore[D] to Isaac,
10 and confirmed to Jacob
as a decree
and to Israel
as an everlasting covenant:
11 "I will give the land of Canaan
to you
as your inherited portion."

12 When they were few
in number,
very few indeed,
and temporary residents
in Canaan,
13 wandering from nation
to nation
and from one kingdom
to another,
14 He allowed no one
to oppress them;

[A]**104:24** Lit *possessions* [B]**104:30** Or *Spirit* [C]**105:5** Lit *judgments of His mouth* [D]**105:9** Lit *and His oath*

He rebuked kings
on their behalf:
15 "Do not touch
My anointed ones,
or harm My prophets."
16 He called down famine
against the land
and destroyed
the entire food supply.
17 He had sent a man ahead
of them—
Joseph, who was sold
as a slave.
18 They hurt his feet
with shackles;
his neck was put in
an iron collar.
19 Until the time his prediction
came true,
the word of the LORD
tested him.
20 The king sent for him
and released him;
the ruler of peoples set him
free.
21 He made him master
of his household,
ruler over all
his possessions—
22 binding[A] his officials at will
and instructing his elders.
23 Then Israel went to Egypt;
Jacob lived as a foreigner
in the land of Ham.[B]
24 The LORD[C] made His people
very fruitful;
He made them
more numerous
than their foes,
25 whose hearts He turned
to hate His people
and to deal deceptively
with His servants.
26 He sent Moses His servant,
and Aaron,
whom He had chosen.
27 They performed
His miraculous signs
among them,
and wonders in the land
of Ham.[B]
28 He sent darkness,
and it became dark—
for did they not defy[D]
His commands?
29 He turned their water
into blood
and caused their fish to die.
30 Their land was overrun
with frogs,
even in their royal chambers.
31 He spoke, and insects came—
gnats
throughout their country.
32 He gave them hail for rain,
and lightning throughout
their land.
33 He struck their vines
and fig trees
and shattered the trees
of their territory.
34 He spoke, and locusts came—
young locusts
without number.
35 They devoured
all the vegetation
in their land
and consumed the produce
of their land.
36 He struck all the firstborn
in their land,
all their first progeny.
37 Then He brought Israel out
with silver and gold,
and no one among
His tribes stumbled.
38 Egypt was glad when they left,
for the dread of Israel[E]
had fallen on them.
39 He spread a cloud
as a covering
and gave a fire to light up
the night.
40 They asked,
and He brought quail
and satisfied them with bread
from heaven.
41 He opened a rock, and water
gushed out;
it flowed like a stream
in the desert.
42 For He remembered
His holy promise
to Abraham His servant.
43 He brought His people out
with rejoicing,
His chosen ones with shouts
of joy.
44 He gave them the lands
of the nations,
and they inherited

105:16-25 These verses summarize the account of Joseph's life (Gn 37–50). **Joseph**, sold by his brothers, became a powerful ruler in Egypt. He saved his people from terrible famine. Jacob and his family came to Egypt to live for the remainder of the famine. There they multiplied and eventually were enslaved. **The land of Ham** is another designation for Egypt (v. 23). Noah's son Ham became the original ancestor of the Egyptians (see Gn 10:6).

105:26-45 These verses recite the history of Israel under the leadership of **Moses**, refreshing the people's memories with the many reasons they had to give thanks to the Lord. The poet recounts the plagues that fell on Egypt before Pharaoh let the Hebrew people go. The final plague was the death of **the firstborn** (v. 36). God provided guidance for His people in a pillar of **cloud** by day and of **fire** by night (v. 39). He cared for them in the wilderness, giving them meat (**quail**), manna (**bread from heaven**), and **water** from the **rock** (vv. 40-41). This recital of Israel's history refreshed the people's memories with the many reasons they had to give thanks to the Lord.

God remembered His **promise** to **Abraham**, again identified as the Lord's **servant** (v. 42; cp. v. 6). The Lord gave to His chosen people the land of Canaan. They enjoyed the fruits of others' labor (v. 44; cp. Dt 6:10-11). Because of all the Lord had done for them, God's people should respond in obedience as an expression of gratitude for His numerous mighty acts on their behalf. They were to keep His laws and observe His statutes (Ps 105:45). Privilege always brings with it responsibility. God's goodness to His people should lead them to obedience as the proper response of a grateful heart.

[A]**105:22** LXX, Syr, Vg read *teaching* [B]**105:23,27** = Egypt [C]**105:24** Lit *He* [D]**105:28** LXX, Syr read *for they did defy* [E]**105:38** Lit *them*

106:1-5 Psalm 106 continues relating incidents from Israel's history. Its focus, however, is on Israel's unfaithfulness to God (cp. Ps 78). That unfaithfulness stands in stark contrast to the **faithful love** (Hb *chesed*, "steadfast covenant loyalty"; see **Word Study**, p. 322) of the Lord. Beginning with a call to praise, the psalmist prayed that God would **remember** him and act with **favor** toward His **people**. The psalmist longed to experience God's **salvation** or deliverance.

106:6-7 Next, the psalmist begins a lengthy confession of sins, piling up phrases that describe the people's unfaithfulness. They had **sinned**, **done wrong**, and **acted wickedly**; this threefold reference to the people's wrongdoing emphasized the completeness of their sin. They had totally missed God's way for them, repeatedly disobeying Him after He had delivered them from Egypt (vv. 7-46). How quickly they forgot the Lord's demonstration of His **faithful love** (Hb *chesed*; see **Word Study**, p. 322). **They rebelled** against God by their unbelief at **the Red Sea**.

106:8-13 Despite their rebellion, God delivered them for the sake of His **name** (v. 8), but **they soon forgot His works** (v. 13). They lusted for the food they had enjoyed in Egypt. In the Lord's wise **counsel** (v. 13), He knows what you need and when you need it. You must learn to wait on His timing.

106:19-23 The people continued in their rebellion by making **a calf** and worshiping it while Moses was on Mount **Horeb**. Foolishly they **exchanged their glory** (here a reference to the Lord) for a man-made **image** of an **ox** (see Rm 1:22-23). The Lord stated that He **would have destroyed them** because of their repeated unfaithfulness **if Moses . . . had not stood . . . in the breach** ((Hb *perets*, "rupture, gap"; see Ex 32:31-32), a military expression referring to the bravery of a soldier who is willing to give his life in repelling the enemy by standing in a breach in the wall (see Ezk 22:30). Moses acted in that capacity, risking and offering his life in defense of those who had sinned grievously against God.

>WORD|*study*

106:14 The word tested (Hb *nasah*, "try, prove, put to the test") has a negative connotation when used for "testing" God (cp. Ex 17:2,7; Dt 6:16). To put God to the test demonstrates willful lack of faith. When one foolishly dares or challenges God to prove Himself, sometimes God brings judgment by allowing her to have her selfish desires.

what other peoples
had worked for.
45 All this happened
so that they might keep
His statutes
and obey His instructions.
•Hallelujah!

Psalm 106
Israel's Unfaithfulness to God

1 •Hallelujah!
Give thanks to the LORD,
for He is good;
His faithful love
endures forever.
2 Who can declare
the LORD's mighty acts
or proclaim all the praise
due Him?
3 How happy are those
who uphold justice,
who practice righteousness
at all times.
4 Remember me, LORD,
when You show favor
to Your people.
Come to me
with Your salvation
5 so that I may enjoy
the prosperity
of Your chosen ones,
rejoice in the joy
of Your nation,
and boast
about Your heritage.
6 Both we and our fathers
have sinned;
we have done wrong
and have acted wickedly.
7 Our fathers in Egypt did not
grasp
the significance of
Your wonderful works
or remember Your many acts
of faithful love;
instead, they rebelled
by the sea—the •Red Sea.
8 Yet He saved them
because of His name,
to make His power known.
9 He rebuked the Red Sea,
and it dried up;
He led them through
the depths as through
a desert.
10 He saved them from the hand
of the adversary;
He redeemed them
from the hand of the enemy.
11 Water covered their foes;
not one of them remained.
12 Then they believed
His promises
and sang His praise.
13 They soon forgot His works
and would not wait
for His counsel.
14 They were seized with craving
in the wilderness
and tested God in the desert.
15 He gave them what
they asked for,
but sent a wasting disease
among them.
16 In the camp
they were envious of Moses
and of Aaron,
the LORD's holy one.
17 The earth opened up
and swallowed Dathan;
it covered the assembly
of Abiram.
18 Fire blazed throughout
their assembly;
flames consumed the wicked.
19 At Horeb they made a calf
and worshiped
the cast metal image.
20 They exchanged their glory[A,B]
for the image of a grass-
eating ox.
21 They forgot God their Savior,
who did great things in Egypt,

[A]**106:20** Alt Jewish tradition reads *His* or *My glory* [B]**106:20** = God

>WORD|*study*

106:39 The verb prostituted (Hb *zanah*) reflects the imagery of Israel as the bride of the Lord who acted unfaithfully to Him. The word is predominantly applied to a woman's committing fornication, pursing a lover other than her husband, or acting as a prostitute. Figuratively, the verb refers to a comparable pursuit of idols, thereby violating the covenant between the Lord and His people (cp. Ex 34:15-16). This imagery particularly applies to the Israelites' participation in the religious prostitution of Canaanite worship (cp. Lv 20:5-6; Dt 23:17-18).

22 wonderful works in the land
of Ham,[A]
awe-inspiring acts
at the Red Sea.
23 So He said He would
have destroyed them—
if Moses His chosen one
had not stood before Him
in the breach
to turn His wrath away
from destroying them.

24 They despised
the pleasant land
and did not believe
His promise.
25 They grumbled in their tents
and did not listen
to the LORD's voice.
26 So He raised His hand
against them with an oath
that He would make them fall
in the desert
27 and would disperse
their descendants[B]
among the nations,
scattering them
throughout the lands.

28 They aligned themselves
with •Baal of Peor
and ate sacrifices offered
to lifeless gods.[C]
29 They provoked the LORD
with their deeds,
and a plague broke out
against them.
30 But Phinehas stood up
and intervened,
and the plague was stopped.
31 It was credited to him
as righteousness
throughout all generations
to come.

32 They angered the LORD
at the waters of Meribah,
and Moses suffered[D]
because of them;
33 for they embittered
his spirit,[E]
and he spoke rashly
with his lips.

34 They did not destroy
the peoples
as the LORD
had commanded them
35 but mingled with the nations
and adopted their ways.
36 They served their idols,
which became a snare
to them.
37 They sacrificed their sons
and daughters to demons.
38 They shed innocent blood—
the blood of their sons
and daughters
whom they sacrificed
to the idols of Canaan;
so the land became polluted
with blood.
39 They defiled themselves
by their actions
and prostituted themselves
by their deeds.

40 Therefore the LORD's anger
burned against His people,
and He abhorred
His own inheritance.
41 He handed them over
to the nations;
those who hated them
ruled them.
42 Their enemies
oppressed them,
and they were subdued
under their power.
43 He rescued them many times,
but they continued
to rebel deliberately
and were beaten down
by their sin.

44 When He heard their cry,
He took note of their distress,

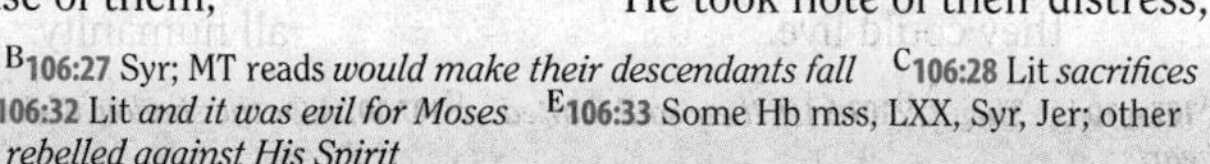
[A]106:22 = Egypt [B]106:27 Syr; MT reads *would make their descendants fall* [C]106:28 Lit *sacrifices for dead ones* [D]106:32 Lit *and it was evil for Moses* [E]106:33 Some Hb mss, LXX, Syr, Jer; other Hb mss read *they rebelled against His Spirit*

106:24-29 When at last the people of Israel reached the land of promise, they refused to believe that the Lord would defeat the inhabitants of that land. As a result the generation that left Egypt, except for Joshua and Caleb, was sentenced to wander in the wilderness until they died. In the wilderness they continued their lifestyle of rebellion, and idol worship.

106:34-39 The next generation who entered the promised land under Joshua's leadership mingled with the inhabitants of Canaan, worshiping their idols.

106:43-47 During the time of the judges the people repeatedly and deliberately revolted against the Lord (cp. Jdg 2:17). Yet the Lord remained faithful to His people. Although He repeatedly disciplined them, He also forgave them and delivered them time and again on the basis of **His faithful love** (Hb *chesed*; see **Word Study**, p. 322). He faithfully kept the covenant despite the unfaithfulness of His people. No wonder the poet issued a call to praise. The psalmist cries out for God's undeserved deliverance at the present time. He asks the Lord to deliver His people in order that they might **give thanks** to His **name**.

106:48 The doxology marks the conclusion to Book IV of the Psalms (cp. 41:13; 72:19; 89:52).

107:1-3 Psalm 107 marks the beginning of Book V, the final book of the Psalms. Two reasons for giving thanks are cited—because of the Lord's goodness and because of His **faithful love** (Hb *chesed*, "steadfast love or covenant loyalty"; see **Word Study**, p. 322), which has run like a theme throughout the Psalter. The Lord is forever faithful to those He has **redeemed** from the **hand** or power of their enemies. God does for His people what they cannot do for themselves. Those who have experienced God's deliverance need to speak up to let others know of their praise to God for His wonderful works of deliverance. The poet then cites a variety of examples of the steadfast, unchanging love of the Lord.

107:4-9 These verses may refer to the Israelites' wandering in the wilderness. They cried out to the Lord in their hunger and thirst, and He **satisfied** their needs. He delivered them from **distress.** Genuine satisfaction can be found not in food or drink, not in material possessions, but in fulfilling the Lord's purpose for your life (cp. Jn 4:34).

107:10-16 The Lord delivers His people when they cry out to Him in repentance, even when they also suffer as a consequence of their sinfulness. God is identified as **the Most High**. The imagery of verses 13-16 depicts every dark and oppressive situation—**distress** (vv. 6,13,19,28), **darkness and gloom and . . . chains, bronze gates and . . . iron bars**.

107:17 Fools (Hb *'ewil*, "one who despises wisdom, is quarrelsome when corrected"; cp. Pr 1:7; 14:9) lacking spiritual discernment fail to see the connection between affliction and rebellion against the Lord. They go astray because they love wrongdoing. Yet even such rebellious ones experience God's healing and deliverance from death when they cry out to Him (Ps 107:20).

45 remembered His covenant
with them,
and relented according to
the riches
of His faithful love.
46 He caused them to be pitied
before all their captors.

47 Save us, •Yahweh our God,
and gather us
from the nations,
so that we may give thanks
to Your holy name
and rejoice in Your praise.

48 May Yahweh, the God
of Israel, be praised
from everlasting
to everlasting.
Let all the people
say, "•Amen!"
Hallelujah!

BOOK V
(Psalms 107:1–150:6)

Psalm 107
Thanksgiving for God's Deliverance

1 Give thanks to the LORD,
for He is good;
His faithful love
endures forever.
2 Let the redeemed
of the LORD proclaim
that He has redeemed them
from the hand of the foe
3 and has gathered them
from the lands—
from the east and the west,
from the north and the south.

4 Some[A] wandered
in the desolate wilderness,
finding no way to a city
where they could live.
5 They were hungry
and thirsty;
their spirits failed[B]
within them.
6 Then they cried out
to the LORD in their trouble;
He rescued them
from their distress.
7 He led them by the right path
to go to a city where
they could live.
8 Let them give thanks
to the LORD
for His faithful love
and His wonderful works for
all •humanity.
9 For He has satisfied
the thirsty
and filled the hungry
with good things.

10 Others[A] sat in darkness
and gloom[C]—
prisoners in cruel chains—
11 because they rebelled
against God's commands
and despised the counsel
of the •Most High.
12 He broke their spirits[D]
with hard labor;
they stumbled, and there was
no one to help.
13 Then they cried out
to the LORD in their trouble;
He saved them
from their distress.
14 He brought them
out of darkness and gloom[C]
and broke their chains apart.
15 Let them give thanks
to the LORD
for His faithful love
and His wonderful works for
all humanity.
16 For He has broken down
the bronze gates
and cut through
the iron bars.

17 Fools suffered affliction
because of
their rebellious ways
and their sins.
18 They loathed all food
and came near the gates
of death.
19 Then they cried out
to the LORD in their trouble;
He saved them
from their distress.
20 He sent His word
and healed them;
He rescued them
from the •Pit.
21 Let them give thanks
to the LORD
for His faithful love
and His wonderful works for
all humanity.

[A]107:4,10 Lit *They* [B]107:5 Lit *their soul fainted* [C]107:10,14 Or *the shadow of death* [D]107:12 Lit *hearts*

22 Let them offer sacrifices
of thanksgiving
and announce His works
with shouts of joy.
23 Others[A] went to sea in ships,
conducting trade
on the vast waters.
24 They saw the LORD's works,
His wonderful works
in the deep.
25 He spoke and raised a tempest
that stirred up the waves
of the sea.[B]
26 Rising up to the sky,
sinking down to the depths,
their courage[C] melting away
in anguish,
27 they reeled and staggered
like drunken men,
and all their skill was useless.
28 Then they cried out
to the LORD in their trouble,
and He brought them
out of their distress.
29 He stilled the storm
to a murmur,
and the waves of the sea[D]
were hushed.
30 They rejoiced
when the waves[E] grew quiet.
Then He guided
them to the harbor
they longed for.
31 Let them give thanks
to the LORD
for His faithful love
and His wonderful works for
all humanity.
32 Let them exalt Him
in the assembly
of the people
and praise Him in the council
of the elders.

33 He turns rivers into desert,
springs of water
into thirsty ground,
34 and fruitful land
into salty wasteland,
because of the wickedness
of its inhabitants.
35 He turns a desert into a pool
of water,
dry land into springs of water.
36 He causes the hungry
to settle there,
and they establish a city
where they can live.
37 They sow fields
and plant vineyards
that yield a fruitful harvest.
38 He blesses them,
and they multiply greatly;
He does not let
their livestock decrease.

39 When they are diminished
and are humbled
by cruel oppression
and sorrow,
40 He pours contempt on nobles
and makes them wander
in a trackless wasteland.
41 But He lifts the needy out of
their suffering
and makes their families
multiply like flocks.
42 The upright see it and rejoice,
and all injustice shuts
its mouth.

43 Let whoever is wise
pay attention
to these things
and consider[F] the LORD's acts
of faithful love.

Psalm 108

A Plea for Victory

A song. A Davidic psalm.

1 My heart is confident, God;[G]
I will sing; I will sing praises
with the whole of my being.[H]
2 Wake up, harp and lyre!
I will wake up the dawn.
3 I will praise You, LORD,
among the peoples;
I will sing praises to You
among the nations.
4 For Your faithful love
is higher than the heavens,
and Your faithfulness reaches
to the clouds.
5 God, be exalted above
the heavens,
and let Your glory be over
the whole earth.
6 Save with Your right hand
and answer me
so that those You love
may be rescued.

107:29-30 The poem vividly depicts rescue from a turbulent **storm** at sea by coming into a quiet **harbor** (cp. Mt 8:23-27; 14:22-33).

107:33-43 The Lord provides streams in the deserts of your life. The bounty described in these verses results from God's blessing. The **needy** are those who wait on the Lord to accomplish His purposes in His time (v. 41). Ultimately God, the just Judge, will right all wrongs. Unlike fools who lack spiritual understanding, those who are **wise . . . consider** (Hb *bin*, "be attentive to, perceive, have understanding," v. 43) how the Lord has demonstrated His **faithful love** (v. 43; cp. v. 21).

108:1-13 Verses 1-5 are found in Ps 57:7-11; verses 6-13 appear in Ps 60:5-12. The psalmist praises God with a steadfast heart. He prays for deliverance and deems the help of human beings worthless. Only God could bring the deliverance for which the poet longed. This psalm, like those immediately preceding it, celebrates God's **faithful love** (Hb *chesed*, v. 4; see **Word Study**, p. 322).

[A]107:23 Lit *They* [B]107:25 Lit *of it* [C]107:26 Lit *souls* [D]107:29 Lit *of them* [E]107:30 Lit *when they* [F]107:43 Lit *and let them consider* [G]108:1 Some Hb mss, LXX, Syr add *my heart is confident* [H]108:1 Lit *praises, even my glory*

109:1-5 The psalmist directly addresses the God whom he praises. He asks that the Lord reject **silent** inactivity and deal with the poet's enemies, identified as **wicked** and deceitful people who have falsely accused him. The psalmist repeatedly emphasizes that he has given his enemies no reason to behave so destructively. They have fought him **without cause**, and they have rewarded his **love** and goodness with **hatred** and **evil** (cp. v. 20; 38:20). In contrast to his enemies, who speak to destroy him, the psalmist engages in prayer. **But I continue to pray** (Hb *wa-ʾani tephillah*, "and I pray") captures the sense of contrast between the destructive speech of the slanderers and the psalmist's refusal to engage in verbal warfare. Instead of lashing out against the **hateful words**, he submits his complaint to the Lord (cp. Pr 10:12).

109:6-21 Judgment, calamity, and curses are invoked upon the guilty party (vv. 6-15). In the New Testament, Peter cites verse 8 and Ps 69:25 as applying to Judas Iscariot (Ac 1:20). According to the psalmist, some specific attitudes and actions displayed by his enemies merit God's judgment (vv. 16-20). The wickedness and evil speech of these enemies was as much a part of them as a garment would be (vv. 18-19). Having asked God to curse his enemies, the psalmist prays for his own deliverance (vv. 20-21). He appeals to the Lord to act on the basis of His **name**—i.e., His character or reputation, His goodness, and His **faithful love** (Hb *chesed*, "covenant loyalty," v. 21; see **Word Study**, p. 322).

109:22-31 The poet depicts his terrible condition and desperate need (vv. 22-25). The harassment of his enemies had taken its toll on him, both physically and psychologically. In response to the Lord's deliverance, the poet vows to offer great praise to Him (vv. 30-31). He promises to witness to others regarding the Lord's power to deliver His people. The Lord stands at the **right hand** (the position of power) of His needy children, to protect and rescue rather than to accuse (v. 31). Psalms such as this one reflect the common belief that the poet's enemies are God's enemies, and the poet's vicious attack on his enemies reflects his concern for God's name or reputation (vv. 21,27).

110:1-4 The initial setting of this psalm may have been the occasion when David brought the ark of the covenant to Jerusalem (2Sm 6:12), where it was viewed as a visible sign that the Lord had established His throne there. When Jesus cited a portion of this psalm, He referred to David as the speaker (Mt 22:41-46). The hymn is messianic since its words were fulfilled in Jesus Christ.

The psalm may be viewed as a message of divine encouragement to

7 God has spoken
in His sanctuary:[A]
"I will triumph!
I will divide up Shechem.
I will apportion the Valley
of Succoth.
8 Gilead is Mine, Manasseh is
Mine,
and Ephraim is My helmet;
Judah is My scepter.
9 Moab is My washbasin;
I throw My sandal on Edom.
I shout in triumph
over Philistia."

10 Who will bring me
to the fortified city?
Who will lead me to Edom?
11 God, haven't You rejected us?
God, You do not march out
with our armies.
12 Give us aid against the foe,
for human help is worthless.
13 With God we will
perform valiantly;
He will trample our foes.

Psalm 109
Prayer Against an Enemy

For the choir director. A Davidic psalm.

1 God of my praise,
do not be silent.

2 For wicked
and deceitful mouths open
against me;
they speak against me
with lying tongues.
3 They surround me
with hateful words
and attack me without cause.
4 In return for my love
they accuse me,
but I continue to pray.[B]
5 They repay me evil for good,
and hatred for my love.

6 Set a wicked person over him;
let an accuser[C] stand
at his right hand.
7 When he is judged, let him
be found •guilty,
and let his prayer be counted
as sin.
8 Let his days be few;
let another take over
his position.
9 Let his children be fatherless
and his wife a widow.
10 Let his children wander
as beggars,
searching for food far[D] from
their demolished homes.
11 Let a creditor seize all he has;
let strangers plunder
what he has worked for.
12 Let no one show him
kindness,
and let no one be gracious
to his fatherless children.
13 Let the line of his descendants
be cut off;
let their name be blotted out
in the next generation.
14 Let his ancestors' guilt
be remembered
before the LORD,
and do not let his mother's sin
be blotted out.
15 Let their sins[E] always remain
before the LORD,
and let Him erase[F]
all memory of them
from the earth.

16 For he did not think to show
kindness,
but pursued the afflicted,
poor, and brokenhearted
in order to put them to death.
17 He loved cursing—let it fall
on him;
he took no delight
in blessing—let it be far
from him.
18 He wore cursing
like his coat—
let it enter his body like water
and go into his bones like oil.
19 Let it be like a robe he wraps
around himself,
like a belt he always wears.
20 Let this be the LORD's payment
to my accusers,
to those who speak evil
against me.
21 But You, •Yahweh my Lord,
deal kindly with me
because of Your name;
deliver me because of
the goodness
of Your faithful love.
22 For I am afflicted and needy;

[A]**108:7** Or *has promised by His holy nature* [B]**109:4** Lit *but I, prayer* [C]**109:6** Or *adversary*
[D]**109:10** LXX reads *beggars, driven far* [E]**109:15** Lit *Let them* [F]**109:15** Or *cut off*

my heart is wounded
within me.
23 I fade away
like a lengthening shadow;
I am shaken off like a locust.
24 My knees are weak
from fasting,
and my body is emaciated.[A]
25 I have become an object
of ridicule to my accusers;[B]
when they see me, they shake
their heads in scorn.

26 Help me, LORD my God;
save me according to
Your faithful love
27 so they may know that this is
Your hand
and that You, LORD,
have done it.
28 Though they curse,
You will bless.
When they rise up, they will be
put to shame,
but Your servant will rejoice.
29 My accusers will be clothed
with disgrace;
they will wear their shame
like a cloak.
30 I will fervently thank the LORD
with my mouth;
I will praise Him
in the presence of many.
31 For He stands
at the right hand of
the needy
to save him from
those who would
condemn him.

Psalm 110
The Priestly King

A Davidic psalm.

1 This is the declaration of the
LORD
to my Lord:
"Sit at My right hand
until I make Your enemies
Your footstool."
2 The LORD will extend
Your mighty scepter
from •Zion.
Rule[C] over
Your surrounding[D] enemies.
3 Your people will volunteer
on Your day of battle.[E]
In holy splendor,
from the womb of the dawn,
the dew of
Your youth belongs to You.[F]
4 The LORD has sworn an oath
and will not take it back:
"Forever, You are a priest
like Melchizedek."

5 The Lord is at Your right hand;
He will crush kings on the day
of His anger.
6 He will judge the nations,
heaping up corpses;
He will crush leaders
over the entire world.
7 He will drink from the brook
by the road;
therefore, He will lift up
His head.

Psalm 111
Praise for the LORD's Works

1 •Hallelujah![G]
I will praise the LORD with all
my heart
in the assembly of the upright
and in the congregation.
2 The LORD's works are great,
studied by all who delight
in them.
3 All that He does is splendid
and majestic;
His righteousness
endures forever.
4 He has caused

[A]**109:24** Lit *denied from fat* [B]**109:25** Lit *to them* [C]**110:2** One Hb ms, LXX, Tg read *You will rule* [D]**110:2** Lit *Rule in the midst of Your* [E]**110:3** Lit *power* [F]**110:3** Hb obscure [G]**111:1** The lines of this poem form an •acrostic.

>WORD|*study*

110:4 To be **a priest like Melchizedek** (Hb, "king of righteousness") signaled exceptional distinction. Melchizedek was the king of Salem (Hb, "peace," a shortened form of "Jerusalem") and priest of God Most High, who blessed Abraham after his rescue of Lot (Gn 14:18-20). The meaning of Melchizedek's name, along with Scripture's silence regarding his origins, make this historical, yet mysterious, figure an apt symbol of the coming Messiah (Heb 7:2-3). The fact that Melchizedek blessed Abraham and received tithes from him demonstrates his superiority over Abraham and his descendants, including the Levitical priesthood (Heb 7:4-19). The word **forever** (Hb *'olam*) indicates that this psalm ultimately refers to the Messiah. Only He is eternally priest and king.

the Davidic king. It emphasizes that the king's authority is conferred by the Lord Himself (i.e., **My right hand** represents the Lord's position of power and honor). Israel's king had a special relationship with God. The phrase **until I make Your enemies Your footstool** does not suggest that the king or Messiah would cease to reign when the enemies had been defeated. Rather, the Messiah's enemies will experience the ultimate defeat for which they are destined (cp. Mt 22:44; Mk 12:36; Lk 20:43; Ac 2:34-35; Heb 1:13; 10:13). The reference to the enemies as a "footstool" is a picture of their complete subjection. According to ancient custom, a victorious king would place his foot on his enemies' necks as a sign of his power over them.

The **scepter** signified power and authority and was an instrument of chastisement. **Zion** (Jerusalem) was the place of the Lord's special presence. There Solomon would build the temple. The king or Messiah ruled as God's special representative. **Rule** (Hb *radah*, "subdue, subjugate"; Gn 1:26,28) has a quality of sternness. The forced obedience of the enemies is contrasted starkly with the voluntary response of the people, which seems to refer to the people's willingness to fight in battle for the king. As God's representative to the people, the Davidic king also had a priestly role given by divine oath (Ps 110:4).

110:5-7 In this battle scene, **the Lord** (Hb *'Adonay*) has been variously viewed as either Yahweh or the Messiah, effecting God's final judgment on the world. The imagery suggests that the hero pauses to drink at a **brook** he crossed. Refreshed, he then presses on to total victory. Ultimately that hero is the Messiah.

The early church recognized the messianic character of this psalm. The New Testament itself frequently refers or alludes to Ps 110 in relation to Christ (e.g., Mt 22:44; Ac 2:34-35; 1 Co 15:25; Heb 1:13; 5:6; 6:20; 7:17; 8:1; 10:12-13). The psalm is a testimony to the faith of God's people. The psalm's original setting as celebrating God's divinely appointed king came to full fruition when Jesus of Nazareth was identified as the Messiah-King. God has indeed set Jesus at His right hand. To Christ alone has been given power and authority, an authority demonstrated by sacrificial love. Jesus is both our great High Priest and King.

111:1-10 Psalm 111 is a good example of a Hebrew acrostic poem. Each of its 22 lines begins with a successive letter of the Hebrew alphabet. The psalmist calls others to praise the Lord and testifies that he will praise the Lord with his whole **heart**, a reference to his entire being (v. 1). He affirms that his praise will not be in secret but rather in the fellowship of believers—the **assembly** or **congregation** (v. 1). The major part of this poem deals with reasons for praising the Lord. The Lord is to be praised for His **wonderful works** (v. 4) on behalf of His people as well as for His nature. He is to be praised both for what He does and for who He is. The works of the Lord include His provisions both to sustain physical life and His **covenant** (vv. 5,9).

The Lord's nature is **gracious and compassionate** (v. 4; cp. Ex 22:27; 34:6). The reference to the Lord's **name** is a reference to His character as **holy and awe-inspiring** (Ps 111:9). The appropriate response to both the Lord's works and His character is reverent obedience. The **fear** that marks the beginning of wisdom is an awesome reverence for God, not a cringing fear (v. 10). Wisdom, which involves knowing the right way to live (Pr 1:7), begins with being rightly related to the Lord.

112:1-10 This psalm is also an acrostic poem (cp. Ps 111) that contrasts the blessings of the righteous with the fate of the wicked (cp. Ps 1). Most of the verses of this poem elaborate on the blessing that belongs to upright people. The emphasis falls on the dependable or stable character of the person living in right relationship with the Lord (vv. 6-8). Such an individual will persevere in doing good even in life's testing times (cp. Jms 1:6-8).

In contrast the punishment of **the wicked man** is described briefly in terms of experiencing frustration, grief, and instability (v. 10).

113:1–118:29 In Jewish tradition, Pss 113–118 are known as the *Hallēl*. These psalms are sung in the morning services of the major Jewish feasts and holy days:

- on the day of the Passover sacrifice;
- at the Festival of Weeks (Pentecost);
- on each of the eight days of the Festival of Booths;
- on each of the eight days of the dedication of the temple.

In addition, they are sung on the night of the Passover meal. Pss 113–114 are sung before the meal and Pss 115–118 are sung after the meal. According to some, Pss 113–116 are to be recited or sung after the *haggadah* (Hb, "telling"), the Passover liturgy recounting the story of the redemption of Israel from Egypt, and Pss 117–118 after the meal (see Mt 26:30).

113:7-9 This great God is also marked by concern for **the poor** and **needy**, societal outcasts, and the **childless woman** (cp. 1Sm 2:8; Lk 1:48,52).

114:1-8 Psalm 114 celebrates God's mighty acts of deliverance on behalf of His people. God delivered His

His wonderful works
to be remembered.
The LORD is gracious
and compassionate.
5 He has provided food for those
who fear Him;
He remembers
His covenant forever.
6 He has shown His people
the power of His works
by giving them the inheritance
of the nations.
7 The works of His hands
are truth and justice;
all His instructions
are trustworthy.
8 They are established forever
and ever,
enacted in truth and in
what is right.
9 He has sent redemption
to His people.
He has ordained
His covenant forever.
His name is holy
and awe-inspiring.

10 The •fear of the LORD is
the beginning of wisdom;
all who follow His
instructions[A] have
good insight.
His praise endures forever.

Psalm 112

The Traits of the Righteous

1 •Hallelujah![B]
Happy is the man who •fears
the LORD,
taking great delight
in His commands.

2 His descendants will be
powerful in the land;
the generation of the upright
will be blessed.
3 Wealth and riches are
in his house,
and his righteousness
endures forever.
4 Light shines in the darkness
for the upright.
He is gracious, compassionate,
and righteous.
5 Good will come to a man
who lends generously
and conducts
his business fairly.
6 He will never be shaken.
The righteous man will be
remembered forever.
7 He will not fear bad news;
his heart is confident,
trusting in the LORD.
8 His heart is assured;
he will not fear.
In the end he will look
in triumph on his foes.
9 He distributes freely
to the poor;
his righteousness
endures forever.
His •horn will be exalted
in honor.

10 The wicked man will see it
and be angry;
he will gnash his teeth
in despair.
The desire of the wicked man
will come to nothing.

Psalm 113

Praise to the Merciful God

1 •Hallelujah!
Give praise, servants
of •Yahweh;
praise the name of Yahweh.
2 Let the name of Yahweh
be praised
both now and forever.
3 From the rising of the sun
to its setting,
let the name of Yahweh
be praised.

4 Yahweh is exalted above
all the nations,
His glory above the heavens.
5 Who is like Yahweh our God—
the One enthroned on high,
6 who stoops down to look
on the heavens and the earth?
7 He raises the poor
from the dust
and lifts the needy
from the garbage pile
8 in order to seat them
with nobles—
with the nobles of His people.
9 He gives the childless woman
a household,
making her the joyful mother
of children.
Hallelujah!

[A]111:10 Lit *follow them* [B]112:1 The lines of this poem form an •acrostic.

Psalm 114

God's Deliverance of Israel

1 When Israel came
out of Egypt—
the house of Jacob
from a people
who spoke
a foreign language—
2 Judah became His sanctuary,
Israel, His dominion.

3 The sea looked and fled;
the Jordan turned back.
4 The mountains skipped
like rams,
the hills, like lambs.
5 Why was it, sea, that you fled?
Jordan, that you turned back?
6 Mountains, that you skipped
like rams?
Hills, like lambs?

7 Tremble, earth,
at the presence of the Lord,
at the presence of the God
of Jacob,
8 who turned the rock
into a pool of water,
the flint into a spring
of water.

Psalm 115

Glory to God Alone

1 Not to us, •Yahweh, not to us,
but to Your name give glory
because of Your faithful love,
because of Your truth.
2 Why should the nations say,
"Where is their God?"
3 Our God is in heaven
and does whatever He pleases.

4 Their idols are silver and gold,
made by human hands.
5 They have mouths
but cannot speak,
eyes, but cannot see.
6 They have ears
but cannot hear,
noses, but cannot smell.
7 They have hands
but cannot feel,
feet, but cannot walk.
They cannot make a sound
with their throats.
8 Those who make them are[A]
just like them,
as are all who trust
in them.

9 Israel,[B] trust in the LORD!
He is their help and shield.
10 House of Aaron,
trust in the LORD!
He is their help and shield.
11 You who •fear the LORD,
trust in the LORD!
He is their help and shield.
12 The LORD remembers us
and will bless us.
He will bless the house
of Israel;
He will bless the house
of Aaron;
13 He will bless those who fear
the LORD—
small and great alike.

14 May the LORD add to
your numbers,
both yours
and your children's.
15 May you be blessed
by the LORD,
the Maker of heaven and earth.
16 The heavens are the LORD's,[C]
but the earth He has given
to the •human race.
17 It is not the dead who praise
the LORD,
nor any of those descending
into the silence of death.
18 But we will praise the LORD,
both now and forever.
•Hallelujah!

Psalm 116

Thanks to God for Deliverance

1 I love the LORD
because He has heard
my appeal for mercy.
2 Because He has turned
His ear to me,
I will call out to Him
as long as I live.

3 The ropes of death
were wrapped around me,
and the torments of •Sheol
overcame me;
I encountered trouble
and sorrow.
4 Then I called on the name
of •Yahweh:
"Yahweh, save me!"

[A]**115:8** Or *May those who make them become Israel* [B]**115:9** Some Hb mss, LXX, Syr read *House of Israel* [C]**115:16** Lit *LORD's heavens*

people from bondage in Egypt. The designations **house of Jacob** and **Judah** (vv. 1-2) are alternate ways of referring to Israel. The Lord parted the sea as His people came out of Egypt and also parted the Jordan River when they entered the promised land. He provided water for His children during their wanderings in the wilderness (v. 8). Nature reverently and joyfully participated in these acts of the Lord (vv. 4-6). God's majestic presence should still prompt His people to **tremble** in awe before Him (v. 7). The participle form of the verb **turned** (Hb *haphak*, "change or convert into something," v. 8) indicates continuing action. To sing these words is to proclaim the continuing presence of the Lord (cp. 107:35; Is 35:7; 41:18).]

115:4-8 The nature of the false gods worshiped by the nations stands in stark contrast to the living Lord. The psalmist further affirms that all who make such **idols**, as well as those who trust in them, are just like the false gods they worship. Those who worship idols are as helpless as the idols themselves. Idol worshipers ultimately will perish with their perishable gods (cp. Ps 135:15-18; Is 40:18-20; 44:9-17).

115:9-11 These verses exhort the people of Israel to put their trust in the Lord as their **help and shield** (Hb *magēn*, the smaller, common type of round shield carried by soldiers). The word translated "help" (Hb *ʿēzer*) generally indicates God's help in the form of military assistance. Although the term is used, particularly in the Psalms, of nonmilitary, personal assistance, the pairing of the term with "shield" in this verse seems to indicate assistance of a military nature. The Lord is called a shield because He protects His servants. He both helps and protects His people.

115:12 Remembers (Hb *zakar*, "is mindful, considers") does not mean that the Lord had at some point forgotten that His people existed. Rather, the Lord is ready to take action on behalf of His people then.

115:17-18 The dead, who cannot **praise the LORD**, are contrasted with the living, who can and should praise Him.

116:1-4 The psalmist cries out to the Lord for deliverance as he faces **death**. God hears his prayer and delivers him. The psalmist vows his **love** (Hb *ʾahav*, "delight in, longing for"; cp. Dt 6:5) and service to the Lord as an expression of gratitude for what the Lord has done for him and of devotion nurtured by answered prayer. That the Lord **heard** and **turned His ear** to the psalmist signifies His deliverance of the one who, in distress, prays to Him. This psalmist had cried out to the Lord in desperation as he felt death encompassing him.

116:5-8 The psalmist celebrated the Lord's **gracious, righteous,** and **compassionate** (Hb *racham*; see **Word Study**, p. 679) nature. The psalmist can **rest** despite turbulence around him because of his trust in the Lord, which is based on what He has experienced in His relationship with the Lord. The Lord had done great things for him.

116:12-19 This psalm expresses the appropriate response to God's deliverance or salvation. The psalmist vows to worship the Lord and to fulfill his vows in the congregation of God's people. He encourages them with his testimony to the Lord's goodness.

117:1-2 This psalm, the shortest in the book of Psalms, nevertheless is a powerful universal call to worship. **All nations** and **peoples**, not just the people of Israel, are called to **praise the LORD** for His **faithful love** (Hb *chesed*, "covenant loyalty"; see **Word Study**, p. 322) and **faithfulness**. Verse 1 is cited in the New Testament in support of an exhortation to believers, both Jews and Gentiles, to "accept one another" (Rm 15:7).

118:1-4 The final psalm of the *Hallēl* praises God for His **faithful love**. According to the Talmud (the traditional interpretation of the Torah), this psalm was sung at the Festival of Booths as well as at Passover. Verses 1-4 comprise a call to thanksgiving. The entire congregation is summoned to **give thanks** because **the LORD . . . is good**. God's faithful love (Hb *chesed*, "covenant loyalty"; see **Word Study**, p. 322) to His people **endures forever**. The psalmist also testifies regarding God's goodness to him personally.

119:1-176 Psalm 119 is the longest poem in the book of Psalms and the longest chapter in the Bible. An acrostic poem, each of the psalm's 22 stanzas begins with a successive letter of the Hebrew alphabet, and the first word of each line in a stanza begins with that particular letter—a technique that can be observed only in the Hebrew text. Notice that the Hebrew letter along with its name is printed at the beginning of each stanza.

The theme of celebrating God's law is readily apparent in the poet's use of eight terms for the law, which appear in almost every verse of the psalm.

119:1-8 begins with the same word as Ps 1: **How happy** (Hb *ʾesher*, a noun meaning "blessedness"; see note on 1:1-2). Here, the "happy" or blessed ones are described with six parallel phrases:

5 The LORD is gracious
and righteous;
our God is compassionate.
6 The LORD guards
the inexperienced;
I was helpless,
and He saved me.
7 Return to your rest, my soul,
for the LORD has been good
to you.
8 For You, LORD, rescued me
from death,
my eyes from tears,
my feet from stumbling.
9 I will walk before the LORD
in the land of the living.
10 I believed, even when I said,
"I am severely afflicted."
11 In my alarm I said,
"Everyone is a liar."

12 How can I repay the LORD
for all the good He has done
for me?
13 I will take the cup of salvation
and call on the name
of Yahweh.
14 I will fulfill my vows
to the LORD
in the presence of all
His people.
15 The death of His faithful ones
is valuable in the LORD's sight.
16 LORD, I am indeed
Your servant;
I am Your servant, the son
of Your female servant.
You have loosened my bonds.

17 I will offer You a sacrifice
of thanksgiving
and call on the name
of Yahweh.
18 I will fulfill my vows
to the LORD
in the presence of all
His people,
19 in the courts
of the LORD's house—
within you, Jerusalem.
•Hallelujah!

Psalm 117
Universal Call to Praise

1 Praise the LORD, all nations!
Glorify Him, all peoples!
2 For His faithful love
to us is great;
the LORD's faithfulness
endures forever.
•Hallelujah!

Psalm 118
Thanksgiving for Victory

1 Give thanks to the LORD,
for He is good;
His faithful love
endures forever.
2 Let Israel say,
"His faithful love
endures forever."
3 Let the house of Aaron say,
"His faithful love
endures forever."
4 Let those who fear the LORD
say,
"His faithful love
endures forever."

5 I called to the LORD
in distress;
the LORD answered me
and put me in a spacious
place.[A]
6 The LORD is for me;
I will not be afraid.
What can man do to me?
7 The LORD is my helper,
Therefore, I will look
in triumph on those
who hate me.

8 It is better to take refuge
in the LORD
than to trust in man.
9 It is better to take refuge
in the LORD
than to trust in nobles.

10 All the nations
surrounded me;
in the name of •Yahweh
I destroyed them.
11 They surrounded me, yes,
they surrounded me;
in the name of Yahweh
I destroyed them.
12 They surrounded me like bees;
they were extinguished
like a fire among thorns;
in the name of Yahweh
I destroyed them.
13 You[B] pushed me[C] hard
to make me fall,

[A]**118:5** Or *answered me with freedom* [B]**118:13** Perhaps the enemy [C]**118:13** LXX, Syr, Jer read *I was pushed*

but the LORD helped me.
14 The LORD is my strength
and my song;
He has become my salvation.

15 There are shouts of joy
and victory
in the tents of the righteous:
"The LORD's right hand
performs valiantly!
16 The LORD's right hand is raised.
The LORD's right hand
performs valiantly!"
17 I will not die, but I will live
and proclaim what the LORD
has done.
18 The LORD disciplined me
severely
but did not give me over
to death.

19 Open the gates
of righteousness for me;
I will enter through them
and give thanks to the LORD.
20 This is the gate of the LORD;
the righteous will enter
through it.
21 I will give thanks to You
because You have
answered me
and have become my salvation.
22 The stone that
the builders rejected
has become the cornerstone.
23 This came from the LORD;
it is wonderful in our eyes.
24 This is the day the LORD
has made;
let us rejoice and be glad in it.

25 LORD, save us!
LORD, please grant us success!
26 He who comes in the name
of the LORD is blessed.
From the house of the LORD
we bless you.
27 The LORD is God and has given
us light.
Bind the festival sacrifice
with cords
to the horns of the altar.
28 You are my God, and I will give
You thanks.
You are my God;
I will exalt You.
29 Give thanks to the LORD,
for He is good;
His faithful love
endures forever.

Psalm 119
Delight in God's Word

א *Alef*

1 How[A] happy are those whose
way is blameless,
who live according
to the LORD's instruction!
2 Happy are those who keep
His decrees
and seek Him with all
their heart.
3 They do nothing wrong;
they follow His ways.
4 You have commanded
that Your precepts
be diligently kept.
5 If only my ways
were committed
to keeping Your statutes!
6 Then I would not
be ashamed
when I think about
all Your commands.
7 I will praise You
with a sincere heart
when I learn
Your righteous judgments.
8 I will keep Your statutes;
never abandon me.

ב *Bet*

9 How can a young man keep
his way pure?
By keeping Your[B] word.

- **those whose way** [Hb *derek*, "way of living or acting; manner or course of life"; cp. vv. 5,14,26,27,29] **is blameless** (Hb *tamim*, "flawless, upright in conduct, characterized by integrity"; cp. 119:80);
- those **who live** [Hb *halak*, literally "walk," referring to one's lifestyle; cp. 119:45) **according to the LORD's instruction** (Hb *torah*; see chart, p. 758).
- **those who keep** [Hb *natsar*, "watch or guard carefully, observe"; cp. 119:22,33-34,56,69,100,115,129,145] **His decrees**;
- those who **seek** [Hb *darash*, "search after; study, follow, practice; consult; go to for answers or help"; cp. 119:10,45,94,155] **Him with all their heart**;
- those who **do nothing wrong**;
- those who **follow** [Hb *halak*; previously translated "live"] **His ways** (Hb *derek*; previously singular).

Like the brief portrait of the one exemplary righteous man in Ps 1, these few verses provide a snapshot of those (plural) who are "happy."

The psalmist lamented his failure to live perfectly by God's law (Ps 119:5-6). That failure brought shame or disgrace as well as a sense of feeling abandoned by the Lord. Thus the psalmist petitioned the Lord not to **abandon** him (v. 8).

119:9-16 The psalmist raises a question, perhaps referring to himself as **a young man**, and then proceeds to answer it. The question is as critical in today's generation as it ever has been, and the answer remains relevant. Keeping one's **way** [Hb *ʾorach*, "path, course or mode of living or acting," v. 15; cp. 119:9,37,101,104, 128] **pure** requires learning *and* obeying what God says (v. 9; cp. 73:13; Pr 20:9).

Significantly, the psalmist answers the question by speaking directly to God, demonstrating recognition that the living God speaks with authority to people through His **word**. Although affirming that he had **sought** (Hb *darash*; see "seek," v. 2) the Lord with his whole being, he acknowledges his tendency to stray from the right path (v. 10b; see vv. 5-6).

In Hebrew, verse 12 begins with the joyful expression **may You be**

[A] **119:1** The stanzas of this poem form an ˙acrostic. [B] **119:9** Or *keeping it according to Your*

>WORD|*study*

119:9 The verb rendered keep . . . pure (Hb *zakah*, "keep clean, cleanse,") is used only eight times in the Old Testament. David says that God is "blameless" (Hb *zakah*) when He judges (51:4). The Lord emphasizes His inability to "excuse" (Hb *zakah*, "count as pure") deception and fraud (Mc 6:11). As two of Job's friends rightly suggest, no one "born of woman" can "be pure" (Hb *zakah*)—i.e., "be righteous" (Jb 15:14)—or "be justified before God" (Jb 25:4; cp. Pr 20:9). However, the one who already walks in covenant relationship with the Lord is expected to recognize and remove "evil deeds" from his life. God commands His people, "Wash yourselves. Cleanse (Hb *zakah*) yourselves" (Is 1:16; cp. Ps 73:13). As one who is joyfully committed to God's covenant—on both personal and national levels, the psalmist's question demonstrates his understanding of his responsibility to "keep his way pure".

Eight Key Words in Psalm 119

	Key Word(s)	Translations
1	*Torah* (Hb, "law, doctrine")	• **The law of the Lord** "the Lord's instruction," (v. 1) • **Your law** ("Your instruction," HCSB; vv. 18,29,34,44,51,53,55,61,70,77, 85,92,97,109,113,126,136,142,150,153,163,165,174); • **instruction from Your lips** (Hb *torah-peh*, "law of [Your] mouth," v. 72)
2	*ʿēdah* (Hb, "divine witness or testimony") *ʿēdut* (Hb, "testimony; precept; the law as synonym for *Torah*, especially the Decalogue")	• **decrees** (*ʿēdah;* vv. 2,22,24,46,59,79,95,119,125, 138,144,146,152,167,168) • **decrees** (*ʿēdut;* vv. 14,31,36,99,111,129,144,157) • **the decree You have spoken** (Hb *ʿēdut-peh*, "testimony of [Your] mouth," v. 88)
3	*piqqud* (Hb, "rule, principle, direction or commandment prescribing a course of action or conduct; injunction regarding moral conduct")	• **precepts** (vv. 4,15,27,40,45,56,63,69,78,87,93,94,100,104,110,128, 134,141,159,168,173)
4	*choq* (Hb, "established law or ordinance; defined limit or boundary") *chuqqah* (Hb, "established law")	• **statutes** (*choq ;* vv. 5,8,12,23,26,33,48,54,64,68, 71,80,83,112,117,118,124, 135,145,155, 171) • **statutes** (*chuqqah ;* v. 16)
5	*mitswah* (Hb, "commandment, precept"; see note on Pr 3:1-8)	• **commands** (vv. 6,10,19,21,32,35,47,48,60,66,73,86,115,131,143, 151,166,176) • **Your command** (vv. 96) • **Your commands** (vv. 127,172)
6	*mishpat* (Hb, "a judgment; law, statute; body of laws—e.g., the law of Moses"; see **Word Study**, p. 218)	• **judgments** (vv. 7,13,20,39,43,52,62,75,91,102,106,108,120,137,156, 160,164,175) • **ordinances** (v. 30)
7	*davar* (Hb, "speech, utterance; promise; law or precept")	• God's **word** (vv. 9,16,17,25,28,42,49,74,81,89,101,105,107,114,147, 160,161,169) • **the word of truth** (v. 43) • **Your words** (vv. 57,130,139) • **as You promised** (v. 65)
8	*ʾimrah* (Hb, "word, speech, utterance;" see **Word Study**, 119:11, p. 759)	• **Your word** (v. 11,67,103,140,158) • **what You said** (v. 38) • **as You promised** (vv. 41,76,154) • **Your promise** (vv. 50,58,116,133,148,162,170,172) • **what You have promised** (v. 82) • **Your righteous promise** (Hb, *ʾimrah tsedeq*, "word of your righteousness," v. 123)

>WORD|*study*

119:11 Given the stanza's introductory question, word (Hb *ʾimrah*) is an especially fitting choice of synonym for God's law in verse 11 since it is often linked with the idea of being "pure" (Hb *tsaraph*, a verb literally denoting the "melting" of precious metals to "refine, purify, or purge" them of impurities, v. 9; 18:30; 119:140; 2Sm 22:31; Pr 30:5). In Ps 12:6, God's "words" (Hb *ʾimrah*) are "pure" (Hb *tahor*, "unmixed, unalloyed" like purified gold; cp. Ex 25:11; Ps 19:10), directly compared with "silver refined" (Hb *tsaraph*; cp. Is 1:25; 48:10; Jr 9:7; Zch 13:9; Mal 3:2-3; cp. the metaphorical sense of "prove, test, or examine," Ps 17:3; 26:2; 66:10). Notably, in Ps 105:19 a description of the ordeal of the patriarch Joseph links "the word (Hb *ʾimrah*) of the Lord" with the latter use of *tsaraph* ("tested"). To combat temptation and avoid sin, the psalmist has "treasured" God's "word" in the fiber of his being (119:11). Although the psalmist does not explicitly use the imagery, the reader finds more clarity in his boast. Stored up in the "heart," God's pure and purifying "word" is the smelter that constantly tests the thoughts, decisions, and emotions to keep the believer from sinning against God (Heb 4:12-13).

119:27 Wonders (Hb *palaʾ*, "that which is extraordinary or wonderful, miraculous,") is used primarily in Scripture to refer to God's acts, either in nature or in history. Such things are beyond human capabilities and evoke astonishment or wonder.

119:25-31 In Hebrew, verses 25 and 31 begin with the same verb, which is more literally rendered as cling (Hb *davaq*, "cleave, adhere," v. 31). Whether speaking of death being close at hand or engaging in hyperbole (exaggeration used for effect), the request follows logically from the description (Ps 119:25b). The psalmist keenly identifies the means by which God would "give [him] life" (Hb *chayah*, "cause to live, make alive, quicken"; cp. 30:3)—through His "word" (v. 25). Similar expressions of this truth are repeated throughout the psalm (see vv. 37,40,50,88,93,107,116,144,149,154,156,159).

10 I have sought You
with all my heart;
don't let me wander
from Your commands.
11 I have treasured Your word
in my heart
so that I may not sin
against You.
12 Lord, may You be praised;
teach me Your statutes.
13 With my lips I proclaim
all the judgments
from Your mouth.
14 I rejoice in the way
revealed by Your decrees
as much as in all riches.
15 I will meditate on
Your precepts
and think about Your ways.
16 I will delight in Your statutes;
I will not forget Your word.

ג *Gimel*

17 Deal generously
with Your servant
so that I might live;
then I will keep Your word.
18 Open my eyes so that
I may contemplate
wonderful things
from Your instruction.
19 I am a stranger on earth;
do not hide Your commands
from me.
20 I am continually overcome
with longing for
Your judgments.
21 You rebuke the proud,
the ones under a curse,
who wander
from Your commands.
22 Take insult and contempt
away from me,
for I have kept Your decrees.
23 Though princes sit together
speaking against me,
Your servant will think
about Your statutes;
24 Your decrees are my delight
and my counselors.

ד *Dalet*

25 My life is down in the dust;
give me life through
Your word.
26 I told You about my life,
and You listened to me;
teach me Your statutes.
27 Help me understand
the meaning of Your precepts
so that I can meditate on
Your wonders.
28 I am weary[A] from grief;
strengthen me through
Your word.
29 Keep me from the way
of deceit
and graciously give me
Your instruction.
30 I have chosen the way
of truth;
I have set Your ordinances
before me.
31 I cling to Your decrees;
Lord, do not put me to shame.
32 I pursue the way of
Your commands,

praised (Hb *barak*, "be continually blessed"; see **Word Study**, p. 744), a preface to the request to be tutored by God in His **statutes** (119:11-12). The psalmist, in turn, will rehearse everything Yahweh says, rejoicing in His testimonies **as much as in all riches** (vv. 13-14). In addition to learning God's Word by heart, the psalmist **will meditate** (Hb *siyach*, "ponder, rehearse, talk about"—with oneself in silent reflection or speaking aloud with others) and **think about** (Hb *navat*, "regard, consider, give attention to") what God has said and done (v. 15). Undergirding the program of learning to keep God's Word, this section of the poem ends with a vow not only to remember but also to take pleasure in God's Word. Love for God is expressed by obedience to His Word in speech, actions, and attitudes.

119:17-32 For the first time in the poem, the psalmist identifies himself as the Lord's **servant** (Hb *ʿeved*, "slave," v. 17)—i.e., one who reverently and humbly binds himself to God's service. The designation, which appears 14 times in Psalm 119, expresses loyalty and submission to the Lord as his source of life.

In order to **contemplate wonderful things** (Hb *palaʾ*, "that which is done in an extraordinary way," i.e., God's miracles; cp. 119:27) in the Torah, the psalmist recognizes that God must **open** (Hb *galah*, "uncover") his eyes, acknowledging his dependence on the Lord for understanding. As the servant of the prophet Elisha experienced (2Kg 6:15-17), the supernatural character of God's deeds is not necessarily evident without His supernatural revelation. Believers likewise need God's revelation and illumination in order to understand His Word. You cannot see the truths God has for you in His Word without the Spirit's work of illumination in your heart and mind (Jn 16:13).

The psalmist begs God not to **hide** (Hb *satar*, "cover, conceal") His **commands** from him, implying an eagerness to know and practice them (Ps 119:19). He does not want to be counted among those who deserve to be reprimanded and is determined to continue to make God's statues His **delight** (Hb *shaʿashuʿim*, "pleasure," v. 24; cp. verb form *shaʿaʿ*, "will delight," 119:16).

Five verses in this stanza begin with the Hebrew word for "way" (Hb *derek*), which, in each case, is translated according to the word's particular context:

- **my life**—lit "My ways (Hb plural of *derek*) I told You about" (v. 26);
- **the meaning** [Hb *derek*] **of Your precepts** (v. 27);
- **the way of deceit** (v. 29);
- **the way of truth** (v. 30);

[A] **119:28** Or *I weep*

- **the way of your commands** (v. 32).
- **Listened** (Hb *ʿanah*, v. 26) suggests the need for "an answer, a response." God not only heard the prayer; He also responded to the psalmist's need.

The psalmist asks the Lord to **strengthen** (Hb "establish," v. 28) him, recognizing that God's Word is the means by which one is anchored and enabled to stand in life's testing times. God's Word renews the believer's strong desire to live in a way pleasing to the Lord. On one hand, the psalmist acknowledged his utter dependence on the Lord (vv. 25-29); on the other hand, he recognized his responsibility to live in obedience to the Lord and to His Word. The verbs **cling** (v. 31) and **pursue** (v. 32) depict the active participation in doing God's will.

119:33-40 The psalmist prays for the commitment for which he longs but cannot maintain in His own strength. Attitudes of dependency and humility characterize the prayer. The power to keep God's law is revealed to be the result of an act of God's grace in the psalmist's life. The psalmist expresses his desire to follow the Lord's instruction with all his **heart** (v. 34), which, in Hebrew thought, represented the mainspring of an individual's life. It was equivalent to the totality of a person's inner nature. An individual's emotions, thoughts, and will were connected with the heart in Old Testament thinking. Thus the heart was viewed as the seat of not only intellect but also decision making and moral responsibility. The psalmist recognizes the constant danger of being lured away from the Lord by material possessions (v. 36; cp. Mk 10:17-25). **Worthless** (Hb *shawʾ*, "emptiness, vanity, falsehood," v. 37) is the same word sometimes translated "vain" in the third commandment (see Ex 20:7).

119:41-48 The psalmist's expression of lifelong devotion to the Lord is an appropriate response to the Lord's **faithful love** (Hb *chesed*) toward His children (vv. 44-48). **Love** (Hb *ʾahav*, vv. 47-48) is the same term in God's command that His people love Him with their entire beings (Dt 6:5).

119:49-56 The poet affirms his commitment to the Lord in the face of **affliction** and opposition (vv. 50-51). To remember the Lord's **name** does not primarily refer to mental recall but rather to the poet's acting in accord with the Lord's character and reputation (v. 55). Even **in the night**, in the times of adversity and difficulty of his life, the poet remained faithful to the Lord and to His commands and teachings.

>WORD|*study*

119:57-64 The psalmist affirms the Lord as his portion (Hb *chēleq*, "lot, share, part," v. 57). This word commonly refers to a share in an inheritance, typically the share of territory given to the various tribes when they entered the promised land. Aaron and the Levites, who received no such territorial allotment, experienced the Lord as their portion and inheritance (Nm 18:20; Dt 10:9). The Lord is the portion of His people and thus their sufficiency (see Ps 73:26).

The psalmist also affirms his whole-hearted devotion to the Lord (119:58). His love for the Lord is expressed by his attentiveness to hear and obey God's Word (v. 60) and by his fellowship with God's people (v. 63). The psalmist recognizes his dependence on the Lord while also affirming his faith that God would eventually act on his behalf, even though that deliverance might seem delayed from the psalmist's perspective (v. 61).

for You broaden
my understanding.[A]

ה *He*

33 Teach me, LORD, the meaning[B]
of Your statutes,
and I will always keep them.[C]
34 Help me understand
Your instruction,
and I will obey it
and follow it with all
my heart.
35 Help me stay on the path
of Your commands,
for I take pleasure in it.
36 Turn my heart
to Your decrees
and not to material gain.
37 Turn my eyes
from looking at
what is worthless;
give me life in Your ways.[D]
38 Confirm what You said
to Your servant,
for it produces reverence
for You.
39 Turn away the disgrace
I dread;
indeed, Your judgments
are good.
40 How I long for Your precepts!
Give me life through
Your righteousness.

ו *Vav*

41 Let Your faithful love
come to me, LORD,
Your salvation,
as You promised.
42 Then I can answer the one
who taunts me,
for I trust in Your word.
43 Never take the word of truth
from my mouth,
for I hope in Your judgments.
44 I will always obey
Your instruction,
forever and ever.
45 I will walk freely
in an open place
because I seek Your precepts.
46 I will speak of Your decrees
before kings
and not be ashamed.
47 I delight in Your commands,
which I love.
48 I will lift up my hands
to Your commands,
which I love,
and will meditate
on Your statutes.

ז *Zayin*

49 Remember Your word
to Your servant;
You have given me hope
through it.
50 This is my comfort
in my affliction:
Your promise has given
me life.
51 The arrogant constantly
ridicule me,
but I do not turn away
from Your instruction.
52 LORD, I remember
Your judgments
from long ago
and find comfort.
53 Rage seizes me because of
the wicked
who reject Your instruction.
54 Your statutes are the theme of
my song
during my earthly life.[E]

[A]119:32 Lit *You enlarge my heart* [B]119:33 Lit *way* [C]119:33 Or *will keep it as my reward*
[D]119:37 Some Hb mss, Tg read *word* [E]119:54 Lit *song in the house of my sojourning*

55 •Yahweh, I remember
Your name in the night,
and I obey Your instruction.
56 This is my practice:
I obey Your precepts.

ח *Khet*

57 The LORD is my portion;[A]
I have promised to keep
Your words.
58 I have sought Your favor
with all my heart;
be gracious to me
according to Your promise.
59 I thought about my ways
and turned my steps back
to Your decrees.
60 I hurried, not hesitating
to keep Your commands.
61 Though the ropes
of the wicked
were wrapped around me,
I did not forget
Your instruction.
62 I rise at midnight
to thank You
for Your righteous judgments.
63 I am a friend to all
who •fear You,
to those who keep
Your precepts.
64 LORD, the earth is filled with
Your faithful love;
teach me Your statutes.

ט *Tet*

65 LORD, You have treated
Your servant well,
just as You promised.
66 Teach me good judgment
and discernment,
for I rely on Your commands.
67 Before I was afflicted
I went astray,
but now I keep Your word.
68 You are good, and You do
what is good;
teach me Your statutes.
69 The arrogant
have smeared me with lies,
but I obey Your precepts
with all my heart.
70 Their hearts are hard
and insensitive,
but I delight in
Your instruction.
71 It was good for me
to be afflicted
so that I could learn
Your statutes.
72 Instruction from Your lips
is better for me
than thousands of gold
and silver pieces.

י *Yod*

73 Your hands made me
and formed me;
give me understanding
so that I can learn
Your commands.
74 Those who fear You
will see me and rejoice,
for I put my hope
in Your word.
75 I know, LORD,
that Your judgments
are just
and that You have afflicted me
fairly.
76 May Your faithful love
comfort me
as You promised Your servant.
77 May Your compassion
come to me
so that I may live,
for Your instruction is
my delight.
78 Let the arrogant be
put to shame
for slandering me with lies;
I will meditate on
Your precepts.
79 Let those who fear You,
those who know Your decrees,
turn to me.
80 May my heart be blameless
regarding Your statutes
so that I will not be put
to shame.

כ *Kaf*

81 I long for Your salvation;
I put my hope in Your word.
82 My eyes grow weary
looking for what
You have promised;
I ask, "When will You
comfort me?"
83 Though I have become
like a wineskin dried
by smoke,
I do not forget Your statutes.

[A]**119:57** Lit *You are my portion, LORD*

119:65-72 This stanza affirms the Lord's goodness. The psalmist recognizes that the affliction he suffered had the positive purpose and outcome of leading him to a greater obedience to and closer fellowship with the Lord (v. 67). The psalmist has seen that the Lord keeps His promises and his faith is strengthened (v. 65). He contrasts his mindset (**heart**) of obedience with that of his enemies, **their hearts are hard and insensitive** (vv. 69-70). The Lord's discipline has changed this psalmist's life because he has responded to it in a positive way. In a world with its primary focus on materialism and its continual devaluation of human life, this poet's affirmation that a right relationship with the Lord (evidenced by the value placed on obedience to His instruction) is of greater value than large sums of gold and silver is a much-needed message (v. 72).

119:73-80 The psalmist acknowledges the Lord's intimate involvement with him from the beginning of his existence. The reference to the Lord's **hands** recalls the account of His forming Adam from the dust of the earth and breathing into him the breath of life (Gn 2:7). The psalmist recognizes the Lord as the source of **understanding** (Hb *bin*, "discernment," v. 73) for learning God's commands. Only the Creator knows best the guidelines that His creation should follow in order to live meaningful, purposeful lives. Do God's people pray for understanding as they diligently apply themselves to the study of His Word? What would be the result? By faithfully learning God's requirements and obeying them, you serve as a source of encouragement to others **who fear** Him (v. 74).

The believer's hope lies in God's Word (v. 74b; cp. 119:43,49). God is faithful even in times of affliction (vv. 75-77). The discipline of His children is one aspect of His **faithful love** (Hb *chesed*, "covenant loyalty," v. 76; see **Word Study**, p. 322). By identifying himself as God's **servant**, the psalmist acknowledges God's lordship in his life (v. 76). He owes his life to the Lord's **compassion** (Hb *racham*, "mercy," v. 77; see **Word Study**, p. 679). While the poet of Psalm 119 prays that his enemies will **be put to shame** (v. 78), he equally requests that the Lord will keep him from being **put to shame** (v. 80). He prays for his **heart**—his entire being with particular emphasis on his mind and will—to be **blameless** (v. 80).

119:81-88 In this stanza, which represents the halfway point of the psalm, the psalmist's longing for the Lord's intervention seems to reach a climax. See **Word Study**, p. 762

119:89-96 In this section the psalmist's focus shifts from his need to the stability and salvation available through God's Word. God's Word is **firmly fixed in heaven**; it stands **forever** (v. 89; cp. Is 40:8; 1 Pt 1:25). There is constancy and order in all of God's creation both in heaven and on **earth** (Ps 119:90). Thus, creation itself, despite the effects of human sin, reflects the Lord's **faithfulness** (v. 90). God established His world with a natural order as well as with a moral order that remains constant (Rm 1:18-25). The psalmist repeatedly identifies himself as the Lord's servant in preceding stanzas (Ps 119:17,23,38,49,65,76,84). In this section he also recognizes that **all things are** the Lord's **servants** (v. 91). The psalmist realizes he would not have survived his ordeal if the Lord's **instruction had not been** his **delight** (v. 92). This preservation of the psalmist's life is connected with his covenantal relationship with the Lord—**I am Yours** (v. 94). God's commands give freedom and a new lease on life to those who obey them (v. 96).

119:97-104 The psalmist continues to praise God's Word, which gives wisdom (vv. 97-98). Even the person considered uneducated by the world's standards can have the wisdom that truly matters by diligently studying God's Word and putting its teachings into practice (vv. 98-100). The truly wise woman is not the one who merely accumulates mental knowledge of God's Word but the one who obeys it. Rejecting God's instruction is equivalent to rejecting the Lord Himself. Following the path of righteousness stands in total opposition to choosing the **evil path** (vv. 101,104). God's Word and accompanying fellowship with Him are **sweet** to those who obey Him (v. 103).

119:105-112 God's Word provides **light** or guidance through life (v. 105; cp. Jn 8:12). The psalmist is committed to obeying God's Word (vv. 106,112) and acknowledges that it is the source of his **life** (v. 107). Although godly living is never easy, the psalmist determines to remain faithful to the Lord even though his life is in constant danger (vv. 109-110). In the midst of difficult circumstances, he experiences joy because of his relationship with the Lord and his commitment to God's Word (v. 111).

>WORD|*study*

119:81-88 The Hebrew text uniquely emphasizes the total anguish the psalmist experienced through the threefold use of the verb *kalah*, a root that basically means "to be finished." The phrase translated I long for (Hb *kalah*, v. 81) is better understood "my soul faints or is finished." Likewise, My eyes grow weary (Hb *kalah*, v. 82) is more literally "my eyes fail" (are finished). Finally, the psalmist acknowledges that his enemies almost ended (Hb *kalah*, v. 87) his life (i.e., they "almost finished me"). The threefold repetition of a single concept in Hebrew thought signifies its totality or significance. This psalmist, therefore, expresses the feeling of being completely overwhelmed by anguish.

Even in this most trying of circumstances, however, the psalmist maintains his commitment to the Lord's Word (vv. 81,83,86-87), his dependence on the Lord as he waited for Him to act (v. 84), and his steadfast faith in the Lord's **faithful love** (Hb *chesed*, "covenant loyalty," v. 88; see **Word Study**, p. 322).

84 How many days must
Your servant wait?
When will You
execute judgment
on my persecutors?
85 The arrogant have dug pits
for me;
they violate Your instruction.
86 All Your commands are true;
people persecute me
with lies—help me!
87 They almost ended my life
on earth,
but I did not abandon
Your precepts.
88 Give me life in accordance
with Your faithful love,
and I will obey the decree
You have spoken.

ל *Lamed*

89 LORD, Your word is forever;
it is firmly fixed in heaven.
90 Your faithfulness is
for all generations;
You established the earth,
and it stands firm.
91 They stand today
in accordance with
Your judgments,
for all things are
Your servants.
92 If Your instruction
had not been my delight,
I would have died
in my affliction.
93 I will never forget
Your precepts,
for You have given me life
through them.
94 I am Yours; save me,
for I have sought
Your precepts.
95 The wicked hope to destroy
me,
but I contemplate
Your decrees.
96 I have seen a limit
to all perfection,
but Your command is
without limit.

מ *Mem*

97 How I love Your instruction!
It is my meditation all
day long.
98 Your commands make me
wiser than my enemies,
for they are always with me.
99 I have more insight than
all my teachers
because Your decrees are
my meditation.
100 I understand more
than the elders
because I obey Your precepts.
101 I have kept my feet
from every evil path
to follow Your word.
102 I have not turned from
Your judgments,
for You Yourself have
instructed me.
103 How sweet Your word is
to my taste—
sweeter than honey in
my mouth.
104 I gain understanding
from Your precepts;
therefore I hate
every false way.

נ *Nun*

105 Your word is a lamp
for my feet
and a light on my path.
106 I have solemnly sworn
to keep
Your righteous judgments.
107 I am severely afflicted;

>WORD|*study*

119:113-120 The word translated **double-minded** (Hb *sēʿēph*, "divided,") occurs only here in the Old Testament. The psalm sharply contrasts those who are "double-minded" persons (who have divided loyalties) with the speaker (who has repeatedly expressed his single-minded devotion to the Lord).

119:114 The psalmist depicts the Lord as his **shelter** (Hb *sether*) and **shield** (Hb *magēn*)—imagery that conveys the idea of protection and testifies, as in other stanzas, that his hope is in God's Word (v. 114; cp. 119:43,49,74,81). "Shelter" conveys the sense of a hiding place, a secret place not known by enemies.

Lord, give me life
through Your word.
108 Lord, please accept
my willing offerings
of praise,
and teach me
Your judgments.
109 My life is constantly
in danger,[A]
yet I do not forget
Your instruction.
110 The wicked have set a trap
for me,
but I have not wandered
from Your precepts.
111 I have Your decrees
as a heritage forever;
indeed, they are the joy
of my heart.
112 I am resolved to obey
Your statutes
to the very end.[B]

ס *Samek*

113 I hate those who are
double-minded,
but I love Your instruction.
114 You are my shelter
and my shield;
I put my hope in Your word.
115 Depart from me,
you evil ones,
so that I may obey
my God's commands.
116 Sustain me as You promised,
and I will live;
do not let me be ashamed
of my hope.
117 Sustain me so that I can
be safe
and always be concerned
about Your statutes.
118 You reject all who stray
from Your statutes,
for their deceit is a lie.
119 You remove all the wicked
on earth
as if they were[C] dross;
therefore, I love Your decrees.
120 I tremble[D] in awe of You;
I fear Your judgments.

ע *Ayin*

121 I have done what is just
and right;
do not leave me to
my oppressors.
122 Guarantee Your servant's
well-being;
do not let the arrogant
oppress me.
123 My eyes grow weary
looking for Your salvation
and for Your righteous
promise.
124 Deal with Your servant
based on Your faithful love;
teach me Your statutes.
125 I am Your servant;
give me understanding
so that I may know
Your decrees.
126 It is time for the Lord to act,
for they have violated
Your instruction.
127 Since I love Your commands
more than gold,
even the purest gold,
128 I carefully follow[E] all
Your precepts
and hate every false way.

פ *Pe*

129 Your decrees are wonderful;
therefore I obey them.
130 The revelation of Your words
brings light
and gives understanding
to the inexperienced.
131 I open my mouth and pant

119:121-128 The psalmist expresses a degree of impatience in waiting on the Lord (vv. 123,126). He identifies his enemies as the Lord's adversaries by stating that they had **violated** God's **instruction** (v. 126). In contrast the speaker's devotion to the Lord is reflected both in his teachable spirit (vv. 124-125) and in his obedience to God's commands (v. 128).

119:129-136 The psalmist is so consumed with zeal for God's Word that he weeps because the people fail to obey it (v. 136).

[A]**119:109** Lit *in my hand* [B]**119:112** Or *statutes; the reward is eternal* [C]**119:119** Some Hb mss, DSS, LXX, Aq, Sym, Jer read *All the wicked of the earth You count as* [D]**119:120** Lit *My flesh shudders* [E]**119:128** Lit *I therefore follow carefully*

119:137-144 Continuing to identify himself as the Lord's **servant** (v. 140), the psalmist affirms the righteousness of the Lord and His Word while expressing his anger over his enemies, who fail to acknowledge it. Despite his experience of trouble and distress, the psalmist continues to find **delight** in God's Word (v. 143). In anguish he clings to his faith in the Lord—not challenging the Lord's integrity but instead humbly praying for understanding (v. 144).

119:145-152 The earnest nature of the petitioner's cry to the Lord for deliverance is expressed in the words **with all my heart,** a reference to the poet's entire being (v. 145). The request for the Lord to **answer** is equivalent to an appeal for Him to act on the psalmist's behalf (v. 145). The psalmist based his confident expectation that the Lord would hear him on the Lord's **faithful love** (Hb *chesed*, "covenant loyalty, steadfast devotion," v. 149; see **Word Study**, p. 322). He affirms God's Word as his source of hope (v. 147; cp. 119:43,49,74,81,114). The poet recognizes the enduring nature of God's Word (v. 152).

119:153-160 This stanza begins with a series of petitions for the Lord to **consider, rescue**, **defend**, **redeem**, and **give . . . life** to the psalmist (vv. 153-154). The psalmist calls attention to the multitude of the Lord's **compassions** (Hb *racham*, v. 156; see **Word Study**, p. 679) and reaffirms his loyalty to God's Word despite his numerous **persecutors and foes** (119:157). In verse 160, as in verse 152, he returned to the theme of the permanence of God's Word.

119:161-168 Godly people can experience joy and blessings even in the midst of persecution. God's **instruction** (Hb *torah*; see note on p. 682 and chart on p. 758)—i.e., His Word—is the source of the poet's deep and abiding joy. Observe the contrast between **falsehood** and the Lord's "instruction" (v. 163)—God's Word is truth. To love this truth is to find **vast treasure** (Hb *shalal*, "spoil, booty," v. 162), a word commonly referring to the plunder taken by those victorious in battle. The psalmist rejoices over the value of God's Word as others rejoice over spoil taken in war. The reference to **seven times** signifies fullness or completion (v. 164). The psalmist knows that all praise belongs to the Lord. He also experiences the abundant peace (Hb *shalom*, "wholeness," v. 165) that characterizes those in right relationship with the Lord. The Hebrew word translated "peace" refers to much more than the absence of conflict. It conveys completeness and well-being. Motivated by love for the Lord, the psalmist faithfully obeys God's laws as

because I long
for Your commands.
132 Turn to me and be gracious
to me,
as is Your practice
toward those who love
Your name.
133 Make my steps steady
through Your promise;
don't let any sin
dominate me.
134 Redeem me
from human oppression,
and I will keep Your precepts.
135 Show favor to Your servant,
and teach me Your statutes.
136 My eyes pour out streams
of tears
because people do not follow
Your instruction.

צ *Tsade*

137 You are righteous, LORD,
and Your judgments are just.
138 The decrees You issue
are righteous
and altogether trustworthy.
139 My anger overwhelms me
because my foes forget
Your words.
140 Your word is completely pure,
and Your servant loves it.
141 I am insignificant
and despised,
but I do not forget
Your precepts.
142 Your righteousness is an
everlasting righteousness,
and Your instruction is true.
143 Trouble and distress
have overtaken me,
but Your commands are
my delight.
144 Your decrees are
righteous forever.
Give me understanding,
and I will live.

ק *Qof*

145 I call with all my heart;
answer me, LORD.
I will obey Your statutes.
146 I call to You; save me,
and I will keep Your decrees.
147 I rise before dawn and cry out
for help;
I put my hope in Your word.
148 I am awake through
each watch of the night
to meditate on Your promise.
149 In keeping with
Your faithful love,
hear my voice.
LORD, give me life
in keeping with
Your justice.
150 Those who pursue evil plans[A]
come near;
they are far from
Your instruction.
151 You are near, LORD,
and all Your commands
are true.
152 Long ago I learned from
Your decrees
that You have established
them forever.

ר *Resh*

153 Consider my affliction
and rescue me,
for I have not forgotten
Your instruction.
154 Defend my cause
and redeem me;
give me life as You promised.
155 Salvation is far
from the wicked
because they do not seek
Your statutes.
156 Your compassions are many,
LORD;
give me life according to
Your judgments.
157 My persecutors and foes
are many.
I have not turned
from Your decrees.
158 I have seen the disloyal
and feel disgust
because they do not keep
Your word.
159 Consider how I love
Your precepts;
LORD, give me life according to
Your faithful love.
160 The entirety of Your word
is truth,
and all Your righteous
judgments endure forever.

[A]**119:150** Some Hb mss, LXX, Sym, Jer read *who maliciously persecute me*

ש Sin/ ש Shin

161 Princes have persecuted me
without cause,
but my heart fears only
Your word.
162 I rejoice over Your promise
like one who finds
vast treasure.
163 I hate and abhor falsehood,
but I love Your instruction.
164 I praise You seven times a day
for Your righteous judgments.
165 Abundant peace belongs
to those
who love Your instruction;
nothing makes them stumble.
166 LORD, I hope for
Your salvation
and carry out
Your commands.
167 I obey Your decrees
and love them greatly.
168 I obey Your precepts
and decrees,
for all my ways are
before You.

ת Tav

169 Let my cry reach You, LORD;
give me understanding
according to Your word.
170 Let my plea reach You;
rescue me according to
Your promise.
171 My lips pour out praise,
for You teach me
Your statutes.
172 My tongue sings
about Your promise,
for all Your commands
are righteous.
173 May Your hand be ready
to help me,
for I have chosen
Your precepts.
174 I long for Your salvation,
LORD,
and Your instruction is
my delight.
175 Let me live, and I will
praise You;
may Your judgments help me.
176 I wander like a lost sheep;
seek Your servant,
for I do not forget
Your commands.

Psalm 120

A Cry for Truth and Peace

A •song of ascents.

1 In my distress I called
to the LORD,
and He answered me.
2 "LORD, deliver me
from lying lips
and a deceitful tongue."

3 What will He give you,
and what will He do to you,
you deceitful tongue?
4 A warrior's sharp arrows
with burning charcoal![A]

5 What misery that I have
stayed in Meshech,[B]
that I have lived among
the tents of Kedar![C]
6 I have lived too long
with those who hate peace.
7 I am for peace;
but when I speak,
they are for war.

Psalm 121

The LORD Our Protector

A •song of ascents.

1 I lift my eyes
toward the mountains.
Where will my help
come from?
2 My help comes from the LORD,
the Maker of heaven
and earth.

3 He will not allow your foot
to slip;
your Protector will not
slumber.
4 Indeed, the Protector of Israel
does not slumber or sleep.
5 The LORD protects you;
the LORD is a shelter right
by your side.[D]
6 The sun will not strike you
by day
or the moon by night.

7 The LORD will protect you
from all harm;
He will protect your life.
8 The LORD will protect
your coming and going
both now and forever.

[A]**120:4** Lit *with coals of the broom bush* [B]**120:5** = a people far to the north of Palestine [C]**120:5** = a nomadic people of the desert to the southeast [D]**121:5** Lit *is your shelter at your right hand*

he awaits the Lord's deliverance (vv. 166-168).

119:169-176 The final stanza of this psalm constitutes a plea for deliverance in order that the psalmist might praise the Lord (v. 175; cp. 51:14-15). He, however, had nothing to offer but a cry and a plea. His words reflect a posture of total dependency on the Lord. His appeal for **understanding** expresses his desire to know God's Word and to discern how to respond to his present difficulties in a manner that reflected his faith in the Lord (v. 169). In faith the psalmist anticipates joyfully expressing thanks for the Lord's answer to his prayer. God's **hand** represents His power to deliver His children (v. 173). This stanza reiterates a common theme of the entire poem—faithfulness to God's Word.

120:1–134:3 This collection of 15 pilgrim psalms is called the Songs of Ascents or the Songs of Degrees. Although the songs of ascents may not have originally been composed for the purpose of being sung by pilgrims on their way to Jerusalem, they probably were also sung by worshipers as they went up to the holy city to celebrate the great festivals each year. Some scholars believe the psalms were sung as the pilgrims actually ascended the steps of the temple itself. Some of the individual psalms reflect other purposes, but as a collection they accurately reflect not only the journey of the pilgrim to Jerusalem but also progression in the Christian life. In addition, these psalms constitute a major part of what are known as the Great *Hallēl* psalms (Pss 120–136).

120:1-7 The psalmist already has received assurance that the Lord will deal with those who oppress him. Yet, finding himself in a hostile environment, he cries out for deliverance from **lying** [Hb *sheqer*, "false, empty, deceptive speech"] **lips and a deceitful** [Hb *remiyah*, "fraudulent"] **tongue** (vv. 2-3). As fitting punishment, the "deceitful tongue" will receive **a warrior's sharp arrows, with burning charcoal** (Hb *gechel*, "live coals" of *rotem*, "broom bush or juniper," v. 4). The psalmist has grown miserable in his current location. Both **Meshech** and **Kedar** refer to places inhabited by people groups the psalmist might have directly described as war-mongering or contentious. Likely he is metaphorically referring to the hostile people of whom he is weary. The psalmist longs for **peace** (Hb *shalom*, "well-being, wholeness," v. 7); his enemies want conflict.

121:1-8 Looking upward to the **mountains**, whether to the hills on which Jerusalem stood or, more generally, in the direction of the highest point at which earth and sky meet, the psalmist's position reflects his realization that the **help** he needs will have to **come** from somewhere else, perhaps from a person or place far outside himself and his resources. The rest of the psalm elaborates on the ways in which **the Lord,** Creator of both the heavens and the earth, which meet at the distant horizon point, is the single answer to his question.

122:1-9 The first song of ascents to be identified as Davidic constitutes a prayer for **the peace** [Hb *shalom*, "wholeness, security, well-being"] **of Jerusalem**. The psalmist rejoices over the opportunity for worship in God's **house** (i.e., the temple) there. Such pilgrimages typically were made three times a year—at the Festivals of Passover, of Firstfruits or Pentecost, and of Booths or Tabernacles. The unity of the city reflected the unity of the tribes of Israel as they came together for worship on these special occasions.

123:1-4 The psalm has characteristics of lament. Having experienced scorn and ridicule, the psalmist appeals to **the One enthroned** [Hb *yashav*, "one who is sitting" as a judge or ruler on his throne, "one who dwells in or inhabits"; cp. Is 6:1] **in heaven** (cp. 121:1-2). Speaking for the community, comprised of both men and women, the psalmist compares their attitude of worship to the fastidious attention of servants who try to anticipate the master's commands and who eagerly yet patiently await the provision and **favor** upon which they are completely dependent.

124:1-8 God receives praise for bringing victory to His people. Vivid imagery of preservation from a flood (vv. 4-5) and escape from a fowler's snare (vv. 6-7) convey the desperation of need met by the Lord.

125:1-5 Unshakable and immovable **Mount Zion**, on which the temple was built, represents God's help, protection, and blessings—the privileges belonging to those in covenant relationship with Him. **Mountains** in general symbolize stability and security. The **scepter of the wicked**—i.e., the power of those who oppose God—and the injustice that characterizes their treatment of God's people is only temporary. Those who choose the straight and right paths stand in contrast to those who choose paths that twist and turn from God's way. Such persons will ultimately reap God's judgment and experience separation from Him.

Psalm 122

A Prayer for Jerusalem

A Davidic •song of ascents.

1 I rejoiced with those who said
to me,
"Let us go to the house
of the LORD."
2 Our feet are standing
within your gates, Jerusalem—

3 Jerusalem, built as a city
should be,
solidly joined together,
4 where the tribes, •Yahweh's
tribes, go up
to give thanks to the name
of Yahweh.
(This is an ordinance
for Israel.)
5 There, thrones for judgment
are placed,
thrones of the house of David.

6 Pray for the peace
of Jerusalem:
"May those who love you
prosper;
7 may there be peace
within your walls,
prosperity
within your fortresses."
8 Because of my brothers
and friends,
I will say, "Peace be with you."
9 Because of the house
of the LORD our God,
I will seek your good.

Psalm 123

Looking for God's Favor

A •song of ascents.

1 I lift my eyes to You,
the One enthroned in heaven.
2 Like a servant's eyes
on his master's hand,
like a servant girl's eyes
on her mistress's hand,
so our eyes are on the LORD
our God
until He shows us favor.

3 Show us favor, LORD, show us
favor,
for we've had more than
enough contempt.
4 We've had more than enough
scorn from the arrogant
and contempt from the proud.

Psalm 124

The Power of the LORD

A Davidic •song of ascents.

1 If the LORD had not been
on our side—
let Israel say—
2 If the LORD had not been
on our side
when men attacked us,
3 then they would have
swallowed us alive
in their burning anger
against us.
4 Then the waters would have
engulfed us;
the torrent would have swept
over us;
5 the raging waters would have
swept over us.

6 Praise the LORD,
who has not let us be
ripped apart by their teeth.
7 We have escaped like a bird
from the hunter's net;
the net is torn,
and we have escaped.
8 Our help is in the name
of •Yahweh,
the Maker of heaven
and earth.

Psalm 125

Israel's Stability

A •song of ascents.

1 Those who trust in the LORD
are like Mount •Zion.
It cannot be shaken;
it remains forever.
2 Jerusalem—the mountains
surround her.
And the LORD surrounds
His people,
both now and forever.

3 The scepter of the wicked
will not remain
over the land allotted
to the righteous,
so that the righteous
will not apply their hands
to injustice.
4 Do what is good, LORD,
to the good,
to those whose hearts
are upright.
5 But as for those

>WORD|*study*

128:3 In most contexts, fruitful (Hb *parah*; cp. Gn 17:6; 28:3; 48:4; Ex 1:7) denotes abundant reproduction and, consequently, increased numbers. This verb appears frequently in God's commands to "be fruitful," often coupled with the parallel imperative to "multiply" (e.g., Gn 1:22,28; 8:17; 9:1,7; 35:11; cp. Lv 26:9). Clearly, the psalmist regards a wife's bearing many healthy **sons** as evidence of the couple's fertility and therefore of their blessedness. The numerous "sons" are compared to **young olive trees**, a symbol of long life and productivity.

128:3 Young (Hb *shetil*, "plant shoots") is from the verb *shalal* (Hb "plant"), which implies intention or deliberate choice (see Ps 1:3; 92:13; Jr 17:8; Ezk 17:8,10,22-23; 19:10,13; Hs 9:13). The sons surrounding a man's dinner *table* represent more than mere progeny. Like a carefully planted olive orchard, these cherished children are being nurtured in the ways of the Lord, the source of blessedness described in the psalm (cp. 144:12). The sons represent hope and the extension of Yahweh's favor to succeeding generations.

who turn aside
to crooked ways,
the LORD will banish them
with the evildoers.

Peace be with Israel.

Psalm 126

Zion's Restoration

A •song of ascents.

1 When the LORD restored
the fortunes of •Zion,[A]
we were like those
who dream.
2 Our mouths were filled
with laughter then,
and our tongues with shouts
of joy.
Then they said
among the nations,
"The LORD has done
great things for them."
3 The LORD had done
great things for us;
we were joyful.

4 Restore our fortunes,[B]
LORD,
like watercourses
in the •Negev.
5 Those who sow in tears
will reap with shouts
of joy.
6 Though one goes along
weeping,
carrying the bag
of seed,
he will surely come back
with shouts of joy,
carrying his sheaves.

Psalm 127

The Blessing of the LORD

A Solomonic •song of ascents.

1 Unless the LORD builds
a house,
its builders labor over it
in vain;
unless the LORD watches over
a city,
the watchman stays alert
in vain.
2 In vain you get up early
and stay up late,
working hard to have
enough food—
yes, He gives sleep to the one
He loves.[C]

3 Sons are indeed a heritage
from the LORD,
children, a reward.
4 Like arrows in the hand
of a warrior
are the sons born in
one's youth.
5 Happy is the man
who has filled his quiver
with them.
Such men will never be put
to shame
when they speak
with their enemies
at the city •gate.

Psalm 128

Blessings for Those Who Fear God

A •song of ascents.

1 How happy is everyone
who •fears the LORD,
who walks in His ways!

[A]126:1 Or *LORD returned those of Zion who had been captives* [B]126:4 Or *Return our captives* [C]127:2 Or *yes, He gives such things to His loved ones while they sleep*

126:1-6 The psalmist focuses on the joyful return of the exiles from captivity in Babylon as permitted by the decree of Cyrus, king of Persia, in 539–538 B.C. (see Ezr 1:1-4). In this **song of ascents**, the psalmist encouraged God's people to persevere, despite the new adversities they encountered, knowing that better days lay ahead (cp. Ps 85).

127:1-2 This is the only **song of ascents** connected with Solomon (cp. Ps 72). **Solomonic** can mean "to Solomon," "for Solomon," or "by Solomon." It conveys the sense of "belonging to" Solomon either in the sense of authorship or of this psalm belonging to his collection.

Without the blessing of the Lord, all human effort is **vain** (Hb *shav'*, "emptiness, worthlessness, futility") morally or materially bankrupt.

127:3-5 The Hebrews regarded children, especially **sons**, as a blessing from the Lord (see Gn 13:16; Ru 4:13-16; 1Sm 1:11). Through the gift of godly sons the perpetuity of the family of faith was assured. **Children**—literally, "fruit (Hb *peri*, "fruit," metaphorically the result of labor) of the womb" (Hb *beten*, "womb"; cp. Gn 30:2; Dt 7:13; 28:4)—are:

- **a heritage** [Hb *nachalah*, "inheritance, allotment, special possession"; cp. 28:9; Pr 19:14] **from the LORD**—a gift to be extended perpetually from one generation to the next; and
- **a reward** (Hb *sakar*, "wages"; cp. Gn 30:18; Ec 4:9)—the positive benefit immediately received in return for one's work.

The Lord provides a sense of security and protection to the families who have faith in Him. The psalmist declares, **Happy** [Hb *'esher*; see note on 1:1-2; cp. 34:8; 40:4; 94:12; 128:4] **is the man** who is like **a warrior** with plenty of **arrows** ready to shoot—either as offensive or defensive weapons. The imagery presupposes that the warrior has a bow and is of sufficient strength and experience to handle it properly. Extending the picture, **they**—presumably such a man "equipped" with his many well-trained and self-controlled sons—constitute a formidable presence that would deter enemy attack.

128:1-6 The shared themes of Ps 127 and Ps 128 invite readers to view them as a pair. Psalm 128 declares the blessings of **everyone who fears the LORD** (v. 1; cp. v. 4; see **Word Study**, p. 784). The positive results of walking **in His ways** and thereby demonstrating authentic reverence for the Lord are depicted in terms of productive work and a thriving family. See **Word Study**, v. 3, p. 767.

129:1-4 In this **song of ascents**, the people of Israel recall those who had afflicted them in the past. God's people had suffered repeatedly at the hands of their enemies, and God again and again had delivered His people (cp. 124:1-2). Agricultural imagery is used to depict how Israel's enemies have treated the people. The **plowmen** represent the adversaries who had inflicted wounds on God's people as severe as deep **furrows** in a long field. Nevertheless, the Lord had delivered His people on the basis of His own righteousness. The imagery then changes to that of a yoked animal whose **ropes** have been **cut** to set it free.

129:5-8 Following a prayer for divine judgment on the enemies of God's people, the psalm concludes with a threefold curse on Israel's enemies, who are viewed also as the Lord's enemies.

130:1-4 This song of ascents is also one of the seven penitential psalms recognized by the ancient church. In the Old Testament, **depths** (Hb *ma'amaqqim*, "deep places") always describes water in the sense of its overwhelming power to drown (69:2,14; Is 51:10; Ezk 27:34). Such "depths" serve as a metaphor for the human experience of trouble, guilt, or destruction, from which there is no possibility of escape or survival without God's intervention (cp. Jonah's experience, Jnh 2:3-5). The psalm links "the depths" with a fear that should grip every human heart: What if the Lord held on to **sins** (Hb *'awon*, "iniquity, depraved action, crime" and often the "guilt" incurred therefrom; one of the main Hebrew terms for sin) with no hope of His ever overlooking them?

130:5-8 Personal and corporate worship are modeled in terms of expressing **hope** (Hb *qawah*, "expect, fix one's hope upon") in the certain fulfillment of God's **word** and His promised **redemption**. The psalmist

2 You will surely eat
what your hands
have worked for.
You will be happy,
and it will go well for you.
3 Your wife will be
like a fruitful vine
within your house,
your sons,
like young olive trees
around your table.
4 In this very way
the man who fears the LORD
will be blessed.

5 May the LORD bless you
from •Zion,
so that you will see
the prosperity of Jerusalem
all the days of your life
6 and will see your children's
children!

Peace be with Israel.

Psalm 129

Protection of the Oppressed

A •song of ascents.

1 Since my youth they
have often attacked me—
let Israel say—
2 Since my youth they have
often attacked me,
but they have not prevailed
against me.
3 Plowmen plowed
over my back;
they made their furrows long.
4 The LORD is righteous;
He has cut the ropes
of the wicked.
5 Let all who hate •Zion
be driven back in disgrace.
6 Let them be like grass
on the rooftops,
which withers before
it grows up[A]
7 and can't even fill the hands
of the reaper
or the arms of the one
who binds sheaves.
8 Then none who pass by
will say,
"May the LORD's blessing be
on you."

We bless you in the name
of •Yahweh.

Psalm 130

Awaiting Redemption

A •song of ascents.

1 Out of the depths I call
to You, •Yahweh!
2 Lord, listen to my voice;
let Your ears be attentive
to my cry for help.

3 Yahweh, if You considered
sins,
Lord, who could stand?
4 But with You there is
forgiveness,
so that You may be revered.

5 I wait for Yahweh; I wait
and put my hope in His word.
6 I wait for the Lord
more than watchmen
for the morning—
more than watchmen
for the morning.

[A]129:6 Or *it can be pulled out*

BIBLICAL WOMANHOOD Monogamy

Because God's basic design for the family is constantly the target of the enemy's efforts to destroy what he cannot have, women who belong to and live for the Lord are wise to embrace His plan as revealed in Scripture (128:1-6). Notably in this psalm, **wife** (Hb *'ishshah*) is singular, reflecting the ideal of monogamous marriage rather than the pattern of taking multiple wives, which was commonly adopted particularly by royalty. In Hebrew, **your**—the noun's possessive ending—is [ma]sculine singular, reflecting an assumption of the [bibli]cal pattern for the family (i.e., that a God-fearing household begins with the marriage of a man and woman). Homosexual partnerships are implicitly excluded from the psalm's snapshot of the household of **the man who fears the LORD** and is, therefore, **blessed**; such deviation is explicitly forbidden elsewhere (Lv 18:22,24; 20:13; Dt 23:17; 1Co 6:9-10; cp. Gn 19 and 2Pt 2:6-10; Jd 7). The comparison of the wife to **a fruitful vine**, immediately followed by the mention of **sons**, makes this implication unmistakable, since non-heterosexual unions cannot produce children.

>WORD|study

130:4 Forgiveness (Hb *selichah*, "pardon"; cp. 25:11; Neh 9:17; Dn 9:9) comes from the verb "forgive" (Hb *salach*, "pardon, be merciful"), which is used in Scripture solely to refer to God's forgiveness of sin. It is never used of people's forgiving one another. God had prescribed sacrificial offerings (e.g., Lv 4:20,26,31,35) as a provisional means of "forgiving" His people's sins.

7 Israel, put your hope
in the LORD.
For there is faithful love
with the LORD,
and with Him is redemption
in abundance.
8 And He will redeem Israel
from all its sins.

Psalm 131
A Childlike Spirit

A Davidic •*song of ascents.*

1 LORD, my heart is not proud;
my eyes are not haughty.
I do not get involved
with things
too great or too difficult
for me.
2 Instead, I have calmed
and quieted myself
like a little weaned child
with its mother;
I am like a little child.

3 Israel, put your hope
in the LORD,
both now and forever.

Psalm 132
The Choice of David and Zion

A •*song of ascents.*

1 LORD, remember David
and all the hardships
he endured,
2 and how he swore an oath
to the LORD,
making a vow
to the Mighty One of Jacob:
3 "I will not enter my house[A]
or get into my bed,[B]
4 I will not allow my eyes
to sleep
or my eyelids to slumber
5 until I find a place
for the LORD,
a dwelling for the Mighty One
of Jacob."

6 We heard of the ark
in Ephrathah;[C]
we found it in the fields
of Jaar.[D]
7 Let us go
to His dwelling place;
let us worship
at His footstool.
8 Rise up, LORD, come to
Your resting place,
You and Your powerful ark.
9 May Your priests be clothed
with righteousness,
and may Your godly people
shout for joy.
10 Because of
Your servant David,
do not reject
Your anointed one.[E]

11 The LORD swore an oath
to David,
a promise He will not
abandon:
"I will set
one of your descendants[F]
on your throne.
12 If your sons keep My covenant
and My decrees
that I will teach them,
their sons will also sit on
your throne forever."

13 For the LORD has chosen
•Zion;
He has desired it
for His home:
14 "This is My resting
place forever;
I will make My home here
because I have desired it.
15 I will abundantly bless
its food;
I will satisfy its needy
with bread.
16 I will clothe its priests
with salvation,
and its godly people will shout
for joy.

[A]**132:3** Lit *enter the tent of my house* [B]**132:3** Lit *into the couch of my bed* [C]**132:6** = Bethlehem
[D]**132:6** = Kiriath-jearim [E]**132:10** = the king [F]**132:11** Lit *set the fruit of your womb*

waits just as expectantly as **watchmen** wait for the dawn in order to experience the Lord's deliverance. In turn, he encourages **Israel** to wait confidently and expectantly for the God who abundantly forgives.

131:1-3 The psalmist used the word picture of a **weaned child with its mother** to describe his newly found serenity. The poet no longer felt torn apart by inner nagging and turmoil. Instead he felt a deep sense of peace and contentment in the presence of the Lord. Based on his own wonderful experience, this psalmist advised the people of **Israel** likewise to trust **in the LORD** and not to depend on themselves. That was and is the only way God's people can know true serenity and security.

132:1-5 The worshipers are reminded of David's desire to build a house for the Lord (cp. 2Sm 7:1-2). This psalm may have been composed specifically to celebrate the bringing of the ark to Jerusalem (see 2Sm 6:12-19). The title **Mighty One of Jacob** signifies the grace the Lord had shown to Jacob in guiding, protecting, and blessing the patriarch (cp. Gn 49:24; 2Sm 7:1). The plea for the Lord to **remember David** is a cry for the Lord to act favorably in keeping with His covenant with David.

132:6-10 David's commitment to the Lord led him to determine to bring the ark of the covenant to Jerusalem and have a temple built to serve as its **dwelling place** (cp. vv. 2-5). David is concerned for the Lord's presence with His people. The bringing of the ark to Jerusalem ushered in a new era of God's rule over His people. The Lord's **footstool** (Hb *hadom*; cp. 99:5; 1Ch 28:2) was a reference to the ark, which represented God's rule on earth. The psalmist prays, on behalf of His **servant David**, that the Lord will not reject His **anointed one** (i.e., Solomon, who carried out David's dream of building the temple) or one of the kings of Judah.

132:11-17 God promised that one of David's **descendants** would occupy the **throne, forever** (cp. 2Sm 7:8-17; 1Ch 17:11-14). The king and his descendants were held responsible to keep the covenant by walking in obedience to the Lord. Since He always keeps all of His promises, the **oath** He swore to David would, without question, be fulfilled. The life, death, and resurrection of Jesus the **anointed one** is the supreme fulfillment of the Davidic covenant (see 1Kg 8:24-25; Lk 1:32; Heb 12:2; Rv 3:21).

The Lord also promised to **make a horn** [Hb *qeren*, a symbol of strength and power; cp. 18:2; Ezk 29:21] **grow for David**, indicating the great vigor of the Davidic dynasty, through which the Lord would establish His kingship and rule the earth. In the New Testament, Zechariah, the father of John the Baptist, interpreted verse 17 as a reference to the Messiah (see Lk 1:69-75).

133:1-3 This song of ascents expresses delight in unity among the members in God's family. The psalmist compares the absence of discord and anger among **brothers** to the special, fragrant **oil** prepared for the tabernacle and used to anoint the priests (cp. Ex 30:22-30). The comparison suggests that the unity of fellowship observed by the psalmist visibly sets apart God's "kingdom of priests" (cp. Ex 19:6; cp. Mt 5:9; Jn 17:22-23; Eph 4:1-6; 1Pt 2:9).

Because of its high altitude and abundant precipitation, Mount **Hermon** was noted for its lush vegetation. The unified fellowship among God's people, observed at the feasts celebrated in Jerusalem, was so refreshing that it was like enjoying the **dew** of Mount Hermon within the walls of **Zion**.

134:1-3 This final song of ascents functions as a fitting conclusion to these 15 psalms. The worshipers are called to **praise the Lord** with a benediction requesting the Lord's blessing on His **servants**. God blesses those who worship Him.

135:1-7 This psalm functions as a call to worship. The **servants of Yahweh** (cp. 113:1; 134:1) are summoned to praise the Lord because He is **good**. His **name** is **delightful** (Hb *na'im*, "pleasant, sweet"; cp. 133:1). Those who have experienced the Lord's electing love know how sweet indeed is a relationship with Him. **Jacob** and **Israel** both refer to God's people, **His treasured possession** (Hb *segullah*, "valued property"; cp. Ex 19:5; Dt 7:6; 14:2; 26:18). With the declaration **I know**, the psalmist praised the Lord in language signifying personal experience and relationship.

135:8-12 In this part of the psalm, the poet celebrated the Lord's deliverance of His people from Egyptian bondage and His protection of them as He led them to the promised land.

135:13-14 The Hebrew word translated as **reputation** (Hb *zeker*, "remembrance, memorial, name by which one is remembered") signals an allusion to God's revelation of His covenant "name" (Hb *shēm*; cp. Ps 30:4; Hs 12:5) to Israel in Ex 3:15. **For** (Hb *ki*, "because"), the word linking verses 13-14, suggests that the ways Yahweh will deal with **His people** are the means by which His name endures from generation to generation:

>WORD|*study*

136:22 The people are mentioned as a corporate unity—as **Israel His** servant (Hb *'eved*, "one who expresses submission or indebtedness to another; one who serves or is subordinate to another; slave"). The phrase is uncommon in the Old Testament but is one that significantly links Israel with the Lord's promises to His people and with the Messiah's fulfillment of the role of "servant" (cp. 1Ch 16:13; Is 41:8-9; 44:1,21; 49:1-7; Jr 30:10; 46:27-28; Lk 1:54; Ac 4:27).

136:23-26 Humiliation (Hb *shephel*, "lowliness," v. 23) is derived from the verb *shaphēl*, meaning to "be humbled or abased, brought low" (e.g., 1Sm 2:7; Ps 18:27; Is 2:11-12,17; Ezk 21:26). The LXX translation (Gk *tapeinōsei*, "low estate, humble condition, humiliation"; cp. Ac 8:33; Php 3:21) appears in Mary's proclamation of the Lord's greatness "because He has looked with favor on the humble condition of His slave," referring both to the first-century status of Israel and to her humble obedience of the Lord (Lk 1:48). Mary's song celebrated the angel's announcement that she would give birth to the long-awaited Messiah as evidence that "His mercy (Gk *eleos*; Lk 1:50,54,58,72,78) is from generation to generation" (Lk 1:50,54-55), a truth matching the refrain of Ps 136. Throughout Israel's history the Lord allowed His people to experience "humiliation"—i.e., to be subjected to the control of ungodly and pagan masters. Repeatedly, He also rescued (Hb *paraq*, "rend, break or tear away"; cp. 7:2; Lm 5:8) them from their **foes** (cp. Lk 1:68-74).

17 There I will make
a •horn grow for David;
I have prepared a lamp for
My anointed one.
18 I will clothe his enemies
with shame,
but the crown he wears[A]
will be glorious."

Psalm 133

Living in Harmony

A Davidic •song of ascents.

1 How good and pleasant it is
when brothers live together
in harmony!
2 It is like fine oil on the head,
running down on the beard,
running down Aaron's beard
onto his robes.
3 It is like the dew of Hermon[B]
falling on the mountains
of •Zion.
For there the Lord
has appointed
the blessing—
life forevermore.

Psalm 134

Call to Evening Worship

A •song of ascents.

1 Now praise the Lord,
all you servants of the Lord
who stand in the Lord's house
at night!
2 Lift up your hands in the
holy place
and praise the Lord!
3 May the Lord,
Maker of heaven and earth,
bless you from •Zion.

Psalm 135

The Greatness of Yahweh

1 •Hallelujah!
Praise the name of •Yahweh.
Give praise, you servants
of Yahweh
2 who stand in the house
of Yahweh,
in the courts of the house
of our God.
3 Praise Yahweh, for Yahweh
is good;
sing praise to His name,
for it is delightful.
4 For Yahweh has chosen Jacob
for Himself,
Israel as His treasured
possession.
5 For I know that Yahweh
is great;
our Lord is greater
than all gods.
6 Yahweh does
whatever He pleases
in heaven and on earth,
in the seas and all the depths.
7 He causes the clouds to rise
from the ends of the earth.
He makes lightning
for the rain
and brings the wind
from His storehouses.
8 He struck down the firstborn
of Egypt,
both man and beast.

[A]**132:18** Lit *but on him his crown* [B]**133:3** The tallest mountain in the region, noted for its abundant precipitation

9 He sent signs and wonders
against you, Egypt,
against Pharaoh and all
his officials.
10 He struck down many nations
and slaughtered
mighty kings:
11 Sihon king of the Amorites,
Og king of Bashan,
and all the kings of Canaan.
12 He gave their land
as an inheritance,
an inheritance to His people
Israel.

13 Yahweh, Your name
endures forever,
Your reputation, Yahweh,
through all generations.
14 For Yahweh will vindicate
His people
and have compassion
on His servants.

15 The idols of the nations are
of silver and gold,
made by human hands.
16 They have mouths
but cannot speak,
eyes, but cannot see.
17 They have ears
but cannot hear;
indeed, there is no breath
in their mouths.
18 Those who make them
are just like them,
as are all who trust in them.

19 House of Israel, praise Yahweh!
House of Aaron,
praise Yahweh!
20 House of Levi, praise Yahweh!
You who revere the LORD,
praise the LORD!
21 May the LORD be praised
from •Zion;
He dwells in Jerusalem.
Hallelujah!

Psalm 136

The Eternality of God's Love

1 Give thanks to the LORD,
for He is good.
His love is eternal.
2 Give thanks to the God
of gods.
His love is eternal.
3 Give thanks to the Lord
of lords.
His love is eternal.
4 He alone does great wonders.
His love is eternal.
5 He made the heavens
skillfully.
His love is eternal.
6 He spread the land
on the waters.
His love is eternal.
7 He made the great lights:
His love is eternal.
8 the sun to rule by day,
His love is eternal.
9 the moon and stars to rule
by night.
His love is eternal.
10 He struck the firstborn
of the Egyptians
His love is eternal.
11 and brought Israel out
from among them
His love is eternal.
12 with a strong hand
and outstretched arm.
His love is eternal.
13 He divided the •Red Sea
His love is eternal.
14 and led Israel through,
His love is eternal.
15 but hurled Pharaoh and
his army into the Red Sea.
His love is eternal.
16 He led His people
in the wilderness.
His love is eternal.
17 He struck down
great kings
His love is eternal.
18 and slaughtered
famous kings—
His love is eternal.
19 Sihon king of the Amorites
His love is eternal.
20 and Og king of Bashan—
His love is eternal.
21 and gave their land as
an inheritance,
His love is eternal.
22 an inheritance to Israel
His servant.
His love is eternal.
23 He remembered us
in our humiliation
His love is eternal.
24 and rescued us
from our foes.
His love is eternal.
25 He gives food
to every creature.
His love is eternal.

- He **will vindicate** (Hb *din*, "rule; plead the cause of, vindicate"; cp. 54:1; 72:2; Is 3:13; Jr 22:16) them, not in the sense of condemning them but in coming to their defense.
- He will also **have compassion** [Hb *nacham*, "pity"] **on His servants**."

Verse 14 borrows, almost verbatim, from Dt 32:36, indicating not only that the "Song of Moses" (Dt 32:1-43) is one of the sources for the construction of this psalm but also that the psalmist likely expects that those who use the psalm in worship will recall and incorporate the entire context of the borrowed verse in the process.

135:15-21 In contrast to the omnipotent God of Israel, the worthless **idols** (Hb *'atsav*, "images"; cp. 115:4-8) are everything the living Lord is not. Those who fashion and worship such man-made objects **are just like them**—i.e., as a rule, you become like the object of your greatest devotion.

136:1-9 Pulsing in every verse of this hymn of praise is a statement expressing the wonder of God's disposition toward man: **His love** [Hb *chesed*, "covenant loyalty, faithfulness"; cp. LXX (Gk *eleos*, "mercy; kindness or good will toward the afflicted, leading to action on their behalf"); see **Word Study**, p. 322] **is eternal**. Examples of God's steadfast love and reasons for praising Him are spelled out in the remainder of this psalm. He should be praised as the great Creator of the universe (vv. 4-9; cp. Gn 1:1,6-10,14-19; Rv 14:7). The **sun**, **moon**, and **stars** are specifically identified as created objects (Ps 136:8-9). They are not to be worshiped; instead their Creator is to be praised (cp. Dt 4:19). One way God demonstrates His eternal love is by providing an appropriate environment for human life.

136:10-24 You also should praise Him as the Deliverer and Redeemer of His people (cp. Ex 12:21-28; 14:10-12).

136:25-26 Verse 25 returns to the theme of God's universal providence for His creation (cp. vv. 1-9; Mt 6:26).

137:1-6 This psalm reflects the disorientation that God's people experienced in exile and captivity in Babylon following the fall of Jerusalem to the Babylonians in 587/586 B.C. They felt abandoned by the Lord and tormented by their captors. Nevertheless, they retained the conviction that their lives were not fully controlled by the Babylonians (cp. 1Kg 8:48-49). The exiles **wept** over their plight. Their **captors** demanded they sing. How could the psalmist **sing . . . the songs of Zion** that proclaimed the Lord's victory and deliverance when they were in captivity and **Jerusalem** lay in ruins? He felt unable to sing, but he vowed never to **forget** his homeland. For this psalmist, love for God and for Jerusalem were interrelated because the temple—the place of God's dwelling—had been built in Jerusalem.

137:7-9 This *imprecatory* portion of the psalm is particularly challenging to interpret (see chart, p. 668). The psalmist desired the Lord to bring judgment on the Babylonians, who had destroyed Jerusalem and taken the people of Judah captive while **the Edomites**, Judah's neighbor to the south, had celebrated the defeat and participated in the city's destruction. The Lord had promised retribution on both oppressors (regarding Babylon, see Is 13:1-22; 47:1-15; Jr 50:1–51:58; regarding the Edomites, see Ezk 25:12-14; 35:2-15; Jl 3:19; Am 1:11; Ob 10-14). The psalmist wants the Lord to fulfill judgment already prophesied against Israel's enemies, who also opposed God Himself (Is 13:16; Hos 13:16). The severity of these statements reflect the psalmist's righteous zeal in wanting to see justice served in a manner equivalent to what harm had been done to Israel.

138:1-5 David announces what he will do to worship the Lord: **I will give You thanks** [Hb *yadah*, "profess or confess" in acknowledgment of benefits received and naturally prompting gratitude, praise, celebration; cp. 118:21,28] **with all my heart** (i.e., with my entire being; cp. 9:1; 86:12; 111:1). Giving thanks will be verbalized with singing and physically demonstrated by prostrating himself toward the temple in Jerusalem, indicating that the psalmist was writing from a different location (cp. 1Kg 8:48; Dn 6:10).

The Lord is extolled for how He has demonstrated His **constant love and truth**. The Lord had made great His **name** and His **promise** [Hb *ʾimrah*, "word"; see **Word Study**, p. 759] **above everything else**. Furthermore, David recognizes that God had **increased** [his] **strength** (Hb *rahav*, "make bold, render courageous" with *ʿoz*, "strength"), responding promptly when he had cried out to the Lord.

26 Give thanks to the God
of heaven!
His love is eternal.

Psalm 137
Lament of the Exiles

1 By the rivers of Babylon—
there we sat down and wept
when we remembered •Zion.
2 There we hung up our lyres
on the poplar trees,
3 for our captors there asked us
for songs,
and our tormentors,
for rejoicing:
"Sing us one of the songs
of Zion."
4 How can we sing
the LORD's song
on foreign soil?
5 If I forget you, Jerusalem,
may my right hand forget
its skill.
6 May my tongue stick
to the roof of my mouth
if I do not remember you,
if I do not exalt Jerusalem
as my greatest joy!
7 Remember, LORD,
what the Edomites said
that day[A] at Jerusalem:
"Destroy it! Destroy it
down to its foundations!"
8 Daughter Babylon,
doomed to destruction,
happy is the one
who pays you back
what you have done to us.
9 Happy is he who takes
your little ones
and dashes them
against the rocks.

Psalm 138
A Thankful Heart

Davidic.

1 I will give You thanks
with all my heart;
I will sing Your praise
before the heavenly beings.[B]
2 I will bow down
toward Your holy temple
and give thanks to Your name

HARD QUESTION

How can Psalm 137:9, which seems to invoke blessing upon the cruel murder of children, be part of a prayer included in Scripture?

As a strategy of warfare in the ancient Near East, destruction of the opposing people's children had the effect of wiping out the next generation. The practice noted here was not unusual (cp. Hos 10:14; Nah 3:10), but Scripture's view of such particularly cruel tactics is illustrated in the weeping of the prophet Elisha over "the evil" that Hazael would do to the people of Israel (2Kg 8:10-15). The immediate context is a psalm (i.e., the prayer of one devoted to upholding the Lord's covenant). In addition, given that the psalmist prays in Babylon, where there were no **rocks** to use for such a purpose, the picture is not intended to refer to the literal action but to convey what was accomplished when the practice was exhibited by a conquering army (2Ch 36:17-20). **He** defers the blessing of being the victor to another, likely implying whatever power would finally bring Babylon's dominance to a complete end. By bringing his outcry to the Lord, the psalmist relinquishes his right to pursue vengeance, which is the Lord's exclusive prerogative (Dt 32:34-43; cp. Rm 12:19).

for Your constant love
and truth.
You have exalted Your name
and Your promise above
everything else.
3 On the day I called,
You answered me;
You increased strength
within me.[C]
4 All the kings on earth
will give You thanks, LORD,
when they hear
what You have promised.[D]
5 They will sing of
the LORD's ways,
for the LORD's glory is great.
6 Though the LORD is exalted,
He takes note of the humble;
but He knows the haughty
from a distance.
7 If I walk into the thick
of danger,
You will preserve my life
from the anger of my enemies.
You will extend Your hand;
Your right hand will save me.
8 The LORD will fulfill
His purpose for me.

[A] **137:7** The day Jerusalem fell to the Babylonians in 586 B.C. [B] **138:1** Or *before the gods*, or *before judges*, or *before kings*; Hb *elohim* [C] **138:3** Hb obscure [D] **138:4** Lit *hear the words of Your mouth*

>WORD|study

138:1 Although the Lord is the primary audience, David will sing Yahweh's praise **before** [Hb *neged*, "in front of, in the presence of"] **the heavenly beings** (Hb *ʾelohim*, "gods"), possibly designating pagan idols (cp. 97:9; 1Ch 16:25-26), other nations' judges or kings (cp. Ps 82:1), or the angels (as translated in the LXX; cp. 1Co 4:9; 11:10; Eph 3:10; Rv 3:5; 14:10). Because the psalmist seems to be away from Jerusalem, the sense may be that either he will worship Yahweh in defiance of the idols of surrounding nations or he will worship openly, "in full view" of heaven.

139:3 The verb **observe** (Hb *zarah*, "scatter, disperse, winnow, sift") is used metaphorically. In saying that the Lord has sifted both his **travels** (Hb *ʾorach*, "path, course or mode of living or acting"; cp. 119:15) and his **rest** (Hb *revaʿ*, "a lying down, stretching out to rest," a *hapax* or term that occurs only once in Scripture), David is reiterating the idea of being thoroughly examined.

139:5 The image of being **encircled** (Hb *tsur*, "press upon, besiege") by the Lord can suggest either the comfort of being surrounded by Him as an impregnable defense or the inescapable pressure of His comprehensive and unceasing scrutiny. This metaphor, combined with the picture of the Lord's **hand** having been **placed . . . on** David, conveys God's nearness and complete control.

LORD, Your love is eternal;
do not abandon the work
of Your hands.

Psalm 139

The All-Knowing, Ever-Present God

For the choir director. A Davidic psalm.

1 LORD, You have searched me
and known me.
2 You know when I sit down
and when I stand up;
You understand my thoughts
from far away.
3 You observe my travels
and my rest;
You are aware of all my ways.
4 Before a word is
on my tongue,
You know all about it, LORD.
5 You have encircled me;
You have placed Your hand
on me.
6 This extraordinary knowledge
is beyond me.
It is lofty; I am unable
to reach it.

7 Where can I go to escape
Your Spirit?
Where can I flee
from Your presence?
8 If I go up to heaven,
You are there;
if I make my bed in •Sheol,
You are there.
9 If I live at the eastern horizon
or settle at the western limits,[A]
10 even there Your hand
will lead me;
Your right hand will hold on
to me.
11 If I say, "Surely the darkness
will hide me,
and the light around me
will be night"—
12 even the darkness is not dark
to You.
The night shines like the day;
darkness and light are alike
to You.

Doctrine ATTRIBUTES OF GOD

The psalmist recognized God's presence, power, and knowledge—in theological language His omnipresence, His omnipotence, and His omniscience (139:1-6). God is limited by nothing. You cannot escape His presence. Everything you do is visible to Him; to hide from Him is impossible. That God is omnipotent means that He has all power to do whatever He pleases whenever He so chooses. God is also omniscient—He knows everything. God knows every move you make; no action is hidden from Him. God knows His creation thoroughly, both good and bad, strengths and weaknesses. He knows intents and motives. The Lord's knowledge of His children involves both objective truth and subjective relationship. He knows you better than you know yourself.

David realized that God thoroughly **searched** (Hb *chaqar*, "examine, investigate, probe," vv. 1,23) him. God misses nothing—no seemingly insignificant details, no cherished sins, no hidden agendas or motives, no unconscious memories or fears escape His notice (cp. 2Sm 10:3; Jb 28:3). He cannot be deceived (cp. Jb 13:9; Ps 44:21). Though the Lord may seem **far away** because He is invisible to earthly eyes, He also perceives the **thoughts** that are inaccessible to others. God's omniscience can evoke either praise or fear. David's response to the reality that God knows all is not fear but faith.

[A]**139:9** Lit *I take up the wings of the dawn; I dwell at the end of the sea*

Both praising the Lord directly and proclaiming His glory and justice, David speaks prophetically of a time when the Lord will receive the universal thanks and acclaim He is due.

138:6-8 Unlike earthly rulers, "the LORD's glory (v. 5) is great" because He gives attention to **the humble** (Hb *shaphal*, "low" in status or "humble" in attitude; cp. Pr 16:19; 29:23; Is 57:15; Mal 2:9) rather than **the haughty** (Hb *gavoahh*, "proud, arrogant, exalted"; cp. 1Sm 2:3; Is 5:15; Lk 16:15).

The past day of distress (v. 3) may have been one in which the psalmist walked **into the thick of danger** (Hb *be-qerev tsarah*, "in the midst of trouble, adversity, distress, anxiety"; cp. Gn 35:3). Just as he declares his worship three times in Ps 138:1-2 (he will "give . . . thanks," "sing . . . praise," and "bow down"), three times in verse 7 he worships the Lord by affirming his security in what God will do for him when threatened by angry enemies:

- **You will preserve my life.**
- **You will extend** [Hb *shalach*, "send or stretch out"] **Your hand**, an idiomatic phrase meaning the Lord will exercise His power in human affairs to crush His enemies and deliver His people (cp. Ex 3:20).
- **Your right hand will save me** (cp. Ex 14:30; Ps 34:6).

Knowing that Yahweh's **love** (Hb *chesed*; see **Word Study**, p. 322) has no end, David could voice his confidence in Him both as a statement of fact—that God would **fulfill** [Hb *gamar*, "complete, finish"; cp. 57:2] **His purpose** for him—and as a prayer that God would **not abandon** (Hb *raphah*, "leave off, cease") His **work** (cp. 100:5; refrain of Ps 136). New Testament believers also can boast of such confidence in the Lord (Rm 8:35; Php 1:6).

139:7-12 Wherever you go, you can have the assurance that God is already **there**. Sometimes you feel guilty and want to **escape** (Hb *yalak*, "go, walk") God's **Spirit** (cp. Neh 9:30) or **flee** (Hb *barach*, "run away, break away"; cp. Ps 3:1; 57:1) from His **presence** (Hb *panim*, literally "face") as did the prophet Jonah when he tried to run away from the Lord (cp. Jnh 1:3). In contrast to the localized presence of a man-made idol, the Creator is omnipresent (i.e., everywhere at once). None can **hide** from God. His omnipresence is an unshakable assurance to those who follow where He leads, especially when following the Lord means going into "dark" places where His enemies think they are hiding from Him. No location, situation, or circumstance is beyond God's grasp. The **light** of His presence penetrates and overcomes, even in **Sheol**, the place of the dead (cp. 23:4; Am 9:2-4; Rm 8:31-39).

139:19-24 The tone of the poem changes dramatically as David's thoughts turn from awe and praise to the enemies of God. Such **bloodthirsty men** are characterized by hostility toward the Lord, violence against those who belong to Him, hypocrisy, deceit, and opposition to His rule. Knowing that God has the power to destroy these adversaries of righteousness, David wants God to do so and aligns himself against God's **enemies**. If the psalm reflects a progression of thought, the abrupt shift to this topic may convey a fitting response to the destructive intrusion of **the wicked**, who resist the reverent response exemplified by David.

After praising God for His unlimited knowledge, power, and presence, the psalmist invited God to search his **heart**. The imperatives translated **search** (Hb *chaqar*) and **know** (Hb *yada'*; see note on Ex 2:24-25, p. 70 see **Word Study**, p. 725) are the same Hebrew verbs that appear in verse 1. David asked God to investigate or analyze him for **any offensive** [Hb *'otsev*, "idol"; cp. Is 48:5] **way**—any hurtful or wicked habit in him. He truly wanted to walk in the Lord's way, enjoying His presence. Every woman is dependent on God to lead her **in the everlasting way**, and He will lead those who have committed themselves to follow His will (Ps 139:24).

140:1-3 In this individual lament, David prays for deliverance from those who oppose God's purposes and from the power of **violent men** (vv. 1,4,11). Paul quoted Ps 140:3 in Rm 3:13, where the apostle was emphasizing that all people are guilty before God. In describing the evildoers,

>WORD|*study*

139:23 Test (Hb *bachan*, "search out, examine, prove") literally applies to refining precious metals and therefore conveys the idea of probing someone's character for proof of integrity (Jb 23:10; Ps 66:10; Jr 9:7). God is the universal Judge and the only one who can judge the human heart correctly (Ps 7:9; 17:3; 26:2; Pr 17:3; Jr 11:20; 12:3; 17:10; 20:12; Zch 13:9).

13 For it was You who created
my inward parts;[A]
You knit me together
in my mother's womb.
14 I will praise You
because I have
been remarkably
and wonderfully made.[B,C]
Your works are wonderful,
and I know this very well.
15 My bones were not hidden
from You
when I was made in secret,
when I was formed
in the depths of the earth.
16 Your eyes saw me when
I was formless;
all my days were written
in Your book and planned
before a single one of them
began.

17 God, how difficult[D]
Your thoughts are
for me to comprehend;
how vast their sum is!
18 If I counted them,
they would outnumber
the grains of sand;
when I wake up,[E] I am still
with You.

19 God, if only You would kill
the wicked—
you bloodthirsty men,
stay away from me—
20 who invoke You deceitfully.
Your enemies swear
by You falsely.
21 LORD, don't I hate those
who hate You,
and detest those who rebel
against You?
22 I hate them
with extreme hatred;
I consider them my enemies.

23 Search me, God, and know
my heart;
test me and know
my concerns.
24 See if there is any
offensive[F] way in me;
lead me in the everlasting way.

[A]139:13 Lit *my kidneys* [B]139:14 DSS, some LXX mss, Syr, Jer read *because You are remarkable and wonderful* [C]139:14 Hb obscure [D]139:17 Or *precious* [E]139:18 Some Hb mss read *I come to an end* [F]139:24 Or *idolatrous*

BIBLICAL WOMANHOOD Sanctity of Life

David's contemplation of his relationship to God, who is omnipresent and omniscient, led to reflection on the beginning of his life, when God personally put him together in his **mother's womb**. Psalm 139:13-16 poetically elaborate on the biblical view that the human embryo is indeed a complete human being uniquely created by God. David consistently refers to himself as a whole person (**I, me, my**)—i.e., not simply to his body but to both his **bones** (Hb *'otsem*, "body, strength," referring to the complete physical frame) and his **inward parts** (Hb *kilyah*, literally "kidneys," metaphorically referring to the seat of emotions, affections, and desires; cp. 73:21; "heart," Jb 19:27; Pr 23:16; Jr 11:20; 17:10; 20:12). When considered in light of such biblical affirmations of life, abortion is rightly understood as destroying a life created in the image of God. David models **praise** as the appropriate response to the wonder of God's ongoing involvement in and purpose for His creation.

Implicitly recognizing God's eternal sovereignty, David also notes that even before his birth—**when I was formless** (Hb *golem*, "embryo," something that is "in the process of being made, not yet fully developed"; a *hapax* or term that appears only once in Scripture)—the Lord **planned** (Hb *yatsar*, "be molded or formed in the mind, devised"; cp. 2Kg 19:25; see **Doctrine** "Creation of Mankind," p. 5) the days of his life, probably referring here to the length of his life (cp. Ex 32:32-33; Jb 14:5). This psalmist further marvels at God's **thoughts** (cp. Ps 139:2), which are **difficult** (Hb *yaqar*, "precious, costly"; cp. 49:8; 72:14; Is 43:4) to understand (cp. Is 55:8-9) and innumerable. The more you learn about the universe and about being human, the more you can marvel at the great contrast between your finite knowledge and God's immeasurable power and creativity. God purposefully and deliberately creates each person and has a plan for each life.

Psalm 140
Prayer for Rescue

For the choir director. A Davidic psalm.

1 Rescue me, LORD,
from evil men.
Keep me safe
from violent men
2 who plan evil in their hearts.
They stir up wars all day long.
3 They make their tongues
as sharp as a snake's bite;
viper's venom is under
their lips.
Selah

4 Protect me, LORD,
from the clutches
of the wicked.
Keep me safe
from violent men
who plan
to make me stumble.[A]
5 The proud hide a trap
with ropes for me;
they spread a net along
the path
and set snares for me. *Selah*
6 I say to the LORD,
"You are my God."
Listen, LORD, to my cry
for help.
7 Lord GOD, my strong Savior,
You shield my head
on the day of battle.
8 LORD, do not grant the desires
of the wicked;
do not let them achieve
their goals.
Otherwise, they will become
proud. *Selah*

9 When those who surround me
rise up,[B]
may the trouble their lips
cause overwhelm them.
10 Let hot coals fall on them.
Let them be thrown
into the fire,
into the abyss, never again
to rise.
11 Do not let a slanderer stay
in the land.
Let evil relentlessly[C]
hunt down a violent man.

12 I[D] know that the LORD upholds
the just cause of the poor,
justice for the needy.
13 Surely the righteous
will praise Your name;
the upright will live in
Your presence.

Psalm 141
Protection from Sin and Sinners

A Davidic psalm.

1 LORD, I call on You; hurry
to help me.
Listen to my voice when I call
on You.
2 May my prayer be set
before You as incense,
the raising of my hands
as the evening offering.

3 LORD, set up a guard
for my mouth;
keep watch at the door
of my lips.
4 Do not let my heart turn
to any evil thing
or perform wicked acts
with men who commit sin.
Do not let me feast
on their delicacies.
5 Let the righteous one
strike me—
it is an act of faithful love;
let him rebuke me—
it is oil for my head;
let me[E] not refuse it.
Even now my prayer
is against
the evil acts of the wicked.[F]
6 When their rulers[G]
will be thrown off
the sides of a cliff,
the people[H] will listen
to my words,
for they are pleasing.

7 As when one plows and
breaks up the soil,
turning up rocks,
so our[I] bones
have been scattered
at the mouth of •Sheol.

[A]**140:4** Lit *to trip up my steps* [B]**140:9** Lit *Head of those who surround me* [C]**140:11** Hb obscure [D]**140:12** Alt Hb tradition reads *You* [E]**141:5** Lit *my head* [F]**141:5** Lit *of them* [G]**141:6** Or *judges* [H]**141:6** Lit *cliff, and they* [I]**141:7** DSS reads *my*; some LXX mss, Syr read *their*

David emphasizes that their evil was premeditated. These wicked persons planned evil deeds and used **their tongues** to destroy others. The tongue is a powerful weapon for evil or for good (see Jms 3:8-12).

140:4-5 David prays to be protected from the **clutches** (Hb *yad*, "hands," representing one's "power") of wicked people, whose goal was to make him **stumble**. They set traps for him just as hunters **set snares** for animals and birds (cp. 141:9).

140:9-13 David also asks for the Lord to render justice by allowing those waging verbal warfare against him to be defeated by their own tactics. David expresses the confident faith that Yahweh would act on behalf of those without means of defending themselves. In response, the people whose lives are characterized by obedience would praise Him and have the privilege of living in His **presence**.

141:1-10 This **Davidic psalm** is difficult to translate. The psalmist apparently fears the influence of evil persons in his life and cries out to the Lord for immediate assistance in dealing with temptation. He prays for protection both from sin (vv. 3-4) and from sinners (v. 9). David requests that his **prayer** be accepted as was the **incense** presented daily to the Lord on the altar of incense, often in connection with **the evening offering** (v. 2; cp. Ex 30:7-8).

141:4-6 Not wanting to speak or even think evil, David asks the Lord to prevent him from saying, pursuing, or doing anything displeasing to Him. Avoiding temptation would require his refusal to keep company with **men who commit sin** and to indulge in the pleasures such men offer. David demonstrates a teachable attitude by welcoming and recognizing the value of the sharp correction or **rebuke** of a virtuous person. He continues praying for the Lord to bring to a decisive end his opponents' wicked deeds and their abuse of power, which would enable the people to see that David had their best interests in mind.

142:1-7 As **a Davidic *Maskil***, Psalm 142 may be understood as a psalm that teaches or gives insight into practical living. This psalm is associated with a specific instance when David **was in the cave**, referring to the time when David was being pursued by Saul and hid in a cave at Adullam (1Sm 22:1,4) or at En-gedi (1Sm 24:1-22).

This psalm models a way to pray through overwhelming feelings of isolation and vulnerability. Although most people have experienced the sense of being all alone with **no one** to notice or care about them and their troubles, hope is available only to those who recognize that the Lord knows both what they are going through and what the outcome will be (cp. 1Pt 5:7).

Significantly, the psalmist acknowledged that he could not, in his own wisdom or strength, escape from his circumstances. Rather than relying on himself, or giving up, or denying that his situation was dire, he put his experience into words and took his **complaint** directly to the Lord. In the psalm, before speaking to the Lord, David reiterates this four times—he cries out **to the Lord; . . . to the Lord . . . before Him; . . . to Him** (v. 1).

143:1-12 This **Davidic psalm** is the last of the seven designated by the ancient church as penitential psalms. Its first words convey a sense of urgency but remain tethered to the basis on which David hopes for the Lord to respond—i.e., God's **faithfulness** (Hb *ʾemunah*, "reliability in keeping promises"; cp. 36:5) and **righteousness**, not on any merits of his own (143:1). Referring to himself as **Your servant**, David appeals to his status as one appointed by the Lord and bound to do His will (vv. 2,12). Since the psalmist admits that **no one alive is righteous** (Hb *tsadaq*, "be just or upright, have a just cause, be justified"; cp. 14:1-3; 53:1-3; Rm 3:9-12,23; Gk [LXX] *dikaiosunē*) before God, the request to be spared from being brought **into judgment** seems futile (v. 2).

However, the argument presented in Rm 3 helps explain the hope expressed in verses 2 and 11; Ps 143, in turn, sheds light on the pattern of thinking in Rm 3. As in Ps 143:2, the psalmist's request in verse 11—**Yahweh, let me live** [Hb *chayah*, "preserve or give life, cause to live, make alive"; cp. 30:4] **. . . deliver me**—is based on the Lord's **righteousness** and for His name's sake. Although Ps 143:11 suggests that the psalmist was probably praying for his life to be spared from earthly **enemies** (cp. vv. 3-4,9), verse 2 broadens the scope of his request.

Romans 3:9-12 confirms that "no one [is] righteous" (see Ps 143:2; cp. 14:1-3; 53:1-3), a truth restated differently in Rm 3:20: No one "will be justified in His sight by the works of the law" (cp. Rm 3:23). The hope for deliverance based on "God's righteousness" (Gk *dikaiosunē*) is ultimately realized in "the redemption that is in Christ Jesus" (see Rm 3:21-26).

144:1-10 This psalm expresses David's exuberant joy in the Lord and his wonder at the blessings of divine providence. David calls for **the Lord . . . [to] be praised** (Hb *barak*, literally "be blessed") for personally training the warrior-king for battle (cp. 18:34,39).

>WORD|*study*

142:3,6 David confesses that he is weak, especially considering the opponents who had **hidden a trap** for him, who pursued him, and who were **too strong** for him. In verse 3, the verb rendered **is weak** (Hb *ʿataph*, "faint, fade away, languish") usually identifies one's **spirit** or soul (i.e., the life **within me**, v. 3). In verse 6 a different verb is translated **am . . . weak** (Hb *dalal*, literally "be low, hang down"; here, "be feeble or languid"; cp. 79:8; 116:6), a word also used to describe the shallow, slow-moving water of a river that is drying up ("dwindle," Is 19:6).

8 But my eyes look to You,
Lord God.
I seek refuge in You; do not
let me die.[A]
9 Protect me from[B] the trap
they have set for me,
and from the snares
of evildoers.
10 Let the wicked fall
into their own nets,
while I pass by safely.

Psalm 142
A Cry of Distress

A Davidic •Maskil.
When he was in the cave.
A prayer.

1 I cry aloud to the Lord;
I plead aloud to the Lord
for mercy.
2 I pour out my complaint
before Him;
I reveal my trouble to Him.
3 Although my spirit is weak
within me,
You know my way.

Along this path I travel
they have hidden a trap
for me.
4 Look to the right and see:[C]
no one stands up for me;
there is no refuge for me;
no one cares about me.

5 I cry to You, Lord;
I say, "You are my shelter,
my portion in the land
of the living."
6 Listen to my cry,
for I am very weak.
Rescue me from those
who pursue me,
for they are too strong
for me.
7 Free me from prison
so that I can praise
Your name.
The righteous will gather
around me
because You deal generously
with me.

Psalm 143
A Cry for Help

A Davidic psalm.

1 Lord, hear my prayer.
In Your faithfulness
listen to my plea,
and in Your righteousness
answer me.
2 Do not bring Your servant
into judgment,
for no one alive is righteous
in Your sight.

3 For the enemy
has pursued me,
crushing me to the ground,
making me live in darkness
like those long dead.
4 My spirit is weak within me;
my heart is overcome
with dismay.

5 I remember the days of old;
I meditate on
all You have done;
I reflect on the work
of Your hands.
6 I spread out my hands to You;
I am like parched land
before You. •*Selah*

7 Answer me quickly, Lord;
my spirit fails.
Don't hide Your face from me,
or I will be like those
going down to the •Pit.
8 Let me experience
Your faithful love
in the morning,
for I trust in You.
Reveal to me the way
I should go
because I long for You.

[A]**141:8** Or *not pour out my life* [B]**141:9** Lit *from the hands of* [C]**142:4** DSS, LXX, Syr, Vg, Tg read *I look to the right and I see*

9 Rescue me from my enemies,
LORD;
I come to You for protection.[A]
10 Teach me to do Your will,
for You are my God.
May Your gracious Spirit
lead me on level ground.

11 Because of Your name,
•Yahweh,
let me live.
In Your righteousness
deliver me from trouble,
12 and in Your faithful love
destroy my enemies.
Wipe out all those
who attack me,
for I am Your servant.

Psalm 144

A King's Prayer

Davidic.

1 May the LORD, my rock,
be praised,
who trains my hands
for battle
and my fingers for warfare.
2 He is my faithful love
and my fortress,
my stronghold
and my deliverer.
He is my shield, and I take
refuge in Him;
He subdues my people[B]
under me.

3 LORD, what is man,
that You care for him,
the son of man, that
You think of him?
4 Man is like a breath;
his days are like
a passing shadow.

5 LORD, part Your heavens
and come down.
Touch the mountains,
and they will smoke.
6 Flash Your lightning
and scatter the foe;[C]
shoot Your arrows and rout
them.
7 Reach down[D] from heaven;
rescue me from deep water,
and set me free
from the grasp of foreigners
8 whose mouths speak lies,
whose right hands
are deceptive.

9 God, I will sing a new song
to You;
I will play on a ten-stringed
harp for You—
10 the One who gives victory
to kings,
who frees His servant David
from the deadly sword.
11 Set me free and rescue me
from the grasp of foreigners
whose mouths speak lies,
whose right hands
are deceptive.

12 Then our sons will be
like plants
nurtured in their youth,
our daughters,
like corner pillars
that are carved
in the palace style.
13 Our storehouses will be full,
supplying all kinds
of produce;
our flocks will increase
by thousands
and tens of thousands in
our open fields.
14 Our cattle will be well fed.[E]
There will be no breach
in the walls,
no going into captivity,[F]
and no cry of lament in
our public squares.
15 Happy are the people with
such blessings.
Happy are the people
whose God is •Yahweh.

[A]**143:9** One Hb ms, LXX; some Hb mss read *I cover myself to You* [B]**144:2** Some Hb mss, DSS, Aq, Syr, Tg, Jer read *subdues peoples*; 2Sm 22:48; Ps 18:47 [C]**144:6** Lit *scatter them* [D]**144:7** Lit *down Your hands* [E]**144:14** Or *will bear heavy loads*, or *will be pregnant* [F]**144:14** Or *be no plague, no miscarriage*

>WORD|*study*

145:20 In the Old Testament, the verb destroy (Hb *shamad*) usually applies to idolatrous places (e.g., Lv 26:30; Nm 33:52) and people—whether worshiping "gods" other than the Lord or rejecting His rule in order to be "in control" personally (Dt 9; Ps 37:38).

Verse 2 describes the Lord using the same metaphors as those in Ps 18:2-3, depicting His strength, stability, and dependability. **Subdues** (Hb *radad*, "conquer," v. 2; cp. Is 45:1), a word rarely used in the Old Testament, more literally means "beat down, tread to pieces, flatten." Figuratively, it conveys the sense of forcing the conquered **people** to lie prostrate on the ground in demonstration of their status as subjects of the dominant power.

All credit for Israel's victories belongs to God (vv. 1-2,10). David marvels that such an almighty, eternal God even gives man a thought. Human beings are like a fleeting **breath** (Hb *hevel*; see **Word Study**, p. 831); a person's lifetime passes like a **shadow** (vv. 3-4; cp. 8:4). The Davidic king called on the Lord to act mightily and thereby rescue him from enemies who appeared to be overwhelming him (vv. 5-8). He called on the Lord to act as He had at Mount Sinai by revealing Himself in such phenomena as **smoke**, **lightning**, and violent shaking (vv. 5-6). The greatly exalted Lord condescends to come down and rescue His own people.

144:12-15 The prosperity of the people in times of peace is as much God's work as God's deliverance of His people in times of war. In ancient Hebrew thought, material prosperity indicated God's blessing on His people. Furthermore, having children, especially sons, indicated God's rich blessing. Thus the Davidic king prayed for vigorous **sons** and stately **daughters**, for bountiful crops and multiplied **flocks**, and for peace in the land.

145:1-21 As an acrostic, each verse of this psalm begins with a successive letter of the Hebrew alphabet. In most Hebrew manuscripts, the verse beginning with *nun* (n) is missing. The Greek (LXX) and Syriac translations, as well as one of the Dead Sea Scrolls, supply a verse, which is included in the second half of verse 13 ("The LORD is faithful . . .").

Overall, the acrostic structure calls attention to the psalm's elevated themes, including the kingship of God and praise of **His holy name** (vv. 1,21). As the last in this group of eight Davidic psalms, like the first such group in Book V of the Psalter (Pss 108–110), this psalm is followed by a grouping of "Hallelujah" psalms. In Jewish tradition, Ps 145 constitutes the bulk of a liturgical piece called "*Ashrei*" (Hb from *ʾesher*, "blessedness"; see note on 1:1-2, p. 667) based on the first word of two verses preceding Ps 145 when recited—Ps 84:5 and 144:15. This use of the psalm in prayer generally closes with Ps 115:18.

Psalm 145 is notably characterized by superlative expressions:

First, the psalmist praises God's name **forever and ever** (Hb *ʿolam* and *ʿad*, vv. 1-2,21; cp. *ʿolam*, "everlasting," v. 13).

Second, the word **all** (Hb *kol*, also translated "every, everyone") appears 16 times in Ps 145 (vv. 9-10,13-18,20-21). All people and **all He has made** are recipients of Yahweh's beneficent reign (v. 9; cp. vv. 14-16). Therefore, the psalmist declares to the Lord that he and all God has made **will praise** Him (vv. 1,10,21; cp. Php 2:9-11). In every attribute, word, and action, the Lord's providence, protection, justice, grace, and righteousness are perfect and reliable. Psalm 145:8 echoes the Lord's testimony about His own character in Ex 34:6-7 and suggests that these attributes constitute, in part, the **glory** of His **kingdom** (Ps 145:11-12).

The Lord's **mighty acts** (Hb *geburah*, "powerful deeds," Ps 145:4,11-12; cp. 106:2; 150:2) reveal His **splendor** and **greatness** (Hb *gedulah*, "majesty, magnificence," 145:3,6; cp. 1Ch 29:11), which is **unsearchable** (Hb *ʾêyn*, "there is no"—a negative particle; with *chêqer*, "investigation," Ps 145:3; cp. Is 40:28). Both what God has done (Ps 145:4-7) and the people **who love Him** (v. 20; cp. vv. 4,18-19)—i.e., **the godly** (vv. 10-12), will publicly glorify the Lord, acclaiming Him both for who He is (vv. 5a,6b-11,12b,13b) and for what He has done (vv. 5b,6a, 12a,13b-19). Such uninhibited **praise** properly characterizes the speech of those who embrace the reign of **God the King** (v. 1) and recognize their complete dependence upon Him (vv. 10-12,21).

Verses 14-16 emphasize utter dependence on the Lord, whether you are aware of it or not. To those **who call out to Him with integrity** (Hb *ʾemet*), however, He **is near** (Hb *qarov*, "nigh, of intimate acquaintance, not far, at hand," Ps 145:18; cp. 34:18; 75:1; 119:151; Dt 4:7). The psalmist implicitly includes himself among **those who fear** (Hb *yarēʾ*, "those who have reverence," Ps 145:19; cp. Gn 22:12; Ps 22:23; 31:9; 33:18; 34:9; Pr 31:30; Mal 4:2) the Lord and genuinely seek Him. They are never disappointed (Ps 145:18-20).

In the context of such exuberant praise, the destruction of **all the wicked** (Hb *rashaʿ*, "unrighteous or guilty, liable to punishment, criminals," v. 20) is mentioned almost in passing, but this detail cannot be left out in such a portrait of God's overwhelming goodness.

Although His mercy and providence are extended to all, those who reject and thereby oppose Him automatically exclude themselves from the presence of the righteous and holy King in whose presence no evil can abide (cp. 1:5-6; 9:16; 141:10; Ezk 18:21-23; Mt 22:1-14; 25:31-46).

>WORD|*study*

145:11-13 The word for kingdom (Hb *malkut*, "royal dominion, realm, a country and people subject to a king, reign") appears four times in verses 11-13 but only twice more in the entire book of Psalms (45:6; 103:19). Elsewhere in the Old Testament the word is used most frequently of the reign or realm of an earthly king (e.g., 1Ch 11:10; Est 1:2; Dn 1:1). However, this is also the term used in the Lord's promise to establish the throne of David's son "forever" (1Ch 22:10; cp. 1Ch 17:11,14; 28:5,7; 2Ch 7:18; Heb 1:8). The messianic significance of the Lord's "kingdom" is evident in the Gospels, in which the same word used in the Greek translation (LXX) of this psalm—*basileia*—appears at least 120 times. For example, "the good news of the kingdom" (Gk *basileia*, Mt 4:23) summarizes the content of Jesus' preaching (cp. Mt 3:2; 4:17). Furthermore, Rv 12:10 indicates that God's "kingdom" and "the authority of His Messiah" will be fully revealed when Satan is "thrown out."

Psalm 145

Praising God's Greatness

A Davidic hymn.

1 I[A] exalt You, my God the King,
and praise Your name
forever and ever.
2 I will praise You every day;
I will honor Your name
forever and ever.
3 •Yahweh is great
and is highly praised;
His greatness is unsearchable.
4 One generation will declare
Your works to the next
and will proclaim
Your mighty acts.
5 I[B] will speak of Your splendor
and glorious majesty
and[C] Your wonderful works.
6 They will proclaim the power
of Your awe-inspiring acts,
and I will declare
Your greatness.[D]
7 They will give a testimony
of Your great goodness
and will joyfully sing
of Your righteousness.

8 The LORD is gracious
and compassionate,
slow to anger and great
in faithful love.
9 The LORD is good to everyone;
His compassion rests
on all He has made.
10 All You have made
will thank You, LORD;
the[E] godly will praise You.
11 They will speak of the glory
of Your kingdom
and will declare Your might,
12 informing all •people
of Your mighty acts
and of the glorious splendor
of Your[F] kingdom.
13 Your kingdom is
an everlasting kingdom;
Your rule is for all
generations.
The LORD is faithful in all
His words
and gracious in all
His actions.[G]
14 The LORD helps all who fall;
He raises up all
who are oppressed.[H]
15 All eyes look to You,
and You give them their food
at the proper time.
16 You open Your hand
and satisfy the desire
of every living thing.

17 The LORD is righteous
in all His ways
and gracious in all His acts.
18 The LORD is near all
who call out to Him,
all who call out to Him
with integrity.
19 He fulfills the desires of those
who •fear Him;
He hears their cry for help
and saves them.
20 The LORD guards all those
who love Him,
but He destroys
all the wicked.
21 My mouth will declare
Yahweh's praise;
let every living thing
praise His holy name forever
and ever.

[A]**145:1** The lines of this poem form an •acrostic. [B]**145:5** LXX, Syr read *They* [C]**145:5** LXX, Syr read *and they will tell of* [D]**145:6** Alt Hb tradition, Jer read *great deeds* [E]**145:10** Lit *Your* [F]**145:12** LXX, Syr, Jer; MT reads *His* [G]**145:13** One Hb ms, DSS, LXX, Syr; some Hb mss omit *The LORD is faithful in all His words and gracious in all His actions.* [H]**145:14** Lit *bowed down*

>WORD|*study*

146:9 Frustrates (Hb *'awath*, lit "bend, curve, pervert, make crooked; turn upside down") metaphorically has the sense of "brings to ruin" by thwarting plans or causing deviations from an intended course (cp. Ec 7:13). The Lord defeats the purposes of **the wicked** and causes their way of life to be found empty.

Psalm 146
The God of Compassion

1 •Hallelujah!
My soul, praise the LORD.
2 I will praise the LORD
all my life;
I will sing to my God
as long as I live.

3 Do not trust in nobles,
in man, who cannot save.
4 When his breath[A] leaves him,
he returns to the ground;
on that day his plans die.

5 Happy is the one whose help
is the God of Jacob,
whose hope is in the LORD
his God,
6 the Maker of heaven
and earth,
the sea and everything
in them.
He remains faithful forever,
7 executing justice
for the exploited
and giving food
to the hungry.
The LORD frees prisoners.
8 The LORD opens the eyes of
the blind.
The LORD raises up those
who are oppressed.[B]
The LORD loves the righteous.
9 The LORD protects foreigners
and helps the fatherless
and the widow,
but He frustrates the ways
of the wicked.

10 The LORD reigns forever;
•Zion, your God reigns
for all generations.
Hallelujah!

Psalm 147
God's Restoration of Jerusalem

1 •Hallelujah!

A 146:4 Or *spirit* B 146:8 Lit *bowed down*

The final word is a call to **every living thing** (Hb *kol basar*, "all flesh, all living creatures, all men") to praise the Lord (Ps 145:21), a call that is answered in Pss 146–150.

147:1-3 In this second "Hallelujah" psalm, the Lord is praised for building up and protecting **Jerusalem**, for creating and sustaining the universe, and particularly for revealing Himself uniquely to the nation of Israel (vv. 12,19). Not only does the Lord bring His **exiled people** back home, but He also **heals** them and tends to their sorrows.

147:4-6 Verses 4-5 celebrate the Lord's faithfulness to His creation. The fact that the Lord **gives names to all** the stars signifies not only His power over them but also His personal interest in all He has created. Verse 6 recognizes the Lord as the righteous Judge who ultimately will right all wrongs.

147:10-11 The Lord **does not value** people the way human beings too often do—by how much **power** they possess. Rather, He rewards those who recognize their weakness and depend on Him in faith.

147:12-20 The psalmist calls on God's people to praise Him because of the benefits with which He blesses His people (vv. 12-14). Sensitivity to God's wonderful works in redemption, in creation, and in revelation should lead His people to praise Him.

148:1-14 This third "Hallelujah" psalm consists of two parts—verses 1-6 and verses 7-14. Each of these two sections

BIBLICAL WOMANHOOD Being a Woman after God's Heart

In Psalm 146, the psalmist exhorts his listeners to **trust** in God, not in people (vv. 1-4). God is the Creator who cares for the needy and helpless. As the psalmist calls on his **soul** (i.e., his entire being) to **praise the LORD**, so women who know Him can tell themselves, even in unhappy circumstances, to celebrate or glorify Christ the Lord, who identified Himself and His mission with the characteristic actions noted in verses 7-8 (cp. Is 61:1-3; Lk 4:16-20). As the psalmist determined to **praise the LORD** and **sing to . . . God as long as** he lived, so women who determine that they will actively recognize and make known the God who can be trusted completely will find in Him everything they need. To focus on the Lord requires a woman to disassociate herself from dependence on human beings to meet her needs—no **man** can meet every need of a woman's heart, but God can (Ps 146:3). People in general will always disappoint you, but the Lord never fails. Even those you most love and trust eventually die; in a moment, all your dreams for your relationship or for your children or the good plans someone has for you can vanish. The Lord, however, is eternal and will always be there—not only until the end of your life but also beyond your grave. Furthermore, though people can betray your trust, the Lord alone **remains faithful forever** (v. 6), and He is and always will be the true King. The **righteous** woman who entrusts her heart and life to this King can trust Him to execute **justice** when she has been wronged, to provide for her physical needs, to lead her out of bondage to sin or painful memories or addictions or oppressive circumstances into the freedom of belonging exclusively and primarily to Him (vv. 7-9). She can count on the Lord to love and protect and help her. In the process of finding the Lord faithful to be who He promises to be in Scripture, the woman in right relationship with Him will become a woman after His own heart, who extends to others the practical and unconditional love and service she has discovered in Him.

begins with a call to **praise the Lord** (vv. 1,7).

148:14 Of all the facets of creation called to praise, appropriately the people who belong to the Lord are noted in this hymn's final and climactic verse.

149:1 In this fourth "Hallelujah" psalm, God receives praise both for His salvation and for His judgment. For the sixth time in the Psalter comes the command to **sing to the Lord a new song** (see 33:3; 40:3; 96:1; 98:1; 144:9), suggesting that what God has just accomplished or is about to do warrants a fresh creative expression of acclaim. The psalmist calls for Him to be praised in **the assembly of the godly** (Hb *chasid*; see 148:14; cp. "the community of the righteous," 1:5)—i.e., among those who can appreciate and join in the rejoicing with sincerity.

149:2-5 These verses describe exuberant, triumphant praise, including **dancing**, making **music**, and shouting **for joy**. The Lord's delight in **His people**, evident in His glorifying **the humble** [Hb *ʿanaw*, "afflicted; meek, gentle"; cp. 22:26; Mt 5:5] **with salvation** (Hb *yeshuʿah*, "deliverance"; cp. 1Sm 2:1; Ps 3:8; Is 25:9; Lk 1:69; see **Word Study**, p. 878) is cause for celebration.

149:6-9 The praise of God extends beyond singing and shouting to the actions involved in being instruments of His **judgment** upon those who have defied His rightful rule (cp. Ps 2; 9:8; 47:3; Rv 20:4). Total victory ultimately belongs to the Lord.

150:1-6 This final "Hallelujah" psalm functions as the doxology of Book V and a fitting conclusion to the entire book of Psalms. The word **praise** (Hb *halal*, "sing praise, celebrate") appears 11 times in the psalm's six verses.

The psalm answers four important questions about worship:

- Where is the Lord to be praised? **In His sanctuary** (i.e., in His house of worship) and, probably referring to the heavenly host, **in His mighty heavens**.
- Why is the Lord to be praised? Both for **His powerful acts**, which are evident both in the world of nature and in human history, and **His abundant greatness** (Hb *godel*, "magnitude, magnificence"; cp. 79:11; Dt 3:24)—i.e., both for what He does and who He is.
- How are we to praise the Lord? A variety of musical instruments were used in offering praise to God in the Old Testament era. The book of Psalms itself functioned as a hymnbook and reveals that

How good it is to sing
to our God,
for praise is pleasant
and lovely.

2 The LORD rebuilds Jerusalem;
He gathers Israel's
exiled people.
3 He heals the brokenhearted
and binds up their wounds.
4 He counts the number
of the stars;
He gives names to all of them.
5 Our Lord is great,
vast in power;
His understanding is infinite.[A]
6 The LORD helps the afflicted
but brings the wicked
to the ground.

7 Sing to the LORD
with thanksgiving;
play the lyre to our God,
8 who covers the sky
with clouds,
prepares rain for the earth,
and causes grass to grow
on the hills.
9 He provides the animals
with their food,
and the young ravens,
what they cry for.

10 He is not impressed
by the strength of a horse;
He does not value the power[B]
of a man.
11 The LORD values
those who fear Him,
those who put their hope
in His faithful love.

12 Exalt the LORD, Jerusalem;
praise your God, •Zion!
13 For He strengthens the bars
of your gates
and blesses your children
within you.
14 He endows your territory
with prosperity;[C]
He satisfies you
with the finest wheat.

15 He sends His command
throughout the earth;
His word runs swiftly.
16 He spreads snow like wool;
He scatters frost like ashes;
17 He throws His hailstones
like crumbs.
Who can withstand His cold?
18 He sends His word
and melts them;
He unleashes His winds,[D]
and the waters flow.

19 He declares His word
to Jacob,
His statutes and judgments
to Israel.
20 He has not done this
for any nation;
they do not know[E]
His judgments.
Hallelujah!

Psalm 148

Creation's Praise of the LORD

1 •Hallelujah!
Praise the LORD
from the heavens;
praise Him in the heights.
2 Praise Him, all His angels;
praise Him, all His •hosts.
3 Praise Him, sun and moon;
praise Him, all
you shining stars.
4 Praise Him, highest heavens,
and you waters above
the heavens.
5 Let them praise the name
of •Yahweh,
for He commanded,
and they were created.
6 He set them in position
forever and ever;
He gave an order
that will never pass away.

7 Praise the LORD
from the earth,
all sea monsters
and ocean depths,
8 lightning[F] and hail,
snow and cloud,
powerful wind that executes
His command,
9 mountains and all hills,
fruit trees and all cedars,
10 wild animals and all cattle,
creatures that crawl
and flying birds,
11 kings of the earth
and all peoples,

[A]**147:5** Lit *understanding has no number* [B]**147:10** Lit *legs* [C]**147:14** Or *peace* [D]**147:18** Or *breath* [E]**147:20** DSS, LXX, Syr, Tg read *He has not made known to them* [F]**148:8** Or *fire*

princes and all judges
of the earth,
12 young men as well as
young women,
old and young together.
13 Let them praise the name
of Yahweh,
for His name alone is exalted.
His majesty covers
heaven and earth.
14 He has raised up a •horn
for His people,
resulting in praise to all
His godly ones,
to the Israelites, the people
close to Him.
Hallelujah!

Psalm 149

Praise for God's Triumph

1 •Hallelujah!
Sing to the LORD a new song,
His praise in the assembly
of the godly.
2 Let Israel celebrate its Maker;
let the children of •Zion
rejoice in their King.
3 Let them praise His name
with dancing
and make music to Him
with tambourine and lyre.
4 For •Yahweh takes pleasure
in His people;
He adorns the humble
with salvation.
5 Let the godly celebrate
in triumphal glory;
let them shout for joy
on their beds.
6 Let the exaltation of God be
in their mouths[A]
and a double-edged sword
in their hands,
7 inflicting vengeance
on the nations
and punishment
on the peoples,
8 binding their kings
with chains
and their dignitaries
with iron shackles,
9 carrying out the judgment
decreed against them.
This honor is for
all His godly people.
Hallelujah!

Psalm 150

Praise for the LORD

1 •Hallelujah!
Praise God in His sanctuary.
Praise Him
in His mighty heavens.
2 Praise Him
for His powerful acts;
praise Him
for His abundant greatness.
3 Praise Him
with trumpet blast;
praise Him with harp
and lyre.
4 Praise Him with tambourine
and dance;
praise Him with flute
and strings.
5 Praise Him
with resounding cymbals;
praise Him
with clashing cymbals.
6 Let everything that breathes
praise the LORD.
Hallelujah!

[A] 149:6 Lit *throat*

songs of lamentation as well as hymns of praise were an accepted part of worship. The **trumpet** (Hb *shophar*, "ram's horn," usually sounded to issue a call to all Israel or the entire army; formally, to signal the Sabbath and the new moon) is the instrument most frequently mentioned in Scripture. The **harp** (Hb *nevel*) and the **lyre** (Hb *kinnor*) often were associated with people of high rank and were made of precious woods and metals. The **tambourine** was the instrument that typically accompanied dancing as a means of praising the Lord (cp. 81:2; 149:3; Ex 15:20; 2Sm 6:5; 1Ch 13:8; Jr 31:4). The **flute** (Hb *'ugav*, "reed-pipe"; cp. Gn 4:21) and stringed instruments also regularly accompanied worship songs of praise. Verse 5 calls for the loud and dramatic use of **cymbals** (Hb *tselatsal*; cp. 2Sm 6:5), signaling the people's great enthusiasm as they worshiped the Lord.

- Finally, who is to praise the Lord? All living creatures—**everything that breathes**—are summoned to burst into spontaneous and unreserved adoration for the Creator. The breath of life itself is a gift of God. This psalm constitutes a pinnacle of praise.

PSALMS… WRITTEN ON MY Heart

The book of Psalms begins appropriately with a wisdom psalm (Ps 1) contrasting the way of blessing (vv. 1-3) with the way of destruction (vv. 4-6). That psalm emphasizes that stability and spiritual productivity belong to the believer who focuses continually on God's Word and chooses a lifestyle of obedience to Him. The Psalter ends appropriately with an extravagant call to praise. A life lived in obedience to the Lord as He has revealed Himself in His Word results in unhindered praise to Him. The psalmist walks through trials and difficulties and is ultimately victorious. Whatever the trials of life, despite the overwhelming sufferings that you may experience as you walk with Him, God provides the comfort needed. The life of obedience is one of freedom for the woman who chooses to delight in the way of the Lord, in which you will discover your true purpose and reason for living. You will experience joyful fellowship with the Lord, and your life itself will be a pinnacle of praise. Your purpose is to bring glory to your Creator, and in so doing you will know life in its abundance, just as the Lord intended (Jn 10:10).

Proverbs

Timeline	994 BC	972–970 BC	970 BC	970 BC
World Events / Biblical Events	Birth of Solomon	Solomon, co-regent with his father David	Solomon, ruler of a united kingdom	Solomon's prayer for wisdom

"The fear of the LORD is the beginning of knowledge" (1:7a).

Who wrote Proverbs?

"Solomon son of David, king of Israel" (1:1; cp. 1Kg 4:29–32) and other contributors (22:17; 24:23; 25:1; 30:1; 31:1)

Who were the recipients?

The people of Israel during Solomon's reign and later generations of anyone who is open to learn

When was Proverbs written?

Most of the book of Proverbs was compiled during the early monarchy period in Israel's history, especially during the tenth century B.C. under the supervision of Solomon, who reigned 40 years (971–931 B.C.). Hezekiah worked to edit and compile a later, and possibly final, form of the book (729–686 B.C.).

Where did it happen?

Israel, particularly during the period of monarchy

What is Proverbs about?

The book applies godly wisdom to many aspects of everyday life. Throughout the book, *wisdom* (i.e., a lifestyle of obeying the Lord) is set in contrast to *folly* (i.e., a lifestyle of turning away from the Lord's commands and priorities).

Why should women read Proverbs?

Women who want to know God and to live in a manner pleasing to Him will discover in the book of Proverbs a wealth of practical guidelines for everyday decision-making as well as for lifelong, life-changing patterns of character development and purpose. The book reveals truths about God and your relationship with Him:

- Who God is—omniscient (15:3,11; 21:2); omnipotent (10:27,29; 12:2);
- What He does—administers justice (2:7-8; 16:2; 17:3; 29:26); keeps His covenant with His people (2:21-22; 3:5-8; 22:19; 29:25); rules as sovereign over all (16:4,9; 19:21; 22:2);
- Your personal responsibility to God (1:7; 3:5).

However, Proverbs also addresses interpersonal relationships, with wisdom regarding:

- Morality and ethics (1:10; 14:30; 16:5,18-19);
- Duties to neighbor (12:26; 14:21);
- Family responsibilities (20:7; 22:6); and
- Civic duty to authorities of government (16:10,12; 20:28).

Throughout the book are treasures of truth that illuminate what a woman's godly obedience looks like in her home and family, as both wife and mother. For example, the book of Proverbs upholds the Lord's standard of joyful monogamous (one man and one woman) union, despite the polygamy prevalent in the surrounding nations and the adultery and other perversions practiced among His people but condemned by God. The author identifies such sins that attack the fiber of the home and warns against falling prey to their appeals. Furthermore, both parents are instructed to train their children to follow Yahweh God (Pr 23:22-25; 29:15,17; cp. Dt 6:4-9).

The book of Proverbs is just as relevant today as when it was written. This collection of sayings represents a distinct worldview that recognizes the world as a battleground between good and evil, wisdom and folly, the righteousness of God and the wickedness of man. Inevitably, every decision brings consequences. In this fallen world, God's justice may be delayed or not readily apparent, but He never fails to keep His promises and accomplish His purposes in His own way and according to His timing.

How do you read Proverbs?

The first nine chapters of the book of Proverbs are easier to read in sections. Although written in the poetical form (see "How do you read Psalms?" p. 666), larger portions of text are clearly connected (e.g., 3:27-35). Also, when you read carefully from 1:1 to 9:18, you will discover repetition of certain themes emphasizing how the wisdom-saturated life is clearly distinguished from the self-indulgent and destructive patterns touted by contemporary culture. Chapter 31 also consists of a longer, unified portion of text.

As you read chapters 10–30, smaller groups of verses seem intended to belong together, but many verses seem to stand alone. Regardless of how many verses or chapters you may read at a time, keeping in mind how proverbs work is essential. Proverbs express observations, down-to-earth illustrations, or insights that are generally applicable; they are not meant to be absolute, for there may be exceptions. Also, proverbs assume the reliability of their message rather than arguing their points. All, however, have a didactic purpose—whether through persuasive admonitions or definitive prohibitions. The method of teaching employed here uses humor and common sense as well as symbolism and other literary devices to help the reader draw from experience, example, or the general body of truth; then to focus on a particular issue; and finally to choose the best course of action. Digesting the book in small bits is helpful, allowing time to ponder and analyze each thought or object lesson. The sayings grip the heart and prick the conscience, so approach the book of Proverbs with a teachable heart, willing for the Lord to change your priorities and perspectives as His wisdom takes root in your life.

968 BC	*967 BC*	*966–931 BC*	*931 BC*	*716–687 BC*
Solomon's exercise of exceptional wisdom in a dispute between two mothers	Solomon's oversight of the building of the temple	Solomon's failure to exercise wisdom in his choice of wives	Solomon's death and an irreparable division in kingdom he was charged to rule	Reign of Hezekiah, compiler of Proverbs 25–29.

Outline

Introduction (1:1-6)

I. Instruction for Young People (1:7–9:18)
  A. The Prelude to True Happiness Through Wisdom (1:7–4:27)
  B. The Prelude to Sin Through Folly (5:1–7:27)
  C. The Personification of Wisdom (8:1–9:18)

II. An Examination of Wisdom Versus Folly (10:1–22:16)

III. A Collection of Additional Proverbs (22:17–24:34)

IV. The Collection by Hezekiah's Men (25:1–29:27)

V. Appendices to the Book (30:1–31:31)
  A. Agur's Words (30:1-33)
  B. Lemuel's Words (31:1-9)
  C. The Acrostic from Lemuel's Mother (31:10-31)

The Purpose of Proverbs (1:1-6)

1 The proverbs of Solomon
son of David, king of Israel:
2 For learning what wisdom
and discipline are;
for understanding
insightful sayings;
3 for receiving
wise instruction
in righteousness, justice,
and integrity;
4 for teaching shrewdness
to the inexperienced,[A]
knowledge and discretion
to a young man—
5 a wise man will listen
and increase
his learning,
and a discerning man
will obtain guidance—
6 for understanding a proverb
or a parable,[B]
the words of the wise,
and their riddles.

[A]1:4 Or *simple*, or *gullible* [B]1:6 Or *an enigma*

>WORD|*study*

1:1 Proverbs (Hb *mashal* [singular form], "wise saying, sentiment, maxim," often taking the form of a similitude, comparison or parable) are authoritative sayings, giving the idea that one's conduct is to be governed or ruled by principles contained within these pithy sayings. The Hebrew root of the word for proverb means "represent, be like" or possibly "rule or have dominion." In this context the sense is "a weighty or wise saying." In general, the book of Proverbs contains sayings that are to rule and govern life. However, these concise, poignant, and carefully crafted sayings, often relying on figures of speech, not only draw the interest of the reader but also make a lasting impression even as they teach important spiritual truths.

1:2 Learning (Hb *yadaᶜ*, "know, realize, perceive, become aware or conscious of" with the sense of both acquiring intellectual knowledge and aligning one's life according to it) such knowledge demands enough personal internalization of the wisdom to make a difference in your life—what you think and what you do.

1:2 The author is committed to the instruction of young people and of those who need **wisdom** (Hb *chokmah*, "skill, acute judgment, a corrective lesson"; cp. Ex 28:3; 31:3,6; 35:26,35; 36:1-2). His goal for this instruction seems twofold. First, attaining and exercising wisdom (i.e., learning what is right and true) is understood in the sense of choosing to keep oneself under the disciplined restraint and control of Yahweh God in order to make wise choices and correct wrong ones in successfully navigating life's journey according to godly principles. Second, achieving discernment between right and wrong and between good and evil makes one useful to God and valuable to the community.

1:2 The idea of **discipline** (Hb *musar*, "training, correction") is inextricably bound to wisdom (cp. v. 7; 3:11; 4:1,13). This word is used not only in the sense of instruction but also with the idea of chastise/spank (cp. 13:24; 22:15; 23:13). The wise person submits willingly to God's loving correction.

Title In the Hebrew Bible, the title is "The Proverbs of Solomon" (*mishlēy* [plural form] *shlomoh*). The Septuagint bears the title *Papoimiai* (Gk, "sayings"). Early Christian writers often called the book *Sophia* (Gk, "wisdom"), but in the Vulgate, Jerome entitled the book *Liber Proverbiorum* (Lat, "book of proverbs").

1:2 In character formation, gaining **wisdom** is no easy task, for it cannot be separated from **discipline**. To learn to obey God's Word takes time and requires a commitment to the disciplines necessary for developing a moral nature pleasing to God. The process of attaining wisdom also requires submission to God's authority and correction, for you will not "get it right" every time.

The other side of instruction in wisdom is **understanding** [Hb *bin*, "explain, teach, perceive, discern"] **insightful** [Hb *binah*, "perceptiveness, discernment"] **sayings** (i.e., internalizing and therefore applying truth to specific circumstances).

1:3-6 The content of **wise instruction** for the student is described as:

- **righteousness** (Hb *tsedeq*, "rightness, straightness, justice, uprightness" in the sense of integrity, virtue, and piety)—conforming oneself to a standard (i.e., in this context, agreeing with the moral standards of God's law). Practicing righteousness involves actively bringing it to all spheres of life.
- **justice** (Hb *mishpat*, "judgment, just weight," using the weight of judgment as with an arbiter who is in litigation to determine what is right)—making decisions by weighing rightly what life brings

you and discerning between the good and the bad.

- **integrity** (Hb *mēshar*, "rectitude, uprightness, equity"; derived from *yashar*, a verbal root meaning "be straight or even")—following a "straight" path of life unsullied by twistedness and corruption (cp. 2:9).

Making wise choices demands the ability to anticipate the coming of evil and prepare effectively to avoid such entrapment. **Shrewdness** (Hb *ʿormah*, cleverness, prudence, subtlety"; cp. 8:5,12) is the ability to discern wickedness in all its manifestations.

1:8 My son, occurring here and often in the initial chapters of the book (cp. vv. 10,15; 2:1; 3:1,11,21; 4:10,20; 5:1,20; 6:1,3,20; 7:1; also cp. 5:7; 7:24; 8:32), indicates, but is not limited to, parental instruction, the most important source of spiritual and moral instruction. Any recipient of instruction—whether biological offspring, spiritual child, or disciple—could be addressed in this intimate way. The phrase is not gender-exclusive in its application and is for all Israel as well as for all followers of Yahweh through the generations.

Here and elsewhere in this book (cp. 6:20; 10:1), both mother and father are assumed to be very much a part of the parental team. Reverencing and honoring both parents—obeying their direction and accepting their discipline—is expected as well. What is taught includes **instruction** (Hb *musar*; see **Word Study**, p. 783) and **teaching** (Hb *torah*, "law," possibly a cognate to the verb meaning "point or direct") which would suggest pointing or guiding the child in the right direction and bringing to the equation the authority of God's law.

1:9 The result of accepting this parental guidance is a **garland of grace** (Hb *chēn*, "charm, favor, elegance"; cp. Pr 4:9; cp. 11:16; 31:30)—the endearing quality making one winsome and agreeable and worn as the reward for victory and success—and a **chain** [Hb *ʿanaq*, "badge of honor or distinction" from a root suggesting "surrounding"] **around your neck**. These metaphors may symbolize protection and display in a figurative sense the results of parental teachings—a combination of ornamentation that enhances and yet a binding connection or the adornment of obedience, as in the neck bowing to authority rather than being "stiff-necked" (29:1).

1:10-19 The word translated as **sinners** (Hb *chattaʾ*, "one who misses the mark, stumbles, falls") speaks to the root of sin (i.e., coming up short of God's standard), which extends to thoughts as well as words and deeds. People who delight in sin as their way of life typically **entice** (Hb *patah*,

>WORD|*study*

1:7 The heart of the book of Proverbs is the concept of **the fear of the Lord** as **the** beginning [Hb *rēʾshit*, "starting point, chief or principal part" in the sense of providing the ground from which wisdom can grow; cognitively an awareness of who God is and what He wants you to do] **of knowledge** (cp. 4:7). Fear [Hb *yirʾah* "reverence, piety, veneration," with the sense of your own weakness and an apprehension of the dangers faced] **of the Lord** motivates people to do the right thing based on an attitude of love and trust that so possesses you that you dare not disobey. Believing what God says He will do, you love Him and in awe draw closer to Him. Believing the warnings about what He forbids, you fear Him and His wrath. Simultaneously you are shrinking back in fear of the wrath of God while moving closer because you are drawn in awe to His presence.

1:7 In contrast, fools (Hb *ʾewil*, "idiot") generally do not seek counsel and, in fact, refuse it when offered. Determined to follow their own desires, their misplaced self-confidence leads to irrational and even wicked actions (12:16). They refuse to make wrongs right (14:9) and have no regard for others (12:16). Fools are not necessarily deficient in intelligence or even in general knowledge; but lacking moral knowledge and discernment, they obstinately refuse to go God's way (12:15; 15:5; 20:3; cp. 17:10).

1:12 Sheol (Hb, "the place of the dead, grave, destruction, wasteland, void, underworld") and **pit** (Hb *bor*, "world of the dead, grave"; cp. 30:16; Jb 17:13) are often paired together and, as here, describe metaphorically a power pursuing its victims with the intent to **swallow them alive** (Pr 1:12; cp. Is 5:14).

The Prelude to True Happiness Through Wisdom (1:7–4:27)

A Warning from Wisdom (1:7-19)

7 The •fear of the Lord
is the beginning of knowledge;
fools despise wisdom
and discipline.

8 Listen, my son,
to your father's instruction,
and don't reject
your mother's teaching,
9 for they will be a garland
of grace on your head
and a gold chain
around your neck.
10 My son, if sinners entice you,
don't be persuaded.
11 If they say—"Come with us!
Let's set an ambush
and kill someone.[A]
Let's attack
some innocent person
just for fun![B]
12 Let's swallow them alive,
like •Sheol,
still healthy as they go down
to the •Pit.
13 We'll find all kinds
of valuable property
and fill our houses
with plunder.
14 Throw in your lot with us,
and we'll all share
our money"[C]—
15 my son, don't travel that road
with them
or set foot on their path,
16 because their feet run
toward trouble
and they hurry
to commit murder.[D]
17 It is foolish to spread a net
where any bird can see it,
18 but they set an ambush
to kill themselves;[E]
they attack their own lives.
19 Such are the paths of all
who make profit dishonestly;
it takes the lives of those
who receive it.[F]

An Invitation from Wisdom (1:20-33)

20 Wisdom calls out in the street;
she raises her voice
in the public squares.
21 She cries out above[G]
the commotion;
she speaks at the entrance
of the city •gates:
22 "How long, foolish ones,
will you love ignorance?
How long will you mockers
enjoy mocking
and you fools hate knowledge?
23 If you respond to
my warning,[H]
then I will pour out my spirit
on you
and teach you my words.
24 Since I called out
and you refused,

[A]1:11 Lit *Let's ambush for blood* [B]1:11 Lit *person for no reason* [C]1:14 Lit *us; one bag will be for all of us* [D]1:16 Lit *to shed blood* [E]1:18 Lit *they ambush for their blood* [F]1:19 Lit *takes the life of its masters* [G]1:21 Lit *at the head of* [H]1:23 Lit *back to my reprimand*

extended my hand and no one
paid attention,
25 since you neglected all
my counsel
and did not accept
my correction,
26 I, in turn, will laugh at
your calamity.
I will mock when terror
strikes you,
27 when terror strikes you
like a storm
and your calamity comes
like a whirlwind,
when trouble and stress
overcome you.
28 Then they will call me,
but I won't answer;
they will search for me,
but won't find me.
29 Because they hated knowledge,
didn't choose to fear the LORD,
30 were not interested
in my counsel,
and rejected all my correction,
31 they will eat the fruit
of their way
and be glutted with
their own schemes.
32 For the turning away
of the inexperienced
will kill them,
and the complacency of fools
will destroy them.
33 But whoever listens to me
will live securely
and be free from the fear
of danger."

The Rewards of Wisdom (2:1–4:27)

2 My son, if you accept my words
and store up my commands
within you,
2 listening closely[A] to wisdom
and directing your heart
to understanding;
3 furthermore, if you call out
to insight
and lift your voice
to understanding,
4 if you seek it like silver
and search for it
like hidden treasure,
5 then you will understand
the •fear of the LORD
and discover the knowledge
of God.
6 For the LORD gives wisdom;
from His mouth
come knowledge
and understanding.
7 He stores up success[B]
for the upright;
He is a shield for those
who live with integrity
8 so that He may guard
the paths of justice
and protect the way
of His loyal followers.
9 Then you will understand
righteousness, justice,
and integrity—
every good path.
10 For wisdom will enter
your mind,
and knowledge will delight
your heart.
11 Discretion will watch over you,
and understanding
will guard you,
12 rescuing you from the way
of evil—
from the one who says
perverse things,

Doctrine SIN

Rescuing (Hb *natsal*, "snatch away, remove, liberate," 2:12; cp. v. 16; see **Word Study**, p. 672) is needed from **the way of evil**, implying that men and women living in opposition to God's good and righteous way are in danger from which they cannot escape on their own. Specific examples of people entrapped in a lifestyle of evil are provided:

- **the one who says perverse** [Hb *tahpukah*, "deceit, fraud," from the root *haphak*, "overturn, overthrow, turn upside down" as in the sense of a topsy-turvy lifestyle] **things**;
- **those who abandon the right** [Hb *yosher*, "straightness"; cp. 4:11; 14:2] **paths**, suggesting that they had once been walking according to God's law but at some point chose to leave that way of life **to walk in ways of darkness** (2:13);
- **those who enjoy doing evil and celebrate perversion** (Hb *tahpukah*, v. 14—see first example above);
- those **whose paths are crooked** (Hb *'iqqēsh*, "twisted, perverse"; cp. 11:20; 22:5) and **devious** (Hb, "perverted," 2:15);
- **a forbidden** [Hb *zur*, "strange, turning aside, deviating, distancing, or removing" in the sense of one outside the covenant community who endangers the entire community because of her behavior, not necessarily a foreigner or an adulteress, though the context does suggest this meaning here] **woman** (2:16).

"persuade someone as in offering an alluring temptation") others to join in their activities. Young people lacking experience and discernment are particularly vulnerable targets for such recruitment (cp. 16:29). The choice to do evil always leads to destruction. Wise parents persistently forewarn their sons and daughters about the evil one's deceptively alluring tactics in order to protect them from the deadly consequences of being gullible and naïve when the temptations emerge.

1:20-23 The personification of wisdom occurs here and in 8:1–9:6. **Wisdom** (Hb *chokmah*; see **Word Study**, p. 783) is plural in the Hebrew, perhaps emphasizing its overwhelming importance and comprehensive scope. It is not private and esoteric but has broad applicability in every sphere of life (vv. 20-21). Descriptions of those addressed move from **foolish ones** (the untutored or naïve) to **mockers** (those who respond with defiance) to **fools** who **hate knowledge** (describing the ungodly and immoral). Each walks in his own way without regard for the message of "wisdom."

2:1-22 These 22 verses are set as a literary acrostic or alphabetic poem. The chapter is styled as one lengthy sentence in which each verse begins with a successive letter of the Hebrew alphabet—a poetic device conveying the completeness of this warning against rejecting wisdom and embracing evil.

2:1-5 The verb translated **store up** (Hb *tsaphan*) here has the sense of concealing something valuable or precious in order to keep it safe (cp. Ps 119:11). The author urges an ardent pursuit of **wisdom** likened to a concentrated search for **hidden treasure** that would have only monetary value. In Hebrew the phrase **listening closely** is more vivid—literally inclining the ear toward a speaker or pricking up one's ears to catch the sound—and conveys both having interest in and giving attention to wisdom. Similarly, **directing** [Hb *natah*] **your heart** pictures actively leaning or stretching out toward, in this case, **understanding** (Hb *tavun*, "competence, discernment"). To know and apply God's Word pays off (cp. Lk 11:10).

2:6-8 The Lord delights in giving wisdom and understanding to those who come to Him, for He is the source of knowledge. **The upright** are, more literally, those who continually "walk" (Hb *halak*) with integrity. For such people, the Lord **stores up** [Hb *tsaphan*; 2:1-5] **success** (Hb *tushiyah*, "sound, reliable wisdom or counsel; cp. 3:21; 8:14; 18:1; Is 28:29). In the New Testament, Jms 1:5 also underscores

[A]2:2 Lit *you, stretching out your ear* [B]2:7 Or *resourcefulness*

that God abundantly provides wisdom to those who seek it from Him.

2:16-19 The dangerous **forbidden woman** is further described as a **stranger** (Hb *nokri*, "one who turns aside, alien, profane, unlawful; one who stands outside the family or even a pagan foreigner"). In this context, a female "stranger" likely refers to a woman practicing either adultery or prostitution because involvement with her brings total moral ruin. She brings not only the harm of sexual infidelity but also **death**. This woman turns aside from her family, her husband (v. 17a), the land (vv. 18,21-22), and the law (v. 17b).

2:20-22 People who are ensnared in evil practices, who enjoy doing wicked things, and who lure others to join in their activities (cp. 1:10-19) ultimately do not share in the blessings of dwelling in the land—as do those who **keep to** [Hb *yathar*, "remain on"] **the paths of the righteous**—but are **cut off** and **uprooted** [Hb *nasach*, "pulled or torn away, plucked up"; cp. Dt 28:63; Ps 52:5] **from it**.

3:1-8 Teaching (Hb *torah*; cp. 1:8), referring to the entire catechism of instruction found in the book is often linked with **commands** (Hb *mitswah*, from the verb *tsawah*, "set up, constitute, charge"; cp. 2:1; 6:20). Wisdom offers the promised rewards of **a full life** and **well-being** (Hb *shalom*, "peace, wholeness"), often manifest in a healthy lifestyle and freedom from anxiety. Just as righteous living tends to offer a happier and healthier life, so unrighteous living brings negative consequences to health and relationships (3:2,8).

To **trust** [Hb *batach*, "rely on, confide in, place hope in, be secure without fear" in the sense of firm and certain confidence in another, v. 5] **in** and **think about** the Lord links earnest persuasion with faithful assurance. This proverb emphasizes exclusivity (i.e., not embracing your own perceptions but fully focusing on God's truth and His ways) and priorities (i.e., choosing God's way before and above your way).

3:9-12 Honor [Hb *kavad*, "be heavy or weighty" in the sense of giving prominence or esteem because of the value of someone] **the Lord** is a reminder that what you give to kingdom causes or to help others is ultimately a way of bringing honor to God, who gave you all that you have. It is also an admonition to give God **the first produce** as an expression of gratitude for His abundant blessings and thanksgiving for His continual care of His creation (i.e., the best, not merely what is left over after you have satisfied all your needs and wants; cp. Ex 22:29; 23:19a; 34:20; Lv 23:10; Lk 11:42).

13 from those who abandon
the right paths
to walk in ways of darkness,
14 from those who enjoy doing evil
and celebrate perversion,
15 whose paths are crooked,
and whose ways are devious.
16 It will rescue you
from a forbidden woman,
from a stranger[A]
with her flattering talk,
17 who abandons the companion
of her youth
and forgets the covenant
of her God;
18 for her house sinks down
to death
and her ways to the land
of the departed spirits.
19 None return who go to her;
none reach the paths of life.
20 So follow the way
of good people,
and keep to the paths
of the righteous.
21 For the upright will inhabit
the land,
and those of integrity
will remain in it;
22 but the wicked will be cut off
from the land,
and the treacherous uprooted
from it.

3 My son, don't forget
my teaching,
but let your heart keep
my commands;
2 for they will bring you
many days, a full life,[B]
and well-being.
3 Never let loyalty
and faithfulness leave you.
Tie them around your neck;
write them on the tablet
of your heart.
4 Then you will find favor
and high regard
in the sight of God and man.

5 Trust in the LORD with all
your heart,
and do not rely on
your own understanding;
6 think about Him in all
your ways,
and He will guide you
on the right paths.[C]

7 Don't consider yourself
to be wise;
•fear the LORD and turn away
from evil.
8 This will be healing
for your body[D]
and strengthening
for your bones.
9 Honor the LORD
with your possessions
and with the first produce
of your entire harvest;
10 then your barns will be
completely filled,
and your vats will overflow
with new wine.
11 Do not despise
the LORD's instruction,
my son,
and do not loathe
His discipline;
12 for the LORD disciplines the one
He loves,
just as a father, the son
he delights in.

HARD QUESTION

Is corporal punishment (spanking) an appropriate way to discipline my children?

Discipline (Hb *musar*, "training, chastening, instruction," 3:11; see **Word Study**, p. 783) is part of the pedagogical process. Whether verbal (1:2) or physical (cp. 13:24; 22:15; 23:13), helping a child to obey sometimes demands a painful correction in order to bring him into the right way. Sometimes corrections become afflictions of love as well as warnings to avoid greater judgment (23:13). If the teacher or parent does not administer this "discipline," he becomes part of the wrongdoing. In the relationship between the Lord and His children, correction is a sign of God's love (cp. Dt 8:5; Heb 12:3-12; Rv 3:19). Discipline, the gentle shaping by a loving heavenly Father and not the vindictive punishment of an irate God, is the means for achieving obedience and the fruit of walking in the way of the Lord.

13 Happy is a man
who finds wisdom
and who acquires
understanding,
14 for she is more profitable
than silver,

[A]2:16 Or *foreign woman* [B]3:2 Lit *days, years of life* [C]3:6 Lit *will make your paths straight* [D]3:8 Lit *navel*

and her revenue is better
than gold.
15 She is more precious
than jewels;
nothing you desire compares
with her.
16 Long life[A] is in her right hand;
in her left, riches and honor.
17 Her ways are pleasant,
and all her paths, peaceful.
18 She is a tree of life to those
who embrace her,
and those who hold on to her
are happy.

19 The LORD founded the earth
by wisdom
and established the heavens
by understanding.
20 By His knowledge
the watery depths
broke open,
and the clouds dripped
with dew.

21 Maintain your competence
and discretion.
My son, don't lose sight
of them.
22 They will be life for you[B,C]
and adornment[D]
for your neck.
23 Then you will go safely
on your way;
your foot will not stumble.
24 When you lie[E] down,
you will not be afraid;
you will lie down,
and your sleep
will be pleasant.
25 Don't fear sudden danger
or the ruin of the wicked
when it comes,
26 for the LORD will be
your confidence[F]
and will keep your foot
from a snare.

27 When it is in your power,[G]
don't withhold good
from the one it belongs to.
28 Don't say to your neighbor,
"Go away! Come back later.
I'll give it tomorrow"—
when it is there with you.
29 Don't plan any harm
against your neighbor,
for he trusts you and lives
near you.
30 Don't accuse anyone
without cause,
when he has done you
no harm.
31 Don't envy a violent man
or choose any of his ways;
32 for the devious are detestable
to the LORD,
but He is a friend[H]
to the upright.
33 The LORD's curse is
on the household
of the wicked,
but He blesses the home
of the righteous;
34 He mocks those who mock,
but gives grace
to the humble.
35 The wise will inherit honor,
but He holds up fools
to dishonor.[I]

4 Listen, my sons,
to a father's discipline,
and pay attention so that you
may gain understanding,
2 for I am giving you
good instruction.
Don't abandon my teaching.
3 When I was a son
with my father,
tender and precious
to my mother,
4 he taught me and said:
"Your heart must hold on
to my words.
Keep my commands and live.
5 Get wisdom, get understanding;
don't forget or turn away
from the words
of my mouth.
6 Don't abandon wisdom,
and she will watch over you;
love her, and she will
guard you.
7 Wisdom is supreme—
so get wisdom.
And whatever else you get,
get understanding.
8 Cherish her, and she will
exalt you;
if you embrace her, she will
honor you.

[A]3:16 Lit *Length of days* [B]3:22 Or *be your throat* [C]3:22 In Hb, *nephesh* can mean throat, soul, or life. [D]3:22 Or *grace* [E]3:24 LXX reads *sit* [F]3:26 Or *be at your side* [G]3:27 Lit *in the power of your hands* [H]3:32 Or *confidential counsel* [I]3:35 Or *but haughty fools dishonor*, or *but fools exalt dishonor*

3:13-35 The teacher moves to an excursus on wisdom (vv. 13-26), in which he praises its value (vv. 13-18), notes again its connection to the Creator (vv. 19-20), and then makes application to the reader by reiterating ways he can embrace and utilize wisdom in his own life (vv. 21-26). Verses 17 and 18 are recited in modern Jewish worship when the Torah is returned to its ark. Wisdom's highest praise comes from God Himself, who possesses wisdom, created the world by wisdom, and continues to govern the world by it (vv. 19-20). The same wisdom God used in creating the world is now a valuable tool for living successfully in that world.

3:27-31 Scripture certainly does not call on you to give what you do not have (cp. 2Co 8:12; Gl 6:10); however, the selflessness of Christ and the Christian emphasis on responding to others does take center stage here. **Your neighbor** (Hb *rēaʿ*, "friend, companion, acquaintance") is your responsibility, and there are five warnings concerning how you relate to him:

- **Don't withhold good**. The dues of life must have attention—repaying what has been borrowed (Ps 37:21), paying a worker for his work (Jms 5:4), or meeting someone's personal need (Ps 82:3-4; 1 Jn 3:17). Kindness is not an option for the believer, and love is not reserved for those who are within the family circle or who are lovable. Sensitivity to the pain and suffering of others, willingness to spend time and energy and resources in meeting needs—these are Christian virtues.
- **Don't** turn away or delay. Response to need is not borne out of a personal timetable or convenience but according to the need and its timing.
- **Don't plan any harm**. Personal rights often awaken retribution. The faults of others or trying to right the wrongs done against others sometimes inspire what may seem to be just recompense for a wronged person. However, God's way is loving forbearance.
- **Don't accuse . . . without cause**. God determines the administration of justice. Believers are cautioned about jumping into quarrels.
- **Don't envy a violent man or choose any of his ways**. You can never honor the Lord even by doing something to correct a wrong when you do it in the world's way.

4:1-9 Discipline (Hb *musar*, "exhortation, warning"; see **Word Study**, p. 783) in this context consists of loving guidance from both father and mother toward self-control. Harsh

>WORD|*study*

4:21 All actions and attitudes come out of the **heart** (Hb *lēvav,* "seat of feeling and affection,") and mind. The Hebrews considered the heart to be the essence of who the person is, which may be different from how she appears to others (cp. 1Ch 28:9; Lk 6:45). What is conceived in the mind becomes the heart's passion and eventually issues in both words and actions. The heart is the control center, the seat of the will and of moral responsibility. For this reason, the heart must be carefully guarded (v. 23).

5:4 **Wormwood** (Hb *la'anah*), a common silvery white plant with an acrid taste found in ancient Palestine, is used in Scripture as a symbol of something bitter and evil or to represent calamity or sorrow (cp. Dt 29:18; Jr 9:15; 23:15; Lm 3:15,19; Am 5:7; Rv 8:11). Here it describes the aftertaste of an illicit union.

5:19 The teacher passionately affirms through erotic language the delights and pleasure of marital love as **satisfying** (Hb *rawah,* "give to drink abundantly, water thoroughly, saturate") and intoxicating (Hb *shagah*, "stagger, swerve, meander" in the sense of being unable to restrain yourself or act under your own power, being overwhelmed with the ecstasies of lovemaking—**be lost in . . . love**). *Shagah* is also translated "infatuated" in a rhetorical question concerning an illicit relationship with the "forbidden woman" (v. 20).

punishment is not in view but rather the fashioning of life under the right governance in order to attain success.

4:10-19 Choosing the **way** [Hb *derek*, "road" as a metaphor for a lifestyle] **of wisdom** (i.e., the right way) leads to prosperity and safety (vv. 11-12). In contrast, the **path of the wicked** is to be avoided at all costs (vv. 13-15). The warning here as elsewhere is to **avoid** the beginning of evil (v. 15; cp. Jms 1:14-15).

4:20-27 The emphasis in this section is not on choosing a path but on the virtues of the right **path for your feet** (v. 26). By pursuing the path **straight ahead**, looking neither to the right nor left, your whole body, motivated and inspired by the "heart," is focused on moving the right way. Your ears hear the teacher's words (v. 20); your **mouth** offers chaste language (v. 24); your **eyes** see the path of righteousness (v. 25); your feet move forward on the right path and do not stray toward **evil** (v. 27); and guarding the heart determines what you say, what you see, and what you do. You must satiate your heart with wisdom and what is good in God's eyes.

5:1-14 **The forbidden** [Hb *zur*, "strange, immoral"] **woman** is the subject of three sections of teaching (5:1-23; 6:20-35; 7:1-27). The woman is identified only as a prostitute, the wife of someone known to the young man, a woman from another country. The young man is married and has been instructed in God's law, but the seductress can effectively allure him to immorality. She identifies and pursues the weakness of her victim with sweet and enticing charms, including hollow praise (5:3), and yet the end brings bitterness and **death** (vv. 4-5).

Education, self-discipline, and all efforts at self-sufficiency are not enough to withstand temptation. The young man is urged to avoid her and **the door of her house** (v. 8) and reminded of the marital bliss available to him with his own wife (vv. 15,18). The teacher speaks of the high cost of being entrapped by this woman:

9 She will place a garland of grace
on your head;
she will give you a crown
of beauty."
10 Listen, my son.
Accept my words,
and you will live many years.
11 I am teaching you the way
of wisdom;
I am guiding you
on straight paths.
12 When you walk, your steps
will not be hindered;
when you run,
you will not stumble.
13 Hold on to instruction;
don't let go.
Guard it, for it is your life.
14 Don't set foot on the path
of the wicked;
don't proceed in the way
of evil ones.
15 Avoid it; don't travel on it.
Turn away from it,
and pass it by.
16 For they can't sleep
unless they have done
what is evil;
they are robbed of sleep
unless they make
someone stumble.
17 They eat the bread
of wickedness
and drink the wine
of violence.
18 The path of the righteous is
like the light of dawn,
shining brighter and brighter
until midday.
19 But the way of the wicked is
like the darkest gloom;
they don't know what makes
them stumble.

20 My son, pay attention
to my words;
listen closely to my sayings.
21 Don't lose sight of them;
keep them within your heart.
22 For they are life to those
who find them,
and health to
one's whole body.
23 Guard your heart
above all else,[A]
for it is the source of life.
24 Don't let your mouth
speak dishonestly,
and don't let your lips
talk deviously.
25 Let your eyes look forward;
fix your gaze[B] straight ahead.
26 Carefully consider the path[C]
for your feet,
and all your ways
will be established.
27 Don't turn to the right
or to the left;
keep your feet away from evil.

A Prelude to Sin Through Folly (5:1–7:27)

The Warning against Falling Prey to Immorality (5:1-23)

5 My son, pay attention
to my wisdom;
listen closely[D]
to my understanding
2 so that you may maintain
discretion
and your lips safeguard
knowledge.
3 Though the lips
of the forbidden woman
drip honey
and her words are[E]
smoother than oil,

[A]4:23 Or *heart with all diligence* [B]4:25 Lit *eyelids* [C]4:26 Or *Clear a path* [D]5:1 Lit *wisdom; stretch out your ear* [E]5:3 Lit *her palate is*

4 in the end she's as bitter
as ·wormwood
and as sharp as
a double-edged sword.
5 Her feet go down to death;
her steps head straight
for ·Sheol.
6 She doesn't consider the path
of life;
she doesn't know
that her ways are unstable.

7 So now, my sons, listen to me,
and don't turn away
from the words
of my mouth.
8 Keep your way far from her.
Don't go near the door
of her house.
9 Otherwise, you will give up
your vitality to others
and your years
to someone cruel;
10 strangers will drain
your resources,
and your earnings will end up
in a foreigner's house.
11 At the end of your life,
you will lament
when your physical body
has been consumed,
12 and you will say,
"How I hated discipline,
and how my heart
despised correction.
13 I didn't obey my teachers
or listen closely[A]
to my mentors.
14 I am on the verge
of complete ruin
before the entire community."

15 Drink water
from your own cistern,
water flowing
from your own well.
16 Should your springs flow
in the streets,
streams of water
in the public squares?
17 They should be for you alone
and not for you to share
with strangers.
18 Let your fountain be blessed,
and take pleasure in the wife
of your youth.
19 A loving doe, a graceful fawn—
let her breasts
always satisfy you;
be lost in her love forever.
20 Why, my son, would you
be infatuated
with a forbidden woman
or embrace the breast
of a stranger?
21 For a man's ways are
before the LORD's eyes,
and He considers
all his paths.
22 A wicked man's iniquities
entrap him;
he is entangled in the ropes
of his own sin.
23 He will die because there is
no discipline,
and be lost because of
his great stupidity.

The Warning Against Being Idle and Deceitful (6:1-19)

6 My son, if you have
put up security
for your neighbor[B]
or entered into an agreement
with[C] a stranger,[D]
2 you have been trapped
by the words of your lips[E]—

[A]5:13 Lit *or turn my ear* [B]6:1 Or *friend* [C]6:1 Lit *or shaken hands for* or *with* [D]6:1 The Hb word for *stranger* can refer to a foreigner, an Israelite outside one's family, or simply to another person. [E]6:2 Lit *mouth*

vitality (Hb *hod*, "bloom of life, majesty, splendor, vigor") and **years**, during which his **resources and . . . earnings** will be lost—whether spent by the woman or given as compensation to her husband, whom she deceived and cheated (vv. 9-10). The deadly effects of this sin mean not only economic loss but also social ruin (vv. 12-13), ostracism from the community (v. 14), and spiritual demise (vv. 21-23). The confession will complete a tragic interruption and destruction of life (vv. 11-14).

5:21-23 This lesson closes with a theological reminder of the all-seeing, omniscient God's watchfulness over all His creation (v. 21); a warning about the entrapment of sin (v. 22); and a promise of justice in the summary judgment that sin, which robs one of true freedom and brings death, will most certainly come—swiftly or over time (v. 23; cp. Gl 6:7).

6:1-5 To **put up security** (Hb *ʿarav*, "pledge yourself and what you have as a guarantee or collateral for the debts of another") can bring ruin. The warning here concerns making yourself accountable through cosigning for the loan of **your neighbor or . . . a stranger**, which could make what you have legally dependent upon the integrity and ability of your neighbor and his creditor, over which you have no direct control (cp. 11:15; 17:18; 20:16; 22:26-27; 27:13). The neighbor cannot afford to incur this debt; to join him in such a venture is doubly foolish. The imperative verbs **free yourself**, **humble yourself**, and **plead** (Hb *rahav*, "storm, assault, press, urge with troublesome persistence") urge a forceful and continued effort to the point of foregoing sleeping or even being willing to humiliate yourself in order to gain release from the unwise obligation.

BIBLICAL WOMANHOOD Marital Intimacy

God's provision for meeting sexual desires—compared in Proverbs 5:15-16 to thirst for water—is within marriage (cp. Gn 2:24). The admonition to drink from one's **own well** underscores the sanctity and exclusivity of physical intimacy within a monogamous marriage; sexual satisfaction is the rightful reward of marriage alone. God's plan is for the tender delights of love and the exciting spontaneity of passion to be woven into the heart of the marital union (cp. Dt 24:5; Ec 9:9). The best protection against the sin of infidelity is to invest full faithfulness and tender, loving affection in your marriage, which provides the opportunity for sexual joy.

6:6-11 In contrast to becoming poor by doing something unwise, the **slacker** (Hb *ʿatsēl*, "lazy or idle person, sluggard"; cp. 10:26; 19:24; 21:25; 22:13; 26:13-16) falls into poverty because he refuses to do anything. The subject of laziness is addressed often through contrasting idleness and work (cp. 10:4; 12:24; 13:4; 15:19; 19:15; 20:4,13; 24:30-34). Unlike the resourceful **ant** as a model of self-motivation and prudent efficiency, this "slacker" does not prepare for the future; and his slothfulness and lack of initiative are criticized. Opportunities are lost, and he slips into severe poverty, losing even the necessities of life because of neglecting his responsibilities.

6:20-24 The parent/teacher again emphasizes that the **father's command** (Hb *mitswah*; cp. 3:1; 6:20) and **mother's teaching** (Hb *torah*, v. 20; cp. 1:8; 3:1-3; 4:1-4; 7:1-3) should be bound **to your heart** and tied **around your neck**—metaphors stressing the importance of keeping something so valuable always close (6:21; cp. 3:3; 7:3; cp. Dt 6:6-9; 11:18-20). In Hebrew thought, the "heart" refers to the center of physical life and spiritual decisions.

Lamp and **light** are metaphors for the wise guidance that comes from godly parents (cp. Ps 119:105), who can teach their children only what they themselves have already learned. **An evil woman** is a **stranger** (Hb *nokri*, "foreign woman, harlot"; cp. 2:16).

>WORD|*study*

6:12 A worthless person, literally "man of Belial" (Hb, "uselessness," a term used to describe an unusually evil man, one who works against all that is good; cp. Dt 13:13; 1Sm 2:12), lives as a "worthless" scoundrel and betrays his lifestyle by his speech and body gestures. He is not a murderer or adulterer, but he "stirs up trouble" (Pr 6:14; cp. v. 19). In the New Testament, Satan is explicitly called "Belial" (2Co 6:15).

6:25 The expanded instruction begins rather than ends with the bottom line: **Don't** lust (Hb *chamad*, "desire"), the same word, in Hebrew, used in the tenth commandment, "Do not covet" (Ex 20:17; Dt 5:21). Jesus likewise bluntly diagnosed adultery as a heart issue (Mt 5:27-28). The parallelism of this verse amplifies the warning to the man—He is responsible for his **heart**. Inevitably the adulterer will bring ruin on himself. He will receive severe punishment, which is a natural outworking of his wrongdoing, and the tragedy for him and others is unending. Although there may be pleasure in the beginning, the end is pain.

ensnared by the words
of your mouth.
3 Do this, then, my son,
and free yourself,
for you have put yourself
in your neighbor's power:
Go, humble yourself,
and plead
with your neighbor.
4 Don't give sleep to your eyes
or slumber to your eyelids.
5 Escape like a gazelle
from a hunter,[A]
like a bird from
a fowler's trap.[A]

6 Go to the ant, you slacker!
Observe its ways
and become wise.
7 Without leader, administrator,
or ruler,
8 it prepares its provisions
in summer;
it gathers its food
during harvest.
9 How long will you stay in bed,
you slacker?
When will you get up
from your sleep?
10 A little sleep, a little slumber,
a little folding of the arms
to rest,
11 and your poverty will come like
a robber,
your need, like a bandit.

12 A worthless person,
a wicked man
goes around
speaking dishonestly,
13 winking his eyes, signaling
with his feet,
and gesturing
with his fingers.
14 He always plots evil
with perversity
in his heart—
he stirs up trouble.
15 Therefore calamity
will strike him suddenly;
he will be shattered
instantly—beyond recovery.

16 The LORD hates six things;
in fact, seven are detestable
to Him:
17 arrogant eyes, a lying tongue,
hands that shed
innocent blood,
18 a heart that plots
wicked schemes,
feet eager to run to evil,
19 a lying witness who gives
false testimony,
and one who stirs up trouble
among brothers.

Another Warning Against Immorality (6:20–7:27)

20 My son, keep
your father's command,
and don't reject
your mother's teaching.
21 Always bind them to your heart;
tie them around your neck.
22 When you walk here and there,
they will guide you;
when you lie down, they will
watch over you;
when you wake up, they will
talk to you.
23 For a command is a lamp,
teaching is a light,
and corrective discipline is
the way to life.
24 They will protect you
from an evil woman,[B]
from the flattering[C] tongue
of a stranger.

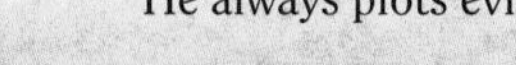

[A]6:5 Lit *hand* [B]6:24 LXX reads *from a married woman* [C]6:24 Lit *smooth*

25 Don't lust in your heart
for her beauty
or let her captivate you
with her eyelashes.
26 For a prostitute's fee is
only a loaf of bread,[A]
but an adulteress[B] goes after
a precious life.
27 Can a man embrace fire[C]
and his clothes not
be burned?
28 Can a man walk
on burning coals
without scorching his feet?
29 So it is with the one
who sleeps with
another man's wife;
no one who touches her
will go unpunished.
30 People don't despise the thief
if he steals
to satisfy himself
when he is hungry.
31 Still, if caught, he must pay
seven times as much;
he must give up all the wealth
in his house.
32 The one who commits adultery[D]
lacks sense;
whoever does so
destroys himself.
33 He will get a beating[E]
and dishonor,
and his disgrace will
never be removed.
34 For jealousy enrages a husband,
and he will show no mercy
when he takes revenge.
35 He will not be appeased
by anything
or be persuaded
by lavish gifts.

7 My son, obey my words,
and treasure my commands.
2 Keep my commands and live;
protect my teachings
as the pupil of your eye.
3 Tie them to your fingers;
write them on the tablet
of your heart.
4 Say to wisdom, "You are
my sister,"
and call understanding
your relative.
5 She will keep you
from a forbidden woman,
a stranger with
her flattering talk.

6 At the window of my house
I looked through my lattice.
7 I saw among the inexperienced,[F]
I noticed among the youths,
a young man lacking sense.
8 Crossing the street
near her corner,
he strolled down the road
to her house
9 at twilight, in the evening,
in the dark of the night.
10 A woman came to meet him
dressed like a prostitute,
having a hidden agenda.[G]
11 She is loud and defiant;
her feet do not stay at home.
12 Now in the street,
now in the squares,
she lurks at every corner.
13 She grabs him and kisses him;
she brazenly says[H] to him,
14 "I've made
•fellowship offerings;[I]
today I've fulfilled my vows.
15 So I came out to meet you,
to search for you,
and I've found you.
16 I've spread coverings
on my bed—
richly colored linen
from Egypt.
17 I've perfumed my bed
with myrrh, aloes,
and cinnamon.
18 Come, let's drink deeply
of lovemaking
until morning.
Let's feast on
each other's love!
19 My husband isn't home;
he went on a long journey.
20 He took a bag of money
with him
and will come home
at the time of the full moon."
21 She seduces him with
her persistent pleading;

7:1-27 This fourth section of instruction brings to a climax the parent/teacher's warnings against the unfaithful wife (2:16-19; 5:1-23; 6:20-33). A metaphor expressing affectionate relationship—**the pupil** of the eye (7:2; cp. Dt 32:10; Ps 17:8; Zch 2:8)—underscores the value of the **commands** (Hb *mitswah*; cp. 3:1) and **teachings** (Hb *torah*; cp. 1:8). The reference to the **heart** (Hb *lēv*, Pr 7:3; see **Word Study**, p. 788) affirms that this wisdom must be planted internally as part of one's character.

This didactic passage graphically describes the ways of the unfaithful wife who seduces an **inexperienced** (Hb *peti*, "naive, foolishly open-minded, gullible," v. 7; cp. 1:4) young man into adultery. The details that unfold lead the listener to recognize the man's utter folly and to identify point after point at which he should have turned around:

- the setting of darkness (v. 9);
- her provocative clothing (v. 10);
- her **loud and defiant** demeanor (v. 11; cp. 9:13);
- her presence everywhere but home (vv. 11-12);
- her bold and aggressive actions to stimulate her victim's sexual appetite (vv. 13,15-18);
- her pseudo-spiritual façade (v. 14);
- her deception of her husband (vv. 19-20);
- her **flattering** speech (v. 21); and
- her heartless move to possess and destroy her prey (vv. 22-23).

[A]6:26 Or *On account of a prostitute, one is left with only a loaf of bread* [B]6:26 Lit *but a wife of a man* [C]6:27 Lit *man take fire to his bosom* [D]6:32 Lit *commits adultery with a woman* [E]6:33 Or *plague* [F]7:7 Or *simple*, or *gullible*, or *naive* [G]7:10 Or *prostitute with a guarded heart* [H]7:13 Lit *she makes her face strong and says* [I]7:14 Meat from a fellowship offering had to be eaten on the day it was offered; therefore she is inviting him to a feast at her house.

8:1-12 Directly contrasting the immoral woman who preys upon the gullible in the secrecy of "the dark of the night" (7:9), wisdom is personified as a woman prominently broadcasting **truth** (Hb *ʾemet*, "that which is true and reliable"—the opposite of falsehood, insincerity, or unfaithfulness; 8:7) to the **inexperienced** (Hb *peti*, v. 5; cp. 7:7) and anyone else who will listen (v. 4). Verses 6-10 elaborate on the reliability and desirability of what Wisdom says, further contrasting her **instruction** with the "flattering talk" of the adulteress (7:13-21). Reiterating 3:15, the listener is reminded of the incomparable value of wisdom. The statement **nothing desirable can compare with it** more literally says that "all things desirable [Hb *kol*, "all" modifying the plural form of *chephets*, "something precious, that which is desired and pursued"; cp. 1Kg 10:13; "delight," Ps 1:2] cannot compare" to wisdom (cp. Is 40:25).

8:13-21 In these verses, **Wisdom** presents an overwhelming list of benefits available to the one who chooses **to fear the Lord** and, therefore **to hate evil** (cp. 3:7; 16:6; Jb 28:28), which is manifested in attitude, action, and speech (Pr 8:13). Wisdom cannot coexist with **arrogant pride** (cp. 16:18) or perversity. Not only are they incompatible, but also one will displace the other. Wisdom yields the greatest dividends—"she" alone is supremely worth one's life-investment (8:14-21). The mention of **riches and honor** is not the enticement of a prosperity gospel but implies a reversal of the deceitful and seductive message that life is all about monetary gain, possessions, and sensual pleasures. Instead, loving and walking in God's way of wisdom brings truly substantive, **lasting wealth**.

8:32-36 Wisdom calls for followers willing to engage in faithful and obedient service. She offers much to those who respond—**life** and the Lord's **favor**. Those who **hate** wisdom are not just foolish; they are twisted and depraved in their value system. To love the Lord is to hate evil (v. 13); conversely, to hate wisdom is to **love death**. Proverbs consistently models discernment between wisdom and folly, good and evil, the (one) way of life and the (many) ways of death.

she lures
with her flattering[A] talk.
22 He follows her impulsively
like an ox going
to the slaughter,
like a deer bounding
toward a trap[B]
23 until an arrow pierces
its[C] liver,
like a bird darting
into a snare—
he doesn't know
it will cost him his life.

24 Now, my sons, listen to me,
and pay attention
to the words of my mouth.
25 Don't let your heart
turn aside to her ways;
don't stray onto her paths.
26 For she has brought many
down to death;
her victims are countless.[D]
27 Her house is the road
to •Sheol,
descending to the chambers
of death.

The Personification of Wisdom (8:1–9:18)

A Description (8:1-36)

8 Doesn't Wisdom call out?
Doesn't Understanding make
her voice heard?
2 At the heights overlooking
the road,
at the crossroads, she takes
her stand.
3 Beside the gates at the entry
to[E] the city,
at the main entrance,
she cries out:
4 "People, I call out to you;
my cry is to mankind.
5 Learn to be shrewd,
you who are inexperienced;
develop common sense,
you who are foolish.
6 Listen, for I speak
of noble things,
and what my lips say is right.
7 For my mouth tells the truth,
and wickedness is detestable
to my lips.
8 All the words of my mouth
are righteous;
none of them are deceptive
or perverse.
9 All of them are clear
to the perceptive,
and right to those
who discover knowledge.
10 Accept my instruction
instead of silver,
and knowledge rather
than pure gold.
11 For wisdom is better
than jewels,
and nothing desirable
can compare with it.
12 I, Wisdom, share a home
with shrewdness
and have knowledge
and discretion.
13 To •fear the Lord is to hate evil.
I hate arrogant pride,
evil conduct,
and perverse speech.
14 I possess good advice
and competence;[F]
I have understanding
and strength.
15 It is by me that kings reign
and rulers enact just law;
16 by me, princes lead,
as do nobles
and all righteous judges.[G]
17 I love those who love me,
and those who search for me
find me.
18 With me are riches and honor,
lasting wealth
and righteousness.
19 My fruit is better
than solid gold,
and my harvest
than pure silver.
20 I walk in the way
of righteousness,
along the paths of justice,
21 giving wealth as an inheritance
to those who love me,
and filling their treasuries.

22 "The Lord made[H] me
at the beginning
of His creation,[I]
before His works of long ago.
23 I was formed
before ancient times,
from the beginning,
before the earth began.

[A]**7:21** Lit *smooth* [B]**7:22** Text emended; MT reads *like a shackle to the discipline of a fool*; Hb obscure [C]**7:23** Or *his* [D]**7:26** Or *and powerful men are all her victims* [E]**8:3** Lit *the mouth of* [F]**8:14** Or *resourcefulness* [G]**8:16** Some Hb mss, LXX read *nobles who judge the earth* [H]**8:22** Or *possessed*, or *begot* [I]**8:22** Lit *way*

24 I was born
when there were
no watery depths
and no springs filled
with water.
25 I was delivered
before the mountains
and hills were established,
26 before He made the land,
the fields,
or the first soil on earth.
27 I was there when He established
the heavens,
when He laid out the horizon
on the surface of the ocean,
28 when He placed the skies above,
when the fountains
of the ocean gushed out,
29 when He set a limit for the sea
so that the waters
would not violate
His command,
when He laid out
the foundations
of the earth.
30 I was a skilled craftsman[A]
beside Him.
I was His[B] delight every day,
always rejoicing before Him.
31 I was rejoicing in
His inhabited world,
delighting in
the •human race.
32 "And now, my sons,
listen to me;
those who keep my ways
are happy.
33 Listen to instruction
and be wise;
don't ignore it.
34 Anyone who listens to me
is happy,
watching at my doors
every day,
waiting by the posts
of my doorway.
35 For the one who finds me
finds life
and obtains favor
from the LORD,
36 but the one who misses me[C]
harms himself;
all who hate me love death."

An Invitation (9:1-18)

9 Wisdom has built her house;
she has carved out
her seven pillars.
2 She has prepared her meat;
she has mixed her wine;
she has also set her table.
3 She has sent out
her female servants;
she calls out from
the highest points
of the city:
4 "Whoever is inexperienced,
enter here!"
To the one who lacks sense,
she says,
5 "Come, eat my bread,
and drink the wine
I have mixed.
6 Leave inexperience behind,
and you will live;
pursue the way
of understanding.
7 The one who corrects a mocker
will bring dishonor
on himself;

[A]8:30 Or *a confidant*, or *a child*, or *was constantly* [B]8:30 LXX; MT omits *His* [C]8:36 Or *who sins against me*

9:1-18 Wisdom (vv. 1-6,11) and **Folly** (vv. 13-18) offer competing invitations. Wisdom builds a house as a resourceful woman should do (v. 1; cp. 14:1; 24:3); prepares a rich, celebratory feast (9:2); and invites many guests (vv. 3-6,11), revealing gracious hospitality. **Seven pillars** may be imagery suggesting perfection or completeness or simply evidence of an unusually large and grand house (v. 1). Wisdom bids the inexperienced to **leave . . . behind** (Hb *'azav*, "forsake, cease") the foolishness of going their own way instead of God's. In contrast, **the woman Folly** (Hb *kesilut*, "insolence, stupidity, inertness, dullness," v. 13) encourages the inexperienced to embrace and justify pursuing what they want. Wisdom reemphasizes fearing the Lord as the beginning of a life of godliness (v. 10); Folly, however, advertises the momentary enjoyment of counterfeit and ill-gained pleasures (vv. 17-18).

BIBLICAL WOMANHOOD Perils of Feminist Interpretation

Some feminists have used Proverbs 8:1–9:18 to endorse the worship or recognition of a wisdom (Gk *Sophia*) goddess, whether independently or as a female counterpart of Yahweh, styled after the polytheistic religions of the ancient Near East. When personified, Wisdom acts and speaks as God mandates, but she is not God. In the book of Job, God's interrogation regarding Job's whereabouts during creation accomplished the intended result of renewing Job's sense of humility and reverence before the omnipotent, eternal God (see Jb 38–41). Similarly, this passage's description of wisdom's presence at creation (in contrast to Job's absence) elevates the status of wisdom as an attribute of the omnipotent, eternal God. This passage implores the listener to pursue "her" instead of illicit sensual and ephemeral pleasures, particularly of the sort described in chapter 7.

In poetic fashion, the personification of God's wisdom variously repeats and thereby emphasizes that wisdom belongs to Yahweh and always has. Wisdom is not a commodity one can have apart from the Lord. God makes it available to everyone, but only those who embrace her and subordinate themselves to her ways actually receive His wisdom (Pr 8:20-21).

10:1-5 Serving as an *inclusio* or "bookends," verses 1 and 5 both contrast the **wise son** and the **foolish son** and the impact of each on the family (cp. 15:20; 17:21,25; 19:13; 23:24-25; 27:11; 28:7). Verses 2-4 in between, as well as verse 5, point out some of the economic consequences of each son's approach to life—one building up and the other squandering, the family resources. The mention of **mother** and **father** affirms that both are involved in the instruction and preparation of their children for life (cp. 1:8; 4:3-4; 6:20).

10:6-10 The contrast between laziness and diligence and especially its effect upon the child's parents is unveiled in antithetical parallels (v. 5). **Name** in a real sense goes beyond mere identification to include character and testimony (v. 7). **A wise heart accepts commands** (Hb *mitswah*), referring to a superior's orders to a subordinate; acceptance of such mandates indicates not only present assent but willing obedience that extends into the future (cp. Mt 21:28-32). In Proverbs, the wise are defined by being open and even eager to receive instruction (cp. 9:8-9).

10:11-32 Communication is a major topic addressed in Proverbs, often signaled by references to the **mouth**, **lips**, and **tongue** as the tools for communication (e.g., vv. 11,13-14,18-21,31-32). Godly communication becomes **a fountain of life** having positive and far-reaching effects of encouragement and correction (v. 11). As a metaphor **pure silver** conveys the trust you can have in the **discerning** and **wise** speech of **the righteous**, whose words have been tested and refined by fire (vv. 13,19-20; cp. 27:21). One who is righteous will produce words of **wisdom** because what is within will be reflected without (v. 31). In contrast, communication of **the wicked** or of **fools** is characterized by deception (vv. 11,18); ill-will (vv. 11, 18); lies (v. 18); **slander** (v. 18); and perversity (vv. 31-32). To **cut out** the tongue is a metaphor depicting the seriousness of perverse speech; yet the penalty of rejection and punishment is clear. In the Old Testament, a talebearer was to receive whatever punishment he described for his victim (v. 31; cp. Dt 19:15-21).

Contrasting the Wise and Foolish Woman in Proverbs

Weaknesses in a Foolish Woman:

- Marked by folly (9:13-18)
  - Clamorous—turbulent and animated by passion (v. 13)
  - Simple—with no shield against evil, no moral fiber to resist temptation (v. 13)
  - Ignorant—lacking knowledge of what is right (v. 13)
  - Embodying the contrast between glamour of life and pathetic reality (vv. 14-18)
- Absorbed with embittering hatred (15:17)
- Characterized by a contentious, nagging spirit (cp. 19:13-14; 21:9,19; 25:24; 30:21-23)

Strengths in the Wise Woman:

- Ravishing as a lover to her husband (5:19)
- Charming discretion in her manner (11:16,22)
- Having strength and worth (12:4; 18:22)
  - Adorning her husband; elevating him in social status and in the esteem of neighbors
  - Choosing to be what God prescribed in creation—a helper fit for him—rather than allowing Satan to call into question and distort God's design for her
- Becoming a woman of wisdom with a determination to build her house (14:1; 31:10-31)
  - Embraces biblical priorities (31:10-12)
  - Willingly works her daily routines to serve her family (31:13-22)
  - Extends her energies to those beyond her family circle (31:23-28)
  - Is rewarded for her faithfulness (31: 29-31)

the one who rebukes
a wicked man will get hurt.[A]
8 Don't rebuke a mocker,
or he will hate you;
rebuke a wise man,
and he will love you.
9 Instruct a wise man, and he will
be wiser still;
teach a righteous man,
and he will learn more.

10 "The •fear of the LORD is
the beginning of wisdom,
and the knowledge
of the Holy One
is understanding.
11 For by Wisdom your days
will be many,
and years will be added
to your life.
12 If you are wise, you are wise
for your own benefit;
if you mock, you alone
will bear the consequences."
13 The woman Folly is rowdy;
she is gullible
and knows nothing.
14 She sits by the doorway
of her house,
on a seat at the highest point
of the city,
15 calling to those who pass by,
who go straight ahead
on their paths:
16 "Whoever is inexperienced,
enter here!"
To the one who lacks sense,
she says,
17 "Stolen water is sweet,
and bread eaten secretly
is tasty!"
18 But he doesn't know
that the departed spirits
are there,
that her guests are
in the depths of •Sheol.

The Contrast Between the Wise and the Foolish (10:1–15:33)

10 Solomon's proverbs:

A wise son brings joy
to his father,
but a foolish son, heartache
to his mother.

[A]9:7 Lit *man his blemish*

2 Ill-gotten gains do not
profit anyone,
but righteousness rescues
from death.

3 The LORD will not let
the righteous go hungry,
but He denies the wicked
what they crave.

4 Idle hands make one poor,
but diligent hands
bring riches.

5 The son who gathers
during summer is prudent;
the son who sleeps
during harvest
is disgraceful.

6 Blessings are on the head
of the righteous,
but the mouth of the wicked
conceals violence.

7 The remembrance
of the righteous is
a blessing,
but the name of the wicked
will rot.

8 A wise heart accepts commands,
but foolish lips
will be destroyed.

9 The one who lives with integrity
lives securely,
but whoever perverts his ways
will be found out.

10 A sly wink of the eye
causes grief,
and foolish lips
will be destroyed.

11 The mouth of the righteous is
a fountain of life,
but the mouth of the wicked
conceals violence.

12 Hatred stirs up conflicts,
but love covers all offenses.

13 Wisdom is found on the lips
of the discerning,
but a rod is for the back
of the one who lacks sense.

14 The wise store up knowledge,
but the mouth of the fool
hastens destruction.

15 A rich man's wealth is
his fortified city;
the poverty of the poor is
their destruction.

16 The labor of the righteous leads
to life;
the activity of the wicked
leads to sin.

17 The one who follows instruction
is on the path to life,
but the one who rejects
correction goes astray.

18 The one who conceals hatred
has lying lips,
and whoever spreads slander
is a fool.

19 When there are many words,
sin is unavoidable,
but the one who controls
his lips is wise.

20 The tongue of the righteous is
pure silver;
the heart of the wicked is
of little value.

21 The lips of the righteous
feed many,
but fools die for lack of sense.

22 The LORD's blessing enriches,
and struggle adds
nothing to it.[A]

23 As shameful conduct is pleasure
for a fool,
so wisdom is for a man
of understanding.

24 What the wicked dreads
will come to him,
but what the righteous desire
will be given to them.

25 When the whirlwind passes,
the wicked are no more,
but the righteous
are secure forever.

26 Like vinegar to the teeth
and smoke to the eyes,
so the slacker is to the one
who sends him
on an errand.

27 The •fear of the LORD
prolongs life,[B]
but the years of the wicked
are cut short.

10:12 Love covers [Hb *kasah*, "pardon"] **offenses** (Hb *pesha'*, "fault, trespass, sin, transgression) by forgiving them (cp. 11:13; 12:16; 17:9; 28:13). The idea is not performing a "cover up" to help someone you love avoid appropriate consequences of wrongdoing. Instead, you choose to value the offending person(s) and the shared relationship enough to absorb, without complaint or grudges or retaliation, the personal cost of being wronged. There is no more beautiful depiction of this "covering" by love than the atonement of Christ, who covered the sins of the world through His death on the cross (1Pt 2:21-24; 4:8). **Hatred**, however, insists on being right and "getting even." With *my* hurt uppermost in mind when *my* rights have been violated or *my* expectations have gone unmet, anger and malice grow, feeding revenge and fueling **conflicts**.

10:22 This proverb states what Yahweh's **blessing** does—it **enriches** (Hb *'ashar*, "makes rich"; cp. 1Sm 2:7) without accompanying **struggle** (Hb *'etsev*, "sorrow, labor"; cp. Gn 3:16). The Lord receives due praise for graciously providing and protecting those who submit to His care, especially when human effort reaches its limit. This proverb does not contradict others warning against idleness or laziness; rather, it distinguishes God-given grace from your personal work (cp. Ps 127:2).

10:23 Shameful conduct is wrong and displeasing to God, but to find **pleasure** (Hb *shechoq*, "laughter, jesting, play, derision") in wrongdoing indicates that one's nature has so conformed to this lifestyle that he finds it satisfying and amusing.

10:27 The fear of the LORD is the identifying mark of those who are wise, and usually the righteous will live longer than the wicked because of their embracing a godly lifestyle, which contributes to health and longevity.

[A]10:22 Or *and He adds no trouble to it* [B]10:27 Lit *LORD adds to days*

Biblical Womanhood A Gracious Woman

A gracious woman is characterized by *chēn* (Hb, "charm, favor, elegance, moral strength, integrity"; 11:16; cp. 31:30). The verb root *chanan* suggests a self-determined and often spontaneous willingness to offer heartfelt actions or a compassionate response, an outpouring of mercy and favor freely extended to others (not on the basis of merit or what is deserved). The word is also used in reference to God Himself, combining purpose and action graciously extended (cp. Gn 33:5,11; Ex 33:19, 2Sm 12:22; 2Kg 13:23; Is 30:18; Mal 1:9). A woman whose personality and actions are notably "gracious" routinely models God's lovingkindness in her tender care for others in His name.

11:1-3 Scales and **weight** refer primarily to business practices—e.g., retail, commerce, and monetary exchange. God Himself is aware of every transaction, and He determines the standards used for weights and measures (16:11; cp. Lv 19:36; Dt 25:13-15; Am 8:5; Mc 6:11). The Lord is pleased with **integrity** (Hb *tummah*, "innocence, complete loyalty"; cp. Jb 2:3,9; 27:5; 31:6), but He despises deception. Use of **dishonest** [Hb *mirmah*, "deceit, guile, treachery"] scales violates the Lord's emphatic command that His people must use "honest" measurements (Lv 19:36).

Warnings about **pride** (Hb *zadon*, "presumptuousness, over-confidence, insolence"; lit "a boiling up," often leading to stepping beyond boundaries and insubordination, described as "self-bestowed divinity") are common in Proverbs.

11:4-31 Several verses in this chapter emphasize the drastically different outcomes of lives characterized by **righteousness** as opposed to wickedness. Righteousness **rescues from death** (vv. 4,6; cp. vv. 8-9,21,23) and makes straight paths (v. 5). **A true reward** and **life** are enjoyed by the righteous (vv. 18-19, 30). In contrast, those who are wicked cannot escape the **day of wrath** (Hb *ʿevrah*, "outpouring of anger," vv. 4,23; cp. Jb 21:30), which may refer to a future day when God unleashes punishment on unrepentant sinners but likely recognizes more generally that being held accountable for sin is inevitable in God's economy (cp. Pr 11:21,28,31; Zph 1:14-15). **The wicked** get in **trouble** (Hb *tsarah*, "distress, adversity," Pr 11:8,28); **fall** (vv. 5,14); and **die** (vv. 10,19; cp. 10:29-30). They will discover too late that the earthly **riches** in which they had trusted come inevitably **to nothing** (vv. 4,28; cp. vv. 18,23).

11:9 The ungodly (Hb *chanēph*, "profane, one defiled in mind and seared in conscience and yet pretending to have zeal and affection for God, one dividing his heart between God and the world"; cp. Jb 27:8) brings devastating

28 The hope of the righteous is joy,
but the expectation
of the wicked
comes to nothing.

29 The way of the Lord
is a stronghold
for the honorable,
but destruction awaits
the malicious.

30 The righteous will never
be shaken,
but the wicked will not remain
on the earth.

31 The mouth of the righteous
produces wisdom,
but a perverse tongue will be
cut out.

32 The lips of the righteous know
what is appropriate,
but the mouth of the wicked,
only what is perverse.

11 Dishonest scales
are detestable to the Lord,
but an accurate weight is
His delight.

2 When pride comes,
disgrace follows,
but with humility
comes wisdom.

3 The integrity of the upright
guides them,
but the perversity
of the treacherous
destroys them.

4 Wealth is not profitable on a day
of wrath,
but righteousness rescues
from death.

5 The righteousness
of the blameless
clears his path,
but the wicked person will fall
because of his wickedness.

6 The righteousness
of the upright rescues them,
but the treacherous
are trapped
by their own desires.

7 When the wicked man dies,
his expectation
comes to nothing,
and hope placed in wealth[A,B]
vanishes.

8 The righteous one is rescued
from trouble;
in his place, the wicked one
goes in.

9 With his mouth the ungodly
destroys his neighbor,
but through knowledge
the righteous are rescued.

10 When the righteous thrive,
a city rejoices,
and when the wicked die,
there is joyful shouting.

11 A city is built up by the blessing
of the upright,
but it is torn down
by the mouth of the wicked.

12 Whoever shows contempt
for his neighbor lacks sense,
but a man with understanding
keeps silent.

13 A gossip goes around revealing
a secret,
but a trustworthy person
keeps a confidence.

14 Without guidance, people fall,

[A]11:7 LXX reads *hope of the ungodly* [B]11:7 Or *strength*

but with many counselors
there is deliverance.

15 If someone puts up security
for a stranger,
he will suffer for it,
but the one who hates
such agreements
is protected.

16 A gracious woman gains honor,
but violent[A] men gain
only riches.

17 A kind man benefits himself,
but a cruel man
brings disaster on himself.

18 The wicked man earns
an empty wage,
but the one
who sows righteousness,
a true reward.

19 Genuine righteousness leads
to life,
but pursuing evil leads
to death.

20 Those with twisted minds
are detestable to the LORD,
but those with blameless
conduct are His delight.

21 Be assured[B] that the wicked
will not go unpunished,
but the offspring
of the righteous will escape.

22 A beautiful woman who rejects
good sense
is like a gold ring
in a pig's snout.

23 The desire of the righteous
turns out well,
but the hope of the wicked
leads to wrath.

24 One person gives freely,
yet gains more;
another withholds what is right,
only to become poor.

25 A generous person
will be enriched,
and the one who gives a drink
of water
will receive water.

26 People will curse anyone
who hoards grain,
but a blessing will come
to the one who sells it.

27 The one who searches
for what is good finds favor,
but if someone looks for
trouble, it will come to him.

28 Anyone trusting in his riches
will fall,
but the righteous will flourish
like foliage.

29 The one who brings ruin
on his household
will inherit the wind,
and a fool will be a slave
to someone whose heart
is wise.

30 The fruit of the righteous is
a tree of life,
but violence[C] takes lives.

31 If the righteous will be repaid
on earth,
how much more the wicked
and sinful.

12 Whoever loves discipline
loves knowledge,
but one who hates correction
is stupid.

2 The good person obtains favor
from the LORD,
but He condemns a man
who schemes.

3 Man cannot be made secure
by wickedness,
but the root of the righteous
is immovable.

4 A capable wife[D] is
her husband's crown,
but a wife who causes shame
is like rottenness in his bones.

[A]**11:16** Or *ruthless* [B]**11:21** Lit *Hand to hand* [C]**11:30** LXX, Syr; MT reads *but a wise one* [D]**12:4** Or *A wife of quality*, or *A wife of good character*

>WORD|*study*

11:2 The word humility (Hb *tsana'*, "be submissive") appears in Scripture only here and in Mc 6:8 as "humbly," an essential one-sentence summary of God's requirements from His people. Choosing to submit to the Lord and to the authorities He places in your life implies a teachable disposition that readily receives His **wisdom**.

harm to **his neighbor**, whether by slander, verbal abuse, or hypocrisy.

11:12 One who **lacks sense** more literally is without "heart" (Hb *lēv*)—devoid of solid convictions, courage, or even understanding and, therefore, easily entrapped in ungodly attitudes, thoughts, and behaviors (cp. 6:32; 7:7; 9:4,16). Such people readily despise, look down on, and openly criticize anyone they do not like. In contrast, people who have learned to see both themselves and others the way God sees them tend to listen instead of condemning and to bear insults without verbal retaliation.

11:13 A gossip (Hb *rakil*, "talebearer, defamer, slanderer") is one who betrays trust and sows destruction (cp. 20:19; Lv 19:16; Jr 9:4). He is both weak, doing his deed deceitfully, and wicked, prompted by a desire to hurt and destroy.

11:14 The phrase **many counselors** (Hb *ya'ats*, "adviser, deliberator who considers action and purpose," implying wisdom, reflection, and skill; cp. 15:22; 24:6) indicates looking beyond yourself, weighing a matter before the Lord, and seeking **guidance** (Hb *tachbulot*, "counsel, art of leading, good advice, prudent measures"; lit "steering") from those around you who are spiritually and experientially prepared to offer godly counsel (cp. Dt 32:28).

11:15 Putting up **security for a stranger** (Hb *zur*, "non-Israelite") is a dangerous action when considered against maintaining personal financial security. Whether the "stranger" is from another country, your own community, or even your extended family, the warning is against making pledges that would put the financial security for your own family at risk.

11:22 In ancient Israel, rings were worn in ears and in the nose (cp. Gn 24:30; 35:4). No adornment, even when worn by **a beautiful woman**, can make up for a lack of **good sense** (Hb *ta'am*, "discretion, judgment, discernment, moral understanding," Pr 11:22; cp. 1Sm 25:33). In fact, inappropriate outward behavior overshadows and negates whatever one may try to project through an attractive appearance. Similarly, no Jew would see a pig as attractive or inviting—whatever the enhancement to its appearance. The picture of an animal, especially the unclean pig, wearing **a gold ring** is ludicrous and beyond belief (v. 22).

12:4 The contrasting example of a wife, however, is compared to **rottenness** [Hb *raqav*, "decay, worm-eaten,"] **in his bones**, an expression for being so fear-stricken that the body becomes

Proverbial Wisdom Regarding Wealth and Possessions

Principles	References in Proverbs
Wisdom is more valuable and desirable than riches.	2:4-5; 3:13-18; 8:10-11,18-21; 16:16; 17:16; 23:23
Honor, a good name, favor, and righteousness are more profitable than riches.	11:4,16,18; 22:1
A poor man with integrity, love, and righteousness is better off than a rich man with dishonesty, hatred, and injustice.	10:3; 11:18; 13:25; 15:6,16-17; 16:8; 19:1,22; 28:6,8
To place one's hope or trust in wealth, which has no enduring value, is unwise.	11:4,7,28; 27:24
Wealth is worthless if obtained by fraud, dishonesty, or oppression.	1:19; 10:2,4; 11:1; 13:11,22; 15:27; 20:17
Diligence, hard work, and humility pay off.	10:4; 12:11,14,24,27; 13:4; 14:23-24; 20:13; 21:5; 22:4; 28:19
Pursuit of sin, laziness, and idleness lead to poverty and loss.	5:7-10; 6:6-11,30-31; 12:24,27; 13:4,18; 14:23; 15:19; 18:9; 20:13; 21:5,17; 22:27; 23:21; 24:32-34; 28:19,22; 29:3
Having wealth brings both benefits and risks.	1:13-14; 10:15; 13:8; 14:20; 18:11; 19:4
Getting rich should not be an end in itself.	23:4; 28:20,22
People who have or pursue wealth are vulnerable to temptations of pride and oppression or mistreatment of others.	16:19; 18:23; 22:16; 28:3,11; 30:14
The Lord commends and blesses those who demonstrate kindness and generosity toward the poor. He enjoins the righteous to "defend the cause of the oppressed and needy" (31:9).	3:27-28; 11:25-26; 14:21,31; 19:17; 22:9; 28:16,27; 29:7,14
The Lord opposes those who oppress or neglect the poor.	17:5; 21:13; 22:16,22; 28:3,27; 29:7; 31:20
The Lord blesses those who honor Him with their possessions.	3:9-10
Bribery is wrong.	15:27; 17:8; 17:23
Follow Scripture's guidelines for borrowing and lending.	11:15; 17:18
Practice good stewardship with your material assets.	27:23
Invest in your family's future.	13:22; 20:21
Be content and trust in God's justice.	11:24; 12:9; 13:7,23; 17:2; 22:2; 29:13; 30:8

>WORD|*study*

12:4 In considering the context, the translation **capable** (Hb *chayil*, "ability or strength"; "integrity, virtue, uprightness") does not adequately describe this exemplary wife (i.e., a strong example of what a wife should be, thus bringing honor to her husband). She is presented in contrast to the opposite, **a wife who causes shame** (Hb *bush*, "put someone to shame"). Proverbs 31:10-31 extols this capable wife as a woman displaying both physical and spiritual "strength." She exemplifies noble and virtuous character, as well as ability and courage (31:10,29; cp. Gn 47:6; Ex 18:21; Ru 3:11; 2Sm 17:10). Such commendable qualities make her a **crown** (Hb *'atarah*, "garland, diadem, ornament") to her husband—like highly visible ornamentation worn outwardly as an expression of his dignity. Typically, a husband is proud of a wife who contributes to his success, elevating him among their neighbors and within the community.

12:8 A **twisted** [Hb *'awah*, a word used only here in Proverbs] **mind** (Hb *lēv*, "heart"—the center of one's will) refers to someone who is "perverse." People who fit this description reject, distort, or turn away from what is right and good. They willfully decide to go against the godly way of wisdom and stubbornly pursue a road to destruction, refusing to heed warnings that they are going the wrong way.

5 The thoughts of the righteous
are just,
but guidance from the wicked
leads to deceit.

6 The words of the wicked are
a deadly ambush,
but the speech of the upright
rescues them.

7 The wicked are overthrown
and perish,
but the house of the righteous
will stand.

8 A man is praised for his insight,
but a twisted mind
is despised.

9 Better to be dishonored,
yet have a servant,
than to act important
but have no food.

10 A righteous man cares about
his animal's health,
but even the merciful acts
of the wicked are cruel.

11 The one who works his land
will have plenty of food,
but whoever chases fantasies
lacks sense.

12 The wicked desire
what evil men have,[A]
but the root of the righteous
produces fruit.

13 An evil man is trapped
by his rebellious speech,
but a righteous one escapes
from trouble.

14 A man will be satisfied
with good
by the words of his mouth,
and the work of a man's hands
will reward him.

15 A fool's way is right
in his own eyes,
but whoever listens
to counsel is wise.

16 A fool's displeasure is known
at once,
but whoever ignores an insult
is sensible.

17 Whoever speaks the truth
declares what is right,
but a false witness, deceit.

18 There is one who speaks rashly,
like a piercing sword;
but the tongue of the wise
brings healing.

19 Truthful lips endure forever,
but a lying tongue,
only a moment.

20 Deceit is in the hearts
of those who plot evil,
but those who promote peace
have joy.

21 No disaster overcomes
the righteous,
but the wicked are full
of misery.

22 Lying lips are detestable
to the LORD,
but faithful people
are His delight.

23 A shrewd person
conceals knowledge,
but a foolish heart
publicizes stupidity.

24 The diligent hand will rule,

[A]**12:12** Or *desire a stronghold of evil*

shaky and wobbly (cp. 14:30; Hab 3:16). In contrast to a crown, this image points to an invisible, deeply embedded weakness undermining all a husband does. Thus, the common adage that the character of a wife will make or break her husband takes on new meaning.

12:5-6 Thoughts are behind words, which bear testimony to what is in your heart (cp. 4:20-27; 23:7; Php 4:8-9). **Words** have great power and once spoken cannot be retrieved, making everyone responsible even for words carelessly spoken (Mt 12:36-37). The phrase **are a deadly ambush** (Hb *'arav-dam*) more literally translated would be "lie in wait for blood," graphically portraying the malicious intent of what is said by people who are unrighteous and defensive about remaining so.

12:15 The contrast established in this pair of descriptions implies that fools do not listen to or heed **counsel**. Rather than taking good advice to heart and adjusting their thoughts and actions accordingly, fools determine to do things their own way (cp. Jdg 21:25). They believe and doggedly insist that their way is the **right** way, thus failing to take the necessary first step toward obeying the Lord—abandoning your own self-will (cp. 3:5-6; Lk 9:23).

12:25 Women, particularly in caregiving roles, have experienced the truth that **anxiety** [Hb *de'agah*, "fear, dread"] **weighs . . . down** (Hb *shachah*, "depress") the heart. Speech is not to be turned only to personal success, but **a good word** is one way to make someone else's life easier. Encouragement in the midst of a trial brings comfort, renewal of strength, creative solutions, and often the motivation necessary to move forward in a positive way.

13:7-8 Great wealth is not counted in money and possessions alone. Some may feel content with what they have and exercise careful stewardship of their resources. Others who are wealthy in property, money, and possessions grapple for more without enjoying or even appreciating what they already have. The contrast is between appearance and reality and depends ultimately on your value system. Money does indicate differences, but even polar opposites may level the ground and bring balance to each other. Perhaps the most important message is the mandate to accept whatever your lot may be and avoid pretense of expressing something that is not true. Honesty and integrity reign over all, and any defrauding is hurtful.

13:24 The verb **hates** figuratively suggests that a parent's refusal to discipline his child betrays a lack of love. By overlooking the child's faults and failing to insist on obedience, a parent encourages the child to pursue his own way (cp. 1:29-31; 3:5-6; 12:15; 16:9,25; 19:18; 21:2; 30:12). Though the child may temporarily escape discomfort, the undisciplined heart will make him vulnerable to sin and generally unwise choices along with their destructive, if not tragic, consequences. Genuine love, however, motivates a parent to help his child achieve obedience to authorities. The ultimate goal is the wisdom and maturity of a son or daughter walking in righteousness, obedient to God's will rather than his own will. Acting in the child's best interest also brings the greatest satisfaction to parents (29:17).

>WORD|*study*

13:10 Proverbs 11:2 notes that "pride" (Hb *zadon*) brings shame. Here arrogance (Hb *zadon*; cp. 21:24) generates strife or conflict. People characterized by *zadon* jump to unwarranted conclusions yet boldly and disrespectfully voice their views, often erupting with defensive anger even in the face of facts proving their view is wrong.

but laziness will lead to
forced labor.

25 Anxiety in a man's heart
weighs it down,
but a good word cheers it up.

26 A righteous man is
careful in dealing
with his neighbor,[A]
but the ways of the wicked
lead them astray.

27 A lazy man doesn't roast
his game,
but to a diligent man,
his wealth is precious.

28 There is life in the path
of righteousness,
but another path leads
to death.[B]

13 A wise son responds to his
father's discipline,
but a mocker doesn't listen
to rebuke.

2 From the words
of his mouth,
a man will enjoy good things,
but treacherous people have
an appetite for violence.

3 The one who guards
his mouth protects his life;
the one who opens his lips
invites his own ruin.

4 The slacker craves,
yet has nothing,
but the diligent is
fully satisfied.

5 The righteous hate lying,
but the wicked
act disgustingly
and disgracefully.

6 Righteousness guards people
of integrity,[C]
but wickedness undermines
the sinner.

7 One man pretends to be rich
but has nothing;
another pretends to be poor
but has great wealth.

8 Riches are a ransom
for a man's life,
but a poor man
hears no threat.

9 The light of the righteous
shines brightly,
but the lamp of the wicked
is put out.

10 Arrogance leads to nothing
but strife,
but wisdom is gained by those
who take advice.

11 Wealth obtained by fraud
will dwindle,
but whoever earns
it through labor[D]
will multiply it.

12 Delayed hope makes
the heart sick,
but fulfilled desire is a tree
of life.

13 The one who has contempt
for instruction will pay
the penalty,
but the one who
respects a command
will be rewarded.

14 A wise man's instruction is
a fountain of life,
turning people away
from the snares of death.

15 Good sense wins favor,
but the way of the treacherous
never changes.[E]

16 Every sensible person
acts knowledgeably,
but a fool displays
his stupidity.

17 A wicked messenger falls
into trouble,
but a trustworthy courier
brings healing.

18 Poverty and disgrace
come to those

[A]**12:26** Or *man guides his neighbor* [B]**12:28** Or *righteousness, and in its path there is no death* [C]**13:6** Lit *guards integrity of way* [D]**13:11** Lit *whoever gathers upon his hand* [E]**13:15** LXX, Syr, Tg read *treacherous will perish*

who ignore discipline,
but the one who accepts
correction will be honored.

19 Desire fulfilled is sweet
to the taste,
but to turn from evil
is an abomination to fools.

20 The one who walks
with the wise
will become wise,
but a companion of fools
will suffer harm.

21 Disaster pursues sinners,
but good rewards
the righteous.

22 A good man leaves
an inheritance
to his[A] grandchildren,
but the sinner's
wealth is stored up
for the righteous.

23 The uncultivated field of the
poor yields abundant food,
but without justice, it is
swept away.

24 The one who will not use
the rod hates his son,
but the one who loves him
disciplines him diligently.

25 A righteous man eats
until he is satisfied,
but the stomach of the wicked
is empty.

14 Every wise woman builds
her house,
but a foolish one tears it down
with her own hands.

2 Whoever lives with integrity
•fears the LORD,
but the one who is devious
in his ways despises Him.

3 The proud speech of a fool
brings a rod of discipline,[B]
but the lips of the wise
protect them.

4 Where there are no oxen, the
feeding trough is empty,[C]
but an abundant harvest comes
through the strength of an ox.

[A]13:22 Or *inheritance: his* [B]14:3 Some emend to *In the mouth of a fool is a rod for his back* [C]14:4 Or *clean*

14:1 The verb **builds** (Hb *banah*, figuratively "cause to prosper, be enlarged") is used in Gn 2:22 for God's creation of woman and elsewhere in the sense of women building a family by bearing children (e.g., Ru 4:11). Women who can be called **wise** are those who focus their energies on shaping their households in conformity with God's purposes. Chapter 31 provides the paradigm for such a **woman**, who, by causing **her house** to thrive, exemplifies fearing the Lord, the foundation for wisdom (cp. v. 2; 31:30).

14:1 See **Word Study**, p. 802.

14:2 Two opposing attitudes toward the Lord correspond to two opposing lifestyles. **Integrity** (Hb *yosher*, "uprightness, virtue") refers to consistent ethical conduct that conforms to the Lord's fixed moral boundaries. A woman characterized by "integrity" takes God seriously and has a healthy respect for His holiness and justice. **Devious** is a synonym for "perverse" (cp. 2:15; 3:32; 10:18). A "devious" woman shows that she **despises** (Hb *bazah*, "regard with contempt") the Lord by consistently turning away from His good **ways**.

14:3 See **Word Study**, p. 802, and **Biblical Womanhood** below.

BIBLICAL WOMANHOOD Motherhood and the Tool of Discipline

A parent who loves her child wisely is willing to endure the pain of applying discipline and to invest time in monitoring the child's behavior and responses. Early and consistent parental discipline gives a child the foundation necessary to cultivate the desire to go God's way throughout his life. However, without loving affection and dedicated responsibility to nurture the child in every sense, the "rod" indeed becomes a means of suffering under tyrannical rule. Under God's plan, the **rod of discipline** can accomplish these goals:

- stop the child's willful rebellion against parental authority (cp. the idea of rebellion against God in 1Sm 15:20-23; Is 53:6);
- express loving concern for guiding a child into the way most helpful to him (Pr 13:24);
- expedite the most effective development of the child in preparation for taking his place in the world (19:18);
- cleanse the child from a spirit of willful disobedience (20:30);
- drive foolishness (the opposite of wisdom) out of the heart of the child (22:15);
- ultimately deliver the child from eternal punishment (23:13-14);
- teach the child (10:13; 29:15);
- communicate to the child his personal responsibility for acts of disobedience (Ps 53:3; Jr 17:10; Ezk 18:4,20; Rm 3:10,23; 14:12; Col 3:20);
- bring the child into voluntary submission to divine authority (cp. Jn 14:15,21,23); and
- reward the parents with rest and satisfaction, knowing they have done their best in rearing their child unto the Lord (Pr 29:17).

The book of Proverbs also presents guidelines for how parents are to use the "rod":

- discipline should be administered promptly in order to correct wrong behavior before patterns are set (Pr 15:10; 19:18; 23:13; Heb 12:11);
- punishment should be administered tenderly and firmly, being certain the child understands the offense clearly (4:3-4,11; 15:32; Jr 17:10; cp. Dt 11:26-28);
- sorrow for the child because of his disobedience should be reflected by the parent (Pr 17:25; Jr 13:17; Mt 23:37; Heb 3:10,17);
- caution should be exercised in avoiding inappropriate severity in punishment (Eph 6:4); and
- the parent should remain with the child after punishment until fellowship has been restored (Ps 51:7-12).

14:12 From a human vantage point, a particular **way**—a direction for life, a choice, a lifestyle—can appear to be good, safe, and prosperous and yet lead instead to disaster and ruin (cp. Pr 12:15; 14:14; 16:25). Happiness and prosperity pursued as ends in themselves are a mirage. Satan is a master at deception, disguising his evil ways and the bitter end to which they lead. **Death** is the true destination of a way that **seems right** (Hb *yashar*, "correct, straight, appealing") only because you have rationalized a sinful pattern of thinking and behavior, convincing yourself that you deserve what you decide to pursue in disobedience or that God will not bother to punish. The true consequence of sin, however, is separation from God (cp. 2:18; 5:5; 7:27; 16:25; Mt 7:13-14).

14:20-21 Having wealth tends to foster contempt for those who are poor. While **the rich** receive favor and, perhaps, take on an air of superiority, **a poor man** may be ignored or mistreated (cp. 10:15; 19:4-7). However, godly wisdom resists this response.

>WORD|*study*

14:1 Wise (Hb *chokmot*, "discriminating between good and evil, receiving instruction, exercising good judgment, shrewd and skillful, intelligent and sensible") is used here in a spiritual sense as a perspective found only by those who seek the Lord (cp. Jms 1:5). The **foolish** woman does the opposite, ignoring biblical commands and principles, pursuing what she wants at the expense of God's purposes for her family, or at times actively undermining what God accomplishes in and through other family members.

14:3 In the book of Proverbs, the rod (Hb *shēvet*, "staff, scepter, tribe") is primarily an instrument for punishment (cp. 10:13; 22:15; 23:13-14; 26:3; 29:15). The term does not imply harsh severity but rather an emphasis on faithful effort to help the child bring his will first under parental control, then under his own control with wise decision-making, and finally under God's control.

Elsewhere *shēvet* is the "staff" used by shepherds to protect their sheep and serves as a metaphor of the Lord's protection of His children walking in the way of righteousness (Ps 23:4). The word also refers to a mark of authority or "scepter" (Gn 49:10; Am 1:5; Zch 10:11) and denotes a tribe or tribal subdivisions within Israel (e.g., Gn 49:28).

5 An honest witness
does not deceive,
but a dishonest witness
utters lies.

6 A mocker seeks wisdom
and doesn't find it,
but knowledge comes easily
to the perceptive.

7 Stay away from a foolish man;
you will gain no knowledge
from his speech.

8 The sensible man's wisdom is
to consider his way,
but the stupidity of fools
deceives them.

9 Fools mock at making
restitution,[A]
but there is goodwill
among the upright.

10 The heart knows
its own bitterness,
and no outsider shares
in its joy.

11 The house of the wicked
will be destroyed,
but the tent of the upright
will stand.[B]

12 There is a way that seems right
to a man,
but its end is the way
to death.

13 Even in laughter a heart
may be sad,
and joy may end in grief.

14 The disloyal one will get
what his conduct deserves,
and a good man,
what his deeds deserve.

15 The inexperienced one believes
anything,
but the sensible one watches[C]
his steps.

16 A wise man is cautious
and turns from evil,
but a fool is easily angered
and is careless.[D]

17 A quick-tempered man
acts foolishly,
and a man who schemes
is hated.

18 The inexperienced inherit
foolishness,
but the sensible are crowned
with knowledge.

19 The evil bow before those
who are good,
the wicked, at the gates
of the righteous.

20 A poor man is hated even
by his neighbor,
but there are many who love
the rich.

21 The one who despises
his neighbor sins,
but whoever shows kindness
to the poor will be happy.

22 Don't those who plan evil
go astray?
But those who plan
good find loyalty
and faithfulness.

[A]**14:9** Or *at guilt offerings* [B]**14:11** Lit *flourish* [C]**14:15** Lit *the prudent understand* [D]**14:16** Or *and falls*

23 There is profit in all hard work,
but endless talk[A] leads only
to poverty.

24 The crown of the wise is
their wealth,
but the foolishness of fools
produces foolishness.

25 A truthful witness rescues lives,
but one who utters lies
is deceitful.

26 In the fear of the LORD one has
strong confidence
and his children have
a refuge.

27 The fear of the LORD is
a fountain of life,
turning people away
from the snares of death.

28 A large population is
a king's splendor,
but a shortage of people is
a ruler's devastation.

29 A patient person shows great
understanding,
but a quick-tempered one
promotes foolishness.

30 A tranquil heart is life
to the body,
but jealousy is rottenness
to the bones.

31 The one who oppresses the poor
person insults his Maker,
but one who is kind
to the needy honors Him.

32 The wicked one is thrown down
by his own sin,
but the righteous one has
a refuge in his death.

33 Wisdom resides in the heart
of the discerning;
she is known[B] even
among fools.

34 Righteousness exalts a nation,
but sin is a disgrace
to any people.

35 A king favors a wise servant,
but his anger falls on
a disgraceful one.

15 A gentle answer
turns away anger,
but a harsh word
stirs up wrath.

2 The tongue of the wise
makes knowledge attractive,
but the mouth of fools
blurts out foolishness.

3 The eyes of the LORD
are everywhere,
observing the wicked
and the good.

4 The tongue that heals is a tree
of life,
but a devious tongue[C]
breaks the spirit.

5 A fool despises
his father's discipline,
but a person who
accepts correction
is sensible.

6 The house of the righteous
has great wealth,
but trouble accompanies
the income of the wicked.

7 The lips of the wise
broadcast knowledge,
but not so the heart of fools.

8 The sacrifice of the wicked
is detestable to the LORD,
but the prayer of the upright
is His delight.

9 The LORD detests the way
of the wicked,
but He loves the one
who pursues righteousness.

10 Discipline is harsh for the one
who leaves the path;
the one who hates correction
will die.

11 •Sheol and •Abaddon lie open
before the LORD—
how much more,
human hearts.

12 A mocker doesn't love one
who corrects him;
he will not consult the wise.

13 A joyful heart makes
a face cheerful,
but a sad heart produces
a broken spirit.

14 A discerning mind
seeks knowledge,

14:26-27 The fear of the LORD engenders security and confidence. This "fear" (Hb *yir'ah*; see **Word Study**, p. 784) is the motivation for godly living. One who is God-fearing lives righteously, walking in the ways of the Lord. **Strong** [Hb *'oz*, "fortified, well-founded strength or might"] **confidence** (Hb *mivtach*, "trust, reliance, security") becomes a **refuge** not only for the one who fears the Lord but also for **his children.** Children inevitably reap the fruit of the faithfulness of their parents (cp. Ex 20:5-6). The image of **a fountain of life** depicts "the fear of the LORD" as a dynamic and dependable source of spiritual vitality and longevity (cp. 13:14; 16:22; Ps 36:9; Jr 2:13; Jn 7:38).

15:1-2 Just as important as what you say is how you say it. A **gentle** [Hb *rak*, "soft, mild, delicate"] **answer** can at times defuse the anger of someone who expects to engage you in an argument or shouting match. Words reveal a woman's character and become her tools for accomplishing what is in her heart. The **tongue** simply verbalizes the thoughts of the heart (15:2,4,7,14,23,26,28).

15:10 This verse warns **the one who leaves the path** of righteousness and wisdom that the kind of **discipline** (Hb *musar*, "chastisement"; see **Word Study**, p. 783) required to effect a course correction will be exceedingly difficult and unpleasant. However, an even worse consequence—death—is reaped by **the one who hates correction**. Instead of being moved to genuine repentance by the efforts made to guide him back to godly living, this person is angered by the light cast on his wrongdoing.

[A]14:23 Lit *but word of lips* [B]14:33 LXX reads *unknown* [C]15:4 Lit *but crookedness in it*

15:16-17 This pair of proverbs implies a relationship between **the fear of the Lord** and the presence of **love** (Hb *ʾahavah*; cp. 10:12) as supreme priorities. Given a choice between earthly prosperity and a life of obedience to the Lord, peace with God and love-empowered relationships are eminently preferable. **Turmoil** (Hb *mehumah*, "commotion, disturbance") within individuals as well as within families is symptomatic of self-centeredness and often accompanies materialism and greed. **A meal of vegetables** representing the unselfish outpouring of love-borne hospitality can be far more palatable than feasting on **a fattened ox** in a house full of dissension and pride (cp. 17:1).

15:25 The Lord brings down the house of the **proud**, who depend upon their own resourcefulness and cunning (cp. Is 2:12); but He **protects** (Hb *natsav*, "cause to stand firm, establish") the needy—the widows, orphans, and poor, who would be a natural prey to thieves and to those more powerful than they. When her husband died, a woman typically lost her source of protection, security, and financial provision. Because a widow is particularly vulnerable to further losses, the Lord Himself guards and defends her **territory** (cp. Ex 22:22, Pss 68:5; 146:9; Jr 49:11; 1Tm 5:5).

16:1-9 The importance of dependence upon the Lord in contrast to looking to your own understandings is again the focus (cp. 1:7; 3:5-6; 9:10). God knows the **reflections** (Hb *maʿarak*, "plan, arrangement") and **motives** of your heart and is not deceived even when you may deceive yourself (v. 2; cp. 15:3); He expedites the **plans** you commit to Him (v. 3); ultimately everything is **prepared . . . for His purpose** (v. 4); He restrains your **enemies** (v. 7); and He **determines** (Hb *kun*, "direct, make firm," v. 9) your **steps**.

but the mouth of fools feeds
on foolishness.

15 All the days of the oppressed
are miserable,
but a cheerful heart has
a continual feast.

16 Better a little with the •fear
of the Lord
than great treasure
with turmoil.

17 Better a meal of vegetables
where there is love
than a fattened ox
with hatred.

18 A hot-tempered man
stirs up conflict,
but a man slow to anger
calms strife.

19 A slacker's way is like
a thorny hedge,
but the path of the upright is
a highway.

20 A wise son brings joy
to his father,
but a foolish man despises
his mother.

21 Foolishness brings joy to one
without sense,
but a man with understanding
walks a straight path.

22 Plans fail when there is
no counsel,
but with many advisers
they succeed.

23 A man takes joy in giving
an answer;[A]
and a timely word—how good
that is!

24 For the discerning the path
of life leads upward,
so that he may avoid
going down to Sheol.

25 The Lord destroys the house
of the proud,
but He protects
the widow's territory.

26 The Lord detests the plans
of an evil man,
but pleasant words are pure.

27 The one who profits dishonestly
troubles his household,
but the one who hates bribes
will live.

28 The mind
of the righteous person
thinks before answering,
but the mouth of the wicked
blurts out evil things.

29 The Lord is far from the wicked,
but He hears the prayer
of the righteous.

30 Bright eyes cheer the heart;
good news strengthens[B]
the bones.

31 One who[C] listens to
life-giving rebukes
will be at home
among the wise.

32 Anyone who ignores discipline
despises himself,
but whoever listens
to correction acquires
good sense.[D]

33 The fear of the Lord is what
wisdom teaches,
and humility comes
before honor.

Spiritual Lessons with Moral and Ethical Applications (16:1–22:16)

16 The reflections of the heart
belong to man,
but the answer of the tongue
is from the Lord.

2 All a man's ways seem right
to him,
but the Lord evaluates
the motives.[E]

3 Commit your activities
to the Lord,
and your plans
will be achieved.

4 The Lord has prepared
everything
for His purpose—
even the wicked for the day
of disaster.

5 Everyone with a proud heart is
detestable to the Lord;

[A]15:23 Lit *in an answer of his mouth* [B]15:30 Lit *makes fat* [C]15:31 Lit *An ear that* [D]15:32 Lit *acquires a heart* [E]16:2 Lit *weighs spirits*

be assured,[A] he will not
go unpunished.

6 Wickedness is •atoned for
by loyalty and faithfulness,
and one turns from evil
by the •fear of the LORD.

7 When a man's ways please
the LORD,
He[B] makes even his enemies
to be at peace with him.

8 Better a little
with righteousness
than great income
with injustice.

9 A man's heart plans his way,
but the LORD determines
his steps.

10 God's verdict is on the lips
of a king;[C]
his mouth should not give
an unfair judgment.

11 Honest balances and scales are
the LORD's;
all the weights in the bag[D] are
His concern.

12 Wicked behavior[E] is detestable
to kings,
since a throne is established
through righteousness.

13 Righteous lips are
a king's delight,
and he loves one
who speaks honestly.

14 A king's fury is a messenger
of death,
but a wise man appeases it.

15 When a king's face lights up,
there is life;
his favor is like a cloud
with spring rain.

16 Get wisdom—
how much better it is
than gold!
And get understanding—
it is preferable to silver.

17 The highway of the upright
avoids evil;
the one who guards his way
protects his life.

18 Pride comes before destruction,
and an arrogant spirit
before a fall.

19 Better to be lowly of spirit
with the humble[F]
than to divide plunder
with the proud.

20 The one who understands
a matter finds success,
and the one who trusts
in the LORD will be happy.

21 Anyone with a wise heart
is called discerning,
and pleasant speech[G]
increases learning.

22 Insight is a fountain of life
for its possessor,
but the discipline of fools
is folly.

23 A wise heart instructs it mouth
and increases learning
with its speech.[H]

24 Pleasant words are
a honeycomb:
sweet to the taste[I] and health
to the body.[J]

25 There is a way that seems right
to a man,
but its end is the way
to death.

26 A worker's appetite works
for him
because his hunger[K]
urges him on.

27 A worthless man digs up evil,
and his speech is like
a scorching fire.

28 A contrary man spreads conflict,
and a gossip separates
close friends.

29 A violent man lures
his neighbor,
leading him in a way that is
not good.

30 The one who narrows his eyes
is planning deceptions;
the one who compresses
his lips brings about evil.

16:15 Spring rain fell in March or April, and the Israelites depended upon this "latter rain" for ripening the grain in preparation for harvest. This simile is used to describe the favor of the king.

16:21-33 Words that come from a woman **with a wise heart** will be **pleasant** and edifying (vv. 21,23-24), life-giving (v. 22), **sweet** and healing (v. 24). In contrast, words of slander and pain or of **conflict** and discord characterize people described as **worthless** and **contrary** (vv. 27-28).

[A]16:5 Lit *hand to hand* [B]16:7 Or *he* [C]16:10 Or *A divination is on the lips of a king*
[D]16:11 Merchants kept the stones for their scales in a bag. [E]16:12 Either the king's or someone else's behavior [F]16:19 Alt Hb tradition reads *afflicted* [G]16:21 Lit *and sweetness of lips*
[H]16:23 Lit *learning upon his lips* [I]16:24 Lit *throat* [J]16:24 Lit *bones* [K]16:26 Lit *mouth*

17:1 There are two comparisons: **peace** versus **strife**; **a dry crust** versus **feasting** (cp. 12:9; 15:16-17; 16:8). The latter reference to food served is not the most important factor, for abundance does not bring peace and satisfaction; rather the emphasis is that, however sumptuous, the feast would not bring happiness if served in the midst of anger and bitterness.

17:6 Family heritage and legacy are important in this generation as they were in the ancient world. Children are still regarded as a blessing (cp. Pss 127:3-5; 128:3-4; 144:12). Elders within the family should live righteously to merit the appropriate honor and respect due them. Three generations are here involved in reciprocal praise as the **elderly** recognize their **grandchildren** as a **crown** and **sons** affirm **pride** in their **fathers**. Of course, foolish children cause grief for their parents (vv. 21,25); but grandparents can find satisfaction in seeing the potential of a legacy in the children of their offspring, and children may see themselves reflected in their parents.

17:9 Responding to the mistakes and shortcomings of others presents a choice: forgiving the **offense** or repeating the gossip (cp. 11:13; 18:8). When **friends** offend, the first option **promotes love**—a relationship damaged by the offense can actually be strengthened when the one who has been hurt chooses to seek reconciliation rather than retaliation. The second option, however, generally proves to be divisive.

17:12 Women who have children know the feeling of rage and the rush of near-supernatural energy, which could fuel an assault on anything or anyone believed to be harming their babies—what some call "the mama bear response." In reality the day you encounter **a bear robbed of her cubs** may be your last. This imagery casts meeting **a fool in his foolishness** as incredibly risky and dangerous. Such a person is irrational, potentially violent, and doggedly focused on expressing his own pain and unleashing his own anger regardless of inflicting harm on others.

31 Gray hair is a glorious crown;
it is found in the way
of righteousness.

32 Patience is better than power,
and controlling one's temper,[A]
than capturing a city.

33 The lot is cast into the lap,
but its every decision is
from the LORD.

17 Better a dry crust with peace
than a house full of feasting
with strife.

2 A wise servant will rule over
a disgraceful son
and share an inheritance
among brothers.

3 A crucible for silver, and
a smelter for gold,
and the LORD is the tester
of hearts.

4 A wicked person listens to
malicious talk;[B]
a liar pays attention to
a destructive tongue.

5 The one who mocks the poor
insults his Maker,
and one who rejoices over
calamity
will not go unpunished.

6 Grandchildren are the crown
of the elderly,
and the pride of sons is
their fathers.

7 Eloquent words are
not appropriate
on a fool's lips;
how much worse are lies
for a ruler.

8 A bribe seems like
a magic stone to its owner;
wherever he turns,
he succeeds.

9 Whoever conceals an offense
promotes love,
but whoever gossips about it
separates friends.

10 A rebuke cuts into
a perceptive person
more than a hundred lashes
into a fool.

11 An evil man seeks
only rebellion;
a cruel messenger[C]
will be sent against him.

12 Better for a man to meet a bear
robbed of her cubs
than a fool in his foolishness.

13 If anyone returns evil for good,
evil will never depart
from his house.

14 To start a conflict is to release
a flood;
stop the dispute before
it breaks out.

15 Acquitting the •guilty
and condemning the just—
both are detestable
to the LORD.

16 Why does a fool have money
in his hand
with no intention
of buying wisdom?

17 A friend loves at all times,
and a brother is born for
a difficult time.

18 One without sense enters
an agreement[D]
and puts up security
for his friend.

19 One who loves to offend
loves strife;
one who builds
a high threshold
invites injury.

20 One with a twisted mind
will not succeed,
and one with deceitful speech
will fall into ruin.

21 A man fathers a fool
to his own sorrow;
the father of a fool has no joy.

22 A joyful heart is good medicine,
but a broken spirit dries up
the bones.

23 A wicked man secretly takes
a bribe
to subvert the course
of justice.

24 Wisdom is the focus
of the perceptive,

[A]**16:32** Lit *and ruling over one's spirit* [B]**17:4** Lit *to lips of iniquity* [C]**17:11** Or *a merciless angel*
[D]**17:18** Lit *sense shakes hands*

but a fool's eyes roam
to the ends of the earth.

25 A foolish son is grief
to his father
and bitterness to the one
who bore him.

26 It is certainly not good to fine
an innocent person
or to beat a noble
for his honesty.[A]

27 The intelligent person restrains
his words,
and one who keeps
a cool head[B]
is a man of understanding.

28 Even a fool is considered wise
when he keeps silent,
discerning when he seals
his lips.

18 One who isolates himself
pursues selfish desires;
he rebels against
all sound judgment.

2 A fool does not delight
in understanding,
but only wants to show off
his opinions.[C]

3 When a wicked man comes,
contempt also does,
and along with dishonor,
disgrace.

4 The words of a man's mouth
are deep waters,
a flowing river, a fountain
of wisdom.[D]

5 It is not good to show partiality
to the •guilty
by perverting the justice
due the innocent.

6 A fool's lips lead to strife,
and his mouth provokes
a beating.

7 A fool's mouth is
his devastation,
and his lips are a trap
for his life.

8 A gossip's words are
like choice food
that goes down
to one's innermost being.[E]

9 The one who is truly lazy
in his work
is brother to a vandal.[F]

10 The name of •Yahweh is
a strong tower;
the righteous run to it
and are protected.[G]

11 A rich man's wealth is
his fortified city;
in his imagination it is
like a high wall.

12 Before his downfall
a man's heart is proud,
but humility comes
before honor.

13 The one who gives an answer
before he listens—
this is foolishness
and disgrace for him.

14 A man's spirit can
endure sickness,
but who can survive
a broken spirit?

15 The mind of the discerning
acquires knowledge,
and the ear of the wise
seeks it.

16 A gift opens doors[H] for a man
and brings him
before the great.

17 The first to state his case
seems right
until another comes
and cross-examines him.

[A]**17:26** Or *noble unfairly* [B]**17:27** Lit *spirit* [C]**18:2** Lit *to uncover his heart* [D]**18:4** Or *waters; a fountain of wisdom is a flowing river.* [E]**18:8** Lit *to the chambers of the belly* [F]**18:9** Lit *master of destruction* [G]**18:10** Lit *raised high* [H]**18:16** Lit *gift makes room*

18:1-7 One of the identifying characteristics of **a fool** is noted in the way he speaks—continually pushing his own opinions and perspectives instead of taking in the wisdom of others (vv. 2,18). His open mouth, absence of self-control, and lack of understanding betray his closed mind and expose his foolishness. He is self-centered and resistant to the process of reasonable investigation of a matter (v. 1). Not only does **a fool's mouth** cause dissension among others, but it also brings trouble upon him (vv. 6-7; cp. Mt 12:34).

18:8 The gossip's words are described as **choice food** (from Hb verb *laham*, "devour greedily," and thus a reference to what is swallowed down voraciously). Like such food consumed ravenously, gossip simply increases the appetite for more (cp. 26:22). The wise person who hears gossip determines to quarantine its malicious message and avoid the company of anyone who shares it.

18:10-11 The protection and security found by **the righteous** when they **run** quickly and decisively to the Lord is set in contrast to the false security of wealth.

>WORD|*study*

17:21 A fool (Hb *kesil*, "one who is stupid or insolent," from the root *kasal*, lit "being fleshy or fat," which in a bad sense becomes "inertness and folly") is an ungodly or impious person so obstinate that he refuses to be moved by reason or counsel (cp. Pr 14:8; 18:2). To have a child who manifests the characteristics of a fool brings parents overwhelming disappointment. In the second line of the couplet, another word is used to describe this son. That word for fool (Hb *naval*, "good-for-nothing, faded or withering, acting stupidly") is used in the second part of this proverb, also with a nuance of "impious and wicked" (see **Word Study**, p. 676).

19:13 Nothing is more tragic than a home marked by foolishness and strife. **A foolish son** brings **ruin** (Hb *hawwah*, "destruction, fall, calamity, disaster"), which can refer to the falling of rain and snow but here metaphorically has the sense of a pouring out of troubles on a family. The Hebrew plural suggests great and continued trials and distress.

Although Old Testament law allowed for the casting out of a foolish son (one who is "stubborn and rebellious," Dt 21:18), **a wife's nagging** (Hb *midyan*, "quarrel, controversy, strife, contention"; cp. 21:9,19; 25:24; 27:15) must be endured (Mt 5:32; 19:9). The comparison to **endless** dripping suggests continual annoyance that cannot be stopped. See **Biblical Womanhood**, p. 813.

19:14 The proximity of verses 13 and 14 implicitly contrasts the contentious wife with one who is **sensible** (Hb *sakal*, "have insight, act circumspectly, behave wisely; make prosperous"; cp. 18:22; Gn 24:14). The more prudent **wife** is able to help her husband think through situations in order to choose a wise course of action. Although wealth may be provided by earthly parents, God alone deserves the credit for providing a wise wife.

19:18 Discipline [Hb *yasar*, "chastise, rebuke, correct, instruct, admonish"] **your son** is a command not merely to chastise for wrongdoing but to fulfill parental responsibility for teaching a child how to live in obedience throughout his life—first to his parents and ultimately to God. The father's focus in discipline is to lead his son to eternal life, the opposite of death. God-inspired discipline is always prompted by love and never has the intention to bring harm (22:6,15; 23:13-14; 29:15). In Proverbs, to ignore discipline is tantamount to a sentence of death (13:24).

>WORD|*study*

18:22 A wife is described as something good [Hb *tov*, "good to the senses, agreeable, pleasant, desirable, delightful, even beautiful, fair; also morally honest, becoming, virtuous, that which is right"] to find. The word can also describe what is precious, prosperous, satisfying, and beneficial—happiness or pleasure in the sense of what is pleasing to God, satisfying to man, and rewarding to all. Note Gn 2:18, "It is not *good* for the man to be alone" (cp. Pr 31:10-31). Parallelism in the second line adds that **favor** [Hb *ratson*, "goodwill"] **from the Lord** is also forthcoming. Clearly the husband does not deserve credit for this delightful addition to his life; she is God's gift to him.

18 Casting the lot ends quarrels
and separates
powerful opponents.

19 An offended brother is
harder to reach[A]
than a fortified city,
and quarrels are like the bars
of a fortress.

20 From the fruit of his mouth
a man's stomach is satisfied;
he is filled with the product
of his lips.

21 Life and death are in the power
of the tongue,
and those who love it will eat
its fruit.

22 A man who finds a wife finds
a good thing
and obtains favor
from the Lord.

23 The poor man pleads,
but the rich one
answers roughly.

24 A man with many friends
may be harmed,[B]
but there is a friend
who stays closer
than a brother.

19 Better a poor man who lives
with integrity
than someone who has
deceitful lips and is a fool.

2 Even zeal is not good
without knowledge,
and the one who acts
hastily[C] sins.

3 A man's own foolishness leads
him astray,
yet his heart rages
against the Lord.

4 Wealth attracts many friends,
but a poor man is separated
from his friend.

5 A false witness will not
go unpunished,
and one who utters lies
will not escape.

6 Many seek a ruler's favor,
and everyone is a friend
of one who gives gifts.

7 All the brothers of a poor man
hate him;
how much more do
his friends
keep their distance from him!
He may pursue them
with words,
but they are not there.[D]

8 The one who acquires
good sense[E] loves himself;
one who safeguards
understanding
finds success.

9 A false witness will not
go unpunished,
and one who utters
lies perishes.

10 Luxury is not appropriate
for a fool—
how much less for a slave
to rule over princes!

11 A person's insight gives
him patience,
and his virtue is to overlook
an offense.

12 A king's rage is like the roaring
of a lion,
but his favor is like dew
on the grass.

13 A foolish son is his father's ruin,
and a wife's nagging is
an endless dripping.

[A]**18:19** LXX, Syr, Tg, Vg read *is stronger* [B]**18:24** Some LXX mss, Syr, Tg, Vg read *friends must be friendly* [C]**19:2** Lit *who is hasty with feet* [D]**19:7** Hb uncertain [E]**19:8** Lit *acquires a heart*

14 A house and wealth
are inherited from fathers,
but a sensible wife is
from the LORD.
15 Laziness induces deep sleep,
and a lazy person
will go hungry.
16 The one who keeps commands
preserves himself;
one who disregards[A] his ways
will die.
17 Kindness to the poor is a loan
to the LORD,
and He will give a reward
to the lender.[B]
18 Discipline your son
while there is hope;
don't be intent
on killing him.[C]
19 A person with great anger bears
the penalty;
if you rescue him, you'll have
to do it again.
20 Listen to counsel
and receive instruction
so that you may be wise
later in life.[D]
21 Many plans are in a man's heart,
but the LORD's decree
will prevail.
22 What is desirable in a man is
his fidelity;
better to be a poor man
than a liar.
23 The •fear of the LORD leads
to life;
one will sleep at night[E]
without danger.
24 The slacker buries his hand
in the bowl;
he doesn't even bring it back
to his mouth.
25 Strike a mocker,
and the inexperienced learn
a lesson;
rebuke the discerning,
and he gains knowledge.
26 The one who assaults his father
and evicts his mother
is a disgraceful
and shameful son.
27 If you stop listening
to correction, my son,
you will stray from the words
of knowledge.
28 A worthless witness
mocks justice,
and a wicked mouth
swallows iniquity.
29 Judgments are prepared
for mockers,
and beatings for the backs
of fools.

20 Wine is a mocker, beer is
a brawler,
and whoever staggers
because of them is not wise.
2 A king's terrible wrath is
like the roaring of a lion;
anyone who provokes him
endangers himself.
3 It is honorable for a man
to resolve a dispute,
but any fool can get himself
into a quarrel.
4 The slacker does not plow
during planting season;[F]
at harvest time he looks,[G]
and there is nothing.
5 Counsel in a man's heart is
deep water;
but a man of understanding
draws it out.
6 Many a man proclaims
his own loyalty,
but who can find
a trustworthy man?
7 The one who lives with integrity
is righteous;
his children[H] who come
after him will be happy.
8 A king sitting on a throne
to judge
sifts out all evil with his eyes.
9 Who can say, "I have kept
my heart pure;
I am cleansed from my sin"?

[A]**19:16** Or *despises*, or *treats lightly* [B]**19:17** Lit *to him* [C]**19:18** Lit *don't lift up your soul to his death* [D]**19:20** Lit *in your end* [E]**19:23** Lit *will spend the night satisfied* [F]**20:4** Lit *plow in winter* [G]**20:4** Lit *inquires* [H]**20:7** Lit *sons*

19:20-21 Your **plans** may be carefully crafted and even produce good results, but God defines what is right by His infinite wisdom and immutable power (2Sm 15:31; 17:14; Neh 4:15).

20:1 With few exceptions, the terms **wine** (Hb *yayin*, "intoxicating drink with fermentation") and **beer** (Hb *shēkar*, "intoxicating drink, strong drink") are used in a negative, unfavorable sense and most often together (cp. Lv 10:9; Dt 14:26; Is 28:7). Here they are personified according to their effects. Drinking intoxicating beverages often results in scornful speech and belligerent behavior. By depicting wine as a **mocker**, the proverb suggests that while a person may indulge in drinking to avoid being mocked or seen as a fool in the eyes of peers, the loss of inhibitions when intoxicated leads to words and actions resulting in reproach and other unexpected damages. Chapters 21 and 23 include a series of warnings against drinking wine (representing intoxicating beverages as a category):

- Wine leads one to poverty (21:17; 23:21).
- Wine brings quarreling, sorrow, gossip, reddened eyes, and wounds (23:29-30).
- Wine deceives and destroys (23:31-32).
- Wine can inspire lust and lead to adultery—"strange things" (Hb *zur*, "forbidden woman, prostitute," 23:33; cp. 2:16).
- Wine is addictive (23:35).

20:4 The **slacker** (Hb *ʿatsēl*, "lazy or idle person, sluggard,") who, though able to work, is criticized throughout Proverbs for his laziness:

- He is not motivated to get up and go (6:9-11).
- He does not complete what he begins (12:27; 19:24; 26:15).
- He will not face his problems and shortcomings (22:13; 26:13-16).
- He is without roots, restless and dissatisfied, worthless (13:4; 18:9).

20:7 The **children** of the **righteous** are often singled out for blessing and commendation (cp. v. 11). A child's character is borne out in his lifestyle and actions. Children before whom **integrity** has been taught and modeled within the family circle are inspired to live out their faith as did their parents before them.

20:13 Sleep itself, which provides needed rest, refreshment, and renewal, is not prohibited. Rather, the proverb points out that avoiding productive activity results in poverty. The second, parallel part of the verse clarifies this message by urging hearers to get up and get to work in order to supply their needs (cp. 2Th 3:10).

20:30 Discipline first and foremost seeks to heal a person's **evil** intent and to lead him unto godliness and good. Physical discipline can bring spiritual healing and can be applied appropriately in order not to break a person's body or spirit but rather to overcome the stubborn resistance to correction and the willful pursuit of destructive patterns of thinking and behavior. Such discipline is not delivered in anger or for the pleasure of the one administering the punishment. There is no hint of abuse, though some remedies are painful and stern. Scripture affirms the value of the child (Ps 127:3-5).

21:1 The figure of speech illustrating the Lord's power is an ancient method of irrigation in which several channels were formed from one stream so that the worker with little effort could direct the flow of each **streams**. Oriental rulers were considered the most powerful human agents with absolute control over their subjects. Yet God, in His sovereignty, had unlimited control over **a king's heart** without interfering with the king's free will—e.g., the Egyptian pharaoh (Ex 10:1-2), Cyrus (Ezr 1:1-4; Is 44:28-45:7), and Artaxerxes (Ezr 7:21-24).

10 Differing weights
and varying measures[A]—
both are detestable
to the LORD.

11 Even a young man is known
by his actions—
if his behavior is pure
and upright.

12 The hearing ear
and the seeing eye—
the LORD made them both.

13 Don't love sleep, or you will
become poor;
open your eyes,
and you'll have
enough to eat.

14 "It's worthless, it's worthless!"
the buyer says,
but after he is on his way,
he gloats.

15 There is gold and a multitude
of jewels,
but knowledgeable lips are
a rare treasure.

16 Take his garment,[B]
for he has put up security
for a stranger;
get collateral if it is
for foreigners.

17 Food gained by fraud is sweet
to a man,
but afterward his mouth
is full of gravel.

18 Finalize plans with counsel,
and wage war with
sound guidance.

19 The one who reveals secrets is
a constant gossip;
avoid someone
with a big mouth.

20 Whoever curses his father
or mother—
his lamp will go out
in deep darkness.

21 An inheritance gained
prematurely
will not be blessed ultimately.

22 Don't say, "I will avenge
this evil!"
Wait on the LORD, and He will
rescue you.

23 Differing weights[C]
are detestable to the LORD,
and dishonest scales
are unfair.

24 A man's steps are determined
by the LORD,
so how can anyone
understand his own way?

25 It is a trap for anyone
to dedicate
something rashly
and later to reconsider
his vows.

26 A wise king separates out
the wicked
and drives
the threshing wheel
over them.

27 The LORD's lamp sheds light on
a person's life,[D]
searching
the innermost parts.[E]

28 Loyalty and faithfulness
deliver a king;
through loyalty he maintains
his throne.

29 The glory of young men is
their strength,
and the splendor of old men
is gray hair.

30 Lashes and wounds
purge away evil,
and beatings cleanse
the innermost parts.[F]

21 A king's heart is like
streams of water
in the LORD's hand:
He directs it wherever
He chooses.

2 All a man's ways seem right
to him,
but the LORD evaluates
the motives.[G]

3 Doing what is righteous
and just
is more acceptable to the LORD
than sacrifice.

[A]**20:10** Lit *Stone and stone, measure and measure* [B]**20:16** A debtor's outer garment was held as collateral. [C]**20:23** Lit *A stone and a stone* [D]**20:27** Lit *breath* [E]**20:27** Lit *the chambers of the belly* [F]**20:30** Lit *beatings the chambers of the belly* [G]**21:2** Lit LORD *weighs the hearts*

4 The lamp[A] that guides
the wicked—
haughty eyes and
an arrogant heart—is sin.

5 The plans of the diligent
certainly lead to profit,
but anyone who is reckless
certainly becomes poor.

6 Making a fortune
through a lying tongue
is a vanishing mist,[B] a pursuit
of death.[C,D]

7 The violence of the wicked
sweeps them away
because they refuse
to act justly.

8 A •guilty man's conduct
is crooked,
but the behavior
of the innocent is upright.

9 Better to live on the corner
of a roof
than to share a house
with a nagging wife.

10 A wicked person desires evil;
he has no consideration[E]
for his neighbor.

11 When a mocker is punished,
the inexperienced
become wiser;
when one teaches a wise man,
he acquires knowledge.

12 The Righteous One considers
the house of the wicked;
He brings the wicked to ruin.

13 The one who shuts his ears
to the cry of the poor
will himself also call out
and not be answered.

14 A secret gift soothes anger,
and a covert bribe,[F]
fierce rage.

15 Justice executed is a joy
to the righteous
but a terror to those
who practice iniquity.

16 The man who strays
from the way of wisdom
will come to rest
in the assembly
of the departed spirits.

17 The one who loves pleasure
will become a poor man;
whoever loves wine and oil
will not get rich.

18 The wicked are a ransom
for the righteous,
and the treacherous,
for[G] the upright.

19 Better to live in a wilderness
than with a nagging
and hot-tempered wife.

20 Precious treasure and oil
are in the dwelling of
a wise person,
but a foolish man consumes
them.[H]

21 The one who pursues
righteousness
and faithful love
will find life, righteousness,
and honor.

22 A wise person went up against
a city of warriors
and brought down
its secure fortress.

23 The one who guards his mouth
and tongue
keeps himself out of trouble.

24 The proud and arrogant person,
named "Mocker,"
acts with excessive pride.

25 A slacker's craving will kill him
because his hands refuse
to work.

26 He is filled with craving[I]
all day long,
but the righteous give
and don't hold back.

27 The sacrifice of a wicked person
is detestable—
how much more so
when he brings it
with ulterior motives!

28 A lying witness will perish,
but the one who listens
will speak successfully.

21:9 A quarrelsome, **nagging wife** creates so much misery and heartache in the home that her husband prefers living on the **roof**, exposed to unseasonable weather, over being with her in his **house**. (cp. v. 19; 19:13; 25:24; 27:15; 2Sm 6:16-23; 1Ch 15:29; Jb 2:9-10; cp. 1Pt 3:4). See **Biblical Womanhood**, p. 813.

21:14 A secret gift does not endorse bribery but is an observation that a **bribe** has been given by one who is tempting its recipient to break God's law (cp. Ex 23:8; Dt 16:19), and it is usually effective in so doing. Scripture condemns bribery (see Pr 15:27; 17:23).

21:17 Self-indulgent **pleasure** (Hb *simchah*, "joy, gladness, revelry," here pursued as an end in itself rather than the reward of righteousness) will not have a good end. The finer things of life are not evil in themselves but may be destructive when they gain a hold on your life. Only being right with God will bring genuine happiness and blessing (10:28). Feasting with **wine and oil**, when expanded to extravagance, can bring a person to poverty and despair (cp. 23:20-21,29-35).

[A]**21:4** Some Hb mss, ancient versions read *tillage* [B]**21:6** Or *a breath blown away* [C]**21:6** Some Hb mss, LXX, Vg read *a snare of death* [D]**21:6** Lit *is vanity, ones seeking death* [E]**21:10** Or *favor* [F]**21:14** Lit *a bribe in the bosom* [G]**21:18** Or *in place of* [H]**21:20** Lit *it* [I]**21:26** Lit *He craves a craving*

22:1 A good name is the fruit of a disciplined life and untarnished character—the result of consistently choosing wisdom and walking with God.

22:6 Although traditionally considered a promise to parents who conscientiously and faithfully nurtured the spiritual development of their children, many godly parents have experienced the pain and disillusionment of watching their children move away from what they were carefully taught in the home and church. Parents do have the responsibility to model what they teach their children and to inspire the child's willing embrace of what is being taught. However, God has given every individual the free will to make his own choices. Some make poor—even bad—choices, despite the spiritual preparation poured into their lives.

The phrase may also be a warning to parents, suggesting that **about the way he should go** refers to the understanding that parents err in allowing a child to have his own way so that a foundation is laid for a self-willed lifestyle, from which the child will never depart. A determination to have his own way keeps a child from becoming obedient to going God's way. Such a pattern is clearly identified in Scripture (12:15; 14:12; 21:2; 29:15; cp. Jdg 21:25; Is 53:6).

22:7 This verse does not pass judgment on borrowing or lending; but by stating the facts, **the borrower** is warned about the bondage engendered by indebtedness.

22:14 A **forbidden woman** (Hb *zur*; see 2:12-16; 5:1-14) either did not belong to or had departed from the covenant community of Israel. Figuratively, then, the word refers to an immoral woman, one with whom a relationship on any level is dangerous because of the power of her words to entice a man to lust after and even pursue her.

22:15 The rod [Hb *shēvet*, "stick, staff for chastising, staff of the shepherd"; see **Word Study**, p. 802] **of discipline** (Hb *musar*, "chastisement, instruction"; see **Word Study**, p. 783) is God's way of turning willfulness

29 A wicked man puts on
a bold face,
but the upright man
considers his way.
30 No wisdom, no understanding,
and no counsel
will prevail against the LORD.
31 A horse is prepared for the day
of battle,
but victory comes
from the LORD.

22 A good name is to be chosen
over great wealth;
favor is better than silver
and gold.
2 The rich and the poor have this
in common:[A]
the LORD made them both.[B]
3 A sensible person sees danger
and takes cover,
but the inexperienced
keep going
and are punished.
4 The result of humility is •fear
of the LORD,
along with wealth, honor,
and life.
5 There are thorns and snares
on the path of the crooked;
the one who guards himself
stays far from them.
6 Teach a youth about the way
he should go;
even when he is old
he will not depart from it.
7 The rich rule over the poor,
and the borrower is a slave
to the lender.
8 The one who sows injustice
will reap disaster,
and the rod of his fury
will be destroyed.
9 A generous person[C]
will be blessed,
for he shares his food
with the poor.
10 Drive out a mocker,
and conflict goes too;
then quarreling and dishonor
will cease.
11 The one who loves
a pure heart
and gracious lips—the king is
his friend.
12 The LORD's eyes keep watch
over knowledge,
but He overthrows the words
of the treacherous.
13 The slacker says,
"There's a lion outside!
I'll be killed
in the public square!"
14 The mouth
of the forbidden woman is
a deep pit;
a man cursed by the LORD
will fall into it.
15 Foolishness is tangled up
in the heart of a youth;
the rod of discipline
will drive it away from him.
16 Oppressing the poor
to enrich oneself,
and giving to the rich—
both lead only to poverty.

The Words of the Wise (22:17–24:34)

17 Listen closely,[D] pay attention
to the words of the wise,
and apply your mind
to my knowledge.
18 For it is pleasing
if you keep them within you
and if[E] they are constantly
on your lips.

[A]22:2 Lit *poor meet* [B]22:2 Lit *all* [C]22:9 Lit *Good of eye* [D]22:17 Lit *Stretch out your ear* [E]22:18 Or *you; let them be*, or *you, so that*

>WORD|*study*

22:6 Teach (Hb *chanak*, "train, initiate, start" from a root associated with the palate or mouth) goes beyond the transfer of facts to speech that imparts wisdom. Some have associated the Hebrew word with a kindred Arabic word used to describe the midwife's massaging date syrup into a newborn baby's gums to encourage the baby's attraction to his mother's breast where he would find nourishment. The word might also be illustrated in the breaking of a wild horse by means of a rope in its mouth. In this sense, wise parents find ways to break their child's willfulness—not to harm the child but to harness the child's potential that flourishes only when willingly submitted to the Lord's control. To allow a child to go his own sin-prone way instead of steering him toward a path of obedience deprives him of the discipline needed from the outside in order to mold his self-discipline within (cp. Heb 12:11). Positive motivation is part of this process as is the example of godly behavior. Elsewhere the word is translated "dedicate" in the sense of setting apart for hallowed usage (cp. Dt 20:5; 1Kg 8:63).

19 I have instructed you
today—even you—
so that your confidence
may be in the LORD.
20 Haven't I written for you
thirty sayings[A]
about counsel and knowledge,
21 in order to teach you true
and reliable words,
so that you may give
a dependable report[B]
to those who sent you?

22 Don't rob a poor man
because he is poor,
and don't crush the oppressed
at the ·gate,
23 for the LORD will take up
their case
and will plunder those
who plunder them.

24 Don't make friends
with an angry man,[C]
and don't be a companion
of a hot-tempered man,
25 or you will learn his ways
and entangle yourself
in a snare.

26 Don't be one of those
who enter agreements,[D]
who put up security for loans.
27 If you have no money to pay,
even your bed will be taken
from under you.

28 Don't move an
ancient boundary marker
that your fathers set up.

29 Do you see a man skilled
in his work?
He will stand in the presence
of kings.
He will not stand
in the presence
of unknown men.

23 When you sit down to dine
with a ruler,
consider carefully what[E] is
before you,
2 and put a knife to your throat
if you have a big[F] appetite;
3 don't desire his choice food,
for that food is deceptive.

4 Don't wear yourself out
to get rich;
stop giving your attention
to it.
5 As soon as your eyes fly to it,
it disappears,
for it makes wings for itself
and flies like an eagle
to the sky.

6 Don't eat
a stingy person's bread,[G]
and don't desire
his choice food,
7 for it's like someone
calculating inwardly.[H]
"Eat and drink,"
he says to you,
but his heart is not with you.
8 You will vomit the little
you've eaten
and waste
your pleasant words.

9 Don't speak to[I] a fool,
for he will despise the insight
of your words.

10 Don't move an
ancient boundary marker,
and don't encroach
on the fields
of the fatherless,
11 for their Redeemer is strong,

and self-direction into submissive obedience to parents and God-control in the life of the child. The rod, a symbol for discipline in the book of Proverbs, was used for remedial or punitive purposes for a child (cp. 13:24; 23:13-14; 29:15). There is no hint of abuse, but this corrective physical spanking administered swiftly and appropriately by a loving parent settles the matter and prevents permissiveness and lawlessness. **Foolishness** is in the heart of a child who goes according to his own way instead of pursuing the wisdom of God's way (cp. Ps 51:5; 1Co 13:11).

23:1-3 A ruler may be any authority or person to whom you relate professionally. Instructions are given concerning etiquette at the table when dining with a person of importance. **Put a knife to your throat** is a hyperbole—a statement or image using exaggeration for effect; here the picture strengthens the admonition to exercise self-control as though your life depended on it (cp. Mt 5:29-30).

23:4-5 Scripture encourages industry and hard work but not for sake of getting **rich**. The warning here to avoid overwork for the sake of material gain also capsulizes the biblical message that wealth is fleeting (cp. 1Tm 6:6-10,17-18).

23:6-8 In hospitality, beware of the hypocritical hostess who appears to welcome but who in reality only begrudgingly offers **choice food**. Her deception will soon become apparent to the guest, who will find the experience nauseating and a waste of time.

23:10-11 The **ancient** property line was important to the widow and orphan. The Lord will not tolerate encroachment on these vulnerable ones under His protection. **Their Redeemer** (Hb *go'ēl*, "one who buys back, kinsman-redeemer"; cp. Ru 4:4,6; 1Kg 16:11)—God Himself (e.g., Pss 19:14; 78:35; Is 41:14; 43:14; 63:16; Jr 50:34)—will protect their borders.

[A]**22:20** Text emended; one Hb tradition reads *you previously*; alt Hb tradition reads *you excellent things*; LXX, Syr, Vg read *you three times* [B]**22:21** Lit *give dependable words* [C]**22:24** Lit *with a master of anger* [D]**22:26** Lit *who shakes hands* [E]**23:1** Or *who* [F]**23:2** Lit *you are the master of an* [G]**23:6** Lit *eat bread of an evil eye* [H]**23:7** LXX reads *it is like someone swallowing a hair in the throat* [I]**23:9** Lit *in the ears of*

BIBLICAL WOMANHOOD Habitual Attitudes of a Wife

Three of the five proverbs that describe a wife as **nagging** (Hb *midyan*, "quarrel, controversy, strife, contention"; 19:13; cp. 21:9,19; 25:24; 27:15) underscore the domestic despair of her husband. A wife's constant bickering, complaining, criticizing, and instigating of arguments makes the atmosphere of her home so unpleasant that her husband might prefer being alone more than being with her. Proverbs 21:19 intensifies the picture by adding the characteristic of being **hot-tempered** (Hb *ka'as*, "anger, provocation").

23:13-14 Parents are admonished again: **Don't withhold discipline from a youth**. The means of correction is the **rod** (Hb *shēvet*; see **Word Study**, p. 802; cp. 22:6). Discipline is not to bring hurt and misery to the child but rather to enable him to live life with the greatest success and joy. **Sheol** is a reference to death, which was considered punishment for wickedness (cp. 1:12). This deliverance includes escaping physical dangers that would be incurred in an undisciplined and foolish lifestyle as well as avoiding spiritual death, which is the end result of rebellion against God.

23:15-18 Nothing thrills the hearts of mothers and fathers like seeing their children walk in the path of wisdom of their own volition (cp. vv. 24-25). Words of praise for children with a godly lifestyle are appropriate and necessary. Their **future and . . . hope** are secure (cp. Jr 29:11).

23:20-21 Children are likewise admonished to listen to the warnings of their parents. Avoiding those who **drink too much wine or . . . gorge themselves on meat** speaks to excess and gluttony and the gratification of unhealthy appetites. The warning against intoxicating beverages appears elsewhere as well (see note on 20:1; cp. Dt 21:20; Is 56:12; Hs 4:18). **Grogginess** is a reference to laziness and slothfulness, which do indeed lead to poverty (Pr 23:21; cp. 6:6-11).

23:27 The reference to **a prostitute** (Hb *zanah*, "one who commits fornication," a word applied primarily to women, whether married or unmarried, indicating active involvement in sexual relations outside marriage"; cp. 6:26; 7:10; 29:3) and to **a stranger** (Hb *nokri*; cp. 2:16) reinforces earlier instruction.

The Hebrew suggests a pun in the contrast between sexual intimacy with one's wife—a joyous and productive **well** blessed of God (5:15-18)—and fornication with a woman who is not your wife—**a deep pit and . . . a narrow well** (cp. 22:14). The path to promiscuity is easy to follow, but once entrapped the escape is difficult and costly (cp. 2:18-19; 5:3-6; 6:24-35; 7:5-23).

23:29-35 Verse 30 answers each question of verse 29. The rest of the passage describes a person who is inebriated as:

- disheveled in appearance;
- having distorted vision, incoherent speech, and staggering steps (vv. 33-35; cp. Jb 12:25; Ps 60:3);
- guilt-ridden and anxious (Pr 23:29-32);
- quarrelsome and combative (20:1);

and He will take up their case
against you.

12 Apply yourself to discipline
and listen to words
of knowledge.

13 Don't withhold discipline
from a youth;
if you beat him with a rod,
he will not die.
14 Strike him with a rod,
and you will rescue his life
from •Sheol.

15 My son, if your heart is wise,
my heart will indeed rejoice.
16 My innermost being will cheer
when your lips say
what is right.

17 Don't let your heart
envy sinners;
instead, always •fear the LORD.
18 For then you will have a future,
and your hope will never fade.

19 Listen, my son, and be wise;
keep your mind
on the right course.
20 Don't associate with those
who drink too much wine
or with those
who gorge themselves
on meat.
21 For the drunkard
and the glutton
will become poor,
and grogginess
will clothe them in rags.

22 Listen to your father who gave
you life,
and don't despise your mother
when[A] she is old.
23 Buy—and do not sell—truth,
wisdom, instruction,
and understanding.
24 The father of a righteous son
will rejoice greatly,
and one who fathers
a wise son will delight
in him.
25 Let your father and mother
have joy,
and let her who gave birth
to you rejoice.

26 My son, give me your heart,
and let your eyes observe
my ways.
27 For a prostitute is a deep pit,
and a stranger is
a narrow well;
28 indeed, she sets an ambush
like a robber
and increases those
among men
who are unfaithful.

29 Who has woe? Who has sorrow?
Who has conflicts?
Who has complaints?
Who has wounds
for no reason?
Who has red eyes?
30 Those who linger over wine,
those who go looking
for mixed wine.
31 Don't gaze at wine
because it is red,
when it gleams in the cup
and goes down smoothly.
32 In the end it bites like a snake
and stings like a viper.
33 Your eyes will see
strange things,
and you will say
absurd things.[B]
34 You'll be like someone sleeping
out at sea
or lying down on the top
of a ship's mast.
35 "They struck me, but[C] I feel
no pain!
They beat me, but I didn't
know it!
When will I wake up?
I'll look for another drink."

24 Don't envy evil men
or desire to be with them,
2 for their hearts
plan violence,
and their words
stir up trouble.

3 A house is built by wisdom,
and it is established
by understanding;
4 by knowledge the rooms
are filled
with every precious
and beautiful treasure.
5 A wise warrior is better
than a strong one,[D]

[A]23:22 Or *because* [B]23:33 Or *will speak perversities* or *inverted things* [C]23:35 LXX, Syr, Tg, Vg read *me," you will say, "But* [D]24:5 LXX, Syr; MT reads *one is in strength*

and a man of knowledge
than one of strength;[A]
6 for you should wage war
with sound guidance—
victory comes
with many counselors.

7 Wisdom is inaccessible
to[B] a fool;
he does not open his mouth
at the •gate.

8 The one who plots evil
will be called a schemer.
9 A foolish scheme is sin,
and a mocker is detestable
to people.

10 If you do nothing
in a difficult time,
your strength is limited.
11 Rescue those being taken off
to death,
and save those stumbling
toward slaughter.
12 If you say, "But we didn't know
about this,"
won't He who weighs hearts
consider it?
Won't He who protects
your life know?
Won't He repay a person
according to his work?

13 Eat honey, my son,
for it is good,
and the honeycomb is sweet
to your palate;
14 realize that wisdom is the same
for you.
If you find it, you will have
a future,
and your hope will never fade.

15 Wicked man, don't set
an ambush,
at the camp
of the righteous man;
don't destroy his dwelling.
16 Though a righteous man falls
seven times,
he will get up,
but the wicked will stumble
into ruin.

17 Don't gloat when your enemy
falls,
and don't let your heart
rejoice when he stumbles,
18 or the LORD will see,
be displeased,
and turn His wrath away
from him.

19 Don't be agitated by evildoers,
and don't envy the wicked.
20 For the evil have no future;
the lamp of the wicked will be
put out.

21 My son, •fear the LORD,
as well as the king,
and don't associate
with rebels,[C]
22 for destruction from them
will come suddenly;
who knows what distress
these two can bring?

23 These sayings also
belong to the wise:
It is not good
to show partiality
in judgment.
24 Whoever says to the •guilty,
"You are innocent"—
people will curse him,
and tribes will denounce him;
25 but it will go well with those
who convict the guilty,
and a generous blessing
will come to them.

26 He who gives an honest answer
gives a kiss on the lips.

27 Complete your outdoor work,
and prepare your field;
afterward, build your house.

28 Don't testify against
your neighbor
without cause.
Don't deceive with your lips.
29 Don't say, "I'll do to him
what he did to me;
I'll repay the man for what
he has done."

30 I went by the field of a slacker
and by the vineyard of a man
lacking sense.
31 Thistles had come up
everywhere,
weeds covered the ground,
and the stone wall was ruined.
32 I saw, and took it to heart;
I looked,
and received instruction:

- vulnerable to abuse while under the influence, unable to remember how or by whom the harm was done but drawn back to alcohol's temporary effect of numbing the pain (23:35).

Since the first drink can launch a lifelong and life-shortening addiction, the admonition is to refuse its enticements totally (vv. 31-32).

24:1-4 From **evil men** come evil plans and deeds. With a metaphor comparing **a house** to a person's life, **wisdom** (i.e., "the fear of the LORD"; cp. 1:7; 9:1), **understanding** (the discernment to apply wise principles in everyday life), and **knowledge** are identified as the means by which beauty, value, and excellence fill each aspect of life. **Built** (Hb *banah*) is the same word used for the wise woman's investment in focusing on her home (Pr 14:1).

24:13-14 Pursuing **wisdom** is hard work, and one who chooses this path will endure correction and discipline along the way. However, like **honey** its rewards are pleasing.

24:26 Integrity of speech is underscored in comparing **an honest answer** to **a kiss** that is an expression of love.

24:27 In an agrarian society, preparing a **field** meant establishing a means of sustenance and income. The proverb counsels concentration on being able to support your family before focusing on building your house, which probably was understood to include marrying and having children.

24:29 Revenge and retaliation are clearly proscribed in this verse. In the context of the entire canon, the attitude and actions of "getting even" are attempts to usurp the Lord's prerogative (cp. Pr 24:12) and, particularly for followers of Christ, constitute disobedience (Rm 12:19).

24:30-34 These verses exemplify a pattern of acquiring wisdom from thoughtful observation, especially when guided by God's perspective and standards. Here, the speaker recognized that a man's laziness and negligence resulted in unsightly and unproductive land. Not only did the speaker see, however, he also **took it to heart**—drew a conclusion and applied the principle to his life (cp. 6:10-11; 20:4).

[A]**24:5** LXX, Syr, Tg; MT reads *knowledge exerts strength* [B]**24:7** Lit *is too high for* [C]**24:21** Or *those given to change*

25:1 Hezekiah, king of Judah evidently had oversight of the men who **copied** (Hb *ʿataq*, "transmit, transfer, transcribe, collect") the wisdom sayings of chapters 25–29. Hezekiah reigned ca 716–687 B.C., about 250 years after Solomon (ca 970–931 B.C.).

25:4-5 The stability of a leader's tenure, reign, or administration depends heavily on the integrity of those who carry out delegated orders or instructions, enforce policy, or simply represent the leader's office. The leader cannot maintain authority and trust as long as unethical people are tolerated. As impurities would compromise the beauty and utility of a silver vessel, so the wicked would weaken an enterprise; therefore, both should be removed.

25:11-12 Verse 11 commends the wisdom of thinking before you speak so that you not only say what is worthy of saying but also speak **at the right time**. Even a reprimand, when given through loving, well-crafted words, should be received in the same spirit.

25:16-17 Good manners or common courtesies that consider the feelings and challenges of others are also affirmed and can be a valuable tool in breaking down opposition encountered.

>WORD|*study*

24:21; 26:11 The warning is given with determination to protect those whom you love against association **with** rebels (Hb *shonim*, "those who change opinion or loyalties, who are unfaithful"; cp. Jr 2:36), who often actively stir up opposition to authority. The root verb *shanah* denotes a change, especially for the worse, in one's character or way of life, inevitably resulting in loss of God's protection as well as the exercise of His justice. Using the same verb, Pr 26:11 depicts the moral degradation of **a fool** who repeats (Hb *shanah*) sinful choices despite the negative consequences already experienced.

33 a little sleep, a little slumber,
a little folding of the arms
to rest,
34 and your poverty will come
like a robber,
your need, like a bandit.

The Collection by Hezekiah's Men (25:1–29:27)

25 These too are proverbs
of Solomon,
which the men of Hezekiah,
king of Judah, copied.

2 It is the glory of God to conceal
a matter
and the glory of kings
to investigate a matter.
3 As the heaven is high
and the earth is deep,
so the hearts of kings cannot
be investigated.

4 Remove impurities from silver,
and a vessel will be produced[A]
for a silversmith.
5 Remove the wicked
from the king's presence,
and his throne
will be established
in righteousness.

6 Don't brag about yourself
before the king,
and don't stand in the place
of the great;
7 for it is better for him to say
to you, "Come up here!"
than to demote you
in plain view of a noble.[B]

8 Don't take a matter
to court hastily.
Otherwise, what will
you do afterward
if your opponent[C]
humiliates you?
9 Make your case
with your opponent[C]
without revealing
another's secret;
10 otherwise, the one who hears
will disgrace you,
and you'll never live it down.[D]

11 A word spoken at the right time
is like gold apples
on a silver tray.[E]
12 A wise correction
to a receptive ear
is like a gold ring
or an ornament of gold.

13 To those who send him,
a trustworthy messenger
is like the coolness of snow
on a harvest day;
he refreshes the life
of his masters.
14 The man who boasts about a gift
that does not exist
is like clouds and wind
without rain.
15 A ruler can be persuaded
through patience,
and a gentle tongue can break
a bone.
16 If you find honey, eat only
what you need;
otherwise, you'll get sick
from it and vomit.
17 Seldom set foot
in your neighbor's house;
otherwise, he'll get sick of you
and hate you.

18 A man giving false testimony
against his neighbor
is like a club, a sword,
or a sharp arrow.
19 Trusting an unreliable person
in a difficult time
is like a rotten tooth
or a faltering foot.

20 Singing songs
to a troubled heart

[A]**25:4** Lit *will come out*; Ex 32:24 [B]**25:7** Lit *you before a noble whom your eyes see* [C]**25:8,9** Or *neighbor* [D]**25:10** Lit *and your evil report will not turn back* [E]**25:11** Or *like apples of gold in settings of silver*

is like taking off clothing
on a cold day
or like pouring vinegar
on soda.[A]

21 If your enemy is hungry,
give him food to eat,
and if he is thirsty, give him
water to drink;
22 for you will heap burning coals
on his head,
and the LORD will reward you.

23 The north wind produces rain,
and a backbiting tongue,
angry looks.
24 Better to live on the corner
of a roof
than to share a house
with a nagging wife.
25 Good news from a distant land
is like cold water
to a parched throat.[B]
26 A righteous person who yields
to the wicked
is like a muddied spring
or a polluted well.
27 It is not good to eat
too much honey
or to seek glory after glory.[C]
28 A man who does not control
his temper
is like a city whose wall
is broken down.

26 Like snow in summer
and rain at harvest,
honor is inappropriate
for a fool.
2 Like a flitting sparrow
or a fluttering swallow,
an undeserved curse
goes nowhere.
3 A whip for the horse, a bridle
for the donkey,
and a rod for the backs
of fools.
4 Don't answer a fool
according to his foolishness
or you'll be like him yourself.
5 Answer a fool according to
his foolishness
or he'll become wise
in his own eyes.
6 The one who sends a message
by a fool's hand
cuts off his own feet
and drinks violence.
7 A proverb in the mouth of a fool
is like lame legs
that hang limp.
8 Giving honor to a fool
is like binding a stone
in a sling.[D]
9 A proverb in the mouth of a fool
is like a stick with thorns,
brandished by[E] the hand
of a drunkard.
10 The one who hires
a fool or who hires
those passing by
is like an archer
who wounds everyone.
11 As a dog returns to its vomit,
so a fool repeats
his foolishness.
12 Do you see a man who is wise
in his own eyes?
There is more hope for a fool
than for him.

13 The slacker says, "There's a lion
in the road—
a lion in the public square!"
14 A door turns on its hinges,
and a slacker, on his bed.
15 The slacker buries his hand
in the bowl;
he is too weary to bring it
to his mouth.
16 In his own eyes, a slacker
is wiser
than seven men
who can answer sensibly.

17 A person who is passing by
and meddles in a quarrel
that's not his
is like one who grabs a dog
by the ears.
18 Like a madman who throws
flaming darts
and deadly arrows,
19 so is the man who deceives
his neighbor
and says, "I was only joking!"
20 Without wood, fire goes out;
without a gossip,
conflict dies down.
21 As charcoal for embers
and wood for fire,
so is a quarrelsome man
for kindling strife.
22 A gossip's words are
like choice food

25:21-22 Kindness and generosity, even to your enemies, inevitably bring the blessing of God (cp. Rm 12:20).

25:24 See **Biblical Womanhood**, p. 813.

26:1-12 The **fool** described here is not merely lacking in intelligence but is enmeshed in his own overconfidence to the point that wisdom passed along to him is futile (vv. 3-5). He cannot be trusted even to deliver a message (v. 6). He misuses **a proverb** or any wisdom that should instruct and correct in favor of justifying his own actions or positions (v. 9). He refuses to learn from the experience of others or himself. He repeats his mistakes in disgusting ways (v. 11). A person who is **wise in his own eyes** is even more hopeless than the common **fool** because he spurns learning in the confidence that he knows it all (v. 12).

26:13-16 **The slacker**, by definition, has no legitimate reasons for putting off his work but typically devises excuses. He is bent on procrastination, seldom beginning or completing anything (cp. 6:6-11; 12:27).

26:17-28 Interpersonal relationships are continually addressed in the book of Proverbs, and a major focus in this discussion is communication within the family circle and in the community. For example, the impact of negative words—even if uttered without evil intent—is overwhelming. Quarrels are fueled or resolved by words (vv. 17,20-21). Destruction of character is more often than not attributed to **gossip** and to the hypocrite who attempts to conceal hatred and hostility under cunning words (vv. 20,22-28).

[A] **25:20** Lit *natron,* or *sodium carbonate* [B] **25:25** Or *a weary person* [C] **25:27** Lit *seek their glory, glory* [D] **26:8** A stone bound in a sling would not release and could harm the person using the sling. A modern equivalent is jamming a cork in a gun barrel. [E] **26:9** Lit *thorn that goes up into*

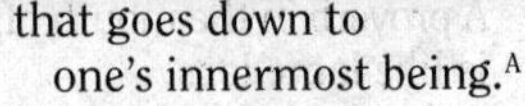

27:1-2 The warning concerning boasting **about tomorrow** in no way suggests that planning for the future is not wise and prudent but more accurately underscores the importance of planning for today and your present season of life. Just as it would be presumptuous to predict the future, so it is to praise yourself (vv. 1-2).

27:5-6 Speaking the truth is often not easy and may appear to jeopardize friendship. **Concealed love** refers to a cowardly way of ignoring the need for rebuke and correction, which are necessary ingredients in a true friendship (cp. v. 17).

27:9-10 The strength found in wise counsel is a recurring theme throughout the book and serves as a protection against **self-counsel**, by which one becomes introverted and close-minded. Friends are commended in different ways, but the use of contrast between friend and family does not suggest any demeaning of a **brother**; rather, sometimes a **friend** is more readily available by mere proximity than is a brother who is **far away**. A friend who acts as a brother should be held in deepest affection and esteem as you would have for a brother.

27:15-16 The warning about a **nagging wife** appears again (vv. 15-16; cp. 19:13; 21:9,19; 25:24); see **Biblical Womanhood**, p. 813. The imagery emphasizes both the difficulty of helping her change and, implicitly, her defiance of any effort to restrain her habitual negativity, impatience, discontentment, and vocalization of her ill-tempered outlook.

that goes down to
one's innermost being.[A]

23 Smooth[B] lips with an evil heart
are like glaze
on an earthen vessel.
24 A hateful person
disguises himself
with his speech
and harbors deceit within.
25 When he speaks graciously,
don't believe him,
for there are
seven abominations
in his heart.
26 Though his hatred is concealed
by deception,
his evil will be revealed
in the assembly.
27 The one who digs a pit will fall
into it,
and whoever rolls a stone—
it will come back on him.
28 A lying tongue hates
those it crushes,
and a flattering mouth
causes ruin.

27 Don't boast about tomorrow,
for you don't know what a day
might bring.

2 Let another praise you, and not
your own mouth—
a stranger, and not
your own lips.

3 A stone is heavy and sand,
a burden,
but aggravation from a fool
outweighs them both.

4 Fury is cruel, and anger a flood,
but who can withstand
jealousy?

5 Better an open reprimand
than concealed love.

6 The wounds of a friend
are trustworthy,
but the kisses of an enemy
are excessive.

7 A person who is full tramples
on a honeycomb,
but to a hungry person,
any bitter thing is sweet.

8 A man wandering
from his home
is like a bird wandering
from its nest.

9 Oil and incense bring joy
to the heart,
and the sweetness of a friend
is better than self-counsel.[C]
10 Don't abandon your friend
or your father's friend,
and don't go
to your brother's house
in your time of calamity;
better a neighbor nearby
than a brother far away.

11 Be wise, my son, and bring
my heart joy,
so that I can answer anyone
who taunts me.

12 A sensible person sees danger
and takes cover;
the inexperienced keep going
and are punished.

13 Take his garment,[D]
for he has put up security
for a stranger;
get collateral if it is
for foreigners.[E]

14 If one blesses his neighbor
with a loud voice early
in the morning,
it will be counted as a curse
to him.

15 An endless dripping
on a rainy day
and a nagging wife are alike.
16 The one who controls her
controls the wind
and grasps oil
with his right hand.

17 Iron sharpens iron,
and one man sharpens
another.[F]

18 Whoever tends a fig tree will eat
its fruit,
and whoever looks after
his master will be honored.

19 As water reflects the face,
so the heart reflects
the person.

[A]26:22 Lit *to the chambers of the belly* [B]26:23 LXX; MT reads *Burning* [C]27:9 LXX reads *heart, but the soul is torn up by affliction* [D]27:13 A debtor's outer garment held as collateral; Dt 24:12-13,17; Jb 22:6; Am 2:8 [E]27:13 Lit *a foreign woman* [F]27:17 Lit *and a man sharpens his friend's face*

20 •Sheol and •Abaddon are
never satisfied,
and people's eyes are
never satisfied.

21 A crucible for silver, and
a smelter for gold,
and a man for the words
of his praise.[A]

22 Though you grind a fool
in a mortar with a pestle
along with grain,
you will not separate
his foolishness from him.

23 Know well the condition
of your flock,
and pay attention
to your herds,
24 for wealth is not forever;
not even a crown lasts
for all time.
25 When hay is removed
and new growth appears
and the grain from the hills
is gathered in,
26 lambs will provide
your clothing,
and goats, the price of a field;
27 there will be enough goat's milk
for your food—
food for your household
and nourishment for your
female servants.

28 The wicked flee when no one
is pursuing them,
but the righteous are as bold
as a lion.

2 When a land is in rebellion,
it has many rulers,
but with a discerning
and knowledgeable person,
it endures.

3 A destitute leader[B]
who oppresses the poor
is like a driving rain
that leaves no food.

4 Those who reject the law
praise the wicked,
but those who keep the law
battle against them.

5 Evil men do not
understand justice,
but those who seek the LORD
understand everything.

6 Better a poor man who lives
with integrity
than a rich man who distorts
right and wrong.[C]

7 A discerning son keeps the law,
but a companion of gluttons
humiliates his father.

8 Whoever increases his wealth
through excessive interest
collects it for one who is kind
to the poor.

9 Anyone who turns his ear
away from hearing the law—
even his prayer is detestable.

10 The one who leads the upright
into an evil way
will fall into his own pit,
but the blameless will inherit
what is good.

11 A rich man is wise in
his own eyes,
but a poor man
who has discernment
sees through him.

12 When the righteous triumph,
there is great rejoicing,[D]
but when the wicked come
to power,
people hide themselves.

13 The one who conceals his sins
will not prosper,
but whoever confesses
and renounces them
will find mercy.

14 Happy is the one who is always
reverent,
but one who hardens
his heart falls into trouble.

15 A wicked ruler over
a helpless people
is like a roaring lion
or a charging bear.

16 A leader who lacks
understanding
is very oppressive,
but one who hates dishonest
profit
prolongs his life.

17 A man burdened by bloodguilt[E]
will be a fugitive until death.
Let no one help him.

27:23-27 Food for your household is a concern for every family. Here the tension seems to be a reminder of the balance between working as hard as you can to provide for your family, while still understanding that God and His providences enable His children to meet their needs.

28:8 Excessive interest is no small concern to the Lord. In fact, Israelites were forbidden to take profit on a loan to a brother in need; rather, according to God's instruction, the loan was to be an act of compassion and interest-free—a practice unheard of in modernity (cp. Ex 22:25; Lv 25:35-37; Dt 23:20). Anyone who took advantage of a brother in poverty would lose whatever gain he received (cp. Pr 22:16; 28:18).

28:9-11 Those who turn a deaf ear to God's law will not be heard by God; likewise, those who lead someone **into an evil way** will **fall into** [their] **own pit**. One who seems to have it all is transparent to **a poor man who has discernment**. The latter has a sound perspective on possessions.

28:13-14 The way you deal with sin determines the way God deals with you. Refusing to admit guilt (i.e., concealing your **sins**) opens the door to severe consequences (Ps 32:3-4). However, confessing and renouncing your sin brings forgiveness and peace (cp. Ps 32:1,5; 1Jn 1:9; Rm 4:7-8). One who does the latter is then **reverent** before the Lord (i.e., he fears the Lord and determines to be obedient to Him).

[A]**27:21** Or *gold, but a man is tested by his praise* [B]**28:3** LXX reads *A wicked man* [C]**28:6** Lit *who twists two ways* [D]**28:12** Lit *glory* [E]**28:17** Lit *the blood of a person*

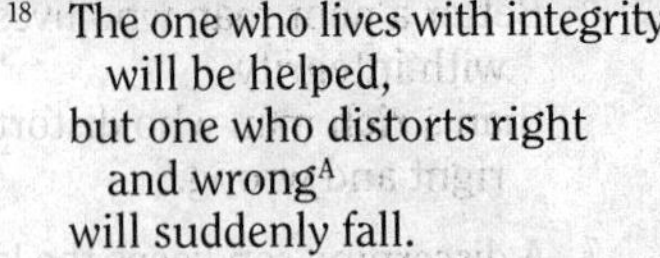

28:21 A piece of bread refers to a bribe offered to one whose position calls for impartiality yet who is willing to give favor or to use his influence in a pending decision by manipulating the circumstances. Being influenced by a bribe destroys justice (cp. Lv 19:15; Dt 1:17; 16:19; Pr 18:5; 24:23). Ultimately, however, God Himself will settle all accounts (cp. Rv 20:12).

28:24 A sense of entitlement prompts children to rob **father or mother**—taking what they believe to be rightfully theirs and arguing that their parents owe them. Solomon wisely compares such children to **a man who destroys** or a murderer (cp. 19:26; 20:20; 30:11,17; Mk 7:11-12).

29:4 A king whose rule is characterized by doing what is right **brings stability** (Hb *'amad*, "cause to stand continually, cause to endure") to his **land**. In contrast, **a man** who cheats, takes bribes, or blackmails people has the opposite effect on his country—he **demolishes it** (Hb *haras*, "pulls down, breaks in pieces, destroys, overthrows, utterly ruins"; cp. 11:11; 14:1; 24:31).

29:11 Self-control and restraint are often affirmed in discussions of wise behavior. The fool is a slave to impulsive responses, while one who is wise is calm and still, resting in his restraint. A **wise man** can calm the storm of **a fool**.

18 The one who lives with integrity
will be helped,
but one who distorts right
and wrong[A]
will suddenly fall.

19 The one who works his land
will have plenty of food,
but whoever chases fantasies
will have his fill of poverty.

20 A faithful man will have
many blessings,
but one in a hurry to get rich
will not go unpunished.

21 It is not good
to show partiality—
yet a man may sin for a piece
of bread.

22 A greedy man[B] is in a hurry
for wealth;
he doesn't know that poverty
will come to him.

23 One who rebukes a person
will later find more favor
than one who flatters[C]
with his tongue.

24 The one who robs his father
or mother
and says, "That's no sin,"
is a companion to a man
who destroys.

25 A greedy person
provokes conflict,
but whoever trusts
in the LORD will prosper.

26 The one who trusts in himself[D]
is a fool,
but one who walks in wisdom
will be safe.

27 The one who gives to the poor
will not be in need,
but one who turns
his eyes away[E]
will receive many curses.

28 When the wicked come
to power,
people hide,
but when they are destroyed,
the righteous flourish.

29 One who becomes
stiff-necked,
after many reprimands
will be shattered instantly—
beyond recovery.

2 When the righteous flourish,
the people rejoice,
but when the wicked rule,
people groan.

3 A man who loves wisdom
brings joy to his father,
but one who consorts
with prostitutes
destroys his wealth.

4 By justice a king brings stability
to a land,
but a man who demands
"contributions"[F]
demolishes it.

5 A man who flatters[G]
his neighbor
spreads a net for his feet.

6 An evil man is caught by sin,
but the righteous one sings
and rejoices.

7 The righteous person knows
the rights[H] of the poor,
but the wicked one
does not understand
these concerns.

8 Mockers inflame a city,
but the wise turn away anger.

9 If a wise man goes to court
with a fool,
there will be ranting
and raving
but no resolution.[I]

10 Bloodthirsty men hate
an honest person,
but the upright care
about him.[J]

11 A fool gives full vent
to his anger,[K]
but a wise man holds it
in check.

12 If a ruler listens to lies,
all his officials will be wicked.

13 The poor and the oppressor
have this in common:[L]

[A]28:18 Lit *who is twisted regarding two ways* [B]28:22 Lit *A man with an evil eye* [C]28:23 Lit *is smooth* [D]28:26 Lit *his heart* [E]28:27 Lit *who shuts his eyes* [F]29:4 The Hb word for "contributions" usually refers to offerings in worship. [G]29:5 Lit *is smooth on* [H]29:7 Lit *justice* [I]29:9 Lit *rest* [J]29:10 Or *person, and seek the life of the upright* [K]29:11 Lit *spirit* [L]29:13 Lit *oppressor meet*

>WORD|*study*

29:11 Anger (Hb *ruach*, "wind, breath, mind") can have the nuance of "the blast of a storm." Here the word metaphorically depicts emotions of aggressiveness and rage (cp. Jdg 8:3; Ec 10:4; Is 25:4; Ezk 3:14).

the LORD gives light
to the eyes of both.

14 A king who judges the poor
with fairness—
his throne will be
established forever.

15 A rod of correction
imparts wisdom,
but a youth left to himself[A]
is a disgrace to his mother.

16 When the wicked increase,
rebellion increases,
but the righteous will see
their downfall.

17 Discipline your son, and
it will bring you
peace of mind
and give you delight.

18 Without revelation[B] people
run wild,
but one who listens
to instruction will be happy.

19 A slave cannot be disciplined
by words;
though he understands,
he doesn't respond.

20 Do you see a man who speaks
too soon?
There is more hope for a fool
than for him.

21 A slave pampered
from his youth
will become arrogant[C]
later on.

22 An angry man stirs up conflict,
and a hot-tempered man[D]
increases rebellion.

23 A person's pride
will humble him,
but a humble spirit
will gain honor.

24 To be a thief's partner is
to hate oneself;
he hears the curse but
will not testify.[E]

25 The fear of man is a snare,
but the one who trusts
in the LORD is protected.[F]

26 Many seek a ruler's favor,
but a man receives justice
from the LORD.

27 An unjust man is detestable
to the righteous,
and one whose way is upright
is detestable to the wicked.

Agur's Words (30:1-33)

30 The words of Agur
son of Jakeh. The oracle.[G]

The man's oration to Ithiel,
to Ithiel and Ucal:[H]

2 I am more stupid than
any other man,[I]
and I lack man's ability
to understand.

3 I have not gained wisdom,
and I have no knowledge
of the Holy One.

4 Who has gone up to heaven
and come down?
Who has gathered the wind
in His hands?
Who has bound up the waters
in a cloak?
Who has established
all the ends of the earth?
What is His name,
and what is the name
of His Son—
if you know?

5 Every word of God is pure;[J]

[A]**29:15** Lit *youth sent away* [B]**29:18** Lit *vision* [C]**29:21** Hb obscure [D]**29:22** Lit *a master of rage* [E]**29:24** When a call for witnesses was made public, anyone with information who did not submit his testimony was under a curse. [F]**29:25** Lit *raised high* [G]**30:1** Or *son of Jakeh from Massa*; Pr 31:1 [H]**30:1** Hb uncertain. Sometimes read with different word division as *oration: I am weary, God, I am weary, God, and I am exhausted*, or *oration: I am not God, I am not God, that I should prevail.* LXX reads *My son, fear my words and when you have received them repent. The man says these things to the believers in God, and I pause.* [I]**30:2** Lit *I am more stupid than a man* [J]**30:5** Lit *refined*

29:15 The **mother** is specifically noted here, as is the father in similar proverbs (e.g., 3:12; 13:1; 17:21). **A rod of correction** is discussed elsewhere (cp. 22:15; see **Word Study**, p. 802). An undisciplined child, left to pursue his own way, will bring judgment on himself and shame to his parents (cp. 22:6; 1Kg 1:6; 2:13-25).

29:17 When words are ignored and authority is spurned, there must be yet another effort to help the child obey. When parents accept the responsibility and bear the burden of this loving and consistent **discipline** (Hb *yasar*, "correct," especially in the sense of a parent's physical punishment of a child [cp. Dt 21:18; 22:18] or verbally admonishing him; see note on 19:18; cp. Dt 8:5), they will receive **peace of mind** (Hb *nuach*, "rest, settle down, be free from anxiety and calamity").

30:1-3 Little is known about **Agur** [Hb, "gathered; one of the assembly," i.e., one of the wise] **son of Jakeh** (Hb, "pious, blameless") except that he was probably a well-known sage or man of wisdom living during Israel's monarchy (cp. 1Kg 4:30-31). **Ithiel** (Hb, "God is with me"; cp. Neh 11:7) and **Ucal** (Hb, "devoured, weary") may have been Agur's sons, companions, or students. Agur humbly noted that even after all his study, he had not yet mastered the subject of **wisdom**.

30:4 The implied answer to the four rhetorical questions is "God alone." The question regarding the name of His Son, therefore, points toward the Messiah to come (cp. Is 53:8-9; Hs 11:1; Mt 2:15).

He is a shield to those
who take refuge in Him.
6 Don't add to His words,
or He will rebuke you,
and you will be proved
a liar.

7 Two things I ask of You;
don't deny them to me
before I die:
8 Keep falsehood
and deceitful words
far from me.
Give me neither poverty
nor wealth;
feed me with the food I need.
9 Otherwise, I might have
too much
and deny You, saying,
"Who is the LORD?"
or I might have nothing
and steal,
profaning[A] the name
of my God.
10 Don't slander a servant
to his master
or he will curse you,
and you will
become •guilty.

11 There is a generation
that curses its father
and does not bless its mother.
12 There is a generation
that is pure in its own eyes,
yet is not washed
from its filth.
13 There is a generation—
how haughty its eyes
and pretentious its looks.[B]
14 There is a generation
whose teeth are swords,
whose fangs are knives,
devouring the oppressed
from the land
and the needy from among
mankind.

15 The leech has two daughters:
"Give, Give!"
Three things are
never satisfied;
four never say, "Enough!":
16 •Sheol; a childless womb;
earth, which is never satisfied
with water;
and fire, which never says,
"Enough!"

17 As for the eye that ridicules
a father
and despises obedience
to a mother,
may ravens of the valley
pluck it out
and young vultures eat it.

18 Three things are beyond me;
four I can't understand:
19 the way of an eagle in the sky,
the way of a snake on a rock,
the way of a ship at sea,
and the way of a man
with a young woman.

20 This is the way of an adulteress:
she eats and wipes her mouth
and says, "I've done
nothing wrong."

21 The earth trembles
under three things;
it cannot bear up under four:
22 a servant
when he becomes king,
a fool when he is stuffed
with food,
23 an unloved woman
when she marries,

[A]30:9 Lit *grabbing* [B]30:13 Lit *and its eyelids lifted up*

>WORD|*study*

30:11-14 Generation (Hb *dor*, "a race among mankind, a class or group of people") in a technical sense refers to a lifetime, beginning from one's conception and extending to the birth of her offspring. Four parallel statements describe metaphorically the moral and spiritual character of **a generation** that is the opposite of one that could be a model (cp. Ps 79:13; Jr 2:31; 7:29). The people who make up this generation (or these four generations):

- dishonor their parents and fail to appreciate them altogether (cp. 20:20; Ex 21:17);
- are self-righteous and religious yet unaware of the failure to repent and receive cleansing from the Lord (cp. Is 1:11-16; Mt 23:27);
- are **haughty** and **pretentious**, embracing an unduly high view of themselves, which then awakens contempt in their hearts for others (cp. Pr 6:16-17; Ps 131:1);
- are cruel and oppressive, even to the most vulnerable in society.

30:7-10 This brief prayer exemplifies a God-centered perspective on what is important in life. The speaker wants most of all to remain humble and truthful, free from any temptation to deny or disparage God's name.

30:15-16 The leech, commonly understood to be a bloodsucker, is an appropriate metaphor for greed and an insatiable demand in the human heart for more.

30:19-20 This numerical saying presents three examples of movement that are untraceable, setting up the fourth and focal consideration of **the way of a young man with a young woman** (Hb *ʿalmah*, "a young woman of marriageable age, yet under the care of her parents, and thus hidden from the public"; cp. Gn 24:43; Sg 1:3; 6:8; see **Doctrine**, p. 870). The pair enter the realm of human sexuality, which may begin with physical attraction but moves toward the highest levels of human intimacy. The physical union is assumed to occur within marriage, especially given the sharp contrast in the proverb that immediately follows. Verse 19 poetically elicits a sense of hushed awe in consideration of the beautiful relationship unfolding, for example, in a honeymoon suite. Verse 20, however, presents **the way of an adulteress**, which earlier passages have accurately traced in lurid detail (5:1-14; 7:6-27) , as brazen, crass, and degenerate in the extreme in the denial of wrongdoing.

30:21-23 This numerical saying notes **four** evils found in an upside-down world—situations in which people suddenly elevated to a higher status in life without reason or preparation, suggesting that their behavior in their new role is intolerable. **An unloved** [Hb *sanēʾ*, "hated," sometimes understood as only a lesser degree of love and regard; "cool and indifferent to, showing less favor to"] **woman** who **marries** may belong in this category because she continues to carry a chip on her shoulder from being rejected or even slighted. The two wives of Elkanah—Hannah, whom he loved though she was barren, and Peninnah, who bore him children—illustrate this situation. Even though Elkanah treated Peninnah with dignity and despite her advantage of having several children, she tried to make life of the beloved wife Hannah miserable (1Sm 1:1-8).

30:24-28 Wisdom is greater than size and strength as is portrayed in **four** small and physically weak creatures who nevertheless show their cleverness in preparing for the future:

- **the ants** are diligent and organized about storing **food**;

>WORD|*study*

31:1 Oracle (Hb *massa'*, "utterance, pronouncement, speech"; more literally "burden, load"; figuratively "what lies heavy on a people"; possibly the name of a province or realm) in this context seems to suggest the sharing of a message coming out of a burdened heart and presented in reasoned argument with the intent for the words to be passed on as a teaching and standard for others. The verb **taught** (Hb *yasar*, "instruct, bind, correct, reform, reprove"; in this context more literally "chastise with words, set right") suggests urgent and persuasive admonition and discipline. This correction results in a learning experience. God's discipline seeks to change lives and bring people into obedience, and this word is used frequently in the book of Proverbs.

and a servant girl
when she ousts her queen.

24 Four things on earth are small,
yet they are extremely wise:
25 the ants are not a strong people,
yet they store up their food
in the summer;
26 hyraxes are not a mighty people,
yet they make their homes
in the cliffs;
27 locusts have no king,
yet all of them march
in ranks;
28 a lizard[A] can be caught
in your hands,
yet it lives in kings' palaces.

29 Three things are stately
in their stride,
even four are stately
in their walk:
30 a lion, which is mightiest
among beasts
and doesn't retreat
before anything,
31 a strutting rooster,[B] a goat,
and a king at the head
of his army.[C]

32 If you have been foolish
by exalting yourself
or if you've been scheming,
put your hand
over your mouth.
33 For the churning of milk
produces butter,
and twisting a nose
draws blood,
and stirring up anger
produces strife.

Lemuel's Words (31:1-9)

31 The words of King Lemuel,
an oracle[D] that his mother
taught him:

2 What should I say, my son?
What, son of my womb?
What, son of my vows?
3 Don't spend your energy
on women
or your efforts on those
who destroy kings.
4 It is not for kings, Lemuel,
it is not for kings
to drink wine
or for rulers to desire beer.
5 Otherwise, they[E] will drink,
forget what is decreed,
and pervert justice for all
the oppressed.[F]
6 Give beer to one who is dying
and wine to one whose life
is bitter.
7 Let him drink so that
he can forget his poverty
and remember his trouble
no more.
8 Speak up[G] for those who have
no voice,[H]
for the justice of all
who are dispossessed.[I]
9 Speak up,[G] judge righteously,
and defend the cause of[J]
the oppressed and needy.

The Acrostic from Lemuel's Mother (31:10-31)

10 Who can find a capable wife?[K]
She is far more precious
than jewels.[L]
11 The heart of her husband
trusts in her,
and he will not lack
anything good.
12 She rewards him with good,
not evil,
all the days of her life.
13 She selects wool and flax
and works with willing hands.

[A]30:28 Or *spider* [B]30:31 Or *a greyhound* [C]30:31 LXX reads *king addressing his people* [D]31:1 Or *of Lemuel, king of Massa*, or *of King Lemuel, a burden* [E]31:5 Lit *he* [F]31:5 Lit *sons of affliction* [G]31:8,9 Lit *Open your mouth* [H]31:8 Lit *who are mute* [I]31:8 Lit *all the sons of passing away* [J]31:9 Lit *and justice for* [K]31:10 Or *a wife of quality*, or *a wife of noble character* [L]31:10 Vv. 10-31 form an •acrostic.

- **hyraxes** or rock badgers are wise in finding a place of safety and security;
- **locusts**, though without a **king** or leader, cooperate to maintain order and discipline;
- **a lizard**, though vulnerable to predators, dwells in **kings' palaces** without fear.

31:1-2 King **Lemuel** (Hb, "unto God or one dedicated to God") may be a reference to Solomon, a symbolic name for an ideal king, or an allusion to a king whose origin is not clearly identified. This name is a mark of his mother's faith. He is not ashamed to acknowledge his mother's influence by giving her credit for this wisdom and her impact on his life, and thus immortalizes her life and wisdom.

Lemuel's **mother** is the inspired messenger. This mother uses endearing epithets: **my son . . . son of my womb . . . son of my vows**, tracing their close and loving relationship back to his conception and growth in the womb. The book of Proverbs begins with wise words from a father (1:8) and now ends with words of wisdom from a mother. Whether or not Lemuel's historic roots are clear is not necessary for understanding the passage.

31:3-9 Lemuel's mother begins with warnings for her son, the king, admonishing him to beware of the dangers of women and wine. **Wine**, especially intemperance or drunkenness, may hinder his judgment (cp. Mk 6:21-28); and **women,** through whom unrestrained sexual gratification and promiscuous relationships, may waste his strength (cp. 5:20-22; 1Kg 11:1-8). Both are distractions from his divinely assigned responsibility of governing his people with justice and righteousness.

Although strong drink might help one in **poverty** or despair to **forget** his circumstances, the most important remedy was for the person charged with judgment and rule to listen and judge righteously and fairly (Pr 31:6-7). The queen mother's call for abstinence from strong drink surely was based on its evil effects and the dangers associated with its overuse. Of course, to make such a suggestion to a monarch in the ancient courts, as in royal households of the present day, would be considered preposterous and unheard of, and yet so would her other warnings in a polygamous and promiscuous society. A king pursuing strange and foreign women would risk losing his integrity and thus destroying his kingship. These warnings occur in different contexts throughout the book and elsewhere in the Old Testament (cp. Pr 7 on the "forbidden woman"; 20:1; 21:17; 23:20-21,31-35; and Gn 9:20-27; Is 5:11; Hos 4:11; Mc 2:11 on the drinking of wine).

CHARACTER PROFILE

The Virtuous Woman of Proverbs 31 Woman of Strength

Purpose of the Portrait

"Who can find a capable wife?" (v. 10). The implied answer is: "No man" can find such a woman. The poem provides an "A to Z" *ideal*, not to prompt despair that no such woman exists but to encourage the pursuit by every woman to the highest standards of excellence. The description should guide:

- single men to seek a wife of excellence,
- husbands to encourage their wives to be women of strength,
- single women to prepare to be excellent wives, and
- wives to determine to please the Lord.

For any reader, man or woman, this poem:

- draws attention to the activities and priorities of "a woman who fears the Lord" (v. 30);
- depicts in detail why "a man who finds a wife . . . obtains favor from the Lord" (18:22). and
- provides a contrast with the "nagging" wife (19:13; 21:9,19) and the "forbidden woman" (5:3-14,20; 6:24-32; 7:6-27).

Her Priorities

- "the Lord" (31:30)
- "her husband" (vv. 11-12,23,28)
- "her sons" (v. 28; cp. vv. 1-9,15,21,26-27)
- "her household" (vv. 15,21,27)
- "her servants" or household workers (v. 15)
- "the poor" (v. 20)
- "the needy" (v. 20)

Her Activities

- She shops for the best quality she can afford (vv. 13-14,22,24).
- She "works with willing hands" (v. 13; cp. "labor," v. 31).
- She provides clothing for her household and for herself (vv. 13,19,21-22).
- She gets up early to make sure everyone has food for the day (v. 15).
- She ensures that her family does not run out of supplies and prepares ahead for harsh circumstances (vv. 11,18,21,25).
- She carefully invests her money and works to profit from her investment (vv. 16,18,24).
- She helps meet the needs of the poor (v. 20).
- She "watches over the activities of her household" (v. 27).

Her Character

She is characterized by:

- trustworthiness (v. 11),
- consistency (vv. 12,18),
- high standards (vv. 13,16),
- industriousness and productivity (vv. 13-16,19,22,24,27),
- initiative (vv. 16,22,20),
- service (vv. 15,20),
- strength (vv. 17,25),
- honor (v. 25),
- compassion (v. 20),
- confidence rather than worry about the future (vv. 21,25), and
- wise words and instruction spoken with love (v. 26).

Her Blessing

- "She is far more precious than jewels" (v. 10).
- "Her sons rise up and call her blessed" (v. 28).
- She is trusted, praised, and prized by her husband (vv. 11-12,28-29).
- The community's respect for her husband is enhanced (vv. 23,31).
- She "will be praised" (v. 30).
- She deserves "the reward for her labor" (v. 31).
- She is known and receives praise for "her works" (v. 31).

14 She is like the merchant ships,
bringing her food
from far away.
15 She rises while it is still night
and provides food
for her household
and portions[A] for
her female servants.
16 She evaluates a field and buys it;
she plants a vineyard
with her earnings.[B]
17 She draws on her strength[C]
and reveals that her arms
are strong.
18 She sees that her profits
are good,
and her lamp never goes out
at night.
19 She extends her hands
to the spinning staff,
and her hands hold
the spindle.
20 Her hands reach[D] out
to the poor,
and she extends her hands
to the needy.
21 She is not afraid
for her household
when it snows,
for all in her household
are doubly clothed.[E]
22 She makes
her own bed coverings;
her clothing is fine linen
and purple.
23 Her husband is known
at the city •gates,
where he sits among
the elders of the land.
24 She makes and sells
linen garments;
she delivers belts[F]
to the merchants.
25 Strength and honor are
her clothing,
and she can laugh at the time
to come.
26 She opens her mouth
with wisdom
and loving instruction[G] is
on her tongue.
27 She watches over the activities
of her household
and is never idle.[H]
28 Her sons rise up
and call her blessed.
Her husband also praises her:
29 "Many women[I] are capable,
but you surpass them all!"

[A]**31:15** Or *tasks* [B]**31:16** Or *vineyard by her own labors* [C]**31:17** Lit *She wraps strength around her like a belt* [D]**31:20** Lit *Her hand reaches* [E]**31:21** LXX, Vg; MT reads *are dressed in scarlet* [F]**31:24** Or *sashes* [G]**31:26** Or *and the teaching of kindness* [H]**31:27** Lit *and does not eat the bread of idleness* [I]**31:29** Lit *daughters*

31:13-24 The text gives no indication of employment or career, which indeed for a woman with husband and children and household to manage would have certainly been an idea foreign to the ancient world culture. Her activities were home-centered. Yet this woman needed and possessed varied skills and diverse giftedness, all of which she used effectively in the management and wise stewardship of her household and in ministries to her family and even to those outside the family circle. She, as wives of the patriarchs in the Old Testament, worked willingly and efficiently with her own hands as well as effectively supervising her household workers (vv. 13,27; cp. Gn 18:6-8; 24:18-20; 29:9-10). Because households in the ancient world were dependent on producing what they needed and bartering through their cottage industries, one should not be surprised to find this woman engaging in trade and purposefully pursuing prosperity in the venues to which she gave oversight in the family.

This "Acrostic from Lemuel's Mother" (31:10-31)—identified as the "Alphabetic Ode," the "Golden ABCs for Women," the "Wife of Many Parts," the "Paradigm for Brides," or even the "Bionic Woman of the Bible"—should encourage every woman to pursue the standard raised with committed energy and creativity. Any woman would do well to mold her life to its model for spiritual and professional excellence.

31:25 The optimism of this extraordinary woman is not expressed

Biblical Womanhood A Paradigm

The closing verses of the book (Pr 31:10-31) comprise a poem of praise for a wise woman whose household included servants and vast resources, which would be far beyond the ordinary woman in any generation. Yet the description moves from the inner character of the woman to how this works itself out, covering such an array of giftedness and activities that every woman may find herself somewhere in the portrait.

The paradigm has its foundation in character and personal virtues (Pr 31:10-12,17,25,30-31), together with her family commitment (vv. 11,23,28) and energetic household management (vv. 13-15,21,27)—as well as an interest in her community (vv. 20,26), personal attractiveness (v. 22), and giftedness (vv. 16,18-19,24). She is set apart as representing a standard of excellence to be admired and emulated. While her husband is the one sitting at the city gates, where the assembly of community leaders did their decision-making and issued their judgments, one notes that this wife's work as a helpful partner makes her husband's leadership in the community more effective as she brings him and their family honor by her own deeds (v. 23; cp. Ru 4:1-12).

Although some suggest that this extraordinary woman merely represents wisdom in an allegory, she is described in vivid detail as a wife and mother and woman whose very diversity in giftedness and skills enables every woman to reach out and touch her in some way. She lifts the standard high and in so doing has been inspiring godly women to excellence throughout the generations.

The poem is fashioned in a literary acrostic, each verse beginning with a successive letter of the Hebrew alphabet, marking its classic literary form for preserving and systematizing the ideals expressed therein and making the verses more memorable. The Jewish husband, or a child in the household, recites the poem on the evening of Sabbath in honor of and expressing gratitude for the wife and mother as she lights the candles for the family meal. The Judeo-Christian community also finds the tribute worthy of celebrations honoring mothers in life or death.

with a flippant lack of concern but rather with the joyful spirit that emanates from within as she can **laugh at the time to come**. She has made her preparations for the future carefully and appropriately.

31:26 This passage shows much contrast between this woman of strength and the "nagging woman" mentioned elsewhere (19:13; 21:9,19). **Wisdom** (Hb *chokmah*; see **Word Study**, p. 783) is the same word Solomon used at the beginning of the book (1:8), and now as another bookend the word appears within the final verses because the whole book is about a search for wisdom. This woman's speech is prudent, cautious practical wisdom arising from discretion and good judgment. **Loving instruction** (Hb *torah*, "law, precept" with *chesed*, "kindness, mercy, loving-kindness") suggests more than love-based teaching, including the idea of covenant and steadfastness, fidelity unshaken by circumstances, and love proactive with determined deeds. For that reason, the translation "law of kindness" should also be considered as supporting the idea of a demand note for a governing of the tongue and for kind deeds produced only by genuine love. There is an element of lifestyle example interwoven in this teaching. The instruction encompasses both spiritual and moral lessons as well as the mundane teachings.

31:28-31 Though praise is most often sought and received from outside the family circle, this woman receives her greatest accolades from those who know her best—her husband and children. The summation may be personal words from her husband or even the author's climactic resolution. Whatever the case, the words are divinely inspired and serve, together with the opening words on the value of "the fear of the LORD" (1:7), as bookends to the entire collection of Proverbs just as the idea of excellence begins this focal passage ("capable wife," 31:10), and then completes it ("capable," but again in the sense of excellence and with the understanding of "woman of

30 Charm is deceptive and beauty
is fleeting,
but a woman who •fears
the LORD will be praised.

31 Give her the reward
of her labor,[A]
and let her works praise her
at the city gates.

[A]31:31 Lit *the fruit of her hands*

PROVERBS . . . WRITTEN ON MY *Heart*

For the woman seeking to grow in Christ-likeness and inner beauty, the book of Proverbs is a wonderful place to find practical and challenging daily workouts. Before any of the admonitions and guidelines, even those you follow "religiously" will truly produce transformation of your character from the inside out. However, you need to be a woman who first and foremost "fears the LORD" (31:30). When you have repented of your sin and received the complete forgiveness of Jesus the Messiah, you also receive His indwelling Holy Spirit, who enables you to turn away from the pursuit of self to the way of wisdom.

In addition to a commitment to lifelong study and application of this book full of God's wisdom, consider focusing some study regarding the "command center" of your mind and will, which Scripture calls your "heart." The word "heart" appears in 65 verses of the book of Proverbs. With a concordance in hand and the Holy Spirit as the Teacher residing in your heart, prayerfully and obediently submit yourself to this set of truths (among many others in the book), and enjoy becoming "heart-healthy" and worthy of the lasting praise of the Lord you love.

BIBLICAL WOMANHOOD Inner Beauty

Charm [Hb *chēn*, "favor, grace, elegance"] **is deceptive** (Hb *sheqer*, "deceit, lie, falsehood," 31:30; cp. 6:17,19) because it is an outer veneer that can change on a personal whim or turn with a disrupting circumstance. **Beauty** [Hb *yophi*, "fair, elegance of shape, symmetry of features, attractive countenance"; cp. 6:25] **is fleeting** (Hb *hevel*, "empty, vain, a puff of air, transitory, what soon vanishes away, vapor or bubble"; cp. 13:11; 21:6; see **Word Study**, "futile," p. 831) and can be marred by the passing of years, the agonies of pain and suffering, the neglect of enhancing one's appearance. There is no decrying of feminine "charm and beauty," which is affirmed elsewhere in Scripture (cp. 4:7-9; 1Sm 25:3; Jb 42:15; Sg 2:14), but rather an elevation of what is most important—a heart set apart in devotion to the Lord (cp. 1Pt 3:4).

>WORD|*study*

31:10 The word capable (Hb *chayil*, "ability, efficiency, wealth, endurance, energy, valor, virtue"; vv. 10,29; cp. Ru 3:11; see **Word Study**, Pr 12:4, p. 799) seems weak in describing this extraordinary woman, whose abilities are overshadowed by more intangible attributes. "Woman of strength" seems much more expressive of her matchless character and spiritual strength and a better nuance of the word as used in this context.

31:21 Doubly [Hb *shani*, "crimson, deep scarlet"] **clothed** has the sense of complete preparation for enduring the elements of weather and climate. However, some commentators note that the Hebrew word is translated in other references as "crimson or scarlet" (e.g., Ex 26:1,31; 28:5-8; Lv 14:4,6,49,51-52; 2Sm 1:24; Is 1:18). The fact that crimson is the color of blood makes it a natural symbol for purification and redemption. There is also the reference elsewhere in Scripture to cleansing from sin as leaving one "whiter than snow" (Ps 51:7; cp. Rv 7:14). Therefore, the latter understanding seems to fit the context better because it uses the metaphor of clothing, which does keep out the cold, to reference figuratively this wise woman's more important assignment of the spiritual protection of her household. This "scarlet" comes from the tola worm, a cochineal-like insect. The deep red or crimson dye produced from the crushing of the tola was greatly honored by the Orientals. This worm (Hb *tola'*, "insect generating crimson or deep scarlet color") is used metaphorically in Ps 22:6, a striking figure for the messianic foretelling of Jesus' suffering. The unusual plural ending could have been used to emphasize that this clothing is the best and is secured at high cost, which only adds strength to the argument in favor of the "scarlet" translation, together with its metaphorical understanding.

strength" or "noble/virtuous woman," 31:29). In Ec 7:28-29, Solomon bemoaned having never met "a true woman," and Pr 31:10 suggests that finding a truly virtuous "woman of strength" (Hb *chayil*) and godliness is like finding a rare and priceless jewel. Verse 29 suggests that Solomon did not look in the right places to find a woman of true excellence, but certainly the ideal woman described in chapter 31 "surpasses" all others (v. 29).

BIBLICAL WOMANHOOD "A Woman Who Fears the LORD"

The powerful phrase "the fear of the LORD" expresses the key to a woman's personal success and praise from others and, most important, her reward from God. "A woman who fears the LORD" (31:30) continues the theme introduced in the beginning of the book where this poignant phrase defines wisdom (1:7; 2:5; 9:10; 15:33; cp. 1:29) and continues throughout to the final reminder (31:30). However, this idea did not just appear in Proverbs but permeates all of Scripture (Ex 19:6–20:20; Dt 10:12; Jb 28:28; Ps 111:10).

Primarily this phrase implies the rightness of your heart toward God rather than the alienation of the heart characteristic of the unbeliever. You cannot fear the Lord without first giving up your own desires and turning from your own way (Pr 3:5; cp. Mt 10:39; 16:24; 19:21,29; Lk 14:33). In so doing you willingly accept God's rebuke and correction and accept His mandates, which in turn lead to personal piety and a life set apart unto Him. The concept is synonymous with intimate knowledge of God and understanding of His ways. It cannot be separated from an understanding of the holiness of God. "A woman who fears the LORD" will be set apart because of these characteristics:

- She has begun a spiritual journey to know the Lord (Pr 1:7);
- She has determined to turn back from going her own way in order to live a life set apart unto the Lord (3:5-7);
- She has entered into deep intimacy and communion with the Lord on a personal level (14:26);
- She experiences genuine joy and satisfaction (31:25);
- She reaps the fruit of a disciplined life (10:27);
- She is determined to serve the Lord with her whole heart (31:30).

To fear the Lord is to move beyond a reverential trust in Him. Rather you know that the Lord is not only watching what you do; but He is also listening to what you say, and He is reading your thoughts before they are verbalized. You are constantly aware that you are in the presence of the holy, just, all-powerful God of the universe. You realize that every thought in your mind, every word from your mouth, every action in your life—all are open before Him and thus will be judged by Him. "Fearing" that you will disappoint or hurt Him whom you love above all others, you deliberately commit your life—mind, heart, and emotions—to learning about Him and what He expects of you. As "a woman who fears the LORD," you devote yourself to Him and His ways in whole-hearted pursuit of pleasing Him.

Ecclesiastes

Timeline	994 BC	972 BC	970 BC	970 BC
World Events / Biblical Events	Birth of Solomon	Solomon rules as co-regent with his father David	Solomon becomes ruler of a united kingdom	Solomon's prayer for wisdom

"I applied my mind to know wisdom and knowledge" (1:17b).

Who wrote Ecclesiastes?

Solomon, the son of David, king of Jerusalem (1:1,12; cp. 1Kg 2:12)

Who were the recipients?

The Teacher was most likely writing to young (11:9–12:1) males (9:9) who lived in or near Jerusalem (i.e., they had access to the temple and to the king, 5:1-8; 8:2-5; 10:4), but "the people" of Israel and "all humanity" are the wider audiences (12:9,13).

When was Ecclesiastes written?

During King Solomon's reign (ca 970–931 B.C.)

Where did it happen?

Jerusalem specifically but in consideration of earthly life in general—life lived "under the sun"

What is Ecclesiastes about?

Many of the themes addressed in the book show dependence upon Genesis (see chart, p. 829), but the most crucial theme for understanding the point of the book is the futility of work because of the curse of sin and death. The ground is cursed; it will now grow thorns and thistles (Gn 3:17-18). Man is cursed; he will now toil all the days of his life, until one day he dies and returns to the same dust out of which he was created (Gn 3:17-19). Then comes the message of Ecclesiastes: Man's subjection to endless toil and work is exceedingly frustrating, for it never seems to render profit comparable to the work required. Death is each person's destiny; it is inevitable and inescapable for all—no matter how a person lives.

Within Judaism, Ecclesiastes is correctly perceived to give incredible insight and understanding to the nature and purpose of life. The book is read on the Sabbath of Sukkot, the Jewish holiday of joy, to put life in perspective and as an antidote to excessive indulgence, stressing the futility of personal pleasures in contrast to the eternality of spiritual pursuits. Closer scrutiny and study of Ecclesiastes yields a much-needed reminder that in an imperfect world full of uncertainty and injustice one may still experience a God-given enjoyment in life within the context of a right relationship to the Lord (12:13-14).

Why should women read Ecclesiastes?

Women dream of living in security, which the world defines in terms of pleasure, possessions, and people. The titles of magazines marketed specifically to women reveal the things to which women give their time, attention, and energies in pursuit of deep and lasting satisfaction and a sense of self-worth. Advertising targets women by appealing to their efforts to be beautiful, to have the best of everything (at least vicariously), to perfect their relationships and image. The book of Ecclesiastes counters the deceptive message that any of these things—anything but a right relationship with God—will make you happy. Rather, the book affirms that the Lord wants you to enjoy life, temporal and fleeting though it is, by adopting His eternal perspective, recognizing the difference between what does not last (all that is "done under the sun", 1:14) and what is of truly lasting value (being a woman "who is pleasing in God's sight," 2:26).

How do you read Ecclesiastes?

In order to understand and interpret the book of Ecclesiastes correctly, one must also have an understanding of the book's genre. Ecclesiastes, Proverbs, and Song of Songs all belong to the biblical wisdom tradition because of their particular approach to reality, as well as their inclusion of certain literary forms and themes. Like other biblical wisdom material, Ecclesiastes focuses on human experience in daily life instead of on Israel's salvation history. Wisdom literature aims to teach people how to navigate through life by living wisely in God's created order. Such wisdom begins with the fear of Yahweh (Jb 28:28; Pr 1:7; Ec 12:13).

In Ecclesiastes, the Teacher—the wisest man who has ever lived (1Kg 3:12)—has intentionally used autobiographical narrative (among other forms) in order to impart wisdom to his hearers. Understanding the book as intentional instruction in wisdom, inspired by God through King Solomon the Teacher, is vital in taking this book seriously and rightly interpreting its meaning.

When you read Ecclesiastes, be prepared to encounter the book's apparently dreary outlook on life. The author seems to portray all of life as meaningless—exactly the opposite of what one wants and expects to hear—especially from the Bible. However, what the Teacher describes as futile applies to life "under the sun," a way of speaking strictly of an earth-bound and rather self-centered existence as opposed to a God-directed life. If you listen carefully to the words of this Teacher, who testifies that he has tried everything in the pursuit of meaning and happiness, you can hear an indictment of the value systems and false promises of any twenty-first century culture or worldview that claims to offer a way to find purpose in life apart from Jesus.

968 BC	*966 BC*	*961 BC*	*966–931 BC*	*931 BC*
Solomon's exercise of exceptional wisdom in a dispute between two mothers	Solomon's oversight of the building of the temple	Solomon's leadership in dedicating the temple	Solomon's failure to exercise wisdom in his choice of wives	Solomon's death and an irreparable division in kingdom he was charged to rule

Outline

Introduction and Thematic Refrain (1:1-11)

I. The Teacher's Experiment (1:12–2:26)
  A. The Pursuit of Wisdom (1:12-18)
  B. The Pursuit of Fleeting Pleasures (2:1-11)
  C. The Value of Wisdom and Work in Light of Death (2:12-23)
  D. Refrain: Enjoy Life! (2:24-26)

II. God's Unchangeable Work and the Mystery of Time (3:1-15)
  A. Discerning Time Appropriately in the Mystery of God's Work (3:1-11)
  B. Refrain: Enjoy Life! (3:12-15)

III. Life's Inevitable Futilities (3:16–7:29)
  A. The Truth about Common Fates (3:16-22)
  B. The Reality of Oppression (4:1-3)
  C. The Loneliness of Wealth and Benefits of Companionship (4:4-16)
  D. The Right Way to Approach God (5:1-7)
  E. The Dissatisfaction and Unreliability of Wealth (5:8–6:9)
  F. What Is Good and Wise for Frail Humanity? (6:10–7:14)
  G. The Elusiveness of Wisdom and True Righteousness (7:15-29)

IV. God's Sovereignty over the Lives of the Righteous and the Wicked (8:1–10:20)
  A. Dealing with Authority (8:1-9)
  B. Inequity in Life under the Sun (8:10-14)
  C. Refrain: Enjoy Life! (8:15-17)
  D. The Absence of Exemption for Any Human Being (9:1-12)
  E. Contrasting Wisdom and Folly (9:13–10:20)

V. The Fleeting Nature of Life (11:1–12:7)
  A. The Challenge to Rejoice and Remember (11:1-6)
  B. Modified Refrain: Rejoice and Remember (11:7-10)
  C. The Approach of Old Age and Death (12:1-7)

Thematic Refrain and Conclusion (12:8-14)

The Teacher's Dependence on Genesis 1–11

Themes about God	**Ecclesiastes**	**Genesis**
Created all that is	7:29; 11:5; 12:1	1:1–2:3
Fixed the order of the world	1:5-8,15; 7:13	1:1–2:3; 8:22
Exercises sovereignty over all	3:10-14; 6:10; 7:13; 9:1	1:28-30; 3:5
Keeps man in his place	3:14; 7:14	3:22; 6:7; 11:1-9
Themes about Mankind		
Was created in the image of God	7:29	1:27
Is limited in knowledge	1:17; 3:11; 7:23-24; 8:7, 16-17; 10:14; 11:5	2:17
Was meant to live in companionship	4:9-12; 9:9	1:27; 2:21-25
Is sinful	7:20,29; 8:11; 9:3	3:1-13; 6:5
Was cursed with tiresome toil	1:3; 2:22-23; 6:7; 5:16-17; 6:7; 8:17	2:5; 3:14-19
Was cursed with death	2:14-16; 3:2,19-21; 9:4-6;11:8; 12:5e-7	2:17; 3:3,19,24; 6:13
Was created from dust and will return to dust	3:20; 12:7	2:7; 3:19

The Bible's Books on the Issues of Life

Book	The questions of life	The world's perspective	God's perspective
Ecclesiastes	When life is empty: • You search for God (Ec 12:1,13). • You reach for faith (Ec 12:1).	Wisdom (Ec 1:12-18) Pleasure (Ec 2:1-3) Ambition (Ec 2:4-17) Work (Ec 2:18-23) People (Ec 4:4-8) Religion (Ec 5:1-7) Wealth (Ec 5:8-20)	Wisdom (Ec 9:16-18) Purity of life (Ec 5:1-6; 9:9) Self-control (Ec 11:10; 12:13) Work (Ec 3:13) Spiritual values (Ec 7:13-15) Wise stewardship (Ec 3:1-8) Friendships (Ec 4:9-12)
Job	When life has suffering: • You struggle with God (Jb 4:4,8-9; 7:11-21). • You pursue hope (Jb 19:25-27).	You take pride in personal wisdom—presuming to know all the answers (Jb 11:1-12:2). You question suffering for the righteous as being unjust (Jb 9:14-24). You make decisions with feelings more than discernment (Jb 9:14-24). You rely on self (Jb 32:10). You demand answers from God (Jb 10:18).	Wisdom—you listen and respond to God (Jb 42:1-6). Suffering—you accept as a channel for edification and spiritual growth (Jb 13:13-19). Providence—you determine that faith in God will govern human feelings (Jb 13:15-16).
Song of Songs	When life has love: • You sense the presence of God (Sg 2:8-10). • You realize joy (Sg 2:3).	Love is a feeling. Love can die. Love is what you do for me. Love is passive. Love never allows suffering.	Love is action (Sg 1:15-16; 2:2-3). Love lives and grows (Sg 4:12,16; 7:12; 8:11-12). Love acts on behalf of another (Sg 8:6). Love requires work (Sg 3:1-2). Love comforts the one suffering (Sg 1:5-6).

Title The Hebrew title is "Qoheleth," the designation given to its author: "The words of the Teacher (Hb *qohelet*; from the root *qahal*, "assembly or congregation," 1:1-2,12; 7:27; 12:8-10), the son of David, king in Jerusalem" (1:1). The word "Qoheleth" likely refers to the office or function of one who assembles people together for the purpose of teaching (cp. Ezk 2:64; Neh 5:13). Hence, the author is identified as "The Teacher." The English title comes from the Greek translation, *ekklēsiastēs*.

1:1 Although this verse does not name the author (cp. Pr 1:1), it implies that King Solomon is **the Teacher** (Hb *qohelet*, "leader of the assembly, speaker who addresses a public assembly, or preacher"; cp. 1:12 and 2:4-9). He is assigned a title, pedigree, position, and locale. The Teacher identifies the writer's authority as well as his intention to impart wisdom.

Introduction and Thematic Refrain (1:1-11)

1 The words of the Teacher,[A] son of
David, king in Jerusalem.

2 "Absolute futility,"
says the Teacher.
"Absolute futility. Everything
is futile."
3 What does a man gain for all
his efforts
that he labors at
under the sun?
4 A generation goes
and a generation comes,
but the earth remains forever.
5 The sun rises
and the sun sets;
panting, it returns
to its place
where it rises.
6 Gusting to the south,
turning to the north,
turning, turning,
goes the wind,
and the wind returns
in its cycles.
7 All the streams flow
to the sea,
yet the sea is never full.
The streams are flowing
to the place,
and they flow there again.

A**1:1** Or *of Qoheleth*, or *of the Leader of the Assembly*

8 All things[A] are wearisome;
man is unable to speak.
The eye is not satisfied
by seeing
or the ear filled with hearing.
9 What has been is what will be,
and what has been done is
what will be done;
there is nothing new
under the sun.
10 Can one say about anything,
"Look, this is new"?
It has already existed
in the ages before us.
11 There is no remembrance
of those who[B] came before;
and of those
who[B] will come after
there will also be
no remembrance
by those who follow them.

The Teacher's Experiment (1:12–2:26)

The Pursuit of Wisdom (1:12-18)

12 I, the Teacher, have been[C] king
over Israel in Jerusalem. 13 I applied my mind to seek and explore
through wisdom all that is done under heaven. God has given •people
this miserable task to keep them occupied. 14 I have seen all the things
that are done under the sun and
have found everything to be futile, a
pursuit of the wind.[D]

15 What is crooked cannot
be straightened;
what is lacking cannot
be counted.

16 I said to myself,[E] "Look, I have
amassed wisdom far beyond all
those who were over Jerusalem
before me, and my mind has thoroughly grasped[F] wisdom and knowledge." 17 I applied my mind to know
wisdom and knowledge, madness
and folly; I learned that this too is a
pursuit of the wind.[D]

18 For with much wisdom is
much sorrow;
as knowledge increases,
grief increases.

The Pursuit of Fleeting Pleasures (2:1-11)

2 I said to myself, "Go ahead, I will
test you with pleasure; enjoy
what is good." But it turned out to
be futile. 2 I said about laughter, "It
is madness," and about pleasure,
"What does this accomplish?" 3 I explored with my mind how to let my
body enjoy life[G] with wine and how
to grasp folly—my mind still guiding me with wisdom—until I could
see what is good for •people to do
under heaven[H] during the few days
of their lives.
4 I increased my achievements. I
built houses and planted vineyards

[A]1:8 Or *words* [B]1:11 Or *of the things that* [C]1:12 Or *Teacher, was* [D]1:14,17 Or *a feeding on wind*, or *an affliction of spirit* [E]1:16 Lit *said with my heart* [F]1:16 Or *discerned* [G]2:3 Lit *to pull my body* [H]2:3 Two Hb mss, LXX, Syr read *the sun*

1:2-3 The Teacher begins and ends with a thematic frame (cp. 12:7), reflecting his assessment of earthly life as meaningless. His rhetorical question is fundamental to the book (cp. 2:22; 3:9; 5:16), guiding the Teacher's own pursuit, as well as giving voice to a search for meaning and (often) a subsequent assessment that hard work does not necessarily reap a profit (Pr 14:23).

1:4-7 In order to illustrate the fruitless, frustrating toil of humanity, the Teacher first uses a poem on the seemingly endless toil observable in nature. The picture is of a cosmos in monotonous repetition, each element continuing to do what it has always done.

1:12-14 Although David had many sons, only Solomon was **king over Israel in Jerusalem**. His quest was comprehensive—he sought to **explore** and understand **all that is done under heaven**. Using his God-given wisdom lens, he wanted to look at how the world operates and the realities of human experience in order to discern meaning in life (cp. 2:3; 6:12, "what is good for people to do under heaven"). He quickly came to regard this quest as a **miserable task** (cp. 4:8), which often increases sorrow and heartache and one which **God** gives people **to keep them occupied**.

2:1-3 The Teacher has already explored wisdom to find meaning (1:16-18). He now turns to explore different forms of **pleasure** (Hb *simchah*, "joy, gladness, mirth"), referring here to all forms of extrinsic material pleasure from which one seeks self-fulfillment and gain (cp. 2:4-8,10) in order to **see what is good for people to do**. This kind of pleasure differs from the lasting gift of inner joy with which God infuses one's

>WORD|*study*

1:2 Futile (Hb *hevel*; cp. 1:14; 2:1,11,15,17,19,21,23,26; 3:19; 4:4,7-8,16; 5:7,10; 6:2,4,9,11; 7:6,15; 8:10,14; 11:8,10; 12:8) has various nuances of meaning, including "meaningless, empty, absurd, vain, transitory, illusory, incomprehensible." Basic to all of these, however, is the idea of "breath" or "vapor," implying that something is fleeting or short-lived, that it does not last (cp. 9:9; 11:10; Pr 21:6; Ps 144:4). Consequently, in describing pleasures that cannot bring fulfillment, *hevel* connotes being "meaningless" (Ec 2:2). In many cases *hevel* has the sense of being "absurd" as the Teacher speaks of an event, action, or situation that defies reason—a reality that does not live up to expectations (e.g., 2:4-15; 8:14).

1:3 The phrase **under the sun** (cp. vv. 9,14; 2:11,17-20,22; 3:16; 4:1,3,7,15; 5:13,18; 6:1,12; 8:9,15,17; 9:3,6,9,13; 10:5; nowhere else in the OT) simply refers to this earthly life. The phrase often serves as an important qualifier, limiting many of the Teacher's observations to the present world. Most of the book is viewed from life on earth, proving that in and of itself life cannot supply the answers. Ultimately, only God can give meaning, purpose, and value to earthly existence.

1:13 Rather than using God's covenant name (Hb *YHWH*; cp. Ex 3:14) throughout the book, the Teacher uses the most general Hebrew name for **God** (Hb *'Elohim*), a name that indicates God's absolute sovereignty. God's covenant name, Yahweh (Ex 3:13-15), usually signaled in the English translation by "LORD" in all capital letters, does not appear in the book of Ecclesiastes, perhaps reflecting the writer's struggle to find meaning in life. Apart from a covenant relationship with "the LORD," who has revealed Himself in Christ, everything "under the sun" does appear to be futile (cp. Rm 5:1-5; 1Co 3:18-20; Eph 2:11-13).

1:14 The phrase translated **pursuit of the wind** (Hb *re'ut ruach*, "chase after the wind [or 'spirit']") occurs nine times in Ecclesiastes. Seven references occur in conjunction with futility (cp. 1:17; 2:11,17,26; 4:4,6,16; 6:9). The phrase implies impossibility, not to mention frustration, for who can chase after and catch the wind? Second, the Teacher soon realized that even he in all his wisdom could not understand all life's happenings or discern its meaning (cp. 3:11; 8:16-17). Lack of understanding only added to his feelings of frustration in observing the way God works in the world. The Teacher understood the source of "this miserable task" to be **God**, who put within every person the desire to know and search out the truth.

for myself. 5 I made gardens and
parks for myself and planted every
kind of fruit tree in them. 6 I constructed reservoirs of water for myself from which to irrigate a grove
of flourishing trees. 7 I acquired
male and female servants and had
slaves who were born in my house.
I also owned many herds of cattle
and flocks, more than all who were
before me in Jerusalem. 8 I also
amassed silver and gold for myself,
and the treasure of kings and provinces. I gathered male and female
singers for myself, and many concubines, the delights of men.[A,B] 9 So
I became great and surpassed all
who were before me in Jerusalem;
my wisdom also remained with me.
10 All that my eyes desired, I did not
deny them. I did not refuse myself
any pleasure, for I took pleasure in
all my struggles. This was my reward
for all my struggles. 11 When I considered all that I had accomplished[C]
and what I had labored to achieve, I
found everything to be futile and a
pursuit of the wind. There was nothing to be gained under the sun.

The Value of Wisdom and Work in Light of Death (2:12-23)

12 Then I turned to consider wisdom, madness, and folly, for what
will the man be like who comes after the king? He[D] will do what has
already been done. 13 And I realized
that there is an advantage to wisdom
over folly, like the advantage of light
over darkness.

14 The wise man has eyes
in his head,
but the fool walks
in darkness.

Yet I also knew that one fate comes
to them both. 15 So I said to myself,
"What happens to the fool will also
happen to me. Why then have I been
overly wise?" And I said to myself
that this is also futile. 16 For, just like
the fool, there is no lasting remembrance of the wise man, since in the
days to come both will be forgotten.
How is it that the wise man dies just
like the fool? 17 Therefore, I hated life
because the work that was done under the sun was distressing to me.
For everything is futile and a pursuit
of the wind.

18 I hated all my work that I labored at under the sun because I
must leave it to the man who comes
after me. 19 And who knows whether
he will be a wise man or a fool? Yet
he will take over all my work that I
labored at skillfully under the sun.
This too is futile. 20 So I began to give
myself over[E] to despair concerning
all my work that I had labored at under the sun. 21 When there is a man
whose work was done with wisdom,
knowledge, and skill, and he must
give his portion to a man who has
not worked for it, this too is futile
and a great wrong. 22 For what does a
man get with all his work and all his
efforts that he labors at under the
sun? 23 For all his days are filled with
grief, and his occupation is sorrowful; even at night, his mind does not
rest. This too is futile.

Refrain: Enjoy Life! (2:24-26)

24 There is nothing better for man
than to eat, drink, and enjoy[F,G] his
work. I have seen that even this is
from God's hand, 25 because who can
eat and who can enjoy life[H] apart
from Him?[I] 26 For to the man who is
pleasing in His sight, He gives wisdom, knowledge, and joy, but to the
sinner He gives the task of gathering
and accumulating in order to give

[A] **2:8** LXX, Theod, Syr read *and male cupbearers and female cupbearers*; Aq, Tg, Vg read *a cup and cups*; Hb obscure [B] **2:8** Or *many treasures that people delight in* [C] **2:11** Lit *all my works that my hands had done* [D] **2:12** Some Hb mss read *They* [E] **2:20** Lit *And I turned to cause my heart* [F] **2:24** Syr, Tg; MT reads *There is no good in man who eats and drinks and enjoys* [G] **2:24** Lit *and his soul sees good* [H] **2:25** LXX, Theod, Syr read *can drink* [I] **2:25** Some Hb mss, LXX, Syr read *me*

everyday activities (vv. 24-26; 5:20). In the end, extrinsic forms of pleasure do not **accomplish** anything lasting. **Laughter**, especially when associated with foolish behavior, is only **madness** (cp. 7:6). Although the Teacher uses the same word for "pleasure" (Hb *simchah*) elsewhere and commends it (cp. 2:26; 5:20; 8:15; 9:7), here he says pleasure is **futile** (Hb *hevel*; see **Word Study**, p. 831).

The Teacher's experiment with pleasure was not for indulgence's sake; it was rationally-controlled for the purpose of seeing if pleasures could provide any profit and true satisfaction. The experiment with **wine** (a symbol of pleasure—Dt 14:26; Ps 104:15) was not for drunkenness (cp. Ec 9:7) but to see if wine were a source of true fulfillment (2:3).

2:4-8 The Teacher found pleasure in achievement. **Concubines** (Hb *ta 'anug*, "delight, delicacy—especially in the sense of sexual pleasure"; 2:8b; cp. Sg 7:6) would fit well with what is known of Solomon (cp. his "300 concubines," 1Kg 11:3).

2:9-11 His achievements and wealth caused him to surpass **all who were before** him **in Jerusalem**, making the conclusion more striking: All accomplishments were **futile** (Hb *hevel*; see **Word Study**, p. 831). **There was nothing to be gained** (Hb *yitron*, "result, advantage"; cp. 1:3)—at least **under the sun** (note the limitation) as he not only had hoped, but *expected*.

2:14-17 If achievements gained through wisdom bring no *ultimate* gain, is there any advantage to being wise? The wise man sees and grasps what has everlasting value. Wisdom's advantage is limited because it cannot prevent the wise from suffering the same **fate** as the foolish—death, the great leveler of all people and pursuits. Since all face death, what difference does it make to be **overly wise?** **. . . this is also futile**. In the *hevel* passages, determining the referent of "this" is often difficult. Is the Teacher concluding here that being "overly wise" is futile (because the wise die just like the foolish), or is he saying that the whole situation (of everyone having the same fate, regardless of their respective lifestyles) is futile (i.e., absurd)? Perhaps both. The Teacher is bothered by the fact that the wise die just like the foolish. Wise actions were supposed to produce good results, and foolish actions were supposed to produce bad results. Instead, the **wise man dies just like the fool**, leaving **no lasting remembrance** (cp. 1:4-11). The Israelites—and even more so, ancient kings—placed a high premium on leaving a legacy for future generations (E.g., Pr 10:7). For the Teacher, death

>WORD | *study*

2:10 In the Old Testament, reward (Hb *chēleq*, "portion, lot") refers to one's assigned share or inheritance (cp. Jos 18:5; 19:9; Nm 18:20; Dt 10:9). The Teacher similarly uses this word (Ec 2:10,21; 3:22; 5:18-19; 9:6,9) to describe what God allots in this life under the sun. Each person's allotment comes with limitations but also with the possibility of joy (cp. 3:22; 5:19; 9:9). If anyone could experience satisfaction or meaning in achievements or wealth, it would have been King Solomon . . . but he did not. Wine (2:3), wealth (2:4-8,10), women (2:8), and entertainment (2:8)—all the usual sources of gratification simply proved their inadequacy (v. 11).

to the one who is pleasing in God's sight. This too is futile and a pursuit of the wind.

God's Unchangeable Work and the Mystery of Time (3:1-15)

Discerning Time Appropriately in the Mystery of God's Work (3:1-11)

3 There is an occasion
for everything,
and a time for every activity
under heaven:
2 a time to give birth and a time
to die;
a time to plant and a time
to uproot;[A]
3 a time to kill and a time
to heal;
a time to tear down
and a time to build;
4 a time to weep and a time
to laugh;
a time to mourn and a time
to dance;
5 a time to throw stones
and a time to gather stones;
a time to embrace and a time
to avoid embracing;
6 a time to search and a time
to count as lost;
a time to keep and a time
to throw away;
7 a time to tear and a time
to sew;
a time to be silent and a time
to speak;
8 a time to love and a time
to hate;
a time for war and a time
for peace.

9 What does the worker gain from
his struggles? 10 I have seen the task
that God has given •people to keep
them occupied. 11 He has made everything appropriate[B] in its time. He
has also put eternity in their hearts,[C]
but man cannot discover the work
God has done from beginning to end.

Refrain: Enjoy Life! (3:12-15)

12 I know that there is nothing better
for them than to rejoice and enjoy
the[D] good life. 13 It is also the gift of
God whenever anyone eats, drinks,
and enjoys all his efforts. 14 I know
that all God does will last forever;
there is no adding to it or taking
from it. God works so that people
will be in awe of Him. 15 Whatever is,
has already been, and whatever will
be, already is. God repeats what has
passed.[E]

Life's Inevitable Futilities (3:16–7:29)

The Truth about Common Fates (3:16-22)

16 I also observed under the sun:
there is wickedness at the place of
judgment and there is wickedness at
the place of righteousness. 17 I said
to myself, "God will judge the righteous and the wicked, since there is
a time for every activity and every
work." 18 I said to myself, "This happens concerning people, so that God
may test them and they may see for
themselves that they are like animals." 19 For the fate of people and
the fate of animals is the same. As
one dies, so dies the other; they all
have the same breath. People have
no advantage over animals since everything is futile. 20 All are going to
the same place; all come from dust,
and all return to dust. 21 Who knows
if the spirit of people rises upward
and the spirit of animals goes downward to the earth? 22 I have seen
that there is nothing better than
for a person to enjoy his activities
because that is his reward. For who
can enable him to see what will happen after he dies?[F]

[A]3:2 Lit *uproot what is planted* [B]3:11 Or *beautiful* [C]3:11 Or *has put a sense of past and future into their minds*, or *has placed ignorance in their hearts* [D]3:12 Lit *his* [E]3:15 Or *God calls the past to account*, or *God seeks what is past*, or *God seeks the persecuted*; lit *God seeks the pursued* [F]3:22 Lit *after him*

("no lasting remembrance") made the pursuit of wisdom seem absurd, for wisdom's advantages were fleeting at best.

2:24-26 The reference to eating and drinking is not a call to hedonism but a reference to the basic functions of life. The one **who is pleasing** (Hb *tov*, "good") to God (i.e., "the one good before God") receives **wisdom, knowledge, and joy** from God. **The sinner** (Hb, active participle of the verb *chata'*, "one who misses the mark"; cp. 7:26; 8:12; 9:2,18; see chart: "Understanding Sin," p. 10), however, receives something different from God: a task of **gathering and accumulating** without the reward of keeping the results of his labor.

3:1-8 God has determined an appropriate **time** and **occasion** (Hb *zeman*, "appointed time") for every **activity** (Hb *chēphets*, "desire, pleasure, pursuit"), implying that human beings do not determine the seasons of life though they can respond to them appropriately with wisdom. The events of life are ultimately ordered by a compassionate, gracious, loving, and faithful God whose sovereignty is the foundation from which His providence springs. His plans do not depend upon human approval (Dt 32:39; Ps 75:2; 102:13).

The poem does not aim to catalog every season God has ordained but to provide a sampling of the various seasons of life (Ec 3:2-8). Each of the 14 contrasting pairs is a merism, a device in which contrasting parts express a totality. These 14 contrasting pairs emphasize the truth that all human life rests under the canopy of God's providential care (cp. Jr 10:23).

3:2-3 The pairs correspond to a life cycle and in this poetic context can be applied both literally and figuratively. To **give birth** and **to plant** refer to the giving of life; to **die** and **to uproot** refer to the taking of life. Similarly, **a time to kill** refers to the ending of a life; **a time to heal** refers to the preservation of life. **To tear down** (Hb *parats*, "break; break through, break down, break into, break open, break away from, break to pieces") and **to build** (Hb *banah*, "erect, restore") are construction terms.

>WORD|*study*

3:10 The Hebrew word translated task (Hb *ʿinyan*, "business, employment") occurs eight times in Ecclesiastes (1:13; 2:23,26; 3:10; 4:8; 5:3,14; 8:16) but nowhere else in Scripture. The root verb is *ʿanah* (Hb, "bestow labor upon"), which also appears in verse 10 as **to keep . . . occupied**. This connotation of the verb is heavily dependent on context and verb form, but it often carries the sense of "afflict, oppress" (e.g., Ex 1:11; Ps 88:7).

4:1 The Teacher's observations on injustice lead to reflections on the **oppressed** (Hb *ʿashaq*, "those who are being treated unjustly, victims of fraud or violence, the needy or helpless), who have all the **tears**, and **those who oppress them**, who have all the **power** (cp. 3:16-17). The situation looks grim for the hurting people who have no one either to console them or to be their advocate in a time of need. Since, in biblical thought, the king was responsible for defending the defenseless (cp. Pr 31:8-9; Jr 22:13-17), the Teacher may have been reflecting upon his own role as king.

4:2-3 The Teacher expresses his grief in a hyperbolic fashion common to the ancient Near East (cp. Jb 3; Jr 20:14-18): The dead are better off than the living, for the dead do not have to see such evil. Even better than the dead or the living is **the one who has not yet existed** (cp. Jb 3:1-22). The living see the oppression; the dead have an advantage for they no longer have to see the oppression; but the one who has not yet been born has the best situation, having never witnessed the **evil activity . . . under the sun.**

4:5-6 Neither being a workaholic nor being lazy is commendable but to be at **rest** (i.e. , at peace, satisfied) in your work. Better to achieve less (**one handful**) but have peace and enjoyment of life than to achieve more (**two handfuls)** by exerting futile effort, missing the enjoyment of your work.

4:7-12 The Teacher tells of another **futility under the sun**: A lone **person** (Hb *ʾechad*, "solitary one") devotes all of his energies to the pursuit of wealth, only to realize that his struggle for wealth serves no real purpose. Although not explicit in the text, the loner has likely isolated himself from all relationships in order to pursue this obsession (and perhaps hoard his earnings). At the very least, clearly he has deprived himself from **good** (i.e., what is enjoyable)—for a temporal, fleeting obsession. The reference to the lone individual brings up the benefits of companionship.

Two are better than one, does not mean that a single individual has no value or that everyone should be married. In context are the benefits of companionship (i.e., friendship or marriage) underscored.

4:14-16 The details that come next contain some ambiguous pronouns (e.g., the antecedent for **he** in verse 14). There are two main possibilities:

- The pronoun "he" refers to the "king": He was **born poor**, was in **prison** for a time, and became **king**. He was later succeeded by

>WORD|*study*

5:1 Obedience (Hb *shamaʿ*, "listen, give heed, obey"; cp. 1Sm 15:22) translates a verb. Since, in the subsequent passage, the Teacher cautions the recipients to let their words be few before God, here *shamaʿ* might best be translated "listen," though still with the connotation of obedience (see also Ec 1:8; 7:5,21; 9:16-17; 12:13).

HARD QUESTION

Can we be certain that there is an afterlife? What about reincarnation or nirvana, for example?

The question **Who knows if . . . ?** (3:21) reflects humanity's limited knowledge about what happens after death, but the question itself nevertheless demonstrates a basic recognition of the difference between **the spirit** [Hb *ruach*, "breath"] **of people** (Hb *ʾadam*, "man, human being, mankind") and **the spirit** [Hb *ruach*] **of animals** (Hb *behemah*, "beast"). Though expressing uncertainty here, the Teacher's question indicates a belief that human beings, unlike animals, are made for God and return to Him when the breath of life is extinguished (see 12:7).

The New Testament clearly affirms that all people face God's judgment when they die (Heb 9:27), whether to enter eternal life (Jn 5:24) or to endure eternal separation from God in death (Mt 25:46; Rv 20:13-14; 21:8). In Scripture, people are generally compared unfavorably to animals (see Ps 49:12,20; 73:22; 2Pt 2:12; Jd 10). In this passage, the human likeness to animals in having been made from dust (Ec 3:20) illustrates man's finite understanding of what happens after death. In addition, the comparison should evoke humility in realizing that God created man and the animals; therefore, God rules all living creatures. Any superiority of man over other creatures is derived from God.

Since with his limitations man cannot know everything that **will happen** after death, **there is nothing better** than simply enjoying one's activities on earth. God's reward for human beings is not to know everything (notice the emphatic **that is his reward** [Hb *chēleq*, "portion"]) but to enjoy life!

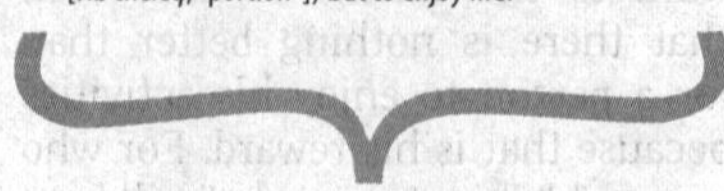

The Reality of Oppression (4:1-3)

4 Again, I observed all the acts of
oppression being done under the
sun. Look at the tears of those who
are oppressed; they have no one to
comfort them. Power is with those
who oppress them; they have no one
to comfort them. 2 So I admired the
dead, who have already died, more
than the living, who are still alive.
3 But better than either of them is
the one who has not yet existed, who
has not seen the evil activity that is
done under the sun.

The Loneliness of Wealth and Benefits of Companionship (4:4-16)

4 I saw that all labor and all skillful work is due to a man's jealousy
of his friend. This too is futile and a
pursuit of the wind.

5 The fool folds his arms
and consumes his own flesh.
6 Better one handful with rest
than two handfuls with effort
and a pursuit of the wind.

7 Again, I saw futility under the
sun: 8 There is a person without a
companion,[A] without even a son or
brother, and though there is no end
to all his struggles, his eyes are still
not content with riches. "So who am
I struggling for," he asks, "and depriving myself from good?" This too
is futile and a miserable task.

9 Two are better than one because
they have a good reward for their efforts. 10 For if either falls, his companion can lift him up; but pity the
one who falls without another to
lift him up. 11 Also, if two lie down
together, they can keep warm; but
how can one person alone keep
warm? 12 And if someone overpowers one person, two can resist him.
A cord of three strands is not easily
broken.

13 Better is a poor but wise youth
than an old but foolish king who no
longer pays attention to warnings.
14 For he came from prison to be
king, even though he was born poor
in his kingdom. 15 I saw all the living, who move about under the sun,
follow[B] a second youth who succeeds him. 16 There is no limit to all
the •people who were before them,
yet those who come later will not rejoice in him. This too is futile and a
pursuit of the wind.

[A]**4:8** Lit *person, but there is not a second,* [B]**4:15** Lit *with*

The Right Way to Approach God (5:1-7)

5 [A] Guard your steps when you go to the house of God. Better to draw near in obedience than to offer the sacrifice as fools do, for they ignorantly do wrong. [2][B]Do not be hasty to speak, and do not be impulsive to make a speech before God. God is in heaven and you are on earth, so let your words be few. [3]For dreams result from much work and a fool's voice from many words. [4]When you make a vow to God, don't delay fulfilling it, because He does not delight in fools. Fulfill what you vow. [5]Better that you do not vow than that you vow and not fulfill it. [6]Do not let your mouth bring •guilt on you, and do not say in the presence of the messenger that it was a mistake. Why should God be angry with your words and destroy the work of your hands? [7]For many dreams bring futility, so do many words. Therefore, •fear God.

The Dissatisfaction and Unreliability of Wealth (5:8–6:9)

[8]If you see oppression of the poor and perversion of justice and righteousness in the province, don't be astonished at the situation, because one official protects another official, and higher officials protect them. [9]The profit from the land is taken by all; the king is served by the field.[C]

[10]The one who loves money is never satisfied with money, and whoever loves wealth is never satisfied with income. This too is futile. [11]When good things increase, the ones who consume them multiply; what, then, is the profit to the owner, except to gaze at them with his eyes? [12]The sleep of the worker is sweet, whether he eats little or much, but the abundance of the rich permits him no sleep.

[13]There is a sickening tragedy I have seen under the sun: wealth kept by its owner to his harm. [14]That wealth was lost in a bad venture, so when he fathered a son, he was empty-handed. [15]As he came from his mother's womb, so he will go again, naked as he came; he will take nothing for his efforts that he can carry in his hands. [16]This too is a sickening tragedy: exactly as he comes, so he will go. What does the one gain who struggles for the wind? [17]What is more, he eats in darkness all his days, with much sorrow, sickness, and anger.

[18]Here is what I have seen to be good: it is appropriate to eat, drink, and experience good in all the labor one does under the sun during the few days of his life God has given him, because that is his reward. [19]Furthermore, every man to whom God has given riches and wealth, He has also allowed him to enjoy them, take his reward, and rejoice in his labor. This is a gift of God, [20]for he does not often consider the days of his life because God keeps him occupied with the joy of his heart.

6 Here is a tragedy I have observed under the sun, and it weighs heavily on humanity:[D] [2]God gives a man riches, wealth, and honor so that he lacks nothing of all he desires for himself, but God does not allow him to enjoy them. Instead, a stranger will enjoy them. This is futile and a sickening tragedy. [3]A man may father a hundred children and live many years. No matter how long he lives,[E] if he is not satisfied by good things and does not even have a proper burial, I say that a stillborn child is better off than he. [4]For he comes in futility and he goes in darkness, and his name is shrouded in darkness. [5]Though a stillborn child does not see the sun and is not conscious, it has more rest than he. [6]And if he lives a thousand years twice, but does not experience happiness, do not both go to the same place?

[7] All man's labor is
for his stomach,[F]
yet the appetite is
never satisfied.

[8]What advantage then does the wise man have over the fool? What advantage is there for the poor person who knows how to conduct himself before others? [9]Better what the eyes see than wandering desire.

[A]**5:1** Ec 4:17 in Hb [B]**5:2** Ec 5:1 in Hb [C]**5:9** Or *An advantage for the land in every respect is a king for a cultivated field*; Hb obscure [D]**6:1** Or *it is common among men* [E]**6:3** Lit *how many years* [F]**6:7** Lit *mouth*

a **second youth**, presumably the **poor but wise youth** of verse 13.

- The pronoun "he" refers to the "poor but wise youth": He was "born poor," was in prison for a time, and succeeded the **old but foolish king**. In this case, the "second youth" would refer either to this same youth or a *third* youth.

Similar ambiguity exists in verse 16 but does not affect the point being made. There is a succession of leaders, each of whom has his period of fame, status, and followers. Although wisdom may commend a king, even the wise kings eventually lose their royal status to successors (cp. 1:9-11). Therefore, to devote one's life to the pursuit of fame, status, and the approval of people is a waste of time; these things are fleeting (Hb *hevel*).

5:1-7 In this passage, the Teacher's view of God is crystal clear: **God is in heaven and you are on earth** (v. 2b). The transcendent greatness of God demands that you approach Him reverently and pray thoughtfully. Also, never make a vow to Him that you do not plan to keep.

When Christ died and the veil of the temple was torn in two (Mt 27:51; Mk 15:38; Lk 23:45), a new era of worship began. Christ's death put an end to the need for sacrifice in communion with God (Heb 9:11-12; 10:10,14), and the torn temple veil symbolized the end of a required *geographical* place for worship. This new era of worship was finally ushered in with the coming of the Holy Spirit, who now inhabits believers so that their bodies might be God's temple (1Co 3:16-17) and their worship might be "in spirit and truth" (Jn 4:19-26).

At the time when the Teacher wrote, however, the **house of God** (temple) was still standing, and you were to **guard your steps** in approaching this plot of sacred space where God had made His dwelling. In bringing a **sacrifice**, you are not to approach God **as fools do**, with many words, too foolish to even know they **do wrong**. Instead, you are to approach God to *listen*.

5:4-6 A vow can be an occasion for irrelevant whims, an irreverent approach to a holy God, or even a way of using profanity. Vows are to be carefully considered with accountability for keeping it (cp. Dt 23:21-23; Mt 5:33).

6:1-2 The **tragedy** (Hb *ra'*, "evil") described in verse 2 seems to contradict 5:19. Actually, however, these are two side-by-side statements that present a universal (a statement that is generally true, 5:19) and a particular (a statement of what is sometimes true, 6:2). In other words, God has richly blessed all people (*every* **man**), allowing them to enjoy the benefits of His blessing (5:19). Yet there are also exceptions. For whatever reason, God has chosen for a **man** *not* to enjoy certain benefits he has been given by God (e.g., Jb 1–2). Sometimes, God may even elect that His benefits be enjoyed by **a stranger** (cp. Ec 2:18-26). This is a truth about God that most do not want to hear; indeed, it **weighs heavily on humanity**. However, it is consonant with scriptural truth elsewhere: God gives, and sometimes God takes away (cp. Jb 1:21; 1Sm 2:6-7). One must remember that these are the actions of the inscrutable God, whose very nature, nonetheless, is love (1Jn 4:8).

6:10-12 Ecclesiastes 6:9 occurs at the midpoint of the book. The Teacher now begins to transition into the second half of the book by reiterating his main theses, all of which highlight the limitations of mankind.

7:1-13 This group of proverbs stands between two theological frames (6:10-12; 7:13-14), both of which emphasize the frailty and finitude of humanity in contrast to the sovereignty of Almighty God. The context considers the fleeting days (6:12), and the subject is what is good (6:12) and wise (7:1-12) for you to think and to do, given your brief lifespan. Two verbs sum up the Teacher's answer: **Take it to heart** (7:2), and **consider** (vv. 13-14). Those who are wise will consider God's work and the limits given to human beings and will take to heart the brevity of life (v. 2). Only then will they learn to appreciate each moment and experience true gladness of heart (v. 3).

7:1 The first part of this proverb is clear enough: Luxurious wealth does not compare to having a good reputation or a lasting name (cp. Pr 22:1; Is 56:5). Among the Hebrews, a name was equated with character and reputation (cp. Pr 22:1). The connection between the first and second part of the proverb is less clear. People of the ancient Near East used fine perfume to bathe newborns and to adorn the bodies of the dead. Since one's reputation was finally secured in **the day of one's death**, perhaps the reference to fine perfume corresponds to **the day of one's birth**. Whatever the connection, the proverb commends a good reputation. The preference of death over birth may underscore the fact that a newborn baby does not have an opportunity to develop testimony and reputation in contrast to the one who dies after a lifetime of earning a good name.

7:3-4 This proverb is not advising that a person should spend life grieving, never

This too is futile and a pursuit of the
wind.

What Is Good and Wise for Frail Humanity? (6:10–7:14)

10 Whatever exists was given its
name long ago,[A] and it is known
what man is. But he is not able to
contend with the One stronger
than he. 11 For when there are many
words, they increase futility. What is
the advantage for man? 12 For who
knows what is good for man in life,
in the few days of his futile life that
he spends like a shadow? Who can
tell man what will happen after him
under the sun?

7 A good name is better than
fine perfume,
and the day of one's death
than the day of one's birth.
2 It is better to go to a house
of mourning
than to go to a house
of feasting,
since that is the end
of all mankind,
and the living should take it
to heart.
3 Grief is better than laughter,
for when a face is sad, a heart
may be glad.
4 The heart of the wise is
in a house of mourning,
but the heart of fools is
in a house of pleasure.
5 It is better to listen to rebuke
from a wise person
than to listen to the song
of fools,
6 for like the crackling
of burning thorns
under the pot,
so is the laughter of the fool.
This too is futile.
7 Surely, the practice
of extortion turns
a wise person into a fool,
and a bribe destroys the mind.
8 The end of a matter is better
than its beginning;
a patient spirit is better
than a proud spirit.
9 Don't let your spirit rush
to be angry,
for anger abides in the heart
of fools.
10 Don't say, "Why were
the former days better
than these?"
since it is not wise of you
to ask this.
11 Wisdom is as good
as an inheritance
and an advantage to those
who see the sun,
12 because wisdom is protection
as money is protection,
and the advantage
of knowledge
is that wisdom preserves
the life of its owner.
13 Consider the work of God,
for who can straighten out
what He has made crooked?

14 In the day of prosperity be joyful,
but in the day of adversity, consider:
God has made the one as well as the
other, so that man cannot discover
anything that will come after him.

The Elusiveness of Wisdom and True Righteousness (7:15-29)

15 In my futile life[B] I have seen everything: there is a righteous man
who perishes in spite of his righteousness, and there is a wicked
man who lives long in spite of his
evil. 16 Don't be excessively righteous, and don't be overly wise.
Why should you destroy yourself?
17 Don't be excessively wicked, and

[A] **6:10** Lit *name already* [B] **7:15** Lit *days*

>WORD|*study*

6:10-12 The Teacher uses the word man (Hb *'adam*) four times in this passage. This general term for humanity recalls the frailty of human existence, for out of the mere dust of the "ground" (Hb *'adamah*, Gn 2:7; 3:19) man was formed. This passage highlights the frailty of man in at least four ways:

- Man is unable to **contend** [Hb *din*, "dispute"] **with** God, who is **stronger than he** (cp. Jb 9:32; 40:1-5). More words simply increase the futility (cp. Ec 5:2-3,7; Jb 35:16). Job learned this lesson the hard way.
- Man is unable to guarantee permanent fruit for his labor (i.e., to gain **advantage**; cp. 1:3; 2:11,18-22; 3:9; 5:13-16).
- Man is limited in knowledge and understanding. **Who knows what is good** (cp. 2:3) or **what will happen after him** (cp. 3:23)?
- Man is finite; he has **few days . . . that he spends like a shadow** on earth (cp. 2:14; 3:19-21; 12:1-7).

don't be foolish. Why should you die
before your time? [18]It is good that
you grasp the one and do not let the
other slip from your hand. For the
one who •fears God will end up with
both of them.

[19] Wisdom makes the wise man
stronger
than ten rulers of a city.
[20] There is certainly
no righteous man
on the earth
who does good and never sins.

[21]Don't pay attention[A] to everything •people say, or you may hear
your servant cursing you, [22]for you
know that many times you yourself
have cursed others.
[23]I have tested all this by wisdom.
I resolved, "I will be wise," but it was
beyond me. [24]What exists is beyond
reach and very deep. Who can discover it? [25]I turned my thoughts
to know, explore, and seek wisdom
and an explanation for things, and
to know that wickedness is stupidity and folly is madness. [26]And I find
more bitter than death the woman
who is a trap, her heart a net, and her
hands chains. The one who pleases
God will escape her, but the sinner
will be captured by her. [27]"Look,"
says the Teacher, "I have discovered
this by adding one thing to another
to find out the explanation, [28]which
my soul continually searches for but
does not find: among a thousand
people I have found one true man,
but among all these I have not found
a true woman. [29]Only see this: I have
discovered that God made people
upright, but they pursued many
schemes."

God's Sovereignty over the Lives of the Righteous and the Wicked (8:1–10:20)

Dealing with Authority (8:1-9)

8 Who is like the wise person, and
who knows the interpretation of
a matter? A man's wisdom brightens
his face, and the sternness of his face
is changed.
[2]Keep[B] the king's command because of your oath made before
God. [3]Do not be in a hurry; leave
his presence, and don't persist in a
bad cause, since he will do whatever

laughing. Rather, sorrow teaches some lessons that cannot be learned any other way. Nothing draws one closer to God than the sorrows and difficulties of life. In addition, a sober assessment of life is better than improper levity (cp. v. 6).

7:7-10 Anger is a form of impatience and suggests an undisciplined and self-driven life rather than a God-controlled spirit. Nostalgic romanticism also comes from an impatient spirit. People begin to glorify **the former days** of their lives when they lack the patience to face present circumstances. This is foolish. Life will always have its difficulties. Reliving the past will only cause one to stop living in the present and thus miss out on God's gift of joy.

7:16 The instruction not to be "excessively" righteous or wise, then, refers to a fanatical kind of righteousness-seeking, motivated by profit or self-glory and ending in self-destruction.

8:1-4 Wisdom has its advantages when dealing with authority. Wisdom helps a person to interpret matters, and it **brightens** a person's face. Elsewhere in Scripture, the shining **face** is God's (cp. Nm 6:25; Pss 31:16; 67:1; 80:3,7,19; 119:135; Dn 9:17), and it represents His manifested favor (as "One . . . dwelling in unapproachable light"; 1Tm 6:16) toward His people.

[A]**7:21** Lit *Don't give your heart* [B]**8:2** Some Hb mss, LXX, Vg, Tg, Syr; other Hb mss read *I, keep*

BIBLICAL WOMANHOOD A True Woman

The context for the Teacher's comments about women (7:26-29) is a description of his search to understand wisdom and folly (vv. 23-25). In Hebrew the verb **find** (*matsa'*, "find out, learn," v. 26) is an active participle, indicating continuous action—having the sense, for example, of "I am finding . . ." or "I am continually finding out . . ." or "I am in the process of discovering . . ." (cp. 1Kg 11:1-6). The Teacher will describe what he is currently learning from observation and/or experience—that a particular type or category of women (**the woman** [Hb *ha'ishshah*], not women in general) is **more bitter than death** (Ec 7:26; cp. Pr 5:4). This conclusion recalls the warnings in Proverbs about the grave dangers of seduction and the attendant lust, sexual immorality, and marital infidelity (cp. Pr 2:16-19; 5:3-23; 6:24-35). The passage also heightens the praise of the virtuous woman in the last chapter of Proverbs, particularly in the rhetorical question, "Who can find (Hb *matsa'*) a capable wife?" (Pr 31:10).

The Teacher notes three characteristics of the type of woman he apparently wishes he had avoided:

- She is **a trap** (Hb *matsod*, "a net spread over a pit"; cp. 22:14; 23:27; 29:5; Pr 9:12) set for capturing prey.
- Her **heart** [is] **a net** (Hb *cheērem*, "an object doomed to destruction").
- Her **hands** [are] **chains** (Hb *'eēsur*, "bondage, prison").

Each metaphor contributes to the stereotype of a woman with whom a man has become entangled so that he cannot get free from her manipulative control. Nevertheless, he implicitly advises **escape** (Hb *malat*, "go away in haste, deliver oneself") by living to please God instead of being a **sinner** who is **captured** (Hb *lakad*, "be caught in a trap," Ec 7:26).

The Teacher has met so many people who cannot be described as "true" that he can think of only one man who was a "real" godly man (**one true man**) but not one woman who was a "real" godly woman (a **true woman**, v. 28). The translators have added the word "true" to convey the sense of the Hebrew wording and the implied meaning in the context of verse 29: **God made people upright** (Hb *yashar*, "straight"), but rare are the men and women who are not so engulfed by the propensity to sin that they can truly reflect God's righteous character.

8:2-4 Because of [Hb *ki*] **your oath . . . before God** is a purpose clause and maintains a parallel in meaning with 10:4. While in the king's presence, one should not be in a hurry to leave (see note on 10:4-7); for the wise person will show both respect and patience (cp. 7:8; 8:6; Pr 25:15). Furthermore, the wise person will **keep the king's command** out of respect for God and because the sovereignty of the king cannot be contested.

8:5-9 Another incentive to keeping the king's command is the prevention of **anything harmful**. Even if **troubles are heavy** and you are tempted to act rashly or contrary to what the king says, the wise person will be patient (cp. 7:8-9), understanding that there is a **right time and procedure** for **every activity** (cp. 3:1,17). Even the wise do not know the future (cp. 3:22; 6:12; 9:1). The Teacher gives four examples of the impotence of human beings in the face of either God or the king's authority (cp. 4:1-3; 5:8-9). They have no control over the **wind** (Hb *ruach*, "life-breath") or the **day of death**. They also lack the power to send a warrior on furlough in the heat of **battle** or prevent the sure consequences of wickedness.

9:7-10 In view of certain death, then, the living should enjoy life. One should come to terms with life's brevity (cp. 7:1-4) without mourning; instead, **white** clothing and an anointed **head** should be constant signs of joy and festivity (cp. 2Sm 12:20; Ps 23:5, in which God anoints or gives joy; Ps 45:8; Pr 27:9; Is 61:3).

9:11-12 Life **under the sun** does not always go according to one's expectations. Success is not guaranteed—even to the **swift** (cp. Asahel the "fast runner," in 2Sm 2:18-23), the **strong**, the **wise**, the **discerning**, and the **skillful**—for this earth-bound life is imperfect because of sin. The reference to **chance** (Hb *pegaʿ*, "incident, event, occurrence, what happens to anyone") here is no indication that the Teacher has abandoned his view of God's sovereignty (e.g. 3:11,14; 7:13-14; 8:17); to human beings, however, life can appear arbitrary. Two examples from nature show how suddenly and unexpectedly calamity may come upon human beings (cp. Pr 7:23).

9:13-18 Another parable illustrates the relative value of wisdom (cp. 4:13-16). A **few men** were confronted by a **great king** who built **large siege works** (Hb *matsod*, usually "net"; here, a "movable assault tower" 9:14; cp. 7:26; Jb 9:26) against the city. The city was saved, however, by a

he wants. 4 For the king's word is
authoritative, and who can say to
him, "What are you doing?" 5 The
one who keeps a command will not
experience anything harmful, and a
wise heart knows the right time and
procedure. 6 For every activity there
is a right time and procedure, even
though man's troubles are heavy on
him. 7 Yet no one knows what will
happen because who can tell him
what will happen? 8 No one has authority over the wind[A] to restrain it,
and there is no authority over the
day of death; there is no furlough in
battle, and wickedness will not allow
those who practice it to escape. 9 All
this I have seen, applying my mind
to all the work that is done under
the sun, at a time when one man has
authority over another to his harm.

Inequity in Life under the Sun (8:10-14)

10 In such circumstances, I saw
the wicked buried. They came and
went from the holy place, and they
were praised[B] in the city where they
did so. This too is futile. 11 Because
the sentence against a criminal act
is not carried out quickly, the heart
of •people is filled with the desire to
commit crime. 12 Although a sinner
commits crime a hundred times and
prolongs his life, yet I also know
that it will go well with God-fearing
people, for they are reverent before
Him. 13 However, it will not go well
with the wicked, and they will not
lengthen their days like a shadow,
for they are not reverent before God.
14 There is a futility that is done
on the earth: there are righteous
people who get what the actions of
the wicked deserve, and there are
wicked people who get what the actions of the righteous deserve. I say
that this too is futile.

Refrain: Enjoy Life! (8:15-17)

15 So I commended enjoyment because there is nothing better for
man under the sun than to eat,
drink, and enjoy himself, for this
will accompany him in his labor
during the days of his life that God
gives him under the sun.
16 When I applied my mind to
know wisdom and to observe the activity that is done on the earth (even
though one's eyes do not close in
sleep day or night), 17 I observed all
the work of God and concluded that
man is unable to discover the work
that is done under the sun. Even
though a man labors hard to explore
it, he cannot find it; even if the wise
man claims to know it, he is unable
to discover it.

The Absence of Exemption for Any Human Being (9:1-12)

9 Indeed, I took all this to heart and
explained it all: the righteous, the
wise, and their works are in God's
hands. •People don't know whether
to expect love or hate. Everything
lies ahead of them. 2 Everything is
the same for everyone: there is one
fate for the righteous and the wicked, for the good and the bad,[C] for the
•clean and the •unclean, for the one
who sacrifices and the one who does
not sacrifice. As it is for the good,
so it is for the sinner; as for the one
who takes an oath, so for the one
who fears an oath. 3 This is an evil in
all that is done under the sun: there
is one fate for everyone. In addition,
the hearts of people are full of evil,
and madness is in their hearts while
they live—after that they go to the
dead. 4 But there is hope for whoever
is joined[D] with all the living, since a
live dog is better than a dead lion.
5 For the living know that they will
die, but the dead don't know anything. There is no longer a reward
for them because the memory of
them is forgotten. 6 Their love, their
hate, and their envy have already
disappeared, and there is no longer
a portion for them in all that is done
under the sun.
7 Go, eat your bread with pleasure,
and drink your wine with a cheerful
heart, for God has already accepted
your works. 8 Let your clothes be
white all the time, and never let oil
be lacking on your head. 9 Enjoy life
with the wife you love all the days
of your fleeting[E] life, which has been
given to you under the sun, all your
fleeting days. For that is your portion in life and in your struggle under the sun. 10 Whatever your hands

[A] **8:8** Or *life-breath* [B] **8:10** Some Hb mss, LXX, Aq, Theod, Sym; other Hb mss read *forgotten* [C] **9:2** LXX, Aq, Syr, Vg; MT omits *and the bad* [D] **9:4** Alt Hb tradition reads *chosen* [E] **9:9** Or *futile*

find to do, do with all your strength,
because there is no work, planning,
knowledge, or wisdom in •Sheol
where you are going.
11 Again I saw under the sun that
the race is not to the swift, or the
battle to the strong, or bread to the
wise, or riches to the discerning,
or favor to the skillful; rather, time
and chance happen to all of them.
12 For man certainly does not know
his time: like fish caught in a cruel
net or like birds caught in a trap, so
people are trapped in an evil time as
it suddenly falls on them.

Contrasting Wisdom and Folly (9:13–10:20)

13 I have observed that this also is
wisdom under the sun, and it is significant to me: 14 There was a small
city with few men in it. A great king
came against it, surrounded it, and
built large siege works against it.
15 Now a poor wise man was found in
the city, and he delivered the city by
his wisdom. Yet no one remembered
that poor man. 16 And I said, "Wisdom is better than strength, but the
wisdom of the poor man is despised,
and his words are not heeded."

17 The calm words of the wise
are heeded
more than the shouts
of a ruler over fools.
18 Wisdom is better
than weapons of war,
but one sinner can destroy
much good.

10 Dead flies make
a perfumer's oil ferment
and stink;
so a little folly outweighs
wisdom and honor.
2 A wise man's heart goes
to the[A] right,
but a fool's heart to the[A] left.
3 Even when the fool walks
along the road, his heart
lacks sense,
and he shows everyone he is
a fool.
4 If the ruler's anger rises
against you, don't leave
your place,
for calmness puts
great offenses to rest.

5 There is an evil I have seen under
the sun, an error proceeding from
the presence of the ruler:

6 The fool is appointed
to great heights,
but the rich remain
in lowly positions.

[A]**10:2** Lit *his*

poor [Hb *miskēn*, "commoner"] **wise man**—how is unclear (Ec 9:16). The advantage of wisdom, then, is being **better than strength** (cp. Pr 21:22); yet, wisdom's value is limited—for it does not guarantee a person lasting remembrance (cp. Ec 1:11; 2:16), respect, or even a hearing by others (9:15-16). The same advantage and limitation are also stated in proverbial form (vv. 17-18). Note the contrast between the **calm words of the wise** and the **shouts of a ruler** [who must also be a fool himself] **over fools**. The limitation of wisdom expressed in 9:18 is emphasized again in 10:1.

10:1-3 Dead flies cannot accomplish anything except to foul up the sweet scent of a **perfumer's oil**. So it is with folly, which can succeed only in spoiling **wisdom and honor**. This proverb emphasizes the point expressed in 9:18 and is similar to the present-day proverb: "One rotten apple spoils the whole barrel." The **heart** (Hb *lēv*, "mind; seat of intelligence") of the wise and of the fool go in opposite directions—to the **right** and to the **left**, respectively—that seem to represent choices in decision-making (cp. Jnh 4:11). The right hand was often associated with advantage and favor, while the left was associated with an inferior position (cp. Gn 48:12-20; Mt 25:31-36). The fool's life journey is guided by a heart that **lacks sense** (Ec 10:3, cp. Pr 6:32; 10:21; 15:21). All he does reveals him to be a fool (cp. Pr 12:23; 13:16).

10:4-7 A person would certainly show himself to be a fool if he left the presence of an angry king. The wise

BIBLICAL WOMANHOOD Marriage

The Teacher charged his young male recipients to pursue enjoyment in their marriages because life goes by so fast (9:9). This advice is directly opposed to the dominant message of people who do not revere the Lord. The temptation of both men and women who begin wrestling with their mortality—young people who have become personally acquainted with the brevity of life or adults going through "a midlife crisis," for example—is to set aside anything and anyone (including a spouse) that does not make them happy. The Teacher has already addressed the futility of pursuing pleasure. Even though Solomon eventually stopped living according to the wisdom God gave him, here he imparts wise advice. He does *not* recommend that in light of how short life is, men should enjoy their wives (plural) or find another one if they are not happy with the one they have. Instead, he directs men to **enjoy life with** [Hb *'im*, the same particle meaning "with" in the name "Immanuel" ("God with us"), Is 7:14; 8:8] **the wife** [singular] **you love** (in Hb, lit "whom you love") from now on, for the rest of your short life. Arranged marriages were the norm for Hebrew culture in Solomon's day, a practice ideally reinforcing the understanding that one's wife was a gift to be cherished. In stark contrast to modern conceptions of love as an emotion or as affection for whatever makes you feel good, "love" (Hb *'ahav*) as used here included actively giving of yourself to the spouse for her benefit and staying faithful to the one with whom you have entered into a covenant relationship. "Love" (Hb *'ahav*, "desire") is here in perfect tense, indicating completed action; the phrase states a fact, an action taken that cannot be undone. For those in the audience who are already married, the Teacher assumes their understanding that the marriage relationship is intended to be not only permanent and lifelong but also *the* greatest enjoyment in life—**your portion in life** (cp. Gn 2:24).

person would remain, for his **calmness** would soothe the angry king (cp. 8:3; Pr 16:14; 25:15). Speaking of fools and of rulers, there is another **evil**, which happens as a result of a ruler's **error** or blunder (cp. Ec 9:3). Sometimes a ruler places a fool in a high position with great responsibility, when obviously he is unworthy of such advancement (i.e., he lacks sense, 10:3). At the same time, the rich—who were expected to hold such positions—do not advance.

Surely the sight of **slaves on horses** (i.e., animals used only by the wealthy and powerful—cp. 2Ch 25:28; Est 6:8-9) and **princes** on foot is a sign of societal instability and upheaval. The Teacher's point here is not so much that slaves should never be treated well or that the rich should be the only ones to hold positions of authority. He is lamenting the fact that sometimes political errors happen (here, the promotion of a fool). Such an error can be costly for a society.

10:10-11 Failing to maintain the tools of your trade costs more time, money, and effort than what might be lost by interrupting a job to sharpen your axe, for example. **Wisdom**, then, can be an **advantage**. However, even the value of wisdom is limited, for a **charmer** (Hb *ba'al*, "owner of an object that embodies his manner, character, or work; master"; *lashon*, "tongue," thus "master of the tongue" or "babbler") can possess all the know-how in charming a **snake**, but the snake can still choose to bite **before it is charmed** (Hb *lo'-lachash*, "without enchantment"; cp. Ps 58:4-5; Jr 8:17).

11:1-2 Your actions cannot be based solely upon what you see or what you think, for **you don't know** (a phrase used four times—vv. 2,5-6) everything, including the work of God. There are two possible meanings for these verses. The Teacher could be encouraging diversification of investments, here in maritime trade, because one never knows when or where a **disaster** might strike. In other words, "Don't put all your eggs in one basket." Another more likely interpretation is that this is an exhortation to be a liberal, risk-taking giver. Compare the Arabic proverb: "Do good, throw your bread on the waters, and one day you will find it." To **send your bread**, then, would be a call to "throw away" a gift or a good deed. One never knows what benefit might be bestowed on others (even in a time of disaster) or when you yourself might **find** the blessing coming back to you (cp. Pr 12:14; 19:17; Lk 6:38).

7 I have seen slaves on horses,
but princes walking
on the ground like slaves.

8 The one who digs a pit
may fall into it,
and the one who breaks
through a wall
may be bitten by a snake.
9 The one who quarries stones
may be hurt by them;
the one who splits trees
may be endangered
by them.
10 If the ax is dull, and one
does not sharpen its edge,
then one must exert
more strength;
however, the advantage
of wisdom is that
it brings success.
11 If the snake bites before
it is charmed,
then there is no advantage
for the charmer.[A]
12 The words from the mouth
of a wise man are gracious,
but the lips of a fool
consume him.
13 The beginning of the words
of his mouth is folly,
but the end of his speaking
is evil madness.
14 Yet the fool multiplies words.
No one knows
what will happen,
and who can tell anyone
what will happen after him?
15 The struggles of fools
weary them,
for they don't know how to go
to the city.
16 Woe to you, land,
when your king is a youth
and your princes feast
in the morning.
17 Blessed are you, land,
when your king is a son
of nobles
and your princes feast
at the proper time—
for strength and not
for drunkenness.
18 Because of laziness the roof
caves in,
and because of
negligent hands
the house leaks.
19 A feast is prepared
for laughter,
and wine makes life happy,
and money is the answer
for everything.
20 Do not curse the king
even in your thoughts,
and do not curse a rich person
even in your bedroom,
for a bird of the sky may carry
the message,
and a winged creature
may report the matter.

The Fleeting Nature of Life (11:1–12:7)

The Challenge to Rejoice and Remember (11:1-6)

11 Send your bread
on the surface of the waters,
for after many days
you may find it.
2 Give a portion to seven
or even to eight,
for you don't know
what disaster may happen
on earth.
3 If the clouds are full,
they will pour out rain
on the earth;
whether a tree falls
to the south or the north,
the place where the tree falls,
there it will lie.
4 One who watches the wind
will not sow,
and the one who looks
at the clouds will not reap.
5 Just as you don't know
the path of the wind,
or how bones develop
in[B] the womb
of a pregnant woman,
so you don't know the work
of God who makes
everything.
6 In the morning sow
your seed,
and at evening do not let
your hand rest,
because you don't know
which will succeed,
whether one or the other,
or if both of them will be
equally good.

[A]**10:11** Lit *master of the tongue* [B]**11:5** Or *know how the life-breath comes to the bones in*

Modified Refrain: Rejoice and Remember (11:7-10)

7 Light is sweet,
and it is pleasing for the eyes
to see the sun.
8 Indeed, if a man lives
many years,
let him rejoice in them all,
and let him remember
the days of darkness,
since they will be many.
All that comes is futile.
9 Rejoice, young man,
while you are young,
and let your heart be glad
in the days of your youth.
And walk in the ways
of your heart
and in the sight of your eyes;
but know that for all
of these things
God will bring you
to judgment.
10 Remove sorrow
from your heart,
and put away pain
from your flesh,
because youth and the prime
of life are fleeting.

The Approach of Old Age and Death (12:1-7)

12 So remember your Creator in the days of your youth:

Before the days of adversity
come,
and the years approach
when you will say,
"I have no delight in them";
2 before the sun and the light
are darkened,
and the moon and the stars,
and the clouds return
after[A] the rain;
3 on the day
when the guardians
of the house tremble,
and the strong men stoop,
the women who grind cease
because they are few,
and the ones who watch
through the windows
see dimly,
4 the doors at the street
are shut
while the sound of the mill
fades;
when one rises at the sound
of a bird,
and all the daughters of song
grow faint.
5 Also, they are afraid of heights
and dangers on the road;
the almond tree blossoms,
the grasshopper loses
its spring,[B]
and the caper berry has
no effect;
for man is headed
to his eternal home,
and mourners will walk
around in the street;
6 before the silver cord
is snapped,[C]
and the gold bowl is broken,
and the jar is shattered
at the spring,
and the wheel is broken
into the well;
7 and the dust returns
to the earth as it once was,
and the spirit returns to God
who gave it.

Thematic Refrain and Conclusion (12:8-14)

8 "Absolute futility," says the Teacher. "Everything is futile."
9 In addition to the Teacher being
a wise man, he constantly taught
the •people knowledge; he weighed,
explored, and arranged many proverbs. 10 The Teacher sought to find
delightful sayings and write words
of truth accurately. 11 The sayings
of the wise are like goads, and those
from masters of collections are like
firmly embedded nails. The sayings
are given by one Shepherd.[D]
12 But beyond these, my son, be
warned: there is no end to the making of many books, and much study
wearies the body. 13 When all has
been heard, the conclusion of the
matter is: •fear God and keep His
commands, because this is for all
humanity. 14 For God will bring every act to judgment, including every
hidden thing, whether good or evil.

11:8-9 The Teacher provides parameters within which life is to be enjoyed (cp. 11:8-9).

12:8-11 The Teacher closes the body of the book the same way he began (1:2): **Everything is futile**. However, one should not miss the irony of verse 10. Although many people through the centuries have been tempted to see the Teacher as a sage of gloom and doom, he **sought to find delightful sayings** for the people and to accurately **write words of truth. The sayings of the wise** are compared to **goads**, pointed sticks—often tipped with **embedded nails**—used to prod cattle in the right direction. Words of wisdom may not seem delightful at the time when you first hear them; truth may, in fact, be painful. However, when wisdom enters the heart, it will eventually be pleasant to the soul (Pr 2:10), for truth brings life and freedom (Jn 8:32). Wisdom comes from the **Shepherd**, Yahweh God, who intends only the best for His sheep (cp. Ps 23).

12:12-14 The warning about going **beyond** these sayings further affirms the reliability of the book (cp. Dt 4:2; 12:32; Rv 22:18-19). Like elsewhere in the book, the Teacher warns about being obsessive in your work (cp. Ec 4:7-8)—this time, in the area of study. The Teacher may frame the body of the book with the theme of futility (1:2; 12:8); however, the **conclusion** of it all is that one should **fear God and keep His commands. . . . For God will bring every act to judgment** (cp. Rm 14:12; 1Pt 4:5). Although the fear of God has not been a major explicit theme of the book (cp. Ec 3:14; 5:7; 7:18; 8:12-13), it has been an implicit theme throughout. The author has given a climactic statement of the overall theme of the book: Whatever the difficulties and inequities of life in the midst of blessings and prosperity, your honoring the Lord and obeying His commands alone will bring happiness and fruitfulness on earth as well as in the life to come.

[A]12:2 Or *with* [B]12:5 Or *grasshopper is weighed down*, or *grasshopper drags itself along*
[C]12:6 Alt Hb tradition reads *removed* [D]12:11 Or *by a shepherd*

BIBLICAL WOMANHOOD Remember Your Creator

To remember the Creator is to remember that He is the Creator, and you are the created (Gn 2:7). He has always been, and you came to be. To remember the Creator is to remember that there is an infinite distinction between Him and you. In view of such greatness, you and I can but bend the knee before this One who alone has all knowledge and all power—confessing all vain attempts to usurp His rightful position as Controller of the Universe. To remember the Creator is to remember that you are a frail creature of dust and that you will return to dust (Ec 3:20; 12:7; cp. Gn 3:19). When you finally begin to accept your limits as a dependent human being and surrender your desires to possess all knowledge and control, you are able to experience the gift of enjoyment that God freely offers (cp. Ec 5:18-20).

The Teacher writes the allegory of old age (12:1-7) to give reason for his injunction: **Remember your Creator in the days of your youth** *because* there will later be **days of adversity** when it is more difficult to find enjoyment in life (**no delight**). The idea is not that the elderly cannot experience enjoyment in life; but admittedly, the deterioration of the human body poses inevitable challenges to one's capacity for enjoyment—challenges that are not present in one's youth. Therefore, these young men are to "seize the day." If "to see the sun" is to live (11:7), then the darkening of the luminaries may be a general symbol for approaching death or the end of life. The lack of vitality in life is seen in the sun's failure to shine even **after the rain**—for the **clouds return** again. On a more particular level, verse 2 could also symbolize the dimming and never quite clearing up (i.e., "the clouds return," of one's vision in old age.

ECCLESIASTES . . . WRITTEN ON MY *Heart* While the assessment of life in this book truthfully reflects the curse of sin on life "under the sun," even the resolve to enjoy life as a God-given gift is only part of the story for today's women, who have the opportunity to know "life . . in abundance" in Jesus Christ (Jn 10:10). However, in order to take to heart God's message in the book of Ecclesiastes, allow the book to remind you of the incomparable worth of your eternal relationship with Christ by refreshing your memory of living without Him or by impressing upon you the void of meaning left in the wake of sin's entry into your life. Consider as well as the wisdom of reevaluating how you spend your time and what your heart is really pursuing with its limited number of heartbeats. In any area of life you discover to be "a chasing after the wind" rather than a God-given gift over which you exercise loving and responsible stewardship, invite your Creator to reorganize your priorities and dreams, lining them up with His eternal perspective, His timing (3:11), and His commands (12:13) setting your hope "on God, who richly provides us with all things to enjoy" (1Tm 6:17).

BIBLICAL WOMANHOOD Antidote for Worry

Women are constantly bombarded with temptations to worry. Ecclesiastes 11:7–12:1 does not specifically mention worry, but the Teacher commends an outlook on life that can serve as an antidote:

- *Life is good* (v. 7). The Teacher affirms that **it is pleasing . . . to see the sun**, a reference to the goodness of simply being alive (11:7; cp. 6:59:4-6). He calls both young (11:9) and old (v. 8) to **rejoice** (Hb *samach*, "be glad"), a verb enlisting active celebration. Worry is not compatible with the attitude of embracing the inherent goodness of life as God's good gift. Doing something that outwardly demonstrates the truth that life itself is good leaves little room for anxiety about how a moment, day, or year will turn out.
- *Life includes dark days* (v. 8). Life is good despite the **days of adversity** (12:1) that everyone experiences. You cannot worry them away. Do **remember the days of darkness**—whether past, present, or future and whether in your life or the lives of others—not as catalysts for worrying but as contrasts enhancing recognition of the inherent goodness of life itself. Worry competes with faith in God's ability to redeem any situation for good (Rm 8:28), with trust in God's faithfulness, and with hope in His promise to render justice in the end (Ec 11:9).
- *Life is short* (v. 10). Here, as throughout the book, the Teacher points out the **fleeting** nature of life and its futility not to incite readers to recoil from life in fear and dread but to recognize that it has meaning only from the Creator's perspective. Whatever threatens to cut life short invites worry. The woman who has addressed the inevitability of death and the aging process (see chap. 12) is better equipped to face with confidence whatever life brings. Discernment between what has eternal value and what does not last can dispel many worries and yield more fruitful investment of mental and emotional energy in God's priorities.
- *Judgment is certain and belongs to God alone* (11:9). Essentially, worry is an effort to control what belongs solely to God's control. No amount of worry can change or undo the past. What you *can* do is to live obediently in the present—bringing your past into the light of God's Word, exercising forgiveness, and both extending and accepting His healing. You cannot, by worrying, determine the future. What you *can* do is to live obediently in the present—especially praying fervently and sharing the gospel so that both the present life and eternal destination of others can be changed. Only God knows the future. Apart from the glimpses He has revealed in His Word and the certainty of the promises He has made, no one is privy to the future. Worrying changes nothing but your health in this earthly life "under the sun." Regarding issues of justice and inexplicable evil, Scripture makes clear that although God does not always intervene or make things right in ways you can see or in your timing, He does hold *everyone* accountable (Rm 14:10-12; 2Co 5:10; Heb 9:27).

Approaching life with an outlook marked by these four truths fits the challenge of Ec 11:1-6 to live soberly, recognizing that "you don't know" what God knows. It also fortifies your heart against the constant temptation to fear (i.e., worry about) everything but God (cp. 12:13-14; **Biblical Womanhood**, p. 827).

Song of Songs

Timeline World Events Biblical Events	*994 BC* Birth of Solomon	*972–970 BC* Solomon, co-regent with his father David	*970 BC* Solomon, ruler of a united kingdom	*970 BC* Solomon's prayer for wisdom

"I belong to my love, and his desire is for me" (7:10).

Who wrote Song of Songs?

Solomon, king of Israel (1:1)

Who were the recipients?

The people of Israel living under Solomon's reign

When was Song of Songs written?

Likely during the early years of Solomon's reign (971–931 B.C.) before he took multiple wives and concubines (see 6:8; 1Kg 11:1-8)

Where did it happen?

Primarily Jerusalem, though the Shulammite was reared southeast of the Sea of Galilee; the gardens of En-gedi, located west of the Dead Sea or Salt Sea, are also mentioned

What is Song of Songs about?

In the Song, sexual love expressed between a man and woman in an exclusive commitment is both natural and restrained by divine boundaries. Biblical sexuality, protected by marriage, is presented as good. The Song is unique in the Bible in its celebration of sexual intimacy—i.e., love expressed within marriage. Sexual language is found elsewhere in Scripture (cp. Pr 7:6-27; 9:17), but here the focus of the entire book is on human love: courtship, sensuous love expressed in conjugal union, and the beauty of marriage. Some dominant themes in the Song of Solomon are:

- *Purity,*
- *Exclusive commitment of marriage,*
- *Joys of marital love.*

Why should women read Song of Songs?

Not every woman is physically beautiful, but all are created for relationship. One of the most glorious yet potentially devastating aspects of a woman's experience—both physically and relationally—is her sexuality. In this sin-filled world, everything good that God has created is under enemy attack. The self-image and ability of a woman to give and receive unconditional love according to divine design are prime targets. In stark contrast to the perverted messages about the purpose for the woman's gift of female sexuality, Song of Songs celebrates God's ideal for the expression of that sexuality—the way He created it to be enjoyed within the covenant relationship of monogamous, heterosexual marriage. Within the context of the whole Bible, the Song's positive portrayal of sexual intimacy affirms God's intention for this gift and thereby implicitly rules out-of-bounds the abuses, extramarital pursuits, and substitutes for His good gifts. For women, reading the Song of Songs can provide an encouraging and challenging picture of God's good design and, though bombarded with the world's lures and lies, assure them of its truth.

How do you read Song of Songs?

The Song is part of the Bible's wisdom literature contained in the Writings (Hb *kethuvim*). The challenges of reading both wisdom literature and poetry apply especially to the Song of Songs, particularly with its heavy concentration of figures of speech and metaphorical language. The dialogue is sometimes difficult to follow because of abrupt changes in speakers, but you will find helpful the way editors of the HCSB text have identified who is speaking. Replete with such rich and evocative imagery, the Song communicates by engaging your imagination and stirring your emotions. Although certain parts of the poetry will sparkle with truth and the possibility of personal application, the overall, composite picture of sexual love as God created it to be enjoyed outshines even these individual jewels.

The "big picture" message of this book comes into focus with several straight-through readings of the whole followed by reading the whole more slowly, at a more contemplative pace, letting the various scenes and portions of dialogue come to life in your mind's eye. Prepare your heart by revisiting the book's theological roots in Genesis 1 and 2. Observe God's placement of the man and his wife in a garden, each transparent to the other, yet without shame (Gn 2:24-25). Instead of allowing the enemy to continue to shape your view of sexual intimacy—whether by falsely exalting it as the supreme expression of love or denigrating it to the level of base instinct, whether perverting its inherent pleasures or insisting on a goal of perfect performance—pray that each time you read the Spirit will line up both mind and heart with His truth. Also pray that the Lord will guide you in accepting His affirmation of your womanhood and your worth and beauty in the eyes of your Creator and Redeemer. Regardless of how close or how far your experience of marital bliss comes to the ideal extolled in the book, the Lord wants to use every part of His Word to conform your view of Him, of you, and of others to His view.

Outline

I. The Beginning of Love: Attraction (1:1–3:5)
   - A. The Shulammite's Expression of Desire (1:1-4)
   - B. The Shulammite's Confession (1:5-7)
   - C. The Assurance of Solomon (1:8-11)
   - D. Lasting Impressions (1:12-17)
   - E. The Deepening of Love (2:1-2)
   - F. The Beginning of the Shulammite's Transformation (2:3-7)
   - G. The Approach of Solomon (2:8-9)
   - H. The Invitation from Solomon (2:10-14)
   - I. The Expression of Mutual Love (2:15-17)
   - J. The Thoughts of the Shulammite (3:1-5)

II. The Building of Love: Commitment (3:6–6:10)
   - A. The Wedding (3:6-11)
   - B. The Honeymoon (4:1-7)
   - C. The Realization of Passion (4:8-16)
   - D. The Celebration in Love (5:1)

970 BC	968 BC	966 BC	966–931 BC
Solomon's engagement and marriage to the Shulammite	Solomon's exercise of exceptional wisdom in a dispute between two mothers	Solomon's oversight of the building of the temple	God's displeasure at Solomon's marriage to an Egyptian princess and other women, taking him away from the Lord

Outline (continued)

- E. The First Conflict (5:2-8)
- F. The Virtues of Solomon (5:9-16)
- G. The Path to Restoration (6:1-3)
- H. The Words of Sweet Forgiveness (6:4-10)

III. The Growing of Love: Faithfulness (6:11–8:14)

- A. A Complete Restoration (6:11-13)
- B. Solomon's View of the Shulammite (7:1-8)
- C. The Expression of Deeper Love (7:9-13)
- D. The Longing for Affection (8:1-4)
- E. The Passion of Unrelenting Love (8:5-7)
- F. The Family's Role of Protection (8:8-12)
- G. The Final Declaration of Love (8:13-14)

The Beginning of Love: Attraction (1:1–3:5)

The Shulammite's Expression of Desire (1:1-4)

1 Solomon's Finest Song.[A]

W[B]
2 Oh, that he would kiss
me with the kisses
of his mouth!
For your[C] love is[D]
more delightful than wine.
3 The fragrance
of your perfume
is intoxicating;
your name is perfume
poured out.
No wonder young women[E]
adore you.
4 Take me with you—
let us hurry.
Oh, that the king
would bring[F] me
to his chambers.

Y We will rejoice and be glad
for you;
we will praise your love
more than wine.

W It is only right that
they adore you.

The Shulammite's Confession (1:5-7)

5 Daughters of Jerusalem,

[A]1:1 Or *The Song of Songs, which is Solomon's* [B]1:2 The **W, M, Y, N,** and **B** indicate the editors' opinions of the changes of speakers: **W** = Woman, **M** = Man, **Y** = Young women of Jerusalem, **N** = Narrator, **B** = Brothers. If a letter is in parenthesis **(W)**, there is a question about the identity of the speaker. [C]1:2 Unexpected change of grammatical persons, here from *he* and *his* to *your*, is a Hb poetic device. [D]1:2 Or *your caresses are*, or *your lovemaking is* [E]1:3 Or *wonder virgins* [F]1:4 Or *The king has brought*

Title This book is known by three different names in English: The Song of Solomon, The Song of Songs, and the Canticles (Lat *Canticum canticorum*, "Song of songs"), originating with the Latin Vulgate. The Song has the distinction of being described by some Jews as the "holy of holies" within the holy writings.

1:1-5 Interestingly, the Shulammite speaks often in the initial verses. She openly expresses her desire for Solomon's affection and explains that his love tops any imaginable pleasure. **For your love** [Hb *dodim*, "the act of making love"; cp. Pr 7:18] **is more delightful than wine** draws a comparison based on the sweetness of her lover's **kisses** and the resulting intoxication, both characteristic of wine (Sg 1:2-3). Wine was a metaphor for all goodness in life and was a treasured commodity.

A **name** (Hb *shēm*) in ancient times expressed the qualities of the person. The Shulammite compares Solomon's outstanding character to the **fragrance** of **perfume**, also highly prized, which

CHARACTER PROFILE

The Shulammite Bride
An Innocent Beauty

Her Background	• She was probably from the town of Shunem, southeast of the Sea of Galilee in the fertile uplands of rich alluvial soil. • She was first seen by the king as he traveled to or from his property in Lebanon (8:11).
Her Story	• Her father was probably dead since the text refers to the house of the Shulammite's mother (3:4; 8:2) and to the authority of her brothers (1:6; 8:2). • She probably had darker skin than the other women of the royal court, which, along with her beauty, set her apart (1:5-6).
Her Character	• Her chastity had been guarded vigorously (8:8-9).
Her Husband	• King Solomon loved her passionately, and she responded in kind (4:16–5:1; 5:3-5; 6:3; 7:6–8:3).

was **poured out** (Hb *ruq*, "be emptied out"; cp. Jr 48:11-12) as an extravagant gesture. When read aloud in Hebrew, repetition of the word translated as perfume (*shemen*, "spiced or fragrant oil" in this context) in such close association with *shēm* ("name") gives this description a musical quality.

The maiden expressed her desire to belong to Solomon and to be a part of his life (1:4). The king's **chambers** (Hb *cheder*, "inner, private apartment") referred to his personal bedroom, the most private room of the palace. The speakers (**We**) in the latter part of the verse were the young unmarried women in the kingdom.

By addressing the young women as **daughters of Jerusalem** (v. 5), the Shulammite maiden establishes the setting in the capital city of Israel.

The Bedouin **tents of Kedar** were made from black goat hair. The fabric is heavy and course, insulating the home from cold wind in the winter and providing shade from the hot sun. The same material was used for sackcloth (cp. Rv 6:12).

1:6 The Shulammite called attention to her sun-darkened skin as a feature that might not have been considered desirable to the king. She admitted that the men in her life, specifically her brothers, did not treat her tenderly and forced her to work in the **vineyards**, exposing her to harsh weather and the bright rays of the sun, which naturally affected her physical appearance. Nevertheless, she also knew that she was "lovely" (Hb *na'weh*, "attractive, beautiful"), like "the curtains of Solomon" (v. 5), which must have been the finest in the kingdom.

1:7 With pastoral imagery the Shulammite expressed her love and desire to be an intimate part of his life. **One who veils herself** refers to the alluring behavior of a prostitute making herself available to the shepherd/king's **companions**. Her questions about **where** to find him in the middle of the day, immediately followed by the third question, indicate her desire to plan and anticipate an appropriate time to enjoy his company instead of adopting the strategies of women who lure men away from their responsibilities.

1:8-11 Solomon answered the Shulammite with extravagant expressions of his affection. To him she is the **most beautiful of women**. He also called her **my darling** (Hb *ra'yah*, "beloved bride"; cp. v. 15; 2:2,10,13; 4;1,7; 5:2; 6:4) and invited her to be a permanent part of his life, promising to provide for all her needs.

He has imagined her to be like his **mare among Pharaoh's chariots**, comparing the Shulammite to one of his most prized possessions—horses (see 1Kg 4:26; 10:26-29; 2Ch 1:14-17; 9:25). The Song's original audience knew that the chariot horses were all stallions. As a mare released among a group of stallions

I am dark like the tents
of Kedar,
yet lovely like the curtains
of Solomon.
6 Do not stare at me because
I am dark,
for the sun has gazed on me.
My mother's sons were angry
with me;
they made me a keeper
of the vineyards.
I have not kept
my own vineyard.[A]
7 Tell me, you, the one I love:
Where do you pasture
your sheep?
Where do you let them rest
at noon?
Why should I be like one
who veils herself[B,C]
beside the flocks
of your companions?

The Assurance of Solomon (1:8-11)

M[D]
8 If you do not know,
most beautiful of women,
follow[E] the tracks
of the flock,
and pasture
your young goats
near the shepherds' tents.
9 I compare you, my darling,
to a[F] mare
among Pharaoh's chariots.[G]
10 Your cheeks are beautiful
with jewelry,
your neck with its necklace.
11 We will make gold jewelry
for you,
accented with silver.

Lasting Impressions (1:12-17)

W 12 While the king is
on his couch,[H]
my perfume[I] releases
its fragrance.
13 My love is a sachet of myrrh
to me,
spending the night
between my breasts.
14 My love is a cluster
of henna blossoms to me,
in the vineyards of En-gedi.[J]

M 15 How beautiful you are,
my darling.
How very beautiful!
Your eyes are doves.

W 16 How handsome you are,
my love.
How delightful!
Our bed is lush with foliage;
17 the beams of our house
are cedars,
and our rafters are cypresses.[K]

The Deepening of Love (2:1-2)

2 I am a rose[L,M] of Sharon,
a lily[N] of the valleys.

M 2 Like a lily among thorns,
so is my darling
among the young women.

The Beginning of the Shulammite's Transformation (2:3-7)

W 3 Like an apricot[O] tree
among the trees
of the forest,
so is my love
among the young men.
I delight to sit in his shade,
and his fruit is sweet
to my taste.
4 He brought me
to the banquet hall,[P]
and he looked on me
with love.[Q]
5 Sustain me with raisins;
refresh me with apricots,[R]
for I am lovesick.
6 His left hand is
under my head,
and his right arm
embraces me.[S]
7 Young women of Jerusalem,
I charge you
by the gazelles
and the wild does
of the field:
do not stir up or awaken love
until the appropriate time.[T]

[A]**1:6** Lit *my vineyard, which is mine* [B]**1:7** Or *who wanders* [C]**1:7** To express shame or grief, or to conceal identity as a prostitute would; Gn 38:14-15 [D]**1:8** Some understand the young women to be the speakers in this verse. [E]**1:8** Lit *go out for yourself into* [F]**1:9** Lit *my* [G]**1:9** Pharaoh's chariot horses were stallions. [H]**1:12** Or *is at his table* [I]**1:12** Lit *nard* [J]**1:14** = Wellspring of the Young Goat [K]**1:17** Or *firs*, or *pines* [L]**2:1** Or *meadow saffron* [M]**2:1** Not the modern flower but a common wildflower in northern Israel [N]**2:1** Or *lotus* [O]**2:3** Or *apple* [P]**2:4** Lit *the house of wine* [Q]**2:4** Or *and his banner over me is love* [R]**2:5** Or *apples* [S]**2:6** Or *Let his left hand be under . . . and his right arm embrace me* [T]**2:7** Lit *until it pleases*

>WORD|*study*

2:4 And he looked on me with love is literally translated, "and his banner (Hb *degel*, "large military standard"; cp. Nm 1:52) over me is love" (Hb *ʾahavah*, "the love properly expressed between husband and wife" in this context, Sg 2:4-5; cp. 5:8; 8:6-7; cp. Gn 29:20). The king cared for the Shulammite as if she sat under a great banner. In that time, banners were used by the military to give direction, protection, and purpose to the troops. They were a vital part of military strategy. The Shulammite was proud to be associated with Solomon and secure in his care for her; she felt as if she were overshadowed by a magnificent banner.

2:12-14 Two specific birds are included in these verses. The **turtledove** (Hb *tor*; cp. Gn 15:9; Lv 1:14; 12:6-8; Jr 8:7) in this context symbolized purity and fidelity because a male and female typically mate for life. Turtledoves migrate and return in the spring. In the Song, the **dove** (Hb *yonah*) appears frequently as a term of endearment (5:2) and a source of imagery. Solomon compares the beautiful eyes of his bride to those of the dove (1:15; 4:1; 5:12). In this passage, he describes her being out of reach (perhaps "playing hard to get") in terms of the rock dove's pattern of nesting in cliffs (2:12; cp. Ps 55:6; Jr 48:28).

The Approach of Solomon (2:8-9)

8 Listen! My love
is approaching.
Look! Here he comes,
leaping over the mountains,
bounding over the hills.
9 My love is like a gazelle
or a young stag.
Look, he is standing
behind our wall,
gazing through the windows,
peering through the lattice.

The Invitation from Solomon (2:10-14)

10 My love calls to me:

M Arise, my darling.
Come away, my beautiful one.
11 For now the winter is past;
the rain has ended
and gone away.
12 The blossoms appear
in the countryside.
The time of singing[A]
has come,
and the turtledove's cooing
is heard in our land.
13 The fig tree ripens its figs;
the blossoming vines give off
their fragrance.
Arise, my darling.
Come away, my beautiful one.

14 My dove, in the clefts
of the rock,
in the crevices of the cliff,
let me see your face,[B]
let me hear your voice;
for your voice is sweet,
and your face is lovely.

The Expression of Mutual Love (2:15-17) (W)

15 Catch the foxes for us—
the little foxes that ruin
the vineyards—
for our vineyards are
in bloom.
W 16 My love is mine and I am his;
he feeds among the lilies.
17 Before the day breaks[C]
and the shadows flee,
turn to me, my love, and be
like a gazelle
or a young stag
on the divided mountains.[D]

The Thoughts of the Shulammite (3:1-5)

3 In my bed at night[E]
I sought the one I love;
I sought him, but did not
find him.[F]
2 I will arise now and go
about the city,
through the streets
and the plazas.
I will seek the one I love.
I sought him, but did not
find him.
3 The guards who go
about the city found me.
I asked them, "Have you seen
the one I love?"
4 I had just passed them
when I found the one I love.
I held on to him
and would not let him go
until I brought him
to my mother's house—
to the chamber of the one
who conceived me.
5 Young women of Jerusalem,
I charge you

[A]2:12 Or *pruning* [B]2:14 Or *form* [C]2:17 Lit *breathes* [D]2:17 Or *the Bether mountains*, or *the mountains of spices*; Hb obscure [E]3:1 Or *bed night after night* [F]3:1 LXX adds *I called him, but he did not answer me*

would excite them, so would the effect be of such a beautiful woman as she in a group of men. Solomon lovingly compared her to the best of the best. He noted the beauty of her face and even commented on the accessories she chose to enhance her appearance. Solomon promised to continue giving her costly **jewelry** to enhance her natural beauty.

1:12-14 Both parties often compared their **love** and affection to perfumes, ointments, and the **fragrance** of these. The book itself lists more than 20 references to nature that would be pleasing to the senses. They viewed their love as springtime and compared it to such excess as that produced by **En-gedi**, a freshwater spring used to produce many perfumes and considered ideal for growing fragrant plants.

2:1-4 Sharon is a fertile plain located between Mount Carmel (north) and Joppa (south) along the coast of the Mediterranean Sea (cp. 1Ch 5:16; 27:29; Is 33:9; 35:2; Ac 9:35). Solomon picked up the flower imagery she used but by imagining a **lily** in a different setting extolled her beauty. In his eyes, she was the opposite of common; rather, he regarded his **darling** (Hb *raʿyah*; see 1:8-11) as such an extraordinary woman that all others, by comparison, were like unsightly and undesirable **thorns**. The Shulammite responded to this adulation by comparing him, in similar fashion, to a choice fruit-bearing tree.

2:5-7 The foods mentioned were considered aphrodisiacs. While the Shulammite might have been referring to literal food eaten at the banquet, apparently she was also expressing her overwhelming desire for Solomon and even the desperation of love she felt for him. The loving expression of total comfort and pleasure was found in the strong protection of her lover's arms.

In Hebrew, the phrase **young women** [Hb *bat*, lit "daughters"] **of Jerusalem** is the same as in 1:5 (cp. 3:5,10-11; 5:8,16; 8:4). **Do not stir up or awaken love until the appropriate time** (cp. 3:5; 8:4) is considered a charge for sexual purity before marriage and fidelity within marriage.

2:15 This couple wisely compared their love to **vineyards**, which could have provision, sustenance, pleasure, and satisfaction only if tended with care. A neglected and unprotected vineyard is easily destroyed. Just as **foxes** could quickly ruin a vineyard so various problems could attack their relationship. They made the commitment to address problems rather than ignore them. They were willing to take risks and gently confronted challenges in order to prune their relationship and allow it to thrive. They realized their love was tender and would require work for preservation.

3:1-5 These verses probably indicate a dream or recurring thoughts that the

Shulammite had before the wedding ceremony, which seems to be the subject of verses 6-11.

In her dream, the Shulammite was startled by the absence of Solomon; it was incredibly distressing to her—so upsetting that she immediately began looking for him, eager to find him and certainly desperate when considering life without him. She searched far and wide, imploring the help of others. Instead of calling Solomon's name, she identified him as **the one I love**.

Although the phrasing seems odd to modern readers, bringing her husband to the bedroom of her mother was an indication of family acceptance and unity. It carried symbolic importance and proved to be a place of comfort for her and for Solomon, so much so that she did not want anyone or anything to disturb that time. She also viewed this choice as a one-time decision and one that should be carefully considered, not awakened **until the appropriate time**. The act of physical intimacy marked an important time for the couple and a milestone in life. This idea stands in contrast to the modern belief that sex is a mere animal instinct and that its exclusive intimacy is not worth preserving or protecting.

3:6-11 These verses describe the **wedding** processional bringing the Shulammite from a distance. This occasion was magnificent and implored the use of extravagance, indicating the importance of the event.

The bride was protected by an entourage of **the mighty** [Hb *gibbor*, "strong, brave man"; cp. 4:4; Jos 6:2; 2Sm 10:7] **of Israel**.

Not only had the king provided for his bride's transportation and honored entrance among the people of Jerusalem, but he had also prepared himself for the wedding day. He, too, proceeded through the city on a royal **sedan chair** (Hb *'appiryon*, "litter, palanquin"), opulently designed and decorated. The queen mother placed on his head a ceremonial **crown**, probably made of a garland of flowers similar to what most grooms would have worn for such occasions. All the effort and ceremony of the day were a reflection of the joy in Solomon's heart.

4:1-3 Chapter 4 seems to describe the couple's wedding night. Affirming his bride's beauty, Solomon first notes her wedding **veil** attracting attention to her eyes. The Shulammite must have had long shiny, slightly curly black hair, which could be compared in a complimentary way to flocks of valuable black **goats** that lived in a chain of mountains called **Mount Gilead** and could often be seen descending. Solomon's compliment of his bride's **teeth** emphasizes that she had a wonderful smile. He continued complimenting the features of her face, noting that her **mouth**, or her speech, was **lovely**. Not only did he shower her with compliments about her outward appearance, but he also noted her

The Daughters of Jerusalem

This phrase also translated "young women of Jerusalem," has been variously understood to identify friends of the bride, women of the royal court of Israel, or an audience for the Shulammite and the king. Yet, if their interactions with the Shulammite are examined from the perspective of a modern bride, the portrait of a bridesmaid emerges.

The friends rejoice.	We are happy for you (1:4).
The bride worries.	I hope he will find me attractive (1:5).
The bride advises.	Wait for the right man at the right time—love is painful when you awaken it too soon (3:5; 8:4).
The friends show their love.	They worked to make the sedan chair beautiful (3:10).
The friends admire the groom.	Come see the groom (3:11).
The friends were messengers.	If you see him, tell him I miss him (5:8).
The bride confides.	He is sweet, desirable, and I love him (5:16).

This phrase is used one other place in Scripture—by Jesus (Lk 23:28). In this reference, the daughters of Jerusalem are still watching the king, but the bridal procession has become the road to the cross, and rejoicing has turned to mourning.

by the gazelles
and the wild does
of the field:
do not stir up or awaken love
until the appropriate time.[A]

The Building of Love: Commitment (3:6–6:10)

The Wedding (3:6-11)

N 6 What is this coming up
from the wilderness
like columns of smoke,
scented with myrrh
and frankincense
from every fragrant powder
of the merchant?
7 It is Solomon's royal litter[B]
surrounded by 60 warriors
from the mighty of Israel.
8 All of them are skilled
with swords
and trained in warfare.
Each has his sword at his side
to guard against the terror
of the night.
9 King Solomon made
a sedan chair[C] for himself
with wood from Lebanon.
10 He made its posts of silver,
its back[D] of gold,
and its seat of purple.
Its interior is inlaid with love[E]
by the young women
of Jerusalem.
11 Come out, young women
of •Zion,
and gaze at King Solomon,
wearing the crown
his mother placed on him
the day of his wedding—
the day of his heart's rejoicing.

The Honeymoon (4:1-7)

M
4 How beautiful you are,
my darling.
How very beautiful!

[A]3:5 Lit *until it pleases* [B]3:7 A conveyance carried on the shoulders of servants [C]3:9 In Hb, the term sedan chair is possibly a synonym for "litter"; it is also called a palanquin. [D]3:10 Or *base*, or *canopy* [E]3:10 Or *leather*

>WORD | *study*

4:8-9 Oddly, he called his bride my sister (Hb *'achot*, applied here in a wider sense as a term of endearment; cp. v. 12; 5:1). The Hebrew meaning of the word can indicate not only a sibling but also a person who has a very close and lasting relationship, such as a bride (Hb *kallah*; implying beauty of dress and appearance).

Behind your veil,
your eyes are doves.
Your hair is like a flock
of goats
streaming down
Mount Gilead.
2 Your teeth are like a flock
of newly shorn sheep
coming up from washing,
each one having a twin,
and not one missing.[A]
3 Your lips are
like a scarlet cord,
and your mouth[B] is lovely.
Behind your veil,
your brow[C] is like a slice
of pomegranate.
4 Your neck is like the tower
of David,
constructed in layers.
A thousand bucklers are hung
on it—
all of them shields
of warriors.[D]
5 Your breasts are
like two fawns,
twins of a gazelle, that feed
among the lilies.
6 Before the day breaks[E]
and the shadows flee,
I will make my way
to the mountain of myrrh
and the hill of frankincense.
7 You are absolutely beautiful,
my darling,
with no imperfection in you.

The Realization of Passion (4:8-16)

8 Come with me
from Lebanon,[F] my bride—
with me from Lebanon!
Descend from the peak
of Amana,
from the summit of Senir
and Hermon,
from the dens of the lions,
from the mountains
of the leopards.
9 You have captured my heart,
my sister,[G] my bride.
You have captured
my heart with one glance
of your eyes,
with one jewel
of your necklace.
10 How delightful your love is,
my sister, my bride.
Your love is much better
than wine,
and the fragrance
of your perfume
than any balsam.
11 Your lips drip sweetness like
the honeycomb, my bride.
Honey and milk are
under your tongue.
The fragrance
of your garments is like
the fragrance of Lebanon.

12 My sister, my bride, you are
a locked garden—
a locked garden[H]
and a sealed spring.
13 Your branches are a paradise[I]
of pomegranates
with choicest fruits,
henna with nard—
14 nard and saffron, calamus
and cinnamon,
with all the trees
of frankincense,
myrrh and aloes,
with all the best spices.
15 You are a garden spring,
a well of flowing water
streaming from Lebanon.

W 16 Awaken, north wind—
come, south wind.
Blow on my garden,
and spread the fragrance
of its spices.
Let my love come
to his garden
and eat its choicest fruits.

The Celebration in Love (5:1)

M

5 I have come
to my garden—my sister,
my bride.
I gather[J] my myrrh
with my spices.
I eat my honeycomb
with my honey.
I drink my wine
with my milk.

N Eat, friends!
Drink, be intoxicated
with love![K]

[A]4:2 Lit *and no one bereaved among them* [B]4:3 Or *speech* [C]4:3 Or *temple*, or *cheek*, or *lips* [D]4:4 Perhaps describing the woman's necklace [E]4:6 Lit *breathes* [F]4:8 In Hb, the word for Lebanon is similar to "frankincense" in Sg 4:6,14,15. [G]4:9 A term of endearment [H]4:12 Some Hb mss read *locked fountain* [I]4:13 Or *park*, or *orchard* [J]5:1 Lit *pluck* [K]5:1 Or *Drink your fill, lovers*

character and the carefulness of her speech. He appreciated both her outward appearance and her inward heart.

4:4-7 Citing her features from head to toe, Solomon identified the confident bearing and elegant beauty of his bride. Comparing her neck to **the tower of David**, Solomon noted the way her jewelry reminded him of the walls of the tower, which was used as an armory—the **bucklers** (i.e., richly ornamented **shields**) were hung there. He was carefully arousing her senses toward him. The **gazelle** symbolized feminine grace, and Solomon appreciated her perfect **breasts**—a compliment with which most women would be somewhat self-conscious, especially in a society where a woman's form was veiled and hidden (v. 5). The most tender and sensitive words appeared where Solomon not only repeated his admiration of her beauty and called her by an endearing name but also explained that she was perfect (v. 7).

4:8-11 The Shulammite was able to enthrall Solomon simply with a glance. The form of the Hebrew verb **captured** (Hb *lavav*) has the sense of "ravish" or even "wound or take away the heart," where the heart includes the mind and will. In colloquial English, he might have said, "The way you look at me blows my mind!" or "Your looking at me absolutely takes my breath away!"

Solomon's invitation to sexual intimacy reflects consideration of his bride. Rather than making demands of her, Solomon displays interest in her pleasure and comfort level as well as his own.

5:1 This verse shows the affirmation and enjoyment of the appropriate expression of conjugal love. Each statement expresses what Solomon does, and each object of his action includes the first person possessive (**my** in English). He speaks figuratively of gathering fragrant herbs and eating and drinking that which would bring consummate pleasure, poetically conveying his complete enjoyment of his bride.

5:2-8 To think that the perfect love and attention to each other continued flawlessly to the end of life would be wonderful indeed. However, this couple, like every other, experienced difficulty. One of their conflicts unfolds here as the Shulammite lay asleep in bed, already clean and comfortable, when Solomon came to her door desiring sexual intimacy. While she loved him deeply, she did not desire to be disturbed and inconvenienced. When she tried to make the situation right, the damage had already been done. Solomon was no longer near. Realizing the effects of her behavior and sensing his absence, the Shulammite was crushed and searched for him in deep distress. This frightening incident—perhaps a dream rather than actual experience—must have made her appreciate and long for Solomon all the more. Apparently the young bride was overcome with sorrow at her hurtful behavior and desired more than anything to be forgiven and restored (v. 8). This plight, together with her own personal longing, consumed her.

5:9 This extensive description of King Solomon also could have been part of the Shulammite's dream. In any case, since the bride had employed the help of the "young women of Jerusalem" (v. 8), they responded to her with a good question: What makes your lover different or more special than any other? Surely this questioning caused the bride to remember and recount why she loved her groom so deeply.

5:10-16 The Shulammite's description reveals her attraction to his physical appearance and strength. His head of **purest gold** may have referred to his wisdom and kingly position (v. 11). From head to foot she admired and loved him completely and was proud to claim him as her **love** and her **friend** (v. 16).

The First Conflict (5:2-8)

W 2 I sleep, but my heart is awake.
A sound! My love is knocking!

M Open to me, my sister,
my darling,
my dove, my perfect one.
For my head is drenched
with dew,
my hair with droplets
of the night.

W 3 I have taken off my clothing.
How can I put it back on?
I have washed my feet.
How can I get them dirty?
4 My love thrust his hand
through the opening,
and my feelings were stirred
for him.
5 I rose to open for my love.
My hands dripped with myrrh,
my fingers with flowing myrrh
on the handles of the bolt.
6 I opened to my love,
but my love had turned
and gone away.
I was crushed[A] that
he had left.[B]
I sought him, but did not
find him.
I called him, but he
did not answer.
7 The guards who go
about the city found me.
They beat and wounded me;
they took my cloak[C] from me—
the guardians of the walls.
8 Young women of Jerusalem,
I charge you:
if you find my love,
tell him that I am lovesick.

The Virtues of Solomon (5:9-16)

Y 9 What makes the one you love
better than another,
most beautiful of women?
What makes him better
than another,
that you would give us
this charge?

W 10 My love is fit and strong,[D]
notable among ten thousand.
11 His head is purest gold.
His hair is wavy[E]
and black as a raven.
12 His eyes are like doves
beside streams of water,
washed in milk
and set like jewels.[F]
13 His cheeks are like beds
of spice,
towers of[G] perfume.
His lips are lilies,
dripping with flowing myrrh.
14 His arms[H] are rods of gold
set[I] with topaz.[J]
His body[K] is an ivory panel
covered with sapphires.
15 His legs are alabaster pillars
set on pedestals of pure gold.
His presence is like Lebanon,
as majestic as the cedars.

[A]**5:6** Lit *My soul went out* [B]**5:6** Or *spoken* [C]**5:7** Or *veil*, or *shawl* [D]**5:10** Or *is radiant and ruddy* [E]**5:11** Or *is like palm leaves*; Hb obscure [F]**5:12** Lit *milk sitting in fullness* [G]**5:13** LXX, Vg read *spice, yielding* [H]**5:14** Lit *hands* [I]**5:14** Lit *filled*; Sg 5:2,12 [J]**5:14** Probably yellow topaz [K]**5:14** Lit *abdomen*

Biblical Womanhood Sexual Purity

Three images refer to the preservation of the woman's virginity until marriage (4:12):

- **a locked** [Hb *na'al*, "bolted shut, barred"] **garden** (Hb *gan*, "enclosed garden"), a place that has been intentionally planted and cultivated;
- **a locked garden** (Hb *gal*, "spring"); and
- **a sealed** [Hb *chatam*, "locked" and so noted with a seal] **spring** (Hb *ma'yan*, "fountain"; metaphorically, the "source of greatest joy, delight, pleasure," Ps 87:7).

Having deliberately protected and excluded all others from the delights of her sexuality, the bride is able freely to invite her beloved to **come to his garden**, for in marriage it belongs exclusively to him. **Choicest** (Hb *meged*) denotes "something very precious or noble" (4:16; cp. 7:13).

Valuing and preserving virginity—by the woman herself as well as by her family and community—reflect God's design, and women who look forward to sex to be enjoyed exclusively in marriage and who carefully guard their purity as an after-the-wedding gift to their husbands as well as a lifestyle of obedience to God should be held in esteem. Nevertheless, the ideal fulfillment of God's intention as presented here and throughout the Song should be upheld without failing to recognize that God's perfect love and grace are sufficient for every woman whose experience or past choices make that ideal impossible. In any case, God is in the business of redeeming, restoring, and healing what has been lost, broken, or stolen—including the goodness of His gift of sexuality.

16 His mouth is sweetness.
He is absolutely desirable.
This is my love, and this is
my friend,
young women of Jerusalem.

The Path to Restoration (6:1-3)

Y

6 Where has your love gone,
most beautiful of women?
Which way has he[A] turned?
We will seek him with you.

W 2 My love has gone down
to his garden,
to beds of spice,
to feed in the gardens
and gather lilies.
3 I am my love's and my love
is mine;
he feeds among the lilies.

The Words of Sweet Forgiveness (6:4-10)

M 4 You are as beautiful
as Tirzah,[B] my darling,
lovely as Jerusalem,
awe-inspiring as an army
with banners.
5 Turn your eyes away from me,
for they captivate me.
Your hair is like a flock
of goats
streaming down from Gilead.
6 Your teeth are like a flock
of ewes
coming up from washing,
each one having a twin,
and not one missing.[C]
7 Behind your veil,
your brow[D] is like a slice
of pomegranate.
8 There are 60 queens
and 80 concubines
and young women[E]
without number.
9 But my dove,
my virtuous one, is unique;
she is the favorite
of her mother,
perfect to the one who gave
her birth.
Women see her and declare
her fortunate;
queens and concubines also,
and they sing her praises:

Y[F]

10 Who is this[G] who shines
like the dawn—
as beautiful as the moon,
bright as the sun,
awe-inspiring as an army
with banners?

The Growing of Love: Faithfulness (6:11–8:14)

A Complete Restoration (6:11-13)

W 11 I came down
to the walnut grove
to see the blossoms
of the valley,
to see if the vines
were budding
and the
pomegranates blooming.
12 Before I knew it,
my desire put me
among the chariots of
my noble people.[H]

Y

13[I] Come back, come back,
Shulammite![J,K]
Come back, come back, that
we may look at you!

M Why are you looking
at the Shulammite,
as you look at the dance
of the two camps?[L]

Solomon's View of the Shulammite (7:1-8)

7 How beautiful are
your sandaled feet,
princess![M]
The curves of your thighs
are like jewelry,
the handiwork of a master.
2 Your navel is a rounded bowl;
it never lacks mixed wine.
Your waist[N] is a mound
of wheat
surrounded by lilies.
3 Your breasts are
like two fawns,
twins of a gazelle.

6:1-3 Again the Shulammite uses the imagery of a **garden** to refer to the reconciliation that culminates in the mutual enjoyment of sexual intimacy. She had the assurance that came with unconditional love and true marital commitment. She again expressed confidence in their union and an unchanging sense of their belonging to each other.

6:7-8 The listing of **60 queens** and **80 concubines** is probably a figurative device of comparison rather than a reference to Solomon's harem. Increasing or ascending numbers were used as a common poetic device, effectively saying here that no woman of any status was as perfect as his bride. There is no clear connection of these women to Solomon. Therefore, likely he was simply saying the Shulammite was better than all other women. Possibly these women were part of David's harem and thus passed to Solomon as part of the royal court, which would not necessarily make them part of Solomon's official harem.

6:9-10 Solomon does call the Shulammite his **virtuous one**, which would seem exclusive. There seems to have been no competition between these other women and the Shulammite, which lends further evidence to the idea that they did not belong to Solomon as wives or concubines.

6:11-12 An interesting transformation was made by this ordinary maiden. She began in the story as someone with low self-esteem and personal doubts. After spending time with Solomon, she was significantly bolstered by his love and truly transformed into a highly desirable, beautiful, and sought-after woman—even when compared to the nation's finest women.

7:1-8 Solomon graphically describes sexual intimacy between him and his wife. The masculinity of the king and femininity of his chosen bride are presented as distinct natures and yet complementary in their intimate relationship. The contrasts served to enhance rather than diminish their love for each other.

7:1-8 Rather than beginning his compliments with her head, Solomon started at her **feet** and described parts of the body he alone would have seen. The Solomon described his wife in regal terms. Her **neck**, **eyes**, **nose**, and **head** symbolized not only outer beauty but also a stateliness of character and appearance (vv. 4-5). Her inward confidence and character caused her outward beauty to be even more distinguished. Nothing seems to have hampered their relationship. The king and his bride thoroughly enjoyed each other.

[A]**6:1** Lit *your love* [B]**6:4** = a mountain city in Manasseh [C]**6:6** Lit *and no one bereaved among them* [D]**6:7** Or *temple*, or *cheek*, or *lips* [E]**6:8** Or *and virgins*; Sg 1:3 [F]**6:10** Some see v. 10 as spoken by **M**. [G]**6:10** In Hb, the word for "this" is feminine. [H]**6:12** Or *of Amminadib*, or *of my people of a prince*; Hb obscure [I]**6:13** Sg 7:1 in Hb [J]**6:13** Or *the peaceable one* [K]**6:13** Perhaps an inhabitant of the town of Shunem, or a feminine form of Solomon's name [L]**6:13** Or *dance of Mahanaim* [M]**7:1** Lit *daughter of a nobleman* or *prince* [N]**7:2** Or *belly*

7:9-13 Fine wine symbolized the most abundant pleasures of life. The woman realized and was grateful for her husband's strong sexual desire for her. The couple reveled in the anticipation and exclusive fulfillment of the other's sexual desires. Verse 10 speaks to the exclusivity of the relationship between the two lovers, underscoring the commitment to a monogamous marriage. The Shulammite exclaimed that she wanted to be with him and for their lives to be intertwined. By mentioning **mandrakes** (v. 13), which were used as an aphrodisiac, the Shulammite was letting Solomon know that she desired his physical intimacy.

8:1-4 Although the Shulammite wanted to express her love openly and at any time, societal rules strictly prohibited such open displays of affection. Again she used the expression **the house of my mother** (v. 2) to refer to approval of their marriage and to the expectation that they would continue to propagate the family line.

8:5 The young women began this section by acknowledging the love and unity of Solomon and his bride, who came **from the wilderness leaning on** each other as if they were the same person. The **apricot tree** could have marked the boundary of the Shulammite's home, and perhaps she experienced her first love at the site of her birth.

8:6-7 The Shulammite asked to be set as **a seal** on the **heart** and **arm** of Solomon. The royal seal marked what belonged exclusively to Solomon. The seal on the heart was a reminder to both that their affections must be only for each other, and the seal on the arm was a sign

4 Your neck is like a tower
of ivory,
your eyes like pools
in Heshbon
by the gate of Bath-rabbim.
Your nose is like the tower
of Lebanon
looking toward Damascus.
5 Your head crowns you[A]
like Mount Carmel,
the hair of your head
like purple cloth—
a king could be held captive
in your tresses.
6 How beautiful you are
and how pleasant,
my love, with such delights!
7 Your stature is
like a palm tree;
your breasts are clusters
of fruit.
8 I said, "I will climb
the palm tree
and take hold of its fruit."
May your breasts be
like clusters of grapes,
and the fragrance
of your breath like apricots.

The Expression of Deeper Love (7:9-13)

9 Your mouth[B] is
like fine wine—
W flowing smoothly for my love,
gliding past my lips
and teeth![C]
10 I belong to my love,
and his desire is for me.
11 Come, my love,
let's go to the field;
let's spend the night among
the henna blossoms.[D]
12 Let's go early to the vineyards;
let's see if the vine
has budded,
if the blossom has opened,
if the pomegranates are
in bloom.
There I will give you my love.
13 The mandrakes give off
a fragrance,
and at our doors is
every delicacy—
new as well as old.
I have treasured them up
for you, my love.

The Longing for Affection (8:1-4)

8 If only I could treat you
like my brother,[E]
one who nursed
at my mother's breasts,
I would find you in public
and kiss you,
and no one would scorn me.
2 I would lead you,
I would take you,

[A]7:5 Lit *head upon you is* [B]7:9 Lit *palate* [C]7:9 LXX, Syr, Vg; MT reads *past lips of sleepers* [D]7:11 Or *the villages* [E]8:1 Lit *Would that you were like a brother to me* [F]8:2 LXX adds *and into the chamber of the one who bore me*

HARD QUESTION

Does the Bible affirm an "anything goes" approach to sexual expression within the bounds of marriage?

The answer becomes clear when you consider what the whole of Scripture says in response to various questions that impinge upon this topic:

- *How does God define "marriage"?* Marriage unites one man with one woman for life. It is a permanent, heterosexual union. Sexual activities involving anyone other than the husband and wife, who are married to each other, are illicit.
- *What purpose does sexual expression serve in marriage?* Song of Songs affirms that God created sexual intimacy to be pleasurable to both the husband and the wife. Procreation is one of its purposes. Another is that sexual intimacy physically enacts the spiritual and legal covenant uniting the man and woman as husband and wife; it gives physical expression to the couple's spiritual, emotional, and relational intimacy. Consequently, both husband and wife should discuss whether or not the form of sexual expression being considered helps or hinders these purposes for marriage.
- *What motive(s) underlie this question in regard to specific sexual activities? Is the motivation in any way addressed by Scripture?* For example, if either spouse recognizes that the motivation for engaging in a particular activity is to fulfill a lust or satisfy a curiosity generated by exposure to pornography, that activity is not justifiable. Sex is not merely a physical act but one that involves a person's entire being—the mind, will, and emotions. As exclusive and private as it is intended to be, God is always the audience, and what the husband and wife do with, for, and to each other affects people outside that intimate union. Sexual intercourse fleshes out the husband and wife's esteem and consideration (or lack thereof) for each other.
- *Does the sexual activity communicate anything contrary to an attitude of holding your spouse in highest esteem?* Would either spouse feel degraded or used, for example? Even if there are no specific biblical prohibitions of the particular activity, the moral parameter in force is that of sacrificial, unconditional, Christ-like love that wants nothing less than God's best for your spouse. Treating each other with such love and respect demands patience with the other's physical limitations, process of healing from past wounds, and preferences.

This list of questions does not cover everything to be considered but does demonstrate that for sinful human beings, even those who follow Jesus Christ, there is no such thing as an "anything goes" marriage—sexually or otherwise. A husband and wife who are Christians are called to honor their respective spouses and, supremely, to honor Christ, particularly in the way they demonstrate love for each other, in every realm of their lives, including the privacy of the marriage bed.

Doctrine GOD'S LOVE

Song 8:6-7 draws attention to the truth that every human couple immersed in romantic love believes or at least hopes that love lasts forever. However, only one man's love has ever proved to be **as strong as death**, incapable of being swept away by the **mighty waters**—the love of Jesus Christ, God incarnate. The rapturous love exhibited in Song of Songs clearly exalts the physical and emotional aspects of human love enjoyed in the right context of marriage, which, as a metaphor of the relationship between God and His people, permeates Scripture. From the beginning, when He created man and woman in His image, to the end, when He finally eliminates every vestige of evil and consummates an eternal relationship with His "bride" (Rv 21:1-9), God's love establishes the intended pattern for marital love and enables human beings to live accordingly (Eph 5:1-3,25-30; 1Jn 3:14; 4:7-21).

to the house of my mother
who taught me.[F]
I would give you spiced wine
to drink
from my pomegranate juice.
3 His left hand is under my head,
and his right arm embraces me.
4 Young women of Jerusalem,
I charge you:
do not stir up or awaken love
until the appropriate time.

The Passion of Unrelenting Love (8:5-7)

Y 5 Who is this coming up
from the wilderness,
leaning on the one she loves?

W I awakened you under
the apricot tree.
There your mother
conceived you;
there she conceived and gave
you birth.
6 Set me as a seal on your heart,
as a seal on your arm.
For love is as strong as death;
ardent love is as unrelenting
as •Sheol.
Love's flames are fiery flames—
the fiercest of all.[A]
7 Mighty waters cannot
extinguish love;
rivers cannot sweep it away.
If a man were to give all
his wealth[B] for love,
it would be utterly scorned.

The Family's Role of Protection (8:8-12)

B 8 Our sister is young;
she has no breasts.
What will we do for our sister
on the day she is spoken for?
9 If she is a wall,
we will build a silver parapet
on it.
If she is a door,
we will enclose it
with cedar planks.[C]

W 10 I am[D] a wall
and my breasts like towers.
So in his eyes I have become
like one who finds peace.[E]
11 Solomon owned a vineyard
in Baal-hamon.
He leased the vineyard
to tenants.
Each was to bring
for his fruit
1,000 pieces of silver.
12 I have my own vineyard.[F]
The 1,000 are for you,
Solomon,
but 200 for those who guard
its fruits.

The Final Declaration of Love (8:13-14)

M 13 You[G] who dwell
in the gardens—
companions are listening
for your voice—
let me hear you!

W 14 Hurry to me, my love,
and be like a gazelle
or a young stag
on the mountains of spices.

[A]**8:6** Or *the blaze of the* LORD [B]**8:7** Lit *all the wealth of his house* [C]**8:8-9** Vv. 8-9 may record what the girl's brothers used to say. [D]**8:10** Or *was* [E]**8:10** In Hb, the word for peace sounds similar to Solomon and Shulammite. [F]**8:12** Lit *My vineyard, which is mine, is before me*; Sg 1:6 [G]**8:13** In Hb, the word for You is feminine.

that these lovers were off limits to others. The Shulammite did not want this seal to be broken because she understood the deep virtue in love and described it with great intensity. The seal was a precious and honorable identification, and this woman wanted the privileges and possession the seal provided.

The Shulammite compares their **love** to the unavoidable reality of **death** and to the most intense **flames** that totally consume and affect every aspect of life—so fierce that nothing could extinguish them. The wealthiest man could not afford to purchase true **love** (Hb *ʾahavah*, "the love properly expressed between husband and wife"; see 2:4-5), an intriguing statement given that Solomon was one of the wealthiest men in all of history. Asking for love as if it could be obtained with any amount of money cheapens the affection. True love can only be given as a free gift.

8:8-9 As mentioned previously, the sexual purity of a bride was of incredibly high value. Her virginity or the loss thereof affected the reputation of the family and the community. Not only was the father seen as an authority figure in the lives of his daughters, but brothers were also expected to protect and defend their sisters. Here, the brothers' affirmation of the purity of their sister is coupled with testimony to their accomplished duty of preserving her most valuable virtue and protecting her future.

These brothers watched the tendencies, spirit, and moral commitment of their sister before she was old enough to make significant choices. They wanted to determine if she was wise, obedient, and godly. If she chose to be a woman of character and remain morally pure until marriage, they would consider her a **wall** that was impregnable and thus deserving of honor and trust. If, however, she chose to be an easily opened **door**, allowing men to pass in and out, they would stand guard and confine her for her own protection.

8:10 The Shulammite proudly proclaimed that she chose wisely. She described herself as the impenetrable **wall**, even comparing her **breasts** to **towers** (i.e., out of reach).

8:11-12 The gift of purity offered by the Shulammite was incredibly valuable—so valuable, in fact, that she compared herself to a profitable **vineyard**, which had been tended by her family and was preserved for Solomon to bring him inestimable pleasure and benefit. She wanted his needs to be met by her, and she acknowledged the help of others in preparing her for a life partner.

8:13-14 Solomon and his wife express their desire for each other, continuing the poetic and playful repartee as each beckoned the other to the mutual pleasures of intimacy.

WRITTEN ON MY *Heart*

SONG OF SONGS . . . In the Song of Songs, God reveals that He affirms the goodness of sexual intimacy as He created it to be enjoyed. In response, may you embrace His view of your sexuality as part of His good design for you, despite whatever the enemy has done to undermine or overemphasize your appreciation of this aspect of who you are as His creation.

Imagery from Nature in Song of Songs

Animals	Plants and Plant Products	Rocks And Minerals
Flock (Hb *ʿēder*): • **of goats** (Hb *ʿēz*, "female goat," 4:1; 6:5); • **of newly shorn sheep** (4:2); • **of ewes** (Hb *rachēl*, "sheep," 6:6) **Flock** (Hb *tsoʾn*, collective noun for "sheep and/or goats," 1:8) Frequent allusions to shepherding reflect a predominantly agricultural economy, intertwining the expressions of love.	**Perfume** (Hb *shemen*, "ointment, spiced or scented oil," 1:3; 4:10) **Perfume** (Hb *nērd*, "nard, spikenard," 1:12; 4:13-14)—an expensive, imported ointment. The fragrance is derived from the aromatic rhizomes (thick, underground stems) of the plant (*Nardostachys jatamansi*), which is grown in the Himalayas of India, China, and Nepal. Also see Mk 14:3; Jn 12:3. **Perfume** (Hb *merqach*, "herbs or flowers with a sweet fragrance," 5:13)	**Gold** (Hb *zahav*, 1:11; 3:10; 5:14)—the common word for the precious metal **Purest gold** (Hb *paz*, 5:11,15)—fine gold that has been purified (cp. Ps 19:10; 19:127; Pr 8:19)
Goats (Hb *gediyah*, "young female goat," 1:8)	**Vineyards** (Hb *kerem*, 1:6,14; 2:15; 7:12; 8:11-12) **Blossoming vines** (Hb *gephen*, 2:13,15; 6:11; 7:8,12)—early stage of grape growth when blossoms are fragrant **Wine** (Hb *yayin*, 1:2,4; 4:10; 5:1; 7:2,9; 8:2) **Mixed wine** (Hb *mezeg*, 7:2) **Clusters** [Hb *ʾeshkol*, 7:7-8] **of grapes**	**Silver** (Hb *keseph*, 1:11; 3:10; 8:9,11)
Mare [Hb *susah*] **among Pharaoh's chariots** (1:9) Solomon imported the finest horses from Egypt. Although Egyptian chariots were drawn by stallions, an Arabian mare was likely the most cherished and beautifully decorated horse of the stables since the quality and value of the Arabian was linked to the purity of its lineage, which was traced through the mare.	**Myrrh** (Hb *mor*, 1:13; 3:6; 4:6,14; 5:1,5,13; cp. Ps 45:8; Pr 7:17)—highly prized aromatic oleo-gum-resin distilled from a stubby tree that grows in Arabia and north and east Africa. Its oil is a perfume fixative. Myrrh was also used as: • an ingredient in holy anointing oil (Ex 30:23); • an element of Esther's "beauty treatments" or purification (Est 2:12); • an analgesic (Mk 15:23); • one of the fragrant materials encasing the body in a burial shroud (Jn 19:39).	**Topaz** (Hb *tarshish*, "beryl," a family of gemstones occurring in a variety of colors including aquamarine and golden beryls, 5:14; Ex 28:20; Ezk 1:16; 10:9; 28:13; Dn 10:6; Rv 21:20; LXX *tharseis*, "chrysolite, golden stone," a translucent, yellow crystal)—often translated as "gems or jewels" because the precise identification of the stone is uncertain. The Hebrew word may refer to the source as Tartessos, a harbor city on the southwest coast of Spain, which, during Solomon's reign, was known for trade with the Phoenicians and is likely identical to Tarshish (see 1Kg 22:48; 2Ch 9:20-21; Ezk 27:12).
Doves (Hb *yonah*): • Comparisons appeal to the dove's beauty and softness (1:15; 4:1; 5:12); • "Rock dove," which hides and nests in hard-to-reach places (2:14; cp. Jr 48:28); • Term of endearment signifying innocence and purity (5:2; 6:9). **Turtledove's** [Hb *tor*, 2:12] **cooing**, which signaled the beginning of the migratory bird's pattern of nesting and claiming territory and therefore heralded the return of spring.	**Henna** (Hb *kopher*, 1:14; 4:13). A paste made from the leaves of this tall shrub were used for hair and nail coloring. Persians used it to dye the hooves and manes of their horses. **Henna blossoms** (Hb *kaphar*, "villages," 7:11)	**Ivory** (Hb *shēn*, 5:14; 7:4; "teeth," 4:2; 6:6; cp. 1Kg 10:18,22; Ps 45:8; Ezk 27:6,15; Am 3:15; 6:4). Ivory, a white carving material produced from elephant tusks, is a mark of wealth and luxury. The imported ivory used by Solomon and other kings of Israel was probably derived from Syrian elephants, which roamed the upper Euphrates and India.

Imagery from Nature in Song of Songs continued

Animals	Plants and Plant Products	Rocks And Minerals
Gazelle (Hb *tsevi*, from 2:7,9,17; 3:5; 8:14)—a symbol of graceful beauty and speed **Fawns** [Hb ʿ*opher*] **. . . of a gazelle** (Hb *tseviyah*, "doe, female gazelle," 4:5; 7:3)	**Cedars** (Hb ʾ*erez*, 1:17; 5:15; 8:9; cp. 1Kg 6:14-38). These majestic coniferous trees, for which Lebanon is famous, grow to 140 feet with a 40-foot girth. The aromatic **wood from Lebanon** (3:9) is esteemed for being lightweight, free from knots, durable, and insect-resistant.	**Sapphires** (5:14; cp. Ex 24:10; 28:18; Ezk 1:26; 10:1; 28:13), an ancient name for lapis lazuli—a deep blue (azure) stone often flecked with shiny gold-colored pyrite (cp. Jb 28:6). An exceedingly precious stone in antiquity, lapis lazuli was imported from India and Afghanistan's Badakshan mines on the north side of the Hindu Kush, the mountain range between modern Afghanistan and Pakistan.
Wild does (Hb ʾ*ayalah*, "female roe deer," 2:7; 3:5) **Young stag** (Hb, ʾ*ayyal*, "roe deer," 2:9,17; 8:14) now extinct but once common on Mount Carmel	**Cypresses** (Hb *berot*,1:17; cp. 1Kg 6:14-38)—evergreen fir or juniper trees, symbolizing the desert's fertility. The wood was used for buildings (2Ch 2:8), ships (Ezk 27:6), and musical instruments (2 Sm 6:5).	**Alabaster** (Hb *shēsh*, "white" marble, 5:15; cp. Est 1:6; 1Ch 29:2)—a close-grained crystalline limestone that was probably white or cream-colored and possibly veined with red or green. It was used for fine statuary and may have been the famed "Parian marble" from the Greek island of Paros.
Foxes (Hb *shu*ʿ*al*, 2:15)—small burrowing canine, possibly a reference to jackals	**Rose** [Hb *chavatstselet*] **of Sharon** (2:1; cp. Is 35:1)—a common wildflower abundant in the plain of Sharon; possibly a meadow saffron with a sweet fragrance like a tulip	
Lions (Hb ʾ*ari*, 4:8)—represented danger lurking in the mountains of Lebanon (cp. Jb 38:39-40; Am 3:4; Nah 2:12).	**Lily** (Hb *shushan*, 2:1-2,16; 4:5; 5:13; 6:2-3; 7:2)—possibly a type of lotus or hyacinth akin to the red anemone; the "madonna lily" is plentiful in Palestine.	
Leopards (Hb *namēr*, 4:8)—a swift predator stalking the mountains of Lebanon (cp. Hs 13:7; Hab 1:8)	**Thorns** (Hb *choach*, 2:2)	
Raven (Hb ʿ*orēv*, 5:11)—sleek black bird	**Apricot tree** (Hb *tappuach*, 2:3; 8:5)—or apple tree; symbol of strength, fragrance, and sweetness **Apricots** (Hb *tappuach*, 2:5; 7:8)	
	Blossoms (Hb *nitstsan*, "flower," 2:12)—wildflowers appearing after the spring rains	
	Raisins (Hb ʾ*ashishah*, 2:5; cp. 2Sm 6:19)—raisin cakes made from grapes pressed together and dried, not baked	
	Fig tree (Hb *te*ʾ*ēnah*, 2:13). **Figs** (Hb *pag*, "green or unripe figs," 2:13), which ripen at various times from August onward, some remaining on the tree through the winter	

Imagery from Nature in Song of Songs continued

Animals	Plants and Plant Products	Rocks And Minerals
	Frankincense (Hb *levonah*, 3:6; 4:6,14). A clear aromatic resin from incisions in the tree's bark hardens into small yellow beads with a strong fragrance. See Ex 30:34-38; Mt 2:11.	
	Pomegranate (Hb *rimmon*, 4:3,13; 6:7,11; 7:12; 8:2; cp. Ex 28:33-34; Dt 8:8)—apple-shaped fruit with thin, hard skin and tart, deeply rose-red pulp **A paradise** [Hb *pardēs*, "garden, plantation," specifically one surrounding a Persian king's palace as an ornamental garden or orchard and habitat for his animals] **of pomegranates** (Sg 4:13).	
	Balsam (Hb *besem*, "spice, perfume, pleasant fragrance," 4:10,14,16; 5:13; 6:2; 8:14; cp. Ex 25:6; 1Kg 10:2; Is 3:24; Ezk 27:22) may refer to the aromatic oil produced from the balsam tree native to southern Arabia. En-gedi became a renowned center of balsam cultivation.	
	Honeycomb (Hb *nophet*, literally, "a dropping down," as of honey from the comb, 4:11; cp. Pr 5:3) **Honey** (Hb *devash*, Sg 4:11; 5:1)	
	Milk (Hb *chalav*, 4:11; 5:1)	
	Saffron (Hb *karkom*, 4:14)—dried, orange-yellow stigma of the autumn crocus (*Crocus sativus*). It produces a unique aroma and orange dye and is used medicinally and as a seasoning.	
	Calamus (Hb *qaneh*, 4:14; cp. Ex 30:23; "aromatic cane," Is 43:24; Ezk 27:19; "sweet cane from a distant land," Jr 6:20)—aromatic reed grown in marshes in India, commonly known as "sweet flag." Its leaves and roots, when crushed, have a cinnamon-like scent.	
	Cinnamon (Hb *qinnamon*, 4:14; cp. Ex 30:23; Pr 7:17)—highly valued spice, particularly for its fragrant oil. The plant's bark yields cinnamon sticks and the ground spice.	

Imagery from Nature in Song of Songs continued

Animals	Plants and Plant Products	Rocks And Minerals
	Aloes (Hb *ʾahalim*, 4:14; cp. Nm 24:6; Ps 45:8; Pr 7:17) or agar wood, likely from northern India, which produces valuable aromatic resin when infected with a rare mold	
	Walnut grove (Hb *ginnah*, "garden"; cp. Est 1:5; 7:7-8) with *ʾegoz*, "nuts," a *hapax* or word used only here in the OT, 6:11) —probably a shady orchard of walnut trees, imported from Persia	
	Palm tree (Hb *tamar*, 7:7-8)—stately tree found in oases. The Judean date palm was a symbol of ancient Israel. Its fruit was used medicinally and as an aphrodisiac. *Hazazon-tamar* (Hb, "city of palm trees," Gn 14:7; 2Ch 20:2) was another name for En-gedi (Sg 1:14).	
	Mandrakes (Hb *dudaʾim*, "love-producing," 7:13; cp. Gn 30:14-16) grew abundantly in Palestine and were used as an aphrodisiac. The low-growing plant has glossy, dark green leaves; a thick, forked root; and purplish flowers that give way to bright red, sweet-smelling fruit the size of a small apple.	

Isaiah

Timeline	740 BC	734–732 BC	732 BC	722 BC	715–701 BC
World Events / Biblical Events	Death of King Uzziah of Judah; call of Isaiah to be a prophet	Tiglath-pileser III's invasions of Israel	Fall of Damascus	Fall of Samaria	Initiation of reforms in Judah by King Hezekiah of Judah

"There is no other God but Me, a righteous God and Savior; . . . . turn to Me and be saved, all the ends of the earth. For I am God, and there is no other" (45:21-22).

Who wrote Isaiah?

This book has sparked much debate regarding a unified or diverse authorship, but significant reasons point to the eighth-century prophet Isaiah's unified authorship of the book (1:1; 2:1; 7:1, etc). First, only one author is mentioned—Isaiah the son of Amoz. Second, the prophecies of the first part of the book give support and validation to the claims and future prophecies of the second part (44:7-8). Third, linguistic and stylistic differences are normal, given the prophet's ministry of four decades. Fourth, there are evidences of the same hand at work throughout the book. For example, the name "The Holy One of Israel" is distinctive and found more frequently in Isaiah than in any other book. Fifth, the Great Isaiah Scroll, the earliest copy of the whole book, shows no discernible break among the "sections" suggested by critical scholars (chaps. 1–39, 40–54, 55–66). In fact, the first line of chapter 40 starts as the last line at the bottom of a scroll in natural continuance from the previous verse. This seems to indicate clearly that Isaiah was circulated as a unity rather than as multiple sections that were turned into one book later. Finally, Jesus and the New Testament writers quoted from each "section" of Isaiah, and authorship is specifically attributed to Isaiah (Mt 3:3; 4:14-16; 8:17; 12:17-21; 13:14-15; 15:7-9; Mk 7:6-8; Lk 3:4-6; 4:17-19; Jn 1:23; 12:38-41; Ac 8:28-34; 28:25-27; Rm 9:27-29).

Who were the recipients?

The initial audience was the nation of Judah, living in Jerusalem before the Babylonian conquest and exile (586 B.C.). In another sense, this work was written for every generation, including the time of the exile and beyond. Highly valued by first-century Jews, for next to Psalms, the book of Isaiah is the most frequently referenced Old Testament book in the New Testament.

When was Isaiah written?

Isaiah's work dates to the time between the last years of Uzziah (792–740 B.C.) through the reign of Hezekiah (729–686 B.C.). Since Sennacherib's death (681 B.C.) is referenced (37:37-38), perhaps Isaiah lived a few years under the sole reign of Manasseh (697–642 B.C.). Therefore, the date of the composition lies approximately between 740 and 700 B.C. Parts of the book were probably written at different times within this period, and Isaiah seemingly edited the whole before his death during the reign of Manasseh.

Where did it happen?

According to Isaiah 1:1, the original setting for the vision occurred during the days of four successive kings of Judah—from Uzziah (792–740 B.C.) through the time of Hezekiah (729–686 B.C., when Manasseh became sole ruler). During Isaiah's formative years, the nation of Judah saw a period of calm and prosperity, which had lulled the people into a misplaced sense of well-being and security. During the span of most of Uzziah's reign, the Assyrian kingdom was ruled by a series of ineffective kings who were preoccupied with enemies to the north and consequently were unable to maintain control of areas as far away as Israel and Judah. At the same time, Egypt was not a threat due to its own internal struggles. With both superpowers preoccupied, Israel and Judah had the chance to prosper unhindered. However, toward the end of Uzziah's reign, in 745 B.C., Tiglath-pileser III assumed the Assyrian throne. With his ascendancy to the Assyrian throne, the balance of power in the region dramatically changed. From that point on, Assyria became a looming threat, finally besieging Samaria and causing the collapse and exile of the northern kingdom in 722/21 B.C. under Shalmaneser V and his son Sargon II. Judah looked on with dismay, trusting in God's deliverance under Hezekiah (chaps. 36–37); however, under his son Manasseh, Judah made the same mistakes as Israel: trusting in alliances with other nations and acknowledging their gods rather than leaning on Yahweh alone. Eventually Judah also fell to the Babylonians in 586 B.C. and returned about 70 years later through the (human) agency of Cyrus the Persian in 539 B.C. Through His servant Isaiah, God had predicted this future event and specified His agent, Cyrus, long before (chaps. 44–45).

What is Isaiah about?

- *Salvation.* The book reflects the heartbeat of a holy God who so hates sin that He brings judgment, yet who so loves humanity that He brings a way of salvation available to all who will repent.
- *Particularity and universality.* In scope, Isaiah's prophecies are both particular (remnant) and universal (Gentiles) regarding sin (which must be judged and punished) and salvation (which is freely offered to repentant people). Judah, Israel, and the nations are all guilty of sin, but all can find a Savior in Yahweh.
- *Attributes of God.* The Uniqueness, Sovereignty and Holiness of the Savior ("Holy One of Israel"). Isaiah affirms throughout his prophecy that Yahweh alone is God: There is no one like Him, and any other so-called deity is categorically denounced as idolatrous. Yahweh's sovereignty applies not only to His dealings with Israel and Judah, but He also holds sway over all the nations of the world and performs the same acts of judgment and restoration equally. The nature of Yahweh as "set apart" and utterly unlike anything in the created universe places on creatures the obligation to worship Him.
- *The Suffering Servant.* The frequent and lyrical messianic passages promise both judgment and jubilation. While God is exalted and transcendent, He is nonetheless also immanent, present with His creatures

705–701 BC	705–701 BC	687 BC	642 BC
Judah's preparations for war against Assyria	King Hezekiah's reception of Merodach-baladan's envoys from Babylon	Death of King Hezekiah; beginning of Manasseh's reign over Judah	Death of Manasseh

and living in their midst as one of them (Immanuel, "God with Us," Is 7:14), suffering in order that "through His stripes" healing from sin and death would be available to all.

Why should women read Isaiah?

Isaiah affirms that the Lord is exalted, high and holy, the unique God who creates, makes covenants, and punishes rebellion, but He loves the rebel deeply and unwaveringly because she is His creation, the "work of His hands." Some definite themes resonate with women in addition to the astonishing acts of redemption God performs and the victorious work of the Suffering Servant; as well as from the lilting passages about the completing work of the Spirit of God in salvation and its availability to all nations—not just Israel. First, haughtiness expressed by self-exaltation and unmitigated pride is despised by the Lord and will be punished (3:16–4:1). The "diva," marked by pride, does not please God and will be condemned as were the "daughters of Jerusalem." Second, hypocrisy masking as piety is rejected by God (chaps. 1 and 58). Israel performed the outward rituals required by God, such as sacrifices, fasting, and festivals, but their hearts were far from God. They fulfilled the letter of the law and had the trappings of piety, but they did not understand or fulfill the spirit of the law and were then puzzled that their prayers went unanswered. Third, Isaiah used metaphors of marriage (covenant-making, 55:3) and divorce (covenant-breaking, chap. 50). Since divorce is growing to be as prevalent in the church as outside it, Isaiah's heavy emphasis on the importance of the covenant is paramount to helping the church understand this critical concept, especially as it applies to marriage. Portraying Himself as a wronged husband, God emphasized that even so, He was not divorcing His wife (chap. 50), only turning away from her for a time while His anger abated, leaving her to reap the consequences of her adultery (chap. 54). However, in His compassion and faithful love (Hb *chesed*), God does not completely break off the relationship but renews it and strengthens the covenant so that it is everlasting (55:3), grounded in and guaranteed by His own eternal nature. Finally, the book of Isaiah closes with a powerfully evocative maternal image, the new Jerusalem portrayed in Is 66 just as in Gl 4:26 as "our mother" (Paul then quotes Is 54:1). Jerusalem is restored, renewed, and comforted after the trials she has undergone, and she is now able to comfort and nourish the redeemed of Israel and every nation, who stream into her as her children, like a mother carrying, cuddling, and playing with her baby boy (66:7-13).

How do you read Isaiah?

Isaiah consists mainly of prophecy written in poetic verse, often with tight parallelism and brilliant imagery. Woven throughout the prophecies are various other genres. There are oracles of judgment against Judah as well as the surrounding nations (1:2–23:18), and there are oracles of salvation like those in 29:17-24 or 30:18-26. In addition, there are hymns (12:1-6; 38:10-20; 42:10-17), laments (26:7-21; 37:16:20; 63:7–64:12), words of wisdom (28:23-29), and various types of songs (5:1-7; 14:4-21; 27:2-6). The most conspicuous genre represented in Isaiah is a section of narrative history, written primarily in prose and located near the middle of the book in chapters 36–39, which serves as a transitional bridge to the entire work. The book begins with oracles of judgment (chaps. 1–5) against Israel, followed by a section called by some the "Book of Immanuel" (chaps. 6–12), containing Isaiah's prophetic call to ministry and various sign-acts he is asked to perform. Some of them involve his children and point to the Child. Two sections of judgment oracles follow, one section against the nations (chaps. 13–24) and the other against God's people (chaps. 25-35). A short prose section (chaps. 36–39) contains the narrative of the Assyrian invasion in Hezekiah's reign. The final two sections contain oracles of salvation for Israel (chaps. 40–54) and oracles of salvation for all nations as Isaiah looks forward to the messianic kingdom (chaps. 55–66). When reading Isaiah, one must bear in mind the idea of prophetic "double fulfillment," that is, many of Isaiah's prophecies were fulfilled both in His day *and* more fully in the Messiah. Additionally, his other prophecies may yet have a future eschatological fulfillment, as revealed to another prophet, the Apostle John, who penned the book of Revelation. The reader, then, is sometimes required to think on three different levels of fulfillment.

Outline

- I. The Case Against Judah (1:1–5:30)
- II. The Fate of Judah (6:1–12:6)
- III. Judgment and Salvation (13:1–35:10)
- IV. The Testing of Judah (36:1–39:8)
- V. Comfort for God's People (40:1–48:22)
- VI. The Salvation of the Lord (49:1–54:17)
- VII. The Call to Repentance (55:1–59:21)
- VIII. The Restoration Brought by the Lord (60:1–66:24)

The Sins of Judah (1:1-15)

1 The vision concerning Judah
and Jerusalem that Isaiah son of
Amoz saw during the reigns[A,B] of Uzziah, Jotham, Ahaz, and Hezekiah,
kings of Judah.

2 Listen, heavens,
and pay attention, earth,
for the LORD has spoken:
"I have raised children[C]
and brought them up,
but they have rebelled
against Me.
3 The ox knows its owner,
and the donkey its master's
feeding trough,
but Israel does not know;
My people do not understand."

4 Oh sinful nation,
people weighed down
with iniquity,
brood of evildoers,
depraved children![C]
They have abandoned the LORD;
they have despised
the Holy One of Israel;
they have turned their backs
on Him.

5 Why do you want
more beatings?
Why do you keep on rebelling?
The whole head is hurt,
and the whole heart is sick.
6 From the sole of the foot
even to the head,
no spot is uninjured—
wounds, welts,
and festering sores
not cleansed, bandaged,
or soothed with oil.

7 Your land is desolate,
your cities burned with fire;
foreigners devour your fields
before your very eyes—
a desolation demolished
by foreigners.
8 Daughter •Zion is abandoned
like a shelter in a vineyard,
like a shack
in a cucumber field,
like a besieged city.
9 If the LORD of •Hosts
had not left us a few survivors,
we would be like Sodom,
we would resemble Gomorrah.

10 Hear the word of the LORD,
you rulers of Sodom!
Listen to the instruction
of our God,
you people of Gomorrah!
11 "What are all your sacrifices
to Me?"
asks the LORD.
"I have had enough
of •burnt offerings and rams

[A]1:1 Lit *saw in the days* [B]1:1 ca 792–686 B.C. [C]1:2,4 Or *sons*

Title: The opening words of Isaiah serve as the Hebrew title for the book: "The Vision of Isaiah, the son of Amoz" (Hb *Chazon Yesha'yahu ben-'Amots*). Second Chronicles 32:32 provides a clear reference to the written work as the "Visions of the Prophet Isaiah, son of Amoz." Shortening the title to reflect only the name of the prophet, the name **Isaiah** (Hb, "Yahweh is salvation") is beautifully fitting as the book's title, which so majestically addresses that theme.

1:1 Verse 1 introduces the **vision** (Hb *chazon*, "revelatory vision granted by God, prophecy") of **Isaiah**, including many themes of the entire prophetic book. In this opening chapter, God clearly outlines the problem: Judah is sinful and under judgment. He calls for repentance and indicates that further judgment will occur; nevertheless, He will save a remnant.

1:2-4 The Lord initiates the trial of Judah by calling upon both the **heavens** and the **earth** to be witnesses (see Dt 17:6; 19:15; 30:19) concerning the shocking behavior of His **children** (Hb plural of *bēn*, "son, offspring, one belonging to a group"). Speaking as judge, prosecuting attorney, and father, Yahweh presents the charge—He had **raised** (Hb *gadal*, "bring up, rear, nurture, train") and **brought . . . up** (Hb *rum*, "raised, attended to needs and training") the people of Israel (i.e., His "children"), but they had **rebelled** (Hb *pasha'*, "revolt, transgress, sin, openly defy authority"; see **Word Study**, p. 924). The people of Judah owed their existence to God, not only as the creator of each individual but also as the founder of their nation Israel. At Mount Sinai, they had voluntarily entered into a covenant with responsibility for obeying the Lord (Dt 26:16–30:20). When the covenant was ratified before entering the land of Canaan, heaven and earth were called to be witnesses concerning the agreement (Dt 30:19). These original witnesses were thus called upon, as in a court of law, to testify to what Israel had committed to do.

1:3-6 The complete illogic of Israel's actions was illustrated by a comparison with how domesticated animals relate to their masters. Oxen and donkeys are not known for their intelligence, yet at least they recognize their owners and know who cares for them. By contrast, **Israel does not know** (Hb *yada'*, "possess information, have personal knowledge from experience," in this case regarding their Lord and their obligations to Him), nor do they **understand** (Hb *bin*, "observe, consider diligently, comprehend information") that the Lord has cared for them.

>WORD|*study*

1:4 Isaiah began by exclaiming **Oh!** (Hb *hoy*, "ah, alas, O, woe"). In the Old Testament this word occurs 52 times, 21 of which are in Isaiah. Except for one instance, *hoy* is used exclusively in prophetic books (1Kg 13:30). Most often it occurs before a warning regarding a judgment in the sense of "woe" (Is 1:24; 5:8,11,18,20-22; 10:1,5; 17:12; 18:1; 28:1; 29:1,15; 30:1; 31:1; 33:1; 45:9-10). Several usages seem to involve an expression of grief or sorrow, most of which directly refer to an individual's death. In a few cases, the word is used to grab attention with a sense of "O" or "Ho" (Is 55:1, KJV). The usage in Is 1:4 conveys a sense of grief and mourning over the rebellious condition of Israel.

1:4 Throughout the book of Isaiah, the prophet used the distinctive name **the Holy One of Israel** (Hb *qedosh yisra'ēl*) for the Lord. The phrase occurs a total of 26 times in Isaiah compared to only six times elsewhere in the Old Testament. It conveys the complete separateness and transcendence of God. For Isaiah the concept of God's holiness included His power and "otherness" as well as His purity and utter goodness (see Is 6:3). The Lord applied this characteristic to Himself and commanded that the children of Israel also adopt it. In Lv 19:2, He commands, "Be holy because I, Yahweh your God, am holy" (Lv 20:7; 1Pt 1:16). Although Israel was to be set apart and consecrated spiritually and morally as a sign of their relationship with their holy God, they had utterly failed. They had rejected the stipulations of the covenant and had rejected God Himself.

1:9 LORD of Hosts (Hb *Yahweh tseva'ot*) is read for *YHWH* (the personal name of God) of hosts. Before the exile, God's name was probably pronounced "Yahweh." After the exile, however, heightened reverence for God's name led the Jews to write it only as the "Tetragrammaton," or "four letters" of God's personal name (*YHWH*), and never to pronounce it, in order to maintain its sanctity. The vowels used by the Masoretic scribes when inserting vowel sounds in the name were the vowels for a different Hebrew word (*'adonay*, "my Lord, Master"), and this word is read in place of the unpronounced true name. *YHWH* ("He is") is the third person of the Hebrew "to be" verb *hayah* and is reflected in God's statement to Moses explaining His name, "I AM" (see Ex 3:14). The word for "hosts" is used throughout Scripture for heavenly and earthly armies as well as in the singular to refer to the sun, moon, and stars. The divine title, "LORD of Hosts," which appears over 250 times in the Old Testament, refers to the sovereignty of God in His control over all these armies and celestial bodies.

The Case Against Judah

Witnesses	Heavens and earth (Is 1:2; cp. Dt 17:6)
Plaintiff Judge	God (Is 1:2,18,24-26)
Defendant	Israel, specifically Judah and Jerusalem—both rulers and people (1:2,4,10)
Charges	• Rebellion (1:2,4) • Corruption (1:15,22-23) • Abandonment of the Lord (1:4,21,29)
Evidence	• Improper worship (1:10-15,29) • Lack of social justice (1:21-23)
Sentence	• Destruction—for the unrepentant (1:20,28-31) • Mercy—for a remnant who would repent (1:19,27)

and the fat of well-fed cattle;
I have no desire for the blood
of bulls,
lambs, or male goats.
12 When you come to appear
before Me,
who requires this from you—
this trampling of My courts?
13 Stop bringing useless offerings.
Your incense is detestable
to Me.
New Moons and Sabbaths,
and the calling
of solemn assemblies—
I cannot stand iniquity
with a festival.
14 I hate your New Moons
and prescribed festivals.
They have become a burden
to Me;
I am tired of putting up
with them.
15 When you lift up your hands
in prayer,
I will refuse to look at you;
even if you offer
countless prayers,
I will not listen.
Your hands are covered
with blood.

The Call to Repentance (1:16-20)

16 "Wash yourselves.
Cleanse yourselves.
Remove your evil deeds
from My sight.
Stop doing evil.
17 Learn to do what is good.
Seek justice.
Correct the oppressor.[A]
Defend the rights
of the fatherless.
Plead the widow's cause.
18 "Come, let us discuss this,"
says the LORD.
"Though your sins are
like scarlet,
they will be as white as snow;
though they are as red
as crimson,
they will be like wool.
19 If you are willing and obedient,
you will eat the good things
of the land.
20 But if you refuse and rebel,
you will be devoured
by the sword."
For the mouth of the LORD
has spoken.

The Sins of Jerusalem (1:21-23)

21 The faithful city—
what an adulteress[B]
she has become!
She was once full of justice.
Righteousness once dwelt
in her—
but now, murderers!
22 Your silver
has become dross,[C]
your beer[D] is diluted
with water.
23 Your rulers are rebels,
friends of thieves.

[A]1:17 Or *Aid the oppressed* [B]1:21 Or *prostitute* [C]1:22 Or *burnished lead* [D]1:22 Or *wine*

Isaiah pleaded with the rebellious children of Israel to stop and think about the consequences of their actions, asking, **Why do you want more beatings?** (Hb *nakah*, "strike, beat, wound" with a passive sense: "Why be beaten again?"). The result of sin was punishment.

1:7-9 The discipline Isaiah had addressed previously is now explained in terms of foreign conquest and occupation. Their land was **desolate** (Hb *shemamah*, "waste, devastation," a word often linked with divine judgment). **Cities** had been **burned** and the harvest of the surrounding **fields** had been consumed by the marauding army. The **Daughter Zion** (Hb *bat tsiyyon*, "daughter of Zion," figurative name for Jerusalem) remained but in a pitiful state.

1:10 Isaiah purposefully used the metaphor of **Sodom** and **Gomorrah** to point out the people's serious sinful condition and the application of the covenant curses taking effect (Dt 29:23-27). The crimes of Sodom and Gomorrah included their well known sexual immorality, general wickedness (Gn 18:20; Jd 7), pride, and a general disregard for the "poor and needy" (Ezk 16:49-50). These crimes were also ascribed to Judah and sanctioned by her leaders (Is 1:21-23).

1:11-14 God utterly rejects worship that lacks righteousness and obedience. Judah followed the ceremonial law, the external forms of religion, without internal righteousness (cp. Is 29:13).

1:21-23 After the call to repentance, Isaiah further elaborated on the sins of Jerusalem, which had once been a **faithful city** but had become an **adulteress**. When faithful, Jerusalem had once been the home of **justice** and **righteousness**. When she turned from the Lord, she became known for harboring **murderers** as well as exhibiting blatant signs of social injustice (1:29; 2:18,20; 41:29; 42:17; 44:9-20; 46:5-13; 56:9–57:12; 59:2-8). Isaiah portrayed her corruption with two illustrations. He said her **silver** had been changed into **dross,** a complete reversal of the normal refinement process in which dross, a dark impurity, was removed from the gleaming white silver through a heating process. Her **beer** (Hb *sove'*, "alcoholic drink, wine") was weakened by water. Both images contrast purity with impurity and speak of a change in essence, not just superficial appearance. Jerusalem had become corrupt and impure. The results of being unfaithful to the covenant were evident religiously and socially—a change rooted within her nature. The leaders of Jerusalem, who were obligated by law to protect the vulnerable and establish justice, were tainted by greed and dishonesty. This blatant disregard for justice was expressly forbidden in the law (Ex 23:3,8; Dt 16:18-19). The actions of the leaders directly violated God's expectation for the behavior of His people (Lv 19:15; Dt 1:16-17; 10:17-18; Is 5:22-23; Mc 3:8-12; 7:2-3). Due to the rulers' greed, the wealthy could easily **bribe** judges for the desired verdict, and those who were the most vulnerable were denied even the hope of a fair hearing.

1:24-26 The depravity of the people led to the pronouncement of the verdict. The word **therefore** signifies the conclusion to the preceding sections and that the "oracle" or "declaration" to follow is based upon the previous statements. Three titles of the Lord at the beginning of this statement of pending judgment are given ascribing the utterance directly to Him, and underscoring His ultimate authority to pass judgment: He calls Himself **the Lord** (Hb *'adon*), a title Isaiah used five times (1:24; 3:1; 10:16; 10:33; 19:4) to convey God's right to rule and judge—He was Master and Ruler (Ex 34:23; Mal 3:1); **God of Hosts** (Hb *YHWH tseva'ot*, Is 1:4,9), a title underscoring God's sovereignty over all forces—natural, human, and angelic; and **the Mighty One of Israel** (Hb *'avir yisra'ēl*), a title appearing six times—only in poetry and always emphasizing the power and strength of the Lord and His special attachment to the people of Israel (see Gn 49:24; Pss 132:2,5; Is 49:26; 60:16). Judah's sin was an affront to the Holy God who had raised them and cared for them. They had disregarded their covenant responsibilities and were subject to the penalty for disobedience. The Lord will personally administer the punishment, but His purpose is to purify and to restore. The intensity of the purging will leave no **dross** or **impurities**. Any rebellious dross will

CHARACTER PROFILE

Widows Defended by God

Situation	The loss of a husband meant the loss of a provider and protector.
Rights	• to glean from fields, orchards, and vineyards following the first harvest • to receive part of a tithe of their sustenance from other Israelites • to be married to a brother of their former husband • to have access to legal help
Examples	• Tamar (Gn 38:6-26) • Ruth (Ru 1:4-5,8-13; 2:2-3,10-12,15-17; 3:1–4:17) • Naomi (Ru 1:3,12) • Abigail (1Sm 25:39-42) • Widow of Zarephath (1Kg 17:8-24) • Widow of a prophet (2Kg 4:1-7) • Anna (Lk 2:36-38) • Widow who gave two tiny coins (Mk 12:41-44; Lk 21:1-4) • Widow of Nain (Lk 7:11-15)

They all love graft
and chase after bribes.
They do not defend the rights
of the fatherless,
and the widow's case
never comes before them.

The Judgment of God (1:24-31)

24 Therefore the Lord GOD
of Hosts,
the Mighty One
of Israel, declares:
"Ah, I will gain satisfaction
from My foes;
I will take revenge
against My enemies.
25 I will turn My hand
against you
and will burn away
your dross[A] completely;[B]
I will remove
all your impurities.
26 I will restore your judges
to what they once were,[C]
and your advisers
to their former state.[D]
Afterward you will be called
the Righteous City,
a Faithful City."
27 Zion will be redeemed
by justice,
her repentant ones
by righteousness.
28 But both rebels and sinners
will be destroyed,
and those who abandon
the LORD will perish.
29 Indeed, they[E] will be ashamed
of the sacred trees
you desired,
and you will be embarrassed
because of the gardens
you have chosen.
30 For you will become
like an oak
whose leaves are withered,
and like a garden
without water.
31 The strong one
will become tinder,
and his work a spark;
both will burn together,
with no one to quench
the flames.

The Future Peace of Zion (2:1-4)

2 The vision that Isaiah son of
Amoz saw concerning Judah and
Jerusalem:

2 In the last days
the mountain
of the LORD's house
will be established
at the top of the mountains
and will be raised
above the hills.

[A]1:25 Or *burnished lead* [B]1:25 Lit *dross as with lye* [C]1:26 Lit *judges as at the first* [D]1:26 Lit *advisers as at the beginning* [E]1:29 Some Hb mss; other Hb mss, Tg read *you*

All nations will stream to it,
3 and many peoples will come
and say,
"Come, let us go up
to the mountain
of the LORD,
to the house of the God
of Jacob.
He will teach us
about His ways
so that we may walk
in His paths."
For instruction will go
out of •Zion
and the word of the LORD
from Jerusalem.
4 He will settle disputes
among the nations
and provide arbitration
for many peoples.
They will turn their swords
into plows
and their spears
into pruning knives.
Nations will not
take up the sword
against other nations,
and they will
never again train for war.

The Current Religious Situation (2:5-9)

5 House of Jacob,
come and let us walk
in the LORD's light.
6 For You have abandoned
Your people,
the house of Jacob,
because they are
full of •divination
from the East
and of fortune-tellers
like the Philistines.
They are in league[A]
with foreigners.

[A]2:6 Or *They teem*, or *They partner*; Hb obscure

>WORD|*study*

1:21 The unfaithful cities of Samaria and Jerusalem have each been identified as an adulteress (Hb *zonah*, "prostitute, harlot") by references to derivations of the Hebrew verb *zanah* ("be a prostitute, harlot, commit fornication") or by the similar word *na'aph* ("commit adultery"). In some cases the words are used interchangeably in the text (e.g., Ezk 16:15-36; 23:43-45). The Hebrew participle *zonah*, carries three basic meanings, one literal and two figurative. First, the term refers to a person, and in all but two cases a woman, who has illicit sexual intercourse. In addition to the literal meaning, there are two figurative meanings with reference to national and religious harlotry. National prostitution entailed interaction with other nations for profit from trade (Is 23:17). The primary figurative meaning was religious prostitution, the most blatant form of which was idolatry, the worship of other gods (Ex 34:16; 2Ch 21:11; Ezk 16:23-25; Hs 3:1; 4:12).

1:27 Zion, or the remnant of Jerusalem and Judah, will be redeemed [Hb *padah*, "ransom, purchase for a price"] by justice. In the Greek Septuagint the root for "will be redeemed" is *sōzō*, the word for "save." Isaiah did not use a passive verb form to describe the future salvation of the remnant by accident. Jerusalem clearly had no way of redeeming herself. Though the call to repentance had been proclaimed, she was thoroughly impure; only through the action of God Himself could she be purged. The **repentant ones** (Hb *shuv*, "turn back, return") would be "redeemed" by the "justice" and **righteousness** of God, not something they had in themselves. This concept is central to the entire book of Isaiah and the thrust of all Scripture. The salvation brought to those who repent comes from the merciful provision of the loving Father, who by His own hand provides a means of deliverance. The details of this deliverance and the Deliverer are developed later in Isaiah, especially in the Servant passages but most fully in the New Testament revelation of Jesus Christ, who is ultimately identified as paying the price for redemption (1Pt 1:18-19).

1:27 This significant event is echoed in the very last verse of Isaiah using the same image of a fire that no one can quench (Hb *kavah*, "be quenched, extinguished, put out"; cp. Is 66:24; Mt 3:8-12; Mk 9:43-48). This root is found only 24 times in the Old Testament with 13 occurrences in the Prophets and two additional uses by a prophetess recorded in the histories. When used by prophets, the word normally refers to God's judgment (2Kg 22:17; 2Ch 34:25; Is 1:31; 34:10; 43:17; 66:24 ; Jr 4:4; 7:20; 17:27; 21:12; Ezk 20:47-48; Am 5:6). In these references the burning fire has an eternal aspect, and assuredly it will not be quenched.

2:1 The phrase the vision [Hb *davar*, "word, thing, matter, happening, event"] that Isaiah son of Amoz saw (Hb *chazah*, "see, behold, perceive") is unusual. In 1:1 Isaiah used both a noun and verb derived from *chazah* and translated respectively "vision" and "saw." In 2:1, he used *davar*, which was commonly tied to revelatory (spoken) words delivered to prophets (e.g., Jr 1:2; Zch 1:1; Jn 1:1). The only similar use linking "word" with "saw" is found in Am 1:1. Still, there are cases when clearly the word of the Lord also included visions that were seen (Is 13:1; Jr 1:11,13; Zch 1:7-8). In this case, Isaiah seemingly received words with accompanying visions concerning the future state of Zion.

2:5 Light (Hb *'or*) may be used figuratively in this instance to denote the ways or teaching of the Lord. A common idea is expressed in Ps 119:105,130, which links "light" to the word of the Lord. In Is 51:4, "light" is tied to the "instruction" (Hb *torah*, "law") and justice of the Lord. "Light" may also express the presence of the Lord and His salvation (Is 9:2; 10:17; 42:6-7,16; 49:6; 51:4; 60:3).

be completely destroyed, but those who emerge from the refinement process will be restored to the faithful ideal God had for His people (see Ezk 22:17-22). At that point, Jerusalem will be transformed—no longer unfaithful and impure; she will instead be known as **Righteous** and **Faithful**, and her leaders will be restored to **what they once were**.

1:27-31 Although one might expect complete destruction, instead the great mercy and grace of the God of Israel comes through. While those who turn back to the Lord have hope, **those who abandon the LORD will perish**. They will have no hope of escape because the destruction comes from the Lord. While Zion observed the external ceremonies of the law (vv. 11-15), she also went after the pagan practices of the people around her. **Sacred trees** and **gardens** referred to the surrounding nations' fertility cults. Often, groves would be set aside for pagan practices, which included Asherah poles, carved images or standing stones for worship, as well as places for sacrifice and offerings. God's judgment is decisive. Israel's situation is like that of trees **withered** and a **garden without water**; one spark and all would be destroyed. Those who rebel against God and refuse to repent will **burn together**—they and their **work**. The New Testament teaches that the works of believers in Christ will also be evaluated in the judgment at the end of this age; however, the difference between the redeemed and the lost is clear. For a believer, enduring works will be rewarded and only unworthy *works* will burn up (1Co 3:12-15). In contrast, the lost have no hope of reward but instead face eternal fire for themselves and their works (Rv 20:12-15).

2:2-6 The revelation regarding Zion in this passage refers to a time in the future. **The mountain of the LORD's house** (Hb *bēt*, "house, dwelling place") would have meant a great deal to Isaiah's audience, who were familiar with the surrounding culture's idea of the mountaintops as the home of their gods. There will come a time when the nations will recognize Yahweh, the God of Israel, as the true God, and Jerusalem as His particular dwelling place—prominent and unrivaled. That people from **all nations** are shown flowing to the **house** of the Lord, seeking to learn about **His ways** (Hb *derek*, "way, path, manner, habit"), is significant. Although this was inaugurated by the coming of Christ, the work of the Holy Spirit, and the subsequent outreach to the Gentiles who began to come to the God of Israel and learn **His paths**, the complete fulfillment of this vision will occur when Christ returns to rule the nations. This text is the first reference in Isaiah to all nations seeking God in the future (Is 60:3-7; 66:23; Jl 3:17; Mc 4:1-3; Zch 8:20-23; 14:8-11,16; Rv 20:4-6; 21:1-3,9-11,22-24). Micah, Isaiah's contemporary, also recorded the vision in Is 2:4 (Mc 4:1-3); the Lord impressed both men with the significance of the events of the latter days. The turning of **swords into plows and . . . spears into pruning knives** is a reversal of the call to arms.

The Lord had **abandoned** the people of Israel because of their involvement in practices displeasing to God. They were **full of divination from the East**, which implies that Judah was full of eastern practices or customs like divination and soothsaying; and they consulted **fortune-tellers** (Hb *ʾanan*, "those who practice sorcery, employing the 'hidden arts' or magic") **like the Philistines**. What type of magic these "fortune-tellers" practiced is not clear, but it has been suggested that somehow they read the cloud formations in a way similar to astrologers' reading of stars because the root meaning of the noun is "cloud." These activities were forbidden in the law (Lv 19:26; Dt 18:9-14). The accusation of being **in league** [Hb *saphaq*, "clasping hands," as in completing formal treaties; "abounding, prospering"] **with foreigners** refers to the fact that dealing with foreigners in the ancient Near East by formal agreements often required the acknowledgment of their gods as witnesses. Military agreements with foreigners, as with the emissaries of Babylon invited by Hezekiah, also meant a refusal to trust in God alone.

2:7-8 Being filled with the East or eastern ways was manifested in a variety of ways. **Their land** was **full of silver and gold**. They had the external signs of wealth and foolishly gloried in their treasures, putting trust in material things rather than God (Dt 17:17; 2Kg 16:5-8; 2Ch 28:21; 32:27-28; Is 39:2-6). It was **full of horses** and **chariots**, referring to the amassing of military strength and putting trust in a human military rather than waiting for heavenly deliverance (Dt 17:15-16; 2Kg 16:5-7; 2Ch 27:5-7; Is 7:2; 31:1-3). Finally, it was **full of idols** (Hb *ʾelilim*, 2:8). By pursuing ways directly opposed to the law of the Lord, Judah had bowed before false gods and invited the Lord's judgment.

2:10-11 Isaiah warned Judah about the coming **terror** [Hb *pachad*] **of the Lord**, which referred to the overwhelming majesty of the Lord's holy presence. Before the power of God, all who had or would exalt themselves through **human pride** would be utterly **humbled** and **brought low** (cp. 5:15-16). Verse 11 is repeated in verse 17 framing a series of pairs of things to be humbled before the glory of the Lord.

7 Their[A,B] land is full of silver
and gold,
and there is no limit
to their treasures;
their land is full of horses,
and there is no limit
to their chariots.
8 Their land is full of idols;
they bow down to the work
of their hands,
to what their fingers
have made.
9 So humanity is brought low,
and man is humbled.
Do not forgive them!

The Coming Day of the Lord (2:10-22)

10 Go into the rocks
and hide in the dust
from the terror of the Lord
and from
His majestic splendor.
11 Human pride[C]
will be humbled,
and the loftiness of men
will be brought low;
the Lord alone will be exalted
on that day.
12 For a day belonging to
the Lord of •Hosts
is coming
against all that is proud
and lofty,
against all that is
lifted up—it will
be humbled—
13 against all the cedars
of Lebanon,
lofty and lifted up,
against all the oaks of Bashan,
14 against all
the high mountains,
against all the lofty hills,
15 against every high tower,
against every fortified wall,
16 against every ship of Tarshish,
and against every splendid
sea vessel.
17 So human pride will be
brought low,
and the loftiness of men
will be humbled;
the Lord alone will be exalted
on that day.
18 The idols
will vanish completely.
19 People will go into caves
in the rocks
and holes in the ground,
away from the terror
of the Lord
and
from His majestic splendor,
when He rises to terrify
the earth.
20 On that day people will throw
their silver and gold idols,
which they made to worship,
to the moles and the bats.
21 They will go into the caves
of the rocks
and the crevices in the cliffs,
away from the terror
of the Lord
and from
His majestic splendor,
when He rises to terrify
the earth.
22 Put no more trust in man,
who has only the breath
in his nostrils.
What is he really worth?

The Judgment Against the Leaders of Judah (3:1-15)

3 Observe this: The Lord God
of •Hosts
is about to remove
from Jerusalem
and from Judah
every kind of security:
the entire supply of bread
and water,

A2:7 Lit *Its* B2:7 = the house of Jacob C2:11 Lit *Mankind's proud eyes*

>WORD|study

3:1 The word security (Hb *mashʿēn umashʿēnah*, "support and staff") is translated from two words, one masculine and one feminine, derived from the same Hebrew verb *shaʿan*, "lean on, trust in." The masculine form occurs only five times and refers to something that a person might depend upon: the Lord (2Sm 22:19; Ps 18:18) or other supports, including **bread** or **water** (Is 3:1 includes three uses of the same word). The feminine form occurs 12 times and usually refers to a literal physical "staff," but there are three figurative uses referring to Egypt as a staff upon which Israel leaned (2Kg 18:21; Is 36:6; Ezk 29:6). The words *mashʿēn umashʿēnah*, which are used together at the beginning of chapter 3, can be seen as reflecting a total removal of any support in which Judah would trust in place of God.

2 the hero and warrior,
the judge and prophet,
the fortune-teller and elder,
3 the commander of 50
and the dignitary,
the counselor,
cunning magician,[A]
and necromancer.[B]
4 "I will make youths
their leaders,
and the unstable[C]
will govern them."
5 The people will oppress
one another,
man against man, neighbor
against neighbor;
the youth will act arrogantly
toward the elder,
and the worthless
toward the honorable.

[A]3:3 Or *skilled craftsman* [B]3:3 Or *medium* [C]3:4 Or *mischief-makers*

3:4-7 This overturning of leadership would lead to a void in Israel and an upheaval of the social order. No longer would there be qualified leaders; instead, **youths** and **the unstable** would be in charge, leading to more general oppression and insecurity. There would come a desperate time when the qualifications for leadership would sink so low that the ownership of a single **cloak** would seem sufficient. Yet even those with the most modest possessions would refuse to take a role in restoring order. The lack of stable civil authority would lead to other economic

Biblical Womanhood Importance of Women to the Moral Fabric of a Nation

When the moral breakdown reaches the nation's women, the most devastating impact is on the home, affecting the most formative influence on the younger generation (3:16–4:1). The last bastion of defense is then crumbling, and God's judgment is imminent. The judgment God pronounced on the women of Isaiah's day, **the daughters of Zion**, indicates a state of unrepentant wickedness on their part and, consequently, their share of responsibility for the desperate social situation. These women were:

- *haughty and arrogant*, manifested by their **walking with heads held high**, with overtones of a desire to be noticed. They exalted themselves, thinking more highly of their own needs and desires than those of others. Self-centered pride led to an improper valuation of their own worth in relation to God and others, so that judgment is imminent (cp. Pss 10:4; 101:5; Pr 16:5,18; 18:12; Ec 7:8; Is 2:11; 5:15).
- *immodest*, going about in a way that attracted attention. They walked with **seductive** [Hb *saqar*, "flirt, ogle, be wanton"] **eyes** and **prancing steps** (Hb *taphaph*, "take quick little steps, mince along, skip"). Their way of going about was not natural or modest; rather they were preoccupied with self-importance, flirting mannerisms, and arrogant embellishments to draw attention to themselves. This attitude contrasts with the behavior the Lord mandates for women (cp. 1Tm 2:9-10; 1Pt 3:3-4).
- *materialistic*, wearing **ankle bracelets** and the long list of accessories the Lord was going to remove indicates that they were wealthy. However, the problem was not the fact of their affluence but their focus on material things coupled with their apparent disregard of the needs of others.
- *self-centered*, lavishing themselves with unnecessary adornments that accentuated their own social status and comfort while ignoring the basic needs around them. Consequently, the selfishness and materialism of the women contributed to the oppression of the poor. Proverbs 31:10-31 commends the contrasting description of a wealthy yet righteous woman who provides for her household and those working for her as well as for the poor (Pr 31:15,20).

The judgment against Jerusalem's haughty women affected all aspects of their lives. The Lord would take away everything in which they had previously placed their trust: physical beauty, material possessions, and confident self-assurance. Their beauty would be marred by **scabs**, **baldness**, and **branding** (Is 3:16,24). They would lose all the material comforts in which they had gloried and the benefits of those who had provided for them. The close connection of the "daughters of Zion" with the "Daughter of Zion," the personified city of Jerusalem, becomes apparent when the Daughter of Zion (figuratively, the city, referenced by **her gates**) is described as grieving her **deserted** state. A coming siege of Jerusalem will leave few men in the city. As a result, **seven women will seize one man** and plead with him, **Take away our disgrace** (Hb *cherpah*, "reproach, state of low status or dishonor" (4:1); cp. Gn 30:23; 2Sm 13:13; Is 54:4). The women would be desperate for a remedy to their vulnerable situation. Being left without a husband or, for some, without even the prospects of a husband meant being without provision and protection and possibly without children. A situation of complete social and economic breakdown occurred with the final destruction of Jerusalem in 586 B.C. and the desperate conditions that followed. Notably, the state of the destroyed city of Jerusalem was described with the same Hebrew word (*cherpah*) as the state of the judged daughters of Zion (Neh 1:2-3; 2:17; 4:4; Dn 9:16). In addition, the people who were not taken into exile were described with the same terminology (Jr 29:16-18; 42:18; 44:8,12; Ezk 5:14-17; 22:4). Sadly, the horrifying shame experienced by the women of Judah reflected the spiritual condition of their hearts when, in their pride, they had embraced a lifestyle that inherently rejected the priorities of the Lord who had provided the **finery** (Hb *tiph'arah*, "splendor, beauty," Is 3:18; see **Word Study**, p. 929) that he had finally taken away (cp. Hs 2:2-13).

difficulties including lack of bread and water (v. 1). This became the state of the city when Jerusalem was defeated by Babylon. Groups of leaders and the elite were deported in 605, 597, and 586 B.C. (2Kg 24:1,8-16; 25:8-12,18-21; 2Ch 36:5-7,10,20; Is 39:6-7; Dn 1:1-5). The leaders were exiled, leaving only the poorest in the land.

3:8-11 Judgment was coming because the people of Judah had **spoken and acted against the LORD**. Their sins were as blatant as those of **Sodom**; but instead of repenting of and mourning over their sins, they gloried in them.

3:12 In the leadership of the day, **youths oppress** [God's] **people, and women rule** [Hb *mashal*, the same word is used in Genesis 3:16 regarding a husband's authority] **over them** (cp. v. 4). Some suggest this passage refers to the reign of Ahaz, who would have been only 20 at the beginning of his sole reign (2Kg 16:2; 2Ch 28:1). Perhaps the queen mother or maybe the harem had influenced him; however, there is nothing in the text to support this position. Others interpret the oppression of children and the rule of women as a reversal of the norm due to the power vacuum that resulted from the exile of leaders; but at this point, Isaiah appeared to be addressing the issues of his own day. Given that 3:16–4:1 deals with the corrupt women of his day and the judgment upon them, Isaiah seemingly referred to a current situation in which the women were exercising a domineering influence over the people—perhaps like the picture presented in Am 4:1.

3:13-15 Once again, legal language was used: The Lord acts as both prosecutor (rising **to argue the case**) and **judge**. He specifically addressed the crimes of the **elders and leaders**. They had **devastated** [Hb *ba'ar*, "consumed, burned"] **the vineyard**, which figuratively represented Israel, the people of the Lord (Is 5:1-7; 27:2-6; Jr 12:10). The leaders of the land had consumed the best for themselves, leaving nothing for the poor. In the case of literal vineyards, according to the law, the poor were supposed to be allowed to glean remnants from the harvest (Ex 23:11; Lv 19:10). Not only did the leaders fail to provide the specified sustenance for the poor, but they even personally profited at the expense of the poor. Their selfishness and materialism caused them to **crush . . . and grind the faces of the poor**. Treatment of the poor was always a kind of barometer for the spiritual health of Israel. God made man not only to care for the earth but also to care for one another. To neglect the poor is to reject a task from God.

6 A man will even seize
his brother
in his father's house, saying:
"You have a cloak—you be
our leader!
This heap of rubble will be
under your control."
7 On that day
he will cry out, saying:
"I'm not a healer.
I don't even have food
or clothing in my house.
Don't make me the leader
of the people!"
8 For Jerusalem has stumbled
and Judah has fallen
because they have spoken
and acted against the LORD,
defying His glorious presence.
9 The look on their faces
testifies against them,
and like Sodom, they flaunt
their sin.
They do not conceal it.
Woe to them,
for they have brought evil
on themselves.
10 Tell the righteous that
it will go well for them,
for they will eat the fruit
of their labor.
11 Woe to the wicked—
it will go badly for them,
for what they have done
will be done to them.
12 Youths oppress My people,
and women rule over them.
My people, your leaders
mislead you;
they confuse the direction
of your paths.

13 The LORD rises to argue
the case
and stands to judge
the people.
14 The LORD brings this charge
against the elders and leaders
of His people:
"You have devastated
the vineyard.
The plunder from the poor is
in your houses.
15 Why do you crush My people
and grind the faces
of the poor?"
This is the declaration
of the Lord GOD of Hosts.

The Judgment Against the Women of Judah (3:16–4:1)

16 The LORD also says:

Because the daughters
of •Zion are haughty,
walking with heads held high
and seductive eyes,
going along
with prancing steps,
jingling their ankle bracelets,
17 the Lord will put scabs
on the heads
of the daughters of Zion,
and the LORD will shave
their foreheads bare.

18 On that day the Lord will
strip their finery: ankle bracelets,
headbands, crescents, 19 pendants,
bracelets, veils, 20 headdresses, ankle
jewelry, sashes, perfume bottles, amulets, 21 signet rings, nose rings, 22 festive robes, capes, cloaks, purses,
23 garments, linen clothes, turbans,
and veils.

24 Instead of perfume
there will be a stench;
instead of a belt, a rope;
instead of beautifully
styled hair, baldness;
instead of
fine clothes, •sackcloth;
instead of beauty, branding.[A]
25 Your men will fall
by the sword,
your warriors in battle.
26 Then her gates will lament
and mourn;
deserted, she will sit
on the ground.

4 On that day seven women
will seize one man, saying,
"We will eat our own bread
and provide our own clothing.
Just let us be called
by your name.
Take away our disgrace."

The Future Holy Remnant of Zion (4:2-6)

2 On that day the Branch of[B] the
LORD will be beautiful and glorious,
and the fruit of the land will be the
pride and glory of Israel's survivors.
3 Whoever remains in •Zion and
whoever is left in Jerusalem will be

[A] **3:24** DSS read *shame* [B] **4:2** Or *plant*

>WORD|*study*

4:3 The word destined (Hb *katav*, "write, record") communicates the sense that only those whose names have been "written down"—i.e., listed in the city's record of its citizens' names—will be permitted to live in Jerusalem. This connects tightly to the teaching regarding the saved being recorded by name in the book of life (Ex 32:32-33; Ps 69:28; Dn 12:1-3; Mal 3:16-18; Lk 10:20; Php 4:3; Heb 12:23; Rv 3:5; 13:8; 20:12-15; 21:27).

called holy—all in Jerusalem who
are destined to live— [4]when the
Lord has washed away the filth of
the daughters of Zion and cleansed
the bloodguilt from the heart of Jerusalem by a spirit of judgment and
a spirit of burning. [5]Then the LORD
will create a cloud of smoke by day
and a glowing flame of fire by night
over the entire site of Mount Zion
and over its assemblies. For there
will be a canopy over all the glory,[A]
[6]and there will be a booth for shade
from heat by day, and a refuge and
shelter from storm and rain.

The Disappointing Vineyard (5:1-7)

5 I will sing about the one
I love,
a song about
my loved one's vineyard:
The one I love had a vineyard
on a very fertile hill.
2 He broke up the soil,
cleared it of stones,
and planted it
with the finest vines.
He built a tower in the middle
of it
and even dug out
a winepress there.
He expected it to yield
good grapes,
but it yielded
worthless grapes.
3 So now,
residents of Jerusalem
and men of Judah,
please judge between Me
and My vineyard.
4 What more could I have done
for My vineyard
than I did?
Why, when I expected a yield
of good grapes,
did it yield worthless grapes?
5 Now I will tell you
what I am about to do
to My vineyard:
I will remove its hedge,
and it will be consumed;
I will tear down its wall,
and it will be trampled.
6 I will make it a wasteland.
It will not be pruned
or weeded;
thorns and briers
will grow up.
I will also give orders
to the clouds
that rain should not fall on it.
7 For the vineyard of the LORD
of •Hosts
is the house of Israel,
and the men[B] of Judah,
the plant He delighted in.
He looked for justice
but saw injustice,
for righteousness,
but heard cries
of wretchedness.

The Judgment Against Judah (5:8-30)

8 Woe to those who add house
to house
and join field to field
until there is no more room
and you alone are left
in the land.

9 I heard the LORD of Hosts say:

Indeed, many houses
will become desolate,
grand and lovely ones
without inhabitants.
10 For a ten-acre[C] vineyard
will yield
only six gallons,[D]
and 10 bushels[E] of seed
will yield
only one bushel.[F]

[A]4:5 Or *For glory will be a canopy over all* [B]5:7 Lit *man* [C]5:10 Lit *ten-yoke* [D]5:10 Lit *one bath* [E]5:10 Lit *one homer* [F]5:10 Lit *one ephah*

4:2-4 Isaiah next provided a contrasting view of the future state of Zion after her purging from sin. Differing views exist concerning the phrase **Branch** [Hb *tsemach*, "sprout, growth"] **of the LORD**. Some scholars suggest that the "branch" and the parallel **fruit of the land** refer to the restoration of actual fruitfulness in Israel; others suggest that the "branch" in this verse refers to Israel, which will eventually be replanted in the land (Hs 14:5-7); and still others view "the branch" as a messianic reference like Is 11:1 (cp. Jr 23:5; 33:15; Zch 3:8; 6:12). If this is so, the next phrase concerning "the fruit of the land" seems to reflect the resumed fruitfulness under the messianic rule, which will be experienced and enjoyed by the redeemed and faithful remnant (cp. Jl 3:17-21; Am 9:11-15). The remnant that survives **will be called holy,** but not by their own actions; only when the Lord **has washed away** the sin of the people of Judah **and cleansed** Jerusalem from **bloodguilt** (Hb *dam*, "blood," often referring to guilt from killing or shedding blood; cp. 1:15; 59:1-3; Ezk 9:9; 22:1-16; 24:6-11; Jl 3:21; Mc 3:9-10; 7:2; Zch 3:8-9).

4:5-6 Echoes of the exodus are clearly intended. The **cloud of smoke** and **flame of fire** from the 40-year wandering manifested the very presence of the Lord with His people (Ex 13:21-22; 14:19,24; 24:16-18; 33:9-10; 40:36-38; Nm 9:15-22; Dt 1:32-33; 31:15).

5:1-10 A **song** concerning the **vineyard** of the Lord prefaces another series of judgments against Israel. In this allegory, a vineyard owner has done everything possible to position his vineyard well for producing quality grapes. He had picked a choice spot, prepared the soil to remove impediments, **planted it with the finest vines**, built up a protective watchtower, and **even dug out a winepress there** (Hb word order "and even *a winepress* he dug out in it," the position of the noun *winepress* is emphatic) because **he expected** (lit "he waited for" or "looked eagerly") that the vineyard would produce a prime vintage. Unfortunately, **it yielded worthless grapes** (Hb *be'ushim*, "rotten, stinking grapes"; most forms of this word convey the concept of a foul odor).

Following the judgment pronouncement on the vineyard, the interpretation of the allegory was given. The **vineyard . . . is the house of Israel, and the men of Judah** (see Jr 12:10). An obvious wordplay accentuates the Lord's disappointment. The fruit He rightly expected was **justice** (Hb *mishpat*), but instead there was **injustice** (Hb *mispach*, "an outpouring of bloodshed, oppression"); He expected **righteousness** (Hb *tsedaqah*) but instead He **heard cries**

of wretchedness (Hb *tsa'aqah*, "an outcry of distress"). God's judgment on His unprofitable people was that they would no longer be protected from the predators around them.

The background of this message was quite possibly a time of general prosperity under King Uzziah. Probably a group of wealthy families gained prominence, and their indulgence led to gross social injustice. They are charged with insatiable greed, which was displayed by a single-minded drive to acquire possessions and land regardless of the hereditary rights of those involved. This action directly contradicted the God-ordained inheritance laws for maintaining land within a family (Lv 25:10, 13-17,23-31; Nm 27:7-11; 36:6-9). The poor were likely dispossessed from their ancestral possessions due to the injustice of the courts (see Am 2:6-8; Mc 2:2). To show disrespect for the inheritance system God had established was to dishonor God Himself. To steal from the proper heirs was to steal from God, the real owner.

5:11-12 Following closely upon the charge of greed was the accusation of self-indulgence expressed by the description of drunkards.

5:13-16 Captivity and death are prescribed as additional judgments (Is 5:13-17). God's **people will go into exile** (Hb *galah*, "remove, depart, be led into captivity") for lack of **knowledge** (Hb *da'at*; cp. Jb 36:12; see note on Gn 2:16-17).

5:24-26 Since the people of Israel had **rejected** the law and **despised the word** of God as an unprofitable vineyard, they would be destroyed.

5:29-30 Isaiah likened the sound of the invaders both to the **roaring** of **lions** and to the **roaring of the sea**. Both images would have struck fear in the hearts of the Israelites. The clouds of dust from the invading army would be so dense that the very **light will be obscured**.

6:1 This chapter conveys the vision of the Lord's majesty and the appropriate response of repentance by Isaiah. It also lays out Isaiah's prophetic commission, which followed his repentance.

6:1-2 The **year . . . King Uzziah died** was about 740 B.C. Isaiah **saw the Lord** who is **high and lofty** upon His **throne**. In Is 57:15, the exact same phrase translated "the High and Exalted One" is used of God Himself. A variation of the phrase (Hb *ram wenissa'* with the same roots, 52:13) is used for the Servant, hinting at the Servant's identity with God, and yielding overtones of Trinitarian doctrine. Isaiah also beheld attending **seraphim** (Hb, "burning, fiery ones"). These heavenly

11 Woe to those who rise early
in the morning
in pursuit of beer,
who linger into the evening,
inflamed by wine.
12 At their feasts they have
lyre, harp,
tambourine, flute, and wine.
They do not perceive
the LORD's actions,
and they do not see the work
of His hands.
13 Therefore My people will go
into exile
because they lack knowledge;
her[A] dignitaries are starving,
and her[A] masses are parched
with thirst.
14 Therefore •Sheol enlarges
its throat
and opens wide
its enormous jaws,
and down go •Zion's
dignitaries, her masses,
her crowds, and those
who carouse in her!
15 Humanity is brought low,
man is humbled,
and haughty eyes
are humbled.
16 But the LORD of Hosts
is exalted by His justice,
and the holy God
is distinguished
by righteousness.
17 Lambs will graze
as if in[B] their own pastures,
and strangers[C] will eat
among the ruins of the rich.
18 Woe to those
who drag wickedness
with cords of deceit
and pull sin along
with cart ropes,
19 to those who say:
"Let Him hurry up and do
His work quickly
so that we can see it!
Let the plan of the Holy One
of Israel take place
so that we can know it!"
20 Woe to those who call
evil good
and good evil,
who substitute darkness
for light
and light for darkness,
who substitute bitter
for sweet
and sweet for bitter.
21 Woe to those who are wise
in their own opinion
and clever in their own sight.[D]
22 Woe to those who are heroes
at drinking wine,
who are fearless
at mixing beer,
23 who acquit the •guilty
for a bribe
and deprive the innocent
of justice.
24 Therefore, as a tongue of fire
consumes straw
and as dry grass shrivels
in the flame,
so their roots will become
like something rotten
and their blossoms
will blow away like dust,
for they have rejected
the instruction of the LORD
of Hosts,
and they have despised
the word of the Holy One
of Israel.
25 Therefore the LORD's anger
burns against His people.
He raised His hand
against them
and struck them;
the mountains quaked,
and their corpses were
like garbage in the streets.
In all this, His anger is
not removed,
and His hand is still raised
to strike.
26 He raises a signal flag
for the distant nations
and whistles for them
from the ends of the earth.
Look—how quickly
and swiftly they come!
27 None of them grows weary
or stumbles;
no one slumbers or sleeps.
No belt is loose
and no sandal strap broken.
28 Their arrows are sharpened,
and all their bows strung.
Their horses' hooves are
like flint;
their chariot wheels are
like a whirlwind.

[A]5:13 Lit *its* [B]5:17 Syr reads *graze in* [C]5:17 LXX reads *sheep* [D]5:21 Lit *clever before their face*

29 Their roaring is like a lion's;
they roar like young lions;
they growl and seize their prey
and carry it off,
and no one can rescue it.
30 On that day they will roar
over it,
like the roaring of the sea.
When one looks at the land,
there will be darkness
and distress;
light will be obscured
by clouds.[A]

The Calling of Isaiah (6:1-13)

The Holiness of the LORD (6:1-4)

6 In the year that King Uzziah died,
I saw the Lord seated on a high
and lofty throne, and His robe[B] filled
the temple. 2 Seraphim[C] were standing above Him; each one had six
wings: with two he covered his face,
with two he covered his feet, and
with two he flew. 3 And one called to
another:

Holy, holy, holy is the LORD
of •Hosts;
His glory fills the whole earth.

4 The foundations of the doorways
shook at the sound of their voices,
and the temple was filled with smoke.

The Repentance and Cleansing of Isaiah (6:5-7)

5 Then I said:

Woe is me for I am ruined[D]
because I am a man
of •unclean lips
and live among a people
of unclean lips,
and because my eyes
have seen the King,
the LORD of Hosts.

6 Then one of the seraphim flew to
me, and in his hand was a glowing
coal that he had taken from the altar
with tongs. 7 He touched my mouth
with it and said:

Now that this has touched
your lips,
your wickedness is removed
and your sin is atoned for.

The Commissioning of Isaiah (6:8-13)

8 Then I heard the voice of the
Lord saying:

Who should I send?
Who will go for Us?

I said:

Here I am. Send me.

9 And He replied:

Go! Say to these people:
Keep listening,
but do not understand;
keep looking,
but do not perceive.
10 Dull the minds[E] of these
people;
deafen their ears and blind
their eyes;
otherwise they might see
with their eyes
and hear with their ears,
understand with their minds,
turn back, and be healed.

[A] 5:30 Lit *its clouds* [B] 6:1 Lit *seam* [C] 6:2 = heavenly beings [D] 6:5 Or *I must be silent* [E] 6:10 Lit *heart*

>WORD|*study*

6:3-4 The phrase Holy, holy, holy (Hb *qadosh, qadosh, qadosh*) is highly significant, conveying an essential attribute of God. Normally a repeated word in Hebrew intensifies the meaning, but this occurrence is one of only three in the Old Testament where one word is repeated three times consecutively (Jr 22:20; Ezk 21:27; cp. Rv 4:2-8). God's unique separateness is emphasized. Originally the word "holy" was used in reference to anything that was "set apart" or "devoted" to deity without necessarily a moral sense. Nevertheless, concerning the God of the Israelites, a unique ethical purity was a part of God's nature and became understood as an element of His holiness. Israelites were commanded to be "holy," ethically pure, separated from evil, because that was a singular trait of God (e.g., Ex 19:6; Lv 11:44-45; 19:2; 20:7,26; 21:6-8; Nm 6:5; 15:40; Dt 7:6; 14:2; 28:9).

6:5 Isaiah saw himself as a man of unclean [Hb *tamē'*] lips who dwelled in the midst of an unclean society. "Unclean" carries the concept of being impure when compared to the standards of God. Only here in the Old Testament are lips connected to the term "unclean," yet various passages link the state and thoughts of one's heart to lips and the words of the mouth (Ps 19:14; Pr 4:23-24; 16:23; 24:2; 26:23; Is 29:13). In the New Testament, Jesus directly linked the thoughts of the heart to sins proceeding from the mouth, saying, "But what comes out of the mouth comes from the heart, and this defiles a man" (Mt 15:18). If Isaiah had been preaching the messages in the previous chapters before this point, perhaps he recognized in God's presence that his actions and heart motivations did not measure up to his words.

creatures with **six wings**, a **face**, feet, and hands were similar to the four-winged cherubim mentioned in Ezk 1 and 10 (cp. Rv 4:6-9). They took coals of fire and touched Isaiah's lips in an act of purification (Is 6:6-7). That the seraphim covered their faces shows the intensity of God's holiness: Even the seraphim would not look upon it. Covering their **feet** was a sign of humility before God.

6:3-4 The seraphim were praising God by exclaiming, **Holy, holy, holy is the LORD of Hosts** (see **Word Study**, 1:9, p. 860). As the seraphim praised God, **the foundations of the doorways shook**. Isaiah's focus was on the foundations, possibly because he was on his face before the presence of the Lord. Often clouds, smoke, and fire are associated with the glory and presence of the Lord, and in this case His presence was manifested as the **temple was filled with smoke** (cp. Is 4:5; cp. Gn 15:17; Ex 19:18; 20:18-19; Ezk 1:27-28; 10:4).

6:5 Before the overwhelming presence of the pure and holy God of Israel, Isaiah recognized his own sinfulness, resulting in an exclamation of dismay, **Woe is me for I am ruined** (Hb *damah*, "be cut off, undone"). Isaiah recognized that his sin had cut him off from God and that he, too, deserved judgment (Is 59:2). He expected his own ruin because of his sin and because his eyes had **seen the King**. Isaiah knew that no one could see the face of God and expect to live (cp. Ex 19:21; 33:20; Jdg 6:22-23; 13:22).

6:6-7 Isaiah's confession of sin prefaced the glorious extension of grace and forgiveness by God. A seraph took **a glowing coal . . . from the altar** and **touched** Isaiah's **lips**. Fire symbolized holiness and purification. The means for purification was a coal from an atoning sacrifice from the altar of God. Isaiah did not cleanse himself; his forgiveness was dependent upon God's mercy and based upon the God-ordained means of providing salvation (cp. Heb 10:1-17).

6:8 Only after Isaiah had received forgiveness and cleansing was he in a position to hear and accept the Lord's call. Once Isaiah's lips were cleansed, he prepared to become the mouthpiece of God. The phrases of the call of the Lord are parallel, **Who should I send? Who will go for Us?** Considering the passage an example of the triune God, referencing Himself in both phrases is appropriate. Some commentators suggest that the "Us" refers to the heavenly assembly as in 1Kg 22:19-23; however, the situations are not the same. In Isaiah, the pronoun "Us" refers to the divine initiators of the call and not the attending seraphim. This phrase bears similarity to Gn 1:26-27 where there also appears to be a reference to plurality in the Godhead.

6:9-13 The Lord knew the message

11 Then I said, "Until when, Lord?"
And He replied:

Until cities lie in ruins
without inhabitants,
houses are without people,
the land is ruined
and desolate,
12 and the LORD drives the people
far away,
leaving great emptiness
in the land.
13 Though a tenth will remain
in the land,
it will be burned again.
Like the terebinth or the oak
that leaves a stump
when felled,
the holy •seed is the stump.

The Rejection of Judah (7:1–8:22)

The Prophecy in Response to the Syro-Israelite Alliance (7:1-9)

7 This took place during the reign
of Ahaz, son of Jotham, son of
Uzziah king of Judah: Rezin king
of Aram, along with Pekah, son of
Remaliah, king of Israel, waged war
against Jerusalem, but he could not
succeed. 2 When it became known
to the house of David that Aram
had occupied Ephraim, the heart of
Ahaz[A] and the hearts of his people
trembled like trees of a forest shaking in the wind.
3 Then the LORD said to Isaiah, "Go
out with your son Shear-jashub to
meet Ahaz at the end of the conduit of the upper pool, by the road
to the Fuller's Field. 4 Say to him:
Calm down and be quiet. Don't be
afraid or cowardly because of these
two smoldering stubs of firebrands,
the fierce anger of Rezin and Aram,
and the son of Remaliah. 5 For Aram,
along with Ephraim and the son of
Remaliah, has plotted harm against
you. They say, 6 'Let us go up against
Judah, terrorize it, and conquer it
for ourselves. Then we can install
Tabeel's son as king in it.'"
7 This is what the Lord GOD says:

It will not happen;
it will not occur.
8 The[B] head of Aram
is Damascus,
the head of Damascus
is Rezin
(within 65 years
Ephraim will be too shattered
to be a people),
9 the head of Ephraim
is Samaria,
and the head of Samaria
is the son of Remaliah.
If you do not stand firm
in your faith,
then you will not stand at all.

The Prophecy of Immanuel (7:10-16)

10 Then the LORD spoke again to
Ahaz: 11 "Ask for a sign from the
LORD your God—from the depths of
•Sheol to the heights of heaven."
12 But Ahaz replied, "I will not ask.
I will not test the LORD."
13 Isaiah said, "Listen, house of David! Is it not enough for you to try
the patience of men? Will you also
try the patience of my God? 14 Therefore, the Lord Himself will give you[C]
a sign: The virgin will conceive,[D]
have a son, and name him Immanuel.[E] 15 By the time he learns to reject what is bad and choose what is
good, he will be eating butter[F] and
honey. 16 For before the boy knows

INCARNATION

Ahaz spurned God's offer, but the Lord gave **a sign** to the **house of David** as proof and promise of what was to come: **The virgin** [Hb *'almah*] **will conceive, have a son, and name him Immanuel** (see 7:10-16). The meaning of the Hebrew word translated "virgin" is hotly debated. Some suggest *'almah* may be applied to any young woman, even in the special sense of virgin, while the word *betulah* was typically used for virgins (although not in Jl 1:8). However, the Old Testament never uses the word *'almah* to refer to a married woman (cp. all seven uses in the OT—here and Gn 24:43; Ex 2:8; Ps 68:25; Pr 30:19; Sg 1:3; 6:8).

The Gospel of Matthew plainly states that Mary's pregnancy with Jesus occurred before her wedding to Joseph and by the divine agency of the Holy Spirit rather than by natural means (cp. Lk 1:26-38). Then, to show that Jesus' conception fulfilled Scripture, Matthew quoted Is 7:14 from the Septuagint (LXX), which translates *'almah* with *parthenos* (Gk, "an unmarried woman past puberty who is still a virgin"; cp. Lk 1:27). Matthew further emphasized that the name "Immanuel" (Hb, "God with us"; cp. Is 8:8,10) referred to Jesus the Messiah (Mt 1:22-23; cp. 1:1).

Isaiah carried would be rejected; however, there seems to be more at work here than just foreknowledge. The people of Israel had rebelled to such a degree that God gave them over to their rebellion and confirmed the hardening of their hearts. The hardening would continue until the prophesied judgment came to pass and **the LORD drives the people far away**. In the declaration of judgment, there was hope for a remnant, a **tenth** who would return and remain in the land but only to be **burned** (in Hb, "to consume"). Yet, out of this remnant, which will be purged, there will be found **holy seed** (i.e., holy offspring left as **the stump**; see notes on 49:19-21; 53:10; 54:3).

Certainly there was a measure of fulfillment when the people were finally carried into exile with only a remnant ultimately left. Still, the greater, final fulfillment came when out of the remnant of the exile a few "holy seed" later came to acknowledge Jesus as the Messiah. Jesus cited Is 6:9-10, applying these words to those who refused to believe Him, saying, "Isaiah's prophecy is fulfilled in them" (Mt 13:13-17; Mk 4:11-12; Lk 8:10). John repeated this understanding (Jn 12:37-41; cp. Ac 28:25-27). Therefore, though the message of Isaiah signified judgment for most Israelites who would harden themselves against God, there was still the promise that some would be spared.

7:1-2 The following passages further illustrate that hardening of the heart was occurring and that God's purpose of salvation for a remnant would prevail. The events of chapter 7 took place during the reign of Ahaz after **Aram** (Syria) and **Israel** united against Jerusalem around 734 B.C. Word came to the king **that Aram had occupied** [with the idea of making an agreement or alliance with] **Ephraim**, a tribe of the northern kingdom of Israel. Here the name referred to the whole kingdom of Israel. All of Judah was frightened by this hostile alliance.

7:3-7 Isaiah was sent by God to encourage Ahaz, and was specifically told to take with him his son, **Shear-jashub** (Hb, "a remnant will return"). Ahaz had refused to join Syria and Israel in rebellion against Assyria. As a result, **Rezin** (the king of Syria) and Pekah (the king of Israel) planned to overthrow Ahaz and install a puppet king, **Tabeel's son**, in his place. This aggressive action was prompted by God, who used the occasion to discipline Judah and to inform Judah about pending future judgment and salvation (2Kg 15:37; 16:2-3). Though Rezin and Pekah had their own plans to depose the king of Judah, God was firmly in control. The Lord assured Ahaz, **It will not happen; it will not occur.**

7:8-9 God revealed ahead of time that

[A]7:2 Lit *Aram has rested upon Ephraim, his heart* [B]7:8 Lit *For the* [C]7:14 In Hb, the word you is pl [D]7:14 Or *virgin is pregnant, will* [E]7:14 = God With Us [F]7:15 Or *sour milk*

CHARACTER PROFILE

The Prophetess Isaiah's Wife

Her Background	• She was described as a prophetess (8:3). • She married Isaiah (8:3).
Her Story	• She bore Isaiah two sons whose names had prophetic significance (8:18): **Shear-jashub** (Hb, "the remnant shall return," 7:3) and **Maher-shalal-hash-baz** (Hb, without the preposition of 8:1, "speed spoil, hasten plunder"). • She witnessed her husband's ministry to kings and to the people of Judah. • She witnessed the fulfillment of the prophecy tied to the name of Maher-shalal-hash-baz when Assyria quickly overwhelmed and plundered Israel (8:4,8).
Life Lesson	She and her husband and children kept themselves free from the sinful rebellion of many of God's people and were thereby used of God to speak truth to their generation.

to reject what is bad and choose
what is good, the land of the two
kings you dread will be abandoned.

The Prophecy of Judgment upon Israel and Judah (7:17–8:22)

17 The LORD will bring on you, your
people, and the house of your father, such a time as has never been
since Ephraim separated from Judah—the king of Assyria is coming."

18 On that day
the LORD will whistle to the fly
that is at the farthest streams
of the Nile
and to the bee that is
in the land of Assyria.
19 All of them will come
and settle
in the steep ravines,
in the clefts of the rocks,
in all the thornbushes, and in
all the water holes.

20 On that day the Lord will use
a razor hired from beyond the Euphrates River—the king of Assyria—to shave the head, the hair on
the legs, and to remove the beard as
well.

21 On that day
a man will raise a young cow
and two sheep,
22 and from the abundant milk
they give
he will eat butter,
for every survivor
in the land will eat butter
and honey.
23 And on that day
every place where there were
1,000 vines,
worth 1,000 pieces of silver,
will become thorns
and briers.
24 A man will go there with bow
and arrows
because the whole land
will be thorns and briers.
25 You will not go to all the hills
that were once tilled
with a hoe,
for fear of the thorns
and briers.
Those hills will be places
for oxen to graze
and for sheep to trample.

8 Then the LORD said to me, "Take
a large piece of parchment[A] and
write on it with an ordinary pen:[B]
Maher-shalal-hash-baz.[C] 2 I have appointed[D] trustworthy witnesses—
Uriah the priest and Zechariah son
of Jeberechiah."
3 I was then intimate with the
prophetess, and she conceived and

[A] 8:1 Hb obscure [B] 8:1 Lit *with the pen of a man* [C] 8:1 = Speeding to the Plunder, Hurrying to the Spoil [D] 8:2 Vg; MT, one DSS ms read *I will appoint*; one DSS ms, LXX, Syr, Tg read *Appoint*

both Syria and Israel were doomed, but he also extended a warning to Ahaz and Judah. God pointed out that each king was **the head** (or "chief") of their capital cities and by extension their countries. God noted that **within** 65 years Ephraim (the power of the whole northern kingdom of Israel) would be **shattered** [Hb *chatat*, "be broken"] as **a people**. Within only a few years, Assyria had invaded both Syria and Israel.

7:10-13 Ahaz refused to test God's ability to provide a sign that would have given early proof that everything God had promised in verses 8 and 9 would also come to pass. He was determined to work out his own solution to the Syro-Israelite problem (2Kg 16:7-8). Isaiah's response clearly indicated that Ahaz's reply was not one of faith.

7:17-19 Judgment was coming not only on Syria and Israel but also upon **Judah**.

7:20-25 The mention of **abundant milk** together with the phrase **butter and honey** reminds one of the goodness found in the promised land, described as "flowing with milk and honey" (e.g., Ex 3:8,17; 13:5; Nm 13:27; 14:8; Dt 6:3; 11:9; Jos 5:6). Even in God's judgment there was grace: Food was available to the survivors, but there was still a sense of loss with regard to the formerly well-maintained fields and fear that they would revert to barren wildernesses. The land would be almost deserted, and even the most fertile and productive land would be overgrown with **thorns and briers**. Eventually after Assyria and later Babylon ravaged the nation and deported first the northern tribes (721 B.C.), then Judah (586 B.C.), the land remained fallow with a God-imposed rest until the exiles were permitted to return and rebuild under Cyrus the Great (539 B.C.; 2Ch 36:20-21).

8:1-4 After the initial prophecy concerning the defeat of Israel and Syria by the hand of Assyria, Isaiah provided more details through the revelation of the Lord. He was commanded to write **Maher-shalal-hash-baz** (Hb, "speeding to the spoil, hastening to the plunder") on a **parchment** in the presence of two **appointed trustworthy witnesses—Uriah . . . and Zechariah.** These men effectively prophesied the destruction of Israel and Syria before the actual event.

Isaiah was **then intimate** [Hb *qarav*, "come near, approach sexually"] **with the prophetess,** his wife. Isaiah's son would serve as a living sign regarding the imminent (before the child could speak and say **father or mother)** defeat of Israel and thus the deliverance of Judah from the harassment of the Syro-Israelite alliance, which was worrying Ahaz and the people of Judah (7:2; 8:18).

8:9-10 The nations are challenged to do their worst against the people of God, but even though they **prepare for war** and **band together,** the outcome will be the same: They will be defeated—**broken** (Hb *chatat*, "be shattered with fear, be confounded"). The Lord was in sovereign control of the situation. Judah had hope, as Isaiah noted, **for God is with us** (Hb *immanu'ēl*; see 7:14).

8:14-15 Isaiah noted that God **will be a sanctuary** (Hb *miqdash*, "holy place"; metaphorically, "a refuge"; cp. Ezk 11:16) for those who wait on the Lord and His deliverance (cp. Ps 91:1-2,9-10). Unfortunately for the **two houses of Israel**, Israel and Judah, most would fail to look to the Lord for deliverance. Instead of a sanctuary, they would find Him **a stone to stumble over and a rock to trip over** (see **Word Study**, p. 884). This certainly applied to Judah and Israel in their failure to seek God and His way; but the ultimate fulfillment of this passage applied to the person of Christ. Various New Testament passages combine the images of this prophecy with Is 28:16 and Ps 118:22 in reference to Jesus (Mt 21:42-44; Lk 2:34; 20:17-18; Rm 9:32-33; 1Co 1:23; 1Pt 2:7-8).

8:16-17 The testimony and **the instruction** (Hb *torah*, "law"; cp. Is 1:10; 2:3; 5:24; 30:9; see chart, p. 758) that had been given to Isaiah were to be bound up, sealed, and passed on to his **disciples** (Hb *limmud*, "one being taught, learner"; cp. Is 50:4; 54:13). Three ideas are present: literally writing down the words of the prophecy; providing a formal legal affirmation of the words; and concealing the full meaning of the words until the future. Although God's deliverance was not immediate or clear, Isaiah was committed **to wait for the Lord.**

8:19-22 Isaiah challenged the people to reject false and forbidden sources of information concerning the future. The sources mentioned were **spirits of the dead** (Hb *'ov*, "medium, soothsayer, one who invokes the dead through incantations") in order to get information about the future (cp. 1Sm 28:3,7-9); and the **spiritists** (Hb *yidde'oni*, "false prophet, wizard"; cp. 19:3), a common word pair. The practice of speaking to the dead or consulting a seer or fortune-teller was strictly forbidden (Lv 19:31; 20:6, 27; Dt 18:10-11; 2Kg 21:6; 23:24; 1Ch 10:13; 2Ch 33:6).

9:1-3 In the Hebrew text, Is 9:1 is the

>WORD|*study*

8:16 The testimony (Hb *te'udah*, "attestation") comes from a verbal root meaning "call to witness" or "warn" (Hb *'ud*). Appearing only in Is 8:16,20 and Ru 4:7, the word in this context connotes a written document effecting a legal transaction. Another word from the same root is *'ēdut*, a synonym for the law (see chart, p. 758). These terms, particularly when used along with others like "commandments" and "statutes," refer to the revealed word of God.

8:18 Isaiah affirmed that both he and his children had been directed by God to be signs (Hb *'ot*, "portent, sign of something future"; cp. "miraculous signs," Ex 10:1) and wonders (Hb *mophēt*, "sign of something future; miraculous proof" of divine action) in Israel. Every time this pair of words "signs and wonders" appears, there is an allusion to the signs and wonders God performed through Moses in Egypt (e.g., Ex 7:3; Dt 4:34; Neh 9:10; Ps 78:43; Jr 32:20). There are two aspects involved: They were wonderful as a means of preparing for deliverance for those who believed, but they were terrible in the sense of foretelling the doom of those who rejected God.

gave birth to a son. The LORD said to
me, "Name him Maher-shalal-hash-
baz, 4 for before the boy knows how
to call out father or mother, the
wealth of Damascus and the spoils
of Samaria will be carried off to the
king of Assyria."
5 The LORD spoke to me again:

6 Because these people rejected
the slowly flowing waters
of Shiloah
and rejoiced with[A] Rezin
and the son of Remaliah,
7 the Lord will certainly bring
against them
the mighty rushing waters
of the Euphrates River—
the king of Assyria
and all his glory.
It will overflow its channels
and spill over all its banks.
8 It will pour into Judah,
flood over it,
and sweep through,
reaching up to the neck;
and its spreading streams[B]
will fill your entire land,
Immanuel!

9 Band together, peoples,
and be broken;
pay attention,
all you distant lands;
prepare for war,
and be broken;
prepare for war,
and be broken.
10 Devise a plan; it will fail.
Make a prediction;
it will not happen.
For God is with us.[C]

11 For this is what the LORD said to
me with great power, to keep[D] me
from going the way of this people:

12 Do not call everything
an alliance
these people say is an alliance.
Do not fear what they fear;
do not be terrified.
13 You are to regard
only the LORD of •Hosts
as holy.
Only He should be •feared;
only He should be held
in awe.
14 He will be a sanctuary;
but for the two houses
of Israel,
He will be a stone
to stumble over
and a rock to trip over,
and a trap and a snare
to the inhabitants
of Jerusalem.
15 Many will stumble
over these;
they will fall and be broken;
they will be snared
and captured.

16 Bind up the •testimony.
Seal up the instruction
among my disciples.
17 I will wait for the LORD,
who is hiding His face
from the house of Jacob.
I will wait for Him.

18 Here I am with the children the
LORD has given me to be signs and
wonders in Israel from the LORD of
Hosts who dwells on Mount •Zion.
19 When they say to you, "Consult the
spirits of the dead and the spiritists
who chirp and mutter," shouldn't a

[A] 8:6 Or *and rejoiced over* [B] 8:8 Or *wings* [C] 8:10 Or *For Immanuel* [D] 8:11 DSS; MT reads *instruct*

people consult their God?[A] Should
they consult the dead on behalf of
the living? 20 To the law and to the
testimony! If they do not speak according to this word, there will be
no dawn for them.
21 They will wander through the
land, dejected and hungry. When
they are famished, they will become
enraged, and, looking upward, will
curse their king and their God.
22 They will look toward the earth
and see only distress, darkness, and
the gloom of affliction, and they will
be driven into thick darkness.

The Deliverance of the Lord (9:1–12:6)

Coming of the Messiah (9:1-7)

9 [B]Nevertheless, the gloom of the distressed land will not be like that of the former times when He humbled the land of Zebulun and the land of Naphtali. But in the future He will bring honor to the Way of the Sea, to the land east of the Jordan, and to Galilee of the nations.

2[C] The people walking in darkness
have seen a great light;
a light has dawned
on those living in the land
of darkness.
3 You have enlarged the nation
and increased its joy.[D]
The people have rejoiced
before You
as they rejoice at harvest time
and as they rejoice
when dividing spoils.
4 For You have shattered
their oppressive yoke
and the rod
on their shoulders,
the staff of their oppressor,
just as You did on the day
of Midian.
5 For the trampling boot
of battle
and the bloodied garments
of war
will be burned as fuel
for the fire.
6 For a child will be born for us,
a son will be given to us,
and the government will be
on His shoulders.
He will be named
Wonderful Counselor,
Mighty God,
Eternal Father,
Prince of Peace.
7 The dominion will be vast,
and its prosperity will
never end.
He will reign on the throne
of David
and over his kingdom,
to establish and sustain it
with justice and
righteousness from now on
and forever.
The zeal of the LORD of •Hosts
will accomplish this.

Judgment against Israel (9:8–10:4)

8 The Lord sent a message
against Jacob;
it came against Israel.
9 All the people—
Ephraim and the inhabitants
of Samaria—will know it.
They will say with pride
and arrogance:
10 "The bricks have fallen,
but we will rebuild
with cut stones;
the sycamores have been
cut down,
but we will replace them
with cedars."
11 The LORD has raised up
Rezin's adversaries
against him
and stirred up his enemies.
12 Aram from the east
and Philistia from the west
have consumed Israel
with open mouths.
In all this, His anger
is not removed,
and His hand is still raised
to strike.
13 The people did not turn
to Him who struck them;
they did not seek the LORD
of Hosts.
14 So the LORD cut off
Israel's head and tail,
palm branch and reed
in a single day.
15 The head is the elder,
the honored one;

[A]**8:19** Or *gods* [B]**9:1** Is 8:23 in Hb [C]**9:2** Is 9:1 in Hb [D]**9:3** Alt Hb tradition reads *have not increased joy*

last verse of the preceding chapter. In the oldest Hebrew manuscript found to date, there is no break until the end of Is 9:2.

9:3-5 The nation would experience great **joy** for three reasons. First, oppression would end. God would deliver the people from oppression as **on the day of Midian**. This referred to the battle fought by Gideon and his 300 men in the face of overwhelming odds. The victory was won by the Lord alone; Gideon's tiny army could claim no credit (Jdg 6:1-16; 7:2-25; 8:10-12). In the future day of deliverance, the Lord would again shatter all oppression, and there would be nobody besides Him to take the credit. Second, war would cease. There would be no need for the garments of war; the implements (**boot**) and results (**bloodied garments**) of warfare will be **fuel for the fire**.

9:6-12 Third, the Messiah would come. The pinnacle of Isaiah's proclamation of hope for Israel in the face of the Assyrian threat lay in the promised ruler who would **reign on the throne of David** and establish **justice and righteousness**. The four compound names given to this **child** (Hb *yeled*, "son") who will **be born** (Hb *yalad*) **for us**, indicate His divinity. He will be a fulfillment of the Immanuel prophecy (7:14). He is a human child who also bears a divine nature. The understanding of the human and divine character of the coming king is further developed by the following four compound names:

- **Wonderful Counselor** (Hb *pele'yo'ēts*) described one who would establish plans, not just advise another. The coming ruler would be wonderful in the origination of His plans (see 11:2; 25:1; 28:29).
- **Mighty God** (Hb *'ēl*, "God"; *gibbor*, "strong, powerful," often used to describe men as proven, elite warriors; cp. 3:2; Jdg 6:12; Jr 51:30), a phrase whose only other occurrence (Is 10:21) clearly applies to Yahweh (Dt 10:17; Neh 9:32; Jr 32:18; Rv 18:8). This reference is to the divinity of the child and accentuates His strength (Lk 11:20-22; Jn 16:33).
- **Eternal Father** (Hb *'avi'ad*, "father of eternity") may emphasize the eternality of the paternal relationship of the coming Messiah with the people (Mt 11:27; 23:9; Rm 8:14-17; Rv 21:7), or the eternality of the Son and His unity with the Godhead (Is 57:15; Mc 5:2; Jn 1:1-3,18; 10:30,33,38; 14:6-11; 16:26-28; 17:5; Col 1:15-17; Rv 22:13).
- **Prince of Peace** (Hb *sar-shalom*) was a title that included the idea of "completeness or wholeness."

Hebrew Words for "Idols" and "Images" in Isaiah

HCSB Translation in Isaiah (Hebrew word)	Definition	Usage
idol (Hb *'elil*)	• something worthless; • false gods, idols	• Is 2:8,18,20; 10:10-11; 19:1,3; 31:7 • cp. Lv 19:4; 26:1
idol (Hb *pasil*)	graven or carved images (from the verb *pasal*, "cut, carve, hew into shape")	• Is 10:10; 21:9; 30:22; 42:8 • cp. "carved images," Jr 8:19 • cp. "carved images," Dt 7:5,25; Jr 50:38; 51:47
idol, image, carved image (Hb *pesel*)	graven, carved, or molten images (from the verb *pasal*, "cut, carve, hew into shape")	• Is 40:19-20; 42:17; 44:9-10,15,17; 45:20; 48:5 • cp. Ex 20:4; Lv 26:1; Dt 4:16,23,25; 5:8; 27:15
idol (Hb *'atsav*)	labor, form, fashion, worship	• Is 10:11; 46:1; Jr 44:19
idol (Hb *'otsev*)	related to *'atsav* above	• Is 48:5
image (Hb *nesek*)	• molten image; • drink offering (from the verb *nasak*, "pour out, cast metal")	• Is 41:29; 48:5
image (Hb *massēkah*)	• casting of metal, molten metal • image (from the verb *nasak*, "pour out, cast metal")	• Is 30:22; 42:17
pillar, sacred pillar (Hb *matstsēvah*)	• statue or monument, • image of an idol	• Is 19:19 • cp. Ex 23:24; 34:13; Lv 26:1; Dt 7:5; 12:3; 16:22; 1Kg 14:23; 2Kg 3:2

The Messiah will bring military peace, but even more important is the peace He established between God and man (v. 5; cp. Is 53:5; 54:10; 57:19; 63:16; 66:12; Zch 9:9-10; Lk 2:14; Jn 14:27; 16:33; 20:21; Rm 5:1; Eph 2:14-18; Php 4:7; Col 1:19-20).

Some view the passage as a royal hymn celebrating the birth of Hezekiah or Josiah. Nevertheless, to limit the interpretation to a purely human king is to disregard the clear language associated with divinity. The incarnation of the Lord Jesus initiated the fulfillment of this passage. He was born of Mary, thus fully human. Yet He was fully God, preexistent before incarnation, heir to the titles and attributes appropriate to the eternal God of Israel. Isaiah foresaw the time when the Lord, as the anointed one, the Messiah, would "reign on the throne of David" forever (cp. Lk 1:32-33). The final fulfillment of verse 7 awaits the return and reign of the Lord Jesus when He will rule with "justice and righteousness from now on and forever" (cp. Rv 22:1-3).

In verses 8-12 Isaiah returned to the theme of God's judgment. God

the tail is the prophet,
  the lying teacher.
16 The leaders of the people
  mislead them,
and those they mislead
  are swallowed up.[A]
17 Therefore the Lord does not
  rejoice
over[B] Israel's young men
and has no compassion
on its fatherless and widows,
for everyone is
  a godless evildoer,
and every mouth speaks folly.
In all this, His anger
  is not removed,
and His hand is still raised
  to strike.

18 For wickedness burns
  like a fire
that consumes thorns
  and briers
and kindles
  the forest thickets
so that they go up
  in a column of smoke.
19 The land is scorched
by the wrath of the LORD
  of Hosts,
and the people are like fuel
  for the fire.
No one has compassion
  on his brother.
20 They carve meat on the right,
but they are still hungry;
they have eaten on the left,
but they are still not satisfied.
Each one eats the flesh
  of his own arm.
21 Manasseh is with Ephraim,
and Ephraim with Manasseh;
together, both are
  against Judah.
In all this, His anger is
  not removed,

A **9:16** Or *are confused* B **9:17** DSS read *not spare*

and His hand is still raised
to strike.

10 Woe to those enacting
crooked statutes
and writing oppressive laws
2 to keep the poor from getting
a fair trial
and to deprive the afflicted
among my people of justice,
so that widows can be
their spoil
and they can plunder
the fatherless.
3 What will you do on the day
of punishment
when devastation comes
from far away?
Who will you run to for help?
Where will you leave
your wealth?
4 There will be nothing to do
except crouch
among the prisoners
or fall among the slain.
In all this, His anger
is not removed,
and His hand is still raised
to strike.

Judgment Against Assyria (10:5-19)

5 Woe to Assyria, the rod
of My anger—
the staff in their hands is
My wrath.
6 I will send him against
a godless nation;
I will command him to go
against a people destined
for My rage,
to take spoils, to plunder,
and to trample them down
like clay in the streets.
7 But this is not
what he intends;
this is not what he plans.
It is his intent to destroy
and to cut off many nations.
8 For he says,
"Aren't all
my commanders kings?
9 Isn't Calno like Carchemish?
Isn't Hamath like Arpad?
Isn't Samaria like Damascus?[A]
10 As my hand seized
the idolatrous kingdoms,
whose idols exceeded
those of Jerusalem
and Samaria,
11 and as I did to Samaria
and its idols
will I not also do to Jerusalem
and its idols?"

12 But when the Lord finishes all
His work against Mount •Zion and
Jerusalem, He will say, "I[B] will punish the king of Assyria for his arrogant acts and the proud look in his
eyes." 13 For he said:

I have done this
by my own strength
and wisdom, for I am clever.
I abolished the borders
of nations
and plundered their treasures;
like a mighty warrior,
I subjugated
the inhabitants.[C]
14 My hand has reached out, as if
into a nest,
to seize the wealth
of the nations.
Like one gathering
abandoned eggs,
I gathered the whole earth.
No wing fluttered;
no beak opened or chirped.

15 Does an ax exalt itself
above the one who chops
with it?
Does a saw magnify itself
above the one who saws
with it?
It would be like a staff waving
the one who lifts[D] it!
It would be like
a rod lifting a man
who isn't wood!
16 Therefore the Lord God
of •Hosts
will inflict
an emaciating disease
on the well-fed of Assyria,
and He will kindle
a burning fire
under its glory.
17 Israel's Light will become
a fire,
and its Holy One, a flame.
In one day it will burn up
Assyria's thorns
and thistles.

presents further indictments: pride, corrupt leadership, wicked disregard for others, and social injustice.

10:1-2 God's final indictment in this group of four sections was against corrupt and oppressive legislators.

10:3-4 Isaiah warned that the oppressors would be punished and their ill-gotten gains would not help them when they were conquered by cruel Assyria.

10:5-6 Isaiah asserted that Assyria, too, would be judged. Again, the sovereignty of God is emphasized. Assyria would be a tool, **the rod** and **the staff**, used by God to accomplish His purpose for Israel.

10:8-11 Still, Assyria would not want to stop her rampage because she would proudly consider victory as a sign of her own strength.

10:12-15 Assyria failed to realize the sovereignty of the God of Israel. God was using Assyria for **His work against Mount Zion and Jerusalem**, but He would not allow Assyria to destroy Jerusalem. The king's pride is vividly portrayed in his arrogant boasting, **I gathered the whole earth**. The more literal Hebrew rendering is, "It was I (and no other) who gathered the whole earth" like **abandoned eggs**. Such arrogance was an explicit affront to God.

Assyria was merely a tool, like an **ax** or a **saw**, which God was using to discipline His people for their unfaithfulness to His covenant (Dt 28:25,29,31-32; 36-41,45-52). Otherwise the Assyrians were powerless. In the end, Assyria would be punished for its own arrogance.

10:16-19 Isaiah artistically used metaphors of sickness and **fire** to describe the effects of the judgment of the Lord. Assyria would no longer have the abundance and glory of the former times. Only a handful of its trees would survive, symbolizing Assyria's diminished presence. The Assyrian royal gardens, filled with exotic trees, were renowned for their glory, which was greatly lessened in 612 B.C. when Nineveh, the capital of Assyria, was overthrown by the Babylonians and Medes. A small group of Assyrians attempted to hold out in Haran, but by 609 B.C. Assyria was no longer an independent nation.

[A] **10:9** Cities conquered by Assyria [B] **10:12** LXX reads *Jerusalem, He* [C] **10:13** Or *I brought down their kings* [D] **10:15** Some Hb mss, Syr, Vg read *wave he who lifts*

>WORD|*study*

10:20 Twelve out of 26 occurrences of the noun **remnant** (Hb *she'ar*, "rest, residue, remainder") in the Old Testament are found in Isaiah. The synonymous cognate form (Hb *she'ērit*) appears six out of 66 times in Isaiah (14:30; 15:9; 37:4,32; 44:17; 46:3). Both derive from the Hebrew verb *sha'ar*, meaning "to remain or be left over." In Isaiah, the word overwhelmingly identifies survivors of God's judgment. King Hezekiah described the surviving Israelites of his time with this word (Is 37:4). Most often Isaiah used the term in a positive sense to describe the future survivors of upcoming judgment. The survivors referenced were usually Israelites, although there are a few cases when the term referred to survivors of other nations (14:22,30; 15:9; 16:14; 17:3; 21:17). In five of the six references to pagan nations, the context indicated that even the survivors would be cut off or suffer further judgment. In 10:19, Isaiah used *she'ar* to describe the leftover trees of Assyria's soon-to-be destroyed forests—symbolic of the nation itself. A unique use of *she'ērit* referred to the leftover wood that idol worshipers carved into an idol (44:17).

10:20 Isaiah returned to one of the great themes in his book: the promise of a **remnant** that would survive the coming judgment.

Perhaps thinking of the effrontery of Ahaz in going to Assyria for help instead of God, Isaiah noted there would come a time when Israel would **no longer depend on the one who struck them** (cp. 2Ch 28:16,20; Hs 14:1-8). Instead, the people would finally depend upon **the Holy One of Israel**.

10:21-23 Isaiah prophesied, **The remnant will return** [Hb *shuv*] **. . . to the Mighty God** (Dt 30:1-4; see **Word Study**, Is 44:21-23). This phrase, "The remnant will return" (Hb *She'ar-yashuv*) is a reminder of the name of Isaiah's son (Is 7:3). Israel is warned that the returning people would be few compared to the original numbers because God was **carrying out a destruction that was decreed** (cp. Dt 28:62). The covenant curses would be fulfilled (see Dt 28:15-68). In the New Testament, Paul specifically applied the final fulfillment of the prophecy of Is 10:22-23 to those Israelites who would believe in the Lord Jesus (Rm 9:27).

10:28-32 The series of cities listed by Isaiah traced the path of the enemy army as they would march and pillage through the land of Judah. Though unclear as to which campaign, the context suggests the Assyrian army. This path of attack differs from that of Sennacherib in 701 B.C. Although the actual campaign remains unidentified, clearly the Assyrians caused terror and misery as they conquered cities. Isaiah noted the enemy would get to **Nob**, within striking distance of Jerusalem, yet no further. The dramatic picture foretold was of the enemy outside of Jerusalem, **shaking his fist at the mountain of Daughter Zion**, which aptly conveyed the frustration later experienced by leaders of Assyria when they failed to conquer the city of Jerusalem (36:1–37:38).

11:1 In this chapter Isaiah provided more particulars about the coming Messiah who would rule Israel. The Messiah would be a descendant of **Jesse . . . a branch** (Hb *nētser*, "sprout, shoot") **from his roots** (Hb *sheresh*,

18 He will completely destroy
the glory of its forests
and orchards
as a sickness consumes
a person.
19 The remaining trees
of its forest
will be so few in number
that a child could count them.

The Return of a Remnant (10:20-23)

20 On that day the remnant of Israel and the survivors of the house
of Jacob will no longer depend on
the one who struck them, but they
will faithfully depend on the LORD,
the Holy One of Israel.

21 The remnant will return,
the remnant of Jacob,
to the Mighty God.
22 Israel, even if your people
were as numerous
as the sand of the sea,
only a remnant of them
will return.
Destruction has been decreed;
justice overflows.
23 For throughout the land
the Lord GOD of Hosts
is carrying out a destruction
that was decreed.

Deliverance from Assyria (10:24-34)

24 Therefore, the Lord GOD of Hosts
says this: "My people who dwell in
Zion, do not fear Assyria, though he
strikes you with a rod and raises his
staff over you as the Egyptians did.
25 In just a little while My wrath will
be spent and My anger will turn to
their destruction." 26 And the LORD of
Hosts will brandish a whip against
him as He did when He struck Midian at the rock of Oreb; and He will
raise His staff over the sea as He did
in Egypt.

27 On that day
his burden will fall
from your shoulders,
and his yoke from your neck.
The yoke will be broken
because of fatness.[A]
28 Assyria has come to Aiath
and has gone
through Migron,
storing his equipment
at Michmash.
29 They crossed over
at the ford, saying,
"We will spend the night
at Geba."
The people of Ramah
are trembling;
those at Gibeah of Saul
have fled.
30 Cry aloud, daughter
of Gallim!
Listen, Laishah!
Anathoth is miserable.
31 Madmenah has fled.
The inhabitants of Gebim
have sought refuge.
32 Today he will stand at Nob,
shaking his fist
at the mountain
of Daughter Zion,
the hill of Jerusalem.
33 Look, the Lord GOD of Hosts
will chop off the branches
with terrifying power,
and the tall trees will be
cut down,
the high trees felled.
34 He is clearing the thickets
of the forest with an ax,
and Lebanon with its majesty
will fall.

The Reign of the Messiah (11:1-16)

11 Then a shoot will grow
from the stump of Jesse,

[A]10:27 Hb obscure

>WORD|*study*

11:10 A **banner** (Hb *nēs*, "something lifted up, an emblem to be seen from far away") or "signal flag" (Ps 60:4; Is 5:26; 31:9; Jr 4:6,21; 50:2; 51:12,27) was usually raised as a rallying point, especially in a military context. When an invading army approached, a banner would show the people or troops where to gather. Distinctive banners identified specific groups—a military unit, tribe, or nation—and their location. In battle, a banner would serve not only as a point of assembly for military personnel but also as the object to which people looked in hope of victory.

and a branch from his roots
will bear fruit.
2 The Spirit of the LORD
will rest on Him—
a Spirit of wisdom
and understanding,
a Spirit of counsel
and strength,
a Spirit of knowledge
and of the •fear of the LORD.
3 His delight will be in the fear
of the LORD.
He will not judge
by what He sees with His eyes,
He will not execute justice
by what He hears
with His ears,
4 but He will judge
the poor righteously
and execute justice
for the oppressed
of the land.
He will strike the land
with discipline[A]
from His mouth,
and He will kill the wicked
with a command[B]
from His lips.
5 Righteousness will be a belt
around His loins;
faithfulness will be a belt
around His waist.
6 The wolf will live
with the lamb,
and the leopard will lie down
with the goat.
The calf, the young
lion, and the fatling
will be together,
and a child will lead them.
7 The cow and the bear
will graze,
their young ones
will lie down together,
and the lion will eat straw
like the ox.
8 An infant will play
beside the cobra's pit,
and a toddler will put
his hand into a snake's den.
9 None will harm or
destroy another
on My entire holy mountain,
for the land will be as full
of the knowledge of the LORD
as the sea is filled with water.

10 On that day the root of Jesse
will stand as a banner
for the peoples.
The nations will seek Him,
and His resting place
will be glorious.

11 On that day the Lord will extend His hand a second time to
recover—from Assyria, Egypt, Pathros, •Cush, Elam, •Shinar, Hamath,
and the coasts and islands of the
west—the remnant of His people
who survive.

12 He will lift up a banner
for the nations
and gather the dispersed
of Israel;
He will collect the scattered
of Judah
from the four corners
of the earth.
13 Ephraim's envy will cease;
Judah's harassment will end.
Ephraim will no longer
be envious of Judah,
and Judah will not harass
Ephraim.
14 But they will swoop down
on the Philistine flank
to the west.
Together they will plunder
the people of the east.
They will extend their power
over Edom and Moab,

[A]**11:4** Lit *the rod* [B]**11:4** Lit *with the breath*

"shoot springing from a root"). Isaiah also called the future ruler "the root (Hb *sheresh*) of Jesse" (11:10; cp. 53:2), who, as the father of King David, is included in the royal lineage of the coming ruler, the Messiah (Mt 1:1,6; Ac 13:22-23; Rm 1:3). In the New Testament, the title "Son of David" is correctly applied in identifying Jesus as the Messiah (e.g., Mt 9:27; 21:9). Jesus personally claimed this heritage as His own in Rv 22:16 when He clearly stated, "I am the Root and Offspring of David, the Bright Morning Star" (cp. Is 4:2; 9:7; 53:2; Jr 23:5-8; 33:14-18; Zch 3:8; 6:12-13; Rv 5:5). The preexistence of Christ is a vital truth inherent in His designation as the "root" and "branch" of David (Mt 22:41-46; Jn 1:1,14). Again, the seeming paradox of being both root and branch is only resolved in the God-man, Jesus Christ.

11:6-9 A figurative reading might describe the new reign of peace in the human realm, while a literal interpretation may suggest that the rule of the Messiah will bring about a complete reversal of fallen natural and human relations. Predators are paired with prey to highlight that animal instinct itself will be changed in a world where the effects of the curse no longer exist (cp. Gn 3:15; Rm 8:18-22). **None will harm** [Hb *ra'a'*, "do evil"] **or destroy**, a reminder of Isaiah's earlier statements concerning the last days (cp. 2:4; 35:9; 65:25; Ezk 34:24-25,28; Hs 2:18; Zch 9:10). The reason for the peace would be that the land will be filled with **the knowledge of the LORD**. This period of peace under the direct reign of the Messiah has not yet been fulfilled but remains for the future (Rv 20:4; 21:1-4).

11:10-12 Isaiah 11:10 serves as the transition between the two sections of this chapter. That this **root of Jesse will stand as a banner for the peoples** points forward to the rest of the passage (see **Word Study**, 11:10). Like such a banner, the Messiah will draw the **nations** (Hb *goyim*, the plural form, "peoples," typically referring to non-Hebrew or Gentile groups, i.e., the surrounding pagan nations) to Himself, in addition to **the remnant** (i.e., **the dispersed of Israel** and **the scattered of Judah**). In the New Testament, Paul quoted verse 10 as a prophecy that the Lord would draw the Gentiles to Himself (Rm 15:8-12).

11:13-16 As the people of both **Ephraim** (northern kingdom) and **Judah** (southern kingdom) return, the old rivalries will be ended (cp. 9:20-21). They will again be one unified nation, inhabiting the Promised Land.

12:1-2 Connected with the preceding passage by the phrase **on that day**, chapter 12 contains songs of joyous praise regarding the certain deliverance to come. Reminiscent of the song of Moses following God's deliverance through the Red Sea (Ex 15:1-18), the theme of **salvation** is prominent, as the people would truly come to trust God for their deliverance.

12:3-6 Furthermore, Isaiah prophesied that they would **joyfully draw water from the springs of salvation**. This contains a depth of meaning. Following the exodus, the Lord, standing above the rock at Massah and Meribah, provided water to the people from the rock (Ex 17:6-7; Nm 20:2-13; cp. 1Co 10:4). Moreover, Christ referred to Himself as the source of the living water (the Holy Spirit), which He would provide to give eternal life (Jn 4:7-14; 7:37-39; cp. Ti 3:4-7). The overwhelming joy resulting from salvation would be expressed in praise to the Lord; His name would be **exalted** (cp. Php 2:9-11). The inhabitants **of Zion** were exhorted to rejoice because **the Holy One of Israel** would be **among** them **in greatness** (Is 12:6; cp. Rv 21:1-4,22-23), another idea linking this passage to the provision of water from the rock, as the people asked whether the LORD was "among us or not" (Ex 17:7).

13:1–35:10 The following chapters alternate between oracles of judgment against the nations and words of encouragement concerning salvation. Israel, like the other nations, would be judged. Nevertheless, all nations had hope in the salvation brought by the arm of God.

13:1-2 This **oracle** (Hb, *massa'*, "utterance"), clearly attributed to the prophet **Isaiah** of the eighth century, was **against Babylon**. Up until this passage, Assyria had been cast as the main enemy and threat. At the time of Isaiah, Assyria—not Babylon—was the dominant power. However, God revealed to Isaiah that Babylon would be the nation to conquer Jerusalem in the future (chap. 39), and He also revealed Babylon's own downfall before it was ever a threat.

13:3-5 God makes a declaration of war (v. 4) and a call to arms (vv. 2-3). He had **chosen ones** and **warriors** who were set apart to use as **weapons of His wrath**.

>WORD|*study*

12:1-2 Isaiah exclaimed that there would come a day when the people would say, "**Indeed, God is my** salvation" (Hb *yeshu'ah*, "deliverance"). The word *yeshu'ah* meaning "salvation" is used 78 times in the Old Testament; 19 occurrences are found in Isaiah, and 45 are found in the Psalms (Is 12:2-3 [3x]; 25:9; 26:1,18; 33:2,6; 49:6,8; 51:6,8; 52:7,10; 56:1; 59:11,17; 60:18; 62:1). Most references are clearly connected with the idea that salvation was provided by God. Through an angelic messenger God instructed Mary and Joseph to name the Messiah Jesus (Gk *Iēsous*, "Savior," Mt 1:21,25; Lk 1:31; 2:21), the Greek version of the Hebrew *Yeshua*. God accomplished salvation and deliverance through Jesus the Savior.

and the Ammonites will be
their subjects.
15 The LORD will divide[A,B]
the Gulf of Suez.[C]
He will wave His hand
over the Euphrates
with His mighty wind
and will split it
into seven streams,
letting people walk through
on foot.
16 There will be a highway
for the remnant
of His people
who will survive from Assyria,
as there was for Israel
when they came up
from the land of Egypt.

Hymns of Praise (12:1-6)

12 On that day you will say:
"I will praise You, LORD,
although You were angry
with me.
Your anger has turned away,
and You have had compassion
on me.
2 Indeed, God is my salvation;
I will trust Him and not
be afraid,
for •Yah, the LORD,
is my strength and my song.
He has become my salvation."
3 You will joyfully draw water
from the springs of salvation,
4 and on that day you will say:
"Give thanks to Yahweh;
proclaim His name!
Celebrate His works
among the peoples.
Declare that His name
is exalted.
5 Sing to Yahweh,
for He has done
glorious things.
Let this be known
throughout the earth.
6 Cry out and sing,
citizen of •Zion,
for the Holy One of Israel is
among you
in His greatness."

Judgment Against Babylon (13:1–14:23)

13 An •oracle against Babylon that
Isaiah son of Amoz saw:

2 Lift up a banner
on a barren mountain.
Call out to them.
Wave your hand,
and they will go
through the gates
of the nobles.
3 I have commanded
My chosen ones;
I have also called My warriors,
who exult in My triumph,
to execute My wrath.
4 Listen, a tumult
on the mountains,
like that of a mighty people!
Listen, an uproar
among the kingdoms,
like nations being
gathered together!
The LORD of •Hosts
is mobilizing an army
for war.
5 They are coming
from a far land,
from the distant horizon—
the LORD and the weapons
of His wrath—
to destroy the whole country.[D]
6 Wail! For the day of the LORD
is near.
It will come like destruction
from the •Almighty.
7 Therefore everyone's hands
will become weak,

[A]11:15 Text emended; MT reads *destroy* [B]11:15 Or *dry up* [C]11:15 Lit *the Sea of Egypt* [D]13:5 Or *earth*

>WORD|*study*

13:9 The day of the LORD (Hb *yom-YHWH*) is a theme often appearing in various prophetic works (Is 13:6,9; cp. Jl 1:15; 2:1,11; 3:14; Am 5:18,20; Ob 15; Zph. 1:7,14; Zch 14:1-15; Mal 4:1,5; 1Th 5:1-4; 2Pt 3:10-13; Rv 6:12-17). References to "the day of the LORD" include imagery of the Lord coming in vengeance to execute judgment on the entire world. His coming is accompanied by cosmic upheaval. Often darkness is connected with the "day of the LORD" (Is 13:10; cp. Jl 2:1-2, 10, 31; Am 5:18,20; Zph 1:15; Rv 6:12). The "day of the LORD" indicates a time when God will set aright the world, when he will finally defeat the unjust and vindicate the just. Often, the "day of the LORD" is connected with the last days when God would judge and punish the wicked permanently (Is 13:11; Jl 1:15; 3:1-16; Ob 15; Zph 1:8-9,12; Mal 4:1; Rv 20:11-15) while lifting up His people.

and every man's heart
will melt.
8 They will be horrified;
pain and agony
will seize them;
they will be in anguish
like a woman in labor.
They will look at each other,
their faces flushed with fear.
9 Look, the day of the LORD
is coming—
cruel, with rage
and burning anger—
to make the earth a desolation
and to destroy the sinners
on it.
10 Indeed, the stars of the sky
and its constellations[A]
will not give their light.
The sun will be dark
when it rises,
and the moon will not shine.
11 I will bring disaster
on the world,
and their own iniquity,
on the wicked.
I will put an end to the pride
of the arrogant
and humiliate the insolence
of tyrants.
12 I will make man scarcer
than gold,
and mankind more rare
than the gold of Ophir.
13 Therefore I will make
the heavens tremble,
and the earth will shake
from its foundations
at the wrath of the LORD
of Hosts,
on the day
of His burning anger.
14 Like wandering gazelles
and like sheep
without a shepherd,
each one will turn
to his own people,
each one will flee
to his own land.
15 Whoever is found
will be stabbed,
and whoever is caught will die
by the sword.
16 Their children will be
smashed to death
before their eyes;
their houses will be looted,
and their wives raped.
17 Look! I am stirring up
the Medes against them,
who cannot be bought off
with[B] silver
and who have no desire
for gold.
18 Their bows will cut
young men to pieces.
They will have no compassion
on little ones;
they will not look with pity
on children.
19 And Babylon, the jewel
of the kingdoms,
the glory of the pride
of the Chaldeans,
will be like Sodom
and Gomorrah
when God overthrew them.
20 It will never be inhabited
or lived in from generation
to generation;
a nomad will not pitch
his tent there,
and shepherds will not let
their flocks rest there.
21 But desert creatures
will lie down there,
and owls will fill the houses.
Ostriches will dwell there,
and wild goats will leap about.
22 Hyenas will howl
in the fortresses,

[A]13:10 Or *Orions* [B]13:17 Lit *who have no regard for*

13:9-11 This passage may indicate the fall of the Babylonian Empire in the sixth century, or there may be a still future prophecy in view.

13:12-16 Based on the context, there was at least a type of fulfillment accomplished by the fall of Babylon to Cyrus; however, perhaps there remains a future final fulfillment regarding the "day of the LORD" (v. 9) and Babylon itself or a typified "Babylon."

13:19-22 Ultimately, Babylon, whether the literal city of antiquity or the symbol of a society in rebellion against God, will be utterly ruined. There will be a swift, violent, and fiery demise reminiscent of **Sodom and Gomorrah** (Gn 19:24-25,28). Left in utter desolation, only the **desert creatures** will go there: unclean birds **and wild goats** [Hb *sa'ir*, "he-goat, demon" see Rv 18:2] **. . . hyenas . . . and jackals** (cp. Is 14:23; 34:9-15; Lv 11:13-19). This passage certainly appears to apply partly to the future overthrow of the "Babylon" mentioned in the book of Revelation (Jr 50:39-40,51; Rv 14:8; 16:19; 17:1–18:24), which includes some of the same imagery Isaiah used to described a land completely forsaken by God.

14:1-2 The language of this passage echoes the first exodus when God brought Israel out of Egyptian bondage and into the land of Canaan. God's promise to the remnant of Israelites was that He would **choose Israel again** and that He would **settle them on their own land**. Notably, the **foreigner** would be allowed to **join them** and be included in **the house of Jacob** (cp. Ex 12:38,48-49). These foreigners joined to Israel would share the rights of native Israelites. Later Isaiah recorded that such foreigners would have "a name better than sons and daughters" (Is 56:3-7; cp. Ezk 47:22-23). This continues to be true for all non-Jewish believers in Jesus. Israel, the remnant and those joined to them, will in that day **rule over their oppressors** (Is 60:12,14). Following captivity in Babylon, Israelites were permitted to return to the land of Israel. This exodus from Babylon and return to the land may also prefigure a greater return and restoration. The New Testament notes that there will be a saved remnant of believing Israelites who will be united with the saved Gentiles who have been "grafted in" to the olive tree, signifying God's covenantal people (Rm 11:17,23-24).

14:3-6 Once the people were released from their bondage, they would reflect on the fall of their former oppressor, **the king of Babylon**. The following song is in the form of a funeral dirge transformed by the content into a taunt song against the king of Babylon. The point of the passage is that God alone is omnipotent and sovereign. The Lord will break the **staff of the wicked**. Although Babylon would rule with relentless persecution, the day would come when its rule would be overturned.

14:9-11 **Sheol**, the place of the dead, is personified as being eager for the arrival of the defeated Babylonian king. In a parody of a kingdom court, **the kings of the nations**, who had preceded the king of Babylon in death, rise in his presence. Some suggest their comments derisively mocked the fallen ruler. Others take their responses as proceeding from shock and amazement that one so powerful would end up exactly as they were. The great and feared ruler would end up being just as weak as all other mortals. The **music of your harps** indicates the luxuries to which the most prosperous had access. The life of the ruler, surrounded by earthly **splendor**, pomp, and luxury, would end ingloriously. **Maggots** and **worms** would be his new attendants.

14:12-13 Isaiah then summarized the absolute pride and arrogance of the ruler. In Canaanite myths, lesser gods attempted to supplant other/greater gods. Perhaps Isaiah knew of these

>WORD|*study*

14:1 A foreigner (Hb *gēr*, "sojourner, stranger") could denote anyone who was dwelling in a land other than his own, as well as a person estranged from his household. At various times the patriarchs and the Israelites were called foreigners. Under the law the foreigner dwelling in Israel shared certain rights with native Israelites like the right to Sabbath rest, rights similar to those of widows and orphans as well as rights to justice, respect, and care (Lv 19:33-34; 25:35; Nm 15:14-16; Dt 10:18; 14:29; 24:17,19-21; 27:19). They were responsible to follow most laws of the Israelites and could face the same penalties (Lv 17:8-13; 18:26; 20:2; Nm 15:29-30; Jos 20:9). Still, certain rights, like the right to celebrate Passover, would not be conferred unless they became full proselytes (Ex 12:48).

14:12 Shining (Hb *hēlēl*) has been translated a variety of ways. Two Hebrew roots could give rise to this word: *halal* (Hb, "shine" or "praise, be boastful") or *yalal* (Hb, "howl"). If *hēlēl* is an imperative verb form of *yalal*, the translation could be "Howl, morning star" (cp. Ezk 21:12; Zch 11:2). However, most scholars take the word in Is 14:12 as a noun derived from *halal*, meaning "shining one, morning star," referring to the brightest star in the heavens, which most now consider to be Venus. When Jerome translated the word in the Latin Vulgate, he chose the word *lucifer* (Lat, "light-bearer, morning star"). Similarly, the word used in the Septuagint (LXX) means "morning star" (Gk *eōsphoros*). In 2Pt 1:19, the similar word *phōsphoros* (Gk, "morning star") is applied to Jesus, who was everything this proud being was not.

and jackals,
in the luxurious palaces.
Babylon's time is almost up;
her days are almost over.

14 For the Lord will have compassion on Jacob and will choose
Israel again. He will settle them on
their own land. The foreigner will
join them and be united with the
house of Jacob. 2 The nations will escort Israel and bring it to its homeland. Then the house of Israel will
possess them as male and female
slaves in the Lord's land. They will
make captives of their captors and
will rule over their oppressors.
3 When the Lord gives you rest
from your pain, torment, and the
hard labor you were forced to do,
4 you will sing this song of contempt
about the king of Babylon and say:

How the oppressor
has quieted down,
and how the raging[A]
has become quiet!
5 The Lord has broken the staff
of the wicked,
the scepter of the rulers.
6 It struck the peoples in anger
with unceasing blows.
It subdued the nations in rage
with relentless persecution.
7 All the earth is calm
and at rest;
people shout
with a ringing cry.
8 Even the cypresses
and the cedars of Lebanon
rejoice over you:
"Since you have been laid low,
no woodcutter has come
against us."
9 •Sheol below is eager to greet
your coming.
He stirs up the spirits
of the departed for you—
all the rulers[B] of the earth.
He makes all the kings
of the nations
rise from their thrones.
10 They all respond
to you, saying:
"You too have become
as weak as we are;
you have become like us!
11 Your splendor has been
brought down to Sheol,
along with the music
of your harps.
Maggots are spread out
under you,
and worms cover you."
12 Shining morning star,[C]
how you have fallen
from the heavens!
You destroyer of nations,
you have been cut down
to the ground.
13 You said to yourself:
"I will ascend to the heavens;
I will set up my throne
above the stars of God.
I will sit on the mount
of the gods' assembly,
in the remotest parts
of the North.[D]
14 I will ascend above
the highest clouds;

[A]14:4 DSS; Hb uncertain [B]14:9 Lit *rams* [C]14:12 Or *Day Star, son of the dawn* [D]14:13 Or *of Zaphon*

I will make myself
like the •Most High."
15 But you will be brought down
to Sheol
into the deepest regions
of the •Pit.
16 Those who see you will stare
at you;
they will look closely at you:
"Is this the man who caused
the earth to tremble,
who shook the kingdoms,
17 who turned the world
into a wilderness,
who destroyed its cities
and would not release
the prisoners
to return home?"
18 All the kings of the nations
lie in splendor,
each in his own tomb.
19 But you are thrown out
without a grave,
like a worthless branch,
covered by those slain
with the sword
and dumped into a rocky pit
like a trampled corpse.
20 You will not join them
in burial,
because you destroyed
your land
and slaughtered
your own people.
The offspring of evildoers
will never be remembered.
21 Prepare a place of slaughter
for his sons,
because of the iniquity
of their fathers.
They will never rise up
to possess a land
or fill the surface of the earth
with cities.

22 "I will rise up against them"—
this is the declaration of the LORD
of •Hosts—"and I will cut off from
Babylon her reputation, remnant,
offspring, and posterity"—this is
the LORD's declaration. 23 "I will
make her a swampland and a region
for screech owls,[A] and I will sweep
her away with a broom of destruction."

This is the declaration
of the LORD of Hosts.

Judgment against Assyria (14:24-27)

24 The LORD of Hosts has sworn:

As I have purposed,
so it will be;
as I have planned it,
so it will happen.
25 I will break Assyria
in My land;
I will tread him down
on My mountain.
Then his yoke will be taken
from them,
and his burden
will be removed
from their shoulders.
26 This is the plan prepared
for the whole earth,
and this is the hand
stretched out
against all the nations.
27 The LORD of Hosts Himself
has planned it;
therefore, who can stand
in its way?
It is His hand
that is outstretched,
so who can turn it back?

Judgment Against Philistia (14:28-32)

28 In the year that King Ahaz died,
this •oracle came:

29 Don't rejoice, all of you
in Philistia,
because the rod of the one
who struck you is broken.
For a viper will come
from the root[B] of a snake,
and from its egg comes
a flying serpent.
30 Then the firstborn of the poor
will be well fed,
and the impoverished
will lie down in safety,
but I will kill your root
with hunger,
and your remnant
will be slain.[C]
31 Wail, you gates! Cry out, city!
Tremble with fear,
all Philistia!
For a cloud of dust is coming
from the north,

[A]14:23 Or *hedgehogs* [B]14:29 Or *stock* [C]14:30 DSS, Syr, Tg; MT reads *and he will kill*

stories and used images from them to make his point without ascribing truth to them. Isaiah noted that this man intended to exalt himself to the status of being equal to God Himself. **I will ascend to the heavens** is mirrored in the comment in verse 14 (cp. 2Sm 22:14; Jb 22:12; 26:9). To reign on a **throne above the stars of God** demonstrates a desire to rule even over other angelic beings (cp. "sons of God," Jb 38:7; "heavenly host," Dn 8:10). Surrounding nations worshiped the heavenly bodies (Dt 4:19; Am 5:26). God was above the stars, and this proud ruler aspired to that position so that he, too, might be worshiped (Jb 22:12). This passage is often interpreted as a description of the fall of Satan, especially when read in light of Jesus' testimony (Lk 10:18).

14:14-20 The highest clouds were regarded by both Canaanites and Israelites as the domain of divinity (cp. 19:1; Ex 19:9; 2Sm 22:10-12; Pss 18:11-12; 68:4; 104:3). By stating **I will make myself like the Most High**, he seeks equality with God, reminiscent of the builders of the Tower of Babel (Gn 11:3-4), also built in ancient Babylon. The ruler's proud desires contrast sharply with his ultimate fate. From the heights of his aspirations, he would be cast into the depths of **Sheol** itself, **into the deepest regions** [Hb *yerēkah*] **of the Pit** (cp. Is 38:18; Jb 20:6-7; Pss 28:1; 143:7). All who saw the fall of this king would ponder the fate of **the man who caused the earth to tremble** by his deeds.

14:22-23 In stark contrast to His plans for rescuing a remnant out of Israel, God declared that He would not even spare a **remnant** from Babylon. All would be destroyed and the land itself would become a **swampland**. The nation would be treated with the same disrespect as the body of the king: The Lord would **sweep her away** like garbage.

14:24-32 Babylon was a distant threat, but Assyria was an imminent threat. However, in the case of both military powers, God was in firm, sovereign control. What He has **planned** and **purposed** is what **will happen**. The fall of Assyria would occur well before the fall of Babylon and provide evidence that God's further plans would also come about. God assured Israel that He would **break** Assyria's power; the enemy nation would find defeat on God's **mountain** (Hb plural, "mountains"). Perhaps this is a reference to the angel of the Lord's future destruction of 185,000 Assyrian soldiers encamped in the land (ca 701 B.C.; 37:36-38; cp. 2Kg 19:35-37). When Assyria would fall by God's design, the **yoke . . . and his burden** would be **removed** from Israel (cp. 9:4; 10:27).

This prophecy against Assyria closed the way it opened, firmly focused on the sovereign plan of God.

King Ahaz died ca 715 B.C. Because of his unfaithfulness, God allowed surrounding nations, including cities of **Philistia**, to attack Judah during his reign (2Ch 28:16-19). Philistia was organized around five cities (Gaza, Ashkelon, Ashdod, Ekron, and Gath), each ruled by its respective king (Jos 13:3; Jdg 3:3). Hezekiah was later able to subdue the Philistines (2Kg 18:8). Likely they exulted over Ahaz's death because Ahaz had pandered to the Assyrians, and his death would weaken Assyria's control in the region.

The Philistines were warned that far worse oppressors would rise up, progressing from a **snake** to a **viper** (Hb *tsepha'*, "poisonous serpent") and then to a **flying serpent** (Hb *saraph*, "fiery serpent"; cp. Nm 21:6). The **poor** and **impoverished** refers to the people of Judah, a remnant whom God would spare from the hand of Assyria. In contrast, the **remnant** of Philistia would **be slain**. Any messengers of Philistia to Judah should be rebuffed. God's provision of **Zion** would be the **refuge** for His people, not a pagan alliance. Around 714 to 711 B.C., a rebellion of the Philistines provoked a renewed Assyrian assault from the north ordered by Sargon II and leading to the capture of Ashdod and Gath (Is 20:1).

15:1-5 Located east of Judah across the Dead Sea, **Moab** had been a thorn in Israel's side since before the conquest of Canaan (Nm 22:1-7; 25:1-3; Jos 24:9; Jdg 3:12-14; 1Sm 12:9; 1Kg 11:7). The Moabites worshiped their god Chemosh on **high places** (Hb *bamah*; see **Word Study**, p. 411). These were often places of worship on hilltops but could also be associated with other areas set aside for worship in a city or elsewhere. Some cultic practices at "high places" included the presentation of incense offerings or sacrifices, prayer, and sometimes cultic prostitution.

As Isaiah named the Moabite cities, he emphasized the general despair throughout the land as the cities fell before their oppressors and the people fled in terror. The passage heavily emphasizes **weeping** and crying out with 11 references to crying and wailing. **Shaved** heads and beards and **sackcloth** were common signs of mourning. Even the speaker's **heart cries out over Moab** (cp. Is 16:9,11; Jr 48:31-33,35-36). Who is the speaker—the Lord or Isaiah? In other first-person references intermingled in the same passage, the speaker is clearly the Lord (Is 15:9; 16:10). Often during prophetic passages, the prophet speaks in unity with the heart of God.

and there is no one missing
from the invader's ranks.
32 What answer will be
given to the messengers
from that nation?
The LORD has founded •Zion,
and His afflicted people
find refuge in her.

Judgment Against Moab (15:1–16:14)

15 An •oracle against Moab:
Ar in Moab is devastated,
destroyed in a night.
Kir in Moab is devastated,
destroyed in a night.
2 Dibon went up to its temple
to weep at its •high places.
Moab wails on Nebo
and at[A] Medeba.
Every head is shaved;
every beard is cut off.
3 In its streets
they wear •sackcloth;
on its rooftops
and in its public squares
everyone wails,
falling down and weeping.
4 Heshbon and Elealeh cry out;
their voices are heard
as far away as Jahaz.
Therefore the soldiers
of Moab cry out,
and they tremble.[B]
5 My heart cries out over Moab,
whose fugitives flee
as far as Zoar,
to Eglath-shelishiyah;
they go up the slope
of Luhith weeping;
they raise a cry of destruction
on the road to Horonaim.
6 The waters of Nimrim
are desolate;
the grass is withered,
the foliage is gone,
and the vegetation
has vanished.
7 So they carry their wealth
and belongings
over the •Wadi of the Willows.
8 For their cry echoes
throughout the territory
of Moab.
Their wailing reaches Eglaim;
their wailing reaches Beer-
elim.
9 The waters of Dibon[C] are full
of blood,
but I will bring on Dibon[C]
even more than this—
a lion for those who escape
from Moab,
and for the survivors
in the land.

16 Send lambs to the ruler
of the land,
from Sela in the desert
to the mountain
of Daughter •Zion.
2 Like a bird fleeing,
forced from the nest,
the daughters of Moab
will be at the fords
of the Arnon.
3 Give us counsel and make
a decision.
Shelter us at noonday
with shade that is as dark
as night.
Hide the refugees;
do not betray the one
who flees.
4 Let my refugees stay
with you;
be a refuge for Moab[D]
from the aggressor.

When the oppressor has gone,
destruction has ended,
and marauders have vanished
from the land.
5 Then in the tent of David
a throne will be established
by faithful love.
A judge who seeks
what is right
and is quick to execute justice
will sit on the throne forever.

6 We have heard
of Moab's pride—
how very proud he is—
his haughtiness, his pride,
his arrogance,
and his empty boasting.
7 Therefore let Moab wail;
let every one of them wail
for Moab.
Mourn, you who are
completely devastated,

[A]**15:2** Or *wails over Nebo and over* [B]**15:4** Lit *out, he trembles within himself* [C]**15:9** DSS, some LXX mss, Vg; MT reads *Dimon* [D]**16:4** Or *you; Moab—be a refuge for him*

for the raisin cakes of Kir-
hareseth.
8 For Heshbon's terraced
vineyards
and the grapevines of Sibmah
have withered.
The rulers of the nations
have trampled its choice vines
that reached as far as Jazer
and spread to the desert.
Their shoots spread out
and reached the Dead Sea.
9 So I join with Jazer
to weep for the vines
of Sibmah;
I drench Heshbon and Elealeh
with my tears.
Triumphant shouts
have fallen silent[A]
over your summer fruit
and your harvest.
10 Joy and rejoicing
have been removed
from the orchard;
no one is singing or shouting
for joy in the vineyards.
No one tramples grapes[B]
in the winepresses.
I have put an end
to the shouting.
11 Therefore I moan like
the sound of a lyre
for Moab,
as does my innermost being
for Kir-heres.
12 When Moab appears
on the ˙high place,
when he tires[C] himself out
and comes to his sanctuary
to pray,
it will do him no good.

13 This is the message that the
LORD previously announced about
Moab. 14 And now the LORD says, "In
three years, as a hired worker counts
years, Moab's splendor will become
an object of contempt, in spite of
a very large population. And those
who are left will be few and weak."

Judgment Against Aram (17:1-3)

17 An ˙oracle against Damascus:
Look, Damascus is no longer
a city.
It has become a ruined heap.
2 The cities of Aroer
are forsaken;
they will be places for flocks.
They will lie down
without fear.
3 The fortress disappears
from Ephraim,
and a kingdom
from Damascus.
The remnant of Aram will be
like the splendor
of the Israelites.
This is the declaration
of the LORD of ˙Hosts.

Judgment Concerning Israel (17:4-14)

4 On that day
the splendor of Jacob
will fade,
and his healthy body[D]
will become emaciated.
5 It will be as if a
reaper had gathered
standing grain—
his arm harvesting the heads
of grain—
and as if one had gleaned
heads of grain
in the Valley of Rephaim.
6 Only gleanings will be left
in Israel,
as if an olive tree
had been beaten—
two or three berries
at the very top of the tree,
four or five
on its fruitful branches.
This is the declaration
of the LORD,
the God of Israel.

7 On that day people will look to
their Maker and will turn their eyes
to the Holy One of Israel. 8 They will
not look to the altars they made
with their hands or to the ˙Asherahs
and incense altars they made with
their fingers.

9 On that day their strong cities
will be
like the abandoned woods
and mountaintops[E]
that were abandoned
because of the Israelites;

[A]16:9 Or *Battle cries have fallen* [B]16:10 Lit *wine* [C]16:12 DSS read *place, he will tire* [D]17:4 Lit *and the fat of his flesh* [E]17:9 Some Hb mss read *like the Horesh and the Amir*; LXX reads *like the Amorites and the Hivites*

16:1-4 Moab was admonished to turn to the ruler of Judah for refuge and told to **send lambs . . . to the mountain of Daughter Zion**. Tribute was sent to rulers as a sign of a vassal kingdom's submission and also when requests were made for protection (2Sm 8:2; 2Kg 3:4; 16:7-8; 18:14-15). Finally, the Moabites will realize that help cannot come from their false gods or themselves; they will need to depend upon the ruler of Zion. The defeat of **the oppressor** will preface the final establishment of the future messianic kingdom.

16:5 Verse 5 rings with the hope of the future ideal messianic ruler from Zion.

16:6-7 In contrast with the future picture of Moab's humility and submission to the Messiah, these verses highlight the **pride** and **arrogance** that would lead to Moab's punishment. Like Babylon, she would be overthrown and her territory **completely devastated**.

17:1-3 Isaiah again took up prophecies against Aram (Syria) and Israel, the coalition partners who had threatened Judah's security.

17:4-6 Using three word pictures for **the splendor of Jacob**, Isaiah described Israel as an **emaciated** (Hb *razah*, "made lean") body, diminished in size and strength just as an extensive illness causes a **healthy body** to waste away; a picked-over field—such as the productive fields in the **Valley of Rephaim** west of Jerusalem—with hardly any grain left (cp. Lv 19:9; 23:22); and **an olive tree** [that] **had been beaten**, left with few olives for gleaning (cp. Dt 24:20). Both Israel and Aram would become weak and few in number. Damascus fell to the Assyrians led by Shalmaneser in 732 B.C. Samaria, the capital of the northern tribes, was likewise besieged by Shalmaneser for three years and fell to Sargon, his successor, in 722 B.C. (2Kg 17:5-6; 19:9-11). The ensuing deportations left only a small Israelite remnant.

17:7-11 At the same time, **on that day people** (Hb *ʾadam*, "man, mankind") would finally **look to their Maker** (i.e., **the Holy One of Israel**; cp. 1:4; 30:15; 2Kg 19:22). Instead of turning to inanimate idols, unauthorized **altars**, which **they made with their hands**, and **Asherahs** (see **Word Study**, p. 884) the people would again recognize and cling to the God who had made them along with all creation (see Dt 4:28-31; 28:64; 32:17-18,39; Jr 2:27). This passage may have been fulfilled among the remnant of the northern tribes following the destruction of Samaria in 722 B.C. During his reforms,

Hezekiah invited them to return to God by joining in the Passover celebration at the Jerusalem temple, an invitation some accepted (2Ch 30:1-11). Other scholars point out that the language of the verse, specifically the mention of mankind generally as looking to God, may refer to a future, more global, turning to God.

17:10 Although the remnant would finally reject the false gods, they would still have to endure the consequences of their previous sin.

17:12-14 Isaiah commented briefly on the fate of those who would be used by God to discipline the children of Israel. Although **the nations** would **rage like the raging of many waters**, they would be ultimately checked by God. They would despoil (**plunder** and **ravage**) Israel, but only briefly—they, too, would be defeated, possibly a reference to the overnight destruction and disappearance of the Assyrian army (37:36-37; cp. 2Kg 19:35-36; 2 Ch 32:21).

18:1-3 Cush was likely located south of Egypt in the area of present-day Ethiopia. During Isaiah's time (ca 715 B.C.) the Cushites assumed control of Egypt. Together, Cush and Egypt did much to try to incite rebellion among the Assyrian-controlled provinces until they lost several key battles, including a battle with Esar-haddon (671 B.C.). Later, they suffered a decisive defeat by Ashurbanipal (663 B.C.), thereby losing control over Egypt (20:4; 37:9; cp. 2Kg 19:9).

In this passage Isaiah portrayed Cush as sending **couriers by sea**. Their destination is not stated, but most scholars suggest that the envoys went to Hezekiah in Jerusalem to solicit his help in revolting against the Assyrians.

18:4-6 Once God's determined time is met, the military might of people and nations would be pruned and overthrown, their corpses exposed to the predators of the natural world. Any notion Israel had of joining in alliance with Cush should have been checked by these words.

18:7 Following the pruning, **a gift will be brought to Yahweh of Hosts** from Cush (cp. 45:14; Ps 68:29-31) like a tribute. The Lord will be at Mount Zion, **the place of the name of Yahweh of Hosts**, an explicit reference to Jerusalem as the place foretold during the wilderness wandering where the Lord would set His name (Dt 12:5-11; 1Kg 8:16-21,29,44,48; 9:3; 2Ch 6:5-10; 7:15-16; 12:13). Corresponding to verse 7, Hezekiah appeared to receive gifts from various nations following the retreat of the army (2Ch 32:23). A possible future fulfillment

>WORD|*study*

17:8 Asherahs were wooden images, either living trees or poles, associated with rites used in the pagan worship of Asherah (or Ashtarte), a Canaanite fertility goddess worshiped by apostate Israelites. In Canaanite literature she was sometimes described as the wife of El, the high god of the pantheon, and sometimes as the wife of Baal. God had commanded His people to destroy such forbidden images (cp. Ex 34:13; Dt 7:5; 12:3; 16:21; Jdg 3:7; 6:25-30; 1Kg 14:15,23; 2Kg 13:6; 17:10,16; 21:3,7; 23:4,6-7,14-15; 2Ch 14:3; 15:16; 34:3-4,7; Is 27:9; Jr 17:2; Mc 5:13).

17:10 Isaiah uses the word **rock** (Hb *tsur*, "cliff") both literally (e.g., Is 2:10) and figuratively (e.g., 8:14). The word "rock" was used for rocky sites of shelter and strength to which refugees could retreat and from which battles could be waged. A rock was a solid foundation that would not give way. The metaphor invites the audience to compare such characteristics of a "rock" with traits of God's character. Echoing the repeated reference to Yahweh as Israel's "Rock" in Moses' song (Dt. 32:4,15,18,30-31; cp. Hab 1:12), "rock of your strength" refers to the Lord. Any pagan god was sarcastically called an ineffective "rock" (Dt 32:31,37), while Yahweh, the God of Israel, was the only sure "Rock"—who is strong, mighty, immovable, and completely trustworthy (Dt 32:30). The metaphor appears frequently in the Old Testament, especially in its poetry (e.g., 1Sm 2:2; 2Sm 22:2,32,47; 23:3; and at least 26 times in Psalms, including Pss 18:2,31,46; 62:2,6-8; 78:35; 89:26; 144:1). In Isaiah, the Lord was also "the rock to trip over" (8:14); "an everlasting rock" (26:4); "the Rock of Israel" (30:29); the "Rock" as the only God (44:8); and "the rock" of origination for Israel (51:1; cp. Dt 32:4).

there will be desolation.
10 For you have forgotten
the God of your salvation,
and you have failed
to remember
the rock of your strength;
therefore you will plant
beautiful plants
and set out cuttings
from exotic vines.
11 On the day that you plant,
you will help them to grow,
and in the morning
you will help your seed
to sprout,
but the harvest will vanish
on the day of disease
and incurable pain.
12 Ah! The roar
of many peoples—
they roar like the roaring
of the seas.
The raging of the nations—
they rage like the raging
of mighty waters.
13 The nations rage
like the raging
of many waters.
He rebukes them,
and they flee far away,
driven before the wind
like chaff on the hills
and like tumbleweeds
before a gale.
14 In the evening—
sudden terror!
Before morning—it is gone!
This is the fate of those
who plunder us
and the lot of those
who ravage us.

Prophecy Concerning Cush (18:1-7)

18 Ah! The land
of buzzing insect wings[A]
beyond the rivers of •Cush
2 sends couriers by sea,
in reed vessels on the waters.

Go, swift messengers,
to a nation tall and smooth-
skinned,
to a people feared
far and near,
a powerful nation
with a strange language,[B]
whose land is divided
by rivers.
3 All you inhabitants
of the world
and you who live
on the earth,
when a banner is raised
on the mountains, look!
When a trumpet sounds,
listen!

4 For, the LORD said to me:

I will quietly look out
from My place,
like shimmering heat
in sunshine,
like a rain cloud
in harvest heat.
5 For before the harvest,
when the blossoming
is over

A 18:1 Or *of sailing ships* B 18:2 Hb obscure

and the blossom becomes
a ripening grape,
He will cut off the shoots
with a pruning knife,
and tear away and remove
the branches.
6 They will all be left
for the birds of prey
on the hills
and for the wild animals
of the land.
The birds will spend
the summer on them,
and all the animals,
the winter on them.

7 At that time a gift will be brought to •Yahweh of •Hosts from[A] a people tall and smooth-skinned, a people feared far and near, a powerful nation with a strange language, whose land is divided by rivers—to Mount •Zion, the place of the name of Yahweh of Hosts.

Judgment Against Egypt (19:1-15)

19 An •oracle against Egypt:

Look, the LORD rides
on a swift cloud
and is coming to Egypt.
Egypt's idols will tremble
before Him,
and Egypt's heart will melt
within it.
2 I will provoke Egypt
against Egypt;
each will fight
against his brother
and each against his friend,
city against city,
kingdom against kingdom.
3 Egypt's spirit will be disturbed
within it,
and I will frustrate its plans.
Then they will seek idols,
ghosts,
spirits of the dead,
and spiritists.
4 I will deliver Egypt
into the hands
of harsh masters,
and a strong king will rule it.
This is the declaration
of the Lord GOD of •Hosts.

5 The waters of the sea
will dry up,
and the river will be parched
and dry.
6 The channels will stink;
they will dwindle,
and Egypt's canals
will be parched.
Reed and rush will die.[B]
7 The reeds by the Nile,
by the mouth of the river,
and all the cultivated areas
of the Nile
will wither, blow away,
and vanish.
8 Then the fishermen
will mourn.
All those who cast hooks
into the Nile will lament,
and those who spread nets
on the water will shrivel up.
9 Those who work with flax
will be dismayed;
the combers and weavers
will turn pale.[C]
10 Egypt's weavers[D]
will be dejected;
all her wage earners
will be demoralized.

11 The princes of Zoan
are complete fools;
Pharaoh's wisest advisers
give stupid advice!
How can you say to Pharaoh,
"I am one[E] of the wise,
a student of eastern[F] kings"?
12 Where then are
your wise men?
Let them tell you and reveal
what the LORD of Hosts
has planned against Egypt.
13 The princes of Zoan
have been fools;
the princes of Memphis
are deceived.
Her tribal chieftains have led
Egypt astray.
14 The LORD has mixed
within her a spirit
of confusion.
The leaders have made Egypt
stagger in all she does,
as a drunkard staggers
in his vomit.
15 No head or tail, palm or reed,

would correspond to other scriptural references regarding the end of the age. The themes of that time are the same. The world will be in tumult with wars and plans for wars (Mt 24:6-7; Rv 16:14-16). There will be a future reaping (Rv 14:14-20). The armies in rebellion against God will be utterly defeated, with their bodies exposed to scavengers for months (Is 66:24; Ezk 39:12-20; Rv 19:17-18). The Lord will reign from Zion (Ezk 48:35; Jl 3:17,21; Zch 2:10-13; 8:3), and nations will come to the mount of the Lord bearing gifts (Ps 72:8-11; Is 2:2-3; 60:3-7; Zch 8:20-23; 14:16).

19:1-2 The Lord heads to Egypt riding **on a swift cloud**. His very presence would strike terror in Egypt. God would bring about internal civil strife, and the Egyptians would end up fighting with each other, **Egypt against Egypt**. Scholars indicate that during the time of Isaiah (eighth century), internal strife in Egypt was prevalent as Cush struggled to control Egypt proper.

19:3-4 In their frustration, the Egyptians would **seek idols** [see chart, p. 874,] **ghosts, spirits of the dead, and spiritists** (see note on 8:19-22). This turn to the occult would be Egypt's desperate recourse. For Jerusalem to align herself with a nation consulting forbidden sources when she had access to God's own counsel through His word and His prophets would not just be unwise; it would be the height of foolishness. Egypt's final fate was to be conquered and dominated by **a strong king**. The Cushite dynasty could not stand up to the power of Assyria. From 671 B.C. onward, Egypt fell time and again under foreign domination—to Assyria, Babylon, Persia and Greece.

19:5-10 Natural disaster (here, a drought) would also distress Egypt, which depended upon the constancy of the Nile River and the predictability of floods in the delta for the land to be productive. The Nile was, simply, the lifeblood of Egypt. But there would be a day when **the river will be parched and dry**.

19:11-13 Just as Egypt trusted in false gods and in the permanency of the Nile, she trusted in the advice of her **wise men**. As Isaiah mockingly pointed out, the wisest counselors of Egypt were useless. Egypt prided itself on its wisdom tradition, yet its seers could not reveal what God was about to do to Egypt (cp. Gn 41:8,16,38; Dn 2:28; 4:18). From **Zoan** in the north of the delta to **Memphis** in the south, throughout all of Egypt, the **princes** were **fools**.

[A] **18:7** DSS, LXX, Vg; MT omits *from* [B] **19:6** Or *wilt*, or *become black* [C] **19:9** DSS, Tg; MT reads *weavers of white cloth* [D] **19:10** Or *foundations* [E] **19:11** Lit *a son* [F] **19:11** Lit *a son of ancient*

19:16-18 Judgment would not be the last word for Egypt. Just as Israel had hope of salvation, so, too, would the nations who learned to fear the Lord, as Egypt would in the future.

19:19-22 Egypt would establish worship to the Lord in her land, demonstrated through the **altar** and **pillar,** evidence of a true heart change. Isaiah pointedly used images reminiscent of Israel's early experience with following the Lord. God would send leaders to deliver them just as he had sent Moses. Through repentance, Egypt, too, would be healed.

19:23-25 Egypt would be at peace with its former enemy, Assyria, and both would worship the Lord. This absolutely shocking statement described two countries who, as archenemies, had been in conflict during most of Isaiah's lifetime (v. 20).

20:1-6 Isaiah historically locates a prophecy centered around a sign-act foretelling imminent judgment on Egypt and Cush. Around 713 B.C., Isaiah was commanded to become a living **sign** for Judah concerning what would happen to **Egypt and Cush**—they would become **exiles** led away in **shame** (cp. 2Sm 10:4-5). Any country trusting in their support would be completely **dismayed and ashamed**. Following God's command he went **naked and barefoot** for **three years**. The word "naked" (Hb *'arom*) did not always mean complete nakedness but could mean stripped of the outer garment, leaving only the undergarments (1Sm 19:24; Jb 24:7; Is 58:7).

21:1-10 The **desert by the sea** refers to the nation of Babylonia. **Babylon**, the capital, was located on the Euphrates River while the nation of Babylonia bordered the Lower Sea (Persian Gulf). Three different explanations exist concerning this chapter's events. Some suggest that the descriptions best fit Babylon's violent destruction by the Assyrians under Sennacherib (ca 689 B.C.). Others suggest that the prophecy was fulfilled when the united Medes and Persians under Cyrus, who incorporated tribes of Elam, overthrew Babylon (ca 539 B.C.). Finally, some argue that although the prophecy was partially fulfilled by the first or second occasion (or both) when historic Babylon fell, there remains a future final fulfillment.

21:3-4 Why seeing the fall of Babylon at this point would have been painful for Isaiah is difficult to understand (39:5-7). Some suggest prophetic empathy; others describe his reaction as dismay about the fact that Israel had put its trust in a nation that would

will be able to do anything
for Egypt.

Future Blessing upon Egypt, Assyria, and Israel (19:16-25)

16 On that day Egypt will be like women. She will tremble with fear because of the threatening hand of the LORD of Hosts when He raises it against her. 17 The land of Judah will terrify Egypt; whenever Judah is mentioned, Egypt will tremble because of what the LORD of Hosts has planned against it.

18 On that day five cities in the land of Egypt will speak the language of Canaan and swear loyalty to the LORD of Hosts. One of the cities will be called the City of the Sun.[A,B]

19 On that day there will be an altar to the LORD in the center of the land of Egypt and a pillar to the LORD near her border. 20 It will be a sign and witness to the LORD of Hosts in the land of Egypt. When they cry out to the LORD because of their oppressors, He will send them a savior and leader, and he will rescue them. 21 The LORD will make Himself known to Egypt, and Egypt will know the LORD on that day. They will offer sacrifices and offerings; they will make vows to the LORD and fulfill them. 22 The LORD will strike Egypt, striking and healing. Then they will return to the LORD and He will hear their prayers and heal them.

23 On that day there will be a highway from Egypt to Assyria. Assyria will go to Egypt, Egypt to Assyria, and Egypt will worship with Assyria. 24 On that day Israel will form a triple alliance with Egypt and Assyria—a blessing within the land. 25 The LORD of Hosts will bless them, saying, "Egypt My people, Assyria My handiwork, and Israel My inheritance are blessed."

Prophecy Against Egypt and Ethiopia (20:1-6)

20 In the year that the chief commander, sent by Sargon king of Assyria, came to Ashdod and attacked and captured it— 2 during that time the LORD had spoken through Isaiah son of Amoz, saying, "Go, take off your •sackcloth[C] and remove the sandals from your feet," and he did so, going naked and barefoot— 3 the LORD said, "As My servant Isaiah has gone naked and barefoot three years as a sign and omen against Egypt and •Cush, 4 so the king of Assyria will lead the captives of Egypt and the exiles of Cush, young and old alike, naked and barefoot, with bared buttocks—to Egypt's shame. 5 Those who made Cush their hope and Egypt their boast will be dismayed and ashamed. 6 And the inhabitants of this coastland will say on that day, 'Look, this is what has happened to those we relied on and fled to for help to rescue us from the king of Assyria! Now, how will we escape?'"

Prophecy of the Fall of Babylon (21:1-10)

21 An •oracle against the desert by the sea:

Like storms that pass
over the •Negev,
it comes from the desert,
from the land of terror.
2 A troubling vision is declared
to me:
"The treacherous one
acts treacherously,
and the destroyer destroys.
Advance, Elam! Lay siege,
you Medes!
I will put an end to all
her groaning."
3 Therefore I am[D] filled
with anguish.
Pain grips me, like the pain
of a woman in labor.
I am too perplexed to hear,
too dismayed to see.
4 My heart staggers;
horror terrifies me.
He has turned
my last glimmer of hope[E]
into sheer terror.
5 Prepare a table,
and spread out a carpet!
Eat and drink!

[A]**19:18** Some Hb mss, DSS, Sym, Tg, Vg, Arabic; other Hb mss read *of Destruction*; LXX reads *of Righteousness* [B]**19:18** = the ancient Egyptian city Heliopolis [C]**20:2** Lit *off the sackcloth from your loins* [D]**21:3** Lit *Therefore my loins are* [E]**21:4** Lit *my twilight*

Rise up, you princes, and oil
the shields!
6 For the Lord has said to me,
"Go, post a lookout;
let him report what he sees.
7 When he sees riders—
pairs of horsemen,
riders on donkeys,
riders on camels—
he must pay close attention."
8 Then the lookout[A] reported,
"Lord, I stand
on the watchtower all day,
and I stay at my post all night.
9 Look, riders come—
horsemen in pairs."
And he answered, saying,
"Babylon has fallen,
has fallen.
All the images of her gods
have been shattered
on the ground."
10 My people who have
been crushed
on the threshing floor,
I have declared to you
what I have heard
from the LORD of •Hosts,
the God of Israel.

Words Concerning Edom (21:11-12)

11 An oracle against Dumah:[B]

One calls to me from Seir,
"Watchman, what is left
of the night?
Watchman, what is left
of the night?"
12 The watchman said,
"Morning has come,
and also night.
If you want to ask, ask!
Come back again."

Judgment Concerning Arabia (21:13-17)

13 An oracle against Arabia:

In the desert[C] brush
you will camp for the night,
you caravans of Dedanites.
14 Bring water for the thirsty.
The inhabitants of the land
of Tema
meet[D] the refugees with food.
15 For they have fled
from swords,
from the drawn sword,
from the bow that is strung,
and from the stress of battle.

16 For the Lord said this to me:
"Within one year, as a hired worker
counts years, all the glory of Kedar
will be gone. 17 The remaining Ke-
darite archers will be few in number." For the LORD, the God of Israel,
has spoken.

Judgment Concerning Jerusalem (22:1-25)

Against the City (22:1-14)

22 An •oracle against the Valley of Vision:

What's the matter with you?
Why have all of you gone up
to the rooftops?
2 The noisy city,
the jubilant town,
is filled with revelry.
Your dead did not die
by the sword;
they were not killed in battle.
3 All your rulers
have fled together,
captured without a bow.
All your fugitives
were captured together;
they had fled far away.
4 Therefore I said,
"Look away from me!
Let me weep bitterly!
Do not try to comfort me
about the destruction
of my dear[E] people."
5 For the Lord GOD of •Hosts
had a day of tumult,
trampling, and confusion
in the Valley of Vision—
people shouting[F] and crying
to the mountains;
6 Elam took up a quiver
with chariots and horsemen,[G]
and Kir uncovered the shield.
7 Your best valleys were full
of chariots,
and horsemen

[A]21:8 DSS, Syr; MT reads *Then a lion* [B]21:11 Some Hb mss, LXX read *Edom* [C]21:13 LXX, Syr, Tg, Vg read *desert at evening* [D]21:14 LXX, Syr, Tg, Vg read *meet* as a command [E]22:4 Lit *of the daughter of my* [F]22:5 Or *Vision—a tearing down of a wall*, or *Vision—Kir raged*; Hb obscure [G]22:6 Lit *chariots of man*

come to naught. Isaiah's distress could have resulted from Hezekiah's (and Judah's) mistake of allying with Babylon (cp. 39:1-4). Isaiah saw that no help would come from Babylon because Babylon would fall.

21:5-7 Daniel 5 recounts that the Babylonian co-regent, Belshazzar, and his companions feasted on the day of the fall, appearing to correspond to the picture of the people feasting until the call to arms (**oil the shields!**).

21:6-10 Most agree that Isaiah himself functioned as the **lookout** and reported his faithfulness at standing watch. His faithfulness was rewarded by confirmation of the upcoming fall of Babylon.

21:11-12 The fate of **Dumah** (Hb, "silence," figuratively connected with death), which is similar in sound to "Edom" (Hb *ʾedom*), appears to be tied closely to the fate of Edom. A direct trade route from Babylon to Edom passed through Dumah. In this oracle, a weary Edomite asked the night **watchman** when the night would end. Isaiah, as the watchman, provided an equivocal answer: **Morning has come, and also night**. While relief from one oppressor was in view, further domination from another still lay ahead (Ezk 25:13; 35:2-15; Am 1:11; 9:12; Mal 1:4). The Edomite was encouraged to ask again in the future, indicating the possibility of another dawn or respite from oppression.

21:13-17 Like Edom, Arabia's fate was directly tied to that of Assyria and Babylon. Arabia included the desert land to the east and southeast of Israel, stretching down the peninsula west and southwest of Babylon.

22:1-7 The **Valley of Vision** may refer symbolically to Jerusalem since it becomes clear that its situation is being described (cp. vv. 8-11). The vagueness of the opening line may indicate a future aspect to the overall oracle, in addition to an immediate application (cp. chap. 21).

22:5-11 Isaiah mourned for Jerusalem's destruction, brought about by the sovereign hand of the **Lord GOD of Hosts**. He foresaw that contingents of soldiers from **Elam** (21:2) and **Kir** (of unknown location; cp. Am 1:5; 9:7) would be a part of the army, possibly as mercenaries fighting with the Babylonian army.

When confronted with an enemy, the people tended to trust more in defenses wrought by their own hands than in God's ability to save. Isaiah decried, **You looked to the weapons** stored **in the House of the Forest**. "You looked" is second-person singular,

were positioned
at the gates.
8 He removed the defenses
of Judah.

On that day you looked to the weapons in the House of the Forest. 9 You saw that there were many breaches in the walls of the city of David. You collected water from the lower pool. 10 You counted the houses of Jerusalem so that you could tear them down to fortify the wall. 11 You made a reservoir between the walls for the waters of the ancient pool, but you did not look to the One who made it, or consider the One who created it long ago.

12 On that day the Lord GOD
of Hosts
called for weeping,
for wailing,
for shaven heads,
and for the wearing
of ·sackcloth.
13 But look: joy and gladness,
butchering of cattle,
slaughtering of sheep,
eating of meat, and drinking
of wine—
"Let us eat and drink,
for tomorrow we die!"
14 The LORD of Hosts has
directly revealed to me:
"This sin of yours
will never[A] be wiped out."
The Lord GOD of Hosts
has spoken.

Against Shebna (22:15-19)

15 The Lord GOD of Hosts said: "Go to Shebna, that steward who is in charge of the palace, and say to him: 16 What are you doing here? Who authorized you to carve out a tomb for yourself here, carving your tomb on the height and cutting a crypt for yourself out of rock? 17 Look, you strong man! The LORD is about to shake you violently. He will take hold of you, 18 wind you up into a ball, and sling you into a wide land.[B] There you will die, and there your glorious chariots will be—a disgrace to the house of your lord. 19 I will remove you from your office; you will be ousted from your position.

Concerning Eliakim (22:20-25)

20 "On that day I will call for my servant, Eliakim son of Hilkiah. 21 I will clothe him with your robe and tie your sash around him. I will put your authority into his hand, and he will be like a father to the inhabitants of Jerusalem and to the House of Judah. 22 I will place the key of the House of David on his shoulder; what he opens, no one can close; what he closes, no one can open. 23 I will drive him, like a peg, into a firm place. He will be a throne of honor for his father's house. 24 They will hang on him the whole burden of his father's house: the descendants and the offshoots—all the small vessels, from bowls to every kind of jar. 25 On that day"—the declaration of the LORD of Hosts—"the peg that was driven into a firm place will give way, be cut off, and fall, and the load on it will be destroyed." Indeed, the LORD has spoken.

Judgment Concerning Tyre (23:1-18)

23 An ·oracle against Tyre:
Wail, ships of Tarshish,
for your haven
has been destroyed.
Word has reached them
from the land of Cyprus.[C]
2 Mourn, inhabitants
of the coastland,
you merchants of Sidon;
your agents have crossed
the sea[D]
3 on many waters.
Tyre's revenue was the grain
from Shihor—
the harvest of the Nile.
She was the merchant
among the nations.
4 Be ashamed Sidon,
the stronghold of the sea,
for the sea has spoken:
"I have not been in labor
or given birth.
I have not raised young men
or brought up
young women."

A 22:14 Lit *will not until you die* B 22:17-18 Hb obscure C 23:1 Hb *Kittim* D 23:2 DSS; MT reads *Sidon, whom the seafarers have filled*

possibly addressed to King Hezekiah. The "House of the Forest" built by Solomon was a 150-by-75-foot cedar building, supported by many cedar columns and housing exotic arms (1Kg 7:2; 10:17; 2Ch 9:16). Hezekiah had likely replenished this armory as the Assyrians neared (2Ch 32:5). Hezekiah had undertaken many building projects to strengthen the city defenses, including strengthening **the wall** and digging a tunnel from the Upper Gihon Spring to a place within the walls to insure a **water** source during a siege (2Kg 20:20; 2Ch 32:2-5,32). Apparently, Hezekiah, along with the people became proud of their man-made provisions with regard to this **reservoir** collecting waters from **the ancient pool** and did not properly **look to the One who made it**.

22:15-19 Shebna had misused his position of steward for his own ambitions instead of serving the people. He would be replaced with a faithful servant.

22:20-25 In contrast to Shebna, **Eliakim** embodied the traits of a faithful servant. God would establish Eliakim, but there was a note of warning. The constancy and ability of Eliakim would be subjected to **the whole burden of his father's house,** and there would come a day when he who had been so firmly established would **be cut off, and fall**. Perhaps in the end, Eliakim would fail with the problems of **the House of David** (Jerusalem) being too much for him. The point seems to be that trusting in anything—defense, politicians, wealth—other than God for protection and well-being is useless. Shebna and Eliakim mentioned here probably are the ones mentioned later in Isaiah (Is 36:3,11,22; 37:2).

23:1-4 Tyre was a prominent city and seaport along the coast of Phoenicia (modern Lebanon). The city, inclusive of both island and coast, was famous for its heavy and profitable international trade. Her destruction would bring mourning by merchants who had profited by trading in her ports. The language regarding the merchants' reactions to Tyre's downfall seems to be incorporated in Rv 18:11-24 (Ezk 27:1–28:19). **Tarshish** was likely Tartessus, a city on Spain's southern coast. **Ships of Tarshish** could refer to any large merchant vessel capable of making long sea voyages. **Cyprus** was an island in the Mediterranean Sea northwest of Tyre. **Sidon** was another main Phoenician coastal city about 25 miles north of Tyre. Tyre had become great by transporting, buying, and selling goods like the **grain from Shihor** ("a branch of the Nile," probably a reference to Egypt; cp. Jos 13:3). Once she had been destroyed, all the people

>WORD|*study*

23:18 The word **dedicated** (Hb *qodesh*, "apartness, sacredness, holiness") draws attention to this astounding result of the Lord's dealings with Tyre. The verbal root *qadash* means to "set apart" as holy or "consecrate" for a sacred use or purpose (Jos 6:19,24; 2Sm 8:11; 1Kg 7:51). Mosaic law explicitly banned bringing a "prostitute's **wages** [Hb *ʾetnan*, always the "payment, fee or earnings" of a prostitute; cp. Ezk 16:31,34; Hs 9:1; Mc 1:7] . . . into the house of the LORD . . . [for they] are detestable to the LORD" (Dt 23:18). There is no indication that the law is changed; the oracle does not speak of such earnings being brought into "the house of the LORD." However, the **wages** (Hb *ʾetnan*) from Tyre's international "business" (Hb *ʾetnan*)—i.e., that which is profane—will be set apart for the sacred purpose of supplying the needs of those whose lives are set apart for Yahweh's glory (cp. Is 18:7; 19:21; 61:6).

5 When the news reaches
Egypt,
they will be in anguish
over the news about Tyre.
6 Cross over to Tarshish;
wail, inhabitants
of the coastland!
7 Is this your jubilant city,
whose origin was
in ancient times,
whose feet have taken her
to settle far away?
8 Who planned this
against Tyre,
the bestower of crowns,
whose traders are princes,
whose merchants are
the honored ones
of the earth?
9 The LORD of •Hosts planned it,
to desecrate all
its glorious beauty,
to disgrace all
the honored ones
of the earth.
10 Overflow[A] your
land like the Nile,
daughter of Tarshish;
there is no longer anything
to restrain you.[B]
11 He stretched out His hand
over the sea;
He made kingdoms tremble.
The LORD has commanded
that the Canaanite fortresses
be destroyed.
12 He said,
"You will not rejoice anymore,
ravished young woman,
daughter of Sidon.
Get up and cross over
to Cyprus—
even there you will have
no rest!"
13 Look at the land
of the Chaldeans—
a people who no longer exist.
Assyria destined it
for desert creatures.
They set up their siege towers
and stripped its palaces.
They made it a ruin.
14 Wail, ships of Tarshish,
because your fortress
is destroyed!

15 On that day Tyre will be forgotten for 70 years—the life span of
one king. At the end of 70 years,
what the song says about the prostitute will happen to Tyre:

16 Pick up your lyre,
stroll through the city,
prostitute forgotten by men.
Play skillfully,
sing many a song,
and you will be thought of
again.

17 And at the end of the 70 years,
the LORD will restore Tyre and she
will go back into business, prostituting herself with all the kingdoms of
the world on the face of the earth.
18 But her profits and wages will be
dedicated to the LORD. They will not
be stored or saved, for her profit will
go to those who live in the LORD's
presence, to provide them with ample food and sacred clothing.

Judgment Concerning the Earth (24:1-23)

24 Look, the LORD is stripping
the earth bare
and making it desolate.
He will twist its surface
and scatter its inhabitants:
2 people and priest alike,
servant and master,
female servant and mistress,
buyer and seller,

(her **young men** and **young women**) who had travelled through or lived in her confines would forsake her and she would be barren.

23:5-7 Among those who would mourn the fall of Tyre would be her distant trade partners, **Egypt** and **Tarshish** (see Jnh 1:3).

23:8-9 The primary agent of destruction was **the LORD of Hosts,** who **planned** to overturn her pride, **to desecrate all its glorious beauty**, literally "the exultation of all beauty." Glory and honor belong to God alone as well as complete authority and sovereignty over even the pagan nations.

23:11-12 He commanded that the **Canaanite fortresses** [Hb *maʿoz*, "place of safety"] **be destroyed**. This verse as well as the repeated reference to Sidon seems to indicate that the destruction would encompass the rest of Phoenicia as well. The prophet pointed out that even in **Cyprus** the inhabitants would have **no rest**.

23:13-14 The mention of the destruction of the **land of the Chaldeans** by **Assyria** is taken by most scholars to refer to the crushing destruction of Babylon in 689 B.C. by Sennacherib in response to the uprising sponsored by Merodach-Baladan (see 21:1-10). Just as Babylon had been ruined, Tyre, too, would be destroyed.

The actual historical fulfillment concerning Tyre is debated. Tyre was besieged a number of times by Assyria, Babylon, and even Persia. Trade was limited, though the island city remained intact. The siege by Nebuchadnezzar lasted 13 years.

Although Phoenicia fell and Tyre paid tribute to Babylon, the island of Tyre was not breached. Tyre (including the island) was finally crushed by Alexander the Great in 332 B.C. Tyre continued to function as a trade port but with diminished influence.

24:1–27:13 Chapters 24 to 27 build upon concepts developed in the oracles of judgment and expand the vision to include the eventual fate of the entire world. This section is known by many scholars as the "Apocalypse of Isaiah." Scholars disagree about whether the fate of all the earth and its inhabitants is intended to be at the end of the age or whether they have been fulfilled by various past events.

24:1-4 Isaiah noted, **the LORD is stripping** (Hb *baqaq*, "empty, lay waste") **the earth** and **making it desolate** (Hb *balaq*, "waste, lay waste"). The judgment to fall will affect the earth as well as all people

[A]23:10 DSS, LXX read *Work* [B]23:10 Or *longer any harbor*

regardless of station in life, illustrated by the six pairs of opposing types.

24:5-6 Judgment falls upon the earth because its inhabitants have violated **teachings** [Hb *torah*, "law, instruction"; see chart, p. 758], **overstepped decrees** [Hb, "statutes"], **and broken the everlasting covenant** (Hb *berit ʿolam*; see **Word Study**, p. 934). This "everlasting covenant" appears to be linked particularly with the one established with Noah and all mankind following the flood sent by God after mankind had utterly corrupted itself, and the earth was "filled with violence" (Gn 6:5,11-12). The passage also seems rooted in the original covenant with mankind at the beginning of time (Gn 2:16-17). Following the fall into sin, curses were pronounced on the natural order and extended to all human descendants (Rm 5:12, 18-19; 8:20-22). The **curse** follows mankind so that all **have become guilty**, and the result of the curse is judgment upon all (cp. Gn 3:14-19; 5:29; 8:21). This curse will be lifted only at the end of time (Rv 22:3).

24:7-9 This judgment would leave only a remnant (vv. 11-13; 2Pt 3:7,10). The land is empty and ruined (Is 24:7-13). The survivors depicted are forlorn, missing the former revelry of music, dancing, and celebrating, and the abundance of wine.

24:12 The **collapsed** gate indicates the city's military vulnerability.

24:14-16 The threat of judgment is balanced with hope concerning a remnant. In marked contrast to the gloom of the city, the saved remnant will sing joyfully to the Lord. The pronoun **they** of verse 14 is emphasized so that the passage literally reads, "They, **they raise their voices**" regarding **the majesty of the Lord**. Praise will resound **from the ends of the earth**. These shown praising the Lord are apparently the ones who were saved, who are possibly scattered abroad in **east** and **west**; they sing **the Splendor of the Righteous One**, better translated as "Glory" or "Honor to the Righteous One." Yet the prophet—possibly overcome by the magnitude of the judgment he had seen leading up to this point—mourned, knowing that much more treachery would follow before peace and praise would reign (21:2).

24:17-20 Reverting to words of judgment, Isaiah asserts that there would be no escape from the impending judgment. Though people might flee, they would **fall into a pit**; and if they managed to escape, they would **be caught in a trap**. Just as a wild animal might be caught, the inhabitants of the earth would

>WORD|*study*

24:1-4 The word translated world [Hb, *tēvēl*] is used around 36 times in the Old Testament, nine in Isaiah (cp. v. 11). Most occurrences of *tēvēl* outside of Isaiah convey a sense of the entire physical world. The word may also refer to all the people of the world and rarely to a possibly smaller inhabited section of the world. When used in parallel form as a synonym for *tēvēl*, *ʾerets* usually means "earth" instead of merely "land" in a regional sense.

lender and borrower,
creditor and debtor.
3 The earth will be stripped
completely bare
and will be totally plundered,
for the Lord has spoken
this message.
4 The earth mourns
and withers;
the world wastes away
and withers;
the exalted people of the earth
waste away.
5 The earth is polluted
by its inhabitants,
for they have transgressed
teachings,
overstepped decrees,
and broken
the everlasting covenant.
6 Therefore a curse
has consumed the earth,
and its inhabitants
have become •guilty;
the earth's inhabitants
have been burned,
and only a few survive.
7 The new wine mourns;
the vine withers.
All the carousers now groan.
8 The joyful tambourines
have ceased.
The noise of the jubilant
has stopped.
The joyful lyre has ceased.
9 They no longer sing
and drink wine;
beer is bitter to those
who drink it.
10 The city of chaos
is shattered;
every house is closed to entry.
11 In the streets they cry[A]
for wine.
All joy grows dark;
earth's rejoicing goes
into exile.
12 Only desolation remains
in the city;
its gate has collapsed in ruins.
13 For this is how it will be
on earth
among the nations:
like a harvested olive tree,
like a gleaning after
a grape harvest.
14 They raise their voices,
they sing out;
they proclaim in the west
the majesty of the Lord.
15 Therefore, in the east
honor the Lord!
In the islands of the west
honor the name of •Yahweh,
the God of Israel.
16 From the ends of the earth
we hear songs:
The Splendor
of the Righteous One.

But I said, "I waste away!
I waste away![B]
Woe is me."
The treacherous
act treacherously;
the treacherous deal
very treacherously.
17 Panic, pit, and trap
await you
who dwell on the earth.
18 Whoever flees at the sound
of panic
will fall into a pit,
and whoever escapes
from the pit
will be caught in a trap.
For the windows are opened
from heaven,
and the foundations
of the earth are shaken.
19 The earth is
completely devastated;
the earth is split open;
the earth is violently shaken.

[A]**24:11** Lit *streets she cries* [B]**24:16** Hb obscure

Covenants

Covenant Type	Bolded Passages Use the Exact Wording of "Everlasting Covenant."
Adamic	Gn 1:28-29; 2:16-17
Noahic	**Gn 9:1-17**
Abrahamic	Gn 12:1-3; **17:4-19; 1Ch 16:14-19; Ps 105:7-12**
Mosaic	Ex 19:5-6; Dt 5:2-21; 28:1–29:9
Sabbath	Ex 31:13-17; Lv 24:5-9
Davidic	2Sm 7:16; **23:5; Is 55:3**
New Covenant	Is 42:6; 49:8; 54:10; **61:8-9**; Jr 31:31-34; **32:37-41; 50:4-5;Ezk 16:60-62; 37:26-28**; Heb 8:8-13

20 The earth staggers
like a drunkard
and sways like a hut.
Earth's rebellion
weighs it down,
and it falls,
never to rise again.
21 On that day the LORD
will punish
the host of heaven above
and kings
of the earth below.
22 They will be
gathered together
like prisoners in a pit.
They will be confined
to a dungeon;
after many days
they will be punished.
23 The moon will be
put to shame
and the sun disgraced,
because the LORD of •Hosts
will reign as king
on Mount •Zion
in Jerusalem,
and He will
display His glory
in the presence of His elders.

Hymn of Praise (25:1-12)

25 •Yahweh, You are my God;
I will exalt You. I will praise
Your name,
for You have accomplished
wonders,
plans formed long ago,
with perfect faithfulness.
2 For You have turned the city
into a pile of rocks,
a fortified city, into ruins;
the fortress of barbarians is
no longer a city;
it will never be rebuilt.
3 Therefore, a strong people
will honor You.
The cities of violent nations
will •fear You.
4 For You have been
a stronghold for the poor,
a stronghold
for the needy person
in his distress,
a refuge from the rain,
a shade from the heat.
When the breath
of the violent
is like rain against a wall,
5 like heat in a dry land,
You subdue the uproar
of barbarians.
As[A] the shade
of a cloud cools the heat
of the day,
so He silences the song
of the violent.
6 The LORD of •Hosts
will prepare a feast
for all the peoples
on this mountain[B]—
a feast of aged wine,

[A]25:5 Lit *In* [B]25:6 = Mount Zion

be caught in the convulsions of final judgment. Verse 18 is similar to Gn 7:11, describing the flood unleashed by God to destroy all on the earth except those in the ark. The same picture of global destruction is evoked. Verse 19 is extremely emphatic with a string of infinitive absolutes paired with finite verbs of the same roots. The picture is of intensive destruction and corresponds to other accounts of the final judgment upon the world (see Rv 6:12-14; 8:5; 16:17-21). The earth will be brought down, **never to rise again**.

24:21-23 The host of heaven above might be used of celestial bodies (stars, planets). "The host" also refers to pagan gods and, on occasion, to the angelic order. Some Scripture references may suggest that the pagan gods were actually demons, the fallen angels. From one end of God's creation to the other, any rebellious elements, whether angelic or human, will be called to account (cp. chap. 14; 2Pt 2:4; Jd 6; Rv 20:1-3). The picture of the rebellious hosts and kings being confined briefly before the final permanent punishment corresponds perfectly to the picture presented in Rv 19:19–20:15. The **reign** of the Lord from **Mount Zion** without need for the **moon** or **sun** fits well with Rv 21:23 regarding the future city of God, illuminated by God's glory and the Lamb. Alternately, the passage could mean that the sun and moon (part of the "host of heaven") will be shown to be unworthy of human worship by comparison to the true king of the universe, or it may be considered an apocalyptic element, on the order of Mk 13:24.

25:1-2 Isaiah voiced his praise to God concerning His sovereign works, which had been planned **long ago** and which had been executed **with perfect faithfulness**.

25:3-5 While those who trusted in man-made fortresses would be brought to ruin, those who trusted in the Lord would find Him **a stronghold . . . a refuge,** and **a shade from the heat** (cp. 1Sm 2:4-10). Those who humbly depended upon the Lord for salvation would find Him sufficient to quell the attacks of **the violent** (see Is 37:36-38).

25:6-8 Just as Isaiah foresaw the ultimate defeat of "the violent," he foresaw a time when **the LORD** would call together all nations and **prepare a feast** for them **on this mountain**, Mount Zion (24:23), the future dwelling place of the Lord and His redeemed people from all nations (Jn 11:50-52; Rv 19:7-9). In addition, God would overthrow death—the last great enemy for His redeemed people. They would no longer need the literal **burial shroud**, nor would death loom over humanity like a shroud. God **will destroy** [Hb *bala'*, "swallow, eat up"] **death forever** (Hb *nētsach*, "perpetuity, victory"), and restore His people to favor before all nations.

25:8-9 God will wipe away the tears from every face (Is 65:19; Rv 7:17; 21:4). By their joyful proclamation of God as Savior, the people will acknowledge that the salvation had been accomplished by God alone (see Is 8:17).

25:10-12 In contrast to the redeemed people of the Lord dwelling on the mountain of the Lord in security and joy, **Moab will be trampled in his place**. In chapters 15 and 16, Moab's pride was mentioned, and here it appears again in the **trickery of his hands**.

26:1-2 In his song of praise in these initial verses of the chapter, Isaiah exults in the assurance of God's strength imparted to the saved community, and in the security and peace they experience. The **strong city** seems to reflect Jerusalem/Zion, where only the saved will be admitted.

26:3-5 Isaiah noted that God would protect with **perfect peace**, literally "peace, peace" (Hb *shalom, shalom*), the one with a **mind that is dependent** on the Lord (cp. Ps 37:39-40). By contrast, the haughty **who live in lofty places** (and depend on self) will be brought down and overthrown. The **rock** indicates strength and dependability.

26:7-12 Isaiah noted **the path of the righteous is level** (Hb *mēshar*, "evenness, uprightness, straightness"). God has ordered and established a straight path for the righteous, and He will enable them to walk it (Pss 27:11; 37:23-24). The path (or way) of the righteous is also drawn from wisdom literature (e.g., Pss 1; 37; Pr 2:7-9; 4:11-15,26-27). The righteous who walk **in the path of** God's **judgments** desire to glorify God (cp. Pss 27:14; 37:3-7a,9,34). By contrast, even when **the wicked man is shown favor**, he chooses to go his own way rather than God's. The wicked person continues in unrighteousness and injustice.

>WORD|*study*

25:8 The word destroy [Hb *bala'*, "swallow, eat up"] is used 49 times in the Old Testament, eight times in Isaiah. The word was used of literal swallowing in the sense of eating (Ex 7:12; Jnh 1:17) as well as figurative swallowing with the sense of destroying (Lm 2:2,5,8). Isaiah noted that God would swallow up or "destroy death." This image stands in pointed contrast to the ravenous picture of Sheol (the grave), figuratively an open mouth to swallow its victims (Is 5:14; see also Ps 69:15; Pr 1:12 for images of the pit). The Greek Septuagint translates *bala'* in Is 25:8 as "swallowed," which is how Paul quotes the passage in 1Co 15:54. Scripture teaches that one day the Lord will put an end to death. The dead who had been redeemed by trusting in the Lord Jesus to save them will be raised up, never to die again (Is 26:19; Hs 13:14; 1Co 15:35-58; Rv 20:6); in contrast, those who died without receiving Jesus Christ as their Savior will ultimately be raised, judged, and cast with death and Hades into the lake of fire forever (1Co 15:26; Rv 20:12-15; 21:8).

choice meat,[A]
finely aged wine.
7 On this mountain
He will destroy
the burial shroud,
the shroud over
all the peoples,
the sheet covering
all the nations;
8 He will destroy
death forever.
The Lord God will wipe away
the tears
from every face
and remove
His people's disgrace
from the whole earth,
for the LORD has spoken.
9 On that day it will be said,
"Look, this is our God;
we have waited for Him,
and He has saved us.
This is the LORD;
we have waited for Him.
Let us rejoice and be glad
in His salvation."
10 For the LORD's power will rest
on this mountain.

But Moab will be trampled
in his place[B]
as straw is trampled
in a dung pile.
11 He will spread out his arms
in the middle of it,
as a swimmer spreads out
his arms to swim.
His pride will be
brought low,
along with the trickery
of his hands.
12 The high-walled fortress
will be brought down,
thrown to the ground,
to the dust.

Song of Salvation (26:1-19)

26 On that day this song will be
sung in the land of Judah:

We have a strong city.
Salvation is established
as walls and ramparts.
2 Open the gates
so a righteous nation
can come in—
one that remains faithful.
3 You will keep the mind that is
dependent on You
in perfect peace,
for it is trusting in You.
4 Trust in the LORD forever,
because in •Yah, the LORD, is
an everlasting rock!
5 For He has humbled
those who live
in lofty places—
an inaccessible city.
He brings it down;
He brings it down
to the ground;
He throws it to the dust.
6 Feet trample it,
the feet of the humble,
the steps of the poor.

7 The path of the righteous
is level;
You clear a straight path
for the righteous.
8 Yes, Yahweh, we wait for You
in the path
of Your judgments.
Our desire is for Your name
and renown.
9 I long for You in the night;
yes, my spirit within me
diligently seeks You,
for when Your judgments are
in the land,
the inhabitants of the world
will learn righteousness.

[A]25:6 Lit *wine, fat full of marrow* [B]25:10 Or *trampled under Him*

>WORD|*study*

26:20-27:1 The name Leviathan (Hb) occurs six times in the Old Testament (Jb 3:8; 41:1-34; Pss 74:13-14; 104:26; Is 27:1). Throughout ancient Near East literature, a great sea monster associated with concepts of evil and chaos was often mentioned. Various names included Lotan, Shalyat, Tiamat, and Tannin. In Scripture, "Leviathan" was the name applied to the ultimate evil sea serpent. Scripture portrays the serpent as a literal creature as in the Job passages; however, the designation is also used symbolically as in Ps 74 where the description appears to represent Egypt. Some interpret the serpent imagery symbolically to indicate various nations that oppressed Israel, including Assyria, Egypt, and Babylon. Others understand the defeat of Leviathan simply to mean that all evil will be defeated in the end. Finally, some connect the image of Leviathan with passages concerning Satan, that great dragon of old, who will be seized by God and slain once and for all (Rv 12:9,15; 20:2). The meaning of the passage is clear; victory against the enemy of God is assured.

10 But if the wicked man is
shown favor,
he does not
learn righteousness.
In a righteous land
he acts unjustly
and does not see the majesty
of the LORD.

11 LORD, Your hand is lifted up
to take action,
but they do not see it.
They will see Your zeal
for Your people,
and they will be
put to shame.
The fire for Your adversaries
will consume them!
12 LORD, You will establish peace
for us,
for You have also done
all our work for us.
13 Yahweh our God, lords
other than You have ruled
over us,
but we remember
Your name alone.
14 The dead do not live;
departed spirits do not rise up.
Indeed, You have visited
and destroyed them;
You have wiped out
all memory of them.
15 You have added
to the nation, LORD.
You have added to the nation;
You are honored.
You have expanded
all the borders of the land.
16 LORD, they went to You
in their distress;
they poured out
whispered prayers
because Your discipline fell
on them.[A]
17 As a pregnant woman
about to give birth
writhes and cries out
in her pains,
so we were before You, LORD.
18 We became pregnant,
we writhed in pain;
we gave birth to wind.
We have won no victories
on earth,
and the earth's inhabitants
have not fallen.

19 Your dead will live;
their bodies[B] will rise.
Awake and sing, you who
dwell in the dust!
For you will be covered
with the morning dew,[C]
and the earth will bring out
the departed spirits.

Coming Judgment (26:20–27:1)

20 Go, my people,
enter your rooms
and close your doors
behind you.
Hide for a little while
until the wrath has passed.
21 For look, the LORD is coming
from His place
to punish the inhabitants
of the earth
for their iniquity.
The earth will reveal
the blood shed on it
and will no longer conceal
her slain.

27 On that day the LORD with His
harsh, great, and strong sword,
will bring judgment on •Leviathan,
the fleeing serpent—Leviathan, the
twisting serpent. He will slay the
monster that is in the sea.

26:14 Verse 14 should be seen together with verse 19. Verse 14 summarizes the fate of the wicked **dead**, while verse 19 rings out with assurance concerning the future resurrection and triumph of the Lord's people ("your dead," v. 19; 25:7-8).

26:16-18 The people were driven to pray to God as they were under His **discipline**, the "lords" (v. 13) possibly being part of that discipline. Though they called out to God, they suffered intensely like a **pregnant woman about to give birth**. Though Israel had struggled as a woman in labor, nothing of substance had come of the labor, they had only given **birth to wind**. The joy of giving birth to a child gives meaning to the long anguish of labor. The image of labor with no child shows the seeming futility of their strenuous efforts. As much as they tried to succeed in their own strength, there were **no victories** for them. These lines may refer to their shattered morale as a conquered nation.

26:19 Nevertheless, there was hope because of the promise of victory beyond this life. Israel was assured that their **dead will live; their bodies will rise**. Various opinions abound regarding Israel's understanding of a physical resurrection. There are indications throughout the Old Testament of at least a partial understanding of some type of resurrection (Jb 19:25-27; Ezk 37:11-14; Dn 12:2). The veiled Old Testament promises of a resurrection for the righteous were unveiled in the New Testament (Mt 22:23-32; Jn 11:21-27; 1Co 15:20-24,35-58; Rv 2:7,10-11; 1Th 4:17).

26:20–27:1 The people of the Lord were encouraged to **hide for a little while until the wrath has passed** (cp. Zph 2:3). The wrath was from **the LORD** who was **coming . . . to punish . . . iniquity**. This passage clearly resembles the night of Passover during which the wrath of God was poured out upon Egypt, but Israel was spared (Ex 12:22-27). In the same way, when the day of God's wrath comes and humanity faces the final judgment, only those covered by the blood of Jesus, the Lamb of God, will be spared (cp. Zph 2:3). On that day, as God judges all creation, He will also **bring judgment on Leviathan, the fleeing serpent**.

[A]**26:16** Hb obscure [B]**26:19** Lit *live; my body they* [C]**26:19** Lit *For your dew is a dew of lights*

27:2-3 The song of the **desirable vineyard** contrasts with the vineyard under God's condemnation in 5:1-7. Whereas in chapter 5 the vineyard bore worthless, the vineyard in chapter 27 has the potential for fruit world-wide (cp. Jn 15:1-8). In both cases the vineyard was tended and protected by the Lord, **so that no one disturbs it**. Whenever the phrase "on that day" is used, two possibilities follow: judgment or vindication and restoration (cp. Is 19:16-24).

27:4-5 In contrast to the picture in 5:25, the Lord is **not angry** with the vineyard of chapter 27. In this song, the wrath of the Lord has been turned from the vineyard. The **thorns and briers** indicate rebellion against God, for which discipline is necessary but for the purpose of restoration rather than total destruction; clearly the hope for peace with God exists. By becoming dependent upon the Lord, even unprofitable people (like **thorns and briers**) might **make peace** with God.

27:7-8 Though Israel had been disciplined, she was different from the other nations rebuked by God. He disciplined Israel to purge her of sin, not utterly to crush her.

27:9 The result of the removal of Israel's **sin** would be the purging of idolatry from the land.

27:10-11 Those who oppose God will be like desolate, abandoned cities, which fall into ruins and become grazing land. They will be like a tree stripped of leaves, left to dry out, eventually **broken** off, and used for firewood.

27:12-13 The purge, as always, would leave only a remnant. **On that day,** God's people will be vindicated and re-gathered as God judges their enemies (**thresh grain**) from **the Euphrates River** to **the Wadi of Egypt,** encompassing the entire land originally given to the children of Israel by God (Gn 15:18).

28:1 Often the drunken participants of revelries wore flower wreaths which would ultimately fade and be trampled. Isaiah used this image of a fading garland to represent Samaria, the capital city of the northern kingdom of Israel, which was located atop a hill overlooking a fertile **valley**.

28:2-4 Self-indulgence and disregard of the Lord would lead to destruction brought by God. This prophecy, which appears to refer to Samaria before its fall, is dated before 722 B.C.

Return of Israel (27:2-13)

2 On that day
sing about
a desirable vineyard:
3 I, ˙Yahweh, watch over it;
I water it regularly.
I guard it night and day
so that no one disturbs it.
4 I am not angry,
but if it produces thorns
and briers for Me,
I will fight against it,
trample it,
and burn it to the ground.
5 Or let it take hold
of My strength;
let it make peace with Me—
make peace with Me.
6 In days to come,
Jacob will take root.
Israel will blossom and bloom
and fill the whole world
with fruit.

7 Did the LORD strike Israel
as He struck the one
who struck Israel?
Was he killed like those killed
by Him?
8 You disputed with her
by banishing and driving her
away.[A]
He removed her
with His severe storm
on the day of the east wind.
9 Therefore Jacob's iniquity
will be purged in this way,
and the result of the removal
of his sin will be this:
when he makes all
the altar stones
like crushed bits of chalk,
no ˙Asherah poles
or incense altars
will remain standing.
10 For the fortified city
will be deserted,
pastures abandoned
and forsaken
like a wilderness.
Calves will graze there,
and there they will spread out
and strip its branches.
11 When its branches dry out,
they will be broken off.
Women will come
and make fires with them,
for they are not a people
with understanding.
Therefore their Maker will not
have compassion on them,
and their Creator will not
be gracious to them.
12 On that day
the LORD will thresh grain
from the Euphrates River
as far as the ˙Wadi of Egypt,
and you Israelites
will be gathered one by one.
13 On that day
a great trumpet will be blown,
and those lost in the land
of Assyria will come,
as well as those dispersed
in the land of Egypt;
and they will worship
the LORD
at Jerusalem
on the holy mountain.

Woe to Ephraim and Jerusalem (28:1–33:24)

28 Woe to the majestic crown
of Ephraim's drunkards,
and to the fading flower
of its beautiful splendor,
which is on the summit above
the rich valley.
Woe to those overcome
with wine.
2 Look, the Lord has a strong
and mighty one—
like a devastating hail storm,
like a storm with strong
flooding waters.
He will bring it across the land
with His hand.
3 The majestic crown
of Ephraim's drunkards
will be trampled underfoot.
4 The fading flower
of his beautiful splendor,
which is on the summit
above the rich valley,
will be like a ripe fig
before the summer harvest.
Whoever sees it
will swallow it
while it is still in his hand.
5 On that day
the LORD of ˙Hosts will become
a crown of beauty
and a diadem of splendor
to the remnant of His people,

[A]27:8 Hb obscure

6 a spirit of justice
to the one who sits
in judgment,
and strength
to those who turn back
the battle at the gate.
7 These also stagger
because of wine
and stumble
under the influence of beer:
priest and prophet stagger
because of beer,
they are confused by wine.
They stumble because of beer,
they are muddled
in their visions,
they stumble
in their judgments.
8 Indeed, all their tables
are covered with vomit;
there is no place
without a stench.
9 Who is he[A] trying to teach?
Who is he[A] trying to instruct?
Infants[B] just weaned
from milk?
Babies[B] removed
from the breast?
10 For he says: "Law after law,
law after law,
line after line, line after line,
a little here, a little there."[C,D]
11 So He will speak
to this people
with stammering speech
and in a foreign language.
12 He had said to them:
"This is the place of rest,
let the weary rest;
this is the place of repose."
But they would not listen.
13 Then the word of the LORD
came to them:
"Law after law, law after law,
line after line, line after line,
a little here, a little there,"[C,E]
so they go
stumbling backward,
to be broken, trapped,
and captured.
14 Therefore hear the word
of the LORD, you mockers
who rule this people
in Jerusalem.
15 For you said, "We have cut
a deal with Death,
and we have made
an agreement with •Sheol;
when the overwhelming
scourge passes through,
it will not touch us,
because we have
made falsehood our refuge
and have hidden
behind treachery."
16 Therefore the Lord GOD said:
"Look, I have laid a stone
in •Zion,
a tested stone,
a precious cornerstone,
a sure foundation;
the one who believes
will be unshakable.[F]
17 And I will make justice
the measuring line
and righteousness
the mason's level."
Hail will sweep away
the false refuge,
and water will flood
your hiding place.
18 Your deal with Death
will be dissolved,
and your agreement
with Sheol will not last.
When the overwhelming
scourge passes through,
you will be trampled.
19 Every time it passes through,
it will carry you away;

[A]28:9 Or *He* [B]28:9 Lit *Those* [C]28:10,13 Hb obscure [D]28:10 Perhaps the mockers of v. 9 are mimicking the prophet's words as baby talk. [E]28:13 The LORD quotes the mockers' words in v. 10 to represent the unintelligible language of the Assyrian invaders. [F]28:16 Lit *will not hurry*

28:6 The Lord would provide His people with **a spirit of justice** for ruling and **strength** to win in battle. The people sought beauty in the midst of over-indulgent living. Isaiah constantly brought in contrasting imagery to correct them. True beauty is to be found in the Lord, in His righteousness and justice.

28:7-10 The indictment here was against the religious leadership of Israel, both **priest and prophet**. The spiritual leaders of Isaiah's time were mocking the repeated simple teachings of the prophet (v. 14), revealing pride and an unteachable spirit by their reaction to God's message. Instead of humbling themselves and seeking the Lord, they took offense (v 9). The unfaithful priests and prophets felt they were beyond Isaiah's simple message; though wise in their own eyes, they were spiritually immature (Heb 5:12-14).

28:11 This passage probably refers to the foreign tongues of the Assyrians or other invaders who would carry Israel away. Israel would be taught through the harsh discipline of oppression rather than the gentle leading of the Lord.

28:12-13 Israel had been given the opportunity for deliverance. Although offered a **place of rest**, tragically, they **would not listen**.

28:16-17 The New Testament writers clearly identified the **precious cornerstone** as Jesus Christ (8:14; Rm 9:33; 10:11; Eph 2:20; 1Pt 2:6-8). For Isaiah's audience, the reference is to God's method of deliverance. With the establishment of God's **sure foundation, justice** would be **the measuring line** (Hb *qaw*) **and righteousness the mason's level**. Anything that could not measure up to His standards of justice and righteousness would fall.

28:18-19 The unfaithful in Jerusalem could bring judgment on themselves, but they could not stop or delay the plans of God. Isaiah warned that they would not escape the coming judgment by any of their self-devised methods of escape. **When the overwhelming** [Hb *shataph*, "overflowing"] **scourge** (Hb *shot*, "calamity") came upon them, they would be **trampled**. In this context, the combined image of a flood and scourge appears related to the Assyrian invaders, previously called a flood (8:7-8). The instability of Israel so that they are swept away **every day and every night** is a far cry from the stability of the "sure foundation" of verse 16.

>WORD|*study*

28:9-10 Some commentators suggest the phrase line after line, line after line (Hb *qaw laqaw, qaw laqaw*) was meaningless babble concocted by the mockers in simple rhyme with the preceding law after law (Hb *tsaw latsaw*) as if communicating in a childish way. *Qaw* is used 21 times in the Old Testament with 12 occurrences found in Isaiah. Though possibly referring to a literal line, the word was often associated with a literal or symbolic standard of measurement (1Kg 7:23; 2Ch 4:2; Jb 38:5; Is 34:17; 44:13; Jr 31:39; Ezk 47:3; Zch 1:16). On various occasions the word was used in reference to the judgment applied to Israel or other nations (2Kg 21:13; Is 34:11; Lm 2:8) and later for the standard of justice the Lord would use (Is 28:17). In Is 28:10 and 13, the meaning may be related to God's standard of measurement, reflecting the mockers' impatience with Isaiah's message regarding God's standards.

28:20-22 Israel would find that their self-devised plans for deliverance would fall uncomfortably short. Because of Israel's rejection of God's provision, instead of being their defense, God would fight against them just as He had previously fought against Israel's enemies at **Perazim** and **Gibeon** (Jos 10:6-14; 2Sm 5:20-25; 1Ch 14:11-16). Mocking would only increase the severity of the coming destruction.

28:23-27 Isaiah used agricultural imagery to illustrate that the proper and measured way to sow and reap a harvest rested in God's hand. **God teaches** the plowman concerning the proper way to sow and reap. Commentators suggest the passage is meant to convey that the harvesting of the people is done with similar great care. The Lord uses varied methods on different occasions to bring about the ultimate goal of a productive harvest.

28:28-29 Although the discipline imposed upon His field might be painful, the results would be worth it (27:2-6). Threshing, which is an image of judgment, will not go on forever, but will have a limit, and will ultimately produce delicious **bread**. Anyone seeking a productive harvest should be willing to learn from the **wonderful advice** of the Lord. The mockers' rejection of God's wisdom was the height of foolishness.

29:1-8 Targeting Jerusalem, Isaiah continued to proclaim woes to the Israelites.

29:3-4 The mention of **earth ramps** and **siege towers** may refer to actual sieges, which God brought against Jerusalem first through Assyria and later Babylon. Walled cities were the refuge of the ancient Near East: Fortified walls were the main protection from invaders. But large armies could build earth ramps and siege towers to overcome even fortified walls, spelling disaster for the city trusting in its mighty fortifications. The point was that the city would be humbled and **brought down** to the point that the **voice** of the city would be as faint and weak as a dead person speaking **from the dust**.

29:5-8 Though God would allow the city to be surrounded by **many foes** and **the ruthless** (Hb *ʿarits*, "terror-striking"; 29:20), He would ultimately deliver the city. Isaiah noted that **in an instant** Jerusalem **will be visited by the Lord of Hosts**, who would be attended by great natural signs (cp. 66:15-16). With the appearance of the Lord, **all the attackers . . . will then be like a dream, a vision in the night**, something that fades away

>WORD|*study*

29:1-2,7 That Ariel (Hb, "lion of God, altar-hearth") refers to Jerusalem is clarified by its being the city where David camped and by the reference to Mount Zion (v. 8). Just as God would overturn Samaria (28:2), the Lord would also "oppress" Ariel (Jerusalem) so she would be "like an Ariel" (i.e., altar hearth, v. 2). Isaiah uses "Ariel" five out of the six times it occurs in the Old Testament. The occurrence in Ezra 8:16 is a personal name, but the meaning of the Isaiah occurrences is debated. Some believe it is a combination of the Hebrew word *ʾari* ("lion") with *ʾēl* ("God") for Judah as lion (Gn 49:9). Others relate the word to the term *ariʾēl* meaning "altar or altar hearth" in Ezk 43:15-16. In that passage the word is actually read in the text with slightly different vowels as *ariʾēl*. Given Isaiah's love of wordplay, perhaps both meanings are in view with the name of Jerusalem reflecting the "lion of God" as well as the "altar-hearth" meaning. When God fought against the city, He made it an "altar hearth" whence the inferno of its destruction would rise, rather than the sacrifices of worship. This would fit well with the introduction of the **city where David encamped** (Is 29:1) as a nostalgic, positive remembrance within a declaration of war (i.e., just as David encamped against and besieged Jerusalem, so would God).

it will pass through
every morning—
every day and every night.
Only terror will cause you
to understand the message.[A]
20 Indeed, the bed is too short
to stretch out on,
and its cover too small
to wrap up in.
21 For the LORD will rise up
as He did at Mount Perazim.
He will rise in wrath,
as at the Valley of Gibeon,
to do His work,
His strange work,
and to perform His task,
His disturbing task.
22 So now, do not mock,
or your shackles
will become stronger.
Indeed, I have heard
from the Lord GOD of Hosts
a decree of destruction
for the whole land.

23 Listen and hear my voice.
Pay attention and hear
what I say.
24 Does the plowman plow
every day to plant seed?
Does he continuously break up
and cultivate the soil?
25 When he has leveled
its surface,
does he not then scatter
black cumin and sow cumin?
He plants wheat in rows
and barley in plots,
with spelt as their border.
26 His God teaches him order;
He instructs him.
27 Certainly black cumin
is not threshed
with a threshing board,
and a cart wheel is not rolled
over the cumin.
But black cumin is beaten out
with a stick,
and cumin with a rod.
28 Bread grain is crushed,
but is not threshed endlessly.
Though the wheel of
the farmer's cart rumbles,
his horses do not crush it.
29 This also comes from the LORD
of Hosts.
He gives wonderful advice;
He gives great wisdom.

29 Woe to Ariel,[B] Ariel,
the city where David camped!
Continue year after year;
let the festivals recur.
2 I will oppress Ariel,
and there will be mourning
and crying,
and she will be to Me
like an Ariel.[B]
3 I will camp in a circle
around you;
I will besiege you
with earth ramps,
and I will set up
my siege towers
against you.
4 You will be brought down;
you will speak
from the ground,
and your words will come
from low in the dust.
Your voice will be like that
of a spirit from the ground;
your speech will whisper
from the dust.

5 Your many foes[C] will be
like fine dust,

[A]28:19 Or *The understanding of the message will cause sheer terror* [B]29:1,2 Or *Altar Hearth*, or *Lion of God*; Hb obscure [C]29:5 Lit *foreigners*

and many of the ruthless,
like blowing chaff.
Then suddenly, in an instant,
6 you will be visited by the LORD
of •Hosts
with thunder, earthquake,
and loud noise,
storm, tempest, and a flame
of consuming fire.
7 All the many nations
going out to battle
against Ariel—
all the attackers, the siege
works against her,
and those who oppress her—
will then be like a dream,
a vision in the night.
8 It will be like a hungry one
who dreams he is eating,
then wakes and is
still hungry;
and like a thirsty one
who dreams he is drinking,
then wakes and is still thirsty,
longing for water.
So it will be for all the
many nations
who go to battle
against Mount •Zion.
9 Stop and be astonished;
blind yourselves
and be blind!
They are drunk,[A] but not
with wine;
they stagger,[B] but not
with beer.
10 For the LORD has poured out
on you
an overwhelming urge
to[C] sleep;
He has shut your
eyes—the prophets,
and covered your
heads—the seers.

11 For you the entire vision will be
like the words of a sealed document.
If it is given to one who can read and
he is asked to read it,[D] he will say,
"I can't read it, because it is sealed."
12 And if the document is given to
one who cannot read and he is asked
to read it,[E] he will say, "I can't read."
13 The Lord said:

Because these people
approach Me
with their mouths
to honor Me with lip-
service[F]—
yet their hearts are far
from Me,
and their worship consists of
man-made rules
learned by rote—
14 therefore I will again
confound these people
with wonder after wonder.
The wisdom of their wise men
will vanish,
and the understanding
of the perceptive
will be hidden.

15 Woe to those who go
to great lengths
to hide their plans
from the LORD.
They do their works
in darkness,
and say, "Who sees us?
Who knows us?"
16 You have turned things
around,
as if the potter were the same
as the clay.
How can what is made say
about its maker,
"He didn't make me"?
How can what is formed
say about the one
who formed it,
"He doesn't understand
what he's doing"?
17 Isn't it true that in just
a little while
Lebanon will become
an orchard,
and the orchard will seem
like a forest?
18 On that day the deaf will hear
the words of a document,
and out of a deep darkness
the eyes of the blind will see.
19 The humble will have joy
after joy in the LORD,
and the poor people
will rejoice
in the Holy One of Israel.

when morning comes. **The many nations who go to battle against Mount Zion** would ultimately fail to destroy God's city. Certainly an initial fulfillment of this prophecy occurred with the supernatural deliverance from Assyria (30:27-31; 37:36-38); however, the passage does not preclude a future fulfillment when the Lord Jesus comes to fight for Jerusalem at the end of the age (Ezk 38:14–39:7; Zch 14:1-16; Mt 24:6-31; Mk 13:8-27; Lk 21:10-28; Rv 16:18-19; 19:11-15).

29:9-12 Isaiah addressed the prophets and seers of his day who were blinded to the meaning of his words. He noted that their failure to understand came from the Lord, fulfilling God's proclamation at Isaiah's calling (6:9-10). As a result, the vision would be incomprehensible to those hearing it. Regardless of whether or not one could read, the meaning of the words would be hidden or **sealed** from their understanding (cp. 29:18; Rm 11:7-8).

29:13-16 Israel's hardness against receiving God's message resulted from their lack of a true relationship with the Lord. Though they gave **lip-service . . . their hearts** were not right (see 1:11-15). The Lord Jesus applied this passage to the religious leaders of His day (Mt 15:7-9; Mk 7:6-9). In both cases worship had ceased to have meaning and was merely a series of **man-made rules**.

Their wisdom would be turned to foolishness as they failed to recognize God's provision of salvation (1Co 1:18-25). The foolishness of the people's arrogance was fittingly captured by Isaiah's example of a lump of **clay** questioning the rights or wisdom of its **maker** (Is 19:16; 45:9-12; cp. Pr 16:4-6; Jr 18:2-11; Rm 9:18-24; 2Tm 2:19-21). To doubt or challenge God's actions, authority, or knowledge was just as ridiculous. God has full rights to do whatever He desires with His creation.

29:17-20 Isaiah continued by addressing the time of future deliverance when the previously sealed teachings would be opened so that **the deaf will hear** and **the blind will see** (cp. 35:5; 42:6-7; Mt 11:3-6). Isaiah noted there would be a time when God's message will no longer fall on deaf ears. He noted joy will come to the **humble** and **poor** who **will rejoice in the Holy One of Israel** (Mt 5:3,5). In addition, both **the ruthless** (Hb *'arits*, "terror-striking one, violent," see **Word Study**, p. 898) as well as **the scorner will disappear** as God's judgment is executed.

[A] **29:9** LXX, Tg, Vg read *Be drunk* [B] **29:9** Tg, Vg read *wine; stagger* [C] **29:10** Lit *you a spirit of* [D] **29:11** Lit *If one gives it to one who knows the document, saying, "Read this, please"* [E] **29:12** Lit *who does not know the document, saying, "Read this, please"* [F] **29:13** Lit *their mouth and honor Me with its lips*

>WORD|*study*

29:20 Isaiah mentioned previously that the ruthless (Hb *'arits*) would surround Jerusalem (29:5). In this passage Isaiah announced that the "ruthless" would be defeated. The word *'arits* occurs 20 times (Jb 6:23; 15:20; 27:13; Pss 37:35; 54:3; 86:14; Pr 11:16; Is 13:11; 25:3,4,5; 29:5,20; 49:25; Jr 15:21; 20:11; Ezk 28:7; 30:11; 31:12; 32:12). Normally, the word is used concerning wicked enemies in general as well as concerning the foreign oppressors of Israel. One verse uniquely uses the word to describe the mighty and awe-inspiring power of God (Jr 20:11). Isaiah most often used the word in reference to external enemies. There would come a time when Israel's external enemies would be eliminated as well as any who scoffed at the Lord.

29:21-23 The redemption of **Abraham** was an act of God, who called him to Himself (Gn 12:1-4; 15:6; Jos 24:2-3). Abraham left the idolatry of his father's house and served the Lord in faith that God would fulfill His promises; they will be completely fulfilled when God Himself redeems Abraham's true descendants (Rm 4:1-25; Gl 3:6-8). At that time, **Jacob will no longer be ashamed** at what has become of his descendants (Is 45:17). God will establish faithful children who **will honor** and **stand in awe** of Him.

30:1-2 Isaiah proclaimed, **Woe to the rebellious children** of Israel because they insisted on pursuing an alliance with Egypt. Instead of taking refuge with God, they sought **Pharaoh's protection**.

30:3-4 Apparently Judah had sent ambassadors to the Egyptian cities of **Zoan** and **Hanes** asking for help. Both cities were probably located in the northeastern area of the Nile delta, where Israel had formerly been enslaved in Egypt. God warned that reliance upon Egypt would bring disappointment; **Egypt** would bring nothing but **shame** (Hb *boshet*, "disgrace, ignominy"; cp. v. 5; 54:4; 61:7).

30:5-7 God also noted that **Egypt's help** was **completely worthless**, and paying tribute to them (as many did, transporting these **treasures** on various animals) was a poor investment. Egypt was scornfully called **Rahab Who Just Sits** (Jb 26:12; Pss 87:4; 89:9-10; Is 51:9-11). Rahab was a sea monster in ancient Near Eastern myths; however, Old Testament writers also used Rahab figuratively to refer to Egypt. This oracle is usually dated to the time following the Ashdod rebellion, which was encouraged by Egypt (see notes on Is 14:24-32). Egypt later failed to follow through with support during the resultant Assyrian crackdown (see notes on Is 20:1-6). The Egyptians even handed over a king of Philistia who had come to them for sanctuary when the rebellion failed. Israel, therefore, sought refuge in a treacherous nation.

30:8-11 Isaiah was commanded to write down the prophecies **in their presence** so that the tablet would **be for the future, forever and ever** (cp. 8:1), as a witness to Isaiah's true prophecies and against the rebelliousness of Israel (cp. 1:2-4), who spoke contemptuously about **the Holy One of Israel** and were dismissive and outright hostile to true **seers** and **prophets**, preferring lies instead (cp. Jr 11:21-22; 14:13-15; 29:21-32; Ezk 13:1-14; Am 2:12; 7:12-13; Mc 2:6-7).

20 For the ruthless one
will vanish,
the scorner will disappear,
and all those who lie in wait
with evil intent
will be killed—
21 those who, with their speech,
accuse a person
of wrongdoing,
who set a trap at the •gate
for the mediator,
and without cause deprive
the righteous of justice.

22 Therefore, the LORD who redeemed
Abraham says this about the house of
Jacob:

Jacob will no longer
be ashamed
and his face will no longer
be pale.
23 For when he sees
his children,
the work of My hands
within his nation,
they will honor My name,
they will honor the Holy One
of Jacob
and stand in awe of the God
of Israel.
24 Those who are confused
will gain understanding,
and those who grumble
will accept instruction.

30 Woe to the rebellious
children!
This is
the LORD's declaration.
They carry out a plan,
but not Mine;
they make an alliance,
but against My will,
piling sin on top of sin.
2 They set out to go down
to Egypt
without asking My advice,
in order to seek shelter
under Pharaoh's protection
and take refuge
in Egypt's shadow.
3 But Pharaoh's protection
will become your shame,
and refuge in Egypt's shadow
your disgrace.
4 For though his[A] princes are
at Zoan
and his messengers reach
as far as Hanes,
5 everyone will be ashamed
because of a people
who can't help.
They are of no benefit,
they are no help;
they are good for nothing
but shame and reproach.

6 An •oracle about the animals of
the •Negev:[B]

Through a land of trouble
and distress,
of lioness and lion,
of viper and flying serpent,
they carry their wealth
on the backs of donkeys
and their treasures
on the humps of camels,
to a people who will not
help them.
7 Egypt's help is
completely worthless;
therefore, I call her:
•Rahab Who Just Sits.
8 Go now, write it on a tablet
in their presence
and inscribe it on a scroll;
it will be for the future,
forever and ever.
9 They are a rebellious people,
deceptive children,
children who do not want to
obey the LORD's instruction.

[A]30:4 Or *Judah's* [B]30:6 Or *Southland*

>WORD|*study*

30:20 The word for Teacher (Hb *morēka*) is debated among commentators as singular or plural. The corresponding verb is singular. Given the context in which the religious leaders of Israel had been criticized, the noun seems best understood as singular. Thus, the "Teacher" would be God, who would reveal Himself in time, providing guidance and care for the people, leading them to reject idolatry (Ezk 39:29). In the New Testament, first Messiah and then the Holy Spirit take on the role of "Teacher" (Mt 23:10; Lk 12:12; Jn 14:26; 1Co 2:12-13). The Holy Spirit teaches a believer how to understand the word of God and how to walk in a way that pleases the Lord.

10 They say to the seers,
"Do not see,"
and to the prophets,
"Do not prophesy the truth
to us.
Tell us flattering things.
Prophesy illusions.
11 Get out of the way!
Leave the pathway.
Rid us of the Holy One
of Israel."
12 Therefore the Holy One
of Israel says:
"Because you have rejected
this message
and have trusted
in oppression and deceit,
and have depended on them,
13 this iniquity of yours will be
like a spreading breach,
a bulge in a high wall
whose collapse will come
in an instant—suddenly!
14 Its collapse will be
like the shattering
of a potter's jar,
crushed to pieces,
so that not even a fragment
of pottery
will be found among
its shattered remains—
no fragment large enough
to take fire from a hearth
or scoop water
from a cistern."
15 For the Lord God,
the Holy One of Israel,
has said:
"You will be delivered
by returning and resting;
your strength will lie
in quiet confidence.
But you are not willing."
16 You say, "No!
We will escape on horses"—
therefore you will escape!—
and, "We will ride
on fast horses"—
but those who pursue you
will be faster.
17 One thousand will flee
at the threat of one,
at the threat of five
you will flee,
until you alone remain
like a solitary pole
on a mountaintop
or a banner on a hill.

18 Therefore the Lord is waiting
to show you mercy,
and is rising up
to show you compassion,
for the Lord is a just God.
All who wait patiently for Him
are happy.

19 For you people will live on ·Zion
in Jerusalem and will never cry
again. He will show favor to you
at the sound of your cry; when He
hears, He will answer you. 20 The
Lord will give you meager bread
and water during oppression, but
your Teacher[A] will not hide Himself[B]
any longer. Your eyes will see your
Teacher,[A] 21 and whenever you turn
to the right or to the left, your ears
will hear this command behind you:
"This is the way. Walk in it." 22 Then
you will defile your silver-plated
idols and your gold-plated images.
You will throw them away like menstrual cloths, and call them filth.
23 Then He will send rain for your
seed that you have sown in the
ground, and the food, the produce of
the ground, will be rich and plentiful. On that day your cattle will graze
in open pastures. 24 The oxen and
donkeys that work the ground will
eat salted fodder scattered with winnowing shovel and fork. 25 Streams
flowing with water will be on every

[A] **30:20** Or *teachers* [B] **30:20** Or *themselves*

30:12-14 As a result, God proclaimed that their sin would be **like a spreading breach**, a defect that would continue to grow until the wall itself would **collapse**.

When the collapse came (which most identify as the final blow struck against Jerusalem by the Babylonian invaders), Israel would be crushed so completely that not even a small **fragment** would be usable. Scraps of pottery were used all the time and are essential to dating in modern archaeology. The uselessness of even the shards of pottery was a picture of the thoroughness of destruction, even down to the smallest detail.

30:15-17 Isaiah reminded them of God's advice to trust Him: **You will be delivered by returning and resting**—reliance upon Him alone. Israel pursued her own methods of deliverance (28:12) and consequently failed to thwart the invasion. They would be so devastated that only the city would survive **like a solitary pole on a mountaintop**. This was the case when Sennacherib overran Judah in 701 B.C., taking all cities and abandoning Jerusalem only after the merciful deliverance of the Lord (2Kg 18:13,17; 19:35-36; Is 36:1; 37:36-37).

30:18-21 Despite Judah's rebelliousness, God was still **waiting** to show them **mercy** upon their **cry** of repentance. Although God is **just** in His punishment, He is yet full of **compassion**. Those who **wait** on Him find happiness (cp. 8:17). Judah would eventually live in Zion again, experience God's **favor**, and be led and instructed by Him as their **Teacher** (cp. 25:8).

30:22-26 With the coming of this outpouring of God's revelation, the **silver-plated idols** as well as the **gold-plated images** will be discarded as unclean. The blessing of the **rain** and agricultural prosperity indicates the restoration of the covenant blessings to the people. Though previously the Lord had given them "meager bread and water" (v. 20), their repentance would prompt abundant provision. For Isaiah's contemporaries, this might refer to the relief following Sennacherib's departure after besieging Jerusalem; it may also correspond to the latter days when the earth's faithful will be blessed by the Lord's reign. A time would come when **the Lord bandages His people's injuries and heals the wounds He inflicted** (cp. 1:5-6)—a time of reversals: instead of disobedience, full obedience; and instead of the suffering and pain resulting from sin, healing and restoration from God's mercy.

30:27-28 This final section is suffused with imagery of heat and fire, indicating God's wrath (**anger burning**) and the **destruction** of enemies, in this case, Assyria. This is typical of Israel's understanding of the Day of the Lord, when God destroys Israel's enemies and exalts Israel as His chosen and favored nation. Isaiah assured Israel that God had already planned the fall of their great enemy Assyria (v. 31). Some also see a reference to the final defeat of the supreme evil among **the nations** in the conflagration of the last days (Is 29:5-8; Rv 19:20; 20:10, 15).

30:29-32 In contrast to the suffering of the Assyrians, Israel will **rejoice** in the presence of the Lord, as if they were attending a **holy festival.** Their rejoicing and singing would be the accompaniment to God's annihilation of the Assyrians.

30:33 God would fight against and ultimately destroy the king of Assyria. **Topheth** (Hb, "place of fire") referred to the Valley of Hinnom located south of Jerusalem where Israelites had sacrificed children to idols by fire (2Kg 23:10; 2Ch 28:3; Jr 7:31; 19:6,11-14). This same valley was called *Gehenna* (Gk) in the New Testament, and its name was figuratively applied to hell (Mk 9:43-48). God related the image of Topheth to the final **funeral pyre** of the pagan king.

31:1 Isaiah repeated the warning against all those who trust in **Egypt** for deliverance instead of the **Holy One of Israel** (Ps 20:6-7). Israel had been instructed never to return to Egypt for **horses** (Dt 17:16). God knew that possession of horses, so powerful in battle, would lead to trusting in their own might.

31:3 The reference to horses and chariots clearly calls to mind the complete overthrow of Pharaoh's soldiers during the exodus of the Israelites from Egypt (Ex 14:23-30; 15:1,4,19). Isaiah reminded Israel that God alone could save and that **Egyptians** were **men, not God.** As during the exodus, He would again destroy both Egypt and those whom they **helped.** In 701 B.C., the Egyptian armies led by Tirhakah did rise to fight against Sennacherib of Assyria but were completely defeated near Ekron (2Kg 19:9; see notes on Is 20:1-6; 37:9).

31:4-5 The enemies of Judah would fall as prey; no one could deter the Lord from His purpose. The Lord Himself, like a **lion,** would defend Jerusalem (cp. Rv 5:5). Isaiah noted that **by protecting it** and **by sparing** [Hb *pasach,* "pass over," the same word used in reference to the Passover; cp. Ex 12:11-13,23,27]

high mountain and every raised hill
on the day of great slaughter when
the towers fall. 26 The moonlight will
be as bright as the sunlight, and the
sunlight will be seven times brighter—like the light of seven days—on
the day that the LORD bandages
His people's injuries and heals the
wounds He inflicted.

27 Look, •Yahweh[A] comes
from far away,
His anger burning and heavy
with smoke.[B]
His lips are full of fury,
and His tongue is
like a consuming fire.
28 His breath is like
an overflowing torrent
that rises to the neck.
He comes to sift the nations
in a sieve of destruction
and to put a bridle on the jaws
of the peoples
to lead them astray.
29 Your singing will be like that
on the night of a holy festival,
and your heart will rejoice
like one who walks
to the music of a flute,
going up to the mountain
of the LORD,
to the Rock of Israel.
30 And the LORD will
make the splendor
of His voice heard
and reveal His arm striking in
angry wrath
and a flame of consuming fire,
in driving rain, a torrent,
and hailstones.
31 Assyria will be shattered
by the voice of the LORD.
He will strike with a rod.
32 And every stroke
of the appointed[C] staff
that the LORD brings down
on him
will be to the sound
of tambourines and lyres;
He will fight against him
with brandished weapons.
33 Indeed! •Topheth
has been ready
for the king for
a long time now.
Its funeral pyre is deep
and wide,
with plenty of fire and wood.
The breath of the LORD,
like a torrent of brimstone,
kindles it.

31 Woe to those who go down
to Egypt for help
and who depend on horses!
They trust in the abundance
of chariots
and in the large number
of horsemen.
They do not look
to the Holy One of Israel
and they do not seek
the LORD's help.
2 But He also is wise
and brings disaster.
He does not go back on what
He says;
He will rise up
against the house
of wicked men
and against the allies
of evildoers.
3 Egyptians are men, not God;
their horses are flesh,
not spirit.
When the LORD
raises His hand to strike,
the helper will stumble
and the one who is helped
will fall;
both will perish together.

4 For this is what the LORD said to
me:

As a lion or young lion growls
over its prey
when a band of shepherds
is called out against it,
and is not terrified
by their shouting
or subdued by their noise,
so the LORD of •Hosts
will come down
to fight on Mount •Zion
and on its hill.
5 Like hovering birds,
so the LORD of Hosts
will protect Jerusalem—
by protecting it,
He will rescue it,
by sparing it,
He will deliver it.

6 Return to the One the Israelites
have greatly rebelled against. 7 For

[A]30:27 Lit *the name Yahweh* [B]30:27 Hb obscure [C]30:32 Some Hb mss read *punishing*

on that day, every one of you will
reject the silver and gold idols that
your own hands have sinfully made.

8 Then Assyria will fall,
but not by human sword;
a sword will devour him,
but not one made by man.
He will flee from the sword;
his young men will be put
to forced labor.
9 His rock[A] will pass away
because of fear,
and his officers will be afraid
because of the signal flag.

This is the LORD's declaration—whose fire is in Zion and whose furnace is in Jerusalem.

32 Indeed, a king
will reign righteously,
and rulers will rule justly.
2 Each will be like a shelter
from the wind,
a refuge from the rain,
like streams of water
in a dry land
and the shade
of a massive rock
in an arid land.
3 Then the eyes of those
who see will not be closed,
and the ears of those
who hear will listen.
4 The reckless mind
will gain knowledge,
and the stammering
tongue will speak clearly
and fluently.
5 A fool will no longer be called
a noble,
nor a scoundrel said
to be important.
6 For a fool speaks foolishness
and his mind plots iniquity.
He lives in a godless way
and speaks falsely
about the LORD.
He leaves the hungry empty
and deprives the thirsty
of drink.
7 The scoundrel's weapons
are destructive;
he hatches plots to destroy
the needy with lies,
even when the poor says
what is right.
8 But a noble person plans
noble things;
he stands up for noble causes.
9 Stand up,
you complacent women;
listen to me.
Pay attention to what I say,
you overconfident daughters.
10 In a little more than a year
you overconfident ones
will shudder,
for the vintage will fail
and the harvest will not come.
11 Shudder,
you complacent ones;
tremble,
you overconfident ones!
Strip yourselves bare
and put •sackcloth
around your waists.
12 Beat your breasts in mourning
for the delightful fields
and the fruitful vines,
13 for the ground of my people
growing thorns and briers,
indeed, for every joyous house
in the joyful city.
14 For the palace
will be forsaken,
the busy city abandoned.
The hill and the watchtower
will become
barren places forever,
the joy of wild donkeys,
and a pasture for flocks,
15 until the Spirit from heaven
is poured out on us.
Then the desert will become
an orchard,
and the orchard will seem
like a forest.
16 Then justice will inhabit
the wilderness,
and righteousness will dwell
in the orchard.
17 The result of righteousness
will be peace;
the effect of righteousness
will be quiet
confidence forever.
18 Then my people will dwell
in a peaceful place,
in safe and secure dwellings.
19 But hail will level the forest,[B]
and the city will sink
into the depths.
20 Those who sow seed are happy

[A]31:9 Perhaps the Assyrian king [B]32:19 Hb obscure

it, He will deliver it. God would spare His people from Assyria as He had from Egypt. Israel would be spared the plague while the soldiers of Sennacherib would be smitten by the "angel of the LORD" (Is 37:36).

31:7 The Lord thus proves His exclusive sovereignty and that He is truly God, unlike the Assyrian **silver and gold idols.**

31:8-9 Thus **Assyria will fall** by God's strength, **not by human sword**. The **rock** of Assyria may be their king or the deity upon whom they depend, and the armies will be intimidated by God's **fire**.

32:1-2 Once again the coming of the messianic kingdom, which would be characterized by righteousness, was announced (9:7; 11:4; 16:5). When the messianic kingdom is established, **rulers** will **rule justly** as opposed to the corrupt and self-serving practices that had been denounced previously (cp. 1:23; 5:7-23). These rulers would also offer effective protection and security (**shelter** and **refuge**).

32:6-8 In both descriptions of the **fool** (Hb *naval*, "impious, wicked"; cp. Nabal, 1Sm 25:3) and the **scoundrel**, their evil deeds were especially destructive for the poor and weak. In contrast, **a noble person** [Hb *nadiv*, "princely" or "noble or generous in mind and character"] **. . . stands up for noble causes**.

32:9-10 Once again Isaiah addresses the indulgent, **overconfident daughters** of Israel with warnings of impending judgment (3:16–4:1). His warning that **in a little more than a year . . . the harvest will not come,** may have been fulfilled in 701 B.C. When the Assyrian armies invaded, they destroyed the fields in the countryside, leaving only Jerusalem standing in the midst of a barren land stripped of any hope of a harvest.

32:11-12 The proper response for these women in the face of his warning should have been **mourning** and repentance. Removal of fancy clothes, donning of **sackcloth**, and beating one's **breasts** are signs of deep grief, here for the lost harvest and productivity. The agricultural failure impacted every **house** (family) in the (formerly) **joyful city**.

32:14-18 Isaiah further noted that the **busy city** would be **abandoned** and **become barren . . . until the Spirit from heaven** was **poured out**. At that point the devastation would be reversed. The life-giving Spirit would bestow supernatural productivity, justice, and righteousness, as well as peace, pictured as **an orchard** that expands and becomes a **forest**, filling the wilderness. The expression "poured out" regarding the Spirit appears in other passages linked to the last days (Ezk 39:29; Jl 2:28-32) and was at least partially fulfilled by the coming of the Spirit at Pentecost (Ac 2:16-21).

33:1-4 In this chapter, Isaiah dealt with the fate of the wicked as well as the future joy of the righteous. Some scholars also consider this as a future event involving a deception of the antichrist (Dn 9:27).

33:6 As Judah waits for God's deliverance, their armory is filled with not only weapons of warfare but also **salvation, wisdom, and knowledge,** indicating a right relationship with, and proper trust in, God. Their treasury is filled not only with gold but with **the fear of the LORD.**

33:7-8 The **messengers of peace** [possibly Judah's ambassadors to the Assyrian king] **weep bitterly** because **an agreement has been broken.** Around 701 B.C., Hezekiah and the kingdom of Judah had been besieged because they had refused to pay tribute to Assyria. When the Assyrian armies poured into Judah, destroying the cities and land, Hezekiah attempted to make a peace treaty with Assyria by sending the demanded tribute. However, the king of Assyria took the tribute and still besieged Jerusalem, to the dismay of the city's inhabitants (2Kg 18:13–19:37; Is 36:1–37:38).

33:10-12 Following the period of desolation, at a specific time conveyed by the threefold repetition of **Now,** the Lord will **rise up** and **be exalted** (cp. chap. 2). He will come in judgment against the unrighteous: **The peoples will be burned to ashes, like thorns cut down and burned in a fire** (cp. 5:24; 9:18-19; 10:16-19; 24:6). Commentators point out that judgment was initially poured out on Assyria, first when God struck down the army around Jerusalem, and later when that kingdom and its capital Nineveh fell (Nah 1:6,10); however, the passage also seems to apply to a future time of final judgment (Mal 4:1; Mt 25:41; 2Th 1:7-10; 2Pt 3:7,10-11).

33:14-17 The coming of the Lord in judgment strikes fear in the hearts of **the sinners** and **ungodly** because they finally recognize the absolute purity of the Holy One of Israel, who comes as **a consuming fire** (cp. Ex 24:17; Dt 4:24; 9:3; Is 29:6; 30:30; Heb 12:29).

33:18-19 Those who are found righteous will enjoy the deliverance of the Lord and will enter the peace of His rule. No longer will they have to pay tribute or fear a foreign enemy like

beside abundant waters;
they let ox and donkey
range freely.

33 Woe, you destroyer
never destroyed,
you traitor never betrayed!
When you have
finished destroying,
you will be destroyed.
When you have
finished betraying,
they will betray you.
2 LORD, be gracious to us!
We wait for You.
Be our strength
every morning
and our salvation in time
of trouble.
3 The peoples flee
at the thunderous noise;
the nations scatter
when You rise
in Your majesty.
4 Your spoil will be gathered
as locusts are gathered;
people will swarm over it
like an infestation
of locusts.
5 The LORD is exalted,
for He dwells on high;
He has filled •Zion with justice
and righteousness.
6 There will be times of security
for you—
a storehouse of salvation,
wisdom, and knowledge.
The •fear of the LORD is
Zion's treasure.
7 Listen! Their warriors
cry loudly in the streets;
the messengers of peace
weep bitterly.
8 The highways are deserted;
travel has ceased.
An agreement has been
broken,
cities[A] despised,
and human life disregarded.
9 The land mourns and withers;
Lebanon is ashamed
and decayed.
Sharon is like a desert;
Bashan and Carmel shake off
their leaves.

10 "Now I will rise up,"
says the LORD.
"Now I will lift Myself up.
Now I will be exalted.
11 You will conceive chaff;
you will give birth to stubble.
Your breath is fire that will
consume you.
12 The peoples will be burned
to ashes,
like thorns cut down
and burned in a fire.
13 You who are far off, hear what
I have done;
you who are near,
know My strength."
14 The sinners in Zion are afraid;
trembling seizes the ungodly:
"Who among us can dwell
with a consuming fire?
Who among us can dwell
with ever-burning flames?"
15 The one who lives righteously
and speaks rightly,
who refuses gain
from extortion,
whose hand never takes a bribe,
who stops his ears
from listening
to murderous plots[B]
and shuts his eyes to avoid
endorsing evil[C]—
16 he will dwell on the heights;
his refuge will be
the rocky fortresses,
his food provided,
his water assured.
17 Your eyes will see the King
in His beauty;
you will see a vast land.
18 Your mind will meditate
on the past terror:
"Where is the accountant?[D]
Where is
the tribute collector?[E]
Where is the one
who spied out
our defenses?"[F]
19 You will no longer see
the barbarians,
a people whose speech
is difficult to comprehend—
who stammer in a language
that is not understood.
20 Look at Zion, the city
of our festival times.

[A]33:8 DSS read *witnesses* [B]33:15 Lit *to bloods* [C]33:15 Lit *eyes from seeing evil* [D]33:18 Lit *counter* [E]33:18 Lit *weigher* [F]33:18 Lit *who counts towers*

Your eyes will see Jerusalem,
a peaceful pasture, a tent
that does not wander;
its tent pegs will not
be pulled up
nor will any of its cords
be loosened.
21 For the majestic One,
our LORD, will be there,
a place of rivers
and broad streams
where ships that are rowed
will not go,
and majestic vessels
will not pass.
22 For the LORD is our Judge,
the LORD is our lawgiver,
the LORD is our King.
He will save us.
23 Your ropes are slack;
they cannot hold the base
of the mast
or spread out the flag.
Then abundant spoil
will be divided,
the lame will plunder it,
24 and none there will say,
"I am sick."
The people who dwell there
will be forgiven their iniquity.

A Summary of Judgment and Salvation (34:1–35:10)

Judgment upon the Nations (34:1-17)

34 You nations, come here
and listen;
you peoples, pay attention!
Let the earth hear, and all
that fills it,
the world and all that comes
from it.
2 The LORD is angry with all
the nations—
furious with all their armies.
He will set them apart
for destruction,
giving them over to slaughter.
3 Their slain will be
thrown out,
and the stench
of their corpses will rise;
the mountains will flow[A]
with their blood.
4 All[B] the heavenly bodies
will dissolve.
The skies will roll up
like a scroll,
and their stars will all wither
as leaves wither on the vine,
and foliage on the fig tree.

5 When My sword has drunk
its fill[C] in the heavens,
it will then come down
on Edom
and on the people I have
•set apart for destruction.
6 The LORD's sword is covered
with blood.
It drips with fat,
with the blood of lambs
and goats,
with the fat of the kidneys
of rams.
For the LORD has a sacrifice
in Bozrah,
a great slaughter in the land
of Edom.
7 The wild oxen
will be struck[D] down
with them,
and young bulls
with the mighty bulls.
Their land will be soaked
with[E] blood,
and their soil will be saturated
with fat.
8 For the LORD has a day
of vengeance,
a time of paying back Edom
for its hostility against •Zion.
9 Edom's streams will be turned
into pitch,

[A]34:3 Or *melt*, or *dissolve* [B]34:4 DSS read *And the valleys will be split, and all* [C]34:5 DSS read *sword will appear* [D]34:7 Or *will go* [E]34:7 Or *will drink its fill of*

>WORD|study

34:2-3 The armies will be **set . . . apart for destruction** (Hb *charam*, "devote to the ban, destruction"; cp. 66:24; Ezk 39:17-20; Rv 19:15-21; 20:7-9). The verb is used 52 times throughout the Old Testament and normally refers to something or someone being dedicated or given over completely to the Lord, expressed by completely destroying the object or being (e.g., Lv 27:28-29; Nm 21:2-3; Dt 2:34). The bulk of occurrences refer to Canaanite cities being set apart to God for destruction. Rarely, the word is used to describe destruction carried out by pagan nations. The verb appears three times in Isaiah (Is 11:15; 34:2; 37:11). This passage notes the armies of rebellious nations will be utterly exterminated.

Assyria, and they will no longer **see the barbarians** (Hb *ya'az*, "arrogant, fierce") speaking a strange language (a reversal of 28:11).

33:20-22 Instead, Jerusalem will be solidly established and the **majestic One, our LORD, will be there** with the righteous. At that point the Lord's rule will be permanently established so that He will be their **Judge**, **lawgiver**, and **King** (cp. 1Sm 8:5-8,18-22; 12:12-13,17-19; Hs 13:9-11).

33:24 The righteous dwelling in the city will be righteous, not because they had been perfect but because they were **forgiven their iniquity** by the grace and mercy of God (Is 33:24; 40:1-2; Jr 50:20; Mc 7:18-20; Rm 3:10,21-26; 1 Jn 1:7-9).

34:1–35:10 In chapters 34 and 35, the dual message of judgment and deliverance is recapped with clear eschatological overtones. Chapter 34 deals with the judgment of the nations, and chapter 35 deals with the salvation of the redeemed.

34:1-4 In this passage Isaiah covered two aspects of that judgment: the destruction of the armies of Israel's enemies and the effect of God's deeds on the created order. There will be two main battles in the last days when the Lord intervenes and completely destroys the rebellious armies—one preceding the Lord's millennial reign and the second following the rebellion of the nations encouraged by Satan at the end of the millennial reign (cp. Rv 16:15-21; 20:7-10).

34:4 The theme of **heavenly bodies** dissolving is found in other apocalyptic and eschatological passages (Is 51:6; Jl 2:30-31; 3:14-16; Mt 24:29; Mk 13:24-25; Lk 21:25-26; 2Pt 3:12; Rv 6:13-14; 8:10; 20:11). Other passages discuss the creation of a new heaven and earth following the destruction of the old (Is 65:17; 66:22; 2Pt 3:13; Rv 21:1).

34:5 Once the judgment against the nations and heavenly bodies has occurred, **Edom** will be marked for particular **destruction** (cp. Jl 3:19).

34:6-11 The language regarding the **sacrifice** of various animals taking place in **Bozrah** (Edom's capital) is taken to refer to the various types of people who would fall to God's sword from the lowest to the highest leaders of the land. Isaiah proclaimed God had **a day of vengeance, a time of paying back** [Hb *shillum*, "requital, retribution"] **Edom for its hostility against Zion** (see note on 63:1; cp. Jr 49:13; Ezk 35:12-15; Am 1:11; Ob 10-14). Around 586 B.C., when Babylon destroyed Jerusalem, Edom joined in the plunder. God warned Edom ahead of time that He would repay the evil the nation committed against Israel in its time of distress (Ob 15).

The image Isaiah gives is of a city losing its people and its natural resources, becoming a barren waste fit only for desert-dwelling creatures.

34:16-17 **The scroll of the Lord** does not have a clear referent, but is perhaps related to the inscription the Lord commanded Isaiah to record so the generations to come would know that this prophecy was fulfilled (30:8).

35:1 Although Edom and defiant nations were slated for destruction, the remnant of Zion was promised redemption and restoration. Even **the desert will rejoice and blossom**. The land's devastation wrought by the enemy would be more than reversed (33:9; 51:3); rather than a wilderness, it will be a garden.

35:4 Again the **vengeance** (Hb *naqam*; see **Word Study**, p. 944) and **retribution** (Hb *gemul*, "recompense") of the Lord are mentioned; but for those who belong to the Lord, His coming means salvation.

35:5-6 Using healing language similar to that in other messianic passages, Isaiah described a complete transformation of the redeemed. **Eyes** would be **opened**, **ears . . . unstopped**, **the lame** would not only walk but would **leap** for joy just as formerly silent tongues would not only talk but **sing for joy**. **Water** would flow representing God's presence and provision of life (cp. 12:3; 32:2; 41:17-18; Jn 4:14). Physical and spiritual transformations were initiated with the first coming of the Messiah, Jesus Christ. The fulfillment will occur when He returns to establish His eternal kingdom.

35:8-9 At that time, there will be a road **called the Holy Way**. Only **the redeemed** [Hb *ga'al*] **will walk on it**, and their progress will be protected.

35:10 Following the "Holy Way," **the redeemed** [Hb *padah*] **. . . will return and come to Zion** (see **Word Study**, p. 863). Isaiah 35:10 is identical to 51:11, which describes the return of the Israelites from the Babylonian captivity to Zion with a reference to the original exodus from Egypt. In all cases, the redemption of the people was brought about solely by the sovereign work of God. For the redeemed, pure **joy** untainted by **sorrow** will be present in Zion (cp. Rv 7:17; 21:4).

36:1 Hezekiah's **fourteenth year** was 701 B.C. Isaiah's account of the Assyrian siege of Jerusalem and God's

her soil into sulfur;
her land will become
burning pitch.
10 It will never go
out—day or night.
Its smoke will go up forever.
It will be desolate,
from generation
to generation;
no one will pass
through it forever and ever.
11 The desert owl[A]
and the screech owl[B]
will possess it,
and the great owl
and the raven
will dwell there.
The LORD will stretch out
a measuring line
and a plumb line over her
for her destruction and chaos.
12 No nobles will be left
to proclaim a king,
and all her princes will come
to nothing.
13 Her palaces will be overgrown
with thorns;
her fortified cities,
with thistles and briers.
She will become a dwelling
for jackals,
an abode[C] for ostriches.
14 The desert creatures
will meet hyenas,
and one wild goat will call
to another.
Indeed, the screech owl
will stay there
and will find a resting place
for herself.
15 The sand partridge[D] will make
her nest there;
she will lay and hatch
her eggs
and will gather her brood
under her shadow.
Indeed, the birds of prey
will gather there,
each with its mate.
16 Search and read the scroll
of the LORD:
Not one of them
will be missing,
none will be lacking its mate,
because He has ordered it
by my[E] mouth,
and He will gather them
by His Spirit.
17 He has ordained a lot
for them;
His hand allotted
their portion
with a measuring line.
They will possess it forever;
they will dwell in it
from generation
to generation.

Salvation by God of the Redeemed (35:1-10)

35 The wilderness
and the dry land
will be glad;
the desert will rejoice
and blossom like a rose.[F][G]
2 It will blossom abundantly
and will also rejoice with joy
and singing.
The glory of Lebanon
will be given to it,
the splendor of Carmel
and Sharon.
They will see the glory
of the LORD,
the splendor of our God.
3 Strengthen the weak hands,
steady the shaking knees!
4 Say to the cowardly:
"Be strong; do not fear!
Here is your God;
vengeance is coming.
God's retribution is coming;
He will save you."
5 Then the eyes of the blind
will be opened,
and the ears
of the deaf unstopped.
6 Then the lame will leap
like a deer,
and the tongue of the mute
will sing for joy,
for water will gush
in the wilderness,
and streams in the desert;
7 the parched ground
will become a pool of water,
and the thirsty land springs
of water.
In the haunt of jackals,
in their lairs,
there will be grass, reeds,
and papyrus.

[A]**34:11** Or *The pelican* [B]**34:11** Or *the hedgehog* [C]**34:13** DSS, LXX, Syr, Tg; MT reads *jackals, grass* [D]**34:15** Or *The arrow snake*, or *The owl* [E]**34:16** Some Hb mss; other Hb mss, DSS, Syr, Tg read *His* [F]**35:1** Or *meadow saffron* [G]**35:1** Not the modern flower but a common wildflower in northern Israel

>WORD|*study*

35:9-10 The concept of redemption is crucial to Isaiah. For the Israelites, this Hebrew verb *ga'al*, occurring around 104 times with 23 references in Isaiah alone, had rich meaning beyond the basic definition of being **redeemed**. The word usually includes the involvement of a close relative or owner who would pay a price to rescue someone or something. A kinsman-redeemer or close relative was obligated to purchase and restore a field, or even a person, that had been sold out of necessity (Lv 25:25-27; Ru 2:20; 3:9,12-13; 4:1-14; see note on Ru 2:19-23). In addition, the word was used when an owner paid a price to redeem something set apart to the Lord (Lv 27:11-33). The participle form of *ga'al* might also be used to describe a near kinsman who was called upon to avenge the life of a relative (Nm 35:12,19,21,24-27). In Isaiah, the word is often used in the context of God's actions to save His people. He takes on the role of kinsman-redeemer to pay a debt His people could not pay in order to restore them (Is 35:9; 43:1,14; 44:6,22-24; 48:17,20; 49:7,26; 52:3,9; 54:5,8; 59:20; 60:16; 62:12; 63:9,16). The Hebrew verb *ga'al* is translated into Greek by "redeem" (Gk *lutroō*, "redeem, set free, liberate"; Is 35:9; 41:14; 43:1,14; 52:3; 62:12; 63:9; cp. Lk 24:21; Ti 2:14; 1Pt 1:18) or "rescue" (Gk *ruomai*, "rescue, save, deliver"; Is 44:6; 47:4; 48:17,20; 49:7,26; 52:9; 54:5,8; 59:20; cp. 2Co 1:10; Col 1:13; 1Th 1:10).

8 A road will be there
and a way;
it will be called the Holy Way.
The •unclean will not travel
on it,
but it will be for the one
who walks the path.
Even the fool will not
go astray.
9 There will be no lion there,
and no vicious beast
will go up on it;
they will not be found there.
But the redeemed will walk
on it,
10 and the redeemed of the LORD
will return
and come to •Zion
with singing,
crowned with unending joy.
Joy and gladness
will overtake them,
and sorrow and sighing
will flee.

Crisis in Judah (36:1–37:20)

36 In the fourteenth year of King
Hezekiah, Sennacherib king
of Assyria attacked all the fortified
cities of Judah and captured them.
2 Then the king of Assyria sent the
•Rabshakeh, along with a massive
army, from Lachish to King Hezekiah at Jerusalem. The Assyrian
stood near the conduit of the upper pool, by the road to the Fuller's
Field. 3 Eliakim son of Hilkiah, who
was in charge of the palace, Shebna
the court secretary, and Joah son of
Asaph, the court historian, came out
to him.

4 The Rabshakeh said to them,
"Tell Hezekiah:

The great king, the king of Assyria, says this: What are you
relying on?[A] 5 I[B] say that your
strategy and military preparedness are mere words. What
are you now relying on that
you have rebelled against me?
6 Look, you are trusting in
Egypt, that splintered reed of a
staff that will enter and pierce
the hand of anyone who leans
on it. This is how Pharaoh king
of Egypt is to all who trust in
him. 7 Suppose you say to me,
'We trust in the LORD our God.'
Isn't He the One whose •high
places and altars Hezekiah has
removed, saying to Judah and
Jerusalem, 'You are to worship
at this altar'?
8 Now make a deal with my
master, the king of Assyria. I'll
give you 2,000 horses if you're
able to supply riders for them!
9 How then can you drive back a
single officer among the weakest of my master's officers and
trust in Egypt for chariots and
horsemen? 10 Have I attacked
this land to destroy it without
the LORD's approval? The LORD
said to me, 'Attack this land
and destroy it.'"

11 Then Eliakim, Shebna, and Joah
said to the Rabshakeh, "Please speak
to your servants in Aramaic, since
we understand it. Don't speak to us
in Hebrew[C] within earshot of the
people who are on the wall."

deliverance (chaps. 36–37) is repeated in 2Kg 18:17–19:37; highlights appear in 2Ch 32:1-23. King Hezekiah had rebelled against Assyria and stopped paying tribute (2Kg 18:7). By 701 B.C. Sennacherib's armies had marched through Israel and Judah, wreaking devastation. Sennacherib boasted on the Bull Inscription that he had conquered 46 cities of Israel as well as many villages (2Kg 18:13). Hezekiah sent a message to the king of Assyria, who was besieging Lachish, a mere 25 miles from Jerusalem, begging for peace, agreeing to pay any amount Sennacherib should assess (2Kg 18:14-16). The king of Assyria set a high price; but, even though Hezekiah emptied the Jerusalem treasury to pay the steep tribute, the Assyrians decided to come against Jerusalem (Is 33:7-9).

36:3 Eliakim, the steward of the palace, **Shebna** and **Joah** appear earlier in 22:15-25. They went out as ambassadors on Judah's behalf to the Rabshekah.

36:4-5 The Rabshakeh began to disparage Judah's two main avenues of deliverance from the Assyrians—the Egyptians and the Lord. He conducted some psychological warfare, intending to demoralize Jerusalem and Hezekiah.

36:7 Making reference to Judah's trust in God, the Rabshakeh commented on the centralized worship place at Jerusalem, referring to Hezekiah's spiritual reformation to restore proper worship throughout the land and especially at the temple in Jerusalem. Hezekiah had attempted to purge the land of improper **high places and altars** in obedience to God's direction (2Kg 18:3-4; 2Ch 31:1). The Rabshakeh would not have understood the necessity to have one site for cultic worship and, therefore, would have perceived Hezekiah's actions to have been against God rather than in obedience to Him. The Rabshakeh incorrectly assumed such actions would have made God angry and unwilling to defend His people (see note on parallel passage, 2Kg 18:13-37).

36:11 The Rabshakeh had been pointedly speaking in Hebrew so that the average person in Jerusalem could understand his demoralizing message. The ambassadors who went out to him requested that he use the current diplomatic language, **Aramaic**, which most Jerusalemites would not have understood at that time.

[A] **36:4** Lit *What is this trust that you trust* [B] **36:5** DSS read *You* [C] **36:11** Lit *Judahite*

12 But the Rabshakeh replied, "Has
my master sent me to speak these
words to your master and to you,
and not to the men who are sitting
on the wall, who are destined with
you to eat their own excrement and
drink their own urine?"
13 Then the Rabshakeh stood and
called out loudly in Hebrew:[A]

Listen to the words of the great
king, the king of Assyria! 14 This
is what the king says: "Don't let
Hezekiah deceive you, for he
cannot deliver you. 15 Don't let
Hezekiah persuade you to trust
in the LORD, saying, 'The LORD
will certainly deliver us! This
city will not be handed over to
the king of Assyria.'"

16 Don't listen to Hezekiah, for
this is what the king of Assyria
says: "Make peace[B] with me and
surrender to me. Then every
one of you may eat from his
own vine and his own fig tree
and drink water from his own
cistern 17 until I come and take
you away to a land like your
own land—a land of grain and
new wine, a land of bread and
vineyards. 18 Beware that Hezekiah does not mislead you by
saying, 'The LORD will deliver
us.' Has any one of the gods of
the nations delivered his land
from the power of the king of
Assyria? 19 Where are the gods
of Hamath and Arpad? Where
are the gods of Sepharvaim?
Have they delivered Samaria
from my power? 20 Who among
all the gods of these lands ever
delivered his land from my
power? So will the LORD deliver
Jerusalem."

21 But they kept silent; they didn't
say anything, for the king's command was, "Don't answer him."
22 Then Eliakim son of Hilkiah, who
was in charge of the palace, Shebna
the court secretary, and Joah son
of Asaph, the court historian, came
to Hezekiah with their clothes torn
and reported to him the words of the
Rabshakeh.

37 When King Hezekiah heard
their report, he tore his
clothes, put on •sackcloth, and went
to the LORD's temple. 2 Then he sent
Eliakim, who was in charge of the
palace, Shebna the court secretary,
and the leading priests, who were
wearing sackcloth, to the prophet
Isaiah son of Amoz. 3 They said to
him, "This is what Hezekiah says:
'Today is a day of distress, rebuke,
and disgrace, for children have
come to the point of birth, and there
is no strength to deliver them. 4 Perhaps •Yahweh your God will hear all
the words of the •Rabshakeh, whom
his master the king of Assyria sent
to mock the living God, and will rebuke him for the words that Yahweh
your God has heard. Therefore offer
a prayer for the surviving remnant.'"
5 So the servants of King Hezekiah
went to Isaiah, 6 who said to them,
"Tell your master this, 'The LORD
says: Don't be afraid because of the
words you have heard, which the
king of Assyria's attendants have
blasphemed Me with. 7 I am about to
put a spirit in him and he will hear
a rumor and return to his own land,
where I will cause him to fall by the
sword.'"
8 When the Rabshakeh heard that
the king of Assyria had left Lachish,
he returned and found him fighting
against Libnah. 9 The king had heard
this about Tirhakah king of •Cush:
"He has set out to fight against
you." So when he heard this, he
sent messengers to Hezekiah, saying, 10 "Say this to Hezekiah king of
Judah: 'Don't let your God, whom
you trust, deceive you by promising that Jerusalem won't be handed
over to the king of Assyria. 11 Look,
you have heard what the kings of Assyria have done to all the countries:
they •completely destroyed them.
Will you be rescued? 12 Did the gods
of the nations that my predecessors
destroyed rescue them—Gozan,
Haran, Rezeph, and the Edenites
in Telassar? 13 Where is the king of
Hamath, the king of Arpad, the king
of the city of Sepharvaim, Hena, or
Ivvah?'"
14 Hezekiah took the letter from
the messengers, read it, then went

[A] **36:13** Lit *Judahite* [B] **36:16** Lit *a blessing*

36:12 The Rabshakeh only intensified his taunts by presenting a grim picture of famine where they would **eat their own excrement and drink their own urine** as a result of the Assyrian siege.

36:16-17 The Rabshakeh demeaned Hezekiah's character and ability to save, while painting a merciful and generous picture of the **king of Assyria.**

36:18-20 A theological appeal was made in his argument that no other nation's gods had been able to withstand Assyria, and he listed cities of Aram (Syria) as well as the city of Samaria.

36:22 Having heard the inflammatory words of the Assyrian officer, the three officials **came to Hezekiah with their clothes torn** as an external sign of their distress and grief.

37:1-2 King Hezekiah's response was to turn in distress to God's prophet.

37:3 The metaphor of the **children** who **come to the point of birth, and there is no strength to deliver them** (26:17-18) clearly conveys the king's **distress**. It pictures a woman in agonizing labor and utter exhaustion who has no remaining ability to deliver her child. All along Hezekiah had been preparing for war and encouraging the people to trust in the Lord and at this point, his anguish was understandable (2Ch 32:1-8). Victory or defeat was near; Jerusalem could not save herself from destruction, but would God deliver?

37:4-7 Hezekiah lamented that not only had Judah been insulted, but also **the living God** had been mocked. The **surviving remnant** were the Judahites who left after enduring the wrath of the Assyrians, specifically those in Jerusalem (1:7-9). The **spirit** from God indicates God's intent to deceive Sennacherib in order to cause his downfall, thus getting vengeance for Assyria's mockery. Isaiah's response referred not just to immediate respite but to the eventual complete deliverance from Assyria, which would occur as documented in verses 36-38.

37:8-13 The Rabshakeh, distracted by news of the Assyrian king's movements, left to join him. Sennacherib first fought against Libnah, formerly under Judah's control (Jos 10:29; 21:13; 2Kg 8:22; 2Ch 21:10), and then had to confront an Egyptian force led by **Tirhakah, king of Cush** (see notes on Is 20:1-6; 31:3). The Assyrians continued their strategy of intimidation and psychological warfare through a letter to Hezekiah.

up to the LORD's temple and spread
it out before the LORD. 15 Then Hezekiah prayed to the LORD:

16 LORD of •Hosts, God of Israel,
who is enthroned above the
•cherubim, You are God—You
alone—of all the kingdoms of
the earth. You made the heavens and the earth. 17 Listen
closely, LORD, and hear; open
Your eyes, LORD, and see. Hear
all the words that Sennacherib
has sent to mock the living
God. 18 LORD, it is true that the
kings of Assyria have devastated all these countries and
their lands. 19 They have thrown
their gods into the fire, for
they were not gods but made
by human hands—wood and
stone. So they have destroyed
them. 20 Now, LORD our God,
save us from his power so that
all the kingdoms of the earth
may know that You are the
LORD—You alone.

Deliverance from the Lord (37:21-38)

21 Then Isaiah son of Amoz sent
a message to Hezekiah: "The LORD,
the God of Israel, says: 'Because you
prayed to Me about Sennacherib
king of Assyria, 22 this is the word the
LORD has spoken against him:

Virgin Daughter •Zion
despises you and scorns you:
Daughter Jerusalem
shakes her head
behind your back.[A]
23 Who is it you have mocked
and blasphemed?
Who have you raised
your voice against
and lifted your eyes in pride?
Against the Holy One
of Israel!
24 You have mocked the LORD
through[B] your servants.
You have said, "With my
many chariots
I have gone up to the heights
of the mountains,
to the far recesses of Lebanon.
I cut down its tallest cedars,
its choice cypress trees.
I came to its distant heights,
its densest forest.
25 I dug wells[C] and drank water.
I dried up all the streams
of Egypt
with the soles of my feet."

26 Have you not heard?
I designed it long ago;
I planned it in days gone by.
I have now brought it to pass,
and you have crushed
fortified cities
into piles of rubble.
27 Their inhabitants have
become powerless,
dismayed, and ashamed.
They are plants of the field,
tender grass,
grass on the rooftops,
blasted by the east wind.[D]

28 But I know[E]
your sitting down,
your going out
and your coming in,
and your raging against Me.
29 Because your raging
against Me
and your arrogance
have reached My ears,
I will put My hook
in your nose
and My bit in your mouth;
I will make you go back
the way you came.

30 "'This will be the sign for you:
This year you will eat what grows on
its own, and in the second year what
grows from that. But in the third
year sow and reap, plant vineyards
and eat their fruit. 31 The surviving
remnant of the house of Judah will
again take root downward and bear
fruit upward. 32 For a remnant will
go out from Jerusalem and survivors, from Mount Zion. The zeal of
the LORD of Hosts will accomplish
this.'
33 "Therefore, this is what the LORD
says about the king of Assyria:

He will not enter this city
or shoot an arrow there
or come before it
with a shield

37:16-19 Hezekiah's prayer affirms his trust in God through several key statements: The **LORD of Hosts** was the **God of Israel . . . enthroned above the cherubim**, angelic beings who, like the seraphim (6:1-2), serve before God. Solomon designed the ark of the covenant with two carved cherubim opposite one another looking down at the mercy seat, the place of atonement covering the ark (Ex 25:19-22; 37:7-9; cp. 1Sm 4:4; 2 Sm 6:2; Pss 18:10; 80:1; 99:1; Ezk 9:3; 10:1-20; 11:22; see **Doctrine**, p. 1058). Recognizing God as "enthroned" acknowledged His kingship even above Hezekiah's and Sennacherib's kingship, and being enthroned "above the cherubim" recognized Him as a divine King rather than an earthly ruler. The God of Israel was sovereign, God of **all the kingdoms of the earth** (Is 43:10-13; 44:6-8; 45:21-22), not just Judah. The common understanding in the ancient Near East was that each people and kingdom had its own local god. In conflicts, the most powerful god generally won, although due to displeasure, gods might permit defeat as punishment for the people of their territory. In contrast to such thinking, Hezekiah asserted that the God of Israel was the only God, and He did not have to strive against other territorial gods. The God of Israel was the Creator of **the heavens and the earth**. God was not **made by human hands** as were the idols of the nations. The Lord God was the sole Creator of all things and so had complete control over His creation (Gn 1:1; Is 40:18-28; Jn 1:1-3).

37:21-23 God's response to Hezekiah shows that He may have intended to punish Judah for its sins, but because of Hezekiah's humility, He decided to spare Judah for a while longer.

37:28-29 In His omniscience, God knew Sennacherib better than he knew himself. The time had come for the arrogance and pride of the Assyrians to fall under God's judgment as well; God would show that He alone raised up and brought low. The Lord said to them, **I will put My hook in your nose and My bit in your mouth** (cp. 30:27-31; see **Word Study**, p. 478). Ancient evidence reveals the humiliating hooks the Assyrians used to lead away their prisoners.

37:30-31 Hezekiah received assurance that Jerusalem would be spared. Assyria would be driven away by the Lord and would never threaten Jerusalem again. The surrounding fields had been scorched by the Assyrians and recovery, though promised, would be gradual. The time span may have covered parts of three years so that the beginning of the second year may have been close to the time of deliverance. In that case, the people of Jerusalem could not

[A]**37:22** Lit *behind you* [B]**37:24** Lit *by the hand of* [C]**37:25** DSS add *in foreign lands* [D]**37:27** DSS; MT reads *rooftops, field before standing grain* [E]**37:28** DSS read *know your rising up and* plant the next harvest. That first year the people would only have what was left, what grew without cultivation, and the following year only what grew from those old roots. However, they were promised that by the third year they would be able to **sow and reap** freely so that things would be back to the normal cycle. Just as the land would recover and bear fruit, so would the population of the **surviving remnant of the house of Judah**.

37:36 Just as the **angel of the Lord** struck the firstborn of the Egyptians, so also he **struck down** 185,000 in the camp of the Assyrians in one night (2Kg 19:35). The surrounding nations may have credited the destruction of the Assyrian army to Hezekiah. Apparently gifts were presented to Hezekiah in connection with this event, and "he was exalted in the eyes of all the nations after that" (2Ch 32:22-23).

37:37-38 Sennacherib was never able to conquer Jerusalem. His own accounts make that quite clear; he could only shut up Hezekiah in Jerusalem "like a bird in a cage."

38:1-3 Commentators have debated the chronology of the events of chapters 38 and 39 with respect to the events of chapters 36 and 37. A good case can be made for the events of chapters 38 and 39 preceding God's mighty deliverance of Jerusalem by nearly a decade. **Hezekiah became terminally ill** (cp. 38:21; 2Kg 20:1-11; 2Ch 32:24) and pleaded with God for his life, pointing to his faithfulness as a reason for divine mercy. Isaiah had not even left "the inner courtyard" before God told him to turn around and deliver a new message (2Kg 20:4).

38:5-6 God's promise of deliverance to Hezekiah during his sickness was the same as the promise in Is 37:35 (2Kg 20:6). God would save both Hezekiah and Jerusalem for His own sake and for the sake of David, His servant—not because of Hezekiah's personal merit.

38:7-8 Hezekiah asked for a **sign** that he would be healed, and the Lord gave him a choice about whether the shadow from Ahaz's stairway should move forward or backwards 10 steps. Hezekiah chose the more difficult option (2Kg 20:9-11; 2Ch 32:24). His willingness to accept the sign of the Lord was in contrast to the unbelief of his father, Ahaz (Is 7:10-14).

38:19 The **father** and the mother were responsible to tell the stories of the Lord's deliverance and to train their **children** to honor the Lord (cp. Dt 4:9; 6:7). Hezekiah was given 15 more years to live. During this time, Manasseh, his son and heir, was born. Although

or build up an assault ramp
against it.
34 He will go back
the way he came,
and he will not enter this city.
This is
the LORD's declaration.

35 I will defend this city
and rescue it
because of Me
and because of
My servant David."

36 Then the angel of the LORD went
out and struck down 185,000 in
the camp of the Assyrians. When
the people got up the next morning—there were all the dead bodies!
37 So Sennacherib king of Assyria
broke camp and left. He returned
home and lived in Nineveh.
38 One day, while he was worshiping in the temple of his god Nisroch,
his sons Adrammelech and Sharezer
struck him down with the sword and
escaped to the land of Ararat. Then
his son Esar-haddon became king in
his place.

The Healing of Hezekiah (38:1-22)

38 In those days Hezekiah became terminally ill. The
prophet Isaiah son of Amoz came
and said to him, "This is what the
LORD says: 'Put your affairs in order,[A]
for you are about to die; you will not
recover.'"[B]
2 Then Hezekiah turned his face to
the wall and prayed to the LORD. 3 He
said, "Please, LORD, remember how
I have walked before You faithfully
and wholeheartedly, and have done
what pleases You."[C] And Hezekiah
wept bitterly.
4 Then the word of the LORD came
to Isaiah: 5 "Go and tell Hezekiah
that this is what the LORD God of
your ancestor David says: I have
heard your prayer; I have seen your
tears. Look, I am going to add 15
years to your life.[D] 6 And I will deliver
you and this city from the power of
the king of Assyria; I will defend this
city. 7 This is the sign to you from
the LORD that He will do what[E] He
has promised:[F] 8 I am going to make
the sun's shadow that goes down on
Ahaz's stairway go back by 10 steps."
So the sun's shadow[G] went back the
10 steps it had descended.
9 A poem by Hezekiah king of Judah after he had been sick and had
recovered from his illness:

10 I said: In the prime[H]
of my life[D]
I must go to the gates
of •Sheol;
I am deprived of the rest
of my years.
11 I said: I will never see
the LORD,
the LORD in the land
of the living;
I will not look on humanity
any longer
with the inhabitants of what
is passing away.[I]
12 My dwelling is plucked up
and removed from me
like a shepherd's tent.
I have rolled up my life
like a weaver;
He cuts me off
from the loom.[J]
You make an end of me
from day until night.
13 I thought until the morning:
He will break all my bones
like a lion;
You make an end of me
day and night.
14 I chirp like a swallow
or a crane;
I moan like a dove.
My eyes grow weak
looking upward.
Lord, I am oppressed;
support me.

15 What can I say?
He has spoken to me,
and He Himself has done it.
I walk along slowly
all my years
because of the bitterness
of my soul,
16 Lord, because of
these promises people live,
and in all of them is the life
of my spirit as well;

[A] 38:1 Lit *Command your house* [B] 38:1 Lit *live days* [C] 38:3 Lit *what is good in Your eyes* [D] 38:5,10 Lit *days* [E] 38:7 Lit *this thing* [F] 38:7 Lit *said* [G] 38:8 Lit *And the sun* [H] 38:10 Lit *quiet* [I] 38:11 Some Hb mss, Tg read *of the world* [J] 38:12 Lit *thrum*

You have restored me
to health
and let me live.
17 Indeed, it was for
my own welfare
that I had
such great bitterness;
but Your love
has delivered me
from the •Pit of destruction,
for You have thrown
all my sins
behind Your back.
18 For Sheol cannot thank You;
Death cannot praise You.
Those who go down to the Pit
cannot hope
for Your faithfulness.
19 The living, only the living
can thank You,
as I do today;
a father will make
Your faithfulness known
to children.
20 The LORD will[A] save me;
we will play
stringed instruments
all the days of our lives
at the house of the LORD.

21 Now Isaiah had said, "Let them take a lump of pressed figs and apply it to his infected skin, so that he may recover." 22 And Hezekiah had asked, "What is the sign that I will go up to the LORD's temple?"

Prophecy of Judgment (39:1-8)

39 At that time Merodach-baladan son of Baladan, king of Babylon, sent letters and a gift to Hezekiah since he heard that he had been sick and had recovered.
2 Hezekiah was pleased with them, and showed them his treasure house—the silver, the gold, the spices, and the precious oil—and all his armory, and everything that was found in his treasuries. There was nothing in his palace and in all his realm that Hezekiah did not show them.
3 Then the prophet Isaiah came to King Hezekiah and asked him, "Where did these men come from and what did they say to you?"

Hezekiah replied, "They came to me from a distant country, from Babylon."
4 Isaiah asked, "What have they seen in your palace?"

Hezekiah answered, "They have seen everything in my palace. There isn't anything in my treasuries that I didn't show them."
5 Then Isaiah said to Hezekiah, "Hear the word of the LORD of •Hosts:
6 'The time will certainly come when everything in your palace and all that your fathers have stored up until this day will be carried off to Babylon; nothing will be left,' says the LORD.
7 'Some of your descendants who come from you will be taken away, and they will become eunuchs in the palace of the king of Babylon.'"
8 Then Hezekiah said to Isaiah, "The word of the LORD that you have spoken is good," for he thought: There will be peace and security during my lifetime.

The Good News for God's People (40:1-11)

40 "Comfort, comfort
My people,"
says your God.
2 "Speak tenderly
to[B] Jerusalem,
and announce to her
that her time of forced labor
is over,
her iniquity has been
pardoned,
and she has received
from the LORD's hand
double for all her sins."

3 A voice of one crying out:

Prepare the way of the LORD
in the wilderness;
make a straight highway
for our God in the desert.
4 Every valley will be lifted up,
and every mountain and hill
will be leveled;
the uneven ground
will become smooth
and the rough places, a plain.
5 And the glory of the LORD
will appear,
and all humanity[C] together
will see it,

Manasseh should have benefited from Hezekiah's training in his early years, he became the worst king Judah ever had (2Kg 21:1-17). Yet, when God punished him with captivity, Manasseh knew enough to repent and humble himself before the Lord (2Ch 33:11-13).

39:1 After his sickness and healing, Hezekiah entertained envoys from Merodach-baladan, son of Baladan, king of Babylon. Merodach-baladan had sent them with **letters and a gift to Hezekiah since he heard that he had been sick and had recovered** (cp. 2Kg 20:12-19; 2Ch 32:24-26,31). The Chronicles account notes that the men from Babylon also came "to inquire about the miraculous sign that happened in the land," perhaps referring to the sign regarding the sun (2Ch 32:31).

39:2 The purpose of the visit was to seek an alliance between Babylon and Judah against Assyria, since Hezekiah had proven himself to be one of the only kings who had both defied and resisted Assyria (2Kg 18:7).

39:4-6 What motivated Hezekiah to show the Babylonians **everything**? Perhaps he was attempting to prove that he was a valuable partner in an alliance with Babylon. The root of the problem with his actions is identified in 2 Chronicles: Hezekiah's "heart was proud" (2Ch 32:24-26).

39:8 Hezekiah accepted the prophecy as certain, displaying none of the tearful mourning he had shown when initially told he would die (38:2-3). He seemed more concerned that it would not happen during his own lifetime than over the fact that it would happen. The account in 2 Chronicles indicates that the king had humbled himself before God regarding his pride; however, perhaps this passage highlights a mark of selfishness in this "good" king.

40:1–48:22 In the preceding chapters, Isaiah clearly highlighted Israel's failure to measure up to God's standards. Even a good king like Hezekiah fell short of the ideal for the king of Israel. Despite God's longsuffering and abundant grace, Judah continued to rely on foreign alliances rather than God for deliverance. As a result, judgment was certain: Babylon would be their eventual oppressor. In the following chapters, Isaiah continued to develop the themes of the incomparability of God and the need for a Savior for Israel as for all the nations.

40:1-5 Comfort, comfort (Hb *nacham, nacham*) means to "alleviate another's sorrow, restore another's hope, bring cheer to someone in

[A]**38:20** Lit *to* [B]**40:2** Lit *Speak to the heart of* [C]**40:5** Lit *flesh*

despair." With this tender and emphatic opening, God announced that the future oppression would not last forever. After Jerusalem had been punished **double for all her sins**, God would forgive her. This news would have brought great comfort to the people in captivity.

The hope of forgiveness was connected with the physical coming of the Lord. Isaiah referred to the **voice of one crying out: Prepare the way of the Lord . . . a straight highway for our God**. Isaiah used imagery of the preparations made for the coming of a great king. Often, to prepare for the entourage attending a king, roads would have to be straightened and cleared to make his travel smooth. This passage was expressly applied to the preaching of John the Baptist regarding repentance as preparing the way for the Lord Jesus, who would accomplish the means of salvation (Mt 3:3; Mk 1:3; Lk 3:4-6; Jn 1:22-23). In Mk 1:3, this passage was combined with the words concerning the coming of the messenger in Mal 3:1. Once the way was prepared, the Lord Jesus came, displaying the glory and image of God (Jn 1:14; Col 1:15; Heb 1:2-3). There will yet be a day when He returns and **all humanity together will see** His glory (cp. Is 35:2; Rv 1:5-7). Although the hope of comfort was proclaimed by Isaiah, the reality of that comfort did not arrive until the physical coming of the Lord, in the person of Jesus.

40:6-8 Commentators suggest that Isaiah was the one encouraged to **cry** out this message. Although humanity decays just as **grass withers**, and humanity's best accomplishments fade away, **the word of our God remains forever** (cp. 1Pt 1:23-26). Humanity is nothing before the ravages of time, and God alone remains eternal and sovereign. Although human life and work are ephemeral, what remains forever is the message of hope and comfort from their God—a comfort to the exiles of Judah since God's judgment was assured, so also was His salvation (cp. Nm 23:19; 1Kg 8:56; Mt 5:18; Ti 1:2-3).

40:9-11 The content of the **good news** was that God Himself was coming. He would come with the power and authority to rule and bring **His reward** (see notes on 62:11; Rv 22:10-15). The **shepherd** imagery is used throughout Scripture to communicate the tender care and protection of the Lord for His people (Pss 23:1-4; 78:52-54; 80:1; Is 53:5-6). Later, the Lord Jesus identified Himself as "the good Shepherd" who cared for and would die for His sheep (i.e., those who believed in Him; Zch 13:7-9; Jn 10:1-5,7-18,25-30; Heb 13:20; 1Pt 2:25).

40:12-15 This passage is reminiscent of the questions that God put to Job as

>WORD|*study*

40:9 The herald of good news (Hb *basar*, "bear tidings, preach") was to proclaim his message loudly from the heights. The word formed from this root, *basar*, which was translated by the Greek Septuagint with the participle of the root *euangelizō*, in English is "good news, gospel." The Hebrew root occurs 24 times in the Old Testament and seven times in Isaiah (Is 40:9 [2x]; 41:27; 52:7 [2x]; 60:6; 61:1). Normally the word is used in the context of bearing good news, although there are cases of the news being negative (1Sm 4:17). Often the word is used in the context of news being related concerning the outcome of military battles (2Sm 4:10; 18:19-20,26,31; 1Kg 1:42; 1Ch 10:9). Isaiah was using the picture of a messenger proclaiming good news in the most conspicuous way possible.

for the mouth of the LORD
has spoken.

6 A voice was saying, "Cry out!"
Another[A] said,
"What should I cry out?"
"All humanity is grass,
and all its goodness is
like the flower of the field.
7 The grass withers,
the flowers fade
when the breath[B] of the LORD
blows on them;[C]
indeed, the people are grass.
8 The grass withers,
the flowers fade,
but the word of our God
remains forever."

9 •Zion, herald of good news,
go up on a high mountain.
Jerusalem, herald
of good news,
raise your voice loudly.
Raise it, do not be afraid!
Say to the cities of Judah,
"Here is your God!"
10 See, the Lord GOD comes
with strength,
and His power establishes
His rule.
His reward is with Him,
and His gifts accompany Him.
11 He protects His flock
like a shepherd;
He gathers the lambs
in His arms
and carries them in the fold
of His garment.
He gently leads those
that are nursing.

The Incomparability of the Lord (40:12–41:29)

12 Who has measured the waters
in the hollow of his hand
or marked off the heavens
with the span of his hand?
Who has gathered the dust
of the earth in a measure
or weighed the mountains
in a balance
and the hills in the scales?
13 Who has directed[D] the Spirit
of the LORD,
or who gave Him His counsel?
14 Who did He consult with?
Who gave Him understanding
and taught Him the paths
of justice?
Who taught Him knowledge
and showed Him the way
of understanding?
15 Look, the nations are
like a drop in a bucket;
they are considered as a speck
of dust in the scales;
He lifts up the islands
like fine dust.
16 Lebanon is not enough
for fuel,
or its animals enough
for a •burnt offering.
17 All the nations are as nothing
before Him;
they are considered by Him
as nothingness
and emptiness.

18 Who will you
compare God with?
What likeness will you
compare Him to?
19 To an idol?—something that
a smelter casts,
and a metalworker plates
with gold
and makes silver welds for it?
20 To one who shapes a pedestal,
choosing wood that
does not rot?[E]

[A]**40:6** DSS, LXX, Vg read *I* [B]**40:7** Or *wind*, or *Spirit* [C]**40:7** Lit *it* [D]**40:13** Or *measured*, or *comprehended* [E]**40:20** Or *who is too poor for such an offering*, or *who chooses mulberry wood as a votive gift*; Hb obscure

He looks for
a skilled craftsman
to set up an idol that will not
fall over.

21 Do you not know?
Have you not heard?
Has it not been declared
to you
from the beginning?
Have you not considered
the foundations of the earth?

22 God is enthroned above
the circle of the earth;
its inhabitants are
like grasshoppers.
He stretches out the heavens
like thin cloth
and spreads them out
like a tent to live in.

23 He reduces princes to nothing
and makes judges of the earth
irrational.

24 They are barely planted,
barely sown,
their stem hardly takes root
in the ground
when He blows on them
and they wither,
and a whirlwind carries them
away like stubble.

25 "Who will you compare Me to,
or who is My equal?"
asks the Holy One.

26 Look up[A] and see:
who created these?
He brings out the starry host
by number;
He calls all of them by name.
Because of His great power
and strength,
not one of them is missing.

27 Jacob, why do you say,
and Israel, why do you assert:
"My way is hidden
from the LORD,
and my claim is ignored
by my God"?

28 Do you not know?
Have you not heard?
•Yahweh is
the everlasting God,
the Creator
of the whole earth.
He never grows faint
or weary;
there is no limit
to His understanding.

29 He gives strength
to the weary
and strengthens
the powerless.

30 Youths may faint
and grow weary,
and young men stumble
and fall,

31 but those who trust
in the LORD
will renew their strength;
they will soar on wings
like eagles;
they will run and not
grow weary;
they will walk and not faint.

41 "Be silent before Me, islands!
And let peoples renew
their strength.
Let them approach,
then let them testify;
let us come together
for the trial.

2 Who has stirred him up
from the east?
He calls righteousness
to his feet.[B]
The LORD hands nations over
to him,
and he subdues kings.
He makes them like dust
with his sword,
like wind-driven stubble
with his bow.

3 He pursues them,
going on safely,
hardly touching the path
with his feet.

4 Who has performed
and done this,
calling the generations
from the beginning?
I, •Yahweh, am the first,
and with the last—I am He."

5 The islands see and are afraid,
the whole earth trembles.
They approach and arrive.

6 Each one helps the other,
and says to another,
"Take courage!"

7 The craftsman encourages
the metalworker;
the one who flattens
with the hammer

He revealed His glorious omnipotence and omniscience (Jb 38:4–39:30; 40:8–41:34). God has no equal; no one can contend with the almighty Creator of all things, who holds the universe in His hand. Compared to the greatness of God, **the nations are like a drop in a bucket**, inconsequential in power.

40:16-20 God could not be compared to the inanimate idols of the nations.

40:22-26 By contrast, the Creator is securely **enthroned** in a universe of His own making. The Lord God created all, knows all, and cannot be contained or even fully understood by mankind. He is sovereign, and He controls the fate of **princes** and **judges** just as He controls the innumerable **starry host**.

40:27-31 Confronted with the omnipotent and omniscient Lord, Israel was rebuked for doubting that God knew their distress (Ps 139:1-16; Is 54:7-8).

41:1-3 The Lord commanded silence so that all might **come together for the trial**. The trial in question had to do with who was worthy to be called God. The Lord faced off against the idols of the nations. This chapter opens and closes with proof of God's omniscience and sovereignty. A ruler **from the east**, who would conquer **nations** through God's empowerment and who would ultimately bring release and thereby good news to the captives of Israel, is foretold (41:25,27). This ruler was later identified as Cyrus the Persian (see notes on 44:28; 45:1-2; 46:11-13).

41:4 Only the Lord God knows and can foretell the **generations from the beginning**. He declared, **I, Yahweh, am the first** [Hb *ri'shon*], **and with the last** (Hb *'acharon*)—**I am He** (Gn 1:1; Is 44:6; 48:12). Expressed in the Greek language, this becomes the Alpha and Omega, the first and last letters of the alphabet. God is both the source and reason ("first") for everything, but also the purpose or end ("last"). All things were made by God in the beginning, for His glory in the end. This key phrase highlights God's uniqueness and is a mark of His deity. That the phrase is clearly used by the Lord Jesus is therefore significant (Rv 1:8,11-18; 2:8; 22:13,16).

41:5-7 Faced with the conqueror mentioned in verses 2-4, the people throughout the earth were afraid. For help, they turned to one another and to worthless idols, which they themselves had built. Again the impotence and vulnerability of an idol is emphasized. Care had to be taken so **it will not fall over** (cp. 40:19-20; 44:13). If an unstable block of wood could not save itself, how could it possibly save its devotees?

[A]**40:26** Lit *Lift up your eyes on high* [B]**41:2** Hb obscure

41:9-12 These verses are reminiscent of the first exodus from Egypt, and are here applied to a second exodus in which Israel is brought home out of the Babylonian exile (cp. Jr 23:7-8).

41:13-14 Israel could take courage because God had chosen them. Israel was assured that all her enemies would be defeated because God said, **Do not fear, I will help you.** Their assurance was based on the fact that their **Redeemer** (Hb *ga'al*, "redeem, act as a kinsman-redeemer"; see **Word Study**, p. 905), the one who purchased them, was God Himself (cp. Ex 3:7-8).

41:15-16 With God's help Israel would be victorious over the nations and would be God's instrument to judge the nations (Gn 12:3). Isaiah used the image of threshing and winnowing at harvest time. God would make Israel into **a sharp threshing board.** As a thresher was forcefully thrust over a plant, the sharp teeth would break the seeds or grains apart from the straw that encased them. Once the grains or seeds were released, winnowing ensued, and everything was tossed up in the air. The light undesirable chaff was blown away leaving the good grain behind. This imagery concerned the time of judgment when worthless, unprofitable people would be destroyed (Mc 4:11-13; Lk 3:17).

41:17-18 The powerful people of the world would be threshed, but the Lord Himself would provide for **the poor and the needy.** The provision would be a miraculous reversal of nature. The Lord would take a dry and barren land and turn it into **springs of water.** These verses are again reminiscent of Israel's experience with God in the desert after the Egyptian exodus. The same powerful God who carried them then will also provide for them a second time.

41:19-20 After providing the source of life, the Lord would plant trees, seven (symbolizing perfection, thus a perfect reversal of barrenness into fruitfulness) varieties, which were all common to the land of Israel. This act of renewing dry land would be done as a witness to all **that the hand of the Lord has done this.**

41:21-29 The Lord challenged the false gods to prove that they were gods by telling either **past** [Hb *ri'shon*] **events** or **coming** [Hb *'acharit*] **events.** Failing that test, they were challenged to do anything at all, whether **good or bad**, to show that they had supernatural ability. Scornfully, the Lord noted: **You are nothing and your work is worthless.** In marked contrast to the worthless idols of the nations, the Lord, who is the first and the last,

>WORD|*study*

41:8 God called Abraham My friend, (Hb *'ahēv*), using the participle form of the Hebrew root, *ahāv* ("love, like"). While the participle carries the meaning "one who loves," at times participial forms of this word are translated using the milder English word "friend" (cp. examples of the participle in Pss 5:11; 38:11; 40:16; 70:4; 97:10; Pr 8:21).

supports the one who strikes
the anvil,
saying of the soldering,
"It is good."
He fastens it with nails so that
it will not fall over.

8 But you, Israel, My servant,
Jacob, whom I have chosen,
descendant of Abraham,
My friend—
9 I brought[A] you from the ends
of the earth
and called you
from its farthest corners.
I said to you: You are
My servant;
I have chosen you and not
rejected you.
10 Do not fear, for I am with you;
do not be afraid, for I am
your God.
I will strengthen you; I will
help you;
I will hold on to you
with My righteous
right hand.
11 Be sure that all
who are enraged
against you
will be ashamed
and disgraced;
those who contend with you
will become as nothing
and will perish.
12 You will look for those
who contend with you,
but you will not find them.
Those who war against you
will become
absolutely nothing.
13 For I, Yahweh your God,
hold your right hand
and say to you: Do not fear,
I will help you.
14 Do not fear, you worm Jacob,
you men[B] of Israel:
I will help you—
this is
the LORD's declaration.
Your Redeemer is
the Holy One of Israel.
15 See, I will make you into
a sharp threshing board,
new, with many teeth.
You will thresh mountains
and pulverize them
and make hills into chaff.
16 You will winnow them
and a wind
will carry them away,
a gale will scatter them.
But you will rejoice
in the LORD;
you will boast in the Holy One
of Israel.

17 The poor and the
needy seek water,
but there is none;
their tongues are parched
with thirst.
I, Yahweh, will answer them;
I, the God of Israel, will not
forsake them.
18 I will open rivers
on the barren heights,
and springs in the middle
of the plains.
I will turn the desert
into a pool of water
and dry land into springs
of water.
19 I will plant cedars
in the desert,
acacias, myrtles,
and olive trees.
I will put juniper trees
in the desert,
elms
and cypress trees together,
20 so that all may see and know,
consider and understand,
that the hand of the LORD
has done this,
the Holy One of Israel
has created it.
21 "Submit your case,"
says the LORD.

[A]41:9 Or *seized* [B]41:14 LXX reads *small number*; DSS read *dead ones*

"Present your arguments,"
says Jacob's King.
22 "Let them come and tell us
what will happen.
Tell us the past events,
so that we may reflect
on them
and know the outcome,
or tell us the future.
23 Tell us the coming events,
then we will know
that you are gods.
Indeed, do something good
or bad,
then we will be in awe[A]
and perceive.
24 Look, you are nothing
and your work is worthless.
Anyone who chooses you
is detestable.

25 "I have raised up one
from the north,
and he has come,
one from the east
who invokes My[B] name.
He will march over rulers as if
they were mud,
like a potter who treads
the clay.
26 Who told about this
from the beginning,
so that we might know,
and from times past,
so that we might say:
He is right?
No one announced it,
no one told it,
no one heard your words.
27 I was the first to say to •Zion:[C]
Look! Here they are!
And I gave a herald
of good news to Jerusalem.
28 When I look, there is no one;
there is no counselor
among them;
when I ask them, they have
nothing to say.
29 Look, all of them are
a delusion;[D]
their works are nonexistent;
their images are wind
and emptiness.

The Servant of the Lord (42:1-17)

42 "This is My Servant;
I strengthen Him,
this is My Chosen One;
I delight in Him.
I have put My Spirit on Him;
He will bring justice[E]
to the nations.
2 He will not cry out or shout
or make His voice heard
in the streets.
3 He will not break
a bruised reed,
and He will not put out
a smoldering wick;
He will faithfully
bring justice.
4 He will not grow weak
or be discouraged
until He has established
justice on earth.
The islands will wait
for His instruction."

5 This is what God,
•Yahweh, says—
who created the heavens
and stretched them out,
who spread out the earth
and what comes from it,
who gives breath
to the people on it
and life[F] to those who walk
on it—
6 "I, Yahweh, have called You
for a righteous purpose,[G]
and I will hold You
by Your hand.
I will keep You and appoint
You
to be a covenant
for the people
and a light to the nations,
7 in order to open blind eyes,
to bring out prisoners
from the dungeon,
and those sitting in darkness
from the prison house.
8 I am Yahweh, that is My name;
I will not give My glory
to another
or My praise to idols.
9 The past events
have indeed happened.
Now I declare new events;

[A]**41:23** DSS read *we may hear* [B]**41:25** DSS read *his* [C]**41:27** Lit *First to Zion* [D]**41:29** DSS, Syr read *are nothing* [E]**42:1** DSS read *His justice* [F]**42:5** Lit *spirit* [G]**42:6** Or *you by My righteousness*; lit *you in righteousness*

not only knows all events but He is also sovereign over the events.

41:25 To prove His omniscience and sovereignty, He shared details about the future before the events occurred. The Lord had **raised up one from the north . . . one from the east** who **invokes** His **name**, a king who would crush the other rulers.

41:26-29 Again the Lord pointed out that no one was able to proclaim events past or present as He could. The proof was that the Lord alone foretold the coming of the ruler who would release Judah from captivity. The Lord noted, **I gave a herald of good news to Jerusalem** [Hb *basar*, see **Word Study**, p. 910]. This prophecy came to pass with the reign of Cyrus, an Elamite prince who became emperor of Persia (near the modern location of Iran). Cyrus conquered and united with the northern nation of Media (41:2-4,25; 44:28; 45:1; 46:11; 48:15). The word used for "herald of good news" repeats the root of "good news" of 40:9, forming an *inclusio*, a kind of literary envelope shaping the two chapters into one unit. In short, the good news is a repudiation of false gods and the welcome of a deliverer sent by God to end the exile. The fullness of this good news comes in the rest of Isaiah.

42:1 Although Israel served as God's servant and although Cyrus acted on God's behalf, another **Servant** was to be proclaimed—One who would perfectly, not imperfectly as all before him, fulfill the role of Servant. The coming Messiah is the perfect Servant portrayed in verses 1-9. The phrase, **My Chosen One; I delight in Him** is specifically applied to Jesus upon His baptism as well as His transfiguration (Mt 3:17; 17:5; Mk 1:11; Lk 9:35; 2Pt 1:16-19). The Gospel of Matthew clearly indicates that this prophecy from Isaiah was fulfilled in the ministry of the Lord (Mt 12:17-21).

42:3-4 The Servant would **bring justice** (Hb *mishpat*, "judgment"; see note on 5:1-10) and deliverance, both physical and spiritual, to all the people.

42:6-7 The coming of the Servant was part of the plan of God, and therefore He would not fail in His mission. God would make Him **a covenant** (Hb *berit*, "pact, treaty, alliance") **for the people and a light to the nations** (49:6,8). The Servant was sent to **open blind eyes**, and to liberate prisoners, a reversal of the judgment proclaimed in chapter 6, applying to both literal physical healings and also the spiritual deliverance wrought by the Lord, giving spiritual sight and delivering those in bondage to sin (cp. 29:18; 35:5; 61:1; Mt 9:27; 11:3-6; Jn 9:6-7; Ac 26:18).

42:8-9 All God had previously foretold had **indeed happened**. Because He is the omniscient true God, He could tell what would come in the future before the events occurred, and their fulfillment was certain.

42:10-12 The emphasis is on a **new song** that the whole earth will join in singing as a result of the work carried out by the Servant. **Kedar**, a tribe of

I announce them to you
before they occur."

10 Sing a new song
to the LORD;
sing His praise from the ends
of the earth,
you who go down to the sea
with all that fills it,
you islands
with your[A] inhabitants.

11 Let the desert
and its cities shout,
the settlements where
Kedar dwells cry aloud.
Let the inhabitants of Sela
sing for joy;

[A]42:10 Lit *their*

The Servant Imagery in Isaiah

Isaiah contains numerous passages referring to a "servant." In some cases scholars are divided about the intended referent during Isaiah's time. Three main possibilities for the identity of this servant are: the nation Israel, a prophet or other man (possibly Isaiah, David, descendant of David, or Cyrus at some points), or the Messiah. In some cases, layers of meanings may be intended by God. One of the primary keys for interpreting whether or not a servant reference ultimately refers to the messianic Servant hangs on how the New Testament authors, inspired by God, applied the passage to Jesus, the Messiah.

Israel, My servant		Messiah, My Servant	
41:8-16	• chosen by God • gathered from ends of earth • strengthened by God • redeemed by God • used to judge the nations	**42:1-7** (vv. 1-4 quoted in Mt 12:18-21 as referring to Jesus)	• chosen by God • strengthened by God • will bring justice to nations • quiet and mild • will become a covenant to nations • will open blind eyes, release prisoners
42:18-21	• blind • deaf • disobedient	**49:1-7;** Lk 2:32; Ac 26:22b-23	• called and named before birth • glorified God as Servant Israel • formed to bring Israel back to God • recognized as God's salvation for all • despised and abhorred • given honor in end
43:10	witnesses to God as Savior	**50:4-11**	• obedient • beaten and abused • justified and helped by God
44:1-5,21	• chosen by God • made by God • descendants given the Spirit of God and His blessing • will belong to the Lord	**2:1–53:12** **53:1** in Jn 12:38 and Rm 10:16; **53:4** quoted in relation to Jesus in Mt 8:17; **53:7-8** applied to Jesus in Ac 8:32-35	• wise • lifted up • disfigured • will sprinkle the nations • grew up before the Lord • despised, rejected, suffered • bore sicknesses, pains for others • pierced for transgressions • crushed for iniquities • brings healing • punished for others • silent leading up to death • died for Israel • died with wicked, buried with rich • died innocently • was a restitution offering • will see seed • will justify many • will be given those for whom he died
		61:1-3	• read by Jesus as fulfilled in Himself, (Lk 4:17-21)

let them cry out
from the mountaintops.
12 Let them give glory
to the LORD
and declare His praise
in the islands.
13 The LORD advances
like a warrior;
He stirs up His zeal
like a soldier.
He shouts, He roars aloud,
He prevails
over His enemies.
14 "I have kept silent
from ages past;
I have been quiet
and restrained Myself.
But now, I will groan
like a woman in labor,
gasping breathlessly.
15 I will lay waste mountains
and hills
and dry up
all their vegetation.
I will turn rivers into islands
and dry up marshes.
16 I will lead the blind by a way
they did not know;
I will guide them on paths
they have not known.
I will turn darkness to light
in front of them
and rough places
into level ground.
This is what I will do
for them,
and I will not
forsake them.
17 They will be turned back
and utterly ashamed—
those who trust in idols
and say to metal-plated
images:
You are our gods!

The Blind and Deaf (42:18-25)

18 "Listen, you deaf!
Look, you blind, so that
you may see.
19 Who is blind but My servant,
or deaf like My messenger
I am sending?
Who is blind
like My dedicated one,[A]
or blind like the servant
of the LORD?
20 Though seeing many things,[B]
you do not obey.
Though his ears are open,
he does not listen."
21 The LORD was
pleased, because of
His righteousness,
to magnify His instruction
and make it glorious.
22 But this is a people plundered
and looted,
all of them trapped in holes
or imprisoned in dungeons.
They have become plunder
with no one to rescue them
and loot, with no one saying,
"Give it back!"
23 Who among you
will pay attention to this?
Let him listen and obey
in the future.
24 Who gave Jacob
to the robber,[C]
and Israel to the plunderers?
Was it not the LORD?
Have we not sinned
against Him?
They were not willing to walk
in His ways,
and they would not listen
to His instruction.
25 So He poured out on Jacob
His furious anger
and the power of war.
It surrounded him with fire,
but he did not know it;
it burned him, but he paid
no attention.[D]

The Redemption by the Lord (43:1–44:5)

43 Now this is what the
LORD says—
the One who created
you, Jacob,
and the One who formed
you, Israel—
"Do not fear, for I have
redeemed you;
I have called you by your
name; you are Mine.
2 I will be with you
when you pass
through the waters,

nomads descended from Ishmael, lived in Arabia; an Arabian region bore the same name (Gn 25:13; Ps 120:5; Sg 1:5; see notes on 21:13-17; Jr 49:28-31). **Sela** was the capital of Edom. Even nations historically antagonistic to Israel are encouraged to join in the praise to God.

42:13-17 Two contrasting images are used of the work of God: He is **like a warrior** (Hb *gibbor*, "mighty, strong one"), conveying His strength and commitment to His plan; and He is like **a woman in labor** (Hb *yalad*, "bear, bring forth in childbirth"). There is no better image to convey that some pain and effort bring tremendous reward. The price for bringing new life into the world is the excruciating pain of labor. The price for the completion of God's plan of salvation included suffering; but God was committed to His people. After the strong actions in verse 15, God would **lead** and **guide** the steps of the **blind,** and He would **not forsake them**, just as a mother leads, guides, and lovingly and faithfully assists her children. He would bring to shame all idolaters (Zch 12:10–13:2).

42:18-20 The reference to **My servant** in this passage refers to God's people, Israel, who suffered from spiritual blindness (41:8-16). They had failed to live up to the full role of servanthood; instead of opening the eyes of the blind, they were themselves blind. How sad that the people who had so much revelation from God walked in darkness. They were to be God's **messenger** to others, but **though seeing many things,** they themselves refused to obey His ways.

42:22-24 God had revealed Himself in a special way to Israel, yet the people consistently rejected His commands. As a result, the covenant curses fell upon them and they became **a people plundered and looted** (Dt 28:28-48). There was no help for them because God Himself gave them over to those who plundered them—first to Assyria and then to Babylon.

43:1-13 As the previous passage made clear, Israel had failed to obey God and, as a result, endured punishment. With wondrous grace and mercy the Lord exclaimed, **Do not fear, for I have redeemed** [Hb *ga'al*; see **Word Study**, p. 905] **you**. The outcome of this redemption is the Lord's presence and protection as well as the gathering of the remnant.

[A] **42:19** Hb obscure [B] **42:20** Alt Hb tradition reads *You see many things;* [C] **42:24** Lit *to loot*
[D] **42:25** Lit *he did not put on heart*

43:3-4 The Lord indicated that Egypt, Cush, and Seba (possibly African or Arabian Sheba) had been given **as a ransom** (Hb *kopher*, "price for a life") for Israel (20:4-5; 45:14). Scholars suggest that this reference indicates that these three nations were given to Persia in return for the release of Israel. They were conquered by Cyrus's son, Cambyses.

43:5-7 The Lord went on to say that He would **bring** their **descendants** and **gather** them from all directions. What is described by this gathering? For Isaiah's time the application is to the return from the Babylonian exile.

43:14-15 For the sake of His people Israel, God would cause Babylon to fall to Persia in 539 B.C. The Babylonians would become **fugitives**. Babylonians used ships on the Tigris and Euphrates rivers as well as the Persian Gulf. The Babylonians would fall because of God, who identified Himself with Israel, as **Yahweh, your Holy One, the Creator of Israel, your King**.

43:16-21 In language clearly harking back to the first exodus from Egypt, the Lord again described a new exodus (40:3-5; 41:17-20; 42:14-16; 43:14-21; 48:20-21; 49:8-12; 51:9-10; 52:11-12; 55:12-13). He would defeat their oppressor just as he overturned the Egyptian army in the Red Sea (Ex 14:15-30). Once again, God would miraculously deliver His people, making **a way** and providing **water in the wilderness** (cp. 48:21; Ex 15:22-25; 17:1-6; Nm 20:2-11). This would be encouraging to the remnant seeking to return to Jerusalem from Babylon because the way back covered more than 500 miles of inhospitable wilderness.

43:22-25 Despite God's mercy, Israel failed to call on God. Israel neglected the basic requirements for worship and maintaining their relationship with God, including the offerings and sacrifices that God commanded. Instead of serving God, Israel **burdened** Him with their **sins**. Yet out of God's mercy, He made a way for them to be restored. The Lord emphatically stated, **It is I** [lit "I, I, am he"] **who sweep** [Hb *machah*, "wipe, blot out"] **away your transgressions** and **remember your sins no more**. What a stunning promise to the people who had failed to follow the Levitical prescriptions for atonement. God would redeem them—not because they earned it but simply out of His sovereign grace.

43:26-28 The identity of the **first father** in question could be Adam, Abraham, or Jacob. In addition Aaron, the first priest, has been proposed since the reference to **mediators** could be

and when you pass
through the rivers,
they will not
overwhelm you.
You will not be scorched
when you walk
through the fire,
and the flame will not
burn you.
3 For I ·Yahweh your God,
the Holy One of Israel,
and your Savior,
give Egypt as a ransom
for you,
·Cush and Seba in your place.
4 Because you are precious
in My sight
and honored, and I love you,
I will give people
in exchange for you
and nations instead of
your life.
5 Do not fear, for I am with you;
I will bring your descendants
from the east,
and gather you from the west.
6 I will say to the north:
Give them up!
and to the south:
Do not hold them back!
Bring My sons from far away,
and My daughters
from the ends of the earth—
7 everyone called by My name
and created for My glory.
I have formed him;
indeed, I have made him."
8 Bring out a people
who are blind,
yet have eyes,
and are deaf, yet have ears.
9 All the nations
are gathered together,
and the peoples
are assembled.
Who among them
can declare this,
and tell us the former things?
Let them present
their witnesses
to vindicate themselves,
so that people may hear
and say, "It is true."
10 "You are My witnesses"—
this is
the LORD's declaration—
"and My servant
whom I have chosen,
so that you may know
and believe Me
and understand that I am He.
No god was formed before Me,
and there will be none
after Me.
11 I, I am Yahweh,
and there is no other Savior
but Me.
12 I alone declared, saved,
and proclaimed—
and not some foreign god[A]
among you.
So you are My witnesses"—
this is
the LORD's declaration—
"and[B] I am God.
13 Also, from today on
I am He alone,
and none can deliver
from My hand.
I act, and who can reverse it?"

14 This is what the LORD, your Redeemer, the Holy One of Israel says:

Because of you, I will send
to Babylon
and bring all of them
as fugitives,[C]
even the Chaldeans
in the ships in which
they rejoice.[D]
15 I am Yahweh, your Holy One,
the Creator of Israel,
your King.
16 This is what the LORD says—
who makes a way in the sea,
and a path
through surging waters,
17 who brings out the chariot
and horse,
the army and
the mighty one together
(they lie down, they do not
rise again;
they are extinguished,
quenched like a wick)—
18 "Do not remember
the past events,
pay no attention to things
of old.
19 Look, I am about to do
something new;

[A] **43:12** Lit *not a foreigner* [B] **43:12** Or *that* [C] **43:14** Or *will break down all their bars* [D] **43:14** Hb obscure

even now it is coming.
Do you not see it?
Indeed, I will make a way
in the wilderness,
rivers[A] in the desert.
20 The animals of the field
will honor Me,
jackals and ostriches,
because I provide water
in the wilderness,
and rivers in the desert,
to give drink
to My chosen people.
21 The people I formed
for Myself
will declare My praise.
22 "But Jacob, you have not
called on Me,
because, Israel, you have
become weary of Me.
23 You have not brought
Me your sheep
for •burnt offerings
or honored Me
with your sacrifices.
I have not burdened you
with offerings
or wearied you with incense.[B]
24 You have not bought Me
aromatic cane with silver,
or satisfied Me
with the fat
of your sacrifices.
But you have burdened Me
with your sins;
you have wearied Me
with your iniquities.
25 "It is I who sweep away
your transgressions
for My own sake
and remember your sins
no more.
26 Take Me to court; let us argue
our case together.
State your case, so that
you may be vindicated.
27 Your first father sinned,
and your mediators
have rebelled against Me.
28 So I defiled the officers
of the sanctuary,
and •set Jacob apart
for destruction
and Israel for abuse.

44 "And now listen,
Jacob My servant,
Israel whom I have chosen.
2 This is the word of the LORD
your Maker who formed you
from the womb;
He[C] will help you:
Do not fear; Jacob is
My servant;
I have chosen Jeshurun.[D]
3 For I will pour water on
the thirsty land
and streams
on the dry ground;
I will pour out My Spirit
on your descendants
and My blessing
on your offspring.
4 They will sprout
among[E] the grass
like poplars by
flowing streams.
5 This one will say, 'I am
the LORD's';
another will call himself
by the name of Jacob;
still another will write
on his hand, 'The LORD's,'
and name himself
by the name of Israel."

The Uniqueness of Yahweh and Futility of Idolatry (44:6-23)

6 This is what the LORD, the King of Israel and its Redeemer, the LORD of •Hosts, says:

I am the first and I am
the last.
There is no God but Me.
7 Who, like Me, can announce
the future?
Let him say so and make
a case before Me,
since I have established
an ancient people.
Let these gods declare[F]
the coming things,
and what will take place.
8 Do not be startled or afraid.
Have I not told you
and declared it long ago?
You are my witnesses!
Is there any God but Me?

taken to refer to their priests. Given his character and the fact that Israel is addressed by the family name of **Jacob** (vv. 22,28), quite possibly Jacob was intended (Gn 27:18-24,35-36; 47:9).

44:1-2 Isaiah emphasized that Israel was made by the Lord **who formed** (Hb *yatsar*, "form, create"; see **Doctrine**: "Creation of Mankind," Gn 2:7-8, p. 5) them **from the womb** (Hb *beten*, "womb"). The One who made them certainly had the power to save them. **Jeshurun** (Hb *yeshurun*) is a poetic designation for Israel, occurring only four times in Scripture (cp. Dt 32:15; 33:5, 26). Some suggest the name is derived from the Hebrew root *yashar*, which conveys a meaning of uprightness. The name of Jeshurun for Israel links this passage to the Song and Blessing of Moses in Dt 32 and 33, passages that share many of the themes found in Is 43 and 44 such as: God is the "Rock" (Dt 32:4, 15, 18, 30-31; Is 44:8); God made and chose Israel (Dt 32:6,18; Is 43:1,7,10,21; 44:1,21,24). Israel corrupts herself through idolatry (Dt 32:5,15-21; Is 43:22-24,27; 44:9-20); God disciplines His people (Dt 32:22-38; Is 43:28); there is no God besides Yahweh (Dt 32:39; 33:26; Is 43:10-13; 44:6,8), and God saves His people (Dt 32:43; 33:26-29; Is 43:1-7,12,25; 44:2-4,22-23). Many of the prophecies in the Song of Moses had been fulfilled, just as God had foretold, providing further assurance of the Lord's sovereignty.

44:3-5 The outpouring of the Lord's **Spirit** upon the descendants of His chosen people was like **water on the thirsty land** (see notes on 32:14-18 and 41:17-20). The coming of the Spirit would renew and revivify just as rain causes life to spring up. The result of the coming of the Spirit would be a people fully identified with the Lord. Other prophets also prophesied a time when the Holy Spirit would be poured out upon people (Ezk 36:27; 37:14; 39:29; Jl 2:28-29; Zch 12:10; cp. Ac 2:1-18).

44:6-8 In chapter 41 God had challenged the idols to prove their worth by telling of things past or present or by doing anything at all (41:21-24). This challenge was repeated in 43:8-13 and in 44:6-8, as God affirms His eternality with the claim, **I am the first and I am the last. There is no God but Me** (see note on 41:4). Proof that He alone is God was His unique ability to **announce the future**, to which the Israelites were ongoing witnesses.

[A]43:19 DSS read *paths* [B]43:23 With demands for offerings and incense [C]44:2 Lit *from the womb, and He* [D]44:2 = Upright One, referring to Israel [E]44:4 Some Hb mss, DSS, LXX read *as among* [F]44:7 Lit *declare them—*

44:9-20 These verses make clear the illogic of worshiping man-made images.

44:12 Isaiah discussed the everyday process for making idols of metal or wood, spending the most time on the latter since wooden objects were cheaper and thus more prevalent. Idols served as representations of the gods who would supposedly indwell them after they were made. Still, even after the point when the "god" was to inhabit the material, there was no sign of life because there was no god but Yahweh (cp. vv. 7-8; 41:21-24,29; 42:8,17; 43:10-12).

44:13-14 Second, the existence of any idol was dependent upon the creativity of man. Idols were outlined, shaped, and made according to a man's conception. By contrast, a human being was formed within the womb by God and was utterly dependent upon Him for life (43:1,7,21; 44:2,21; Ps 115:4-8). Also, idols had to be fashioned out of existing materials. Though artisans might choose the finest **cedars**, **cypress**, **oak**, or **laurel**, the very trees he used were created by God and sustained by God's **rain** (Gn 1:1; Jb 5:8-10; 37:5-6; Ps 147:7-8; Jn 1:1-3).

44:18-20 Sadly, the Israelites had not turned to the Creator God to deliver them, trusting instead in alliances formed in their own wisdom, in the security of possessions, and even in lifeless blocks of wood to save. The same phenomenon occurs whenever people purposely harden themselves to God's truth (cp. Jesus' application at Mk 4:10-12; 8:17-18).

44:21-23 The only hope for Israel was to be found in the great mercy of the God who **formed** (Hb *yatsar*) them for His purpose. Though they forgot the Lord, the Israelites would **never be forgotten** by God. Though His people could not save themselves, the Lord had **swept away** (Hb *machah*, "wipe, blot out") their **transgressions like a cloud**, and their **sins like a mist**. A response to His offer of grace was required, as the Lord exhorted then to repent and **return** to Him, their Redeemer.

The details of how the redemption was to be effected only appear later in Is 52:13–53:12 (cp. Rm 5:8-11). Still, a response of pure joy and adulation by all creation is encouraged following God's redemptive action, which Isaiah prophetically saw as a completed action.

44:24-27 A very pointed prophecy about the coming deliverance of Israel appears here. Israel was reminded again that God had **formed** them as He had **made everything**. On the one hand, God **destroys the omens**

There is no other Rock;
I do not know any.

9 All who make idols
are nothing,
and what they treasure
does not profit.
Their witnesses do not see
or know anything,
so they will be put to shame.
10 Who makes a god or casts
a metal image
for no profit?
11 Look, all its worshipers
will be put to shame,
and the craftsmen
are humans.
They all will assemble
and stand;
they all will be startled
and put to shame.

12 The ironworker labors
over the coals,
shapes the idol
with hammers,
and works it
with his strong arm.
Also he grows hungry
and his strength fails;
he doesn't drink water
and is faint.
13 The woodworker stretches out
a measuring line,
he outlines it with a stylus;
he shapes it with chisels
and outlines it
with a compass.
He makes it according to
a human likeness,
like a beautiful person,
to dwell in a temple.
14 He cuts down[A] cedars
for his use,
or he takes a cypress
or an oak.
He lets it grow strong
among the trees
of the forest.
He plants a laurel,
and the rain makes it grow.
15 It serves as fuel for man.
He takes some of it
and warms himself;
also he kindles a fire
and bakes bread;
he even makes it into a god
and worships it;
he makes an idol from it
and bows down to it.
16 He burns half of it in a fire,
and he roasts meat
on that half.
He eats the roast
and is satisfied.
He warms himself
and says, "Ah!
I am warm, I see the blaze."
17 He makes a god or his idol
with the rest of it.
He bows down to it
and worships;
He prays to it, "Save me, for
you are my god."
18 Such people[B]
do not comprehend
and cannot understand,
for He has shut their eyes[C]
so they cannot see,
and their minds
so they cannot understand.
19 No one reflects,
no one has the perception
or insight to say,
"I burned half of it in the fire,
I also baked bread on its coals,
I roasted meat and ate.
I will make
something detestable
with the rest of it,
and I will bow down to a block
of wood."
20 He feeds on[D] ashes.
His deceived mind
has led him astray,
and he cannot deliver himself,
or say, "Isn't there a lie
in my right hand?"

21 Remember these things,
Jacob,
and Israel, for you are
My servant;
I formed you, you are
My servant;
Israel, you will never
be forgotten by Me.[E]
22 I have swept away
your transgressions
like a cloud,
and your sins like a mist.
Return to Me,
for I have redeemed you.
23 Rejoice, heavens, for the LORD
has acted;

[A]44:14 Lit *To cut down for himself* [B]44:18 Lit *They* [C]44:18 Or *for their eyes are shut* [D]44:20 Or *He shepherds* [E]44:21 DSS, LXX, Tg read *Israel, do not forget Me*

>WORD|*study*

44:21-23 The word root for return (Hb *shuv*, "turn back") is one of the most common verbs in the Old Testament, occurring more than 1,000 times. The most frequent meaning involves a physical turning or returning to a person or place (e.g., 1:25; 37:7-8,29,34,37). The word takes on a special nuance when used regarding the relationship between God and people in the context of redemption. This usage contains the idea of repentance, a turning away from sin and turning to God. The word occurs with this added meaning several times in Isaiah (1:27; 6:10; 9:13; 19:22; 30:15; 31:6; 44:22; 55:7; 59:20). In addition, the root *shuv* is used regarding the return to Jerusalem from exile, which could incorporate both the physical and spiritual understanding of the term (10:21-22; 35:10; see also **Word Study**, p. 956).

shout, depths of the earth.
Break out
into singing, mountains,
forest, and every tree in it.
For the LORD
has redeemed Jacob,
and glorifies Himself
through Israel.

Cyrus as the Instrument of the Lord (44:24–45:13)

24 This is what the LORD, your Redeemer who formed you from the womb, says:

I am •Yahweh,
who made everything;
who stretched out
the heavens by Myself;
who alone spread out
the earth;
25 who destroys the omens
of the false prophets
and makes fools of diviners;
who confounds the wise
and makes their
knowledge foolishness;
26 who confirms the message
of His servant
and fulfills the counsel
of His messengers;
who says to Jerusalem,
"She will be inhabited,"
and to the cities of Judah,
"They will be rebuilt,"
and I will restore her ruins;
27 who says to the depths
of the sea, "Be dry,"
and I will dry up your rivers;
28 who says to Cyrus,
"My shepherd,
he will fulfill all My pleasure"
and says to Jerusalem,
"She will be rebuilt,"
and of the temple,
"Its foundation will be laid."

45 The LORD says this to Cyrus,
His anointed,
whose right hand
I have grasped
to subdue nations before him,
to disarm[A] kings,
to open the doors before him
and the gates will not be shut:
2 "I will go before you
and level the uneven places;[B]
I will shatter the bronze doors
and cut the iron bars in two.
3 I will give you the treasures
of darkness
and riches from secret places,
so that you may know that I,
•Yahweh,
the God of Israel call you
by your name.

HARD QUESTION

Is prophecy real?

Some scholars reject the idea that the eighth-century prophet Isaiah could have so accurately predicted the name of the future king over 150 years before the events occurring during his reign; but these scholars are baffled that the prediction is genuine. The whole point of these passages is that God is the one true God because He alone could predict the future. Also, the people of Israel were to be **witnesses** of the fact that they had been told of future events **long ago** (44:8). The argument made for Yahweh's supremacy would not have made sense had the prediction been an intuitive guess by a writer living in the exile, as some scholars speculate. In reality, the accuracy of the prophecy in 44:28–45:1 validates Isaiah as a true prophet and provides proof that Yahweh, who holds all history in His hand, alone is God. Through Scripture, as well as the historical events inscribed in stone and written down by historians, linguists, and archaeologists (some of whom are unbelievers), even in the twenty-first century you can confidently bear witness that Yahweh alone is God and knows the end from the beginning.

[A]45:1 Lit *unloosen the loins* [B]45:2 DSS, LXX read *the mountains*

of the false prophets and on the other He **confirms the message of His servant**. In Israel, the true prophet was to be known by his prophetic message, which would be confirmed by its fulfillment, and would not lead the people into idolatry (Dt 13:1-3; 18:21-22; Zch 1:6).

Isaiah prophesied through the inspiration of God that **Jerusalem** and **Judah** would be **rebuilt**. Even as he had delivered the Israelites from Egypt by parting the Red Sea, the Lord could dry up the rivers to prepare the way for Israel's release from Babylon.

44:28 Isaiah's prophecy identified the name of the man whom God would use to accomplish His purpose—**Cyrus**, whom the Lord called His **shepherd**, a common ancient Near Eastern metaphor for a ruler (see 41:2-4,25; 45:1-6; 46:11; cp. Ezk 34). Shortly after his conquest of Media ca 550 B.C., Cyrus assumed the title King of Persia as he continued his conquests. Around 539 B.C., Cyrus attacked Babylonia and soon was able to take Babylon without a fight (see notes on 13:12-16; 21:1-10). Herodotus records that Cyrus took the city of Babylon by diverting the Euphrates River so that his troops were able to enter the city by the river bed during the night. On the night of the banquet when God spoke against Babylon by writing on the palace wall, Belshazzar (who had been co-reigning with his father Nabonidus) was killed (Dn 5:30-31). According to Isaiah's prophecy, Cyrus would facilitate the rebuilding of Jerusalem and the **temple** (Is 44:28). This was fulfilled after Cyrus conquered Babylon. During his first year in power, he issued an edict permitting the Israelites to return to Jerusalem. He also encouraged the rebuilding of the temple (2Ch 36:22-23; Ezr 1:1-11).

45:1-2 The Lord's appellation of Cyrus as **His anointed** is quite surprising. Only kings, priests, and prophets of Israel are typically referenced by that designation. The term clearly indicated that Cyrus was hand-picked by the Lord to accomplish His purpose. Cyrus rose to power because God took him by the **right hand**, the favored stronger hand, indicating His support (cp. Ps 75:6-7). By God's design and help, Cyrus was able to conquer nations.

45:3-4 **Cyrus** was a pagan king. Although he was evidently tolerant of various religions, there is no indication that he had an experiential relationship with the Lord; yet his actions underscored the sovereignty of the one true God. The Cyrus Cylinder ascribes Cyrus's victories to Marduk, the high Babylonian god, and acknowledges Nebo in addition to other gods (see chap. 42). Cyrus instigated a policy to restore to their homelands all the religious articles the Babylonians had carried away, for both political and religious reasons, to encourage stability and contentment within his empire (Ezk 1:7-11).

45:5 Cyrus did encounter the true God, as his edict indicates, even if he failed to trust exclusively in **Yahweh**. God still used Cyrus in order to glorify His name so all would know He alone is God. The phrase or part of the phrase **I am Yahweh, and there is no other** is repeated seven times within chapters 45 and 46 (45:5-6,14,18,21-22; 46:9).

45:6-8 By fully disclosing His plans for Cyrus well over a hundred years before their fulfillment, God proved His sovereignty. God is not restricted to working among and through believers. God's sovereignty is a characteristic concomitant with His omnipotence, as He is the originator of the created universe (**light** and **darkness**) as well as its providential workings—**success, righteousness,** and **salvation**, but also **disaster**.

45:9-10 The people of Israel may have resisted the idea that the right to rebuild their temple would be given by a pagan king. Still, as the Lord pointed out, for the creature to question the intentions of the Creator makes no sense. It is just as ludicrous as a **clay pot** questioning the intent of the potter or a child questioning the intent of his parents (see 29:16; Rm 9:18-21). In both cases, the things being formed or made called into question their maker's wisdom.

45:11-13 Just as the Lord chose to use a pagan nation to destroy Israel, He would also use a pagan king to help restore the people.

45:14 The three nations mentioned in 43:3, **Egypt . . . Cush and the Sabeans** are once again referenced together. Isaiah noted **they will come over in chains and bow down to you**. The pronoun "you" is feminine singular, so Cyrus is not the one referenced. Instead, the referent apparently is redeemed Israel. The time in view appears to have shifted as well to encompass the time of the last days when, as earlier and later passages prophesy, all people would acknowledge the one true God of Israel and would bring the wealth of the nations to Israel (2:2-4; 19:18-24; 60:3-18).

45:15-17 Who actually makes the statement, **You are a God who hides Himself**. Was it voiced by the nations, by Israel, or by Isaiah? Each of these would have had cause to be puzzled by the character and actions of the God of Israel. The pagans could be making a

4 I call you by your name,
because of Jacob My servant
and Israel My chosen one.
I give a name to you,
though you do not know Me.
5 I am Yahweh, and there is
no other;
there is no God but Me.
I will strengthen[A] you,
though you do not know Me,
6 so that all may know
from the rising of the sun
to its setting
that there is no one but Me.
I am Yahweh, and there is
no other.
7 I form light
and create darkness,
I make success
and create disaster;
I, Yahweh, do all these things.

8 "Heavens, sprinkle
from above,
and let the skies
shower righteousness.
Let the earth open up
so that salvation will sprout
and righteousness will
spring up with it.
I, Yahweh, have created it.

9 "Woe to the one who argues
with his Maker—
one clay pot among many.[B]
Does clay say to the one
forming it,
'What are you making?'
Or does your work say,
'He has no hands'?[C]
10 How absurd is the one
who says to his father,
'What are you fathering?'
or to his mother,
'What are you
giving birth to?'"
11 This is what the LORD,
the Holy One of Israel
and its Maker, says:
"Ask Me what is to happen
to[D] My sons,
and instruct Me
about the work
of My hands.
12 I made the earth,
and created man on it.
It was My hands
that stretched out
the heavens,
and I commanded
all their host.
13 I have raised him up
in righteousness,
and will level all roads
for him.
He will rebuild My city,
and set My exiles free,
not for a price or a bribe,"
says the LORD of ·Hosts.

God Alone and Set Apart (45:14–46:13)

14 This is what the LORD says:

The products of Egypt
and the merchandise
of ·Cush
and the Sabeans,
men of stature,
will come over to you
and will be yours;
they will follow you,
they will come over in chains
and bow down to you.
They will confess[E] to you:
God is indeed with you,
and there is no other;
there is no other God.

15 Yes, You are a God
who hides Himself,
God of Israel, Savior.
16 All of them are put to shame,
even humiliated;
the makers of idols
go in humiliation together.
17 Israel will be saved
by the LORD
with an everlasting salvation;
you will not be put to shame
or humiliated
for all eternity.
18 For this is
what the LORD says—
God is the Creator
of the heavens.
He formed the earth
and made it.
He established it;
He did not create it
to be empty,
but formed it
to be inhabited—
"I am Yahweh,

[A]**45:5** Lit *gird* [B]**45:9** Lit *a clay pot with clay pots of the ground* [C]**45:9** Or *making? Your work has no hands.* [D]**45:11** Or *Me the coming things about* [E]**45:14** Lit *pray*

Yahweh vs. Babylonian Gods Isaiah 46

Yahweh	Idols
He is *one* ("there is no other," v. 9).	The Babylonian gods are *many* ("Bel . . . Nebo . . . idols . . . gods . . . they," vv. 1-2).
He carries the remnant of Israel (vv. 3-4).	Idols are carried by animals and men (vv. 1,7).
He made men ("I have made you," v. 4).	Idols are made *by* men ("a goldsmith . . . makes it [gold] into a god," v. 6).
He reveals the future and fulfills all His plans ("I declare the end from the beginning . . . I have planned it; I will also do it," vv. 10- 11).	They cannot move or speak ("it [a man-made 'god'] does not budge . . . it doesn't answer," v. 7).
He saves His people ("I will . . . save you"; "My salvation will not delay," vv. 4,13).	"It [a man-made 'god'] saves no one" (v. 7); the idols "are not able to rescue . . . they themselves go into captivity," v. 2).

and there is no other.
19 I have not spoken in secret,
somewhere in a land
of darkness.
I did not say
to the descendants of Jacob:
Seek Me in a wasteland.
I, Yahweh, speak truthfully;
I say what is right.
20 "Come, gather together,
and draw near, you fugitives
of the nations.
Those who carry
their wooden idols,
and pray to a god
who cannot save,
have no knowledge.
21 Speak up and present
your case[A]—
yes, let them
take counsel together.
Who predicted this long ago?
Who announced it
from ancient times?
Was it not I, Yahweh?
There is no other God but Me,
a righteous God and Savior;
there is no one except Me.
22 Turn to Me and be saved,
all the ends of the earth.
For I am God,
and there is no other.
23 By Myself I have sworn;
Truth has gone
from My mouth,
a word that will not
be revoked:
Every knee will bow to Me,
every tongue will
swear allegiance.
24 It will be said to Me:
Righteousness and strength
is only in the LORD."
All who are enraged
against Him
will come to Him and be
put to shame.
25 All the descendants of Israel
will be justified and find glory
through the LORD.

46 Bel crouches; Nebo cowers.
Their idols are consigned
to beasts and cattle.
The images you carry
are loaded,
as a burden
for the weary animal.
2 The gods cower;
they crouch together;
they are not able to rescue
the burden,
but they themselves go
into captivity.
3 "Listen to Me, house of Jacob,
all the remnant of the house
of Israel,

[A]45:21 Lit *and approach*

statement about the fact that the God of Israel refused to have images made of Himself, in effect hiding Himself from worshipers. Their statement could reflect a final rejection of idolatry, an understanding that the God of Israel could not be represented by a man-made image. Israel could have been speaking in a more symbolic way about the inscrutability of the actions of God. God acts but sometimes His plan seems hidden to man.

45:18-19 The Lord speaks again and reminds all who are willing to listen that He had **not spoken in secret**. He had not left the **descendants of Jacob** in the dark concerning what His plans were or His desires for them. Israel had revelation about who God was and how they were to relate to Him. God's interactions with Israel had not been hidden to the nations. Various times God acted so that the nations might recognize that He was truly God (Ex 7:3-5; 11:9; 14:4; 1Sm 17:46-47; 2Kg 5:15; Dn 2:28-29).

45:22 In a simple and direct message, the Lord extends repentance to all nations, not just Israel. He calls to the nations, **Turn to Me and be saved, all the ends of the earth. For I am God, and there is no other**. Yahweh is not a territorial god of Israel, as so many in the ancient world believed. He is the only God, and therefore He is God for all people.

45:23-24 Paul quoted this passage regarding the judgment seat of Christ (Rm 14:11), and likely the apostle had this passage in mind when he penned Php 2:10-11. For those who reject His call, though they will one day acknowledge His supremacy, they **will come to Him and be put to shame** (Dn 12:1-3; Rv 20:11-15).

45:25 In the New Testament, those who bend the knee to the lordship of God through Jesus will become a part of the true descendants of Israel (see notes on 14:1-2; Rm 10:9-13). As a result, on that great day when all will bow before Him, those who are heirs to the promise of Abraham as His true descendants **will be justified and find glory through the LORD** (Gl 3:6-9,26-29).

46:1-2 **Bel** (Hb, "lord") was a name used for Marduk, the highest god in the Babylonian pantheon. **Nebo** (Hb, "speaker" or "he who has called") was the son of Marduk. Nebo was the Babylonian god of wisdom and writing who normally was arrayed in his temple in Borsippa. Ironically, the helpless idols being worshiped had to be carried as helpless burdens. Isaiah portrays idols haphazardly being loaded into ox carts to be hauled off unceremoniously as

they themselves go into captivity. They could not save themselves, much less Babylon.

46:3-7 By contrast, **the remnant . . . Israel** was assured in no uncertain terms that they themselves had been **sustained** and **carried** [Hb *nasa'*; the same word used of the idols being borne by people] **along since birth** by the one true God. The unchangeable God would be there to bear them even as they grew old. God alone would **bear** [Hb *saval*, "bear a heavy load"] **and save** (Hb *malat*, "cause to escape, deliver from danger") them (v. 4).

46:11-13 The **bird of prey from the east** is another reference to Cyrus. The emphasis is once again upon the absolute sovereignty of God.

47:1-3 In previous chapters, the people had been prepared to expect deliverance from Babylon. Chapter 47 is a taunt song against their captors. Like Judah and other nations who were personified as virgin daughters, Babylon was portrayed as the **Virgin** [Hb *betulah*] **Daughter Babylon** (cp. 23:12; 37:22; Jr 14:17; 46:11; Lm 2:13; Am 5:2). The sense of "virgin" conveyed the idea of a formerly unconquered city that was suddenly thrown down and violated. No longer would she reign proudly and untouched; she would lose her throne and her self-indulgent comfort. Forced to **take millstones and grind meal** like a menial laborer stripped of her adornments, the shame of her fall would be visible to all (for similar judgment on Israel, see Is 3:16–4:1).

47:5-6 God had used Babylon to punish Israel (**My possession**); however, Babylon ruled as if her reign would never end. She failed to acknowledge that her destiny was in God's hands, not her own. Babylon's merciless rule would end, and God already had appointed the means for her destruction as punishment for her excesses. For example, Babylon had made her **yoke very heavy on the elderly**, a taskmaster who showed no compassion for the most vulnerable.

47:8 Babylon's military conquests had made the nation wealthy. She was self-indulgent, a **lover of luxury**. With prosperity came the tendency to overindulge fleshly appetites because they could afford it, for example, Belshazzar's lavish banquet the night Babylon fell, where the king and "1,000 of his nobles" drank wine from the gold vessels from Solomon's temple (Dn 5:1-4). The Hanging Gardens of Babylon, one of the Seven Wonders of the Ancient World, are another example of Babylon's might and ostentatious wealth. Seven times in chapters 45 and 46 the Lord had stated in various

who have been sustained
from the womb,
carried along since birth.
4 I will be the same
until your old age,
and I will bear you up
when you turn gray.
I have made you,
and I will carry you;
I will bear and save you.

5 "Who will you compare Me
or make Me equal to?
Who will you
measure Me with,
so that we should be
like each other?
6 Those who pour out
their bags of gold
and weigh out silver
on scales—
they hire a goldsmith
and he makes it into a god.
Then they kneel
and bow down to it.
7 They lift it to their shoulder
and bear it along;
they set it in its place,
and there it stands;
it does not budge
from its place.
They cry out to it
but it doesn't answer;
it saves no one
from his trouble.
8 "Remember this
and be brave;[A]
take it to heart,
you transgressors!
9 Remember what happened
long ago,
for I am God, and there is
no other;
I am God, and no one is
like Me.
10 I declare the end
from the beginning,
and from long ago what is
not yet done,
saying: My plan
will take place,
and I will do all My will.
11 I call a bird of prey[B]
from the east,
a man for My purpose
from a far country.
Yes, I have spoken;
so I will also bring it about.
I have planned it;
I will also do it.
12 Listen to me,
you hardhearted,
far removed from justice:
13 I am bringing My justice near;
it is not far away,
and My salvation
will not delay.
I will put salvation in •Zion,
My splendor in Israel.

The Fall of Babylon (47:1-15)

47 "Go down and sit in the dust,
Virgin Daughter Babylon.
Sit on the ground
without a throne,
Daughter Chaldea!
For you will no longer
be called pampered
and spoiled.
2 Take millstones
and grind meal;
remove your veil,
strip off your skirt,
bare your thigh,
wade through the streams.
3 Your nakedness
will be uncovered,
and your shame
will be exposed.
I will take vengeance;
I will spare no one.[A]
4 The Holy One of Israel is
our Redeemer;
•Yahweh of •Hosts is
His name.

5 "Daughter Chaldea,
sit in silence and go
into darkness.
For you will no longer
be called mistress
of kingdoms.
6 I was angry with My people;
I profaned My possession,
and I placed them
under your control.
You showed them no mercy;
you made your yoke
very heavy on the elderly.
7 You said, 'I will be
the mistress forever.'
You did not take these things
to heart
or think about their outcome.

[A] **46:8; 47:3** Hb obscure [B] **46:11** = Cyrus

8 "So now hear this,
lover of luxury,
who sits securely,
who says to herself,
'I exist, and there is
no one else.
I will never be a widow
or know the loss of children.'
9 These two things will happen
to you
suddenly, in one day:
loss of children
and widowhood.
They will happen to you
in their entirety,
in spite of
your many sorceries
and the potency
of your spells.
10 You were secure
in your wickedness;
you said, 'No one sees me.'
Your wisdom and knowledge
led you astray.
You said to yourself,
'I exist, and there is
no one else.'
11 But disaster will happen
to you;
you will not know how
to avert it.
And it will fall on you,
but you will be unable to ward
it off.[A]
Devastation will happen
to you suddenly
and unexpectedly.
12 So take your stand
with your spells
and your many sorceries,
which you have
wearied yourself with
from your youth.
Perhaps you will be able
to succeed;
perhaps you will
inspire terror!
13 You are worn out with
your many consultations.
So let them stand
and save you—
the astrologers,[B] who observe
the stars,
who predict monthly
what will happen to you.
14 Look, they are like stubble;
fire burns them up.
They cannot
deliver themselves
from the power[C] of the flame.
This is not a coal
for warming themselves,
or a fire to sit beside!
15 This is what they are to you—
those who have wearied you
and have traded with you
from your youth—
each wanders on his own way;
no one can save you.

The Exodus from Babylon (48:1-22)

48 "Listen to this,
house of Jacob—
those who are called
by the name Israel
and have descended
from[D] Judah,
who swear by the name
of •Yahweh
and declare the God of Israel,
but not in truth
or righteousness.
2 For they are named
after the Holy City,
and lean on the God of Israel;
His name is Yahweh of •Hosts.
3 I declared the past events
long ago;
they came out of My mouth;
I proclaimed them.
Suddenly I acted,
and they occurred.
4 Because I know
that you are stubborn,
and your neck is iron[E]
and your forehead bronze,
5 therefore I declared to you
long ago.
I announced it to you
before it occurred,
so you could not claim,
'My idol caused them;
my carved image and cast idol
control them.'
6 You have heard it.
Observe it all.
Will you not acknowledge it?
From now on I will announce
new things to you,
hidden things that
you have not known.
7 They have been created now,
and not long ago;

combinations, "I am God, and there is no other; I am God, and no one is like Me" (46:9; see also 45:5-6,14,18,21-22). The similarity in phrasing highlights Babylon's pride in claiming a supremacy that God alone could claim.

47:9-14 Occult practices were widespread in Babylon, as her wise men were renowned (Dn 2:2; 5:7). Yet confronted with the supreme God of the universe, they were helpless (Dn 2:10-11; 5:8,15; cp. Ex 7:11-12). She was wicked and trusted in her **sorceries**.

God mockingly challenged Babylon to see if her **spells** and **sorceries** could save her. Babylon trusted **astrologers** to tell her the future just as people today turn to horoscopes. Sorcery and astrology were and are worthless and despised by God (cp. Dt 18:10-12; 2 Ch 33:6; Jr 10:2; 27:9; Mc 5:12; Nah 3:4-5; Mal 3:5). Occultic practitioners could not even **deliver themselves**, much less anyone else.

47:15 Although Isaiah initially had in view the Babylon that fell to Cyrus, "Babylon" became symbolic for the height of human sin and idolatry. Revelation 18 adopts some of the same language to reflect the attitude found in the great Babylon of the last days (Rv 18:7-8,23; cp. Is 13:9-18). The heart of Babylon's sin was her pride, expressed by the assumption that she alone was in control of her fate and unanswerable for any of her deeds. Such an attitude rejects the sovereignty and authority of God, in essence deifying oneself (the height of idolatry) and inviting the full measure of God's wrath.

48:1-2 The Lord God addressed specifically those **descended from Judah**, the primary tribe of the southern kingdom from whom the kings came and whose capital was Jerusalem, **the Holy City** (cp. Gn 49:8-12). The Lord addressed them while they were yet in their sinful state. They gave lip service to the Lord and called themselves His people, but their declarations were still not made in **truth or righteousness** (cp. Is 1:10-20; Zch 7:5-11).

48:3 The Lord pointed out again that His revelation of the future was done so that everyone would know without a doubt that He had done it.

48:4-7 He took into account the fact that Israel was **stubborn** (Hb *qasheh*, "hard") and tended to ascribe God's actions to other sources (cp. Ex 32:1-9; 1 Kg 12:28). A common description for Israel in the wilderness following the Exodus was "stiff-necked" (Ex 32:9; 33:3,5; 34:9; Dt 9:6,13).

[A]**47:11** Or *to atone for it* [B]**47:13** Lit *dividers of the heavens* [C]**47:14** Lit *hand* [D]**48:1** Lit *have come from the waters of* [E]**48:4** Lit *is an iron sinew*

48:8 The Lord accused the offspring of Jacob of being **very treacherous** (Hb *bagod tivgod*, "act deceitfully, unfaithfully"). Two verbs from the same root convey the completeness of the treachery. Israel was also **known as a rebel from birth.**

48:9-11 The Lord had punished Israel for her transgressions. He had **refined** (Hb *tsaraph*) her, but the process was not complete (cp. 1:25; Pss 17:3; 66:10). Although there was still impurity found within His people, God planned to deliver her from Babylon anyway for His **own sake**. There would be a further future purging, which would be completed in those coming to the Lord Jesus (Dn 12:10; Zch 13:9; Mal 3:2-3).

48:12-15 The Lord notes, **I am He; I am the first** [Hb *ri'shon*], **I am also the last** (Hb *'acharon*; see notes on 41:4; 44:6-8). In the New Testament, this identification is adopted by the Lord Jesus as an expression of His divinity and of His unity with God the Father (Rv 1:8,17; 2:8; 22:13). The creation of the world is the work of God alone, and He is always sovereign over His creation. Scholars suggest that verse 14 refers to Cyrus as the one whom God would use against Babylon (45:1-2).

48:16 The words of this verse possibly came from one speaker. On this understanding, only the Messiah (whose coming fulfilled the Servant passages) could be the speaker. His pre-existence as well as the involvement of the Spirit in His life and ministry are clearly delineated in the Gospels (pre-existence, Jn 1:1-3,14-18; on the Spirit, cp. Jn 1:29-34; 14:16-18; 15:26; 16:7-15; Ac 2:1-4,33,38). Possibly verse 14 transitions from Cyrus, the conqueror of historical Babylon, to a greater conqueror of symbolic Babylon, the Messiah, who would one day deliver Israel from all her enemies forever. This good news will be the topic of the passages to follow.

48:22 In contrast to the joy and peace of the redeemed, the Lord warned: **There is no peace for the wicked.** This last warning seems to be given to those fleeing Babylon as a somber warning about the future for any who continued to walk in wickedness. It may also serve as a concluding note for the first division, chapters 40–48 (cp. 57:21 and the similar image in 66:24).

49:1–54:17 The previous chapter discussed the sinfulness of Israel even following the captivity. Although Israel would be physically delivered from exile by the actions of Cyrus, the people would still need spiritual redemption from the bondage of sin. The following passages further develop the theme of the coming Servant of the Lord who

>WORD|*study*

48:8 The word rebel (Hb root *pasha'*, participle meaning "rebel, transgress," cp. Dt 9:6,24; see note on 48:8) is used 41 times in the Old Testament and conveys the sense of breaking or violating an agreement or relationship. The word was used in a political sense when nations rebelled against other nations (1Kg 12:19; 2Kg 1:1; 3:5,7; 8:20, 22; 2Ch 10:19; 21:8,10). The word was also used when Israel violated the laws or crossed the boundaries that God had outlined for them. Isaiah used the verbal root nine times, always in the spiritual sense of the breaking of God's laws by Israel or other nations (Is 1:2,28; 43:27; 46:8; 48:8; 53:12 [2x]; 59:13; 66:24). The noun derivative *pasha'* carries the sense of "transgression" and is one of the words used to convey the concept of "sin" (24:20; 43:25; 44:22; 50:1; 53:5,8; 57:4; 58:1; 59:12,20).

you have not heard of them
before today,
so you could not claim,
'I already knew them!'
8 You have never heard;
you have never known;
For a long time your ears
have not been open.
For I knew that you
were very treacherous,
and were known as a rebel
from birth.
9 I will delay My anger
for the honor of My name,
and I will restrain
Myself for your benefit
and for My praise,
so that you will not be
destroyed.
10 Look, I have refined you,
but not as silver;
I have tested[A] you
in the furnace of affliction.
11 I will act for My own sake,
indeed, My own,
for how can I[B] be defiled?
I will not give My glory
to another.

12 "Listen to Me, Jacob,
and Israel, the one called
by Me:
I am He; I am the first,
I am also the last.
13 My own hand founded
the earth,
and My right hand spread out
the heavens;
when I summoned them,
they stood up together.
14 All of you, assemble
and listen!
Who among the idols[C]
has declared these things?
The LORD loves him;[D]
he will accomplish His will
against Babylon,
and His arm will be against
the Chaldeans.
15 I—I have spoken;
yes, I have called him;
I have brought him,
and he will succeed
in his mission.
16 Approach Me and listen
to this.
From the beginning
I have not spoken in secret;
from the time anything
existed, I was there."
And now the Lord GOD
has sent me and His Spirit.

17 This is what the LORD, your Redeemer, the Holy One of Israel says:

I am Yahweh your God,
who teaches you
for your benefit,
who leads you in the way
you should go.
18 If only you had paid attention
to My commands.
Then your peace
would have been like a river,
and your righteousness
like the waves of the sea.
19 Your descendants
would have been
as countless as the sand,
and the offspring of your body
like its grains;
their name would not
be cut off
or eliminated
from My presence.

20 Leave Babylon,
flee from the Chaldeans!
Declare with a shout of joy,
proclaim this,
let it go out to the end
of the earth;
announce,

A48:10 Or *chosen* B48:11 DSS, Syr; MT reads *it* C48:14 Lit *among them* D48:14 = Cyrus

"The LORD has redeemed
His servant Jacob!"
21 They did not thirst
when He led them
through the deserts;
He made water flow for them
from the rock;
He split the rock, and water
gushed out.
22 "There is no peace
for the wicked,"
says the LORD.

The Servant's Salvation for All Nations (49:1-26)

49 Coastlands,[A] listen to me;
distant peoples, pay attention.
The LORD called me
before I was born.
He named me while I was
in my mother's womb.
2 He made my words
like a sharp sword;
He hid me in the shadow
of His hand.
He made me
like a sharpened arrow;
He hid me in His quiver.
3 He said to me, "You are
My Servant, Israel;
I will be glorified in him."
4 But I myself said:
I have labored in vain,
I have spent my strength
for nothing and futility;
yet my vindication is
with the LORD,
and my reward is
with my God.
5 And now, says the LORD,
who formed me
from the womb to be
His Servant,
to bring Jacob back to Him
so that Israel
might be gathered to Him;
for I am honored in the sight
of the LORD,
and my God is my strength—
6 He says,
"It is not enough for you to be
My Servant
raising up the tribes of Jacob
and restoring
the protected ones of Israel.
I will also make you a light
for the nations,
to be My salvation to the ends
of the earth."
7 This is what the LORD,
the Redeemer of Israel,
his Holy One, says
to one who is despised,
to one abhorred by people,[B]
to a servant of rulers:
"Kings will see and stand up,
and princes[C] will bow down,
because of the LORD,
who is faithful,
the Holy One of Israel—and
He has chosen you."
8 This is what the LORD says:
I will answer you in a time
of favor,
and I will help you in the day
of salvation.
I will keep you,
and I will appoint you
to be a covenant
for the people,
to restore the land,
to make them possess
the desolate inheritances,
9 saying to the prisoners:
Come out,
and to those who
are in darkness:
Show yourselves.
They will feed
along the pathways,
and their pastures will be
on all the barren heights.
10 They will not hunger
or thirst,
the scorching heat or sun
will not strike them;
for their compassionate One
will guide them,
and lead them to springs
of water.
11 I will make all My mountains
into a road,
and My highways will be
raised up.
12 See, these will come
from far away,
from the north
and from the west,[D]
and from the land of Sinim.[E,F]
13 Shout for joy, you heavens!
Earth, rejoice!

[A]**49:1** Or *Islands* [B]**49:7** Or *by the nation* [C]**49:7** Lit *princes and they* [D]**49:12** Lit *sea* [E]**49:12** DSS read *of the Syenites* [F]**49:12** Perhaps modern Aswan in southern Egypt

would provide the final salvation that all people, not just Israel, needed.

49:1-13 This chapter contains the second of four "Servant Songs" in Isaiah. Initial details are provided about the work of the coming Servant, the Messiah and His mission in 42:1-7. Matthew clearly identified Jesus Christ as the Servant of chapter 42 (see notes on 42:1-7; Mt 12:17-21). In Is 42, God addresses the Servant, but in Is 49 the Servant speaks first and God concludes. Scholars have observed many similarities between chapters 42 and 49.

The Servant says He was **called** before birth and **named** in the **womb** (cp. 42:1; Mt 1:20-23; Lk 1:31-35). This man was not just one who "rose to the top"; God designated Him before birth to a particular calling.

49:4 The Servant expends great effort and feels discouraged, but He maintains, **My vindication** [Hb *mishpat*] **is with the LORD and my reward is with my God** (see 42:4, where *mishpat* is translated "justice"; cp. 53:10-12). The Servant Songs in 50:4-11 and 52:13–53:12 deal in greater detail with the suffering of the Messiah, identified by the New Testament as Jesus of Nazareth. He experienced deep sorrow and even abandonment when God the Father turned away as the sins of the world were laid upon Him as He hung on the cross; yet the Lord Jesus persevered, completing the plan and will of God (Mt 26:37-42,46,50; Lk 22:41-44; Jn 19:30). His **reward** (Hb *pe'ullah*, "recompense") may be linked with the redemption and salvation of those who would trust in Him (Is 40:10; 53:10-11; see notes on 62:10-12; Rv 22:10-15).

49:6 God would make His Servant **a light for the nations** (Hb *le'or goyim*, only used in 42:6 and 49:6; cp. "a light to the nations" [Hb *'am*, "a people or nation," 51:4]; 60:1-5). This was a radical departure from ancient Near Eastern theology. Gods were territorial and specific to a given people. But this Servant would be a universal light, deliverer, and leader—not just for Israel, but also **to the ends of the earth**. Simeon recognized Jesus as the fulfillment of these words (Lk 2:27-32). Jesus was identified as the light of the world on various occasions (Jn 1:4-5; 8:12; 9:5; 12:34-36,46). Paul and Barnabas claimed their ministry to the Gentiles (the Greek translation for "nations") fulfilled this verse (Ac 13:47). In this text, there is no room for pluralism or multiple paths to God. There is one Servant, who is the light for all nations.

49:13 Despite the prophet's present position in the gloom of captivity, he could break out in elation, enjoining creation to **rejoice** over the redemption provided by the Lord. God had revealed His plan for the future, and Isaiah trusted Him fully to do all He promised (cp. Jr 29:11-14).

49:14-16 Although personified Zion (Jerusalem) expresses a sense of abandonment by the Lord, the Lord responds fervently, **Can a woman forget her nursing child, or lack compassion for the child of her womb?** There is extreme discomfort, to the point of excruciating pain, for a woman who suddenly stops nursing a child. For a woman to forget her child would be extraordinary; however, even if that should happen, God would never forget Zion. He exclaimed, **Look, I have inscribed you on the palms of My hands**.

49:18 God's commitment to Zion and the restored people who would populate Zion is permanent. The city was assured that the time of desolation would end. The city would be restored just as her redeemed people would **gather together** and **come** to her. Zion will proudly display the redeemed **children** who come to inhabit God's holy city in the same way a **bride** puts on prized jewelry for the wedding ceremony (see 61:10; 62:4-5).

49:19-21 Instead of being barren and **desolate**, the land will be filled with the restored people (54:1-13). Zion will question from whence all the **children** came since her own had been taken away (into captivity) and she had no chance to bear others naturally. Scholars note that the returning children are those born in Babylon (54:1). Others suggest this gathering may also be fulfilled in an assembling yet to come, which would include the redeemed people of both Jews and Gentiles at the initiation of the millennial reign (see 62:11-12; 66:18-21). This interpretation would provide added meaning to Zion's question concerning the origination of the children; the children would include believers who did not descend physically from Abraham but were adopted into the family of Abraham as spiritual offspring and became united with the redeemed of Israel (see notes on 54:1-2,3; Gl 3:29). Both the redeemed Jews and Gentiles are the Servant's reward, the result of His salvific work on the cross (cp. Eph 2:14-19).

49:26 God will cause those who oppressed Israel to destroy themselves, and ultimately **all flesh will know** that the Lord is the **Savior**, **Redeemer**, and **Mighty One of Jacob** (cp. 60:16). The picture is grotesque but simply reveals the truth that those whom God redeems will have limitless joy, but those whom God does not redeem

Mountains break
into joyful shouts!
For the LORD has comforted
His people,
and will have compassion
on His afflicted ones.
14 •Zion says, "The LORD
has abandoned me;
The Lord has forgotten me!"
15 "Can a woman forget
her nursing child,
or lack compassion
for the child of her womb?
Even if these forget,
yet I will not forget you.
16 Look, I have inscribed you
on the palms of My hands;
your walls are continually
before Me.
17 Your builders[A] hurry;
those who destroy
and devastate you
will leave you.
18 Look up, and look around.
They all gather together;
they come to you.
As I live"—
this is
the LORD's declaration—
"you will wear
all your children[B] as jewelry,
and put them on
as a bride does.
19 For your waste
and desolate places
and your land marked
by ruins—
will now be indeed too small
for the inhabitants,
and those who swallowed
you up will be far away.
20 Yet as you listen, the children
that you have been
deprived of will say,
'This place is too small
for me;
make room for me so that
I may settle.'
21 Then you will say
within yourself,
'Who fathered these for me?
I was deprived of my children
and unable to conceive,
exiled and wandering—
but who brought them up?
See, I was left by myself—
but these, where did they
come from?'"[C]
22 This is what the Lord GOD says:
Look, I will lift up My hand
to the nations,
and raise My banner
to the peoples.
They will bring your sons
in their arms,
and your daughters
will be carried
on their shoulders.
23 Kings will be
your foster fathers,
and their queens[D]
your nursing mothers.
They will bow down to you
with their faces to the ground,
and lick the dust at your feet.
Then you will know that I am
•Yahweh;
those who put their hope
in Me
will not be put to shame.
24 Can the prey be taken
from the mighty,
or the captives
of the righteous[E]
be delivered?
25 For this is what the LORD says:
"Even the captives
of a mighty man
will be taken,
and the prey of a tyrant
will be delivered;
I will contend with the one
who contends with you,
and I will save your children.
26 I will make your oppressors
eat their own flesh,
and they will be drunk
with their own blood
as with sweet wine.
Then all flesh will know
that I, Yahweh,
am your Savior,
and your Redeemer,
the Mighty One of Jacob."

The Behavior of Israel and the Servant (50:1-11)

50 This is what the LORD says:
Where is your mother's
divorce certificate

[A]49:17 DSS, Aq, Theod, Vg; MT, Syr, Sym read *sons* [B]49:18 Lit *all of them* [C]49:21 Lit *where are they* [D]49:23 Lit *princesses* [E]49:24 DSS, Syr, Vg read *fearsome one*, or *tyrant*

that I used to send
her away?
Or who were My creditors
that I sold you to?
Look, you were sold
for your iniquities,
and your mother was
put away
because of
your transgressions.
2 Why was no one there
when I came?
Why was there no one
to answer when I called?
Is My hand too short
to redeem?
Or do I have no power
to deliver?
Look, I dry up the sea
by My rebuke;
I turn the rivers
into a wilderness;
their fish rot because of lack
of water
and die of thirst.
3 I dress the heavens in black
and make •sackcloth
their clothing.

4 The Lord God has given Me
the tongue of those
who are instructed
to know how to sustain
the weary with a word.
He awakens Me
each morning;
He awakens My ear to listen
like those being instructed.
5 The Lord God has opened
My ear,
and I was not rebellious;
I did not turn back.
6 I gave My back to those
who beat Me,
and My cheeks to those
who tore out My beard.
I did not hide My face
from scorn and spitting.
7 The Lord God
will help Me;
therefore I have not
been humiliated;
therefore I have set My face
like flint,
and I know I will not
be put to shame.
8 The One who vindicates Me
is near;
who will contend with Me?
Let us confront each other.[A]
Who has a case against Me?[B]
Let him come near Me!
9 In truth, the Lord God
will help Me;
who will condemn Me?
Indeed, all of them
will wear out
like a garment;
a moth will devour them.
10 Who among you •fears
the LORD,
listening to the voice
of His Servant?
Who among you walks
in darkness,
and has no light?
Let him trust in the name
of •Yahweh;
let him lean on his God.
11 Look, all you who kindle
a fire,
who encircle yourselves
with[C] firebrands;
walk in the light of your fire
and in the firebrands
you have lit!
This is what you'll get
from My hand:
you will lie down in a place
of torment.

The Lord's Comfort and Redemption (51:1–52:12)

51 Listen to Me, you
who pursue righteousness,
you who seek the LORD:
Look to the rock from which
you were cut,
and to the quarry from which
you were dug.
2 Look to Abraham your father,
and to Sarah who gave birth
to you in pain.
When I called him, he was
only one;
I blessed him
and made him many.
3 For the LORD
will comfort •Zion;
He will comfort
all her waste places,
and He will make
her wilderness like Eden,
and her desert like the garden
of the LORD.

will have equally limitless misery and suffering. To turn from the redemption of God is not a light thing.

50:1 The Lord asks His people about their **mother's divorce certificate** in order to point out that there had been no official permanent separation between God and His people (i.e., the covenant or "marriage" was still in effect). In Israel, a man could divorce his wife if he discovered "something improper" (unclean or immoral) about her (Dt 24:1-4). To make the divorce official, a written document was given to the woman, and the man was forbidden ever to take her back, but she was permitted to remarry. Right before the Assyrian exile, God declared that He had served the apostate northern kingdom of Israel with divorce papers; but, though Jerusalem had played the harlot with false gods just as Samaria had, He did not mention divorcing Judah (Jr 3:1,6-10; Hs 1:6-7; 2:2).

50:4 This passage constitutes the third Servant Song. Though the people of Israel had been sinful and rebellious to God's call, the Servant exhibited complete obedience. The Servant had **the tongue of those who are instructed**, learning from God and speaking His message to the people (Jn 5:19-20, 30; 12:49-50; 14:10, 24; 15:15; 17:7-8).

51:1-3 Addressing those **who seek the LORD,** the speaker directs them to consider their heritage. The Lord is often referenced as the Rock; however, in this context **rock** (Hb *tsur*; see **Word Study**, p. 884) seems to point to God's deliberate act of choosing Abraham and Sarah to be the parents of His chosen people since Is 51:1b and 2a express parallel thoughts. Abraham was **only one** when God choose Him to become heir to the promises of land, descendants, and blessing (Gn 12:1-3,7). As God had miraculously raised up a nation from Abraham and his barren wife Sarah (Gn 18:11-14), the same God would also **comfort Zion** and restore her **waste places** (Hb *chorbah*, "ruins"). The Lord would miraculously make the barren land fruitful and fill it with joy and gladness (Is 35:1-2; 58:11-12; 61:4; 64:10-11; 65:17-19).

[A]**50:8** Lit *us stand* [B]**50:8** Lit *Who is lord of My judgment* [C]**50:11** Syr reads *who set ablaze*

51:4 Due to similarities in phrasing between this passage and other Servant songs, some commentators suggest that the speaker is still the Servant, although displaying His divine rather than human nature. The emphasis is upon His future establishment of **instruction** (Hb *torah*, "law") and **justice for a light to the nations** (Hb *le'or 'ammim*, "for the peoples"; see note on 49:6).

51:5-6 There will be an eternal quality to both the Servant's **righteousness** and His **salvation**—not the righteousness and salvation enacted by earthly kingdoms, which quickly fade. The imagery of cosmic upheaval was often used to describe socio-political regime changes. Understanding this, the deliverance mentioned initially was fulfilled in the release of the people from Babylonian captivity. The mentions of **forever** and a deliverance **never to be shattered** point to a later time when even the **nations** (Hb *'am mim*, "people") and the **coastlands** (Hb *'i*, "seashore, island") **will put their hope** in the Lord (Is 42:4; 49:1). The reference to the destruction of the **heavens**, **earth**, and all **inhabitants** also points to the end of time (13:9-13; 24:17-23; 34:2-4; cp. Ps 102:25-28; Heb 1:10-12; 2Pt 3:10). In contrast to creation's temporality, God's **salvation will last forever** (cp. Mt 24:35).

51:7-8 The Lord encouraged all those who would suffer humiliation at the hands of **men** to remember their tormentor's mortality as opposed to God's eternal promises (cp. 50:9). They should not fear what man could do but instead should cling to God's eternal **righteousness** and **salvation** (cp. 45:17; Mt 10:28).

51:9–52:6 This passage is structured around four sections beginning with double imperatives (51:9,17; 52:1,11).

51:9 The first emphatic double imperatives, **Wake up, wake up** (Hb *'ur, 'ur*, "rouse oneself") and the plea to **put on . . . strength** are addressed to **the Lord's power** (Hb *zeroa'*, "arm, shoulder, strength"). **The Lord's power** is literally translated "the arm of the Lord," especially in view of the following reference of the Lord's arm hacking apart **Rahab** and piercing **the sea monster** (Hb *tannin*, "serpent, dragon"). Likely Rahab and Tannin are references to Egypt as well as to a sea monster of chaos like the Babylonian sea monster, Tiamat (see note on 26:20–27:1). In both cases, God conquered victoriously.

51:10-11 During the first exodus, the Lord had **dried up the sea . . . for the redeemed to pass over** (cp. 63:12). If God could do it in the past, He could

Joy and gladness will be found
in her,
thanksgiving
and melodious song.

4 Pay attention to Me,
My people,
and listen to Me, My nation;
for instruction will come
from Me,
and My justice for a light
to the nations.
I will bring it about quickly.
5 My righteousness is near,
My salvation appears,
and My arms will bring justice
to the nations.
The coastlands[A] will put
their hope in Me,
and they will look
to My strength.[B]
6 Look up to the heavens,
and look at the earth beneath;
for the heavens will vanish
like smoke,
the earth will wear out
like a garment,
and its inhabitants will die
like gnats.[C]
But My salvation
will last forever,
and My righteousness
will never be shattered.

7 Listen to Me, you who
know righteousness,
the people in whose heart is
My instruction:
do not fear disgrace by men,
and do not be shattered
by their taunts.
8 For the moth
will devour them
like a garment,
and the worm will eat them
like wool.
But My righteousness
will last forever,
and My salvation
for all generations.

9 Wake up, wake up!
Put on the strength
of the LORD's power.
Wake up as in days past,
as in generations of long ago.
Wasn't it You
who hacked •Rahab
to pieces,
who pierced the sea monster?
10 Wasn't it You who dried up
the sea,
the waters of the great deep,
who made the sea-bed
into a road
for the redeemed to pass over?
11 And the redeemed of the LORD
will return
and come to Zion
with singing,
crowned with unending joy.
Joy and gladness
will overtake them,
and sorrow and sighing
will flee.

12 I—I am the One
who comforts you.
Who are you that you should
fear man who dies,
or a son of man
who is given up like grass?
13 But you have forgotten
the LORD, your Maker,
who stretched out
the heavens
and laid the foundations
of the earth.
You are in constant dread
all day long
because of the fury
of the oppressor,
who has set himself
to destroy.
But where is the fury
of the oppressor?
14 The prisoner[D] is soon to be
set free;
he will not die and go
to the •Pit,
and his food will not
be lacking.
15 For I am •Yahweh your God
who stirs up the sea so that
its waves roar—
His name is Yahweh of •Hosts.
16 I have put My words
in your mouth,
and covered you
in the shadow of My hand,
in order to plant[E] the heavens,
to found the earth,
and to say to Zion, "You are
My people."

[A]51:5 Or *islands* [B]51:5 Lit *arm* [C]51:6 Or *die in like manner* [D]51:14 Hb obscure [E]51:16 Syr reads *to stretch out*

17 Wake yourself,
wake yourself up!
Stand up, Jerusalem,
you who have drunk the cup
of His fury
from the hand of the LORD;
you who have drunk
the goblet to the dregs—
the cup that causes people
to stagger.
18 There is no one to guide her
among all the children
she has raised;
there is no one to take hold
of her hand
among all the offspring
she has brought up.
19 These two things
have happened to you:
devastation and destruction,
famine and sword.
Who will grieve for you?
How can I[A] comfort you?
20 Your children have fainted;
they lie at the head
of every street
like an antelope in a net.
They are full
of the LORD's fury,
the rebuke of your God.

21 So listen to this, afflicted
and drunken one—but not
with wine.
22 This is what your Lord says—
Yahweh, even your God,
who defends His people—
"Look, I have removed
the cup of staggering
from your hand;
that goblet, the cup
of My fury.
You will never drink it again.
23 I will put it into the hands
of your tormentors,
who said to you:
Lie down, so we can walk
over you.
You made your back
like the ground,
and like a street for those
who walk on it.

52 "Wake up, wake up;
put on your strength, •Zion!
Put on
your beautiful garments,
Jerusalem, the Holy City!
For the uncircumcised
and the •unclean
will no longer enter you.
2 Stand up, shake the dust
off yourself!
Take your seat, Jerusalem.
Remove the bonds[B]
from your neck,
captive Daughter Zion."
3 For this is what the LORD says:
"You were sold for nothing,
and you will be redeemed
without silver."
4 For this is what
the Lord GOD says:
"At first My people went down
to Egypt to live there,
then Assyria oppressed them
without cause.[C]

[A]**51:19** DSS, LXX, Syr, Vg read *you? Who can* [B]**52:2** Alt Hb tradition reads *The bonds are removed*
[C]**52:4** Or *them at last*, or *them for nothing*

also do it in the future. The prophet merged the exodus language with the future return from the Babylonian exile when **the redeemed of the LORD will return and come to Zion with singing** (see 35:10; cp. Ex 15:1-21), delivered once more from bondage.

51:12-16 God's response to Isaiah's double plea to "wake up," was emphatic, **I—I am the One** [Hb *hu'*, "he"] **who comforts you** (cp. 40:1). The comfort He provided was grounded in His identity as the sovereign Creator of the world and the **Maker** of the nation of Israel. God promised deliverance would soon come to His people in exile, and He had both the power and will to save. The Lord addressed one who will speak His **words** and will be instrumental in the establishment of the **heavens** and the **earth** and the redeemed of **Zion** (cp. 65:17). Seemingly the one being addressed in verse 16 is the Servant, who is ultimately fulfilled in Christ.

In Is 50:4 the Servant was given words from God for the people, and in 49:2 the Servant was hidden by the shadow of God's hand. In addition, some scholars note the coming of Jesus brought about the assurance of a new heaven and earth and a redeemed Zion, of whom He would say, **You are My people** (cp. 65:17-19; Hs 2:23; Zch 8:7-8; 13:9; Rv 21:1-4).

51:21-23 They were drunk, **not with wine** but from the judgment of the Lord. Yet, God would deliver them and remove the **cup of** His **fury** from them so that they **will never drink it again**. Instead, the cup of judgment would be drunk by their **tormentors** who had oppressed them (cp. Rv 18:6).

52:1 The third pair of imperatives encouraged Zion to **wake up** and **put on . . . strength** and **beautiful garments** in token of her redemption and rededication as the **Holy City**.

52:2 Jerusalem was encouraged to rise from her former position of humiliation and grief and **shake the dust off** (cp. 51:23; in contrast to Babylon, 47:1). She would sit enthroned as God's "Holy City" (52:1). No longer would she be oppressed and in bondage, for the Daughter of Zion was told to **remove the bonds from** her **neck**, which was possible only through the redemption of the Lord.

52:4-5 The history of Israel's captivities are reviewed. The Lord had delivered the nation from Egypt with a mighty hand to bring glory to His name. In Isaiah's time, the Lord delivered Jerusalem from the Assyrian oppression for the glory of His name.

>WORD|*study*

52:1 Beautiful (Hb *tiph'arah*, "beauty, glory"), occurring 51 times in the Old Testament, is often used to describe God (46:13; 60:19; 63:12,14; cp. 1Ch 29:11,13; Ps 71:8) or His temple or dwelling place (1Ch 22:5; 2Ch 3:6; Is 60:7; 63:15; 64:11). Occasionally, the word is used concerning the honor or glory of a nation (Dt 26:19; Is 10:12; 13:19; 20:5; Lm 2:1). The word is also connected with crowns, ornaments, or finery (Pr 4:9; 16:31; Is 3:18; 62:3; Ezk 16:12,17,39). In the only other case where it is linked with "garments," the reference is to the clothes worn by the high priests (Ex 28:2,40). Jerusalem and her inhabitants were to be separated and prepared for priestly service before God (Is 61:6). In addition, Jerusalem would be adorned with the redeemed who were clothed with salvation and righteousness (see notes on 49:18 and 61:9; Rv 21:1-4).

52:1 The renewed city would be free from any unclean influences: **The** uncircumcised [Hb *'arel*, often referring to any non-Israelites, like the Philistines, who were outside of the covenant; Ex 12:48; Jdg 14:3; 1Sm 17:26,36] **and the unclean will no longer enter**. Additionally, in the Old Testament there was a concept of being spiritually "uncircumcised" (Lv 26:40-45; Jr 9:26; Ezk 44:6-9). Circumcision of the heart implied openness and dedication to God (Dt 10:16; 30:6; Jr 4:4). In the New Testament, Paul pointed out that true circumcision was of the heart and that was accomplished by faith in Jesus Christ (Rm 2:28-29; Eph 2:11-22; Col 2:11-14). The uncircumcised will have no place in God's redeemed kingdom but are reserved for destruction (Ezk 31:18; 32:19-32). This complete separation from anything unclean will be fulfilled in the final establishment of Jerusalem following the return and reign of Christ (Rv 21:1-2,8,27).

52:6 In the understanding of the day, the strongest "god" won in confrontations between nations (Ezk 36:16-28). For His own glory, the Lord would deliver His people and reestablish Israel in their land (Dt 32:26-29). His people would know His name; He would clearly reveal Himself as the One who says **Here I am** (Hb *hinnēni*; see Is 65:1).

52:7 In contemplating the glorious news of God's pending self-revelation and deliverance, Isaiah exulted joyfully concerning the message of one **who proclaims peace . . . brings news of good things** (Hb *basar*, "one who bears or announces good news or glad tidings"; see **Word Study**, p. 910; cp. 41:27; 61:1) and **salvation** (Hb *yeshu'ah*; see **Word Study**, p. 878). The good news for the Babylonian exiles from Jerusalem was that they were free; they would know experientially that their **God reigns**. The Apostle Paul clearly connected the good news of peace and salvation in 52:7 with the news that salvation came to those who put their faith in Christ (Rm 10:9-15; Eph 2:13-17; 6:15). Paul used a similar metaphor—"How **beautiful** (Gk *hōraios*, "pleasant, timely") are the feet"—to describe those who proclaim the gospel of Jesus Christ (Rm 10:15). Paul also exhorted the soldier of Christ to "take up the full armor of God . . . . sandaled with readiness for the gospel ["good news"] of peace" (Eph 6:13-15).

52:8-9 The **watchmen** were lookouts posted on the city wall to warn of any threats. They would naturally be the first witnesses to the Lord's return to His people, but in addition **every eye will see**. The Lord's return to Jerusalem (or in Isaiah's time, the *promise* of His return) brought the people comfort.

52:10 Just as Israel was disciplined publicly before **all the nations**, so they were also publicly redeemed and restored to their land after the Babylonian exile.

52:12 In contrast to the hurried flight of the exodus, those leaving Babylon were told **you will not leave in a hurry** (cp. Ex 12:33-34, 39; Ezr 1:1-11).

52:13 The fourth "Servant Song," 52:13—53:12, is considered by most scholars as the core of the last half of the book.

52:14-15 The Servant would be **so disfigured,** so severely abused as to be unrecognizable. In previous chapters there had also been hints about the fact that the Servant would be mistreated (42:4; 49:4,7; 50:6-9); with ever increasing detail, the Lord outlined the degree and purpose for the suffering.

>WORD|*study*

52:15 The word here translated sprinkle (Hb *nazah*) occurs only 22 times in the Old Testament. Some uses concern the purification or consecration of people or holy items by sprinkling blood, oil, or water (Ex 29:21; Lv 6:27; 8:11,30; 14:7,16,27,51; Nm 8:7; 19:18,19,21). Most of the other uses are connected with blood sprinkled in the course of offering sacrifice for sin (Lv 4:6,17; 5:9; 16:14, 15,19; Nm 19:4). In Is 52:15, based on the New Testament understanding, the sprinkling referred to the blood sacrifice made by Jesus Christ for the sins of all people (cp. 63:3; Heb 9:12-15,18-22,24-28; 10:1-14,19-22; 12:24; 1Pt 1:2).

53:1 The exact phrase, the arm [Hb *zeroa'*, "shoulder, strength"] of the LORD occurs only two times in the Old Testament (Is 51:9; 53:1); however, there are many occurrences of *zeroa'* being used anthropomorphically to explain the strength and power of God's works. Several times the term refers to God's deliverance of Israel from Egypt (e.g., 63:12; Ex 6:6; 15:16; Dt 4:34; Ps 77:15). This prototypical deliverance assured Israel that the God who once delivered His people from Egypt will deliver them again from other troubles. In many other cases, the idea of God's strength or power to deliver is linked to His "arm" (Pss 89:13; 98:1; Is 33:2; 40:10; 51:9; 52:10; 63:5; Ezk 20:33). In this passage "arm of the LORD" or strength of God is manifested through the Suffering Servant, Jesus, to all those who saw or heard of Him.

53:3-4 Suffering (Hb *mak'ov*, lit "pain"—physical, emotional, mental) is the same word translated pains (v. 4). Likewise, sickness (Hb *choli*, v. 3) is the same as sicknesses (v. 4). Scholars point out that the **sicknesses** could have been either physical or spiritual, much like the "pains."

5 So now what have I here"—
this is
the LORD's declaration—
"that My people
are taken away for nothing?
Its rulers wail"—
this is
the LORD's declaration—
"and My name is continually
blasphemed all day long.
6 Therefore My people
will know My name;
therefore they will know
on that day
that I am He who says:
Here I am."

7 How beautiful
on the mountains
are the feet of the herald,
who proclaims peace,
who brings news
of good things,
who proclaims salvation,
who says to Zion,
"Your God reigns!"
8 The voices
of your watchmen—
they lift up their voices,
shouting for joy together;
for every eye will see
when the LORD returns
to Zion.
9 Be joyful, rejoice together,
you ruins of Jerusalem!
For the LORD has comforted
His people;
He has redeemed Jerusalem.
10 The LORD has displayed
His holy arm
in the sight of all the nations;
all the ends of the earth
will see
the salvation of our God.

11 Leave, leave, go out
from there!
Do not touch
anything unclean;
go out from her,
purify yourselves,
you who carry the vessels
of the LORD.
12 For you will not leave
in a hurry,
and you will not have
to take flight;
because the LORD is going
before you,
and the God of Israel is
your rear guard.

The Work of the Servant (52:13–53:12)

13 See, My Servant[A]
will act wisely;[B]
He will be raised and lifted up
and greatly exalted.
14 Just as many were appalled
at You[C]—
His appearance
was so disfigured
that He did not look
like a man,
and His form did not resemble
a human being—

[A]52:13 Tg adds *the Messiah* [B]52:13 Or *will be successful* [C]52:14 Some Hb mss, Syr, Tg read *Him*

15 so He will sprinkle[A,B]
many nations.[C]
Kings will shut their mouths
because of Him,
For they will see what
had not been told them,
and they will understand
what they had not heard.

53 Who has believed
what we have heard?[D]
And who has the arm
of the LORD
been revealed to?
2 He grew up before Him
like a young plant
and like a root out of
dry ground.
He didn't have an
impressive form
or majesty that we
should look at Him,
no appearance that we should
desire Him.
3 He was despised and rejected
by men,
a man of suffering who knew
what sickness was.
He was like someone
people turned away from;[E]
He was despised,
and we didn't value Him.

4 Yet He Himself bore
our sicknesses,
and He carried our pains;
but we in turn
regarded Him stricken,
struck down by God,
and afflicted.
5 But He was pierced because of
our transgressions,
crushed because of
our iniquities;
punishment for our peace was
on Him,
and we are healed
by His wounds.
6 We all went astray like sheep;
we all have turned
to our own way;
and the LORD
has punished Him
for[F] the iniquity of us all.
7 He was oppressed and afflicted,
yet He did not open
His mouth.
Like a lamb led
to the slaughter
and like a sheep silent
before her shearers,
He did not open His mouth.
8 He was taken away because of
oppression and judgment;
and who considered His fate?[G]
For He was cut off
from the land of the living;

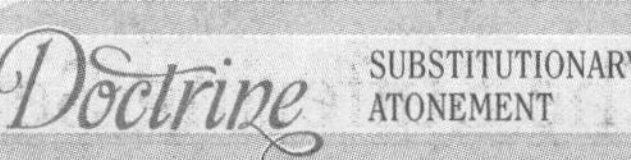

Doctrine: SUBSTITUTIONARY ATONEMENT

The Servant's suffering (53:3-6) was propitiatory and redemptive. Although He Himself was sinless (2Co 5:21; Heb 4:15; 1Jn 3:5), He suffered on behalf of mankind. He bore **our pains, transgressions**, and **iniquities**. The physical and spiritual healing ministry of Jesus has fulfilled Isaiah's prophecy (Mt 8:16-17). When Jesus healed others, He was taking on Himself the battle and the consequences of sin (disease, all kinds of infirmities), bearing the cost of others' pains and sicknesses. Instead of understanding that His suffering was on our behalf, however, those around Him assumed that He suffered because God **afflicted** Him.

The language of pain and sickness (the results of sin) gives way to the plain language of sin itself. **He was pierced** [Hb *chalal*, "wound fatally, bore through"] for **our transgressions** (Hb *pesha'*; see **Word Study**, p. 924). Elsewhere in the Old Testament, Hebrew synonyms for *chalal* are used to describe the piercing of the Messiah (Ps 22:16-17; Zch 12:10). This was ultimately fulfilled in the crucifixion, foreshadowing the thorns upon His brow, nails that pierced His flesh, and the spear thrust into His side (Mk 15:17; Jn 19:34-37; Rv 1:7). The Servant was **crushed** [Hb *daka'*, "be broken in pieces, bruised, smitten"; cp. Is 53:10] **because of our iniquities** (Hb *'awon*; cp. Is 50:1). The verb "crush" conveys the spiritual agony the Lord Jesus experienced as the sins of the world were placed upon Him as He hung upon the cross (Mk 15:33-34). Far greater than the physical pain was the spiritual separation from God the Father, as the Son was abandoned to pay the price of humanity's sin, expressed in the cry of dereliction, "My God, My God, why have You forsaken Me?" (Mk 15:34; Ps 22:1). Healing from the fatal sickness of sin is available only **by His wounds** (Hb *chabburah*, "bruise, strip, blow," as from being whipped; cp. Ex 21:25; Is 1:6)—because Christ suffered and died in our place.

We all went astray like sheep; we all have turned to our own way (notes on Is 40:9-11; cp. Ps 14:3; Rm 3:23;1 Pt 2:24-25). All humanity (not just Israel) is guilty of violating God's righteous standards and could not be ultimately justified until the Servant took the punishment **for the iniquity of us all** (cp. Is 53:12; Rm 3:21-26; 4:24-25; 1Pt 1:18-21; 2:21).

Nevertheless, through His actions, He would **sprinkle many nations** (Hb *goyim*). Ultimately kings would **understand** what they had previously **not heard**. Complete reversal would happen. The sufferings of this Servant were not only for Israel, to whom the law had been revealed, but for all nations. Paul quoted this passage in relation to his call to take the good news of salvation to the Gentiles (Rm 15:20-21).

53:1 The opening verse of this awe-inspiring chapter is quoted directly two times in the New Testament in relation to Jesus Christ (Jn 12:37-38; Rm 10:16). John clearly pointed out that the failure to believe of those who witnessed the works of Jesus fulfilled this passage, and Paul similarly referred to it concerning the good news about Jesus Christ.

53:2 The **young plant** and **root** imagery recalls earlier plant references concerning the Messiah (11:1,10). The **dry ground** is an unflattering commentary on the environment in which the Servant grew up, but it did not hinder Him; He grew nonetheless. But He was undesirable based on human standards of mere outward appearance.

53:7 These verses fully explain the mission of the Servant—to die for sinners. Imagery of **a sheep silent before her shearers** describes how the Servant allowed Himself to be led to death without resistance because His death was the necessary atonement to cover sins and bring redemption. The Ethiopian eunuch was reading this passage when Philip overheard him (Ac 8:30-37) and "proceeded to tell him the good news about Jesus" (Ac 8:35). The Lord Jesus fulfilled this passage as He silently submitted to the abuse of His interrogators (Mt 26:62-63; 27:11-14; Mk 14:60-61; 15:3-5; Lk 23:8-9; Jn 19:9). His submission to death was purposeful obedience to God's will (Mt 16:21; 17:12,22-23; 20:17-19; Mk 8:31; 9:31; Lk 9:22; 18:31-33; 24:44-47; Jn 12:23-27,31-33). The **lamb** imagery conveys humble submission and also refers to Jesus' role as the sacrificial "Lamb of God, who takes away the sin of the world" (Jn 1:29; Ac 8:32, 35; 1Pt 1:18-20; Rv 5:5-14; 13:8). The blood of this Lamb cleanses believers and makes reconciliation with the Holy God possible (Rv 5:9; 7:14; 12:10-11; 19:7-9; 21:2-3, 9-10).

53:8 The Servant was to be **cut off from the land of the living**; He was to die **because** of the **people's rebellion** (Hb *pesha'*; see related **Word Study**, p.924).

[A] **52:15** Or *startle* [B] **52:15** As the blood of a sacrifice is sprinkled on the altar on behalf of the people [C] **52:15** LXX reads *so many nations will marvel at Him* [D] **53:1** Or *believed our report* [E] **53:3** Lit *And like a hiding of faces from Him* [F] **53:6** Or *has placed on Him*; lit *with* [G] **53:8** Or *and as for His generation, who considered Him?*

53:9 Isaiah specifically prophesied that people would make the grave of the Servant **with the wicked,** and His death **with a rich man**. This was fulfilled in the death and unusual burial of Jesus: crucified between two criminals (Mk 15:27-28; Lk 23:32-33,39-41) and buried in the new rock-hewn tomb of the wealthy Sanhedrin member, Joseph of Arimathea (Mt 27:57-60; Mk 15:43-46; Lk 23:50-53; Jn 19:38-41). The suffering did *not* indicate God's condemnation. He died ignobly **although He had done no violence** (Hb *chamas*, "wrong"). With this passage Peter encourages believers to endure patiently their own suffering (1Pt 2:21-25).

53:10 Obedient to God's will, the Servant would be exalted after His suffering. According to God's design, the Servant became a **restitution offering** (Hb *ʾasham*, "guilt, trespass, sin offering"; see notes on vv. 7,8, and 9). The results of His perfect and acceptable offering would be **seed** (Hb *zeraʿ*, "offspring"; see notes on 6:9-13; 49:19-21; Jn 1:9-13; 1Pt 1:22-25; 1Jn 3:4-10). Jesus had no children while on earth, but by His death He opened the way for the adoption of all believers as children of God.

53:11 And although Jesus' life on earth was cut short, He would conquer that death and prolong His days—live forever—in the resurrection. Death would not be able to deprive Him of life. Success for the Servant was decreed; although there would be **anguish**, the Servant would **be satisfied with His knowledge**. The Servant was satisfied that His work was effective, and He would **justify many** by bearing **their iniquities** (Jn 11:51-52; Rm 3:21-26; 5:6-21; Heb 12:2; 1Jn 2:1-2; 4:9-10).

53:12 Just as the opening verse in this chapter was directly quoted as applying to Jesus, so also was the final verse. Jesus quoted from Is 53:12—"He was counted among the outlaws," indicating that the passage was to be fulfilled in Himself (Lk 22:37). Mark noted that prophecy was fulfilled as the Lord Jesus hung upon the cross between the two criminals (Mk 15:27-28). From the opening verse to the closing verse, Is 53 details the suffering and victory wrought by God's Servant, Jesus Christ. When Jesus, God incarnate, sinless and pure, purposefully bled and died in the place of sinners, **He bore the sin of many and interceded for the rebels**. His sacrifice was effective once and for all (Heb 7:25; 10:10), and redemption from sin is available to all who will believe (Ac 3:26; 1Co 15:3; 2Co 5:18-21; 1Pt 2:21, 24; Rv 1:5-6).

54:1-2 The response to the work of the Servant can only be jubilant celebration. The same joy Zion felt at

The Suffering Servant Revealed

The Suffering Servant (Isaiah 52–53)	The Lord Jesus (NT)
"He will be raised and lifted up and greatly exalted" (52:13).	Jn 3:14; 12:32-33; Php 2:8-9
"His appearance was so disfigured" (52:14).	Mt 26:67; 27:26,30; Lk 18:32-33
"He will sprinkle many nations" (52:15).	Heb 10:19-22; 12:24; 1Pt 1:2
"They will understand what they had not heard" (52:15).	Rm 15:20-21
"He was despised and rejected" (53:3).	Mk 8:31; Lk 9:22; 17:25; Jn 12:37-38
"He Himself bore our sicknesses, and He carried our pains" (53:4).	Mt 8:17; Rm 4:25; 1 Pt 2:24-25
"He was pierced because of our transgressions" (53:5).	Jn 19:34-37; Rv 1:7
"We are healed by His wounds" (53:5).	1Pt 2:24
"The Lord has punished Him for the iniquity of us all" (53:6; cp. vv. 10-12).	Rm 3:23-25; 2Co 5:21; 1Jn 2:2
"He did not open His mouth" (53:7).	Mt 26:63; 27:12-14; Mk 14:61; 15:5
"He was cut off from the land of the living" (53:8; cp. v. 12).	Mk 15:37-39; Lk 23:46; Rm 5:6-8; 14:9
"He had done no violence and had not spoken deceitfully" (53:9).	1Pt 2:21-22
"They made His grave with the wicked, and with a rich man at His death" (53:9).	Mt 27:38,57-60; Lk 23:33; Jn 19:38-41
"He will see His seed" (53:10).	Jn 1:12-13; 1 Jn 3:9; Ac 17:28-29
"He bore the sin of many" (53:12).	Jn 1:29; 1Co 15:3-4; Heb 9:28; 1Pt 2:24

He was struck because of
my people's rebellion.
9 They[A] made His grave
with the wicked
and with a rich man
at His death,
although He had done
no violence
and had not
spoken deceitfully.
10 Yet the LORD was pleased
to crush Him severely.[B]
When[C] You make Him
a •restitution offering,
He will see His •seed,
He will prolong His days,
and by His hand, the
LORD's pleasure
will be accomplished.
11 He will see it[D]
out of His anguish,
and He will be satisfied
with His knowledge.

[A]53:9 DSS; MT reads *He* [B]53:10 Or *Him; He made Him sick.* [C]53:10 Or *If* [D]53:11 DSS, LXX read *see light*

>WORD|*study*

54:1-2 The word for **childless** (Hb *'aqar*, "barren") occurs 12 times in the Old Testament (Gn 11:30; 25:21; 29:31; Ex 23:26; Dt 7:14 [2x]; Jdg 13:2-3; 1Sm 2:5; Jb 24:21; Ps 113:9; Is 54:1). Sarai, Rebekah, Rachel, Hannah, and the wife of Manoah (Samson's mother) are each described as barren at some stage in life. In each of these cases, the Lord intervened, enabling conception. Barrenness was one of the most powerful ways in which God intervened in people's lives, demonstrating His authority and sovereignty. He could seal a woman's womb and, when it suited His purpose, miraculously provide her with a child. Any couple who struggles with infertility knows the anguish and despair of barrenness; and those who have subsequently borne children know the overwhelming surprise and joy accompanying that extraordinary gift. The absence of life is suddenly replaced with life as God's work in miniature—bringing life where there was none (see **Hard Question**, p. 68.)

My righteous Servant
will justify many,
and He will carry
their iniquities.
12 Therefore I will give Him[A]
the many as a portion,
and He will receive[B]
the mighty as spoil,
because He submitted
Himself to death,
and was counted
among the rebels;
yet He bore the sin of many
and interceded
for the rebels.

The Covenant of Peace (54:1-17)

54 "Rejoice, childless one,
who did not give birth;
burst into song and shout,
you who have not been
in labor!
For the children
of the forsaken one
will be more
than the children
of the married woman,"
says the LORD.
2 "Enlarge the site of your tent,
and let your tent curtains
be stretched out;
do not hold back;
lengthen your ropes,
and drive your pegs deep.
3 For you will spread out
to the right and to the left,
and your descendants
will dispossess nations
and inhabit
the desolate cities.
4 "Do not be afraid,
for you will not
be put to shame;
don't be humiliated,
for you will not
be disgraced.
For you will forget the shame
of your youth,
and you will
no longer remember
the disgrace
of your widowhood.
5 Indeed, your husband is
your Maker—
His name is
•Yahweh of •Hosts—
and the Holy One of Israel is
your Redeemer;
He is called the God of all
the earth.
6 For the LORD has called you,
like a wife deserted
and wounded in spirit,
a wife of one's youth
when she is rejected,"
says your God.
7 "I deserted you
for a brief moment,
but I will take you back
with great compassion.
8 In a surge of anger
I hid My face from you
for a moment,
but I will have compassion
on you
with everlasting love,"
says the LORD your Redeemer.
9 "For this is like the days[C]
of Noah to Me:
when I swore that the waters
of Noah
would never flood
the earth again,
so I have sworn that I will not
be angry with you
or rebuke you.
10 Though the mountains move
and the hills shake,

the miraculous appearance of new children (49:20-21) is also found in chapter 54 at the abundant redemption accomplished by the Servant. Zion, portrayed here as the wife of Yahweh, is called **forsaken** and **childless** (Hb *'aqar*); through exile she had lost her children. She was told, **Enlarge the site of your tent** because the great number of children she would eventually have (i.e., they were going to return) would create the need for more living space (49:20).

54:3 Zion was promised that the Lord would provide **descendants** (Hb *zera'*, "offspring") who would re-settle the land. Following the exile, the Israelites born in Babylon would return to the land and **inhabit the desolate cities** (see notes on 49:19-21; 53:10). However, this was only the precursor to a greater fulfillment. Paul applied verse 1 of this passage to all the spiritual children of promise, those Jews and Gentiles who believed in Christ (Gl 3:26-29; 4:21-28).

54:4 Scholars suggest the **shame** of her **youth** was the time of slavery in Egypt, while **the disgrace of** her **widowhood** referred to the exile. Perhaps the shame included the time of Israel's disgraceful apostasy after entering a covenant relationship with Yahweh in the wilderness at the time of her youth (Ezk 16:4-43,58-63; Hs 2:2-23).

54:5-6 Israel's spiritual adultery led to the Lord's temporary rejection of her. His **wife** had cheated on Him, so He **deserted** and **rejected** her. Isaiah 50:1 made it clear that Zion was not divorced but temporarily set aside, and her people were sent into exile because of their sins. Zion's restoration was certain because of the character and nature of her faithful **husband** who was also her **Maker**.

54:7 The mighty God of Israel had the power and inclination to redeem the fallen nation. The good news was that the rejection was only **for a brief moment**. As prophesied later by Jeremiah, the Babylonian exile would last only 70 years (2Ch 36:21; Jr 25:11-12; 29:10), a relatively brief moment in the full span of time. Israel was assured there would be a time when the Lord would take back the remnant **with great compassion**, an undeserved kindness to this wayward spouse.

54:9-10 The character of God's commitment to the redeemed people was like the nature of the Noahic covenant following the destruction of the earth by the flood (Gn 9:12-17; see notes on Is 24:5-6). The Lord made an everlasting covenant never again to inundate the whole earth despite

[A]**53:12** Or *Him with* [B]**53:12** Or *receive with* [C]**54:9** DSS, Cairo Geniza; MT, LXX read *waters*

human wickedness. The new covenant through the Lord's redemptive work would be just as eternal. Though the **mountains** themselves would one day **be removed**, the **covenant of peace** (Hb *berit shalom*) would never cease (cp. Ezk 37:26).

54:11-12 With tenderness, God assured Jerusalem of a bright future; the Lord Himself would rebuild the city. The design of the city, especially in reference to the precious gems, recalls the New Jerusalem passages (Rv 21:10-21; see also Is 49:18; 52:1). The gems would be **set . . . in black mortar** (Hb *puk*, "antimony," a silvery grey mineral). The list of precious stones conveys the wealth and luxury of the city. There would be no poverty or lack; the city would abound in everything good and rich. Harking back to marriage imagery, the jewels could also indicate a restoration of favor toward the wife and her reinstatement as one who is loved and cherished (cp. Ezk 16:11-13).

54:13 The **children**, the inhabitants of the holy city, would be **taught by the Lord** (cp. 2:3; Jr 31:33-34; Mc 4:2; Jn 6:44-45). In this new relationship between God and His people, He will engage with His children, personally teaching them His ways.

54:14-17 In those days the city would be securely founded on **righteousness**. The final status of the city would be one of unqualified peace.

55:1 While chapter 54 celebrated the covenant of peace wrought by the Redeemer's work (chap. 53), chapter 55 marvels at the terms of the new covenant, which extends the call of repentance to everyone. Those responding positively will be granted the privilege of joining with God in an everlasting covenant. He extended the invitation to **everyone** [Hb *kol*, "all"] **who is thirsty**. In this case, thirst referred to a deep longing for spiritual fulfillment (Mt 5:6). The reference to **waters** affirms earlier passages concerning water supplied by God (see notes on Is 12:3-6; 43:16-21; 44:3-5). The summons was for those **without money**, without a means in themselves to meet their own need (41:17). They were encouraged to **buy wine and milk**, elements that represented the best of the land, symbolizing abundance.

55:2 In the context of Isaiah's day, the people had spent everything they had in vain, seeking satisfaction and deliverance apart from God. The end result led to exile. Yet God's call still extended to His people to return to Him for their sustenance. He would provide those who turned to Him for **the choicest of foods**. Jesus gave a

My love will not be removed
from you
and My covenant of peace
will not be shaken,"
says your compassionate
Lord.
11 "Poor Jerusalem, storm-
tossed, and not comforted,
I will set your stones
in black mortar,[A]
and lay your foundations
in sapphires.[B]
12 I will make
your fortifications[C]
out of rubies,
your gates out of
sparkling stones,
and all your walls out of
precious stones.
13 Then all your children
will be taught by the Lord,
their prosperity will be great,
14 and you will be established
on a foundation of
righteousness.
You will be far
from oppression,
you will certainly not
be afraid;
you will be far from terror,
it will certainly not
come near you.
15 If anyone attacks you,
it is not from Me;
whoever attacks you
will fall before you.
16 Look, I have created
the craftsman
who blows on
the charcoal fire
and produces
a weapon suitable
for its task;
and I have created
the destroyer
to cause havoc.
17 No weapon formed
against you will succeed,
and you will refute
any accusation[D]
raised against you in court.
This is the heritage
of the Lord's servants,
and their righteousness is
from Me."
This is
the Lord's declaration.

God's Everlasting Covenant (55:1–56:8)

55 "Come, everyone
who is thirsty,
come to the waters;
and you without money,
come, buy, and eat!
Come, buy wine and milk
without money
and without cost!
2 Why do you spend money
on what is not food,
and your wages on what
does not satisfy?
Listen carefully to Me, and eat
what is good,
and you will enjoy
the choicest of foods.[E]
3 Pay attention and come
to Me;
listen, so that you will live.
I will make
an everlasting covenant
with you,

[A]54:11 Lit *in antimony* [B]54:11 Or *lapis lazuli* [C]54:12 Lit *suns*; perhaps *shields*; Ps 84:11
[D]54:17 Lit *refute every tongue* [E]55:2 Lit *enjoy fatness*

>WORD|*study*

55:3 The phrase everlasting covenant (Hb *berit 'olam*) is found repeatedly in the Old Testament to describe various covenants. It first appears in reference to God's promise never again to destroy mankind and the whole earth by deluge (Gn 9:16; also Is 24:5). This phrase is also used to refer to the Abrahamic covenant concerning relationship, land, and offspring (Gn 17:7,13,19; also 1Ch 16:17; Ps 105:10); the observation of the Sabbath (Ex 31:16; Lv 24:8); and the promise to David to establish his house and throne forever (2Sm 23:5 regarding 2Sm 7:16; also Is 55:3). The everlasting promise of favor and relationship finds its final expression in the new covenant God promised to establish with His people following the work of Messiah (cp. 61:8; Jr 32:40; 50:5; Ezk 16:60; 37:26). This final new covenant would fulfill and complete all the earlier promises.

Paul used Is 55:3 in reference to Jesus' resurrection, never to see corruption, in order to provide forgiveness of sins for those who believe (Ac 13:32-38). Jesus would rule eternally on David's throne, fulfilling the covenantal promise to David of a perpetual heir on the throne (2Sm 7:16; Ps 89:28-29,34-36). Moreover, by His death and resurrection, Jesus enabled any who believed on Him to also participate in the covenant promises.

the promises assured
to David.
4 Since I have made him
a witness to the peoples,
a leader and commander
for the peoples,
5 so you will summon a nation
you do not know,
and nations who do not
know you will run to you.
For the LORD your God,
even the Holy One of Israel,
has glorified you."
6 Seek the LORD
while He may be found;
call to Him while He is near.
7 Let the wicked one abandon
his way
and the sinful one
his thoughts;
let him return to the LORD,
so He may have compassion
on him,
and to our God, for He will
freely forgive.
8 "For My thoughts are not
your thoughts,
and your ways are not
My ways."
This is
the LORD's declaration.
9 "For as heaven is higher
than earth,
so My ways are higher
than your ways,
and My thoughts
than your thoughts.
10 For just as rain and snow fall
from heaven
and do not return there
without saturating the earth
and making it germinate
and sprout,
and providing seed to sow
and food to eat,
11 so My word that comes
from My mouth
will not return to Me empty,
but it will accomplish
what I please
and will prosper
in what I send it to do."
12 You will indeed go out
with joy
and be peacefully guided;
the mountains and the hills
will break into singing
before you,
and all the trees of the field
will clap their hands.
13 Instead of the thornbush,
a cypress will come up,
and instead of the brier,
a myrtle will come up;
it will make a name
for •Yahweh
as an everlasting sign
that will not be destroyed.

56 This is what the LORD says:
Preserve justice and do
what is right,
for My salvation
is coming soon,
and My righteousness
will be revealed.
2 Happy is the man
who does this,
anyone who maintains this,
who keeps the Sabbath
without desecrating it,
and keeps his hand
from doing any evil.
3 No foreigner who has
joined himself to the LORD
should say,
"The LORD will exclude me
from His people";
and the eunuch
should not say,
"Look, I am a dried-up tree."
4 For the LORD says this:
"For the eunuchs who keep
My Sabbaths,
and choose what pleases Me,
and hold firmly
to My covenant,
5 I will give them, in My house
and within My walls,
a memorial and a name
better than sons
and daughters.
I will give each of them
an everlasting name
that will never be cut off.
6 And the foreigners who join
themselves to the LORD
minister to Him,
love the name of •Yahweh
and become His servants,
all who keep the Sabbath
without desecrating it
and who hold firmly
to My covenant—
7 I will bring them
to My holy mountain

similar invitation, linking the picture of the water and bread He provided to the free gift of eternal life, which He would give to those who believed in Him (Jn 4:10-14; Jn 6:27,32-58; Jn 7:37-38; Rv 21:6; 22:17).

55:3 The words of God give life (cp. Jn 6:63,68). Those responding to the invitation of the Lord would be participants in the **everlasting covenant** of God, which would include **the promises assured to David** (see **Doctrine:** "The Davidic Covenant," p. 378).

55:4-5 Scholars offer various suggestions about the identity of those mentioned here. Were the words about David, the Messiah, or the redeemed people? Certainly, the Messiah, the Lord Jesus, is the eternal and ideal Davidic Prince who bore witness before the world and draws people of all nations to Himself, thus exercising total rule (Dn 9:25; Jn 3:11,26-36; 12:32; Rv 1:5). However, the redeemed people would also serve as witnesses to God's wondrous work—first of the release from exile and second of the release from sin.

55:8-9 Sinners are called to imitate in their **ways** and **thoughts** the infinitely exalted **thoughts** and **ways** of God. In two beautiful chiastically arranged verses, God's sovereignty and transcendence are celebrated and held up for marvel.

55:13 Because God had spoken it, the provision of physical release from exile and spiritual release from the curse of sin was certain.

56:3-4 Strict guidelines determined who could enter into the assembly of the Lord (Dt 23:1,3,8). Eunuchs and certain foreigners were excluded. However, a startling and inclusive promise is now made to the foreigner and the eunuch who have **joined himself to the LORD** and kept His **covenant**.

56:5 God promised to establish eunuchs within His dwelling place and to provide them **a memorial** and posterity **better than sons and daughters**. A eunuch physically had no hope of siring offspring to perpetuate his name beyond death, which was vitally important in the ancient Near Eastern mind (2Sm 18:18). However, those who were redeemed would be given an **everlasting name that will never be cut off** (cp. Rv 3:5). This promise was especially meaningful for those from the Judean nobility who had been forcefully castrated during their captivity in Babylon (Is 39:7). The promise was that if they were faithful, though emasculated, they would not be cut off from God.

56:7 This verse rings out with the promise, **My house will be called a house of prayer for all nations** (cp. Mt 21:12-13; Mk 11:15-17; Lk 19:45-46).

56:10-12 The comparison of Israel's religious leaders to **blind watchmen, mute dogs** who love to lay around and **sleep,** and **shepherds** without **discernment** (cp. Jr 12:10; Ezk 34:1-10, 22-31; Mc 3:1-7; Zch 11:3-5) indicates the inability of the nation's prophets and priests to warn of the threat of judgment for covenantal violation.

57:3 In Is 1:2, the people were identified as children of the Lord who had rebelled. Now God identified them as the **sons of a sorceress** and the **offspring of an adulterer and a prostitute**.

57:4 By practicing sorcery and religious prostitution/ idolatry, they behaved as if they were sired by wicked parents, rejecting the upright teachings of the Lord.

57:10 Efforts to secure their future by attempting to communicate with the dead or other means of sorcery were in vain and took their toll; yet, they irrationally continued. They **did not say, "I give up"** (Hb *ya'ash*, "despair"), or "There is no hope" (KJV). Israel's spiritual leaders resorted to improper methods of divining the future to allay their fears rather than addressing the sin problem, calling for repentance, and relying on God alone for deliverance (Jr 23:16-22; note the contrasting messages of peace in Is 57:19,21).

57:11 Throughout Israel's history, God had shown by His acts that there was "no other" who could rival Him; yet the people denied their heritage and failed to remember or **fear** Him. During God's silence, they turned from Him to false gods. The thrust of God's questions to them is, who could possibly be greater and more worthy of fear than He? When He finally moved against them in judgment, they would find their devotion to false gods worthless (65:6-7).

57:13 God taunted, **let your collection of idols deliver you** (cp. v. 6; Dt 32:36-39). The idols were useless; nothing could deliver from the wrath of the Almighty God of the universe. In contrast, God would faithfully save those who trusted Him, and they alone would **inherit the land and possess** His **holy mountain** (cp. Is 65:8-9; Ac 26:17-18)—i.e., worship before Him in the temple.

and let them rejoice
in My house of prayer.
Their •burnt offerings
and sacrifices
will be acceptable on My altar,
for My house will be called
a house of prayer
for all nations."
8 This is the declaration
of the Lord God,
who gathers
the dispersed of Israel:
"I will gather to them
still others
besides those
already gathered."

Condemnation of the Wicked (56:9–57:21)

9 All you animals of the field
and forest,
come and eat!
10 Israel's[A] watchmen are blind,
all of them,
they know nothing;
all of them are mute dogs,
they cannot bark;
they dream, lie down,
and love to sleep.
11 These dogs have
fierce appetites;
they never have enough.
And they are shepherds
who have no discernment;
all of them turn
to their own way,
every last one
for his own gain.
12 "Come, let me get some wine,
let's guzzle some beer;
and tomorrow will be
like today,
only far better!"

57 The righteous one perishes,
and no one takes it to heart;
faithful men are swept away,
with no one realizing
that the righteous one
is swept away
from the presence[B] of evil.
2 He will enter into peace—
they will rest on their beds[C]—
everyone who lives uprightly.
3 But come here,
you sons of a sorceress,
offspring of an adulterer
and a prostitute![D]
4 Who is it you are mocking?
Who is it you are opening
your mouth
and sticking out
your tongue at?
Isn't it you,
you rebellious children,
you race of liars,
5 who burn with lust
among the oaks,
under every green tree,
who slaughter children
in the •wadis
below the clefts of the rocks?
6 Your portion is
among the smooth stones
of the wadi;
indeed, they are your lot.
You have even poured out
a •drink offering to them;
you have offered
a •grain offering;
should I be satisfied
with these?
7 You have placed your bed
on a high and lofty mountain;
you also went up there
to offer sacrifice.
8 You have set up
your memorial
behind the door and doorpost.
For away from Me,
you stripped,
went up, and made
your bed wide,
and you have made a bargain[E]
for yourself with them.
You have loved their bed;
you have gazed on
their genitals.[FG]
9 You went to the king with oil
and multiplied
your perfumes;
you sent your couriers
far away
and sent them down
even to •Sheol.
10 You became weary
on your many journeys,
but you did not say,
"I give up!"
You found a renewal
of your strength;[H]

[A]**56:10** Or *His*, or *Its* [B]**57:1** Or *away because* [C]**57:2** Either their deathbeds or their graves [D]**57:3** Lit *and she acted as a prostitute* [E]**57:8** Lit *you cut* [F]**57:8** Lit *hand* [G]**57:8** In Hb, the word hand is probably a euphemism for "genitals." [H]**57:10** Lit *found life of your hand*

therefore you did not
grow weak.
11 Who was it you dreaded
and feared,
so that you lied and didn't
remember Me
or take it to heart?
Have I not kept silent for such
a long time[A]
and you do not •fear Me?
12 I will expose
your righteousness,
and your works—
they will not profit you.
13 When you cry out,
let your collection of idols
deliver you!
The wind will carry
all of them off,
a breath will take them away.
But whoever takes refuge
in Me
will inherit the land
and possess
My holy mountain.
14 He said,
"Build it up, build it up,
prepare the way,
remove every obstacle
from My people's way."
15 For the High and Exalted One
who lives forever, whose name
is Holy says this:
"I live in a high
and holy place,
and with the oppressed
and lowly of spirit,
to revive the spirit
of the lowly
and revive the heart
of the oppressed.
16 For I will not
accuse you forever,
and I will not always be angry;
for then the spirit
would grow weak before Me,
even the breath of man,
which I have made.
17 Because of his sinful greed
I was angry,
so I struck him; I was angry
and hid;[B]
but he went on turning back
to the desires of his heart.
18 I have seen his ways,
but I will heal him;
I will lead him and
restore comfort
to him and his mourners,
19 creating words of praise."[C]
The LORD says,
"Peace, peace to the one
who is far or near,
and I will heal him.
20 But the wicked are
like the storm-tossed sea,
for it cannot be still,
and its waters churn up mire
and muck.
21 There is no peace
for the wicked,"
says my God.

True Fasting (58:1-14)

58 "Cry out loudly,[D]
don't hold back!
Raise your voice
like a trumpet.
Tell My people
their transgression
and the house of Jacob
their sins.
2 They seek Me day after day
and delight to know My ways,
like a nation that does
what is right
and does not abandon
the justice of their God.
They ask Me
for righteous judgments;
they delight in the nearness
of God."
3 "Why have we fasted,
but You have not seen?
We have denied ourselves,
but You haven't noticed!"[E]
"Look, you do as you please
on the day of your fast,
and oppress
all your workers.
4 You fast with contention
and strife
to strike viciously
with your fist.
You cannot fast
as you do today,
hoping to make your voice
heard on high.
5 Will the fast I choose
be like this:
A day for a person
to deny himself,
to bow his head like a reed,

57:14 For those who trusted God for deliverance, He would prepare their way so they might return physically from exile.

57:15-18 Though God is most exalted, in compassion He also makes His dwelling with those who are **oppressed** [Hb *dakka'*, "crushed, contrite"; 53:5] **and lowly of spirit** (cp. 1Co 3:11-17; 2Co 6:16; Eph 2:4-9,19-22). God would **revive** [Hb *chayah*, "preserve"] **the spirit of the lowly** and **the heart of the oppressed**. He will relent in His anger, so that His creatures would not become utterly discouraged and despair of their relationship with their Maker.

57:19 For all who would humble themselves and accept the way of the Lord's salvation, He would pronounce **peace, peace to the one who is far or near**, and He would heal them (53:5). The restoration of the people of Israel from the exile prefigures the restoration of those who would believe in Jesus Christ and thereby be rightly related to God (Eph 2:13-18). The future restoration from sin would include both the "near" Jews and the "far" Gentiles; all who confess Christ would be brought near to God.

57:20-21 In contrast to the comfort provided the repentant (v. 2), the rebellious were again warned, **There is no peace for the wicked** (cp. 48:22).

58:1 Isaiah was told to **cry out loudly** with a **voice like a trumpet**, in contradistinction to the "mute" watchmen of Israel (56:10).

58:3-4 Although the people felt justified in their own eyes by their spiritual practices, God pointed out the hypocrisy of their Sabbath worship and their ritualistic fasts. On the surface the people appeared spiritual, but their actions were hollow because they lacked inward repentance. Still they expected God to respond favorably to them just because they **fasted** and **denied** themselves. The main thrust of the accusation is aimed at the rulers of the land, who would have had the power to "oppress" those under them.

58:5-6 The ideal fast does not consist exclusively of abasing or making oneself miserable (i.e., of abject and pious self-denial) but required accompanying social justice. Israel was to end oppression (cp. v. 9), which may have consisted of the unjust enslavement of their brothers or of abuse of legal slaves through a disregard of the Sabbath laws or other laws concerning servants (Ex 20:9-10; 21:1-11,26-27; 23:12; Lv 25:39-43; Dt 15:12-18; Jr 34:8-11).

A **57:11** LXX reads *And I, when I see you, I pass by* B **57:17** Lit *him; hiding and I am angry* C **57:19** Lit *creating fruit of the lips* D **58:1** Lit *with throat* E **58:3** These are Israel's words to God.

58:7-8 Israel was to provide for **the poor** (vv. 7,10a) by generously sharing food, shelter, and clothing with those in need (Ex 22:22-27; Lv 25:35-38; Dt 15:7-11). The same concern is repeated in the New Testament (Mt 25:33-46; Jms 2:15-16; 1Jn 3:16-19).

God indicated that if Israel would show signs of true self-denial by providing for their needy brothers, then **their light will appear like the dawn**. He would heal them and provide ongoing protection. Their righteousness would precede them and **the Lord's glory** would be their **rear guard** (see note on 52:12).

58:11-12 Not all would respond in obedience to the Lord, but those who did would have the blessing of God's presence and provision. Some would participate in the restoration of the **ancient ruins**. The redeemed remnant who returned to Jerusalem from the exile were able to see the restoration of the old city wall to some extent (Neh 6:15). In the future, there will be a greater restoration of Zion as the called-out remnant of the children of Israel are a part of the rebuilding of "the fallen booth of David" (Am 9:11-12; Ac 15:14-17).

58:13-14 In response to the people's faithful observance of the Sabbath, the Lord would cause the people to prevail and **enjoy the heritage of** their **father Jacob** (i.e., their land, Dt 32:9-14).

59:1-2 When the people questioned why God had failed to answer their prayers (58:3), Isaiah reaffirmed that **the Lord's hand is not too short** [Hb *qatsar*, "ineffective, powerless"] **to save** (cp. v. 16; 50:2), nor was **His ear** unable to hear. Instead, the people's sins had **built barriers** [Hb *badal*, "to divide, separate"] **between** the Israelites and God (cp. 1:15). God purposefully refused to respond to the sin-laden people due to their lack of repentance.

59:3-6 The indictment of being **defiled with blood** graphically conveyed the people's unclean status. They had willfully shed innocent blood in the land (Nm 35:33-34; Is 1:15,21; Jr 2:30,34; Lm 4:13-14; Ezk 7:23; Hs 4:2). Lying and injustice also were singled out as offenses—sins that were linked with oppression through the court system. The imagery of hatching **viper's eggs** and weaving **spider's webs** referred to wicked plotting that brought forth deadly results. Regardless of the intricacy of their schemes, ultimately the wicked would not prosper because **their works** were **sinful**.

59:7-8 Paul quoted these verses as part of his description of universal human sinfulness (cp. Rm 3:15-17). All people are separated from God by their sins

and to spread out •sackcloth
and ashes?
Will you call this a fast
and a day acceptable
to the LORD?
6 Isn't the fast I choose:
To break the chains
of wickedness,
to untie the ropes
of the yoke,
to set the oppressed free,
and to tear off every yoke?
7 Is it not to share your bread
with the hungry,
to bring the poor
and homeless
into your house,
to clothe the naked
when you see him,
and not to ignore[A]
your own flesh and blood?
8 Then your light will appear
like the dawn,
and your recovery
will come quickly.
Your righteousness will go
before you,
and the LORD's glory will be
your rear guard.
9 At that time, when you call,
the LORD will answer;
when you cry out, He will say,
'Here I am.'
If you get rid of the yoke
among you,[B]
the finger-pointing
and malicious speaking,
10 and if you offer yourself[C]
to the hungry,
and satisfy the afflicted one,
then your light will shine
in the darkness,
and your night will be
like noonday.
11 The LORD will always lead you,
satisfy you in a parched land,
and strengthen your bones.
You will be
like a watered garden
and like a spring
whose waters never run dry.
12 Some of you will rebuild
the ancient ruins;
you will restore
the foundations laid
long ago;[D]
you will be called the repairer
of broken walls,
the restorer of streets
where people live.
13 "If you keep from desecrating[E]
the Sabbath,
from doing whatever
you want on My holy day;
if you call the Sabbath
a delight,
and the holy day
of the LORD honorable;
if you honor it, not going
your own ways,
seeking your own pleasure,
or talking too much;[F]
14 then you will delight yourself
in the LORD,
and I will make you ride
over the heights of the land,
and let you enjoy the heritage
of your father Jacob."
For the mouth of the LORD
has spoken.

Sin and Redemption (59:1–21)

59 Indeed, the LORD's hand is not
too short to save,
and His ear is not too deaf
to hear.
2 But your iniquities
have built barriers
between you and your God,
and your sins have made Him
hide His face from you
so that He does not listen.
3 For your hands are defiled
with blood
and your fingers,
with iniquity;
your lips have spoken lies,
and your tongues
mutter injustice.
4 No one makes claims justly;
no one pleads honestly.
They trust in empty
and worthless words;
they conceive trouble
and give birth to iniquity.
5 They hatch viper's eggs
and weave spider's webs.
Whoever eats their eggs
will die;
crack one open, and a viper
is hatched.

[A]**58:7** Lit *not hide yourself from* [B]**58:9** Lit *yoke from your midst* [C]**58:10** Some Hb mss, LXX, Syr read *offer your bread* [D]**58:12** Lit *foundations generation and generation* [E]**58:13** Lit *keep your foot from* [F]**58:13** Lit *or speak a word*

6 Their webs cannot
become clothing,
and they cannot
cover themselves
with their works.
Their works are sinful works,
and violent acts are
in their hands.
7 Their feet run after evil,
and they rush to shed
innocent blood.
Their thoughts are
sinful thoughts;
ruin and wretchedness are
in their paths.
8 They have not known
the path of peace,
and there is no justice
in their ways.
They have made
their roads crooked;
no one who walks on them
will know peace.

9 Therefore justice is far
from us,
and righteousness does not
reach us.
We hope for light,
but there is darkness;
for brightness, but we live
in the night.
10 We grope along a wall
like the blind;
we grope like those
without eyes.
We stumble at noon
as though it were twilight;
we are like the dead
among those
who are healthy.
11 We all growl like bears
and moan like doves.
We hope for justice,
but there is none;
for salvation, but it is
far from us.
12 For our transgressions
have multiplied before You,
and our sins testify
against us.
For our transgressions are
with us,
and we know our iniquities:
13 transgression and deception
against the LORD,
turning away from following
our God,
speaking oppression
and revolt,
conceiving and uttering
lying words from the heart.
14 Justice is turned back,
and righteousness stands
far off.
For truth has stumbled
in the public square,
and honesty cannot enter.
15 Truth is missing,
and whoever turns from evil
is plundered.

The LORD saw that there was
no justice,
and He was offended.
16 He saw that there was
no man—
He was amazed that there was
no one interceding;
so His own arm
brought salvation,
and His own righteousness
supported Him.
17 He put on righteousness
like a breastplate,
and a helmet of salvation
on His head;
He put on garments
of vengeance for clothing,
and He wrapped Himself
in zeal as in a cloak.
18 So He will repay according to
their deeds:
fury to His enemies,
retribution to His foes,
and He will repay
the coastlands.
19 They will •fear the name
of •Yahweh in the west
and His glory in the east;
for He will come
like a rushing stream

>WORD|*study*

59:17 God wrapped Himself in zeal (Hb *qin'ah*, "ardour, jealousy"). The masculine noun form appears six times and only in relation to God's intense desire for the devotion of Israel (e.g., Ex 20:5). The feminine form used here, however, conveys an intense feeling of desire and is often found in reference to jealousy in a marital situation, or as an expression of one's passion for God or against an enemy. It also conveys God's passionate commitment to save the redeemed and/or to punish the wicked (Is 42:13-16; Zch 1:14-17; 8:2).

(cp. Rm 3:23). The prophet assured the people of Israel that any who followed such wicked **paths** would not **know peace** (cp. Is 48:22; 57:21). The idea of an unrighteous "path" seems to be appropriated from wisdom literature and the teaching of the "two ways": the way of wisdom and life, and the way of foolishness and death (cp. Ps 1; Pr 1:10-19; 2:1-22). There will be no **peace** for a person who chooses to walk in a lifestyle of rebellion from God's ways.

59:9-10 Isaiah identified with His people, resulting in a corporate admission of guilt. He continued with a sincere confession, which deliberately began with language relating back to the covenantal curses (Dt 28:28-29). Sin has resulted in a people who are spiritually blinded despite having God's revelation through the covenant.

59:11 The imagery of growling **bears** and moaning **doves** conveyed both the irritation and despondency of a frustrated people. Isaiah mournfully acknowledged the guilt of His people in rebelling against God.

59:13-15a Rejection of God's laws always leads to social injustice and depravity. When there is no truth in **the heart**, societal consequences follow. Without an absolute moral standard founded in the righteousness of the almighty God, morality is abandoned, ultimately causing **justice** to be **turned back** and **righteousness** to be inhibited. In such a society, one who repents of evil and tries to follow God's moral guidelines is **plundered** by the rebellious.

59:15b-16 The message of hope to the truly repentant was that God **saw that there was no justice, and He was offended**. Because of His deep compassion for human beings who were given over to sin and helpless, He Himself made a way for reconciliation to occur (57:18-19), since there was no one to mediate or intercede for them. God provided salvation by Himself, through **His own arm** (cp. 40:10; 51:9; 52:10; 53:1, 10-12).

59:17 The Lord clothed Himself with His own **righteousness like a breastplate** and placed **a helmet of salvation on His head**. The military imagery conveys the sense of the power and intent of God to provide the promised salvation for His people as well as to cause the overthrow of His enemies. Paul later used the same imagery to describe how believers should behave (Eph 6:14,17; 1Th 5:8-9).

59:18-19 At the time of His choosing, the Lord would **repay** (Hb *shalam*) His enemies **according to their deeds** (Hb *gemulah*; cp. 65:6-7; Rm 6:23; Rv 20:12-15).

59:20-21 Verses 20-21 are quoted by Paul in reference to the final salvation of Israel (Rm 11:26-27). This passage is also similar to the promise of a new covenant made in Jeremiah: God would write His law upon the hearts of His people (Jr 31:33; Heb 8:10; 10:16). The inscription of the law upon the heart is accomplished through the ministry of the Holy **Spirit** in a believer's life. God does not redeem His people and then forget about them; He redeems them and sends His Spirit to indwell them, to teach them. Here is the fuller explanation of "your children will be taught by the Lord" (54:13).

60:1–66:24 In the final chapters of Isaiah, the themes initiated at the end of chapter 59 concerning salvation and vengeance are further developed.

60:1 Chapters 60 through 63:14 celebrate the glorious reversal of darkness addressed in chapter 59.

60:2 From the outset, the prophet seems to look further than the immediate restoration of Israel from the Babylonian captivity. There is a global cast to the phrasing regarding the darkness of **earth** and all **the peoples**.

60:3 Not only will the redeemed of Israel experience God's light, but also **nations will come** to the **light** and participate in the final glory of Zion. The source of the light is the Redeemer who will shine upon the redeemed of Zion, who in turn will reflect His glory.

60:5 Ultimately **the wealth of the nations** will stream to Zion. In the time foretold, even nations normally hostile to Israel would praise the Lord and find acceptance before Him (56:7-8).

60:6-7 The nations of **Midian**, **Ephah**, and **Sheba** were all descended from Abraham through Keturah, whom he married after Sarah died (cp. Gn 25:1-4; see Is 9:4; 10:26). **Kedar** and **Nebaioth** were descendants of Ishmael, Abraham's son by Hagar, Sarah's Egyptian slave (cp. Gn 25:12-13). Originally, these other sons of Abraham were excluded from the covenant and blessing bestowed upon Isaac (Gn 17:18-21; 25:5-6). Nevertheless, the time would come when they and all the nations would again bring gifts as they had done in the time of Solomon, and even their **praises**, offerings, sacrifices, and prayers would be acceptable before the Lord.

60:10 The prophecy uttered here was fulfilled by Cyrus and the provisions he made for the freed exiles. (Ezr 1:4,6-11; 6:3-5).

60:11 Once the walls of Jerusalem had been restored following the exile, they

driven by the wind
of the LORD.
20 "The Redeemer will come
to •Zion,
and to those
in Jacob who turn
from transgression."
This is
the LORD's declaration.

21 "As for Me, this is My covenant with
them," says the LORD: "My Spirit who is
on you, and My words that I have put
in your mouth, will not depart from
your mouth, or from the mouth of
your children, or from the mouth of
your children's children, from now on
and forever," says the LORD.

God's Glory in Zion (60:1-22)

60 Arise, shine, for your light
has come,
and the glory
of the LORD shines
over you.[A]
2 For look, darkness
covers the earth,
and total darkness
the peoples;
but the LORD will shine
over you,
and His glory will appear
over you.
3 Nations will come
to your light,
and kings to the brightness
of your radiance.
4 Raise your eyes
and look around:
they all gather and come
to you;
your sons will come
from far away,
and your daughters
will be carried on the hip.
5 Then you will see
and be radiant,
and your heart will tremble
and rejoice,[B]
because the riches of the sea
will become yours
and the wealth of the nations
will come to you.
6 Caravans of camels will cover
your land[C]—
young camels of Midian
and Ephah—
all of them will come
from Sheba.
They will carry gold
and frankincense
and proclaim the praises
of the LORD.
7 All the flocks of Kedar
will be gathered to you;
the rams of Nebaioth
will serve you
and go up on My altar
as an acceptable sacrifice.
I will glorify
My beautiful house.
8 Who are these who fly
like a cloud,
like doves to their shelters?
9 Yes, the islands will wait
for Me
with the ships of Tarshish
in the lead,
to bring your children
from far away,
their silver and gold
with them,
for the honor of the LORD
your God,
the Holy One of Israel,
who has glorified you.
10 Foreigners will build up
your walls,
and their kings will serve you.
Although I struck you
in My wrath,
yet I will show mercy to you
with My favor.
11 Your gates will always
be open;
they will never be shut
day or night
so that the wealth
of the nations
may be brought into you,
with their kings being led
in procession.
12 For the nation
and the kingdom
that will not serve
you will perish;
those nations
will be annihilated.
13 The glory of Lebanon
will come to you—
its pine, fir,
and cypress together—
to beautify the place
of My sanctuary,

[A]60:1 = Jerusalem [B]60:5 Lit *expand* [C]60:6 Lit *cover you*

and I will glorify
My dwelling place.[A]
14 The sons of your oppressors
will come and bow down
to you;
all who reviled you
will fall facedown
at your feet.
They will call you the City
of the LORD,
•Zion of the Holy One
of Israel.
15 Instead of your being deserted
and hated,
with no one passing through,
I will make you an object
of eternal pride,
a joy from age to age.
16 You will nurse on the milk
of nations,
and nurse at the breast
of kings;
you will know that I, •Yahweh,
am your Savior
and Redeemer,
the Mighty One of Jacob.
17 I will bring gold
instead of bronze;
I will bring silver
instead of iron,
bronze instead of wood,
and iron instead of stones.
I will appoint peace
as your guard
and righteousness
as your ruler.
18 Violence will never again
be heard of in your land;
devastation and destruction
will be gone
from your borders.
But you will name
your walls salvation
and your gates, praise.
19 The sun will no longer be
your light by day,
and the brightness
of the moon will not shine
on you;
but the LORD will be
your everlasting light,
and your God will be
your splendor.
20 Your sun will no longer set,
and your moon will not fade;
for the LORD will be
your everlasting light,
and the days of your sorrow
will be over.
21 Then all your people
will be righteous;
they will possess
the land forever;
they are the branch
I planted,
the work of My[B] hands,
so that I may be glorified.
22 The least will become
a thousand,
the smallest a mighty nation.
I am Yahweh;
I will accomplish it quickly
in its time.

Year of Favor (61:1-11)

61 The Spirit of the Lord GOD is
on Me,
because the LORD
has anointed Me
to bring good news
to the poor.
He has sent Me to heal[C]
the brokenhearted,
to proclaim liberty
to the captives
and freedom
to the prisoners;
2 to proclaim the year
of the LORD's favor,
and the day
of our God's vengeance;
to comfort all who mourn,
3 to provide for those
who mourn in •Zion;
to give them a crown
of beauty instead of ashes,
festive oil
instead of mourning,

[A]**60:13** Lit *glorify the place of My feet* [B]**60:21** LXX, DSS read *His* [C]**61:1** Lit *bind up*

>WORD|*study*

61:1 He would heal [Hb *chavash*, "bind up"] the brokenhearted (Hb *shavar*). The Servant was "to bind" their hearts, which are figuratively conveyed as being broken. The Hebrew verb *chavash* carries a concept of healing in addition to the general sense of just tying something together. The purpose of the binding is to facilitate healing. This healing could be emotional healing or the healing for one who is broken and contrite over sin.

were carefully guarded and shut tightly at night (Neh 7:1-3). By contrast, in the city Isaiah describes, the **gates will always be open; they will never be shut day or night**.

60:17-18 The new city would be resplendent with the best of things—**gold**, **silver**, **bronze**, and **iron** would be common. Unlike the restored city of Jerusalem, which was again destroyed in A.D. 70 by the Romans, following the exile the future land of Zion under the Lord's reign would never again face **violence** (Hb *chamas*, v. 18; cp. 53:9), devastation, or destruction. The city would be protected by **salvation** (Hb *yeshu'ah*) and **praise** in the promised kingdom (26:1-3).

60:20-21 This appears to find its final fulfillment in the glorious future city of the New Jerusalem where God "will wipe away every tear" (Rv 21:4) and only the righteous will be present (Is 65:17-19; Rv 21:27). God's promise to Abraham will be complete; for Abraham's descendants, those redeemed by the Messiah, **will possess the land forever** (Gn 12:7; 13:15).

61:1-3 Jesus read this text on a Sabbath in his synagogue in Nazareth (Lk 4:16-30) The picture of the Spirit of God resting upon the Servant carries the understanding that the Servant is being enabled to accomplish specific tasks (see notes on Is 42:1; 48:16). The Servant notes that the Spirit rests upon Him because He has been **anointed** (Hb *mashach*) for a specific task. The conjunction **because** carries with it the idea of "purpose or intention." In the Old Testament, the language of being "anointed" was used in connection with the prophetic (1Kg 19:16), priestly (Nm 35:25), and kingly (1Sm 16:13; 2Sm 2:4) offices. In this passage, it seems the Servant's anointing serves a prophetic function as His specific task is to **bring good news** [Hb *basar*; see **Word Study**, p. 910] **to the poor**. The specific aspects of the good news are outlined in the following lines.

The captives could include the physically captive (e.g., slaves) as well as the spiritually captive (e.g., the demon-possessed). The phrase "to proclaim liberty" is used elsewhere in conjunction with the Jubilee Year, when slaves were set free according to the law (49:9; Lv 25:10; Jr. 34:8,15,17). The **freedom** He proclaimed **to prisoners** could mean being literally released from bondage and also carries the concept of coming from darkness to light. The year of the **LORD's favor** (Hb *ratson*; cp. 49:8) refers back to the Year of Jubilee, while the **day of our God's vengeance** refers to a future judgment, elsewhere called the "Day of the LORD." The juxtaposition of deliverance and vengeance is not unusual (cp. chap. 2; 59:17-18; 63:3-6).

The vengeance will be carried out quickly, but the Lord's favor will endure.

The ones **who mourn** refers to those who mourned due to their spiritual condition and the condition of **Zion**. The Servant would transform their mourning to joy, giving **them a crown of beauty** (Hb *pe'ēr*, "turban, tiara, garland worn on the head"; cp. 61:10) **instead of ashes** (Hb *'ēpher*); a word play on these two items emphasizes the exchange being made. In times of mourning the head was customarily covered with ashes (Jb 2:8, 12); the opposite, then, was a beautiful headdress covering (Ezk 24:17). **Festive oil** would replace the ashes upon their heads, indicating blessing and rejoicing. Also the mourners would be given **splendid clothes** (Hb *ma'atēh tehillah*, more literally "garment" or "mantle of praise") **instead of despair** (Hb *ruach kēheh*, "dim, faint spirit").

61:9 The resulting redemption and restoration of Israel culminates in the nations' acknowledgement of Israel's relationship with the Lord and the blessings flowing from that relationship. Israel will be unique, and the source of her blessings will be properly seen as coming from her relationship with the Lord.

61:11 The Servant relates his confidence in the fruit of His labors by a comparison to the predictability of an earthly harvest. The phrase, **so the Lord God will cause righteousness and praise to spring up**, emphasizes the fact that God is responsible for the increase. The words "righteousness and praise" (cp. v. 3) represent the spiritual harvest that can only happen by God's bestowal through the Servant. The increase of fruit will bear testimony to the nations of God's power and faithful compassion.

62:1 The speaker in these verses may be the Servant of chapter 61, expressing His commitment to Jerusalem; or it might be the prophet expressing his devotion to Zion. Having received God's glorious plan for the city of Jerusalem and her inhabitants, he longed for God to hasten the fulfillment of His plans for Jerusalem's **salvation** (2Pt 2:11-13; Ti 2:11-14; Rv 22:20).

62:2-3 In the day of Zion's transformation, her **righteousness** and **glory** will be seen by all. At that time, the Lord will call Zion **by a new name**, and she will **be a glorious crown in the Lord's hand** (see 28:5; Zch 9:16).

62:4 Names were extremely important in the Old Testament, often reflecting the character of the individual or the circumstance. Zion's new name would reflect her redeemed status. She would

>WORD|*study*

61:10 Using bridal language, the Servant links His being covered with salvation and righteousness to the picture of a bridegroom wearing his **turban** (Hb *pe'ēr*, "headdress"). The same word is translated as "splendid clothes," connoting beauty, joy, and ornamentation (61:3). This fairly rare word was also used to describe the headdress worn by the priests (Ex 39:28; Ezk 44:18), which seems like an apt connection because of the unique wording used for how the bridegroom **wears** (Hb *cahan*, "to act as a priest") the head covering (Is 61:10). "Wears" is linked with the word for "priest" (Hb *kohēn*). The verb is used elsewhere only in connection with the priestly office.

and splendid clothes
instead of despair.[A]
And they will be called
righteous trees,
planted by the LORD
to glorify Him.

4 They will rebuild
the ancient ruins;
they will restore
the former devastations;
they will renew
the ruined cities,
the devastations
of many generations.
5 Strangers will stand and feed
your flocks,
and foreigners will
be your plowmen
and vinedressers.
6 But you will be called
the LORD's priests;
they will speak of you
as ministers of our God;
you will eat the wealth
of the nations,
and you will boast
in their riches.
7 Because your shame
was double,
and they cried out,
"Disgrace is their portion,"
therefore, they will possess
double in their land,
and eternal joy will be theirs.

8 For I •Yahweh love justice;
I hate robbery and injustice;[B]
I will faithfully reward them
and make
an everlasting covenant
with them.
9 Their descendants
will be known
among the nations,
and their posterity
among the peoples.
All who see them
will recognize
that they are a people
the LORD has blessed.

10 I greatly rejoice in the LORD,
I exult in my God;
for He has clothed me
with the garments
of salvation
and wrapped me in a robe
of righteousness,
as a groom wears a turban
and as a bride adorns herself
with her jewels.
11 For as the earth produces
its growth,
and as a garden enables
what is sown to spring up,
so the Lord GOD
will cause righteousness
and praise
to spring up
before all the nations.

Restoration of Zion (62:1-12)

62 I will not keep silent
because of •Zion,
and I will not keep still
because of Jerusalem,
until her righteousness
shines like a bright light
and her salvation,
like a flaming torch.
2 Nations will see
your righteousness
and all kings, your glory.
You will be called
by a new name
that the LORD's mouth
will announce.
3 You will be a glorious crown
in the LORD's hand,
and a royal diadem
in the palm of your God.
4 You will no longer
be called Deserted,

[A]61:3 Lit *a dim spirit* [B]61:8 Some Hb mss, DSS, LXX, Syr, Tg, Vg; other Hb mss read *robbery with a burnt offering*

The Redeemed City of God: New Names

"The Righteous City, a Faithful City"	Is 1:26
"My Delight is in Her" and her land called "Married"	Is 62:4
"Cared For" and "A City Not Deserted"	Is 62:12
"Yahweh Our Righteousness"	Jr 33:16
"Yahweh is There"	Ezk 48:35
"The Faithful City, the mountain of the LORD of Hosts, and the Holy Mountain"	Zch 8:3

and your land will not
be called Desolate;
instead, you will be called
My Delight is in Her,[A]
and your land Married;[B]
for the LORD delights in you,
and your land will be married.
5 For as a young man marries
a young woman,
so your sons will marry you;
and as a groom rejoices[C]
over his bride,
so your God will rejoice
over you.

6 Jerusalem,
I have appointed watchmen
on your walls;
they will never be silent,
day or night.
There is no rest for you,
who remind the LORD.
7 Do not give Him rest
until He establishes
and makes Jerusalem
the praise of the earth.

8 The LORD has sworn
with His right hand
and His strong arm:
I will no longer give
your grain
to your enemies for food,
and foreigners will not drink
your new wine
you have labored for.
9 For those who gather grain
will eat it
and praise the LORD,
and those who harvest
the grapes will drink
the wine
in My holy courts.
10 Go out, go out
through the gates;
prepare a way for the people!
Build it up, build up
the highway;
clear away the stones!
Raise a banner
for the peoples.
11 Look, the LORD
has proclaimed
to the ends of the earth,
"Say to Daughter Zion:
Look, your salvation
is coming,
His reward is with Him,
and His gifts
accompany Him."
12 And they will be called[D]
the Holy People,
the LORD's Redeemed;
and you will be called
Cared For,
A City Not Deserted.

The Vengeance of the Lord (63:1-6)

63 Who is this coming
from Edom
in crimson-stained garments
from Bozrah—
this One who is splendid
in His apparel,
rising up proudly[E]
in His great might?

[A]62:4 Or *Hephzibah* [B]62:4 Or *Beulah* [C]62:5 Lit *and the rejoicing of the groom* [D]62:12 Lit *will call them* [E]63:1 Syr, Vg read *apparel, striding forward*

no longer be named **Deserted** or **Desolate**, for the Lord would restore to the city its inhabitants, drawing her back to Himself with faithful love. Isaiah noted she **will be called My Delight is in Her** (Hb *chephtsi-bah*), and the land would be called **Married** (Hb *be'ulah*). These names indicate the restoration of Zion's intimate relationship with the Lord (54:4-8).

62:5 Bridal language is used to reflect God's rejoicing over Zion (see note on 54:5-6; Hs 2:19-20). The joyous return from exile and the reestablishment of the people in the land prefigures the restoration of redeemed Zion at the end of time. Bridal imagery is specifically applied to the relationship between Christ and His bride, the redeemed, "holy Jerusalem" (Rv 19:7-9; 21:2, 9-10; cp. also Eph 5:24-32). Additionally, the imagery of a bridegroom was specifically applied to Jesus (Mt 9:15; 25:1-13; Mk 2:19-20; Lk 5:34-35; Jn 3:28-29).

62:8-9 The certain hope of the prophet is that God's promises are reliable. For **The LORD** swearing an oath **with His right hand and His strong arm** (see note on 51:9; cp. Heb 6:13).

62:10-11 As in 57:14, the authoritative call went out to prepare a way for the people. The **banner** connects the passage to 49:22, in which the Lord promised Zion He would initiate the return of her people by raising His "banner to the peoples."

62:12 The designation of Israel as **the Holy People, the LORD's Redeemed** invokes the background of the Sinai covenant when God told the people if they obeyed Him and kept His covenant, He would make them "My kingdom of priests and My holy nation" (Ex 19:5; see notes on Is 61:1-3; 1Pt 2:4-10). The sanctified people of the Lord would inhabit the transformed city of Zion. Two additional names for the future city: **Cared For** (often translated "sought out" from the Hebrew passive participle form of *darash*, "seek") and **A City Not Deserted** emphasize the final reversal of their current state ("Deserted" and "Desolate," Is 62:4).

63:1 Throughout Isaiah, the idea of salvation for the remnant is interwoven with the image of God's vengeance (1:24-28; 34:8; 35:4; 59:17-18; 61:1-3). **Edom**, a nation whose people descended from Esau, was located southeast of Judah. Edom may represent all nations who scorned the rule of the Lord and His people (Gn 25:24, 30-34; see note on Is 34:5). God had previously prophesied Edom's destruction as a part of His greater judgment against all nations, which accompanied salvation for the remnant (Is 34:1-5; 35:4). God is vividly and majestically attired **in crimson-stained garments**, coming from **Bozrah**, a main city of **Edom** (Hb *'edom*, "red").

63:2 The metaphor of trampling grapes in a **winepress** describes judgment upon the nations. A winepress consisted of a simple flat surface, generally either of hewn rock or a construction of mortared stones upon which ripe grapes were crushed, causing the juice to flow through a channel into waiting containers. The practice of treading a winepress required that a person literally tread upon the grapes, destroying them in the process and staining anything in contact with the juice.

Using this image, God graphically showed Isaiah how He **alone** would finally pour out His **anger** and **fury** against the nations.

This passage is often understood as ultimately fulfilled in the final outpouring of God's wrath in the last days (Lk 21:20-28, 36; Rv 14:14-20). Specifically, the Lord Jesus, wearing "a robe stained with blood . . . . will also trample the winepress of the fierce anger of God, the Almighty" (Rv 19:11-16).

63:7 Isaiah's hymn of praise blends into a lament concerning the condition of Israel and culminates in a confession of sin and prayer for God to have mercy. God's actions with Israel proceeded primarily from His **faithful love** (Hb *chesed*; see **Word Study**, p. 322) and **compassion**, not from anything Israel had done. The word *chesed* is central to the verse as well as fundamental to God's relationship with Israel.

63:8 Through His covenant, God established Israel as His **people** and **children who will not be disloyal** (Lv 26:12; Dt 29:13), and out of divine compassion, **He became their Savior**. This verse and the succeeding verses refer to Israel's exodus from Egypt.

63:9 The Angel of His Presence (Hb *panim*, "face") refers to the physical manifestation of God's presence (Ex 33:14).

63:10-11 Though the people had seen God's deliverance, they still **rebelled** and **grieved** (Hb *'atsav*, "vex") **His Holy Spirit** (Ps 78:40-42; Eph 4:30). The exact phrase **Holy Spirit** is rare in the Old Testament, occurring only here and in Ps 51:11. The rebellion began as the people wandered in the wilderness and continued throughout their history in the land (e.g., Ex 16:4, 20, 27-28). Even in the wilderness the Israelites experienced the wrath of God (Ex 32:35; Nm 16:30-35, 45-48; 21:6-7) as God **became their enemy** (cp. 1:24; Lv 26:14-39; Dt 32:23-25; Jr

>WORD|*study*

63:2 Scripture insists that vengeance (Hb *naqam*, "righting a wrong, bringing about a just and righteous punishment") belongs to the Lord (Dt 32:35). In the majority of the passages containing this word, God brings the vengeance against a variety of offenders from Israel herself to the heathen nations (Lv 26:25; Dt 32:41, 43; Ps 58:10; Mc 5:15). The noun *naqam* is used six times in Isaiah, and the verb form only appears once in the first chapter (Is 1:24; 34:8; 35:4; 47:3; 59:17; 61:2; 63:4). In every case in Isaiah, God is the agent of vengeance. Except for its use in 1:24, each reference in Isaiah deals with vengeance taken upon the enemies of Israel, a frequent accompaniment to the salvation of the remnant.

It is I,
proclaiming vindication,[A]
powerful to save.

2 Why are Your clothes red,
and Your garments like one
who treads a winepress?

3 I trampled
the winepress alone,
and no one from the nations
was with Me.
I trampled them in My anger
and ground them underfoot
in My fury;
their blood spattered
My garments,
and all My clothes
were stained.

4 For I planned the day
of vengeance,[B]
and the year
of My redemption[C] came.

5 I looked, but there was no one
to help,
and I was amazed
that no one assisted;
so My arm accomplished
victory for Me,
and My wrath assisted Me.

6 I crushed nations
in My anger;
I made them drunk
with My wrath
and poured out their blood
on the ground.

Remembrance and Repentance (63:7–64:12)

7 I will make known
the LORD's faithful love
and the LORD's
praiseworthy acts,
because of all the LORD
has done for us—
even the many good things
He has done for the house
of Israel
and has done for them
based on His compassion
and the abundance of
His faithful love.

8 He said, "They are indeed
My people,
children who will not
be disloyal,"
and He became their Savior.

9 In all their suffering,
He suffered,[D]
and the Angel of His Presence
saved them.
He redeemed them
because of His love
and compassion;
He lifted them up
and carried them
all the days of the past.

10 But they rebelled
and grieved His Holy Spirit.
So He became their enemy
and fought against them.

11 Then He[E] remembered
the days of the past,
the days of Moses
and his people.
Where is He who
brought them out of the sea
with the shepherds[F]
of His flock?
Where is He who
put His Holy Spirit
among the flock?

12 He sent His glorious arm
to be at Moses' right hand,
divided the waters
before them
to obtain eternal fame
for Himself,

13 and led them
through the depths
like a horse in the wilderness,
so that they did not stumble.

[A]63:1 Or *righteousness* [B]63:4 Lit *For day of vengeance in My heart* [C]63:4 Or *blood revenge*
[D]63:9 Alt Hb tradition reads *did not suffer* [E]63:11 Or *he*, or *they* [F]63:11 LXX, Tg, Syr read *shepherd*

>WORD|*study*

64:5-6 The prophet recognized that the people's best actions were like a **polluted** [Hb *ʿiddah,* "menstruation"] **garment**, thereby ruling out any possibility of their acceptance by God. The pieces of cloth or undergarments used by a menstruating woman would have been treated as "unclean" both in the sense of being permanently soiled (no amount of washing could make them suitable for any other use) and in the sense of ritual impurity (see Lv 15:19-33). The comparison of "best" in one category to the concrete image of "worst" in another makes the desperate situation of the sinner unmistakable—there is no hope of achieving God's standard of perfect righteousness (cp. Ps 14:1-3; Rm 3:10-12). True righteousness comes from God alone (see notes on Is 54:14-17; cp. Eph 4:24; Php 3:9).

14 Like cattle that go down
into the valley,
the Spirit of the LORD
gave them[A] rest.
You led Your people this way
to make a glorious name
for Yourself.
15 Look down from heaven
and see
from Your lofty
home—holy and beautiful.
Where is Your zeal
and Your might?
Your yearning[B]
and Your compassion
are withheld from me.
16 Yet You are our Father,
even though Abraham
does not know us
and Israel doesn't
recognize us.
You, •Yahweh, are
our Father;
from ancient times,
Your name is our Redeemer.
17 Why, Yahweh, do
You make us stray
from Your ways?
You harden our hearts
so we do not •fear[C] You.
Return, because of
Your servants,
the tribes of Your heritage.
18 Your holy people
had a possession[D]
for a little while,
but our enemies
have trampled down
Your sanctuary.
19 We have become like those
You never ruled over,
like those not called
by Your name.

64 [E]If only You would tear
the heavens open
and come down,
so that mountains
would quake
at Your presence—
2[F] as fire kindles
the brushwood,
and fire causes water
to boil—
to make Your name known
to Your enemies,
so that nations will tremble
at Your presence!
3 When You did
awesome works
that we did not expect,
You came down,
and the mountains quaked
at Your presence.
4 From ancient times no one
has heard,
no one has listened,
no eye has seen any God
except You,
who acts on behalf of the one
who waits for Him.
5 You welcome the one
who joyfully does
what is right;
they remember You
in Your ways.
But we have sinned, and You
were angry.
How can we be saved if we
remain in our sins?[G]
6 All of us have become
like something •unclean,
and all our righteous acts are
like a polluted[H] garment;
all of us wither like a leaf,
and our iniquities carry us
away like the wind.
7 No one calls on Your name,
striving to take hold of You.
For You have hidden
Your face from us

[A] **63:14** Lit *him* [B] **63:15** Lit *The agitation of Your inward parts* [C] **63:17** Lit *our heart from fearing*
[D] **63:18** Or *Your people possessed Your holy place* [E] **64:1** Is 63:19b in Hb [F] **64:2** Is 64:1 in Hb
[G] **64:5** Lit *angry; in them continually and we will be saved*; Hb obscure [H] **64:6** Lit *menstrual*

30:14-15). Whenever they rebelled, they placed themselves in line for a fulfillment of the covenantal curses: God **fought against them** (Pss 78:17-64; 106:7-48).

63:17 Isaiah found his call difficult because he prophesied to a people who would not listen, and he knew that his message would even **harden hearts** (see notes on 6:9-13). Isaiah asked, **Why, LORD, do You make us stray from Your ways?** God did harden the people's hearts, but the people were responsible for their own actions. When people initially harden their hearts against God, there comes a point when God abandons them to their rebellion and further hardens their hearts so that repentance is no longer possible (Rm 1).

64:1-2 Isaiah continued His prayerful lament to the Lord by again reflecting upon the greatness of God's revelation in the past and His mighty deeds. The prophet longed for God to **come down** and exercise His power on behalf of Israel so the enemies of God would be rebuked and **tremble** at God's **presence**. The imagery of quaking mountains and fire is a reminder of God's encounter with Israel at Mount Sinai (Ex 19:16-20; 20:18-21).

64:3 At that key point in Israel's history God revealed His mighty power in a very personal way to the children of Israel, through the smoke and flames on Mount Sinai. He had also shown His presence by His **awesome works**.

64:4 Isaiah affirmed again that God was unique; He is all-powerful, transcendent, and invisible, but reveals Himself to **the one who waits for Him** (cp. 45:5-6,14,18,21; 46:9; Dt 32:39; 1Co 2:9).

64:5-6 God accepts **the one who joyfully does what is right**. Representing His people, Isaiah fully recognized and confessed **we have sinned** (Ec 7:20).

64:7 The picture Isaiah painted was one of total depravity, a complete enslavement to sin. The phrase, **No one calls on Your name,** resonates with the Apostle Paul, who emphasized the sinfulness of all Jews and Gentiles alike (cp. Rm 3:9-24; Pss 14:1-3; 53:1-3).

64:8-9 Again, Isaiah repeated, **You are our Father** (cp. 63:16).

65:1–66:24 Isaiah had confessed the sins of his people and interceded for them before God (63:15–64:12). Isaiah needed reassurance, as would the people, that God would have mercy and restore them. In chapters 65–66, the Lord provided a reply that elevated Isaiah's perspective beyond the relatively near fate of Israel alone and included promises regarding the final culmination of God's plans for all people, both faithful and unfaithful.

65:1 God's response to Isaiah's prayer affirms a new work that God would do among the nations.

65:2 Repeating a theme initiated in the opening verses of the book of Isaiah, the Lord once again addressed Israel as a **rebellious people** (1:2-5).

65:3 The sins the Lord highlighted revolved around improper worship and hypocrisy. **Sacrificing in gardens** and **burning incense on bricks** were illegitimate ways to worship Yahweh, even if the people asserted they were only worshiping the God of Israel. Once the Solomonic temple had been built, sacrifices were to be performed exclusively at the temple (Dt 12:2-5,11-14; 1Kg 8:29; 9:3), and altars were to be made of earth or unhewn stone (Ex 20:24-25; Dt 27:5-6). In addition, religious practices in gardens were often pagan and tantamount to blatant idolatry (see notes on Is 1:27-31; 65:11-12).

65:4 Sitting among the graves may refer to the pagan practice of consulting the dead regarding the future (see note on 8:19-22; also see notes on 57:10; Dt 18:21-22). Eating **the meat of pigs** and the **polluted broth** refer to pagan practices that are unknown to us. In addition, even the foods themselves were forbidden (Lv 11:7-8). The people "dedicated" and "purified" themselves to participate in these unholy practices (Is 66:17).

65:5 From the depths of self-deception, the people hypocritically saw themselves as **too holy** for others, failing to see the corruption within. Such actions inflamed the righteous wrath of the holy God of Israel.

65:6 Isaiah ended his prayer in chapter 64 with the question, "Will You keep silent and afflict severely" (64:12). God responded, No, He would **not keep silent but** He would **repay** [Hb *shalam*, more literally "repay into their bosom/lap"; cp. 59:18-20; Dt 32:35] **them fully**.

65:9 The Lord noted He would spare a cluster of grapes for the sake of **My**

and made us melt
because of[A,B] our iniquity.
8 Yet LORD, You are our Father;
we are the clay, and You are
our potter;
we all are the work
of Your hands.
9 LORD, do not be terribly angry
or remember
our iniquity forever.
Please look—all of us are
Your people!
10 Your holy cities have become
a wilderness;
•Zion has become
a wilderness,
Jerusalem a desolation.
11 Our holy
and beautiful[C] temple,
where our fathers
praised You,
has been burned with fire,
and all that was dear to us lies
in ruins.
12 LORD, after all this, will You
restrain Yourself?
Will You keep silent
and afflict severely?

God's Discipline and Redemption of a Remnant (65:1-25)

65 "I was sought by those
who did not ask;[D]
I was found by those
who did not seek Me.
I said: Here I am, here I am,
to a nation that was not called
by[E] My name.
2 I spread out My hands
all day long
to a rebellious people
who walk in the wrong path,
following their own thoughts.
3 These people
continually provoke Me
to My face,
sacrificing in gardens,
burning incense on bricks,
4 sitting among the graves,
spending nights
in secret places,
eating the meat of pigs,
and putting polluted broth
in their bowls.[F]
5 They say, 'Keep to yourself,
don't come near me, for I am
too holy for you!'
These practices are smoke
in My nostrils,
a fire that burns all day long.
6 It is written before Me:
I will not keep silent,
but I will repay;
I will repay them fully[G]
7 for your iniquities
and the iniquities
of your[H] fathers together,"
says the LORD.
"Because they burned incense
on the mountains
and reproached Me
on the hills,
I will reward them fully[I]
for their former deeds."

8 The LORD says this:

As the new wine is found
in a bunch of grapes,
and one says,
'Don't destroy it,
for there's some good[J] in it,'
so I will act because of
My servants
and not destroy them all.
9 I will produce descendants
from Jacob,
and heirs to My mountains
from Judah;
My chosen ones
will possess it,
and My servants
will dwell there.
10 Sharon will be a pasture
for flocks,
and the Valley of Achor
a place for cattle
to lie down,
for My people
who have sought Me.
11 But you who abandon
the LORD,
who forget My holy mountain,
who prepare a table
for Fortune
and fill bowls of mixed wine
for Destiny,[K]

[A]64:7 LXX, Syr, Vg, Tg read *and delivered us into the hand of* [B]64:7 Lit *melt by the hand* [C]64:11 Or *glorious*; Is 60:7 [D]65:1 LXX, Syr, DSS, Tg read *ask for Me* [E]65:1 LXX, Syr, DSS, Tg, Vg read *that did not call on* [F]65:3-4 These vv. describe pagan worship. [G]65:6 Lit *repay into their lap* [H]65:7 LXX, Syr read *for their iniquities and the iniquities of their* [I]65:7 Lit *reward into their lap* [J]65:8 Or *there's a blessing* [K]65:11 Pagan gods

12 I will destine you
for the sword,
and all of you will kneel down
to be slaughtered,
because I called
and you did not answer,
I spoke and you did not hear;
you did what was evil
in My sight
and chose what I did not
delight in.

13 Therefore, this is what the Lord
God says:

My servants will eat,
but you will be hungry;
My servants will drink,
but you will be thirsty;
My servants will rejoice,
but you will be put to shame.
14 My servants will shout for joy
from a glad heart,
but you will cry out
from an anguished heart,
and you will lament out of
a broken spirit.
15 You will leave
your name behind
as a curse for My chosen ones,
and the Lord God will kill you;
but He will give His servants
another name.
16 Whoever is blessed in the land
will be blessed by the God
of truth,
and whoever swears
in the land
will swear by the God
of truth.
For the former troubles
will be forgotten
and hidden from My sight.

17 "For I will create
a new heaven
and a new earth;
the past events will not
be remembered or come
to mind.
18 Then be glad
and rejoice forever
in what I am creating;
for I will create Jerusalem
to be a joy
and its people to be a delight.
19 I will rejoice in Jerusalem
and be glad in My people.
The sound of weeping
and crying
will no longer be heard in her.
20 In her, a nursing infant
will no longer live
only a few days,[A]
or an old man not live out
his days.
Indeed, the youth will die
at a hundred years,
and the one who misses
a hundred years
will be cursed.
21 People will build houses
and live in them;
they will plant vineyards
and eat their fruit.
22 They will not build
and others live in them;
they will not plant
and others eat.
For My people's lives will be
like the lifetime of a tree.
My chosen ones
will fully enjoy
the work of their hands.
23 They will not labor
without success
or bear children destined
for disaster,
for they will be a people
blessed by the Lord
along with their descendants.
24 Even before they call,
I will answer;
while they are still speaking,
I will hear.
25 The wolf and the lamb
will feed together,[B]
and the lion will eat straw
like the ox,
but the serpent's food
will be dust!
They will not do what is evil
or destroy
on My entire holy mountain,"
says the Lord.

The Final Judgment and Establishment of Worship (66:1-24)

66 This is what the Lord says:

Heaven is My throne,
and earth is My footstool.
What house could you
possibly build for Me?

servants (Hb *'eved*). The masculine plural form of *'eved* suggests the remnant of Israel. On the identity of **My chosen ones** and **My servants**, some argue the passage discusses only the rescue from exile of Jacob's biological descendants, so that the passage's primary meaning was fulfilled with the nation's post-exilic restoration. Others maintain that the passage refers additionally to both the physical descendants of Jacob and those mentioned in verse 1 who also "sought" and "found" the Lord (see note on 14:1-2).

65:10 These servants will inherit the land originally promised from **Sharon** (north and west extending from Carmel to Joppa) to the **Valley of Achor** spanning the southeast in the vicinity of Jericho north of Jerusalem (Ezk 47:21-23). Scholars suggest the mention of Sharon and Achor stands symbolically for the whole land.

65:25 The curse will be reversed from the natural realm. The instincts of predators will be reversed, bringing peace even into the realm of nature (see note on 11:6-9). Even though the natural realm is transformed, dust will remain **the serpent's food** (Gn 3:14). There will be peace in God's **entire holy mountain** (Is 11:9; Mc 4:3). The realities initiated for the people of God in the millennial reign will be carried through to the creation of the new heavens and earth. All the expectations of redemption will culminate in the final promise in the book of Revelation: "There will no longer be any curse" (Rv 22:3).

66:1-24 This final chapter concludes the Lord's response to Isaiah and brings together the major themes developed from the opening chapter throughout the book. God emphasized His transcendence and detailed what type of person He would accept as opposed to those He would treat as enemies. The dual themes of salvation for the remnant and judgment for the rebellious are central to this chapter as they are to the entire book.

66:1 God declared, **Heaven is My throne, and earth is My footstool** (Mt 5:34-35). The ark and the temple were referenced at times as the footstool of God (1Ch 28:2; Pss 99:5; 132:7). Isaiah had mourned the destruction of the temple, which was seen as God's house (Is 63:18; 64:11); yet, God reminded His people of the truth of His utter transcendence. He cannot be contained by any man-made structure although He condescended to fill the temple of Jerusalem with His presence (1Kg 8:27; 9:3; cp. Ac 7:44-50).

[A] **65:20** Lit *her, no longer infant of days* [B] **65:25** Lit *as one*

66:2 The type of person pleasing to God **is humble** (Hb *'ani*, "poor, afflicted;" cp. 29:19; 61:1). The adjective *'ani* can describe those who are poor, oppressed, or humble. The word describes a person who recognizes his own deep need (Pss 25:16,18; 40:17; 70:5; 86:1; 109:22) and who sees himself as dependent upon the great mercy of God, trusting Him to deliver (Is 41:17; Jms 4:8-10).

One . . . who trembles is a phrase connected with the concept of real fear (Jdg 7:3; 1Sm 4:13). As the proverb aptly states, "The fear of the Lord is the beginning of wisdom" (Ps 111:10; Pr 1:7; 9:10). A proper fear of God consists of awe and reverence that affects how you treat His **word** and commands (Ezr 9:4; 10:3; Is 66:2,5). The words of God are never to be treated lightly or disregarded.

66:3 The Lord described the actions of those who rebelled against Him. The exact meaning of the series of eight participles is uncertain. On a straight literal translation of the text, the series could be an indictment of religious syncretism. **One slaughters an ox, one kills a man** may indicate the people were following the rituals prescribed by God while at the same time participating in pagan practices (1:29; 2:6-8). The participle phrase, "one [who] kills a man" may refer to killing in a cultic context, in the sense of human sacrifice. Both **dogs** and **swine** were considered unclean, and the practices mentioned probably had to do with pagan rituals (Dt 14:8; Is 57:6; 65:4; 66:17).

66:7-9 The childbirth metaphor is most often used to convey the pain and difficulty of labor (Ps 48:6; Is 13:8; 21:3-4; 26:17-18; 37:3; 42:14; Jr 4:31; Hs 13:13; Mc 4:9-10; Jn 16:19-21; 1Th 5:3; Rv 12:2,5). In this case, the entire event is surprising; the birth takes place before **labor** and **pain**. The event described happened suddenly and abnormally. This unnatural birth appears to be related to the children unexpectedly given to Zion after the period of her estrangement (see notes on Is 54:1-2; 62:4-5; Gl 4:21-31).

66:10-11 The returning exiles would come home to their mother, Jerusalem, who had borne them (v. 7) and would nourish them **from her glorious breasts**. The maternal imagery of comfort at the mother's bosom extends to all believing Jews and Gentiles, who together would constitute Zion's new offspring (7:14; 49:21; 53:10; 54:1-3; Mc 5:3; Gl 3:28-29). Those who were a part of the new nation God raised up for Himself would **rejoice** in Jerusalem's restoration. The final Jerusalem is once again the New Jerusalem of the last days, which is to be populated by the redeemed from all nations.

>WORD|*study*

66:2 The adjective of this phrase, submissive in spirit (Hb *nekēh-ruach*, "stricken" or "broken of spirit") is only used two other times in the Old Testament (2Sm 4:4; 9:3). In both the references in 2 Samuel, the phrase conveys brokenness with regard to the feet (i.e., lameness) of Mephibosheth. A similar expression, "broken in heart" (Hb *nik'ēh lēvav*) appears in the Psalms parallel to *'ani* (Ps 109:16). In Is 66:2, the phrase probably conveys the sense of being broken over your spiritual state. Brokenness over sin precedes repentance (Jl 2:12-13; 2Co 7:9-10).

And what place could be
My home?
2 My hand made
all these things,
and so they all came
into being.
This is
the LORD's declaration.
I will look favorably
on this kind of person:
one who is humble,
submissive[A] in spirit,
and trembles at My word.
3 One slaughters an ox,
one kills a man;
one sacrifices a lamb,
one breaks a dog's neck;
one offers a •grain offering,
one offers pig's blood;
one offers incense, one praises
an idol—
all these have chosen
their ways
and delight
in their detestable practices.
4 So I will choose
their punishment,
and I will bring on them
what they dread
because I called
and no one answered;
I spoke and they didn't hear;
they did what was evil
in My sight
and chose
what I didn't delight in.

5 You who tremble at His word,
hear the word of the LORD:
"Your brothers who hate
and exclude you
because of Me have said,
'Let the LORD be glorified
so that we can see your joy!'
But they will be
put to shame."
6 A sound of uproar
from the city!
A voice from the temple—
the voice of the LORD,
paying back His enemies
what they deserve!

7 Before •Zion was in labor,
she gave birth;
before she was in pain,
she delivered a boy.
8 Who has heard of such a thing?
Who has seen such things?
Can a land be born in one day
or a nation be delivered
in an instant?
Yet as soon as Zion was
in labor,
she gave birth to her sons.
9 "Will I bring a baby
to the point of birth
and not deliver it?"
says the LORD;
"or will I who deliver,
close the womb?"
says your God.
10 Be glad for Jerusalem
and rejoice over her,
all who love her.
Rejoice greatly with her,
all who mourn over her—
11 so that you may nurse
and be satisfied
from her comforting breast
and drink deeply
and delight yourselves
from her glorious breasts.

12 For this is what the LORD says:

I will make peace flow to her
like a river,
and the wealth[B] of nations
like a flood;
you will nurse and be carried
on her hip
and bounced on her lap.
13 As a mother comforts her son,
so I will comfort you,
and you will be comforted
in Jerusalem.

[A]66:2 Lit *broken* [B]66:12 Or *glory*

>WORD|*study*

66:18-19 The **survivors** (Hb *pelêtim*) gathered by the Lord will be sent "to the nations." The noun *palit* occurs 19 times in the Old Testament. It is overwhelmingly used in reference to those who do or do not survive a military conflict (Gn 14:13; Jos 8:22; 2Kg 9:15) and is often used specifically regarding a surviving Israelite or a remnant of Israelites (Ezk 6:8-9; 24:26-27; 33:21-22). At times the fate of the survivors of a conflict is still death (Jdg 12:4-6; Am 9:1; Ob 14). The word appears twice in Isaiah. The occurrence in Is 45:20 specifically refers to the "fugitives of the nations."

14 You will see, you will rejoice,
and you[A] will flourish
like grass;
then the LORD's power
will be revealed
to His servants,
but He will show His wrath
against His enemies.
15 Look, the LORD will come
with fire—
His chariots are
like the whirlwind—
to execute His anger with fury
and His rebuke with flames
of fire.
16 For the LORD
will execute judgment
on all flesh
with His fiery sword,
and many will be slain
by the LORD.

17 "Those who dedicate and purify themselves to enter the groves following their leader,[B] eating meat from pigs, vermin, and rats, will perish together."

This is
the LORD's declaration.
18 "Knowing[C] their works and their thoughts, I have come to gather all nations and languages; they will come and see My glory. 19 I will establish a sign among them, and I will send survivors from them to the nations—to Tarshish, Put,[D] Lud (who are archers), Tubal, Javan, and the islands far away—who have not heard of My fame or seen My glory. And they will proclaim My glory among
the nations. 20 They will bring all your brothers from all the nations as a gift to the LORD on horses and chariots, in litters, and on mules and camels, to My holy mountain Jerusalem," says the LORD, "just as the Israelites bring an offering in a •clean vessel to the house of the LORD. 21 I will also take
some of them as priests and Levites," says the LORD.

22 "For just as the new heavens
and the new earth,
which I will make,
will endure before Me"—
this is
the LORD's declaration—
"so your offspring
and your name will endure.
23 All mankind will come
to worship Me
from one New Moon
to another
and from one Sabbath
to another,"
says the LORD.

24 "As they leave, they will see the dead bodies of the men who have rebelled against Me; for their worm will never die, their fire will never go out, and they will be a horror to all mankind."

[A]66:14 Lit *your bones* [B]66:17 Hb obscure [C]66:18 LXX, Syr; MT omits *Knowing* [D]66:19 LXX; MT reads *Pul*

66:15 In that day, **the LORD will come with fire** to execute wrath against His foes (see 29:6). This passage bears a clear similarity to the vision John had of Christ's return when He would slay the rebellious nations with "a sharp sword" (Rv 19:11-15,21).

66:17 When the Lord comes with judgment, all those who had participated in pagan worship (entering **groves** for idolatrous prostitution, and polluting themselves through the consumption of unclean **meat**) **will perish together** (see notes on 65:3-4. The same themes raised initially in 1:27-31 regarding salvation for God's people find their consummation concurrently with the destruction of the rebellious in 66:14-17.

66:22 The new heavens and earth will be eternal just as the redeemed **offspring** and their **name** will **endure** (see notes on 53:10 and 55:13; Rv 22:3-5). In this new world, all those who live will come to worship God (Rv 15:4).

66:23 In contrast to the rejection of worship as first portrayed in Isaiah 1, the worship of the redeemed people offered **from one New Moon to another, and from one Sabbath to another** would be accepted by the Lord God for eternity (see note on 1:11-14). This glorious depiction of the future culmination of all the Lord's plans for His people is amplified by descriptions in the book of Revelation. The Lord will dwell with the people He has redeemed, and they will faithfully serve and joyfully reign with Him forever (Rv 22:5).

66:24 Tragically, there will be people from every nation and language who reject God's call to salvation (Is 45:22). For these, the end of judgment will be that **their fire will never go out** (cp. 1:31; Mk 9:43-48), possibly a description of the Valley of Hinnom. Unforgiven sin will lead to eternal punishment in the lake of fire (Rv 20:10-15). For those who die without trusting in God's provision for their sin, there will be no hope (Rm 6:23).

ISAIAH… WRITTEN ON MY *Heart*

Isaiah contains a wealth of spiritual riches. Two major themes prevail, and they are themes to take to heart. There is a personal and particular aspect of Isaiah, as well as global or missiological import. The personal aspect has to do with the individual. Although Israel and Judah are addressed as a nation, they are often treated as a corporate individual, like God's son Jacob or God's youthful wife Jerusalem. The nation was composed of thousands of individuals, but this literary treatment is a reminder that each person individually is responsible for sin before God, and each person is responsible to keep covenant faith with God. The covenant with God is not composed primarily of ritual; rather, the ritual symbolizes and flows gladly out of a heart of love and a passionate commitment to God. "Cheating" via idolatry is not tolerated, is deemed unacceptable, and is punishable by abandonment to the consequences of your own sinful choices. There is forgiveness and restoration after punishment, however, because other aspects of the divine covenant include compassion and mercy, taking back the erring partner.

Jeremiah

Timeline	621 BC	605 BC	594–593 BC	586 BC
World Events Biblical Events	Consultation with Huldah the prophetess (2Kg 22:13-20)	Nebuchadnezzar's defeat of the Egyptians at the Battle of Carchemish	Delivery of the scroll of Jeremiah's prophecies to Babylon (Jr 51:59-64)	Destruction of Jerusalem (Jr 39 and 52)

"This is the covenant I will make with the house of Israel after those days. . . . I will put my teaching within them and write it on their hearts. I will be their God and they will be My people" (31:33).

Who wrote Jeremiah?

Jeremiah of Anathoth is the accepted author of the book bearing his name (Jr 1:1). Anathoth was a small town in the territory of Benjamin, about 5 miles northeast of Jerusalem. He was from the priestly family of Hilkiah (1Kg 2:26-27).

Who were the recipients?

The recipients were chiefly the people of Judah. Jeremiah addressed himself to those who dwelt in Jerusalem, as well as to a group who had already been deported to Babylon.

When was Jeremiah written?

The dates of the prophecies found in this book encompass the years 627–586 B.C., the time of Jeremiah's ministry. Some scholars believe Jeremiah began writing down his prophecies around 605 B.C. His final messages were probably delivered around 585–82 B.C.

Where did it happen?

The events of Jeremiah's life and ministry took place in Judah, in and around Jerusalem. The superpowers of the day vied for control of the ancient Near East in a time of political and military turmoil. Assyria, which had dominated the region since the eighth century B.C., felt its hold weakening on its vassal and tributary kingdoms such as Egypt, Judah, and Chaldea, all of which believed the time was ripe to throw off the cruel Assyrian yoke. In about 612 B.C., the Babylonians dealt a final blow to the Assyrian Empire. From then on, they and the Egyptians were the largest powers in the area. Egypt had oppressed Judah as its vassal, and King Josiah decided to ride out against Pharaoh Neco at the Battle of Megiddo in 609 B.C., but he failed and was killed by Neco.

In addition to the geographical, political, and historical setting, there is a spiritual setting. Jeremiah's ministry unfolded against the backdrop of King Josiah's sweeping religious reform, prompted by the discovery of the book of the law (Deuteronomy) found in the temple by one of Josiah's priests in 621 B.C. Josiah saw that the people fell far short of God's requirements for holy living; and after consulting with the priests and the prophetess Huldah (2Ch 34:22-28), he took the drastic measures delineated in 2Kg 23:4-15. Tragically, Josiah's successors did not follow in their father's footsteps and instead led the people back into idolatry, eventually precipitating the Babylonian exile—the ultimate covenant curse.

What is Jeremiah about?

- *The new covenant of the heart.* Unlike what the Mosaic covenant had become, the new covenant would be written on the heart rather than in stone. A person's relationship with God must be internal and relationship-based, not external and ritual-based.
- *Call to repentance.* Jeremiah uses variations of the word indicating "turning" back or "returning" (Hb *shuv*) to God more than any other OT prophet. Thoroughgoing repentance is essential to the maintenance of the new covenant.
- *Sovereignty of God.* Through His prophet, God's will for the nation's "uprooting and tearing down" (destruction) as well as its "building and planting" (reconstruction) would be revealed. The theme also applies to the surrounding nations, not solely to Judah, as God is sovereign over *all* nations.
- *Powerful nature of the words of God.* God's words revealed to and through the prophet are powerful, vital, active, certain, and reliable.

Why should women read Jeremiah?

This book deals with the final punishment for idolatry and other sins stemming from it. Sin is the pervasive problem of humanity for men and women alike. Some interesting passages include the prophecy of Rachel weeping for her children; the prophetic warnings against idolatry aimed specifically at women (wives and mothers); and clues to understanding women's religious roles within their own households in Judah, and also more broadly in the ancient Near East. Although women, together with children, are often portrayed as victims of political, economic, military, and religious ferment, apparently Jeremiah did hold women in Judah accountable for some of the nation's religious decline into idolatry, especially with regard to the domestic sphere where they wielded substantial influence (Jr 7:18; 44:15-25).

A further reason to read this book is to know the heart of God. God is loving and patient. He wants to have a heart relationship with you, not an outward relationship of religious formalities and platitudes. While God is longsuffering and warns continuously of sin's consequences, He will nevertheless punish His children if they do not repent of sin and return to God for forgiveness and restoration.

How do you read Jeremiah?

Jeremiah's book is of the prophetic genre, so over half the book is written in a kind of lyrical poetry. Jeremiah was known as the "weeping prophet," since both his prophecy and his life were fraught with tragedy and heartbreak. The book carries themes of both prophecy and poetry. Prophetic aspects not only involve the prediction of the future of Jerusalem and other nations but also boldly speak forth an unpopular message from the Lord to the powerful rulers of his day. Much of the prophetic material consists of warnings to return to the Lord wholeheartedly. Poetic features include a vast panoply

586 BC	582 BC	568–567 BC	539 BC
Gedaliah's governorship	Jeremiah's escape to Egypt	Invasion of Egypt by Nebuchadnezzar	Daniel's reading of the prophecy of Jeremiah concerning the 70-year exile (Dn 9:2; Jr 25:11-13; 29:10)

of metaphors, word images, parallelisms, word plays, fervent prayers, and anguished laments. There are also many narrative chapters, which usually involve going somewhere or encountering someone in order to do (sign-act) or say (oracle) something prophetic, so that narrative and prophecy are constantly interrelated. One may also approach the book of Jeremiah in terms of a collection of "books," not expected to be read in chronological order.

Jeremiah opens with the prophet's call to ministry by the Lord, followed by about 18 chapters detailing Judah's sins against God, as well as warnings of punishment and constant pleas for repentance. Some have labeled chapters 11–20 the "Confessions" of Jeremiah, passages which provide insight into Jeremiah's inner anguish over his nation's unrepentant attitude, and also over his own rejection as a prophet of the Lord. A brief narrative section (chaps. 20–21) displays a prophetic "show-down," followed by several more prophetic chapters (22–25). Chapters 26–29 provide yet another brief narrative, again containing a prophetic "show-down," giving way to the unfurling of God's blueprint for a new covenant of the heart. Seemingly these chapters (20–29) might be grouped as a more specifically prophetic section, the two "showdowns" functioning parenthetically around the prophetic warning material. Chapters 30–33 are known as the "Book of Consolation" and reveal God's heart of compassion and forgiveness toward His people. As noted in this "Book," however, God's love does not preclude punishment for sin. Following the new covenant material are 12 chapters of narrative, which indicate clearly to the reader that Judah is indeed headed for exile and will certainly bear the consequences of violating their covenant with Yahweh through idolatry. Consistent with Jeremiah's appointment as a prophet "over nations and kingdoms" (Jr 1:10), he rounds out his book with a group of prophecies known as the "Oracles against the Nations" (chaps. 46–51), warning of destruction (and sometimes restoration) of surrounding nations and world powers, whom God judges for their sins, thus demonstrating that God is sovereign over *all* nations and kingdoms, not just Judah. The final tragic chapter details Jerusalem's ultimate capitulation to the Babylonian siege.

If you were to identify a crucial passage for understanding the Gospel, it would have to be the Book of Consolation (Jr 30–33). In the midst of prophetic warnings, accusations, and predictions of dire national consequences, God reveals through Jeremiah that His fervent love for His people is sure. Although the Jews had the written law of Moses, they benefited from very little since it was not allowed to penetrate their hearts: Their obedience to God came from obligation rather than as an outflow of a love relationship. Although Judah broke covenant faith, God maintains and even extends His love through a new covenant work. This work is of an internal nature. God's word will one day be written on their hearts, and they will know God from within rather than only from without (Jr 31:31-34). This promise culminates in the saving ministry of Jesus, who is the Mediator of this new covenant (Rm 11:27; Heb 8:8-13; 10:16-17), inaugurating it through His atoning sacrifice (Lk 22:20). Extending the impact of this salvific achievement of God to the church, Paul writes in 2 Corinthians 3 that he is a minister of the new covenant in his preaching of the Gospel, and also that believers must live a "new covenant" life of holiness as ones who are set apart for and in relationship with the Lord (2Co 6). Finally, the Book of Consolation also contains a number of Messianic prophecies concerning a Davidic "Righteous Branch," who will one day rule over the united and restored house of Israel and will shepherd them in righteousness (23:5; 30:9,21; 33:15-22).

Outline

- I. Jeremiah's Call and Commission (1:1-19)
  - A. Jeremiah's Pedigree and Divine Call (1:1-8)
  - B. The Prophet's Visions Confirming His Commission (1:9-15)
  - C. The Lord's Equipping of the Prophet for the Task (1:16-19)
- II. The Lord's Warnings and Judgment on Judah (2:1–25:38)
  - A. God's Lawsuit Against Israel (2:1-37)
  - B. The People's Apostasy and the Prophet's Call to Repentance (3:1–4:4)
  - C. The Warnings and Threats of Coming Judgment (4:5–7:34)
  - D. Jeremiah's Lamentation over the People's Doom (8:1–10:25)
  - E. The Punishment for Violation of the Covenant (11:1–12:17)
  - F. The Consequences of Apostasy (13:1–15:9)
  - G. Jeremiah's Complaint and Rebuke (15:10-21)
  - H. Jeremiah's Loneliness and the Nation's Devastation and Hope (16:1-21)
  - I. The Sin and Punishment of Judah (17:1-27)
  - J. The Lessons from Pottery (18:1–19:15)
  - K. Jeremiah's Maltreatment (20:1-18)
  - L. The Warning and Judgment Concerning the Kings (21:1–22:30)
  - M. The Condemnation of False Prophets (23:1-40)
  - N. The Vision of Good and Bad Figs (24:1-10)
  - O. The 70-Year Exile (25:1-38)
- III. Jeremiah's Life before the Captivity (26:1–38:28)
  - A. True Versus False Prophecy (26:1–29:32)
  - B. The Book of Consolation (30:1–33:26)
  - C. The Warning to Zedekiah and Indictment of Judah (34:1–35:19)
  - D. Jeremiah, Jehoiakim, and the Scroll of God's Word (36:1-32)
  - E. The Royal Summons and Incarcerations (37:1–38:28)
- IV. Jeremiah's Life after the Fall of Jerusalem (39:1–45:5)
- V. The Prophet's Oracles Against Foreign Nations (46:1–51:64)
- VI. Details Concerning the Fall of Jerusalem (52:1-34)

Title: Jeremiah (Hb "may Yahweh lift up or establish") He was sometimes known as "the weeping prophet."

1:1-3 Jeremiah had a priestly pedigree, as the **son of Hilkiah,** a priest from **Anathoth**, although he himself is not called a priest. Jeremiah's prophetic ministry spanned the reigns of three kings: Josiah and his two sons—Jehoiakim and Zedekiah.

1:4 Jeremiah's call, as every valid call to ministry, was initiated by God. Parallels exist with other calling stories: Isaiah (Is 6:1-13), Servant of the Lord (Is 49:1-7), Ezekiel (Ezk 2:1–3:10), and Paul (Gl 1:11-16).

1:5 God initiates this call with four action verbs: God **chose** (Hb *yada'*, "know," especially in the sense of intimate, personal knowledge; see note on Ex 2:24-25 and **Word Study**, p. 725) him; **formed** (Hb *yatsar*, "form, shape," as a potter "fashions" clay; see **Doctrine**: "Creation of Mankind," p. 5) him; **set** him **apart** (Hb *qadash*, "consecrate, declare as holy"; see note on Ex 13:1-3); and **appointed** (Hb *natan*, "give; set or put in place; make or constitute someone to be something") him **a prophet**, not only to Israel but even beyond them, **to the nations**.

1:6 Jeremiah, as Moses (Ex 4:10-11), protested that he was inadequate for this calling; but when God calls, God equips His servants.

1:8-9 God promises protection as well as a divine message. The prophet's words are now **My** (the Lord's) **words** (cp. Is 6:6-7; Ezk 3:1-4).

1:10 Jeremiah would speak God's words to his own nation and to any other nation to which he was sent. The words describing the impact of Jeremiah's words recur throughout the text and tie the book together by explaining the rise and fall of nations via this metaphor portraying Israel as God's vineyard (Jr 1:10; cp. 18:7; 31:28; 45:4; Is 5:1-7; Ezk 19:10-14): **to uproot** [Hb *natash*, "pluck up" as one would pull weeds out of the ground; cp. Dt 29:28; 1Kg 14:15; 2Ch 27:20; Jr 12:14-15,17; 18:14; Mc 5:14] **and tear down** [Hb *natats*, "pull or break down, destroy"; cp. Ex 34:13; Dt 7:5; 12:3], **to destroy** [Hb *'avad*, "cut off, devastate, perish"; cp. Ex 10:7; Ps 2:12; 5:6; Is 60:12] **and demolish** [Hb *haras*, "pull down, destroy"; cp. 1Kg 19:10,14; Lm 2:2; Ezk 16:39; 36:36], **to build** [Hb *banah*; see **Doctrine**: "Creation of Mankind," p. 5] **and plant** (Hb *nata'*, "set upright so [the plant] is fixed in the ground"; cp. Ex 15:17; 2Sm 7:10; 1Ch 17:9; Pss 44:2; 80:8,15; Is 40:24; 51:16; Jr 2:21; 11:17; 12:2; 18:9; 24:6; 32:41; 42:10; 45:4; Am 9:14-15).

>WORD|*study*

1:11-12 Almond tree (Hb *shaqēd*) derives from the verb **watch over** (Hb *shaqad*, "be sleepless or wakeful, attend to"; cp. 31:28; Ps 127:1) in the sense that this tree is the first to "awaken" from its winter sleep. Anathoth was particularly known (and still is today) for almond growing, so this must have been a particularly vivid and familiar sight to Jeremiah. God promised to fix His attention on His **word to accomplish** (Hb *'asah*, "perform, do, effect, complete," Jr 1:12; see **Doctrine**: "Creation of Mankind", p. 5) it, meaning He would take upon Himself the responsibility (i.e., be vigilant) for ensuring that His will prevailed, giving the sense that the events Jeremiah would prophesy are imminent and certain. Just as the almond blossoms indicate the sure arrival of spring, God's words coming forth from His prophet indicate the sure arrival of the predicted disaster.

Jeremiah's Pedigree and Divine Call (1:1-8)

1 The words of Jeremiah, the son of
Hilkiah, one of the priests living
in Anathoth in the territory of Benjamin. 2 The word of the LORD came
to him in the thirteenth year of the
reign of Josiah son of Amon, king
of Judah. 3 It also came throughout
the days of Jehoiakim son of Josiah,
king of Judah, until the fifth month
of the eleventh year of Zedekiah son
of Josiah, king of Judah, when the
people of Jerusalem went into exile.
4 The word of the LORD came to me:

5 I chose you
before I formed you
in the womb;
I set you apart
before you were born.
I appointed you a prophet
to the nations.

6 But I protested, "Oh no, Lord
GOD! Look, I don't know how to
speak since I am only a youth."
7 Then the LORD said to me:

Do not say, "I am only
a youth,"
for you will go to everyone
I send you to
and speak whatever I tell you.
8 Do not be afraid of anyone,
for I will be with you
to deliver you.

This is
the LORD's declaration.

The Prophet's Visions: Confirming His Commission (1:9-15)

9 Then the LORD reached out His
hand, touched my mouth, and told
me:

I have now filled your mouth
with My words.
10 See, I have
appointed you today
over nations and kingdoms
to uproot and tear down,
to destroy and demolish,
to build and plant.

11 Then the word of the LORD came
to me, asking, "What do you see, Jeremiah?"
I replied, "I see a branch of an almond tree."
12 The LORD said to me, "You have
seen correctly, for I watch over My
word to accomplish it." 13 Again the
word of the LORD came to me inquir-
ing, "What do you see?"
And I replied, "I see a boiling pot,
its lip tilted from the north to the
south."
14 Then the LORD said to me, "Disaster will be poured out[A] from the
north on all who live in the land.
15 Indeed, I am about to summon
all the clans and kingdoms of the
north."

This is
the LORD's declaration.

They will come, and each king
will set up his throne
at the entrance
to Jerusalem's gates.
They will attack
all her surrounding walls
and all the other cities
of Judah.

The LORD's Equipping of the Prophet for the Task (1:16-19)

16 "I will pronounce My judgments
against them for all the evil they did
when they abandoned Me to burn
incense to other gods and to worship the works of their own hands.
17 "Now, get ready. Stand up and

[A]1:14 LXX reads *will boil*

tell them everything that I command you. Do not be intimidated by them or I will cause you to cower before them. 18 Today, I am the One who has made you a fortified city, an iron pillar, and bronze walls against the whole land—against the kings of Judah, its officials, its priests, and the population. 19 They will fight against you but never prevail over you, since I am with you to rescue you."

This is
the LORD's declaration.

God's Lawsuit Against Israel (2:1-37)

2 The word of the LORD came to me: 2 "Go and announce directly to Jerusalem that this is what the LORD says:

I remember the loyalty
of your youth,
your love as a bride—
how you followed Me
in the wilderness,
in a land not sown.
3 Israel was holy to the LORD,
the •firstfruits of His harvest.
All who ate of it found
themselves •guilty;
disaster came on them."
This is
the LORD's declaration.
4 Hear the word of the LORD,
house of Jacob
and all families of the house
of Israel.
5 This is what the LORD says:

What fault did your fathers
find in Me
that they went so far
from Me,
followed worthless idols,
and became worthless
themselves?
6 They stopped asking,
"Where is the LORD
who brought us from the land
of Egypt,
who led us
through the wilderness,
through a land of deserts
and ravines,
through a land of drought
and darkness,[A]
a land no one
traveled through
and where no one lived?"
7 I brought you to
a fertile land
to eat its fruit and bounty,
but after you entered,
you defiled My land;
you made
My inheritance detestable.
8 The priests quit asking,
"Where is the LORD?"
The experts in the law
no longer knew Me,
and the rulers rebelled
against Me.
The prophets prophesied
by[B] •Baal
and followed useless idols.

9 Therefore, I will bring a case
against you again.
This is
the LORD's declaration.
I will bring a case
against your children's
children.
10 Cross over to Cyprus[C]
and take a look.
Send someone to Kedar
and consider carefully;
see if there has ever been
anything like this:
11 Has a nation ever exchanged
its gods?

[A]2:6 Or *shadow of death* [B]2:8 = in the name of [C]2:10 Lit *to the islands of Kittim*

>WORD|*study*

2:8 Baal (Hb *ba'al*, "lord, master, owner; husband") was a Canaanite fertility god, also known as a god of the thunderstorm. His goddess consort was Asherah, mother of Canaanite deities, and sometimes Ashtoreth (or Ashtaroth), his sister. The worship of Baal had always proven a snare to the people of Israel, who were all too prone to desire to be like the surrounding nations, despite the covenant that God had made with them, by virtue of which they were to be a holy nation and a "kingdom of priests" (Ex 19:5-6). The worship of Baal involved rites of sacred prostitution in which worshipers had sexual relationships with prostitutes dedicated to Baal in order to promote agricultural fertility. Other times, priestly men and women re-enacted the union of Baal with his consorts to ensure agricultural abundance. It was believed that the ritual sexual union in imitation of Baal and his consort would actualize the union of the lord of nature with mother earth.

1:11-12 The Lord affirms Jeremiah's calling via two visions. In the first, a pun is used to convey meaning.

1:13-15 The vision of a **boiling pot** tilting away **from the north** (i.e., toward Judah in the south) was an image of terrible, inescapable **disaster**, which would certainly come from Babylon, the invaders of Judah from the north.

1:16 Judah's egregious crime was clear: She had violated the covenant through gross idolatry.

1:17-19 Jeremiah was not to be intimidated by his prophetic task before the people and national leaders; otherwise God would cause him **to cower** [Hb *chatat*, "frighten, put to shame"] **before them.** Jeremiah received power from the Lord, who had made him **a fortified city, an iron pillar, and bronze walls against . . . the kings of Judah, its officials, its priests, and the population** (cp. Ezk 3:8-9).

2:1-2 This chapter constitutes a lawsuit brought against Judah by the Lord, so the tone is accusatory throughout. When Israel was first rescued from Egyptian bondage, a "honeymoon" period ensued. She followed the Lord, **as a bride**, deeply in love, **followed** her groom anywhere, even **in the wilderness**—such was the depth of her loyalty and devotion at that time.

2:3 The Lord protected her, and she followed Him. This reference is to the travels in the wilderness where the Lord provided for the people's every need.

2:5-7 Eventually, the wife became unfaithful to and disinterested in her husband and redeemer, and she turned away from the provider who had brought her into a bountiful, **fertile land.**

2:8 Israel's apostasy into idolatry was complete, led by the spiritual and political leaders—including the priests, legal experts, rulers, and most tragically, the prophets. This latter group was specifically entrusted to speak the Lord's message truthfully, yet they **prophesied by Baal.**

2:9-10 Because of her unfaithfulness to the covenant made at Mount Sinai, the Lord would bring a lawsuit against Israel, accusing her of breaking her allegiance to her former vows.

2:11-12 His people had **exchanged** [Hb *mur*; cp. Gk (LXX) *allassō*, Rm 1:23] **their Glory**, i.e., the divine presence, **for useless idols** (Hb *lo'-ya'al*, "worth or profiting nothing," Jr 2:11; cp. v. 8; 12:13; 16:19; 23:32; 1 Sm 12:21). To denounce Israel's rejection of Him, God addressed the **heavens** as the courtroom's jury/witnesses, who should be **horrified** [Hb *shamēm*, "astonish, put to silence, stun"] **. . . shocked** [Hb *saʿar*, "shudder with horror," especially as the skin quivers when one is terror-stricken; cp. Ezk 27:35; 32:10] **and utterly appalled** (Hb *charav*, literally "be desolate or laid waste," Jr 2:12) at what Israel had done.

2:13 In abandoning **the fountain of living water** for **cracked cisterns that cannot hold water**, Israel made a terrible deal—she exchanged something living (God) for something lifeless (idols); something life-giving and vital for something stale, stagnant, and disappointing.

2:14-17 Whereas in the past Israel had enjoyed freedom and God's protection (v. 3), Israel now falls prey to nations (**lions**) who would enslave her. Egypt and Assyria are likely in view here, as **Memphis** and **Tahpanhes** are in Egypt, and about 130 years prior Assyria had devastated Israel, the Northern Kingdom. God had freed Israel from bondage in Egypt, but Israel had in effect re-enslaved herself by foolishly making treaties with the neighboring nations and paying tribute to them in exchange for protection, thereby deeming as insufficient their covenant or "treaty" with God.

2:18-19 An attitude where **fear of** the Lord is absent has brought Israel back to this point.

2:20 A string of vivid similes describe Israel's apostasy. Israel threw off God's laws in exchange for serving idols, which God considered spiritual prostitution. Like a rebellious ox breaking its **yoke**, Israel asserted that she would no longer **serve** a master.

2:21 The next metaphor is of a **choice vine** (Hb *sorēq*, "preferred species of grapevine, fruit-bearing vine," v. 21; cp. Jn 15:1-5) that had been **planted** (Hb *nataʿ*; cp. 11:17; 12:2; Is 5:2) by God Himself **from the very best** [Hb *kol*, "completely," modifying *ʾemeth*, "faithful, true"] **seed**. This carefully cultivated vine had turned wild.

2:22 Judah's rebellion is like a stain that no detergent can purge. It is a permanent **stain** (Hb *katam*, "defiled, soiled, filthy, or deeply stained," used only here in the Old Testament) of sin in God's sight.

2:23-25 Finally, Israel is compared to a **young camel**, which moves around spasmodically and erratically, completely unpredictable in its course (in effect, running around but not getting anywhere) and a **wild donkey**

>WORD|*study*

2:20 The yoke (Hb *ʿol*) is a curved piece of wood fitted to the working animal's neck and attached to a pole or beam for pulling a load or a plow (Nm 19:2). A "yoke" figuratively represents servitude or bondage (cp. Gn 27:40; Lv 26:13; Dt 28:48; Jr 27). Chains (Hb *mosēr*, "bonds"), the metal bands of a yoke, likewise signify enslavement. In both Jr 2:20 and 5:5 (cp. Ps 2:3), the imagery of breaking or tearing off God's "yoke" depicts blatant defiance against the Lord, as though His lordship restricts freedom. To reject His rule, however, is to choose enslavement to sin (Rm 6:16) and to pervert God's identity as the One who liberates people from sin and its consequent forms of enslavement (see Ezk 34:27); who "broke their **chains** (Hb *mosēr*) apart" (Ps 107:14); who promised to "break off his [Assyria's] yoke . . . and tear off your shackles" (Hb *mosēr*, Nah 1:13); who "was like one who eases the yoke (Hb *ʿol*) from their jaws" (Hs 11:4); and, in the incarnate Son, declares that His "yoke is easy" (Mt 11:29-30; cp. Gl 5:1).

(But they were not gods!)
Yet My people have exchanged
their[A] Glory
for useless idols.
12 Be horrified at this, heavens;
be shocked
and utterly appalled.
This is
the LORD's declaration.
13 For My people
have committed
a double evil:
They have abandoned Me,
the fountain of living water,
and dug cisterns
for themselves,
cracked cisterns that cannot
hold water.
14 Is Israel a slave?
Was he born into slavery?[B]
Why else has he become
a prey?
15 The young lions have roared
at him;
they have roared loudly.
They have laid waste his land.
His cities are in ruins,
without inhabitants.
16 The men of Memphis
and Tahpanhes
have also broken your skull.
17 Have you not brought this
on yourself
by abandoning the LORD
your God
while He was leading you
along the way?
18 Now what will you gain
by traveling along the way
to Egypt
to drink the waters
of the Nile?[C]
What will you gain
by traveling along the way
to Assyria
to drink the waters
of the Euphrates?
19 Your own evil
will discipline you;
your own apostasies
will reprimand you.
Think it over and see how evil
and bitter it is
for you to abandon the LORD
your God
and to have no •fear of Me.
This is the declaration
of the Lord GOD
of •Hosts.
20 For long ago I[D] broke
your yoke;
I[D] tore off your chains.
You insisted,
"I will not serve!"
On every high hill
and under every green tree
you lie down like a prostitute.
21 I planted you, a choice vine
from the very best seed.
How then could you turn into
a degenerate, foreign vine?
22 Even if you wash with lye
and use a great amount
of soap,
the stain of your sin is still
in front of Me.
This is
the Lord GOD's declaration.
23 How can you protest, "I am
not defiled;
I have not followed
the Baals"?
Look at your behavior
in the valley;
acknowledge
what you have done.

A2:11 Ancient Jewish tradition reads *My* B2:14 Lit *born of a house* C2:18 Lit *of Shihor*
D2:20 LXX reads *you*

You are a swift young camel
twisting and turning
on her way,
24 a wild donkey at home[A]
in the wilderness.
She sniffs the wind
in the heat of her desire.
Who can control her passion?
All who look for her will not
become tired;
they will find her
in her mating season.[B]
25 Keep your feet
from going bare
and your throat from thirst.
But you say, "It's hopeless;
I love strangers,
and I will continue
to follow them."
26 Like the shame of a thief
when he is caught,
so the house of Israel
has been put to shame.
They, their kings,
their officials,
their priests,
and their prophets
27 say to a tree, "You are
my father,"
and to a stone,
"You gave birth to me."
For they have
turned their back to Me
and not their face,
yet in their time of disaster
they beg,
"Rise up and save us!"
28 But where are your gods
you made for yourself?
Let them rise up and save you
in your time of disaster
if they can,
for your gods are as numerous
as your cities, Judah.

29 Why do you bring a case
against Me?
All of you have rebelled
against Me.
This is
the LORD's declaration.
30 I have struck down
your children in vain;
they would not
accept discipline.
Your own sword has devoured
your prophets
like a ravaging lion.
31 Evil generation,
pay attention to the word
of the LORD!
Have I been a wilderness
to Israel
or a land of dense darkness?
Why do My people claim,
"We will go where we want;[C]
we will no longer come
to You"?
32 Can a young woman forget
her jewelry
or a bride her wedding sash?
Yet My people
have forgotten Me
for countless days.
33 How skillfully
you pursue love;
you also teach evil women
your ways.
34 Moreover, your skirts
are stained
with the blood
of the innocent poor.
You did not catch them
breaking and entering.
But in spite of all these things
35 you claim, "I am innocent.
His anger is sure to turn away
from me."
But I will certainly judge you
because you have said, "I have
not sinned."
36 How unstable you are,
constantly changing
your ways!
You will be put to shame
by Egypt
just as you were put to shame
by Assyria.
37 Moreover, you will be led out
from here
with your hands on your head
since the LORD has rejected
those you trust;
you will not succeed
even with their help.[D]

The People's Apostasy and the Prophet's Call to Repentance (3:1–4:4)

3 If[E] a man divorces his wife
and she leaves him
to marry another,
can he ever return to her?

in **heat**, looking with uncontrollable **desire** for a mate, having lost all decency and propriety. Like an addict who knows she is addicted, Israel resigns herself to spiritual adultery, saying, **It's hopeless** (cp. 18:12).

2:26-28 The leaders of the people brought **shame** upon Israel by embracing pantheistic and animistic religion. Ludicrously attributing their origin to nature, they had **turned their back** (Hb *'oreph*, "neck") on the Creator, at least until they got into trouble (cp. 32:33). For this hypocrisy, God mocked the impotence of the **numerous** gods in which Judah had trusted. The **tree** may refer to the goddess Asherah, whose worship involved pole-like representations of her, and the **stone** may refer to the Baal idols. However, the terms may also be somewhat more generic in the fashion of Is 44:14-17, which highlights the insanity of garnering raw materials like wood (or stone), shaping and fashioning them, then worshiping them as gods (cp. Jr 3:9).

2:29-31 Israel seems to protest their discipline by the Lord, but they have no case; rather they are so hardened **they would not accept discipline**. They are incorrigible, brazen children, who flout God's discipline and continue in their rebellion.

2:32-34 For God's people to **forget** (Hb *shakach*, "ignore, not care about"; cp. Jr 3:21; 13:25; 18:15) Him was as ridiculous as a **young woman** forgetting **her jewelry or a bride her wedding sash** (her gown). Israel even had expert advice for **evil women**, not only as adulteresses but also as murderers.

2:35 Evil deeds, murders (v. 30), and injustice seem no impediment to Israel's continued denial of guilt (**I am innocent**).

2:36-37 God will judge Israel by means of **Egypt**, as He had also used **Assyria** in the past, punishments which have evidently taught them very little. They will be invaded, captured, and led out of the land like slaves.

3:1 The metaphor of marriage is used by the Lord to compare Judah and Israel, who had both been unfaithful to Him. If a divorced woman, after having married another man, must not be taken back by her former husband (Dt 24:1-4), then Israel, whose pursuit of idols is depicted as playing **the prostitute** [Hb *zanah*, "commit fornication or adultery, act as a harlot"; cp. 2:20; 3:6,8] **with many partners**, certainly had no right to expect the Lord to take her back.

[A]2:24 Lit *donkey taught* [B]2:24 Lit *her month* [C]2:31 Or *We have taken control*, or *We can roam* [D]2:37 Lit *with them* [E]3:1 One Hb ms, LXX, Syr; other Hb mss read *Saying: If*

3:2-3 God's land was **defiled** (Hb *chanēph*, "pollute, corrupt, degrade; profane, treat irreverently or contemptuously, violate the sanctity of a place") by Israel's unfaithfulness, so the needed rains had been withheld. The lack of **rain** not only demonstrated Yahweh's withdrawal of blessing but also the impotence of Baal, the Canaanite "thunderstorm" god. Confronted with her shameful behavior, Israel, nevertheless, appears defiant. The word refuse (Hb *maʾēn*, "be unwilling") appears several times in Jeremiah, presenting overwhelming evidence of Israel's obstinate resistance to the Lord's warnings and discipline (5:3; 8:5; 9:6; 11:10).

3:4-5 To call God **My Father** is to address Him with familial intimacy; to call Him **my friend in my youth** (Hb *ʾalluph*, "familiar, intimate friend; husband, as the friend from [her] youth") acknowledges a marriage-like relationship between Israel and the Lord. The **evil** aspect of this lay in Israel's duplicity in assuming she could play the prostitute without harming her relationship with the Lord.

3:6 **In the days of King Josiah** resets the prophetic message within the historical framework. Jeremiah received the message here during Josiah's reign (see 2Kg 22:1–23:30; 2Ch 34:1–35:27).

3:7-10 The Lord had given the northern kingdom of Israel **a certificate of divorce** (Hb *sēpher*, "written legal document"; *keritut*, "a cutting off from marriage;" cp. Dt 24:1,3; Is 50:1) because she was **unfaithful** (Hb *meshuvah*, "turning away, defection," Jr 3:6,8,11-12; cp. "waywardness," Pr 1:32; "apostasies," Jr 2:19), having both **prostituted herself** and **committed adultery** (Hb *naʾaph*; cp. 5:7; 23:14). Baal worship constituted infidelity to the one true God, Israel's "husband," and Judah was no better, (2:26-27). Her shallow **pretense** of repentance probably refers to the reforms executed by Josiah (see 2Kg 23:4-25; 2Ch 34:3-8). Although the king ordered the removal of all visible evidence of idolatrous practices and repaired the temple, inwardly the people's loyalties did not change (2Kg 23:26-27,31-32,36-37; 2Ch 36:5,8-21).

3:11-13 Israel had been living in **the north** (Assyrian exile) since 722 B.C. **Under every green tree** probably refers to the custom of setting up Baal shrines under luxuriant, green, healthy trees.

3:14-15 The Lord's assertion, **I am your master** (Hb *baʿal*) as a verb, in this context, has the meaning "take a wife." God was declaring that He was Israel's husband, (i.e., that He had entered a binding covenant relationship with Israel

>WORD|*study*

3:10 Jeremiah frequently employs the word return (Hb *shuv*, "repent") and various words derived from it. In this chapter alone he uses the variations at least 15 times: **return** (Hb *shuv*, "repent," 3:1,7,10,12,14,22); turn away (Hb *shuv*, 3:19); faithless (Hb *shovav*, "falling away, rebellious, unrepentant, backsliding," 3:14,22); and unfaithful (Hb *meshuvah*, "backsliding, backslidden state," 3:6,8,11-12). Inherent in this word and its many variants is the active response of "turning" and its application primarily to relational contexts—turning away from someone (giving them your back) or turning toward someone.

3:14-15 They would shepherd (Hb *raʿah*, "feed, pasture"; cp. 23:2,4; "protect," Is 40:11) the people **with knowledge** " (Hb *dēʿah*, Jr 3:15; cp. Is 28:9). The LXX translates this word as higher knowledge (Gk *epistēmōn*, "understanding," Jms 3:13), the experiential knowledge of an expert. The Hebrew word is used only six times in the Old Testament, in each case denoting "knowledge" that belongs to or comes directly from Yahweh. In her prayer, Hannah describes Yahweh as "a God of knowledge" (1Sm 2:3). In the book of Job, Elihu boasts of having "perfect knowledge," a ridiculous claim (Jb 36:4; cp. the related word *deaʿ*, all five instances appearing in Elihu's speeches: Jb 32:6,10,17; 36:3; 37:16). Psalm 73:11 reveals the bold and willful sinfulness of "the wicked" in their question, "Does the Most High know everything?" (the implied answer being, "Yes, He does!"). Like Jeremiah's prophetic description of the future in 3:14-18, Isaiah describes the coming reign of the Messiah as bringing Eden-like peace, when "the land will be . . . full of the knowledge of the LORD" (Is 11:9).

Wouldn't such a land[A] become
totally defiled?
But you!
You have played the prostitute
with many partners—
can you return to Me?
This is
the LORD's declaration.
2 Look to the barren heights
and see.
Where have you not
been immoral?
You sat waiting for them
beside the highways
like a nomad in the desert.
You have defiled the land
with your prostitution
and wickedness.
3 This is why the showers
haven't come—
why there has been
no spring rain.
You have the brazen look
of a prostitute[B]
and refuse to be ashamed.
4 Have you not lately
called to Me, "My Father.
You were my friend
in my youth.
5 Will He bear a grudge forever?
Will He be
endlessly infuriated?"
This is what you have said,
but you have done
the evil things
you are capable of.

6 In the days of King Josiah the
LORD asked me, "Have you seen what
unfaithful Israel has done? She has
ascended every high hill and gone
under every green tree to prostitute
herself there. 7 I thought: After she
has done all these things, she will
return to Me. But she didn't return,
and her treacherous sister Judah
saw it. 8 I[C] observed that it was because unfaithful Israel had committed adultery that I had sent her away
and had given her a certificate of
divorce. Nevertheless, her treacherous sister Judah was not afraid but
also went and prostituted herself.
9 Indifferent to[D] her prostitution,
she defiled the land and committed
adultery with stones and trees. 10 Yet
in spite of all this, her treacherous
sister Judah didn't return to Me with
all her heart—only in pretense."
This is
the LORD's declaration.
11 The LORD announced to me,
"Unfaithful Israel has shown herself
more righteous than treacherous
Judah. 12 Go, proclaim these words
to the north, and say:

Return, unfaithful Israel.
This is
the LORD's declaration.
I will not look on you
with anger,[E]
for I am unfailing in My love.
This is
the LORD's declaration.
I will not be angry forever.
13 Only acknowledge
your •guilt—

[A]3:1 LXX reads *woman* [B]3:3 Lit *have a prostitute's forehead* [C]3:8 One Hb ms, Syr read *She* [D]3:9 Lit *From the lightness of* [E]3:12 Lit *not cause My face to fall on you*

you have rebelled
against the LORD your God.
You have scattered
your favors to strangers
under every green tree
and have not obeyed My voice.
This is
the LORD's declaration.

14 "Return, you faithless children"—this is the LORD's declaration—"for I am your master, and I
will take you, one from a city and
two from a family, and I will bring
you to •Zion. 15 I will give you shepherds who are loyal to Me,[A] and they
will shepherd you with knowledge
and skill. 16 When you multiply
and increase in the land, in those
days"—the LORD's declaration—"no
one will say any longer, 'The ark of
the LORD's covenant.' It will never
come to mind, and no one will remember or miss it. It will never
again be made. 17 At that time Jerusalem will be called, •Yahweh's
Throne, and all the nations will be
gathered to it, to the name of Yahweh in Jerusalem. They will cease
to follow the stubbornness of their
evil hearts. 18 In those days the house
of Judah will join with the house of
Israel, and they will come together
from the land of the north to the
land I have given your ancestors to
inherit."

19 I thought: How I long
to make you My sons
and give you a desirable land,
the most beautiful
inheritance of all
the nations.
I thought: You will call Me,
my Father,
and never turn away from Me.
20 However, as a woman
may betray her lover,[B]
so you have betrayed Me,
house of Israel.
This is
the LORD's declaration.

21 A sound is heard
on the barren heights,
the children of Israel weeping
and begging for mercy,
for they have perverted
their way;
they have forgotten the LORD
their God.
22 Return, you faithless children.
I will heal
your unfaithfulness.
"Here we are, coming to You,
for You are the LORD our God.
23 Surely, falsehood comes
from the hills,
commotion
from the mountains,
but the salvation of Israel
is only in the LORD our God.
24 From the time of our youth
the shameful one[C]
has consumed
what our fathers
have worked for—
their flocks and their herds,
their sons
and their daughters.
25 Let us lie down in our shame;
let our disgrace cover us.
We have sinned
against the LORD our God,
both we and our fathers,
from the time of our youth
even to this day.
We have not obeyed the voice
of the LORD our God."

4 If you return,[D] Israel—
this is
the LORD's declaration—
you will return to Me,
if you remove
your detestable idols
from My presence
and do not waver,
2 then you can swear,
"As the LORD lives,"
in truth, in justice,
and in righteousness,
then the nations
will be blessed[E] by Him
and will pride themselves
in Him.

3 For this is what the LORD says to
the men of Judah and Jerusalem:

Break up
the unplowed ground;
do not sow among the thorns.
4 Circumcise yourselves
to the LORD;
remove the foreskin
of your hearts,

like that of marriage). See **Word Study**, p. 289. The Lord promised to **bring** (Hb *bo'*, "lead or cause to come in"; cp. Gn 43:17; Ex 6:8; special usage meaning "take as a wife," Jdg 12:9) them to **Zion** (i.e., Jerusalem),the city of David (cp. Ps 132:13). The people's relationship with God would be renewed, and they would have new leadership—**shepherds who are loyal** to God—literally, "according to My heart."

3:16-17 At that time, the Lord Himself would be present among His people. **The ark of the Lord's covenant**, symbolizing Yahweh's presence, would be unnecessary, He will dwell freely with a holy people. **Jerusalem** (Zion) would be called **Yahweh's Throne**, signifying His righteous and incontestable rule over **all the nations** (Hb *goy*, "people," especially "non-Hebrews, Gentiles"), who would **be gathered** (Hb *qawah*; cp. Gk [LXX] *sunachthēsontai*, also used in Mt 25:32 to the city (cp. Rv 21:2-3,22-27).

3:20-22 By serving idols, Israel **betrayed** the Lord **as a woman may betray** [Hb *bagad*, "deal treacherously with"; see vv. 7-11] **her lover** or husband. Israel appeared to express repentance and announced her return to the Lord, who promised to **heal** her **unfaithfulness** (Hb *meshuvah*, "backsliding, turning away, defection"; see **Word Study**, 3:10; p. 956).

3:23-25 References to the **hills** and **mountains** probably signify elevated places where shrines to Baal were traditionally built. The people confessed that for a long time they had allowed **the shameful one** (a euphemism for Baal, worshiped at shrines built on high places) to devour both their possessions and their families. They were both shameful and ashamed of themselves and now wanted to lie down, taking the normal position of penitent mourners.

4:1-2 The Lord called Israel not only to repentance but also back to their original mission. **If** Israel was serious about returning to Him, putting away her **detestable idols** (Hb *shiqquts*, "impure, abominable things," referring here to the Canaanite idols; cp. 2Kg 23:24; Ezk 20:7-8; Nah 3:6; Zch 9:7), and making oaths reflecting the covenant with Yahweh, **then the nations** [Hb *goy*; see Jr 3:17] **will be blessed by Him** as first expressed in the Abrahamic covenant (Gn 12:3). Such repentance must be deeper than before (cp. Jr 3:10).

4:3-4 Break up the unplowed ground (Hb *nir*, "newly cultivated field, virgin soil," 4:3)—i.e., start over, begin anew. This step is the first in preparing a field for planting—God's ultimate desire for Israel ("to build and plant," Jr 1:10).

[A] **3:15** Lit *shepherds according to My heart* [B] **3:20** Lit *friend* [C] **3:24** = Baal [D] **4:1** Or *Repent*
[E] **4:2** Or *will bless themselves*

The extent of syncretism in Israel and Judah may also be archaeologically demonstrated. An interesting set of inscriptions discovered in Israel from Khirbet el-Qom in Judah (inscribed on a tomb) and Kuntillet ʿAjrud (inscribed on pottery) mention Yahweh along with Asherah (e.g., "I bless you by Yahweh of Samaria and by his [or its] Asherah"), demonstrating the embedded nature of idolatry into Yahweh worship.

Do not sow among the thorns (cp Hs 10:12) reiterates the command to pursue a fresh start. After harvest, the thorns that had grown alongside the crop were effectively planted when the ground was tilled for new seed. To "sow among the thorns," then, would signify an attempt to reincorporate Yahweh worship into Israel's religious life, fraught as it was with idolatrous practices, rather than completely rejecting the false gods and removing every vestige of past associations with them, stamping out syncretism (cp. 2Sm 23:6; Is 32:13; 33:12).

4:5-8 If the people refused to repent, disaster would ensue (**lion, destroyer of nations**), possibly referring to Babylon.

4:11-13 The Babylonians—"the disaster from the north"—are described metaphorically as a **searing wind**—not a useful and desirable wind that separates wheat from chaff (good from evil) but a full force gale that only destroys. Yahweh's **dear people** (Hb *bath-ʿami*, "daughter of My people," cp. 6:26; 8:11,19,21; 9:1; 14:17) are clearly the target of the judgment coming through the Babylonians, whose **chariots** advanced **like a storm,** i.e., ominously, threateningly, and furiously. God identifies himself as the agent of this judgment.

4:14 Although deliverance was still available if Jerusalem would **wash the evil from** their **heart**, the imperative to do so is followed immediately by an expression of anguish that Judah continued to **harbor** (Hb *lun*, "cherish, cause to continue or remain in any condition") their vain ways of thinking **within** (Hb *qerev*, "interior, inner part, in one's heart or mind"; cp. "inwardly," 9:8). Both parts of verse 14 locate Judah's problem in the core of her identity—in a recalcitrant heart, which God promises to correct (31:33).

4:15-16 **Dan** is in the north of Israel, while **Mount Ephraim** is in the south, closer to the border with Judah. The invaders from the north can be heard from afar.

4:19-22 Jeremiah empathized with his people, agonizing over the tragic

men of Judah and residents
of Jerusalem.
Otherwise, My wrath
will break out like fire
and burn with no one
to extinguish it
because of your evil deeds.

The Warnings and Threats of Coming Judgment (4:5–7:34)

Judgment from the North (4:5-18)

5 Declare in Judah, proclaim in Jerusalem, and say:

Blow the ram's horn
throughout the land.
Cry out loudly and say:
Assemble yourselves,
and let's flee
to the fortified cities.
6 Lift up a signal flag
toward •Zion.
Run for cover!
Don't stand still!
For I am bringing disaster
from the north—
a great destruction.
7 A lion has gone up
from his thicket;
a destroyer of nations
has set out.
He has left his lair
to make your land a waste.
Your cities will be reduced
to uninhabited ruins.
8 Because of this,
put on •sackcloth;
mourn and wail,
for the LORD's burning anger
has not turned away from us.

9 "On that day"—this is the LORD's
declaration—"the king and the officials will lose their courage. The
priests will tremble in fear, and the
prophets will be scared speechless."
10 I said, "Oh no, Lord GOD, You
have certainly deceived this people
and Jerusalem, by announcing, 'You
will have peace,' while a sword is at[A]
our throats."
11 "At that time it will be said to this
people and to Jerusalem, 'A searing
wind blows from the barren heights
in the wilderness on the way to My
dear[B] people. It comes not to winnow or to sift; 12 a wind too strong
for this comes at My call.[C] Now I will
also pronounce judgments against
them.'"

13 Look, he advances like clouds;
his chariots are like a storm.
His horses are
swifter than eagles.
Woe to us, for we are ruined!
14 Wash the evil
from your heart, Jerusalem,
so that you will be delivered.
How long will you harbor
malicious thoughts
within you?
15 For a voice announces
from Dan,
proclaiming malice
from Mount Ephraim.
16 Warn the nations: Look!
Proclaim to Jerusalem:
Those who besiege
are coming
from a distant land;
they raise their voices
against the cities of Judah.
17 They have her surrounded
like those who guard a field,
because she has rebelled
against Me.
This is
the LORD's declaration.
18 Your way of life
and your actions
have brought this on you.
This is your punishment. It is
very bitter,
because it has reached
your heart!

[A]4:10 Lit *sword touches* [B]4:11 Lit *to the daughter of My* [C]4:12 Lit *comes for Me*

>WORD|*study*

4:10,18 The phrase at [Hb *nagaʿ*, "touch, get, or reach as far as"] our throats (Hb *nephesh*, "soul") vividly depicts how near the threat of destruction had come. This announcement of judgment closes with a similar phrase using the verb *nagaʿ*—has reached—to make explicit the cause of the impending disaster. The people's offense lay within themselves, their rebellious actions stemming from unrepentant hearts. The consequences could not be superficial but must be **bitter** enough to penetrate the **heart** (v. 18).

Jeremiah's Lamentation (4:19-31)

19 My anguish, my anguish![A]
I writhe in agony!
Oh, the pain in[B] my heart!
My heart pounds;
I cannot be silent.
For you, my soul,
have heard the sound
of the ram's horn—
the shout of battle.
20 Disaster after disaster
is reported
because the whole land
is destroyed.
Suddenly my tents
are destroyed,
my tent curtains,
in a moment.
21 How long must I see
the signal flag
and hear the sound
of the ram's horn?

22 "For My people are fools;
they do not know Me.
They are foolish children,
without understanding.
They are skilled in doing
what is evil,
but they do not know how
to do what is good."

23 I looked at the earth,
and it was formless
and empty.
I looked to the heavens,
and their light was gone.
24 I looked at the mountains,
and they were quaking;
all the hills shook.
25 I looked, and no man was left;
all the birds of the sky
had fled.
26 I looked, and the fertile field
was a wilderness.
All its cities were torn down
because of the LORD
and His burning anger.

27 For this is what the LORD says:

The whole land will be
a desolation,
but I will not finish it off.
28 Because of this, the earth
will mourn;
the skies above
will grow dark.
I have spoken;
I have planned,
and I will not relent
or turn back from it.
29 Every city flees
at the sound of the horseman
and the archer.
They enter the thickets
and climb among the rocks.
Every city is abandoned;
no inhabitant is left.
30 And you, devastated one,
what are you doing
that you dress yourself
in scarlet,
that you adorn yourself
with gold jewelry,
that you enlarge your eyes
with paint?
You beautify yourself
for nothing.
Your lovers reject you;
they want to take your life.
31 I hear a cry like a woman
in labor,
a cry of anguish
like one bearing
her first child.
The cry of Daughter Zion
gasping for breath,
stretching out her hands:
Woe is me, for my life
is weary
because of the murderers!

The Depravity of Jerusalem (5:1-13)

5 Roam through the streets
of Jerusalem.
Look and take note;
search in her squares.
If you find one person,
any who acts justly,
who seeks to be faithful,
then I will forgive her.
2 When they say,
"As the LORD lives,"
they are swearing falsely.
3 LORD, don't Your eyes
look for faithfulness?
You have struck them,
but they felt no pain.
You finished them off,
but they refused
to accept discipline.
They made their faces harder
than rock,
and they refused to return.

consequence of their sin, the physical destruction of their homeland.

4:23-26 These verses read like a dramatic reversal of the creation account. **The earth . . . was formless and empty** (cp. Gn 1:2), and there was no **light** in the **heavens** (cp. Gn 1:3-5; 2:1). The **mountains** and **hills** trembled—imagery frequently conveying the terrifying power of God's wrath (cp. Nah 1:5). No humans or animals remained, and the **fertile field** (Hb *karmel*, "cultivated garden, fruitful place"; cp. 2:7) was a **wilderness**. The people had precipitated God's **burning anger**, which would leave them utterly devastated.

4:27-28 What God has determined, He will perform. He will not **relent** from the destruction He had promised, and He would not **turn back** [Hb *shuv*; see **Word Study**, 3:10; p. 956] **from it**. However, a note of hope is sounded in the Lord's promise not to inflict total destruction (i.e., **finish it off**).

4:29-31 The final image of Jerusalem's fate is that of a prostitute who, amid devastation at every turn, foolishly dresses up in alluring fashion for her **lovers**; they are no longer smitten with her, however, and will betray and murder her (v. 30). The Lord was not deaf to the **anguish** (Hb *tsarah*, "distress, trouble") of Jerusalem. Calling the city **Daughter Zion** further suggests the Lord's thoughts of compassion toward the doomed city (in Jeremiah, used only here and in 6:2,23).

5:1-3 As the Lord had promised to spare Sodom and Gomorrah for just ten righteous people (Gn 18:22-32), so here the tragic fact of the matter is that it is hard to find anyone **who seeks to be faithful**. The unrepentant people were so hardened that the Lord's correction was meaningless to them—**they felt no pain. . . . They made their faces harder than rock, and they refused to return.**

A 4:19 Lit *My inner parts, my inner parts* B 4:19 Lit *the walls of*

5:4-6 Jeremiah approached the leaders of the people (i.e., **the powerful**, thinking they might **know the way of the LORD**). But even they were stubborn-hearted. Images of predatory animals (**lion, wolf**, and **leopard**) refer to the northern threat and are related to the image of an ox that had escaped its master's **yoke** (Hb *'ol*; see **Word Study**, p. 954), thereby leaving itself vulnerable to attack.

5:7 God would give up the city and not spare it. The people had turned to idols and lived a concomitantly depraved lifestyle. **Gashed themselves** refers to Canaanite religious practices, as practiced by the prophets of Baal in 1Kg 18:28, and the worshipers from Shechem, Shiloh, and Samaria, who came to worship in Jerusalem after the fall of the city (Jr 41:5).

5:8-10 Language of sexual immorality is embodied in the image of **eager stallions**, depicting adultery among the people. Violating the first of the Ten Commandments (Ex 20:3) resulted in a downward spiral, leading to further violations of the second commandment (against graven images), the seventh (against adultery), and the tenth (against coveting your neighbor's wife). Despite Judah's sin, however, God would **not finish them off** (cp. 5:18) but would merely prune them severely, as a vinedresser thoroughly prunes his vineyard.

5:11-14 The Lord had promised to watch over His word to fulfill it (1:12). In contrast, the words of Israel's false prophets were lies contradicting God's warning. Jeremiah ridiculed them as being full of **wind** (Hb *ruach*, "spirit, breath, wind") rather than the spirit of God; effectively they are nothing more than "windbags" because **the LORD's word is not in them**. The true words of God, which had been placed into the mouth of Jeremiah (1:9), would now become a consuming **fire** symbolic of God's judgment, destroying the people with the prediction of impending disaster (5:14-17).

5:18-19 The ultimate sparing of the people is reiterated (cp. 3:12-25; 4:27; 5:10), and the reason for their dire punishment is spelled out, citing Dt 29:24-28.

5:20-21 **Eyes, but they don't see, ... ears, but they don't hear** picks up on a prophetic theme in Isaiah 6:9-10. Unrepentant people will never learn except through punishment. The lack of hearing and seeing has to do with spiritual insight and spiritual understanding. Jesus expected this

4 Then I thought:

They are just the poor;
they have played the fool.
For they don't understand
the way of the LORD,
the justice of their God.
5 I will go to the powerful
and speak to them.
Surely they know the way
of the LORD,
the justice of their God.
However, these also
had broken the yoke
and torn off the chains.
6 Therefore, a lion
from the forest
will strike them down.
A wolf from an arid plain
will ravage them.
A leopard keeps watch over
their cities.
Anyone who leaves them
will be torn to pieces
because their rebellious acts
are many,
their unfaithful deeds
numerous.
7 Why should I forgive you?
Your children
have abandoned Me
and sworn by those who are
not gods.
I satisfied their needs, yet they
committed adultery;
they gashed themselves
at the[A] prostitute's house.
8 They are well-fed,[B]
eager[C] stallions,
each neighing after
someone else's wife.
9 Should I not punish them
for these things?
This is
the LORD's declaration.
Should I not avenge Myself
on such a nation as this?

10 Go up among
her vineyard terraces
and destroy them,
but do not finish them off.
Prune away her shoots,
for they do not belong
to the LORD.
11 They, the house of Israel
and the house of Judah,
have dealt very treacherously
with Me.
This is
the LORD's declaration.
12 They have contradicted
the LORD
and insisted,
"It won't happen.[D]
Harm won't come to us;
we won't see sword
or famine."
13 The prophets become
only wind,
for the LORD's word is not
in them.
This will in fact happen
to them.

Coming Judgment (5:14-31)

14 Therefore, this is what the Lord
GOD of •Hosts says:

Because you have spoken
this word,
I am going to make My words
become fire in your mouth.
These people are the wood,
and the fire
will consume them.
15 I am about to bring a nation
from far away against you,
house of Israel.
This is
the LORD's declaration.
It is an established nation,
an ancient nation,
a nation whose language
you do not know
and whose speech
you do not understand.
16 Their quiver is
like an open grave;
they are all mighty warriors.
17 They will consume
your harvest and your food.
They will consume your sons
and your daughters.
They will consume
your flocks and your herds.
They will consume your vines
and your fig trees.
They will destroy
with the sword
your fortified cities in which
you trust.

18 "But even in those days"—this
is the LORD's declaration—"I will

[A] 5:7 Or *adultery and trooped to the*, or *adultery and lodged at the*; Hb obscure [B] 5:8 Lit *well-equipped*; Hb obscure [C] 5:8 Lit *early-rising*; Hb obscure [D] 5:12 Lit *He does not exist*

not finish you off. [19]When people
ask, 'For what offense has the LORD
our God done all these things to us?'
You will respond to them: Just as
you abandoned Me and served foreign gods in your land, so will you
serve strangers in a land that is not
yours.

[20]"Declare this in the house of Jacob; proclaim it in Judah, saying:

21 Hear this,
you foolish
and senseless[A] people.
They have eyes,
but they don't see.
They have ears,
but they don't hear.
22 Do you not •fear Me?
This is
the LORD's declaration.
Do you not tremble
before Me,
the One who set the sand
as the boundary of the sea,
an enduring barrier that
it cannot cross?
The waves surge, but they
cannot prevail.
They roar but cannot
pass over it.
23 But these people
have stubborn
and rebellious hearts.
They have turned aside
and have gone away.
24 They have not said
to themselves,
'Let's fear the LORD our God,
who gives the rain, both early
and late, in its season,
who guarantees to
us the fixed weeks
of the harvest.'
25 Your •guilty acts have diverted
these things from you.
Your sins have withheld
My bounty from you,
26 for wicked men live
among My people.
They watch like fowlers
lying in wait.[B]
They set a trap;
they catch men.
27 Like a cage full of birds,
so their houses are full
of deceit.
Therefore they have
grown powerful and rich.
28 They have become fat
and sleek.
They have also excelled
in evil matters.
They have not taken up cases,
such as the case
of the fatherless,
so they might prosper,
and they have not defended
the rights of the needy.
29 Should I not punish them
for these things?
This is
the LORD's declaration.
Should I not avenge Myself
on such a nation as this?

30 A horrible, terrible thing
has taken place in the land.
31 The prophets prophesy falsely,
and the priests rule
by their own authority.
My people love it like this.
But what will you do
at the end of it?

Threatened Siege of Jerusalem (6:1-8)

6 "Run for cover, Benjaminites,
out of Jerusalem!
Sound the ram's horn
in Tekoa;
raise a smoke signal
over Beth-haccherem,[C]
for disaster threatens
from the north,
even great destruction.
2 Though she is beautiful
and delicate,
I will destroy[D] Daughter •Zion.
3 Shepherds and their flocks
will come against her;
they will pitch their tents
all around her.
Each will pasture
his own portion.
4 Set them apart for war
against her;
rise up, let's attack at noon.
Woe to us, for the day
is passing;
the evening shadows
grow long.
5 Rise up, let's attack by night.
Let us destroy her fortresses."

[6]For this is what the LORD of •Hosts
says:

reaction from the people whom He taught only in parables, and He even rebuked His disciples for the same spiritual hardening, indicating their weak faith (Mk 4:11-12; 8:17-21).

5:22-25 The people's foolishness was manifested in their perverse refusal to worship the Creator who is sovereign over nature, the seasons, and agricultural bounty. Instead, they persisted in worshiping Baal, who, they believed, provided **rain** for the harvest season. God has **withheld** the rain and agricultural **bounty** because of the people's rejection of Him in favor of idols.

5:26-31 Righteousness and justice for the poor and orphaned were completely lacking throughout the cities of Judah, and the **prophets** and **priests** contributed to the denial of responsibility for the upcoming tragedy. Tragically, God's people **love it like this**. Ominously, the question hangs, **But what will you do at the end of it?**

6:1-5 The answer to the question in 5:31 was not long in coming: **Run for cover, Benjaminites, out of Jerusalem!** The threat of impending doom from the north loomed closer. The **shepherds** coming against Judah were the enemy fighters, so bent on war and destruction that they were prepared to attack at any time of the day (**noon**) or night (**evening**). They would besiege and **destroy** Jerusalem.

[A]**5:21** Lit *without heart* [B]**5:26** Hb obscure [C]**6:1** = House of the Vineyard [D]**6:2** Or *silence*

6:6-10 Judah deserved her fate, as she oppressed her own people, pouring out **evil**, **violence**, and **destruction**. Another **warning** was issued in terms of gleaning a grapevine thoroughly (cp. 5:10). Although God gave repeated warnings, the people were unable to **pay attention**, because **their ear is uncircumcised**, (i.e., unreceptive to the Word of the Lord, who had commanded circumcision of both the body and the heart). They refused to heed God's warning because His **word . . . has become contemptible to them—they find no pleasure in it**. Judah was so hardened that the covenant with and commands of her God meant nothing to her, so disobedience came easily.

6:11-15 God's punishment would come upon all His people, **young** and old, husbands and **wives**, and **children**. The prophets and priests had been like doctors who treated **brokenness** (Hb *shevar*, from the verb *shavar*, "break or tear to pieces, fracture, shatter"; cp. 8:21)— i.e., a serious wound treated as if it were not serious. They prophesied falsely that **peace, peace** (Hb *shalom, shalom*) would come, but peace was not what God had planned. The lying prophets would perish along with the people.

6:16-17 The people were advised by five imperative action verbs: **Stand by the roadways** (i.e., stop what you are doing and give attention to the options that lie before you); **look** (i.e., examine or see for yourself the choices people are making); **ask about the ancient paths** (i.e., the people should look back at the covenant laws of God; cp. v. 19); **take** it (i.e., the **way to what is good**); and **find rest** [Hb *margowa*ᶜ; a *hapax*, or word used only here in the OT, from the verb *raga*ᶜ, "be still, dwell quietly"; cp. 31:2; 50:34; Dt 28:65] **for yourselves**. But the people stubbornly refused to obey God's counsel. They even refused the warnings of God's **watchmen** (Hb *tsaphah*, "lookout, positioned to see and warn of approaching danger; metaphor for "prophet"; cp. Ezk 3:16-21; 33:1-20), saying, **We won't listen!** (Hb *qashav*, "hearken, give heed, pay attention," Jr 6:10,17,19; cp. Is 48:18).

6:18-21 As a result of their willful disobedience, God would **bring disaster** on them. Often the word **therefore** indicates that judgment follows (e.g., 2:9; 5:6,14). God pronounced judgment before the nations and the heavens as witnesses. Sacrifices and expensive spices do not please God when there is disobedience.

Cut down the trees;
raise a siege ramp
against Jerusalem.
This city must be punished.
There is nothing
but oppression within her.
7 As a well gushes out its water,
so she pours out her evil.[A]
Violence and destruction
resound in her.
Sickness and wounds
keep coming
to My attention.
8 Be warned, Jerusalem,
or I will turn away from you;
I will make you a desolation,
a land without inhabitants.

Wrath on Israel (6:9-15)

9 This is what the LORD of Hosts
says:

Glean the remnant of Israel
as thoroughly as a vine.
Pass your hand once more
like a grape gatherer
over the branches.
10 Who can I speak to and give
such a warning[B]
that they will listen?
Look, their ear
is uncircumcised,[C]
so they cannot pay attention.
See, the word of the LORD
has become contemptible
to them—
they find no pleasure in it.
11 But I am full
of the LORD's wrath;
I am tired of holding it back.
Pour it out on the children
in the street,
on the gang of young men
as well.
For both husband and wife
will be captured,
the old with the very old.[D]
12 Their houses will be
turned over to others,
their fields and wives as well,
for I will stretch out
My hand
against the inhabitants
of the land.
This is
the LORD's declaration.
13 For from the least
to the greatest of them,
everyone is making
profit dishonestly.
From prophet to priest,
everyone deals falsely.
14 They have treated My people's
brokenness superficially,
claiming, "Peace, peace,"
when there is no peace.
15 Were they ashamed
when they acted
so abhorrently?
They weren't
at all ashamed.
They can no longer
feel humiliation.
Therefore, they will fall
among the fallen.
When I punish them,
they will collapse,
says the LORD.

Disaster Because of Disobedience (6:16-21)

16 This is what the LORD says:

Stand by the roadways
and look.
Ask about the ancient paths:
Which is the way to what
is good?
Then take it
and find rest for yourselves.
But they protested,
"We won't!"
17 I appointed watchmen
over you
and said: Listen for the sound
of the ram's horn.
But they protested,
"We won't listen!"
18 Therefore listen,
you nations
and you witnesses,
learn what the charge is
against them.
19 Listen, earth!
I am about to bring disaster
on these people,
the fruit
of their own plotting,
for they have paid
no attention to My word.
They have rejected
My instruction.

[A]6:7 Or *well keeps its water fresh, so she keeps her evil fresh* [B]6:10 Or *and bear witness*
[C]6:10 They are unresponsive to God. [D]6:11 Lit *with fullness of days*

[20] What use to Me is
frankincense from Sheba
or sweet cane
from a distant land?
Your •burnt offerings
are not acceptable;
your sacrifices do not
please Me.
[21] Therefore, this is what
the LORD says:
I am going to place
stumbling blocks
before these people;
fathers and sons together
will stumble over them;
friends and neighbors
will also perish.

A Cruel Nation from the North (6:22-26)

[22] This is what the LORD says:

Look, an army is coming
from a northern land;
a great nation
will be awakened
from the remote regions
of the earth.
[23] They grasp bow and javelin.
They are cruel and show
no mercy.
Their voice roars
like the sea,
and they ride on horses,
lined up like men
in battle formation
against you, Daughter Zion.
[24] We have heard about it,
and we are discouraged.[A]
Distress has seized us—
pain like a woman in labor.
[25] Don't go out to the fields;
don't walk on the road.
For the enemy has a sword;
terror is on every side.
[26] My dear[B] people,
dress yourselves
in •sackcloth
and roll in the dust.
Mourn as you would for
an only son,
a bitter lament,
for suddenly the destroyer
will come on us.

Jeremiah Appointed as an Examiner (6:27-30)

[27] I have appointed you
to be an assayer
among My people—
a refiner[C]—
so you may know and assay
their way of life.
[28] All are stubborn rebels
spreading slander.
They are bronze and iron;
all of them are corrupt.
[29] The bellows blow,
blasting the lead with fire.
The refining is completely
in vain;
the evil ones are not
separated out.
[30] They are called
rejected silver,
for the LORD
has rejected them.

False Trust in the Temple (7:1-11)

7 This is the word that came to
Jeremiah from the LORD: [2] "Stand
in the gate of the house of the LORD
and there call out this word: Hear
the word of the LORD, all you people
of Judah who enter through these
gates to worship the LORD.
[3] "This is what the LORD of •Hosts,
the God of Israel, says: Correct your
ways and your deeds, and I will allow you to live in this place. [4] Do
not trust deceitful words, chanting:
This is the temple of the LORD, the
temple of the LORD, the temple of the
LORD. [5] Instead, if you really change
your ways and your actions, if you
act justly toward one another,[D] [6] if
you no longer oppress the foreigner,
the fatherless, and the widow and no
longer shed innocent blood in this
place or follow other gods, bringing
harm on yourselves, [7] I will allow
you to live in this place, the land I
gave to your ancestors long ago and
forever. [8] But look, you keep trusting
in deceitful words that cannot help.
[9] "Do you steal, murder, commit
adultery, swear falsely, burn incense
to •Baal, and follow other gods that
you have not known? [10] Then do you
come and stand before Me in this
house called by My name and say,
'We are delivered, so we can continue

6:22-26 The destruction at the hand of the cruel Babylonians—**a great nation . . . from the remote regions of the earth**—is described vividly. Judah, personified as **Daughter Zion**, should mourn and lament the coming destruction.

6:27-30 The Lord **appointed** Jeremiah as an **assayer** (Hb *bachan*, "search out, examine; test or refine" metals; cp. Zch 13:9) over the people to try to sort out the wicked from the good. This effort proved to be **completely in vain**. Imagery of smelting and refining ore is used to show that the spiritual purification process did not yield any purity because nothing good was left or because the impurities (**evil ones**) stuck to the metal and could not be separated.

7:1-10 This section is referred to as a "Temple Sermon" because these words were preached in the **gate of the house of the LORD** in Jerusalem. Some material is repeated in chapter 26. Apparently, worshipers repeated three times the formulaic chant, **the temple of the LORD**, which was supposed to give a sense of safety, protection, and security from punishment. But the Lord desired a spurning of evil deeds—oppression of foreigners, orphans, and widows; murder; and idolatry—not empty chants. The people broke the Ten Commandments, and then came to the temple, believing that they could hold onto a formulaic incantation involving the temple and be **delivered** from punishment. They placed false hope in the temple's presence among them as an indicator of God's favor and protection, treating it as a sort of good luck charm. Their attitude reflects gross presumption and willful misunderstanding of covenant faithfulness: Standing in the temple, they say, **We are delivered, so we can continue doing all these detestable acts** (v. 10).

[A] 6:24 Lit *and our hands fail* [B] 6:26 Lit *Daughter of My* [C] 6:27 Text emended; MT reads *fortress* [D] 7:5 Lit *justly between a man and his neighbor*

7:11 By their attitude, they degrade God's holy house, making it into a **den of robbers**. The metaphor suggests the image of thieves who temporarily hide out in a cave until their next opportunity to go out and commit crime.

7:12-15 As a warning, God pointed to the fate of **Shiloh**, the Old Testament city in the northern kingdom of Israel, in which the tabernacle and the ark of the covenant were first located during the days of the judges. The ark, which represented God's presence among His people, was mistakenly regarded as a talisman. Shiloh was completely destroyed by the Philistines around 1050 B.C., and clearly the ensuing disaster was God's doing. In the same way, God would allow the temple's destruction. The people must not rely on a symbol (the temple, the ark); rather their trust must be in the God who inhabits the temple. Judah believed the temple was wholly inviolable; so when it was looted and destroyed, the people's shock was palpable (cp. Lm 2:6-7; 5:18). Its destruction was simply not considered possible.

7:16-20 God instructed Jeremiah not to intercede for the people. God purposely would **not listen**. They have provoked Him with idolatry within their family units in the worship of the **queen of heaven**, also known as Ishtar by the Babylonians and Astarte/Ashtoreth by the Egyptians and Canaanites. The queen of heaven was a fertility goddess, and all members of the Judean household were involved in her service, thereby making them all guilty: the children gathered wood, the fathers lit the fire, and the women kneaded the dough to bake cakes for her to ensure fertility (cp. Hs 7:4).

7:20 As the people **pour out** [Hb *nasak*, "pour out libations"; cp. v. 18; Ps 16:4] **drink offerings** to idols—Ishtar, as well as **other gods**—God's **burning wrath is about to be poured out** (Hb *natak*, "poured forth, melted"; cp. Jr 42:18; 44:6; 2Ch 34:21,25; Ezk 22:21-22; Nah 1:6) over them and all their land. Jeremiah 8 and 44 will add further information about the Judean women's participation in these idolatrous practices.

7:21-24 Despite consistent warnings through prophets, the people had deliberately ignored God; now God would ignore the prayers of the people.

7:25-29 The urgency of the prophetic warnings is expressed in the phrase **time and time again**, literally "each day rising early and sending" the prophets. The people were stubborn and disobedient, and God indicated

>WORD|*study*

7:11 The word robbers (Hb *parits*), comes from a verbal root (Hb *parats*, meaning "break down or destroy") and denotes "violent men," not merely those who steal (cp. Ezk 7:22; 18:10; Dn 11:14). Jesus cited Jr 7:11 when He cleansed the temple (cp. Mt 21:13; Mk 11:17; Lk 19:46). Likewise, many people in this generation think that their wickedness during the week may be overcome with lip-service in occasional worship or by ownership of religious items—whether crosses, Bibles, or other spiritual paraphernalia.

doing all these detestable acts'? 11 Has this house, which is called by My name, become a den of robbers in your view? Yes, I too have seen it."

This is
the LORD's declaration.

Shiloh as a Warning (7:12-15)

12 "But return to My place that was at Shiloh, where I made My name dwell at first. See what I did to it because of the evil of My people Israel. 13 Now, because you have done all these things"—this is the LORD's declaration—"and because I have spoken to you time and time again[A] but you wouldn't listen, and I have called to you, but you wouldn't answer, 14 what I did to Shiloh I will do to the house that is called by My name—the house in which you trust—the place that I gave you and your ancestors. 15 I will drive you from My presence, just as I drove out all of your brothers, all the descendants of Ephraim.

Not Praying for Judah (7:16-20)

16 "As for you, do not pray for these people. Do not offer a cry or a prayer on their behalf, and do not beg Me, for I will not listen to you. 17 Don't you see how they behave in the cities of Judah and in the streets of Jerusalem? 18 The sons gather wood, the fathers light the fire, and the women knead dough to make cakes for the queen of heaven,[B] and they pour out •drink offerings to other gods so that they provoke Me to anger. 19 But are they really provoking Me?" This is the LORD's declaration. "Isn't it they themselves being provoked to disgrace?"

20 Therefore, this is what the Lord GOD says: "Look, My anger—My burning wrath—is about to be poured out on this place, on man and beast, on the tree of the field, and on the produce of the land. My wrath will burn and not be quenched."

Obedience over Sacrifice (7:21-26)

21 This is what the LORD of Hosts, the God of Israel, says: "Add your •burnt offerings to your other sacrifices, and eat the meat yourselves, 22 for when I brought your ancestors out of the land of Egypt, I did not speak with them or command them concerning burnt offering and sacrifice. 23 However, I did give them this command: Obey Me, and then I will be your God, and you will be My people. You must follow every way I command you so that it may go well with you. 24 Yet they didn't listen or pay attention but followed their own advice and according to their own stubborn, evil heart. They went backward and not forward. 25 Since the day your ancestors came out of the land of Egypt until this day, I have sent all My servants the prophets to you time and time again.[C] 26 However, they wouldn't listen to Me or pay attention but became obstinate;[D] they did more evil than their ancestors.

A Lament for Disobedient Judah (7:27-34)

27 "When you speak all these things to them, they will not listen to you. When you call to them, they will not answer you. 28 You must therefore declare to them: This is the nation that would not listen to the voice of the LORD their God and would not accept discipline. Truth[E] has perished—it has disappeared from their mouths. 29 Cut off the hair of your sacred vow[F] and throw

[A]7:13 Lit *you rising early and speaking* [B]7:18 = a pagan goddess [C]7:25 Lit *you, each day rising early and sending* [D]7:26 Lit *but stiffened their neck* [E]7:28 Or *Faithfulness* [F]7:29 Lit *off your consecration*

it away. Raise up a dirge on the barren heights, for the LORD has rejected and abandoned the generation
under His wrath.
30 "For the Judeans have done what
is evil in My sight." This is the LORD's
declaration. "They have set up their
detestable things in the house that
is called by My name and defiled it.
31 They have built the •high places of
•Topheth[A] in the Valley of Hinnom[B]
in order to burn their sons and
daughters in the fire, a thing I did
not command; I never entertained
the thought.[C]
32 "Therefore, take note! Days are
coming"—the LORD's declaration—
"when this place will no longer be
called Topheth and the Valley of Hinnom, but the Valley of Slaughter.
Topheth will become a cemetery,[D]
because there will be no other burial
place. 33 The corpses of these people
will become food for the birds of the
sky and for the wild animals of the
land, with no one to scare them away.
34 I will remove from the cities of Judah and the streets of Jerusalem the
sound of joy and gladness and the
voices of the groom and the bride,
for the land will become a desolate
waste.

Jeremiah's Lamentation over the People's Doom (8:1–10:25)

Death over Life (8:1-7)

8 "At that time"—this is the LORD's
declaration—"the bones of the
kings of Judah, the bones of her
officials, the bones of the priests,
the bones of the prophets, and the
bones of the residents of Jerusalem
will be brought out of their graves.
2 They will be exposed to the sun,
the moon, and the whole heavenly
•host, which they have loved, served,
followed, consulted, and worshiped.
Their bones will not be collected and
buried but will become like manure
on the surface of the soil. 3 Death
will be chosen over life by all the
survivors of this evil family, those
who remain wherever I have banished them." This is the declaration
of the LORD of Hosts.

4 "You are to say to them: This is
what the LORD says:

Do people fall and not
get up again?
If they turn away, do they
not return?
5 Why have these people
turned away?
Why is Jerusalem always
turning away?
They take hold of deceit;
they refuse to return.
6 I have paid careful attention.
They do not speak
what is right.
No one regrets his evil,
asking, 'What have I done?'
Everyone has stayed
his course
like a horse rushing into battle.
7 Even the stork in the sky
knows her seasons.
The turtledove, swallow,
and crane[E]
are aware of their migration,
but My people do not know
the requirements of the LORD.

Punishment for Judah's Leaders (8:8-13)

8 "How can you claim,
'We are wise;
the law of the LORD is with us'?
In fact, the lying pen
of scribes
has produced falsehood.
9 The wise will be put to shame;
they will be dismayed
and snared.
They have rejected the word
of the LORD,
so what wisdom do they
really have?
10 Therefore, I will give
their wives to other men,
their fields to new occupants,
for from the least
to the greatest,
everyone is making
profit dishonestly.
From prophet to priest,
everyone deals falsely.
11 They have treated
superficially the brokenness
of My dear[F] people,
claiming, 'Peace, peace,'
when there is no peace.

that they had defiled themselves. **Cut off the hair of your sacred vow** refers to a Nazirite, whose long hair was a sign of dedication to God, as defiling himself by touching a dead body (cp. Nm 6:5-12). Cutting the hair was also a sign of mourning.

7:30-31 The reason for defilement followed—a complete and idolatrous abomination within the family and community: The people had sacrificed their own children by burning them as an offering to the god Molech at **Topheth** (Hb, "fireplace") in the **Valley of Hinnom** (Hb, "lamentation").

7:32-34 God's judgment on the people is indicated by the change of name from "Valley of Hinnom" to **Valley of Slaughter**, where the people who performed such crimes would themselves be murdered and their corpses left unburied. This scene represented the pinnacle of the disaster that Judah had brought upon herself. She had destroyed her own community—family by family—as idolatrous practices bound the family in their joint participation in worship and also divided the family as they worshiped through child sacrifice. Consequently, the family would be completely subverted by a removal of both the solemnity and respect characterizing proper funerals and by the joy of weddings. By Jesus' day, this valley (named Ge-hinnom) had become a dump where garbage was burned, and it was known as Gehenna (Gk *geenna*, "hellfire"; e.g., see textual note on Mt 5:22), Jesus' image for hell.

8:1-3 As part of the coming judgment (7:32), the bones of Judah's leaders would be exhumed and exposed to the elements, ironically, the very elements they worshiped, the **sun, the moon, and the whole heavenly host**. Their bodies would remain unburied, and those who survived the disaster would prefer death to life.

8:4-5 Multiple variations of the word **turn** (Hb *shuv*) are used in these verses. The Lord lamented that Jerusalem was **always turning away** but does **not return** (i.e., she was unwilling to repent, choosing instead to continue pursuing evil and **deceit**, of which she had now taken **hold**).

8:7 Even migratory birds instinctively obey the will of the Lord—they know their **seasons**; but the people of God do not obey because they **do not know the requirements of the LORD**.

8:8-11 The religious leaders who thought they were **wise** were actually foolish, being unwise in the way of God; they lacked true, spiritual wisdom. Their worldly wisdom led only to selfish

A7:31 Lit *of the fireplace* B7:31 A valley south of Jerusalem C7:31 Lit *command, and it did not arise on My heart* D7:32 Lit *They will bury in Topheth* E8:7 Hb obscure F8:11 Lit *of the daughter of My*

gain at the expense of the well-being of the people. They will experience punishment by having all of their ill-gotten gain and much more (**wives, fields**) taken away (i.e., by the coming invaders).

The religious leaders neither saw nor cared to see the true spiritual needs of the people (repentance), thereby treating their **brokenness** as nothing serious.

8:13-17 Their punishment was their own loss of life (**I will . . . bring them to an end**; i.e., they will not be spared like the remnant; cp. note on 5:18-19) and loss of the land's fertility—**even the leaf will wither**, presumably from a drought more fully described in chapter 14. Judah seemed to have resigned herself to the reality of the coming destruction, which began to dawn on her as she imagined hearing the sounds of war coming **from Dan** in the north. Metaphors of war and destruction are used to convey the dread of the Babylonians' invasion (**mighty steeds** coming to **devour the land** and its **residents** as well as **poisonous vipers**).

8:18–9:3 This lament is one of several prompting the epithet of "weeping prophet" for Jeremiah. He seems to speak both for himself as well as for the Lord.

8:19 Jeremiah might be referring here to the imagined cries of those already deported to Babylon.

8:21 Jeremiah's heartfelt anguish over his people's fate was overwhelming. Unlike false prophets who "have treated superficially the brokenness of My dear people" (8:11), the Lord's prophet was **broken by the brokenness of** [His] **dear people**.

8:22 Their sin is described as an illness for which no cure can be found—not even in **Gilead**, a region renowned for its healing **balm** (or balsam) and the quality of its physicians. The answer to the two rhetorical questions here is "Yes, but to no avail," for even that famous ointment and those renowned physicians would be of no benefit for the grave illness of being unrepentant.

9:1-2 The depth of Jeremiah's "grief" (Hb *yagon*, "great sorrow," v. 18; cp. 20:18; 31:13; 45:3; Gn 42:38; Rm 9:2) is hyperbolized: **If my head were water, my eyes a fountain of tears, I would weep day and night** over Judah's situation. At the same time, the prophet experienced conflicting feelings. He was both grieved and repulsed by the people's actions and would like to separate himself from them, for they were liars, **adulterers**, and evildoers.

12 Were they ashamed
when they acted
so abhorrently?
They weren't at all ashamed.
They can no longer
feel humiliation.
Therefore, they will fall
among the fallen.
When I punish them,
they will collapse,"
says the LORD.

13 I will gather them
and bring them to an end.[A]
This is
the LORD's declaration.
There will be no grapes
on the vine,
no figs on the fig tree,
and even the leaf will wither.
Whatever I have given them
will be lost to them.

God's Unrepentant People (8:14-17)

14 Why are we just sitting here?
Gather together; let us enter
the fortified cities
and perish there,[B]
for the LORD our God
has destroyed[C] us.
He has given us
poisoned water to drink,
because we have sinned
against the LORD.
15 We hoped for peace,
but there was nothing good;
for a time of healing,
but there was only terror.

16 From Dan the snorting
of horses is heard.
At the sound of the neighing
of mighty steeds,
the whole land quakes.
They come to devour the land
and everything in it,
the city and all its residents.
17 Indeed, I am about to send
snakes among you,
poisonous vipers that cannot
be charmed.
They will bite you.
This is
the LORD's declaration.

Lament over Judah (8:18—9:3)

18 My joy has flown away;
grief has settled on me.
My heart is sick.
19 Listen—the cry
of my dear[D] people
from a far away land,
"Is the LORD no longer
in •Zion,
her King not within her?"
Why have they provoked me
to anger
with their carved images,
with their worthless
foreign idols?
20 Harvest has passed,
summer has ended,
but we have not been saved.
21 I am broken
by the brokenness
of my dear[D] people.
I mourn; horror has
taken hold of me.
22 Is there no balm in Gilead?
Is there no physician there?
So why has the healing
of my dear[D] people
not come about?

9[E] If my head were a spring of
water,
my eyes a fountain of tears,
I would weep day and night
over the slain
of my dear[F] people.
2[G] If only I had a traveler's
lodging place
in the wilderness,
I would abandon my people
and depart from them,
for they are all adulterers,
a solemn assembly
of treacherous people.
3 They bent their tongues
like their bows;
lies and not faithfulness
prevail in the land,
for they proceed from one evil
to another,
and they do not take Me
into account.
This is
the LORD's declaration.

Imminent Ruin and Exile (9:4-16)

4 Everyone has to be on guard
against his friend.
Don't trust any brother,
for every brother will
certainly deceive,

[A] **8:13** Lit *Gathering I will end them* [B] **8:14** Or *there be silenced* [C] **8:14** Or *silenced* [D] **8:19,21,22** Lit *of the daughter of my* [E] **9:1** Jr 8:23 in Hb [F] **9:1** Lit *slain among the daughter of my* [G] **9:2** Jr 9:1 in Hb

and every friend
spread slander.
5 Each one betrays his friend;
no one tells the truth.
They have taught
their tongues to speak lies;
they wear themselves out
doing wrong.
6 You live in a world
of deception.[A]
In their deception they refuse
to know Me.
This is
the LORD's declaration.

7 Therefore, this is what the LORD
of •Hosts says:

I am about to refine them
and test them,
for what else can I do
because of
My dear[B] people?[C]
8 Their tongues are
deadly arrows—
they speak deception.
With his mouth
a man speaks peaceably
with his friend,
but inwardly he sets up
an ambush.
9 Should I not punish them
for these things?
This is
the LORD's declaration.
Should I not avenge Myself
on such a nation as this?
10 I will raise weeping
and a lament
over the mountains,
a dirge over the wilderness
grazing land,
for they have been
so scorched
that no one passes through.
The sound of cattle is
no longer heard.
From the birds of the sky
to the animals,
everything has
fled—they have gone away.
11 I will make Jerusalem a heap
of rubble,
a jackals' den.
I will make the cities of Judah
a desolation,
an uninhabited place.

12 Who is the man wise enough
to understand this? Who has the
LORD spoken to, that he may explain
it? Why is the land destroyed and
scorched like a wilderness, so no
one can pass through?
13 The LORD said, "It is because they
abandoned My instruction that I set
in front of them and did not obey My
voice or walk according to it. 14 Instead, they followed the stubbornness of their hearts and followed
after the •Baals as their fathers
taught them." 15 Therefore, this is
what the LORD of Hosts, the God of
Israel, says: "I am about to feed this
people •wormwood and give them
poisonous water to drink. 16 I will
scatter them among the nations
that they and their fathers have not
known. I will send a sword after
them until I have finished them off."

Mourning over Judah (9:17-22)

17 This is what the LORD of Hosts
says:

Consider, and summon
the women who mourn;
send for the skillful women.
18 Let them come quickly
to raise a lament over us
so that our eyes may overflow
with tears,
our eyelids soaked
with weeping.
19 For a sound of lamentation
is heard from •Zion:
How devastated we are.
We are greatly ashamed,
for we have abandoned
the land;
our dwellings have been
torn down.
20 Now hear the word
of the LORD, you women.
Pay attention to[D] the word
of His mouth.
Teach your daughters
a lament
and one another a dirge,
21 for Death has climbed
through our windows;
it has entered our fortresses,
cutting off children
from the streets,
young men from the squares.

9:3-6 The entrenchment of sins of the tongue (slander, deceit, falsehood, betrayal) prevented the people from knowing the Lord. That **every brother will certainly deceive** indicated that the people were living up to the heritage of their ancestor Jacob, who deceived his brother Esau (9:4; cp. Gn 27).

9:7-11 Due to the pervasiveness of falsehood among the people, the Lord had no choice but to **refine** [Hb *tsaraph*; cp. 6:29; see note on Ps 66:10-12] **them and test** [Hb *bachan*; see Jr 6:27] **them**, and He did so by the destruction of their land, which was scorched and burned beyond any use—the wildlife fled, and the city remained a desolate pile of **rubble,** inhabited only by **jackals** (cp. Lm 5:18).

9:12-13 The wise person would understand that Judah's abandonment of her God was the cause of this national and natural tragedy.

9:15-16 Wormwood (Hb *la'anah*, "noxious or poisonous herb"; cp. 23:15; Dt 29:18; Pr 5:4) and **poisonous water** (Hb *mayim*, "waters" of *ro'sh*, "gall, poison"; cp. 8:14; Dt 29:18; 32:32; Ps 69:21) indicated that the punishment would be bitter and deadly. The sins of the tongue, which were symptomatic of the people's spiritual corruption, tore down the community and contributed to its disintegration (cp. Jms 1:26).

9:17-20 Mourning was a form of employment for many **women** in ancient Israel; these women wailed loudly, beat their breasts, tore their hair, and chanted a **dirge** or song of grief. This profession was passed on to the next generation of **daughters**. These women's **tears**, which overflowed and **soaked** their eyes (as well as Jeremiah's own "fountain of tears," 9:1), stood in stark contrast to the drought (14:1).

9:21-22 Death is personified as an intruder who has penetrated the city and taken the lives of both weak **children** and strong **young men**. Death is also like a **reaper** who thoroughly cuts down the grain in a field, then leaves it out in the open, subject to the elements; this is possibly the origin of the "Grim Reaper" in Western tradition. Stark imagery of **manure** and **newly cut grain** left in the open and subject to the elements indicates bodies left to decay without the dignity of burial.

[A]9:6 LXX reads *Oppression on oppression, deceit on deceit* [B]9:7 Lit *of the daughter of My* [C]9:7 LXX, Tg read *because of their evils* [D]9:20 Lit *Your ears must receive*

9:23-24 Too many people in Judah thought **wealth**, **wisdom**, or **strength** was sufficient for a secure life, but the Lord insists that one can boast only in the knowledge of the Lord whose covenant qualities (**faithful love, justice, and righteousness**) alone are sufficient for life.

9:25-26 An unfavorable comparison is set forth of the chosen people with other nations who also practiced circumcision for various reasons. Israelites practiced it as a sign of their covenant with the Lord (cp. Gn 17:10-14), while their neighbors were circumcised only for the sake of their flesh (Rm 2:25-29). God's people did not keep that covenant in their hearts and were thus equally rejected and punished along with the surrounding nations.

10:1-2 A hymn about the incomparable nature of God follows, alternating in its stanzas between the vanity of idols and the powerful majesty of Israel's God. **The way of the nations** and **signs in the heavens** refer to superstitious pagans who place stock in omens.

10:3-5 The worthlessness of idols and the folly of idolatry are then highlighted. What begins as **a tree from the forest** is fashioned by a skilled artisan as a god to be worshiped, though it is no more frightening than lifeless "scarecrows."

10:5 The futility of worshiping idols is underscored by four negative action verbs: the idols **cannot speak** or **walk**; they **can do no harm** and **cannot do any good**. In short, they are dead and ineffective. Everything of value in an idol—its craftsmanship, decoration, and garment—comes from a human being.

10:6-9 The Lord, by contrast, is a powerful **King**, who should be feared. He is living and eternal (v. 10). The power, vitality, and creativity of the Lord are juxtaposed with the lifelessness, sterility, and futility of idols. This paean of praise to Yahweh as the God over the elements possibly constitutes an additional criticism of Baal.

10:10-11 The gods that did not make the heavens and the earth is a defining phrase. False gods stand in stark contrast to **the true God, living** and **eternal**, who is identified in Scripture (OT and NT) as the Maker of the heavens and the earth (Gn 1:1; Ps 102:25; Is 40:21-22; Rom 1:20; Col 1:16; Heb 11:3; Rv 4:11).

22 Speak as follows:
This is what the LORD says:

Human corpses will fall
like manure on the surface
of the field,
like newly cut grain
after the reaper
with no one to gather it.

Boasting in the LORD (9:23-26)

23 This is what the LORD says:

The wise man must not boast
in his wisdom;
the strong man
must not boast
in his strength;
the wealthy man
must not boast
in his wealth.
24 But the one who boasts
should boast in this,
that he understands
and knows Me—
that I am •Yahweh,
showing faithful love,
justice, and righteousness
on the earth,
for I delight in these things.
This is
the LORD's declaration.

25 "The days are coming"—the
LORD's declaration—"when I will
punish all the circumcised yet uncircumcised: 26 Egypt, Judah, Edom,
the Ammonites, Moab, and all the
inhabitants of the desert who clip
the hair on their temples.[A] All these
nations are uncircumcised, and the
whole house of Israel is uncircumcised in heart."

Contrasting False Gods with the Creator (10:1-16)

10 Hear the word that the LORD
has spoken to[B] you, house of
Israel. 2 This is what the LORD says:

Do not learn the way
of the nations
or be terrified by signs
in the heavens,
although the nations
are terrified by them,
3 for the customs of the peoples
are worthless.
Someone cuts down a tree
from the forest;
it is worked by the hands
of a craftsman with a chisel.
4 He decorates it with silver
and gold.
It is fastened with hammer
and nails,
so it won't totter.
5 Like scarecrows
in a cucumber patch,
their idols cannot speak.
They must be carried because
they cannot walk.
Do not fear them for they
can do no harm—
and they cannot do any good.

6 •Yahweh, there is no one
like You.
You are great;
Your name is great in power.
7 Who should not •fear You,
King of the nations?
It is what You deserve.
For among all the wise people
of the nations
and among
all their kingdoms,
there is no one like You.
8 They are both stupid
and foolish,
instructed by worthless idols
made of wood!
9 Beaten silver is brought
from Tarshish,
and gold from Uphaz[C]
from the hands
of a goldsmith,
the work of a craftsman.
Their clothing is blue
and purple,
all the work
of skilled artisans.
10 But Yahweh is the true God;
He is the living God
and eternal King.
The earth quakes
at His wrath,
and the nations
cannot endure His rage.

11 You are to say this to them, "The
gods that did not make the heavens
and the earth will perish from the
earth and from under these heavens."[D]

[A] 9:26 Or *who live in distant places* [B] 10:1 Or *against* [C] 10:9 Or *Ophir* [D] 10:11 This is the only Aram v. in Jr.

12 He made the earth
by His power,
established the world
by His wisdom,
and spread out the heavens
by His understanding.
13 When He thunders,[A]
the waters in the heavens
are in turmoil,
and He causes the clouds
to rise
from the ends of the earth.
He makes lightning
for the rain
and brings the wind
from His storehouses.
14 Everyone is stupid
and ignorant.
Every goldsmith
is put to shame
by his carved image,
for his cast images are a lie;
there is no breath in them.
15 They are worthless, a work
to be mocked.
At the time
of their punishment
they will be destroyed.
16 Jacob's Portion[B] is not
like these
because He is the One
who formed all things.
Israel is the tribe
of His inheritance;
Yahweh of •Hosts is His name.

Exile after the Siege (10:17-18)

17 Gather up your belongings[C]
from the ground,
you who live under siege.

18 For this is what the LORD says:

Look, I am slinging out
the land's residents
at this time
and bringing them
such distress
that they will feel it.

Jeremiah's Grief (10:19-25)

19 Woe to me because of
my brokenness—
I am severely wounded!
I exclaimed, "This is
my intense suffering,
but I must bear it."
20 My tent is destroyed;
all my tent cords are snapped.
My sons have departed
from me and are no more.
I have no one to pitch
my tent again
or to hang up my curtains.
21 For the shepherds are stupid:
they don't seek the LORD.
Therefore they have not
prospered,
and their whole flock
is scattered.
22 Listen!
A noise—it is coming—
a great commotion
from the land to the north.
The cities of Judah will be
made desolate,
a jackals' den.

23 I know, LORD,
that a man's way of life is not
his own;
no one who walks determines
his own steps.
24 Discipline me, LORD,
but with justice—
not in Your anger,
or You will reduce me
to nothing.
25 Pour out Your wrath
on the nations
that don't recognize You
and on the families
that don't call on Your name,
for they have consumed
Jacob;
they have consumed him
and finished him off
and made his homeland
desolate.

The Punishment for Violation of the Covenant (11:1–12:17)

Reminder of the Covenant (11:1-23)

11 This is the word that came to
Jeremiah from the LORD: 2 "Listen to the words of this covenant
and tell them to the men of Judah
and the residents of Jerusalem. 3 You
must tell them: This is what the
LORD, the God of Israel, says: 'Let a
curse be on the man who does not
obey the words of this covenant,
4 which I commanded your ancestors when I brought them out of
the land of Egypt, out of the iron

10:12-16 This song of praise to the Creator God is repeated in Jr 51:15-19. **Jacob's portion** and **inheritance** both refer to the Lord, **the One who formed all things**.

10:17-18 Jeremiah predicted the severe punishment of coming exile. The people may be speaking here, or Jeremiah may be expressing grief on their behalf, identifying with them.

10:19-20 Brokenness, being **severely** [Hb *chalah*, "grievous," so bad as to be unlikely to heal"; cp. 14:17; 30:12] **wounded** (Hb *makkah*, "blow, wound from being struck"; cp. 6:7), and **intense suffering** (Hb *choli*, "disease, sickness, affliction, grief," from *chalah* [above]; cp. Is 1:5; 53:3-4)—brought about by invasion, siege, and exile—are expressed through domestic imagery. **My tent** [Hb *ʾohel*, "nomad's moveable house; tabernacle"] **is destroyed** (Hb *shadad*, "be laid waste, devastated, ruined"; cp. 4:13; Is 15:1; 23:1; Nah 3:7)—possibly a reference to the destruction of the temple and/or tabernacle, and there was no one to reestablish worship according to God's prescription, represented by the tabernacle—i.e., the **tent** and its **curtains** (Hb *yeriʿah*; see note on Ex 26:1-6).

10:21-22 The **shepherds**, or civil leaders, **are stupid** (Hb *baʿar*, "insensible, carnal, or cruel"; cp. v. 14; 51:17). Having failed to **seek the LORD**, their sheep had **scattered** (Hb *puts*, "be dispersed"; cp. Ezk 34:6)—figurative reference to what had happened to the people without spiritually competent leadership.

10:23-25 This action is the people's last attempt to appease either God's wrath or Jeremiah's prayer. The theme of these verses also appears in Jb 10:2-9 and the exilic Ps 79:5-7. The repetition of words indicating destruction—**consumed** (Hb *ʾakal*, "devour"), **finished . . . off** (Hb *kalah*, "consume, destroy"), and **made . . . desolate** (Hb *shamēm*, "lay waste")—emphasizes the complete and utter devastation of the city.

11:1-2 Commentators sometimes refer to Jr 11–20 as the "Confessions (or complaints) of Jeremiah." **This covenant** (vv. 2-3,6,8) seems to imply something more recent than the original Sinai covenant—likely a reference to the rediscovery of the book of Deuteronomy during the reign of Josiah, who initiated a covenant renewal ceremony and a program of religious reform (cp. 2Kg 22:1–23:30).

[A]**10:13** Lit *At His giving of the voice* [B]**10:16** = the LORD [C]**10:17** Lit *bundle*

11:3-8 The repetition of terms like **covenant**, **curse**, and **obey** lend further credence to the idea that Jeremiah refers here to Deuteronomy, where the covenant blessings (**you will be My people and I will be your God,** and also a **land flowing with milk and honey**) as well as the **curses** are clearly laid out (Dt 26:16–30:20).

11:9-11 The **conspiracy** may refer to those who did not desire to participate in the covenant renewal under Josiah. The Lord, in turn, rejected His people, and will no longer **hear them**.

11:13 The altars you have set up to Shame compared to the number of their **streets** might have the sense of "an idol on every corner."

11:14 The beginning of the end came when God forbade Jeremiah to intercede for the people (Jr 7:16; 14:11). The means of repentance and restoration were eliminated.

11:15-17 Although the Lord called His people **My beloved** (Hb *yedid*; cp. Dt 33:12; Pss 60:5; 108:6; 127:2; Is 5:1), they had **carried out so many evil schemes** (Hb *mezimmah*, "evil plan, thought, or counsel; lewdness") that they could not possibly be allowed in His **house**. Yahweh's rejection included the temple sacrifices, which were defiled in His sight because of the people's evil. The **olive tree**—an image of Judah's experiencing God's blessings under the covenant—connotes beauty, health, abundance, and prosperity. God would **set fire to it**—a common image of destruction—as a consequence of His anger at their idolatry (cp. 2Kg 22:13,17); not only were the blessings removed, but also the curses enacted nearly destroyed the nation altogether.

11:18-25 God reveals to Jeremiah a conspiracy against him from his very own townspeople. The conspiracies against God and against Jeremiah stood somewhat parallel; disloyalty to the Lord led to a rejection of His spokesman. Their desire was to destroy both Jeremiah and his message (**the tree with its fruit**). Jeremiah compared himself to **a docile** [Hb *ʾalluph*, "domesticated, gentle, tame"] **lamb led** [Hb *yaval*, "brought"; cp. Is 53:7] **to slaughter,** to underscore that he learned of the **plots** to destroy him from Yahweh Himself. The Lord pronounces judgment on **the people of Anathoth**, who are trying to silence His message and messenger. Jeremiah will not be **cut . . . off** and **no longer . . . remembered** (v. 19); rather, the people will be killed by **sword** and **famine,** and **they will have no remnant.**

furnace.' I declared: 'Obey Me, and do everything that I command you, and you will be My people, and I will be your God,' 5 in order to establish the oath I swore to your ancestors, to give them a land flowing with milk and honey, as it is today."

I answered, "•Amen, LORD."

6 The LORD said to me, "Proclaim all these words in the cities of Judah and in the streets of Jerusalem: Obey the words of this covenant and carry them out. 7 For I strongly warned your ancestors when I brought them out of the land of Egypt until today, warning them time and time again,[A] 'Obey My voice.' 8 Yet they would not obey or pay attention; each one followed the stubbornness of his evil heart. So I brought on them all the curses of this covenant, because they had not done what I commanded them to do."

9 The LORD said to me, "A conspiracy has been discovered among the men of Judah and the residents of Jerusalem. 10 They have returned to the sins of their ancestors who refused to obey My words and have followed other gods to worship them. The house of Israel and the house of Judah broke My covenant I made with their ancestors.

11 "Therefore, this is what the LORD says: I am about to bring on them disaster that they cannot escape. They will cry out to Me, but I will not hear them. 12 Then the cities of Judah and the residents of Jerusalem will go and cry out to the gods they have been burning incense to, but they certainly will not save them in their time of disaster. 13 Your gods are indeed as numerous as your cities, Judah, and the altars you have set up to Shame[B]—altars to burn incense to •Baal—as numerous as the streets of Jerusalem.

14 "As for you, do not pray for these people. Do not raise up a cry or a prayer on their behalf, for I will not be listening when they call out to Me at the time of their disaster.

15 What right does
My beloved have
to be in My house,
having carried out so many
evil schemes?
Can holy meat[C] prevent
your disaster[D]
so you can rejoice?
16 The LORD named you
a flourishing olive tree,
beautiful with
well-formed fruit.
He has set fire to it,
and its branches
are consumed[E]
with a great roaring sound.

17 "The LORD of •Hosts who planted you has decreed disaster against you, because of the harm the house of Israel and the house of Judah brought on themselves, provoking Me to anger by burning incense to Baal."

18 The LORD informed me,
so I knew.
Then You helped me to see
their deeds,
19 for I was like a docile[F] lamb
led to slaughter.
I didn't know that they had
devised plots against me:
"Let's destroy the tree
with its fruit;[G]
let's cut him off from the land
of the living
so that his name will
no longer be remembered."
20 But, LORD of Hosts,
who judges righteously,
who tests heart[H] and mind,
let me see Your vengeance
on them,
for I have presented my case
to You.

21 Therefore, here is what the LORD says concerning the people of Anathoth who want to take your life. They warn, "You must not prophesy in the name of •Yahweh, or you will certainly die at our hand." 22 Therefore, this is what the LORD of Hosts says: "I am about to punish them. The young men will die by the sword; their sons and daughters will die by famine. 23 They will have no remnant, for I will bring disaster on the people of Anathoth in the year of their punishment."

[A]11:7 Lit *today, rising early and warning* [B]11:13 = Baal [C]11:15 = sacrificial meat [D]11:15 LXX; MT reads *meat pass from you* [E]11:16 Vg; MT reads *broken* [F]11:19 Or *pet* [G]11:19 Lit *bread* [H]11:20 Lit *kidneys*

Jeremiah's Complaint (12:1-4)

12 You will be righteous, LORD,
even if I bring a case
against You.
Yet, I wish to contend
with You:
Why does the way
of the wicked prosper?
Why do all the treacherous
live at ease?
2 You planted them, and they
have taken root.
They have grown
and produced fruit.
You are ever on their lips,[A]
but far from
their conscience.[B]
3 As for You, LORD,
You know me; You see me.
You test whether my heart is
with You.
Drag the wicked away
like sheep to slaughter
and set them apart for the day
of killing.
4 How long will the land mourn
and the grass of every field
wither?
Because of the evil
of its residents,
animals and birds have been
swept away,
for the people have said,
"He cannot see what our end
will be."[C]

The Lord's Response (12:5-17)

5 If you have raced
with runners
and they have worn you out,
how can you compete
with horses?
If you stumble[D]
in a peaceful land,
what will you do
in the thickets
of the Jordan?
6 Even your brothers—your
own father's household—
even they were treacherous
to you;
even they have
cried out loudly after you.
Do not have confidence
in them,
though they speak well
of you.
7 I have abandoned My house;
I have deserted
My inheritance.
I have given the love of My life
into the hands
of her enemies.
8 My inheritance has acted
toward Me
like a lion in the forest.
She has roared against Me.
Therefore, I hate her.
9 Is My inheritance
like a hyena[E] to Me?
Are birds of prey circling her?
Go, gather all
the wild animals;
bring them to devour her.
10 Many shepherds
have destroyed My vineyard;
they have trampled My plot
of land.
They have turned
My desirable plot
into a desolate wasteland.
11 They have made it
a desolation.
It mourns, desolate,
before Me.
All the land is desolate,
but no one takes it to heart.
12 Over all the barren heights
in the wilderness
the destroyers have come,
for the LORD has a sword
that devours
from one end of the earth
to the other.
No one has peace.
13 They have sown wheat
but harvested thorns.
They have exhausted
themselves but have
no profit.
Be put to shame
by your harvests
because of the LORD's
burning anger.

14 This is what the LORD says:
"Concerning all My evil neighbors
who attack the inheritance that I
bequeathed to My people, Israel, I
am about to uproot them from their
land, and I will uproot the house of
Judah from them. 15 After I have uprooted them, I will once again have
compassion on them and return

[A]12:2 Lit *are near in their mouth* [B]12:2 Lit *kidneys* [C]12:4 LXX reads *see our ways* [D]12:5 Or *you are secure* [E]12:9 Hb obscure

12:1 Jeremiah poses the age-old enigma of the prosperity of the **wicked**. Perhaps he was referring to "the people of Anathoth" (11:21), but not necessarily, for wicked and **treacherous** people existed throughout the land (cp. 9:2-6). The question could be a general one, as in the wisdom writings (Job, Psalms, Proverbs, Ecclesiastes), not directed at specific individuals.

12:5-6 Worse trials were still to come for Jeremiah. **Thickets of the Jordan** refers to the marshy, overgrown, dangerous area along the riverbanks, especially common during the rainy season when there was extensive flooding (cp. Jos 3:15). Until this point in his ministry, Jeremiah had encountered relatively mild opposition (as far as he was aware). If he struggled with a **peaceful** situation, the Lord asked him how he would handle a more precarious one? His own kin were against him, paying him only lip service—a parallel to Israel's attitude toward the Lord.

12:7-10 This section uses several metaphors to depict the relationship between God and Judah:

- a **house** (Hb *bayit*), here referring not to the temple but to the nation, the "house of Israel" in the sense of a household or royal dynasty, a nation instated by God;
- **inheritance**, indicating that Judah was God's personal possession (vv. 7-9,14-15);
- **love** [Hb *yedidut*, "one dearly loved, beloved, delight"; from *yedid*, e.g., 11:15] **of My life**, indicating that God was Judah's husband and had a unique relationship with her—she was *not* like all the other nations; and
- **My vineyard** and **My plot of land,** which indicate that God is the vinedresser and farmer who tends and cares for His property, making it fruitful and prosperous.
- **Like a lion**, Judah had **roared against** her spouse—the one who cared for her. He would, therefore, abandon her to her enemies, who gathered around like **birds of prey** to **devour her**.

12:12-13 Behind the work of the destroyers was the Lord's **sword that devours** as punishment. Nevertheless, the attackers' evil deeds were not exempt from punishment.

12:14-16 Both Judah and the attackers had desolated and devoured the Lord's land and inheritance, and the Lord would punish (**uproot**) them by taking away their land. The **evil neighbors** would be punished along with Judah, but they could be redeemed if they turned to the Lord and would **learn the ways of My people**, a reversal of Jr 10:2-3 where

Judah followed the "way of the nations." The land was central to the promise of restoration. The punishment consisted of being uprooted from the land; the restoration consisted of returning to the land and being **built up among My people**. This passage amounts to an offer extended to Gentiles for inclusion among the people of God, if they would give allegiance to the Lord, swearing by His name, **As Yahweh lives** (cp. Rm 11:11; 19-32).

13:1-6 The oracle concerning the **linen undergarments** (Hb *'ēzor*, "belt, girdle, waistband") was a sign-act for which God provided an interpretation. The "linen underwear" in its composition represented priestliness (the priests usually wore linen) and close intimacy because of its position next to the wearer. The **Euphrates** (Hb *perat*, "fruitfulness," vv. 4-7) River was 350 miles from Jerusalem. Some believe that *Perath*, the Hebrew designation, may refer to another location, a spring that was only about four miles from Anathoth.

13:7-11 Just as Jeremiah's linen garment was **ruined** and **of no use at all**, so Israel had become useless. God had intended an intimate and holy relationship between Himself and Israel/Judah, yet the people had rotted and become useless for such a relationship because of idolatrous disobedience.

13:12-14 The second oracle of the jars **filled with wine** came via verbal metaphor only. This oracle involved imagery of smashing the wine jars representing wealth, joy, and blessing. **Drunkenness**, however, indicated a good situation gone bad—i.e., confusion, vulnerability, and weakness. The leaders, as well as the people, would be drunk on God's wrath and vulnerable to invading destroyers.

13:15-16 Jeremiah pointed to pride as a reason for continuing disobedience and refusal to return to God.

13:18-20 The royalty embodied a self-sufficient pride that spurns submission to the Lord, and God directed a message to **the king** (probably Jehoiachin) and **the queen mother** (Nehushta) that their loss of the throne and the takeover of their kingdom (**the flock entrusted to you**) by another nation had been decided.

13:22-26 The images of destruction are not only tragic but also violent, shocking, and disturbing. Judah had been publicly disgraced because of her preference for the sensually depraved worship of Baal, whose character is personified as **Falsehood**—as an idol he is but a lie, a deception that disappoints and betrays his worshipers (cp. 9:3-8; 16:19, which describe how God's people had become like the object of their worship).

each one to his inheritance and to
his land. 16 If they will diligently
learn the ways of My people—to
swear by My name, 'As •Yahweh
lives,' just as they taught My people
to swear by •Baal—they will be built
up among My people. 17 However, if
they will not obey, then I will uproot
and destroy that nation."
This is
the LORD's declaration.

The Consequences of Apostasy (13:1–15:9)

Linen Underwear (13:1-11)

13 This is what the LORD said to
me: "Go and buy yourself a lin-
en undergarment and put it on,[A] but
do not put it in water." 2 So I bought
underwear as the LORD instructed
me and put it on.
3 Then the word of the LORD came
to me a second time: 4 "Take the
underwear that you bought and
are wearing,[B] and go at once to the
Euphrates[C] and hide it in a rocky
crevice." 5 So I went and hid it by the
Euphrates, as the LORD commanded
me.
6 A long time later the LORD said
to me, "Go at once to the Euphrates
and get the underwear that I commanded you to hide there." 7 So I
went to the Euphrates and dug up
the underwear and got it from the
place where I had hidden it, but it
was ruined—of no use at all.
8 Then the word of the LORD came
to me: 9 "This is what the LORD says:
Just like this I will ruin the great
pride of both Judah and Jerusalem.
10 These evil people, who refuse to
listen to Me, who follow the stubbornness of their own hearts, and
who have followed other gods to
serve and worship—they will be
like this underwear, of no use at all.
11 Just as underwear clings to one's
waist, so I fastened the whole house
of Israel and of Judah to Me"—this
is the LORD's declaration—"so that
they might be My people for My
fame, praise, and glory, but they
would not obey.

The Wine Jars (13:12-14)

12 "Say this to them: This is what
the LORD, the God of Israel, says:
Every jar should be filled with wine.
Then they will respond to you,
'Don't we know that every jar should
be filled with wine?' 13 And you will
say to them: This is what the LORD
says: I am about to fill all who live
in this land—the kings who reign
for David on his throne, the priests,
the prophets and all the residents of
Jerusalem—with drunkenness. 14 I
will smash them against each other,
fathers and sons alike"—this is the
LORD's declaration. "I will allow no
mercy, pity, or compassion to keep
Me from destroying them."

The Lord's Warning (13:15-20)

15 Listen and pay attention.
Do not be proud,
for the LORD has spoken.
16 Give glory to the LORD
your God
before He brings darkness,
before your feet stumble
on the mountains at dusk.
You wait for light,
but He brings darkest gloom[D]
and makes thick darkness.
17 But if you will not listen,
my innermost being will weep
in secret
because of your pride.
My eyes will overflow
with tears,
for the LORD's flock has been
taken captive.

18 Say to the king
and the queen mother:
Take a humble seat,
for your glorious crowns
have fallen from your heads.
19 The cities of the •Negev are
under siege;
no one can help them.
All of Judah has been taken
into exile,
taken completely into exile.
20 Look up and see
those coming from the north.
Where is the flock entrusted
to you,
the sheep that were
your pride?

[A] **13:1** Lit *around your waist* [B] **13:4** Lit *wearing around your waist* [C] **13:4-7** Perhaps a place near Anathoth with the same spelling as river [D] **13:16** Or *brings a shadow of death*

The Destiny of Jerusalem (13:21-27)

21 What will you say
when He appoints
close friends as leaders
over you,
ones you yourself trained?
Won't labor pains seize you,
as they do a woman in labor?
22 And when you ask yourself,
"Why have these things
happened to me?"
It is because of
your great •guilt
that your skirts have been
stripped off,
your body exposed.[A]
23 Can the •Cushite change
his skin,
or a leopard his spots?
If so, you might be able to do
what is good,
you who are instructed
in evil.
24 I will scatter you[B]
like drifting chaff
before the desert wind.
25 This is your lot,
what I have decreed for you—
this is
the LORD's declaration—
because you have
forgotten Me
and trusted in Falsehood.[C]
26 I will pull your skirts up
over your face
so that your shame
might be seen.
27 Your adulteries and
your lustful neighing,
your heinous prostitution
on the hills, in the fields—
I have seen
your detestable acts.
Woe to you, Jerusalem!
You are •unclean—
for how long yet?

The Drought (14:1-10)

14 The word of the LORD that came to Jeremiah concerning the drought:

2 Judah mourns;
her gates languish.
Her people are on the ground
in mourning;
Jerusalem's cry rises up.
3 Their nobles send
their servants[D] for water.
They go to the cisterns;
they find no water;
their containers
return empty.
They are ashamed
and humiliated;
they cover their heads.
4 The ground is cracked
since no rain has fallen
on the land.
The farmers are ashamed;
they cover their heads.
5 Even the doe in the field
gives birth and abandons
her fawn
since there is no grass.
6 Wild donkeys stand
on the barren heights
panting for air like jackals.
Their eyes fail
because there are
no green plants.
7 Though our •guilt testifies
against us,
•Yahweh, act for
Your name's sake.
Indeed, our rebellions
are many;
we have sinned against You.
8 Hope of Israel,
its Savior in time of distress,
why are You like a foreigner
in the land,
like a traveler stopping only
for the night?
9 Why are You
like a helpless man,
like a warrior unable to save?
Yet You are among us,
Yahweh,
and we are called
by Your name.
Don't leave us!

10 This is what the LORD says concerning these people:

Truly they love to wander;
they never rest their feet.
So the LORD does not
accept them.
Now He will remember
their guilt
and punish their sins.

[A]13:22 Lit *your heels have suffered violence* [B]13:24 Lit *them* [C]13:25 = Baal [D]14:3 Lit *little ones*

Furthermore, Judah will never change, as a **leopard** does not change **his spots**. Jerusalem is figuratively portrayed as a woman whose guilt has been exposed. The imagery is shocking: Her **skirts** [Hb *shul*, "flowing skirt or train of a robe, the hem of a robe"; cp. Ex 28:33-34; Lm 1:9] **have been stripped off** (Hb *galah*, "uncovered or revealed, made naked"; cp. Is 47:3; Ezk 16:36; 23:29); her **body** (Hb *ʿaqēv*, "heels") has been **exposed** (Hb *chamas*, "violently made naked, treated with violence"). The Lord says, **I will pull** [Hb *chasaph*, "strip off a covering, make bare," v. 2; cp. Is 47:2; Jl 1:7] **your skirts up over your face**.

13:27 Her **adulteries**—i.e., idolatrous practices—are compared to the **neighings** of copulating horses. The severity of the punishment further points to the egregious nature of Judah's sin of idolatry, which started with devaluing her unique relationship with God. He would let her have her way, removing His protection and care and leaving her helpless before the lovers-turned-predators. The exile was still to come, but a more immediate punishment was the devastating drought described in chapter 14, a harsh blow to those who trusted in the storm god Baal to send the necessary water for their crops (see 3:3; 5:24; 14:22).

14:1 The **drought** (Hb *batstsoret*, "restraint" as in the holding back of rain; appears only here and 17:8) occurred on two levels—physical and spiritual.

14:2-4 Physically, the land was actually parched; no rain had fallen for so long that even the reservoirs (**cisterns**), which should have carried the nation through in times of drought, had dried up completely.

14:5-6 Even the doe, who instinctively protects her young, abandoned the fawns to their fate. **Wild donkeys,** normally able to survive in the desert, experienced difficulty during this drought.

14:7 The people's desperate cry to God to save them from this devastating situation was in vain. They themselves identified the cause of the drought—their sins, **guilt**, and **rebellions**.

14:8-9 The metaphors used for God indicate the people's perspective. He seemed like: **a foreigner** [Hb *gēr*, "stranger, foreigner, person living outside his own country"] **in the land**, one who is not invested in His people; **a traveler** passing through and therefore not present in their time of distress; **a helpless man** (Hb *daham*, "one confounded by sudden calamity"); and **a warrior unable to save**.

14:10-12 God saw the people's insincerity and fickleness and responded with harsh truth: The people were unfaithful and deserved their punishment. God would not even be impressed or moved if they fasted or brought sacrifices.

14:13-16 The false **prophets** led the people into complacency over their sin. They deceived the people into believing that the consequences of sin, "sword, famine, and plague" (v. 12) could be avoided, or that even without turning to God there would always be **peace**. God's oracle asserted that both the lying prophets and those deceived by them would perish by the very means they sought to avoid; worse yet, their bodies would remain unburied (cp. 9:22).

14:17-18 Jeremiah's lament for Judah takes the form of a dirge. He wept, both in retrospect and in anticipation, for the nation's calamity—the exile was either in progress or imminent. Already people had been slain, drought had resulted in **famine**, and people were being deported to Babylon.

14:21-22 Jeremiah confessed the people's sin, pleading for God's mercy on account of His **name**, **glorious throne**, and **covenant**. He acknowledged that Yahweh alone was the living God, who bore responsibility for the drought, and he indicated by his questions the cause for the devastating lack of rain: **Can any of the worthless idols of the nations bring rain?** This question is reminiscent to the confrontation between Elijah and King Ahab, whose wife Jezebel was a Baal worshiper. The confrontation between Elijah and those priests came within the context of another three-year drought that resulted in famine. Following the slaughter of the prophets of Baal, Elijah prayed for rain. The drought broke when the true God of Israel sent a thunderstorm (1Kg 17–18).

15:3-4 One reason for their horrible fourfold punishments (v. 2) was the deeds of King **Manasseh**, Josiah's grandfather (cp. 2Kg 21:1-17; 2Ch 33:1-20). Manasseh led the nation into idolatry after his father **Hezekiah** had purged the land, and he also sacrificed his children to idols in the Valley of Hinnom. When the exile came in Jeremiah's day, God reminded the people of the detestable practices leading Him to withdraw His compassion from His unrepentant people, abandoning them to their violent fate.

15:5-7 Jeremiah 15:5-9 constitutes a war lament, summed up in the terrible effect of war on Judah's women (cp. Jdg 5:28-30, a mocking lament). The implied answer to the three rhetorical questions in verse 5 is "no one." Jerusalem could count on no one for sympathy or commiseration when judgment fell because, Yahweh asserted, *she* was

Punishment of False Prophets (14:11-16)

11 Then the LORD said to me, "Do
not pray for the well-being of these
people. 12 If they fast, I will not hear
their cry of despair. If they offer
•burnt offering and •grain offering,
I will not accept them. Rather, I will
finish them off by sword, famine,
and plague."

13 And I replied, "Oh no, Lord GOD!
The prophets are telling them, 'You
won't see sword or suffer famine. I
will certainly give you true peace in
this place.'"

14 But the LORD said to me, "These
prophets are prophesying a lie in My
name. I did not send them, nor did
I command them or speak to them.
They are prophesying to you a false
vision, worthless •divination, the deceit of their own minds.

15 "Therefore, this is what the LORD
says concerning the prophets who
prophesy in My name, though I did
not send them, and who say, 'There
will never be sword or famine in this
land.' By sword and famine these
prophets will meet their end. 16 The
people they are prophesying to will
be thrown into the streets of Jerusalem because of the famine and the
sword. There will be no one to bury
them—they, their wives, their sons,
and their daughters. I will pour out
their own evil on them."

Jeremiah's Request (14:17-22)

17 You are to speak this word
to them:
Let my eyes overflow
with tears;
day and night may they
not stop,
for the virgin daughter
of my people
has been destroyed
by a great disaster,
an extremely severe wound.

18 If I go out to the field,
look—those slain
by the sword!
If I enter the city,
look—those ill from famine!
For both prophet and priest
travel to a land
they do not know.

19 Have You completely
rejected Judah?
Do You detest •Zion?
Why do You strike us
with no hope of healing
for us?
We hoped for peace,
but there was nothing good;
for a time of healing,
but there was only terror.

20 We acknowledge
our wickedness, LORD,
the guilt of our fathers;
indeed, we have sinned
against You.

21 Because of Your name,
don't despise us.
Don't disdain
Your glorious throne.
Remember Your covenant
with us;
do not break it.

22 Can any of the worthless idols
of the nations bring rain?
Or can the skies alone
give showers?
Are You not the LORD
our God?
We therefore put our hope
in You,
for You have done
all these things.

The Lord's Negative Response (15:1-9)

15 Then the LORD said to me:
"Even if Moses and Samuel
should stand before Me, My compassions would not reach out to these
people. Send them from My presence, and let them go. 2 If they ask
you, 'Where will we go?' you must
tell them: This is what the LORD says:

Those destined for death,
to death;
those destined for the sword,
to the sword.
Those destined for famine,
to famine;
those destined for captivity,
to captivity.

3 "I will ordain four kinds[A] of judgment for them"—this is the LORD's
declaration—"the sword to kill, the
dogs to drag away, and the birds
of the sky and the wild animals of
the land to devour and destroy. 4 I

A 15:3 Lit *families*

will make them a horror to all the kingdoms of the earth because of Manasseh son of Hezekiah, the king of Judah, for what he did in Jerusalem.

5 Who will have pity on you,
Jerusalem?
Who will show sympathy
toward you?
Who will turn aside
to ask about your welfare?
6 You have left Me.
This is
the LORD's declaration.
You have turned your back,
so I have stretched out
My hand against you
and destroyed you.
I am tired of
showing compassion.
7 I scattered them
with a winnowing fork
at the gates of the land.
I made them childless;
I destroyed My people.
They would not turn
from their ways.
8 I made their widows
more numerous
than the sand of the seas.
I brought a destroyer at noon
against the mother
of young men.
I suddenly released on her
agitation and terrors.
9 The mother of seven
grew faint;
she breathed her last breath.
Her sun set while it was
still day;
she was ashamed
and humiliated.
The rest of them I will
give over to the sword
in the presence
of their enemies."
This is
the LORD's declaration.

Jeremiah's Complaint and Rebuke (15:10-21)

10 Woe is me, my mother,
that you gave birth to me,
a man who incites dispute
and conflict
in all the land.
I did not lend or borrow,
yet everyone curses me.

11 The LORD said:

I will certainly set you free
and care for you.[A]
I will certainly intercede
for you
in a time of trouble,
in your time of distress,
with the enemy.
12 Can anyone smash iron,
iron from the north,
or bronze?
13 I will give up your wealth
and your treasures as plunder,
without cost, for all your sins
in all your borders.
14 Then I will make you serve
your enemies[B]
in a land you do not know,
for My anger will kindle a fire
that will burn against you.

15 You know, LORD;
remember me and take note
of me.
Avenge me
against my persecutors.
In Your patience,[C]
don't take me away.
Know that I suffer disgrace
for Your honor.
16 Your words were found,
and I ate them.
Your words became a delight
to me
and the joy of my heart,
for I am called by Your name,
•Yahweh God of •Hosts.
17 I never sat with the band
of revelers,
and I did not celebrate
with them.
Because Your hand was
on me, I sat alone,
for You filled me
with indignation.
18 Why has my pain
become unending,
my wound incurable,
refusing to be healed?
You truly have become
like a mirage to me—
water that is not reliable.

19 Therefore, this is what the LORD says:

[A]15:11 Lit *free for good* [B]15:14 Some Hb mss, LXX, Syr, Tg; other Hb mss read *you pass through*
[C]15:15 Lit *In the slowness of Your anger*

the one who left Him. Therefore, the Lord had **stretched out** [His] **hand**, manifesting His power in judgment (cp. 21:5; 51:25; Is 5:25; 23:11; Ezk 6:14; Zph 1:4; 2:13). Despite punishment sent by the Lord, Judah **turned** (Hb *ʾachor*, "backward," the direction of the verb *yalak*, "go, walk"; cp. 7:24) her **back** on the Lord, refusing to **turn from** (Hb *shuv*; see **Word Study**, p. 956) her ways.

15:8-9 The deaths of so many warriors is indicated by a striking reversal of the Lord's promise to Abraham—that his offspring would outnumber the grains of sand on the shore (Gn 22:17). Instead, **widows** would be incredibly numerous. **Mother of seven** (the number of perfection) refers to a woman fulfilled in childbearing, in the pride and joy of having many children. The woman who thought she had found this blessing would suddenly be **ashamed** and **humiliated** rather than proud. Her remaining days would be suddenly dark with grief, as if the **sun** had **set** prematurely, changing the noonday to darkness. The proliferation of children and the joy of marriage were the epitome of a flourishing community, but the weeping of widows and bereaved mothers epitomized the failing community.

15:10-11 A dialogue ensued between the Lord and Jeremiah, as Jeremiah struggled with the consequences of fulfilling his calling. As a prophet of doom, Jeremiah was not well-liked and was the victim of plotting by his own household (11:18-19; 12:6). In deep anguish, Jeremiah wished he were either dead or had never been born (cp. Jb 3:1-11). As Jeremiah lamented, the Lord comforted and reassured him.

15:12 The answer to this rhetorical question is that no one can **smash iron . . . or bronze**, particularly not **iron from the north**, probably referring to the Babylonians, God's invincible instruments of judgment.

15:15-17 Jeremiah's lament/complaint resumed, as he prayed for vengeance against his **persecutors**. Jeremiah's acceptance of his commission (cp. 1:9; Ezk 3:1-3) gives **joy**, in contrast to the previous and subsequent expressions of suffering and despair.

15:18 While his prophetic calling yielded joy, knowing that he identified with God, his identification with his own people yielded only hardship, alienation, loneliness, heaviness, and **pain.** Jeremiah's experience ought to come as no surprise to servants of God, as suffering accompanies joy even in the ministry of Paul (2Co 11:24-31; Php 1:3; 4:1). In his discouragement, Jeremiah felt that God, in some instances, had not

If you return,
 I will restore you;
you will stand in My presence.
And if you speak noble words,
 rather than worthless ones,
you will be My spokesman.
It is they who must return
 to you;
you must not return to them.
20 Then I will make you
 a fortified wall of bronze
to this people.
They will fight against you
but will not overcome you,
for I am with you
to save you and deliver you.
This is
the LORD's declaration.
21 I will deliver you
 from the power
 of evil people
and redeem you
 from the control
 of the ruthless.

Jeremiah's Loneliness and the Nation's Devastation and Hope (16:1-21)

16 The word of the LORD came to
me: 2 "You must not marry or
have sons or daughters in this place.
3 For this is what the LORD says concerning sons and daughters born in
this place as well as concerning the
mothers who bear them and the fathers who father them in this land:
4 They will die from deadly diseases.
They will not be mourned or buried
but will be like manure on the face
of the earth. They will be finished off
by sword and famine. Their corpses
will become food for the birds of the
sky and for the wild animals of the
land.
5 "For this is what the LORD says:
Don't enter a house where a mourning feast is taking place.[A] Don't go to
lament or sympathize with them, for
I have removed My peace from these
people"—this is the LORD's declaration—"as well as My faithful love
and compassion. 6 Both great and
small will die in this land without
burial. No lament will be made for
them, nor will anyone cut himself
or shave his head for them.[B] 7 Food
won't be provided for the mourner
to comfort him because of the dead.
A cup of consolation won't be given
him because of the loss of his father
or mother. 8 You must not enter the
house where feasting is taking place
to sit with them to eat and drink.
9 For this is what the LORD of •Hosts,
the God of Israel, says: I am about
to eliminate from this place, before
your very eyes and in your time, the
sound of joy and gladness, the voice
of the groom and the bride.
10 "When you tell these people all
these things, they will say to you,
'Why has the LORD declared all this
great disaster against us? What is
our •guilt? What is our sin that we
have committed against the LORD
our God?' 11 Then you will answer
them: Because your fathers abandoned Me"—this is the LORD's declaration—"and followed other gods,
served them, and worshiped them.
Indeed, they abandoned Me and did
not keep My instruction. 12 You did
more evil than your fathers. Look,
each one of you was following the
stubbornness of his evil heart, not
obeying Me. 13 So I will hurl you
from this land into a land that you
and your fathers are not familiar
with. There you will worship other
gods both day and night, for I will
not grant you grace.[C]
14 "However, take note! The days
are coming"—the LORD's declaration—"when it will no longer be
said, 'As the LORD lives who brought
the Israelites from the land of Egypt,'
15 but rather, 'As the LORD lives who
brought the Israelites from the land
of the north and from all the other
lands where He had banished them.'
For I will return them to their land
that I gave to their ancestors.
16 "I am about to send for many
fishermen"—this is the LORD's declaration—"and they will fish for
them. Then I will send for many
hunters, and they will hunt them
down on every mountain and hill
and out of the clefts of the rocks,
17 for My gaze takes in all their ways.
They are not concealed from Me,
and their guilt is not hidden from
My sight. 18 I will first repay them
double for their guilt and sin be-

been **reliable**—like a brook that only sometimes gives water.

15:19-21 The Lord, in His gracious way, told Jeremiah to **return** (repent), admonishing him to continue to speak God's authoritative words rather than his own **worthless** words derived from his personal despondency. He was encouraged to pursue the acceptance of the Lord rather than of the people. The Lord again assured His **spokesman** of protection in words that reiterated His promise at the time of Jeremiah's prophetic commissioning.

16:1-9 The Lord commanded Jeremiah to enact three parables (sign-acts) by obeying three restrictions: Jeremiah was not to marry or have his own children **in this place** (i.e., in Judah); he must not go to a funeral; and he must not attend a feast. The point was to communicate that the routines of community life were over.

16:2-4 There will no longer be in the land the joy brought by marriage, family, and feasting. Jeremiah was not to marry because God would soon cut off the lives of men, women, and children by pestilence and famine: Better not to marry or have offspring than to endure this fate.

16:5-7 Jeremiah was not to offer any comfort at mourning feasts because God had no more pity or compassion for His people. There will no longer be any **comfort** or **consolation** for mourners in their grief.

16:8-9 Jeremiah was not to rejoice at any feasts because God had cut off joy from the land. Jeremiah's actions signaled a social breach in a system in which marriage, children, family, weddings and funerals were vital community acts. The acts and institutions that signified God's blessing were to be withdrawn, as Jeremiah himself withdrew from them.

16:10-15 While verses 10-13 reiterate other passages about Israel's sin of idolatry and consequent exile, verses 14-15 offer a glimmer of hope for the nation. Covenant language, which reiterates the curses concomitant with covenant violation, is used (cp. Dt 29:18-21, 24-28). The curse of being thrown or hurled [Hb *tul*, "cast out violently"] into a foreign land is about to be fulfilled for Judah.

After administering punishment, **however**, the Lord will accomplish something superseding the exodus, the defining event of Israel's nationhood (v. 15). The image of restoration and return appeared, as God promised to **return** each one to the **land**, which He had given to **their ancestors** (i.e., the

[A] **16:5** Lit *house of mourning* [B] **16:6** This custom demonstrated pagan mourning rituals.
[C] **16:13** Or *compassion*

>WORD|*study*

16:19-21 God's intent to reveal Himself and have a relationship with formerly idolatrous nations is shown by His use of three forms of the verb know (Hb *yada'*; see note on Jb 38:4-38): inform ["cause to know, teach"] **them**; make them know, and **they** will know. These terms emphasize a deeper knowledge of God that is relational and covenantal.

cause they have polluted My land. They have filled My inheritance with the lifelessness of their detestable and abhorrent idols."

19 LORD, my strength
and my stronghold,
my refuge in a time
of distress,
the nations will come to You
from the ends of the earth,
and they will say,
"Our fathers inherited
only lies,
worthless idols of no benefit
at all."
20 Can one make gods
for himself?
But they are not gods.
21 "Therefore, I am about
to inform them,
and this time I will
make them know
My power and My might;
then they will know
that My name is •Yahweh."

The Sin and Punishment of Judah (17:1-27)

17 The sin of Judah is written
with an iron stylus.
With a diamond point
it is engraved on the tablet
of their hearts
and on the horns
of their[A] altars,
2 while their children
remember their altars
and their •Asherah poles,
by the green trees
on the high hills—
3 My mountains
in the countryside.
I will give up your wealth
and all your treasures
as plunder
because of the sin
of your •high places[B]
in all your borders.
4 You will, on your own,
relinquish your inheritance
that I gave you.
I will make you serve
your enemies
in a land you do not know,
for you have set My anger
on fire;
it will burn forever.
5 This is what the LORD says:

The man who trusts
in mankind,
who makes human flesh
his strength
and turns his heart
from the LORD is cursed.
6 He will be like a juniper
in the •Arabah;
he cannot see
when good comes
but dwells
in the parched places
in the wilderness,
in a salt land
where no one lives.
7 The man who trusts
in the LORD,
whose confidence indeed is
the LORD, is blessed.
8 He will be like a tree planted
by water:
it sends its roots out
toward a stream,
it doesn't fear
when heat comes,
and its foliage remains green.
It will not worry in a year
of drought
or cease producing fruit.

9 The heart is more deceitful
than anything else,
and incurable—
who can understand it?
10 I, •Yahweh, examine the mind,
I test the heart[C]
to give to each according to
his way,

[A]17:1 Some Hb mss, Syr, Vg; other Hb mss read *your of sin* [C]17:10 Lit *kidneys* [B]17:3 Lit *plunder, your high places because*

blessing expressed via the promise of land would be restored).

16:19-21 LORD, also *Yahweh*, the name of God affirmed by Jeremiah, appears in verse 19. The last word of the passage is **Yahweh,** a self-affirmation by God. This "Yahweh parenthesis" encloses a brief confession that idols are useless and ineffective as well as reflecting the foolish idea that men can manufacture gods.

17:1 Various forms of poetry and some narrative prose concerning Sabbath observance comprise most of this chapter. The poetic portions may be classified as a prophetic oracle (vv. 1-4), wisdom sayings (vv. 5-13), and a lament (or complaint) of Jeremiah (vv. 14-18).

17:1-4 Judah's sin is metaphorically described as indelible. Tragically, their **sin . . . is engraved on the tablet of their hearts** (the rightful place of the new covenant with God) and on their **altars** (the place reserved for atonement and forgiveness for sin). **Asherah poles** symbolized a Canaanite fertility goddess. Israel has brought judgment upon herself through idolatry.

17:5-13 The three groups of sayings may have been directed at King Jehoiakim or intended to apply more generally to any other person.

17:5-6 Two trees are contrasted. The first represents the **man** who trusts in **human . . . strength,** who is isolated, dry, and barren like a desert shrub.

17:7-8 The one who trusts the Lord is like a continually fruitful, abundant, and flourishing tree because it draws on a reliable source of water. The imagery here is strikingly reminiscent of Ps 1:3.

17:9-13 The next group of sayings asserts that God tests and examines both the heart and the mind. The **heart** is the seat of thought and reason, while the **mind** (Hb *kilyah*, literally "kidneys") is the seat of emotions. A person's thoughts result in either worthy or unworthy actions, which will be justly recompensed by God, as in the case of the man who became rich through injustice. Possibly, Jehoiakim is in view here, as one who abandoned God, became wealthy unjustly, lost his material riches and power, and was **put to shame**. In this way, he had become like the "juniper in the Arabah" desert (v. 6) because he had abandoned the **fountain of living water**, which could have resulted in the production of abundant fruit.

17:14-18 Jeremiah trusted in God for healing, salvation, and protection from those who scorned him and his divinely given message. As the prophet pleaded with God for protection from persecutors, he reminded God of His previous promises given at his commissioning (1:8,17-19).

17:19-23 The people—leaders and subjects alike—had consistently violated the Sabbath by transacting their own business, going in and out of **the gates of Jerusalem**. Honoring the Sabbath is the fourth commandment of the Mosaic covenant, a central pillar of a relationship with the Creator and covenant-making God. As the people had violated other commandments (against adultery, idolatry, lying, etc.), so they violated this one.

17:24-26 The conditional nature of the covenant may be observed in the various consequences appropriate to their actions. Honoring the **Sabbath** as God intended would lead to the continuity of David's dynasty and thriving worship at the temple, which would include Israelites from all regions of Judah.

18:4 Jeremiah watched the potter at his wheel for a while, observing his skill and mastery over the clay. The potter planned to mold the clay into a certain vessel; but, depending upon the quality of the clay, the potter exercised his freedom to pursue an alternate plan according to what he deemed appropriate.

according to what
his actions deserve.
11 He who makes
a fortune unjustly
is like a partridge
that hatches eggs
it didn't lay.
In the middle of his days
his riches will abandon him,
so in the end he will be a fool.

12 A throne of glory
on high from the beginning
is the place of our sanctuary.
13 LORD, the hope of Israel,
all who abandon You
will be put to shame.
All who turn away from Me
will be written in the dirt,
for they have abandoned
the LORD, the fountain
of living water.

14 Heal me, LORD,
and I will be healed;
save me, and I will be saved,
for You are my praise.
15 Hear how they keep
challenging me,
"Where is the word
of the LORD?
Let it come!"
16 But I have not run away
from being Your shepherd,
and I have not longed for
the fatal day.
You know my words
were spoken
in Your presence.
17 Don't become a terror to me.
You are my refuge in the day
of disaster.
18 Let my persecutors be
put to shame,
but don't let me be
put to shame.
Let them be terrified,
but don't let me be terrified.
Bring on them the day
of disaster;
shatter them
with total[A] destruction.

19 This is what the LORD said to me,
"Go and stand at the People's Gate,
through which the kings of Judah
enter and leave, as well as at all the
gates of Jerusalem. 20 Announce to
them: Hear the word of the LORD,
kings of Judah, all Judah, and all the
residents of Jerusalem who enter
through these gates. 21 This is what
the LORD says: Watch yourselves;
do not pick up a load and bring it
in through the gates of Jerusalem
on the Sabbath day. 22 You must not
carry a load out of your houses on
the Sabbath day or do any work,
but you must consecrate the Sabbath day, just as I commanded your
ancestors. 23 They wouldn't listen or
pay attention but became obstinate,
not listening or accepting discipline.
24 "However, if you listen to Me,
says the LORD, and do not bring
loads through the gates of this city
on the Sabbath day and consecrate
the Sabbath day and do no work on
it, 25 kings and princes will enter
through the gates of this city. They
will sit on the throne of David, riding
in chariots and on horses with their
officials, the men of Judah, and the
residents of Jerusalem. This city will
be inhabited forever. 26 Then people
will come from the cities of Judah
and from the area around Jerusalem,
from the land of Benjamin and from
the Judean foothills, from the hill
country and from the •Negev bringing •burnt offerings and sacrifice,
•grain offerings and frankincense,
and thank offerings to the house of
the LORD. 27 If you do not listen to Me
to consecrate the Sabbath day by not
carrying a load while entering the
gates of Jerusalem on the Sabbath
day, I will set fire to its gates, and it
will consume the citadels of Jerusalem and not be extinguished."

The Lessons from Pottery (18:1–19:15)

18 This is the word that came to
Jeremiah from the LORD: 2 "Go
down at once to the potter's house;
there I will reveal My words to you."
3 So I went down to the potter's
house, and there he was, working
away at the wheel.[B] 4 But the jar
that he was making from the clay
became flawed in the potter's hand,
so he made it into another jar, as it
seemed right for him to do.
5 The word of the LORD came to me:
6 "House of Israel, can I not treat you

A 17:18 Lit *double* B 18:3 Lit *pair of stones*

>WORD|*study*

18:2-3 God told Jeremiah He would **reveal** [His] **words** to him at **the potter's house**. In Hebrew, the word potter is the active participle form of the verb *yatsar* ("form, fashion")—"one who forms or fashions." The verb is often used of God as the Creator (Ps 94:9; Is 43:1; see **Doctrine**, "Creation of Mankind", p. 5). The potter's **wheel** (Hb *ʾovnayim*, "pair of stones, two stones,") probably consisted of two disk-shaped stones. The larger upper stone, on which the clay was thrown and turned, was constructed to pivot on the lower one, or both stones may have been attached to an axle.

18:4; 19:1,7,10-11 The word for clay (Hb *chomer*, 18:4) denotes the raw, still malleable material from which the pots are formed. In 19:1, a different word for clay (Hb *cheres*) identifies the vessel as baked or dried-out earthenware (cp. 32:14; cp. Ps 22:15). In other contexts, the word frequently refers to a "potsherd," a worthless fragment of broken pottery (cp. Jb 2:8). Unlike wet clay on a potter's wheel, which can still be reshaped (18:4), a broken "clay pot" could not be repaired but was thrown away or its shards used like pieces of scrap paper. Potsherd [Hb *charsut*] Gate (19:2) may have been named for its use as a dumping ground for worthless, broken pottery (cp. Neh 2:13). The visual metaphor was particularly significant, given God's instructions in the law to "break" (Hb *shavar*, "break in pieces, shatter") clay pots that became "unclean" (see Lv 6:28; 11:33; 15:12). Likewise, the Lord would **shatter** [Hb *shavar*] **these people and this city** as Jeremiah would **shatter** [Hb *shavar*] the **jar** (Hb *baqbuq*, "bottle, flask,") from the verb *baqaq* ("pour out to empty," 19:10-11). The earthenware vessel Jeremiah was instructed to buy was probably designed for storing or serving something liquid. The verb itself appears as a wordplay in the Lord's pledge to spoil (Hb *baqaq*, "make empty, cancel") Judah's plans (19:7).

as this potter treats his clay?"—this
is the LORD's declaration. "Just like
clay in the potter's hand, so are you
in My hand, house of Israel. 7 At one
moment I might announce concerning a nation or a kingdom that
I will uproot, tear down, and destroy
it. 8 However, if that nation I have
made an announcement about turns
from its evil, I will relent concerning the disaster I had planned to do
to it. 9 At another time I announce
that I will build and plant a nation
or a kingdom. 10 However, if it does
what is evil in My sight by not listening to My voice, I will relent concerning the good I had said I would
do to it. 11 So now, say to the men of
Judah and to the residents of Jerusalem: This is what the LORD says: I
am about to bring harm to you and
make plans against you. Turn now,
each from your evil way, and correct
your ways and your deeds. 12 But
they will say, 'It's hopeless. We will
continue to follow our plans, and
each of us will continue to act according to the stubbornness of his
evil heart.'"
13 Therefore, this is what the LORD
says:

Ask among the nations,
Who has heard things
like these?
Virgin Israel has done
a most terrible thing.
14 Does the snow
of Lebanon ever leave
the highland crags?
Or does cold water flowing
from a distance ever fail?
15 Yet My people
have forgotten Me.
They burn incense
to false idols
that make them stumble
in their ways
on the ancient roads
and walk on new paths,
not the highway.
16 They have made their land
a horror,
a perpetual object of scorn;[A]
everyone who passes by it
will be horrified
and shake his head.

DIVINE SOVEREIGNTY

The chief theme of the enacted metaphor in 18:1-2 is the sovereignty of God in shaping national destinies (18:1-2). His sovereignty extends over all nations, although this text pertains particularly to Judah. Sovereignty does not equal determinism: God allows room for human response—whether obedience or disobedience. The compatibility of divine sovereignty with human freedom is well illustrated in this text, which shows the inconsistency and fickleness of humanity. However, human actions do not nullify God's plans. God remains sovereign and ultimately fulfills His purposes, despite human failure to comply. God's response is consistent: Sin brings punishment, but repentance brings blessing. He taught this lesson to Jonah in his experience with the Ninevites (Assyrians), showing that the principle applies to any nation, not just Israel (Jnh 3). In the passage at hand, God indicates that even though Judah is far gone and is bringing retribution upon herself, it is never too late to repent.

18:7-10 The Lord's explanation of the potter's actions reiterates the prophetic theme first announced in 1:10. Jeremiah was called to be God's spokesman, conveying His plans to **uproot, tear down, and destroy**, but also to **build and plant a nation or a kingdom** (cp. 31:28). The different destinies would depend upon that nation's repentance or continued rebellion.

18:11-12 The Lord invited Judah to **turn** from its **evil** and **correct your ways and your deeds,** indicating that He was willing to "build and plant" them. Judah, however, responded in willful disobedience, acting according to its **evil heart** (cp. 17:9-10).

18:15-17 Judah had turned away from **ancient roads**, i.e., the ways of faithful obedience to the Lord. Instead, the people walked on side roads—rough, dirt paths, representing their idolatry—as opposed to the straight **highway** of worshiping the true and living God. Consequently, Judah had chosen doom and destruction. Since she rejected God, God would also reject her in **the day of . . . calamity**, turning His **back** on her.

A 18:16 Lit *hissing*

18:18-23 This lament of Jeremiah was occasioned by another plot against him. Previously, he had interceded for the people of Judah, but now he pleaded with God to destroy them. Israel's persistent faithlessness and rejection of God took visible form in their rejection of His prophet Jeremiah, who was personally experiencing in miniature the same rejection God had experienced.

19:1 This passage contains another enacted parable in which a **clay jar** (symbolizing Judah) is smashed as a visual illustration of how God will irreparably shatter His people for their disobedience. See **Word Study**, p. 979.

19:2-7 The **Valley of Hinnom** or **Topheth** (vv. 11-14) was a place where pagan rituals and child sacrifices were practiced by the Israelites (cp. 7:30-34). King Josiah had made it into a dump where garbage was burned (2Kg 23:1-20). This oracle was addressed to the entire house of Judah, past and present, including the previous kings whose actions had led the nation into apostasy. The place was made **foreign** or alien in the sense of being non-Israelite, since Israel was inextricably bound in a covenant with her God. Disaster would come upon Israel because of idolatry, murder, and the offering of child sacrifices to Baal. On **Potsherd Gate**, (v. 2) and **spoil** (v. 7), see **Word Study**, p. 979.

19:8-9 The Lord described the appalling conditions during the siege of Jerusalem when desperation would lead to cannibalism. The covenant curses of Dt 5–6, 10–12, and 26–28 graphically describe the very situation that befell Judah at this time (especially Dt 28:45-57). Jeremiah's prophecy was fulfilled in 586 B.C. when Nebuchadnezzar invaded Judah and besieged Jerusalem (cp. Jr 52:4-6; Lm 2:20).

19:10-13 Like the jar shattered beyond repair, the city of Jerusalem was to become as vile and **impure** a place as **Topheth;** in fact, people themselves had defiled their city by practicing idolatry not only in the valley but also on the flat roofs of their own houses. Jeremiah repeated his message in the temple court, publicly addressing the people and citing their stubborn disobedience as the cause of the prophesied disasters.

17 I will scatter them
before the enemy
like the east wind.
I will show them[A] My back
and not My face
on the day of their calamity.

18 Then certain ones said, "Come,
let's make plans against Jeremiah,
for instruction will never be lost
from the priest, or counsel from the
wise, or an •oracle from the prophet.
Come, let's denounce him[B] and pay
no attention to all his words."

19 Pay attention to me, LORD.
Hear what my opponents
are saying!
20 Should good be repaid
with evil?
Yet they have dug a pit
for me.
Remember how I stood
before You
to speak good on their behalf,
to turn Your anger
from them.
21 Therefore, hand their children
over to famine,
and pour the sword's power
on them.
Let their wives
become childless
and widowed,
their husbands slain
by deadly disease,[C]
their young men struck down
by the sword in battle.
22 Let a cry be heard
from their houses
when You suddenly
bring raiders against them,
for they have dug a pit
to capture me
and have hidden snares
for my feet.
23 But You, LORD, know
all their deadly plots
against me.
Do not wipe out their •guilt;
do not blot out their sin
before You.
Let them be forced to stumble
before You;
deal with them in the time
of Your anger.

19 This is what the LORD says: "Go,
buy a potter's clay jar. Take[D]
some of the elders of the people and
some of the leading priests 2 and go
out to the Valley of Hinnom near
the entrance of the Potsherd Gate.
Proclaim there the words I speak
to you. 3 Say: Hear the word of the
LORD, kings of Judah and residents
of Jerusalem. This is what the LORD
of •Hosts, the God of Israel, says: I
am going to bring such disaster on
this place that everyone who hears
about it will shudder[E] 4 because they
have abandoned Me and made this a
foreign place. They have burned incense in it to other gods that they,
their fathers, and the kings of Judah
have never known. They have filled
this place with the blood of the innocent. 5 They have built •high places to •Baal on which to burn their
children in the fire as burnt offerings to Baal, something I have never
commanded or mentioned; I never
entertained the thought.[F]

6 "Therefore, take note! The days
are coming"—this is the LORD's
declaration—"when this place will
no longer be called Topheth and the
Valley of Hinnom, but the Valley of
Slaughter. 7 I will spoil the plans of
Judah and Jerusalem in this place.
I will make them fall by the sword
before their enemies, by the hand of
those who want to take their life. I
will provide their corpses as food for
the birds of the sky and for the wild
animals of the land. 8 I will make
this city desolate, an object of scorn.
Everyone who passes by it will be
horrified and scoff because of all its
wounds. 9 I will make them eat the
flesh of their sons and their daughters, and they will eat each other's
flesh in the siege and distress that
their enemies, those who want to
take their life, inflict on them.

10 "Then you are to shatter the jar
in the presence of the people traveling with you, 11 and you are to proclaim to them: This is what the LORD
of Hosts says: I will shatter these
people and this city, like one shatters
a potter's jar that can never again be
mended. They will bury the dead in

[A] **18:17** LXX, Lat, Syr, Tg; MT reads *will look at them* [B] **18:18** Lit *let's strike him with the tongue* [C] **18:21** Lit *by death* [D] **19:1** Syr, Tg; MT omits *Take* [E] **19:3** Lit *shudder their ears*; 1Sm 3:11; 2Kg 21:12 [F] **19:5** Lit *mentioned, and it did not arise on My heart*

Topheth because there is no other place for burials. 12 I will do so to this place"—this is the declaration of the LORD—"and to its residents, making this city like Topheth. 13 The houses of Jerusalem and the houses of the kings of Judah will become impure like that place Topheth—all the houses on whose rooftops they have burned incense to the whole heavenly host and poured out •drink offerings to other gods."

14 Jeremiah came back from Topheth, where the LORD had sent him to prophesy, stood in the courtyard of the LORD's temple, and proclaimed to all the people, 15 "This is what the LORD of Hosts, the God of Israel, says: 'I am about to bring on this city—and on all its dependent villages—all the disaster that I spoke against it, for they have become obstinate, not obeying My words.'"

Jeremiah's Maltreatment (20:1-18)

20 Pashhur the priest, the son of Immer and chief official in the temple of the LORD, heard Jeremiah prophesying these things. 2 So Pashhur had Jeremiah the prophet beaten and put him in the stocks at the Upper Benjamin Gate in the LORD's temple. 3 The next day, when Pashhur released Jeremiah from the stocks, Jeremiah said to him, "The LORD does not call you Pashhur, but Magor-missabib,[A] 4 for this is what the LORD says, 'I am about to make you a terror to both yourself and those you love. They will fall by the sword of their enemies before your very eyes. I will hand Judah over to the king of Babylon, and he will deport them to Babylon and put them to the sword. 5 I will give away all the wealth of this city, all its products and valuables. Indeed, I will hand all the treasures of the kings of Judah over to their enemies. They will plunder them, seize them, and carry them off to Babylon. 6 As for you, Pashhur, and all who live in your house, you will go into captivity. You will go to Babylon. There you will die, and there you will be buried, you and all your friends that you prophesied falsely to.'"

7 You deceived me, LORD,
and I was deceived.
You seized me and prevailed.
I am a laughingstock
all the time;
everyone ridicules me.
8 For whenever I speak,
I cry out,
I proclaim, "Violence
and destruction!"
because the word of the LORD
has become for me
constant disgrace
and derision.
9 If I say, "I won't mention Him
or speak any longer
in His name,"
His message becomes
a fire burning in my heart,
shut up in my bones.
I become tired of holding
it in,
and I cannot prevail.
10 For I have heard the gossip
of many people,
"Terror is on every side![B]
Report him; let's report him!"
Everyone I trusted[C] watches
for my fall.
"Perhaps he will be deceived
so that we might prevail
against him
and take our vengeance
on him."
11 But the LORD is with me
like a violent warrior.
Therefore, my persecutors
will stumble
and not prevail.
Since they have not
succeeded, they will be
utterly shamed,
an everlasting humiliation
that will never be forgotten.
12 LORD of •Hosts, testing
the righteous
and seeing the heart[D]
and mind,
let me see Your vengeance
on them,
for I have presented my case
to You.
13 Sing to the LORD!
Praise the LORD,

[A]20:3 = Terror Is on Every Side; Jr 6:25; 20:10; 46:5 [B]20:10 Hb *Magor-missabib*; Jr 20:3
[C]20:10 Lit *Every man of my peace* [D]20:12 Lit *kidneys*

20:1-2 When **Pashhur the priest** heard Jeremiah's prophecy upon his return from Topheth/Hinnom, he had the prophet beaten and incarcerated. The **Upper Benjamin Gate** was probably an entrance to the temple on its north side, since the territory of Benjamin lay directly north of Jerusalem (cp. Ezk 8:14; 9:2). Perhaps Pashhur was one of the "certain ones" of 18:18 who plotted against Jeremiah, confident that he and the current religious leadership of Judah (priests, wise counselors, and prophets) would always have the true words of God.

20:3-6 Pashhur brought disaster upon himself, drawing from Jeremiah a prophecy of captivity in Babylon for himself and his household. He also drew an accusation of false prophecy. Jeremiah renamed Pashhur **Magor-missabib** (Hb, "terror is on every side"; cp. *magor*, "terror, fear, dread" in 20:10; 46:5; 49:29; Ps 31:30; Lm 2:22), intending to prophesy Pashhur's future. Ironically, while Pashhur reacted violently against Jeremiah's message, he fell prey to his own actions, becoming **a terror** (Hb *magor*, v. 4) to his own household.

20:7-11 Jeremiah then lamented his treatment and the difficulty of his prophetic assignment. After prophesying that Pashhur would be associated with terror on every side, in his own experience he himself was the one for whom terror was on every side! The **word of the LORD**—the message he preached—brought only **disgrace and derision** to the messenger. But the prophetic mandate was compelling. Verse 9 is critically important for understanding the motivation that drove the prophet to continue to preach a loathsome, offensive message of slaughter, plague, and exile: He is unable *not* to proclaim the message that is like a **fire burning** within him because it consists of God's words, not his own (cp. 1:9).

20:14 Jeremiah's confidence in the Lord's protection (20:11-13) did not alter or lessen his current suffering. Like Job, at times he wished for death. In this lament of Jeremiah, he was not suicidal but rather a despised, lonely, and broken-spirited man whose pain and grief were profound. He cursed the day of his birth since it marked the beginning of his misery.

20:15-17 He cursed the messenger who announced his birth as if it were good news (he did not curse his own parents, for that was forbidden by law), and he wondered bitterly why he could not have been aborted or stillborn.

21:1 Chapters 21 onward are not necessarily in chronological order. After Josiah's death, two of his sons (Shallum/Jehoahaz and Eliakim/Jehoiakim) reigned, then his grandson (Jehoiachin/Jeconiah, Jehoiakim's son); then another son, Mattaniah/**Zedekiah,** was the last king of Judah. Each one took a throne name when he became king. This chapter gives an oracle against Zedekiah.

21:2-5 Zedekiah inquired of Jeremiah for a word from the Lord, hoping to presume upon God's power and past deliverances in this time of crisis as the Babylonians were upon them. Ironically, God reversed a formula—"with a strong hand and an outstretched arm" (Dt 5:15; Ps 136:12)—often used to indicate deliverance from enemies, turning it against Zedekiah and Jerusalem: **I will fight against you with an outstretched hand and a mighty arm**.

21:6-7 The repeated use of "I" by the Lord reinforces the primary agency of God. As God had personally delivered them in the past *from* Egyptian captivity, He would now personally deliver them and their king *into* Babylonian captivity (cp. Lm 4:20).

21:8-10 Jeremiah's message to the **people** seemed to offer a glimmer of hope, but it was faint and conditional. They had to choose between the **way of life and the way of death**, a Deuteronomic theme (cp. Dt 30:15, 19); but living involved surrender and submission to their enemies, since Jerusalem's doom had already been decided.

21:11-12 The kings of Judah had violated the requirements of the Lord concerning **justice** in the land, thus incurring God's **anger**, symbolized as an unquenchable **fire**. The frequent condemnation of kings for widespread injustice highlights the chief duty of the kingly office (cp. Pr 31:4-5,8-9). Injustice characterized the reigns of all four kings after Josiah, until God's **anger** came against Judah, resulting in destruction, captivity, and exile.

HARD QUESTION

How should I handle discouragement and depression?

How should we understand these disturbing sentiments? Jeremiah was deeply discouraged (20:15-17). While he was certain of God's calling into the prophetic ministry, he felt that his message had brought only pain and rejection; moreover, none of his prophecies had yet been fulfilled. His dejection was real—the normal, and possibly appropriate, response to his situation. Verbalizing it before God was part of his relationship with the Lord. Since all along God had been putting Jeremiah through experiences mimicking God's own, the implied depth of God's disappointment and dejection over the situation was obvious. In his despair, Jeremiah believed that his life and work were meaningless—death would be preferable.

In the womb was precisely the place in which God's calling was affirmed, even before Jeremiah's birth; but in his anguish, Jeremiah characterized that time not as joyous but as tragic as the destruction of Sodom and Gomorrah. This lament is Jeremiah's final "complaint," and apparently the Lord did not rebuke him for his thoughts.

As with Job, God permits His servants to express deep grief at their human frailty and inability to endure the demands of God's will. The powerful (and perhaps shocking) sentiments recorded here show Jeremiah as a frail man whose faith sometimes wavered and whose God is patient and sovereign in His intent to fulfill the words He has spoken through His servant.

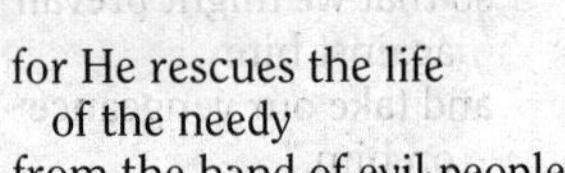

for He rescues the life
of the needy
from the hand of evil people.
14 May the day I was born
be cursed.
May the day my mother
bore me
never be blessed.
15 May the man be cursed
who brought the news
to my father, saying,
"A male child is born to you,"
bringing him great joy.
16 Let that man be like the cities
the LORD demolished
without compassion.
Let him hear an outcry
in the morning
and a war cry at noontime
17 because he didn't kill me
in the womb
so that my mother
might have been my grave,
her womb eternally pregnant.
18 Why did I come out
of the womb
to see only struggle
and sorrow,
to end my life in shame?

The Warning and Judgment Concerning the Kings (21:1–22:30)

21 This is the word that came to Jeremiah from the LORD when King Zedekiah sent Pashhur son of Malchijah and the priest Zephaniah son of Maaseiah to Jeremiah, asking,
2 "Ask the LORD on our behalf, since Nebuchadnezzar[A] king of Babylon is making war against us. Perhaps the LORD will perform for us something like all His past wonderful works so that Nebuchadnezzar will withdraw from us."

3 But Jeremiah answered, "This is what you are to say to Zedekiah:
4 'This is what the LORD, the God of Israel, says: I will repel the weapons of war in your hands, those you are using to fight the king of Babylon and the Chaldeans[B] who are besieging you outside the wall, and I will bring them into the center of this
city. 5 I will fight against you with an outstretched hand and a mighty arm, with anger, rage, and great
wrath. 6 I will strike the residents of this city, both man and beast. They will die in a great plague. 7 After-
ward'"—this is the LORD's declaration—"'King Zedekiah of Judah, his officers, and the people—those in this city who survive the plague, the sword, and the famine—I will hand over to King Nebuchadnezzar of Babylon, to their enemies, yes, to those who want to take their lives. He will put them to the sword; he won't spare them or show pity or compassion.'

8 "But you must say to this people, 'This is what the LORD says: Look, I am presenting to you the way of life and the way of death.
9 Whoever stays in this city will die by the sword, famine, and plague, but whoever goes out and surrenders to the Chaldeans who are besieging you will live and will retain his life

[A]21:2 Lit *Nebuchadrezzar* [B]21:4 = Babylonians

like the spoils of war. 10 For I have
turned[A] against this city to bring
disaster and not good'"—this is the
LORD's declaration. "'It will be handed over to the king of Babylon, who
will burn it down.'
11 "And to the house of the king of
Judah say this: 'Hear the word of the
LORD! 12 House of David, this is what
the LORD says:

Administer justice
every morning,
and rescue the victim
of robbery
from the hand
of his oppressor,
or My anger will flare up
like fire
and burn unquenchably
because of their evil deeds.
13 Beware! I am against you,
you who sit above the valley,
you atop the rocky plateau—
this is
the LORD's declaration—
you who say, "Who can
come down against us?
Who can enter our
hiding places?"
14 I will punish you according to
what you have done—
this is
the LORD's declaration.
I will kindle a fire in its forest
that will consume everything
around it.'"

22 This is what the LORD says: "Go
down to the palace of the king
of Judah and announce this word
there. 2 You are to say: Hear the word
of the LORD, king of Judah, you who
sit on the throne of David—you,
your officers, and your people who
enter these gates. 3 This is what the
LORD says: Administer justice and
righteousness. Rescue the victim
of robbery from the hand of his oppressor. Don't exploit or brutalize
the foreigner, the fatherless, or the
widow. Don't shed innocent blood in
this place. 4 For if you conscientiously carry out this word, then kings
sitting on David's throne will enter
through the gates of this palace riding on chariots and horses—they,
their officers, and their people.
5 But if you do not obey these words,
then I swear by Myself"—this is the
LORD's declaration—"that this house
will become a ruin."
6 For this is what the LORD says
concerning the house of the king of
Judah:

You are like Gilead to Me,
or the summit of Lebanon,
but I will certainly turn you
into a wilderness,
uninhabited cities.
7 I will appoint destroyers
against you,
each with his weapons.
They will cut down
the choicest of your cedars
and throw them into the fire.

8 "Many nations will pass by this
city and ask one another, 'Why did
the LORD do such a thing to this
great city?' 9 They will answer, 'Because they abandoned the covenant
of •Yahweh their God and worshiped
and served other gods.'"

10 Do not weep for the dead;
do not mourn for him.
Weep bitterly for the one[B]
who has gone away,
for he will never return again
and see his native land.

11 For this is what the LORD says
concerning Shallum son of Josiah,
king of Judah, who became king in
place of his father Josiah: "He has
left this place—he will never return
here again, 12 but he will die in the
place where they deported him, never seeing this land again."

13 Woe for the one who builds
his palace
through unrighteousness,
his upper rooms
through injustice,
who makes his fellow man
serve without pay
and will not give him
his wages,
14 who says, "I will build myself
a massive palace,
with spacious upper rooms."
He will cut windows[C] in it,
and it will be paneled
with cedar
and painted with vermilion.

21:13-14 Instead of justice in Jerusalem there was found only pride at her alleged invincibility; but God's punishment for pride is assured, again symbolized by a consuming **fire**.

22:1-3 This chapter consists of a collection of oracles against Judah's royalty; in particular, it contains warnings and judgments for the three kings who followed Josiah: Jehoahaz, Jehoiakim, and Jehoiachin. The imperative to **administer justice** is reiterated and expanded to include other victims: **the foreigner, the fatherless,** and **the widow**. The shedding of **innocent blood** was one of the gravest sins of King Manasseh of Judah (Josiah's grandfather), and his example may have been followed by his great-grandsons (cp. 22:17; 2Kg 24:1-4).

22:4-7 The political blessings that could result from acts of justice pleasing to God are the same as those resulting from respect for the Sabbath in Jr 17:24-27. **Gilead** and **Lebanon** were known for their lush forests, especially Lebanon, which was renowned for its **cedars**. A stark contrast exists between that lush vegetation and the **wilderness** resulting from the ravages of **destroyers**.

22:8-9 The reason for this destruction once again appears (in Deuteronomic terms) as idolatry and abandonment of the **covenant**.

22:10-12 An oracle against Jehoahaz/Shallum: The dead King Josiah was not to be mourned; rather his son, who was exiled without the possibility of return, was to be pitied; in other words, to be dead would be better than to be exiled. Jehoahaz ruled as king only three months before Pharaoh Neco deported him to Egypt, where he eventually died (2Kg 23:31-34).

22:13-15 The oracle against Jehoiakim is the longest in this chapter. Jehoiakim reigned for 11 years. Unlike his father Josiah, he failed to rule justly and righteously, the standards by which God measured a king. The sins of pride and presumption (mentioned in chap. 21) are intertwined with his kingly failure, as he used **unrighteousness** and **injustice** to build **his palace** and **his upper rooms**, oppressing his **fellow man** by not paying him his wages. In the manner of a tyrant, Jehoiakim had used forced, unpaid labor to build and remodel his palace.

Jehoiakim had a vision of royal splendor for himself, the **cedar** beams and paneling of his palace representing strength and magnificence reminiscent of the days of Solomon (cp. 1Kg 7:2-11).

[A]**21:10** Lit *set My face* [B]**22:10** = Shallum (Jehoahaz) in v. 11 [C]**22:14** Lit *My windows*

22:16-17 However, he neglected God and did not **know** Him (i.e., he had no true relationship with God as Josiah had). Knowing God involves practicing justice and righteousness, since these qualities characterize God Himself, and He delights in them (cp. 9:24).

22:24 The final oracle in this section comes against Jehoiachin, also called Jeconiah or **Coniah**, the **son of Jehoiakim**. The Lord metaphorically described Jehoiachin as a **signet ring** on His **right hand**. As a signature seal, the signet ring's face, when pressed into wet clay or hot wax, left a unique impression authenticating or showing ownership of a document. Such a ring, as a symbol of authority, was always kept on the king's person. The Lord said He would **tear** Jehoiachin from His hand—i.e., no longer would the Lord rule Israel through this king.

22:26-27 Jehoiachin followed in the evil footsteps of his predecessors; thus, God would **hurl** [Hb *tul* "cast out violently"] Jehoiachin to Babylon, along with his mother, Nehushta, who evidently was unable or unwilling to influence him for good.

22:28-30 Jehoiachin would be like a **despised, shattered** [Hb *naphats*, "broken, dashed to pieces"; cp. 13:14; 48:12; 51:20-23; Jdg 7:19; Ps 2:9] **pot** [Hb *ʿetsev*, "earthen vessel"], **a jar** [Hb *keli*, "vessel, container"; cp. Jr 14:3] **no one wants . . . hurled** (Hb *tul* "cast out violently") and **cast** (Hb *shalak*, "thrown out") into a foreign land, subject to his enemies. This language accords well with Jr 16:13 ("I will hurl [Hb *tul*, "cast out violently"] you" into exile); the sign act of Jr 19:10 (the throwing down and shattering of the clay jar); and the covenant curse of exile (Dt 29:28, "The LORD . . . threw [Hb *shalak*, "thrown out"] them into another land"). God emphatically called the **earth** to witness the truth of His prophet's declaration (cp. Dt 30:19). Separation from one's homeland and death in a foreign land was the final, worst covenant curse. Consequently, **none of his descendants** would rule after him, so he was as good as **childless**, the most disgraceful consequence that a person in the ancient world could experience.

23:1-4 After pronouncing judgment on the kings for having fallen short of God's standards, attention moves to the other leaders of the people ("shepherds," cp. 22:22) and to the (false) prophets of Judah, who received the most thorough invective. This passage bears a strong thematic resemblance to Ezekiel 34, in which the leaders are compared with **shepherds who destroy** and **scatter** the flock. Only the Lord can properly shepherd (attend to) His flock, and in the future

15 Are you a king
because you excel in cedar?
Didn't your father
eat and drink
and administer justice
and righteousness?
Then it went well with him.
16 He took up the case
of the poor and needy,
then it went well.
Is this not what it means
to know Me?
This is
the LORD's declaration.
17 But you have eyes and a heart
for nothing
except your own
dishonest profit,
shedding innocent blood
and committing extortion
and oppression.

18 Therefore, this is what the LORD says concerning Jehoiakim son of Josiah, king of Judah:

They will not mourn
for him, saying,
"Woe, my brother!" or "Woe,
my sister!"
They will not mourn
for him, saying,
"Woe, lord! Woe, his majesty!"
19 He will be buried
like a donkey,
dragged off and thrown
outside the gates
of Jerusalem.
20 Go up to Lebanon
and cry out;
raise your voice in Bashan;
cry out from Abarim,
for all your lovers[A]
have been crushed.
21 I spoke to you when
you were secure.
You said, "I will not listen."
This has been your way
since youth;
indeed, you have
never listened to Me.
22 The wind will take charge
of[A] all your shepherds,
and your lovers[B] will go
into captivity.
Then you will be ashamed
and humiliated
because of all your evil.
23 You residents of Lebanon,
nestled among the cedars,
how you will groan[C]
when labor pains
come on you,
agony like a woman in labor.

24 "As I live," says the LORD,
"though you, Coniah[D] son of Jehoiakim, the king of Judah, were a signet
ring on My right hand, I would tear
you from it. 25 In fact, I will hand you
over to those you dread, who want
to take your life, to Nebuchadnezzar
king of Babylon and the Chaldeans.
26 I will hurl you and the mother who
gave birth to you into another land,
where neither of you were born, and
there you will both die. 27 They will
never return to the land they long
to return to."

28 Is this man Coniah
a despised, shattered pot,
a jar no one wants?
Why are he
and his descendants
hurled out
and cast into a land
they have not known?
29 Earth, earth, earth,
hear the word of the LORD!

30 This is what the LORD says:

Record this man as childless,
a man who will not
be successful in his lifetime.
None of his descendants
will succeed
in sitting on the throne
of David
or ruling again in Judah.

The Condemnation of False Prophets (23:1-40)

23 "Woe to the shepherds who destroy and scatter the sheep of
My pasture!" This is the LORD's declaration. 2 "Therefore, this is what
the LORD, the God of Israel, says
about the shepherds who shepherd
My people: You have scattered My
flock, banished them, and have not
attended to them. I will attend to
you because of your evil acts"—this
is the LORD's declaration. 3 "I will
gather the remnant of My flock from
all the lands where I have banished

[A]22:20,22 Or *friends*, or *allies* [B]22:22 Lit *will shepherd* [C]22:23 LXX, Syr, Vg; MT reads *will be pitied* [D]22:24 = Jehoiachin

them, and I will return them to
their grazing land. They will become
fruitful and numerous. [4] I will raise
up shepherds over them who will
shepherd them. They will no longer
be afraid or dismayed, nor will any
be missing." This is the LORD's declaration.

5 "The days are coming"—this
is the LORD's declaration—
"when I will raise
up a Righteous
Branch of David.
He will reign wisely as king
and administer justice and
righteousness in the land.
6 In His days Judah will
be saved,
and Israel will dwell securely.
This is what He will
be named:
•Yahweh Our Righteousness.

7 "The days are coming"—the
LORD's declaration—"when it will
no longer be said, 'As the LORD lives
who brought the Israelites from the
land of Egypt,' [8] but, 'As the LORD
lives, who brought and led the descendants of the house of Israel
from the land of the north and from
all the other countries where I[A] had
banished them.' They will dwell
once more in their own land."

9 Concerning the prophets:

My heart is broken within me,
and all my bones tremble.
I have become
like a drunkard,
like a man overcome by wine,
because of the LORD,
because of His holy words.
10 For the land is full
of adulterers;
the land mourns because
of the curse,
and the grazing lands
in the wilderness
have dried up.
Their way of life[B]
has become evil,
and their power is not
rightly used
11 because both prophet
and priest are ungodly,
even in My house
I have found their evil.
This is
the LORD's declaration.
12 Therefore, their way will be
to them
like slippery paths
in the gloom.
They will be driven away
and fall down there,
for I will bring disaster
on them,
the year of their punishment.
This is
the LORD's declaration.
13 Among the prophets
of Samaria
I saw something disgusting:
They prophesied by[C] •Baal
and led
My people Israel astray.
14 Among the prophets
of Jerusalem also
I saw a horrible thing:
They commit adultery
and walk in lies.
They strengthen the hands
of evildoers,
and none turns his back
on evil.
They are all like Sodom
to Me;
Jerusalem's residents are
like Gomorrah.

15 Therefore, this is what the
LORD of •Hosts says concerning the
prophets:

I am about
to feed them •wormwood
and give them poisoned water
to drink,
for from the prophets
of Jerusalem
ungodliness[D] has spread
throughout the land.

16 This is what the LORD of Hosts
says: "Do not listen to the words
of the prophets who prophesy to
you. They are making you worthless. They speak visions from their
own minds, not from the LORD's
mouth. [17] They keep on saying to
those who despise Me, 'The LORD has
said: You will have peace.' They have
said to everyone who follows the

He will raise up a righteous king from David's line who will ensure the safety of Israel (cp. Ezk 34:1-31).

23:5-6 A word of messianic prophecy is inaugurated by the phrase **the days are coming**, and the use of the title **Branch** [Hb *tsemach*, literally "sprout, that which is produced by a living plant"; figuratively, "offspring"] **of David** (cp. 33:15; Is 4:2; Zch 3:8; 6:12). A legitimate **king** will be appointed by God, one who will exhibit the true kingly virtues of wisdom, **justice and righteousness**; in fact, his name will be **Yahweh Our Righteousness** (Hb *YHWH-tsidqēnu*). The fact that the future legitimate ruler embodies righteousness emphasizes the unrighteousness (and illegitimacy) of the kings previously addressed.

23:7-8 The Lord's work in regathering His people will be renowned, surpassing the miracle of the exodus, so much so that a popular oath formula would be altered to reflect the Lord's newest act of deliverance and resettlement of His people in their promised land (cp. 16:14-15).

23:9-14 The prophets are condemned for several reasons. God's judgment upon these unholy prophets was imminent. The **prophets of Samaria** were Israel's prophets—the northern kingdom, whose capital was Samaria. Comparison of the two capital cities emphasizes Judah's stubborn refusal to repent. Rather than abiding within a covenant relationship, Judah chose to break the commandments. Therefore, God regarded them as incorrigible as **Sodom** and **Gomorrah**, pagans with whom God had no covenant relationship and whose sin brought about the archetypal judgment of sudden total destruction by fire and brimstone.

23:15 Jerusalem imitated Samaria's deeds despite witnessing its destruction and the deportation of its inhabitants (cp. 3:6-11; Ezk 23). The false prophets would bear the burden of God's punishment for leading the people into idolatry and **ungodliness** (Hb *chanuphah*, "pollution"; from the verb *chanēph*, "be profaned or defiled"; cp. 3:1-2,9; Nm 35:33; Ps 106:38).

23:16-17 The Lord warned His people against prophets who offer false security, those who preach messages of **peace** and **no harm** to unrepentant people. In reality, God's "wrath" comes against "the wicked," and His "anger will not turn back" until their punishment is complete. His anger against their sin was as unstoppable as a hurricane.

[A] **23:8** LXX reads *He* [B] **23:10** Lit *Their manner of running* [C] **23:13** = in the name of [D] **23:15** Or *pollution*

23:18-22 Twice the **council** [Hb *sod*, "assembly," referring to a group of heavenly beings who gather in God's presence, receiving information about God's intended plans and His wisdom; cp. Ps 89:7] **of the LORD** is mentioned. The false prophets knew nothing of either the Lord or His council because they had not consulted with God.

23:23-27 The Lord had neither commissioned them nor given them a message; they spoke apart from Him, only from **their own minds** and their own **dreams**. The Lord's punishment of His people is inescapable because God is present everywhere: **near** and **far away**, **in secret places** as well as in the open—**the heavens and the earth**. God condemned the **prophets prophesying lies** for deceitfully claiming dreams as the source of authority for their message.

23:28-32 Although dreams were acceptable modes of prophetic revelation, **the LORD's declaration** compared the relative worth of **a dream** and His **word** to that of **straw** (Hb *teven*, "chaff, dried grass eaten by cattle and horses") and **grain** (Hb *bar*, "corn or wheat"), a substantive food source and basis of the people's diet. Yahweh further compared His own **word** to **fire** and **a hammer that pulverizes rock**. His word as delivered by the genuine prophet was one of destruction and judgment upon those **leading** [His] **people astray**.

23:33-35 In these verses, **burden** (Hb *massa'*; see **Word Study**, p. 823) is a wordplay, which can refer not only to a "load" that is carried but also to an "oracle or utterance." The **people** and their prophets and priests had been trusting in false oracles, so for assurance they asked for the latest oracle (i.e., more assurance). God answered that there was no oracle, only a non-reassuring burden. In fact, *they* were the "burden," one that He would discard.

23:36-39 The Lord prohibited the use of the phrase **burden of the LORD** because the people were inventing their own revelation from God, thereby perverting **the words of the living God**. God threatened to **throw** them **away from** His **presence** (or to "unburden" Himself of them), for they had spoken lies in His name.

24:1-4 The vision of the **two baskets of figs** took place during the reign of Zedekiah, after the deportation of Jehoiachin. It was intended to distinguish between the exiles already in Babylon and those who remained in Judah. The Lord Himself interpreted this vision. He interprets **good figs** in terms reminiscent of His original

stubbornness of his heart, 'No harm
will come to you.'"

18 For who has stood
in the council of the LORD
to see and hear His word?
Who has paid attention
to His word and obeyed?
19 Look, a storm from the LORD!
Wrath has gone out,
a whirling storm.
It will whirl about the heads
of the wicked.
20 The LORD's anger will not
turn back
until He has completely
fulfilled the purposes
of His heart.
In time to come you will
understand it clearly.

21 I did not send these prophets,
yet they ran with a message.
I did not speak to them,
yet they prophesied.
22 If they had really stood
in My council,
they would have enabled
My people to hear My words
and would have
turned them back
from their evil ways
and their evil deeds.

23 "Am I a God who is only
near"—this is the LORD's declaration—"and not a God who is far
away? 24 Can a man hide himself
in secret places where I cannot
see him?"—the LORD's declaration.
"Do I not fill the heavens and the
earth?"—the LORD's declaration.
25 "I have heard what the prophets who prophesy a lie in My name
have said, 'I had a dream! I had a
dream!' 26 How long will this continue in the minds of the prophets
prophesying lies, prophets of the deceit of their own minds? 27 Through
their dreams that they tell one another, they plan to cause My people
to forget My name as their fathers
forgot My name through Baal worship. 28 The prophet who has only a
dream should recount the dream,
but the one who has My word should
speak My word truthfully, for what is
straw compared to grain?"—this is
the LORD's declaration. 29 "Is not My
word like fire"—this is the LORD's
declaration—"and like a hammer
that pulverizes rock? 30 Therefore,
take note! I am against the prophets"—the LORD's declaration—"who
steal My words from each other.
31 I am against the prophets"—the
LORD's declaration—"who use their
own tongues to make a declaration.
32 I am against those who prophesy
false dreams"—the LORD's declaration—"telling them and leading My
people astray with their falsehoods
and their boasting. It was not I who
sent or commanded them, and they
are of no benefit at all to these people"—this is the LORD's declaration.
33 "Now when these people or a
prophet or a priest asks you, 'What
is the burden of the LORD?' you will
respond to them: What is the burden? I will throw you away"—this
is the LORD's declaration. 34 "As for
the prophet, priest, or people who
say, 'The burden of the LORD,' I will
punish that man and his household.
35 This is what each man is to say to
his friend and to his brother, 'What
has the LORD answered?' or 'What has
the LORD spoken?' 36 But no longer
refer to[A] the burden of the LORD, for
each man's word becomes his burden and you pervert the words of the
living God, the LORD of Hosts, our
God. 37 You must say to the prophet:
What has the LORD answered you?
and What has the LORD spoken? 38 But
if you say, 'The burden of the LORD,'
then this is what the LORD says: Because you have said, 'The burden of
the LORD,' and I specifically told you
not to say, 'The burden of the LORD,'
39 I will surely forget you[B] and throw
away from My presence both you and
the city that I gave you and your fathers. 40 I will bring on you everlasting shame and humiliation that will
never be forgotten."

The Vision of Good and Bad Figs (24:1-10)

24 After Nebuchadnezzar king of
Babylon had deported Jeconiah[C] son of Jehoiakim king of Judah, the officials of Judah, and the
craftsmen and metalsmiths from

[A] **23:36** Or *longer remember* [B] **23:39** Some Hb mss; other Hb mss, LXX, Syr, Vg read *surely lift you up* [C] **24:1** = Jehoiachin

>WORD|*study*

25:10 The Hebrew word *qol* is thrice repeated, translated as both sound and voice. **Joy, gladness**, and the sounds of daily activities of the daytime (**millstones**) and nighttime (**light of the lamp**) would all be eliminated, marking the complete desolation of the land.

Jerusalem and had brought them
to Babylon, the LORD showed me
two baskets of figs placed before
the temple of the LORD. 2 One basket
contained very good figs, like early
figs, but the other basket contained
very bad figs, so bad they were inedible. 3 The LORD said to me, "What
do you see, Jeremiah?" I said, "Figs!
The good figs are very good, but the
bad figs are extremely bad, so bad
they are inedible."
4 The word of the LORD came to me:
5 "This is what the LORD, the God of
Israel, says: Like these good figs, so
I regard as good the exiles from Judah I sent away from this place to
the land of the Chaldeans. 6 I will
keep My eyes on them for their good
and will return them to this land. I
will build them up and not demolish
them; I will plant them and not uproot them. 7 I will give them a heart
to know Me, that I am •Yahweh.
They will be My people, and I will be
their God because they will return
to Me with all their heart.
8 "But as for the bad figs, so bad
they are inedible, this is what the
LORD says: in this way I will deal
with king Zedekiah of Judah, his
officials, and the remnant of Jerusalem—those remaining in this land
and those living in the land of Egypt.
9 I will make them an object of horror and disaster to all the kingdoms
of the earth, a disgrace, an object of
scorn, ridicule, and cursing, wherever I have banished them. 10 I will
send the sword, famine, and plague
against them until they have perished from the land I gave to them
and their ancestors."

The 70-Year Exile (25:1-38)

25 This is the word that came to
Jeremiah concerning all the
people of Judah in the fourth year
of Jehoiakim son of Josiah, king of
Judah (which was the first year of
Nebuchadnezzar king of Babylon).
2 The prophet Jeremiah spoke concerning all the people of Judah and
all the residents of Jerusalem as follows: 3 "From the thirteenth year of
Josiah son of Amon, king of Judah,
until this very day—23 years—the
word of the LORD has come to me,
and I have spoken to you time
and time again,[A] but you have not
obeyed. 4 The LORD sent all His servants the prophets to you time
and time again,[B] but you have not
obeyed or even paid attention.[C] 5 He
announced, 'Turn, each of you, from
your[D] evil way of life and from your
evil deeds. Live in the land the LORD
gave to you and your ancestors long
ago and forever. 6 Do not follow other gods to serve them and to worship them, and do not provoke Me
to anger by the work of your hands.
Then I will do you no harm.
7 "'But you would not obey
Me'—this is the LORD's declaration—'in order that you might
provoke Me to anger by the work
of your hands and bring disaster on
yourselves.'
8 "Therefore, this is what the LORD
of •Hosts says: 'Because you have
not obeyed My words, 9 I am going
to send for all the families of the
north'—this is the LORD's declaration—'and send for My servant Nebuchadnezzar king of Babylon, and
I will bring them against this land,
against its residents, and against
all these surrounding nations, and
I will •completely destroy them
and make them a desolation, a derision, and ruins forever. 10 I will
eliminate the sound of joy and gladness from them—the voice of the
groom and the bride, the sound of
the millstones and the light of the
lamp. 11 This whole land will become

intent for Jeremiah's mission (cp. 1:10). The purpose of the two kinds of figs was to dramatize the nature of their situation—the figs were either good or bad, with nothing in between. Similarly, there was either hope (for the exiles) or no hope at all (for those in the land), but there was nothing in between.

24:5-7 The exiles already in Babylon constituted the remnant who would **return** to Israel. God would **build them up and not demolish them** (cp. 42:10). In addition to returning to the land, they would also **return** to God **with all their heart**, and God would accept them once more as His covenant people. Their return was made possible by God's work: He would **give them a heart to know** Him, evidencing one of the most important themes of Jeremiah—that the new covenant is written internally on the heart, not just externally on stone tablets.

24:8-10 By contrast, those who were left will be wiped out, not because God arbitrarily plays favorites but because of their own rebellion against God's word. The punishment of those remaining in the land would have been surprising for Jeremiah's hearers since they considered those already exiled as the ones being punished, while those who remained were favored by God.

25:1-7 The prophecies contained here date to the **fourth year of Jehoiakim**, around 605/604 B.C. By this time, Jeremiah had been preaching God's message to Judah for **23 years** without a positive response. Through him, the Lord had urged repentance, obedience, and a turning away from **the work of your hands** (i.e., idolatry, but Judah refused to listen).

25:8-10 Therefore, the Lord would stir up **all the families of the north** (the Babylonians), who would completely destroy the land and leave it in ruins. This passage clearly illustrates God's sovereignty over all nations, not just His own people. God called Nebuchadnezzar, a pagan Gentile, **My servant**, the one to whom would be entrusted the task of punishing Judah for her sins. Nebuchadnezzar did this unwittingly, even as Cyrus the Persian, called "My Shepherd" (Is 44:28) and "His anointed" (Is 45:1), would serve as God's instrument for the restoration of His people to their land and to their city Jerusalem, whose ruins would be rebuilt (Is 44:24–45:6). Cyrus did this while he did not know Yahweh (Is 45:4-5), and indeed God initiated and performed the actions, as indicated both in Jeremiah 25 and in Isaiah 45 by the repeated first-person verbs (identified in English by the phrase **I will**).

[A]**25:3** Lit *you; rising early and speaking even inclined your ears* [B]**25:4** Lit *prophets, rising early and sending* [C]**25:4** Lit *even inclined your ears* [D]**25:5** Lit *his*

25:13-14 The period of the exile is foretold as **70 years**, thereby giving the land its Sabbath rest (cp. 2Ch 36:21). Many years later, the Lord's words through Jeremiah were read by Daniel, a younger contemporary. Daniel (who was taken into captivity with the very first group of exiles) ascertained from "the books according to the word of the Lord to Jeremiah the prophet that the number of years for the desolation of Jerusalem would be 70" (Dn 9:2). When Judah's punishment was complete, a similar judgment would come upon Babylon. Indeed, not only would Babylon suffer, but also **all the nations** against whom **Jeremiah prophesied** would be punished for their wickedness and idolatry.

25:15-26 The nations to be punished are listed in verses 18-26. Their punishment was signaled by the **cup of the wine of wrath** from the Lord. The **cup** symbolizes God's wrath in other places in the Scriptures (cp. Jb 21:20; Is 51:17; Ezk 23:31; Mt 26:39; Mk 10:38-39; Rv 14:10; 16:19). In this instance it symbolizes not only wrath but also the effects of God's judgment by **the sword** (war), a devastating punishment beginning with God's own people, **Judah** (cp. vv. 27,29), and culminating in the devastation of **Sheshach**, a code name for Babylon. Some suggest the passage is metaphorical, while others hold that Jeremiah may have approached political delegates or foreign ambassadors from the countries listed.

25:27-38 God's judgment is not limited to His own people (**the city that bears My name**) and the surrounding nations, but is **against all the inhabitants of the earth**. In His sovereignty, God judges **all flesh**. Several metaphors convey the magnitude of the Lord's judgment. The first and final threatening images of the roaring lion (**the Lord roars** and **He has left His den like a lion**) serve as parentheses for the intervening metaphors. The image of the winepress denoted judgment rather than the festal joy of the grape harvest. This may relate to the earlier cup imagery and to other violent images that use winepress imagery (Is 63:2-6; Rv 14:19-20), paralleling wine with blood and associating these with divine judgment and wrath.

Shepherds and **leaders** refer to the kings of the nations listed in verses 18-26. They would not escape judgment, and their **pasture** or **grazing land** (their kingdoms) would be utterly destroyed by the Lord.

a desolate ruin, and these nations
will serve the king of Babylon for 70
years. 12 When the 70 years are completed, I will punish the king of Babylon and that nation'—this is the
Lord's declaration—'the land of the
Chaldeans, for their •guilt, and I will
make it a ruin forever. 13 I will bring
on that land all My words I have spoken against it, all that is written in
this book that Jeremiah prophesied
against all the nations. 14 For many
nations and great kings will enslave
them, and I will repay them according to their deeds and the work of
their hands.'"

15 This is what the Lord, the God
of Israel, said to me: "Take this cup
of the wine of wrath from My hand
and make all the nations I am sending you to, drink from it. 16 They will
drink, stagger,[A] and go out of their
minds because of the sword I am
sending among them."

17 So I took the cup from the Lord's
hand and made all the nations drink
from it, everyone the Lord sent me
to. 18 These included:

Jerusalem and the other
cities of Judah, its kings and
its officials, to make them a
desolate ruin, an object of
scorn and cursing—as it is
today;
19 Pharaoh king of Egypt, his
officers, his leaders, all his
people,
20 and all the mixed peoples;
all the kings of the land of Uz;
all the kings of the land of the
Philistines—Ashkelon, Gaza,
Ekron, and the remnant of
Ashdod;
21 Edom, Moab, and the
Ammonites;
22 all the kings of Tyre,
all the kings of Sidon,
and the kings of the
coastlands across the sea;
23 Dedan, Tema, Buz, and
all those who shave their
temples;[B]
24 all the kings of Arabia,
and all the kings of the mixed
peoples who have settled in
the desert;
25 all the kings of Zimri,
all the kings of Elam,
and all the kings of Media;
26 all the kings of the north,
both near and far from one
another;
that is, all the kingdoms of
the world which are on the
face of the earth.
Finally, the king of Sheshach[C]
will drink after them.

27 "Then you are to say to them:
This is what the Lord of Hosts, the
God of Israel, says: Drink, get drunk,
and vomit. Fall down and never get
up again, as a result of the sword I
am sending among you. 28 If[D] they
refuse to take the cup from you
and drink, you are to say to them:
This is what the Lord of Hosts says:
You must drink! 29 For I am already
bringing disaster on the city that
bears My name, so how could you
possibly go unpunished? You will
not go unpunished, for I am summoning a sword against all the inhabitants of the earth"—this is the
declaration of the Lord of Hosts.

30 "As for you, you are to prophesy
all these things to them, and say to
them:

The Lord roars from heaven;
He raises His voice
from His holy dwelling.
He roars loudly
over His grazing land;
He calls out with a shout,
like those who tread grapes,
against all the inhabitants
of the earth.
31 The tumult reaches
to the ends of the earth
because the Lord brings
a case against the nations.
He enters into judgment
with all flesh.
As for the wicked,
He hands them over
to the sword—
this is
the Lord's declaration.

32 "This is what the Lord of Hosts
says:

Pay attention!
Disaster spreads

[A]**25:16** Or *vomit* [B]**25:23** Or *who live in distant places* [C]**25:26** Probably a name for Babylon
[D]**25:28** Or *When*

from nation to nation.
A great storm is stirred up
from the ends of the earth."

33 Those slain by the LORD on that
day will be spread from one end of
the earth to the other. They will not
be mourned, gathered, or buried.
They will be like manure on the surface of the ground.

34 Wail, you shepherds,
and cry out.
Roll in the dust,[A] you leaders
of the flock.
Because the days
of your slaughter
have come,
you will fall
and become shattered
like a precious vase.
35 Flight will be impossible
for the shepherds,
and escape, for the leaders
of the flock.
36 Hear the sound
of the shepherds' cry,
the wail of the leaders
of the flock,
for the LORD is destroying
their pasture.
37 Peaceful grazing land
will become lifeless
because of
the LORD's burning anger.
38 He has left His den like a lion,
for their land has become
a desolation
because of the sword[B]
of the oppressor,
because of His burning anger.

True Versus False Prophecy (26:1–29:32)

26 At the beginning of the reign
of Jehoiakim son of Josiah,
king of Judah, this word came
from the LORD: 2 "This is what the
LORD says: Stand in the courtyard of
the LORD's temple and speak all the
words I have commanded you to
speak to all Judah's cities that are
coming to worship there. Do not
hold back a word. 3 Perhaps they
will listen and return—each from
his evil way of life—so that I might
relent concerning the disaster that
I plan to do to them because of the
evil of their deeds. 4 You are to say
to them: This is what the LORD says:
If you do not listen to Me by living
according to My instruction that I
set before you 5 and by listening to
the words of My servants the prophets I have been sending you time
and time again,[C] though you did
not listen, 6 I will make this temple
like Shiloh. I will make this city an
object of cursing for all the nations
of the earth."

7 The priests, the prophets, and all
the people heard Jeremiah speaking these words in the temple of the
LORD. 8 He finished the address the
LORD had commanded him to deliver
to all the people. Then the priests,
the prophets, and all the people
took hold of him, yelling, "You must
surely die! 9 How dare you prophesy in the name of •Yahweh, 'This
temple will become like Shiloh and
this city will become an uninhabited
ruin'!" Then all the people assembled against Jeremiah at the LORD's
temple.

10 When the officials of Judah
heard these things, they went from
the king's palace to the LORD's temple and sat at the entrance of the
New Gate.[D] 11 Then the priests and
prophets said to the officials and
all the people, "This man deserves
the death sentence because he has
prophesied against this city, as you
have heard with your own ears."

12 Then Jeremiah said to all the
officials and the people, "The LORD
sent me to prophesy all the words
that you have heard against this
temple and city. 13 So now, correct
your ways and deeds and obey the
voice of the LORD your God so that
He might relent concerning the disaster that He warned about. 14 As
for me, here I am in your hands; do
to me what you think is good and
right. 15 But know for certain that if
you put me to death, you will bring
innocent blood on yourselves, on
this city, and on its residents, for
it is certain the LORD has sent me
to speak all these things directly to
you."

26:1-24 Although Jeremiah seems like a lone figure, the following chapters place him in the context of other prophetic contemporaries. This chapter at once summarizes the temple sermon of chapter 7 and expands on that incident. While chapter 7 provides a full presentation of the sermon itself, chapter 26 provides a fuller presentation of the trial of Jeremiah.

26:1-6 The thrust of Jeremiah's message was that if Judah refused to repent, the Jerusalem temple would be destroyed as the tabernacle at Shiloh had been destroyed by the Philistines around 1050 B.C. Jerusalem's destruction would serve as an object lesson to **all the nations of the earth**.

26:7-11 Because of his words against the temple, Jeremiah drew threats against his life. Indeed, **the priests, the prophets, and all the people** took Jeremiah's prophecy as a lie blasphemously delivered **in the name Yahweh**. According to Deuteronomic law, the false prophet must die (as will be the case in the coming chapters). Jeremiah's words were probably considered demoralizing and treasonous.

26:12-15 Jeremiah defended himself by reiterating his call to repentance, insisting that his message bore divine authority.

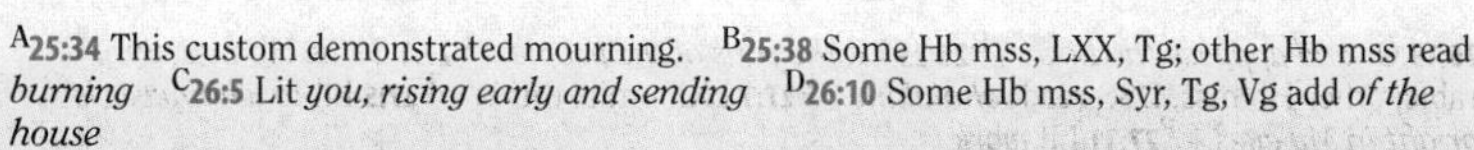

[A] **25:34** This custom demonstrated mourning. [B] **25:38** Some Hb mss, LXX, Tg; other Hb mss read *burning* [C] **26:5** Lit *you, rising early and sending* [D] **26:10** Some Hb mss, Syr, Tg, Vg add *of the house*

16 Then the officials and all the people told the priests and prophets, "This man doesn't deserve the death sentence, for he has spoken to us in the name of Yahweh our God!"

17 Some of the elders of the land stood up and said to all the assembled people, 18 "Micah the Moreshite prophesied in the days of Hezekiah king of Judah and said to all the people of Judah, 'This is what the LORD of •Hosts says:

> •Zion will be plowed
> like a field,
> Jerusalem will become ruins,
> and the temple mount
> a forested hill.'

19 Did Hezekiah king of Judah and all the people of Judah put him to death? Did he not •fear the LORD and plead for the LORD's favor,[A] and did not the LORD relent concerning the disaster He had pronounced against them? We are about to bring great harm on ourselves!"

20 Another man was also prophesying in the name of Yahweh—Uriah son of Shemaiah from Kiriath-jearim. He prophesied against this city and against this land in words like all those of Jeremiah. 21 King Jehoiakim, all his warriors, and all the officials heard his words, and the king tried to put him to death. When Uriah heard, he fled in fear and went to Egypt. 22 But King Jehoiakim sent men to Egypt: Elnathan son of Achbor and certain other men with him went to Egypt. 23 They brought Uriah out of Egypt and took him to King Jehoiakim, who executed him with the sword and threw his corpse into the burial place of the common people.[B]

24 But Ahikam son of Shaphan supported Jeremiah, so he was not handed over to the people to be put to death.

27 At the beginning of the reign of Zedekiah[C] son of Josiah, king of Judah, this word came to Jeremiah from the LORD:[D] 2 "This is what the LORD said to me: Make chains and yoke bars for yourself and put them on your neck. 3 Send word to the king of Edom, the king of Moab, the king of the Ammonites, the king of Tyre, and the king of Sidon through messengers who are coming to Zedekiah king of Judah in Jerusalem. 4 Command them to go to their masters, saying: This is what the LORD of •Hosts, the God of Israel, says: This is what you must say to your masters: 5 By My great strength and outstretched arm, I made the earth, and the people, and animals on the face of the earth. I give it to anyone I please.[E] 6 So now I have placed all these lands under the authority of My servant Nebuchadnezzar, king of Babylon. I have even given him the wild animals to serve him. 7 All nations will serve him, his son, and his grandson until the time for his own land comes, and then many nations and great kings will enslave him.

8 "As for the nation or kingdom that does not serve Nebuchadnezzar king of Babylon and does not place its neck under the yoke of the king of Babylon, that nation I will punish by sword, famine, and plague"—this is the LORD's declaration—"until through him I have destroyed it. 9 But as for you, do not listen to your prophets, diviners, dreamers, fortune-tellers, or sorcerers who say to you, 'Don't serve the king of Babylon!' 10 for they prophesy a lie to you so that you will be removed from your land. I will banish you, and you will perish. 11 But as for the nation that will put its neck under the yoke of the king of Babylon and serve him, I will leave it in its own land, and that nation will cultivate[F] it and reside in it." This is the LORD's declaration.

12 I spoke to Zedekiah king of Judah in the same way: "Put your necks under the yoke of the king of Babylon, serve him and his people, and live! 13 Why should you and your people die by the sword, famine, or plague as the LORD has threatened against any nation that does not serve the king of Babylon? 14 Do not listen to the words of the prophets

[A]**26:19** Or *and appease the LORD* [B]**26:23** Lit *the sons of the people* [C]**27:1** Some Hb mss, Syr, Arabic; other Hb mss, DSS read *Jehoiakim* [D]**27:1** LXX omits this v. [E]**27:5** Lit *to whomever is upright in My eyes* [F]**27:11** Lit *work*

26:16-19 The **officials** and **elders** formed a kind of jury or defense council, reminding Jeremiah's accusers that **Micah the Moreshite** preached an identical message, yet his life was spared by King **Hezekiah**.

26:20-24 By contrast, the fate of **Uriah son of Shemaiah** proved tragic. Uriah's message was apparently the same as Jeremiah's, but seemingly he had no one to defend him. Jeremiah stood his ground, had a trial, and was additionally protected by an influential courtier, **Ahikam son of Shaphan**. Uriah fled to Egypt for asylum, but Judah and Egypt shared laws of extradition since Jehoiakim was a vassal ruler. Uriah was considered a false prophet and a traitor, and he was therefore extradited, executed, and denied a proper burial in a family tomb. His body was thrown into a **burial place of the common people**, perhaps in the Kidron Valley.

27:1-3 The enacted parable of the **yoke** of Babylon occurred in the reign of **Zedekiah**, the last Judean king before Jerusalem's final collapse (1Kg 24:17–25:7). The Lord commanded Jeremiah physically to act out the prophetic oracle. He was to make a yoke and wear it. It appears that foreign ambassadors from **Edom**, **Moab**, Ammon, **Tyre**, and **Sidon** had come to Jerusalem to discuss with **Zedekiah** how to join forces against the king of Babylon. Jeremiah advised the political gathering to submit to the "yoke of the king of Babylon" (cp. vv. 8-15).

27:4-8 The Lord asserts His own sovereignty over all the earth as creator and ruler. Again, Nebuchadnezzar is called **My servant** and given rulership over all kingdoms—yet his time would also come to be overthrown and enslaved (cp. 25:9).

27:9-17 The Lord advised the surrounding nations to disregard the false **prophets, diviners, dreamers, fortune-tellers**, and **sorcerers**—which were forbidden in Judah—whose advice contradicted "the Lord's declaration" (vv. 1-8,11). Twice Jeremiah rejected the advice to rebel against Babylon, and once he condemned the prophecies regarding the temple articles that had been taken to Babylon. The other prophetic messages were encouraging but false; Jeremiah's message from the Lord was discouraging but true. He reiterated the Lord's message preached under the previous kings, Jehoiakim and Jehoiachin: **Put your necks under the yoke of the king of Babylon, serve him and his people, and live!** The **articles of the LORD's temple** taken by Nebuchadnezzar were gold utensils and vessels used for temple worship (cp. 2Kg 24:13). These vessels

who are telling you, 'You must not serve the king of Babylon,' for they are prophesying a lie to you. 15 'I have not sent them'—this is the LORD's declaration—'and they are prophesying falsely in My name; therefore, I will banish you, and you will perish—you and the prophets who are prophesying to you.'"

16 Then I spoke to the priests and all these people, saying, "This is what the LORD says: 'Do not listen to the words of your prophets. They are prophesying to you, claiming, "Look, very soon now the articles of the LORD's temple will be brought back from Babylon." They are prophesying a lie to you. 17 Do not listen to them. Serve the king of Babylon and live! Why should this city become a ruin? 18 If they are indeed prophets and if the word of the LORD is with them, let them intercede with the LORD of Hosts not to let the articles that remain in the LORD's temple, in the palace of the king of Judah, and in Jerusalem go to Babylon.' 19 For this is what the LORD of Hosts says about the pillars, the sea, the water carts, and the rest of the articles that still remain in this city, 20 those Nebuchadnezzar king of Babylon did not take when he deported Jeconiah[A] son of Jehoiakim, king of Judah, from Jerusalem to Babylon along with all the nobles of Judah and Jerusalem. 21 Yes, this is what the LORD of Hosts, the God of Israel, says about the articles that remain in the temple of the LORD, in the palace of the king of Judah, and in Jerusalem: 22 'They will be brought to Babylon and will remain there until I attend to them again.' This is the LORD's declaration. 'Then I will bring them up and restore them to this place.'"

28 In that same year, at the beginning of the reign of King Zedekiah of Judah, in the fifth month of the fourth year, the prophet Hananiah son of Azzur from Gibeon said to me in the temple of the LORD in the presence of the priests and all the people, 2 "This is what the LORD of •Hosts, the God of Israel, says: 'I have broken the yoke of the king of Babylon. 3 Within two years I will restore to this place all the articles of the LORD's temple that King Nebuchadnezzar of Babylon took from here and transported to Babylon. 4 And I will restore to this place Jeconiah[A] son of Jehoiakim, king of Judah, and all the exiles from Judah who went to Babylon'—this is the LORD's declaration—'for I will break the yoke of the king of Babylon.'"

5 The prophet Jeremiah replied to the prophet Hananiah in the presence of the priests and all the people who were standing in the temple of the LORD. 6 The prophet Jeremiah said, "•Amen! May the LORD do so. May the LORD make the words you have prophesied come true and may He restore the articles of the LORD's temple and all the exiles from Babylon to this place! 7 Only listen to this message I am speaking in your hearing and in the hearing of all the people. 8 The prophets who preceded you and me from ancient times prophesied war, disaster,[B] and plague against many lands and great kingdoms. 9 As for the prophet who prophesies peace—only when the word of the prophet comes true will the prophet be recognized as one the LORD has truly sent."

10 The prophet Hananiah then took the yoke bar from the neck of Jeremiah the prophet and broke it. 11 In the presence of all the people Hananiah proclaimed, "This is what the LORD says: 'In this way, within two years I will break the yoke of King Nebuchadnezzar of Babylon from the neck of all the nations.'" Jeremiah the prophet then went on his way.

12 The word of the LORD came to Jeremiah after Hananiah the prophet had broken the yoke bar from the neck of Jeremiah the prophet: 13 "Go say to Hananiah: This is what the LORD says, 'You broke a wooden yoke bar, but in its place you will make an iron yoke bar.' 14 For this is what the LORD of Hosts, the God of Israel, says, 'I have put an iron yoke on the neck of all these nations that they might serve King Nebuchadnezzar of Babylon, and they will serve him.

had been made by Solomon during the construction of the temple (1Kg 7:48-51). Their removal was of particular concern for the priests, and on this subject Jeremiah addressed them.

27:18-22 The false prophets had attempted to reassure the priests that the vessels would be restored soon, but Jeremiah insisted that the city's doom was assured. Those prophets would be better off interceding with God that nothing worse would happen to the remaining bronze vessels (cp. 1Kg 7:15-47 for their origin). God had already determined that the bronze items would be **brought to Babylon**, but in time they would be restored to the Jerusalem temple. Jeremiah's prophecy was fulfilled in 52:17-23 and Ezra 1:7-11.

28:1-4 The confrontation with **Hananiah** in the temple must have perplexed those who witnessed it, for their exchange was one of prophet against prophet, both claiming to speak truthfully for God and both using identical oracular formulae: **This is what the LORD of Hosts, the God of Israel, says** (v. 2) and "this is what the LORD says" (v. 11). Hananiah, who appears only here, flatly contradicted Jeremiah, using Jeremiah's enacted parable to make his own point. Hananiah's prophecy may have been motivated by a desire to curry favor with the king and other ambassadors.

28:5-9 After engaging in some sarcasm, Jeremiah pointed out that Hananiah's message was inconsistent with his own and with that of his predecessors (perhaps a reference to Isaiah and Micah). He also reminded hearers of Dt18:15-22, in which true prophets are known by the fulfillment of their message: Time would tell who was the true prophet.

28:10-12 Jeremiah was apparently still wearing **the yoke** God instructed him to make and wear for an unspecified time. In the face of Hananiah's counter-prophecy and sign act, Jeremiah seemed to retreat; but when he received a word from the Lord concerning Hananiah, he spoke out once more.

28:13-17 Ironically, the one who predicted peace (v. 9) and restoration within two years (v. 11) was judged and dead within two months. False prophecy incurred the death penalty, and the Lord Himself initiated Hananiah's punishment. Also ironic is the wording of Hananiah's sentence: The one who was not "sent" (v. 9) by the Lord to preach would now be sent by the Lord to his death.

[A]**27:20; 28:4** = Jehoiachin [B]**28:8** Some Hb mss, Vg read *famine*

29:1-3 Jeremiah was instructed to write a prophetic oracle in the form of a **letter** to the exilic community (**elders, priests, prophets,** and **all the people**) already in **Babylon** (ca 597 B.C.). The letter was by a delegation of sorts (probably carrying tribute) sent **to Nebuchadnezzar** by King **Zedekiah.**

29:4-7 The first of three letters in this chapter concerns God's plan for the exiles. God was the instigator of the exile through Nebuchadnezzar, His agent. God was also the One who would restore them from exile. The divine first person is used continually with the action verbs: **I deported** [the exiles] **from Jerusalem to Babylon**. The message to the exiles is a fulfillment of God's intention as expressed to Jeremiah at his commissioning (1:10): **Build** and **plant**; marry and **multiply**; **pray** for the **welfare** of the captors' land in order to ensure their own **prosperity.**

29:8-9 This message to settle down in a foreign land must have confused the exiles, especially in light of the optimistic predictions of the prophets among them. Some of the exiled prophets set themselves up as true prophets, but in fact they misled the people. Jeremiah addresses this issue, calling them false prophets **not sent** by the Lord.

29:10-14 The Lord gave the people an oracle, which—for a change—was positive, yet not immediately gratifying. Although this celebrated passage is widely beloved, few realize that this hopeful message is set in a context of hopelessness. The One responsible for Judah's punishment and rejection was also responsible for Judah's eventual restoration. In the midst of self-inflicted **disaster**, God promised **a future and a hope**. Whereas most recently God turned His back on His people, forbidding Jeremiah to intercede for them, in the future God would **listen to** them. The condition for seeking and finding God lies in the **heart**. The search must be wholehearted for the people's restoration to be complete.

29:15-19 These verses expand on chapter 24, comparing those left behind in Jerusalem with rotten figs. **The king sitting on David's throne** refers to Zedekiah, the current ruler. God corrects the people's incorrect interpretation of themselves as the cursed ones and those left in Jerusalem as favored.

29:20-23 Two particular false prophets—**Ahab** and **Zedekiah**—are singled out at the end of the letter. These were also adulterers who would be punished by incineration, the same Babylonian punishment that was used against

I have also put the wild animals under him.'"
15 The prophet Jeremiah said to the
prophet Hananiah, "Listen, Hananiah! The LORD did not send you, but
you have led these people to trust
in a lie. 16 Therefore, this is what the
LORD says: 'I am about to send you
off the face of the earth. You will die
this year because you have spoken
rebellion against the LORD.'" 17 And
the prophet Hananiah died that year
in the seventh month.

29 This is the text of the letter
that Jeremiah the prophet sent
from Jerusalem to the rest of the
elders of the exiles, the priests, the
prophets, and all the people Nebuchadnezzar had deported from Jerusalem to Babylon. 2 This was after
King Jeconiah,[A] the queen mother,
the court officials, the officials of Judah and Jerusalem, the craftsmen,
and the metalsmiths had left Jerusalem. 3 The letter was sent by Elasah
son of Shaphan and Gemariah son
of Hilkiah whom Zedekiah king of
Judah had sent to Babylon to Nebuchadnezzar king of Babylon. The
letter stated:

4 This is what the LORD of
•Hosts, the God of Israel, says
to all the exiles I deported from
Jerusalem to Babylon: 5 "Build
houses and live in them. Plant
gardens and eat their produce.
6 Take wives and have sons and
daughters. Take wives for your
sons and give your daughters
to men in marriage so that they
may bear sons and daughters.
Multiply there; do not decrease.
7 Seek the welfare of the city I
have deported you to. Pray to
the LORD on its behalf, for when
it has prosperity, you will prosper."

8 For this is what the LORD of
Hosts, the God of Israel, says:
"Don't let your prophets who
are among you and your diviners deceive you, and don't listen
to the dreams you elicit from
them, 9 for they are prophesying falsely to you in My name. I
have not sent them." This is the
LORD's declaration.

10 For this is what the LORD says:
"When 70 years for Babylon are
complete, I will attend to you
and will confirm My promise
concerning you to restore you
to this place. 11 For I know the
plans I have for you"—this is
the LORD's declaration—"plans
for your welfare, not for disaster, to give you a future and a
hope. 12 You will call to Me and
come and pray to Me, and I will
listen to you. 13 You will seek Me
and find Me when you search
for Me with all your heart. 14 I
will be found by you"—this is
the LORD's declaration—"and I
will restore your fortunes[B] and
gather you from all the nations
and places where I banished
you"—this is the LORD's declaration. "I will restore you to the
place I deported you from."

15 You have said, "The LORD has
raised up prophets for us in
Babylon!" 16 But this is what
the LORD says concerning the
king sitting on David's throne
and concerning all the people
living in this city—that is,
concerning your brothers who
did not go with you into exile. 17 This is what the LORD of
Hosts says: "I am about to send
against them sword, famine,
and plague and will make them
like rotten figs that are inedible because they are so bad. 18 I
will pursue them with sword,
famine, and plague. I will make
them a horror to all the kingdoms of the earth—a curse and
a desolation, an object of scorn
and a disgrace among all the
nations where I have banished
them. 19 I will do this because
they have not listened to My
words"—this is the LORD's declaration—"that I sent to them
with My servants the prophets
time and time again.[C] And you
too have not listened." This is
the LORD's declaration.

[A] **29:2** = Jehoiachin [B] **29:14** Or *will end your captivity* [C] **29:19** Lit *prophets, rising up early and sending*

20 Hear the word of the LORD,
all you exiles I have sent from
Jerusalem to Babylon. 21 This
is what the LORD of Hosts, the
God of Israel, says to Ahab son
of Kolaiah and to Zedekiah son
of Maaseiah, the ones prophesying a lie to you in My name:
"I am about to hand them over
to Nebuchadnezzar king of
Babylon, and he will kill them
before your very eyes. 22 Based
on what happens to them, all
the exiles of Judah who are in
Babylon will create a curse that
says, 'May the LORD make you
like Zedekiah and Ahab, whom
the king of Babylon roasted in
the fire!' 23 because they have
committed an outrage in Israel
by committing adultery with
their neighbors' wives and have
spoken a lie in My name, which
I did not command them. I am
He who knows, and I am a witness." This is the LORD's declaration.

24 To Shemaiah the Nehelamite
you are to say, 25 "This is what
the LORD of Hosts, the God of
Israel, says: You[A] in your own
name have sent out letters to all
the people of Jerusalem, to the
priest Zephaniah son of Maaseiah, and to all the priests, saying: 26 'The LORD has appointed
you priest in place of Jehoiada
the priest to be the chief officer in the temple of the LORD,
responsible for every madman
who acts like a prophet. You
must confine him in the stocks
and an iron collar. 27 So now,
why have you not rebuked Jeremiah of Anathoth who has been
acting like a prophet among
you? 28 For he has sent word to
us in Babylon, claiming, "The
exile will be long. Build houses
and settle down. Plant gardens
and eat their produce."'"

29 Zephaniah the priest read this letter in the hearing of Jeremiah the
prophet.
30 Then the word of the LORD came
to Jeremiah: 31 "Send a message to
all the exiles, saying: This is what
the LORD says concerning Shemaiah
the Nehelamite. Because Shemaiah
prophesied to you, though I did not
send him, and made you trust a lie,
32 this is what the LORD says: I am
about to punish Shemaiah the Nehelamite and his descendants. There
will not be even one of his descendants living among these people,
nor will any ever see the good that
I will bring to My people"—this
is the LORD's declaration—"for he
has preached rebellion against the
LORD."

The Book of Consolation (30:1–33:26)

Restoration from Captivity (30:1—31:30)

30 This is the word that came to
Jeremiah from the LORD. 2 This
is what the LORD, the God of Israel,
says: "Write down on a scroll all the
words that I have spoken to you, 3 for
the days are certainly coming"—this
is the LORD's declaration—"when I
will restore the fortunes[B] of My people Israel and Judah"—the LORD's
declaration. "I will restore them to
the land I gave to their ancestors
and they will possess it."

4 These are the words the LORD
spoke to Israel and Judah. 5 Yes, this
is what the LORD says:

We have heard a cry of terror,
of dread—there is no peace.
6 Ask and see
whether a male
can give birth.
Why then do I see every man
with his hands on his stomach
like a woman in labor
and every face turned pale?
7 How awful that day will be!
There will be none like it!
It will be a time of trouble
for Jacob,
but he will be delivered
out of it.

8 "On that day"—this is the declaration of the LORD of •Hosts—"I will
break his yoke from your neck and
tear off your chains so strangers will
never again enslave him. 9 They will

Shadrach, Meshach, and Abed-nego for not worshiping the pagan king (Dn 3).

29:24-32 The second letter singles out another false prophet—**Shemaiah the Nehelamite**.

Shemaiah wrote to **the priest Zephaniah** in response to Jeremiah's letter (vv. 4-14). He objected to his message that **the exile will be long**, and that the people should **settle down** in Babylon. For this opposition, the Lord declares that Shemaiah's **descendants** would die out—none would return from exile. Similarities appear between Shemaiah and Hananiah, Jeremiah's previous opponent (cp. chap. 28). None of these three false prophets is mentioned elsewhere in the Old Testament.

30:1–33:26 This so-called "Book of Consolation" (chaps. 30–33), which Jeremiah was instructed to record **on a scroll** (1:2), holds out hope for both Israel and Judah; but their future hope does not preclude the punishing disaster that has already been determined by the Lord. The theme from Jeremiah's prophetic commissioning is reiterated throughout (1:10). The judgment portions are examples of uprooting, tearing down, and overthrowing, while messages of hope and restoration are examples of building up (i.e., edifying and planting; establishing in a right relationship/covenant).

30:5-7 The sheer dread, panic, and fear occasioned by their punishment are graphically illustrated by the image of **a woman in labor**; labor pains are excruciating and unavoidable. The brief moments of respite between contractions are filled with the dread of the next one, and there is nothing that can be done to escape them. The end will come but only after escalating pain for what seems an unbearable time. Before the days of modern medicine, there was no certainty that a woman would survive labor; death during childbirth was common. Experiencing the labor of childbirth was a terrifying time.

30:8-9 The time of trouble would pass, however, and the Lord would deliver His people from it after they had suffered. Two phrases—"the days are certainly coming" (v. 3) and **on that day**—indicated a future time of deliverance from enemies, of restoration to their own land, and of a return to governance by their own king, **David**, under the protection of their own God, whom **they will serve**. The people's deliverance was guaranteed by the Lord, yet their sins must be punished. Both actions demonstrate God's just and merciful love.

[A] **29:25** Lit *Because you* [B] **30:3** Or *will end the captivity*

30:10-11 Eventually there would be **calm and quiet with no one to frighten** them, but first they must endure the terror, dread, and time of trouble (v. 4). Although God loved His people deeply and would destroy the invading nations, He would nevertheless **discipline . . . justly**.

30:12-17 The punishment of those who carried out God's judgment upon Judah is re-emphasized in verse 16 with the devouring of the devourers, the destruction of the destroyers, and the raiding of the raiders. The Lord punishes, but also saves; though He strikes His people **as an enemy would**, He also brings **health**, healing their wounds as only He is able to do; for, apart from Him, the **wounds** of **Zion** on account of her sins are **incurable**.

30:18-20 The promised restoration of the land involved the physical reconstruction of Judah's cities. There would again be a **sound of celebration.** Whereas they would shortly be decimated, the future promises expansion, prosperity, and **honor**. The nation (**his congregation**) would be restored in their relationship with God: They would be **established in** [His] **presence**.

30:21 A messianic passage promising a future **leader**, who would **be one of them**, not a foreigner—David their king (v. 9). This **ruler** would be a priest-king, one who enters the presence of God at God's invitation, not on his own initiative. His mediation would result in renewing the nation's covenant with God (as King Josiah, cp. 2Kg 23:1-3) according to God's original intention.

30:22 The formula in verse 22 (cp. Ex 19:6; Lv 26:12; Hs 2:23) is a covenant formula, encapsulating everything the covenant means—a mutual relationship between God and His people, through which each has both privileges and responsibilities.

30:23-24 These verses could refer to the punishment about to befall Judah or possibly to the Babylonians who would shortly crush and oppress Judah. God's wrath is described as a **storm**—an unstoppable whirlwind, which will accomplish God's **purposes**. On the eve of bereavement and devastation, Judah may not have understood God's justice, though it was tempered by love; with hindsight, they would understand.

serve the LORD their God and I will
raise up David their king for them."

10 As for you, My servant Jacob,
do not be afraid—
this is
the LORD's declaration—
and do not
be dismayed, Israel,
for without fail I will save you
from far away,
your descendants,
from the land
of their captivity!
Jacob will return
and have calm and quiet
with no one to frighten him.
11 For I will be with you—
this is
the LORD's declaration—
to save you!
I will bring destruction
on all the nations
where I have scattered you;
however, I will not
bring destruction on you.
I will discipline you justly,
and I will by no means
leave you unpunished.

12 For this is what the LORD says:

Your injury is incurable;
your wound most severe.
13 No one takes up the case
for your sores.
There is no healing for you.
14 All your lovers
have forgotten you;
they no longer look for you,
for I have struck
you as an enemy would,
with the discipline
of someone cruel,
because of
your enormous •guilt
and your innumerable sins.
15 Why do you cry out
about your injury?
Your pain has no cure!
I have done these things
to you
because of
your enormous guilt
and your innumerable sins.
16 Nevertheless, all
who devoured you
will be devoured,
and all your
adversaries—all of them—
will go off into exile.
Those who plunder you
will be plundered,
and all who raid you
will be raided.
17 But I will bring you health
and will heal you
of your wounds—
this is
the LORD's declaration—
for they call you Outcast,
•Zion whom no one
cares about.

18 This is what the LORD says:

I will certainly restore
the fortunes[A]
of Jacob's tents
and show compassion
on his dwellings.
Every city will be rebuilt
on its mound;
every citadel will stand
on its proper site.
19 Thanksgiving will come
out of them,
a sound of celebration.
I will multiply them,
and they will not decrease;
I will honor them,
and they will not
be insignificant.
20 His children will be
as in past days;
his congregation
will be established
in My presence.
I will punish
all his oppressors.
21 Jacob's leader will be
one of them;
his ruler will issue from him.
I will invite him to Me,
and he will approach Me,
for who would otherwise
risk his life to approach Me?
This is
the LORD's declaration.
22 You will be My people,
and I will be your God.

23 Look, a storm from the LORD!
Wrath has gone out,
a churning storm.
It will whirl about the heads
of the wicked.

[A]**30:18** Or *certainly end the captivity*

24 The LORD's burning anger
will not turn back
until He has
completely fulfilled
the purposes of His heart.
In time to come you will
understand it.

31 "At that time"—this is the
LORD's declaration—"I will be
the God of all the families of Israel,
and they will be My people."
2 This is what the LORD says:

They found favor
in the wilderness—
the people who survived
the sword.
When Israel went to find rest,
3 the LORD appeared to him[A]
from far away.
I have loved you
with an everlasting love;
therefore, I have continued
to extend faithful love
to you.
4 Again I will build you so that
you will be rebuilt,
Virgin Israel.
You will take up
your tambourines again
and go out in joyful dancing.
5 You will plant vineyards again
on the mountains of Samaria;
the planters will plant
and will enjoy the fruit.
6 For there will be a day
when watchmen
will call out
in the hill country
of Ephraim,
"Get up, let's go up to •Zion,
to •Yahweh our God!"

7 For this is what the LORD says:

Sing with joy for Jacob;
shout for the chief
of the nations!
Proclaim, praise, and say,
"LORD, save Your people,
the remnant of Israel!"
8 Watch! I am going
to bring them
from the northern land.
I will gather them
from remote regions
of the earth—
the blind and the lame will be
with them,
along with those
who are pregnant and those
about to give birth.
They will return here
as a great assembly!
9 They will come weeping,
but I will bring them back
with consolation.[B]
I will lead them to •wadis
filled with water
by a smooth way where
they will not stumble,
for I am Israel's Father,
and Ephraim is My firstborn.
10 Nations, hear the word
of the LORD,
and tell it among the
far off coastlands!
Say: The One who scattered
Israel will gather him.
He will watch over
him as a shepherd
guards his flock,
11 for the LORD has ransomed
Jacob
and redeemed him
from the power of one
stronger than he.
12 They will come and shout
for joy on the heights
of Zion;
they will be radiant with joy
because of
the LORD's goodness,
because of the grain,
the new wine, the fresh oil,
and because of the young
of the flocks and herds.
Their life will be
like an irrigated garden,
and they will no longer
grow weak from hunger.
13 Then the young woman will
rejoice with dancing,
while young and old men
rejoice together.
I will turn their mourning
into joy,
give them consolation,
and bring happiness
out of grief.
14 I will refresh the priests
with an abundance,[C]

31:1-3 This passage is forward-looking and hopeful, referring to the day of Israel's restoration. God's **faithful love** (Hb *chesed*, God's "covenant loyalty, faithful lovingkindness"; see **Word Study**, p. 322) has always been manifested to Israel and is **everlasting**. He promises an incredible blessing—the reunification of Israel (northern and southern kingdoms) under Yahweh.

31:4 A variation of the initial theme appears, namely, God's promise to **build** and rebuild Israel, whose joy would be restored. Illustrating this joy is the image of singing women with **tambourines** (cp. Ex 15:20-21). The building may refer to the multiplication of the nation after it had dwindled due to war and exile. The image of rebuilding a family is suggested in Genesis by the use of this term by Sarai and Rachel, when each gave her servant/concubine to her respective husband to produce children in her behalf, saying, "Through her I too can build a family" (Gn 30:3; cp. Gn 16:2).

31:5-6 Israel would also **plant . . . again**, and the land would produce abundant fruit. The references to **Samaria** and **Ephraim** make it clear that the northern kingdom's restoration of Yahweh's worship is in view.

31:7-9 God promised a joyful homecoming for His scattered, exiled people, like a new exodus out of the land of the north. The returning remnant will include even weak, vulnerable people (those who are **blind, lame, pregnant,** and **about to give birth**), indicating that no one would be left behind or excluded. God comforted His people who returned weeping, leading them back home **by a smooth way** rather than a rough way, which could lead to stumbling. As God has identified Himself as a husband to Israel (v. 32; cp. Is 54:5; Hs 2:16), He also identified Himself as a **Father** to Israel (**Ephraim** is another name for Israel; cp. Hs 11).

31:10-14 The regathering of Israel to its home served as a witness before other nations to God's sovereignty (**One who scattered**), protection (shepherd imagery), and power as He ransomed Israel from a powerful oppressor. **Joy**, as a contrast to weeping and discouragement, emerges prominently in this lyrical passage. This joy stemmed from God's goodness demonstrated through abundant agricultural production and the consolation prompted by their return to their homeland and by their spiritual restoration to God.

A **31:3** LXX; MT reads *me* B **31:9** LXX; MT reads *supplications* C **31:14** Lit *fatness*

31:15-17 The citation of this verse in Mt 2:18 combines the idea of Rachel as sorrowful matriarch of Israel with the association of her place of death somewhere near Bethlehem. The infants slaughtered were those "in and around Bethlehem" (Mt 2:16). The weeping of Rachel, therefore, is taken up and echoed by the mother of Bethlehem. **Ramah** (Hb, "hill, heights"), though perhaps the location of Rachel's tomb, was a site to which Babylonians transplanted exiles. **Rachel**, Jacob's second wife, was associated with the southern tribes and northern tribes—with the southern tribes through Benjamin and with the northern tribes through Joseph's children, Ephraim and Manasseh. She wept, therefore, for all Israel, both the northern kingdom (already exiled to Assyria) and the southern kingdom, whose exile was imminent. **Weeping** seems tied to Rachel's difficult and fatal delivery of Benjamin, whom she originally had named "Ben-oni," meaning "Son of My Sorrow." The image is of Rachel, dead from the travails of childbirth, weeping in her grave because her children, too, are gone. She is comforted by the Lord who promised her children a hopeful future, but only after they had endured discipline as they deserved (cp. Jr 29:11).

31:18-20 This passage contains numerous uses of the Hebrew word *shuv* ("turn"; see **Word Study**, 3:10, p. 956) in the terms **repented**, **return**, and **restore**. **I struck my thigh** refers to a gesture of sorrow and remorse; the meaning parallels "I repented." God's compassion toward Israel is communicated by emotionally intense vocabulary. **My inner being** [Hb *mē'ah*, "bowels, heart," as metaphors of one's "inmost soul"; cp. Lm 1:20] **yearns** [Hb *hamah*, "groaning," referring to the churning of deep emotions; cp. "turmoil," Ps 42:5] **for him**; one might say, comparably, "My very heart trembles." The verb **will truly have compassion** (Hb *racham*, used twice for emphasis) is related to the word "womb" (see **Word Study**, p. 584). This usage ties the passage nicely together as Rachel's intense emotion of grief for her children's exile culminates in Yahweh's intense emotion of "compassion" toward His spiritually wayward child.

31:21-22 The Lord replied to Ephraim's repentance by advising action—setting up indicators that would lead to the straight way, the direct road back to God. **Virgin Israel** was urged to **return . . . return . . . how long will you turn here and there?** Israel had strayed so far that drastic measures were required on behalf of Yahweh, who **creates** [Hb *bara'*, "produce"; cp. Gn 1:1] **something new in the land.** An unheard-of situation

and My people will be satisfied
with My goodness.
This is
the LORD's declaration.

15 This is what the LORD says:

A voice was heard in Ramah,
a lament
with bitter weeping—
Rachel weeping
for her children,
refusing to be comforted
for her children
because they are no more.

16 This is what the LORD says:

Keep your voice from weeping
and your eyes from tears,
for the reward for your work
will come—
this is
the LORD's declaration—
and your children will return
from the enemy's land.
17 There is hope
for your future—
this is
the LORD's declaration—
and your children will return
to their own territory.
18 I have heard
Ephraim moaning,
"You disciplined me,
and I have been disciplined
like an untrained calf.
Restore me, and I will return,
for you, LORD, are my God.
19 After I returned, I repented;
After I was instructed,
I struck my thigh in grief.
I was ashamed and humiliated
because I bore the disgrace
of my youth."
20 Isn't Ephraim a precious son
to Me,
a delightful child?
Whenever I speak
against him,
I certainly still think
about him.
Therefore, My inner being
yearns for him;
I will truly have compassion
on him.
This is
the LORD's declaration.

21 Set up road markers
for yourself;
establish signposts!
Keep the highway in mind,
the way you have traveled.
Return, Virgin Israel!
Return to these cities
of yours.
22 How long will you turn
here and there,
faithless daughter?
For the LORD creates
something new
in the land[A]—
a female[B] will shelter[C] a man.

23 This is what the LORD of •Hosts,
the God of Israel, says: "When I restore their fortunes,[D] they will once
again speak this word in the land of
Judah and in its cities, 'May the LORD
bless you, righteous settlement,
holy mountain.' 24 Judah and all its
cities will live in it together—also
farmers and those who move[E] with
the flocks— 25 for I satisfy the thirsty
person and feed all those who are
weak."
26 At this I awoke and looked
around. My sleep had been most
pleasant to me.
27 "The days are coming"—this
is the LORD's declaration—"when
I will sow the house of Israel and
the house of Judah with the seed of
man and the seed of beast. 28 Just as I
watched over them to uproot and to
tear them down, to demolish and to
destroy, and to cause disaster, so will
I be attentive to build and to plant
them," says the LORD. 29 "In those
days, it will never again be said:

The fathers have eaten
sour grapes,
and the children's teeth
are set on edge.

30 Rather, each will die for his own
wrongdoing. Anyone who eats sour
grapes—his own teeth will be set on
edge.

The New Covenant (31:31-40)

31 "Look, the days are coming"—this is the LORD's declaration—"when I will make a new
covenant with the house of Israel
and with the house of Judah. 32 This

A 31:22 Or *new on earth* B 31:22 Or *woman* C 31:22 Or *female surrounds*, or *female courts*; Hb obscure D 31:23 Or *I end their captivity* E 31:24 Tg, Vg, Aq, Sym; MT reads *and they will move*

>WORD|*study*

31:31-33 New (Hb *chadash*) means, in part, that the covenant would be different than the previous one. It will not be breakable or external like the Sinai covenant. The phrase "new covenant" does not appear elsewhere in the Old Testament, but other passages may refer to it (cp. 32:40-41; Ezk 11:19-20). Its fulfillment is in the blood of Jesus as an atoning sacrifice (Mt 26:28; Mk 14:24; Lk 22:20; 1Co 11:25); it is preached by the new covenant community, the church (Rm 11:27; 2Co 3:6-11; Heb 8:7-13; 9:15; 10:11-18). Rather than "My law" (Hb *torah*; see note on Ps 19:6-13) written in stone, it will be "within them," written "on their hearts."

one will not be like the covenant I
made with their ancestors when
I took them by the hand to bring
them out of the land of Egypt—a
covenant they broke even though I
had married them"—the LORD's declaration. 33 "Instead, this is the covenant I will make with the house of
Israel after those days"—the LORD's
declaration. "I will put My teaching within them and write it on
their hearts. I will be their God, and
they will be My people. 34 No longer
will one teach his neighbor or his
brother, saying, 'Know the LORD,'
for they will all know Me, from the
least to the greatest of them"—this
is the LORD's declaration. "For I will
forgive their wrongdoing and never
again remember their sin."
35 This is what the LORD says:

The One who gives the sun
  for light by day,
the fixed order of moon
  and stars for light by night,
who stirs up the sea
  and makes its waves roar—
Yahweh of Hosts is His name:
36 If this fixed order departs
  from My presence—
      this is
  the LORD's declaration—
then also Israel's descendants
  will cease
to be a nation
  before Me forever.

37 This is what the LORD says:

If the heavens above
  can be measured
and the foundations
  of the earth below explored,
I will reject all of
  Israel's descendants
  because of
  all they have done—
      this is
  the LORD's declaration.

38 "Look, the days are coming"
—the LORD's declaration— "when
the city[A] from the Tower of Hananel
to the Corner Gate will be rebuilt
for the LORD. 39 A measuring line
will once again stretch out straight
to the hill of Gareb and then turn
toward Goah. 40 The whole valley—the corpses, the ashes, and all
the fields as far as the Kidron Valley
to the corner of the Horse Gate to
the east—will be holy to the LORD.
It will never be uprooted or demolished again."

Jeremiah's Land Purchase (32:1-44)

32 This is the word that came to
Jeremiah from the LORD in the
tenth year of Zedekiah king of Judah, which was the eighteenth year
of Nebuchadnezzar. 2 At that time,
the army of the king of Babylon was
besieging Jerusalem, and Jeremiah
the prophet was imprisoned in the
guard's courtyard in the palace of
the king of Judah. 3 Zedekiah king
of Judah had imprisoned him, saying: "Why are you prophesying,
'This is what the LORD says: Look, I
am about to hand this city over to
Babylon's king, and he will capture
it. 4 Zedekiah king of Judah will not
escape from the Chaldeans; indeed,
he will certainly be handed over to
Babylon's king. They will speak face
to face[B] and meet eye to eye. 5 He will
take Zedekiah to Babylon where he
will stay until I attend to him'—this
is the LORD's declaration. 'You will
fight the Chaldeans, but you will not
succeed'?"
6 Jeremiah replied, "The word
of the LORD came to me: 7 Watch!

deemed impossible by the social conventions of the time would come about: **A female** (Hb *neqēvah*, word for "female" gender; cp. Gn 1:27) would **shelter** [Hb *savav*, "surround, encircle, enfold, protect," here in the sense of faithful and encompassing love; cp. Dt 32:10] **a man.** As unbelievable as this gender role reversal sounds, the new covenant would be just as unbelievable and shocking. God would need a new act of creation to restore His people completely.

31:23-40 Four eschatological promises follow. First, God promises Israel and Judah to shepherd them back into their homeland. Yahweh will bless them and fellowship with them (vv. 23-25).

31:27-30 In the second promise, Yahweh declared that although His people had been demolished, destroyed, uprooted, and torn down, He would yet **build** and **plant** them. Their destruction (then and currently) could not be blamed on previous generations; rather, they suffered the consequences of their own sins.

31:31-33 The third promise constitutes the heart of Jeremiah's preaching, the message for which he is best known: God's **new covenant** with His people. See **Word Study**, above.

31:34 Teaching God's law to one another was an obligation in order to pass the knowledge of God from generation to generation (Dt 6:1-9; 11:18-21). With the advent of the "new covenant" inscribed internally on minds and hearts, teaching about God would become obsolete since all would **know the LORD**, a reversal of the conditions that resulted in punishment and exile (Jr 9:4-6).

31:35-37 The covenant's permanence is grounded in the **fixed order** of the cosmos, for the One who brought the cosmos into being also brought Israel as a **nation** into being and has bound Himself to her by this new spiritual covenant, which will endure eternally.

31:38-40 The fourth future prophecy mentions specific Jerusalem landmarks, which would be rebuilt and which denoted an area (i.e., the entire city) to be sanctified for God. **The . . . valley** may refer to the Hinnom Valley, which (unbelievably in light of its history of pagan ritual sacrifices) would also be consecrated to God. A reversal of the prophetic mandate appears here in the promise that the city will **never be uprooted or demolished again.**

32:1-3 Zedekiah (588/587 B.C.) questioned Jeremiah's loyalty since the message he preached seemed pro-Babylonian and, therefore, treasonous.

[A]**31:38** = Jerusalem [B]**32:4** Lit *His mouth will speak with his mouth*

Jeremiah relates an enacted prophecy, which transpired while he was still **imprisoned in the guard's courtyard**.

32:8-9 In light of the imminent destruction of Jerusalem (it was then under siege), Jeremiah's purchase of land was laughable as a seeming waste of money and denial of reality.

32:10-14 The two parties carried out the legal procedure for such a transaction, complete with **witnesses** and all the proper documentation. An **earthen storage jar** was commonly used to preserve documents, as the Dead Sea Scrolls had been stored in clay jars to protect them for 20 centuries.

32:15 The explanation of this enacted prophecy appears here and in verses 42-44: Jeremiah's action constituted faith in God's promise of the future restoration of the inhabitants to their land. It was not a denial of reality but the recognition of a greater, future reality—that one day the people would be returned to their land.

32:16-23 Jeremiah's prayer begins with praise for the Creator, who is faithful, loving, and omniscient. He reviews Israel's salvation history and her subsequent apostasy and punishment.

32:24-26 Jeremiah struggled to grasp the implications of the land purchase. Even to him, it seemed like a denial of the present reality, although he had been preaching it for many years. Jeremiah had spent "17 shekels of silver"—money that could have bought food—for a parcel of land destined for certain destruction by an enemy's army (v. 9). He even had **witnesses** to his apparent foolishness (v. 12). This sign-act seemed to be what the false prophets were doing—predicting that all would be well rather than what God had been telling Jeremiah to prophesy.

32:27 The Lord responded to Jeremiah by reaffirming His identity as **Yahweh**, sovereign and universal **God of all flesh**, not just of Israel. Jeremiah had affirmed that "nothing is too difficult for You" (v. 17), yet he still seemed to doubt God's words. God asked him, **Is anything too difficult for Me?** The fullness of God's message was that destruction and judgment would come but not permanent destruction.

32:28-35 The cause of the people's destruction follows. As the people had **burned** incense to **Baal** and even burned their children as sacrifices to **Molech**, so the land, houses, and entire city would be **set . . . on fire** (cp. 7:30-31). The punishment would fit the crime. The fire was both destructive

Hanamel, the son of your uncle Shallum, is coming to you to say, 'Buy my field in Anathoth for yourself, for you own the right of redemption to buy it.'

8 "Then my cousin Hanamel came to the guard's courtyard as the LORD had said and urged me, 'Please buy my field in Anathoth in the land of Benjamin, for you own the right of inheritance and redemption. Buy it for yourself.' Then I knew that this was the word of the LORD. 9 So I bought the field in Anathoth from my cousin Hanamel, and I weighed out to him the money—17 •shekels[A] of silver. 10 I recorded it on a scroll, sealed it, called in witnesses, and weighed out the silver in the scales. 11 I took the purchase agreement—the sealed copy with its terms and conditions and the open copy— 12 and gave the purchase agreement to Baruch son of Neriah, son of Mahseiah. I did this in the sight of my cousin[B] Hanamel, the witnesses who were signing the purchase agreement, and all the Judeans sitting in the guard's courtyard.

13 "I instructed Baruch in their sight, 14 'This is what the LORD of •Hosts, the God of Israel, says: Take these scrolls—this purchase agreement with the sealed copy and this open copy—and put them in an earthen storage jar so they will last a long time. 15 For this is what the LORD of Hosts, the God of Israel, says: Houses, fields, and vineyards will again be bought in this land.'

16 "After I had given the purchase agreement to Baruch, son of Neriah, I prayed to the LORD: 17 Oh, Lord GOD! You Yourself made the heavens and earth by Your great power and with Your outstretched arm. Nothing is too difficult for You! 18 You show faithful love to thousands but lay the fathers' sins on their sons' laps after them, great and mighty God whose name is •Yahweh of Hosts, 19 the One great in counsel and mighty in deed, whose eyes are on all the ways of the sons of men in order to give to each person according to his ways and the result of his deeds. 20 You performed signs and wonders in the land of Egypt and do so to this very day both in Israel and among mankind. You made a name for Yourself, as is the case today. 21 You brought Your people Israel out of Egypt with signs and wonders, with a strong hand and an outstretched arm, and with great terror. 22 You gave them this land You swore to give to their ancestors, a land flowing with milk and honey. 23 They entered and possessed it, but they did not obey Your voice or live according to Your instructions. They failed to perform all You commanded them to do, and so You have brought all this disaster on them. 24 Look! Siege ramps have come against the city to capture it, and the city, as a result of the sword, famine, and plague, has been handed over to the Chaldeans who are fighting against it. What You have spoken has happened. Look, You can see it! 25 Yet You, Lord GOD, have said to me: Buy the field with silver and call in witnesses—even though the city has been handed over to the Chaldeans!"

26 Then the word of the LORD came to Jeremiah: 27 "Look, I am Yahweh, the God of all flesh. Is anything too difficult for Me? 28 Therefore, this is what the LORD says: I am about to hand this city over to the Chaldeans, to Babylon's king Nebuchadnezzar, and he will capture it. 29 The Chaldeans who are going to fight against this city will come, set this city on fire, and burn it along with the houses where incense has been burned to •Baal on their rooftops and where •drink offerings have been poured out to other gods to provoke Me to anger. 30 From their youth, the Israelites and Judeans have done nothing but what is evil in My sight! They have done nothing but provoke Me to anger by the work of their hands"—this is the LORD's declaration— 31 "for this city has caused My wrath and fury from the day it was built until now. I will therefore remove it from My presence, 32 because of all the evil the Israelites and Judeans have done to provoke Me to anger—they, their kings, their officials, their priests, and their prophets, the men of Ju-

A 32:9 About 7 ounces B 32:12 Some Hb mss, LXX, Syr; other Hb mss read *uncle*

dah, and the residents of Jerusalem. 33 They have turned their backs to Me and not their faces. Though I taught them time and time again,[A] they do not listen and receive discipline. 34 They have placed their detestable things in the house that is called by My name and have defiled it. 35 They have built the •high places of Baal in the Valley of Hinnom to make their sons and daughters pass through the fire to •Molech—something I had not commanded them. I had never entertained the thought[B] that they do this detestable act causing Judah to sin!

36 "Now therefore, this is what the LORD, the God of Israel, says to this city about which you said, 'It has been handed over to Babylon's king through sword, famine, and plague': 37 I am about to gather them from all the lands where I have banished them in My anger, rage and great wrath, and I will return them to this place and make them live in safety. 38 They will be My people, and I will be their God. 39 I will give them one heart and one way so that for their good and for the good of their descendants after them, they will •fear Me always.

40 "I will make an everlasting covenant with them: I will never turn away from doing good to them, and I will put fear of Me in their hearts so they will never again turn away from Me. 41 I will take delight in them to do what is good for them, and with all My heart and mind I will faithfully plant them in this land.

42 "For this is what the LORD says: Just as I have brought all this great disaster on these people, so am I about to bring on them all the good I am promising them. 43 Fields will be bought in this land about which you are saying, 'It's a desolation without man or beast; it has been handed over to the Chaldeans!' 44 Fields will be purchased with silver, the transaction written on a scroll and sealed, and witnesses will be called on in the land of Benjamin, in the areas surrounding Jerusalem, and in Judah's cities—the cities of the hill country, the cities of the Judean foothills, and the cities of the •Negev—because I will restore their fortunes."[C]

This is
the LORD's declaration.

Israel's Restoration (33:1-26)

33 While he was still confined in the guard's courtyard, the word of the LORD came to Jeremiah a second time: 2 "The LORD who made the earth,[D] the LORD who forms it to establish it, •Yahweh is His name, says this: 3 Call to Me and I will answer you and tell you great and incomprehensible things you do not know. 4 For this is what the LORD, the God of Israel, says concerning the houses of this city and the palaces of Judah's kings, the ones torn down for defense against the siege ramps and the sword: 5 The people coming to fight the Chaldeans will fill the houses with the corpses of their own men that I strike down in My wrath and rage. I have hidden My face from this city because of all their evil. 6 Yet I will certainly bring health and healing to it and will indeed heal them. I will let them experience the abundance[E] of peace and truth. 7 I will restore the fortunes[C] of Judah and of Israel and will rebuild them as in former times. 8 I will purify them from all the wrongs they have committed against Me, and I will forgive all the wrongs they have committed against Me, rebelling against Me. 9 This city will bear on My behalf a name of joy, praise, and glory before all the nations of the earth, who will hear of all the good I will do for them. They will tremble with awe because of all the good and all the peace I will bring about for them.

10 "This is what the LORD says: In this place, which you say is a ruin, without man or beast—that is, in Judah's cities and Jerusalem's streets that are a desolation without man, without inhabitant, and without beast—there will be heard again 11 a sound of joy and gladness, the voice of the groom and the bride, and the voice of those saying,

A 32:33 Lit *them, rising up early and teaching* B 32:35 Lit *them, and it did not arise on My heart* C 32:44; 33:7 Or *will end their captivity* D 33:2 LXX; MT reads *made it* E 33:6 Or *fragrance*; Hb obscure

and purifying, since their practices had defiled God's house (cp. 6:27-30). Whereas in 7:30-34 the people's depravity earned harsh destruction, here a note of restoration is sounded.

32:37-39 God's wrath, rage, and great fury had **banished them**, but He planned to restore them to their own land and to claim them again as His people. New covenant language appears: **They will be My people, and I will be their God**. In addition to the covenant's newness, its superiority to the previous covenant, and its internal nature, the covenant would unify the people one with another and with God.

32:40-41 Yahweh would **faithfully plant them**, and the covenant grounded in His fixed and firm intention would be **everlasting** (cp. 1:10).

32:42-44 Just as certain as their punishment would be God's future restoration. The meaning of Jeremiah's sign-act is clarified as being certain to be accomplished.

33:1-3 This final chapter of the Book of Consolation continues the promises of future good despite the tragic events of the present. This chapter smoothly follows the previous one, as God's word came to Jeremiah while he was **still confined in the guard's courtyard**. God promises to tell Jeremiah **great and incomprehensible things you do not know**. "Incomprehensible" (Hb *batsar*, "that which is wondrous, a secret or a mystery") has the sense of something "fenced in" or "inaccessible."

33:4-14 A word of doom was spoken regarding Judah and Jerusalem, as God said ominously, **I have hidden My face from this city** as a show of disfavor and rejection (cp. 2:27; 32:33). Yet God would **heal** them, give them abundant **peace**, end their captivity, and **restore the fortunes** of the entire nation (i.e., of both Judah and Israel). These blessings would serve as a witness to surrounding nations of the Lord's awesome might and of His desire and willingness to forgive.

Agricultural prosperity and temple worship would be restored, and sounds of vitality and **joy . . . the voice of the groom and the bride** would once again ring out. After His people had reaped the destruction they sowed in rebellion against God, the Lord promised to **bring health and healing . . . restore . . . rebuild . . . purify . . . forgive . . . and fulfill** [His] **good promises**.

33:15-22 The Davidic covenant (which would seem to be abrogated by the impending exile) is reaffirmed, and 23:5-8 is partially repeated. Despite minor differences, the import is identical. A righteous ruler of David's dynasty would rule in Judah, and **Jerusalem** would be called by His name, **Yahweh Is Our Righteousness**. Yahweh reaffirmed His covenant promises to David and the **Levitical** line, which would continue perpetually. God is forever faithful to His covenant promises (cp. Gn 9:13). The most likely understanding of these prophecies is messianic rather than literal-historical. In His role as Priest-King, Christ fulfilled the promise to Israel. He was born of David's lineage in David's city (Lk 2:10), and would receive "the throne of His father David. He will reign over the house of Jacob forever, and His kingdom will have no end" (Lk 1:32-33). Christ took on the Levitical role as well, actually superseding the Levitical priesthood, as the covenant in His blood superseded the previous covenant (Heb 7:11-28; 8:6-13).

33:24-26 As in Jeremiah 31:35-37, God's promise was grounded in His covenants with the natural order, the **day** and the **night**, and the **fixed order of heaven and earth**, promising that He would never reject Israel, represented by the **seed of Jacob** and Judah and **My servant David**. One might say that their restoration was as likely as would be the coming up of the sun tomorrow.

34:1-3 A **word . . . from the LORD** came to Jeremiah for King **Zedekiah**: The king of Judah would go to Babylon along with the other exiles after meeting Nebuchadnezzar **eye to eye** and **face to face**. In other words, he would not escape as he in fact attempted to do (39:4-6).

34:4-7 **Zedekiah** would not be killed but would die a natural death, complete with a ceremony and lamentation befitting royalty. Although he would not escape, yet he would survive the siege.

Praise the LORD of •Hosts,
for the LORD is good;
His faithful love
endures forever

as they bring thank offerings to the temple of the LORD. For I will restore the fortunes[A] of the land as in former times, says the LORD.

12 "This is what the LORD of Hosts says: In this desolate place—without man or beast—and in all its cities there will once more be a grazing land where shepherds may rest flocks. 13 The flocks will again pass under the hands of the one who counts them in the cities of the hill country, the cities of the Judean foothills, the cities of the •Negev, the land of Benjamin—the cities surrounding Jerusalem and Judah's cities, says the LORD.

14 "Look, the days
are coming"—
this is
the LORD's declaration—
"when I will fulfill
the good promises
that I have spoken
concerning the
house of Israel
and the house of Judah.
15 In those days and at that time
I will cause
a Righteous Branch
to sprout up for David,
and He will administer justice
and righteousness in the land.
16 In those days Judah
will be saved,
and Jerusalem
will dwell securely,
and this is what she
will be named:
Yahweh Our Righteousness.

17 "For this is what the LORD says: David will never fail to have a man sitting on the throne of the house of Israel. 18 The Levitical priests will never fail to have a man always before Me to offer •burnt offerings, to burn •grain offerings, and to make sacrifices."

19 The word of the LORD came to Jeremiah: 20 "This is what the LORD says: If you can break My covenant with the day and My covenant with the night so that day and night cease to come at their regular time, 21 then also My covenant with My servant David may be broken so that he will not have a son reigning on his throne, and the Levitical priests will not be My ministers. 22 The hosts of heaven cannot be counted; the sand of the sea cannot be measured. So, too, I will make the descendants of My servant David and the Levites who minister to Me innumerable."

23 The word of the LORD came to Jeremiah: 24 "Have you not noticed what these people have said? They say, 'The LORD has rejected the two families He had chosen.' My people are treated with contempt and no longer regarded as a nation among them. 25 This is what the LORD says: If I do not keep My covenant with the day and with the night and fail to establish the fixed order of heaven and earth, 26 then I might also reject the •seed of Jacob and of My servant David—not taking from his descendants rulers over the descendants of Abraham, Isaac, and Jacob. Instead, I will restore their fortunes[B] and have compassion on them."

The Warning to Zedekiah and Indictment of Judah (34:1–35:19)

34 This is the word that came to Jeremiah from the LORD when Nebuchadnezzar, king of Babylon, all his army, all the earthly kingdoms under his control, and all other nations were fighting against Jerusalem and all its surrounding cities: 2 "This is what the LORD, the God of Israel, says: Go, speak to Zedekiah, king of Judah, and tell him: This is what the LORD says: I am about to hand this city over to the king of Babylon, and he will burn it down. 3 As for you, you will not escape from his hand but are certain to be captured and handed over to him. You will meet the king of Babylon eye to eye and speak face to face;[C] you will go to Babylon.

4 "Yet hear the LORD's word, Zedekiah, king of Judah. This is what the LORD says concerning you: You

[A]33:11 Or *will end the captivity* [B]33:26 Or *Instead, I will end their captivity* [C]34:3 Lit *and his mouth will speak to your mouth*

will not die by the sword; 5 you will die peacefully. There will be a burning ceremony for you just like the burning ceremonies for your fathers, the former kings who preceded you. 'Our king is dead!'[A] will be the lament for you, for I have spoken this word." This is the LORD's declaration.

6 So Jeremiah the prophet related all these words to Zedekiah king of Judah in Jerusalem 7 while the king of Babylon's army was attacking Jerusalem and all of Judah's remaining cities—against Lachish and Azekah, for they were the only ones left of Judah's fortified cities.

8 This is the word that came to Jeremiah from the LORD after King Zedekiah made a covenant with all the people who were in Jerusalem to proclaim freedom to them, 9 so each man would free his male and female Hebrew slaves and no one would enslave his Judean brother. 10 All the officials and people who entered into covenant to free their male and female slaves—in order not to enslave them any longer—obeyed and freed them. 11 Afterward, however, they changed their minds and took back their male and female slaves they had freed and forced them to become slaves again.

12 Then the word of the LORD came to Jeremiah from the LORD: 13 "This is what the LORD, the God of Israel, says: I made a covenant with your ancestors when I brought them out of the land of Egypt, out of the place of slavery, saying: 14 At the end of seven years, each of you must free his Hebrew brother who sold himself[B] to you. He may serve you six years, but then you must send him out free from you. But your ancestors did not obey Me or pay any attention. 15 Today you repented and did what pleased Me, each of you proclaiming freedom for his neighbor. You made a covenant before Me at the temple called by My name. 16 But you have changed your minds and profaned My name. Each has taken back his male and female slaves who had been freed to go wherever they wanted, and you have again subjugated them to be your slaves.

17 "Therefore, this is what the LORD says: You have not obeyed Me by proclaiming freedom, each man for his brother and for his neighbor. I hereby proclaim freedom for you"—this is the LORD's declaration—"to the sword, to plague, and to famine! I will make you a horror to all the earth's kingdoms. 18 As for those who disobeyed My covenant, not keeping the terms of the covenant they made before Me, I will treat them like the calf they cut in two in order to pass between its pieces. 19 The officials of Judah and Jerusalem, the court officials, the priests, and all the people of the land who passed between the pieces of the calf 20 will be handed over to their enemies, to those who want to take their life. Their corpses will become food for the birds of the sky and for the wild animals of the land. 21 I will hand Zedekiah king of Judah and his officials over to their enemies, to those who want to take their lives, to the king of Babylon's army that is withdrawing. 22 I am about to give the command"—this is the LORD's declaration—"and I will bring them back to this city. They will fight against it, capture it, and burn it down. I will make Judah's cities a desolation, without inhabitant."

35 This is the word that came to Jeremiah from the LORD in the days of Jehoiakim son of Josiah, king of Judah: 2 "Go to the house of the Rechabites, speak to them, and bring them to one of the chambers of the temple of the LORD to offer them a drink of wine."

3 So I took Jaazaniah son of Jeremiah, son of Habazziniah, and his brothers and all his sons—the entire house of the Rechabites— 4 and I brought them into the temple of the LORD to a chamber occupied by the sons of Hanan son of Igdaliah, a man of God, who had a chamber near the officials' chamber, which was above the chamber of Maaseiah son of Shallum the doorkeeper. 5 I set jars filled with wine and some cups before the sons of the house of the Rechabites and said to them, "Drink wine!"

34:8-11 These verses refer to a situation in which owners of indentured servants freed them, only to renege later. The operative phrases are **made a covenant** and **proclaim freedom**. The decision to release slaves may have been prompted by a desperate wish to please God during the Babylonian siege. Their reason for reneging is unclear.

34:17-20 Yahweh pronounced two punishments. First, those who failed to **proclaim freedom** (Hb *deror*, "freedom"; cp. Lv 25:10; Is 61:1; Ezk 46:17) to their slaves would be "freed" of God's protection, making them vulnerable to **the sword, to plague, and to famine**. Second, those who broke the covenant would be made **like the calf they cut in two;** this refers to the ceremonial making (literally "cutting") of a covenant (cp. Gn 15:10-18), in which each partner cursed himself with the same fate as the slaughtered animals if he did not faithfully carry out his part of the covenant. Zedekiah and the people of Jerusalem may have performed this ancient covenant ritual **at the temple** (v. 15).

34:21-22 They would fall prey to those who would take their lives. Breaking the covenant is a profanation of God's name, a sacrilege.

35:1-19 The **Rechabites**, also known as Kenites (cp. Jdg 4:11), were a family of scribes and descendants of Hammath, the father of the house of Rechab (1Ch 2:55). They were living temporarily in Jerusalem, having sought asylum there when Nebuchadnezzar began to harass Jerusalem's outlying cities (Jr 35:11). These actions between the prophet and the **Rechabites** constitute a sign-act. Jeremiah offered them wine and they refused it out of deference to their ancestor, **Jonadab**.

[A] 34:5 Lit *Alas, lord* [B] 34:14 Or *who was sold*

35:13-17 This narrative is an object lesson for the **men of Judah and the residents of Jerusalem**. The Rechabites over many generations had obeyed a human mandate not to drink wine and to live a nomadic lifestyle. By contrast, God's people had disobeyed and even rejected a divine mandate to **turn, each one from his evil way of life, and correct** [Hb *yatav*, "do well or rightly, make good or pleasing, adjust"; cp. Gn 4:7; cp. 7:3,5; 18:11; 25:5; 26:13] **your actions**. By their rebellion, the people of Judah had sealed their fate; their destruction was certain.

35:18-19 The obedient Rechabites had obtained favor in God's eyes, and God promised to preserve their household as the reward for their example of obedience.

36:1-32 This chapter uniquely records the inscripturation of oral prophecy into a form to be passed down to future readers.

36:1-3 Jeremiah's message was intended for **Israel, Judah, and all the nations**. At this point in Jeremiah's prophetic ministry, a chance for repentance, forgiveness, and the averting of disaster still exists. The year was 605 B.C. Nebuchadnezzar had just ascended the throne of Babylon, and he was not yet bent on Judah's destruction.

36:4 The **scroll** may have been made of papyrus since the other conventional material, leather, would have been more difficult to cut and burn as described in verse 23. Jeremiah used a scribe, **Baruch** [Hb, "blessed"] **son of Neriah**, whose name appears on one of about 250 clay seals found in 1975 in Israel, approximately 44 miles southwest of Jerusalem. The seal, which served as the person's official signature, bears the inscription: "Berekhyahu son of Neriyahu the scribe." The collection also includes a seal for "'Elishama' servant of the king" (vv. 10-12) and "Yerahme'el, son of the king" (i.e., Jerahmeel, son of Jehoiakim, v. 26). A clay seal for "Gemariah, son of Shaphan" (vv. 10-12, 25) was found in 1978.

36:5-7 **Baruch** is mentioned in chapter 32, but this occasion is earlier than that one. The collaboration between him and Jeremiah had lasted through three kings' reigns. Baruch was to take Jeremiah's dictation onto the scroll, and read it aloud in the temple in the hearing of local residents as well as pilgrims. Perhaps **on a day of fasting**, their hearts would be receptive to His word, and they would repent and obey. The call for national fasting could come in times of national crisis.

6 But they replied, "We do not drink wine, for Jonadab, son of our ancestor Rechab, commanded: 'You and your sons must never drink wine. 7 You must not build a house or sow seed or plant a vineyard. Those things are not for you. Rather, you must live in tents your whole life, so you may live a long time on the soil where you stay as a temporary resident.' 8 We have obeyed the voice of Jonadab, son of our ancestor Rechab, in all he commanded us. So we haven't drunk wine our whole life—we, our wives, our sons, and our daughters. 9 We also have not built houses to live in and do not have vineyard, field, or seed. 10 But we have lived in tents and have obeyed and done as our ancestor Jonadab commanded us. 11 However, when Nebuchadnezzar king of Babylon marched into the land, we said: Come, let's go into Jerusalem to get away from the Chaldean and Aramean armies. So we have been living in Jerusalem."

12 Then the word of the LORD came to Jeremiah: 13 "This is what the LORD of •Hosts, the God of Israel, says: Go, say to the men of Judah and the residents of Jerusalem: Will you not accept discipline by listening to My words?"—this is the LORD's declaration. 14 "The words of Jonadab, son of Rechab, have been carried out. He commanded his sons not to drink wine, and they have not drunk to this very day because they have obeyed their ancestor's command. But I have spoken to you time and time again,[A] and you have not obeyed Me! 15 Time and time again[B] I have sent you all My servants the prophets, proclaiming: Turn, each one from his evil way of life, and correct your actions. Stop following other gods to serve them. Live in the land that I gave you and your ancestors. But you would not pay attention or obey Me. 16 Yes, the sons of Jonadab son of Rechab carried out their ancestor's command he gave them, but these people have not obeyed Me. 17 Therefore, this is what the LORD, the God of Hosts, the God of Israel, says: I will certainly bring to Judah and to all the residents of Jerusalem all the disaster I have pronounced against them because I have spoken to them, but they have not obeyed, and I have called to them, but they would not answer."

18 Jeremiah said to the house of the Rechabites: "This is what the LORD of Hosts, the God of Israel, says: 'Because you have obeyed the command of your ancestor Jonadab and have kept all his commands and have done all that he commanded you, 19 this is what the LORD of Hosts, the God of Israel, says: Jonadab son of Rechab will never fail to have a man to always stand before Me.'"

Jeremiah, Jehoiakim, and the Scroll of God's Word (36:1-32)

36 In the fourth year of Jehoiakim son of Josiah, king of Judah, this word came to Jeremiah from the LORD: 2 "Take a scroll, and write on it all the words I have spoken to you concerning Israel, Judah, and all the nations from the time I first spoke to you during Josiah's reign until today. 3 Perhaps when the house of Judah hears about all the disaster I am planning to bring on them, each one of them will turn from his evil way. Then I will forgive their wrongdoing and their sin."

4 So Jeremiah summoned Baruch son of Neriah. At Jeremiah's dictation,[C] Baruch wrote on a scroll all the words the LORD had spoken to Jeremiah. 5 Then Jeremiah commanded Baruch, "I am restricted; I cannot enter the temple of the LORD, 6 so you must go and read from the scroll—which you wrote at my dictation[D]—the words of the LORD in the hearing of the people at the temple of the LORD on a day of fasting. You must also read them in the hearing of all the Judeans who are coming from their cities. 7 Perhaps their petition will come before the LORD, and each one will turn from his evil way, for the anger and fury that the LORD has pronounced against this people are great." 8 So Baruch son of Neriah did everything Jeremiah the prophet had commanded him. At the LORD's

[A] **35:14** Lit *you, rising up early and speaking* [B] **35:15** Lit *Rising up early and sending* [C] **36:4** Lit *From Jeremiah's mouth* [D] **36:6** Lit *wrote from my mouth*

temple he read the LORD's words from the scroll.

9 In the fifth year of Jehoiakim son of Josiah, king of Judah, in the ninth month, all the people of Jerusalem and all those coming in from Judah's cities into Jerusalem proclaimed a fast before the LORD. 10 Then at the LORD's temple, in the chamber of Gemariah son of Shaphan the scribe, in the upper courtyard at the opening of the New Gate of the LORD's temple, in the hearing of all the people, Baruch read Jeremiah's words from the scroll.

11 When Micaiah son of Gemariah, son of Shaphan, heard all the words of the LORD from the scroll, 12 he went down to the scribe's chamber in the king's palace. All the officials were sitting there—Elishama the scribe, Delaiah son of Shemaiah, Elnathan son of Achbor, Gemariah son of Shaphan, Zedekiah son of Hananiah, and all the other officials. 13 Micaiah reported to them all the words he had heard when Baruch read from the scroll in the hearing of the people. 14 Then all the officials sent word to Baruch through Jehudi son of Nethaniah, son of Shelemiah, son of Cushi, saying, "Bring the scroll that you read in the hearing of the people, and come." So Baruch son of Neriah took the scroll and went to them. 15 They said to him, "Sit down and read it in our hearing." So Baruch read it in their hearing.

16 When they had heard all the words, they turned to each other in fear and said to Baruch, "We must surely tell the king all these things." 17 Then they asked Baruch, "Tell us—how did you write all these words? At his dictation?"[A]

18 Baruch said to them, "At his dictation.[A] He recited all these words to me while I was writing on the scroll in ink."

19 The officials said to Baruch, "You and Jeremiah must hide yourselves and tell no one where you are." 20 Then they came to the king at the courtyard, having deposited the scroll in the chamber of Elishama the scribe, and reported everything in the hearing of the king. 21 The king sent Jehudi to get the scroll, and he took it from the chamber of Elishama the scribe. Jehudi then read it in the hearing of the king and all the officials who were standing by the king. 22 Since it was the ninth month, the king was sitting in his winter quarters with a fire burning in front of him. 23 As soon as Jehudi would read three or four columns, Jehoiakim would cut the scroll[B] with a scribe's knife and throw the columns into the blazing fire until the entire scroll was consumed by the fire in the brazier. 24 As they heard all these words, the king and all of his servants did not become terrified or tear their garments. 25 Even though Elnathan, Delaiah, and Gemariah had urged the king not to burn the scroll, he would not listen to them. 26 Then the king commanded Jerahmeel the king's son, Seraiah son of Azriel, and Shelemiah son of Abdeel to seize Baruch the scribe and Jeremiah the prophet, but the LORD had hidden them.

27 After the king had burned the scroll with the words Baruch had written at Jeremiah's dictation,[C] the word of the LORD came to Jeremiah: 28 "Take another scroll, and once again write on it the very words that were on the original scroll that Jehoiakim king of Judah burned. 29 You are to proclaim concerning Jehoiakim king of Judah: This is what the LORD says: You have burned the scroll, saying, 'Why have you written on it: The king of Babylon will certainly come and destroy this land and cause it to be without man or beast?' 30 Therefore, this is what the LORD says concerning Jehoiakim king of Judah: He will have no one to sit on David's throne, and his corpse will be thrown out to be exposed to the heat of day and the frost of night. 31 I will punish him, his descendants, and his officers for their wrongdoing. I will bring on them, on the residents of Jerusalem, and on the men of Judah all the disaster, which I warned them about but they did not listen."

32 Then Jeremiah took another scroll and gave it to Baruch son of

36:9-10 A **fast before the LORD** was called the following year; Baruch took this occasion to read the scroll as Jeremiah had instructed him.

36:11-12 **Micaiah** and **Gemariah** were grandson and son, respectively, of **Shaphan**, Josiah's court secretary, who had read aloud to the king the book of the law found in the temple by Hilkiah the priest (cp. 2Kg 22:8-10).

36:14-16 The reaction of the people is unrecorded, but the reaction of other **officials** and scribes was immediate and striking: They responded with **fear**. Seemingly they accepted the words as from the Lord, regarding Jeremiah as a genuine prophet.

36:17-18 Because of their respect for Jeremiah, they wanted to ensure that the words were directly from him. They inquired of Baruch whether the words were **at his dictation** (Hb, literally "from his mouth"). Perhaps scribes occasionally took liberties with the material they copied or recorded. Baruch assured them that all these words are Jeremiah's ("from his mouth"), the literal translation harking back to the call of Jeremiah when God touched Jeremiah's mouth, and told him: "I have now filled your mouth with My words" (1:9).

36:19 Upon Baruch's confirmation of Jeremiah's authorship, the scribes and officials acted decisively. The king would be displeased; therefore, Baruch and Jeremiah must hide themselves.

36:22-23 Jehoiakim used a scribe's knife to cut the scroll into pieces before burning it in the open fire that heated his winter apartment (the **ninth month** was December).

36:24-25 Jehoiakim's systematic destruction of the scroll demonstrated his disbelief in the divine pronouncement. He evinced no remorse or sign of repentance. By contrast with the officials' reaction of fear, Jehoiakim and his servants **did not become terrified or tear their garments**, as his father Josiah had done when confronted with God's word (cp. 2Kg 22:11). There is an unmistakable comparison between the irreverent Jehoiakim and the God-fearing Josiah.

36:27-31 Because of his disregard of God's warning, a curse was pronounced against Jehoiakim, whose royal lineage would cease. As for Jeremiah, the Lord instructed him to rewrite the scroll, again **at Jeremiah's dictation** with the aid of Baruch.

[A]**36:17,18** Lit *From his mouth* [B]**36:23** Lit *columns, he would tear it* [C]**36:27** Lit *written from Jeremiah's mouth*

37:1-3 The events recorded in this chapter probably took place before those in the related narrative of chapter 32. For the second time, seemingly, Zedekiah asked Jeremiah to **pray** [Hb *palal*, "intercede, interpose as a mediator"; cp. Gn 20:7,17; Nm 11:12; 21:7; Jb 42:8] **to the LORD our God for us**, despite the fact that neither he nor **the people of the land** obeyed **the words of the LORD**. Perhaps the king's request was made in derision (which might explain Jeremiah's taunting in return, v. 19), since Judah's ally, Egypt, might succeed in saving Judah from her enemy, whereas Jeremiah had been preaching certain doom.

37:4-5 Zedekiah must have been desperate, since Jerusalem was besieged at that time, and Pharaoh's army distracted the attention of the **Chaldeans** (Babylonians) from Judah (vv. 9-11).

37:7-10 The Lord's answer indicated certain captivity and destruction of the city by the Babylonians. The message is clinched by hyperbole: Even if all the Babylonians were **badly wounded** (Hb, "pierced, thrust through," i.e., mortally wounded; cp. Jdg 9:54), they would still **capture** and **burn . . . down** Jerusalem.

37:11-14 Upon the temporary lifting of the siege, Jeremiah tried to leave the city but was **apprehended** at the city gate and accused of deserting to the Babylonians. Since his message demoralized those around him, he was seen as a traitor.

37:15-21 The **officials** (who may have represented a pro-Egyptian party at court) beat Jeremiah and imprisoned him in **a cell in the dungeon** located in the **house of Jonathan the scribe.** The king again inquired of the Lord (secretly this time), but the message was still the same. Jeremiah was compelled to convey God's message in all its unpleasantness, despite the cost of pain and suffering to him. He was probably mistreated in the dungeon and would have eventually died of abuse and starvation. He was thus allowed to remain in the **guard's courtyard** and was given a ration of a **loaf of bread each day** from "Baker Street" until there was none left in the city because of the siege.

38:1-4 This chapter and the previous one highlight the king's indecision. Zedekiah was afraid to confront his own officials, showing little or no confidence in his advisors since he continued secretly consulting Jeremiah. Possibly, he had come to believe that Jeremiah was a true prophet (37:19). As Jeremiah continued to preach the same pro-Babylonian message, the

Neriah, the scribe, and he wrote on it at Jeremiah's dictation[A] all the words of the scroll that Jehoiakim, Judah's king, had burned in the fire. And many other words like them were added.

The Royal Summons and Incarcerations (37:1–38:28)

37 Zedekiah son of Josiah reigned as king in the land of Judah in place of Jehoiachin[B] son of Jehoiakim, for Nebuchadnezzar king of Babylon made him king. 2 He and his officers and the people of the land did not obey the words of the LORD that He spoke through Jeremiah the prophet.

3 Nevertheless, King Zedekiah sent Jehucal son of Shelemiah and Zephaniah son of Maaseiah, the priest, to Jeremiah the prophet, requesting, "Please pray to the LORD our God for us!" 4 Jeremiah was going about his daily tasks[C] among the people, for they had not yet put him into the prison. 5 Pharaoh's army had left Egypt, and when the Chaldeans, who were besieging Jerusalem, heard the report, they withdrew from Jerusalem.

6 The word of the LORD came to Jeremiah the prophet: 7 "This is what the LORD, the God of Israel, says: This is what you will say to Judah's king, who is sending you to inquire of Me: Watch: Pharaoh's army, which has come out to help you, is going to return to its own land of Egypt. 8 The Chaldeans will then return and fight against this city. They will capture it and burn it down. 9 This is what the LORD says: Don't deceive yourselves by saying, 'The Chaldeans will leave us for good,' for they will not leave. 10 Indeed, if you were to strike down the entire Chaldean army that is fighting with you, and there remained among them only the badly wounded[D] men, each in his tent, they would get up and burn this city down."

11 When the Chaldean army withdrew from Jerusalem because of Pharaoh's army, 12 Jeremiah started to leave Jerusalem to go to the land of Benjamin to claim his portion there among the people. 13 But when he was at the Benjamin Gate, an officer of the guard was there, whose name was Irijah son of Shelemiah, son of Hananiah, and he apprehended Jeremiah the prophet, saying, "You are deserting to the Chaldeans."

14 "That's a lie," Jeremiah replied. "I am not deserting to the Chaldeans!" Irijah would not listen to him but apprehended Jeremiah and took him to the officials. 15 The officials were angry at Jeremiah and beat him and placed him in jail in the house of Jonathan the scribe, for it had been made into a prison. 16 So Jeremiah went into a cell in the dungeon and stayed there many days.

17 King Zedekiah later sent for him and received him, and in his house privately asked him, "Is there a word from the LORD?"

"There is," Jeremiah responded, and he continued, "You will be handed over to the king of Babylon." 18 Then Jeremiah said to King Zedekiah, "How have I sinned against you or your servants or these people that you have put me in prison? 19 Where are your prophets who prophesied to you, claiming, 'The king of Babylon will not come against you and this land'? 20 So now please listen, my lord the king. May my petition come before you. Don't send me back to the house of Jonathan the scribe, or I will die there."

21 So King Zedekiah gave orders, and Jeremiah was placed in the guard's courtyard. He was given a loaf of bread each day from the baker's street until all the bread was gone from the city. So Jeremiah remained in the guard's courtyard.

38 Now Shephatiah son of Mattan, Gedaliah son of Pashhur, Jucal[E] son of Shelemiah, and Pashhur son of Malchijah heard the words Jeremiah was speaking to all the people: 2 "This is what the LORD says: 'Whoever stays in this city will die by the sword, famine, and plague, but whoever surrenders to the Chaldeans will live. He will

[A]**36:32** Lit *it from Jeremiah's mouth* [B]**37:1** = Coniah [C]**37:4** Lit *was coming in and going out* [D]**37:10** Lit *the pierced* [E]**38:1** = Jehucal in Jr 37:3

>WORD|*study*

38:4 Weakening the morale (Hb *raphah*, "let down" with the object *yad*, "hand") effectively expresses the meaning of the literal phrase, "letting down the hand" (cp. Ezr 4:4). The idiom conveys the sense of deserting people in time of need and thereby destroying their courage.

keep his life like the spoils of war
and will live.' 3 This is what the LORD
says: 'This city will most certainly be
handed over to the king of Babylon's
army, and he will capture it.'"
4 The officials then said to the
king, "This man ought to die, because he is weakening the morale
of the warriors who remain in this
city and of all the people by speaking to them in this way. This man
is not seeking the well-being of this
people, but disaster."
5 King Zedekiah said, "Here he is;
he's in your hands since the king
can't do anything against you." 6 So
they took Jeremiah and dropped
him into the cistern of Malchiah the
king's son, which was in the guard's
courtyard, lowering Jeremiah with
ropes. There was no water in the cistern, only mud, and Jeremiah sank
in the mud.
7 But Ebed-melech, a •Cushite
court official employed in the king's
palace, heard Jeremiah had been put
into the cistern. While the king was
sitting at the Benjamin Gate, 8 Ebed-
melech went from the king's palace
and spoke to the king: 9 "My lord the
king, these men have been evil in
all they have done to Jeremiah the
prophet. They have dropped him
into the cistern where he will die
from hunger, because there is no
more bread in the city."
10 So the king commanded Ebed-
melech, the Cushite, "Take from
here 30 men under your authority
and pull Jeremiah the prophet up
from the cistern before he dies."
11 So Ebed-melech took the men
under his authority and went to
the king's palace to a place below
the storehouse.[A] From there he
took old rags and worn-out clothes
and lowered them by ropes to Jeremiah in the cistern. 12 Ebed-melech
the Cushite cried out to Jeremiah,
"Place these old rags and clothes between your armpits and the ropes."
Jeremiah did so, 13 and they pulled
him up with the ropes and lifted him
out of the cistern, but he continued
to stay in the guard's courtyard.
14 King Zedekiah sent for Jeremiah
the prophet and received him at the
third entrance of the LORD's temple.
The king said to Jeremiah, "I am going to ask you something; don't hide
anything from me."
15 Jeremiah replied to Zedekiah,
"If I tell you, you will kill me, won't
you? Besides, if I give you advice,
you won't listen to me anyway."
16 King Zedekiah swore to Jeremiah in private, "As the LORD lives, who
has given us this life, I will not kill
you or hand you over to these men
who want to take your life."
17 Jeremiah therefore said to Zedekiah, "This is what the LORD, the
God of •Hosts, the God of Israel,
says: 'If indeed you surrender to
the officials of the king of Babylon,
then you will live, this city will not
be burned down, and you and your
household will survive. 18 But if you
do not surrender to the officials of
the king of Babylon, then this city
will be handed over to the Chaldeans. They will burn it down, and
you yourself will not escape from
them.'"
19 But King Zedekiah said to Jeremiah, "I am worried about the
Judeans who have deserted to the
Chaldeans. They may hand me over
to the Judeans to abuse me."
20 "They will not hand you over,"
Jeremiah replied. "Obey the voice of
the LORD in what I am telling you, so
it may go well for you and you can
live. 21 But if you refuse to surrender,
this is the verdict[B] that the LORD has
shown me: 22 'All the women[C] who
remain in the palace of Judah's king
will be brought out to the officials
of the king of Babylon and will say:

[A]**38:11** Or *treasury* [B]**38:21** Or *promise*; lit *word* [C]**38:22** Or *wives*

king's **officials** called for Jeremiah's life because he was **weakening the morale of the warriors**.

38:5-6 The weakling ruler allowed these men to do whatever they pleased with Jeremiah. During his third incarceration, the prophet was thrown into a muddy **cistern** (Hb *bor*, "pit, prison"), which must have been quite deep since they had to lower him with ropes.

38:7-13 God rescued Jeremiah through an unlikely source. **Ebed-melech** (Hb, "servant of the king"), a **Cushite court official** who may have been an Ethiopian eunuch in charge of the harem, solicited the king on Jeremiah's behalf. The king granted a party of 30 men to rescue Jeremiah, transferring him once again to the **guard's courtyard**.

38:14-18 Zedekiah's third conversation with Jeremiah follows the same lines as previously. Seemingly Zedekiah still had opportunity to obey the Lord's word and save his people.

38:19 Apparently some warriors had followed Jeremiah's advice and **deserted** [Hb *naphal*, "fall away"] **to the Chaldeans** (cp. 37:13-14). It was not uncommon for captured kings to be subjected to harsh treatment and possible mutilation.

38:20-23 If he did not obey, Zedekiah would be derided by the women of his harem as they and his sons were **brought out to the Chaldeans**, and he himself would be captured. Even with the threat of capture, Zedekiah was still unwilling to obey God.

Your trusted friends[A]
misled[B] you
and overcame you.
Your feet sank into the mire,
and they deserted you.

23 All your wives and sons will be brought out to the Chaldeans. You yourself will not escape from them, for you will be seized by the king of Babylon and this city will burn down.'"

24 Then Zedekiah warned Jeremiah, "Don't let anyone know about these things or you will die. 25 If the officials hear that I have spoken with you and come and demand of you, 'Tell us what you said to the king; don't hide anything from us and we won't kill you. Also, what did the king say to you?' 26 then you will tell them, 'I was bringing before the king my petition that he not return me to the house of Jonathan to die there.'" 27 When all the officials came to Jeremiah and questioned him, he reported the exact words to them the king had commanded, and they quit speaking with him because nothing had been heard. 28 Jeremiah remained in the guard's courtyard until the day Jerusalem was captured, and he was there when it happened.[C]

The Final Collapse of Jerusalem (39:1–40:6)

39 In the ninth year of Zedekiah king of Judah, in the tenth month, King Nebuchadnezzar of Babylon advanced against Jerusalem with his entire army and laid siege to it. 2 In the fourth month of Zedekiah's eleventh year, on the ninth day of the month, the city was broken into. 3 All the officials of the king of Babylon entered and sat at the Middle Gate: Nergal-sharezer, Samgar, Nebusarsechim[D] the Rab-saris, Nergal-sharezer the Rab-mag, and all the rest of the officials of Babylon's king.

4 When he saw them, Zedekiah king of Judah and all the soldiers fled. They left the city at night by way of the king's garden through the gate between the two walls. They left along the route to the •Arabah. 5 However, the Chaldean army pursued them and overtook Zedekiah in the plains[E] of Jericho, arrested him, and brought him to Nebuchadnezzar, Babylon's king, at Riblah in the land of Hamath. The king passed sentence on him there.

6 At Riblah the king of Babylon slaughtered Zedekiah's sons before his eyes, and he also slaughtered all Judah's nobles. 7 Then he blinded Zedekiah and put him in bronze chains to take him to Babylon. 8 The Chaldeans next burned down the king's palace and the people's houses and tore down the walls of Jerusalem. 9 Nebuzaradan, the commander of the guards, deported the rest of the people to Babylon—those who had remained in the city and those deserters who had defected to him along with the rest of the people who had remained. 10 However, Nebuzaradan, the commander of the guards, left in the land of Judah some of the poor people who owned nothing, and he gave them vineyards and fields at that time.

11 Speaking through Nebuzaradan, captain of the guard, King Nebuchadnezzar of Babylon gave orders concerning Jeremiah, saying: 12 "Take him, look after him, and don't let any harm come to him; do for him whatever he says." 13 Nebuzaradan, captain of the guard, Nebushazban the Rab-saris, Nergal-sharezer the Rab-mag, and all the captains of the king of Babylon 14 had Jeremiah brought from the guard's courtyard and turned him over to Gedaliah son of Ahikam, son of Shaphan, to take him home. So he settled among his own people.

15 Now the word of the LORD had come to Jeremiah when he was confined in the guard's courtyard: 16 "Go tell Ebed-melech the •Cushite: This is what the LORD of •Hosts, the God of Israel, says: I am about to fulfill My words for harm and not for good against this city. They will take place before your eyes on that day. 17 But I will rescue you on that day"—this is the LORD's declaration—"and you

38:24-28 To his credit, Jeremiah keeps the king's confidence. The chapter concludes with Jeremiah's witness to the fulfillment of his prophecies.

39:1-18 Although this chapter parallels the account of chapter 52, it includes information on Jeremiah's circumstances, while chapter 52 provides details about the destruction of the temple and the plundering of its vessels. Zedekiah's **ninth year** was approximately 589/588 B.C., the year when the siege began. It lasted about 18 months, after which the city wall was breached in the **eleventh** year, around 587 B.C. The people had been worn down by the siege; the food supplies were exhausted (38:9; 52:4-6).

39:1-13 After the Babylonians had breached the wall, their officials entered the city. Some uncertainty remains concerning the exact translations of the titles (which are in Akkadian, the language of the Babylonians), but they are surely official military titles. Many of the names, like **Nebuchadnezzar** ("may Nebo protect the crown,") include Nebo (Hb), the name of a Babylonian deity. Nergal was a solar deity portrayed as a god of war, associated with the planet Mars, and regarded as ruler of the underworld. The names of these officials generally indicate their provenance and rank: **Nergal-sharezer the Rab-mag** ("may Nergal protect the king"); **Samgar** ("sword of Nebo"); **Nebusarsechim** ("chief or princes of the eunuchs") **the Rab-saris** (a title meaning "head chief"; cp. 2Kg 18:17); (a title meaning "high official"); **Nebushazban** ("may Nebo save me," v. 13); **Nebuzaradan** ("the leader whom Nebo favors; Nebo has given offspring," vv. 9-13; cp. 40:1; 41:10; 52:12,15-16,26,30; 2Kg 25:8,11,20).

39:4-7 Riblah was a Syrian town located near Kadesh on the Orontes and near the Babylonian border where Nebuchadnezzar had probably set up his headquarters (52:9-10,26-27; cp. Nm 34:11; 2Kg 23:33; 25:6,20-21). Jeremiah had predicted that Zedekiah would be seized, handed over to the Babylonians, and "meet the king of Babylon eye to eye and speak face to face" (Jr 34:3; cp. 32:4). Zedekiah eventually died in Babylon(cp. 52:9-11).

39:8-10 The Babylonian officials' second order of business was to destroy Jerusalem completely. They destroyed **the walls**, **burned . . . the king's palace**, the temple, the nobles' houses, and **the people's houses** (39:8-9; cp. 52:12-14). Understanding the Babylonians' utter destruction of Jerusalem gives a better appreciation of the enormous task of reconstruction that lay before Ezra, Nehemiah,

[A] **38:22** Lit *The men of your peace* [B] **38:22** Or *incited* [C] **38:28** Or *captured. This is what happened when Jerusalem was captured:* [D] **39:3** LXX; MT reads *Samgar-nebu, Sarsechim* [E] **39:5** Lit *Arabah*

will not be handed over to the men
you fear. 18 Indeed, I will certainly
deliver you so that you do not fall by
the sword. Because you have trusted
in Me, you will keep your life like
the spoils of war." This is the LORD's
declaration.

40 This is the word that came to
Jeremiah from the LORD after
Nebuzaradan, captain of the guard,
released him at Ramah. When he
found him, he was bound in chains
with all the exiles of Jerusalem and
Judah who were being exiled to
Babylon. 2 The captain of the guard
took Jeremiah and said to him, "The
LORD your God decreed this disaster
on this place, 3 and the LORD has fulfilled it. He has done just what He
decreed. Because you people have
sinned against the LORD and have
not obeyed Him, this thing has happened. 4 Now pay attention: Today I
am setting you free from the chains
that were on your hands. If it pleases
you to come with me to Babylon,
come, and I will take care of you.
But if it seems wrong to you to come
with me to Babylon, go no farther.[A]
Look—the whole land is in front of
you. Wherever it seems good and
right for you to go, go there." 5 When
Jeremiah had not yet turned to go,
Nebuzaradan said to him: "Return[B]
to Gedaliah son of Ahikam, son of
Shaphan, whom the king of Babylon
has appointed over the cities of Judah, and stay with him among the
people or go wherever you want to
go." So the captain of the guard gave
him a ration and a gift and released
him. 6 Jeremiah therefore went to
Gedaliah son of Ahikam at Mizpah,
and he stayed with him among the
people who remained in the land.

The Governorship of Gedaliah (40:7–41:18)

7 When all the commanders of the
armies in the field—they and their
men—heard that the king of Babylon had appointed Gedaliah son of
Ahikam over the land and that he
had put him in charge of the men,
women, and children from the poorest of the land who had not been
deported to Babylon, 8 they came
to Gedaliah at Mizpah. The commanders included Ishmael son of
Nethaniah, Johanan and Jonathan
the sons of Kareah, Seraiah son of
Tanhumeth, the sons of Ephai the
Netophathite, and Jezaniah son of
the Maacathite—they and their
men.

9 Gedaliah son of Ahikam, son of
Shaphan, swore an oath to them and
their men, assuring them, "Don't
be afraid to serve the Chaldeans.
Live in the land and serve the king
of Babylon, and it will go well for
you. 10 As for me, I am going to live
in Mizpah to represent[C] you before
the Chaldeans who come to us. As
for you, gather wine, summer fruit,
and oil, place them in your storage
jars, and live in the cities you have
captured."

11 When all the Judeans in Moab
and among the Ammonites and in
Edom and in all the other lands also
heard that the king of Babylon had
left a remnant in Judah and had appointed Gedaliah son of Ahikam, son
of Shaphan, over them, 12 they all
returned from all the places where
they had been banished and came
to the land of Judah, to Gedaliah
at Mizpah, and harvested a great
amount of wine and summer fruit.

13 Meanwhile, Johanan son of
Kareah and all the commanders of
the armies in the field came to Gedaliah at Mizpah 14 and warned him,
"Don't you realize that Baalis, king
of the Ammonites, has sent Ishmael
son of Nethaniah to kill you?" But
Gedaliah son of Ahikam would not
believe them. 15 Then Johanan son
of Kareah suggested to Gedaliah in
private at Mizpah, "Let me go kill
Ishmael son of Nethaniah. No one
will know it. Why should he kill
you and scatter all of Judah that has
gathered to you so that the remnant
of Judah would perish?"

16 But Gedaliah son of Ahikam responded to Johanan son of Kareah,
"Don't do that! What you're saying
about Ishmael is a lie."

41 In the seventh month, Ishmael son of Nethaniah, son
of Elishama, of the royal family
and one of the king's chief officers,

Zerubbabel, Zechariah, and Haggai. Most of those remaining in Jerusalem were **deported**, but the indigent were left to tend the land (52:15-16).

39:11-14 Jeremiah was apparently known to the Babylonians. That this ill-treated prophet of the Lord was the subject of discussion among the highest Babylonian officials, including the king himself, was nothing short of astounding. Jeremiah was sent to **Gedaliah**, with whose family he was already familiar (cp. 26:24; 2Kg 22:3-20).

39:15-18 This short section is not in chronological order, but probably takes place before the breach of the wall. **Ebed-melech** is informed that his life will be spared because of his faith (**you have trusted in Me**).

40:1-6 Seemingly Jeremiah was released into the general population, then accidentally recaptured and taken along with a group of **exiles** to **Ramah**, a city used as a gathering point for those going into exile. **Nebuzaradan** found and recognized Jeremiah and released him again. In these verses, Nebuzaradan appears as the Lord's mouthpiece, even though he was a Gentile and Israel's enemy. When Jeremiah was given complete freedom, he preferred to remain among his own people in his own land. Although the future of Israel lay with the exiles going to Babylon, Jeremiah chose to stay behind.

40:11-12 As word spread about Gedaliah's governorship, other **Judeans** scattered among the surrounding nations returned to **Mizpah.** Perhaps the "commanders of the armies" (v. 13) also felt assured of safety since one of their own (a Judean) had been installed as governor. These commanders were probably among those who had fled with Zedekiah but were scattered (**banished**) to avoid capture; those who did not escape were slaughtered at Riblah (52:8-10).

40:13-16 The warning to Gedaliah of the plot against his life underscores the fallout from the political void in Judah as well as the people's persistent rebellion against God's command to submit to the Babylonians. Gedaliah apparently failed to recognize the depth of sin and rebellion among the people he governed. **Baalis, king of the Ammonites** planned to take advantage of the remnant's vulnerability through **Ishmael son of Nethaniah**.

41:1-3 Ishmael's plot was not countered, and with the murder of Gedaliah, Ishmael set off on a spree of violence. Of royal descent, he almost

[A] **40:4** Lit *Babylon, stop* [B] **40:5** LXX reads *But if not, run, return*; Hb obscure [C] **40:10** Lit *to stand*

certainly was attempting to restore the Davidic throne, throwing off the Babylonian yoke. He had found an ally in Baalis and thought the time had come to dispense with Gedaliah, a "sell-out" to the Babylonians. Ishmael killed all those in Gedaliah's house, including the **Chaldean soldiers**, probably a small detachment.

41:4-5 The following day, **80** pilgrims came to Jerusalem from the north (**Shechem, Shiloh, and Samaria**) to celebrate the Festival of Booths (or the ingathering of the harvest). As their appearance indicated, they were obviously in mourning, most likely for the destruction of the temple. Despite this, they came to Jerusalem since even the ruins of the temple were considered sacred. Signs of syncretism appear as the mourners are gashing themselves.

41:8-10 Ten men were able to save themselves through bribery, offering **wheat, barley, oil, and honey**—items that may have been scarce at that time. Ishmael then took all he had captured from Mizpah and set out for Ammon.

41:11-18 Johanan, who had originally offered to eliminate Ishmael, took charge, along with the other **commanders of the armies**. Ishmael eluded capture, escaping to the Ammonites, while those in the remnant rescued by Johanan began their journey southward toward Egypt, seeking to escape certain retribution by Babylon for the murder of its representative and detachment of soldiers.

42:1-6 Many commentators believe that the exchange between prophet and people is significant in terms of the use of the phrase **the LORD your God**. After the people had referred to God as "your God," Jeremiah replied in like terms. After the people once more used the phrase to Jeremiah, they finally acknowledged **the LORD our God** twice, promising obedience to His **word**. Evidently Jeremiah is still recognized as God's prophet among the **remnant**.

came with 10 men to Gedaliah son
of Ahikam at Mizpah. They ate a
meal together there in Mizpah, 2 but
then Ishmael son of Nethaniah and
the 10 men who were with him got
up and struck down Gedaliah son of
Ahikam, son of Shaphan, with the
sword; he killed the one the king of
Babylon had appointed in the land.
3 Ishmael also struck down all the
Judeans who were with Gedaliah at
Mizpah, as well as the Chaldean soldiers who were there.

4 On the second day after he had
killed Gedaliah, when no one knew
yet, 5 80 men came from Shechem,
Shiloh, and Samaria who had
shaved their beards, torn their garments, and gashed themselves,
and who were carrying •grain and
incense offerings to bring to the
temple of the LORD. 6 Ishmael son
of Nethaniah came out of Mizpah
to meet them, weeping as he came.
When he encountered them, he said:
"Come to Gedaliah son of Ahikam!"
7 But when they came into the city,
Ishmael son of Nethaniah and the
men with him slaughtered them and
threw them into[A] a cistern.

8 However, there were 10 men
among them who said to Ishmael,
"Don't kill us, for we have hidden
treasure in the field—wheat, barley, oil, and honey!" So he stopped
and did not kill them along with
their companions. 9 Now the cistern
where Ishmael had thrown all the
corpses of the men he had struck
down was a large one[B] that King
Asa had made in the encounter with
Baasha king of Israel. Ishmael son of
Nethaniah filled it with the slain.

10 Then Ishmael took captive all
the remnant of the people of Mizpah including the daughters of the
king—all those who remained in
Mizpah over whom Nebuzaradan,
captain of the guard, had appointed
Gedaliah son of Ahikam. Ishmael
son of Nethaniah took them captive
and set off to cross over to the Ammonites.

11 When Johanan son of Kareah and
all the commanders of the armies
with him heard of all the evil that
Ishmael son of Nethaniah had done,
12 they took all their men and went to
fight with Ishmael son of Nethaniah
and found him by the great pool in
Gibeon. 13 When all the people with
Ishmael saw Johanan son of Kareah
and all the commanders of the army
with him, they rejoiced, 14 and all
the people whom Ishmael had taken
captive from Mizpah turned around
and rejoined Johanan son of Kareah. 15 But Ishmael son of Nethaniah
escaped from Johanan with eight
men and went to the Ammonites.
16 Johanan son of Kareah and all
the commanders of the armies with
him then took from Mizpah all the
remnant of the people whom he
had recovered from Ishmael son of
Nethaniah after Ishmael had killed
Gedaliah son of Ahikam—men, soldiers, women, children, and court
officials whom he brought back
from Gibeon. 17 They left, stopping
in Geruth Chimham, which is near
Bethlehem, in order to make their
way into Egypt, 18 away from the
Chaldeans. For they feared them
because Ishmael son of Nethaniah
had struck down Gedaliah son of
Ahikam, whom the king of Babylon
had appointed in the land.

Jeremiah's Counsel Requested and Rejected (42:1–43:7)

42 Then all the commanders of
the armies, along with Johanan son of Kareah, Jezaniah son
of Hoshaiah, and all the people from
the least to the greatest, approached
2 Jeremiah the prophet and said,
"May our petition come before you;
pray to the LORD your God on our
behalf, on behalf of this entire remnant (for few of us remain out of the
many, as you can see with your own
eyes), 3 that the LORD your God may
tell us the way we should walk and
the thing we should do."

4 So Jeremiah the prophet said to
them, "I have heard. I will now pray
to the LORD your God according to
your words, and every word that the
LORD answers you I will tell you; I
won't withhold a word from you."

5 And they said to Jeremiah, "As for
every word the LORD your God sends
you to tell us, if we don't act accordingly, may the LORD be a true and

[A]41:7 Syr; MT reads *slaughtered them in* [B]41:9 LXX; MT reads *down by the hand of Gedaliah*

faithful witness against us. 6 Whether it is pleasant or unpleasant, we
will obey the voice of the LORD our
God to whom we are sending you so
that it may go well with us. We will
certainly obey the voice of the LORD
our God!"
7 Now at the end of 10 days, the
word of the LORD came to Jeremiah,
8 and he summoned Johanan son
of Kareah, all the commanders of
the armies who were with him, and
all the people from the least to the
greatest.
9 He said to them, "This is what the
LORD says, the God of Israel to whom
you sent me to bring your petition
before Him: 10 'If you will indeed stay
in this land, then I will rebuild and
not demolish you, and I will plant
and not uproot you, because I relent
concerning the disaster that I have
brought on you. 11 Don't be afraid of
the king of Babylon whom you now
fear; don't be afraid of him'—this
is the LORD's declaration—'because
I am with you to save you and deliver you from him. 12 I will grant
you compassion, and he[A] will have
compassion on you and allow you to
return to your own soil. 13 But if you
say, 'We will not stay in this land,' so
as not to obey the voice of the LORD
your God, 14 and if you say, 'No, instead we'll go to the land of Egypt
where we will not see war or hear the
sound of the ram's horn or hunger
for food, and we'll live there,' 15 then
hear the word of the LORD, remnant
of Judah! This is what the LORD of
•Hosts, the God of Israel, says: If you
are firmly resolved to go to Egypt
and live there for a while, 16 then
the sword you fear will overtake you
there in the land of Egypt, and the
famine you are worried about will
follow on your heels[B] there to Egypt,
and you will die there. 17 All who resolve to go to Egypt to live there for
a while will die by the sword, famine, and plague. They will have no
one escape or survive from the disaster I will bring on them.'
18 "For this is what the LORD of
Hosts, the God of Israel, says: 'Just
as My anger and fury were poured
out on Jerusalem's residents, so will
My fury pour out on you if you go
to Egypt. You will become an object
of cursing, scorn, execration, and
disgrace, and you will never see this
place again.' 19 The LORD has spoken
concerning you, remnant of Judah: 'Don't go to Egypt.' Know for
certain that I have warned you today! 20 You have led your own selves
astray because you are the ones who
sent me to the LORD your God, saying, 'Pray to the LORD our God on
our behalf, and as for all that the
LORD our God says, tell it to us, and
we'll act accordingly.' 21 For I have
told you today, but you have not
obeyed the voice of the LORD your
God in everything He has sent me to
tell you. 22 Now therefore, know for
certain that by the sword, famine,
and plague you will die in the place
where you desired to go to live for
a while."

43 When Jeremiah had finished
speaking to all the people all
the words of the LORD their God—all
these words the LORD their God had
sent him to give them— 2 then Azariah[C] son of Hoshaiah, Johanan son
of Kareah, and all the other arrogant
men responded to Jeremiah, "You
are speaking a lie! The LORD our God
has not sent you to say, 'You must
not go to Egypt to live there for a
while!' 3 Rather, Baruch son of Neriah is inciting you against us to hand
us over to the Chaldeans to put us to
death or to deport us to Babylon!"
4 So Johanan son of Kareah and
all the commanders of the armies
did not obey the voice of the LORD to
stay in the land of Judah. 5 Instead,
Johanan son of Kareah and all the
commanders of the armies took
the whole remnant of Judah, those
who had returned from all the nations where they had been banished
to live in the land of Judah for a
while— 6 the men, women, children, king's daughters, and everyone whom Nebuzaradan, captain of
the guard, had allowed to remain
with Gedaliah son of Ahikam son of
Shaphan, along with Jeremiah the
prophet and Baruch son of Neriah—
7 and they went to the land of Egypt
because they did not obey the voice

42:7-8 Interestingly, the prophet waited until he heard from God and did not speak until then, even though it required **10 days**. Jeremiah waited for the Lord's timing, not that of impatient or desperate men. His words were not to the people's liking, and his advice to remain in Judah and not go to Egypt seemed to contradict human wisdom and strategic thinking.

42:9-12 Babylon did not readily accept rebellion. God's promise of blessing to those who obeyed Him and remained reiterates the prophetic theme of building, planting, demolishing, and uprooting. God promised deliverance from Nebuchadnezzar and that He would **rebuild** and **plant** them (cp. 33:7).

42:13-18 However, going to Egypt would not help them escape war and hunger; rather, these would **overtake** [them] **there in the land of Egypt**. God told them clearly not to go to Egypt, or the remnant would be completely obliterated.

43:1-3 **Azariah** and **Johanan**, the leaders of the people, responded defiantly. **Arrogant** [Hb *zēd*, "proud, inflated"; one might say 'hotheads'] **men** thought they knew what God would and would not do, despite God's message through Jeremiah (cp. Ps 119:69,78,85; Is 13:11; Mal 4:1). They blamed **Baruch** for **inciting** Jeremiah against them, delivering a pro-Babylonian message.

43:4-7 The **commanders** disobeyed God's word, and decided to take everyone to **Egypt**—including **Jeremiah** and **Baruch**.

[A]**42:12** LXX reads *I* [B]**42:16** Lit *will cling after you* [C]**43:2** = Jezaniah

43:8-13 At **Tahpanhes** (northern Egyptian border) the Lord spoke to His disobedient people about the fate of Egypt via another sign-act. In accordance with God's plan, Nebuchadnezzar would soundly defeat Egypt and kill and/or capture her people. Egypt's fate would be the same as Judah's, and Nebuchadnezzar would accomplish his task effortlessly (this is the effect of the vivid metaphor used), destroying both Egypt and her gods, referring here specifically to the sun god, Re, while the **sacred pillars** are no doubt obelisks.

44:1-2 God addressed Himself to the people, invoking His covenant name as divine warrior, **the LORD** [Hb *Yahweh*] **of Hosts** (Hb *tsava'*, "army"), and His right to speak as the **God of Israel**.

44:3-8 The recurring problem of idolatry had plagued Israel and Judah throughout their history in the promised land, and was the reason for the disaster they had just witnessed in Jerusalem. The people were **burning incense to serve other gods**, gods such as Baal, Anat, and Astarte/Ishtar. Out of mercy, God had sent the prophets to warn Judah, but the people stubbornly persisted in disobedience. The blame for disaster, therefore, rested squarely with the people; by their idolatry, they **provoked** God and are **cutting off . . . a remnant**.

44:9-14 Possibly there is an allusion here to child sacrifice (see Jr 7:30-31). They continued to practice idolatry in Egypt. Despite the devastation of Jerusalem, the people neither humbled themselves nor repented. The text mentions specifically that both men and women had participated actively in idolatrous practices. **Therefore** indicates that a judgment will follow: God purposed that all except a few fugitives would be wiped out in Egypt: the covenant curses would follow them.

44:15-19 Jeremiah specifies that responsibility for both past and future disaster is shared among the men and **their wives. The queen of heaven** likely refers to Ishtar (Akkadian)/Ashtoreth (Assyrian, Canaanite)/Astarte (Canaanite, Egyptian). The elements of their worship to her consisted of burning **incense**, a sweet-smelling perfume to please the goddess; bringing **drink offerings** (usually **poured out** on the ground or over the sacrifice on the altar) of wine; and presenting **cakes** for the goddess to eat. The cakes are further described as being **in her image**, suggesting that they may have been imprinted or stamped with her image, that there was a deity-shaped mold used to bake the cakes, or that the cakes were star-shaped to represent Ishtar as an astral deity. Perhaps they were baked in

of the LORD. They went as far as Tahpanhes.

God's Judgment on His People in Egypt (43:8–44:30)

8 Then the word of the LORD came
to Jeremiah at Tahpanhes: 9 "Pick up
some large stones and set them in
the mortar of the brick pavement
that is at the opening of Pharaoh's
palace at Tahpanhes. Do this in the
sight of the Judean men 10 and tell
them: This is what the LORD of •Hosts,
the God of Israel, says: I will send for
My servant Nebuchadnezzar king of
Babylon, and I will place his throne
on these stones that I have embedded, and he will pitch his pavilion
over them. 11 He will come and strike
down the land of Egypt—those destined for death, to death; those destined for captivity, to captivity; and
those destined for the sword, to the
sword. 12 I[A] will kindle a fire in the
temples of Egypt's gods, and he will
burn them and take them prisoner.
He will •clean the land of Egypt as a
shepherd picks lice off[B] his garment,
and he will leave there unscathed.
13 He will smash the sacred pillars
of the sun temple[C,D] in the land of
Egypt and burn down the temples of
the Egyptian gods."

44 This is the word that came to
Jeremiah for all the Jews living in the land of Egypt—at Migdol,
Tahpanhes, Memphis, and in the
land of Pathros: 2 "This is what the
LORD of •Hosts, the God of Israel,
says: You have seen all the disaster
I brought against Jerusalem and all
Judah's cities; look, they are a ruin
today without an inhabitant in them
3 because of their evil ways that provoked Me to anger, going and burning incense to serve other gods that
they, you, and your fathers did not
know. 4 So I sent you all My servants
the prophets time and time again,[E]
saying: Don't do this detestable
thing that I hate. 5 But they did not
listen or pay attention; they did not
turn from their evil or stop burning
incense to other gods. 6 So My fierce
wrath poured out and burned in Judah's cities and Jerusalem's streets
so that they became the desolate
ruin they are today.

7 "So now, this is what the LORD,
the God of Hosts, the God of Israel,
says: Why are you doing such great
harm to yourselves? You are cutting off man and woman, child and
infant from Judah, leaving yourselves without a remnant. 8 You are
provoking Me to anger by the work
of your hands. You are burning incense to other gods in the land of
Egypt where you have gone to live
for a while. As a result, you will
be cut off and become an object of
cursing and insult among all the nations of earth. 9 Have you forgotten
the evils of your fathers, the evils
of Judah's kings, the evils of their
wives, your own evils, and the evils
of your wives that were committed in the land of Judah and in the
streets of Jerusalem? 10 They have
not become humble to this day, and
they have not •feared or followed My
instruction or My statutes that I set
before you and your ancestors.

11 "Therefore, this is what the LORD
of Hosts, the God of Israel, says: I am
about to turn against you to bring
disaster, to cut off all Judah. 12 And I
will take away the remnant of Judah,
those who have resolved to go to the
land of Egypt to live there for a while;
they will meet their end. All of them
in the land of Egypt will fall by the
sword; they will meet their end by
famine. From the least to the greatest, they will die by the sword and
by famine. Then they will become
an object of cursing, scorn, execration, and disgrace. 13 I will punish
those living in the land of Egypt just
as I punished Jerusalem by sword,
famine, and plague. 14 Then the
remnant of Judah—those going to
live for a while there in the land of
Egypt—will have no fugitive or survivor to return to the land of Judah
where they are longing[F] to return to
live, for they will not return except
for a few fugitives."

15 However, all the men who
knew that their wives were burning incense to other gods, all the

[A] **43:12** LXX, Syr, Vg read *He* [B] **43:12** Or *will wrap himself in the land of Egypt as a shepherd wraps himself in* [C] **43:13** Or *Beth-shemesh* [D] **43:13** = of Heliopolis [E] **44:4** Lit *prophets, rising up early and sending* [F] **44:14** Lit *lifting up their soul*

women standing by—a great assembly—and all the people who
were living in the land of Egypt at
Pathros answered Jeremiah, 16“As
for the word you spoke to us in the
name of •Yahweh, we are not going
to listen to you! 17Instead, we will do
everything we said we would: burn
incense to the queen of heaven[A] and
offer •drink offerings to her just as
we, our fathers, our kings, and our
officials did in Judah's cities and
in Jerusalem's streets. Then we
had enough food and good things
and saw no disaster, 18but from the
time we ceased to burn incense to
the queen of heaven and to offer
her drink offerings, we have lacked
everything, and through sword and
famine we have met our end.”
19And the women said,[B] “When
we burned incense to the queen of
heaven and poured out drink offerings to her, was it apart from our
husbands' knowledge that we made
sacrificial cakes in her image and
poured out drink offerings to her?”
20But Jeremiah responded to all
the people—the men, women, and
all the people who were answering him: 21“As for the incense you
burned in Judah's cities and in Jerusalem's streets—you, your fathers,
your kings, your officials, and the
people of the land—did the LORD
not remember them? He brought
this to mind. 22The LORD can no
longer bear your evil deeds and the
detestable acts you have committed,
so your land has become a waste, a
desolation, and an object of cursing,
without inhabitant, as you see today.
23Because you burned incense and
sinned against the LORD and didn't
obey the LORD's voice and didn't follow His instruction, His statutes,
and His testimonies, this disaster
has come to you, as you see today.”
24Then Jeremiah said to all the
people, including all the women,
“Hear the word of the LORD, all Judah who are in the land of Egypt.
25This is what the LORD of Hosts, the
God of Israel, says: ‘As for you and
your wives, you women have spoken
with your mouths, and you men fulfilled it by your deeds, saying, “We
will keep our vows that we have
made to burn incense to the queen
of heaven and to pour out drink offerings for her.” Go ahead, confirm
your vows! Pay your vows!’
26“Therefore, hear the word of the
LORD, all you Judeans who live in the
land of Egypt: ‘I have sworn by My
great name, says Yahweh, that My
name will never again be invoked
by anyone of Judah in all the land
of Egypt, saying, “As the Lord GOD
lives.” 27I am watching over them
for disaster and not for good, and every man of Judah who is in the land
of Egypt will meet his end by sword
or famine until they are finished off.
28Those who escape the sword will
return from the land of Egypt to the
land of Judah only few in number,
and the whole remnant of Judah,
the ones going to the land of Egypt
to live there for a while, will know
whose word stands, Mine or theirs!
29This will be a sign to you'—this is
the LORD's declaration—‘that I am
about to punish you in this place,
so you may know that My words of
disaster concerning you will certainly come to pass. 30This is what
the LORD says: I am about to hand
over Pharaoh Hophra, Egypt's king,
to his enemies, to those who want
to take his life, just as I handed over
Judah's King Zedekiah to Babylon's
King Nebuchadnezzar, who was his
enemy, the one who wanted to take
his life.'”

The Message to Baruch (45:1-5)

45 This is the word that Jeremiah
the prophet spoke to Baruch
son of Neriah when he wrote these
words on a scroll at Jeremiah's dictation[C] in the fourth year of Jehoiakim son of Josiah, king of Judah:
2“This is what the LORD, the God of
Israel, says to you, Baruch: 3‘You
have said, “Woe is me, because the
LORD has added misery to my pain!
I am worn out with[D] groaning and
have found no rest.”'
4“This is what you are to say to
him: ‘This is what the LORD says:
What I have built I am about to
demolish, and what I have planted

a mold as the one found in the palace kitchen at Mari, a Babylonian city. The mold showed a feminine figure with wide hips, her hands supporting her breasts—physical indicators of fertility. Judean women may have practiced rites of goddess-worship on the rooftops of their houses (8:2; 19:13; cp. 32:29). Worship of Ashtoreth at local shrines may have involved ritual prostitution to simulate the fertility rite between her and Baal (cp. 2:20; 3:6). Shockingly, there were even Asherah (another consort of Baal in mythology) poles set up in the Jerusalem temple until Josiah purged it (see "Where did it happen?" in the Introduction, p. 950).

43:20-25 Jeremiah's specific mention of the **women** (vv. 15,19) and wives (vv. 9,15) in this passage is interesting and unusual. In a patriarchal society, the men were held accountable for the spiritual welfare of the household, while the women were responsible for its management. The men "knew that their wives were burning incense to other gods", v. 15 and approved it, thus becoming participants in idolatry, together with their wives, for the sake of the protection, fertility, and prosperity of the household (v. 15). Men and women together defied God's stipulation against idolatry. In addition to the crowd of men, the women were specifically addressed five times (vv. 15-25), indicating that they functioned actively in their households as priestesses of this idolatrous cult. The equal share of blame for sin serves as an example of the theme of individual spiritual responsibility for sin (cp. 31:29-30).

44:26-30 **Therefore** indicates a pronouncement of judgment (44:11). God swore by His own **name** that the majority of the remnant would perish and, in fact, would not experience protection and prosperity in the land to which they fled, for Egypt's pharaoh would soon be defeated. As in the beginning of the book, God declared that He was **watching** [Hb *shaqad*, "be sleepless or wakeful, be alert"] **over** the Judeans in Egypt to ensure that His promise to **punish** them would be fulfilled.

45:1-4 This oracle's date is debated, as is the occasion of Baruch's lament. In the **fourth year of Jehoiakim** (605/604 B.C.), Babylon defeated Egypt at the Battle of Carchemish, thus making Jehoiakim, who had been a vassal of Egypt, a servant of Babylon (cp. 46:2). Additionally, that year Jehoiakim had cut up and burned the **scroll** of God's word dictated to Baruch by Jeremiah. Perhaps Baruch was overwhelmed by the realization that the fulfillment of Jeremiah's prophecy of doom was near. Given his loyalty to Jeremiah, Baruch may have expected

[A]**44:17** = Ashtoreth, or Astarte [B]**44:19** LXX, Syr; MT omits *And the women said* [C]**45:1** Lit *scroll from Jeremiah's mouth* [D]**45:3** Lit *I labored in my*

special treatment (salvation from disaster). His question expressed his belief about the fate of the wicked—**no rest**, and he lamented that he, a righteous man, had received that fate unjustly.

45:5 The Lord upbraided Baruch for this desire to be exempt from the coming exile. What God had determined would certainly come to pass. How could Baruch hope to receive special consideration? Nonetheless, he would at least escape with his life (and that in itself was a generous concession). There is a hint that perhaps Baruch would also go into exile, a conclusion that seems likely since Baruch's brother, Seraiah, was also taken to Babylon (51:59-64).

46:1 The oracles against Egypt take the form of a mocking taunt song. The passage refers to events which took place in 605/604 B.C., the Battle of Carchemish. Archaeological evidence (Egyptian artifacts and indications of destruction around 600 B.C.) has shown the biblical dating to be correct.

46:2-9 Egypt was encouraged to make all preparations necessary for battle, but despite these efforts their army was **terrified**, defeated, and fled the battle. In their rush to **escape** devastation by the Babylonians, the warriors stumbled over one another. Egypt, figuratively depicted as rising **like the Nile** to take over other kingdoms, is identified with **Pharaoh Neco**, who mustered his entire fighting force, including foreign mercenaries from **Cush** (Nubia or modern Sudan), **Put** (Libya), and **Ludim** (possibly Lydia).

46:10-11 All was in vain, however, because **that day belongs to the Lord, the GOD of Hosts**. The routed Egyptians were like sacrificial victims slaughtered by the Lord, the true victorious warrior. Sarcastically, Egypt (which was famous for healing arts) was urged to go get some **balm** from **Gilead**, but alas, **there is no healing for you**.

I am about to uproot—the whole
land! 5 But as for you, do you seek
great things for yourself? Stop seeking! For I am about to bring disaster
on every living creature'—this is
the LORD's declaration—'but I will
grant you your life like the spoils of
war wherever you go.'"

Oracles Against Foreign Nations (46:1–51:64)

Against Egypt (46:1-28)

46 The word of the LORD that came to Jeremiah the prophet about the nations:

2 About Egypt and the army of
Pharaoh Neco, Egypt's king, which
was defeated at Carchemish on the
Euphrates River by Nebuchadnezzar
king of Babylon in the fourth year
of Judah's King Jehoiakim son of
Josiah:

3 Deploy small shields
and large;
draw near for battle!
4 Harness the horses;
mount the steeds;[A]
take your positions
with helmets on!
Polish the lances;
put on armor!
5 Why have I seen this?
They are terrified,
they are retreating,
their warriors are crushed,
they flee headlong,
they never look back,
terror is on every side!
This is
the LORD's declaration.
6 The swift cannot flee,
and the warrior
cannot escape!
In the north by the bank
of the Euphrates River,
they stumble and fall.

7 Who is this,
rising like the Nile,
like rivers
whose waters churn?
8 Egypt rises like the Nile,
and its waters churn
like rivers.
He boasts, "I will go up,
I will cover the earth;
I will destroy cities
with their residents."
9 Rise up, you cavalry!
Race furiously, you chariots!
Let the warriors go out—
•Cush and Put,
who are able
to handle shields,
and the Ludim,
who are able to handle
and string the bow.
10 That day belongs to the Lord,
the GOD of •Hosts,
a day of vengeance
to avenge Himself

HARD QUESTION

How can God raise up a nation as a "destroyer," then judge and punish that nation for its actions?

This section, known as the Oracles (or Prophecies) against the Nations, was composed at various times, gathered together, and placed at the end of the book (46:1–51:64). Although they are not in chronological order within the book of Jeremiah, their appearance at the end is nonetheless appropriate. After Judah's doom was fulfilled, the surrounding nations that perpetrated oppression, destruction, harassment, and exile on Judah would also receive their due from the God who is sovereign over all nations. A number of these nations were also involved in the anti-Babylonian coalition convened by Zedekiah in 594 B.C. (27:3).

Egypt and **Babylon**, the two major military powers of the time, serve in the current passage as bookends, while the other nations are dealt with from west to east. The issue arises of God's use of foreign nations, notably Babylon, as political and military instruments to discipline and punish sinful Judah and then as recipients of His subsequent punishment of those nations. God's attributes of justice, sovereignty, and love seem to interact and perhaps conflict; but this is not the case. God's love for His covenant people is primary here.

In the Abrahamic covenant, God promised that all the families of the earth would have access to God's blessing (Gn 12:3). God claimed Israel as His special possession, and nations hostile to Israel would be judged. Although God could allow a nation to oppress His wayward people as a means of chastisement, that nation would yet be punished for its own sins.

In a number of oracles, for example, idolatry and inhumanity in warfare are mentioned as offenses against God. Babylon received harsh punishment for its plunder of the temple in Jerusalem. Finally, the oracles represent one aspect of God's call to Jeremiah: God had set him "over nations and kingdoms to uproot and tear down, to destroy and demolish, to build and plant" (1:10). Most oracles pronounced destruction on a nation, but many of them also sounded a hopeful note.

[A] 46:4 Or *mount up, riders*

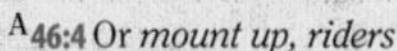

against His adversaries.
The sword will devour
and be satisfied;
it will drink its fill
of their blood,
because it will be a sacrifice
to the Lord, the GOD
of Hosts,
in the northern land
by the Euphrates River.

11 Go up to Gilead and get balm,
Virgin Daughter Egypt!
You have multiplied remedies
in vain;
there is no healing for you.
12 The nations have heard
of your dishonor,
and your outcry
fills the earth,
because warrior stumbles
against warrior
and together both of them
have fallen.

13 This is the word the LORD spoke
to Jeremiah the prophet about the
coming of Nebuchadnezzar king of
Babylon to defeat the land of Egypt:

14 Announce it in Egypt,
and proclaim it in Migdol!
Proclaim it in Memphis
and in Tahpanhes!
Say: Take positions!
Prepare yourself,
for the sword devours
all around you.
15 Why have your strong ones
been swept away?
Each has not stood,
for the LORD
has thrust him down.
16 He continues to stumble.
Indeed, each falls
over the other.
They say, "Get up! Let's return
to our people
and to the land of our birth,
away from the sword
that oppresses."
17 There they will cry out,
"Pharaoh king of Egypt
was all noise;
he let the
opportune moment pass."
18 As I live—
this is
the King's declaration;
•Yahweh of Hosts is
His name.
He will come like Tabor
among the mountains
and like Carmel by the sea.
19 Get your bags ready for exile,
inhabitant of Daughter Egypt!
For Memphis will become
a desolation,
uninhabited ruins.
20 Egypt is
a beautiful young cow,
but a horsefly from the north
is coming against her.[A]
21 Even her mercenaries
among her
are like stall-fed calves.
They too will turn back;
together they will flee;
they will not take their stand,
for the day of their calamity
is coming on them,
the time of their punishment.
22 Egypt will hiss
like a slithering snake,[B]
for the enemy will come
with an army;
with axes they will come
against her
like those who cut trees.
23 They will cut down
her forest—
this is
the LORD's declaration—
though it is dense,
for they are more numerous
than locusts;
they cannot be counted.
24 Daughter Egypt will be
put to shame,
handed over
to a northern people.

25 The LORD of Hosts, the God of
Israel, says: "I am about to punish
Amon, god of Thebes, along with
Pharaoh, Egypt, her gods, and her
kings—Pharaoh and those trusting in him. 26 I will hand them over
to those who want to take their
lives—to Nebuchadnezzar king of
Babylon and his officers. But after

46:13-15 In this passage, the Lord is the chief opponent of Egypt, despite the information that the oracle refers to Nebuchadnezzar's coming. A terrifying announcement would be made in several main Egyptian cities that **the sword devours all around you**. The true source of this destruction was not Nebuchadnezzar, but **the LORD** [who] **has thrust him down.**

46:17-19 At the heart of this chapter, which speaks of two earthly kings, the true **King** swore by His own name, **Yahweh of Hosts**, that He would hand over one king to another. **Tabor** and **Carmel** provide images of the one who **will come.** Both are massive, intimidating mountains—Tabor towering over other heights and Carmel jutting out into the sea.

46:20-21 Egypt and her **mercenaries** are portrayed as cattle (i.e., dumb and helpless), not warring animals at all. Egypt was vulnerable to the stinging **horsefly** coming against her (i.e., an invading army). The Egyptian mercenaries regretted their situation and decided to abandon Pharaoh.

46:22-24 The enemy—**an army . . . with axes**—is further compared to **locusts**, insects that devastate a landscape by utterly consuming its foliage. After suffering crushing, humiliating defeat of her armies, people, and land, **Daughter Egypt** would be taken into exile by a **northern people**.

46:25 Pharaoh, his gods (**Amon** and others), and his retinue (**those trusting in him**) would be handed over **to Nebuchadnezzar . . . and his officers.** Thus Egypt and all nations would know that true kingship belongs to the Lord. Often, Egyptian kings were worshiped as gods, and in this respect the Lord demonstrates through the events of history that He is both God and King, worthy of the worship of all nations.

46:26 Finally, this King declared a brief message of hope for Egypt. The phrase recurs in several oracles and relates to Jeremiah's original mission: The sovereign God is powerful not only to "uproot and tear down, to destroy and demolish" but also "to build and plant" Israel or any other nation (1:10).

[A]**46:20** Some Hb mss, LXX, Syr; other Hb mss read *is coming, coming* [B]**46:22** Lit *Her sound, she will go like a snake*

46:27-28 The Lord also promised that a remnant would be preserved in exile and would return to the land to a future of **calm and quiet**. Twice Judah was told, **do not be afraid**, for two reasons: the Lord would **save** them and would **be with** His people, destroying their oppressors, while justly punishing Judah (**Jacob**) for his sins and giving him a hopeful future.

47:1-7 This brief oracle is directed against long-time enemies of Judah, the **Philistines**, as both nations shared the land of Canaan. By Jeremiah's time the Philistines were not politically significant, but their territory was strategically located between Egypt and Babylon; indeed, as this oracle suggests, Philistia had become a satellite of Egypt so that this oracle's placement seems something of a continuation of chapter 46. Lack of evidence prevents an accurate identification of the **Pharaoh** mentioned here.

47:2-3 The thrust of this oracle is to warn Philistia of the impending threat from the north described in terms of rising and **overflowing** waters, the thundering of horse-drawn war **chariots**, and the destruction of the "sword of the Lord." The force of these armies was so overwhelming that the Philistines would be incapable of protecting even their own families.

47:4-5 Tyre and **Sidon** were Philistine allies. **Gaza** could expect only **baldness** (Hb *qorchah*; cp. Is 15:2; Ezk 7:18; Am 8:10), probably referring either to the common funerary practice of shaving the head in mourning (cp. Jr 48:37; verb root *qarach*, "make bald," 16:6; Ezk 27:31) or, figuratively, to complete destruction of the city. **Ashkelon will become silent** (Hb *damah*, "is cut off or devastated"; cp. Is 15:1; Hs 10:7). In 604 B.C., the two chief cities—Ashkelon and Gaza—were destroyed by Nebuchadnezzar (cp. Jdg 1:18; Am 1:8; Zph 2:4,7; 9:5). In both cities the inhabitants would **gash** (Hb *gadad*, "cut oneself"; cp. Dt 14:1; 1Kg 18:28; Jr 16:6; 41:5) themselves as a sign of mourning or as an attempt to appease their gods.

47:6-7 These verses possibly represents a question asked by the Philistines, who received the answer that the sword would only **rest** once it had completed its assignment from the Lord; (i.e., destruction was commanded and fully executed at the Lord's initiative). A glimmer of hope for Philistia is notably absent.

48:1-47 Although **Moab** had little political leverage in Jeremiah's day, the oracle against Moab is particularly long and virulent, second in length

this, it will be inhabited again as in
ancient times."
This is
the LORD's declaration.

27 But you, My servant Jacob,
do not be afraid,
and do not
be discouraged, Israel,
for without fail I will save you
from far away
and your descendants,
from the land
of their captivity!
Jacob will return
and have calm and quiet
with no one to frighten him.
28 And you, My servant Jacob,
do not be afraid—
this is
the LORD's declaration—
for I will be with you.
I will bring destruction
on all the nations
where I have banished you,
but I will not
bring destruction on you.
I will discipline you
with justice,
and I will by no means
leave you unpunished.

Against the Philistines (47:1-7)

47 This is the word of the LORD that came to Jeremiah the prophet about the Philistines before Pharaoh defeated Gaza. 2 This is what the LORD says:

Look, waters are rising
from the north
and becoming
an overflowing •wadi.
They will overflow the land
and everything in it,
the cities
and their inhabitants.
The people will cry out,
and every inhabitant
of the land will wail.
3 At the sound
of the stomping hooves
of his stallions,
the rumbling of his chariots,
and the clatter
of their wheels,
fathers will not turn back
for their sons,
because they will be
utterly helpless[A]
4 on account of the day
that is coming
to destroy all the Philistines,
to cut off from Tyre and Sidon
every remaining ally.
Indeed, the LORD is
about to destroy
the Philistines,
the remnant of the islands
of Caphtor.[B]
5 Baldness is coming to Gaza.
Ashkelon will become silent,
a remnant of their valley.
How long will you
gash yourself?
6 Oh, sword of the LORD!
How long will you be restless?
Go back to your sheath;
be still; be silent!
7 How can it[C] rest
when the LORD has given it
a command?
He has assigned it
against Ashkelon
and the shore of the sea.

Against the Moabites (48:1-47)

48 About Moab, this is what the LORD of •Hosts, the God of Israel, says:

Woe to Nebo, because it is
about to be destroyed;
Kiriathaim will be
put to shame; it will be
taken captive.
The fortress will be
put to shame and dismayed!
2 There is no longer praise
for Moab;
they plan harm against her
in Heshbon:
Come, let's cut her off
from nationhood.
Also, Madmen,[D] you will
be silenced;
the sword will pursue you.
3 A voice cries out
from Horonaim,
"devastation
and great disaster!"
4 Moab will be shattered;
her little ones will cry out.

[A]**47:3** Lit *because of laziness of hands* [B]**47:4** Probably Crete [C]**47:7** LXX, Vg; MT reads *you* [D]**48:2** A city in Moab

5 For on the Ascent to Luhith
they will be
weeping continually,[A]
and on the descent
to Horonaim
will be heard cries of distress
over the destruction:
6 Flee! Save your lives!
Be like a juniper bush[B]
in the wilderness.
7 Because you trust
in your works[C]
and treasures,
you will be captured also.
Chemosh will go into exile
with his priests and officials.
8 The destroyer will move
against every town;
not one town will escape.
The valley will perish,
and the plain
will be annihilated,
as the LORD has said.
9 Make Moab a salt marsh,[D]
for she will run away;[E]
her towns will become
a desolation,
without inhabitant.
10 The one who does
the LORD's business
deceitfully[F] is cursed,
and the one who withholds
his sword from bloodshed
is cursed.
11 Moab has been left quiet
since his youth,
settled like wine on its dregs.
He hasn't been poured
from one container
to another
or gone into exile.
So his taste has remained
the same,
and his aroma
hasn't changed.
12 Therefore look, the days
are coming—
this is
the LORD's declaration—
when I will send those to him,
who will pour him out.
They will empty
his containers
and smash his jars.
13 Moab will be put to shame
because of Chemosh,
just as the house of Israel was
put to shame
because of Bethel
that they trusted in.
14 How can you say,
"We are warriors—
mighty men ready for battle"?
15 The destroyer of Moab
and its towns
has come up,[G]
and the best of its young men
have gone down to slaughter.
This is
the King's declaration;
•Yahweh of Hosts is
His name.
16 Moab's calamity is near
at hand;
his disaster is rushing swiftly.
17 Mourn for him, all
you surrounding nations,
everyone who knows
his name.
Say: How the mighty scepter
is shattered,
the glorious staff!
18 Come down from glory;
sit on parched ground,
resident of the daughter
of Dibon,
for the destroyer of Moab
has come against you;
he has destroyed
your fortresses.
19 Stand by the highway
and look,
resident of Aroer!
Ask him who is fleeing or her
who is escaping:
What happened?
20 Moab is put to shame,
indeed dismayed.
Wail and cry out!
Declare by the Arnon
that Moab is destroyed.

21 "Judgment has come to the land
of the plateau—to Holon, Jahzah,
Mephaath, 22 Dibon, Nebo, Beth-dib-
lathaim, 23 Kiriathaim, Beth-gamul,
Beth-meon, 24 Kerioth, Bozrah, and
all the towns of the land of Moab,

[A]48:5 Lit *Luhith, weeping goes up with weeping* [B]48:6 Or *like Aroer*; Is 17:2; Jr 48:19 [C]48:7 LXX reads *strongholds* [D]48:9 LXX reads *a sign*; Vg reads *a flower*; Syr, Tg read *a crown* [E]48:9 Hb obscure [F]48:10 Or *negligently* [G]48:15 Or *Moab is destroyed; he has come up against its city*

only to the anti-Babylonian oracles. Throughout the chapter, names of a several cities that remain unidentified appear. In short, Moab was bound for destruction, devastation, and disaster from the Lord because of its sins of pride and idolatrous worship of Chemosh.

48:1-5 Nebo in this reference is a Moabite city, not the mountain (v. 22; Nm 32:38; Is 15:2). Complete **devastation** is indicated by the poetic use of merisms or opposites to indicate the entirety of something. **Weeping** and **distress** are predicted in the land, both **on the Ascent to Luhith** and **on the descent to Horonaim** (cp. Is 15:5). Both the valley and the plain—i.e., everywhere—would be laid waste.

48:6-8 Moab's sin was uncovered: The nation had trusted itself and its own strength. By the pronouncement of exile for Moab and its god **Chemosh**, the oracle shows that Moab actually had no strength. Chemosh together with the cult priests would be taken into captivity by **the destroyer**. Chemosh was a god (probably an astral deity) who could not save even himself, let alone his devotees, the people of Chemosh (v. 46).

48:9-12 After Moab's devastation, her land would be rendered useless and infertile by means of the sowing of **salt**. It appears that Babylon was the agent of destruction who must complete the task assigned by the Lord. Moab became complacent because it had not experienced exile or been "shaken up" (**poured from one container to another**). At the Lord's initiative, men would come against Moab, who would **pour him out . . . [and] empty his containers and smash his jars**.

48:13 An identical metaphor was used, through Jeremiah's sign-act (19:10-11), to communicate to Judah its shattering without any hope of being mended. Moab would realize that it had been deceived by its trust in **Chemosh**, who could not save any more than **Bethel** (either a bull god or a place of idol worship in Israel) could save Israel.

48:15 The Lord directly asserted His sovereignty shortly in the events to surround Moab (cp. 46:18).

48:18 Daughter of Dibon metaphorically represents the nation of Moab (cp. "Daughter Egypt," 46:11,19,24; "daughter of my people," 14:7; "Daughter Zion," 6:23). The feminine figure is weak and vulnerable. She realized the exile would shortly come upon her and acted as a figure of mourning and lament, consistent

those far and near. 25 Moab's •horn is
chopped off; his arm is shattered."
This is
the LORD's declaration.
26 "Make him drunk, because he
has exalted himself against the LORD.
Moab will wallow in his own vomit,
and he will also become a laughingstock. 27 Wasn't Israel a laughingstock to you? Was he ever found
among thieves? For whenever you
speak of him you shake your head."

28 Abandon the towns!
Live in the cliffs,
residents of Moab!
Be like a dove
that nests inside the mouth
of a cave.

29 We have heard
of Moab's pride,
great pride, indeed—
his insolence, arrogance,
pride,
and haughty heart.
30 I know his outburst.
This is
the LORD's declaration.
It is empty.
His boast is empty.
31 Therefore, I will wail
over Moab.
I will cry out for Moab,
all of it;
he will moan for the men
of Kir-heres.
32 I will weep for you,
vine of Sibmah,
with more than the weeping
for Jazer.
Your tendrils have extended
to the sea;
they have reached to the sea
and to Jazer.[A]
The destroyer has fallen
on your summer fruit
and grape harvest.
33 Joy and celebration are taken
from the fertile field
and from the land of Moab.
I have stopped
the flow of wine
from the winepresses;
no one will tread with shouts
of joy.
The shouting is not a shout
of joy.

34 "There is a cry from Heshbon to
Elealeh; they raise their voices as far
as Jahaz—from Zoar to Horonaim
and Eglath-shelishiyah—because
even the waters of Nimrim have
become desolate. 35 In Moab, I will
stop"—this is the LORD's declaration—"the one who offers sacrifices on the •high place and burns
incense to his gods. 36 Therefore, My
heart moans like flutes for Moab,
and My heart moans like flutes for
the people of Kir-heres. And therefore, the wealth he has gained has
perished. 37 Indeed, every head is
bald and every beard clipped; on
every hand is a gash and •sack-
cloth around the waist. 38 On all the
rooftops of Moab and in her public
squares, everyone is mourning because I have shattered Moab like a
jar no one wants." This is the LORD's
declaration. 39 "How broken it is!
They wail! How Moab has turned
his back! He is ashamed. Moab will
become a laughingstock and a shock
to all those around him."
40 For this is what the LORD says:

He will swoop down
like an eagle
and spread his wings
against Moab.
41 The towns
have[B] been captured,
and the strongholds seized.
In that day the heart
of Moab's warriors
will be like the heart
of a woman
with contractions.
42 Moab will be destroyed
as a people
because he has
exalted himself
against the LORD.
43 Panic, pit, and trap
await you, resident of Moab.
This is
the LORD's declaration.
44 He who flees from the panic
will fall in the pit,
and he who climbs
from the pit
will be captured in the trap,
for I will bring against Moab

[A]48:32 Some Hb mss read *reached as far as Jazer*
[B]48:41 Or *Kerioth has*

with female mourners. In grief, she sat **on parched ground**, lamenting the destruction of her nation and its **fortresses**, waiting to be led away into captivity.

48:21-27 A string of Moabite cities is mentioned, but not all are identified. **Horn** and **arm** symbolize power, and the number of destroyed cities indicates that Moab had been completely sapped of all her strength. The Lord had compelled Moab to drink the cup of God's wrath until the nation was so **drunk** it became an object of scorn (**laughingstock**), even as the Lord had previously scorned Israel (cp. 25:15-16,27-29). In this punishment, there seems to be a reminder of the terms of the Abrahamic covenant (Gn 12:3).

48:28-29 Moab's chief sin is reiterated and expanded by means of several synonyms (cp. Is 16:6): **insolence** (Hb *govahh*, "pride, arrogance"; literally "height"), **arrogance** (Hb *ga'awah*, "rising up, haughtiness"; cp. Pr 29:23), **pride** (Hb *ga'on*; cp. Pr 16:18), and a **haughty** [Hb *rum*; cp. Pr 21:4; Is 2:11, 17] **heart**.

48:32-33 All agricultural prosperity and fertility (as indicated by the **vine** metaphor) would disappear from Moab by divine initiative (cp. Is 16:8-9). The **shouts of joy** normally accompanying harvest festivals when the grapes were trodden in the winepress had disappeared. There was indeed **shouting . . . not a shout of joy** but rather the cries as of wailing or of the enemy's victory, variously interpreted by scholars.

48:34-37 Some commentators interpret this section as Jeremiah's personal lament over Moab, but there are several indications that this entire speech is the Lord's (vv. 35,38,40,43-44,47). By conducting what is essentially a legal prosecution, indictment, execution, and national funeral (**flutes** were normally used at funerals and indicated mourning, as did the **bald head**, **clipped beard**, **gash**, and **sackcloth**) in poetic language, the Lord expressed His sorrow over Moab's sins of pride and idolatry, which had drawn down divine punishment.

48:38-39 The utter shattering of the nation is lamentable. God does not rejoice in destruction for its own sake. The same metaphor of devastation and shattering is used of King Jehoiachin (22:28).

48:40-41 The Lord (or the invaders) would attack Moab **like an eagle**. Moab's **warriors** would experience the same dread as the men of Philistia (47:3) and the same dread of impending pain as **a woman with**

the year of their punishment.
This is
the LORD's declaration.
45 Those who flee
will stand exhausted
in Heshbon's shadow
because fire has come out
from Heshbon
and a flame
from within Sihon.
It will devour
Moab's forehead
and the skull
of the noisemakers.
46 Woe to you, Moab!
The people of Chemosh
have perished
because your sons have been
taken captive
and your daughters have gone
into captivity.
47 Yet, I will restore
the fortunes[A] of Moab
in the last days.
This is
the LORD's declaration.
The judgment on Moab
ends here.

Against the Ammonites (49:1-6)

49 About the Ammonites, this is what the LORD says:

Does Israel have no sons?
Is he without an heir?
Why then has •Milcom[B,C]
dispossessed Gad
and his people settled
in their cities?
2 Therefore look, the days
are coming—
this is
the LORD's declaration—
when I will make the shout
of battle heard
against Rabbah
of the Ammonites.
It will become
a desolate mound,
and its villages will be
burned down.
Israel will dispossess
their dispossessors,
says the LORD.
3 Wail, Heshbon, for Ai
is devastated;
cry out,
daughters of Rabbah!
Clothe yourselves
with •sackcloth,
and lament;
run back and forth
within your walls,[D]
because Milcom will go
into exile
together with his priests
and officials.
4 Why do you brag
about your valleys,
your flowing valley,[E]
you faithless daughter?
You who trust
in your treasures
and boast,
"Who can attack me?"
5 Look, I am about
to bring terror on you—
this is
the declaration of
the Lord GOD of •Hosts—
from all those
around you.
You will be banished,
each man headlong,
with no one to gather up
the fugitives.
6 But after that, I will restore
the fortunes[A]
of the Ammonites.
This is
the LORD's declaration.

Against the Edomites (49:7-22)

7 About Edom, this is what the LORD of Hosts says:

Is there no longer wisdom
in Teman?[F]
Has counsel perished
from the prudent?
Has their wisdom
rotted away?
8 Run! Turn back! Lie low,
residents of Dedan,
for I will bring
Esau's calamity on him
at the time I punish him.
9 If grape harvesters
came to you,
wouldn't they leave
some gleanings?

contractions, a common metaphor for describing the people's reaction to an impending, inescapable fate (cp. 49:22).

48:43-47 Anywhere they might turn, their **punishment** followed them, expressed as **panic, pit, and trap**. Surprisingly, the Lord ended on a note of hope and restoration after exile.

49:1 Two rhetorical questions (the answer to both of which is "no") indicate tensions between the two nations over land ownership, which had existed since the time of the judges in Israel. **Milcom** (or Molech), as the national god, represents the **Ammonites**, who had taken over some land belonging to the tribe of **Gad**, filling the vacuum in the region left by the collapse of the northern kingdom of Israel.

49:2 **Rabbah** was Ammon's capital, and **Heshbon** and **Ai** were both Ammonite cities.

Land could easily be lost or seized with the change of power in a region. As Israel was dispossessed by Ammon, so God would shape the power politics so **their dispossessors** would themselves be dispossessed.

49:3 Wailing, lamentation, **sackcloth**, and running **back and forth** as sheep in their pens all have to do with mourning or desperation.

49:4 Ammon's own resources gave it relative independence from the dominant empires, allying itself with one or another nation when convenient or rebelling at will.

49:5 God solemnly declared that Ammon's days of national boasting were over. Its people would be **banished.** This particular oracle was likely fulfilled when Nebuchadnezzar punished Ammon for its complicity in the assassination of Gedaliah by Ishmael (40:14; 41:10).

49:6 Just as authoritatively, Yahweh declared the reversal—at His pleasure—of Ammon's fate, from exile to restoration.

49:7-11 The oracle against **Edom** (interchangeable with Esau; cp. Gn 25:30) is the lengthiest in chapter 49. Some sections parallel material in Obadiah. Edom was traditionally known as a place of **wisdom**. Unlike **harvesters** or **thieves** who only take what they want, God would take everything (**strip Esau bare**), devastating the nation so that they would be unable even to protect those weak and vulnerable among them (i.e., the **widows** and **fatherless**).

[A]**48:47; 49:6** Or *will end the captivity* [B]**49:1** LXX, Syr, Vg; MT reads *Malkam* [C]**49:1** = Molech
[D]**49:3** Or *sheep pens* [E]**49:4** Or *about your strength, your ebbing strength* [F]**49:7** = a region or city in Edom

49:12-16 They and other nations who had been caught up in the violence and destruction of regional geopolitical power plays were forced to **drink the cup** of punishment.

Edom's sin consisted of a **presumptuous** [Hb *zadon*, "pride, haughtiness"; cp. 50:31-32; Pr 11:2; 13:10; Ob 3] **heart**. When God came against them, there would be no hiding, not even in the **clefts of the rock** or high on a **mountain summit**, geographical features pervasive in rocky, mountainous Edom.

49:17-22 Edom's devastation is cast metaphorically by three threatening images: **Sodom and Gomorrah** and their well-known fate; a ravaging **lion**, whom no leader (**shepherd**) can withstand; and an **eagle swooping down** to capture its prey. The force coming against Edom would make even its **warriors** fainthearted.

49:23-25 Hamath and Arpad are cities in Syria, which, along with **Damascus**, represent the country of Syria in this oracle (cp. 2Kg 18:34; 19:13; Is 10:9; 36:19; 37:13). **The sea** probably refers figuratively to the mythical, cosmic image of destructive chaos, as the sea was believed to harbor Leviathan, the great sea monster (cp. Jb 41; Pss 74:13-14; 77:16; 104:26; 114:3,5). **Panic . . . distress, and labor pains** were in store for the city, which was once joyful.

49:26-27 Damascus would be reduced to complete defenselessness as all her **young men** and **warriors** are killed and her **wall** and fortresses are incinerated. No hope is in store for the city.

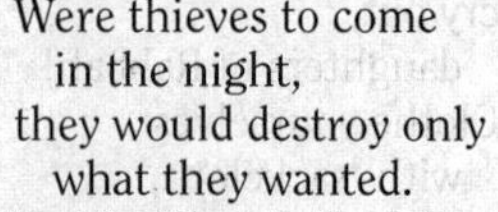

Were thieves to come
in the night,
they would destroy only
what they wanted.
10 But I will strip Esau bare;
I will uncover
his secret places.
He will try to hide himself,
but he will be unable.
His descendants
will be destroyed
along with his relatives
and neighbors.
He will exist no longer.
11 Abandon your fatherless;
I will preserve them;
let your widows trust in Me.

12 "For this is what the LORD says:
If those who do not deserve to drink
the cup must drink it, can you possibly remain unpunished? You will
not remain unpunished, for you
must drink it too. 13 For by Myself I
have sworn"—this is the LORD's declaration—"Bozrah[A] will become a
desolation, a disgrace, a ruin, and a
curse, and all her cities will become
ruins forever."

14 I have heard a message
from the LORD;
a messenger has been sent
among the nations:
Assemble yourselves to come
against her.
Rise up for war!

15 Look, I will certainly
make you insignificant
among the nations,
despised among humanity.
16 As to the terror you cause,[B]
your presumptuous heart
has deceived you.
You who live in the clefts
of the rock,[C]
you who occupy
the mountain summit,
though you elevate your nest
like the eagle,
even from there I will bring
you down.
This is
the LORD's declaration.

17 "Edom will become a desolation.
Everyone who passes by her will be
horrified and scoff because of all her
wounds. 18 As when Sodom and Gomorrah were overthrown along with
their neighbors," says the LORD, "no
one will live there; no human being
will even stay in it as a temporary
resident.

19 "Look, it will be like a lion coming from the thickets[D] of the Jordan
to the watered grazing land. Indeed,
I will chase Edom away from her
land in a flash. I will appoint whoever is chosen for her. For who is like
Me? Who will summon Me? Who is
the shepherd who can stand against
Me?"

20 Therefore, hear the plans that
the LORD has drawn up against
Edom and the strategies He has devised against the people of Teman:
The flock's little lambs will certainly
be dragged away, and their grazing
land will be made desolate because
of them. 21 At the sound of their fall
the earth will quake; the sound of
her cry will be heard at the •Red Sea.
22 Look! It will be like an eagle soaring upward, then swooping down
and spreading its wings over Bozrah. In that day the hearts of Edom's
warriors will be like the heart of a
woman with contractions.

Against Damascus (49:23-27)

23 About Damascus:

Hamath and Arpad are
put to shame,
for they have heard
a bad report
and are agitated;
in the sea there is anxiety
that cannot be calmed.
24 Damascus has become weak;
she has turned to run;
panic has gripped her.
Distress and labor pains
have seized her
like a woman in labor.
25 How can the city of praise
not be abandoned,
the town that brings Me joy?
26 Therefore, her young
men will fall
in her public squares;
all the warriors will perish
in that day.
This is the declaration of
the LORD of Hosts.

[A] **49:13** = Edom's capital [B] **49:16** Lit *Your horror* [C] **49:16** = Petra [D] **49:19** Lit *pride*

>WORD|*study*

49:32 Two different words for "side" in this verse form a kind of wordplay. One is *'ēber* (Hb, "side," usually in a geographical sense). The other is *pē'ah* (Hb, "side, edge" in a physical sense), which refers to the side of the head (i.e., sideburns, or edge of the beard). As the idolatrous people shaved their temples (Hb, *'ēber*), God would bring calamity upon their borders (Hb, *pē'ah*).

27 I will set fire to the wall
of Damascus;
it will consume
Ben-hadad's citadels.

Against Kedar and Hazor (49:28-33)

28 About Kedar and the kingdoms
of Hazor, which Nebuchadnezzar,
Babylon's king, defeated, this is
what the LORD says:

Rise up, go against Kedar,
and destroy the people
of the east!
29 They will take their tents
and their flocks
along with their tent curtains
and all their equipment.
They will take their camels
for themselves.
They will call out to them:
Terror is on every side!
30 Run! Escape quickly! Lie low,
residents of Hazor—
this is
the LORD's declaration—
for Nebuchadnezzar
king of Babylon
has drawn up a plan
against you;
he has devised a strategy
against you.
31 Rise up, go up against
a nation at ease,
one living in security.
This is
the LORD's declaration.
They have no doors, not even
a gate bar;
they live alone.
32 Their camels will
become plunder,
and their massive herds
of cattle will become spoil.
I will scatter them to the wind
in every direction,
those who shave
their temples;
I will bring calamity on them
across all their borders.
This is
the LORD's declaration.
33 Hazor will become
a jackals' den,
a desolation forever.
No one will live there;
no human being
will even stay in it as a
temporary resident.

Against Elam (49:34-39)

34 This is the word of the LORD that
came to Jeremiah the prophet about
Elam[A] at the beginning of the reign
of Zedekiah king of Judah. 35 This is
what the LORD of Hosts says:

I am about to shatter
Elam's bow,
the source[B] of their might.
36 I will bring the four winds
against Elam
from the four corners
of the heavens,
and I will scatter them
to all these winds.
There will not be a nation
to which
Elam's banished ones
will not go.
37 I will devastate Elam
before their enemies,
before those who want to take
their lives.
I will bring disaster on them,
My burning anger.
This is
the LORD's declaration.
I will send the sword
after them
until I finish them off.
38 I will set My throne in Elam,
and I will destroy the king
and officials from there.
This is
the LORD's declaration.

[A]**49:34** = modern Iran [B]**49:35** Lit *first*

49:28-31 Kedar and **Hazor** were nomadic peoples living in the Arabian Desert (cp. Ps 120:5; Sg 1:5; Ezk 27:21). The Kedarites were descendants of Kedar, the son of Ishmael, son of Abraham and Hagar (Gn 25:13; 1Ch 1:29). Despite living out in the open, they are described as **a nation at ease, one living in security**.

49:32-33 Jeremiah regarded Kedar and Hazor as pagan nations, describing their people as **those who shave their temples**, a pagan practice forbidden to Jews (cp. 2:10; Lv 19:27; Is 21:16-17). Kedar received specific warning of Nebuchadnezzar's coming, but the Lord promised to **scatter** them with no assurance of future hope.

49:34-39 Along the northeastern shores of the Persian Gulf, **Elam** became the Persian province in which Susa, the capital city, was located (cp. Ezr 4:9; Dn 8:2). The region is now the southwestern part of Iran. The oracle was given at the beginning of Zedekiah's reign (ca 597 B.C.). Although no specific reason is given for its destruction by the Lord, Elam had been an enemy of Israel for some time and had allied itself in the past with Assyria against Judah. All of the first person pronouns indicate that the Lord was the chief agent and architect of their destruction. In the end, however, better days awaited Elam, after the true King had set up His **throne** among the people.

50:1–51:58 This unit of prophecies is part of a document given to Seraiah, the brother of Baruch, to take with him to **Babylon** (51:61-64). The message against Babylon was directed to the Judean exiles. Seraiah served as both a political and religious delegate for Zedekiah, ironically carrying two conflicting messages—a tribute of political submission and a prophecy of destruction.

50:1-3 A word came to the nations who had just been doomed. The one who came against them as a destroying aggressor would herself be destroyed by a **nation from the north**. Babylon would be punished for her own sins, including idolatry and arrogance against God. **Bel** was a title meaning "lord" or "master" (51:44; Is 46:1), which came to be associated with **Marduk** (or Merodach). Babylon's deities had failed to protect the empire, and its punishment signaled hope for the exiles' return.

50:4-7 The **Israelites and Judeans** would return home, **weeping**, seeking the Lord, and asking about their homeland. In addition to their restoration to the land, the new and **everlasting covenant that will never be forgotten** (promised in the Book of Consolation) would be implemented. In pastoral metaphors, the people of Israel are described as **lost sheep**, whose **shepherds** (leaders) have misled them, leaving them vulnerable to any who desired to devour them. The Lord portrays Himself as their **resting place** and as their **righteous grazing land**, from whence (i.e., whom) they had strayed.

50:7-10 The tone of the **adversaries** (Babylonians) seems somewhat self-serving, shifting blame away from themselves for the devastation wrought on Judah and citing instead Judah's sins **against the Lord**. Now that the adversaries were destroyed, Judah was urged to **be like the rams that lead the flock** (i.e., to take initiative for strong leadership), to lead the people in abandoning the doomed Babylon.

50:11-15 **Like a young cow** and **like stallions**, Babylon has acted according to her own appetites in plundering and destroying. However, a day of accountability was set for her: Babylon would pay for her own sins, for she had also **sinned against the Lord**. She would be humiliated and shamed for the wanton acts she had perpetrated: **This is the Lord's vengeance . . . as she has done, do the same to her**. This passage illustrates God's sovereignty and providence versus human freedom. Babylon was allowed to destroy and punish other sinful nations, as it served Yahweh's divine purposes, but she did these things

39 In the last days,
I will restore the fortunes[A]
of Elam.
This is
the LORD's declaration.

Against Babylon (50:1–51:58)

50 The word the LORD spoke about Babylon, the land of the Chaldeans, through Jeremiah the prophet:

2 Announce to the nations;
proclaim and raise up
a signal flag;
proclaim, and hide nothing.
Say: Babylon is captured;
Bel is put to shame;
Marduk is devastated;
her idols are put to shame;
her false gods, devastated.
3 For a nation from the north
will come against her;
it will make
her land desolate.
No one will be living in it—
both man and beast
will escape.[B]
4 In those days
and at that time—
this is
the LORD's declaration—
the Israelites and Judeans
will come together,
weeping as they come,
and will seek the LORD
their God.
5 They will ask about •Zion,
turning their faces
to this road.
They will come
and join themselves[C]
to the LORD
in an everlasting covenant
that will never be forgotten.

6 My people are lost sheep;
their shepherds have
led them astray,
guiding them the wrong way
in the mountains.
They have wandered
from mountain to hill;
they have forgotten
their resting place.
7 All who found them
devoured them.
Their adversaries said,
"We're not •guilty;
instead, they have sinned
against the LORD,
their righteous grazing land,
the hope of their ancestors,
the LORD."

8 Escape from Babylon;
depart from
the Chaldeans' land.
Be like the rams that lead
the flock.
9 For I will soon stir up
and bring against Babylon
an assembly of great nations
from the north country.
They will line up
in battle formation
against her;
from there she
will be captured.
Their arrows will be like those
of a skilled[D] warrior
who does not return
empty-handed.
10 The Chaldeans will
become plunder;
all Babylon's plunderers
will be fully satisfied.
This is
the LORD's declaration.
11 Because you rejoice,
because you sing
in triumph—
you who plundered
My inheritance—
because you frolic
like a young cow
treading grain
and neigh like stallions,
12 your mother will be
utterly humiliated;
she who bore you will be
put to shame.
Look! She will lag behind
all[E] the nations—
a dry land, a wilderness,
an •Arabah.
13 Because of the LORD's wrath,
she will not be inhabited;
she will become a desolation,
every bit of her.
Everyone who passes
through Babylon
will be horrified

[A]49:39 Or *will end the captivity* [B]50:3 Lit *escape; they will walk* [C]50:5 LXX; MT reads *Come and join yourselves* [D]50:9 Some Hb mss, LXX, Syr; other Hb mss read *bereaving* [E]50:12 Lit *Look! The last of*

and scoff because of
all her wounds.
14 Line up in battle formation
around Babylon,
all you archers!
Shoot at her! Do not spare
an arrow,
for she has sinned
against the LORD.
15 Raise a war cry against her
on every side!
She has thrown up her hands
in surrender;
her defense towers
have fallen;
her walls are demolished.
Since this is
the LORD's vengeance,
take out your vengeance
on her;
as she has done, do the same
to her.
16 Cut off the sower
from Babylon
as well as him who wields
the sickle at harvest time.
Because of
the oppressor's sword,
each will turn
to his own people,
each will flee to his own land.

17 Israel is a stray lamb,
chased by lions.
The first who devoured him
was the king of Assyria;
the last one who crushed
his bones
was Nebuchadnezzar
king of Babylon.

18 Therefore, this is what the LORD
of •Hosts, the God of Israel, says: "I
am about to punish the king of Babylon and his land just as I punished
the king of Assyria.

19 I will return Israel
to his grazing land,
and he will feed on Carmel
and Bashan;
he will be satisfied
in the hill country of Ephraim
and of Gilead.
20 In those days
and at that time—
this is
the LORD's declaration—
one will search
for Israel's guilt,
but there will be none,
and for Judah's sins,
but they will not be found,
for I will forgive those I leave
as a remnant.

21 "Go against the land
of Merathaim,
and against those living
in Pekod.
Put them to the sword;
•completely destroy them—
this is
the LORD's declaration—
do everything I have
commanded you.
22 The sound of war is
in the land—
a great destruction.
23 How the hammer
of the whole earth
is cut down and smashed!
What a horror Babylon
has become
among the nations!
24 Babylon, I laid a trap for you,
and you were caught,
but you did not even know it.
You were found and captured
because you fought
against the LORD.
25 The LORD opened His armory
and brought out His weapons
of wrath,
because it is a task
of the Lord GOD of Hosts
in the land of the Chaldeans.
26 Come against her from
the most distant places.[A]
Open her granaries;
pile her up like mounds
of grain
and completely destroy her.
Leave her no survivors.
27 Put all her young bulls
to the sword;
let them go down
to the slaughter.
Woe to them,
because their day has come,
the time of their punishment.

28 "There is a voice of fugitives
and those who escape
from the land of Babylon
announcing in Zion

freely according to her own imperialistic agenda; therefore, her punishment was just.

50:17-19 Again in pastoral metaphors, Israel (used to denote both kingdoms) is described as a **stray lamb**, while its oppressors (first **Assyria**, then **Nebuchadnezzar**) are **lions**. God, the protective shepherd, would therefore treat one aggressor as the other. Babylon would be treated by Yahweh the same as Assyria, while Israel would be shepherded in the rich, lush grazing lands of its own country: **Carmel**, **Bashan**, **Ephraim**, and **Gilead**.

50:20 Israel not only would be nurtured physically but also would be restored spiritually in a way similar to David's description of the Lord as shepherd (Ps 23:1-3). **Israel's guilt** and **Judah's sins** would be forgiven.

50:24-25 Babylon's punishment would continue, as war is declared against her, not only by the northern aggressor described above but also by the Lord Himself: **I laid a trap for you, and you were caught . . . . you fought against the LORD**. Babylon's fight **against the LORD** refers to its destruction of God's people and the Jerusalem temple (cp. v. 28). Having **opened His armory**, God is now Babylon's foe.

50:27 The reference to **all her young bulls** probably denotes male warriors.

[A] **50:26** Lit *from the end*

50:29-32 Three times Babylon is described as **arrogant** (Hb *zadon*, "swollen with pride"; cp. 49:6) or acting **arrogantly** (Hb *zud*, "act insolently, proudly, presumptuously"), emphasizing the logical relationship between the nation's attitude toward God and its manifestation in the wholesale plunder of His temple and its holy articles (52:1-23), for which He now took "vengeance" (50:28). The Babylonian King Belshazzar further desecrated these articles when he ordered the gold and silver vessels to be used as drinking cups at his feast, during which he, his nobles, and his entourage worshiped their idols (Dn 5:1-4).

50:33-34 The idea of the Kinsman-Redeemer and His work on behalf of the oppressed Israel are evident. The LORD Himself was the **Redeemer** of the **Israelites and Judeans**.

50:35-38 These verses are sometimes called the "Song of the Sword" (cp. "Song of the Hammer," 51:20-23). As part of His avenging work, the Lord had set **a sword** over the political leaders, wise men, diviners, **warriors**, **horses and chariots**, mercenaries, and **treasuries** of Babylon, a **land of carved images** (i.e., idolatry).

50:39-40 He predicted the desertion of superstitious Babylon by all living things and compared its future to **Sodom and Gomorrah**, which had become a byword for utter judgment and destruction.

50:41-43 Portrayed here are the northern aggressor(s) and Babylon's distress, which is likened to **a woman in labor**, paralleling and reversing the fate awaiting Judah via Babylon's agency (6:22-24). The tables will be turned on Babylon.

the vengeance of the LORD
our God,
the vengeance for His temple.
29 Summon the archers
to Babylon,
all who string the bow;
camp all around her;
let none escape.
Repay her according to
her deeds;
just as she has done,
do the same to her,
for she has acted arrogantly
against the LORD,
against the Holy One of Israel.
30 Therefore, her young men
will fall
in her public squares;
all the warriors will perish
in that day.
This is
the LORD's declaration.
31 Look, I am against you,
you arrogant one—
this is the declaration of
the Lord GOD of Hosts—
because your day has come,
the time when I will
punish you.
32 The arrogant will stumble
and fall
with no one to pick him up.
I will set fire to his cities,
and it will
consume everything
around him."

33 This is what the LORD of Hosts
says:

Israelites and Judeans alike
have been oppressed.
All their captors
hold them fast;
they refuse to release them.
34 Their Redeemer is strong;
•Yahweh of Hosts is His name.
He will fervently
plead their case
so that He might bring rest
to the earth
but turmoil to those who live
in Babylon.
35 A sword is
over the Chaldeans—
this is
the LORD's declaration—
against those who live
in Babylon,
against her officials,
and against her sages.
36 A sword is
against the diviners,
and they will act foolishly.
A sword is
against her heroic warriors,
and they will be terrified.
37 A sword is against his horses
and chariots
and against all the foreigners
among them,
and they will be like women.
A sword is
against her treasuries,
and they will be plundered.
38 A drought will come
on her waters,
and they will be dried up.
For it is a land
of carved images,
and they go mad because of
terrifying things.[A]
39 Therefore, desert creatures[B]
will live with hyenas,
and ostriches will also live
in her.
It will never again
be inhabited
or lived in
through all generations.
40 Just as God
demolished Sodom
and Gomorrah
and their neighboring
towns—
this is
the LORD's declaration—
so no one will live there;
no human being
will even stay in it
as a temporary resident.

41 Look! A people comes
from the north.
A great nation
and many kings will be
stirred up
from the remote regions
of the earth.
42 They grasp bow and javelin.
They are cruel and show
no mercy.
Their voice roars like the sea,
and they ride on horses,

[A]**50:38** Or *of dreaded gods* [B]**50:39** Or *desert demons*

>WORD|*study*

51:1 Stir up (Hb *ʿur*, "arouse, wake from sleep") has the sense of "inciting or provoking" something to action. **Destructive** [Hb *shachat*, "destroyer"; cp. Ex 12:23; 2Sm 24:16] **wind** (Hb *ruach*, "breath, spirit") is a vivid metaphor for the swift, unstoppable disaster to be unleashed on Babylon.

51:2 Strangers (Hb *zur*, "turn aside"; a participle meaning "those who turn aside") acquired its meaning from the sense of turning aside from a road to be a guest in someone's home. The plural form (*zarim*) with different vowels would read *zorim* (Hb, "winnowers") from the verb "scatter" (Hb *zarah*, "winnow, disperse, sift"). The "destructive wind" of verse 1 is the same force called "strangers" in verse 2, so a wordplay is possible. "Winnowers" will be sent to Babylon, who will use the wind not only to separate wheat from chaff but to "strip her land bare" (cp. Jr 51:33; 15:7; cp. Is 41:16; Ezk 5:2).

lined up like men
in battle formation
against you, Daughter
Babylon.
43 The king of Babylon has heard
reports about them,
and his hands fall helpless.
Distress has seized him—
pain, like a woman in labor.

44 "Look, it will be like a lion coming from the thickets[A] of the Jordan
to the watered grazing land. Indeed,
I will chase Babylon[B] away from her
land in a flash. I will appoint whoever is chosen for her. For who is like
Me? Who will summon Me? Who is
the shepherd who can stand against
Me?"

45 Therefore, hear the plans that
the LORD has drawn up against
Babylon and the strategies He has
devised against the land of the Chaldeans: Certainly the flock's little
lambs will be dragged away; certainly the grazing land will be made
desolate because of them. 46 At the
sound of Babylon's conquest the
earth will quake; a cry will be heard
among the nations.

Instructions to Seraiah (51:59-64)

51 This is what the LORD says:
I am about to stir up
a destructive wind[C]
against Babylon
and against the population
of Leb-qamai.[D,E]
2 I will send strangers
to Babylon
who will scatter her and strip
her land bare,
for they will come against her

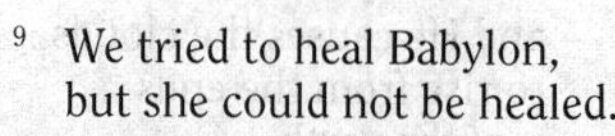

from every side in the day
of disaster.
3 Don't let the archer string
his bow;
don't let him put on[F]
his armor.
Don't spare her young men;
•completely destroy
her entire army!
4 Those who were slain
will fall in the land
of the Chaldeans,
those who were
pierced through,
in her streets.
5 For Israel and Judah are not
left widowed
by their God, the LORD
of •Hosts,
though their land is
full of •guilt
against the Holy One of Israel.

6 Leave Babylon;
save your lives, each of you!
Don't perish because of
her guilt.
For this is the time
of the LORD's vengeance—
He will pay her
what she deserves.
7 Babylon was a gold cup
in the LORD's hand,
making the whole earth
drunk.
The nations drank her wine;
therefore, the nations go mad.
8 Suddenly Babylon fell
and was shattered.
Wail for her;
get balm for her wound—
perhaps she can be healed.

9 We tried to heal Babylon,
but she could not be healed.

50:44-46 These verses parallel 49:19-22 from the prophecy against Edom. In another pastoral metaphor, the Lord is an overpowering predator (**lion**) which no **shepherd** can withstand. Babylon is a flock whose **little lambs will be dragged away,** and the flock will be scared away from its pasture, which will subsequently become a wasteland.

51:1-2 The rejoicing over Babylon's doom continues. Throughout this chapter, the ironies of Babylon's reversed circumstances—as brought about by the Lord—are cause for exultation. **Leb-qamai** (Hb *lēv*, "heart"; *qum*, "one who rises up as opposition"; cp. Gn 4:8) refers to rebellious Babylon.

51:6-9 At the coming of the Lord's **vengeance**, the exiles, and perhaps other captive nations, were urged to **leave Babylon** to avoid suffering her fate along with her. **She could not be healed**, and her "life thread is cut" (i.e., her time had come to be cut off). The phrase **Babylon was a gold cup in the LORD's hand** means that Babylon was used by God to mete out to **the nations** their portion of punishment (**her wine**). Suddenly, however, Babylon fell like a cup thrown down and shattered beyond repair.

[A]50:44 Lit *pride* [B]50:44 Lit *them* [C]51:1 Or *stir up the spirit of a destroyer* [D]51:1 Lit *heart of my adversaries* [E]51:1 = Chaldeans [F]51:3 Hb obscure

51:10-13 Through their return to their own land, Israel would witness God's **vindication** (Hb *tsedeqah*, "justice, righteousness") as well as God's **vengeance** [Hb *neqamah*, vv. 6,11; cp. 50:28] **for His temple**. These things would be accomplished through **the kings of the Medes**. Media was probably located in the area of northwestern Iran. After making an alliance with the Babylonians against Assyria, the Medes eventually turned against them. The reference to **many waters** may indicate Babylon's location on the Euphrates River, a waterway that allowed access to foreign traders' commercial activities (cp. Rv 18:11-19), making the city **rich in treasures**.

51:14-19 A doxology extolling the Creator's superiority over **carved** and **cast images** insists that the Lord (**Jacob's Portion**) **formed all things** in the natural order. He is the giver of life, whereas idols are breathless, **worthless**, and **a lie**.

51:20-26 The diatribe against idols is followed by the so-called "Song of the Hammer." The Medes invading from the north seem to be the referent. Formerly, Babylon was "the hammer," but Babylon had been "cut down and smashed" by a new enemy (50:23). The Lord had declared His opposition to Babylon, the **devastating** [Hb *mashchit*, "destruction," from the verb *shachath*; cp. 2 Kg 23:12-14] **mountain** who abused her power (cp. 46:18).

Consequently, rather than a dominating, overpowering mountain, Babylon would become like a burned-out volcano (**charred mountain**). Her destruction would be such that her building stones would not even be reusable.

Abandon her!
Let each of us go
to his own land,
for her judgment extends
to the sky
and reaches as far
as the clouds.

10 The LORD has brought about
our vindication;
come, let's tell in •Zion
what the LORD our God
has accomplished.

11 Sharpen the arrows!
Fill the quivers!
The LORD has put it
into the mind
of the kings of the Medes
because His plan is aimed
at Babylon
to destroy her,
for it is the LORD's vengeance,
vengeance for His temple.
12 Raise up a signal flag
against the walls of Babylon;
fortify the watch post;
set the watchmen in place;
prepare the ambush.
For the LORD has both planned
and accomplished
what He has threatened
against those who live
in Babylon.
13 You who reside
by many waters,
rich in treasures,
your end has come,
your life thread is cut.

14 The LORD of Hosts has sworn by Himself:

I will fill you up with men
as with locusts,
and they will sing
the victory song over you.

15 He made the earth
by His power,
established the world
by His wisdom,
and spread out the heavens
by His understanding.
16 When He thunders,[A]
the waters in the heavens are
in turmoil,
and He causes the clouds
to rise from the ends
of the earth.
He makes lightning
for the rain
and brings the wind
from His storehouses.

17 Everyone is stupid
and ignorant.
Every goldsmith
is put to shame
by his carved image,
for his cast images are a lie;
there is no breath in them.
18 They are worthless, a work
to be mocked.
At the time
of their punishment
they will be destroyed.
19 Jacob's Portion[B] is not
like these
because He is the One
who formed all things.
Israel is the tribe
of His inheritance;
•Yahweh of Hosts is His name.

20 You are My battle club,
My weapons of war.
With you I will smash
nations;
with you I will bring
kingdoms to ruin.
21 With you I will smash
the horse and its rider;
with you I will smash
the chariot and its rider.
22 With you I will smash man
and woman;
with you I will smash
the old man and the youth;
with you I will smash
the young man
and the young woman.
23 With you I will smash
the shepherd and his flock;
with you I will smash
the farmer and his
ox-team.[C]
With you I will smash
governors and officials.

24 "I will repay Babylon and all the residents of Chaldea for all their evil they have done in Zion before your very eyes."

This is
the LORD's declaration.

[A]**51:16** Lit *At His giving of the voice* [B]**51:19** = the LORD [C]**51:23** Lit *yoke*

>WORD|*study*

51:33 Babylon is compared to **a threshing floor** (Hb *goren*), a leveled tract of ground on which grain was trodden to break the heads of grain from the stalks and husks (cp. Is 41:15-16). Here, the threshing floor was a place sometimes used for holding court (1Kg 22:10), and here the harvest and its metaphors symbolize judgment, a theme reflected also in New Testament passages such as Mt 3:7-12 (which refers to "the coming wrath") and Rv 14:14-20 (which contains similar imagery).

25 Look, I am against you,
devastating mountain—
this is
the LORD's declaration—
you devastate the whole earth.
I will stretch out My hand
against you,
roll you down from the cliffs,
and turn you into
a charred mountain.
26 No one will be able to retrieve
a cornerstone
or a foundation stone
from you,
because you will become
desolate forever.
This is
the LORD's declaration.
27 Raise a signal flag in the land;
blow a ram's horn
among the nations;
set apart the nations
against her.
Summon kingdoms
against her—
Ararat, Minni, and Ashkenaz.
Appoint a marshal
against her;
bring up horses like a swarm[A]
of locusts.
28 Set apart the nations
for battle against her—
the kings of Media,
her governors
and all her officials,
and all the lands they rule.
29 The earth quakes
and trembles
because the LORD's intentions
against Babylon stand:
to make the land of Babylon
an uninhabited desolation.
30 Babylon's warriors have
stopped fighting;
they sit in their strongholds.
Their might is exhausted;
they have become
like women.
Babylon's homes have been
set ablaze,
her gate bars are shattered.
31 Messenger races
to meet messenger,
and herald to meet herald,
to announce to the king
of Babylon
that his city
has been captured
from end to end.
32 The fords have been seized,
the marshes set on fire,
and the soldiers are terrified.

33 For this is what the LORD of
Hosts, the God of Israel, says:

Daughter Babylon is
like a threshing floor
at the time it is trampled.
In just a little while
her harvest time will come.

34 "Nebuchadnezzar of Babylon
has devoured me;
he has crushed me.
He has set me aside
like an empty dish;
he has swallowed me
like a sea monster;
he filled his belly
with my delicacies;
he has vomited me out,"[B]
35 says the inhabitant of Zion;
"Let the violence done to me
and my family be done
to Babylon.
Let my blood be
on the inhabitants
of Chaldea,"
says Jerusalem.

36 Therefore, this is what the LORD
says:

I am about to plead your case
and take vengeance
on your behalf;
I will dry up her sea

51:27-30 There is mention once more of God's instrument, the **kings of Media**, as well as of those lands and people over whom they ruled and from whom they drew soldiers to staff their armies: the **kingdoms** of **Ararat, Minni, and Ashkenaz**, located in the areas of modern day Armenia, Turkey, Iran, and Iraq. Her fate was unavoidable because **the LORD's intentions** [Hb *machashavah*, "thought, plan"; cp. 29:11; 49:20; 50:45] **against Babylon stand**. Her **warriors** were exhausted and had **become like women**, i.e., they had become non-combatants.

51:33 The chain of destructive images and metaphors is rounded off with a harvest theme once more.

51:34-40 God is an advocate for His oppressed people. Consistent with and more explicit than 49:23 is the image of Babylon (or Nebuchadnezzar) as a devouring and ravaging **sea monster** (also possible are images of a serpent or dragon, all symbols of the power of evil). The Lord is an avenger who would transform the monster's home into a **jackals' den** (cp. Kedar and Hazor, 49:33; Zion in Lam 5:18). He would serve them lethal wine at a deadly banquet so that they would get **drunk . . . fall asleep forever and never wake up** (cp. v. 57), possibly fulfilled in Daniel 5:30-31.

[A] **51:27** Hb obscure [B] **51:34** Lit *has rinsed me off*

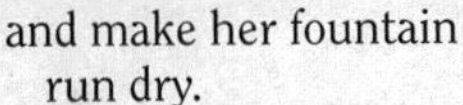

51:41-44 Sheshach is a code name for Babylon. **The sea**—the abode of the monster—had **risen over Babylon**; its powers of chaos were now a threat to her, and she would be punished for her idolatry, including her idol **Bel** and all the rest of **Babylon's carved images** (cp. vv. 47,52). Babylon's wall is mentioned twice (vv. 44, 58). Its massive, thick walls were legendary and considered virtually impregnable.

51:45-50 These verses are directed to the Jewish exiles in Babylon. The Lord assured Israel that **destroyers** from the north would assail Babylon, and He Himself would be the agent who initiated that invasion (v. 53). Israel was urged to flee the doomed city, and not panic when they heard **the report . . . in the land**, presumably of political infighting, insurrections, and revolts, which would signal Babylon's demise.

51:51-58 As they fled, the exilic community lamented as they remembered Jerusalem, their God, and the desecration of the **Lord's temple** (cp. 51:6; Ps 137). As **retribution** by God, all of Babylon's defenses would be utterly stripped from her—**warriors**, political leaders, **thick walls**, and **high gates** (Jr 51:56-58). Babylon later became a biblical symbol for an arrogant adversary of God, a greedy destroyer who was, in turn, utterly devastated, and over whose fate heaven rejoiced. The total destruction of an unnamed nation is prophesied in the book of Revelation using terms of Babylon's defeat. Similar symbolism occurs of a drinking cup, winepresses, and the cup of God's wrath (Rv 18:1–19:5).

and make her fountain
run dry.
37 Babylon will become a heap
of rubble,
a jackals' den,
a desolation and an object
of scorn,
without inhabitant.
38 They will roar together
like young lions;
they will growl like lion cubs.
39 While they are flushed
with heat, I will serve them
a feast,
and I will make them drunk
so that they revel.[A]
Then they will fall
asleep forever
and never wake up.
This is
the LORD's declaration.
40 I will bring them down
like lambs to the slaughter,
like rams together
with male goats.

41 How Sheshach
has been captured,
the praise
of the whole earth seized.
What a horror Babylon
has become
among the nations!
42 The sea has risen
over Babylon;
she is covered
with its turbulent waves.
43 Her cities have become
a desolation,
a dry and arid land,
a land where no one lives,
where no human being
passes through.
44 I will punish Bel in Babylon.
I will make him vomit
what he swallowed.
The nations will
no longer stream to him;
even Babylon's wall will fall.

45 Come out from among her,
My people!
Save your lives, each of you,
from the LORD's
burning anger.
46 May you not become cowardly
and fearful
when the report is proclaimed
in the land,
for the report will come
one year,
and then another
the next year.
There will be violence
in the land
with ruler against ruler.
47 Therefore, look, the days
are coming
when I will punish
Babylon's carved images.
Her entire land
will suffer shame,
and all her slain will lie fallen
within her.
48 Heaven and earth
and everything in them
will shout for joy
over Babylon
because the destroyers
from the north
will come against her.
This is
the LORD's declaration.
49 Babylon must fall because of
the slain of Israel,
even as the slain of all
the earth fell
because of Babylon.
50 You who have escaped
the sword,
go and do not stand still!
Remember the LORD
from far away,
and let Jerusalem come
to your mind.

51 We are ashamed
because we have
heard insults.
Humiliation covers our faces
because foreigners
have entered
the holy places
of the LORD's temple.

52 Therefore, look, the days
are coming—
this is
the LORD's declaration—
when I will punish
her carved images,
and the wounded will groan
throughout her land.
53 Even if Babylon should ascend
to the heavens

[A]51:39 LXX reads *pass out*

and fortify her tall fortresses,
destroyers will come
against her from Me.
This is
the LORD's declaration.

54 The sound of a cry
from Babylon!
The sound
of great destruction
from the land
of the Chaldeans!
55 For the LORD is going
to devastate Babylon;
He will silence
her mighty voice.
Their waves roar
like abundant waters;
the tumult
of their voice resounds,
56 for a destroyer is coming
against her,
against Babylon.
Her warriors will be captured,
their bows shattered,
for the LORD is a God
of retribution;
He will certainly repay.
57 I will make her princes
and sages drunk,
along with her governors,
officials, and warriors.
Then they will fall
asleep forever
and never wake up.
This is
the King's declaration;
Yahweh of Hosts is
His name.

58 This is what Yahweh of Hosts
says:

Babylon's thick walls will be
totally demolished,
and her high gates consumed
by fire.
The peoples will have labored
for nothing;
the nations will
exhaust themselves
only to feed the fire.

59 This is what Jeremiah the prophet commanded Seraiah son of Neriah
son of Mahseiah, the quartermaster,
when he went to Babylon with King
Zedekiah of Judah in the fourth
year of Zedekiah's reign. 60 Jeremiah
wrote on one scroll about all the disaster that would come to Babylon;
all these words were written against
Babylon.
61 Jeremiah told Seraiah, "When
you get to Babylon, see that you
read all these words aloud. 62 You
must say, 'LORD, You have threatened to cut off this place so that no
one will live in it—man or beast.
Indeed, it will remain desolate forever.' 63 When you have finished
reading this scroll, tie a stone to it
and throw it into the middle of the
Euphrates River. 64 Then say, 'In the
same way, Babylon will sink and
never rise again because of the disaster I am bringing on her. They
will grow weary.'"

The words of Jeremiah end here.

Details Concerning the Fall of Jerusalem (52:1-34)

52 Zedekiah was 21 years old
when he became king and
reigned 11 years in Jerusalem. His
mother's name was Hamutal daughter of Jeremiah; she was from Libnah. 2 Zedekiah did what was evil in
the LORD's sight just as Jehoiakim
had done. 3 Because of the LORD's
anger, it came to the point in Jerusalem and Judah that He finally
banished them from His presence.
Nevertheless, Zedekiah rebelled
against the king of Babylon.
4 In the ninth year of Zedekiah's
reign, on the tenth day of the tenth
month, King Nebuchadnezzar of
Babylon advanced against Jerusalem
with his entire army. They laid siege
to the city and built a siege wall all
around it. 5 The city was under siege
until King Zedekiah's eleventh year.
6 By the ninth day of the fourth
month the famine was so severe in
the city that the people of the land
had no food. 7 Then the city was broken into, and all the warriors fled.
They left the city by night by way
of the gate between the two walls
near the king's garden, though the
Chaldeans surrounded the city. They
made their way along the route to
the •Arabah. 8 The Chaldean army
pursued the king and overtook Zedekiah in the plains of Jericho. Zedekiah's entire army was scattered
from him. 9 The Chaldeans seized
the king and brought him to the
king of Babylon at Riblah in the land

51:59-62 In these final recorded words of Jeremiah, **Seraiah** brother of Baruch was commissioned by the prophet to take to Babylon on a **scroll . . . all the disaster that would come to Babylon**. The message probably consisted of the oracles against Babylon in chapters 50–51.

51:63-64 Jeremiah instructed Seraiah to perform a sign-act in Babylon, similar to other sign-acts that Jeremiah had performed in Jerusalem (chaps. 19, 27). In carrying out this sign-act, there is again a parallel with Revelation. After the prophecy of Babylon's doom, a "mighty angel picked up a stone . . . and threw it into the sea, saying: In this way, Babylon the great city will be thrown down violently and never be found again" (Rv 18:21). At the same time that Seraiah's tribute acknowledged the lordship of Nebuchadnezzar, the prophecy he carries powerfully affirms the lordship of the true King.

52:1-34 This chapter details the fall of Jerusalem. It parallels and overlaps with chapter 39, as well as accounts found in 2Kg 25 and 2Ch 36:15-21, although the latter only summarizes the events. Chapter 52 differs from 39 by focusing on Nebuchadnezzar's plundering of the temple, including a catalog of the articles taken.

52:1-16 This passage is a parallel account of 39:1-10. The **Jeremiah** mentioned here, of course, is not the prophet. Due to **Zedekiah**'s disobedience and wickedness, the Lord **finally banished** Judah **from His presence**. Thus the reasons for defeat and exile are summarized.

52:4-11 The siege lasted about 18 months (588–587 B.C.), after which a severe famine ensued. At that point, the enemy broke in, and **all the warriors fled**. Even Zedekiah fled but was overtaken and captured at **Jericho**. Severe punishment was meted out to him, his sons, and his officials at **Riblah**, after which Zedekiah was also deported.

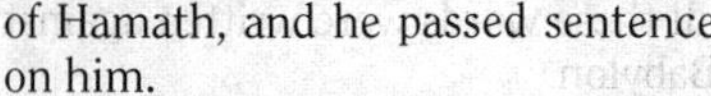

52:12-14 The fate of the temple, palace, and city walls is described here.

52:17-23 This passage parallels 2Kg 25:13-17 in describing the plunder of the temple and the sacred vessels. The **gold** and **silver** vessels were taken, as well as an inestimable amount of **bronze** contained in some enormous articles that had to be broken into pieces in order to be transported. Notably 2Kg 24:13 and 2Ch 36:10 describe a looting of the temple that would have occurred earlier in 597 B.C., when other gold and silver utensils were taken to Babylon.

52:24-29 Verses 24-27 specify 74 more men singled out for execution at Riblah (cp. 2Kg 25:18-21). The number of deported Jews reported in verses 28-29 constitute the only available numerical information concerning the final deportation to Babylon after the fall of Jerusalem.

52:30-34 Both this final passage as well as 2Kg 25:27-30 tell the story of King Jehoiachin's release by **Evil-merodach** (or Amel-Marduk). This addition or inclusion, in illustrating the fulfillment of Jeremiah's prophecy, vindicates the prophet as a genuine messenger of God. However, ending on a note of hope, the conclusion indicates that just as Jeremiah's message of doom was fulfilled, so his message of hope would also come to pass. One gets the sense that the end of Jehoiachin's story is not the end of the story for Israel, nor the last word regarding God's promises to the house of David.

of Hamath, and he passed sentence
on him.
10 At Riblah the king of Babylon
slaughtered Zedekiah's sons before
his eyes and also slaughtered the Judean commanders. 11 Then he blinded Zedekiah and bound him with
bronze chains. The king of Babylon
brought Zedekiah to Babylon, where
he kept him in custody[A] until his dying day.
12 On the tenth day of the fifth
month—which was the nineteenth
year of King Nebuchadnezzar, king
of Babylon—Nebuzaradan, the commander of the guards, entered Jerusalem as the representative of[B] the
king of Babylon. 13 He burned the
LORD's temple, the king's palace, all
the houses of Jerusalem, and all the
houses of the nobles. 14 The whole
Chaldean army with the commander
of the guards tore down all the walls
surrounding Jerusalem. 15 Nebuzaradan, the commander of the
guards, deported some of the poorest
of the people, as well as the rest of
the people who were left in the city,
the deserters who had defected to the
king of Babylon, and the rest of the
craftsmen. 16 But some of the poorest
people of the land Nebuzaradan, the
commander of the guards, left to be
vinedressers and farmers.
17 Now the Chaldeans broke into
pieces the bronze pillars for the
LORD's temple and the water carts
and the bronze reservoir that were
in the LORD's temple, and carried all
the bronze to Babylon. 18 They took
the pots, shovels, wick trimmers,
sprinkling basins, dishes, and all the
bronze articles used in the temple
service. 19 The commander of the
guards took away the bowls, firepans, sprinkling basins, pots, lampstands, pans, and •drink offering
bowls—whatever was gold or silver.
20 As for the two pillars, the one reservoir, and the 12 bronze bulls under
the water carts that King Solomon
had made for the LORD's temple, the
weight of the bronze of all these articles was beyond measure. 21 One
pillar was 27 feet[C] tall, had a circumference of 18 feet,[D] was hollow—four
fingers thick— 22 and had a bronze
capital on top of it. One capital, encircled by bronze latticework and
pomegranates, stood $7\frac{1}{2}$ feet[E] high.
The second pillar was the same,
with pomegranates. 23 Each capital
had 96 pomegranates all around it.
All the pomegranates around the latticework numbered 100.
24 The commander of the guards
also took away Seraiah the chief
priest, Zephaniah the priest of the
second rank, and the three doorkeepers. 25 From the city he took a
court official who had been appointed over the warriors; seven trusted
royal aides[F] found in the city; the
secretary of the commander of
the army, who enlisted the people
of the land for military duty; and
60 men from the common people
who were found within the city.
26 Nebuzaradan, the commander of
the guards, took them and brought
them to the king of Babylon at Riblah. 27 The king of Babylon put them
to death at Riblah in the land of Hamath. So Judah went into exile from
its land.
28 These are the people Nebuchadnezzar deported: in the seventh
year, 3,023 Jews; 29 in his eighteenth
year,[G] 832 people from Jerusalem;
30 in Nebuchadnezzar's twenty-third
year, Nebuzaradan, the commander
of the guards, deported 745 Jews. All
together 4,600 people were deported.
31 On the twenty-fifth day of the
twelfth month of the thirty-seventh
year of the exile of Judah's King
Jehoiachin, Evil-merodach king of
Babylon, in the first year of his
reign, pardoned King Jehoiachin of
Judah and released him from prison.
32 He spoke kindly to him and set
his throne above the thrones of the
kings who were with him in Babylon. 33 So Jehoiachin changed his
prison clothes, and he dined regularly in the presence of the king of
Babylon for the rest of his life. 34 As
for his allowance, a regular allowance was given to him by the king of
Babylon, a portion for each day until
the day of his death, for the rest of
his life.

[A]**52:11** Lit *in a house of guards* [B]**52:12** Lit *Jerusalem; he stood before* [C]**52:21** Lit *18 cubits* [D]**52:21** Lit *12 cubits* [E]**52:22** Lit *five cubits* [F]**52:25** Lit *seven men who look on the king's face* [G]**52:29** Some Hb mss, Syr add *he deported*

JEREMIAH . . . WRITTEN ON MY *Heart* Much is to be learned from this book in terms of the faithful proclamation of God's messages to people and culture, not forgetting that God is sovereign over all and might send you to proclaim His word to other cultures as well. You have much to learn about yourself in terms of accepting personal responsibility for sin. Despite having so many advantages over the Jews in Jeremiah's time, too often you act as they did and turn away from God to your own ways. You have God's written Word, whereas in the sixth century B.C., the Word was continuing to be written, a task undertaken with much anguish and suffering on Jeremiah's part.

A further great advantage of this generation involves the new covenant of the heart. Jeremiah's contemporaries just hoped for such a day, whereas those on the other side of the cross may enter into, experience, and benefit from this new covenant through Jesus Christ and the ministry of the Holy Spirit who seals believers. Perhaps you may learn from the fate of Jerusalem not to sin presumptuously, for God's compassion as well as His justice is real and will definitely be applied to His (new) covenant people. May you also find comfort that after judgment and repentance, restoration to God is still possible.

Women in the Major Prophets

BOOK	MESSAGES
Isaiah	• Lament that women were ruling over God's people (3:12) • Denouncement of the pride of Judah's women (3:16-17) • Warning of tragedy when women outnumber men (4:1) • Warning against complacency and self-sufficiency (32:9-14) • God's reference to Zion/Jerusalem as His "Virgin Daughter," whom He promised to defend (37:21-23) • Comparison of God's judgment on Babylon to the tragedy of a woman's • sudden "loss of children and widowhood" (47:1-10) • Also consider applications of contemporary feminism to false teachings (5:20-21; 22:11; 29:16; 45:9-13,18-19; 47:1-10)
Jeremiah	• Incredulity over the way Israel had forgotten the Lord by contrast to the way "a young woman" never forgets "her jewelry" and "a bride" never forgets "her wedding sash" (2:32) • God's condemnation of His people's oppression of widows (7:5-7; 22:3) • Summons of women to mourn the tragic consequences of abandoning the Lord (9:17-22) • Effects on women of God's judgment of Israel (15:5-9; 38:21-23) • Restoration of hope and joy as experienced and expressed by women (31:1-4, 8,13,15-17,21-22) • Accountability of women to God for their idolatry (44:15-25) • Use of imagery of women in childbirth to describe the experience of distressed enemies (49:22,24; 50:43) • Also consider application of God's prohibition and warnings against the shedding of "innocent blood" and the Canaanite practice of sacrificing children to Molech to the contemporary sin of abortion (2:33-35; 7:5-10; 9:20-21; 22:3,17; 32:35; cp. Ezk 16:20-21; 20:26)
Lamentations	• Personification of Jerusalem as a grieving woman (e.g., 1:1-11) • Failure to consider the consequences of sin (1:9) • Depth of moral depravity (2:20; 4:4,10)
Ezekiel	• Identification of women's participation in idolatry as one of the "detestable" practices that prompted the Lord to judge His people (8:13-14) • Prophecy against "women . . . who prophesy out of their own imagination" (13:17-23) • Portrayal of Israel's unfaithfulness to the Lord in terms of adultery and prostitution (chaps. 16 and 23) • Listing of crimes against women among the "detestable practices" for which God would judge His people (22:8,10-11)

Lamentations

Timeline	605 BC	597 BC	587/586 BC	586 BC
World Events Biblical Events	Rise of Nebuchadnezzar; first deportation (Daniel and friends)	Siege of Jerusalem; second deportation (Ezekiel)	Destruction, burning of Jerusalem; third deportation	Governorship of Gedaliah

"Even if He causes suffering, He will show compassion according to His abundant, faithful love" (3:32).

Who wrote Lamentations?

According to strong ancient tradition, both Jewish (Talmud) and Christian (LXX, Latin Vulgate), the author of this book is Jeremiah, although he is not specifically named in the text. There is some thematic similarity between the two books, especially the incessant and bitter weeping for Judah's plight (Jr 8:18–9:1; 14:17; Lm 3:48-51).

Who were the recipients?

This brief but intense work was possibly used in temple worship even after its destruction. Jeremiah 41 seems to describe a group of pilgrims who came to worship in the temple ruins, indicating its continued sanctity for Judah.

When was Lamentations written?

This book was written between 586 and 582 B.C., between the fall of Jerusalem (586 B.C.) and Jeremiah's forcible flight to Egypt (ca 582 B.C.).

Where did it happen?

The events to which Lamentations refers took place in Jerusalem, the capital of Judah, the southern kingdom of the nation of Israel. The Babylonian king Nebuchadnezzar had begun to deport Jews in 605 B.C., as soon as he ascended the throne. Others were deported in 597 and 586 B.C., after an 18-month siege and the devastation of Jerusalem and its walls, leaving it a ruin.

What is Lamentations about?

Lamentations is chiefly a song of grief over the events of Jerusalem's destruction. The mourner, as a representative of the nation, expresses deep grief not only over the tragic events that transpired but also over the situation precipitating those events. Rather than citing geopolitics or national upheavals as the major reasons for Judah's demise, the author cites spiritual reasons instead. Judah's worst enemy was her own willful sin, having violated the covenant many times over.

One particularly poignant theme is the sense of shock expressed by the mourners at the desecration and depredation of the temple. The cloud of gloom is pierced by one bright ray at the heart of the book, a lyrical passage in which the author evinces hope and a certainty that God's covenant love will temper His just wrath with mercy; God will chastise but will not utterly destroy His people (Lm 3:21-33).

Why should women read Lamentations?

One of the oldest professions conferred upon women by ancient society was functioning as funerary mourners. As givers of life, in a sense, women felt particularly deeply the loss of life, and even Jeremiah seems to understand this as he summons women to mourn over the city and to teach their daughters to lament as well because their children and young men would soon perish (cp. Jr 9:17-21). In antiquity, the nearest female relatives of the deceased were responsible for the washing and anointing of the body, for perfuming it with spices, and for preparing it for viewing. The practice was common in both the ancient Near East generally (e.g., Greece) as well as in Jewish tradition (e.g., the resurrection accounts in the Gospels). Additionally, the main speaker in Lamentations is "Daughter Zion," the feminine personification of the city, who weeps for the fate of her citizens in a manner akin to Rachel weeping for her children (Jr 31:15; Mt 2:16-18). Of course the imagery is not exclusively feminine, as its author is traditionally Jeremiah (note Lm 3:1); however, the predominant image of the city cast as the grief-stricken Daughter Zion can especially draw in women.

How do you read Lamentations?

This brief five-chapter poetic composition delivers a devastating blow. This impact is due as much to the subject matter as to its literary format. Its subject concerns the siege, fall, and destruction of Jerusalem. The assault left the Jews reeling and utterly devastated. The city grieves as much for loss of life as loss of homeland and as much for the broken walls and the temple ruins as for the broken covenant and a relationship with God that is in spiritual ruins. The metaphors used can at times shock the reader, but strong images convey strong emotions. The book is composed of five poems, four of which are acrostics. The first line begins with the initial letter of the Hebrew alphabet (alef), the next line with the following letter (bet), and proceeds thus through the 22-letter alphabet. Chapter 3, the heart and culmination of the book, is actually a triple acrostic, containing 66 verses. Chapter 5 is not an acrostic but still consists of 22 verses/couplets. In a book of such brevity, images are packed together succinctly for a powerful effect. It is vital to note that the author frames the tragedy of Daughter Zion in theological (specifically, covenantal) terms, in effect helping the exiles and anyone left behind (like Jeremiah) to make sense of their plight and the horrors of defeat, captivity, and exile. It also provides a way for any mourner to frame the aftermath of sin in her life by following Lamentations' pattern of expression of grief and admission of guilt, followed by hope in God's love and mercy, and finally by prayers of praise and repentance and a petition for full restoration to God.

>WORD|*study*

1:7,10-11 In verses 7, 10, and 11, Jerusalem's precious belongings (Hb *machmud*; from the verb *chamad*, "desire, delight in") probably refers to the temple treasures, which were taken as plunder when the Babylonians entered, sacked, and burned the temple (cp. 2Kg 24:13; 25:13-17; 2Ch 36:18-19; Jr 52:17-23). In Lamentations 1:11, **precious belongings** renders a near doubling of the word (Hb *machmad*, "object of desire, something precious" with *machmud*). The additional word elsewhere refers to the temple furnishings (2Ch 36:19; Is 64:11; Jl 3:5). Here, however, the **precious belongings** exchanged **for food** may refer to children who were cannibalized during the siege or later sold into slavery (cp. 2:20; 4:10; Dt 28:53-57; 2Kg 6:28-29).

586/585 BC	582 BC	568–567 BC	538 BC
Insurrection of Ishmael	Flight to Egypt and final words of Jeremiah (see timeline in Jeremiah)	Nebuchadnezzar's invasion of Egypt in fulfillment of prophecies by both Jeremiah and Ezekiel	Decree issued by Cyrus allowing the Jews to return to Judah.

Outline

I. The Lament over Jerusalem (1:1-22)
  A. The Lament for the City's Abject Situation (1:1-11)
  B. The Disconsolation of Daughter Judah (1:12-22)
II. The Judgment on Jerusalem (2:1-22)
  A. The City's Utter Destruction (2:1-9)
  B. The Weeping of Judah's Inhabitants over Their Devastation (2:10-22)
III. Hope Through God's Mercy (3:1-66)
  A. The LORD: Jerusalem's Enemy (3:1-20)
  B. The LORD: Compassionate and Just (3:21-33)
  C. The LORD: Punisher of Judah (3:34-54)
  D. The LORD: Defender and Avenger of Judah (3:55-66)
IV. Terrors of the Besieged City (4:1-22)
  A. The Curse of Destruction and Famine (4:1-11)
  B. Jerusalem's Sins as the Cause of Her Collapse (4:12-22)
V. Prayer for Restoration (5:1-22)
  A. Repentance of the Nation (5:1-18)
  B. Prayer for Restoration of the Nation (5:19-22)

The Lament over Jerusalem (1:1-22)

The Lament for the City's Abject Situation (1:1-11)

א *Alef*

1 How[A] she sits alone,
the city once crowded
with people!
She who was great
among the nations
has become like a widow.
The princess
among the provinces
has been put to forced labor.

ב *Bet*

2 She weeps aloud
during the night,
with tears on her cheeks.
There is no one to offer
her comfort,
not one from all her lovers.[B]
All her friends
have betrayed her;
they have become her enemies.

ג *Gimel*

3 Judah has gone into exile
following[C] affliction
and harsh slavery;
she lives among the nations
but finds no place to rest.
All her pursuers
have overtaken her
in narrow places.

ד *Dalet*

4 The roads to •Zion mourn,
for no one comes
to the appointed festivals.
All her gates are deserted;
her priests groan,
her young women grieve,
and she herself is bitter.

ה *He*

5 Her adversaries have become
her masters;
her enemies are at ease,
for the LORD has made
her suffer
because of her
many transgressions.
Her children have gone away
as captives before the adversary.

ו *Vav*

6 All her splendor has vanished
from Daughter Zion.
Her leaders are like stags
that find no pasture;
they walk away exhausted
before the hunter.

[A]1:1 The stanzas in Lm 1–4 form an •acrostic. [B]1:2 = Jerusalem's political allies [C]1:3 Or *because of*

Title: The title of the book in most English translations comes from the Latin Vulgate (*Lamenta*) and is descriptive of the content. In the Hebrew Bible, it is called, "Alas! How . . ." the initial phrase in chaps. 1, 2, and 4.

1:1-2 Jerusalem is personified as a feminine figure, according to the gender of the word "city" in Hebrew. At times she is described as an abandoned mother or a widow, while at other times as a lonely woman, an adulteress deserted by **her lovers**, weeping over her change of fortune. Whereas in former days she was **crowded**, now she is deserted and forsaken as a **widow**, and the **princess** has become a slave. Jerusalem's **lovers** and **friends** refer most likely to nations such as Egypt, with whom she formed political alliances to serve her own military interests, defying God's command to the contrary (cp. 5:6).

1:4 Grief extends even to inanimate objects such as the **roads to Zion** and **her gates.** Pilgrims and visitors would have come to festivals on these roads, and the gates would normally throng with people coming to worship at the temple. This verse might hint at the use of Lamentations in worship at the temple ruins, which were still revered (cp. Jr 41:5).

1:5 The LORD (Yahweh) is identified as the agent of punishment.

1:6 Judah's leaders were weak spiritually and militarily, described here as **stags that find no pasture**. Hunger leads to exhaustion, resulting in vulnerability before the enemy. Perhaps the author had in mind the attempted flight of Zedekiah and his men, who were overtaken and severely punished.

1:8-9 Nakedness refers to the punishment of being stripped down in order to humiliate a prostitute or a captive. **Uncleanness** indicates impurity and may refer to blood stains of innocents she has killed, or perhaps the image is linked to the sin of adultery (cp. Jr 2:34; 3:2). The **stains** on **her skirts** do not here refer to menstrual impurity.

1:10 The temple was desecrated and plundered by idolatrous Gentiles.

1:12-15 Jerusalem mourns loss of life brought about as a result of her **transgressions**, which were so numerous they could form an oppressive and enslaving **yoke**.

ז *Zayin*

7 During the days
of her affliction
and homelessness
Jerusalem remembers all
her precious belongings
that were hers in days of old.
When her people fell
into the adversary's hand,
she had no one to help.
The adversaries looked at her,
laughing over her downfall.

ח *Khet*

8 Jerusalem has
sinned grievously;
therefore, she has become
an object of scorn.[A]
All who honored her
now despise her,
for they have seen
her nakedness.
She herself groans
and turns away.

ט *Tet*

9 Her uncleanness stains
her skirts.
She never considered her end.
Her downfall was astonishing;
there was no one
to comfort her.
LORD, look on my affliction,
for the enemy triumphs!

י *Yod*

10 The adversary has seized
all her precious belongings.
She has even seen the nations
enter her sanctuary—
those You had forbidden
to enter Your assembly.

כ *Kaf*

11 All her people groan
while they search for bread.
They have traded
their precious belongings
for food
in order to stay alive.
LORD, look and see
how I have become despised.

The Disconsolation of Daughter Judah (1:12-22)

ל *Lamed*

12 Is this nothing to you, all you
who pass by?
Look and see!
Is there any pain like mine,
which was dealt out to me,
which the LORD
made me suffer
on the day of His
burning anger?

מ *Mem*

13 He sent fire from heaven
into my bones;
He made it descend.[B]
He spread a net for my feet
and turned me back.
He made me desolate,
sick all day long.

נ *Nun*

14 My transgressions
have been formed
into a yoke,[C,D]
fastened together
by His hand;
they have been placed
on my neck,
and the Lord has broken
my strength.

[A] **1:8** Or *become impure* [B] **1:13** DSS, LXX; MT reads *bones, and it prevailed against them* [C] **1:14** Some Hb mss, LXX read *He kept watch over my transgressions* [D] **1:14** Or *The yoke of my transgressions is bound*; Hb obscure

>WORD|*study*

1:17 Judah had become something impure (Hb *niddah*, "something unclean or filthy"). In the context of Levitical law, the word *niddah* most often refers to "menstrual impurity" (Lv 12:2; 15:19-20,24-26,33; 18:19) or other uncleanness (Lv 12:5; 20:21). Some translations regard the sentence here as a metaphor comparing Judah's sinfulness to the uncleanness of a menstruating woman (cp. Ezk 18:6; 36:17). However, in this context, comprehensively, the impurity is the sin of spiritual adultery rather than a reference to menstrual uncleanness. The word means "something unclean" or "uncleanness" in the sense of sin, which cannot abide in God's holy presence. After the exile, Ezra used *niddah* to describe the Canaanites (before Israel's conquest) as having "filled" the land "with their uncleanness" (Hb *niddah*, Ezr 9:11). Similarly, King Hezekiah of Judah once ordered the priests and Levites to get rid of "everything detestable" (Hb *niddah*, 2Ch 29:5,10) found in the temple in order to prepare for its restoration. Though referring especially to idols, he also referenced anything that did not belong in the presence of God, who is supremely holy (cp. Ezk 7:19-20; Zch 1:1). The use of *niddah* here suggests a dreadful reversal of what God intended Israel to be. In line with the root meaning of *niddah*—"separation or removal" prompted by an encounter with something repulsive—Judah's pursuit of other gods not only demanded the Lord's judgment but also motivated her enemies to remove her from the land.

He has handed me over
to those I cannot withstand.

ס *Samek*

15 The Lord has rejected
all the mighty men
within me.
He has summoned an army[A]
against me
to crush my young warriors.
The Lord has trampled
Virgin Daughter Judah
like grapes in a winepress.

ע *Ayin*

16 I weep because of
these things;
my eyes flow[B] with tears.
For there is no one nearby
to comfort me,
no one to keep me alive.
My children are desolate
because the enemy
has prevailed.

פ *Pe*

17 Zion stretches out her hands;
there is no one
to comfort her.
The LORD has issued a decree
against Jacob
that his neighbors should be
his adversaries.
Jerusalem has become
something impure
among them.

צ *Tsade*

18 The LORD is just,
for I have rebelled
against His command.
Listen, all you people;
look at my pain.
My young men and women
have gone into captivity.

A1:15 Or *has announced an appointed time* B1:16 Lit *my eye, my eye flows*

1:16 Judah's weeping over her **children** may parallel Rachel's weeping over hers (Jr 31:15-17).

1:17-20 Jerusalem is referred to in both feminine and masculine terms.

1:18-19 Jerusalem appeals to **people** to witness the pain brought on by sin/rebellion.

Biblical Womanhood Feminine Imagery

Feminist interpreters have sometimes suggested that the imagery employed in chapter 1 for Jerusalem/Judah as **Daughter Zion** speaks to the plight of battered women in contemporary society (Lm 1:6), depicting God as the abusive husband and Daughter Zion as the victim who is both the cause of, and a collaborator in, her own suffering. These feminists, referring to the description of Jerusalem's impurity, **her nakedness**, and the **uncleanness** that **stains her skirts** (1:8-9,17), further argue that the language of uncleanness throughout the book leads to hatred for and the devaluation of the female body and to claims that women alone are blamed for the fall of Jerusalem.

Several errors are immediately apparent in these arguments. First, to suggest that throughout the book uncleanness is always associated with menstruation is incorrect. In fact, even feminist interpreters note that the initial references to uncleanness in the book are tied to Judah's adultery and sin (vv. 2,5). God is not guilty because the actions taken against Jerusalem/Judah and her inhabitants do not constitute abuse; rather, these actions are properly seen as the discipline of a holy God. When adultery is understood as the metaphor for the *nation's* unfaithfulness to God, clearly this is in no way restricted to women. Recalling Ezekiel, the male priests actually bore much of the blame for spiritual unfaithfulness. Interestingly, even when uncleanness is associated with blood, the reference is far more often linked to bloodshed of the innocent rather than a woman's menstrual cycle. The claim that all guilt is placed on women is misleading at best.

Second, the claim that the structure of Lamentations places blame solely on the shoulders of women or that the writer portrays the female images only in a negative light simply does not withstand scrutiny. While much of the blame is charged to the expression "Daughter Zion" and "Daughter Judah" and though the female imagery is the most common in the book, the use of masculine images as negative depictions of the nation of Judah are also present. For example, the imagery of Jacob is used throughout (cp. 2:2-3). Chapter 3 contains some very violent imagery, and from the outset the speaker is male—"the man who has seen affliction" (3:1).

Third, to try to apply the standards of modern society to the sixth century BC regarding responses to adultery is anachronistic. In the Torah (the Jewish Law), adultery was a capital offense for both offenders, not just for the woman—the absence of the man in John 8 may be a reason why Jesus offered the woman mercy. The prescribed punishment at the time was stoning. Thus, the judgment upon Jerusalem/Judah for her unfaithfulness may well be merciful in that she has hope of restoration and cleansing from her sins.

1:20-22 The city appeals for vindication and retribution to the Lord. She accepts the responsibility for sin and faces the reality of its consequences. Sin leads to pain, betrayal, heartbreak, slaughter, death, heartsickness, and lack of comfort.

2:1-2 Israel's glory may refer to the temple's destruction. God is depicted in His anger as Judah's enemy. The theme of having no comfort and being **without compassion** continues from the previous chapter and becomes intensified (1:2,17,21). Not only does Judah lack compassion from the Lord, but she is also **overshadowed** by the fullness of His **anger**. Words like **anger, wrath, fierce, blazed,** and **flaming fire** appear clustered in verses 1-6 and 21-22.

2:3 Imagery of **enemy** attack prevails here (vv. 3-5). Instead of protecting His people with **His right hand**, the Lord withdraws and uses it against Judah.

2:4-5 The phrase **swallowed up** (2:16) appears in other passages dealing with Babylon's attack of Jerusalem (e.g., Jr 51:34).

2:6-8 Clearly expressed here is the unfathomable fact that the Lord Himself rejected and brought about the destruction of the temple, here called **Israel's glory . . . His footstool** (v. 1), **His place of meeting** (v. 6), **His altar, . . . His sanctuary . . .** [and] **the house of the Lord** (v. 7), thus fulfilling Jeremiah's warnings (Jr 7:1-15).

ק *Qof*

19 I called to my lovers,
but they betrayed me.
My priests and elders
perished in the city
while searching for food
to keep themselves alive.

ר *Resh*

20 LORD, see how I am in distress.
I am churning within;
my heart is broken,[A]
for I have been
very rebellious.
Outside, the sword takes
the children;
inside, there is death.

ש *Shin*

21 People have heard
me groaning,
but there is no one
to comfort me.
All my enemies have heard
of my misfortune;
they are glad that
You have caused it.
Bring on the day
You have announced,
so that they may become
like me.

ת *Tav*

22 Let all their wickedness come
before You,
and deal with them
as You have dealt with me
because of all
my transgressions.
For my groans are many,
and I am sick at heart.

The Judgment on Jerusalem (2:1-22)

The City's Utter Destruction (2:1-9)

א *Alef*

2 How the Lord
has overshadowed
Daughter ·Zion
with His anger!
He has thrown down
Israel's glory
from heaven to earth.
He has abandoned
His footstool[B]
in the day of His anger.

ב *Bet*

2 Without compassion the Lord
has swallowed up
all the dwellings of Jacob.
In His wrath
He has demolished
the fortified cities
of Daughter Judah.
He brought them
to the ground
and defiled the kingdom
and its leaders.

ג *Gimel*

3 He has cut off every ·horn
of Israel
in His burning anger
and withdrawn His right hand
in the presence of the enemy.
He has blazed against Jacob
like a flaming fire
that consumes everything.

ד *Dalet*

4 He has bent His bow
like an enemy;
His right hand is positioned
like an adversary.
He has killed everyone
who was loved,[C]
pouring out His wrath
like fire
on the tent of Daughter Zion.

ה *He*

5 The Lord is like an enemy;
He has swallowed up Israel.
He swallowed up
all its palaces
and destroyed
its fortified cities.
He has multiplied mourning
and lamentation
within Daughter Judah.

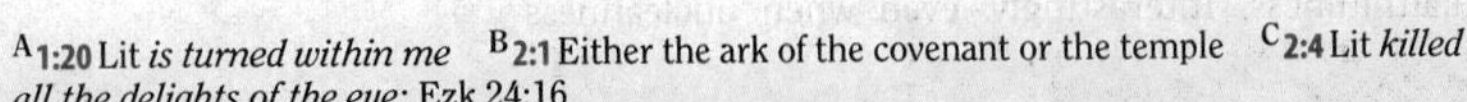
[A]**1:20** Lit *is turned within me* [B]**2:1** Either the ark of the covenant or the temple [C]**2:4** Lit *killed all the delights of the eye*; Ezk 24:16

>WORD|*study*

2:11 The writer, perhaps personifying himself as the city, expresses acute agony at Jerusalem's plight: **My heart** [Hb *kavēd*, "liver"] **is poured out in grief**. A different word is more frequently used for "heart" (Hb *lēv*, vv. 18-19; cp. 1:20). When not referring literally to the bodily organ (e.g., Ex 29:13), *kavēd* indicates the organ that is "heavy" (Hb *kavod*), i.e., "important." Metaphorically, it indicates that which is "grievous or burdensome." Since being "poured out" connotes death, the statement speaks of the way mourning is physically overwhelming, as would be a wound to this very important organ. In the contemporary idiom, one might say, "I'm dying on the inside."

ו *Vav*

6 He has done violence
to His temple[A]
as if it were a garden booth,
destroying His place
of meeting.
The LORD has abolished
appointed festivals
and Sabbaths in Zion.
He has despised king
and priest
in His fierce anger.

ז *Zayin*

7 The Lord has rejected
His altar,
repudiated His sanctuary;
He has handed the walls
of her palaces
over to the enemy.
They have raised a shout
in the house of the LORD
as on the day
of an appointed festival.

ח *Khet*

8 The LORD determined
to destroy
the wall of Daughter Zion.
He stretched out
a measuring line
and did not restrain Himself
from destroying.
He made the ramparts
and walls grieve;
together they waste away.

ט *Tet*

9 Zion's gates have fallen
to the ground;
He has destroyed
and shattered the bars
on her gates.
Her king and her leaders live
among the nations,
instruction[B] is no more,
and even her prophets receive
no vision from the LORD.

The Weeping of Judah's Inhabitants over Their Devastation (2:10-22)

י *Yod*

10 The elders of Daughter Zion
sit on the ground in silence.
They have thrown dust
on their heads
and put on •sackcloth.
The young women
of Jerusalem
have bowed their heads
to the ground.

כ *Kaf*

11 My eyes are worn out
from weeping;
I am churning within.
My heart is poured out
in grief[C]
because of the destruction
of my dear people,
because children
and infants faint
in the streets of the city.

ל *Lamed*

12 They cry out to their mothers:
Where is the grain and wine?
as they faint like the wounded
in the streets of the city,
as their lives fade away
in the arms of their mothers.

מ *Mem*

13 What can I say
on your behalf?
What can I compare you to,
Daughter Jerusalem?
What can I liken you to,

2:9 The city's **leaders** were humiliated by being scattered **among the nations**, godless Gentiles. Those who embodied the Law (Torah) are exiled; therefore, **instruction** [Hb *torah*] **is no more**. Additionally, a second mode of revelation, the **vision**, perished when the prophets received none or turned false (e.g., Jr 27–28). In effect, God stopped speaking to His people, a sign of rejection.

2:11-13 The mourner expresses profound grief through incessant weeping (vv. 18-19) for the most innocent victims of the siege, the **children and infants** who starved to death.

[A]2:6 Lit *booth* [B]2:9 Or *the law* [C]2:11 Lit *My liver is poured out on the ground*

2:14 See Jr 14:14, 23:16.

2:16 Note the use of the phrase **swallowed her up** to describe Judah's military enemies.

2:19-22 Glimpses of the horrors of the Babylonian siege are provided here. **Children** and **infants** are starving and are victims of cannibalism by the desperate besieged population (cp. the siege of Samaria in 857 B.C. in 2Kg 6:26-29).

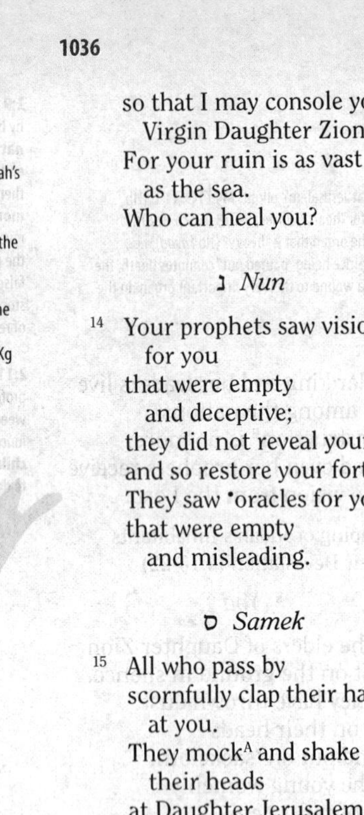

so that I may console you,
Virgin Daughter Zion?
For your ruin is as vast
as the sea.
Who can heal you?

נ *Nun*

14 Your prophets saw visions
for you
that were empty
and deceptive;
they did not reveal your •guilt
and so restore your fortunes.
They saw •oracles for you
that were empty
and misleading.

ס *Samek*

15 All who pass by
scornfully clap their hands
at you.
They mock[A] and shake
their heads
at Daughter Jerusalem:
Is this the city that was called
the perfection of beauty,
the joy of the whole earth?

פ *Pe*

16 All your enemies
open their mouths
against you.
They hiss and gnash
their teeth,
saying, "We have swallowed
her up.
This is the day
we have waited for!
We have lived to see it."

ע *Ayin*

17 The LORD has done
what He planned;
He has accomplished
His decree,
which He ordained in days
of old.
He has demolished
without compassion,
letting the enemy gloat
over you
and exalting the horn
of your adversaries.

HARD QUESTION

How can a loving God destroy His own people and bring about the atrocities delineated here?

To answer this question, one must understand the nature of God's relationship with His people. God and Judah were in a covenantal relationship initiated by God, who desired to dwell among His people and "be their God" (Ex 25:8; Dt 29:13; Jr 30:22; 31:1,33). The problem was Judah's violation of the covenant: She had broken her oath of love and loyalty. In a common prophetic metaphor, Judah betrayed the Lord, her spouse (Jr 3:1-5; 31:32; Ezk 16:1-63; 23:1-49; Hs 2:2-23). Clearly Judah understood that the devastation she experienced came about by **the LORD's** agency; He accomplished His plan and His **decree** from **days of old** (Lm 2:17). This "decree" is found at the original making of the covenant as well as at its renewal (Dt 4:1–8:20; 11:13-17,26-28). Obedience to the covenant brought blessings while violation of the covenant resulted in curses. Among other curses, the worst was exile; and when destruction and exile resulted from Judah's many transgressions against her covenant God, there was no doubt concerning agency. While the Babylonians, and the Assyrians before them, were agents of punishment in God's hand, the primary agent was God, who honored His own covenant conditions by following through with punishment (Lm 2:17; see Dt 29:24-28). God does not capriciously or maliciously destroy His chosen people, or any people for that matter (Lm 3:32-33). God defines His own nature and character as "compassionate and gracious" and simultaneously just, not leaving the guilty "unpunished" (Ex 34:6-7). In Lm 3:31-33 God's punishment is intended to discipline, purge, and restore His people, not ultimately to obliterate them (cp. Ezk 36:25-29).

צ *Tsade*

18 The hearts of the people
cry out to the Lord.
Wall of Daughter Zion,
let your tears run down
like a river
day and night.
Give yourself no relief
and your[B] eyes no rest.

ק *Qof*

19 Arise, cry out in the night
from the first watch
of the night.
Pour out your heart like water
before the Lord's presence.
Lift up your hands to Him
for the lives of your children
who are fainting from hunger
on the corner of every street.

[A] **2:15** Lit *hiss* [B] **2:18** Lit *and the daughter of your*

ר *Resh*

20 LORD, look and consider
who You have done this to.
Should women eat
their own children,
the infants they
have nurtured?[A]
Should priests and prophets
be killed
in the Lord's sanctuary?

ש *Shin*

21 Both young and old
are lying on the ground
in the streets.
My young men and women
have fallen by the sword.
You have killed them
in the day of Your anger,
slaughtering
without compassion.

ת *Tav*

22 You summoned my attackers[B]
on every side,
as if for an appointed
festival day;
on the day of the LORD's anger
no one escaped or survived.
My enemy has destroyed
those I nurtured[C] and reared.

Hope Through God's Mercy (3:1-66)

The LORD: Jerusalem's Enemy (3:1-20)

א *Alef*

3 I am the man
who has seen affliction
under the rod of God's wrath.
2 He has driven me away
and forced me to walk
in darkness instead of light.
3 Yes, He repeatedly
turns His hand
against me all day long.

ב *Bet*

4 He has worn away my flesh
and skin;
He has shattered my bones.
5 He has laid siege against me,
encircling me with bitterness
and hardship.
6 He has made me dwell
in darkness
like those who have been dead
for ages.

ג *Gimel*

7 He has walled me in
so I cannot escape;
He has weighed me down
with chains.
8 Even when I cry out and plead
for help,
He rejects my prayer.
9 He has walled in my ways
with cut stones;
He has made
my paths crooked.

ד *Dalet*

10 He is[D] a bear waiting
in ambush,
a lion in hiding.
11 He forced me off my way
and tore me to pieces;
He left me desolate.
12 He strung His bow
and set me as the target
for His arrow.

ה *He*

13 He pierced my kidneys
with His arrows.
14 I am a laughingstock
to all my people,[E]
mocked by their songs
all day long.
15 He filled me with bitterness,
satiated me with •wormwood.

ו *Vav*

16 He ground my teeth on gravel
and made me cower[F]
in the dust.
17 My soul has been deprived[G]
of peace;
I have forgotten
what happiness is.
18 Then I thought: My future[H]
is lost,

3:1 This chapter presents the Lord as both for and against Judah. He destroys and humiliates Judah like an enemy, yet Judah can count on God's faithfulness to His own covenantal love. **I am the man** strengthens the idea of Jeremianic authorship. The **rod of God's wrath** refers to Babylon, God's agent of punishment.

3:2-6 The poet is like a living dead man. Death and **darkness** connote both the specter of Sheol, the place of the dead, and the idea of being cut off from the presence of God. The poet is alive but he might as well be dead, physically and spiritually.

3:7-9 God acts like a besieging, enslaving conqueror, surrounding him and weighing him **down with chains**.

3:10-13 Violent metaphors for God's actions here include a predatory beast (**bear, lion**), which rips its victim to shreds, and a warrior who shoots lethal **arrows**, which unerringly hit the target, namely, the victim's vital organs, the **kidneys**.

3:16-22 The cumulative effect of vv. 2-16 is that the imagery pushes the speaker lower and lower until he is bowled over, trampled face down in the **dust** and eating **gravel** (v. 16). He is completely despondent and **depressed** (v. 20), dismissing any **future** or **hope** (v. 18). The pairing of these two ideas (**hope** and **future**) harks back to God's words to the exiles through Jeremiah in the beloved promise of Jr 29:11.

[A]2:20 Or *infants in a healthy condition*; Hb obscure [B]2:22 Or *terrors* [C]2:22 Or *I bore healthy*; Hb obscure [D]3:10 Lit *is to me* [E]3:14 Some Hb mss, LXX, Vg; other Hb mss, Syr read *all peoples* [F]3:16 Or *and trampled me* [G]3:17 Syr, Vg; MT reads *You deprived my soul* [H]3:18 Or *splendor*

3:21-22 Suddenly, the speaker recalls God's **faithful love** (Hb *chesed*; see **Word Study**, p. 322), upon which one can always rely. For the first time in this chapter, the author invokes God's covenant name, **Lord** (Hb *YHWH*, "Yahweh," vv. 22,24-26). The thought of God's love gives the speaker renewed optimism that with God there is an endless supply of mercy and compassion. This testimony of the providential goodness of God is the brightest spot in this book.

3:23-24 The covenant-breaker does not deserve compassion, but the faithful covenant God gives **new** "mercies" **every morning;** when all other comforts are removed, the Lord as **my portion** is sufficient.

3:27-33 How should one deal with divine discipline? It should be borne in quiet waiting, seeking, bearing **the yoke** (cp. 1:14) in silence and even alone. This description of patient, hopeful suffering has messianic overtones, being found in one of the Servant Songs of Isaiah (Is 50:6), knowing that one is not forever abandoned by the Lord, who **does not enjoy bringing affliction or suffering on mankind**.

3:34-36 God is displeased with injustice and punishes it. Perhaps Judah is at fault here, or perhaps the poet is describing military injustices perpetrated upon Judah by the invaders.

3:37-39 This strong view of God's providence is akin to material in Job 2:10.

3:40-42 A heartfelt prayer of confession and repentance seems to begin here, as Judah addresses God as **You**, expresses a desire for conversion (**turn back to the Lord**), and extends herself toward Him both outwardly (**hands**) and inwardly (**Let us lift up our hearts**).

3:43-47 As Judah recounts God's punishments, she weeps continually, not only for herself but also for the violated covenant and its disastrous results among the nations.

as well as my hope
from the LORD.

ז *Zayin*

19 Remember[A] my affliction
and my homelessness,
the wormwood
and the poison.
20 I continually remember them
and have become depressed.[B]

The LORD: Compassionate and Just (3:21-33)

21 Yet I call this to mind,
and therefore I have hope:

ח *Khet*

22 Because of the LORD's
faithful love
we do not perish,[C]
for His mercies never end.
23 They are new every morning;
great is Your faithfulness!
24 I say: The LORD is my portion,
therefore I will put my hope
in Him.

ט *Tet*

25 The LORD is good to those
who wait for Him,
to the person who seeks Him.
26 It is good to wait quietly
for deliverance from the LORD.
27 It is good for a man to bear
the yoke
while he is still young.

י *Yod*

28 Let him sit alone
and be silent,
for God has disciplined him.
29 Let him put his mouth
in the dust—
perhaps there is still hope.
30 Let him offer his cheek
to the one
who would strike him;
let him be filled with shame.

כ *Kaf*

31 For the Lord
will not reject us forever.
32 Even if He causes suffering,
He will show compassion
according to His abundant,
faithful love.
33 For He does not enjoy
bringing affliction
or suffering on •mankind.

The LORD: Punisher of Judah (3:34-54)

ל *Lamed*

34 Crushing all the prisoners
of the land[D]
beneath one's feet,
35 denying justice to a man
in the presence
of the •Most High,
36 or suppressing
a person's lawsuit—
the Lord does not approve
of these things.

מ *Mem*

37 Who is there who speaks
and it happens,
unless the Lord
has ordained it?
38 Do not both adversity
and good
come from the mouth
of the Most High?
39 Why should any living
person complain,
any man, because
of the punishment
for his sins?

נ *Nun*

40 Let us search out
and examine our ways,
and turn back to the LORD.
41 Let us lift up our hearts
and our hands
to God in heaven:
42 We have sinned
and rebelled;
You have not forgiven.

ס *Samek*

43 You have covered Yourself
in anger and pursued us;
You have killed
without compassion.
44 You have covered Yourself
with a cloud

[A] 3:19 Or *I remember* [B] 3:20 Ancient Jewish tradition reads *and You cause me to collapse*
[C] 3:22 One Hb mss, Syr, Tg read *The LORD's faithful love, indeed, does not perish* [D] 3:34 Or *earth*

so that no prayer
can pass through.
45 You have made
us disgusting filth
among the peoples.

פ *Pe*

46 All our enemies
open their mouths against us.
47 We have experienced panic
and pitfall,
devastation and destruction.
48 My eyes flow with streams
of tears
because of the destruction
of my dear people.

ע *Ayin*

49 My eyes overflow unceasingly,
without end,
50 until the LORD looks down
from heaven and sees.
51 My eyes bring me grief
because of the fate of
all the women in my city.

צ *Tsade*

52 For no apparent reason,
my enemies[A]
hunted me like a bird.
53 They dropped me alive
into[B] a pit
and threw stones at me.
54 Water flooded over my head,
and I thought: I'm going
to die!

The LORD: Defender and Avenger of Judah (3:55-66)

ק *Qof*

55 I called
on Your name, •Yahweh,
from the
depths of the •Pit.
56 You hear my plea:
Do not ignore my cry
for relief.
57 You come near when I call
on You;
You say: "Do not be afraid."

ר *Resh*

58 You defend my cause, Lord;
You redeem my life.
59 LORD, You see the wrong
done to me;
judge my case.
60 You see all their malice,
all their plots against me.

שׂ *Sin*/ שׁ *Shin*

61 LORD, You hear their insults,
all their plots against me.
62 The slander[C] and murmuring
of my opponents
attack me all day long.
63 When they sit and when
they rise, look,
I am mocked by their songs.

ת *Tav*

64 You will pay them back
what they deserve, LORD,
according to the work
of their hands.
65 You will give them a heart
filled with anguish.[D]
May Your curse be on them!
66 You will pursue them
in anger and destroy them
under Your heavens.[E,F]

Terrors of the Besieged City (4:1-22)

The Curse of Destruction and Famine (4:1-11)

א *Alef*

4 How the gold
has become tarnished,
the fine gold become dull!
The stones of the temple[G]
lie scattered
at the corner of every street.

ב *Bet*

2 •Zion's precious people—
once worth their weight
in pure gold—
how they are regarded
as clay jars,
the work of a potter's hands!

3:51 Whether the **fate of all the women** has to do with defenselessness and captivity or refers to the loss of their children in various ways is unclear here.

3:52-57 These verses could refer to Jeremiah's experience of unjust persecution and being thrown into the pit (Jr 38). Otherwise, the metaphors of the **pit** and of overwhelming floodwaters express fear that death is imminent (eg., Ps 88:3-7).

3:58-59 Judah's punishment has overwhelmed her, and she appeals for vindication from the just Judge.

3:60-66 The plaintiff recounts how she has been insulted, attacked, and mocked. Her plea for vindication is akin to imprecatory material in the Psalms, as Judah requests that her enemies will be pursued **in anger** just as she had been.

4:1-2 The terrors of destruction and famine are recounted here. **Zion's precious people** once gleamed like **gold** but are now dull and broken like a **clay** jar.

A3:52 Or *Those who were my enemies for no reason* B3:53 Or *They ended my life in*; Hb obscure C3:62 Lit *lips* D3:65 Or *them an obstinate heart*; Hb obscure E3:66 LXX, Syr, Vg read *heavens, LORD* F3:66 Lit *under the LORD's heavens* G4:1 Or *The sacred gems*

4:3-4 There is no food in the city during the siege, and famine affects everyone, especially the children, who are fully dependent upon their parents to feed them. **Ostriches** were proverbial for their lack of maternal care (cp. Jb 39:13-18; 4-6). Bitter ironies are put forth: Formerly refined and wealthy people are homeless and tattered. Noteworthy citizens who were in their prime are now unrecognizable, wizened, and emaciated.

4:9-11 Conditions in the city are so severe that death would be merciful, as it came **in an instant** upon **Sodom** (v. 6); better to be **slain by the sword** than starving. In a nightmarish, horrifying turn, **compassionate women** are killing their **children** and cooking them. A mother's intimate connection to her own child during pregnancy, often risking her own life and health in delivery, creates a bond that is only strengthened as she personally gives the child nourishment. In view of this, a mother cooking her child is the height of humanity gone wrong. Judah feels that God's **wrath** has been **exhausted** on them (i.e., they have experienced the full measure of **His burning anger** for their sins).

4:12-14 The author expresses disbelief that an enemy successfully invaded the Lord's chosen city. Yet the cause is manifest: **the sins of her prophets and the guilt of her priests, who shed the blood of the righteous**, described in the language of uncleanness and defilement—again, a reference to bloodguilt, not menstruation.

4:15-20 Judah's spiritual leaders (prophets, **priests**, and **elders**), her military and political leaders (specifically her king, Zedekiah, **the Lord's anointed**), and her foreign allies, like Egypt (**a nation that refused to help**) all failed her miserably. The **breath of our life** probably refers to the king, whose very person was considered sacrosanct.

ג *Gimel*

3 Even jackals
offer their breasts
to nurse their young,
but my dear people
have become cruel
like ostriches
in the wilderness.

ד *Dalet*

4 The nursing infant's tongue
clings to the roof
of his mouth from thirst.
Little children beg for bread,
but no one gives them any.

ה *He*

5 Those who used
to eat delicacies
are destitute in the streets;
those who were reared
in purple garments
huddle in garbage heaps.

ו *Vav*

6 The punishment
of my dear people
is greater than that of Sodom,
which was overthrown
in an instant
without a hand laid on it.

ז *Zayin*

7 Her dignitaries were brighter
than snow,
whiter than milk;
their bodies[A] were more ruddy
than coral,
their appearance
like sapphire.[B]

ח *Khet*

8 Now they appear darker
than soot;
they are not recognized
in the streets.
Their skin has shriveled
on their bones;
it has become dry like wood.

ט *Tet*

9 Those slain by the sword are
better off
than those slain by hunger,
who waste away,
pierced with pain
because the fields
lack produce.

י *Yod*

10 The hands
of compassionate women
have cooked
their own children;
they became their food
during the destruction
of my dear people.

כ *Kaf*

11 The Lord has exhausted
His wrath,
poured out
His burning anger;
He has ignited a fire in Zion,
and it has consumed
her foundations.

Jerusalem's Sins: the Cause of Her Collapse (4:12-22)

ל *Lamed*

12 The kings of the earth
and all the world's inhabitants
did not believe
that an enemy or adversary
could enter Jerusalem's gates.

מ *Mem*

13 Yet it happened because of
the sins of her prophets
and the •guilt of her priests,
who shed the blood
of the righteous
within her.

נ *Nun*

14 Blind, they stumbled
in the streets,
defiled by this blood,
so that no one dared
to touch their garments.

A 4:7 Lit *bones* B 4:7 Or *lapis lazuli*

ס *Samek*

15 "Stay away! •Unclean!"
people shouted at them.
"Away, away! Don't touch us!"
So they wandered aimlessly.
It was said among the nations,
"They can stay here
no longer."

פ *Pe*

16 The LORD Himself
has scattered them;
He regards them no more.
The priests are not respected;
the elders find no favor.

ע *Ayin*

17 All the while our eyes
were failing
as we looked in vain
for assistance;
we watched from our towers
for a nation[A] that refused
to help.

צ *Tsade*

18 Our steps
were closely followed
so that we could not walk
in our streets.
Our end drew near; our time
ran out.
Our end had come!

ק *Qof*

19 Those who chased us
were swifter
than eagles in the sky;
they relentlessly pursued us
over the mountains
and ambushed us
in the wilderness.

ר *Resh*

20 The LORD's anointed,[B]
the breath of our life,[C]
was captured in their traps.
We had said about him,
"We will live
under his protection
among the nations."

ש *Sin*

21 So rejoice and be glad,
Daughter Edom,
you resident of the land of Uz!
Yet the cup will pass to you
as well;
you will get drunk
and expose yourself.

ת *Tav*

22 Daughter Zion,
your punishment
is complete;
He will not lengthen
your exile.[D]
But He will punish
your iniquity,
Daughter Edom,
and will expose your sins.

Prayer for Restoration (5:1-22)

Repentance of the Nation (5:1-18)

5 •Yahweh, remember
what has happened to us.
Look, and see our disgrace!
2 Our inheritance
has been turned over
to strangers,
our houses to foreigners.
3 We have become
orphans, fatherless;
our mothers are widows.
4 We must pay for the water
we drink;
our wood comes at a price.
5 We are closely pursued;
we are tired, and no one
offers us rest.
6 We made a treaty with[E] Egypt
and with Assyria,
to get enough food.
7 Our fathers sinned;
they no longer exist,
but we bear
their punishment.
8 Slaves rule over us;
no one rescues us
from their hands.
9 We secure our food at the risk
of our lives
because of the sword
in the wilderness.
10 Our skin is as hot[F] as an oven
from the ravages of hunger.

4:21-22 Edom, a long-time enemy of Judah, is singled out for harsh punishment, consistent with Jr 49:12. In both passages, Edom must drink **the cup** of the Lord's punishment, just like Judah did. Unlike Judah, however, Edom's situation shows no hope of recovery (Jr 49:17-18).

5:1-5 The final stanza of this lament concludes as an appeal to **Yahweh** to act on the nation's behalf. Possibly this section describes living conditions of those poor people who remained in Jerusalem (left by Nebuchadnezzar) after the fall of the city. They are displaced, devastated, and destitute.

5:6-9 The current generation is reaping the consequences of their **fathers**' sins of idolatry, which led to allegiances to godless nations. The situation is one of difficulty and servitude, where the conqueror reigns supreme (also vv. 4,13), and obtaining food is expensive and dangerous, perhaps due to enemy raids (**sword in the wilderness**).

A4:17 Probably Egypt B4:20 = King Zedekiah C4:20 Lit *nostrils* D4:22 Or *not deport you again* E5:6 Lit *We gave the hand to* F5:10 Or *black*; Hb obscure

5:10-12 In the destruction of Jerusalem, people of all ages and ranks were abused; none were unaffected, from **women** and **girls** to **princes** and **elders.**

5:13-18 Various evidences of desolation include lack of **elders** at the **city gate**, lack of youth and **music**, lack of **joy** and **dancing,** and lack of pride (**the crown has fallen from our head**). Especially distressing is the desolation of Mount **Zion**, where the ruins of the temple remind the citizens of God's anger toward them.

5:19-22 This lengthy, poetic death wail ends with an expression of triumph that the **Lord** is **enthroned forever**, inspiring hope that He sees Judah's plight and hears her supplication. Judah pleads for restoration and return (both of which have *shuv* as their Hb root) to the Lord and a renewal of her former status.

11 Women are raped in •Zion,
girls in the cities of Judah.
12 Princes are hung up
by their hands;
elders are shown no respect.
13 Young men labor
at millstones;
boys stumble
under loads of wood.
14 The elders have left
the city •gate,
the young men, their music.
15 Joy has left our hearts;
our dancing has turned
to mourning.
16 The crown has fallen
from our head.
Woe to us,
for we have sinned.
17 Because of this, our heart
is sick;
because of these, our eyes
grow dim:
18 because of Mount Zion,
which lies desolate
and has jackals
prowling in it.

Prayer for Restoration of the Nation (5:19-22)

19 You, LORD,
are enthroned forever;
Your throne endures
from generation
to generation.
20 Why have You
forgotten us forever,
abandoned us
for our entire lives?
21 LORD, restore us to Yourself,
so we may return;
renew our days
as in former times,
22 unless You have completely
rejected us
and are intensely angry
with us.

LAMENTATIONS... WRITTEN ON MY Heart Daughter Zion certainly lays out a heart-rending story of suffering and brokenness. Often, a woman's nurturing instinct leads her to empathize, comfort, and encourage a sufferer by minimizing the pain. That is a Christian response and is compatible with Paul's injunction for those within the body of Christ to "weep with those who weep" (Rm 12:15). It is worth asking, however, whether the suffering that you or others experience might constitute divine discipline brought on as a consequence of personal sins. More specifically, among children of the heavenly Father, you should expect to be disciplined when you violate your covenant with Him. Above all, you must remind yourself and others that God disciplines as a loving and compassionate Father and that He does not intend to destroy His children but rather to spur them to repentance, renewal, and restoration. God's discipline is "for our benefit, so that we can share His holiness" (Heb 12:10). Take a cue from Judah, and examine yourself when you are beset by suffering and distress, whether in greater or lesser capacities, and respond to the covenant God with humility, confession, and repentance, claiming God's "mercies" and the hope of full restoration.

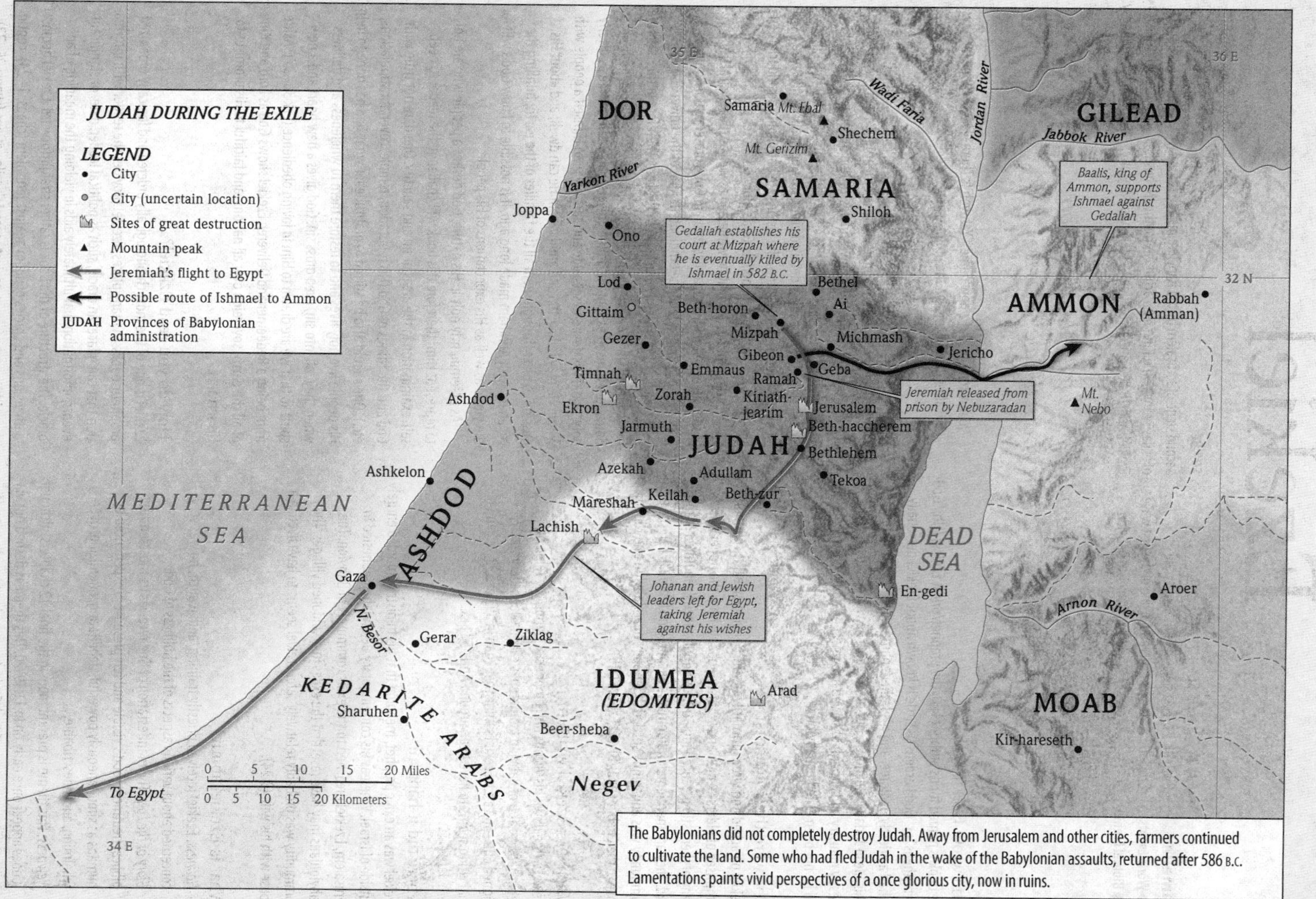

The Babylonians did not completely destroy Judah. Away from Jerusalem and other cities, farmers continued to cultivate the land. Some who had fled Judah in the wake of the Babylonian assaults, returned after 586 B.C. Lamentations paints vivid perspectives of a once glorious city, now in ruins.

Ezekiel

Timeline World Events Biblical Events	623 BC Birth of Ezekiel	605 BC First siege of Jerusalem by the Babylonians and taking of the first wave of exiles, including Daniel, to Babylon	597 BC Second siege of Jerusalem by the Babylonians and second wave of exiles—including King Jehoiachin, his mother Nehushta, Ezekiel, and 10,000 citizens of Judah—taken to Babylon	593 BC God's calling of Ezekiel, then 30 years old, to prophesy

"I will give you a new heart . . . I will place My Spirit within you . . . then you will live" (36:26-28).

Who wrote Ezekiel?

The book is named for its author (1:3), the prophet/priest Ezekiel (Hb, "God strengthens" or "God hardens"). Little is known about Ezekiel personally. He had a priestly pedigree, and his father's name was Buzi. The dating of his life in Judah is unknown, but presumably he was prepared for the priestly ministry and either had served as a priest or would have done so, had he not been exiled to Babylon in 597 B.C.

Who were the recipients?

Ezekiel preached and wrote primarily for the Babylonian exilic community comprised of elders—men and women probably from the upper classes. Many of them still practiced idolatry, yet simultaneously inquired of the Lord. They are mentioned in Jeremiah's encouraging letter (Jr 29). The exilic community was apparently settled at Tel-abib, near Babylon and Nippur, close to the Chebar Canal/River (Ezk 3:11,15).

When was Ezekiel written?

Ezekiel wrote down his visions and prophecies during the reign of Nebuchadnezzar II of Babylon (sometimes called "Nebuchadrezzar"; reigned 605–562 B.C.). Ezekiel's ministry began in 592 or 593 B.C., and his final vision seems to have been around April, 571 B.C.

Where did it happen?

Ezekiel was an exilic prophet, meaning that his ministry unfolded entirely outside of Israel. Whereas his contemporary, Jeremiah, prophesied in Jerusalem, Ezekiel preached to the exilic community in Babylon. The Babylonians may have resettled the exiles in abandoned villages. Their community was probably relatively safe. Ezekiel seems to have lived in a house with his wife (3:24).

What is Ezekiel about?

- *Holiness*. Ezekiel received priestly training, and as such, he was very concerned about various aspects of the holiness of God.
- *Glory of the Lord*. The manifestation of God receives its most lengthy biblical treatment. God's visible and felt presence is experienced by humans as simultaneously powerful, debilitating, energizing, overwhelming, and indescribable.
- *Newness*: This theme is present more in the final 12 chapters, although it does appear once early on in 11:19-20. This theme is fleshed out via several concrete actions of God. Ezekiel writes about Israel's restoration to God through the event of a new exodus (gathered from the nations), and regeneration through the gift of a new heart and new spirit. The land would be renewed and made fruitful, and the new city would have a new temple and a new name, "Yahweh Is There." Finally, hope for new life after death came via the promise of resurrection.

Why should women read Ezekiel?

All sincere believers, whether male or female, yearn for a glimpse of God's glory. Ezekiel offers the most powerful description of God's unbelievable might, majesty, power, and holiness since Moses encountered God on Mount Sinai. The only other detailed visions of God in all His glory are found in Daniel and Revelation. The visions are both uplifting and frightening, and while we desire to behold God's glory (as Moses did, Ex 33:18), Ezekiel's descriptions of what he witnessed as well as the physical impact of such an overwhelming manifestation of God's presence is a reminder that we are responsible to the omnipotent King of the universe.

Ezekiel contains mainly oracles from the Lord; therefore in this book we can hear God clearly speaking to and through Ezekiel, revealing information about Himself as supreme in the universe; about His nature as utterly holy; about His desire to set aside and sanctify unto Himself a people with whom He may fellowship and amid whom He can dwell; and about His mission to bless through them all the families of the earth, fulfilling the covenant with Abraham made long ago. It *is* possible to know God's will for the world as well as His expectations of His people.

As preeminently holy in His nature, God desires a people who are holy to represent Him; therefore this book will challenge the reader to deep self-examination in the areas of sin and sanctity. One dare not trifle with God and the things of God (His reputation, temple, covenant stipulations, etc.). One should also be stirred to gratitude for what God has done to help His people live holy lives and to restore them to wholeness and holiness when they fall into sin, even gross sin. God gives a new heart and a new spirit so that we are drawn to Him in loving obedience (Ezk 36–37). Aside from being a Redeemer and Deliverer, Ezekiel shows God as Lord and King of all the earth, sovereign over all nations, and faithful to His promises to His servants.

How do you read Ezekiel?

Ezekiel is one of the most chronologically ordered and logically organized prophetic books. In many places, Ezekiel provides the reader with information that can "place" an oracle, such as political leader, date, or significant events, information that ultimately aids in yielding the meaning of an oracle. The structure of the book is rather straightforward. Ezekiel begins with visions and oracles of doom against Jerusalem (chaps. 1–24), continues with oracles of doom against several Gentile nations (chaps. 25–32), and then continues for the remainder of the book with oracles of hope for the exiles, culminating in a glorious description and "tour" of a new temple in a restored and Edenic Israel (chaps. 33–48).

588 BC	586 BC	587–586 BC	538 BC	515 BC
Death of Ezekiel's wife	Destruction of the walls of Jerusalem and the temple after a two-year siege; taking of the third wave of exiles to Babylon	Nebuchadnezzar's invasion of Egypt in fulfillment of prophecies by both Jeremiah and Ezekiel	Decree issued by Cyrus allowing the Jews to return to Judah	Dedication of the new temple

Much prophetic, oracular material is poetic in nature and seems at times to be a riddle, making some of the passages inaccessible without study helps. Poetry is not always meant to be taken literally. It employs metaphor and personification as literary devices to convey truth. Ezekiel contains several lyrical/ poetic passages, which include several "songs": of the sword, of the pot, and of the cup. There is also the use of several allegories/parables: the useless vine (chap. 15), the eagles (chap. 17), the two immoral sisters (chap. 23), and God's tragic romance with Jerusalem (chap. 16). The latter two bear some comment concerning their portrayal of women. Some of the descriptions are graphic and vivid, leaving no doubt as to the author's meaning. The text is intended to shock the reader/Israelite into repulsion, remorse, and repentance upon realization of the heinous nature of sin. The reader also is made aware of the disgusting nature of sin in God's sight. The intent is *not* to denigrate women, marriage, or sex or to single out women for violent treatment or abuse.

Poetry is grounded in history, and the reader should bear in mind that the historical background to Ezekiel, and indeed all the prophetic books, is found in the historical books of the Bible, especially in Kings and Chronicles, while the theological background is found mainly in the first five books (Pentateuch) of Moses, and especially the covenant passages in Deuteronomy. One final word ought to be said regarding Ezekiel's personal history. Ezekiel's own life unfolded in tandem with his own people and his own prophecies. As he prophesied to the exiles, he spoke as one of them, suffering the reproach of exile alongside them. As he performed sign-acts before the people, Ezekiel himself became a sign-act on one occasion; his wife died, and he was prohibited from mourning. His wife, as the "delight of his eyes" was clearly likened to the Jerusalem temple, the "delight" of Yahweh's eyes, which would shortly be devastated (Ezk 24:16,21). When Ezekiel received the final grand vision of the new temple, one cannot help but wonder if the hopeful and reassuring messages of resurrection from the grave and the certainty of a "resurrected" temple gave Ezekiel hope that one day that promise might become a reality for his wife, so that she too might live again.

Outline

I. Visions of God's Glory (1:1–11:25)
   A. Ezekiel's Call to Ministry (1:1–3:27)
   B. Prophecy Against Israel's Sin (4:1–5:17)
   C. Condemnation and Hope (6:1-14)
   D. A Declaration of Finality (7:1-27)
   E. Ezekiel's Vision of Jerusalem (8:1–11:25)

II. Oracles of Judgment Against Israel and Judah (12:1–24:27)
   A. A Dramatization of the Exile (12:1-28)
   B. An Oracle Against False Prophets (13:1-23)
   C. An Oracle Against Idolatrous Elders (14:1-23)
   D. The Parable of the Useless Vine (15:1-8)
   E. The Parable of the Adulterous Wife (16:1-63)
   F. The Demise of the Last Rulers of Judah (17:1–19:14)
   G. Rebellion and Restoration (20:1-49)
   H. The Sword of Judgment (21:1-32)
   I. Oracles against Jerusalem (22:1–24:27)

III. Oracles Against the Nations (25:1–32:32)
   A. Oracles Against Surrounding Nations (25:1-17)
   B. Oracles Against Tyre (26:1–28:26)
   C. Oracles Against Egypt (29:1–32:32)

IV. The Restoration of Israel (33:1–39:29)
   A. The Vocation of Ezekiel (33:1-33)
   B. The Good Shepherd (34:1-31)
   C. Judgment and the Restoration of Mountains (35:1–36:15)
   D. A Restoration of the People (36:16–37:28)
   E. Prophecies Against Gog of Magog (38:1–39:29)

V. The New/Heavenly Temple (40:1–48:35)
   A. The Temple and Its Measurements (40:1–42:20)
   B. The Return of the LORD's Glory and the Altar (43:1-27)
   C. Sacrificial and Property Stipulations Pertaining to the Prince (44:1–46:24)
   D. The Healing and Reallotment of the Land (47:1–48:29)
   E. The New City (48:30-35)

Title: The book is named for its author, Ezekiel, whose name means "God strengthens" or "God hardens." His name becomes a play on words when God compares the stubbornness of the people of Judah with the strengthening of Ezekiel for his ministry task to the Judean exiles in Babylon. See **Word Study**, 3:9-10,14, on p. 1048. He was both prophet and priest living in the sixth-century B.C. All that is known of Ezekiel derives from his book. He was a son of Buzi (1:3), taken captive to Babylon in 597 B.C., along with King Jehoiachin and 10,000 others, including political and military leaders and skilled craftsmen (2Kg 24:14-16). He lived in his own house near the river Chebar, an irrigation canal that channeled the Euphrates River into surrounding arid areas. He was married and ministered from his own home (3:24; 8:1; 33:30-33). His wife died suddenly (24:18), but he was not allowed to mourn the loss. Ezekiel was a priest before God called him to a prophetic ministry. In Jerusalem, he would have inherited the priestly office and prepared for it by traditional means. However, in exile the call came dramatically and directly from God. In a vision he was called into divine service and ushered into the presence of God. In autobiographical notes Ezekiel described his reactions to events with priestly sensitivities, especially to issues involving cleanness and uncleanness (4:14). Some of the actions God assigned to him were appropriate only for a priest: "bearing the iniquity" of the people (4:4-6) and not mourning the death of his wife (24:15-27; cp. Lv 21:4-5).

1:1-2 Two dates are given—**the fifth year of King Jehoiachin's exile** (i.e., 592 B.C.), and **the thirtieth year**. The meaning of the second date is unclear. The **Chebar Canal** was a tributary of the great Euphrates River, which fed the whole of Babylon and was used for agricultural irrigation. Although this reference could be simply stating Ezekiel's location at the time of his call, it is also worth noting that other prophets received visions and revelations by fresh water sources (Elijah, Elisha, Daniel, etc.), and in the Ancient Near East, *water* often represents life.

1:3 The word of the LORD came [a phrase used 50 times in the book of Ezekiel, more than any other OT book] **directly to Ezekiel** communicates that Ezekiel was given God's words. The test of legitimacy for the ministries of Old Testament prophets was the accuracy of the message they delivered because the words of the Lord can never be wrong. The book repeatedly assures its readers that Ezekiel preached God's words, not his own. The phrase **the LORD's hand was on** Ezekiel recurs whenever Ezekiel receives visions and revelations (3:22; 8:1; 33:22; 37:1; 40:1).

1:4 Ezekiel's visions began with his sighting of **a whirlwind coming from the north**, within which the Lord manifested Himself. A common belief in the ancient Near East was that a conquering nation's god(s) were more powerful than the conquered nation's god(s), that the human military defeat paralleled a spiritual/heavenly battle. Thus, perhaps the Jews believed that the god(s) of Babylon had defeated the Lord. Clearly, the immense power of this vision demonstrated that Yahweh was not defeated. That the whirlwind came from the **north** may be a reference to Mount Zaphon (Hb, "north"), the supposed abode of Baal (also adopted by the Babylonians), and serves as an assertion of Yahweh's power over Baal. The Lord is not a localized deity, limited to Jerusalem or the geographical boundaries of Israel. The King of the universe comes from and goes wherever He pleases.

1:5-10 These four mysterious creatures are described as having **four faces—of a man . . . a lion . . . an ox . . . and . . . an eagle**. Scholars disagree on the meaning or significance of the different faces. Some have suggested that the ox or bull represents fertility and/or harvest, the lion signifies strength, the eagle represents nobility, and the man embodies the image of God. Others have suggested that the eagle represents the creatures of the air; the lion, creatures of the wild; the bull, domesticated creatures; and the man, the pinnacle of creation. In any case, the little information available in the text remains difficult to interpret.

>WORD|*study*

1:4 Whirlwind (Hb *ruach*, "wind, breath, spirit" combined with *sa'ar*, "storm, tempest, whirlwind"; cp. 13:11,13) refers literally to a great storm cloud with attendant winds, possibly a tornado, displaying the great strength and power of the Lord. The "whirlwind" imagery is also associated with the "Spirit" (Hb *ruach*, 1:12) of God, who animated the vision, directing the movement of the "living creatures" (see **Doctrine,** "Angels: Cherubim and Living Creatures," p.1058) and inhabiting the "wheels" (vv. 12,20-21). The imagery is similar to the description of the coming of the Holy Spirit at Pentecost (Ac 2) and to the language of Jesus in His conversation with Nicodemus (Jn 3).

1:5 Here, the details are intended to convey Ezekiel's overall impression of the appearance (Hb *mar'eh*, "form, sight, vision; like," used 36 times in the book, 15 in chap. 1) of the form (Hb *demut*, "likeness," used nine times in chap. 1) of the LORD's glory" (1:28). The concentrated use of these two Hebrew words throughout chapter 1 (including four times in v. 28) is striking. Repeated use of these words underscores the fact that the prophet saw things so completely out of the ordinary that he lacked the vocabulary to compose a direct description. To convey what he saw required heavy reliance on comparison. As the primary author of Scripture, the Holy Spirit has allowed the mysterious character of this and other prophetic visions (cp. Dn 8:15-17,27) to persist rather than providing such thorough explanations that men would mistakenly believe they were capable of completely understanding the Lord and His ways (cp. Is 55:8-9).

Ezekiel's Call to Ministry (1:1–3:27)

His Vision of the LORD (1:1-28)

1 In the thirtieth year, in the fourth month, on the fifth day of the month, while I was among the exiles by the Chebar Canal, the heavens opened and I saw visions of God. 2 On the fifth day of the month—it was the fifth year of King Jehoiachin's exile— 3 the word of the LORD came directly to Ezekiel the priest, the son of Buzi, in the land of the Chaldeans by the Chebar Canal. And the LORD's hand was on him there.

4 I looked and there was a whirlwind coming from the north, a great cloud with fire flashing back and forth and brilliant light all around it. In the center of the fire, there was a gleam like amber. 5 The form of four living creatures came from it. And this was their appearance: They had human form, 6 but each of them had four faces and four wings. 7 Their legs were straight, and the soles of their feet were like the hooves of a calf, sparkling like the gleam of polished bronze. 8 They had human hands under their wings on their four sides. All four of them had faces and wings. 9 Their wings were touching. The creatures did not turn as they moved; each one went straight ahead. 10 The form of each of their faces was that of a man, and each of the four had the face of a lion on the right, the face of an ox on the left, and the face of an eagle. 11 That is what their faces were like. Their wings were spread upward; each had two wings touching that of another and two wings covering its body. 12 Each creature went straight ahead. Wherever the Spirit[A] wanted to go, they went without turning as they moved.

13 The form of the living creatures was like the appearance of burning coals of fire and torches. Fire was moving back and forth between the living creatures; it was bright, with lightning coming out of it. 14 The creatures were darting back and forth like flashes of lightning.

15 When I looked at the living creatures, there was one wheel on the ground beside each creature that had four faces. 16 The appearance of the wheels and their craftsmanship was like the gleam of beryl, and all four had the same form. Their appearance and craftsmanship was like a wheel within a wheel. 17 When they moved, they went in any of the four directions, without pivoting as they moved. 18 Their rims were large and frightening. Each of their four rims were full of eyes all around. 19 So when the living creatures moved, the wheels moved beside them, and when the creatures rose from the earth, the wheels also rose. 20 Wherever the Spirit[A] wanted to go, the creatures went in the direction the Spirit was moving. The wheels rose alongside them, for the spirit of the living creatures was in the wheels. 21 When the creatures moved, the wheels moved; when the creatures stood still, the wheels stood still;

A 1:12,20 Or *spirit*

>WORD|*study*

1:26 The Hebrew word translated human in Ezk 1:5,8,26 is the word *ʾadam*, first used in Scripture in Gn 1:26—"And God said, 'Let Us make man in Our image, according to Our likeness'"; verse 27 then clarifies that "God created man in His own image . . . male and female" (see **Word Study**, Gn 2:18, p. 7). The word *ʾadam*, as a term of comparison in Ezk 1 (and 10:8,14,21), refers to the generic or collective concept of "man," implicitly including both men and women, who, together rather than separately, comprise mankind. In English, both "mankind" and "human" are always generic in this sense. In the context of Ezekiel's visions, however, the prophet does not compare the appearance of either the creatures or God the King to an undefined human being but to the features of a man:

- *ʾAdam* is translated as "man" in verse 10, perhaps reflecting its parallel in Rv 4:7, which translates the Greek word *anthrōpos* as "man" because it is used there in reference to a particular individual, "the third living creature." Like *ʾadam*, *anthrōpos* can also be used in a gender-inclusive, generic sense, but it ordinarily refers to a male human and, when used in reference to individuals, never denotes a female. *Anthrōpos* is used to translate the word *ʾadam* throughout the Septuagint, the first translation of Ezekiel.
- The immediate context of Ezk 1 does not leave any question marks about what sort of human form the prophet saw. In verse 27, both instances of the word **waist** (Hb *motenayim*, "loins") have a masculine possessive ending, denoting *his* (a man's) waist. The translators have also capitalized "His" to indicate Ezekiel's understanding, noted in verse 28, that he was seeing a vision of God as King, who then speaks to the prophet.
- *ʾAdam* appears at least 130 times in Ezekiel, more often than in any other Old Testament book, most often (93 times) in the phrase "son of man," with which the Lord addressed the prophet (e.g., 2:1,6).

1:27 The term for amber (Hb *chashmal*) occurs in Scripture only in the book of Ezekiel (1:4,27; 8:2). It could refer to glowing metal or to a precious stone. The detail seems to convey both the purity and great worth of the Lord. It also contributes to the brilliance and intensity of the vision of the majesty of the Lord.

and when the creatures rose from
the earth, the wheels rose alongside them, for the spirit of the living
creatures was in the wheels.
22 The shape of an expanse, with
a gleam like awe-inspiring crystal,
was spread out over the heads of the
living creatures. 23 And under the
expanse their wings extended one
toward another. Each of them also
had two wings covering their bodies. 24 When they moved, I heard the
sound of their wings like the roar of
mighty waters, like the voice of the
•Almighty, and a sound of commotion like the noise of an army. When
they stood still, they lowered their
wings.
25 A voice came from above the
expanse over their heads; when
they stood still, they lowered their
wings. 26 The shape of a throne with
the appearance of sapphire[A] stone
was above the expanse.[B] There was
a form with the appearance of a
human on the throne high above.
27 From what seemed to be His waist
up, I saw a gleam like amber, with
what looked like fire enclosing it
all around. From what seemed to
be His waist down, I also saw what
looked like fire. There was a brilliant
light all around Him. 28 The appearance of the brilliant light all around
was like that of a rainbow in a cloud
on a rainy day. This was the appearance of the form of the LORD's glory.
When I saw it, I fell facedown and
heard a voice speaking.

His Commission (2:1–3:15)

2 He said to me, "Son of man, stand
up on your feet and I will speak
with you." 2 As He spoke to me, the
Spirit entered me and set me on my
feet, and I listened to the One who
was speaking to me. 3 He said to
me: "Son of man, I am sending you
to the Israelites, to[C] the rebellious

Doctrine THEOPHANY

A theophany means literally a showing or appearance of God. Ezekiel describes a manifestation of God's glory in time and space, hovering over the Chebar Canal (chaps. 1–3), abandoning the city of Jerusalem (chap. 10), and later returning in triumphant procession to the new temple and filling up the holy of holies (chap. 43). The associated imagery is consistent and includes: fire/hot coals, lightning, loud noise, an overpowering physical presence, smoke/cloud, whirlwind/storm/tornado and sometimes various combinations of these elements (cp. Jb 36:22–38:3; Dn 8:18,27; 10:5-19; Rv 1:9-20; 4:1-11). For example, in Rv 4, God appears on His throne surrounded by living creatures with six wings and covered with eyes. In Rv 15:1-8 the glass/crystal platform appears as in Ezk 1:22-23,25-26. The usual effect of a theophany is to manifest God's omnipotence and visible presence in a captivating and powerful way.

1:12-14 In light of the fact that Judah found herself in exile, the fire imagery probably indicates God's judgment against the people's sin, and His pure holiness contrasted with their defilement.

1:15-21 This extended description of the **wheels** seems curious. Their depiction adds to the fascinating symmetry of this image within a constantly moving whirlwind. In addition to the four faces and four wings, there are four wheels with **rims**, which were **large and frightening** and **full of eyes all around**. This imagery foreshadows John's vision of God's throne room in Rv 4, in which the living creatures are covered with eyes "around and inside" (Rv 4:8) rather than the wheels being covered with eyes. For more on this comparison see **Doctrine**, p. 1058. There is constant movement effected by the wheels, which are powered by the life energy of the **living creatures**, so that the chariot-throne rises and descends at will in any direction.

1:22 Ezekiel describes an **expanse** (Hb *raqiyaʿ*, from the verb *ragaʿ*—"hammered or pounded out, like a metal plate; spread out") as something like icy **crystal**, a glassy platform.

1:22-28 Ultimately, Ezekiel's vision set the stage for his entire ministry. This commissioning foreshadowed the message he would be given to proclaim. The imagery of the Lord as a warrior-king riding His awe-inspiring chariot and coming with flaming fire and lightning flashes speaks to the judgment that has already been poured out upon the Jews because of their sin. This imagery also points to the future judgment coming upon the nations who seek to destroy the Lord's people and defile the land. This same imagery, though, is also associated with the deliverance of the Jews from the nations (cp. Ps 18, especially vv. 10,16-24). Ezekiel's ministry will be one of judgment upon all who deny the Lord, but it will also offer hope to the people of God, if they will turn back to the Lord.

2:1 The One speaking to Ezekiel was the Lord, the One whose "voice came from above the expanse" (1:25).

2:2 The description of the **Spirit** (Hb *ruach*) entering Ezekiel could possibly be as innocuous as Ezekiel regaining his breath (*ruach*) after having the wind knocked out of him. The phrase **set me on my feet** would then be understood as a Hebraic expression referring to regaining one's composure. However, more likely God's Spirit (*ruach*) animates Ezekiel's body in a way similar to the Spirit's control and

[A]1:26 Or *lapis lazuli* [B]1:26 Lit *expanse that was over their head* [C]2:3 Or *Israelites and to*

guidance of the living creatures. Thus, Ezekiel's ministry begins with divine empowerment.

2:3-5 The phrase, **This is what the Lord God says** (cp. 3:11) indicates the true source of the prophet's authority, which might have been doubted by those living so far from the land of Israel. The Lord repeatedly characterized the Israelites as **rebellious** (Hb *marad*, "stubbornly perverse, willfully disobedient;" cp. 17:15; 20:38; *meri*, "obstinately disobedient," vv. 5-8; cp. 3:9,26-27; 12:2-3,9,25; 17:12; 24:3; 44:6).

2:6–3:3 Ezekiel's message would be rejected, and he himself would encounter hostility, indicated by the imagery of **briers and thorns** and **scorpions.** He was commanded to eat the **scroll**, which **a hand** extended to him and **unrolled** (2:10). **Words** are a theme throughout—words of rejecting the prophetic judgment and words of the divine-human encounter within the prophet as a willing vessel (cp. 2:10; 3:4,5-6,10). The word of the Lord is sweet to **eat** (3:1; cp. Ps 119:103), but proclaiming its message of judgment on his own people would be a bitter task (cp. Rv 10:9-10). The eating of the scroll symbolized the prophet's internalizing of God's message.

3:7-9 Israel's rejection of Ezekiel's message reflected their rejection of God Himself. Although the text emphasizes the house of Israel as the intended recipients of the message, Ezekiel's ministry also extended to the nations, especially seen in chapters 25–32 (cp. Jr 46–51).

3:12-14 Interestingly, Ezekiel **left** the presence of God's glory **in bitterness and in an angry** [Hb *chêmah*, "heat, rage, fury"; used over 25 times in the book, always referring to *God's* "wrath" (e.g., 5:13)—except in this verse] **spirit**.

3:15 For **seven days**, Ezekiel **sat there . . . stunned** (Hb *shamêm*, "astonished"; cp. 32:10), apparently trying to make sense of what the Lord had revealed to him and commanded him to do. Ezekiel was overwhelmed by the visions he had witnessed.

3:16-17 The length of **seven days** may be related to the consecration time for the priests (cp. Lv 8:1-33). Ezekiel's responsibility to warn sinners **when** he would **hear a word from** God's **mouth** carried the threat of death if he failed in his mission because he was given a direct revelation from God for the people. God commissioned Ezekiel as a **watchman over the house of Israel**. Although the priests of Israel were supposed to serve this function,

>WORD|*study*

2:4 In the Hebrew text, the word heart (*lēv*) occurs 41 times, referring most often to Israel's spiritual condition. In Hebrew thought, "heart" refers to a person's will—the mind, imagination, and faculty of planning and decision-making. The book of Ezekiel continually describes the Israelites' sin in terms of their hearts:

- departure from the Lord—having "promiscuous hearts that turned away" from Him (6:9);
- pursuit of "idols" (6:9; 20:16) and "dishonest profit" (33:31);
- desire for "detestable things and practices" (11:21);
- pride (28:2,6,17); and
- surrender to the control of "idols," having "set [them] up [Hb *ʿalah*, "elevate, exalt"] in their hearts" (14:3-5,7).

Having compromised and utterly defiled their hearts, therefore, the Lord promised to give them (11:19; cp. 18:31):

- "one heart" (i.e., characterized by integrity and single-minded devotion to the Lord, by fidelity as opposed to divided loyalty); and
- "a heart of flesh," replacing their hardened determination to defy God's purposes (see **hardhearted** below, 3:9-10,14) with a will that is alive and pliable, easily molded to the Lord's design.

2:4–3:14 It is interesting to note the language of *hardness* in chapters 2 and 3. God told **Ezekiel**, whose name means "God hardens," that his audience would be:

- **hardhearted** (Hb *chazaq*, "firm," of *lēv*, "heart," 2:4),
- **obstinate** (Hb *qasheh*, "stiff," of *panim*, "face"—i.e., "impudent," 2:4; 3:7),
- **hardheaded** (Hb *chazaq*, "firm," of *metsach*, "forehead"), and
- **hardhearted** (Hb *qasheh*, "stiff," of *lēv*, "heart," 3:7).

3:9-10,14 The Lord reassured Ezekiel that He had equipped the prophet to withstand the people's recalcitrant opposition to his message. The prophet's **face** and **forehead** would be harder (Hb *chazaq*, appearing three more times in 3:8-9), in fact, **like a diamond, harder than flint.** Rather than being "hardhearted" like his audience, Ezekiel was instructed to **take . . . to heart** what God spoke to him (3:10) and not to be discouraged [Hb *chatat*, "broken down with fear, dismayed"] **by the look on their faces** (2:6; 3:9; cp. Jr 1:17). Finally, as a means of compelling Ezekiel to carry out his assigned task, **the Lord's hand was on** [him] powerfully (Hb *chazaq*, "be strong, firm; hold fast," 3:14). Jeremiah also was promised God's strength and support, but this same language is not used (Jr 1:17-19). Hardness of heart and mind together with hardness of face (internal hardness, which produces external hardness) are paired together logically with **rebellion** numerous times throughout this commissioning section.

pagans[A] who have rebelled against
Me. The Israelites and their ancestors have transgressed against Me
to this day. 4 The children are obstinate[B] and hardhearted. I am sending you to them, and you must say
to them, 'This is what the Lord God
says.' 5 Whether they listen or refuse to listen—for they are a rebellious house—they will know that a
prophet has been among them.
6 "But you, son of man, do not
be afraid of them or their words,
though briers and thorns are beside you and you live among scorpions. Don't be afraid of their words
or be discouraged by the look on
their faces, for they are a rebellious
house. 7 But speak My words to them
whether they listen or refuse to listen, for they are rebellious.
8 "And you, son of man, listen to
what I tell you: Do not be rebellious
like that rebellious house. Open
your mouth and eat what I am giving you." 9 So I looked and saw a
hand reaching out to me, and there
was a written scroll in it. 10 When He
unrolled it before me, it was written
on the front and back; words of lamentation, mourning, and woe were
written on it.

3 He said to me: "Son of man,
eat what you find here. Eat this
scroll, then go and speak to the
house of Israel." 2 So I opened my
mouth, and He fed me the scroll.
3 "Son of man," He said to me, "eat[C]
and fill your stomach with this scroll
I am giving you." So I ate it, and it
was as sweet as honey in my mouth.
4 Then He said to me: "Son of man,
go to the house of Israel and speak
My words to them. 5 For you are not
being sent to a people of unintelligible speech or difficult language
but to the house of Israel. 6 You are
not being sent to many peoples of
unintelligible speech or difficult

[A] 2:3 LXX omits *to the rebellious pagans* [B] 2:4 Lit *hard of face* [C] 3:3 Lit *feed your belly*

language, whose words you cannot
understand. No doubt, if I sent you
to them, they would listen to you.
7 But the house of Israel will not
want to listen to you because they
do not want to listen to Me. For the
whole house of Israel is hardheaded
and hardhearted. 8 Look, I have made
your face as hard as their faces and
your forehead as hard as their foreheads. 9 I have made your forehead
like a diamond, harder than flint.
Don't be afraid of them or discouraged by the look on their faces, even
though they are a rebellious house."
10 Next He said to me: "Son of man,
listen carefully to all My words that I
speak to you and take them to heart.
11 Go to your people, the exiles, and
speak to them. Tell them, 'This is
what the Lord God says,' whether
they listen or refuse to listen."
12 The Spirit then lifted me up,
and I heard a great rumbling sound
behind me—praise the glory of the
Lord in His place!— 13 with the[A]
sound of the living creatures' wings
brushing against each other and the
sound of the wheels beside them, a
great rumbling sound. 14 So the Spirit lifted me up and took me away. I
left in bitterness and in an angry
spirit, and the Lord's hand was on
me powerfully. 15 I came to the exiles
at Tel-abib, who were living by the
Chebar Canal, and I sat there among
them stunned for seven days.

His Responsibility (3:16-27)

16 Now at the end of seven days
the word of the Lord came to me:
17 "Son of man, I have made you a
watchman over the house of Israel.
When you hear a word from My
mouth, give them a warning from
Me. 18 If I say to the wicked person,
'You will surely die,' but you do not
warn him—you don't speak out to
warn him about his wicked way in
order to save his life—that wicked
person will die for his iniquity. Yet
I will hold you responsible for his
blood. 19 But if you warn a wicked
person and he does not turn from
his wickedness or his wicked way,
he will die for his iniquity, but you
will have saved your life. 20 Now if
a righteous person turns from his
righteousness and practices iniquity, and I put a stumbling block in
front of him, he will die. If you did
not warn him, he will die because of
his sin and the righteous acts he did
will not be remembered. Yet I will
hold you responsible for his blood.
21 But if you warn the righteous person that he should not sin, and he
does not sin, he will indeed live because he listened to your warning,
and you will have saved your life."
22 Then the hand of the Lord was
on me there, and He said to me, "Get
up, go out to the plain, and I will
speak with you there." 23 So I got up
and went out to the plain. The Lord's
glory was present there, like the glory I had seen by the Chebar Canal,
and I fell facedown. 24 The Spirit entered me and set me on my feet. He
spoke with me and said: "Go, shut
yourself inside your house. 25 And
you, son of man, they will put ropes
on you and bind you with them so
you cannot go out among them. 26 I
will make your tongue stick to the
roof of your mouth, and you will be

[A] 3:12-13 Some emend to *behind me as the glory of the Lord rose from His place:* [13] *the*

clearly many of them were not performing this sacred duty.

3:18-21 God charged Ezekiel with warning two specific groups of people—those who were **wicked** and sinning and those who were **righteous** but had begun sinning. While there are minor differences in the wording of God's role in warning and executing judgment—the unrighteous are told, **You will surely die** (cp. 33:8,14; Gn 2:17), and the sinning righteous have **a stumbling block** placed in front of them—the result is the same. If those in either group fail to repent, death follows. The text does not clarify whether God actively judges the righteous who sin while passively judging the unrighteous. Either way, every sector of Judean society was affected by sin, and all people—both the wicked and the righteous—had turned from the Lord. Ezekiel was responsible for calling the people to repentance, and he would incur some form of bloodguilt (**responsible for** their **blood**; cp. 33:8) if he failed to warn them; in fact, it could result in his own death. God clearly told Ezekiel that if he did warn the people, even if they continued in their sin, he would have **saved** (Hb *natsal*, "deliver"; see **Word Study**, Ps 7:1-2, p. 672) his own **life** (cp. Ezk 33:9).

3:22-23 As the **Lord's glory** manifested itself again in another location (**the plain**), the control of the Spirit of God is again evident: first, with the control of the Lord's chariot-throne and then with the work of the Spirit in/through Ezekiel.

3:24-27 God offers a somewhat strange command to Ezekiel, along with a warning. He tells Ezekiel to withdraw from society and warns him that he will be persecuted by the people (**bind you**), presumably because of his confrontational message.

The Lord informs Ezekiel that He will prevent him from preaching on his own, seemingly in order to protect the integrity of the proclamation. Only when the Lord speaks with Ezekiel will he be able to preach to the people; otherwise, he will be **mute (tongue** stuck to **the roof of** his **mouth)**. It seems that the order to **shut** himself **inside** his **house** is another provision to protect the integrity of the proclamation. If Ezekiel's only words to the people are the words directly from the Lord—divine revelation—then the people are without excuse. If, however, the divine revelation were intermixed with Ezekiel's own ideas, then there could be a possibility of erroneous teaching, giving the people an excuse for not following God's wishes. God makes it clear to Ezekiel that few, if any, will listen to his

>WORD|*study*

3:17 The Lord addresses the prophet as son of man (Hb *bên-'adam*) throughout the book. The phrase highlights Ezekiel's identity as an ordinary, sinful, mortal human being, in contrast to the supernatural God, the Lord of glory. However, to be called "son of man" also reflects the dignity of being created in God's image. Of great significance is the fact that Jesus, the Son of God, most often referred to Himself as "the Son of Man" (e.g., Mt 24:27; Mk 8:38; 14:62; Jn 1:51; 13:31; see also Dn 7:13-14).

3:17 A watchman (Hb *tsaphah*) is one who bends or inclines forward, training his eyes on what can be seen from the wide view afforded by the height of the watch tower. A **watchman** was a guard tasked with warning (Hb *zahar*, "admonish, dissuade from," vv. 17-21; cp. 33:3-9; 2Kg 6:10; 2Ch 19:10) the inhabitants of a city when an enemy army approached. If the watchman fell asleep at his post or failed to warn the people, he was held personally responsible for any losses. Metaphorically, the prophet's role involved declaring future events that God has revealed. As a prophet, Ezekiel's job included guarding the Israelites from their own sin and warning them of the coming destruction and judgment on their rebellion.

mute and unable to rebuke them, for they are a rebellious house. 27 But when I speak with you, I will open your mouth, and you will say to them, 'This is what the Lord God says.' Let the one who listens, listen, and let the one who refuses, refuse—for they are a rebellious house.

Prophecy Against Israel's Sin (4:1–5:17)

Symbolic Act I: The Siege of Jerusalem (4:1-8)

4 "Now you, son of man, take a brick, set it in front of you, and draw the city of Jerusalem on it. 2 Then lay siege against it: construct a siege wall, build a ramp, pitch military camps, and place battering rams against it on all sides. 3 Take an iron plate and set it up as an iron wall between yourself and the city. Turn your face toward it so that it is under siege, and besiege it. This will be a sign for the house of Israel.

4 "Then lie down on your left side and place the iniquity[A] of the house of Israel on it. You will bear their iniquity for the number of days you lie on your side. 5 For I have assigned you the years of their iniquity according to the number of days you lie down, 390 days; so you will bear the iniquity of the house of Israel. 6 When you have completed these days, lie down again, but on your right side, and bear the iniquity of the house of Judah. I have assigned you 40 days, a day for each year. 7 You must turn your face toward the siege of Jerusalem with your arm bared, and prophesy against it. 8 Be aware that I will put cords on you so you cannot turn from side to side until you have finished the days of your siege.

Symbolic Act II: The Eating of Unclean Food (4:9-17)

9 "Also take wheat, barley, beans, lentils, millet, and spelt. Put them in a single container and make them into bread for yourself. You are to eat it during the number of days you lie on your side, 390 days. 10 The food you eat each day will be eight ounces[B] by weight; you will eat it from time to time.[C] 11 You are also to drink water by measure, a sixth of a gallon,[D] which you will drink from time to time. 12 You will eat it as you would a barley cake and bake it over dried human excrement in their sight." 13 The Lord said, "This is how the Israelites will eat their bread—ceremonially •unclean—among the nations where I will banish them."

14 But I said, "Oh, Lord God, I have never been defiled. From my youth until now I have not eaten anything that died naturally or was mauled by wild beasts. And impure meat has never entered my mouth."

15 He replied to me, "Look, I will let you use cow dung instead of human excrement, and you can make your bread over that." 16 Then He said to me, "Son of man, I am going to cut off the supply of bread in Jerusalem. They will anxiously eat bread rationed by weight and in dread drink water by measure. 17 So they will lack bread and water; everyone will be devastated and waste away because of their iniquity.

Symbolic Act III: The Cutting of Hair (5:1-4)

5 "Now you, son of man, take a sharp sword, use it as you would a barber's razor, and shave your head and beard. Then take a set of scales and divide the hair. 2 You are to burn up a third of it in the city when the days of the siege have ended; you are to take a third and slash it with the sword all around the city; and you are to scatter a third to the wind, for I will draw a sword to chase after them. 3 But you are to take a few strands from the hair and secure them in the folds of your robe. 4 Take some more of them, throw them into the fire, and burn them in it. A fire will spread from it to the whole house of Israel.

The Godlessness of Judah/Israel and the Fall of Jerusalem (5:5-10)

5 "This is what the Lord God says: I have set this Jerusalem in the center of the nations, with countries all around her. 6 But she has rebelled against My ordinances with more

message because the people of Judah are **rebellious**.

4:1–5:17 Ezekiel was commanded to perform three symbolic acts depicting the coming judgment on Judah: the siege, the eating of defiled food, and the shaving of his head. Symbolic actions were particularly appropriate for Ezekiel at this time because of his inability to speak (cp. 3:26), but they also served as powerful means of communication.

4:1-3 Taking a **brick** symbolizing Jerusalem, Ezekiel set up a mock attack against it, complete with ramparts and siege works, as **a sign** of the coming **siege** of the city.

4:4-7 He was then told to lie on his **left side** to **bear** Israel's **iniquity** (Hb *'awon*, "depraved action, crime, guilt, punishment") and to lie on his **right side . . .** to **bear** Judah's **iniquity**. The significance of the days (representing years of the people's iniquity)—390 days for Israel, and 40 days for Judah—and their intention of literal or symbolic representation is unclear. The significance of the 390 years is difficult to establish, especially in relation to the northern kingdom of Israel. Subtracting 390 from the time of the fall of Jerusalem (586 B.C.), one arrives at a date of 976 B.C., during the reign of Solomon and prior to the existence of a distinct northern kingdom of Israel. The time of Israel's iniquity may be related to Solomon's apostasy in allowing the worship of foreign gods in the promised land. With respect to the second number, 40 years prior to Ezekiel's ministry would have been during the reign of Josiah, before the book of the law was found, not a particularly significant year for Judah. However, the number 40 is significant in biblical imagery for denoting times of testing, refinement, or judgment (e.g., rains of judgment, Gn 9; Moses on Mount Sinai, Ex 34:28; Elijah's fasting, 1Kg 19:8; Jesus' testing, Lk 4). The two lengths of time together may indicate symbolically the nation's apostasy (**iniquity**) and punishment (exile), or the 40 years can be viewed as a parallel to the Israelites' wilderness wandering (Nm 14:34), since from other texts the exile lasted 70 years. Symbolically, the exile would be long enough in duration to ensure that the current generation would pass away and a new generation would be given a fresh start. Thus, after a lengthy iniquity and a short punishment, God's mercy would again be offered and restoration to the land would be possible.

4:9-11 This act has a double meaning: first, as a sign of the people's deportation from the promised land; second, as a symbol of the famine Judah would experience during the Babylonian siege.

[A]4:4 Or *punishment* [B]4:10 Lit *20 shekels* [C]4:10 Or *it at set times* [D]4:11 Lit *hin*

wickedness than the nations, and against My statutes more than the countries that surround her. For her people have rejected My ordinances and have not walked in My statutes.

[7] "Therefore, this is what the Lord God says: Because you have been more insubordinate than the nations around you—you have not walked in My statutes or kept My ordinances; you have not even kept the ordinances of the nations around you— [8] therefore, this is what the Lord God says: See, I am against you, Jerusalem, and I will execute judgments within you in the sight of the nations. [9] Because of all your detestable practices, I will do to you what I have never done before and what I will never do again. [10] As a result, fathers will eat their sons within Jerusalem,[A] and sons will eat their fathers. I will execute judgments against you and scatter all your survivors to every direction of the wind.

A Description of the Fall of Jerusalem (5:11-17)

[11] "Therefore, as I live"—this is the declaration of the Lord God—"I am going to cut you off and show you no pity, because you have defiled My sanctuary with all your detestable practices and abominations. Yes, I will not spare you. [12] A third of your people will die by plague and be consumed by famine within you; a third will fall by the sword all around you; and I will scatter a third to every direction of the wind, and I will draw a sword to chase after them. [13] When My anger is spent and I have vented My wrath on them, I will be appeased. Then after I have spent My wrath on them, they will know that I, •Yahweh, have spoken in My jealousy.

[14] "I will make you a ruin and a disgrace among the nations around you, in the sight of everyone who passes by. [15] So you[B] will be a disgrace and a taunt, a warning and a horror, to the nations around you when I execute judgments against you in anger, wrath, and furious rebukes. I, Yahweh, have spoken. [16] When I shoot deadly arrows of famine at them, arrows for destruction that I will send to destroy you, inhabitants of Jerusalem, I will intensify the famine against you and cut off your supply of bread. [17] I will send famine and dangerous animals against you. They will leave you childless, Jerusalem. Plague and bloodshed will sweep through you, and I will bring a sword against you. I, Yahweh, have spoken."

Condemnation and Hope (6:1-14)

Prophecy Against the Land (6:1-7)

6 The word of the Lord came to me: [2] "Son of man, turn your face toward the mountains of Israel and prophesy against them. [3] You are to say: Mountains of Israel, hear the word of the Lord God! This is what the Lord God says to the mountains and the hills, to the ravines and the valleys: I am about to bring a sword against you, and I will destroy your •high places. [4] Your altars will be desolated and your incense altars smashed. I will throw down your slain in front of your idols. [5] I will lay the corpses of the Israelites in front of their idols and scatter your bones around your altars. [6] Wherever you live the cities will be in ruins and the high places will be desolate, so that your altars will lie in ruins and be desecrated,[C] your idols smashed and obliterated, your incense altars cut down, and your works wiped out. [7] The slain will fall among you, and you will know that I am •Yahweh.

The Remnant (6:8-10)

[8] "Yet I will leave a remnant when you are scattered among the nations, for throughout the countries there will be some of you who will escape the sword. [9] Then your survivors will remember Me among the nations where they are taken captive, how I was crushed by their promiscuous hearts that turned away from Me and by their eyes that lusted after their idols. They will loathe themselves because of the evil things they did, their detestable practices of every kind. [10] And they will know that I am the Lord; I did

[A]5:10 Lit *you* [B]5:15 DSS, LXX, Syr, Tg, Vg; MT reads *she* [C]6:6 Hb obscure

4:16-17 Clearly, a scarcity of quality produce and water in the city would result from the sins of the people (cp. 12:18-19; Jr. 37:21). God would **cut off the supply of bread** (Hb *shavar*, "break" with the object *matteh-lechem*, "staff of bread"; cp. 5:16; 14:13).

5:1-3 In the third symbolic act, Ezekiel was to **shave** his **head and beard** and **divide** his hair into three equal parts. One **third** was to be burned, one third slashed **with the sword**, and one third scattered in **the wind**. Ezekiel was also told to withhold **a few strands** and secure them **in the folds of . . . [his] robe**, serving as a picture of God's preservation of a remnant of Israelites who would remain faithful to Him and who would continue to be the progeny of the Lord's covenant promises to Abraham.

5:11-17 God poured out His wrath not merely to punish but also to reveal to the people of Israel His holiness and **jealousy**—**they will know that . . . Yahweh** has **spoken** (v. 13).

6:3 Ezekiel's prophecy was not only against the **mountains of Israel** but also against **the hills, the ravines and the valleys**. The thrust of the prophecy was a condemnation of the Israelites' use of **high places** (Hb *bamah*; see **Word Study**, p. 411), sites used for pagan worship practices often intermixed with Yahweh worship. The preferred places of worship were elevated areas (mountaintops), where Israelites would set up altars and sometimes use idols in their rituals.

6:4-6 The prophecy here repudiates the validity of all such worship—the false altars **will lie in ruins and be desecrated** and the idols will be destroyed. As a final act of irony, the bodies of the people would lie exposed around the rubble of the false altars. For the ancient Israelites the failure to receive a proper burial meant humiliation and ritual defilement. Thus, just as the people defiled themselves while alive by worshiping in improper ways or practicing idolatry, so they would be defiled in death by having their corpses exposed to the elements and the wild beasts.

6:8-10 As earlier, God promised to preserve **a remnant** for the sake of His unconditional covenant promises to Abraham. Clearly, those who do survive will turn from their sins and **will remember** the Lord. The language here is particularly personal—God appears as a lover whose heart has been **crushed** (Hb *shavar*, "break"; cp. "smashed," 6:4,6; "shattered," 30:8) by the promiscuity of His lover (i.e., the people who **turned away** from Him and **lusted after their idols**). Thus,

Real Women vs. Images of Women in Ezekiel

Woman	Type	Text(s)	Significance
Jerusalem	**Image:** • Jerusalem and its inhabitants are metaphorically represented • It is labeled City of Blood/ "Bloodshed City"	5:5 22:1-16, 23-31	Jerusalem is portrayed as a mother with recalcitrant, incorrigible and corrupt children. She has become polluted by the idolatry, covenant-breaking, and crimes of those "in her." She and her inhabitants will therefore suffer the consequences of God's wrath.
Idolatrous Women	**Real:** Actual women engaged in the worship of fertility deities by weeping for Tammuz, a type of seasonal dying and rising god, whose cult is similar to Adonis among the Greeks	8:14-15	These women serve as one of four examples shown to Ezekiel of idolatrous practices occurring at the temple of the Lord. Their engagement in a Tammuz cult shows that both men and women were responsible for Judah's spiritual demise and its descent into syncretism. Perhaps they felt abandoned by Yahweh, and so felt compelled to appeal to additional deities for fertility and prosperity.
Temple (Solomon's) and New Heavenly Temple	**Image:** God refers to the Temple in the same way one refers to one's darling or sweetheart, as "the delight of your eyes" and "the desire of your heart." Some have suggested feminine imagery in the descriptions of life-giving waters flowing from out of the New Temple.	24:15-27 40:1–48:35 (cp. Is 66:7-13; Rv 21:1–22:4)	The temple has been rejected by the Lord and will be devastated because of its defilement and pollution by idolatry. God has abandoned it, but later He will rebuild it, making it perfect and holy. Comparable passages in Isaiah and Revelation use feminine imagery that overlaps with Ezekiel's descriptions of the new temple, although they describe the city as new Jerusalem, strictly speaking. In Rv 21:22, God Himself and the Lamb are the temple.
False Women Prophets	**Real:** Actual women, either in Jerusalem or among the exiles, practiced a kind of witchcraft. Their tools were magical bracelets and veils. These women are deadly to the people spiritually.	13:17-23	Ezekiel strongly condemns them right alongside false male prophets. Their practices constitute a further example of syncretism in Israel. They have concocted prophetic messages that deceive and discourage the righteous, while encouraging the wicked to remain in sin. They have ensnared the people like hunters trap birds.
God's Unfaithful Spouse	**Image:** The extended parable pictures Jerusalem as an unfaithful wife.	Chap. 16	Ezekiel recounts in allegorical form the tragic romance of God with Jerusalem. The story presents God's choice and redemption of Jerusalem, who was an unwanted baby, cast out and despised by her pagan parents. God established and prospered her, and married her, making her a queen. Her rejection of God and preference for the idolatrous ways of the nations are portrayed in terms of sexual promiscuity and adultery. She is abandoned and punished by God, but, in the end, atoned for and restored in keeping with God's covenant faithfulness.

Real Women vs. Images of Women in Ezekiel

Woman	Type	Text(s)	Significance
The Lioness and the Vine	**Imaged and Real:** An allegory of the royal line of David or queen mothers of the House of Judah	Chap. 19	Although there is disagreement about individual or corporate interpretations in this chapter, in the nation's demise the role played by ambitious royal women—who seemed no godlier than their sons, the kings in charge—is highlighted. Some scholars believe Hamutal, (mother of Jehoahaz and Zedekiah) is in view as the lioness, and others believe that Nehushta (mother of Jehoiachin) may qualify as the vine, since she is mentioned specifically as being deported with her son, only three months into his reign. Mothers as well as fathers have obligations to train children according to God's commands, and both can be culpable for failure to do so. Josiah was a godly father, but these women may have had more ambitious plans for their children, plans that eventually collapsed.
God's Adulterous Wives, Oholah and Oholibah	**Images:** The "wives" represent the sister cities of Jerusalem and Samaria.	Chap. 23	These cities represent the kingdoms of Israel and Judah. Both forsook God spiritually, in favor of Baal worship and other idols to whom children were sacrificed; and politically, in favor of alliances with surrounding nations and world powers of the time (Assyria, Egypt, Babylon/ Chaldea). This parable recounts the nation's history: Israel's demise came first at the hands of the Assyrians, and Judah's demise followed at the hands of the Babylonians.
Ezekiel's Wife	**Real:** Ezekiel's wife died in exile. Although prohibited from mourning for her, he was allowed to groan quietly. As the faithful wife of a priest, she was a stark contrast to the 'wives' of Yahweh, so horrifically memorialized in the previous chapter.	Chap. 24	Ezekiel's unnamed wife is called the "delight of your eyes," indicating God's intimate love for Jerusalem and the temple, as a man dearly loves his wife and takes pleasure in being in her company. She literally died, and served as a symbol of the "death" or removal of the temple.
Cities of Surrounding Nations (Tyre, Sidon, Egypt, Assyria, Elam, Edom)	**Images:** Cities are portrayed in the feminine, their inhabitants being like "children."	Chaps. 26–28; 32:18-32	These nations are mentioned in close proximity, especially in the passage on their presence in Sheol, which reads like a roll call of nations of the ancient Near East.
Women Mourners	**Imaged and Real:** Women mourn, weep, and lament with funeral dirges. Mourning was a well-known profession for women in the ancient world.	32:16	Egypt's downfall will be so devastating that all nations will mourn for her via their women. These may be the women of the nations represented in Sheol. The mourning means that Egypt will die, as indicated in the subsequent passage; the funeral has begun before the death, but the death is certain.

the people would **remember** (Hb *zakar*; see note on 1Sm 1:19)—i.e., "turn toward" or "give personal attention to"—the Lord once they have been taken into exile. The people would **know that I am the Lord**, demonstrating God's purpose not merely to punish but to show forth the truth—He alone is God; His people rightfully belonged only to Him. At the same time, punishment was justified (not **without a reason**), and the people knew this.

6:11-14 The theme of chastisement as revelation of God's nature and character carries over into the final verses. Ezekiel mentions twice that the result of Judah's destruction is **they will know that I am Yahweh**. Three responses to the sins of Israel were prescribed for Ezekiel—clapping of hands, stomping of feet, and crying out. All three were gestures of pain, remorse, or anguish. The sins of Israel caused Ezekiel pain, especially since he had been given knowledge of the desolation of Jerusalem and the nation, resulting from Israel's disobedience.

7:1-6 Unlike the preceding prose sections, this section uses a number of poetic devices to create a rousing, shocking effect—even panic—in the hearer. **End** (Hb *qēts*, "destruction; point of termination, extremity, or limit"; cp. Gn 6:13; Am 8:2) is repeated five times in brief, punching lines as if meant to deliver blows (Ezk 7:2-3,6), and a note of finality.

7:7-15 The repetition of **none** (Hb *lo'*, "no," v. 11) indicates the completeness of the destruction of the people. There is some debate regarding the referent of **rod** (Hb *matteh*, "staff, spear, rod of chastisement," v. 10; cp. Is 9:4; Mc 6:9). However, it seems to relate to "the wicked of the earth" and the "violent men" (Ezk 7:21-22), likely referring to Nebuchadnezzar and his invading army. The other reference to a rod that blossoms is the almond staff of Aaron (Nm 17:8), but this is found in a positive context, while the current context concerns **doom** (Hb *tsephirah*, "morning," literally "circle, circuit," thus having the sense of something that has finally "come around," Ezk 7:7,10).

Verses 12-13 provide a concrete illustration of the futility of hoping that God would relent. The city's imminent doom would overshadow and cut short the financial transactions of a normal day. For those who did not heed the prophet's warning, "business as usual" would come to a halt.

7:16 Ezekiel 7 has marked affinities with Zph 1 and Is 2, 13, and 22 regarding warnings about an appointed

>WORD|*study*

7:5-12 The warning's urgency is also conveyed by repetition of the verb come (Hb *bo'*), emphasizing the imminent arrival of an appointed judgment. Of the 10 incidences, four are active participles (vv. 5,6b,7b,10), indicating continuous, ongoing action—the "coming" is in progress. Six are in the form "has come" (vv. 2,6a,7a,12), indicating completed action—the decision is made and will not be reversed (cp. v. 13). Repeated temporal expressions contribute to the sense of urgency:

- **the time** [Hb *'ēt*, "proper time," whether happy or calamitous] **has come** (vv. 7,12);
- **the day is near** (Hb *qarov*, "close, short," from the verb *qarav*, "approach, come near," v. 7);
- **very soon** (Hb *qarov*, v. 8; cp. 30:3); **the day is coming** (7:10); and
- **the day has arrived** (Hb *naga'*, "draw near," v. 12).

The refrain regarding judgment—**sword . . . plague and famine**—is also repeated (7:15; cp. 5:12,17; 6:11-12; 12:16; 14:21; 1Ch 21:12; Jr 34:17; Rv 6:8).

not threaten to bring this disaster
on them without a reason.

A Lament over the Destruction of God's People (6:11-14)

11 "This is what the Lord God says:
Clap your hands, stamp your feet,
and cry out over all the evil and
detestable practices of the house of
Israel, who will fall by the sword,
famine, and plague. 12 The one who
is far off will die by plague; the one
who is near will fall by the sword;
and the one who remains and is
spared[A] will die of famine. In this
way I will exhaust My wrath on
them. 13 You will all know that I am
Yahweh when their slain lie among
their idols around their altars, on
every high hill, on all the mountaintops, and under every green tree and
every leafy oak—the places where
they offered pleasing aromas to all
their idols. 14 I will stretch out My
hand against them, and wherever
they live I will make the land a desolate waste, from the wilderness to
Diblah.[B] Then they will know that I
am Yahweh."

A Declaration of Finality (7:1-27)

7 And the word of the Lord came
to me: 2 "Son of man, this is what
the Lord God says to the land of Israel:

An end! The end has come
on the four corners
of the land.
3 The end is now upon you;
I will send My anger
against you
and judge you according to
your ways.
I will punish you for all
your detestable practices.
4 I will not look on you
with pity or spare you,
but I will punish you
for your ways
and for your
detestable practices
within you.
Then you will know that I am
•Yahweh."

5 This is what the Lord God says:

Look, one disaster
after another is coming!
6 An end has come; the end
has come!
It has awakened against you.
Look, it is coming!
7 Doom[C] has come on you,
inhabitants of the land.
The time has come; the day
is near.
There will be panic
on the mountains
and not celebration.
8 I will pour out My wrath
on you very soon;
I will exhaust My anger
against you
and judge you
according to your ways.
I will punish you for all your
detestable practices.
9 I will not look on you
with pity or spare you.
I will punish you
for your ways
and for your

[A]6:12 Or *besieged* [B]6:14 Some Hb mss, some LXX mss read *Riblah*; 2Kg 23:33; Jr 39:5 [C]7:7 Hb obscure

detestable practices
within you.
Then you will know
that it is I, Yahweh,
who strikes.

10 Look, the day is coming!
Doom has gone out.
The rod has blossomed;
arrogance has bloomed.
11 Violence has grown into a rod
of wickedness.
None of them will remain:
none of their multitude,
none of their wealth,
and none of the eminent[A]
among them.
12 The time has come; the day
has arrived.
Let the buyer not rejoice
and the seller not mourn,
for wrath is on all her masses.
13 The seller will certainly
not return
to what was sold
as long as he and the buyer
remain alive.[B]
For the vision concerning
all its people
will not be revoked,
and none of them
will preserve
his life because of his iniquity.

14 They have blown the trumpet
and prepared everything,
but no one goes to war,
for My wrath is on all
her masses.
15 The sword is on the outside;
plague and famine are
on the inside.
Whoever is in the field will die
by the sword,
and famine and plague
will devour
whoever is in the city.

16 The survivors among them
will escape
and live on the mountains
like doves of the valley,
all of them moaning,
each over his own iniquity.
17 All their hands
will become weak,
and all their knees will turn
to water.
18 They will put on •sackcloth,
and horror will
overwhelm them.
Shame will cover all
their faces,
and all their heads
will be bald.
19 They will throw their silver
into the streets,
and their gold will seem like
something filthy.
Their silver and gold
will be unable to save them
in the day of the LORD's wrath.
They will not satisfy
their appetites
or fill their stomachs,
for these were
the stumbling blocks
that brought
about their iniquity.
20 He appointed
His beautiful ornaments
for majesty,
but[C] they made
their abhorrent images
from them,
their detestable things.
Therefore, I have made these
into something filthy
for them.
21 I will hand these things over
to foreigners as plunder
and to the wicked of the earth
as spoil,
and they will profane them.
22 I will turn My face
from the wicked
as they profane
My treasured place.
Violent men will enter it
and profane it.

23 Forge the chain,
for the land is filled
with crimes of bloodshed,
and the city is filled
with violence.
24 So I will bring the most evil
of nations
to take possession
of their houses.
I will put an end to the pride
of the strong,
and their sacred places
will be profaned.

"day" of judgment for which Israel longed as a day of vindication, reward, and great blessing. The prophets described this "day" as one of strife, doom, and judgment on sin. In Ezk 7, the "day" that is coming is described negatively, as a violently destructive event bringing judgment and manifesting God's wrath against Judah for her abominable behavior. **The mountains** would normally serve as a place of refuge for those fleeing the disaster, but Ezekiel warned that there would be "panic . . . and not celebration" (cp. v. 7) even among the **survivors** who manage to **escape**. There would be no relief, only a realization that they had barely escaped a well-deserved punishment for sins, over which they would moan **like doves.**

7:17-18 Wearing **sackcloth** and shaving one's head are signs of mourning.

7:19-22 They apparently refers to the survivors (vv. 16,19-22,24-27). Their money would now be worthless, even disgusting to them, since the gathering of riches and spending them on their own pleasures had **brought about their iniquity**. Other treasures, such as those of the temple, were defiled and rendered worthless because they had been used for idolatry. They would consequently be further defiled because God would allow a foreign nation to **profane** the temple not only by entering it but also by taking its treasures as **plunder**.

7:23-27 The temple's defilement would be a final reveille to the people who had prophesied that the "day of the LORD's" wrath (v. 19) was indeed upon them, and they would seek out **prophets** and **priests** to confirm the bad news. By then, it would be too late, and they would finally realize that God is indeed sovereign: **I am Yahweh.**

[A]**7:11** Some Hb mss, Syr, Vg read *and no rest* [B]**7:13** Lit *sold, while still in life is their life*
[C]**7:20** Or *They turned their beautiful ornaments into objects of pride, and*

8:1-2 Fourteen months after Ezekiel's call to ministry, the prophet had another encounter with God. This vision encompasses chapters 8–11 and includes four abominations and two judgments.

8:3-6 The Lord took hold of Ezekiel's **hair**, and **the Spirit** transported him **in visions of God to Jerusalem**. The fact that Ezekiel had hair long enough to grab indicates that he was ritually pure. The shaving of hair was forbidden for the priests and was an indicator of uncleanness.

Ezekiel arrived in Jerusalem at the northern gate where the first abomination was evident. An **offensive statue** [Hb *semel*, "image, idol"] **that provokes jealousy** had been set up **at the entrance** to the courtyard. Ezekiel may have been given a glimpse of Manasseh's statue of Asherah, the mother of Baal in Canaanite mythology, which Manasseh set up in the temple (cp. 2Ch 33:7,15). Manasseh later removed this image, and it was destroyed during Josiah's reforms 30 years prior to Ezekiel's vision (2Kg 23). Whatever Ezekiel saw in the vision, whether it represented an actual circumstance or was symbolic of Israel's rejection of the Lord, it signified only one of the **detestable things** in which Israel actively engaged. The Lord cited these as the reason He **must depart from** [His] **sanctuary** (cp. Ezk 10:18-19; 11:22-23).

8:10 The second abomination was inside the temple building. Not only were **idols** being worshiped, but the idols were images of ritually unclean animals.

8:11-13 Seventy is reminiscent of the number of men who were appointed to help Moses in ruling the people of Israel during the theocracy (Ex 24:1,9; Nm 11:16,24-25). The **elders from the house of Israel** were supposed to be leaders in social, cultural, and religious matters. However, they had no legitimate role in the temple, and such idolatrous worship in the Lord's sanctuary would have been unthinkable to Ezekiel. He recognized **Jaazaniah** (Hb "Yahweh listens"), whose name becomes ironic when the Lord told Ezekiel that He would refuse to "listen to them" (v. 18). If the family name **Shaphan** refers to the man who was a secretary for Josiah (2Kg 22:3-14; 2Ch 34:8-20), then Jaazaniah's idolatry conflicted with his family's loyalty to Jeremiah (see Jr 26:24; 29:3; 36:10-12) and illustrated the extent of spiritual degradation in Judah. **Each** elder was burning **incense**, but the legitimate place for a particular formula of incense to be burned in the temple was the altar of incense, not where these elders were (see Ex 30:1-10,34-38).

>WORD|*study*

8:11 In Scripture the word firepan (Hb *miqteret*, "censer") appears only here and in the account of what happened to King Uzziah of Judah when he burned incense in the temple, thereby claiming for himself a privilege that belonged only to the priests (2Ch 26:19). Illegitimate incense burning was also at issue in the account of Korah's rebellion (Nm 16), a significant event in Israel's history of rebellion that seems to have been in view in Ezk 7:10 (cp. Nm 17). Furthermore, the burning of incense to other gods was one of the specific manifestations of Israel's rebellion against Yahweh (cp. 2Kg 22:17; Jr 11:12-13, 17; 18:15).

25 Anguish is coming!
They will seek peace,
but there will be none.
26 Disaster after disaster
will come,
and there will be rumor
after rumor.
Then they will seek a vision
from a prophet,
but instruction will perish
from the priests
and counsel from the elders.
27 The king will mourn;
the prince will be clothed
in grief;
and the hands of the people
of the land will tremble.
I will deal with
them according to
their own conduct,
and I will judge them
by their own standards.
Then they will know that I am
Yahweh.

Ezekiel's Vision of Jerusalem (8:1–11:25)

The Vision of God (8:1-4)

8 In the sixth year, in the sixth month, on the fifth day of the month, I was sitting in my house and the elders of Judah were sitting in front of me, and there the hand of the Lord God came down on me. 2 I looked, and there was a form that had the appearance of a man.[A] From what seemed to be His waist down was fire, and from His waist up was something that looked bright, like the gleam of amber. 3 He stretched out what appeared to be a hand and took me by the hair of my head. Then the Spirit lifted me up between earth and heaven and carried me in visions of God to Jerusalem, to the entrance of the inner gate that faces north, where the offensive statue that provokes jealousy was located. 4 I saw the glory of the God of Israel there, like the vision I had seen in the plain.

The Godlessness of the People (8:5-18)

5 The Lord said to me, "Son of man, look toward the north." I looked to the north, and there was this offensive statue north of the altar gate, at the entrance. 6 He said to me, "Son of man, do you see what they are doing here, more detestable things that the house of Israel is committing, so that I must depart from My sanctuary? You will see even more detestable things."

7 Then He brought me to the entrance of the court, and when I looked there was a hole in the wall. 8 He said to me, "Son of man, dig through the wall." So I dug through the wall, and there was a doorway. 9 He said to me, "Go in and see the terrible and detestable things they are committing here." 10 I went in and looked, and there engraved all around the wall was every form of detestable thing, crawling creatures and beasts, as well as all the idols of the house of Israel.

11 Seventy elders from the house of Israel were standing before them, with Jaazaniah son of Shaphan standing among them. Each had a firepan in his hand, and a fragrant cloud of incense was rising up. 12 Then He said to me, "Son of man, do you see what the elders of the house of Israel are doing in the darkness, each at the shrine of his idol? For they are saying, 'The Lord does not see us. The Lord has abandoned the land.'" 13 Again He said to me, "You will see even more detest-

[A] 8:2 LXX; MT, Vg read *of fire*

>WORD|*study*

9:4 The word translated **mark** (Hb *taw*, "sign," transliterated into English as "t") is the name of the last letter in the Hebrew alphabet, which was written in the form of an "X." Later it was written as a cross, especially in the Greek alphabet, which borrowed from the Semitic alphabet of the Phoenicians. Rabbinic commentaries noted the link between this mark in Ezk 9 and the marking of the doorposts on the night of the inaugural Passover event (Ex 12) until early church interpreters recognized the parallel in Christian terms—i.e., that those who follow Jesus have repented of their sin, are forgiven and counted as righteous because of Christ's blood shed on the cross (cp. Jb 31:35, "signature"; Php 3:9; Rv 7:2-3; 14:1).

able things, which they are committing."
14 So He brought me to the entrance of the north gate of the LORD's house, and I saw women sitting there weeping for Tammuz.
15 And He said to me, "Do you see this, son of man? You will see even more detestable things than these."
16 So He brought me to the inner court of the LORD's house, and there were about 25 men at the entrance of the LORD's temple, between the portico and the altar, with their backs to the LORD's temple and their faces turned to the east. They were bowing to the east in worship of the sun.
17 And He said to me, "Do you see this, son of man? Is it not enough for the house of Judah to commit the detestable things they are practicing here, that they must also fill the land with violence and repeatedly provoke Me to anger, even putting the branch to their nose?[A,B]
18 Therefore I will respond with wrath. I will not show pity or spare them. Though they cry out in My ears with a loud voice, I will not listen to them."

The LORD's Response: Judgment upon the People (9:1-11)

9 Then He called to me directly with a loud voice, "Come near, executioners of the city, each of you with a destructive weapon in his hand."
2 And I saw six men coming from the direction of the Upper Gate, which faces north, each with a war club in his hand. There was another man among them, clothed in linen, with writing equipment at his side. They came and stood beside the bronze altar.
3 Then the glory of the God of Israel rose from above the •cherub where it had been, to the threshold of the temple. He called to the man clothed in linen with the writing equipment at his side.
4 "Pass throughout the city of Jerusalem," the LORD said to him, "and put a mark on the foreheads of the men who sigh and groan over all the detestable practices committed in it."

[A]8:17 Ancient Jewish tradition reads *My nose* [B]8:17 Possibly a pagan ritual or a euphemism for offensive behavior

8:14-15 At **the entrance of the north gate,** Ezekiel saw the third abomination—women **weeping for Tammuz**, an ancient Akkadian fertility god.

8:16 The fourth abomination took place in **the inner court**, the holy place, though not the holy of holies. The 25 men Ezekiel saw with their backs to the altar facing **east in worship of the sun** may have been priests, who would be expected to be in this part of the temple, but they are not identified as such. Sun worship symbolized the nation's rejection of Yahweh, as the men prostrated themselves, possibly with words of veneration, and simultaneously turned their backs to the **altar** and **temple**, an obvious sign of disrespect and rejection.

8:17-18 The religious practices of the people deserved the Lord's condemnation, but additionally, they provoked Him **to anger** through injustice and the shedding of innocent blood. A curious practice is cited here—**putting the branch** [Hb *zemorah*, "pruned vine-branch or shoot"; cp. 15:2] **to their nose**. Most modern scholars believe this was a practice associated with pagan ritual, but this interpretation seems to ignore its placement in the narrative. The indictment of the Lord against the people has shifted from religious to ethical sins. Thus, the phrase seems to be tied to the violence perpetrated by the people against one another. It may also be an ancient colloquialism akin to a defiant gesture against God.

9:1-4 The six **executioners** called forth are described as men wielding warriors' clubs, most likely angelic beings. A seventh **man** (using the number representing completeness) came with them. He was **clothed in linen**, the clothing worn by priests

BIBLICAL WOMANHOOD Role of Women in Ancient Near Eastern Religion

The role of women in the cult of **Tammuz** was similar to many of the pagan religions of the ancient Near East. The harvest supposedly died each year when the vines withered and then revived with the beginning of new growth in the spring. Thus, the women's **weeping** in 8:14 had a twofold purpose: it showed evidence of cultic ties with pagan worship, and also indicated a legitimate concern over the lack of vegetation. This vision can be placed in the August/September time frame when the land in Palestine is parched. While the practice of organized and ritualistic mourning in the fall seems relatively harmless (at least with respect to its physical effects upon the practitioners), the activities associated with the coming of spring could be viewed as exploitive and even abusive. The rising of Tammuz and the revitalization of the harvest were celebrated and entreated (viewed as something akin to prayer) by means of ritualistic orgies in which temple prostitutes slept with multiple partners. Temple prostitutes were common, so the religion was based on the exploitation of women. This worship may be seen as more detestable than the previous two because of its lewd perversion of sexuality.

when they performed their duties (vv. 2-3,11; 10:2,6-7). Rather than wielding a **club**, however, he carried a scribe's tablet. He was told to go into Jerusalem and place **a mark on the foreheads of the men who sigh** [Hb *ʾanach*, "groan"; cp. 21:6-7; Ex 2:23; Pr 29:2] **and groan** [Hb *ʾanaq*, "be in anguish, the cries prompted by extreme anguish"] **over all the detestable practices** (cp. 26:15; Jr 51:52).

9:5-6 The executioners' work symbolized the spiritual cleansing of the city, and the temple (**My sanctuary**) had become the center of the nation's odious spiritual condition. The purification, therefore, would begin with God's own house.

9:8-11 This chapter illustrates the interplay between God's wrath and mercy. Noticeably pained by the destruction brought upon the people, Ezekiel attempted to intercede for them, although to no avail. The role of intercessor was appropriate for him, given his priestly background. Ezekiel's query itself reflects God's mercy. He referred to the **remnant** (Hb *sheʾērit*, "remaining survivors," especially after a slaughter; cp. 5:10; 11:13), a concept tied to the covenant faithfulness of Yahweh, who will fulfill His promises to Abraham regardless of the actions of the people. Twice God made it clear that He wanted no mercy to be shown to the people, perhaps to communicate the gravity of the situation (9:5,10). The work of **the man clothed in linen** presents God's grace at the beginning of the chapter, as does the report of his fulfilled mission at the end of the chapter, serving to couch the wrath of God as executed by the warriors in terms of the Lord's mercy and grace. Just as the Lord said He would show no mercy, the angelic scribe returned with the news that he had sealed all of the faithful for protection.

10:1-2 After the wicked were killed by the six executioners, Ezekiel saw the **throne** of God moving higher. The scattering of **hot coals . . . over the city**, is reminiscent of the destruction by fire of the unrighteous Sodom and Gomorrah (Gn 19:13,24-25). Here, the burning anger of the Lord is manifest and may literally indicate the burning of the city by the invaders.

10:3-5 Here the cherubim were at the **south of the temple**, most likely because the abominations were being perpetrated on the north side. The **glory** [Hb *kavod*; see **Word Study**, p. 688] **of the Lord** moved from the holy place to the **threshold of the temple**. This movement indicated that the Lord was moving out of His house, as it had been defiled by idolatry, bloodshed, and dead bodies (cp. 8:6; 9:7). The **cloud** and the **glory** of the Lord filling the temple harks

5 He spoke as I listened to the others, "Pass through the city after him and start killing; do not show pity or spare them! 6 Slaughter the old men, the young men and women, as well as the older women and little children, but do not come near anyone who has the mark. Now begin at My sanctuary." So they began with the elders who were in front of the temple. 7 Then He said to them, "Defile the temple and fill the courts with the slain. Go!" So they went out killing people in the city.

8 While they were killing, I was left alone. And I fell facedown and cried out, "Oh, Lord God! Are You going to destroy the entire remnant of Israel when You pour out Your wrath on Jerusalem?"

9 He answered me: "The iniquity of the house of Israel and Judah is extremely great; the land is full of bloodshed, and the city full of perversity. For they say, 'The LORD has abandoned the land; He does not see.' 10 But as for Me, I will not show pity or spare them. I will bring their actions down on their own heads." 11 Then the man clothed in linen with the writing equipment at his side reported back, "I have done as You commanded me."

The Departure of God's Glory from the Temple (10:1-22)

10 Then I looked, and there above the expanse over the heads of the •cherubim was something like sapphire[A] stone resembling the shape of a throne that appeared above them. 2 The LORD spoke to the man clothed in linen and said, "Go inside the wheelwork beneath the cherubim. Fill your hands with hot coals from among the cherubim and scatter them over the city." So he went in as I watched.

3 Now the cherubim were standing to the south of the temple when the man went in, and the cloud filled the inner court. 4 Then the glory of the LORD rose from above the cherub to the threshold of the temple. The temple was filled with the cloud, and the court was filled with the brightness of the LORD's glory. 5 The sound of the cherubim's wings could be heard as far as the outer court; it was like the voice of •God Almighty when He speaks.

6 After the LORD commanded the man clothed in linen, saying, "Take fire from inside the wheelwork, from among the cherubim," the man went in and stood beside a wheel. 7 Then the cherub reached out his hand to the fire that was among them. He took some, and put it into the hands of the man clothed in linen, who took it and went out.

[A]**10:1** Or *lapis lazuli*

Doctrine — ANGELS: CHERUBIM AND LIVING CREATURES

Perhaps the most interesting and intimidating aspect of the book of Ezekiel is the prophet's description of his vision(s) of **the LORD's glory** (10:4) and the **cherubim** that accompany Him (chaps. 1, 9, 10, 11). Ezekiel had worked as a priest in the temple and was familiar with the images of cherubim on the ark of the covenant. Their wings covered the mercy seat on top of the ark, and the cloud of the Lord's presence would rest between them (Ex 25:18-22; Nm 7:89; 2Sm 6:2; 1Kg 6:23-28; 8:6-7; 2Kg 19:15; 1Ch 13:6; 28:18; 2Ch 3:10-13; 5:7-8; Pss 80:1; 99:1; Is 37:16). The **living creatures** (Hb *chay*, "that which has life," Ezk 10:15,17,20; cp. 1:5,13,15,19-22; 3:13) of Ezekiel's vision seem to have a function similar to that of the "living creatures" in John's vision of heaven (Rv 4:6,8-9; 5:6,8,11,14; 6:1,6; 7:11; 8:9; 14:3; 15:7; 19:4). In both visions they are described as winged creatures, which are covered with **eyes all around** (Ezk 1:18; 10:12; cp. Rv 4:6,8); extremely close to the Lord's **throne** and the **expanse** (Hb *raqiyaʿ*, "firmament" of heaven spread out like a vaulted ceiling from an earthly perspective, Ezk 1:22-23,25-26; 10:1; cp. Gn 1:6-7; Rv 4:6, "something like a sea of glass, similar to crystal"); with four **faces** (Ezk 1:10; cp. Rv 4:7)—of a lion, an eagle, a man, and an **ox** (Hb *shor*; Gk *moschos*, "calf" in the LXX and Rv 4:7); of **a cherub, . . . a man, . . . a lion, and . . . an eagle** (Ezk 10:14). These similarities, along with the fact that the One seated on the throne in both visions is clearly the Lord, suggest that the creatures in the two visions are the same. Ezekiel identifies the **living creatures** as **cherubim** (vv. 20-22). Some seeming discrepancies in the descriptions of Ezekiel and John include the number of **wings** on the creatures (four in Ezk 10:21; six in Rv 4:8), the number of faces of each creature (four in Ezekiel; in Revelation, four single-faced creatures), and the wheels of Ezekiel's description, and they may be due to the fact that in John's vision, God is not moving or going into battle but instead is holding court in heaven. Thus, the chariot-throne is neither needed nor observed in motion. Of course, John simply may not have mentioned some of the details he saw; his vision is not meant to be taken as a comprehensive description. These details can only serve as descriptions of the specific manifestations that the prophets experienced at that time.

[8] The cherubim appeared to have the form of human hands under their wings.

[9] I looked, and there were four wheels beside the cherubim, one wheel beside each cherub. The luster of the wheels was like the gleam of beryl. [10] In appearance, all four had the same form, like a wheel within a wheel. [11] When they moved, they would go in any of the four directions, without pivoting as they moved. But wherever the head faced, they would go in that direction,[A] without pivoting as they went. [12] Their entire bodies, including their backs, hands, wings, and the wheels that the four of them had, were full of eyes all around. [13] As I listened the wheels were called "the wheelwork." [14] Each one had four faces: the first face was that of a cherub, the second that of a man, the third that of a lion, and the fourth that of an eagle.

[15] The cherubim ascended; these were the living creatures I had seen by the Chebar Canal. [16] When the cherubim moved, the wheels moved beside them, and when they lifted their wings to rise from the earth, even then the wheels did not veer away from them. [17] When the cherubim stood still, the wheels stood still, and when they ascended, the wheels ascended with them, for the spirit of the living creatures was in them.

[18] Then the glory of the LORD moved away from the threshold of the temple and stood above the cherubim. [19] The cherubim lifted their wings and ascended from the earth right before my eyes; the wheels were beside them as they went. The glory of the God of Israel was above them, and it stood at the entrance to the eastern gate of the LORD's house.

[20] These were the living creatures I had seen beneath the God of Israel by the Chebar Canal, and I recognized that they were cherubim. [21] Each had four faces and each had four wings, with the form of human hands under their wings. [22] Their faces looked like the same faces I had seen by the Chebar Canal. Each creature went straight ahead.

An Oracle Against Israel's Corrupt Leaders and the Promise of Israel's Restoration (11:1-25)

11 The Spirit then lifted me up and brought me to the eastern gate of the LORD's house, which faces east, and at the gate's entrance were 25 men. Among them I saw Jaazaniah son of Azzur, and Pelatiah son of Benaiah, leaders of the people. [2] The LORD said to me, "Son of man, these are the men who plan evil and give wicked advice in this city. [3] They are saying, 'Isn't the time near to build houses?[B] The city is the pot, and we are the meat.' [4] Therefore, prophesy against them. Prophesy, son of man!"

[5] Then the Spirit of the LORD came on me, and He told me, "You are to say: This is what the LORD says: That is what you are thinking, house of Israel; and I know the thoughts that arise in your mind. [6] You have multiplied your slain in this city, filling its streets with the dead.

[7] "Therefore, this is what the Lord GOD says: The slain you have put within it are the meat, and the city is the pot, but I[C] will remove you from it. [8] You fear the sword, so I will bring the sword against you." This is the declaration of the Lord GOD. [9] "I will bring you out of the city and hand you over to foreigners; I will execute judgments against you. [10] You will fall by the sword, and I will judge you at the border of Israel. Then you will know that I am •Yahweh. [11] The city will not be a pot for you, and you will not be the meat within it. I will judge you at the border of Israel, [12] so you will know that I am Yahweh, whose statutes you have not followed and whose ordinances you have not practiced. Instead, you have acted according to the ordinances of the nations around you."

[13] Now while I was prophesying, Pelatiah son of Benaiah died. Then I fell facedown and cried out with a loud voice: "Oh, Lord GOD! Will You bring to an end the remnant of Israel?"

[14] The word of the LORD came to me again: [15] "Son of man, your own relatives, those who have the right to

back to the guiding and revelatory cloud in the Exodus travels (Ex 13:21-22; 14:19-24; 16:6-10; 33:9-11; Nm 9:15-23), the filling of the tabernacle (Ex 40:34-35), the filling of the temple at its dedication (1Kg 8:10), and the theophany visible to Isaiah (Is 6:3-4).

10:8-22 As in chapter 1, Ezekiel described the cherubim and God's chariot throne in detail, indicating that God continued moving out of the temple, from the **threshold** to the **eastern gate** temple entrance, and eventually out of Jerusalem completely and east to the Mount of Olives (vv. 18-19; cp. 11:22-23).

11:1 The 25 **leaders** are probably not the same men from the inner court who were worshiping the sun. Two of the men are identified. The **Jaazaniah** identified here does not seem to be the same as the one in the darkened room worshiping the icons on the walls (8:11-12). This seems to be a ring of political leaders.

11:2-6 The meaning of the two sayings is not completely clear. They could each have two interpretations. The first saying can be rendered in the affirmative, but posed as a rhetorical question or in the negative, presented as a statement. In the first, by suggesting that it is a good time **to build houses**, these men were claiming social and political stability for the people when the city was clearly doomed. This may reference the **wicked advice** for which they were indicted. The second interpretation could refer to the greed of these men, who may have been taking the homes of others (either the previous leaders of the city who were deported to Babylon or the innocent in the city who were slain by the hands and/or schemes of these men, cp. Mc 2:1-2).

The second saying about the **city, the pot,** and **the meat** can be dually interpreted as well. In a positive interpretation, these men are choice cuts of meat, worthy to be included in the pot (i.e., live in the city). Perhaps they regarded some people as unworthy of owning houses in the holy city, presumably those who were killed unjustly by them. Interpreted negatively, the saying could mean that just as meat is trapped in a pot to be cooked, so also the people are trapped in Jerusalem and will be destroyed if they do not act (e.g., make an alliance with Egypt against Babylon). The positive interpretation is clearly what was in view; to be meat in the pot, in this instance, was a good thing. However, it should be noted that this analogy will be turned on its head later in Ezekiel (chap. 24).

11:12-18 As Ezekiel again intercedes on behalf of the **remnant** (cp. note

[A] **10:11** Lit *go after it* [B] **11:3** Or *The time is not near to build houses.* [C] **11:7** Some Hb mss, LXX, Syr, Tg, Vg; other Hb mss read *He*

redeem you,[A,B] and the entire house of Israel, all of them, are those that the residents of Jerusalem have said this to, 'Stay away from the LORD; this land has been given to us as a possession.'

16 "Therefore say: This is what the Lord GOD says: Though I sent them far away among the nations and scattered them among the countries, yet for a little while I have been a sanctuary for them in the countries where they have gone.

17 "Therefore say: This is what the Lord GOD says: I will gather you from the peoples and assemble you from the countries where you have been scattered, and I will give you the land of Israel.

18 "When they arrive there, they will remove all its detestable things and practices from it. 19 And I will give them one heart and put a new spirit within them; I will remove their heart of stone from their bodies[C] and give them a heart of flesh, 20 so they may follow My statutes, keep My ordinances, and practice them. Then they will be My people, and I will be their God. 21 But as for those whose hearts pursue their desire for detestable things and practices, I will bring their actions down on their own heads." This is the declaration of the Lord GOD.

22 Then the •cherubim, with the wheels beside them, lifted their wings, and the glory of the God of Israel was above them. 23 The glory of the LORD rose up from within the city and stood on the mountain east of the city.[D] 24 The Spirit lifted me up and brought me to Chaldea and to the exiles in a vision from the Spirit of God. After the vision I had seen left me, 25 I spoke to the exiles about all the things the LORD had shown me.

A Dramatization of the Exile (12:1-28)

12 The word of the LORD came to me: 2 "Son of man, you are living among a rebellious house. They have eyes to see but do not see, and ears to hear but do not hear, for they are a rebellious house.

3 "Son of man, get your bags ready for exile and go into exile in their sight during the day. You will go into exile from your place to another place while they watch; perhaps they will understand, though they are a rebellious house. 4 During the day, bring out your bags like an exile's bags while they look on. Then in the evening go out in their sight like those going into exile. 5 As they watch, dig through the wall and take the bags out through it. 6 And while they look on, lift the bags to your shoulder and take them out in the dark; cover your face so that you cannot see the land. For I have made you a sign to the house of Israel."

7 So I did just as I was commanded. In the daytime I brought out my bags like an exile's bags. In the evening I dug through the wall by hand; I took them out in the dark, carrying them on my shoulder in their sight.

8 Then the word of the LORD came to me in the morning: 9 "Son of man, hasn't the house of Israel, that rebellious house, asked you, 'What are you doing?' 10 Say to them: This is what the Lord GOD says: This •oracle is about the prince[E] in Jerusalem and all the house of Israel who are living there.[F] 11 You are to say, 'I am a sign for you. Just as I have done, so it will be done to them; they will go into exile, into captivity.' 12 The prince who is among them will lift his bags to his shoulder in the dark and go out. They[G] will dig through the wall to bring him out through it. He will cover his face so he cannot see the land with his eyes. 13 But I will spread My net over him, and he will be caught in My snare. I will bring him to Babylon, the land of the Chaldeans, yet he will not see it, and he will die there. 14 I will also scatter all the attendants who surround him and all his troops to every direction of the wind, and I will draw a sword to chase after them. 15 They will know that I am •Yahweh when I disperse them among the nations and scatter them among the

at 9:8), he is informed that those left in Jerusalem (contrary to outward appearances) are not the remnant. Instead, the remnant is made up of many who had been exiled. The **residents of Jerusalem** viewed the exiles as somehow stricken by God for their sins, and saw themselves as blessed by God because they were not taken in the first two deportations. On the contrary, the remnant will return from exile to the **land of Israel** and will remove all the objects of false worship.

11:19-20 In the new covenant (cp. chaps. 36–37), God promises to perform a supernatural work on the people—giving them **one heart**, which enables them to follow His Torah. He will also place a **new spirit within them**. The language used here about the Spirit differs from the language throughout the Old Testament, where the Spirit of God temporarily "came on" particular men (e.g., Othniel, Jdg 3:10). Only Ezekiel says, "The Spirit *entered* me" (Ezk 2:2; 3:24). Yet the Lord indicates that all the remnant will have an indwelling spirit. The phrases, **heart of stone** and **heart of flesh** indicate a change of demeanor and spiritual attitude. Whereas previously the people were described as "hardheaded" and "hardhearted" (2:4, an indication of rebellious sin), the remnant will have a heart of flesh, a soft, pliable heart to obey God's **ordinances, and practice them**.

11:22-24 The **mountain east of the city** is identified as the Mount of Olives.

12:1–24:27 Chapter 12 begins a segment of judgment oracles against Israel and Judah. Often, the formula, **The word of the LORD came to me**, sets apart the coming message from the others. Ezekiel presents 10 separate prophecies in this section, via words and/or sign acts.

12:2-6 Ezekiel followed the Lord's instructions to dramatize the **exile** as a **sign** of the coming third deportation and to stop a faithless "proverb" (vv. 21-28; cp. 24:24, 27). The Lord warned Ezekiel that the people may or may not **understand** what he was doing because their **rebellious** spirit would not allow them to consider that these military defeats at the hands of godless men (i.e., the Babylonians) were from the Lord (cp. Dt 29:4).

12:7-13 Ezekiel's actions symbolized those of King Zedekiah of Judah in Jerusalem, who tried to sneak out of the city during the Babylonian siege. He was captured, taken to Babylon, and forced to watch as all of his sons were executed. His eyes were then put out, and he lived in captivity until his

A **11:15** LXX, Syr read *your relatives, your fellow exiles* B **11:15** Or *own brothers, your relatives* C **11:19** Lit *flesh* D **11:23** = the Mount of Olives E **12:10** = King Zedekiah F **12:10** Lit *are among them* G **12:12** LXX, Syr read *He*

countries. 16 But I will spare a few of them from the sword, famine, and plague so they can tell about all their detestable practices among the nations where they go. Then they will know that I am Yahweh."

17 The word of the LORD came to me: 18 "Son of man, eat your bread with trembling and drink your water with shaking and anxiety. 19 Then say to the people of the land: This is what the Lord GOD says about the residents of Jerusalem in the land of Israel: They will eat their bread with anxiety and drink their water in dread, for their[A,B] land will be stripped of everything in it because of the violence of all who live there. 20 The inhabited cities will be destroyed, and the land will become a desolation. Then you will know that I am Yahweh."

21 Again the word of the LORD came to me: 22 "Son of man, what is this proverb you people have about the land of Israel, which goes:

> The days keep passing by,
> and every vision fails?

23 Therefore say to them: This is what the Lord GOD says: I will put a stop to this proverb, and they will not use it again in Israel. But say to them: The days draw near, as well as the fulfillment of every vision. 24 For there will no longer be any false vision or flattering •divination within the house of Israel. 25 But I, Yahweh, will speak whatever message I will speak, and it will be done. It will no longer be delayed. For in your days, rebellious house, I will speak a message and bring it to pass." This is the declaration of the Lord GOD.

26 The word of the LORD came to me: 27 "Son of man, notice that the house of Israel is saying, 'The vision that he sees concerns many years from now; he prophesies about distant times.' 28 Therefore say to them: This is what the Lord GOD says: None of My words will be delayed any longer. The message I speak will be fulfilled." This is the declaration of the Lord GOD.

An Oracle Against False Prophets (13:1-23)

13 The word of the LORD came to me: 2 "Son of man, prophesy against the prophets of Israel who are prophesying. Say to those who prophesy out of their own imagination: Hear the word of the LORD! 3 This is what the Lord GOD says: Woe to the foolish prophets who follow their own spirit and have seen nothing. 4 Your prophets, Israel, are like jackals among ruins. 5 You did not go up to the gaps or restore the wall around the house of Israel so that it might stand in battle on the day of the LORD. 6 They see false visions and speak lying •divinations. They claim, 'This is the LORD's declaration,' when the LORD did not send them, yet they wait for the fulfillment of their message. 7 Didn't you see a false vision and speak a lying divination when you proclaimed, 'This is the LORD's declaration,' even though I had not spoken?

8 "Therefore, this is what the Lord GOD says: I am against you because you have spoken falsely and had lying visions." This is the declaration of the Lord GOD. 9 "My hand will be against the prophets who see false visions and speak lying divinations. They will not be present in the fellowship of My people or be recorded in the register of the house of Israel, and they will not enter the land of Israel. Then you will know that I am the Lord •Yahweh.

10 "Since they have led My people astray saying, 'Peace,' when there is no peace, for when someone builds a wall they plaster it with whitewash, 11 therefore, tell those who plaster it that it will fall. Torrential rain will come, and I will send hailstones plunging[C] down, and a windstorm will be released. 12 Now when the wall has fallen, will you not be asked, 'Where is the coat of whitewash that you put on it?'

13 "So this is what the Lord GOD says: I will release a windstorm in My wrath. Torrential rain will come in My anger, and hailstones will fall in destructive fury. 14 I will tear down the wall you plastered

[A]**12:19** Lit *its* [B]**12:19** = Jerusalem's [C]**13:11** One Hb ms, LXX, Vg; other Hb mss read *and you, hailstones, will plunge*

death (2Kg 25:6-7; 2Ch 36:11; Jr 39:5-7; 52:9-11).

12:16 Those who survived the threefold judgment of **sword, famine, and plague** would bear witness to their punishment by the Lord for their **detestable practices**.

12:17-20 Ezekiel was told to **eat** and **drink** with the outward signs of great fear, visibly foreshadowing the overwhelming fear with which the inhabitants of Jerusalem would eat their food because of the siege. This prophecy, like the others, revealed God's character and affirmed that He does not tolerate sin.

12:21-22 This saying was apparently popular in Ezekiel's day, indicating the lackadaisical attitude of the people.

12:23-28 The meaning was that the prophecies were so far into the future that they were of no concern or relevance to the people's daily lives. Ezekiel was told to correct both misconceptions—the horrors that he prophesied would come quickly and in his lifetime.

13:3 The overarching accusation against these prophets is that they are liars who purposely deceive. They **follow** [Hb *halak*, "walk, proceed," an active word, indicating continuous or characteristic activity; cp. Pr 6:12] **their own spirit** (not God's Spirit), although they **have seen nothing**.

13:6-9 They see **false** [Hb *shav'*, "falsehood, what is not true, emptiness"; cp. 12:24; 21:23,29; 22:28; Lm 2:14; Zch 10:2] **visions** and speak **lying** [Hb *kazav*, "falsehood, that which deceives or incites false hope"; cp. 21:29; 22:28] **divinations** (Hb *qesem*, "use of occultic or supernatural means to try to foretell future events"; cp. 21:21-22; Dt 18:10; Jr 14:14) and **have spoken falsely** (Hb *shav'*), claiming to speak **the LORD's declaration,** though He **had not spoken** and had not sent them. These false prophets claimed to have a word from the Lord but in fact did not.

13:10-14 In sum, these prophets **have led** [God's] **people astray** (Hb *ta'ah*, "seduce, cause to wander or stray") by their message of safety, security, and blessing, despite the people's faithlessness: **peace** [Hb *shalom*]**, when there is no peace** (vv. 10,16; cp. Jr 8:10-11). These men are compared to those who strengthen a wall with paint (**whitewash**) rather than mortar. The wall (which represents the people's false confidence) was so flimsy that a strong flood or hailstorm (representing God's **wrath, anger,** and **destructive fury**) could overturn it, hardly a defensive wall to keep out a hostile force. This false sense of security, bolstered by the wishful thinking of the false prophets, would be the people's undoing.

13:17-19 Next Ezekiel confronted **women** prophesying **out of their own imagination** (Hb *lēv*, "heart"; cp. v. 2). They were apparently practicing divination or witchcraft by means of magical amulets, making and wearing arm bands or bracelets as well as some kind of head gear, whether veils, bonnets, or shawls. These women took advantage of gullible people who believed their lying prophecies, claiming to help clients with personal issues but also wielding a measure of control over them. **Handfuls of barley and scraps of bread** may refer to the food they bought with the money they gained. When bread became scarce during the siege of Jerusalem or when the exiles were trying to survive, the food may have been a payment from clients.

13:20-23 These sorceresses had deceived the righteous and had encouraged the wicked to continue in their iniquity, perhaps ensnaring both groups by a dependence upon themselves. The Lord threatened to **deliver** the people from the black magic of these witches.

14:1-5 As some of the elders visit Ezekiel to inquire of the Lord, Ezekiel is advised that these elders are currently practicing idolatry and are unworthy to consult God. The only answer they will receive is judgment, according to their idolatry.

14:6-8 Yet judgment was not total; redemption was still a possibility. Ezekiel was told to call the people to repentance and to warn those who did not repent of the destruction to come. There was still the hope of mercy for those who followed the admonition to **turn away from** their **idols**. As before, God made Himself known by means of His judgment upon the ungodly.

14:9-11 These verses refer back to the judgments pronounced upon false prophets in chapter 13. Here the shocking statement that the deception of the false prophet was from the Lord can be understood in light of the story of Micaiah and the false prophets of Ahab (1Kg 22). In that instance, the false prophets had no intention of giving a negative oracle for the king; no matter what God told them, they were going to prophesy victory for the combined army. Even Micaiah was urged to prophesy favorably (1Kg 22:13). The text also makes it clear that Ahab was not going to listen to any prophet who told him something

with whitewash and knock it to the ground so that its foundation is exposed. The city will fall, and you will be destroyed within it. Then you will know that I am Yahweh. 15 After I exhaust My wrath against the wall and against those who plaster it with whitewash, I will say to you: The wall is no more and neither are those who plastered it— 16 those prophets of Israel who prophesied to Jerusalem and saw a vision of peace for her when there was no peace." This is the declaration of the Lord GOD.

17 "Now, son of man, turn[A] toward the women of your people who prophesy out of their own imagination. Prophesy against them 18 and say: This is what the Lord GOD says: Woe to the women who sew magic bands on the wrist of every hand and who make veils for the heads of people of every height in order to ensnare lives. Will you ensnare the lives of My people but preserve your own? 19 You profane Me in front of My people for handfuls of barley and scraps of bread; you kill those who should not die and spare those who should not live, when you lie to My people, who listen to lies.

20 "Therefore, this is what the Lord GOD says: I am against your magic bands that you ensnare people with like birds, and I will tear them from your arms. I will free the people you have ensnared like birds. 21 I will also tear off your veils and deliver My people from your hands, so that they will no longer be prey in your hands. Then you will know that I am Yahweh. 22 Because you have disheartened the righteous person with lies, even though I have not caused him grief, and because you have encouraged the wicked person not to turn from his evil way to save his life, 23 therefore you will no longer see false visions or practice divination. I will deliver My people from your hands. Then you will know that I am Yahweh."

An Oracle Against Men of Israel (14:1-23)

14 Some of the elders of Israel came to me and sat down in front of me. 2 Then the word of the LORD came to me: 3 "Son of man, these men have set up idols in their hearts and have put sinful stumbling blocks before their faces. Should I be consulted by them at all?

4 "Therefore, speak to them and tell them: This is what the Lord GOD says: When anyone from the house of Israel sets up idols in his heart, puts a sinful stumbling block before his face, and then comes to the prophet, I, •Yahweh, will answer him appropriately.[B] I will answer him according to his many idols, 5 so that I may take hold of the house of Israel by their hearts. They are all estranged from Me because of their idols.

6 "Therefore, say to the house of Israel: This is what the Lord GOD says: Repent and turn away from your idols; turn your faces away from all your detestable things. 7 For when anyone from the house of Israel or from the foreigners who reside in Israel separates himself from Me, setting up idols in his heart and putting a sinful stumbling block before his face, and then comes to the prophet to inquire of Me,[C] I, Yahweh, will answer him Myself. 8 I will turn against that one and make him a sign and a proverb; I will cut him off from among My people. Then you will know that I am Yahweh.

9 "But if the prophet is deceived and speaks a message, it was I, Yahweh, who deceived that prophet. I will stretch out My hand against him and destroy him from among My people Israel. 10 They will bear their punishment—the punishment of the one who inquires will be the same as that of the prophet— 11 in order that the house of Israel may no longer stray from following Me and no longer defile themselves with all their transgressions. Then they will be My people and I will be their God." This is the declaration of the Lord GOD.

12 The word of the LORD came to

[A]13:17 Lit *set your face* [B]14:4 Alt Hb tradition reads *him who comes* [C]14:7 Lit *Me for himself*

me: 13 "Son of man, if a land sins against Me by acting faithlessly, and I stretch out My hand against it to cut off its supply of bread, to send famine through it, and to wipe out both man and animal from it, 14 even if these three men—Noah, Daniel, and Job—were in it, they would deliver only themselves by their righteousness." This is the declaration of the Lord GOD.

15 "If I allow dangerous animals to pass through the land and depopulate it so that it becomes desolate, with no one passing through it for fear of the animals, 16 even if these three men were in it, as I live"—the declaration of the Lord GOD—"they could not deliver their sons or daughters. They alone would be delivered, but the land would be desolate.

17 "Or if I bring a sword against that land and say: Let a sword pass through it, so that I wipe out both man and animal from it, 18 even if these three men were in it, as I live"—the declaration of the Lord GOD—"they could not deliver their sons or daughters, but they alone would be delivered.

19 "Or if I send a plague into that land and pour out My wrath on it with bloodshed to wipe out both man and animal from it, 20 even if Noah, Daniel, and Job were in it, as I live"—the declaration of the Lord GOD—"they could not deliver their son or daughter. They would deliver only themselves by their righteousness.

21 "For this is what the Lord GOD says: How much worse will it be when I send My four devastating judgments against Jerusalem—sword, famine, dangerous animals, and plague—in order to wipe out both man and animal from it! 22 Even so, there will be survivors left in it, sons and daughters who will be brought out. Indeed, they will come out to you, and you will observe their conduct and actions. Then you will be consoled about the devastation I have brought on Jerusalem, about all I have brought on it. 23 They will bring you consolation when you see their conduct and actions, and you will know that it was not without cause that I have done what I did to it." This is the declaration of the Lord GOD.

The Parable of the Useless Vine (15:1-8)

15 Then the word of the LORD came to me: 2 "Son of man, how does the wood of the vine, that branch among the trees of the forest, compare to any other wood? 3 Can wood be taken from it to make something useful? Or can anyone make a peg from it to hang things on? 4 In fact, it is put into the fire as fuel. The fire devours both of its ends, and the middle is charred. Can it be useful for anything? 5 Even when it was whole it could not be made into a useful object. How much less can it ever be made into anything useful when the fire has devoured it and it is charred!

6 "Therefore, this is what the Lord GOD says: Like the wood of the vine among the trees of the forest, which I have given to the fire as fuel, so I will give up the residents of Jerusalem. 7 I will turn against them. They may have escaped from the fire, but it will still consume them. And you will know that I am •Yahweh when I turn against them. 8 I will make

>WORD|*study*

15:8 God announced that He would **make the land** desolate (Hb *shemamah*, "that which is laid waste," from the verb *shamēm*, "lay waste, make desolate," both of which, in the OT, are used most often in the book of Ezekiel). The word's root meaning connects a sense of comprehensive destruction with the primary idea of silence both in terms of a place made devoid of the sounds of life and of the human reaction to such devastation—being stunned, appalled, left speechless (cp. 3:15; Jb 18:20; 21:5). The word appears only three times in the Old Testament before its repeated use in the prophetic books. At Sinai, God explained to the people whom He had recently redeemed from Egypt how He would drive out the Canaanites from the promised land to prevent it from becoming "desolate" (Ezk 14:15-16; cp. Ex 23:29). Second, in explaining to the people the consequences of their disobedience and rebellion against Him, God said that their "land will become desolate" (Lv 26:33-35,43), and Ezekiel's audience was experiencing these consequences. Finally, the word was used to describe the city of Ai after Joshua conquered and burned it (Jos 8:28). Unlike the permanent desolation of Ai, however, restoration is promised to Israel (Ezk 36:33-36; cp. Is 62:4; Lv 26:43-45).

he did not want to hear. Thus, God did not instigate the false prophesying. By sending a lying spirit, He only bolstered the prophets' confidence in their own sin, so He could make a statement. Here, God used the obstinacy of the false prophets to reveal Himself. As the prophets and those who inquired of them were punished, the rest of Israel saw and returned to the Lord and experienced the blessings of the covenant relationship with God (cp. Jms 1:13-15).

14:12-20 The tone of the prophecy changes abruptly. God lists four judgments: **famine** (v. 13); **dangerous animals** (v. 15); **sword** (v. 17); and **plague** (v. 19). The inescapability of the coming punishment was made clear in a somewhat strange fashion: Even if the righteous men **Noah** (Gn 6:8-9,17-18,22; 7:5; 9:1; Heb 11:7; 2Pt 2:5), **Daniel** (Dn 1:8; 6:2-5,23; 10:11-12,19), and **Job** (Jb 1) were in the land, only they would escape; for their righteousness would be effectual only for themselves and not for the preservation of anyone else (Ezk 14:14,16,18,20). These statements may be taken as God's extended answer to Ezekiel's repeated attempts to intercede for the people. Each of these men intervened on behalf of others as part of his righteous acts: Noah delivered his sons and their families from the wrath of the flood; Job prayed for his friends; and Daniel put in a good word with the king for Shadrach, Meschach, and Abednego. In order to show the severity of Judah's situation, God declared that no such intercession would help this time.

14:22-23 Some people would survive but only as an example of the sinfulness of the nation.

15:2-6 This brief oracle reinforces God's emphasis on His purpose for sending his "four devastating judgments" (14:12-23) against **Jerusalem**. In the Hebrew text, verses 4 and 5 both begin with a word often translated "behold" (Hb *hinnēh*, "look, see"), calling the audience's attention to the metaphor that illustrates their own condition. The city's **residents** are compared to **the wood of the vine**, which is good only as **fuel** (Hb *ʾoklah*, "food," vv. 3, 6; cp. 21:32; 29:5; 34:5, 8, 10) for a fire. It is useless as a natural resource for construction; one cannot make from it even a small object like **a peg** (cp. Is 22:23-25). Like the wood of a grapevine, Judah was fit only to be burned and would be given up as fuel for fire.

the land desolate because they have acted unfaithfully." This is the declaration of the Lord GOD.

The Parable of the Adulterous Wife (16:1-63)

16 The word of the LORD came to me again: 2 "Son of man, explain Jerusalem's detestable practices to her. 3 You are to say: This is what the Lord GOD says to Jerusalem: Your origin and your birth were in the land of the Canaanites. Your father was an Amorite and your mother a Hittite. 4 As for your birth, your umbilical cord wasn't cut on the day you were born, and you weren't washed •clean[A] with water. You were not rubbed with salt or wrapped in cloths. 5 No one cared enough about you to do even one of these things out of compassion for you. But you were thrown out into the open field because you were despised on the day you were born.

6 "I passed by you and saw you lying in your blood, and I said to you as you lay in your blood: Live! Yes, I said to you as you lay in your blood: Live![B] 7 I made you thrive[C] like plants of the field. You grew up and matured and became very beautiful.[D] Your breasts were formed and your hair grew, but you were stark naked.

8 "Then I passed by you and saw you, and you were indeed at the age for love. So I spread the edge of My garment over you and covered your nakedness. I pledged Myself to you, entered into a covenant with you, and you became Mine." This is the declaration of the Lord GOD. 9 "I washed you with water, rinsed off your blood, and anointed you with oil. 10 I clothed you in embroidered cloth and provided you with leather sandals. I also wrapped you in fine linen and covered you with silk. 11 I adorned you with jewelry, putting bracelets on your wrists and a chain around your neck. 12 I put a ring in your nose, earrings on your ears, and a beautiful tiara on your head. 13 So you were adorned with gold and silver, and your clothing was made of fine linen, silk, and embroidered cloth. You ate fine flour, honey, and oil. You became extremely beautiful and attained royalty. 14 Your fame spread among the nations because of your beauty, for it was perfect through My splendor, which I had bestowed on you." This is the declaration of the Lord GOD.

15 "But you were confident in your beauty and acted like a prostitute because of your fame. You lavished your sexual favors on everyone who passed by. Your beauty became his.[A] 16 You took some of your garments and made colorful •high places for yourself, and you engaged in prostitution on them. These places should not have been built, and this should never have happened![A] 17 You also took your beautiful jewelry made from the gold and silver I had given you, and you made male images so that you could engage in prostitution with them. 18 Then you took your embroidered garments to cover them, and set My oil and incense before them. 19 You also set before

[A]16:4,15,16 Hb obscure [B]16:6 Some Hb mss, LXX, Syr omit *Yes, I said to you as you lay in your blood: Live!* [C]16:7 LXX reads *Thrive; I made you of ornaments* [D]16:7 Or *matured and developed the loveliest*

16:1-63 The Lord employed a lengthy allegory to ensure Jerusalem's full understanding of her conduct toward Him and, therefore, of the necessity of punishment. Allegory (or extended metaphor) is a literary device that employs concrete images to represent and illuminate abstract ideas, principles, or truths. Readers should not expect an exact correspondence between representative characters or elements of the story and the reality being illustrated. This allegory portrays Jerusalem as the wife of Yahweh, vividly making the Lord's case against her.

16:1-3 In the story, Jerusalem is cast as an unwanted, "despised," (v. 5) baby girl, whose parents represent two Canaanite nations (cp. v. 5; Gn 10:16; 15:13-21). Jerusalem was originally an **Amorite** city (cp. Jos 10:5-8; 1Kg 21:26) and was inhabited by both Amorites and Hittites (Jebusites, Jos 15:63; Jdg 1:8,21; 1Sm 17:54; 2Sm 5:6-7; 1Kg 11:13,32,36) when conquered by David.

16:4-6 In the metaphorical story, no one performed the typical acts of caring for a newborn child, not even the basic procedure of cutting the **umbilical cord** or washing off the blood and birth fluids.

16:7 Just as in the story Jerusalem **grew up and matured** into a **very beautiful** young woman, likewise David "built . . . up [the city] all the way around from the supporting terraces inward," transforming a strategically located "stronghold" into a lovely capital city (2Sm 5:9-10). That she was **stark naked** (Hb, the adjective *'erom*, "naked," with the noun *'eryah*, "nakedness, want"; cp. Ezk 16:22,39) implies moral vulnerability and possibly shame (cp. 23:29; Gn 3:7,10-11; Dt 28:48), perhaps reflecting the city's morally shameful pagan background.

16:8-9 Again, God acted on her behalf by entering into a marriage **covenant** with her: He **spread the edge of** [His] **garment over** her (cp. Ru 3:9) and **covered** [her] **nakedness** (Hb *'erwah*, "external genitals," implying shameful exposure; cp. Ezk 16:37; 23:10,18,29; Lv 18:7-19; 20:17-21; Is 47:3; Lm 1:8; Hs 2:9); He **washed** [her] **with water**, possibly part of the marriage ritual (cp. Eph 5:26-27), and **rinsed off** [her] **blood**, which may refer to "virginal bleeding," signaling her new identity as a wife. He **anointed** [her] **with oil**, a common practice after bathing, possibly comparable to applying lotion to avoid dry skin. The oil may have been perfumed as well. By marrying the young woman, the Lord extended to her the most highly favored status for a woman in the ancient world. For a God-fearing Israelite man, her Gentile heritage and upbringing would

>WORD|*study*

16:15 The word translated lavished (Hb *shaphak*, "pour out") appears 33 times in Ezekiel—more often than in any other Old Testament book. Usually the verb speaks of the Lord pouring out His "wrath" or "indignation" on rebellious Israel (7:8; 9:8; 20:8,13,21,33-34; 21:31; 22:22,31; 36:18; cp. 30:15; Rv 16) or refers to the shedding of blood (Ezk 16:38; 18:10; 22:3-4,6,9,12,27; 23:45; 24:7; 33:25; 36:18). Only in 16:15,36 and 23:8 is *shaphak* used to convey the extent of Israel's pursuit of idolatry and sexual promiscuity. However, one instance of the verb signals God's commitment to redemption—His promise to "pour out . . . [His] Spirit on the house of Israel" (39:29; cp. Jl 2:28-29; Zch 12:10). The Septuagint (Greek translation of the OT) uses the verb *ekcheō* (Gk, "pour out"), which appears both in Ac 2:17-18, noting the fulfillment of Joel 2:28-29, and in other passages referring to the work of the Holy Spirit (see Ac 2:33; 10:45; Rm 5:5; Ti 3:6).

16:15 Acted like a prostitute (Hb *zanah*, "be a harlot, commit fornication"; cp. 1Kg 3:16; Pr 23:27; Jr 3:1; see **Word Study**, Is 1:21, p. 863), Jerusalem liberally poured out sexual favors (Hb *taznut*, "fornications, whoredom," Ezk 16:15,20,22,25-26,29,33-34,36; metaphorically, the "worship of idols," 16:25-26,29; 23:7-8,11,14,17-29,35,43). Used only by Ezekiel in the Old Testament, this word is derived from the verb *zanah*.

them as a pleasing aroma the food
I gave you—the fine flour, oil, and
honey that I fed you. That is what
happened." This is the declaration of
the Lord God.
20 "You even took your sons and
daughters you bore to Me and sacrificed them to these images as food.
Wasn't your prostitution enough?
21 You slaughtered My children and
gave them up when you passed them
through the fire to the images. 22 In
all your detestable practices and acts
of prostitution, you did not remember the days of your youth when you
were stark naked and lying in your
blood.
23 "Then after all your evil—Woe,
woe to you!"—the declaration of the
Lord God— 24 "you built yourself a
mound and made yourself an elevated place in every square. 25 You built
your elevated place at the head of
every street and turned your beauty
into a detestable thing. You spread
your legs to everyone who passed
by and increased your prostitution. 26 You engaged in promiscuous
acts with Egyptian men, your well-
endowed neighbors, and increased
your prostitution to provoke Me to
anger.
27 "Therefore, I stretched out My
hand against you and reduced your
provisions. I gave you over to the
desire of those who hate you, the
Philistine women, who were embarrassed by your indecent behavior.
28 Then you engaged in prostitution
with the Assyrian men because you
were not satisfied. Even though you
did this with them, you were still
not satisfied. 29 So you extended your
prostitution to Chaldea, the land of
merchants, but you were not even
satisfied with this!
30 "How your heart was inflamed
with lust"—the declaration of the
Lord God—"when you did all these
things, the acts of a brazen prostitute, 31 building your mound at the
head of every street and making your
elevated place in every square. But
you were unlike a prostitute because
you scorned payment. 32 You adulterous wife, who receives strangers
instead of her husband! 33 Men give
gifts to all prostitutes, but you gave
gifts to all your lovers. You bribed

HARD QUESTION

How can passages like these on child sacrifice practiced by some primitive idol—worshiping religions apply to 21st-century readers?

Child sacrifice more commonly characterized some religions that are no longer practiced. However, not only are there places where such ritual sacrifice is still practiced but also the human motivation behind other forms of behavior toward children still appears in the most advanced nations, making appropriate the fairly direct application of such passages. For example, child sacrifice is practiced unlawfully in Uganda. A person who wants to become wealthy goes to the witchdoctor, whose prescription may be sacrificing a child, who does not have to be the parent's own child. Government enforcement of China's one-child policy and the preference for having male children also results not only in infanticide but also in gender-targeted infanticide, which also takes place in India, for example.

Biblical passages addressing child sacrifice either simply report on what has taken place in history (e.g., Jdg 11:29-40) or depict God's character in His response to the practice as in this text (Ezk 16:20-22; cp. Jr 7:31-34; 19:1-15). Ironically, Jerusalem (metaphorically portrayed as Yahweh's wayward wife) forgot that she also had at one time been like a vulnerable child, an unwanted infant thrown out to be exposed, yet God rescued her, saved her life, and married her. She, in turn, lacks compassion for her own children, who in fact are Yahweh's children (Ezk 16:22).

Child sacrifice not only constituted idolatry and the profaning of God's name (Lv 20:3) but also showed a shocking denigration of the most vulnerable human life. Its effects were not only personal or for the family involved but rather extended to the community, who were held accountable to punish such atrocities. The consequences for failure in this regard included a "pollution" of the land, which would "vomit" out its inhabitants (Lv 18:25,27-28). As the Canaanites who had practiced this ritual were purged when Israel entered the land, so Israel would suffer the same fate, as they themselves would be removed from the land by two exiles (Ezk 36:16-19).

Western readers can too easily denounce the horrors of child sacrifice in primitive religions and the injustice of gender-selective or government-forced abortion practices of other nations while overlooking the facts regarding abortions being performed legally in America and other nations. The circumstances and techniques of clinical abortions differ from the ritual slaughtering of children already born, but the results are the same. Motivations of personal convenience, "choice," or even greed effectively display the idolatry of replacing God with selfish desires. Women who follow Christ must not only recognize with wisdom and discernment the various contemporary forms of child sacrifice across the globe but also advocate for the voiceless victims. Biblical passages addressing child sacrifice and idolatry reveal God's view of these practices (cp. Mt 18:5-7) and can be applied in numerous ways that reflect not only upholding the value of children but also championing the value of the women, men, and communities for whom Christ has made possible complete rescue and healing from any sin.

preclude such a marriage; the story, then, illustrates the unconditional grace of the Lord in making a city such as Jerusalem the place where His name would dwell (see Dt 12:11; 14:23; 16:2,6,11; 1Kg 5:5; 8:16-20,29; 2Ch 7:20; 33:4-7; Jr 34:15). David brought the ark of the covenant to Jerusalem, and the Lord established a new covenant that entailed Solomon's construction of the temple (cp. Ezk 43:6-12).

16:10-13 The gifts lavished upon Jerusalem by the Lord effectively constituted a dowry.

16:14-19 Jerusalem perverted everything good that had been lavished on her by the Lord. By using those good gifts in the worship of idols and participating in the sexual practices of Canaanite religions, the city betrayed the Lord in the most shocking ways.

16:20-22 Most appalling of all was the "wife's" sacrifice of her own children to idols. This passage addresses the abhorrent practices of child sacrifice that characterized many ancient Canaanite and other ancient Near Eastern religions.

16:24-29 The promiscuous wife of the narrative even pursued prostitution as a business venture. **Mound** (Hb *gav*, "rounded or convex shape") is understood in the Septuagint as a brothel (Gk *oikēma pornikon*, "house of prostitution"; *porneias*, "place of illicit sexual intercourse"). An **elevated place** (Hb *ramah*, "high place"; cp. vv. 31,39) was likely a platform or rooftop position from which one could advertise or catch the attention of travelers.

The description of this woman's scandalous sexual promiscuity is intentionally shocking so that, as a metaphor of Jerusalem's political alliances—with Egypt (cp. 20:7; 1Kg 3:1; 9:16; Is 30:1-7; 31:1-3; Jr 2:18; Hs 12:1), Assyria (cp. 2Kg 16:1-18), and **Chaldea** (cp. 2Kg 20:12-19)—the audience will recognize the enormity of the sins provoking God's imminent judgment. Even Jerusalem's enemies, cast in the narrative as **the Philistine women**, responded to her **indecent behavior** (Hb *zimmah*, "wickedness," especially "lewdness, fornication"; cp. Ezk 16:43,58; 22:9,11; 23:21,27,29,35,44,48-49; 24:13; Lv 19:29; Jr 13:27; Hs 6:9) with embarrassment.

16:30-34 Despite the removal of His abundant blessings (v. 27), Jerusalem continued her relentless pursuit of worldly wealth and recognition (vv. 28-29; cp. Is 55:2). Jerusalem acted as both a **prostitute** (Ezk 16:3-31) and an **adulterous wife**, yet she was even worse than a harlot—rather than charging her clients a fee, she perversely **gave gifts** (Hb *nadan*, "large gift," with the sense of being freely cast before the recipient) to them—i.e., paid them to accept her **sexual favors** (Hb *taznut*; see **Word Study**, 16:15; p. 1064). This bribery refers to Judah's voluntary contributions to such nations as Egypt (cp. 17:7-9; Hs 12:1; Jr 2:18,36) and Assyria (cp. 2Kg 16:7-9; 18:14-16) in order to solicit their help.

16:35-43 Therefore signals judgment about to fall. The adulteress who behaved worse than a harlot would be shamed and exposed before all her **lovers**, both those she **loved** and those she **hated** (vv. 36-37; such as the Philistines, v. 27). She would be charged not only with adultery but also with murder—both capital crimes punishable by stoning (vv. 38-40; cp. Lv 20:1-5,10-12; Dt 17:2-5; 22:22; Jn 8:5). Punishment would actually be meted out by her former lovers (i.e., pagan nations), who would humiliate, plunder, destroy, and burn the city to the ground (Ezk 16:37-42). Readers who interpret the violent imagery as a description of what a husband could do, with biblical justification, to an adulterous wife miss the point of the passage. In the vivid, concrete language of metaphor, the Lord described what He would do to Jerusalem, the only city in which He had caused His name to dwell, by withdrawing the blessing and protection of His presence, which Israel has spurned. The extreme and exaggerated events, announced as though happening to a woman, graphically represented Egypt's treatment of Judah since the death of King Josiah and Babylon's catastrophic destruction of Jerusalem. The city would finally experience the frightening consequences of the inexcusable violations of her covenant with the Lord (v. 43; cp. Lv 26:30).

16:44-47 By means of a **proverb** (Hb *mashal*; see **Word Study**, Pr 1:1; p. 783), in which the **daughter** represents Jerusalem, the Lord continued to prosecute His case against the city by recalling both her past and current idolatry.

16:48-52 Usually the sexual immorality of Sodom is highlighted, but the Lord identified several sins not emphasized in Genesis of which Jerusalem was also guilty.

16:53-55 A note of hope was sounded when God promised to **restore** [the] **fortunes of** Sodom, Samaria, and Jerusalem and declared that all three sinful "sisters" would **return to their former state**.

16:58-63 Before restoration, however, the consequences for sin had to

them to come to you from all around for your sexual favors. 34 So you were the opposite of other women in your acts of prostitution; no one solicited you. When you paid a fee instead of one being paid to you, you were the opposite.

35 "Therefore, you prostitute, hear the word of the LORD! 36 This is what the Lord GOD says: Because your lust was poured out and your nakedness exposed by your acts of prostitution with your lovers, and because of all your detestable idols and the blood of your children that you gave to them, 37 I am therefore going to gather all the lovers you pleased—all those you loved as well as all those you hated. I will gather them against you from all around and expose your nakedness to them so they see you completely naked. 38 I will judge you the way adulteresses and those who shed blood are judged. Then I will bring about your bloodshed in wrath and jealousy. 39 I will hand you over to them, and they will level your mounds and tear down your elevated places. They will strip off your clothes, take your beautiful jewelry, and leave you stark naked. 40 They will bring a mob against you to stone you and cut you to pieces with their swords. 41 Then they will burn down your houses and execute judgments against you in the sight of many women. I will stop you from being a prostitute, and you will never again pay fees for lovers. 42 So I will satisfy My wrath against you, and My jealousy will turn away from you. Then I will be silent and no longer angry. 43 Because you did not remember the days of your youth but enraged Me with all these things, I will also bring your actions down on your own head." This is the declaration of the Lord GOD. "Haven't you committed immoral acts in addition to all your detestable practices?

44 "Look, everyone who uses proverbs will say this proverb about you:

Like mother, like daughter.

45 You are the daughter of your mother, who despised her husband and children. You are the sister of your sisters, who despised their husbands and children. Your mother was a Hittite and your father an Amorite. 46 Your older sister was Samaria, who lived with her daughters to the north of you, and your younger sister was Sodom, who lived with her daughters to the south of you. 47 Didn't you walk in their ways and do their detestable practices? It was only a short time before you behaved more corruptly than they did.[A]

48 "As I live"—the declaration of the Lord GOD—"your sister Sodom and her daughters have not behaved as you and your daughters have. 49 Now this was the iniquity of your sister Sodom: she and her daughters had pride, plenty of food, and comfortable security, but didn't support the poor and needy. 50 They were haughty and did detestable things before Me, so I removed them when I saw this.[B] 51 But Samaria did not commit even half your sins. You have multiplied your detestable practices beyond theirs and made your sisters appear righteous by all the detestable things you have committed. 52 You must also bear your disgrace, since you have been an advocate for your sisters. For they appear more righteous than you because of your sins, which you committed more abhorrently than they did. So you also, be ashamed and bear your disgrace, since you have made your sisters appear righteous.

53 "I will restore their fortunes, the fortunes of Sodom and her daughters and those of Samaria and her daughters. I will also restore[C] your fortunes among them, 54 so you will bear your disgrace and be ashamed of all you did when you comforted them. 55 As for your sisters, Sodom and her daughters and Samaria and her daughters will return to their former state. You and your daughters will also return to your former state. 56 Didn't you treat your sister Sodom as an object of scorn when you were proud, 57 before your wickedness was exposed? It was like the time you were scorned by the daughters of Aram[D] and all those around her, and by the daughters of

[A] **16:47** Lit *they in all your ways* [B] **16:50** Or *them as you have seen* [C] **16:53** LXX, Vg; MT reads *Samaria and her daughters and the fortunes of* [D] **16:57** Some Hb mss, Syr read *Edom*

the Philistines—those who treated
you with contempt from every side.
58 You yourself must bear the consequences of your indecency and
detestable practices"—this is the
LORD's declaration.
59 "For this is what the Lord GOD
says: I will deal with you according
to what you have done, since you
have despised the oath by breaking
the covenant. 60 But I will remember
the covenant I made with you in the
days of your youth, and I will establish an everlasting covenant with
you. 61 Then you will remember your
ways and be ashamed when you[A] receive your older and younger sisters.
I will give them to you as daughters,
but not because of your covenant.
62 I will establish My covenant with
you, and you will know that I am
•Yahweh, 63 so that when I make
•atonement for all you have done,
you will remember and be ashamed,
and never open your mouth again
because of your disgrace." This is
the declaration of the Lord GOD.

The Demise of the Last Rulers of Judah (17:1–19:14)

A Parable of Eagles, Cedars, and a Vine (17:1-24)

17 The word of the LORD came to
me: 2 "Son of man, pose a riddle
and speak a parable to the house of
Israel. 3 You are to say: This is what
the Lord GOD says:

A great eagle
with great wings,
long pinions,
and full plumage
of many colors
came to Lebanon and took
the top of the cedar.
4 He plucked off
its topmost shoot,
brought it to the land
of merchants,
and set it in a city of traders.
5 Then he took some
of the land's seed
and put it in a fertile field;
he set it like a willow,
a plant[B] by abundant waters.
6 It sprouted and became
a spreading vine,
low in height
with its branches turned
toward him,
yet its roots stayed under it.
So it became a vine,
produced branches,
and sent out shoots.
7 But there was another
great eagle
with great wings
and thick plumage.
And this vine bent its roots
toward him!
It stretched out its branches
to him
from its planting bed,
so that he might water it.
8 It had been planted
in a good field
by abundant waters
in order to produce branches,
bear fruit, and become
a splendid vine.

9 You are to say: This is what the
Lord GOD says:

Will it flourish?
Will he not tear out its roots
and strip off its fruit
so that it shrivels?
All its fresh leaves will wither!
Great strength
and many people
will not be needed to pull it
from its roots.
10 Even though it is planted,
will it flourish?
Won't it completely wither
when the east wind strikes it?
It will wither on the bed
where it sprouted."

11 The word of the LORD came to
me: 12 "Now say to that rebellious
house: Don't you know what these
things mean? Tell them: The king of
Babylon came to Jerusalem, took its
king and officials, and brought them
back with him to Babylon. 13 He took
one of the royal family and made a
covenant with him, putting him
under oath. Then he took away the
leading men of the land, 14 so the
kingdom might be humble and not
exalt itself but might keep his covenant in order to endure. 15 However, this king revolted against him
by sending his ambassadors to Egypt

be borne. Afterwards, God would reestablish His **covenant** (referring to the Sinai covenant) with Jerusalem. He would take back and forgive His adulterous wife after she had endured the consequences of her actions. Nevertheless, Jerusalem was unable to expunge her own sins. God made **atonement for all you have done**, and on the basis of this atonement, a new and **everlasting covenant** could be established.

17:1-2 The removal of the last four kings of Judah is depicted through poetic imagery (chaps. 17,19). God instructed Ezekiel to **pose a riddle and speak a parable** (Hb *mashal*; see **Word Study**, Pr 1:1; p. 783) regarding the relationships among Zedekiah, king of Judah; Nebuchadnezzar, king of Babylon; and Apries (or Hophra), pharaoh of Egypt. Zedekiah (Mattaniah; renamed by Nebuchadnezzar), the son of Josiah and Hamutal, and the full brother of Jehoahaz, reigned 11 years. Zedekiah was 21 years old when the king of Babylon placed him on the throne in place of his nephew Jehoiachin, whose rebellion had provoked the siege of Jerusalem and deportation of over 10,000 Israelites (2Kg 24:17-19; Jr 37:1).

17:3-4 Nebuchadnezzar is represented as **a great eagle** who took the **topmost shoot** of a **cedar** tree (i.e., Jehoiachin) to the **land of merchants**, Babylon (cp. v. 12; 2Kg 24:10-16). Jehoiachin, the son of Jehoiakim, was 18 years old when he became king and reigned three months and 10 days (2Kg 24:6-17; 2Ch 36:9-10; Jr 24:1). He was captured by Nebuchadnezzar and deported to Babylon. He later received favor from Nebuchadnezzar's successor, Evil-merodach (Ezk 19:6-9; cp. 2Kg 24:9-12,15; Jr 52:31-33). A young treetop is appropriate imagery for Jehoiachin, given his young age when he became king and his foolish attempt to rebel against Babylon.

17:5-10 Zedekiah and his household are described as **seed** that the king of Babylon had planted **in a fertile field**, where he flourished for awhile (see v. 13; cp. 2Kg 24:17-20) like a **vine**. He had all he needed, but then he turned toward **another great eagle**, the pharaoh of Egypt (see v. 15; cp. 2Kg 24:7). For violating his treaty with Babylon, Zedekiah would be greatly punished (see vv. 16-18; cp. 2Kg 24:20; 25:1-7).

17:12-16 Nebuchadnezzar, the **king of Babylon**, removed Jehoiachin in about 597 B.C., and made a treaty with Zedekiah by placing him under an **oath** of loyalty. Zedekiah also **revolted** against Nebuchadnezzar in 589 B.C. or 588 B.C., and Jerusalem was besieged,

[A]**16:61** Some LXX mss, Syr read *I* [B]**17:5** Hb obscure

finally falling in 586 B.C. Zedekiah was deported to Babylon and died there in captivity.

17:19 Zedekiah's unfaithfulness to his covenant with Nebuchadnezzar becomes an image of the unfaithfulness of God's people to their own covenant.

17:20-23 God would execute judgment especially upon the king for his godlessness. When Jerusalem fell in 586 B.C., Zedekiah and some of his men fled but were pursued and captured. They were then taken to Riblah, where Zedekiah's sons were executed, and Zedekiah's eyes were gouged out. Ezekiel's message prepared the exiles for what was to come and justified Zedekiah's punishment before the people. Nevertheless, the message of judgment was not without hope.

A comparison contrasting Babylon's treatment of Judah with God's future treatment follows. God would make sure that all **will know** that *He* is **Yahweh** and that *He* has **spoken** (cp. v. 24). The enormous predatory bird representing Babylon had "planted" the captives of Israel within the empire "in order to . . . become a splendid [Hb *ʾadderet*, "glorious, magnificent"] vine" (i.e., a trophy, v. 8). Similarly, God would **take** (Hb *laqach*, "lay hold of, seize, snatch"; cp. vv. 3,5,12-13; 16:16-20) a shoot from the **cedar** tree and **plant** it on **Israel's high mountain**. However, this shoot would become not merely a lovely garden vine, "low in height," but a **majestic** [Hb *ʾaddir*, "glorious, magnificent, mighty"] **cedar**, a towering tree under which **birds of every kind** can dwell (cp. vv. 6,8; Gn 7:14). The famous cedars of Lebanon can reach heights of 130 feet with trunks that are eight feet in diameter. For an audience familiar with both grapevines and cedars, these verses announce remarkable reversals that would be impossible, even unimaginable, apart from the sovereignty and grace of Yahweh (Ezk 17:21-24).

Although a return of the exiles to the land of Israel may have been immediately in view, a messianic interpretation makes better sense of this expansive picture. Just as the initial metaphors referred to individual persons, so also in this picture the shoot from the cedar tree refers to the Messiah. He will be the fulfillment of the Abrahamic, Davidic, and Mosaic covenants and will usher in the kingdom of God. Jesus used similar imagery in the parable comparing the kingdom of God to the growth of a mustard seed (cp. Mt 13:31-32; Mk 4:30-32; Lk 13:18-19).

17:24 The further imagery of **trees—the tall tree** being brought down, **the low tree** being made tall, **the green tree** withering, and **the withered**

so they might give him horses and a large army. Will he flourish? Will the one who does such things escape? Can he break a covenant and still escape?

16 "As I live"—this is the declaration of the Lord God—"he will die in Babylon, in the land of the king who put him on the throne, whose oath he despised and whose covenant he broke. 17 Pharaoh will not help him with his great army and vast horde in battle, when ramps are built and siege walls constructed to destroy many lives. 18 He despised the oath by breaking the covenant. He did all these things even though he gave his hand in pledge. He will not escape!"

19 Therefore, this is what the Lord God says: "As I live, I will bring down on his head My oath that he despised and My covenant that he broke. 20 I will spread My net over him, and he will be caught in My snare. I will bring him to Babylon and execute judgment on him there for the treachery he committed against Me. 21 All the fugitives[A] among his troops will fall by the sword, and those who survive will be scattered to every direction of the wind. Then you will know that I, •Yahweh, have spoken."

22 This is what the Lord God says:

I will take a sprig
from the lofty top of the cedar
and plant it.
I will pluck a tender sprig
from its topmost shoots,
and I will plant it
on a high towering mountain.
23 I will plant it on Israel's
high mountain
so that it may bear branches,
produce fruit,
and become a majestic cedar.
Birds of every kind will nest
under it,
taking shelter in the shade
of its branches.
24 Then all the trees of the field
will know
that I am Yahweh.
I bring down the tall tree,
and make the low tree tall.
I cause the green tree
to wither
and make
the withered tree thrive.
I, Yahweh, have spoken
and I will do it.

A Call for Personal Responsibility for Sin (18:1-32)

18 The word of the Lord came to me: 2 "What do you mean by using this proverb concerning the land of Israel:

The fathers eat sour grapes,
and the children's teeth
are set on edge?

3 As I live"—this is the declaration of the Lord God—"you will no longer use this proverb in Israel. 4 Look, every life belongs to Me. The life of the father is like the life of the son—both belong to Me. The person who sins is the one who will die.

5 "Now suppose a man is righteous and does what is just and right: 6 He does not eat at the mountain shrines or raise his eyes to the idols of the house of Israel. He does not defile his neighbor's wife or come near a woman during her menstrual impurity. 7 He doesn't oppress anyone but returns his collateral to the debtor. He does not commit robbery, but gives his bread to the hungry and covers the naked with clothing. 8 He doesn't lend at interest or for profit but keeps his hand from wrongdoing and carries out true justice between men. 9 He follows My statutes and keeps My ordinances, acting faithfully. Such a person is righteous; he will certainly live." This is the declaration of the Lord God.

10 "Now suppose the man has a violent son, who sheds blood and does any of these things, 11 though the father has done none of them. Indeed, when the son eats at the mountain shrines and defiles his neighbor's wife, 12 and when he oppresses the poor and needy, commits robbery, and does not return collateral, and when he raises his eyes to the idols, commits detestable acts, 13 and lends at interest or for profit, will he live? He will not live! Since he has committed all these detestable acts, he

A 17:21 Some Hb mss, LXX, Syr, Tg read *choice men*

will certainly die. His blood will be on him.

14 “Now suppose he has a son who sees all the sins his father has committed, and though he sees them, he does not do likewise. 15 He does not eat at the mountain shrines or raise his eyes to the idols of the house of Israel. He does not defile his neighbor’s wife. 16 He doesn’t oppress anyone, hold collateral, or commit robbery. He gives his bread to the hungry and covers the naked with clothing. 17 He keeps his hand from harming the poor, not taking interest or profit on a loan. He practices My ordinances and follows My statutes. Such a person will not die for his father’s iniquity. He will certainly live.

18 “As for his father, he will die for his own iniquity because he practiced fraud, robbed his brother, and did what was wrong among his people. 19 But you may ask, ‘Why doesn’t the son suffer punishment for the father’s iniquity?’ Since the son has done what is just and right, carefully observing all My statutes, he will certainly live. 20 The person who sins is the one who will die. A son won’t suffer punishment for the father’s iniquity, and a father won’t suffer punishment for the son’s iniquity. The righteousness of the righteous person will be on him, and the wickedness of the wicked person will be on him.

21 “Now if the wicked person turns from all the sins he has committed, keeps all My statutes, and does what is just and right, he will certainly live; he will not die. 22 None of the transgressions he has committed will be held against him. He will live because of the righteousness he has practiced. 23 Do I take any pleasure in the death of the wicked?” This is the declaration of the Lord God. “Instead, don’t I take pleasure when he turns from his ways and lives? 24 But when a righteous person turns from his righteousness and practices iniquity, committing the same detestable acts that the wicked do, will he live? None of the righteous acts he did will be remembered. He will die because of the treachery he has engaged in and the sin he has committed.

25 “But you say, ‘The Lord’s way isn’t fair.’ Now listen, house of Israel: Is it My way that is unfair? Instead, isn’t it your ways that are unfair? 26 When a righteous person turns from his righteousness and practices iniquity, he will die for this. He will die because of the iniquity he has practiced. 27 But if a wicked person turns from the wickedness he has committed and does what is just and right, he will preserve his life. 28 He will certainly live because he thought it over and turned from all the transgressions he had committed; he will not die. 29 But the house of Israel says, ‘The Lord’s way isn’t fair.’ Is it My ways that are unfair, house of Israel? Instead, isn’t it your ways that are unfair?

30 “Therefore, house of Israel, I will judge each one of you according to his ways.” This is the declaration of the Lord God. “Repent and turn from all your transgressions, so they will not be a stumbling block that causes your punishment. 31 Throw off all the transgressions you have committed, and get yourselves a new heart and a new spirit. Why should you die, house of Israel? 32 For I take no pleasure in anyone’s death.” This is the declaration of the Lord God. “So repent and live!

A Lament for Israel’s Princes (19:1-14)

19 “Now, lament for the princes of Israel 2 and say:

>WORD|*study*

18:31 The command to get [Hb *‘asah*, “do, commit”] yourselves [Hb *lakem*, “for you” (plural)] **a new heart and a new spirit** does not assume that the people are capable of such radical reform. The common verb “make” in this context may have the sense of “prepare, make ready, or offer” (cp. 43:25,27; 45:22-25; Ex 29:36; Jdg 6:19; 1Kg 18:23; Hs 2:8), or “effect, execute, bring to pass” (cp. 12:25; 16:41; Is 30:1; Dn 8:24; Pss 22:31; 37:5; 52:9). Later in the book, the Lord promises a “new heart and . . . a new spirit” to Israel as a gift (Ezk 36:26-27). The command emphasized the nation’s responsibility for the consequences of their sins as well as their freedom to receive this gift when the promise is fulfilled (cp. Dt 10:16; 30:6).

tree being made to thrive—suggests God’s sovereign hand in the rise and fall of earthly kingdoms. Also, such divine promises to manifest, someday, how things are ordered in His economy invite faith in His lordship over all. **Bring down** (Hb *shaphēl*, “make low, cast down”) appears in several such passages—e.g., 1Sm 2:7; 2Sm 22:28; Pss 18:27; 75:7; 147:6; Is 2:11-18; 40:4; Ezk 21:26; Mt 23:12; Jms 4:10.

18:1-18 This chapter calls people to accept personal responsibility for sin. Persons in every generation must accept personal responsibility for sin and not blame their punishment on a prior generation. In the early days of Israel’s nationhood, God had already established this principle (cp. Ex 32:31-33). Three examples are offered to illustrate this point.

18:21-24 While the Lord clearly states that the unrighteous will suffer punishment for their sins and the righteous will be rewarded for their good deeds, the process should not be seen as wooden or static; allowance must be made for judgment and consideration by God. Even if one has sinned, he can receive forgiveness if he repents. As long as one lives, hope is available and forgiveness is possible. In addition, God reveals His desire for the repentance of sinners rather than for their condemnation in this rhetorical question:—**Do I take any pleasure** [Hb *chaphēts*, “delight in, favor”; cp. v. 32; 33:11; Is 1:11; Mc 7:18] **in the death of the wicked.** Similarly, **a righteous person** who turns to sin is still in danger of judgment.

18:25-29 Amazingly, the people complained that God would punish those who abandoned righteousness to pursue sin and would show mercy to those who changed their ways and repented of their sins (cp. 33:17,20).

18:30-32 The Lord calls the people to **repent**. In turning away from and forsaking their **transgressions** (Hb *pesha‘*, “trespass, rebellious act”) they were mercifully given a way to avoid death and were shown the way to truly **live**.

19:1 This entire chapter is a **lament for the princes** [Hb *nasi’*, “ruler, chief or leader of a tribe”; cp. 45:8-9] **of Israel** and should be used as a lament—a funeral dirge, a song of mourning usually chanted by professional mourners in a procession taking the body of the deceased to the tomb (v. 14). Two images depict the fall of the last kings of the Davidic dynasty: a lioness and her cubs (vv. 2-9) and a vine and its branches (vv. 10-14).

19:2-4 Judah is depicted as **a lioness** (cp. Gn 49:9) that bore two particularly aggressive **cubs**. The first cub represents Jehoahaz, who was imprisoned by Pharaoh Neco, then deported to **Egypt** (v. 4; cp. 2Kg 23:32-34).

19:5-7 Although each of the three kings of Judah following Jehoahaz has been proposed as the referent of the second cub, Jehoiachin for the second **young lion** is the most likely candidate.

19:8-9 As Jehoahaz was deported to Egypt, Jehoachin was **led . . . away to the king of Babylon**, deported by Nebuchadnezzar. In later years, under his successor, Evil-Merodach (or Amel-Marduk) released him and allowed him to dine with the king (2Kg 25:27-29).

19:10-11 In the second image, Judah (or the nation of Israel more broadly) is compared to **a vine,** using language that draws on Moses' prophetic blessing of the tribe (cp. Gn 49:8-12). The growth of this vine is exaggerated (**its height . . . among the clouds**), serving as a caricature of Judah's arrogance. When it flourished, this vine was **full of branches** (Hb *'anêph*, from the noun *'anaph*, "branch, bough" used only here; Ezk 17:8,23; 36:8; Ps 80:8-10) and was known for **its many branches** (Hb *daliyah*, "bough"; Ezk 17:6-7,23; 19:11; Jr 11:6); it **had strong branches** (Hb *matteh*, "staff, rod"; cp. Ps 110:2) suitable for use as **scepters** (Hb *shêvet*; see note on Gn 49:8-12; **Word Study**, Pr 14:3; p. 802), lending credence to the view that the vine is the royal house of Judah.

19:12-14 The Lord imposed fitting consequences for arrogance.

20:1-3 Chapter 20 begins a new series of prophecies by Ezekiel. It has been just over two years since Ezekiel's original vision. Ezekiel's initiation to prophetic office dates to "the fifth year of King Jehoiachin's exile" (1:1-3). Chapter 8 dates another set of visions to "the sixth year." Ezekiel notes that "the elders of Judah" were there and that "the hand of the Lord God came down on" him (8:1-2). The occasion of this series, like the previous one, is an inquiry of the Lord by several of **Israel's elders**. To **consult** [Hb *darash*, "seek"; lit "tread or trample with the feet," lending the idea of "beating a path" to a place, of "frequenting" or going regularly to a place] **the Lord** is to "go to" Him constantly for direction (see Dt 4:29; 1Ch 28:8-9; Ps 9:10; Mt 6:32-33; Heb 11:6; 13:14). On this occasion, **the word of the Lord came to** Ezekiel, instructing him to address **the elders of Israel**.

>WORD|*study*

19:12 The word uprooted (Hb *natash*, "be plucked up or rooted out"), in particular, signals that the judgment prophesied here would also fulfill God's covenant promises to punish Israel for turning away from Him to worship other gods (Dt 29:28; 1Kg 14:15; 2Ch 7:19-20). It also reflects God's promises of hope for Israel's future (Jr 24:6; 31:28, 40; 42:10; Am 9:15).

What was your mother?
A lioness!
She lay down
among the lions;
she reared her cubs
among the young lions.
3 She brought up one
of her cubs,
and he became a young lion.
After he learned to tear prey,
he devoured people.
4 When the nations
heard about him,
he was caught in their pit.
Then they led him away
with hooks
to the land of Egypt.

5 When she saw that she waited
in vain,
that her hope was lost,
she took another of her cubs
and made him a young lion.
6 He prowled among the lions,
and he became a young lion.
After he learned to tear prey,
he devoured people.
7 He devastated
their strongholds[A]
and destroyed their cities.
The land and everything
in it shuddered
at the sound of his roaring.
8 Then the nations from
the surrounding provinces
set out against him.
They spread their net
over him;
he was caught in their pit.
9 They put a wooden yoke
on him[B] with hooks
and led him away to the king
of Babylon.
They brought him into the
fortresses
so his roar could no longer
be heard
on the mountains of Israel.

10 Your mother was like a vine
in your vineyard,[C]
planted by the water;
it was fruitful and full
of branches
because of plentiful waters.
11 It had strong branches, fit for
the scepters of rulers;
its height towered
among the clouds.[D]
So it was conspicuous
for its height
as well as its many branches.
12 But it was uprooted in fury,
thrown to the ground,
and the east wind dried up
its fruit.
Its strong branches were
torn off and dried up;
fire consumed them.
13 Now it is planted
in the wilderness,
in a dry and thirsty land.
14 Fire has gone out from its
main branch[E]
and has devoured its fruit,
so that it no longer has
a strong branch,
a scepter for ruling.

This is a lament and should be used as a lament."

Rebellion and Restoration (20:1-49)

20 In the seventh year, in the fifth month, on the tenth day of the month, some of Israel's elders came to consult the Lord, and they sat down in front of me. 2 Then the word of the Lord came to me: 3 "Son of man, speak with the elders of Israel and tell them: This is what the Lord God says: Are you coming to consult Me? As I live, I will not be consulted by you." This is the declaration of the Lord God.

4 "Will you pass judgment against them, will you pass judgment, son

[A]19:7 Tg, Aq; MT reads *knew their widows* [B]19:9 Or *put him in a cage* [C]19:10 Some Hb mss; other Hb mss read *blood* [D]19:11 Or *thick foliage* [E]19:14 Lit *from the branch of its parts*

of man? Explain the detestable practices of their fathers to them. 5 Say to them: This is what the Lord God says: On the day I chose Israel, I swore an oath[A] to the descendants of Jacob's house and made Myself known to them in the land of Egypt. I swore to them, saying: I am •Yahweh your God. 6 On that day I swore[B] to them that I would bring them out of the land of Egypt into a land I had searched out for them, a land flowing with milk and honey, the most beautiful of all lands. 7 I also said to them: Each of you must throw away the detestable things that are before your eyes and not defile yourselves with the idols of Egypt. I am Yahweh your God.

8 "But they rebelled against Me and were unwilling to listen to Me. None of them threw away the detestable things that were before their eyes, and they did not forsake the idols of Egypt. So I considered pouring out My wrath on them, exhausting My anger against them within the land of Egypt. 9 But I acted because of My name, so that it would not be profaned in the eyes of the nations they were living among, in whose sight I had made Myself known to Israel by bringing them out of Egypt.

10 "So I brought them out of the land of Egypt and led them into the wilderness. 11 Then I gave them My statutes and explained My ordinances to them—the person who does them will live by them. 12 I also gave them My Sabbaths to serve as a sign between Me and them, so they will know that I am Yahweh who sets them apart as holy.

13 "But the house of Israel rebelled against Me in the wilderness. They did not follow My statutes and they rejected My ordinances—the person who does them will live by them. They also completely profaned My Sabbaths. So I considered pouring out My wrath on them in the wilderness to put an end to them. 14 But I acted because of My name, so that it would not be profaned in the eyes of the nations in whose sight I had brought them out. 15 However, I swore[B] to them in the wilderness that I would not bring them into the land I had given them—the most beautiful of all lands, flowing with milk and honey— 16 because they rejected My ordinances, profaned My Sabbaths, and did not follow My statutes. For their hearts went after their idols. 17 But I spared them from destruction and did not bring them to an end in the wilderness.

18 "Then I said to their children in the wilderness: Don't follow the statutes of your fathers, defile yourselves with their idols, or keep their ordinances. 19 I am Yahweh your God. Follow My statutes, keep My ordinances, and practice them. 20 Keep My Sabbaths holy, and they will be a sign between Me and you, so you may know that I am Yahweh your God.

21 "But the children rebelled against Me. They did not follow My statutes or carefully keep My ordinances—the person who does them will live by them. They also profaned My Sabbaths. So I considered pouring out My wrath on them and exhausting My anger against them in the wilderness. 22 But I withheld My hand and acted because of My name, so that it would not be profaned in the eyes of the nations in whose sight I brought them out. 23 However, I swore[B] to them in the wilderness that I would disperse them among the nations and scatter them among the countries. 24 For they did not practice My ordinances but rejected My statutes and profaned My Sabbaths, and their eyes were fixed on their fathers' idols. 25 I also gave them statutes that were not good and ordinances they could not live by. 26 When they made every firstborn pass through the fire, I defiled them through their gifts in order to devastate them so they would know that I am Yahweh.

27 "Therefore, son of man, speak to the house of Israel, and tell them: This is what the Lord God says: In this way also your fathers blasphemed Me by committing treachery against Me: 28 When I brought them into the land that I swore[B] to give them and they saw any high hill or leafy tree, they offered their sacrifices and presented their offensive

[A]**20:5** Lit *I lifted My hand* [B]**20:6,15,23,28** Lit *lifted My hand*

20:4-6 Ezekiel's answer begins with a long explanation of God's troubled relationship with the people.

20:8-9 The Lord's indictment against Israel was presented in a pattern repeated three times. Israel had rebelled against Him on several occasions (cp. vv. 13,21), but He had not destroyed them **because of** [His] **name** (cp. vv. 14,22), leading them instead into the promised land. They continued to rebel even there, worshiping false gods. Idolatry is presented as a defilement that offends God. The concern for God's **name** (that **it would not be profaned in the eyes of the nations**) speaks to God's desire to protect His own witness before pagan nations. He had entered into a covenant with Israel in the **sight** of other nations, showing Himself to be a Redeemer, Savior, and a loving, gracious, and personal God who keeps His promises from generation to generation.

20:10-12 The language of sanctity looms large here, not surprisingly from a priestly author.

20:13-17 Two of these cycles of redemption, rebellion, and withholding of the deserved punishment appear. These verses refer to God's redemption via the Exodus, the giving of the law at Sinai, and the people's rebellion in worshiping the golden calf. God spared the people solely due to Moses' mediation on their behalf (Ex 32:7-14).

20:18-26 A second generation of Israelites is advised to obey the Lord's statutes, but they also rebel. No specifics are given here, but two famous incidents of rebellion in which God was prepared to strike the entire community but was prevented by the intercession of Moses are found in Nm 14:11-19 (refusing to enter Canaan) and Nm 16:22,43 (Korah's rebellion). Although God spared them despite their idolatry, they came under the threat of dispersal to other nations. They also came under God's wrath in that God gave them over to **statutes that were not good and ordinances they could not live by**. The Israelites preferred the idolatrous religious practices of the surrounding nations (like child sacrifice) and stubbornly refused to obey God's statutes and ordinances, which were intended to bring life (cp. vv. 11,13; Rm 1:24-29).

20:27-29 The behavior of the next generation of Israelites in Canaan was no better than their ancestors. They adapted themselves to Canaanite religion, offering sacrifices at every **high place** they could set up. This was the case even **to this day**, up to the time of Ezekiel's conversation, bringing the listeners back to the present.

20:30-31 The Lord accuses the current generation of the same blasphemies and atrocities as the previous generations. Thus the Lord says that He will not allow the people to consult Him (cp. v. 3). In order to consult the **Lord, God**, one must first purge himself of idolatry and anything God deems sinful.

20:32-34 Despite Israel's defilement with idols, God will not allow the nation to be completely lost. To save the nation, judgment must come. The formulaic expression, **a strong hand, an outstretched arm, and outpoured wrath** is used twice to communicates this truth. It is not meant to suggest that the Lord *forces* people to worship Him or serve Him against their wills, but rather that when He judges the iniquity of the people, at least some will repent and turn back to Him.

20:35-38 God assures His people that He is faithful to His covenant promises, that He is providential and sovereign, and He will ensure that His people are preserved as a nation. This will be accomplished through the **rod** of **judgment** in two ways. First, some will recognize the hand of God, repent, and "listen" to God (v. 39). Second, some (presumably those who would not repent) will be removed from Israel by means of death. This is the meaning of the language of purging and exclusion from the land of Israel. The place for this judgment will be **the wilderness of the peoples**, a reference to the exile in which they are scattered among foreigners. It is a type of wilderness experience for them, corresponding to the previous examples of God's dealings with Israel in the desert.

20:39-41 While some individuals will be allowed to engage in idolatry, the whole nation will not be allowed to reject the Lord completely (v. 32) because some will turn back to God after judgment. Ezekiel's words are both passionate and compassionate as the promise and hope of grace, forgiveness, and restoration are presented.

21:42-44 A shift occurs here in the use of the language of revelation. Whereas previously the punishment and judgment of God was seen as revelatory—the formulaic expression, **you will know that I am Yahweh,** was used extensively with respect to the destruction of Jerusalem and the deportation of its inhabitants—now the knowledge of the Lord comes by means of His restoration of the people to the land. The fall of Jerusalem and subsequent exile reveal God's holiness and wrath, while the preservation and restoration of the remnant reveal God's mercy, grace, and faithfulness. God will not deal with the people according to their actions, according to what they deserve, but instead will deal with them according to His Name. He will

>WORD|*study*

20:33 The phrase a strong hand, an outstretched arm, and outpoured wrath (Hb *chēmah;* see 3:12-14) is used twice. This particular group of three expressions does not occur elsewhere in the Old Testament. "A strong hand," sometimes coupled with "an outstretched arm," often appears in references to God's deliverance from Egypt (e.g., Dt 5:15). Only three verses combine these two phrases with a third (Hb *mora'*, "terror, terrifying power," Dt 4:34; 26:8; Jr 32:21)—also in describing what God did in the exodus. The third word (Hb *chēmah*) in this expression should have prompted fear in Ezekiel's audience since this word is used to describe God's judgment of Sodom and Gomorrah (Dt 29:23) and to express His promise to judge His people if they abandoned His covenant (cp. Dt 9:19; 29:28). The closest parallel is found in the Lord's word to King Zedekiah: "I will fight against you with an outstretched hand and a mighty arm, with anger, rage (Hb *chēmah*), and great wrath" (Jr 21:5).

offerings there. They also sent up their pleasing aromas and poured out their •drink offerings there. 29 So I asked them: What is this •high place you are going to? And it is called High Place to this day.

30 "Therefore say to the house of Israel: This is what the Lord God says: Are you defiling yourselves the way your fathers did, and prostituting yourselves with their detestable things? 31 When you offer your gifts, making your children pass through the fire, you continue to defile yourselves with all your idols to this day. So should I be consulted by you, house of Israel? As I live"—this is the declaration of the Lord God—"I will not be consulted by you!

32 "When you say, 'Let us be like the nations, like the peoples of other countries, worshiping wood and stone,' what you have in mind will never happen. 33 As I live"—the declaration of the Lord God—"I will rule over you with a strong hand, an outstretched arm, and outpoured wrath. 34 I will bring you from the peoples and gather you from the countries where you were scattered, with a strong hand, an outstretched arm, and outpoured wrath. 35 I will lead you into the wilderness of the peoples and enter into judgment with you there face to face. 36 Just as I entered into judgment with your fathers in the wilderness of the land of Egypt, so I will enter into judgment with you." This is the declaration of the Lord God. 37 "I will make you pass under the rod and will bring you into the bond of the covenant. 38 And I will also purge you of those who rebel and transgress against Me. I will bring them out of the land where they live as foreign residents, but they will not enter the land of Israel. Then you will know that I am Yahweh.

39 "As for you, house of Israel, this is what the Lord God says: Go and serve your idols, each of you. But afterward you will surely listen to Me, and you will no longer defile My holy name with your gifts and idols. 40 For on My holy mountain, Israel's high mountain"—the declaration of the Lord God—"there the entire house of Israel, all of them, will serve Me in the land. There I will accept them and will require your contributions and choicest gifts, all your holy offerings. 41 When I bring you from the peoples and gather you from the countries where you have been scattered, I will accept you as a pleasing

Doctrine HOLINESS

The priestly language of holiness and cleanliness permeates the entire book of Ezekiel. Holiness is a preeminent attribute of God. Discussions of the holy versus the profane, contamination, defilement, or pollution of the land due to sin recur often throughout the book. Holiness is intertwined with the covenant: Israel is to be a holy people set apart in thought, worship, and action, reflecting God's holiness. The Ten Commandments point to this, with commands deploring polytheism and idolatry (graven images), as well as commands to venerate God's name. The latter was being profaned among the nations because of Israel's behavior (chaps. 20, 36). A number of images of burning appear in the book, indicating purification and wrath, and these two are intertwined. God's wrath is directed at sin, which is unholiness, impurity, and defilement. For example, Ezekiel was shown that the holy of holies overseen by cherubim had been defiled, as had the temple or God's holy place, a situation so despicable that God abandoned Jerusalem to the Babylonians. In order to guard against the repeating of this defilement, in the new temple of the new city, the Levites will be careful to instruct the people about the distinction between the holy and the common, the sacred and the profane (cp. 22:26 and 44:23).

aroma. And I will demonstrate My holiness through you in the sight of the nations. 42 When I lead you into the land of Israel, the land I swore[A] to give your fathers, you will know that I am Yahweh. 43 There you will remember your ways and all your deeds that you have defiled yourselves with, and you will loathe yourselves for all the evil things you have done. 44 You will know that I am Yahweh, house of Israel, when I have dealt with you because of My name rather than according to your evil ways and corrupt acts." This is the declaration of the Lord GOD.

45[B] The word of the LORD came to me: 46 "Son of man, face the south and preach against it. Prophesy against the forest land in the •Negev, 47 and say to the forest there: Hear the word of the LORD! This is what the Lord GOD says: I am about to ignite a fire in you, and it will devour every green tree and every dry tree in you. The blazing flame will not be extinguished, and every face from the south to the north will be scorched by it. 48 Then all people will see that I, Yahweh, have kindled it. It will not be extinguished."

49 Then I said, "Oh, Lord GOD, they are saying of me, 'Isn't he just posing riddles?'"

The Sword of Judgment (21:1-32)

21[C] The word of the LORD came to me again: 2 "Son of man, turn your face toward Jerusalem and preach against the sanctuaries. Prophesy against the land of Israel, 3 and say to it: This is what the LORD says: I am against you. I will draw My sword from its sheath and cut off both the righteous and the wicked from you. 4 Since I will cut off[D] both the righteous and the wicked, My sword will therefore come out of its sheath against everyone from the south to the north. 5 So all the people will know that I, •Yahweh, have taken My sword from its sheath—it will not be sheathed again.

6 "But you, son of man, groan! Groan bitterly with a broken heart[E] right before their eyes. 7 And when they ask you, 'Why are you groaning?' then say: Because of the news that is coming. Every heart will melt, and every hand will become weak. Every spirit will be discouraged, and every knee will turn to water. Yes, it is coming and it will happen." This is the declaration of the Lord GOD.

8 The word of the LORD came to me: 9 "Son of man, prophesy: This is what the Lord says! You are to proclaim:

A sword! A sword is sharpened
and also polished.
10 It is sharpened for slaughter,
polished to flash
like lightning!
Should we rejoice?
The scepter of My son,
the sword despises
every tree.[F]
11 The sword is given
to be polished,
to be grasped in the hand.
It is sharpened, and it
is polished,
to be put in the hand
of the slayer.
12 Cry out and wail, son of man,
for it is against My people.
It is against all the princes
of Israel!
They are given
over to the sword
with My people.
Therefore strike your thigh
in grief.
13 Surely it will be a trial!
And what if the sword
despises even the scepter?
The scepter will
not continue.[F]
This is the declaration
of the Lord GOD.
14 Therefore, son of
man, prophesy
and clap your hands together.
Let the sword strike
two times, even three.
It is a sword for massacre,
a sword for great massacre—
it surrounds[G] them!

[A]20:42 Lit *lifted My hand* [B]20:45 Ezk 21:1 in Hb [C]21:1 Ezk 21:6 in Hb [D]21:4 Lit *off from you* [E]21:6 Lit *with broken loins* [F]21:10,13 Hb obscure [G]21:14 Or *penetrates*

honor His unconditional promise to Abraham by ensuring that a remnant survives and is faithful, and thus His people will be a light to the nations.

20:45-49 A theological explanation is given of a forest fire **in the Negev**. Perhaps not a literal fire, it is nonetheless descriptive of the coming judgment upon Jerusalem. Interestingly, the people complain that Ezekiel's messages are too cryptic. This is ironic because, while some of the symbols used by Ezekiel are admittedly difficult to follow, his message of the coming doom of Jerusalem due to the people's gross immorality and religious harlotry is far too clear to be ignored, so the complaint is unfounded. Second, the desire for *relevant* messages, and the rejection of messages with content seems to be as common in contemporary churches as in Ezekiel's own day.

21:1-2 In response to the people's charge that Ezekiel's messages were irrelevant (20:49), the Lord gave the prophet a word that would be fulfilled in their lifetimes. The command to preach against the **sanctuaries** is unclear since most of the message here is against the city of Jerusalem.

21:3-4 Disaster does not necessarily indicate God's displeasure with a particular person or nation. Oftentimes, those who are innocent suffer because of the actions of the guilty. This fact is apparent in the lives of faithful men like Daniel, Jeremiah, Baruch, and Ezekiel himself, all of whom were negatively impacted by the Babylonian invasions.

21:6-7 Ezekiel was told to mourn, groaning **bitterly**—a sign that would prompt the people to ask why he mourned. The fact that the mourning was a sign did not diminish the actual horror and grief Ezekiel felt for the people and the city: His **heart** was **broken** due to the people's sin and the overwhelming devastation of God's impending judgment—hearts would **melt**, hands would be **weak**, spirits would be **discouraged**, and knees would buckle (**turn to water**).

21:8-13 The first of two prophetic *songs* in this chapter is a song of the sword of judgment against Israel (vv. 9-17,25-27; cp. Jeremiah's song of the sword against Babylon, Jr 50:35-37, and song of the sword against Philistia, Jr 47:6-7). Here, the sword is not against other nations, but specifically against **all the princes of Israel**, who neglected their role(s) to lead the people in proper reverence of the Lord. By stating that **the scepter will not continue**, the **Lord GOD** indicated that the removal of Zedekiah would end the monarchy.

21:14-17 After the sword has been prepared (**sharpened** and **polished**), it is ready to do its bloody work: to **strike, massacre, slaughter,** and **slash**. The sword virtually takes on a life of its own. The references to clapping and turning to the **right** and **left** might indicate some kind of sword dance accompanying these lyrics.

21:19-20 In the midst of this sword song, Nebuchadnezzar appears, graphically described at a fork in the road, deciding on his next military offensive: Should he strike Judah or Ammon? As a sign-act, Ezekiel drew a sand table of sorts with a military map, complete with signposts to Jerusalem and Rabbah, the capitals of the respective countries. That the wielder of the sword (the "slayer" of v. 11) and God's agent of judgment will be Nebuchadnezzar becomes clear.

21:21-24 The **divination** methods mentioned here were commonly practiced in the ancient Near East and are not exclusively Babylonian. In the shaking of **arrows**, arrows were marked with names, placed in a quiver, shaken up and then drawn out like straws. In the second method, miniature statuettes of ancestral gods (**idols**) are probably in view, although exactly how they were used is uncertain. The third method was highly popular in Babylon, and even carried over into the Roman Empire, as priests examined the markings on the **liver**, kidneys, or other entrails before a battle. While pagans used divination to make their decision, the Lord used the process and the pagans to bring judgment upon the Judeans.

21:25-27 The second refrain made the monarchy's demise even clearer, commanding Zedekiah to **remove** his **turban** and **crown** because **things will not remain as they are.** The threefold repetition of the city's destruction (**a ruin, a ruin, . . . a ruin!**) indicates that the fate of the king and his city has been sealed.

21:28-32 Even though Jerusalem was to be attacked, Rabbah and the Ammonites would not escape unscathed. The second *sword song* was against Ammon. For the time being, the sword had been put in its **sheath**, but the Lord would use the Babylonians, **brutal men** who were **skilled at destruction**, to judge the Ammonites at a later time. They, like the Judeans, would be devastated in their own land because of their ungodliness and hatred of Israel (cp. Ezk 25), and possibly because they had also rebelled against Babylon.

22:1-24:14 Chapters 22 and 24 mark the beginning and the end of a literary unit called an *inclusio*, a literary device that signals a unit with a common

15 I have appointed a sword
for slaughter[A]
at all their gates,
so that their hearts may melt
and many may stumble.
Yes! It is ready to flash
like lightning;
it is drawn[A] for slaughter.
16 Slash to the right;
turn to the left—
wherever your blade
is directed.
17 I also will clap
My hands together,
and I will satisfy My wrath.
I, Yahweh, have spoken."

18 Then the word of the LORD came
to me: 19 "Now you, son of man, mark
out two roads that the sword of Babylon's king can take. Both of them
should originate from the same
land. And make a signpost at the
fork in the road to each city. 20 Mark
out a road that the sword can take
to Rabbah of the Ammonites and to
Judah into fortified Jerusalem. 21 For
the king of Babylon stands at the
split in the road, at the fork of the
two roads, to practice •divination:
he shakes the arrows, consults the
idols, and observes the liver. 22 The
answer marked[B] Jerusalem appears
in his right hand, indicating that he
should set up battering rams, give
the order to[C] slaughter, raise a battle
cry, set battering rams against the
gates, build a ramp, and construct
a siege wall. 23 It will seem like false
divination in the eyes of those who
have sworn an oath to the Babylonians,[D] but it will draw attention to
their •guilt so that they will be captured.
24 "Therefore, this is what the Lord
GOD says: Because you have drawn
attention to your guilt, exposing
your transgressions, so that your
sins are revealed in all your actions,
since you have done this, you will be
captured by them.

25 And you, profane
and wicked prince of Israel,[E]
the day has come
for your punishment."[F]

26 This is what the Lord GOD says:

Remove the turban,
and take off the crown.
Things will not remain
as they are;[G]
exalt the lowly
and bring down
the exalted.
27 A ruin, a ruin,
I will make it a ruin!
Yet this will not happen
until He comes;
I have given the judgment
to Him.[H]

28 "Now prophesy, son of man, and
say: This is what the Lord GOD says
concerning the Ammonites and
their contempt. You are to proclaim:

A sword! A sword
is drawn for slaughter,
polished to consume, to flash
like lightning.
29 While they offer false visions
and lying divinations
about you,
the time has come to put you
to the necks of the profane
wicked ones;
the day has come
for your punishment.[F]

30 Return it to its sheath!

I will judge you[I]
in the place
where you were created,
in the land of your origin.
31 I will pour out My indignation
on you;
I will blow the fire of My fury
on you.
I will hand you over
to brutal men,
skilled at destruction.
32 You will be fuel for the fire.
Your blood will be spilled
in the land.
You will not
be remembered,
for I, Yahweh, have spoken."

[A]**21:15** Hb obscure [B]**21:22** Lit *The divination for them* [C]**21:22** Lit *rams, open the mouth in* [D]**21:23** Lit *them* [E]**21:25** = King Zedekiah [F]**21:25,29** Lit *come in the time of the punishment of the end* [G]**21:26** Lit *This not this* [H]**21:27** Or *comes to whom it rightfully belongs, and I will give it to Him* [I]**21:30** = the Ammonites

Oracles Against Jerusalem (22:1–24:27)

The City's Bloodshed and Idolatry (22:1-31)

22 The word of the LORD came to me: 2 "As for you, son of man, will you pass judgment? Will you pass judgment against the city of blood? Then explain all her detestable practices to her. 3 You are to say: This is what the Lord GOD says: A city that sheds blood within her walls so that her time of judgment has come and who makes idols for herself so that she is defiled! 4 You are •guilty of the blood you have shed, and you are defiled from the idols you have made. You have brought your judgment days near and have come to your years of punishment. Therefore, I have made you a disgrace to the nations and a mockery to all the lands. 5 Those who are near and those far away from you will mock you, you infamous one full of turmoil.

6 "Look, every prince of Israel within you has used his strength to shed blood. 7 Father and mother are treated with contempt, and the foreign resident is exploited within you. The fatherless and widow are oppressed in you. 8 You despise My holy things and profane My Sabbaths. 9 There are men within you who slander in order to shed blood. People who live in you eat at the mountain shrines; they commit immoral acts within you. 10 Men within you have sexual intercourse with their father's wife and violate women during their menstrual impurity. 11 One man within you commits a detestable act with his neighbor's wife; another wickedly defiles his daughter-in-law; and yet another violates his sister, his father's daughter. 12 People who live in you accept bribes in order to shed blood. You take interest and profit on a loan and brutally extort your neighbors. You have forgotten Me." This is the declaration of the Lord GOD.

13 "Now look, I clap My hands together against the dishonest profit you have made and against the blood shed among you. 14 Will your courage endure or your hands be strong in the days when I deal with you? I, •Yahweh, have spoken, and I will act. 15 I will disperse you among the nations and scatter you among the countries; I will purge your uncleanness. 16 You[A] will be profaned in the sight of the nations. Then you will know that I am Yahweh."

17 The word of the LORD came to me: 18 "Son of man, the house of Israel has become dross to Me. All of them are copper, tin, iron, and lead inside the furnace; they are the dross of silver. 19 Therefore, this is what the Lord GOD says: Because all of you have become dross, I am about to gather you into Jerusalem. 20 Just as one gathers silver, copper, iron, lead, and tin into the furnace to blow fire on them and melt them, so I will gather you in My anger and wrath, put you inside, and melt you. 21 Yes, I will gather you together and blow on you with the fire of My fury, and you will be melted within the city. 22 As silver is melted inside a furnace, so you will be melted inside the city. Then you will know that I, Yahweh, have poured out My wrath on you."

23 The word of the LORD came to me: 24 "Son of man, say to her: You are a land that has not been cleansed, that has not received rain in the day of indignation. 25 The conspiracy of her prophets within her is[B] like a roaring lion tearing its prey: they devour people, seize wealth and valuables, and multiply the widows within her. 26 Her priests do violence to My instruction and profane My holy things. They make no distinction between the holy and the common, and they do not explain the difference between the •clean and the •unclean. They disregard[C] My Sabbaths, and I am profaned among them.

27 "Her officials within her are like wolves tearing their prey, shedding blood, and destroying lives in order to make profit dishonestly. 28 Her prophets plaster with whitewash for them by seeing false visions and lying •divinations, and they say, 'This is what the Lord GOD says,' when the

[A] **22:16** One Hb ms, LXX, Syr, Vg read *I* [B] **22:24-25** LXX reads *indignation,* [25] *whose princes within her are* [C] **22:26** Lit *close their eyes from*

theme. In this case, Jerusalem as **the city of blood** (22:2) and **city of bloodshed** (24:6) serve as brackets of the *inclusio*, with chapter 23 as the center carrying the same themes. Chapter 23 closely links the themes of adultery/idolatry with defilement and bloodshed. Most often an *inclusio* is far more evident in the original language (i.e., Hebrew in this text) than in translations.

22:1-5 Jerusalem had continually been involved in two major sins—bloodshed and idolatry, for which she would be so greatly punished that she would be a byword of iniquity, an **infamous one** to godless **nations**. Shedding of blood is mentioned eight times in chapter 22 and four times in chapter 24.

22:6-9 Specified in detail are the crimes of which Judah was guilty.

22:10-12 The outrages mentioned here violate the Levitical holiness code (Lv 18–20) so that part of the rationale for the language of bloodshed may be that blood stains defile a person, making him ritually unclean. This may be bolstered by the verdict: "You are a land that has not been cleansed" (v. 24).

22:13-15 The punishment for bloodshed and **dishonest profit** were coming in the impending exile.

22:17-22 Sandwiched between two indictments of the prosecution is a "postcard" view of Jerusalem, appropriately and ominously portrayed as a smelting oven. It is bracketed by verses 15 and 24 regarding the need for purging and cleansing. To God, the people had all become as **dross**, the impurity that needed to be burned off.

22:24-26 Specifically indicted were the rapacious **prophets within her**, who conspired to kill and rob. The **priests** who despised the holiness laws had failed to teach them to the people and had not taught people the difference between **the holy and the common** and **the clean and the unclean**. Consequently, the people had profaned God.

22:27-28 The **officials** sought to **profit dishonestly** and are described as **wolves** even as the prophets had been described as "a roaring lion," (v. 25) both dangerous predators. For the phrase **plaster with whitewash**, see note on 13:10-14.

22:29-31 As a result of the leaders' spiritual and moral failures, the **people of the land** have followed their terrible example, committing extortion, oppressing the poor, and abusing immigrants. All the leadership was guilty, and consequently no one was worthy to mediate between God and the people (cp. chap. 14).

23:1-4 This chapter is an extended parable about the cities of Jerusalem and Samaria, the two capital cities of the Israelite nation, portrayed as the two adulterous wives of the Lord (cp. chap. 16, focusing chiefly on Jerusalem but including comparisons with the "sister cities" of Sodom and Samaria; Jr 3:1-13). Their names connote their spiritual natures: **Oholah** (Hb, "her tent") and **Oholibah** (Hb, "my tent is in her") seem to be Canaanite names related to Esau's wife Oholibamah (Hb, "tent of the high place," Gn 36:2,5), a name suggestive of the idolatry of Canaan. The similarity of the names may simply highlight the sister-like relationship between the cities. The **two . . . daughters of the same mother** had committed harlotries since their adolescence in **Egypt**, where they lost their virginity. This sexual history haunted them throughout their religious and political history (Ezk 23:8,19-21,27; cp. Ps 78). God "married" them (**They became Mine**), and they increased the family or nation. In this sometimes graphic parable, idolatry and adultery are taken to be interchangeable (cp. Ex 32:6-8; 34:15-16). The powerful temptations and urges associated with idol worship (spiritual adultery) are illustrated in terms of sexual lust and degeneracy (adultery and profligacy).

23:5-10 Sexual imagery depicts political alliances with godless foreign nations, alliances that bore disastrous spiritual results—the importing of these nations' idolatrous practices, as well as reliance on the strength of foreign treaties and foreign warriors rather than on the Lord. Samaria's involvement with the Assyrians led to her downfall as they turned against her, enslaved her (Israel became a vassal state, paying tribute to the Assyrians under Jehu, Menahem, and Hoshea, 2Kg 15:19; 17:3), and finally conquered her population, taking her into captivity in 722 B.C. under Shalmaneser V (Ezk 23:5-10; cp. 2Kg 17:6-23). The Assyrian exile rendered the 10 tribes of Israel (represented by Samaria) essentially defunct. As a result of her captivity and demise, **she became notorious among women**.

23:11-21 Meanwhile, Jerusalem learned nothing from the disaster she observed. Instead, she outdid her sister in wanton acts of lasciviousness (v. 11). She engaged in even more

LORD has not spoken. 29 The people of the land have practiced extortion and committed robbery. They have oppressed the poor and needy and unlawfully exploited the foreign resident. 30 I searched for a man among them who would repair the wall and stand in the gap before Me on behalf of the land so that I might not destroy it, but I found no one. 31 So I have poured out My indignation on them and consumed them with the fire of My fury. I have brought their actions down on their own heads." This is the declaration of the Lord GOD.

The Two Adulterous Wives of Yahweh (23:1-49)

23 The word of the LORD came to me again: 2 "Son of man, there were two women, daughters of the same mother, 3 who acted like prostitutes in Egypt, behaving promiscuously in their youth. Their breasts were fondled there, and their virgin nipples caressed. 4 The older one was named Oholah,[A] and her sister was Oholibah.[B] They became Mine and gave birth to sons and daughters. As for their names, Oholah represents Samaria and Oholibah represents Jerusalem.

5 "Oholah acted like a prostitute even though she was Mine. She lusted after her lovers, the Assyrians: warriors 6 dressed in blue, governors and prefects, all of them desirable young men, horsemen riding on steeds. 7 She offered her sexual favors to them; all of them were the elite of Assyria. She defiled herself with all those she lusted after and with all their idols. 8 She didn't give up her promiscuity that began in Egypt, when men slept with her in her youth, caressed her virgin nipples, and poured out their lust on her. 9 Therefore, I handed her over to her lovers, the Assyrians she lusted for. 10 They exposed her nakedness, seized her sons and daughters, and killed her with the sword. Since they executed judgment against her, she became notorious among women.

11 "Now her sister Oholibah saw this, but she was even more depraved in her lust than Oholah, and made her promiscuous acts worse than those of her sister. 12 She lusted after the Assyrians: governors and prefects, warriors splendidly dressed, horsemen riding on steeds, all of them desirable young men. 13 And I saw that she had defiled herself; both of them had taken the same path. 14 But she increased her promiscuity when she saw male figures carved on the wall, images of the Chaldeans, engraved in vermilion, 15 wearing belts on their waists and flowing turbans on their heads; all of them looked like officers, a depiction of the Babylonians in Chaldea, the land of their birth. 16 At the sight of them[C] she lusted after them and sent messengers to them in Chaldea. 17 Then the Babylonians came to her, to the bed of love, and defiled her with their lust. But after she was defiled by them, she turned away from them in disgust. 18 When she flaunted her promiscuity and exposed her nakedness, I turned away from her in disgust just as I turned away from her sister. 19 Yet she multiplied her acts of promiscuity, remembering the days of her youth when she acted like a prostitute in the land of Egypt 20 and lusted after their lovers, whose sexual members were like those of donkeys and whose emission was like that of stallions. 21 So you revisited the indecency of your youth, when the Egyptians caressed your nipples to enjoy your youthful breasts.

22 "Therefore Oholibah, this is what the Lord GOD says: I am going to incite your lovers against you, those you turned away from in disgust. I will bring them against you from every side: 23 the Babylonians and all the Chaldeans; Pekod, Shoa, and Koa; and all the Assyrians with them—desirable young men, all of them governors and prefects, officers and administrators, all of them riding on horses. 24 They will come against you with an alliance of nations and with weapons, chariots, and[D] wagons. They will set themselves against you on every side with shields, bucklers, and helmets.

A **23:4** = Her Tent B **23:4** = My Tent Is in Her C **23:16** Lit *of her eyes* D **23:24** LXX reads *nations, from the north, chariots and*; Hb obscure

I will delegate judgment to them,
and they will judge you by their own
standards. 25 When I vent My jealous rage on you, they will deal with
you in wrath. They will cut off your
nose and ears, and your descendants
will fall by the sword. They will seize
your sons and daughters, and your
descendants will be consumed by
fire. 26 They will strip off your clothes
and take your beautiful jewelry. 27 So
I will put an end to your indecency
and sexual immorality, which began
in the land of Egypt, and you will not
look longingly at them or remember
Egypt anymore.

28 "For this is what the Lord God
says: I am going to hand you over to
those you hate, to those you turned
away from in disgust. 29 They will
treat you with hatred, take all you
have worked for, and leave you stark
naked, so that the shame of your debauchery will be exposed, both your
indecency and promiscuity. 30 These
things will be done to you because
you acted like a prostitute with the
nations, defiling yourself with their
idols. 31 You have followed the path
of your sister, so I will put her cup
in your hand."

32 This is what the Lord God says:

You will drink
your sister's cup,
which is deep and wide.
You will be an object
of[A] ridicule and scorn,
for it holds so much.
33 You will be filled
with drunkenness and grief,
with a cup of devastation
and desolation,
the cup of your
sister Samaria.
34 You will drink it and drain it;
then you will gnaw
its broken pieces,
and tear your breasts.
For I have spoken.
This is the declaration
of the Lord God.

35 Therefore, this is what the Lord
God says: "Because you have forgotten Me and cast Me behind your
back, you must bear the consequences of your indecency and promiscuity."

36 Then the Lord said to me: "Son
of man, will you pass judgment
against Oholah and Oholibah? Then
declare their detestable practices
to them. 37 For they have committed adultery, and blood is on their
hands; they have committed adultery with their idols. They have even
made the children they bore to Me
pass through the fire as food for the
idols. 38 They also did this to Me: they
defiled My sanctuary on that same
day and profaned My Sabbaths. 39 On
the same day they slaughtered their
children for their idols, they entered
My sanctuary to profane it. Yes, that
is what they did inside My house.

40 "In addition, they sent for men
who came from far away when
a messenger was dispatched to
them. And look how they came!
You bathed, painted your eyes,
and adorned yourself with jewelry
for them. 41 You sat on a luxurious
couch with a table spread before it,
on which you had set My incense and
oil. 42 The sound of a carefree crowd
was there. Drunkards[B] from the
desert were brought in, along with
common men. They put bracelets
on the women's hands and beautiful
crowns on their heads. 43 Then I said
concerning this woman worn out by
adultery: Will they now have illicit
sex with her, even her? 44 Yet they
had sex with her as one does with a
prostitute. This is how they had sex
with Oholah and Oholibah, those
obscene women. 45 But righteous
men will judge them the way adulteresses and those who shed blood
are judged, for they are adulteresses
and blood is on their hands.

46 "This is what the Lord God says:
Summon[C] an assembly against
them and consign them to terror
and plunder. 47 The assembly will
stone them and cut them down with
their swords. They will kill their
sons and daughters and burn their
houses with fire. 48 So I will put an
end to indecency in the land, and
all the women will be admonished
not to imitate your indecent behavior. 49 They will repay you for your

alliances with foreign nations, whose concomitant idolatry was implanted among her population. She made treaties with Assyria (v. 12) and Chaldea (Babylon; vv. 14-16), and behaved with them as she had back in **Egypt** (vv. 19-21). Her nymphomaniacal lust disgusted and enraged the Lord, her husband.

23:22-24 This **alliance of nations** would come against Jerusalem and destroy her.

23:25-30 The Lord allowed these nations to function as agents of His wrath. Included in God's judgment upon both cities was the same kind of treatment meted out to the adulteress in chapter 16. Physical brutality and mutilation of an adulteress by her husband is attested in ancient Near Eastern laws. The point of cutting **off** her **nose** was to make her ugly and an example to others. In the legal codes of other nations, the male participant in adultery is also punished, so that legally, adultery apparently was considered a two-sided affair.

23:31-35 This portion, a so-called "Song of the Cup," is a violent poem, perhaps based upon a drinking song. In its substance, it is akin to the "cup of the wine of wrath" (Jr 25:15-17). The **cup** was full to the brim, and Oholibah would drink it down to the dregs. Since Jerusalem patterned her deeds after her sister Samaria, her cup would be the same. In what appears to be a cruel extension of the breast-beating of the mourning ritual, Jerusalem in her grief will go much further than that, tearing her breasts after having gnawed the shards of the broken cup.

23:36-39 Two interrelated accusations against the cities are here reiterated—their spiritual **adultery,** which led to bloodshed as they sacrificed their children to **idols**. Seemingly the residents of Jerusalem saw little contradiction in the concurrent worship of idols and Yahweh (cp. 2Kg 17:24-40 concerning the people of Samaria, who worshiped the Lord as well as their own native gods; Jr 7:9-11).

23:40-45 The Lord also complained about Oholibah's lovers. Although they would be the agents of His wrath and judgment, they were not righteous men, but were themselves immoral.

23:48 This kind of **indecency** could only be purged from the land by the destruction of its perpetrators. The two sisters would become an example to **all the women** that such obscene behavior would have dire consequences.

[A] **23:32** Or *It will bring* [B] **23:42** Or *Sabeans* [C] **23:46** Or *I will summon*

24:1-2 The siege of Jerusalem had begun on the very day of this prophecy (589/588 B.C.), thus bringing to fulfillment Ezekiel's messages and warnings.

24:3-5 This event is interpreted for **the rebellious house** of Israel through **a parable** (vv. 3-14) and **a sign** (vv. 15-27). The image of the boiling pot is reminiscent of a previous saying and its divine interpretation (11:3,7-12). The **pot** symbolized the city of Jerusalem, and the **pieces of meat . . . every good piece** represented its inhabitants.

24:6-10 The pot, however, was defective: It was covered with thick **rust**, resistant to cleaning (cp. v. 12) and symbolizing uncleanness due to bloodshed, since Jerusalem is again labeled **city of bloodshed.**

24:11-14 From the imagery used here, the symbolic equivalents seem to be roughly as follows: Jerusalem is the pot, its residents are the meat and bones, the rust represents its defilement due to sin, the "cook" is the Lord, the kindling that stokes the fire represents His wrath, fury, and judgment, which increases the intensity of the fire in an effort to purge the city (**pot**) of its defilement (**rust**). The resistant rust **has frustrated every effort**, and therefore drastic measures, namely destruction, are necessary to clean the pot.

indecency, and you will bear the consequences for your sins of idolatry. Then you will know that I am the Lord •Yahweh."

The Boiling Pot and the Death of Ezekiel's Wife (24:1-27)

24 The word of the LORD came to me in the ninth year, in the tenth month, on the tenth day
of the month: 2 "Son of man, write down today's date, this very day. The king of Babylon has laid siege to Jerusalem this very day.
3 Now speak a parable to the rebellious house. Tell them: This is what the Lord GOD says:

Put the pot on the fire—
put it on,
and then pour water into it!
4 Place the pieces of meat in it,
every good piece—
thigh and shoulder.
Fill it with choice bones.
5 Take the choicest of the flock
and also pile up the fuel[A]
under it.
Bring it to a boil
and cook the bones in it."

6 Therefore, this is what the Lord GOD says:

Woe to the city of bloodshed,
the pot that has rust inside it,
and whose rust will not
come off!
Empty it piece by piece;
lots should not be cast
for its contents.
7 For the blood she shed[B] is still
within her.
She put it out
on the bare rock;
she didn't pour it
on the ground
to cover it with dust.
8 In order to stir up wrath
and take vengeance,
I have put her blood
on the bare rock,
so that it would not
be covered.

9 Therefore, this is what the Lord GOD says:

Woe to the city of bloodshed!
I Myself will make the pile
of kindling large.
10 Pile on the logs and kindle
the fire!
Cook the meat well
and mix in the spices![C,D]
Let the bones be burned!
11 Set the empty pot on its coals
so that it becomes hot
and its copper glows.
Then its impurity will melt
inside it;

[A]24:5 Lit *bones* [B]24:7 Lit *For her blood* [C]24:10 Some Hb mss read *well; remove the broth*; LXX reads *fire so that the meat may be cooked and the broth may be reduced* [D]24:10 Or *and stir the broth*

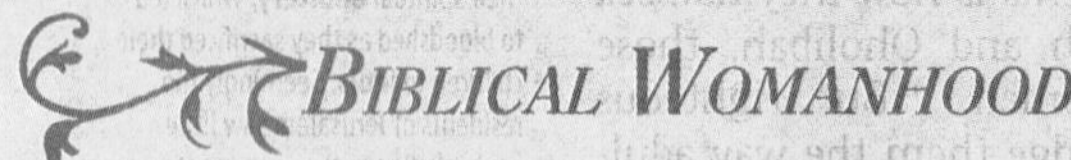

BIBLICAL WOMANHOOD Sexuality, Social Ethics, and Hermeneutics

Regarding Ezekiel 16 and 23, feminist commentators have voiced concern that the association of female sexuality with sin could be used to justify violence against or murder of women, particularly as a way for an enraged husband to deal with marital infidelity. According to this perspective, the violent parable-allegories seem to be offered as an admonition against adultery exclusively directed to women (16:41; 23:48). However, to read the biblical text as misogynistic or as promoting violence against women on any level is erroneous. The context clearly identifies God as the speaker in both narratives (cp. 16:1-3,14,19,23,30,35,43; 23:1,28,32,34-36,46). Although God adopts the persona of a husband dealing with an adulterous wife, the genre is also clearly metaphorical with the purpose of illustrating the appalling nature of Israel's sins, not of depicting a paradigm for dealing with marital infidelity (cp. 16:15-26,28-36; 23:3-21,31-45).

Additionally, these texts emphasize that the perpetrators of violence are the ones with whom Israel has been promiscuous; God warns that He will hand over the adulteresses to the "lovers" whom they have chosen to pursue (cp. 16:27,37-41,56-59; 23:22-30,46-49). By means of withdrawing His protection and unleashing the consequences of the sinful retaliation against His goodness, God intended not merely to respond with rage but to purge His people of the sinful entanglements of their hearts and to restore them (cp. 16:53-55,60-63; 23:27,48-49).

CHARACTER PROFILE

The Wife of Ezekiel A Beloved Wife

Her Background	Her identity is unknown (24:15-27).
Her Story	• She died as a sign to God's people, illustrating the grief they would experience upon the future destruction of Jerusalem (24:15-27). • Ezekiel was commanded not to mourn outwardly (24:17). • She was loved by her husband (24:15). • No one mourned her death (24:17-18).
Life Lessons	• The prophets were often required to deliver very difficult messages, sometimes sacrificing their own well-being. • By establishing the parallel between Ezekiel's unexpressed bereavement and the people's imminent sorrows, God implicitly affirmed the depth of affection He intends for a husband to have for his wife.

its rust will be consumed.
12 It has frustrated
every effort;[A]
its thick rust will not
come off.
Into the fire with its rust!
13 Because of the indecency
of your uncleanness—
since I tried to purify you,
but you would not be purified
from your uncleanness—
you will not be pure again
until I have satisfied My wrath
on you.
14 I, °Yahweh, have spoken.
It is coming, and I will do it!
I will not refrain, I will not
show pity,
and I will not relent.
I[B] will judge you
according to your ways
and deeds.
This is the declaration
of the Lord God.

15 Then the word of the Lord came
to me: 16 "Son of man, I am about to
take the delight of your eyes away
from you with a fatal blow. But you
must not lament or weep or let your
tears flow. 17 Groan quietly; do not
observe mourning rites for the dead.
Put on your turban and strap your
sandals on your feet; do not cover
your mustache or eat the bread of
mourners."[C]
18 I spoke to the people in the morning, and my wife died in the evening.
The next morning I did just as I was
commanded. 19 Then the people asked
me, "Won't you tell us what these
things you are doing mean for us?"
20 So I answered them: "The word
of the Lord came to me: 21 'Say to the
house of Israel: This is what the Lord
God says: I am about to desecrate My
sanctuary, the pride of your power,
the delight of your eyes, and the desire of your heart. Also, the sons and
daughters you left behind will fall by
the sword. 22 Then you will do just as
I have done: You will not cover your
mustache or eat the bread of mourners.[C] 23 Your turbans will remain on
your heads and your sandals on your
feet. You will not lament or weep but
will waste away because of your sins
and will groan to one another. 24 Now
Ezekiel will be a sign for you. You
will do everything that he has done.
When this happens, you will know
that I am the Lord Yahweh.
25 "'Son of man, know that on the
day I take their stronghold from
them, their pride and joy, the delight of their eyes and the longing
of their hearts, as well as their sons
and daughters, 26 on that day a fugitive will come to you and report the
news. 27 On that day your mouth will
be opened to talk with him; you will
speak and no longer be mute. So you
will be a sign for them, and they will
know that I am Yahweh.'"

24:15-17 Ezekiel was informed of the impending death of his wife (**the delight of your eyes**) and instructed not to perform any rites of grief such as lamenting, weeping, crying, groaning, wearing of sackcloth and ashes, going barefoot, covering the lower part of the face (**mustache**), or eating **the bread of mourners**.

24:18-24 Whereas on other occasions Ezekiel performed signs pregnant with meaning for the exiles, in which case Ezekiel himself became a sign for them by his lack of mourning.

24:25-27 The phrase **the delight of their eyes** encompasses both Ezekiel's wife (vv. 16,18) and the temple (cp. v. 21), which was not only an object of national pride but of powerful emotion, also described as **the longing of their hearts** (cp. v. 20). Ezekiel apparently was made **mute** at some point, possibly right after his delivery of chapter 24—from the time of the siege to the fall of the city (33:21-22).

[A]24:12 Hb obscure [B]24:14 Some Hb mss, LXX, Syr, Tg, Vg; other Hb mss read *They*
[C]24:17,22 Lit *men*

Oracles Against Surrounding Nations (25:1-17)

25 Then the word of the LORD came to me: 2 "Son of man, turn your face toward the Ammonites and prophesy against them. 3 Say to the Ammonites: Hear the word of the Lord GOD: This is what the Lord GOD says: Because you said, 'Good!' about My sanctuary when it was desecrated, about the land of Israel when it was laid waste, and about the house of Judah when they went into exile, 4 therefore I am about to give you to the people of the east as a possession. They will set up their encampments and pitch their tents among you. They will eat your fruit and drink your milk. 5 I will make Rabbah a pasture for camels and Ammon a sheepfold. Then you will know that I am •Yahweh."

6 For this is what the Lord GOD says: "Because you clapped your hands, stamped your feet, and rejoiced over the land of Israel with wholehearted contempt, 7 therefore I am about to stretch out My hand against you and give you as plunder to the nations. I will cut you off from the peoples and eliminate you from the countries. I will destroy you, and you will know that I am Yahweh."

8 This is what the Lord GOD says: "Because Moab and Seir said, 'Look, the house of Judah is like all the other nations,' 9 therefore I am about to expose Moab's flank beginning with its[A] frontier cities, the pride of the land: Beth-jeshimoth, Baal-meon, and Kiriathaim. 10 I will give it along with Ammon to the people of the east as a possession, so that Ammon will not be remembered among the nations. 11 So I will execute judgments against Moab, and they will know that I am Yahweh."

12 This is what the Lord GOD says: "Because Edom acted vengefully against the house of Judah and incurred grievous •guilt by taking revenge on them, 13 therefore this is what the Lord GOD says: I will stretch out My hand against Edom and cut off both man and animal from it. I will make it a wasteland; they will fall by the sword from Teman to Dedan. 14 I will take My vengeance on Edom through My people Israel, and they will deal with Edom according to My anger and wrath. So they will know My vengeance." This is the declaration of the Lord GOD.

15 This is what the Lord GOD says: "Because the Philistines acted in vengeance and took revenge with deep contempt, destroying because of their ancient hatred, 16 therefore this is what the Lord GOD says: I am about to stretch out My hand against the Philistines, cutting off the Cherethites and wiping out what remains of the coastal peoples.[B] 17 I will execute great vengeance against them with furious rebukes. They will know that I am Yahweh when I take My vengeance on them."

Oracles Against Tyre (26:1–28:26)

26 In the eleventh year, on the first day of the month, the word of the LORD came to me: 2 "Son of man, because Tyre said about Jerusalem, 'Good! The gateway to the peoples is shattered. She has been turned over to me. I will be filled now that she lies in ruins,' 3 therefore this is what the Lord GOD says: See, I am against you, Tyre! I will raise up many nations against you, just as the sea raises its waves. 4 They will destroy the walls of Tyre and demolish her towers. I will scrape the soil from her and turn her into a bare rock. 5 She will become a place in the sea to spread nets, for I have spoken." This is the declaration of the Lord GOD. "She will become plunder for the nations, 6 and her villages on the mainland will be slaughtered by the sword. Then they will know that I am •Yahweh."

7 For this is what the Lord GOD says: "See, I am about to bring King Nebuchadnezzar of Babylon, king of kings, against Tyre from the north with horses, chariots, cavalry, and a vast company of troops. 8 He will slaughter your villages on the mainland with the sword. He will set up siege works against you, and will build a ramp[C] and raise a wall of shields against you. 9 He will di-

25:1-6 Chapter 25 begins a series of prophecies against the nations that rejoiced at Judah's fall. The first to receive notice of condemnation was the nation mentioned as an alternative to Judah for Babylon's invasion (chap. 21)—Ammon. The stated reason for judgment was the joy the Ammonites expressed at Judah's defeat by the Babylonian army; they **clapped** their **hands, stamped** their **feet**, and rejoiced with **contempt**. Interestingly, Ezekiel was told to perform these actions as a sign of the coming judgment. The Ammonites would be destroyed.

25:8-11 When the Babylonians took Ammon, they also swept through Moab, and the judgment was for much the same reason. Nebuchadnezzar destroyed Moab in 582 B.C.

25:12-14 Edom would also come under judgment. The Edomites were the descendants of Esau, as the Israelites were the descendants of Jacob. The Edomites prevented the Israelites from crossing their land during the exodus from Egypt (Nm 20:20-21), yet God commanded Israel to treat Edom as a brother (Dt 23:7-8). This relationship made Edom's sins heinous. However, Edom's demise was also tied to the apparent failure to show no mercy to the Israelites during the invasion by Babylon (cp. Obadiah).

An interesting difference between Edom and the other condemned nations was that the instrument of God's wrath did not seem to be the Babylonian army but the Israelite army. This did not happen in Ezekiel's day, as the Israelite armies were not in a position to engage any army in combat, but according to Old Testament eschatology, Israel will one day possess the land of the Edomites (Nm 24:18; Am 9:12).

25:15-16 The Philistines took advantage of Judah's situation. Their vengeful actions may have been motivated by racism (**ancient hatred**) or old prejudices, or unforgiveness may have served as the impetus for Philistine aggression. According to archaeological finds, the Philistines were far superior to the Israelites in material culture, and seemingly this spawned a haughty attitude on the Philistines' part. Whatever the cause, the Philistines would find themselves under a cloud of judgment.

26:2 Chapters 26–28 constitute a description of God's judgment against the ancient island city of **Tyre**, located in modern Lebanon. Appended is a prophecy against the city of Sidon (28:20-26). These cities became the epitome of unbelief and pride in the Old Testament. Jesus cited

[A]**25:9** Lit *with the cities, with its* [B]**25:16** Lit *the seacoast* [C]**26:8** Lit *ramp against you*

rect the blows of his battering rams
against your walls and tear down
your towers with his iron tools.
10 His horses will be so numerous that their dust will cover you.
When he enters your gates as an
army entering a breached city, your
walls will shake from the noise of
cavalry, wagons, and chariots. 11 He
will trample all your streets with the
hooves of his horses. He will slaughter your people with the sword, and
your mighty pillars will fall to the
ground. 12 They will take your wealth
as spoil and plunder your merchandise. They will also demolish your
walls and tear down your beautiful
homes. Then they will throw your
stones, timber, and soil into the water. 13 I will put an end to the noise
of your songs, and the sound of your
lyres will no longer be heard. 14 I will
turn you into a bare rock, and you
will be a place to spread nets. You
will never be rebuilt, for I, Yahweh,
have spoken." This is the declaration
of the Lord God.
15 This is what the Lord God says to
Tyre: "Won't the coasts and islands
quake at the sound of your downfall, when the wounded groan and
slaughter occurs within you? 16 All
the princes of the sea will descend
from their thrones, remove their
robes, and strip off their embroidered garments. They will clothe
themselves with trembling; they will
sit on the ground, tremble continually, and be appalled at you. 17 Then
they will lament for you and say of
you:

How you have perished,
city of renown,
you who were populated
from the seas![A]
She who was powerful
on the sea,
she and all of her inhabitants
inflicted their terror.[B]
18 Now the coastlands tremble
on the day of your downfall;
the islands in the sea
are alarmed by your demise."

19 For this is what the Lord God
says: "When I make you a ruined city
like other deserted cities, when I
raise up the deep against you so that
the mighty waters cover you, 20 then
I will bring you down to be with
those who descend to the •Pit, to
the people of antiquity. I will make
you dwell in the underworld[C] like[D]
the ancient ruins, with those who
descend to the Pit, so that you will
no longer be inhabited or display
your splendor[E] in the land of the living. 21 I will make you an object of
horror, and you will no longer exist.
You will be sought but will never be
found again." This is the declaration
of the Lord God.

27 The word of the Lord came
to me: 2 "Now, son of man, lament for Tyre. 3 Say to Tyre, who is
located at the entrance of the sea,
merchant of the peoples to many
coasts and islands: This is what the
Lord God says:

Tyre, you declared,
'I am perfect in beauty.'
4 Your realm was in the heart
of the sea;
your builders perfected
your beauty.
5 They constructed
all your planking
with pine trees from Senir.[F]
They took a cedar
from Lebanon
to make a mast for you.
6 They made your oars of oaks
from Bashan.
They made your deck
of cypress wood
from the coasts of Cyprus,
inlaid with ivory.
7 Your sail was made of
fine embroidered linen
from Egypt,
and served as your banner.
Your awning was of blue
and purple fabric
from the coasts of Elishah.
8 The inhabitants of Sidon
and Arvad
were your rowers.
Your wise men were
within you, Tyre;
they were your captains.

[A]26:17 Some LXX mss read *How you were destroyed from the seas, city of renown!* [B]26:17 Lit *and all her inhabitants who put their terror on all her inhabitants*; Hb obscure [C]26:20 Lit *the lower parts of the earth* [D]26:20 Some Hb mss, LXX; other Hb mss, Syr read *in* [E]26:20 LXX reads *or appear* [F]27:5 = Mount Hermon

them in condemning Chorazin and Bethsaida, comparing the faith of their inhabitants to those of Tyre and Sidon (Mt 11:21-22; Lk 10:13-14). In this condemnation of Tyre, the city rejoices at the fall of Jerusalem, believing that it could profit thereby. Jerusalem, **the gateway to the peoples**, may have been strategically situated for economic advantage, thus drawing Tyre's envy.

26:3-6 This chapter primarily describes the city's destruction. The power and numerical advantage of the invading army would simply overwhelm the people of **Tyre** (Hb, "rock"). Incredibly, this prosperous city, renowned for international trade through its strength as a maritime power, would be reduced to **a bare rock** and a **place . . . to spread nets** as expressed in a tragic play on its name.

26:7-13 Although the Babylonian army would execute this judgment of God, they did not ultimately defeat and destroy Tyre. While Nebuchadnezzar did lay siege to the city for 13 years, he did not destroy it. In fact, there is widespread disagreement over exactly what happened (29:17-21). The eventual destruction of the city, as described in the prophecy, occurred approximately 250 years later when Alexander the Great built a bridge to lay siege to the island fortress. This may be why the prophecy includes a reference to successive invasions by "many nations" (26:3).

26:14 Ezekiel declared that Tyre would **never be rebuilt.** Some interpreters have expressed concern about this, since there is a city in modern Lebanon by the same name. Some scholars have argued that the modern city of Tyre is not built at the same location as the ancient city. In any case, Tyre was never the imperial (Phoenician) city it once was.

26:15-18 Other maritime city-states, possibly trading partners (the **princes of the sea**), who aspired to Tyre's greatness and prosperity, would be **appalled**, expressing grief and shock.

26:19-20 This once secure island built on a rock is shown metaphorically to be sinking into the sea, like an Atlantis, covered over by **mighty waters**. The **underworld** was thought to be under the waters (cp. Jb 26:5-6); from its once lofty position, Tyre sinks down to the place of the dead, to the grave or **Pit**, no longer to enjoy its former prestige **in the land of the living**.

27:3-11 As a poetic depiction of the fall of the city, chapter 27 is sometimes viewed as a funeral dirge for the city, since much of it is composed in the meter of a lament. **Tyre** was an important coastal town, wealthy beyond many of its neighbors because of a thriving import and trade business through commercial shipping. However, Tyre allowed itself to become haughty and proud: **I am perfect in beauty** (v. 3).

The Tyrians had all of the finest products of the countries of the ancient Near East. A multi-ethnic city whose splendor and beauty were well known (vv. 3-4,11), Tyre also had a powerful navy, which, along with the city's wealth, may have contributed to the hubris of the inhabitants whom the prophecy condemned (v. 3). Ezekiel depicts Tyre as a beautifully-crafted sailing vessel, proudly riding the sea.

The imagery of a ship was particularly appropriate for this maritime city, and Ezekiel continues to describe the **rowers** (v. 8), **captains** (v. 8), **sailors** (v. 9), and **warriors** (mercenaries, v. 10) who guided and protected Tyre, and **perfected** [her] **beauty** (v. 11; cp. v. 3).

27:12-25 Tyre is shown being served with the most exquisite products of all her trading partners, including **Judah and the land of Israel** (v. 17). These verses read like a trade catalogue. An ominous note is sounded as the ship is so **heavily loaded** that its demise seems foreshadowed (v. 25).

27:26-34 Ultimately, even the best-built vessels are vulnerable, and the city's fall is described as a ship in trouble, sinking to the bottom of the sea. The phrase **in the heart of the sea** (vv. 4,25- 27,32; cp. 28:2,8) is a refrain through the lament, extending even into the next chapter. The sea is instrumental in both building Tyre's prosperity as well as causing her demise (27:34). As a naval power, Tyre ruled the seas, but God sent against it an **east wind**, causing this once proud and stately ship to be overcome and destroyed by the same sea (v. 26). Rather than reveling in her position "in the heart of the sea," Tyre now was shipwrecked and sank helplessly into the sea to be lamented by all who witnessed her tragedy (vv. 27-34).

27:35-36 All the other coastal people should learn from the tragedy of Tyre. Good economic relationships, secure flanks, money, and power cannot ensure safety. The Lord's hand would be evident in the city's destruction.

28:1-19 Two prophecies concerning **the ruler of Tyre** appear here. The first (vv. 1-10) describes his fall from power; the second (vv. 11-19) is a dirge for him on the occasion of his death. The first describes his fall in more literal terms, while the second is usually interpreted as an allegory of the fall of Satan. The king of Tyre fell from a position of

9 The elders of Gebal and its
wise men
were within you,
repairing your leaks.
All the ships of the sea
and their sailors
came to[A] you to barter
for your goods.
10 Men of Persia, Lud, and Put
were in your army, serving
as your warriors.
They hung shields
and helmets in you;
they gave you splendor.
11 Men of Arvad and Helech
were stationed on your walls
all around,
and Gammadites were
in your towers.
They hung their shields[B]
all around your walls;
they perfected your beauty.
12 "Tarshish was your trading partner because of your great wealth of
every kind. They exchanged silver,
iron, tin, and lead for your merchandise. 13 Javan, Tubal, and Meshech
were your merchants. They exchanged slaves[C] and bronze utensils for your goods. 14 Those from
Beth-togarmah exchanged horses,
war horses, and mules for your merchandise. 15 Men of Dedan[D] were also
your merchants; many coasts and
islands were your regular markets.
They brought back ivory tusks and
ebony as your payment. 16 Aram[E,F]
was your trading partner because of
your numerous products. They exchanged turquoise,[G] purple and embroidered cloth, fine linen, coral,[G]
and rubies[G] for your merchandise.
17 Judah and the land of Israel were
your merchants. They exchanged
wheat from Minnith, meal,[H] honey, oil, and balm, for your goods.
18 Damascus was also your trading
partner because of your numerous
products and your great wealth of
every kind, trading in wine from
Helbon and white wool.[I] 19 Vedan[J]
and Javan from Uzal[G] dealt in your
merchandise; wrought iron, cassia,
and aromatic cane were exchanged
for your goods. 20 Dedan was your
merchant in saddlecloths for riding.
21 Arabia and all the princes of Kedar
were your business[K] partners, trading with you in lambs, rams, and
goats. 22 The merchants of Sheba and
Raamah traded with you. They exchanged gold, the best of all spices,
and all kinds of precious stones for
your merchandise. 23 Haran, Can-
neh, Eden, the merchants of Sheba,
Asshur, and Chilmad traded with
you. 24 They were your merchants in
choice garments, cloaks of blue and
embroidered materials, and multi-
colored carpets,[G] which were bound
and secured with cords in your marketplace. 25 Ships of Tarshish were
the carriers for your goods.
So you became full
and heavily loaded[L]
in the heart of the sea.
26 Your rowers have brought you
onto the high seas,
but the east wind
has shattered you
in the heart of the sea.
27 Your wealth, merchandise,
and goods,
your sailors and captains,
those who repair your leaks,
those who barter
for your goods,
and all the warriors
within you,
with all the other people
on board,[M]
sink into the heart of the sea
on the day of your downfall.
28 The countryside shakes
at the sound
of your sailors' cries.
29 All those who handle an oar
disembark from their ships.
The sailors and
all the captains of the sea
stand on the shore.
30 They raise their voices
over you
and cry out bitterly.
They throw dust
on their heads;
they roll in ashes.
31 They shave their heads
because of you

[A]**27:9** Lit *sailors were with* [B]**27:11** Or *quivers*; Hb obscure [C]**27:13** Lit *souls of men* [D]**27:15** LXX reads *Rhodes* [E]**27:16** Some Hb mss, Aq, Syr read *Edom* [F]**27:16** = Syria [G]**27:16,19,24** Hb obscure [H]**27:17** Or *resin*; Hb obscure [I]**27:18** Or *and wool from Zahar* [J]**27:19** Or *Dan* [K]**27:21** Lit *trading* [L]**27:25** Or *and very glorious* [M]**27:27** Lit *with all your assembly among you*

and wrap themselves
in •sackcloth.
They weep over you
with deep anguish
and bitter mourning.

32 In their wailing they lament
for you,
mourning over you:
Who was like Tyre,
silenced[A] in the middle
of the sea?

33 When your merchandise
was unloaded from the seas,
you satisfied many peoples.
You enriched the kings
of the earth
with your abundant wealth
and goods.

34 Now you are shattered
by the sea
in the depths of the waters;
your goods and the people
within you
have gone down.

35 All the inhabitants
of the coasts and islands
are appalled at you.
Their kings shudder with fear;
their faces are contorted.

36 Those who trade
among the peoples
mock[B] you;
you have become an object
of horror
and will never exist again."

28 The word of the LORD came to
me: 2 "Son of man, say to the
ruler of Tyre: This is what the Lord
GOD says:

Your[C] heart is proud,
and you have said,
'I am a god;
I sit in the seat of gods
in the heart of the sea.'
Yet you are a man and not
a god,
though you have regarded
your heart
as that of a god.

3 Yes, you are wiser
than Daniel;
no secret is hidden from you!

4 By your wisdom
and understanding
you have acquired wealth
for yourself.
You have acquired gold
and silver
for your treasuries.

5 By your great skill in trading
you have increased
your wealth,
but your heart has
become proud
because of your wealth."

6 Therefore this is what the Lord
GOD says:

Because you regard
your heart as that of a god,

7 I am about to bring strangers
against you,
ruthless men
from the nations.
They will draw their swords
against your
magnificent wisdom
and will defile your splendor.

8 They will bring you down
to the •Pit,
and you will die
a violent death
in the heart of the sea.

9 Will you still say,
'I am a god,'
in the presence of those
who kill[D] you?
Yet you will be only a man,
not a god,
in the hands of those
who kill you.

10 You will die the death
of the uncircumcised
at the hands of strangers.
For I have spoken.
This is the declaration
of the Lord GOD.

11 The word of the LORD came to
me: 12 "Son of man, lament for the
king of Tyre and say to him: This is
what the Lord GOD says:

You were the seal[E]
of perfection,[A]
full of wisdom and perfect
in beauty.

13 You were in Eden, the garden
of God.
Every kind of precious stone
covered you:

[A]27:32; 28:12 Hb obscure [B]27:36 Lit *hiss* [C]28:2 Lit *Because your* [D]28:9 Some Hb mss, LXX, Syr, Vg; other Hb mss read *of the one who kills* [E]28:12 Or *sealer*

power and beauty, a position which should have been regarded as God's blessing, and died at the hands of an invader sent by God. Likewise, Satan fell from his position as an angel of God in the heavenly council and became the enemy of God and His people. Ultimately, his final judgment will include condemnation to hell.

28:2-5 The first message concerning Tyre's king clearly emphasizes his humanity, contrasting his mortality with his claims of divinity (cp. vv. 9-10). While he believes he has the **heart . . . of a god** (cp. v. 6), in reality his heart is full of pride. While he believes himself to be wise, in reality, his pride shows that he is not wise because it has deceived him into believing that he is untouchable. By the time of Ezekiel's ministry, **Daniel** already had a reputation for superior **wisdom**. Verse 3 appears to be sarcastic in tone, indicating that although the king of Tyre may have been shrewd in his financial decisions, he was *not* particularly wise with regard to his beliefs about himself or God. His position as ruler over a wealthy and diverse people and over a beautiful and secure city, has led him to exalt himself to a position equal to **a god**.

28:6-7 In reality, though, he will be shown his lowly position when his city is overrun and destroyed, his people are ravaged and dispersed, his wealth conscripted, and his life is at the mercy of a merciless enemy (**ruthless men**), who will not spare him.

28:8-10 Being brought **down to the Pit** and dying a **violent death in the heart of the sea** show an association present elsewhere in Scripture. Sea waters are sometimes regarded as symbolic of forces of evil and/or chaos and are associated with death as in Pss 18:4,16; 69:1-2; 88:3-7, 16-18; 124:4-5; 144:7. The kind of fall from greatness experienced by the King of Tyre finds a similar description in Lk 10:13-15, as Jesus rebukes Capernaum, where he began His ministry and performed miracles.

28:11-19 The second message about **the king of Tyre** takes the form of a funeral dirge lamenting his movement from such a lofty position to such a lowly end. While the lament clearly includes figurative language, it is still meant to refer to the disappointment associated with the man's fall from a God-given position of power and influence, perhaps to perform some important work. He **became proud** and wicked (vv. 15,17), and greed apparently became a motivation, as **violence** is associated with his business and **trade** and his demise (vv. 16,18). Because some of the imagery and language used cannot be read as referring literally to any human being, many commentators view this message as an allegory for Satan's fall from heaven: He is called **perfect** twice (v. 12) and **blameless** once (v. 15) and is said to have been in the garden of **Eden** (v. 13). He is called a **guardian cherub** who walks **among the fiery stones** (vv. 14,16; see also **Doctrine**, p. 1058). From **the holy mountain of God**, he was cast **down to the earth** (vv. 14,16-17). Interestingly, Jesus' description of the fall of Satan is tied to His condemnation of Chorazin and Bethsaida for having less faith than Tyre and Sidon (Lk 10:13-20). Those who believe that this prophecy does refer to the fall of Satan offer some possible conclusions regarding Satan's function and status. He appears to have been an angel of high standing, who served in a capacity close to God—"among the fiery stones" of the Lord's glory (v. 14). He was beautiful, adorned with precious stones and had some sort of role in Eden (vv. 13,17). His **beauty** became his downfall, and he was filled with pride (vv. 12,17). His own greed and lust for power consumed him (v. 18). The description of the fates of Assyria and Egypt (chap. 31) draw notice for their striking similarity. These three cities are comparable in their high, divinely-appointed positions, their hubris and ensuing demise, even their expulsion from that lofty status and association with God, who cast them into the depths of Sheol. And the passages concerning Assyria and Egypt are definitely interpreted as having only human referents.

28:20-23 The judgment poured out on **Sidon** by means of invasion and disease was clearly meant to reveal God's power and holiness. When the city fell, the people would know that Yahweh is God.

28:24-26 The destruction of all who had persecuted God's people was also meant to call Israel back to God. The Lord's promise to restore His people will find complete fulfillment in the end-times. The reference to building **houses** and planting **vineyards** reveals both divine grace and divine judgment associated with keeping God's covenant (cp. Jr 1:10; 18:9; 24:6). The promise associated with the Mosaic covenant was *conditional*. If the people were obedient, the Israelites' occupation of the promised land would include the blessings of living in houses they did not build, drinking from cisterns they did not dig, and eating from vineyards they did not plant (Dt 6:10-12). Because of their covenant violations, the people clearly deserved punishment and the terrible consequences associated with their infidelity. In the covenant with Abraham, however, the promises of divine protection were *unconditional* (cp. Gn 12:3). While Ezekiel's immediate audience had rejected the Mosaic

carnelian, topaz,
and diamond,[A]
beryl, onyx, and jasper,
sapphire,[B] turquoise[C]
and emerald.[D]
Your mountings and settings
were crafted in gold;
they were prepared on the day
you were created.
14 You were an anointed
guardian cherub,
for[E] I had appointed you.
You were on
the holy mountain of God;
you walked among
the fiery stones.
15 From the day you
were created
you were blameless
in your ways
until wickedness was found
in you.
16 Through the abundance
of your trade,
you were filled with violence,
and you sinned.
So I expelled you in disgrace
from the mountain of God,
and banished you,
guardian cherub,[F]
from among the fiery stones.
17 Your heart became proud
because of your beauty;
For the sake of your splendor
you corrupted your wisdom.
So I threw you down
to the earth;
I made you a spectacle
before kings.
18 You profaned your sanctuaries
by the magnitude
of your iniquities
in your dishonest trade.
So I made fire come
from within you,
and it consumed you.
I reduced you to ashes
on the ground
in the sight of everyone
watching you.
19 All those who know you
among the nations
are appalled at you.
You have become an object
of horror
and will never exist again."

20 The word of the LORD came to
me: 21 "Son of man, turn your face
toward Sidon and prophesy against
it. 22 You are to say: This is what the
Lord GOD says:

Look! I am against
you, Sidon,
and I will display My glory
within you.
They will know that
I am •Yahweh
when I execute judgments
against her
and demonstrate My holiness
through her.
23 I will send a plague
against her
and bloodshed in her streets;
the slain will fall within her,
while the sword is
against her[G] on every side.
Then they will know that
I am Yahweh.

24 "The house of Israel will no
longer be hurt by[H] prickly briers or
painful thorns from all their neighbors who treat them with contempt.
Then they will know that I am the
Lord Yahweh.
25 "This is what the Lord GOD says:
When I gather the house of Israel
from the peoples where they are
scattered and demonstrate My holiness through them in the sight of
the nations, then they will live in
their own land, which I gave to My
servant Jacob. 26 They will live there
securely, build houses, and plant
vineyards. They will live securely
when I execute judgments against
all their neighbors who treat them
with contempt. Then they will know
that I am Yahweh their God."

Oracles Against Egypt (29:1–32:32)

29 In the tenth year, in the tenth
month on the twelfth day of
the month, the word of the LORD
came to me: 2 "Son of man, turn
your face toward Pharaoh king of
Egypt and prophesy against him and
against all of Egypt. 3 Speak to him
and say: This is what the Lord GOD
says:

[A]28:13 Hb obscure [B]28:13 Or *lapis lazuli* [C]28:13 Or *malachite*, or *garnet* [D]28:13 Or *beryl* [E]28:14 Or *With an anointed guardian cherub* [F]28:16 Or *and the guardian cherub banished you* [G]28:23 Or *within her by the sword* [H]28:24 Lit *longer have*

Look, I am against you,
Pharaoh king of Egypt,
the great monster[A] lying
in the middle of his Nile,
who says, 'My Nile is my own;
I made it for myself.'
4 I will put hooks in your jaws
and make the fish
of your streams
cling to your scales.
I will haul you up
from the middle of your Nile,
and all the fish
of your streams
will cling to your scales.
5 I will leave you in the desert,
you and all the fish
of your streams.
You will fall on
the open ground
and will not be taken away
or gathered for burial.
I have given you
to the beasts of the earth
and the birds of the sky
as food.

6 Then all the inhabitants
of Egypt
will know that I am •Yahweh,
for they[B] have been a staff
made of reed
to the house of Israel.
7 When Israel grasped you
by the hand,
you splintered, tearing all
their shoulders;
when they leaned on you,
you shattered and made all
their hips unsteady.[C]

8 "Therefore this is what the Lord
God says: I am going to bring a
sword against you and wipe out man
and animal from you. 9 The land of
Egypt will be a desolate ruin. Then
they will know that I am Yahweh.
Because you[D] said, 'The Nile is my
own; I made it,' 10 therefore, I am
against you and your Nile. I will turn
the land of Egypt into ruins, a desolate waste from Migdol to Syene, as
far as the border of •Cush. 11 No human foot will pass through it, and
no animal foot will pass through it.
It will be uninhabited for 40 years.
12 I will make the land of Egypt a
desolation among[E] desolate lands,
and its cities will be a desolation
among[F] ruined cities for 40 years. I
will disperse the Egyptians among
the nations and scatter them across
the countries.

13 "For this is what the Lord God
says: At the end of 40 years I will
gather the Egyptians from the nations where they were dispersed. 14 I
will restore the fortunes of Egypt
and bring them back to the land of
Pathros, the land of their origin.
There they will be a lowly kingdom. 15 Egypt will be the lowliest of
kingdoms and will never again exalt
itself over the nations. I will make
them so small they cannot rule over
the nations. 16 It will never again be
an object of trust for the house of Israel, drawing attention to their sin
of turning to the Egyptians. Then
they will know that I am the Lord
Yahweh."

17 In the twenty-seventh year in
the first month, on the first day of
the month, the word of the Lord
came to me: 18 "Son of man, Nebuchadnezzar king of Babylon made
his army labor strenuously against
Tyre. Every head was made bald and
every shoulder chafed, but he and
his army received no compensation
from Tyre for the labor he expended
against it. 19 Therefore this is what
the Lord God says: I am going to give
the land of Egypt to Nebuchadnezzar king of Babylon, who will carry
off its wealth, seizing its spoil and
taking its plunder. This will be his
army's compensation. 20 I have given
him the land of Egypt as the pay he
labored for, since they worked for
Me." This is the declaration of the
Lord God. 21 "In that day I will cause
a •horn to sprout for the house of Israel, and I will enable you to speak
out among them. Then they will
know that I am Yahweh."

30 The word of the Lord came to
me: 2 "Son of man, prophesy
and say: This is what the Lord God
says:

Wail: Woe for the day!
3 For a day is near;

[A]29:3 Or *crocodile* [B]29:6 LXX, Syr, Vg read *you* [C]29:7 LXX, Syr, Vg; MT reads *and you caused their hips to stand* [D]29:9 LXX, Syr, Vg; MT reads *he* [E]29:12 Or *Egypt the most desolate of* [F]29:12 Or *be the most desolate of*

covenant by following after idols and had thus been excluded from covenantal blessings, and even incurred covenantal curses, the nation was not completely lost because of God's promises to Abraham. Therefore, there was hope because of the promise of return (cp. Jr 32:40-44), but there was also a reminder of the exclusion of these people from the Mosaic covenant.

29:1–30:26 Chapter 29 begins an extended section spanning four chapters, composed of a series of prophecies against Egypt. The first prophecy against Egypt predates the prophecies against Tyre by at least two months (cp. 29:1 and 26:1). Yet, immediately following this message from the **tenth year** (29:1), Ezekiel recounts a further prophecy against Egypt, which he received in the **twenty-seventh year** (29:17). After that, a message from the **eleventh year** is presented (30:20). The messages are apparently not chronological, but rather arranged thematically.

29:3-5 The first prophecy against Egypt offers an initial theological explanation for the impending invasion by the Babylonians. Pharaoh's claim to ownership of the Nile (cp. v. 9) was more than a mere territorial statement; it was a pronouncement of his belief in his own elevated status as a god. The claim of ownership of the Nile was tied to the claim that Pharaoh *created* it (**I made it for myself**).

29:6-12 Egypt's hubris, coupled with its unreliability as an ally to the Israelites (cp. v. 16), had led to the destruction of Egypt (cp. Jr 46:7-8).

29:13-16 While the doom of Egypt was sure and devastating, it would not be total or final. The Lord offered Egypt a message of hope and restoration.

29:17-21 The second prophecy against Egypt is dated 17 years later and offers an additional behind-the-scenes explanation for Egypt's fall to Babylon. Amazingly, God told Ezekiel that Nebuchadnezzar would be given Egypt as a sort of compensation for his army's labors against Tyre because he did not take the city and gain its riches. Yet, in waging war against Tyre, Nebuchadnezzar was an instrument of God's wrath.

30:2-3 Chapter 30 describes the defeat of the Egyptian armies by Nebuchadnezzar's forces in June of 587 B.C., when Pharaoh Hophra was defeated by Nebuchadnezzar as the former tried to help Zedekiah by breaking the Babylonian siege of Jerusalem. The repetition of **day** serves as an ominous indicator of doom on the horizon. It is similar to the idea of the "day of the LORD," a day of judgment and destruction, discussed in many of the prophets (cp. Is 2; Jl 2; Am 5).

30:4-6 The mercenary armies employed by Pharaoh—including those of Cush, Put, Lud, and Libya—would fail in their defense of Egypt's border, and the whole of North Africa would fear the Babylonian Empire. **The men of the covenant land** most likely refers to Israel, indicating that God's chosen people will also come under judgment along with the Gentiles, a message consistent with the aforementioned prophets.

30:7-8 The phrase **set fire to Egypt**, repeated in verse 16, is also found in Jeremiah's condemning prophecy in Jr 43:12, as some survivors from the fall of Jerusalem fled to Egypt after overturning Babylon's establishment of a representative governor loyal to them in Judah. God specifically condemned Egypt's sun worship (Jr. 43:13).

30:9-17 As Egypt's **day** of doom approaches, Ezekiel makes it clear that the great cities of Egypt—Memphis, Thebes (which had been the national capital and the headquarters of worship of the sun-god, Amon), Pathros, and Pelusium, among others—would all fall to the Babylonian army (vv. 13-17). Some would be burned, some people would be deported (v. 17), and many would die. God's primary role as the acting agent in this judgment is emphasized in the repetition of the word **I**.

30:18-19 On, another city devoted to the worship of the sun, was also known as "Heliopolis," Sun City. Pharaoh had a palace with a temple for sun worship at **Tehaphnehes**, likely the "Tahpanhes" mentioned in Jr 43:7-13. The destruction of these places would demonstrate God's true lordship to Egypt.

30:20-22 In a particularly violent metaphor for the defeat of Egypt by the Babylonians, the two rulers, Pharaoh Hophra and King Nebuchadnezzar, representing their two nations, are pictured in one-on-one combat. The Lord depicts Pharaoh's defeat with the concrete picture of breaking both of his arms so that he could no longer brandish a sword or carry a shield to protect himself. With two broken arms, he would be virtually as helpless as a newborn infant, completely exposed and at the mercy of his adversary, who could easily finish him off. This highly ironic description is a deliberate play on Hophra's name/title, which was "Possessor of a Strong Arm."

30:23-26 The Egyptian people would

a day belonging to the LORD
is near.
It will be a day of clouds,
a time of doom
for the nations.
4 A sword will come
against Egypt,
and there will be anguish
in •Cush
when the slain fall in Egypt,
and its wealth is taken away,
and its foundations
are torn down.
5 Cush, Put, and Lud,
and all the various
foreign troops,[A]
plus Libya[B] and the men
of the covenant land[C]
will fall by the sword
along with them.
6 This is what the LORD says:
Those who support Egypt
will fall,
and its proud strength
will collapse.
From Migdol to Syene
they will fall within it
by the sword.
This is the declaration
of the Lord GOD.
7 They will be desolate
among[D] desolate lands,
and their cities will lie
among ruined[E] cities.
8 They will know that
I am •Yahweh
when I set fire to Egypt
and all its allies are shattered.

9 On that day, messengers will go out
from Me in ships to terrify confident
Cush. Anguish will come over them
on the day of Egypt's doom. For indeed it is coming."
10 This is what the Lord GOD says:

I will put an end
to the hordes[F] of Egypt
by the hand of
Nebuchadnezzar
king of Babylon.
11 He along with his people,
ruthless men
from the nations,
will be brought in to destroy
the land.
They will draw their swords
against Egypt
and fill the land
with the slain.
12 I will make the streams dry
and sell the land
into the hands of evil men.
I will bring desolation
on the land and everything
in it
by the hands of foreigners.
I, Yahweh, have spoken.

13 This is what the Lord GOD says:

I will destroy the idols
and put an end
to the false gods in Memphis.
There will no longer be
a prince from the land
of Egypt.
So I will instill fear
in that land.
14 I will make Pathros desolate,
set fire to Zoan,
and execute judgments
on Thebes.
15 I will pour out My wrath
on Pelusium,
the stronghold of Egypt,
and will wipe out the crowds[F]
of Thebes.
16 I will set fire to Egypt;
Pelusium will writhe
in anguish,
Thebes will be breached,
and Memphis will face foes
in broad daylight.[G]
17 The young men of On[H]
and Pi-beseth
will fall by the sword,
and those cities[I] will go
into captivity.
18 The day will be dark[J]
in Tehaphnehes,
when I break the yoke
of Egypt there
and its proud strength
comes to an end in the city.
A cloud will
cover Tehaphnehes,[K]
and its villages will go
into captivity.
19 So I will execute judgments
against Egypt,

[A]30:5 Or *all Arabia* [B]30:5 Lit *Cub*; Hb obscure [C]30:5 Probably Israel [D]30:7 Or *be the most desolate of* [E]30:7 Or *will be the most ruined of* [F]30:10,15 Or *pomp, or wealth* [G]30:16 Or *foes daily* [H]30:17 LXX, Vg; MT reads *iniquity* [I]30:17 Or *and the women*; lit *and they* [J]30:18 Some Hb mss, LXX, Syr, Tg, Vg; other Hb mss read *will withhold* [K]30:18 Or *Egypt*

and they will know that
I am Yahweh.

20 In the eleventh year, in the first
month, on the seventh day of the
month, the word of the LORD came
to me: 21 "Son of man, I have broken
the arm of Pharaoh king of Egypt.
Look, it has not been bandaged—no
medicine has been applied and
no splint put on to bandage it so
that it can grow strong enough to
handle a sword. 22 Therefore this is
what the Lord GOD says: Look! I am
against Pharaoh king of Egypt. I
will break his arms, both the strong
one and the one already broken,
and will make the sword fall from
his hand. 23 I will disperse the Egyptians among the nations and scatter them among the countries. 24 I
will strengthen the arms of Babylon's king and place My sword in
his hand. But I will break the arms
of Pharaoh, and he will groan before him as a mortally wounded
man. 25 I will strengthen the arms of
Babylon's king, but Pharaoh's arms
will fall. They will know that I am
Yahweh when I place My sword in
the hand of Babylon's king and he
wields it against the land of Egypt.
26 When I disperse the Egyptians
among the nations and scatter
them among the countries, they
will know that I am Yahweh."

31 In the eleventh year, in the
third month, on the first day
of the month, the word of the LORD
came to me: 2 "Son of man, say to
Pharaoh king of Egypt and to his
hordes:

Who are you like
in your greatness?
3 Think of Assyria, a cedar
in Lebanon,
with beautiful branches
and shady foliage
and of lofty height.
Its top was among
the clouds.[A]
4 The waters caused it to grow;
the underground springs
made it tall,
directing their rivers
all around
the place where the tree
was planted
and sending their channels
to all the trees of the field.
5 Therefore the cedar
became greater in height
than all the trees of the field.
Its branches multiplied,
and its boughs grew long
as it spread them out
because of the plentiful water.
6 All the birds of the sky
nested in its branches,
and all the animals
of the field
gave birth beneath its boughs;
all the great nations lived
in its shade.
7 It was beautiful
in its greatness,
in the length of its limbs,
for its roots extended
to abundant water.
8 The cedars in God's garden
could not rival it;
the pine trees couldn't
compare with its branches,
nor could the plane trees
match its boughs.
No tree in the garden of God
could compare with it
in beauty.
9 I made it beautiful with its
many limbs,
and all the trees of Eden,
which were in God's garden,
envied it.

10 "Therefore this is what the Lord
GOD says: Since it[B] became great in
height and set its top among the
clouds,[A] and it[C] grew proud on account of its height, 11 I determined
to hand it over to a ruler of nations;
he would surely deal with it. I banished it because of its wickedness.
12 Foreigners, ruthless men from the
nations, cut it down and left it lying.
Its limbs fell on the mountains and
in every valley; its boughs lay broken in all the earth's ravines. All the
peoples of the earth left its shade and
abandoned it. 13 All the birds of the
sky nested on its fallen trunk, and all
the animals of the field were among
its boughs. 14 This happened so that
no trees planted beside water would
become great in height and set their

be deported in much the same way as the Judeans. The parallel language of God's primary agency in Egypt's defeat together with Nebuchadnezzar as God's tool continues: **I place My sword in the hand of Babylon's king and he wields it against the land of Egypt**.

31:1-2 The message of chapter 31, given two months after the previous message, compares Egypt to Assyria. The prophecies against Egypt apparently had not produced any response of humility or repentance by Pharaoh. The consistent theme of the tall, luxuriant, growing cedar that is felled, collapsing and descending into Sheol, ties together this devastating chapter. The tall cedar brought low is also a theme in chapter 17, demonstrating God's sovereignty (esp. 17:24).

31:3-7 The image of a Lebanese **cedar** is used to depict the beauty, strength, and power of **Assyria**. The familiar language of the tree's sheltering **shade** and the refuge of its **boughs** suggests Assyria's potential as a blessed nation. The **great nations** refer to allied (whether voluntary or compelled) nations that became dependent on Assyria. A similar image is used for Babylon/Nebuchadnezzar in the king's dream (Dn 4:10-23); another similar but more sinister parallel reference to Nebuchadnezzar is given in Is 14:4-22. The **top . . . among the clouds** is reminiscent of the Tower of Babel (Gn 11), and again brings to mind the sin of pride and self-exaltation, which consistently draws God's censure.

31:8-11 Assyria was the most powerful nation of the eighth century B.C., surpassing the ancient empires—even ancient Egypt—in strength and splendor. Several references to the beauty and splendor of **the garden of God** or **Eden** show that God was the One who had made Assyria the beautiful and powerful cedar she had become, the envy of the other trees. Yet, despite its potential, **it grew proud** (lit, "its heart grew proud"), and therefore became subject to divine judgment.

31:12-14 The felled tree's crash was felt world-wide as its debris lay strewn around in the **earth's ravines**, **mountains**, and in **every valley**. Its allies and dependents (**all the peoples of the earth**) all fled, leaving the tree **abandoned.** Its fall became an example of how pride goes before a fall. Its punishment was so dramatic that the tree was not merely cast down to earth but banished even deeper to **the Pit**, the **underworld**.

[A] **31:3,10** Or *thick foliage* [B] **31:10** Syr, Vg; MT, LXX read *you* [C] **31:10** Lit *its heart*

tops among the clouds,[A] and so that
no other well-watered trees would
reach them in height. For they have
all been consigned to death, to the
underworld, among the •people who
descend to the •Pit.
15 "This is what the Lord GOD says:
I caused grieving on the day the cedar went down to •Sheol. I closed
off the underground deep because
of it:[B] I held back the rivers of the
deep, and its abundant waters were
restrained. I made Lebanon mourn
on account of it, and all the trees
of the field fainted because of it.
16 I made the nations quake at the
sound of its downfall, when I threw
it down to Sheol to be with those
who descend to the Pit. Then all the
trees of Eden, all the well-watered
trees, the choice and best of Lebanon, were comforted in the underworld. 17 They too descended with it
to Sheol, to those slain by the sword.
As its allies[C,D] they had lived in its
shade among the nations.
18 "Who then are you like in glory
and greatness among Eden's trees?
You also will be brought down to
the underworld to be with the trees
of Eden. You will lie among the
uncircumcised with those slain by
the sword. This is Pharaoh and all
his hordes"—the declaration of the
Lord GOD.

32 In the twelfth year, in the
twelfth month, on the first day
of the month, the word of the LORD
came to me: 2 "Son of man, lament
for Pharaoh king of Egypt and say
to him:

You compare yourself
to a lion of the nations,
but[E] you are like a monster
in the seas.
You thrash about
in your rivers,
churn up the waters
with your feet,
and muddy the[F] rivers."

3 This is what the Lord GOD says:

I will spread My net over you
with an assembly
of many peoples,
and they[G] will haul you up
in My net.
4 I will abandon you
on the land
and hurl you
on the open field.
I will cause all the birds
of the sky
to settle on you
and let the beasts
of the entire earth
eat their fill of you.
5 I will put your flesh
on the mountains
and fill the valleys
with your carcass.
6 I will drench the land
with the flow of your blood,
even to the mountains;
the ravines will be filled
with your gore.

7 When I snuff you out,
I will cover the heavens
and darken their stars.
I will cover the sun
with a cloud,
and the moon will not give
its light.
8 I will darken all
the shining lights
in the heavens over you,
and will bring darkness
on your land.
This is the declaration
of the Lord GOD.

9 I will trouble the hearts
of many peoples,
when I bring about
your destruction
among the nations,
in countries you do not know.
10 I will cause many nations
to be appalled at you,
and their kings will shudder
with fear because of you
when I brandish My sword
in front of them.
On the day of your downfall
each of them will tremble
every moment for his life.

11 For this is what the Lord GOD
says:

The sword of Babylon's king

[A]31:14 Or *thick foliage* [B]31:15 Or *I covered it with the underground deep* [C]31:17 LXX, Syr read *offspring* [D]31:17 Lit *arm* [E]32:2 Or *Lion of the nations, you are destroyed;* [F]32:2 Lit *their* [G]32:3 LXX, Vg read *I*

31:15-17 God's control over the **abundant waters** is emphasized, indicating that it was because of God's graciousness that these waters had fed the tree(s) and caused their luxuriant growth. As God had previously provided water generously, He now **restrained** them, resulting in the deaths of the other **trees** as well. The phrase **I made Lebanon mourn** is an idiom for clothing Lebanon in black (mourning) garments. These **trees of the field** died and went to the **Pit**, to **Sheol**. They symbolize Assyria's **allies**, whose demise resulted from Assyria's defeat. Their meager comfort stemmed from the fact of equality in death—no one is exalted, but rather all are humbled and laid low. Assyria is no longer a threat, nor is it in an enviable position.

31:18 Within this poetic structure is a rather straightforward logical argument that Pharaoh was asked to consider: If the more powerful Assyria had fallen to the Babylonians, on what basis could Egypt expect to withstand an assault by Nebuchadnezzar? Pharaoh seems to believe his possession of the Nile will prove a decisive advantage (29:3,9), but Assyria also held powerful waters (i.e., the Tigris and Euphrates rivers), and these proved to be of no advantage. Egypt will fall just as Assyria did.

32:1-4 Almost two years later (March, 585 B.C.), **the word of the LORD came** to Ezekiel concerning the fall of Egypt, again compared to a crocodile that is captured, brought out of the Nile, placed on the land, slaughtered, and left for the animals to eat (cp. 29:4-5).

32:5-6 The amount of blood—enough to fill the **mountains**, **valleys**, and **ravines**—indicates that death reached beyond one man (e.g., Pharaoh) to the whole of Egypt.

32:7-10 The imagery of **darkness** over the **land** has several corollaries in the Old Testament. First, and most obviously, darkness is almost always associated with negativity, whether sin, evil, judgment, doom, or destruction. Second, darkness—when due to cataclysmic events in the heavens—is often associated with the coming "Day of the LORD" (cp. 30:2-3; Jl 2:2,10). Third, and most relevant for Egypt, darkness enveloping the land was the ninth plague brought on by Pharaoh's refusal to release the Israelites to worship the Lord in the wilderness (Ex 10:20-27), the final plague before the crushing death of all the firstborn sons. Any one or all three of these may be in view, but clearly Egypt would fall to Babylon, and all the other nations of the region would **be appalled** and fear Nebuchadnezzar's might.

will come against you!
12 I will make your hordes fall
by the swords of warriors,
all of them ruthless men
from the nations.
They will ravage
Egypt's pride,
and all its hordes
will be destroyed.
13 I will slaughter all its cattle
that are beside many waters.
No human foot
will churn them again,
and no cattle hooves
will disturb them.
14 Then I will let their
waters settle
and will make their rivers
flow like oil.
This is the declaration
of the Lord GOD.
15 When I make the land
of Egypt a desolation,
so that it is emptied of
everything in it,
when I strike down all
who live there,
then they will know that
I am •Yahweh.

16 "This is a lament that will be
chanted; the women of the nations
will chant it. They will chant it over
Egypt and all its hordes." This is the
declaration of the Lord GOD.
17 In the twelfth year,[A] on the fifteenth day of the month, the word
of the LORD came to me: 18 "Son of
man, wail over the hordes of Egypt
and bring Egypt and the daughters
of mighty nations down to the underworld,[B] to be with those who descend to the •Pit:

19 Who do you surpass
in loveliness?
Go down and be laid to rest
with the uncircumcised!
20 They will fall
among those slain
by the sword.
A sword is appointed!
They drag her and all
her hordes away.
21 Warrior leaders will speak
from the middle of •Sheol
about him[C] and his allies:
They have come down;
the uncircumcised lie
slain by the sword.
22 Assyria is there with all
her company;
her graves are all around her.
All of them are slain, fallen
by the sword.
23 Her graves are set
in the deepest regions
of the Pit,
and her company is all around
her burial place.
All of them are slain, fallen
by the sword—
those who once spread terror
in the land of the living.

24 Elam is there
with all her hordes
around her grave.
All of them are slain, fallen
by the sword—
those who went down
to the underworld[B]
uncircumcised,
who once spread
their terror
in the land of the living.
They bear their disgrace
with those who descend
to the Pit.
25 Among the slain
they prepare a resting place
for Elam
with all her hordes.
Her graves are all around her.
All of them are
uncircumcised,
slain by the sword,
although their terror
was once spread
in the land of the living.
They bear their disgrace
with those who descend
to the Pit.
They are placed
among the slain.

26 Meshech and Tubal[D] are there,
with all their hordes.
Their graves are all
around them.
All of them are
uncircumcised,
slain by the sword,
although their terror was
once spread

32:15-16 Once again, total destruction due to the Lord's judgment reveals God's sovereignty; He will bring down any nation that exalts itself and excludes God. The **lament** over Egypt **will be chanted** by professional mourners, the **women of the nations**. Mourning was most often a women's profession in the ancient Near East (cp. Jr 9:17-20).

32:17-32 Verses 19-32 constitute a poem or dirge about the descent of Pharaoh and his warriors to the realm of the dead, Sheol, or **the Pit**. Pharaoh is questioned as he was in 31:18. He envisions his Egypt as equal to the great empires like Assyria (31:2-3), but in reality he will share their fall. Rather than praising him, they will actually welcome him to the **underworld**.

32:19-21 The picture is of a cemetery sectioned nation by nation. Egyptians would lie among **the uncircumcised**, even though they practiced the rite of circumcision (v. 32). The reference to lying among **the uncircumcised** probably was meant to communicate the equality of all persons in death—no matter what their stature, they would end in the same place.

32:22-25 Various nations and kingdoms that were once powerful would also lie in the dust (vv. 22-30). These included the Assyrians, who were defeated by the Babylonians in 612 B.C., and the Edomites, who also practiced circumcision (cp. v. 29). Multiple references to the fear formerly instilled by these nations underscores that death envelops even the mightiest of warriors and nations (cp. vv. 26-27,30).

32:26-28 Because of their sins, the soldiers of **Meshech and Tubal** are not allowed to **lie down** with the uncircumcised soldiers of renown, who were buried with full military honors, their **swords . . . placed under their heads**.

A 32:17 LXX reads *year, in the first month,* B 32:18,24 Lit *the lower parts of the earth*
C 32:21 Either Pharaoh or Egypt D 32:26 Lit *Meshech-tubal*

32:29-32 Despite their strength (as in the case of **Edom**), Pharaoh and the Egyptians can and would die; they were just one among many nations—like the **Sidonians,** whose **strength** inspired **terror**—that falsely conceived of themselves as invincible. Pharaoh's comfort apparently lies in seeing that he is not alone; all these great nations shared his fate. The poem intends to call Pharaoh and Egypt to humility, and simultaneously to rid Judah of any delusions they might harbor that Pharaoh could deliver on his promises of protection for Jerusalem or on his claims of supremacy over Babylon.

33:1-6 With this chapter, Ezekiel's oracles take on a more hopeful tone for his nation. The narrative of chapter 33 begins where chapter 24 concludes—before the oracles against the nations. It is set off parenthetically by two vocations of Ezekiel: the preacher as watchman (sentry) and the preacher as entertainer. The former is his God-given vocation, while the latter is an unwilling role in which the people have cast him. Ezekiel again offers a description of the watchman's duty—if he sees a **sword** (i.e., an invading army) coming, he is to blow a **trumpet** to warn the people (vv. 2-3). Those who ignore **the warning** and die are at fault and are responsible for their own death; if the watchman fails to warn, then he is accountable (cp. chap. 3). The use of repetition, which is common in the prophets, here may set parentheses around the material included between chapters 3 and 33. It could also be used to introduce a new phase of Ezekiel's ministry. The first assignment as watchman begins Ezekiel's ministry of delivering messages of judgment, and the second assignment begins his ministry of delivering messages of hope.

33:7-9 Ezekiel was a spiritual **watchman** for the house of Israel. He was obligated to warn the wicked of their fate if they did not repent and turn to the Lord. Clearly, the **wicked person** refers to Israel, and the "sound of the trumpet" (v. 5) symbolizes Ezekiel's prophetic oracles.

33:10-11 The parallel passage (3:16-21) does not have an equivalent to verses 10-11, in which the Lord encouraged the people to choose repentance and life rather than continue in sin leading to death. This passage speaks to the love, patience, and grace God demonstrates toward sinners. He does not relish their death, the natural consequence of their sins. Instead, He sends prophets to warn sinners of their fate and to call them to repentance and life.

33:12-16 A parallel passage focusing on taking personal responsibility for

in the land of the living.
27 They do not lie down
with the fallen warriors
of the uncircumcised,[A]
who went down to Sheol
with their weapons of war,
whose swords were placed
under their heads.[B]
The punishment for their sins
rested on their bones,
although the terror
of these warriors
was once in the land
of the living.
28 But you will be shattered
and will lie down
among the uncircumcised,
with those slain by the sword.

29 Edom is there, her kings
and all her princes,
who, despite their strength,
have been placed
among those slain
by the sword.
They lie down
with the uncircumcised,
with those who descend
to the Pit.
30 All the leaders of the north
and all the Sidonians
are there.
They went down in shame
with the slain,
despite the terror
their strength inspired.
They lie down uncircumcised
with those slain by the sword.
They bear their disgrace
with those who descend
to the Pit.

31 Pharaoh will see them
and be comforted over all
his hordes—
Pharaoh and all his army,
slain by the sword.
This is the declaration
of the Lord GOD.

32 For I will spread My[C] terror
in the land of the living,
so Pharaoh and all his hordes
will be laid to rest
among the uncircumcised,
with those slain
by the sword."
This is the declaration
of the Lord GOD.

The Vocation of Ezekiel (33:1-33)

Ezekiel as a Watchman (33:1-20)

33 The word of the LORD came to
me: 2 "Son of man, speak to
your people and tell them: Suppose
I bring the sword against a land,
and the people of that land select
a man from among them, appointing him as their watchman, 3 and
he sees the sword coming against
the land and blows his trumpet to
warn the people. 4 Then, if anyone
hears the sound of the trumpet but
ignores the warning, and the sword
comes and takes him away, his blood
will be on his own head. 5 Since he
heard the sound of the trumpet but
ignored the warning, his blood is
on his own hands.[D] If he had taken
warning, he would have saved his
life. 6 However, if the watchman
sees the sword coming but doesn't
blow the trumpet, so that the people
aren't warned, and the sword comes
and takes away their lives, then
they have been taken away because
of their iniquity, but I will hold the
watchman accountable for their
blood.
7 "As for you, son of man, I have
made you a watchman for the house
of Israel. When you hear a word
from My mouth, give them a warning from Me. 8 If I say to the wicked,
'Wicked one, you will surely die,' but
you do not speak out to warn him
about his way, that wicked person
will die for his iniquity, yet I will
hold you responsible for his blood.
9 But if you warn a wicked person
to turn from his way and he doesn't
turn from it, he will die for his iniquity, but you will have saved your
life.
10 "Now as for you, son of man,
say to the house of Israel: You have
said this, 'Our transgressions and
our sins are heavy on us, and we are
wasting away because of them! How
then can we survive?' 11 Tell them: As
I live"—the declaration of the Lord

[A]32:27 LXX reads *of antiquity* [B]32:27 Or *Do they not . . . heads?* [C]32:32 Alt Hb tradition, LXX, Syr read *his* [D]33:5 Lit *on him*

God—"I take no pleasure in the death of the wicked, but rather that the wicked person should turn from his way and live. Repent, repent of your evil ways! Why will you die, house of Israel?

12 "Now, son of man, say to your people: The righteousness of the righteous person will not save him on the day of his transgression; neither will the wickedness of the wicked person cause him to stumble on the day he turns from his wickedness. The righteous person won't be able to survive by his righteousness on the day he sins. 13 When I tell the righteous person that he will surely live, but he trusts in his righteousness and commits iniquity, then none of his righteousness will be remembered, and he will die because of the iniquity he has committed.

14 "So when I tell the wicked person, 'You will surely die,' but he repents of his sin and does what is just and right— 15 he returns collateral, makes restitution for what he has stolen, and walks in the statutes of life without practicing iniquity—he will certainly live; he will not die. 16 None of the sins he committed will be held against him. He has done what is just and right; he will certainly live.

17 "But your people say, 'The Lord's way isn't fair,' even though it is their own way that isn't fair. 18 When a righteous person turns from his righteousness and commits iniquity, he will die on account of this. 19 But if a wicked person turns from his wickedness and does what is just and right, he will live because of this. 20 Yet you say, 'The Lord's way isn't fair.' I will judge each of you according to his ways, house of Israel."

The Fall of Jerusalem and Continued Rebellion by Israel (33:21-33)

21 In the twelfth year of our exile, in the tenth month, on the fifth day of the month, a fugitive from Jerusalem came to me and reported, "The city has been taken!" 22 Now the hand of the Lord had been on me the evening before the fugitive arrived, and He opened my mouth before the man came to me in the morning. So my mouth was opened and I was no longer mute.

23 Then the word of the Lord came to me: 24 "Son of man, those who live in the[A] ruins in the land of Israel are saying, 'Abraham was only one person, yet he received possession of the land. But we are many; the land has been given to us as a possession.' 25 Therefore say to them: This is what the Lord God says: You eat meat with blood in it, raise your eyes to your idols, and shed blood. Should you then receive possession of the land? 26 You have relied on your swords, you have committed detestable acts, and each of you has defiled his neighbor's wife. Should you then receive possession of the land?

27 "Tell them this: This is what the Lord God says: As surely as I live, those who are in the ruins will fall by the sword, those in the open field I have given to wild animals to be devoured, and those in the strongholds and caves will die by plague. 28 I will make the land a desolate waste, and its proud strength will come to an end. The mountains of Israel will become desolate, with no one passing through. 29 They will know that I am •Yahweh when I make the land a desolate waste because of all the detestable acts they have committed.

30 "Now, son of man, your people are talking about you near the city walls and in the doorways of their houses. One person speaks to another, each saying to his brother, 'Come and hear what the message is that comes from the Lord!' 31 So My people come to you in crowds,[B] sit in front of you, and hear your words, but they don't obey them. Although they express love with their mouths, their hearts pursue dishonest profit. 32 Yes, to them you are like a singer of love songs who has a beautiful voice and plays skillfully on an instrument. They hear your words, but they don't obey them. 33 Yet when it comes—and it will definitely come—then they will know that a prophet has been among them."

sin can be found in 18:11-32. The Lord holds out hope to the wicked who mend their ways, and shares a warning to the righteous to avoid relying on their past righteous deeds to balance out their transgressions. Trusting in past good deeds cannot be used as an excuse for living a sinful lifestyle (cp. Gn 2:17; Rm 6:23).

33:17-20 Despite God's gracious warnings and His patience with the people, they accused God of unfairness (cp. 18:25-29).

33:21-22 The fall of **Jerusalem** is reported to Ezekiel, who had been **mute**, possibly since the death of his wife (approximately two years). Just before the **fugitive** arrived from Jerusalem with the news, Ezekiel's tongue was loosed.

33:23-24 This section seems to be directed partly toward those who survived the destruction of Jerusalem and partly toward the exiles among whom Ezekiel exercised his ministry. Restoration to **the land** is a theological construct grounded in the Lord's covenantal promise to Abraham and his descendants (Gn 12:1-3). The people understood that God's promise to give Abraham the land of Canaan applied to themselves as his descendants (Is 51:2).

33:25-29 Some who survived the fall of Jerusalem appear to have been scattered, while others remained there, living **in the ruins**; some were living **in the open field**, others **in the strongholds and caves**. Despite the ruins, pilgrims still came to bring offerings to the temple, signifying that the ruins themselves were still venerated (Jr 41:5). Perhaps these persons looked down upon those either slaughtered or deported, believing themselves to be more righteous and the true recipients of the land. The Lord's answer indicates that they had not been spared because of their righteousness, as they still practiced idolatry and defiled themselves. Their fate was still to come and would be deadly—by **sword, wild animals,** and **plague**—rather than triumphant. No relief was in sight for this wicked, sinful remnant, only imminent disaster. These claims of righteousness and entitlement to covenant blessings based on physical descent from Abraham are echoed in the audience of John the Baptist. Some who came to hear him preach on repentance believed that they were exempt "from the coming wrath" (Lk 3:7-8).

33:30-33 As a preacher (God's watchman), whose commission was to warn Israel of sin and spur them to true repentance, Ezekiel was compelled to perform sign-acts to

A **33:24** Lit *these* B **33:31** Lit *you like the coming of a people*

convey His message visually. Although the message pertained to a life-and-death situation, the listeners regarded Ezekiel's ministry as entertainment.

34:1-4 The **shepherds** refer to the leaders of the people, specifically the kings whose symbolic anointing was part of the coronation ritual. Although a shepherd could refer to anyone in a leadership position (i.e., to other officials), the reference to kings is preferable, since the Lord is both King and Shepherd, and He promised to appoint another king to shepherd His people. This prophecy was given after the fall of the city and could refer to the present leadership (Gedaliah and others more abusive, e.g., Ishmael; cp. Jr 41). The nation's kings had been derelict in their duties as caregivers and nurturers of those entrusted to them, treating them with cruelty rather than compassion.

34:5-6 The "scattering" of the flock could be a literal reference to exile or a figurative/spiritual reference to idolatry, especially when associated with the phrases **all the mountains** and **every high hill**, commonly associated with worship at Baal shrines.

34:8-13 The Lord—the true Shepherd—would depose the shepherds and **rescue** His **flock**. The shepherds not only neglected the flock but also fed **themselves rather than** [God's] **flock**. God Himself provides the model for a shepherd as one who seeks out the lost, nurtures the injured and the weak, rescues the scattered, and protects them from harm.

34:14-16 God will bring His people home to **Israel's lofty mountains**. He will ensure bountiful grazing pasture and will **let them lie down**, giving them rest and restoration (cp. Ps 23:2). **Justice** is the hallmark of His leadership.

34:17-22 After rebuking the leaders, God judged the **flock** as well, since the sheep themselves were not blameless. Injustice was being perpetrated even within the ranks of the flock by the larger, stronger members (**the fat sheep**) who oppressed the weaker members (**the lean sheep**). They pushed and shoved and bullied, taking first pick of the pasture and clear water and leaving the leftovers for the weaker members. These strong sheep (administrators and officials) would also be judged, removed, and ultimately replaced by a worthy shepherd, the Messiah.

34:23-24 The ideal shepherd-king is modeled by **David**, who composed Ps 23, in which he identifies Yahweh as his shepherd (cp. 1Sm 17:34-37). Through

The Good Shepherd (34:1-31)

34 The word of the LORD came to me: 2 "Son of man, prophesy against the shepherds of Israel. Prophesy, and say to them: This is what the Lord GOD says to the shepherds: Woe to the shepherds of Israel, who have been feeding themselves! Shouldn't the shepherds feed their flock? 3 You eat the fat, wear the wool, and butcher the fattened animals, but you do not tend the flock. 4 You have not strengthened the weak, healed the sick, bandaged the injured, brought back the strays, or sought the lost. Instead, you have ruled them with violence and cruelty. 5 They were scattered for lack of a shepherd; they became food for all the wild animals when they were scattered. 6 My flock went astray on all the mountains and every high hill. They were scattered over the whole face of the earth, and there was no one searching or seeking for them.

7 "Therefore, you shepherds, hear the word of the LORD. 8 As I live"—the declaration of the Lord GOD—"because My flock has become prey and food for every wild animal since they lack a shepherd, for My shepherds do not search for My flock, and because the shepherds feed themselves rather than My flock, 9 therefore, you shepherds, hear the word of the LORD!

10 "This is what the Lord GOD says: Look, I am against the shepherds. I will demand My flock from them[A] and prevent them from shepherding the flock. The shepherds will no longer feed themselves, for I will rescue My flock from their mouths so that they will not be food for them.

11 "For this is what the Lord GOD says: See, I Myself will search for My flock and look for them. 12 As a shepherd looks for his sheep on the day he is among his scattered flock, so I will look for My flock. I will rescue them from all the places where they have been scattered on a cloudy and dark day. 13 I will bring them out from the peoples, gather them from the countries, and bring them into their own land. I will shepherd them on the mountains of Israel, in the ravines, and in all the inhabited places of the land. 14 I will tend them with good pasture, and their grazing place will be on Israel's lofty mountains. There they will lie down in a good grazing place; they will feed in rich pasture on the mountains of Israel. 15 I will tend My flock and let them lie down." This is the declaration of the Lord GOD. 16 "I will seek the lost, bring back the strays, bandage the injured, and strengthen the weak, but I will destroy[B] the fat and the strong. I will shepherd them with justice.

17 "The Lord GOD says to you, My flock: I am going to judge between one sheep and another, between the rams and male goats. 18 Isn't it enough for you to feed on the good pasture? Must you also trample the rest of the pasture with your feet? Or isn't it enough that you drink the clear water? Must you also muddy the rest with your feet? 19 Yet My flock has to feed on what your feet have trampled, and drink what your feet have muddied.

20 "Therefore, this is what the Lord GOD says to them: See, I Myself will judge between the fat sheep and the lean sheep. 21 Since you have pushed with flank and shoulder and butted all the weak ones with your horns until you scattered them all over, 22 I will save My flock, and they will no longer be prey for you. I will judge between one sheep and another. 23 I will appoint over them a single shepherd, My servant David, and he will shepherd them. He will tend them himself and will be their shepherd. 24 I, *Yahweh, will be their God, and My servant David will be a prince among them. I, Yahweh, have spoken.

25 "I will make a covenant of peace with them and eliminate dangerous animals in the land, so that they may live securely in the wilderness and sleep in the forest. 26 I will make them and the area around My hill a blessing: I will send down showers in their season—showers[C] of blessing. 27 The trees of the field will give their fruit, and the land will yield

[A]**34:10** Lit *their hand* [B]**34:16** Some Hb mss, LXX, Syr, Vg read *watch over* [C]**34:26** Lit *season; they will be showers*

>WORD|*study*

34:25 The Lord promised to make it possible for His people to **live securely** (Hb *betach*, "without fear or danger, safely"; cp. 28:26; Jr 32:37; 33:16; 39:26; Zch 14:11), a phrase used in the Torah to describe the rewards of obedience—both generally, in the people's occupation of the promised land (Lv 26:3-5; Dt 12:10), and particularly, in the Year of Jubilee (Lv 25:18-19). In Psalm 4:8 David used both this word and the parallel idea of being able to **sleep** (Hb *yashēn*) to express his assurance that Yahweh alone is the source of peace and safety (cp. Ps 3:5).

its produce; My flock will be secure
in their land. They will know that I
am Yahweh when I break the bars of
their yoke and rescue them from the
hands of those who enslave them.
28 They will no longer be prey for the
nations, and the wild animals of the
land will not consume them. They
will live securely, and no one will
frighten them. 29 I will establish for
them a place renowned for its agriculture,[A] and they will no longer be
victims of famine in the land. They
will no longer endure the insults of
the nations. 30 Then they will know
that I, Yahweh their God, am with
them, and that they, the house of
Israel, are My people." This is the
declaration of the Lord God. 31 "You
are My flock, the human flock of My
pasture, and I am your God." This is
the declaration of the Lord God.

Judgment and the Restoration of Mountains (35:1–36:15)

Judgment Against Mount Seir of Edom (35:1-15)

35 The word of the Lord came to
me: 2 "Son of man, turn your
face toward Mount Seir and prophesy against it. 3 Say to it: This is what
the Lord God says:

Look! I am against you,
Mount Seir.
I will stretch out My hand
against you
and make you
a desolate waste.
4 I will turn your cities
into ruins,
and you will become
a desolation.
Then you will know that
I am Yahweh.

5 "Because you maintained an ancient hatred and handed over the
Israelites to the power of the sword
in the time of their disaster, the time
of final punishment, 6 therefore, as I
live"—this is the declaration of the
Lord God—"I will destine you for
bloodshed, and it will pursue you.
Since you did not hate bloodshed, it
will pursue you. 7 I will make Mount
Seir a desolate waste and will cut off
from it those who come and go. 8 I
will fill its mountains with the slain;
those slain by the sword will fall on
your hills, in your valleys, and in
all your ravines. 9 I will make you
a perpetual desolation; your cities
will not be inhabited. Then you will
know that I am Yahweh.
10 "Because you said, 'These two
nations and two lands will be mine,
and we will possess them'—though
the Lord was there— 11 therefore, as
I live"—the declaration of the Lord
God—"I will treat you according to
the anger and jealousy you showed
in your hatred of them. I will make
Myself known among them[B] when
I judge you. 12 Then you will know
that I, Yahweh, have heard all the
blasphemies you uttered against
the mountains of Israel, saying,
'They are desolate. They have been
given to us to devour!' 13 You boasted
against Me with your mouth, and
spoke many words against Me. I
heard it Myself!
14 "This is what the Lord God says:
While the whole world rejoices, I
will make you a desolation. 15 Just
as you rejoiced over the inheritance
of the house of Israel because it became a desolation, so I will deal with
you: you will become a desolation,
Mount Seir, and so will all Edom
in its entirety. Then they will know
that I am Yahweh.

Ezekiel the Lord promised to **appoint** a descendant of David to shepherd His flock (cp. Mt 9:35-36). As that promised shepherd (Mt 2:6; Jn 10:11-14), Jesus sacrificed His own life for the sheep (Mk 14:27-28; Jn 10:11,17-18), unlike the unjust, greedy, exploitative kings of Israel in Ezekiel's day.

34:25-31 Because Yahweh initiates and effects the restored relationship with His people, they and the land—particularly His **hill**, referring to Mount Zion or Jerusalem—would receive **blessing** from Him and be **a blessing** to the surrounding nations. To provide such comprehensive security—from the barren **wilderness** to the thickly vegetated **forest**—the Lord promised, under His lordship and the kingship of His servant David, to **make a covenant of peace with them** (cp. 37:26). Divine wrath would cease, and the Lord would restore wholeness and harmony between Himself and the people as well as land (cp. Nm 25:12-13; Is 54:10). The Lord would also **eliminate dangerous animals in the land** (cp. 14:15; Is 35:9).

The description of Israel as God's **human flock** closely fits the description of covenant blessings promised in Lv 26:4-13 and Dt 28:2-14. Under this unilateral covenant of peace, however, abundant life will be guaranteed by what God does (Rm 5:1,9-11; 11:26-27; Heb 7:22; 8:6-12; 9:11-14; 13:20-21; cp. Jr 31:31-34; Ezk 11:19; 36:26; Jn 10:10). The covenantal formula is also reiterated here as God's gracious acts on His nation's behalf are intended to reveal that the covenantal blessings are once again in effect: **You are My flock . . . and I am your God** (cp. Ps 100:3; Jr 30:22; 32:38).

35:5-15 There had been a long history of hostility (**an ancient hatred**) between Israel and Edom (cp. 2Ch 21:8-10a; 28:16-17). The Edomites aided invading armies against the Israelites, even killing some Israelite warriors as they fled. Specifically, God would judge Edom for four sins: their hatred (Hb *ʾēyvah*, "enmity, hostile mindset," v. 5; used only here and 25:15; Gn 3:15; Nm 35:21-22; Hb *sinʾah*, Ezk. 35:11; cp. 23:29) of Israel and their role in the defeat of Israel (v. 5); for their treatment of the Israelites (vv. 10-15; cp. Ps 137:7); their lusting after Israel's land (Ezk 35:10); and their disregard for the Lord (v. 13). Many of these same sins were those perpetrated by Esau (Edom)—he hated his brother Jacob; he sought to kill his brother; he wished to take back his inheritance (land); and he showed disregard for the Lord. The **desolation** of Edom would demonstrate the truth and holiness of the Lord to **the whole world** (vv. 14-15).

A **34:29** LXX, Syr read *a plant of peace* B **35:11** LXX reads *you*

The Restoration of the Mountains of Israel (36:1-15)

36 "Son of man, prophesy to the mountains of Israel and say: Mountains of Israel, hear the word of the LORD. 2 This is what the Lord GOD says: Because the enemy has said about you, 'Good! The ancient heights have become our possession,' 3 therefore, prophesy and say: This is what the Lord GOD says: Because they have made you desolate and have trampled you from every side, so that you became a possession for the rest of the nations and an object of people's gossip and slander, 4 therefore, mountains of Israel, hear the word of the Lord GOD. This is what the Lord GOD says to the mountains and hills, to the ravines and valleys, to the desolate ruins and abandoned cities, which have become plunder and a mockery to the rest of the nations all around.

5 "This is what the Lord GOD says: Certainly in My burning zeal I speak against the rest of the nations and all of Edom, who took[A] My land as their own possession with wholehearted rejoicing and utter contempt so that its pastureland became[B] plunder. 6 Therefore, prophesy concerning the land of Israel and say to the mountains and hills, to the ravines and valleys: This is what the Lord GOD says: Look, I speak in My burning zeal because you have endured the insults of the nations. 7 Therefore this is what the Lord GOD says: I swear[C] that the nations all around you will endure their own insults.

8 "You, mountains of Israel, will produce your branches and bear your fruit for My people Israel, since their arrival is near. 9 Look! I am on your side; I will turn toward you, and you will be tilled and sown. 10 I will fill you with people, with the whole house of Israel in its entirety. The cities will be inhabited and the ruins rebuilt. 11 I will fill you with people and animals, and they will increase and be fruitful. I will make you inhabited as you once were and make you better off than you were before. Then you will know that I am •Yahweh. 12 I will cause people, My people Israel, to walk on you; they will possess you, and you will be their inheritance. You will no longer deprive them of their children.

13 "This is what the Lord GOD says: Because people are saying to you, 'You devour men and deprive your nation of children,' 14 therefore, you will no longer devour men and deprive your nation of children."[D] This is the declaration of the Lord GOD. 15 "I will no longer allow the insults of the nations to be heard against you, and you will not have to endure the reproach of the peoples anymore; you will no longer cause your nation to stumble."[E] This is the declaration of the Lord GOD.

A Restoration of the People (36:16–37:28)

Cleaning and Purging (36:16-38)

16 The word of the LORD came to me: 17 "Son of man, while the house of Israel lived in their land, they defiled it with their conduct and actions. Their behavior before Me was like menstrual impurity. 18 So I poured out My wrath on them because of the blood they had shed on the land, and because they had defiled it with their idols. 19 I dispersed them among the nations, and they were scattered among the countries. I judged them according to their conduct and actions. 20 When they came to the nations where they went, they profaned My holy name, because it was said about them, 'These are the people of Yahweh, yet they had to leave His land in exile.' 21 Then I had concern for My holy name, which the house of Israel profaned among the nations where they went.

22 "Therefore, say to the house of Israel: This is what the Lord GOD says: It is not for your sake that I will act, house of Israel, but for My holy name, which you profaned among the nations where you went. 23 I will honor the holiness of My great name, which has been profaned among the nations—the name you have profaned among them. The nations will know that I am Yah-

36:1-5 References to the mountains of Edom and Israel serve as symbols of these nations and picture the future of both. While Mount Seir in Edom received condemnation, the **mountains of Israel** receive a promise of restoration and fruitfulness (cp. vv. 8,10).

36:6-7 Although God was the one punishing His people, the surrounding nations who insulted His people and His land (by taking it over) elicited God's **burning zeal**.

36:8-14 The destiny of the **mountains of Israel** will be exactly opposite to those of Edom. Their abundant fruitfulness and agricultural fertility will be restored. Their inhabitants and cattle will also be restored and God's covenant people will dwell there. The reference to depriving the **nation of children** might hark back to 5:11-17, where natural disasters (along with a few man-made threats) were said to leave Jerusalem childless.

36:16-19 Once the land is restored and made fruitful again, the spiritual and geographical restoration of the people follows. The land had been **defiled** by the people's idolatry, incurring God's wrath and judgment. The metaphor of **menstrual impurity** signifies defilement and pollution, but in a way that shows the land is not morally culpable, any more than a woman is morally blameworthy for her monthly discharge. The other charges of bloodshed and idolatry (cp. chap. 22) fit well together as a possible reference to child sacrifice.

36:20-23 Even in exile, the people called by His name had **profaned** that holy name **among the nations** by continuing to engage in idolatry (e.g., chaps. 14 and 20). God, therefore, promised to "cleanse" Israel of sins (vv. 25,33). As with the allegorical wife in chapter 16, God Himself would make atonement for the people's sins so that the covenant blessings could be realized. By returning His duly chastised people to the land and making them prosper again, the Lord demonstrated His holiness "among the nations," who had disparaged the strength of Israel's God as being unable to prevent their exile. The Lord shows His strength by the very fact of His people's destruction, removal from the land, and exile. In His holiness, God will not stand for defilement of His land and violation of His covenant; He will not flinch at punishing even His own, for **the holiness of** [His] **great name** demands justice, which will be a testimony to the nations.

36:24-27 The Lord promised not only to restore His people to the land, but

[A]**36:5** Lit *gave* [B]**36:5** Or *contempt, to empty it of*; Hb obscure [C]**36:7** Lit *lift up My hand* [D]**36:14** Alt Hb tradition reads *and cause your nation to stumble* [E]**36:15** Some Hb mss, Tg read *no longer bereave your nation of children*

weh"—the declaration of the Lord
GOD—"when I demonstrate My holiness through you in their sight.
24 "For I will take you from the nations and gather you from all the
countries, and will bring you into
your own land. 25 I will also sprinkle
clean water on you, and you will be
•clean. I will cleanse you from all
your impurities and all your idols.
26 I will give you a new heart and put
a new spirit within you; I will remove
your heart of stone[A] and give you a
heart of flesh. 27 I will place My Spirit
within you and cause you to follow
My statutes and carefully observe
My ordinances. 28 Then you will live
in the land that I gave your fathers;
you will be My people, and I will be
your God. 29 I will save you from all
your uncleanness. I will summon
the grain and make it plentiful, and
will not bring famine on you. 30 I will
also make the fruit of the trees and
the produce of the field plentiful, so
that you will no longer experience
reproach among the nations on account of famine.
31 "Then you will remember your
evil ways and your deeds that were
not good, and you will loathe yourselves for your iniquities and detestable practices. 32 It is not for your
sake that I will act"—the declaration of the Lord GOD—"let this
be known to you. Be ashamed and
humiliated because of your ways,
house of Israel!
33 "This is what the Lord GOD says:
On the day I cleanse you from all
your iniquities, I will cause the cities to be inhabited, and the ruins
will be rebuilt. 34 The desolate land
will be cultivated instead of lying
desolate in the sight of everyone
who passes by. 35 Then they will say,
'This land that was desolate has become like the garden of Eden. The
cities that were once ruined, desolate, and destroyed are now fortified
and inhabited.' 36 Then the nations
that remain around you will know
that I, Yahweh, have rebuilt what
was destroyed and have replanted
what was desolate. I, Yahweh, have
spoken and I will do it.
37 "This is what the Lord GOD says:

Doctrine HOLY SPIRIT

Ezekiel 36:24–37:1-14 is an especially amazing and hopeful passage, not only for the Judean exiles, but for all people, especially those in the exile of sin. The New Testament teaches that the Holy Spirit, the Third Person of the Trinity, performs several characteristic tasks in the life of a believer. First, the Spirit convicts of sin and the need for cleansing and forgiveness. The Spirit helps sinners understand the reasons for their separation from a holy and awesome God. Atonement has already been graciously accomplished by the Son, the Second Person of the Trinity, thus making restoration and fellowship with God possible. When sinners accept that atonement made on their behalf, the Holy Spirit performs the work of regeneration, what Jesus called being "born again" (Jn 3:3). Further, the Holy Spirit of God takes up residence in and continues to sanctify the believer.

This passage in Ezekiel indicates that these works performed by the Holy Spirit are not just a New Testament idea. Although the indwelling function did not actually come to pass until after Christ's completed work of atonement, other features of God's work through the Holy Spirit are already evident in the Old Testament. Ezekiel writes that when the people witness God's amazing work of deliverance from exile and restoration to their own land, thus vindicating God's holy Name, the people will respond with shame and humiliation, being convicted of their sin (36:31-32). Full restoration will require cleansing by the sprinkling of clean water on them, images of washing and sanctification by the blood of a sacrifice (36:25). The new heart and new spirit express the necessary changes within a woman, in order to relate properly to God. The current "heart of stone" indicates deadness, as well as stubborn, unyielding rebellion and an inability to love God properly; someone who cannot love or obey is basically dead. On the other hand, a "heart of flesh" is alive, sensitive, and able to respond in loving obedience (36:26). Furthermore, God will place a "new spirit" within the believer, namely, His Spirit, to ensure careful attention to and fulfillment of God's law (36:27).

This "heart transplant" and Spirit "implant" combine as a beautiful picture of regeneration, wrought by God's Spirit, so that the one "born again," as Jesus teaches Nicodemus, is "born of water and the Spirit," the former to cleanse and the latter to revive (Jn 3:5). This amazing promise is full of hope not only for Judah and for the exiles but also for all God's people who call themselves by His name. It is a promise of cleansing from sin, of gracious granting of new life by the Spirit, and of the Spirit remaining within the believer. In Ezekiel, God's Spirit inhabits the new temple and dwells among His people (43:1-7; 48:35), while in the New Testament the Spirit indwells believers, who become a bodily sanctuary (Jn 7:38-39, approximating Ezk 47:1-12; 1Co 3:16-17; 2Co 6:16). The promise of newness also encourages believers who fall into sin that there is still hope for restoration. Such restoration does not remove the temporal consequences of sin, but it restores the believer to fellowship with God.

In this chapter and the following several chapters, the amount of material in the first person by the Lord increases. He is the protagonist in the entire epic of destruction and restoration of the people. They (as we) were unable to overcome temptations to sin, "stumbling blocks," and are therefore unable to change themselves or save themselves. The work of restoration, of renewal and regeneration, and of salvation has to do first and foremost with God and the manifestation of His glory and His holiness. Although we have been faithless, God's power can and will accomplish our restoration on the condition of conviction and repentance. It is His work through His regenerating Spirit, who gives new life to the land and new life to the people. This latter is spectacularly portrayed in Ezekiel's awesome and famous vision of the valley of dry bones (chap. 37).

I will respond to the house of Israel
and do this for them: I will multiply
them in number like a flock.[B] 38 So
the ruined cities will be filled with
a flock of people, just as the flock of
sheep for sacrifice is filled[C] in Jerusalem during its appointed festivals.
Then they will know that I am Yahweh."

The Vision of the Valley of Dry Bones (37:1-14)

37 The hand of the LORD was on
me, and He brought me out by
His Spirit and set me down in the
middle of the valley; it was full of
bones. 2 He led me all around them.

also to cleanse them from idolatry, and to give them a new heart and a **new spirit**.

36:29-32 To be **ashamed** and **humiliated** indicates conviction and repentance.

36:33-38 By judging and cleansing rather than merely destroying His people, the Lord had acted and would continue to act according to His word (cp. Lv 26:40-45). Only the one true God (Yahweh) could turn desolation into beauty like that of **the garden of Eden**. Only He would rebuild and replant and **multiply**, reversing the emptiness and destruction that resulted from His people's disobedience (cp. Jr 31:28).

37:1-6 Scripture does not specify a particular geographical location for **the valley** (Hb *biq'ah*, "plain"; cp. 3:22;

[A] **36:26** Lit *stone from your flesh* [B] **36:37** Lit *flock of people* [C] **36:38** Lit *the flock of consecrated things, as the flock*

8:4) to which God's **Spirit** took Ezekiel. It is simply described as the scene of a battle in which countless Israelites died, their bodies left unburied. That the remaining skeletons were **very dry** underscored the lifelessness of the audience to which Ezekiel was commanded to **prophesy**.

God emphasizes that this impossible feat will be His work alone, driven by His will to restore life and His power as the giver of life.

37:7-10 He exemplifies faith both in his answer to the Lord's question (v. 3) and in his obedience to deliver God's message to dead, dry **bones**. Even when the bones were reassembled and the physical bodies were completely restored, however, they remained lifeless without **breath**. Therefore, Ezekiel was commanded to prophesy to **the breath** to come into and thereby give life to the **vast army**.

37:11 Rather than a military "army," the bones represented the utter lifelessness of **the whole house of Israel**. The three sayings that follow are worded as though no remedy were possible:

- **Our bones are dried up** (i.e., "We are lifeless or good for nothing");
- **Our hope has perished** (Hb *ʾavad*, "fail, be lost, come to nothing"; cp. 12:22; Pr 10:28; 11:7);
- **We are cut off** (Hb *gazar*, "be taken away, perish; be excluded or separated from"; cp. 2Ch 26:21; Ps 88:6; Is 53:8; Lm 3:54).

Indeed, death is final—no one but God can make dead men live.

37:12-14 The Lord encourages His people that He will do the impossible. He will resurrect His people from the dead by instilling His **Spirit** in them. This work foreshadows the New Testament work of the Holy Spirit in regenerating believers and indwelling them. This empowers them to walk in new life after having died to an old life of sin (Rm 6:4-11). Only by God's Spirit within are believers able to live a God-pleasing life of obedience and holiness. This promise of the gift of the indwelling Spirit is something quite new for Ezekiel's listeners, for the usual role of God's Spirit was external (kings, prophets, etc.); He was poured out *upon* persons rather than dwelling *within* them. This passage is also one of the rare mentions of resurrection in the Old Testament (cp. Dn 12:2,13).

37:15-25 The Lord further promises a reunification of the kingdom of Israel, which had been divided since the time of Solomon's successor (v. 22). It was symbolized by two rods (Ephraim and Judah) becoming one. The **single stick** may refer to a shepherd's staff since the one who will lead the reunified

There were a great many of them on the surface of the valley, and they were very dry. 3 Then He said to me, "Son of man, can these bones live?"

I replied, "Lord God, only You know."

4 He said to me, "Prophesy concerning these bones and say to them: Dry bones, hear the word of the Lord! 5 This is what the Lord God says to these bones: I will cause breath to enter you, and you will live. 6 I will put tendons on you, make flesh grow on you, and cover you with skin. I will put breath in you so that you come to life. Then you will know that I am •Yahweh."

7 So I prophesied as I had been commanded. While I was prophesying, there was a noise, a rattling sound, and the bones came together, bone to bone. 8 As I looked, tendons appeared on them, flesh grew, and skin covered them, but there was no breath in them. 9 He said to me, "Prophesy to the breath,[A] prophesy, son of man. Say to it: This is what the Lord God says: Breath, come from the four winds and breathe into these slain so that they may live!" 10 So I prophesied as He commanded me; the breath[A] entered them, and they came to life and stood on their feet, a vast army.

11 Then He said to me, "Son of man, these bones are the whole house of Israel. Look how they say, 'Our bones are dried up, and our hope has perished; we are cut off.' 12 Therefore, prophesy and say to them: This is what the Lord God says: I am going to open your graves and bring you up from them, My people, and lead you into the land of Israel. 13 You will know that I am Yahweh, My people, when I open your graves and bring you up from them. 14 I will put My Spirit in you, and you will live, and I will settle you in your own land. Then you will know that I am Yahweh. I have spoken, and I will do it." This is the declaration of the Lord.

The Reunification of Israel (37:15-28)

15 The word of the Lord came to me: 16 "Son of man, take a single stick and write on it: Belonging to Judah and the Israelites associated with him. Then take another stick and write on it: Belonging to Joseph—the stick of Ephraim—and all the house of Israel associated with him. 17 Then join them together into a single stick so that they become one in your hand. 18 When your people ask you, 'Won't you explain to us what you mean by these things?'— 19 tell them: This is what the Lord God says: I am going to take the stick of Joseph, which is in the hand of Ephraim, and the tribes of Israel associated with him, and put them together with the stick of Judah. I will make them into a single stick so that they become one in My hand.

20 "When the sticks you have written on are in your hand and in full view of the people, 21 tell them: This is what the Lord God says: I am going to take the Israelites out of the nations where they have gone. I will gather them from all around and bring them into their own land. 22 I will make them one nation in the land, on the mountains of Israel, and one king will rule over all of them. They will no longer be two nations and will no longer be divided into two kingdoms. 23 They will not defile themselves anymore with their idols, their detestable things, and all their transgressions. I will save them from all their apostasies by which[B] they sinned, and I will cleanse them. Then they will be My people, and I will be their God. 24 My servant David will be king over them, and there will be one shepherd for all of them. They will follow My ordinances, and keep My statutes and obey them.

25 "They will live in the land that I gave to My servant Jacob, where your fathers lived. They will live in it forever with their children and grandchildren, and My servant David will be their prince forever. 26 I will make a covenant of peace with them; it will be an everlasting covenant with them. I will establish and multiply them and will set My sanctuary among them forever. 27 My

[A]37:9,10 Or *wind*, or *spirit* [B]37:23 Some Hb mss, LXX, Sym; other Hb mss read *their settlements where*

dwelling place will be with them; I will be their God, and they will be My people. 28 When My sanctuary is among them forever, the nations will know that I, Yahweh, sanctify Israel."

Prophecies Against Gog of Magog (38:1–39:29)

38 The word of the LORD came to me: 2 "Son of man, turn your face toward Gog, of the land of Magog, the chief prince of[A] Meshech and Tubal. Prophesy against him 3 and say: This is what the Lord GOD says: Look, I am against you, Gog, chief prince of Meshech and Tubal. 4 I will turn you around, put hooks in your jaws, and bring you out with all your army, including horses and riders, who are all splendidly dressed, a huge company armed with shields and bucklers, all of them brandishing swords. 5 Persia, •Cush, and Put are with them, all of them with shields and helmets; 6 Gomer with all its troops; and Beth-togarmah from the remotest parts of the north along with all its troops—many peoples are with you.

7 "Be prepared and get yourself ready, you and all your company who have been mobilized around you; you will be their guard. 8 After a long time you will be summoned. In the last years you will enter a land that has been restored from war[B] and regathered from many peoples to the mountains of Israel, which had long been a ruin. They were brought out from the peoples, and all of them now live securely. 9 You, all of your troops, and many peoples with you will advance, coming like a thunderstorm; you will be like a cloud covering the land.

10 "This is what the Lord GOD says: On that day, thoughts will arise in your mind, and you will devise an evil plan. 11 You will say, 'I will go up against a land of open villages; I will come against a tranquil people who are living securely, all of them living without walls and without bars or gates— 12 in order to seize spoil and carry off plunder, to turn your hand against ruins now inhabited and against a people gathered from the nations, who have been acquiring cattle and possessions and who live at the center of the world.' 13 Sheba and Dedan and the merchants of Tarshish with all its rulers[C] will ask you, 'Have you come to seize spoil? Have you assembled your hordes to carry off plunder, to make off with silver and gold, to take cattle and possessions, to seize great spoil?'

14 "Therefore prophesy, son of man, and say to Gog: This is what the Lord GOD says: On that day when My people Israel are dwelling securely, will you not know this 15 and come from your place in the remotest parts of the north—you and many peoples with you, who are all riding horses—a mighty horde, a huge army? 16 You will advance against My people Israel like a cloud covering the land. It will happen in the last days, Gog, that I will bring you against My land so that the nations may know Me, when I show Myself holy through you in their sight.

17 "This is what the Lord GOD says: Are you the one I spoke about in former times through My servants, the prophets of Israel, who for years prophesied in those times that I would bring you against them? 18 Now on that day, the day when Gog comes against the land of Israel"—this is the declaration of the Lord GOD—"My wrath will flare up.[D] 19 I swear in My zeal and fiery rage: On that day there will be a great earthquake in the land of Israel. 20 The fish of the sea, the birds of the sky, the animals of the field, every creature that crawls on the ground, and every human being on the face of the earth will tremble before Me. The mountains will be thrown down, the cliffs will collapse, and every wall will fall to the ground. 21 I will call for a sword against him on all My mountains"—the declaration of the Lord GOD—"and every man's sword will be against his brother. 22 I will execute judgment on him with plague and bloodshed. I will pour out torrential rain, hailstones, fire, and brimstone on him, as well as his troops and the many peoples

nation will be a **shepherd**, namely, **my servant David**, a messianic reference. Christ was from the line of David (vv. 19,24-25).

37:26-28 A new **covenant** would replace the Mosaic covenant, which the people had violated grossly and repeatedly, and God promised to dwell with His people once more as He re-established the temple in the land. Finally, Israel will be clean, sanctified, and the work will have been completely the Lord's doing from start to finish (cp. Rv 21:3).

38:1-5 Ezekiel is told to prophesy against King **Gog** of **Meshech** and **Tubal**, two cities mentioned previously in Ezekiel as trading partners with Tyre and as having warriors who were not going to receive a proper burial because of atrocities against the Judeans (cp. 27:13; 32:26). He proclaims defeat for the armies that Gog commands, including his allies from **Persia** (Iran) and North Africa. They will be enslaved.

38:6-11 The land of Magog, from which Gog came, is described as being from the **north** (cp. v. 15), and Ezekiel notes that it will attack people living in peace in the **mountains of Israel**. The picture here is of a vast army descending upon the Israelites *after* the restoration prophesied previously (e.g., 36:16–37:28). The people of Israel will have such a sense of security that their cities will not have the typical defense mechanisms in place (**gates, bars**, and **walls**) but instead will trust in the Lord (cp. 39:29).

38:12-16 Greed seems to have been the primary motivation for the invasion, with the expectation of easy victory. The Lord will fight the battle for Israel, defeating the hordes of invaders through both supernatural and natural means. Verse 16 seems to indicate the Lord's agency: He purposely brings in the evil and greedy invaders in order to destroy them. Thus He will show Himself **holy** in the **sight** of the **nations**.

38:17-23 Many of the invaders will be killed by cataclysmic events that the Lord will bring about—a massive **earthquake, torrential rain, hailstones, fire, and brimstone**. This destruction will reveal the Lord's **greatness** and **holiness** to **many nations**. Many will also die through an opposing army's efforts, disease, and even insurrection within the unit.

[A] **38:2** Or *the prince of Rosh,* [B] **38:8** Lit *from the sword* [C] **38:13** Lit *young lions,* or *villages*
[D] **38:18** Lit *up in My anger*

39:2-3 The Lord's agency in invasion of **the mountains of Israel** for the purpose of defeat is further reinforced.

39:6-8 Those living on **coasts** and **islands** may be associates, allies, or dependents of **Magog**. A concept like the Day of the Lord (**the day I have spoken about**) seems to be referenced when Israel's enemies are routed and destroyed.

39:9-13 The defeat of this army led by Gog will be so devastating that it will take the Israelites **seven months** to bury all the enemy soldiers, and it will signify the end of strife in the land of Israel. The Israelites will burn the implements of war belonging to these enemy soldiers, warming their homes for **seven years**. Some commentators have argued that these durations are figurative, and this could be the case; seven is a number typically signifying completion, but the lengths of time taken more or less literally—about seven months of burying and about seven years of burning. There is no indication in the text that Ezekiel did not mean for the terms to be understood in this way. The *amount* of time allotted for each activity, the specific length notwithstanding, points to the great size of the invading army.

39:14-16 The concept of cleansing the land is surely important for Ezekiel's message and has a dual meaning here. On one hand, it refers to the removal of the carcasses of the invading army. Under Mosaic law and Levitical holiness rules, dead bodies were sources of ceremonial uncleanness, and to leave a dead body exposed was an abomination (Lv 17:15; 21:11; Nm 5:2; 6:6; 9:7-10). Additionally, rotting corpses strewn throughout the land would produce a putrid odor and would breed disease. Therefore, their removal would be described as a cleansing of the land. On the other hand, it could also refer to finally ridding the land of idolaters such as all those associated with Magog (see **Doctrine**, this page).

39:21-29 God Himself will force the land to be cleansed by raising up a combined army of the descendants of the Canaanites and then summarily destroying them. This interpretation leads to two startling conclusions. First, the identity of Magog seems to be one of, or a combination of, the people groups who originally inhabited the land of Canaan. Second, the destruction of these peoples fulfills the original intent of the Mosaic covenant, but the Lord meets His own righteous requirement. This is to be viewed as a reaffirmation of the Abrahamic covenant's validity. The people of Israel will dwell in the land promised to Abraham, and they will be at peace because the Lord will

who are with him. [23]I will display
My greatness and holiness, and will
reveal Myself in the sight of many
nations. Then they will know that I
am •Yahweh.

39 "As for you, son of man, prophesy against Gog and say: This
is what the Lord God says: Look, I
am against you, Gog, chief prince
of[A] Meshech and Tubal. [2]I will turn
you around, drive you on, and lead
you up from the remotest parts of
the north. I will bring you against
the mountains of Israel. [3]Then I
will knock your bow from your left
hand and make your arrows drop
from your right hand. [4]You, all your
troops, and the peoples who are with
you will fall on the mountains of Israel. I will give you as food to every
kind of predatory bird and to the
wild animals. [5]You will fall on the
open field, for I have spoken." This
is the declaration of the Lord God.
[6]"I will send fire against Magog
and those who live securely on the
coasts and islands. Then they will
know that I am •Yahweh. [7]So I will
make My holy name known among
My people Israel and will no longer
allow it to be profaned. Then the nations will know that I am Yahweh,
the Holy One in Israel. [8]Yes, it is
coming, and it will happen." This
is the declaration of the Lord God.
"This is the day I have spoken about.
[9]"Then the inhabitants of Israel's
cities will go out, kindle fires, and
burn the weapons—the bucklers
and shields, the bows and arrows,
the clubs and spears. For seven
years they will use them to make
fires. [10]They will not gather wood
from the countryside or cut it down
from the forests, for they will use
the weapons to make fires. They will
take the loot from those who looted
them and plunder those who plundered them." This is the declaration
of the Lord God.
[11]"Now on that day I will give Gog
a burial place there in Israel—the
Valley of the Travelers[B] east of the
Sea. It will block those who travel
through, for Gog and all his hordes
will be buried there. So it will be
called the Valley of Hamon-gog.[C]

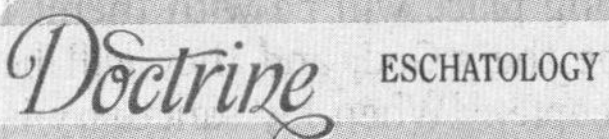

ESCHATOLOGY

The identity of Gog and Magog has proven elusive. The references to the "last years" (38:8) and "the day" God has "spoken about" (39:8) have led many commentators to view these events as still future (i.e., the final Day of the Lord). John briefly refers to "Gog and Magog" in the book of Revelation, in which the destruction of the army from Magog takes place after the millennial reign of Christ, and the leader of the army is the devil himself (Rv 20:7-10). Interpreting these places solely within an end-times framework is problematic, however. For example, in Revelation, the Day of the Lord takes place *before* this uprising; in fact, it is the judgment of God poured out in the bowl, seal, and trumpet judgments, all of which take place before the millennium.

Thus, while there are similarities between Ezekiel's account of the destruction of this army and John's description of the last stand of Satan, they should not be identified *as the same events*. Instead, a type/antitype relationship is more likely (i.e., the destruction of the army of Gog, prophesied by Ezekiel, prefigures the final defeat of Satan and his forces). In addition to burying the corpses so as to cleanse the land from the defilement of death, the concept of cleansing the land seems to have a more subtle meaning that is commensurate with the whole of Ezekiel's message. Much of the book addresses the failure of the Israelites to live up to the requirements of the Mosaic covenant. In the judgment against the nations, Ezekiel included hope of restoration for some and absolute destruction for others. Egypt, for example, is promised restoration, while Meshach and Tubal are not (32:26-27). These promises of restoration and lack thereof seem to be tied to the identities of the peoples. Before the Israelites entered the promised land, they were commanded to destroy completely all the peoples dwelling there, but they failed to do so (Dt 20:17; Jos 13:13; 15:63; 16:10; 17:12-13). Instead, in many cases, they made treaties with or enslaved the local populace. This failure led to significant problems for the Israelites, including their eventual slide into idolatry, just as Moses had predicted (Dt 31:14-29). Thus, the failure of the Israelites to cleanse the land of the idolatrous people had to be rectified if they were to possess the land in proper relationship to the Lord as the fulfillment of the Abrahamic covenant.

[12]The house of Israel will spend sev-
en months burying them in order
to cleanse the land. [13]All the people
of the land will bury them and their
fame will spread on the day I display
My glory." This is the declaration of
the Lord God.
[14]"They will appoint men on a full-
time basis to pass through the land
and bury the invaders[D] who remain
on the surface of the ground, in
order to cleanse it. They will make
their search at the end of the seven
months. [15]When they pass through

[A]**39:1** Or *Gog, prince of Rosh,* [B]**39:11** Hb obscure [C]**39:11** = Hordes of Gog [D]**39:14** Or *basis, some to pass through the land, and with them some to bury those*

the land and one of them sees a human bone, he will set up a marker
next to it until the buriers have buried it in the Valley of Hamon-gog.
16 There will even be a city named
Hamonah[A] there. So they will
cleanse the land.
17 "Son of man, this is what the
Lord God says: Tell every kind of
bird and all the wild animals: Assemble and come! Gather from all
around to My sacrificial feast that
I am slaughtering for you, a great
feast on the mountains of Israel; you
will eat flesh and drink blood. 18 You
will eat the flesh of mighty men and
drink the blood of the earth's princes: rams, lambs, male goats, and all
the fattened bulls of Bashan. 19 You
will eat fat until you are satisfied and
drink blood until you are drunk, at
My sacrificial feast that I have prepared for you. 20 At My table you will
eat your fill of horses and riders, of
mighty men and all the warriors."
This is the declaration of the Lord
God.
21 "I will display My glory among
the nations, and all the nations will
see the judgment I have executed
and the hand I have laid on them.
22 From that day forward the house
of Israel will know that I am Yahweh
their God. 23 And the nations will
know that the house of Israel went
into exile on account of their iniquity, because they dealt unfaithfully
with Me. Therefore, I hid My face
from them and handed them over
to their enemies, so that they all fell
by the sword. 24 I dealt with them
according to their uncleanness and
transgressions, and I hid My face
from them.
25 "So this is what the Lord God
says: Now I will restore the fortunes
of Jacob and have compassion on
the whole house of Israel, and I will
be jealous for My holy name. 26 They
will feel remorse for[B,C] their disgrace
and all the unfaithfulness they committed against Me, when they live
securely in their land with no one to
frighten them. 27 When I bring them
back from the peoples and gather
them from the countries of their
enemies, I will demonstrate My holiness through them in the sight of
many nations. 28 They will know that
I am Yahweh their God when I regather them to their own land after
having exiled them among the nations. I will leave none of them behind.[D] 29 I will no longer hide My face
from them, for I will pour out My
Spirit on the house of Israel." This
is the declaration of the Lord God.

The Temple and Its Measurements (40:1–42:20)

40 In the twenty-fifth year of our
exile, at the beginning of the
year, on the tenth day of the month
in the fourteenth year after Jerusalem had been captured, on that very
day the LORD's hand was on me, and
He brought me there. 2 In visions of
God He took me to the land of Israel and set me down on a very high
mountain. On its southern slope was
a structure resembling a city. 3 He
brought me there, and I saw a man
whose appearance was like bronze,
with a linen cord and a measuring
rod in his hand. He was standing
by the gate. 4 He spoke to me: "Son
of man, look with your eyes, listen
with your ears, and pay attention to
everything I am going to show you,
for you have been brought here so
that I might show it to you. Report
everything you see to the house of
Israel."
5 Now there was a wall surrounding the outside of the temple. The
measuring rod in the man's hand
was six units of 21 inches;[E] each unit
was the standard length plus three
inches.[F] He measured the thickness
of the wall structure; it was about 10
feet,[G] and its height was the same.[G]
6 Then he came to the gate that faced
east and climbed its steps. He measured the threshold of the gate; it
was 10 feet deep—the first threshold was 10 feet deep. 7 Each recess
was about 10 feet[G] long and 10 feet[H]
deep, and there was a space of 8¾
feet[I] between the recesses. The inner
threshold of the gate on the temple
side next to the gate's portico was

[A] **39:16** In Hb, Hamonah is related to the word "horde." [B] **39:26** Some emend to *will forget* [C] **39:26** Lit *will bear* [D] **39:28** Lit *behind there any longer* [E] **40:5** = a long cubit [F] **40:5** Lit *six cubits by the cubit and a handbreadth* [G] **40:5,7** Lit *was one rod* [H] **40:7** Lit *and one rod* [I] **40:7** Lit *five cubits*

destroy their enemies, and by doing so He will display His holiness to all (vv. 25,28-29).

40:1–48:35 Chapters 40–48 form a unit that could be considered part of the book's third section of oracles or visions of restoration. These descriptions are the most extensive elaborations on the temple, surpassing any material concerning the construction of the tabernacle, or the temple of Solomon, or even John's description of the heavenly Jerusalem (Rv 21–22). The theme of holiness is pronounced in this section, as all things in the new temple must be fit for the holiness of its divine resident. To this end, gradations of holiness are evident in the arrangements of various rooms and the functions of certain people. Holiness, as the quintessential attribute of God, is expressed concretely in the arrangements of the heavenly temple. Along the pathway to the holy of holies from the east gate, the area is progressively holy, as are those allowed to traverse the area. Gradations of holiness are also evident vertically; not only are the temple and the holy city located atop a mountain (40:2), but the number of stairs increases as one approaches the elevation of the holy of holies.

40:1-2 The twenty-fifth year of our exile would have been 573 B.C., 14 years after the fall of Jerusalem. **The beginning of the year** (Hb *ro'sh hashanah)* was New Year's, and the first month was Nisan (April). The timing of this vision is significant since 25 years was halfway to the 50-year Jubilee mark. Perhaps this vision and the hope it inspired indicated to the exiles that they had "turned a corner" in their time of exile. Ezekiel received a vision of a new Jerusalem, focusing especially on the new temple and its measurements. The prophet describes it as a **structure resembling a city**, consistent with John's descriptions of the new Jerusalem (Rv 21).

40:3-4 A heavenly messenger (**a man whose appearance was like bronze**; cp. Dn 10:6) told him to record everything he saw and **report** back to the exiles, who may have received words of a plan for a new, enduring temple with joy and relief (and later, conviction of sin; cp. Ezk 43:10-12). This chapter consists largely of measurements of various areas of sacred space around the temple and in the temple complex. The movement is from outside to the inside, from the outer wall into the Holy of Holies (chaps. 40–43).

40:5-37 Ezekiel witnessed the measuring of the outer **wall** surrounding the temple (v. 5) and of three other **gates** on the **east** (vv.

6-19), **north** (vv. 20-23), and **south** (vv. 24-27) sides of the wall. The **recess** in the gates (six for each) was probably a place where a guard was stationed to keep watch over the sacred space and maintain order. **All** of the outer gates' measurements were identical, as were those of the **inner** gates (vv. 28-37). This thick outer wall with its fortified inner and outer gates was like a fortress containing a palace. The **palm trees** decorating the tops of the pillars are an aesthetic detail reminiscent of the décor of Solomon's temple and perhaps symbolizing the tree of life (cp. Gn 2:9; 3:22-24; Rv 2:7; 22:2,14).

40:38-46 Next, Ezekiel was shown **four tables** for the preparation of sacrificial offerings inside the north gate (vv. 38-43). Further, he saw **chambers** facing each other **for the singers** and **priests** (vv. 44-46). Priests, generally Levites, who were in charge of guarding the temple were distinguished from priests who were allowed to minister at the altar—namely, Levites specifically from the line of **Zadok**, priest of the tabernacle under David and Solomon (v. 46). The mention of the Zadokite priests in this chapter is a second measure against the recurrence of idolatry in the temple and temple complex. The first measure involved the gate rooms, which accommodated guards for the sacred precinct. In this second measure, the Zadokite Levites are chosen specifically because historically their loyalty to the Davidic kingship and to Yahweh worship never waned; they were never corrupted by idols. Possibly, guards for all four gates in the sacred precinct plus guards for the altar were taken from the Zadokites (cp. vv. 5-37).

about 10 feet.[A] 8 Next he measured the portico of the gate; 9 it[B] was 14 feet,[C] and its pilasters were 3½ feet.[D] The portico of the gate was on the temple side.

10 There were three recesses on each side of the east gate, each with the same measurements, and the pilasters on either side also had the same measurements. 11 Then he measured the width of the gate's entrance; it was 17½ feet,[E] while the width[F] of the gateway was 22¾ feet.[G] 12 There was a barrier of 21 inches[H] in front of the recesses on both sides, and the recesses on each side were 10½ feet[I] square. 13 Then he measured the gateway from the roof of one recess to the roof of the opposite one; the distance was 43¾ feet.[J] The openings of the recesses faced each other. 14 Next, he measured the pilasters—105 feet.[K] The gate extended around to the pilaster of the court.[L] 15 The distance from the front of the gate at the entrance to the front of the gate's portico on the inside was 87½ feet.[M] 16 The recesses and their pilasters had beveled windows all around the inside of the gateway. The porticoes also had windows all around on the inside. Each pilaster was decorated with palm trees.

17 Then he brought me into the outer court, and there were chambers and a paved surface laid out all around the court. Thirty chambers faced the pavement, 18 which flanked the gates and corresponded to the length of the gates; this was the lower pavement. 19 Then he measured the distance from the front of the lower gate to the exterior front of the inner court; it was 175 feet.[N] This was the east; next the north is described.

20 He measured the gate of the outer court facing north, both its length and width. 21 Its three recesses on each side, its pilasters, and its portico had the same measurements as the first gate: 87½ feet[M] long and 43¾ feet[J] wide. 22 Its windows, portico, and palm trees had the same measurements as those of the gate that faced east. Seven steps led up to the gate, and its portico was ahead of them. 23 The inner court had a gate facing the north gate, like the one on the east. He measured the distance from gate to gate; it was 175 feet.[N]

24 He brought me to the south side, and there was also a gate on the south. He measured its pilasters and portico; they had the same measurements as the others. 25 Both the gate and its portico had windows all around, like the other windows. It was 87½ feet[M] long and 43¾ feet[J] wide. 26 Its stairway had seven steps, and its portico was ahead of them. It had palm trees on its pilasters, one on each side. 27 The inner court had a gate on the south. He measured from gate to gate on the south; it was 175 feet.[N]

28 Then he brought me to the inner court through the south gate. When he measured the south gate, it had the same measurements as the others. 29 Its recesses, pilasters, and portico had the same measurements as the others. Both it and its portico had windows all around. It was 87½ feet[M] long and 43¾ feet[J] wide. 30 (There were porticoes all around, 43¾ feet long and 8¾ feet[O] wide.[P]) 31 Its portico faced the outer court, and its pilasters were decorated with palm trees. Its stairway had eight steps.

32 Then he brought me to the inner court on the east side. When he measured the gate, it had the same measurements as the others. 33 Its recesses, pilasters, and portico had the same measurements as the others. Both it and its portico had windows all around. It was 87½ feet[M] long and 43¾ feet[J] wide. 34 Its portico faced the outer court, and its pilasters were decorated with palm trees on each side. Its stairway had eight steps.

35 Then he brought me to the north gate. When he measured it,

[A]**40:7** Lit *was one rod* [B]**40:8-9** Some Hb mss, Syr, Vg; other Hb mss read *gate facing the temple side; it was one rod. 9 Then he measured the portico of the gate; it* [C]**40:9** Lit *eight cubits* [D]**40:9** Lit *two cubits* [E]**40:11** Lit *10 cubits* [F]**40:11** Lit *length* [G]**40:11** Lit *13 cubits* [H]**40:12** Lit *one cubit* [I]**40:12** Lit *six cubits* [J]**40:13,21,25,29,33** Lit *25 cubits* [K]**40:14** Lit *60 cubits* [L]**40:14** Hb obscure [M]**40:15,21,25,29,33** Lit *50 cubits* [N]**40:19,23,27** Lit *100 cubits* [O]**40:30** Lit *five cubits* [P]**40:30** Some Hb mss, LXX omit v. 30

it had the same measurements as the others, 36 as did its recesses, pilasters, and portico. It also had windows all around. It was 87½ feet[A] long and 43¾ feet[B] wide. 37 Its portico[C] faced the outer court, and its pilasters were decorated with palm trees on each side. Its stairway had eight steps.

38 There was a chamber whose door opened into the portico of the gate.[D] The •burnt offering was to be washed there. 39 Inside the portico of the gate there were two tables on each side, on which to slaughter the burnt offering, •sin offering, and •restitution offering. 40 Outside, as one approaches the entrance of the north gate, there were two tables on one side and two more tables on the other side of the gate's portico. 41 So there were four tables inside the gate and four outside, eight tables in all on which the slaughtering was to be done. 42 There were also four tables of cut stone for the burnt offering, each 31½ inches[E] long, 31½ inches wide, and 21 inches[F] high. The utensils used to slaughter the burnt offerings and other sacrifices were placed on them. 43 There were three-inch[G] hooks[H] fastened all around the inside of the room, and the flesh of the offering was to be laid on the tables.

44 Outside the inner gate, within the inner court, there were chambers for the singers:[I] one[J] beside the north gate, facing south, and another beside the south[K] gate, facing north. 45 Then the man said to me: "This chamber that faces south is for the priests who keep charge of the temple. 46 The chamber that faces north is for the priests who keep charge of the altar. These are the sons of Zadok, the ones from the sons of Levi who may approach the LORD to serve Him." 47 Next he measured the court. It was square, 175 feet[L] long and 175 feet wide. The altar was in front of the temple.

48 Then he brought me to the portico of the temple and measured the pilasters of the portico; they were 8¾ feet[M] thick on each side. The width of the gateway was 24½ feet,[N] and the side walls of the gate were[O] 5¼ feet[P] wide on each side. 49 The portico was 35 feet[Q] across and 21[R] feet[S] deep, and 10 steps led[T] up to it. There were pillars by the pilasters, one on each side.

41 Next he brought me into the great hall and measured the pilasters; on each side the width of the pilaster was 10½ feet.[U,V] 2 The width of the entrance was 17½ feet,[W] and the side walls of the entrance were 8¾ feet[M] wide on each side. He also measured the length of the great hall, 70 feet,[X] and the width, 35 feet.[Q] 3 He went inside the next room and measured the pilasters at the entrance; they were 3½ feet[Y] wide. The entrance was 10½ feet[V] wide, and the width of the entrance's side walls on each side[Z] was 12¼ feet.[AA] 4 He then measured the length of the room adjacent to the great hall, 35 feet,[Q] and the width, 35 feet. And he said to me, "This is the most holy place."

5 Then he measured the wall of the temple; it was 10½ feet[V] thick. The width of the side rooms all around the temple was seven feet.[AB] 6 The side rooms were arranged one above another in three stories of 30 rooms each.[AC] There were ledges on the wall of the temple all around to serve as supports for the side rooms, so that the supports would not be in the temple wall itself. 7 The side rooms surrounding the temple widened at each successive story, for the structure surrounding the temple went up by stages. This was the reason for the temple's broadness as it

41:1-13 Ezekiel was taken further into the temple complex and into the temple itself. He saw an outer room in the **great hall** (Hb *hēykal*, "large, magnificent building; temple, palace," v. 1), a word usually used in contexts referring to the luxurious rooms of a king's palace, denoting one of the purposes for the new temple as God's palace. Ezekiel saw the man measuring out the space for the holy of holies, where the ark of the covenant had originally been set. The ark is conspicuous here for its absence; perhaps this absence signifies the fulfillment of Jr 3:16-17, when the ark is no longer the Lord's throne, but rather "Jerusalem will be called, Yahweh's Throne." There is also no mention of the two enormous cherubim crafted by Solomon to be above the ark (1Kg 6:23-28). The many **side rooms** are not accorded a specific function, but they may have been used for storage (vv. 5-11). The temple itself measured a perfect square (vv. 12-13).

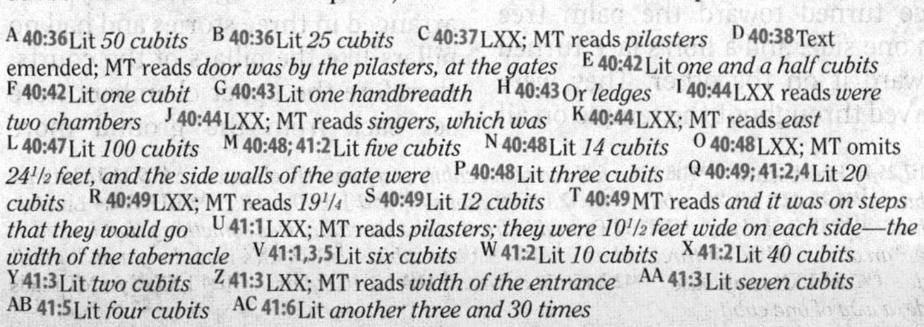

A **40:36** Lit *50 cubits* B **40:36** Lit *25 cubits* C **40:37** LXX; MT reads *pilasters* D **40:38** Text emended; MT reads *door was by the pilasters, at the gates* E **40:42** Lit *one and a half cubits* F **40:42** Lit *one cubit* G **40:43** Lit *one handbreadth* H **40:43** Or *ledges* I **40:44** LXX reads *were two chambers* J **40:44** LXX; MT reads *singers, which was* K **40:44** LXX; MT reads *east* L **40:47** Lit *100 cubits* M **40:48; 41:2** Lit *five cubits* N **40:48** Lit *14 cubits* O **40:48** LXX; MT omits *24½ feet, and the side walls of the gate were* P **40:48** Lit *three cubits* Q **40:49; 41:2,4** Lit *20 cubits* R **40:49** LXX; MT reads *19¼* S **40:49** Lit *12 cubits* T **40:49** MT reads *and it was on steps that they would go* U **41:1** LXX; MT reads *pilasters; they were 10½ feet wide on each side—the width of the tabernacle* V **41:1,3,5** Lit *six cubits* W **41:2** Lit *10 cubits* X **41:2** Lit *40 cubits* Y **41:3** Lit *two cubits* Z **41:3** LXX; MT reads *width of the entrance* AA **41:3** Lit *seven cubits* AB **41:5** Lit *four cubits* AC **41:6** Lit *another three and 30 times*

41:17-20 The interior temple walls were paneled with a certain design (like wallpaper). The pattern was of **cherubim and palm trees**, with a **palm tree between each pair of cherubim**. The fact that they are used to decorate the wall is in striking contrast to the depictions earlier in the book of unclean animals that the 70 men were worshiping in the inner room in Ezekiel's vision of the idolatry in Jerusalem (8:10-11). These cherubim are appropriately located, as they may be reminiscent of the cherubim on the mercy seat of the ark or of the two enormous cherubim overlooking the ark. The descriptions of these cherubim are somewhat different from others, as they appear to have only two faces—one of a **human** and the other of a lion (see **Doctrine**, p. 1058).

41:21-26 Ezekiel is then shown the wooden **altar**. The **double doors** for moving between the sanctuary and great hall were also adorned with **cherubim and palm trees**, reminiscent of Solomon's temple, adorned by "cherubim, palm trees, and flowering blossoms" (1Kg 6:31-32; cp. Ex 26:1,31).

42:1-14 Ezekiel saw a number of priestly **chambers** (vv. 1-13). On either side of **the outer court** of the temple were two sets of rooms used for eating the meat of the sacrifices (v. 13). These rooms were also used as changing rooms so the priests could change out of their vestments, which they wore to serve in the holy place (v. 14). In the Hebrew concept, holiness was something that could be transmitted between persons and objects (cp. 44:19). What became holy due to contact with God had to remain in the holy place, not to be taken outside into a profane, public place.

rose. And so, one would go up from the lowest story to the highest by means of the middle one.[A]

8 I saw that the temple had a raised platform surrounding it; this foundation for the side rooms was 10½ feet high.[B] 9 The thickness of the outer wall of the side rooms was 8¾ feet.[C] The free space between the side rooms of the temple 10 and the outer chambers was 35 feet[D] wide all around the temple. 11 The side rooms opened into the free space, one entrance toward the north and another to the south. The area of free space was 8¾ feet[C] wide all around.

12 Now the building that faced the temple yard toward the west was 122½ feet[E] wide. The wall of the building was 8¾ feet[C] thick on all sides, and the building's length was 157½ feet.[F]

13 Then the man measured the temple; it was 175 feet[G] long. In addition, the temple yard and the building, including its walls, were 175 feet long. 14 The width of the front of the temple along with the temple yard to the east was 175 feet. 15 Next he measured the length of the building facing the temple yard to the west, with its galleries[H] on each side; it was 175 feet.

The interior of the great hall and the porticoes of the court— 16 the thresholds, the beveled windows, and the balconies all around with their three levels opposite the threshold—were overlaid with wood on all sides. They were paneled from the ground to the windows (but the windows were covered), 17 reaching to the top of the entrance, and as far as the inner temple and on the outside. On every wall all around, on the inside and outside, was a pattern 18 carved with •cherubim and palm trees. There was a palm tree between each pair of cherubim. Each cherub had two faces: 19 a human face turned toward the palm tree on one side, and a lion's face turned toward it on the other. They were carved throughout the temple on all sides. 20 Cherubim and palm trees were carved from the ground to the top of the entrance and on the wall of the great hall.

21 The doorposts of the great hall were square, and the front of the sanctuary had the same appearance. 22 The altar was[I] made of wood, 5¼ feet[J] high and 3½ feet[K] long.[L] It had corners, and its length[M] and sides were of wood. The man told me, "This is the table that stands before the LORD."

23 The great hall and the sanctuary each had a double door, 24 and each of the doors had two swinging panels. There were two panels for one door and two for the other. 25 Cherubim and palm trees were carved on the doors of the great hall like those carved on the walls. There was a wooden canopy[A] outside, in front of the portico. 26 There were beveled windows and palm trees on both sides, on the side walls of the portico, the side rooms of the temple, and the canopies.[A]

42 Then the man led me out by way of the north gate into the outer court. He brought me to the group of chambers opposite the temple yard and opposite the building to the north. 2 Along the length of the chambers, which was 175 feet,[G] there was an entrance on the north; the width was 87½ feet.[N] 3 Opposite the 35 foot space[D] belonging to the inner court and opposite the paved surface belonging to the outer court, the structure rose gallery by gallery in three tiers. 4 In front of the chambers was a walkway toward the inside, 17½ feet[O] wide and 175 feet[G] long,[P] and their entrances were on the north. 5 The upper chambers were narrower because the galleries took away more space from them than from the lower and middle stories of the building. 6 For they were arranged in three stories and had no pillars like the pillars of the courts; therefore the upper chambers were set back from the ground more

[A]**41:7,25,26** Hb obscure [B]**41:8** Lit *a full rod of six cubits of a joint*; Hb obscure [C]**41:9,11,12** Lit *five cubits* [D]**41:10; 42:3** Lit *20 cubits* [E]**41:12** Lit *70 cubits* [F]**41:12** Lit *90 cubits* [G]**41:13; 42:2,4** Lit *100 cubits* [H]**41:15** Or *ledges* [I]**41:21-22** Or *and in front of the sanctuary was something that looked like* [22] *an altar* [J]**41:22** Lit *three cubits* [K]**41:22** Lit *two cubits* [L]**41:22** LXX reads *long and 3½ feet wide* [M]**41:22** LXX reads *base* [N]**42:2** Lit *50 cubits* [O]**42:4** Lit *10 cubits* [P]**42:4** LXX, Syr; MT reads *wide, a way of one cubit*

than the lower and middle stories.
[7]A wall on the outside ran in front
of the chambers, parallel to them,
toward the outer court; it was 87½
feet[A] long. [8]For the chambers on
the outer court were 87½ feet long,
while those facing the great hall
were 175 feet[B] long. [9]At the base of
these chambers there was an entryway on the east side as one enters
them from the outer court.

[10]In the thickness of the wall of the
court toward the south,[C] there were
chambers facing the temple yard
and the western building, [11]with a
passageway in front of them, just
like the chambers that faced north.
Their length and width, as well as
all their exits, measurements, and
entrances, were identical. [12]The entrance at the beginning of the passageway, the way in front of the
corresponding[D] wall as one enters
on the east side, was similar to the
entrances of the chambers that were
on the south side.

[13]Then the man said to me, "The
northern and southern chambers
that face the temple yard are the
holy chambers where the priests
who approach the LORD will eat the
most holy offerings. There they will
deposit the most holy offerings—the
•grain offerings, •sin offerings, and
•restitution offerings—for the place
is holy. [14]Once the priests have entered, they must not go out from the
holy area to the outer court until
they have removed the clothes they
minister in, for these are holy. They
are to put on other clothes before
they approach the public area."

[15]When he finished measuring inside the temple complex, he led me
out by way of the gate that faced east
and measured all around the complex.

[16]He measured the east side
with a measuring rod;
it was 875 feet[E] by the
measuring rod.[F]
[17]He[G] measured the north side;
it was 875 feet[E] by the
measuring rod.[F]
[18]He[H] measured the south
side;
it was 875 feet[E] by the
measuring rod.[F]
[19]Then he turned to the west
side
and measured 875 feet[E] by
the measuring rod.[F]

[20]He measured the temple complex
on all four sides. It had a wall all
around it, 875 feet long and 875 feet
wide, to separate the holy from the
common.

The Return of the LORD's Glory and the Altar (43:1-27)

43 He led me to the gate, the one
that faces east, [2]and I saw the
glory of the God of Israel coming from
the east. His voice sounded like the
roar of mighty waters, and the earth
shone with His glory. [3]The vision I
saw was like the one I had seen when
He[I] came to destroy the city, and like
the ones I had seen by the Chebar Canal. I fell facedown. [4]The glory of the
LORD entered the temple by way of the
gate that faced east. [5]Then the Spirit
lifted me up and brought me to the
inner court, and the glory of the LORD
filled the temple.

[6]While the man was standing beside me, I heard someone speaking
to me from the temple. [7]He said to
me: "Son of man, this is the place
of My throne and the place for the
soles of My feet, where I will dwell
among the Israelites forever. The
house of Israel and their kings will
no longer defile My holy name by
their religious prostitution and by
the corpses[J] of their kings at their
•high places.[K] [8]Whenever they
placed their threshold next to My
threshold and their doorposts beside
My doorposts, with only a wall between Me and them, they were defiling My holy name by the detestable
acts they committed. So I destroyed
them in My anger. [9]Now let them
remove their prostitution and the
corpses[J] of their kings far from Me,
and I will dwell among them forever.

[10]"As for you, son of man, describe

[A]42:7 Lit *50 cubits* [B]42:8 Lit *100 cubits* [C]42:10 LXX; MT reads *east* [D]42:12 Or *protective*; Hb obscure [E]42:16,17,18,19 Lit *500 in rods* [F]42:16,17,18,19 Lit *rod all around* [G]42:17 LXX reads *Then he turned to the north and* [H]42:18 LXX reads *Then he turned to the south and* [I]43:3 Some Hb mss, Theod, Vg; other Hb mss, LXX, Syr read *I* [J]43:7,9 Or *monuments* [K]43:7 Some Hb mss, Theod, Tg read *their death*

42:20 The final verse elaborates on this concept, stating that the (perfectly square) wall around the temple complex was intended **to separate the holy from the common.** In these chapters, this instance is one of many in which God's transcendence, His awesome "otherness" is emphasized; however, there is simultaneously an insistence upon His immanence or presence with His people (e.g., 34:30-31; 43:7).

43:1-5 In this chapter, another restoration is detailed—that of Yahweh to His land and to His "throne" (v. 7) in His sanctuary. As Ezekiel had seen God abandon the temple defiled by idolatry, so he saw the Lord's glory returning to the new temple, which God Himself prepared. **The glory of the God of Israel** inspired as much awe and terror in him as during his initial visions at the **Chebar Canal.** Once more Ezekiel collapsed to the ground in awe and worship, and was eventually **lifted** up by the **Spirit.** He entered through **the gate . . . that faced east,** and Ezekiel saw the Lord's glory once more fill the temple, as in the days of Solomon when it was first dedicated, and even during Aaron's ministry in the wilderness tabernacle. This detail is significant since the east gate was also the gate through which God's glory had departed (chaps. 10–11). As Yahweh re-entered His palace/temple to take up residence as the rightful king, He did so by moving down the sacred path from the east gate in a straight line, past the altar, and to the holy of holies.

43:7-9 This place was to be His palace, the **place for the soles of . . .** [His] **feet.** God promises to **dwell among the Israelites forever** since this temple will never be defiled as the previous one had been. Three accusations surface here. The first—ritual **prostitution**—is clear from what has gone before. The second and third are more obscure. The reference to the **corpses of their kings** seems to indicate a royal cult of the dead, not actual burial places in the temple space. The reference to **thresholds** and **doorposts** is a violation of sacred space and could refer to the palace-sponsored building of altars and shrines to idols in the temple precincts. Up to this point, there is no human participation in the reconstruction of this heavenly temple. God alone builds it according to exact specifications, and He returns to **dwell among them forever** by His own gracious initiative. He prepared Himself a place without human assistance. The proximity of the king's palace (**only a wall between Me and them**) also possibly violated God's space, and in the new temple the walls would be thicker and the courtyard of the temple would be completely enclosed without direct and open access to the king's palace.

43:10-12 These verses contain the rationale for sharing these measurements and specifications with the exiles. When they hear an account and see what Ezekiel writes or draws **in their sight** of all that he had seen, they will be convicted of their sins. The exiles will be **ashamed** or humiliated when they consider how far short of the divine ideal they have fallen in their worship practices, specifically their lack of concern for preserving God's sanctity.

43:13-27 This portion describes the procedure necessary to cleanse and make atonement for **the altar** (v. 26). Before being restored to its proper function, the altar had to be properly consecrated by the Zadokite priests.

44:1-2 After His entrance from the outside through the east gate, the gate was closed and would remain closed to symbolize the permanence of the Lord's residence there.

44:3 This section gives some indication of the position of the monarchy with respect to the new order inaugurated by the Lord. In general, the monarchy is prohibited from carrying out priestly functions. The king will be indicted for injustice (chaps. 11, 45).

44:4 Once again Ezekiel's response to God's presence filling the temple is complete prostration, or perhaps he is overcome by the Lord's proximity.

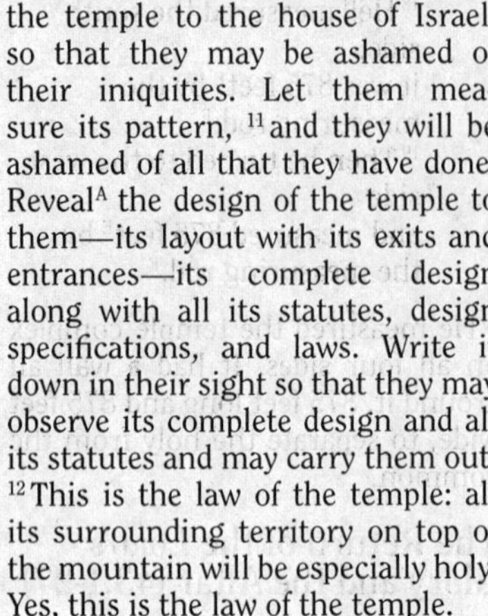

the temple to the house of Israel,
so that they may be ashamed of
their iniquities. Let them measure its pattern, 11 and they will be
ashamed of all that they have done.
Reveal[A] the design of the temple to
them—its layout with its exits and
entrances—its complete design
along with all its statutes, design
specifications, and laws. Write it
down in their sight so that they may
observe its complete design and all
its statutes and may carry them out.
12 This is the law of the temple: all
its surrounding territory on top of
the mountain will be especially holy.
Yes, this is the law of the temple.

13 "These are the measurements
of the altar in units of length (each
unit being the standard length plus
three inches):[B] the gutter is 21 inches[C] deep and 21 inches wide, with
a rim of nine inches[D] around its
edge. This is the base[E] of the altar.
14 The distance from the gutter on
the ground to the lower ledge is 3½
feet,[F] and the width of the ledge is 21
inches.[C] There are seven feet[G] from
the small ledge to the large ledge,
whose width is also 21 inches. 15 The
altar hearth[H] is seven feet[G] high,
and four horns project upward from
the hearth. 16 The hearth is square,
21 feet[I] long by 21 feet wide. 17 The
ledge is 24½ feet[J] long by 24½ feet
wide, with four equal sides. The rim
all around it is 10½ inches,[K] and its
gutter is 21 inches[C] all around it.
The altar's steps face east."

18 Then He said to me: "Son of man,
this is what the Lord God says: These
are the statutes for the altar on the
day it is constructed, so that •burnt
offerings may be sacrificed on it and
blood may be sprinkled on it: 19 You
are to give a bull from the herd as a
•sin offering to the Levitical priests
who are from the offspring of Zadok,
who approach Me in order to serve
Me." This is the declaration of the
Lord God. 20 "You must take some
of its blood and apply it to the four
horns of the altar, the four corners
of the ledge, and all around the rim.
In this way you will purify the altar
and make •atonement for it. 21 Then
you must take away the bull for the
sin offering, and it must be burned
outside the sanctuary in the place
appointed for the temple.

22 "On the second day you are to
present an unblemished male goat
as a sin offering. They will purify
the altar just as they did with the
bull. 23 When you have finished the
purification, you are to present a
young, unblemished bull and an
unblemished ram from the flock.
24 You must present them before the
Lord; the priests will throw salt on
them and sacrifice them as a burnt
offering to the Lord. 25 You will offer a goat for a sin offering each day
for seven days. A young bull and a
ram from the flock, both unblemished, must also be offered. 26 For
seven days the priests are to make
atonement for the altar and cleanse
it. In this way they will consecrate
it[L] 27 and complete the days of purification. Then on the eighth day and
afterward, the priests will offer your
burnt offerings and •fellowship offerings on the altar, and I will accept
you." This is the declaration of the
Lord God.

Sacrificial and Property Stipulations Pertaining to the Prince (44:1–46:24)

44 The man then brought me
back toward the sanctuary's
outer gate that faced east, and it
was closed. 2 The Lord said to me:
"This gate will remain closed. It
will not be opened, and no one
will enter through it, because the
Lord, the God of Israel, has entered
through it. Therefore it will remain
closed. 3 The prince himself will sit
in the gateway to eat a meal before
the Lord. He must enter by way
of the portico of the gate and go out
the same way."

4 Then the man brought me by
way of the north gate to the front of
the temple. I looked, and the glory
of the Lord filled His temple. And I
fell facedown. 5 The Lord said to me:

A 43:10-11 LXX, Vg; MT reads *pattern.* 11 *And if they are ashamed . . . done, reveal* B 43:13 Lit *in cubits (a cubit being a cubit plus a handbreadth)* C 43:13,14,17 Lit *one cubit* D 43:13 Lit *one span* E 43:13 LXX reads *height* F 43:14 Lit *two cubits* G 43:14,15 Lit *four cubits* H 43:15 Hb obscure I 43:16 Lit *12 cubits* J 43:17 Lit *14 cubits* K 43:17 Lit *one-half cubit* L 43:26 Lit *will fill its hands*

“Son of man, pay attention; look
with your eyes and listen with your
ears to everything I tell you about all
the statutes and laws of the LORD’s
temple. Take careful note of the entrance of the temple along with all
the exits of the sanctuary.
6 “Say to the rebellious people,
the house of Israel: This is what the
Lord GOD says: I have had enough of
all your detestable practices, house
of Israel. 7 When you brought in
foreigners, uncircumcised in both
heart and flesh, to occupy My sanctuary, you defiled My temple while
you offered My food—the fat and
the blood. You[A] broke My covenant
by all your detestable practices.
8 You have not kept charge of My
holy things but have appointed others to keep charge of My sanctuary
for you.
9 “This is what the Lord GOD says:
No foreigner, uncircumcised in
heart and flesh, may enter My sanctuary, not even a foreigner who is
among the Israelites. 10 Surely the
Levites who wandered away from
Me when Israel went astray, and
who strayed from Me after their
idols, will bear the consequences
of their sin. 11 Yet they will occupy
My sanctuary, serving as guards at
the temple gates and ministering at
the temple. They will slaughter the
•burnt offerings and other sacrifices
for the people and will stand before them to serve them. 12 Because
they ministered to the house of Israel before their idols and became
a sinful stumbling block to them,
therefore I swore an oath[B] against
them”—this is the declaration of
the Lord GOD—“that they would
bear the consequences of their sin.
13 They must not approach Me to
serve Me as priests or come near any
of My holy things or the most holy
things. They will bear their disgrace
and the consequences of the detestable acts they committed. 14 Yet I will
make them responsible for the duties of the temple—for all its work
and everything done in it.
15 “But the Levitical priests descended from Zadok, who kept
charge of My sanctuary when the
Israelites went astray from Me, will
approach Me to serve Me. They will
stand before Me to offer Me fat and
blood.” This is the declaration of the
Lord GOD. 16 “They are the ones who
may enter My sanctuary and draw
near to My table to serve Me. They
will keep My mandate. 17 When they
enter the gates of the inner court
they must wear linen garments;
they must not have on them anything made of wool when they minister at the gates of the inner court
and within it. 18 They must wear
linen turbans on their heads and
linen undergarments around their
waists. They are not to put on anything that makes them sweat. 19 Before they go out to the outer court,[C]
to the people, they must take off the
clothes they have been ministering
in, leave them in the holy chambers,
and dress in other clothes so that
they do not transmit holiness to the
people through their clothes.
20 “They may not shave their heads
or let their hair grow long, but must
carefully trim their hair. 21 No priest
may drink wine before he enters the
inner court. 22 He is not to marry
a widow or a divorced woman, but
must marry a virgin from the offspring of the house of Israel, or a
widow who is the widow of a priest.
23 They must teach My people the
difference between the holy and
the common, and explain to them
the difference between the •clean
and the •unclean.
24 “In a dispute, they will offici-
ate as judges and decide the case
according to My ordinances. They
must observe My laws and statutes
regarding all My appointed festivals, and keep My Sabbaths holy.
25 A priest may not come near a dead
person so that he becomes defiled.
However, he may defile himself for
a father, a mother, a son, a daughter,
a brother, or an unmarried sister.
26 After he is cleansed, he is to count
off seven days for himself. 27 On the
day he goes into the sanctuary, into
the inner court to minister in the
sanctuary, he must present his •sin
offering.” This is the declaration of
the Lord GOD.

44:6-9 The Lord brings some strong accusations against the priestly order, which had previously failed to respect God’s holiness by allowing **foreigners** to enter the temple. Those to whom Ezekiel refers here are unclear and unspecified, but possible referents might include the Gibeonites, who were assigned some lower-level temple duties (Jos 9:27), serving the Lord’s altar; or the Carites, from Caria in Asia Minor, who were recruited as royal guards who had access even to the temple (2Kg 11:4-11). By their presence, these **uncircumcised** foreigners defiled God’s sacred space, but the real culprits were the Israelites and the Levites who allowed this situation.

44:10-14 The precise occasions of the Levite’s apostasy are unspecified. Perhaps they had failed to protect/guard the sacred precinct as they were charged; therefore they will be demoted in a way, bearing the **consequences** of their apostasy. However, God does not completely reject them, and in the new temple they will serve as **guards at the temple gates,** ostensibly fulfilling their original assignment.

44:15-27 The Zadokite Levites are singled out for their loyalty to the Lord, and they are privileged to have charge of God’s “holy things” (v. 8). They alone would enter the sanctuary to minister before God. They had to keep themselves holy according to priestly specifications concerning dress, hair, diet, and ethics (vv. 17-23). They must also abide by the Holiness Code with respect to defilement by contact with a corpse (25-27). They were also charged with judging disputes in accordance with covenantal laws, and teaching the people **the difference between the holy and the common** so that God’s name and sanctuary would not be profaned as it had been previously (v. 23). This pattern is in stark contrast to what had transpired in the past, as illustrated by Ezekiel’s visions of abominations in the temple (chap. 8).

[A]**44:7** LXX, Syr, Vg; MT reads *They* [B]**44:12** Lit *I lifted My hand* [C]**44:19** Some Hb mss, LXX, Syr, Vg; other Hb mss read *court, to the outer court*

45:1-5 Provisions for dwellings were made for the Levites, who did not receive a tribal portion of land. Instead, their portion was the Lord and everything that belongs to Him (44:28-29; cp. Jos 14:4; 18:7).

45:7-12 While one tract was designated as the crown's land, the prince would be restricted from acquiring other land in order to guard against the crown's perpetrating property injustices against his subjects. These included **violence and oppression**, **evictions**, and the use of dishonest weights and measures or overcharging in the collection of taxes.

45:13-17 The prince was also entitled to sacrificial contributions (a kind of sacrifice tax) from the people, with which he would perform various seasonal sacrifices **on behalf of the house of Israel**. .

45:18-25 A ceremony is required for regular decontamination of the temple area to maintain its holiness and keep it cleansed from the people's sins (cp. Lv 16:19). The sacrifices, in which the **prince** participates, as during **Passover** and the Festival of Booths, are further sketched in verses 21-25.

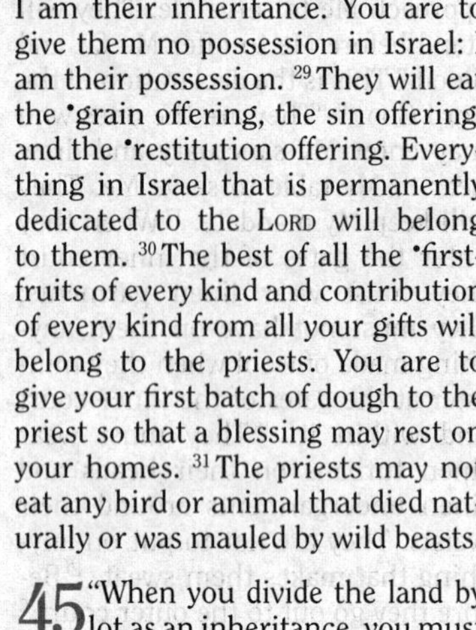

28 "This will be their inheritance: I am their inheritance. You are to give them no possession in Israel: I am their possession. 29 They will eat the •grain offering, the sin offering, and the •restitution offering. Everything in Israel that is permanently dedicated to the LORD will belong to them. 30 The best of all the •firstfruits of every kind and contribution of every kind from all your gifts will belong to the priests. You are to give your first batch of dough to the priest so that a blessing may rest on your homes. 31 The priests may not eat any bird or animal that died naturally or was mauled by wild beasts.

45 "When you divide the land by lot as an inheritance, you must set aside a donation to the LORD, a holy portion of the land, 8⅓ miles[A] long and 6⅔ miles[B] wide. This entire tract of land will be holy. 2 In this area there will be a square section[C] for the sanctuary, 875 by 875 feet,[D] with 87½ feet[E] of open space all around it. 3 From this holy portion,[F] you will measure off an area 8⅓ miles[A] long and 3⅓ miles[G] wide, in which the sanctuary, the most holy place, will stand.[H] 4 It will be a holy area of the land to be used by the priests who minister in the sanctuary, who draw near to serve the LORD. It will be a place for their houses, as well as a holy area for the sanctuary. 5 There will be another area 8⅓ miles[A] long and 3⅓ miles[G] wide for the Levites who minister in the temple; it will be their possession for towns to live in.[I]

6 "As the property of the city, you must set aside an area 1⅔ of a mile[J] wide and 8⅓ miles[A] long, adjacent to the holy donation of land. It will be for the whole house of Israel. 7 And the prince will have the area on each side of the holy donation of land and the city's property, adjacent to the holy donation and the city's property, stretching to the west on the west side and to the east on the east side. Its length will correspond to one of the tribal portions from the western boundary to the eastern boundary. 8 This will be his land as a possession in Israel. My princes will no longer oppress My people but give the rest of the land to the house of Israel according to their tribes.

9 "This is what the Lord GOD says: You have gone too far,[K] princes of Israel! Put away violence and oppression and do what is just and right. Put an end to your evictions of My people." This is the declaration of the Lord GOD. 10 "You must have honest scales, an honest dry measure,[L] and an honest liquid measure.[M] 11 The dry measure[N] and the liquid measure[O] will be uniform, with the liquid measure containing 5½ gallons[P] and the dry measure holding half a bushel.[P] Their measurement will be a tenth of the standard larger capacity measure.[Q] 12 The •shekel will weigh 20 *gerahs*. Your mina will equal 60 shekels.

13 "This is the contribution you are to offer: Three quarts[R] from five bushels[S] of wheat and[T] three quarts from five bushels of barley. 14 The quota of oil in liquid measures[U] will be one percent of every[V] cor. The cor equals 10 liquid measures or one standard larger capacity measure,[W] since 10 liquid measures equal one standard larger capacity measure. 15 And the quota from the flock is one animal out of every 200 from the well-watered pastures of Israel. These are for the •grain offerings, •burnt offerings, and •fellowship offerings, to make •atonement for the people." This is the declaration of the Lord GOD. 16 "All the people of the land must take part in this contribution for the prince in Israel. 17 Then the burnt offerings, grain offerings, and •drink offerings for the festivals, New Moons, and Sabbaths—for all the appointed times of the house of Israel—will be the prince's responsibility. He will provide the •sin

[A] **45:1,3,5,6** Lit *25,000 cubits* [B] **45:1** LXX reads *20,000 cubits*; MT reads *10,000 cubits* [C] **45:2** Lit *square all around* [D] **45:2** Lit *500 by 500 cubits* [E] **45:2** Lit *50 cubits* [F] **45:3** Lit *this measured portion* [G] **45:3,5** Lit *10,000 cubits* [H] **45:3** Lit *be* [I] **45:5** LXX; MT, Syr, Tg, Vg read *possession—20 chambers* [J] **45:6** Lit *5,000 cubits* [K] **45:9** Lit *Enough of you* [L] **45:10** Lit *an honest ephah* [M] **45:10** Lit *and an honest bath* [N] **45:11** Lit *the ephah* [O] **45:11** Lit *the bath* [P] **45:11** Lit *one-tenth of a homer* [Q] **45:11** Lit *be based on the homer* [R] **45:13** Lit *One-sixth of an ephah* [S] **45:13** Lit *a homer* [T] **45:13** LXX, Vg; MT reads *and you are to give* [U] **45:14** Lit *oil, the bath, the oil* [V] **45:14** Lit *be a tenth of the bath from the* [W] **45:14** Lit *10 baths, a homer*

offerings, grain offerings, burnt offerings, and fellowship offerings to make atonement on behalf of the house of Israel.

18 "This is what the Lord God says: In the first month, on the first day of the month, you are to take a young, unblemished bull and purify the sanctuary. 19 The priest must take some of the blood from the sin offering and apply it to the temple doorposts, the four corners of the altar's ledge, and the doorposts of the gate to the inner court. 20 You must do the same thing on the seventh day of the month for everyone who sins unintentionally or through ignorance. In this way you will make atonement for the temple.

21 "In the first month, on the fourteenth day of the month, you are to celebrate the •Passover, a festival of seven days during which unleavened bread will be eaten. 22 On that day the prince will provide a bull as a sin offering on behalf of himself and all the people of the land. 23 During the seven days of the festival, he will provide seven bulls and seven rams without blemish as a burnt offering to the Lord on each of the seven days, along with a male goat each day for a sin offering. 24 He will also provide a grain offering of half a bushel[A] per bull and half a bushel per ram, along with a gallon[B] of oil for every half bushel. 25 At the festival that begins on the fifteenth day of the seventh month,[C] he will provide the same things for seven days—the same sin offerings, burnt offerings, grain offerings, and oil.

46 "This is what the Lord God says: The gate of the inner court that faces east must be closed during the six days of work, but it will be opened on the Sabbath day and opened on the day of the New Moon. 2 The prince should enter from the outside by way of the gate's portico and stand at the doorpost of the gate while the priests sacrifice his •burnt offerings and •fellowship offerings. He will bow in worship at the threshold of the gate and then depart, but the gate must not be closed until evening. 3 The people of the land will also bow in worship before the Lord at the entrance of that gate on the Sabbaths and New Moons.

4 "The burnt offering that the prince presents to the Lord on the Sabbath day is to be six unblemished lambs and an unblemished ram. 5 The •grain offering will be half a bushel[A] with the ram, and the grain offering with the lambs will be whatever he wants to give, as well as a gallon[B] of oil for every half bushel. 6 On the day of the New Moon, the burnt offering is to be a young, unblemished bull, as well as six lambs and a ram without blemish. 7 He will provide a grain offering of half a bushel[A] with the bull, half a bushel with the ram, and whatever he can afford with the lambs, together with a gallon[B] of oil for every half bushel. 8 When the prince enters, he must go in by way of the gate's portico and go out the same way.

9 "When the people of the land come before the Lord at the appointed times,[D] whoever enters by way of the north gate to worship must go out by way of the south gate, and whoever enters by way of the south gate must go out by way of the north gate. No one must return through the gate by which he entered, but must go out by the opposite gate. 10 When the people enter, the prince will enter with them, and when they leave, he will leave. 11 At the festivals and appointed times, the grain offering will be half a bushel[A] with the bull, half a bushel with the ram, and whatever he wants to give with the lambs, along with a gallon[B] of oil for every half bushel.

12 "When the prince makes a freewill offering, whether a burnt offering or a fellowship offering as a freewill offering to the Lord, the gate that faces east must be opened for him. He is to offer his burnt offering or fellowship offering just as he does on the Sabbath day. Then he will go out, and the gate must be closed after he leaves.

13 "You must offer an unblemished year-old male lamb as a daily burnt

46:1-9 The Lord explained how **the Sabbath day and . . . the day of the New Moon** should be observed and how **the people of the land** should **come before the Lord at the appointed times** (v. 9). There is a pronounced focus on **the prince** and his movements within the temple complex at times of worship (cp. vv. 4,8,10,12,16-18). As previously, although the prince received certain privileges, his movements were also restricted, and his status as cultic functionary would be associated more with the people (laity) than with the priests. The east gate into the inner court was opened on these feast days, and the prince entered from the outer court and stood in the doorway while his sacrifices were being offered. He was prohibited from going any further inside, worshiping only from the threshold. The people were also permitted the privilege of worshiping from that gate, thereby associating the king with the "people of the land" (commoners) rather than with the priesthood.

46:4-15 Verses 4-8 and 11-15 detail the sacrifices offered for Sabbaths, New Moons, and daily observances. Verses 9-10 seem to specify certain patterns of movement within the outer courtyard for the sake of symmetry and order. These movements characterize the entire new temple and new city, or possibly these movements were required for the more practical reasons of crowd control at particularly busy worship times. Again, the prince's solidarity with the **people of the land** is shown as he and they entered and left together (v. 10).

[A]45:24; 46:5,7,11 Lit *an ephah* [B]45:24; 46:5,7,11 Lit *a hin* [C]45:25 = the Festival of Booths [D]46:9 Or *the festivals*

46:16-24 By ensuring that crown land remained within the ownership and purview of the king, the Lord guaranteed that the people would never again be **displaced from** [their] **own property** (v. 18). The Lord showed Ezekiel the kitchens where sacrificial meals were cooked. These two kitchens contribute to the theme of gradations of sanctity within the temple complex. One kitchen, used only by the priests, was in the inner court, manifesting a concern to preserve holiness (v. 20). The other kitchen in the outer court was used to **cook the people's sacrifices** (v. 24).

47:1-2 A beautiful section in this chapter describes the healing of the land by the life-giving river, followed by the reallotment of the tribal territories. Ezekiel had prophesied that the land would be healed and would become "like the garden of Eden" (36:35). In this chapter, a glimpse is given as to how this is fulfilled. The similarity of imagery between 47:1-12, and Gn 2:8-10 on the one side, and Rv 22:1-21 on the other side is unmistakable. The river of Gn 2:10 is in the primordial past; the "river of living water" of Rv 22:1 awaits the apocalyptic future, while the life-giving river of Ezekiel's vision perhaps stands somewhere in between. Several similarities and distinctions are worth noting in the text. First, the **river** of Ezk 47:9 flows out from **under the threshold of the temple**. Similarly, in Rv 22:1 the river flows from under the throne of God and the Lamb (representing both the sacrificial system *and* its supersession by the once-for-all atoning sacrifice of Christ, the Lamb of God).

47:3-5 The river deepens substantially every **third of a mile,** quickly becoming deep enough for swimming. If it continued at that rate, Ezekiel is left to marvel at the size and depth and power of such a river, which began as a trickle.

47:7-10 The reference to Eden in Ezk 36:35 ties it to Gn 2. In Ezekiel the river flows out from the temple and out of the holy city, watering and reviving the entire countryside all the way down to the **sea of foul water** (the Dead Sea), which will become **fresh**, allowing multitudes of **fish** and other water **creatures** to live and thrive. The deadness of the land (desert) and sea (Salt Sea) is healed by the life-giving river.

offering to the LORD; you will offer
it every morning. 14 You must also
prepare a grain offering every morning along with it: three quarts,[A] with
one-third of a gallon[B] of oil to moist-
en the fine flour—a grain offering
to the LORD. This is a permanent
statute to be observed regularly.
15 They will offer the lamb, the grain
offering, and the oil every morning
as a regular burnt offering.
16 "This is what the Lord GOD says:
If the prince gives a gift to each of
his sons as their inheritance, it will
belong to his sons. It will become
their property by inheritance. 17 But
if he gives a gift from his inheritance to one of his servants, it will
belong to that servant until the year
of freedom, when it will revert to the
prince. His inheritance belongs only
to his sons; it is theirs. 18 The prince
must not take any of the people's inheritance, evicting them from their
property. He is to provide an inheritance for his sons from his own
property, so that none of My people
will be displaced from his own property."
19 Then he brought me through
the entrance that was at the side
of the gate, into the priests' holy
chambers, which faced north. I saw
a place there at the far western end.
20 He said to me, "This is the place
where the priests will boil the •resti-
tution offering and the •sin offering,
and where they will bake the grain
offering, so that they do not bring
them into the outer court and transmit holiness to the people." 21 Next
he brought me into the outer court
and led me past its four corners.
There was a separate court in each
of its corners. 22 In the four corners
of the outer court there were enclosed[C] courts, 70 feet[D] long by 52½
feet[E] wide. All four corner areas had
the same dimensions. 23 There was
a stone wall[F] around the inside of
them, around the four of them, with
ovens built at the base of the walls
on all sides. 24 He said to me: "These
are the kitchens where those who
minister at the temple will cook the
people's sacrifices."

The Healing and Reallotment of the Land (47:1–48:29)

The River of Life (47:1-12)

47 Then he brought me back to
the entrance of the temple and
there was water flowing from under
the threshold of the temple toward
the east, for the temple faced east.
The water was coming down from
under the south side of the threshold of the temple, south of the altar.
2 Next he brought me out by way of
the north gate and led me around
the outside to the outer gate that
faced east; there the water was trick-
ling from the south side. 3 As the
man went out east with a measuring line in his hand, he measured
off a third of a mile[G] and led me
through the water. It came up to
my ankles. 4 Then he measured off a
third of a mile[G] and led me through
the water. It came up to my knees.
He measured off another third of a
mile[G] and led me through the water.
It came up to my waist. 5 Again he
measured off a third of a mile[G], and
it was a river that I could not cross
on foot. For the water had risen; it
was deep enough to swim in, a river
that could not be crossed on foot.
6 He asked me, "Do you see this,
son of man?" Then he led me back
to the bank of the river. 7 When I had
returned, I saw a very large number
of trees along both sides of the riverbank. 8 He said to me, "This water
flows out to the eastern region and
goes down to the •Arabah. When it
enters the sea, the sea of foul water,[H,I] the water of the sea becomes
fresh. 9 Every kind of living creature
that swarms will live wherever the
river flows,[J] and there will be a huge
number of fish because this water
goes there. Since the water will become fresh, there will be life everywhere the river goes. 10 Fishermen
will stand beside it from En-gedi
to En-eglaim.[K] These will become
places where nets are spread out to

[A] **46:14** Lit *one-sixth of an ephah* [B] **46:14** Lit *one-third of a hin* [C] **46:22** Hb obscure [D] **46:22** Lit *40 cubits* [E] **46:22** Lit *30 cubits* [F] **46:23** Or *a row* [G] **47:3,4,5** Lit *1,000 cubits* [H] **47:8** Or *enters the sea, being brought out to the sea*; Hb obscure [I] **47:8** = the Dead Sea [J] **47:9** LXX, Vg; MT reads *the two rivers flow* [K] **47:10** Two springs near the Dead Sea

dry. Their fish will consist of many
different kinds, like the fish of the
Mediterranean Sea. 11 Yet its swamps
and marshes will not be healed; they
will be left for salt. 12 All kinds of
trees providing food will grow along
both banks of the river. Their leaves
will not wither, and their fruit will
not fail. Each month they will bear
fresh fruit because the water comes
from the sanctuary. Their fruit will
be used for food and their leaves for
medicine."

Geographical Borders and Tribal Allotments (47:13–48:29)

13 This is what the Lord God says:
"This is[A] the border you will use to
divide the land as an inheritance
for the 12 tribes of Israel. Joseph
will receive two shares. 14 You will
inherit it in equal portions, since I
swore[B] to give it to your ancestors.
So this land will fall to you as an inheritance.
15 "This is to be the border of the
land:

On the north side it will extend
from the Mediterranean Sea
by way of Hethlon and Lebo-
hamath to Zedad,[C] 16 Berothah,
and Sibraim (which is between
the border of Damascus and
the border of Hamath), as far
as Hazer-hatticon, which is on
the border of Hauran. 17 So the
border will run from the sea
to Hazar-enon at the border of
Damascus, with the territory of
Hamath to the north. This will
be the northern side.

18 On the east side it will run between Hauran and Damascus,
along the Jordan between Gilead and the land of Israel; you
will measure from the northern border to the eastern sea.[D]
This will be the eastern side.

19 On the south side it will run
from Tamar to the waters of
Meribath-kadesh,[E] and on to
the Brook of Egypt as far as the
Mediterranean Sea. This will be
the southern side.

20 On the west side the Mediterranean Sea will be the border,
from the southern border up to
a point opposite Lebo-hamath.
This will be the western side.

21 "You are to divide this land
among yourselves according to the
tribes of Israel. 22 You will allot it as
an inheritance for yourselves and
for the foreigners living among
you, who have fathered children
among you. You will treat them[F]
like native-born Israelites; along
with you, they will be allotted an inheritance among the tribes of Israel.
23 In whatever tribe the foreigner
lives, you will assign his inheritance
there." This is the declaration of the
Lord God.

48 "Now these are the names of
the tribes:

From the northern end, along
the road of Hethlon, to Lebo-
hamath as far as Hazar-enon,
at the northern border of
Damascus, alongside Hamath
and extending from the
eastern side to the sea, will be
Dan—one portion.
2 Next to the territory of Dan,
from the east side to the west,
will be Asher—one portion.
3 Next to the territory
of Asher, from the east
side to the west, will be
Naphtali—one portion.
4 Next to the territory of
Naphtali, from the east
side to the west, will be
Manasseh—one portion.
5 Next to the territory of
Manasseh, from the east
side to the west, will be
Ephraim—one portion.
6 Next to the territory of
Ephraim, from the east
side to the west, will be
Reuben—one portion.
7 Next to the territory of
Reuben, from the east side to
the west, will be Judah—one
portion.

8 "Next to the territory of Judah,
from the east side to the west, will
be the portion you donate to the

47:12 The trees along the **banks of the river** are not identified as "the tree of life" in Ezekiel (v. 7). In Gn 3:22-24, however, the tree of life is in the center; and in Rv 22:2, the tree of life grows along the banks of the river down the streets of the city (cp. Rv 2:7; 22:14,19). The trees provide food every month as they are watered from the sanctuary, the source of their life. Their **leaves will not wither** and will be used **for medicine** (cp. "for healing," Rv 22:2). The beautiful images of living water flowing out of the temple in Ezekiel and Revelation are fulfilled in Christ, who referred to His own body as the temple (Jn 2:21) and promised that "streams of living water [i.e., the Holy Spirit, would] flow from deep within" those who believe in Him (Jn 7:37-39). The imagery of Ezekiel also speaks to the Spirit's work of regeneration and of Jesus' admonition to Nicodemus that one must be "born of water and the Spirit" (Jn 3:3,5-8).

47:13-23 This section outlines the new divisions of the land, followed by tribal allotments. First, the total boundaries of the land are given (vv. 13-20), making some provision for **foreigners living among** them as well (v. 21). These non-ethnic Israelites are different than those who pollute the sacred space (43:9). Rather, these are proselytes who have **fathered children** and who participate in the spiritual life of the community.

48:1-14 Once the boundaries of the land had been determined, specific lots are assigned to the tribes (vv. 1-7,23-29). Levi possessed only the sacred land (44:28; 48:13-14), while the two half-tribes of Joseph (named after his sons Ephraim and Manasseh) each received a portion of land. The divisions are listed from north (near **Hamath**) to south and down to Kadesh-barnea, with a swath of land between Benjamin and Judah reserved for the Lord, and specifically for the Zadokite priests (vv. 8-12), adjacent to land for the Levites (vv. 13-14). The Lord's land is measured, indicating a completely square area.

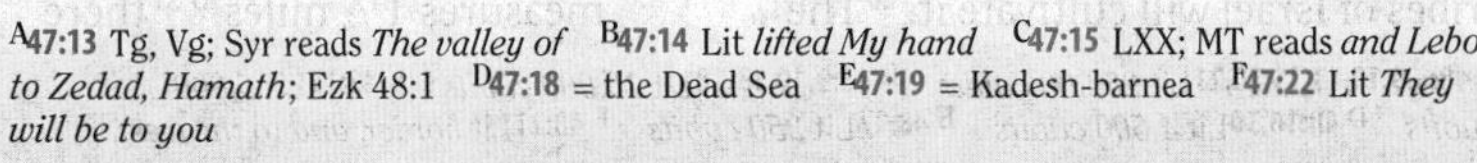
A 47:13 Tg, Vg; Syr reads *The valley of to Zedad, Hamath*; Ezk 48:1 B 47:14 Lit *lifted My hand* C 47:15 LXX; MT reads *and Lebo* D 47:18 = the Dead Sea E 47:19 = Kadesh-barnea F 47:22 Lit *They will be to you*

48:15-22 Within it stands the city, whose measurements also result in a perfect square. Alongside the holy, priestly portion of land, there was a portion of cultivated land to produce food for **the city's workers** (vv. 18-19), and the remaining area was to be crown property.

LORD, $8\frac{1}{3}$ miles[A] wide, and as long as
one of the tribal portions from the
east side to the west. The sanctuary
will be in the middle of it.
9 "The special portion you donate to
the LORD will be $8\frac{1}{3}$ miles[A] long and
$3\frac{1}{3}$ miles[B] wide. 10 This holy donation
will be set apart for the priests alone.
It will be $8\frac{1}{3}$ miles[A] long on the
northern side, $3\frac{1}{3}$ miles[B] wide on the
western side, $3\frac{1}{3}$ miles[B] wide on the
eastern side, and $8\frac{1}{3}$ miles[A] long on
the southern side. The LORD's sanctu-
ary will be in the middle of it. 11 It is
for the consecrated priests, the sons
of Zadok, who kept My charge and
did not go astray as the Levites did
when the Israelites went astray. 12 It
will be a special donation for them
out of the holy donation of the land,
a most holy place adjacent to the territory of the Levites.
13 "Next to the territory of the
priests, the Levites will have an area
$8\frac{1}{3}$ miles[A] long and $3\frac{1}{3}$ miles[B] wide.
The total length will be $8\frac{1}{3}$ miles[A]
and the width $3\frac{1}{3}$ miles.[B] 14 They
must not sell or exchange any of
it, and they must not transfer this
choice part of the land, for it is holy
to the LORD.
15 "The remaining area, $1\frac{2}{3}$ of a
mile[C] wide and $8\frac{1}{3}$ miles[A] long, will
be for common use by the city, for
both residential and open space.
The city will be in the middle of it.
16 These are the city's measurements:

$1\frac{1}{2}$ miles[D] on the north side;
$1\frac{1}{2}$ miles[D] on the south side;
$1\frac{1}{2}$ miles[D] on the east side;
and $1\frac{1}{2}$ miles[D] on the west
side.

17 The city's open space will extend:

425 feet[E] to the north,
425 feet[E] to the south,
425 feet[E] to the east,
and 425 feet[E] to the west.

18 "The remainder of the length
alongside the holy donation will be
$3\frac{1}{3}$ miles[B] to the east and $3\frac{1}{3}$ miles[B]
to the west. It will run alongside
the holy donation. Its produce will
be food for the workers of the city.
19 The city's workers from all the
tribes of Israel will cultivate it. 20 The
entire donation will be $8\frac{1}{3}$ miles[A] by
$8\frac{1}{3}$ miles;[A] you are to set apart the
holy donation along with the city
property as a square area.
21 "The remaining area on both
sides of the holy donation and the
city property will belong to the
prince. He will own the land adjacent to the tribal portions, next to
the $8\frac{1}{3}$ miles[A] of the donation as
far as the eastern border and[F] next
to the $8\frac{1}{3}$ miles[A] of the donation as
far as the western border. The holy
donation and the sanctuary of the
temple will be in the middle of it.
22 Except for the Levitical property
and the city property in the middle
of the area belonging to the prince,
the area between the territory of
Judah and that of Benjamin will belong to the prince.
23 "As for the rest of the tribes:

From the east side to the
west, will be Benjamin—one
portion.
24 Next to the territory of
Benjamin, from the east
side to the west, will be
Simeon—one portion.
25 Next to the territory of
Simeon, from the east
side to the west, will be
Issachar—one portion.
26 Next to the territory of
Issachar, from the east
side to the west, will be
Zebulun—one portion.
27 Next to the territory of
Zebulun, from the east side
to the west, will be Gad—one
portion.

28 Next to the territory of Gad toward
the south side, the border will run
from Tamar to the waters of Meribath-kadesh, to the Brook of Egypt,
and out to the Mediterranean Sea.
29 This is the land you are to allot as
an inheritance to Israel's tribes, and
these will be their portions." This is
the declaration of the Lord GOD.

The New City (48:30-35)

30 "These are the exits of the city:

On the north side, which
measures $1\frac{1}{2}$ miles,[D] 31 there

A **48:8,9,10,13,15,20,21** Lit *25,000 cubits* B **48:9,10,13,18** Lit *10,000 cubits* C **48:15** Lit *5,000 cubits* D **48:16,30** Lit *4,500 cubits* E **48:17** Lit *250 cubits* F **48:21** Lit *border, and to the west,*

will be three gates facing
north, the gates of the city
being named for the tribes
of Israel: one, the gate of
Reuben; one, the gate of
Judah; and one, the gate of
Levi.
32 On the east side, which is
$1\frac{1}{2}$ miles,[A] there will be three
gates: one, the gate of Joseph;
one, the gate of Benjamin;
and one, the gate of Dan.
33 On the south side, which
measures $1\frac{1}{2}$ miles,[A] there
will be three gates: one, the
gate of Simeon; one, the gate
of Issachar; and one, the gate
of Zebulun.
34 On the west side, which is
$1\frac{1}{2}$ miles,[A] there will be three
gates: one, the gate of Gad;
one, the gate of Asher; and
one, the gate of Naphtali.

35 The perimeter of the city will be
six miles,[B] and the name of the city
from that day on will be: •Yahweh Is
There."

[A]48:32,33,34 Lit *4,500 cubits* [B]48:35 Lit *18,000 cubits*

48:30-35 The final image is of the new city, a prospect for which Ezekiel's listeners yearned. Each of the **gates of the city** is named for a tribe, looking forward to the "new Jerusalem" (Rv 21:2,9-14), with three gates on each of the four sides of the city's walls. Appropriately, the book of Ezekiel concludes with one final new thing. After giving His people a new heart and new spirit, constructing a new temple in a new city surrounded by renewed land fed by a river of new life, the Lord sealed the city with a new name. Rather than the old name, Jerusalem, the city is named **Yahweh Is There**, compounding the significance and reiterating the hope of the Lord's presence with His people. This prophecy finds its ultimate fulfillment for the church in Jesus the Messiah, who is Immanuel, "God with us" (Is 7:14; Mt 1:23).

EZEKIEL... WRITTEN ON MY *Heart*

Ezekiel is a hard book to digest. Over half of it contains harsh condemnation and judgment against Israel and other nations. At times, these judgments are allegorized in feminine terms. However, several gems are gleaned from this amazing book. Ezekiel affirms that God is perfectly holy and is concerned about His people's holiness; this was also Ezekiel's concern as a priest and ought to be the concern of those in the church, which 1Pt 2:9 calls "a royal priesthood" and "a holy nation." As Christian women, we ought to be vitally concerned and intentional about maintaining personal holiness regarding our morality, sexual ethics, appearance, and demeanor in order to please the holy God. As Christian mothers, we ought to invest ourselves in being proactive with respect to teaching and building personal holiness in our children, and encouraging it lovingly in our husbands. As ministry workers, we should mentor women—both young and old, married and single—being wise to teach them "the difference between the holy and the common" (Ezk 44:23), and we must model it ourselves. As one who kept himself holy even in exile away from the temple, which was to be his life's work, Ezekiel stood in stark contrast to his countrymen, who were idolaters both "back home" in Jerusalem as well as "abroad" in exile in Babylon. These exiles (and our culture) had little clue about the meaning of holiness. In a sense, we too are exiles in the world, as "our citizenship is in Heaven" (Php 3:20). In our world, we can be agents of a renewed understanding of and emphasis upon holiness. Like Ezekiel (and his contemporary Daniel), we also must keep ourselves holy and unstained in the midst of what Paul called "a crooked and perverted generation" among whom we are to "shine like stars in the world" (Php 2:15). To this end, we are at an advantage compared to Ezekiel's audience. We are not alone in the struggle for personal holiness, nor is the struggle against sin hopeless. After providing forgiveness and atonement for us, God has given His Spirit to renew, restore, and assist us in reflecting His holiness with the hope of future resurrection and complete transformation of our sinful lives. We engage in the effort toward holiness knowing that our bodies are a sanctuary for the Holy Spirit (1Co 6:19-20); and as God emphasized the absolute necessity for holiness in the new temple (Ezk 40–48), we need to maintain our own sanctuary in purity and holiness if we are to experience the blessing of our Holy God and the glory of His presence.

Daniel

Timeline

- World Events
- Biblical Events

620 BC	605 BC	602 BC	586 BC	573–566 BC
Birth of Daniel	Fall of Jerusalem to Nebuchadnezzar during Jehoiakim's reign	Daniel's interpretation of Nebuchadnezzar's statue dream	Destruction of the temple in Jerusalem	Nebuchadnezzar's seven years of insanity

"I saw One like a son of man coming with the clouds of heaven . . . . His dominion is an everlasting dominion that will not pass away" (7:13-14).

Who wrote Daniel?

The book of Daniel bears the name of its author (1:6; 7:2; 8:1; 9:2; 10:2; 12:5). Daniel was a teenager when he was taken to Babylon about 605 B.C. He and his three friends were of noble or royal Judean lineage (1:3). He served in the Babylonian administration during the successive reigns of several Babylonian and Medo-Persian kings.

Who were the recipients?

The book of Daniel is written both in classical Hebrew and in Aramaic. The former was Daniel's native language, and its use points to a primarily Jewish audience. Aramaic was the official and legal language of the empire, giving evidence that the Gentiles using that language were included among the book's intended readers.

When was Daniel written?

Although many modern critical scholars contest Danielic authorship and posit a second-century BC author (ca 165 B.C.), the traditional view asserts that the book was composed in the sixth century B.C., at the time of the events described, over the course of the prophet Daniel's long life (ca 620–530 B.C.). Both manuscript and linguistic evidence supports the sixth-century dating.

Where did it happen?

The contents of the book take place in Babylon during the Babylonian exile, which began under King Nebuchadnezzar. Daniel opens with a description of the events when he and his friends were taken to Babylon (ca 605 B.C.) and ends in the reign of Cyrus of Persia (third year of his reign, ca 536 B.C.).

What is Daniel about?

- *God's sovereignty over all nations.* Daniel's perspective on the Babylonian exile indicates that God is the agent who "handed Jehoiakim king of Judah" to Nebuchadnezzar (1:2). Daniel tells Nebuchadnezzar that he is "king of kings" because "the God of heaven has given you sovereignty" (2:37). Daniel also affirms in prayer that God "changes the times and seasons; He removes kings and establishes kings" (2:21).
- *God's providence in a foreign land.* God was faithful to His covenant with Abraham (9:4), having brought Israel to the promised land of Canaan. God is also just and righteous, and He punishes according to the stipulations of the Mosaic covenant (Dt 29; Dn 9:11-14). Despite their sin, God still had plans to prosper His people (Jr 29:11), to cleanse, forgive, and restore them (Ezk 36:22-28), promises that were made even before they entered the land (Dt 30:1-10, especially v. 6). Daniel claimed these promises and even lived to see the beginning of their fulfillment in the return of the exiles to Jerusalem (Dan 9:2,17-19; 10:1). Jeremiah advised the Jews to pray for their Babylonian overlords (Jr 29:4-7) so that both nations would prosper. Indeed, God raised up faithful leaders such as Daniel, as well as encouraging him with visions through his ministry.
- *Encouragement for God's people to be uncompromising in their worship and devotion.* The young men could have used their exile, distance from Jerusalem, and indeed, the destruction of their worship sanctuary as excuses for why the rules of their faith and practice no longer applied. Yet in the years of their youth as much as in adulthood and old age, Daniel and his companions demonstrate uncompromising faith, even at the risk of their lives (1:8; 3:18; 6:10). God had called Israel to be a nation set apart (holy) as a witness to the Gentiles, and this group of exiles determined to remain holy even as their nation was disciplined by the Babylonian subjugation.
- *God's sovereignty over history, as He reveals the future to His servant.* God is not bound by the circumstances of human history, political exigencies, or imperialistic ambitions. As the "Ancient of Days" who changes times, seasons, and rulers (2:21; 7:9-10), God is above the flow of time and human history. As the Jews have been captured and engulfed once again by a Gentile nation, God reveals from the throne room of heaven His plan to fulfill His covenantal promises. These plans are assured and non-negotiable and will be carried out in God's own time by His messengers and heavenly agents (10:13,21). Two parallel worlds appear in this book, one earthly and temporal, the other heavenly and eternal. The kings of the earth may hold sway at one period or another, but the "Most High" God and His Messiah hold eternal sway over the universe and its destiny. Daniel's visions provide glimpses of this supernatural parallel universe.

Why should women read Daniel?

Women as well as men derive comfort and assurance that God is in control of the times, of nations and governments. This book encourages the faithful to trust God: He is taking history to the conclusion He has planned for it, and its destiny is something good that glorifies Him. Such a perspective also encourages believers to look beyond personal circumstances and take an eternal perspective, praying for divine insight into God's dealings with the world and what role he would assign to each believer. The book follows Daniel on his life journey, from a young man (teenager) to an old man, all the while living a life without compromise as an exile in a foreign land. His life of faithful and uncompromising devotion gained him favor with

562 BC	560 BC	556 BC	553 BC
Evil-merodach, the son of Nebuchadnezzar, assumes the throne.	Murder of Evil-merodach by Nergal-sharezer, Nebuchadnezzar's son-in-law, who takes the throne	Leadership turnover in Babylon until Nabonidus assumes the throne (Nergal-sharezer dies; Nebuchadnezzar's grandson Labashi-marduk becomes king but is assassinated); birth of Belshazzar, son of Nabonidus	First year of Belshazzar's reign as co-regent

God and the privilege of receiving powerful visions, which encouraged the Jews that God was with His people and revealed Himself to them even in their time of punishment. His life of integrity as a wise man distinguished him from his administrative peers and garnered the respect of the ruling authorities.

Another aspect of the book has to do with Daniel's unseen and unknown parents. Jeremiah's description of the covenant compromises in Judah in the decades before Jerusalem's fall indicates that idolatry was often a family affair, with the participation of both parents and children (Jr 7:17-20). Daniel's determination to remain pure in an apostate culture that did not acknowledge God as Lord is all the more amazing, and may be attributed to godly parents, and quite possibly to godly leaders such as the zealous King Josiah, whose religious reforms may have been sincerely heeded by the noble families of Daniel and his friends and others. The critical value of faithful parents and leaders is here underscored. If the next generation is to be equipped to face the challenges of a sinful culture that seduces with promises of greatness in exchange for moral and spiritual compromise, parents must take their assignment to prepare the next generation very seriously.

How do you read Daniel?

The book of Daniel is generally divided into two distinct sections. The first, containing accounts of Daniel and his friends, is primarily historical narrative. The second, featuring the dreams and visions of the future, is primarily prophetic and belongs to the genre of apocalyptic literature. The Greek word *apokalupsis* suggests an "unveiling of that which has been concealed; a revelation, disclosure." Like prophetic material, apocalyptic literature features God-given revelation concerning future events. Through visions saturated with symbolism, the apocalyptic section heavily emphasizes what will happen "at the time of the end," a refrain in chapters 11 and 12. For the modern reader, unaware of the history of the Jews in the second century B.C., the final few chapters can prove confusing and foreign. However, perseverance in reading the text, along with notes on its background, will yield a fruitful understanding of the book's message for Daniel's future as well as for the modern era; indeed, some of the events related have not yet taken place. Not least among these promised events "at the end of days" is the resurrection of the dead to either "eternal life" or "eternal contempt." Resurrection in these terms (which approximate the NT teaching so closely) appears only in Daniel 12 in the Old Testament canon. Written in the midst of persecution, oppression, or crisis, apocalyptic literature offers assurance of God's sovereignty over all history and the promise of His ultimate triumph over all evil powers.

Another way to divide the book is linguistically. Daniel's material has been recorded in two languages: Dn 1:1-2:4 and 8:1–12:13 are written in classical Hebrew and are apparently directed at the captive Israelites; Dn 2:4–7:28 is written in Aramaic, the official and legal language of the Persian empire, giving evidence that the Gentiles using that language were included among the book's intended readers. This feature strengthens the book's theme that God is interested in revealing Himself to and among Gentiles as well as His own people and that His sovereignty extends over all people.

Within the context of the biblical canon, Daniel is important for his descriptions of the "Ancient of Days" and the "son of man" (Dn 7:9-10, 13); imagery from these passages is applied to the risen Jesus in the book of Revelation (1:13-18; 2:18). Also, in the apostolic preaching of Stephen, his final vision was that of the exalted Jesus, whom he clearly identified as the "Son of Man, standing at the right hand of God" (Acts 7:56). Jesus Himself took on the appellation "Son of Man," which He considered a Messianic title when He predicted His second coming (e.g., Mt 24:30; Mk 13:26). He thereby validated Daniel's visions as predictive prophecy.

Outline

- I. Daniel's Service in Babylon (1:1–6:28)
  - A. The Capture of Jerusalem and the Deportation of Youth to Babylon (1:1-21)
  - B. Nebuchadnezzar's Dream (2:1-49)
  - C. The Gold Statue (3:1-30)
  - D. Nebuchadnezzar's Insanity (4:1-37)
  - E. The Great Feast of Belshazzar (5:1-30)
  - F. The Lions' Den (5:31–6:28)
- II. Daniel's Visions (7:1–12:13)
  - A. Daniel's First Vision (7:1-28)
  - B. Daniel's Second Vision (8:1-27)
  - C. The Prayer of Daniel (9:1-19)
  - D. The 70 Weeks of Years (9:20-27)
  - E. The Future of Israel and the End-Times (10:1–12:13)

Title: The Hebrew name Daniel means "God is my judge" or "God is Judge." In the Hebrew canon, Daniel is included in the third section known as the Writings (Hb *Ketuvim*) rather than the second section called the Prophets (Hb *Neviʾim*) probably because Daniel was not considered a prophet. Vocationally, Daniel was a government official. He was counted among the wise men (Aram *chakkim*, 2:13,48) in Babylon.

1:1 This **siege** of Jerusalem (cp. 2Kg 23:36–24:5; 2Ch 36:5-8), probably took place in 605 B.C. and may have been very brief, since Nebuchadnezzar was occupied with the Battle of Carchemish, his father's death, and his own accession to the Babylonian throne that was imminent (604 B.C.).

1:2 Nebuchadnezzar had power to control Jerusalem and ransack the temple because **the Lord** [Hb *ʾAdonay*, "sovereign ruler, owner"] **handed Jehoiakim... over** to him (cp. 2Kg 24:2-4; 2Ch 36:4-8; Jr 1:3; 26:1-6,20-23; 35:17). By seizing the temple vessels and putting them in the temple **treasury** of his own god, Nebuchadnezzar suggested that his god had defeated the God of Israel. Capture of the vessels was the Babylonians' way of "capturing" Israel's God since there were no statues of Yahweh to capture. The mention of the vessels sets the stage for the story of Belshazzar's drunken feast in Dn 5.

1:3 Daniel and his friends were probably around 15 years of age.

1:4-5 The four companions were given a literary, linguistic, cultural, and probably a political education. One of the empire's strategies was to train such young men according to **Chaldean** culture and **language**, then to place them in leadership positions among their own people, thereby minimizing the chances of insurrection.

1:6-7 The young men were accorded Chaldean names, an important aspect of their immersion in the new culture: **Daniel** (see note on **Title**) was renamed **Belteshazzar** (Chald, "protect his life," a petition to the god Bel or Marduk). **Hananiah** (Hb, "Yahweh is gracious") was renamed **Shadrach** (Chald, "command of Aku," the Sumerian moon god). **Mishael** (Hb, "who is like God") was given the name **Meshach** (Chald, "who is what Aku is?" or "salvation by Aku"). **Azariah** (Hb, "Yahweh is my helper") received the name **Abednego** (Chald, "servant of Nebo").

1:8 A clear transition is marked here from a description of circumstances beyond their control to an account of their own decisions.

>WORD|*study*

1:2 Two phrases magnify the contrast between Yahweh, the one true God, and the Babylonian gods. Nebuchadnezzar took vessels **from the house of** God [Hb *ha-ʾelohim*, "the God"] **... to the house of his** god (Hb *ʾelohim*, "god or gods"), probably referring to Marduk. Daniel consistently used the definite article "the" with "God," signifying that there is only one.

1:17 Understand (Hb *bin*, "discern, perceive; declare, explain") in this context has the sense of interpreting, explaining, or articulating the meaning of something. The word appears 19 times in the book, most often in relation to visions (8:5,16-17,27; 9:22-23; 10:1,11-12,14; 12:8,10). In 1:4, however, the same word is translated more generally as "perceptive," one of the criteria for selecting young noblemen such as Daniel. For example, compare Daniel with Joseph, whose unparalleled discernment and intelligence were displayed in his interpretation of dreams and led to the pharaoh's appointment of him as prime minister of Egypt (Gn 41:33,39). In the case of both Joseph and Daniel, the text clearly indicates that the gift of interpretation of dreams and visions comes from God (Gn 40:8, 41:16; Dn 1:17; 2:19-23,28). This ability goes beyond human intelligence and hard work.

The Capture of Jerusalem and the Deportation of Youth to Babylon (1:1-21)

An Introduction to the Young Men and Setting (1:1-7)

1 In the third year of the reign of Jehoiakim king of Judah, Nebuchadnezzar[A] king of Babylon came to Jerusalem and laid siege to it. 2 The Lord handed Jehoiakim king of Judah over to him, along with some of the vessels from the house of God. Nebuchadnezzar carried them to the land of Babylon,[B] to the house of his god,[C] and put the vessels in the treasury of his god.

3 The king ordered Ashpenaz, the chief of his court officials,[D] to bring some of the Israelites from the royal family and from the nobility— 4 young men without any physical defect, good-looking, suitable for instruction in all wisdom, knowledgeable, perceptive, and capable of serving in the king's palace—and to teach them the Chaldean language and literature. 5 The king assigned them daily provisions from the royal food and from the wine that he drank. They were to be trained for three years, and at the end of that time they were to serve in the king's court.[E] 6 Among them, from the descendants of Judah, were Daniel, Hananiah, Mishael, and Azariah. 7 The chief official gave them other names: he gave the name Belteshazzar to Daniel, Shadrach to Hananiah, Meshach to Mishael, and Abednego to Azariah.

Courage of the Young Men in Difficult Circumstances (1:8-16)

8 Daniel determined that he would not defile himself with the king's food or with the wine he drank. So he asked permission from the chief official not to defile himself. 9 God had granted Daniel favor and compassion from the chief official, 10 yet he said to Daniel, "My lord the king assigned your food and drink. I'm afraid of what would happen if he saw your faces looking thinner than those of the other young men your age. You would endanger my life[F] with the king."

11 So Daniel said to the guard whom the chief official had assigned to Daniel, Hananiah, Mishael, and Azariah, 12 "Please test your servants for 10 days. Let us be given vegetables to eat and water to drink. 13 Then examine our appearance and the appearance of the young men who are eating the king's food, and deal with your servants based on what you see." 14 He agreed with them about this and tested them for 10 days. 15 At the end of 10 days they looked better and healthier[G] than all the young men who were eating the king's food. 16 So the guard continued to remove their food and the wine they were to drink and gave them vegetables.

The Excellence of God's Chosen Men (1:17-21)

17 God gave these four young men knowledge and understanding in every kind of literature and wisdom. Daniel also understood visions and

[A] **1:1** Or *Nebuchadrezzar* [B] **1:2** Lit *Shinar* [C] **1:2** Or *gods* [D] **1:3** Or *his eunuchs* [E] **1:5** Lit *to stand before the king* [F] **1:10** Lit *would make my head guilty* [G] **1:15** Lit *fatter of flesh*

dreams of every kind. [18]At the end of the time that the king had said to present them, the chief official presented them to Nebuchadnezzar. [19]The king interviewed them, and among all of them, no one was found equal to Daniel, Hananiah, Mishael, and Azariah. So they began to serve in the king's court. [20]In every matter of wisdom and understanding that the king consulted them about, he found them 10 times[A] better than all the diviner-priests and mediums in his entire kingdom. [21]Daniel remained there until the first year of King Cyrus.

Nebuchadnezzar's Dream (2:1-49)

The Failure of the Chaldeans (2:1-23)

2 In the second year of his reign, Nebuchadnezzar had dreams that troubled him, and sleep deserted him. [2]So the king gave orders to summon the diviner-priests, mediums, sorcerers, and Chaldeans[B] to tell the king his dreams. When they came and stood before the king, [3]he said to them, "I have had a dream and am anxious to understand it."

[4]The Chaldeans spoke to the king (Aramaic[C] begins here): "May the king live forever. Tell your servants the dream, and we will give the interpretation."

[5]The king replied to the Chaldeans, "My word is final: If you don't tell me the dream and its interpretation, you will be torn limb from limb,[D] and your houses will be made a garbage dump. [6]But if you make the dream and its interpretation known to me, you'll receive gifts, a reward, and great honor from me. So make the dream and its interpretation known to me."

[7]They answered a second time, "May the king tell the dream to his servants, and we will give the interpretation."

[8]The king replied, "I know for certain you are trying to gain some time, because you see that my word is final. [9]If you don't tell me the dream, there is one decree for you. You have conspired to tell me something false or fraudulent until the situation changes. So tell me the dream and I will know you can give me its interpretation."

[10]The Chaldeans answered the king, "No one on earth can make known what the king requests. Consequently, no king, however great and powerful, has ever asked anything like this of any diviner-priest, medium, or Chaldean. [11]What the king is asking is so difficult that no one can make it known to him except the gods, whose dwelling is not with mortals." [12]Because of this, the king became violently angry and gave orders to destroy all the wise men of Babylon. [13]The decree was issued that the wise men were to be executed, and they searched for Daniel and his friends, to execute them.

[14]Then Daniel responded with tact and discretion to Arioch, the commander of the king's guard,[E] who had gone out to execute the wise men of Babylon. [15]He asked Arioch, the king's officer, "Why is the decree from the king so harsh?"[F] Then Arioch explained the situation to Daniel. [16]So Daniel went and asked the king to give him some time, so

[A]1:20 Lit *hands* [B]2:2 In this chap. Chaldeans are influential Babylonian wise men. [C]2:4 Dn 2:4–7:28 is written in Aram. [D]2:5 Lit *be made into limbs* [E]2:14 Or *executioners* [F]2:15 Or *urgent*

>WORD|*study*

2:5 By saying, **My word is** final (Aram *ʾazad*, "go away, go out, depart," also v. 8), Nebuchadnezzar announced that his word or judgment on the matter would not be recalled after it left his mouth. However, if the word was borrowed from the Persian language, it may instead mean "certain" or "public knowledge." In this case, the king was probably asserting that he had made a "firm" decision regarding his demand that the one giving the correct interpretation would be proven reliable by first recounting the dream itself. Some interpreters believe there is a suggestion in this phrase that Nebuchadnezzar has forgotten the dream, which might explain his irascibility. However, seemingly the better translation indicates the king's firm decision to put his wise men to the test of relating the dream as well as its meaning.

2:13-16 By describing Nebuchadnezzar's orders as harsh (Aram *chatsaph*, "hasty, urgent, sharp, showing insolence"), Daniel appealed to Arioch's judgment about the encounter between the king and his senior advisers. The word suggests that while Daniel was not trying to defy authority, the king's interest was best served to be sure the order's severity was warranted.

1:9-10 God's providence is evident as a reward for those who wish to honor the covenant even in adverse circumstances.

1:11-14 The guard assigned by Ashpenaz **agreed** to replace the meals allotted to Daniel and the other three friends with **vegetables** (Hb, *zēroʿim*, "seeds," foods from plants) and water **for 10 days**.

1:19-20 These men stood out in comparison to the other captives in training, as well as their vocational peers, the **diviner-priests** (Hb *chartom*, "sacred scribe") and **mediums** (Hb and Chald *ʾashshaph*, "enchanter, necromancer, conjurer"; cp. Gn 41:8,16,38-39; Ex 7:10-12; 1Kg 3:7-12; 4:29-31).

1:21 Daniel's wisdom and special abilities allowed him longevity of service in the royal court throughout the exile, and he lived into **the first year** of the reign of **King Cyrus** (539 B.C.), the Medo-Persian king who allowed the Jews to return to Israel and rebuild the temple (cp. 2Ch 36:22-23; Is 44:28–45:4).

2:1 The second year of Nebuchadnezzar's **reign** was about 603–602 B.C.

2:2-3 As one who recently ascended the throne, perhaps he was overwhelmed and disturbed when conquered people in his realm resisted his rule, as some commentators suggest the *Babylonian Chronicle* seems to indicate was the case in the first few years of his reign.

2:4 Beginning with the report of the Chaldeans' reply, the language of the narrative switches to Aramaic, the most widely spoken language of the ancient Near East.

2:9-11 These men possibly relied on historical dreams such as those found in Babylonian dream manuals. The king's demand was impossible apart from genuine divine revelation from **the gods,** since in order to use the manuals, the diviners first needed the dream. While the king's challenge was highly unusual, **the Chaldeans'** inability to meet it made him **violently angry,** one of the first samplings of Nebuchadnezzar's impulsive and volatile behavior. Nebuchadnezzar accused his advisers of stalling for time and of coming up with **something false** [Aram *kedav*, "lying, deceptive"] **or fraudulent** (Aram *shechat*, "corrupt"; cp. 6:4)—i.e., of committing a crime deserving of death.

2:13-16 Although **Daniel and his friends** apparently were not among the **wise men** directly addressed by

Nebuchadnezzar, they were included in the execution order given to **Arioch** (Aram, "lion-like"). Daniel's response **with tact and discretion** is commendable under these critical circumstances.

2:17 As Daniel and **his friends** prepared to pray to their covenant God, appropriately their Hebrew names are used.

2:19 In the original language, the first word of this verse is **then** (Aram *'edayin*, "afterward"), clearly marking the sequence of events: God revealed **the mystery** to Daniel sometime after the young men prayed.

2:20-23 Daniel exalted God's name and recounted God's unique powers as the source of **wisdom and power.** Daniel also thanked the Lord for giving him **wisdom and power** and for specifically revealing **the king's mystery**.

2:26-28 God providentially **reveals mysteries** to a powerful pagan king about **the last days** (Aram *'acharit yom*, "end of the days or era, latter days"), using Daniel as a channel of revelation (cp. Joseph in Gn 41). This phrase may best be understood as describing the kingdoms following Nebuchadnezzar, including both the life of Christ on earth and the still future return of Christ.

2:31-35 Nebuchadnezzar's dream showed a **colossal** and **terrifying** statue (not an idol) composed of various materials. Even more terrifying was the force of the **stone**, which seemingly appeared out of nowhere and crushed the statue to dust (**chaff**), easily borne away by the **wind**. Perhaps the king worried about an unknown opponent toppling his kingdom. The **tall and dazzling** statue was replaced by the **great mountain**.

2:36-38 As Daniel turned to the dream's **interpretation**, he hailed Nebuchadnezzar as the greatest earthly king, **the head of gold**, but carefully placed the extent of the king's power in perspective. **The God of heaven**—i.e., the God of Israel and of Daniel, not Marduk or any other figure in the Babylonian pantheon—had sovereignly exalted Nebuchadnezzar. The effect of this is to encourage humility in this proud king, since he falls under a power he cannot fully understand or control. The Babylonian Empire lasted approximately from 605–539 B.C.

2:39 Most conservative scholars agree on the identification of the kingdoms succeeding Babylon. The **kingdom** following Nebuchadnezzar—the

>WORD|*study*

2:13-16 Here the word time (Aram *zeman*, "set time, season") has a more specific meaning than the word in verse 8, in which Nebuchadnezzar accused his wise men of "trying to gain some time" (Aram *'iddan*), knowing they could not meet his demand and therefore hoping that the king would relent and describe the dream. Daniel, however, was granted an appointed length of time—apparently at least overnight or perhaps a day (v. 19)—to provide the interpretation. What Daniel did with the time was to gather his friends to pray, as the lives of all four were at stake (v. 18).

that he could give the king the interpretation.

17 Then Daniel went to his house and told his friends Hananiah, Mishael, and Azariah about the matter, 18 urging them to ask the God of heaven for mercy concerning this mystery, so Daniel and his friends would not be killed with the rest of Babylon's wise men. 19 The mystery was then revealed to Daniel in a vision at night, and Daniel praised the God of heaven 20 and declared:

May the name of God
be praised forever and ever,
for wisdom and power belong
to Him.
21 He changes the times
and seasons;
He removes kings
and establishes kings.
He gives wisdom to the wise
and knowledge to those
who have understanding.
22 He reveals the deep
and hidden things;
He knows what is
in the darkness,
and light dwells with Him.
23 I offer thanks and praise
to You,
God of my fathers,
because You have given me
wisdom and power.
And now You have
let me know
what we asked of You,
for You have let us know
the king's mystery.[A]

The Approach of Daniel to the King (2:24-30)

24 Therefore Daniel went to Arioch, whom the king had assigned to destroy the wise men of Babylon. He came and said to him, "Don't kill the wise men of Babylon! Bring me before the king, and I will give him the interpretation."

25 Then Arioch quickly brought Daniel before the king and said to him, "I have found a man among the Judean exiles who can let the king know the interpretation."

26 The king said in reply to Daniel, whose name was Belteshazzar, "Are you able to tell me the dream I had and its interpretation?"

27 Daniel answered the king: "No wise man, medium, diviner-priest, or astrologer is able to make known to the king the mystery he asked about. 28 But there is a God in heaven who reveals mysteries, and He has let King Nebuchadnezzar know what will happen in the last days. Your dream and the visions that came into your mind as you lay in bed were these: 29 Your Majesty, while you were in your bed, thoughts came to your mind about what will happen in the future.[B] The revealer of mysteries has let you know what will happen. 30 As for me, this mystery has been revealed to me, not because I have more wisdom than anyone living, but in order that the interpretation might be made known to the king, and that you may understand the thoughts of your mind.

Daniel's Interpretation (2:31-45)

31 "My king, as you were watching, a colossal statue appeared. That statue, tall and dazzling, was standing in front of you, and its appearance was terrifying. 32 The head of the statue was pure gold, its chest and arms were silver, its stomach and thighs were bronze, 33 its legs were iron, and its feet were partly iron and partly fired clay. 34 As you were watching, a stone broke off without a hand touching it,[C] struck the stat-

A 2:23 Lit *matter* B 2:29 Lit *happen after this* C 2:34 Lit *off not by hands*

ue on its feet of iron and fired clay, and crushed them. [35]Then the iron, the fired clay, the bronze, the silver, and the gold were shattered and became like chaff from the summer threshing floors. The wind carried them away, and not a trace of them could be found. But the stone that struck the statue became a great mountain and filled the whole earth.

[36]"This was the dream; now we will tell the king its interpretation. [37]Your Majesty, you are king of kings. The God of heaven has given you sovereignty, power, strength, and glory. [38]Wherever people live—or wild animals, or birds of the air—He has handed them over to you and made you ruler over them all. You are the head of gold.

[39]"After you, there will arise another kingdom, inferior to yours, and then another, a third kingdom, of bronze, which will rule the whole earth. [40]A fourth kingdom will be as strong as iron; for iron crushes and shatters everything, and like iron that smashes, it will crush and smash all the others.[A] [41]You saw the feet and toes, partly of a potter's fired clay and partly of iron—it will be a divided kingdom, though some of the strength of iron will be in it. You saw the iron mixed with clay, [42]and that the toes of the feet were partly iron and partly fired clay—part of the kingdom will be strong, and part will be brittle. [43]You saw the iron mixed with clay—the peoples will mix with one another[B] but will not hold together, just as iron does not mix with fired clay.

[44]"In the days of those kings, the God of heaven will set up a kingdom that will never be destroyed, and this kingdom will not be left to another people. It will crush all these kingdoms and bring them to an end, but will itself endure forever. [45]You saw a stone break off from the mountain without a hand touching it,[C] and it crushed the iron, bronze, fired clay, silver, and gold. The great God has told the king what will happen in the future.[D] The dream is true, and its interpretation certain."

The Response of the King (2:46-49)

[46]Then King Nebuchadnezzar fell down, paid homage to Daniel, and gave orders to present an offering and incense to him. [47]The king said to Daniel, "Your God is indeed God of gods, Lord of kings, and a revealer of mysteries, since you were able to reveal this mystery." [48]Then the king promoted Daniel and gave him many generous gifts. He made him ruler over the entire province of Babylon and chief governor over all the wise men of Babylon. [49]At Daniel's request, the king appointed Shadrach, Meshach, and Abednego to manage the province of Babylon. But Daniel remained at the king's court.

The Gold Statue (3:1-30)

Nebuchadnezzar's Statue (3:1-7)

3 King Nebuchadnezzar made a gold statue, 90 feet high and nine feet wide.[E] He set it up on the plain of Dura in the province of Babylon. [2]King Nebuchadnezzar sent word to assemble the satraps, prefects, governors, advisers, treasurers, judges, magistrates, and all the rulers of the provinces to attend the dedication of the statue King Nebuchadnezzar had set up. [3]So the satraps, prefects, governors, advisers, treasurers, judges, magistrates, and all the rulers of the provinces assembled for the dedication of the statue the king had set up. Then they stood before the statue Nebuchadnezzar had set up.

[4]A herald loudly proclaimed, "People of every nation and language, you are commanded: [5]When you hear the sound of the horn, flute, zither,[F] lyre,[G] harp, drum,[H] and every kind of music, you are to fall down and worship the gold statue that King Nebuchadnezzar has set up. [6]But whoever does not fall down and worship will immediately be thrown into a furnace of blazing fire."

[7]Therefore, when all the people heard the sound of the horn, flute, zither, lyre, harp, and every kind of music, people of every nation and

[A]2:40 Lit *all these* [B]2:43 Lit *another in the seed of men* [C]2:45 Lit *mountain, not by hands* [D]2:45 Lit *happen after this* [E]3:1 Lit *statue, its height 60 cubits, its width six cubits* [F]3:5 Or *lyre* [G]3:5 Or *sambuke* [H]3:5 Or *pipe*

Medo-Persian Empire— lasted more than two centuries (539–331 B.C.). **A third kingdom of bronze**, described as ruling **the whole earth**, represents Greece led by Alexander the Great, who invaded Persia in 332 B.C. (cp. 7:6; 8:5; 11:3-4). Greek domination lasted nearly two centuries (331–146 B.C.).

2:40 The kingdom **as strong as iron** represents the Roman republic (509–ca 27 B.C.), which crushed, shattered, and smashed all opposition. Some view this kingdom as the entire period of Roman domination under both the republican and imperial rule.

2:41-43 The history of the Roman Empire also generally matches this picture of strength—in terms of military conquest and strong imperial government—mixed with the inherently debilitating weakness of internal power struggles, an influx of foreigners among the workforce, government, and military, and growing threats of invasion along the borders.

2:44-45 The symbolism of the stone seems to be an interpretive key to Nebuchadnezzar's dream. The stone caused the successive empires to be obliterated. If a messianic interpretation is correct, the stone may portray the complete victory of Christ over all known and "future" earthly powers.

Then this stone, which broke off (Aram *gezar*, "cut away," corresponding to Hb *gazar*, "cut off," Is 53:8; Ezk 37:11) **from the mountain**, grew to become "a great mountain . . . [that] filled the whole earth" (Dn 2:34-35,45). In the interpretation of the dream, the "stone" is identified with the **kingdom** that God **will set up**. The time frame given for the kingdom is during the time when the rulers represented by the statue's feet and toes are exercising power. Its duration is **forever**, echoing the Lord's promise to David (2Sm 7:16) as well as an idea emphasized elsewhere in the book of Daniel (Dn 4:3,34; 6:26; 7:14,18,26-27).

Some believe the kingdom is a spiritual one, established by Jesus during His earthly life, while others believe the stone signifies Christ's return at the end of time when He will set up an eternal kingdom. Seemingly the former would more naturally fit the chronological sequence of the rest of the dream. With the dawn of the first century A.D.—in the last days of the "kings" of the Roman republic and the first decades of the Roman emperors—came the birth of Jesus the Messiah. His kingdom alone, what Scripture calls "the kingdom of God," fits the description here of an everlasting kingdom and an enduring reign that supersedes all earthly powers and fills "the whole earth" (2:34-35,44-45; cp. Mt 28:18; Mk 1:15; 1Pt 3:22; cp. Mt 21:42-44; Ac 1:8; 13:47; Eph 4:10).

3:8 Some Chaldeans undoubtedly resented Daniel's promotion as their governor and Shadrach, Meshach, and Abednego as provincial rulers (2:48-49). They now had the opportunity to **maliciously accuse** them (the phrase means to "eat pieces of flesh torn off from someone else's body"). Daniel's whereabouts are not mentioned, but his royal duties likely kept him at the palace in the capital city while the king and the other officials assembled on the plain of Dura (2:49–3:3).

3:15-18 Nebuchadnezzar's fury and hubris have previously manifested themselves. Here they are shown in the arrogant and threatening question, **who is the god who can rescue you from my power?**

3:20-25 The extreme heat of the fire did not even singe the men who were thrown into the furnace (vv. 19,22,27). The king was astonished not only to observe the men **walking around in the fire unharmed** but also to count four men rather than three. The fourth man he described as **like a son of the gods**.

3:26-28 The king concluded that the **Most High God** had **sent His angel** to rescue the men he had tried to execute. Most scholars agree that Nebuchadnezzar saw a pre-incarnate appearance of Christ or a Christophany. The king then realized that although his laws were binding in his kingdom, yet his power was not absolute.

3:29-30 Nebuchadnezzar's **decree** served to legitimize Jewish monotheism, but it did not eliminate polytheism. Despite receiving revelation through a miraculous deliverance, Nebuchadnezzar failed to acknowledge the exclusivity of the God of the Hebrews.

4:1-3 King Nebuchadnezzar shared what could be considered the most humiliating experience of his life. The public testimony is recounted by Daniel or may have been written or dictated by the king himself in the form of a "confession" rather than an official proclamation. Both its introduction (v. 3) and its conclusion (4:34-35) contain elements of doxology, thus underscoring the purpose of the story—to recognize and praise God as "the King of heaven" (v. 37); in so doing he reiterates the major theme in Daniel of God's sovereignty over kings and nations, as well as the unstoppable **mighty** and **eternal** nature of **His kingdom**.

4:4-5 This dream probably came late in his reign, around 30 years after the events of chapter 3. Daniel would have been about 50 years old.

language fell down and worshiped the gold statue that King Nebuchadnezzar had set up.

God's Miraculous Deliverance (3:8-30)

8 Some Chaldeans took this occasion to come forward and maliciously accuse[A] the Jews. 9 They said to King Nebuchadnezzar, "May the king live forever. 10 You as king have issued a decree that everyone who hears the sound of the horn, flute, zither, lyre, harp, drum, and every kind of music must fall down and worship the gold statue. 11 Whoever does not fall down and worship will be thrown into a furnace of blazing fire. 12 There are some Jews you have appointed to manage the province of Babylon: Shadrach, Meshach, and Abednego. These men have ignored you, the king; they do not serve your gods or worship the gold statue you have set up."

13 Then in a furious rage Nebuchadnezzar gave orders to bring in Shadrach, Meshach, and Abednego. So these men were brought before the king. 14 Nebuchadnezzar asked them, "Shadrach, Meshach, and Abednego, is it true that you don't serve my gods or worship the gold statue I have set up? 15 Now if you're ready, when you hear the sound of the horn, flute, zither, lyre, harp, drum, and every kind of music, fall down and worship the statue I made. But if you don't worship it, you will immediately be thrown into a furnace of blazing fire—and who is the god who can rescue you from my power?"

16 Shadrach, Meshach, and Abednego replied to the king, "Nebuchadnezzar, we don't need to give you an answer to this question. 17 If the God we serve exists,[B] then He can rescue us from the furnace of blazing fire, and He can rescue us from the power of you, the king. 18 But even if He does not rescue us,[C] we want you as king to know that we will not serve your gods or worship the gold statue you set up."

19 Then Nebuchadnezzar was filled with rage, and the expression on his face changed toward Shadrach, Meshach, and Abednego. He gave orders to heat the furnace seven times more than was customary, 20 and he commanded some of the strongest soldiers in his army to tie up Shadrach, Meshach, and Abednego and throw them into the furnace of blazing fire. 21 So these men, in their trousers, robes, head coverings,[D] and other clothes, were tied up and thrown into the furnace of blazing fire. 22 Since the king's command was so urgent[E] and the furnace extremely hot, the raging flames[F] killed those men who carried Shadrach, Meshach, and Abednego up. 23 And these three men, Shadrach, Meshach, and Abednego fell, bound, into the furnace of blazing fire.

24 Then King Nebuchadnezzar jumped up in alarm. He said to his advisers, "Didn't we throw three men, bound, into the fire?"

"Yes, of course, Your Majesty," they replied to the king.

25 He exclaimed, "Look! I see four men, not tied, walking around in the fire unharmed; and the fourth looks like a son of the gods."[G]

26 Nebuchadnezzar then approached the door of the furnace of blazing fire and called: "Shadrach, Meshach, and Abednego, you servants of the •Most High God—come out!" So Shadrach, Meshach, and Abednego came out of the fire. 27 When the satraps, prefects, governors, and the king's advisers gathered around, they saw that the fire had no effect on[H] the bodies of these men: not a hair of their heads was singed, their robes were unaffected, and there was no smell of fire on them. 28 Nebuchadnezzar exclaimed, "Praise to the God of Shadrach, Meshach, and Abednego! He sent His angel[I] and rescued His servants who trusted in Him. They violated the king's command and risked their lives rather than serve or worship any god except their own God. 29 Therefore I issue a decree that anyone of any

[A]**3:8** Lit *and eat the pieces of* [B]**3:17** They do not doubt God's existence as 3:18 shows. The "if" is part of an argument used to defend their refusal to serve Babylonian gods. [C]**3:18** Lit *But if not* [D]**3:21** The identity of these articles of clothing is uncertain. [E]**3:22** Or *harsh* [F]**3:22** Lit *the flame of the fire* [G]**3:25** Or *of a divine being* [H]**3:27** Lit *fire had not overcome* [I]**3:28** Or *messenger*

people, nation, or language who says anything offensive against the God of Shadrach, Meshach, and Abednego will be torn limb from limb and his house made a garbage dump. For there is no other god who is able to deliver like this." [30] Then the king rewarded Shadrach, Meshach, and Abednego in the province of Babylon.

Nebuchadnezzar's Insanity (4:1-37)

King Nebuchadnezzar's Proclamation (4:1-18)

4 [A] King Nebuchadnezzar,

To those of every people, nation, and language, who live in all the earth:

May your prosperity increase. [2] I am pleased to tell you about the miracles and wonders the •Most High God has done for me.

[3] How great are His miracles,
and how mighty His wonders!
His kingdom is
an eternal kingdom,
and His dominion is
from generation
to generation.

[4] [B] I, Nebuchadnezzar, was at ease in my house and flourishing in my palace. [5] I had a dream, and it frightened me; while in my bed, the images and visions in my mind alarmed me. [6] So I issued a decree to bring all the wise men of Babylon to me in order that they might make the dream's interpretation known to me. [7] When the diviner-priests, mediums, Chaldeans, and astrologers came in, I told them the dream, but they could not make its interpretation known to me.

[8] Finally Daniel, named Belteshazzar after the name of my god—and the spirit of the holy gods is in him—came before me. I told him the dream: [9] "Belteshazzar, head of the diviners, because I know that you have a spirit of the holy gods and that no mystery puzzles you, explain to me the visions of my dream that I saw, and its interpretation.

[10] In the visions of my mind as I was lying in bed, I saw this:

There was a tree in the middle
of the earth,
and its height was great.
[11] The tree grew large
and strong;
its top reached to the sky,
and it was visible to the ends
of the[C] earth.
[12] Its leaves were beautiful,
its fruit was abundant,
and on it was food for all.
Wild animals found shelter
under it,
the birds of the air lived
in its branches,
and every creature was fed
from it.

[13] "As I was lying in my bed, I also saw in the visions of my mind an observer, a holy one,[D] coming down from heaven. [14] He called out loudly:

Cut down the tree
and chop off its branches;
strip off its leaves and scatter
its fruit.
Let the animals flee
from under it,
and the birds
from its branches.
[15] But leave the stump
with its roots
in the ground,
and with a band of iron
and bronze around it,
in the tender grass
of the field.
Let him be drenched with dew
from the sky
and share the plants
of the earth
with the animals.
[16] Let his mind be changed
from that of a man,
and let him be given the mind
of an animal
for seven periods of time.[E,F]
[17] This word is by decree
of the observers;
the matter is a command
from the holy ones.
This is so the living will know
that the Most High is ruler
over the kingdom of men.

A4:1 Dn 3:31 in Hb B4:4 Dn 4:1 in Hb C4:11 Lit *of all the* D4:13 = an angel E4:16 Lit *animal as seven times pass over him* F4:16 Perhaps 7 years

The king had completed his greatest building projects (v. 30) and settled down without conflicts on the horizon. Although he had achieved great success and contentment, he was greatly troubled by a **dream**.

4:6-9 Dreams or visions are only one method God uses to reveal Himself. After the **wise men** once again proved unable to give **the dream's interpretation**, Nebuchadnezzar turned to **Daniel,** recognizing his gifting from God for the specific purpose of interpreting dreams and noting three times that Daniel had the **spirit of the holy gods** (cp. v. 18). Evidently Nebuchadnezzar remains a polytheist. Although he respected the messenger of the "Most High God" (v. 2), he worshiped the god Bel, after whom he named Daniel.

4:11-12 The high tree whose **top reached to the sky** invites comparison with the tower of Babel, which had been built in Babylon in olden times (Shinar, cp. 1:2; Gn 11:2-9). The tree was enormous, healthy, and housed and fed animals and birds (cp. Lk 13:18-19 for comparable imagery referring to the kingdom of God).

4:13-15 An observer (Aram *ʿir*, "watcher, guardian," vv. 13,23) refers to an angel. The order given and carried out for this healthy, fruitful, and beautiful tree to be cut down is shocking. Such destruction of a tree was typically reserved for those that had died or were persistently unfruitful. The command included a limitation, however, that allowed hope for regrowth. **The stump** is left **with its roots in the ground** and is protected by the metal **band** or fencing around it (vv. 15,23). Some commentators see the band as a kind of shackle rather than protection.

4:16-17 The imagery shifts here from a tree to a **man**, whose mind will be adversely affected. The condition described is either lycanthropy or boanthropy. Lycanthropy (Gk *lukos*, "wolf," and *anthrōpos*, "man") is a temporary insanity during which time a man thinks he is some animal. For **seven periods of time**—whether days, months, seasons, or years—the king was deranged, acting as an animal and forced, therefore, "to live with the wild animals" (vv. 23-25). The purpose of this action is clearly decreed by **the observers** on behalf of **the Most High** so that **the living will know** who is truly sovereign **over the kingdom of men** (cp. vv. 24-25, 32). As Nebuchadnezzar had made decrees that were binding on all his subjects, he would learn that on behalf of the heavenly King there are binding decrees on Nebuchadnezzar, the earthly king.

4:19 The introductory words of **Belteshazzar** (Daniel) demonstrated his respect for the king and the peril of approaching him with bad news.

4:22 In the dream, the great **tree** represented Nebuchadnezzar and his expansive empire (**reaches the sky**, like the tower of Babel, Gn 11:1-9) encompassing many peoples, nations, and languages (cp. v. 1; 3:29).

4:24-25 The **sentence** pronounced against Nebuchadnezzar was exile. He would be **driven away** from society until he had learned humility under the rule of the **Most High,** the true **ruler over the kingdom of men**.

4:27 This punishment as well as Daniel's urging of the king to repent also mitigate against a positive assessment of the enormous tree and its all-encompassing branches.

4:29-33 The text does not explain what happened during the ensuing **12 months**. Perhaps the king took the dream's warning and Daniel's advice to heart. However, as soon as the king openly boasted of his own **majestic glory** and accomplishments, the judgment was announced by **a voice** [that] **came from heaven**, and insanity struck him. His case of lycanthropy was so overwhelming that he was driven out of the palace and far from the people over whom he had ruled.

4:34 By looking **up to heaven** Nebuchadnezzar acknowledged that he was subject to God (i.e., "that the Most High is ruler" and "that Heaven rules," 4:25-26,32). Nebuchadnezzar learned that although his earthly "dominion" was expansive geographically (4:22), it was temporal in scope. In contrast, the **dominion** of **the Most High** is **an everlasting dominion** because He **lives forever**.

4:35 The ability to do **what He wants** is synonymous with absolute power. The heavenly King possesses this ability whereas earthly kings do not. Those in positions of power must always bear this lesson in mind lest they come under the discipline of God.

4:37 God rewards humility but **humbles those who walk in pride** (cp. 1Sm 2:7-8; Lk 1:51-52). As Daniel was rewarded, Nebuchadnezzar was humbled.

5:1 Nebuchadnezzar died in 562 B.C. Nabonidus, who was not of royal descent, assumed the throne about six years later. Liberal scholars have attempted to use this chapter to

He gives it to anyone
He wants
and sets the lowliest of men
over it.

18 This is the dream that I, King Nebuchadnezzar, had. Now, Belteshazzar, tell me the interpretation, because none of the wise men of my kingdom can make the interpretation known to me. But you can, because you have the spirit of the holy gods."

Daniel's Interpretation (4:19-27)

19 Then Daniel, whose name is Belteshazzar, was stunned for a moment, and his thoughts alarmed him. The king said, "Belteshazzar, don't let the dream or its interpretation alarm you."

Belteshazzar answered, "My lord, may the dream apply to those who hate you, and its interpretation to your enemies! 20 The tree you saw, which grew large and strong, whose top reached to the sky and was visible to all the earth, 21 whose leaves were beautiful and its fruit abundant—and on it was food for all, under it the wild animals lived, and in its branches the birds of the air lived— 22 that tree is you, the king. For you have become great and strong: your greatness has grown and even reaches the sky, and your dominion extends to the ends of the earth.

23 "The king saw an observer, a holy one, coming down from heaven and saying, 'Cut down the tree and destroy it, but leave the stump with its roots in the ground and with a band of iron and bronze around it, in the tender grass of the field. Let him be drenched with dew from the sky, and share food with the wild animals for seven periods of time.' 24 This is the interpretation, Your Majesty, and this is the sentence of the Most High that has been passed against my lord the king: 25 You will be driven away from people to live with the wild animals. You will feed on grass like cattle and be drenched with dew from the sky for seven periods of time, until you acknowledge that the Most High is ruler over the kingdom of men, and He gives it to anyone He wants. 26 As for the command to leave the tree's stump with its roots, your kingdom will be restored[A] to you as soon as you acknowledge that Heaven[B] rules. 27 Therefore, may my advice seem good to you my king. Separate yourself from your sins by doing what is right, and from your injustices by showing mercy to the needy. Perhaps there will be an extension of your prosperity."

Nebuchadnezzar's Rebellion (4:28-33)

28 All this happened to King Nebuchadnezzar. 29 At the end of 12 months, as he was walking on the roof of the royal palace in Babylon, 30 the king exclaimed, "Is this not Babylon the Great that I have built by my vast power to be a royal residence and to display my majestic glory?"

31 While the words were still in the king's mouth, a voice came from heaven: "King Nebuchadnezzar, to you it is declared that the kingdom has departed from you. 32 You will be driven away from people to live with the wild animals, and you will feed on grass like cattle for seven periods of time, until you acknowledge that the Most High is ruler over the kingdom of men, and He gives it to anyone He wants."

33 At that moment the sentence against Nebuchadnezzar was executed. He was driven away from people. He ate grass like cattle, and his body was drenched with dew from the sky, until his hair grew like eagles' feathers and his nails like birds' claws.

The Restoration of Nebuchadnezzar (4:34-37)

34 But at the end of those days, I, Nebuchadnezzar, looked up to heaven, and my sanity returned to me. Then I praised the Most High and honored and glorified Him who lives forever:

For His dominion is
an everlasting dominion,
and His kingdom is
from generation
to generation.

A 4:26 Lit *enduring* B 4:26 = God

35 All the inhabitants
of the earth are counted
as nothing,
and He does what He wants
with the army of heaven
and the inhabitants
of the earth.
There is no one
who can hold back His hand
or say to Him,
"What have You done?"

36 At that time my sanity returned to me, and my majesty and splendor returned to me for the glory of my kingdom. My advisers and my nobles sought me out, I was reestablished over my kingdom, and even more greatness came to me. 37 Now I, Nebuchadnezzar, praise, exalt, and glorify the King of heaven, because all His works are true and His ways are just. He is able to humble those who walk in pride.

The Great Feast of Belshazzar (5:1-30)

Belshazzar's Pride and the Writing on the Wall (5:1-24)

5 King Belshazzar held a great feast for 1,000 of his nobles and drank wine in their presence. 2 Under the influence of[A] the wine, Belshazzar gave orders to bring in the gold and silver vessels that his predecessor[B] Nebuchadnezzar had taken from the temple in Jerusalem, so that the king and his nobles, wives, and concubines could drink from them. 3 So they brought in the gold[C] vessels that had been taken from the temple, the house of God in Jerusalem, and the king and his nobles, wives, and concubines drank from them. 4 They drank the wine and praised their gods made of gold and silver, bronze, iron, wood, and stone.

5 At that moment the fingers of a man's hand appeared and began writing on the plaster of the king's palace wall next to the lampstand. As the king watched the hand[D] that was writing, 6 his face turned pale,[E] and his thoughts so terrified him that his hip joints shook and his knees knocked together. 7 The king called out to bring in the mediums, Chaldeans, and astrologers. He said to these wise men of Babylon, "Whoever reads this inscription and gives me its interpretation will be clothed in purple, have a gold chain around his neck, and have the third highest position in the kingdom." 8 So all the king's wise men came in, but none could read the inscription or make its interpretation known to him. 9 Then King Belshazzar became even more terrified, his face turned pale,[F] and his nobles were bewildered.

10 Because of the outcry of the king and his nobles, the queen[G] came to the banquet hall. "May the king live forever," she said. "Don't let your thoughts terrify you or your face be pale.[H] 11 There is a man in your kingdom who has the spirit of the holy gods in him. In the days of your predecessor he was found to have insight, intelligence, and wisdom like the wisdom of the gods. Your predecessor, King Nebuchadnezzar, appointed him chief of the diviners, mediums, Chaldeans, and astrologers. Your own predecessor, the king, 12 did this because Daniel, the one the king named Belteshazzar, was found to have an extraordinary spirit, knowledge and perception, and the ability to interpret dreams, explain riddles, and solve problems. Therefore, summon Daniel, and he will give the interpretation."

13 Then Daniel was brought before the king. The king said to him, "Are you Daniel, one of the Judean exiles that my predecessor the king

[A]5:2 Or *When he tasted* [B]5:2 Or *father*, or *grandfather* [C]5:3 Theod, Vg add *and silver* [D]5:5 Lit *part of the hand* [E]5:5-6 Lit *writing, 6 the king's brightness changed* [F]5:9 Lit *his brightness changed on him* [G]5:10 Perhaps the queen mother [H]5:10 Lit *your brightness change*

>WORD|*study*

5:5 The phrase at that moment (Aram *sha'ah*, "the same hour, in a moment's time, suddenly"; cp. 3:6; 4:33) conveys a sense of immediacy and suggests a cause-effect relationship between these evidences of pride and God's astounding message. The verb **appeared** (Aram *nephaq*, "go out, come out") suggests that **the fingers** were extended or came forth from God to write on the palace wall.

buttress their claims that the Bible contains errors and to strike one more blow at the historicity of the book, arguing that no **King Belshazzar** (Aram, "Bel protect the king") existed. Nabonidus was recognized as Babylon's last king, and when the kingdom fell to the Medo-Persians, he was not killed but was offered a pension. However, archaeological discoveries have proven that Belshazzar was the firstborn son of Nabonidus and the acting ruler or co-regent in Babylon, while his father spent several years of his reign pursuing religious and archaeological interests in Arabia.

In August 539 B.C., Cyrus defeated Babylonian troops at Opis on the west bank of the Tigris River. Further south toward Babylon, without a battle, he seized Sippar, from which Nabonidus fled to Babylon. Ugbaru (Gubaru or Gobryas), the governor of Gutium, joined Cyrus's army and led the troops into Babylon, taking the city without opposition and capturing Nabonidus. On October 29, 539 B.C., Cyrus entered Babylon. Apparently unwavering in the belief that Babylon was impregnable, **Belshazzar held a great feast**.

5:2-4 The king's public desecration of the **vessels** from the **temple in Jerusalem**, using them in the worship of pagan **gods**, exhibited a level of extreme irreverence for the one true God. Belshazzar's pride rather than his political foolishness—feasting when hostile armies were camped within striking distance—assured his sudden downfall (vv. 22-23).

5:5 Excavations of Babylonian palaces show that there was some tiling on one wall of a particular banquet room, but the remaining walls were mostly made of white **plaster**, so the **writing** on the wall would have been clearly seen.

5:10 The fear intensified when none could interpret the writing, and **the outcry** [Aram *millah*, "word, speech"] **of the king and his nobles** reached beyond the banquet hall. As with Nebuchadnezzar's dreams, these men recognized that they were dealing with supernatural power beyond their expertise (cp. 2:10-11,27). The actual position or identity of **the queen** cannot be determined. The king's other "wives and concubines" were already present (v. 2). "The queen" may have been Nebuchadnezzar's widow, or daughter, or Belshazzar's mother (the wife of Nabonidus), grandmother, or wife. In any case, she arrived on the scene with the solution.

5:11-12 Daniel was much older by this point, around 80 years old. His reputation was still intact, however, and the queen remembered him as one who had **wisdom like the wisdom of the gods** and an **extraordinary spirit.** Belshazzar himself had heard that Daniel had **the spirit of the holy gods** in him (cp. Gn 41:38; Joseph was also said to have the "spirit of God [or the gods] in him").

5:16-17 Daniel's lack of desire for reward is a critical trait for a prophet of God.

5:18-19 Daniel gave a little history lesson about the king's **predecessor,** Nebuchadnezzar, reminding the king that **the Most High God** both gives and removes earthly sovereignty, mentioning here the power over life and death, and the power to **exalt** and **humble**.

5:25-28 The **interpretation** was not positive in any way for Belshazzar. Although the common meaning of the three verbs was understood, their prophetic application required Daniel's special insight for understanding:

- **MENE, MENE**: God had **numbered** (Aram *menah*, "review, appoint") the days of the Babylonian **kingdom**. That the time of Babylon's rule had reached its limit was a non-negotiable fact.
- **TEKEL** (Aram, "weigh"): The king was shown to be **deficient** (Aram *chassir*, "wanting, too light") in God's estimation. The imagery of a balance depicts the emptiness of Belshazzar's pride and his false sense of security.
- **PARSIN**: Babylon's end had already been determined by God. The nation had **been divided** (Aram *peras*, "break in two") and given to her conquerors, the Persians and Medes (cp. v. 23). **Peres** could also be a wordplay on "Persia." *Peres* is the singular form of Parsin.

5:30 That very night (October 11, 539 B.C.) Belshazzar lost his life. The Greek writers Herodotus and Xenophon (fifth century B.C.) explain that the Persians diverted the Euphrates River (which flowed beneath the impregnable double wall and into the city) into a nearby swamp. With the water level lowered, they entered the city under the walls, and both the *Cyrus Cylinder* and the *Nabonidus Chronicle* report that the city was taken without a battle. Nabonidus, the real king, was arrested but not harmed; the crown prince Belshazzar was executed, however, possibly as revenge for his prior murder of the son of Cyrus's general, Gobryas (or Ugbaru) while hunting.

5:31 There has been much controversy and uncertainty regarding **Darius the**

brought from Judah? 14 I've heard
that you have the spirit of the gods
in you, and that you have insight,
intelligence, and extraordinary wisdom. 15 Now the wise men and mediums were brought before me to
read this inscription and make its
interpretation known to me, but
they could not give its interpretation. 16 However, I have heard about
you that you can give interpretations and solve problems. Therefore,
if you can read this inscription and
give me its interpretation, you will
be clothed in purple, have a gold
chain around your neck, and have
the third highest position in the
kingdom."
17 Then Daniel answered the king,
"You may keep your gifts, and give
your rewards to someone else; however, I will read the inscription for
the king and make the interpretation known to him. 18 Your Majesty,
the •Most High God gave sovereignty, greatness, glory, and majesty to
your predecessor Nebuchadnezzar.
19 Because of the greatness He gave
him, all peoples, nations, and languages were terrified and fearful of
him. He killed anyone he wanted
and kept alive anyone he wanted; he
exalted anyone he wanted and humbled anyone he wanted. 20 But when
his heart was exalted and his spirit
became arrogant, he was deposed
from his royal throne and his glory
was taken from him. 21 He was driven
away from people, his mind was like
an animal's, he lived with the wild
donkeys, he was fed grass like cattle,
and his body was drenched with dew
from the sky until he acknowledged
that the Most High God is ruler over
the kingdom of men and sets anyone
He wants over it.
22 "But you his successor, Belshazzar, have not humbled your heart,
even though you knew all this.
23 Instead, you have exalted yourself
against the Lord of heaven. The vessels from His house were brought
to you, and as you and your nobles,
wives, and concubines drank wine
from them, you praised the gods
made of silver and gold, bronze,
iron, wood, and stone, which do
not see or hear or understand. But
you have not glorified the God who
holds your life-breath in His hand
and who controls the whole course
of your life.[A] 24 Therefore, He sent
the hand, and this writing was inscribed.

The Interpretation of the Inscription (5:25-30)

25 "This is the writing that was inscribed:

MENE, MENE, TEKEL, PARSIN.

26 This is the interpretation of the
message:

MENE[B] means that God has
numbered the days of your
kingdom and brought it to
an end.
27 TEKEL[C] means that you
have been weighed in the
balance and found deficient.
28 PERES[D,E] means that your
kingdom has been divided
and given to the Medes and
Persians."

29 Then Belshazzar gave an order,
and they clothed Daniel in purple,
placed a gold chain around his neck,
and issued a proclamation concerning him that he should be the third
ruler in the kingdom.
30 That very night Belshazzar the
king of the Chaldeans was killed,

The Lions' Den (5:31–6:28)

Continuing Threats to Daniel's Life (5:31–6:9)

31[F] and Darius the Mede received the
kingdom at the age of 62.

6 Darius decided[G] to appoint 120
satraps over the kingdom, stationed throughout the realm, 2 and
over them three administrators, including Daniel. These satraps would
be accountable to them so that the
king would not be defrauded. 3 Daniel[H] distinguished himself above the
administrators and satraps because
he had an extraordinary spirit, so
the king planned to set him over
the whole realm. 4 The administrators and satraps, therefore, kept try-

A5:23 Lit *and all your ways belong to Him* B5:26 Or *a mina* C5:27 Or *a shekel* D5:28 Or *half a shekel* E5:28 In Aram, the word *peres* is the sg form of "parsin" in v. 25. F5:31 Dn 6:1 in Hb G6:1 Lit *It was pleasing before Darius* H6:3 Lit *Now this Daniel*

>WORD|*study*

6:6 These disgruntled people joined forces and presented a united front. The verb went together (Aram *regash*, "run together with tumult, gather in a tumultuous throng"; cp. "went as a group," v. 11; "went," v. 15) depicts Daniel's enemies as loud, obnoxious schemers. The attack came from people who coveted the favor Daniel received and who resisted enforcement of the ethical standards he upheld.

ing to find a charge against Daniel regarding the kingdom. But they could find no charge or corruption, for he was trustworthy, and no negligence or corruption was found in him. 5 Then these men said, "We will never find any charge against this Daniel unless we find something against him concerning the law of his God."

6 So the administrators and satraps went together to the king and said to him, "May King Darius live forever. 7 All the administrators of the kingdom, the prefects, satraps, advisers, and governors have agreed that the king should establish an ordinance and enforce an edict that for 30 days, anyone who petitions any god or man except you, the king, will be thrown into the lions' den. 8 Therefore, Your Majesty, establish the edict and sign the document so that, as a law of the Medes and Persians, it is irrevocable and cannot be changed." 9 So King Darius signed the document.

The Lions' Den Experience (6:10-18)

10 When Daniel learned that the document had been signed, he went into his house. The windows in its upper room opened toward Jerusalem, and three times a day he got down on his knees, prayed, and gave thanks to his God, just as he had done before. 11 Then these men went as a group and found Daniel petitioning and imploring his God. 12 So they approached the king and asked about his edict: "Didn't you sign an edict that for 30 days any man who petitions any god or man except you, the king, will be thrown into the lions' den?"

The king answered, "As a law of the Medes and Persians, the order stands and is irrevocable."

13 Then they replied to the king, "Daniel, one of the Judean exiles, has ignored you, the king, and the edict you signed, for he prays three times a day." 14 As soon as the king heard this, he was very displeased; he set his mind on rescuing Daniel and made every effort until sundown to deliver him.

15 Then these men went to the king and said to him, "You as king know it is a law of the Medes and Persians that no edict or ordinance the king establishes can be changed."

16 So the king gave the order, and they brought Daniel and threw him into the lions' den. The king said to Daniel, "May your God, whom you serve continually, rescue you!" 17 A stone was brought and placed over the mouth of the den. The king sealed it with his own signet ring and with the signet rings of his nobles, so that nothing in regard to Daniel could be changed. 18 Then the king went to his palace and spent the night fasting. No diversions[A] were brought to him, and he could not sleep.

The Preservation of Daniel's Life (6:19-24)

19 At the first light of dawn the king got up and hurried to the lions' den. 20 When he reached the den, he cried out in anguish to Daniel. "Daniel, servant of the living God," the king said,[B] "has your God whom you serve continually been able to rescue you from the lions?"

21 Then Daniel spoke with the king: "May the king live forever. 22 My God sent His angel and shut the lions' mouths. They haven't hurt me, for I was found innocent before Him. Also, I have not committed a crime against you my king."

23 The king was overjoyed and gave orders to take Daniel out of the den. So Daniel was taken out of the den, uninjured, for he trusted in his God. 24 The king then gave the command,

[A]**6:18** Hb obscure [B]**6:20** Lit *said to Daniel*

Mede. According to the *Nabonidus Chronicle* (which recounts the reign of Nabonidus and the overthrow of Babylon), on the sixteenth day of Tishri (October 12, 539 B.C.), Gobryas the governor of Gutium led Cyrus's army to take the city of Babylon. Belshazzar was killed. Cyrus himself entered the city almost two weeks later on October 29, 539 B.C., assuming control without resistance. "Darius" may have been a title for Cyrus himself, but Daniel 6:28 seems to distinguish Darius and "Cyrus the Persian" as two individuals.

6:1-5 Darius retained Daniel, then in his early eighties, as a high-ranking government administrator.

6:8-9 As the new ruler of Babylon, perhaps Darius welcomed the governors' proposal as a kind of loyalty test and also an affirmation of his powerful rule, as he would be acknowledged as semi-divine (note similarities in Dn 3).

6:10-11 Daniel showed no sign of alarm or fear, but continued doing what **he had done before** (i.e., **petitioning** God rather than the king).

6:13-16 The plot against Daniel was perfectly executed, as the king was trapped by his own legal system.

6:17 This **den** of lions may have been a pit in the ground with a top and a side entrance. Animals were brought in through the side and food (or victim) was cast in from the top. So that Daniel could not escape, a **stone** covered the exit and the **king** and the **nobles** pressed their **signet rings** into soft clay placed over chains that had been draped over the stone.

6:19-21 The narrative clearly indicates the king's personal affection for Daniel. As Darius has thoughts of life and death on his mind, he calls out in the hope that **the living God**, whom Daniel serves, has rescued his life. Daniel responds by wishing the king a long life.

6:22-23 Many scholars believe that the **angel** spoken of here is another Christophany, the Angel of the Lord, as is possibly also the case in Dn 3:25,28. As with his three youthful companions, Daniel emerged from the place of testing unharmed (**uninjured**, without wounds). The reason for his preservation is the same as theirs: **he trusted in his God** (cp. Dn 3:28) and refused spiritual compromise for political power or expediency or even self-preservation.

6:24 This verse is at once interesting and tragic. The same terms are used here as in 3:8 for the phrase

maliciously accused, meaning "to eat pieces of [someone]." In Daniel's case, those who tried to tear him to shreds by conspiring to frame him and have him executed were themselves torn to shreds. Not only, however, would they suffer for their crime; a heinous Persian practice was to execute the family members of criminals as well, so **their children and their wives** were included.

6:26-27 Whereas the king had no power to change the previous decree he had issued, God was able to overturn its effectiveness by saving Daniel's life.

6:28 As there was prosperity in the land, **Daniel prospered** also in his time of exile. This verse seems to indicate two separate persons, but the **and** can also mean "even," "namely," or "that is," bolstering the view of some scholars that Darius and Cyrus were one and the same person.

7:1 Chapter 7 is a pivotal chapter in the book of Daniel. The narrative material in chapters 1–6 establishes not only the setting in which Daniel received the visions recorded in chapters 7–12 but also Daniel's credibility and positions of prominence in Babylon. The vision recorded here has influenced most subsequent apocalyptic writings. Chapter 7 forms an outline of future events, giving meaning to prophecy regarding Christ's kingdom and His return.

7:2-8 For a summary of Daniel's vision in this chapter and its relationship to Nebuchadnezzar's vision in ch 2 and Daniel's subsequent vision (ch 8) see the chart on p. 1127.

7:9-10 Suddenly, Daniel's vision switched to a parallel universe; the judgment scene he sees is the heavenly counterpart to the earthly rule of the beasts/kings. The true King, **the Ancient of Days** (an expression used only here in Scripture—Dn 7:9,13,22), possesses overarching authority and supreme power. In contrast to the pagan rulers depicted as beasts, God is described in human terms as inherently superior. His **clothing** of **white** reflects His holiness (cp. Mt 17:2; 28:3; Mk 9:3; Lk 9:29) and the whiteness of his **hair** draws attention to His eternal life and wisdom (Dn 7:9; cp. Rv 1:14). Three times the word **fire** is used in the description of the Lord's **throne** where He takes His seat as the Judge, suggesting the unapproachable purity of His holy presence. The description of the throne as having **wheels** is reminiscent of Ezk 1:15-21. In this **court**/throne room, the judgments are decisive and cannot be overturned by human beings.

>WORD|*study*

7:7 Horn (Hb *qeren*) figuratively signifies a person's strength and power to dominate or rule (cp. Jr 48:25). As the interpreter makes clear, the "horns" in Daniel's vision represent kings—men who "rise" to positions of power. The source of a ruler's exalted status is significant in Scripture. God refers to the boastful and arrogant speech of the wicked when He commands, "'Do not lift up your horn against heaven" (Ps 75:4-5). Both before and after his view of the Lord's court (Aram *din*, "judgment, supreme tribunal," Dn 7:10,26), Daniel noted the "arrogant" speech of the little "horn" (vv. 8,11; cp. Rv 13:1-6). God's sovereign authority ensures that "the holy ones of the Most High," rather than the defiant kings of the earth, will be given His kingdom, and this possession will never be taken away (Dn 7:18,22,26-27; cp. Pss 89:5-24; 132:17-18).

and those men who had maliciously
accused Daniel[A] were brought and
thrown into the lions' den—they,
their children, and their wives. They
had not reached the bottom of the
den before the lions overpowered
them and crushed all their bones.

Daniel's Prosperity (6:25-28)

25 Then King Darius wrote to those
of every people, nation, and language who live in all the earth: "May
your prosperity abound. 26 I issue a
decree that in all my royal dominion, people must tremble in fear before the God of Daniel:

For He is the living God,
and He endures forever;
His kingdom will never
be destroyed,
and His dominion has no end.
27 He rescues and delivers;
He performs signs
and wonders
in the heavens
and on the earth,
for He has rescued Daniel
from the power of the lions."

28 So Daniel prospered during the
reign of Darius and[B] the reign of
Cyrus the Persian.

Daniel's First Vision (7:1-28)

The Four Beasts (7:1-17)

7 In the first year of Belshazzar
king of Babylon, Daniel had a
dream with visions in his mind as he
was lying in his bed. He wrote down
the dream, and here is the summary[C] of his account. 2 Daniel said,
"In my vision at night I was watching, and suddenly the four winds
of heaven stirred up the great sea.
3 Four huge beasts came up from the
sea, each different from the other.
4 "The first was like a lion but had
eagle's wings. I continued watching
until its wings were torn off. It was
lifted up from the ground, set on its
feet like a man, and given a human
mind.
5 "Suddenly, another beast appeared, a second one, that looked
like a bear. It was raised up on one
side, with three ribs in its mouth between its teeth. It was told, 'Get up!
Gorge yourself on flesh.'
6 "While I was watching, another
beast appeared. It was like a leopard
with four wings of a bird on its back.
It had four heads and was given authority to rule.
7 "While I was watching in the
night visions, a fourth beast appeared, frightening and dreadful,
and incredibly strong, with large
iron teeth. It devoured and crushed,
and it trampled with its feet whatever was left. It was different from
all the beasts before it, and it had 10
horns.
8 "While I was considering the
horns, suddenly another horn, a
little one, came up among them,
and three of the first horns were uprooted before it. There were eyes in
this horn like a man's, and it had a
mouth that spoke arrogantly.
9 "As I kept watching,

thrones were set in place,
and the Ancient of Days
took His seat.
His clothing was white
like snow,
and the hair of His head
like whitest wool.
His throne was flaming fire;
its wheels were blazing fire.
10 A river of fire was flowing,
coming out
from His presence.
Thousands upon thousands
served Him;

[A] 6:24 Lit *had eaten his pieces* [B] 6:28 Or *Darius, even* [C] 7:1 Lit *beginning*

ten thousand times
ten thousand
stood before Him.
The court was convened,
and the books were opened.

11 "I watched, then, because of the
sound of the arrogant words the
horn was speaking. As I continued
watching, the beast was killed and
its body destroyed and given over
to the burning fire. 12 As for the rest
of the beasts, their authority to rule
was removed, but an extension of
life was granted to them for a certain period of time. 13 I continued
watching in the night visions,

and I saw One like a son
of man
coming with the clouds
of heaven.
He approached the Ancient
of Days
and was escorted before Him.
14 He was given authority
to rule,
and glory, and a kingdom;
so that those of every people,
nation, and language
should serve Him.
His dominion is
an everlasting dominion
that will not pass away,
and His kingdom is one
that will not be destroyed.

15 "As for me, Daniel, my spirit
was deeply distressed within me,[A]
and the visions in my mind terrified
me. 16 I approached one of those who
were standing by and asked him the
true meaning of all this. So he let
me know the interpretation of these
things: 17 'These huge beasts, four in
number, are four kings who will rise
from the earth.

The Angel's Interpretation (7:18-28)

18 But the holy ones of the •Most High
will receive the kingdom and possess
it forever, yes, forever and ever.'
19 "Then I wanted to know the
true meaning of the fourth beast,
the one different from all the others, extremely terrifying, with iron
teeth and bronze claws, devouring, crushing, and trampling with
its feet whatever was left. 20 I also
wanted to know about the 10 horns
on its head and about the other horn
that came up, before which three
fell—the horn that had eyes, and a
mouth that spoke arrogantly, and
that was more visible than the others. 21 As I was watching, this horn
waged war against the holy ones and
was prevailing over them 22 until the
Ancient of Days arrived and a judgment was given in favor of the holy
ones of the Most High, for the time
had come, and the holy ones took
possession of the kingdom.
23 "This is what he said: 'The
fourth beast will be a fourth kingdom on the earth, different from all
the other kingdoms. It will devour
the whole earth, trample it down,
and crush it. 24 The 10 horns are 10
kings who will rise from this kingdom. Another, different from the
previous ones, will rise after them
and subdue three kings. 25 He will
speak words against the Most High
and oppress[B] the holy ones of the
Most High. He will intend to change
religious festivals[C] and laws, and the
holy ones will be handed over to him
for a time, times, and half a time.[D]
26 But the court will convene, and his
dominion will be taken away, to be
completely destroyed forever. 27 The
kingdom, dominion, and greatness
of the kingdoms under all of heaven
will be given to the people, the holy
ones of the Most High. His kingdom
will be an everlasting kingdom, and
all rulers will serve and obey Him.'

A7:15 Lit *was distressed in the middle of its sheath* B7:25 Lit *wear out* C7:25 Lit *change times*
D7:25 Or *for three and a half years*

>WORD|*study*

7:15 Daniel's expression, **My spirit was deeply** distressed [Aram *kara'*, "pained, grieved"] **within me**, more literally translated would be, "My spirit was distressed in the midst of its sheath." Figuratively, a sword in its sheath represented the soul or spirit within the body. In English idiom, Daniel might have said something like, "I was shaken to the core." Saying that he was terrified (Aram *behal*, "frighten"; corresponding to Hb *bahal*, "tremble" with fear, "be stricken with terror"; cp. v. 28; "trembling," Ex 15:15; "dismayed," 2 Sm 4:1; "shaking," Ps 6:2) by what he saw reinforces the powerful impact of the visions on Daniel and his reaction to what God revealed in them.

7:13-14 Finally, the **son of man** was given the **authority to rule** a true and eternal kingdom. Several descriptors indicate the deity of the **One like a son of man.**

Most importantly, Jesus personally assumed the title "Son of Man" in reference to Himself (Mt 24:30; 26:63-64; Mk 13:26; 14:62). The title reflects His incarnation and identification with humankind. Because of the obedience of the Son of Man "to the point of death—even to death on a cross," God "gave Him the name that is above every name," at which all people will one day bow (Php 2:5-11; cp. Dn 7:27).

7:18 The holy ones of the Most High would ultimately **receive the kingdom and possess it forever** (vv. 18-19,21-22,25,27), although these holy ones are not clearly identified. They are the servants of the true God who will reign with Him eternally.

7:24-25 The interpreter explains that the fourth beast is a kingdom from which **10 kings** will emerge. The little horn rising up among these 10 also symbolizes a kingdom, **different from the previous ones**, which will **subdue** [Aram *shephal*, "humble"; corresponding to Hb *shaphēl*, "humble, bring low," used most frequently of God's power and plan to humble those who are proud; e.g., 4:37; 5:19,22; Is 2:11-17] **three kings**. Its characteristics include having eyes "like a man's" (cp. v. 8); being arrogant vocally (cp. vv. 8,11,20; Rv 13:5) in his appearance, perhaps exalting himself to public prominence (Dn 7:20) and in his policies, attempting to redefine religious traditions and systems (v. 25). He actively opposed God and His **holy ones** (cp. v. 21; Rv 11:7; 13:3b-4,7).

Most conservative scholars agree that aspects of Daniel's vision have not yet been fulfilled, particularly when considered in connection with very similar apocalyptic imagery in the book of Revelation (e.g., Rv 13:1-2,11).

7:25-27 God establishes and enforces a fixed limitation of time during which this kingdom is allowed to operate (cp. vv. 11,22,25). Many interpret the length of time stated as **a time, times, and half a time** to be three and a half years—adding "a time" (one year), plus "times" (two years) and "half a time" (a half-year)—and correlate this with an apparent three-and-a-half-year "Great Tribulation" (Rv 11:2-3; 12:14; 13:5). After this reign of terror, Christ will reconcile and rule the earth along with His people (Rv 20:4; 21:27; 22:3-4,14). This powerful vision must have been enormously comforting to the Jewish exiles.

28 "This is the end of the interpretation. As for me, Daniel, my thoughts terrified me greatly, and my face turned pale,[A] but I kept the matter to myself."

Daniel's Second Vision (8:1-27)

A Ram, a Goat, and a Little Horn (8:1-22)

8 In the third year of King Belshazzar's reign, a vision appeared to me, Daniel, after the one that had appeared to me earlier. 2 I saw the vision, and as I watched, I was in the fortress city of Susa, in the province of Elam. I saw in the vision that I was beside the Ulai Canal. 3 I looked up,[B] and there was a ram standing beside the canal. He had two horns. The two horns were long, but one was longer than the other, and the longer one came up last. 4 I saw the ram charging to the west, the north, and the south. No animal could stand against him, and there was no rescue from his power. He did whatever he wanted and became great.

5 As I was observing, a male goat appeared, coming from the west across the surface of the entire earth without touching the ground. The goat had a conspicuous horn[C] between his eyes. 6 He came toward the two-horned ram I had seen standing beside the canal and rushed at him with savage fury. 7 I saw him approaching the ram, and infuriated with him, he struck the ram, shattering his two horns, and the ram was not strong enough to stand against him. The goat threw him to the ground and trampled him, and there was no one to rescue the ram from his power. 8 Then the male goat became very great, but when he became powerful, the large horn was shattered. Four conspicuous horns came up in its place, pointing toward the four winds of heaven.

9 From one of them a little horn emerged and grew extensively toward the south and the east and toward the beautiful land.[D] 10 It grew as high as the heavenly •host, made some of the stars and some of the host fall to the earth, and trampled them. 11 It made itself great, even up to the Prince of the host; it removed His daily sacrifice and overthrew the place of His sanctuary. 12 Because of rebellion, a host, together with the daily sacrifice, will be given over. The horn will throw truth to the ground and will be successful in whatever it does.

13 Then I heard a holy one speaking, and another holy one said to the speaker, "How long will the events of this vision last—the daily sacrifice, the rebellion that makes desolate, and the giving over of the sanctuary and of the host to be trampled?"

14 He said to me,[E] "For 2,300 evenings and mornings; then the sanctuary will be restored."

15 While I, Daniel, was watching the vision and trying to understand it, there stood before me someone who appeared to be a man. 16 I heard a human voice calling from the middle of the Ulai: "Gabriel, explain the vision to this man."

17 So he approached where I was standing; when he came near, I was terrified and fell facedown. "Son of man," he said to me, "understand that the vision refers to the time of the end." 18 While he was speaking to me, I fell into a deep sleep, with my face to the ground. Then he touched me, made me stand up, 19 and said, "I am here to tell you what will happen at the conclusion of the time of wrath, because it refers to the appointed time of the end. 20 The two-horned ram that you saw represents the kings of Media and Persia. 21 The shaggy goat represents the king of Greece, and the large horn between his eyes represents the first king.[F] 22 The four horns that took the place of the shattered horn represent four kingdoms. They will rise from that nation, but without its power.

An Insolent King (8:23-27)

23 Near the end
of their kingdoms,
when the rebels have reached
the full measure of their sin,[G]
an insolent king, skilled
in intrigue,[H]
will come to the throne.

[A] **7:28** Lit *my brightness changed on me* [B] **8:3** Lit *I lifted my eyes and looked* [C] **8:5** Lit *a horn of a vision* [D] **8:9** = Israel [E] **8:14** LXX, Theod, Syr, Vg read *him* [F] **8:21** = Alexander the Great [G] **8:23** Lit *have become complete* [H] **8:23** Lit *king, and understanding riddles*

8:1-2 Beginning with this chapter, Daniel reverts back to Hebrew, indicating the rest of the book's primary intent for his own people. This **vision** came around 550 B.C., about two years after the one in chapter 7; both occurred during **King Belshazzar's reign**, before the Medo-Persians conquered Babylon.

8:3-4 There is a dual aspect to the **ram**—his **horns** and successful **charging** in all directions. The angel Gabriel (Hb, "warrior of God; God's mighty one," v. 16; cp. 9:21; Lk 1:19,26) explained that the two horns of the **ram** symbolized "the kings of Media and Persia" (Dn 8:20). The **longer** horn indicated Persia's dominance. "Charging" from the east in every direction, Persian armies expanded the empire in all directions. Numerous uprisings against the Persian Empire failed.

8:5-8 Gabriel identified the **goat** with the **conspicuous horn** as the "king of Greece" (v. 21). Alexander the Great fulfilled this description when he overcame the Medes and Persians in 331 B.C. The description of the goat's rapid movement conveys the speed of the Greek Empire's conquest of every kingdom in its path.

When Alexander died at the height of his career (**the large horn was shattered**), his kingdom was divided among his four generals (i.e., the **four conspicuous horns**; cp. 7:6).

8:9-11 These verses describe the political power and spiritual arrogance of the one identified as the **little horn** and generally considered to be Antiochus IV Epiphanes (175–163 B.C.), a brutal Seleucid ruler who persecuted the Jews—those living in **the beautiful** [Hb *tsevi*, "splendor, glory, honor"; cp. 11:16,41; Ezk 20:6,15] **land**.

8:12 First and Second Maccabees, written during the second and first centuries B.C., tell of the Syrian tyrant's "deeds of murder" and acts of sacrilege. In addition, they describe the unfaithfulness of many in Israel, who, **because of rebellion** (Hb *pesha'*, "revolt, defection; sin, transgression") and idolatry, would **be given over** to such suffering.

8:14 While the events would be horrendous, they would be limited to **2,300 evenings and mornings**, a way of expressing the concept of literal 24-hour days (cp. 8:26; Gn 1:5). The end point is the restoration of the temple (**sanctuary**), which took place on December 14, 164 B.C., when Judas Maccabeus captured the temple mount, destroyed the statue and altar of Zeus, and restored the daily sacrifices on a newly rebuilt altar. The

Dreams and Visions in the Book of Daniel

	Nebuchadnezzar's Dream (2:1-45)	Daniel's Dream with Visions (7:1-14)	Daniel's Vision (8:1-27)	Kingdom Represented
Imagery	"a colossal statue" (v. 31)	"four huge beasts" (v. 3)	"a ram," "a male goat," and "a little horn" (vv. 3,5,9)	
Imagery	"head of gold" (2:32,38)	like a lion but had eagle's wings (v. 4)		Babylon
Imagery	silver chest and arms (2:32,39)	"like a bear" (v. 5)	"two-horned ram, one horn longer than the other" (vv. 3,6-7)	Medo-Persia
Imagery	"stomach and thighs of bronze" (vv. 32,39)	"like a leopard with four wings of a bird" "and four heads" (v. 6)	male goat with "a conspicuous horn" (8:5), then "four horns" (8:8,22)	Greece
Imagery	iron legs (vv. 33,40) feet "partly iron and partly fired clay" (v. 42)	"dreadful beast with iron teeth" and "10 horns" (vv. 7,11) a little horn (v. 8)	a little horn (8:9-11)	Rome
Imagery	"a stone" (vv. 33-35; 41-43)	throne room of "the Ancient of Days" (vv. 9-10,13-14)		eternal kingdom of Christ
Interpretation	Successive world empires that would ultimately be defeated by God's kingdom	Successive world empires with emphasis on the ultimate triumph of God's "everlasting kingdom" and His "holy ones" (7:27)	Greece would conquer the Medo-Persian Empire.	

[24] His power will be great,
but it will not be his own.
He will cause
terrible destruction
and succeed in whatever
he does.
He will destroy the powerful
along with the holy people.
[25] He will cause deceit
to prosper
through his cunning
and by his influence,
and in his own mind he will
make himself great.
He will destroy many in a
time of peace;
he will even stand
against the Prince
of princes.
Yet he will be
shattered—not by
human hands.
[26] The vision of the evenings
and the mornings
that has been told is true.
Now you must seal up
the vision
because it refers to many days
in the future."

[27] I, Daniel, was overcome and lay
sick for days. Then I got up and went
about the king's business. I was
greatly disturbed by the vision and
could not understand it.

The Prayer of Daniel (9:1-19)

9 In the first year of Darius, the
son of Ahasuerus, a Mede by
birth, who was ruler over the kingdom of the Chaldeans: [2] In the first
year of his reign, I, Daniel, understood from the books according to
the word of the LORD to Jeremiah

date of December 16, 167 B.C., when Antiochus IV desecrated the temple occurred less than 1,150 days prior to this event. However, 2,300 days—six years and four months—before the reconsecration of the temple (autumn of 170 B.C.), the murder of the former high priest, Onias III, marked the beginning of intensified persecution of the Jews and their religion.

9:1-2 The setting is around 538 B.C., about 12 years after the vision in chapter 8. Daniel was more than 80 years old, and had been in Babylon for over 65 years. **Darius** is identified as **the son of Ahasuerus**, more widely known by the Greek name Xerxes I (reigned 486–465/64 B.C.; see note on 5:31 and textual note on Est 1:1). Babylon's sudden demise and the installment of Darius over **the kingdom of the Chaldeans** likely prompted many Jews in exile to wonder if the political change might bring any change to their status as captives.

Daniel had access to **the books** (Hb *sepharim*, "writings, scriptures"), the Hebrew writings, regarded as divinely inspired and already including **the word of the LORD to Jeremiah** whose prophecy specified **70** as **the number of years for the desolation** [Hb *chorbah*, "ruins, place that has been laid waste"] **of Jerusalem** and were recorded before the first deportation to Babylon (605 B.C.; Jr 25:11-12) and restated after 597 B.C. during the exile (cp. Jr 29:10). Jerusalem and its temple were destroyed by the Babylonians. The second temple, constructed by Zerubbabel, was dedicated 70 years later in 516 B.C. Daniel must have recognized that he would not live to see the fulfillment of the prophecy.

9:3-4 Daniel's **fasting, sackcloth, and ashes** indicated humility before the Lord and personal mourning. He both **prayed** (Hb *palal*, "supplicate, intercede") and **confessed** (Hb *yadah*, "show oneself as guilty") to **the LORD** (Hb *YHWH*, "Yahweh," God's covenant name, Dn 9:4,8,10,13; see Ex 3:15).

9:4-6 Although Daniel has been described in the text as upright and faithful, his prayer is one of corporate confession; he also identifies with the corporate sin of the people. Their sinful rebellion and repeated ignoring of **prophets** like Jeremiah led to their current situation.

9:7-10 Daniel contrasted the Lord's **righteousness** (cp. vv. 14,16), **compassion**, and **forgiveness** (cp. v. 18) with the **public shame** (cp. v. 16) and **disloyalty** (cp. vv. 11,15) of the people. Daniel understood that sin both constituted a *personal* affront against God and led to *public* disgrace.

9:11-14 In His righteousness, Yahweh carries out the consequences prescribed in the law (cp. vv. 7,16), specifically the climactic **curse** of Dt 27–30, a passage that sets out the covenant blessings and curses. Exile was the worst and final curse for covenant violation. In response to Solomon's temple dedication prayer, God reminded him of the curses for disobedience, specifying that the temple would be "rejected" and Israel would "become an object of scorn and ridicule among all the peoples" (see 1Kg 9:6-9).

9:15-18 Daniel appealed to the defining act of redemption, requesting the redemption of **Jerusalem** and asking God once again to deliver His people from the slavery of exile as He had delivered them from Egypt. The request for favor and restoration was not founded upon Israel's own **righteous acts** but rather on God's **abundant compassion**. Even in the Old Testament, forgiveness and salvation come by grace, not works (cp. Eph 2:1-5).

the prophet that the number of years for the desolation of Jerusalem would be 70. 3 So I turned my attention to the Lord God to seek Him by prayer and petitions, with fasting, •sackcloth, and ashes.

4 I prayed to the LORD my God and confessed:

Ah, Lord—the great and awe-inspiring God who keeps His gracious covenant with those who love Him and keep His commands— 5 we have sinned, done wrong, acted wickedly, rebelled, and turned away from Your commands and ordinances. 6 We have not listened to Your servants the prophets, who spoke in Your name to our kings, leaders, fathers, and all the people of the land.

7 Lord, righteousness belongs to You, but this day public shame belongs to us: the men of Judah, the residents of Jerusalem, and all Israel—those who are near and those who are far, in all the countries where You have dispersed them because of the disloyalty they have shown toward You. 8 LORD, public shame belongs to us, our kings, our leaders, and our fathers, because we have sinned against You. 9 Compassion and forgiveness belong to the Lord our God, though we have rebelled against Him 10 and have not obeyed the voice of the LORD our God by following His instructions that He set before us through His servants the prophets.

11 All Israel has broken Your law and turned away, refusing to obey You. The promised curse[A] written in the law of Moses, the servant of God, has been poured out on us because we have sinned against Him. 12 He has carried out His words that He spoke against us and against our rulers[B] by bringing on us so great a disaster that nothing like what has been done to Jerusalem has ever been done under all of heaven. 13 Just as it is written in the law of Moses, all this disaster has come on us, yet we have not appeased the LORD our God by turning from our iniquities and paying attention to Your truth. 14 So the LORD kept the disaster in mind and brought it on us, for the LORD our God is righteous in all He has done. But we have not obeyed Him.

15 Now, Lord our God, who brought Your people out of the land of Egypt with a mighty hand and made Your name renowned as it is this day, we have sinned, we have acted wickedly. 16 Lord, in keeping with all Your righteous acts, may Your anger and wrath turn away from Your city Jerusalem, Your holy mountain; for because of our sins and the iniquities of our fathers, Jerusalem and Your people have become an object of ridicule to all those around us.

17 Therefore, our God, hear the prayer and the petitions of Your servant. Show Your favor to Your desolate sanctuary for the Lord's sake. 18 Listen,[C] my God, and hear. Open Your eyes and see our desolations and the city called by Your name. For we are not presenting our petitions before You based on our righteous acts, but based on Your abundant compassion. 19 Lord, hear! Lord, forgive! Lord, listen and act! My God, for Your own sake, do not delay, because Your city and Your people are called by Your name.

The 70 Weeks of Years (9:20-27)

The Prophecy of the 70 Weeks (9:20-23)

20 While I was speaking, praying, confessing my sin and the sin of my people Israel, and presenting my petition before •Yahweh my God concerning the holy mountain of my God— 21 while I was praying, Gabriel, the man I had seen in the

[A] 9:11 Lit *The curse and the oath* [B] 9:12 Lit *against rulers who ruled us* [C] 9:18 Lit *Stretch out Your ear*

>WORD|*study*

9:21 For Daniel, **weariness** (Hb *ya'aph*, "be fatigued, worn out, exhausted") probably resulted from both physical investment in fervent prayer accompanied by fasting (cp. 9:3; Is 44:12; Hab 2:13) and the expression of intense emotions poured into such a prayer of confession (cp. Is 50:4). Daniel's grief is evident both in the words of his prayer and in his choice of "sackcloth and ashes" as outward signs of mourning (cp. Dn 9:3; Est 4:1,3).

9:26 Messiah (Hb *mashiyach*, "anointed one") signified a priest, king, or prophet who had been consecrated to the Lord. Oil was poured on the man's head to "anoint" (Hb *mashach*) him for one of these offices (e.g., Ex 29:7; 30:30; 1Sm 15:1; 16:12; 1Kg 1:34; 19:16). Only in Leviticus the term "anointed" appears with a definite article ("the") to describe the priest (Lv 4:3,5,16; 6:22). In every other instance in the Old Testament, except for Dn 9:25-26, the "anointed one" always has a possessive pronoun referring to the Lord ("My" or "Your") or the phrase "the LORD's" (cp. 2Sm 23:1) to indicate that he belonged to or was set apart unto the Lord (e.g., 1Sm 2:10,35; 2Sm 1:14; Ps 132:17; Is 45:1). In Dn 9:25-26, Gabriel merely refers to "Messiah" as the endpoint of the **62 weeks** and as one who **will be cut off** (Hb *karat*, "punishment by death or exile," Dn 9:26; cp. Ex 12:15; 31:14). Perhaps Gabriel's unprecedented use of the term "Messiah" (i.e., with no modifiers) supports the traditional understanding of the passage as referring to Jesus Christ (Gk *christos*, "anointed"; cp. Mt 1:16-17; Jn 20:31). In addition, one of the six purposes given for the decree of 70 weeks—"to anoint the most holy place" (Dn 9:24)—suggests that this event of re-consecrating the holy of holies was closely linked to the man designated as an "anointed one." When Jesus the Messiah died on the cross (was "cut off"), the veil barring entrance to the holy of holies in the temple was torn in two, signaling that Christ Himself constituted "the new and living way" to forgiveness of sins and the presence of God (Heb 10:19-20; cp. 9:11-12,24; Mk 15:38). Messiah's decisive victory on the cross has precipitated the expansion of God's kingdom, in which "rebellion [will ultimately be brought] to an end," in which He will "put a [final] stop to sin" and "wipe away [Hb *kaphar*, "cover over, pardon, atone for"; cp. Ps 79:9] iniquity"; He has brought in "everlasting righteousness" (cp. Ps 119:142) and sealed up (i.e., signed and authenticated or completed, fulfilled) "vision and prophecy" (Dn 9:24; cp. Heb 1:1-2).

first vision, came to me in my extreme weariness, about the time of the evening offering. 22 He gave me this explanation: "Daniel, I've come now to give you understanding. 23 At the beginning of your petitions an answer went out, and I have come to give it, for you are treasured by God. So consider the message and understand the vision:

The Prayer of the Prophet (9:24-27)

24 Seventy weeks[A] are decreed
about your people
and your holy city—
to bring the rebellion
to an end,
to put a stop to sin,
to wipe away iniquity,
to bring in
everlasting righteousness,
to seal up vision
and prophecy,
and to anoint
the most holy place.
25 Know and understand this:
From the issuing
of the decree
to restore
and rebuild Jerusalem
until •Messiah the Prince[B]
will be seven weeks
and 62 weeks.[C]
It will be rebuilt with a plaza
and a moat,
but in difficult times.
26 After those 62 weeks[D]
the Messiah will be cut off
and will have nothing.
The people
of the coming prince
will destroy the city
and the sanctuary.
The[E] end will come
with a flood,
and until the end
there will be[F] war;
desolations are decreed.
27 He will make
a firm covenant[G]
with many for one week,[H]
but in the middle of the week
he will put a stop to sacrifice
and offering.
And the abomination
of desolation
will be on a wing
of the temple[I,J]
until the decreed destruction
is poured out
on the desolator."

[A]**9:24** = 490 years [B]**9:25** Or *until an anointed one, a prince* [C]**9:25** = 49 years and 434 years [D]**9:26** = 434 years [E]**9:26** Lit *Its*, or *His* [F]**9:26** Or *end of a* [G]**9:27** Or *will enforce a covenant* [H]**9:27** = 7 years [I]**9:27** LXX; MT reads *of abominations* [J]**9:27** Or *And the desolator will be on the wing of abominations*, or *And the desolator will come on the wings of monsters* (or *of horror*); Hb obscure

9:19-21 While Daniel was engaged in fasting, regular prayer, confession of sin, and reading of the Scriptures, the messenger **Gabriel** again brought revelation to him. **The time of the evening offering** may denote a regular time of prayer (around 3:00 to 4:00 in the afternoon; cp. Ezr 9:4-5; Ps 141:2), when the evening sacrifice had usually been offered at the temple, a ritual now defunct due to the temple's destruction.

9:23 That God's word **went out** before Daniel had finished praying underscores the speed with which He responds to prayer, whether or not the one praying is aware of God's activities. **The vision** mentioned here perhaps refers to the one recorded in chapter 8 (see 8:27). Gabriel pointed out that Daniel was **treasured** [Hb *chemdah*, "that in which one takes delight; deemed precious, of great value"; cp. 10:11,19] **by God**. God had not forgotten or neglected him; in Daniel's struggle and distress, God heard him and loved him.

9:24-26 These verses present some interpretive challenges. Although competing views have been advanced, the **seventy weeks** are best understood literally as "70 sevens" or 490 years. Because of the eschatological and messianic overtone of these verses, the six reasons for the events of these weeks have been partially fulfilled in Jesus the Messiah, with the remaining fulfillment still to come. The end point for this period of time (ca A.D. 26) was probably the year that Jesus—**Messiah the Prince**—was baptized and began His public ministry.

9:26-27 This passage stands as a part of a whole eschatological chain of events—namely, God's program of the desolation of Jerusalem and the time of tribulation. God frequently used other nations as the instruments by which He would punish His own people, Israel. After the Messiah comes, Jerusalem will be destroyed like a **flood**, a metaphorical description of the overwhelming way the city was destroyed. An explanation is given of the events of the last **weeks** (seven years). These are the years known as the tribulation. During the tribulation, the **coming prince**, also the antichrist, **will destroy the city and the sanctuary**. Presumably, therefore, sometime after Christ died and before the tribulation, the temple in Jerusalem will be rebuilt. The church is waiting, even now, for the seventieth week. Therefore, interest in a new temple will certainly be a sign of eschatological events.

10:1 The **third year of Cyrus king of Persia** was ca 536 B.C., two years after the vision of chapter 9. Although some exiles had returned to Jerusalem, Daniel remained in Babylon. The Jews had begun to rebuild the temple, but the work had temporarily stopped. The **conflict** referenced here could be spiritual/angelic or earthly, and indeed both are possible as seen from the substance of the following chapters.

10:2 The period of time in which Daniel **was mourning** (21 days) coincided with the season of Passover.

10:4-8 The twenty-fourth day of the first month—Nisan (March–April)—would have been three days after the seven-day celebration of Passover or the Festival of Unleavened Bread had ended (cp. Ex 12:15,18; Lv 23:5-8; Dt 16:1-8). Daniel was standing by the **Tigris** [Old Persian, "the fast one"; Hb *chiddeqel*, "rapid"] **River**, meaning he was away from the city of Babylon. With Daniel were some men who **did not see** the vision but were struck by **a great terror** (Hb *charadah*, "panic, fear expressed by trembling or quaking"; cp. 1Sm 14:15; Is 21:4; Ezk 26:16) and fled, leaving him alone (Dn 10:7).

The Future of Israel and the End-Times (10:1–12:13)

Daniel's Vision of the Glorious One (10:1-14)

10 In the third year of Cyrus king
of Persia, a message was revealed to Daniel, who was named
Belteshazzar. The message was true
and was about a great conflict. He
understood the message and had
understanding of the vision.
2 In those days I, Daniel, was
mourning for three full weeks. 3 I
didn't eat any rich food, no meat
or wine entered my mouth, and I
didn't put any oil on my body until the three weeks were over. 4 On
the twenty-fourth day of the first
month,[A] as I was standing on the
bank of the great river, the Tigris,
5 I looked up, and there was a man
dressed in linen, with a belt of gold
from Uphaz[B] around his waist. 6 His
body was like topaz,[C] his face like the
brilliance of lightning, his eyes like
flaming torches, his arms and feet
like the gleam of polished bronze,
and the sound of his words like the
sound of a multitude.
7 Only I, Daniel, saw the vision.
The men who were with me did
not see it, but a great terror fell on
them, and they ran and hid. 8 I was
left alone, looking at this great vision. No strength was left in me; my
face grew deathly pale,[D] and I was
powerless. 9 I heard the words he
said, and when I heard them I fell
into a deep sleep,[E] with my face to
the ground.
10 Suddenly, a hand touched me
and raised me to my hands and
knees. 11 He said to me, "Daniel, you
are a man treasured by God. Understand the words that I'm saying to
you. Stand on your feet, for I have
now been sent to you." After he said
this to me, I stood trembling.
12 "Don't be afraid, Daniel," he said
to me, "for from the first day that
you purposed to understand and to
humble yourself before your God,
your prayers were heard. I have
come because of your prayers. 13 But
the prince of the kingdom of Persia

[A]10:4 = Nisan (March–April) [B]10:5 Some Hb mss read *Ophir* [C]10:6 The identity of this stone is uncertain. [D]10:8 Lit *my splendor was turned on me to ruin* [E]10:9 Lit *a sleep on my face*

The Prophecy of Seventy Weeks (490 years) – Interpretation 1

This interpretation takes as its starting point, Artaxerxes' decree to Nehemiah in 444 B.C. (Neh 2:1-8). From 444 B.C. to A.D. 33 the number of years is calculated to be 478 years rather than the 483 years required. However, one must note that this calculation is based upon the Gregorian solar calendar of 365 days (as used in this modern era) instead of the Jewish lunar calendar with 360 days. Adjusting the two calendars, which must be done for accuracy, leaves a difference of about eight years. When this is considered, as well as noting the additional year for transition (1 B.C. to A.D. 1), the date of A.D. 33 is clearly the date at the end of the 69th week when Christ was welcomed to Jerusalem as King.

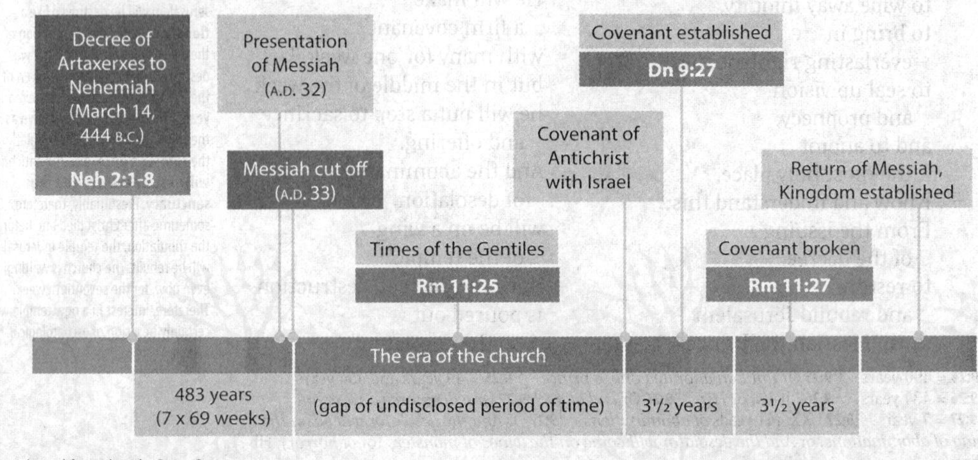

Adapted from chart by Paige Patterson

opposed me for 21 days. Then Michael, one of the chief princes, came to help me after I had been left there with the kings of Persia. 14 Now I have come to help you understand what will happen to your people in the last days, for the vision refers to those days."

The Revelation of Conflict (10:15-21)

15 While he was saying these words to me, I turned my face toward the ground and was speechless. 16 Suddenly one with human likeness touched my lips. I opened my mouth and said to the one standing in front of me, "My lord, because of the vision, anguish overwhelms me and I am powerless. 17 How can someone like me, your servant,[A] speak with someone like you, my lord? Now I have no strength, and there is no breath in me."

18 Then the one with human likeness touched me again and strengthened me. 19 He said, "Don't be afraid, you who are[B] treasured by God. Peace to you; be very strong!"

As he spoke to me, I was strengthened and said, "Let my lord speak, for you have strengthened me."

20 He said, "Do you know why I've come to you? I must return at once to fight against the prince of Persia, and when I leave, the prince of Greece will come. 21 No one has the courage to support me against them except

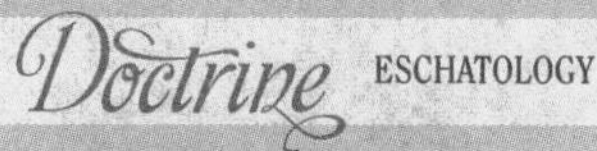

ESCHATOLOGY

10:11-14 *Eschatology* refers to the study of the last things. Eschatological events constitute the main theme of this **vision** (or at least the description and interpretation given here). Some events shown to Daniel took place in the third and second centuries B.C. Other events predicted in 11:36-45 have not yet come to pass and possibly refer to the time of antichrist in the end (or "last") times—i.e., in the *eschaton*.

The speaker (angel) mentioned was **sent** in response to Daniel's **prayers**, honoring his intention to **understand** and **humble** himself. He also came to help Daniel understand the future, specifically regarding his people, the Jews. **The prince** [Hb *sar*, "one who commands"] **. . . of Persia** likely refers to an angelic being capable of standing against an angel of God and having a territorial assignment, not to the earthly "prince," Cyrus. The conflict is in the spiritual realm (cp. Eph 6:12). This opposing angel had withstood God's messenger **for 21 days**—the same length of time during which Daniel had been mourning. God's messenger also mentioned being **left there with the kings of Persia** (beings whose purpose was to frustrate the purposes of God), implying that he had contended additionally with multiple spiritual rulers over Persia (cp. 1Co 2:6,8). The word "prince" is also used to identify **Michael** (Hb, "who is like God"), a high-ranking archangel. As **one of the chief princes** or archangels, Michael intervened and apparently ended the standoff so that his colleague could go to Daniel.

10:5 Many regard this vision as a Christophany (cp. Dn 3:25; Is 6:1-5; Rv 1:1-3,17). The **man** Daniel saw was **dressed in linen**, the white clothing of priests (Lv 16:4; 1Ch 15:27; 2Ch 5:12) and of the angels and armies of heaven (cp. Rv 15:6; 19:14), denoting purity and holiness.

[A]**10:17** Lit *Can I, a servant of my lord* [B]**10:19** Lit *afraid, man*

The Prophecy of Seventy Weeks (490 years) – Interpretation 2

Although at least four competing views are held, the **seventy weeks** (9:24) are best understood literally as "70 sevens" or 490 years. This period of time was **decreed** (Hb *chatak*, literally "cut, divide"; here "decide, determine," in the sense that God had "cut out" this particular period of time), and it began with a particular historical event. **The issuing** [Hb *motsa'* "a going out or putting into effect; open declaration or proclamation"] **of the decree to restore and rebuild Jerusalem** likely referred to one of two decrees given by Artaxerxes I, who ruled the Persian empire from 464-424 B.C. This chart is based on the assumption that the relevant decree to restore and rebuild Jerusalem was the one Artaxerxes I gave to Ezra in 457 B.C. Based on this assumption, the 69 weeks (69 x 7) or 483 years would have as an end point A.D. 26, the year Jesus was baptized and inaugurated His public ministry.

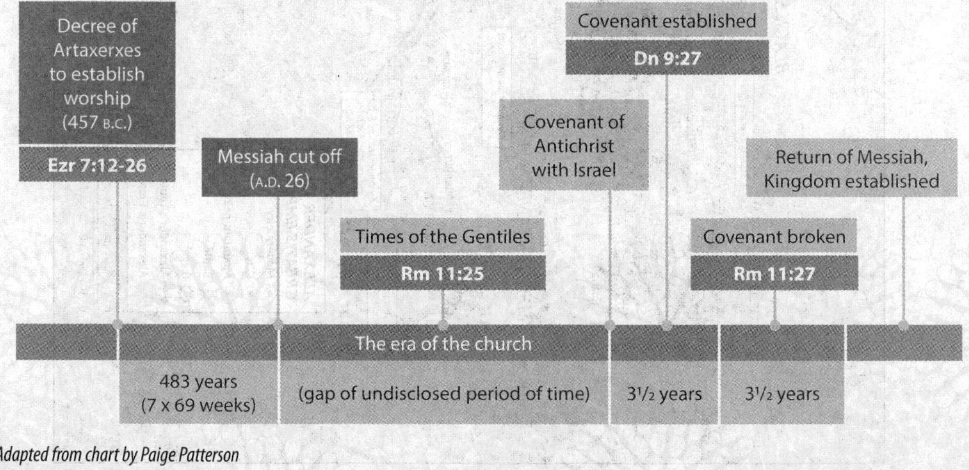

Adapted from chart by Paige Patterson

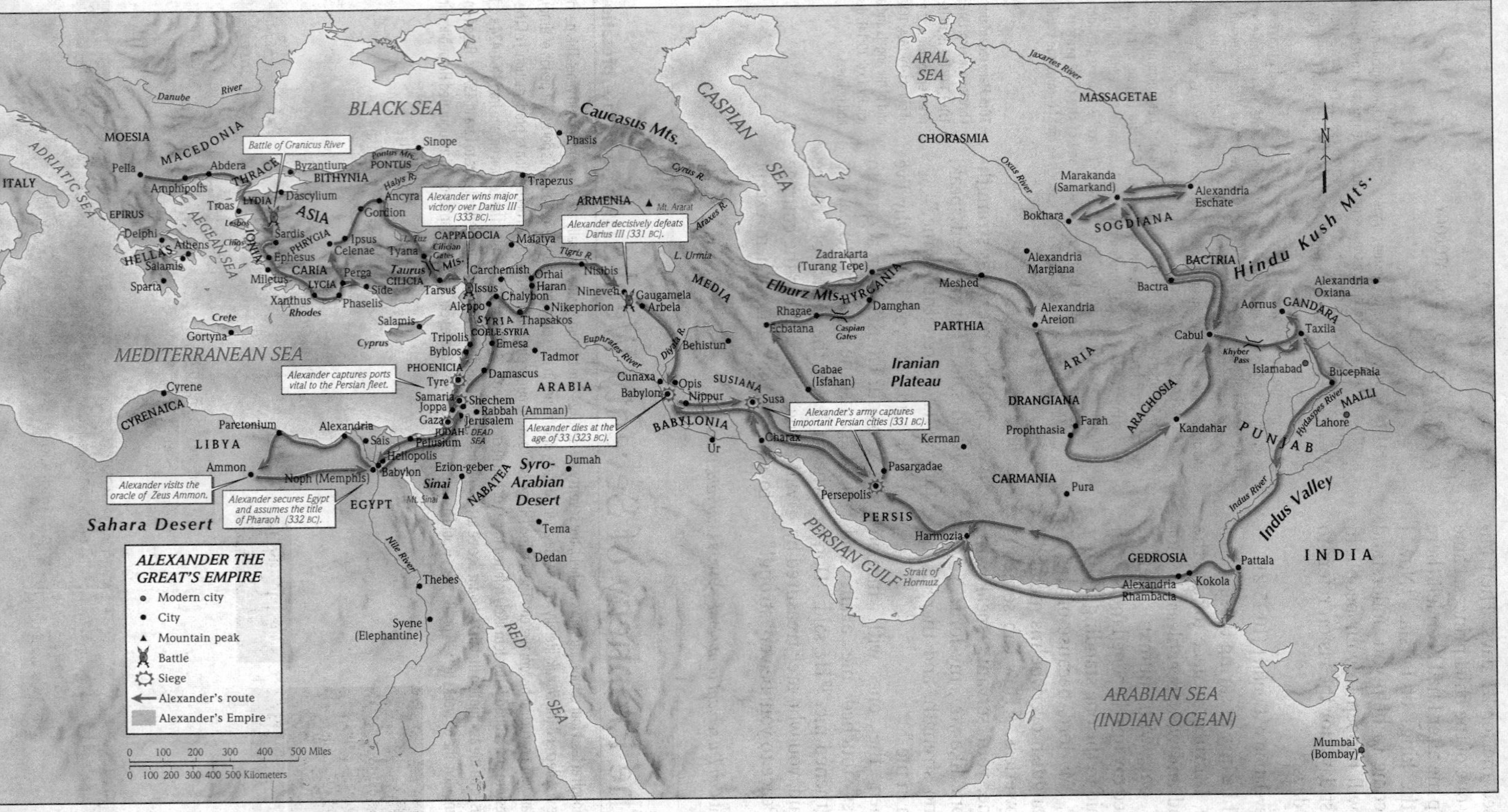
ALEXANDER THE GREAT'S EMPIRE
Modern city
City
Mountain peak
Battle
Siege
Alexander's route
Alexander's Empire
0 100 200 300 400 500 Miles
0 100 200 300 400 500 Kilometers
Battle of Granicus River
Alexander wins major victory over Darius III (333 BC).
Alexander decisively defeats Darius III (331 BC).
Alexander captures ports vital to the Persian fleet.
Alexander dies at the age of 33 (323 BC).
Alexander's army captures important Persian cities (331 BC).
Alexander visits the oracle of Zeus Ammon.
Alexander secures Egypt and assumes the title of Pharaoh (332 BC).
BLACK SEA
CASPIAN SEA
ARAL SEA
MEDITERRANEAN SEA
AEGEAN SEA
ADRIATIC SEA
RED SEA
PERSIAN GULF
ARABIAN SEA (INDIAN OCEAN)
Strait of Hormuz
Caucasus Mts.
Elburz Mts.
Hindu Kush Mts.
Taurus Mts.
Iranian Plateau
Sahara Desert
Syro-Arabian Desert
Indus Valley
ITALY
MOESIA
MACEDONIA
THRACE
EPIRUS
HELLAS
LYDIA
IONIA
CARIA
LYCIA
PHRYGIA
ASIA
BITHYNIA
PONTUS
CAPPADOCIA
CILICIA
ARMENIA
SYRIA
COELE-SYRIA
PHOENICIA
JUDAH
ARABIA
NABATEA
MEDIA
SUSIANA
BABYLONIA
HYRCANIA
PARTHIA
ARIA
DRANGIANA
ARACHOSIA
CARMANIA
PERSIS
GEDROSIA
CHORASMIA
MASSAGETAE
SOGDIANA
BACTRIA
GANDARA
PUNJAB
MALLI
INDIA
LIBYA
CYRENAICA
EGYPT
Sinai
Danube River
Halys R.
Tigris R.
Euphrates River
Diyala R.
Cyrus R.
Araxes R.
Oxus River
Jaxartes River
Nile River
Hydaspes River
Indus River
L. Urmia
Mt. Ararat
Mt. Sinai
Cilician Gates
Caspian Gates
Khyber Pass
Pella
Amphipolis
Abdera
Troas
Lesbos
Chios
Delphi
Athens
Salamis
Sparta
Crete
Gortyna
Rhodes
Byzantium
Dascylium
Sardis
Ephesus
Miletus
Xanthus
Phaselis
Perga
Side
Celenae
Ipsus
Gordion
Ancyra
Sinope
Tyana
Tarsus
Issus
Trapezus
Phasis
Malatya
Carchemish
Aleppo
Chalybon
Orhai
Haran
Nisibis
Nineveh
Gaugamela
Arbela
Nikephorion
Thapsakos
Salamis
Cyprus
Tripolis
Byblos
Emesa
Tadmor
Damascus
Tyre
Samaria
Shechem
Joppa
Rabbah (Amman)
Gaza
Jerusalem
DEAD SEA
Pelusium
Heliopolis
Babylon
Noph (Memphis)
Sais
Alexandria
Paretonium
Ammon
Cyrene
Ezion-geber
Dumah
Tema
Dedan
Thebes
Syene (Elephantine)
Cunaxa
Opis
Babylon
Nippur
Ur
Behistun
Susa
Charax
Ecbatana
Rhagae
Gabae (Isfahan)
Zadrakarta (Turang Tepe)
Damghan
Pasargadae
Persepolis
Kerman
Harmozia
Meshed
Alexandria Margiana
Alexandria Areion
Prophthasia
Farah
Pura
Kandahar
Alexandria Rhambacia
Kokola
Pattala
Bokhara
Marakanda (Samarkand)
Alexandria Eschate
Bactra
Cabul
Aornus
Alexandria Oxiana
Taxila
Islamabad
Bucephala
Lahore
Mumbai (Bombay)
N

Michael, your prince. However, I will tell you what is recorded in the book

The Continuation of the Vision (11:1-4)

11 of truth. 1 In the first year of Darius the Mede, I stood up to strengthen and protect him. 2 Now I will tell you the truth.

"Three more kings will arise in Persia, and the fourth will be far richer than the others. By the power he gains through his riches, he will stir up everyone against the kingdom of Greece. 3 Then a warrior king will arise; he will rule a vast realm and do whatever he wants. 4 But as soon as he is established, his kingdom will be broken up and divided to the four winds of heaven, but not to his descendants; it will not be the same kingdom that he ruled, because his kingdom will be uprooted and will go to others besides them.

The King of the South (11:5-20)

5 "The king of the South will grow powerful, but one of his commanders will grow more powerful and will rule a kingdom greater than his. 6 After some years they will form an alliance, and the daughter of the king of the South will go to the king of the North to seal the agreement. She will not retain power, and his strength will not endure. She will be given up, together with her entourage, her father,[A] and the one who supported her during those times. 7 In the place of the king of the South, one from her family[B] will rise up, come against the army, and enter the fortress of the king of the North. He will take action against them and triumph. 8 He will take even their gods captive to Egypt, with their metal images and their precious articles of silver and gold. For some years he will stay away from the king of the North, 9 who will enter the kingdom of the king of the South and then return to his own land.

10 "His sons will mobilize for war and assemble a large number of armed forces. They will advance, sweeping through like a flood,[C] and will again wage war as far as his fortress. 11 Infuriated, the king of the South will march out to fight with the king of the North who will raise a large army but they will be handed over to his enemy. 12 When the army is carried off, he will become arrogant and cause tens of thousands to fall, but he will not triumph. 13 The king of the North will again raise a multitude larger than the first. After some years[D] he will advance with a great army and many supplies.

14 "In those times many will rise up against the king of the South. Violent ones among your own people will assert themselves to fulfill a vision, but they will fail. 15 Then the king of the North will come, build up an assault ramp, and capture a well-fortified city. The forces of the South will not stand; even their select troops will not be able to resist. 16 The king of the North who comes against him will do whatever he wants, and no one can oppose him. He will establish himself in the beautiful land[E] with total destruction in his hand. 17 He will resolve to come with the force of his whole kingdom and will reach an agreement with him.[F] He will give him a daughter in marriage[G] to destroy it,[H] but she will not stand with him or support him. 18 Then he will turn his attention to the coasts and islands[I] and capture many. But a commander will put an end to his taunting; instead, he will turn his taunts against him. 19 He will turn his attention back to the fortresses of his own land, but he will stumble, fall, and be no more.

20 "In his place one will arise who will send out a tax collector for the glory of the kingdom; but within a few days he will be shattered, though not in anger[J] or in battle.

The King of the North (11:21-28)

21 "In his place a despised person will arise; royal honors will not be given to him, but he will come during a time of peace[K] and seize the kingdom by intrigue. 22 A flood

[A]**11:6** Some Hb mss, Theod read *the child*; Syr, Vg read *her children* [B]**11:7** Lit *from the shoot of her roots* [C]**11:10** Lit *advance and overflow and pass through* [D]**11:13** Lit *At the end of the times* [E]**11:16** = Israel [F]**11:17** = the king of the South [G]**11:17** Lit *him the daughter of women* [H]**11:17** Perhaps the kingdom [I]**11:18** of the Mediterranean [J]**11:20** Or *not openly* [K]**11:21** Or *come without warning*

11:1 The first year of Darius (539/538 B.C.) links this section with chapter 9. In that year, Cyrus the Persian incorporated Babylon as a province of his empire (cp. 5:30 and 9:1). Under Cyrus's rule the Jews were allowed to return to Jerusalem and begin rebuilding the temple. The prophecies about Persia and Greece are so historically accurate that many have questioned the dating of the book of Daniel, assuming it must have been written after the events actually occurred. However, evidence—particularly from the portions of text discovered among the Dead Sea Scrolls—points to the antiquity of the book, undermining theories that it was composed during the second century B.C.

11:3 When Antiochus stopped in Jerusalem on his way back to Syria, he encountered a rebellion incited by the hellenization (adoption of Greek culture and religion) forced upon the city by the priests he appointed—Jason and Menelaus. Therefore, favoring and sparing "those who abandon the holy covenants" (i.e., apostates who embraced the changes that replaced or corrupted Jewish religious practices; 11:30), his troops killed or enslaved tens of thousands of Jews—men, women, and children—and plundered the temple.

11:5 The four divisions of the empire conquered by Alexander are identified geographically in relation to the land of Israel, which lay between these warring nations. These verses cover almost 200 years of conflict among them. **The king of the South** was Ptolemy I Soter (323–285 B.C.), who established the Ptolemaic Dynasty of Egypt (323–30 B.C.). Seleucus I Nicator became **one of his commanders** in Egypt after losing control of Babylonia to a general named Antigonus, whose success incited opposition on several fronts. The defeat of Antigonus's son Demetrius at Gaza in 312 B.C. led to Seleucus's recovery of power. The Seleucid Dynasty ruled over **a kingdom greater than** Ptolemy's, eventually including Babylonia, Syria, and Media.

11:21-22 Antiochus IV Epiphanes was the **despised person** (Hb *bazah*, "one who is vile") of verse 21 and the "little horn" of Dn 8:9-12. The throne should have belonged to Demetrius I Soter; but while he was still a Roman hostage, Antiochus IV was able to **seize the kingdom by intrigue** (Hb *chalqlaqqot*, "words or actions intended to flatter, ingratiate, entice, or coax"; literally, "slippery"). The verbs **will be swept away** (Hb *shataph*, "be overwhelmed or rinsed out") and **will be shattered** (Hb *shavar*, "be broken, wrecked, or torn to pieces") vividly depict his triumph over every opponent, whether political rivals or the Jews resisting his heavy-handed promotion of hellenization in Judea. The identity of **the covenant prince** is uncertain, but the legitimate high priest Onias III is a likely candidate.

11:23-24 Accepting a bribe from Onias's brother Jason, Antiochus made him the high priest, the person invested with the greatest authority for implementing not only Jewish law (Torah) but also the king's political control. Having formed an **alliance** with the Jewish leader, Antiochus then acted **deceitfully** when, three years later, he replaced Jason with Menelaus, a man of unknown heritage who also bribed Antiochus for the position. Jason fled, and Onias III was assassinated. Antiochus was politically ambitious and a manipulator of persons, rewarding them for their loyalty with **plunder, loot, and wealth**. According to the prophetic word given to Daniel, this activity would last **only for a time** (i.e., only as long as the sovereign God allowed).

11:25-26 The **king of the South** was Ptolemy VI Philometer, one of two sons of Ptolemy V Epiphanes and Cleopatra I, the daughter of Antiochus III (the Great).

11:28 On his way back to Syria after having taken **great wealth** out of Egypt, Antiochus turned to persecuting the Jews (**against the holy covenant**). He pillaged the city of Jerusalem, looting the gold and silver of the temple treasury and killing many of his opponents there. He also replaced Jason with Menelaus as high priest (see 11:23-24).

11:31 Antiochus banned circumcision and **the daily sacrifice**, even sacrificing a pig on the sacred altar and setting up a statue to Zeus within the temple courts. The Jews called this the **abomination of desolation**, to which Jesus referred in Mt 24:15. This is also a preview of what would happen during the times of the antichrist.

The harsh treatment of the Jews by Antiochus and his desecration of their temple incited the Jews to revolt (165 B.C.).

11:32-33 Conditions were so oppressive that many faithful Jews (**people who know their God**), led by Judas Maccabeus, successfully revolted (were **strong** and took **action**), though many died as martyrs.

11:35 Clearly God uses even persecution to accomplish His purposes of **refining, purifying, and cleansing**. The **time of the end** identifies some eschatological teaching for the reader. Here the antichrist, or "the little horn," and the last days before the return of Christ are predicted (cp. 10:14).

>WORD|*study*

11:30 Two words underscore the fury of the "king of the North." First, he had been **intimidated** (Hb *kaʾah*, "rebuked, cast out, dejected"; cp. Ps 109:16; Ezk 13:22). The Romans had interfered with his ambitious plans. He was returning home in humiliation rather than glory. Second, he would **rage** (Hb *zaʿam*, "pour out anger, often intending to punish; be indignant or defiant") against the Jews **(holy covenant)** when he stopped in Jerusalem on his way back to Syria. The Septuagint translates this word with *thumoō* (Gk, "become incensed or angry," Mt 2:16), a verb which appears only once in the New Testament, expressing the great fury that Herod unleashed on Bethlehem when he ordered all the male children two years and under to be slaughtered (Mt 2:16; cp. use of the noun *thumos* in Rv 12:12).

of forces will be swept away before
him; they will be shattered, as well
as the covenant prince. 23 After an
alliance is made with him, he will
act deceitfully. He will rise to power with a small nation.[A] 24 During a
time of peace,[B] he will come into the
richest parts of the province and do
what his fathers and predecessors
never did. He will lavish plunder,
loot, and wealth on his followers,
and he will make plans against fortified cities, but only for a time.
25 "With a large army he will stir up
his power and his courage against
the king of the South. The king of
the South will prepare for battle
with an extremely large and powerful army, but he will not succeed,
because plots will be made against
him. 26 Those who eat his provisions
will destroy him; his army will be
swept away, and many will fall slain.
27 The two kings, whose hearts are
bent on evil, will speak lies at the
same table but to no avail, for still
the end will come at the appointed
time. 28 The king of the North will
return to his land with great wealth,
but his heart will be set against the
holy covenant;[C] he will take action,
then return to his own land.

The Appointed Time (11:29-35)

29 "At the appointed time he will
come again to the South, but this
time[D] will not be like the first.
30 Ships of Kittim[E] will come against
him, and being intimidated, he will
withdraw. Then he will rage against
the holy covenant and take action.
On his return, he will favor those
who abandon the holy covenant.
31 His forces will rise up and desecrate the temple fortress. They
will abolish the daily sacrifice and
set up the abomination of desolation. 32 With flattery he will corrupt
those who act wickedly toward the
covenant, but the people who know
their God will be strong and take action. 33 Those who are wise among
the people will give understanding
to many, yet they will die by sword
and flame, and be captured and
plundered for a time. 34 When defeated, they will be helped by some,
but many others will join them in-
sincerely. 35 Some of the wise will fall
so that they may be refined, purified,
and cleansed until the time of the
end, for it will still come at the appointed time.

The King's Magnification of Himself (11:36-39)

36 "Then the king will do whatever
he wants. He will exalt and magnify
himself above every god, and he will
say outrageous things against the
God of gods. He will be successful
until the time of wrath is completed, because what has been decreed
will be accomplished. 37 He will not
show regard for the gods[F] of his fathers, the god longed for by women,
or for any other god, because he will
magnify himself above all. 38 Instead,
he will honor a god of fortresses—a
god his fathers did not know—with
gold, silver, precious stones, and
riches. 39 He will deal with the strongest fortresses with the help of a
foreign god. He will greatly honor
those who acknowledge him,[G] making them rulers over many and distributing land as a reward.

The Time of the End (11:40-45)

40 "At the time of the end, the
king of the South will engage him
in battle, but the king of the North

[A]**11:23** Or *a few people* [B]**11:24** Or *Without warning* [C]**11:28** Or *the Jewish people and religion* [D]**11:29** Lit *but the last* [E]**11:30** = the Romans [F]**11:37** Or *God* [G]**11:39** Or *those he acknowledges*

will storm against him with chariots, horsemen, and many ships. He
will invade countries and sweep
through them like a flood. 41 He will
also invade the beautiful land, and
many will fall. But these will escape from his power: Edom, Moab,
and the prominent people[A] of the
Ammonites. 42 He will extend his
power against the countries, and
not even the land of Egypt will escape. 43 He will get control over the
hidden treasures of gold and silver
and over all the riches of Egypt. The
Libyans and •Cushites will also be in
submission.[B] 44 But reports from the
east and the north will terrify him,
and he will go out with great fury to
annihilate and •completely destroy
many. 45 He will pitch his royal tents
between the sea and[C] the beautiful
holy mountain, but he will meet his
end with no one to help him.

Michael's Prophecy (12:1-4)

12 At that time
Michael the great prince
who stands watch
over your people
will rise up.
There will be a time
of distress
such as never has occurred
since nations came into being
until that time.
But at that time all
your people
who are found written
in the book will escape.
2 Many of those who sleep
in the dust
of the earth will awake,
some to eternal life,
and some to shame
and eternal contempt.
3 Those who are wise will shine
like the bright expanse
of the heavens,
and those who lead many
to righteousness,
like the stars forever and ever.

4 "But you, Daniel, keep these
words secret and seal the book until the time of the end. Many will
roam about, and knowledge will increase."[D]

Final Instructions for Daniel (12:5-13)

5 Then I, Daniel, looked, and two
others were standing there, one on
this bank of the river and one on the
other. 6 One of them said to the man
dressed in linen, who was above the
waters of the river, "How long until the end of these extraordinary
things?" 7 Then I heard the man
dressed in linen, who was above the
waters of the river. He raised both
his hands[E] toward heaven and swore
by Him who lives eternally that it
would be for a time, times, and half
a time. When the power of the holy
people is shattered, all these things
will be completed.

8 I heard but did not understand.
So I asked, "My lord, what will be the
outcome of these things?"

9 He said, "Go on your way, Daniel, for the words are secret and
sealed until the time of the end.
10 Many will be purified, cleansed,
and refined, but the wicked will act
wickedly; none of the wicked will
understand, but the wise will understand. 11 From the time the daily
sacrifice is abolished and the abomination of desolation is set up, there
will be 1,290 days. 12 The one who
waits for and reaches 1,335 days is
blessed. 13 But as for you, go on your
way to the end;[F] you will rest, then
rise to your destiny at the end of the
days."

[A] **11:41** Lit *the first* [B] **11:43** Lit *Cushites at his steps* [C] **11:45** Or *the seas at* [D] **12:4** LXX reads *and the earth will be filled with unrighteousness* [E] **12:7** Lit *raised his right and his left* [F] **12:13** LXX omits *to the end*

11:36-39 This section marks a transition to discussion of the antichrist, who arrogantly **magnifies** himself above all, even the one true God. God allows the success of the antichrist for a time until He extends His **wrath** at the end of time. This man will be more evil than any other and will not worship any known gods. The phrase "the desire of women" (HCSB, **longed for by women**) has been interpreted many ways. Possibly this reference is to the Messiah, since every Jewish woman desired to be the mother of the Messiah, and the king would show no regard for the Messiah. He will worship **himself** and force others to worship him. His god, or religion, will be himself, power, and war for which he will expend great efforts; and he will **reward** those who support him. Perhaps this fixation with war as a means of growing powerful draws the description of his devotion to **a god of fortresses** by whose help he will take even **the strongest fortresses**.

11:45 This campaign of annihilation will prove to be a fatal move for the antichrist, who will set up **between the sea and the beautiful holy mountain** (i.e., Zion) where the temple would make the land beautiful and holy. His location is also between the seas; the Mediterranean and the Dead Sea border Israel on the east and west. So the antichrist will make his last stand in Jerusalem and invade the temple itself (2Th 2:4). Possibly in this intrusion, he will commit the abomination of desolation (Mt 24:15). However, the battle itself will be in close proximity. Some scholars see a parallel between this passage and Ezekiel 38–39, the battle of Armageddon, the last great battle on earth. Here the antichrist is ultimately defeated and slain.

12:1 This verse brings fearful anticipation but also an encouraging twofold promise. The **time of distress** is an allusion to "the great tribulation" (Rv 7:14), a time of trouble **such as never has occurred** before or since, when the antichrist will make war with God's people. Matthew describes it as a "great tribulation, the kind that hasn't taken place from the beginning of the world until now and never will again" (Mt 24:21). In order to protect His people, God sends **Michael** the **great prince** (cp. Mt 24:22; Rv 12:7-8). The first part of the promise is that those **written in the book** will be saved (Dn 7:10; cp. "the book of life," Rv 20:12; "the Lamb's book of life," Rv 21:27—both depict security for the believer).

12:4 The book with Daniel's prophecies would remain sealed to the majority of the Jewish nation until the end-times, during which people will grow in their understanding of Daniel's prophecy as they hurry to seek its meaning, possibly during the tribulation period. The command to **seal the book** need not indicate complete secrecy but rather preservation and protection until such time as the prophecies became relevant and sought out by those of whom it spoke.

12:13 Daniel is reminded that his ministry will not be forever. He should keep going, trusting in the full reality of this revelation, which for the moment he and others to come would only partially understand. **You will rest** implies death (i.e., resting in the grave), and **rise to your destiny** notes that he would stand and receive an allotted inheritance. He would be one who (as v. 2) would rise to eternal life at the eschatological **end of the days,** a wonderful and hope-filled promise for this faithful, life-long servant of God.

DANIEL... WRITTEN ON MY *Heart*

There is an "itch" of curiosity that Daniel partially scratches. Consequently, one may be tempted to overindulge in speculation as to the nature of prophetic fulfillment. Instead, Christians ought to prepare themselves and others for the return of Christ. The mysterious timing of His reappearance should motivate believers to share the gospel and invest themselves in the work of the kingdom of God. When the disciples pressed Jesus on specifics of the end-times (Ac 1:1-8), he responded with two ideas. First, the end of all things is set by God, who has the authority to do so. Second, until that time, Christians are to be consumed with making others ready. Even Daniel was encouraged to seek understanding and lead others into righteousness (Dn 11:33; 12:3). He was allowed to ask questions, and certainly God encourages believers to study His Word and find answers; however, some things will remain secret until the end of time (12:9). God has shrouded end-time events in mystery, which can only lead the believer to have greater faith and confidence in God.

Readers can take great comfort in the fact that Daniel's prophecies have been proven by history to be accurate and, therefore, trustworthy in what describes the future. While many may disagree on exact interpretations, this apocalyptic literature is exciting and inspiring to believers who realize the moral decline of the world and who desire Christ's rule. Daniel explained that this rulership was guaranteed to come. For Christians, this great triumph is an encouragement. Believers in this generation (like Daniel) should perceive life on earth focused through the lens of a heavenly perspective, a view which brings purpose, contentment, and hope.

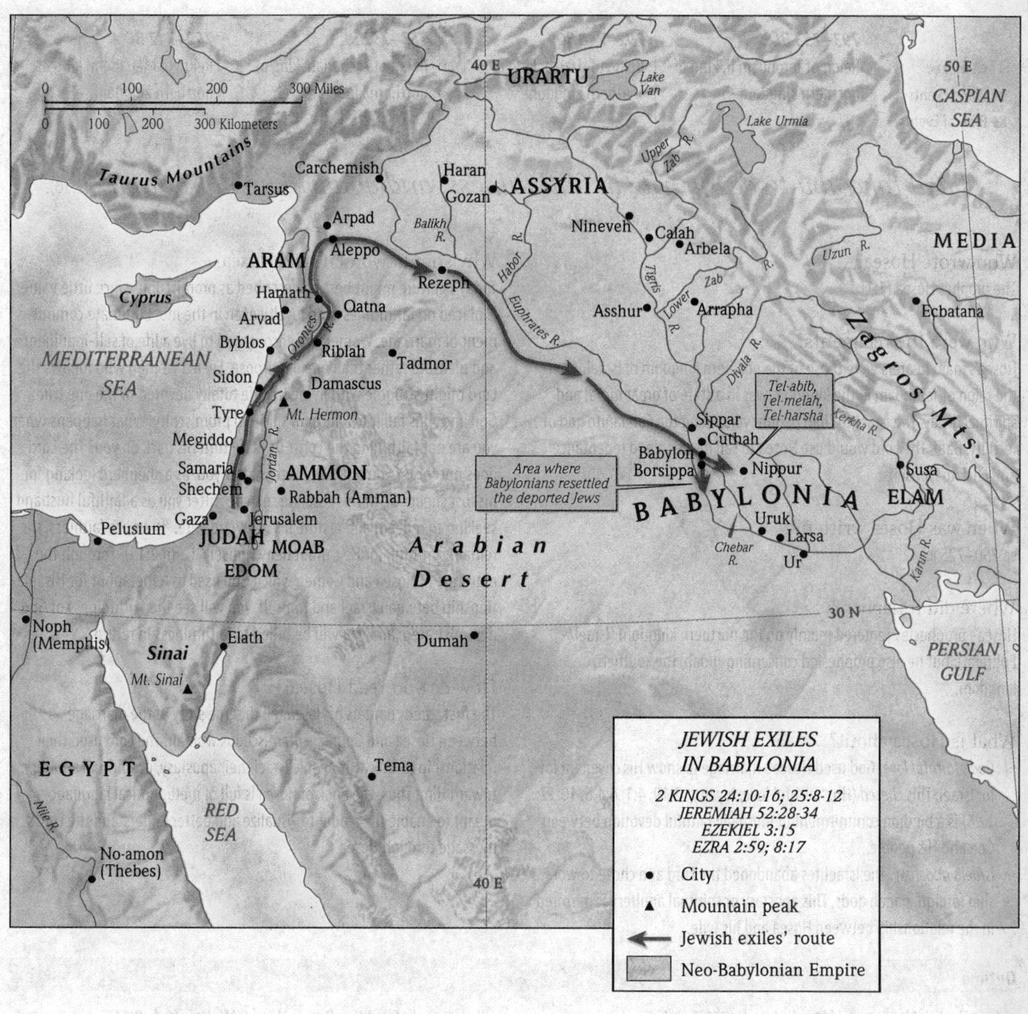
JEWISH EXILES IN BABYLONIA
2 KINGS 24:10-16; 25:8-12
JEREMIAH 52:28-34
EZEKIEL 3:15
EZRA 2:59; 8:17
City
Mountain peak
Jewish exiles' route
Neo-Babylonian Empire
0 100 200 300 Miles
0 100 200 300 Kilometers
40 E
50 E
30 N
URARTU
Lake Van
Lake Urmia
CASPIAN SEA
Taurus Mountains
Tarsus
Carchemish
Haran
Gozan
ASSYRIA
Arpad
Balikh R.
Habor R.
Nineveh
Calah
Arbela
Upper Zab R.
Lower Zab R.
Tigris R.
Uzun R.
MEDIA
ARAM
Aleppo
Rezeph
Euphrates R.
Cyprus
Hamath
Qatna
Arvad
Orontes R.
Byblos
Riblah
Tadmor
Asshur
Arrapha
Ecbatana
Zagros Mts.
MEDITERRANEAN SEA
Sidon
Damascus
Mt. Hermon
Diyala R.
Tyre
Megiddo
Jordan R.
Samaria
Shechem
AMMON
Rabbah (Amman)
Tel-abib, Tel-melah, Tel-harsha
Sippar
Cuthah
Kerkha R.
Babylon
Borsippa
Nippur
Susa
Area where Babylonians resettled the deported Jews
BABYLONIA
ELAM
Gaza
Jerusalem
Pelusium
JUDAH
MOAB
EDOM
Arabian Desert
Uruk
Larsa
Ur
Chebar R.
Karun R.
Noph (Memphis)
Sinai
Mt. Sinai
Elath
Dumah
PERSIAN GULF
EGYPT
Tema
Nile R.
RED SEA
No-amon (Thebes)

Hosea

Timeline	793–753 BC	792–740 BC	753–752 BC	752–742 BC
World Events Biblical Events	Reign of Jeroboam II, king of northern kingdom	Reign of Uzziah, king of southern kingdom	Reign of Zechariah, king of northern kingdom	Reign of Menahem, king of northern kingdom

"I will take you to be My wife in faithfulness, and you will know Yahweh" (2:20).

Who wrote Hosea?

The prophet Hosea (1:1)

Who were the recipients?

Hosea's main hearers were those of the northern kingdom of Israel. After the reign of Jeroboam II, the kingdom was in a state of great moral and spiritual decay. The Israelites had begun worshiping the Canaanite god of fertility, Baal. The Lord would use Hosea to call his people to repentance and back to Himself.

When was Hosea written?

ca 750–725 B.C.

Where did it happen?

Hosea's prophecies centered mainly on the northern kingdom (Israel/ Ephraim), but he also prophesied concerning Judah, the southern kingdom.

What is Hosea about?

- *God's faithful love*. God used Hosea's marriage to show His covenant love for Israel. This *chesed* (Hb, "faithful love, loyalty," 2:19; 4:1; 6:4,6; 10:12; 12:6) is a binding commitment of mutually faithful devotion between God and His people.
- *Israel's apostasy*. The Israelites abandoned the Lord and chose to worship foreign, pagan gods. This apostasy or spiritual adultery is mirrored in the relationship between Hosea and his wife.

Why should women read Hosea?

Today's culture might best be described as promiscuous since little value is placed on faithfulness and loyalty even in the most intimate commitment of marriage. Women are encouraged to live a life of self-indulgence and pleasure rather than one of purpose. Even a woman who follows the Lord might struggle with living her life totally devoted to the one true God and thus fall into a form of spiritual promiscuity. What happens when you are not faithful to the Lord? Does He turn His back on you? The Lord does not forget you but rather seeks after you, as a shepherd looking for his lost sheep. Or, in this case, He searches after you as a faithful husband seeking to redeem and restore his wayward wife. "If we are faithless, He remains faithful, for He cannot deny Himself" (2Tm 2:13). Through the marriage of Hosea and Gomer, which God used as a metaphor for His relationship between Israel and Himself, you will see the faithfulness of God demonstrated, and you will be called to faithfulness in return.

How do you read Hosea?

The first three chapters of Hosea tell the true story of the marriage between Hosea and Gomer, a promiscuous woman. The Lord used their relationship to show His people Israel their apostasy, or spiritual adultery, toward Him. Thus, the book of Hosea is full of metaphorical language meant to enable the reader to visualize and better understand the Lord's message through Hosea.

Outline

I. Hosea's Marriage and Israel's Apostasy (1:1–3:5)
   - A. Hosea Marries Gomer (1:1-11)
   - B. God Promises to Restore Israel (2:1)
   - C. God Details Israel's Punishment (2:2-13)
   - D. God Describes Israel's Future Restoration (2:14-23)
   - E. Hosea Restores Gomer (3:1-3)
   - F. Restoration also Required for Israel (3:4-5)

II. Hosea's Messages (4:1–6:3)
   - A. Israel's Apostasy Defined (4:1-19)
   - B. God's Warnings and Judgments for Israel (5:1-15)
   - C. God's Call to Repentance (6:1-3)

III. Israel's Condition During Hosea's Ministry (6:4–8:14)
   - A. God Considers Israel's Condition (6:4-11a)
   - B. Israel's Failures as a Nation (6:11b–7:16)
   - C. Israel's Self-Serving Behavior Results in Destruction (8:1-14)

IV. Prophecies and Judgments for Israel (9:1–13:16)
   - A. Prophecies About Israel's Future (9:1-17)
   - B. More Accusations Against Israel (10:1-15)
   - C. God's Love for Israel (11:1-11)
   - D. Israel's Apostasy Compared to Jacob's Life (11:12–12:14)
   - E. Further Judgment on Israel (13:1-16)

V. The Final Plea for Israel's Repentance (14:1-9)

Title: The book of Hosea (Hb, "help, deliverance, salvation") is named for the prophet whose oracle it contains and is canonically the first of the Minor Prophets or "The Twelve."

1:1 God took the initiative in revealing His truth to **Hosea**, a contemporary of the prophets Isaiah and Amos. The list of kings suggests that Hosea was a young man when **the word of the** **Lord** came to him. Apart from Hs 1:1 and Is 1:1, only the genealogy of Jesus in Mt 1:8-9 lists in such close sequence these four kings of Judah, who traced their lineage from King David.

1:2 The words **when the Lord first** [Hb *techillah*, "beginning," a noun] **spoke** suggest that the first message from the Lord **to Hosea** was God's verbatim command to **marry a promiscuous**

750–731 BC	750–725 BC	742–740 BC	735–716 BC
Reign of Jotham, king of southern kingdom	Hosea's prophetic ministry	Reign of Pekahiah, king of northern kingdom	Reign of Ahaz, king of southern kingdom

Hosea's Marriage and Israel's Apostasy (1:1–3:5)

Hosea Marries Gomer (1:1-11)

1 The word of the LORD that came
to Hosea son of Beeri during the
reigns of Uzziah, Jotham, Ahaz, and
Hezekiah, kings of Judah, and of
Jeroboam son of Jehoash, king of
Israel.
2 When the LORD first spoke to Hosea, He said this to him:

> Go and marry
> a promiscuous wife
> and have children
> of promiscuity,
> for the land is committing
> blatant acts of promiscuity
> by abandoning the LORD.

3 So he went and married Gomer
daughter of Diblaim, and she conceived and bore him a son. 4 Then
the LORD said to him:

> Name him Jezreel,
> for in a little while
> I will bring the bloodshed
> of Jezreel
> on the house of Jehu
> and put an end
> to the kingdom of the house
> of Israel.
> 5 On that day I will break
> the bow of Israel
> in the Valley of Jezreel.[A]

6 She conceived again and gave
birth to a daughter, and the LORD
said to him:

> Name her No Compassion,[B]
> for I will no longer
> have compassion
> on the house of Israel.
> I will certainly
> take them away.
> 7 But I will have compassion
> on the house of Judah,
> and I will deliver them by
> the LORD their God.
> I will not deliver them
> by bow, sword, or war,
> or by horses and cavalry.

8 After Gomer had weaned No
Compassion, she conceived and gave
birth to a son. 9 Then the LORD said:

> Name him Not My People,[C]
> for you are not My people,
> and I will not be your God.[D]
> 10E Yet the number
> of the Israelites
> will be like the sand
> of the sea,
> which cannot be measured
> or counted.

[A]1:5 = God sows [B]1:6 Or *Lo-ruhamah* [C]1:9 Or *Lo-ammi* [D]1:9 Lit *not be yours* [E]1:10 Hs 2:1 in Hb

>WORD|*study*

1:2 Promiscuous (Hb *zenunim*, "adulteries, whoredoms"; cp. Gn 38:24; 2 Kg 9:22; Ezk 23:11,29; Hs 2:2; 4:12; 5:4; Nah 3:4) literally denotes sexual relations with someone other than one's spouse or prostitution. It can refer figuratively to "idolatry," especially in the verb form of the word (Hb *zanah*, translated "has been promiscuous" in Hs 1:2; see **Word Study**, Is 1:21, p. 863; notes on 1 Ch 5:23-26 and Pr 23:27), which occurs more frequently in Scripture and 13 times in the book of Hosea. **Children of promiscuity** (Hb *zenunim*) may refer either to their being fathered by someone other than Hosea or to the fact that they bore the disgrace of their mother's behavior.

1:6-7 To have compassion (Hb *racham*) on someone is to treat that person with tender affection as an expression of deep love. In the Old Testament, the word is used primarily of God's commitment to care for and deliver His people, particularly when they do not deserve His mercy or kindness (see Ex 33:19; Dt 13:17; 30:3; 1Kg 8:50; 2Kg 13:23; Ps 102:13; 116:5; Is 54:8,10; 55:7; 60:10; Jr 12:15; 30:18; 31:20; Lm 3:32; Ezk 39:25; Mc 7:19; Zch 10:6).

wife, which explains Hosea's inexplicable choice of such a wife.

1:4-5 Jezreel (Hb, "God sows; what is scattered") is the only child clearly designated as Hosea's child. The name drew attention not only to **that day** of judgment on Israel but also to God's promise to restore His relationship with His people. For Jezreel, Yahweh declares that He will "sow" Israel "in the land" for Himself (2:23).

The Lord announced His intent to bring bloodshed upon **the house of Jehu** in order to avenge **the bloodshed of Jezreel**, the town where Jehu had brought God's judgment on the house of Omri (2Kg 9:1–10:31; cp. 1Kg 21:23). Therefore, the Lord promised that as at Jezreel, where Jehu had violently annihilated a wicked and idolatrous dynasty, so He would, **in the Valley of Jezreel**, violently remove **the kingdom of the house of Israel**.

1:6-7 The identity of the daughter's father is open to question. Yahweh commanded Hosea to name the girl **No Compassion** (Hb *Lo' Ruchamah*, "not pitied, not loved; no mercy"; cp. Is 9:17; 13:18; 14:1; 27:11; Jr 13:14; 15:1-7) as a living testimony to His disposition toward Israel, particularly in contrast to His decision to **have compassion on the house of Judah** (cp. Is 30:18; 49:10,13,15).

1:8-11 Since children were not **weaned** until three or four years of age, the two births are seemingly separated by about that length of time. The father of Gomer's son is not identified, but the Lord commanded that the boy be named **Not My People** (Hb *Lo'-'ammi*) to convey to Israel that He was temporarily suspending His covenant with the northern kingdom. This demarcation indicates the reversal of God's protection of the Israelites from Egypt when He announced that He would rescue them from slavery: "I will take you as My people, and I will be your God" (Ex 6:7; cp. Lv 26:12; Dt 27:9; Jr 7:23; 11:4).

And in the place where
they were told:
You are not My people,
they will be called:
Sons of the living God.
11 And the Judeans
and the Israelites
will be gathered together.
They will appoint
for themselves a single ruler
and go up from[A] the land.
For the day of Jezreel
will be great.

God Promises to Restore Israel (2:1)

2[B] Call[C] your brothers: My People
and your sisters: Compassion.

God Details Israel's Punishment (2:2-13)

2 Rebuke your mother;
rebuke her.
For she is not My wife
and I am not her husband.
Let her remove
the promiscuous look
from her face
and her adultery
from between her breasts.
3 Otherwise, I will strip her naked
and expose her as she was
on the day of her birth.
I will make her like a desert
and like a parched land,
and I will let her die of thirst.
4 I will have no compassion
on her children
because they are the children
of promiscuity.
5 Yes, their mother
is promiscuous;
she conceived them
and acted shamefully.
For she thought, "I will go
after my lovers,
the men who give me my food
and water,
my wool and flax, my oil
and drink."
6 Therefore, this is what I will do:
I will block her[D] way
with thorns;
I will enclose her with a wall,
so that she cannot find
her paths.
7 She will pursue her lovers
but not catch them;
she will seek them
but not find them.
Then she will think,
"I will go back
to my former husband,
for then it was better for me
than now."
8 She does not recognize
that it is I who gave her
the grain,
the new wine, and the oil.
I lavished silver and gold
on her,
which they used for •Baal.
9 Therefore, I will take back
My grain in its time
and My new wine
in its season;
I will take away My wool
and linen,
which were to cover
her nakedness.
10 Now I will expose her shame
in the sight of her lovers,
and no one will rescue her
from My hands.
11 I will put an end to all
her celebrations:
her feasts, New Moons,
and Sabbaths—
all her festivals.
12 I will devastate her vines
and fig trees.
She thinks that these are
her wages
that her lovers have given her.
I will turn them
into a thicket,
and the wild animals
will eat them.

[A]**1:11** Or *and flourish in*; Hb obscure [B]**2:1** Hs 2:3 in Hb [C]**2:1** Lit *Say to* [D]**2:6** LXX, Syr; MT reads *your*

>WORD|*study*

2:2 Adultery (Hb *na'aphuphim*) is a plural noun—appearing in Scripture only here—of the verb for committing adultery (Hb *na'aph*). In the Old Testament, the verb first appears in the Ten Commandments (Ex 20:14; Dt 5:18), explicitly forbidding sexual relations with someone other than one's spouse. Leviticus 20:10 prescribed the death penalty for both parties committing adultery. Particularly in the books of Jeremiah, Ezekiel, and Hosea, "adultery" is a metaphor illustrating Israel's turning away from the Lord to worship idols, figuratively pursuing other "lovers" (e.g., Jr 3:8-9; 5:7; Ezk 16:32,38; 23:37,45; cp. Rm 2:22).

2:1 The reversal of the prophetic meaning of the children's names is completed in the future restoration of Israel, to whom the Lord has extended His **Compassion**. This command anticipates a future act or the development of a present condition.

2:2 The command to **rebuke** [Hb *riv*, "strive or contend with, plead one's cause"] **your mother** presumably is addressed to the mother's children—likely, here, to the sons and daughters of Israel who, though still worshiping the Lord, lived among morally and spiritually corrupt people. Speaking to Israel in the persona of a devoted husband whose wife is actively pursuing adulterous relationships, the Lord insists that the ongoing betrayal of this adulterous wife must cease.

2:3 If Israel refused to end the illicit relationships, the Lord would **expose** (Hb *yatsag*, "place, set, leave") Israel in the sense of abandoning her rather than protecting her from the devastating consequences of her choices. Reference to **her birth** links this warning with Ezk 16, which describes with similar imagery the Lord's rescue, cleansing, and marriage of Israel.

2:4-5 Children of promiscuity were born of the adulterous unions of the wayward wife and her **lovers**. These illegitimate children figuratively represent the idolatrous Israelites, who had no right to identify themselves as God's sons and daughters.

2:6-7 The Lord intentionally acted to deter the Israelites from worshiping other gods by making their adulterous pursuits unpleasant, unrewarding, and unsuccessful.

2:7-13 The adulterous wife is described as one who has been deceptively convinced that her lovers, rather than her faithful husband, have provided for her. However, a wife's seeking elsewhere for the provision that her husband was obligated to give her (Ex 21:10) constituted betrayal and rejection of her husband. Israel had done this, having deserted the Lord and looked to idols for benefits they supposedly could supply. As the **former husband** (v. 7), the Lord laments Israel's failure to **recognize** and appreciate the truth that everything she enjoyed, basic provisions as well as luxuries, was given by Him (v. 8).

Not only did she spurn the Lord's provision, but she also took for herself what He had given her and used it in her worship of **Baal** (Hb, "lord, master," v. 16), the Canaanite god of fertility believed to be responsible for fruitful harvests (v. 8). Yahweh would make a mockery of this fertility cult

>WORD|*study*

2:13 Forgot (Hb *shakach*; cp. 4:6; 8:14; 13:6) implies that something or someone is known but is not given appropriate attention. God's warnings to His people not to forget Him indicate that the word denotes not merely a mental slip but a willful ignorance or setting aside of what should remain "front and center" (Dt 6:12; 8:11,14,19; Jdg 3:7; 1 Sm 12:9). To "forget" the Lord is to stop caring about Him and what He says. Such neglect inevitably leads to blatant disrespect and sinful, destructive choices (cp. Jr 3:21; 13:25-27; 18:15).

2:15 The name **Valley of Achor** (Hb, "trouble") was given to the place where the sin of a man named Achan had brought "trouble" upon "the Israelites" as a whole following the battle of Jericho (cp. 1Ch 2:7). Achan did not confess his sin of taking some of what was "set apart" until the Lord singled him out (Jos 7:1,16-23; for God's instructions, see Jos 6:16-19). "A large pile of rocks" was set up at the place where Achan and all his family and possessions consequently were destroyed (Jos 7:24-26). This memorial of past "trouble" would give way to the expectation of good things to come in the future (Hs 2:15).

13 And I will punish her
for the days of the Baals
when she burned incense
to them,
put on her rings and jewelry,
and went after her lovers,
but forgot Me.
This is
the LORD's declaration.

God Describes Israel's Future Restoration (2:14-23)

14 Therefore, I am going
to persuade her,
lead her to the wilderness,
and speak tenderly to her.[A]
15 There I will give her vineyards
back to her
and make the Valley of Achor[B]
into a gateway of hope.
There she will respond
as she did
in the days of her youth,
as in the day she came out
of the land of Egypt.
16 In that day—
this is
the LORD's declaration—
you will call Me,
"My husband,"
and no longer call Me,
"My Baal."[C]
17 For I will remove the names
of the Baals
from her mouth;
they will no longer
be remembered
by their names.
18 On that day I will make
a covenant for them
with the wild animals,
the birds of the sky,
and the creatures that crawl
on the ground.
I will shatter bow, sword,
and weapons of war
in the land[D]
and will enable the people
to rest securely.
19 I will take you to be
My wife forever.
I will take you to be My wife
in righteousness,
justice, love, and compassion.
20 I will take you to be My wife
in faithfulness,
and you will know •Yahweh.
21 On that day I will respond—
this is
the LORD's declaration.
I will respond to the sky,
and it will respond
to the earth.
22 The earth will respond
to the grain,
the new wine, and the oil,
and they will respond
to Jezreel.
23 I will sow her[E] in the land
for Myself,
and I will have compassion
on No Compassion;
I will say to Not My People:
You are My people,
and he will say, "You are
My God."

Hosea Restores Gomer (3:1-3)

3 Then the LORD said to me, "Go
again; show love to a woman who
is loved by another man and is an
adulteress, just as the LORD loves the
Israelites though they turn to other
gods and love raisin cakes."

[A]2:14 Lit *speak to her heart* [B]2:15 = Trouble [C]2:16 Or *My master* [D]2:18 Or *war on the earth* [E]2:23 = Israel

by withdrawing from the land and its sinful people the agricultural and other material blessings that should be attributed to Him alone.

Furthermore, the Lord would **expose** (Hb *galah*, "uncover, make naked," usually used with the word for "nakedness" as an idiom for having sexual intercourse) Israel's **shame** (Hb *navlut*, "disgrace," from the word *naval*, "ungodly, wicked"), humiliation, and devastation (cp. Jr 14:1-10). Although the Lord can **rescue** (Hb *natsal*, "snatch, deliver," v. 10; see **Word Study**, Ps 7:1-2, p. 672) His people from anyone or anything, **no one** can "rescue" God's people out of His hands.

2:14-15 Although remembered as a place where the people grumbled against the Lord, the **wilderness** was also a place in which the people had to rely on God alone to provide for them, and they saw Him do it. God would return to Israel what He had stripped away, even declaring that He would **make the Valley of Achor . . . a gateway of hope.**

2:19-20 Citing five of the Lord's attributes characterizing His commitment to His people—comparable to payment of the bride price, the Lord three times repeated His promise to them (cp. Ex 6:7): **I will take you to be My wife** (Hb *ʾaras*, "espouse, betroth," the first step toward marriage and binding contract; cp. description of the "new covenant," Jr 31:31-34; Zch 8:7-8; Heb 8:10). **Righteousness** and **justice** denote God's perfect fairness in His treatment of Israel (Hs 2:19). **Love** (Hb *chesed*, "steadfast love, covenant loyalty"; see **Word Study**, p. 322) and **compassion** describe God's unwavering devotion to Israel (Hs 2:19). God's **faithfulness** contrasted Baal's fickleness and Israel's unfaithfulness.

3:1-3 Although the text does not name the **adulteress** (Hb *naʾaph*; see **Word Study**, p. 1140), clearly the audience is expected to assume that the symbolism of Hosea's marriage to Gomer continues here. Hosea is commanded, **Go again** (Hb *ʿod*, "still"), indicating repetition and return. The woman toward whom the prophet must **show love** (Hb *ʾahav*, "do acts of love for, be loyal to, treat with affection and tenderness, prefer") is identified both as an "adulteress" and as **a woman who is loved** [Hb *ʾahav*] **by another man** (Hb *rēaʿ*, "lover, companion, friend"; cp. Sg 5:16; Jr 3:20). The Lord's explanation for such a difficult instruction sustains the parallel He established between Hosea's marriage to Gomer and His relationship with His people. Just as Gomer has given herself to the desires of "another man," Yahweh's people were turning to **other gods**.

3:2 That Hosea **bought her** indicates that whatever Gomer's status, someone accepted the payment specified, which exceeded the price of a female slave (cp. Ex 21:32; Lv 27:4). She may have become a slave to pay an overwhelming debt. Perhaps her lover insisted on payment before allowing Hosea to take her home. In any case, the transaction gave Hosea the legal right to do with her as he pleased, even to put her to death for adultery. Yet his response was to take her again as his wife.

3:3-5 The parameters established by Hosea for Gomer's return to his household were intended to illustrate the way **the Israelites** would be restored to the Lord and again receive His love and goodness (v. 5; cp. Jr 30:9). Gomer would be required to stay home with Hosea, curtailing any opportunity to develop illicit relationships with other men. Hosea apparently took deliberate measures as well to demonstrate his own continued faithfulness to her. Likewise, the Israelites would be deprived of every possible rival to the lordship of Yahweh (i.e., including their human leaders and the objects associated with pagan worship).

An **ephod** was a garment worn by the priests in the temple (Ex 28:28-34), but other ephods had been fashioned for use in divination and pagan worship (Hs 3:4; Jdg 8:27; 17:5).

3:5 The focus of the text shifts from Hosea's experience to the intended result of removing from **the people of Israel** everything in which they had trusted instead of trusting the Lord.

4:1 Chapter 4 begins a series of messages delivered by Hosea to Israel. Thus God commands them to listen to what He has to say, and He presents His **case** [Hb *riv*, "contention or quarrel presented in court"] **against the inhabitants of the land**, the place God had promised to give His people when they came into covenant relationship with Him.

>WORD|*study*

3:1 Turn (Hb *panah*) is not the same word translated "turn," "return," and "repent" (Hb *shuv*), which is repeatedly used in 3:5 and in prophetic passages such as Ezekiel 14:6,8. *Panah* denotes "turning oneself" in the sense of physically turning one's eyes, head, or body to look away from someone. It is sometimes used figuratively to convey a choice of the will to stop listening to God. The Lord warned His people that turning away from Him would result in their being "led astray to bow down to other gods and worship them" (Dt 30:17; cp. 29:17). In turning "to other gods," Israel had grievously betrayed the Lord, who "loves" (Hb *ʾahavah*, "devoted love that takes great delight in another," Hs 3:1; cp. 11:4; Gn 29:20; Dt 7:8; 2 Ch 9:8; Ps 109:5; Jr 2:2) His people, just as a cheating wife would wound the "one-woman man" who has devotedly loved her.

4:8 The example noted in verse 8 regards their feeding on the sin (Hb *chattaʾat*) of God's people. The word translated "sin" also denotes the "sin offering" (e.g., Lv 4:25), one of the sacrifices from which the priest and his sons were granted a portion to eat (Lv 7:28-37). The priests' failure to teach the people the law and knowledge of God promoted their sinfulness, indicating the need for more "sin offerings," from which the priests benefited. Metaphorically, the priests were indulging an "appetite for their transgressions."

2 So I bought her for 15 •shekels of
silver and five bushels of barley.[A,B] 3 I
said to her, "You must live with me
many days. Don't be promiscuous or
belong to any man, and I will act the
same way toward you."

Restoration Is also Required for Israel (3:4-5)

4 For the Israelites must live many
days without king or prince, without sacrifice or sacred pillar, and
without •ephod or household idols.
5 Afterward, the people of Israel
will return and seek the LORD their
God and David their king. They will
come with awe to the LORD and to
His goodness in the last days.

Hosea's Messages (4:1–6:3)

Israel's Apostasy Defined (4:1-19)

4 Hear the word of the LORD,
people of Israel,
for the LORD has a case
against the inhabitants
of the land:
There is no truth,
no faithful love,
and no knowledge of God
in the land!
2 Cursing, lying,
murder, stealing,
and adultery are rampant;
one act of bloodshed
follows another.
3 For this reason
the land mourns,
and everyone who lives
in it languishes,
along with the wild animals
and the birds of the sky;
even the fish
of the sea disappear.
4 But let no one dispute;
let no one argue,
for My case is
against you priests.[C,D]
5 You will stumble by day;
the prophet will also stumble
with you by night.
And I will destroy
your mother.
6 My people are destroyed
for lack of knowledge.
Because you have
rejected knowledge,
I will reject you from serving
as My priest.
Since you have forgotten
the law of your God,
I will also forget your sons.
7 The more they multiplied,
the more they sinned
against Me.
I[E] will change their honor[F]
into disgrace.
8 They feed on the sin[G]
of My people;
they have an appetite
for their transgressions.
9 The same judgment
will happen
to both people and priests.
I will punish them
for their ways
and repay them
for their deeds.
10 They will eat
but not be satisfied;

[A] 3:2 LXX reads *barley and a measure of wine* [B] 3:2 Lit *silver, a homer of barley, and a lethek of barley* [C] 4:4 Text emended; MT reads *argue, and your people are like those contending with a priest* [D] 4:4 Hb obscure [E] 4:7 Alt Hb tradition, Syr, Tg read *They* [F] 4:7 Ancient Jewish tradition reads *My honor* [G] 4:8 Or *sin offerings*

they will be promiscuous
but not multiply.
For they have abandoned
their devotion to the LORD.
11 Promiscuity, wine,
and new wine
take away one's understanding.

12 My people consult
their wooden idols,
and their divining rods
inform them.
For a spirit of promiscuity
leads them astray;
they act promiscuously
in disobedience to[A] their God.
13 They sacrifice
on the mountaintops,
and they burn offerings
on the hills,
and under oaks, poplars,
and terebinths,
because their shade
is pleasant.
And so your daughters
act promiscuously
and your daughters-in-law
commit adultery.
14 I will not punish
your daughters
when they act promiscuously
or your daughters-in-law
when they commit adultery,
for the men themselves go off
with prostitutes
and make sacrifices
with cult prostitutes.
People without discernment
are doomed.

15 Israel, if you
act promiscuously,
don't let Judah
become •guilty!
Do not go to Gilgal
or make a pilgrimage
to Beth-aven,[B]
and do not swear an oath:
As the LORD lives!
16 For Israel is as obstinate
as a stubborn cow.
Can the LORD now
shepherd them
like a lamb
in an open meadow?
17 Ephraim is attached to idols;
leave him alone!
18 When their drinking is over,
they turn to promiscuity.
Israel's leaders[C] fervently
love disgrace.[D]
19 A wind with its wings will
carry them off,[E]
and they will be ashamed
of their sacrifices.

God's Warnings and Judgments for Israel (5:1-15)

5 Hear this, priests!
Pay attention, house of Israel!
Listen, royal house!
For the judgment applies
to you
because you have been
a snare at Mizpah
and a net spread out on Tabor.
2 Rebels are deeply involved
in slaughter;
I will be a punishment
for all of them.[D]
3 I know Ephraim,
and Israel is not hidden
from Me.
For now, Ephraim,
you have
acted promiscuously;
Israel is defiled.
4 Their actions do not
allow them
to return to their God,
for a spirit of promiscuity
is among them,
and they do not know
the LORD.
5 Israel's arrogance testifies
against them.[F]
Both Israel
and Ephraim stumble
because of their wickedness;
even Judah will stumble
with them.
6 They go with their flocks
and herds
to seek the LORD
but do not find Him;
He has withdrawn from them.
7 They betrayed the LORD;
indeed, they gave birth
to illegitimate children.
Now the New Moon
will devour them
along with their fields.
8 Blow the horn in Gibeah,
the trumpet in Ramah;

4:11-14 Both alcohol consumption and attempts to satisfy sexual desires with anyone or anything other than one's spouse are addictive behaviors. They **take away one's understanding** (Hb *lēv*, "heart," the center not only of the mind but also of the will and the emotions), and **people without discernment are doomed** (Hb *lavat*, "fall down, perish, be thrown down headlong," v. 14).

5:1 The Lord emphatically and comprehensively demanded Israel's attention, then proceeded to elaborate on the reasons why they could expect His **judgment** to fall upon them. Compared to **a snare . . . and a net**, Israel's leaders had deceitfully led the people into the trap of idolatry, from which they could not free themselves (cp. Jos 23:13); and the Lord would begin His judgment with the king and the priests, who were primarily responsible for covenant-keeping leadership. **Mizpah**, of the two possible sites, was probably a reference to the city located on Samuel's regular circuit for judging the people (cp. 1Sm 7:5-11), and **Tabor** was a mountain in north central Palestine, south of the Lebanese border and near the Sea of Galilee (probably the location within the tribe of Benjamin).

5:5-6 Israel's **arrogance**, resulting from attempts at self-reliance, is proof of an unrepentant heart. All of Israel, including Judah, had chosen to treat God as just another god to whom they could offer sacrifices. The Israelites were sacrificing animals but doing so with arrogance and shallow intentions; therefore, their attempts **to seek the LORD** failed.

5:7 The women of Israel were delivering **illegitimate** [Hb *zur*, "prohibited, strange, foreign"] **children**. The Israelite apostasy had given rise to a generation identified more accurately as children of Baal than as children of the Lord. **The New Moon** is probably a reference to the festivals or monthly sacrifices that were part of the Canaanite worship. Clearly, God was warning wayward Israel of a disastrous judgment.

5:8 The **horn** and **trumpet** serve here as military signals to alert people to take cover and prepare for battle. The attack would most likely come from the south because the three places mentioned were progressively farther north from Jerusalem.

[A]**4:12** Lit *promiscuously from under* [B]**4:15** = House of Wickedness [C]**4:18** Lit *Her shields*; Ps 47:9; 89:18 [D]**4:18; 5:2** Hb obscure [E]**4:19** Lit *wind will bind it in its wings* [F]**5:5** Lit *against his face*

5:9 The phrase **among the tribes of Israel** indicates that the coming devastation would impact both the northern and southern kingdoms.

5:10 Moving the **boundary markers** was a covert way to gain territory illegally, bringing the perpetrator under God's curse (cp. Dt 27:17).

5:13 Ephraim and Judah believed the cure for their problems would come from Assyria. The **great king** may be a reference to Tiglath-pileser III (Pul) of Assyria (cp. 10:6; also called King Yareb, an epithet meaning "contender").

6:1 The phrase **return to the Lord** calls Israel away from her pilgrimage to seek help from Assyria (cp. 5:13).

6:2-3 Although Israel appears to accept God's judgment on them as just, they still have not admitted personal guilt. **Two days** and **the third day**, as well as the verbs **revive** and **raise** certainly emphasize the assurance of restoration.

6:6 The Israelites were following their own rituals rather than obeying God out of the sincere devotion in their hearts. His desire was for an outward manifestation of an inner heart commitment (cp. Mt 9:13; 12:7). **Sacrifice** in itself was meaningless unless it pictured a devotion or **loyalty** within.

6:7-9 Within this list cataloging sins, **Adam** refers to God's creation in the Garden of Eden. **Gilead** was a place where wickedness occurred (cp. Gn 31:25-26; Jdg 11:1-40). **Shechem** also was notorious for wickedness (see Gn 34).

6:10–7:2 The restoration of Israel involves the exposure and healing of their sins. God remembers each sin as if it were vividly reenacted before Him.

raise the war cry
in Beth-aven:
After you, Benjamin!
9 Ephraim will become
a desolation
on the day of punishment;
I announce what is certain
among the tribes of Israel.
10 The princes of Judah are
like those
who move boundary markers;
I will pour out My fury
on them like water.
11 Ephraim is oppressed,
crushed in judgment,
for he is determined to follow
what is worthless.[A]
12 So I am like rot to Ephraim
and like decay to the house
of Judah.
13 When Ephraim saw
his sickness
and Judah his wound,
Ephraim went to Assyria
and sent a delegation
to the great king.[B]
But he cannot cure you
or heal your wound.
14 For I am like a lion to Ephraim
and like a young lion
to the house of Judah.
Yes, I will tear them to pieces
and depart.
I will carry them off,
and no one can rescue them.
15 I will depart and return
to My place
until they recognize
their •guilt and seek
My face;
they will search for Me
in their distress.

God's Call to Repentance (6:1-3)

6 Come, let us return
to the Lord.
For He has torn us,
and He will heal us;
He has wounded us,
and He will bind up
our wounds.
2 He will revive us
after two days,
and on the third day
He will raise us up
so we can live in His presence.
3 Let us strive to know the Lord.
His appearance is as sure as
the dawn.
He will come to us
like the rain,
like the spring showers
that water the land.

Israel's Condition During Hosea's Ministry (6:4–8:14)

God Considers Israel's Condition (6:4-11a)

4 What am I going to do
with you, Ephraim?
What am I going to do
with you, Judah?
Your loyalty is like
the morning mist
and like the early dew
that vanishes.
5 This is why I have used
the prophets
to cut them down;[C]
I have killed them
with the words
of My mouth.
My judgment strikes
like lightning.[D]
6 For I desire loyalty
and not sacrifice,
the knowledge of God
rather than •burnt offerings.
7 But they, like Adam,[E]
have violated the covenant;
there they have betrayed Me.
8 Gilead is a city of evildoers,
tracked
with bloody footprints.
9 Like raiders who wait
in ambush for someone,
a band of priests murders
on the road to Shechem.
They commit atrocities.
10 I have seen something
horrible in the house
of Israel:
Ephraim's promiscuity
is there; Israel is defiled.
11 A harvest is also appointed
for you, Judah.

Israel's Failures as a Nation (6:11b–7:16)

When I[F] return My people
from captivity,

[A]5:11 Or *follow a command*; Hb obscure [B]5:13 Or *to King Yareb* [C]6:5 Or *have cut down the prophets* [D]6:5 LXX, Syr, Tg; MT reads *Your judgments go out as light* [E]6:7 Or *they, as at Adam*, or *they, like men,* [F]6:11 Or *you. Judah, when I*

7

[1] when I heal Israel,
the sins of Ephraim
and the crimes of Samaria
will be exposed.
For they practice fraud;
a thief breaks in;
a raiding party
pillages outside.
2 But they never consider
that I remember
all their evil.
Now their sins are
all around them;
they are right in front
of My face.

3 They please the king
with their evil,
the princes with their lies.
4 All of them commit adultery;
they are like an oven heated
by a baker
who stops stirring the fire
from the kneading
of the dough
until it is leavened.
5 On the day of our king,
the princes are sick
with the heat of wine—
there is a conspiracy
with traitors.[A]
6 For they—their hearts
like an oven—
draw him into their oven.
Their anger smolders
all night;
in the morning it blazes
like a flaming fire.
7 All of them are as hot
as an oven,
and they consume
their rulers.
All their kings fall;
not one of them calls on Me.[B]

8 Ephraim has allowed
himself to get mixed up
with the nations.
Ephraim is unturned bread
baked on a griddle.
9 Foreigners consume
his strength,
but he does not notice.
Even his hair is streaked
with gray,
but he does not notice.
10 Israel's arrogance testifies
against them,[C]
yet they do not return to
•Yahweh their God,
and for all this, they do not
seek Him.

11 So Ephraim has become
like a silly, senseless dove;
they call to Egypt, and they go
to Assyria.
12 As they are going, I will spread
My net over them;
I will bring them down
like birds of the sky.
I will discipline them
in accordance
with the news that reaches[D]
their assembly.

13 Woe to them, for they fled
from Me;
destruction to them,
for they rebelled against Me!
Though I want
to redeem them,
they speak lies against Me.
14 They do not cry to Me
from their hearts;
rather, they wail
on their beds.
They slash themselves[E]
for grain and new wine;
they turn away from Me.
15 I trained and strengthened
their arms,
but they plot evil against Me.
16 They turn, but not to what
is above;[F]
they are like a faulty bow.
Their leaders will fall
by the sword
because of the cursing
of their tongue.

[A]**7:5** Lit *wine—he stretches out his hand to scorners*; Hb obscure [B]**7:3-7** These vv. may refer to a king's assassination; Hb obscure. [C]**7:10** Lit *against his face* [D]**7:12** Lit *news to* [E]**7:14** Some Hb mss, LXX; other Hb mss read *They stay* [F]**7:16** Some emend to *turn to what is useless*

>WORD|*study*

7:11 Senseless (Hb *patah*, "being simple, gullible, without expertise") refers to one who does not have the heart or discernment to make right choices, one who is easily influenced by unwise counsel.

7:3 **They** is probably a reference to the priesthood since Hosea continues to lay ultimate blame for the downfall of Israel at the feet of the corrupt priests.

7:4-7 **Adultery** was not limited to the spiritual sense of unfaithfulness on the part of the people to the Lord but also included their breaking of marital vows, especially through cultic prostitution. The metaphor or imagery of the **oven** and a **baker** is used to portray the releasing of all moral restraint, which now characterized the people. With the heating of unleavened bread in the baker's oven, which was so hot that it did not have to be stirred from the time the dough started to rise until the bread was baked. So it was with the passions of the people of the Northern Kingdom.

The baking metaphor continues, explaining the progression of the plot to dethrone the king. Though a baker ought to tend the fire properly to cook the food, here the baker, the oven, and the fire become symbolic of the traitors and their sinful behavior, which resulted in the plot to dethrone the king. The unattended fire, in the process, begins to lose control. The neglected oven resulted in an uncontrollable fire. **All their kings fall; not one of them calls on Me** is an expression of the downfall of the king. The traitors have killed, or at least dethroned, the king without ever consulting God.

7:8 The **unturned bread** refers to round, flat bread slapped into the side of the oven, thus burnt on one side and undone on the other and, therefore, useless and inedible.

7:9-10 The powers in whom the Israelites trusted consumed them, and the Israelites did not even realize they had lost their power or that their **hair** was **streaked with gray**. Again Israel's failure to repent because of her own **arrogance** will result in her demise.

7:16 Israel's trust in human protection was like having faith in a **faulty bow**, which not only could not produce the intended results but also could leave them vulnerable in situations.

8:1 The **eagle** (Hb *nesher*, "vulture") personifies an enemy who would quickly swoop down in judgment. Though the enemy is nameless, the sin of the Israelites is specific: They have broken God's **covenant** and rebelled against His **law**.

8:4 The Israelites did not seek God's counsel when appointing their leaders, resulting in catastrophe, and they constructed idols (cp. Jn 4:24).

8:5-6 The **calf-idol** in Samaria, housed in a royal shrine in Bethel, probably refers to the golden calf set up by Jeroboam I (cp. 1Kg 12:28-29). Having made these idols to take the place of Yahweh, the people aroused the Lord's anger. God refused their counterfeit worship.

8:7-10 Dishonoring the Lord brought consequences both agriculturally and militarily. Only Yahweh made the people unique and powerful among nations. When Israel deserted the Lord, her people had only the value of **discarded pottery**.

8:9-10 A **wild donkey going off on its own** can bray loudly, making itself obnoxious. Israel has chosen a lonely path. Ephraim, too, has become a lonely creature left to fend for itself. Finally, Ephraim is pictured as paying the fees prostitutes require to get their favors. However, the money paid is a fruitless endeavor because Ephraim's destiny belongs to Yahweh. God would allow Israel to fall under the domination of the foreign nations whose protection Israel sought to purchase.

8:13 Genuine sacrifices were intended to bring people closer to God, yet the Israelites' participation in pagan sacrifices resulted in greater sin.

8:14 Even the **palaces** and **fortified cities** are against God's will because they are mere human efforts to provide security and represent attempts by Israel and Judah to save themselves instead of calling upon God for their deliverance. God would destroy the things they had built to take His place.

9:1-2 Israel had committed adultery against the Lord by celebrating harvest festivals, focusing on Baal to provide prosperity and blessings for the nation. These rituals of Baal worship, probably including sexual promiscuity with temple prostitutes on the **threshing floor**, were thought to ensure a good harvest. A **wine vat** was carved from stone to hold the grapes on which the harvesters stomped to produce the juice of the fruit.

They will be ridiculed for this
in the land of Egypt.

Israel's Self-Serving Behavior Results in Destruction (8:1-14)

8 Put the horn to your mouth!
One like an eagle comes
against the house of the LORD,
because they transgress
My covenant
and rebel against My law.
2 Israel cries out to Me,
"My God, we know You!"
3 Israel has rejected
what is good;
an enemy will pursue him.

4 They have installed kings,
but not through Me.
They have appointed leaders,
but without My approval.
They make their silver
and gold
into idols for themselves
for their own destruction.[A]
5 Your calf-idol[B]
is rejected, Samaria.
My anger burns against them.
How long will they be
incapable of innocence?
6 For this thing is from Israel—
a craftsman made it,
and it is not God.
The calf of Samaria
will be smashed to bits!

7 Indeed, they sow the wind
and reap the whirlwind.
There is no standing grain;
what sprouts fails
to yield flour.
Even if they did,
foreigners would
swallow it up.
8 Israel is swallowed up!
Now they are
among the nations
like discarded pottery.
9 For they have gone up
to Assyria
like a wild donkey going off
on its own.
Ephraim has paid for love.
10 Even though they hire lovers
among the nations,
I will now round them up,
and they will begin
to decrease in number
under the burden of the king
and leaders.

11 When Ephraim multiplied
his altars for sin,
they became his altars
for sinning.
12 Though I were to write out
for him
ten thousand points
of My instruction,
they would be[C] regarded
as something strange.
13 Though they offer
sacrificial gifts[D]
and eat the flesh,
the LORD does not
accept them.
Now He will remember
their •guilt
and punish their sins;
they will return to Egypt.
14 Israel has forgotten his Maker
and built palaces;
Judah has also multiplied
fortified cities.
I will send fire on their cities,
and it will consume
their citadels.

Prophecies and Judgments for Israel (9:1–13:16)

Prophecies about Israel's Future (9:1-17)

9 Israel, do not
rejoice jubilantly
as the nations do,
for you have acted
promiscuously,
leaving your God.
You have loved the wages
of a prostitute
on every
grain-threshing floor.
2 Threshing floor and wine vat
will not sustain them,
and the new wine
will fail them.
3 They will not stay in the land
of the LORD.
Instead, Ephraim will return
to Egypt,
and they will eat
•unclean food in Assyria.

4 They will not pour out
their wine offerings
to the LORD,

[A]8:4 Lit *themselves that it might be cut off* [B]8:5 Lit *calf* [C]8:12 Or *Though I wrote out . . . instruction, they are* [D]8:13 Hb obscure

and their sacrifices
will not please Him.
Their food will be
like the bread of mourners;
all who eat it become defiled.
For their bread will be
for their appetites alone;
it will not enter the house
of the LORD.
5 What will you do
on a festival day,
on the day of the LORD's feast?
6 For even if they flee
from devastation,
Egypt will gather
them, and Memphis
will bury them.
Thistles will take possession
of their precious silver;
thorns will invade their tents.

7 The days of punishment
have come;
the days of retribution
have come.
Let Israel recognize it!
The prophet is a fool,
and the inspired man
is insane,
because of the magnitude
of your •guilt and hostility.
8 Ephraim's watchman is
with my God.
The prophet encounters
a fowler's snare
on all his ways.
Hostility is in the house
of his God!
9 They have deeply
corrupted themselves
as in the days of Gibeah.
He will remember their guilt;
He will punish their sins.
10 I discovered Israel
like grapes in the wilderness.
I saw your fathers
like the first fruit
of the fig tree
in its first season.
But they went to Baal-peor,
consecrated themselves
to Shame,[A]
and became detestable,
like the thing they loved.
11 Ephraim's glory will fly away
like a bird:
no birth, no gestation,
no conception.
12 Even if they raise children,
I will bereave them
of each one.
Yes, woe to them
when I depart from them!
13 I have seen Ephraim like Tyre,
planted in a meadow,
so Ephraim will bring out
his children
to the executioner.
14 Give them, LORD—
What should You give?
Give them a womb
that miscarries
and breasts that are dry!

15 All their evil appears at Gilgal,
for there I came to hate them.
I will drive them
from My house
because of their evil,
wicked actions.
I will no longer love them;
all their leaders are rebellious.
16 Ephraim is struck down;
their roots are withered;
they cannot bear fruit.
Even if they bear children,
I will kill the precious
offspring of their wombs.
17 My God will reject them
because they have not
listened to Him;
they will become wanderers
among the nations.

[A]**9:10** = Baal

9:3 Egypt and **Assyria** are references to the exile of the Israelites, who would find themselves in Assyria where they would eat **unclean food** (food that had not been prepared according to their laws).

9:4 The Israelites' **offerings**, whether unacceptable in choice or non-existent, were unacceptable to God because they were honoring a pagan god. The **bread of mourners** is a reference to those in mourning, who would be unclean because of their association with a dead body and thus contaminators of any food they touched, making all unfit as an offering to God.

9:6 Memphis, a city located in northern Egypt, has long been associated with burial grounds, including some significant pyramids still standing. Their idols and possessions would be abandoned and forgotten with only **thistles** and **thorns** remaining.

9:7 Ridiculing the prophets for their behavior, beliefs, and preaching was common among the Israelites. Hosea merely turned these taunts sarcastically against Israel.

9:8 Hosea defined his role as a prophet by describing himself as **Ephraim's watchman**. He understood **hostility is in the house of his God**, affirming that Israel did not welcome him and wanted to do him harm.

9:9 Hosea compared Israel with **Gibeah**, which is associated with the horrific rape and murder of the Levite's concubine by members of the tribe of Benjamin, which brought ongoing destructive results on the tribe (cp. Jdg 19–21).

9:11-13 Since **Ephraim's glory** was her children, judgment included an infertility that would strip them of this "glory." Even if children were conceived, they would die. Children alive at that time were considered part of God's judgment. How ironic that Israel had been worshiping Baal to achieve fertility in agriculture and to produce descendants; yet the Lord's judgment brought them their greatest losses in these areas. Future generations would be cut off from the land.

9:15 At Gilgal . . . I came to hate them is a statement reminiscent of the history of how Gilgal has been at the heart of much of Israel's disobedience.

9:16 Barrenness and famine continue as God's judgment (cp. 10:1; 14:8). The bearing of a child is futile under such judgment. To **kill** (Hb *mut*, "die") may refer to accidental death or to violent death. Death is the ultimate consequence of and punishment for sin.

>WORD|*study*

9:15 Hate (Hb *sanē'*) is not always understood as the strongest aversion, i.e., as an emotional feeling inciting a desire to harm without reason. The word can mean a lesser degree of love or even a coldness and indifference.

9:15 Love (Hb *'ahavah*) suggests an ardent and devoted commitment conveying deep affection and tenderness. The word is used to describe the unspeakable devotion and tender mercies God Himself shows to His people. However, this word does not have the binding and unconditional implications of "lovingkindness" (Hb *chesed*), which refers to God's covenant love. God does not withhold His covenant love from Israel despite their rejection of Him.

10:4-6 The loss of the **calf of Beth-aven** was evidence that their false religion had failed them. The idol was meant to be **an offering to the great king** (or King Yareb; see note on 5:13). **Samaria** had not found security in their alliances with other nations; they had sowed the seeds of their own judgment (10:4). Ephraim and Israel would feel shame because of their Baal worship. What they worshiped and believed was the source of their good fortune became the possession of the Assyrian king. The complete ineffectiveness of Baal was evident to the people.

10:7 The use of **foam** (Hb *qetseph*, "twig, splinter, or stick") accentuated the fact that as Samaria's king appeared, he would just as quickly disappear or be swept away, like a twig or "foam" in the ocean. The king had no power in himself to impact historical events.

10:8 The **high places of Aven** (Hb, "wickedness"), a reference to Bethel, would be destroyed. Here the Israelites had congregated in their apostasy, which began to lose its significance as **thorns and thistles** grew **over their altars**. The imagery of the **mountains** and **hills** falling on them is used later by Jesus to describe the reaction of the Jews to the Roman destruction of Jerusalem (Lk 23:30). Likewise this imagery is used at the coming great tribulation (cp. Rv 6:16).

10:9 The days of Gibeah was to the people of Israel a reminder of their many years of disobedience since the incident involving the concubine and civil war (cp. Jdg 19–21). Israel had continued in its disobedience. The city represented both Israel's decadence and its dependence on violent force.

10:10 Though previously God had protected His people from the attacks of other nations, this time He was permitting other nations to punish Israel **for their two crimes**, which are not named.

10:13-14 Israel's trust in military strength and power was misplaced. The destruction resulting from this battle is compared with **Shalman's destruction of Beth-arbel.** Likely Shalman is Shalmaneser V of Assyria, who succeeded Tiglath-pileser III (cp. 2Kg 17:3-5). The destruction would be so horrific that even mothers and their children would be brutally killed.

More Accusations against Israel (10:1-15)

10 Israel is a lush[A] vine;
it yields fruit for itself.
The more his fruit increased,
the more he increased
the altars.
The better his land produced,
the better they made
the sacred pillars.
2 Their hearts are devious;[B]
now they must bear
their •guilt.
The LORD will break down
their altars
and demolish
their sacred pillars.
3 In fact, they are now saying,
"We have no king!
For we do not •fear the LORD.
What can a king do for us?"
4 They speak mere words,
taking false oaths
while making covenants.
So lawsuits break out
like poisonous weeds
in the furrows of a field.

5 The residents of Samaria
will have anxiety
over the calf of Beth-aven.
Indeed, its idolatrous priests
rejoiced over it;
the people will mourn over it,
over its glory.
It will certainly depart
from them.
6 The calf itself will be taken
to Assyria
as an offering
to the great king.[C]
Ephraim will
experience shame;
Israel will be ashamed
of its counsel.
7 Samaria's king will disappear[D]
like foam[E] on the surface
of the water.
8 The •high places of Aven,
the sin of Israel,
will be destroyed;
thorns and thistles will grow
over their altars.
They will say
to the mountains,
"Cover us!"
and to the hills, "Fall on us!"

9 Israel, you have sinned
since the days of Gibeah;
they have taken
their stand there.
Will not war against
the unjust
overtake them in Gibeah?
10 I will discipline them
at My discretion;
nations will be gathered
against them
to put them in bondage[F]
for their two crimes.

11 Ephraim is a well-trained calf
that loves to thresh,
but I will place a yoke on[G] her
fine neck.
I will harness Ephraim;
Judah will plow;
Jacob will do the
final plowing.
12 Sow righteousness
for yourselves
and reap faithful love;
break up
your unplowed ground.
It is time to seek the LORD
until He comes
and sends righteousness
on you like the rain.

13 You have plowed wickedness
and reaped injustice;
you have eaten the fruit
of lies.
Because you have trusted
in your own way[H]
and in your large number
of soldiers,
14 the roar of battle will rise
against your people,
and all your fortifications
will be demolished
in a day of war,
like Shalman's destruction
of Beth-arbel.
Mothers will be dashed
to pieces
along with their children.
15 So it will be done
to you, Bethel,
because of your extreme evil.
At dawn the king of Israel
will be totally destroyed.

[A]10:1 Or *ravaged* [B]10:2 Or *divided* [C]10:6 Or *to King Yareb* [D]10:7 Or *will be cut off* [E]10:7 Or *a stick* [F]10:10 LXX, Syr, Vg read *against them when they are disciplined* [G]10:11 Lit *will pass over* [H]10:13 LXX reads *your chariots*

God's Love for Israel (11:1-11)

11 When Israel was a child,
I loved him,
and out of Egypt I called
My son.
2 The more they[A] called them,[B]
the more they[B] departed
from Me.[C]
They kept sacrificing
to the •Baals
and burning offerings
to idols.
3 It was I who taught Ephraim
to walk,
taking them[D] in My arms,
but they never knew
that I healed them.
4 I led them with human cords,
with ropes of love.
To them I was like one
who eases the yoke
from their jaws;
I bent down
to give them food.
5 Israel will not return
to the land of Egypt
and Assyria will be his king,
because they refused
to repent.
6 A sword will whirl
through his cities;
it will destroy and devour
the bars of his gates,[E]
because of their schemes.
7 My people are bent on turning
from Me.
Though they call to Him
on high,
He will not exalt them at all.

8 How can I give you
up, Ephraim?
How can I surrender
you, Israel?
How can I make you
like Admah?
How can I treat you
like Zeboiim?
I have had a change of heart;
My compassion is stirred!
9 I will not vent the full fury
of My anger;
I will not turn back
to destroy Ephraim.
For I am God and not man,
the Holy One among you;
I will not come in rage.[F]
10 They will follow the LORD;
He will roar like a lion.
When He roars,
His children
will come trembling
from the west.
11 They will be roused like birds
from Egypt
and like doves from the land
of Assyria.
Then I will settle them
in their homes.
This is
the LORD's declaration.

Israel's Apostasy Compared to Jacob's Life (11:12–12:14)

12G Ephraim surrounds me
with lies,
the house of Israel,
with deceit.
Judah still wanders with God
and is faithful
to the holy ones.[H,I]

12 Ephraim chases[J] the wind
and pursues the east wind.
He continually multiplies lies
and violence.
He makes a covenant
with Assyria,
and olive oil is carried
to Egypt.
2 The LORD also has a dispute
with Judah.
He is about to punish Jacob
according to his ways;
He will repay him based on
his actions.
3 In the womb he grasped
his brother's heel,
and as an adult he wrestled
with God.
4 Jacob struggled with the Angel
and prevailed;
he wept and sought
His favor.
He found him[K] at Bethel,
and there He spoke
with him.[L]
5 •Yahweh is the God of •Hosts;
Yahweh is His name.

11:5-9 The **sword** represents what **Assyria** would do to Israel, whom, despite their unfaithfulness and wrongdoing, God still identified as **My people**. For the Lord to **give . . . up Ephraim** or **surrender . . . Israel** means that He allows them to experience the consequences of their unfaithfulness, which could include slavery, torture, and death.

11:8 Admah and **Zeboiim**, together with Sodom and Gomorrah, are among the cities of the plain destroyed (cp. Gn 10:19; 19:24-25). God did not want to see this destruction fall upon His people and affirmed that He would not unleash His wrath to the extent that He did with these evil cities.

11:12 Judah, too, was demonstrating apostasy. The inhabitants of the southern kingdom appeared devoted to God, but they had been influenced by the Canaanite cults. El was the chief Canaanite god, and the **holy ones** referred to the Canaanite pantheon of idols.

12:2-4 God addressed Judah about her forefather **Jacob**, thus showing a connection with the northern kingdom. The prophet reviewed the life of Jacob and his grabbing the heel of his brother while still in the womb. As the man Jacob **wrestled with God**, he **struggled with the Angel and prevailed**. Hosea underscores God's gracious initiative with Jacob at Bethel despite Jacob's pattern of treachery (Gn 28:10-22).

[A] **11:2** Perhaps the prophets [B] **11:2** = Israel [C] **11:2** LXX; MT reads *them* [D] **11:3** LXX, Syr, Vg; MT reads *him* [E] **11:6** Or *devour his empty talkers*, or *devour his limbs*; Hb obscure [F] **11:9** Or *come into any city*; Hb obscure [G] **11:12** Hs 12:1 in Hb [H] **11:12** Or *to the Holy One*; Hb obscure [I] **11:12** Possibly angels, or less likely, pagan gods or idols [J] **12:1** Or *feeds on*, or *tends* [K] **12:4** Or *Him* [L] **12:4** LXX, Syr; MT reads *us*

12:9 The **festival days** referred to the Festival of Tabernacles or Booths, during which the Israelites lived in tents to commemorate the time God cared for them in the wilderness. The discomfort they experienced in tent life would return as judgment for their apostasy.

12:10 The prophets functioned as mouthpieces for God, declaring God's warnings and judgments and announcing His appointments to leadership. Despite the presence of these men of God, throughout Israel's history, the people repeatedly went astray.

12:14 Continually **Ephraim** betrayed God with the worship of other gods, ultimately resulting in their experiencing God's **bitter anger**.

13:1-2 Ephraim's choice to worship **Baal** resulted in death (Hs 13:1). To **kiss the calves** was part of the pagan ritual (cp. 1Kg 19:18).

13:5 The fact that the Israelites received God's provision in **the land of drought** stresses the abundance of care God provided.

13:6 The word **satisfied** conveys the sense of complacency, leading to a false sense of self-reliance so that **their hearts became proud**. Despite God's provision, the people forgot Him and failed to express gratitude for His providential care.

6 But you must return
to your God.
Maintain love and justice,
and always put your hope
in God.

7 A merchant loves to extort
with dishonest scales
in his hands.
8 But Ephraim says:
"How rich I have become;
I made it all myself.
In all my earnings,
no one can find any crime
in me
that I can be punished for!"[A]
9 I have been Yahweh your God
ever since[B] the land of Egypt.
I will make you live
in tents again,
as in the festival days.
10 I spoke through the prophets
and granted many visions;
I gave parables
through the prophets.
11 Since Gilead is full of evil,
they will certainly come
to nothing.
They sacrifice bulls in Gilgal;
even their altars will be
like heaps of rocks
on the furrows of a field.

12 Jacob fled to the land of Aram.
Israel worked to earn a wife;
he tended flocks for a wife.
13 The LORD brought Israel
from Egypt by a prophet,
and Israel was tended
by a prophet.

14 Ephraim has provoked
bitter anger,
so his Lord will leave
his bloodguilt on him
and repay him
for his contempt.

Further Judgment on Israel (13:1-16)

13 When Ephraim spoke,
there was trembling;
he was exalted in Israel.
But he incurred •guilt
through •Baal and died.

2 Now they continue to sin
and make themselves
a cast image,
idols skillfully made
from their silver,
all of them the work
of craftsmen.
People say about them,
"Let the men who sacrifice[C]
kiss the calves."
3 Therefore, they will be
like the morning mist,
like the early dew
that vanishes,
like chaff blown
from a threshing floor,
or like smoke from a window.

4 I have been •Yahweh your God
ever since[D] the land of Egypt;
you know no God but Me,
and no Savior exists
besides Me.
5 I knew[E] you in the wilderness,
in the land of drought.
6 When they had pasture,
they became satisfied;
they were satisfied,
and their hearts became proud.
Therefore they forgot Me.
7 So I will be like a lion to them;
I will lurk like a leopard
on the path.
8 I will attack them
like a bear robbed of her cubs
and tear open the rib cage
over their hearts.
I will devour them there
like a lioness,

[A]12:8 Lit *crime which is sin* [B]12:9 LXX reads *God who brought you out of* [C]13:2 Or *Those who make human sacrifices* [D]13:4 DSS, LXX read *God who brought you out of* [E]13:5 LXX, Syr read *fed*

>WORD|*study*

12:14 The term **bloodguilt** (Hb *dam*, "the guilt of murder, an atrocious crime") implies a crime offensive enough to merit death. The Israelites would experience God's full wrath for their continual disrespect and uncaring lack of loyalty to Yahweh.

13:4 The word **know** (Hb *yada'*, "come to knowledge by seeing, hearing, and experience"; cp. note on Ex 2:24) refers to an intimate relationship. Hosea uses the word to return to the understanding of intimacy between a husband and wife and compares this knowledge to God's relationship with Israel. One cannot *know* what is nonexistent; therefore, Yahweh is the only God Israel had ever *known*.

like a wild beast that
would rip them open.
9 I will destroy you, Israel;
you have no help but Me.[A]

10 Where now is your king,[B]
that he may save you in all
your cities,
and the[C] rulers[D] you
demanded, saying,
"Give me a king and leaders"?
11 I give you a king in My anger
and take away a king
in My wrath.
12 Ephraim's guilt is preserved;
his sin is stored up.
13 Labor pains come on him.
He is not a wise son;
when the time comes,
he will not be born.[E]

14 I will ransom them
from the power of •Sheol.
I will redeem[F] them
from death.
Death, where are your barbs?
Sheol, where is your sting?
Compassion is hidden
from My eyes.
15 Although he flourishes
among his brothers,[G]
an east wind will come,
a wind from the LORD
rising up from the desert.
His water source will fail,
and his spring will run dry.
The wind[H] will plunder
the treasury
of every precious item.

16[I] Samaria will bear her guilt
because she has rebelled
against her God.
They will fall by the sword;
their little ones will be dashed
to pieces,
and their pregnant women
ripped open.

The Final Plea for Israel's Repentance (14:1-9)

14 Israel, return to •Yahweh
your God,
for you have stumbled
in your sin.
2 Take words of repentance
with you
and return to the LORD.
Say to Him: "Forgive all
our sin
and accept what is good,
so that we may repay You
with praise[J] from our[K] lips.
3 Assyria will not save us,
we will not ride on horses,
and we will no longer
proclaim, 'Our gods!'
to the work of our hands.
For the fatherless
receives compassion in You."

4 I will heal their apostasy;
I will freely love them,
for My anger will have turned
from him.
5 I will be like the dew to Israel;
he will blossom like the lily
and take root like
the cedars of Lebanon.
6 His new branches will spread,
and his splendor will be
like the olive tree,
his fragrance, like
the forest of Lebanon.
7 The people will return
and live beneath his shade.
They will grow grain
and blossom like the vine.
His renown will be
like the wine of Lebanon.

8 Ephraim, why should I[L] have
anything more
to do with idols?
It is I who answer and watch
over him.
I am like
a flourishing pine tree;
your fruit comes from Me.

9 Let whoever is wise
understand these things,
and whoever is insightful
recognize them.
For the ways of the LORD
are right,
and the righteous walk
in them,
but the rebellious stumble
in them.

13:13 The metaphor of a woman giving birth provides a clear picture of a child who refuses to act upon the **labor pains** of coming birth and ends up stillborn. Thus the judgments that came upon Israel to refine and correct could have been a path to new birth and restoration.

13:15 The **east wind** coming to dry out and wither Ephraim's bounty represents the power of God's justice.

13:16 God would bring on Samaria such destruction that any hope of rebuilding would be lost. **Their little ones will be dashed to pieces, and their pregnant women ripped open** is a vivid picture of destruction that extends even to the generations to come.

14:1-8 Hosea issued a final call for Israel to repent. Their offense was breaking their covenant with God. God explained the necessary steps for restoration in a clear, concise manner: Repent of specific sins; accept God's goodness; and reject help from any source other than what God provides.

14:5-6 To **blossom like the lily**, a flower of extravagant fragrance and beauty, was a beautiful picture of ultimate restoration. **The olive tree**, providing food, medicine, and even hair products, represented life and emphasized quality more than quantity.

14:8 The prophet used **a flourishing pine tree** as a simile to show the futility of Baal's fertility. The worship of this idol was associated with a wooden image or pole, and now clearly its effectiveness was nil (cp. 4:12-13). God alone is the source of fertility in every area of life.

14:9 The obedient prophet Hosea took "a promiscuous wife" (1:2) and, despite Gomer's actions in breaking their covenant of marriage, restored her to himself. In the same way, Yahweh God will continue to love His people Israel with an everlasting love and restore them to Himself—not because of their merit but because of His covenant commitment.

[A]**13:9** LXX reads *At your destruction, Israel, who will help you?* [B]**13:10** LXX, Syr, Vg; MT reads *I will be your king* [C]**13:10** Lit *your* [D]**13:10** Or *judges* [E]**13:13** Lit *he will not present himself at the opening of the womb for sons* [F]**13:14** Or *Should I ransom . . . Should I redeem . . . ?* [G]**13:15** Or *among reeds* [H]**13:15** Probably the Assyrian king [I]**13:16** Hs 14:1 in Hb [J]**14:2** LXX reads *with the fruit* [K]**14:2** Lit *repay the bulls of our* [L]**14:8** LXX reads *he*

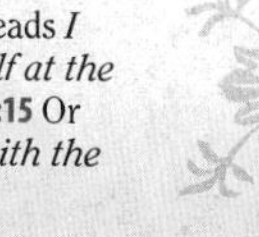

CHARACTER PROFILE

Gomer A Selfish Harlot

Her Background

- The daughter of Diblaim (1:2-8)
- The wife of Hosea (1:3)
- The mother of Jezreel, No Compassion, and Not My People (1:3-10)

Her Story

- She shamelessly committed adultery with numerous men (1:2; 3:1; cp. 2:2,5).
- Her pursuit of "lovers" outside her marriage to Hosea resulted in captivity (3:1-2).
- Her true husband redeemed her from slavery and brought her back home (3:2-3).
- Hosea's instructions suggest that Gomer's full restoration of marital privileges would follow a period of time during which her addiction to adultery would be supplanted by renewed commitment to covenant faithfulness (3:2).

Life Lessons

- This story pictures God's compassionate love for His people and His anger at their disobedience.
- However, Gomer's life also illustrates the depth of God's forgiveness and restoration.

HOSEA... WRITTEN ON MY Heart

Perhaps you do not bow down to a hand-carved idol as the Israelites were doing, but you may find yourself serving and worshiping at the feet of self or the world from time to time. God's faithful love does not falter even in the midst of your deplorable trysts away from Him. He still loves you and often brings discipline to your life through sin's consequences. Hosea reminds his readers that redemption is never too far away to receive. Some may feel their sins are too great or too many, but God's grace is there to restore even the worst of sinners. Hosea points all to Christ's love. While Hosea went to great lengths to restore his marriage with Gomer, the Lord went even further for you. He did not even spare His own Son, Jesus, but gave Him so that you and I might come into a right relationship with God Himself.

Women in the Minor Prophets

Prophet	Approximate Date of Ministry	Key Female Figure
Hosea	755–725 B.C.	**Gomer**, the "promiscuous wife" (Hs 1:2) and "adulteress" (3:1) whom the Lord told the prophet to marry and redeem as a picture of His relationship with His people
Joel	835 B.C. or 445–400 B.C.	**Daughters** and **female slaves** upon whom God promised to pour out His Spirit (Jl 2:28-29)
Amos	767–753 B.C.	**Cows of Bashan**, a metaphor depicting the women of Israel "who oppress the poor and crush the needy, who say to their husbands, 'Bring us something to drink'" (Am 4:1)
Obadiah	586 B.C.	
Jonah	800–750 B.C.	
Micah	750–686 B.C.	**Daughter Zion**, whose sin is lamented (Mc 1:13) yet whose rescue, redemption, and ultimate triumph over enemies are assured (4:6-13)
Nahum	663–612 B.C.	**Nineveh**, the capital city of Assyria, portrayed as a "prostitute" and "mistress of sorcery" (Nah 3:4-7; cp. Zph 2:13-15)
Habakkuk	625–587 B.C.	
Zephaniah	640–609 B.C.	**Jerusalem**, punished as a "rebellious and defiled . . . oppressive city" (Zph 3:1-8); **Daughter Zion**/Daughter Jerusalem, representing "the remnant of Israel," restored by the Lord to a favored position of "fame and praise" (3:10-20)
Haggai	520 B.C.	
Zechariah	520–480 B.C.	**Wickedness**, represented in the prophet's seventh vision as a woman sitting in a measuring basket with a lead cover, which two winged women carry to set on a pedestal "in the land of Shinar" (5:5-11) **Daughter Zion**/**Daughter Jerusalem**, chosen as the Lord's "holy dwelling" (Zch 2:10-13) and called to rejoice in her future coming King (9:9-17)
Malachi	458–435 B.C.	**The daughter of a foreign god**, forbidden as a legitimate marriage partner for Jewish men (Mal 2:11-12; cp. Dt 7:3-4) **The wife of your youth**/your marriage partner/your wife by covenant, whose being divorced by their husbands is regarded by the Lord as treachery (Mal 2:14-16)

Joel

Timeline World Events Biblical Events	***722 BC*** Samaria, capital of the northern kingdom, fell to the Assyrians.	***722–605 BC*** If an early date is assumed, Joel likely prophesied between 722 and 605 B.C.	***700 BC*** Greeks established trading posts in Philistine territory on the Mediterranean coast (Jl 3:6).	***700 BC*** Philistines and Phoenicians sold the people of Judah and Jerusalem as slaves to the Greeks.

"After this I will pour out My Spirit on all humanity; then your sons and your daughters will prophesy, your old men will have dreams, and your young men will see visions" (2:28).

Who wrote Joel?

The prophet Joel (1:1)

Who were the recipients?

The immediate context of Joel suggests the recipients as those living in and around Jerusalem and Judah. But the overall eschatological message of Joel is intended for all generations of believers, and many argue that the message extends beyond the prophecies.

When was Joel written?

Suggested dates range from 800 B.C. (preexilic) to 400 B.C. (postexilic)

Where did it happen?

The book of Joel takes place in Judah after a horrific locust plague had delivered destruction on the economy and society at a time when Judah (the southern kingdom) was experiencing spiritual decay. There is much debate as to the dating of Joel, but its message is not dependent on an exact date.

What is Joel about?

- *Judgment*. The people of Israel were reaping the consequences of their sin and would experience further punishment unless they heeded the voice of Joel.
- *Repentance*. Joel called the people of Israel to turn from sin and return to the Lord.
- *The future "Day of the Lord."* Joel gives some details of God's judgment in the last days and describes the final restoration of Judah and Jerusalem.

Why should women read Joel?

Before repentance comes confrontation. Joel is a lesson in confrontation. The people in Joel's day were experiencing the judgment of God in their lives through a locust plague. Had they heeded the warnings about their disobedience earlier and repented, perhaps judgment would have been delayed or even averted. Just as the people of Judah in Joel's day, women have a tendency to avoid confrontation, but a Christ-following woman must learn to be thankful for confrontation when it comes from the Holy Spirit. Your spiritual growth will be stunted if you avoid dealing with sin, but perhaps worse, short or prolonged disobedience leads to the Lord's discipline in your life. The book of Joel reminds women to welcome prophetic confrontation about sin in their lives.

How do you read Joel?

The book of Joel should be read as poetic prophecy. Yet it has a specific purpose—to proclaim a message from God and confront His people with their sins. There is imagery and metaphor. For example, the locust plague is an image of the judgment of God on Judah. Joel's recipients had experienced a disastrous locust plague that affected the economy and every level of society. Joel differs from other prophets. He does not give much attention to specific sins. Rather, he focuses on the motivation behind the sin. Their faith had become empty religious ritual. As with any prophetic book, Joel calls on his readers to change their hearts and to return to the Lord. The first two chapters of Joel deal with the devastating locust plague and the need for repentance, while chapter 3 reveals some details of God's judgment in the last days and describes the final restoration of Judah and Jerusalem. The end of chapter two constitutes the beginning of the second part of Joel's book. The events described in this part of the book are set almost entirely in the future. The nations' destructive behavior toward Israel and their future destruction are discussed in this part of the book. This second part of the book is dominated by themes of material and spiritual blessings given to Israel.

God reveals Himself as both a God of judgment and faithful love. The Lord's goal in confronting sin is not to be vindictive but rather to redeem and restore. Jesus Himself confronted the people of His day with their sin and continues to do so today. There is no godly repentance without godly sorrow, which is inspired by the Word of God. Read and meditate on His Word daily, so you may, as did Joel, confront the sin in your life and so be restored through the love and grace found in Jesus Christ.

Outline

I. The Locusts in the Land (1:1-14)
  A. The Call to Attention (1:1-4)
  B. The Call to Mourn (1:5-14)
II. God's Judgment on the Land (1:15–2:11)
  A. The Devastation of the Locust Invasion (1:15-20)
  B. The Invasion of the LORD's Army (2:1-11)
III. God's Mercy on the Land (2:12-27)
  A. A Call to Repentance (2:12-17)
  B. The LORD's Response (2:18-27)
IV. God's Wonders in the Earth (2:28-32)
V. God's Judgment on the Earth (3:1-21)

605–586 BC	538 BC	536 BC	445–400 BC
Nebuchadnezzar invaded Judah three times and took many into exile.	Cyrus allowed return of Jews from exile.	Construction of the second temple began.	If a late date is assumed, Joel likely prophesied from 445–400 B.C.

>WORD|*study*

1:2 Elders (Hb *zaqēn*, "old men;" cp. 1:14) may refer to the tribal or family leaders governing the Jewish remnant in Israel after the exile. If so, the audience included both the leaders and all the people who lived in the land (cp. Is 3:14; Lm 2:10). The term may refer, however, to the senior citizens of the community since the message begins with a rhetorical question appealing to the memory of the audience (cp. "the aged," Jl 2:16; "old men," 2:28). The implied answer to the question is that nothing "like this [had] ever happened."

1:6 Powerful (Hb *'atsum*, "strong, mighty, numerous"), especially when coupled with the phrase "without number," indicates the overwhelming numerical strength of this ferocious and violent force, whether people or insects. Elsewhere in the book of Joel, the word describes "a great and *strong* people" (2:2), a "*mighty* army" (2:5), and "those who carry out His command . . . [as] *powerful*" (2:11).

The Locusts in the Land (1:1-14)

The Call to Attention (1:1-4)

1 The word of the LORD that came to Joel son of Pethuel:

2 Hear this, you elders;
listen, all you inhabitants
of the land.
Has anything like this
ever happened in your days
or in the days
of your ancestors?
3 Tell your children about it,
and let your children
tell their children,
and their children
the next generation.
4 What the devouring locust
has left,
the swarming locust
has eaten;
what the swarming locust
has left,
the young locust has eaten;
and what the young locust
has left,
the destroying locust
has eaten.

The Call to Mourn (1:5-14)

5 Wake up, you drunkards,
and weep;
wail, all you wine drinkers,
because of the sweet wine,
for it has been taken
from your mouth.
6 For a nation has invaded
My land,
powerful
and without number;
its teeth are the teeth
of a lion,
and it has the fangs
of a lioness.
7 It has devastated My grapevine
and splintered My fig tree.
It has stripped off its bark
and thrown it away;
its branches have turned white.
8 Grieve like a young woman
dressed in •sackcloth,
mourning for the husband
of her youth.
9 •Grain and •drink offerings
have been cut off
from the house of the LORD;
the priests, who are ministers
of the LORD, mourn.
10 The fields are destroyed;
the land grieves;
indeed, the grain
is destroyed;
the new wine is dried up;
and the olive oil fails.
11 Be ashamed, you farmers,
wail, you vinedressers,[A]

[A]1:11 Or *The farmers are dismayed, the vinedressers wail*

Title: The book is named for its prophet, Joel (Hb, "The Lord is God").

1:1-3 The word of the LORD called the people to heed His explanation of the unprecedented events they had experienced and to pass this understanding down to their children as a witness to subsequent generations.

God commanded this audience to make sure the story of these remarkable events became part of their family and national history and thus never forgotten.

1:4-11 Most scholars conclude that this passage describes the aftermath of an actual locust plague that caused unprecedented destruction (cp. Am 4:9).

1:7 The use of **grapevine** (Hb *gephen*), used in several passages, is a metaphor for God's people Israel (cp. Jl 1:12; cp. 2:22; Ps 80:8-16; Jr 2:21; Hs 10:1). To sit under one's own grapevine and fig tree was an idiom for living in security (cp. 1Kg 4:25; 2Kg 18:31; Mc 4:4). Here, however, the Lord asserted His ownership of all that was destroyed. The calamity He brought upon His people involved devastation of what personally belonged to Him, not merely an impersonal administration of punishment.

1:8-10 In commanding the "drunkards" (v. 5) to "grieve" the loss of the vines, which would have produced wine for future consumption, the Lord uses the particularly poignant image of a disconsolate woman. **Young woman** (Hb *betulah*) in Hebrew denotes a "virgin." **The husband of her youth** is the man to whom the bride price had been paid and to whom she, therefore, had been betrothed. However, the woman publicly mourning her loss is not a widow *per se* but a bride bereft of her groom before the consummation of her marriage and thus with little hope for the joys of marital bliss.

Even **the land grieves** (Hb *ʾaval*) because of its loss of produce (cp. Jl 2:21). Those who knew the covenant promises in the book of Deuteronomy (cp. Dt 7:12-13; 11:14) would have recognized that this loss was due to the people's disobedience.

1:13-14 The **priests** are implored to lead in a deliberate season of mourning. Mention of **the house of . . . God** and of **the house of the Lord** as a place to which the people were summoned to meet for corporate fasting and prayer (cp. v. 16) suggests that Joel prophesied either before the destruction of the first temple (pre-exilic) or after the second temple had been built (postexilic). God prescribed how the people, under the direction of their religious leaders, should respond to the disastrous experience of judgment—they were to **cry out to the Lord**.

Joel believed that the first responsibility for calling for repentance rested with the spiritual leaders whom God had appointed for the people. Without the means to offer sacrifices, expressing their desire for mercy and a reconciled relationship with God depended entirely on the sincerity of their plea and on His grace (cp. 2:13,17-19).

1:15-20 Between two admonitions for the people to repent (1:13-14; 2:12-17) are warnings about the nearness of **the Day of the Lord** (cp. 2:1). Historical references to "the Day of the Lord" serve as God's warning about "the Day of the Lord" in the end-times. This reference is first and foremost a warning of judgment, but secondarily it is a message of restoration. The **devastation** (Hb *shod*, "desolation, destruction," the only use of the word in the book of Joel; cp. Is 13:6; Hs 7:13) following the locust plague (or the repeated enemy invasions) clearly demonstrated the sort of desperate circumstances that God would allow to get His people's attention.

1:19-20 The first person pronoun **I** presumably refers to the prophet Joel, who called out to Yahweh at the sight of what **fire** and **flames** had destroyed. Joel's message initially was delivered to his peers as he boldly identified their sins and called them to repentance. But he did not stop there, pointing to the future coming of the Holy Spirit (cp. 2:28-32).

2:1-11 The Day of the Lord has two key features: It **is near** (Jl 1:15; 2:1; 3:14; cp. Ob 15; Zph 1:7,14), and it brings unimaginable destruction

>WORD|*study*

1:11-12 The Lord also commanded those who cultivated these crops to **be ashamed** (Hb *yavēsh*, lit "be dried up") because of the extensive agricultural losses. Here the word signifies "withered" hope and confidence as it does in the phrase **joy** [that] **has dried up**. *Yavēsh* is also used several times with its literal meaning—new wine being "dried up," the grapevine being "dried up" and the orchards having **withered** (cp. "withered" grain, v. 17)—indicating wordplay. The **farmers** (Hb *ʾikkar*, "husbandman, plowman) should **be ashamed** not because their efforts had failed but because the catastrophic circumstances displayed God's judgment against the nation and therefore exposed their moral failure and unfaithfulness to His covenant.

1:19-20 Twice Joel lamented the loss of **the pastures of the wilderness** (Hb *naʾah*, "where flocks lie down—i.e., a safe place," with *midbar*, "uninhabited plain"), a phrase that appears only six times in the Old Testament, including Jl 1:19-20; 2:22. That God's gift of abundance was seen in how "the wilderness pastures overflow" (Ps 65:12) makes sense of Yahweh's call elsewhere for a funeral "dirge" (cp. Jr 9:10) to be played and/or sung over the "scorched" earth left in place of "the wilderness grazing land." This loss is a result of Yahweh's judgment on "the cities of Judah" for abandoning His law to follow idols (cp. Dt 32:22). Similarly, "the grazing lands in the wilderness . . . dried up" and "the land mourns" because it was "full of adulterers" (Jr 23:10).

over the wheat and the barley,
because the harvest
of the field has perished.
12 The grapevine is dried up,
and the fig tree is withered;
the pomegranate,
the date palm,
and the apple—
all the trees of the orchard—
have withered.
Indeed, human joy
has dried up.

13 Dress in sackcloth and lament,
you priests;
wail, you ministers
of the altar.
Come and spend the night
in sackcloth,
you ministers of my God,
because grain
and drink offerings
are withheld from the house
of your God.
14 Announce a sacred fast;
proclaim an assembly!
Gather the elders
and all the residents
of the land
at the house of the Lord
your God,
and cry out to the Lord.

God's Judgment on the Land (1:15–2:11)

The Devastation of the Locust Invasion (1:15-20)

15 Woe because of that day!
For the Day of the Lord
is near
and will come as devastation
from the •Almighty.
16 Hasn't the food been cut off
before our eyes,
joy and gladness
from the house of our God?
17 The seeds lie shriveled
in their casings.[A]
The storehouses are in ruin,
and the granaries are
broken down,
because the grain has
withered away.
18 How the animals groan!
The herds of cattle wander
in confusion
since they have no pasture.
Even the flocks of sheep
suffer punishment.
19 I call to You, Lord,
for fire has consumed
the pastures of the wilderness,
and flames have devoured
all the trees
of the countryside.
20 Even the wild animals cry out
to[B] You,
for the river beds are dried up,
and fire has consumed
the pastures of the wilderness.

The Invasion of the Lord's Army (2:1-11)

2 Blow the horn in •Zion;
sound the alarm
on My holy mountain!
Let all the residents
of the land tremble,
for the Day of the Lord
is coming;
in fact, it is near—
2 a day of darkness and gloom,

[A]1:17 Or *clods*; Hb obscure [B]1:20 Or *animals pant for*; Hb obscure

a day of clouds
and dense overcast,
like the dawn spreading
over the mountains;
a great
and strong people appears,
such as never existed
in ages past
and never will again
in all the generations
to come.

3 A fire destroys[A] in front of them,
and behind them
a flame devours.
The land in front of them
is like the Garden of Eden,
but behind them,
it is like a desert wasteland;
there is no escape from them.
4 Their appearance is like that
of horses,
and they gallop
like war horses.
5 They bound on the tops
of the mountains.
Their sound is like the sound
of chariots,
like the sound of fiery flames
consuming stubble,
like a mighty army deployed
for war.

6 Nations writhe in horror
before them;
all faces turn pale.
7 They attack as warriors attack;
they scale walls as men
of war do.
Each goes on his own path,
and they do not change
their course.
8 They do not push each other;
each man proceeds
on his own path.
They dodge the arrows,
never stopping.
9 They storm the city;
they run on the wall;
they climb into the houses;
they enter
through the windows
like thieves.

10 The earth quakes before them;
the sky shakes.
The sun and moon grow dark,
and the stars cease
their shining.

11 The LORD raises His voice
in the presence of His army.
His camp is very large;
Those who carry out
His command are powerful.
Indeed, the Day of the LORD
is terrible and dreadful—
who can endure it?

God's Mercy on the Land (2:12-27)

A Call to Repentance (2:12-17)

12 Even now—
this is
the LORD's declaration—
turn to Me with all
your heart,
with fasting, weeping,
and mourning.
13 Tear your hearts,
not just your clothes,
and return to the LORD
your God.
For He is gracious
and compassionate,
slow to anger,
rich in faithful love,
and He relents
from sending disaster.
14 Who knows? He may turn
and relent
and leave a blessing
behind Him,
so you can offer grain
and wine
to the LORD your God.
15 Blow the horn in Zion!
Announce a sacred fast;
proclaim an assembly.
16 Gather the people;
sanctify the congregation;
assemble the aged;[B]
gather the children,
even those nursing
at the breast.
Let the groom
leave his bedroom,
and the bride
her honeymoon chamber.
17 Let the priests,
the LORD's ministers,
weep between the portico
and the altar.
Let them say:
"Have pity
on Your people, LORD,

(Jl 2:11; cp. Am 5:18-20). For Joel's immediate audience, "the Day of the LORD" had come in the form of a locust plague or enemy invasions prophesied through Jeremiah and others. The audience's fresh experience of God's judgment provided a foretaste of another future "Day of the LORD" (i.e., if they were in a state of ruin, what would happen to them when the final "Day of the LORD" is revealed).

2:1 To **blow the horn** and **sound the alarm** usually meant that danger was imminent and action had to be taken immediately to protect the city and its inhabitants (cp. Zph 1:16). If the approaching enemies were formidable, fear could easily grip the hearts of the people. The Lord's command called for the people of Jerusalem (**Zion**, the Lord's **holy mountain**) to recognize that He was orchestrating events to fulfill His promised judgments against His people (cp. Dt 28:15,25,38-42,49-51; 29:24-27). To **tremble** at the announcement of the coming "Day of the LORD" would be an appropriate response.

2:2-11 Overall, "the Day of the LORD" is presented in military terms, with the attacking army headed by the Lord Himself. The prospect of such a **terrible and dreadful** (Hb *yarē'*, "inciting fear, terrifying"; cp. v. 31) day of judgment should have motivated the people to repent. The implied answer to the question in verse 11 is that no one **can endure** (Hb *kul*, "bear, hold up under") "the Day of the LORD" (cp. Jr 10:10; Mal 3:2). There is no defense against the **voice** of the Lord. The only preparation Joel's audience could make was obedience and repentance as described in verses 12-27. The people of Judah needed a change of heart.

2:12-14 This poignant appeal from Joel is one of the strongest and most urgent calls to repentance found in Scripture. These verses describe behaviors that exhibit repentance while clearly defining it as a change of heart.

Yahweh commanded repentance in both first person (**turn to Me**), calling the people to Himself, and in third person, reminding the people that restoration depended on His character, which He revealed when He established His covenant with them (cp. Ex 34:6-7; 2Ch 30:9; Neh 9:17,31; Ps 86:15; 103:8; Jnh 4:2). The Lord would not be obligated by their repentance to **relent**, but they could be sure He would send **disaster** unless they did repent.

2:15-17 The Lord commanded **the priests, the LORD's ministers**, to gather all the people, without exception, and lead them in prayer. Even those usually exempt, such as nursing mothers and children, would not be excused.

[A]**2:3** Lit *consumes* [B]**2:16** Or *elders*

2:18-27 The text does not explicitly say that the people repented, but the Lord's gracious response suggests that the people had turned to Him.

The Lord had instructed the priests to pray that He would not make His **inheritance a disgrace** (Hb *cherpah*, "reproach, that which is despised; an embarrassment," 2:17-19), **an object of scorn** subject to the ridicule of the Gentiles. The Lord's response contains three parts (vv. 19-27). First, He promised to restore the crops and announced that He would remove the invaders, whether locusts or foreign rulers, bringing an end to their **disgrace** (Hb *cherpah*, vv. 18-20). He promised that His people would **never again be put to shame** (Hb *bush*, "be ashamed," vv. 26-27; Ps 22:5; 25:2-3,20). Second, the Lord commanded the land and His people, whom He addressed as **children of Zion**, to **rejoice** in what He had done and to **be glad** in Him, the source of the restored abundance (Jl 2:21-24). Third, the Lord committed to **repay** (Hb *shalam*, "restore" what has been stolen or lost) His people for the **years** eaten by the **locust** (v. 25; cp. v. 11). What a promise for the people who had wasted years in disobedience and experienced the resultant judgment. They were now assured that with their repentance and God's forgiveness would come full restoration of the joy and security resulting from God's grace and mercy.

2:26 For having traded God's goodness and security for empty idols and fear, they did not deserve to be called "children of Zion" (i.e., people reflecting the righteous character of the Lord, to whom Jerusalem belonged, v. 23). Instead, God restored what had been destroyed through Israel's failures—He **dealt wondrously** with them.

2:28 After this seems to refer to events coming after the fulfillment of the restoration Yahweh promised in verses 18-27.

2:28-32 The New Testament clarifies that redemption and thus the indwelling of God's Spirit is available to all, but only through Jesus Christ (cp. Jn 3:5-7,13-16,34-36; 7:39; Ac 2:21). The New Testament also affirms that salvation is equally available to both men and women, to both young and old, to **slaves** as well as to **sons and . . . daughters**, to both Jews and Gentiles (**everyone who calls on the name of Yahweh**; cp. Ac 10:38-47; Gl 3:28).

Peter quoted Jl 2:28-32 as context for what Jews from across the Roman Empire experienced on the day of Pentecost (Ac 2:16-17). He cited Pentecost as partial fulfillment of Joel's prophecy and prelude to **the great and awe-inspiring Day of the Lord** that is still to come (Jl 2:31). On that

and do not make
Your inheritance a disgrace,
an object of scorn
among the nations.
Why should it be said
among the peoples,
'Where is their God?'"

The Lord's Response (2:18-27)

18 Then the Lord became jealous
for His land and spared His people.
19 The Lord answered His people:

Look, I am about to send you
grain, new wine, and olive oil.
You will be satiated
with them,
and I will no longer make you
a disgrace among the nations.

20 I will drive the northerner
far from you
and banish him to a dry
and desolate land,
his front ranks
into the Dead Sea,
and his rear guard
into the Mediterranean Sea.
His stench will rise;
yes, his rotten smell will rise,
for he has done
catastrophic things.

21 Don't be afraid, land;
rejoice and be glad,
for the Lord has done
great things.

22 Don't be afraid, wild animals,
for the wilderness pastures
have turned green,
the trees bear their fruit,
and the fig tree
and grapevine yield
their riches.

23 Children of Zion, rejoice
and be glad
in the Lord your God,
because He gives you
the autumn rain
for your vindication.[A]
He sends showers for you,
both autumn and spring rain
as before.

24 The threshing floors
will be full of grain,
and the vats will overflow
with new wine and olive oil.

25 I will repay you for the years
that the swarming locust ate,
the young locust,
the destroying locust,
and the devouring locust—
My great army that I sent
against you.

26 You will have plenty to eat
and be satisfied.
You will praise the name
of •Yahweh your God,
who has dealt wondrously
with you.
My people will never again be
put to shame.

27 You will know that I am present
in Israel
and that I am Yahweh
your God,
and there is no other.
My people will never again be
put to shame.

God's Wonders in the Earth (2:28-32)

28[B] After this
I will pour out My Spirit
on all humanity;
then your sons

[A]2:23 Or *righteousness* [B]2:28 Jl 3:1 in Hb

>WORD|*study*

2:28 God's promise to pour out His Spirit **on all** humanity (Hb *basar*, "flesh") has been variously interpreted. In other contexts in which *basar* refers to all living creatures, the HCSB uses "flesh" in the account of Noah and the flood (Gn 7:15-16); "every creature" (Gn 6:17,19; 7:21; 8:17; 9:11,15-17; Ps 136:25); and "every living thing" (Ps 145:21)—even though "humanity" in some instances would be a better translation when moral agency is ascribed to all flesh (e.g., Gn 6:12-13). Both "all humanity" (Hb *basar*) and "all flesh" (Hb *basar*) appear in various prophetic passages, which, like Jl 2:28, also emphasize that the Lord's redemptive work in Jesus the Messiah is available to all—regardless of age, sex, or social class—and/or that He will reveal His glory and execute judgment upon His return (Is 40:5; 66:16,23-24; Jr 25:31; cp. "all people," Zch 2:13).

2:28 In the Old Testament, the object of the verb pour out (Hb *shaphak*, "spill, shed") is usually blood (Ezk 22:3-4; 36:18) or God's wrath (e.g., Is 42:25; Lm 4:11; Ezk 7:8; Hs 5:10; Zph 3:8). Whatever mental picture the word "pour" suggests to the audience, the sense is that something is given or distributed liberally, flowing down from a container above (analogous to heaven, where God reigns; cp. Is 32:15) into or onto something below it (analogous to earthly inhabitants—"all humanity"; cp. Is 44:3).

>WORD|*study*

3:1-12 To **restore the** fortunes (Hb *shevut*, "captivity," from the verb *shavah*, "take or lead away captive") conveys the broad idea of returning to a formerly secure and prosperous position. However, the Hebrew idiom more specifically refers to the restoration of a nation that has been held in captivity—i.e., the reversal or end of the captivity.

The Lord draws attention to future circumstances, integrally linking His judgment of the nations to **Judah and Jerusalem** (Zion; vv. 1,6,16-18,20-21) in terms of:

- timing (when He reverses the captivity of "Judah and Jerusalem," vv. 1,17);
- what the nations had done to His **people**, His **inheritance** (vv. 2-3,6-8,19);
- the nations' theft of the wealth and sustenance of His temple (v. 5);
- the nations' **wickedness** (v. 13; cp. vv. 3,19); and
- the strength and security of Zion because of His presence there (vv. 16-17,20-21).

and your daughters
will prophesy,
your old men
will have dreams,
and your young men
will see visions.
29 I will even pour out
My Spirit
on the male and female slaves
in those days.
30 I will display wonders
in the heavens and on
the earth:
blood, fire, and columns
of smoke.
31 The sun will be turned
to darkness
and the moon to blood
before the great
and awe-inspiring Day
of the LORD comes.
32 Then everyone who calls
on the name of Yahweh
will be saved,
for there will be an escape
for those on Mount Zion
and in Jerusalem,
as the LORD promised,
among the survivors
the LORD calls.

God's Judgment on the Earth (3:1-21)

3[A] Yes, in those days
and at that time,
when I restore the fortunes
of Judah and Jerusalem,
2 I will gather all the nations
and take them to the Valley
of Jehoshaphat.[B]
I will enter into judgment
with them there
because of My people,
My inheritance Israel.
The nations have scattered
the Israelites
in foreign countries
and divided up My land.
3 They cast lots for My people;
they bartered a boy
for a prostitute
and sold a girl for wine
to drink.

4 And also: Tyre, Sidon, and all
the territories of Philistia—what
are you to Me? Are you paying Me
back or trying to get even with Me?
I will quickly bring retribution on
your heads. 5 For you took My silver and gold and carried My finest
treasures to your temples. 6 You sold
the people of Judah and Jerusalem
to the Greeks to remove them far
from their own territory. 7 Look, I
am about to rouse them up from the
place where you sold them; I will
bring retribution on your heads. 8 I
will sell your sons and daughters
into the hands of the people of Judah, and they will sell them to the
Sabeans,[C] to a distant nation, for the
LORD has spoken.

9 Proclaim this
among the nations:
Prepare for holy war;
rouse the warriors;
let all the men of war advance
and attack!
10 Beat your plows into swords
and your pruning knives
into spears.
Let even the weakling say,
"I am a warrior."

[A]3:1 Jl 4:1 in Hb [B]3:2 = The LORD Will Judge [C]3:8 Probably the south Arabian kingdom of Sheba (modern Yemen)

day widespread signs and wonders will occur on earth and in the heavens (vv. 30-31; Ac 2:19-20), and the captives of Judah will be restored.

3:1-12 In this final section of the second half of Joel's book, the ultimate fate of many of the nations surrounding Judah receives focus, while the glorious destiny of God's people also is revealed. The Gentile nations would experience the full strength of God's wrath while Israel would be enveloped by His blessings.

The Lord announced that He would **gather** [Hb *qavats*, "assemble, collect," v. 2; cp. "round them up," Hs 8:10] **all the nations** to a place of reckoning. The **Valley of Jehoshaphat** (Hb, "Yahweh judges, the Lord will judge," Jl 3:2,12) may or may not denote a geographical place. In any case, the name carries the imagery of armies clashing in a valley—the nations' **warriors** (vv. 9-10) fighting in vain against Yahweh's warriors (v. 11). Isaiah and Micah had prophesied that "in the last days," the Lord would resolve conflicts "among the nations," using vivid imagery to describe an end to war (Is 2:4; Mc 4:3). In Joel 3:10, the Lord reverses this imagery, taunting the nations to take up arms against Him.

3:13-16 These verses function like a quick graphic presentation of six images, which illustrate cumulatively what these nations will encounter when they confront the Lord.

The swift, decisive harvesting of a vineyard and the trampling of the grapes until **the wine vats overflow** depicts the Lord's power against the nations' wickedness (cp. Is 63:3). There will be the overwhelming sight of **multitudes** awaiting imminent judgment (**the Day of the Lord**) in **the valley of decision** (Hb *charuts*, "being brought to a sharp point of judgment"). There will be darkness. Finally, there will be Yahweh's lion-like **roar from Zion**, which will overpower the roaring of the nations (cp. Is 5:26-30; Jr 2:14-15; 25:30-31; Am 1:2), and cause the violent trembling of earth and sky (cp. Jl 2:10; 2 Sm 22:8; Is 13:13; Jr 10:10; Hg 2:7,21). Yahweh's people will be protected from harm because they are hidden in Him as the **refuge** and **stronghold** for His people.

3:17-21 In contrast to the results of judgment for such nations as **Egypt** and **Edom**, Jerusalem and Judah will experience nearly indescribable blessings of being the dwelling place of Yahweh. The benefits of His presence include holiness (v. 17; cp. 1 Pt 2:9), provision beyond necessity (v. 18; cp. Am 9:13), freedom from foreign control (v. 20; cp. Rm 6:14), and **pardon** (v. 21).

3:21 The book of Joel closes with an emphasis on the Lord's removal of His people's **bloodguilt** in order to take up residence in Zion. The book of Revelation marks the arrival of the New Jerusalem with the triumphant announcement, "Look! God's dwelling is with men" ("humanity," HCSB, Rv 21:3).

11 Come quickly,[A] all
you surrounding nations;
gather yourselves.
Bring down
Your warriors there, LORD.
12 Let the nations be roused
and come to the Valley
of Jehoshaphat,
for there I will sit down
to judge all
the surrounding nations.
13 Swing the sickle
because the harvest is ripe.
Come and trample
the grapes
because the winepress is full;
the wine vats overflow
because the wickedness
of the nations is great.
14 Multitudes, multitudes
in the valley of decision!
For the Day of the LORD
is near
in the valley of decision.
15 The sun and moon
will grow dark,
and the stars will cease
their shining.
16 The LORD will roar from •Zion
and raise His voice
from Jerusalem;
heaven and earth will shake.
But the LORD will be a refuge
for His people,
a stronghold for the Israelites.
17 Then you will know
that I am •Yahweh
your God,
who dwells in Zion,
My holy mountain.
Jerusalem will be holy,
and foreigners will never
overrun it again.
18 In that day
the mountains will drip
with sweet wine,
and the hills will flow
with milk.
All the streams of Judah
will flow with water,
and a spring will issue
from the LORD's house,
watering the Valley
of Acacias.[B]
19 Egypt will
become desolate,
and Edom a desert wasteland,
because of the violence done
to the people of Judah
in whose land they shed
innocent blood.
20 But Judah will be
inhabited forever,
and Jerusalem
from generation
to generation.
21 I will pardon
their bloodguilt,[C]
which I have not pardoned,
for the LORD dwells in Zion.

[A] **3:11** LXX, Syr, Tg read *Gather yourselves and come*; Hb obscure [B] **3:18** Or *Shittim* [C] **3:21** LXX, Syr read *I will avenge their blood*

JOEL... WRITTEN ON MY *Heart* Too often utter devastation must occur in a woman's life before she turns to the Lord. Only after a locust plague had ravaged God's people and judgment was looming did they turn and repent. Being humble enough to have God search your heart daily for sin will help you avoid seeking God's forgiveness only as a last resort. But, while you fall short, He does not. The Lord's faithful love, patience, and grace are painted throughout Joel and point to the salvation available in Christ. Paul quotes Jl 2:32 in Rm 10:13. Only in Jesus Christ can salvation and forgiveness be found.

Biblical Womanhood Repentance and Restoration

Within the book of Joel, the Lord makes a profound promise to "His people" (2:18): "I will repay you for the years that the swarming locust ate" (v. 25). Consider the metaphor of the locust. There are nine different Hebrew words for **locust**. Attempts to identify the scientific species to which the four different Hebrew words used in Jl 1:4-11 and 2:28 might refer have not been particularly helpful in interpreting the verse. They are descriptive of common characteristics of the locust. More likely, the use of repetition with some variety builds the rhetorical effect of emphasizing the extent to which the creatures had destroyed all vegetation in the land. Certainly such a picture of a literal swarming of locusts would prepare Joel's hearers for chapter 2 and the invading armies described. Such metaphoric use is effective, for example, in describing Assyria's destruction of the northern kingdom of Israel, which was followed by repeated foreign invasions:

- Egyptian domination (2Kg 23:29,33-35);
- "Chaldean, Aramean, Moabite, and Ammonite raiders," as well as Babylon's seizure of control from Egypt (2Kg 24:1-7);
- Babylon's siege of Jerusalem and deportation of the city's residents;
- Babylon's destruction of Jerusalem and of the temple, leaving only "some of the poorest of the land to be vinedressers and farmers" (2Kg 24:20–25:26; 2Ch 36:17-20).

Joel does not spell out, as do some of the other prophets, what Israel had done to incur the devastating consequences described in Jl 1:2–2:11. His immediate audience undoubtedly knew the reasons. You or a woman you know may have experienced or may be currently struggling through devastating circumstances that may be the result of years of rebellion and disobedience, years of trying to do life in your own way. Although the Lord's judgment is to be feared, the God of Scripture declares that "He is gracious and compassionate, slow to anger, rich in faithful love, and He relents from sending disaster" (2:13). To continue doing life in your own way leads away from the Father's loving arms and into hopeless dead ends of sin. However, God pleads with women to give up hoping for self-made happiness and instead to

- "turn" to Him "with all your heart" (v. 12);
- "tear your hearts" (i.e., publicly declare your spiritual bankruptcy, v. 13; cp. Mt 5:3), acknowledging that doing life your way instead of God's way is hopeless; and
- "return to the Lord your God" (v. 13).

This is a picture of repentance. When women turn their devastated, hopeless, "locust-consumed" lives over to God's Son, Jesus Christ, He is faithful not only to forgive sin but to restore the wholeness, peace, joy, and hope previously devoured by the enemy (vv. 25-27; cp. Rm 8:28; 1Jn 1:9).

Amos

Timeline	793–753 BC	792–740 BC	767–753 BC	765–760 BC
➡ World Events ➡ Biblical Events	Reign of Jeroboam II, northern kingdom	Reign of Uzziah, southern kingdom	Amos's prophetic ministry	Earthquake at Hazor

"For the LORD *says to the house of Israel: Seek Me and live!"* (5:4).

Who wrote Amos?

The prophet Amos (1:2; 7:14)

Who were the recipients?

While the book of Amos mentions surrounding nations, the heart of its message is aimed at the northern kingdom of Israel, which was engaging in idolatry and unjust social practices.

When was Amos written?

767–753 B.C.

Where did it happen?

Amos, a prophet from Judah, did not proclaim God's words to his own people so much as he did to those in the northern kingdom of Israel and particularly to those in Samaria. This was during a time of prosperity for Israel and most likely a time of peace between the two kingdoms during the reigns of Uzziah and Jeroboam II.

What is Amos about?

- Injustice is a major theme in the book of Amos, which testifies to Israel's guilt over rejecting God's covenant.
- The Lord is awesome and is to be greatly feared. The Lord's judgment upon Israel and her enemies is terrifying to behold.

Why should women read Amos?

"Fat and happy" is a phrase that describes the people and more specifically the women in Amos. The self-indulgent and self-focused women of Judah had no concern for the poor and needy around them. The prophet, speaking the words of God, called them "cows." Amos is a reminder to women that God is not so much concerned with our happiness as He is our holiness or right living. While the Israelites were the "people of God" in name, their actions belied such a blessed title. As you read, ask yourself, "Am I living to please myself or the Lord?"

How do you read Amos?

Nearly the entire prophecy of Amos is poetic. Amos draws on vivid images from the animal kingdom and from agriculture. He also uses a wide variety of literary forms, including numerical sayings in order to express the fullness of iniquity (1:3,6,9), rhetorical questions (3:3-8), imperatives (3:9), irony (4:4-5), humor (5:19-20), personification (5:2-3), and hyperbole (5:21-23).

Amos is among the "writing prophets," who left behind books bearing their names (e.g., Amos, Isaiah, Jeremiah). The message of Amos was not an easy one to hear for two important reasons. First, Amos was from the southern kingdom (Judah), yet his main message was aimed at the northern kingdom (Israel). Second, the message was given to a people who were living quite well, a people who were free from external oppression and blessed with wealth and prosperity. Amos was calling the northern kingdom of Israel to repent of their social injustices and their empty religious practices or else go into exile.

The book of Amos can be roughly divided into three main parts. The first section (chaps. 1–2) announced that Israel's sins demanded swift judgment. The nation could not call for any special treatment in light of the egregious sins they had committed against the covenant. The second section (chaps. 3–6) is the Lord's judgment upon the nations, Judah, and Israel. The final section (chaps. 7–9) ends on a note of hope. The question remained in the end: Will God abandon His people? The answer of the book of Amos is a resounding "No!" The final message of Amos is that God will show mercy and compassion to Israel and remain faithful to His covenant. But this does not mean that Israel will not suffer consequences for its unfaithfulness.

Outline

I. Amos and His Message (1:1–2:16)
  A. Heading and Theme (1:1-2)
  B. Israel's Guilt and Judgment (1:3–2:16)
II. Words of Warning and Woe (3:1–6:14)
  A. Breach of the Covenant (3:1-15)
  B. Failure to Repent (4:1-13)
  C. Choice of Life or Death (5:1-17)
  D. Woe to Zion (5:18–6:14)
III. Visions of Judgment and Salvation (7:1–9:15)
  A. The Lord Has Spared (7:1-6).
  B. The Lord Will Spare No Longer (7:7–8:14).
  C. The Lord Will Spare None (9:1-6).
  D. The Lord Will Restore His People (9:7-15).

750 BC	*750–710 BC*	*740 BC*	*722 BC*	*716–687 BC*
Micah's call to prophetic ministry	Hosea's prophetic ministry	Isaiah's call to be a prophet	Fall of Samaria to the Assyrians	Hezekiah's reign in Judah

Amos and His Message (1:1–2:16)

Heading and Theme (1:1-2)

1 The words of Amos, who was one of the sheep breeders[A] from Tekoa—what he saw regarding Israel in the days of Uzziah, king of Judah, and Jeroboam son of Jehoash, king of Israel, two years before the earthquake.

2 He said:

The LORD roars from ·Zion
and raises His voice
from Jerusalem;
the pastures
of the shepherds mourn,[B]
and the summit
of Carmel withers.

Israel's Guilt and Judgment (1:3–2:16)

3 The LORD says:

I will not relent
from punishing Damascus
for three crimes, even four,
because they threshed Gilead
with iron sledges.
4 Therefore, I will send fire
against Hazael's palace,
and it will consume
Ben-hadad's citadels.
5 I will break down the gates[C]
of Damascus.
I will cut off the ruler
from the Valley of Aven,
and the one who wields
the scepter
from Beth-eden.
The people of Aram
will be exiled to Kir.
The LORD has spoken.

6 The LORD says:

I will not relent
from punishing Gaza
for three crimes, even four,
because they exiled
a whole community,
handing them over to Edom.
7 Therefore, I will send fire
against the walls of Gaza,
and it will consume
its citadels.
8 I will cut off the ruler
from Ashdod,
and the one who wields
the scepter from Ashkelon.
I will also turn My hand
against Ekron,

[A]1:1 Or *the shepherds* [B]1:2 Or *dry up* [C]1:5 Lit *gate bars*

Title: The title "Amos" (Hb, "burdened" or "burden bearer") reflects the name of the author to whom this prophecy is attributed. His name suggests that he is "one sustained by the Lord." The author identifies himself as a sheep breeder from Tekoa, a small Judean city located about 10 miles from Jerusalem. He lets his readers know in his introduction that his words are the words of the Lord (1:2). He was not a trained prophet and clearly had no intention of ever becoming a prophet (7:14). Some claim that Amos was penned by more than one author. However, the internal evidence of the book is strong evidence for a single author.

The strongest argument for this view is that most of the book was written in first person narrative: the heading (1:1); the introduction (1:2); and the encounter between Amos and Amaziah at Bethel (7:10-17). There are only two sentences in the entire book that indicate a third person narrative: "Then Amaziah said to Amos . . ." (7:12) and "So Amos answered Amaziah . . ." (7:14). There are at least three possible explanations for this shift to the third person. First, Amos himself might have written this passage in the third person. There is evidence in other books of the Bible that this was a common practice (cp. Dn 1–6 vs. Dn 7–12). Second, Amos may have written the book and organized the material, but the section concerning Amos and Amaziah may have been added by someone else. Third, a secretary working for Amos may have recorded the entire book (as did Baruch at times for Jeremiah). Whatever the case, based on external and internal evidence, the prophet Amos wrote and/or organized the book that bears his name.

1:1 Amos introduces himself, his occupation before his prophetic call, and the political situation in Israel at the time of his call. The special mention of **Judah** in this context indicates the close relationship between the northern and southern kingdoms and indicates that God's dealings with Judah are also important to Israel. They will both once again be united under David's rule (9:11). The prophet says he **saw** the words he recorded to make clear the divine origin of his thoughts. The **earthquake** referenced by Amos was so significant that it was mentioned two centuries later by the prophet Zechariah (Zch 14:5).

1:3–2:16 Before beginning His indictment against Israel, the Lord outlined the guilt of the surrounding nations. For the immediate audience in Israel, each announcement of the Lord's refusal to withhold punishment from one of the pagan nations would have been applauded. The people of the northern kingdom could certainly see the sins of the surrounding nations; but to any extent that the Israelites condemned their neighbors, they could only condemn themselves because they were just as guilty.

1:3-5 The Lord begins explaining why He would **not relent from punishing** six pagan nations: Damascus, Gaza, Tyre, Edom, Ammon, and Moab. He begins with **Damascus**, the capital of the Aramean (Syrian) kingdom, which was judged for its cruelty against the people of **Gilead**, the region east of the Jordan and south of Damascus ruled by Hazael. Aram had been a bitter enemy of Israel for many years, but the conflicts described in 2Kg 13:1-7 may have been specifically in view. The location of **the Valley of Aven** (Hb, "sin, wickedness, calamity"; or, alluding to idolatry, "emptiness, vanity," Am 1:5; cp. "Beth-aven," Hs 4:15; 10:5; "Aven," Hs 10:8) is uncertain. **Beth-eden** (Hb, "house of pleasure"), however, likely refers to Bit-Adini, an Aramean state east of the Euphrates River near the mouth of its tributary, the Khabur River.

1:6-8 Gaza, representing the Philistines, was also a bitter enemy of Israel. The Philistines deported an entire community of people from their homes, **handing them over to Edom** (2:1-3). The Philistines were known and feared not only for cruelty toward their captives but also for selling their captives as slaves to other nations.

>WORD|*study*

1:2 **The Lord** roars [Hb *sha'ag*, "make a roaring sound"] **from Zion** implies a comparison between the Lord's raising "His voice from Jerusalem" and the roaring of a lion. The roar of a male lion powerfully announces his presence in and claim over his own territory. By roaring, the lion both defends his territory, warning any would-be intruders of his presence. The intended effect of the comparison of the Lord's voice to a lion's roar is captured in 3:8, "A lion has roared; who will not fear? The Lord God has spoken" (3:4; cp. Jr 25:30; Hs 11:10; Jl 3:16). The repeated phrases, "the Lord says" (Am 1:3,6,9,11,13; 2:1,4,6), "the Lord has spoken" (1:5,8,15; 2:3; 5:17), and "the Lord's declaration" (2:11,16; 3:10,13,15; 4:3,5-6,8-11; 6:14; 8:3,9,11; 9:7-8,12-13) reverberate like a lion's mighty roar throughout the book, asserting God's sovereignty over all nations and exercising His particular claim upon Israel and Judah.

1:2 The noun translated pastures (Hb *na'ah*, "place where flocks lie down and rest") is used only 12 times in the Old Testament, eight of these by the prophets. The grazing lands of Israel were beautiful as well as necessary for sustaining flocks of sheep. Therefore, the prophets lamented their destruction because of the Lord's burning anger (Jr 25:36-38; cp. Jr 9:10; 23:10; Jl 1:19-20). Here, the pastures are personified as able to mourn (Hb *'aval*, "languish, hang one's head down in visible expression of grief," Am 1:2), imagery that also resonates with the other prophetic books in which "the land" or "the earth" is said to "mourn" (e.g., Is 24:4; 33:9; Jr 23:10; Hs 4:3; Jl 1:10). One effect of this imagery is to broaden the audience's perspective on the effects of sin. Even the land suffered the destructive consequences of Israel's apostasy.

A specific example was Mount **Carmel** (Hb, "garden of God," Am 1:2), located in the northern kingdom. Well known for its lush landscape, Carmel symbolized God's blessings of abundance and beauty (e.g., Is 35:2). Therefore, the destruction of its choice grazing lands signaled the intensity of God's wrath against the apostasy of His people.

This eighth-century B.C. house in Israel has been reconstructed (Am 3:15; 6:11). Archaeological excavations in the area bear out the society of Samaria and the northern kingdom in the eighth century. Houses in the tenth-century strata are uniform. The eighth-century stratum shows great contrast between large houses of the affluent and small structures in which the poor lived.

>WORD|*study*

1:9 The phrase for three crimes, even four is not intended to convey the idea that God waited until the offending nation had reached a limit of doing three or even four things wrong before receiving punishment. Instead, the second part of the expression, **even four**, suggests that the list of sins was not limited to a specific number but that God had withheld punishment long enough—not unlike a parent counting to three and even to four to give a child ample opportunity to correct his behavior. The multiple crimes of these nations constituted more than sufficient justification for whatever punishment the Lord inflicted upon them.

At last, when the Lord finally addressed Israel's "crimes," her sins appeared even more egregious because, unlike the other nations, they knew the law of God. Judah's crimes were presented in general terms of their rejection of God's law. The indictment of Israel emphasized the concrete evidence of their betrayal of God's covenant (2:6-8,12).

and the remainder
of the Philistines
will perish.
The Lord God has spoken.

9 The Lord says:

I will not relent
from punishing Tyre
for three crimes, even four,
because they handed over
a whole community of exiles
to Edom
and broke[A] a treaty
of brotherhood.
10 Therefore, I will send fire
against the walls of Tyre,
and it will consume
its citadels.

11 The Lord says:

I will not relent
from punishing Edom
for three crimes, even four,
because he pursued
his brother with the sword.
He stifled his compassion,
his anger tore
at them continually,
and he harbored
his rage incessantly.
12 Therefore, I will send fire
against Teman,
and it will consume
the citadels of Bozrah.

13 The Lord says:

I will not relent
from punishing
the Ammonites
for three crimes, even four,
because they ripped open
the pregnant women of Gilead
in order to enlarge
their territory.
14 Therefore, I will set fire
to the walls of Rabbah,
and it will consume
its citadels.
There will be shouting
on the day of battle
and a violent wind on the day
of the storm.
15 Their king and his princes
will go into exile together.
The Lord has spoken.

2 The Lord says:

I will not relent
from punishing Moab
for three crimes, even four,
because he burned the bones
of the king of Edom to lime.
2 Therefore, I will send fire
against Moab,
and it will consume
the citadels of Kerioth.
Moab will die with a tumult,
with shouting and the sound
of the ram's horn.
3 I will cut off the judge
from the land
and kill all its officials
with him.
The Lord has spoken.

4 The Lord says:

I will not relent
from punishing Judah
for three crimes, even four,
because they have rejected
the instruction of the Lord
and have not kept
His statutes.
The lies that
their ancestors followed
have led them astray.
5 Therefore, I will send fire
against Judah,

[A]1:9 Lit *and did not remember*

1:9-10 The Phoenician port city of **Tyre** also handed a whole community of exiles over to Edom and thus broke a **treaty** of trust among brothers.

1:11-12 Likewise, **Edom** (Hb, "red," v. 11; Gn 25:30) pursued his brother with a sword (Obadiah), stifled compassion, and raged incessantly against him. The people of Edom and Israel (Nm 20:14-21) trace their history of bitter animosity back to Esau, the brother of Jacob/Israel (Gn 35:29–36:43).

1:13-15 In graphic language portraying unspeakable cruelty and an utter contempt of the powerful for the powerless, **the Ammonites . . . ripped open the pregnant women of Gilead**. The Ammonites, who were descendants of Lot, Abraham's nephew (Gn 19:36-38; Dt 2:19), occupied territory on Gilead's border east of the Jordan River and had been battling Israel for control of Gilead since the days of the judges (Jdg 11:4-33).

2:1-3 **Moab** (also descendants of Abraham's nephew, Lot; Gn 19:36-38) would be punished for unwarranted cruelty against the king of Edom. To burn the enemy's remains to ash was a supreme insult, perhaps suggesting the denial of a resurrected body.

2:4-5 The first six nations addressed in this context are judged for their cruelty against humanity. Then the Lord addressed **Judah**, which had forsaken the law of God and had not kept His decrees. They followed lies, which led them astray.

2:6-8 By placing Israel's indictment in the final, climactic position, the Lord intended for the compact description of Israel's crimes against her own people to be heard as the worst of all. The Lord charged Israel with three specific offenses which, escalated in perversity. First, Israel was oppressing the poor. Second, they were **profaning** (Hb *chalal*, "treat as common that which is holy; lay open, give access to that which is supposed to remain set apart") Yahweh's name with gross immorality. Third, they were flaunting in idolatrous worship what they had acquired by fraud and treachery.

2:8 The third indictment involved both wrongfully acquired **garments** and **wine** and idolatrous worship indicated by multiple altars. Also, the LORD spoke of **the house of *their* God**. Exodus 22:26-27 prohibited keeping a "neighbor's cloak [taken] as collateral" beyond sunset. Disobeying this regulation signaled the people's exploitation of those who were unable to repay a loan immediately (cp. Dt 24:17). The law also made provision for imposing **fines**—but only as restitution, not as arbitrary penalties or means of extortion (see Ex 21:22; Dt 22:19). The drinking of wine associated with the place of worship was foreign to Yahweh's law (Lv 10:9). The behavior was even worse because what they drank had been acquired by illegitimate means.

2:9-16 The second part of the speech consists of two sections identified as **the LORD's declaration** (Hb *neʾum*, "utterance, that which has been said," vv. 11,16), i.e., emphatically spoken with divine authority. In light of what Yahweh had done for His people, their offenses were elevated to the level of outright betrayal and would be punished. Israel existed only because the Lord had driven out the Amorites because of their "iniquity" (Gn 15:16; cp. Ex 3:8; 23:23). Israel's covenant relationship with the Lord had remained open only because the Lord had continued to speak through prophets and to call out **Nazirites** to model radical holiness demonstrated in their abstinence from **wine** (Am 2:11-12; cp. Nm 6). Instead of gratitude and obedience, however, Israel had effectively told God to stop speaking to her either through words (**the prophets**; cp. Is 30:10-11) or the testimony of holy living , (v. 12; see chart, p. 307).

3:1-15 One can get an overall understanding of chapter 3 by imagining a courtroom scene in which a lawsuit is being leveled against Israel. In the "opening statement," the Lord calls Israel to hear the charges He is leveling against them in order to understand the call for Israel's punishment and the rationale for the charges He is bringing against them. Then He calls foreign nations as witnesses against Israel's behavior. The opening statement concludes with a pronouncement of judgment against the

>WORD|*study*

2:6 Three different words are used in these verses for people who are materially poor. Needy person (Hb *ʾevyon*, "poor, oppressed," describing one who works in order to survive on a day-to-day basis, 2:6-7) is also used in:

- **4:1,** which addressed Israelite women who "crush the needy";
- **5:12,** in which the Lord indicted Israel for depriving "the poor of justice";
- **8:4,** in which the Lord addressed His people as those who "do away with the poor of the land"; and
- **8:6,** which echoes 2:6 in recalling that Israel boasted of buying "the needy for a pair of sandals."

Instead of being generous to meet the needs of the poor as the Lord had commanded, Israel was taking advantage of them, treating them as objects rather than as brothers (Ex 23:6; Dt 15:7-8,11; 24:14-15; Pr 14:31). The Lord had also promised to "rise up" in response to the "groaning of the poor" (Ps 12:5).

In the book of Amos, the Lord also criticized the Israelite women for oppressing the poor (Hb *dal*, "powerless, weak, low"; cp. 4:1) and "the house of Israel" for trampling on and overtaxing them (5:1,11). Also echoing 2:6, the Lord condemned the Israelites' boast that they could "buy the poor with silver" (8:6). By mistreating the poor, Israel was both forfeiting the Lord's promises of blessing for generosity (Ps 41:1; Pr 19:17; 22:9) and ignoring His warnings against oppression (Pr 21:13; 22:16,22; 28:3; 29:7). Furthermore, Israel's contempt for "the poor" as described in Am 2:7 reflected the opposite of the Lord's disposition toward them: "He raises the poor from the dust and lifts the needy from the garbage pile" (1Sm 2:8; Ps 113:7). Similarly, to **block** [Hb *natah*, "push out of the way"] **the path of the** needy (Hb *ʿanav*, "afflicted, miserable") put Israel in the category of "the wicked," who "push (Hb *natah*) the needy off the road" (Jb 24:2-4), rather than likening their character to that of the Lord and His Messiah (cp. Ps 147:6; Is 11:4; 61:1).

Regarding the second accusation, some interpreters assume that girl (Hb *naʿarah*) refers to a prostitute—either a temple prostitute employed in the fertility cults Israel had embraced, as suggested by the religious context of verse 8, or a common prostitute for hire. However, in Scripture the Hebrew word never has this meaning. Rather, it generically denotes a "young woman" of marriageable age, usually implying an unmarried "girl" who is a "virgin." In some contexts the word can also refer to a "servant girl" or "handmaid."

In the context of Am 2:6-8, the accusation that **a man and his father** had both slept with the same prostitute seems unlikely. That both had **sexual relations** with a servant girl (who had been purchased legally, though unjustly, to settle her family's debts) makes more sense. Just as the Lord had given His people instructions in the law for their treatment of the poor, so He had also specified just treatment of such women, both when a man "chose her for himself" and when he "chooses her for his son." The regulations even included the man's obligations "if he takes an additional wife" (Ex 21:7-11). For both a father and son to use the woman may have been so unthinkable as not to be mentioned in Exodus. Similar sexual unions are clearly forbidden in Leviticus 18:8 and 15 (cp. Lv 20:11-12; cp. Dt 21:10-14; 27:20) and appear in a list of practices by which the surrounding nations had "defiled themselves" (Lv 18:24-30).

and it will consume
the citadels of Jerusalem.

6 The LORD says:

I will not relent
from punishing Israel
for three crimes, even four,
because they sell
a righteous person for silver
and a needy person for a pair
of sandals.
7 They trample the heads
of the poor
on the dust of the ground
and block the path
of the needy.
A man and his father
have sexual relations
with the same girl,
profaning My holy name.
8 They stretch out beside
every altar
on garments taken
as collateral,
and in the house of their God,
they drink wine obtained
through fines.
9 Yet I destroyed the Amorite
as Israel advanced;
his height was like the cedars,
and he was as sturdy
as the oaks;
I destroyed his fruit above
and his roots beneath.
10 And I brought you
from the land of Egypt
and led you 40 years
in the wilderness
in order to possess the land
of the Amorite.
11 I raised up some of your sons
as prophets
and some of your young men
as Nazirites.
Is this not the case, Israelites?
This is
the LORD's declaration.
12 But you made the Nazirites
drink wine
and commanded
the prophets,
"Do not prophesy."
13 Look, I am about to crush[A] you
in your place

[A]2:13 Or *hinder*; Hb obscure

as a wagon full of sheaves
crushes grain.
14 Escape will fail the swift,
the strong one will not prevail
by his strength,
and the brave will not save
his life.
15 The archer will not stand
his ground,
the one who is swift of foot
will not save himself,
and the one riding a horse
will not save his life.
16 Even the most courageous
of the warriors
will flee naked on that day—
this is
the LORD's declaration.

Words of Warning and Woe (3:1–6:14)

Breach of the Covenant (3:1-15)

3 Listen to this message that the LORD has spoken against you, Israelites, against the entire clan that I brought from the land of Egypt:

2 I have known only you
out of all the clans
of the earth;
therefore, I will punish you
for all your iniquities.
3 Can two walk together
without agreeing to meet?[A]
4 Does a lion roar in the forest
when it has no prey?
Does a young lion growl
from its lair
unless it has
captured something?
5 Does a bird land in a trap
on the ground
if there is no bait for it?
Does a trap spring
from the ground
when it has caught nothing?
6 If a ram's horn is blown
in a city,
aren't people afraid?
If a disaster occurs in a city,
hasn't the LORD done it?
7 Indeed, the Lord GOD
does nothing
without revealing His counsel
to His servants the prophets.
8 A lion has roared;
who will not fear?
The Lord GOD has spoken;
who will not prophesy?
9 Proclaim on the citadels
in Ashdod
and on the citadels in the land
of Egypt:
Assemble on the mountains
of Samaria
and see the great turmoil
in the city
and the acts of oppression
within it.
10 The people are incapable
of doing right—
this is
the LORD's declaration—
those who store up violence
and destruction
in their citadels.

11 Therefore, the Lord GOD says:

An enemy will surround
the land;
he will destroy
your strongholds
and plunder your citadels.

12 The LORD says:

As the shepherd snatches
two legs
or a piece of an ear
from the lion's mouth,
so the Israelites who live
in Samaria
will be rescued
with only the corner of a bed
or the[B] cushion[C] of a couch.[D]

[A]3:3 LXX reads *without meeting* [B]3:12 Or *Israelites will be rescued, those who sit in Samaria on a corner of a bed or a* [C]3:12 Hb obscure [D]3:12 LXX, Aq, Sym, Theod, Syr, Tg, Vg read *or in Damascus*

land, the people, "the altars of Bethel," and the homes of the rich (vv. 11-15).

3:1 By addressing the **Israelites** as the people He had **brought from the land of Egypt**, the Lord highlighted His redemptive work of rescuing the people of Israel from bondage and forging a covenant with them.

3:2 The uniqueness of this relationship between God and the people He had made His own (Dt 7:6; 10:15; 14:2) is implicitly compared to the marriage relationship: **I have known only you** (cp. Hs 13:4-5). Because the Lord had revealed Himself to and through Israel, the people had greater responsibility for their **iniquities** than did the surrounding pagan nations, and they would be punished accordingly.

3:3-8 The Lord asked seven rhetorical questions, illustrating the improbability of certain events if some other event had not taken place beforehand. The relationships depicted are not so much cause-and-effect as they are action-and-result. The emphatic statement of verse 7 makes the connection plain: When the Lord chooses to act in Israel, He will reveal His plans to his prophets, as He had done with Amos. The final two questions compel the readers to listen and apply to themselves what was heard.

3:9 The Lord cried out against the ungodliness of His people by summoning their enemies to come see for themselves what was going on in the northern kingdom, represented by the capital city of **Samaria**. **Ashdod** was one of the five chief cities of the Philistines, located on the coast of the Mediterranean. To be put on display before their enemies—the Philistines or **Egypt**—would have represented the height of embarrassment (cp. Ezk 22:1-5).

3:11-15 The land would be surrounded by **an enemy**, successfully attacking the material defenses and destroying the places of idol worship upon which Israel relied in place of the Lord. This attack would demolish the material comforts and luxuries the Israelites preferred to enjoy instead of obeying the Lord. Only a remnant of the people would survive.

>WORD|*study*

3:9 The word turmoil (Hb *mehumah*, "disturbance, tumult, confusion") appears only 12 times in the Old Testament. It is used twice in the account of the "great panic" that broke out among the Philistines when they captured the ark of the covenant (1Sm 5:9,11) and once in the account of the "great confusion" of Philistines fighting against each other, the event by which "the LORD saved Israel" from her enemies (1Sm 14:20,23; cp. Zch 14:13). Use of the word *mehumah* would recall not only these two instances of God's judgment on Israel's enemies but also the Lord's covenant promise to drive out these nations. If Israel would obey the Lord, He would "throw them [the pagan nations] into great confusion (Hb *mehumah*) until they are destroyed" (Dt 7:23). However, if Israel abandoned the Lord, He would send against His people "curses, confusion (Hb *mehumah*), and rebuke . . . until you are destroyed" (Dt 28:20). To describe the condition of Samaria with this term underscored that "the city" deserved and was already experiencing God's judgment.

4:1-2a This section opens by singling out wealthy women whose actions were habitually to **oppress** [Hb *ʿashaq*, "treat unjustly, financially exploit," used only here in Amos; cp. Dt 24:14; Pr 14:31; 22:16; Ezk 22:29] **the poor**; **crush** [Hb *ratsats*, "break, break down," used only here in Amos; figuratively, "oppress, treat violently"; cp. Dt 28:33; Is 58:6] **the needy**; and invite **their husbands** (Hb *ʾadon*, usually "lord, master," but cp. Gn 18:12; Jdg 19:26; Ps 45:11) to **bring** the desired beverages and come **drink** with them, making the women complicit with the men of Israel in the pursuit of personal pleasure at the expense of the poor.

The metaphor **cows of Bashan** would have brought to mind the pampered, well-fed cattle of the lushly vegetated region of Bashan located north of the Yarmuk River and east and northeast of the Sea of Galilee (cp. Dt 32:14; Ezk 39:18). In comparison, certain women of Samaria enjoyed a rich, carefree lifestyle. The imagery may also figuratively depict Israel's worship of a cow as the female counterpart of Baal represented by the bull's power and fertility. The unusual use of the word *ʾadon* (Hb, "lord, master") for "husband" functions as a wordplay contrasting the apostate men ("lords") catering to their wives and ***the* Lord** [Hb *ʾAdonay*] **God** who **has sworn by His holiness** to judge them both (cp. Ps 89:35).

4:2b-3 Each woman would be held accountable. These verses likely describe prophetically the Assyrian conquest of Samaria, when thousands of people were deported from the city (cp. 2Kg 17:1-6). The Assyrians were notorious for leading their captives by hooks inserted through the nose or other part of the face. Translation difficulties make Am 4:2 difficult to interpret. If it is extending the metaphor of verse 1, then it depicts the women as being led single-file through the gaps in the city wall where the conquerors had broken through.

4:3 Harmon may simply denote the "fortress or palace" of the Assyrian king.

4:4-5 These verses continue the reminder that each is **the Lord's declaration** (cp. vv. 3,6,8-11; 2:9-16). The Lord sarcastically called the people to **rebel** (Hb *pashaʿ*, "revolt, sin, transgress; fall or break away from someone, especially to break one's covenant," 4:4) at their pagan sanctuaries. Jeroboam I, the first king of the northern kingdom of Israel, had set up golden calves at **Bethel** and Dan to provide worship centers rivaling the worship of the Lord at the temple in Jerusalem (see 1Kg 12:26-30). **Gilgal** was the site where Israel first worshiped after crossing the Jordan to enter the promised land (Jos 4:1–5:10). Before the Lord established worship exclusively at the temple in Jerusalem, sacrifices to the Lord were offered there (1Sm 7:15-16; 10:8; 11:14-15; 13:7-15; 15:21). However, both Bethel and Gilgal were illegitimate places of worship after the temple was built (1Kg 3:2; 8:10-11; cp. Dt 12:5-6,10-14).

4:6-11 Chapter 4 highlights the Israelites' failure to repent of their social and spiritual corruption. Each of the remaining five sections marked as "the Lord's

13 Listen and testify
against the house
of Jacob—
this is the declaration
of the Lord God,
the God of •Hosts.
14 I will punish the altars of Bethel
on the day I punish Israel
for its crimes;
the horns of the altar will be
cut off
and fall to the ground.
15 I will demolish the winter house
and the summer house;
the houses inlaid with ivory
will be destroyed,
and the great houses
will come to an end.
This is
the Lord's declaration.

Failure to Repent (4:1-13)

4 Listen to this message,
you cows of Bashan
who are on the hill
of Samaria,
women who oppress the poor
and crush the needy,
who say to their husbands,
"Bring us something
to drink."

2 The Lord God has sworn by His holiness:

Look, the days are coming[A]
when you will be taken away
with hooks,
every last one of you
with fishhooks.
3 You will go through breaches
in the wall,
each woman straight ahead,
and you will be driven along
toward Harmon.
This is
the Lord's declaration.
4 Come to Bethel and rebel;
rebel even more at Gilgal!
Bring your sacrifices
every morning,
your tenths every three days.
5 Offer leavened bread as
a thank offering,
and loudly proclaim
your freewill offerings,
for that is what you Israelites
love to do!
This is
the Lord's declaration.
6 I gave you absolutely nothing
to eat[B]
in all your cities,
a shortage of food in all
your communities,
yet you did not return to Me.
This is
the Lord's declaration.
7 I also withheld the rain
from you
while there were still
three months until harvest.
I sent rain on one city
but no rain on another.
One field received rain
while a field
with no rain withered.
8 Two or three cities staggered
to another city to drink water
but were not satisfied,
yet you did not return to Me.
This is
the Lord's declaration.

[A]4:2 Lit *coming on you* [B]4:6 Lit *you cleanness of teeth*

>WORD|*study*

4:2-3 If the hooks should be understood as meat hooks for butchered cattle or the hooks on which the Assyrians were known to impale people, then verse 2 depicts another outcome. The common translation of the verb **driven** (Hb *shalak*, "throw away, cast off or down") may indicate that the dead bodies of the women would be "cast or thrown out" of the city or "cast off" along or at the end of the march northward.

4:11; 5:8 To overthrow (Hb *haphak*, "overturn, overthrew"; "convert, change," 5:7-8; 6:12; 8:10) is to change something from its intended use or identity into the opposite. The Lord accused Israel of turning righteousness and justice, in which the Lord delights (Jr 9:24), into something distasteful at best, deadly at worst (6:12; cp. Dt 29:18). In pursuit of their own ways, Israel corrupted the good systems of government, which the Lord had established for making exemplary the nation's treatment of people according to His law. Government had become a means of oppression and extortion. Sin perverts God's good gifts, deceptively "turning" them to evil purposes. However, the Lord at no point yielded His sovereign power over Israel. Rather, He would "turn" Israel's religious festivals into occasions for "mourning" and "lamentation," thereby exposing the destructive ends of their perversions (8:10). Later, however, He would restore His people and "turn" their sorrows into joy (see Ps 30:11; Jr 31:13). In Am 5:8 the verb again highlights the Lord's sovereign power and control by identifying Him as **the One . . . who** turns [Hb *haphak*] **darkness into dawn**.

9 I struck you with blight
and mildew;
the locust devoured
your many gardens
and vineyards,
your fig trees and olive trees,
yet you did not return to Me.
This is
the LORD's declaration.

10 I sent plagues like those
of Egypt;
I killed your young men
with the sword,
along with
your captured horses.
I caused the stench
of your camp
to fill your nostrils,
yet you did not return to Me.
This is
the LORD's declaration.

11 I overthrew some of you
as I[A] overthrew Sodom
and Gomorrah,
and you were
like a burning stick
snatched from a fire,
yet you did not return
to Me—
this is
the LORD's declaration.

12 Therefore, Israel, that is what
I will do to you,
and since I will do that to you,
Israel, prepare to meet
your God!

13 He is here:
the One who forms
the mountains,
creates the wind,
and reveals His[B] thoughts
to man,
the One who makes the dawn
out of darkness
and strides on the heights
of the earth.
•Yahweh, the God of •Hosts,
is His name.

Choice of Life or Death (5:1-17)

5 Listen to this message that I am
singing for you, a lament, house
of Israel:

2 She has fallen;
Virgin Israel will never
rise again.
She lies abandoned
on her land,
with no one to raise her up.

3 For the Lord GOD says:

The city that marches out
a thousand strong
will have only a hundred left,
and the one that marches out
a hundred strong
will have only ten left
in the house of Israel.

4 For the LORD says to the house of
Israel:

Seek Me and live!
5 Do not seek Bethel
or go to Gilgal
or journey to Beer-sheba,
for Gilgal will certainly go
into exile,
and Bethel will come
to nothing.
6 Seek •Yahweh and live,
or He will spread like fire
throughout the house
of Joseph;
it will consume everything,
with no one at Bethel
to extinguish it.
7 Those who turn justice
into •wormwood
throw righteousness
to the ground.

8 The One who made the Pleiades
and Orion,
who turns darkness[C]
into dawn
and darkens day into night,
who summons the waters
of the sea
and pours them out
over the face of the earth—
Yahweh is His name.
9 He brings destruction[D]
on the strong,[E]
and it falls on the stronghold.

10 They hate the one who convicts
the •guilty
at the city •gate
and despise the one
who speaks with integrity.
11 Therefore, because you
trample on the poor

[A]4:11 Lit *God* [B]4:13 Or *his* [C]5:8 Or *turns the shadow of death* [D]5:9 Hb obscure [E]5:9 Or *stronghold*

declaration" ends with the refrain, **yet you did not return to Me**, showing the Israelites' hardness of heart and the reason for God's judgment. The Lord's discipline and wooing of Israel back to Himself were to no avail. Judgment was inevitable.

4:12-13 The people indulged in idolatry at multiple "high places" (e.g., 1Kg 13:32-33), but *God* **strides** [Hb *darak*, "tread, trample," an active participle indicating characteristic action or action in progress; cp. Mc 1:3] **on the heights** [Hb *bamah*, "high places, mountain tops"] **of the earth** (i.e., He is larger, so to speak, than anyone can imagine). He is "on the move," and totally overpowers every purported rival. If there were any question about the identity of this God to whom Israel rightfully belonged, He declared His name: **Yahweh, the God of Hosts** (Hb *tsava'*, "army"), a title drawing attention to His invincibility and therefore suggesting the folly of going to war against Him.

5:1-2 Virgin Israel personifies the nation as a young woman who has never been physically united with a man and so is or can be betrothed in purity to a man as his bride. The imagery intensifies the sense of anguish expressed with the **lament**, or outcry of sorrow, over the fall of one who is full of promise and yet who will never realize the fruits of that potential (cp. 8:14). The parallel description—**She lies abandoned** (Hb *natash*, "be cast down"), utterly alone and beyond help—further emphasizes the tragedy of Israel's refusal to return to the Lord (cp. Jr 14:17; 18:13; 31:21).

5:1-17 The first half of chapter 5 contains the only direct call to repentance in the book of Amos. Arranged in a chiastic structure, focusing on the center, it draws the reader into the key idea of the hymn to the Lord (vv. 8-9). The Lord remained at the center of Israel's existence, whether they chose to acknowledge Him or not. Judgment on Israel would be swift and certain.

5:4-6 Before this tragedy became a reality, the Lord explained to His people the way of escape (cp. 1Co 10:13). The Israelites were to **seek** (Hb *darash*, literally "tread" a path to, Am 5:4,6; cp. Ps 119:1-3) Him and **good** rather than evil (Am 5:14). This command is in all three cases linked with the result—to **live** rather than die (Am 5:4,6,14; cp. Dt 16:20; 30:16; Heb 11:6). They were also told **do not seek** [Hb *darash*] **... or go to ... or journey to** any of the illegitimate places of worship, which will all be eliminated by the Lord.

5:7 The two words **justice** and **righteousness** were commonly used together to summarize the king's responsibility for ruling Israel according to the demands of the covenant (2Sm 8:15; 1Kg 10:9; 1Ch 18:14; 2Ch 9:8). To change the ideal of administering justice into something bitter and poisonous is to **throw** (Hb *yanach*, "put down and abandon") down righteousness like something worthless, thus grievously insulting the Lord.

5:10-12 Compounding their sins, Israel spurned those who spoke the truth or words of rebuke. The people chose to persist in their **crimes**, so the Lord would frustrate their plans to enjoy what they had acquired through oppression of **the poor** and **the righteous**.

5:18–6:13 Having pleaded with Israel to repent, the Lord pronounced two woes. The people had no idea how wretched they had become. They were relying on their outward show of religion (5:21-27), their material wealth (6:1,4-6), and military might (6:13). However, Israel was deceiving herself. Amos 5:18-27 reveals the truth about their false beliefs.

5:18-20 For the people of Israel to **long** [Hb *ʾawah*, "have strong desire"; often denoting lust or "craving" (Ps 106:14) or having the sense of "covet" (Dt 5:21)] **for the Day of the Lord** was to be eager for God's judgment on all the other nations and exaltation of His chosen people (cp. Ob 5). Here the Lord shattered such expectations. He asked a question to which they were giving the wrong answer (Am 5:18b). Correcting their notion of what "the Day of the Lord" was about, He clarified: **For you**—i.e., for Israel, "the Day of the Lord" would not shine a spotlight on their place of privilege but would rather eclipse their complacency and self-indulgence (cp. 6:1-6).

5:21-27 God denounced and rejected the empty religious practices of His people, calling instead for **justice . . . and righteousness** (cp. v. 15 and notes on v. 7; Mt 23:14,23,25). The Lord pointed out that their **sacrifices and grain offerings**, although presented to Him, could not be equated with keeping His covenant while they were carrying around idols. The One who created the stars (Am 5:8) could not allow His people to worship **star gods**—namely, **Sakkuth** (Mesopotamian astral deity) and **Kaiwan** (another idol associated with Saturn)—and remain in the land He had given them.

5:13 In the Hebrew text, days (Hb *ʿet*) is the same word translated as "time" in verse 13. More literally, **the days are** evil (Hb *raʿ*, "bad, wicked, unfortunate") would be "an evil time." As used here, the phrase likely has the same sense as in Jr 2:27-28 and 11:12, which note that only in "their time of disaster" (Hb *raʿ*) did God's people call to Him for help (cp. Ec 9:12). The Lord promises, however, that in such "times of adversity" (Hb *raʿ*), "the blameless . . . will not be disgraced" (Ps 37:18-19).

5:16-17 The military context continues both in the elaborate announcement of the One speaking—**Yahweh, the God of** Hosts [Hb *tsavaʾ*, "army"], **the Lord**—and in His plan to pass among [Hb *ʿavar* "pass or march over, cross" with *qerev*, "midst, interior," together denoting "pass over or through, go through"] the people. The Lord's movement through Israel may have been comparable to that of the military officers who "went through" the Israelites' camp in their days of conquest, commanding them to get ready for battle (Jos 1:11; 3:2). Although without *qerev*, the verb *ʿavar* appears, significantly, in the description of the Lord's movement through Egypt to "strike every firstborn male" (Ex 12:12). As in Egypt, the coming destruction lamented here would be God's doing.

and exact a grain tax
from him,
you will never live
in the houses of cut stone
you have built;
you will never drink the wine
from the lush vineyards
you have planted.
12 For I know your crimes
are many
and your sins innumerable.
They oppress the righteous,
take a bribe,
and deprive the poor of justice
at the gates.
13 Therefore, the wise person
will keep silent[A]
at such a time,
for the days are evil.

14 Seek good and not evil
so that you may live,
and the Lord, the God
of ·Hosts,
will be with you,
as you have claimed.
15 Hate evil and love good;
establish justice in the gate.
Perhaps the Lord, the God
of Hosts, will be gracious
to the remnant of Joseph.

16 Therefore Yahweh, the God of
Hosts, the Lord, says:

There will be wailing in all
the public squares;
they will cry out in anguish[B]
in all the streets.
The farmer will be called on
to mourn,
and professional mourners[C]
to wail.
17 There will be wailing in all
the vineyards,
for I will pass among you.
The Lord has spoken.

Woe to Zion (5:18–6:14)

18 Woe to you who long for
the Day of the Lord!
What will the Day of the Lord
be for you?
It will be darkness
and not light.
19 It will be like a man who flees
from a lion
only to have a bear
confront him.
He goes home and
rests his hand
against the wall
only to have a snake
bite him.
20 Won't the Day of the Lord
be darkness
rather than light,
even gloom
without any brightness
in it?
21 I hate, I despise
your feasts!
I can't stand the stench
of your solemn assemblies.
22 Even if you offer Me
your ·burnt offerings
and ·grain offerings,
I will not accept them;
I will have no regard
for your ·fellowship offerings
of fattened cattle.
23 Take away from Me the noise
of your songs!
I will not listen to the music
of your harps.

[A]5:13 Or *the prudent will perish* [B]5:16 Lit *will say, "Alas! Alas!"* [C]5:16 Lit *and those skilled in lamentation*

[24] But let justice flow
like water,
and righteousness,
like an unfailing stream.

[25]"House of Israel, was it sacrifices and grain offerings that you
presented to Me during the 40 years
in the wilderness? [26]But you have
taken up[A] Sakkuth[B,C] your king[D] and
Kaiwan[E] your star god, images you
have made for yourselves. [27]So I will
send you into exile beyond Damascus." Yahweh, the God of Hosts, is
His name. He has spoken.

6 Woe to those who are at ease
in •Zion
and to those who feel secure
on the hill of Samaria—
the notable people in this first
of the nations,
those the house of Israel
comes to.

[2] Cross over to Calneh and see;
go from there
to great Hamath;
then go down to Gath
of the Philistines.
Are you better than
these kingdoms?
Is their territory larger
than yours?

[3] You dismiss any thought
of the evil day
and bring in a reign
of violence.

[4] They lie on beds
inlaid with ivory,
sprawled out
on their couches,
and dine on lambs
from the flock
and calves from the stall.

[5] They improvise songs[F]
to the sound of the harp
and invent[G] their own
musical instruments
like David.

[6] They drink wine by the bowlful
and anoint themselves
with the finest oils
but do not grieve
over the ruin of Joseph.

[7] Therefore, they will now go
into exile
as the first of the captives,
and the feasting of those
who sprawl out
will come to an end.

[8]The Lord God has sworn by Himself—this is the declaration of •Yah-
weh, the God of •Hosts:

I loathe Jacob's pride
and hate his citadels,
so I will hand over the city
and everything in it.

[9]And if there are 10 men left in
one house, they will die. [10]A close
relative[H] and burner[I] will remove his
corpse[J] from the house. He will call
to someone in the inner recesses of
the house, "Any more with you?"

That person will reply, "None."

Then he will say, "Silence, because Yahweh's name must not be
invoked."

[11]For the Lord commands:

The large house
will be smashed to pieces,
and the small house
to rubble.

[12] Do horses gallop on the cliffs;
does anyone plow there
with oxen?[K]
Yet you have turned justice
into poison
and the fruit of righteousness
into •wormwood—

[13] you who rejoice over Lo-debar
and say, "Didn't we
capture Karnaim
for ourselves by our
own strength?"

[14] But look, I am raising up
a nation
against you, house of Israel—
this is the declaration
of the Lord,
the God of Hosts—
and they will oppress you
from the entrance of Hamath[L]
to the Brook of the •Arabah.[M]

6:1-7 The Lord elaborated on why Israel would be taken captive **into exile**, citing the arrogance of both Judah (**Zion** or Jerusalem) and Israel (**Samaria**, the capital of the northern kingdom). The accusation of being **at ease** (Hb *sha'anan*, "arrogant, complacent") was also leveled specifically against the women of Judah (see Is 32:9,11), amplified with the parallel word "overconfident," which is here translated as feeling **secure** (Hb *batach*, "trust, set one's hope and confidence upon").

6:2 Calneh (cp. Gn 10:10; "Calno," Is 10:9) and **Hamath** were fortified cities in Syria. These cities, **Gath**, and eventually Samaria, were all conquered by the Assyrians; Israel was no **better than these kingdoms** when God's judgment was necessary.

6:8 For the injustices already cited and described, the Lord declared in the strongest terms, swearing **by Himself**, that He was going to **hand over** (Hb *sagar*, "deliver into another's power"; cp. Dt 32:30) Samaria. The Lord had announced seven times regarding six enemy nations and Judah that He would destroy their "citadels" (Am 1:4,7,10,12,14; 2:2,5). Here He links His disposition toward **Jacob's pride** with His opposition to Israel's **citadels** (Hb *'armon*, "fortress, palace," i.e., a place that is "lofty or elevated," both physically in terms of location and figuratively in terms of attitude).

6:9-14 Verse 9 is a snapshot of the devastation predicted in verse 3, as well as the sense of fear even of mentioning **Yahweh's name** after He had punished His people so severely (cp. 8:2). The understood answer to the rhetorical question of 6:12 is, "Of course not." What Israel had done in general and the arrogance of claiming to have succeeded in her **own strength** were just as inconceivable. What the Lord would do in response would be comprehensive, reaching to Israel's borders (cp. 2 Kg 14:25,28).

[A]**5:26** Or *you will lift up* [B]**5:26** LXX, Sym, Syr, Vg read *the tent*; Ac 7:43 [C]**5:26** Probably a Mesopotamian war god also called Adar or Ninurta [D]**5:26** LXX reads *up the tent of Molech and Rephan*; Ac 7:43 [E]**5:26** Probably a Mesopotamian god identified with Saturn [F]**6:5** Hb obscure [G]**6:5** Or *compose on* [H]**6:10** Lit *His uncle* [I]**6:10** A burner of incense, a memorial fire, or a body; Hb obscure [J]**6:10** Lit *remove bones* [K]**6:12** Some emend to *plow the sea* [L]**6:14** Or *from Lebo-hamath* [M]**6:14** Probably the Valley of Zared at the southeast end of the Dead Sea

7:1-6 In this third and final section of the book, Amos describes five visions that demonstrate the Lord's judgment. These first two visions revealed that although the Lord would certainly judge His people, He was not willing to destroy them completely.

7:4-5 In the second vision, God showed the prophet His **calling for a judgment** [Hb *riv*, "contend or strive," whether literally to fight against or to plead a cause in court] **by fire**, which **consumed** all the water in the land (cp. Is 66:16).

The close relationship between the prophet and God comes into focus, a relationship that benefits the people of God. The Lord gave the prophet an occasion to pray, giving Him an opportunity to demonstrate His reluctance to threaten **Jacob's** survival and His willingness to listen and show mercy.

7:7-9 In contrast to the first two visions, God **showed** Amos two visions revealing judgment that would not be turned back (cp. 8:1-3). The Lord would destroy places of illicit worship in the northern kingdom, and He would demolish the dynasty of Jeroboam II.

The first vision involved a **plumb line**, a builder's tool for checking the alignment of a wall. A plumb line consisted of a metal or stone weight attached to the end of a string. When suspended from the top of a building, it made visible the precisely perpendicular line from the ground upward. Use of a plumb line, therefore, would show crooked walls that needed to be replaced. In this vision, Israel had been tested and found wanting. Mercy was no longer an option. Jeroboam's kingdom would be destroyed.

7:10-15 The prophecy concerning the downfall of King Jeroboam prompted **Amaziah the priest of Bethel** to alert the king and then to confront Amos, telling him to go back to Judah. Israel's rejection of Amos is central to the book. Despite Israel's rejection of his message, Amos continued to obey God in revealing His displeasure with His people.

7:15-17 Amos urged the false priest to **hear the word of the Lord**. Like Peter and John in the New Testament, Amos refused to be silenced (cp. Ac 4:18-20). Amaziah was powerless either to forbid God's prophet from speaking or to stop his prophecies from being realized. Regardless of what Amaziah thought about Amos's prophecies, **exile** for Israel was certain (cp. 5:5; 6:7). In addition, for trying to contend against rather than faithfully to serve the one true God, the false priest had surrendered any divine protection of his family, of his possessions and heritage (**land**), as well as of his life.

>WORD|*study*

7:6 Relented (Hb *nacham*, "lament, grieve—either because of one's own actions or because of the suffering of others," vv. 3,6) is sometimes translated "repent" (e.g., KJV, RSV). However, when God is the subject, the verb conveys His compassion for the unnecessary suffering of His people and His sorrow over the consequences coming to a man who has chosen sin, including the resulting consequences over God's intended good (cp. "regret," Gn 6:6-7; "moved to pity," Jdg 2:18; 1Sm 15:11,35; "have compassion," Ps 90:13; 135:14; "take it back," Ps 110:4). Heeding Amos's plea regarding the extent of suffering His punishment would bring, the Lord refrained from sending such devastating famine and drought (Am 7:2-3,5-6; cp. 2Sm 24:16; 1Ch 21:15; Ps 106:45; Jr 4:28; 26:3,13,19; 42:10; Ezk 24:14; Jl 2:13-14; Jnh 3:9-10; 4:2; Zch 8:14; see note on Ex 32:14).

7:14 Amos had worked not only as a shepherd but as one who **took care** [Hb *balas*, "one who gathers, plucks, cultivates"] **of sycamore figs**, likely the *Ficus sycomorus* originally cultivated in Egypt and central Africa. In the Greek translation of the Old Testament (LXX), Amos was "one who pierces" (Gk *knizōn*) the sycamore fruit, likely referring to the ancient practice of cutting or gashing the figs while they are still hard and green. The procedure releases a plant hormone that induces more rapid ripening of the fruit and makes it juicier.

Visions of Judgment and Salvation (7:1–9:15)

The Lord Has Spared (7:1-6)

7 The Lord God showed me this: He
was forming a swarm of locusts
at the time the spring crop first began to sprout—after the cutting of
the king's hay. 2 When the locusts
finished eating the vegetation of the
land, I said, "Lord God, please forgive! How will Jacob survive since
he is so small?"
3 The Lord relented concerning
this. "It will not happen," He said.
4 The Lord God showed me this:
The Lord God was calling for a judgment by fire. It consumed the great
deep and devoured the land. 5 Then I
said, "Lord God, please stop! How will
Jacob survive since he is so small?"
6 The Lord relented concerning
this. "This will not happen either,"
said the Lord God.

The Lord Will Spare No Longer (7:7–8:14)

7 He showed me this: The Lord was
standing there by a vertical wall with
a plumb line in His hand. 8 The Lord
asked me, "What do you see, Amos?"
I replied, "A plumb line."
Then the Lord said, "I am setting a
plumb line among My people Israel;
I will no longer spare them:

9 Isaac's •high places
will be deserted,
and Israel's sanctuaries
will be in ruins;
I will rise up against
the house of Jeroboam
with a sword."

10 Amaziah the priest of Bethel
sent word to Jeroboam king of Israel, saying, "Amos has conspired
against you right here in the house
of Israel. The land cannot endure all
his words, 11 for Amos has said this:
'Jeroboam will die by the sword, and
Israel will certainly go into exile
from its homeland.'"
12 Then Amaziah said to Amos, "Go
away, you seer! Flee to the land of Judah. Earn your living[A] and give your
prophecies there, 13 but don't ever
prophesy at Bethel again, for it is the
king's sanctuary and a royal temple."
14 So Amos answered Amaziah, "I
was[B] not a prophet or the son of a
prophet;[C] rather, I was[B] a herdsman,
and I took care of sycamore figs.
15 But the Lord took me from following the flock and said to me, 'Go,
prophesy to My people Israel.'"
16 Now hear the word of the Lord.
You say:

Do not prophesy
against Israel;
do not preach
against the house of Isaac.

17 Therefore, this is what the Lord
says:

Your wife will be a prostitute
in the city,
your sons and daughters
will fall by the sword,
and your land will be
divided up
with a measuring line.
You yourself will die
on pagan[D] soil,

[A]7:12 Lit *Eat bread* [B]7:14 Or *am* [C]7:14 = a prophet's disciple or a member of a prophetic guild [D]7:17 Lit *unclean*

>WORD|*study*

8:1-2 Particularly when gathered in the harvester's basket, **summer fruit** (Hb *qayits*, "harvest, i.e., cutting off, of fruits," especially figs and grapes, cp. Mc 7:1) represented the **end** (Hb *qēts*, having special reference to the "time of destruction" of a people; cp. Ezk 7:1-4) of the season. The similar sound of these two words likely reinforced the message of the vision for the prophet's immediate audience.

8:4 The word **trample** (Hb *sha'aph*, literally "breathe hard, pant," suggesting haste or eager desire for something) depicts not merely the figurative notion of "walking on" someone of lower status or, in American idiom, treating someone "like a doormat." The verb more strongly characterizes the breathless pursuit of "the needy" in terms of a "bloodthirsty" animal chasing down its prey (cp. Ps 56:1-2; 57:3; Ezk 36:3).

and Israel will certainly go
into exile
from its homeland.

8 The Lord God showed me this:
A basket of summer fruit. 2He
asked me, "What do you see, Amos?"
I replied, "A basket of summer
fruit."
The Lord said to me, "The end has
come for My people Israel; I will no
longer spare them. 3In that day the
temple[A] songs will become wailing"—this is the Lord God's declaration. "Many dead bodies, thrown
everywhere! Silence!"

4 Hear this, you who trample
on the needy
and do away with the poor
of the land,
5 asking, "When will
the New Moon be over
so we may sell grain,
and the Sabbath,
so we may market wheat?
We can reduce the measure
while increasing the price[B]
and cheat
with dishonest scales.
6 We can buy the poor with silver
and the needy for a pair
of sandals
and even sell the chaff!"

7The Lord has sworn by the Pride
of Jacob:[C]

I will never forget
all their deeds.
8 Because of this,
won't the land quake
and all who dwell
in it mourn?
All of it will rise like the Nile;
it will surge and then subside
like the Nile in Egypt.

9 And in that day—
this is the declaration
of the Lord God—
I will make the sun go down
at noon;
I will darken the land
in the daytime.
10 I will turn your feasts
into mourning
and all your songs
into lamentation;
I will cause everyone[D]
to wear •sackcloth
and every head to be shaved.
I will make that grief
like mourning for an only son
and its outcome
like a bitter day.

11 Hear this! The days
are coming—
this is the declaration
of the Lord God—
when I will send a famine
through the land:
not a famine of bread
or a thirst for water,
but of hearing the words
of the Lord.
12 People will stagger from sea
to sea
and roam from north to east,
seeking the word of the Lord,
but they will not find it.
13 In that day
the beautiful young women,
the young men also, will faint
from thirst.
14 Those who swear by the •guilt
of Samaria
and say,
"As your god lives, Dan,"
or "As the way[E,F]
of Beer-sheba lives"—
they will fall,
never to rise again.

8:1-2 Like the vision of the plumb line, the vision of the **basket of summer fruit** signified that Israel would be spared **no longer**.

8:2-3 Amos was not speaking on his own. The explanation of the vision is introduced as what **the Lord said** to Amos, and the phrase **the Lord God's declaration** is inserted in the announcement of Israel's "end" (cp. vv. 9,11). **That day** would bring the dramatic reversal of Israel's disobedient pursuits. Enjoyment of illicit worship (cp. 5:23) would **become wailing** (Hb *yalal*, "cry out, lament, howl"; cp. 8:10; Is 13;6; Jr 4:8; Jl 1:5,11,13); the nation in which God's people lived life on their own terms rather than His would become a scene of carnage; noisy backtalk (e.g., Am 7:10-13) would cease at God's command.

8:7-10 **Their deeds** were so repulsive that **the land** itself would heave, and mourning would visit Israelites of every social stratum. The **grief** to come **in that day** of judgment would be evidence of the Lord's supreme authority over every aspect of their lives.

8:11-14 Compounding the immeasurable grief to come would be the future **famine of . . . hearing the words of the Lord**. God's people would realize that what they had ignored and treated as dispensable was, in fact, what they could not do without. Tragically, this desperation for the Lord would come too late.

[A]8:3 Or *palace* [B]8:5 Lit *reduce the ephah and make the shekel great* [C]8:7 = the Lord or the promised land [D]8:10 Lit *every loin* [E]8:14 LXX reads *god* [F]8:14 Or *power*

9:1-6 In each of the previous four visions Amos reported that the Lord showed him something. In this fifth vision, however, Amos **saw the Lord standing beside the altar** and commanding the complete destruction of the temple and the people, beginning with the place of Israel's fundamental offense against the Lord—worship of other gods at places other than Jerusalem. As promised in His description of "the Day of the LORD" in 5:19, God Himself would pursue the people and hunt them down wherever they tried to hide or escape (cp. Ps 139:7-10). As the Lord declared in Am 8:8—that because of Israel's sins the land would "rise like the Nile" and "quake and all who dwell in it [would] mourn"—so He reiterated His sovereignty over the earth to make it rise and subside "like the Nile" and cause the earth to melt so that **all who dwell in it mourn**.

9:8 The sinful kingdom seems to refer collectively to the Gentile nations, which God **will destroy**, a group to which the Israelites should belong because of their sinful rebellion. Though Israel was undeserving, the Lord promised that He would **not totally destroy** the people.

9:9-10 The metaphor of shaking a **sieve** vividly illustrates God's plan. The sieve was a course piece of cloth used at harvest time. It was shaken in order to separate the grain from stones and other foreign objects. The grain passed through the sieve, but the stones would be trapped and then discarded. The sieve initially holds all the Israelites. **All the sinners** counted on their identity as God's chosen people to assure their protection from **disaster**. God's sifting process would separate Israelites faithful to the covenant from those who were Israelites by birth and would guarantee a right relationship to Yahweh despite the condition of their hearts. If the people of God rejected Him, judgment would fall on them.

9:11-12 The phrase **in that day** marks the time of restoration following judgment. Just as the Lord insisted that what would befall Israel, though at the hand of other nations, would be His doing, so He Himself would do the rebuilding.

The Lord Will Spare None (9:1-6)

9 I saw the Lord standing beside the altar, and He said:

Strike the capitals
of the pillars
so that the thresholds shake;
knock them down
on the heads of all
the people.
Then I will kill the rest
of them with the sword.
None of those who flee
will get away;
none of the fugitives
will escape.
2 If they dig down to •Sheol,
from there My hand
will take them;
if they climb up to heaven,
from there I will
bring them down.
3 If they hide themselves
on the top of Carmel,
from there I will track
them down
and seize them;
if they conceal themselves
from My sight
on the sea floor,
from there I will command
the sea serpent to bite them.
4 And if they are driven
by their enemies
into captivity,
from there I will command
the sword to kill them.
I will fix My eyes on them
for harm and not for good.

5 The Lord, the GOD of •Hosts—
He touches the earth;
it melts, and all who dwell
in it mourn;
all of it rises like the Nile
and subsides like the Nile
of Egypt.
6 He builds His upper chambers
in the heavens
and lays the foundation
of His vault
on the earth.
He summons the waters
of the sea
and pours them out
on the face of the earth.
•Yahweh is His name.

The Lord Will Restore His People (9:7-15)

7 Israelites, are you not
like the •Cushites to Me?
This is
the LORD's declaration.
Didn't I bring Israel
from the land of Egypt,
the Philistines
from Caphtor,[A]
and the Arameans from Kir?
8 Look, the eyes of the Lord GOD
are on the sinful kingdom,
and I will destroy it
from the face of the earth.
However, I will not
totally destroy
the house of Jacob—
this is
the LORD's declaration—
9 for I am about to give
the command,
and I will shake the house
of Israel
among all the nations,
as one shakes a sieve,
but not a pebble will fall
to the ground.
10 All the sinners
among My people
who say: "Disaster
will never overtake[B]
or confront us,"
will die by the sword.

11 In that day
I will restore the fallen booth
of David:
I will repair its gaps,
restore its ruins,
and rebuild it as in the days
of old,
12 so that they may possess
the remnant of Edom
and all the nations
that are called by My name[C]—
this is
the LORD's declaration—

He will do this.

13 Hear this! The days
are coming—
this is
the LORD's declaration—
when the plowman
will overtake the reaper

[A]9:7 Probably Crete [B]9:10 Or *You will not let disaster come near* [C]9:12 LXX reads *so that the remnant of man and all the nations . . . may seek Me*; Ac 15:17

>WORD|*study*

9:15 The verb uprooted (Hb *natash*) literally denotes the action of pulling, plucking, or yanking weeds out of the ground. Figuratively, therefore, the word most often conveyed the Lord's promise to "expel" or "destroy" Israel for their disobedience (e.g., Dt 29:28; 1Kg 14:15; 2Ch 7:20; Jr 12:14-17; 45;4; Mc 5:14). The sense of permanence conveyed in God's promise that He would never again forcibly remove His people from their land is echoed in the new covenant promises found in Jr 31:31-34 and Ezk 11:18-19.

and the one
who treads grapes,
the sower of seed.
The mountains will drip
with sweet wine,
and all the hills will flow
with it.
14 I will restore the fortunes
of My people Israel.[A]
They will rebuild and occupy
ruined cities,
plant vineyards and drink
their wine,
make gardens and eat
their produce.
15 I will plant them
on their land,
and they will never again
be uprooted
from the land I have
given them.
Yahweh your God has spoken.

[A]**9:14** Or *restore My people Israel from captivity*

AMOS... WRITTEN ON MY *Heart* The riches of this life are likely to produce spiritual apathy and a total disregard for right living. The remedy for self-indulgence and selfishness is found in Amos. You must remember your need for the Lord and turn to Him. Living your life for yourself and disregarding the purposes of God is to live in disobedience. Just as the actions taken by those in Amos' day revealed the attitude of their hearts, so do yours. Your inner worship of the Lord is no good unless it produces outward worship that is pleasing to Him. Amos shouts that love for the Lord produces love for others. Amos is a reminder to be generous because the Lord has been generous to you. Give to others your time, money, and food—meet the needs of the unfortunate. But most of all do not be stingy with Jesus. Share the good news of His forgiveness and grace with anyone and everyone!

9:12-15 The future would bring undeserved plenty. In exaggerated imagery, the time comes for the **plowman** and the **sower of seed** to begin their work even before those who reap and process the harvest have been able to take care of the overabundance produced in the previous season. With imagery shared by the prophet Joel, grape production would so exceed expectations that one might say **sweet wine** constantly oozes from the **mountains** and **hills** (cp. Jl 3:18).

God Himself would **restore the fortunes** of His people, enabling them to rebuild their cities and **plant vineyards** and **gardens** again. There would be an abundance of food and drink in the land, and they would **never again be uprooted**.

The passage features two emphatic statements of the absolute certainty that the prophecies are true. First, **He** [Yahweh] **will do** what He said He would do (Am 9:12). Second, the book ends with the appropriate final statement of assurance that the Lord would remain faithful to His covenant commitment to His people, both then and forevermore: **Yahweh** [God's covenant name] **your God has spoken.**

Obadiah

Timeline World Events Biblical Events	*1900 BC* Esau, son of Isaac and Rebekah, is the father of the Edomites.	*1406 BC* Edomites refuse to allow Israel passage through their territory on the last phase of their journey from Egypt to Canaan.	*1040 BC* Saul, Israel's first king, fights against the Edomites.	*990 BC* David's forces gain a decisive victory against 18,000 Edomites in the Valley of Salt.

"For the Day of the Lord is near, against all the nations. As you have done, so it will be done to you; what you deserve will return on your own head" (v. 15).

Who wrote Obadiah?

The prophet Obadiah (v. 1)

Who were the recipients?

The author does not note his audience, but likely the message is for those who experienced the anger and opposition of the Edomites during Judah's conflict with Nebuchadnezzar, king of Babylon. The prophecy is in response to a time when Jerusalem was ransacked by her enemies and when Edom was collaborating with Jerusalem's foes.

When was Obadiah written?

586–539 B.C.

Where did it happen?

Obadiah takes place in Judah, more specifically in Jerusalem, during a time of great political upheaval and a period of conflict between both Nebuchadnezzar of Babylon and the Edomites.

What is Obadiah about?

- There are consequences for those who choose to oppose the Lord.
- The sovereignty of God is evidenced through his control and judgment of the nations.

Why should women read Obadiah?

True strength comes by relying not on oneself but on the Lord. While the world of Obadiah may seem too far off to be of any relevance, the truths of Scripture stand the test of time. Edom, like many women, was found to be deceptive and full of pride. Judah was weak enough to put its faith in Edom rather than the Lord for protection. This book serves as a warning not to rely on your own abilities or those of any other that would set you in direct opposition to the Lord. And, while you may be able to deceive others, you live your life in plain sight of a just God.

How do you read Obadiah?

Obadiah is prophetic literature with a message of coming judgment and hope. Understand that this prophetic book had both a very immediate message to its hearers as well as having spiritual applications for the reader today. The structure of Obadiah revolves around the central verses 10-14 and the judgment of Edom. The recipients of Obadiah's message were given hope of justice after having been deceived by Edom.

Outline

I. The Judgment of God on Edom (vv. 1-9)

II. The Basis for the Judgment of Edom (vv. 10-14)

III. The Day of the Lord (vv. 15-21)

- A. God's Judgment on the Nations (vv. 15-16)
- B. God's Deliverance of Israel (vv. 17-21)

>WORD|*study*

Edom

v. 1 The rocky relationship between Edom and Israel started in the womb of Rebekah, wife of Isaac (Gn 25:23). God's word was fulfilled when (Hb, "red") came out first with Jacob (Israel) grasping his heel. When the boys were adults, Esau sold his birthright to Jacob for food (Gn 25:27-34). Not long after this incident, Jacob stole the blessing that belonged to Esau as the firstborn son, making Jacob "lord" over his brother (Gn 27:27-29). Not until the time of the early monarchy did Edom come under the control of Israel. Saul fought against the Edomites (1Sm 14:47), and David subjugated them (2Sm 8:14). Jehoshaphat, king of Judah, had the Edomites under his control (2Ch 20:10). The Edomites rebelled during the reign of Jehoram, Jehoshaphat's son and the king of Judah (2Kg 8:20-22), at which time they set up an independent monarchy. Amaziah killed 10,000 Edomites during his reign; but apparently their monarchy remained intact. During the last days of Judah, Edom joined them and many other nations in a rebellion against Nebuchadnezzar, king of Babylon (Jr 27:1-11). When Nebuchadnezzar attacked Judah, the allies, including Edom, deserted her. For this reason, many of the Old Testament writers criticize Edom (Ps 137:7; Lm 4:21). The Lord's promise to His people is that justice will be served.

850 BC	700 BC	597 BC	586 BC	586 BC
Edom gains the upper hand against Judah during the reign of Judah's King Joram.	Edom becomes a vassal state of Assyria.	Edom sends envoys to meet with King Zedekiah of Judah to consider an alliance against the Babylonians.	Edom joins Babylon in the destruction of Judah.	Obadiah prophesies against Edom.

The Judgment of God on Edom (vv. 1-9)

The vision of Obadiah.

This is what the Lord God has said about Edom:

We have heard a message
from the Lord;
a messenger has been sent
among the nations:
"Rise up, and let us go to war
against her."[A]
2 Look, I will make
you insignificant
among the nations;
you will be deeply despised.
3 Your presumptuous heart
has deceived you,
you who live in clefts
of the rock[B,C]
in your home on the heights,
who say to yourself,
"Who can bring me down
to the ground?"
4 Though you seem to soar[D]
like an eagle
and make your nest
among the stars,
even from there I will
bring you down.
This is
the Lord's declaration.

5 If thieves came to you,
if marauders by night—
how ravaged you would be!—
wouldn't they steal only
what they wanted?
If grape pickers came to you,
wouldn't they leave
some grapes?
6 How Esau will be pillaged,
his hidden treasures
searched out!
7 Everyone who has a treaty
with you
will drive you to the border;
everyone at peace with you
will deceive and conquer you.
Those who eat your bread
will set[E] a trap for you.
He will be unaware of it.
8 In that day—
this is
the Lord's declaration—
will I not eliminate
the wise ones of Edom
and those who understand
from the hill country of Esau?
9 Teman,[F] your warriors
will be terrified
so that everyone from
the hill country of Esau
will be destroyed by slaughter.

The Basis for the Judgment of Edom (vv. 10-14)

10 You will be covered
with shame
and destroyed forever
because of violence done
to your brother Jacob.
11 On the day you stood aloof,
on the day strangers captured
his wealth,[G]

[A]1 = Edom [B]3 Or *in Sela*; probably = Petra [C]3 Probably Petra [D]4 Or *to build high* [E]7 Some LXX mss, Sym, Tg, Vg; MT reads *They will set your bread as* [F]9 = a region or city in Edom [G]11 Or *forces*

Title: The prophet Obadiah (Hb, "servant or worshiper of the Lord"), to whom the Lord gave this vision, inspires the title.

v. 1 In Obadiah's **vision**, he saw clearly the Lord's vision about the fate of Edom.

v. 3 Deceived by perceived invincibility, Edom's pride would ultimately be its downfall.

v. 4 From on high, the Lord would **bring** [the nation] **down**. Edom was located south of the Dead Sea. Though the exact borders are unknown, the area surrounding Edom was indeed rugged and steep, God would search out the Edomites and leave nothing behind.

vv. 7-9 This judgment is the first on Edom. The nations who were once friendly to Edom would do as Edom had done to Israel.

>WORD|*study*

v. 3 The reference to **rock** (Hb *selaʿ*, "cliff, crag,") may be a play on words because Edom's capital Sela was built on a hill in the midst of steep cliffs.

vv. 15-16 Edom would be judged by the nations and then by the Lord Himself and by His people. The first (v. 8) and last (v. 15) mention of "Day" by Obadiah refer to the time when the Lord will lash out against those who have betrayed His people. All references to "Day" in between these two points refer to the oppression experienced by Jerusalem and Judah. Edom and all the other nations who caused this suffering will feel the full force of God's wrath in the period of time known as the **Day of the Lord**, which is a term frequently used by the prophets in reference to a time in history when God acts in a unique and spectacular way to show His glory (v. 15; see **Word Study**, p. 879). Undoubtedly this reference is to the final day when all unbelievers will be judged.

vv. 17-21 Obadiah speaks of a great reversal. Israel and Judah will be reunited, and they will once again possess the land the Lord had promised them.

v. 20 The location of **Sepharad**, identified in the Targum (an Aramaic translation of the Hebrew Bible) as Spain, is uncertain. Spanish Jews call themselves Sephardim.

v. 21 In the end, the kingdom of God will stand and endure forever.

while foreigners entered
his •gate
and cast lots for Jerusalem,
you were just like one
of them.
12 Do not[A] gloat over
your brother
in the day of his calamity;
do not rejoice over the people
of Judah
in the day of their destruction;
do not boastfully mock[B]
in the day of distress.
13 Do not enter the gate
of My people
in the day of their disaster.
Yes, you—do not gloat
over their misery
in the day of their disaster
and do not appropriate
their possessions
in the day of their disaster.
14 Do not stand
at the crossroads[C]
to cut off their fugitives,
and do not hand over
their survivors
in the day of distress.

The Day of the Lord (vv. 15-21)

God's Judgment on the Nations (vv. 15-16)

15 For the Day of the Lord
is near,
against all the nations.
As you have done, so it will be
done to you;
what you deserve will return
on your own head.
16 As you have drunk
on My holy mountain,
so all the nations will
drink continually.
They will drink and
gulp down
and be as though they had
never been.

God's Deliverance of Israel (vv. 17-21)

17 But there will be a deliverance
on Mount •Zion,
and it will be holy;
the house of Jacob
will dispossess
those who
dispossessed them.[D]
18 Then the house of Jacob
will be a blazing fire,
and the house of Joseph,
a burning flame,
but the house of Esau
will be stubble;
Jacob[E] will set them on fire
and consume Edom.[F]
Therefore no survivor
will remain
of the house of Esau,
for the Lord has spoken.
19 People from the •Negev
will possess
the hill country of Esau;
those from the Judean
foothills will possess
the land of the Philistines.
They[G] will possess
the territories of Ephraim
and Samaria,
while Benjamin
will possess Gilead.
20 The exiles of the Israelites
who are in Halah[H]
and who are among
the Canaanites
as far as Zarephath
as well as the exiles
of Jerusalem who are
in Sepharad
will possess the cities
of the Negev.
21 Saviors[I] will ascend
Mount Zion
to rule over the hill country
of Esau,
but the kingdom will be
the Lord's.

[A]**12-14** Or *You should not* throughout vv. 12-14 [B]**12** Lit *not make your mouth big* [C]**14** Hb obscure [D]**17** DSS, LXX, Syr, Vg, Tg; MT reads *Jacob will possess its inheritance* [E]**18** Lit *they* [F]**18** Lit *them* [G]**19** = The house of Jacob [H]**20** Or *of this host of the Israelites*; Hb obscure [I]**21** Or *Those who have been delivered*

OBADIAH... WRITTEN ON MY *Heart*

Life may seem unfair at times. Evil appears to triumph or even prosper over good. There is a constant struggle going on in the world between good and evil, a war for your own soul. However, just as Obadiah ends on a note of hope, so you can have hope. The Lord is just and will repay all evil, and in the end, the Lord wins! Let that also serve as a reminder to live for the Lord while you have breath.

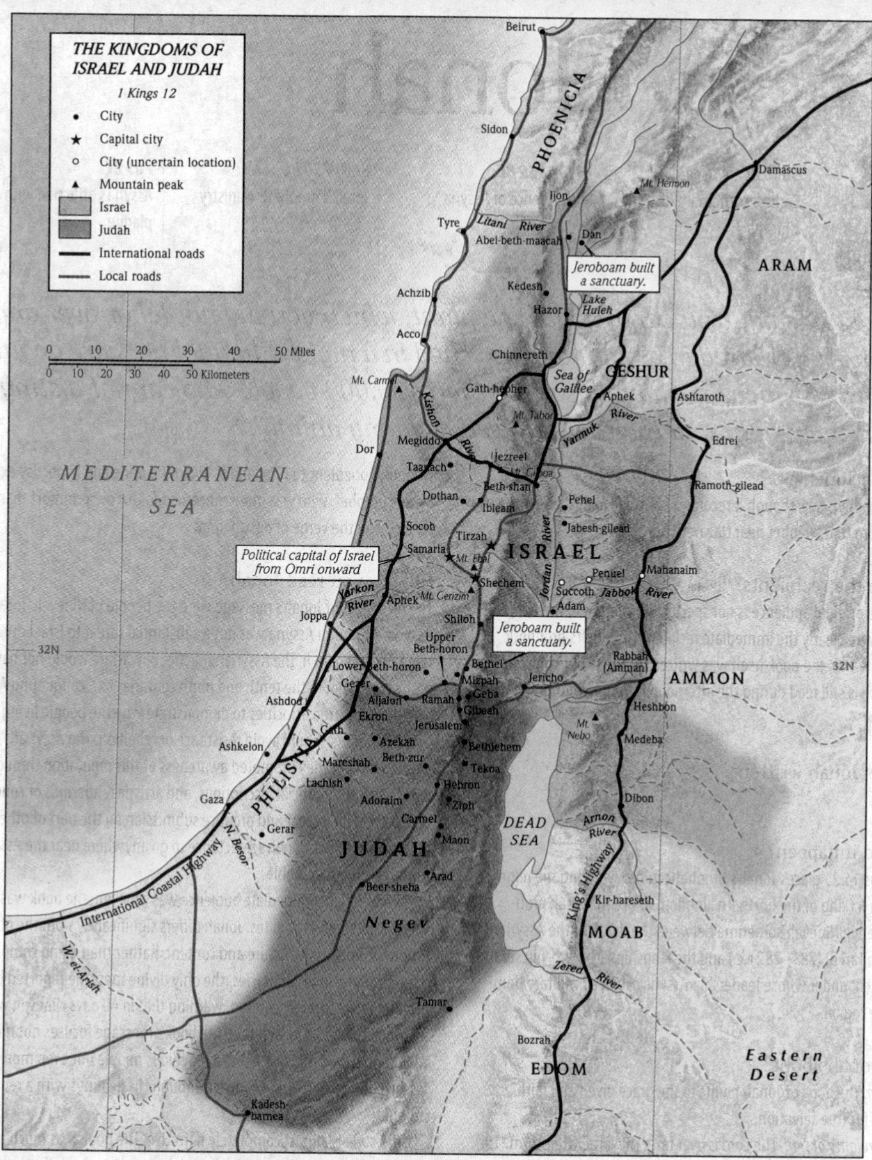

Edom was southeast of Judah. Bozrah, its capital, was about 200 miles from Jerusalem.

Jonah

Timeline	5000 BC	911–859 BC	800–750 BC	765 BC
World Events Biblical Events	Earliest settlement of Nineveh	Resurgence of Assyria	Jonah's prophetic ministry	Assyria's affliction with a plague

"So the LORD said, 'You cared about the plant, which you did not labor over and did not grow. It appeared in a night and perished in a night. Should I not care about the great city of Nineveh, which has more than 120,000 people who cannot distinguish between their right and their left, as well as many animals?' " (4:10-11).

Who wrote Jonah?

The book is anonymous, though it records a narrative about Jonah, the son of Amittai from Gath-hepher near Nazareth (2Kg 14:25).

Who were the recipients?

Although the original audience is not specifically identified, the people of Nineveh were clearly the immediate recipients of Jonah's prophetic message. However, the book itself was written for the people of Israel. The book of Jonah is still read during the afternoon of Yom Kippur or the Day of Atonement.

When was Jonah written?

800–750 B.C.

Where did it happen?

Second Kings 14:25 places Jonah's prophetic ministry during the reign of Jeroboam II (king of the northern kingdom of Israel). Jonah probably preached in Nineveh sometime between the death of the Assyrian ruler Adad-nirari III (783–782 B.C.) and the kingship of Tiglath-pileser III (745–727 B.C.), under whose leadership Assyria achieved military dominance of the region.

What is Jonah about?

- *Salvation*. The book of Jonah points to the grace given and faith required for true salvation.
- *The sovereignty of God*. The Lord is over both the large (the storm, 1:4) and the small (the worm, 4:7).
- *The compassion of God*. The Lord's love and mercy reaches out and seeks to bring to repentance even those who are not His people.

Why should women read Jonah?

Probably the best known of the 12 Minor Prophets, the book of Jonah is not just a story for children. Rather, Jonah reminds women that often obedience to God comes at the cost of your own comfort. In the context of the entire biblical canon, the book of Jonah challenges followers of Christ to revisit their sometimes inadequate view of God, to be radically (and willingly) obedient to Him, and to avoid the pride and hypocrisy exhibited by this prophet, who was more concerned for his own comfort than he was for a city on the verge of destruction.

How do you read Jonah?

The recipients of Jonah's message were the people of Nineveh, located in Assyria. Although Assyria was not a substantial threat to Israel during the reign of Jeroboam II, the Assyrians' tactics of warfare would not have been easily forgotten. In the tenth and ninth centuries B.C., conquering Assyrian armies committed atrocities to demonstrate why the people living in other military targets should avoid resistance or rebellion. The Assyrians' cruelty was legendary. They promoted awareness of this reputation through word-of-mouth, official inscriptions, and artistic renderings of conquest designed to incite fear and produce submission on the part of other nations. Therefore, Jonah's reluctance to go anywhere near the Assyrian capital is understandable.

While Jonah's immediate audience was Nineveh, the book was written specifically for the Israelites. Jonah differs significantly from the other prophetic books in structure and content. Rather than being comprised of a series of messages or oracles, the only divine message reported by the prophet is the succinct sermon, warning that in 40 days Nineveh would be overthrown (3:4). Therefore, the book's message focuses not merely on the prophetic word delivered to a rebellious people but even more on the lessons God reveals about Himself through His dealings with a rebellious prophet.

The style is almost completely narrative. The book is as much about the story of the prophet as it is about what was prophesied concerning Nineveh. Only Jonah's prayer (chap. 2) is in poetic form. Many literary features allow the book of Jonah to be read as satire without denying any of its historicity. Satire is characterized by its didactic and corrective purpose. Typically aimed at exposing the pervasive and destructive vices of pride and hypocrisy, satire frequently uses irony, exaggeration, and humor to elicit the audience's recognition and rejection of the vice(s) being criticized. The way Jonah's story is told in Scripture intensifies the instructive aims of the prophetic book, not only for the Israelites' narrow understanding of God but also for the Christian reader's worldview.

Outline

I. The Disobedient Prophet on the Run (1:1–2:10)
   A. Jonah's Flight (1:1-16)
   B. Jonah's Rescue and Intercession (1:17–2:10)

II. The Obedient Prophet and His Task (3:1–4:11)
   A. Jonah's Preaching (3:1-10)
   B. Jonah's Anger (4:1-4)
   C. God's Loving Rebuke of Jonah (4:5-11)

763 BC	759 BC	745–727 BC	722 BC
Assyria's experience of a total eclipse	Assyria's second plague	Tiglath-pileser III's expansion of Assyria's borders and reduction of Israel's territory	Capture of Samaria by Assyria's Sargon II

The Disobedient Prophet on the Run (1:1–2:10)

Jonah's Flight (1:1-16)

1 The word of the LORD came to Jonah son of Amittai: 2 "Get up! Go to
the great city of Nineveh and preach
against it, because their wickedness
has confronted[A] Me." 3 However, Jonah got up to flee to Tarshish from
the LORD's presence. He went down
to Joppa and found a ship going to
Tarshish. He paid the fare and went
down into it to go with them to Tarshish, from the LORD's presence.
4 Then the LORD hurled a violent
wind on the sea, and such a violent
storm arose on the sea that the ship
threatened to break apart. 5 The sailors
were afraid, and each cried out to his
god. They threw the ship's cargo into
the sea to lighten the load. Meanwhile,
Jonah had gone down to the lowest
part of the vessel and had stretched
out and fallen into a deep sleep.
6 The captain approached him and
said, "What are you doing sound
asleep? Get up! Call to your god.[B]
Maybe this god will consider us, and
we won't perish."
7 "Come on!" the sailors said to
each other. "Let's cast lots. Then
we'll know who is to blame for this
trouble we're in." So they cast lots,
and the lot singled out Jonah. 8 Then
they said to him, "Tell us who is
to blame for this trouble we're in.
What is your business and where are
you from? What is your country and
what people are you from?"
9 He answered them, "I'm a Hebrew. I worship[C] •Yahweh, the God
of the heavens, who made the sea
and the dry land."
10 Then the men were even more
afraid and said to him, "What is this
you've done?" The men knew he was
fleeing from the LORD's presence, because he had told them. 11 So they said
to him, "What should we do to you to
calm this sea that's against us?" For
the sea was getting worse and worse.
12 He answered them, "Pick me up
and throw me into the sea[D] so it may
quiet down for you, for I know that I'm
to blame for this violent storm that is
against you." 13 Nevertheless, the men
rowed hard to get back to dry land, but
they couldn't because the sea was raging against them more and more.
14 So they called out to the LORD:
"Please, Yahweh, don't let us perish
because of this man's life, and don't
charge us with innocent blood! For
You, Yahweh, have done just as You
pleased." 15 Then they picked up
Jonah and threw him into the sea,
and the sea stopped its raging. 16 The
men •feared the LORD even more,
and they offered a sacrifice to the
LORD and made vows.

Jonah's Rescue and Intercession (1:17–2:10)

17 [E]Now the LORD had appointed a

[A]1:2 Or *has come up to* [B]1:6 Or *God* [C]1:9 Or *fear* [D]1:12 Lit *sea that's against you* [E]1:17 Jnh 2:1 in Hb

>WORD|*study*

1:17 The verb appointed (Hb *manah*, "order, cause, prepare, assign, ordain") appears four times in the book of Jonah. In each case "the LORD" is the subject who commands the various members of the natural world to do His bidding. The instant "obedience" of these non-human creatures magnifies the prophet's defiant disobedience. Here, the Lord "appointed a huge fish to swallow Jonah." In chapter 4, He "appointed a plant . . . to provide shade . . . to ease his [Jonah's] discomfort (4:6); "a worm" to destroy the plant (4:7); and finally, "a scorching east wind" (4:8).

Title: The book is named for its author and principal character, the prophet Jonah (Hb, "dove").

1:1 The story begins abruptly and personally with **the word of the LORD**, the covenant God of Israel, to the prophet **Jonah**.

1:2-3 The Lord issued several commands to Jonah. (1) **Get up!** (Hb *qum*, "arise, stand"; cp. v. 6)—an idiom for shifting from one's current, familiar position to a posture of readiness for action. (2) **Go** [Hb *yalak*, "proceed, walk"] **to . . . Nineveh**. (3) **Preach** [Hb *qara'*, "cry or call out, proclaim"] **against** Nineveh (cp. 3:2,4). Instead, Jonah tried to get as far away from Assyria and Israel as he could go—to **Tarshish** (from the Semitic root "to smelt," indicating the central trade of its people), probably Tartessus in Spain. He **went down to Joppa**, a port city located on the Mediterranean coast, about 30 miles northwest of Jerusalem. There he **went down** into **a ship going to Tarshish** (vv. 3,5). With God figuratively understood as being "above" in the heavens, Jonah was fleeing both horizontally (west instead of east) and vertically (down, away from God).

1:4-8 The narrator identifies Yahweh as the source of the **violent storm** that prompted each sailor to cry out to his god. The ship was probably run by Phoenicians, the most skilled seafaring people of the time. The gods in ancient Near Eastern mythology, were considered a constant threat for sailors, who needed to curry favor with their gods in order to avert destruction.

1:9-16 Ironically, during the tempest that threatened to destroy the ship, the pagan crew aroused Jonah from a deep sleep commanding him to **Get up!** (Hb *qum*; cp. v. 2) and pray to his God as the rest of the crew had done to no avail. However, there is no clear confirmation that Jonah prayed at all until the fish had swallowed him (2:1). He did not take responsibility for the danger that the entire crew faced until the lot **singled** [him] **out** and the other men anxiously questioned him.

Jonah identified himself as **a Hebrew**, the title by which the

Israelites were known among the surrounding nations. Jonah's country of origin would signify to the sailors what god might be stirred against him. He identified "his god" as **Yahweh** (Hb, "God's covenant name," Ex 3:15), who is **the God of the heavens** (the supreme deity, greater than all gods and not subject to the forces of chaos) and the Creator. Although Jonah claimed to **worship** (Hb *yarē'*, "fear"; see **Word Study**, p. 37) the one true God, he did not repent of his disobedience. In contrast, the sailors **were even more afraid** (more literally, "feared with great fear") than when the storm began because they did not know Jonah's God, whose power over the sea grew more terrifying by the minute (1:10-11,13).

Jonah seems to have been determined to stick with his plan of getting away from God, even if it meant drowning in the sea. However, the solution Jonah offered betrays his cowardice. Despite the admission that he deserved death, Jonah did not offer to jump overboard but instructed the crew to **pick** [him] **up and throw** [him] **into the sea**.

Ironically, the sailors did what Jonah did not—**they called out** [Hb *qara'*, "cry out, call upon"; see **Word Study**, p. 119] **to the LORD** (cp. v. 6; 3:8). Having pleaded with God not to **charge** them with murder, the men did what Jonah instructed them to do, and the sea calmed (more literally, "ceased her raging"; cp. v. 12), confirming Jonah's testimony that **Yahweh** is the God of all and prompting an outpouring of worship by the Gentile sailors.

1:17–2:9 From the belly of **the fish** (Hb *dag*), Jonah **prayed to the LORD his God**, and the Lord heard his voice. In this psalm of thanksgiving, the reader hears a grateful and repentant Jonah. The message is clear: Salvation is from the Lord. While Jonah's prayer is unique, it contains expressions that are reminiscent of the psalms indicated in the chart above.

Jonah's Psalm and the Book of Psalms

Jonah	Psalms	Jonah	Psalms
2:2a	3:4; 120:1	2:6b	49:15
2:2b	18:4-5; 30:3	2:7a	18:6
2:3a	88:6-7	2:8a	31:6
2:3b	31:22	2:9a	50:14
2:4a	5:7	2:9c	3:8
2:5a	69:1-2		

huge fish to swallow Jonah, and Jonah was in[A] the fish three days and three nights.

2 Jonah prayed to the LORD his God from inside[B] the fish:

2 I called to the LORD
in my distress,
and He answered me.
I cried out for help
in the belly of ·Sheol;
You heard my voice.
3 You threw me into the depths,
into the heart of the seas,
and the current[C]
overcame me.
All Your breakers
and Your billows
swept over me.
4 But I said: I have been banished
from Your sight,
yet I will look once more[D]
toward Your holy temple.
5 The waters engulfed me up
to the neck;[E]
the watery depths
overcame me;
seaweed was wrapped
around my head.
6 I sank to the foundations
of the mountains;
the earth with its prison bars
closed behind me forever!
But You raised my life
from the ·Pit, LORD my God!
7 As my life was fading away,
I remembered ·Yahweh.
My prayer came to You,
to Your holy temple.
8 Those who cling
to worthless idols
forsake faithful love,
9 but as for me, I will sacrifice
to You
with a voice of thanksgiving.
I will fulfill
what I have vowed.
Salvation[F] is from the LORD!

10 Then the LORD commanded the fish, and it vomited Jonah onto dry land.

The Obedient Prophet and His Task (3:1–4:11)

Jonah's Preaching (3:1-10)

3 Then the word of the LORD came to Jonah a second time: 2 "Get up! Go to the great city of Nineveh and preach the message that I tell you." 3 So Jonah got up and went

A1:17 Lit *in the belly of* B2:1 Lit *from the belly of* C2:3 Lit *river* D2:4 LXX reads *said: Indeed, will I look . . . ?* E2:5 Or *me, threatening my life* F2:9 Or *Deliverance*

>WORD|*study*

3:5 Believed (Hb *'aman*, "trust in") has the sense of "being firm or sure." Certain factors could have prompted this repentance:
- the power of God's word (Is 55:11);
- the testimony of Jonah's experience (Lk 11:30); and
- the political decline and natural disasters affecting Assyria.

3:10 So God relented (Hb *nacham*, "pity, have compassion") is not to be confused with changing the will as in the repentance of men; rather with God comes the willing of a change. When you change your will from going away from God, He wills a change to draw you to Him.

to Nineveh according to the LORD's
command.
Now Nineveh was an extremely
large city,[A] a three-day walk.[B] 4Jonah
set out on the first day of his walk in
the city and proclaimed, "In 40 days
Nineveh will be demolished!" 5The
men of Nineveh believed in God.[C]
They proclaimed a fast and dressed
in •sackcloth—from the greatest of
them to the least.
6When word reached the king of
Nineveh, he got up from his throne,
took off his royal robe, put on sackcloth, and sat in ashes. 7Then he issued a decree in Nineveh:

> By order of the king and his
> nobles: No man or beast, herd
> or flock, is to taste anything at
> all. They must not eat or drink
> water. 8Furthermore, both man
> and beast must be covered with
> sackcloth, and everyone must
> call out earnestly to God. Each
> must turn from his evil ways
> and from the violence[D] he is
> doing.[E] 9Who knows? God may
> turn and relent; He may turn
> from His burning anger so that
> we will not perish.

10Then God saw their actions—
that they had turned from their evil
ways—so God relented from the
disaster He had threatened to do to
them. And He did not do it.

Jonah's Anger (4:1-4)

4 But Jonah was greatly displeased
and became furious. 2He prayed
to the LORD: "Please, LORD, isn't this
what I said while I was still in my
own country? That's why I fled toward Tarshish in the first place. I
knew that You are a merciful and
compassionate God, slow to become
angry, rich in faithful love, and One
who relents from sending disaster.
3And now, LORD, please take my life
from me, for it is better for me to die
than to live."
4The LORD asked, "Is it right for
you to be angry?"

God's Loving Rebuke of Jonah (4:5-11)

5Jonah left the city and sat down
east of it. He made himself a shelter
there and sat in its shade to see what
would happen to the city. 6Then the
LORD God appointed a plant,[F] and it
grew up to provide shade over Jonah's head to ease his discomfort.[G]
Jonah was greatly pleased with the
plant. 7When dawn came the next
day, God appointed a worm that attacked the plant, and it withered.
8As the sun was rising, God appointed a scorching east wind. The
sun beat down so much on Jonah's
head that he almost fainted, and he
wanted to die. He said, "It's better
for me to die than to live."
9Then God asked Jonah, "Is it
right for you to be angry about the
plant?"
"Yes," he replied. "It is right. I'm
angry enough to die!"
10So the LORD said, "You cared
about the plant, which you did not
labor over and did not grow. It appeared in a night and perished in
a night. 11Should I not care about
the great city of Nineveh, which
has more than 120,000 people[H] who
cannot distinguish between their
right and their left, as well as many
animals?"

[A] **3:3** Or *was a great city to God* [B] **3:3** Probably the time required to cover the city on foot [C] **3:5** Or *believed God* [D] **3:8** Or *injustice* [E] **3:8** Lit *violence in their hands* [F] **4:6** A castor-oil plant or a climbing gourd [G] **4:6** Lit *to deliver him from his evil* [H] **4:11** Or *men*

3:1-4 The phrase **a second time** is interesting in this context. Perhaps that is highlighted because God's sovereignty, not man's failure, is one of the primary themes of the book of Jonah. This unique situation is certainly not meant to suggest that God sometimes overlooks disobedience.

4:1-4 Divine mercy was shown to the Ninevites based on their repentance, which is consistent with the Lord's treatment of those who turn to Him (2Sm 12:14-23; 1Kg 21:27-29); yet Jonah was displeased that God would extend mercy to the wicked Ninevites. The Assyrians had brutally oppressed the Israelites, and Jonah believed that the Israelites would suffer even more at their hands in the future. However, Jonah knew God's character—that He is slow to anger and abounding in love to all who respond to Him.

4:5-9 Appointed (Hb *manah*, "number, assign") affirms the divine initiative in Jonah's life (cp. 1:17). The **plant** was probably the *elkeroa*, a broad-leafed shrub that reaches a tall height and thrives in sandy soil. The **worm** first appeared to be an antagonist by destroying Jonah's shade. However, God used the worm to deliver His message of loving rebuke to the prophet (4:10-11).

4:10-11 Jonah, who knew well the Lord's character, had grown apathetic toward the outside world. God's compassion reached far beyond the borders of Israel. The Lord's lesson in mercy and forgiveness should be for believers in every age. Jesus Himself referred to the story of Jonah as a historical event and used it effectively as an object lesson for His hearers (Mt 12:38-41; Lk 11:29-30,32).

JONAH... WRITTEN ON MY *Heart*

When your heart grows weak at the Lord's command and disobedience seems more appealing, hitting your knees rather than your feet will save you from the belly of the "huge fish." Jonah reminds you and me of our own weaknesses and failings, even as followers of Christ. Instead of seeing with our eyes and feeling with our hearts, we must see with God's eyes and love with His heart. The message of salvation is for all. Whether the Lord sends you to those in your own home, down the block, or halfway across the world, your response should be to get up and go do as He commanded.

Micah

Timeline	793 BC	760 BC	750 BC	740 BC
■ World Events ■ Biblical Events	Period of prosperity during the reign of Israel's Jeroboam II	Calling of Amos the prophet	Calling of Micah the prophet	Calling of Isaiah the prophet

"Who is a God like You, removing iniquity and passing over rebellion for the remnant of His inheritance? He does not hold on to His anger forever, because He delights in faithful love" (7:18).

Who wrote Micah?

The prophet Micah, the Moreshite (1:1,14)

Who were the recipients?

Micah, while delivering his message primarily to Judah, addressed both Samaria and Jerusalem. Micah was not a court prophet like Isaiah but spoke to leaders and common people alike.

When was Micah written?

750–686 B.C.

Where did it happen?

Micah, from a small town in Judah, lived in a time of great political upheaval. The Assyrian Empire had begun to dominate the ancient Near East around 740 B.C. Israel and Judah became vassals of this new political power and were engaging in idolatry. God declared through Micah that he would send Assyria to judge both the northern and southern kingdoms for their sin. Micah witnessed the fall of Samaria in the north and the revival under Hezekiah in the south. However, many cities of Judah were destroyed, and Jerusalem was besieged but did not fall at that time (2Kg 18–19).

What is Micah about?

- *The spiritual, moral, and ethical corruption of Judah and Israel*. The people had mixed idolatrous practices with worship of the Lord and its effects were far reaching.
- *The sovereignty of God*. The Lord is not some local deity concerned only with the destiny of His own people. He is, rather, the sovereign Lord of the universe who works through all nations to bring about His purposes. God's people will ultimately triumph, and then all nations will be subject to the Lord.
- *The LORD's faithfulness to His covenantal obligations*. There is the well-known promise of divine blessing under the Ruler from Bethlehem, which is an inextricable part of this covenant. This promise, together with his emphasis on God's sovereignty, shows the urgency of Micah's message. The Lord, though He punishes His people, will not give up on them. Thus, Micah gives his readers a true theology of hope.

Why should women read Micah?

The book of Micah speaks especially to women who enjoy checklists and have organized their lives to such a point that they live to check off a list rather than living for the highest purpose. For the Israelites, the obligation to worship and complete the task of temple sacrifice had become more important than living their daily lives as a sacrifice to the Lord. Women who read Micah will be reminded that their confession and conduct are intertwined. To do outward acts of devotion but have no inner heart of submission to the Lord results in religiosity rather than true worship.

How do you read Micah?

Micah's unity is affirmed in its outline. It is comprised of three sections (1:1–2:13; 3:1–5:15; 6:1–7:20). Each main section begins with an exhortation to listen, followed by a prophecy of judgment, and ending with a message of encouragement and hope. There is no good reason to doubt the book's unity and the power of its message. Micah is written entirely in poetry. It is marked by alliteration and vivid and powerful imagery. Although best known for its prophecy concerning the birthplace of the Messiah (5:20), the book of Micah is primarily concerned with the spiritual apostasy of both Israel and Judah and includes many of the same themes found in Amos.

Though he often stands in the shadow of Isaiah, his more famous contemporary, Micah's message is no less important than Isaiah's. He preached against the social and ethical injustices of his day and warned the people of the coming exile. But he also foretold a time of restored blessing under the divine Ruler of Bethlehem.

Micah states at the beginning of his book that what he saw concerns both Samaria and Jerusalem. Therefore, while delivered primarily to Judah, his message concerned both kingdoms. Micah was not a court prophet like Isaiah, but his message is for both leaders and common people alike. In relation to the whole of Scripture, Micah's treatment of the remnant of God's people is noteworthy. He prophesies that this remnant will become a powerful force in the world under their divine Ruler, the Messiah, and thus he continually points readers to the Messiah.

Outline

732 BC	722 BC	701 BC	686 BC	605 BC
Fall of Damascus to the Assyrians	Capture of Samaria, capital of the northern kingdom, and the taking of many of its people into exile by the Assyrians	Revolt of Judah's King Hezekiah against Assyria followed by the destruction of many cities in Judah, sparing Jerusalem	End of Micah's ministry	The Babylonians as the dominant power in the region

God's Coming Judgment on Israel and Judah (1:1–2:13)

The Prophet's Call to Attention: God's Anger Against Samaria and Judah (1:1-16)

1 The word of the LORD that came
to Micah the Moreshite—what he
saw regarding Samaria and Jerusalem in the days of Jotham, Ahaz, and
Hezekiah, kings of Judah.

2 Listen, all you peoples;
pay attention, earth[A]
and everyone in it!
The Lord GOD will be
a witness against you,
the Lord,
from His holy temple.
3 Look, the LORD is leaving
His place
and coming down to trample
the heights[B] of the earth.
4 The mountains will melt
beneath Him,
and the valleys will split apart,
like wax near a fire,
like water cascading down
a mountainside.
5 All this will happen because of
Jacob's rebellion
and the sins of the house
of Israel.
What is the rebellion
of Jacob?
Isn't it Samaria?
And what is the •high place
of Judah?
Isn't it Jerusalem?
6 Therefore, I will
make Samaria
a heap of ruins
in the countryside,
a planting area for a vineyard.
I will roll her stones
into the valley
and expose her foundations.
7 All her carved images
will be smashed to pieces;
all her wages will be burned
in the fire,
and I will destroy all her idols.
Since she collected the wages
of a prostitute,
they will be used again
for a prostitute.

8 Because of this I will lament
and wail;
I will walk barefoot
and naked.
I will howl like the jackals
and mourn like ostriches.[C]
9 For her wound is incurable
and has reached even Judah;
it has approached the gate
of my people,
as far as Jerusalem.

10 Don't announce it in Gath,
don't weep at all.
Roll in the dust in Beth-
leaphrah.
11 Depart in
shameful nakedness,
you residents of Shaphir;
the residents of Zaanan
will not come out.
Beth-ezel is lamenting;
its support[D] is taken from you.
12 Though the residents
of Maroth
anxiously wait for
something good,
disaster has come
from the LORD
to the gate of Jerusalem.
13 Harness the horses
to the chariot,

[A]1:2 Or *land* [B]1:3 Or *high places* [C]1:8 Or *eagle owls*; lit *daughters of the desert* [D]1:11 Lit *its standing place*; Hb obscure

Title: This book is named for the author, "Micah" (Hb, a shortened form of Micaiah, literally "Who is like Yahweh?"), an eighth-century prophet—not Micaiah, the son of Imlah, the northern kingdom prophet during the reign of Ahab (874–853 B.C.; cp. 1Kg 22:8-28; 2Ch 18:3-27).

1:1 Micah the Moreshite was from Moresheth, a small rural village in Judah. Micah was a contemporary of Isaiah in the southern kingdom, which may explain why many of their prophecies overlap (Mc 2; cp. Is 2).

1:1-7 Though Micah's vision specifically concerns Israel and Judah, the entire **earth** will be affected. Describing the cosmic nature of God's judgment, Micah is appealing to God's sovereignty, one of his major themes. The judgment of **Samaria** and **Jerusalem** would be a strong **witness** to the peoples on earth that the sovereign Lord does not tolerate idolatry.

1:10-16 The irony of this section is that it begins by recalling David's lament for Saul, and ends with the name of the cave in which David fled from Saul. Though never mentioned directly, David is a shadowy figure in the background. The destruction of the two kingdoms spells the end of David's kingdom. Like David, Israel and Judah are destined for the cave of Adullam.

1:10-12 Gath is similar to the Hebrew word "announce or tell." "Don't announce it in Gath" is reminiscent of David's lament at Saul's death (2Sm 1:20). In **Beth-leaphrah** (Hb, "house of dust"), the people are to **roll in the dust** as a sign of mourning. The people of **Shaphir** (Hb, "beautiful") are to experience the opposite of what their name means. They will be shamed and dishonored. **Beth-ezel** possibly means "standing place." If so, this city close to Jerusalem would no longer be a **support** to them. **Maroth** (Hb, "bitter") will not experience the good for which they are waiting because God's judgment is coming.

1:13 The people of **Lachish** are to **harness the horses to the chariot.**

The wordplay here is between "horses" and "Lachish." The **residents** of that city are to flee the coming judgment like steeds.

1:14 Moresheth-gath possibly means "betrothed." If this is correct, the wordplay is found in the connection between **farewell gifts** and "Moresheth-gath." Parting gifts were given to brides as dowries. The idea, then, is that Moresheth-gath would soon be departing from Judah as a bride departs from her family.

1:15-16 The name **Mareshah** is similar to the word "possess." Thus, the town whose name means "conqueror" or "one who possesses" will be conquered (dispossessed) by its enemies. Like David, the people will be forced to flee to **Adullam**. As a result, there will be great mourning for the exiled people.

2:1-5 Micah declares God's indictments of his people by mentioning the specific offenses committed by certain groups. At this time, the rich were brutally oppressing the poor, even devising wicked schemes against the poor in the dead of night. They ruthlessly took from those who could not defend themselves. The unjust seizure of land was especially heinous because God had divided the land among the respective tribes as their divinely assigned **inheritance** (cp. 1Kg 21). Those who committed such acts would no longer be able to participate in covenantal activities.

2:6-13 The false prophets of Micah's day were commanding that prophesying be stopped. The true prophets, like Micah, were considered troublemakers, whose **preaching** was considered dangerous to society. The true prophets were humiliating the rich by their words; thus their prophesying must be stopped. But the Lord through Micah adamantly declares that His **words bring good to the one who walks** [Hb *halak*, "follow a manner of life"; cp. Ex 16:4; Ps 1:1; 15:2; 119:3,45] **uprightly** (Hb *yashar*, "honest, right")—one whose lifestyle can be described as obedient to the Lord.

The people, however, were anything but upright at this time (cp. 1Kg 11:33,38). Micah describes the ways in which the poor were treated like enemies. They were stripped of their garments. **Women** (probably widows) and **their children** were forced from **their . . . homes**. The "prophet" for these unrighteous people is one who preaches the ways in which they can continue in their debauchery.

Micah ends this first oracle with a message of hope. A remnant will be gathered, and the Lord will be their leader, creating a sharp contrast with the false prophets and their message

you residents of Lachish.
This was the beginning of sin
for Daughter •Zion,
because Israel's acts of
rebellion can be traced
to you.
14 Therefore, send farewell gifts
to Moresheth-gath;
the houses of Achzib are
a deception
to the kings of Israel.
15 I will again bring a conqueror
against you who live
in Mareshah.
The nobility[A] of Israel
will come to Adullam.
16 Shave yourselves bald
and cut off your hair
in sorrow for your
precious children;
make yourselves as bald
as an eagle,
for they have been taken
from you into exile.

The Lord's Restoration of Israel's Remnant (2:1-13)

2 Woe to those who dream
up wickedness
and prepare evil plans
on their beds!
At morning light they
accomplish it
because the power is
in their hands.
2 They covet fields
and seize them;
they also take houses.
They deprive a man
of his home,
a person of his inheritance.

3 Therefore, the Lord says:
I am now planning a disaster
against this nation;
you cannot free your necks
from it.
Then you will not walk
so proudly
because it will be an evil time.
4 In that day one will take up
a taunt against you,
and lament
mournfully, saying,
"We are totally ruined!
He measures out
the allotted land
of my people.
How He removes it from me!
He allots our fields
to traitors."
5 Therefore, there will be
no one
in the assembly of the Lord
to divide the land
by casting lots.[B]

6 "Quit your preaching,"
they[C] preach.
"They should not preach
these things;
shame will not overtake us."[D]
7 House of Jacob, should it
be asked,
"Is the Spirit
of the Lord impatient?
Are these the things
He does?"
Don't My words bring good
to the one who
walks uprightly?
8 But recently My people
have risen up
like an enemy:
You strip off the splendid robe
from those who are passing
through confidently,
like those returning from war.
9 You force the women
of My people
out of their
comfortable homes,
and you take My blessing[E]
from their children forever.
10 Get up and leave,
for this is not your place
of rest,
because defilement
brings destruction—
a grievous destruction!
11 If a man of wind[F] comes
and invents lies:
"I will preach to you
about wine and beer,"
he would be just the preacher
for this people!

12 I will indeed gather all
of you, Jacob;
I will collect the remnant
of Israel.
I will bring them together
like sheep in a pen,

[A]1:15 Lit *glory* [B]2:5 Lit *Lord stretching the measuring line by lot* [C]2:6 = the prophets [D]2:6 Text emended; MT reads *things. Shame will not depart.* [E]2:9 Perhaps the land [F]2:11 Or *spirit*

like a flock in the middle
of its fold.
It will be noisy with people.
13 One who breaks open the way
will advance before them;
they will break out, pass
through the gate,
and leave by it.
Their King will pass through
before them,
the LORD as their leader.

God's Merciful Deliverance (3:1–5:15)

The Judgment of Unjust Leaders and False Prophets (3:1-8)

3 Then I said, "Now listen,
leaders of Jacob,
you rulers of the house
of Israel.
Aren't you supposed to know
what is just?
2 You hate good and love evil.
You tear off people's skin
and strip their flesh
from their bones.
3 You eat the flesh of my people
after you strip their skin
from them
and break their bones.
You chop them up
like flesh for the cooking pot,
like meat in a cauldron."
4 Then they will cry out
to the LORD,
but He will not answer them.
He will hide His face
from them at that time
because of the crimes
they have committed.

5 This is what the LORD says
concerning the prophets
who lead my people astray,
who proclaim peace
when they have food to sink
their teeth into
but declare war
against the one
who puts nothing
in their mouths.
6 Therefore, it will be night
for you—
without visions;
it will grow dark for you—
without •divination.
The sun will set on
these prophets,
and the daylight
will turn black over them.
7 Then the seers will
be ashamed
and the diviners disappointed.
They will all cover
their mouths[A]
because there will be
no answer from God.

8 As for me, however, I am filled
with power
by the Spirit of the LORD,
with justice and courage,
to proclaim to Jacob
his rebellion
and to Israel his sin.

The Destruction of Zion (3:9-12)

9 Listen to this, leaders
of the house of Jacob,
you rulers of the house
of Israel,
who abhor justice
and pervert everything
that is right,
10 who build •Zion
with bloodshed
and Jerusalem with injustice.
11 Her leaders issue rulings
for a bribe,
her priests teach for payment,
and her prophets
practice divination
for money.
Yet they lean
on the LORD, saying,
"Isn't the LORD among us?
No disaster will overtake us."
12 Therefore, because of you,
Zion will be plowed
like a field,
Jerusalem will become ruins,
and the hill of the
temple mount
will be a thicket.

The Deliverance of a Remnant (4:1–5:15)

4 In the last days
the mountain
of the LORD's house
will be established
at the top of the mountains
and will be raised
above the hills.
Peoples will stream to it,
2 and many nations will come
and say,

of "hope," which says only what corrupt people want to hear.

3:1-8 Micah begins his second oracle by summoning the people to pay attention to his indictments. The **leaders** are those who should know **what is just**. But their behavior toward the poor reflects that they know nothing but evil and injustice. Micah describes just how harshly these leaders have treated the poor. They are the ones who should protect the poor; instead, they are the ones responsible for cruelty against them. Micah then turns his attention to the false **prophets** who **proclaim peace** while Micah and those like him preach doom. But the end will come for these false prophets. They and their **visions** will be plunged into eternal darkness (v. 6). When disaster comes, they will receive **no answer from God**, unlike Micah who receives his message from God.

3:9-12 The blatant disobedience of Judah's **leaders** will result in the total destruction of **Zion**. In this period of time "Zion" became a synonym for the city of Jerusalem in the poetic and prophetic literature. **Priests** offered ministry only for profit, and **prophets** delivered a message only if they were paid. That the prophet Jeremiah quotes Micah's words when he is predicting the destruction of Jerusalem lends credence to this view (see Jr 26:18). Micah also describes the destruction of the temple in this context. The temple, the visible sign of God on earth, was doomed to be destroyed along with the people of God.

4:1-8 Micah describes the future glory of Zion. The temple mount will be exalted **in the last days**. With power and great glory **the LORD will rule** from Zion, the center of God's dealings with all the peoples of the earth. Micah is likely the source of this prophecy, which is an integral part of his vision of the future Jerusalem. Also, Micah's description is much longer, an indication that Isaiah may have adopted a portion of it to fit his purposes. The prophets corroborate each other with unbelievable accuracy.

[A] 3:7 Lit *mustache*

4:9-13 Micah once again centers his attention on the current crisis in Jerusalem. He foresees the Babylonian exile when the Jews will go into captivity. First, they will leave the city; then they will camp out in the open fields; finally, they **will go to Babylon**, which in this context may not mean the literal city. Micah makes it clear that the nations rejoicing over the exile of the Jews do not understand the Lord's plans or how His people fit into those plans within the providence of God. The day will come when they will be broken by the **horns** of Israel. Throughout the Old Testament, the word "horn" represents strength. The **wealth** of the nations will be brought to the Lord, the God of Israel.

5:1-15 Micah follows his pattern of first doom, and then hope, in order to emphasize his message. He first warns Israel to protect herself against the coming attacks, in which the king will be insulted by his enemies. This dire warning is followed by the glorious hope of a future King who will protect his people.

5:2 The King's influence will extend throughout the world. **Ephrathah** is the ancient name of **Bethlehem** and is used to distinguish it from the Bethlehem in Zebulun (cp. Jos 19:15). The Bethlehem in Judah was David's hometown (1Sm 17:12), and clearly a king from David's line is in view (cp. 2Sm 7:16; Is 11:1). This future **ruler**, the Messiah, will come forth from ancient Bethlehem, and He will be closely allied with the purposes of the Lord.

Micah's wording indicates that he was expecting a divine person, in keeping with the prophecies of Is 9:6, where the future King is referred to as God. Both prophets agree that this future King will bring eternal peace. Christ is the fulfillment of both of these predictions as indicated where this passage is specifically quoted (Mt 2:6). The eternality of Christ is taught throughout the New Testament (cp. Jn 1:1-2; 17:5; Php 2:6; Col 1:15-19; Rv 1:17) as His preexistence is affirmed here.

"Come, let us go up
to the mountain
of the LORD,
to the house of the God
of Jacob.
He will teach us
about His ways
so we may walk in His paths."
For instruction will go out
of •Zion
and the word of the LORD
from Jerusalem.
3 He will settle disputes
among many peoples
and provide arbitration
for strong nations
that are far away.
They will beat their swords
into plows,
and their spears
into pruning knives.
Nation will not take up
the sword against nation,
and they will never
again train for war.
4 But each man will sit
under his grapevine
and under his fig tree
with no one to frighten him.
For the mouth of the LORD
of •Hosts
has promised this.
5 Though all the peoples
each walk
in the name of their gods,
we will walk in the name
of •Yahweh our God
forever and ever.

6 On that day—
this is
the LORD's declaration—
I will assemble the lame
and gather the scattered,
those I have injured.
7 I will make the lame
into a remnant,
those far removed
into a strong nation.
Then the LORD will rule
over them in Mount Zion
from this time on and forever.
8 And you, watchtower
for the flock,
fortified hill[A]
of Daughter Zion,
the former rule will come
to you,
sovereignty will come
to Daughter Jerusalem.
9 Now, why are you
shouting loudly?
Is there no king with you?
Has your counselor perished
so that anguish grips you
like a woman in labor?
10 Writhe and cry out,[B]
Daughter Zion,
like a woman in labor,
for now you will leave the city
and camp in the open fields.
You will go to Babylon;
there you will be rescued;
there the LORD
will redeem you
from the power
of your enemies!
11 Many nations have
now assembled against you;
they say, "Let her be defiled,
and let us feast our eyes
on Zion."
12 But they do not know
the LORD's intentions
or understand His plan,
that He has gathered them
like sheaves
to the threshing floor.
13 Rise and thresh,
Daughter Zion,
for I will make
your horns iron
and your hooves bronze,
so you can crush
many peoples.
Then you[C] will •set apart
their plunder
to the LORD for destruction,
their wealth to the Lord of all
the earth.

5[D] Now, daughter who is
under attack,
you slash yourself in grief;
a siege is set against us!
They are striking the judge
of Israel
on the cheek with a rod.
2[E] Bethlehem Ephrathah,
you are small
among the clans of Judah;
One will come from you
to be ruler over Israel for Me.

[A] **4:8** Or *flock, Ophel* [B] **4:10** Hb obscure [C] **4:13** LXX, Syr, Tg; MT reads *I* [D] **5:1** Mc 4:14 in Hb
[E] **5:2** Mc 5:1 in Hb

His origin[A] is from antiquity,
from eternity.[B]
3 Therefore, He will abandon
them until the time
when she who is in labor
has given birth;
then the rest of His brothers
will return
to the people of Israel.
4 He will stand
and shepherd them
in the strength of •Yahweh,
in the majestic name
of Yahweh His God.
They will live securely,
for then His greatness
will extend
to the ends of the earth.
5 He will be their peace.
When Assyria invades
our land,
when it marches
against our fortresses,
we will raise against it
seven shepherds,
even eight leaders of men.
6 They will shepherd the land
of Assyria with the sword,
the land of Nimrod
with a drawn blade.[C]
So He will rescue us
from Assyria
when it invades our land,
when it marches
against our territory.
7 Then the remnant of Jacob
will be among many peoples
like dew from the LORD,
like showers on the grass,
which do not wait for anyone
or linger for •mankind.
8 Then the remnant of Jacob
will be among the nations,
among many peoples,
like a lion among animals
of the forest,
like a young lion
among flocks of sheep,
which tramples and tears
as it passes through,
and there is no one
to rescue them.
9 Your hand will be lifted up
against your adversaries,
and all your enemies
will be destroyed.
10 In that day—
this is
the LORD's declaration—
I will remove your horses
from you
and wreck your chariots.
11 I will remove the cities
of your land
and tear down all
your fortresses.
12 I will remove sorceries
from your hands,
and you will not have
any more fortune-tellers.
13 I will remove
your carved images
and sacred pillars from you
so that you will not bow
down again
to the work of your hands.
14 I will pull up the •Asherah
poles from among you
and demolish your cities.[D]
15 I will take vengeance in anger
and wrath
against the nations that
have not obeyed Me.

God's Triumph in Righteousness (6:1–7:20)

The Case of God Against Judah (6:1-16)

6 Now listen to what the LORD is saying:

[A]5:2 Lit *His going out* [B]5:2 Or *from ancient times* [C]5:6 Aq, Vg; MT, Sym read *Nimrod at its gateways* [D]5:14 Or *shrines*

5:7-8 This reign of eternal peace is also characterized by the gathering of **the remnant** (Hb *she'ērit*, "survivors; those who remain, especially after a slaughter"; cp. Is 37:32), a concept that is very important to Micah's overall theology (cp. Mc 2:12; 5:8; 7:18).

The vivid metaphor of **a lion** stalking does not mean that the remnant will achieve victory by bloodshed; the metaphor, rather, portrays the remnant as having a power that cannot be resisted. The triumph of the remnant will not be achieved by the power of the nations; Micah states that **the nations** will not be able to withstand the power of the remnant. Both metaphors testify to the gathering triumph and power of the remnant.

6:1-2 The Lord was calling His people to answer the accusations of His **case** against them. **The mountains** and **the hills**, even the **enduring foundations of the earth** (all creation, from the heights to the depths) would be His witnesses. The Lord reversed the typical question of accusation, "What have you done?" (cp. Gn 3:13; 4:10; Jdg 2:2; 1Sm 13:11), and demanded that His people explain what *He* had done to *them* (cp. Ex 14:11). The implied answer is that the Lord had done nothing to deserve the people's scorn. What had He *not* done on their behalf?

>WORD|*study*

6:1 Now (Hb *na'*, "please, I pray or implore"; cp. Is 38:3; Am 7:2,5) lends urgency to the command to heed God's speech. In the Hebrew text, the word also strengthens the appeal made in Mc 3:1,9 and 6:5, even though the HCSB translation of 1:9 and 6:5 does not reflect this.

6:1 Saying (Hb *'amar*, "speak") is a very common verb in the Old Testament, especially with "the LORD" as the subject. However, the active participial form used here does not frequently appear with God as the subject. Usually, as in 2:3 ("The LORD says"), the verb form indicates a completed action. Here, the participial form lends a sense of immediacy to the command to "listen." As God's people were sitting in the courtroom where the Lord was already in the process of presenting His case without interruption, they were ignoring Him and therefore had to be prompted to sit up and pay attention.

6:4-5 The Israelites have no defense as the Lord rehearses what He had done for them. **The Lord's righteous acts** (cp. Jdg 5:11; Ps 103:6) were manifest in the account of Balaam, as well as in the present case. The people who had been given instructions for taking possession of the promised land while camped in Acacia Grove (cp. Nm 33:49–35:34) had demonstrated their capacity for sin and failure there as well (cp. Nm 25:1-13). Likewise, **Gilgal**, where the Israelites had first celebrated their presence in the promised land (see Jos 5:10-12), became a symbol of the nation's abject failures to fulfill their covenant obligations (see Jdg 2) and maintain righteous leadership (cp. 1Sm 11:14-15; 13:8-15; 15:10-33). Both Hosea and Amos, prophets primarily to the northern kingdom of Israel, directly linked Gilgal with Israel's apostasy (see Hs 4:15; 9:15; 12:12; Am 4:4; 5:5).

6:6-8 Verse 8 answers the questions posed in verses 6-7 regarding what sacrifice would be costly enough to please the Lord and obtain forgiveness for one's **transgression**. These questions were unnecessary, however, given that the Lord had already revealed **what is good** and what He **requires** (Hb *darash*, an active participle here, indicating continuous, uninterrupted action: "is demanding or asking") of His people:

- **to act justly** (i.e., to do what is right [cp. 3:1,9; Lv 18:4-5; Pr 21:7; Jr 7:5-7; Hs 12:6; Am 5:15] because God does [Gn 18:25; Is 30:18]).
- **to love** [Hb *ʾahavah*, a noun, "delight, wholehearted devotion"] **faithfulness** (Hb *chesed*, "unfailing love"; see **Word Study**, p. 322) because it characterizes God (Ex 34:6-7; Nm 14:18-19);
- **to walk humbly** [Hb *tsanaʿ*, "act submissively, recognizing one's position of lowliness," only here and Pr 11:2] **with your God**, reflecting man's position before the Almighty. God rewards such attitudes and actions (Ps 25:9; 37:11; 149:4; 1Pt 5:6).

6:9-16 The Lord forcefully issued another command, specifically to Jerusalem, to **pay attention** to His judgment. The Lord asked two rhetorical questions requiring at least an unspoken admission of guilt and acknowledgment of the necessity of punishment. The implied answer to the first question is "yes"—unethical financial practices were ongoing. The implied answer to the second is "no"—God cannot **excuse** (Hb *zakah*, "justify, clear") such wickedness and deception.

God would break down their self-sufficient pride by thwarting every effort not only to be materially successful but also to meet basic

Rise, plead your case
before the mountains,
and let the hills hear
your voice.
2 Listen to the LORD's lawsuit,
you mountains
and enduring foundations
of the earth,
because the LORD has a case
against His people,
and He will argue it
against Israel.
3 My people, what have I done
to you,
or how have I wearied you?
Testify against Me!
4 Indeed, I brought you up
from the land of Egypt
and redeemed you
from that place of slavery.
I sent Moses, Aaron,
and Miriam ahead of you.
5 My people,
remember what Balak
king of Moab proposed,
what Balaam son of Beor
answered him,
and what happened from
the Acacia Grove[A] to Gilgal
so that you may acknowledge
the LORD's righteous acts.

6 What should I bring
before the LORD
when I come to bow
before God on high?
Should I come before Him
with •burnt offerings,
with year-old calves?
7 Would the LORD be pleased
with thousands of rams
or with ten thousand streams
of oil?
Should I give my firstborn
for my transgression,
the child of my body
for my own sin?

8 Mankind, He has told you
what is good
and what it is the LORD
requires of you:
to act justly,
to love faithfulness,
and to walk humbly
with your God.

9 The voice of •Yahweh calls out
to the city[B]
(and it is wise to •fear
Your name):
"Pay attention to the rod
and the One who ordained it.[C]
10 Are there still[D] the treasures
of wickedness
and the accursed
short measure
in the house of the wicked?
11 Can I excuse wicked scales
or bags of deceptive weights?
12 For the wealthy of the city
are full of violence,
and its residents speak lies;
the tongues in their mouths
are deceitful.

13 "As a result, I have begun
to strike you severely,[E]
bringing desolation
because of your sins.
14 You will eat but not
be satisfied,
for there will be hunger
within you.
What you acquire,
you cannot save,
and what you do save,
I will give to the sword.[D]
15 You will sow but not reap;
you will press olives
but not anoint yourself
with oil;
and you will tread grapes
but not drink the wine.
16 The statutes of Omri
and all the practices
of Ahab's house
have been observed;
you have followed
their policies.
Therefore, I will make you
a desolate place
and the city's[F] residents
an object of contempt;[G]
you will bear the scorn
of My people."[H]

The Moral Decline of Israel (7:1-7)

7 How sad for me!
For I am like one who—
when the summer fruit
has been gathered

[A]6:5 Or *Shittim* [B]6:9 = Jerusalem [C]6:9 Or *attention, you tribe. Who has ordained it?*; Hb obscure [D]6:10,14 Hb obscure [E]6:13 LXX, Aq, Theod, Syr, Vg; MT reads *I have made you sick by striking you down* [F]6:16 Lit *and its* [G]6:16 Lit *residents a hissing* [H]6:16 LXX reads *of the peoples*

after the gleaning
of the grape harvest—
finds no grape cluster to eat,
no early fig, which I crave.
2 Godly people have vanished
from the land;
there is no one upright
among the people.
All of them wait in ambush
to shed blood;
they hunt each other
with a net.
3 Both hands are good
at accomplishing evil:
the official and the judge
demand a bribe;
when the powerful
man communicates
his evil desire,
they plot it together.
4 The best of them is
like a brier;
the most upright is worse
than a hedge of thorns.
The day of your watchmen,
the day of your punishment,
is coming;
at this time their panic
is here.
5 Do not rely on a friend;
don't trust
in a close companion.
Seal your mouth
from the woman who lies
in your arms.
6 Surely a son considers
his father a fool,
a daughter opposes
her mother,
and a daughter-in-law is
against her mother-in-law;
a man's enemies are the men
of his own household.
7 But I will look to the LORD;
I will wait for the God
of my salvation.
My God will hear me.

The Vindication of Zion (7:8-20)

8 Do not rejoice over me,
my enemy!
Though I have fallen,
I will stand up;
though I sit in darkness,
the LORD will be my light.
9 Because I have sinned
against Him,
I must endure the LORD's rage
until He argues my case
and establishes justice for me.
He will bring me
into the light;
I will see His salvation.[A]
10 Then my enemy will see,
and she will be covered
with shame,
the one who said to me,
"Where is the LORD
your God?"
My eyes will look at her
in triumph;
at that time she
will be trampled
like mud in the streets.

11 A day will come for rebuilding
your walls;
on that day your boundary
will be extended.
12 On that day people will come
to you
from Assyria and the cities
of Egypt,
even from Egypt
to the Euphrates River
and from sea to sea
and mountain to mountain.
13 Then the earth will become
a wasteland
because of its inhabitants
and as a result of
their actions.

14 Shepherd Your people
with Your staff,
the flock that is
Your possession.
They live alone
in a woodland
surrounded by pastures.
Let them graze in Bashan
and Gilead
as in ancient times.

[A]**7:9** Or *righteousness*

>WORD|*study*

7:14 In petitioning the Lord to **shepherd** (Hb *ra'ah*, "feed, tend, pasture" a flock of sheep; figuratively "guard, care for, rule, govern") His people, Micah used imagery that characterizes God as a shepherd who cares for His own "flock" (Mc 7:14; Ps 28:9; Is 40:11; Jr 31:10; Ezk 34:11-16,23). The same imagery marks the character of the Messiah (cp. Mc 5:2 and Mt 2:6; Jn 10:11-16; Rv 7:17).

needs. He reiterated the reason for making His nation **a desolate place** (Hb *shammah*, "an object of horror, execration, or scorn"; cp. Dt 28:37; 2Ch 29:8; Jr 42:18). They had willingly participated in the evil, idolatrous, and unethical practices promoted by two kings of Israel, **Omri** and his son Ahab, who were notorious for leading Israel astray (see 1Kg 16:25-26,30; 21:25-26; cp. 12:28-33).

7:1-7 Micah himself lamented the moral and spiritual condition of his people. The prophet communicated his anguish at not being able to find a person devoted to the Lord. Micah likened his grievous disappointment with the experience of waiting all summer to savor the juicy sweetness of the season's ripened fruit but not coming up with so much as a cluster of grapes or an early fig. Micah assured his audience that the day was **coming** when God would make good on His promise to punish His people for their wickedness.

In such a time of **panic** (Hb *mebukah*, "confusion, perplexity"; cp. Is 22:5), when **godly people** are nowhere to be found, those who remain faithful to the Lord cannot afford to depend on or trust anyone else, not even family. Jesus included this verse in His instructions to the 12 disciples, warning them against the assumption that the purpose of His coming was "to bring peace on earth" (Mt 10:34-39). Jesus' appropriation of the passage signaled His identity as the Messiah and underscored His message, "Repent, because the kingdom of heaven has come near!" (Mt 4:17).

In contrast to the **watchmen** (Hb *tsaphah*, "one who looks out for, observes closely") for the unfaithful, who are promised sight of their **punishment** headed their way, Micah determined to **look** [Hb *tsaphah*, "watch, expect"] **to the LORD**, confident that He would both **hear** and deliver him (cp. Ps 18:42).

7:8-13 Speaking in the persona of Jerusalem, Micah prophesied about the restoration of God's city. Such good news is only effective, however, in the context of the confession that one has **sinned against** the Lord and an acknowledgment that His wrath and punishment are just, reflecting His righteousness. When the **darkness** and sin had been overcome by the **light** of the Lord's presence and His **justice**, Zion would **triumph** over the **enemy** (cp. 2Sm 22:29; Ps 18:43; 107:10,14; Is 9:2). The Lord's dominion, represented by Jerusalem, **on that day** will be evident in the places of origin from which people come to the center of His domain (cp. Mc 4:1-8; Ps 72:8; Is 2:2; Zch 9:10).

7:15-17 The Lord answered Micah's prayer. He promised to display the kind of miraculous power by which He had delivered Israel from bondage in Egypt. As a result, the Gentiles would be compelled to come into the light of His presence, trembling with reverence—willingly or not.

7:18-19 Micah, whose name means "Who is like the Lord?" asks, **Who is a God like You?** The central attribute upon which the prophet elaborates is the forgiveness God extends to the people whom He has purified through the exile—**the remnant of His inheritance**—the objects of His faithful love (Hb *chesed*; **Word Study**, p. 322). God's people could count on the Lord to continue to keep His covenantal obligations, rooted in His **loyalty** and promise of faithful love to Abraham and his descendants through Jacob (i.e., Israel, Mc 7:20). Verse 19 is a vivid description of what Christ's crucifixion and resurrection accomplished. This Ruler from Bethlehem has thereby fulfilled Micah's confidence in the Lord to **vanquish** [Hb *kavash*, "subject, subdue, trample underfoot"] **our iniquities** and completely do away with **our sins** (cp. Ps 103:12).

15 I will perform miracles
for them[A]
as in the days of your exodus
from the land of Egypt.
16 Nations will see
and be ashamed
of[B] all their power.
They will put their hands
over their mouths,
and their ears will
become deaf.
17 They will lick the dust
like a snake;
they will come trembling
out of their hiding places
like reptiles slithering
on the ground.
They will tremble
in the presence of •Yahweh
our God;
they will stand in awe of You.
18 Who is a God like You,
removing iniquity
and passing
over rebellion
for the remnant
of His inheritance?
He does not hold on
to His anger forever,
because He delights
in faithful love.
19 He will again
have compassion on us;
He will vanquish
our iniquities.
You will cast all our[C] sins
into the depths of the sea.
20 You will show loyalty
to Jacob
and faithful love to Abraham,
as You swore to our fathers
from days long ago.

[A]**7:15** = Israel [B]**7:16** Or *ashamed in spite of* [C]**7:19** Some Hb mss, LXX, Syr, Vg; other Hb mss read *their*

MICAH... WRITTEN ON MY *Heart*

There should be no compartmentalization of your relationship with the Lord from the rest of your life. This problem of the Israelites in Micah's day led to sin's triumph in their lives. Their public worship did not agree with their private worship and way of life. Perhaps you are a woman who struggles with being religious when it suits you. The Lord does not want a woman who tries to attain righteousness on her own but rather one who gives herself up to Him in every area of her life. Learn from the Israelites and ask the Lord to change your heart, for He requires justice, mercy, and humility (6:6-8), not vain outward attempts to appease Him.

>WORD|*study*

5:2 When the "wise men from the east" arrived in Jerusalem seeking to worship the one who had "been born King of the Jews," Herod consulted "the chief priests and scribes" about the birthplace of the Messiah (Mt 2:1-6). Knowing the Scriptures, they knew the answer. According to what was written by the prophet Micah, the coming **ruler over Israel** would be born in Bethlehem [Hb, "House of Bread"] Ephrathah (Hb, "Fruitful"). Both parts are significant, not merely because of what the words mean but because of the way each recalls significant portions of biblical history (i.e., of the recorded history of God's relationship with mankind). Note how each of the following threads with which the story of this place is woven in Scripture prominently features a *woman:*

- On Jacob's way from Bethel to "Ephrath (that is, Bethlehem)" (Gn 35:19), his beloved wife *Rachel* died as she gave birth to his twelfth, and youngest, son Benjamin (Gn 35:16-20; 48:7). *Rachel's* tomb was near Ramah on the border between the tribal territories of Ephraim and Benjamin (1Sm 10:2; Jr 31:15).
- When Herod realized the wise men had not reported back to him, he "gave orders to massacre all the male children in and around Bethlehem who were two years old and under (Mt 2:16). The horrific result also fulfilled Jeremiah's prophetic words:

  "A voice was heard in Ramah,
  weeping, and great mourning,
  Rachel weeping for her children;
  and she refused to be consoled,
  because they were no more" (Mt 2:18).

- Instead of Jacob/Israel weeping over the death of *Rachel*, the mother of Joseph and Benjamin is depicted as the representative mother grieving inconsolably over the sons slaughtered by Herod's soldiers.
- *Ruth* left Moab with her mother-in-law *Naomi* on her return to Israel where she and her deceased husband and sons "were Ephrathites from Bethlehem in Judah" (Ru 1:2).
- There, *Ruth* married Boaz (a descendant of *Rahab*, Jos 2; Ru 4:13; Mt 1:5).
- "The elders and all the people who were at the gate" of the town blessed the marriage of Boaz and *Ruth*:

  "May the Lord make the woman who is entering your house like *Rachel* and Leah, who together built the house of Israel. May you be powerful in Ephrathah and famous in Bethlehem. May your house become like the house of Perez, the son *Tamar* bore to Judah, because of the offspring the Lord will give you by this young woman" (Ru 4:11-12; see Gn 38; Mt 1:3).

The book of Ruth concludes with a brief genealogical account noting the places of *Naomi, Ruth*, and Boaz in the lineage of King David (Ru 4:13-22).

- The Lord sent Samuel to Bethlehem to anoint David as King Saul's successor (1Sm 16:1-13). As the youngest son in his family, God's choice of David was surprising (cp. 1Sm 17:12-15,57-58). Jesus is called "Son of David" at least a dozen times in the Gospels.
- Although it was "least among the leaders of Judah," David's hometown, Bethlehem Ephrathah, was God's surprising choice for the birthplace of the Messiah (cp. Mt 2:6; Lk 2:4,15; Jn 7:42).

Nahum

Timeline World Events Biblical Events	*841 BC* Assyria exacts tribute from Jehu of Israel.	*750 BC* Jonah reluctantly preaches in Nineveh and the people repent.	*732 BC* Damascus falls to Assyria.	*722 BC* Sargon II of Assyria destroys Samaria and takes many from Israel into exile.	*701 BC* Assyria invades Judah, destroys many cities, but Jerusalem is spared.

"The LORD is slow to anger but great in power; the LORD will never leave the guilty unpunished. His path is in the whirlwind and storm, and clouds are the dust beneath His feet" (1:3).

Who wrote Nahum?

The prophet Nahum (1:1)

Who were the recipients?

While Nahum's prophecy is about the coming destruction of Nineveh, its message also brings hope to the people of Judah, who were suffering under Assyrian oppression, reminding them of Assyria's eventual defeat.

When was Nahum written?

663–612 B.C.

Where did it happen?

Nahum's prophecy must be understood against the backdrop of the painful oppression of Israel and Judah by Assyria. The northern kingdom of Israel had already been conquered by Assyria (722 B.C.). Now Judah was experiencing the Assyrian cruelty. Just as God had appointed Assyria to judge Judah for their sin, the cup of His wrath would be poured on Nineveh, the Assyrian capital, when the city fell to the Medes and the Babylonians (612 B.C.).

What is Nahum about?

- *God is faithful to His people, even though they have repeatedly turned away from Him.*
- *Evildoers will ultimately be destroyed.* Reasons for divine judgment on Nineveh are given: the inhumane oppression administered by the Assyrian army (2:12) and the wickedness of the city (3:4).

Why should women read Nahum?

Nahum is a reminder to women that God is a God of justice. He does not allow evil to go unpunished. While perhaps at times the evil seem to get away unscathed, in the end the Lord will right all. There will be eternal punishment for those who do not repent and turn to Him. Those who seek to live godly lives in Christ Jesus will experience persecution. But in the midst of oppression, you can rejoice that God is for you.

How do you read Nahum?

Nahum appropriately describes his prophecy as an oracle and a vision. His message is characterized by vivid imagery and picturesque language. Nahum's name (Hb, "comfort") and Isaiah's thematic verse, "Comfort, comfort My people" (Is 40:1), suggest common ground. The reason for the comfort is God's faithfulness—both to His own people, to restore them, and to their avengers (Assyria), to destroy them.

The Assyrian oppression caused God's people to question how He could tolerate such evil. The Lord's word through Nahum to the people of Judah was vivid and precise. Assyria's hand had been heavy on Judah, but her own end was near. God was going to judge her. The book opens with an affirmation of God's awesome power and an announcement of His coming wrath on Nineveh.

While the book of Nahum is unpleasant in many ways, its message does give hope to the people of Judah. Having been subjected to the harsh oppression of the Assyrians for more than a century, they were despondent. But, through Nahum's message, their hope would be renewed. They would again embrace the truth that their God is a God of justice. And He does come to the aid of those who trust in Him.

Outline

I. The Case Against Nineveh (1:1-15)
   A. The Evidence (1:1-8)
   B. The Confrontation (1:9-11)
   C. The Judgment (1:12-15)
II. The Destruction of Nineveh (2:1-13)
   A. The Siege of the City (2:1-6)
   B. The Degrading of the City (2:7-13)
III. The Humiliation of Nineveh (3:1-19)
   A. The Destruction (3:1-5a)
   B. The Shame (3:5b-17)
   C. The Epitaph (3:18-19)

663–612 BC	612 BC	331 BC	AD 1850
Nahum prophesies the destruction of Nineveh.	Nineveh falls to the Babylonians and the Medes.	So great was the destruction of Nineveh that when Alexander the Great was on the site (Battle of Arbela), he was unable to detect that there had ever been a city there.	A.A. Layard and other archaeologists begin to uncover the ruins of Nineveh.

The Case Against Nineveh (1:1-15)

The Evidence (1:1-8)

1 The •oracle concerning Nineveh. The book of the vision of Nahum the Elkoshite.

2 The LORD is a jealous
and avenging God;
the LORD takes vengeance
and is fierce in[A] wrath.
The LORD takes vengeance
against His foes;
He is furious
with His enemies.
3 The LORD is slow to anger
but great in power;
the LORD will never leave
the •guilty unpunished.
His path is in the whirlwind
and storm,
and clouds are the dust
beneath His feet.
4 He rebukes the sea so that
it dries up,
and He makes all the rivers
run dry.
Bashan and Carmel wither;
even the flower
of Lebanon withers.
5 The mountains quake
before Him,
and the hills melt;
the earth trembles[B,C]
at His presence—
the world and all who live
in it.
6 Who can withstand
His indignation?
Who can endure
His burning anger?
His wrath is poured out
like fire,
even rocks are shattered
before Him.
7 The LORD is good,
a stronghold in a day
of distress;
He cares for those
who take refuge in Him.
8 But He will completely
destroy Nineveh[D]
with an overwhelming flood,
and He will chase His enemies
into darkness.

The Confrontation (1:9-11)

9 Whatever you[E] plot
against the LORD,
He will bring it
to complete destruction;
oppression will not rise up
a second time.
10 For they will be consumed
like entangled thorns,
like the drink of a drunkard
and like straw that is
fully dry.[F]
11 One has gone out from you,[G]

[A]1:2 Lit *is a master of* [B]1:5 Some emend to *earth is laid waste* [C]1:5 Lit *lifts* [D]1:8 Lit *her place* [E]1:9 = Nineveh [F]1:10 Hb obscure [G]1:11 Possibly Nineveh

>WORD|*study*

1:2-3 Because of His absolute holiness, He is a **jealous** (Hb *qanno'*, "inflamed, burn with zeal"; cp. Jos 24:19) God, **slow to anger, but great in power.** God's holiness is both positive in the sense of passionate advocacy for the well-being of His people and negative in refusing to ignore wrong and demanding justice. This jealousy is essential to God's nature and expresses itself in God's actions against evil and idolatry (cp. Jms 4:4-5). His jealousy is simply His holiness protecting what is His.

Title: This book is named for its author, Nahum (Hb, "comfort" or "consolation"). God called Nahum to warn the Assyrians of their pride and their coming destruction. The Assyrians had captured Thebes in Egypt in 667 B.C., a clear demonstration of their military might. But their pride would be their downfall. The words of Nahum were fulfilled in 612 B.C. when Nineveh was completely destroyed. A century before, the people of Nineveh repented as a result of Jonah's testimony and witness. But their repentance was short-lived; and, in this sequel to the account of Jonah's journey to Nineveh (see the book of Jonah, pp. 1180–1183), Nahum prophesied that God would once and for all put an end to their cruelty by utterly destroying them.

1:1 Little is known about **Nahum** himself. He is an **Elkoshite**, possibly a native of Elkosh, which Arab tradition has identified with "Al Qosh," a small village in Iraq. Others suggest Capernaum, literally "village of Nahum." But its exact location is uncertain.

1:3-8 Even when Israel sinned, God gave them many opportunities to repent. But just as His patience could run out with His own people, so, too, it had a time limit with Assyria. Shortly after its fall to the Medes, Babylonians, and Scythians, Assyria was assimilated into the Babylonian Empire. God would by no means leave the guilty unpunished.

1:9-11 Assyria had long been a menace to the people of Judah. God allowed Assyria to attack Judah because of His people's disobedience. Now that Judah's judgment was complete, God's fierce anger was turned toward Nineveh, the capital of Assyria, located on the Tigris River and built upon the foundation of the city established by Nimrod (cp. Gn 10:11-12). The means of God's judgment is described in metaphorical language. The Ninevites will be consumed completely.

1:12-15 The judgment represents a complete reversal of the final destinies of Assyria and Judah. Assyria's political and military power will be completely destroyed while their bondage over Judah will be broken. Assyria's religion will be rejected, while Judah's faith will be renewed.

2:1-5 The prophet uses military language to warn of the tough battle coming. The rest of the book is devoted to the Lord's destruction of Nineveh.

2:6 The Babylonian Chronicle records that Nineveh fell because of breaches in the city's defenses from flooding waters.

2:7-10 Nineveh would be a city in complete disarray upon her destruction. In the ancient Near East, **stripped** would indicate complete humiliation, and **beat their breasts** suggested overwhelming sorrow and mourning.

2:11-13 These verses are a metaphor interpreting verses 7-10. The kings of Assyria often compared themselves to lions in the flaunting of their fierce power. Like **lions**, who, with their marauding pride, wreak destruction, Nineveh had been free to inflict havoc throughout the known world. The lion is also a symbol of destruction in the Old Testament; and Assyria had been referred to as a "lion," an agent of God's judgment on Judah (Is 5:29-30). Now the Assyrians were being held accountable for their ruthless actions—the Lord is **against** them.

who plots evil
against •Yahweh,
and is a wicked counselor.

The Judgment (1:12-15)

12 This is what the LORD says:

Though they are strong[A]
and numerous,
they will still be mowed down,
and he[B] will pass away.
Though I have afflicted you,[C]
I will afflict you no longer.
13 For I will now break off
his yoke from you
and tear off your shackles.

14 The LORD has issued an order
concerning you:

There will be no offspring
to carry on your name.[D]
I will eliminate the carved idol
and cast image
from the house of your gods;
I will prepare your grave,
for you are contemptible.

15E Look to the mountains—
the feet of one
bringing good news
and proclaiming peace!
Celebrate
your festivals, Judah;
fulfill your vows.
For the wicked one
will never again
march through you;
he will be entirely wiped out.

The Destruction of Nineveh (2:1-13)

The Siege of the City (2:1-6)

2 One who scatters
is coming up against you.
Man the fortifications!
Watch the road!
Brace[F] yourself!
Summon all your strength!

2 For the LORD will restore
the majesty of Jacob,
yes,[G] the majesty of Israel,
though ravagers
have ravaged them
and ruined
their vine branches.

3 The shields of his[H] warriors
are dyed red;
the valiant men are dressed
in scarlet.
The fittings
of the chariot flash like fire
on the day
of its battle preparations,
and the spears are brandished.
4 The chariots dash madly
through the streets;
they rush around
in the plazas.
They look like torches;
they dart back and forth
like lightning.
5 He gives orders to his officers;
they stumble as they advance.
They race to its wall;
the protective shield is set
in place.
6 The river gates are opened,
and the palace erodes away.

The Degrading of the City (2:7-13)

7 Beauty[I] is stripped,[J]
she is carried away;
her ladies-in-waiting moan
like the sound of doves,
and beat their breasts.
8 Nineveh has been like a pool
of water
from her first days,[J]
but they are fleeing.
"Stop! Stop!" they cry,
but no one turns back.
9 "Plunder the silver!
Plunder the gold!"
There is no end
to the treasure,
an abundance
of every precious thing.
10 Desolation, decimation,
devastation!
Hearts melt,
knees tremble,
loins shake,
every face grows pale!
11 Where is the lions' lair,
or the feeding ground
of the young lions,
where the lion
and lioness prowled,
and the lion's cub,

A **1:12** Lit *intact* B **1:12** Either the king of Assyria or his army C **1:12** = Judah D **1:14** Lit *It will not be sown from your name any longer* E **1:15** Nah 2:1 in Hb F **2:1** Lit *Strengthen* G **2:2** Or *like* H **2:3** = the army commander attacking Nineveh I **2:7** Text emended; MT reads *Huzzab* J **2:7,8** Hb obscure

with nothing to frighten
them away?
12 The lion mauled whatever
its cubs needed
and strangled prey
for its lionesses.
It filled up its dens
with the kill,
and its lairs with mauled prey.
13 Beware, I am against you.
This is the declaration
of the LORD of •Hosts.
I will make your chariots
go up in smoke[A]
and the sword will devour
your young lions.
I will cut off your prey
from the earth,
and the sound
of your messengers
will never be heard again.

The Humiliation of Nineveh (3:1-19)

The Destruction (3:1-5a)

3 Woe to the city of blood,
totally deceitful,
full of plunder,
never without prey.
2 The crack of the whip
and rumble of the wheel,
galloping horse
and jolting chariot!
3 Charging horseman,
flashing sword,
shining spear;
heaps of slain,
mounds of corpses,
dead bodies without end—
they stumble over their dead.
4 Because of the
continual prostitution
of the prostitute,
the attractive mistress
of sorcery,
who betrays nations
by her prostitution
and clans by her witchcraft,
5 I am against you.
This is the declaration
of the LORD of •Hosts.

The Shame (3:5b-17)

I will lift your skirts
over your face
and display your nakedness
to nations,
your shame to kingdoms.
6 I will throw filth on you
and treat you with contempt;
I will make a spectacle of you.
7 Then all who see you
will recoil from you, saying,
"Nineveh is devastated;
who will show sympathy
to her?"
Where can I find anyone
to comfort you?

8 Are you better than Thebes[B]
that sat along the Nile
with water surrounding her,
whose rampart was the sea,
the river[C,D] her wall?
9 •Cush and Egypt were
her endless source
of strength;
Put and Libya were
among her[E] allies.
10 Yet she became an exile;
she went into captivity.
Her children were also dashed
to pieces
at the head of every street.
They cast lots
for her dignitaries,
and all her nobles were bound
in chains.
11 You[F] also will become drunk;
you will hide yourself.[G]
You also will seek refuge
from the enemy.

12 All your fortresses are
fig trees
with figs that ripened first;
when shaken, they fall—
right into the mouth
of the eater!

13 Look, your troops
are like women among you;
the gates of your land
are wide open
to your enemies.
Fire will devour the bars
of your gates.

14 Draw water for the siege;
strengthen your fortresses.
Step into the clay and tread
the mortar;
take hold of the brick-mold!
15 The fire will devour you there;
the sword will cut you down.

3:1-4 Assyria had often hired out their military forces in order to defeat small, defenseless nations. Then they would turn on and destroy their allies. Nineveh, acting as a harlot, had pulled many nations under her control through her mighty armies as well as by her prosperous economy (cp. 2Kg 18:29-35). Assyria indulged in occult practices on a regular basis. The allusion to **witchcraft** suggests that demonic means were being used to ensnare nations.

3:8-11 The Ninevites believed they were invincible. So Nahum reminds them of the defeat of **Thebes**, now known as Luxor (the cult center with the Karnak temple of Amun, the main deity of Egypt 1570–1225 B.C. during the 18th and 19th dynasties) and located about 400 miles south of Cairo. The point of Nahum's analogy is that Nineveh will suffer the same fate as Thebes. The irony here is that Nahum refers to one of the cities that Assyria itself had toppled. The Ninevites will prove powerless against their future enemies, just as their past enemies were powerless against them.

[A] **2:13** Lit *will burn her chariots in smoke* [B] **3:8** Or *No-amon* [C] **3:8** LXX, Syr, Vg read *water*
[D] **3:8** Lit *sea from sea* [E] **3:9** Lit *your* [F] **3:11** = Nineveh [G] **3:11** Or *will be overcome*

3:18-19 Those who claim to serve Nineveh, the Assyrian aristocracy, have turned against her by being absent in her time of need.

It will devour you
like the young locust.
Multiply yourselves
like the young locust,
multiply like
the swarming locust!
16 You have made
your merchants
more numerous than
the stars of the sky.
The young locust strips[A]
the land
and flies away.
17 Your court officials are
like the swarming locust,
and your scribes like clouds
of locusts,
which settle on the walls
on a cold day;
when the sun rises,
they take off,
and no one knows
where they are.

The Epitaph (3:18-19)

18 King of Assyria,
your shepherds slumber;
your officers sleep.
Your people are scattered
across the mountains
with no one to gather
them together.
19 There is no remedy
for your injury;
your wound is severe.
All who hear the news
about you
will clap their hands
because of you,
for who has not experienced
your constant cruelty?

[A] **3:16** Or *sheds its skin*

NAHUM... WRITTEN ON MY *Heart* Maybe you are experiencing the hand of heavy persecution for following Christ or feeling the subtle and slow pull of peer pressure to love the world a little more and Jesus a little less. Jesus Himself said, "You will be hated by everyone because of My name" (Mt 10:22). To follow the Lord is to suffer as He did (see 1Pt 4:13-14). Your suffering for the sake of Christ is not in vain. The Lord will receive glory for your endurance and you can rest knowing there will be justice in the end.

CHARACTER PROFILE

Nineveh A City (Personified as a Harlot) Spared, Shamed, and Swept Away

Her Background

- Founded by Nimrod, "the first powerful man on earth. . . . a powerful hunter in the sight of the LORD" (Gn 10:8-9)
- Located on the east bank of the Tigris River (facing Mosul, Iraq on the west bank)
- By 1800 B.C., the Mesopotamian center of the worship of Ishtar (fertility goddess of love and war, Astarte in Babylon), which included ritual prostitution
- Expansion of territory and architecture with the rise of the Neo-Assyrian Empire under Ashurnasirpal II (883–859 B.C.)
- By the eighth century, "an extremely large city, a three-day walk" from one end to the other (Jnh 3:3) and occupied by at least 120,000 people (Jnh 4:11)
- Capital of the Assyrian Empire under the rule of Sennacherib (705–681 B.C.), who planted a botanical garden with trees and herbs from all parts of the empire

Her Story

- God sent the reluctant Israelite prophet Jonah to preach to Nineveh during the reign of Israel's King Jeroboam II (793–853 B.C.).
- In response to Jonah's preaching, "The men of Nineveh believed in God," and "the king of Nineveh . . . issued a decree in Nineveh" ordering everyone to fast, "call out earnestly to God," and turn from their "evil ways and from the violence" they were doing (Jnh 3:5-8).
- When the people of Nineveh "turned from their evil ways . . . God relented from the disaster He had threatened to do to them (Jnh 3:10; cp. Jonah's message, v. 4).
- Sennacherib invaded Judah and laid siege to Jerusalem during the reign of King Hezekiah (729–686 B.C.), who prayed to God for deliverance. Isaiah reported God's answer to Hezekiah (2Kg 19:20-34; Is 37:21-35). After "the angel of the LORD went out and struck down 185,000 in the camp of the Assyrians . . . Sennacherib king of Assyria broke camp and left. He returned home and lived in Nineveh" (2Kg 19:35-36; Is 37:36-37).
- In 681 B.C., "while he was worshiping in the temple of his god Nisroch," Sennacherib was murdered by his two sons, and "his son Esar-haddon became king in his place" (2Kg 19:37; Is 37:38).
- Through the prophet Zephaniah (640–609 B.C.), God promised to "make Nineveh a desolate ruin," describing the Assyrian capital as a "self-assured city that lives in security, that thinks to herself: I exist, and there is no one else" (Zph 2:13-15).
- The prophet Nahum (663–612 B.C.) delivered "the oracle concerning Nineveh," in which God predicted that He would "completely destroy Nineveh with an overwhelming flood" (Nah 1:1,8; cp. 1:14; 3:7).
- Around 613–612 B.C., Nineveh was besieged by the Babylonians, Medes, and Scythians.
- The Khosr River—a tributary of the Tigris River running through the city—flooded, breaking down part of the wall and allowing the conquering armies to penetrate the city (Nah 1:8; 2:6; 3:13).
- As Nahum prophesied (1:8-9), in 612 B.C., Nineveh was completely destroyed.

Life Lessons

- In reference to Nineveh, both Jnh 4:2 and Nah 1:3 affirm that God is "slow to anger," but He is also holy and therefore "will never leave the guilty unpunished" (Nah 1:1-3). God demonstrated His compassion toward even the cruel Assyrians whom Jonah hated when they repented; God demonstrated His "great . . . power" (v. 3) and goodness (v. 7) by judging the city of Nineveh for persistently opposing Him (v. 11) and turning to idols (v. 14).
- No one can prevail against God, nor can anyone escape or thwart His judgment (Nah 1:12-14; 2:13; 3:4-7,19).
- Although the Lord extends the same offer of salvation, love, mercy, and forgiveness to prostitutes and preachers alike (e.g., Mt 21:31; Jn 3:16; 8:2-11; Rm 6:23; Heb 11:31), His view of prostitution is evident in the metaphors describing His judgment of Nineveh (see Nah 2:7-10; 3:1-7).

Habakkuk

Timeline	687–648 BC	628 BC	626 BC	625–587 BC	612 BC
■ World Events ■ Biblical Events	Manasseh leads Judah during a time of great apostasy.	Josiah, grandson of Manasseh, leads Judah in spiritual reform.	With the death of Ashurbanipal, Assyria's two centuries of dominating Babylon shows signs of weakening.	Habakkuk prophesies.	Assyria's capital, Nineveh, falls to the Babylonians and the Medes.

"Yahweh my Lord is my strength; He makes my feet like those of a deer and enables me to walk on mountain heights!" (3:19).

Who wrote Habakkuk?

The prophet Habakkuk (1:1; 3:1)

Who were the recipients?

Because Habakkuk asked God questions and received answers, he is set apart from the other prophets. Indeed he spoke to God about the people. The people of Judah living in the time just before Nebuchadnezzar's attacks obviously received his words, and that message continues to be heard until the present era.

When was Habakkuk written?

625–587 B.C.

Where did it happen?

Habakkuk prophesies in Judah after the death of King Josiah, who had tried to reform a society, which was reeling from the moral corruption caused by Manasseh and Amon. But Josiah's reform efforts perished with him, and moral and spiritual corruption plagued Judean society once again. Babylon was a growing threat to Judah. In the book of Habakkuk, they are referred to as the Chaldeans, named after the region of their rulers. These Chaldeans were led at this time by Nebuchadnezzar and were used by the Lord as His instrument of judgment upon His people.

What is Habakkuk about?

- *The nature of God*. God is holy. God is faithful. God's wisdom is far above ours.
- *Good versus evil*. The Lord will not let wickedness stand, even if He chooses to use others who are wicked to accomplish His purposes. All will be judged by the righteous Judge.
- *The triumph of faith over adversity*. Habakkuk did not always understand the ways of God but trusted God's character in the midst of crisis.

Why should women read Habakkuk?

The book of Habakkuk is far from "minor" in terms of its influence. Those who lived in the Dead Sea caves and penned what are known today as the Dead Sea Scrolls identified this book as one of their favorites. The book had a tremendous influence on the Apostle Paul, providing part of his framework for understanding the righteousness available through Jesus Christ. And through Paul's writings, Martin Luther, the father of the Reformation, was awakened by the truth that the righteous will live by faith and not by their own merits. Those who glibly speak of living by faith would do well to return to the original context of Habakkuk—distress, injustice and terror, in the midst of which God's goodness and greatness shine through all the more.

How do you read Habakkuk?

Habakkuk, though prophecy, is set apart from other prophetic books because of its dialogue format in which the prophet asks God questions and receives answers. Noted for its literary excellence, chapter 3 is a psalm (including musical instruction). The book also contains many vivid metaphors and idiomatic phrases.

Habakkuk reveals some mysterious aspects of the character of God, while at the same time many questions remain unanswered. For example, when Habakkuk asked God questions about the nature of evil and His methods of punishment, God answered by revealing His plan of action. The prophet's response is an appropriate one and can be found in 2:4: "The righteous one will live by his faith." The Apostle Paul used this quotation as Old Testament support for his claim that salvation is by faith alone (Rm 1:17; Gl 3:11-12).

Outline

I. Habakkuk's Questions and the LORD's Answers (1:1–2:4)
  A. Habakkuk's First Complaint (1:1-4)
  B. God's First Response (1:5-11)
  C. Habakkuk's Second Complaint (1:12–2:1)
  D. God's Second Response (2:2-4)

II. God's Judgments Against Evil Rulers (2:5-20)

III. Habakkuk's Prayer of Faith and Trust (3:1-19)

609 BC	605 BC	605 BC	588–86 BC
With Josiah's death, his reforms come to an end.	Babylonians continue to gain strength, defeating an alliance of Assyria and Egypt at Carchemish.	Babylon's crown prince Nebuchadnezzar II makes the first of several attacks on Judah and Jerusalem, taking Daniel and other Hebrew young men to Babylon.	Babylonians destroy Jerusalem and the temple.

Habakkuk's Questions and the LORD's Answers (1:1–2:5)

Habakkuk's First Complaint (1:1-4)

1 The •oracle that Habakkuk the prophet saw.

2 How long, LORD, must I call
for help
and You do not listen
or cry out to You
about violence
and You do not save?
3 Why do You force me to look
at injustice?
Why do You
tolerate[A] wrongdoing?
Oppression and violence
are right in front of me.
Strife is ongoing,
and conflict escalates.
4 This is why the law
is ineffective
and justice never emerges.
For the wicked restrict
the righteous;
therefore, justice
comes out perverted.

God's First Response (1:5-11)

5 Look at the nations[B]
and observe—
be utterly astounded!
For something is taking place
in your days
that you will not believe
when you hear about it.
6 Look! I am raising up
the Chaldeans,[C]
that bitter, impetuous nation
that marches across
the earth's open spaces
to seize territories
not its own.
7 They are fierce and terrifying;
their views of justice
and sovereignty
stem from themselves.
8 Their horses are swifter
than leopards
and more fierce[D] than wolves
of the night.
Their horsemen
charge ahead;
their horsemen come
from distant lands.
They fly like an eagle,
swooping to devour.
9 All of them come
to do violence;
their faces are set
in determination.[E]
They gather prisoners
like sand.
10 They mock kings,
and rulers are a joke to them.
They laugh at every fortress
and build siege ramps
to capture it.
11 Then they sweep by
like the wind
and pass through.
They are •guilty;[F]
their strength is their god.

Habakkuk's Second Complaint (1:12–2:1)

12 Are You not from eternity,
•Yahweh my God?
My Holy One,
You[G] will not die.
LORD, You appointed them
to execute judgment;
my Rock, You destined them
to punish us.
13 Your eyes are too pure to look
on evil,
and You cannot
tolerate wrongdoing.

A 1:3 Lit *observe* B 1:5 DSS, LXX, Syr read *Look, you treacherous people* C 1:6 = the Babylonians D 1:8 Or *and quicker* E 1:9 Hb obscure F 1:11 Or *wind, and transgress and incur guilt* G 1:12 Ancient Jewish tradition reads *we*

Title: The book is named for the author. Nothing is known about Habakkuk (Hb, "embrace, embracer") outside of this book (1:1; 3:1). "Habakkuk" is not a typical Hebrew name and occurs only in this book. Some rabbis relate the name to the Hebrew *chavaq*, translated "embrace" (see 2Kg 4:16), suggesting that the prophet loved his people and sought to draw them to himself in comfort.

1:1 Habakkuk begins with a phrase that serves as a header for his message. He uses the term translated as **oracle** (Hb *massa'*, "burden or heavy load"; see **Word Study**, p. 823, and notes on Jr 23:33-39) to describe his prophecy. God Himself is the author of this vision.

1:3 Habakkuk began to doubt the goodness of God. As he watched the spiritual decline of Judah, he struggled with his own faltering faith and despair over the perversion of justice: Why didn't God intervene? Why do the righteous suffer when the guilty seem to prosper? The silence of an all-powerful, all-loving God in the midst of chaos and destruction is hard to understand.

1:5-11 God is not offended by questions or expressions of confusion and concern. He willingly responded to Habakkuk's questions. God does see. He commanded Habakkuk to look away from his own people and to look at the nations (v. 5). God is going to do something quite unbelievable by judging Judah, and using a nation far more wicked than she—the Babylonians—to do so.

1:12–2:1 Habakkuk was shocked. Where was the justice in punishing Judah by a far more wicked nation? Habakkuk understood the character of God: He is eternal and He is holy. He cannot tolerate evil. Yahweh is Habakkuk's God. Habakkuk is committed to Him. However, Habakkuk did not fully understand God's ways with man. The Babylonians worshiped their own strength. How could such a people teach *anything* to God's nation? Rather, they would only be encouraged to continue to destroy other nations.

Habakkuk spoke honestly with God and desired to understand more about God's ways. Like Jonah, when he waited outside the gates of Nineveh in order to see what God would do to the city (Jnh 4), Habakkuk **will watch to see** how God will answer his own complaint.

2:2-3 God responded to Habakkuk by giving him a vision. He was to write it down **on tablets**, recalling the tablets of Moses. Writing on tablets was done to preserve a message: The covenant was not ephemeral, but it was to last, and the tablets were the official record. Such tablets bore public announcements to be exhibited in the marketplace. They were conspicuously displayed and easily read to all passing by (cp. Is 8:1; 30:8). Writing on tablets also indicates the certainty of the vision even though its realization is far off. God will be faithful to make it happen.

2:4 The outcome of this warning is certain because God sees the inflated ego of those He is about to judge. This situation calls for patient endurance: **The righteous one will live by his faith**. Faith is needed because the judgment on the Babylonians will take place in the unforeseeable future, and the delay in judgment will not make sense from a human perspective.

2:5-20 Though protected by what was believed to be impregnable—walls 85 feet thick and 11 miles long, Babylon would fall to the Medes and Persians in 539 B.C. The Babylonian king would be too **arrogant** to recognize when his time of power was over. Five "woes" are covered concerning the judgment against Babylon. The list of woes comes to a close, recalling that regardless of the Babylonians and their wickedness, the Lord is still enthroned in power **in His holy temple** as He so determines; every tongue will **be silent in His presence**—including Babylon (cp. Ps 68:5; Zph 1:7). This final verse hints at the closing for the entire book (cp. Hab 3:16-19). In the midst of all circumstances, God remains in power and sovereign over all, and His people can entrust to Him all vengeance as well as their deliverance.

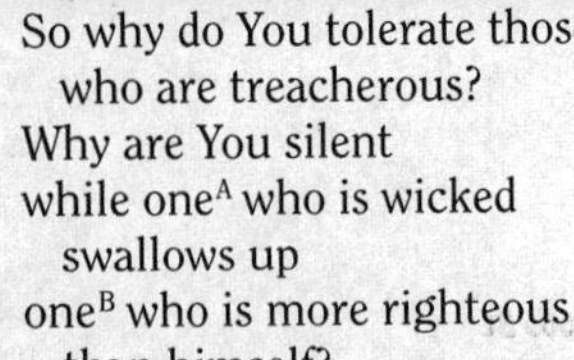

So why do You tolerate those
who are treacherous?
Why are You silent
while one[A] who is wicked
swallows up
one[B] who is more righteous
than himself?
14 You have made mankind
like the fish of the sea,
like marine creatures
that have no ruler.
15 The Chaldeans pull them all
up with a hook,
catch them in their dragnet,
and gather them
in their fishing net;
that is why they are glad
and rejoice.
16 That is why they sacrifice
to their dragnet
and burn incense
to their fishing net,
for by these things
their portion is rich
and their food plentiful.
17 Will they therefore empty
their net[C]
and continually slaughter
nations without mercy?

2 I will stand at my guard post
and station myself
on the lookout tower.
I will watch to see what
He will say to me
and what I should[D] reply
about my complaint.

God's Second Response (2:2-4)

2 The LORD answered me:

Write down this vision;
clearly inscribe it on tablets
so one may easily read it.[E]
3 For the vision is yet
for the appointed time;
it testifies about the end
and will not lie.
Though it delays, wait for it,
since it will certainly come
and not be late.
4 Look, his ego is inflated;[F]
he is without integrity.
But the righteous one
will live by his faith.[G]

God's Judgments Against Evil Rulers (2:5-20)

5 Moreover, wine[H] betrays;
an arrogant man is never
at rest.[I]
He enlarges his appetite
like ·Sheol,
and like Death he is
never satisfied.
He gathers all the nations
to himself;
he collects all the peoples
for himself.
6 Won't all of these take up
a taunt against him,
with mockery and riddles
about him?
They will say:

Woe to him who amasses
what is not his—
how much longer?—
and loads himself with goods
taken in pledge.
7 Won't your creditors
suddenly arise,
and those who disturb you
wake up?
Then you will become spoil
for them.
8 Since you have plundered
many nations,
all the peoples who remain
will plunder you—
because of human bloodshed
and violence
against lands, cities,
and all who live in them.

9 Woe to him
who dishonestly makes
wealth for his house[J]
to place his nest on high,
to escape from the reach
of disaster!
10 You have planned shame
for your house
by wiping out many peoples
and sinning against
your own self.
11 For the stones will cry out
from the wall,
and the rafters
will answer them
from the woodwork.

[A] **1:13** = Babylon [B] **1:13** = Judah [C] **1:17** DSS read *sword* [D] **2:1** Syr reads *what He will* [E] **2:2** Lit *one who reads in it may run* [F] **2:4** Hb obscure [G] **2:4** Or *faithfulness* [H] **2:5** DSS read *wealth* [I] **2:5** Or *man does not endure*; Hb obscure [J] **2:9** Or *dynasty*

>WORD|*study*

3:1 Shigionoth (Hb), in the header, is a musical term describing a dithyramb or type of music marked by quick changes of rhythm and emotion. Its Hebrew root suggests a man who moves as one intoxicated, and it is used here to note the prophet's strong emotional passion.

12 Woe to him who builds a city
with bloodshed
and founds a town
with injustice!
13 Is it not from the LORD
of •Hosts
that the peoples labor
only to fuel the fire
and countries
exhaust themselves
for nothing?
14 For the earth will be filled
with the knowledge
of the LORD's glory,
as the waters cover the sea.

15 Woe to him who gives
his neighbors drink,
pouring out your wrath[A]
and even making them drunk,
in order to look
at their nakedness!
16 You will be filled
with disgrace
instead of glory.
You also—drink,
and expose
your uncircumcision![B]
The cup in the LORD's
right hand
will come around to you,
and utter disgrace will cover
your glory.
17 For your violence
against Lebanon
will overwhelm you;
the destruction of animals
will terrify you[C]
because of your human
bloodshed and violence
against lands, cities, and all
who live in them.

18 What use is a carved idol
after its craftsman carves it?
It is only a cast image,
a teacher of lies.
For the one who crafts
its shape trusts in it
and makes idols
that cannot speak.
19 Woe to him who says to wood:
Wake up!
or to mute stone: Come alive!
Can it teach?
Look! It may be plated
with gold and silver,
yet there is no breath in it
at all.
20 But the LORD is
in His holy temple;
let everyone on earth
be silent in His presence.

Habakkuk's Prayer of Faith and Trust (3:1-19)

3 A prayer of Habakkuk the prophet. According to *Shigionoth*.[D]

2 LORD, I have heard the report
about You;
LORD, I stand in awe
of Your deeds.
Revive Your work
in these years;
make it known in these years.
In Your wrath
remember mercy!

3 God comes from Teman,
the Holy One
from Mount Paran. •*Selah*
His splendor covers
the heavens,
and the earth is full
of His praise.
4 His brilliance is like light;
rays are flashing
from His hand.
This is where His power
is hidden.
5 Plague goes before Him,
and pestilence follows
in His steps.
6 He stands and shakes[E]
the earth;
He looks and startles
the nations.

2:14 The prophet shares a glimpse of the messianic kingdom to come.

3:1-19 Habakkuk's prayer is arranged in a chiastic structure (see "How do you read Ruth?", p. 322), highlighting the importance of this revelation.

3:1-2 Habakkuk finally understood God's answer and responded with a **prayer** of **awe**. He was not sure that all his needs would be met or that he himself would avoid suffering at the hands of the Babylonians, but no longer concerned about mundane matters, he focused on the character of his God and affirmed that he could trust Yahweh God to **remember mercy**.

3:3-15 Habakkuk recalled God's workings in the past, His deliverance of the people of Israel out of Egypt. His prayer was situated in the past in order to appeal to God for help in the present.

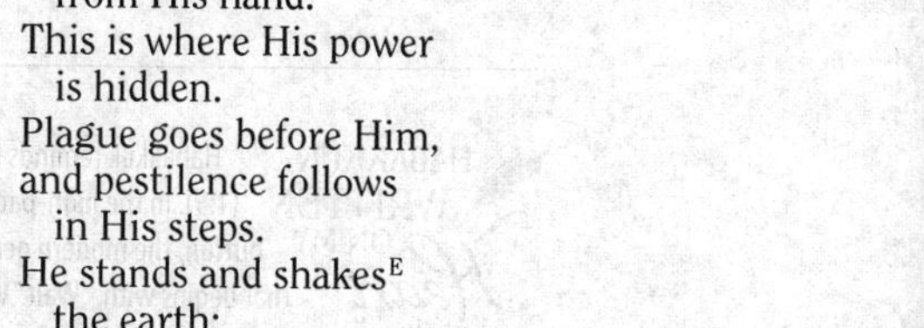

A 2:15 Or *venom* B 2:16 DSS, LXX, Aq, Syr, Vg read *and stagger* C 2:17 DSS, LXX, Aq, Syr, Tg, Vg; MT reads *them* D 3:1 Perhaps a passionate song with rapid changes of rhythm, or a dirge E 3:6 Or *surveys*

3:16-19 The prophet's prayer communicates the contrast between the magnificent past with the coming demonstration of God's awesome power in the midst of the present distress. He was overwhelmed with the revelation of God's faithfulness in the past and the assurance that He also controls the present. Because of God's goodness, He exercises His power in behalf of His people. He is faithful even when they have been unfaithful. Habakkuk found God sufficient! The one who has faith overcomes all circumstances (cp. 1 Jn 5:4-5).

The age-old mountains
break apart;
the ancient hills sink down.
His pathways are ancient.
7 I see the tents of Cushan[A]
in distress;
the tent curtains of the land
of Midian tremble.
8 Are You angry
at the rivers, LORD?
Is Your wrath
against the rivers?
Or is Your rage
against the sea
when You ride
on Your horses,
Your victorious chariot?
9 You took the sheath
from Your bow;
the arrows are ready[B]
to be used
with an oath.[C] *Selah*
You split the earth
with rivers.
10 The mountains see You
and shudder;
a downpour of water
sweeps by.
The deep roars with its voice
and lifts its waves[D] high.
11 Sun and moon stand still
in their lofty residence,
at the flash
of Your flying arrows,
at the brightness
of Your shining spear.
12 You march across the earth
with indignation;
You trample down the nations
in wrath.
13 You come out to save
Your people,
to save Your anointed.[E]
You crush the leader
of the house of the wicked
and strip him from foot[F]
to neck. *Selah*
14 You pierce his head
with his own spears;
his warriors storm out
to scatter us,
gloating as if ready
to secretly devour the weak.
15 You tread the sea
with Your horses,
stirring up the great waters.

16 I heard,
and I trembled within;
my lips quivered at the sound.
Rottenness entered my bones;
I trembled where I stood.
Now I must quietly wait
for the day of distress
to come against the people
invading us.
17 Though the fig tree
does not bud
and there is no fruit
on the vines,
though the olive crop fails
and the fields produce
no food,
though there are no sheep
in the pen
and no cattle in the stalls,
18 yet I will triumph in •Yahweh;
I will rejoice in the God
of my salvation!
19 Yahweh my Lord
is my strength;
He makes my feet like those
of a deer
and enables me to walk
on mountain heights!

For the choir director: on[G] stringed instruments.

[A]**3:7** = Midian [B]**3:9** Or *set* [C]**3:9** Hb obscure [D]**3:10** Lit *hands* [E]**3:13** The Davidic king or the nation of Israel [F]**3:13** Lit *foundation* [G]**3:19** Lit *on my*

HABAKKUK… WRITTEN ON MY *Heart* Habakkuk reminds his readers that the Lord's silence does not mean indifference (1:5). In the high-paced, high-tech world where everything comes at the push of a button, the modern generation has become impatient with any answer from the Lord that begins with, "Wait." Whenever the silence is deafening, remember that the Lord is still working, and most important—He is working on you. Though your circumstances and crises will change, God will remain the same. Hold steadfastly to Him and His Word, and you will see Him work.

Habakkuk: Links in Scripture

Old Testament	Habakkuk		New Testament
	Reference	**Link**	
	1:5	The coming of God's judgment, though not evident now	Ac 13:41
	2:3	God's purpose in "delay"	2Pt 3:9
	2:4	Living by faith	Rm 1:17 Gl 3:11 Heb 10:38
Is 44:9-20	2:18-19	The foolishness of worshiping idols	1Co 12:2
Ex 7:1–12:32 Ex 19:16-20 Dt 33:2 Ps 18:7-15	3:3-6	The majesty and terror of God's coming and His judgment	
Ex 14:15–15:16 Ps 74:12-17 Ps 77:16-20	3:8-15	God's power to defend His people	
Jos 10:12-13	3:11	God's power over the sun and moon	
1Sm 2:10 Ps 2:1-6 Ps 20:6 Ps 68:21 Zch 14:1-11	3:13-15	God's invincible power to defeat the enemies of His people and exalt His "anointed"	Col 2:13-15
Gn 35:3 Ps 138:7	3:16-17	The day of trouble and distress	
Ps 28:7 Ps 31:7	3:18	Choosing to rejoice in the God who saves	
Dt 33:29 2Sm 22:34 Ps 18:33	3:19	Strength and security in the Lord	

Zephaniah

Timeline	722 BC	716–687 BC	695–640 BC	640–609 BC
World Events / Biblical Events	Samaria, the capital of the northern kingdom, falls to the Assyrians.	Hezekiah is king of Judah and ancestor of Zephaniah.	Judah experiences years of great apostasy during the reign of Manasseh and his son Amon.	Prophecy of Zephaniah is probably influential on the young King Josiah.

"Yahweh your God is among you, a warrior who saves. He will rejoice over you with gladness. He will bring you quietness with His love. He will delight in you with shouts of joy" (3:17).

Who wrote Zephaniah?

The prophet Zephaniah (1:1)

Who were the recipients?

The immediate recipients of Zephaniah's message were the people of Judah.

When was Zephaniah written?

640–609 B.C.

Where did it happen?

Zephaniah takes place in Judah, after a long, dark period of spiritual decline. Josiah's reign and reforms were most likely concurrent with Zephaniah's ministry.

What is Zephaniah about?

- *The Day of the Lord*. This expression is used more often than in other prophetic books, but as the others, it refers to the Lord's providential intervention in the affairs of His people and the pagan nations.
- *Purification from sin and the preparation of a remnant*. Though Judah's sin and spiritual decay were offensive to the Lord, in His grace He still desired to cleanse them and even save a remnant of the faithful (3:9).

Why should women read Zephaniah?

As with all the Lord's true prophets, Zephaniah was not a tickler of ears. His unminced words of future destruction were meant to bring restoration, though to those in Judah they would have been unwelcome. Zephaniah was giving the people one last chance to return to the Lord and be faithful to Him. Just as the Lord desired Judah's loyalty, so He is calling for ladies to be faithful followers of Jesus Christ.

How do you read Zephaniah?

Though almost entirely poetic in form, the book is a prophetic declaration.

Zephaniah's recipients were in Judah, which along with some of the early discourses by Jeremiah and the history recorded in 2Kg 21–23, depicts the social, moral, and religious condition in Judah at that time. It is important to understand that the moral condition of Judah was in decline for more than 50 years. Samaria, the capital of the northern kingdom of Israel, had fallen to the Assyrians in 722 B.C. because of her own wickedness. During this time Josiah launched his massive reforms. He even moved into the territory of the northern kingdom in an attempt to take back some of the land lost to Assyria.

The first chapter focuses on God's judgment upon Judah; in the second chapter, after imploring the people to repent, judgments are pronounced against some of Judah's neighbors, including Philistia, Moab, Ammon, and Assyria; the last chapter continues themes of judgment specifically upon Jerusalem, while also promising her future glory.

Outline

I. The Day of Judgment (1:1–2:15)
   - A. The Universal Nature of the Judgment (1:1-3)
   - B. The Judgment of Judah (1:4–2:3)
   - C. The Judgment on Neighboring Nations (2:4-15)

II. The Sins of Jerusalem (3:1-8)
   - A. The Sins of the Leaders (3:1-5)
   - B. The Sins of Unrepentant Hearts (3:6-8)

III. The Promise of Restoration (3:9-20)
   - A. The Worshiping Nations (3:9-10)
   - B. The Faithful Remnant (3:11-20)

>WORD|*study*

1:2-3 Zephaniah's language is reminiscent of the language used by Moses with regard to the great flood during Noah's time (Gn 6:7; 7:23) and by Isaiah (Is 24) when he described the devastation that would be coming upon the whole earth (Zph 1:2). Three times Zephaniah speaks of the Lord's purpose to sweep away (Hb *suph*, "consume"), emphasizing the extensive and all-encompassing aspect of the wrath of the Lord. By using the language of creation and enumerating the different species of life, the Lord emphasizes that no created being will escape judgment.

640 BC	628 BC	621 BC	621 BC	605–586 BC
At the death of Amon, his son Josiah becomes king of Judah at the age of eight.	Josiah leads a spiritual reformation in Judah.	Judah's spiritual reformation intensifies when the Book of the Law is found in the temple.	Huldah the prophetess brought the word from Yahweh that He would bring disaster on Judah after the reign of Josiah.	Babylonians attack and destroy Jerusalem.

The Day of Judgment (1:1–2:15)

The Universal Nature of the Judgment (1:1-3)

1 The word of the LORD that came to Zephaniah son of Cushi, son of Gedaliah, son of Amariah, son of Hezekiah, in the days of Josiah son of Amon, king of Judah.

2 I will completely
sweep away everything
from the face of the earth—
this is
the LORD's declaration.
3 I will sweep away man
and animal;
I will sweep away the birds
of the sky
and the fish of the sea,
and the ruins[A] along with
the wicked.
I will cut off mankind
from the face of the earth.
This is
the LORD's declaration.

The Judgment of Judah (1:4–2:3)

4 I will stretch out My hand
against Judah
and against all the residents
of Jerusalem.
I will cut off every vestige
of •Baal
from this place,
the names
of the pagan priests
along with the priests;
5 those who bow in worship
on the rooftops
to the heavenly host;
those who bow
and pledge loyalty
to the LORD
but also pledge loyalty
to •Milcom;[B]
6 and those who turn back
from following the LORD,
who do not seek the LORD
or inquire of Him.
7 Be silent in the presence
of the Lord GOD,
for the Day of the LORD
is near.
Indeed, the LORD has prepared
a sacrifice;
He has consecrated
His guests.
8 On the day
of the LORD's sacrifice
I will punish the officials,
the king's sons,
and all who are dressed
in foreign clothing.
9 On that day I will punish
all who skip over
the threshold,[C]
who fill their master's house
with violence and deceit.
10 On that day—
this is
the LORD's declaration—
there will be an outcry
from the Fish Gate,
a wailing
from the Second District,
and a loud crashing
from the hills.
11 Wail, you residents
of the Hollow,[D]
for all the merchants[E]
will be silenced;
all those loaded with silver
will be cut off.

[A]1:3 Perhaps objects connected with idolatry [B]1:5 Some LXX mss, Syr, Vg; MT, other LXX mss read *their king* [C]1:9 Hb obscure [D]1:11 Or *the market district* [E]1:11 Or *Canaanites*

Title: Though the exact meaning of Zephaniah (Hb) remains uncertain, most scholars assign its meaning as "Yahweh, or the Lord, has hidden or treasured." If so, it might refer to a recurring theme of hiddenness as in 2:3, "Perhaps you will be concealed on the day of the LORD's anger"—i.e., a wish that the Lord would hide His people from the dreadful consequences of His wrath, which was about to be poured out. Three other men in Scripture had this name (cp. 1Ch 6:36; Jr 21:1; Zch 6:10,14). Zephaniah was the great-great-grandson of one named Hezekiah, whom most scholars believe was the popular king of Judah. If this is correct, then Zephaniah was a member of the royal family.

1:1 Zephaniah is the only minor prophet to give such an extended record of his lineage. If he were a descendant of the great king Hezekiah, he would have had personal insight into the activities of Judah's leaders.

1:4-5 Zephaniah turns specifically to **Judah**. The people of Judah and **Jerusalem** were guilty of **Baal** (Hb, "master, husband, possessor") worship and of swearing to **Milcom**, the god of the Ammonites (cp. 1Kg 11:5; 2Kg 23:13). Introduced to Israel by King Ahab, eradicated by Hezekiah (2Kg 21:1-3), Baal worship was a pagan cult, widely practiced during the reign of Manasseh. This Canaanite deity was believed to control all fertility.

1:7-8 Zephaniah used the metaphor of a **sacrifice** ritual and terms closely associated with the sacrificial meals well known to the Jews so they might understand the judgment. The victim in the sacrifice is Judah while the **guests** are the Babylonians, who are God's instrument to bring judgment on them (cp. Is 34:6; Jr 46:10; Ezk 39:17-19). The Lord will especially punish the king's children (perhaps the sons of Josiah—Jehoahaz, Jehoiakim, and Zedekiah), who are wearing **foreign clothing**—a sign demonstrating just how far from God they had wandered.

1:9 The leaders of Judah had even adopted the superstitious Philistine ritual of jumping **over the threshold** at Dagon's temple; or worse still, they eagerly leaped over thresholds in order to plunder others, especially the poor and defenseless among them.

1:12 The people believed their behavior would be overlooked by the Lord; but the Lord would **search Jerusalem with lamps**—there would be no hiding for the wicked.

1:15-18 Drawing upon the imagery used by many of the prophets before him (Jl 2:11; Is 2:5-22; Is 24), Zephaniah described **the Day of the Lord** with the darkest of terms (Zph 1:14), vividly portraying its destruction with the terms of military conflict. It will encompass **the whole earth**. The reason the Lord brings such devastation is stated concisely—**mankind** has **sinned against the Lord**.

2:3 The only way to escape God's wrath is to repent. Zephaniah called specifically upon the **humble of the earth**, those who carry out God's commands. Though the day of judgment cannot be avoided, Zephaniah encouraged the righteous who acknowledge the Lord's standard of justice to continue in faithfulness so that those who honored the Lord would be protected in the midst of the inevitable destruction to come.

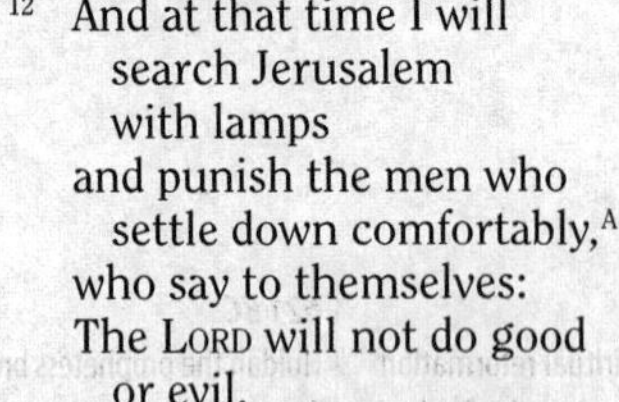

12 And at that time I will
search Jerusalem
with lamps
and punish the men who
settle down comfortably,[A]
who say to themselves:
The LORD will not do good
or evil.
13 Their wealth will
become plunder
and their houses a ruin.
They will build houses
but never live in them,
plant vineyards
but never drink their wine.

14 The great Day of the LORD
is near,
near and rapidly approaching.
Listen, the Day of the LORD—
then the warrior's cry
is bitter.
15 That day is a day of wrath,
a day of trouble and distress,
a day of destruction
and desolation,
a day of darkness and gloom,
a day of clouds and blackness,
16 a day of trumpet blast
and battle cry
against the fortified cities,
and against
the high corner towers.
17 I will bring distress
on mankind,
and they will walk
like the blind
because they have sinned
against the LORD.
Their blood will be poured out
like dust
and their flesh like dung.
18 Their silver and their gold
will not be able
to rescue them
on the day
of the LORD's wrath.
The whole earth
will be consumed
by the fire of His jealousy.
For He will make a complete,
yes, a horrifying end
of all the inhabitants
of the earth.

2 Gather yourselves together;
gather together,
undesirable[B] nation,
2 before the decree takes effect
and the day passes like chaff,
before the burning
of the LORD's anger
overtakes you,
before the day
of the LORD's anger
overtakes you.
3 Seek the LORD, all you humble
of the earth,
who carry out
what He commands.
Seek righteousness,
seek humility;
perhaps you will be concealed
on the day of the LORD's anger.

The Judgment on Neighboring Nations (2:4-15)

4 For Gaza will be abandoned,
and Ashkelon will become
a ruin.
Ashdod will be driven out
at noon,
and Ekron will be uprooted.
5 Woe, inhabitants
of the seacoast,
nation of the Cherethites![C]
The word of the LORD is
against you,
Canaan, land
of the Philistines:
I will destroy you until
there is no one left.
6 The seacoast will
become pasturelands
with caves for shepherds
and folds for sheep.
7 The coastland will belong
to the remnant of the house
of Judah;
they will find pasture there.
They will lie down
in the evening
among the houses
of Ashkelon,
for the LORD their God
will return to them
and restore their fortunes.

8 I have heard the taunting
of Moab
and the insults
of the Ammonites,
who have taunted My people
and threatened their territory.
9 Therefore, as I live—
this is the declaration
of the LORD of •Hosts,
the God of Israel—

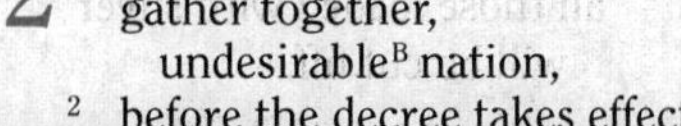

[A]1:12 Lit *who thicken on their dregs* [B]2:1 Or *shameless* [C]2:5 = Sea Peoples

Moab will be like Sodom
and the Ammonites
like Gomorrah—
a place overgrown with weeds,
a salt pit,
and a perpetual wasteland.
The remnant of My people
will plunder them;
the remainder of My nation
will dispossess them.
10 This is what they get
for their pride,
because they have taunted
and acted arrogantly
against the people of the LORD
of Hosts.
11 The LORD will be terrifying
to them
when He starves all the gods
of the earth.
Then all
the distant coastlands
of the nations
will bow in worship to Him,
each in its own place.

12 You •Cushites will also
be slain by My sword.

13 He will also stretch out
His hand against the north
and destroy Assyria;
He will make Nineveh
a desolate ruin,
dry as the desert.
14 Herds will lie down
in the middle of it,
every kind of wild animal.[A]
Both the desert owl[B]
and the screech owl[C]
will roost in the capitals
of its pillars.
Their calls will sound[D]
from the window,
but devastation[E] will be
on the threshold,
for He will expose
the cedar work.[F]
15 This is the self-assured city
that lives in security,
that thinks to herself:
I exist, and there is
no one else.
What a desolation
she has become,
a place for wild animals
to lie down!
Everyone who passes by her
jeers[G] and shakes his fist.

The Sins of Jerusalem (3:1-8)

The Sins of the Leaders (3:1-5)

3 Woe to the city
that is rebellious[H]
and defiled,
the oppressive city!
2 She has not obeyed;
she has not
accepted discipline.
She has not trusted
in •Yahweh;
she has not drawn near
to her God.
3 The[I] princes within her are
roaring lions;
her judges are wolves
of the night,
which leave nothing
for[J] the morning.
4 Her prophets are reckless—
treacherous men.
Her priests profane
the sanctuary;
they do violence
to instruction.
5 The righteous LORD is in her;
He does no wrong.
He applies His justice
morning by morning;
He does not fail at dawn,
yet the one who does wrong
knows no shame.

The Sins of Unrepentant Hearts (3:6-8)

6 I have cut off nations;
their corner towers
are destroyed.
I have laid waste their streets,
with no one to pass through.
Their cities lie devastated,
without a person,
without an inhabitant.
7 I thought: You
will certainly •fear Me
and accept correction.
Then her dwelling place[K]
would not be cut off
based on
all that I had allocated
to her.
However, they became
more corrupt
in all their actions.

2:4-15 Like other prophets who gave specific judgments for the surrounding nations, Zephaniah used universal/narrow, present/future literary oppositions. In this way he demonstrated that God is truly in control of all events for all time. After the Lord destroys both the nations dependent on their man-made gods and their false idols, every nation will recognize and worship Yahweh as the one true God (cp. Is 45:23; Mal 1:11). The nations mentioned in this section are the **Philistines** to the west, **Moab** and Ammon to the east, **Cushites** to the south, and **Assyria**, whose path of invasion was from the north. Using nations from the four points of the earth was representative of the universality of the coming judgment.

3:1-5 Indictments are given, specifically against the leaders of Jerusalem. Sandwiched between references to Jerusalem are the leaders' crimes. Disobedient Jerusalem is contrasted with the faithful Lord who dwells within her. **They do violence to instruction** speaks of the twisting and distorting of God's Word to justify their wickedness (cp. Jr 7:8).

3:6-8 Zephaniah vividly reminded the people that God had **cut off** [other] **nations**. The people should have feared Him and heeded His correction, but they were so steeped in their sin and waywardness that they acted even more corruptly. Therefore, the day will come when the whole earth will be consumed by His wrath. Though the Day of the Lord is not specifically mentioned in this context, it is surely what is referenced.

[A] **2:14** Lit *every wild animal of a nation* [B] **2:14** Or *the pelican* [C] **2:14** Or *the hedgehog* [D] **2:14** Lit *sing* [E] **2:14** LXX, Vg read *ravens* [F] **2:14** Hb obscure [G] **2:15** Or *hisses* [H] **3:1** Or *filthy* [I] **3:3** Lit *Her* [J] **3:3** Or *that had nothing to gnaw in* [K] **3:7** LXX, Syr read *her eyes*

3:9 The Day of the Lord brings destruction upon the earth, but it will also cleanse and **restore** a remnant from every nation who will worship the Lord in holiness. Their speech will be purified, and they will serve the Lord with a single heart. Some suggest that **pure speech** is meant to be a reversal of the Tower of Babel event (Gn 11:1-9).

3:11-13 The future restoration of God's people is described even in the midst of the devastation prophesied. Pride and boastfulness will be far removed. Only the meek and humble, those who trust fully in the Lord, will remain.

3:14 Daughter (Hb *bat*) is sometimes confirmed with the name of a place as a figure of speech representing the inhabitants of that place (cp. Is 23:10,12; Jr 46:11). Here the word is linked to **Zion**, referring to the people of Jerusalem or the city of David, which was built on Mount Zion. Here (Zph 3:14-20), the messianic age is described as marked by resounding joy and gladness throughout Zion. Judgment and restoration are in the Lord's hands.

8 Therefore, wait for Me—
this is
the LORD's declaration—
until the day I rise up
for plunder.[A]
For My decision is
to gather nations,
to assemble kingdoms,
in order to pour out
My indignation on them,
all My burning anger;
for the whole earth
will be consumed
by the fire of My jealousy.

The Promise of Restoration (3:9-20)

The Worshiping Nations (3:9-10)

9 For I will then restore
pure speech to the peoples
so that all of them may call
on the name of Yahweh
and serve Him
with a single purpose.[B]
10 From beyond the rivers
of •Cush
My supplicants,
My dispersed people,
will bring an offering to Me.

The Faithful Remnant (3:11-20)

11 On that day you[C] will not
be put to shame
because of everything
you have done
in rebelling against Me.
For then I will remove
your proud, arrogant people
from among you,
and you will never again
be haughty
on My holy mountain.
12 I will leave
a meek and humble people
among you,
and they will take refuge
in the name of Yahweh.
13 The remnant of Israel will
no longer
do wrong or tell lies;
a deceitful tongue will not
be found
in their mouths.
But they will pasture
and lie down,
with nothing to make
them afraid.
14 Sing for joy, Daughter •Zion;
shout loudly, Israel!
Be glad and rejoice with all
your heart,
Daughter Jerusalem!
15 The LORD has removed
your punishment;
He has turned back
your enemy.
The King of Israel, Yahweh,
is among you;
you need no longer fear harm.
16 On that day it will be said
to Jerusalem:
"Do not fear;
Zion, do not let your hands
grow weak.
17 Yahweh your God
is among you,
a warrior who saves.
He will rejoice over you
with gladness.
He will bring you quietness[D]
with His love.
He will delight in you
with shouts of joy."
18 I will gather those
who have been driven
from the appointed festivals;
they will be a tribute
from you[E]
and a reproach on her.[F]

[A]**3:8** LXX, Syr read *for a witness*; Vg reads *up forever* [B]**3:9** Lit *with one shoulder* [C]**3:11** = Israel [D]**3:17** LXX, Syr read *He will renew you* [E]**3:18** = Jerusalem [F]**3:18** Hb obscure

19 Yes, at that time
I will deal with all
who afflict you.
I will save the lame
and gather the scattered;
I will make those
who were disgraced
throughout the earth
receive praise and fame.

20 At that time I will bring
you[A] back,
yes, at the time
I will gather you.
I will give you fame and praise
among all the peoples
of the earth,
when I restore your fortunes
before your eyes.
Yahweh has spoken.

3:18-20 I will bring you back are words of promise referring to the remnant whom God would bring back to Jerusalem from Babylon after 70 years of exile. This return began when Cyrus issued his decree in 538 B.C. That glorious return to the land was promised to God's people in fulfillment of Zephaniah's prophecy, foreshadowing God's final redemption of His creation. This promise is sealed by words with divine authority—**Yahweh has spoken**.

[A] **3:20** = people of Israel

ZEPHANIAH… WRITTEN ON MY *Heart*

The people of Judah had been in the miry pit of spiritual destitution and apathy for years. Just as Zephaniah's call to repent was meant to save them from the Lord's great wrath, so, too, the call of repentance echoes true today. The Lord is calling for you to **seek** after Him for He will be found (2:3). When you turn to Jesus, He promises full restoration. Whether you are coming to Jesus out of lostness and a life of sin or returning to Jesus after a period of neglect, He waits with open arms to forgive you and give you life abundantly.

Haggai

Timeline	538 BC	538–457 BC	526 BC	520–518 BC
World Events Biblical Events	Cyrus's decree allowing the Jews to return to Judah and begin rebuilding the temple	Events in Ezra	Opposition, discouragement, and cessation of work on the temple	Challenge from Haggai and Zechariah to resume construction of the temple

"'The final glory of this house will be greater than the first,' says the LORD of Hosts. 'I will provide peace in this place'—this is the declaration of the LORD of Hosts" (2:9).

Who wrote Haggai?

The prophet Haggai (1:1,13)

Who were the recipients?

The recipients for Haggai's four messages are plainly stated in the text. He addresses Zerubbabel, the governor of Judah; Joshua, the high priest; and the "remnant" or returned exiles in Israel.

Where did it happen?

Haggai takes place in Jerusalem. In 538 B.C., King Cyrus of Persia allowed any Jewish person in his kingdom to return to Jerusalem to help rebuild the temple. In 537 B.C., the first group of exiles, numbering close to 50,000 (see Ezr 1–4), arrived in Jerusalem. In 536 B.C., the foundation of the temple was laid, but the work ceased until Haggai called them back to the task at hand.

When was Haggai written?

ca 520 B.C.

What is Haggai about?

- *God as the LORD of Hosts*. God's power is over all things on earth and in heaven.
- *The rebuilding of the temple*. The temple lay in ruins and Haggai's message was for God's people to remember the things of God.

Why should women read Haggai?

Haggai reminds women that the material and spiritual cannot be totally separated. Often the material things of life are revelatory of one's spiritual life. The remnant's indifference toward God's house lying in ruins revealed that their hearts were far from Him. Enemies and everyday life had distracted God's people from what He had called them to do. Haggai delivered God's message to God's people in God's time about the things of God.

How do you read Haggai?

This brief book with only 38 verses is included in the postexilic books, one of the 12 books identified as the Minor Prophets. The recipients for Haggai's four messages are plainly stated in the text. He addresses Zerubbabel, the governor of Judah; Joshua, the high priest; and the "remnant" or returned exiles in Judah. As the Israelites began to rebuild, they faced opposition from their enemies in the surrounding lands. The Jewish remnant became discouraged and left the work God called them to do and concentrated on building their own houses. Sixteen years later in 520 B.C., God sent His prophet Haggai to call His people back to the task, and over a four-month period Haggai delivered four messages to the people calling them to consider their ways, be convicted of their sins, be encouraged by God's faithfulness, and be assured of God's promised blessing (see Ezr 5–6).

Outline

I. The First Message: Rebuild the Temple (1:1-15)
   A. Haggai's Challenge (1:1-11)
   B. The People's Response (1:12-15)

II. The Second Message: Encouragement and Promise (2:1-9)

III. The Third Message: From Defilement to Blessing (2:10-19)

IV. The Fourth Message: Promise to Zerubbabel (2:20-23)

August 29, 520 BC	October 17,520 BC	December 18, 520 BC	March 12, 515 BC	445 BC
Haggai's first message	Haggai's second message	Haggai's third and fourth messages	Completion of the temple	Completion of the walls of Jerusalem under Nehemiah's leadership

The First Message: Rebuild the Temple (1:1-15)

Haggai's Challenge (1:1-11)

1 In the second year of King Darius,[A] on the first day of the sixth month, the word of the LORD came through Haggai the prophet to Zerubbabel son of Shealtiel, the governor of Judah, and to Joshua son of Jehozadak, the high priest: 2 "The LORD of •Hosts says this: These people say: The time has not come for the house of the LORD to be rebuilt."

3 The word of the LORD came through Haggai the prophet: 4 "Is it a time for you yourselves to live in your paneled houses, while this house[B] lies in ruins?" 5 Now, the LORD of Hosts says this: "Think carefully about[C] your ways:

6 You have planted much
but harvested little.
You eat
but never have enough
to be satisfied.
You drink
but never have enough
to become drunk.
You put on clothes
but never have enough
to get warm.
The wage earner
puts his wages
into a bag with a hole in it."

7 The LORD of Hosts says this: "Think carefully about[C] your ways. 8 Go up into the hills, bring down lumber, and build the house. Then I will be pleased with it and be glorified," says the LORD. 9 "You expected much, but then it amounted to little. When you brought the harvest to your house, I ruined[D] it. Why?" This is the declaration of the LORD of Hosts. "Because My house still lies in ruins, while each of you is busy with his own house.

10 So on your account,[E]
the skies have withheld
the dew
and the land its crops.
11 I have summoned a drought
on the fields and the hills,
on the grain, new wine,
olive oil,
and whatever
the ground yields,
on man and beast,
and on all that
your hands produce."

The People's Response (1:12-15)

12 Then Zerubbabel son of Shealtiel, the high priest Joshua son of Jehozadak, and the entire remnant of the people obeyed the voice of the LORD their God and the words of the prophet Haggai, because the LORD their God had sent him. So the people •feared the LORD.

13 Haggai, the LORD's messenger, delivered the LORD's message to the people, "I am with you"—this is the LORD's declaration.

14 The LORD stirred up the spirit of Zerubbabel son of Shealtiel, governor of Judah, the spirit of the high priest Joshua son of Jehozadak, and the spirit of all the remnant of the people. They began work on the house of •Yahweh of Hosts, their God, 15 on the twenty-fourth day of the sixth month, in the second year of King Darius.

[A] **1:1** King of Persia reigned 522–486 B.C. [B] **1:4** = the temple [C] **1:5,7** Lit *Place your heart on* [D] **1:9** Lit *blew on* [E] **1:10** Or *So above you*

Title: The book bears the name of its author Haggai (Hb, "feast or festival"), a prophet (Hg 1:1) and the Lord's messenger (Hg 1:13), who ministered for a brief period of four months and then disappeared from recorded biblical history. Consequently, not much is known about this prophet. He was a contemporary of Zechariah (Ezr 5:1; 6:14), though neither prophet mentions the other. Scholars debate whether Haggai was born in Israel and then taken into exile, born in Babylon during the exile, or a resident of Israel who never went into exile. However, Haggai was familiar with the situation in Jerusalem, and God used the prophet to motivate His people to resume the task of rebuilding the temple.

1:1-2 Haggai gives a precise date for his message: **in the second year of King Darius, on the first day of the sixth month**, which would have been about August 29, 520 B.C. The first day of each month was a holy day when people would give a special offering to the Lord at the altar (Nm 28:11-13). Haggai, questioning the people's priorities, begins by addressing the leaders: Zerubbabel, the governor, and Joshua the high priest. They have not only neglected the work of rebuilding the temple but also the task of leading the people. Haggai speaks for the **LORD of Hosts**, a reference to the powerful nature of God, the same God who had protected the Israelites and preserved the remnant, the God whom the Israelites had disobeyed.

1:4 They are living in **paneled houses**, referring to either the roofs or highly decorated walls, while God's house **lies in ruins**.

1:5-11 Haggai outlines the adversities the people had faced as a result of their disobedience. The key phrase **think carefully about your ways** (or "consider," vv. 5,7) is one of Haggai's favorite expressions to urge the Israelites to reflect carefully on their lives and their decisions.

1:12-13 God used Haggai's message to convict the people and cause them to resume the work. Zerubbabel, Joshua, and **the entire remnant** of the people **obeyed the voice of the Lord.** Haggai's reference to the people, once they respond in obedience to God's Word, as the "remnant" is significant. These were those who feared the Lord in the sense that they chose to honor and reverence him. As the people began their work, He encouraged them through Haggai, reassuring them that He was with them.

1:15 There is some question about why the work resumed 23 days (**on the twenty-fourth day of the sixth month**) after the delivery of Haggai's message. While some have suggested that this date is a mistake, one must note that harvesting was done during the sixth month. All able-bodied people would be in the fields to harvest the crops and thus would be unable to work on the temple. However, as soon as the crop was harvested, the people began on the temple.

2:1-4 About a month later, Haggai delivered his second message **on the twenty-first day of the seventh month**, the last day of the Festival of Booths (or Tabernacles), which lasted seven days. The Lord instructed Haggai to ask the people if anyone remembered **its former glory**. The people who remembered the temple knew that the present temple was nothing like Solomon's temple, which had been dedicated 440 years earlier during the Festival of Booths (see 1Kg 8:2). Nevertheless, the Lord encouraged them to **be strong** because God was with them.

2:9 The future promise, which the Lord gave the people through Haggai, is that this temple would be filled with His glory and that **peace** would be provided in this temple.

2:10-14 The third message **on the twenty-fourth day of the ninth month** is an exhortation to holiness. In the first message, God encouraged the people to consider their ways and resume their work. In the second, He urged them to be strong; in this third message, God addressed purity and impurity. God asked a series of questions to show that holiness cannot be caught or transmitted by touch.

2:15-18 Haggai asked the people several times to **reflect** and **consider carefully** the fact that their disobedience made them unclean before the Lord, and he explained why they did not immediately receive blessings once they returned to the Lord's work. The Lord would bless them from this day forward because the punishment had made its point, but Haggai did not want them to forget that their previous disobedience did

The Second Message: Encouragement and Promise (2:1-9)

2 On the twenty-first day of the seventh month, the word of the LORD came through Haggai the prophet: 2 "Speak to Zerubbabel son of Shealtiel, governor of Judah, to the high priest Joshua son of Jehozadak, and to the remnant of the people: 3 Who is left among you who saw this house in its former glory? How does it look to you now? Doesn't it seem like nothing to you?[A] 4 Even so, be strong, Zerubbabel"—this is the LORD's declaration. "Be strong, Joshua son of Jehozadak, high priest. Be strong, all you people of the land"—this is the LORD's declaration. "Work! For I am with you"—the declaration of the LORD of •Hosts. 5 "This is the promise I made to you when you came out of Egypt, and My Spirit is present among you; don't be afraid."

6 For the LORD of Hosts says this: "Once more, in a little while, I am going to shake the heavens and the earth, the sea and the dry land. 7 I will shake all the nations so that the treasures of all the nations will come, and I will fill this house with glory," says the LORD of Hosts. 8 "The silver and gold belong to Me"—this is the declaration of the LORD of Hosts. 9 "The final glory of this house[B] will be greater than the first," says the LORD of Hosts. "I will provide peace in this place"—this is the declaration of the LORD of Hosts.

The Third Message: From Defilement to Blessing (2:10-19)

10 On the twenty-fourth day of the ninth month, in the second year of Darius, the word of the LORD came to Haggai the prophet: 11 "This is what the LORD of Hosts says: Ask the priests for a ruling. 12 If a man is carrying consecrated meat in the fold of his garment, and it touches bread, stew, wine, oil, or any other food, does it become holy?"

The priests answered, "No."

13 Then Haggai asked, "If someone defiled by contact with a corpse touches any of these, does it become defiled?"

The priests answered, "It becomes defiled."

14 Then Haggai replied, "So is this people, and so is this nation before Me"—this is the LORD's declaration. "And so is every work of their hands; even what they offer there is defiled.

15 "Now, reflect back from this day: Before one stone was placed on another in the LORD's temple, 16 what state were you in?[C] When someone came to a grain heap of 20 measures, it only amounted to 10; when one came to the winepress to dip 50 measures from the vat, it only amounted to 20. 17 I struck you—all the work of your hands—with blight, mildew, and hail, but you didn't turn to Me"—this is the LORD's declaration. 18 "Consider carefully from this day forward; from the twenty-fourth day of the ninth month, from the day the foundation of the LORD's temple was laid; consider it carefully. 19 Is there still seed left in the granary? The vine, the fig, the pomegranate, and the olive tree have not yet produced. But from this day on I will bless you."

The Fourth Message: Promise to Zerubbabel (2:20-23)

20 The word of the LORD came to Haggai a second time on the twenty-fourth day of the month: 21 "Speak to Zerubbabel, governor of Judah: I am going to shake the heavens and the earth. 22 I will overturn royal thrones and destroy the power of the Gentile kingdoms. I will overturn chariots and their riders. Horses and their riders will fall, each by his brother's sword. 23 On that day"—this is the declaration of the LORD of Hosts—"I will take you, Zerubbabel son of Shealtiel, My servant"—this is the LORD's declaration—"and make you like My signet ring, for I have chosen you." This is the declaration of the LORD of Hosts.

[A]2:3 Lit *Is it not in your eyes?* [B]2:9 Or *The glory of this latter house* [C]2:16 Hb obscure

HAGGAI ... WRITTEN ON MY *Heart*

The saying, "Good is the enemy of the best," is true. Good things like church or family activities can distract from spiritual priorities such as prayer and devotional time. Just as the Israelites were busy about their lives while God's temple lay in ruins, you can miss God's vision for your life. Haggai told the Israelites to refocus their eyes on the Lord. Taking your eyes off the Lord even for a second can mean choosing a good but, in the end, vain path. When you stay attentive to the Lord, He gives you clear vision and the best and most meaningful work.

>WORD|*study*

2:23 The Hebrew word for signet ring (*chotam*, "seal, seal-ring"; cp. Sg 8:6) comes from the verb *chatam* (Hb, "seal, shut, complete"). For example, the unique image impressed on clay or wax signified, for example, that a document had been officially authorized or written by the king himself. The book of Esther notes the importance of the Persian king's signet ring, which gave Haman authority to draft a document that, once sealed, would bear the irreversible authority of the king (Est 3:10-12; cp. Rv 5:1-9). As the king later explained, when extending the same authority to Mordecai (who sought to rectify what Haman had done in the king's name, Est 8:2,10): "A document written in the king's name and sealed with the royal signet ring cannot be revoked" (Est 8:8). Also, when Daniel was thrown into the lions' den, "A stone was brought and placed over the mouth of the den. The king sealed it with his own signet ring and with the signet rings of his nobles, so that nothing in regard to Daniel could be changed" (Dn 6:17; cp. Mt 27:66; Rv 20:3). Significantly, the Lord *chose* (Hb *bachar*, "select as approved or as having been examined and proved to be excellent, take delight in"; cp. Ex 18:25; Dt 4:37; 1Kg 8:16; Lk 9:35) Zerubbabel and *made* (Hb *sum*, "put, place") him like His signet ring. Only in God's service, at God's command, did Zerubbabel lead with authority.

have consequences. God has control over every aspect of life, and He had caused them to have difficulty with their crops because of their sinfulness.

2:20-23 The final message took place on the same day as the third message and was specifically addressed to Zerubbabel. The purpose of this message was to proclaim God's intention to raise up a leader for His people. **Zerubbabel**, a descendant of the Davidic line, was a type of the Lord Jesus Christ, and the fact that Zerubbabel, and not Joshua, is addressed suggests that this message has royal implications. God would overthrow the rulers of the nations and turn them against one another. Once that happened, Zerubbabel, called **My servant**, a title that is often messianic in the Old Testament (see 1Kg 11:34; Ezk 34:23-24), would become like a **signet ring**.

A signet ring was used to designate royal authority, and Zerubbabel's grandfather Jehoiachin was also called God's signet ring (Jr 22:24-25); yet he was removed by Nebuchadnezzar when he went into exile. However, God had placed Zerubbabel back on His hand figuratively; and Zerubbabel, as a descendant of David, served as a symbol of God's authority. Whereas the promises to David, of an eternal dynasty and kingship over Israel, had seemed to be broken through the exile, God proclaimed His faithfulness through this message to the current member of David's lineage. The victory promised in Hg 2:21-22 would be accomplished through one of Zerubbabel's descendants, the perfect son of David, Jesus Christ (cp. 1Kg 11:34).

Zechariah

Timeline	539 BC	538 BC	536 BC	522–486 BC
➡ World Events ➡ Biblical Events	Cyrus's capture of Babylon	Cyrus's decree allowing the Jews to rebuild the temple in Jerusalem	Start of construction on the temple in Jerusalem	Reign of Darius I

"I will put this third through the fire; I will refine them as silver is refined and test them as gold is tested. They will call on My name, and I will answer them. I will say: They are My people, and they will say: Yahweh is our God" (13:9).

Who wrote Zechariah?

The prophet Zechariah (1:1)

Who were the recipients?

Zechariah spoke to the people who had returned from Babylonian exile to Jerusalem and Judah. About 50,000 people arrived in Jerusalem and the surrounding area in 538–537 B.C.

Where did it happen?

Zechariah's ministry takes place in Judah at the time of the return to Jerusalem by the Babylonian exiles, known as the postexilic period. When the time in exile was complete (Is 40:2), God prompted Cyrus, the king of Persia, to allow Judah to return to the promised land and rebuild the temple of the Lord (Is 44:28). Zechariah's ministry began with Cyrus's capture of Babylon (539 B.C.) and continued through the restoration of the temple. Shortly thereafter, Cyrus allowed Judah to return to the land of Israel and rebuild the temple (2Ch 36:21-23; Ezr 1:1-4; 6:3-5). According to Ezra, the first group of exiles returning to the land laid the foundation of the temple but then encountered many obstacles, which brought construction to a halt.

When was Zechariah written?

520–480 B.C.

What is Zechariah about?

- *The people's need to return to the Lord*. The prophet's eight visions reveal that God was calling His people to return wholeheartedly to Him.
- *The coming of the Messiah*. Zechariah is arguably the most messianic book in the Old Testament.

Why should women read Zechariah?

God does not desire His army of saints to be unprepared or unfit for battle. Obedience to the Lord often comes with opposition from the Devil. Women are not exempt from spiritual warfare—the war over souls. Even in the midst of great hostility, a past fraught with sin and disobedience by Israel's ancestors and a present heavily burdened with oppression, Zechariah's message is one of repentance in the face of the enemy. Zechariah is a reminder that there is great hope in the Lord for those who follow Him, and our ultimate hope is in Christ. There will be victory!

How do you read Zechariah?

Like the books of Daniel, Revelation, and portions of Ezekiel, Zechariah is an example of apocalyptic literature. It communicates revelations through visions or symbols and describes the consummation of history with graphic imagery. Zechariah spoke to the people who had returned from Babylonian exile to Jerusalem and Judah. Through Zechariah, the Lord exhorted the high priest Joshua and the people to be obedient and to complete the temple.

Zechariah's visions have both present and future implications. The book's chiastic structure reveals the central focus of each vision (see "How do you read Ruth?", p. 322 for discussion of chiasm):

(A) Jerusalem is comforted /Anger toward the nations is displayed (1:8-17).
 (B) The enemies of Jerusalem/Judah are judged (1:18-21).
  (C) Jerusalem is restored (2:1-13).
   (D) Joshua foreshadows the high priesthood of Christ, the Branch (3:1-10).
   (D′) The power of the Spirit of the Lord (4:1-14).
  (C′) Sinners are removed from Jerusalem (5:1-4).
 (B′) Wickedness is removed to Babylon (5:5-11).
(A′) The nations are judged, and Jerusalem's rightful King is restored (6:1-15).

The book, which many falsely believe is too difficult to understand, is essentially one of encouragement regarding God's final victory over the forces of darkness and evil in this world. The Gospel writers quoted from the book of Zechariah more than from any other book of the Minor Prophets because Zechariah foretold the ultimate triumph of the Messiah. Chapters 1–8 address how Israel will return to her God, and chapters 9–14 reflect how God will return to Israel, penultimately in Christ and ultimately in the eschaton. The book demonstrates that the Lord remembers His covenant promises to Israel and works to fulfill them.

Outline

I. Visions in the Night (1:1–6:15)
  A. A Call to Repentance (1:1-6)
  B. Eight Visions (1:7–6:15)
    1. The First Vision: Horsemen (1:7-17)
    2. The Second Vision: Four Horns and Craftsmen (1:18-21)
    3. The Third Vision: Surveyor (2:1-13)
    4. The Fourth Vision: High Priest and Branch (3:1-10)
    5. The Fifth Vision: Gold Lampstand (4:1-14)
    6. The Sixth Vision: Flying Scroll (5:1-4)
    7. The Seventh Vision: Woman in the Basket (5:5-11)
    8. The Eighth Vision: Four Chariots (6:1-15)

II. Covenant Expectations and Blessing (7:1–8:23)
  A. A Question About Fasting (7:1-3)
  B. A Perspective of the Past and the Future (7:4–8:23)

October/November, 520 BC	*February 15, 519 BC*	*December 7, 518 BC*	*March 12, 515 BC*	*445 BC*
Zechariah's first prophetic message	Zechariah's night visions	Zechariah's message on fasting	Completion of the temple	Reconstruction of Jerusalem's walls under Nehemiah's leadership

Outline (continued)

III. The Coming of the Messiah (9:1–11:17)
- A. Judgment on Zion's Enemies (9:1-8)
- B. The Coming of Zion's King (9:9-17)
- C. The LORD Restores His People (10:1-12)
- D. Israel's Shepherds: Good and Bad (11:1-17)

IV. The Return of the Messiah (12:1–14:21)
- A. Judah's Security (12:1-9)
- B. Mourning for the Pierced One (12:10-14)
- C. The Cleansing of God's People (13:1-9)
- D. The Establishment of the LORD's Kingdom(14:1-21)

A Call to Repentance (1:1-6)

1 In the eighth month, in the
second year of Darius, the word
of the LORD came to the prophet
Zechariah son of Berechiah, son
of Iddo: 2 "The LORD was extremely
angry with your ancestors. 3 So tell
the people: This is what the LORD of
•Hosts says: Return to Me"—this
is the declaration of the LORD of
Hosts—"and I will return to you,
says the LORD of Hosts. 4 Do not
be like your ancestors; the earlier
prophets proclaimed to them: This
is what the LORD of Hosts says: Turn
from your evil ways and your evil
deeds. But they did not listen or pay
attention to Me"—this is the LORD's
declaration. 5 "Where are your ancestors now? And do the prophets
live forever? 6 But didn't My words
and My statutes that I commanded
My servants the prophets overtake
your ancestors? They repented and
said: As the LORD of Hosts purposed
to deal with us for our ways and
deeds, so He has dealt with us."

Eight Visions (1:7–6:15)

The First Vision: Horsemen (1:7-17)

7 On the twenty-fourth day of the
eleventh month, which is the month
of Shebat, in the second year of Darius, the word of the LORD came to the
prophet Zechariah son of Berechiah,
son of Iddo:
8 I looked out in the night and saw
a man riding on a red horse. He was
standing among the myrtle trees
in the valley. Behind him were red,
sorrel, and white horses. 9 I asked,
"What are these, my lord?"

The angel who was talking to me

Title: The book is named for its author Zechariah (Hb, "the Lord remembers").

1:1-6 Zechariah records a date for many of his prophecies. Reference to **the eighth month** (*Marcheshvan* on "Jewish Calendar," p. 618) places them in relationship to those of Haggai (Hg 1:1,15; 2:1,10,20). **In the second year of Darius** (520 B.C.—see Timeline), God spoke through Zechariah to the Jews who were rebuilding the temple. The first temple had been completed "in the eighth month" of the eleventh year of King Solomon's reign (1Kg 6:38). God warned His people not to be like their **ancestors** (Hb *'av*, "father"; cp. 8:14), who had followed Jeroboam's plan of worshiping idols in Bethel and Dan rather than the Lord at the temple in Jerusalem (1Kg 12:26-30). Jeroboam had also substituted a religious feast for the Festival of Booths observed in the seventh month (1Kg 12:32-33; cp. Lv 23:34; Neh 8:14; Zch 14:16-19).

1:8-17 The key figure in Zechariah's first vision was **a man riding on a**

>WORD|*study*

1:2 Extremely angry (cp. "fiercely angry," v. 15; "provoked . . . to anger," 8:14) captures the emphasis of the Hebrew sentence, which begins with the verb (Hb *qatsaph*, "break out, break forth" into anger)—"he was angry"—and ends with its nominal form (Hb *qetseph*, "anger"; cp. 7:12). Use of either the noun or verb typically conveys a level of anger that moves someone to action. Such anger cannot be contained as an emotion or expressed only in words. Therefore, the word is used of God's wrath, particularly when He inflicts punishment or is likely to demonstrate His anger in acts of judgment (e.g., Nm 16:46; Jos 22:20; 2Ch 24:18; 32:25-26; Ps 38:1; Is 34:2). Even though in the Old Testament these two forms of the word (i.e., the verb with its "cognate" as an object) appear together only in Zch 1:2 and 15, God's disposition toward Israel's **ancestors** was the result of the nation's apostasy as predicted in Dt 29:24-28.

1:3 The command to **return** (Hb *shuv*) conveys what happens when people repent. They stop walking away from the Lord and "turn around." Abandoning their disobedient and rebellious way of life, they receive God's grace and embrace His standards of holiness. The Lord's promise to "return" (Hb *shuv*) recognizes that God, who is holy, turns His back on sin but longs for restored fellowship with those who will do the same. Therefore, He had told His people through "the earlier prophets" to "turn (Hb *shuv*) from [their] evil ways and . . . evil deeds" (cp. 2Kg 17:13; Jr 18:11; 25:5; 35:15; Ezk 33:11). These "ancestors" had "repented" (Hb *shuv*, Zch 1:6) but not in time to escape His judgment (see Ezr 9:1-10:17; Dn 9:1-19).

1:6 The verb **overtake** (Hb *nasag*, "reach, attain"; cp. Gn 44:4; Ex 14:9) vividly depicts the covenant promises of the eternal God pursuing or chasing down His people as they tried to get away from Him and go their own way. God had done what He had **purposed** (Hb *zamam*, "have in mind," Zch 1:6; cp. 8:14-15) to do in the description of the blessings (Dt 28:2) and curses (Dt 28:15,45), which would "overtake" His people according to their faithfulness or unfaithfulness to the covenant (cp. Jr 4:28; 51:12; Lm 2:17).

red horse, who seems to be the same **man** as the one **standing among the myrtle trees**. If so, Zechariah saw a figure seated on a horse but not in motion. This "man" seems to be identified in the passage as **the Angel of the Lord** (likely a pre-incarnate appearance of the Son of God, or *theophany*; cp. Gn 16:7-13; Ex 3:1-6; Nm 22:22-23; 1Ch 21:16; Ps 34:7). Zechariah apparently addressed his question about the other **horses** to this man, but another speaker, whom he consistently calls **the angel who was speaking with me**, answered (cp. Zch 6:4-5). This angel served as a guide and interpreter through the series of visions presented to the prophet that night (cp. 1:19; 2:3; 4:1; 5:5; 6:4-5).

In the vision, the horses' report implies an absence of war or rebellion. Perhaps voicing the question of the people who knew the exile would be limited to **70 years** (Jr 25:11-12; Dn 9:2), "the Angel of the Lord" asked the **Lord of Hosts** a question implicitly reflecting a desperate hope for reconciliation with Yahweh.

The Lord described His disposition toward **Jerusalem and Zion** in the present tense—He is **extremely jealous** for His people—and, in present tense, the Lord declared that He is **fiercely angry with the nations that are at ease** (Hb *sha'anan*, having a negative sense here, "careless, proud, arrogant"; cp. Ps 123:4; Is 32:9,11; Am 6:1) with an anger that had intensified as they continually refused His lordship and oppressed His people (Zch 1:5). Because the Lord said so, He **in mercy** [Hb *be-rachamim* (plural; cp. v. 12), "with compassions or mercies"] **returned** (Hb *shuv*; see **Word Study**, 1:3, p. 1217) to Jerusalem and made sure that the temple would be rebuilt there.

1:18-21 The vision shows how God will punish the nations—symbolized by **four horns**—that had **scattered** [Hb *zarah*, "disperse, spread out"; cp. Lv 26:33; 1 Kg 14:15; Ps 44:11; Ezk 22:15] **Judah, Israel, and Jerusalem**. The four nations represented may be Babylon, Medo-Persia, Greece, and Rome. The **four craftsmen** seem to represent the nations God had used in the past to overthrow Israel's enemies, who—past, present, and future—will ultimately be defeated.

2:1-13 A third vision depicts the growth and prosperity of **Jerusalem**, extending into the messianic period.

3:1-2 The vision of **Joshua the high priest**—"Jeshua" in Ezr 3:2—clearly differs from the others in that Zechariah does not report asking any questions or the angel's providing any explanations. Either the angel or the Lord Himself presented this vision to Zechariah. The rhetorical question included in the

>WORD | *study*

1:10 The form of the verb patrol (Hb *halak*, "walk, go") suggests "walk to and fro, walk around, go about." In Zechariah's eighth vision, also, the prophet saw horses about which he asked the angel the same question and received a similar explanation—under the Lord's sovereign command "they patrolled the earth" (see 6:1-7). The appearance of the same form of the verb in Job 1:6-7 (see **Word Study**, p. 622) and 2:2, in which Satan described his activities as "walking around on" the earth, invites a contrast between the divine assignment of the horses in Zechariah's visions and Satan's personal surveillance of the earth as though it were his domain. Although both answered to the Lord (cp. Zch 6:5,7; Jb 1:6-12; 2:1-8), the horses **sent** by the Lord represent, in military terms, His supremacy over all creation.

1:17 Four times in this verse a word is used suggesting the extravagance of God's restoration. Zechariah is told to deliver a message that further (Hb *'owd*, "more") extended the Lord's promise of grace. Again (Hb *'owd*), once more (Hb *'owd*), the Lord would make His own **cities** prosper, **comfort Zion** (cp. Is 40:1; 51:3) and **choose** [Hb *bachar*, "select, approve, delight in"; cp. 2:12; 3:2; Dt 16:6] **Jerusalem**."

replied, "I will show you what they
are."
10 Then the man standing among
the myrtle trees explained, "They
are the ones the LORD has sent to patrol the earth."
11 They reported to the Angel of
the LORD standing among the myrtle
trees, "We have patrolled the earth,
and right now the whole earth is
calm and quiet."
12 Then the Angel of the LORD responded, "How long, LORD of Hosts,
will You withhold mercy from Jerusalem and the cities of Judah that
You have been angry with these 70
years?" 13 The LORD replied with kind
and comforting words to the angel
who was speaking with me.
14 So the angel who was speaking
with me said, "Proclaim: The LORD of
Hosts says: I am extremely jealous for
Jerusalem and •Zion. 15 I am fiercely
angry with the nations that are at
ease, for I was a little angry, but they
made it worse. 16 Therefore, this is
what the LORD says: In mercy, I have
returned to Jerusalem; My house will
be rebuilt within it"—this is the declaration of the LORD of Hosts—"and a
measuring line will be stretched out
over Jerusalem.
17 "Proclaim further: This is what
the LORD of Hosts says: My cities will
again overflow with prosperity; the
LORD will once more comfort Zion
and again choose Jerusalem."

The Second Vision: Four Horns and Craftsmen (1:18-21)

18[A] Then I looked up and saw four
•horns. 19 So I asked the angel who was
speaking with me, "What are these?"
And he said to me, "These are the
horns that scattered Judah, Israel,
and Jerusalem."
20 Then the LORD showed me four
craftsmen. 21 I asked, "What are they
coming to do?"
He replied, "These are the horns
that scattered Judah so no one could
raise his head. These craftsmen have
come to terrify them, to cut off the
horns of the nations that raised
their horns against the land of Judah to scatter it."

The Third Vision: Surveyor (2:1-13)

2[B] I looked up and saw a man with
a measuring line in his hand. 2 I
asked, "Where are you going?"
He answered me, "To measure Jerusalem to determine its width and
length."
3 Then the angel who was speaking
with me went out, and another angel went out to meet him. 4 He said
to him, "Run and tell this young
man: Jerusalem will be inhabited
without walls because of the number of people and livestock in it."
5 The declaration of the LORD: "I will
be a wall of fire around it, and I will
be the glory within it."
6 "Get up! Leave the land of the
north"—this is the LORD's declaration—"for I have scattered you like
the four winds of heaven"—this is
the LORD's declaration. 7 "Go, •Zion!
Escape, you who are living with
Daughter Babylon." 8 For the LORD
of •Hosts says this: "He has sent Me[C]
for His glory against the nations
who are plundering you, for anyone
who touches you touches the pu-
pil[D] of His[E] eye. 9 I will move against
them with My[F] power, and they will
become plunder for their own ser-

[A] **1:18** Zch 2:1 in Hb [B] **2:1** Zch 2:5 in Hb [C] **2:8** Or *me* [D] **2:8** Or *apple* [E] **2:8** Ancient Jewish tradition reads *My* [F] **2:9** Or *my*

vants. Then you will know that the LORD of Hosts has sent Me.[A]

10 "Daughter Zion, shout for joy and be glad, for I am coming to dwell among you"—this is the LORD's declaration. 11 "Many nations will join themselves to the LORD on that day and become My[B] people. I will dwell among you, and you will know that the LORD of Hosts has sent Me[A] to you. 12 The LORD will take possession of Judah as His portion in the Holy Land, and He will once again choose Jerusalem. 13 Let all people be silent before the LORD, for He is coming from His holy dwelling."

The Fourth Vision: High Priest and Branch (3:1-10)

3 Then he showed me Joshua the high priest standing before the Angel of the LORD, with Satan[C] standing at his right side to accuse him. 2 The LORD[D] said to Satan: "The LORD rebuke you, Satan! May the LORD who has chosen Jerusalem rebuke you! Isn't this man a burning stick snatched from the fire?"

3 Now Joshua was dressed with filthy[E] clothes as he stood before the Angel. 4 So the Angel of the LORD[F] spoke to those[G] standing before Him, "Take off his filthy clothes!" Then He said to him, "See, I have removed your •guilt from you, and I will clothe you with splendid robes."

5 Then I said, "Let them put a •clean turban on his head." So a clean turban was placed on his head, and they clothed him in garments while the Angel of the LORD was standing nearby.

6 Then the Angel of the LORD charged Joshua: 7 "This is what the LORD of •Hosts says: If you walk in My ways and keep My instructions, you will both rule My house and take care of My courts; I will also grant you access among these who are standing here.

8 "Listen, Joshua the high priest, you and your colleagues sitting before you; indeed, these men are a sign that I am about to bring My servant, the Branch. 9 Notice the stone I have set before Joshua; on that one stone are seven eyes. I will engrave an inscription on it"—this is the declaration of the LORD of Hosts—"and I will take away the guilt of this land in a single day. 10 On that day, each of you will invite his neighbor to sit under his vine and fig tree." This is the declaration of the LORD of Hosts.

The Fifth Vision: Gold Lampstand (4:1-14)

4 The angel who was speaking with me then returned and roused me as one awakened out of sleep. 2 He asked me, "What do you see?"

I replied, "I see a solid gold lampstand there with a bowl on its top. It has seven lamps on it and seven channels for each of[H] the lamps on its top. 3 There are also two olive trees beside it, one on the right of the bowl and the other on its left."

4 Then I asked the angel who was speaking with me, "What are these, my lord?"

5 "Don't you know what they are?" replied the angel who was speaking with me.

I said, "No, my lord."

6 So he answered me, "This is the word of the LORD to Zerubbabel: 'Not by strength or by might, but by My Spirit,' says the LORD of •Hosts. 7 'What are you, great mountain? Before Zerubbabel you will become a plain. And he will bring out the capstone accompanied by shouts of: Grace, grace to it!'"

8 Then the word of the LORD came to me: 9 "Zerubbabel's hands have laid the foundation of this house, and his hands will complete it. Then you will know that the LORD of Hosts has sent me to you. 10 For who scorns the day of small things? These seven eyes of the LORD, which scan throughout the whole earth, will rejoice when they see the plumb line[I] in Zerubbabel's hand."

11 I asked him, "What are the two olive trees on the right and left of the lampstand?" 12 And I questioned him further, "What are the two olive branches beside the two gold conduits, from which golden oil pours out?"

[A]2:9,11 Or *me* [B]2:11 LXX, Syr read *His* [C]3:1 Or *the adversary* [D]3:2 Syr reads *The Angel of the LORD* [E]3:3 Probably stained with human excrement [F]3:4 Lit *He* [G]3:4 = the angels [H]4:2 Or *seven lips to* [I]4:10 Lit *the tin stone*

LORD's **rebuke** called for the answer that Joshua, representing the postexilic remnant of Israel, could indeed be described as a **burning stick** [Hb *ʾud*, "log, brand, fire-brand"] **snatched from** [Hb *natsal*, "be plucked out or delivered"; see **Word Study**, Ps 7:1-2, p. 672] **the fire**. The metaphor makes sense when read in light of Am 4:11, in which Yahweh compares His punishing "some" of His people to His overthrowing Sodom and Gomorrah and likens this chastened group of Israelites to "a burning stick snatched from a fire," who, nevertheless, "did not return" to Him. In the scene viewed by Zechariah, Joshua represented people who would have been obliterated by their enemies if the Lord, before whom this high priest stood, had not rescued them. Though still "burning"—influenced and afflicted by the dominant pagan culture from which the Lord was removing them—God's people were not subject to Satan's efforts to thwart God's purpose for them.

3:3-5 Zechariah called for a **clean turban** (Hb *tsaniph*; cp. Jb 29:14; Ex 28:39 [*mitsnephet*]; Is 62:3 [*ʿatarah*, "crown"]) as well, indicating that Joshua was likely clothed in the priestly garments designed for service in the official capacity of high priest (cp. Ex 28).

3:6-8 With language similar to the charge to Solomon (from his father David, 1Kg 2:3-4; from the Lord, 1Kg 3:14), the Lord commissioned Joshua the high priest and promised that faithful obedience would be rewarded with authority over both the Lord's **house** (Hb *bayit*; see **Word Study**, p. 377) and **courts** (cp. Ezk 44:15-16; 48:11). **These men** likely represent the priesthood, the purpose and duties of which served as **a sign** of the coming Messiah, whom the Angel of the Lord identified as **My servant** [cp. Jb 1:8-12; Is 41:8-20; Ezk 37:15-28], **the Branch** (Hb *tsemach*, lit "sprout, that which is produced by a living plant"; figuratively "offspring," Zch 3:8). The "Branch" metaphor appears again in the account of the crowning of Joshua (6:9-15) and links both passages with other key messianic texts (Is 4:2; 11:1; Jr 23:5; 33:15).

3:9-10 A single **stone**, engraved by the Lord Himself, was placed where Joshua could see it. Instead of the high priest's bearing the names of the individual tribes of Israel (i.e., symbolically bearing their guilt day after day while continually offering sacrifices to atone for it), this stone is linked to the Lord's announcement that He would get rid of it once and for all—the achievement of Christ's crucifixion (cp. Lv 16:22; Heb 7:26-27; 10:11-12).

4:1-14 This vision encouraged Joshua and Zerubbabel in the work of rebuilding the temple and vindicated them before the community with the assurance that God's Spirit would empower them. The **gold lampstand** represents the idea of testimony, and the **two olive branches** are Joshua and Zerubbabel, who testify to God's power. The **golden oil** represents the Spirit of God. The number seven symbolizes perfection or completion. Just as there was a constant supply of oil without human aid, so Zerubbabel's work would not be completed by human hands but by God's power. The **seven eyes of the LORD** probably suggests that God is all-seeing and all-knowing.

The fourth and fifth visions reveal a time of spiritual renewal for the people of Judah and Jerusalem, which will find its completion in the messianic kingdom. These two visions also make clear that God's work faces opposition from both spiritual and physical enemies whose efforts, nevertheless, will fail.

5:1-4 The themes of spiritual cleansing and renewal are continued in this sixth vision. The land must be purged of its evil. On the **flying scroll** were written the sins of the people living in the land. Because the scroll was open, the sins of the people were not hidden; because the scroll was on the move, the sins were known and read by all. Idolatry was not cited as an offense, as was primarily the case before the exile. Instead, the sins had to do with theft and swearing falsely, both of which encompass violations against the two greatest commandments: loving God and loving others (cp. Dt 6:5; Lv 19:18). In the postexilic period there is a renewed desire to read the Old Testament law, and those who committed such offenses against the law had to be **removed** from the land.

5:5-11 The removal of sin from the land takes on a deeper meaning in the seventh vision. Not only must sinners be removed from the land, but the entire system of sin must be eliminated and brought back to its symbolic place of origin—to Babylon. Babylon, representing the origin and stronghold of sin, is most prominent in Revelation. **Shinar** is another word for Babylonia (cp. Gn 10:10). Zechariah saw **a measuring basket** containing a woman who personified **Wickedness**.

6:1-8 The eighth vision bears many similarities to the first. Though there are some differences between the two visions with regard to the order and color of the horses, the two visions represent the Lord as the One who sovereignly controls the events of history. The nations that had attacked Israel would be overthrown. The **chariots** are instruments of God's judgment on the nations. The **two**

13 Then he inquired of me, "Don't you know what these are?"

"No, my lord," I replied.

14 "These are the two anointed ones,"[A] he said, "who stand by the Lord of the whole earth."

The Sixth Vision: Flying Scroll (5:1-4)

5 I looked up again and saw a flying scroll. 2 "What do you see?" he asked me.

"I see a flying scroll," I replied, "30 feet[B] long and 15 feet[C] wide."

3 Then he said to me, "This is the curse that is going out over the whole land, for every thief will be removed according to what is written on one side, and everyone who swears falsely will be removed according to what is written on the other side. 4 I will send it out,"—this is the declaration of the LORD of •Hosts—"and it will enter the house of the thief and the house of the one who swears falsely by My name. It will stay inside his house and destroy it along with its timbers and stones."

The Seventh Vision: Woman in the Basket (5:5-11)

5 Then the angel who was speaking with me came forward and told me, "Look up and see what this is that is approaching."

6 So I asked, "What is it?"

He responded, "It's a measuring basket[D] that is approaching." And he continued, "This is their iniquity[E] in all the land." 7 Then a lead cover was lifted, and there was a woman sitting inside the basket. 8 "This is Wickedness," he said. He shoved her down into the basket and pushed the lead weight over its opening. 9 Then I looked up and saw two women approaching with the wind in their wings. Their wings were like those of a stork, and they lifted up the basket between earth and sky.

10 So I asked the angel who was speaking with me, "Where are they taking the basket?"

11 "To build a shrine for it in the land of •Shinar," he told me. "When that is ready, the basket will be placed there on its pedestal."

The Eighth Vision: Four Chariots (6:1-15)

6 Then I looked up again and saw four chariots coming from between two mountains. And the mountains were made of bronze. 2 The first chariot had red horses, the second chariot black horses, 3 the third chariot white horses, and the fourth chariot dappled horses—all strong horses. 4 So I inquired of the angel who was speaking with me, "What are these, my lord?"

5 The angel told me, "These are the four spirits[F] of heaven going out after presenting themselves to the Lord of the whole earth. 6 The one with the black horses is going to the land of the north, the white horses are going after them, but the dappled horses are going to the land of the south." 7 As the strong horses went out, they wanted to go patrol the earth, and the LORD said, "Go, patrol the earth." So they patrolled the earth. 8 Then He summoned me saying, "See, those going to the land of the north have pacified My Spirit in the northern land."

9 The word of the LORD came to me: 10 "Take an offering from the exiles, from Heldai, Tobijah, and Jedaiah, who have arrived from Babylon, and go that same day to the house of Josiah son of Zephaniah. 11 Take silver and gold, make crowns and place them on the head of Joshua son of Jehozadak, the high priest. 12 You are to tell him: This is what the LORD

[A] **4:14** = Joshua and Zerubbabel [B] **5:2** Lit *20 cubits* [C] **5:2** Lit *10 cubits* [D] **5:6** Lit *It's an ephah* [E] **5:6** One Hb ms, LXX, Syr; other Hb mss read *eye* [F] **6:5** Or *winds*

>WORD|*study*

5:8 Wickedness (Hb *rish'ah*, "unrighteousness, wicked deed, guilt"; cp. Dt 9:4-5; Pr 11:5; 13:6) denotes religious, moral, and civil evil. It is the opposite of righteousness. Feminists have tried to argue that this imagery somehow portrays the patriarchal, male-dominated approach of the Bible. Even though the Hebrew word is feminine, which may explain why the concept is depicted as a woman in this context, the context does not support the accusation of gender bias in the language of the text.

of •Hosts says: Here is a man whose name is Branch; He will branch out from His place and build the LORD's temple. 13 Yes, He will build the LORD's temple; He will be clothed in splendor and will sit on His throne and rule. There will also be a priest on His throne, and there will be peaceful counsel between the two of them. 14 The crown will reside in the LORD's temple as a memorial to Heldai, Tobijah, Jedaiah, and Hen[A] son of Zephaniah. 15 People who are far off will come and build the LORD's temple, and you will know that the LORD of Hosts has sent Me to you. This will happen when you fully obey the LORD your God."

A Question About Fasting (7:1-3)

7 In the fourth year of King Darius, the word of the LORD came to Zechariah on the fourth day of the ninth month, which is Chislev. 2 Now the people of Bethel had sent Sharezer, Regem-melech, and their men to plead for the LORD's favor 3 by asking the priests who were at the house of the LORD of •Hosts as well as the prophets, "Should we mourn and fast in the fifth month as we have done these many years?"

A Perspective of the Past and the Future (7:4–8:23)

4 Then the word of the LORD of Hosts came to me: 5 "Ask all the people of the land and the priests: When you fasted and lamented in the fifth and in the seventh months for these 70 years, did you really fast for Me? 6 When you eat and drink, don't you eat and drink simply for yourselves? 7 Aren't these the words that the LORD proclaimed through the earlier prophets when Jerusalem was inhabited and secure,[B] along with its surrounding cities, and when the southern region and the Judean foothills were inhabited?"

8 The word of the LORD came to Zechariah: 9 "The LORD of Hosts says this: Make fair decisions. Show faithful love and compassion to one another. 10 Do not oppress the widow or the fatherless, the foreigner or the poor, and do not plot evil in your hearts against one another. 11 But they refused to pay attention and turned a stubborn shoulder; they closed their ears so they could not hear. 12 They made their hearts like a rock so as not to obey the law or the words that the LORD of Hosts had sent by His Spirit through the earlier prophets. Therefore great anger came from the LORD of Hosts. 13 Just as He had called, and they would not listen, so when they called, I would not listen," says the LORD of Hosts. 14 "I scattered them with a windstorm over all the nations that had not known them, and the land was left desolate behind them, with no one coming or going. They turned a pleasant land into a desolation."

8 The word of the LORD of •Hosts came: 2 "The LORD of Hosts says this: I am extremely jealous for •Zion; I am jealous for her with great wrath." 3 The LORD says this: "I will return to Zion and live in Jerusalem. Then Jerusalem will be called the Faithful City, the mountain of the LORD of Hosts, and the Holy Mountain." 4 The LORD of Hosts says this: "Old men and women will again sit along the streets of Jerusalem, each with a staff in hand because of advanced age. 5 The streets of the city will be filled with boys and girls playing in them." 6 The LORD of Hosts says this: "Though it may seem incredible to the remnant of this people in those days, should it also seem incredible to Me?"—this is the declaration of the LORD of Hosts. 7 The LORD of Hosts says this: "I will save My people from the land of the east and the land of the west. 8 I will bring them back to live in Jerusalem. They will be My people, and I will be their faithful and righteous God."

9 The LORD of Hosts says this: "Let your hands be strong, you who now hear these words that the prophets spoke when the foundations were laid for the rebuilding of the temple, the house of the LORD of Hosts. 10 For prior to those days neither man nor beast had wages. There was no safety from the enemy

mountains . . . of bronze are most likely symbolic for Mount Zion and the Mount of Olives with the Kidron Valley lying between them.

The **second chariot** [with] **black horses** (possibly representing death as the outcome of God's judgment), which went **to the land of the north** (likely referring to Babylon), **pacified** (Hb *nuach*, "cause to rest"; figuratively here, "satisfy or accomplish one's wrath"; cp. Ezk 5:13; 16:42) God's **Spirit** there. The divine judgment unleashed upon Judah's captors had accomplished its purpose of satisfying His holy anger against this nation that persisted in paganism and idolatry (cp. Is 13:1–14:23; 21:1-10; 47:1-15).

6:9-15 The reestablishment of a throne in Jerusalem was not intended. Rather Joshua clearly represents the future messianic Priest- King. The **Branch** (i.e., the crowned priest) would build the temple and would supersede and transcend what was accomplished in Zechariah's day (cp. 3:8-10). These two offices—the king and the priest—would come together for the first time in the messianic age. As Priest, He would build the temple; as King, He would rule (cp. Ps 110).

The making of this **crown** and its placement in the **temple**, through which the crown became **a memorial**, were meant to act as a reminder giving to those living in Zechariah's day hope that these things would surely come to pass. The crown's placement on **the high priest** Joshua is meant to dismiss any misunderstanding of the significance made clear by uniting the spiritual (priest) and civil (king) authority in the Messiah, Jesus Christ (cp. Heb 5:5-10; Rv 3:21; 5:9-14; 11:15; 20:4-6). God had not forsaken His covenantal promise that He would dwell with His people. The temple, too, was a form of surety for the Lord's covenant.

7:1-3 The specific date is December 7, 518 B.C., almost two years after the night visions recorded by Zechariah. Zechariah's concern for the spiritual renewal of his community heightens, and he presses home the point that, in light of all the past judgments and future glory, his people must live holy and righteous lives. They were not fulfilling this purpose, so the Lord used an inquiry about fasting as an occasion to make clear His covenantal expectations.

Bethel (Hb, "house of God"), a small town in Israel, may be a reference to the origin of this delegation rather than to a generic location for God's presence since the term is not used that way elsewhere in the Old Testament.

7:4–8:23 Though the people faithfully observed fasts four times a year, God was not happy with mere rituals.

[A] **6:14** Probably Josiah [B] **7:7** Or *prosperous*

He demanded **faithful love** that prompted obedience to His word.

Zechariah helped the people to reflect on whether their fasting and feasting was merely self-focused or done to honor God (cp. Mc 6:8). What ought to have been a time of reflection and repentance of past sins turned into empty ritual. Then Zechariah encouraged the exiles who had returned to the land to live in obedience to the Lord, demonstrating the authority of promised blessings with the use of some variation of the phrase **the Lord of Hosts says this** (Zch 8:1-2,3,4,6,7,9,11,14,18-19,20,23). There is clearly a millennial reminder since until now the Jews had not been regathered from all over the world and restored in righteousness—a magnificent promise reserved for the future when Messiah reigns over the land as the **faithful and righteous God** (8:8). The people who heard this promise ought to live righteously because of future blessings.

8:19 God wanted to change the sorrow of fasting, which had been prompted by their own disobedience and sin, into the **joy** of feasting on His blessings.

9:1-17 Oracle appears as a subheading for chapters 9 and 12 (9:1 and 12:1). These oracles have a wide range of prophecies concerning the Messiah, including the judgments and blessings that will occur with the coming of the Messiah. However, even in the midst of judgment, there is deliverance (9:1-8). As blessings come to Israel (9:9–10:12), so her sorrow increases (11:1-17). When the Messiah comes, amazingly He is rejected. The temple had been rebuilt, and even the formidable Persian Empire had begun to fall.

The judgment in the first oracle covers a broad geographic area, beginning north of Palestine and winding down the coast of Syro-Palestine (cp. Am 1:3-10). **The land of Hadrach** seems to be a reference to a region in Syria near its capital Damascus. The Philistine cities of **Ashkelon**, **Gaza**, **Ekron**, and **Ashdod** were included. The Lord affirmed that He would convert the Philistines. Israel will be spared to behold her Messiah. Alexander the Great is the Lord's instrument of judgment in this oracle. After defeating the Persians, Alexander moved on to Egypt and to Syria. He did not destroy Jerusalem, seemingly because of divine intervention. Intense battle and war are described. Then the people of God are commanded to rejoice and shout for joy at the coming of their King, a specific messianic prophecy. Ultimately, the **prisoners**, remaining exiles in Babylon, would be set free because of the covenant they have with Yahweh God. Jesus referred to Himself as the sacrifice because by the shedding of His blood freedom

for anyone who came or went, for I
turned everyone against his neighbor. 11 But now, I will not treat the
remnant of this people as in the former days"—this is the declaration
of the LORD of Hosts. 12 "For they will
sow in peace: the vine will yield its
fruit, the land will yield its produce,
and the skies will yield their dew. I
will give the remnant of this people
all these things as an inheritance.
13 As you have been a curse among
the nations, house of Judah and
house of Israel, so I will save you,
and you will be a blessing. Don't be
afraid; let your hands be strong."
14 For the LORD of Hosts says this: "As
I resolved to treat you badly when
your fathers provoked Me to anger,
and I did not relent," says the LORD
of Hosts, 15 "so I have resolved again
in these days to do what is good to
Jerusalem and the house of Judah.
Don't be afraid. 16 These are the
things you must do: Speak truth to
one another; make true and sound
decisions within your •gates. 17 Do
not plot evil in your hearts against
your neighbor, and do not love per-
jury, for I hate all this"—this is the
LORD's declaration.

18 Then the word of the LORD of
Hosts came to me: 19 "The LORD
of Hosts says this: The fast of the
fourth month, the fast of the fifth,
the fast of the seventh, and the fast
of the tenth will become times of
joy, gladness, and cheerful festivals
for the house of Judah. Therefore,
love truth and peace." 20 The LORD
of Hosts says this: "Peoples will yet
come, the residents of many cities;
21 the residents of one city will go
to another, saying: Let's go at once
to plead for the LORD's favor and to
seek the LORD of Hosts. I am also
going. 22 Many peoples and strong
nations will come to seek the LORD
of Hosts in Jerusalem and to plead
for the LORD's favor." 23 The LORD of
Hosts says this: "In those days, 10
men from nations of every language
will grab the robe of a Jewish man
tightly, urging: Let us go with you,
for we have heard that God is with
you."

Judgment on Zion's Enemies (9:1-8)

9 An •Oracle

The word of the LORD
is against the land
of Hadrach,
and Damascus is
its resting place—
for the eyes of men
and all the tribes of Israel
are on the LORD[A]—
2 and also against Hamath,
which borders it,
as well as Tyre and Sidon,
though they are very shrewd.
3 Tyre has built herself
a fortress;
she has heaped up silver
like dust
and gold like the dirt
of the streets.
4 Listen! The Lord will
impoverish her
and cast her wealth
into the sea;
she herself will be consumed
by fire.
5 Ashkelon will see it
and be afraid;
Gaza too, and will writhe
in great pain,
as will Ekron, for her hope
will fail.
There will cease to be a king
in Gaza,
and Ashkelon will
become uninhabited.
6 A mongrel people will live
in Ashdod,
and I will destroy the pride
of the Philistines.
7 I will remove the blood
from their mouths
and the detestable things
from between their teeth.
Then they too will become
a remnant for our God;
they will become like a clan
in Judah
and Ekron like the Jebusites.
8 I will set up camp at My house
against an army,[B]
against those who march
back and forth,
and no oppressor will march
against them again,

[A] 9:1 Or *eyes of the LORD are on mankind—* [B] 9:8 Or *house as a guard*

for now I have seen
with My own eyes.

The Coming of Zion's King (9:9-17)

9 Rejoice greatly,
Daughter •Zion!
Shout in triumph,
Daughter Jerusalem!
Look, your King is coming
to you;
He is righteous
and victorious,[A]
humble and riding
on a donkey,
on a colt, the foal of a donkey.
10 I will cut off the chariot
from Ephraim
and the horse
from Jerusalem.
The bow of war
will be removed,
and He will proclaim peace
to the nations.
His dominion will extend
from sea to sea,
from the Euphrates River
to the ends of the earth.
11 As for you,
because of the blood
of your covenant,
I will release your prisoners
from the waterless cistern.
12 Return to a stronghold,
you prisoners who have hope;
today I declare that
I will restore double to you.
13 For I will bend Judah
as My bow;
I will fill that bow
with Ephraim.
I will rouse your sons, Zion,
against your sons, Greece.[B]
I will make you
like a warrior's sword.
14 Then the LORD will appear
over them,
and His arrow will fly
like lightning.
The Lord GOD will sound
the trumpet
and advance
with the southern storms.
15 The LORD of •Hosts will
defend them.
They will consume
and conquer
with slingstones;
they will drink and be rowdy
as if with wine.
They will be as full as
the sprinkling basin,
like those at the corners
of the altar.
16 The LORD their God will
save them on that day
as the flock of His people;
for they are like jewels
in a crown,
sparkling over His land.
17 How lovely and beautiful
they will be!
Grain will make
the young men flourish,
and new wine,
the young women.

The LORD Restores His People (10:1-12)

10 Ask the LORD for rain
in the season of spring rain.
The LORD makes
the rain clouds,
and He will give them
showers of rain
and crops in the field
for everyone.
2 For the idols speak falsehood,
and the diviners see illusions;
they relate empty dreams
and offer empty comfort.
Therefore the people wander
like sheep;
they suffer affliction because
there is no shepherd.
3 My anger burns
against the shepherds,
so I will punish the leaders.[C]
For the LORD of •Hosts
has tended His flock,
the house of Judah;
He will make them
like His majestic steed
in battle.
4 The cornerstone will come
from Judah.[D]
The tent peg will come
from them
and also the battle bow and
every[E] ruler.
Together 5 they will be
like warriors in battle

would be possible for all who would come to Him in faith (Mk 14:24).

After announcing the coming of the King, Zechariah goes on to describe the Messiah's triumphant entry into Jerusalem (cp. Mt 21:1-5; Jn 12:12-16). He is righteous and humble, and He will proclaim peace to all nations. His crucifixion is not explicitly referenced here, but His resurrection is assumed in what follows. Before His reign of peace can begin, He must destroy all His enemies. The Lord will strengthen the hands of both Judah and Ephraim (the northern kingdom), and they will conquer their enemies. God's people will ultimately defeat their enemies by the power of the Lord (cp. Rv 20:1-6).

10:1-12 Zechariah warned Israel's leaders about their idolatry, while encouraging the people. The worship of **idols** (Hb *teraphim*, "statuette, mask"; revered and used as gods within the household) by the Israelites had led to the Babylonian captivity. The **shepherds** and **leaders** were symbolic of the rulers of the pagan nations that oppressed Israel (cp. Ezk 34). The Lord promises to make His people invincible and to unify His nation. God's people are successful despite overwhelming odds against them. While undoubtedly partial fulfillment may have been achieved in the Maccabean period, the ultimate fulfillment of this promise is messianic and for the future. The prophet continued this messianic hope with his description of steadfast strength as **the cornerstone . . . the tent peg . . . the battle bow** in the hands of a warrior. The promise is for a final regathering before the messianic kingdom is established (cp. Is 11:11-16).

[A]9:9 Or *and has salvation* [B]9:13 Lit *Javan* [C]10:3 Lit *male goats* [D]10:4 Lit *them* [E]10:4 Lit *also from them the . . . , from them every*

11:1-17 Verses 1-3, which are a lament and unlike the prose in the remainder of the chapter, concern the devastation coming to Israel in A.D. 70—an event recorded by Josephus as the Roman siege in which more than one million Jews lost their lives in the midst of the destruction of Jerusalem. This destruction came because Israel rejected the Good Shepherd despite His tender care for a rebellious **flock intended for slaughter**.

The rejection of the Messiah was the reason for Israel's judgment. Zechariah was instructed by the Lord to act the part of the good shepherd over the flock of Israel. The result of the people's rejection of the Messiah is symbolized by the breaking of the staffs called **Favor** (Hb *no'am* as in the name Naomi, "kindness, favor, delightfulness, pleasantness"; cp. Ru 1:2) and **Union** (Hb *chabal*, the participial form denoting "a tying or binding together," thus "cord, harmony"). The Messiah would reign in a way pleasant to Israel, and He would bind them together.

Zechariah explained that breaking the first staff signified God's **annulling the covenant . . . with all the peoples**. The breaking of the **second staff** signified the division between Judah and Israel. These disobedient people who had suffered under bad leaders then rejected all godly leaders. The utter rejection of the Good Shepherd is dramatically demonstrated with a request for severance pay, to which Israel responded by offering **30 pieces of silver**. This amount offered for a slave in ancient Israel, is meant to show the disdain Israel had for their Good Shepherd (Ex 21:32).

The Gospel of Matthew refers to this scene, describing its literal fulfillment in the condemnation of Jesus (Mt 26:14-15; 27:3-10). There are some textual differences between the accounts of Zechariah and Matthew, likely because Matthew combined the prophecies in Jr 32:6-9 and Zch 11:12-13. He mentioned only the account from Jeremiah, perhaps because Jeremiah was the more prominent prophet and better known than Zechariah.

12:1-9 The **oracle** announces Israel's triumph over the surrounding nations. Rather than "Judah" or "Jerusalem," the prophet references **Israel** in his introductory statement. Nevertheless, Jerusalem is clearly the focal point.

The oracle begins with a description of the Lord's sovereign reign over the created universe, giving Him the power and authority to carry out what is detailed in the rest of the oracle. Though every nation will gather to suck the life out of Jerusalem, the tiny nation will be strong in that day because the Lord will protect her. **A**

trampling down the mud
of the streets.
They will fight because
the LORD is with them,
and they will put horsemen
to shame.
6 I will strengthen the house
of Judah
and deliver the house
of Joseph.[A]
I will restore[B] them
because I have compassion
on them,
and they will be
as though I had never
rejected them.
For I am •Yahweh their God,
and I will answer them.
7 Ephraim will be like a warrior,
and their hearts will be glad
as if with wine.
Their children will see it
and be glad;
their hearts will rejoice
in Yahweh.
8 I will whistle and gather them
because I have
redeemed them;
they will be as numerous as
they once were.
9 Though I sow them
among the nations,
they will remember Me
in the distant lands;
they and their children
will live and return.
10 I will bring them back
from the land of Egypt
and gather them from Assyria.
I will bring them to the land
of Gilead
and to Lebanon,
but it will not be enough
for them.
11 Yahweh[C] will pass through
the sea of distress
and strike the waves
of the sea;
all the depths of the Nile
will dry up.
The pride of Assyria will be
brought down,
and the scepter of Egypt
will come to an end.
12 I will strengthen them
in Yahweh,
and they will march
in His name—
this is
Yahweh's declaration.

Israel's Shepherds: Good and Bad (11:1-17)

11 Open your gates, Lebanon,
and fire will consume
your cedars.
2 Wail, cypress, for the cedar
has fallen;
the glorious trees
are destroyed!
Wail, oaks of Bashan,
for the stately forest
has fallen!
3 Listen to the wail
of the shepherds,
for their glory is destroyed.
Listen to the roar
of young lions,
for the thickets of the Jordan
are[D] destroyed.

4 •Yahweh my God says this: "Shepherd the flock intended for slaughter.
5 Those who buy them slaughter them
but are not punished. Those who sell
them say: Praise the LORD because I
have become rich! Even their own
shepherds have no compassion for
them. 6 Indeed, I will no longer have
compassion on the inhabitants of the
land"—this is the LORD's declaration.
"Instead, I will turn everyone over to
his neighbor and his king. They will
devastate the land, and I will not deliver it from them."
7 So I shepherded the flock intended for slaughter, the afflicted
of the flock.[E] I took two staffs, calling one Favor and the other Union,
and I shepherded the flock. 8 In one
month I got rid of three shepherds.
I became impatient with them, and
they also detested me. 9 Then I said,
"I will no longer shepherd you. Let
what is dying die, and let what is
going astray go astray; let the rest
devour each other's flesh." 10 Next I
took my staff called Favor and cut it
in two, annulling the covenant I had
made with all the peoples. 11 It was
annulled on that day, and so the afflicted of the flock[F] who were watching me knew that it was the word of

[A]**10:6** = the northern kingdom [B]**10:6** Other Hb mss, LXX read *settle* [C]**10:11** Lit *He* [D]**11:3** Lit *for the majesty of the Jordan is* [E]**11:7** LXX reads *slaughter that belonged to the sheep merchants* [F]**11:11** LXX reads *and the sheep merchants*

the LORD. 12 Then I said to them, "If
it seems right to you, give me my
wages; but if not, keep them." So
they weighed my wages, 30 pieces
of silver.
13 "Throw it to the potter,"[A] the
LORD said to me—this magnificent
price I was valued by them. So I
took the 30 pieces of silver and
threw it into the house of the LORD,
to the potter.[B] 14 Then I cut in two
my second staff, Union, annulling
the brotherhood between Judah and
Israel.
15 The LORD also said to me: "Take
the equipment of a foolish shepherd.
16 I am about to raise up a shepherd in
the land who will not care for those
who are going astray, and he will not
seek the lost[C] or heal the broken. He
will not sustain the healthy,[D] but he
will devour the flesh of the fat sheep
and tear off their hooves.

17 Woe to
the worthless shepherd
who deserts the flock!
May a sword strike[E] his arm
and his right eye!
May his arm wither away
and his right eye go
completely blind!"

Judah's Security (12:1-9)

12 An •Oracle
The word of the LORD
concerning Israel.
A declaration of the LORD,
who stretched out
the heavens,
laid the foundation
of the earth,
and formed the spirit of man
within him.

2 "Look, I will make Jerusalem a
cup that causes staggering for the
peoples who surround the city. The
siege against Jerusalem will also
involve Judah. 3 On that day I will
make Jerusalem a heavy stone for all
the peoples; all who try to lift it will
injure themselves severely when
all the nations of the earth gather
against her. 4 On that day"—this is
the LORD's declaration—"I will strike
every horse with panic and its rider
with madness. I will keep a watchful
eye on the house of Judah but strike
all the horses of the nations with
blindness. 5 Then each of the leaders of Judah will think to himself:
The residents of Jerusalem are my
strength through the LORD of •Hosts,
their God. 6 On that day I will make
the leaders of Judah like a firepot
in a woodpile, like a flaming torch
among sheaves; they will consume
all the peoples around them on the
right and the left, while Jerusalem
continues to be inhabited on its site,
in Jerusalem. 7 The LORD will save
the tents of Judah first, so that the
glory of David's house and the glory
of Jerusalem's residents may not be
greater than that of Judah. 8 On that
day the LORD will defend the inhabitants of Jerusalem, so that on that
day the one who is weakest among
them will be like David on that day,
and the house of David will be like
God, like the Angel of the LORD, before them. 9 On that day I will set out
to destroy all the nations that come
against Jerusalem.

Mourning for the Pierced One (12:10-14)

10 "Then I will pour out a spirit[F] of
grace and prayer on the house of David and the residents of Jerusalem,
and they will look at[G] Me whom they
pierced. They will mourn for Him
as one mourns for an only child
and weep bitterly for Him as one
weeps for a firstborn. 11 On that day
the mourning in Jerusalem will be
as great as the mourning of Hadad-
rimmon in the plain of Megiddo.
12 The land will mourn, every family
by itself: the family of David's house
by itself and their women by themselves; the family of Nathan's[H] house
by itself and their women by themselves; 13 the family of Levi's house
by itself and their women by themselves; the family of Shimei[I] by itself
and their women by themselves;
14 all the remaining families, every
family by itself, and their women by
themselves.

cup that causes staggering is a metaphor for divine judgment (cp. Is 51:17,21-22; Jr 25:15-28). This same metaphor is used to describe the judgment Jesus would take upon Himself for all who would believe (cp. Jn 18:11). God will give Israel the strength to prevail against her enemies. Divine intervention is apparent, and the Lord's protection of His people shines as a beacon of light, discouraging all who would come against her.

12:10-14 In the context of spiritual renewal and deliverance, the Lord promises the empowerment of His Spirit to His people. The Jewish people, both individually and corporately, will repent and accept the Messiah, whom they previously had rejected, confirming what had been previously prophesied by other prophets (cp. Is 32:15; 44:3; 59:20-21; Jr 31:31,33; Ezk 36:26-27; 39:29; Jl 2:28-29). The convicting work of the Spirit will move the entire nation of Israel to **look** upon their Messiah with great mourning, a sign of their repentance (cp. Lk 23:48), turning to Him and putting their faith in Him as their Messiah. John quoted this verse at the time of Christ's crucifixion (cp. Jn 19:37) as a partial fulfillment of Zechariah's prophecy with its final fulfillment for a future time (Rm 11:25-27).

The **mourning of Hadad-rimmon** may refer to the Syrian gods of storms and fertility and the rites of mourning associated with this idolatrous worship (cp. Ezk 8:14). Perhaps the sorrowful repentance of Israel was compared to the rites of mourners that were an abomination to the Lord at **Megiddo**, a place often associated with Josiah, the righteous king who died from his battle wounds at Megiddo (2Ch 35:20-25). Or perhaps mourning took place at another nearby site named for their pagan god. The site cannot be identified with certainty but seemingly was associated with ungodly mourning. **Their women by themselves** is a phrase repeated five times, probably emphasizing that there were no professional mourners here. Their overwhelming sorrow was a sign of genuine repentance.

A11:13 Syr reads *treasury* B11:13 One Hb ms, Syr read *treasury* C11:16 Lit *young* D11:16 Or *exhausted* E11:17 Lit *be against* F12:10 Or *out the Spirit* G12:10 Or *to* H12:12 = a son of David I12:13 = a descendant of Levi

The Cleansing of God's People (13:1-9)

13 "On that day a fountain will be opened for the house of David and for the residents of Jerusalem, to wash away sin and impurity. 2 On that day"—this is the declaration of the LORD of •Hosts—"I will erase the names of the idols from the land, and they will no longer be remembered. I will remove the prophets[A] and the •unclean spirit from the land. 3 If a man still prophesies, his father and his mother who bore him will say to him: You cannot remain alive because you have spoken falsely in the name of •Yahweh. When he prophesies, his father and his mother who bore him will pierce him through. 4 On that day every prophet will be ashamed of his vision when he prophesies; they will not put on a hairy cloak in order to deceive. 5 He will say: I am not a prophet; I work the land, for a man purchased[B] me as a servant since my youth. 6 If someone asks him: What are these wounds on your chest?[C]—then he will answer: I received the wounds in the house of my friends.

7 Sword, awake
against My shepherd,
against the man who is
My associate—
this is the declaration
of the LORD of Hosts.
Strike the shepherd,
and the sheep
will be scattered;
I will also turn My hand
against the little ones.
8 In the whole land—
this is
the LORD's declaration—
two-thirds[D] will be cut off
and die,
but a third will be left in it.
9 I will put this third
through the fire;
I will refine them as silver
is refined
and test them as gold
is tested.
They will call on My name,
and I will answer them.
I will say: They are My people,
and they will say: Yahweh is
our God."

The Establishment of the LORD's Kingdom (14:1-21)

14 A day of the LORD is coming when your plunder will be divided in your presence. 2 I will gather all the nations against Jerusalem for battle. The city will be captured, the houses looted, and the women raped. Half the city will go into exile, but the rest of the people will not be removed from the city.

3 Then the LORD will go out to fight against those nations as He fights on a day of battle. 4 On that day His feet will stand on the •Mount of Olives, which faces Jerusalem on the east. The Mount of Olives will be split in half from east to west, forming a huge valley, so that half the mountain will move to the north and half to the south. 5 You will flee by My mountain valley,[E] for the valley of the mountains will extend to Azal. You will flee as you fled[F] from the earthquake in the days of Uzziah king of Judah. Then the LORD my God will come and all the holy ones with Him.[G]

6 On that day there will be no light; the sunlight and moonlight[H] will diminish.[I] 7 It will be a day known only to •Yahweh, without day or night, but there will be light at evening.

8 On that day living water will flow out from Jerusalem, half of it toward the eastern sea[J] and the other half toward the western sea,[K] in summer and winter alike. 9 On that day Yahweh will become King over all the earth—Yahweh alone, and His name alone. 10 All the land from Geba to Rimmon south of Jerusalem will be changed into a plain. But Jerusalem will be raised up and will remain[L] on its site from the Benjamin Gate to the place of the First Gate,[M] to the Corner Gate, and from the Tower of

[A] **13:2** = false prophets [B] **13:5** Or *sold* [C] **13:6** Lit *wounds between your hands* [D] **13:8** Lit *two-thirds in it* [E] **14:5** Some Hb mss, LXX, Sym, Tg read *You will be blocked—the valley of My mountains—* [F] **14:5** LXX reads *It will be blocked as it was blocked* [G] **14:5** Some Hb mss, LXX, Vg, Tg, Syr; other Hb mss read *you* [H] **14:6** Lit *light; the precious things* [I] **14:6** LXX, Sym, Syr, Tg, Vg read *no light or cold or ice* [J] **14:8** = the Dead Sea [K] **14:8** = the Mediterranean Sea [L] **14:10** Or *will be inhabited* [M] **14:10** Or *the former gate*

13:1-7 The **fountain** is symbolic of an unending supply of water available for spiritual cleansing (cp. Jn 4:14; 7:38; Rv 21:6). As a result of the spiritual cleansing, the land will be completely purged of idols and false prophets. The reference to seeming harshness on the part of **father and . . . mother** underlined the seriousness of the matter for one who persisted in delivering false prophecy. A remnant of the Lord's people would emerge, purified and refined by the Lord's consuming fire (cp. Is 11:11; Rm 11:27-29). Self-inflicted **wounds** identified one with a practice characteristic of idolatry (cp. 1 Kg 18:28).

My shepherd . . . the man who is My associate (Hb *ʿamit*, "neighbor" in the sense of an equal; "confidant"; cp. Lv 6:2) and **the shepherd** to be struck refer to the Messiah, who will die at the command of **the LORD of Hosts** (cp. Jn 10:11,18), affirming the deity of the Messiah, especially in Jesus' application of this prophecy to Himself (Mt 26:31).

14:1-21 The Lord's kingdom is established visibly on earth in **Jerusalem**, which becomes the most important city in the world. Chapter 14 begins with the invasion of the holy city and ends with its glorification through the return of the Messiah . The chiastic structure of chapter 14 reveals the dramatic reversal of events, turning Jerusalem from crushing defeat and a place of darkness to victory and a new role as the source of light, with the Day of the Lord as its central focus in verse seven.

Those **nations** uniting against Jerusalem are described in Rv 16:13-16 as "the battle for the great day of God" or Battle of "Armageddon." **The Mount of Olives**, dominating the range of hills running from north to southeast of Jerusalem, remains a prime spot for viewing the city. The prophet pictured this mountain **split in half,** creating a **valley** of escape from the city. This "valley" could be the Valley of Jehoshaphat (cp. Jl 3:12), but certainly this reference is to the final return of Christ (cp. Ac 1:9-12; Rv 19:11-16). **Azal** has not been identified but is located east of Jerusalem. The **holy ones** may include both the redeemed and the angels (cp. Mt 24:31; 1 Th 3:13; Rv 19:14). The **eastern sea** refers to the Dead Sea, and the **western sea** is the Mediterranean Sea. **Geba** is the northern boundary (cp. 2Kg 23:8), and **Rimmon** is located at the entry to the Negev in the south. Geographically **Jerusalem** becomes the high point.

The **Festival of Booths**, also called the Feast of Tabernacles, now finds its fulfillment, just as have Passover and Pentecost. This "festival" is a celebration of thanksgiving for

Hananel to the royal winepresses.
11 People will live there, and never
again will there be a curse of •com-
plete destruction. So Jerusalem will
dwell in security.
12 This will be the plague the LORD
strikes all the peoples with, who
have warred against Jerusalem:
their flesh will rot while they stand
on their feet, their eyes will rot in
their sockets, and their tongues will
rot in their mouths. 13 On that day
a great panic from the LORD will be
among them, so that each will seize
the hand of another, and the hand
of one will rise against the other.
14 Judah will also fight at Jerusalem,
and the wealth of all the surrounding nations will be collected: gold,
silver, and clothing in great abundance. 15 The same plague as the
previous one will strike[A] the horses,
mules, camels, donkeys, and all the
animals that are in those camps.
16 Then all the survivors from the
nations that came against Jerusalem
will go up year after year to worship
the King, the LORD of •Hosts, and
to celebrate the Festival of Booths.
17 Should any of the families of the
earth not go up to Jerusalem to worship the King, the LORD of Hosts,
rain will not fall on them. 18 And if
the people[B] of Egypt will not go up
and enter, then rain will not fall on
them; this will be the plague the
LORD inflicts on the nations who do
not go up to celebrate the Festival
of Booths. 19 This will be the punishment of Egypt and all the nations
that do not go up to celebrate the
Festival of Booths.
20 On that day, the words

HOLY TO THE LORD

will be on the bells of the horses. The
pots in the house of the LORD will be
like the sprinkling basins before the
altar. 21 Every pot in Jerusalem and
in Judah will be holy to the LORD of
Hosts. Everyone who sacrifices will
come and take some of the pots to
cook in. And on that day there will
no longer be a Canaanite[C] in the
house of the LORD of Hosts.

the harvest, which finds its ultimate fulfillment during the millennial kingdom under the reign of Messiah (cp. Lv 23:33-44; Dt 16:13-15; 31:10; Neh 8:17-18; Rv 20:1-6). **HOLY TO THE LORD**, words engraved on the turban of the high priest, will characterize the messianic kingdom (cp. Ex 28:36-38). Now the ordinary things of mundane life would be set apart as dedicated to the Lord and consecrated to His service. There will be no **Canaanite** because no one outside the Lord's covenant would enter His house.

[A]**14:15** Lit *be on* [B]**14:18** Lit *family* [C]**14:21** Or *merchant*

ZECHARIAH ... WRITTEN ON MY *Heart*

The book of Zechariah provides a guide to spiritual renewal for individual hearts. Spiritual renewal begins with an inner decision to turn to the Lord and then proactive steps, which include prayer and fasting, to rid your life of sin. There is a spiritual battle that rages for the very souls of women and men, and any attempt to turn to the Lord is attacked. Paul says that, "our battle is not against flesh and blood, but against the rulers, against the authorities, against the world powers of this darkness, against the spiritual forces of evil in the heavens" (Eph 6:12). While the evil of this world is against you, Zechariah reminds his readers that Christ, the Victor, fights *for* you.

Malachi

Timeline World Events Biblical Events	***538 BC*** Cyrus's decree allowing the return of exiled Jews from Babylon to Judah	***526 BC*** Opposition, discouragement, and cessation of work on the temple	***520–518 BC*** Challenge from Haggai and Zechariah to resume construction of the temple	***March 12, 515 BC*** Completion of the temple

"'I have loved you," says the Lord. But you ask: 'How have You loved us?' 'Wasn't Esau Jacob's brother?' This is the Lord's declaration. 'Even so, I loved Jacob, but I hated Esau'" (1:2-3a).

Who wrote Malachi?

Whether its author was Ezra or a prophet named Malachi is still debated. However, most evidence points to a prophet, and most likely a priest named Malachi.

Who were the recipients?

The postexilic people of Judah are the immediate audience for the book of Malachi. They were given a strong rebuke in order to motivate them to return to a covenant relationship with their God. Since believers in every age need to be reminded of that covenant relationship, the danger of half-hearted commitment is always relevant.

When was Malachi written?

458–435 B.C.

Where did it happen?

The book of Malachi is postexilic, occurring in Judah after the rebuilding of the temple. Though the people had recommitted themselves to the Lord, considerable time had passed, and they returned to their sinful ways.

What is Malachi about?

- God's covenant love for Israel, despite her waywardness
- God's demand for wholehearted obedience to His Word and complete commitment on the part of His people to fulfill their covenant
- The sanctity of the marriage commitment
- The coming Day of the Lord, the coming of Christ's forerunner, and the coming of Christ Himself

Why should women read Malachi?

Have you ever resented serving the Lord? Perhaps you taught Sunday School for years and are the one always asked to serve because you are a "yes" woman. The priests in Malachi's day were experiencing spiritual burnout. The repetition of the sacrifices made the priests resent their service to God and give to Him the very minimum required. Malachi reminds his readers that repetition for its own sake does not equal spiritual excellence.

How do you read Malachi?

Malachi is comprised of a series of first person, prophetic discourses, each of which begins with "yet you ask" or "but you ask" (1:2,6; 2:14,17; 3:7,13). The Lord Himself is directly addressing His people. The postexilic people of Judah are the immediate audience for the book of Malachi. They were given a strong rebuke in order to motivate them to return to a covenant relationship with their God. Malachi deals with the destruction of Edom, a corrupt priesthood, half-hearted worship and careless offerings, and intermarriages with daughters of a foreign god (2:11). The concerns of the book are closely related to those raised by Nehemiah (cp. Neh 13:23-27).

Outline

I. God's Choice of Israel as His People (1:1-5)
II. The Failure of God's People to Keep His Covenant (1:6–2:17)
   A. Spiritual Apathy in Unholy Offerings (1:6–2:9)
   B. Personal Moral Failure in Unholy Marriages (2:10-17)
III. A Prophecy of the Last Day (3:1–4:6)
   A. The Prophecy of the Coming Messiah (3:1-6)
   B. The Breaking of the Divine Covenant (3:7–4:6)

Similar Themes in Malachi and Nehemiah

The Theme	Malachi	Nehemiah
Perversion of the priesthood	1:6–2:9	13:4-9
Intermarriage with foreigners	2:11-16	13:23-27
Problems in society	3:5	5:1-13
Disobedience of principles governing giving	8:8-11	13:10-14

486–465 BC	460 BC	458 BC	445 BC	445 BC
Events in Esther	Malachi's prophecy	Ezra's journey from Babylon to Jerusalem	Walls of Jerusalem completed under Nehemiah's leadership	Study of Torah in Jerusalem under Ezra's leadership

God's Choice of Israel as His People (1:1-5)

1 An •oracle: The word of the LORD
to Israel through Malachi.[A]
2 "I have loved you," says the LORD.
But you ask: "How have You loved
us?"
"Wasn't Esau Jacob's brother?"
This is the LORD's declaration. "Even
so, I loved Jacob, 3 but I hated Esau.
I turned his mountains into a wasteland, and gave his inheritance to the
desert jackals."
4 Though Edom says: "We have
been devastated, but we will rebuild[B]
the ruins," the LORD of •Hosts says
this: "They may build, but I will demolish. They will be called a wicked
country and the people the LORD has
cursed[C] forever. 5 Your own eyes will
see this, and you yourselves will say,
'The LORD is great, even beyond[D] the
borders of Israel.'

The Failure of God's People to Keep His Covenant (1:6–2:17)

Spiritual Apathy in Unholy Offerings (1:6–2:9)

6 "A son honors his father, and a
servant his master. But if I am a father, where is My honor? And if I am
a master, where is your •fear of Me?
says •Yahweh of Hosts to you priests,
who despise My name."
Yet you ask: "How have we despised Your name?"
7 "By presenting defiled food on
My altar."
You ask: "How have we defiled
You?"
When you say: "The LORD's table is
contemptible."
8 "When you present a blind animal for sacrifice, is it not wrong?
And when you present a lame or sick
animal, is it not wrong? Bring it to
your governor! Would he be pleased
with you or show you favor?" asks
the LORD of Hosts. 9 "And now ask
for God's favor. Will He be gracious
to us? Since this has come from
your hands, will He show any of
you favor?" asks the LORD of Hosts.
10 "I wish one of you would shut the
temple doors, so you would no longer kindle a useless fire on My altar!
I am not pleased with you," says the
LORD of Hosts, "and I will accept no
offering from your hands.
11 "For My name will be great

[A]1:1 = My Messenger [B]1:4 Or *will return and build* [C]1:4 Or *LORD is angry with* [D]1:5 Or *great over*

Title: "Malachi" (Hb "My messenger") may be a proper name for the book's author or a common noun used as a title. The book of Malachi (Hb, "my messenger or my angel") gives no precise information about its author apart from the record of his name (1:1). Whether "Malachi" is a proper name or a common noun, and thus a title is not known. If the name of the author is not known, Malachi would be the only prophetic oracle to be anonymous. Tradition suggests that Ezra the scribe may be the author; however, Ezra never referred to himself as a prophet. If Malachi were a proper name, he was likely a priest, given the content of his book. The evidence seems to affirm that the prophet named Malachi is the human author.

1:2 But you ask is the prophet's way of bringing the people into conversation with the Lord. **Jacob** represented Israel.

1:4 Edom (see note on Gn 25:24-34), located southeast of Jerusalem, was the nation of Esau's descendants, and thus its people were kinsmen of Israel, the nation of Jacob's descendants. The nations were enemies throughout history.

1:6-14 God's major complaint against the people in general and the **priests** in particular is unfaithfulness. In natural familial relationships, **a son honors his** father and a **servant** honors **his master.** Yet the priests do not honor God, the King of heaven as well as their Master. They dishonor God by offering

>WORD|*study*

1:2 Loved (Hb *'ahav*, "that in which one delights or that which one earnestly desires") in the sense of passionate devotion as well as tender affection is a perfect expression of the tender mercies of Yahweh for His people, which He confirms in His covenant with them. Only God's love is unconditional despite the fact that it is undeserved. Because of this love, He determined to bring Israel back to the land He had promised them.

1:3 Hated (Hb *sanē'*) must be understood here as expressing a lesser degree of love and esteem or having less favor toward one. Indeed in the salvific sense the descendants of Esau could be saved just as those coming through Jacob, God's chosen nation Israel, could be lost because of their rejection of Him (cp. Rm 9:6). The term "hated" is then used as a hyperbole to affirm God's choice of Jacob to inherit the covenant blessing over Esau, who remained outside the Lord's covenant (cp. Gn 25:29-34; 27:1-40). Thus, the contrast: Jacob was "loved" and Esau was "hated."

God had not chosen **Esau** in the same way He had chosen Jacob. His choice, however, is to be understood in a national rather than an individual sense and as temporal rather than eternal. God's choice shows priority for Jacob over Esau, with whom God had no covenant relationship. Jesus does much the same thing when He notes that those who love father or mother more than Him are not worthy of Him (Mt 10:37). The idea is priority rather than the despising of one person or, in this case, nation.

unacceptable sacrifices—ones that not even their own governor would accept. The Lord had forbidden the sacrifice of animals with any defect or blemish (Lv 22:22,24; Dt 15:21). Thus, the priests showed just how corrupt they had become.

2:1-9 These verses are the Lord's rebuke of His **priests**. God's covenant was based on faithfulness and truth. The mouths of the priests were to speak knowledge, and their words were intended to instruct the people about the things of God. So complete was the corruption of the priests that God promised to humiliate them before the people.

2:5-7 In the time of Malachi, the people's offerings at the temple were so scarce that the Levites, God's servants who cared for His temple, could not support themselves. **My covenant** is a reference to God's promise to Levi and the priesthood making up his tribe within Israel: to honor Him with their fear of the Lord; to give these **instructions** or accurate teachings of His Word; to walk with Him **in peace** and **fairness**; and to draw people to hear God's truth (i.e., to practice what they were teaching). Then the Lord would give to them **life and peace**.

2:14-15 The sanctity of marriage and its covenant nature are important to the Lord, who is an ever-present witness to the sacred covenant (cp. Gn 31:50; Pr 2:17). Marriages with those from pagan nations were against the law of Moses (Dt 7:1-4). To marry among their own people was part of Israel's covenant relationship with God. Marriage to a foreigner would increase the risk of idolatry. Foreigners were allowed to marry into the nation if they had forsaken their gods and if they committed to worship the Lord only (Ru 1:16). In Malachi's day, some of the men were marrying foreign women who were still practicing idolatry, a behavior that was a sign of the spiritual compromise permeating the community. At the heart of the marriage covenant is God's intent for the union to produce godly offspring.

2:16 Divorce, though allowed under certain circumstances by legal authorities (cp. Dt 24:1; see note on Dt 24:5), was also a serious problem at this time. Throughout the ancient Near East, all marriages were considered bound by law, but Yahweh was especially clear with His people about the lifelong commitment demanded by this spiritual covenant. Though the law of Moses permitted divorce (Dt 24:1-4), God, as clearly presented in this context, despises the breaking of the sacred covenant.

The alternate reading in the HCSB footnote has overwhelmingly been

among the nations, from the rising of the sun to its setting. Incense[A] and pure offerings will be presented in My name in every place because My name will be great among the nations,"[B] says Yahweh of Hosts.

12 But you are profaning it when you say: "The Lord's table is defiled, and its product, its food, is contemptible." 13 You also say: "Look, what a nuisance!" "And you scorn[C] it,"[D] says the LORD of Hosts. "You bring stolen,[E] lame, or sick animals. You bring this as an offering! Am I to accept that from your hands?" asks the LORD.

14 "The deceiver is cursed who has an acceptable male in his flock and makes a vow but sacrifices a defective animal to the Lord. For I am a great King," says Yahweh of Hosts, "and My name[F] will be feared among the nations.

2 "Therefore, this decree is for you priests: 2 If you don't listen, and if you don't take it to heart to honor My name," says •Yahweh of •Hosts, "I will send a curse among you, and I will curse your blessings. In fact, I have already begun to curse them because you are not taking it to heart.

3 "Look, I am going to rebuke your descendants, and I will spread animal waste[G] over your faces, the waste from your festival sacrifices, and you will be taken away with it. 4 Then you will know that I sent you this decree so My covenant with Levi may continue," says the LORD of Hosts. 5 "My covenant with him was one of life and peace, and I gave these to him; it called for reverence, and he revered Me and stood in awe of My name. 6 True instruction was in his mouth, and nothing wrong was found on his lips. He walked with Me in peace and fairness and turned many from sin. 7 For the lips of a priest should guard knowledge, and people should seek instruction from his mouth, because he is the messenger of the LORD of Hosts.

8 "You, on the other hand, have turned from the way. You have caused many to stumble by your instruction. You have violated[H] the covenant of Levi," says the LORD of Hosts. 9 "So I in turn have made you despised and humiliated before all the people because you are not keeping My ways but are showing partiality in your instruction."

Personal Moral Failure in Unholy Marriages (2:10-17)

10 Don't all of us have one Father? Didn't one God create us? Why then do we act treacherously against one another, profaning the covenant of our fathers? 11 Judah has acted treacherously, and a detestable thing has been done in Israel and in Jerusalem. For Judah has profaned the LORD's sanctuary,[I] which He loves, and has married the daughter of a foreign god.[J] 12 To the man who does this, may the LORD cut off any descendants[K,L] from the tents of Jacob, even if they present an offering to the LORD of Hosts.

13 And this is another thing you do: you cover the LORD's altar with tears, with weeping and groaning, because He no longer respects your offerings or receives them gladly from your hands.

14 Yet you ask, "For what reason?" Because the LORD has been a witness between you and the wife of your youth. You have acted treacherously against her, though she was your marriage partner and your wife by covenant. 15 Didn't the one God make us with a remnant of His life-breath? And what does the One seek?[M] A godly •offspring. So watch yourselves carefully,[N] and do not act treacherously against the wife of your youth.

16 "If he hates and divorces his wife," says the LORD God of Israel, "he[O] covers his garment with injustice," says the LORD of Hosts. There-

[A]1:11 Or *Burnt offerings* [B]1:11 Or *is great . . . are presented . . . is great* [C]1:13 Lit *blow at* [D]1:13 Ancient Jewish tradition reads *Me* [E]1:13 Or *injured* [F]1:14 Or *Because I am . . . Yahweh of Hosts, My name* [G]2:3 Dung or entrails [H]2:8 Lit *corrupted* [I]2:11 Or *profaned what is holy to the LORD* [J]2:11 = a woman who worshiped a foreign god [K]2:12 One Hb ms, LXX, DSS read *off one witnessing or answering* [L]2:12 Lit *off one waking or answering*; Hb obscure [M]2:15 Or *Did the One not make them? So their flesh and spirit belong to Him*, or *No one who does this even has a remnant of the Spirit in him*; Hb obscure [N]2:15 Lit *So guard yourselves in your spirit* [O]2:16 Or *The LORD God of Israel says that He hates divorce and the one who*

fore, watch yourselves carefully,[A] and do not act treacherously.

[17]You have wearied the LORD with your words.

Yet you ask, "How have we wearied Him?"

When you say, "Everyone who does what is evil is good in the LORD's sight, and He is pleased with them," or "Where is the God of justice?"

A Prophecy of the Last Day (3:1–4:6)

The Prophecy of the Coming Messiah (3:1-6)

3 "See, I am going to send My messenger, and he will clear the way before Me. Then the Lord you seek will suddenly come to His temple, the Messenger of the covenant you desire—see, He is coming," says the LORD of •Hosts. [2]But who can endure the day of His coming? And who will be able to stand when He appears? For He will be like a refiner's fire and like cleansing lye. [3]He will be like a refiner and purifier of silver; He will purify the sons of Levi and refine them like gold and silver. Then they will present offerings to the LORD in righteousness. [4]And the offerings of Judah and Jerusalem will please the LORD as in days of old and years gone by.

[5]"I will come to you in judgment, and I will be ready to witness against sorcerers and adulterers; against those who swear falsely; against those who oppress the widow and the fatherless, and cheat the wage earner; and against those who deny justice to the foreigner. They do not •fear Me," says the LORD of Hosts. [6]"Because I, •Yahweh, have not changed, you descendants of Jacob have not been destroyed.

The Breaking of the Divine Covenant (3:7–4:6)

[7]"Since the days of your fathers, you have turned from My statutes; you have not kept them. Return to Me, and I will return to you," says the LORD of Hosts.

But you ask: "How can we return?"

[8]"Will a man rob God? Yet you are robbing Me!"

You ask: "How do we rob You?"

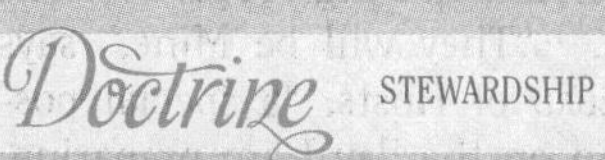

Doctrine STEWARDSHIP

A steward is someone who cares for someone else's property. Whatever the Lord gives, whether wealth, children, talents, or abilities makes us stewards. Stewards are to protect and even increase what their master entrusted to them. The Lord, in Mal 3:9-11, gives direct commands in regard to being good stewards of money. In Malachi, God makes it clear that Israel's refusal to obey His instructions about tithing (given in Lv 27:30-33; Nm 8:8-32; Dt 14:22-29; 26:12-15) is one of the acts of disobedience from which Malachi calls God's people to repent. The tithe, giving ten percent of your gross income to the Lord, is an act of worship acknowledging the Lord who gave you all that you have. The people in Malachi's day were withholding their tithes and by so doing missing out on the blessings of God. Tithing tests a person's heart as to whether she is in obedience to the Lord. Then the Lord Himself even invites you to test His goodness in responding to your needs (Mal 3:10). What you pour out in submission and thanks, He returns in abundant blessing.

"By not making the payments of the tenth and the contributions. [9]You are suffering under a curse, yet you—the whole nation—are still robbing Me. [10]Bring the full tenth into the storehouse so that there may be food in My house. Test Me in this way," says the LORD of Hosts. "See if I will not open the floodgates of heaven and pour out a blessing for you without measure. [11]I will rebuke the devourer[B] for you, so that it will not ruin the produce of your land and your vine in your field will not fail to produce fruit," says the LORD of Hosts. [12]"Then all the nations will consider you fortunate, for you will be a delightful land," says the LORD of Hosts.

[13]"Your words against Me are harsh," says the LORD.

Yet you ask: "What have we spoken against You?"

[14]You have said: "It is useless to serve God. What have we gained by keeping His requirements and walking mournfully before the LORD of Hosts? [15]So now we consider the arrogant to be fortunate. Not only do those who commit wickedness prosper, they even test God and escape."

[16]At that time those who feared the LORD spoke to one another. The LORD took notice and listened. So a book of remembrance was written before Him for those who feared

the preferred translation, "the LORD God of Israel says that He hates divorce" (Hb *shalach*, "send out, put hand to something with force"). The words have a stronger force because of the careful balance in the Hebrew text between the lines of verses 15b and verse 16 as well as two clauses affirming **says the LORD**. Also "divorce" was the breaking of the marriage covenant, which itself had been witnessed by God.

3:1-2 The people had clearly lost sight of the value of their relationship with the Lord. Thus, He promised to purge them of their sins by cleansing them with **a refiner's fire**, a metaphor for spiritual cleansing.

3:7-10 The Lord implored the people to **return** to Him, for they had been **robbing** Him. The people had become so apathetic toward the things of God that they did not understand how they could have been robbing Him. The people questioned God's holiness. But the Lord promised that if they brought in their whole tithe, He would bless them and God's favor on all nations would be bestowed.

3:13–4:3 The people were claiming that there was no difference between those who worshiped God and those who did not. Those who were wicked prospered and those who were faithful suffered. But God knew the difference and took note of it. The Day of the Lord will consume the wicked. But for those who fear the Lord, this day will be joyous.

[A]2:16 Lit *Therefore, guard yourselves in your spirit* [B]3:11 Perhaps locusts

4:4-6 Malachi closes with reference to the law of Moses. The promise of the coming of Elijah offered hope that God would still speak to Israel. Jesus declared John the Baptist to be this Elijah (Mt 11:13-14; 17:12; Mk 9:11-13). God's promise to Israel will be fulfilled in Jesus.

Yahweh and had high regard for His
name. [17] "They will be Mine," says
the LORD of Hosts, "a special possession on the day I am preparing.
I will have compassion on them as
a man has compassion on his son
who serves him. [18] So you will again
see the difference between the righteous and the wicked, between one
who serves God and one who does
not serve Him.

4 [A] "For indeed, the day is coming,
burning like a furnace, when
all the arrogant and everyone who
commits wickedness will become
stubble. The coming day will consume them," says the LORD of •Hosts,
"not leaving them root or branches.
[2] But for you who •fear My name, the
sun of righteousness will rise with
healing in its wings, and you will go
out and playfully jump like calves
from the stall.[B] [3] You will trample the
wicked, for they will be ashes under
the soles of your feet on the day I am
preparing," says the LORD of Hosts.
[4] "Remember the instruction of
Moses My servant, the statutes and
ordinances I commanded him at
Horeb for all Israel. [5] Look, I am going to send you Elijah the prophet
before the great and awesome Day of
the LORD comes. [6] [C] And he will turn
the hearts of fathers to their children and the hearts of children to
their fathers. Otherwise, I will come
and strike the land[D] with a curse."

[A] **4:1** Mal 3:19 in Hb [B] **4:2** Or *like stall-fed calves* [C] **4:6** Mal 3:24 in Hb [D] **4:6** Or *earth*

MALACHI … WRITTEN ON MY *Heart*

Half-hearted obedience is disobedience. Spiritual apathy and vain religiosity do not receive the blessing of a holy and worthy God. Though you might attempt to hide the true attitude of your heart and keep areas of your life from the touch of God, His gaze pierces the deepest recesses of your heart, and His mighty arms reach the things we keep farthest from Him. Malachi reminds you that you are to worship the Lord fearfully and wholly with your hearts, lives, and money, lest you rob Him of what of what He deserves.

The
New Testament

Matthew

Timeline ■ World Events ■ Biblical Events	*2166–1991 BC* Life of Abraham	*1010–970 BC* Reign of King David over Israel	*586–538 BC* Babylonian exile	*63 BC* Beginning of Roman dominance of Israel

"But seek first the kingdom of God and His righteousness" (6:33).

Who wrote Matthew?

The Apostle Matthew, also called Levi (Mk 2:14-15; Lk 5:28-29), who left his career as tax collector to follow Jesus the Messiah (see Mt 9:9-13)

Who were the recipients?

Matthew wrote primarily for Jewish Christians but also for Gentiles and Jews who did not yet know or believe in Jesus. The primary destination is generally understood to be Antioch in Syria.

When was Matthew written?

Sometime in the 60s of the first century A.D., before the fall of the temple (A.D. 70)

Where did it happen?

In Israel, except for the months when Jesus, as an infant, was in Egypt (1:13-15)

What is Matthew about?

Matthew portrays Jesus as the long-awaited Messiah-King, the Son of David, whose kingdom God had promised would last forever.

Why should women read Matthew?

The Gospel of Matthew introduces women to the God of history who spotlights rather than sidesteps the importance of women in His orchestration of the history of Israel as the people from whom the Messiah-King would be given (1:1,3,5-6,17-23). This account of the life, death, and resurrection of Jesus the Messiah is the story of "God with us" (1:23), of the divine King who came into the world through a young virgin's womb (1:18-25) and entrusted women with the first news report of His resurrection (28:1-10). Matthew especially underscores the way the story of Jesus fulfills Scripture (e.g., 1:22-23; 2:5-6,15,17-18,23; esp. 5:17), proving that all God's promises are true and therefore making especially precious the resurrected Lord's promise to those who follow Him: "I am with you always, to the end of the age" (28:20).

How do you read Matthew?

The Gospel of Matthew presents Jesus as the Jewish Messiah, the Anointed One who came to fulfill the Old Testament Law and the Prophets (5:17). Preferably, read through the entire book at least once to gain a sense of the overall portrait of Christ being presented, paying attention to the kind of king Jesus presents Himself to be. Take note not only of what He says and does but also of how people respond to Him and what they say about Him. Also note the many Old Testament references and quotations, and spend some time reading these verses in their original contexts. Consider recording or in some way marking all the uses of the word "fulfill" in this Gospel. Always as you read, listen for the Spirit's application of Jesus' teachings (this Gospel contains five sermons or discourses) and observe Jesus' life. Matthew especially highlights the impossibly high standards of righteousness that are met only in Christ, who bestows His righteousness on those who follow Him (cp. Mt 6:33; Rm 3:20-25).

Outline

I. The Identification of Jesus: Who He Is (1:1–4:11)
   - A. The Genealogy and Birth of Jesus (1:1–2:23)
   - B. The Preparation for Jesus' Ministry (3:1–4:11)

II. The Development of Jesus' Ministry: What He Did (4:12–16:20)
   - A. The Beginning of Ministry (4:12-25)
   - B. Preaching: The Sermon on the Mount (5:1–7:29)
   - C. Healing the People (8:1–9:38)
   - D. The Opposition to Jesus' Mission (10:1–12:50)
   - E. Predicting Progressive Opposition Toward Jesus (13:1–16:20)

III. The Climax of Jesus' Ministry (16:21–28:20)
   - A. A Focus on Coming Death and Resurrection (16:21–18:35)
   - B. The Road to Jerusalem: The Coming Judgment (19:1–25:46)
   - C. An Account of Jesus' Ultimate Destiny (26:1–28:20)

>WORD|*study*

1:1-16 Matthew begins telling the good news by providing the historical record (Gk *biblos geneseōs*, "book of [one's] generation or source," v. 1)—the lineage or ancestry—of the Messiah (v. 16). Matthew aimed to show that Jesus (Gk transliteration of Hb *Yehoshua*—i.e., "Joshua"—meaning "Yahweh saves") was the messianic Son of David—the Davidic king whose throne would be established forever (see 2Sm 7:12-16; Is 9:6-7). This **Jesus** is also identified, therefore, by the title Christ (Gk *christou*, "anointed one")—i.e., "Messiah." Furthermore, as the Son of Abraham, Jesus is presented as the consummate fulfillment of God's covenant promises to Abraham (see Gn 12:3; 17:7-8; 18:18; 22:18), the true Israelite through whom all the nations would be blessed. Matthew includes in this "historical record" a number of Gentile women representative of "the nations" partaking in the kingdom blessings. Four of the five women named in the genealogy were Gentiles: **Tamar, Rahab, Ruth**, and **Uriah's wife** (Bathsheba).

Fathered (Gk *egennēsen*) is a verb properly used of men "begetting" children. It is followed by *ek* (Gk, "by") and the mother's name when she is identified, as in verses 3,5,6. Although in this genealogy most of the wives and mothers of the patriarchs are not mentioned by name, readers familiar with the Hebrew Scriptures knew well the stories of women such as Sarah, Abraham's wife. In the Greek text of verse 16, the phrase translated as **Mary, who** gave birth to **Jesus** literally reads, "Mary, from (*ek*, "out of," here a reference to origin or source) whom (*hēs*) was born Jesus." The relative pronoun *hēs* is feminine, making it clear that only Mary was Jesus' biological parent.

5 BC	*4 BC*	*AD 29*	*March 28–April 3, AD 33*
Birth of Jesus	Death of Herod the Great	Beginning of the ministries of John the Baptist and of Jesus	Passover week leading to Jesus' crucifixion

The Genealogy and Birth of Jesus (1:1–2:23)

From Abraham to David (1:2-6a)

1 The historical record[A] of Jesus Christ, the Son of David, the Son of Abraham:

2 Abraham fathered[B] Isaac,
Isaac fathered Jacob,
Jacob fathered Judah
and his brothers,
3 Judah fathered
Perez and Zerah by Tamar,
Perez fathered Hezron,
Hezron fathered Aram,
4 Aram fathered Amminadab,
Amminadab fathered
Nahshon,
Nahshon fathered Salmon,
5 Salmon fathered Boaz
by Rahab,
Boaz fathered Obed by Ruth,
Obed fathered Jesse,
6 and Jesse fathered King David.

From David to the Babylonian Exile (1:6b-11)

Then[C] David fathered Solomon
by Uriah's wife,
7 Solomon fathered Rehoboam,
Rehoboam fathered Abijah,
Abijah fathered Asa,[D]
8 Asa[D] fathered Jehoshaphat,
Jehoshaphat fathered Joram,[E]
Joram fathered Uzziah,
9 Uzziah fathered Jotham,
Jotham fathered Ahaz,
Ahaz fathered Hezekiah,
10 Hezekiah fathered Manasseh,
Manasseh fathered Amon,[F]
Amon fathered Josiah,
11 and Josiah fathered Jechoniah
and his brothers
at the time of the exile
to Babylon.

From the Exile to the Messiah (1:12-17)

12 Then after the exile to Babylon
Jechoniah fathered Shealtiel,
Shealtiel fathered Zerubbabel,
13 Zerubbabel fathered Abiud,
Abiud fathered Eliakim,
Eliakim fathered Azor,
14 Azor fathered Zadok,
Zadok fathered Achim,
Achim fathered Eliud,
15 Eliud fathered Eleazar,
Eleazar fathered Matthan,
Matthan fathered Jacob,
16 and Jacob fathered Joseph
the husband of Mary,
who gave birth to[G] Jesus
who is called the •Messiah.

17 So all the generations from Abraham to David were 14 generations; and from David until the exile to Babylon, 14 generations; and from the exile to Babylon until the Messiah, 14 generations.

The Birth of the Messiah (1:18-25)

18 The birth of Jesus Christ came

[A]1:1 Or *The book of the genealogy* [B]1:2 In vv. 2-16 either a son, as here, or a later descendant, as in v. 8 [C]1:6 Other mss add *King* [D]1:7,8 Other mss read *Asaph* [E]1:8 = Jehoram [F]1:10 Other mss read *Amos* [G]1:16 Lit *Mary, from whom was born*

1:5 **Rahab** was the prostitute who protected the spies Joshua sent into the city of Jericho before Israel attacked (see Jos 2). As she requested, Rahab and her family were spared when the city was destroyed. She committed herself to the God of Israel and became the mother of kings.

Ruth, a Moabite woman, married a Jew who had immigrated with his family to her homeland (see Ru 1–4). Her husband died, and as a widow she moved to Judah with her mother-in-law Naomi. **Boaz**, a distant relative of Ruth's first husband, who owned land in Judah, became Ruth's kinsman-redeemer and husband.

1:6 **Uriah's wife** was Bathsheba, the woman with whom King **David** committed adultery (see 2Sm 11–12). David arranged for Uriah's certain death in battle and took Bathsheba to be one of his wives. The child born of this adultery died, but Bathsheba conceived again and gave birth to **Solomon**, who became one of the greatest kings of Israel.

1:7 The Old Testament identifies the mother of **Rehoboam** (Gk *Rhoboam*, "enlarger of the people") three times as "Naamah the Ammonite," another Gentile woman (1Kg 4:21,31; 2Ch 12:13).

1:11 The Jews who were exiled were taken captive to Babylon in three waves of conflict. One group (including Daniel) was exiled in 605 B.C., another (including the prophet Ezekiel) in 597 B.C., and finally in 586 B.C. when Babylon destroyed the walls of Jerusalem and the temple (see 2Ch 36:11-21).

Title: The Greek title (*Kata Maththaion*, "According to Matthew") reflects the early church's conviction that the apostle Matthew is this gospel's author.

1:2-3 The Messiah would come from the tribe of **Judah**. Judah married a Canaanite woman by whom he had three sons. He arranged for his oldest son Er to marry **Tamar** (see Gn 38 for the entire account). When Er died (the Lord "put him to death" because he "was evil in the LORD's sight"), the second son Onan was responsible, according to the laws of levirate marriage (Dt 25:5-6), to marry and provide an heir for his deceased brother. The Lord "put . . . to death" Onan for his "evil" behavior in spurning this obligation. Judah was afraid to give his third son as a husband to Tamar and put off the marriage past the son's being old enough to fulfill his duty. Tamar disguised herself as a prostitute and became pregnant by Judah, her father-in-law. Her actions secured for him the continued existence of the tribe as well as the lineage of David and the Messiah (see Gn 49:8-12).

1:20-25 As a righteous man, Joseph obeyed the Lord. Joseph knew that Mary's child was not his, but he believed what the Lord revealed to him in a dream about the conception being **by the Holy Spirit**. Not only did he stop pursuing the divorce but he married her and did not exercise his right, as her husband, to sexual intimacy until after Jesus was born, thereby honoring and preserving her virginity. By prescribing the name **Jesus** (Gk equivalent of Joshua—Hb, "*Yahweh* is salvation"), the Lord asserted His authority over the child (cp. Lk 1:31).

Matthew recognized the significance of **all this**—the circumstances he has summarized in these verses. The events surrounding Jesus' conception fulfilled the prophecy quoted (Is 7:14).

2:1-2 See **Map**, p. 1238. The **wise men** were probably an educated group of philosophers, scientists, or astrologers—possibly from a priestly class, coming from Persia or Babylon. The word describing these "magi" was also used of Babylonian priests or men who were especially gifted in the interpretation of dreams and stars and was used in the Septuagint in Dn 2:2 to describe the "diviner-priests" to whom King Nebuchadnezzar gave orders to interpret his dream. Although the text does not record the number of wise men, the fact that three gifts were presented has led to the tradition of "three" wise men.

2:2-4 When the magi came to Jerusalem, looking for the one who had been **born King of the Jews**, **King Herod** and the whole city were **disturbed** (Gk *etarachthē*, "stirred, unsettled and thrown into confusion, frightened"). Herod was one of the cruelest rulers of all time, and he did not hesitate even to murder members of his own family if they appeared to be a threat to his throne. In fact, Caesar Augustus, the Roman Emperor, used a Greek play-on-words to say that it was safer to be Herod's pig (Gk *hus*) than Herod's son (Gk *huios*).

The **chief priests** included past high priests and the current high priest, most of whom were Sadducees (see chart, p. 1242). Their position required working with Herod. Most of the **scribes** were Pharisees. They were summoned for their biblical expertise. These select groups, along with "the elders," comprised the Great Sanhedrin (i.e., the Jewish supreme court; see 16:21).

The Journeys of Mary

Location	Purpose	Reference
Bethlehem	Mary traveled with Joseph to be registered in his ancestral village. There Christ was born.	Lk 2:1-7
Jerusalem	Jesus was presented at the temple and the prophetess Anna bore witness to Him.	Lk 2:22-38
Bethlehem	The magi visited Jesus.	Mt 2:1-11
Egypt	Joseph and Mary, with Jesus, fled Bethlehem for safety.	Mt 2:13-15
Nazareth	The family returned home.	Mt 2:19-23

about this way: After His mother
Mary had been •engaged to Joseph,
it was discovered before they came
together that she was pregnant by
the Holy Spirit. 19 So her husband
Joseph, being a righteous man, and
not wanting to disgrace her publicly,
decided to divorce her secretly.
20 But after he had considered these
things, an angel of the Lord suddenly appeared to him in a dream,
saying, "Joseph, son of David, don't
be afraid to take Mary as your wife,
because what has been conceived in
her is by the Holy Spirit. 21 She will
give birth to a son, and you are to
name Him Jesus,[A] because He will
save His people from their sins."
22 Now all this took place to fulfill what was spoken by the Lord
through the prophet:

23 **See, the virgin will**
become pregnant
and give birth to a son,
and they will
name Him Immanuel,[B]

which is translated "God is with us."
24 When Joseph got up from sleeping, he did as the Lord's angel had
commanded him. He married her
25 but did not know her intimately
until she gave birth to a son.[C] And
he named Him Jesus.

Wise Men and the King (2:1-12)

2 After Jesus was born in Bethlehem of Judea in the days of King
•Herod, •wise men from the east
arrived unexpectedly in Jerusalem,
2 saying, "Where is He who has been
born King of the Jews? For we saw
His star in the east[D] and have come
to worship Him."[E]
3 When King Herod heard this, he
was deeply disturbed, and all Jerusalem with him. 4 So he assembled all
the •chief priests and •scribes of the
people and asked them where the
•Messiah would be born.
5 "In Bethlehem of Judea," they
told him, "because this is what was
written by the prophet:

6 **And you, Bethlehem,**
in the land of Judah,
are by no means **least**
among the leaders
of Judah:
because out of you will come
a leader
who will shepherd My people
Israel."[F]

7 Then Herod secretly summoned
the wise men and asked them the
exact time the star appeared. 8 He
sent them to Bethlehem and said,
"Go and search carefully for the
child. When you find Him, report
back to me so that I too can go and
worship Him."[G]
9 After hearing the king, they went
on their way. And there it was—the
star they had seen in the east![H] It
led them until it came and stopped
above the place where the child
was. 10 When they saw the star, they
were overjoyed beyond measure.

[A] **1:21** *Jesus* is the Gk form of the Hb name "Joshua," which = "The LORD saves" or "Yahweh saves." [B] **1:23** Is 7:14 [C] **1:25** Other mss read *to her firstborn son* [D] **2:2** Or *star at its rising* [E] **2:2** Or *to pay Him homage* [F] **2:6** Mc 5:2 [G] **2:8** Or *and pay Him homage* [H] **2:9** Or *star . . . at its rising*

Biblical Womanhood

Sexual Purity: The Example of Jewish Betrothal

In first-century Jewish culture, being **engaged** (Gk *mnēsteutheisēs,* "be promised in marriage, be betrothed, be espoused") was a legally binding relationship that could be dissolved only through an official, legal divorce (1:18-19). An "engaged" or betrothed woman was bound by a marriage contract (Hb *ketubah*; see **Biblical Womanhood**, p. 106). The consequences of infidelity during the betrothal period were the same as those after the wedding and consummation of the marriage. Although the obligations for the betrothed couple were the same as if they were married, they did not live together but remained sexually pure. Therefore, the discovery before they came together that Mary **was pregnant** demanded that Joseph terminate the betrothal on grounds of Mary's apparent unfaithfulness. Jewish, Roman, and Greek law made it virtually impossible for a man to retain his honor and do anything other than **divorce** the betrothed wife. Not to do so raised suspicions that he had acted immorally by having slept with her himself before the wedding.

Matthew describes **Joseph** as **a righteous man** because, despite the extreme disappointment and pain of apparent betrayal presented by the circumstances and the confusion of Mary's unbelievable explanation, he did not want **to disgrace** [Gk *paradeigmatisai,* "expose, make an example of, humiliate publicly"] **her publicly** (i.e., subject her to the shame of public divorce proceedings). By pursuing the divorce privately, Joseph demonstrated godly compassion (also see 3:15; 5:20 regarding the importance of righteousness in Matthew). Furthermore, he forfeited the bride price and dowry (the assets Mary brought into the marriage) promised to her in the *ketubah;* the only way to recover these would be to prove her adultery in a public divorce trial. Nevertheless, to end the betrothal would mean drafting an official certificate of divorce, which required the signature of two witnesses. Once in her hands the bill of divorce was final; and because of the presumed infidelity, Joseph could not thereafter take her back as his wife.

As an example of Jewish law and custom, the circumstances imposed on Mary and Joseph by her pregnancy **by the Holy Spirit** (v. 20) challenge the prevailing views of engagement and marriage in contemporary secular cultures. Sexual intimacy was rightfully enjoyed only within marriage—after, absolutely not before, the public wedding. The betrothed or engaged couple were not customarily allowed to be alone together in order to protect them from accusation as well as temptation. Even in the absence of such protections and in the face of immense pressure from society, peers, entertainment, and even non-Christian parents or other family members and friends, Christian women who determine to maintain sexual purity as a gift to be enjoyed only after the wedding can establish clear guidelines for themselves (and their daughters). By writing down such guidelines and treating them as concrete provisions of a contract you will keep to honor the Lord, you will not only be more likely to follow them but you can also articulate and explain your reasons for them. You can also share them with someone who will hold you accountable.

2:9-11 The phrase, **entering the house** (Gk *oikian*, "residence," usually inhabited by a family), indicates that when the magi arrived, Mary and Joseph had moved to a permanent dwelling in Bethlehem. Additionally, Jesus was referred to as a **child** (Gk *paidon*) instead of as a "baby" (Gk *brephos*; see Lk 2:16), suggesting that Jesus could then have been about two years old.

The wise men presented the child with **gifts** befitting a king. **Gold** was prized for its beauty and worth. **Frankincense**, a fragrant spice, was taken from the bark of trees and used in incense. **Myrrh** was a costly perfume often used for embalming the dead.

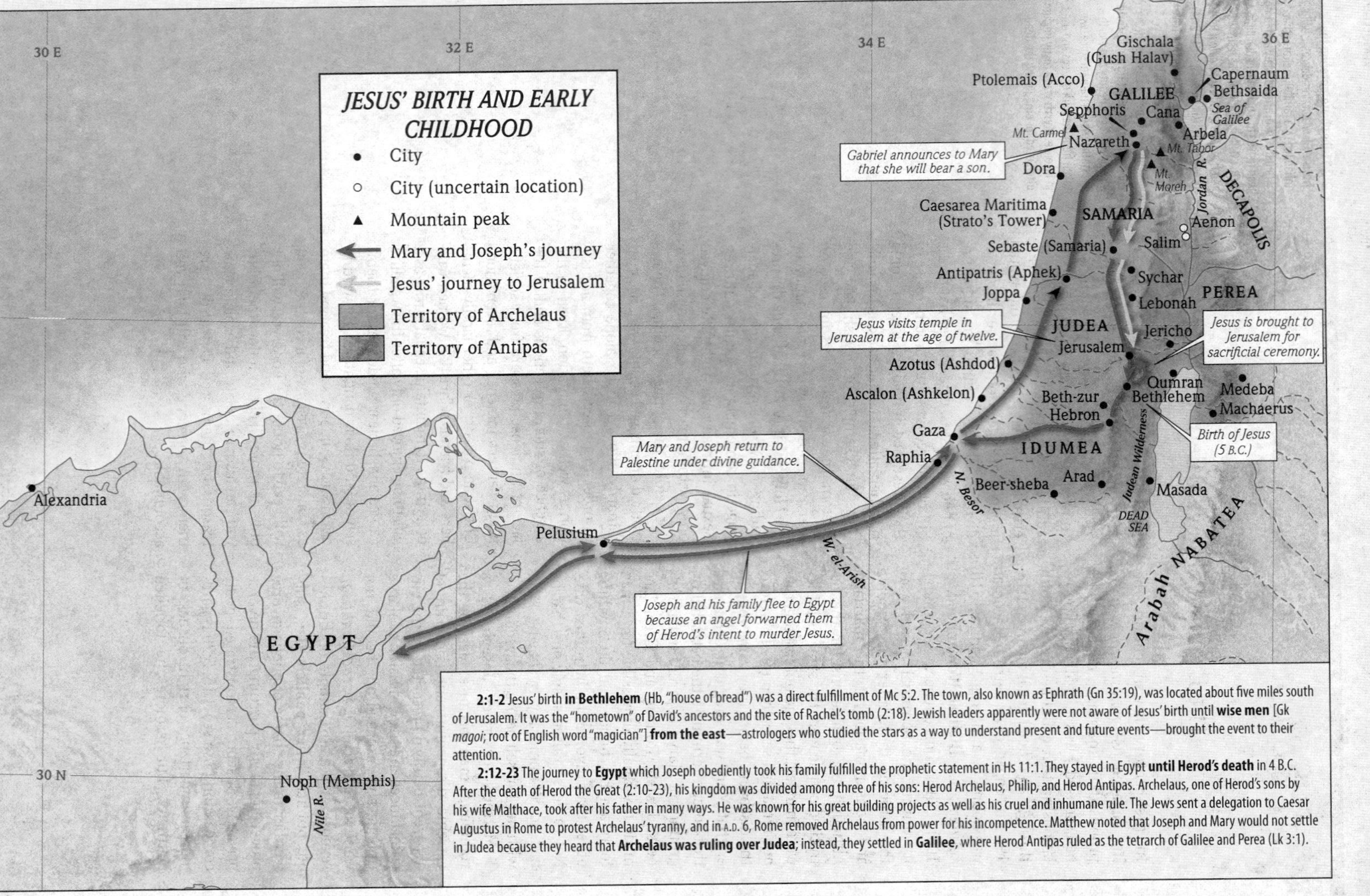

2:1-2 Jesus' birth **in Bethlehem** (Hb, "house of bread") was a direct fulfillment of Mc 5:2. The town, also known as Ephrath (Gn 35:19), was located about five miles south of Jerusalem. It was the "hometown" of David's ancestors and the site of Rachel's tomb (2:18). Jewish leaders apparently were not aware of Jesus' birth until **wise men** [Gk *magoi*; root of English word "magician"] **from the east**—astrologers who studied the stars as a way to understand present and future events—brought the event to their attention.

2:12-23 The journey to **Egypt** which Joseph obediently took his family fulfilled the prophetic statement in Hs 11:1. They stayed in Egypt **until Herod's death** in 4 B.C. After the death of Herod the Great (2:10-23), his kingdom was divided among three of his sons: Herod Archelaus, Philip, and Herod Antipas. Archelaus, one of Herod's sons by his wife Malthace, took after his father in many ways. He was known for his great building projects as well as his cruel and inhumane rule. The Jews sent a delegation to Caesar Augustus in Rome to protest Archelaus' tyranny, and in A.D. 6, Rome removed Archelaus from power for his incompetence. Matthew noted that Joseph and Mary would not settle in Judea because they heard that **Archelaus was ruling over Judea**; instead, they settled in **Galilee**, where Herod Antipas ruled as the tetrarch of Galilee and Perea (Lk 3:1).

The Wives of Herod the Great, King of Judea

Wife	Description	Children	Descendants
Mariamne II	Daughter of the high priest Simon	Herod Philip	Salome (daughter of Herod Philip and Herodias, Mt 14:1-12; Mk 6:17)
Mariamne I	Hasmonean princess and Herod's favorite wife	Salampsio Alexander Cypros Aristobulus	Herod Agrippa I (King of Judea, Ac 12:1-24) Bernice (Ac 25:13; 26:30) Drusilla (Ac 24:24) Herod Agrippa II (King of Judea, Ac 25:13–26:32) Mariamne
Malthace	A Samaritan	Herod Antipas (tetrarch of Galilee) Archelaus (King of Judea, Mt 2:22)	
Cleopatra		Herod Philip (tetrarch of Iturea; Lk 3:1)	
Doris		Antipater	
5 other wives	Unnamed	Other children	

11 Entering the house, they saw the
child with Mary His mother, and falling to their knees, they worshiped
Him.[A] Then they opened their treasures and presented Him with gifts:
gold, frankincense, and myrrh. 12 And
being warned in a dream not to go
back to Herod, they returned to their
own country by another route.

The Flight into Egypt (2:13-15)

13 After they were gone, an angel
of the Lord suddenly appeared to
Joseph in a dream, saying, "Get up!
Take the child and His mother, flee
to Egypt, and stay there until I tell
you. For Herod is about to search
for the child to destroy Him." 14 So
he got up, took the child and His
mother during the night, and escaped to Egypt. 15 He stayed there
until Herod's death, so that what
was spoken by the Lord through the
prophet might be fulfilled: **Out of
Egypt I called My Son.**[B]

The Massacre of the Innocents (2:16-18)

16 Then Herod, when he saw that
he had been outwitted by the wise
men, flew into a rage. He gave orders
to massacre all the male children
in and around Bethlehem who were
two years[C] old and under, in keeping
with the time he had learned from
the wise men. 17 Then what was spoken through Jeremiah the prophet
was fulfilled:

18 **A voice was heard in Ramah,**
weeping,[D] and
great mourning,
Rachel weeping
for her children;
and she refused
to be consoled,
because they were no more.[E]

The Holy Family in Nazareth (2:19-23)

19 After Herod died, an angel of the
Lord suddenly appeared in a dream
to Joseph in Egypt, 20 saying, "Get
up! Take the child and His mother
and go to the land of Israel, because
those who sought the child's life are
dead." 21 So he got up, took the child
and His mother, and entered the
land of Israel. 22 But when he heard
that Archelaus[F] was ruling over Judea in place of his father Herod, he
was afraid to go there. And being

[A]2:11 Or *they paid Him homage* [B]2:15 Hs 11:1 [C]2:16 Lit *were from two years* [D]2:18 Other mss read *Ramah, lamentation, and weeping,* [E]2:18 Jr 31:15 [F]2:22 A son of Herod the Great who ruled a portion of his father's kingdom 4 B.C.–A.D. 6

2:12-15 The journey **to Egypt** on which Joseph obediently took his family fulfilled the prophetic statement in Hs 11:1. They stayed in Egypt **until Herod's death** in 4 B.C.

2:16-17 Herod had slaughtered two of his own sons, Aristobulus and Alexander, and their mother, Mariamne I, even though she was considered the favorite of his 10 wives.

Herod's acute paranoia claimed victim after victim. When he realized that the **wise men** had bypassed him on their return journey, Herod **flew into a rage** (Gk *ethumōthē lian*—the adverb *lian*, "exceedingly, greatly," modifying the verb *ethumōthē*, "be provoked to anger," stressed the intensity of Herod's violent reaction). Determined to eliminate the life of the child who would be expected by those who knew of him to become "King of the Jews" (Herod's position), Herod ordered the slaughtering of all male children who would be close to Jesus' age in Bethlehem.

2:18 Women at the time of the exile were mourning the loss of their children (Jr 31:15). **Rachel** was a wife of Jacob and the mother of Joseph and Benjamin (see Gn 29–31). She was a "type" of all Israelite women who mourned the loss of their children. Matthew applied this theme at the time of Herod's slaughter to the mothers of Bethlehem who lost their children age two years and under. Rachel herself died in childbirth on the way to Bethlehem (Gn 35:16-20).

2:23 The precise wording, **He will be called a Nazarene**, is nowhere to be found in the Old Testament. But Matthew introduced the quote as representing the teachings not of one prophet, but of the **prophets** in general, concerning the obscurity of the place of Christ's birth and childhood.

3:1-3 John the Baptist preached in **the Wilderness of Judea**, rocky desert region west of the Dead Sea. With an average rainfall of less than two inches, the land produces almost no vegetation and has long been inhabited primarily by Bedouin.

3:9-12 John pointed out to the Jewish leaders that they could not appeal to their ancestry as **children** [of] **Abraham** to save them. Genuine repentance would produce the **fruit** of righteousness, and John demanded this proof before he would baptize anyone. He was not saying that a person was saved by works but that a person's lifestyle would demonstrate whether or not he had truly forsaken his sins.

John used two metaphors to describe the reality of judgment for anyone who did not repent: the **ax** and **fire** (v. 10) and the **winnowing shovel** (v. 12). A **tree** that no longer produced fruit would be **cut down** with an ax and burned with **fire**. Fire often represented judgment in Scripture. John also proclaimed that when Christ came, He would divide the **wheat** and the **chaff** (the empty shells that covered the grain). When harvest time arrived, farmers would gather up and bring the wheat with the chaff to the **threshing floor**. In order to separate the grain from the chaff, the farmer would take the forklike winnowing shovel and throw his harvested grain into the air. The grain would fall to the ground as the worthless chaff blew away in the wind.

Only Matthew recorded Jesus' response to John's protest concerning His request for baptism (v. 15). Jesus did not need to confess or repent of sin. By being baptized, however, Jesus publicly endorsed John's ministry and message, and He personally displayed obedience to the will of God the Father, who verbally expressed His approval of Jesus' baptism. Each person of the Trinity was represented as Jesus formally entered into His messianic ministry: God the Son in His incarnation, God the Father as **a voice from heaven**, and God the Holy **Spirit . . . descending like a dove**.

warned in a dream, he withdrew
to the region of Galilee. 23 Then he
went and settled in a town called
Nazareth to fulfill what was spoken
through the prophets, that He will
be called a •Nazarene.

The Preparation for Jesus' Ministry (3:1–4:11)

The Messiah's Herald (3:1-12)

3 In those days John the Baptist
came, preaching in the Wilderness of Judea 2 and saying, "Repent,
because the kingdom of heaven has
come near!" 3 For he is the one spoken of through the prophet Isaiah,
who said:

A voice of one crying out
in the wilderness:
Prepare the way
for the Lord;
make His paths straight![A]

4 John himself had a camel-hair
garment with a leather belt around
his waist, and his food was locusts
and wild honey. 5 Then people from
Jerusalem, all Judea, and all the vicinity of the Jordan were flocking
to him, 6 and they were baptized by
him in the Jordan River as they confessed their sins.
7 When he saw many of the •Phari-
sees and •Sadducees coming to the
place of his baptism,[B] he said to
them, "Brood of vipers! Who warned
you to flee from the coming wrath?
8 Therefore produce fruit consistent
with[C] repentance. 9 And don't presume to say to yourselves, 'We have
Abraham as our father.' For I tell
you that God is able to raise up children for Abraham from these stones!
10 Even now the ax is ready to strike
the root of the trees! Therefore, every tree that doesn't produce good
fruit will be cut down and thrown
into the fire.
11 "I baptize you with[D] water for repentance,[E] but the One who is coming after me is more powerful than
I. I am not worthy to remove[F] His
sandals. He Himself will baptize you
with[D] the Holy Spirit and fire. 12 His
winnowing shovel[G] is in His hand,
and He will clear His threshing floor
and gather His wheat into the barn.
But the chaff He will burn up with
fire that never goes out."

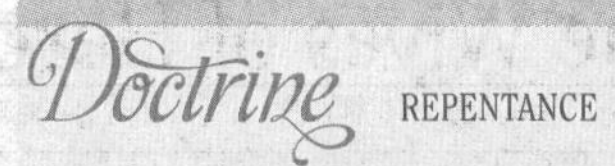

REPENTANCE

The heart of John's message was **Repent**! (Gk *metanoeite*, "have a change of heart, change one's ways," 3:1). The idea of **repentance** links sorrow for personal actions with making a complete turnaround and embracing new actions (v. 8). The biblical call to repentance involves being sorry for your actions but goes far beyond feeling guilt or regret to turning your back on sin and heading in the opposite direction. To repent is the necessary prerequisite for receiving forgiveness and salvation.

John urged people to repent because of the imminence of the **kingdom of heaven**. His ministry was foretold in Is 40:3, which portrays his mission as that of a herald running ahead of a king and his entourage as they approached. Like a herald, who would not only announce the king's arrival but would also call for people to clear the pathway of any obstacles, John announced the coming of the Messiah-King and called for people to prepare their hearts to receive Him. To bow before this righteous King and accept His lordship, you must be willing to *turn away from* being your own boss and *turn toward* Him, ready to do whatever *He* says.

[A]3:3 Is 40:3 [B]3:7 Lit *to his baptism* [C]3:8 Lit *fruit worthy of* [D]3:11 Or *in* [E]3:11 Baptism was the means by which repentance was expressed publicly. [F]3:11 Or *to carry* [G]3:12 A wooden farm implement used to toss threshed grain into the wind so the lighter chaff would blow away and separate from the heavier grain

>WORD|*study*

3:13-17 Baptize (Gk *baptizō*, "immerse, submerge") originally meant "to dip under," with the idea of totally enveloping one substance in another. In the first century, baptism was a well-known ceremony performed as a sign of repentance. For a Christian, baptism is a public testimony that symbolizes putting off the old life and identifying with the new life in Christ. It has a threefold significance:

- A public confession that Jesus died and rose again, picturing His death, burial, and resurrection.
- A public testimony of the experience of regeneration, showing death to an old life and resurrection to walk in the newness of life in Christ. Only the believer who has experienced the new birth is a candidate for baptism.
- A declaration of the believer's confidence that he will be raised from his own death and burial when Christ returns.

The Baptism of Jesus (3:13-17)

13 Then Jesus came from Galilee to
John at the Jordan, to be baptized by
him. 14 But John tried to stop Him,
saying, "I need to be baptized by
You, and yet You come to me?"
15 Jesus answered him, "Allow it
for now, because this is the way for
us to fulfill all righteousness." Then
he allowed Him to be baptized.
16 After Jesus was baptized, He
went up immediately from the water. The heavens suddenly opened
for Him,[A] and He saw the Spirit of
God descending like a dove and
coming down on Him. 17 And there
came a voice from heaven:

> This is My beloved Son.
> I take delight in Him!

[A]3:16 Other mss omit *for Him*

Jewish Sects in the New Testament

PHARISEES

Name	Date of Existence	Origin	Segments of Society
Pharisees = "the Separated Ones" with three possible meanings: • separating themselves from people • separating themselves to the study of the law ("dividing" or "separating" the truth) • separating themselves from pagan practices	Existed under Jonathan (160–143 B.C.) Declined in power under John Hyrcanus (134–104 B.C.) Began resurgence under Salome Alexandra (76 B.C.)	Probably spiritual descendants of the Hasidim (religious freedom fighters of the time of Judas Maccabeus)	Largest of the Jewish parties (or sects) Probably descendants of the Hasidim—scribes and lawyers Members of the middle class—mostly businessmen (merchants and tradesmen)

Beliefs	Selected Biblical References	Activities
Monotheistic Viewed entirety of the Old Testament (Torah, Prophets, and Writings) as authoritative Believed that the study of the law was true worship Accepted both the written and oral law More liberal in interpreting the law than were the Sadducees Quite concerned with the proper keeping of the Sabbath, tithing, and purification rituals Believed in life after death and the resurrection of the body (with divine retribution and reward) Believed in the reality of demons and angels Revered humanity and human equality Missionary-minded regarding the conversion of Gentiles Believed that individuals were responsible for how they lived	Mt 3:7-10; 5:20; 9:14; 16:1,6-12; 22:15-22,34-46; 23:2-36 Mk 3:6; 7:3-5; 8:15; 12:13-17 Lk 6:7; 7:36-39; 11:37-44; 18:9-14 Jn 3:1; 9:13-16; 11:46-47; 12:19 Ac 23:6-10 Php 3:4b-6	Developers of oral tradition Taught that the way to God was through obedience to the law Changed Judaism from a religion of sacrifice to a religion of law Progressive thinkers regarding the adaptation of the law to new situations Opposed Jesus because He would not accept the teachings of the oral law as binding Established and controlled synagogues Exercised great control over general population Served as religious authorities for most Jews Took several ceremonies from the temple to the home Emphasized ethical as opposed to theological action Legalistic and socially exclusive (shunned non-Pharisees as unclean) Tended to have a self-sufficient and haughty attitude

Jewish Sects in the New Testament (continued)

SADDUCEES

Name	Date of Existence	Origin	Segments of Society
Sadducees = Three possible translations: • "the Righteous Ones"—based on the Hebrew consonants for the word righteous • "ones who sympathize with Zadok," or "Zadokites"—based on their possible link to Zadok the high priest • "syndics," "judges," or "fiscal controllers"—based on the Greek word *syndikoi*	Probably began about 200 B.C. Demise occurred in A.D. 70 (with the destruction of the temple)	Unknown origin Claimed to be descendants of Zadok—high priest under David (see 2Sm 8:17; 15:24) and Solomon (see 1Kg 1:34-35; 1Ch 12:28) Had a possible link to Aaron Were probably formed into a group about 200 B.C. as the high priest's party	Aristocracy—the rich descendants of the high-priestly line (however, not all priests were Sadducees) Possibly descendants of the Hasmonean priesthood Probably not as refined as their economic position in life would suggest

Beliefs	Selected Biblical References	Activities
Accepted only the Torah (Genesis through Deuteronomy—the written law of Moses) as authoritative Practiced literal interpretation of the law Rigidly conservative towards the law Stressed strict observance of the law Observed past beliefs and tradition Opposed oral law as obligatory or binding Believed in the absolute freedom of human will—that people could do as they wished without attention from God Denied divine providence Denied the concept of life after death and the resurrection of the body Denied the concept of reward and punishment after death Denied the existence of angels and demons Materialistic	2Sm 8:17; 15:24 1 Kg 1:34 1Ch 12:26-28 Ezk 40:45-46; 43:19; 44:15-16 Mt 3:7-10; 16:1,6-12; 22:23-34 Mk 12:18-27 Lk 20:27-40 Jn 11:47 Ac 4:1-2; 5:17-18; 23:6-10	In charge of the temple and its services Politically active Exercised great political control through the Sanhedrin, of which many were members Supported the ruling power and the status quo Leaned toward Hellenism (the spreading of Greek influence)—and were thus despised by the Jewish populace Opposed both the Pharisees and Jesus because these lived by a larger canon (The Pharisees and Jesus both considered more than only Genesis through Deuteronomy as authoritative.) Opposed Jesus specifically for fear their wealth/position would be threatened if they supported him.

ZEALOTS

Name	Date of Existence	Origin	Segments of Society
Refers to their religious zeal Josephus used the term in referring to those involved in the Jewish revolt against Rome in A.D. 6—led by Judas of Galilee	Three possibilities for their beginning: • during the reign of Herod the Great (about 37 B.C.) • during the revolt against Rome (A.D. 6) • traced to the Hassidim or the Maccabees (about 168 B.C.) Their certain demise occurred around A.D. 70–73 with Rome's conquering of Jerusalem.	The Zealots began with Judas (the Galilean), son of Ezekias, who led a revolt in A.D. 6 because of a census done for tax purposes, according to Josephus.	The extreme wing of the Pharisees

Jewish Sects in the New Testament (continued)

ZEALOTS

Beliefs	Selected Biblical References	Activities
Similar to the Pharisees with this exception: believed strongly that only God had the right to rule of the Jews Patriotism and religion became inseparable. Believed that total obedience (supported by drastic physical measures) must be apparent before God would bring in the Messianic Age Were fanatical in their Jewish faith and in their devotion to the law—to the point of martyrdom	Mt 10:4 Mk 3:18 Lk 6:15 Ac 1:13	Extremely opposed to Roman rule over Palestine Rejected peace with Rome Refused to pay taxes Demonstrated against the use of the Greek language in Palestine Engaged in terrorism against Rome and others with whom they disagreed politically Sicarii or Assassins were an extremist Zealot group who carried out acts of terrorism against Rome.

HERODIANS

Name	Date of Existence	Origin	Segments of Society
Based on their support of the Herodian rulers (Herod the Great or his dynasty)	Existed during the time of the Herodian dynasty (which began with Herod the Great in 37 B.C.) Uncertain demise	Exact origin uncertain	Wealthy, politically influential Jews who supported Herod Antipas (or any descendant of Herod the Great) as ruler over Palestine (Judea and Samaria were under Roman governors at this time).

Beliefs	Selected Biblical References	Activities
Not a religious but a political group Membership was probably comprised of representatives of varied theological perspectives	Mt 22:5-22 Mk 3:6; 8:15; 12:13-17	Supported Herod and the Herodian dynasty Accepted Hellenization Accepted foreign rule

ESSENES

Name	Date of Existence	Origin	Segments of Society
Unknown origin	Probably began during Maccabean times (about 168 B.C.)—around the same time as the Pharisees and the Sadducees organized Uncertain demise—probably in A.D. 68–70 with the collapse of Jerusalem	Possibly developed as a reaction to the corrupt Sadducean priesthood Have been identified with various groups: Hasidim, Zealots, Greek influence, or Iranian influence	Scattered throughout the villages of Judea (possibly including the community of Qumran) About 4,000 in Palestinian Syria according to Philo and Josephus

Beliefs	Selected Biblical References	Activities
Very strict ascetics Monastic, usually took vow of celibacy (adopting male children in order to perpetuate the group), but some did marry for the purpose of procreation Rigidly adherent to the law (including a strict rendering of the ethical teachings) Considered other literature as authoritative (in addition to the Hebrew Scripture) Believed and lived as pacifists Rejected temple worship and temple offerings as corrupted Believed in the immortality of the soul with no bodily resurrection Apocalyptically oriented	None	Devoted to the copying and studying of the manuscript of the law Lived in a community sense with communal property Required a long probationary period and ritual baptisms of those wishing to join Highly virtuous and righteous Extremely self-disciplined Diligent manual laborers Assigning great importance to daily worship Upholding rigid Sabbath laws Commitment to a non-Levitical priesthood Rejected worldly pleasures as evil Refused matrimony—but did not forbid others to marry

A typical synagogue of the first century A.D. showing the large inner room where the men gathered and its loft above where the women gathered. This particular drawing is patterned after the synagogue at Capernaum in Israel.

4:1-11 The Synoptic Gospels all place the temptation of Jesus after His baptism, indicating the sequence of these events is significant. God the Father acknowledged Jesus to be His Son (3:17); then, even **the Devil** referred to Him as **the Son of God**.

The word **tempted** (Gk *peirasthēnai*, "put to the test," in order to determine quality or to see how someone will react or behave; "to try one's faith, character, or virtue by enticing to sin") here means "solicit to sin." As the final "Law Giver" and final "Prophet," Jesus fasted 40 days and 40 nights in the wilderness—in the same general region where John had been preaching. He was tempted in three significant ways: to turn **stones** into **bread**, to be rescued supernaturally from death, and to receive **all the kingdoms of the world**. Jesus accomplished what Adam, in his Edenic paradise, could not do when faced with temptation. Jesus resisted the Devil and thus became the "Greater Adam." In every instance, He used Scripture to defend Himself against the enemy's attacks (Dt 8:3; 6:16; 6:13).

The Temptation of Jesus (4:1-11)

4 Then Jesus was led up by the
Spirit into the wilderness to be
tempted by the Devil. 2 After He had
fasted 40 days and 40 nights, He
was hungry. 3 Then the tempter approached Him and said, "If You are
the Son of God, tell these stones to
become bread."
4 But He answered, "It is written:

Man must not live
on bread alone
but on every word that comes
from the mouth of God."[A]

5 Then the Devil took Him to the
holy city,[B] had Him stand on the
pinnacle of the temple, 6 and said
to Him, "If You are the Son of God,
throw Yourself down. For it is written:

He will give His angels
orders concerning you,
and they will support you
with their hands
so that you will not strike
your foot against a stone."[C]

7 Jesus told him, "It is also written:
Do not test the Lord your God."[D]
8 Again, the Devil took Him to a
very high mountain and showed
Him all the kingdoms of the world
and their splendor. 9 And he said to
Him, "I will give You all these things
if You will fall down and worship
me."[E]
10 Then Jesus told him, "Go away,[F]
Satan! For it is written:

Worship the Lord your God,
and serve only Him."[G]

11 Then the Devil left Him, and im-

[A] **4:4** Dt 8:3 [B] **4:5** = Jerusalem [C] **4:6** Ps 91:11-12 [D] **4:7** Dt 6:16 [E] **4:9** Or *and pay me homage* [F] **4:10** Other mss read *Get behind Me* [G] **4:10** Dt 6:13

mediately angels came and began to
serve Him.

The Beginning of Ministry (4:12–9:38)

Ministry in Galilee (4:12-25)

12 When He heard that John had
been arrested, He withdrew into
Galilee. 13 He left Nazareth behind
and went to live in Capernaum by
the sea, in the region of Zebulun and
Naphtali. 14 This was to fulfill what
was spoken through the prophet
Isaiah:

15 **Land of Zebulun and land**
of Naphtali,
along the sea road,
beyond the Jordan,
Galilee of the Gentiles!
16 **The people who live**
in darkness
have seen a great light,
and for those living
in the shadowland of death,
light has dawned.[A,B]

17 From then on Jesus began to
preach, "Repent, because the kingdom of heaven has come near!"

The First Disciples (4:18-22)

18 As He was walking along the Sea
of Galilee, He saw two brothers, Simon, who was called Peter, and his
brother Andrew. They were casting
a net into the sea, since they were
fishermen. 19 "Follow Me," He told
them, "and I will make you fish for[C]
people!" 20 Immediately they left
their nets and followed Him.
21 Going on from there, He saw
two other brothers, James the son
of Zebedee, and his brother John.
They were in a boat with Zebedee
their father, mending their nets, and
He called them. 22 Immediately they
left the boat and their father and followed Him.

Teaching, Preaching, and Healing (4:23-25)

23 Jesus was going all over Galilee, teaching in their •synagogues,
preaching the good news of the
kingdom, and healing every[D] disease

[A]**4:16** Lit *dawned on them* [B]**4:15-16** Is 9:1-2 [C]**4:19** Lit *you fishers of* [D]**4:23** Or *every kind of*

In each temptation Jesus was enticed to use His divine Sonship in a way inconsistent with His mission. Jesus knew that obedience to God's Word was more necessary than eating bread. He did not test God by protecting Himself, but He relied on His confidence in God's promise of constant protection. Jesus did not in any way swerve from His undivided allegiance to God the Father. The Son was to be King, but He was also to live in complete submission to the Father's authority.

4:18-22 Two sets of **brothers, Simon** and **Andrew**, together with **James** and **John**, were among the first men Jesus called to follow Him. Simon and Andrew were **fishermen** by trade and probably knew Jesus before this encounter by the **Sea of Galilee** (Jn 1:40-42). When Jesus called them to **fish for people**, they **immediately** (Gk *eutheōs*, "at once, soon") left their business and accepted His call. The other set of brothers, James and John, were in their boat with their father **mending their nets**, and they immediately left their boat and their father to follow Christ.

4:23-25 These verses display the threefold ministry of Christ of **teaching, preaching**, and **healing** while He was on the earth. He taught **in their synagogues**

Jesus' Ministry as Fulfillment of Scripture in the Gospel of Matthew

Aspects of His Ministry	Fulfillment Passage in Matthew	OT Prophecy
His virgin birth and role as God with us	1:18,22-23	Is 7:14
His birth in Bethlehem and role as shepherd	2:4-6	Mc 5:2-4
His exile years in Egypt and messianic role as God's Son	2:14-15	Hs 11:1
His upbringing in Nazareth and role as Messiah (Hb *nētser*, "branch")	2:23	Is 11:1
His preaching ministry in Galilee and role as Light to the Gentiles	4:12-16	Is 9:1-2
His healing ministry and role as God's Servant	8:16-17	Is 53:4
His reluctance to attract attention and His role as God's chosen and loved Servant	12:16-21	Is 42:1-4
His teaching in parables and His role in proclaiming God's sovereign rule	13:34-35	Ps 78:2
His humble entry into Jerusalem and role as King	21:1-5	Zch 9:9
His betrayal, arrest, and death and His role as Suffering Servant	26:50,56	The prophetic writings as a whole

(Gk *sunagōgais*, "assemblies"). During the exile the Jewish nation was cut off from worshiping in the temple, so synagogues became the centers of worship, community, discipline, and religious instruction. Even after the temple was restored, synagogues remained an important part of the religious life of the Jews, who formally gathered in these buildings to offer prayers and to listen to the reading and teaching of Scripture. These assemblies occurred weekly on the Sabbath and on feast days, as well as on the second and fifth days of each week.

Christ's preaching and healing ministry was well underway before He delivered the Sermon on the Mount. News about Him had spread as far as the region of **Syria** with its heavy Gentile population. The "darkness" that plagued the people of **Galilee** and beyond was demonstrated by the various kinds of sufferings and ailments Christ healed (cp. Is 9:1-2).

5:1–7:29 The Sermon on the Mount is one of the most well-known biblical texts, quoted often by both believers and unbelievers. Though believers have never been able to meet perfectly the demands of Jesus' words, they have been challenged to strive toward the standard He set, through the power of the Holy Spirit, demonstrating in every way full submission to Jesus. The Sermon on the Mount, then, is not about righteousness by works but about living a life consistent with genuine repentance, which then bears fruit.

The Sermon was meticulously structured to communicate Jesus' demand for a greater righteousness (5:17-20). The teachings are essentially grouped into units of three. The Beatitudes and the "salt and light" passages formed the introduction (5:3-16). Six illustrations of the greater righteousness followed, contrasting the Old Testament Law with Christ's ethic (5:21-48), then three examples of true piety (6:1-18), followed by three teachings about money and anxiety (6:19-34) and then by three sections on how to treat others (7:1-12). Jesus concluded His sermon with three examples, focusing on the only two responses possible for those who heard Him—acceptance or rejection (7:13-27).

The greater righteousness, then, involved a total and complete change of heart. Righteousness goes beyond mere works by producing good fruit consistent with this heart change (5:20). It involves seeking God's kingdom and His righteousness first (6:33) and treating others as you would want to be treated (7:12). Righteousness holds God's will to be supreme, (7:21), and unswerving allegiance to Jesus Christ produces security in Him (7:24-25).

In every way, the Sermon on the Mount was designed to demonstrate

and sickness among the people.
24 Then the news about Him spread
throughout Syria. So they brought
to Him all those who were afflicted,
those suffering from various diseases and intense pains, the demon-
possessed, the epileptics, and the
paralytics. And He healed them.
25 Large crowds followed Him from
Galilee, •Decapolis, Jerusalem, Judea, and beyond the Jordan.

Preaching: The Sermon on the Mount (5:1–7:29)

5 When He saw the crowds, He
went up on the mountain, and after He sat down, His disciples came
to Him. 2 Then[A] He began to teach
them, saying:

The Beatitudes (5:3-12)

3 "The poor in spirit are blessed,
for the kingdom of heaven
is theirs.
4 Those who mourn are blessed,
for they will be comforted.
5 The gentle are blessed,
for they will inherit the earth.
6 Those who hunger and
thirst for righteousness
are blessed,
for they will be filled.
7 The merciful are blessed,
for they will be shown mercy.
8 The pure in heart are blessed,
for they will see God.
9 The peacemakers are blessed,
for they will be called
sons of God.
10 Those who are persecuted
for righteousness
are blessed,
for the kingdom of heaven
is theirs.

11 "You are blessed when they insult and persecute you and falsely
say every kind of evil against you
because of Me. 12 Be glad and rejoice,
because your reward is great in heav-
en. For that is how they persecuted
the prophets who were before you.

Believers Are Salt and Light (5:13-16)

13 "You are the salt of the earth. But
if the salt should lose its taste, how
can it be made salty? It's no longer
good for anything but to be thrown
out and trampled on by men.
14 "You are the light of the world. A
city situated on a hill cannot be hidden. 15 No one lights a lamp and puts
it under a basket,[B] but rather on a
lampstand, and it gives light for all
who are in the house. 16 In the same
way, let your light shine[C] before
men, so that they may see your good
works and give glory to your Father
in heaven.

Christ Fulfills the Law (5:17-20)

17 "Don't assume that I came to
destroy the Law or the Prophets. I
did not come to destroy but to fulfill.
18 For •I assure you: Until heaven and
earth pass away, not the smallest
letter[D] or one stroke of a letter will
pass from the law until all things are
accomplished. 19 Therefore, whoever
breaks one of the least of these commands and teaches people to do so
will be called least in the kingdom
of heaven. But whoever practices
and teaches these commands will
be called great in the kingdom of
heaven. 20 For I tell you, unless your
righteousness surpasses that of the
•scribes and •Pharisees, you will
never enter the kingdom of heaven.

Murder Begins in the Heart (5:21-26)

21 "You have heard that it was said
to our ancestors,[E] **Do not murder**,[F]
and whoever murders will be subject
to judgment. 22 But I tell you, everyone who is angry with his brother[G]
will be subject to judgment. And

[A]5:2 Lit *Then opening His mouth* [B]5:15 A large basket used to measure grain [C]5:16 Or *way, your light must shine* [D]5:18 Or *not one iota; iota* is the smallest letter of the Gk alphabet. [E]5:21 Lit *to the ancients* [F]5:21 Ex 20:13; Dt 5:17 [G]5:22 Other mss add *without a cause*

>WORD|*study*

5:1-12 Blessed (Gk *makarioi*, "blessed, fortunate") is usually understood to mean "happy," but this concept does not capture its real meaning. More precisely the word suggests the idea of being congratulated because God's favor is granted to the individual. The source and point of reference for this blessedness is God.

Biblical Womanhood The Blessed Woman

Jesus presented an upside-down kingdom. The very things valued by the Greco-Roman world—wealth and fame—were devalued in Christ's kingdom. **Blessed** (Gk *makarioi,* "blessed, fortunate") is usually understood to mean "happy," but more precisely the word suggests the idea of "being congratulated" because God's favor is granted to the individual. The blessedness described in the Beatitudes is not a quality characteristic of human beings but a trait of God Himself. Only God imparts this blessedness—not on demand or as the result of your fulfilling prescribed conditions. Blessedness is a characteristic exclusively available to believers. Since this blessedness comes from within, it is neither caused nor affected by outside circumstances. Social and spiritual aspects of life are woven through each Beatitude. Believers are characterized by their humility and confidence in God. Through the Beatitudes Christ explained His personhood and His ministry, which were marked by humility and sacrifice. The world despised anyone who was considered weak, but Jesus taught that anyone who recognizes his own spiritual poverty and helplessness is ready for spiritual growth.

The **poor** [Gk *ptōchoi*, from the root meaning "crouch," suggesting a beggar who kneels in hope that his need will be supplied by another] **in spirit** (v. 5) could refer to those who are both spiritually impoverished and socially and economically oppressed. Nowhere in Scripture is poverty or absence of possessions declared to be the path to spiritual blessing. The emphasis was upon emptying yourself to make room for God. One who is poor cannot satisfy her own needs; she is driven by her poverty to dependence upon God. When self-sufficiency and pride are stripped away, you are ready to be responsive to God, His word, and the gracious ministries He sends to meet your need. As with most godly character traits, the pattern is found in the life of Jesus. He came into the world in a humble setting—a stable manger in an insignificant village. There is no way into the kingdom of God other than with the poverty of spirit that comes from emptying yourself of pride, self-reliance, and self-sufficiency and in contrast filling yourself with God, His strength, and God-sufficiency. The emphasis is on God's power instead of your resourcefulness.

The New Testament uses the phrase **kingdom of heaven** (v. 3) in three ways. Here all can be included in the meaning:

- the kingdom of God within the heart of a believer (Mt 6:33);
- the body that includes all believers on earth (Lk 11:2);
- the kingdom prepared for believers after death (Mt 16:19; Lk 9:62).

In each case God ushers in the kingdom, and Jesus reigns over it. Only the poor in spirit, claiming no personal merit, can enter because grace, and not works, opens the door.

Those who mourn (v. 4) echoed Isaiah 61:1. The meaning cannot be confined to sorrow over sin. Again the reader finds a paradox since most people do not recognize sorrow as a blessing. Followers of Christian Science even deny the existence of physical illness and suffering. Yet sorrow and death will always be present. Still this Beatitude does not suggest that physical suffering or loss of a loved one or any other tragedy of life would bring blessing merely as a payment for grief. Spiritual mourning indicates a sensitive consciousness of sin and an accompanying sorrow because of that sin (Jms 4:9). Those who mourn recognize who they are; they see purpose in sorrow and suffering; they allow that sorrow to give glory to God. Tragedies become stepping stones to the heart of God and His comfort (Ps 63:6-8; 77:2-6). Grief prompted by the sin itself, rather than only by the consequences of the sin that might have affected you adversely, produced sanctified sorrow. They will be **comforted** (Gk *paraklēthēsontai,* "encourage, console, cheer up," from the same root as *paraklētos*, "the one called alongside" and the name identifying the Holy Spirit). The Holy Spirit enables you to cry out for help because He not only brings conviction but also awakens within you sorrow over sin (Jn 16:7-11). As the believer mourns over her sin, the Holy Spirit who abides within does His work to give comfort and joy and enables her to persevere, even in the midst of sorrow and suffering. The Greek verb is in the passive voice and the future tense, implying not only assurance for the present but also security for the future. The cycle of comfort will be continuous because the Holy Spirit dwells now and forever in the believer's heart. The blessedness should not be construed as coming from the path of sorrow itself but from the comfort accompanying the believer in the journey (2Co 1:3-4).

The **gentle** (Gk *praeis,* "humble, meek," v. 5) were not the weak or cowardly. They were those who, under the pressures of life, had learned to bend their wills and to set aside their own notions as they stood before the greatness and grace of God. They were characterized by humble trust rather than arrogant independence as they exercised self-control of life and actions, submitting to the authority of Christ. Your focus must move from dependence on your own gifts and abilities to genuine dependence upon God. In humble recognition of her sinfulness, the believer has emptied her life and now stands before the Lord, seeking to please and serve Him by cheerfully obeying His commands and graciously submitting to the authorities God has placed in her life. Again the paradox is clear: The world associates gentleness with weakness, but in God's eyes strength characterizes the one who harnesses her life in order to maintain God-control. Gentle self-control prepares the way for God-control. Just as inheritance of the land was an expression of God's intervention and deliverance for Israel (Dt 4:1; 16:20), to **inherit the earth** was a temporal manifestation of the heavenly kingdom to come and another way to express God's sovereign rule. Enjoying that inheritance is possible because of a God-given spirit of contentment (Ps 37:16; Pr 15:16).

The first four Beatitudes describe the character of one who has been awakened and filled with the Spirit of God:

- Being poor in spirit affirms your own inadequacy and humility before the Lord.
- You are conscious of your sinfulness and mourn.
- You are gentle and allow God to control your life.
- You are not self-righteous, but realize only God Himself can offer what is needed. Your spiritual sensitivity brings a complete change of perspective.

Each Beatitude builds upon the previous one and prepares for those that follow.

Those who **hunger and thirst for righteousness** (Gk *dikaiosunēn*, "what God requires, what is right, what is just," v. 6) have a craving for righteousness, comparable to such physical hunger and thirst as was known only in lands where people died for want of food or water. God has placed in His creation an insatiable hunger for Himself—a God-shaped vacuum only He can fill. "Righteousness" equaled the will of God. Matthew used this word seven times in his Gospel, and five times the word was used in the Sermon on the Mount (3:15; 5:6,10,20; 6:1,33; 21:32). In the Greek text the noun was prefaced by the article (lit "the righteousness"), demanding a character from which right actions flowed. God's standard for righteousness is the life of the Lord Jesus. The text does not say that the person full of righteousness would be blessed; rather the one blessed would "hunger and thirst" or yearn after righteousness, realizing the journey of spiritual nurture never ends. The desire for spiritual sustenance must be renewed daily even as in your physical appetite. The word for **filled** (Gk *chortasthēsontai*, "feed, be satisfied, eat one's fill") is in the passive voice, indicating that the filling was to be done by an outside agent. The Lord did the filling. The verb is in the future tense, affirming that the filling was not a one-time event. God means for the filling to continue to supply nourishment and satisfaction. The emphasis turns from character to how character is shown in relationship to others.

The **merciful** (Gk *eleēmones*,"sympathetic") are moved to pity and compassion—sympathetic to the suffering of another. However, this mercy is not merely pity or an emotional response. To extend mercy God's way is an act of the will, and once extended, mercifulness draws more mercy. The religious leaders of Jesus' day prided themselves in doing deeds of service, but their hearts were often indifferent to the sufferings of others (Mk 3:1-6). Mercy ruled out merit and overshadowed other attributes of God. God's justice was satisfied by the sacrifice of His Son, and that was mercy.

The **pure** [Gk *katharoi*, "clean, guiltless"] **in heart** (v. 8) are people who are morally upright and holy and not just ritually cleansed. They have a lifestyle not only different and set apart in what they do but also marked by a difference in thought and motivation. To be "pure in heart" is to be obsessed by God and controlled by Him. This purity is an inner fountain that feeds all you do and say. The pure in heart do not harbor ill intentions toward anyone and are obsessed with pursuing genuine godliness. Those whose debt has been paid by Christ on the cross will indeed see God. Having been redeemed, they enter His holy presence and see things as God sees them. Many of the religious leaders in Jesus' day observed the laws concerning ritual cleanliness of the body, but only a person who turns to Christ to cleanse him of his sins will ever **see God** (Heb 12:14).

The **peacemakers** (Gk *eirēnopoioi*, v. 9) strive for harmony in all areas of life as a reflection on the inner peace that God brings to His children. Jesus taught that peace will only come when people have peace with God. This Beatitude raises the bar to the highest intimacy with the heavenly Father (Mt 5:45). The word moves beyond the idea of political and economic stability to include total well-being in the spiritual realm as well. Peacemakers want more than an end of conflict. They want healing among the people, ultimately dependent on reconciliation with God. This derivation of the Greek word for peacemakers is used only here in the New Testament. It refers to one who makes peace and seeks reconciliation rather than to one who is passive and seeking peace at any cost. A peacemaker separates herself from her own interests and whims and what is best for her. She becomes others-oriented with a deep concern for how the kingdom would be impacted by her actions. She is willing to suffer injustice in order for peace to reign and Christ to be magnified. To be **called sons of God** (v. 9) was not a gender assignment but an honorable title that went beyond personal identification to acknowledge publicly your relationship to the Lord and your place in His family.

Those **persecuted for righteousness** will have the **kingdom of heaven** (v. 10), having come full circle to offer the same reward as the first beatitude and best displaying the paradoxical nature of Christ's kingdom. Persecution was considered a blessing in Christ's kingdom because it allowed a person to empathize with the sufferings of Christ. Jesus did not promise vindication, but a reward in heaven awaited the person who persevered. Persecution begins when you commit yourself to Christ and it intensifies as you become more and more like the Savior. The world expects compromise and the path of least resistance, but Christ demands a gentle spirit and purity of heart and life in view of these three persecutions:

- **insult** (Gk *oneidisōsin*, "reproach, revile, heap insults upon");
- **persecute** (Gk *diōxōsin*, "seek after, strive for," and in its root meaning "pursue") in the sense that the world was running after believers to cause them suffering;
- **falsely say every kind of evil against you** (Gk *pseudomenoi*,"lying") referred to defamation of character or deception by falsehood. The tense of each of these verbs describing these categories of suffering suggests that the event happened at a particular time in the past instead of being an ongoing and continual action. Persecution happens, but it is not necessarily a continuous experience. There is a window of hope for earthly relief and the assurance of ultimate heavenly deliverance. In verse 12 Jesus used a strong word to express rejoicing (Gk *chairete* from the root meaning "grace"), and it was amplified with another verb, suggesting increasing intensity of joy (Gk *agalliasthe*, "rejoice greatly, jump for joy"). The persecution in itself does not bring joy but often affirms that you belonged to Christ, giving you a unique opportunity to glorify Christ and bear your testimony for Him. DKP

"Be-Attitudes for Women"

Blessed are...	Character Quality	Description	References
"the poor in spirit" (Mt 5:3).	Humility	Stripped of pride and sensitive to God's ministry in their behalf	Is 61:1; Lk 4:16-21; 7:22
"those who mourn" (Mt 5:4).	Sensitivity	Responsive to personal sinfulness and tenderhearted toward one another	Is 61:2; Ec 3:1-8; Lk 19:41; Jn 11:33,35
"the gentle" (Mt 5:5).	Gentleness	Demonstration of self-control and submission	Mt 6:33; 1Pt 3:1-7
"those who hunger and thirst for righteousness" (Mt 5:6).	Obedience	Desire to hear and do the will of God	Lk 1:53
"the merciful" (Mt 5:7).	Compassion	Outworking of faith to meet the needs of others	Lk 1:58
"the pure in heart" (Mt 5:8).	Holiness	Lifestyle of set-apartness, including thoughts and actions	Ps 24:4-6
those who are peacemakers (Mt 5:9).	Reconciliation	Forbearance instead of retaliation; forgiveness of wrongs; restoration of fellowship	Rm 3:25; 12:18; Eph 4:32; Php 1:3-5; Ti 3:2; 1Jn 1:7
"those who are persecuted for righteousness" (Mt 5:10).	Commitment	Steadfast loyalty that cannot be broken	Lk 13:34-35; 2Th 2:15-17; 2Tm 2:3
those who are insulted and persecuted because of Christ (Mt 5:11).	Patience	Willingness to endure suffering	1Pt 2:19-21; 3:14; Rv 12:11

whoever says to his brother, 'Fool!'[A]
will be subject to the •Sanhedrin.
But whoever says, 'You moron!' will
be subject to •hellfire.[B] 23 So if you
are offering your gift on the altar,
and there you remember that your
brother has something against you,
24 leave your gift there in front of the
altar. First go and be reconciled with
your brother, and then come and offer your gift. 25 Reach a settlement
quickly with your adversary while
you're on the way with him, or your
adversary will hand you over to the
judge, the judge to[C] the officer, and
you will be thrown into prison. 26 I
assure you: You will never get out
of there until you have paid the last
penny![D]

Adultery in the Heart (5:27-30)

27 "You have heard that it was said,
Do not commit adultery.[E] 28 But I
tell you, everyone who looks at a
woman to lust for her has already
committed adultery with her in his
heart. 29 If your right eye •causes
you to sin, gouge it out and throw
it away. For it is better that you lose
one of the parts of your body than
for your whole body to be thrown
into hell. 30 And if your right hand
causes you to sin, cut it off and
throw it away. For it is better that
you lose one of the parts of your
body than for your whole body to go
into hell!

Censuring of Divorce Practices (5:31-32)

31 "It was also said, **Whoever divorces his wife must give her a
written notice of divorce.**[F] 32 But
I tell you, everyone who divorces
his wife, except in a case of sexual

[A]5:22 Lit *Raca*, an Aram term of abuse similar to "airhead" [B]5:22 Lit *the gehenna of fire* [C]5:25 Other mss read *judge will hand you over to* [D]5:26 Lit *quadrans*, the smallest and least valuable Roman coin, worth 1/64 of a daily wage [E]5:27 Ex 20:14; Dt 5:18 [F]5:31 Dt 24:1

Jesus' authority as the final "Law Giver." Reminiscent of Moses' trek up Mount Sinai to receive the Law from the God of Israel, Jesus went up to the mountain, sat down, and delivered His message. But unlike Moses, He did not receive His message from a higher authority—Christ *is* the higher authority (7:29). Jesus—the Son of David, the Son of Abraham (1:1)—is greater than Moses. When Moses came down from the mountain, the people of Israel responded negatively to him, and judgment fell upon them. When Jesus came down from the mountain, the people followed Him, and He demonstrated His authority (and His greater righteousness) by various healings and miracles. Clearly, then, Matthew intended to show that, based on who Christ is, all believers must strive to embrace the greater righteousness about which He taught.

5:31-32 The Old Testament allowed a man to give his wife a certificate of **divorce** if he found "something improper about her" (Dt 24:1). This allowance was often abused, and men divorced their wives for many different reasons. Jesus rejected this practice on the grounds of the sanctity

immorality,[A] causes her to commit
adultery. And whoever marries a divorced woman commits adultery.

Telling the Truth (5:33-37)

33 "Again, you have heard that it
was said to our ancestors,[B] **You must
not break your oath, but you must
keep your oaths to the Lord.**[C] 34 But
I tell you, don't take an oath at all:
either by heaven, because it is God's
throne; 35 or by the earth, because it
is His footstool; or by Jerusalem, because it is the city of the great King.
36 Neither should you swear by your
head, because you cannot make a
single hair white or black. 37 But let
your word 'yes' be 'yes,' and your
'no' be 'no.'[D] Anything more than
this is from the evil one.

Going the Second Mile (5:38-42)

38 "You have heard that it was said,
An eye for an eye and **a tooth for a
tooth.**[E] 39 But I tell you, don't resist[F]
an evildoer. On the contrary, if anyone slaps you on your right cheek,
turn the other to him also. 40 As for
the one who wants to sue you and
take away your shirt,[G] let him have
your coat[H] as well. 41 And if anyone
forces[I] you to go one mile, go with
him two. 42 Give to the one who asks
you, and don't turn away from the
one who wants to borrow from you.

Loving Your Enemies (5:43-48)

43 "You have heard that it was said,
Love your neighbor[J] and hate your
enemy. 44 But I tell you, love your
enemies[K] and pray for those who[L]
persecute you, 45 so that you may
be[M] sons of your Father in heaven.
For He causes His sun to rise on the
evil and the good, and sends rain on
the righteous and the unrighteous.
46 For if you love those who love you,
what reward will you have? Don't
even the tax collectors do the same?
47 And if you greet only your •broth-
ers, what are you doing out of the
ordinary?[N] Don't even the Gentiles[O]
do the same? 48 Be perfect, therefore,
as your heavenly Father is perfect.

How to Give (6:1-4)

6 "Be careful not to practice your
righteousness[P] in front of people, to be seen by them. Otherwise,
you will have no reward from your
Father in heaven. 2 So whenever
you give to the poor, don't sound
a trumpet before you, as the hypocrites do in the •synagogues and on
the streets, to be applauded by people. •I assure you: They've got their
reward! 3 But when you give to the
poor, don't let your left hand know
what your right hand is doing, 4 so
that your giving may be in secret.
And your Father who sees in secret
will reward you.[Q]

How to Pray (6:5-8)

5 "Whenever you pray, you must
not be like the hypocrites, because
they love to pray standing in the
synagogues and on the street corners to be seen by people. I assure
you: They've got their reward! 6 But
when you pray, go into your private
room, shut your door, and pray to
your Father who is in secret. And
your Father who sees in secret will
reward you.[R] 7 When you pray, don't
babble like the idolaters,[S] since they
imagine they'll be heard for their

[A] **5:32** Gk *porneia* = fornication, or possibly a violation of Jewish marriage laws [B] **5:33** Lit *to the ancients* [C] **5:33** Lv 19:12; Nm 30:2; Dt 23:21 [D] **5:37** Say what you mean and mean what you say [E] **5:38** Ex 21:24; Lv 24:20; Dt 19:21 [F] **5:39** Or *don't set yourself against*, or *don't retaliate against* [G] **5:40** Lit *tunic*; = inner garment [H] **5:40** Or *garment*; lit *robe*; = outer garment [I] **5:41** Roman soldiers could require people to carry loads for them. [J] **5:43** Lv 19:18 [K] **5:44** Other mss add *bless those who curse you, do good to those who hate you,* [L] **5:44** Other mss add *mistreat you and* [M] **5:45** Or *may become*, or *may show yourselves to be* [N] **5:47** Or *doing that is superior*; lit *doing more* [O] **5:47** Other mss read *tax collectors* [P] **6:1** Other mss read *charitable giving* [Q] **6:4** Other mss read *will Himself reward you openly* [R] **6:6** Other mss add *openly* [S] **6:7** Or *Gentiles*, or *nations*, or *heathen*, or *pagans*

of marriage (see Mt 19). He continues to call His followers to a higher standard than what the Jewish law demanded. **Sexual immorality** (Gk *porneias*, "unlawful sexual intercourse, unchastity, fornication") is exhibited in various ways in the New Testament:

- voluntary sexual intercourse between a man and woman who are not married (1Co 7:2; 1Th 4:3);
- all forms of unchastity (Jn 8:41; Ac 15:20,29; 1Co 5:1; 6:13,18; Eph 5:3);
- prostitution (Rv 2:14,20-21).

5:33-37 Jesus teaches that all stated commitments are uttered in the presence of God and thus considered binding. He also condemned the hypocritical use of **oaths** by the religious leaders who taught that oaths omitting God's name were not binding and could be broken. Some, fearing they would not be able to keep a promise, might **swear** by something less than God's name, such as **heaven** or **earth** or **Jerusalem**. Jesus totally rejected this practice because a person of integrity has no need for oaths since his word should be trustworthy.

5:38-48 Jesus quotes from Lv 24:20 and teaches that His followers are not to **resist** evil with evil. He does not deny the common *lex talionis* (law of retaliation) as a principle of legal justice. The law insisted upon adequate punishment. However, the standard for Jesus' kingdom is higher. A slap across the **cheek** was intended to insult a person considered to be inferior. In contrast to the behavior of the Pharisees, disciples of Christ were to accept insults and were to go an extra mile when forced by the Romans to carry a load **one mile**. The ultimate principle is **love** of one's **enemies**, a standard still applicable, even mandatory, for every believer. The rabbis had corrupted the statement of summary of the law by adding to Scripture the words, "**and hate your enemy**" (v. 43; see Lv 19:18). By tampering with God's Word they were able to define **neighbor** to eliminate the hated **Gentiles** and Samaritans. On the other hand, Jesus called for unconditional love toward all just as God's love extended to all (v. 45).

6:1-4 The greater righteousness demands that acts of religious devotion not be merely external but truly motivated from a heart that is right before the Lord. Religious acts that issue from a pure heart are done **in secret**; the **Father**—and not the response of people—is the focus. Public prayer and fasting and even good deeds were not forbidden, but Jesus was cautioning against wrong motivation. Giving **to the poor** was not required by Jewish law, yet it was

>WORD|*study*

6:5 Jesus denounced as hypocrites (Gk *hupokritai*, "pretenders, actors, anyone who impersonated another") people who pretended to be pious. The root verb *hupokrinomai* was a theatrical term for "playing a part" onstage and thus "impersonating, wearing a mask, pretending, feigning."

Teachings from the Lord's Prayer

Phrase	Meaning	References
"Our Father in heaven" (Mt 6:9)	Recognize who God is.	Rm 8:15
"Your name be honored as holy" (Mt 6:9)	Worship Him because of who He is.	Ps 18:3; 96:8
"Your Kingdom come/Your will be done" (Mt 6:10)	Seek the will of God and do it. His Word is the path to finding His will.	1Jn 5:14
"Give us today our daily bread" (Mt 6:11)	Ask God to meet even your most mundane needs to accomplish your spiritual duties.	Php 4:9
"And forgive us our debts" (Mt 6:12)	Ask God to forgive your debts and your failures to obey Him.	Ps 66:18; Hs 14:2
"And do not bring us into temptation, but deliver us from the evil one" (Mt 6:13)	Seek a way of escape from the evil of temptation—protection, not removal from any trials but rather from judgment that comes when you are overcome by trials.	1Co 10:13; Jms 1:2-3
"For Yours is the kingdom" (Mt 6:13)	This benediction acts as a doxology.	1Ch 29:11

many words.
8 Don't be like them, because your Father knows the things you need before you ask Him.

The Model Prayer (6:9-15)

9 "Therefore, you should pray like this:

Our Father in heaven,
Your name be honored as holy.
10 Your kingdom come.
Your will be done
on earth as it is in heaven.
11 Give us today our daily bread.[A]
12 And forgive us our debts,
as we also have forgiven
our debtors.
13 And do not bring us
into[B] temptation,
but deliver us
from the evil one.[C]
[For Yours is the kingdom
and the power
and the glory
forever. •Amen.][D]

14 "For if you forgive people their wrongdoing,[E] your heavenly Father will forgive you as well.
15 But if you don't forgive people,[F] your Father will not forgive your wrongdoing.[E]

How to Fast (6:16-18)

16 "Whenever you fast, don't be sad-faced like the hypocrites. For they make their faces unattractive[G] so their fasting is obvious to people. I assure you: They've got their reward!
17 But when you fast, put oil on your head, and wash your face,
18 so that you don't show your fasting to people but to your Father who is in secret. And your Father who sees in secret will reward you.[H]

God and Possessions (6:19-24)

19 "Don't collect for yourselves treasures[I] on earth, where moth and rust destroy and where thieves break in and steal.
20 But collect for yourselves treasures in heaven, where neither moth nor rust destroys, and where thieves don't break in and steal.
21 For where your treasure is, there your heart will be also.
22 "The eye is the lamp of the body. If your eye is good, your whole body will be full of light.
23 But if your eye is bad, your whole body will be full of darkness. So if the light within you is darkness—how deep is that darkness!

[A]6:11 Or *our necessary bread*, or *our bread for tomorrow* [B]6:13 Or *do not cause us to come into* [C]6:13 Or *from evil* [D]6:13 Other mss omit bracketed text [E]6:14,15 Or *trespasses* [F]6:15 Other mss add *their wrongdoing* [G]6:16 Or *unrecognizable*, or *disfigured* [H]6:18 Other mss add *openly* [I]6:19 Or *valuables*

considered especially praiseworthy. Some people would **sound a trumpet** (a figurative way of calling attention to your deeds) when they gave to the poor so they would be commended for their acts. The offering chests in the temple were shaped like trumpets or funnels. Once coins were dropped in the mouth they were inaccessible to any thieving hands. Throwing the coins in the coffer in such a way that the "trumpet" reverberated with the noise was a way to call attention to one's generosity.

6:9-13 The model prayer illustrated *how* to pray rather than prescribing necessary words to use. This prayer, summarizing the teachings of Jesus about God's kingdom, is also known as the "Disciple's Prayer" or the "Lord's Prayer." Jesus addressed God as **Father** (Gk *patēr*); presenting God as an accessible, caring parent was unheard of in the first century.

God's forgiveness cannot be earned. It is a gift. But God's forgiveness can be blocked by your unwillingness to forgive those who have sinned against you.

6:16-24 As the disciples are told to perform their good deeds in *public* so that others might praise the Father (5:16), so they are now told to do their religious deeds in *private* in order that the deeds will not be motivated by human praise. The point is the same. In both cases, to bring praise to the Father is paramount. If good deeds in general are not performed in public, the Father is not praised. If religious deeds are performed merely in public, the

Father is not praised. Hypocrisy must be avoided in both cases.

Fasting (Gk *nesteuontes*, "abstaining from food") is a spiritual discipline exclusively between a believer and God, serving to draw a believer closer to God. Jesus assumed that His disciples would fast. He fasted for 40 days to prepare for ministry and strengthen His soul for the confrontation with Satan (Mt 4:1-2). Jesus stresses that God is not moved by fasting itself but rather by the turning of the hearts of His people to Him. Fasting must come from a right motive, or it loses its significance.

God, not possessions, must be at the center of the disciple's life. If not, no amount of "good" behavior will account for anything. What a disciple values reveals where his **treasure** is, and you cannot hide where your true loyalty lies. The **eye**, which is the mirror of the soul, will reveal the truth. It will show whether you serve **light** or **darkness**, **God** or **money**.

6:27 The **cubit** is a measurement defined as the length of a man's forearm from the inside of the elbow to the end of his longest finger—about 18 inches.

6:33 The true disciple must **seek . . . God and His righteousness** before all else and trust God to provide for her needs.

7:1-12 Christ's disciples are to treat others as they wanted to be treated (v. 12). The religious leaders failed to do this. However, only by treating others well will the greater righteousness be served and **the Law and the Prophets** fulfilled. Those committed to God and His righteousness must not be like the hypocrites and **judge** others without first judging themselves. A disciple must use discernment.

In this context, the disciple's priority is to seek God continually. If you ask God to meet your daily needs and if you treat others as you want to be treated, then the two greatest commands—to love God supremely and to love your neighbor as yourself—would be fulfilled in your life as a disciple. The "Golden Rule" and its principle of reciprocity summarize the moral and ethical requirements for those who choose to follow Christ.

7:13-29 With three illustrations—the two gates (vv. 13-14); the two trees (vv. 15-23); the two foundations (vv. 24-28)—Christ shows that there are only two ways to respond to His message—either to accept Him or to reject Him. There is no middle road.

7:13-14 The **gate** leading to **life** is a **narrow** one—allowing passage of one person at a time (i.e., you are not

24 "No one can be a •slave of two masters, since either he will hate one and love the other, or be devoted to one and despise the other. You cannot be slaves of God and of money.

The Cure for Anxiety (6:25-34)

25 "This is why I tell you: Don't worry about your life, what you will eat or what you will drink; or about your body, what you will wear. Isn't life more than food and the body more than clothing? 26 Look at the birds of the sky: They don't sow or reap or gather into barns, yet your heavenly Father feeds them. Aren't you worth more than they? 27 Can any of you add a single •cubit to his height[A] by worrying? 28 And why do you worry about clothes? Learn how the wildflowers of the field grow: they don't labor or spin thread. 29 Yet I tell you that not even Solomon in all his splendor was adorned like one of these! 30 If that's how God clothes the grass of the field, which is here today and thrown into the furnace tomorrow, won't He do much more for you—you of little faith? 31 So don't worry, saying, 'What will we eat?' or 'What will we drink?' or 'What will we wear?' 32 For the idolaters[B] eagerly seek all these things, and your heavenly Father knows that you need them. 33 But seek first the kingdom of God[C] and His righteousness, and all these things will be provided for you. 34 Therefore don't worry about tomorrow, because tomorrow will worry about itself. Each day has enough trouble of its own.

Judging Others (7:1-6)

7 "Do not judge, so that you won't be judged. 2 For with the judgment you use,[D] you will be judged, and with the measure you use,[E] it will be measured to you. 3 Why do you look at the speck in your brother's eye but don't notice the log in your own eye? 4 Or how can you say to your brother, 'Let me take the speck out of your eye,' and look, there's a log in your eye? 5 Hypocrite! First take the log out of your eye, and then you will see clearly to take the speck out of your brother's eye. 6 Don't give what is holy to dogs or toss your pearls before pigs, or they will trample them with their feet, turn, and tear you to pieces.

Asking, Searching, Knocking (7:7-12)

7 "Keep asking,[F] and it will be given to you. Keep searching,[G] and you will find. Keep knocking,[H] and the door[I] will be opened to you. 8 For everyone who asks receives, and the one who searches finds, and to the one who knocks, the door[J] will be opened. 9 What man among you, if his son asks him for bread, will give him a stone? 10 Or if he asks for a fish, will give him a snake? 11 If you then, who are evil, know how to give good gifts to your children, how much more will your Father in heaven give good things to those who ask Him! 12 Therefore, whatever you want others to do for you, do also the same for them—this is the Law and the Prophets.[K]

Entering the Kingdom (7:13-23)

13 "Enter through the narrow gate. For the gate is wide and the road is broad that leads to destruction, and there are many who go through it. 14 How narrow is the gate and difficult the road that leads to life, and few find it.

15 "Beware of false prophets who come to you in sheep's clothing but inwardly are ravaging wolves. 16 You'll recognize them by their fruit. Are grapes gathered from thornbushes or figs from thistles? 17 In the same way, every good tree produces good fruit, but a bad tree produces bad fruit. 18 A good tree can't produce bad fruit; neither can a bad tree produce good fruit. 19 Every tree that doesn't produce good fruit is cut down and thrown into the fire. 20 So you'll recognize them by their fruit.

21 "Not everyone who says to Me, 'Lord, Lord!' will enter the kingdom of heaven, but only the one who

[A] **6:27** Or *add one moment to his life-span* [B] **6:32** Or *Gentiles*, or *nations*, or *heathen*, or *pagans* [C] **6:33** Other mss omit *of God* [D] **7:2** Lit *you judge* [E] **7:2** Lit *you measure* [F] **7:7** Or *Ask* [G] **7:7** Or *Search* [H] **7:7** Or *Knock* [I] **7:7** Lit *and it* [J] **7:8** Lit *knocks, it* [K] **7:12** When capitalized, the Law and the Prophets = the OT

does the will of My Father in heaven. 22 On that day many will say to Me, 'Lord, Lord, didn't we prophesy in Your name, drive out demons in Your name, and do many miracles in Your name?' 23 Then I will announce to them, 'I never knew you! **Depart from Me, you lawbreakers!**'[A,B]

The Two Foundations (7:24-29)

24 "Therefore, everyone who hears these words of Mine and acts on them will be like a sensible man who built his house on the rock. 25 The rain fell, the rivers rose, and the winds blew and pounded that house. Yet it didn't collapse, because its foundation was on the rock. 26 But everyone who hears these words of Mine and doesn't act on them will be like a foolish man who built his house on the sand. 27 The rain fell, the rivers rose, the winds blew and pounded that house, and it collapsed. And its collapse was great!"

28 When Jesus had finished this sermon,[C] the crowds were astonished at His teaching, 29 because He was teaching them like one who had authority, and not like their •scribes.

Healing the People (8:1–9:38)

A Cleansed Man (8:1-4)

8 When He came down from the mountain, large crowds followed Him. 2 Right away a man with a serious skin disease came up and knelt before Him, saying, "Lord, if You are willing, You can make me •clean."

3 Reaching out His hand He touched him, saying, "I am willing; be made clean." Immediately his disease was healed.[D] 4 Then Jesus told him, "See that you don't tell anyone; but go, show yourself to the priest, and offer the gift that Moses prescribed, as a testimony to them."

A Centurion's Faith (8:5-13)

5 When He entered Capernaum, a •centurion came to Him, pleading with Him, 6 "Lord, my servant is lying at home paralyzed, in terrible agony!"

7 "I will come and heal him," He told him.

8 "Lord," the centurion replied, "I am not worthy to have You come under my roof. But only say the word, and my servant will be cured. 9 For I too am a man under authority, having soldiers under my command.[E] I say to this one, 'Go!' and he goes; and to another, 'Come!' and he comes; and to my •slave, 'Do this!' and he does it."

10 Hearing this, Jesus was amazed and said to those following Him, "I assure you: I have not found anyone in Israel with so great a faith! 11 I tell you that many will come from east and west, and recline at the table with Abraham, Isaac, and Jacob in the kingdom of heaven. 12 But the sons of the kingdom will

A7:23 Lit *you who work lawlessness* B7:23 Ps 6:8 C7:28 Lit *had ended these words* D8:3 Lit *cleansed* E8:9 Lit *under me*

Doctrine HELL

Jesus' description of this **place** [where] **there will be weeping and gnashing of teeth** is found six times in Matthew (8:12; 13:42,50; 22:13; 24:51; 25:30) and once in Luke (13:28). In each case, including those that are parables, God is consigning certain people to eternal condemnation. In Mt 8, particularly following so closely after Jesus' assertion of His divine authority to deny "lawbreakers" entrance in heaven and receive only those He knows (7:13-23), Jesus clearly speaks about "the kingdom of heaven" as the place where He and His Father rule. The criterion by which people, apparently sometime in the future, will be included or excluded from this kingdom is whether or not Jesus knows them (7:23), which is a matter of faith—the reason the centurion will be there but "the sons of the kingdom" will be cast out.

In Mt 13:36-43, Jesus describes a time "at the end of the age" when the angels sent by "the Son of Man" (i.e., Jesus) will "throw . . . into the blazing furnace" whatever "causes sin and those guilty of lawlessness." In verses 47-50, the angels again do the same with "the evil people." In Jesus' parable of the king's wedding banquet (Mt 22:1-14), the king orders a man to be thrown "into the outer darkness" because he had tried to attend without the proper "wedding clothes," signifying what God requires of men to enter His kingdom—repentance and genuine faith (i.e., evident in obedience). Also compare the accounts in chapters 24 and 25 and Lk 13:22-30.

These passages do not include the most common words for "hell" (e.g., Mt 10:28; 11:23), but each is describing a place to which people are forcibly taken away. Although these people want to enjoy the blessings of living under God's rule, they have denied God's right to rule over them. Jesus clearly refers to this place of exclusion from His kingdom (i.e., hell) as a real place, the experience of which suggests an overwhelming sense of regret, loss, hopelessness, and isolation.

received through the gate because you belong to a believing family or church, for example), each of whom must leave behind whatever might hinder their entrance through that one small gate (cp. Jn 10:9). The **road** leading to life is **difficult** (Gk *tethlimmenē*, "compressed"; metaphorically, "be afflicted, troubled, or distressed"; cp. "pressured," 2Co 4:8; "troubled," 2Co 7:5; "afflicted," 2Co 1:6; Heb 11:37).

7:15-20 There are many who will endeavor to lead a disciple astray, but Christ assures His followers that **false prophets** will be recognized **by their fruit**.

7: 21-27 Jesus gives His would-be followers a most stern warning. He will recognize His true disciples by their obedience. Only those who do the will of the Father **will enter the kingdom of heaven**, and the Father's **will** is for His followers to believe in the One He sent. Jesus' command, "Repent because the kingdom of heaven has come near" (4:17), must be met with seriousness and with genuine, fruit-bearing repentance. Jesus' words call for a decision. The popular opinion is that virtually all would be saved, but Jesus suggested the opposite. Only a few will be saved.

8:1–9:38 In this narrative sequence, Matthew introduces two very important matters:

- As the sovereign interpreter of the Law, Jesus demonstrated His authority by performing various miracles. He also demonstrated His greater righteousness by living under the Law (8:4) and by extending its boundaries in His interpretation (9:30; see 6:1).
- The greater righteousness is attained by *faith*. Faith is explicitly mentioned five times in this narrative sequence (8:10,26; 9:2,22,29). Jesus praised and rewarded all who exercised faith in Him, but He rebuked those who exercised little faith (8:26).

8:1-13 The **man with a serious skin disease** (Gk *lepros*, "a leper") was considered unclean, and anyone who touched him would also become unclean from the encounter. This man, both by his actions and words, demonstrated remarkable faith. Despite the social constraints and, likely, the physical difficulties of his condition, he found a way to approach Jesus and **knelt** [Gk *prosekunei*, "show homage to one of superior rank, kneel or prostrate oneself to show reverence or make supplication"] **before Him**. Not only did Jesus heal him, but **He touched him** as well, demonstrating His tender compassion for the man's suffering and His authority over sickness and disease. By instructing the man to go directly

Women Healed by Jesus

Woman	Faith	Jesus' Response	Her Response	References
Peter's mother-in-law	The faith of her family was demonstrated.	He healed her fever.	After being healed, she arose and served those present.	Mt 8:14,15; Mk 1:30,31; Lk 4:38,39
All who were sick	In faith, people came to Jesus for healing.	He healed all who were sick and cast out spirits as well.	None is given.	Mt 8:16-17; Mk 1:32-34
The hemorrhaging woman	Jesus was impressed with her faith.	After feeling her touch Him, He saw her and healed her.	She received the healing she sought and must have rejoiced.	Mt 9:20-22; Mk 5:25-34; Lk 8:43-48
The Canaanite woman's daughter	The mother was persistent and worshiped Jesus.	Her request was heard and answered when He healed her daughter.	None is given.	Mt 15:21-28; Mk 7:24-30
The infirm woman	Not stated	Upon seeing her, He called to her and healed her.	She was healed in being made straight and began glorifying God.	Lk 13:11-13

to the priest, Jesus was asking him to obey the law regarding his healing (see Lv 14:3-4,10).

Capernaum is on the northwestern shore of the Sea of Galilee, two and a half miles from the point where the Jordan River enters the Sea of Galilee. In Jesus' day the town was a poor fishing village just east of which was a small military garrison under the command of a Roman **centurion**, an officer in charge of 100 **soldiers**. As a Gentile, this man was considered unclean to the Jews, but he demonstrated remarkable confidence in the **authority** and power of Jesus' spoken word to heal his **servant**. Jesus commended the centurion for his faith and confirmed that the Gentiles would have a place with the Jewish patriarchs **in the kingdom of heaven**, while **the sons of the kingdom** (the Jews who did not believe Him; cp. Jn 1:12) would **be thrown into the outer darkness**.

8:14-22 So far in chapter 8, Matthew has recorded the healings of:

- a Gentile, traditionally excluded from the blessings of God's people, who had an incurable disease that had cut him off from society and from temple worship;
- a woman, who was not highly valued in Jewish or Greco-Roman society. Although regarded as a rabbi, Jesus even **touched her hand**—a detail that is particularly significant since Matthew has just noted Jesus' power to heal by saying the word (v. 8). By openly placing value upon women, Jesus was doing

be thrown into the outer darkness.
In that place there will be weeping
and gnashing of teeth." 13 Then Jesus
told the centurion, "Go. As you have
believed, let it be done for you." And
his servant was cured that very moment.[A]

Healings at Capernaum (8:14-17)

14 When Jesus went into Peter's
house, He saw his mother-in-law
lying in bed with a fever. 15 So He
touched her hand, and the fever left
her. Then she got up and began to
serve Him. 16 When evening came,
they brought to Him many who were
demon-possessed. He drove out the
spirits with a word and healed all
who were sick, 17 so that what was
spoken through the prophet Isaiah
might be fulfilled:

> **He Himself took**
> **our weaknesses**
> **and carried our diseases.**[B]

Following Jesus (8:18-22)

18 When Jesus saw large crowds[C]
around Him, He gave the order to
go to the other side of the sea.[D] 19 A
•scribe approached Him and said,
"Teacher, I will follow You wherever
You go!"
20 Jesus told him, "Foxes have dens
and birds of the sky have nests, but
the Son of Man has no place to lay
His head."
21 "Lord," another of His disciples
said, "first let me go bury my father."[E]
22 But Jesus told him, "Follow Me,
and let the dead bury their own
dead."

Obedience of Wind and Waves (8:23-27)

23 As He got into the[F] boat, His
disciples followed Him. 24 Suddenly,
a violent storm arose on the sea, so
that the boat was being swamped by
the waves. But He was sleeping. 25 So
the disciples came and woke Him
up, saying, "Lord, save us! We're going to die!"
26 But He said to them, "Why are
you fearful, you of little faith?" Then
He got up and rebuked the winds
and the sea. And there was a great
calm.
27 The men were amazed and asked,
"What kind of man is this?—even
the winds and the sea obey Him!"

The Driving Out of Demons by the Master (8:28-34)

28 When He had come to the
other side, to the region of the

[A] **8:13** Or *that hour*; lit *very hour* [B] **8:17** Is 53:4 [C] **8:18** Other mss read *saw a crowd* [D] **8:18** = Sea of Galilee [E] **8:21** Not necessarily meaning his father was already dead [F] **8:23** Other mss read *to a*

Gadarenes,[A] two demon-possessed men met Him as they came out of the tombs. They were so violent that no one could pass that way. 29 Suddenly they shouted, "What do You have to do with us,[B,C] Son of God? Have You come here to torment us before the time?"

30 Now a long way off from them, a large herd of pigs was feeding. 31 "If You drive us out," the demons begged Him, "send us into the herd of pigs."

32 "Go!" He told them. So when they had come out, they entered the pigs. And suddenly the whole herd rushed down the steep bank into the sea and perished in the water. 33 Then the men who tended them fled. They went into the city and reported everything—especially what had happened to those who were demon-possessed. 34 At that, the whole town went out to meet Jesus. When they saw Him, they begged Him to leave their region.

Forgiveness and Healing by the Son of Man (9:1-8)

9 So He got into a boat, crossed over, and came to His own town. 2 Just then some men[D] brought to Him a paralytic lying on a mat. Seeing their faith, Jesus told the paralytic, "Have courage, son, your sins are forgiven."

3 At this, some of the •scribes said among themselves, "He's blaspheming!"

4 But perceiving their thoughts, Jesus said, "Why are you thinking evil things in your hearts?[E] 5 For which is easier: to say, 'Your sins are forgiven,' or to say, 'Get up and walk'? 6 But so you may know that the •Son of Man has authority on earth to forgive sins"—then He told the paralytic, "Get up, pick up your mat, and go home." 7 And he got up and went home. 8 When the crowds saw this, they were awestruck[F,G] and gave glory to God who had given such authority to men.

The Call of Matthew (9:9-13)

9 As Jesus went on from there, He saw a man named Matthew sitting at the tax office, and He said to him, "Follow Me!" So he got up and followed Him.

10 While He was reclining at the table in the house, many tax collectors and sinners came as guests to eat[H] with Jesus and His disciples. 11 When the •Pharisees saw this, they asked His disciples, "Why does your Teacher eat with tax collectors and sinners?"

12 But when He heard this, He said, "Those who are well don't need a doctor, but the sick do. 13 Go and learn what this means: **I desire mercy and not sacrifice.**[I] For I didn't come to call the righteous, but sinners."[J]

A Question About Fasting (9:14-17)

14 Then John's disciples came to Him, saying, "Why do we and the Pharisees fast often, but Your disciples do not fast?"

15 Jesus said to them, "Can the wedding guests[K] be sad while the groom is with them? The time[L] will come when the groom will be taken away from them, and then they will fast. 16 No one patches an old garment with unshrunk cloth, because the patch pulls away from the garment and makes the tear worse. 17 And no one puts[M] new wine into old wineskins. Otherwise, the skins burst, the wine spills out, and the skins are ruined. But they put new wine into fresh wineskins, and both are preserved."

A Girl Restored and a Woman Healed (9:18-26)

18 As He was telling them these things, suddenly one of the leaders[N] came and knelt down before Him, saying, "My daughter is near death,[O] but come and lay Your hand on her, and she will live." 19 So Jesus and His disciples got up and followed him.

20 Just then, a woman who had suffered from bleeding for 12 years

[A]8:28 Other mss read *Gergesenes* [B]8:29 Other mss add *Jesus* [C]8:29 Lit *What to us and to You* [D]9:2 Lit *then they* [E]9:4 Or *minds* [F]9:8 Other mss read *amazed* [G]9:8 Lit *afraid* [H]9:10 Lit *came, they were reclining* (at the table); at important meals the custom was to recline on a mat at a low table and lean on the left elbow. [I]9:13 Hs 6:6 [J]9:13 Other mss add *to repentance* [K]9:15 Lit *the sons of the bridal chamber* [L]9:15 Lit *days* [M]9:17 Lit *And they do not put* [N]9:18 A leader of a synagogue; Mk 5:22 [O]9:18 Lit *daughter has now come to the end*

something new in Israel. Jesus does not show partiality; the benefits of His kingdom are for everyone who will come to Him in faith.

8:17 Christ's healing ministry was a fulfillment of Is 53:4.

8:20 Jesus referred to Himself as **the Son of Man**, a phrase occurring in the Greek text 81 times in the Gospels, 69 of which are found in the Synoptics. In every instance Jesus referred to Himself. The title carries with it supernatural overtones, drawing on its usage in a prophetic description of the Messiah (Dn 7:13-14; cp. Mt 26:63-64).

8:23–9:9 Jesus demonstrated His power over nature and the demonic realm. He manifested His authority to forgive sins, to raise the dead, to heal the chronically ill, to open the eyes of the blind, and to loose the tongues of those unable to speak. There were a variety of responses to His deeds, manifesting strong faith, faltering faith, or open rejection of faith.

Jesus' calming of the wind and the waves prompted His disciples to ask, **What kind of man is this?** (8:27). But the demons knew exactly who He was and what He could do (8:31). The scribes accused Jesus of blasphemy because He claimed the power to forgive sins (9:6). But the healing of the paralytic provided ample proof of His authority in this arena. To solidify this proof, **Matthew** included an account of his own calling to follow Jesus (9:9).

9:14-15 Then the followers of John the Baptist asked Jesus about fasting, the religious practice of abstaining from food. In His answer, Jesus compared Himself to a **groom** during the days leading up to His wedding, a time of joyous preparation during which fasting would be inappropriate.

9:16-17 With these two related parables, Jesus emphasized that He was doing a new thing in Israel. Both the **old** and the **new** would be preserved and restored in Him and in the covenant He would inaugurate.

9:18-26 The **woman who had suffered from bleeding for 12 years** was healed because of her **faith**, and the life of the ruler's **daughter** was restored because of her father's faith. The woman's disease was obviously not life-threatening, but it made her unclean and, therefore, an outcast in society (see Lv 15:19-28). Her effort to touch Jesus for healing displayed extraordinary faith, which Jesus acknowledged. He also addressed her with the endearing and relational term, **daughter**, which must have brought emotional healing as well to a woman whose condition had likely been a source of shame not only for her but for her father and perhaps for a husband who could not tolerate her disease or the infertility that added to her despair (Mt 9:22).

9:27-34 The next two miracles Matthew recorded show Jesus responding to true faith, opening the eyes of **the blind** and driving out a **demon** who robbed a man of speech. The response of the people linked these healings with the previous question about fasting and the subsequent healings of the woman and the girl: **Nothing like this has ever been seen in Israel!** (cp. vv. 26).

9:35-38 Verse 35 summarizes Jesus' earthly ministry. In the crowds Jesus saw the aimless and desperate wandering of sin-ravaged people who, like lost **sheep**, needed Him to shepherd them. Part of His mission for accomplishing this was to train His disciples to minister to people as He did and likewise to multiply themselves.

10:1-4 Matthew first mentioned Jesus' 12 disciples (Gk *mathētas*, "learners") at this point, but one may safely assume that these men had been with Jesus before He delivered the Sermon on the Mount. Matthew calls these men **apostles** (Gk *apostolōn*, "one sent forth with orders, messenger, delegate"). He sent workers out fully equipped by His power and given **authority** to minister as He had done, which included driving out **unclean spirits** and to healing **every disease and sickness**.

In each list of **the 12 apostles** found in the Gospels (see also Mk 3:16-19 and Lk 6:14-16), **Peter** is listed first and **Judas Iscariot** is listed last.

10:5-15 Jesus' next sermon was divided into two sections, giving instructions specifically for ministry during His lifetime and words of wisdom for future generations of disciples who would come after His death and resurrection (vv. 16-42). The Twelve were to go only to the **lost sheep** of Israel (a reference to Jesus' concern for the "sheep without a shepherd," 9:36). There was a sense of urgency with regard to getting the message out. It would be better for the sinful cities of **Sodom and Gomorrah** than for any of the lost sheep of Israel who refused to welcome these sent by the Lord, an allusion that emphasized the certainty and magnitude of God's judgment.

approached from behind and touched the •tassel on His robe, 21 for she said to herself, "If I can just touch His robe, I'll be made well!"[A]

22 But Jesus turned and saw her. "Have courage, daughter," He said. "Your faith has made you well."[B] And the woman was made well from that moment.[C]

23 When Jesus came to the leader's house, He saw the flute players and a crowd lamenting loudly. 24 "Leave," He said, "because the girl isn't dead, but sleeping." And they started laughing at Him. 25 But when the crowd had been put outside, He went in and took her by the hand, and the girl got up. 26 And this news spread throughout that whole area.

Healing the Blind (9:27-31)

27 As Jesus went on from there, two blind men followed Him, shouting, "Have mercy on us, Son of David!"

28 When He entered the house, the blind men approached Him, and Jesus said to them, "Do you believe that I can do this?"

"Yes, Lord," they answered Him.

29 Then He touched their eyes, saying, "Let it be done for you according to your faith!" 30 And their eyes were opened. Then Jesus warned them sternly, "Be sure that no one finds out!"[D] 31 But they went out and spread the news about Him throughout that whole area.

Driving out a Demon (9:32-34)

32 Just as they were going out, a demon-possessed man who was unable to speak was brought to Him. 33 When the demon had been driven out, the man[E] spoke. And the crowds were amazed, saying, "Nothing like this has ever been seen in Israel!"

34 But the Pharisees said, "He drives out demons by the ruler of the demons!"

The Lord of the Harvest (9:35-38)

35 Then Jesus went to all the towns and villages, teaching in their •synagogues, preaching the good news of the kingdom, and healing every[F] disease and every sickness.[G] 36 When He saw the crowds, He felt compassion for them, because they were weary and worn out, like sheep without a shepherd. 37 Then He said to His disciples, "The harvest is abundant, but the workers are few. 38 Therefore, pray to the Lord of the harvest to send out workers into His harvest."

The Opposition to Jesus' Mission (10:1–12:50)

Commissioning the Twelve (10:1-15)

10 Summoning His 12 disciples, He gave them authority over •unclean spirits, to drive them out and to heal every[F] disease and sickness. 2 These are the names of the 12 apostles:

First, Simon, who is called Peter,
and Andrew his brother;
James the son of Zebedee,
and John his brother;
3 Philip and Bartholomew;[H]
Thomas and Matthew the tax collector;
James the son of Alphaeus,
and Thaddaeus;[I]
4 Simon the Zealot,[J]
and Judas Iscariot,[K]
who also betrayed Him.

5 Jesus sent out these 12 after giving them instructions: "Don't take the road leading to other nations, and don't enter any •Samaritan town. 6 Instead, go to the lost sheep of the house of Israel. 7 As you go, announce this: 'The kingdom of heaven has come near.' 8 Heal the sick, raise the dead, cleanse those with skin diseases, drive out demons. You have received free of charge; give free of charge. 9 Don't take along gold, silver, or copper for your money-belts. 10 Don't take a traveling bag for the road, or an extra shirt, sandals, or a walking stick, for the worker is worthy of his food.

11 "When you enter any town or village, find out who is worthy, and stay there until you leave. 12 Greet a household when you enter it, 13 and if the household is worthy, let your peace be on it. But if it is unworthy,

[A] **9:21** Or *be delivered* [B] **9:22** Or *has saved you* [C] **9:22** Lit *hour* [D] **9:30** Lit *no one knows* [E] **9:33** Lit *the man who was unable to speak* [F] **9:35; 10:1** Or *every kind of* [G] **9:35** Other mss add *among the people* [H] **10:3** Probably the Nathanael of Jn 1:45-51 [I] **10:3** Other mss read *and Lebbaeus, whose surname was Thaddaeus* [J] **10:4** Lit *the Cananaean* [K] **10:4** *Iscariot* is probably "a man of Kerioth," a town in Judea.

Jesus' Disciples 10:1-4

Name	Description	References
Simon [Hb, "hearing"] **. . . Peter** or **Cephas** (Aram, "rock"; Jn 1:42)	He was a strong leader and among the first called by Jesus as a disciple. He was the brother of Andrew and worked in his father's fishing business. He wrote 1 and 2 Peter.	Mt 10:2; 16:16; Mk 3:16; 13:3; Lk 5:8; 6:14; Jn 1:42; Ac 1:13
Andrew (Gk, "manliness")	Originally a fisherman, he was also a disciple of John the Baptist but later followed Christ. He brought his brother, Simon Peter, to Christ.	Mt 4:18; 10:2; Mk 3:18; 13:3; Lk 6:14; Jn 1:40-44; Ac 1:13
James [Hb (Jacob), "he who grasps the heel"] **the son of Zebedee**	He was a fisherman who worked with his brother John and his father. Jesus nicknamed James and John the "Sons of Thunder." James was later executed by Herod Agrippa I.	Mt 4:21; 10:2; Mk 1:19; 3:13,17; 13:3; Lk 6:14; Ac 1:13
John (Hb, "the Lord is gracious"), a son of Zebedee	He was the brother of James and was part of the inner circle. The fourth Gospel, several epistles or letters, and the book of Revelation have been attributed to him. John was called "the beloved disciple," and Jesus singled him out from the cross to assign to him the care of His mother Mary.	Mt 4:21; 10:2; Mk 1:19; 13:3; Lk 6:14; Ac 1:13
Philip (Gk, "horse lover")	He was a disciple who came to Jesus early. He was from the same town (Bethsaida in Galilee) as Peter and Andrew.	Mt 10:3; Mk 3:18; Lk 6:14; Jn 1:43-48; Ac 1:13
Bartholomew (Aram, "son of Tolmai"), also known as **Nathanael**	He was Philip's companion on several missionary journeys. Possibly Bartholomew is the Nathanael whom Philip brings to Christ (Jn 1:44-51).	Mt 10:3; Mk 3:18; Lk 6:14; Jn 1:44-51; Ac 1:13
Thomas (Hb, "twin")	He is most famous for doubting the resurrection of Jesus.	Mt 10:3; Mk 3:18; Lk 6:15; Jn 14:5; 20:24-29; Ac 1:13
Matthew (Aram, "gift of God"), also known as **Levi**	A former tax collector; the Gospel of Matthew has been attributed to him.	Mt 9:9-13; 10:3; Mk 3:18; Lk 6:15; Ac 1:13
James [Hb (Jacob), "he who grasps the heel"] **the son of Alphaeus**	Little is known about him, other than that he was called James "the younger" or "the less" in order to distinguish him from the son of Zebedee.	Mt 10:3; Mk 3:18; Lk 6:15; Ac 1:13
Thaddaeus (Hb, "chest or heart"), also identified as **Judas the son of James**	Possibly he was known by his nickname, Thaddaeus, because of the disgrace that was attached to the name *Judas*.	Mt 10:3; Mk 3:18; Lk 6:16; Ac 1:13
Simon [Hb, "hearing"] **the Zealot** (Gk, "zealous one")	He was one of the lesser known apostles. His nickname, "the Zealot," could have been used to distinguish him from Simon Peter or could refer to his personality or political allegiance.	Mt 10:4; Mk 3:18; Lk 6:15; Ac 1:13
Judas Iscariot (Hb, "man of Kerioth")	Some take his name as that of cities in Judea and Moab, but others take it to mean *assassin* or *false one*. He is infamous for betraying Jesus and then hanging himself out of guilt and regret.	Mt 10:4; Mk 3:19; Lk 6:16; 22:3; Jn 13:26-30

10:16-42 Several things come into focus concerning the later generations of disciples. First, there would be hostility toward them simply because they were associated with Jesus' **name** (v. 22). This hostility would be widespread, ranging from the synagogue to the streets to the homes. If **the Son of Man** had been persecuted, His followers were sure to be, too. The only proper response to such persecution was to fear God. Looking back to His teachings concerning reliance on God in the Sermon on the Mount (6:25-34), Jesus reassured the disciples that God was in control (10:26). Therefore, His disciples must fear Him alone. He reminded them that death was not final for the believer (v. 28), and He continued to express His loving care for all of His creation (vv. 29-31).

Reminiscent again of the Sermon on the Mount, Jesus declared that there are only two responses to the Gospel—acceptance or rejection (7:13-27). There is no middle road. The depiction of family strife must be understood in this context. Those who profess to follow Him must have unswerving allegiance to Him, even if that brings alienation from family or if it costs your own life. His call is to single-minded devotion, even in the midst of division. Ultimately, all will be judged by their obedience to Christ (7:21-23).

Christ never disregards or devalues family relationships. God created family and gave clear instructions throughout Scripture concerning His will for families. However, concerning Christ and devotion to Him, all else must take second place (v. 37). The first command is always to love God with all your being.

11:1-30 The sermon portion of this second sermon-narrative sequence predicts future opposition to the disciples' mission. This narrative section emphasizes the rising opposition to Christ's mission. Chapter 11 begins with a segment that tied the importance of John the Baptist to his role in Jesus' ministry.

11:1-6 While sitting in prison, **John** had begun to have questions about Jesus' identity, so he sent some of his **disciples** to ask Jesus about his concerns. Christ answered John's question indirectly by pointing to the miracles He was performing.

11:7-24 Jesus praised John as far greater than the Old Testament prophets and as the one who fulfilled the prophecies concerning **Elijah** (v. 14). However, John's understanding was not complete. The disciples would witness Jesus' crucifixion, resurrection, and His ascension, and they would have an even more complete witness to share. Jesus praised John, but He

let your peace return to you. 14 If anyone will not welcome you or listen to your words, shake the dust off your feet when you leave that house or town. 15 •I assure you: It will be more tolerable on the day of judgment for the land of Sodom and Gomorrah than for that town.

Persecutions Predicted (10:16-25)

16 "Look, I'm sending you out like sheep among wolves. Therefore be as shrewd as serpents and as harmless as doves. 17 Because people will hand you over to sanhedrins[A] and flog you in their •synagogues, beware of them. 18 You will even be brought before governors and kings because of Me, to bear witness to them and to the nations. 19 But when they hand you over, don't worry about how or what you should speak. For you will be given what to say at that hour, 20 because you are not speaking, but the Spirit of your Father is speaking through you.

21 "Brother will betray brother to death, and a father his child. Children will even rise up against their parents and have them put to death. 22 You will be hated by everyone because of My name. But the one who endures to the end will be delivered.[B] 23 When they persecute you in one town, escape to another. For I assure you: You will not have covered the towns of Israel before the •Son of Man comes. 24 A disciple[C] is not above his teacher, or a •slave above his master. 25 It is enough for a disciple to become like his teacher and a slave like his master. If they called the head of the house 'Beelzebul,' how much more the members of his household!

Fear God (10:26-31)

26 "Therefore, don't be afraid of them, since there is nothing covered that won't be uncovered and nothing hidden that won't be made known. 27 What I tell you in the dark, speak in the light. What you hear in a whisper,[D] proclaim on the housetops. 28 Don't fear those who kill the body but are not able to kill the soul; rather, fear Him who is able to destroy both soul and body in •hell. 29 Aren't two sparrows sold for a penny?[E] Yet not one of them falls to the ground without your Father's consent.[F] 30 But even the hairs of your head have all been counted. 31 So don't be afraid therefore; you are worth more than many sparrows.

Acknowledging Christ (10:32-39)

32 "Therefore, everyone who will acknowledge Me before men, I will also acknowledge him before My Father in heaven. 33 But whoever denies Me before men, I will also deny him before My Father in heaven. 34 Don't assume that I came to bring peace on the earth. I did not come to bring peace, but a sword. 35 For I came to turn

a man against his father,
a daughter against
her mother,
a daughter-in-law against
her mother-in-law;
36 **and a man's enemies will be**
the members
of his household.[G]

37 The person who loves father or mother more than Me is not worthy of Me; the person who loves son or daughter more than Me is not worthy of Me. 38 And whoever doesn't take up his cross and follow[H] Me is not worthy of Me. 39 Anyone finding[I] his life will lose it, and anyone losing[J] his life because of Me will find it.

A Cup of Cold Water (10:40-42)

40 "The one who welcomes you welcomes Me, and the one who welcomes Me welcomes Him who sent Me. 41 Anyone who[K] welcomes a prophet because he is a prophet[L] will receive a prophet's reward. And anyone who[M] welcomes a righteous person because he's righteous[N] will receive a righteous person's reward. 42 And whoever gives just a cup of cold water to one of these little ones

[A] **10:17** Local Jewish courts or local councils [B] **10:22** Or *saved* [C] **10:24** Or *student* [D] **10:27** Lit *in the ear* [E] **10:29** Gk *assarion*, a small copper coin [F] **10:29** Lit *ground apart from your Father* [G] **10:35-36** Mc 7:6 [H] **10:38** Lit *follow after* [I] **10:39** Or *The one who finds* [J] **10:39** Or *and the one who loses* [K] **10:41** Or *The one who* [L] **10:41** Lit *prophet in the name of a prophet* [M] **10:41** Or *And the one who* [N] **10:41** Lit *person in the name of a righteous person*

because he is a disciple[A]—I assure you: He will never lose his reward!"

In Praise of John the Baptist (11:1-15)

11 When Jesus had finished giving orders to His 12 disciples, He moved on from there to teach and preach in their towns. 2 When John heard in prison what the •Messiah was doing, he sent a message by his disciples 3 and asked Him, "Are You the One who is to come, or should we expect someone else?"

4 Jesus replied to them, "Go and report to John what you hear and see: 5 the blind see, the lame walk, those with skin diseases are healed,[B] the deaf hear, the dead are raised, and the poor are told the good news. 6 And if anyone is not •offended because of Me, he is blessed."

7 As these men went away, Jesus began to speak to the crowds about John: "What did you go out into the wilderness to see? A reed swaying in the wind? 8 What then did you go out to see? A man dressed in soft clothes? Look, those who wear soft clothes are in kings' palaces. 9 But what did you go out to see? A prophet? Yes, I tell you, and far more than a prophet. 10 This is the one it is written about:

> **Look, I am sending**
> **My messenger**
> **ahead of You;**[C]
> **he will prepare Your way**
> **before You.**[D]

11 "•I assure you: Among those born of women no one greater than John the Baptist has appeared,[E] but the least in the kingdom of heaven is greater than he. 12 From the days of John the Baptist until now, the kingdom of heaven has been suffering violence,[F] and the violent have been seizing it by force. 13 For all the prophets and the Law prophesied until John; 14 if you're willing to accept it, he is the Elijah who is to come. 15 Anyone who has ears[G] should listen!

An Unresponsive Generation (11:16-24)

16 "To what should I compare this generation? It's like children sitting in the marketplaces who call out to each other:

> 17 We played the flute for you,
> but you didn't dance;
> we sang a lament,
> but you didn't mourn![H]

18 For John did not come eating or drinking, and they say, 'He has a demon!' 19 The •Son of Man came eating and drinking, and they say, 'Look, a glutton and a drunkard, a friend of tax collectors and sinners!' Yet wisdom is vindicated[I] by her deeds."[J]

20 Then He proceeded to denounce the towns where most of His miracles were done, because they did not repent: 21 "Woe to you, Chorazin! Woe to you, Bethsaida! For if the miracles that were done in you had been done in Tyre and Sidon, they would have repented in •sackcloth and ashes long ago! 22 But I tell you, it will be more tolerable for Tyre and Sidon on the day of judgment than for you. 23 And you, Capernaum, will you be exalted to heaven? You will go down to •Hades. For if the miracles that were done in you had been done in Sodom, it would have remained until today. 24 But I tell you, it will be more tolerable for the land of Sodom on the day of judgment than for you."

The Son Gives Knowledge and Rest (11:25-30)

25 At that time Jesus said, "I praise[K] You, Father, Lord of heaven and earth, because You have hidden these things from the wise and learned and revealed them to infants. 26 Yes, Father, because this was Your good pleasure.[L] 27 All things have been entrusted to Me by My Father. No one knows[M] the Son except the Father, and no one knows the Father except the Son and anyone to whom the Son desires[N] to reveal Him.

28 "Come to Me, all of you who are

rebuked the Jewish people for refusing to respond to the message of Jesus and John. Foreshadowing the openness of the Gentiles to His message, Jesus condemned the heavily populated Jewish towns where He ministered for their lack of repentance.

11:25-30 By contrast, Jesus praised the **Father** for His way of revealing Himself to people. Here is a paradox. God's revelation was **hidden** from those who seemed most likely to understand, but pride and self-sufficiency kept them from getting it. On the other hand, **infants** are dependent by nature and tend to have a desire to learn. The good news of the gospel was available to all who wanted to listen and learn. Yet underlying this discussion was Jesus' clear affirmation of the Father's will. Jesus had an exclusive relationship with the Father and delighted to do the will of the Father.

Jesus taught another lesson in discipleship, using the common **yoke** as a metaphor. The yoke is Jesus' life and teachings—not the law. Followers of Christ are indeed free from the law, but they are not free to do as they please. They are to be harnessed to Christ. The yoke is a harness in which two animals pull together. One harness often is larger, designed for the stronger and more experienced animal, so that the younger animal can be trained and guided by its mentor. Jesus invites **all** who are **weary and burdened** to come to Him for **rest**. In the context, **all** seems to refer to both Jews and Gentiles, stressing Christ's mission to both groups. And this could be the ultimate point Matthew intended to make.

[A] 10:42 Lit *little ones in the name of a disciple* [B] 11:5 Lit *cleansed* [C] 11:10 Lit *messenger before Your face* [D] 11:10 Mal 3:1 [E] 11:11 Lit *arisen* [F] 11:12 Or *has been forcefully advancing* [G] 11:15 Other mss add *to hear* [H] 11:17 Or *beat your breasts* [I] 11:19 Or *declared right* [J] 11:19 Other mss read *children* [K] 11:25 Or *thank* [L] 11:26 Lit *was well-pleasing in Your sight* [M] 11:27 Or *knows exactly* [N] 11:27 Or *wills*, or *chooses*

12:1-45 In this section, opposition to Jesus' mission is apparent. The rising clamor began with Jesus' claims about Himself as being **greater than the temple** (v. 6), **Jonah** the prophet (v. 41), and King **Solomon** (v. 42). His miracles provided ample evidence for His claims (v. 13). The healing that He performed on the Sabbath caused the Pharisees to want to **destroy Him** (v. 14). When Jesus learned of their plot, He **withdrew**.

With these events, Matthew claimed that Isaiah's prophecy was **fulfilled** (v. 17; Is 42:1-4). In this context, Christ's character was contrasted with that of the Pharisees. Unlike the religious leaders, the true servant of the Lord was gentle and merciful (see also 11:29; 12:7). The Gentile **nations** would put their **hope** in this humble **Servant** of the Lord, corroborating the testimony Jesus gave of Himself (12:18-21).

12:22-32 In light of Jesus' healing of **a demon-possessed man who was blind and unable to speak**, the Pharisees accused Him of being empowered by the Devil. Jesus clearly showed them that their accusation could not be true because a kingdom divided against itself would not stand. Jesus again showed that there are only two ways to respond to Him: acceptance or rejection (v. 30). Those who reject Him can be forgiven if they repent and accept Him. But blasphemy **against the Holy Spirit** or attributing to Satan the work of the Holy Spirit—which the Pharisees were indeed doing—would not be forgiven (vv. 31-32).

12:33-37 The religious leaders were clearly an example of the bad trees mentioned in the Sermon on the Mount (7:15-20). Jesus blatantly called them **evil**, for their evil words revealed their evil hearts. While the warning about words in this context was meant for the Pharisees, it stands as a warning to all who use their words without thought of eternal and/or temporal consequences.

12:38-42 When the Pharisees asked for **a sign**, Jesus compared Himself to **the prophet Jonah**, alluding to His own death and resurrection. These words were the first specific mention of His future suffering. Jesus rebuked the Pharisees by citing historical examples of the willingness of the Gentiles to listen to Jonah and Solomon. People recognized the importance of the messages of these mere men; yet here stood Jesus, the awaited Messiah, and the religious leaders who studied the Scriptures could not recognize the One before them.

12:43-45 The hardness of this generation of Jews was more sharply defined as Jesus described the **unclean**

weary and burdened, and I will give you rest. 29 All of you, take up My yoke and learn from Me, because I am gentle and humble in heart, and you will find rest for yourselves. 30 For My yoke is easy and My burden is light."

Lord of the Sabbath (12:1-8)

12 At that time Jesus passed through the grainfields on the Sabbath. His disciples were hungry and began to pick and eat some heads of grain. 2 But when the •Pharisees saw it, they said to Him, "Look, Your disciples are doing what is not lawful to do on the Sabbath!"

3 He said to them, "Haven't you read what David did when he and those who were with him were hungry— 4 how he entered the house of God, and they ate[A] the •sacred bread, which is not lawful for him or for those with him to eat, but only for the priests? 5 Or haven't you read in the Law[B] that on Sabbath days the priests in the temple violate the Sabbath and are innocent? 6 But I tell you that something greater than the temple is here! 7 If you had known what this means: **I desire mercy and not sacrifice,**[C] you would not have condemned the innocent. 8 For the •Son of Man is Lord of the Sabbath."

The Man with the Paralyzed Hand (12:9-14)

9 Moving on from there, He entered their •synagogue. 10 There He saw a man who had a paralyzed hand. And in order to accuse Him they asked Him, "Is it lawful to heal on the Sabbath?"

11 But He said to them, "What man among you, if he had a sheep[D] that fell into a pit on the Sabbath, wouldn't take hold of it and lift it out? 12 A man is worth far more than a sheep, so it is lawful to do what is good on the Sabbath."

13 Then He told the man, "Stretch out your hand." So he stretched it out, and it was restored, as good as the other. 14 But the Pharisees went out and plotted against Him, how they might destroy Him.

The Servant of the Lord (12:15-21)

15 When Jesus became aware of this, He withdrew from there. Huge crowds[E] followed Him, and He healed them all. 16 He warned them not to make Him known, 17 so that what was spoken through the prophet Isaiah might be fulfilled:

18 **Here is My Servant**
whom I have chosen,
My beloved in whom
My soul delights;
I will put My Spirit on Him,
and He will proclaim justice
to the nations.
19 **He will not argue or shout,**
and no one will hear
His voice in the streets.
20 **He will not break**
a bruised reed,
and He will not put out
a smoldering wick,
until He has led justice
to victory.[F]
21 **The nations will put**
their hope in His name.[G]

A Divided House (12:22-32)

22 Then a demon-possessed man who was blind and unable to speak was brought to Him. He healed him, so that the man[H] could both speak and see. 23 And all the crowds were astounded and said, "Perhaps this is the Son of David!"

24 When the Pharisees heard this, they said, "The man drives out demons only by •Beelzebul, the ruler of the demons."

25 Knowing their thoughts, He told them: "Every kingdom divided against itself is headed for destruction, and no city or house divided against itself will stand. 26 If Satan drives out Satan, he is divided against himself. How then will his kingdom stand? 27 And if I drive out demons by Beelzebul, who is it your sons drive them out by? For this reason they will be your judges. 28 If I drive out demons by the Spirit of God, then the kingdom of God has come to you. 29 How can someone enter a strong man's house and steal his possessions unless he first ties up the strong man? Then he can rob

A 12:4 Other mss read *he ate* B 12:5 = The Torah (the Pentateuch) C 12:7 Hs 6:6 D 12:11 Or *had one sheep* E 12:15 Other mss read *Many* F 12:20 Or *until He has successfully put forth justice* G 12:18-21 Is 42:1-4 H 12:22 Lit *mute*

his house. 30 Anyone who is not with Me is against Me, and anyone who does not gather with Me scatters. 31 Because of this, I tell you, people will be forgiven every sin and blasphemy, but the blasphemy against[A] the Spirit will not be forgiven.[B] 32 Whoever speaks a word against the Son of Man, it will be forgiven him. But whoever speaks against the Holy Spirit, it will not be forgiven him, either in this age or in the one to come.

A Tree and Its Fruit (12:33-37)

33 "Either make the tree good and its fruit good, or make the tree bad[C] and its fruit bad; for a tree is known by its fruit. 34 Brood of vipers! How can you speak good things when you are evil? For the mouth speaks from the overflow of the heart. 35 A good man produces good things from his storeroom of good,[D] and an evil man produces evil things from his storeroom of evil. 36 I tell you that on the day of judgment people will have to account for every careless word they speak.[E] 37 For by your words you will be acquitted, and by your words you will be condemned."

The Sign of Jonah (12:38-42)

38 Then some of the •scribes and Pharisees said to Him, "Teacher, we want to see a sign from You."

39 But He answered them, "An evil and adulterous generation demands a sign, but no sign will be given to it except the sign of the prophet Jonah. 40 For as Jonah was in the belly of the huge fish three days and three nights, so the Son of Man will be in the heart of the earth three days and three nights. 41 The men of Nineveh will stand up at the judgment with this generation and condemn it, because they repented at Jonah's proclamation; and look—something greater than Jonah is here! 42 The queen of the south will rise up at the judgment with this generation and condemn it, because she came from the ends of the earth to hear the wisdom of Solomon; and look—something greater than Solomon is here!

An Unclean Spirit's Return (12:43-45)

43 "When an •unclean spirit comes out of a man, it roams through waterless places looking for rest but doesn't find any. 44 Then it says, 'I'll go back to my house that I came from.' And returning, it finds the house vacant, swept, and put in order. 45 Then off it goes and brings with it seven other spirits more evil than itself, and they enter and settle down there. As a result, that man's last condition is worse than the first. That's how it will also be with this evil generation."

True Relationships (12:46-50)

46 He was still speaking to the crowds when suddenly His mother and brothers were standing outside wanting to speak to Him. 47 Someone told Him, "Look, Your mother and Your brothers are standing outside, wanting to speak to You."[F]

48 But He replied to the one who told Him, "Who is My mother and who are My brothers?" 49 And stretching out His hand toward His disciples, He said, "Here are My mother and My brothers! 50 For whoever does the will of My Father in heaven, that person is My brother and sister and mother."

Predicting Progressive Opposition Toward Jesus (13:1–16:20)

The Parable of the Sower (13:1-9)

13 On that day Jesus went out of the house and was sitting by the sea. 2 Such large crowds gathered around Him that He got into a boat and sat down, while the whole crowd stood on the shore.

3 Then He told them many things in parables, saying: "Consider the sower who went out to sow. 4 As he was sowing, some seed fell along the path, and the birds came and ate them up. 5 Others fell on rocky ground, where there wasn't much soil, and they sprang up quickly since the soil wasn't deep. 6 But when the sun came up they were scorched, and since they had no root, they withered. 7 Others fell among thorns, and the thorns came

[A] **12:31** Or *of* [B] **12:31** Other mss add *people* [C] **12:33** Or *decayed*; lit *rotten* [D] **12:35** Other mss read *from the storehouse of his heart* [E] **12:36** Lit *will speak* [F] **12:47** Other mss omit this v.

spirit that left and then returned to a man who had been cleansed. This reference was to the "cleansing" power of His ministry. When the demon returned, the **condition** of that man would be worse than at first—an indication of just how hardened this generation would become.

12:46-50 Jesus poignantly described the characteristics of a person who was for Him and not against Him. The one who was for Him would be doing **the will of** His **Father in heaven**. In this way, Jesus elevated spiritual relationships above natural/biological relationships. Jesus was not denigrating His **mother** and **brothers**; He was simply giving priority to the will of His Father over all human relationships.

13:1-52 This third sermon-narrative sequence represented a crucial turning point in Christ's ministry. Only those who would do the Father's will were true followers of Christ (12:46-50). From this point the polarization, explained through parables, between those who would follow Christ and those who would not came into sharp contrast. **Parables** (Gk *parabolais*, "proverb, figure, symbol") are basically metaphorical narratives. Two Greek words are linked—*para* ("near, beside, along") and *ballō* ("throw, put, place, bring")—with the sense of literally "bringing alongside." Jesus' parables are distinctive in that they are composed in particular contexts so that the main point can be discovered if that same point is translated into a contemporary context. The overall function of a parable is to call forth a response from the hearer. The kind of response evoked really depends on the heart of the listener. In this section Jesus began to separate His listeners into outsiders (those who did not have responsive hearts) and insiders (those who responded favorably).

Also, Jesus' parables were vehicles for proclaiming the kingdom, which lay at the heart of Jesus' message. **The kingdom of heaven** could refer to different ideas:

- a covenant into which one enters,
- a future entity yet to be fully established,
- an unexpected coming event separating the righteous from the wicked,
- the establishment of a recognizable social order,
- a present experience of Jesus' words and deeds,
- an entity over which God reigned as King.

The kingdom of God, according to Jesus, most certainly has present and future dimensions. By the power of the Holy Spirit, a believer simply cannot underestimate what he can do now. However, she has to be realistic about the kinds of things she can truly accomplish. Believers in this world are still in enemy territory.

13:10-17 Parables have been described as "an earthly story with a heavenly meaning." Indeed Jesus did often use examples drawn from daily life (13:24-30,45-46) or from nature (13:1-7,31-32) to teach spiritual truths. The details used to tell the story are not necessarily significant, though often they play a part in the lesson to be taught. The audience did not always understand what Jesus was teaching, but the truths conveyed are as relevant and applicable to life today as they were when spoken by Jesus.

13:18-23 The **parable of the sower** provides a key to understanding not only Jesus' other parables but also His teachings in general. This parable indicated the kind of hearers who had been around Jesus since the beginning of His ministry; but in that late hour, the weeding-out process had to begin. This particular parable has been interpreted in many ways, but clearly the only harvest in which a farmer would be truly interested would be the one that produced good, mature fruit (vv. 8,23), which was the main point of the story.

Before Jesus explained the meaning of this parable, His disciples asked Him why He was speaking in such terms. Here the division between insiders and outsiders was made plain. Parables were for insiders. Clearly, too, according to other passages, outsiders also understood His stories; but the difference between the insiders and outsiders lay in the fact that the latter did not respond appropriately. True spiritual understanding is characterized by a willing heart. Once the meaning of the story has been made clear, an unwilling heart will only become more hostile. The Isaiah quote makes clear that, with regard to the outsiders, Jesus was speaking to a people who were already hostile to His message (Is 6:9-10; Mt 13:14-15).

13:24-50 Parables of the **wheat** and **weeds** (vv. 24-30), and of the **large net** (vv. 47-50) described events surrounding the Judgment Day. Although at times evil might appear to be winning out and seemingly there was little difference between God's people and those who followed the evil one, God's purposes ultimately would not be thwarted.

The **mustard seed** and **yeast** reveal that God's **kingdom** will be much larger than expected, especially considering the way in which it began. The reference to the birds likely referred to the Gentile believers (see Ezk 17:23).

13:44-52 The treasure and the **one priceless pearl** represent the immeasurable value of the kingdom. They are worth sacrificing all to attain them.

up and choked them. 8 Still others
fell on good ground and produced a
crop: some 100, some 60, and some
30 times what was sown. 9 Anyone
who has ears[A] should listen!"

Jesus' Use of Parables (13:10-17)

10 Then the disciples came up and
asked Him, "Why do You speak to
them in parables?"
11 He answered them, "Because the
•secrets of the kingdom of heaven
have been given for you to know, but
it has not been given to them. 12 For
whoever has, more will be given to
him, and he will have more than
enough. But whoever does not have,
even what he has will be taken away
from him. 13 For this reason I speak
to them in parables, because looking
they do not see, and hearing they do
not listen or understand. 14 Isaiah's
prophecy is fulfilled in them, which
says:

You will listen and listen,
yet never understand;
and you will look and look,
yet never perceive.
15 **For this people's heart**
has grown callous;
their ears are hard
of hearing,
and they have shut
their eyes;
otherwise they might see
with their eyes
and hear with their ears,
understand with their hearts
and turn back—
and I would cure them.[B]

16 "But your eyes are blessed because they do see, and your ears because they do hear! 17 For •I assure
you: Many prophets and righteous
people longed to see the things
you see yet didn't see them; to hear
the things you hear yet didn't hear
them.

Explaining the Parable of the Sower (13:18-23)

18 "You, then, listen to the parable of the sower: 19 When anyone
hears the word[C] about the kingdom
and doesn't understand it, the evil
one comes and snatches away what
was sown in his heart. This is the
one sown along the path. 20 And the
one sown on rocky ground—this
is one who hears the word and immediately receives it with joy. 21 Yet
he has no root in himself, but is
short-lived. When pressure or persecution comes because of the word,
immediately he stumbles. 22 Now the
one sown among the thorns—this
is one who hears the word, but the
worries of this age and the seduction[D] of wealth choke the word, and
it becomes unfruitful. 23 But the one
sown on the good ground—this is
one who hears and understands the
word, who does bear fruit and yields:
some 100, some 60, some 30 times
what was sown."

The Parable of the Wheat and the Weeds (13:24-30)

24 He presented another parable
to them: "The kingdom of heaven
may be compared to a man who
sowed good seed in his field. 25 But
while people were sleeping, his enemy came, sowed weeds[E] among the
wheat, and left. 26 When the plants
sprouted and produced grain, then
the weeds also appeared. 27 The landowner's •slaves came to him and
said, 'Master, didn't you sow good
seed in your field? Then where did
the weeds come from?'
28 "'An enemy did this!' he told
them.
"'So, do you want us to go and
gather them up?' the slaves asked
him.
29 "'No,' he said. 'When you gather
up the weeds, you might also uproot
the wheat with them. 30 Let both
grow together until the harvest.
At harvest time I'll tell the reapers:
Gather the weeds first and tie them
in bundles to burn them, but store
the wheat in my barn.'"

The Parables of the Mustard Seed and of the Yeast (13:31-33)

31 He presented another parable
to them: "The kingdom of heaven
is like a mustard seed that a man
took and sowed in his field. 32 It's the
smallest of all the seeds, but when
grown, it's taller than the vegetables

[A]13:9 Other mss add *to hear* [B]13:14-15 Is 6:9-10 [C]13:19 Gk *logos* = *word*, or *message*, or *saying*, or *thing* [D]13:22 Or *pleasure*, or *deceitfulness* [E]13:25 Or *darnel*, a weed similar in appearance to wheat in the early stages

and becomes a tree, so that the birds of the sky come and nest in its branches."

33 He told them another parable: "The kingdom of heaven is like yeast that a woman took and mixed into 50 pounds[A] of flour until it spread through all of it."[B]

Fulfillment of Prophecy by Using Parables (13:34-35)

34 Jesus told the crowds all these things in parables, and He would not speak anything to them without a parable, 35 so that what was spoken through the prophet might be fulfilled:

> **I will open My mouth**
> **in parables;**
> **I will declare things**
> **kept secret**
> **from the foundation**
> **of the world.**[C]

Jesus' Interpretation of the Wheat and the Weeds (13:36-43)

36 Then He dismissed the crowds and went into the house. His disciples approached Him and said, "Explain the parable of the weeds in the field to us."

37 He replied: "The One who sows the good seed is the •Son of Man; 38 the field is the world; and the good seed—these are the sons of the kingdom. The weeds are the sons of the evil one, 39 and the enemy who sowed them is the Devil. The harvest is the end of the age, and the harvesters are angels. 40 Therefore, just as the weeds are gathered and burned in the fire, so it will be at the end of the age. 41 The Son of Man will send out His angels, and they will gather from His kingdom everything that causes sin[D] and those •guilty of lawlessness.[E] 42 They will throw them into the blazing furnace where there will be weeping and gnashing of teeth. 43 Then the righteous will shine like the sun in their Father's kingdom. Anyone who has ears[F] should listen!

The Parables of the Hidden Treasure and of the Priceless Pearl (13:44-46)

44 "The kingdom of heaven is like treasure, buried in a field, that a man found and reburied. Then in his joy he goes and sells everything he has and buys that field.

45 "Again, the kingdom of heaven is like a merchant in search of fine pearls. 46 When he found one priceless[G] pearl, he went and sold everything he had, and bought it.

The Parable of the Net (13:47-50)

47 "Again, the kingdom of heaven is like a large net thrown into the sea. It collected every kind of fish, 48 and when it was full, they dragged it ashore, sat down, and gathered the good fish into containers, but threw out the worthless ones. 49 So it will be at the end of the age. The angels will go out, separate the evil people from the righteous, 50 and throw them into the blazing furnace. In that place there will be weeping and gnashing of teeth.

The Storehouse of Truth (13:51-53)

51 "Have you understood all these things?"[H]

"Yes," they told Him.

52 "Therefore," He said to them, "every student of Scripture[I] instructed in the kingdom of heaven is like a landowner who brings out of his storeroom what is new and what is old." 53 When Jesus had finished these parables, He left there.

Rejection at Nazareth (13:54-58)

54 He went to His hometown and began to teach them in their •synagogue, so that they were astonished and said, "How did this wisdom and these miracles come to Him? 55 Isn't this the carpenter's son? Isn't His mother called Mary, and His brothers James, Joseph,[J] Simon, and Judas? 56 And His sisters, aren't they all with us? So where does He get all these things?" 57 And they were •offended by Him.

But Jesus said to them, "A prophet is not without honor except in his hometown and in his household."

Once the crowd was dismissed (13:36), Jesus fully explained to His disciples the meaning of these parables. The discerning (Jewish) disciple, who had been instructed in the kingdom, could now understand the ways in which Jesus' teachings were similar or dissimilar to Jewish law.

13:53-58 As the narrative section of this third sequence began, the hardness of the Jewish leaders and people was more pronounced, and Jesus now focused on the Gentiles. The highs and lows of the disciples' faith have also been highlighted in this section. In fact, faith, unbelief, rebellion, and acceptance all have been placed side by side throughout this entire section. Jesus was first rejected by the people in His hometown of Nazareth. He did not perform many miracles there because of their **unbelief** (v. 58).

[A] **13:33** Lit *3 sata*; about 40 quarts [B] **13:33** Or *until all of it was leavened* [C] **13:35** Ps 78:2
[D] **13:41** Or *stumbling* [E] **13:41** Or *those who do lawlessness* [F] **13:43** Other mss add *to hear*
[G] **13:46** Or *very precious* [H] **13:51** Other mss add *Jesus asked them* [I] **13:52** Or *every scribe*
[J] **13:55** Other mss read *Joses*; Mk 6:3

14:1-12 Herod the tetrarch (Herod Antipas) was ultimately responsible for the cruel and inhumane murder of **John the Baptist**. "Herod," a title, described a number of rulers. He, as other members of his family, was a ruthless and paranoid tyrant. His father Herod the Great had been responsible for the slaughter of innocent babies in Bethlehem following the visit of the magi (2:16). His murder of John was prompted by John's condemnation of Herod's adulterous and incestuous relationship with **Herodias,** the wife of **his brother Philip** (14:3-4). Herod may have been intrigued by John, but Herodias hated him. She forced Herod's hand and achieved her goal of getting rid of John (14:6-11).

14:13-36 The rebellion and unbelief of the Roman officials was apparent in the account of the beheading of John the Baptist (14:1-12). Several miracles were sandwiched in between this account of Roman hostility and the rebellion by Jewish leaders against God's Word in favor of their tradition (15:1-9). In contrast to this wicked behavior, Jesus fed the 5,000 and healed many who were sick (14:13-21,34-36). He was overwhelmed by **compassion** for these people (v. 14). The One who performed these miracles and walked on the water was none other than **the Son of God** (v. 33). The proclamation came from the lips of the disciples themselves, and they **worshiped Him** (v. 33). The Messiah's power, compassion, and authority stood in stark contrast to the evil behavior of the secular and religious authorities. Peter's **little faith** (v. 31) was also contrasted with the disciple's proclamation to highlight further the disequilibrium caused by Jesus' ministry.

CHARACTER PROFILE

Herodias A Power-Hungry Woman

Her Background	• Member of the Herodian dynasty • Wife of Philip, then of Herod Antipas • Mother of Salome
Her Story	• Divorced Philip and married his brother Herod Antipas (14:3-4) • Hated John the Baptist due to his public condemnation of her unlawful marriage • Cleverly urged Salome to ask Herod for the head of John the Baptist (14:8-10)
Life Lesson	Her devious, evil character makes her the New Testament counterpart of Jezebel of the Old Testament.

See also Mk 6:14-24; Lk 3:19-20.

58 And He did not do many miracles
there because of their unbelief.

Beheading of John the Baptist (14:1-12)

14 At that time •Herod the tetrarch heard the report about
Jesus. 2 "This is John the Baptist!"
he told his servants. "He has been
raised from the dead, and that's why
supernatural powers are at work in
him."
3 For Herod had arrested John,
chained[A] him, and put him in prison
on account of Herodias, his brother
Philip's wife, 4 since John had been
telling him, "It's not lawful for you
to have her!" 5 Though he wanted to
kill him, he feared the crowd, since
they regarded him as a prophet.
6 But when Herod's birthday celebration came, Herodias's daughter
danced before them[B] and pleased
Herod. 7 So he promised with an
oath to give her whatever she might
ask. 8 And prompted by her mother,
she answered, "Give me John the
Baptist's head here on a platter!"
9 Although the king regretted it, he
commanded that it be granted because of his oaths and his guests.
10 So he sent orders and had John
beheaded in the prison. 11 His head
was brought on a platter and given
to the girl, who carried it to her
mother. 12 Then his disciples came,
removed the corpse,[C] buried it, and
went and reported to Jesus.

Feeding of the 5,000 (14:13-21)

13 When Jesus heard about it, He
withdrew from there by boat to a
remote place to be alone. When the
crowds heard this, they followed
Him on foot from the towns. 14 As
He stepped ashore,[D] He saw a huge
crowd, felt compassion for them,
and healed their sick.
15 When evening came, the disciples approached Him and said,
"This place is a wilderness, and it is
already late.[E] Send the crowds away
so they can go into the villages and
buy food for themselves."
16 "They don't need to go away,"
Jesus told them. "You give them
something to eat."
17 "But we only have five loaves and
two fish here," they said to Him.
18 "Bring them here to Me," He
said. 19 Then He commanded the
crowds to sit down[F] on the grass. He
took the five loaves and the two fish,
and looking up to heaven, He blessed
them. He broke the loaves and gave
them to the disciples, and the disciples gave them to the crowds. 20 Everyone ate and was filled. Then they
picked up 12 baskets full of leftover
pieces! 21 Now those who ate were
about 5,000 men, besides women
and children.

[A]14:3 Or *bound* [B]14:6 Lit *danced in the middle* [C]14:12 Other mss read *body* [D]14:14 Lit *Coming out* (of the boat) [E]14:15 Lit *and the time* (for the evening meal) *has already passed* [F]14:19 Lit *to recline*

Walking on the Water (14:22-33)

22 Immediately He[A] made the disciples get into the boat and go ahead
of Him to the other side, while He
dismissed the crowds. 23 After dismissing the crowds, He went up on
the mountain by Himself to pray.
When evening came, He was there
alone. 24 But the boat was already
over a mile[B] from land,[C] battered
by the waves, because the wind was
against them. 25 Around three in the
morning,[D] He came toward them
walking on the sea. 26 When the disciples saw Him walking on the sea,
they were terrified. "It's a ghost!"
they said, and cried out in fear.

27 Immediately Jesus spoke to
them. "Have courage! It is I. Don't
be afraid."

28 "Lord, if it's You," Peter answered Him, "command me to come
to You on the water."

29 "Come!" He said.

And climbing out of the boat, Peter started walking on the water and
came toward Jesus. 30 But when he
saw the strength of the wind,[E] he was
afraid. And beginning to sink he cried
out, "Lord, save me!"

31 Immediately Jesus reached out
His hand, caught hold of him, and
said to him, "You of little faith,
why did you doubt?" 32 When they
got into the boat, the wind ceased.
33 Then those in the boat worshiped
Him and said, "Truly You are the
Son of God!"

Miraculous Healings (14:34-36)

34 Once they crossed over, they
came to land at Gennesaret. 35 When
the men of that place recognized
Him, they alerted[F] the whole vicinity and brought to Him all who were
sick. 36 They were begging Him that
they might only touch the •tassel on
His robe. And as many as touched it
were made perfectly well.

The Tradition of the Elders (15:1-9)

15 Then •Pharisees and •scribes
came from Jerusalem to Jesus
and asked, 2 "Why do Your disciples
break the tradition of the elders? For
they don't wash their hands when
they eat!"[G]

3 He answered them, "And why
do you break God's commandment
because of your tradition? 4 For God
said:[H]

Honor your father
and your mother;[I] and,
The one who speaks evil
of father or mother
must be put to death.[J]

5 But you say, 'Whoever tells his father or mother, "Whatever benefit
you might have received from me is
a gift committed to the temple"—
6 he does not have to honor his father.'[K] In this way, you have revoked
God's word[L] because of your tradition. 7 Hypocrites! Isaiah prophesied
correctly about you when he said:

8 **These people**[M] **honor Me**
with their lips,
but their heart is far
from Me.
9 **They worship Me in vain,**
teaching as doctrines
the commands of men."[N]

Defilement from Within (15:10-20)

10 Summoning the crowd, He told
them, "Listen and understand: 11 It's
not what goes into the mouth that
defiles a man, but what comes out of
the mouth, this defiles a man."

12 Then the disciples came up and
told Him, "Do You know that the
Pharisees took offense when they
heard this statement?"

13 He replied, "Every plant that My
heavenly Father didn't plant will be
uprooted. 14 Leave them alone! They
are blind guides.[O] And if the blind
guide the blind, both will fall into a
pit."

15 Then Peter replied to Him, "Explain this parable to us."

16 "Are even you still lacking in
understanding?" He[A] asked. 17 "Don't
you realize[P] that whatever goes into
the mouth passes into the stomach

15:1-20 After Jesus rebuked the religious leaders for their blatant disregard of God's Word, He denounced them. The confused disciples were concerned that Jesus had offended the Pharisees (15:12), but Jesus rebuked the disciples for their lack of understanding (15:16-20).

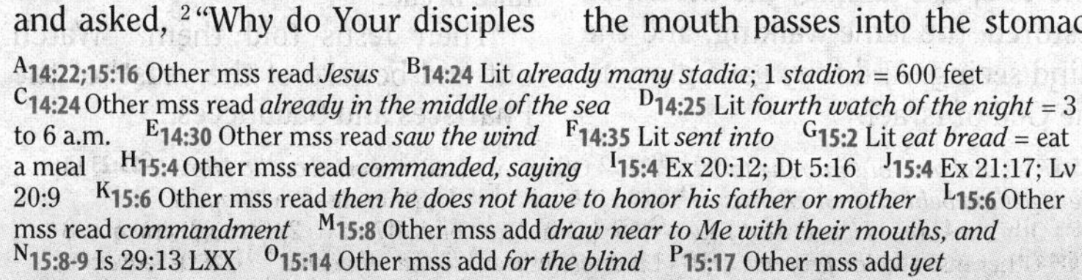

[A]**14:22;15:16** Other mss read *Jesus* [B]**14:24** Lit *already many stadia*; 1 *stadion* = 600 feet [C]**14:24** Other mss read *already in the middle of the sea* [D]**14:25** Lit *fourth watch of the night* = 3 to 6 a.m. [E]**14:30** Other mss read *saw the wind* [F]**14:35** Lit *sent into* [G]**15:2** Lit *eat bread* = eat a meal [H]**15:4** Other mss read *commanded, saying* [I]**15:4** Ex 20:12; Dt 5:16 [J]**15:4** Ex 21:17; Lv 20:9 [K]**15:6** Other mss read *then he does not have to honor his father or mother* [L]**15:6** Other mss read *commandment* [M]**15:8** Other mss add *draw near to Me with their mouths, and* [N]**15:8-9** Is 29:13 LXX [O]**15:14** Other mss add *for the blind* [P]**15:17** Other mss add *yet*

15:21-28 Matthew contrasted the disciples' *lack of understanding* with the Gentile woman's *understanding* of Jesus. This **Canaanite woman** lived in the Gentile region of **Tyre and Sidon**. She referred to Jesus as the **Son of David**, a sure recognition of His identity as the Messiah, and then begged Him to heal her **daughter**. As the disciples wanted to send the people away to the villages to get food (showing their lack of faith, 14:15), they also urged Jesus to **send her away** (15:23). The disciples still did not understand fully the nature of Christ's ministry. But He would not be deterred; nor would the Gentile woman.

The Lord tested the Canaanite woman's faith by claiming He had come only for **the lost sheep of the house of Israel**. Her response revealed a still greater faith. Although she understood that as a Gentile she was despised by the Jews, she was not deterred; she admitted her unworthy status before Christ. Rather than turning her away, Jesus rewarded her faith and healed her daughter. So, with a Gentile woman's perseverance and faith, Christ began His ministry to the Gentiles.

15:29-31 Jesus moved from Tyre and Sidon to Galilee of the Gentiles, climbed up a mountain, and sat down. Crowds came to Him and He healed them all; and the people **gave glory to the God of Israel**, indicating that the people were probably primarily Gentile. There was a clear connection between this scene and Jesus' ministry which was strictly to the Jews just before the Sermon on the Mount (4:23-25).

15:32-39 Again driven by **compassion**, Jesus fed the 4,000. This time the people were primarily Gentiles, testifying again to the change in the focus of His ministry. But one thing had not yet changed: the disciples' fledgling faith. They were concerned about the apparent lack of bread. After the feeding, Jesus left for **Magadan** (or Magdala), a site near the Sea of Galilee (15:39).

16:1-12 Jesus was approached by the Pharisees and Sadducees, who asked Him for another **sign** (16:1). But this time none would be given. Jesus then warned His disciples about **the yeast of the Pharisees and Sadducees** (vv. 6,12). But they did not yet understand, and Jesus rebuked them (vv. 8-11). After Jesus recounted His miracles with the bread, they finally got Jesus' point.

This narrative section is clearly characterized by contrasts. The most striking is the one juxtaposing the Gentile woman's faith with the consistent lack of understanding on the part of the disciples, who had witnessed so much of the ministry of Christ and yet continued to exhibit a

and is eliminated?[A] 18 But what comes out of the mouth comes from the heart, and this defiles a man. 19 For from the heart come evil thoughts, murders, adulteries, sexual immoralities, thefts, false testimonies, blasphemies. 20 These are the things that defile a man, but eating with unwashed hands does not defile a man."

A Gentile Mother's Faith (15:21-28)

21 When Jesus left there, He withdrew to the area of Tyre and Sidon. 22 Just then a Canaanite woman from that region came and kept crying out,[B] "Have mercy on me, Lord, Son of David! My daughter is cruelly tormented by a demon."

23 Yet He did not say a word to her. So His disciples approached Him and urged Him, "Send her away because she cries out after us."[C]

24 He replied, "I was sent only to the lost sheep of the house of Israel."

25 But she came, knelt before Him, and said, "Lord, help me!"

26 He answered, "It isn't right to take the children's bread and throw it to their dogs."

27 "Yes, Lord," she said, "yet even the dogs eat the crumbs that fall from their masters' table!"

28 Then Jesus replied to her, "•Woman, your faith is great. Let it be done for you as you want." And from that moment[D] her daughter was cured.

Healing of Many People (15:29-31)

29 Moving on from there, Jesus passed along the Sea of Galilee. He went up on a mountain and sat there, 30 and large crowds came to Him, having with them the lame, the blind, the deformed, those unable to speak, and many others. They put them at His feet, and He healed them. 31 So the crowd was amazed when they saw those unable to speak talking, the deformed restored, the lame walking, and the blind seeing. And they gave glory to the God of Israel.

Feeding 4,000 (15:32-39)

32 Now Jesus summoned His disciples and said, "I have compassion on the crowd, because they've already stayed with Me three days and have nothing to eat. I don't want to send them away hungry; otherwise they might collapse on the way."

33 The disciples said to Him, "Where could we get enough bread in this desolate place to fill such a crowd?"

34 "How many loaves do you have?" Jesus asked them.

"Seven," they said, "and a few small fish."

35 After commanding the crowd to sit down on the ground, 36 He took the seven loaves and the fish, and He gave thanks, broke them, and kept on giving them to the disciples, and the disciples gave them to the crowds. 37 They all ate and were filled. Then they collected the leftover pieces—seven large baskets full. 38 Now those who ate were 4,000 men, besides women and children. 39 After dismissing the crowds, He got into the boat and went to the region of Magadan.[E]

The Yeast of the Pharisees and the Sadducees (16:1-12)

16 The •Pharisees and •Sadducees approached, and as a test, asked Him to show them a sign from heaven.

2 He answered them: "When evening comes you say, 'It will be good weather because the sky is red.' 3 And in the morning, 'Today will be stormy because the sky is red and threatening.' You[F] know how to read the appearance of the sky, but you can't read the signs of the times.[G] 4 An evil and adulterous generation demands a sign, but no sign will be given to it except the sign of[H] Jonah." Then He left them and went away.

5 The disciples reached the other shore,[I] and they had forgotten to take bread.

6 Then Jesus told them, "Watch out and beware of the yeast[J] of the Pharisees and Sadducees."

A15:17 Lit *and goes out into the toilet* B15:22 Other mss read *and cried out to Him* C15:23 Lit *she is yelling behind us* or *after us* D15:28 Lit *hour* E15:39 Other mss read *Magdala* F16:3 Other mss read *Hypocrites! You* G16:2-3 Other mss omit *When* (v. 2) through end of v. 3 H16:4 Other mss add *the prophet* I16:5 Lit *disciples went to the other side* J16:6 Or *leaven*

CHARACTER PROFILE

The Syro-Phoenician Woman

A Desperate Mother

Her Background	• She lived in area northwest of the Sea of Galilee, near cities of Tyre and Sidon (modern day Lebanon). • She was a Canaanite—a Gentile.
Her Story	• Her daughter was demon-possessed, and she begged Jesus to help her (15:22). • She referred to Jesus by His messianic title "Son of David." • Her response to Jesus revealed her faith in His power and compassion for all people (15:27). • Jesus commended her for her faith and healed her daughter (15:28).
Life Lesson	A mother's persistent prayer for her children is her highest duty and privilege.

See also Mk 7:24-30.

7 And they discussed among themselves, "We didn't bring any bread."
8 Aware of this, Jesus said, "You of
little faith! Why are you discussing
among yourselves that you do not
have bread? 9 Don't you understand
yet? Don't you remember the five
loaves for the 5,000 and how many
baskets you collected? 10 Or the
seven loaves for the 4,000 and how
many large baskets you collected?
11 Why is it you don't understand
that when I told you, 'Beware of the
yeast of the Pharisees and Sadducees,' it wasn't about bread?" 12 Then
they understood that He did not tell
them to beware of the yeast in bread,
but of the teaching of the Pharisees
and Sadducees.

Peter's Confession of the Messiah (16:13-20)

13 When Jesus came to the region
of Caesarea Philippi,[A] He asked His
disciples, "Who do people say that
the •Son of Man is?"[B]
14 And they said, "Some say John
the Baptist; others, Elijah; still others, Jeremiah or one of the prophets."
15 "But you," He asked them, "who
do you say that I am?"
16 Simon Peter answered, "You are
the •Messiah, the Son of the living
God!"
17 And Jesus responded, "Simon
son of Jonah,[C] you are blessed because flesh and blood did not reveal
this to you, but My Father in heav-
en. 18 And I also say to you that you
are Peter,[D] and on this rock[E] I will
build My church, and the forces[F] of
•Hades will not overpower it. 19 I will
give you the keys of the kingdom of
heaven, and whatever you bind on
earth is already bound[G] in heaven,
and whatever you loose on earth is
already loosed[H] in heaven."
20 And He gave the disciples orders
to tell no one that He was[I] the Messiah.

A Focus on Coming Death and Resurrection (16:21–18:35)

Prediction of Jesus' Death and Resurrection (16:21-23)

21 From then on Jesus began to
point out to His disciples that He
must go to Jerusalem and suffer
many things from the elders, •chief
priests, and •scribes, be killed, and
be raised the third day. 22 Then Peter
took Him aside and began to rebuke

[A] 16:13 A town north of Galilee at the base of Mount Hermon [B] 16:13 Other mss read *that I, the Son of Man, am* [C] 16:17 Or *son of John* [D] 16:18 *Peter* (Gk *Petros*) = a specific stone or rock [E] 16:18 *Rock* (Gk *petra*) = a rocky crag or bedrock [F] 16:18 Lit *gates* [G] 16:19 Or *earth will be bound* [H] 16:19 Or *earth will be loosed* [I] 16:20 Other mss add *Jesus*

lack of faith. But Matthew intended to show their growth, too.

16:13-20 In the very next scene, for the moment at least, their faith began to take on a much stronger character. In **the region of Caesarea Philippi**, well known for its pagan worship, Simon Peter made his great confession concerning Jesus' identity, **You are the Messiah, the Son of the living God!** (v. 16). Jesus affirmed Peter's confession and acknowledged that God the **Father** was responsible for revealing this truth. Jesus also changed Simon's name to **Peter** (Gk *Petros*, "a specific rock") and claimed that He would **build** His **church** on the foundation of Peter's confession of Jesus' identity as not only the Messiah but also the Son of God (**this rock** [Gk *petra*, "a rocky crag, massive rock"], v. 16). Firmly established on this truth, even **the forces of Hades** [Gk, "underworld" or "place of the dead"] **will not overpower** (Gk *katischusousin*, "prevail, be victorious over") Christ's church (v. 18). Alternatively, the reference to Peter as a "rock" might simply be a recognition of his leadership role among the apostles. The word **church** (Gk *ekklēsian*, "assembly") refers to those who have been called out. In the New Testament, the word became the designation for Christians who joined together in a common purpose. The **keys of the kingdom** is a metaphor for the gospel (v. 19). Peter used these "keys" at Pentecost (Ac 2:14), at Samaria (Ac 8:14), and as a witness to Cornelius (Ac 10). In Greek the verb tense is most accurately expressed as "will have already been bound" (in the sense of *forbid*) and "will have been already loosed" (in the sense of *permit*). Peter certainly was not given authority to forgive sins, but his pronouncement was that the forgiveness of sins was dependent upon what heaven had already willed.

16:21-23 Jesus called Peter **an offense** when for a brief moment, Peter became an instrument of **Satan** because he tried to dissuade Jesus from the way of the cross.

16:24-28 Jesus' message emphasizes the radical commitment needed to follow in His steps. There can be no neutral ground. Those who would follow Him must be willing to lose everything in this life for His sake—the true nature of discipleship. Anyone who follows Christ must be willing to suffer. But Jesus assures His disciples that they will be rewarded when He returns in the glory of His kingdom.

17:1-13 In the transfiguration, **Peter, James, and . . . John** were given the opportunity to see Christ in His glory. They were singled out for this opportunity because they were the closest to Christ; they formed His "inner circle" of companions. During this amazing experience, they saw **Moses** and **Elijah**, the giver of the law and the greatest prophet, talking with Jesus. Although Peter objected, Moses and Elijah were taken away, and Jesus was left there alone. The disciples learned of the true supremacy of Christ—worthy of whole-hearted discipleship. In language similar to what was uttered at the baptism of Jesus, God the Father acknowledged Jesus as His **beloved Son** in whom He took **delight**. But this time He told Peter, James, and John to listen to Jesus alone. True discipleship entails unswerving devotion to the Son of God. The disciples now **understood** that **John the Baptist**, the forerunner of Christ, was the Elijah who was to come.

17:14-23 A **mustard seed** was the smallest seed known in that region. Because the time was near when Jesus would no longer be with them physically, the disciples' needed to exercise their faith more than ever. They would have to learn to depend solely on His unseen presence. Jesus reminded them again that He was **about to be betrayed**, killed, and **on the third day**, He would be **raised up**. The fact that the disciples were **deeply distressed** showed that the mustard seed of faith had yet to take root.

17:24-27 In verse 24, the Jewish temple tax for the upkeep of the sanctuary—not a Roman tax—was being considered (Ex 30:12-14; 38:26; 2Ch 24:6). The amount required was the didrachma or **double-drachma**, the equivalent of wages for about two days' work. Verse 25 involved a question concerning civil taxes. The main point of the question was that, just as royal sons are exempt from the taxes imposed by their fathers, so Jesus was exempt from the tax imposed by His Father. Jesus, in other words, acknowledged the temple tax to be an obligation to God; but as God's Son, He was exempt. But so as not to offend, Jesus would pay the tax. Jesus paid Peter's tax, too (v. 27). Jesus extended sonship to all who followed

Him, "Oh no,[A] Lord! This will never happen to You!"

23 But He turned and told Peter, "Get behind Me, Satan! You are an offense to Me because you're not thinking about God's concerns,[B] but man's."

Taking Up Your Cross (16:24-28)

24 Then Jesus said to His disciples, "If anyone wants to come with Me, he must deny himself, take up his cross, and follow Me. 25 For whoever wants to save his •life will lose it, but whoever loses his life because of Me will find it. 26 What will it benefit a man if he gains the whole world yet loses his life? Or what will a man give in exchange for his life? 27 For the Son of Man is going to come with His angels in the glory of His Father, and then He will reward each according to what he has done. 28 •I assure you: There are some standing here who will not taste death until they see the Son of Man coming in His kingdom."

The Transfiguration (17:1-13)

17 After six days Jesus took Peter, James, and his brother John and led them up on a high mountain by themselves. 2 He was transformed[C] in front of them, and His face shone like the sun. Even His clothes became as white as the light. 3 Suddenly, Moses and Elijah appeared to them, talking with Him.

4 Then Peter said to Jesus, "Lord, it's good for us to be here! If You want, I will make[D] three •tabernacles here: one for You, one for Moses, and one for Elijah."

5 While he was still speaking, suddenly a bright cloud covered[E] them, and a voice from the cloud said:

> This is My beloved Son.
> I take delight in Him.
> Listen to Him!

6 When the disciples heard it, they fell facedown and were terrified.

7 Then Jesus came up, touched them, and said, "Get up; don't be afraid." 8 When they looked up they saw no one except Him[F]—Jesus alone. 9 As they were coming down from the mountain, Jesus commanded them, "Don't tell anyone about the vision until the •Son of Man is raised[G] from the dead."

10 So the disciples questioned Him, "Why then do the •scribes say that Elijah must come first?"

11 "Elijah is coming[H] and will restore everything," He replied.[I] 12 "But I tell you: Elijah has already come, and they didn't recognize him. On the contrary, they did whatever they pleased to him. In the same way the Son of Man is going to suffer at their hands."[J] 13 Then the disciples understood that He spoke to them about John the Baptist.

The Power of Faith over a Demon (17:14-21)

14 When they reached the crowd, a man approached and knelt down before Him. 15 "Lord," he said, "have mercy on my son, because he has seizures[K] and suffers severely. He often falls into the fire and often into the water. 16 I brought him to Your disciples, but they couldn't heal him."

17 Jesus replied, "You unbelieving and rebellious[L] generation! How long will I be with you? How long must I put up with you? Bring him here to Me." 18 Then Jesus rebuked the demon,[M] and it[N] came out of him, and from that moment[O] the boy was healed.

19 Then the disciples approached Jesus privately and said, "Why couldn't we drive it out?"

20 "Because of your little faith," He[P] told them. "For •I assure you: If you have faith the size of[Q] a mustard seed, you will tell this mountain, 'Move from here to there,' and it will move. Nothing will be impossible for you. [21 However, this kind does not come out except by prayer and fasting.]"[R]

[A]**16:22** Lit *Mercy to You = May God have mercy on You* [B]**16:23** Lit *about the things of God* [C]**17:2** Or *transfigured* [D]**17:4** Other mss read *wish, let's make* [E]**17:5** Or *enveloped*; Ex 40:34-35 [F]**17:8** Other mss omit *Him* [G]**17:9** Other mss read *Man has risen* [H]**17:11** Other mss add *first* [I]**17:11** Other mss read *Jesus said to them* [J]**17:12** Lit *suffer by them* [K]**17:15** Lit *he is moonstruck*; thought to be a form of epilepsy [L]**17:17** Or *corrupt*, or *perverted*, or *twisted*; Dt 32:5 [M]**17:18** Lit *rebuked him* or *it* [N]**17:18** Lit *the demon* [O]**17:18** Lit *hour* [P]**17:20** Other mss read *your unbelief," Jesus* [Q]**17:20** Lit *faith like* [R]**17:21** Other mss omit bracketed text; Mk 9:29

The Second Prediction of Jesus' Death (17:22-23)

22 As they were meeting[A] in Galilee,
Jesus told them, "The Son of Man is
about to be betrayed into the hands
of men. 23 They will kill Him, and on
the third day He will be raised up."
And they were deeply distressed.

Payment of the Temple Tax (17:24-27)

24 When they came to Capernaum,
those who collected the double-
drachma tax[B] approached Peter and
said, "Doesn't your Teacher pay the
double-drachma tax?"

25 "Yes," he said.

When he went into the house,
Jesus spoke to him first,[C] "What do
you think, Simon? Who do earthly
kings collect tariffs or taxes from?
From their sons or from strangers?"[D]

26 "From strangers," he said.[E]

"Then the sons are free," Jesus
told him. 27 "But, so we won't •offend
them, go to the sea, cast in a fish-
hook, and take the first fish that you
catch. When you open its mouth
you'll find a coin.[F] Take it and give it
to them for Me and you."

Identification of the Greatest? (18:1-9)

18 At that time[G] the disciples
came to Jesus and said, "Who is
greatest in the kingdom of heaven?"

2 Then He called a child to Him
and had him stand among them.
3 "•I assure you," He said, "unless
you are converted[H] and become
like children, you will never enter
the kingdom of heaven. 4 Therefore,
whoever humbles himself like this
child—this one is the greatest in
the kingdom of heaven. 5 And whoever welcomes[I] one child like this in
My name welcomes Me.

6 "But whoever •causes the downfall of one of these little ones who
believe in Me—it would be better
for him if a heavy millstone[J] were
hung around his neck and he were
drowned in the depths of the sea!
7 Woe to the world because of •of-
fenses. For offenses must come, but
woe to that man by whom the offense comes. 8 If your hand or your
foot causes your downfall, cut it off
and throw it away. It is better for you
to enter life maimed or lame, than
to have two hands or two feet and
be thrown into the eternal fire. 9 And
if your eye causes your downfall,
gouge it out and throw it away. It is
better for you to enter life with one
eye, rather than to have two eyes
and be thrown into •hellfire![K]

The Parable of the Lost Sheep (18:10-14)

10 "See that you don't look down on
one of these little ones, because I tell
you that in heaven their angels continually view the face of My Father
in heaven. [11 For the •Son of Man
has come to save the lost.][L] 12 What
do you think? If a man has 100
sheep, and one of them goes astray,
won't he leave the 99 on the hillside
and go and search for the stray?
13 And if he finds it, I assure you: He
rejoices over that sheep[M] more than
over the 99 that did not go astray.
14 In the same way, it is not the will
of your Father in heaven that one of
these little ones perish.

Process for Restoring a Brother (18:15-20)

15 "If your brother sins against
you,[N] go and rebuke him in private.[O]
If he listens to you, you have won
your brother. 16 But if he won't listen, take one or two more with you,
so that **by the testimony**[P] **of two or
three witnesses every fact may be
established.**[Q] 17 If he pays no attention to them, tell the church.[R] But
if he doesn't pay attention even to
the church, let him be like an unbeliever[S] and a tax collector to you.
18 I assure you: Whatever you bind on
earth is already bound[T] in heaven,
and whatever you loose on earth is
already loosed[U] in heaven. 19 Again,
I assure you: If two of you on earth
agree about any matter that you[V]
pray for, it will be done for you[W] by
My Father in heaven. 20 For where

Him; therefore, the sons were exempt from the temple tax, too.

18:1-35 In this fourth sermon, Jesus dealt with what His death and resurrection would mean for the church—humility and forgiveness, characteristics most perfectly emulated by Christ.

18:1-9 The **greatest** in Christ's **kingdom** is one who models childlike dependence on God. The idea is not "childishness," implying a perpetual state of immaturity; but childlike, implying that the mature or "perfect" believer is one who is completely dependent on God to meet all of his needs (6:25-34). Believers ought to do all they can to avoid causing even a child, one of the least of Christ's followers, to stumble. God has His eye on all of His flock, no matter how "insignificant" they might appear to others.

18:10-14 The parable of the lost **sheep** illustrates Jesus' saving activity as a shepherd's diligent **search for the stray** and celebration of finding it. The Father's **will** (Gk *thelēma*, "what one wishes or has determined will be done") is His purpose or desire. The heart of Jesus' mission of carrying out on earth the will of the **Father in heaven** was this "search-and-rescue" effort for the wayward souls of men.

18:15-20 Jesus taught His disciples how to resolve disputes among believers (vv. 15-17). Forgiveness is essential for **the church**. When one believer sins against another, the one offended is to go to that believer and point out the wrong. If the offending believer is unrepentant, church discipline must be invoked. If there is still no repentance, excluding the unrepentant one from fellowship is appropriate (cp. 1Co 6:1-11).

[A] **17:22** Other mss read *were staying* [B] **17:24** Jewish men paid this tax to support the temple; Ex 30:11-16. A double-drachma could purchase 2 sheep. [C] **17:25** Lit *Jesus anticipated him by saying* [D] **17:25** Or *foreigners* [E] **17:26** Other mss read *Peter said to Him* [F] **17:27** Gk *stater*, worth 2 double-drachmas [G] **18:1** Lit *hour* [H] **18:3** Or *are turned around* [I] **18:5** Or *receives* [J] **18:6** A millstone turned by a donkey [K] **18:9** Lit *gehenna of fire* [L] **18:11** Other mss omit bracketed text [M] **18:13** Lit *over it* [N] **18:15** Other mss omit *against you* [O] **18:15** Lit *him between you and him alone* [P] **18:16** Lit *mouth* [Q] **18:16** Dt 19:15 [R] **18:17** Or *congregation* [S] **18:17** Or *like a Gentile* [T] **18:18** Or *earth will be bound* [U] **18:18** Or *earth will be loosed* [V] **18:19** Lit *they* [W] **18:19** Lit *for them*

18:21-35 With the parable of the unforgiving **slave,** Jesus taught that true repentance must *always* be met with forgiveness. The rabbis taught that a sin, when there was repentance, should be forgiven a few times but then there was to be no forgiveness. Peter's suggestion that you should forgive **seven times** would have been considered generous, but Jesus taught unlimited forgiveness.

The comparison between what was owed the king and what was owed the servant was ridiculous. This parable does not contradict the previous teaching on church discipline. The key here is *true* repentance. The one who truly changes his behavior ought to be forgiven one-hundredfold. But where true repentance was not manifested, judgment would be unrelenting. God has forgiven believers an overwhelming **debt**; how could those same believers refuse to forgive the small offenses of others?

19:1 As the cross loomed closer, teachings on the meaning of true discipleship and the condemnation of the Jewish leaders who had rejected Him took on new urgency.

By heading toward **Judea** (v. 1), Jesus deliberately put Himself even closer to Jerusalem, where He had already predicted He would be killed (16:21).

two or three are gathered together in My name, I am there among them."

Parable of the Unforgiving Slave (18:21-35)

21 Then Peter came to Him and said, "Lord, how many times could my brother sin against me and I forgive him? As many as seven times?"

22 "I tell you, not as many as seven," Jesus said to him, "but 70 times seven.[A] 23 For this reason, the kingdom of heaven can be compared to a king who wanted to settle accounts with his •slaves. 24 When he began to settle accounts, one who owed 10,000 talents[B] was brought before him. 25 Since he had no way to pay it back, his master commanded that he, his wife, his children, and everything he had be sold to pay the debt.

26 "At this, the slave fell facedown before him and said, 'Be patient with me, and I will pay you everything!' 27 Then the master of that slave had compassion, released him, and forgave him the loan.

28 "But that slave went out and found one of his fellow slaves who owed him 100 •denarii.[C] He grabbed him, started choking him, and said, 'Pay what you owe!'

29 "At this, his fellow slave fell down[D] and began begging him, 'Be patient with me, and I will pay you back.' 30 But he wasn't willing. On the contrary, he went and threw him into prison until he could pay what was owed. 31 When the other slaves saw what had taken place, they were deeply distressed and went and reported to their master everything that had happened.

32 "Then, after he had summoned him, his master said to him, 'You wicked slave! I forgave you all that debt because you begged me. 33 Shouldn't you also have had mercy on your fellow slave, as I had mercy on you?' 34 And his master got angry and handed him over to the jailers to be tortured until he could pay everything that was owed. 35 So My heavenly Father will also do to you if each of you does not forgive his brother[E] from his[F] heart."

The Road to Jerusalem: The Coming Judgment (19:1–25:46)

The Question of Divorce (19:1-12)

19 When Jesus had finished this instruction, He departed from Galilee and went to the region of Judea across the Jordan. 2 Large crowds followed Him, and He healed them there. 3 Some •Pharisees approached Him to test Him. They asked, "Is it lawful for a man to divorce his wife on any grounds?"

4 "Haven't you read," He replied, "that He who created[G] them in the beginning **made them male and female,**"[H] 5 and He also said:

"For this reason a man will leave
his father and mother
and be joined to his wife,
and the two will become one flesh?[I]

6 So they are no longer two, but one flesh. Therefore, what God has

[A]18:22 Or *but 77 times* [B]18:24 A huge sum of money that could never be repaid by a slave; a talent = 6,000 denarii [C]18:28 A small sum compared to 10,000 talents [D]18:29 Other mss add *at his feet* [E]18:35 Other mss add *his trespasses* [F]18:35 Lit *your* [G]19:4 Other mss read *made* [H]19:4 Gn 1:27; 5:2 [I]19:5 Gn 2:24

Reasons God Rejects Divorce

- Marriage is the divine institution used by the Lord to teach His children about their relationships to Him (Gn 1:27; Mt 19:4-5).
- Marriage is God's design, operates under His authority, and carries His imprimatur (Mt 19:4-5).
- Marriage brings two people together as one flesh, testifying to the permanence God planned for this most intimate union (Mt 19:6).
- Jesus pointed to the example of the first couple (Mt 19:8).
- Remarriage following divorce often compounds sin (Mt 19:9).

HARD QUESTION

Is divorce ever okay for a follower of Jesus?

The particular question **asked** by the **Pharisees** emerged in a culture in which only **a man** could initiate divorce and could do so for just about any reason (19:3). Their question specifically reflected a debate going on between the Pharisaic schools of Shammai and Hillel. Moses allowed a man to divorce his wife in such cases where he found "something improper" about her (Dt 24:1). The controversy was over whether this injunction was limited to sexual unfaithfulness or could be applied in a wider context. The Shammai school took the strict view that divorce was allowed only in cases of sexual immorality. The Hillel school held that the statute could be applied to practically any action that displeased a husband. In the modern era, such a position would have provided grounds for putting away or seeking divorce even if a wife burned her husband's breakfast toast. The Pharisees had taken the permission of the law granted by Moses and made it a command. In the process they had allowed human choices and circumstances to circumvent God's plan and purpose. Therefore, rather than citing the teachings of one of the popular rabbis Jesus returned to the creation account to support His rejection of divorce (Mt 19:4-6). Jesus also defined uncleanness as **sexual immorality** (Gk *porneia*, referring to a broad range of forbidden sexual practices, v. 9).

Because marriage was a metaphor used by the Lord to illustrate His own relationship to believers and to the church, He had a stern word for any who broke the vows of marriage. Ultimately, then, God's answer to this problematic issue was not found in laws or legal codes or traditions or even human choices. God returned to His creative design for the man and the woman, their holy and committed union, and His plan to use that sacred union as a tool for revealing Himself and His faithfulness. God cannot and will not compromise His principles; nor does He lower His standards. However, God redeems and restores all who seek Him and His forgiveness. Jesus came not to reduce the law's demands but to enable those who rely on Him to live according to God's high standards. In His reply, Jesus appealed to neither view.

Jesus certainly did not recommend or require **divorce** (Gk *apostasiou*, "repudiation") under any circumstances. He never suggested that the innocent spouse must **send . . . away** (Gk *apoluō*, "dismiss, bid depart"; cp. 1:19) the one guilty of unfaithfulness (see Hs 3:1-3). Rather, He acknowledged the permission Moses granted for a bill of divorcement (Dt 24:1-4), noting that such would be used only because of hardened **hearts** (Mt 19:8).

Faithfulness to marriage vows, in accordance with the creation commandment, must be a top priority. God's plan was permanent monogamy (v. 5; cp. Gn 2:24; Mk 10:7-8). The modern application of Jesus' teaching on divorce must heed these considerations:

- God's primary intention for marriage is life-long commitment; therefore, maintaining the marital union is absolutely essential (Mt 19:6).
- Jesus put the rights of husband and wife on equal footing (Mk 10:11-12).
- Some Christians may never marry, which does not mean they are settling for second best; Paul the apostle was single (1Co 7:7-9).
- Divorce may be permitted (though not mandated) if a believing spouse is deserted by an unbelieving spouse (1Co 7:10-16).
- Physical, sexual, or emotional abuse in a marriage situation must be dealt with in a compassionate and firm manner within the context of church discipline.

joined together, man must not separate."

[7] "Why then," they asked Him, "did Moses command us to give divorce papers and to send her away?"

[8] He told them, "Moses permitted you to divorce your wives because of the hardness of your hearts. But it was not like that from the beginning. [9] And I tell you, whoever divorces his wife, except for sexual immorality, and marries another, commits adultery."[A]

[10] His disciples said to Him, "If the relationship of a man with his wife is like this, it's better not to marry!"

[11] But He told them, "Not everyone can accept this saying, but only those it has been given to. [12] For there are eunuchs who were born that way from their mother's womb, there are eunuchs who were made by men, and there are eunuchs who have made themselves that way because of the kingdom of heaven. Let anyone accept this who can."

Blessing the Children (19:13-15)

[13] Then children were brought to Him so He might put His hands on them and pray. But the disciples rebuked them. [14] Then Jesus said, "Leave the children alone, and don't try to keep them from coming to Me, because the kingdom of heaven is made up of people like this."[B] [15] After putting His hands on them, He went on from there.

The Rich Young Ruler (19:16-22)

[16] Just then someone came up and asked Him, "Teacher, what good must I do to have eternal life?"

[17] "Why do you ask Me about what is good?"[C] He said to him. "There is only One who is good.[D] If you want to enter into life, keep the commandments."

[18] "Which ones?" he asked Him. Jesus answered:

Do not murder;
do not commit adultery;
do not steal;

[A] 19:9 Other mss add *Also whoever marries a divorced woman commits adultery*; Mt 5:32
[B] 19:14 Lit *heaven is of such ones*
[C] 19:17 Other mss read *Why do you call Me good?*
[D] 19:17 Other mss read *No one is good but One—God*

19:3-12 Clearly the Pharisees had evil intentions when they questioned Jesus about **divorce**. The word for **test** (Gk *peirazontes*, "try"; in a negative sense, "test maliciously" with the intent to "prove" one's feelings or judgments, v. 3) is the same word used of Jesus' being tempted by the Devil (4:1).

19:13-15 Children were then brought to Jesus in order to receive His blessing, but **the disciples rebuked** [Gk *epetimēsan*, "admonish or charge sharply, censure severely, chide, reprove"] **them**. The **kingdom of heaven** belongs to those who are childlike, and Jesus Himself loved the children (Mt 19:14).

19:16-30 The rich young ruler was concerned about his eternal destiny and questioned Jesus about the **good** things he must **do to have eternal life**. Jesus' rhetorical question in response probed the man's heart, pushing him to consider what assumptions he already had about Him. In quoting from the Ten Commandments Jesus was trying to point the ruler to the ultimate standard of goodness. The man admitted **lack** but did not, at least at that point, follow Jesus' instructions for dealing with it. Jesus did not command His followers to sell all their possessions and follow Him while living a life of utter poverty. His point was that if your possessions are keeping you from full allegiance to Christ, you must immediately divest yourself of these things. Jesus' emphasis was always on the heart within rather than the possessions or position.

Jesus did not condemn people because they had wealth, but earthly prosperity could not earn entrance into **the kingdom of heaven**. Not even altruism or any humanitarianism, without commitment to Christ, counts for anything toward eternity. Those who have left everything to follow Him will receive certain blessings in this life (primarily through the fellowship of God's people) and in the life to come, including participation in judging the world (1Co 6:2-3).

20:1-16 The parable of the vineyard **workers** supports Jesus' statement in 19:30, to which He returns in 20:16. Comparing Himself to the **landowner,** Jesus stresses the equality of all believers, regardless of when they come to Him. Jesus assigns rank or position as well as rewards and opportunities. He determines what is to be required. The parable also shows that God is interested in more than how much work would be done; He requires faithfulness to the task assigned.

20:17-19 For the third time since Peter's confession (16:16), Jesus told His disciples that He was going to suffer in **Jerusalem**, be killed, and **on the third day** be raised to life.

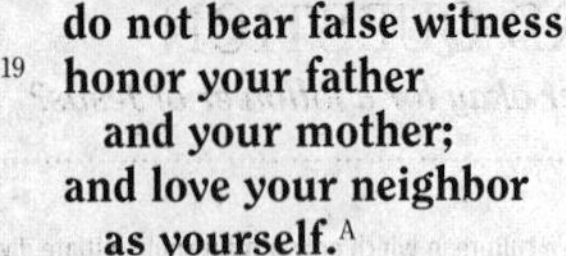

do not bear false witness;
19 **honor your father**
and your mother;
and love your neighbor
as yourself.[A]

20 "I have kept all these,"[B] the young man told Him. "What do I still lack?"

21 "If you want to be perfect,"[C] Jesus said to him, "go, sell your belongings and give to the poor, and you will have treasure in heaven. Then come, follow Me."

22 When the young man heard that command, he went away grieving, because he had many possessions.

Possessions and the Kingdom (19:23-30)

23 Then Jesus said to His disciples, "•I assure you: It will be hard for a rich person to enter the kingdom of heaven! 24 Again I tell you, it is easier for a camel to go through the eye of a needle than for a rich person to enter the kingdom of God."

25 When the disciples heard this, they were utterly astonished and asked, "Then who can be saved?"

26 But Jesus looked at them and said, "With men this is impossible, but with God all things are possible."

27 Then Peter responded to Him, "Look, we have left everything and followed You. So what will there be for us?"

28 Jesus said to them, "I assure you: In the Messianic Age,[D] when the •Son of Man sits on His glorious throne, you who have followed Me will also sit on 12 thrones, judging the 12 tribes of Israel. 29 And everyone who has left houses, brothers or sisters, father or mother,[E] children, or fields because of My name will receive 100 times more and will inherit eternal life. 30 But many who are first will be last, and the last first.

The Parable of the Vineyard Workers (20:1-16)

20 "For the kingdom of heaven is like a landowner who went out early in the morning to hire workers for his vineyard. 2 After agreeing with the workers on one •denarius for the day, he sent them into his vineyard. 3 When he went out about nine in the morning,[F] he saw others standing in the marketplace doing nothing. 4 To those men he said, 'You also go to my vineyard, and I'll give you whatever is right.' So off they went. 5 About noon and at three,[G] he went out again and did the same thing. 6 Then about five[H] he went and found others standing around,[I] and said to them, 'Why have you been standing here all day doing nothing?'

7 "'Because no one hired us,' they said to him.

"'You also go to my vineyard,' he told them.[J] 8 When evening came, the owner of the vineyard told his foreman, 'Call the workers and give them their pay, starting with the last and ending with the first.'[K]

9 "When those who were hired about five[L] came, they each received one denarius. 10 So when the first ones came, they assumed they would get more, but they also received a denarius each. 11 When they received it, they began to complain to the landowner: 12 'These last men put in one hour, and you made them equal to us who bore the burden of the day and the burning heat!'

13 "He replied to one of them, 'Friend, I'm doing you no wrong. Didn't you agree with me on a denarius? 14 Take what's yours and go. I want to give this last man the same as I gave you. 15 Don't I have the right to do what I want with my business?[M] Are you jealous[N] because I'm generous?'[O]

16 "So the last will be first, and the first last."[P]

The Third Prediction of Jesus' Death (20:17-19)

17 While going up to Jerusalem, Jesus took the 12 disciples aside privately and said to them on the way: 18 "Listen! We are going up to Jerusalem. The •Son of Man will be handed over to the •chief priests and

[A] **19:18-19** Ex 20:12-16; Lv 19:18; Dt 5:16-20 [B] **19:20** Other mss add *from my youth* [C] **19:21** Or *complete* [D] **19:28** Lit *the regeneration* [E] **19:29** Other mss add *or wife* [F] **20:3** Lit *about the third hour* [G] **20:5** Lit *about the sixth hour and the ninth hour* [H] **20:6** Lit *about the eleventh hour* [I] **20:6** Other mss add *doing nothing* [J] **20:7** Other mss add *'and you'll get whatever is right.'* [K] **20:8** Lit *starting from the last until the first* [L] **20:9** Lit *about the eleventh hour* [M] **20:15** Lit *with what is mine* [N] **20:15** Lit *Is your eye evil*; an idiom for jealousy or stinginess [O] **20:15** Lit *good* [P] **20:16** Other mss add *For many are called, but few are chosen."*

CHARACTER PROFILE

Zebedee's Wife An Ambitious Mother

Her Background	• Mother of disciples James and John • Possibly Salome (see Mark 15:40) • A devout follower of Jesus
Her Story	• She asked Jesus to favor her two sons when He took His rightful throne in heaven (20:21). • This understandably caused jealousy and resentment among the other disciples (20:24). • Jesus used her petition to explain humility and service in God's kingdom to the disciples and others present (20:25-28).
Life Lesson	Ambition, even if it is well intentioned, can cloud good judgment.

See also Mt 27:56; Mk 10:35-45; 15:40; 16:1.

•scribes, and they will condemn Him
to death. 19 Then they will hand Him
over to the Gentiles to be mocked,
flogged,[A] and crucified, and He will
be resurrected[B] on the third day."

Suffering and Service (20:20-28)

20 Then the mother of Zebedee's
sons approached Him with her
sons. She knelt down to ask Him for
something. 21 "What do you want?"
He asked her.

"Promise,"[C] she said to Him, "that
these two sons of mine may sit, one
on Your right and the other on Your
left, in Your kingdom."

22 But Jesus answered, "You don't
know what you're asking. Are you
able to drink the cup[D] that I am
about to drink?"[E]

"We are able," they said to Him.

23 He told them, "You will indeed
drink My cup.[F] But to sit at My right
and left is not Mine to give; instead,
it belongs to those for whom it
has been prepared by My Father."
24 When the 10 disciples heard this,
they became indignant with the two
brothers. 25 But Jesus called them
over and said, "You know that the
rulers of the Gentiles dominate
them, and the men of high position
exercise power over them. 26 It
must not be like that among you.
On the contrary, whoever wants to
become great among you must be
your servant, 27 and whoever wants
to be first among you must be your
•slave; 28 just as the Son of Man did
not come to be served, but to serve,
and to give His life—a ransom for
many."

Healing of Two Blind Men (20:29-34)

29 As they were leaving Jericho, a
large crowd followed Him. 30 There
were two blind men sitting by the
road. When they heard that Jesus
was passing by, they cried out,
"Lord, have mercy on us, Son of
David!" 31 The crowd told them to
keep quiet, but they cried out all the
more, "Lord, have mercy on us, Son
of David!"

32 Jesus stopped, called them, and
said, "What do you want Me to do
for you?"

33 "Lord," they said to Him, "open
our eyes!" 34 Moved with compassion,
Jesus touched their eyes. Immediately
they could see, and they
followed Him.

The Triumphal Entry (21:1-11)

21 When they approached Jerusalem
and came to Bethphage at
the •Mount of Olives, Jesus then sent
two disciples, 2 telling them, "Go
into the village ahead of you. At once
you will find a donkey tied there,

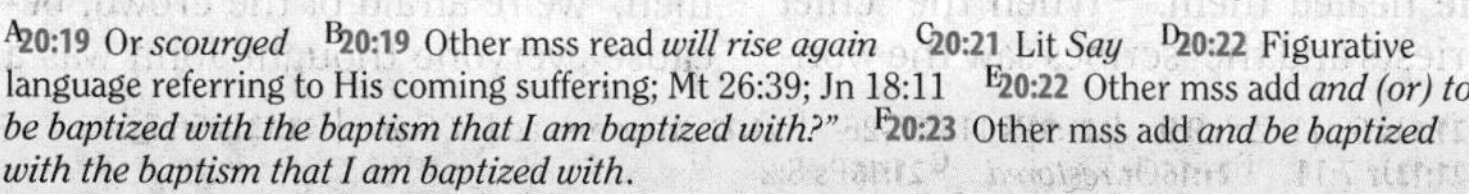

[A]20:19 Or *scourged* [B]20:19 Other mss read *will rise again* [C]20:21 Lit *Say* [D]20:22 Figurative language referring to His coming suffering; Mt 26:39; Jn 18:11 [E]20:22 Other mss add *and (or) to be baptized with the baptism that I am baptized with?"* [F]20:23 Other mss add *and be baptized with the baptism that I am baptized with.*

20:20-28 Despite Jesus' repeated warnings about His upcoming suffering (metaphorically represented by **the cup**) and His teachings on humility, James and John and seemingly their **mother** as well, were still concerned about prestige and power (v. 21). With great sensitivity, Jesus did not abruptly reject this devoted mother's request. Rather, He used the question as a springboard for correcting her misunderstanding and teaching valuable lessons, such as humility and servanthood (vv. 26-28). True discipleship involved submission and service. Jesus' disciples were to follow in the footsteps of their Master who **did not come to be served, but to serve, and to give His life—a ransom for many** (v. 28). Salome (see Mk 15:40) came to get something, but she left the Savior's presence having made the supreme sacrifice for any mother by giving her two sons to Christ. James was martyred (Ac 12:2) for following Christ. Though John outlived the other apostles, he, too, suffered persecution (Rv 1:9).

20:29-34 The healing of the **two blind men** was an example of Christ's servanthood and a testimony of faith and true discipleship. As the healing of two demon-possessed men in the Gadarenes was recorded at the beginning of Christ's ministry, coming after Jesus' rebuke of the little faith displayed by the disciples (see 8:26), so Matthew mentioned at the end of Christ's earthly ministry the healing of two blind men immediately after a demonstration of the disciples' still faltering faith (17:20).

The demons identified Christ clearly, though they were certainly not His disciples (cp. 8:29). Similarly, these blind men recognized Jesus as the **Son of David**. After their healing, **they followed Him**.

21:1-11 The triumphal entry marked the beginning of the end of Christ's earthly ministry. His entrance into Jerusalem was a fulfillment of Is 62:11 and Zch 9:9. As He rode on the **donkey**, large crowds lined the road to Jerusalem **shouting: *"Hosanna* to the Son of David!"** clearly recognizing His kingly status (v. 9; cp. v. 15). As He entered Jerusalem, however, the crowds referred to Him as **the prophet Jesus from Nazareth in Galilee**.

21:11-17 Jesus immediately challenged the practices in **the temple complex** by driving the **money changers** from His Father's house. His healing of **the blind and the lame** enabled them to come into the temple complex. The scribes and the Pharisees were indignant toward the children for acclaiming Jesus as the **Son of David**, but the Old Testament Scripture quoted by Jesus confirmed the wisdom of the children (see Ps 8:2).

21:18-22 The curse of the barren **fig tree** served two purposes in this context:

- Israel is often likened to a fig tree (Jr 8:13; 24:1-8), and the reference was symbolic of the coming judgment upon Israel.
- This lesson on **faith** was the last lesson given to the disciples before the Lord's suffering came.

21:23-45 In this section, the harsher condemnation of the Jewish leaders was highlighted with a series of their questions challenging Jesus' authority. Jesus answered them with a series of parables and baffled His enemies with some of His own questions.

Jesus' question concerning the nature of **John's baptism** (referring to John the Baptist and his baptism of repentance) forced the religious leaders to take an agnostic stance (vv. 23-27). Then Jesus shared three parables in which He made perfectly clear that **the kingdom of God** was being **taken away** from the Jews **and given to** a people who would listen (vv. 31,45)—most notably the very people that the religious leaders despised. The parable of the two sons, peculiar to Matthew, disclosed that the religious leaders rejected the **way of righteousness**, but the **tax collectors and prostitutes** accepted it; therefore, the kingdom of heaven would be theirs (vv. 28-32).

and a colt with her. Untie them and
bring them to Me. 3 If anyone says
anything to you, you should say that
the Lord needs them, and immediately he will send them."
4 This took place so that what was
spoken through the prophet might
be fulfilled:

5 **Tell Daughter •Zion,**
"Look, your King is coming
to you,
gentle, and mounted
on a donkey,
even on a colt,
the foal of a
beast of burden."[A]

6 The disciples went and did just as
Jesus directed them. 7 They brought
the donkey and the colt; then they
laid their robes on them, and He sat
on them. 8 A very large crowd spread
their robes on the road; others were
cutting branches from the trees and
spreading them on the road. 9 Then
the crowds who went ahead of Him
and those who followed kept shouting:

•Hosanna to the Son of David!
He who comes in the name
of the Lord is
the blessed One![B]
Hosanna
in the highest heaven!

10 When He entered Jerusalem, the
whole city was shaken, saying, "Who
is this?" 11 And the crowds kept saying, "This is the prophet Jesus from
Nazareth in Galilee!"

Cleansing of the Temple Complex (21:12-13)

12 Jesus went into the •temple
complex[C] and drove out all those
buying and selling in the temple.
He overturned the money changers'
tables and the chairs of those selling
doves. 13 And He said to them, "It is
written, **My house will be called a**
house of prayer.[D] But you are making it **a den of thieves**!"[E]

Children's Praise of Jesus (21:14-17)

14 The blind and the lame came
to Him in the temple complex, and
He healed them. 15 When the •chief
priests and the •scribes saw the wonders that He did and the children
shouting in the temple complex,
"*Hosanna* to the Son of David!" they
were indignant 16 and said to Him,
"Do You hear what these children
are saying?"
"Yes," Jesus told them. "Have you
never read:

You have prepared[F] **praise**
from the mouths of children
and nursing infants?"[G]

17 Then He left them, went out of the
city to Bethany, and spent the night
there.

The Barren Fig Tree (21:18-22)

18 Early in the morning, as He was
returning to the city, He was hungry. 19 Seeing a lone fig tree by the
road, He went up to it and found
nothing on it except leaves. And He
said to it, "May no fruit ever come
from you again!" At once the fig tree
withered.
20 When the disciples saw it, they
were amazed and said, "How did the
fig tree wither so quickly?"
21 Jesus answered them, "•I assure
you: If you have faith and do not
doubt, you will not only do what was
done to the fig tree, but even if you
tell this mountain, 'Be lifted up and
thrown into the sea,' it will be done.
22 And if you believe, you will receive
whatever you ask for in prayer."

Challenging of Messiah's Authority (21:23-27)

23 When He entered the temple
complex, the chief priests and the
elders of the people came up to Him
as He was teaching and said, "By
what authority are You doing these
things? Who gave You this authority?"
24 Jesus answered them, "I will also
ask you one question, and if you answer it for Me, then I will tell you
by what authority I do these things.
25 Where did John's baptism come
from? From heaven or from men?"
They began to argue among themselves, "If we say, 'From heaven,' He
will say to us, 'Then why didn't you
believe him?' 26 But if we say, 'From
men,' we're afraid of the crowd, because everyone thought John was a

[A] **21:5** Is 62:11; Zch 9:9 [B] **21:9** Ps 118:25-26 [C] **21:12** Other mss add *of God* [D] **21:13** Is 56:7 [E] **21:13** Jr 7:11 [F] **21:16** Or *restored* [G] **21:16** Ps 8:2

prophet." 27 So they answered Jesus, "We don't know."

And He said to them, "Neither will I tell you by what authority I do these things.

The Parable of the Two Sons (21:28-32)

28 "But what do you think? A man had two sons. He went to the first and said, 'My son, go, work in the vineyard today.'

29 "He answered, 'I don't want to!' Yet later he changed his mind and went. 30 Then the man went to the other and said the same thing.

"'I will, sir,' he answered. But he didn't go.

31 "Which of the two did his father's will?"

"The first," they said.

Jesus said to them, "I assure you: Tax collectors and prostitutes are entering the kingdom of God before you! 32 For John came to you in the way of righteousness, and you didn't believe him. Tax collectors and prostitutes did believe him, but you, when you saw it, didn't even change your minds then and believe him.

The Parable of the Vineyard Owner (21:33-46)

33 "Listen to another parable: There was a man, a landowner, who planted a vineyard, put a fence around it, dug a winepress in it, and built a watchtower. He leased it to tenant farmers and went away. 34 When the grape harvest[A] drew near, he sent his •slaves to the farmers to collect his fruit. 35 But the farmers took his slaves, beat one, killed another, and stoned a third. 36 Again, he sent other slaves, more than the first group, and they did the same to them. 37 Finally, he sent his son to them. 'They will respect my son,' he said.

38 "But when the tenant farmers saw the son, they said among themselves, 'This is the heir. Come, let's kill him and take his inheritance!' 39 So they seized him, threw him out of the vineyard, and killed him. 40 Therefore, when the owner of the vineyard comes, what will he do to those farmers?"

41 "He will completely destroy those terrible men," they told Him, "and lease his vineyard to other farmers who will give him his produce at the harvest."[B]

42 Jesus said to them, "Have you never read in the Scriptures:

> **The stone that**
> **the builders rejected**
> **has become the cornerstone.**[C]
> **This came from the Lord**
> **and is wonderful**
> **in our eyes?**[D]

43 Therefore I tell you, the kingdom of God will be taken away from you and given to a nation producing its[E] fruit. [44 Whoever falls on this stone will be broken to pieces; but on whoever it falls, it will grind him to powder!]"[F]

45 When the chief priests and the •Pharisees heard His parables, they knew He was speaking about them. 46 Although they were looking for a way to arrest Him, they feared the crowds, because they[G] regarded Him as a prophet.

The Parable of the Wedding Banquet (22:1-14)

22 Once more Jesus spoke to them in parables: 2 "The kingdom of heaven may be compared to a king who gave a wedding banquet for his son. 3 He sent out his •slaves to summon those invited to the banquet, but they didn't want to come. 4 Again, he sent out other slaves, and said, 'Tell those who are invited: Look, I've prepared my dinner; my oxen and fattened cattle have been slaughtered, and everything is ready. Come to the wedding banquet.'

5 "But they paid no attention and went away, one to his own farm, another to his business. 6 And the others seized his slaves, treated them outrageously and killed them. 7 The king[H] was enraged, so he sent out his troops, destroyed those murderers, and burned down their city.

8 "Then he told his slaves, 'The banquet is ready, but those who were invited were not worthy. 9 Therefore go to where the roads exit the city and invite everyone you find to the banquet.' 10 So those slaves went out

22:1-14 The parable of the **wedding banquet** also demonstrated how the religious leaders paid no attention to the call of God. The invitation for everyone to join the banquet was a reference to the Gentiles and to all whom the religious leaders would certainly deem unworthy for such an occasion. The invitation was broad, but all did not respond positively to the message. There were requirements to the divine invitation. The **chosen** were the ones who committed to do the will of the Father (v. 14; see 7:21).

A **21:34** Lit *the season of fruits* B **21:41** Lit *him the fruits in their seasons* C **21:42** Lit *the head of the corner* D **21:42** Ps 118:22-23 E **21:43** = the kingdom's F **21:44** Other mss omit bracketed text G **21:46** = the crowds H **22:7** Other mss read *But when the (that) king heard about it he*

22:15-33 This section recounts a series of confrontations with leaders from three groups: **The Pharisees** (vv. 15-22,34-45), **the Herodians** (vv. 16-22), and **the Sadducees** (vv. 23-32). For a brief description of these groups, see pp. 1241-1243. When these groups came together to test Jesus, His answer tested them (vv. 19-22,41-46). They were so **amazed** (Gk *ethaumasan*, "wondered at, marveled with admiration," v. 22; cp. 8:27; 9:33; 15:31; Ac 4:13) that all they could do was to withdraw from Him.

22:23-33 The Sadducees' question appealed to the tradition of levirate marriage (Dt 25:5-6) in which a brother married the childless widow of his deceased brother in order to secure the property for and ensure the lineage of his deceased brother. Jesus quickly pointed out their ignorance of Scripture and showed them that the Torah, which they held as the Word of God, actually affirmed the resurrection. Although marriage as experienced on earth will not exist in heaven, happiness will not be absent because of the absence of sexual intimacy. Heavenly relationships, in fact, will surpass even the most intimate relationships on earth. This time Matthew pointed out that the crowds were **astonished** [Gk *exeplēssonto*, "were blown away, struck with amazement"; cp. 7:28; 13:54; Ac 13:12] **at His teaching** (22:33).

22:34-40 For the Jewish people, to **love** God was fundamental to all life, and the command from Dt 6:5 was well known. Hillel taught that Lv 19:18, which commanded love of one's **neighbor**, was also a fundamental mandate. But Jesus put both of these commandments together in such a way that for one to do otherwise would be nonsense. For Jesus said, **all the Law and the Prophets depend** [Gk *kremantai*, "hang, be suspended"] **on these two commands**. A right relationship to God is prerequisite to producing a right relationship to others.

22:41-46 Jesus asked the Pharisees a question: How could they view **the Messiah** as merely a human descendant of **David**? Jesus quoted Ps 110, widely understood to be written by David. The psalm mentions two "lords"—the first clearly referring to *Yahweh* (the personal name of God), the second possibly referring to an earthly master. However, since there had been no human being in Israel with a position higher than King David, the reference must have been to the Messiah. Therefore, the Messiah must be higher than David. The title "Son of David" had often been used to show the descent of Messiah, but few people realized that the Messiah would also be God's **Son**. Jesus illustrated that in these verses. Unable to refute such

on the roads and gathered everyone they found, both evil and good. The wedding banquet was filled with guests.[A] 11 But when the king came in to view the guests, he saw a man there who was not dressed for a wedding. 12 So he said to him, 'Friend, how did you get in here without wedding clothes?' The man was speechless.

13 "Then the king told the attendants, 'Tie him up hand and foot,[B] and throw him into the outer darkness, where there will be weeping and gnashing of teeth.'

14 "For many are invited, but few are chosen."

God and Caesar (22:15-22)

15 Then the ·Pharisees went and plotted how to trap Him by what He said.[C] 16 They sent their disciples to Him, with the ·Herodians. "Teacher," they said, "we know that You are truthful and teach truthfully the way of God. You defer to no one, for You don't show partiality.[D] 17 Tell us, therefore, what You think. Is it lawful to pay taxes to Caesar or not?"

18 But perceiving their malice, Jesus said, "Why are you testing Me, hypocrites? 19 Show Me the coin used for the tax." So they brought Him a ·denarius. 20 "Whose image and inscription is this?" He asked them.

21 "Caesar's," they said to Him.

Then He said to them, "Therefore give back to Caesar the things that are Caesar's, and to God the things that are God's." 22 When they heard this, they were amazed. So they left Him and went away.

The Sadducees and the Resurrection (22:23-33)

23 The same day some ·Sadducees, who say there is no resurrection, came up to Him and questioned Him: 24 "Teacher, Moses said, **if a man dies, having no children, his brother is to marry his wife and raise up offspring for his brother.**[E] 25 Now there were seven brothers among us. The first got married and died. Having no offspring, he left his wife to his brother. 26 The same happened to the second also, and the third, and so to all seven.[F] 27 Then last of all the woman died. 28 In the resurrection, therefore, whose wife will she be of the seven? For they all had married her."[G]

29 Jesus answered them, "You are deceived, because you don't know the Scriptures or the power of God. 30 For in the resurrection they neither marry nor are given in marriage but are like[H] angels in heaven. 31 Now concerning the resurrection of the dead, haven't you read what was spoken to you by God: 32 **I am the God of Abraham and the God of Isaac and the God of Jacob**?[I] He[J] is not the God of the dead, but of the living."

33 And when the crowds heard this, they were astonished at His teaching.

The Primary Commands (22:34-40)

34 When the Pharisees heard that He had silenced the Sadducees, they came together. 35 And one of them, an expert in the law, asked a question to test Him: 36 "Teacher, which command in the law is the greatest?"[K]

37 He said to him, "**Love the Lord your God with all your heart, with all your soul, and with all your mind.**[L] 38 This is the greatest and most important[M] command. 39 The second is like it: **Love your neighbor as yourself.**[N] 40 All the Law and the Prophets depend[O] on these two commands."

The Question About the Messiah (22:41-46)

41 While the Pharisees were together, Jesus questioned them, 42 "What do you think about the ·Messiah? Whose Son is He?"

"David's," they told Him.

43 He asked them, "How is it then that David, inspired by the Spirit,[P] calls Him 'Lord':

> 44 **The Lord declared to my Lord,**
> **'Sit at My right hand**
> **until I put Your enemies**
> **under Your feet'?**[Q,R]

[A] 22:10 Lit *those reclining* (to eat) [B] 22:13 Other mss add *take him away* [C] 22:15 Lit *trap Him in a word* [D] 22:16 Lit *don't look on the face of men*; that is, on the outward appearance [E] 22:24 Dt 25:5 [F] 22:26 Lit *so until the seven* [G] 22:28 Lit *all had her* [H] 22:30 Other mss add *God's* [I] 22:32 Ex 3:6,15-16 [J] 22:32 Other mss read *God* [K] 22:36 Lit *is great* [L] 22:37 Dt 6:5 [M] 22:38 Lit *and first* [N] 22:39 Lv 19:18 [O] 22:40 Or *hang* [P] 22:43 Lit *David in Spirit* [Q] 22:44 Other mss read *until I make Your enemies Your footstool* [R] 22:44 Ps 110:1

45"If David calls Him 'Lord,' how then can the Messiah be his Son?" 46No one was able to answer Him at all,[A] and from that day no one dared to question Him anymore.

Rebuke of Religious Hypocrites (23:1-26)

23 Then Jesus spoke to the crowds and to His disciples: 2"The •scribes and the •Pharisees are seated in the chair of Moses.[B] 3Therefore do whatever they tell you, and observe it. But don't do what they do,[C] because they don't practice what they teach. 4They tie up heavy loads that are hard to carry[D] and put them on people's shoulders, but they themselves aren't willing to lift a finger[E] to move them. 5They do everything[F] to be observed by others: They enlarge their phylacteries[G] and lengthen their •tassels.[H] 6They love the place of honor at banquets, the front seats in the •synagogues, 7greetings in the marketplaces, and to be called '•Rabbi' by people.

8"But as for you, do not be called 'Rabbi,' because you have one Teacher,[I] and you are all •brothers. 9Do not call anyone on earth your father, because you have one Father, who is in heaven. 10And do not be called masters either, because you have one Master,[J] the •Messiah. 11The greatest among you will be your servant. 12Whoever exalts himself will be humbled, and whoever humbles himself will be exalted.

13"But woe to you, scribes and Pharisees, hypocrites! You lock up the kingdom of heaven from people. For you don't go in, and you don't allow those entering to go in.

[14"Woe to you, scribes and Pharisees, hypocrites! You devour widows' houses and make long prayers just for show.[K] This is why you will receive a harsher punishment.][L]

15"Woe to you, scribes and Pharisees, hypocrites! You travel over land and sea to make one •proselyte, and when he becomes one, you make him twice as fit for •hell[M] as you are!

16"Woe to you, blind guides, who say, 'Whoever takes an oath by the sanctuary, it means nothing. But whoever takes an oath by the gold of the sanctuary is bound by his oath.'[N] 17Blind fools![O] For which is greater, the gold or the sanctuary that sanctified the gold? 18Also, 'Whoever takes an oath by the altar, it means nothing. But whoever takes an oath by the gift that is on it is bound by his oath.'[P] 19Blind people![Q] For which is greater, the gift or the altar that sanctifies the gift? 20Therefore, the one who takes an oath by the altar takes an oath by it and by everything on it. 21The one who takes an oath by the sanctuary takes an oath by it and by Him who dwells in it. 22And the one who takes an oath by heaven takes an oath by God's throne and by Him who sits on it.

23"Woe to you, scribes and Pharisees, hypocrites! You pay a tenth of[R] mint, dill, and cumin,[S] yet you have neglected the more important matters of the law—justice, mercy, and faith. These things should have been done without neglecting the others. 24Blind guides! You strain out a gnat, yet gulp down a camel!

25"Woe to you, scribes and Pharisees, hypocrites! You •clean the outside of the cup and dish, but inside they are full of greed[T] and self-indulgence! 26Blind Pharisee! First clean the inside of the cup,[U] so the outside of it[V] may also become clean.

Jesus' Lamentation over Jerusalem (23:27-39)

27"Woe to you, scribes and Pharisees, hypocrites! You are like whitewashed tombs, which appear beautiful on the outside, but inside

logic, the Pharisees walked away speechless.

In every confrontation, Jesus responded with supreme logic and Scripture. With such weapons, the religious leaders were humiliated and defeated, which fueled their rage against Him.

23:1-39 This fifth and final sermon includes a scathing diatribe against the Jewish leaders. Jesus first spoke to the crowds and His disciples (vv. 1-12). Then he unleashed a series of woes directed to the Pharisees (vv. 13-36). Its inclusion in the Gospel of Matthew is consistent with Matthew's overall purpose to present Jesus as the Messiah—the sole, authoritative interpreter of the Law and the Prophets. Jesus showed how the Pharisees failed to practice the greater righteousness (cp. chaps. 5–6 with 23:2-22). They did not practice what they preached. Everything they did was for the eyes of men. They neglected the deeper matters of the Law—justice, mercy, and faith. Inside they were full of hypocrisy and lawlessness.

Jesus' diatribe was very similar to the preaching of many Old Testament prophets, who decried the deeds of wayward Israel and Judah. Jesus did not attack the task of teaching in the synagogues. His words of criticism were for the self-righteous teachers, condemning their preoccupation with external things and their neglect of inward things. Jesus also lamented over Jerusalem, calling for nothing more than His people's willingness to accept Him. The return of Christ came into focus here as well.

23:2-3 The chair of Moses was probably a reference to the stone chair located at the front of the synagogue. The teacher occupied this chair of honor and influence, and to be **seated** there would suggest becoming the honored teacher's successor. Jesus respected the position of authority represented by this seat, explaining that the people should honor **the scribes and the Pharisees** who were seated there. In actuality, however, only Jesus was qualified to sit in the chair of Moses.

23:5 Phylacteries, leather boxes containing Scripture written on small scrolls, were worn on the left arm and on the forehead by Jewish men—a practice continued among orthodox Jewish men even in the modern era (Ex 13:9,16; Dt 6:8; 11:18). Some of these religious leaders had turned what was to be a personal reminder of God's words into a public spectacle to draw attention to their supposed spiritual devotion.

[A]**22:46** Lit *answer Him a word* [B]**23:2** Perhaps a special chair for teaching in synagogues, or a metaphorical phrase for teaching with Moses' authority [C]**23:3** Lit *do according to their works* [D]**23:4** Other mss omit *that are hard to carry* [E]**23:4** Lit *lift with their finger* [F]**23:5** Lit *do all their works* [G]**23:5** Small leather boxes containing OT texts, worn by Jews on their arms and foreheads [H]**23:5** Other mss add *on their robes* [I]**23:8** Other mss add *the Messiah* [J]**23:10** Or *Teacher* [K]**23:14** Or *prayers with false motivation* [L]**23:14** Other mss omit bracketed text [M]**23:15** Lit *twice the son of gehenna* [N]**23:16** Lit *is obligated* [O]**23:17** Lit *Fools and blind* [P]**23:18** Lit *is obligated* [Q]**23:19** Other mss read *Fools and blind* [R]**23:23** Or *You tithe* [S]**23:23** A plant whose seeds are used as a seasoning [T]**23:25** Or *full of violence* [U]**23:26** Other mss add *and dish* [V]**23:26** Other mss read *of them*

24:1-3 When Jesus' **disciples** praised the magnificence of the temple buildings, Jesus prophesied the total destruction of the temple, which occurred in A.D. 70. Having directed the disciples' attention to the future, they wanted to know what would signal His **coming** and **the end of the age** (cp. 13:39-40,49; 28:20).

24:4-5 Before answering the disciples' questions (v. 3) more directly, Jesus warned them against being deceived by imposters—false messiahs claiming to speak or act in Jesus' **name** or actually claiming to be **the Messiah**. Jesus reiterates the need for His followers to beware in verses 11,23-28.

24:6-8 Jesus instructed His disciples not be deceived (vv. 4-5) but also *not* to be **alarmed** (Gk *throeisthe*, "troubled, frightened"; from the verb *throeō*, wanting to "wail, cry aloud, lament" because terrified; "thrown into an emotional uproar"; cp. Mk 13:7; 2Th 2:2). Many tragic conflicts and cataclysmic events that normally and understandably elicit such anxiety and confusion would happen with increasing frequency and intensity—like **the beginning of birth pains** (Gk *ōdinōn*, "intolerable anguish or travail" of childbirth; cp. Mk 13:8; 1Th 5:3).

24:9-14 Widespread **persecution** (Gk *thlipsin*, "intense pressure, affliction, tribulation," vv. 9,21,29; cp. 13:21; Jn 16:21) of the disciples would come, along with conflict, hatred, **false prophets**, **lawlessness**, and a waning of the passionate, unconditional love that marks the followers of Jesus. Nevertheless, the gospel would continue to spread. Finally, Jesus answers, in part, the disciples' question about when **the end will come**.

24:15-22 The **abomination that causes desolation** refers to Dn 9:27; 11:31; 12:11. An early fulfillment of this prophecy came with the desecration of the temple, when Antiochus Epiphanes erected a statue of Zeus and sacrificed a swine on the altar (168 B.C.). Jesus spoke of another similar act of desecration that would take place in the future (e.g., Lk 21:20; Rv 21:27), as well as unprecedented **tribulation** (v. 21).

are full of dead men's bones and
every impurity. 28 In the same way,
on the outside you seem righteous
to people, but inside you are full of
hypocrisy and lawlessness.
29 "Woe to you, scribes and Pharisees, hypocrites! You build the
tombs of the prophets and decorate
the monuments of the righteous,
30 and you say, 'If we had lived in
the days of our fathers, we wouldn't
have taken part with them in shedding the prophets' blood.'[A] 31 You,
therefore, testify against yourselves
that you are sons of those who murdered the prophets. 32 Fill up, then,
the measure of your fathers' sins![B]
33 "Snakes! Brood of vipers! How
can you escape being condemned to
hell?[C] 34 This is why I am sending you
prophets, sages, and scribes. Some
of them you will kill and crucify, and
some of them you will flog in your
synagogues and hound from town
to town. 35 So all the righteous blood
shed on the earth will be charged to
you,[D] from the blood of righteous
Abel to the blood of Zechariah, son
of Berechiah, whom you murdered
between the sanctuary and the altar.
36 •I assure you: All these things will
come on this generation!
37 "Jerusalem, Jerusalem! She who
kills the prophets and stones those
who are sent to her. How often I
wanted to gather your children together, as a hen gathers her chicks[E]
under her wings, yet you were not
willing! 38 See, your house is left to
you desolate. 39 For I tell you, you
will never see Me again until you
say, '**He who comes in the name of
the Lord is the blessed One**'!"[F]

Prediction of the Destruction of the Temple (24:1-2)

24 As Jesus left and was going out
of the •temple complex, His
disciples came up and called His
attention to the temple buildings.
2 Then He replied to them, "Don't
you see all these things? •I assure
you: Not one stone will be left here
on another that will not be thrown
down!"

Signs of the End of the Age (24:3-8)

3 While He was sitting on the
•Mount of Olives, the disciples approached Him privately and said,
"Tell us, when will these things happen? And what is the sign of Your
coming and of the end of the age?"
4 Then Jesus replied to them:
"Watch out that no one deceives you.
5 For many will come in My name,
saying, 'I am the •Messiah,' and they
will deceive many. 6 You are going
to hear of wars and rumors of wars.
See that you are not alarmed, because these things must take place,
but the end is not yet. 7 For nation
will rise up against nation, and kingdom against kingdom. There will be
famines[G] and earthquakes in various
places. 8 All these events are the beginning of birth pains.

Prediction of Persecutions (24:9-14)

9 "Then they will hand you over for
persecution,[H] and they will kill you.
You will be hated by all nations because of My name. 10 Then many will
•take offense, betray one another
and hate one another. 11 Many false
prophets will rise up and deceive
many. 12 Because lawlessness will
multiply, the love of many will grow
cold. 13 But the one who endures to
the end will be delivered.[I] 14 This
good news of the kingdom will be
proclaimed in all the world[J] as a testimony to all nations. And then the
end will come.

The Great Tribulation (24:15-28)

15 "So when you see **the abomination that causes desolation**,[K,L]
spoken of by the prophet Daniel,
standing in the holy place" (let the
reader understand[M]), 16 "then those
in Judea must flee to the mountains!
17 A man on the housetop[N] must not
come down to get things out of his
house. 18 And a man in the field must
not go back to get his clothes. 19 Woe
to pregnant women and nursing
mothers in those days! 20 Pray that

[A] **23:30** Lit *have been partakers with them in the blood of the prophets* [B] **23:32** Lit *the measure of your fathers* [C] **23:33** Lit *escape from the judgment of gehenna* [D] **23:35** Lit *will come on you* [E] **23:37** Or *as a mother bird gathers her young* [F] **23:39** Ps 118:26 [G] **24:7** Other mss add *epidemics* [H] **24:9** Or *tribulation*, or *distress* [I] **24:13** Or *be saved* [J] **24:14** Or *in all the inhabited earth* [K] **24:15** Or *abomination of desolation*, or *desolating sacrilege* [L] **24:15** Dn 9:27 [M] **24:15** These are, most likely, Matthew's words to his readers. [N] **24:17** Or *roof*

your escape may not be in winter or on a Sabbath. 21 For at that time there will be great tribulation, the kind that hasn't taken place from the beginning of the world until now and never will again! 22 Unless those days were limited, no one would[A] survive.[B] But those days will be limited because of the elect.

23 "If anyone tells you then, 'Look, here is the Messiah!' or, 'Over here!' do not believe it! 24 False messiahs[C] and false prophets will arise and perform great signs and wonders to lead astray, if possible, even the elect. 25 Take note: I have told you in advance. 26 So if they tell you, 'Look, He's in the wilderness!' don't go out; 'Look, He's in the inner rooms!' do not believe it. 27 For as the lightning comes from the east and flashes as far as the west, so will be the coming of the •Son of Man. 28 Wherever the carcass is, there the vultures[D] will gather.

The Coming of the Son of Man (24:29-31)

29 "Immediately after the tribulation of those days:

> The sun will be darkened,
> and the moon will not shed
> its light;
> the stars will fall from the sky,
> and the celestial powers
> will be shaken.

30 "Then the sign of the Son of Man will appear in the sky, and then all the peoples of the earth[E] will mourn;[F] and they will see the Son of Man coming on the clouds of heaven with power and great glory. 31 He will send out His angels with a loud trumpet, and they will gather His elect from the four winds, from one end of the sky to the other.

The Parable of the Fig Tree (24:32-35)

32 "Now learn this parable from the fig tree: As soon as its branch becomes tender and sprouts leaves, you know that summer is near. 33 In the same way, when you see all these things, recognize[G] that He[H] is near—at the door! 34 I assure you: This generation will certainly not pass away until all these things take place. 35 Heaven and earth will pass away, but My words will never pass away.

Uncertainty of the Day or Hour (24:36-44)

36 "Now concerning that day and hour no one knows—neither the angels in heaven, nor the Son[I]—except the Father only. 37 As the days of Noah were, so the coming of the Son of Man will be. 38 For in those days before the flood they were eating and drinking, marrying and giving in marriage, until the day Noah boarded the ark. 39 They didn't know[J] until the flood came and swept them all away. So this is the way the coming of the Son of Man will be: 40 Then two men will be in the field: one will be taken and one left. 41 Two women will be grinding at the mill: one will be taken and one left. 42 Therefore be alert, since you don't know what day[K] your Lord is coming. 43 But know this: If the homeowner had known what time[L] the thief was coming, he would have stayed alert and not let his house be broken into. 44 This is why you also must be ready, because the Son of Man is coming at an hour you do not expect.

Faithful Service to the Messiah (24:45-51)

45 "Who then is a faithful and sensible •slave, whom his master has put in charge of his household, to give them food at the proper time? 46 That slave whose master finds him working when he comes will be rewarded. 47 I assure you: He will put him in charge of all his possessions. 48 But if that wicked slave says in his heart, 'My master is delayed,' 49 and starts to beat his fellow slaves, and eats and drinks with drunkards, 50 that slave's master will come on a day he does not expect and at an hour he does not know. 51 He will cut him to pieces[M] and assign him a place with the hypocrites. In that

24:27-31 But there would be no mistaking the return of Christ, **the Son of Man** (cp. Ezk 2:3; Dn 7:13-14; Mt 26:64). The Messiah came the first time in humility and obscurity (Lk 2:4-7), seeking to save the lost. But when He returns, He will light up the sky, announcing the coming judgment.

24:32-35 The **parable** of the **fig tree** was especially important in this context. **This generation** (Gk *genea*, "nation, race, offspring") may refer to the nation of Israel, reaffirming her continued existence until the last days, or the expression may simply suggest "age" or "time period" in general. The word may also suggest a particular time frame, as a 30- or 40-year period, in which case these signs described in the text would have begun to be fulfilled before that generation passed away (see also Mt 11:16; 12:39,41-42,45; 16:4; 17:17; and 23:36).

24:36-51 In this section of the sermon, Jesus stressed three very important points:

- **No one . . . except the Father** knows the day or hour of Christ's return.
- Disciples should be watchful and ready for His return in all circumstances.
- While waiting for the King to return, the disciples' watchfulness must be manifested in service.

24:42–25:46 A genuine disciple is consistently practicing watchfulness and service (24:51; 25:12,30,46). Finally addressing directly the disciples' question about the coming of **the Son of Man** (24:3,37,39), Jesus compared His sudden arrival to the flood that came unexpectedly upon the people who had spurned the preaching of Noah. Instead, Jesus urged His followers to **be alert** (vv. 42-43; 25:13; cp. Rv 3:2).

24:45-51 The faithful slave was prepared at all times, faithful even when his master's delay was long (v. 46). In the end, he would be greatly **rewarded** (Gk *makarios*, "blessed, happy"; cp. 5:3-11). The **wicked slave**, on the other hand, was lax in his responsibilities and would be **cut . . . to pieces** (Gk *dichotomēsei*, lit "cut in two;" here, "cut" in the sense of "scourge severely").

[A]**24:22** Lit *short, all flesh would not* [B]**24:22** Or *be saved* or *delivered* [C]**24:24** Or *False christs* [D]**24:28** Or *eagles* [E]**24:30** Or *all the tribes of the land* [F]**24:30** Lit *will beat*; that is, beat their breasts [G]**24:33** Or *things, you know* [H]**24:33** Or *it*; that is, summer [I]**24:36** Other mss omit *nor the Son* [J]**24:39** They didn't know the day and hour of the coming judgment. [K]**24:42** Other mss read *hour*; = time [L]**24:43** Lit *watch*; a division of the night in ancient times [M]**24:51** Lit *him in two*

25:1-30 The parable of the **10 virgins** (bridesmaids) also addresses delay of **the groom**, again representing the return of the Son of Man. The parables illustrate what Jesus' followers should and should not do while they wait for His return, which could occur at any time, perhaps when they least expect it. In this parable, five **sensible** (Gk *phronimoi*, "thoughtful, wise") virgins took extra oil for their lamps; the other five virgins did not make sufficient preparation ahead of time and suffered the consequences. These "sensitive" virgins are better understood to be women who indeed used good sense and reasoning but even more were marked by genuine wisdom and understanding—for believers, spiritual sensitivity (Pr 14:1).

place there will be weeping and gnashing of teeth.

The Parable of the 10 Virgins (25:1-13)

25 "Then the kingdom of heaven will be like 10 virgins[A] who took their lamps and went out to meet the groom. 2 Five of them were foolish and five were sensible. 3 When the foolish took their lamps, they didn't take olive oil with them. 4 But the sensible ones took oil in their flasks with their lamps. 5 Since the groom was delayed, they all became drowsy and fell asleep.

6 "In the middle of the night there was a shout: 'Here's the groom! Come out to meet him.'

7 "Then all those virgins got up and trimmed their lamps. 8 But the foolish ones said to the sensible ones, 'Give us some of your oil, because our lamps are going out.'

9 "The sensible ones answered, 'No, there won't be enough for us and for you. Go instead to those who sell, and buy oil for yourselves.'

10 "When they had gone to buy some, the groom arrived. Then those who were ready went in with him to the wedding banquet, and the door was shut.

11 "Later the rest of the virgins also came and said, 'Master, master, open up for us!'

12 "But he replied, '•I assure you: I do not know you!'

13 "Therefore be alert, because you don't know either the day or the hour.[B]

The Parable of the Talents (25:14-30)

14 "For it is just like a man going on a journey. He called his own •slaves and turned over his possessions to them. 15 To one he gave five talents;[C] to another, two; and to another, one—to each according to his own ability. Then he went on a journey. Immediately 16 the man who had received five talents went, put them to work, and earned five more. 17 In the same way the man with two earned two more. 18 But the man who had received one talent went off, dug a hole in the ground, and hid his master's money.

19 "After a long time the master of those slaves came and settled accounts with them. 20 The man who had received five talents approached, presented five more talents, and said, 'Master, you gave me five talents. Look, I've earned five more talents.'

21 "His master said to him, 'Well done, good and faithful slave! You were faithful over a few things; I will put you in charge of many things. Share your master's joy!'

22 "Then the man with two talents also approached. He said, 'Master, you gave me two talents. Look, I've earned two more talents.'

23 "His master said to him, 'Well done, good and faithful slave! You were faithful over a few things; I will put you in charge of many things. Share your master's joy!'

24 "Then the man who had received one talent also approached and said, 'Master, I know you. You're a difficult man, reaping where you haven't sown and gathering where you haven't scattered seed. 25 So I was afraid and went off and hid your talent in the ground. Look, you have what is yours.'

26 "But his master replied to him,

[A] **25:1** Or *bridesmaids* [B] **25:13** Other mss add *in which the Son of Man is coming.* [C] **25:15** Worth a very large sum of money; a talent = 6,000 •denarii

>WORD|*study*

25:1-30 The Greek word for foolish (*mōros*), from which is derived the English word "moron," has a range of meaning depending on context. For example, it can mean "without learning, uneducated" (1Co 1:27) or "empty, useless, senseless" (2Tm 2:23). In the New Testament the word does not have the same connotation of "stupid" except figuratively in a moral sense. In this parable, the "foolish" virgins are "without forethought or wisdom." In biblical wisdom literature—e.g., Proverbs and Ecclesiastes—"foolish" (Hb *naval*; see **Word Study**, p. 807) describes someone who rejects God's ways and a lifestyle of righteousness, choosing instead his own way and, therefore, a lifestyle of wickedness and opposition to God. This is why behaviors and choices that may seem like instances merely of irresponsibility, forgetfulness, immaturity, or laziness—which typically might be considered excusable in the reader's life experiences—are treated as serious, punishable, and inexcusable offenses in wisdom literature and parables (cp. 7:26; 23:17,19).

'You evil, lazy slave! If you knew
that I reap where I haven't sown and
gather where I haven't scattered,
27 then[A] you should have deposited
my money with the bankers. And
when I returned I would have received my money[B] back with interest.
28 "'So take the talent from him
and give it to the one who has 10
talents. 29 For to everyone who has,
more will be given, and he will have
more than enough. But from the
one who does not have, even what
he has will be taken away from him.
30 And throw this good-for-nothing
slave into the outer darkness. In
that place there will be weeping and
gnashing of teeth.'

The Sheep and the Goats (25:31-46)

31 "When the •Son of Man comes
in His glory, and all the angels[C] with
Him, then He will sit on the throne
of His glory. 32 All the nations[D] will
be gathered before Him, and He will
separate them one from another,
just as a shepherd separates the
sheep from the goats. 33 He will put
the sheep on His right and the goats
on the left. 34 Then the King will say
to those on His right, 'Come, you
who are blessed by My Father, inherit the kingdom prepared for you
from the foundation of the world.

35 For I was hungry
and you gave Me something
to eat;

25:31-46 This story has some parabolic elements (sheep, goats, and the shepherd) but actually illustrates metaphorically the truth that God knows who belongs to Him (cp. 10:40-42). **The least of these brothers of Mine** likely refers not generally to the poor or societal outcasts but more specifically to Christ's disciples (25:40). The fate of the nations is determined by how they have treated Christ's followers, who endure severe suffering for the gospel's sake (cp. Ac 9:5). Those who treated His followers with kindness would be rewarded; those who neglected or ignored them would themselves be ignored and rejected in the end. To respond to Jesus' love is to obey His commands. To obey His commands is to reach out to others in love. Christ's divine authority over all nations, which comes into sharp focus in chapter 28, is briefly highlighted here.

[A]25:26-27 Or *So you knew . . . scattered? Then* (as a question) [B]25:27 Lit *received what is mine* [C]25:31 Other mss read *holy angels* [D]25:32 Or *the Gentiles*

Women and the Parables of Jesus

Parable	Audience	Application	Reference
The lamp under a basket	The disciples	All of your words and actions should give testimony to God's redemptive and transforming grace.	Mt 5:14-16; Mk 4:21-22; Lk 8:16-17
The marriage	The Pharisees and the disciples of John the Baptist	In Christ's companionship, joy will be found.	Mt 9:15; Mk 2:19-20; Lk 5:34-35
The patched garment	The Pharisees and the disciples of John the Baptist	Jesus came to make all things new.	Mt 9:16; Mk 2:21; Lk 5:36
The children in the marketplace	The multitudes concerning John the Baptist	Those who rejected Jesus and John could not be satisfied. Beware of focusing on personal whims.	Mt 11:16-17; Lk 7:31-32
The leaven	The multitude on the seashore	Beware of sin, for it makes its way into life, corrupting and drawing away from the good and true.	Mt 13:33; Lk 13:20-21
The pearl of great price	The disciples	The value of the gospel greatly exceeds all else.	Mt 13:45-46
The wedding garment	The chief priests and the Pharisees	Your life must be kept pure and holy.	Mt 22:10-14
The sensible (i.e., wise) and foolish virgins	The disciples on the Mount of Olives	Be prepared and watchful for Jesus' return.	Mt 25:1-13
The wedding feast	The chief priests and the Pharisees	Do not reject God's invitation to salvation.	Mt 22:2-9; Lk 14:16-23
The lost coin	The Pharisees and scribes	Christ's love is for sinners, and He is determined to draw them to Himself.	Lk 15:8-10
The persistent widow	The disciples	Pray fervently and persistently.	Lk 18:1-8

26:1-56 The plot against Jesus was twofold. First, the Jewish leaders **conspired** to **kill Him** (vv. 3-5). Second, **Judas Iscariot**, spurred on by what he considered a **waste** of **oil** for Jesus' anointing in preparation for burial (vv. 8-9,14-16; cp. Jn 12:3-6), plotted with the Jewish leaders to **hand** [Jesus] **over** to them. The 30 pieces of silver paid to Judas would have been the value of a male or female slave gored to death by an ox (Mt 26:15; see Ex 21:32). Sandwiched between these two acts of treachery was the one act of faith in this entire section: Jesus' anointing in Bethany—an act performed by a woman (vv. 6-13). Compare the juxtaposition, in 15:21-28, of a Gentile woman's faith with the rebellion of the Jewish leaders and the unbelief of the disciples.

At this last **Passover**, Jesus predicted Judas' betrayal (vv. 21-25,46) as well as Peter's denial and the disciples' abandonment of Him (vv. 31-35). The Passover, celebrated every year, is a very important feast commemorating the delivery of Israel out of Egypt. The elements of the ceremony observed by the Jews included the following:

- a blessing and the first cup of wine: "I will deliver you . . ." (Ex 6:6);
- the meal of unleavened bread, bitter herbs, greens, and roasted lamb, each symbolizing details associated with the first Passover;
- a second cup of wine: "I will . . . free you from slavery to them . . ." (Ex 6:6);
- the singing of a song of praise (Ps 113–114);
- the breaking of bread and the eating of the meal;
- a third cup of wine and the end of meal: "I will redeem you . . ." (Ex 6:6);
- the singing of another song of praise (Ps 115–118).
- a fourth cup of wine: "I will take you as My people, and I will be your God . . ." (Ex 6:7).

CHARACTER PROFILE

The Wise and Foolish Virgins

Their Background	These women were characters in one of Jesus' parables.
Their Story	• They were bridesmaids in a wedding party (25:1). • They were to have their lamps lit for the bridal procession, whenever the groom arrived (25:3-4). • Due to his delay, five of them did not have enough oil for their lamps and left the wedding to purchase more. While they were gone, the groom arrived for the bride (25:10). • They were left out of the wedding celebration (25:10).
Life Lesson	Spiritual preparation must be made ahead of Christ's return; it cannot be made at the last minute.

I was thirsty
and you gave Me something
to drink;
I was a stranger and you
took Me in;
36 I was naked and you
clothed Me;
I was sick and you took care
of Me;
I was in prison and you
visited Me.'

37 "Then the righteous will answer Him, 'Lord, when did we see You hungry and feed You, or thirsty and give You something to drink?
38 When did we see You a stranger and take You in, or without clothes and clothe You? 39 When did we see You sick, or in prison, and visit You?'
40 "And the King will answer them, 'I assure you: Whatever you did for one of the least of these ·brothers of Mine, you did for Me.' 41 Then He will also say to those on the left, 'Depart from Me, you who are cursed, into the eternal fire prepared for the Devil and his angels!

42 For I was hungry
and you gave Me nothing to eat;
I was thirsty
and you gave Me nothing
to drink;
43 I was a stranger
and you didn't take Me in;
I was naked
and you didn't clothe Me,
sick and in prison
and you didn't take care
of Me.'

44 "Then they too will answer, 'Lord, when did we see You hungry, or thirsty, or a stranger, or without clothes, or sick, or in prison, and not help You?'
45 "Then He will answer them, 'I assure you: Whatever you did not do for one of the least of these, you did not do for Me either.'
46 "And they will go away into eternal punishment, but the righteous into eternal life."

An Account of Jesus' Ultimate Destiny (26:1–28:20)

The Plot to Kill Jesus (26:1-5)

26 When Jesus had finished saying all this, He told His disciples, 2 "You know[A] that the ·Passover takes place after two days, and the ·Son of Man will be handed over to be crucified."
3 Then the ·chief priests[B] and the elders of the people assembled in the palace of the high priest, who was called Caiaphas, 4 and they conspired to arrest Jesus in a treacherous way and kill Him. 5 "Not during the festival," they said, "so there won't be rioting among the people."

The Anointing at Bethany (26:6-16)

6 While Jesus was in Bethany at the house of Simon, a man who had a serious skin disease, 7 a woman approached Him with an alabaster jar

[A] **26:2** Or *Know* (as a command) [B] **26:3** Other mss add *and the scribes*

Women with Jesus in His Last Days

The Woman	The Event	Her Ministry to Jesus	Reference
Mary, unnamed in Matthew but identified in John	Jesus' anointing at Bethany	She anointed Jesus' head with expensive and fragrant oil.	Mt 26:6-13; Jn 11:1-44
Unnamed female servants	Peter's testing	They questioned Peter about his association with Jesus.	Mt 26:69,70-72
Pilate's wife	Jesus' trial	She pleaded with her husband to release Jesus, whom she believed was righteous.	Mt 27:17-19
Unnamed women	The journey to the crucifixion site	They mourned for Jesus.	Lk 23:26-29
Mary Magdalene; Mary (Jesus' mother, possibly identified as the mother of James and Joseph in Mt 27:55-56); Salome (the wife of Zebedee, and the mother of disciples James and John); Mary (the wife of Clopas and the sister of Mary and thus the aunt of Jesus.	Jesus' crucifixion and burial	They remained with Jesus through His time of suffering and prepared His body for burial.	Mt 27:55-56; Jn 19:25-28
Mary Magdalene; Mary (the mother of James); Joanna	Jesus' resurrection	They announced His resurrection to the disciples.	Mt 28:1-10; Lk 24:1-12

of very expensive fragrant oil. She
poured it on His head as He was reclining at the table. 8 When the disciples saw it, they were indignant.
"Why this waste?" they asked. 9 "This
might have been sold for a great deal
and given to the poor."
10 But Jesus, aware of this, said to
them, "Why are you bothering this
woman? She has done a noble thing
for Me. 11 You always have the poor
with you, but you do not always have
Me. 12 By pouring this fragrant oil on
My body, she has prepared Me for
burial. 13 •I assure you: Wherever this
gospel is proclaimed in the whole
world, what this woman has done
will also be told in memory of her."
14 Then one of the Twelve—the
man called Judas Iscariot—went to
the chief priests 15 and said, "What
are you willing to give me if I hand
Him over to you?" So they weighed
out 30 pieces of silver for him. 16 And
from that time he started looking for
a good opportunity to betray Him.

Betrayal at the Passover (26:17-25)

17 On the first day of •Unleavened
Bread the disciples came to Jesus
and asked, "Where do You want us
to prepare the Passover so You may
eat it?"
18 "Go into the city to a certain man,"
He said, "and tell him, 'The Teacher
says: My time is near; I am celebrating the Passover at your place[A] with
My disciples.'" 19 So the disciples did
as Jesus had directed them and prepared the Passover. 20 When evening
came, He was reclining at the table
with the Twelve. 21 While they were
eating, He said, "I assure you: One of
you will betray Me."
22 Deeply distressed, each one began
to say to Him, "Surely not I, Lord?"
23 He replied, "The one who dipped
his hand with Me in the bowl—he
will betray Me. 24 The Son of Man will
go just as it is written about Him,

[A] **26:18** Lit *Passover with you*

26:26-28 While reciting this liturgy, Jesus proclaimed that a new Passover was about to be inaugurated by the shedding of His blood. Jesus then instituted the Lord's Supper by using two symbols—the unleavened **bread** (a reminder of the hasty departure of God's people from Egypt [Ex 12] and a symbol of His body, which would be broken at His death) and the **fruit of the vine** (symbolic of His blood, which would be shed on the cross). This celebratory event looked back to Jesus' death on the cross and forward to His return.

26:36-56 Gethsemane (lit "oil press," v. 36) was the garden located across the Kidron Valley at the foot of the Mount of Olives. **Peter**, James and John (**the two sons of Zebedee**) had also been with Jesus at His transfiguration (v. 37; see 17:1-13). **Judas** greeted Jesus with the traditional **kiss** of friendship (26:48-49) to identify Him to **the chief priests and elders** leading the armed **mob** to arrest Him.

To highlight further Jesus' loyalty to the Father's will, Matthew added the words of Jesus concerning the **legions of angels** whom His Father would send upon His request for deliverance (v. 53) and His commitment to fulfill **the Scriptures** (v. 54).

but woe to that man by whom the
Son of Man is betrayed! It would
have been better for that man if he
had not been born."
25 Then Judas, His betrayer, replied, "Surely not I, •Rabbi?"
"You have said it," He told him.

The First Lord's Supper (26:26-30)

26 As they were eating, Jesus took
bread, blessed and broke it, gave it to
the disciples, and said, "Take and eat
it; this is My body." 27 Then He took a
cup, and after giving thanks, He gave
it to them and said, "Drink from it,
all of you. 28 For this is My blood that
establishes the covenant;[A] it is shed
for many for the forgiveness of sins.
29 But I tell you, from this moment I
will not drink of this fruit of the vine
until that day when I drink it in a new
way[B] in My Father's kingdom with
you." 30 After singing psalms,[C] they
went out to the •Mount of Olives.

Prediction of Peter's Denial (26:31-35)

31 Then Jesus said to them, "Tonight all of you will run away[D] because of Me, for it is written:

I will strike the shepherd,
and the sheep of the flock
will be scattered.[E]

32 But after I have been resurrected, I
will go ahead of you to Galilee."
33 Peter told Him, "Even if everyone runs away because of You, I will
never run away!"
34 "I assure you," Jesus said to him,
"tonight, before the rooster crows,
you will deny Me three times!"
35 "Even if I have to die with You,"
Peter told Him, "I will never deny
You!" And all the disciples said the
same thing.

The Prayer in the Garden (26:36-46)

36 Then Jesus came with them to
a place called Gethsemane,[F] and He
told the disciples, "Sit here while I
go over there and pray." 37 Taking
along Peter and the two sons of Zebedee, He began to be sorrowful and
deeply distressed. 38 Then He said
to them, "My soul is swallowed up
in sorrow[G]—to the point of death.[H]
Remain here and stay awake with
Me." 39 Going a little farther,[I] He fell
facedown and prayed, "My Father! If
it is possible, let this cup pass from
Me. Yet not as I will, but as You will."
40 Then He came to the disciples
and found them sleeping. He asked
Peter, "So, couldn't you[J] stay awake
with Me one hour? 41 Stay awake and
pray, so that you won't enter into
temptation. The spirit is willing, but
the flesh is weak."
42 Again, a second time, He went
away and prayed, "My Father, if
this[K] cannot pass[L] unless I drink it,
Your will be done." 43 And He came
again and found them sleeping, because they could not keep their eyes
open.[M]
44 After leaving them, He went
away again and prayed a third time,
saying the same thing once more.
45 Then He came to the disciples and
said to them, "Are you still sleeping
and resting?[N] Look, the time is near.
The Son of Man is being betrayed
into the hands of sinners. 46 Get up;
let's go! See, My betrayer is near."

The Judas Kiss (26:47-56)

47 While He was still speaking,
Judas, one of the Twelve, suddenly
arrived. A large mob, with swords
and clubs, was with him from the
chief priests and elders of the people. 48 His betrayer had given them a
sign: "The One I kiss, He's the One;
arrest Him!" 49 So he went right up
to Jesus and said, "Greetings, Rabbi!" and kissed Him.
50 "Friend," Jesus asked him, "why
have you come?"[O]
Then they came up, took hold of
Jesus, and arrested Him. 51 At that
moment one of those with Jesus
reached out his hand and drew his
sword. He struck the high priest's
•slave and cut off his ear.
52 Then Jesus told him, "Put your
sword back in its place because all

[A] **26:28** Other mss read *new covenant* [B] **26:29** Or *drink new wine*; lit *drink it new* [C] **26:30** Pss 113–118 were sung during and after the Passover meal. [D] **26:31** Or •*stumble* [E] **26:31** Zch 13:7 [F] **26:36** A garden east of Jerusalem at the base of the Mount of Olives; Gethsemane = olive oil press [G] **26:38** Or *I am deeply grieved*, or *I am overwhelmed by sorrow*; Ps 42:6,11; 43:5 [H] **26:38** Lit *unto death* [I] **26:39** Other mss read *Drawing nearer* [J] **26:40** = all 3 disciples because the verb in Gk is pl [K] **26:42** Other mss add *cup* [L] **26:42** Other mss add *from Me* [M] **26:43** Lit *because their eyes were weighed down* [N] **26:45** Or *Sleep on now and take your rest.* [O] **26:50** Or *Jesus told him, "do what you have come for."* (as a statement)

who take up a sword will perish by a
sword. 53 Or do you think that I cannot call on My Father, and He will
provide Me at once with more than
12 legions[A] of angels? 54 How, then,
would the Scriptures be fulfilled
that say it must happen this way?"
55 At that time Jesus said to the
crowds, "Have you come out with
swords and clubs, as if I were a
criminal,[B] to capture Me? Every day
I used to sit, teaching in the •temple
complex, and you didn't arrest Me.
56 But all this has happened so that
the prophetic Scriptures[C] would be
fulfilled." Then all the disciples deserted Him and ran away.

Jesus Before the Sanhedrin (26:57-68)

57 Those who had arrested Jesus
led Him away to Caiaphas the high
priest, where the •scribes and the elders had convened. 58 Meanwhile, Peter was following Him at a distance
right to the high priest's courtyard.[D]
He went in and was sitting with the
temple police[E] to see the outcome.[F]
59 The chief priests and the whole
•Sanhedrin were looking for false
testimony against Jesus so they
could put Him to death. 60 But they
could not find any, even though
many false witnesses came forward.[G]
Finally, two[H] who came forward
61 stated, "This man said, 'I can demolish God's sanctuary and rebuild
it in three days.'"
62 The high priest then stood up
and said to Him, "Don't You have
an answer to what these men are
testifying against You?" 63 But Jesus
kept silent. Then the high priest said
to Him, "By the living God I place
You under oath: tell us if You are the
•Messiah, the Son of God!"
64 "You have said it,"[I] Jesus told
him. "But I tell you, in the future[J]
you will see **the Son of Man seated
at the right hand** of the Power and
coming on the clouds of heaven."[K]
65 Then the high priest tore his
robes and said, "He has blasphemed!
Why do we still need witnesses?
Look, now you've heard the blasphemy! 66 What is your decision?"[L]
They answered, "He deserves
death!" 67 Then they spit in His face
and beat Him; others slapped Him
68 and said, "Prophesy to us, Messiah!
Who hit You?"

Peter's Denial (26:69-75)

69 Now Peter was sitting outside in
the courtyard. A servant approached
him and she said, "You were with
Jesus the Galilean too."
70 But he denied it in front of everyone: "I don't know what you're
talking about!"
71 When he had gone out to the
gateway, another woman saw him
and told those who were there, "This
man was with Jesus the •Nazarene!"

26:57-68 Jesus was condemned by the **Sanhedrin**, denied by Peter, handed over to Pilate, and eventually crucified on what has long been called "Good" Friday. Matthew highlighted the fact that Jesus went to the Jews first, where He was placed under oath and asked if He were the **Messiah, the Son of God**. Jesus answered affirmatively and announced His return in power and glory (v. 64; cp. Dn 7:13-14).

[A]**26:53** A Roman legion contained up to 6,000 soldiers. [B]**26:55** Lit *as against a criminal* [C]**26:56** Or *the Scriptures of the prophets* [D]**26:58** Or *high priest's palace* [E]**26:58** Or *the officers*, or *the servants* [F]**26:58** Lit *end* [G]**26:60** Other mss add *they found none* [H]**26:60** Other mss add *false witnesses* [I]**26:64** Or *That is true*, an affirmative oath; Mt 27:11; Mk 15:2 [J]**26:64** Lit *you, from now* [K]**26:64** Ps 110:1; Dn 7:13 [L]**26:66** Lit *What does it seem to you?*

CHARACTER PROFILE

Female Servants

Their Background	They were servants in the house of Caiaphas the high priest.
Their Story	• Their duties included greeting guests. • They identified Peter as a follower of Jesus (26:69,71).
Life Lesson	Peter had defended Jesus in the garden of Gethsemane before armed men (Jn 18:3-11), yet he denied Jesus before two insignificant servants. Sometimes the small pressures of life can be more difficult to handle than the large ones.

See also Mk 14:66-68; Lk 22:56-57; Jn 18:17.

27:1-14 Then Jesus was sent to a Gentile, the Roman leader **Pilate**, where He was again placed under oath and asked if He were **the King of the Jews** (v. 11; cp. v. 37). Jesus acknowledged that fact. During both inquisitions, to the amazement of His opponents, Jesus' demeanor was one of quiet acceptance and gentle response, in keeping with the prophecies spoken about Him (Is 42:1-4). Before both the Jews and the Gentiles, Jesus had made His confession to being the Messiah, the Son of God, the King of Israel.

27:3-10 In contrast to Peter's sorrow over having denied Jesus (26:75), Judas was full of **remorse** (Gk *metamelētheis*, "regret, be sorry; change of mind"), and he even returned the money he received for betraying Jesus (27:3-5). However, he did not repent. **Blood money** could not be placed in **the temple treasury** (27:6-7); so the legalistic religious leaders, wanting to observe the letter of the law, used the money to buy a **field** in which foreigners would be buried.

72 And again he denied it with an
oath, "I don't know the man!"
73 After a little while those standing there approached and said to Peter, "You certainly are one of them,
since even your accent[A] gives you
away."
74 Then he started to curse[B] and to
swear with an oath, "I do not know
the man!" Immediately a rooster
crowed, 75 and Peter remembered
the words Jesus had spoken, "Before
the rooster crows, you will deny Me
three times." And he went outside
and wept bitterly.

Plot to Execute Jesus (27:1-2)

27 When daybreak came, all the
•chief priests and the elders of
the people plotted against Jesus to
put Him to death. 2 After tying Him
up, they led Him away and handed
Him over to •Pilate,[C] the governor.

Suicide of Judas Iscariot (27:3-10)

3 Then Judas, His betrayer, seeing
that He had been condemned, was
full of remorse and returned the 30
pieces of silver to the chief priests
and elders. 4 "I have sinned by betraying innocent blood," he said.
"What's that to us?" they said.
"See to it yourself!"
5 So he threw the silver into the
sanctuary and departed. Then he
went and hanged himself.
6 The chief priests took the silver
and said, "It's not lawful to put it
into the temple treasury,[D] since it is
blood money."[E] 7 So they conferred
together and bought the potter's
field with it as a burial place for foreigners. 8 Therefore that field has
been called "Blood Field" to this day.
9 Then what was spoken through the
prophet Jeremiah was fulfilled:

They took the 30 pieces of silver, the price of Him whose

HARD QUESTION

Is God's sovereignty compatible with your freedom to choose?

If the betrayal and suicide of Judas were prophesied in Scripture and had to be fulfilled, did Judas really have a choice?

God knew what Judas would do. Nevertheless, Judas made his own choices (27:3). He had every opportunity to repent, but he chose to go his own way (vv. 14,25,48-50). Judas later regretted what he did and went back to his conspirators, who would offer no help. Judas is one example of the theological tension between divine foreknowledge and sovereignty on one hand and human responsibility on the other. God is in control of all—past, present, and future. You are responsible for the choices you makes and their consequences. Both statements are true, even though that does not seem possible. The interpretive stance that most closely adheres to the biblical text is one that recognizes the truth of both and works within that tension instead of trying to argue one truth against the other.

[A]26:73 Or *speech* [B]26:74 To call down curses on himself if what he said weren't true [C]27:2 Other mss read *Pontius Pilate* [D]27:6 See Mk 7:11 where the same Gk word (*Corban*) means a gift pledged to the temple. [E]27:6 Lit *the price of blood*

CHARACTER PROFILE

Pilate's Wife An Intuitive Woman

Her Background	Wife of Pontius Pilate, Roman governor of Judea
Her Story	• She sent Pilate an urgent note in the midst of the proceedings, imploring him to release Jesus (27:19). • She had a painful dream about Jesus. • She believed Him to be a "righteous man." • Although dreams at that time were thought to be messages from the gods, Pilate did not heed her warning (27:26). • Her appeal to Pilate shows her to be one of Jesus' last advocates before his crucifixion.
Life Lesson	Defend the innocent, no matter how lost the cause may be.

price was set by the Israelites,
[10] **and they gave them for the**
potter's field, as the Lord di-
rected me.[A]

Jesus Before the Governor (27:11-14)

[11] Now Jesus stood before the
governor. "Are You the King of the
Jews?" the governor asked Him.
Jesus answered, "You have said
it."[B] [12] And while He was being accused by the chief priests and elders,
He didn't answer.
[13] Then Pilate said to Him, "Don't
You hear how much they are testifying against You?" [14] But He didn't
answer him on even one charge,
so that the governor was greatly
amazed.

Jesus or Barabbas (27:15-26)

[15] At the festival the governor's
custom was to release to the crowd a
prisoner they wanted. [16] At that time
they had a notorious prisoner called
Barabbas.[C] [17] So when they had gathered together, Pilate said to them,
"Who is it you want me to release
for you—Barabbas,[C] or Jesus who
is called •Messiah?" [18] For he knew
they had handed Him over because
of envy.
[19] While he was sitting on the
judge's bench, his wife sent word to
him, "Have nothing to do with that
righteous man, for today I've suffered terribly in a dream because of
Him!"
[20] The chief priests and the elders,
however, persuaded the crowds to
ask for Barabbas and to execute
Jesus. [21] The governor asked them,
"Which of the two do you want me
to release for you?"
"Barabbas!" they answered.
[22] Pilate asked them, "What should
I do then with Jesus, who is called
Messiah?"
They all answered, "Crucify
Him!"[D]
[23] Then he said, "Why? What has
He done wrong?"
But they kept shouting, "Crucify
Him!" all the more.
[24] When Pilate saw that he was
getting nowhere,[E] but that a riot
was starting instead, he took some
water, washed his hands in front of
the crowd, and said, "I am innocent
of this man's blood.[F] See to it yourselves!"
[25] All the people answered, "His
blood be on us and on our children!" [26] Then he released Barabbas to them. But after having Jesus
flogged,[G] he handed Him over to be
crucified.

Mocking of Jesus (27:27-31)

[27] Then the governor's soldiers

[A] **27:9-10** Jr 32:6-9; Zch 11:12-13 [B] **27:11** Or *That is true*, an affirmative oath; Mt 26:64; Mk 15:2 [C] **27:16,17** Other mss read *Jesus Barabbas* [D] **27:22** Lit *"Him—be crucified!"* [E] **27:24** Lit *that it availed nothing* [F] **27:24** Other mss read *this righteous man's blood* [G] **27:26** Roman flogging was done with a whip made of leather strips embedded with pieces of bone or metal that brutally tore the flesh.

27:15-26 The inclusion of the words from Pilate's **wife** concerning the innocence of Christ (v. 19) and the crowd's statement claiming responsibility for Jesus' death were also peculiar to Matthew's passion account (v. 25). Pilate himself evidently believed Jesus was innocent, since he tried to **release** Him by offering His accusers a deal he thought they could not resist. Pilate offered to release one of two prisoners: **Barabbas**, a violent insurrectionist, or Jesus. The people chose the hardened criminal

The crowd answered Pilate by saying, **"His blood be on us and on our children!"** These words have often been used to promote the view that the Jewish people and their descendents were solely responsible for the death of Jesus. This belief has fueled anti-Semitic causes and crimes for two thousand years. This view is a grave distortion of Scripture. According to Scripture, all people through every generation until today had a role in the death of Jesus. Isaiah 53 (especially vv. 4-5,10) identified as the heart of God's message of redemption in Scripture, spoke to the role of God and of mankind in Jesus' suffering and death. In addition to the perspective expressed by the prophet Isaiah, Jesus spoke of His own death as a choice He actively embraced (see Jn 10:18).

Although Matthew's Gospel showed the prominence of the Jewish leaders in the death of Jesus, their role has to be interpreted in a much wider context. God's grace is offered regardless of the part any individual played in the death of His Son. In the 30 years following Jesus' resurrection, the most ardent disciple of Jesus, Saul of Tarsus, was a man of the same mindset as those crying, **"Crucify Him!"** (Mt 27:22-23). He had given his full energies to persecuting followers of Christ until he himself met Christ and sought His forgiveness (see Ac 9:1-31).

CHARACTER PROFILE

Mary, Mother of James **A Faithful Follower**

Her Background	• Mother of James and Joseph • Follower of Jesus who supported His ministry in Galilee • Referred to as "the other Mary"
Her Story	• She, together with Mary Magdalene, witnessed Jesus' crucifixion and burial (27:55-56,61). • They went to the tomb to anoint His body after the Sabbath (28:1; Mk 16:1). • An angel appeared to them, announcing Jesus' resurrection (Mt 28:2).
Life Lesson	Mary was one of the first to hear and see the resurrected Christ. God rewards His faithful servants.

See also Mk 15:40,47; 16:1; Lk 24:10.

27:27-66 Matthew gave careful details of Jesus' crucifixion, of His burial, and of the measures taken to ensure that no one stole Jesus' body from the tomb given by Joseph of Arimathea. He also gave attention to some of the cosmic events surrounding the death of Jesus (vv. 39-44,51-53).

took Jesus into •headquarters and gathered the whole •company around Him. 28 They stripped Him and dressed Him in a scarlet military robe. 29 They twisted together a crown of thorns, put it on His head, and placed a reed in His right hand. And they knelt down before Him and mocked Him: "Hail, King of the Jews!" 30 Then they spit on Him, took the reed, and kept hitting Him on the head. 31 When they had mocked Him, they stripped Him of the robe, put His clothes on Him, and led Him away to crucify Him.

Crucifixion Between Two Criminals (27:32-44)

32 As they were going out, they found a Cyrenian man named Simon. They forced this man to carry His cross. 33 When they came to a place called *Golgotha* (which means Skull Place), 34 they gave Him wine[A] mixed with gall to drink. But when He tasted it, He would not drink it. 35 After crucifying Him they divided His clothes by casting lots.[B] 36 Then they sat down and were guarding Him there. 37 Above His head they put up the charge against Him in writing:

THIS IS JESUS
THE KING OF THE JEWS.

38 Then two criminals[C] were crucified with Him, one on the right and one on the left. 39 Those who passed by were yelling insults at[D] Him, shaking their heads 40 and saying, "The One who would demolish the sanctuary and rebuild it in three days, save Yourself! If You are the Son of God, come down from the cross!" 41 In the same way the chief priests, with the •scribes and elders,[E] mocked Him and said, 42 "He saved others, but He cannot save Himself! He is the King of Israel! Let Him[F] come down now from the cross, and we will believe in Him. 43 He has put His trust in God; let God rescue Him now—if He wants Him![G] For He said, 'I am God's Son.'" 44 In the same way even the criminals who were crucified with Him kept taunting Him.

The Death of Jesus (27:45-56)

45 From noon until three in the afternoon[H] darkness came over the whole land.[I] 46 About three in the afternoon Jesus cried out with a loud voice, "***Elí, Elí, lemá***[J] ***sabachtháni?***" that is, "**My God, My God, why have You forsaken**[K] **Me?**"[L]

47 When some of those standing there heard this, they said, "He's calling for Elijah!"

48 Immediately one of them ran and got a sponge, filled it with sour wine, fixed it on a reed, and offered Him a drink. 49 But the rest said, "Let's see if Elijah comes to save Him!"

50 Jesus shouted again with a loud voice and gave up His spirit. 51 Suddenly, the curtain of the sanctuary[M] was split in two from top to bottom; the earth quaked and the rocks were split. 52 The tombs were also opened and many bodies of the •saints who had fallen •asleep were raised. 53 And they came out of the tombs after His resurrection, entered the holy city, and appeared to many.

54 When the •centurion and those with him, who were guarding Jesus, saw the earthquake and the things that had happened, they were terrified and said, "This man really was God's Son!"[N]

55 Many women who had followed Jesus from Galilee and ministered to Him were there, looking on from a distance. 56 Among them were •Mary Magdalene, Mary the mother of James and Joseph, and the mother of Zebedee's sons.

The Burial of Jesus (27:57-61)

57 When it was evening, a rich man from Arimathea named Joseph came, who himself had also become a disciple of Jesus. 58 He approached

[A]**27:34** Other mss read *sour wine* [B]**27:35** Other mss add *that what was spoken by the prophet might be fulfilled: "They divided My clothes among them, and for My clothing they cast lots."* [C]**27:38** Or *revolutionaries* [D]**27:39** Lit *passed by blasphemed* or *were blaspheming* [E]**27:41** Other mss add *and Pharisees* [F]**27:42** Other mss read *If He . . . Israel, let Him* [G]**27:43** Or *if He takes pleasure in Him* [H]**27:45** Lit *From the sixth hour to the ninth hour* [I]**27:45** Or *whole earth* [J]**27:46** Some mss read *lama*; other mss read *lima* [K]**27:46** Or *abandoned* [L]**27:46** Ps 22:1 [M]**27:51** A heavy curtain separated the inner room of the temple from the outer. [N]**27:54** Or *the Son of God*

Pilate and asked for Jesus' body. Then Pilate ordered that it[A] be released. [59] So Joseph took the body, wrapped it in •clean, fine linen, [60] and placed it in his new tomb, which he had cut into the rock. He left after rolling a great stone against the entrance of the tomb. [61] Mary Magdalene and the other Mary were seated there, facing the tomb.

The Closely Guarded Tomb (27:62-66)

[62] The next day, which followed the preparation day, the chief priests and the •Pharisees gathered before Pilate [63] and said, "Sir, we remember that while this deceiver was still alive He said, 'After three days I will rise again.' [64] Therefore give orders that the tomb be made secure until the third day. Otherwise, His disciples may come, steal Him, and tell the people, 'He has been raised from the dead.' Then the last deception will be worse than the first."

[65] "You have[B] a guard of soldiers,"[C] Pilate told them. "Go and make it as secure as you know how." [66] Then they went and made the tomb secure by sealing the stone and setting the guard.[D]

Resurrection Morning (28:1-10)

28 After the Sabbath, as the first day of the week was dawning, •Mary Magdalene and the other Mary went to view the tomb. [2] Suddenly there was a violent earthquake, because an angel of the Lord descended from heaven and approached the tomb. He rolled back the stone and was sitting on it. [3] His appearance was like lightning, and his robe was as white as snow. [4] The guards were so shaken from fear of him that they became like dead men.

[5] But the angel told the women, "Don't be afraid, because I know you are looking for Jesus who was crucified. [6] He is not here! For He has been resurrected, just as He said. Come and see the place where He lay. [7] Then go quickly and tell His disciples, 'He has been raised from the dead. In fact, He is going ahead of you to Galilee; you will see Him there.' Listen, I have told you."

[8] So, departing quickly from the tomb with fear and great joy, they ran to tell His disciples the news. [9] Just then[E] Jesus met them and said, "Good morning!" They came up, took hold of His feet, and worshiped Him. [10] Then Jesus told them, "Do not be afraid. Go and tell My brothers to leave for Galilee, and they will see Me there."

The Bribing of the Soldiers (28:11-15)

[11] As they were on their way, some of the guards came into the city and reported to the •chief priests everything that had happened. [12] After the priests[F] had assembled with the elders and agreed on a plan, they gave the soldiers a large sum of money [13] and told them, "Say this, 'His disciples came during the night and stole Him while we were sleeping.' [14] If this reaches the governor's ears,[G] we will deal with[H] him and keep you out of trouble." [15] So they took the money and did as they were instructed. And this story has been spread among Jewish people to this day.

The Great Commission (28:16-20)

[16] The 11 disciples traveled to Galilee, to the mountain where Jesus had directed them. [17] When they saw Him, they worshiped,[I] but some doubted. [18] Then Jesus came near and said to them, "All authority has been given to Me in heaven and on earth. [19] Go, therefore, and make disciples of[J] all nations, baptizing them in the name of the Father and of the Son and of the Holy Spirit, [20] teaching them to observe everything I have commanded you. And remember,[K] I am with you always,[L] to the end of the age."

[A]**27:58** Other mss read *that the body* [B]**27:65** Or *"Take* [C]**27:65** It is uncertain whether this guard consisted of temple police or Roman soldiers. [D]**27:66** Lit *stone with the guard* [E]**28:9** Other mss add *as they were on their way to tell the news to His disciples* [F]**28:12** Lit *After they* [G]**28:14** Lit *this is heard by the governor* [H]**28:14** Lit *will persuade* [I]**28:17** Other mss add *Him* [J]**28:19** Or *and disciple*; lit *and instruct* [K]**28:20** Lit *look* [L]**28:20** Lit *all the days*

28:1-20 Only Matthew recorded the visit of the chief priests and the Pharisees to Pilate. They asked for a guard to secure Christ's tomb. Christ's teaching concerning His resurrection was well known, even among His enemies. Matthew recorded that the women conquered their fears and ran back to report to the 11 disciples the good news of Christ's resurrection. On their way the risen Christ met them, and they worshiped Him (v. 9).

Uniquely in Matthew, the scheme of the Jewish leaders to explain away Christ's resurrection was recorded (vv. 11-15). Matthew undoubtedly recorded this event to counter this story. Known as the "Great Commission," verses 16-20 summarized Matthew's main themes found throughout his Gospel: the importance of discipleship, the universal mission of the church, Christ's commandments as a reflection of God's will for all believers, and the perpetual teaching ministry of Christ as the final and sovereign Interpreter of the Law.

The risen Savior's strategy, simple yet profound, was explained clearly. Jesus first called His disciples to Himself. He took time to teach them; He let them learn about Him by spending time with Him. Then He sent them out. The structure of the passage indicated that the heart of disciple-making was simple to understand:

- going out in evangelism in order to make disciples (v. 19a);
- **baptizing** the converts—those who have accepted Christ (v. 19b);
- **teaching** the baptized disciples to grow through obedience to the Lord's standards (v. 20a).

Sharing the gospel was vitally important, but Jesus also challenged His disciples to lead those who embraced the gospel into obedience to Christ through believer's baptism and through learning the disciplines of the Christian life.

Matthew's Gospel includes mention of the women who were involved in Jesus' final days and post-resurrection appearances. Women followed Christ from afar to the cross and to the tomb (27:55-56). They were present at both the crucifixion (27:55-56) and burial (27:61) of Jesus. The women at the empty tomb were the first to witness the resurrection and were instructed by Christ to tell the apostles of His resurrection (28:5-10). In effect, they were commissioned by the risen Lord to announce His resurrection to His disciples (28:8-10). The devoted women who remained with Jesus at the cross and followed Him to the tomb were in the right place at the right time to deliver the glorious news of His resurrection. The Lord honored their faithfulness by entrusting them with these wonderful words of hope and victory to be delivered to the disciples.

Biblical Womanhood Women and the Great Commission

The best way to appreciate the presence of women disciples in the New Testament is to study the Great Commission in context. The female disciples were not only there at the most difficult and dangerous point in Jesus' ministry, but they also became indispensable as models of how Christ's followers were to pursue His marching orders for the church, even until the end of the age. Yet, although you may understand the vital parts of the Great Commission, you may still easily miss the important role of the women disciples. Certainly, the presence of women in the various passages that led to the challenging commissioning appeal is obvious. But just how closely these events tie the women to those statements is frequently overlooked. When Jesus gave His apostles the command to witness and make disciples, He used contextual examples of women disciples to illustrate what it means to be a disciple and to share a witness. Therefore, you must consider the presence and roles of the women seen in the broad context surrounding the words of the Great Commission. Striking artistic portraits of women disciples have been blended together to make a wonderful composite of devotion to Christ and a commitment to share the gospel. As a woman in the modern era, you have an open door and the divine anointing to direct your energies and creativity into using every opportunity to share the gospel with those who cross your path.

Matthew… Written on My Heart

What is your reaction to Jesus? In Mt 2:1-11 Herod the Great and all Jerusalem, the chief priests and scribes, and the wise men were all confronted with the reality of Christ. When Herod heard about this new King of the Jews, he reacted in anger and condemnation because he felt Jesus posed a threat to his throne and his way of life.

Unfortunately, many people in contemporary society react the same way when they come face to face with the truth of Jesus the Savior—they reject Him because they feel He threatens their way of life. The chief priests and scribes had been looking for the coming Messiah for hundreds of years, but because Jesus did not fit their mold, they rejected Him. Only the wise men accepted Christ as the promised King and worshiped Him in reverence.

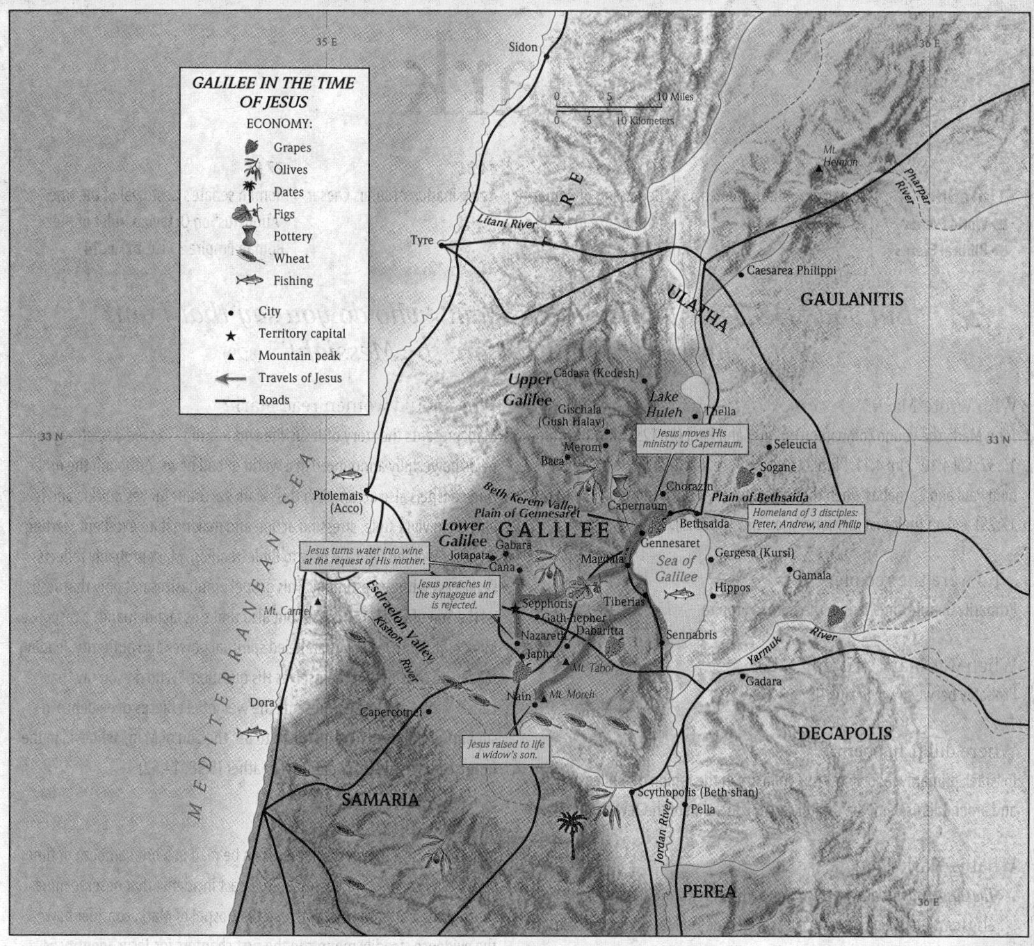
GALILEE IN THE TIME OF JESUS
ECONOMY:
Grapes
Olives
Dates
Figs
Pottery
Wheat
Fishing
City
Territory capital
Mountain peak
Travels of Jesus
Roads
0 5 10 Miles
0 5 10 Kilometers
35 E
36 E
33 N
Sidon
Tyre
Litani River
TYRE
Mt. Hermon
Pharpar River
Caesarea Philippi
ULATHA
GAULANITIS
Upper Galilee
Cadasa (Kedesh)
Lake Huleh
Thella
Gischala (Gush Halav)
Merom
Baca
Jesus moves His ministry to Capernaum.
Seleucia
Sogane
Chorazin
Plain of Bethsaida
Capernaum
Bethsaida
Homeland of 3 disciples: Peter, Andrew, and Philip
Ptolemais (Acco)
Beth Kerem Valley
Plain of Gennesaret
Lower Galilee
GALILEE
Gennesaret
Gabara
Jotapata
Jesus turns water into wine at the request of His mother.
Cana
Magdala
Sea of Galilee
Gergesa (Kursi)
Gamala
Hippos
Jesus preaches in the synagogue and is rejected.
Mt. Carmel
Esdraelon Valley
Kishon River
Sepphoris
Gath-hepher
Tiberias
Nazareth
Dabaritta
Sennabris
Japha
Mt. Tabor
Yarmuk River
Gadara
Nain
Mt. Moreh
Dora
Capercotnei
MEDITERRANEAN SEA
DECAPOLIS
Jesus raised to life a widow's son.
SAMARIA
Scythopolis (Beth-shan)
Pella
Jordan River
PEREA

Mark

Timeline World Events Biblical Events	**740–680 BC** Isaiah's prophetic ministry	**63 BC** Beginning of Roman dominance in Israel	**44 BC** Assassination of Julius Caesar	**27 BC** Roman senate's bestowal of the title "Augustus" on Octavian, ruler of the Roman Empire 31 B.C. to A.D. 14

"'But you,' He [Jesus] asked them again, 'who do you say that I am?' Peter answered Him, 'You are the Messiah!'" (8:29).

Who wrote Mark?

John Mark, the young companion of Peter and Paul (Ac 12:12,25; 13:5,13; 15:37; Col 4:10; 2Tm 4:11; Phm 24; 1Pt 5:13; cp. Mk 14:51). He accompanied Paul and Barnabas when they returned to Antioch from Jerusalem (Ac 12:25) and on their first missionary journey (Ac 13:5).

Who were the recipients?

Primarily Gentile Christians in the Roman Empire

When was Mark written?

Probably between A.D. 64 and 68

Where did it happen?

In Israel, primarily following Jesus' ministry in the region of Galilee and in and around Jerusalem, the capital city and location of the Jewish temple

What is Mark about?

- *The Gospel about Jesus as Good News*. The Greek word (*euangelion*, also translated *good news*) occurs seven times in Mark, four times in Matthew, and never in Luke or John.
- *Jesus' identity as the divine Son of God.* Mark announces this conviction in the opening sentence and notes this realization of the Roman centurion who witnessed the death of Jesus on the cross and observed the various signs accompanying that event (15:39). Both God the Father (1:11; 9:7) and the demons (3:11; 5:7) confronted by Jesus spoke audibly regarding Jesus' identity. Jesus Himself taught this truth in a parable (12:1-12), alluded to this relationship to deity in 13:32, and confirmed the high priest's accusation that He believed this about Himself (14:61-62).

Why should women read Mark?

Mark presents the story of Jesus' life and teachings as *the gospel*—good news powerfully announced in a world of bad news. Although the other three gospels also accomplish this, Mark's account moves quickly and is written in vivid style, stressing action and making it an excellent starting place for women who are new to Bible-reading. Mark probably reflects Peter's eyewitness testimony. This gospel emphasizes not only that Jesus is "the Son of God" (1:1; 15:39) but also that this fact demands a response. Mark highlights Jesus' unparalleled spiritual power and authority, leading readers to consider for themselves His question, "Who do you say that I am?" Mark's gospel also presents the weightiest pieces of evidence in support of the truth of Jesus' claim to be "the Son of Man," who will in the future come in the glory of God His Father (8:38; 14:62).

How do you read Mark?

Mark's narrative moves quickly and can be read in a brief amount of time. The brevity can make it easy to breeze past incidents that deserve more concentrated attention. As you read the Gospel of Mark, consider how the evidence steadily mounts in the first chapters for Jesus' identity as the Jewish Messiah and the divine Son of God while affirming Jesus' full humanity as well. In addition, Mark emphasizes both the character of Jesus as servant (8:31-34; 10:45) and Jesus' authority (e.g., 1:27; 5:1-17). Ultimately, Mark intends for the presentation of who Jesus is to lead readers to acknowledge Him, find salvation in Him, and follow Him. Therefore, as you read, do not ignore the prodding of the Holy Spirit to refresh your commitment to follow Jesus in specific ways or, perhaps, first to entrust your life to the incarnate Son of God who gave His life to ransom yours (10:45).

Outline

I. A Prologue to the Gospel (1:1-13)
   - A. Preparing the Way by John the Baptist (1:1-8)
   - B. Going Through the Waters of Baptism (1:9-11)
   - C. Experiencing Temptation in the Wilderness (1:12-13)

II. The Ministry of Christ in Galilee (1:14–8:30)
   - A. The Authority of Jesus and the Blindness of the Pharisees (1:14–3:6)
   - B. The Parables and Signs of Jesus and the Blindness of the People (3:7–6:6a)
   - C. Jesus' Ministry to the Gentiles and the Blindness of His Disciples (6:6b–8:30)

III. The Passion of Christ (8:31–16:20)
   - A. Predictions of Death and Defining of Discipleship (8:31–10:52)
   - B. Jesus' Teachings at the Temple (11:1–13:37)
   - C. The Climax of Jesus' Life (14:1–16:20)

AD 4–34	*AD 26–36*	*AD 29–30*	*AD 33*	*AD 37*
Rule of Caesarea Philippi by Philip (a son of Herod the Great) as tetrarch	Rule of Pilate as prefect of the Roman province of Judea	Imprisonment and execution of John the Baptist; beginning of Jesus' public ministry	Jesus' crucifixion and resurrection	Death of Tiberius and succession of Caligula as emperor of Rome

Preparing the Way by John the Baptist (1:1-8)

1 The beginning of the gospel of
Jesus Christ, the Son of God. 2 As
it is written in Isaiah the prophet:[A]

Look, I am sending
My messenger ahead
of You,
who will prepare Your way.[B]
3 **A voice of one crying out**
in the wilderness:
Prepare the way for the Lord;
make His paths straight![C]

4 John came baptizing[D] in the wilderness and preaching a baptism of repentance[E] for the forgiveness of
sins. 5 The whole Judean countryside and all the people of Jerusalem were flocking to him, and they were baptized by him in the Jordan River
as they confessed their sins. 6 John
wore a camel-hair garment with a leather belt around his waist and
ate locusts and wild honey. 7 He was
preaching: "Someone more powerful than I will come after me. I am not worthy to stoop down and untie the strap of His sandals. 8 I have
baptized you with[F] water, but He will baptize you with the Holy Spirit."

Going Through the Waters of Baptism (1:9-11)

9 In those days Jesus came from Nazareth in Galilee and was baptized
in the Jordan by John. 10 As soon as
He came up out of the water, He saw the heavens being torn open and the Spirit descending to Him like a dove.
11 And a voice came from heaven:

You are My beloved Son;
I take delight in You![G]

Experiencing Temptation in the Wilderness (1:12-13)

12 Immediately the Spirit drove
Him into the wilderness. 13 He was
in the wilderness 40 days, being tempted by Satan. He was with the wild animals, and the angels began to serve Him.

The Ministry of Christ in Galilee (1:14–8:30)

14 After John was arrested, Jesus
went to Galilee, preaching the good
news[H,I] of God:[J] 15 "The time is ful-
filled, and the kingdom of God has come near. Repent and believe in the good news!"

The First Disciples (1:16-20)

16 As He was passing along by the
Sea of Galilee, He saw Simon and

A1:2 Other mss read *in the prophets* B1:2 Other mss add *before You* C1:2-3 Is 40:3; Mal 3:1 D1:4 Or *John the Baptist came*, or *John the Baptizer came* E1:4 Or *a baptism based on repentance* F1:8 Or *in* G1:11 Or *In You I am well pleased* H1:14 Other mss add *of the kingdom* I1:14 Or *gospel* J1:14 Either *from God* or *about God*

>WORD|*study*

1:14 The kingdom of God (or "the kingdom of heaven" in Matthew) was central to Jesus' teachings with both a present and future aspect. In Jesus, God's rule was present on earth. But the kingdom also had a future dimension (Mt 8:11). Soon after the announcement of the kingdom, Jesus called and commissioned 12 men to follow Him and carry His mission forward into the future, giving people an opportunity to be rescued from impending judgment. The situation was urgent, so the men immediately left everything and followed Christ.

Title: The lengthy opening phrase in the Greek text provided the work's title, "Gospel (Gk *euaggelion*, "good news") according to Mark."

1:1 Christ (Gk *Christos*, "anointed one") is equivalent to the Hebrew *Mashiach*, a title so closely associated with Jesus that it became part of His name. As **the Son of God**, Jesus addressed God as "Father," and the Father referred to Jesus as "My beloved Son" (1:11; 9:7).

1:2-3 As it is written recognizes the truth and reliability of the Scriptures (here combined from Is 40:3, Mal 3:1, and Ex 23:20). The true Messiah fulfills Old Testament prophecy. The verb "is written," in the perfect tense, affirms that the truth of the prophets' words continues into the future.

1:4-6 Baptism of repentance can be interpreted two ways: baptism produced by repentance or baptism characterized by repentance. John's straightforward call to repentance cannot be construed as suggesting that baptism itself produced forgiveness. The meaning of the phrase **for** [Gk *eis*, "into, to; in, at, on, upon, by, near; among; concerning"] **the forgiveness of sins** hinges on the preposition *eis*. Logically, the sense seems to be that forgiveness of sins is the end result of repentance.

Baptism is an outer, symbolic manifestation offering a clear, public testimony that the inner work of repentance has already taken place. John's baptism called for repentance of sins before he would administer baptism, which thus signaled a deliberate turning from the old path to a new. It symbolized a life cleansed from sin (i.e., that repentance had already occurred).

1:9-15 Two events pinpoint the beginning of Jesus' public ministry: His baptism and His temptation. Jesus did not need John's baptism of repentance because Jesus was sinless (Heb 4:15). However, by submitting to John's baptism He humbled Himself to identify with those He came to save. God the Father's **voice came from heaven**.

He clearly expressed the Son's essential identity (**My beloved Son**). Jesus did not become God's Son at His baptism. The words **You are** emphasized the eternal and essential relationship between the Father and Son. The Father also affirmed His approval of the Son's role: **I take delight** [Gk *eudokēsa*, "be well-pleased with, take pleasure in"; cp. 1Co 10:5; Col 1:19; Heb 10:6; 2Pt 1:17] **in You**, implying His approval of the Son's performance of a particular function in history. Jesus was not forced **into the wilderness** because of His reluctance. This testing was a necessary event in the divine plan. **The time is fulfilled** (Gk *kairos*, "a favorable, opportune, significant time") was not a reference to chronological time (Gk *chronos*, "extension or period of time") but to the time appointed and foretold through the prophets for God's activity on earth.

1:21-34 Miracles were an important testimony of the power of the gospel. Mark recorded 17 miracles and alluded to others. Here Mark grouped together three healing miracles (vv. 21-28; vv. 29-31; and vv. 32-34) to portray Christ's divine power. These events seem to have taken place on one particular Sabbath day. **Capernaum**, Peter's hometown, became a base for Jesus' Galilean ministry.

1:21-28 Jesus ultimately came to destroy the Devil's work, and He encountered an evil spirit early in His ministry. The spirit knew Jesus and what He came to do. Jesus cast out the **unclean spirit** with a simple command (v. 25). Because Jesus was teaching with incomparable **authority**, the crowds were **amazed** (Gk *ethambēthēsan*) a verb form having the sense that as long as Jesus taught, the crowds would keep on being amazed.

1:29-34 The phrases **as soon as** and **at once** show the urgency of the illness suffered by **Simon's mother-in-law**. Once she was well, she served **them**, all who were present. Matthew says that she served Jesus, choosing to identify specifically the most important one she served, while Mark's reference was more general.

1:35-39 Jesus drew His strength and power for ministry from His Father. After a busy night of healings and exorcisms, Jesus arose **early in the morning** to seek His Father. Mark specifically notes Jesus' spending time in prayer when facing a crisis (6:46; 14:32-41). Here, the people seemed interested only in being healed. However, the primary purpose for Jesus' coming was to **preach** the good news.

1:40-45 By law this **man with a**

CHARACTER PROFILE

Simon's Mother-in-Law A Willing Servant

Her Background	She was the mother of Simon Peter's wife.
Her story	• She was in Simon's home in Capernaum in bed, sick with a fever (1:29–30). • Jesus went to her, took her hand, and her fever disappeared (1:31). • She arose and began serving the guests.
Life Lesson	The right response to Jesus is to serve others.

See also Mt 8:14-18; Lk 4:38-41.

Andrew, Simon's brother. They were casting a net into the sea, since they were fishermen.

17 "Follow Me," Jesus told them, "and I will make you fish for[A] people!" 18 Immediately they left their nets and followed Him. 19 Going on a little farther, He saw James the son of Zebedee and his brother John. They were in their boat mending their nets. 20 Immediately He called them, and they left their father Zebedee in the boat with the hired men and followed Him.

Driving out an Unclean Spirit (1:21-28)

21 Then they went into Capernaum, and right away He entered the •synagogue on the Sabbath and began to teach. 22 They were astonished at His teaching because, unlike the •scribes, He was teaching them as one having authority.

23 Just then a man with an •unclean spirit was in their synagogue. He cried out,[B] 24 "What do You have to do with us,[C] Jesus—Nazarene? Have You come to destroy us? I know who You are—the Holy One of God!"

25 But Jesus rebuked him and said, "Be quiet,[D] and come out of him!" 26 And the unclean spirit convulsed him, shouted with a loud voice, and came out of him.

27 Then they were all amazed, so they began to argue with one another, saying, "What is this? A new teaching with authority![E] He commands even the unclean spirits, and they obey Him." 28 News about Him then spread throughout the entire vicinity of Galilee.

Healings at Capernaum (1:29-34)

29 As soon as they left the synagogue, they went into Simon and Andrew's house with James and John. 30 Simon's mother-in-law was lying in bed with a fever, and they told Him about her at once. 31 So He went to her, took her by the hand, and raised her up. The fever left her,[F] and she began to serve them.

32 When evening came, after the sun had set, they began bringing to Him all those who were sick and those who were demon-possessed. 33 The whole town was assembled at the door, 34 and He healed many who were sick with various diseases and drove out many demons. But He would not permit the demons to speak, because they knew Him.

Preaching in Galilee (1:35-39)

35 Very early in the morning, while it was still dark, He got up, went out, and made His way to a deserted place. And He was praying there. 36 Simon and his companions went searching for Him. 37 They found Him and said, "Everyone's looking for You!"

38 And He said to them, "Let's go on to the neighboring villages so that I may preach there too. This

[A]**1:17** Lit *you to become fishers of* [B]**1:23** Other mss add to the beginning of v. 24: *"Leave us alone.* [C]**1:24** Lit *What to us and to You* [D]**1:25** Or *Be muzzled* [E]**1:27** Other mss read *What is this? What is this new teaching? For with authority* [F]**1:31** Other mss add *at once*

is why I have come." [39] So He went into all of Galilee, preaching in their synagogues and driving out demons.

Cleansing of a Man (1:40-45)

[40] Then a man with a serious skin disease came to Him and, on his knees,[A] begged Him: "If You are willing, You can make me •clean."

[41] Moved with compassion, Jesus reached out His hand and touched him. "I am willing," He told him. "Be made clean." [42] Immediately the disease left him, and he was healed.[B] [43] Then He sternly warned him and sent him away at once, [44] telling him, "See that you say nothing to anyone; but go and show yourself to the priest, and offer what Moses prescribed for your cleansing, as a testimony to them." [45] Yet he went out and began to proclaim it widely and to spread the news, with the result that Jesus could no longer enter a town openly. But He was out in deserted places, and they would come to Him from everywhere.

Doctrine CHRISTOLOGY

The use of **Son of Man** more than 14 times (2:10,28; 8:31,38; 9:9,12,31; 10:33-34; 13:26; 14:21 [twice], 41,62) made this title the most frequent Christological designation in Mark's Gospel. In the Gospels, Jesus always used this phrase as a self-descriptor with three different connotations. First, "Son of Man" is future-oriented and is strongly linked to Daniel's use of the expression (Dn 7:13). The Son of Man will come on the clouds of heaven with great power and majesty (Mk 8:38; 13:26). Second, Jesus refers to Himself as the Son of Man when He speaks of His imminent suffering, death, and resurrection (8:31; 9:31; 10:33-34). Finally, Jesus often uses the expression rather than the pronoun "I" to refer to His humanity and His present ministry. But even in this sense, the Son of Man is not just human but is Lord of the Sabbath (Mt 12:8) and claims the authority to forgive sins (Mk 2:10). This expression serves well the purpose of communicating Jesus' full humanity and full deity.

The Son of Man's Authority to Forgive and Heal (2:1-12)

2 When He entered Capernaum again after some days, it was reported that He was at home. [2] So many people gathered together that there was no more room, not even in the doorway, and He was speaking the message to them. [3] Then they came to Him bringing a paralytic, carried by four men. [4] Since they were not able to bring him to[C] Jesus because of the crowd, they removed the roof above where He was. And when they had broken through, they lowered the mat on which the paralytic was lying.

[5] Seeing their faith, Jesus told the paralytic, "Son, your sins are forgiven."

[6] But some of the •scribes were sitting there, thinking to themselves:[D] [7] "Why does He speak like this? He's blaspheming! Who can forgive sins but God alone?"

[8] Right away Jesus understood in His spirit that they were thinking like this within themselves and said to them, "Why are you thinking these things in your hearts?[E] [9] Which is easier: to say to the paralytic, 'Your sins are forgiven,' or to say, 'Get up, pick up your mat, and walk'? [10] But so you may know that the •Son of Man has authority on earth to forgive sins," He told the paralytic, [11] "I tell you: get up, pick up your mat, and go home."

[12] Immediately he got up, picked up the mat, and went out in front of everyone. As a result, they were all astounded and gave glory to God, saying, "We have never seen anything like this!"

The Call of Matthew (2:13-14)

[13] Then Jesus went out again beside the sea. The whole crowd was coming to Him, and He taught them. [14] Then, moving on, He saw Levi the son of Alphaeus sitting at the tax office, and He said to him, "Follow Me!" So he got up and followed Him.

Dining with Sinners (2:15-17)

[15] While He was reclining at the table in Levi's house, many tax collectors and sinners were also guests[F] with Jesus and His disciples, because there were many who were following Him. [16] When the scribes of the •Pharisees[G] saw that He was

[A]**1:40** Other mss omit *on his knees* [B]**1:42** Lit *made clean* [C]**2:4** Other mss read *able to get near* [D]**2:6** Or *thinking in their hearts* [E]**2:8** Or *minds* [F]**2:15** Lit *reclining* (at the table); at important meals the custom was to recline on a mat at a low table and lean on the left elbow. [G]**2:16** Other mss read *scribes and Pharisees*

serious skin disease (Gk *lepros*) was required to wear torn clothes, let his hair be unkempt, and then cry out, "Unclean!" to warn people to stay away from him (see Lv 13:45-46). Mark notes that Jesus was **moved with compassion**. The leper disobeyed Jesus. Because of the crowd, Jesus was forced to leave the towns and go to a deserted place.

2:1–3:6 Five incidents are described in which Jesus challenged important Jewish traditions, bringing Him into conflict with the Jewish leaders in Galilee. These leaders felt threatened because Jesus seemed to know their thoughts before they spoke, and He exposed their true character. Mark also recorded a similar series of five controversies that took place when Jesus was in Jerusalem (11:27–12:37). These incidents are grouped topically (rather than chronologically) to record conflicts between Jesus and His opponents.

2:1-12 In the first controversy, which occurred at the healing of **a paralytic** (v. 3), Jesus showed that He was able **to forgive sins** (v. 10). The Pharisees found this idea blasphemous because they failed to accept Jesus as who He truly was—God in flesh (vv. 6-7). **Blaspheming** (Gk *lalei blasphemias*, lit "speaking blasphemies") refers to profane and irreverent speech about God (cp. 14:64; Jn 10:33). The Old Testament penalty for blasphemy was death (Lv 24:16).

In Jewish teaching, even the Messiah could not forgive sin. Nevertheless, Jesus proved His **authority** by doing the work only God could do (v. 10). This act of healing actually had three miraculous elements:

- Jesus knew the scribes' thoughts before they spoke (v. 8);
- Jesus performed a physical healing for the paralytic (v. 11);
- Jesus forgave the paralytic's sins (v. 5).

The house where so many **gathered** probably consisted of a few rooms and a courtyard with an outside stairway leading to a flat roof, often fashioned from branches and mud. Creating an opening in such a roof would not be difficult.

2:13-17 The sinners whom Jesus came to forgive included tax collectors like **Levi the son of Alphaeus** and others who realized their need for a spiritual healing. There is a strong, almost universal tradition that Levi and Matthew are one and the same (see parallel account in Mt 9:9). Some have suggested that Levi was his given name and Matthew (meaning "gift of God") was the name he was given when he became an apostle. Name changes often accompanied dramatic changes in life. Levi was a tax collector for Herod Antipas, the tetrarch of Galilee, and was despised by the Jews. There was a major route from Damascus to the Mediterranean coast for which Capernaum would have been a strategic site for a tax booth collecting the custom tax on goods and produce entering Galilee. When Levi was called out by Jesus, he most certainly knew there would be no turning back to his old profession with its financial security.

The **Pharisees** or "separated ones" were developers of what came to be known as the oral tradition (the *Talmud* and *Mishnah*). They were the official interpreters of the Law. They were very legalistic and obsessed with observing the Sabbath in certain ways and performing rituals.

Jesus likened His ministry to that of a physician. The sinners, or spiritually **sick**, realized their need; the **righteous** did not.

2:15 Although first-century Jews sat for everyday meals, a festive or formal meal was an occasion for leaning on the left elbow while reclining on a mat at a low table.

2:18-22 Jesus clarified the purpose of **fasting**. Familiar key elements were involved in the metaphors Jesus used in response to the question about fasting:

- Jesus rejected fasting because the **groom** (a metaphor for God in the Old Testament) was there. But when the groom had gone away, then fasting would begin. (Jesus' death was not specifically mentioned here because the timing was not yet right for such a revelation.)
- The metaphors of the **cloth** as well as of the **wine** and **wineskins** reflected that a new age had come, one in which the old Mosaic law would not suffice.

2:23-28 In the fourth and fifth controversies, Jesus challenged the Pharisees' understanding of the purpose of the Sabbath. Mark's reference to **Abiathar** is not in conflict with the Old Testament account in which Ahimelech is identified as the priest (1Sm 21:1-6). As the son of Ahimelech (1Sm 23:6), Abiathar was evidently involved in the incident as well since both were priests at the time. David's close association with Abiathar would prompt Jesus to mention him with David.

Jesus did not declare the law itself invalid but simply interpreted it properly to include exceptions under certain conditions. Sabbath rest and the ceasing of normal pursuits were intended to give opportunity for refreshing renewal and for special worship and service to God.

3:1-6 Later, at the synagogue, Jesus also established that it was lawful

eating with sinners and tax collectors, they asked His disciples, "Why
does He eat[A] with tax collectors and
sinners?"
17 When Jesus heard this, He told
them, "Those who are well don't
need a doctor, but the sick do need
one. I didn't come to call the righteous, but sinners."

A Question About Fasting (2:18-22)

18 Now John's disciples and the
Pharisees[B] were fasting. People
came and asked Him, "Why do
John's disciples and the Pharisees'
disciples fast, but Your disciples do
not fast?"
19 Jesus said to them, "The wedding guests[C] cannot fast while the
groom is with them, can they? As
long as they have the groom with
them, they cannot fast. 20 But the
time[D] will come when the groom
is taken away from them, and then
they will fast in that day. 21 No one
sews a patch of unshrunk cloth on
an old garment. Otherwise, the new
patch pulls away from the old cloth,
and a worse tear is made. 22 And no
one puts new wine into old wineskins. Otherwise, the wine will burst
the skins, and the wine is lost as well
as the skins.[E] But new wine is for
fresh wineskins."

Lord of the Sabbath (2:23-28)

23 On the Sabbath He was going
through the grainfields, and His
disciples began to make their way
picking some heads of grain. 24 The
Pharisees said to Him, "Look, why
are they doing what is not lawful on
the Sabbath?"
25 He said to them, "Have you never
read what David and those who were
with him did when he was in need
and hungry— 26 how he entered the
house of God in the time of Abiathar
the high priest and ate the •sacred
bread—which is not lawful for anyone to eat except the priests—and
also gave some to his companions?"
27 Then He told them, "The Sabbath
was made for[F] man and not man for[F]
the Sabbath. 28 Therefore, the Son of
Man is Lord even of the Sabbath."

The Man with the Paralyzed Hand (3:1-6)

3 Now He entered the •synagogue
again, and a man was there who
had a paralyzed hand. 2 In order
to accuse Him, they were watching Him closely to see whether He
would heal him on the Sabbath.
3 He told the man with the paralyzed
hand, "Stand before us."[G] 4 Then He
said to them, "Is it lawful on the
Sabbath to do what is good or to do
what is evil, to save life or to kill?"
But they were silent. 5 After looking
around at them with anger and sorrow at the hardness of their hearts,
He told the man, "Stretch out your
hand." So he stretched it out, and
his hand was restored. 6 Immediately
the •Pharisees went out and started
plotting with the •Herodians against
Him, how they might destroy Him.

[A]2:16 Other mss add *and drink* [B]2:18 Other mss read *the disciples of John and of the Pharisees* [C]2:19 Lit *The sons of the bridal chamber* [D]2:20 Lit *the days* [E]2:22 Other mss read *the wine spills out and the skins will be ruined* [F]2:27 Or *because of* [G]3:3 Lit *Rise up in the middle*

>WORD|*study*

3:5 Jesus looked at them **with anger and sorrow at the** hardness [Gk *pōrōsei*, "dullness, insensibility"] **of their hearts.** A vivid description of Christ's feelings of anger and sorrow was expressed uniquely in Mark's Gospel. The emotion of anger (Gk *orgēs*, "wrath, retribution") in Jesus was not an impulsive outburst or uncontrolled explosion with the intent of seeking revenge. Rather, divine anger is always a righteous response to sin—what one might call righteous indignation or what a righteous man feels in the presence of full-blown evil.

Anger itself is never a sin, for a believer's senses and emotions should prompt action when there is injustice or evil. The key is for anger, as with all emotions, to be under God's control. Jesus had a settled disposition against evil and hypocrisy, but His response was always governed by His own character. Jesus healed the man. The extent of the hardness of the religious leaders became clear when they conspired on how to **destroy Him.**

3:17 James and **John**, the sons of Zebedee, were assigned the nickname Boanerges (Gk, "sons of thunder") perhaps because of their impetuous personalities (see 9:38; 10:35-45; Lk 9:54) or maybe even because of their thunderous preaching.

Ministering to the Multitude (3:7-12)

7 Jesus departed with His disciples
to the sea, and a large crowd followed from Galilee, Judea, 8 Jerusalem, Idumea, beyond the Jordan,
and around Tyre and Sidon. The
large crowd came to Him because
they heard about everything He was
doing. 9 Then He told His disciples
to have a small boat ready for Him,
so the crowd would not crush Him.
10 Since He had healed many, all who
had diseases were pressing toward
Him to touch Him. 11 Whenever
the •unclean spirits saw Him, those
possessed fell down before Him and
cried out, "You are the Son of God!"
12 And He would strongly warn them
not to make Him known.

The 12 Apostles (3:13-19)

13 Then He went up the mountain
and summoned those He wanted,
and they came to Him. 14 He also appointed 12—He also named them
apostles[A]—to be with Him, to send
them out to preach, 15 and to have
authority to[B] drive out demons.
16 He appointed the Twelve:[C]

To Simon, He gave
the name Peter;
17 and to James the son
of Zebedee,
and to his brother John,
He gave
the name "Boanerges"
(that is, "Sons of Thunder");
18 Andrew;
Philip and Bartholomew;

[A]3:14 Other mss omit *He also named them apostles to* [C]3:16 Other mss omit *He appointed the Twelve* [B]3:15 Other mss add *heal diseases, and*

to do . . . good on the Sabbath by healing a man with **a paralyzed hand**. When Jesus asked the religious leaders a question concerning good and evil with regard to the Sabbath, they had no reply.

3:7-12 Having demonstrated the authority of Jesus by describing the blindness and hostility of the Jewish religious leaders, Mark next illustrated the blindness of the people. Mark did not say specifically why Jesus withdrew, but Matthew noted that Jesus was aware of a plot to kill him (Mt 12:14-15). Jesus' fame had spread as far as the southern part of Judea. Demons (**unclean spirits**) shouted Christ's identity; but He silenced them, striving to keep the focus on His ultimate destiny, the cross.

3:13-19 Jesus prepared **12** men to share directly in His earthly ministry and to prepare them for their future ministry after His death and resurrection. None of the disciples was a trained religious leader.

Controversial Encounters Found in Mark

Controversy	Reference in Mark
Over Jesus' right to forgive sins	2:1-12
Over Jesus' fellowship with tax collectors and "sinners"	2:13-17
Over the disciples' freedom from fasting	2:18-22
Over the disciples' picking grain on the Sabbath	2:23-27
Over Jesus' right to do good on the Sabbath	3:1-6
Over the nature of Jesus' family	3:20-21,31-35
Over the source of Jesus' power to exorcise evil spirits	3:22-30
Over the disciples eating with unwashed hands	7:1-5,14-23
Over setting aside the commands of God on the part of the Pharisees and teachers of the law of God in order to observe their own tradition	7:6-13
Over the legality of divorce and God's intention for marriage	10:1-12
Over Jesus' authority to cleanse the temple and John's authority to baptize	11:27-33
Over paying taxes to Caesar and giving God His due	12:13-17
Over marriage in the resurrection, the power of God, and the witness of Scripture	12:18-27
Over the most important commandment	12:28-34
Over the nature of the Messiah—the son of David or David's Lord	12:35-37

3:20-35 By using Jesus' hostile encounter with the scribes to divide the narrative concerning His encounters with His family (3:20-21 and 3:31-35), Mark contrasted Jesus' disciples with His opponents, drawing attention to the events by using one to offset the other. With the reactions of Jesus' family presented as bookends surrounding the hostility of the scribes, the skepticism of Jesus' own biological family was seen more clearly. Members of His own family said, **"He's out of His mind,"** revealing how little His family understood Him (v. 21). So who are the relatives of Jesus? Only the one, whether biologically related or not, who determined to do the will of God (vv. 33-35). In a culture that valued family relations above all else, Jesus' claims were radical indeed. Nevertheless, there is no hint that Jesus was undermining the family and its relationships, for the family was commissioned by the Creator God, and Jesus was the agent of creation (Gn 2:8-25; Jn 1:1). Jesus simply used the visit of His family to teach a spiritual truth.

4:1-20 This section is one of the few that Mark devoted strictly to the teachings of Jesus. Its importance lies in revealing what **the kingdom of God** is like, how it grows, and who can actually enter the kingdom. Jesus used **parables** (a transliteration of Gk *parabolais*, "proverb, figure, symbol"; from *para*, "beside," and *ballō*, "throw," lit to "throw beside," v. 2) as His primary tool for teaching truths. Parables use comparison, placing a concrete situation readily known by the pupil next to a biblical truth or spiritual lesson.

Some parables were easily understood and readily revealed truth (12:12); others required an explanation for understanding (4:13-20). Jesus did sometimes veil the truth from those who heard Him, such as those who persisted in unbelief and those seeking to end His ministry or destroy His message. Parables were used so that believers would understand immediately or with an explanation, while unbelievers would not grasp the meaning. The hearing without understanding was the result, not the purpose, of the message (see Is 6:9-10). The fact that the parable contained an admonition to **listen** at the beginning (Mk 4:3) and end (v. 9) would seem to affirm that the parable's meaning is not always readily clear.

In the parable of the sower, the only harvest about which the farmer cared was the one that produced mature fruit. **The sower** and what was sown were the same in each planting, but the soils were different. The emphasis was on the different kinds of soil and the ways the gospel was received in each. Accordingly, only true disciples yield fruit. Jesus used parables to reveal secrets (v. 11) not

Matthew and Thomas;
James the son of Alphaeus,
and Thaddaeus;
Simon the Zealot,[A]
19 and Judas Iscariot,[B]
who also betrayed Him.

A House Divided (3:20-30)

20 Then He went home, and the
crowd gathered again so that they
were not even able to eat.[C] 21 When
His family heard this, they set out
to restrain Him, because they said,
"He's out of His mind."
22 The •scribes who had come down
from Jerusalem said, "He has •Beel-
zebul in Him!" and, "He drives out
demons by the ruler of the demons!"
23 So He summoned them and
spoke to them in parables: "How can
Satan drive out Satan? 24 If a kingdom is divided against itself, that
kingdom cannot stand. 25 If a house
is divided against itself, that house
cannot stand. 26 And if Satan rebels
against himself and is divided, he
cannot stand but is finished![D]

HARD QUESTION

How do I know I have not committed "an eternal sin" (i.e., "the unpardonable sin")?

First examine the context of the passage in which this phrase appears. **The scribes** admitted that Jesus performed miracles, but they charged that Jesus must be empowered by the devil or be demon-possessed in order to cast out the devil (3:22). Their charge was both self-contradictory and self-condemning. **Satan** (vv. 23,26) would not thwart his own work; other Jewish exorcists were casting out demons by the power of God. The point Jesus ultimately made was that attributing God's work to demons is blasphemous and could not be forgiven (vv. 28-30). You cannot commit "the unpardonable sin" (a sin for which there is no **forgiveness**, v. 20) unless you know what you are doing. Before this tragic step from which there is no turning back, you become so hardened in unbelief that despite knowledge and understanding, you make a conscious choice to adopt a pattern of willful defiance toward God. The Pharisees reached this point when they attributed the work of **the Holy Spirit** to Satan (v. 29). In light of this opposition, Jesus began to "weed out" those who were against Him from those who were with Him.

27 "On the other hand, no one can
enter a strong man's house and rob
his possessions unless he first ties up
the strong man. Then he will rob his
house. 28 •I assure you: People will be
forgiven for all sins[E] and whatever
blasphemies they may blaspheme.
29 But whoever blasphemes against
the Holy Spirit never has forgiveness, but is •guilty of an eternal
sin"[F]— 30 because they were saying,
"He has an unclean spirit."

True Relationships (3:31-35)

31 Then His mother and His brothers came, and standing outside, they
sent word to Him and called Him.
32 A crowd was sitting around Him
and told Him, "Look, Your mother,
Your brothers, and Your sisters[G] are
outside asking for You."
33 He replied to them, "Who are
My mother and My brothers?" 34 And
looking about at those who were
sitting in a circle around Him, He
said, "Here are My mother and My
brothers! 35 Whoever does the will
of God is My brother and sister and
mother."

The Parable of the Sower (4:1-9)

4 Again He began to teach by the
sea, and a very large crowd gathered around Him. So He got into a
boat on the sea and sat down, while
the whole crowd was on the shore
facing the sea. 2 He taught them
many things in parables, and in His
teaching He said to them: 3 "Listen!
Consider the sower who went out
to sow. 4 As he sowed, this occurred:
Some seed fell along the path, and
the birds came and ate it up. 5 Other
seed fell on rocky ground where it
didn't have much soil, and it sprang
up right away, since it didn't have
deep soil. 6 When the sun came up,
it was scorched, and since it didn't
have a root, it withered. 7 Other seed
fell among thorns, and the thorns
came up and choked it, and it didn't
produce a crop. 8 Still others fell
on good ground and produced a
crop that increased 30, 60, and 100
times what was sown." 9 Then He

[A] **3:18** Lit *the Cananaean* [B] **3:19** *Iscariot* is probably "a man of Kerioth," a town in Judea. [C] **3:20** Or *eat a meal*; lit *eat bread* [D] **3:26** Lit *but he has an end* [E] **3:28** Lit *All things will be forgiven the sons of men* [F] **3:29** Other mss read *is subject to eternal judgment* [G] **3:32** Other mss omit *and Your sisters*

said, "Anyone who has ears to hear should listen!"

Why Jesus Used Parables (4:10-12)

10 When He was alone with the Twelve, those who were around Him asked Him about the parables. 11 He answered them, "The •secret of the kingdom of God has been given to you, but to those outside, everything comes in parables 12 so that

they may look and look,
yet not perceive;
they may listen and listen,
yet not understand;
otherwise, they might
turn back—
and be forgiven."[A,B]

The Parable of the Sower Explained (4:13-20)

13 Then He said to them: "Don't you understand this parable? How then will you understand any of the parables? 14 The sower sows the word. 15 These[C] are the ones along the path where the word is sown: when they hear, immediately Satan comes and takes away the word sown in them.[D] 16 And these are[E] the ones sown on rocky ground: when they hear the word, immediately they receive it with joy. 17 But they have no root in themselves; they are short-lived. When pressure or persecution comes because of the word, they immediately •stumble. 18 Others are sown among thorns; these are the ones who hear the word, 19 but the worries of this age, the seduction[F] of wealth, and the desires for other things enter in and choke the word, and it becomes unfruitful. 20 But the ones sown on good ground are those who hear the word, welcome it, and produce a crop: 30, 60, and 100 times what was sown."

Using Your Light (4:21-25)

21 He also said to them, "Is a lamp brought in to be put under a basket or under a bed? Isn't it to be put on a lampstand? 22 For nothing is concealed except to be revealed, and nothing hidden except to come to light. 23 If anyone has ears to hear, he should listen!" 24 Then He said to them, "Pay attention to what you hear. By the measure you use,[G] it will be measured and added to you. 25 For to the one who has, it will be given, and from the one who does not have, even what he has will be taken away."

The Parable of the Growing Seed (4:26-29)

26 "The kingdom of God is like this," He said. "A man scatters seed on the ground; 27 he sleeps and rises—night and day, and the seed sprouts and grows—he doesn't know how. 28 The soil produces a crop by itself—first the blade, then the head, and then the ripe grain on the head. 29 But as soon as the crop is ready, he sends for the sickle, because the harvest has come."

The Parable of the Mustard Seed (4:30-32)

30 And He said: "How can we illustrate the kingdom of God, or what parable can we use to describe it? 31 It's like a mustard seed that, when sown in the soil, is smaller than all the seeds on the ground. 32 And when sown, it comes up and grows taller than all the vegetables, and produces large branches, so that the birds of the sky can nest in its shade."

Using Parables (4:33-34)

33 He would speak the word to them with many parables like these, as they were able to understand. 34 And He did not speak to them without a parable. Privately, however, He would explain everything to His own disciples.

Authority over Wind and Waves (4:35-41)

35 On that day, when evening had come, He told them, "Let's cross over to the other side of the sea." 36 So they left the crowd and took Him along since He was already in the boat. And other boats were with Him. 37 A fierce windstorm arose, and the waves were breaking over the boat, so that the boat was already being swamped. 38 But He was in the

previously understood. For those who were already on the **outside** (i.e., out of touch with God, persistent unbelievers), the message of the kingdom would further alienate them. But for those who were open to Jesus' message, greater maturity and discipleship would result.

4:21-34 The next three parables concerned spiritual perception of the message of the kingdom and the specific growth of the kingdom. The parables of the **lamp** and **measure** in Mark were stern exhortations to be spiritually perceptive. Jesus did not come for His kingdom to be hidden but to be revealed fully to all. The more you appropriate spiritual truth now, the more you will receive in the future. If you do not make spiritual perceptiveness a high priority now, even the little spiritual perception you think you have will be taken from you. In other words, you had better wonder if you have truly made a commitment to Christ and are counted as His disciple if pursuing spiritual understanding is not a priority. Those who do not have an interest in spiritual things will soon find themselves falling further away from the kingdom (v. 25).

The parable of the secretly growing **seed**, which is unique to Mark, had to do with the mysterious way **the kingdom of God** grows. All a farmer could do was plant the seed. He would not understand how the seed grows. The kingdom of God was like the **mustard seed** because the kingdom, too, appeared weak and insignificant in the beginning. But in the end its size and significance would exceed what would be expected at the beginning.

The summary statement on the parables emphasized again that Jesus' disciples, the ones on the "inside," were privy to the secrets of the kingdom in a way that no others were. Moreover, true insiders are characterized by a spiritual hunger for the things that have to do with the kingdom of God. If this hunger is not present, you must question whether or not you are truly on the inside.

4:35–6:6a In a dramatic display of miraculous powers, Mark showed Jesus' triumph over hostile forces in nature (4:35-41), in the demonic realm (5:1-20), and in death and chronic illness (5:21-43). Jesus' tremendous display of divine power made the blindness and hostility of the world look ludicrous. Though Jesus' message and ministry were powerful, He was still ultimately rejected. Mark was preparing his readers for the cross.

4:35-41 Jesus often demonstrated His power over nature itself by harnessing its elements. With the calming of the storm, the disciples were desperately fearful, and they were compelled to ask, **Who then is this**? Their faith still

[A]**4:12** Other mss read *and their sins be forgiven them* [B]**4:12** Is 6:9-10 [C]**4:15** Some people [D]**4:15** Other mss read *in their hearts* [E]**4:16** Other mss read *are like* [F]**4:19** Or *pleasure*, or *deceitfulness* [G]**4:24** Lit *you measure*

left much to be desired. **The wind and the sea** knew the voice of their Master, but the disciples had yet to learn to recognize it.

5:1-20 Healing of demon-possession showed the victory of the supernatural over unusually powerful forces of evil. The demons (wicked, unclean spirit-beings) also knew His voice. They did not need to ask who He was. But they had to ask Him for permission to go where they wanted to go.

Jesus did not engage in lengthy conversations with demons and frequently forbade them from speaking (1:34). Mark paid extraordinary attention to the details surrounding the healing of the man possessed by the legion of demons. Some would question Jesus' assigning these animals to destruction. Of course, the demons, not Jesus, actually destroyed the swine (5:13).

Nevertheless, Jesus always showed that He cared more for mankind, created in His own image and redeemed by His own blood, than for animals. The demons, of course, were determined to destroy. When they could not destroy the man, they settled for the pigs. The account is riveting precisely because Mark gives the reader an up-close view of all with which Jesus had to contend in a single day (vv. 2-5).

Believers need not look for demons, but they must be aware of their existence and influence and be prepared to stand against them (Eph 6:10-12; 1Pt 5:8-9). The only permanent protection from demon possession is to be born again, which includes the permanent indwelling of

stern, sleeping on the cushion. So
they woke Him up and said to Him,
"Teacher! Don't You care that we're
going to die?"
39 He got up, rebuked the wind,
and said to the sea, "Silence! Be
still!" The wind ceased, and there
was a great calm. 40 Then He said to
them, "Why are you fearful? Do you
still have no faith?"
41 And they were terrified and
asked one another, "Who then is
this? Even the wind and the sea obey
Him!"

Demons Driven out by the Master (5:1-20)

5 Then they came to the other
side of the sea, to the region of
the Gerasenes.[A] 2 As soon as He got
out of the boat, a man with an •un-
clean spirit came out of the tombs
and met Him. 3 He lived in the
tombs. No one was able to restrain
him anymore—even with chains—
4 because he often had been bound
with shackles and chains, but had
snapped off the chains and smashed
the shackles. No one was strong
enough to subdue him. 5 And always, night and day, he was crying
out among the tombs and in the
mountains and cutting himself with
stones.
6 When he saw Jesus from a distance, he ran and knelt down before
Him. 7 And he cried out with a loud
voice, "What do You have to do with
me,[B] Jesus, Son of the Most High
God? I beg[C] You before God, don't
torment me!" 8 For He had told him,
"Come out of the man, you unclean
spirit!"
9 "What is your name?" He asked
him.
"My name is Legion,"[D] he answered Him, "because we are many."
10 And he kept begging Him not to
send them out of the region.
11 Now a large herd of pigs was
there, feeding on the hillside. 12 The
demons[E] begged Him, "Send us to
the pigs, so we may enter them."
13 And He gave them permission.
Then the unclean spirits came out
and entered the pigs, and the herd of
about 2,000 rushed down the steep
bank into the sea and drowned there.
14 The men who tended them[F] ran off
and reported it in the town and the
countryside, and people went to see
what had happened. 15 They came

A **5:1** Some mss read *Gadarenes*; other mss read *Gergesenes* B **5:7** Lit *What to me and to You* C **5:7** Or *adjure* D **5:9** A Roman legion contained up to 6,000 soldiers; here legion indicates a large number. E **5:12** Other mss read *All the demons* F **5:14** Other mss read *tended the pigs*

Demons 5:1-20

Information	Reference
Could act as personal and intelligent beings	Ac 16:16-18
Sought to express themselves through another living creature	Mt 12:43-45
Could achieve supernatural strength	Lk 8:29; Ac 19:13-16
Were aware of the destiny God planned for them	Mt 8:29; 2Pt 2:4
Were apparently fallen angels who took part in Satan's rebellion	Is 14:12-15; Ezk 28:14-15; Jd 6
Can attack through temptation, direct opposition to God's work, and by influence, oppression, and possession	Mt 4:1-11; Mk 5:1-5; Lk 13:10-17; Ac 16:16-18
Can cause physical illness	Mt 12:22; 17:14-18; Mk 9:17-25
Can generate emotional turmoil	1Sm 16:14; Mk 5:1-5
Can deceive, causing people to believe lies	Ac 5:3
Can draw people to embrace worldly wisdom	Jms 3:13-16
Can entice people to accept doctrinal error in the place of truth	1Tm 4:1-5

to Jesus and saw the man who had
been demon-possessed by the legion, sitting there, dressed and in
his right mind; and they were afraid.
16 The eyewitnesses described to
them what had happened to the demon-possessed man and told about
the pigs. 17 Then they began to beg
Him to leave their region.
18 As He was getting into the boat,
the man who had been demon-possessed kept begging Him to be with
Him. 19 But He would not let him;
instead, He told him, "Go back home
to your own people, and report to
them how much the Lord has done
for you and how He has had mercy
on you." 20 So he went out and began
to proclaim in the •Decapolis how
much Jesus had done for him, and
they were all amazed.

A Girl Restored and a Woman Healed
(5:21-43)

21 When Jesus had crossed over
again by boat to the other side, a
large crowd gathered around Him
while He was by the sea. 22 One of the
•synagogue leaders, named Jairus,
came, and when he saw Jesus, he fell
at His feet 23 and kept begging Him,
"My little daughter is at death's
door.[A] Come and lay Your hands on
her so she can get well and live."
24 So Jesus went with him, and a
large crowd was following and pressing against Him. 25 A woman suffering from bleeding for 12 years 26 had
endured much under many doctors.
She had spent everything she had
and was not helped at all. On the
contrary, she became worse. 27 Having heard about Jesus, she came behind Him in the crowd and touched
His robe. 28 For she said, "If I can just
touch His robes, I'll be made well!"
29 Instantly her flow of blood ceased,
and she sensed in her body that she
was cured of her affliction.
30 At once Jesus realized in Himself
that power had gone out from Him.
He turned around in the crowd and
said, "Who touched My robes?"
31 His disciples said to Him, "You
see the crowd pressing against You,
and You say, 'Who touched Me?'"
32 So He was looking around to see
who had done this. 33 Then the woman, knowing what had happened to
her, came with fear and trembling,
fell down before Him, and told Him
the whole truth. 34 "Daughter," He
said to her, "your faith has made you
well.[B] Go in peace and be free[C] from
your affliction."
35 While He was still speaking, people came from the synagogue leader's house and said, "Your daughter
is dead. Why bother the Teacher
anymore?"
36 But when Jesus overheard what

[A]5:23 Lit *My little daughter has it finally*; = to be at the end of life [B]5:34 Or *has saved you* [C]5:34 Lit *healthy*

CHARACTER PROFILE

Woman with the Issue of Blood

A Woman of Faith

Her Background	• She had suffered for 12 years from chronic bleeding (5:25). • She had sought treatment, but her condition had worsened (5:26). • She had spent all her resources.
Her Story	• She approached Jesus from behind, unnoticed (5:27). • She believed she could be healed if she only touched His robe (5:28). • Jesus turned around, looking to find who had touched Him (5:30). • He called her "Daughter," an expression of tenderness, and commended her for her faith (5:34).
Life Lesson	Jesus had compassion on all people, regardless of their age or station in life.

See also Mt 9:18-26; Lk 8:43-48.

the Holy Spirit from that day forward (1 Co 6:19). The believer is to put aside sinful practices and remove any demonic influences. Incorporating the disciplines of prayer and Bible study prepare a believer for battle against Satan and his demons.

The Decapolis was a league of 10 Greek cities largely populated by Gentiles (thus the presence of a herd of pigs would not be surprising) and located to the east of the Sea of Galilee and the Jordan River (5:20). In 6:6b–8:30, Jesus launched His ministry to the Gentiles, and the man possessed with demons was in Gentile territory.

5:21-43 As **one of the synagogue leaders, Jairus**, whose name was omitted in the Matthean account (Mt 9:18), was a layman with responsibility for supervising worship, education, and synagogue-building (v. 22). Jairus probably knew Jesus only by reputation. Yet he believed Jesus could heal his young **daughter** (v. 23). His request for Jesus to **lay** [His] **hands on her so she can get well** [Gk *sōthē*, save] **and live** (v. 23) was a commonly understood prelude to healing among the Jews (6:5; 7:32; 8:23,25). The use of the Greek verb meaning "save" was appropriate since in all Jesus' miracles recorded in Mark 5, physical healing served as a metaphor for spiritual deliverance from sin and was understood in a theological sense as ultimate healing or salvation.

When the message came that Jarius' daughter was **dead** (v. 35), Jesus was undeterred. **The people weeping and wailing loudly** at Jarius' house (v. 38) were probably professional mourners who would have been summoned even without a direct word from Jairus because of his prominence in the community. Even the death of a poor man would merit some public display of mourning. Jesus gave the family **strict orders that no one should know about this** (v. 43) to prevent the dramatic news from multiplying the demands of both the curious and incredulous.

The **woman suffering from bleeding** endured both a physical burden and serious spiritual and social consequences (v. 25). Because this condition made her unclean, she lived as an outcast (cp. Lv 15:25-30). Since Jewish law mandated that contact with graves, blood, or death made one ceremonially unclean, the woman's plan for getting near Jesus involved great risk—anyone she touched was considered unclean, and she had to work her way through a moving crowd to get to Jesus. Finally, when she touched Jesus' robe, she became clean even without conscious effort on Jesus' part (vv. 27-29). Jesus not only healed her physically and removed the cause of social rejection, but He also met her spiritual needs, assuring her,

"**Daughter, . . . your faith has made you well**" (Gk *sesōken*, "save").

6:1-6 The wind and the waves, demons, sickness, and death all responded to Christ. They recognized His authority and had to respond. But the people from Nazareth could not see what was so special about the man from their hometown. To them Jesus was merely a carpenter, Mary's son. Though He was invited to speak at the synagogue (He was well known as a teacher) and though His preaching was just as powerful there as anywhere else, the people of Nazareth took offense at Him. And Jesus was amazed at their lack of faith.

Although Jesus' family lived in Nazareth, He went there as a rabbi with His disciples. His mission was to preach the good news. How unfortunate that the people of Nazareth allowed their everyday knowledge about Jesus (who came from the home of an ordinary craftsman) to block the spiritual understanding He offered to them. The rejection He experienced there was a sign of what was to come. Even His family joined in this rejection (see also 3:20-21,31-35).

One should not be shaken by Mark's statement that **He was not able to do any miracles there**. Of course the entire Gospel, and the New Testament as a whole, point clearly to the omnipotence of God. God and His Son (also fully God) could do anything, but Mark acknowledged that Jesus chose to limit Himself based on the response of the people. One is again reminded that Jesus was not setting out to impress people as a miracle worker. His miracles were kingdom-centered. In an atmosphere of unbelief, Jesus chose not to exercise His power through miracles. Throughout His ministry, His miracles were in response to faith. Those who were true disciples responded to His teachings on the kingdom of God, but the world in general rejected these truths.

6:7-13 As a result of the success of His village ministry, Jesus commissioned **the Twelve** to assist in His endeavors. He had been preparing them for this ministry. They were originally called to "fish for people" (1:17); Jesus gave them special attention on several occasions (3:7,13; 4:10). They had seen His amazing miracles and heard His powerful teaching. What they needed to do now was to have complete trust in God to meet all their needs on their journey. The mission assignment to the Twelve was patterned after Jesus' ministry—preaching the necessity of repentance (6:12), casting out demons (v. 13), and healing the sick (v. 13).

6:14-29 **King Herod** heard of all that Jesus was doing and feared that **John the Baptist** had **been raised** from

CHARACTER PROFILE

Jairus's Daughter A Young Woman Healed

Her Background	• She was the daughter of Jairus, an important official of the synagogue (5:22). • She was 12 years old (5:42).
Her Story	• She was on her deathbed (5:23). • Jairus begged Jesus to come and heal her. • His servants then appeared and reported that she had died (5:35). • Jesus went to her bedside with Peter, James, John, and her parents (5:40). • He took her by the hand, raised her up and told them to get her something to eat (5:43).
Life Lesson	"Don't be afraid. Only believe . . ." (Lk 8:50).

See also Mt 9:18-26; Lk 8:41-56.

was said, He told the synagogue
leader, "Don't be afraid. Only believe." 37 He did not let anyone accompany Him except Peter, James,
and John, James's brother. 38 They
came to the leader's house, and He
saw a commotion—people weeping
and wailing loudly. 39 He went in and
said to them, "Why are you making a
commotion and weeping? The child
is not dead but asleep."
40 They started laughing at Him,
but He put them all outside. He
took the child's father, mother,
and those who were with Him, and
entered the place where the child
was. 41 Then He took the child by
the hand and said to her, "*Talitha
koum!*"[A] (which is translated, "Little
girl, I say to you, get up!"). 42 Immediately the girl got up and began to
walk. (She was 12 years old.) At this
they were utterly astounded. 43 Then
He gave them strict orders that no
one should know about this and said
that she should be given something
to eat.

Rejection at Nazareth (6:1-6a)

6 He went away from there and
came to His hometown, and His
disciples followed Him. 2 When the
Sabbath came, He began to teach
in the •synagogue, and many who
heard Him were astonished. "Where
did this man get these things?" they
said. "What is this wisdom given to
Him, and how are these miracles
performed by His hands? 3 Isn't this
the carpenter, the son of Mary, and
the brother of James, Joses, Judas,
and Simon? And aren't His sisters
here with us?" So they were •offend-
ed by Him.
4 Then Jesus said to them, "A
prophet is not without honor except in his hometown, among his
relatives, and in his household." 5 So
He was not able to do any miracles[B]
there, except that He laid His hands
on a few sick people and healed
them. 6 And He was amazed at their
unbelief.

Commissioning the Twelve (6:6b-13)

Now He was going around the
villages in a circuit, teaching. 7 He
summoned the Twelve and began
to send them out in pairs and gave
them authority over •unclean spirits. 8 He instructed them to take
nothing for the road except a walking stick: no bread, no traveling bag,
no money in their belts. 9 They were
to wear sandals, but not put on an
extra shirt. 10 Then He said to them,
"Whenever you enter a house, stay
there until you leave that place. 11 If
any place does not welcome you and
people refuse to listen to you, when
you leave there, shake the dust off

A 5:41 An Aram expression B 6:5 Lit *miracle*

your feet as a testimony against
them."[A]
12 So they went out and preached
that people should repent. 13 And
they were driving out many demons,
anointing many sick people with olive oil, and healing them.

Beheading of John the Baptist (6:14-29)

14 King •Herod heard of this, because Jesus' name had become well
known. Some[B] said, "John the Baptist has been raised from the dead,
and that's why supernatural powers
are at work in him." 15 But others
said, "He's Elijah." Still others said,
"He's a prophet[C]—like one of the
prophets."
16 When Herod heard of it, he said,
"John, the one I beheaded, has been
raised!" 17 For Herod himself had
given orders to arrest John and to
chain him in prison on account of
Herodias, his brother Philip's wife,
whom he had married. 18 John had
been telling Herod, "It is not lawful
for you to have your brother's wife!"
19 So Herodias held a grudge against
him and wanted to kill him. But she
could not, 20 because Herod was in
awe of[D] John and was protecting
him, knowing he was a righteous
and holy man. When Herod heard
him he would be very disturbed,[E] yet
would hear him gladly.
21 Now an opportune time came
on his birthday, when Herod gave
a banquet for his nobles, military
commanders, and the leading men
of Galilee. 22 When Herodias's own
daughter[F] came in and danced,
she pleased Herod and his guests.
The king said to the girl, "Ask me
whatever you want, and I'll give it
to you." 23 So he swore oaths to her:
"Whatever you ask me I will give
you, up to half my kingdom."
24 Then she went out and said to
her mother, "What should I ask for?"
"John the Baptist's head!" she
said.
25 Immediately she hurried to the
king and said, "I want you to give
me John the Baptist's head on a platter—right now!"
26 Though the king was deeply distressed, because of his oaths and the
guests[G] he did not want to refuse
her. 27 The king immediately sent for
an executioner and commanded him
to bring John's head. So he went and
beheaded him in prison, 28 brought
his head on a platter, and gave it to
the girl. Then the girl gave it to her
mother. 29 When his disciples[H] heard
about it, they came and removed his
corpse and placed it in a tomb.

Feeding 5,000 (6:30-44)

30 The apostles gathered around
Jesus and reported to Him all that
they had done and taught. 31 He
said to them, "Come away by yourselves to a remote place and rest
for a while." For many people were
coming and going, and they did not
even have time to eat. 32 So they
went away in the boat by themselves
to a remote place, 33 but many saw
them leaving and recognized them.
People ran there by land from all the
towns and arrived ahead of them.[I]
34 So as He stepped ashore, He saw a
huge crowd and had compassion on
them, because they were like sheep
without a shepherd. Then He began
to teach them many things.
35 When it was already late, His
disciples approached Him and said,
"This place is a wilderness, and it
is already late! 36 Send them away,
so they can go into the surrounding countryside and villages to buy
themselves something to eat."

[A] **6:11** Other mss add *I assure you, it will be more tolerable for Sodom or Gomorrah on judgment day than for that town.* [B] **6:14** Other mss read *He* [C] **6:15** Lit *Others said, "A prophet* [D] **6:20** Or *Herod feared* [E] **6:20** Other mss read *When he heard him, he did many things* [F] **6:22** Other mss read *When his daughter Herodias* [G] **6:26** Lit *and those reclining at the table* [H] **6:29** = John's disciples [I] **6:33** Other mss add *and gathered around Him*

the dead to haunt him. Herod's concern about John's being raised from the dead was not as motivated by Jesus' ministry per se as by a guilty conscience over his murder of John. Traditionally, according to the Jewish historian Josephus, John was imprisoned and executed at Machaerus, a fortress located in modern-day Jordan (ancient southern Perea). Indeed, John's death did foreshadow the death of Jesus. John the Baptist had refused to overlook the blatant adultery of Herod Antipas and Herodias. The daughter of Aristobulus, a son of Herod the Great and Mariamne, **Herodias** had married her uncle Philip, also a son of Herod the Great. Herodias' husband Philip was the half-brother of Herod Antipas, who was ruling during the days of John; but she was living out of wedlock with Herod Antipas. Although Herod was embarrassed when John denounced his adulterous relationship, he himself seemed intrigued by John and even protected him for a time. Herodias, however, was furious and immediately sought to destroy the prophet. Her daughter Salome not only showed no surprise with her mother's request to her to ask for John's beheading but added two enhancements of her own: She wanted the head **right now** and **on a platter** (v. 25).

Mark's Gospel has two passion (suffering) narratives—the passion of John and the passion of Jesus. A passion narrative presents the story of someone's death. There are interesting parallels between these two passion narratives:

- The respect for John the Baptist and Jesus by Roman rulers—Herod and Pilate, respectively (v. 20; 15:5,14);
- The hatred experienced by John and by Jesus from their enemies—Herodias and the Jewish religious leaders respectively (6:24; 11:18);
- The yielding to pressure to kill John and Jesus by Herod and Pilate, respectively (6:26; 15:15);
- The mention of disciples coming for the body and burial in a tomb (6:29; 15:43-46).

6:30-44 Apart from Jesus' resurrection, the feeding of the 5,000 was the only miracle recorded in all four Gospels (cp. Mt 14:13-21; Lk 9:12-17; Jn 6:5-13). Again pointing to the kingdom, Jesus showed Himself to be a man of compassion, a supplier of needs when resources were unavailable, and the One whose authority extended to the natural world. The numbering was based on counting the men. Adding women and children would have greatly increased the number.

>WORD|*study*

6:34 Had compassion (Gk, *esplagchnisthē* "have pity, feel sympathy, be moved") in the New Testament is used only by or about Jesus (Mt 18:27; Lk 10:33). The word goes beyond pity and encompasses the idea of supplying help.

7:1-7 This section, similar to the accounts of conflict in 2:1–3:6 and ultimately showing why Jesus was turning to the Gentiles, served as an introduction to Jesus' ministry among the Gentiles. Jewish ritual and tradition had to be put into perspective to move forward with reaching Gentiles with the gospel.

7:9-13 The example Jesus gave the Pharisees affirmed the Fifth Commandment (Ex 20:12). Anyone who cursed his mother or father would receive the death penalty (Lv 20:9). Jesus then demonstrated how **tradition** added by the religious leaders subverted this command.

According to the tradition, a son only had to declare what he intended to give his father or mother as *Corban*—a **gift** committed to the temple. No longer could the son be required to use the designated gift to assist his parents. In the practice of *Corban,* the Pharisees effectively nullified for children the commandment to honor their parents. If the son later regretted his gift of *Corban*, the Pharisees would then demand that his earlier vow be kept (see Nm 30:2). Evidently this gift, when assigned to the temple, did not have to be surrendered immediately. The child could continue to use the property until his own death when the remainder would then go to the temple. The son denied his parents, enriched himself, and then gave God what was left. God's intent in giving the command had been negated by the tradition of man (v. 13). The Pharisees in effect used the letter of one commandment to invalidate the intent of another commandment. By such a declaration, a son legally excluded his parents from benefiting from the gift. In other words, he dedicated something to God but then disobeyed God's mandate in using it. Again, stressing the letter of the law and adhering to the Pharisees' interpretation and additions to the law subverted the true intent of the law.

This interchange revealed the seriousness of God's commandments and the wickedness of anyone who was seeking to get around them. A stern warning was addressed to anyone who wanted to shirk his responsibilities.

7:14-23 Specific food regulations had been expanded to the point that some religious leaders wanted to determine whether a person was righteous or unrighteous by the food he ate. Jesus condemned them because real uncleanness is decided by the heart, not food (7:18-23). True defilement is internal (in the heart) and not external (determined by what you do or do not do). Uncleanness was determined by moral principles, not by routine ritual. Food and drink did not make one unclean, even if imbibed with unclean hands or declared unclean by food laws. Rather, evil thoughts and

[37] "You give them something to eat," He responded.

They said to Him, "Should we go and buy 200 •denarii worth of bread and give them something to eat?"

[38] And He asked them, "How many loaves do you have? Go look."

When they found out they said, "Five, and two fish."

[39] Then He instructed them to have all the people sit down[A] in groups on the green grass. [40] So they sat down in ranks of hundreds and fifties. [41] Then He took the five loaves and the two fish, and looking up to heaven, He blessed and broke the loaves. He kept giving them to His disciples to set before the people. He also divided the two fish among them all. [42] Everyone ate and was filled. [43] Then they picked up 12 baskets full of pieces of bread and fish. [44] Now those who ate the loaves were 5,000 men.

Walking on the Water (6:45-52)

[45] Immediately He made His disciples get into the boat and go ahead of Him to the other side, to Bethsaida, while He dismissed the crowd. [46] After He said good-bye to them, He went away to the mountain to pray. [47] When evening came, the boat was in the middle of the sea, and He was alone on the land. [48] He saw them being battered as they rowed,[B] because the wind was against them. Around three in the morning[C] He came toward them walking on the sea and wanted to pass by them. [49] When they saw Him walking on the sea, they thought it was a ghost and cried out; [50] for they all saw Him and were terrified. Immediately He spoke with them and said, "Have courage! It is I. Don't be afraid." [51] Then He got into the boat with them, and the wind ceased. They were completely astounded,[D] [52] because they had not understood about the loaves. Instead, their hearts were hardened.

Miraculous Healings (6:53-56)

[53] When they had crossed over, they came to land at Gennesaret and beached the boat. [54] As they got out of the boat, people immediately recognized Him. [55] They hurried throughout that vicinity and began to carry the sick on mats to wherever they heard He was. [56] Wherever He would go, into villages, towns, or the country, they laid the sick in the marketplaces and begged Him that they might touch just the •tassel of His robe. And everyone who touched it was made well.

The Tradition of the Elders (7:1-23)

7 The •Pharisees and some of the •scribes who had come from Jerusalem gathered around Him. [2] They observed that some of His disciples were eating their bread with •unclean—that is, unwashed—hands. [3] (For the Pharisees, in fact all the Jews, will not eat unless they wash their hands ritually, keeping the tradition of the elders. [4] When they come from the marketplace, they do not eat unless they have washed. And there are many other customs they have received and keep, like the washing of cups, jugs, copper utensils, and dining couches.[E]) [5] Then the Pharisees and the scribes asked Him, "Why don't Your disciples live according to the tradition of the elders, instead of eating bread with ritually unclean[F] hands?"

[6] He answered them, "Isaiah prophesied correctly about you hypocrites, as it is written:

> **These people honor Me**
> **with their lips,**
> **but their heart is far**
> **from Me.**
> [7] **They worship Me in vain,**
> **teaching as doctrines**
> **the commands of men.**[G]

[8] Disregarding the command of God, you keep the tradition of men."[H] [9] He also said to them, "You completely invalidate God's command in order to maintain[I] your tradition! [10] For Moses said:

[A]**6:39** Lit *people recline* [B]**6:48** Or *them struggling as they rowed* [C]**6:48** Lit *Around the fourth watch of the night* = 3 to 6 a.m. [D]**6:51** Lit *were astounded in themselves* [E]**7:4** Other mss omit *and dining couches* [F]**7:5** Other mss read *with unwashed* [G]**7:6-7** Is 29:13 [H]**7:8** Other mss add *The washing of jugs, and cups, and many other similar things you practice.* [I]**7:9** Other mss read *to establish*

>WORD|*study*

7:6 Hypocrites (a transliteration of Gk *hupokritōn*, "one who pretends to be other than what he is") originated as a Greek theatrical term describing someone who acted the part of another. The Greek root *krinō*, meaning "judge," is linked to the Greek preposition *hupo*, meaning "under" and thus having the sense of "judging under." The actors of the ancient world wore a series of masks as they assumed the identities of the characters they were playing. In other words, the Pharisees were masking their internal beliefs behind their external rituals. Their insincerity and radical inconsistency, although covered by pretense, was uncovered by Jesus.

Honor your father
and your mother;[A] and
Whoever speaks evil of father
or mother
must be put to death.[B]

11 But you say, 'If a man tells his father or mother: Whatever benefit
you might have received from me
is Corban'" (that is, a gift committed to the temple), 12 "you no longer
let him do anything for his father or
mother. 13 You revoke God's word by
your tradition that you have handed down. And you do many other
similar things." 14 Summoning the
crowd again, He told them, "Listen
to Me, all of you, and understand:
15 Nothing that goes into a person
from outside can defile him, but the
things that come out of a person are
what defile him. [16 If anyone has
ears to hear, he should listen!]"[C]
17 When He went into the house
away from the crowd, the disciples asked Him about the parable.
18 And He said to them, "Are you
also as lacking in understanding?
Don't you realize that nothing going into a man from the outside
can defile him? 19 For it doesn't go
into his heart but into the stomach
and is eliminated."[D] (As a result,
He made all foods •clean.[E]) 20 Then
He said, "What comes out of a person—that defiles him. 21 For from
within, out of people's hearts, come
evil thoughts, sexual immoralities,
thefts, murders, 22 adulteries, greed,
evil actions, deceit, promiscuity,
stinginess,[F] blasphemy, pride, and
foolishness. 23 All these evil things
come from within and defile a person."

A Gentile Mother's Faith (7:24-30)

24 He got up and departed from
there to the region of Tyre and
Sidon.[G] He entered a house and did
not want anyone to know it, but He
could not escape notice. 25 Instead,
immediately after hearing about
Him, a woman whose little daughter
had an unclean spirit came and fell
at His feet. 26 Now the woman was
Greek, a Syrophoenician by birth,
and she kept asking Him to drive
the demon out of her daughter. 27 He
said to her, "Allow the children to be
satisfied first, because it isn't right
to take the children's bread and
throw it to the dogs."
28 But she replied to Him, "Lord,
even the dogs under the table eat
the children's crumbs."
29 Then He told her, "Because of
this reply, you may go. The demon
has gone out of your daughter."
30 When she went back to her home,
she found her child lying on the bed,
and the demon was gone.

Jesus' Astonishing Deeds (7:31-37)

31 Again, leaving the region of
Tyre, He went by way of Sidon to the
Sea of Galilee, through[H] the region
of the •Decapolis. 32 They brought
to Him a deaf man who also had a
speech difficulty, and begged Jesus
to lay His hand on him. 33 So He took
him away from the crowd privately.
After putting His fingers in the
man's ears and spitting, He touched
his tongue. 34 Then, looking up to
heaven, He sighed deeply and said
to him, *"Ephphatha!"*[I] (that is, "Be
opened!"). 35 Immediately his ears
were opened, his speech difficulty
was removed,[J] and he began to speak
clearly. 36 Then He ordered them to
tell no one, but the more He would

wicked behavior from the heart made one unclean. Jesus was fulfilling the law in the Old Testament. If all foods were clean, ritual washings were not necessary, and the barriers between Jews and Gentiles were abolished.

The disciples did not understand this idea. Mark explains Jesus' teaching to his readers (v. 19b). Mark wanted to emphasize the freedom of Gentiles by plainly stating Jesus' rejection of Jewish ceremonial law as the path to righteousness (Col 2:20-23).

7:24-30 Typically, the Jews had no relationships with Gentiles because of ritual uncleanness. But Jesus distanced Himself from the Jewish oral traditions; and, in contrast to these traditions, He revealed the true nature of uncleanness. Jesus' rejection of the ceremonial law would have encouraged the Gentiles to believe that the gospel was for them as much as it was for the **Syrophoenician** woman, who came to Jesus with an urgent request. Her daughter was suffering terribly from demon possession. Jesus' first response to her at a glance seemed uncharacteristically harsh. However, Jesus was neither indifferent nor insensitive; rather, He wanted to test the faith of this Gentile woman and use her faith as a testimony to the disciples. The Jews often referred to the Gentiles as **dogs**, but here the reference is a diminutive form, meaning small dogs kept as household pets rather than scavengers of the streets.

More amazing than Jesus' initial response to the woman was her response to Him. Clearly she understood Jesus' messianic mission. Matthew noted in his parallel passage (Mt 15:21-28) that she referred to Jesus as the "Son of David" and indicated that Jesus viewed His ministry as being first to the Jews and then to the Gentiles (Mt 15:24; Ac 13:46; Rm 1:16).

7:31-37 Only Mark includes the healing of the deaf and mute man. This passage is one of only three in which Jesus used saliva in order to heal someone (see also Mk 8:23; Jn 9:6). Although impossible at this point in His ministry, Jesus still wanted to keep His identity unknown and do His work apart from curious crowds (Mk 7:24,36).

[A] **7:10** Ex 20:12; Dt 5:16 [B] **7:10** Ex 21:17; Lv 20:9 [C] **7:16** Other mss omit bracketed text [D] **7:19** Lit *goes out into the toilet* [E] **7:19** Other mss read *is eliminated, making all foods clean."* [F] **7:22** Lit *evil eye* [G] **7:24** Other mss omit *and Sidon* [H] **7:31** Or *into* [I] **7:34** An Aram expression [J] **7:35** Lit *opened, the bond of his tongue was untied*

order them, the more they would proclaim it.

37 They were extremely astonished and said, "He has done everything well! He even makes deaf people hear, and people unable to speak, talk!"

Feeding 4,000 (8:1-10)

8 In those days there was again a large crowd, and they had nothing to eat. He summoned the disciples and said to them, 2 "I have compassion on the crowd, because they've already stayed with Me three days and have nothing to eat. 3 If I send them home hungry,[A] they will collapse on the way, and some of them have come a long distance."

4 His disciples answered Him, "Where can anyone get enough bread here in this desolate place to fill these people?"

5 "How many loaves do you have?" He asked them.

"Seven," they said. 6 Then He commanded the crowd to sit down on the ground. Taking the seven loaves, He gave thanks, broke the loaves, and kept on giving them to His disciples to set before the people. So they served the loaves to the crowd. 7 They also had a few small fish, and when He had blessed them, He said these were to be served as well. 8 They ate and were filled. Then they collected seven large baskets of leftover pieces. 9 About 4,000 men were there. He dismissed them 10 and immediately got into the boat with His disciples and went to the district of Dalmanutha.[B]

The Yeast of the Pharisees and Herod (8:11-21)

11 The •Pharisees came out and began to argue with Him, demanding of Him a sign from heaven to test Him. 12 But sighing deeply in His spirit, He said, "Why does this generation demand a sign? •I assure you: No sign will be given to this generation!" 13 Then He left them, got on board the boat again, and went to the other side.

14 They had forgotten to take bread and had only one loaf with them in the boat. 15 Then He commanded them: "Watch out! Beware of the yeast of the Pharisees and the yeast of •Herod."

16 They were discussing among themselves that they did not have any bread. 17 Aware of this, He said to them, "Why are you discussing that you do not have any bread? Don't you understand or comprehend? Is your heart hardened? 18 **Do you have eyes, and not see, and do you have ears, and not hear?**[C] And do you not remember? 19 When I broke the five loaves for the 5,000, how many baskets full of pieces of bread did you collect?"

"Twelve," they told Him.

20 "When I broke the seven loaves for the 4,000, how many large baskets full of pieces of bread did you collect?"

"Seven," they said.

21 And He said to them, "Don't you understand yet?"

Healing a Blind Man (8:22-26)

22 Then they came to Bethsaida. They brought a blind man to Him and begged Him to touch him. 23 He took the blind man by the hand and brought him out of the village. Spitting on his eyes and laying His hands on him, He asked him, "Do you see anything?"

24 He looked up and said, "I see people—they look to me like trees walking."

25 Again Jesus placed His hands on the man's eyes, and he saw distinctly. He was cured and could see everything clearly. 26 Then He sent him home, saying, "Don't even go into the village."[D]

Peter's Confession of Faith (8:27-30)

27 Jesus went out with His disciples to the villages of Caesarea Philippi. And on the road He asked His disciples, "Who do people say that I am?"

28 They answered Him, "John the Baptist; others, Elijah; still others, one of the prophets."

29 "But you," He asked them again, "who do you say that I am?"

Peter answered Him, "You are the •Messiah!"

30 And He strictly warned them to tell no one about Him.

8:1-10 As happened earlier in Jesus' ministry, large crowds followed Him. **They had nothing to eat**; and out of compassion He wanted to feed them. He did feed them and, as always, what He provided was sufficient—and the people were satisfied (v. 8). Jesus was still in Gentile territory, so He was performing the same miracle for the Gentiles He had done for the Jews (6:31-44). The theme uniting these parallel events was spiritual understanding or the lack of it. Jesus sounds a call to spiritual understanding in 7:14-18, but the disciples fail to understand after each feeding miracle (6:52; 8:14-21). The miracles of healing—the opening of the ears of the deaf man (7:31-36) and the eyes of the blind man (8:22-26)—may be symbolic of and prepare the way for the opening of the spiritual understanding of the disciples.

8:27-30 Caesarea Philippi was built on the site of ancient Paneas (also called Banias) by Philip the tetrarch. Its ruins remain a popular archaeological site and are located at the foot of Mount Hermon with beautiful gushing springs that are identified as one of the sources of the Jordan River. Jesus asked a question first of the disciples. Contrary to what some modern scholars have said, the fact that Jesus hesitated to reveal Himself as Messiah early in His ministry does not mean He did not believe Himself to be the Messiah. He clearly accepted the title as expressing His true connection to the Old Testament and to the people of God (8:29).

8:31-33 The third and final section in the Gospel of Mark was built around Jesus' three predictions concerning His suffering and death (8:31; 9:31; 10:33-34). The "secret" was now out in the open. The **Son of Man** must go to Jerusalem, suffer, die, and on the third day be raised to life.

Jesus had alluded to His coming suffering and death, but the disciples still did not understand. Here Jesus became more direct to be sure they understood what He had been saying. Peter rebuked Jesus because he did not understand the true mission of the Messiah. Jesus saw Peter's effort to divert Him on His path to the cross as the same temptation Satan offered in the wilderness when Jesus began His ministry. In His stinging rebuke of Peter, Jesus still refused to act on His own apart from the Father's will. Jesus did not demand martyrdom to secure salvation. However, He was clear that one who comes to Christ must remove all hindrances so that Christ is in complete control.

9:1-13 Jesus' puzzling statement did not necessarily imply that some standing before Him would not die.

[A] 8:3 Or *fasting* [B] 8:10 Probably on the western shore of the Sea of Galilee [C] 8:18 Jr 5:21; Ezk 12:2 [D] 8:26 Other mss add *or tell anyone in the village*

Predictions of Death and Defining of Discipleship (8:31–10:52)

Prediction of Jesus' Death and Resurrection (8:31-33)

31 Then He began to teach them
that the •Son of Man must suffer
many things and be rejected by the
elders, the •chief priests, and the
•scribes, be killed, and rise after
three days. 32 He was openly talking
about this. So Peter took Him aside
and began to rebuke Him.

33 But turning around and looking
at His disciples, He rebuked Peter
and said, "Get behind Me, Satan,
because you're not thinking about
God's concerns,[A] but man's!"

Taking Up Your Cross (8:34–9:1)

34 Summoning the crowd along
with His disciples, He said to them,
"If anyone wants to be My follower,
he must deny himself, take up his
cross, and follow Me. 35 For whoever
wants to save his •life will lose it,
but whoever loses his life because
of Me and the gospel will save it.
36 For what does it benefit a man to
gain the whole world yet lose his
life? 37 What can a man give in exchange for his life? 38 For whoever
is ashamed of Me and of My words
in this adulterous and sinful generation, the Son of Man will also be
ashamed of him when He comes in
the glory of His Father with the holy
angels."

9 Then He said to them, "•I assure
you: There are some standing
here who will not taste death until
they see the kingdom of God come
in power."

The Transfiguration (9:2-13)

2 After six days Jesus took Peter,
James, and John and led them up
on a high mountain by themselves
to be alone. He was transformed[B] in
front of them, 3 and His clothes became dazzling—extremely white as
no launderer on earth could whiten
them. 4 Elijah appeared to them with
Moses, and they were talking with
Jesus.

5 Then Peter said to Jesus, "•Rabbi,
it's good for us to be here! Let us
make three •tabernacles: one for
You, one for Moses, and one for Elijah"— 6 because he did not know
what he should say, since they were
terrified.

7 A cloud appeared, overshadowing them, and a voice came from the
cloud:

> This is My beloved Son;
> listen to Him!

8 Then suddenly, looking around,
they no longer saw anyone with
them except Jesus alone.

9 As they were coming down from
the mountain, He ordered them to
tell no one what they had seen until
the •Son of Man had risen from the
dead. 10 They kept this word to themselves, discussing what "rising from
the dead" meant.

11 Then they began to question
Him, "Why do the •scribes say that
Elijah must come first?"

12 "Elijah does come first and restores everything," He replied. "How
then is it written about the Son of
Man that He must suffer many
things and be treated with contempt? 13 But I tell you that Elijah
really has come, and they did whatever they pleased to him, just as it is
written about him."

The Power of Faith over a Demon (9:14-29)

14 When they came to the disciples,
they saw a large crowd around them
and scribes disputing with them.
15 All of a sudden, when the whole
crowd saw Him, they were amazed[C]
and ran to greet Him. 16 Then He
asked them, "What are you arguing
with them about?"

17 Out of the crowd, one man answered Him, "Teacher, I brought
my son to You. He has a spirit that
makes him unable to speak. 18 Wherever it seizes him, it throws him
down, and he foams at the mouth,
grinds his teeth, and becomes rigid.
So I asked Your disciples to drive it
out, but they couldn't."

19 He replied to them, "You unbelieving generation! How long will I
be with you? How long must I put
up with you? Bring him to Me." 20 So
they brought him to Him. When
the spirit saw Him, it immediately

Rather, He was saying that some, but not all, standing there would witness the transfiguration. More than anything these words offered encouragement and anticipation for the coming kingdom (v. 1).

Peter's suggestion of erecting tabernacles would not only indicate that Elijah and Moses were of the same importance as Jesus but also would have diverted Jesus from the cross in the process (v. 5). The transfiguration (Gk *metemorphōthē*, "changed in form") was an actual event that showed Christ's glory. Truths were illuminated through this extraordinary event:

- Jesus was the fulfillment of the Law (represented by Moses) and of the prophets (represented by Elijah);
- Jesus prefigured the glory that would be His at the time of His return;
- All believers were represented (Moses represented those who had died and been buried, Dt 34:5-6; Elijah was translated without dying and represented those who remain alive at the time of Christ's return, 2Kg 2:11);
- This event demonstrated beyond doubt that Jesus was more than He appeared to be (i.e., God in human flesh).
- The transfiguration was also meant for the spiritual training of those who were with Him. Jesus' words, **Elijah really has come** (v. 13) referred to John the Baptist who "will go before Him in the spirit and power of Elijah" (Lk 1:17), thus fulfilling the prophecy of the forerunner who was to prepare the way for Messiah (See Is 40:3; Mal 3:1-2; 4:5).

9:14-32 Mark told the story of the demon-possessed boy with urgency, dramatic detail, and intense emotion. Only Mark recorded Jesus' question to the father (v. 21). And only Mark recorded the father's desperate plea: **I do believe! Help my unbelief** (v. 24). This plea for help demonstrated what the disciples needed to do in order to cast out the demon in the first place: they needed to seek God in prayer and ask for help as a true disciple would do. Perhaps the disciples had begun to believe that the power to cast out demons was their own, or perhaps they assumed that they controlled the power and thus determined when it would be used. The disciples had had success in casting out demons (6:13). Jesus gave an instructive reply, reminding the disciples of the real source of power, which is available to all believers through prayer.

[A] **8:33** Lit *about the things of God* [B] **9:2** Or *transfigured* [C] **9:15** Or *surprised*

9:33-37 Jesus called out the most humble, helpless, vulnerable, and seemingly insignificant one in the kingdom—a young **child**—to illustrate the demeanor demanded in discipleship and to provide an opportunity for Jesus to affirm His love for and recognition of the value of children (v. 37). Jesus made clear again that greatness in His kingdom was not determined by position or possessions but by having a servant's heart and humble spirit.

9:38-41 Jesus by no means erased the exclusivity of the gospel. There is only one way for salvation (Rm 10:9,13). However, within the body of believers should be an inclusive spirit of love—not to violate one's conscience by supporting what you believe to be contrary to Scripture (Ac 5:29) but by being loving and kind in the way you interact with those whose approach is different than your own. Two cannot walk together unless they have agreed on the non-negotiables, the great doctrines of faith, but there is a place for diversity of methodology. He may have been warning the Twelve that they were not His only disciples. Others had committed themselves to follow Christ and to do His work.

9:42-48 Jesus stressed that the destructive nature of evil demanded a radical offensive action. He was certainly not calling for mutilation of the body; rather, He was emphasizing the necessity of avoiding eternal punishment or jeopardizing one's right standing with God whatever the cost.

9:49-50 Verse 49 must be connected to verse 43. Therefore, Jesus was affirming the eternal fire awaiting unbelievers in the day of punishment. Since the disciples had already been told that they were the "salt of the earth" (Mt 5:13) to preserve against decay and to season the world with Christlike character, the mention of **salt** here was meant to illustrate a vivid contrast. The tragedy of the lack of salt would become readily apparent. Here it represented purification. Jesus admonished His followers to prevent decay and to preserve life.

10:1-12 In their interchange with Jesus, the Pharisees were not interested in answers to difficult questions; they wanted only to entrap Jesus (v. 2, **to test Him**). Perhaps they remembered that Herod Antipas had murdered John the Baptist because of John's condemnation of Herod's marriage to Herodias and thought Herod would get rid of Jesus for the same reason. **Divorce** remains a challenging issue to consider. The Jews generally were one-minded in allowing divorce, but they differed on the acceptable grounds for divorce. The religious leaders

>WORD|*study*

9:29 Fasting (Gk *nēsteia*, "going without food"), although not included in all early manuscripts, is a natural response when one's entire focus of body and mind turned to God. Prayer and fasting often go hand in hand because in praying with your heart and mind fixed upon God, the mundane needs of the body are overshadowed with the urgency of the spiritual battle before you. Fasting for the Jews was observed for different reasons:

- As part of observing the Day of Atonement (Lv 23:27-32);
- As a sign of mourning (1Sm 31:13; Est 4:1-3);
- As personal or corporate repentance (1Sm 7:6; Dn 9:3-19);
- As a way of calling out to God during suffering or sickness (2Sm 12:16-23);
- As part of important decision-making (2Ch 20:1-18; Est 4:16).

Fasting was never meant to be a perfunctory ritual to attract the attention of others but rather a very private and personal means of drawing a believer closer to God.

convulsed the boy. He fell to the
ground and rolled around, foam-
ing at the mouth. 21 "How long has
this been happening to him?" Jesus
asked his father.
"From childhood," he said. 22 "And
many times it has thrown him into
fire or water to destroy him. But if
You can do anything, have compassion on us and help us."
23 Then Jesus said to him, "'If You
can'?[A,B] Everything is possible to the
one who believes."
24 Immediately the father of the
boy cried out, "I do believe! Help my
unbelief."
25 When Jesus saw that a crowd
was rapidly coming together, He
rebuked the •unclean spirit, saying
to it, "You mute and deaf spirit,[C] I
command you: come out of him and
never enter him again!"
26 Then it came out, shrieking and
convulsing him[D] violently. The boy
became like a corpse, so that many
said, "He's dead." 27 But Jesus, taking
him by the hand, raised him, and he
stood up.
28 After He went into a house, His
disciples asked Him privately, "Why
couldn't we drive it out?"
29 And He told them, "This kind
can come out by nothing but prayer
[and fasting]."[E]

The Second Prediction of Jesus' Death (9:30-32)

30 Then they left that place and
made their way through Galilee, but
He did not want anyone to know it.
31 For He was teaching His disciples
and telling them, "The Son of Man
is being betrayed[F] into the hands of
men. They will kill Him, and after
He is killed, He will rise three days
later." 32 But they did not understand
this statement, and they were afraid
to ask Him.

The Essence of Greatness (9:33-37)

33 Then they came to Capernaum.
When He was in the house, He
asked them, "What were you arguing about on the way?" 34 But they
were silent, because on the way they
had been arguing with one another
about who was the greatest. 35 Sitting down, He called the Twelve and
said to them, "If anyone wants to be
first, he must be last of all and servant of all." 36 Then He took a child,
had him stand among them, and
taking him in His arms, He said to
them, 37 "Whoever welcomes[G] one
little child such as this in My name
welcomes Me. And whoever welcomes Me does not welcome Me, but
Him who sent Me."

Driving out Demons (9:38-41)

38 John said to Him, "Teacher, we
saw someone[H] driving out demons
in Your name, and we tried to stop
him because he wasn't following
us."
39 "Don't stop him," said Jesus,
"because there is no one who will
perform a miracle in My name who
can soon afterward speak evil of Me.
40 For whoever is not against us is for
us. 41 And whoever gives you a cup of

A9:23 Other mss add *believe* B9:23 Jesus appears to quote the father's words in v. 22 and then comment on them. C9:25 A spirit that caused the boy to be deaf and unable to speak D9:26 Other mss omit *him* E9:29 Other mss omit bracketed text F9:31 Or *handed over* G9:37 Or *Whoever receives* H9:38 Other mss add *who didn't go along with us*

>WORD|*study*

9:42-48 Hell (Gk *geennan*) is derived from the Valley of Hinnom (Hb *geʾhinnom*), which lies southwest of what is known as the Old City of Jerusalem. During the monarchy, occult practices—even cremation of babies as sacrifices to pagan gods like Baal and Molech (2Kg 23:10; Jr 7:31-32; 32:35)—were followed here by apostatizing Jews. In later years the place became a trash dump and was known as the place of destruction by fire, Gehenna (Jr 31:40). The place continued as a dumping ground for garbage and sewage during the intertestamental time. This metaphor was Jesus' most effective description to warn His hearers that the torments of hell are real and eternal and thus should be avoided at all cost.

water to drink because of My name,[A] since you belong to the •Messiah—I assure you: He will never lose his reward.

Warnings from Jesus (9:42-50)

42 "But whoever •causes the downfall of one of these little ones who believe in Me—it would be better for him if a heavy millstone[B] were hung around his neck and he were thrown into the sea.
43 And if your hand causes your downfall, cut it off. It is better for you to enter life maimed than to have two hands and go to •hell—the unquenchable fire, [
44 where

> **Their worm does not die,**
> **and the fire is**
> **not quenched.**][C,D]

45 And if your foot causes your downfall, cut it off. It is better for you to enter life lame than to have two feet and be thrown into hell— [the unquenchable fire,
46 where

> **Their worm does not die,**
> **and the fire is**
> **not quenched.**][C,D]

47 And if your eye causes your downfall, gouge it out. It is better for you to enter the kingdom of God with one eye than to have two eyes and be thrown into hell,
48 where

> **Their worm does not die,**
> **and the fire is not quenched.**[D]

49 For everyone will be salted with fire.[E,F]
50 Salt is good, but if the salt should lose its flavor, how can you make it salty? Have salt among yourselves and be at peace with one another."

The Question of Divorce (10:1-12)

10 He set out from there and went to the region of Judea and across the Jordan. Then crowds converged on Him again and, as He usually did, He began teaching them once more.
2 Some •Pharisees approached Him to test Him. They asked, "Is it lawful for a man to divorce his wife?"

[A]**9:41** Lit *drink in the name* [B]**9:42** A millstone turned by a donkey [C]**9:44,46** Other mss omit bracketed text [D]**9:44,46,48** Is 66:24 [E]**9:49** Other mss add *and every sacrifice will be salted with salt* [F]**9:49** Lv 2:13; Ezk 43:24

themselves were divided into two camps and could not agree:

- Shammai and his followers interpreted "something improper" (Dt 24:1) more strictly as being immorality, such as adultery.
- Hillel and his followers believed that anything the husband found distasteful in his wife fell in this category.

Jesus' response was a classic rebuke in which He cut to the heart of the issue by answering their question with one of His own. Again the Pharisees were willing to disregard the intent of the law (see 2:23–3:6; 7:1-23). God established the first union between one man and one woman as a permanent covenant commitment. Jesus knew the religious leaders would appeal to Moses, and He did not question or throw out the law in His answer. However, He noted that Moses' permission to divorce (10:4) was accommodating human weakness (v. 5). Jesus not only returned to the creation account and God's first unveiling of His plan for marriage, but He also noted that divorce was a concession to human stubbornness—**hardness of your hearts**. There is forever a tension in the Creator God's perfect will and the actions of His sinful creation.

Jesus also leveled the ground between husband and wife in the arena of marital commitment (vv. 10-12). Jesus again went beyond the Jewish religious leaders because He acknowledged that for a man to commit infidelity against his wife made him an adulterer as well. The moral obligation within the marriage covenant in the teachings of Jesus was the same for husband and wife. Jesus even recognized the right of a wife to divorce her husband, which had not been allowed in Judaism.

Jesus not only went to the heart of the problem—human rebellion was shifting the focus from divine plans—

Biblical Womanhood Christlike Service

In another lesson on discipleship, Jesus discussed the meaning of true greatness, which was never the advancing of oneself but rather the pouring out of one's life in service to others (9:33-34). Although contemporary cultures applaud people who sacrifice themselves on behalf of others—including mothers who invest their lives in serving their families and communities—in daily life the pressure is to pursue what builds your self-esteem and gains the recognition of others. Followers of Jesus do well to discern and establish in their thought life the criterion of Jesus' teaching and example. When the goal of looking your best becomes a pursuit of being *the* best-looking woman in the room, recall the way Jesus focused on the needs of others without losing His identity. Instead of entertaining even a twinge of resentment and jealousy within your heart when another woman seems to enjoy what your heart desires or receives recognition while your efforts remain unnoticed or unappreciated, consider how you can demonstrate Christ's selfless love toward someone in need. Wives can take particular delight in appropriately serving their husbands and families, and single women desiring to be married can find joy in practicing Christlike service. As Jesus' earthly ministry demonstrates, such servanthood always involves concrete actions on behalf of people with needs.

but He also lifted the discussion beyond Mosaic law to God's original plan at creation. God intended for one man and one woman to become inseparably one being, mirroring the unity within the Godhead (Gn 1:27). Indeed, Jesus condemned all divorce, whether by husband or wife, as being contrary to His plan.

10:13-16 Jesus emphasized the importance of childlike faith, in which dependence upon the Lord was mandated over self-reliant trust in one's personal strength and ability. Jesus also clearly embraced the children with loving affection. He underlined the sanctity of each life as precious and valuable.

10:17-31 Jesus loved the wealthy young man and revealed to him the weaknesses in his spiritual understanding. Jesus looked into the heart of this confident young man; He knew the self-reliant young man was putting his possessions in first place in his life. To put Christ first in his life, the man must first get rid of the things that commanded his greatest devotion and upon which he depended for security. Jesus illustrated the truth through irony and hyperbole (v. 25). The warning was serious, but it was presented in a humorous way.

The disciples were truly puzzled since the Jews placed great emphasis on wealth as a divine blessing. On the other hand, Jesus saw wealth as a diversion of trust from God to self. The final word affirms again that salvation is totally the work of God, and no one can achieve entrance to the kingdom with his own efforts. Jesus never tried to whitewash the Christian life, but He promised believers:

- They would receive more than they gave up (vv. 29-30).
- They would experience difficulties and **persecutions** (v. 30).
- They would have **eternal life** (v. 30).
- They would see some surprising reversals (v. 31).

10:32-34 Jesus then gave His third prediction of His own passion, offering more details of what He would experience as He and His disciples walked to Jerusalem: betrayal, sentence of death; delivery to Gentiles; being mocked, **spit** upon, flogged, executed, and resurrected.

10:35-45 Jesus presented a second lesson on greatness (see 9:33-37), which was also a third lesson on discipleship. Rather than focusing on position and prominence for yourself, Jesus defined another paradox, reversing human reasoning and defining greatness as serving others.

The death of Christ is the redemption of one who trusts in Christ

3 He replied to them, "What did Moses command you?"

4 They said, "Moses permitted us to write divorce papers and send her away."

5 But Jesus told them, "He wrote this command for you because of the hardness of your hearts. 6 But from the beginning of creation God[A] **made them male and female.**[B]

7 **For this reason a man**
will leave
his father and mother
[and be joined to his wife],[C]
8 **and the two will become**
one flesh.[D]

So they are no longer two, but one flesh. 9 Therefore what God has joined together, man must not separate."

10 Now in the house the disciples questioned Him again about this matter. 11 And He said to them, "Whoever divorces his wife and marries another commits adultery against her. 12 Also, if she divorces her husband and marries another, she commits adultery."

Blessing the Children (10:13-16)

13 Some people were bringing little children to Him so He might touch them, but His disciples rebuked them. 14 When Jesus saw it, He was indignant and said to them, "Let the little children come to Me. Don't stop them, for the kingdom of God belongs to such as these. 15 •I assure you: Whoever does not welcome[E] the kingdom of God like a little child will never enter it." 16 After taking them in His arms, He laid His hands on them and blessed them.

The Rich Young Ruler (10:17-22)

17 As He was setting out on a journey, a man ran up, knelt down before Him, and asked Him, "Good Teacher, what must I do to inherit eternal life?"

18 "Why do you call Me good?" Jesus asked him. "No one is good but One—God. 19 You know the commandments:

Do not murder;
do not commit adultery;
do not steal;
do not bear false witness;
do not defraud;
honor your father
and mother."[F]

20 He said to Him, "Teacher, I have kept all these from my youth."

21 Then, looking at him, Jesus loved him and said to him, "You lack one thing: Go, sell all you have and give to the poor, and you will have treasure in heaven. Then come,[G] follow Me." 22 But he was stunned[H] at this demand, and he went away grieving, because he had many possessions.

Possessions and the Kingdom (10:23-31)

23 Jesus looked around and said to His disciples, "How hard it is for those who have wealth to enter the kingdom of God!" 24 But the disciples were astonished at His words. Again Jesus said to them, "Children, how hard it is[I] to enter the kingdom of God! 25 It is easier for a camel to go through the eye of a needle than for a rich person to enter the kingdom of God."

26 So they were even more astonished, saying to one another, "Then who can be saved?"

27 Looking at them, Jesus said, "With men it is impossible, but not with God, because all things are possible with God."

28 Peter began to tell Him, "Look, we have left everything and followed You."

29 "I assure you," Jesus said, "there is no one who has left house, brothers or sisters, mother or father,[J] children, or fields because of Me and the gospel, 30 who will not receive 100 times more, now at this time—houses, brothers and sisters, mothers and children, and fields, with persecutions—and eternal life in the age to come. 31 But many who are first will be last, and the last first."

The Third Prediction of Jesus' Death (10:32-34)

32 They were on the road, going up

[A]10:6 Other mss omit *God* [B]10:6 Gn 1:27; 5:2 [C]10:7 Other mss omit bracketed text [D]10:7-8 Gn 2:24 [E]10:15 Or *not receive* [F]10:19 Ex 20:12-16; Dt 5:16-20 [G]10:21 Other mss add *taking up the cross, and* [H]10:22 Or *he became gloomy* [I]10:24 Other mss add *for those trusting in wealth* [J]10:29 Other mss add *or wife*

>WORD|*study*

10:43-45 Jesus clearly said that one who would be great in His kingdom would be a servant (Gk *diakonos*, "one who executes the commands of another," cp. 9:45) and a slave (Gk *doulos*, metaphorically "one who gives himself up wholly to another's will")—not just to Jesus Himself but **to all**. Jesus Himself would lay down His life as a ransom (Gk *lutron*, "price paid for release, means for redeeming") or what is paid to free someone from bondage.

to Jerusalem, and Jesus was walking ahead of them. They were astonished, but those who followed Him were afraid. Taking the Twelve aside again, He began to tell them the things that would happen to Him.

33 "Listen! We are going up to Jerusalem. The •Son of Man will be handed over to the •chief priests and the •scribes, and they will condemn Him to death. Then they will hand Him over to the Gentiles, 34 and they will mock Him, spit on Him, flog[A] Him, and kill Him, and He will rise after three days."

Suffering and Service (10:35-45)

35 Then James and John, the sons of Zebedee, approached Him and said, "Teacher, we want You to do something for us if we ask You."

36 "What do you want Me to do for you?" He asked them.

37 They answered Him, "Allow us to sit at Your right and at Your left in Your glory."

38 But Jesus said to them, "You don't know what you're asking. Are you able to drink the cup I drink or to be baptized with the baptism I am baptized with?"

39 "We are able," they told Him.

Jesus said to them, "You will drink the cup I drink, and you will be baptized with the baptism I am baptized with. 40 But to sit at My right or left is not Mine to give; instead, it is for those it has been prepared for." 41 When the other 10 disciples heard this, they began to be indignant with James and John.

42 Jesus called them over and said to them, "You know that those who are regarded as rulers of the Gentiles dominate them, and their men of high positions exercise power over them. 43 But it must not be like that among you. On the contrary, whoever wants to become great among you must be your servant, 44 and whoever wants to be first among you must be a •slave to all. 45 For even the Son of Man did not come to be served, but to serve, and to give His life—a ransom for many."[B]

A Blind Man Healed (10:46-52)

46 They came to Jericho. And as He was leaving Jericho with His disciples and a large crowd, Bartimaeus (the son of Timaeus), a blind beggar, was sitting by the road. 47 When he heard that it was Jesus the •Nazarene, he began to cry out, "Son of David, Jesus, have mercy on me!" 48 Many people told him to keep quiet, but he was crying out all the more, "Have mercy on me, Son of David!"

49 Jesus stopped and said, "Call him."

So they called the blind man and said to him, "Have courage! Get up; He's calling for you." 50 He threw off his coat, jumped up, and came to Jesus.

51 Then Jesus answered him, "What do you want Me to do for you?"

"Rabbouni,"[C] the blind man told Him, "I want to see!"

52 "Go your way," Jesus told him. "Your faith has healed you." Immediately he could see and began to follow Him on the road.

Jesus' Teachings at the Temple (11:1–13:37)

The Triumphal Entry (11:1-11)

11 When they approached Jerusalem, at Bethphage and Bethany near the •Mount of Olives, He sent two of His disciples 2 and told them, "Go into the village ahead of you. As soon as you enter it, you will find a young donkey tied there, on which no one has ever sat. Untie it and bring it here. 3 If anyone says to you, 'Why are you doing this?' say, 'The

[A] **10:34** Or *scourge* [B] **10:45** Or *in the place of many*; Is 53:10-12 [C] **10:51** Hb word for *my teacher*

and seeks forgiveness of sin (see Rm 6:20-23; Heb 2:14-18; 1Pt 1:18-19). Also significant is the allusion to the substitutionary nature of His atonement in the phrase **for many** (Gk *antipollōn*, "in the place of, instead of many").

Mark also uniquely paralleled the request of James and John (vv. 35-45) with their discussion on who would be the greatest (9:30-37). Both discussions defined true greatness, and both followed a prediction of Jesus' passion. Both accounts revealed just how spiritually blind the disciples were at times.

10:46-52 The accounts of Matthew and Mark were often parallel on this part of Jesus' Judean ministry. In Matthew there were two blind men in Jericho begging for healing (Mt 20:29-34). There was no contradiction when Mark focused his discussion on one of the blind men evidently for reasons specific to his purpose. Matthew recorded that Jesus and the disciples met these blind men "as they were leaving Jericho" (Mt 20:29); Mark noted that they met the men as **they came to Jericho**. In Jesus' day there was a Jericho dating back to the Old Testament era and another Jericho that thrived in the New Testament period. The old Jericho was largely abandoned, but the new one was larger and much more populated. Even now one can visit both of these archaeological sites, which are close together but not identical. The healings may have taken place somewhere between these locations of Jericho.

Mark names one of the blind men—**Bartimaeus**—and describes the details surrounding this event (vv. 49-50). Bartimaeus referred to Jesus as the **Son of David**, a messianic title that appears only twice in Mark's Gospel (see 12:35, in which Jesus uses this title to describe Himself). The fact that Jesus did not silence Bartimaeus indicates that He accepted the title.

When Jesus was near Jerusalem and the fulfillment of His mission, keeping His identity secret was no longer necessary. The opening of the blind man's eyes stands in contrast to the blindness of the religious leaders with whom Jesus was about to engage in Jerusalem.

11:1-11 Bethphage (Aram, "house of unripe figs," v. 1) must have been close to Jerusalem, but its location is not noted on maps. **Bethany** was only two miles east of Jerusalem and seemed a popular stop for Jesus as He often stayed in the home of His friends Lazarus, Mary, and Martha (v. 1; Mt. 21:17; Jn 12:1).

With regard to the importance of the triumphal entry, the unique way in which Jesus entered the city combined hints of His messiahship as the Son of David. Moreover, He was the fulfillment of prophecy, and He brought deliverance, although not in the political ways the people envisioned. This entry was humble and lowly as prophesied (Zch 9:9) and stands in contrast to His victorious return to usher in His kingdom (Rv 19:11).

11:12-14 The nation of Israel and her hypocritical religious leaders were represented by the barren **fig tree**, which looked good on the outside but bore no fruit. Jesus cursed the tree, and it "withered from the roots up," prefiguring God's judgment on Israel (v. 21). Some question Jesus' response because of Mark's interjection concerning the season for harvesting fruit. One does well to remember that such a statement could merely serve as a device to alert the reader to consider the lesson in the event.

11:15-19 Particularly during Passover week, the temple was taken over by the charlatan money-makers who found their profit in dishonest practices—and all in the name of religion. They charged inflated prices for sacrificial animals, excluding the participation of poor people in offering sacrifices.

The priests had allowed politics to enter the spiritual realm. The chief priests had been descendants of Zadok (see 1Ch 24) from the days of Solomon until the time of Antiochus IV. From that time onward each conquering ruler selected the high priest. Officers of the temple then came from the wealthy and influential families of Jewish society.

11:23-26 Jesus used the hyperbole—a figure of speech that makes a point through exaggeration—of being able to throw a mountain into the sea to emphasize that God is able to do anything. Yet faith includes an element of submission to the Father and to His will. To pray believing includes submitting yourself to accept whatever God wills when you pray.

As far as your posture when praying, the text does not mandate standing since in Scripture both standing and kneeling are mentioned as acceptable positions for praying. More important is the relationship between prayer and forgiveness. Nothing negates prayer as much as an unforgiving heart (see Mt 6:13-14; 7:7; 17:20; 18:19; Lk 11:9; 17:6). This forgiveness is certainly not to be interpreted as questioning the security of the salvation of one who has been redeemed, which offers absolute assurance of one's position in Christ for all eternity. On the other hand, your fellowship with other believers and with the Father is dependent upon your having a heart pure before Him. If you harbor an unforgiving spirit toward your brother or sister in the Lord, you are impeding your fellowship with the Father as well. Your position in Christ

>WORD|*study*

11:9-10 *Hosanna* (Hb, "save now") was first used to call for God's power to save, but by this time the word had become a joyous shout of praise or call for victory.

Lord needs it and will send it back here right away.'"

4 So they went and found a young donkey outside in the street, tied by a door. They untied it, 5 and some of those standing there said to them, "What are you doing, untying the donkey?" 6 They answered them just as Jesus had said, so they let them go. 7 Then they brought the donkey to Jesus and threw their robes on it, and He sat on it.

8 Many people spread their robes on the road, and others spread leafy branches cut from the fields.[A] 9 Then those who went ahead and those who followed kept shouting:

•Hosanna!
He who comes in the name
of the Lord is
the blessed One![B]
10 The coming kingdom
of our father David is blessed!
Hosanna
in the highest heaven!

11 And He went into Jerusalem and into the •temple complex. After looking around at everything, since it was already late, He went out to Bethany with the Twelve.

Cursing the Barren Fig Tree (11:12-14)

12 The next day when they came out from Bethany, He was hungry. 13 After seeing in the distance a fig tree with leaves, He went to find out if there was anything on it. When He came to it, He found nothing but leaves, because it was not the season for figs. 14 He said to it, "May no one ever eat fruit from you again!" And His disciples heard it.

Cleansing the Temple Complex (11:15-19)

15 They came to Jerusalem, and He went into the temple complex and began to throw out those buying and selling in the temple. He overturned the money changers' tables and the chairs of those selling doves, 16 and would not permit anyone to carry goods through the temple complex.

17 Then He began to teach them: "Is it not written, **My house will be called a house of prayer for all nations**?[C] But you have made it **a den of thieves**!"[D] 18 Then the •chief priests and the •scribes heard it and started looking for a way to destroy Him. For they were afraid of Him, because the whole crowd was astonished by His teaching.

19 And whenever evening came, they would go out of the city.

Withering the Barren Fig Tree (11:20-26)

20 Early in the morning, as they were passing by, they saw the fig tree withered from the roots up. 21 Then Peter remembered and said to Him, "•Rabbi, look! The fig tree that You cursed is withered."

22 Jesus replied to them, "Have faith in God. 23 •I assure you: If anyone says to this mountain, 'Be lifted up and thrown into the sea,' and does not doubt in his heart, but believes that what he says will happen, it will be done for him. 24 Therefore I tell you, all the things you pray and ask for—believe that you have received[E] them, and you will have them. 25 And whenever you stand praying, if you have anything against anyone, forgive him, so that your Father in heaven will also forgive you your wrongdoing. [26 But if you don't forgive, neither will your Father in heaven forgive your wrongdoing.]"[F,G]

[A]**11:8** Other mss read *others were cutting leafy branches from the trees and spreading them on the road* [B]**11:9** Ps 118:26 [C]**11:17** Is 56:7 [D]**11:17** Jr 7:11 [E]**11:24** Some mss read *you receive*; other mss read *you will receive* [F]**11:26** Other mss omit bracketed text [G]**11:25-26** These are the only uses of this word in Mk. It means "the violation of the Law" or "stepping over a boundary" or "departing from the path" or "trespass."

Messiah's Authority Challenged (11:27-33)

27 They came again to Jerusalem.
As He was walking in the temple
complex, the chief priests, the
scribes, and the elders came 28 and
asked Him, “By what authority
are You doing these things? Who
gave You this authority to do these
things?”
29 Jesus said to them, “I will ask
you one question; then answer Me,
and I will tell you by what authority I am doing these things. 30 Was
John's baptism from heaven or from
men? Answer Me.”
31 They began to argue among
themselves: “If we say, ‘From heav-
en,’ He will say, ‘Then why didn't
you believe him?’ 32 But if we say,
‘From men’”—they were afraid
of the crowd, because everyone
thought that John was a genuine
prophet. 33 So they answered Jesus,
“We don't know.”
And Jesus said to them, “Neither
will I tell you by what authority I do
these things.”

The Parable of the Vineyard Owner (12:1-12)

12 Then He began to speak to
them in parables: “A man
planted a vineyard, put a fence
around it, dug out a pit for a winepress, and built a watchtower. Then
he leased it to tenant farmers and
went away. 2 At harvest time he sent
a •slave to the farmers to collect
some of the fruit of the vineyard
from the farmers. 3 But they took
him, beat him, and sent him away
empty-handed. 4 Again he sent another slave to them, and they[A] hit
him on the head and treated him
shamefully.[B] 5 Then he sent another,
and they killed that one. He also
sent many others; they beat some
and they killed some.
6 “He still had one to send, a beloved son. Finally he sent him to
them, saying, ‘They will respect my
son.’
7 “But those tenant farmers said
among themselves, ‘This is the heir.
Come, let's kill him, and the inheritance will be ours!’ 8 So they seized
him, killed him, and threw him out
of the vineyard.
9 “Therefore, what will the owner[C]
of the vineyard do? He will come
and destroy the farmers and give the
vineyard to others. 10 Haven't you
read this Scripture:

The stone that
the builders rejected
has become the cornerstone.[D]
11 **This came from the Lord**
and is wonderful in
our eyes?”[E]

12 Because they knew He had said
this parable against them, they were
looking for a way to arrest Him, but
they were afraid of the crowd. So
they left Him and went away.

God and Caesar (12:13-17)

13 Then they sent some of the
•Pharisees and the •Herodians to
Him to trap Him by what He said.[F]
14 When they came, they said to Him,
“Teacher, we know You are truthful
and defer to no one, for You don't
show partiality[G] but teach truthfully
the way of God. Is it lawful to pay
taxes to Caesar or not? 15 Should we
pay, or should we not pay?”
But knowing their hypocrisy, He
said to them, “Why are you testing
Me? Bring Me a •denarius to look
at.” 16 So they brought one. “Whose
image and inscription is this?” He
asked them.
“Caesar's,” they said.
17 Then Jesus told them, “Give
back to Caesar the things that are
Caesar's, and to God the things that
are God's.” And they were amazed at
Him.

The Sadducees and the Resurrection (12:18-27)

18 Some •Sadducees, who say there
is no resurrection, came to Him
and questioned Him: 19 “Teacher,
Moses wrote for us that **if a man's**
brother dies, leaves his wife behind,
and **leaves no child, his brother**
should take the wife and produce
•offspring for his brother.[H] 20 There
were seven brothers. The first took

[A]12:4 Other mss add *threw stones and* [B]12:4 Other mss add *and sent him off* [C]12:9 Or *lord* [D]12:10 Lit *the head of the corner* [E]12:10-11 Ps 118:22-23 [F]12:13 Lit *trap Him in (a) word* [G]12:14 Lit *don't look on the face of men*; that is, on the outward appearance [H]12:19 Gn 38:8; Dt 25:5

is secure, but your separation from the delights of fellowship with Him is not to be taken lightly.

11:27–12:44 With respect to these teachings and debates, Matthew and Mark contain similar accounts of this section (see Mt 21:23–22:46 on Christ's interchange with the religious leaders), except that Matthew recorded the parable of the wedding banquet not found in Mark's Gospel (Mt 22:1-14). However, Matthew omitted the story about the widow's coins found in Mark (Mk 12:41-44).

12:1-12 Jesus used this parable to expose the plot on His life and the coming divine judgment on all who rejected Him. The **man** represented God; the **tenant farmers** represented Israel; the **slave**[s] represented the prophets; the **beloved son** represented Jesus. Clearly this parable seemed to be directed against the religious leaders who opposed Jesus' ministry from its inception. The Messianic implications were there. Jesus was understood to be the son in the parable. He applied the quotation from Ps 118:22-23 to Himself (Mk 12:10-11). He presented His coming rejection by the people themselves and His death at their hands.

12:13-17 The **Herodians** (identified as men who supported Herod) and the **Pharisees** were not usually united, but here they joined forces in an attempt to **trap** (Gk *agreusōsin*, "catch off guard"), a word implying deceit, often used to describe catching an animal in a trap. Again Jesus was in conflict with the religious leaders. Using flattery, they addressed an issue that did seem to present an impossible dilemma for Jesus. If He instructed the people to pay taxes they thought unfair, they would undoubtedly turn on Him; if He suggested anarchy against the Roman government, He would be arrested. The Herodians paid taxes willingly to gain favor with government leaders, but the Pharisees did so only grudgingly. Jesus acknowledged the responsibility of the people and their spiritual leaders to their government, but He did not fail to affirm that any obligation due the state was less important than their foremost responsibility to God.

12:18-27 The **Sadducees**, mentioned only here in Mark's Gospel, did not believe in the **resurrection**. Some historians have claimed that they accepted only the Pentateuch as Scripture, but all are agreed that they did not accept the oral tradition of the scribes and Pharisees. The Sadducees tried to entrap Jesus with a question about the resurrection. Jesus responded with a counter-question showing their lack of understanding of the Scripture and ignorance concerning **the power of God**. The question alluded to the

Jewish law of levirate marriage in which a wife whose husband died without a male heir would marry her husband's brother in order to produce an heir and preserve her deceased husband's name and property. Jesus corrected the Sadducees on their misunderstanding of the resurrection, affirming that there would be no marriage in heaven, which made their question moot.

12:28-34 When one of the scribes asked Jesus, **"Which command is the most important of all?"** Jesus answered him directly, quoting from Dt 6:4-5 (Mk 12:29-30) and Lv 19:18 (Mk 12:31). This Jewish confession of faith, known as the *Shema* (Hb, *shema'*, "hear, listen"), was recited then and now by devout Jews both evening and morning. The reference to **most important** (Gk *prōtē*, "leading, foremost, first") may refer to significance more than to sequence. Jesus not only answered His critics, but He confounded them. Their response changed from one encounter to the next:

- "They left Him and went away" (v. 12);
- "They were amazed at Him" (v. 17);
- **No one dared to question Him any longer** (v. 34).

12:35-37 Jesus fulfilled all Scripture. In reversing the question and answer session, Jesus posed His own question. He understood that the question here was not concerning the validity of Scripture itself but rather an attempt to determine how Scripture should be interpreted. Even in the modern era, within the kingdom this challenge remains at the forefront. Since David was speaking of his descendant as his **Lord**, not a characteristic way for fathers to refer to their sons, he must have had in mind someone who was more than a son or descendant. Jesus did not deny His Davidic descent, but He was correcting the misunderstanding, among His followers and the people, that the Messiah was to be a liberating ruler. Jesus showed that He was more than the Son of David. As the Son of Man, Jesus represented not only the Jews but also humanity.

12:38-40 Often there is misunderstanding of the difference between clergy and laity. Here the religious leaders showed their pride and arrogance by wearing garments associated with their ecclesiastical office and by demanding and receiving a special deference from the people. They also had special seating in the synagogues and experienced prestigious expressions of honor and protocol at festive events. They forgot that they themselves were servants of God who should be seeking to honor Him and serve others in behalf of Him.

a wife, and dying, left no offspring. 21 The second also took her, and he died, leaving no offspring. And the third likewise. 22 So the seven[A] left no offspring. Last of all, the woman died too. 23 In the resurrection, when they rise,[B] whose wife will she be, since the seven had married her?"[C]

24 Jesus told them, "Are you not deceived because you don't know the Scriptures or the power of God? 25 For when they rise from the dead, they neither marry nor are given in marriage but are like angels in heaven. 26 Now concerning the dead being raised—haven't you read in the book of Moses, in the passage about the burning bush, how God spoke to him: **I am the God of Abraham and the God of Isaac and the God of Jacob**?[D] 27 He is not God of the dead but of the living. You are badly deceived."

The Primary Commandment (12:28-31)

28 One of the •scribes approached. When he heard them debating and saw that Jesus answered them well, he asked Him, "Which command is the most important of all?"[E]

29 "This is the most important,"[F] Jesus answered:

> **Listen, Israel! The Lord our God, the Lord is One.**[G] 30 **Love the Lord your God with all your heart, with all your soul, with all your mind, and with all your strength.**[H,I]

31 "The second is: **Love your neighbor as yourself.**[J] There is no other command greater than these."

The Question about Messiah (12:32-37)

32 Then the scribe said to Him, "You are right, Teacher! You have correctly said that He is One, and there is no one else except Him. 33 And to love Him with all your heart, with all your understanding,[K] and with all your strength, and to love your neighbor as yourself, is far more important than all the burnt offerings and sacrifices."

34 When Jesus saw that he answered intelligently, He said to him, "You are not far from the kingdom of God." And no one dared to question Him any longer.

35 So Jesus asked this question as He taught in the •temple complex, "How can the scribes say that the •Messiah is the Son of David? 36 David himself says by the Holy Spirit:

> **The Lord declared to**
> **my Lord,**
> **'Sit at My right hand**
> **until I put Your enemies**
> **under Your feet.'**[L]

37 David himself calls Him 'Lord'; how then can the Messiah be his Son?" And the large crowd was listening to Him with delight.

Warning Against the Scribes (12:38-40)

38 He also said in His teaching, "Beware of the scribes, who want to go around in long robes, and who want greetings in the marketplaces, 39 the front seats in the •synagogues, and the places of honor at banquets. 40 They devour widows' houses and say long prayers just for show. These will receive harsher punishment."

The Widow's Gift (12:41-44)

41 Sitting across from the temple treasury, He watched how the crowd dropped money into the treasury. Many rich people were putting in large sums. 42 And a poor widow came and dropped in two tiny coins worth very little.[M] 43 Summoning His disciples, He said to them, "•I assure you: This poor widow has put in more than all those giving to the temple treasury. 44 For they all gave out of their surplus, but she out of her poverty has put in everything she possessed—all she had to live on."

Destruction of the Temple Predicted (13:1-2)

13 As He was going out of the •temple complex, one of His disciples said to Him, "Teacher,

[A]12:22 Other mss add *had taken her and* [B]12:23 Other mss omit *when they rise* [C]12:23 Lit *the seven had her as a wife* [D]12:26 Ex 3:6,15-16 [E]12:28 Lit *Which command is first of all?* [F]12:29 Other mss add *of all the commands* [G]12:29 Or *The Lord our God is one Lord.* [H]12:30 Other mss add *This is the first commandment.* [I]12:30 Dt 6:4-5; Jos 22:5 [J]12:31 Lv 19:18 [K]12:33 Other mss add *with all your soul* [L]12:36 Ps 110:1 [M]12:42 Lit *dropped in two lepta, which is a quadrans*; the *lepton* was the smallest and least valuable Gk coin in use. The *quadrans*, 1/64 of a daily wage, was the smallest Roman coin.

CHARACTER PROFILE

The Widow Who Gave Two Coins

A Generous Giver

Her Background	She was a widow, the lowest station in the social strata of biblical times. Unless a widow received support from her family or others, she was usually destitute and powerless.
Her Story	• She was bringing her offering to the temple (12:42). • She gave two small coins of very little value, all she had. • Jesus noticed her generosity and pointed out her sacrificial offering to the disciples (12:43-44).
Life Lesson	When you give, God looks at the attitude of your heart, not the amount.

See also Luke 21:1-4.

look! What massive stones! What impressive buildings!"
2 Jesus said to him, "Do you see these great buildings? Not one stone will be left here on another that will not be thrown down!"

Signs of the End of the Age (13:3-8)

3 While He was sitting on the •Mount of Olives across from the temple complex, Peter, James, John, and Andrew asked Him privately,
4 "Tell us, when will these things happen? And what will be the sign when all these things are about to take place?"
5 Then Jesus began by telling them: "Watch out that no one deceives you.
6 Many will come in My name, saying, 'I am He,' and they will deceive many.
7 When you hear of wars and rumors of wars, don't be alarmed; these things must take place, but the end is not yet.
8 For nation will rise up against nation, and kingdom against kingdom. There will be earthquakes in various places, and famines.[A] These are the beginning of birth pains.

Prediction of Persecutions (13:9-13)

9 "But you, be on your guard! They will hand you over to sanhedrins,[B] and you will be flogged in the •synagogues. You will stand before governors and kings because of Me, as a witness to them.
10 And the good news[C] must first be proclaimed to all nations.
11 So when they arrest you and hand you over, don't worry beforehand what you will say. On the contrary, whatever is given to you in that hour—say it. For it isn't you speaking, but the Holy Spirit.
12 Then brother will betray brother to death, and a father his child. Children will rise up against parents and put them to death.
13 And you will be hated by everyone because of My name. But the one who endures to the end will be delivered.[D]

The Great Tribulation (13:14-23)

14 "When you see the **abomination that causes desolation**[E] standing where it should not" (let the reader understand[F]), "then those in Judea must flee to the mountains!
15 A man on the housetop must not come down or go in to get anything out of his house.
16 And a man in the field must not go back to get his clothes.
17 Woe to pregnant women and nursing mothers in those days!
18 Pray it[G] won't happen in winter.
19 For those will be days of tribulation, the kind that hasn't been from the beginning of the world,[H] which God created, until now and never will be again!
20 Unless the Lord limited those days, no one would survive.[I] But He

They were to be supported by the people, but they had again abused this practice for unlawful gain and at the expense of those most vulnerable among the people.

12:41-44 After Jesus' encounters with the religious leaders, He sat down in the temple court. Interestingly, He was in the court of women, a place in which both men and women could gather and also where the **treasury** was located. **A poor widow** caught His attention. She put in the box **two tiny coins** (Gk *lepta*, the smallest coin in Palestine, each valued at about one-eighth of a cent), the smallest currency in circulation among the Jews at that time. Yet her gift was genuinely sacrificial. Jesus paid attention even to the smallest details. This scene is sharply contrasted with the disciples, who, upon visiting the same temple, noticed the **impressive buildings** (13:1). The amount of a gift was not as important as the attitude of the heart (2Co 9:6-7).

13:1-37 See **Doctrine**, p. 1316.

[A] **13:8** Other mss add *and disturbances* [B] **13:9** Local Jewish courts or local councils [C] **13:10** Or *the gospel* [D] **13:13** Or *saved* [E] **13:14** Dn 9:27 [F] **13:14** These are, most likely, Mark's words to his readers. [G] **13:18** Other mss read *pray that your escape* [H] **13:19** Lit *creation* [I] **13:20** Lit *days, all flesh would not survive*

14:1-72 A series of events led to Jesus being delivered over to the Romans to be executed:

- the betrayal by Judas, one of His inner circle (vv. 10-11);
- the desertion of most of those closest to Jesus (vv. 27-31,50);
- the religious and civil trials (vv. 53-65; 15:1-5);
- His crucifixion (15:16-41).

14:1-2 None of these events took Jesus by surprise. He knew from eternity past His mission (10:45) and the ultimate victory that would be His (16:6,19-20). **The Passover** (Gk *pascha*) and **the Festival of Unleavened Bread** (Gk *ta azuma*, without yeast, with the article *ta* or "the" used to describe the feast), which was celebrated subsequent to Passover, were important to the Jews. The Passover reminded the Jews of that last night their forefathers spent in Egypt when the angel of death killed all the firstborn in Egypt but "passed over" the homes of all who displayed the blood of the slain lamb over the doorpost. All the Jewish households who were obedient and trusted God's Word were spared. The subsequent Festival lasted seven days and commemorated the exodus from Egypt (see Ex 12:1-51).

ESCHATOLOGY

Jesus' discourse on the last days, delivered on **the Mount of Olives** and known as the Olivet Discourse (v. 3), is by far the longest teaching segment in Mark's Gospel. The discourse is part of the apocalyptic (from Gk root *apokaluptō*, "reveal, disclose," and thus claiming to reveal the future) genre and is also identified as "The Little Apocalypse." In addition to the discussion of what is to come, Mark's Gospel is a testimony, including the words of Jesus Himself. Jesus encourages and exhorts His followers to prepare for His imminent return and warns them against the deceivers who would come to pull them away. This teaching leaves for the generations to come a legacy of instruction for living the Christian life with expectancy.

Jesus warned His disciples about the danger of being deceived and listed some of the signs that would indicate that judgment and His return are drawing near:

- **Many will come in My name** (i.e., false messiahs, v. 6).
- There will be **wars and rumors of wars** (vv. 7-8), with the most immediate example being the coming war with Rome, which resulted in the destruction of Jerusalem in A.D. 70, followed by a host of conflicts, until the present era.
- **Earthquakes . . . and famines** will be widespread (v. 8).
- Persecution will escalate against Jesus' disciples but will continue throughout the generations of those who honor Christ (vv. 9-13). The phrase **hand you over** (Gk *paradōsousi*) runs as a thread through verses 9-12, appearing three times in the Greek text. In verse 12 the word is translated **betray**, and the same word is used repeatedly in chapters 14 and 15 in reference to the betrayal of Jesus and His being handed over to His enemies.

The signs announcing the end of the age are confined to a remote future, but these signs began in the generation contemporaneous with Jesus. Yet the signs continued into the future and notably are not exhausted or ended in the present era, underscoring the absolute reliability of Jesus' words not only for the time in which He lived but until now and into the future.

Jesus spoke of the near future, which would be the destruction of Jerusalem and the temple in A.D. 70, and of the distant future or the "Great Tribulation." Mark's record of the teaching of Jesus' last days was also full of exhortations and imperatives concerning practical, ethical living. The discourse was not delivered merely to satisfy curiosity about the future. Rather, Jesus combined information on what was coming in the future with an exhortation to live and bear witness in a hostile world. The emphasis was on being vigilant and spiritually alert since **no one knows** the time of Jesus' return (vv. 32-33).

Jesus referred to the **abomination that causes desolation** (see vv. 14-23; cp. Dn 9:27; 11:31; 12:11; Mt 24:15) and the appearance of antichrist. The first fulfillment came in 168–167 B.C. when Antiochus Epiphanes, a Syrian ruler, erected an altar to Zeus and sacrificed a pig on it, defiling the temple altar of burnt offering. **Abomination** (Gk *bdelugma*, "something detestable, sacrilegious object," Mk 13:14) refers to anything that is repulsive to God, especially idolatrous practices and immorality (Dt 29:16-17; 1Kg 11:6-7; Ezk 8:9-18). Then a second fulfillment came with the destruction of the temple in A.D. 70, and final fulfillment will come when the antichrist desecrates the temple and breaks his covenant with Israel in the middle of the great tribulation (see Dn 9:24-27; 2Th 2:3-4; Rv 13:14-15).

Jesus clearly told His disciples that they would not know the date and time set by **the Father** (Mk 13:32-33; cp. Ac 1:7). No one but the Father **knows** the **day or hour** of Christ's return. Focus on the future could hinder the mission of Christ's followers to preach the good news. The coming of Christ described in Mk 13:24-27 is not the rapture or translation of the church (1Th 4:13-18; 1Co 15:51-58) but the return of Christ following the great tribulation (Mk 13:14-23) and inauguration of the millennial kingdom (Rv 19:11-21).

limited those days because of the elect, whom He chose.
21 "Then if anyone tells you, 'Look, here is the •Messiah! Look—there!' do not believe it! 22 For false messiahs[A] and false prophets will rise up and will perform signs and wonders to lead astray, if possible, the elect.
23 And you must watch! I have told you everything in advance.

The Coming of the Son of Man (13:24-27)

24 "But in those days, after that tribulation:

> The sun will be darkened,
> and the moon will not shed
> its light;
> 25 the stars will be falling
> from the sky,
> and the celestial powers
> will be shaken.

26 Then they will see the •Son of Man coming in clouds with great power and glory. 27 He will send out the angels and gather His elect from the four winds, from the end of the earth to the end of the sky.

The Parable of the Fig Tree (13:28-31)

28 "Learn this parable from the fig tree: As soon as its branch becomes tender and sprouts leaves, you know that summer is near. 29 In the same way, when you see these things happening, know[B] that He[C] is near—at the door! 30 •I assure you: This generation will certainly not pass away until all these things take place.
31 Heaven and earth will pass away, but My words will never pass away.

[A]13:22 Or *false christs* [B]13:29 Or *you know* [C]13:29 Or *it*; = summer

Uncertainty of the Day or Hour (13:32-37)

32 “Now concerning that day or
hour no one knows—neither the
angels in heaven nor the Son—except the Father. 33 Watch! Be alert![A]
For you don’t know when the time
is coming. 34 It is like a man on a
journey, who left his house, gave
authority to his •slaves, gave each
one his work, and commanded the
doorkeeper to be alert. 35 Therefore
be alert, since you don’t know when
the master of the house is coming—whether in the evening or at
midnight or at the crowing of the
rooster or early in the morning.
36 Otherwise, he might come suddenly and find you sleeping. 37 And
what I say to you, I say to everyone:
Be alert!”

The Climax of Jesus’ Life (14:1–16:20)

The Plot to Kill Jesus (14:1-2)

14 After two days it was the •Pass-
over and the Festival of •Un-
leavened Bread. The •chief priests
and the •scribes were looking for a
treacherous way to arrest and kill
Him. 2 “Not during the festival,”
they said, “or there may be rioting
among the people.”

The Anointing at Bethany (14:3-11)

3 While He was in Bethany at the
house of Simon who had a serious
skin disease, as He was reclining at
the table, a woman came with an
alabaster jar of pure and expensive
fragrant oil of nard. She broke the
jar and poured it on His head. 4 But
some were expressing indignation
to one another: “Why has this fragrant oil been wasted? 5 For this oil
might have been sold for more than
300 •denarii and given to the poor.”
And they began to scold her.
6 Then Jesus said, “Leave her
alone. Why are you bothering her?
She has done a noble thing for Me.
7 You always have the poor with
you, and you can do what is good
for them whenever you want, but
you do not always have Me. 8 She
has done what she could; she has
anointed My body in advance for
burial. 9 •I assure you: Wherever the
gospel is proclaimed in the whole
world, what this woman has done
will also be told in memory of her.”
10 Then Judas Iscariot, one of the
Twelve, went to the chief priests to
hand Him over to them. 11 And when
they heard this, they were glad and
promised to give him silver.[B] So he
started looking for a good opportunity to betray Him.

Preparation for Passover (14:12-16)

12 On the first day of Unleavened
Bread, when they sacrifice the Passover lamb, His disciples asked Him,
“Where do You want us to go and
prepare the Passover so You may eat
it?”
13 So He sent two of His disciples
and told them, “Go into the city, and
a man carrying a water jug will meet
you. Follow him. 14 Wherever he enters, tell the owner of the house, ‘The
Teacher says, “Where is the guest
room for Me to eat the Passover with
My disciples?”’ 15 He will show you a
large room upstairs, furnished and
ready. Make the preparations for us
there.” 16 So the disciples went out,
entered the city, and found it just as
He had told them, and they prepared
the Passover.

Betrayal at the Passover (14:17-21)

17 When evening came, He arrived
with the Twelve. 18 While they were
reclining and eating, Jesus said, “I
assure you: One of you will betray
Me—one who is eating with Me!”
19 They began to be distressed and
to say to Him one by one, “Surely
not I?”
20 He said to them, “It is one of
the Twelve—the one who is dipping
bread with Me in the bowl. 21 For
the •Son of Man will go just as it is
written about Him, but woe to that
man by whom the Son of Man is betrayed! It would have been better for
that man if he had not been born.”

The First Lord’s Supper (14:22-26)

22 As they were eating, He took
bread, blessed and broke it, gave it
to them, and said, “Take it;[C] this is
My body.”
23 Then He took a cup, and after

14:3-9 Jesus’ sufferings were highlighted in this section by betrayal and denial. Like Matthew, Luke, and John, Mark highlighted Mary’s devotion to Christ as she anointed Jesus in preparation for His **burial**. She was identified as Mary of Bethany. In the midst of this dark hour in Jesus’ life, she stood out as a model of committed devotion. Mary gave her attention to Jesus and ministered to Him; He in turn expressed gratitude to her and recorded her testimony for generations to come.

14:10-26 Perhaps because Judas went immediately to betray Jesus, he was identified as one of those who questioned Mary’s use of extravagant oil to anoint Jesus (vv. 4-5; Jn 12:4-6). **Betray** (Gk *paradoi*, “hand over”) was not only a deceitful act, but the one who would hand over a friend was without honor. Especially would this dishonor fall upon one who would eat a meal (an important act of friendship) with the man he intended to betray (Mk 14:20). A comparison of the accounts of this final meal Jesus had with His disciples suggests that Judas evidently did leave the meal before the institution of the memorial supper by the Lord (Mk 14:20-21). Judas had not questioned Mary’s extravagance because of his concern for the poor but because of his own greed (Jn 12:4-6).

Jesus used two familiar symbols when He instituted the Lord’s Supper with His disciples: **bread** (Mk 14:22) and the **cup** or **fruit of the vine** (vv. 23-25). The reference to drinking of the cup **in the kingdom of God** must point to a time beyond Jesus’ crucifixion and resurrection and to the Lord’s return to establish His glorious kingdom (v. 25).

[A] **13:33** Other mss add *and pray* [B] **14:11** Or *money*; in Mt 26:15 it is specified as 30 pieces of silver; see Zch 11:12-13 [C] **14:22** Other mss add *eat;*

giving thanks, He gave it to them, and so they all drank from it. 24 He said to them, "This is My blood that establishes the covenant;[A] it is shed for many. 25 I assure you: I will no longer drink of the fruit of the vine until that day when I drink it in a new way[B] in the kingdom of God." 26 After singing psalms,[C] they went out to the •Mount of Olives.

Prediction of Peter's Denial (14:27-31)

27 Then Jesus said to them, "All of you will run away,[D,E] because it is written:

> **I will strike the shepherd,**
> **and the sheep**
> **will be scattered.**[F]

28 But after I have been resurrected, I will go ahead of you to Galilee."

29 Peter told Him, "Even if everyone runs away, I will certainly not!"

30 "I assure you," Jesus said to him, "today, this very night, before the rooster crows twice, you will deny Me three times!"

31 But he kept insisting, "If I have to die with You, I will never deny You!" And they all said the same thing.

Jesus' Prayer in the Garden (14:32-42)

32 Then they came to a place named Gethsemane, and He told His disciples, "Sit here while I pray." 33 He took Peter, James, and John with Him, and He began to be deeply distressed and horrified. 34 Then He said to them, "My soul is swallowed up in sorrow[G]—to the point of death. Remain here and stay awake." 35 Then He went a little farther, fell to the ground, and began to pray that if it were possible, the hour might pass from Him. 36 And He said, "•*Abba*, Father! All things are possible for You. Take this cup away from Me. Nevertheless, not what I will, but what You will."

37 Then He came and found them sleeping. "Simon, are you sleeping?" He asked Peter. "Couldn't you stay awake one hour? 38 Stay awake and pray so that you won't enter into temptation. The spirit is willing, but the flesh is weak."

39 Once again He went away and prayed, saying the same thing. 40 And He came again and found them sleeping, because they could not keep their eyes open.[H] They did not know what to say to Him. 41 Then He came a third time and said to them, "Are you still sleeping and resting? Enough! The time has come. Look, the Son of Man is being betrayed into the hands of sinners. 42 Get up; let's go! See—My betrayer is near."

The Judas Kiss (14:43-52)

43 While He was still speaking, Judas, one of the Twelve, suddenly arrived. With him was a mob, with swords and clubs, from the chief priests, the scribes, and the elders. 44 His betrayer had given them a signal. "The One I kiss," he said, "He's the One; arrest Him and take Him away under guard." 45 So when he came, he went right up to Him and said, "•Rabbi!"—and kissed Him. 46 Then they took hold of Him and arrested Him. 47 And one of those who stood by drew his sword, struck the high priest's •slave, and cut off his ear.

48 But Jesus said to them, "Have you come out with swords and clubs, as though I were a criminal,[I] to capture Me? 49 Every day I was among you, teaching in the •temple complex, and you didn't arrest Me. But the Scriptures must be fulfilled." 50 Then they all deserted Him and ran away.

51 Now a certain young man,[J] having a linen cloth wrapped around his naked body, was following Him. They caught hold of him, 52 but he left the linen cloth behind and ran away naked.

Jesus and the Sanhedrin (14:53-65)

53 They led Jesus away to the high priest, and all the chief priests, the elders, and the scribes convened. 54 Peter followed Him at a distance, right into the high priest's courtyard. He was sitting with the temple

[A]14:24 Other mss read *the new covenant* [B]14:25 Or *drink new wine*; lit *drink it new* [C]14:26 Pss 113–118 were sung during and after the Passover meal. [D]14:27 Other mss add *because of Me this night* [E]14:27 Or •*stumble* [F]14:27 Zch 13:7 [G]14:34 Or *I am deeply grieved* [H]14:40 Lit *because their eyes were weighed down* [I]14:48 Lit *as against a criminal* [J]14:51 Perhaps John Mark who later wrote this Gospel

14:27-31 Jesus again quoted Zch 13:7 to present a poignant picture of the desertion of the disciples during His hour of suffering and death. He used the metaphor of the shepherd to describe Himself in relation to the disciples (His **sheep**). The difficulty lies in understanding **run away**, which in some versions is translated "fall away" (Gk *skandalisthesesthē*, "cause to sin, be led into sin, desert, have doubts"). The verb has a wide range of meanings, but the context, especially the quote from Zechariah, does help in interpreting the meaning here. Nothing interprets Scripture as effectively as another passage of Scripture. The disciples would not lose their salvation (a premise clear throughout the whole of Scripture, Jn 10:28-29); rather, they will falter in their faith and thus abandon Jesus for a time. Few people realize their weaknesses, and Peter certainly fit this model. Despite the bold disciple's interruption and rebuttal, Jesus announced that Peter would not only fulfill the prophecy but would do it soon and repeatedly (Mk 14:30). Jesus even used one of His favorite words for emphasis (Gk *amen*, "truly, indeed"), translated here **I assure you**.

14:32-42 Gethsemane (Gk, "oil press") was a garden located on the Mount of Olives. Jesus often went there to pray. This prayer was not uttered by one who was weak or fearful. No matter how much Jesus suffered from knowing the temporary alienation from the Father was coming, He chose the path of obedience with determination, knowing the divine necessity for His death to make atonement for all who would turn to Him in faith.

14:43-52 Evidently those who were sent to arrest Jesus did not know Him. His popularity at that time may have made it difficult for the religious leaders to find people who really knew Him and had watched His ministry who would betray Jesus in this way. Rabbis were often greeted by their disciples with the common sign of affection and esteem—the **kiss** (vv. 44-45). Judas probably feared for his own life and thus chose this deceptive means of identifying Jesus for those who sought to do Him harm. This action in itself showed how little Judas knew about the Savior. Judas expected resistance. **One of those** is a reference to Simon Peter (v. 47; Jn 18:10). Many believe the **certain young man** who left naked was an autobiographical reference to Mark since such trivia would be an unusual inclusion unless it was imbedded in the mind of the author himself (Mk 14:51), and its inclusion served to add to the authenticity of the entire book.

14:53-64 Jesus had two trials: one

police,[A] warming himself by the fire.[B]

[55] The chief priests and the whole •Sanhedrin were looking for testimony against Jesus to put Him to death, but they could find none. [56] For many were giving false testimony against Him, but the testimonies did not agree. [57] Some stood up and were giving false testimony against Him, stating, [58] "We heard Him say, 'I will demolish this sanctuary made by human hands, and in three days I will build another not made by hands.'" [59] Yet their testimony did not agree even on this.

[60] Then the high priest stood up before them all and questioned Jesus, "Don't You have an answer to what these men are testifying against You?" [61] But He kept silent and did not answer anything. Again the high priest questioned Him, "Are You the •Messiah, the Son of the Blessed One?"

[62] "I am," said Jesus, "and all of you[C] will see **the Son of Man seated at the right hand** of the Power and **coming with the clouds of heaven**."[D]

[63] Then the high priest tore his robes and said, "Why do we still need witnesses? [64] You have heard the blasphemy! What is your decision?"[E]

And they all condemned Him to be deserving of death. [65] Then some began to spit on Him, to blindfold Him, and to beat Him, saying, "Prophesy!" The temple police also took Him and slapped Him.

Peter's Denial of His Lord (14:66-72)

[66] While Peter was in the courtyard below, one of the high priest's servants came. [67] When she saw Peter warming himself, she looked at him and said, "You also were with that •Nazarene, Jesus."

[68] But he denied it: "I don't know or understand what you're talking about!" Then he went out to the entryway, and a rooster crowed.[F]

[69] When the servant saw him again she began to tell those standing nearby, "This man is one of them!"

[70] But again he denied it. After a little while those standing there said to Peter again, "You certainly are one of them, since you're also a Galilean!"[G]

[71] Then he started to curse[H] and to swear with an oath, "I don't know this man you're talking about!"

[72] Immediately a rooster crowed a second time, and Peter remembered when Jesus had spoken the word to him, "Before the rooster crows twice, you will deny Me three times." When he thought about it, he began to weep.[I]

Jesus Before Pilate (15:1-5)

15 As soon as it was morning, the •chief priests had a meeting with the elders, •scribes, and the whole •Sanhedrin. After tying Jesus up, they led Him away and handed Him over to •Pilate.

[2] So Pilate asked Him, "Are You the King of the Jews?"

He answered him, "You have said it."[J]

[3] And the chief priests began to accuse Him of many things. [4] Then Pilate questioned Him again, "Are You not answering anything? Look how many things they are accusing You of!" [5] But Jesus still did not answer anything, so Pilate was amazed.

Jesus or Barabbas (15:6-15)

[6] At the festival it was Pilate's custom to release for the people a prisoner they requested. [7] There was one named Barabbas, who was in prison with rebels who had committed murder during the rebellion. [8] The crowd came up and began to ask Pilate to do for them as was his custom. [9] So Pilate answered them, "Do you want me to release the King of the Jews for you?" [10] For he knew it was because of envy that the chief priests had handed Him over. [11] But the chief priests stirred up the crowd so that he would release Barabbas to them instead.

[12] Pilate asked them again, "Then what do you want me to do with the One you call the King of the Jews?"

religious and another civil. The religious trial involved a progression:

- Before Annas, a former high priest and the father-in-law of the current high priest Caiaphas (Jn 18:19-24);
- Then Caiaphas, **the high priest**, who had assembled **all the chief priests, the elders, and the scribes** (Mk 14:53-65);
- Formal condemnation by the Sanhedrin (Lk 22:66-71).

In the religious trials Jesus was charged with blasphemy because He affirmed that He was indeed the Son of God (Mk 14:61-64). Jesus also appeared before Pilate in a civil trial, without which He would not have been crucified (15:1-15). Although the Jews, especially their religious leaders, had much freedom to pursue their own ends, only the Roman government could carry out sentences for capital crimes. Here Jesus was accused of treason and of causing a public insurrection against the Roman government, and Jesus did indeed affirm that He was **King of the Jews** (15:2).

14:65-72 Peter did show his deep affection for and commitment to Jesus by following Him into an area where he also would be at risk. However, as with many believers, he allowed his human fears to overcome his spiritual resources, which were available to give him strength for the difficult times. Even after Peter's denial, he did not flee the scene but simply retreated into the shadows (v. 66).

15:1-20 The Roman government had a tradition of releasing **a prisoner** for the Jews during the Festival of Unleavened Bread because of its commemoration of the release of the Hebrews from Egyptian bondage as a gesture of goodwill. **Pilate** believed they would choose Jesus for release over the criminal **Barabbas** (vv. 11-15). However, once the Jews made their choice of Barabbas, Pilate proceeded not only to condemn Jesus to death by crucifixion but also to call for flogging and scourging, a barbaric and senseless cruel punishment in which the victim was stripped to the waist with his hands bound to a stationary pole while he was mercilessly whipped (v. 15). The whip itself was a torturous instrument consisting of a handle with attached leather thongs weighted with jagged pieces of bone and rock. The victim was most assuredly disfigured and often died from this ordeal (v. 15).

[A]14:54 Or *the officers*; lit *the servants* [B]14:54 Lit *light* [C]14:62 Lit *and you* [D]14:62 Ps 110:1; Dn 7:13 [E]14:64 Lit *How does it appear to you?* [F]14:68 Other mss omit *and a rooster crowed* [G]14:70 Other mss add *and your speech shows it* [H]14:71 To call down curses on himself if what he said weren't true [I]14:72 Or *he burst into tears*, or *he broke down* [J]15:2 Or *That is true*, an affirmative oath; Mt 26:64; 27:11

15:21-39 Even the Romans recognized crucifixion as the most hideous death. **Golgotha** (Gk *Golgothan*, the Aramaic name of a hill near the site of Jerusalem in Jesus' day) was the place of execution, located outside the city walls. The name means the **Skull Place** (Gk *kraniou*, "skull," v. 22; Mt 27:33; Lk 23:33; Jn 19:17). Jesus refused the sedative drink traditionally offered by the Romans in the execution detail to make the excruciating pain more bearable for the victim (Mk 15:23). Unknowingly the Roman soldiers themselves fulfilled the ancient prophecy (see Ps 22:18), which they would never have done purposefully (Mk 15:24).

The taunt, **"Look, He's calling for Elijah!"** likely recalls the Jews' understanding that the prophet Elijah (Hb, "my God is Yahweh") would prepare the way for the Messiah (Mk 9:11-13; see also Mt 17:3). At the time of His transfiguration Jesus had spoken with Elijah (Mk 9:4; see also Lk 9:30-31).

The order of events culminating in Jesus' death is gleaned from a summary of the accounts found in all four of the Gospels:

- The Passover meal that Jesus ate with the disciples (Mk 14:12-21; Lk 22:14-16,24-30);
- Jesus' washing of the disciples' feet (Jn 13:1-20);
- Judas' departure from the Upper Room (Jn 13:21-30);
- Jesus' institution of the memorial supper (Mk 14:22-26; Lk 22:17-20);
- Jesus' prayer in Gethsemane (Mk 14:26,32-42);
- Judas' betrayal of Jesus (14:43-46; Jn 18:2-12);
- Jesus' appearance before Annas, the former high priest (Jn 18:12-14,19-23);
- Jesus' condemnation by the high priest Caiaphas and the Sanhedrin (Mk 14:53,55-65);
- Peter's denial of the Lord (14:66-72; Jn 18:15-18,25-27);
- Jesus' formal sentencing before the Sanhedrin (Lk 22:66-71);
- Jesus in the court of Pilate (Mk 15:1-15; Jn 18:28-38);
- Jesus before Herod Antipas (Lk 23:6-12);
- Jesus' sentence delivered by Pilate (Mk 15:6-15; Lk 23:13-25);
- Jesus' flogging (Mk 15:15-20; Jn 19:1-14);
- Jesus' crucifixion (Mk 15:23-32);
- Jesus' death (15:37);
- The tearing of the curtain of the sanctuary (15:37-38; Mt 27:50-54);
- The piercing of Jesus' side (Jn 19:31-37).

The tearing of the **curtain of the sanctuary . . . from top to bottom** made clear that God was in control and was a reminder that through Christ's

13 Again they shouted, "Crucify Him!"

14 Then Pilate said to them, "Why? What has He done wrong?"

But they shouted, "Crucify Him!" all the more.

15 Then, willing to gratify the crowd, Pilate released Barabbas to them. And after having Jesus flogged,[A] he handed Him over to be crucified.

Mocking by the Soldiers (15:16-20)

16 Then the soldiers led Him away into the courtyard (that is, •headquarters) and called the whole •company together. 17 They dressed Him in a purple robe, twisted together a crown of thorns, and put it on Him. 18 And they began to salute Him, "Hail, King of the Jews!" 19 They kept hitting Him on the head with a reed and spitting on Him. Getting down on their knees, they were paying Him homage. 20 When they had mocked Him, they stripped Him of the purple robe, put His clothes on Him, and led Him out to crucify Him.

Crucifixion Between Two Criminals (15:21-32)

21 They forced a man coming in from the country, who was passing by, to carry Jesus' cross. He was Simon, a Cyrenian, the father of Alexander and Rufus. 22 And they brought Jesus to the place called *Golgotha* (which means Skull Place). 23 They tried to give Him wine mixed with myrrh, but He did not take it. 24 Then they crucified Him and divided His clothes, casting lots for them to decide what each would get. 25 Now it was nine in the morning[B] when they crucified Him. 26 The inscription of the charge written against Him was:

THE KING OF THE JEWS.

27 They crucified two criminals[C] with Him, one on His right and one on His left. [28 So the Scripture was fulfilled that says: **And He was counted among outlaws.**][D,E] 29 Those who passed by were yelling insults at[F] Him, shaking their heads, and saying, "Ha! The One who would demolish the sanctuary and build it in three days, 30 save Yourself by coming down from the cross!" 31 In the same way, the chief priests with the scribes were mocking Him to one another and saying, "He saved others; He cannot save Himself! 32 Let the •Messiah, the King of Israel, come down now from the cross, so that we may see and believe." Even those who were crucified with Him were taunting Him.

The Death of Jesus (15:33-41)

33 When it was noon,[G] darkness came over the whole land[H] until three in the afternoon.[I] 34 And at three[I] Jesus cried out with a loud voice, ***"Eloi, Eloi, lemá***[J] ***sabachtháni?"*** which is translated, "**My God, My God, why have You forsaken Me?**"[K]

35 When some of those standing there heard this, they said, "Look, He's calling for Elijah!" 36 Someone ran and filled a sponge with sour wine, fixed it on a reed, offered Him a drink, and said, "Let's see if Elijah comes to take Him down!"

37 But Jesus let out a loud cry and breathed His last. 38 Then the curtain of the sanctuary[L] was split in two from top to bottom. 39 When the •centurion, who was standing opposite Him, saw the way He[M] breathed His last, he said, "This man really was God's Son!"[N]

40 There were also women looking on from a distance. Among them were •Mary Magdalene, Mary the mother of James the younger and of Joses, and Salome. 41 When He was in Galilee, they would follow Him and help Him. Many other women had come up with Him to Jerusalem.

The Burial of Jesus (15:42-47)

42 When it was already evening, because it was preparation day (that is, the day before the Sabbath), 43 Jo-

[A]**15:15** Roman flogging was done with a whip made of leather strips embedded with pieces of bone or metal that brutally tore the flesh. [B]**15:25** Lit *was the third hour* [C]**15:27** Or *revolutionaries* [D]**15:28** Other mss omit bracketed text [E]**15:28** Is 53:12 [F]**15:29** Lit *passed by blasphemed* [G]**15:33** Lit *the sixth hour* [H]**15:33** Or *whole earth* [I]**15:33,34** Lit *the ninth hour* [J]**15:34** Some mss read *lama*; other mss read *lima* [K]**15:34** Ps 22:1 [L]**15:38** A heavy curtain separated the inner room of the temple from the outer. [M]**15:39** Other mss read *saw that He cried out like this and* [N]**15:39** Or *the Son of God*; Mk 1:1

seph of Arimathea, a prominent member of the Sanhedrin who was himself looking forward to the kingdom of God, came and boldly went in to Pilate and asked for Jesus' body. 44 Pilate was surprised that He was already dead. Summoning the centurion, he asked him whether He had already died. 45 When he found out from the centurion, he gave the corpse to Joseph. 46 After he bought some fine linen, he took Him down and wrapped Him in the linen. Then he placed Him in a tomb cut out of the rock, and rolled a stone against the entrance to the tomb. 47 Now Mary Magdalene and Mary the mother of Joses were watching where He was placed.

Resurrection Morning (16:1-8)

16 When the Sabbath was over, ·Mary Magdalene, Mary the mother of James, and Salome bought spices, so they could go and anoint Him. 2 Very early in the morning, on the first day of the week, they went to the tomb at sunrise. 3 They were saying to one another, "Who will roll away the stone from the entrance to

HARD QUESTION

Should Mark 16:9-20 be read as authoritative Scripture or not?

Modern translations like the HCSB bracket this passage because there is evidence leaning both ways. The evidence is not conclusive; there is enough to raise legitimate questions about the authorship of the passage but not enough to eliminate it from the canon of Scripture with confidence. Consequently, general readers as well as scholars must engage both their minds in weighing the evidence and their hearts in heeding the Holy Spirit if or when He speaks through this portion of the text.

These last verses of Mark's Gospel have been closely scrutinized and have caused considerable debate. A number of textual critics (specialists in studying manuscripts in order to establish the one[s] closest to the original) have questioned whether or not these concluding verses were penned by the Gospel's author or added by an editor at a later time. The two earliest manuscripts, and generally the ones most respected as reliable, as well as others, do not include verses 9-20. These critics primarily appeal to internal evidence (e.g., a difference between verses 9-20 and the remainder of the Gospel). Others note that to end with verse 8 would be an abrupt and inappropriate ending. Yet as has been wisely noted by some, the abrupt ending follows an abrupt beginning of the Gospel. Mark hardly notes anything in Jesus' life before moving into the events of His ministry. Throughout the Gospel He is not concerned with smooth transitions. Also, Mark may have wanted an "open" ending as evidence that the story of Christ was not complete. By ending with the announcement that the women told no one (v. 8), perhaps Mark admonishes readers to proclaim the good news themselves.

Many who maintain verse 8 as the ending of the Gospel in surviving early manuscripts further argue that final verses penned by Mark must then have been lost. The majority of the extant manuscripts of the Gospel do contain the full twenty verses; but most of these manuscripts are late in dating. What is most important for anyone seeking to interpret these verses is that whatever the precise ending of Mark may be, the verses in the canon of Scripture entrusted to believers in subsequent generations, when properly interpreted, will not cause confusion or generate erroneous doctrine. No doctrine is built upon one isolated passage; thus you must continue to search the whole counsel of God in interpreting Scripture. These verses essentially summarize the post-resurrection appearances of Christ, including the Great Commission. Other Gospels record the same events.

Verses 17-18 have been particularly controversial. The apostles had recorded instances describing their power to exorcise demons (Ac 16:16-18). There was also a phenomenon at Pentecost in which the apostles communicated with people in languages they had never studied or those hearing the gospel understood languages with which they were not familiar. Whether a gift of speaking or hearing or both, a linguistic miracle happened at Pentecost (Ac 2:1-12). Trampling on snakes was associated with the powers accorded the Seventy who were sent out by the Lord (Lk 10:18), and the apostle Paul shook off a poisonous viper on Malta (Ac 28:3-6). These happenings recorded in Acts were Pentecost and post-Pentecost events, but the point is that although such occasional phenomena are noted, they were not the norm, even if extended beyond the apostolic circle to include other believers. Neither were such miracles the focus. Jesus and the good news of the gospel occupied center stage in Mark and throughout the New Testament.

In the providence of God, the Lord promised to watch over and care for His people in their missionary endeavors. This protective care included God's occasional intervention on behalf of His servants. The fact that Peter and Paul evidently died as martyrs is indicative that the Lord did not intervene in every crisis, but incidents recorded from their lives and the lives of others showed that sometimes God did intervene in miraculous ways.

There is evidence of the existence of Mk 16:9-20 as early as Irenaeus (second century), who regarded the verses as genuine. Whatever the final verdict will be concerning the ending verses of Mark, one can have full confidence that the presence or absence of these verses does not affect the overall integrity of the book or compromise any major doctrine associated with the historic Christian faith. Amazingly God's Word has been so carefully preserved that even in debate and uncertainties among scholars, its authenticity in authority and lack of contradiction reigns supreme.

death all would have direct access to God (Mk 15:38; see Heb 10:19-22). Even the **centurion**, the Roman soldier in charge of the band of soldiers assigned to keep order among the people and execute the ordered crucifixion, recognized that Jesus is the Son of God (Mk 15:39), a fact that would have special significance in Mark's Gospel, since it was primarily directed to a Gentile audience. This seasoned military officer was strangely moved and drawn to Jesus. Whether or not the military official realized the full meaning of his words, he clearly identified Jesus as the Son of God.

15:40–16:13 There are more similarities than differences between the contents of the Gospels penned by Mark and Matthew. However, some of the differences may be important in understanding the role of the women who were disciples of Jesus Christ. Those differences included one significant addition to Matthew's account, two seemingly purposeful deletions, and another long-debated possible deletion or change.

The addition has to do with Mark's description of the women disciples viewing the crucifixion. After naming the same three women as in Mt 27:56, if Salome was the mother of James and John, the sons of Zebedee, Mark refers to many other **women** [who] **had come up with Him to Jerusalem** (Mk 15:40-41). Though not specifically numbered or named, other women, beyond those specifically named in the Gospel passages, followed Jesus.

The first omission has to do with any mention of the Jewish leaders or Roman guards, both of whom played prominent roles in Matthew's account (Mt 27:62-66; 28:2-4,11-15). In their absence, the narrative starting at Mk 15:40 describes only those who were disciples of Jesus. The attention paid to the women disciples, including identifying them by name (15:40-41; 15:47–16:10), was remarkable during a time when women were not at the forefront in public gatherings.

The second deletion, which is more subtle, has to do with the mention of the women being **afraid** (Gk *ephobounto*, "be afraid, worship, reverence," 16:8) without the allusion to "great joy" recorded in Mt 28:8. Fear on the part of the women fit the unusual encounter they experienced. However, **don't be alarmed** (Gk *ekthambeisthe*, "greatly surprised or distressed," Mk 16:6) has a different connotation. The women experienced awe and reverence for the risen Christ. Especially in the latter case, the women were not in any sense portrayed in a bad light but with a very positive report of their reverence for Christ. In fact, the women also fled from the tomb just as the male disciples had run away from Christ and had failed to stand by Him at the time of His arrest, trial, and crucifixion. Even more tragic is the fact that the women **said nothing to anyone** (v. 8).

There is no need, as some feminists attempt to read into the account a victim mentality or to compare these women with the men who were disciples. First, Paul himself warned believers not to compare themselves with others (2Co 10:12). More important, for women and men the goal is always to glorify Christ. Each woman must bear her own faithful testimony to Him. These women ultimately did just that (Mk 16:10). Jesus, remembering the loving acts of devotion from women who faithfully served Him, entrusted to the women disciples the message of His resurrection (16:7-8), not based on their merit or performance but as a gracious gift and opportunity.

the tomb for us?" [4] Looking up, they
observed that the stone—which was
very large—had been rolled away.
[5] When they entered the tomb, they
saw a young man[A] dressed in a long
white robe sitting on the right side;
they were amazed and alarmed.
[6] "Don't be alarmed," he told
them. "You are looking for Jesus
the •Nazarene, who was crucified.
He has been resurrected! He is not
here! See the place where they put
Him. [7] But go, tell His disciples and
Peter, 'He is going ahead of you to
Galilee; you will see Him there just
as He told you.'"
[8] So they went out and started
running from the tomb, because
trembling and astonishment overwhelmed them. And they said
nothing to anyone, since they were
afraid.

Appearances of the Risen Lord (16:9-13)

[[9] Early on the first day of the
week, after He had risen, He appeared first to Mary Magdalene, out
of whom He had driven seven demons. [10] She went and reported to
those who had been with Him, as
they were mourning and weeping.
[11] Yet, when they heard that He was
alive and had been seen by her, they
did not believe it. [12] Then after this,
He appeared in a different form to
two of them walking on their way
into the country. [13] And they went
and reported it to the rest, who did
not believe them either.

The Great Commission (16:14-18)

[14] Later, He appeared to the Eleven
themselves as they were reclining at
the table. He rebuked their unbelief and hardness of heart, because
they did not believe those who saw
Him after He had been resurrected.
[15] Then He said to them, "Go into all
the world and preach the gospel to
the whole creation. [16] Whoever believes and is baptized will be saved,
but whoever does not believe will be
condemned. [17] And these signs will
accompany those who believe: In My
name they will drive out demons;
they will speak in new languages;
[18] they will pick up snakes;[B] if they
should drink anything deadly, it
will never harm them; they will lay
hands on the sick, and they will get
well."

The Ascension (16:19-20)

[19] Then after speaking to them,
the Lord Jesus was taken up into
heaven and sat down at the right
hand of God. [20] And they went out
and preached everywhere, the Lord
working with them and confirming the word by the accompanying
signs.][C]

[A] **16:5** In Mt 28:2, the young man = an angel [B] **16:18** Other mss add *with their hands*
[C] **16:9-20** Other mss omit bracketed text

MARK… WRITTEN ON MY *Heart*

Following Jesus includes serving in the same way He taught His first disciples to serve (10:35-45). Living Jesus' way in the world does not come naturally and is frequently met with opposition. The Christian woman who serves as Jesus demonstrated in word and deed stands out. Her attitude is not one of entitlement, self-gratification, or superiority; her actions do not include exalting her accomplishments, "bossing" other people around, or putting down those who fail to meet her expectations. As the Gospel of Mark soaks into your heart and mind, may you willingly follow Jesus, allowing Him both to ransom your life and to transform your approach to life—becoming a woman who willingly gives her life to meet the needs of others as Jesus would. Your prayer to be more and more like Jesus will, in this way—His way—be answered.

Women Ministering to Jesus

Woman	Her Ministry	Practical Application	Reference
Mary	Nurturing Jesus as He grew into manhood	Mothers are to rear their children by nurturing them in the Lord.	Lk 21:51-52 Eph 6:4
Susanna	Supporting Jesus' ministry with her energies and resources	Women have opportunity to invest time, energy, and resources.	Lk 8:1-3 1Tm 6:17-19
Mary of Bethany	Listening to Jesus as He taught spiritual truth	Women must take time to study God's Word and to listen for His voice.	Lk 10:39 2Tm 2:15 Heb 4:12
Samaritan woman	Hearing Jesus share the gospel, accepting His grace, sharing her testimony with others	Women, too, have the responsibility to share the good news of the gospel.	Jn 4:28-30 1Pt 3:15
The mother-in-law of Simon Peter	Extending hospitality to Jesus and His disciples	In a sense, all hospitality is offered ultimately to Jesus.	Mk 1:29-31 Col 3:17,23-24
The widow with two tiny coins	Generously supporting the kingdom	The Lord never expects you to give more than you have—only to be generous with what has been entrusted to you.	Mk 12:41-44 Heb 6:10
Mary of Bethany	Preparing Jesus' body for burial	Even mundane tasks are important.	Mt 26:6-13 Mk 14:8
Mary Magdalene	Staying with Jesus even when He was rejected, giving the first proclamation to His resurrection	Women must stand firm in the faith even in times of discouragement and persecution. They must be ready to share the good news of the resurrection.	Mt 27:55; Jn 19:25; 20:1-18 Rm 8:35-39 2Co 3:23 1Pt 3:15

Luke

Timeline ■ World Events ■ Biblical Events	*27 BC* Beginning of Augustus Caesar's reign over the Roman Empire	*39 BC* Roman Senate's declaration of Herod as "king of the Jews"	*6–4 BC* Imperial census in territory governed by Herod	*5 BC* Birth of Jesus

"For the Son of Man has come to seek and to save the lost" (19:10).

Who wrote Luke?

A Gentile follower of Christ named Luke, a physician who traveled with the apostle Paul (Ac 16:10-17; 20:5-15; 21:1-18; 27:1–28:16; Col 4:14; Phm 24; 2Tm 4:11)

Who were the recipients?

The text is addressed to Theophilus (Gk, "one who loves God"), but overall this gospel is written with a Gentile-Christian audience predominantly in mind.

When was Luke written?

A.D. 59–63

Where did it happen?

In Israel, although Luke also locates the gospel's events in a broader historical and geographical context than do the other three gospels:

- "In the days of King Herod of Judea" (1:5);
- During the reign of Caesar Augustus over "the whole [Roman] empire" (2:1); and
- "While Quirinius was governing Syria" (2:2).

What is Luke about?

- *Salvation for all people.* Luke expressly intended to provide a trustworthy account of the Christian faith based on eyewitness reports and on his own careful investigation of other written accounts (1:1-4). The central and overriding theme is that Jesus is the Son of God and Savior of all who turn to Him in faith for salvation—regardless of ethnicity, gender, or socioeconomic status (2:10-11; 19:10).
- *The activity of the Holy Spirit.* Luke mentions the Holy Spirit far more frequently than the other gospel writers, and the work of the Holy Spirit is also a dominant theme throughout the book of Acts, in which the Spirit is mentioned about 70 times (Ac 1:4-5,8; 2:4,17-18,38; 10:19,38,44). The Spirit overshadowed Mary in the conception of Jesus (Lk 1:35) and filled both John the Baptist (1:15) and his mother Elizabeth (1:41). The Spirit "guided" Simeon and inspired him to prophesy about the future of the Messiah (2:25-35). Jesus was "full of the Holy Spirit, and was led by the Spirit in the wilderness . . . to be tempted by the Devil" (4:1-2). Jesus, quoting from Isaiah, testified that the "Spirit of the Lord" was upon Him (4:18). Jesus promised the Holy Spirit as an answer to prayer (11:13).
- *Prayer.* Closely linked to Luke's awareness of the Spirit's activity is his emphasis on the role of prayer in Jesus' ministry (e.g., 3:21; 5:15; 6:1; 9:18,29; 11:1-13; 18:1-8).

Why should women read Luke?

In addition to Luke's portrayal of Jesus as the compassionate Savior of sinners (e.g., 4:18; chap. 15; 18:9-14; 19:1-10), Luke, among the four Gospels, gives the most attention to the women involved in Jesus' life and to those who received healing and mercy from Him. For example, Mary and Elizabeth are prominent in Luke's detailed account of the events surrounding Jesus' birth (chaps. 1–2).

Some suggest that Luke composed Mary's hymn (1:39-56), implying that the literary masterpiece could not have come from a young peasant girl. Such a conjecture dismisses divine inspiration, which by definition surpasses human ability and giftedness. Whether the song came to her in a moment of inspiration or over time in private meditation, Mary was noted by Luke as the human composer of these meaningful and beautifully fashioned words that have been recorded for the generations. The mother of the Lord Jesus was indeed an extraordinary woman.

Only Luke includes the encounter at the temple with Anna, who prophesied about Christ (2:36-38). Luke also acknowledges the women who supported Christ during His earthly ministry (8:1-3) and announced the resurrection (23:27-31; 23:55–24:11).

How do you read Luke?

Read the Gospel of Luke all the way through at least once, engaging your imagination to picture the dramatic scenes unfolding in the various events within the larger stories of Jesus' ministry and teachings. Luke claims up front to have arranged the narrative in "an orderly sequence" (1:3) that will contribute to its intention to build his audience's confidence in the truth of the gospel—"the events that have been fulfilled among us" (1:1). Then read this Gospel through again and again, each time paying closer attention to one of the important aspects of its content (see "What is Luke about?"). Note the way Luke builds this book's portrait of Jesus, and explore the ways this historical record of what Jesus did and taught also challenges followers of Christ to be like Him.

Also read its sequel, the book of Acts; the two books are really two parts of a continuous story. The "end" of "Part 1," the Gospel of Luke, is actually the beginning of "Part 2," the book of Acts, in which the Holy Spirit guides Christ's followers to proclaim the gospel of Jesus Christ everywhere they go. Prayerfully listen to what the Lord teaches you about Himself and obey Him.

AD 18–36	Summer, AD 29	AD 31-32	April 1, AD 33	April 3, AD 33
Years that Caiaphas served as high priest	Jesus' baptism and wilderness temptation	Jesus' Galilean ministry	Jesus' crucifixion	Jesus' resurrection

Outline

- I. Introduction to Jesus' Ministry (1:1-4:13)
  - A. Preface to the Gospel (1:1-4)
  - B. The Birth and the Infancy of Jesus (1:5–2:52)
  - C. Preparation for Jesus' Ministry (3:1–4:13)
- II. Ministry in and Around Galilee (4:14–9:50)
  - A. Preaching in Nazareth (4:14-30)
  - B. Beginning a Healing Ministry (4:31-44)
  - C. Calling the First Disciples (5:1-11)
  - D. Participating in Controversies with the Jewish Leaders (5:12–6:11)
  - E. Formalizing the Call to Discipleship (6:12-49)
  - F. Focusing on the Question of Jesus' Identity (7:1–8:3)
  - G. Hearing the Word of God Correctly (8:4-21)
  - H. Illustrating Jesus' Authoritative Word (8:22-56)
  - I. Coming to the Christological Climax (9:1-50)
- III. Jesus' Teaching En Route to Jerusalem (9:51–18:34)
  - A. Discipleship in the Shadow of the Cross (9:51-62)
  - B. The Mission of the Seventy (10:1-24)
  - C. The Mandate for Double Love (10:25-42)
  - D. The Teaching About Prayer (11:1-13)
  - E. The Controversy with a Pharisee (11:14-54)
  - F. The Preparation for Judgment (12:1–13:9)
  - G. Kingdom Reversals (13:10–14:24)
  - H. The Cost of Discipleship (14:25-35)
  - I. The Seeking and Saving of the Lost (15:1-32)
  - J. The Use and Abuse of Riches (16:1-31)
  - K. The Teachings on Faith (17:1-19)
  - L. The Coming of the Kingdom (17:20–18:8)
  - M. The Requirements for Entering the Kingdom (18:9-30)
  - N. Conclusion and Transition (18:31-34)
- IV. Jesus in Judea: Ministry Near and in Jerusalem (18:35–21:38)
  - A. From Jericho to Jerusalem (18:35–19:27)
  - B. Entry into Jerusalem (19:28-48)
  - C. Jesus' Teaching during the Final Week (20:1–21:38)
- V. The Climax of Jesus' Life (22:1–24:53)
  - A. Passover (22:1-71)
  - B. Crucifixion (23:1-56)
  - C. Resurrection (24:1-53)

Preface to the Gospel (1:1-4)

1 Many have undertaken to compile
a narrative about the events that
have been fulfilled[A] among us, 2 just
as the original eyewitnesses and
servants of the word handed them
down to us. 3 It also seemed good to
me, since I have carefully investigated everything from the very first, to
write to you in an orderly sequence,
most honorable Theophilus, 4 so
that you may know the certainty
of the things about which you have
been instructed.[B]

The Birth and the Infancy of Jesus (1:5–2:52)

The Annunciation of the Birth of the Forerunner John (1:5-25)

5 In the days of King •Herod of
Judea, there was a priest of Abijah's
division[C] named Zechariah. His wife
was from the daughters of Aaron,
and her name was Elizabeth. 6 Both
were righteous in God's sight, living
without blame according to all the
commands and requirements of the
Lord. 7 But they had no children[D] because Elizabeth could not conceive,[E]

[A]1:1 Or *events that have been accomplished*, or *events most surely believed* [B]1:4 Or *informed* [C]1:5 One of the 24 divisions of priests appointed by David for temple service; 1Ch 24:10 [D]1:7 Lit *child* [E]1:7 Lit *Elizabeth was sterile* or *barren*

>WORD|*study*

1:1 The root of the verb **have been fulfilled** (Gk *peplērophorēmenōn*) is *plēroō* (Gk, "fill up, render full or complete, accomplish"), which is used repeatedly in the New Testament to highlight the occurrence of circumstances that had been prophesied in the Old Testament (e.g., Mt 1:22; Lk 1:20; 4:21; Jn 12:38; Ac 1:16). Although similar in meaning, the verb in Lk 1:1 combines this root with the verb *phoreō* (Gk, "wear constantly") to include the sense of persuading—"cause something to be shown completely, fill with conviction or certainty." The **events** (Gk *pragma*, "that which has been done, accomplished fact"; in a forensic sense, a "case, matter, issue") to which Luke refers do constitute fulfilled prophecies, but this verb suggests that their reliability has also been made evident.

Title: The Greek text acquired the title "According to Luke," recognizing Luke as its human author.

1:1 Following the rhetorical pattern for introducing a written work, Luke begins a formal preface explaining the rationale for his work.

1:1-4 Luke's purpose was to give an "orderly account" of the person and works of Jesus. Rather than a strictly chronological account, however, the order is more thematic. In fact, his purpose had more to do with thematic order. He intended to detail salvific or theological history and to give his readers a firm basis for the knowledge they had received. **Most honorable Theophilus** (Gk, "one who loves God") was probably a person of distinction, but his exact identity is unknown. The name may also have served as a literary device for addressing all believers (those who "love God").

1:5-6 The description of **Zechariah** and **Elizabeth** as **righteous in God's sight** precluded their infertility as being the result of their sin. Although imperfect because of their humanity, they were truly devoted to God and faithfully served Him (vv. 5-6). The unexpected reversal of her infertility served as another way of pointing to God's miraculous intervention in what would be impossible—humanly speaking.

Luke is unique among the four Gospels in showing the familial relationship between John and Jesus. Luke highlighted both similarities and differences between John and Jesus, he also wanted to show clearly the significant differences between them. With respect to similarities, John's birth is foretold (v. 13) as was the birth of Jesus (vv. 26-33). Then the relationship between Elizabeth and Mary was clarified (vv. 39-56), followed by a narration of the birth and growth of both John (vv. 57-80) and Jesus (2:1-52). Both came from godly Jewish parents who were visited by angels; both mothers experienced the power of the Holy Spirit and were told of the salvific significance of their children, whose ministries would offer spiritual consolation and even social changes to both Jews and Gentiles (1:11-17,26-35). Both sets of parents experienced some disbelief but were eventually filled with joy and praise at the working of God in their lives (vv. 39-56). Luke also detailed the circumcision, naming, and maturation of both John and Jesus (vv. 57-80; 2:21-52).

As for differences, Luke pointed out at least two ways in which Jesus is greater than John:

- The virgin birth clearly sets Jesus above John;
- John was the forerunner to Jesus, who is the only Savior, the Christ, and the Lord of all.

1:8 There were approximately 18,000 priests in Israel at the time Zechariah was called to minister in the temple; so this was definitely a once-in-a-lifetime opportunity for him.

1:11-14 The appearance of **an angel of the Lord** was a supernatural event specifically noted and thus affirming its historicity. Although Zechariah may have been praying for the long awaited messianic redemption, more probably the **prayer . . . heard** was that of a godly couple for a child to continue the generations, further enhanced with the prophetic announcement of the child's name **John** (Gk *Iōannēs*, linking the Hb name of God with *chanan*, "showing favor, being gracious"). **Joy** [Gk *chara*, "gladness"] **and delight** (Gk *agalliasis*, "exultation," "extreme joy") regarding this **birth** are followed by an allusion to **many** [who] **will rejoice** (Gk *charēsontai*, "show favor, bestow").

1:15 Since some of the requirements for a Nazirite are not mentioned (Nm 6:2-15), the more logical explanation seems to be that John was called to live a set-apart life, including a commitment to serve God in a unique way (Lv 10:9).

CHARACTER PROFILE

Elizabeth

Mother of John the Baptist

Her Background	• The wife of Zechariah, from the lineage of Aaron (1:5-7) • Childless • A righteous woman
Her Story	• An angel appeared to Zechariah while serving in the temple, saying their prayers would be answered and they would have a son (1:11-17). • Elizabeth conceived and was in seclusion for five months (1:24). • She was visited by her cousin, Mary, who was pregnant with Jesus (1:39). • She and her unborn child recognized Jesus the Messiah in utero (1:41-45). • She gave birth to John the Baptist, whom Jesus called the greatest of all men (Mt 11:11).
Life Lesson	Waiting on the Lord often brings unexpected blessings.

and both of them were well along in years.[A]
8 When his division was on duty
and he was serving as priest before
God, 9 it happened that he was chosen by lot, according to the custom
of the priesthood, to enter the sanctuary of the Lord and burn incense.
10 At the hour of incense the whole
assembly of the people was praying
outside. 11 An angel of the Lord appeared to him, standing to the right
of the altar of incense. 12 When Zechariah saw him, he was startled and
overcome with fear.[B] 13 But the angel
said to him:

Do not be afraid, Zechariah,
because your prayer
has been heard.
Your wife Elizabeth will bear
you a son,
and you will name him John.
14 There will be joy and delight
for you,
and many will rejoice
at his birth.
15 For he will be great
in the sight of the Lord
and will never drink wine
or beer.
He will be filled
with the Holy Spirit
while still in his
mother's womb.
16 He will turn many
of the sons of Israel
to the Lord their God.
17 And he will go before Him
in the spirit and power
of Elijah,
to turn the hearts of fathers
to their children,
and the disobedient
to the understanding
of the righteous,
to make ready for the Lord
a prepared people.

18 "How can I know this?" Zechariah asked the angel. "For I am an
old man, and my wife is well along
in years."[C]
19 The angel answered him, "I am
Gabriel, who stands in the presence
of God, and I was sent to speak to
you and tell you this good news.
20 Now listen! You will become silent
and unable to speak until the day
these things take place, because you
did not believe my words, which will
be fulfilled in their proper time."
21 Meanwhile, the people were
waiting for Zechariah, amazed that
he stayed so long in the sanctuary.
22 When he did come out, he could
not speak to them. Then they realized that he had seen a vision in the
sanctuary. He kept making signs
to them and remained speechless.

[A] **1:7** Lit *in their days* [B] **1:12** Lit *and fear fell on him* [C] **1:18** Lit *in her days*

CHARACTER PROFILE

Mary of Nazareth

Mother of Jesus

Her Background	• Lived in Nazareth (1:26) • Engaged to Joseph (1:27) • Related to Elizabeth (1:36) • Descended from King David (3:31) • Eventually had other children (Mk 3:31-32)
Her Story	• An angel appeared to her, announcing she had been chosen to give birth to Jesus (Lk 1:30-33). • She submitted herself to God's will (1:38). • The angel's message was confirmed by Elizabeth (1:42-45). • She gave birth to Jesus in a stable in Bethlehem (2:4-7). • She participated in the ministry of Christ (Jn 2: 1-5). • She was at the cross and given by Jesus into the care of John (Jn 19:25-27). • She prayed with other believers for the Spirit in Jerusalem (Ac 1:12-14).
Life Lesson	Mary modeled an attitude of obedience and trust.

See also Mt 1:16-25.

23 When the days of his ministry were
completed, he went back home.
24 After these days his wife Elizabeth conceived and kept herself in
seclusion for five months. She said,
25 "The Lord has done this for me. He
has looked with favor in these days
to take away my disgrace among the
people."

The Annunciation of the Birth of Jesus (1:26-38)

26 In the sixth month, the angel
Gabriel was sent by God to a town
in Galilee called Nazareth, 27 to a
virgin •engaged to a man named
Joseph, of the house of David. The
virgin's name was Mary. 28 And the
angel came to her and said, "Rejoice, favored woman! The Lord is
with you."[A] 29 But she was deeply
troubled by this statement, wondering what kind of greeting this could
be. 30 Then the angel told her:

Do not be afraid, Mary,
for you have found favor
with God.
31 Now listen:
You will conceive
and give birth to a son,
and you will call
His name Jesus.
32 He will be great
and will be called the Son of
the Most High,
and the Lord God
will give Him
the throne of His father
David.
33 He will reign over the house
of Jacob forever,
and His kingdom will have
no end.

34 Mary asked the angel, "How can
this be, since I have not been intimate with a man?"[B]
35 The angel replied to her:

"The Holy Spirit will come
upon you,
and the power
of the Most High
will overshadow you.
Therefore, the holy One
to be born
will be called the Son of God.

36 And consider your relative Elizabeth—even she has conceived a son
in her old age, and this is the sixth
month for her who was called childless. 37 For nothing will be impossible with God."
38 "I am the Lord's •slave,"[C] said

[A]1:28 Other mss add *blessed are you among women* [B]1:34 Lit *since I do not know a man*
[C]1:38 Lit *Look, the Lord's slave*

More important than what was forbidden for John was what was promised by God. In the Old Testament the Holy Spirit came upon a prophet later in life, but John the Baptist would **be filled with the Holy Spirit while still in his mother's womb**, showing again God's supernatural intervention as well as giving subtle affirmation to life in the womb as worthy of divine protection and as receiving an endowment for service.

1:16-17 John's message would include the straightforward admonition to families to restore godly leadership in the home. He would call fathers to turn to their children with love and compassion, persuading their offspring to look to God.

1:24-25 For Elizabeth to keep **herself in seclusion for five months** would hide her pregnancy from public view (v. 24). Whether this action was her choice because of innuendos from curious neighbors was not apparent. Even Mary was unaware of the pregnancy of her relative Elizabeth (v. 36). On the other hand, this seclusion may have been God's plan to follow His timing on these glorious events. In any case, when Elizabeth did appear, she was quick to acknowledge with humble gratitude what God had done in removing the stigma of her barren womb and giving her new usefulness in His divine purpose (v. 25).

1:26-38 Mary, too, was approached by an angel, and she questioned how this birth could come about, since she had never "known" a man. Zechariah had expressed his doubt (v. 20) with a seemingly innocent question. But on Mary's part this question was not so much an indication of unbelief as it was a sincere inquiry concerning how conception could possibly come about any other way (v. 34). God's power over reproduction was at work respectively in the wombs of both Mary and Elizabeth and was completely consistent with His supernatural powers revealed elsewhere (vv. 35-36). In Elizabeth's case there were clearly Old Testament examples of barren women becoming pregnant (Sarah, Gn 21:1-7; Hannah, 1Sm 1:1-19); but with Mary, what she was being promised by the angel was unprecedented. **Virgin** (Gk *parthenos*), although sometimes translated with a broader meaning as "maid," is clear here in its more restrictive sense. Many argue that the people of the first century did not understand the laws of nature and thus were gullible to believe in the supernatural, especially in the idea of a miraculous "virgin birth." However, precisely because Mary understood the laws of nature, she questioned the angel. An understanding of the supernatural is enhanced by an understanding of the natural. Mary clearly knew that what Gabriel had promised her could not come about naturally (v. 34).

Luke refers to the Holy Spirit repeatedly in the first four chapters (1:41,67,80; 2:25-27). In the description of conception, the Holy Spirit would **overshadow** (Gk *episkiasei*, "cast a shadow, cover") Mary, suggesting the powerful presence of God (1:35). The same word is used in the accounts of the transfiguration (9:34; Mt 17:5; Mk 9:7) to describe the overshadowing of the cloud from which God spoke, identifying Jesus as His Son.

A woman cannot help but be touched by Mary's servant heart. She submitted to the inevitable shame and suffering that would accompany a premarital pregnancy. Her submission was to God (Lk 1:48) and served as the crowning touch to her humble confidence in the Lord (v. 38).

1:39-56 Throughout this narrative Luke has interwoven the lives of the two women—different in age and in season of life but the same in their spirit of commitment, which prompted each to offer herself to the Savior. Both mothers were told of the place their sons would hold in the divine economy, and each accepted her own role and that of her son with humble obedience. As soon as the sound of Mary's voice was heard, John **leaped inside** the womb of his mother, and Elizabeth was **filled with the Holy Spirit** (v. 41). Nowhere is Mary called the "Mother of God," but she is clearly identified as the mother of Jesus, the Messiah (v. 43).

Mary responded to Elizabeth with a hymn of praise, one similar in context to the words spoken by Hannah in 1Sm 2:1-10. Mary's hymn, known as the *Magnificat*, spoke of the deliverance of Israel, both spiritual and physical; but it also told of the illumination that would come to the Gentiles. The hymn was marked by these distinctions:

- many Old Testament phrases and references (Lk 1:54; Ps 98:3);
- evidence of the deep piety of Mary with character traits appropriate for the mother of the Lord (vv. 47-48);
- affirmation of her personal knowledge about the Old Testament (vv. 50-53);
- call to action in meeting physical needs (vv. 51-53);
- consciousness of her own role in the divine economy (vv. 46-49).

Some suggest that Luke composed this hymn, implying that the literary masterpiece could not have come from a young peasant girl. Such conjecture dismisses the matter of divine inspiration, which by definition surpasses human ability and giftedness, and is able to place a heavenly message in an earthly vessel. Although one would assume that Mary, as most

Mary. "May it be done to me according to your word." Then the angel left her.

Mary's Visit to Elizabeth (1:39-56)

39 In those days Mary set out and
hurried to a town in the hill country of Judah 40 where she entered
Zechariah's house and greeted
Elizabeth. 41 When Elizabeth heard
Mary's greeting, the baby leaped
inside her,[A] and Elizabeth was filled
with the Holy Spirit. 42 Then she exclaimed with a loud cry:

"You are the most blessed
  of women,
and your child
  will be blessed![B]

43 How could this happen to me,
that the mother of my Lord should
come to me? 44 For you see, when
the sound of your greeting reached
my ears, the baby leaped for joy inside me![C] 45 She who has believed is
blessed because what was spoken to
her by the Lord will be fulfilled!"
46 And Mary said:

My soul proclaims
  the greatness of[D] the Lord,
47 and my spirit has rejoiced
  in God my Savior,
48 because He has looked
  with favor
on the humble condition
  of His slave.
Surely, from now on
  all generations
will call me blessed,
49 because the Mighty One
has done great things for me,
and His name is holy.
50 His mercy is from generation
  to generation
on those who fear Him.
51 He has done a mighty deed
  with His arm;
He has scattered the proud
because of the thoughts
  of their hearts;
52 He has toppled the mighty
  from their thrones
and exalted the lowly.
53 He has satisfied the hungry
  with good things
and sent the rich away empty.
54 He has helped
  His servant Israel,
mindful of His mercy,[E]
55 just as He spoke
  to our ancestors,
to Abraham and his
  descendants[F] forever.

56 And Mary stayed with her about
three months; then she returned to
her home.

The Birth of John the Baptist (1:57-80)

57 Now the time had come for Elizabeth to give birth, and she had a
son. 58 Then her neighbors and relatives heard that the Lord had shown
her His great mercy,[G] and they rejoiced with her.
59 When they came to circumcise
the child on the eighth day, they
were going to name him Zechariah,
after his father. 60 But his mother
responded, "No! He will be called
John."
61 Then they said to her, "None of
your relatives has that name." 62 So
they motioned to his father to find
out what he wanted him to be called.
63 He asked for a writing tablet and
wrote:

HIS NAME IS JOHN.

And they were all amazed. 64 Immediately his mouth was opened and
his tongue set free, and he began to
speak, praising God. 65 Fear came on
all those who lived around them, and
all these things were being talked
about throughout the hill country
of Judea. 66 All who heard about him
took it to heart, saying, "What then
will this child become?" For, indeed,
the Lord's hand was with him.
67 Then his father Zechariah was
filled with the Holy Spirit and
prophesied:

68 Praise the Lord, the God
  of Israel,
because He has visited
and provided •redemption
  for His people.
69 He has raised up a •horn
  of salvation[H] for us

[A]**1:41** Lit *leaped in her abdomen* or *womb* [B]**1:42** Lit *and the fruit of your abdomen* (or *womb*) *is blessed* [C]**1:44** Lit *in my abdomen* or *womb* [D]**1:46** Or *soul magnifies* [E]**1:54** Because He remembered His mercy; Ps 98:3 [F]**1:55** Or *offspring*; lit *seed* [G]**1:58** Lit *the Lord magnified His mercy with her* [H]**1:69** = a strong Savior

in the house of His servant
David,
70 just as He spoke by the mouth
of His holy prophets
in ancient times;
71 salvation from our enemies
and from the clutches[A]
of those who hate us.
72 He has dealt mercifully
with our fathers
and remembered
His holy covenant—
73 the oath that He swore
to our father Abraham.
He has given us the privilege,
74 since we have been rescued
from our enemies' clutches,[B]
to serve Him without fear
75 in holiness and righteousness
in His presence all our days.
76 And child, you will be called
a prophet of the Most High,
for you will go
before the Lord
to prepare His ways,
77 to give His people knowledge
of salvation
through the forgiveness
of their sins.
78 Because of our God's merciful
compassion,
the Dawn from on high
will visit us
79 to shine on those who live
in darkness
and the shadow of death,
to guide our feet into the way
of peace.

80 The child grew up and became
spiritually strong, and he was in the
wilderness until the day of his public
appearance to Israel.

The Birth of Jesus (2:1-20)

2 In those days a decree went out
from Caesar Augustus[C] that the
whole empire[D] should be registered.
2 This first registration took place
while[E] Quirinius was governing
Syria. 3 So everyone went to be registered, each to his own town.
4 And Joseph also went up from
the town of Nazareth in Galilee, to
Judea, to the city of David, which is
called Bethlehem, because he was of
the house and family line of David,
5 to be registered along with Mary,
who was •engaged to him[F] and was
pregnant. 6 While they were there,
the time came for her to give birth.
7 Then she gave birth to her firstborn
Son, and she wrapped Him snugly
in cloth and laid Him in a feeding
trough—because there was no room
for them at the lodging place.
8 In the same region, shepherds
were staying out in the fields and
keeping watch at night over their
flock. 9 Then an angel of the Lord
stood before[G] them, and the glory
of the Lord shone around them, and
they were terrified.[H] 10 But the angel
said to them, "Don't be afraid, for
look, I proclaim to you good news
of great joy that will be for all the
people:[I] 11 Today a Savior, who is
•Messiah the Lord, was born for you
in the city of David. 12 This will be
the sign for you: You will find a baby
wrapped snugly in cloth and lying in
a feeding trough."
13 Suddenly there was a multitude
of the heavenly host with the angel,
praising God and saying:

14 Glory to God
in the highest heaven,
and peace on earth to people
He favors![J,K]

15 When the angels had left them
and returned to heaven, the shepherds said to one another, "Let's go
straight to Bethlehem and see what
has happened, which the Lord has
made known to us."
16 They hurried off and found both
Mary and Joseph, and the baby who
was lying in the feeding trough. 17 After seeing them, they reported the
message they were told about this
child, 18 and all who heard it were
amazed at what the shepherds said
to them. 19 But Mary was treasur-
ing up all these things[L] in her heart
and meditating on them. 20 The
shepherds returned, glorifying and

[A]**1:71** Lit *the hand* [B]**1:74** Lit *from the hand of enemies* [C]**2:1** Emperor who ruled the Roman Empire 27 B.C.–A.D. 14; also known as Octavian, he established the peaceful era known as the *Pax Romana*; Caesar was a title of Roman emperors. [D]**2:1** Or *the whole inhabited world* [E]**2:2** Or *This registration was the first while*, or *This registration was before* [F]**2:5** Other mss read *was his engaged wife* [G]**2:9** Or *Lord appeared to* [H]**2:9** Lit *they feared a great fear* [I]**2:10** Or *the whole nation* [J]**2:14** Other mss read *earth good will to people* [K]**2:14** Or *earth to men of good will* [L]**2:19** Lit *these words*

young women in her peer group, was uneducated, the text does not say so. She, as the chosen vessel to nurture the Messiah, may have had some unique opportunities for learning; she may have had extraordinary giftedness with the ability to recall the Old Testament Scripture, which she probably had heard repeatedly in her home and in the synagogue. Whether the song came to her in a moment of inspiration or over time in private meditation, Mary was noted by Luke as the human composer of these meaningful and beautifully fashioned words that have been recorded for the generations. The mother of the Lord Jesus was indeed an extraordinary woman.

Mary actually described herself as the **slave** (Gk *doulēs*, "female servant") of the Lord. There is no hint of an oppressive bondage imposed by another but rather a self-determined submission to God's will (vv. 38,48).

1:57-80 After John was born, Elizabeth's relatives **were going to name him** after his father **Zechariah**. But Elizabeth protested, claiming that his name was to be **John**. When her relatives asked her husband Zechariah about it, he quickly agreed with his wife. At that moment, Zechariah's tongue was loosed and he gave praise to God. His hymn is commonly called the *Benedictus* (Lat, "blessed"). Like Mary's hymn, it speaks of rescue from Israel's physical enemies, of spiritual restoration, and of blessings to the Gentiles (vv. 68-79). The covenant God made with Abraham was being fulfilled, and this covenant included blessings to all nations. John's childhood and adult years were briefly mentioned, specifying that he resided **in the wilderness**. This description of the forerunner cleared the way for the entrance of the Messiah.

2:8-20 The timing of Jesus' birth almost certainly was not during December since the **shepherds were staying out in the fields** (v. 8). The months spent out in the fields began as early as March but must have ended by November because of the weather. Luke emphasized the humble beginnings of the Savior even further by recording the announcement made to the shepherds. Shepherds were despised in the first century for their lifestyles; some had the reputation of being thieves. Nevertheless, to such lowly people, the angels announced the birth of God's Son, **a Savior, who is Messiah the Lord** (vv. 10-11). "Savior" is the most distinctive title for Jesus in Luke, while "Lord" is more prevalent in Acts. The **heavenly host** presented a doxology with heavenly and earthly components: **Glory** (Gk *doxa*, "splendor, brightness") belongs to God, but His favor (Gk *eudoxia*, "good will, good pleasure") rests upon His people (v. 14). These very humble and ordinary men—**shepherds**—became the first evangelists to proclaim the Savior's birth. They delivered **the message they were told about this child** (v. 17).

2:21-24 During childbirth a woman became unclean because the flow of blood and the bodily discharge associated with the birth were considered impure. **Eight days** was the set period for preparing for the **circumcision** of a male child, at which time medical science has since affirmed that the coagulants reach their maximum effectiveness, making that day the safest time for the minor surgical procedure. Both Jesus and His forerunner John were circumcised according to Jewish law (v. 21; 1:59), embracing the covenant mark God had given to Abraham (Gn 17:12-14; 21:4; Lv 12:3). Circumcision occurred on the eighth day. For a male child the mother was considered unclean for an additional 33 days (Lv 12:1-5) or a total of 40 days. Then the mother had to offer a sacrifice and present her first son to the Lord (Nm 18:15). Luke was careful to note that Mary and Joseph fulfilled the Law:

- **He was named Jesus** (Lk 2:21; cp. 1:31);
- He was circumcised on the eighth day (2:21);
- Mary completed her days of **purification** (v. 22);
- Mary and Joseph presented Jesus, the firstborn male, to the Lord in Jerusalem (vv. 22-23);
- They offered a sacrifice of **a pair of turtledoves or two young pigeons** (v. 24), as expected from a humble, poor family (Lv 2:6-8).

2:25-40 Mary's first visit to the temple after Jesus' birth took place on the eighth day, the appointed time to circumcise Him.

2:36-40 Anna the elderly **prophetess** also thanked God for Jesus and spoke about Him in her own words of testimony **to all who were looking for the redemption of Jerusalem**. The words of Simeon and Anna set Jesus apart from John by showing that the ministry of Jesus was destined to surpass the ministry of John. Simeon saw the Christ child and was ready to die (v. 29); Anna saw Him and began to bear witness to those who would listen (v. 38).

Anna A Prophetess

Her Background	• She was a prophetess from the tribe of Asher (2:36). • She was married for seven years and a widow for 84 years, or she was a widow until age 84, depending on how the text is understood (vv. 36-37). • She lived in the temple compound, fasting and praying daily (v. 37).
Her Story	• She arrived at the moment Simeon was blessing baby Jesus and prophesying about Him (vv. 36-38). • She also recognized the Christ child and began praising God (v. 38).
Life Lesson	God's perfect timing is found when you are sensitive to His Spirit and follow His promptings.

praising God for all they had seen
and heard, just as they had been
told.

The Presentation of Jesus in the Temple (2:21-40)

21 When the eight days were completed for His circumcision, He was
named Jesus—the name given by
the angel before He was conceived.[A]
22 And when the days of their purification according to the law of Moses
were finished, they brought Him up
to Jerusalem to present Him to the
Lord 23 (just as it is written in the law
of the Lord: **Every firstborn male**[B]
will be dedicated[C] **to the Lord**[D])
24 and to offer a sacrifice (according
to what is stated in the law of the
Lord: **a pair of turtledoves or two
young pigeons**[E]).
25 There was a man in Jerusalem
whose name was Simeon. This man
was righteous and devout, looking
forward to Israel's consolation,[F] and
the Holy Spirit was on him. 26 It had
been revealed to him by the Holy
Spirit that he would not see death
before he saw the Lord's Messiah.
27 Guided by the Spirit, he entered[G]
the •temple complex. When the parents brought in the child Jesus to
perform for Him what was customary under the law, 28 Simeon took
Him up in his arms, praised God,
and said:

29 Now, Master,
You can dismiss Your •slave
in peace,
as You promised.
30 For my eyes have seen
Your salvation.
31 You have prepared it
in the presence
of all peoples—
32 a light for revelation
to the Gentiles[H]
and glory
to Your people Israel.

33 His father and mother[I] were
amazed at what was being said about
Him. 34 Then Simeon blessed them
and told His mother Mary: "Indeed,
this child is destined to cause the
fall and rise of many in Israel and
to be a sign that will be opposed[J]—
35 and a sword will pierce your own
soul—that the thoughts[K] of many
hearts may be revealed."
36 There was also a prophetess,
Anna, a daughter of Phanuel, of the
tribe of Asher. She was well along
in years,[L] having lived with her
husband seven years after her marriage,[M] 37 and was a widow for 84
years.[N] She did not leave the temple
complex, serving God night and day

[A]**2:21** Or *conceived in the womb* [B]**2:23** Lit *"Every male that opens a womb* [C]**2:23** Lit *be called holy* [D]**2:23** Ex 13:2,12 [E]**2:24** Lv 5:11; 12:8 [F]**2:25** The coming of the Messiah with His salvation for the nation; Is 40:1; 61:2; Lk 2:26,30 [G]**2:27** Lit *And in the Spirit, he came into* [H]**2:32** Or *the nations* [I]**2:33** Other mss read *But Joseph and His mother* [J]**2:34** Or *spoken against* [K]**2:35** Or *schemes* [L]**2:36** Lit *in many days* [M]**2:36** Lit *years from her virginity* [N]**2:37** Or *she was a widow until the age of 84*

with fasting and prayers. 38 At that
very moment,[A] she came up and began to thank God and to speak about
Him to all who were looking forward
to the •redemption of Jerusalem.[B]
39 When they had completed everything according to the law of the
Lord, they returned to Galilee, to
their own town of Nazareth. 40 The
boy grew up and became strong,
filled with wisdom, and God's grace
was on Him.

The Childhood of Jesus (2:41-52)

41 Every year His parents traveled to Jerusalem for the •Passover
Festival. 42 When He was 12 years
old, they went up according to the
custom of the festival. 43 After those
days were over, as they were returning, the boy Jesus stayed behind in
Jerusalem, but His parents[C] did not
know it. 44 Assuming He was in the
traveling party, they went a day's
journey. Then they began looking
for Him among their relatives and
friends. 45 When they did not find
Him, they returned to Jerusalem to
search for Him. 46 After three days,
they found Him in the temple complex sitting among the teachers,
listening to them and asking them
questions. 47 And all those who heard
Him were astounded at His understanding and His answers. 48 When
His parents saw Him, they were
astonished, and His mother said to
Him, "Son, why have You treated
us like this? Your father and I have
been anxiously searching for You."
49 "Why were you searching for
Me?" He asked them. "Didn't you
know that I had to be in My Father's
house?"[D] 50 But they did not understand what He said to them.
51 Then He went down with them
and came to Nazareth and was obedient to them. His mother kept all
these things in her heart. 52 And
Jesus increased in wisdom and stature, and in favor with God and with
people.

Preparation for Jesus' Ministry (3:1–4:13)

The Work of John (3:1-20)

3 In the fifteenth year of the reign
of Tiberius Caesar,[E] while Pontius •Pilate was governor of Judea,
•Herod was tetrarch[F] of Galilee, his
brother Philip tetrarch of the region
of Iturea[G] and Trachonitis,[G] and Ly-
sanias tetrarch of Abilene,[H] 2 during
the high priesthood of Annas and
Caiaphas, God's word came to John
the son of Zechariah in the wilderness. 3 He went into all the vicinity
of the Jordan, preaching a baptism
of repentance[I] for the forgiveness of
sins, 4 as it is written in the book of
the words of the prophet Isaiah:

A voice of one crying out
in the wilderness:
Prepare the way for the Lord;
make His paths straight!
5 **Every valley will be filled,**
and every mountain and hill
will be made low;[J]
the crooked
will become straight,
the rough ways smooth,
6 **and everyone**[K] **will see**
the salvation of God.[L]

7 He then said to the crowds who
came out to be baptized by him,
"Brood of vipers! Who warned you to
flee from the coming wrath? 8 Therefore produce fruit consistent with
repentance. And don't start saying
to yourselves, 'We have Abraham as
our father,' for I tell you that God is
able to raise up children for Abraham from these stones! 9 Even now
the ax is ready to strike[M] the root of
the trees! Therefore, every tree that
doesn't produce good fruit will be
cut down and thrown into the fire."
10 "What then should we do?" the
crowds were asking him.
11 He replied to them, "The one
who has two shirts[N] must share with
someone who has none, and the one
who has food must do the same."
12 Tax collectors also came to
be baptized, and they asked him,
"Teacher, what should we do?"

2:41-52 The incident between the young boy Jesus and the erudite Jewish leaders in the temple, recorded only by Luke, sheds light on an event in the life of Jesus before He officially began his ministry. He astounded the religious leaders by **asking** penetrating **questions** (v. 46). Luke does not attempt to give a detailed account of Jesus' early years, but he did provide this brief vignette showing Jesus' humanity.

When Joseph and Mary finally **found** Jesus **in the temple** and expressed their anxiety about looking for him, Jesus' response drew attention to His unique identity as the Son of God (v. 49). Although she and Joseph **did not understand** this at the time, Mary added this incident to her heart's treasury of evidence of His divinity (v. 51). The boy Jesus submitted to His parents by going home with them. And, under their nurture, He grew and matured, honoring Mary and Joseph as other children were expected to honor their parents.

3:1-22 Luke's introduction of John the Baptist not only reflects historical precision and accuracy but also bears much similarity with some of the introductions of the Old Testament prophets (Is 1:1; Jr 1:1-3; Hs 1:1; Am 1:1).

Luke's opening chapters present many of the same themes as Matthew but appealing to a broader Gentile audience. For example, in quoting Is 40, Matthew only quotes verse 3, while Luke includes verses 4 and 5 and the words **everyone will see the salvation of God**. Matthew singles out the Pharisee and Sadducees as those who came to hear John and who were addressed by him, but Luke records John's address to the crowd. Luke gives the fuller account in which John the Baptist raised the question concerning what they should do to bear fruit in keeping with repentance. The people, the **tax collectors**, and the **soldiers** were all instructed by John the Baptist concerning how they should live their daily lives. They were to **share with** those who were in need. They were not to be greedy but were to live as a people of integrity. Luke emphasizes the practical and concrete. He is concerned about the social aspects of the life of faith. Even in Jesus' baptism (Lk 3:21-22), only Luke mentions that **the Holy Spirit descended on Him** [Jesus] **in a physical appearance like a dove** (3:22).

[A]**2:38** Lit *very hour* [B]**2:38** Other mss read *in Jerusalem* [C]**2:43** Other mss read *but Joseph and His mother* [D]**2:49** Or *be involved in My Father's interests* (or *things*), or *be among My Father's people* [E]**3:1** Emperor who ruled the Roman Empire A.D. 14–37 [F]**3:1** Or *ruler* [G]**3:1** A small province northeast of Galilee [H]**3:1** A small Syrian province [I]**3:3** Or *baptism based on repentance* [J]**3:5** Lit *be humbled* [K]**3:6** Lit *all flesh* [L]**3:4-6** Is 40:3-5 [M]**3:9** Lit *the ax lies at* [N]**3:11** Lit *tunics*

3:23-38 The genealogy presented in Luke appealed to a broader audience than the one in Matthew. Luke emphasizes Christ's humanity and His universal appeal. Luke does not begin Jesus' genealogy with Abraham (as does Matthew); he traces Jesus' lineage with an emphasis on His humanity, showing that Jesus was the **son of Adam** as well as the divine Son of God. Some scholars have suggested that Luke presents Christ's natural and royal ancestry through Mary while Matthew presents Christ's legal and royal ancestry through Joseph. Yet Luke still substantiates His messianic claim by noting Jesus' descent from David. Only the ancestors from **Heli** (v. 23) to **Zerubbabel** (v. 27) are found in other accounts. Luke seems primarily concerned with presenting Jesus as the Savior of all people, not just the Jews. With the exception of verses 23-27, you can find the genealogy in the Old Testament (Gn 5:3-32; 11:10-26; Ru 4:18-22; 1Ch 1:1-4,24-28; 2:1-15).

Some have commented extensively on the differences between the genealogies in Mt 1:1-17 and here in Lk 3:23-38. In summary, consider these options for explaining the differences:

- One gives legal descent and the other physical descent, which occurred especially when the law of levirate marriage was involved (Dt 25:5); or
- Both Mary and **Joseph** descended from David but by different branches of the family.

The latter seems more likely as noted in earlier discussion.

4:1-13 The **40 days** (v. 2) probably served as a reminder of the 40-year wilderness experience of Israel after the exodus (Nm 14:33; 32:13; Dt 2:7) or of the 40 days Moses spent on the mountain (Dt 9:9). With Israel, God was testing His people; with Jesus, Satan was allowed to tempt the Son of God (cp. Mt 4:1-11). Here the one who opposes God is called the **Devil** (Gk *diabolou*, a compound of *dia*, "through," and *ballō*, "throw, cast"), "the one who casts through" (Lk 4:2). Luke records that the Devil left Him only **for a time** (v. 13).

Clearly, Satan's power is always limited. God Himself never *tempts* His people (Jms 1:13) in the sense of trying to get them to sin or to do evil. That would be contrary to His divine nature. He *allows* Satan to tempt His children since nothing happens unless God lifts His hand and allows it. In this sense, God tests His people by letting them make choices.

13 He told them, "Don't collect any
more than what you have been authorized."
14 Some soldiers also questioned
him: "What should we do?"
He said to them, "Don't take
money from anyone by force or false
accusation; be satisfied with your
wages."
15 Now the people were waiting
expectantly, and all of them were
debating in their minds[A] whether
John might be the •Messiah. 16 John
answered them all, "I baptize you
with[B] water, but One is coming who
is more powerful than I. I am not
worthy to untie the strap of His sandals. He will baptize you with[B] the
Holy Spirit and fire. 17 His winnowing shovel[C] is in His hand to clear
His threshing floor and gather the
wheat into His barn, but the chaff
He will burn up with a fire that
never goes out." 18 Then, along with
many other exhortations, he proclaimed good news to the people.
19 But Herod the tetrarch, being rebuked by him about Herodias, his
brother's wife, and about all the evil
things Herod had done, 20 added this
to everything else—he locked John
up in prison.

The Baptism of Jesus (3:21-22)

21 When all the people were baptized, Jesus also was baptized. As He
was praying, heaven opened, 22 and
the Holy Spirit descended on Him
in a physical appearance like a dove.
And a voice came from heaven:

You are My beloved Son.
I take delight in You!

The Genealogy of Jesus (3:23-38)

23 As He began His ministry, Jesus
was about 30 years old and was
thought to be[D] the

son of Joseph, son[E] of Heli,
24 son of Matthat, son of Levi,
son of Melchi, son of Jannai,
son of Joseph,
25 son of Mattathias,
son of Amos, son of Nahum,
son of Esli, son of Naggai,
26 son of Maath,
son of Mattathias,
son of Semein, son of Josech,
son of Joda, 27 son of Joanan,
son of Rhesa,
son of Zerubbabel,
son of Shealtiel, son of Neri,
28 son of Melchi, son of Addi,
son of Cosam,
son of Elmadam,
son of Er, 29 son of Joshua,
son of Eliezer, son of Jorim,
son of Matthat, son of Levi,
30 son of Simeon, son of Judah,
son of Joseph, son of Jonam,
son of Eliakim, 31 son of Melea,
son of Menna, son of Mattatha,
son of Nathan, son of David,
32 son of Jesse, son of Obed,
son of Boaz, son of Salmon,[F]
son of Nahshon,
33 son of Amminadab,
son of Ram,[G] son of Hezron,
son of Perez, son of Judah,
34 son of Jacob, son of Isaac,
son of Abraham, son of Terah,
son of Nahor, 35 son of Serug,
son of Reu, son of Peleg,
son of Eber, son of Shelah,
36 son of Cainan,
son of Arphaxad,
son of Shem, son of Noah,
son of Lamech,
37 son of Methuselah,
son of Enoch, son of Jared,
son of Mahalaleel,
son of Cainan,
38 son of Enos, son of Seth,
son of Adam, son of God.

The Temptation of Jesus (4:1-13)

4 Then Jesus returned from the
Jordan, full of the Holy Spirit,
and was led by the Spirit in the wilderness 2 for 40 days to be tempted
by the Devil. He ate nothing during those days, and when they were
over,[H] He was hungry. 3 The Devil
said to Him, "If You are the Son
of God, tell this stone to become
bread."
4 But Jesus answered him, "It is
written: **Man must not live on bread
alone.**"[I,J]

[A]**3:15** Or *hearts* [B]**3:16** Or *in* [C]**3:17** A wooden farm implement used to toss threshed grain into the wind so the lighter chaff would blow away and separate from the heavier grain [D]**3:23** People did not know about His virgin birth; Mt 1:18-25; Lk 1:26-38 [E]**3:23** The relationship in some cases may be more distant than a son. [F]**3:32** Other mss read *Sala* [G]**3:33** Other mss read *Amminadab, son of Aram, son of Joram*; other mss read *Amminadab, son of Admin, son of Arni* [H]**4:2** Lit *were completed* [I]**4:4** Other mss add *but on every word of God* [J]**4:4** Dt 8:3

5 So he took Him up[A] and showed
Him all the kingdoms of the world in
a moment of time. 6 The Devil said to
Him, "I will give You their splendor
and all this authority, because it has
been given over to me, and I can give
it to anyone I want. 7 If You, then,
will worship me,[B] all will be Yours."
8 And Jesus answered him,[C] "It is
written:

Worship the Lord your God,
and serve Him only."[D]

9 So he took Him to Jerusalem,
had Him stand on the pinnacle of
the temple, and said to Him, "If You
are the Son of God, throw Yourself
down from here. 10 For it is written:

He will give His angels
orders concerning you,
to protect you,[E] 11 and
they will support you
with their hands,
so that you will not strike
your foot against a stone."[F]

12 And Jesus answered him, "It
is said: **Do not test the Lord your
God."**[G]
13 After the Devil had finished every temptation, he departed from
Him for a time.

Ministry in and Around Galilee (4:14–9:50)

Preaching in Nazareth (4:14-30)

14 Then Jesus returned to Galilee
in the power of the Spirit, and news
about Him spread throughout the
entire vicinity. 15 He was teaching in
their •synagogues, being acclaimed[H]
by everyone.
16 He came to Nazareth, where
He had been brought up. As usual,
He entered the synagogue on the
Sabbath day and stood up to read.
17 The scroll of the prophet Isaiah
was given to Him, and unrolling the
scroll, He found the place where it
was written:

18 **The Spirit of the Lord is**
on Me,
because He has anointed Me
to preach good news
to the poor.
He has sent Me[I]
to proclaim freedom[J]
to the captives
and recovery of sight
to the blind,
to set free the oppressed,
19 **to proclaim the year**
of the Lord's favor.[K,L]

20 He then rolled up the scroll,
gave it back to the attendant, and
sat down. And the eyes of everyone
in the synagogue were fixed on Him.
21 He began by saying to them, "Today as you listen, this Scripture has
been fulfilled."
22 They were all speaking well of
Him[M] and were amazed by the gracious words that came from His
mouth, yet they said, "Isn't this Joseph's son?"
23 Then He said to them, "No doubt
you will quote this proverb[N] to Me:
'Doctor, heal yourself. So all we've
heard that took place in Capernaum,
do here in Your hometown also.'"
24 He also said, "•I assure you: No
prophet is accepted in his hometown. 25 But I say to you, there were
certainly many widows in Israel in
Elijah's days, when the sky was shut
up for three years and six months
while a great famine came over all
the land. 26 Yet Elijah was not sent
to any of them—but to a widow at
Zarephath in Sidon. 27 And in the
prophet Elisha's time, there were
many in Israel who had serious skin
diseases, yet not one of them was
healed[O]—only Naaman the Syrian."
28 When they heard this, everyone in the synagogue was enraged.
29 They got up, drove Him out of
town, and brought Him to the edge[P]
of the hill that their town was built
on, intending to hurl Him over the
cliff. 30 But He passed right through
the crowd and went on His way.

Beginning a Healing Ministry (4:31-44)

31 Then He went down to Capernaum, a town in Galilee, and was
teaching them on the Sabbath.

4:14-30 Luke is the only writer to emphasize that Jesus began His ministry in Galilee **in the power of the Spirit**. This scene concerning Jesus' visit, and ultimate rejection, at His hometown in Nazareth, is described with more detail than Matthew and is perfectly fitted for Luke's overall purpose. The event took place during Jesus' Galilean ministry.

When Jesus **entered the synagogue** He **was given** the **scroll** of Isaiah, and He found the passage that described His overall mission (Is 61:1-2; see also 58:6). Both the physical and spiritual aspects of the Messiah's ministry were seen in these few verses. The people **were amazed** at His words, but their questions concerning His identity as **Joseph's son** (Lk 4:22) hint at their unbelief. Jesus' response was harsh, a **proverb** (v. 23) that was undoubtedly well known by the common people. Jesus used it to make a crucial point (v. 24). Those who are recognized as great in other places are not recognized as such at home.

Jesus implicitly put Himself in the same category of authority as the Old Testament prophets **Elijah** and Elisha (vv. 25-27). Also, by highlighting God's ministry to Gentiles through these prophets—having sent Elijah to meet the needs of a **widow** living outside Israel and having brought a foreign general to Elisha for healing—Jesus underscored His intention to fulfill God's mission of extending the offer of salvation to all people (i.e., including Gentiles among **the poor**, **the captives**, **the blind**, and **the oppressed**; vv. 18-19). As the Jews had rejected the prophets of the Old Testament, so the infuriated Jews rejected Jesus in His **hometown** synagogue (vv. 28-30).

4:31-44 Following on the heels of Jesus' proclamation of the purpose of His mission in Nazareth came a demonstration of its truth. Jesus entered a synagogue in **Capernaum**, His new hometown. His **authority** was revealed when a demon-possessed man addressed Him **with a loud voice**, begging to be left alone. Jesus silenced the demon and cast him out (v. 35). As at Nazareth, the people were amazed at His teaching and authority (v. 32). But there was a difference in their response. His identity was not questioned. In fact, the demons verified that He is the Son of God. Unbelief was not immediately evident in this context; therefore, Jesus' healing ministry advanced and culminated with the healings at Simon Peter's house.

Peter's **mother-in-law** was the first to draw Jesus' attention (v. 38). After He **rebuked** her **fever**, she served those present (cp. Mk 1:29-31). Soon her house was filled with those who needed the Master's touch.

[A]**4:5** Other mss read *So the Devil took Him up on a high mountain* [B]**4:7** Lit *will fall down before me* [C]**4:8** Other mss add *"Get behind Me, Satan!* [D]**4:8** Dt 6:13 [E]**4:10** Ps 91:11 [F]**4:11** Ps 91:12 [G]**4:12** Dt 6:16 [H]**4:15** Or *glorified* [I]**4:18** Other mss add *to heal the brokenhearted,* [J]**4:18** Or *release*, or *forgiveness* [K]**4:19** The time of messianic grace [L]**4:18-19** Is 61:1-2 [M]**4:22** Or *They were testifying against Him* [N]**4:23** Or *parable* [O]**4:27** Lit *cleansed* [P]**4:29** Lit *brow*

5:1-11 The calling of the first disciples is paralleled in Mt 4:18-22 and Mk 1:16-20, but Luke gives a fuller and more interesting account of the event. Because **the crowd was pressing in on Jesus**, He got into Simon's boat and taught the people from a position away from the shore. Luke makes clear that those first disciples had a good chance to hear Jesus teach just before He called them. They had heard Him before this time (Jn 1:40-42), but perhaps this insight from Luke indicated that their decision to follow Jesus was not one made impulsively but after hearing His teachings. Further, Jesus actually helped these poor fishermen by guiding them to the catch of their lives. They had **worked hard all night**, but with nothing to show for it. At Jesus' command, however, they **let down** their **nets** and brought in such a large load that their boats **began to sink** (Lk 5:6-7).

Simon Peter's confession concerning his own true nature is highly significant. Peter shows here an understanding not only of his own inadequacy but also of his own sinfulness (v. 8). Luke often focuses on an individual in order to draw attention to Jesus. Here Jesus' holiness and power are contrasted with Peter's weakness and sinfulness.

The radical nature of discipleship is also emphasized here. Luke alone mentions that the disciples **left everything** to follow Jesus (v. 11).

5:12–6:11 As in Matthew and Mark, Luke is concerned to show the reasons why Christianity went beyond ancient Judaism. Luke shows Jesus' conflicts with the religious leaders in order to demonstrate the Lord's authority to heal and to forgive sins and to reveal His superiority over the old traditions of Judaism.

5:12-16 First, Jesus healed the leper, which demonstrated His authority over disease and His compassion for the sick. **Serious skin disease** seemed to be synonymous with leprosy. The disease is not necessarily equivalent to modern-day Hansen's disease, but its victims were repulsive to society, and there was no known cure. In the eyes of the people, the most astounding thing Jesus did was to touch the man (5:13) since lepers were considered unclean (cp. Lv 13:9-11,45-46). Obviously this simple gesture communicated concern in a way nothing else would. The man's humble statement, **"Lord, if You are willing, You can make me clean,"** by which words he affirmed his confidence in Jesus' ability to heal and thus Jesus' divinity, His authority, and His power. Jesus not only responded with **"I am willing,"** but He gave instructions to the man seeking help with the message **be made clean** (Gk *katharisthēti*, "purify, declare ritually

32 They were astonished at His teaching because His message had authority. 33 In the synagogue there was a man with an •unclean demonic spirit who cried out with a loud voice, 34 "Leave us alone![A] What do You have to do with us,[B] Jesus—•Nazarene? Have You come to destroy us? I know who You are—the Holy One of God!"

35 But Jesus rebuked him and said, "Be quiet and come out of him!"

And throwing him down before them, the demon came out of him without hurting him at all. 36 Amazement came over them all, and they kept saying to one another, "What is this message? For He commands the unclean spirits with authority and power, and they come out!" 37 And news about Him began to go out to every place in the vicinity.

38 After He left the synagogue, He entered Simon's house. Simon's mother-in-law was suffering from a high fever, and they asked Him about her. 39 So He stood over her and rebuked the fever, and it left her. She got up immediately and began to serve them.

40 When the sun was setting, all those who had anyone sick with various diseases brought them to Him. As He laid His hands on each one of them, He would heal them. 41 Also, demons were coming out of many, shouting and saying, "You are the Son of God!" But He rebuked them and would not allow them to speak, because they knew He was the •Messiah.

42 When it was day, He went out and made His way to a deserted place. But the crowds were searching for Him. They came to Him and tried to keep Him from leaving them. 43 But He said to them, "I must proclaim the good news about the kingdom of God to the other towns also, because I was sent for this purpose." 44 And He was preaching in the synagogues of Galilee.[C]

Calling the First Disciples (5:1-11)

5 As the crowd was pressing in on Jesus to hear God's word, He was standing by Lake Gennesaret.[D] 2 He saw two boats at the edge of the lake;[E] the fishermen had left them and were washing their nets. 3 He got into one of the boats, which belonged to Simon, and asked him to put out a little from the land. Then He sat down and was teaching the crowds from the boat.

4 When He had finished speaking, He said to Simon, "Put out into deep water and let down[F] your nets for a catch."

5 "Master," Simon replied, "we've worked hard all night long and caught nothing! But at Your word, I'll let down the nets."[G]

6 When they did this, they caught a great number of fish, and their nets[G] began to tear. 7 So they signaled to their partners in the other boat to come and help them; they came and filled both boats so full that they began to sink.

8 When Simon Peter saw this, he fell at Jesus' knees and said, "Go away from me, because I'm a sinful man, Lord!" 9 For he and all those with him were amazed[H] at the catch of fish they took, 10 and so were James and John, Zebedee's sons, who were Simon's partners.

"Don't be afraid," Jesus told Simon. "From now on you will be catching people!" 11 Then they brought the boats to land, left everything, and followed Him.

Participating in Controversies with the Jewish Leaders (5:12–6:11)

12 While He was in one of the towns, a man was there who had a serious skin disease all over him. He saw Jesus, fell facedown, and begged Him: "Lord, if You are willing, You can make me •clean."

13 Reaching out His hand, He touched him, saying, "I am willing; be made clean," and immediately the disease left him. 14 Then He ordered him to tell no one: "But go and show yourself to the priest, and offer what Moses prescribed for your cleansing as a testimony to them."

15 But the news[I] about Him spread even more, and large crowds would

[A]**4:34** Or *Ha!*, or *Ah!* [B]**4:34** Lit *What to us and to You* [C]**4:44** Other mss read *Judea* [D]**5:1** = Sea of Galilee [E]**5:2** Lit *boats standing by the lake* [F]**5:4** Lit *and you* (pl in Gk) *let down* [G]**5:5,6** Other mss read *net* (Gk sg) [H]**5:9** Lit *For amazement had seized him and all those with him* [I]**5:15** Lit *the word*

Doctrine DEITY OF CHRIST

Evidently the **Pharisees and teachers of the law** had heard enough about the popularity of Jesus as a teacher that they felt it necessary to hear and judge what He was teaching the people (5:17). Here Jesus' power to heal is coupled with His power to forgive sins. Luke showed his own keen theological understanding when he included **alone** (Gk *monos*, "only") to indicate the uniqueness of Jesus' authority to **forgive sins**, which was reserved for God alone (v. 21). Luke uses this opportunity to make clear that Jesus is indeed God. Blasphemies were capital crimes and called for stoning of the perpetrators (Lv 24:14-16). This act described not merely speaking against God but insulting or slandering the character of God. The religious leaders believed Jesus had committed blasphemy because they did not accept Him as God but clearly understood that Jesus claimed to do what only God can do (Mk 2:7).

come together to hear Him and to
be healed of their sicknesses. 16 Yet
He often withdrew to deserted places and prayed.
17 On one of those days while He
was teaching, •Pharisees and teachers of the law were sitting there who
had come from every village of Galilee and Judea, and also from Jerusalem. And the Lord's power to heal
was in Him. 18 Just then some men
came, carrying on a mat a man who
was paralyzed. They tried to bring
him in and set him down before
Him. 19 Since they could not find a
way to bring him in because of the
crowd, they went up on the roof and
lowered him on the mat through
the roof tiles into the middle of the
crowd before Jesus.
20 Seeing their faith He said,
"Friend,[A] your sins are forgiven
you."
21 Then the •scribes and the Pharisees began to think: "Who is this
man who speaks blasphemies? Who
can forgive sins but God alone?"
22 But perceiving their thoughts,
Jesus replied to them, "Why are
you thinking this in your hearts?[B]
23 Which is easier: to say, 'Your sins
are forgiven you,' or to say, 'Get up
and walk'? 24 But so you may know
that the •Son of Man has authority
on earth to forgive sins"—He told
the paralyzed man, "I tell you: Get
up, pick up your mat, and go home."
25 Immediately he got up before
them, picked up what he had been
lying on, and went home glorifying
God. 26 Then everyone was astounded, and they were giving glory to
God. And they were filled with awe
and said, "We have seen incredible
things today!"
27 After this, Jesus went out and
saw a tax collector named Levi sitting at the tax office, and He said
to him, "Follow Me!" 28 So, leaving
everything behind, he got up and
began to follow Him.
29 Then Levi hosted a grand banquet for Him at his house. Now there
was a large crowd of tax collectors
and others who were guests[C] with
them. 30 But the Pharisees and their
scribes were complaining to His disciples, "Why do you eat and drink
with tax collectors and sinners?"
31 Jesus replied to them, "The
healthy don't need a doctor, but the
sick do. 32 I have not come to call
the righteous, but sinners to repentance."
33 Then they said to Him, "John's
disciples fast often and say prayers,
and those of the Pharisees do the
same, but Yours eat and drink."[D]
34 Jesus said to them, "You can't
make the wedding guests[E] fast while
the groom is with them, can you?
35 But the time[F] will come when
the groom will be taken away from
them—then they will fast in those
days."
36 He also told them a parable: "No
one tears a patch from a new garment and puts it on an old garment.
Otherwise, not only will he tear the
new, but also the piece from the new
garment will not match the old.
37 And no one puts new wine into old
wineskins. Otherwise, the new wine
will burst the skins, it will spill, and
the skins will be ruined. 38 But new
wine should be put into fresh wineskins.[G] 39 And no one, after drinking
old wine, wants new, because he
says, 'The old is better.'"[H]

[A]5:20 Lit *Man* [B]5:22 Or *minds* [C]5:29 Lit *were reclining* (at the table); at important meals the custom was to recline on a mat at a low table and lean on the left elbow. [D]5:33 Other mss read *"Why do John's . . . drink?"* (as a question) [E]5:34 Or *the friends of the groom*; lit *sons of the bridal chamber* [F]5:35 Lit *days* [G]5:38 Other mss add *And so both are preserved.* [H]5:39 Other mss read *is good*

acceptable"), and the leper was healed **immediately** (Gk *eutheōs*), the word used so commonly in Mark's fast-moving Gospel.

News about Jesus **spread** quickly despite His admonition to **tell no one**, and the crowds following Him were overwhelming. Jesus never called for silence to forbid the spread of the gospel but rather to allow Him to do the work the Father had given Him before His time for the cross came. He felt a constant urgency to do His work. The news of healings increased His popularity but hindered His work. Jesus, in order to escape the crowds, went to lonely places to pray.

Second, Jesus manifested His authority to forgive sins, which drew heavy criticism from the Jewish leaders. Not only did Jesus heal, but the healing validated His claim that He could forgive sins.

5:27-32 Jesus bestowed favor on those who seemed least worthy and helped them. First a demoniac received Christ's touch (4:31-37), then a paralytic (5:17-26), and finally **a tax collector** (vv. 29-32). When Jesus called, Levi (Matthew) left **everything behind** and followed Him. Only Luke emphasizes this total obedience on the part of Levi. In all three Synoptic Gospels, Levi's dinner and **guests** led to questions about religious practices. The outcome was that Jesus' mission involved a radical break with traditional religious practices. He did not come merely to add to what was already practiced. His ministry involved something that was radically new. This profound difference was seen in the company He kept.

5:33-39 The bridal metaphor is used here and elsewhere throughout Scripture. In the Old Testament Israel was the unfaithful bride (Hs 3:1), and in the New Testament the church was compared to a bride in her relationship to Christ, the Bridegroom (Jn 3:29). Jesus' answer was radical as He contrasted the joy of the **wedding** with the sorrow that would come with the absence of the bridegroom. He anticipated His coming death (v. 35). Jesus used both garments (a **new**, unwashed, and thus unshrunk, cloth that was sewn into an old and seasoned garment) and **wineskins**, which, because when sewn together they were watertight, were often used to hold liquids. The new skins had good elasticity and could adjust to the volume of the liquid during the aging process. However, the **old** skins were rigid and could easily burst under pressure. The gospel Jesus brought could not be absorbed into Judaism because it was radically new.

6:1-5 Although defined as Sabbath-violating work, in this incident plucking the **grain** was prompted by the need for food. Jesus maintained that ceremonial law ought only to be the means to an end and so should become a servant to any higher moral law. When accused of **doing what is not lawful on the Sabbath**, Jesus questioned whether his accusers had even **read** the Scripture they claimed to uphold, applying to the case at hand a particular example from the life of King David (1Sm 21:1-6).

6:6-11 When Jesus healed **the man with the paralyzed hand**, apparently taking the initiative rather than waiting for the man's request, the religious leaders were so infuriated at His brazen defiance of the Sabbath that they began **discussing . . . what they might do** to him. The man's illness was not life-threatening, or rabbinical law would have allowed him medical help. However, Jesus' point was that when healing can be provided, it should not be delayed. Jesus clearly established that He, not the Pharisees and other religious leaders, was "Lord of the Sabbath" (v. 5) and, therefore, rightfully would rule and properly interpret how the Sabbath would be observed.

6:12-19 Jesus now gained momentum in His ministry with the appointment of the Twelve as apostles (see Mt 4:18-21 for further discussion on the calling out of the Twelve). Jesus spent the entire **night in prayer**, an indication of His feeling great need in the challenges before Him. As Jesus' ministry advanced, the controversy with the religious leaders heated up. Jesus needed the wisdom and guidance of the Father. Even Jesus was probably not in the habit of praying all night (Lk 6:12). But on this occasion, nothing less than a lengthy and extended night of prayer could suffice for the Son of God. What a scene when Jesus and His disciples came down from the mountain! Multitudes gathered to Him to hear Him and to be healed by Him (v. 17). Unlike Matthew, Luke stresses that **the whole crowd was trying to touch** Jesus **because power was coming out from Him**. The night of prayer had energized Him with the power of God, which resonated and overflowed through the crowd.

6:20-49 Although the setting for this sermon and the Sermon on the Mount in Matthew (Mt 5–7) is considered the same by many, others believe the difference in content suggests two different settings of the sermon. Of course, there are very logical choices:

- The same location and sermon but described by two men from their different perspectives;

6 On a Sabbath,[A] He passed through
the grainfields. His disciples were
picking heads of grain, rubbing
them in their hands, and eating
them. 2 But some of the •Pharisees
said, "Why are you doing what is not
lawful on the Sabbath?"
3 Jesus answered them, "Haven't
you read what David and those who
were with him did when he was hungry— 4 how he entered the house of
God, and took and ate the •sacred
bread, which is not lawful for any
but the priests to eat? He even gave
some to those who were with him."
5 Then He told them, "The •Son of
Man is Lord of the Sabbath."
6 On another Sabbath He entered
the •synagogue and was teaching. A man was there whose right
hand was paralyzed. 7 The •scribes
and Pharisees were watching Him
closely, to see if He would heal on
the Sabbath, so that they could
find a charge against Him. 8 But He
knew their thoughts and told the
man with the paralyzed hand, "Get
up and stand here."[B] So he got up
and stood there. 9 Then Jesus said to
them, "I ask you: Is it lawful on the
Sabbath to do what is good or to do
what is evil, to save life or to destroy
it?" 10 After looking around at them
all, He told him, "Stretch out your
hand." He did so, and his hand was
restored.[C] 11 They, however, were
filled with rage and started discussing with one another what they
might do to Jesus.

Formalizing the Call to Discipleship (6:12-49)

12 During those days He went out
to the mountain to pray and spent all
night in prayer to God. 13 When daylight came, He summoned His disciples, and He chose 12 of them—He
also named them apostles:

14 Simon, whom He also
named Peter,
and Andrew his brother;
James and John;
Philip and Bartholomew;
15 Matthew and Thomas;
James the son of Alphaeus,
and Simon called the Zealot;
16 Judas the son of James,
and Judas Iscariot,
who became a traitor.

17 After coming down with them,
He stood on a level place with a large
crowd of His disciples and a great
number of people from all Judea and
Jerusalem and from the seacoast of
Tyre and Sidon. 18 They came to hear
Him and to be healed of their diseases; and those tormented by •unclean
spirits were made well. 19 The whole
crowd was trying to touch Him, because power was coming out from
Him and healing them all.
20 Then looking up at[D] His disciples, He said:

You who are poor are blessed,

HARD QUESTION

How can Jesus legitimately claim both to fulfill the law (Mt 5:17) and yet break one of the Ten Commandments by violating the Sabbath?

The Gospels include three **Sabbath** controversies—two in Lk 6:1-11 and another in Jn 5. The origin of the Sabbath is not only rooted in the creation account and in the Ten Commandments of the Old Testament but was also deeply grounded in the Jewish rabbinic tradition upheld particularly by the Pharisees. Realizing that in the Babylonian captivity God was punishing His people for defying the law, a body of oral law and commentaries on the law emerged to protect the people from breaking it. By the first century A.D., this burgeoning interpretive tradition was revered as having the same authority as Scripture and was even attributed to Moses. Regulations for keeping the Sabbath (and other areas of Jewish life) were practiced and enforced with a ferocious sense of legalism that entirely obscured God's intention for the function and application of the law. Jesus did not break God's law, but He forcefully denounced the legalism of the Jewish religious leaders and refused to bow to equate their rules with God's Word. Weekly observance of the Sabbath (the seventh day of every week reserved for worship and rest) provided fertile ground for public conflict between the religious leaders and Jesus. Jesus observed the Sabbath but not according to their oral traditions and ceremonial additions to the law. For Him it remained a day of rest and worship.

In the conflicts regarding the Sabbath, Jesus made several points:

- the Sabbath is for man's benefit (Mk 2:27);
- **the Son of Man is Lord of the Sabbath** (Lk 6:5);
- the Sabbath is for good deeds (v. 9);
- God the Father and the Son both work on the Sabbath (Jn 5).

[A] **6:1** Other mss read *a second-first Sabbath*; perhaps a special Sabbath [B] **6:8** Lit *stand in the middle* [C] **6:10** Other mss add *as sound as the other* [D] **6:20** Lit *Then lifting up His eyes to*

because the kingdom of God
is yours.
21 You who are now hungry
are blessed,
because you will be filled.
You who now weep
are blessed,
because you will laugh.
22 You are blessed when people
hate you,
when they exclude you,
insult you,
and slander your name as evil
because of the Son of Man.

23 "Rejoice in that day and leap for
joy! Take note—your reward is great
in heaven, for this is the way their
ancestors used to treat the prophets.

24 But woe to you who are rich,
for you have received
your comfort.
25 Woe to you who are now full,
for you will be hungry.
Woe to you[A]
who are now laughing,
for you will mourn and weep.
26 Woe to you[A]
when all people speak well
of you,
for this is the way
their ancestors
used to treat
the false prophets.

27 "But I say to you who listen:
Love your enemies, do what is good
to those who hate you, 28 bless those
who curse you, pray for those who
mistreat you. 29 If anyone hits you on
the cheek, offer the other also. And
if anyone takes away your coat, don't
hold back your shirt either. 30 Give to
everyone who asks you, and from
one who takes your things, don't ask
for them back. 31 Just as you want
others to do for you, do the same for
them. 32 If you love those who love
you, what credit is that to you? Even
sinners love those who love them.
33 If you do what is good to those who
are good to you, what credit is that
to you? Even sinners do that. 34 And
if you lend to those from whom you
expect to receive, what credit is that
to you? Even sinners lend to sinners
to be repaid in full. 35 But love your
enemies, do what is good, and lend,
expecting nothing in return. Then
your reward will be great, and you
will be sons of the Most High. For
He is gracious to the ungrateful and
evil. 36 Be merciful, just as your Father also is merciful.

37 "Do not judge, and you will not
be judged. Do not condemn, and
you will not be condemned. Forgive,
and you will be forgiven. 38 Give,
and it will be given to you; a good
measure—pressed down, shaken
together, and running over—will be
poured into your lap. For with the
measure you use,[B] it will be measured back to you."

39 He also told them a parable:
"Can the blind guide the blind?
Won't they both fall into a pit? 40 A
disciple is not above his teacher, but
everyone who is fully trained will be
like his teacher.

41 "Why do you look at the speck in
your brother's eye, but don't notice
the log in your own eye? 42 Or how
can you say to your brother, 'Brother, let me take out the speck that
is in your eye,' when you yourself
don't see the log in your eye? Hypocrite! First take the log out of your
eye, and then you will see clearly to
take out the speck in your brother's
eye.

43 "A good tree doesn't produce
bad fruit; on the other hand, a bad
tree doesn't produce good fruit.
44 For each tree is known by its own
fruit. Figs aren't gathered from
thornbushes, or grapes picked from
a bramble bush. 45 A good man produces good out of the good storeroom of his heart. An evil man
produces evil out of the evil storeroom, for his mouth speaks from
the overflow of the heart.

46 "Why do you call Me 'Lord,
Lord,' and don't do the things I say?
47 I will show you what someone is
like who comes to Me, hears My
words, and acts on them: 48 He is
like a man building a house, who
dug deep[C] and laid the foundation
on the rock. When the flood came,
the river crashed against that house
and couldn't shake it, because it was
well built. 49 But the one who hears
and does not act is like a man who

- The same location but two different, yet similar, messages were delivered to different audiences;
- Two similar sermons were delivered by Jesus in different locations with the heart of the message, namely, the nature of the Christian life, being the same but with varying content—a situation common among modern-day itinerant preachers who each tends to have a keynote message.

The context of this passage and of Mt 5–7 is undoubtedly the same even though the content recorded differs considerably. There is no reason to question the trustworthiness of Luke's account since to do so is to question Scripture itself. Such questioning is not warranted when you keep in mind that Luke's purpose in presenting the material was seemingly quite different than Matthew's, and his audience was different as well.

The first thing noted in terms of differences between the sermon as recorded in Mt 5–7 (see extensive discussion in commentary on Mt) and in Lk 6 is that Luke adds several woes in his listing of the Beatitudes. Luke includes what are called "kingdom reversal" passages, which became more prevalent in the central section of his book, where he nailed down the rigorous demands of discipleship. However, this short introduction to such reversals describes what the call to discipleship entails.

Luke emphasizes not only the spiritual but also the physical and practical aspects of discipleship, as in his mention of the **poor** and **hungry** in the negative section on woes. Also Luke's use of **laugh** (Gk *gelasete*, v. 21) has a different nuance than Matthew's "be comforted" (Mt 5:4). The promise of great **reward** in heaven (Lk 6:23) does not suggest a works salvation but rather the Lord's blessing and personal vindication for faithfulness under fire. The **rich** are not singled out to receive **woe** because of their wealth but rather because they have chosen to seek fulfillment of their desires on earth instead of future kingdom blessings (v. 24). They do not see value in spiritual disciplines.

The second significant difference is that, unlike Matthew, Luke does not mention anything concerning the law and the Pharisees. The entire section of the Sermon on the Mount concerning Christ and His relationship to the law, as well as His discussion on prayer and fasting (Mt 5:17-42; 6:1-18) was omitted by Luke. Some conclude that this omission was made because Luke was writing primarily to a Gentile audience. Gentiles would not have been as concerned about the law and Christ's response to it. Luke did record the sections in the Sermon on the Mount

[A] **6:25,26** Other mss omit *to you* [B] **6:38** Lit *you measure* [C] **6:48** Lit *dug and went deep*

concerning prayer as well as Jesus' discussion on God and possessions but not until his central section (Lk 11:1-13; 12:22-34), where the meaning of these passages takes on a slightly different character than they did in Matthew.

With regard to formalizing the call to discipleship, Luke found these four elements of utmost importance:

- blessings and woes (6:20-26);
- love for enemies (6:27-36);
- judging others (6:37-42);
- a test to prove the genuineness of professing to be a disciple given in two illustrations: a tree and its fruit (6:43-45) and then the wise and foolish builders (6:46-49).

7:1-10 Both Matthew (8:5-13) and Luke record the healing of the centurion's servant, but with slightly different details. Luke, as is often the case, gives a more complete narrative than Matthew. Luke records that the man sent **Jewish elders** to make the request on his behalf, reflecting an ancient custom of allowing a person to speak through his agents; Matthew does not mention the Jewish elders' involvement. Also Luke's account of the healing of the centurion more clearly foreshadows Christ's ministry to the Gentiles and strikingly resembles the conversion account of the Gentile centurion Cornelius in Ac 10.

7:11-17 With Jesus' authority in focus, Luke deals with the question concerning Jesus' identity. The people of Nain viewed Him as a "prophet"—and only a prophet—even though Jesus had just raised the widow's son from the dead. Much has been said about Christ's **compassion** for this woman, considering that the young man was her **only son** and that **she was a widow**, an important point. The raising of the widow's son is similar to Elisha's raising of the Shunammite's son (2Kg 4:8-37). Luke seems to recognize this similarity as evidenced by his comment that the crowd responded to this miracle by saying, **"A great prophet has arisen among us"** (Lk 7:16). Also, only in Luke does Jesus refer to Himself as a prophet (13:33; cp. Dt 18:15).

7:18-35 Jesus' ministry raised questions in the mind of another "prophet"—**John the Baptist**. John sent messengers to ask questions of Jesus. Jesus sent them back to John with the assurance that He (Jesus) is **the One** who was **to come** (vv. 22-23). Then Jesus praised John the Baptist to the crowd. While John indeed came in the spirit and power of Elijah, Luke wanted his readers to know that Jesus was the great prophet unparalleled by any other (vv. 21-23).

built a house on the ground without a foundation. The river crashed against it, and immediately it collapsed. And the destruction of that house was great!"

Focusing on the Question of Jesus' Identity (7:1–8:3)

7 When He had concluded all His sayings in the hearing of the people, He entered Capernaum. 2 A •centurion's •slave, who was highly valued by him, was sick and about to die. 3 When the centurion heard about Jesus, he sent some Jewish elders to Him, requesting Him to come and save the life of his slave. 4 When they reached Jesus, they pleaded with Him earnestly, saying, "He is worthy for You to grant this, 5 because he loves our nation and has built us a •synagogue." 6 Jesus went with them, and when He was not far from[A] the house, the centurion sent friends to tell Him, "Lord, don't trouble Yourself, since I am not worthy to have You come under my roof. 7 That is why I didn't even consider myself worthy to come to You. But say the word, and my servant will be cured.[B] 8 For I too am a man placed under authority, having soldiers under my command.[C] I say to this one, 'Go!' and he goes; and to another, 'Come!' and he comes; and to my slave, 'Do this!' and he does it."

9 Jesus heard this and was amazed at him, and turning to the crowd following Him, He said, "I tell you, I have not found so great a faith even in Israel!" 10 When those who had been sent returned to the house, they found the slave in good health.

11 Soon afterward He was on His way to a town called Nain. His disciples and a large crowd were traveling with Him. 12 Just as He neared the gate of the town, a dead man was being carried out. He was his mother's only son, and she was a widow. A large crowd from the city was also with her. 13 When the Lord saw her, He had compassion on her and said, "Don't cry." 14 Then He came up and touched the open coffin,[D] and the pallbearers stopped. And He said, "Young man, I tell you, get up!"

15 The dead man sat up and began to speak, and Jesus gave him to his mother. 16 Then fear[E] came over everyone, and they glorified God, saying, "A great prophet has risen among us," and "God has visited[F] His people." 17 This report about Him went throughout Judea and all the vicinity.

18 Then John's disciples told him about all these things. So John summoned two of his disciples 19 and sent them to the Lord, asking, "Are You the One who is to come, or should we look for someone else?"

20 When the men reached Him, they said, "John the Baptist sent us to ask You, 'Are You the One who is to come, or should we look for someone else?'"

21 At that time Jesus healed many people of diseases, plagues, and evil spirits, and He granted sight to

[A] **7:6** Lit *and He already was not far from* [B] **7:7** Other mss read *and let my servant be cured* [C] **7:8** Lit *under me* [D] **7:14** Or *the bier* [E] **7:16** Or *awe* [F] **7:16** Or *come to help*

CHARACTER PROFILE

The Widow of Nain
A Grieving Woman

Her Background	• She lived in the village of Nain, south of Nazareth (Lk 7:11). • She was a widow (v. 12).
Her Story	• Her only child, a son, had died (v. 12). • She was left not only heartbroken but destitute as well. • Upon seeing the funeral procession, Jesus had compassion upon her and raised her son from the dead.
Life Lesson	This widow witnessed the resurrection power of Christ before anyone else.

CHARACTER PROFILE

The Sinful Woman **Forgiven Sinner**

Her Background	• She is referred to as a "sinner," perhaps a prostitute. • This woman should not be confused with Mary of Bethany (Mt 26:6-13; Jn 12:1-8).
Her Story	• She approached Jesus at Simon's home, bringing a jar of fragrant oil with which to anoint Him. • She washed His feet with her tears, wiping them with her hair and anointing them with the oil. • Jesus defended her and used her as an example of "loving much."
Life Lesson	She fully understood the forgiveness of Christ and was unashamed to show her love for Him.

many blind people. 22 He replied to
them, "Go and report to John the
things you have seen and heard:
The blind receive their sight, the
lame walk, those with skin diseases
are healed,[A] the deaf hear, the dead
are raised, and the poor are told the
good news. 23 And anyone who is not
•offended because of Me is blessed."
24 After John's messengers left, He
began to speak to the crowds about
John: "What did you go out into the
wilderness to see? A reed swaying
in the wind? 25 What then did you
go out to see? A man dressed in soft
robes? Look, those who are splendidly dressed[B] and live in luxury are
in royal palaces. 26 What then did you
go out to see? A prophet? Yes, I tell
you, and far more than a prophet.
27 This is the one it is written about:

> **Look, I am sending**
> **My messenger**
> **ahead of You;**[C]
> **he will prepare Your way**
> **before You.**[D]

28 I tell you, among those born
of women no one is greater than
John,[E] but the least in the kingdom
of God is greater than he."
29 (And when all the people, including the tax collectors, heard
this, they acknowledged God's way
of righteousness,[F] because they had
been baptized with John's baptism.
30 But since the •Pharisees and experts in the law had not been baptized by him, they rejected the plan
of God for themselves.)
31 "To what then should I compare
the people of this generation, and
what are they like? 32 They are like
children sitting in the marketplace
and calling to each other:

> We played the flute for you,
> but you didn't dance;
> we sang a lament,
> but you didn't weep!

33 For John the Baptist did not come
eating bread or drinking wine, and
you say, 'He has a demon!' 34 The
•Son of Man has come eating and
drinking, and you say, 'Look, a glutton and a drunkard, a friend of tax
collectors and sinners!' 35 Yet wisdom is vindicated[G] by all her children."
36 Then one of the Pharisees invited Him to eat with him. He entered
the Pharisee's house and reclined
at the table. 37 And a woman in the
town who was a sinner found out
that Jesus was reclining at the table
in the Pharisee's house. She brought
an alabaster jar of fragrant oil 38 and
stood behind Him at His feet, weeping, and began to wash His feet with
her tears. She wiped His feet with
the hair of her head, kissing them

A 7:22 Lit *cleansed* B 7:25 Or *who have glorious robes* C 7:27 Lit *messenger before Your face* D 7:27 Mal 3:1 E 7:28 Other mss read *women is not a greater prophet than John the Baptist* F 7:29 Lit *they justified God* G 7:35 Or *wisdom is declared right*

7:36-50 Unlike Matthew, Luke records the kind of people who responded to John's message—"tax collectors and sinners" (v. 34). They were the ones who acknowledged God's way of righteousness. Then Luke provides an extended example of the kind of person who responded to Jesus, namely, the sinful woman.

Jesus was at the house of a Pharisee, one who "rejected the plan of God" for himself (v. 30). When the sinful woman entered the Pharisee's home, she did not go to the Pharisee, but she immediately directed her attention and service to Jesus (vv. 37-38). The Pharisee retorted **to himself** that **if** Jesus truly were a prophet, He **would know who and what kind of woman** she was (v. 39). Luke is showing the challenge made to Jesus' identity.

Jesus responded to Simon's complaint with a parable about **two debtors**, one who had been forgiven a small debt and the other a much larger one. Jesus intended to compare the woman with the debtor who was forgiven more and then to show that her sins were forgiven. The woman **loved much**. Because of this devotion, Jesus proclaimed that her sins were forgiven. She had demonstrated that Jesus' forgiveness awakened in her heart the desire to serve Him more sacrificially (vv. 47-48).

Interestingly, the woman's focus was on Jesus' **feet** (v. 38). In 14 short verses, Jesus' feet are mentioned seven times. Prophesying about the salvation that would come to Israel through the Messiah, Isaiah had said, "How beautiful on the mountains are the *feet* of the herald, who proclaims peace, who brings news of good things, who proclaims salvation, who says to Zion, 'Your God reigns!'" (Is 52:7, italics added). Jesus' ministry to the sinful woman beautifully demonstrates the fulfillment of Isaiah's prophecy. A Pharisee, who was quite learned in the Word of God, did not recognize this truth. But a sinful woman, an outcast, acknowledged the prophecy and demonstrated her understanding of it by focusing on the *feet* of the greatest *Prophet,* the One destined to bring her peace and salvation (Lk 7:50). Luke in this passage was demonstrating a kingdom reversal at its finest.

8:4-21 Those who are true disciples will not only hear the Word, but they will put its truths into practice. The practical side of Christian living is extremely important for Luke. The first-century Romans were intensely practical as well. So this message would have resonated with them.

Parables were a popular tool used by Jesus (5:36-39; 6:39,44-45,47-49; 7:41-42), and the account of the **parable** of the **sower** is found in all three Synoptic Gospels (Mt 13:1-23; Mk 4:1-20; Lk 8:4-15) but in some ways more detailed and extended in Luke. However, Luke seems to abbreviate the account with some notable omissions. In each case the author interjected a brief section on the purpose for parables between the presentation of the parable and the explanation of its meaning.

Parables had a dual function: to reveal truth to the disciples (called by some "the insiders") or genuine seekers and to conceal the message from enemies (also called "outsiders") or those who sought to harm Jesus (v. 10). The central theme in Jesus' parables was **the kingdom of God**. Jesus used metaphors that would be understood by those who wanted to find meaning in His message.

Luke's focus seems to be on enduring in the faith and bearing fruit, ideas that find their fullness in Lk 14:25-34, where the cost of discipleship is fully disclosed. Luke intended to leave his readers with no doubts concerning the nature of discipleship. If true disciples were not enduring and bearing fruit, they must be ready to lose even what they think they might have. They must take an internal inventory

and anointing them with the fragrant oil.
39 When the Pharisee who had
invited Him saw this, he said to
himself, "This man, if He were a
prophet, would know who and what
kind of woman this is who is touching Him—she's a sinner!"
40 Jesus replied to him, "Simon, I
have something to say to you."
"Teacher," he said, "say it."
41 "A creditor had two debtors. One
owed 500 •denarii, and the other 50.
42 Since they could not pay it back,
he graciously forgave them both. So,
which of them will love him more?"
43 Simon answered, "I suppose the
one he forgave more."
"You have judged correctly," He
told him. 44 Turning to the woman,
He said to Simon, "Do you see this
woman? I entered your house; you
gave Me no water for My feet, but
she, with her tears, has washed
My feet and wiped them with her
hair. 45 You gave Me no kiss, but
she hasn't stopped kissing My feet
since I came in. 46 You didn't anoint
My head with olive oil, but she has
anointed My feet with fragrant oil.
47 Therefore I tell you, her many sins
have been forgiven; that's why[A] she
loved much. But the one who is forgiven little, loves little." 48 Then He
said to her, "Your sins are forgiven."
49 Those who were at the table
with Him began to say among themselves, "Who is this man who even
forgives sins?"
50 And He said to the woman, "Your
faith has saved you. Go in peace."

8 Soon afterward He was traveling from one town and village to
another, preaching and telling the
good news of the kingdom of God.
The Twelve were with Him, 2 and
also some women who had been
healed of evil spirits and sicknesses:
Mary, called •Magdalene (seven demons had come out of her); 3 Joanna
the wife of Chuza, •Herod's steward;
Susanna; and many others who were
supporting them from their possessions.

Hearing the Word of God Correctly (8:4-21)

4 As a large crowd was gathering,
and people were flocking to Him
from every town, He said in a parable: 5 "A sower went out to sow his
seed. As he was sowing, some fell
along the path; it was trampled on,
and the birds of the sky ate it up.
6 Other seed fell on the rock; when
it sprang up, it withered, since it
lacked moisture. 7 Other seed fell

[A]7:47 Her love shows that she has been forgiven

BIBLICAL WOMANHOOD Women Who Followed Jesus

Unique to Luke is this account of the women who supported Christ's work, yet another example of the unlikely people who responded to Christ and His message (8:1-3). These women were **healed** of various diseases and illnesses by Jesus. Seven demons had come out of **Mary Magdalene**. Luke does not specify how **Joanna, the wife of Chuza**, and **Susanna** were healed; but they were among the many **supporting** Jesus **from their** own **possessions**. Luke emphasized the sacrifice and commitment made by these women. For women to be a part of the party traveling with itinerant preachers in the first century was uncommon.

Jesus had large crowds following Him in groups—probably for protection and possibly even for fellowship. When the young boy Jesus was thought to be part of the group traveling from the temple, the entourage was large enough that Mary and Joseph did not initially realize Jesus was not in the group (Lk 2:41-52).

Women never traveled alone and did not travel as much as men because of the difficulties and dangers as well as their responsibilities in the home. In this case, for women to be included in the large entourage would not have been as unusual as the fact that they were obviously considered among the inner circle of disciples and were specifically named as part of the group. There is no indication in the text as to the length of travel or distance covered or how far they went from their homes. From the high value Jesus placed on children and the home, you can be sure that He was not encouraging women to neglect their home responsibilities. (Note the frequency with which He used the family metaphor in His teaching.) Jesus recognized women as full-fledged disciples, something completely unheard of in His day. These women not only gave sacrificially of their resources, but they also exhibited extraordinary devotion and selfless service to Jesus, giving of their time and energy to be a part of His traveling ministry. There were many generous women who contributed to the ministry of Christ.

CHARACTER PROFILE

Joanna and Susanna **Faithful Followers**

Their Background	Two of several women who followed Jesus, along with His disciples (8:3).
Their Story	• They and other unnamed women supported Jesus' ministry from their own resources. • Joanna was the wife of Chuza, Herod's steward. • Joanna may have been at the burial of Jesus (Luke 23:55). • No other information is given on Susanna.
Life Lesson	A woman with a generous spirit will freely share what she has.

among thorns; the thorns sprang
up with it and choked it. 8 Still other
seed fell on good ground; when it
sprang up, it produced a crop: 100
times what was sown." As He said
this, He called out, "Anyone who has
ears to hear should listen!"
9 Then His disciples asked Him,
"What does this parable mean?"
10 So He said, "The •secrets of the
kingdom of God have been given for
you to know, but to the rest it is in
parables, so that

> **Looking they may not see,**
> **and hearing they may**
> **not understand.**[A]

11 "This is the meaning of the parable:[B] The seed is the word of God.
12 The seed along the path are those
who have heard and then the Devil
comes and takes away the word from
their hearts, so that they may not believe and be saved. 13 And the seed on
the rock are those who, when they
hear, welcome the word with joy.
Having no root, these believe for a
while and depart in a time of testing. 14 As for the seed that fell among
thorns, these are the ones who, when
they have heard, go on their way and
are choked with worries, riches, and
pleasures of life, and produce no mature fruit. 15 But the seed in the good
ground—these are the ones who,[C]
having heard the word with an honest and good heart, hold on to it and
by enduring, bear fruit.
16 "No one, after lighting a lamp,
covers it with a basket or puts it under a bed, but puts it on a lampstand
so that those who come in may see
its light. 17 For nothing is concealed
that won't be revealed, and nothing
hidden that won't be made known
and come to light. 18 Therefore take
care how you listen. For whoever
has, more will be given to him; and
whoever does not have, even what
he thinks he has will be taken away
from him."
19 Then His mother and brothers came to Him, but they could
not meet with Him because of the
crowd. 20 He was told, "Your mother
and Your brothers are standing outside, wanting to see You."
21 But He replied to them, "My
mother and My brothers are those
who hear and do the word of God."

Illustrating Jesus' Authoritative Word (8:22-56)

22 One day He and His disciples got
into a boat, and He told them, "Let's
cross over to the other side of the
lake." So they set out, 23 and as they
were sailing He fell asleep. Then
a fierce windstorm came down on
the lake; they were being swamped
and were in danger. 24 They came
and woke Him up, saying, "Master,
Master, we're going to die!" Then He
got up and rebuked the wind and the
raging waves. So they ceased, and
there was a calm. 25 He said to them,
"Where is your faith?"
They were fearful and amazed, asking one another, "Who can this be?[D]

in order to verify to whom they really belong (8:16-18).

Jesus in no way dishonored His family (vv. 19-20), but here He is affirming those who obey God (v. 21). The way to be close to Jesus—as close as His own family—is to **hear** His Word and **do** it. The Word of God is the final authority in the life of every believer. In other words, those who belong to Christ hear Him and obey Him (vv. 19-21).

8:22-56 Jesus, the Savior of outcasts and sinners, demonstrated His divine authority exercising power over nature (vv. 22-25), over demons (vv. 26-39), and over sickness and death (vv. 40-53), and He commanded complete obedience from His followers. In these passages, Luke provided illustrations of Jesus' authoritative Word.

Jesus raised some interesting questions during each miracle. After calming the winds and the waves, Jesus asked His disciples, **Where is your faith?** (v. 25). **Fearful and amazed**, they responded with their own question, **Who can this be?** (v. 25), which showed that the disciples continued to be slow in understanding Jesus' true identity.

[A] **8:10** Is 6:9 [B] **8:11** Lit *But this is the parable:* [C] **8:15** Or *these are the kind who* [D] **8:25** Lit *Who then is this?*

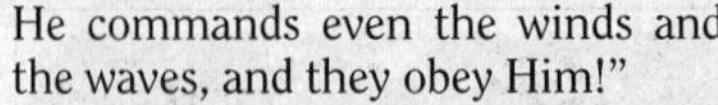

8:38-39 Before casting legions of demons from the possessed man, Jesus asked the demons, **What is your name?** (v. 30). Luke gives a vivid account of the destructive nature of demon possession. The man, when he was set free, begged to go with Jesus; but, instead, Jesus **sent him away** to his hometown so that he could bear witness about what had happened to him (see further discussion in Mk 5:1-20).

8:43-48 When the **woman suffering from bleeding** touched him, Jesus asked, **Who touched Me?** (v. 45). The woman came to Him trembling with fear and confessed what had happened. He sent her away with the assurance that her faith made her well (8:48; see further discussion in parallel passage on the healing of the bleeding woman as well as on the resurrection to life of Jairus's daughter in Mk 5:21-43). The significance was not in what Christ's questions revealed about Him but in what His questions revealed within the hearts of His hearers. They trembled at His words and deeds. And this awesome power was precisely what Luke wanted to communicate about Christ and His authority.

He commands even the winds and the waves, and they obey Him!"

26 Then they sailed to the region of the Gerasenes,[A] which is opposite Galilee. 27 When He got out on land, a demon-possessed man from the town met Him. For a long time he had worn no clothes and did not stay in a house but in the tombs. 28 When he saw Jesus, he cried out, fell down before Him, and said in a loud voice, "What do You have to do with me,[B] Jesus, You Son of the Most High God? I beg You, don't torment me!" 29 For He had commanded the •unclean spirit to come out of the man. Many times it had seized him, and though he was guarded, bound by chains and shackles, he would snap the restraints and be driven by the demon into deserted places.

30 "What is your name?" Jesus asked him.

"Legion," he said—because many demons had entered him. 31 And they begged Him not to banish them to the •abyss.

32 A large herd of pigs was there, feeding on the hillside. The demons begged Him to permit them to enter the pigs, and He gave them permission. 33 The demons came out of the man and entered the pigs, and the herd rushed down the steep bank into the lake and drowned. 34 When the men who tended them saw what had happened, they ran off and reported it in the town and in the countryside. 35 Then people went out to see what had happened. They came to Jesus and found the man the demons had departed from, sitting at Jesus' feet, dressed and in his right mind. And they were afraid. 36 Meanwhile, the eyewitnesses reported to them how the demon-possessed man was delivered. 37 Then all the people of the Gerasene region[A] asked Him to leave them, because they were gripped by great fear. So getting into the boat, He returned.

38 The man from whom the demons had departed kept begging Him to be with Him. But He sent him away and said, 39 "Go back to your home, and tell all that God has done for you." And off he went, proclaiming throughout the town all that Jesus had done for him.

40 When Jesus returned, the crowd welcomed Him, for they were all expecting Him. 41 Just then, a man named Jairus came. He was a leader of the •synagogue. He fell down at Jesus' feet and pleaded with Him to come to his house, 42 because he had an only daughter about 12 years old, and she was at death's door.[C]

While He was going, the crowds were nearly crushing Him. 43 A woman suffering from bleeding for 12 years, who had spent all she had on doctors[D] yet could not be healed by any, 44 approached from behind and touched the •tassel of His robe. Instantly her bleeding stopped.

45 "Who touched Me?" Jesus asked.

When they all denied it, Peter[E] said, "Master, the crowds are hemming You in and pressing against You."[F]

46 "Someone did touch Me," said Jesus. "I know that power has gone out from Me." 47 When the woman saw that she was discovered,[G] she came trembling and fell down before Him. In the presence of all the people, she declared the reason she had touched Him and how she was instantly cured. 48 "Daughter," He said to her, "your faith has made you well.[H] Go in peace."

49 While He was still speaking, someone came from the synagogue leader's house, saying, "Your daughter is dead. Don't bother the Teacher anymore."

50 When Jesus heard it, He answered him, "Don't be afraid. Only believe, and she will be made well." 51 After He came to the house, He let no one enter with Him except Peter, John, James, and the child's father and mother. 52 Everyone was crying and mourning for her. But He said, "Stop crying, for she is not dead but asleep."

53 They started laughing at Him, because they knew she was dead. 54 So He[I] took her by the hand and called out, "Child, get up!" 55 Her spirit returned, and she got up at

[A]**8:26,37** Other mss read *the Gadarenes* [B]**8:28** Lit *What to me and to You* [C]**8:42** Lit *she was dying* [D]**8:43** Other mss omit *who had spent all she had on doctors* [E]**8:45** Other mss add *and those with him* [F]**8:45** Other mss add *and You say, 'Who touched Me?'* [G]**8:47** Lit *she had not escaped notice* [H]**8:48** Or *has saved you* [I]**8:54** Other mss add *having put them all outside*

once. Then He gave orders that she be given something to eat. 56 Her parents were astounded, but He instructed them to tell no one what had happened.

Coming to the Christological Climax (9:1-50)

9 Summoning the Twelve, He gave them power and authority over all the demons, and power to heal[A] diseases. 2 Then He sent them to proclaim the kingdom of God and to heal the sick.

3 "Take nothing for the road," He told them, "no walking stick, no traveling bag, no bread, no money; and don't take an extra shirt. 4 Whatever house you enter, stay there and leave from there. 5 If they do not welcome you, when you leave that town, shake off the dust from your feet as a testimony against them." 6 So they went out and traveled from village to village, proclaiming the good news and healing everywhere.

7 •Herod the tetrarch heard about everything that was going on. He was perplexed, because some said that John had been raised from the dead, 8 some that Elijah had appeared, and others that one of the ancient prophets had risen. 9 "I beheaded John," Herod said, "but who is this I hear such things about?" And he wanted to see Him.

10 When the apostles returned, they reported to Jesus all that they had done. He took them along and withdrew privately to a[B] town called Bethsaida. 11 When the crowds found out, they followed Him. He welcomed them, spoke to them about the kingdom of God, and cured[C] those who needed healing.

12 Late in the day,[D] the Twelve approached and said to Him, "Send the crowd away, so they can go into the surrounding villages and countryside to find food and lodging, because we are in a deserted place here."

13 "You give them something to eat," He told them.

"We have no more than five loaves and two fish," they said, "unless we go and buy food for all these people." 14 (For about 5,000 men were there.)

Then He told His disciples, "Have them sit down[E] in groups of about 50 each." 15 They did so, and had them all sit down. 16 Then He took the five loaves and the two fish, and looking up to heaven, He blessed and broke them. He kept giving them to the disciples to set before the crowd. 17 Everyone ate and was filled. Then they picked up[F] 12 baskets of leftover pieces.

18 While He was praying in private and His disciples were with Him, He asked them, "Who do the crowds say that I am?"

19 They answered, "John the Baptist; others, Elijah; still others, that one of the ancient prophets has come back."[G]

20 "But you," He asked them, "who do you say that I am?"

Peter answered, "God's •Messiah!"

21 But He strictly warned and instructed them to tell this to no one, 22 saying, "The •Son of Man must suffer many things and be rejected by the elders, •chief priests, and •scribes, be killed, and be raised the third day."

23 Then He said to them all, "If anyone wants to come with[H] Me, he must deny himself, take up his cross daily,[I] and follow Me. 24 For whoever wants to save his •life will lose it, but whoever loses his life because of Me will save it. 25 What is a man benefited if he gains the whole world, yet loses or forfeits himself? 26 For whoever is ashamed of Me and My words, the Son of Man will be ashamed of him when He comes in His glory and that of the Father and the holy angels. 27 I tell you the truth: There are some standing here who will not taste death until they see the kingdom of God."

[A] **9:1** In this passage, different Gk words are translated as heal. In Eng, "to heal" or "to cure" are synonyms with little distinction in meaning. Technically, we do not heal or cure diseases. People are healed or cured from diseases. [B] **9:10** Other mss add *deserted place near a* [C] **9:11** Or *healed*; in this passage, different Gk words are translated as heal. In Eng, "to heal" or "to cure" are synonyms with little distinction in meaning. Technically, we do not heal or cure diseases. People are healed or cured from diseases. [D] **9:12** Lit *When the day began to decline* [E] **9:14** Lit *them recline* [F] **9:17** Lit *Then were picked up by them* [G] **9:19** Lit *has risen* [H] **9:23** Lit *come after* [I] **9:23** Other mss omit *daily*

9:1-9 In this section, Luke basically follows the accounts of Matthew and Mark concerning events leading up to Peter's confession of Christ, but there are some significant differences to be mentioned. Unlike Matthew, Luke gives a truncated version of the commissioning of the Twelve (vv. 1-6), perhaps because of his intended Gentile audience and overall purpose. The lengthier version was especially appropriate for Matthew who was writing to a Jewish audience. The section concerning only "the lost sheep of . . . Israel" (Mt 10:6) would not have fit Luke's overall purpose. The instructions recorded would certainly heighten the importance and urgency of the task assigned (Lk 9:3-5).

The passage concerning Herod's desire to see Jesus is unique to Luke (vv. 7-9). For John the Baptist to be on Herod's mind and conscience was not surprising. Herod did not see Jesus at this time but did come face-to-face with Him when Pilate sent Jesus to him (23:8-11). Since Luke sought to reveal Jesus as the greatest prophet, these verses might have been important for Luke's overall purpose because of the references to **Elijah** and **the ancient prophets** (9:8).

9:10-36 The feeding of the **5,000** is recorded in all the Gospels (Mk 6:30-44). Jesus had intended to go away with His apostles for some rest; but, instead, **the crowds** discovered His whereabouts and came to Him. Jesus had compassion on them, healed their sick, and fed all of them with **five loaves and two fish** (Lk 9:13-17). Luke in his account specified that Jesus **spoke to them about the kingdom of God** (v. 11), an important concept for Luke. This event appears just before Peter's confession (vv. 18-20), Jesus' prediction of His death (vv. 21-22), Jesus' teaching on discipleship (vv. 23-27), and the demonstration of the kingdom's power in the transfiguration (vv. 28-36).

9:18-27 After Peter made his confession (vv. 18-20; see further discussion at note on Mt 16:13-20), Jesus told His followers what it would cost them to follow Him (Lk 9:23-27). When Jesus posed the question concerning His identity to His disciples, He most assuredly expected more from them than the rumors floating among the people or the innuendos coming from the religious leaders (v. 20). Peter's succinct answer came: **God's Messiah** (Gk *ton Christon tou Theou*, lit "the Christ of the God" or "the anointed one of God"). Luke does not include the more explicit words "the Son of the living God" (Mt 16:16), but he does emphasize the divine nature of Messiah in the phrase "God's Messiah" (Lk 9:20). Luke adds that the **cross** was to be taken up **daily** (v. 23). This addition unique to Luke fits his emphasis on the practical side of Christian living, which is to be lived out daily and in every way.

9:28-36 The transfiguration of Christ was the most significant event between His birth and His passion. All of the Synoptic Gospels recorded this phenomenal event. Luke's account contains several elements that have significance within the biblical accounts of two events—one past (the exodus, Ex 24) and one future (the return of Christ, 1Th 4:16-17; Rv 1:7) that serve as frames of references shedding light on the overall purpose of the transfiguration:

- The **mountain** (v. 28)—God spoke both to Moses (Ex 19:1-6,20; 24:12-18; 31:18; cp. Dt 5:2) and Elijah (1Kg 19:8-18) on "Horeb, the mountain of God" (Ex 3:1; 1Kg 19:8), also referenced as "Mount Sinai" (e.g., Ex 19:20).
- Jesus' **death** [Gk *exodon* (form of *exodus*), lit "exit"; metaphorically, "decease, departure from life," v. 31], **which He was about to accomplish** [Gk *plēroun*, "fulfill, render full or complete, consummate"] **in Jerusalem**. When Jesus willingly laid down His life on the cross (and returned to life), He fulfilled the Law (represented by **Moses**) and the Prophets (represented by **Elijah**)—see Mt 5:17; Lk 24:44; Jn 1:45; Ac 28:23. Only Luke mentions Jerusalem in the context of the transfiguration, which prefigured Jesus' determination to set out for Jerusalem (Lk 9:51).
- The **tabernacles** (Lk 9:33)—Peter's suggestion was answered forcefully by God the Father's audible command to **listen to** His **Son**, whom He identified as **the Chosen One** (vv. 34-35; cp. 3:22; 20:13; Mt 12:15-18; Heb 9:11-12).
- The **cloud** (v. 34)—God made known His presence on Mount Sinai (e.g., Ex 24:16), in His tabernacle (e.g., Ex 40:34; Nm 9:17), and later in the temple (e.g., 1Kg 8:10-11) by descending upon and filling each with a cloud. After the resurrection, Jesus ascended to heaven in the clouds and promised to return in the same manner (Ac 1:9-11).

9:37-43 The healing of the demon-possessed boy further demonstrated the power and **greatness of God** (v. 43). Although the physical effects were similar to those caused by epilepsy; the boy's father and Jesus focused on the demonic source of the boy's suffering.

9:51–18:34 While some of the material used by Luke in this central section has also been recorded in Matthew and Mark, the arrangement of the material in Luke is uniquely his. Some of the most beloved and well-known passages of Scripture, such as the good Samaritan

28 About eight days after these words, He took along Peter, John, and James and went up on the mountain to pray. 29 As He was praying, the appearance of His face changed, and His clothes became dazzling white. 30 Suddenly, two men were talking with Him—Moses and Elijah. 31 They appeared in glory and were speaking of His death,[A] which He was about to accomplish in Jerusalem.

32 Peter and those with him were in a deep sleep,[B] and when they became fully awake, they saw His glory and the two men who were standing with Him. 33 As the two men were departing from Him, Peter said to Jesus, "Master, it's good for us to be here! Let us make three •tabernacles: one for You, one for Moses, and one for Elijah"—not knowing what he said.

34 While he was saying this, a cloud appeared and overshadowed them. They became afraid as they entered the cloud. 35 Then a voice came from the cloud, saying:

> This is My Son,
> the Chosen One;[C]
> listen to Him!

36 After the voice had spoken, only Jesus was found. They kept silent, and in those days told no one what they had seen.

37 The next day, when they came down from the mountain, a large crowd met Him. 38 Just then a man from the crowd cried out, "Teacher, I beg You to look at my son, because he's my only child. 39 Often a spirit seizes him; suddenly he shrieks, and it throws him into convulsions until he foams at the mouth;[D] wounding[E] him, it hardly ever leaves him. 40 I begged Your disciples to drive it out, but they couldn't."

41 Jesus replied, "You unbelieving and rebellious[F] generation! How long will I be with you and put up with you? Bring your son here."

42 As the boy was still approaching, the demon knocked him down and threw him into severe convulsions. But Jesus rebuked the •unclean spirit, cured the boy, and gave him back to his father. 43 And they were all astonished at the greatness of God.

While everyone was amazed at all the things He was doing, He told His disciples, 44 "Let these words sink in:[G] The Son of Man is about to be betrayed into the hands of men."

45 But they did not understand this statement; it was concealed from them so that they could not grasp it, and they were afraid to ask Him about it.[H]

46 Then an argument started among them about who would be the greatest of them. 47 But Jesus, knowing the thoughts of their hearts, took a little child and had him stand next to Him. 48 He told them, "Whoever welcomes[I] this little child in My name welcomes Me. And whoever welcomes Me welcomes Him who sent Me. For whoever is least among you—this one is great."

49 John responded, "Master, we saw someone driving out demons in Your name, and we tried to stop him because he does not follow us."

50 "Don't stop him," Jesus told him, "because whoever is not against you is for you."[J]

Jesus' Teaching En Route to Jerusalem (9:51–18:34)

Discipleship in the Shadow of the Cross (9:51-62)

51 When the days were coming to a close for Him to be taken up,[K] He determined[L] to journey to Jerusalem. 52 He sent messengers ahead of Him, and on the way they entered a village of the •Samaritans to make preparations for Him. 53 But they did not welcome Him, because He determined to journey to Jerusalem. 54 When the disciples James and John saw this, they said, "Lord, do You want us to call down fire from heaven to consume them?"[M]

55 But He turned and rebuked

[A] **9:31** Or *departure*; Gk *exodus* [B] **9:32** Lit *were weighed down with sleep* [C] **9:35** Other mss read *the Beloved* [D] **9:39** Lit *convulsions with foam* [E] **9:39** Or *bruising*, or *mauling* [F] **9:41** Or *corrupt*, or *perverted*, or *twisted*; Dt 32:5 [G] **9:44** Lit *Put these words in your ears* [H] **9:45** Lit *about this statement* [I] **9:48** Or *receives*, throughout the verse [J] **9:50** Other mss read *against us is for us* [K] **9:51** His ascension [L] **9:51** Lit *He stiffened His face to go*; Is 50:7 [M] **9:54** Other mss add *as Elijah also did*

them,[A] 56 and they went to another
village.
57 As they were traveling on the
road someone said to Him, "I will
follow You wherever You go!"
58 Jesus told him, "Foxes have
dens, and birds of the sky[B] have
nests, but the Son of Man has no
place to lay His head." 59 Then He
said to another, "Follow Me."
"Lord," he said, "first let me go
bury my father."[C]
60 But He told him, "Let the dead
bury their own dead, but you go and
spread the news of the kingdom of
God."
61 Another also said, "I will follow
You, Lord, but first let me go and say
good-bye to those at my house."
62 But Jesus said to him, "No one
who puts his hand to the plow and
looks back is fit for the kingdom of
God."

The Mission of the Seventy (10:1-24)

10 After this, the Lord appointed
70[D] others, and He sent them
ahead of Him in pairs to every town
and place where He Himself was
about to go. 2 He told them: "The
harvest is abundant, but the workers
are few. Therefore, pray to the Lord
of the harvest to send out workers into His harvest. 3 Now go; I'm
sending you out like lambs among
wolves. 4 Don't carry a money-bag,
traveling bag, or sandals; don't greet
anyone along the road. 5 Whatever
house you enter, first say, 'Peace to
this household.' 6 If a son of peace[E]
is there, your peace will rest on
him; but if not, it will return to you.
7 Remain in the same house, eating
and drinking what they offer, for the
worker is worthy of his wages. Don't
be moving from house to house.
8 When you enter any town, and
they welcome you, eat the things set
before you. 9 Heal the sick who are
there, and tell them, 'The kingdom
of God has come near you.' 10 When
you enter any town, and they don't
welcome you, go out into its streets
and say, 11 'We are wiping off as a
witness against you even the dust
of your town that clings to our feet.
Know this for certain: The kingdom
of God has come near.' 12 I tell you,
on that day it will be more tolerable
for Sodom than for that town.
13 "Woe to you, Chorazin! Woe to
you, Bethsaida! For if the miracles
that were done in you had been
done in Tyre and Sidon, they would
have repented long ago, sitting in
•sackcloth and ashes! 14 But it will
be more tolerable for Tyre and
Sidon at the judgment than for you.
15 And you, Capernaum, will you be
exalted to heaven? No, you will go
down to •Hades! 16 Whoever listens
to you listens to Me. Whoever rejects you rejects Me. And whoever
rejects Me rejects the One who sent
Me."
17 The Seventy[F] returned with joy,
saying, "Lord, even the demons submit to us in Your name."
18 He said to them, "I watched Satan fall from heaven like a lightning
flash. 19 Look, I have given you the
authority to trample on snakes and
scorpions and over all the power of
the enemy; nothing will ever harm
you. 20 However, don't rejoice that[G]
the spirits submit to you, but rejoice that your names are written in
heaven."
21 In that same hour He[H] rejoiced
in the Holy[I] Spirit and said, "I
praise[J] You, Father, Lord of heaven
and earth, because You have hidden
these things from the wise and the
learned and have revealed them to
infants. Yes, Father, because this was
Your good pleasure.[K] 22 All things
have[L] been entrusted to Me by My
Father. No one knows who the Son
is except the Father, and who the Father is except the Son, and anyone
to whom the Son desires[M] to reveal
Him."
23 Then turning to His disciples
He said privately, "The eyes that
see the things you see are blessed!
24 For I tell you that many prophets

[A] **9:55-56** Other mss add *and said, "You don't know what kind of spirit you belong to.* [56] *For the Son of Man did not come to destroy people's lives but to save them,"* [B] **9:58** Wild birds, as opposed to domestic birds [C] **9:59** Not necessarily meaning his father was already dead [D] **10:1** Other mss read *72* [E] **10:6** A peaceful person; one open to the message of the kingdom [F] **10:17** Other mss read *The Seventy-two* [G] **10:20** Lit *don't rejoice in this, that* [H] **10:21** Other mss read *Jesus* [I] **10:21** Other mss omit *Holy* [J] **10:21** Or *thank*, or *confess* [K] **10:21** Lit *was well-pleasing in Your sight* [L] **10:22** Other mss read *And turning to the disciples, He said, "Everything has* [M] **10:22** Or *wills*, or *chooses*

(10:30-37) and the prodigal son (15:11-31), are found in this section.

9:51-62 Jesus **sent messengers ahead**, and they entered a Samaritan village, but they were quickly turned away, much to the displeasure of James and John. When the disciples wanted **to call down fire** on the village, Jesus **rebuked them** and then moved on **to another village**. Jesus was entering Samaritan territory, an indication of the beginning of His Gentile ministry. Throughout this section Jesus ministered in Samaria and Judea. While relatively little is said about Jesus' traveling from one place to another, there are indications that He was on His way to **Jerusalem** (Lk 9:51,53; 10:38; 13:22,32-33; 17:11).

The cost of following Jesus is laid out early in this lengthy section. Letting someone else bury your father or saying good-bye to your family was akin to saying that Jesus has priority over familial and even customary religious duties. Jesus' pointed response, though short, ought not to be taken lightly (v. 62). To follow Jesus means a radical transfer of your loyalty.

10:1-24 In an event unique to Luke, Jesus sent out messengers to go into **every town and place** where Jesus was planning to go to prepare the way for Him. The word **others** seemed to indicate that the 70 were in addition to the Twelve, who may have remained with Jesus.

The commissioning of the 70 closely parallels the commissioning of the Twelve in Mt 10:5-15. If Jesus was in Perea at this time, His presence could have indicated that this mission was especially to Gentiles. The fact that the 70 were representative of the Gentile nations listed in Gn 10 seems to support this conclusion. Sending the men **in pairs** (Lk 10:1) enabled them to help and support one another, but there was another reason. Jewish law required two witnesses for the condemnation described (vv. 10-11; Dt 19:15).

There was an urgency to this missionary task. They were to put aside the usual extra items with which one would travel. Even time-consuming greetings along the road were to be bypassed, not as a discourteous response to those encountered but as a means of moving forward with an urgent task. On the other hand, a prescribed greeting was given for those who received them (v. 5). That greeting centered around **peace** (Gk *eirēnē*, "harmony," "order"), the traditional Hebrew greeting. The word is also a synonym for the blessing of salvation. **Son of peace** (v. 6) denoted a believer. Of course, if the household did not have believers, the blessing would not be effective.

10:12-16 God's judgment on **Sodom**, one of the cities destroyed with burning sulfur (Gn 19:24), was well-known. Jesus indicated that God's judgment on these cities mentioned would be far greater than what happened to Sodom.

Jesus' visit to **Chorazin**, whose location is uncertain, is mentioned only here. **Tyre** and **Sidon** were pagan cities. They would not escape condemnation for their unbelief, but the cities of Galilee had greater responsibility because they had the advantage of the ministry of Jesus Himself.

Bethsaida was near the site for the feeding of the 5,000 (cp. 9:10-17). **Capernaum**, located on the western side of the Sea of Galilee had also been the site of ministries by Jesus. For these cities of Galilee to reject Jesus after His ministries and teaching among them would mean greater judgment than what God had poured out on the pagan cities.

10:25-42 This section contains what are considered two of the best known events in Scripture: the parable of the good Samaritan and the account of Jesus as a guest in the home of Mary and Martha. Luke seems to link these two passages to the question from the **expert in the law**. Jesus told the parable of the good Samaritan in response to the legal expert's question: Who is your **neighbor**? The basic lesson was that you must show compassion to all who are in need, even to your worst enemy. Clearly the priest and the Levite did not understand this concept. The shocking point of this story is that even your enemy is to be treated as your neighbor.

How does the predicament of **Mary** and **Martha** fit into this context? The key to understanding Mary and Martha can be found in the first of the greatest commandments: love for God. As was shown in the parable of the good Samaritan, loving your neighbor is vitally important; but such sacrifice can draw attention away from appropriate love for God. Therefore, Luke shares the story of Mary and Martha in order to show that love and devotion to God ought never to be compromised, not even for good deeds. Defying all social norms of His day, Jesus proclaimed that Mary had chosen to sit and learn from Him, and her **right choice** would not be **taken away from** her (v. 42). Even for Gentile believers, the two greatest commandments, which originated in the Jewish Old Testament, were vitally important, and their importance has been vividly illustrated.

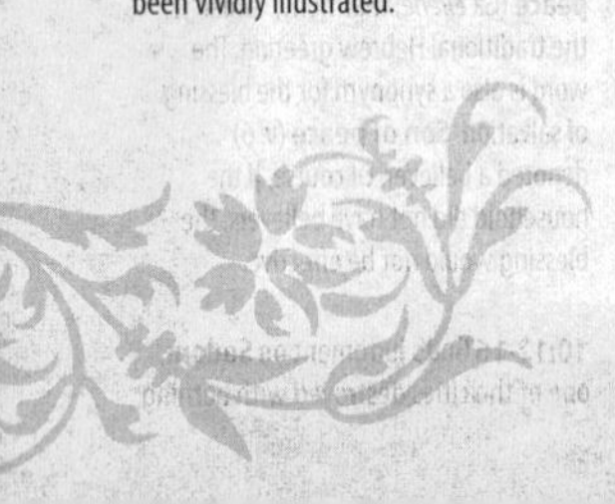

and kings wanted to see the things you see yet didn't see them; to hear the things you hear yet didn't hear them."

The Mandate for Double Love (10:25-42)

25 Just then an expert in the law stood up to test Him, saying, "Teacher, what must I do to inherit eternal life?"

26 "What is written in the law?" He asked him. "How do you read it?"

27 He answered:

> **Love the Lord your God with all your heart, with all your soul, with all your strength, and with all your mind;** and **your neighbor as yourself.**[A]

28 "You've answered correctly," He told him. "Do this and you will live."

29 But wanting to justify himself, he asked Jesus, "And who is my neighbor?"

30 Jesus took up the question and said: "A man was going down from Jerusalem to Jericho and fell into the hands of robbers. They stripped him, beat him up, and fled, leaving him half dead. 31 A priest happened to be going down that road. When he saw him, he passed by on the other side. 32 In the same way, a Levite, when he arrived at the place and saw him, passed by on the other side. 33 But a •Samaritan on his journey came up to him, and when he saw the man, he had compassion. 34 He went over to him and bandaged his wounds, pouring on olive oil and wine. Then he put him on his own animal, brought him to an inn, and took care of him. 35 The next day[B] he took out two •denarii, gave them to the innkeeper, and said, 'Take care of him. When I come back I'll reimburse you for whatever extra you spend.'

36 "Which of these three do you think proved to be a neighbor to the man who fell into the hands of the robbers?"

37 "The one who showed mercy to him," he said.

Then Jesus told him, "Go and do the same."

38 While they were traveling, He entered a village, and a woman named Martha welcomed Him into her home.[C] 39 She had a sister named Mary, who also sat at the Lord's[D] feet and was listening to what He said.[E] 40 But Martha was distracted by her many tasks, and she came up and asked, "Lord, don't You care that my sister has left me to serve alone? So tell her to give me a hand."[F]

41 The Lord[G] answered her, "Martha, Martha, you are worried and upset about many things, 42 but one thing is necessary. Mary has made the right choice,[H] and it will not be taken away from her."

The Teaching About Prayer (11:1-13)

11 He was praying in a certain place, and when He finished, one of His disciples said to Him, "Lord, teach us to pray, just as John also taught his disciples."

2 He said to them, "Whenever you pray, say:

> Father,[I]
> Your name be honored
> as holy.
> Your kingdom come.[J]
> 3 Give us each day
> our daily bread.[K]
> 4 And forgive us our sins,
> for we ourselves also
> forgive everyone
> in debt to us.[L]
> And do not bring us
> into temptation."[M]

5 He also said to them: "Suppose one of you[N] has a friend and goes to him at midnight and says to him, 'Friend, lend me three loaves of bread, 6 because a friend of mine on a journey has come to me, and I don't have anything to offer him.'[O] 7 Then he will answer from inside and say, 'Don't bother me! The door is already locked, and my children and I have gone to bed. I can't get

[A]**10:27** Lv 19:18; Dt 6:5 [B]**10:35** Other mss add *as he was leaving* [C]**10:38** Other mss omit *into her home* [D]**10:39** Other mss read *at Jesus'* [E]**10:39** Lit *to His word* or *message* [F]**10:40** Or *tell her to help me* [G]**10:41** Other mss read *Jesus* [H]**10:42** Lit *has chosen the good part* [I]**11:2** Other mss read *Our Father in heaven* [J]**11:2** Other mss add *Your will be done on earth as it is in heaven* [K]**11:3** Or *our bread for tomorrow* [L]**11:4** Or *everyone who wrongs us* [M]**11:4** Other mss add *But deliver us from the evil one* [N]**11:5** Lit *Who of you* [O]**11:6** Lit *I have nothing to set before him*

up to give you anything.' 8 I tell you,
even though he won't get up and
give him anything because he is his
friend, yet because of his friend's·
persistence,[A] he will get up and give
him as much as he needs.
9 "So I say to you, keep asking,[B] and
it will be given to you. Keep searching,[C] and you will find. Keep knocking,[D] and the door will be opened
to you. 10 For everyone who asks
receives, and the one who searches
finds, and to the one who knocks,
the door will be opened. 11 What father among you, if his son[E] asks for a
fish, will give him a snake instead of
a fish? 12 Or if he asks for an egg, will
give him a scorpion? 13 If you then,
who are evil, know how to give good
gifts to your children, how much
more will the heavenly Father give[F]
the Holy Spirit to those who ask
Him?"

The Controversy with a Pharisee (11:14-54)

14 Now He was driving out a demon
that was mute.[G] When the demon
came out, the man who had been
mute, spoke, and the crowds were
amazed. 15 But some of them said,
"He drives out demons by •Beelze-
bul, the ruler of the demons!" 16 And
others, as a test, were demanding of
Him a sign from heaven.
17 Knowing their thoughts, He
told them: "Every kingdom divided
against itself is headed for destruction, and a house divided against
itself falls. 18 If Satan also is divided
against himself, how will his kingdom stand? For you say I drive out
demons by Beelzebul. 19 And if I drive
out demons by Beelzebul, who is it
your sons[H] drive them out by? For
this reason they will be your judges.
20 If I drive out demons by the finger
of God, then the kingdom of God
has come to you. 21 When a strong
man, fully armed, guards his estate,
his possessions are secure.[I] 22 But
when one stronger than he attacks
and overpowers him, he takes from
him all his weapons[J] he trusted in,
and divides up his plunder. 23 Anyone who is not with Me is against
Me, and anyone who does not gather
with Me scatters.
24 "When an •unclean spirit comes
out of a man, it roams through waterless places looking for rest, and
not finding rest, it then[K] says, 'I'll
go back to my house where I came
from.' 25 And returning, it finds
the house swept and put in order.
26 Then it goes and brings seven other spirits more evil than itself, and
they enter and settle down there. As
a result, that man's last condition is
worse than the first."
27 As He was saying these things,
a woman from the crowd raised her
voice and said to Him, "The womb
that bore You and the one who
nursed You are blessed!"
28 He said, "Even more, those who
hear the word of God and keep it are
blessed!"
29 As the crowds were increasing,
He began saying: "This generation
is an evil generation. It demands a
sign, but no sign will be given to it
except the sign of Jonah.[L] 30 For just
as Jonah became a sign to the people
of Nineveh, so also the •Son of Man
will be to this generation. 31 The
queen of the south will rise up at
the judgment with the men of this
generation and condemn them, because she came from the ends of the
earth to hear the wisdom of Solomon, and look—something greater
than Solomon is here! 32 The men of
Nineveh will rise up at the judgment
with this generation and condemn
it, because they repented at Jonah's
proclamation, and look—something greater than Jonah is here!
33 "No one lights a lamp and puts it
in the cellar or under a basket,[M] but
on a lampstand, so that those who
come in may see its light. 34 Your eye
is the lamp of the body. When your
eye is good, your whole body is also
full of light. But when it is bad, your
body is also full of darkness. 35 Take
care then, that the light in you is not
darkness. 36 If, therefore, your whole

[A] 11:8 Or *annoying persistence*, or *shamelessness* [B] 11:9 Or *you, ask* [C] 11:9 Or *Search* [D] 11:9 Or *Knock* [E] 11:11 Other mss read *son asks for bread, would give him a stone? Or if he* [F] 11:13 Lit *the Father from heaven will give* [G] 11:14 A demon that caused the man to be mute [H] 11:19 Your exorcists [I] 11:21 Lit *his possessions are in peace* [J] 11:22 Gk *panoplia*, the armor and weapons of a foot soldier; Eph 6:11,13 [K] 11:24 Other mss omit *then* [L] 11:29 Other mss add *the prophet* [M] 11:33 Other mss omit *or under a basket*

11:1-13 The well-known prayer Jesus taught His disciples can also be found in Mt 6:9-13. The prayer is a pattern for believers since the prayer began with **Father**, a noun of address for God reserved exclusively for Jesus and His followers. Jesus, of course, had a unique relationship with the Father reserved only for Himself. However, the term is also a special one for believers because the endearing name with the intimacy and respect engendered is a beautiful way to affirm the link Jesus established between the Father and His children, who come to Him through their relationship with Jesus, the Son of God. Anyone who accepts Jesus' atoning death on the cross is reconciled to God by becoming His spiritual child.

The first petitions relate to God—the honoring of His **name** through your worship and adoration and the acknowledging of His rule in your life (v. 2). The second group of petitions relate to the individual—provision of sufficient food for sustenance (v. 3), forgiveness of your **sins** and your forgiveness of others to make possible your personal fellowship with God (v. 4a), faithfulness in God's protection during times of testing (v. 4b). God does not seek to lure His children into doing evil (Jms 1:1-15), but He allows testing to strengthen character and nurture commitment.

The parable involved a reluctant host and persistent visitor. The visitor was asking for **bread** because he had been on a long **journey**, but at first the host refused to give the petitioner anything. However, because of the petitioner's persistence, not his friendship, the host acquiesced to the request. **Persistence** (Gk *anaideia*, "shamelessness, impudence," v. 8) essentially connoted the idea of annoying persistence. Jesus promised that God will **give good gifts** (in this case, **the Holy Spirit**) to those who shamelessly and boldly ask of Him. In this context, Luke intends that his readers focus not so much on God's response as on the response of the believer. Believers are to love God and their neighbors, and they are to be bold in prayer. Perhaps the ultimate picture presented in this vivid parable is the contrast between the way God answers the prayers of His children in contradistinction to the way believers respond to the petitions of one another.

11:14-54 These passages concerning the conflicts between Jesus and the Pharisees have parallels in both Matthew and Mark (see Mt 12:1-45 for a more in-depth treatment). For the Pharisees to attribute Christ's miracles to the work of Satan called into question not only Christ's authority but also the authority of the Word of God itself. Perhaps for that reason, Luke adds within this context a passage concerning the woman who blessed

the womb that bore Jesus (Lk 11:27-28). Jesus responded by saying that true blessedness is found in hearing the Word of God and keeping it.

Jonah's message had brought immediate and far-reaching repentance (vv. 29-30; Jn 3:5-10). The **queen of the south** (of Sheba, 1Kg 10:1-13) had traveled a great distance just **to hear the wisdom of Solomon** (Lk 11:31). Jesus was far **greater than Jonah** or Solomon, and His message was far more powerful. The people of Nineveh and the foreign queen represent Gentiles who responded correctly to the light they were given about God, unlike most of the Jews to whom Jesus preached. Jonah (a Jewish prophet) and Solomon (a Jewish king) exemplify God's determination to use His people as bearers of the **light** (e.g., Is 42:6; 60:3; cp. Mt 5:14), pointing the way to the one true God in whom salvation from sin (i.e., **darkness**) is found.

In this context, Jesus uses the people's understanding of the **eye** as the body's means of receiving and shining forth light to support His observation that overall His immediate audience was **an evil generation** (Lk 11:29). As such, their "eye" was **bad** (i.e., unreceptive to the light of truth embodied in Christ Himself and His words) and could be like neither Jonah nor Solomon. Although they claimed to uphold the light by following the law, the lives of God's people were characterized instead by darkness (v. 34). In verses 37-52, Jesus elaborates on this hypocrisy, particularly of the **Pharisees**, who had become so obsessed with ceremonial cleanness and with fulfilling rituals such as tithing that they failed to recognize "the light of the world" among them (Jn 1:4,9-12; 8:12; 1Jn 1:5).

Rue was a shrub with stringent odor growing on hills in the Holy Land (v. 42). Jesus affirmed the Pharisees' commitment to tithing even their garden herbs and vegetables, but He also warned that stewardship went beyond this ritualistic practice to include attitude of heart and discipline of life. This inconsistency seemed to be the overall point of this entire section. Jesus' controversies with the Pharisees exposed their religious hypocrisy, which would soon be judged.

12:1-3 The previously mentioned judgment is seen in full light here. The disciples and the crowds are warned against religious **hypocrisy** (vv. 1-3). Jesus used **yeast**, a rising agent in bread, to continue His discussion of the Pharisees' hypocrisy, which was spreading through their teachings as yeast did in dough.

12:4-12 Jesus exhorted His listeners to fear God alone and to acknowledge Christ. Jesus was emphasizing the value of all of His creation by pointing

body is full of light, with no part of
it in darkness, it will be entirely illuminated, as when a lamp shines its
light on you."[A]
37 As He was speaking, a •Pharisee
asked Him to dine with him. So He
went in and reclined at the table.
38 When the Pharisee saw this, he was
amazed that He did not first perform
the ritual washing[B] before dinner.
39 But the Lord said to him: "Now
you Pharisees •clean the outside of
the cup and dish, but inside you are
full of greed and evil. 40 Fools! Didn't
He who made the outside make the
inside too? 41 But give from what is
within to the poor,[C] and then everything is clean for you.
42 "But woe to you Pharisees! You
give a tenth[D] of mint, rue, and every
kind of herb, and you bypass[E] justice
and love for God.[F] These things you
should have done without neglecting the others.
43 "Woe to you Pharisees! You love
the front seat in the •synagogues
and greetings in the marketplaces.
44 "Woe to you![G] You are like unmarked graves; the people who walk
over them don't know it."
45 One of the experts in the law answered Him, "Teacher, when You say
these things You insult us too."
46 Then He said: "Woe also to you
experts in the law! You load people
with burdens that are hard to carry,
yet you yourselves don't touch these
burdens with one of your fingers.
47 "Woe to you! You build monuments[H] to the prophets, and your fathers killed them. 48 Therefore, you
are witnesses that you approve[I] the
deeds of your fathers, for they killed
them, and you build their monuments.[J] 49 Because of this, the wisdom of God said, 'I will send them
prophets and apostles, and some of
them they will kill and persecute,'
50 so that this generation may be
held responsible for the blood of all
the prophets shed since the foundation of the world[K]— 51 from the
blood of Abel to the blood of Zechariah, who perished between the altar
and the sanctuary.
"Yes, I tell you, this generation
will be held responsible.[L]
52 "Woe to you experts in the law!
You have taken away the key of
knowledge! You didn't go in yourselves, and you hindered those who
were going in."
53 When He left there,[M] the •scribes
and the Pharisees began to oppose
Him fiercely and to cross-examine
Him about many things; 54 they were
lying in wait for Him to trap Him in
something He said.[N]

The Preparation for Judgment (12:1–13:9)

12 In these circumstances,[O] a
crowd of many thousands
came together, so that they were
trampling on one another. He began to say to His disciples first: "Be
on your guard against the yeast[P]
of the •Pharisees, which is hypocrisy. 2 There is nothing covered that
won't be uncovered, nothing hidden
that won't be made known. 3 Therefore, whatever you have said in the
dark will be heard in the light, and
what you have whispered in an ear
in private rooms will be proclaimed
on the housetops.
4 "And I say to you, My friends,
don't fear those who kill the body,
and after that can do nothing more.
5 But I will show you the One to
fear: Fear Him who has authority to
throw people into •hell after death.
Yes, I say to you, this is the One to
fear! 6 Aren't five sparrows sold for
two pennies?[Q] Yet not one of them
is forgotten in God's sight. 7 Indeed,
the hairs of your head are all counted. Don't be afraid; you are worth
more than many sparrows!
8 "And I say to you, anyone who
acknowledges Me before men, the
•Son of Man will also acknowledge
him before the angels of God, 9 but
whoever denies Me before men will

[A] **11:36** Or *shines on you with its rays* [B] **11:38** Lit *He did not first wash* [C] **11:41** Or *But donate from the heart as charity* [D] **11:42** Or *a tithe* [E] **11:42** Or *neglect* [F] **11:42** Lit *the justice and the love of God* [G] **11:44** Other mss read *you scribes and Pharisees, hypocrites!* [H] **11:47** Or *graves* [I] **11:48** Lit *witnesses and approve* [J] **11:48** Other mss omit *their monuments* [K] **11:50** Lit *so that the blood of all . . . world may be required of this generation,* [L] **11:51** Lit *you, it will be required of this generation* [M] **11:53** Other mss read *And as He was saying these things to them* [N] **11:54** Other mss add *so that they might bring charges against Him* [O] **12:1** Or *Meanwhile,* or *At this time,* or *During this period* [P] **12:1** Or *leaven* [Q] **12:6** Lit *two assaria*; the *assarion* (sg) was a small copper coin

be denied before the angels of God. 10 Anyone who speaks a word against the Son of Man will be forgiven, but the one who blasphemes against the Holy Spirit will not be forgiven. 11 Whenever they bring you before •synagogues and rulers and authorities, don't worry about how you should defend yourselves or what you should say. 12 For the Holy Spirit will teach you at that very hour what must be said."

13 Someone from the crowd said to Him, "Teacher, tell my brother to divide the inheritance with me."

14 "Friend,"[A] He said to him, "who appointed Me a judge or arbitrator over you?" 15 He then told them, "Watch out and be on guard against all greed because one's life is not in the abundance of his possessions."

16 Then He told them a parable: "A rich man's land was very productive. 17 He thought to himself, 'What should I do, since I don't have anywhere to store my crops? 18 I will do this,' he said. 'I'll tear down my barns and build bigger ones and store all my grain and my goods there. 19 Then I'll say to myself, "You[B] have many goods stored up for many years. Take it easy; eat, drink, and enjoy yourself."'

20 "But God said to him, 'You fool! This very night your •life is demanded of you. And the things you have prepared—whose will they be?'

21 "That's how it is with the one who stores up treasure for himself and is not rich toward God."

22 Then He said to His disciples: "Therefore I tell you, don't worry about your life, what you will eat; or about the body, what you will wear. 23 For life is more than food and the body more than clothing. 24 Consider the ravens: They don't sow or reap; they don't have a storeroom or a barn; yet God feeds them. Aren't you worth much more than the birds? 25 Can any of you add a •cubit to his height[C] by worrying? 26 If then you're not able to do even a little thing, why worry about the rest?

27 "Consider how the wildflowers grow: They don't labor or spin thread. Yet I tell you, not even Solomon in all his splendor was adorned like one of these! 28 If that's how God clothes the grass, which is in the field today and is thrown into the furnace tomorrow, how much more will He do for you—you of little faith? 29 Don't keep striving for what you should eat and what you should drink, and don't be anxious. 30 For the Gentile world eagerly seeks all these things, and your Father knows that you need them.

31 "But seek His kingdom, and these things will be provided for you. 32 Don't be afraid, little flock, because your Father delights to give you the kingdom. 33 Sell your possessions and give to the poor. Make money-bags for yourselves that won't grow old, an inexhaustible treasure in heaven, where no thief comes near and no moth destroys. 34 For where your treasure is, there your heart will be also.

35 "Be ready for service[D] and have your lamps lit. 36 You must be like people waiting for their master to return[E] from the wedding banquet so that when he comes and knocks, they can open the door for him at once. 37 Those •slaves the master will find alert when he comes will

HARD QUESTION

Am I guilty of greed or outright disobedience if I do not sell everything I own and give it to the poor, as Jesus commands?

Jesus' admonition (see 12:31-34) has been interpreted by some as a suggestion that the disciples get rid of possessions that might deter their service to Christ. Others interpret it as a call to help those less fortunate than they by their own personal sacrifice. Jesus seems to be emphasizing what His disciples treasure in their hearts. Giving priority to material possessions is incompatible with devoting your life to Christ. The Lord does not lead every follower to **sell** everything to **give to the poor**, but He does expect every follower to be willing to do so without hesitation, knowing that the only **treasure** of any value is whatever is eternal—the souls of people. The issue is not how much you have but how what you have affects your commitment to Christ.

to one of the most insignificant—the sparrow, which was used for food by the poor. These words served as a reminder of God's providential care, which extended even to the smallest details of life (vv. 6-7). **One who blasphemes against the Holy Spirit** has a hardened heart toward God and opposes God's work with a full understanding of what he is doing (Lk 12:10). (See note on Mt 12:22-32 concerning blasphemy against the Holy Spirit.) Jesus' disciples were warned about greed and exhorted instead to do good works, knowing that if they did not, they would be punished based upon the level of their knowledge of their master's will (vv. 13-48).

12:13-21 Greed is a self-centered desire for wealth or possessions (v. 15). Greed generally escalates as a person acquires more possessions. The man's greedy character becomes apparent in his own actions (vv. 17-19). Religious leaders were frequently called upon to mediate disputes concerning inheritances; but Jesus refused to be drawn into dividing up possessions, not because He did not have the right or authority to decide the dispute or because He was insensitive to the problem. Jesus directed His remarks to matters of the heart.

12:22-30 Just as with greed, **worry** can affect anyone, whatever his position in life. An attitude of anxiety is destructive to the physical life and hurtful to spiritual testimony (vv. 22-26). **Height** (Gk *hēlikian*, "stature, years, maturity," v. 25) in this context seems to suggest the span of life. Again Jesus clearly noted the value of every life and the loving care He poured out on all His creation (v. 24). To use your energies in worry over things you cannot control—whether great or small—is futile and inappropriate. God does not overlook the necessities of His children according to His plan for their lives. When He allows suffering or even deprivation, such is never wasted in the divine economy. Drinking of the cup of His sufferings is never to be taken lightly. The privilege must be embraced for the opportunity of testimony and means of glorifying the Father.

12:31-34 Alongside right attitudes is the mandate for God-given priorities. Not only does God provide what is needed, whether in abundant outpouring or measured inner strength, but He also has given a clear pattern for right priorities. Clearly God demands your first and foremost allegiance.

12:35-48 Jesus noted again the importance of readiness for His **return**, using the metaphor of a **master** and his **slaves**, who were responsible for protecting and caring for their master's

[A]**12:14** Lit *Man* [B]**12:19** Lit *say to my soul, "Soul, you* [C]**12:25** Or *add one moment to his life-span* [D]**12:35** Lit *Let your loins be girded*; an idiom for tying up loose outer clothing in preparation for action; Ex 12:11 [E]**12:36** Lit *master, when he should return*

household and being ready or **alert** for his return (v. 37).

The severity of punishment for unfaithfulness is clear. Whether the phrase **cut him to pieces** is a means of portraying severe punishment or, more likely, a metaphor for emphasizing the separation from God and His people is not as important as the understanding that the penalty for unfaithfulness is great indeed (v. 46). The idea of degrees of punishment is presented here (v. 48). One who sins in ignorance does not have the same responsibility as one with full knowledge and understanding. God is absolutely just in administering His wrath. However, the main tragedy is separation from God; and that is the penalty for all who reject Him.

12:49–13:9 Fire is used to symbolize divine judgment or refining purification or the coming of the Holy Spirit (12:49). The context seems to point to judgment. The reference to **baptism** (12:50) as in Mk 10:38 seems to be used as a reference to His coming death, at which time He would be immersed in His suffering on the cross. When Jesus spoke of **division** in contrast to **peace**, He was alluding to the separation of believers from unbelievers (Lk 12:51). Elsewhere Jesus does talk about bringing peace (1:78-79; 2:14; 7:50). Indeed Jesus' coming brought the opposite of peace—division even among families and friends (12:52-53)—because some not only would reject Christ themselves but would be angry with any who received Him.

People are forced to make a choice: Either they are for Christ or against Him. There is no middle ground. Those who do not understand this choice and its consequences have a lack of discernment concerning the times in which they live. Therefore, Jesus' followers must do everything they can to be reconciled with God, who is here described as their **adversary** (12:57-59) because anyone who does not take personal responsibility and repent, will perish (13:1-5).

Repentance and fruit-bearing are both necessary; or judgment will come (13:6-8). Some very stern warnings against hypocrisy and indifference—warnings, which, unfortunately, the modern Western church has ceased to heed, are recorded in this section. Jesus must be feared, loved, and obeyed.

13:1–14:24 This section points to a reversal of the expectation concerning who will enter the kingdom. Christ rebuked those who sought to put God in their debt and promised eternal reward to those who followed Him without expecting something in return (14:14b,15-24).

13:1-9 Regarding the incident reported to Him, Jesus did not assign blame

be blessed. •I assure you: He will get ready,[A] have them recline at the table, then come and serve them. 38 If he comes in the middle of the night, or even near dawn,[B] and finds them alert, those slaves are blessed. 39 But know this: If the homeowner had known at what hour the thief was coming, he would not have let his house be broken into. 40 You also be ready, because the Son of Man is coming at an hour that you do not expect."

41 "Lord," Peter asked, "are You telling this parable to us or to everyone?"

42 The Lord said: "Who then is the faithful and sensible manager his master will put in charge of his household servants to give them their allotted food at the proper time? 43 That slave whose master finds him working when he comes will be rewarded. 44 I tell you the truth: He will put him in charge of all his possessions. 45 But if that slave says in his heart, 'My master is delaying his coming,' and starts to beat the male and female slaves, and to eat and drink and get drunk, 46 that slave's master will come on a day he does not expect him and at an hour he does not know. He will cut him to pieces[C] and assign him a place with the unbelievers.[D] 47 And that slave who knew his master's will and didn't prepare himself or do it[E] will be severely beaten. 48 But the one who did not know and did things deserving of blows will be beaten lightly. Much will be required of everyone who has been given much. And even more will be expected of the one who has been entrusted with more.[F]

49 "I came to bring fire on the earth, and how I wish it were already set ablaze! 50 But I have a baptism to be baptized with, and how it consumes Me until it is finished! 51 Do you think that I came here to give peace to the earth? No, I tell you, but rather division! 52 From now on, five in one household will be divided: three against two, and two against three.

53 **They will be divided, father**
against son,
son against father,
mother against daughter,
daughter against mother,
mother-in-law against
her daughter-in-law,
and daughter-in-law
against mother-in-law."[G]

54 He also said to the crowds: "When you see a cloud rising in the west, right away you say, 'A storm is coming,' and so it does. 55 And when the south wind is blowing, you say, 'It's going to be a scorcher!' and it is. 56 Hypocrites! You know how to interpret the appearance of the earth and the sky, but why don't you know how to interpret this time?

57 "Why don't you judge for yourselves what is right? 58 As you are going with your adversary to the ruler, make an effort to settle with him on the way. Then he won't drag you before the judge, the judge hand you over to the bailiff, and the bailiff throw you into prison. 59 I tell you, you will never get out of there until you have paid the last cent."[H]

13 At that time, some people came and reported to Him about the Galileans whose blood •Pilate had mixed with their sacrifices. 2 And He[I] responded to them, "Do you think that these Galileans were more sinful than all Galileans because they suffered these things? 3 No, I tell you; but unless you repent, you will all perish as well! 4 Or those 18 that the tower in Siloam fell on and killed—do you think they were more sinful than all the people who live in Jerusalem? 5 No, I tell you; but unless you repent, you will all perish as well!"

6 And He told this parable: "A man had a fig tree that was planted in his vineyard. He came looking for fruit on it and found none. 7 He told the vineyard worker, 'Listen, for three years I have come looking for fruit on this fig tree and haven't found any. Cut it down! Why should it even waste the soil?'

[A] **12:37** Lit *will gird himself* [B] **12:38** Lit *even in the second or third watch* [C] **12:46** Lit *him in two* [D] **12:46** Or *unfaithful*, or *untrustworthy* [E] **12:47** Lit *or do toward his will* [F] **12:48** Or *much* [G] **12:53** Mc 7:6 [H] **12:59** Gk *lepton*, the smallest and least valuable copper coin in use [I] **13:2** Other mss read *Jesus*

CHARACTER PROFILE

The Disabled Woman **Healed and Thankful**

Her Background	She was disabled and had a curvature of the spine, unable to straighten up (13:11).
Her Story	• She heard Jesus teaching at the synagogue on the Sabbath. • He noticed her, called out to her, and instantly healed her (13:12-13). • She immediately began to praise God.
Life Lesson	Legalism can cause you to be blind to the needs of others around you.

8 "But he replied to him, 'Sir,[A]
leave it this year also, until I dig
around it and fertilize it. 9 Perhaps it
will bear fruit next year, but if not,
you can cut it down.'"

Kingdom Reversals (13:10–14:24)

10 As He was teaching in one of
the •synagogues on the Sabbath,
11 a woman was there who had been
disabled by a spirit[B] for over 18
years. She was bent over and could
not straighten up at all.[C] 12 When
Jesus saw her, He called out to her,[D]
"•Woman, you are free of your disability." 13 Then He laid His hands on
her, and instantly she was restored
and began to glorify God.

14 But the leader of the synagogue,
indignant because Jesus had healed
on the Sabbath, responded by telling
the crowd, "There are six days when
work should be done; therefore
come on those days and be healed
and not on the Sabbath day."

15 But the Lord answered him and
said, "Hypocrites! Doesn't each one
of you untie his ox or donkey from
the feeding trough on the Sabbath
and lead it to water? 16 Satan has
bound this woman, a daughter of
Abraham, for 18 years—shouldn't
she be untied from this bondage on
the Sabbath day?"

17 When He had said these things,
all His adversaries were humiliated,
but the whole crowd was rejoicing
over all the glorious things He was
doing.

18 He said, therefore, "What is the
kingdom of God like, and what can
I compare it to? 19 It's like a mustard
seed that a man took and sowed in
his garden. It grew and became a
tree, and the birds of the sky nested
in its branches."

20 Again He said, "What can I compare the kingdom of God to? 21 It's
like yeast that a woman took and
mixed into 50 pounds[E] of flour until
it spread through the entire mixture."[F]

22 He went through one town
and village after another, teaching
and making His way to Jerusalem.
23 "Lord," someone asked Him, "are
there few being saved?"[G]

He said to them, 24 "Make every
effort to enter through the narrow
door, because I tell you, many will
try to enter and won't be able 25 once
the homeowner gets up and shuts
the door. Then you will stand[H] outside and knock on the door, saying,
'Lord, open up for us!' He will answer you, 'I don't know you or where
you're from.' 26 Then you will say,[I]
'We ate and drank in Your presence,
and You taught in our streets!' 27 But
He will say, 'I tell you, I don't know
you or where you're from. Get away
from Me, all you workers of unrighteousness!' 28 There will be weeping
and gnashing of teeth in that place,
when you see Abraham, Isaac, Jacob,
and all the prophets in the kingdom
of God, but yourselves thrown out.
29 They will come from east and west,

[A]13:8 Or *Lord* [B]13:11 Lit *had a spirit of disability* [C]13:11 Or *straighten up completely* [D]13:12 Or *He summoned her* [E]13:21 Lit *3 sata*; about 40 quarts [F]13:21 Or *until all of it was leavened* [G]13:23 Or *are the saved few?* (in number); lit *are those being saved few?* [H]13:25 Lit *you will begin to stand* [I]13:26 Lit *you will begin to say*

solely to **Pilate** or to **the Galileans** who suffered. Regarding the incident **in Siloam**, Jesus did not confirm what many if not all in His audience assumed—that those who died must have been very sinful to receive such divine punishment. Instead, Jesus' response to these bad-news headlines precluded the typical speculation about how sinful the victims of such terrible events (whether the result of human intention or seemingly by inexplicable misfortune) must have been. He turned the attention of the audience away from trying to make sense of suffering and toward evaluating their own spiritual condition—the need for all to **repent** lest they **perish** [Gk *apoleisthe*, "be destroyed or put to death, be given over to eternal misery, incur loss of eternal life"; cp. 4:34; 9:56; 15:6,9,17,24,32; 21:18] **as well** (13:3,5).

Jesus then used the familiar **fig tree** to represent Israel. Despite its lack of fruit, the tree received an additional year of grace (v. 8). However, Israel remained in danger of God's judgment if the nation continued to reject her Messiah.

13:10-17 In the first mention of the Sabbath, Luke recorded that a woman **who had been disabled by a spirit for over** 18 years had been set free. Evidently she had a spinal problem, which had crippled her body (v. 11). Demonic activity seemed to be responsible for her chronic and lengthy illness (vv. 11,16), although Luke does not say that the woman was demon-possessed. Ultimately all evil and sickness would be attributed to Satan. Here Jesus initiated the healing without a request from the woman (v. 12), showing His compassion. She was healed immediately, and all knew the healing was of God (v. 13). **The leader of the synagogue** was indignant; he rebuked Jesus, though not directly addressing Him, for healing on the Sabbath (v. 14). Jesus likewise answered him with a general statement to all who would elevate ritualistic observances over extending healing and mercy. He used their willingness to extend mercy to an animal instead of to one of God's people as an example of their hypocrisy (v. 15). After Jesus' questions concerning what was most important to do on the Sabbath, the Jewish leader, and not Jesus, was humiliated. The phrase **daughter of Abraham** indicated her Jewish heritage (v. 16).

13:18-30 This scene was followed by two parables about **the kingdom**. One points out its unlikely beginnings, and another exhorts believers to make every effort to stay on the narrow path leading to the kingdom. The idea is not so much emphasizing the growing process as noting how what seems very insignificant can be the beginning of something great and wonderful. A tiny **seed** becomes a mighty tree (vv. 18-19); a small amount of **yeast** can change a measuring of **flour** by spreading itself through the **mixture** and increasing its volume (vv. 20-21). Jesus clearly presented the responsibility and accountability of the individual (v. 24). **Many will try to enter and won't be able** has nothing to do with personal merit or diligence. Jesus had already made clear that the key was personal repentance (13:3,5). Even to be at the table with Jesus (**we ate and drank in Your presence**, v. 26) was not enough. The closing proverb in this section probably would have been understood by Luke's audience as the inclusion of the Gentiles and a recognition of the unbelief in Israel. However, the article used in the Greek text is omitted in the English version, indicating that the designation was not meant to suggest all Gentiles would now **be first** and all Jews **last**, for some Jews did believe, and many Gentiles did not believe (v. 30).

13:31-35 After Jesus received the Pharisees' warning that **Herod** was trying **to kill** Him, He referred to Himself as a **prophet** and claimed that a true prophet could not die **outside of Jerusalem**. He then lamented over Jerusalem—the city of His future passion. Nevertheless, Jesus was still "on his way" to Jerusalem. Nothing would deter Him, not even Herod (Is 50:7).

14:1-6 On the second mention of the Sabbath, Luke described the healing of a man **whose body was swollen with fluid**. This condition is described with Greek *hudrōpikos*, "dropsy or edema." The text does not indicate whether this man was an invited guest, an intruding man seeking help, or someone planted by the Pharisees to entrap Jesus. The matter of healing on the Sabbath was further complicated with the obvious elevation of rituals and traditions above concern for the well-being of people. Again Jesus' wisdom left the religious leaders speechless.

14:7-24 This scene is followed by Jesus' teachings on humility, followed by the parable of the **large banquet** (vv. 16-24). **Those who were invited** (the Jews) made **excuses** for not coming. Therefore, those who gathered at this great table were the most unlikely: **the poor, maimed, blind, and lame** (v. 21; cp. v. 13). **Humiliation** is often the result of a lack of humility (v. 9), which is essential for entering God's kingdom. There is no coercion in the strong invitation **make them come in** (v. 23); rather there is strong persuasion for those who might feel hesitant to come to the great banquet because of their own personal unworthiness.

from north and south, and recline at the table in the kingdom of God. 30 Note this: Some are last who will be first, and some are first who will be last."

31 At that time some •Pharisees came and told Him, "Go, get out of here! •Herod wants to kill You!"

32 He said to them, "Go tell that fox, 'Look! I'm driving out demons and performing healings today and tomorrow, and on the third day[A] I will complete My work.'[B] 33 Yet I must travel today, tomorrow, and the next day, because it is not possible for a prophet to perish outside of Jerusalem!

34 "Jerusalem, Jerusalem! She who kills the prophets and stones those who are sent to her. How often I wanted to gather your children together, as a hen gathers her chicks under her wings, but you were not willing! 35 See, your house[C] is abandoned to you. And I tell you, you will not see Me until the time comes when you say, **'He who comes in the name of the Lord is the blessed One'!"**[D]

14 One Sabbath, when He went to eat[E] at the house of one of the leading •Pharisees, they were watching Him closely. 2 There in front of Him was a man whose body was swollen with fluid.[F] 3 In response, Jesus asked the law experts and the Pharisees, "Is it lawful to heal on the Sabbath or not?" 4 But they kept silent. He took the man, healed him, and sent him away. 5 And to them, He said, "Which of you whose son or ox falls into a well, will not immediately pull him out on the Sabbath day?" 6 To this they could find no answer.

7 He told a parable to those who were invited, when He noticed how they would choose the best places for themselves: 8 "When you are invited by someone to a wedding banquet, don't recline at the best place, because a more distinguished person than you may have been invited by your host.[G] 9 The one who invited both of you may come and say to you, 'Give your place to this man,' and then in humiliation, you will proceed to take the lowest place.

10 "But when you are invited, go and recline in the lowest place, so that when the one who invited you comes, he will say to you, 'Friend, move up higher.' You will then be honored in the presence of all the other guests. 11 For everyone who exalts himself will be humbled, and the one who humbles himself will be exalted."

12 He also said to the one who had invited Him, "When you give a lunch or a dinner, don't invite your friends, your •brothers, your relatives, or your rich neighbors, because they might invite you back, and you would be repaid. 13 On the contrary, when you host a banquet, invite those who are poor, maimed, lame, or blind. 14 And you will be blessed, because they cannot repay you; for you will be repaid at the resurrection of the righteous."

15 When one of those who reclined at the table with Him heard these things, he said to Him, "The one who will eat bread in the kingdom of God is blessed!"

16 Then He told him: "A man was giving a large banquet and invited many. 17 At the time of the banquet, he sent his •slave to tell those who were invited, 'Come, because everything is now ready.'

18 "But without exception[H] they all began to make excuses. The first one said to him, 'I have bought a field, and I must go out and see it. I ask you to excuse me.'

19 "Another said, 'I have bought five yoke of oxen, and I'm going to try them out. I ask you to excuse me.'

20 "And another said, 'I just got married,[I] and therefore I'm unable to come.'

21 "So the slave came back and reported these things to his master. Then in anger, the master of the house told his slave, 'Go out quickly into the streets and alleys of the city, and bring in here the poor, maimed, blind, and lame!'

22 "'Master,' the slave said, 'what

[A] **13:32** Very shortly [B] **13:32** Lit *I will be finished* [C] **13:35** Probably the temple; Jr 12:7; 22:5
[D] **13:35** Ps 118:26 [E] **14:1** Lit *eat bread*; = eat a meal [F] **14:2** Afflicted with dropsy or edema
[G] **14:8** Lit *by him* [H] **14:18** Lit *And from one* (voice) [I] **14:20** Lit *I have married a woman*

CHARACTER PROFILE

The Woman with the Lost Coin

Her Background	She is a character in Jesus' parable on the lost coin (15:8-10).
Her Story	• She had lost a coin from her headdress, which was probably from her dowry or had been a wedding gift. • The coin would have had not only monetary value but also sentimental value. • She swept the house, searching for the coin. • She found it and called her neighbors to celebrate with her.
Life Lesson	This woman's joy is a picture of the angels' joy when even one sinner repents.

you ordered has been done, and there's still room.'
23 "Then the master told the slave, 'Go out into the highways and lanes and make them come in, so that my house may be filled.
24 For I tell you, not one of those men who were invited will enjoy my banquet!'"

The Cost of Discipleship (14:25-35)

25 Now great crowds were traveling with Him. So He turned and said to them:
26 "If anyone comes to Me and does not hate his own father and mother, wife and children, brothers and sisters—yes, and even his own life—he cannot be My disciple.
27 Whoever does not bear his own cross and come after Me cannot be My disciple.
28 "For which of you, wanting to build a tower, doesn't first sit down and calculate the cost to see if he has enough to complete it?
29 Otherwise, after he has laid the foundation and cannot finish it, all the onlookers will begin to make fun of him,
30 saying, 'This man started to build and wasn't able to finish.'
31 "Or what king, going to war against another king, will not first sit down and decide if he is able with 10,000 to oppose the one who comes against him with 20,000?
32 If not, while the other is still far off, he sends a delegation and asks for terms of peace.
33 In the same way, therefore, every one of you who does not say good-bye to[A] all his possessions cannot be My disciple.
34 "Now, salt is good, but if salt should lose its taste, how will it be made salty?
35 It isn't fit for the soil or for the manure pile; they throw it out. Anyone who has ears to hear should listen!"

The Seeking and Saving of the Lost (15:1-32)

15 All the tax collectors and sinners were approaching to listen to Him.
2 And the •Pharisees and •scribes were complaining, "This man welcomes sinners and eats with them!"
3 So He told them this parable:
4 "What man among you, who has 100 sheep and loses one of them, does not leave the 99 in the open field[B] and go after the lost one until he finds it?
5 When he has found it, he joyfully puts it on his shoulders,
6 and coming home, he calls his friends and neighbors together, saying to them, 'Rejoice with me, because I have found my lost sheep!'
7 I tell you, in the same way, there will be more joy in heaven over one sinner who repents than over 99 righteous people who don't need repentance.
8 "Or what woman who has 10 silver coins,[C] if she loses one coin, does not light a lamp, sweep the house, and search carefully until she finds it?
9 When she finds it, she calls her women friends and

[A]14:33 Or *does not renounce* or *leave* [B]15:4 Or *the wilderness* [C]15:8 Gk *10 drachmas*; a *drachma* was a silver coin = a •denarius

14:25-35 Parables recorded only in Luke form the heart of this section. Jesus emphasizes that the cost of discipleship is high; those who desire to enter the kingdom ought to reflect deeply on the sacrifice that is necessary in order to do so (v. 27). He also gave stern warnings to any who would use family responsibilities as an excuse to abandon a radical commitment to Him. Jesus did not suggest dishonoring parents or neglecting family responsibilities. Love for Jesus should be so great that love of family would seem like hatred by comparison. All other loyalties are subordinate to your devotion to Christ. Sometimes to follow Christ means giving up even the most precious earthly relationships. Ultimately you must be willing to lay down your life for Christ since to **bear** your **own cross** was often an expression indicating death (v. 27). Only those who have committed themselves to Christ and who have persevered over the long term are truly saved. Here the text does call for giving up all. Genuine believers give up ownership and control of their lives and possessions and instead become God's steward of these. Christ must be set above everyone and everything in a person's life. Nothing less will do. While **the cost** of following Christ is high (vv. 28-30), the cost of not following Him is higher still (vv. 31-32).

15:1-32 The trilogy of parables illustrates the deep love God has for wayward sinners and affirms the joy of the heavenly Father when the lost are recovered. First and foremost, God forgives and restores. The tragedy of lostness is vividly portrayed but is always overshadowed by the joy of finding the precious object that has been lost.

15:1-7 The religious leaders complained about the **tax collectors** because they considered them thieves and thus linked them with all who were immoral or **sinners**. To eat at the same table with them would have been unthinkable. Jesus was not suggesting that anyone did not need repentance. Rather He was describing the Pharisees and scribes as so self-righteous that they had not realized their need for **repentance**. There are some interesting analogies in this parable. The shepherd sought his **lost sheep**, and Jesus actively seeks anyone who is lost (19:10). Also even as the shepherd called for a celebration when he found the lost sheep, Jesus rejoices over receiving a sinner who comes home in repentance.

15:8-10 Women who married in the ancient world often wore headpieces that were adorned with valuable coins. Perhaps the coins were part of her dowry, the savings she had put aside, ornaments to accessorize her head covering, or some combination of these. In any case, **10 silver coins** (Gk *deka*, "ten"; *drachmēn*, "silver coins") would have been a treasured possession. Since these coins are mentioned only here in the New Testament, their exact value is uncertain, but some have suggested the number of coins probably meant they were all she had. One coin would have been typically one day's wages. To lose something this valuable would have been considered a shameful and irresponsible act.

Undoubtedly the scene was a humble home, probably few if any windows, explaining the diligence of her search. When she found the lost treasure, her joy had to be shared with all. The lesson in this parable comes at several points. First, the seeking **woman** is a model of every woman's search for the treasure of the gospel, the inheritance awaiting those who will repent and believe and trust Jesus for salvation. Second, the joy engendered by the woman's happy celebration over finding her lost coin is compared to the **joy in the presence of God's angels over one sinner who repents**. Nowhere is there any indication that the woman in this parable is to represent God. Jesus clearly unveiled the lesson as being found in the joy over finding the precious coin as parallel to the joy in heaven over a sinner who repents.

15:11-32 According to Dt 21:17 in a family of two brothers, the **older son** would receive a double portion or two thirds of his father's estate.

The gifts of the **father** carried symbolism: **the best robe**, a sign of important position; **a ring**, a symbol denoting authority; and **sandals**, usually suggesting luxury since servants and common people did not usually have them (v. 22). Also **the fattened calf** was indicative of a special occasion since meat was not regularly included in the ordinary diet (v. 23).

The heart of this parable was to showcase God's unconditional love in receiving sinners who have repented and His joyous celebration on their return (vv. 20-24). However, the lesson of the parable is not complete without a look at the older brother who sharply criticized not only his brother but also his father. The father remained constant and faithful. He did not condemn his older son, but he continued to emphasize the joy over receiving the younger son who had repented and returned home (15:31-32).

16:1-13 This section contains parables that are unique to Luke, and they are among the most difficult to interpret. The subject is possessions and wealth.

16:5-8 Rather than considering the words of commendation as endorsing

neighbors together, saying, 'Rejoice
with me, because I have found the
silver coin I lost!' 10 I tell you, in the
same way, there is joy in the presence of God's angels over one sinner
who repents."

11 He also said: "A man had two
sons. 12 The younger of them said
to his father, 'Father, give me the
share of the estate I have coming
to me.' So he distributed the assets[A] to them. 13 Not many days later,
the younger son gathered together
all he had and traveled to a distant
country, where he squandered his
estate in foolish living. 14 After he
had spent everything, a severe famine struck that country, and he had
nothing.[B] 15 Then he went to work
for[C] one of the citizens of that country, who sent him into his fields to
feed pigs. 16 He longed to eat his fill
from[D] the carob pods[E] the pigs were
eating, but no one would give him
any. 17 When he came to his senses,[F]
he said, 'How many of my father's
hired hands have more than enough
food, and here I am dying of hunger![G] 18 I'll get up, go to my father,
and say to him, Father, I have sinned
against heaven and in your sight.
19 I'm no longer worthy to be called
your son. Make me like one of your
hired hands.' 20 So he got up and
went to his father. But while the son
was still a long way off, his father
saw him and was filled with compassion. He ran, threw his arms around
his neck,[H] and kissed him. 21 The son
said to him, 'Father, I have sinned
against heaven and in your sight.
I'm no longer worthy to be called
your son.'

22 "But the father told his •slaves,
'Quick! Bring out the best robe and
put it on him; put a ring on his finger[I] and sandals on his feet. 23 Then
bring the fattened calf and slaughter
it, and let's celebrate with a feast,
24 because this son of mine was dead
and is alive again; he was lost and is
found!' So they began to celebrate.

25 "Now his older son was in the
field; as he came near the house,
he heard music and dancing. 26 So
he summoned one of the servants
and asked what these things meant.
27 'Your brother is here,' he told him,
'and your father has slaughtered the
fattened calf because he has him
back safe and sound.'[J]

28 "Then he became angry and
didn't want to go in. So his father
came out and pleaded with him.
29 But he replied to his father, 'Look,
I have been slaving many years for
you, and I have never disobeyed
your orders, yet you never gave me a
young goat so I could celebrate with
my friends. 30 But when this son of
yours came, who has devoured your
assets[K] with prostitutes, you slaughtered the fattened calf for him.'

31 "'Son,'[L] he said to him, 'you
are always with me, and everything I have is yours. 32 But we had
to celebrate and rejoice, because
this brother of yours was dead and
is alive again; he was lost and is
found.'"

The Use and Abuse of Riches (16:1-31)

16 He also said to the disciples:
"There was a rich man who
received an accusation that his
manager was squandering his possessions. 2 So he called the manager
in and asked, 'What is this I hear
about you? Give an account of your
management, because you can no
longer be my manager.'

3 "Then the manager said to himself, 'What should I do, since my
master is taking the management
away from me? I'm not strong
enough to dig; I'm ashamed to beg.
4 I know what I'll do so that when I'm
removed from management, people
will welcome me into their homes.'

5 "So he summoned each one of
his master's debtors. 'How much do
you owe my master?' he asked the
first one.

6 "'A hundred measures of olive
oil,' he said.

"'Take your invoice,' he told him,
'sit down quickly, and write 50.'

7 "Next he asked another, 'How
much do you owe?'

[A]15:12 Or *living*; lit *livelihood* [B]15:14 Lit *and he began to be in need* [C]15:15 Lit *went and joined with* [D]15:16 Other mss read *to fill his stomach with* [E]15:16 Seed casings of a tree used as food for cattle, pigs, and sometimes the poor [F]15:17 Lit *to himself* [G]15:17 Or *dying in the famine*; v. 14 [H]15:20 Lit *He ran, fell on his neck* [I]15:22 Lit *hand* [J]15:27 Lit *him back healthy* [K]15:30 Lit *livelihood*, or *living* [L]15:31 Or *Child*

"'A hundred measures of wheat,'
he said.
"'Take your invoice,' he told him,
'and write 80.'
8 "The master praised the unrighteous manager because he had acted
astutely. For the sons of this age are
more astute than the sons of light
in dealing with their own people.[A]
9 And I tell you, make friends for
yourselves by means of the unrighteous money so that when it fails,[B]
they may welcome you into eternal
dwellings. 10 Whoever is faithful in
very little is also faithful in much,
and whoever is unrighteous in very
little is also unrighteous in much.
11 So if you have not been faithful
with the unrighteous money, who
will trust you with what is genuine?
12 And if you have not been faithful
with what belongs to someone else,
who will give you what is your own?
13 No household slave can be the
•slave of two masters, since either he
will hate one and love the other, or
he will be devoted to one and despise
the other. You can't be slaves to both
God and money."
14 The •Pharisees, who were lovers
of money, were listening to all these
things and scoffing at Him. 15 And
He told them: "You are the ones who
justify yourselves in the sight of others, but God knows your hearts. For
what is highly admired by people is
revolting in God's sight.
16 "The Law and the Prophets
were[C] until John; since then, the
good news of the kingdom of God
has been proclaimed, and everyone
is strongly urged to enter it.[D] 17 But
it is easier for heaven and earth to
pass away than for one stroke of a
letter in the law to drop out.
18 "Everyone who divorces his wife
and marries another woman commits adultery, and everyone who
marries a woman divorced from her
husband commits adultery.
19 "There was a rich man who
would dress in purple and fine linen,
feasting lavishly every day. 20 But
a poor man named Lazarus, covered with sores, was left at his gate.
21 He longed to be filled with what

HELL

The rich man was described as **being in torment**, which indicated that death for an unbeliever does not mean annihilation; rather there is continual consciousness while enduring the perpetual torment (16:23-26). Although these vivid words fall within a parable and thus are not an actual description of hell, they do coincide with other biblical information on the place of torment (Is 66:24; Mt 18:8-9; 25:41). There are some clear statements concerning the nature of hell:

- the awareness of what was forfeited;
- the flame (v. 24);
- the memory of opportunities ignored (v. 25);
- the separation from God and the blessings accompanying His presence (v. 26);
- the permanence of this condition (v. 26).

The rich man did not suffer the penalties of separation from God because of his wealth but because of his attitude toward his wealth.

fell from the rich man's table, but
instead the dogs would come and
lick his sores. 22 One day the poor
man died and was carried away by
the angels to Abraham's side.[E] The
rich man also died and was buried.
23 And being in torment in •Hades,
he looked up and saw Abraham a
long way off, with Lazarus at his
side. 24 'Father Abraham!' he called
out, 'Have mercy on me and send
Lazarus to dip the tip of his finger in
water and cool my tongue, because I
am in agony in this flame!'
25 "'Son,'[F] Abraham said, 'remember that during your life you
received your good things, just as
Lazarus received bad things, but
now he is comforted here, while you
are in agony. 26 Besides all this, a
great chasm has been fixed between
us and you, so that those who want
to pass over from here to you cannot; neither can those from there
cross over to us.'
27 "'Father,' he said, 'then I beg you
to send him to my father's house—
28 because I have five brothers—to
warn them, so they won't also come
to this place of torment.'
29 "But Abraham said, 'They have
Moses and the prophets; they should
listen to them.'
30 "'No, father Abraham,' he said.
'But if someone from the dead goes
to them, they will repent.'

[A] **16:8** Lit *own generation* [B] **16:9** Other mss read *when you fail* or *pass away* [C] **16:16** Perhaps *were proclaimed*, or *were in effect* [D] **16:16** Or *everyone is forcing his way into it* [E] **16:22** Or *to Abraham's bosom*; lit *to the fold of Abraham's robe*; Jn 13:23 [F] **16:25** Lit *Child*

dishonest action, you could consider the exact wording of the text, **because he had acted astutely**, as merely praising the manager for acting with prudence in collecting what he could.

16:18 Only a brief part of Jesus' teaching on divorce and remarriage is recorded by Luke. You cannot purport to accept the accuracy and authority of Scripture and suggest that there is internal contradiction. Luke and Matthew present the same teaching with minor differences, which would be expected from reports by two different people. Luke omits the phrase "except in a case of sexual immorality" (Mt 5:32); he records that **everyone who divorces his wife and marries another woman commits adultery** rather than Matthew's words "causes her to commit adultery" (a case in which Luke does not refute what Matthew says any more than Matthew is differing with Luke; both are true, but the emphasis of each writer varies from the other).

In each account, the man who "marries a divorced woman" (Mt 5:32) or who **marries a woman divorced from her husband** commits adultery. Although neither Matthew nor Luke discussed a wife's divorcing her husband, which would have been very unusual in Israel, Mark did (Mk 10:12). There is no attempt to suggest a woman divorced by her husband was penalized. These words are addressed to serious followers of Christ who want their lives to be totally consistent with the standards of Christ. They are well aware that this standard is more demanding, and they know that they cannot always understand the ways of God (Is 55:8-9).

16:19-22 In the parable of the rich man and Lazarus, the **rich man** was a lover of money who was an unfaithful steward of his possessions. He never repented during his lifetime. He knew well the Old Testament commands to care for the poor and needy, but he ignored such commands. On the other hand, **Lazarus** (from Hb *Eleazar*, "he whom God has helped") was **a poor man** who had been blessed for his faithfulness. The phrase **Abraham's side** became an expression for "heaven."

16:23-31 Jesus again returned to the supremacy of Scripture when He described the rich man's plea for the resurrection of Lazarus as a messenger to his family to warn them of the penalty of rejecting God. Abraham's response pointed to an attitude of unbelief. Rejecting the Scriptures would not be changed even by one who had risen from the grave (v. 31), as would be even more evident when Jesus Himself arose **from the dead**.

17:1-19 Luke continues with more teachings on faith as he returns to the warnings concerning sin, repentance, and forgiveness that Jesus delivered to His disciples. The relationship between faith and duty was unveiled in the short parable of the unworthy servant, which was unique to Luke and which provided a perfect illustration of salvation by grace through faith alone.

17:1-2 The term **offenses** (Gk *skandala*, "trap, temptation, that which offends, stumbling block") was also used to describe traps used to catch animals, but in the New Testament it is most often a metaphor for whatever leads people into sin. A **millstone** was a substantially heavy round stone used to grind grain. Women sometimes used the smaller ones, but often an animal's strength was required to accomplish the task. **These little ones** could refer to children, but the context seems to identify them as new or perhaps weak believers.

17:3-6 The number of times forgiveness is to be offered was not the issue but rather the importance of being willing to forgive others. Perhaps **the apostles** felt they needed an extra portion of faith in order to be forgiving. The **mustard seed** provided an object lesson for how little faith would be required to accomplish even what seemed impossible.

17:10 Jesus returned to the theme of servanthood, emphasizing how diametrically opposed to the world His teachings are. Instead of trying to rule or lord it over others, Jesus calls for humble service as the path to greatness in His kingdom. To be Christlike calls for going beyond duty.

17:11-19 Only **one** leper returned to say thank you, and he was **a Samaritan**. Jesus acknowledged the man's **faith**. Nothing anyone can do can repay Christ for His grace; the only response for those who have received His grace is to offer gratitude, and the Samaritan did precisely that.

17:20-37 Jesus answered the Pharisee that the kingdom would not come visibly, but would be **among you** (v. 21). The discussion is parallel to what is found in Matthew and Mark about the appearance of the kingdom of God (Mt 24; Mk 13). Jesus' emphasis does not preclude the kingdom as seen in a different way in the consummation at the end of time, but rather there is also a sense in which the kingdom comes in the lives of those who accept God's rule in their lives. On the one hand, the kingdom of God was already at work in the earthly ministry of Jesus; on the other hand, it was yet to come in fullness and power (vv. 22-37). The

31 "But he told him, 'If they don't listen to Moses and the prophets, they will not be persuaded if someone rises from the dead.'"

The Teachings on Faith (17:1-19)

17 He said to His disciples, "Offenses[A] will certainly come,[B] but woe to the one they come through! 2 It would be better for him if a millstone[C] were hung around his neck and he were thrown into the sea than for him to cause one of these little ones to •stumble. 3 Be on your guard. If your brother sins,[D] rebuke him, and if he repents, forgive him. 4 And if he sins against you seven times in a day, and comes back to you seven times, saying, 'I repent,' you must forgive him."

5 The apostles said to the Lord, "Increase our faith."

6 "If you have faith the size of[E] a mustard seed," the Lord said, "you can say to this mulberry tree, 'Be uprooted and planted in the sea,' and it will obey you.

7 "Which one of you having a •slave tending sheep or plowing will say to him when he comes in from the field, 'Come at once and sit down to eat'? 8 Instead, will he not tell him, 'Prepare something for me to eat, get ready,[F] and serve me while I eat and drink; later you can eat and drink'? 9 Does he thank that slave because he did what was commanded?[G] 10 In the same way, when you have done all that you were commanded, you should say, 'We are good-for-nothing slaves; we've only done our duty.'"

11 While traveling to Jerusalem, He passed between[H] Samaria and Galilee. 12 As He entered a village, 10 men with serious skin diseases met Him. They stood at a distance 13 and raised their voices, saying, "Jesus, Master, have mercy on us!"

14 When He saw them, He told them, "Go and show yourselves to the priests." And while they were going, they were healed.[I]

15 But one of them, seeing that he was healed, returned and, with a loud voice, gave glory to God. 16 He fell facedown at His feet, thanking Him. And he was a •Samaritan.

17 Then Jesus said, "Were not 10 cleansed? Where are the nine? 18 Didn't any return[J] to give glory to God except this foreigner?" 19 And He told him, "Get up and go on your way. Your faith has made you well."[K]

The Coming of the Kingdom (17:20–18:8)

20 Being asked by the •Pharisees when the kingdom of God will come, He answered them, "The kingdom of God is not coming with something observable; 21 no one will say,[L] 'Look here!' or 'There!' For you see, the kingdom of God is among you."

22 Then He told the disciples: "The days are coming when you will long to see one of the days of the •Son of Man, but you won't see it. 23 They will say to you, 'Look there!' or 'Look here!' Don't follow or run after them. 24 For as the lightning flashes from horizon to horizon and lights up the sky, so the Son of Man will be in His day. 25 But first He must suffer many things and be rejected by this generation.

26 "Just as it was in the days of Noah, so it will be in the days of the Son of Man: 27 People went on eating, drinking, marrying and giving in marriage until the day Noah boarded the ark, and the flood came and destroyed them all. 28 It will be the same as it was in the days of Lot: People went on eating, drinking, buying, selling, planting, building. 29 But on the day Lot left Sodom, fire and sulfur rained from heaven and destroyed them all. 30 It will be like that on the day the Son of Man is revealed. 31 On that day, a man on the housetop, whose belongings are in the house, must not come down to get them. Likewise the man who is in the field must not turn back. 32 Remember Lot's wife! 33 Whoever tries to make his •life secure[M,N] will lose it, and whoever loses his life will

[A]**17:1** Or *Traps*, or *Bait-sticks*, or *Causes of stumbling*, or *Causes of sin* [B]**17:1** Lit *It is impossible for offenses not to come* [C]**17:2** Large stone used for grinding grains into flour [D]**17:3** Other mss add *against you* [E]**17:6** Lit *faith like* [F]**17:8** Or *eat, gird yourself*; lit *eat, tuck in your robe* [G]**17:9** Other mss add *I don't think so* [H]**17:11** Or *through the middle of* [I]**17:14** Lit *cleansed* [J]**17:18** Lit *Were they not found returning* [K]**17:19** Or *faith has saved you* [L]**17:21** Lit *they will not say* [M]**17:33** Other mss read *to save his life* [N]**17:33** Or *tries to retain his life*

CHARACTER PROFILE

The Persistent Widow — A Woman Under Attack

Her Background	She is a character in Jesus' parable on prayer.
Her Story	• She repeatedly went to a heartless judge, begging for justice. • He first refused to listen to her, but finally relented. • Hearing her case was not motivated by his desire for justice but giving her what she wanted so she would leave him alone.
Life Lesson	Persevere in prayer; do not give up or become discouraged. God is not an uncaring judge but a righteous and loving Father.

preserve it. 34 I tell you, on that night two will be in one bed: One will be taken and the other will be left. 35 Two women will be grinding grain together: One will be taken and the other left. [36 Two will be in a field: One will be taken, and the other will be left.][A]

37 "Where, Lord?" they asked Him.

He said to them, "Where the corpse is, there also the vultures will be gathered."

18 He then told them a parable on the need for them to pray always and not become discouraged: 2 "There was a judge in a certain town who didn't fear God or respect man. 3 And a widow in that town kept coming to him, saying, 'Give me justice against my adversary.'

4 "For a while he was unwilling, but later he said to himself, 'Even though I don't fear God or respect man, 5 yet because this widow keeps pestering me,[B] I will give her justice, so she doesn't wear me out[C] by her persistent coming.'"

6 Then the Lord said, "Listen to what the unjust judge says. 7 Will not God grant justice to His elect who cry out to Him day and night? Will He delay to help them?[D] 8 I tell you that He will swiftly grant them justice. Nevertheless, when the •Son of Man comes, will He find that faith[E] on earth?"

The Requirements for Entering the Kingdom (18:9-30)

9 He also told this parable to some who trusted in themselves that they were righteous and looked down on everyone else: 10 "Two men went up to the •temple complex to pray, one a •Pharisee and the other a tax collector. 11 The Pharisee took his stand[F] and was praying like this: 'God, I thank You that I'm not like other people[G]—greedy, unrighteous, adulterers, or even like this tax collector. 12 I fast twice a week; I give a tenth[H] of everything I get.'

13 "But the tax collector, standing far off, would not even raise his eyes to heaven but kept striking his chest[I] and saying, 'God, turn Your wrath from me[J]—a sinner!' 14 I tell you, this one went down to his house •justified rather than the other; because everyone who exalts himself will be humbled, but the one who humbles himself will be exalted."

15 Some people were even bringing infants to Him so He might touch them, but when the disciples saw it, they rebuked them. 16 Jesus, however, invited them: "Let the little children come to Me, and don't stop them, because the kingdom of God belongs to such as these. 17 •I assure you: Whoever does not welcome the

[A]17:36 Other mss omit bracketed text [B]18:5 Lit *widow causes me trouble* [C]18:5 Or *doesn't give me a black eye*, or *doesn't ruin my reputation* [D]18:7 Or *Will He put up with them?* [E]18:8 Or *faith*, or *that kind of faith*, or *any faith*, or *the faith*, or *faithfulness*; the faith that persists in prayer for God's vindication [F]18:11 Or *Pharisee stood by himself* [G]18:11 Or *like the rest of men* [H]18:12 Or *give tithes* [I]18:13 = mourning [J]18:13 Lit *God, be propitious to me*; = May Your wrath be turned aside by the sacrifice

suddenness of His return is further affirmed in Jesus' examples of Noah (vv. 26-27) and Lot's wife (v. 28). Lot's wife was a reminder of what happens to one who is obsessed with material possessions—she lost everything (Gn 19:26).

18:1-8 The message of the parable about the persistent **widow** is not that you should bombard the Lord again and again with every request or desire you have. Rather, you see God's working through His masterful timing and the way He teaches His children, building their character and virtue, in the process of struggle. God wants you to bring your petitions to Him. He is moved by your sufferings and the misunderstandings you experience.

The **judge . . . who didn't fear God or respect man** would be typical of the pagan secularist in the judicial world. As a local judge, he was easily accessible to the people. The phrase **wear me out** (Gk *hupōpiazē*, "treat roughly," lit "seize or arrest under") has the sense of "holding down" or "gaining control." Idiomatically the phrase can be understood as "damaging the reputation of someone."

The contrast between a corrupt judge and a helpless woman cannot be overlooked. Of course, God cannot be compared to a crooked and corrupt judge, but the difference in power between God and His creation is far greater than between a judge and his subject. Yet God patiently listens to His children in their hours of trial, and He is moved by their pleas. If an unjust judge is moved by a lowly widow, how much more a loving heavenly Father by His children. If even unjust judges could be persuaded to give justice through persistent intercession, then certainly God would be faithful to mete out justice. In other words, the kingdom of God will not be shut to those who persistently seek entry according to God's terms .

18:9-14 The parable of the **Pharisee** and the **tax collector** is a powerful and poignant example of one who received the mercy and favor of God—not the one who, as the Pharisee, boasted in his own righteousness—but the one who, as the tax collector, acknowledged that he was a sinner and in need of mercy. He who was seeking mercy gained entrance into the kingdom of God.

18:15-17 The one who was humble as a child belonged in the kingdom of God. Jesus never suggested that children would become part of the kingdom just because they were children. However, childlike humility and faith were attitudes necessary for receiving God's grace.

18:18-30 The **ruler** may have been a member of the prestigious Sanhedrin or perhaps the leader of a synagogue since he began his conversation with Jesus by trying to flatter Him. The one who would come to God on divine terms and then willingly follow Jesus would be a true member of the kingdom of God. Indeed, for the rich **to enter the kingdom of God** was **hard** (v. 24). The wealth in and of itself was not evil; rather, what that wealth could potentially do to the human heart was the issue. Luke was not claiming that everyone must be materially poor to enter the kingdom; but certainly all must put Christ first, above all people and possessions, in order to enter the kingdom. Riches must remain in their proper place, that is, subservient to Christ and His authority.

This young man tried to justify himself by his deeds, testifying that he had kept the law from his youth (vv. 20-21). Yet no one can keep these laws. Even this young man fell easily before the commandment against covetousness (Ex 20:17) because he could not part with his material possessions (Lk 18:22-23). Ultimately he depended more on what his wealth provided than what God offered. Some commentators have suggested that **the eye of a needle** was an especially narrow gate into Jerusalem, but there is no archaeological evidence for this. More likely the expression is simply a figure of speech emphasizing how difficult it would be for a man enchained in material possessions to enter the kingdom (vv. 24-25).

18:31-34 Jesus predicted His death for the third time. He reiterated that He would be **handed over to the Gentiles**, mocked, spit upon, flogged, and finally killed. Then He would **rise on the third day**. But His disciples did not grasp what He said. Still Jesus expressed a strong sense of destiny as He quickly approached Jerusalem.

18:35-43 Luke and Mark record these events in similar ways, but Luke makes some significant additions. The healing of the **blind man** near Jericho demonstrated that Jesus was the **Son of David** and the Messiah. Only Luke described this incident as moving the newly healed man and the people to give glory to God through the work of Jesus (v. 43). The blind man knew Jesus even when He could not see Him (vv. 38-39). He not only was healed physically, but he also received spiritual sight. He came to know Jesus (vv. 41-43).

19:1-10 The account of **Zacchaeus**, unique to Luke, contains what many believe is the key verse in all of Luke, **For the Son of Man has come to seek and to save the lost** (v. 10). The

kingdom of God like a little child will never enter it."

18 A ruler asked Him, "Good Teacher, what must I do to inherit eternal life?"

19 "Why do you call Me good?" Jesus asked him. "No one is good but One—God. 20 You know the commandments:

> **Do not commit adultery;**
> **do not murder;**
> **do not steal;**
> **do not bear false witness;**
> **honor your father**
> **and mother.**"[A]

21 "I have kept all these from my youth," he said.

22 When Jesus heard this, He told him, "You still lack one thing: Sell all that you have and distribute it to the poor, and you will have treasure in heaven. Then come, follow Me."

23 After he heard this, he became extremely sad, because he was very rich.

24 Seeing that he became sad,[B] Jesus said, "How hard it is for those who have wealth to enter the kingdom of God! 25 For it is easier for a camel to go through the eye of a needle than for a rich person to enter the kingdom of God."

26 Those who heard this asked, "Then who can be saved?"

27 He replied, "What is impossible with men is possible with God."

28 Then Peter said, "Look, we have left what we had and followed You."

29 So He said to them, "I assure you: There is no one who has left a house, wife or •brothers, parents or children because of the kingdom of God, 30 who will not receive many times more at this time, and eternal life in the age to come."

Conclusion and Transition (18:31-34)

31 Then He took the Twelve aside and told them, "Listen! We are going up to Jerusalem. Everything that is written through the prophets about the Son of Man will be accomplished. 32 For He will be handed over to the Gentiles, and He will be mocked, insulted, spit on; 33 and after they flog Him, they will kill Him, and He will rise on the third day."

34 They understood none of these things. This saying[C] was hidden from them, and they did not grasp what was said.

Jesus in Judea: Ministry Near and in Jerusalem (18:35–21:38)

A Blind Man Who Receives Sight (18:35-43)

35 As He drew near Jericho, a blind man was sitting by the road begging. 36 Hearing a crowd passing by, he inquired what this meant. 37 "Jesus the •Nazarene is passing by," they told him.

38 So he called out, "Jesus, Son of David, have mercy on me!" 39 Then those in front told him to keep quiet,[D] but he kept crying out all the more, "Son of David, have mercy on me!"

40 Jesus stopped and commanded that he be brought to Him. When he drew near, He asked him, 41 "What do you want Me to do for you?"

"Lord," he said, "I want to see!"

42 "Receive your sight!" Jesus told him. "Your faith has healed you."[E] 43 Instantly he could see, and he began to follow Him, glorifying God. All the people, when they saw it, gave praise to God.

Jesus' Visit to Zacchaeus (19:1-10)

19 He entered Jericho and was passing through. 2 There was a man named Zacchaeus who was a chief tax collector, and he was rich. 3 He was trying to see who Jesus was, but he was not able because of the crowd, since he was a short man. 4 So running ahead, he climbed up a sycamore tree to see Jesus, since He was about to pass that way. 5 When Jesus came to the place, He looked up and said to him, "Zacchaeus, hurry and come down because today I must stay at your house."

6 So he quickly came down and welcomed Him joyfully. 7 All who saw it began to complain, "He's gone to lodge with a sinful man!"

8 But Zacchaeus stood there and said to the Lord, "Look, I'll give[F] half

[A] **18:20** Ex 20:12-16; Dt 5:16-20 [B] **18:24** Other mss omit *he became sad* [C] **18:34** The meaning of the saying [D] **18:39** Or *those in front rebuked him* [E] **18:42** Or *has saved you* [F] **19:8** Or *I give*

of my possessions to the poor, Lord! And if I have extorted anything from anyone, I'll pay[A] back four times as much!"

9 "Today salvation has come to this house," Jesus told him, "because he too is a son of Abraham. 10 For the •Son of Man has come to seek and to save the lost."[B]

The Parable of the 10 Minas (19:11-27)

11 As they were listening to this, He went on to tell a parable because He was near Jerusalem, and they thought the kingdom of God was going to appear right away.

12 Therefore He said: "A nobleman traveled to a far country to receive for himself authority to be king[C] and then return. 13 He called 10 of his •slaves, gave them 10 minas,[D] and told them, 'Engage in business until I come back.'

14 "But his subjects hated him and sent a delegation after him, saying, 'We don't want this man to rule over us!'

15 "At his return, having received the authority to be king,[E] he summoned those slaves he had given the money to, so he could find out how much they had made in business. 16 The first came forward and said, 'Master, your mina has earned 10 more minas.'

17 "'Well done, good[F] slave!' he told him. 'Because you have been faithful in a very small matter, have authority over 10 towns.'

18 "The second came and said, 'Master, your mina has made five minas.'

19 "So he said to him, 'You will be over five towns.'

20 "And another came and said, 'Master, here is your mina. I have kept it hidden away in a cloth 21 because I was afraid of you, for you're a tough man: you collect what you didn't deposit and reap what you didn't sow.'

22 "He told him, 'I will judge you by what you have said,[G] you evil slave! If you knew I was a tough man, collecting what I didn't deposit and reaping what I didn't sow, 23 why didn't you put my money in the bank? And when I returned, I would have collected it with interest!' 24 So he said to those standing there, 'Take the mina away from him and give it to the one who has 10 minas.'

25 "But they said to him, 'Master, he has 10 minas.'

26 "'I tell you, that to everyone who has, more will be given; and from the one who does not have, even what he does have will be taken away. 27 But bring here these enemies of mine, who did not want me to rule over them, and slaughter[H] them in my presence.'"

The Triumphal Entry (19:28-40)

28 When He had said these things, He went on ahead, going up to Jerusalem. 29 As He approached Bethphage and Bethany, at the place called the •Mount of Olives, He sent two of the disciples 30 and said, "Go into the village ahead of you. As you enter it, you will find a young donkey tied there, on which no one has ever sat. Untie it and bring it here. 31 If anyone asks you, 'Why are you untying it?' say this: 'The Lord needs it.'"

32 So those who were sent left and found it just as He had told them. 33 As they were untying the young donkey, its owners said to them, "Why are you untying the donkey?"

34 "The Lord needs it," they said. 35 Then they brought it to Jesus, and after throwing their robes on the donkey, they helped Jesus get on it. 36 As He was going along, they were spreading their robes on the road. 37 Now He came near the path down the Mount of Olives, and the whole crowd of the disciples began to praise God joyfully with a loud voice for all the miracles they had seen:

38 **The King who comes**
in the name of the Lord[I,J]
is the blessed One.
Peace in heaven
and glory
in the highest heaven!

[A]19:8 Or *I pay* [B]19:10 Or *save what was lost* [C]19:12 Lit *to receive for himself a kingdom* or *sovereignty* [D]19:13 = Gk coin worth 100 drachmas or about 100 days' wages [E]19:15 Lit *to receive for himself a kingdom* or *sovereignty* [F]19:17 Or *capable* [G]19:22 Lit *you out of your mouth* [H]19:27 Or *execute* [I]19:38 Luke substitutes "the King" for "He" in Ps 118:26. [J]19:38 Ps 118:26

story also showcases several primary themes of this Gospel:

- the universal nature of the gospel (vv. 2-4);
- the problem of wealth (v. 2);
- Christ's ministry to tax collectors and sinners (v. 7);
- the joy of giving to the poor (v. 8); and
- salvation (vv. 9-10).

Jericho was an important toll site in ancient Palestine. Zacchaeus's response to Jesus indicates that his heart was ready (v. 8). Tax collectors were known for their fraud. They could officially collect whatever amount they chose and keep anything above what was required by the government. The law, in cases of fraud, required only the return of the amount defrauded plus one fifth (Lv 6:5; Nm 5:6). However, theft had a stiffer penalty—restoration of at least four times the amount stolen (Ex 22:1). Zacchaeus was under such conviction that he immediately recognized what he had done as theft and committed to **pay back four times as much** (Lk 19:8). Also when he spoke of giving **half of** his **possessions to the poor**, he was not talking about his income but rather all that he had (v. 8). The change in his life had been dramatic and inclusive of every area of lifestyle.

19:11-27 The **parable** of the **10 minas** is linked to the story of Zacchaeus by the words, **As they were listening to this** (v. 11). Luke again deals with Jesus' teaching about the future and God's purpose in history. The **mina** was a Greek monetary unit. Each slave received about three months' wages. They understood that this money was to be used to **engage in business** (v. 13). Jesus commented on three of the slaves, two of whom did well (vv. 16,18). The third slave was ruled by his fear of the nobleman and did nothing (vv. 20-21). Then he defended his irresponsibility by attacking the character of the nobleman (v. 21), who simply turned the tables and reacted as the slave said he would (vv. 22-24).

Portraying the coming rejection and future return of Jesus, the parable of the 10 minas (cp. Mt 25:14-30) ties the appearance of **the kingdom of God** (v. 11) to the return of Christ (the **nobleman**) from **a far country**, having received **authority to be king** (v. 12). The parable also delineates the role of a disciple in the time between Jesus' ascension and His return.

19:28-44 Bethany is on the eastern slope of the Mount of Olives about two to three miles from Jerusalem. It is still so identified today. **Bethphage** was near Bethany, but its exact location remains unknown (v. 28). The **Mount of Olives,** still well known in Jerusalem, is strategically important as an eastern route coming down the mountain (2,660 feet above sea level) into the Kidron Valley and then through the Eastern or Golden Gate on to the temple mount (v. 37).

19:40-44 Luke's account of Jesus approaching Jerusalem does not contradict the accounts of Matthew and Mark, both of which clearly emphasize Jesus' entry to Jerusalem. Rather, Luke makes a theological point—that Jesus was moving toward the place of rejection, which would be the city of Jerusalem.

Jesus stated that **the stones would cry out** if His disciples did not recognize the importance of this day and were silent (v. 40; Hab 2:11). Then Jesus Himself **wept** over the city that would reject Him. Luke zeroed in on Jesus' concern for the city of Jerusalem and also recorded His prediction of its future destruction (Lk 19:43-44). **The time of your visitation** referred to the time when salvation and blessing would come.

19:45-48 Jesus had spent much time teaching in the temple, an emphasis in Luke's Gospel. Now in His role as Messiah He came to cleanse the temple. Here Luke noted the first clear reference to the efforts of Jesus' enemies to kill Him. At this point the people did not share the feelings of their religious leaders.

Those who were selling referred to the merchants who sold animals and other things to be used for sacrifices and offerings. Commercial activity in **the temple complex** was awkward at best; but without competition or controls, there were unequal exchange rates and exorbitant prices.

20:9-19 In the parable of the vineyard owner, in the accounts by Matthew and Mark, one of the servants is killed. In Luke, only the killing of the son is mentioned. The allegorical nature of the parable is readily noted:

- The **vineyard** represents Israel (Is 5:1-7);
- the **owner** represents God (Lk 20:13);
- the **slave(s)**, the Old Testament prophets (vv. 10-12);
- the **son**, Jesus (vv. 13-15);
- the **tenant farmers**, the religious leaders (vv. 9-12); and
- the **others**, the Gentiles (v. 16).

The response of Jesus' listeners may suggest that they understood the allegory's forecast of the destruction of Jerusalem (v. 16). Jesus then used Ps 118:22 to add a prediction of His death and again to refute the popular notions concerning His messiahship (Lk 20:17). Jesus knew that He was to be the stone over which Israel would stumble and then **be broken** (v. 18). The **cornerstone** was unique, bearing the weight and stress where two walls

39 Some of the ·Pharisees from the crowd told Him, "Teacher, rebuke Your disciples."

40 He answered, "I tell you, if they were to keep silent, the stones would cry out!"

Jesus' Love for Jerusalem (19:41-44)

41 As He approached and saw the city, He wept over it, 42 saying, "If you knew this day what would bring peace—but now it is hidden from your eyes. 43 For the days will come on you when your enemies will build an embankment against you, surround you, and hem you in on every side. 44 They will crush you and your children within you to the ground, and they will not leave one stone on another in you, because you did not recognize the time of your visitation."

Cleansing of the Temple Complex (19:45-48)

45 He went into the ·temple complex and began to throw out those who were selling,[A] 46 and He said, "It is written, **My house will be a house of prayer,** but you have made it **a den of thieves!**"[B]

47 Every day He was teaching in the temple complex. The ·chief priests, the ·scribes, and the leaders of the people were looking for a way to destroy Him, 48 but they could not find a way to do it, because all the people were captivated by what they heard.[C]

Challenges to Jesus' Authority (20:1-47)

20 One day[D] as He was teaching the people in the ·temple complex and proclaiming the good news, the ·chief priests and the ·scribes, with the elders, came up 2 and said to Him: "Tell us, by what authority are You doing these things? Who is it who gave You this authority?"

3 He answered them, "I will also ask you a question. Tell Me, 4 was the baptism of John from heaven or from men?"

5 They discussed it among themselves: "If we say, 'From heaven,' He will say, 'Why didn't you believe him?' 6 But if we say, 'From men,' all the people will stone us, because they are convinced that John was a prophet."

7 So they answered that they did not know its origin.[E]

8 And Jesus said to them, "Neither will I tell you by what authority I do these things."

9 Then He began to tell the people this parable: "A man planted a vineyard, leased it to tenant farmers, and went away for a long time. 10 At harvest time he sent a ·slave to the farmers so that they might give him some fruit from the vineyard. But the farmers beat him and sent him away empty-handed. 11 He sent yet another slave, but they beat that one too, treated him shamefully, and sent him away empty-handed. 12 And he sent yet a third, but they wounded this one too and threw him out.

13 "Then the owner of the vineyard said, 'What should I do? I will send my beloved son. Perhaps[F] they will respect him.'

14 "But when the tenant farmers saw him, they discussed it among themselves and said, 'This is the heir. Let's kill him, so the inheritance will be ours!' 15 So they threw him out of the vineyard and killed him.

"Therefore, what will the owner of the vineyard do to them? 16 He will come and destroy those farmers and give the vineyard to others."

But when they heard this they said, "No—never!"

17 But He looked at them and said, "Then what is the meaning of this Scripture:[G]

> **The stone that**
> **the builders rejected—**
> **this has become**
> **the cornerstone?**[H,I]

18 Everyone who falls on that stone will be broken to pieces, and if it falls on anyone, it will grind him to powder!"

19 Then the scribes and the chief priests looked for a way to get their hands on Him that very hour, because they knew He had told this parable against them, but they feared the people.

[A]19:45 Other mss add *and buying in it* [B]19:46 Is 56:7; Jr 7:11 [C]19:48 Lit *people hung on what they heard* [D]20:1 Lit *It happened on one of the days* [E]20:7 Or *know where it was from* [F]20:13 Other mss add *when they see him* [G]20:17 Lit *What then is this that is written* [H]20:17 Lit *the head of the corner* [I]20:17 Ps 118:22

20 They[A] watched closely and sent
spies who pretended to be righteous,[B] so they could catch Him in
what He said,[C] to hand Him over to
the governor's rule and authority.
21 They questioned Him, "Teacher,
we know that You speak and teach
correctly, and You don't show partiality,[D] but teach truthfully the way
of God. 22 Is it lawful for us to pay
taxes to Caesar or not?"
23 But detecting their craftiness,
He said to them,[E] 24 "Show Me a •de-
narius. Whose image and inscription does it have?"
"Caesar's," they said.
25 "Well then," He told them, "give
back to Caesar the things that are
Caesar's and to God the things that
are God's."
26 They were not able to catch Him
in what He said[C] in public,[F] and being amazed at His answer, they became silent.
27 Some of the •Sadducees, who
say there is no resurrection, came
up and questioned Him: 28 "Teacher,
Moses wrote for us that **if a man's
brother** has a wife, and **dies childless, his brother should take the
wife and produce •offspring for his
brother.**[G] 29 Now there were seven
brothers. The first took a wife and
died without children. 30 Also the
second[H] 31 and the third took her.
In the same way, all seven died
and left no children. 32 Finally, the
woman died too. 33 In the resurrection, therefore, whose wife will the
woman be? For all seven had married her."[I]
34 Jesus told them, "The sons of
this age marry and are given in marriage. 35 But those who are counted
worthy to take part in that age and
in the resurrection from the dead
neither marry nor are given in marriage. 36 For they cannot die anymore, because they are like angels
and are sons of God, since they are
sons of the resurrection. 37 Moses
even indicated in the passage about
the burning bush that the dead are
raised, where he calls the Lord **the
God of Abraham and the God of
Isaac and the God of Jacob.**[J] 38 He is
not God of the dead but of the living,
because all are living to[K] Him."
39 Some of the scribes answered,
"Teacher, You have spoken well."
40 And they no longer dared to ask
Him anything.
41 Then He said to them, "How can
they say that the •Messiah is the Son
of David? 42 For David himself says in
the Book of Psalms:

The Lord declared
to my Lord,
'Sit at My right hand
43 **until I make Your enemies**
Your footstool.'[L]

44 David calls Him 'Lord'; how then
can the Messiah be his Son?"
45 While all the people were listening, He said to His disciples, 46 "Beware of the scribes, who want to go
around in long robes and who love
greetings in the marketplaces, the
front seats in the •synagogues, and
the places of honor at banquets.
47 They devour widows' houses and
say long prayers just for show. These
will receive greater punishment."[M]

The Widow's Gift (21:1-4)

21 He looked up and saw the rich
dropping their offerings into
the temple treasury. 2 He also saw
a poor widow dropping in two tiny
coins.[N] 3 "I tell you the truth," He
said. "This poor widow has put in
more than all of them. 4 For all these
people have put in gifts out of their
surplus, but she out of her poverty
has put in all she had to live on."

Prediction of the Destruction of the Temple (21:5-6)

5 As some were talking about
the •temple complex, how it was
adorned with beautiful stones and
gifts dedicated to God,[O] He said,
6 "These things that you see—the
days will come when not one stone
will be left on another that will not
be thrown down!"

are joined and without which the entire structure would collapse (v. 17).

20:20-26 The **denarius**, a small silver Roman coin bearing the image of the ruling emperor on its face, was equivalent to a day's wages in value. Jews ages 14 to 65 were required to pay a tax **to Caesar** (Tiberius) and to the government of Rome. Of course, the Jews resented greatly having to pay these **taxes**, which collectively often amounted to over one third of a person's income.

20:27-40 There will be no death in heaven, which makes the Sadducees' issue moot since there will be no need for births to continue the generations (vv. 34-36; see notes on Mt 22:23-33 and Mk 12:18-27).

20:41-44 David, the second king of Israel, was identified as the one through whose lineage **the Messiah** would come. In His humanity, Jesus was a descendant of David (Lk 3:31) when He came in His incarnation as a baby in Bethlehem. He was also clearly David's **Lord** in that as the eternal Son of God, He had existed before David. The section of Ps 110 quoted here was undoubtedly coming from what Luke considered a messianic psalm. The psalm does in fact affirm that the Messiah is indeed greater than and possesses more authority than David, who was considered Israel's greatest king.

20:45-47 Jesus made universal application with His warnings concerning the religious leaders. Spurning the poor, they even neglected responsibilities to their own parents (Mk 7:9-13) and lacked sensitivity to widows. Perhaps when serving as executors of the estates of these helpless women, they would squander their humble estates through assessing fees and collecting expenses.

21:1-4 The **temple treasury** had 13 trumpet-shaped treasure boxes according to the Talmud. Since they were located in the court of the women, the widow could have entered without being noticed. Yet Jesus saw her and immediately knew of her sacrificial gift of **two tiny coins**, worth only a fraction of a day's wages—but all she had (vv. 2-4).

[A]**20:20** The scribes and chief priests of v. 19 [B]**20:20** Or *upright*; that is, loyal to God's law [C]**20:20,26** Lit *catch Him in a word* [D]**20:21** Lit *You don't receive a face* [E]**20:23** Other mss add *"Why are you testing Me?* [F]**20:26** Lit *in front of the people* [G]**20:28** Dt 25:5 [H]**20:30** Other mss add *took her as wife, and he died without children* [I]**20:33** Lit *had her as wife* [J]**20:37** Ex 3:6,15 [K]**20:38** Or *with* [L]**20:42-43** Ps 110:1 [M]**20:47** Or *judgment* [N]**21:2** Lit *two lepta*; the *lepton* was the smallest and least valuable Gk coin in use. [O]**21:5** Gifts given to the temple in fulfillment of vows to God

21:8-21 Jesus gave a straightforward warning about the false teachers, some of whom would claim to be the Messiah, and many who would make predictions about the end-times. He also warned about the coming persecution from the Gentiles and from the Jews. These warnings began to be fulfilled with a very intense time of persecution for believers between the death of Jesus and the destruction of Jerusalem in A.D. 70. Luke includes an extended explanation of the destruction of Jerusalem (vv. 20-24). His description is vivid and intense. Jesus described events that would take place in the immediate future (A.D. 70) and in the distant future (the time of His return).

Jesus did not promise escape from death for His disciples or any of His followers (v. 18). In fact, He affirmed that some would die (v. 16). Rather He was emphasizing that they would be lovingly carried through these sufferings by the Lord and ultimately have life eternal with Him (v. 19).

The prophecy concerning the temple's destruction was fulfilled in A.D. 70 when the Roman general Titus captured Jerusalem and destroyed the temple (vv. 5-6). Jesus also noted the long siege of Jerusalem by the Romans before the fall of the city (v. 20). Evidently, according to Eusebius, the Christians fled Jerusalem and took refuge at Pella, a town near the Sea of Galilee and east of the Jordan River (v. 21).

21:22-23 Pregnant women and nursing mothers would certainly be among the most vulnerable in war. Being uprooted from their homes or surviving a siege would be difficult enough by yourself. Having children and being concerned about their many needs would be a source of almost unbearable pressure. A condition that usually brought joy and life would mean sorrow and death.

21:24 The phrase **the times of the Gentiles** indicates that the Gentiles would have control over Jerusalem until God determined the end of that rule. This domination of Jerusalem and Palestine would continue up to and including the last three and a half years of the great tribulation (Rv 11:1-2). Antichrist would annul the covenant made with Israel at the beginning of the great tribulation. He would then pour out his wrath against the Jews until Christ intervenes upon His return to establish His earthly kingdom.

21:28-36 All things (v. 32) must be in reference to the destruction of Jerusalem and thus **this generation** would have the most natural understanding, a reference to those who were listening to Jesus speak. Jesus did seem to move in His

Signs of the End of the Age (21:7-19)

7 "Teacher," they asked Him, "so
when will these things be? And what
will be the sign when these things
are about to take place?"
8 Then He said, "Watch out that
you are not deceived. For many will
come in My name, saying, 'I am He,'
and, 'The time is near.' Don't follow
them. 9 When you hear of wars and
rebellions,[A] don't be alarmed. Indeed, these things must take place
first, but the end won't come right
away."
10 Then He told them: "Nation
will be raised up against nation,
and kingdom against kingdom.
11 There will be violent earthquakes,
and famines and plagues in various
places, and there will be terrifying
sights and great signs from heaven.
12 But before all these things, they
will lay their hands on you and persecute you. They will hand you over
to the •synagogues and prisons, and
you will be brought before kings and
governors because of My name. 13 It
will lead to an opportunity for you
to witness.[B] 14 Therefore make up
your minds[C] not to prepare your defense ahead of time, 15 for I will give
you such words[D] and a wisdom that
none of your adversaries will be able
to resist or contradict. 16 You will
even be betrayed by parents, brothers, relatives, and friends. They will
kill some of you. 17 You will be hated
by everyone because of My name,
18 but not a hair of your head will be
lost. 19 By your endurance gain[E] your
•lives.

The Destruction of Jerusalem (21:20-24)

20 "When you see Jerusalem surrounded by armies, then recognize
that its desolation has come near.
21 Then those in Judea must flee to
the mountains! Those inside the
city[F] must leave it, and those who
are in the country must not enter
it, 22 because these are days of vengeance to fulfill all the things that
are written. 23 Woe to pregnant wom-
en and nursing mothers in those
days, for there will be great distress
in the land[G] and wrath against this
people. 24 They will fall by the edge of
the sword and be led captive into all
the nations, and Jerusalem will be
trampled by the Gentiles[H] until the
times of the Gentiles are fulfilled.

The Coming of the Son of Man (21:25-28)

25 "Then there will be signs in the
sun, moon, and stars; and there will
be anguish on the earth among nations bewildered by the roaring sea
and waves. 26 People will faint from
fear and expectation of the things
that are coming on the world, because the celestial powers will be
shaken. 27 Then they will see the
•Son of Man coming in a cloud with
power and great glory. 28 But when
these things begin to take place,
stand up and lift up your heads, because your •redemption is near!"

The Parable of the Fig Tree (21:29-33)

29 Then He told them a parable:
"Look at the fig tree, and all the trees.
30 As soon as they put out leaves you
can see for yourselves and recognize
that summer is already near. 31 In
the same way, when you see these
things happening, recognize[I] that
the kingdom of God is near. 32 •I assure you: This generation will certainly not pass away until all things
take place. 33 Heaven and earth will
pass away, but My words will never
pass away.

The Need for Watchfulness (21:34-38)

34 "Be on your guard, so that your
minds are not dulled[J] from carousing,[K] drunkenness, and worries of
life, or that day will come on you
unexpectedly 35 like a trap. For it will
come on all who live on the face of
the whole earth. 36 But be alert at all
times, praying that you may have
strength[L] to escape all these things
that are going to take place and to
stand before the Son of Man."
37 During the day, He was teaching in the temple complex, but in
the evening He would go out and
spend the night on what is called

[A]21:9 Or *insurrections*, or *revolutions* [B]21:13 Lit *lead to a testimony for you* [C]21:14 Lit *Therefore place* (determine) *in your hearts* [D]21:15 Lit *you a mouth* [E]21:19 Other mss read *endurance you will gain* [F]21:21 Lit *inside her* [G]21:23 Or *the earth* [H]21:24 Or *nations* [I]21:31 Or *you know* [J]21:34 Lit *your hearts are not weighed down* [K]21:34 Or *hangovers* [L]21:36 Other mss read *you may be counted worthy*

the •Mount of Olives. 38 Then all
the people would come early in the
morning to hear Him in the temple
complex.

The Climax of Jesus' Life (22:1–24:53)

The Plot to Kill Jesus (22:1-6)

22 The Festival of •Unleavened
Bread, which is called •Pass-
over, was drawing near. 2 The •chief
priests and the •scribes were looking
for a way to put Him to death, because they were afraid of the people.
3 Then Satan entered Judas, called
Iscariot, who was numbered among
the Twelve. 4 He went away and discussed with the chief priests and
temple police how he could hand
Him over to them. 5 They were glad
and agreed to give him silver.[A] 6 So
he accepted the offer and started
looking for a good opportunity to
betray Him to them when the crowd
was not present.

Preparation for Passover (22:7-13)

7 Then the Day of Unleavened
Bread came when the Passover lamb
had to be sacrificed. 8 Jesus sent Peter and John, saying, "Go and prepare the Passover meal for us, so we
can eat it."
9 "Where do You want us to prepare it?" they asked Him.
10 "Listen," He said to them, "when
you've entered the city, a man carrying a water jug will meet you. Follow him into the house he enters.
11 Tell the owner of the house, 'The
Teacher asks you, "Where is the
guest room where I can eat the Passover with My disciples?"' 12 Then he
will show you a large, furnished
room upstairs. Make the preparations there."
13 So they went and found it just as
He had told them, and they prepared
the Passover.

The First Lord's Supper (22:14-23)

14 When the hour came, He reclined at the table, and the apostles
with Him. 15 Then He said to them,
"I have fervently desired to eat this
Passover with you before I suffer. 16 For I tell you, I will not eat
it again[B] until it is fulfilled in the
kingdom of God." 17 Then He took
a cup, and after giving thanks, He
said, "Take this and share it among
yourselves. 18 For I tell you, from
now on I will not drink of the fruit
of the vine until the kingdom of God
comes."
19 And He took bread, gave thanks,
broke it, gave it to them, and said,
"This is My body, which is given for
you. Do this in remembrance of Me."
20 In the same way He also took the
cup after supper and said, "This cup
is the new covenant established by
My blood; it is shed for you.[C] 21 But
look, the hand of the one betraying
Me is at the table with Me! 22 For the
•Son of Man will go away as it has
been determined, but woe to that
man by whom He is betrayed!"
23 So they began to argue among
themselves which of them it could
be who was going to do this thing.

The Dispute over Greatness (22:24-30)

24 Then a dispute also arose among
them about who should be considered the greatest. 25 But He said to
them, "The kings of the Gentiles
dominate them, and those who have
authority over them are called[D]
'Benefactors.'[E] 26 But it must not be
like that among you. On the contrary, whoever is greatest among
you must become like the youngest,
and whoever leads, like the one serving. 27 For who is greater, the one at
the table or the one serving? Isn't it
the one at the table? But I am among
you as the One who serves. 28 You are
the ones who stood by Me in My trials. 29 I bestow on you a kingdom,
just as My Father bestowed one on
Me, 30 so that you may eat and drink
at My table in My kingdom. And you
will sit on thrones judging the 12
tribes of Israel.

Jesus' Prayer for Peter (22:31-34)

31 "Simon, Simon,[F] look out!
Satan has asked to sift you[G] like
wheat. 32 But I have prayed for you[H]

[A]**22:5** Or *money*; Mt 26:15 specifies 30 pieces of silver; Zch 11:12-13 [B]**22:16** Other mss omit *again* [C]**22:19-20** Other mss omit *which is given for you* (v. 19) through the end of v. 20 [D]**22:25** Or *them call themselves* [E]**22:25** Title of honor given to those who benefited the public good [F]**22:31** Other mss read *Then the Lord said, "Simon, Simon* [G]**22:31** In Gk, the word you is pl [H]**22:32** In Gk, the word you is sg

discussion from **that day** as a reference to the destruction of Jerusalem as a type of judgment to come (v. 34) and the final judgment, which would come at the consummation of all things.

Jesus' words concerning false messiahs are left out in this context but are recorded in 17:23. Also missing from Luke's description of the end-times is an account of the gathering of the elect (Mt 24:31; Mk 13:27). Instead, Luke records Jesus' teaching concerning future **redemption** (v. 28). The account ends with Jesus' exhortation for the need of watchfulness (v. 36). Only Luke records the details of this watchfulness. Believers were to be on guard (vv. 34-36).

22:1-6 The Festival of Unleavened Bread followed immediately after the **Passover** (observed Nisan 14-15, which came in early spring) and lasted 7 days (vv. 1,7). The Jews ate unleavened bread to commemorate their deliverance from the slavery of Egypt since their ancestors had done this on the night of their hasty departure from Egypt (Ex 12). Luke begins his account with a description of Judas's plot **to betray Him** (Lk 22:3-6). Only Luke mentions that this betrayal was ultimately the work of Satan. Luke was careful to show that Jesus' mission meant the ultimate demise of the Devil. Throughout his narrative, Luke has referred to Satan's activity and to his ultimate downfall (10:18-20). But in this context Satan was still at work, causing dissension and seeking to interfere with Jesus' mission (22:23). **Satan entered Judas** in order to move him to betray Jesus (v. 3). Judas then became the instrument of Satan to accomplish his purpose of trying to destroy Jesus' life and ministry.

22:7-30 In preparing for Passover, Jesus noted that the disciples were to follow **a man carrying a water jug** (v. 10). Since carrying water was done by women, a man doing this task would be easily spotted. The meal would have been eaten **when the hour came**, which would have been immediately after sundown on the 15th of Nisan (v. 14). Both at the table and in the garden, Luke captured Jesus' intense feelings concerning all that was happening to Him. As He reclined at the table, Jesus said, **I have fervently desired to eat this Passover with you before I suffer** (v. 15). In Greek these words are intense—more literally, "with desire I have desired."

During the Passover meal, four cups were shared, of which Luke mentioned two—one before and after the bread:

- A cup of thanksgiving before sharing the bread (v. 17);
- A cup of **the new covenant** after supper (v. 20; Mt 26:27-29; Mk 14:23-25; 1Co 11:25-26).

Paul focuses attention on one cup: a "cup of blessing" (1Co 10:16), which ties the Passover and the Lord's Supper together. Luke probably combines his descriptions of Jesus' Passover in the company of His disciples with the Lord's institution of the Lord's Supper. This explains the reference to two cups.

The Lord's Supper brought new significance to the ancient Passover meal. The disciples clearly understood the metaphor Jesus used, speaking of the **bread**, which was broken as His **body** would be, and of **the fruit of the vine** as the **blood** He would shed in His vicarious atonement (1Co 11:23-26).

The **new covenant** is one of grace and forgiveness based upon the sacrificial death of Christ on behalf of sinners (Lk 22:20; cp. Jr 31:31-34). Although Judas was present at the time of the Supper (Lk 22:21), apparently he did not actually partake of the elements (Jn 13:26-30). Luke had received an account of the information Jesus shared with the apostles at the time of the Passover celebration; but even if he knew the exact order of events, he was not bound to follow that order. Thus some slight differences in the accounts do occur.

22:31-34 Satan asked Jesus **to sift** Peter as **wheat**. **You**, however, is plural, a reference to all the disciples. But Jesus prayed specifically for **Peter** (**you** is singular in v. 32). Peter's leadership among the other disciples was evident as Jesus instructed him to **strengthen** his **brothers** after he **turned back** to the Lord.

22:35-38 Jesus gave instructions to the disciples, including an update on their itinerant ministries. Although some have suggested that Jesus was now calling for an armed revolt, the context, as well as Jesus' overall teaching, does not support this interpretation. Jesus could have been using irony in suggesting that some disciples who had considered His way adequate and the best now wanted to abandon it because of difficulties encountered. However, more likely Jesus knew that far greater persecution than any they had known was coming, and He wanted to admonish them to prepare for it. He ended the discussion abruptly because of the lack of understanding on the part of His disciples. Rather than a reversal of any earlier instructions, Jesus was more likely addressing an exception or plan for a time of crisis as symbolic of the upheaval to come.

22:39-46 In the garden, Jesus' **sweat became like drops of blood falling to the ground**, indicating the immense stress and agony He was experiencing. **This cup** was a figurative way of describing that which was allotted to a person. The expression

that your faith may not fail. And you, when you have turned back, strengthen your brothers."
33 "Lord," he told Him, "I'm ready to go with You both to prison and to death!"
34 "I tell you, Peter," He said, "the rooster will not crow today until[A] you deny three times that you know Me!"

Readiness for Trouble (22:35-38)

35 He also said to them, "When I sent you out without money-bag, traveling bag, or sandals, did you lack anything?"

"Not a thing," they said.

36 Then He said to them, "But now, whoever has a money-bag should take it, and also a traveling bag. And whoever doesn't have a sword should sell his robe and buy one.
37 For I tell you, what is written must be fulfilled in Me: **And He was counted among the outlaws.**[B] Yes, what is written about Me is coming to its fulfillment."

38 "Lord," they said, "look, here are two swords."

"Enough of that!"[C] He told them.

Jesus' Prayer in the Garden (22:39-46)

39 He went out and made His way as usual to the •Mount of Olives, and the disciples followed Him.
40 When He reached the place, He told them, "Pray that you may not enter into temptation."
41 Then He withdrew from them about a stone's throw, knelt down, and began to pray,
42 "Father, if You are willing, take this cup away from Me—nevertheless, not My will, but Yours, be done."

[43 Then an angel from heaven appeared to Him, strengthening Him.
44 Being in anguish, He prayed more fervently, and His sweat became like drops of blood falling to the ground.][D]
45 When He got up from prayer and came to the disciples, He found them sleeping, exhausted from their grief.[E]
46 "Why are you sleeping?" He asked them. "Get up and pray, so that you won't enter into temptation."

The Judas Kiss (22:47-53)

47 While He was still speaking, suddenly a mob was there, and one of the Twelve named Judas was leading them. He came near Jesus to kiss Him,
48 but Jesus said to him, "Judas, are you betraying the Son of Man with a kiss?"

49 When those around Him saw what was going to happen, they asked, "Lord, should we strike with the sword?"
50 Then one of them struck the high priest's •slave and cut off his right ear.

51 But Jesus responded, "No more of this!"[F] And touching his ear, He healed him.
52 Then Jesus said to the chief priests, temple police, and the elders who had come for Him, "Have you come out with swords and clubs as if I were a criminal?[G]
53 Every day while I was with you in the •temple complex, you never laid a hand on Me. But this is your hour—and the dominion of darkness."

Peter's Denial of His Lord (22:54-62)

54 They seized Him, led Him away, and brought Him into the high priest's house. Meanwhile Peter was following at a distance.
55 They lit a fire in the middle of the courtyard and sat down together, and Peter sat among them.
56 When a servant saw him sitting in the firelight, and looked closely at him, she said, "This man was with Him too."

57 But he denied it: "Woman, I don't know Him!"

58 After a little while, someone else saw him and said, "You're one of them too!"

"Man, I am not!" Peter said.

59 About an hour later, another kept insisting, "This man was certainly with Him, since he's also a Galilean."

60 But Peter said, "Man, I don't know what you're talking about!" Immediately, while he was still speaking, a rooster crowed.
61 Then the Lord turned and looked at Peter. So Peter remembered the word of the Lord, how He had said to him, "Before the rooster crows today, you will deny Me three times."
62 And he went outside and wept bitterly.

[A] **22:34** Other mss read *before* [B] **22:37** Is 53:12 [C] **22:38** Or *It is enough!* [D] **22:43-44** Other mss omit bracketed text [E] **22:45** Lit *sleeping from grief* [F] **22:51** Lit *Permit as far as this* [G] **22:52** Lit *as against a criminal*

Jesus' Hour of Agony (22:63-65)

63 The men who were holding Jesus started mocking and beating Him. 64 After blindfolding Him, they kept[A] asking, "Prophesy! Who hit You?" 65 And they were saying many other blasphemous things against Him.

Jesus Before the Sanhedrin (22:66-71)

66 When daylight came, the elders[B] of the people, both the chief priests and the scribes, convened and brought Him before their •Sanhedrin. 67 They said, "If You are the •Messiah, tell us."

But He said to them, "If I do tell you, you will not believe. 68 And if I ask you, you will not answer. 69 But from now on, the Son of Man will be seated at the right hand of the Power of God."

70 They all asked, "Are You, then, the Son of God?"

And He said to them, "You say that I am."

71 "Why do we need any more testimony," they said, "since we've heard it ourselves from His mouth?"

Jesus with Pilate (23:1-5)

23 Then their whole assembly rose up and brought Him before •Pilate. 2 They began to accuse Him, saying, "We found this man subverting our nation, opposing payment of taxes to Caesar, and saying that He Himself is the •Messiah, a King."

3 So Pilate asked Him, "Are You the King of the Jews?"

He answered him, "You have said it."[C]

4 Pilate then told the •chief priests and the crowds, "I find no grounds for charging this man."

5 But they kept insisting, "He stirs up the people, teaching throughout all Judea, from Galilee where He started even to here."

Jesus and Herod Antipas (23:6-12)

6 When Pilate heard this,[D] he asked if the man was a Galilean. 7 Finding that He was under •Herod's jurisdiction, he sent Him to Herod, who was also in Jerusalem during those days. 8 Herod was very glad to see Jesus; for a long time he had wanted to see Him because he had heard about Him and was hoping to see some miracle[E] performed by Him. 9 So he kept asking Him questions, but Jesus did not answer him. 10 The chief priests and the •scribes stood by, vehemently accusing Him. 11 Then Herod, with his soldiers, treated Him with contempt, mocked Him, dressed Him in a brilliant robe, and sent Him back to Pilate. 12 That very day Herod and Pilate became friends.[F] Previously, they had been hostile toward each other.

Jesus or Barabbas (23:13-25)

13 Pilate called together the chief priests, the leaders, and the people, 14 and said to them, "You have brought me this man as one who subverts the people. But in fact, after examining Him in your presence, I have found no grounds to charge this man with those things you accuse Him of. 15 Neither has Herod, because he sent Him back to us. Clearly, He has done nothing to deserve death. 16 Therefore, I will have Him whipped[G] and then release Him." [17 For according to the festival he had to release someone to them.][H]

18 Then they all cried out together, "Take this man away! Release Barabbas to us!" 19 (He had been thrown into prison for a rebellion that had taken place in the city, and for murder.)

20 Pilate, wanting to release Jesus, addressed them again, 21 but they kept shouting, "Crucify! Crucify Him!"

22 A third time he said to them, "Why? What has this man done wrong? I have found in Him no grounds for the death penalty. Therefore, I will have Him whipped and then release Him."

23 But they kept up the pressure, demanding with loud voices that He be crucified. And their voices[I] won out. 24 So Pilate decided to grant

[A]22:64 Other mss add *striking Him on the face and* [B]22:66 Or *council of elders* [C]23:3 Or *That is true*; an affirmative oath [D]23:6 Other mss read *heard "Galilee"* [E]23:8 Or *sign* [F]23:12 Lit *friends with one another* [G]23:16 Gk *paideuo*; to discipline or "teach a lesson"; 1Kg 12:11,14 LXX; 2Ch 10:11,14; perhaps a way of referring to the Roman scourging; Lat *flagellatio* [H]23:17 Other mss omit bracketed text [I]23:23 Other mss add *and those of the chief priests*

was a reminder of the Passover supper already past and of the crucifixion death still to come.

22:47-71 With a grand entrance and with a **kiss** (a customary greeting between friends in the Middle East), Judas betrayed his master while Jesus was literally in mid-sentence in the garden of Gethsemane, located at the Mount of Olives (v. 47). A student might also kiss his teacher or rabbi as a sign of respect and honor. For Judas to betray Jesus **with a kiss** made his act even more unconscionable. The "holy kiss" was also a greeting in the early church, offering blessing and expressing unity within the body (Rm 16:16; 2Co 13:12; 1Th 5:26). Jesus reminded Judas, **this is your hour**, an acknowledgment of more than the **darkness** of night at the time of Jesus' arrest (Lk 22:53). Satan was at work. Although Satan seemed to have victory in this **hour**, Jesus would have the ultimate hour of victory. The **temple police** whisked Jesus away and **brought Him** to the **house** of the high priest. In the passage concerning Peter's denial, Luke records that Jesus **turned and looked at Peter** (v. 61), a detail capturing the intensity of the moment in which a friend denied a friend.

Not long after this, Jesus was mocked and beaten. He was then brought **before** the **Sanhedrin** where He was questioned about His identity. Here Jesus made His great confession that He is **the Messiah**, the **Son of Man**, the One who will be **seated at the right hand** of God.

23:1-56 The **whole assembly** referred to the Sanhedrin (v. 1). There were a few unique contributions Luke made to the crucifixion narrative. First, he mentions that when **Pilate** (Pontius Pilate, Roman governor, A.D. 26-36) found out that Jesus **was a Galilean**, he **sent Him to Herod**, who was **in Jerusalem** at the time (vv. 6-12). Herod interrogated Jesus, **mocked Him**, and then **sent Him back to Pilate**. That day, Luke noted that **Herod and Pilate** had become **friends** (v. 12).

Second, Luke records Jesus' words to the **Daughters of Jerusalem**, a tender and affectionate designation (vv. 28-31). Jesus told them not to **weep** for Him but for their great city, which would be destroyed. Barren women who had no children would be fortunate in the sense that they would not have to see their children suffer and die in the awful destruction coming (v. 29). An indication of this was seen in what they were doing to Him. Luke's concern for the future of Jerusalem was clearly evident here.

Third, Luke alone mentions that **one of the criminals** crucified with Christ repented and actually acknowledged Jesus as God. He knew that Jesus was innocent, and he also had heard about the kingdom Jesus was about to enter (vv. 41-43). **Paradise** was a Persian word that had come over into Greek meaning "garden" or "park" (v. 43). In the New Testament it was used as a synonym for heaven, and in the Septuagint (Gk translation of the OT), it was used to describe the garden of Eden.

The splitting of the curtain in two was symbolic of the fact that Jesus' death made the sacrificial system unnecessary because now the people could have direct access to God through Christ and His supreme sacrifice on the cross (v. 45; Rm 5:2).

Luke mentions **the women** as part of the larger crowd **watching** Jesus suffer on the cross (Lk 23:49), noting that they **had followed** (Gk *sunakolouthēsasai*, "follow together with others, accompany") Jesus **from Galilee** (Lk 23:49). Significantly, out of **all who knew Him**, the women were specifically mentioned. These women disciples did not turn away or distance themselves after Jesus died. They courageously **followed** Joseph of Arimathea to **the tomb** (v. 55).

As a good historian, Luke assures his readers of the credentials of the one who offered to bury Jesus. **Joseph** of Arimathea (ancient Ramah, which belonged to Samaria in Old Testament times and Judea in the New Testament period; Jr 31:15) **was a good and righteous man**, one who could confirm that Jesus was indeed a just man, and in this way, could by inference validate the trustworthiness of Christianity (Lk 23:50-51). He was a wealthy **member of the Sanhedrin** and evidently a secret follower of Christ. Jewish law would not allow a body to remain on the cross after sunset on the Sabbath. Crucified criminals were usually dumped in common burial grounds, but Joseph gave up the newly carved stone **tomb** he had prepared for himself. Preparation of the body would have included wrapping it in strips of **linen** that had been interwoven with **spices** (v. 53).

their demand 25 and released the one
they were asking for, who had been
thrown into prison for rebellion and
murder. But he handed Jesus over to
their will.

The Way to the Cross (23:26-31)

26 As they led Him away, they
seized Simon, a Cyrenian, who was
coming in from the country, and
laid the cross on him to carry behind Jesus. 27 A large crowd of people followed Him, including women
who were mourning and lamenting
Him. 28 But turning to them, Jesus
said, "Daughters of Jerusalem, do
not weep for Me, but weep for yourselves and your children. 29 Look,
the days are coming when they will
say, 'The women without children,
the wombs that never bore and the
breasts that never nursed, are fortunate!' 30 Then they will begin **to
say to the mountains, 'Fall on us!'
and to the hills, 'Cover us!'**[A] 31 For if
they do these things when the wood
is green, what will happen when it
is dry?"

The Crucifixion of Jesus Between Two Criminals (23:32-43)

32 Two others—criminals—were
also led away to be executed with
Him. 33 When they arrived at the
place called The Skull, they crucified
Him there, along with the criminals,
one on the right and one on the left.
[34 Then Jesus said, "Father, forgive
them, because they do not know
what they are doing."][B] And they divided His clothes and cast lots.
35 The people stood watching, and
even the leaders kept scoffing: "He
saved others; let Him save Himself
if this is God's Messiah, the Chosen
One!" 36 The soldiers also mocked
Him. They came offering Him sour
wine 37 and said, "If You are the King
of the Jews, save Yourself!"
38 An inscription was above Him:[C]

**THIS IS
THE KING OF THE JEWS.**

39 Then one of the criminals hanging there began to yell insults at[D]
Him: "Aren't You the Messiah? Save
Yourself and us!"
40 But the other answered, rebuking him: "Don't you even fear God,
since you are undergoing the same
punishment? 41 We are punished
justly, because we're getting back
what we deserve for the things we
did, but this man has done nothing
wrong." 42 Then he said, "Jesus, remember me[E] when You come into
Your kingdom!"
43 And He said to him, "•I assure
you: Today you will be with Me in
paradise."

The Death of Jesus (23:44-49)

44 It was now about noon,[F] and
darkness came over the whole land[G]
until three,[H] 45 because the sun's
light failed.[I] The curtain of the sanctuary was split down the middle.
46 And Jesus called out with a loud
voice, "Father, **into Your hands I
entrust My spirit.**"[J] Saying this, He
breathed His last.
47 When the •centurion saw what
happened, he began to glorify God,
saying, "This man really was righteous!" 48 All the crowds that had
gathered for this spectacle, when
they saw what had taken place, went
home, striking their chests.[K] 49 But
all who knew Him, including the
women who had followed Him from
Galilee, stood at a distance, watching these things.

The Burial of Jesus (23:50-56)

50 There was a good and righteous
man named Joseph, a member of the
•Sanhedrin, 51 who had not agreed
with their plan and action. He was
from Arimathea, a Judean town, and
was looking forward to the kingdom
of God. 52 He approached Pilate and
asked for Jesus' body. 53 Taking it
down, he wrapped it in fine linen and
placed it in a tomb cut into the rock,
where no one had ever been placed.[L]
54 It was preparation day, and the
Sabbath was about to begin.[M] 55 The
women who had come with Him
from Galilee followed along and observed the tomb and how His body

[A] **23:30** Hs 10:8 [B] **23:34** Other mss omit bracketed text [C] **23:38** Other mss add *written in Greek, Latin, and Hebrew letters* [D] **23:39** Or *began to blaspheme* [E] **23:42** Other mss add *Lord* [F] **23:44** Lit *about the sixth hour* [G] **23:44** Or *whole earth* [H] **23:44** Lit *the ninth hour* [I] **23:45** Other mss read *three, and the sun was darkened* [J] **23:46** Ps 31:5 [K] **23:48** = mourning [L] **23:53** Or *interred,* or *laid* [M] **23:54** Lit *was dawning*; not in the morning but at sundown Friday

was placed. [56]Then they returned and prepared spices and perfumes. And they rested on the Sabbath according to the commandment.

Resurrection Morning (24:1-12)

24 On the first day of the week, very early in the morning, they[A] came to the tomb, bringing the spices they had prepared. [2]They found the stone rolled away from the tomb. [3]They went in but did not find the body of the Lord Jesus. [4]While they were perplexed about this, suddenly two men stood by them in dazzling clothes. [5]So the women were terrified and bowed down to the ground.[B]

"Why are you looking for the living among the dead?" asked the men. [6]"He is not here, but He has been resurrected! Remember how He spoke to you when He was still in Galilee, [7]saying, 'The •Son of Man must be betrayed into the hands of sinful men, be crucified, and rise on the third day'?" [8]And they remembered His words.

[9]Returning from the tomb, they reported all these things to the Eleven and to all the rest. [10]•Mary Magdalene, Joanna, Mary the mother of James, and the other women with them were telling the apostles these things. [11]But these words seemed like nonsense to them, and they did not believe the women. [12]Peter, however, got up and ran to the tomb. When he stooped to look in, he saw only the linen cloths.[C] So he went home, amazed at what had happened.

The Emmaus Disciples (24:13-35)

[13]Now that same day two of them were on their way to a village called[D] Emmaus, which was about seven miles[E] from Jerusalem. [14]Together they were discussing everything that had taken place. [15]And while they were discussing and arguing, Jesus Himself came near and began to walk along with them. [16]But they[F] were prevented from recognizing Him. [17]Then He asked them, "What is this dispute that you're having[G] with each other as you are walking?" And they stopped walking and looked discouraged.

[18]The one named Cleopas answered Him, "Are You the only visitor in Jerusalem who doesn't know the things that happened there in these days?"

[19]"What things?" He asked them.

So they said to Him, "The things concerning Jesus the •Nazarene, who was a Prophet powerful in action and speech before God and all the people, [20]and how our •chief priests and leaders handed Him over to be sentenced to death, and they crucified Him. [21]But we were hoping that He was the One who was about to •redeem Israel. Besides all this, it's the third day since these things happened. [22]Moreover, some women from our group astounded us. They arrived early at the tomb, [23]and when they didn't find His body, they came and reported that they had seen a vision of angels who said He was alive. [24]Some of those who were with us went to the tomb and found it just as the women had said, but they didn't see Him."

[25]He said to them, "How unwise and slow you are to believe in your hearts all that the prophets have spoken! [26]Didn't the •Messiah have to suffer these things and enter into His glory?" [27]Then beginning with Moses and all the Prophets, He interpreted for them the things concerning Himself in all the Scriptures.

[28]They came near the village where they were going, and He gave the impression that He was going farther. [29]But they urged Him: "Stay with us, because it's almost evening, and now the day is almost over." So He went in to stay with them.

[30]It was as He reclined at the table with them that He took the bread, blessed and broke it, and gave it to them. [31]Then their eyes were opened, and they recognized Him, but He disappeared from their sight. [32]So they said to each other, "Weren't our hearts ablaze within us while He was talking with us on

[A]**24:1** Other mss add *and other women with them* [B]**24:5** Lit *and inclined their faces to the ground* [C]**24:12** Other mss add *lying there* [D]**24:13** Lit *village, which name is* [E]**24:13** Lit *about 60 stadia*; 1 *stadion* = 600 feet [F]**24:16** Lit *their eyes* [G]**24:17** Lit *What are these words that you are exchanging*

24:1-53 As soon as restrictions associated with reverence for the Sabbath permitted, several women disciples returned to **the tomb** (23:56–24:1). The women were visiting the tomb, not to confirm Jesus' resurrection as He had announced, but they were coming to be sure that His body had been prepared properly for burial (v. 1). They did not expect to find an empty tomb (vv. 2-3). Two angels appeared, telling them of the resurrection and reminding them that Jesus had predicted this event (vv. 4-7). The women, according to Luke's account, were the only disciples present at the first appearance of the resurrected Jesus. They then were privileged to go immediately and inform the apostles about what had happened (vv. 8-9).

Each of the three Synoptic Gospels speaks to a truly surprising degree on the presence of women disciples at the crucifixion and resurrection of Jesus. They were present at Jesus' lowest point at the cross, and they were honored to be the first witnesses to His resurrection. These women provided a wonderful testimony of faithful service and witness.

Luke's extended account of the resurrection of Jesus provides an astounding conclusion to the major theme developed throughout the Gospel—the *saving mission of Christ*. Luke also sets the stage for the development of the early church in the book of Acts. No one account captures the essence of Jesus' saving mission better that the Emmaus story (vv. 13-35). The **first day of the week** (v. 1) is Sunday. The Sabbath ended the week for Jews. Sunday became the day of worship for believers (Ac 20:7), showing the importance of the resurrection to the Christians of the first century. Unique to Luke, this moving account sent a clear message concerning the nature and fulfillment of Jesus' mission. **Emmaus** (modern-day Kubeibeh) was located about seven miles northwest from Jerusalem.

Six major themes emerge from this final section:

- Jesus is the fulfillment of Scripture (Lk 24:26-27,44-48).
- Jesus was made known during fellowship at the table, possibly a reminder of the last supper (vv. 30-35).
- The reality of Christ's humanity and of His bodily resurrection is emphasized (vv. 36-43).
- Luke's overall interest in the power of the Holy Spirit is manifested in the prediction of the Spirit's role at Pentecost (vv. 48-49).
- All of the resurrection appearances in Luke happened in Jerusalem and at the time the disciples returned to the temple. Jerusalem had an important role in God's redemptive plan (vv. 52-53; Ac 1:8).
- Only Luke mentions the ascension of Jesus (Lk 24:50-51).

24:37-43 The disciples were overwhelmed with the reality of Jesus' resurrection (v. 37). Jesus proved Himself to be alive by showing them **His** pierced **hands and feet** and asking them to touch Him (v. 39). Then He asked for food and ate (vv. 41-43), not because He needed nourishment but to affirm the reality of His physical presence among them.

24:44-53 Luke's concluding verses (vv. 46-53) provided transition to his second volume, the book of Acts. Luke then continued his historical record, taking up in the book of Acts where the Gospel of Luke ended.

the road and explaining the Scriptures to us?" 33 That very hour they
got up and returned to Jerusalem.
They found the Eleven and those
with them gathered together, 34 who
said,[A] "The Lord has certainly been
raised, and has appeared to Simon!"
35 Then they began to describe what
had happened on the road and how
He was made known to them in the
breaking of the bread.

The Reality of the Risen Jesus (24:36-49)

36 And as they were saying these
things, He Himself stood among
them. He said to them, "Peace to
you!" 37 But they were startled and
terrified and thought they were seeing a ghost. 38 "Why are you troubled?" He asked them. "And why do
doubts arise in your hearts? 39 Look
at My hands and My feet, that it is I
Myself! Touch Me and see, because a
ghost does not have flesh and bones
as you can see I have." 40 Having said
this, He showed them His hands
and feet. 41 But while they still were
amazed and unbelieving because of
their joy, He asked them, "Do you
have anything here to eat?" 42 So
they gave Him a piece of a broiled
fish,[B] 43 and He took it and ate in
their presence.
44 Then He told them, "These are
My words that I spoke to you while
I was still with you—that everything written about Me in the Law
of Moses, the Prophets, and the
Psalms must be fulfilled." 45 Then He
opened their minds to understand
the Scriptures. 46 He also said to
them, "This is what is written:[C] The
Messiah would suffer and rise from
the dead the third day, 47 and repentance for[D] forgiveness of sins would
be proclaimed in His name to all the
nations, beginning at Jerusalem.
48 You are witnesses of these things.
49 And look, I am sending you[E] what
My Father promised. As for you, stay
in the city[F] until you are empowered[G] from on high."

The Ascension of Jesus (24:50-53)

50 Then He led them out as far as
Bethany, and lifting up His hands
He blessed them. 51 And while He
was blessing them, He left them and
was carried up into heaven. 52 After worshiping Him, they returned
to Jerusalem with great joy. 53 And
they were continually in the •temple
complex praising God.[H]

[A]**24:34** Gk is specific that this refers to the Eleven and those with them. [B]**24:42** Other mss add *and some honeycomb* [C]**24:46** Other mss add *and thus it was necessary that* [D]**24:47** Other mss read *repentance and* [E]**24:49** Lit *upon you* [F]**24:49** Other mss add *of Jerusalem* [G]**24:49** Lit *clothed with power* [H]**24:53** Other mss read *praising and blessing God. Amen.*

LUKE … WRITTEN ON MY *Heart*

Luke recognized that the driving force in history—both in the world and in the lives of individual believers—is God's Holy Spirit. The empowerment and direction of the Holy Spirit evident throughout the Gospel of Luke is available only in surrendering your life to Christ in repentance and faith. If you already know Jesus as Savior and Lord, prioritize prayer and consistent Bible reading in fellowship with other committed followers of Christ. These disciplines keep you "in tune" with and aware of what the Holy Spirit is doing in and around you. He will also change you from the inside out, making your life look more and more like Jesus. Many of the changes He makes will require uncomfortable, even painful decisions (consider memorizing 9:23), but He promises to be worth any cost—and He keeps all His promises.

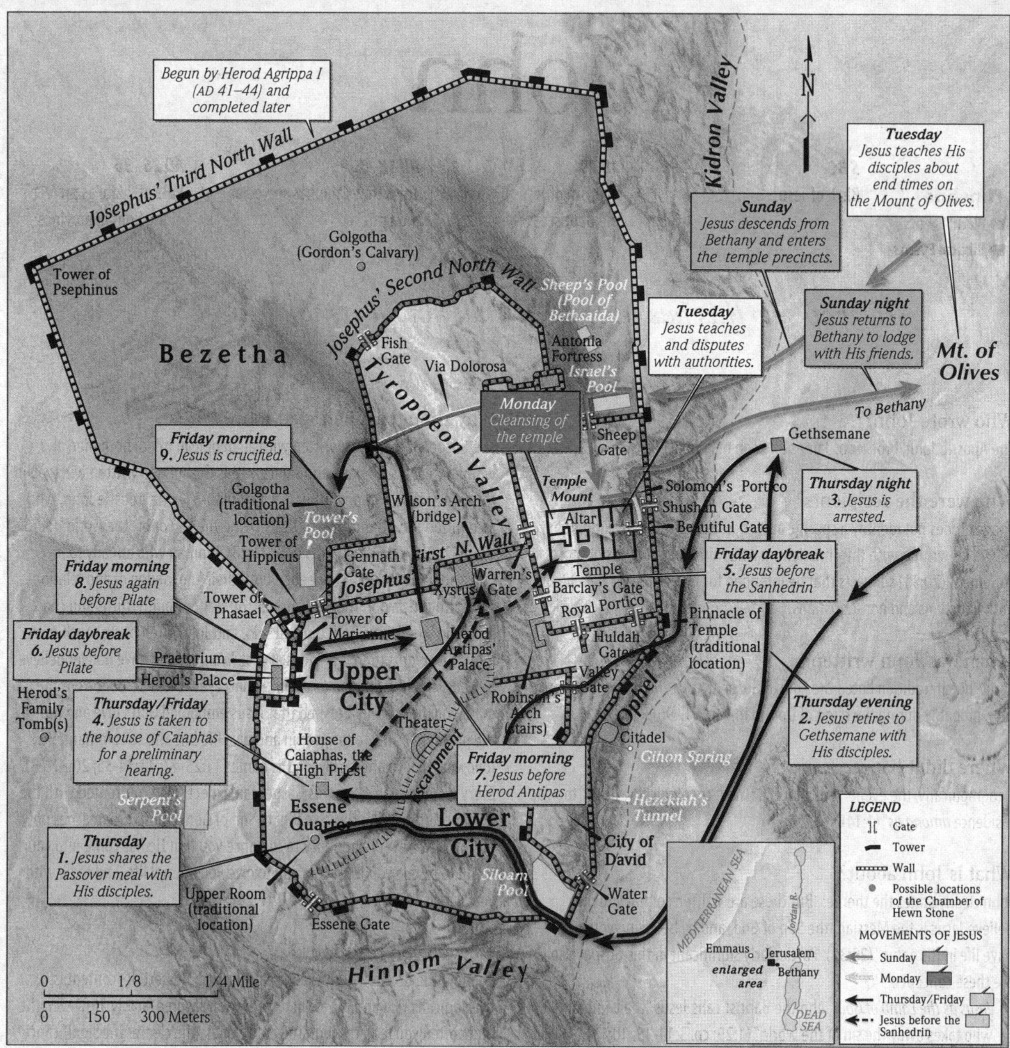
Begun by Herod Agrippa I (AD 41–44) and completed later
Josephus' Third North Wall
Kidron Valley
N
Tuesday
Jesus teaches His disciples about end times on the Mount of Olives.
Sunday
Jesus descends from Bethany and enters the temple precincts.
Golgotha (Gordon's Calvary)
Tower of Psephinus
Josephus' Second North Wall
Sheep's Pool (Pool of Bethsaida)
Tuesday
Jesus teaches and disputes with authorities.
Sunday night
Jesus returns to Bethany to lodge with His friends.
Mt. of Olives
Bezetha
Fish Gate
Antonia Fortress
Israel's Pool
Tyropoeon Valley
Via Dolorosa
Monday
Cleansing of the temple
To Bethany
Sheep Gate
Gethsemane
Friday morning
9. Jesus is crucified.
Temple Mount
Solomon's Portico
Shushan Gate
Beautiful Gate
Thursday night
3. Jesus is arrested.
Golgotha (traditional location)
Tower's Pool
Wilson's Arch (bridge)
Altar
Tower of Hippicus
Gennath Gate
Josephus' First N. Wall
Warren's Gate
Temple
Friday daybreak
5. Jesus before the Sanhedrin
Friday morning
8. Jesus again before Pilate
Xystus
Barclay's Gate
Royal Portico
Tower of Phasael
Tower of Mariamne
Herod Antipas' Palace
Huldah Gates
Pinnacle of Temple (traditional location)
Friday daybreak
6. Jesus before Pilate
Praetorium
Herod's Palace
Upper City
Valley Gate
Ophel
Herod's Family Tomb(s)
Thursday/Friday
4. Jesus is taken to the house of Caiaphas for a preliminary hearing.
Theater
Robinson's Arch (stairs)
Citadel
Thursday evening
2. Jesus retires to Gethsemane with His disciples.
House of Caiaphas, the High Priest
Escarpment
Friday morning
7. Jesus before Herod Antipas
Gihon Spring
Hezekiah's Tunnel
Serpent's Pool
Essene Quarter
Lower City
City of David
Thursday
1. Jesus shares the Passover meal with His disciples.
Siloam Pool
Upper Room (traditional location)
Water Gate
Essene Gate
Hinnom Valley
0 1/8 1/4 Mile
0 150 300 Meters
MEDITERRANEAN SEA
Jordan R.
Emmaus
Jerusalem
Bethany
enlarged area
DEAD SEA
LEGEND
Gate
Tower
Wall
Possible locations of the Chamber of Hewn Stone
MOVEMENTS OF JESUS
Sunday
Monday
Thursday/Friday
Jesus before the Sanhedrin

The Passion Week in Jerusalem

John

Timeline World Events Biblical Events	*5 BC* Birth of Jesus	*AD 29* Baptism of Jesus by John the Baptist	*AD 18–36* Years that Caiaphas served as high priest	*AD 26–36* Rule of Pilate as prefect of the Roman province of Judea

"He who saw this has testified so that you also may believe" (19:35a).

Who wrote John?

The Apostle John, brother of James and son of Zebedee

Who were the recipients?

The text does not identify a specific audience. Historically speaking, John likely was writing with the Christians in Asia Minor in mind. His purpose statement (20:31) suggests that he intended for his account to be read by both Christians and non-Christians.

When was John written?

Early church tradition dated the Fourth Gospel to the end of the first century, probably during the reign of Domitian (A.D. 81–96).

Where did it happen?

Geographically, the events took place in Israel; theologically, Jesus "took up residence *among us*" (1:14).

What is John about?

John clearly states the theme: "But these are written so that you may believe Jesus is the Messiah, the Son of God, and by believing you may have life in His name" (20:31). Particularly significant in this Gospel also are these concepts:

- *Jesus as the Lamb of God.* John the Baptist calls Jesus "the Lamb of God, who takes away the sin of the world" (1:29; cp. 3:14-15; 10:11).
- *The deity of Christ.* All seven "I am" statements of Christ allude to His divine nature:
  - "the bread of life" (6:35);
  - "the light of the world" (8:12);
  - "the door of the sheep" (10:7);
  - "the good shepherd" (10:11);
  - "the resurrection and the life" (11:25);
  - "the way, the truth, and the life" (14:6);
  - "the true vine" (15:1).
- *The Holy Spirit.* Particularly in chapters 14–16, the Holy Spirit is described as fulfilling several roles benefiting the believer:
  - "Counselor" (14:16,26; 15:26; 16:7);
  - "Spirit of truth" (14:17; 15:26; 16:13);
  - teacher (14:25)
  - witness (15:26);
  - prosecutor (16:7-11); and
  - revealer (16:12-15).
- *Miracles as "signs"* (e.g., 2:11; 4:53-54; 20:30).

Why should women read John?

The Gospel of John was written with all people in mind, both men and women; seekers, sinners, and saints—this Gospel was written with *you* in the mind of the human author (19:35; 20:30-31), the Apostle John, who recognized the significance of Jesus' being the Savior of "the world" (3:16-17; 4:42; 6:63,51; 12:47; 14:31; 17:21,23). Women who already follow Christ should read John to deepen both their knowledge of and relationship with the Savior. They will also encounter profound truths and challenges in what Jesus both did and said, and John often packs much more into a few words than is obvious at first. Women who have not yet believed in Jesus should read John as a compelling eyewitness account from the man who most firmly grasped that Jesus embodied God's love and has the power not only to forgive sin and give life but also to command His followers to love and forgive in His name (11:25-27; 13:34-35; 20:21-23). Every woman who reads this Gospel can expect to be confronted with the uncompromising yet compassionate Son of God, whose love reaches powerfully across every boundary to convince you that He has come into your world to rescue you from your sin, to give you eternal life, and to be with you always (3:16-17; 8:12; 14:17; 17:24).

How do you read John?

Reading the Gospel of John is like eating a rich dessert. Its content is theologically rich and is best digested when savored slowly. However, the more often you read through the entire book, the clearer the significance of each aspect of this overview of Jesus' life and teachings will become. The Gospel can be divided thematically into two parts (chaps. 1–11 and chaps. 12–21)—the first focusing on Jesus' deeds (the "signs"), the second revealing His passion and glory. The prologue of John (chap. 1) stresses Jesus' pre-existence and His incarnation and presents the testimony of John the Baptist. Chapters 2–11 consist of seven miracles performed by Jesus, accompanied by seven lengthy discourses. These function as "signs" of Jesus' authority so that people may believe. Chapters 12–21 contain two major sections. After a brief introduction in chapter 12 describing the events that will lead to Jesus' death, chapters 13–17 recount Jesus' farewell discourse to His disciples. Chapters 18–21 then narrate the Lord's crucifixion, resurrection, and the reinstatement of the disciples.

In addition, the more familiar you become with the Old Testament, the more you will understand. The discourses of Jesus also presuppose knowledge of the symbolism behind the Jewish festivals (2:13,23 ; 4:45; 6:4; 7:2,8,10-11,14,37; 10:22; 11:55-56; 12:1,12,20). Continually reading through both Old and New Testaments is fundamental for increased understanding of each book in the canon.

Passover, AD 30	Winter, AD 33	Monday, March 28, AD 33	Friday, April 1, AD 33	Sunday, April 3, AD 33
Jesus' cleansing of the temple.	Jesus' raising of Lazarus from death	Jesus' second cleansing of the temple	Jesus' crucifixion	Jesus' resurrection

Outline

- I. Introductory Testimony (1:1-51)
  - A. The Prologue (1:1-18)
  - B. The Testimony (1:19-51)
- II. The Testimony of Signs and Discourses (2:1–11:57)
  - A. Jesus and Jewish Institutions (2:1–4:54)
  - B. Jesus and Jewish Festivals (5:1–10:21)
  - C. Jesus as the Resurrection and the Life (11:1-57)
- III. The Testimony of Death and Resurrection (12:1–20:31)
  - A. Actions in Preparation for Death (12:1-50)
  - B. Teaching in Preparation for Death (13:1–17:26)
  - C. Events Surrounding Jesus' Death (18:1–20:31)
- IV. Concluding Testimony (21:1-25)
  - A. The Reinstatement of the Disciples (21:1-23)
  - B. Epilogue (21:24-25)

The Prologue (1:1-18)

1 In the beginning was the Word,[A]
and the Word was with God,
and the Word was God.
2 He was with God
in the beginning.
3 All things were created
through Him,
and apart from Him
not one thing was created
that has been created.
4 Life was in Him,[B]
and that life was the light
of men.
5 That light shines
in the darkness,
yet the darkness did not
overcome[C] it.

 FAITH

The apostle John consistently points to the goal of presenting the Gospel **so that all might believe** (Gk *pisteusōsin*, "actively trust or place one's confidence in," 1:7) in Jesus. The verb "believe" includes the idea of mental assent, but its use in Scripture is better understood as an active demonstration of its root word, "faith" (Gk *pistis*). Likewise, although the truth of the Gospel confronts people with the demand for a decision or choice ("Do you believe . . . ?" e.g., v. 50; 3:35), "belief" always involves commitment that is actively demonstrated—both positively in identifying oneself as a follower of Christ and negatively in renouncing and forsaking the path of sin (see 1Jn 1:5-10; cp. Jn 8:31).

6 There was a man named John
who was sent from God.

[A]1:1 The *Word* (Gk *Logos*) is a title for Jesus as the communication and the revealer of God the Father; Jn 1:14,18; Rv 19:13. [B]1:3-4 Other punctuation is possible: . . . *not one thing was created. What was created in Him was life* [C]1:5 Or *grasp*, or *comprehend*, or *overtake*; Jn 12:35

>WORD|*study*

1:1 In this context, particularly as used by John, Word (Gk *logos*, "a thing uttered, speech, language") incorporates both Old Testament usage and the idea of *logos* belonging to Greek philosophy. Repeatedly in the Old Testament, the authenticity of God's speaking to a person and the inspiration of the prophets' messages are endorsed by the phrase, "The word [Hb *davar*] of the LORD came to . . ." (e.g., Gn 15:1,4; 1Sm 15:10; Jr 1:2,4,11,13), in which the verb "came" suggests the personality and initiative of "the word." As a term in ancient Greek philosophy, *logos* generally refers to a fixed principle of order in a world of change, the source of order and being in the universe or the source of intelligence and reason.

1:5 Overcome (Gk *katelaben*) has several nuances of meaning, each of which illuminates a facet of the truth that Jesus is God incarnate:

- "lay hold of to make one's own" (cp. Php 3:12; "receives" and "win," 1Co 9:24);
- "seize upon, take possession of" (cp. "overtake," Jn 12:35);
- "lay hold of with the mind, perceive, understand, comprehend" (cp. Eph 3:18).

Title: The simple title in the Greek text, "According to John" (Gk *kata Iōannēn*), identifying by name the apostle who, writing under the inspiration of the Holy Spirit, bears witness to Jesus the Christ.

1:1-5 The introductory phrase, **in the beginning** (Gk *archē*, "starting point," referring to the time before creation), deliberately recalls the opening words of Genesis, implicitly emphasizing the identity of Jesus Christ—**the Word**—with the God who is the preexistent Creator. The translators have capitalized "word" to reflect their conviction that John is referring to Jesus Christ, whom he later identifies as "the Son" (v. 14). Verse 2 explicitly reinforces Christ's divine nature by asserting His integral role in creation both **with God** (indicating His distinction of identity) and as God (recognizing His equality as deity Himself). Logically, then, "the Word" was *not* created; He already **was** when this beginning occurred. Rather, Christ is the source of all there is.

1:5 Verse 5 previews the victorious outcome of Christ's work on the cross— overpowering darkness (i.e., the forces of evil in the world) with light (i.e., the truth, who is God Himself). John—both in this Gospel and in his letters—brings into focus the mutual exclusivity of life (Gk *zōe*) and death and of **light** (Gk *phōs*) and **darkness** (Gk *skotia*, "darkness that is due to the absence of daylight"; cp. 8:12; 12:46; 1Jn 1:5; 2:8-9,11). Often, "light" and "darkness" metaphorically express the truth, goodness, and holiness of God ("light") in stark contrast to wickedness and rebellion—anyone and anything opposing Him.

1:6-8 That John the Baptist was **sent** [Gk *apestalmenos*, "commission"] **from**

God conveys this prophet's sense of authority as a personal representative of the Lord. The primary function of John the Baptist was **to testify** [Gk *marturēsē*, "bear witness, affirm what one has experienced firsthand or received as revelation"] **about the light** (i.e., Jesus Christ), serving, therefore, as a **witness** (Gk *marturian*, "one who testifies; testimony"; cp. v. 19) concerning Jesus. The Greek word is the source of the later English word "martyr," a reference to one who suffers or dies for his beliefs.

1:9-13 Christ is presented as **the true** [Gk *alēthinon*, "real, genuine, authentic"] **light**. The emphasis here is on completeness and clarity, as if coming out of the shadows. Under the radiance and brightness of Christ, all else seems dim and inadequate. Ultimately, revelation is only in and through Him. The phrase **gives light** (Gk *phōtizei*, "shed light, instruct") emphasizes His purpose of revealing God **to everyone** (cp. 3:16).

The failure of **the world** (Gk *kosmos*) to **recognize** (Gk *egnō*, "know") "the true light" does not mean that Christ's divine character was not made evident. The term is volitional, involving a deliberate choice to stay in the "comfort zone" of sin instead of submitting to the authority of God in Christ (cp. 3:19). Generally, people—although created by God—do not "know," acknowledge, or "recognize" Him in the sense of giving Him the honor He is due because they have consciously determined to reject God's revelation of Himself in Christ.

The word **children** (Gk *tekna*) suggests endearment and connection. These were not linked biologically **of blood** or by human decision (i.e., **the will of the flesh**); they were not natural children of God. But by believing and receiving, they became His children; the relationship was spiritual.

1:18 The Son is said to be **at the Father's side** (Gk *eis ton kolpon*, lit being "in the bosom"), a Hebrew idiom denoting the intimate relationship between a child and his parents. **Is** (Gk *ōn*, a present participle, "being, existing") implies not only pre-incarnate existence but also constant and continual association. No statement more clearly expresses intimate association and close following and thus God's compassion for the world.

The verb in the phrase **He has revealed Him** (Gk *exēgēsato*, "explain or interpret") is transliterated into English as *exegesis*. The incarnation is the ultimate teaching or expounding of God's Word and was often used to proclaim divine secrets. God cannot be understood by ordinary human senses, but the life and words of Jesus provide all one needs to know God and His

>WORD|*study*

1:11 Interestingly the two occurrences of the word translated His own are different in gender. The first (Gk *idia*) is a neuter reference to one's personal belongings (i.e., the land of Israel); the other (Gk *idioi*), a masculine form, refers to His people. Jesus created the world, and it belonged to Him; but the people He created rejected Him.

1:11-12 In direct contrast to the rejection of Christ, believe (Gk *pisteuousin*) indicates an active and continual commitment to Christ. Belief **in His** [Jesus'] **name** is not merely head knowledge but is inextricably linked with receiving (Gk *parelabon*, "taking to one's side or welcoming") which includes confidence that the giver is trustworthy.

7 He came as a witness
to testify about the light,
so that all might believe
through him.[A]
8 He was not the light,
but he came to testify
about the light.
9 The true light, who gives light
to everyone,
was coming into the world.[B]

10 He was in the world,
and the world was created
through Him,
yet the •world did not
recognize Him.
11 He came to His own,[C]
and His own people[C]
did not receive Him.
12 But to all who did
receive Him,
He gave them the right to be[D]
children of God,
to those who believe
in His name,
13 who were born,
not of blood,[E]
or of the will of the flesh,
or of the will of man,[F]
but of God.

14 The Word became flesh[G]
and took up residence[H]
among us.
We observed His glory,
the glory as the
•One and Only Son[I]
from the Father,
full of grace and truth.

15 (John testified
concerning Him
and exclaimed,

Doctrine INCARNATION

Although Gnosticism did not appear until later, reaching its full strength in the second and third centuries, John battled what might be called "incipient Gnosticism," which claimed that Jesus only *seemed* to be human since a sinless Christ could not have become human. Gnostics regarded the spiritual as inherently good and the earthly (i.e., the created world, as evil). Gnostics refused to see any connection between the sins of the body and spiritual things. Therefore, in their thinking they could worship on a spiritual level while remaining free to do as they pleased in everyday living. John countered with unveiling Christ's humanity (4:6-7; 11:35; 12:27; 19:30). Jesus took His human nature at His incarnation, but He did not lose any of His deity. He was truly the God-Man. In Jn 1:1, "the Word" refers to eternal deity; in 1:4 **the Word became flesh** refers to the incarnation by which God the Son entered into the domain of humanity.

Through His birth, Jesus **took up residence** (Gk *eskēnōsen*, "live in a tent, take temporary residence," 1:14) as the executor of His Father's will in human flesh. John is comparing the incarnation to the time when God's presence was among His people, "tabernacling" with them in the wilderness of Sinai. His fleshly tent was God's residence, replacing the ancient tabernacle in the wilderness (Ex 24:16). Yet, Jesus' glory has a unique dimension in that He is the only Son.

The incarnation was the most perfect and complete revelation of the **Only Son** (Gk *monogenous*, "unique," Jn 1:14), literally a "one of a kind" Son. With no equal from all of humanity, He alone was able to reveal the Father fully. John asserts having **observed His glory**, indicating a reality personally experienced (v. 14; cp. 1Jn 1:1; 4:14).

[A]**1:7** Or *through it* (the light) [B]**1:9** Or *The true light who comes into the world gives light to everyone*, or *The true light enlightens everyone coming into the world.* [C]**1:11** The same Gk adjective is used twice in this verse: the first refers to all that Jesus owned as Creator (*to His own*); the second refers to the Jews (*His own people*). [D]**1:12** Or *become* [E]**1:13** Lit *bloods*; the pl form of *blood* occurs only here in the NT. It may refer either to lineal descent (that is, blood from one's father and mother) or to the OT sacrificial system (that is, the various blood sacrifices). Neither is the basis for birth into the family of God. [F]**1:13** Or *not of human lineage, or of human capacity, or of human volition* [G]**1:14** The eternally existent Word (vv. 1-2) took on full humanity but without sin; Heb 4:15. [H]**1:14** Or *and dwelt in a tent*; lit *and tabernacled*; this word occurs only here in John. A related word, referring to the Festival of Tabernacles, occurs only in 7:2; Ex 40:34-38. [I]**1:14** *Son* is implied from the reference to the Father and from Gk usage.

"This was the One of whom
I said,
'The One coming after me
has surpassed me,
because He existed
before me.'")
16 Indeed, we have all received
grace after grace
from His fullness,
17 for the law was given
through Moses,
grace and truth came
through Jesus Christ.
18 No one has ever seen God.[A]
The One and Only Son[B]—
the One who is
at the Father's side[C]—
He has revealed Him.

The Testimony (1:19-51)

19 This is John's testimony when
the •Jews from Jerusalem sent
priests and Levites to ask him, "Who
are you?"
20 He did not refuse to answer, but
he declared: "I am not the •Messiah."
21 "What then?" they asked him.
"Are you Elijah?"
"I am not," he said.
"Are you the Prophet?"[D]
"No," he answered.
22 "Who are you, then?" they asked.
"We need to give an answer to those
who sent us. What can you tell us
about yourself?"
23 He said, "I am a **voice of one
crying out in the wilderness: Make
straight the way of the Lord**[E]—just
as Isaiah the prophet said."
24 Now they had been sent from
the •Pharisees. 25 So they asked him,
"Why then do you baptize if you
aren't the Messiah, or Elijah, or the
Prophet?"
26 "I baptize with[F] water," John
answered them. "Someone stands
among you, but you don't know
Him. 27 He is the One coming after
me,[G] whose sandal strap I'm not
worthy to untie."
28 All this happened in Bethany[H]
across the Jordan,[I] where John was
baptizing.
29 The next day John saw Jesus
coming toward him and said, "Here
is the Lamb of God, who takes away
the sin of the world! 30 This is the
One I told you about: 'After me
comes a man who has surpassed me,
because He existed before me.' 31 I
didn't know Him, but I came baptizing with[F] water so He might be
revealed to Israel."
32 And John testified, "I watched
the Spirit descending from heaven
like a dove, and He rested on Him.
33 I didn't know Him, but He[J] who
sent me to baptize with[F] water told
me, 'The One you see the Spirit descending and resting on—He is the
One who baptizes with[F] the Holy
Spirit.' 34 I have seen and testified
that He is the Son of God!"[K]
35 Again the next day, John was
standing with two of his disciples.
36 When he saw Jesus passing by, he
said, "Look! The Lamb of God!"
37 The two disciples heard him
say this and followed Jesus. 38 When
Jesus turned and noticed them following Him, He asked them, "What
are you looking for?"
They said to Him, "•Rabbi" (which
means "Teacher"), "where are You
staying?"

Doctrine — CHRISTOLOGY

John the Baptist did know Jesus; they were relatives (Lk 1:36). However, he had not known Him as Messiah; and here, for John, the Holy Spirit began to unveil Jesus as the Christ, the Messiah (Jn. 1:31). This section summarizes John's theological presentation of Jesus as the Messiah:

- Jesus is the Passover **Lamb** (v. 36), the sacrifice meeting Old Testament requirements.
- Jesus was preexistent—fully God and fully Man in His incarnation (v. 30).
- Jesus identified Himself with the Holy Spirit as the intercessor for believers (v. 33).
- Jesus as the "only Son" truly embodied God and yet clothed Himself with humanity (v. 14).
- He was the one described in the Law and the Prophets (v. 45).

purposes for life. God as a being is so beyond human comprehension that He cannot be seen. Only through spiritual eyes can you know Him. However, He chose to reveal Himself in physical form through Jesus. Thus, John reveals in his prologue that Jesus is both divine and human.

1:19-51 John the Baptist's primary function was to testify of Jesus. He clearly stated that he was **not the Messiah**. He was the one who was to testify concerning the Messiah. There is no explicit mention of Jesus' baptism by John in this Gospel. The focus is exclusively on Jesus. The apostle John may have been attempting to combat a sect worshiping John the Baptist in his community.

1:27 John the Baptist understood his role in contradistinction to that of Jesus the Christ. Untying sandals was the menial task of a slave, and thus the Baptist did not see himself even as worthy of being a slave of Jesus, emphasizing again the exalted nature of Jesus.

1:28 Bethany across the Jordan is not the same village (located near Jerusalem) in which Lazarus and Mary and Martha lived. Since the site has not been identified with any certainty, some suggest that it is Betharba (lit "the place of crossing"). However, the only sure information about the village is that it was not a populated area, which may be why the location is uncertain.

1:30 A significant change sets this verse apart from verse 15 with the words **after me comes a man** (Gk *anēr*, "man or husband," emphasizing maleness more than does the generic term *anthrōpos*). Some commentators see this distinction as alluding to the headship of Christ over His followers as paralleled in the husband's headship over the wife in marriage (see 1Co 11:3; Eph 5:22-23), a principle clearly taught in the Pauline epistles.

1:29-50 This section records a series of happenings that occurred on successive days:

First, John testified to Jesus' identity (vv. 29-34).

Second, John the Baptist introduced Jesus to his own disciples (vv. 35-42). He announced that Jesus is **the Lamb of God, who takes away the sin of the world**; two disciples took notice (vv. 35-37). One was **Andrew**; the other was not named. They quickly turned from following John the Baptist to following Jesus. Andrew called Peter (vv. 40-42).

Third, Jesus left for Galilee (vv. 43-51). **Jesus found Philip**, who then brought **Nathanael** to Jesus. This initial calling in Judea seems to have occurred before the formal calling

[A]**1:18** Since God is an infinite being, no one can see Him in His absolute essential nature; Ex 33:18-23. [B]**1:18** Other mss read *God* [C]**1:18** Lit *is in the bosom of the Father* [D]**1:21** Probably the Prophet in Dt 18:15 [E]**1:23** Is 40:3 [F]**1:26,31,33** Or *in* [G]**1:27** Other mss add *who came before me* [H]**1:28** Other mss read *in Bethabara* [I]**1:28** Another Bethany, near Jerusalem, was the home of Lazarus, Martha, and Mary; Jn 11:1. [J]**1:33** *He* refers to God the Father, who gave John a sign to help him identify the Messiah. Vv. 32-34 indicate that John did not know that Jesus was the Messiah until the Spirit descended upon Him at His baptism. [K]**1:34** Other mss read *is the Chosen One of God*

of the disciples by the Sea of Galilee, which is recorded in the Synoptic Gospels (Mt 10:1-15; Mk 3:13-19; Lk 6:12-16).

Many titles were used to describe Jesus in the Law and the Prophets (v. 45):

- **the Lamb of God** (a picture of the Passover lamb slain when the children of Israel were delivered from Egypt, Ex 12:12-13);
- **Rabbi** (lit "master or teacher," a title of respect used by students in addressing a wise and honored teacher, v. 38),
- **Messiah** (lit "anointed one," v. 41);
- **the Son of God** (v. 49); and
- **the King of Israel** (v. 49).

1:42 Cephas, a Greek transliteration of an Aramaic term meaning "rock," was not commonly used as a proper name in either language. The Greek equivalent is used in Matthew's Gospel (Mt 16:18). The term is used as a nickname and became so popular (perhaps because it seemed to suit him well) that his given name **Simon** became secondary in importance. Note also the common way of identification—referring to a boy or a man with the phrase **son of** (Hb *bēn* or Aram *bar*) attached to the name of his father.

1:47-51 Jesus referred to **Nathanael** as **a true Israelite** in whom there was **no deceit**. Perhaps here there is a play on words between two names—Jacob and Israel. Jacob means "deceiver," and yet here Jesus identified a man from Israel (i.e., the House of Jacob) as one without deceit. Overwhelmed with wonder at the omniscience of Jesus, Nathanael called Him **the Son of God** and **the King of Israel**. Jesus' description of **the angels of God ascending and descending on the Son of Man** recalls Jacob's dream about the ladder to heaven (Gn 28:10-12). As Jacob received an overwhelming blessing from God despite his deceitful life, so Nathanael, in whom there was **no deceit**, could anticipate even more (Jn 1:47,51).

2:4 Woman (Gk *gunai*) was a polite form of address that Jesus used elsewhere to address other women (4:21; 20:13; Mt 15:28; Lk 13:12). His use of this formal noun of address seemed to push the event into a more formalized and thus less intimate relationship. His public ministry had already begun. Family members often use more generic designations of one another in public settings. Jesus might also have been consciously trying to change Mary's thinking as a mother in order to spare her additional suffering when His hour would come. Jesus was still her son during His last hours on the cross, but He was now her Lord as well.

Clearly Mary was not offended by her Son's words, and with confidence she still anticipated that he would

39 "Come and you'll see," He replied. So they went and saw where He was staying, and they stayed with Him that day. It was about 10 in the morning.[A]

40 Andrew, Simon Peter's brother, was one of the two who heard John and followed Him. 41 He first found his own brother Simon and told him, "We have found the Messiah!"[B] (which means "Anointed One"), 42 and he brought Simon to Jesus.

When Jesus saw him, He said, "You are Simon, son of John.[C] You will be called •Cephas" (which means "Rock").

43 The next day He[D] decided to leave for Galilee. Jesus found Philip and told him, "Follow Me!"

44 Now Philip was from Bethsaida, the hometown of Andrew and Peter. 45 Philip found Nathanael[E] and told him, "We have found the One Moses wrote about in the Law (and so did the prophets): Jesus the son of Joseph, from Nazareth!"

46 "Can anything good come out of Nazareth?" Nathanael asked him.

"Come and see," Philip answered.

47 Then Jesus saw Nathanael coming toward Him and said about him, "Here is a true Israelite; no deceit is in him."

48 "How do you know me?" Nathanael asked.

"Before Philip called you, when you were under the fig tree, I saw you," Jesus answered.

49 "Rabbi," Nathanael replied, "You are the Son of God! You are the King of Israel!"

50 Jesus responded to him, "Do you believe only because I told you I saw you under the fig tree? You[F] will see greater things than this." 51 Then He said, "•I assure you: You[G] will see heaven opened and the angels of God ascending and descending on the •Son of Man."

Jesus and Jewish Institutions (2:1–4:54)

Water into Wine—A New Joy (2:1-12)

2 On the third day a wedding took place in Cana of Galilee. Jesus' mother was there, and 2 Jesus and His disciples were invited to the wedding as well. 3 When the wine ran out, Jesus' mother told Him, "They don't have any wine."

4 "What has this concern of yours to do with Me,[H] •woman?" Jesus asked. "My hour[I] has not yet come."

5 "Do whatever He tells you," His mother told the servants.

6 Now six stone water jars had been set there for Jewish purification. Each contained 20 or 30 gallons.[J]

7 "Fill the jars with water," Jesus told them. So they filled them to the brim. 8 Then He said to them, "Now draw some out and take it to the chief servant."[K] And they did.

9 When the chief servant tasted the water (after it had become wine), he did not know where it came from—though the servants who had drawn the water knew. He called the groom 10 and told him, "Everyone sets out the fine wine first, then, after people have drunk freely, the inferior. But you have kept the fine wine until now."

11 Jesus performed this first sign[L] in Cana of Galilee. He displayed His glory, and His disciples believed in Him.

12 After this, He went down to Capernaum, together with His mother, His brothers, and His disciples, and they stayed there only a few days.

[A]**1:39** Lit *about the tenth hour*. Various methods of reckoning time were used in the ancient world. John probably used a different method from the other 3 Gospels. If John used the same method of time reckoning as the other 3 Gospels, the translation would be: *It was about four in the afternoon.* [B]**1:41** In the NT, the word Messiah translates the Gk word *Christos* ("Anointed One"), except here and in Jn 4:25 where it translates *Messias.* [C]**1:42** Other mss read *Simon, son of Jonah* [D]**1:43** Or *he*, referring either to Simon Peter (vv. 41-42) or Andrew (vv. 40-41) [E]**1:45** Probably the Bartholomew of the other Gospels and Acts [F]**1:50** In Gk, the word you is sg and refers to Nathanael. [G]**1:51** In Gk, the word you is pl and refers to Nathanael and the other disciples. [H]**2:4** Or *You and I see things differently*; lit *What to Me and to you*; Mt 8:29; Mk 1:24; 5:7; Lk 8:28 [I]**2:4** The time of His sacrificial death and exaltation; Jn 7:30; 8:20; 12:23,27; 13:1; 17:1 [J]**2:6** Lit *2 or 3 measures* [K]**2:8** Lit *ruler of the table*; perhaps *master of the feast*, or *headwaiter* [L]**2:11** Lit *this beginning of the signs*; Jn 4:54; 20:30. Seven miraculous signs occur in John's Gospel and are so noted in the headings.

Temple Cleansing—A New Temple (2:13-25)

13 The Jewish •Passover was near, so Jesus went up to Jerusalem. 14 In the •temple complex He found people selling oxen, sheep, and doves, and He also found the money changers sitting there. 15 After making a whip out of cords, He drove everyone out of the temple complex with their sheep and oxen. He also poured out the money changers' coins and overturned the tables. 16 He told those who were selling doves, "Get these things out of here! Stop turning My Father's house into a marketplace!"[A]

17 And His disciples remembered that it is written: **Zeal for Your house will consume Me.**[B]

18 So the •Jews replied to Him, "What sign of authority will You show us for doing these things?"

19 Jesus answered, "Destroy this sanctuary, and I will raise it up in three days."

20 Therefore the Jews said, "This sanctuary took 46 years to build, and will You raise it up in three days?"

21 But He was speaking about the sanctuary of His body. 22 So when He was raised from the dead, His disciples remembered that He had said this. And they believed the Scripture and the statement Jesus had made.

23 While He was in Jerusalem at the Passover Festival, many trusted in His name when they saw the signs He was doing. 24 Jesus, however, would not entrust Himself to them, since He knew them all 25 and because He did not need anyone to testify about man; for He Himself knew what was in man.

Jesus, Nicodemus, and the Baptist—A New Birth (3:1-36)

3 There was a man from the •Pharisees named Nicodemus, a ruler of the •Jews. 2 This man came to Him at night and said, "•Rabbi, we know that You have come from God as a teacher, for no one could perform these signs You do unless God were with him."

3 Jesus replied, "•I assure you: Unless someone is born again,[C] he cannot see the kingdom of God."

4 "But how can anyone be born when he is old?" Nicodemus asked Him. "Can he enter his mother's womb a second time and be born?"

5 Jesus answered, "I assure you: Unless someone is born of water and the Spirit,[D] he cannot enter the kingdom of God. 6 Whatever is born of the flesh is flesh, and whatever is born of the Spirit is spirit. 7 Do not be amazed that I told you that you[E] must be born again. 8 The wind[F] blows where it pleases, and you hear its sound, but you don't know where it comes from or where it is going. So it is with everyone born of the Spirit."

9 "How can these things be?" asked Nicodemus.

10 "Are you a teacher[G] of Israel and don't know these things?" Jesus replied. 11 "I assure you: We speak what We know and We testify to what We have seen, but you[H] do not accept Our testimony.[I] 12 If I have told you about things that happen on earth and you don't believe, how will you

Doctrine SALVATION

In Jn 3:16 **life** (Gk *zōēn,* "living thing" in contrast to Gk *bios*, "manner of life" or "period of duration of life") is modified by **eternal** (Gk *aiōnion*, "unending, everlasting, for all time"), a word used only by John in conjunction with life (see vv. 15,36; 4:14,36; 5:24,39; 6:27,40,47,54,68; 10:28; 12:25,50; 17:2-3). The biblical concept of eternal life includes more than immortality. It emphasizes the enduring nature of a quality of life that includes not only the soul but also the body. God created mankind for life and not death. Clearly this concept of eternal life involves an eschatological or future dimension as well as the present reality (3:36; 5:24; 6:47; 1Jn 5:13).

Salvation is a gift for all who believe and trust in the Lord. God is the sole author of salvation. Yet each person has a choice on how he responds. Those who **perish**—i.e., who are confined to eternal punishment—will experience its suffering throughout eternity (Jn 3:16). The experience is one that can never be exhausted because it is perpetual.

intervene in some way, which indeed He did. But He chose to do so without calling attention to the miracle.

2:13-25 This cleansing symbolized that **the temple**, along with the ceremonies and rituals that accompany it, was about to be replaced. Jesus' body represented the new temple.

3:1-3 Nicodemus (Gk, "innocent of blood"), a pious and respected teacher who was a Pharisee and a member of the Sanhedrin, is an example of a person who merely believed in signs without truly understanding Jesus' message (3:1-12). His coming to Jesus **at night** could have been for secrecy to protect his own reputation, to avoid delay of crowds, to ensure privacy in conservation, or simply because he could not wait. The phrase **I assure you** (Gk *amēn*, "truly" or "indeed") is commonly used for emphasis and personal affirmation (vv. 3,5,11).

3:3-8 To be **born** [Gk *gennēthēnai*, "born, begotten"] **again** (Gk *anōthen*, "from above or from heaven, again or anew") includes both the idea of a new beginning and of heavenly source, emphasizing the origin of salvation (Gl 4:19). Nicodemus knew a rebirth was impossible physically, but Jesus pointed to the necessity of spiritual birth as a parallel to physical birth. He used the word **Spirit** (Gk *pneuma*, "power, wind, breath") to carry a double entendre with the emphasis on the power brought with the Spirit as He enters a life. The reference to **water** is not so easily explained. These options are to be considered:

- Water baptism is regenerative in itself, an idea antithetical to the New Testament teaching of salvation by grace. Verse 5 emphatically does not teach baptismal regeneration. One of the most basic principles for interpreting Scripture is that difficult passages must be interpreted in light of what is crystal clear—e.g., Jn 3:16 and Eph 2:8-9.
- Water is a reference to the natural physical birth, which is accompanied by a flow of water.
- Water is a metaphor for God's Word, which does have cleansing quality (Jn 15:3; 1Pt 1:23).
- Water is a metaphor for the washing of regeneration and renewing of the Holy Spirit (Ti 3:5), suggesting that one enters the kingdom of heaven through this process.

Both the second and last options fit within the whole of Scripture.

[A]2:16 Lit *a house of business* [B]2:17 Ps 69:9 [C]3:3 The same Gk word can mean again or from above (also in v. 7). [D]3:5 Or *spirit*, or *wind*; the Gk word *pneuma* can mean *wind*, *spirit*, or *Spirit*, each of which occurs in this context. [E]3:7 The pronoun is pl in Gk. [F]3:8 The Gk word *pneuma* can mean wind, spirit, or Spirit, each of which occurs in this context. [G]3:10 Or *the teacher* [H]3:11 In Gk, the word you is pl here and throughout v. 12. [I]3:11 The pronouns we and our refer to Jesus and His authority to speak for the Father.

3:14-24 Jesus used history to illustrate the salvific message He was preparing to share (v. 14). Moses in the wilderness prefigured the crucifixion by lifting up the bronze serpent in the midst of people who were dying from the venomous bites of the serpents (Nm 21:4-9). The Old Testament event pointed to Jesus who would be lifted up on the cross as the sacrifice necessary for salvation (Jn 3:16-18; 8:28; 12:32-34).

4:1-2 Jesus obviously honored, encouraged, and participated in baptism, having been baptized Himself by John the Baptist (Mt 3:13-17). Yet by His own words, He **was not baptizing**, suggesting this conclusion—baptism is important and not optional but is not necessary for salvation.

4:4-6 John's record that Jesus **had to** [Gk *edei* "must, necessarily, ought, should"] **travel through Samaria**, is a reminder that Jesus never traveled at His own pleasure or because of human pressure; He waited for and received direction from the Father (Ps 40:8).

Located on the main road between Judea and Galilee, about 40 miles north of Jerusalem, **Samaria** was the capital of the territory occupied by the 10 northern tribes of Israel. Israelites living in the northern kingdom did not worship at the Jerusalem temple. They set up a sacrificial system in their own territory. The area has remained hated by the Jews and a trouble spot even in the modern era. The Jews preferred to avoid the route, and most seemed to take alternate routes despite the longer distance.

The Samaritans, a remnant of Jews who intermarried with Gentiles during the Assyrian captivity of the northern kingdom (2Kg 17:5-6,24), were considered by the Jews to be half-breeds. The monotheism of Israel did become dominant, but with innovations, including a rival temple on Mount Gerizim about 40 miles north of Jerusalem (Jn 4:20). A small Samaritan community still worships there. The Samaritans traditionally celebrate Passover outdoors under a full moon to reenact the first Passover as faithfully as possible. At sunset male heads of households take their Passover lambs to the area for sacrifice where their throats are cut simultaneously; the blood is drained from the carcasses; the animals are skinned and roasted. The meal begins about midnight.

Although **Jacob's well** is not mentioned in the Old Testament, the traditional site in ancient **Sychar** is identified in the modern era as it has been for centuries. Gathering water was usually done in early morning or late afternoon and not at noon, the hottest part of the day. Some commentators identify **about six in the evening** as the sixth hour, which

believe if I tell you about things of heaven? 13 No one has ascended into heaven except the One who descended from heaven—the •Son of Man.[A] 14 Just as Moses lifted up the snake in the wilderness, so the Son of Man must be lifted up, 15 so that everyone who believes in Him will[B] have eternal life.

16 "For God loved the world in this way:[C] He gave His •One and Only Son, so that everyone who believes in Him will not perish but have eternal life. 17 For God did not send His Son into the world that He might condemn the world, but that the world might be saved through Him. 18 Anyone who believes in Him is not condemned, but anyone who does not believe is already condemned, because he has not believed in the name of the One and Only Son of God.

19 "This, then, is the judgment: The light has come into the world, and people loved darkness rather than the light because their deeds were evil. 20 For everyone who practices wicked things hates the light and avoids it,[D] so that his deeds may not be exposed. 21 But anyone who lives by[E] the truth comes to the light, so that his works may be shown to be accomplished by God."[F]

22 After this, Jesus and His disciples went to the Judean countryside, where He spent time with them and baptized. 23 John also was baptizing in Aenon near Salim, because there was plenty of water there. People were coming and being baptized, 24 since John had not yet been thrown into prison.

25 Then a dispute arose between John's disciples and a Jew[G] about purification. 26 So they came to John and told him, "Rabbi, the One you testified about, and who was with you across the Jordan, is baptizing—and everyone is flocking to Him."

27 John responded, "No one can receive a single thing unless it's given to him from heaven. 28 You yourselves can testify that I said, 'I am not the •Messiah, but I've been sent ahead of Him.' 29 He who has the bride is the groom. But the groom's friend, who stands by and listens for him, rejoices greatly[H] at the groom's voice. So this joy of mine is complete. 30 He must increase, but I must decrease."

31 The One who comes from above is above all. The one who is from the earth is earthly and speaks in earthly terms.[I] The One who comes from heaven is above all. 32 He testifies to what He has seen and heard, yet no one accepts His testimony. 33 The one who has accepted His testimony has affirmed that God is true. 34 For God sent Him, and He speaks God's words, since He[J] gives the Spirit without measure. 35 The Father loves the Son and has given all things into His hands. 36 The one who believes in the Son has eternal life, but the one who refuses to believe in the Son will not see life; instead, the wrath of God remains on him.

Jesus, the Samaritan Woman, and the Official's Son—A New Diversity of Followers (4:1-54)

4 When Jesus[K] knew that the •Pharisees heard He was making and baptizing more disciples than John 2 (though Jesus Himself was not baptizing, but His disciples were), 3 He left Judea and went again to Galilee. 4 He had to travel through Samaria, 5 so He came to a town of Samaria called Sychar near the property[L] that Jacob had given his son Joseph. 6 Jacob's well was there, and Jesus, worn out from His journey, sat down at the well. It was about six in the evening.[M]

7 A woman of Samaria came to draw water.

"Give Me a drink," Jesus said to her, 8 for His disciples had gone into town to buy food.

[A] **3:13** Other mss add *who is in heaven* [B] **3:15** Other mss add *not perish, but* [C] **3:16** The Gk word *houtos*, commonly translated in Jn 3:16 as "so" or "so much" occurs over 200 times in the NT. Almost without exception it is an adverb of manner, not degree (for example, see Mt 1:18). It only means "so much" when modifying an adjective (see Gl 3:3; Rv 16:18). Manner seems primarily in view in Jn 3:16, which explains the HCSB's rendering. [D] **3:20** Lit *and does not come to the light* [E] **3:21** Lit *who does* [F] **3:21** It is possible that Jesus' words end at v. 15. Ancient Gk did not have quotation marks. [G] **3:25** Other mss read *and the Jews* [H] **3:29** Lit *with joy rejoices* [I] **3:31** Or *of earthly things* [J] **3:34** Other mss read *since God* [K] **4:1** Other mss read *the Lord* [L] **4:5** Lit *piece of land* [M] **4:6** Lit *the sixth hour*; see note at Jn 1:39; an alt time reckoning would be *noon*

CHARACTER PROFILE

The Samaritan Woman Changed by Christ

Her Background	• She lived in Samaria, the region between Judea and Galilee (4:7). • The Samaritans were considered unclean by the Jews.
Her Story	• She came to Jacob's well, in Sychar, to draw water (4:7). • Jesus, who was resting there, asked her to give Him a drink (4:8-26). • She was surprised He would speak to her, since He was a Jewish man and she was a Samaritan woman (4:9). • Jesus engaged her in conversation and offered her "living water" (4:10-14). • She quickly ran into town to tell others about Jesus, the Messiah (4:28-29).
Life Lesson	Anyone whose life has been changed by Christ will want to share that news.

9 "How is it that You, a Jew, ask for a drink from me, a •Samaritan woman?" she asked Him. For Jews do not associate with[A] Samaritans.[B]

10 Jesus answered, "If you knew the gift of God, and who is saying to you, 'Give Me a drink,' you would ask Him, and He would give you living water."

11 "Sir," said the woman, "You don't even have a bucket, and the well is deep. So where do You get this 'living water'? 12 You aren't greater than our father Jacob, are You? He gave us the well and drank from it himself, as did his sons and livestock."

13 Jesus said, "Everyone who drinks from this water will get thirsty again. 14 But whoever drinks from the water that I will give him will never get thirsty again—ever! In fact, the water I will give him will become a well[C] of water springing up within him for eternal life."

15 "Sir," the woman said to Him, "give me this water so I won't get thirsty and come here to draw water."

16 "Go call your husband," He told her, "and come back here."

17 "I don't have a husband," she answered.

"You have correctly said, 'I don't have a husband,'" Jesus said. 18 "For you've had five husbands, and the man you now have is not your husband. What you have said is true."

19 "Sir," the woman replied, "I see that You are a prophet. 20 Our fathers worshiped on this mountain,[D] yet

[A]4:9 Or *do not share vessels with Samaritans.* [B]4:9 Other mss omit *For Jews do not associate with Samaritans.* [C]4:14 Or *spring* [D]4:20 Mount Gerizim, where there had been a Samaritan temple that rivaled Jerusalem's

if determined from 6 a.m. would mean noon; but according to the Roman plan, the time would be reclaimed either from midnight or noon, making the hour—whether early morning or late afternoon—more appropriate for hauling water. Whether the woman was fetching water at the usual time or deliberately going midday to avoid other people matters not. The fact that the presence of others was not mentioned might make the latter a more reasonable explanation.

4:7-9 Perhaps the phrase, **for Jews do not associate** [Gk *sugchrōntai*, "having dealings with or associating on friendly terms"] **with Samaritans,** had more to do with sharing vessels for food or, as here, for drink. However, Jesus broke social and religious norms in three significant ways:

- He spoke to **a woman**;
- He interacted with someone from a different ethnic and religious background (and one despised by the Jews);
- He associated with someone who had indulged in immoral behavior (v. 17).

John showed the absolute impartiality of the gospel message, which ignores social and religious boundaries and is extended to all.

4:10-15 Jesus turned the conversation to spiritual matters. For Jewish purification rituals, flowing water was often preferred to well water, and the reference may mean "flowing [i.e., "living"] water." In the Old Testament *Yahweh* is referred to as "the fountain of living water" (Jr 2:13; 17:13). Jesus compared the indwelling of the Holy Spirit to "streams of living water" (Jn 7:38)—an endless supply.

4:16-42 Jesus then focused on the woman's personal life (vv. 16-19). Not only does Jesus' omniscience come into play, but Jesus also demonstrated His compassion even for the outcasts of society. Yet He required them to repent since repentance is the necessary condition for all who come to him. The woman was impressed by Jesus' ability

BIBLICAL WOMANHOOD A Woman's Worth and Mission

Jesus' disciples were shocked to find Him **talking with a woman** (4:27). John does not leave out the equally challenging details about the power of her testimony bringing **the men** (vv. 28-30) and **many Samaritans** from her town to believe in Jesus as the Messiah and **Savior of the world** (vv. 39-42). Jesus' deliberate interaction with the Samaritan woman and His categorizing His conversation with her as doing His Father's will and work (v. 34) reveal God's love for each woman as an individual, a person of inestimable value. Jesus exhorted His disciples to recognize the **fields . . . ready for** [spiritual] **harvest** (v. 35), emphasizing the urgency of harvesting souls. Not only is the good news of salvation in Christ intended for women, but the Lord of the harvest takes delight in expanding His kingdom through the testimony of women who have experienced His life-transforming forgiveness and will proclaim—joyfully, unabashedly, and without hesitation—who Jesus is and what He has done.

to penetrate her life and thoughts. She not only responded to the invitation to take the "living water," but she also went out and told everyone she saw that she had met a man who told her everything she ever did (vv. 28-29).

Despite the woman's attempt to change the subject, she was moved to take the conversation precisely where Jesus wanted it to go (vv. 20-24). As a result, Jesus accomplished His purpose to bring her to salvation. John's purpose was also served: He showed Jesus Himself as being the replacement for all holy places. Jesus described **God** as **Spirit**. He has no limitations of time and space (i.e., He is omnipresent).

Jesus revealed Himself as the **Messiah** whom the Jews of Samaria were expecting because there were prophecies about Him in the Pentateuch (vv. 25-26). He came into the world as one from the lineage of David and from the tribe of Judah (v. 22). However, because they rejected the rest of the Old Testament, their understanding was flawed and incomplete. Jesus identified Himself as **the One** (v. 26). The woman acknowledged this but with little understanding of what that meant. Even the disciples called Jesus "Messiah" before they came to an adequate understanding of what that designation really meant. The title "Messiah" in the Old Testament, as the title "Christ" in the New Testament, was connected to the announcement of a coming "anointed one." Jesus continued to reveal Himself as the woman began to grow in her understanding of who He is. How affirming of John's stated purpose (Jn 20:31) for other Samaritans to come to believe through her testimony (4:42).

4:46-54 Since John identifies this event as the **second sign Jesus performed after He came from Judea to Galilee** (v. 54), the two events in Cana (cp. 2:11) would seem to be related in some way. Whether a Jew or Gentile, the **royal official** surprisingly sought the help of Jesus, the son of a humble carpenter (vv. 46-47). Like the healing of the centurion's servant (Mt 8:5-13; Lk 7:1-10), Jesus healed the man's son only by saying the word (cp. Mt 8:8). This event demonstrates that miraculous signs can produce faith. In the ancient world, a man's **whole household** would include his immediate and extended family as well as servants (Jn 4:53). The head of the household would obviously be very influential in determining the spiritual direction of those who found shelter under his roof. Certainly there was no way to enter the household of faith without believing, and the verb (Gk *pisteusen*, "believe") would affirm that understanding.

5:1–10:21 Chapters 5–10 represent another literary unit, describing the

you Jews say that the place to worship is in Jerusalem."

21 Jesus told her, "Believe Me, •woman, an hour is coming when you will worship the Father neither on this mountain nor in Jerusalem. 22 You Samaritans[A] worship what you do not know. We worship what we do know, because salvation is from the Jews. 23 But an hour is coming, and is now here, when the true worshipers will worship the Father in spirit and truth. Yes, the Father wants such people to worship Him. 24 God is spirit, and those who worship Him must worship in spirit and truth."

25 The woman said to Him, "I know that •Messiah[B] is coming" (who is called Christ). "When He comes, He will explain everything to us."

26 "I am He," Jesus told her, "the One speaking to you."

27 Just then His disciples arrived, and they were amazed that He was talking with a woman. Yet no one said, "What do You want?" or "Why are You talking with her?"

28 Then the woman left her water jar, went into town, and told the men, 29 "Come, see a man who told me everything I ever did! Could this be the Messiah?" 30 They left the town and made their way to Him.

31 In the meantime the disciples kept urging Him, "•Rabbi, eat something."

32 But He said, "I have food to eat that you don't know about."

33 The disciples said to one another, "Could someone have brought Him something to eat?"

34 "My food is to do the will of Him who sent Me and to finish His work," Jesus told them. 35 "Don't you say, 'There are still four more months, then comes the harvest'? Listen to what I'm telling you: Open[C] your eyes and look at the fields, for they are ready[D] for harvest. 36 The reaper is already receiving pay and gathering fruit for eternal life, so the sower and reaper can rejoice together. 37 For in this case the saying is true: 'One sows and another reaps.' 38 I sent you to reap what you didn't labor for; others have labored, and you have benefited from[E] their labor."

39 Now many Samaritans from that town believed in Him because of what the woman said[F] when she testified, "He told me everything I ever did." 40 Therefore, when the Samaritans came to Him, they asked Him to stay with them, and He stayed there two days. 41 Many more believed because of what He said.[G] 42 And they told the woman, "We no longer believe because of what you said, for we have heard for ourselves and know that this really is the Savior of the world."[H]

43 After two days He left there for Galilee. 44 Jesus Himself testified that a prophet has no honor in his own country. 45 When they entered Galilee, the Galileans welcomed Him because they had seen everything He did in Jerusalem during the festival. For they also had gone to the festival.

46 Then He went again to Cana of Galilee, where He had turned the water into wine. There was a certain royal official whose son was ill at Capernaum. 47 When this man heard that Jesus had come from Judea into Galilee, he went to Him and pleaded with Him to come down and heal his son, for he was about to die.

48 Jesus told him, "Unless you people see signs and wonders, you will not believe."

49 "Sir," the official said to Him, "come down before my boy dies!"

50 "Go," Jesus told him, "your son will live." The man believed what[I] Jesus said to him and departed.

51 While he was still going down, his •slaves met him saying that his boy was alive. 52 He asked them at what time he got better. "Yesterday at seven in the morning[J] the fever left him," they answered. 53 The father realized this was the very hour at which Jesus had told him, "Your son will live." Then he himself be-

[A]**4:22** *Samaritans* is implied since the Gk verb and pronoun are pl. [B]**4:25** In the NT, the word Messiah translates the Gk word *Christos* ("Anointed One"), except here and in Jn 1:41 where it translates *Messias*. [C]**4:35** Lit *Raise* [D]**4:35** Lit *white* [E]**4:38** Lit *you have entered into* [F]**4:39** Lit *because of the woman's word* [G]**4:41** Lit *because of His word* [H]**4:42** Other mss add *the Messiah* [I]**4:50** Lit *the word* [J]**4:52** Or *seven in the evening*; lit *at the seventh hour*; see note at Jn 1:39; an alt time reckoning would be *at one in the afternoon*

lieved, along with his whole household.

54 This, therefore, was the second
sign Jesus performed after He came
from Judea to Galilee.

Jesus and Jewish Festivals (5:1–10:21)

Healing The Paralytic and Imitating the Father (5:1-47)

5 After this, a Jewish festival took
place, and Jesus went up to Jerusalem. 2 By the Sheep Gate in
Jerusalem there is a pool, called
Bethesda[A] in •Hebrew, which has
five colonnades.[B] 3 Within these lay
a large number of the sick—blind,
lame, and paralyzed [—waiting for
the moving of the water, 4 because
an angel would go down into the
pool from time to time and stir up
the water. Then the first one who
got in after the water was stirred up
recovered from whatever ailment he
had].[C]

5 One man was there who had been
sick for 38 years. 6 When Jesus saw
him lying there and knew he had
already been there a long time, He
said to him, "Do you want to get
well?"

7 "Sir," the sick man answered,
"I don't have a man to put me into
the pool when the water is stirred
up, but while I'm coming, someone
goes down ahead of me."

8 "Get up," Jesus told him, "pick up
your mat and walk!" 9 Instantly the
man got well, picked up his mat, and
started to walk.

Now that day was the Sabbath,
10 so the •Jews said to the man who
had been healed, "This is the Sabbath! It's illegal for you to pick up
your mat."

11 He replied, "The man who made
me well told me, 'Pick up your mat
and walk.'"

12 "Who is this man who told you,
'Pick up your mat and walk'?" they
asked. 13 But the man who was cured
did not know who it was, because
Jesus had slipped away into the
crowd that was there.[D]

14 After this, Jesus found him in
the •temple complex and said to
him, "See, you are well. Do not sin
anymore, so that something worse
doesn't happen to you." 15 The man
went and reported to the Jews that
it was Jesus who had made him well.

16 Therefore, the Jews began persecuting Jesus[E] because He was doing
these things on the Sabbath. 17 But
Jesus responded to them, "My Father is still working, and I am working also." 18 This is why the Jews
began trying all the more to kill
Him: Not only was He breaking the
Sabbath, but He was even calling
God His own Father, making Himself equal with God.

19 Then Jesus replied, "•I assure
you: The Son is not able to do anything on His own, but only what He
sees the Father doing. For whatever
the Father[F] does, the Son also does
these things in the same way. 20 For
the Father loves the Son and shows
Him everything He is doing, and He
will show Him greater works than
these so that you will be amazed.
21 And just as the Father raises the
dead and gives them life, so the Son
also gives life to anyone He wants to.
22 The Father, in fact, judges no one
but has given all judgment to the
Son, 23 so that all people will honor
the Son just as they honor the Father. Anyone who does not honor
the Son does not honor the Father
who sent Him.

24 "I assure you: Anyone who hears
My word and believes Him who sent
Me has eternal life and will not come
under judgment but has passed
from death to life.

25 "I assure you: An hour is coming, and is now here, when the dead
will hear the voice of the Son of God,
and those who hear will live. 26 For
just as the Father has life in Himself,
so also He has granted to the Son to
have life in Himself. 27 And He has
granted Him the right to pass judgment, because He is the •Son of
Man. 28 Do not be amazed at this, because a time is coming when all who
are in the graves will hear His voice
29 and come out—those who have
done good things, to the resurrection of life, but those who have done

[A]5:2 Other mss read *Bethzatha*; other mss read *Bethsaida* [B]5:2 Rows of columns supporting a roof [C]5:3-4 Other mss omit bracketed text [D]5:13 Lit *slipped away, there being a crowd in that place* [E]5:16 Other mss add *and trying to kill Him* [F]5:19 Lit *whatever that One*

events that took place when Jesus was in Jerusalem for the religious festivals and supplementing the Synoptic record of Jesus' Galilean ministry. John meticulously shows that Jesus is the fulfillment of the Jewish festivals: Passover, Tabernacles, and Hanukkah (Dedication). In John's Gospel the feeding of the 5,000 and Jesus' walking on water, which did not occur in Jerusalem, are recorded as taking place around the time of the Passover and followed by Jesus' discourse on "the bread of life" (chap. 6), in which the symbolism is closely related to the bread of the Passover meal.

5:1-18 The healing of this paralytic on the Sabbath sparked a controversy with the Jewish leaders, who began to plot how they might kill Jesus (vv. 17-18).

The Sheep Gate was one of the entrances carved into Jerusalem's city wall. The pools were actually deep stone reservoirs collecting rainwater to be used for drinking and other necessities. Water has always been a precious resource in the Middle East. The **pool** named **Bethesda** (Hb, "house of mercy, house of flowing water") was especially prominent as a gathering place for **the sick** and maimed because the people believed healing properties were in its waters (v. 3). The tradition concerning **the moving of the water** is not found in extant Greek manuscripts dated prior to A.D. 400. This brief section (parts of vv. 3-4) may have been based on popular tradition and thus have been added by a scribe as an effort to explain the bubbly flow of the water that occurred from time to time (v. 7). This insignificant textual problem does not undercut the miracle or clear meaning of the text in any way.

Near the modern church of St. Anne is a group of pools many archaeologists have identified as this popular ancient site. At this pool Jesus singled out a man and asked if he wanted to **get well** (v. 6). Jesus presupposed a relationship between the man's illness and past sin (v. 14). What that sin might have been is not indicated. John made no mention of the man's response to Jesus after their second encounter but reported that the Jews began to persecute Jesus as a result of His healing the man on the Sabbath. The man's negative attitude was apparent and seemingly did not change. He was so indifferent and ungrateful that he did not even inquire about Jesus' identity (v. 13).

5:16-41 Jesus' disregard for Sabbath regulations was not the only thing upsetting the Jewish religious leaders. They actually sought His life because of His **calling God His own Father**, thus **making Himself equal with God** (v. 18). John, of course, states his own purpose as showing that Jesus is indeed the Son of God (20:31).

The parallel between **the Son** and **the Father** is continually asserted by John. Never is the Son purported to be in charge of the Father, but He is sent by the Father, obedient to the Father, committed to glorifying the Father (5:23,27,30; 6:44; 8:28-29). The Son was given power by the Father to render judgment (5:27). Jesus describes His relationship with the Father as being one in which He is *ontologically* (of the same essence or being) equal with the Father yet *functionally* subordinate to Him.

Human action is a manifestation of human commitment (v. 29; see also Eph 2:10; Jms 2:14-17). But there is no hint of a salvation by works. These verses are among the few eschatological references in John. The idea is that human works simply bear testimony to decisions in the hearts of individuals—whether to follow righteousness or wickedness.

Jesus presented four witnesses that affirmed His claims (Jn 5:31-47): **John** the Baptist (vv. 33-35); His own **works** (v. 36); **the Father** (vv. 37-38); and **the Scriptures** (vv. 39-47). The Jews were tied to the legacy of the great lawgiver **Moses** (v. 45).

Jesus affirmed that Moses **wrote** Scripture (v. 46), and these verses are critically important to affirming Jesus' view of Scripture. He believed that Moses wrote the Pentateuch. Either He was wrong or He accommodated Himself to the Jewish tradition or He was correct in affirming the Mosaic authorship of the Torah. The latter, of course, is the only option consistent with His deity.

6:1-15 The **mountain** Jesus ascended was east of the **Sea of Galilee**, an area known as the Golan Heights (v. 3). The feeding of the 5,000 is the one miracle recorded by all the Gospel writers (Mt 14:15; Mk 6:35; Lk 9:12).

6:16-21 The **disciples** still showed spiritual immaturity as in the midst of a storm Jesus came to them, still reassuring (v. 19). Characteristically, John uses these fourth and fifth miraculous signs to introduce another lengthy discourse from Jesus. Only Luke does not mention the "walking on the water miracle" (Mt 14:25; Mk 6:48).

6:22-26 This "Bread of Life" discourse (6:22-40) functions in John's narrative in much the same way that the parable of the sower did in the Synoptic Gospels. Jesus used this discourse as a "weeding out" tool to separate true believers from those who followed Him merely to benefit from His miracles. Also, the discourse clearly communicates that Jesus, as the Bread of Life, is the true fulfillment of the Passover, a festival mentioned elsewhere in John (2:13,23; 7:2; 11:55; 12:1; 13:1; 18:28,39; 10:14).

wicked things, to the resurrection of judgment.

30 "I can do nothing on My own. I judge only as I hear, and My judgment is righteous, because I do not seek My own will, but the will of Him who sent Me.

31 "If I testify about Myself, My testimony is not valid.[A] 32 There is Another who testifies about Me, and I know that the testimony He gives about Me is valid.[B] 33 You have sent messengers to John, and he has testified to the truth. 34 I don't receive man's testimony, but I say these things so that you may be saved. 35 John[C] was a burning and shining lamp, and for a time you were willing to enjoy his light.

36 "But I have a greater testimony than John's because of the works that the Father has given Me to accomplish. These very works I am doing testify about Me that the Father has sent Me. 37 The Father who sent Me has Himself testified about Me. You have not heard His voice at any time, and you haven't seen His form. 38 You don't have His word living in you, because you don't believe the One He sent. 39 You pore over[D] the Scriptures because you think you have eternal life in them, yet they testify about Me. 40 And you are not willing to come to Me so that you may have life.

41 "I do not accept glory from men, 42 but I know you—that you have no love for God within you. 43 I have come in My Father's name, yet you don't accept Me. If someone else comes in his own name, you will accept him. 44 How can you believe? While accepting glory from one another, you don't seek the glory that comes from the only God. 45 Do not think that I will accuse you to the Father. Your accuser is Moses, on whom you have set your hope. 46 For if you believed Moses, you would believe Me, because he wrote about Me. 47 But if you don't believe his writings, how will you believe My words?"

The True Passover: The Bread of Life (6:1-71)

6 After this, Jesus crossed the Sea of Galilee (or Tiberias). 2 And a huge crowd was following Him because they saw the signs that He was performing by healing the sick. 3 So Jesus went up a mountain and sat down there with His disciples.

4 Now the •Passover, a Jewish festival, was near. 5 Therefore, when Jesus looked up and noticed a huge crowd coming toward Him, He asked Philip, "Where will we buy bread so these people can eat?" 6 He asked this to test him, for He Himself knew what He was going to do.

7 Philip answered, "Two hundred •denarii worth of bread wouldn't be enough for each of them to have a little."

8 One of His disciples, Andrew, Simon Peter's brother, said to Him, 9 "There's a boy here who has five barley loaves and two fish—but what are they for so many?"

10 Then Jesus said, "Have the people sit down."

There was plenty of grass in that place, so they sat down. The men numbered about 5,000. 11 Then Jesus took the loaves, and after giving thanks He distributed them to those who were seated—so also with the fish, as much as they wanted.

12 When they were full, He told His disciples, "Collect the leftovers so that nothing is wasted." 13 So they collected them and filled 12 baskets with the pieces from the five barley loaves that were left over by those who had eaten.

14 When the people saw the sign[E] He had done, they said, "This really is the Prophet who was to come into the world!" 15 Therefore, when Jesus knew that they were about to come and take Him by force to make Him king, He withdrew again[F] to the mountain by Himself.

16 When evening came, His disciples went down to the sea, 17 got into a boat, and started across the sea to Capernaum. Darkness had already set in, but Jesus had not yet come to them. 18 Then a high wind

[A] **5:31** Or *not true* [B] **5:32** Or *true* [C] **5:35** Lit *That man* [D] **5:39** In Gk this could be a command: *Pore over . . .* [E] **6:14** Other mss read *signs* [F] **6:15** A previous withdrawal is mentioned in Mk 6:31-32, an event that occurred just before the feeding of the 5,000.

arose, and the sea began to churn. 19 After they had rowed about three or four miles,[A] they saw Jesus walking on the sea. He was coming near the boat, and they were afraid.

20 But He said to them, "It is I.[B] Don't be afraid!" 21 Then they were willing to take Him on board, and at once the boat was at the shore where they were heading.

22 The next day, the crowd that had stayed on the other side of the sea knew there had been only one boat.[C] They also knew that Jesus had not boarded the boat with His disciples, but that His disciples had gone off alone. 23 Some boats from Tiberias came near the place where they ate the bread after the Lord gave thanks. 24 When the crowd saw that neither Jesus nor His disciples were there, they got into the boats and went to Capernaum looking for Jesus.

25 When they found Him on the other side of the sea, they said to Him, "•Rabbi, when did You get here?"

26 Jesus answered, "•I assure you: You are looking for Me, not because you saw[D] the signs, but because you ate the loaves and were filled. 27 Don't work for the food that perishes but for the food that lasts for eternal life, which the •Son of Man will give you, because God the Father has set His seal of approval on Him."

28 "What can we do to perform the works of God?" they asked.

29 Jesus replied, "This is the work of God—that you believe in the One He has sent."

30 "What sign then are You going to do so we may see and believe You?" they asked. "What are You going to perform? 31 Our fathers ate the manna in the wilderness, just as it is written: **He gave them bread from heaven to eat.**"[E,F]

32 Jesus said to them, "I assure you: Moses didn't give you the bread from heaven, but My Father gives you the real bread from heaven. 33 For the bread of God is the One who comes down from heaven and gives life to the world."

34 Then they said, "Sir, give us this bread always!"

35 "I am the bread of life," Jesus told them. "No one who comes to Me will ever be hungry, and no one who believes in Me will ever be thirsty again. 36 But as I told you, you've seen Me,[G] and yet you do not believe. 37 Everyone the Father gives Me will come to Me, and the one who comes to Me I will never cast out. 38 For I have come down from heaven, not to do My will, but the will of Him who sent Me. 39 This is the will of Him who sent Me: that I should lose none of those He has given Me but should raise them up on the last day. 40 For this is the will of My Father: that everyone who sees the Son and believes in Him may have eternal life, and I will raise him up on the last day."

41 Therefore the •Jews started complaining about Him because He said, "I am the bread that came down from heaven." 42 They were saying, "Isn't this Jesus the son of Joseph, whose father and mother we know? How can He now say, 'I have come down from heaven'?"

43 Jesus answered them, "Stop complaining among yourselves. 44 No one can come to Me unless the Father who sent Me draws[H] him, and I will raise him up on the last day. 45 It is written in the Prophets: **And they will all be taught by God.**[I] Everyone who has listened to and learned from the Father comes to Me— 46 not that anyone has seen the Father except the One who is from God. He has seen the Father.

47 "I assure you: Anyone who believes[J] has eternal life. 48 I am the bread of life. 49 Your fathers ate the manna in the wilderness, and they died. 50 This is the bread that comes down from heaven so that anyone may eat of it and not die. 51 I am the living bread that came down from heaven. If anyone eats of this bread he will live forever. The bread that I

6:30-33 One must have faith in Jesus Himself. Faith based on the performing of miracles is not enough. A contrast is made between Jesus and Moses, under whose leadership God supplied **manna** to feed the Israelites as they left Egypt and made their journey through **the wilderness** for 40 years. "Manna"—a small, round wafer that appeared with the morning dew—was gathered by the people, made into cakes, and baked or boiled (Ex 16:13-36). The Old Testament "manna" was a prototype pointing to Jesus, the **real bread from heaven** who would provide unfailing sustenance and satisfaction (Jn 6:32-33).

6:35 "I am the bread of life" is the first of seven "I am" axioms, which are recorded only in John. The metaphors Jesus used include:

- "the bread of life" (6:35,41,48,51);
- "the light of the world" (8:12);
- "door of the sheep" (10:7,9);
- "the good shepherd" (10:11,14);
- "the resurrection and the life" (11:25);
- "the way, truth, and the life" (14:6); and
- "the true vine" (15:1,5).

6:37-40 True followers of Christ have great assurance because Christ will not lose a single one the Father **has given** Him. These verses support the eternal security of the believer. However, one must not ignore the immediate context of these verses. Only those who are true believers are secure. Hence, you must make sure that your faith is based solely on Christ Himself and not merely on His miracles.

6:51-58 There has been much debate concerning the meaning of eating Christ's **flesh** and drinking His **blood**. Some have argued that these words are a reference to the Eucharist. However, nothing in the immediate context warrants this interpretation. Rather, eating Christ's flesh and drinking His blood are vivid metaphors describing the kind of relationship true believers must have with Christ. The necessity of food intake in the physical realm carries over as analogous to receiving Christ (i.e., partaking of His body in a figurative sense, in order to have spiritual life). Jesus' followers must be willing to identify with Him and assimilate His life within their own lives so that they will be willing to suffer and die with Him.

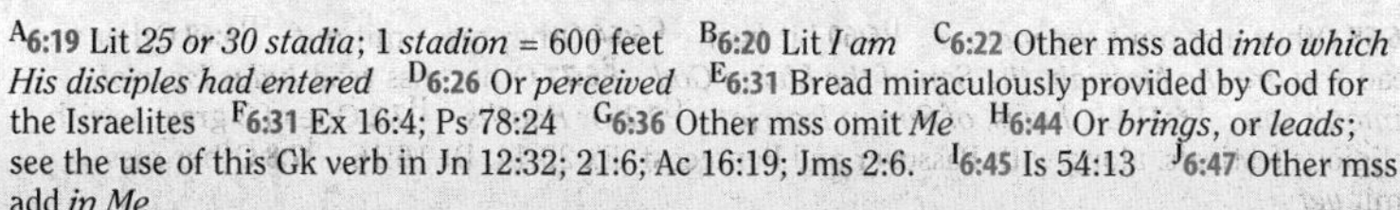
[A]**6:19** Lit *25 or 30 stadia*; 1 *stadion* = 600 feet [B]**6:20** Lit *I am* [C]**6:22** Other mss add *into which His disciples had entered* [D]**6:26** Or *perceived* [E]**6:31** Bread miraculously provided by God for the Israelites [F]**6:31** Ex 16:4; Ps 78:24 [G]**6:36** Other mss omit *Me* [H]**6:44** Or *brings*, or *leads*; see the use of this Gk verb in Jn 12:32; 21:6; Ac 16:19; Jms 2:6. [I]**6:45** Is 54:13 [J]**6:47** Other mss add *in Me*

6:60-67 Clearly not many who were following Jesus at the time were willing to so identify themselves with Him. Many walked away because the teaching was too **hard**. After this, Jesus addressed **the Twelve**.

6:68-71 These verses represent the kind of confession given by Peter in the Synoptic Gospels. Jesus is **the Holy One of God**, and He alone has **the words of eternal life**. Thus, John was presenting the Twelve as *true* followers of Christ because they were the ones who stuck with Him.

7:1–9:41 Chapters 7–9 are intended to show Jesus as the fulfillment of the Festival of Tabernacles or Festival of Ingathering or Festival of Booths, celebrated "on the fifteenth day of the seventh month" (Lv 23:34) and beginning five days after the Day of Atonement (*Yom Kippur*) for seven days (Lv 23:33-36; Dt 16:13-17). Each family gathered in Jerusalem and built temporary shelters or booths in which they would live during the entire festival. This temporary housing was symbolic of the years the Israelites spent wandering in the desert after leaving slavery in Egypt before entering Canaan, and these dwellings represented shelter and protection. The festival was a time of thanksgiving for the harvest that marked their transition from nomadic living to more permanent housing in their own land. John's allusion to the festivals highlighted the way Jesus fulfilled the Old Testament celebration and added to them ongoing spiritual significance.

7:1-9 John begins this section by juxtaposing the true belief of the disciples (6:68-71) with the unbelief of Jesus' own brothers (7:1-5). The perpetual virginity of Mary advocated by some is certainly challenged in the references to **His** [Jesus'] **brothers**—other sons of Mary and Joseph (v. 3; 2:12; Mk 3:21,31-35; 6:3). A similar scene is recorded in Mk 3:20-35, in which Jesus' family members came to silence Him because they believed He was out of His mind. In John's narrative, this contrast between belief and unbelief, displayed respectively by the Twelve and by Jesus' brothers, foreshadows similar things to come as Jesus later went alone to the festival (Jn 7:10).

7:10-24 Jesus responded to the question concerning the origin of His teachings (vv. 15-16). The Jewish leaders could not understand how Jesus could know the Scripture so thoroughly, teach with clarity, and speak with authority without formal training in rabbinical schools.

Jesus responded quickly and decisively that His **teaching** was vested in the authority of **the One who sent** Him (v. 16). Jesus also placed squarely

will give for the life of the world is My flesh."

52 At that, the Jews argued among themselves, "How can this man give us His flesh to eat?"

53 So Jesus said to them, "I assure you: Unless you eat the flesh of the Son of Man and drink His blood, you do not have life in yourselves. 54 Anyone who eats My flesh and drinks My blood has eternal life, and I will raise him up on the last day, 55 because My flesh is real food and My blood is real drink. 56 The one who eats My flesh and drinks My blood lives in Me, and I in him. 57 Just as the living Father sent Me and I live because of the Father, so the one who feeds on Me will live because of Me. 58 This is the bread that came down from heaven; it is not like the manna[A] your fathers ate—and they died. The one who eats this bread will live forever."

59 He said these things while teaching in the •synagogue in Capernaum.

60 Therefore, when many of His disciples heard this, they said, "This teaching is hard! Who can accept[B] it?"

61 Jesus, knowing in Himself that His disciples were complaining about this, asked them, "Does this •offend you? 62 Then what if you were to observe the Son of Man ascending to where He was before? 63 The Spirit is the One who gives life. The flesh doesn't help at all. The words that I have spoken to you are spirit and are life. 64 But there are some among you who don't believe." (For Jesus knew from the beginning those who would not[C] believe and the one who would betray Him.) 65 He said, "This is why I told you that no one can come to Me unless it is granted to him by the Father."

66 From that moment many of His disciples turned back and no longer accompanied Him. 67 Therefore Jesus said to the Twelve, "You don't want to go away too, do you?"

68 Simon Peter answered, "Lord, who will we go to? You have the words of eternal life. 69 We have come to believe and know that You are the Holy One of God!"[D]

70 Jesus replied to them, "Didn't I choose you, the Twelve? Yet one of you is the Devil!" 71 He was referring to Judas, Simon Iscariot's son,[E,F] one of the Twelve, because he was going to betray Him.

The True Tabernacles: Living Water and Light of the World (7:1–9:41)

7 After this, Jesus traveled in Galilee, since He did not want to travel in Judea because the •Jews were trying to kill Him. 2 The Jewish Festival of Tabernacles[G,H] was near, 3 so His brothers said to Him, "Leave here and go to Judea so Your disciples can see Your works that You are doing. 4 For no one does anything in secret while he's seeking public recognition. If You do these things, show Yourself to the world." 5 (For not even His brothers believed in Him.)

6 Jesus told them, "My time has not yet arrived, but your time is always at hand. 7 The world cannot hate you, but it does hate Me because I testify about it—that its deeds are evil. 8 Go up to the festival yourselves. I'm not going up to the festival yet,[I] because My time has not yet fully come." 9 After He had said these things, He stayed in Galilee.

10 After His brothers had gone up to the festival, then He also went up, not openly but secretly. 11 The Jews were looking for Him at the festival and saying, "Where is He?" 12 And there was a lot of discussion about Him among the crowds. Some were saying, "He's a good man." Others were saying, "No, on the contrary, He's deceiving the people." 13 Still, nobody was talking publicly about Him because they feared the Jews.

14 When the festival was already half over, Jesus went up into the •temple complex and began to teach. 15 Then the Jews were amazed and said, "How does He know the Scriptures, since He hasn't been trained?"

16 Jesus answered them, "My teaching isn't Mine but is from the One

[A]6:58 Other mss omit *the manna* [B]6:60 Lit *hear* [C]6:64 Other mss omit *not* [D]6:69 Other mss read *You are the Messiah, the Son of the Living God* [E]6:71 Other mss read *Judas Iscariot, Simon's son* [F]6:71 Lit *Judas, of Simon Iscariot* [G]7:2 Or *Booths* [H]7:2 One of 3 great Jewish religious festivals, along with Passover and Pentecost; Ex 23:14; Dt 16:16 [I]7:8 Other mss omit *yet*

who sent Me. 17 If anyone wants to do
His will, he will understand whether
the teaching is from God or if I am
speaking on My own. 18 The one who
speaks for himself seeks his own
glory. But He who seeks the glory of
the One who sent Him is true, and
there is no unrighteousness in Him.
19 Didn't Moses give you the law? Yet
none of you keeps the law! Why do
you want to kill Me?"
20 "You have a demon!" the crowd
responded. "Who wants to kill You?"
21 "I did one work, and you are all
amazed," Jesus answered. 22 "Consider this: Moses has given you circumcision—not that it comes from
Moses but from the fathers—and
you circumcise a man on the Sabbath. 23 If a man receives circumcision on the Sabbath so that the law
of Moses won't be broken, are you
angry at Me because I made a man
entirely well on the Sabbath? 24 Stop
judging according to outward appearances; rather judge according
to righteous judgment."
25 Some of the people of Jerusalem were saying, "Isn't this the man
they want to kill? 26 Yet, look! He's
speaking publicly and they're saying nothing to Him. Can it be true
that the authorities know He is the
•Messiah? 27 But we know where this
man is from. When the Messiah
comes, nobody will know where He
is from."
28 As He was teaching in the temple complex, Jesus cried out, "You
know Me and you know where I am
from. Yet I have not come on My
own, but the One who sent Me is
true. You don't know Him; 29 I know
Him because I am from Him, and He
sent Me."
30 Then they tried to seize Him. Yet
no one laid a hand on Him because
His hour[A] had not yet come. 31 However, many from the crowd believed
in Him and said, "When the Messiah comes, He won't perform more
signs than this man has done, will
He?"
32 The •Pharisees heard the crowd
muttering these things about Him,
so the •chief priests and the Pharisees sent temple police to arrest
Him.
33 Then Jesus said, "I am only with
you for a short time. Then I'm going to the One who sent Me. 34 You
will look for Me, but you will not
find Me; and where I am, you cannot come."
35 Then the Jews said to one another, "Where does He intend to go
so we won't find Him? He doesn't intend to go to the Dispersion[B] among
the Greeks and teach the Greeks,
does He? 36 What is this remark He
made: 'You will look for Me, and you
will not find Me; and where I am,
you cannot come'?"
37 On the last and most important
day of the festival, Jesus stood up
and cried out, "If anyone is thirsty,
he should come to Me[C] and drink!
38 The one who believes in Me, as
the Scripture has said,[D] will have
streams of living water flow from
deep within him." 39 He said this
about the Spirit. Those who believed
in Jesus were going to receive the
Spirit, for the Spirit[E] had not yet
been received[F,G] because Jesus had
not yet been glorified.
40 When some from the crowd
heard these words, they said, "This
really is the Prophet!"[H] 41 Others
said, "This is the Messiah!" But
some said, "Surely the Messiah
doesn't come from Galilee, does He?
42 Doesn't the Scripture say that the
Messiah comes from David's offspring[I] and from the town of Bethlehem, where David once lived?"
43 So a division occurred among the
crowd because of Him. 44 Some of
them wanted to seize Him, but no
one laid hands on Him.
45 Then the temple police came
to the chief priests and Pharisees,
who asked them, "Why haven't you
brought Him?"
46 The police answered, "No man
ever spoke like this!"[J]

upon His accusers the responsibility for determining "the work of God" (6:28-29), which if they had done would have revealed that indeed His teaching was from God (vv. 17-18). In so doing Jesus reached to the heart of their challenging His teaching by raising His own counter-questions concerning their understanding of the law and their willingness to manipulate it. He used their desire **to kill** Him (v. 19), which did not sync with the prohibition of murder in the Decalogue (Ex 20:13), as placing them contra their own standard. Jesus also noted that **the law** forbade all but emergency medical attention; however, the religious leaders allowed **circumcision** but not healing **on the Sabbath** (Jn 7:21-24).

7:37-52 Rituals accompanying the feasts often included the pouring out of water to picture God's provision of water to the people during their wandering in the wilderness (Ex 17:6) and in times of drought in the land (1Kg 18:45). This provision of water was temporary relief to their thirst. Therefore, considering their life in an arid, desert terrain, the people would understand the metaphor of Jesus' offer of thirst-quenching water as ultimate sustenance and satisfaction. **Living water** was imagery Jesus took from the Old Testament (cp. Is 32:15; 44:3; Ezk 39:29; Jl 2:28-32) to use as a metaphor for the gift of the Holy Spirit to be poured out on the disciples after Jesus' death and resurrection. Obviously the people were ignorant of the fact that Jesus was born in Bethlehem (Jn 7:41-42).

Nicodemus appeared again and attempted to protect Jesus from His accusers (vv. 50-52), which probably indicated that he had indeed been converted in his earlier encounter with Jesus (3:1-3). Nicodemus here intervened openly in behalf of Jesus even in the midst of the hostile religious establishment of which he had been a part.

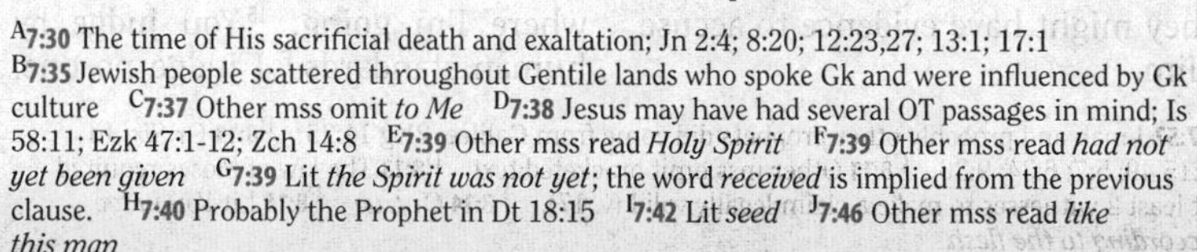

[A]**7:30** The time of His sacrificial death and exaltation; Jn 2:4; 8:20; 12:23,27; 13:1; 17:1
[B]**7:35** Jewish people scattered throughout Gentile lands who spoke Gk and were influenced by Gk culture [C]**7:37** Other mss omit *to Me* [D]**7:38** Jesus may have had several OT passages in mind; Is 58:11; Ezk 47:1-12; Zch 14:8 [E]**7:39** Other mss read *Holy Spirit* [F]**7:39** Other mss read *had not yet been given* [G]**7:39** Lit *the Spirit was not yet*; the word *received* is implied from the previous clause. [H]**7:40** Probably the Prophet in Dt 18:15 [I]**7:42** Lit *seed* [J]**7:46** Other mss read *like this man*

7:53–8:11 This is an incomparable example of how Jesus dealt with the legalistic critics who were testing His commitment to the law and attempting to entrap Him while reaching out to the sinful woman in her need. He never glossed over moral standards but graciously extended mercy. No one could bring together what seemed to be polar opposites as did Jesus.

Only the woman is presented (v. 4) in this account; whereas in the Torah both the man and the woman (if betrothed or engaged) were to be put to death by stoning (Dt. 22:23-24) and by an unspecified method if the woman were married (Lv 20:10; Dt 22:22). Jesus' conclusion was not what they expected but continued to confound them (Jn 8:7). Jesus in no way ignored sin and its consequences, but here He saw the hearts and motivation of these self-righteous accusers who were using a woman to accomplish their own purpose of seeking to entrap Him. In Jewish law the witness was to cast the first stone when capital punishment was involved (Dt 17:5-7). The accusing group slowly departed, beginning with the most revered members and the **older men** (Gk *presbuterōn*). Surely this woman must have been shocked and overwhelmed to meet a man who instead of exploiting and using her for his own lustful and selfish purposes, showed loving concern and extended forgiving grace. Jesus not only refused to condemn her, but He redeemed and restored her. Only Jesus as the sinless One could forgive her sin (Jn 1:29).

8:12-20 John did not indicate the exact timing of these words from Jesus, but they were delivered during His visit to Jerusalem and possibly sometime after the Festival of Tabernacles. While in the temple complex, Jesus made a second proclamation: **I am the light of the world** (v. 12). During the Festival of Tabernacles the great Menorah or lampstand was lighted. The special lighting in the court of the women initiated the Festival on the first night and probably continued except on the eve of the Sabbath. The lights, of course, were symbolic, reminding the people of the pillar of fire that led them through the wilderness (Ex 13:21; Nm 9:15-23).

The question from the Pharisees (Jn 8:19) could have been a legitimate inquiry reflecting the confusion in their own minds just as easily as an insult to Jesus' paternity. One is always wise to move slowly when considering judging motivations in the hearts of others. Nevertheless, even when Jesus answered, they refused to acknowledge His connection to the **Father**; and they continued to ask the same questions (v. 25) and ignore His answers. Despite their hostility, Jesus was protected from them until His work was completed (v. 20).

CHARACTER PROFILE

The Adulteress A Forgiven Woman

Her Background

An unnamed woman in Jerusalem

Her Story

- She was caught in the act of adultery and brought to the temple to be accused before Jesus and the Pharisees (8:2-3).
- The Pharisees were attempting to trap Jesus into disregarding the law or breaking it (8:5-6).
- He wrote something in the dirt with His finger, then challenged anyone without sin to throw the first stone (8:6-7).
- They departed, one at a time (8:9).
- He did not condemn her and told her to go and stop sinning (8:11).

Life Lesson

Your job is not to condemn sinners but to point them to Jesus.

47 Then the Pharisees responded to them: "Are you fooled too? 48 Have any of the rulers or Pharisees believed in Him? 49 But this crowd, which doesn't know the law, is accursed!"

50 Nicodemus—the one who came to Him previously, being one of them—said to them, 51 "Our law doesn't judge a man before it hears from him and knows what he's doing, does it?"

52 "You aren't from Galilee too, are you?" they replied. "Investigate and you will see that no prophet arises from Galilee."[A]

[53 So each one went to his house.

8 1 But Jesus went to the •Mount of Olives.

2 At dawn He went to the •temple complex again, and all the people were coming to Him. He sat down and began to teach them.

3 Then the •scribes and the •Pharisees brought a woman caught in adultery, making her stand in the center. 4 "Teacher," they said to Him, "this woman was caught in the act of committing adultery. 5 In the law Moses commanded us to stone such women. So what do You say?" 6 They asked this to trap Him, in order that they might have evidence to accuse Him. Jesus stooped down and started writing on the ground with His finger. 7 When they persisted in questioning Him, He stood up and said to them, "The one without sin among you should be the first to throw a stone at her."

8 Then He stooped down again and continued writing on the ground. 9 When they heard this, they left one by one, starting with the older men. Only He was left, with the woman in the center. 10 When Jesus stood up, He said to her, "•Woman, where are they? Has no one condemned you?"

11 "No one, Lord,"[B] she answered.

"Neither do I condemn you," said Jesus. "Go, and from now on do not sin anymore."][C]

12 Then Jesus spoke to them again: "I am the light of the world. Anyone who follows Me will never walk in the darkness but will have the light of life."

13 So the Pharisees said to Him, "You are testifying about Yourself. Your testimony is not valid."[D]

14 "Even if I testify about Myself," Jesus replied, "My testimony is valid,[E] because I know where I came from and where I'm going. But you don't know where I come from or where I'm going. 15 You judge by human standards.[F] I judge no one.

[A]**7:52** Jonah and probably other prophets did come from Galilee; 2Kg 14:25 [B]**8:11** Or *Sir*; Jn 4:15,49; 5:7; 6:34; 9:36 [C]**8:11** Other mss omit bracketed text [D]**8:13** The law of Moses required at least 2 witnesses to make a claim legally valid (v. 17). [E]**8:14** Or *true* [F]**8:15** Lit *You judge according to the flesh*

16 And if I do judge, My judgment is
true, because I am not alone, but I
and the Father who sent Me judge
together. 17 Even in your law it is
written that the witness of two men
is valid. 18 I am the One who testifies
about Myself, and the Father who
sent Me testifies about Me."
19 Then they asked Him, "Where is
Your Father?"
"You know neither Me nor My Father," Jesus answered. "If you knew
Me, you would also know My Father." 20 He spoke these words by the
treasury,[A] while teaching in the temple complex. But no one seized Him,
because His hour[B] had not come.
21 Then He said to them again, "I'm
going away; you will look for Me,
and you will die in your sin. Where
I'm going, you cannot come."
22 So the •Jews said again, "He
won't kill Himself, will He, since He
says, 'Where I'm going, you cannot
come'?"
23 "You are from below," He told
them, "I am from above. You are of
this world; I am not of this •world.
24 Therefore I told you that you will
die in your sins. For if you do not
believe that I am He,[C] you will die in
your sins."
25 "Who are You?" they questioned.
"Precisely what I've been telling
you from the very beginning," Jesus
told them. 26 "I have many things to
say and to judge about you, but the
One who sent Me is true, and what I
have heard from Him—these things
I tell the world."
27 They did not know He was
speaking to them about the Father.
28 So Jesus said to them, "When you
lift up the •Son of Man, then you
will know that I am He, and that I do
nothing on My own. But just as the
Father taught Me, I say these things.
29 The One who sent Me is with Me.
He has not left Me alone, because I
always do what pleases Him."
30 As He was saying these things,
many believed in Him. 31 So Jesus
said to the Jews who had believed
Him, "If you continue in My word,[D]
you really are My disciples. 32 You
will know the truth, and the truth
will set you free."
33 "We are descendants[E] of Abraham," they answered Him, "and we
have never been enslaved to anyone.
How can You say, 'You will become
free'?"
34 Jesus responded, "•I assure you:
Everyone who commits sin is a •slave
of sin. 35 A slave does not remain in
the household forever, but a son
does remain forever. 36 Therefore,
if the Son sets you free, you really
will be free. 37 I know you are descendants[E] of Abraham, but you are trying to kill Me because My word[D] is
not welcome among you. 38 I speak
what I have seen in the presence of
the Father;[F] therefore, you do what
you have heard from your father."
39 "Our father is Abraham!" they
replied.
"If you were Abraham's children,"
Jesus told them, "you would do what
Abraham did. 40 But now you are trying to kill Me, a man who has told
you the truth that I heard from God.
Abraham did not do this! 41 You're
doing what your father does."
"We weren't born of sexual immorality," they said. "We have one
Father—God."
42 Jesus said to them, "If God were
your Father, you would love Me,
because I came from God and I am
here. For I didn't come on My own,
but He sent Me. 43 Why don't you
understand what I say? Because you
cannot listen to[G] My word. 44 You are
of your father the Devil, and you
want to carry out your father's desires. He was a murderer from the
beginning and has not stood in the
truth, because there is no truth in
him. When he tells a lie, he speaks
from his own nature,[H] because he is
a liar and the father of liars.[I] 45 Yet
because I tell the truth, you do not
believe Me. 46 Who among you can
convict Me of sin? If I tell the truth,
why don't you believe Me? 47 The one
who is from God listens to God's

Thirteen trumpet-shaped containers were placed in the **treasury** as a place for receiving offerings from the people (see Mk 12:41-44 and the account of the widow who gave her "two tiny coins"). The treasury is commonly noted as being in the court of women within reach of women whose sacrificial giving has been a matter of record through the generations.

8:21-29 Throughout the Gospel of John there is a path to the cross. **When you lift up the Son of Man** is another marker (v. 28; cp. 12:32). "Lift up" (Gk *hupsōsete*, "raise high, exalt") was used in reference to the cross (3:14) with which Jesus compared the "pole" on which the "bronze serpent" was mounted in the wilderness (Nm 21:9). The word often has the sense of setting something in a place of prominence or exalting.

The Jews knew exactly what Jesus was claiming—He declared Himself to be the Old Testament "I AM that I AM"—God Himself. The words **I am** (Gk *egō eimi*) are significant, occurring three times in this discourse (8:24,28,58). Some commentators believe these words are alluding to the title of God, revealed to Moses when he was commissioned by *Yahweh* God to lead the enslaved Israelites out of Egypt (Ex 3:14). Jesus' claim cannot be missed: Jesus is *Yahweh* God of the Old Testament. Rich in meaning, the title affirms preexistence and eternality. But the lesson does not stop with this affirmation of unity with the Father. The following phrase **I do nothing on My own** (Jn 8:28) affirms yet again the Son's subordination, as the redeemer and bearer of the message of salvation, to the Father. Four times Jesus noted that He had been sent by the Father (vv. 16,18,26,29). The Son's devotion to the Father and His voluntary obedience to the will of the Father provide a perfect model for biblical submission. Equality in being but uniqueness in role is again affirmed. Here is a climatic declaration of the gospel and a beautiful unfolding of the theological foundations for the Godhead.

[A]**8:20** A place for offerings to be given, perhaps in the court of women [B]**8:20** The time of His sacrificial death and exaltation; Jn 2:4; 7:30; 12:23,27; 13:1; 17:1 [C]**8:24** Jesus claimed to be deity, but the Pharisees didn't understand His meaning. [D]**8:31,37** Or *My teaching*, or *My message* [E]**8:33,37** Or *offspring*; lit *seed*; Jn 7:42 [F]**8:38** Other mss read *of My Father* [G]**8:43** Or *cannot hear* [H]**8:44** Lit *from his own things* [I]**8:44** Lit *of it*

8:48-59 To accuse Jesus of being a demon-possessed **Samaritan** is an expression of heightened hostility and determined opposition as well as a double slur against His character. With the "Samaritan" designation, which in itself was a figure of speech expressing dishonor, the Jews probably were referencing Jesus' differences with their traditional interpretations of the law since they viewed any differences as heresy. In John's Gospel, Jesus was accused of demon-possession three times (7:20; 8:52; 10:20), a label probably understood as meaning "deranged" or "crazy." Such disrespectful name-calling was typical of mob reaction. Jesus was straightforward in refuting their allegations concerning His character, and He was clear in connecting Himself with the Father and in revealing that His purpose was to glorify the Father and accomplish His will above all else (8:49-51).

The Jews had no understanding of eternal life and considered that concept ridiculous and nonsensical. Jesus distinguished between physical death and spiritual death and simply affirmed that one who believed in Him would not suffer spiritual death but would in fact inherit life everlasting (v. 52; see also Rv 2:11; 20:6).

Jesus was often subtle in the verbal affirmations of His deity. He chose to live His life and do His work so that His deity would not be questioned with any objective consideration. He never denied that He was God, but He did continually point to the Father and glorify Him, knowing that in so doing He would be vindicating Himself.

His reference to **My day** was looking forward to His redemptive work on the cross (Jn 8:56). He did allude to His deity in a veiled way, **before Abraham was, I am** (v. 58), implying continuing existence without beginning or end. "I am" in the Jewish mind was recognized as a title of deity (Ex 3:14). Obviously the crowd, perhaps inflamed by the religious leaders in their midst, understood exactly what Jesus was saying. They tried to stone Him, and He simply vanished from them, not because of fear or intimidation, but because His time had not yet come (Jn 8:59; see 7:30).

9:1-41 Jesus once again healed on the **Sabbath** (v. 14). The one He healed had been blind all his life. Jesus healed in an unusual way (v. 6). Using this method, Jesus could be accused not only of breaking the Old Testament law concerning Sabbath but also of breaking the Pharisaic law forbidding the use of spittle on the Sabbath. The man whose sight was restored confessed faith in Jesus, and even proceeded to worship Him. He clearly had seen the light. His **sight** (faith or belief) is now juxtaposed with the Pharisee's "blindness" (unbelief).

Doctrine SATAN

The people did not respond with obedience and commitment to Jesus because their allegiance was to another. They belonged to their **father the Devil**. Here Jesus gave a clear warning concerning the Devil and described his work in detail (8:44):

- His name **Devil** (Gk *diabolou*, "slanderer") describes his work. The Greek preposition *dia*, meaning "through," is combined with the Greek verb *ballō*, meaning "throw or cast" or even "assault, strike." The Devil then is the one who "casts through" or slanders.
- He is the father of those who oppose God.
- **He was a murderer** [Gk *anthrōpoktonos*—*anthrōpos*, "man" combined with *kteinō*, "slay or kill"] **from the beginning**. He deceived Adam, robbed him and all who came after of life and immortality (cp. 10:10).
- **He has not stood in the truth**. "Stood" (Gk *estēken*, "stand firm") suggests a steadfast stance, which might allow some wiggle room; but Jesus reinforced the devil's assault against truth by adding **because there is no truth in him**. Lying was a pattern for his life (i.e., **he speaks from his own nature**).
- **He is a liar and the father of liars**. The Devil uttered the first lie in the Garden of Eden, and he continues to breed deceit into everyone with whom he has influence or control (Gn 3:4).

words. This is why you don't listen,
because you are not from God."
48 The Jews responded to Him,
"Aren't we right in saying that
You're a •Samaritan and have a demon?"
49 "I do not have a demon," Jesus
answered. "On the contrary, I honor
My Father and you dishonor Me. 50 I
do not seek My glory; the One who
seeks it also judges. 51 I assure you: If
anyone keeps My word, he will never
see death—ever!"
52 Then the Jews said, "Now we
know You have a demon. Abraham
died and so did the prophets. You
say, 'If anyone keeps My word, he
will never taste death—ever!' 53 Are
You greater than our father Abraham who died? Even the prophets
died. Who do You pretend to be?"[A]
54 "If I glorify Myself," Jesus answered, "My glory is nothing. My Father—you say about Him, 'He is our
God'—He is the One who glorifies
Me. 55 You've never known Him, but
I know Him. If I were to say I don't
know Him, I would be a liar like you.
But I do know Him, and I keep His
word. 56 Your father Abraham was
overjoyed that he would see My day;
he saw it and rejoiced."
57 The Jews replied, "You aren't 50
years old yet, and You've seen Abraham?"[B]
58 Jesus said to them, "I assure you:
Before Abraham was, I am."[C]
59 At that, they picked up stones
to throw at Him. But Jesus was hidden[D] and went out of the temple
complex.[E]

9 As He was passing by, He saw a
man blind from birth. 2 His disciples questioned Him: "•Rabbi, who
sinned, this man or his parents, that
he was born blind?"
3 "Neither this man nor his parents
sinned," Jesus answered. "This came
about so that God's works might be
displayed in him. 4 We[F] must do the
works of Him who sent Me[G] while it
is day. Night is coming when no one
can work. 5 As long as I am in the
world, I am the light of the world."
6 After He said these things He
spit on the ground, made some mud
from the saliva, and spread the mud
on his eyes. 7 "Go," He told him,
"wash in the pool of Siloam" (which
means "Sent"). So he left, washed,
and came back seeing.
8 His neighbors and those who formerly had seen him as a beggar said,
"Isn't this the man who sat begging?" 9 Some said, "He's the one."
"No," others were saying, "but he
looks like him."
He kept saying, "I'm the one!"
10 Therefore they asked him, "Then
how were your eyes opened?"
11 He answered, "The man called
Jesus made mud, spread it on my
eyes, and told me, 'Go to Siloam and
wash.' So when I went and washed I
received my sight."
12 "Where is He?" they asked.
"I don't know," he said.
13 They brought the man who used
to be blind to the •Pharisees. 14 The
day that Jesus made the mud and
opened his eyes was a Sabbath. 15 So
again the Pharisees asked him how
he received his sight.

[A]**8:53** Lit *Who do You make Yourself?* [B]**8:57** Other mss read *and Abraham has seen You?* [C]**8:58** *I AM* is the name God gave Himself at the burning bush; Ex 3:13-14; see note at Jn 8:24. [D]**8:59** Or *Jesus hid Himself* [E]**8:59** Other mss add *and having gone through their midst, He passed by* [F]**9:4** Other mss read *I* [G]**9:4** Other mss read *sent us*

HARD QUESTION

Am I suffering (e.g., illness, loss, pain, etc.) because God is punishing me?

In the view of the Jews, whether from a birth defect, infection, advanced age, or as a side effect from another illness, blindness was the result of sin. Some Jews believed in prenatal sin—i.e., that the man could have sinned while still in his mother's womb, or he could have sinned before his conception (an idea from the Greek philosopher Plato). On the other hand, perhaps the sin of his parents brought this affliction upon their son (9:1-2; see Ex 20:5; 34:7; Nm 14:18).

The Bible does trace suffering to moral causes. For example, death came ultimately to all because of Adam's sin (Rm 5:12-21). Children do sometimes suffer because of the sins of their parents (Ex 34:7). One of the greatest tragedies of sin comes in its far-reaching effect, hurting the innocent as well as the guilty. Personal sin can also cause suffering (Dt 28:15-68; Jr 31:30). However, biblical teachings have been distorted and misunderstood. Often, we press the question "Why does God allow suffering?" or complain that the person who is suffering does not deserve it. Jesus' reply that this man's blindness had been allowed to fulfill the purpose of God confirms that God is aware of but does not intervene to prevent every negative result of living in a sin-damaged world. However, Jesus does not merely make a statement but acts on it. With the blind man's cooperation (Jn 9:7) and his simple, unwavering testimony, Jesus not only turned the man's physical disability into the eternal gain of knowing "the light of the world" (v. 5) but also continues to use the story of what He did for and through this man to demonstrate that He is indeed the Messiah and that to deny Him is to remain "blind" in one's sin (vv. 35-41). What a comforting blessing to know that in suffering one can exalt Christ (Rm 8:28; 1Pt 2:21).

"He put mud on my eyes," he told
them. "I washed and I can see."
16 Therefore some of the Pharisees
said, "This man is not from God, for
He doesn't keep the Sabbath!" But
others were saying, "How can a sinful man perform such signs?" And
there was a division among them.
17 Again they asked the blind man,[A]
"What do you say about Him, since
He opened your eyes?"
"He's a prophet," he said.
18 The •Jews did not believe this
about him—that he was blind and
received sight—until they summoned the parents of the one who
had received his sight.
19 They asked them, "Is this your
son, the one you say was born blind?
How then does he now see?"
20 "We know this is our son and
that he was born blind," his parents
answered. 21 "But we don't know
how he now sees, and we don't know
who opened his eyes. Ask him; he's
of age. He will speak for himself."
22 His parents said these things because they were afraid of the Jews,
since the Jews had already agreed
that if anyone confessed Him as
•Messiah, he would be banned from
the •synagogue. 23 This is why his
parents said, "He's of age; ask him."
24 So a second time they summoned the man who had been blind
and told him, "Give glory to God.[B]
We know that this man is a sinner!"
25 He answered, "Whether or not
He's a sinner, I don't know. One
thing I do know: I was blind, and
now I can see!"
26 Then they asked him, "What did
He do to you? How did He open your
eyes?"
27 "I already told you," he said, "and
you didn't listen. Why do you want
to hear it again? You don't want to
become His disciples too, do you?"
28 They ridiculed him: "You're that
man's disciple, but we're Moses'
disciples. 29 We know that God has
spoken to Moses. But this man—we
don't know where He's from!"
30 "This is an amazing thing," the
man told them. "You don't know
where He is from, yet He opened my
eyes! 31 We know that God doesn't
listen to sinners, but if anyone is
God-fearing and does His will, He
listens to him. 32 Throughout history[C] no one has ever heard of someone opening the eyes of a person
born blind. 33 If this man were not
from God, He wouldn't be able to do
anything."
34 "You were born entirely in sin,"
they replied, "and are you trying
to teach us?" Then they threw him
out.[D]
35 When Jesus heard that they had
thrown the man out, He found him
and asked, "Do you believe in the
•Son of Man?"[E]

Blindness was undoubtedly common in the ancient world. Jesus had healed others who were blind (Mt 9:27-31; 12:22; 15:30; 21:14; Mk 8:22-26; 10:46-52). In this healing, Jesus not only showed His power to restore physical sight, but He also revealed His power to give spiritual sight and light. He used another "I am" metaphor—**I am the light of the world** (Jn 9:5).

The **pool of Siloam** (v. 7), located just inside the southeastern wall, was in itself an engineering masterpiece created in connection with the construction of Hezekiah's tunnel, which had been designed to divert the waters from Siloam to the Gihon Spring. The 583-yard tunnel had been dug through solid rock at the command of King Hezekiah to divert water into the city in the event of a siege by his enemies. The Siloam pool, measuring 20 by 30 feet, is used as a source of water even today. An adventure that can still be experienced in Jerusalem is to wade through the winding tunnel from Gihon to Siloam.

The fact of the man's healing could not be disputed. Too many family members and friends who knew of his lifelong affliction now saw that condition completely reversed (v. 8) so that even Jesus' enemies had to acknowledge what had happened; yet their unbelief was set (v. 16). The skepticism of the stubborn and hard-hearted religious leaders did not deter the man who had been healed, who now with physical sight restored had also received spiritual sight and responded with gratitude and praise (vv. 25,38). The Pharisees could see physically, but they chose to remain blind spiritually (vv. 40-41). They refused to act on the revelation of truth they had received.

God listens to **anyone** who **is God-fearing** [Gk *theosebēs*, "devout, religious, pious"] **and does His will** (v. 31). *Theosebēs* combines *theos* ("God") with the verb *sebō* ("revere, worship") to convey the sense of reverencing God, describing one who is a sincere worshiper of God. One who is "God-fearing" does God's will. The "fear of the Lord" is interwoven throughout Scripture as a mark of one who has set herself apart unto the Lord (see **Word Study**, p. 784). It is more than reverential awe, including a loving devotion on the part of one toward another who is so loved and respected that you cannot bear to disappoint that exalted one in your heart and mind.

A **9:17** = the man who had been blind B **9:24** *Give glory to God* was a solemn charge to tell the truth; Jos 7:19. C **9:32** Lit *From the age* D **9:34** = they banned him from the synagogue; v. 22
E **9:35** Other mss read *the Son of God*

36 “Who is He, Sir, that I may believe in Him?” he asked.
37 Jesus answered, “You have seen
Him; in fact, He is the One speaking
with you.”
38 “I believe, Lord!” he said, and he
worshiped Him.
39 Jesus said, “I came into this
world for judgment, in order that
those who do not see will see and
those who do see will become blind.”
40 Some of the Pharisees who were
with Him heard these things and
asked Him, “We aren't blind too, are
we?”
41 “If you were blind,” Jesus told
them, “you wouldn't have sin.[A] But
now that you say, ‘We see’—your sin
remains.

The Good Shepherd and Oneness with the Father (10:1-42)

10 “•I assure you: Anyone who
doesn't enter the sheep pen by
the door but climbs in some other
way, is a thief and a robber. 2 The one
who enters by the door is the shepherd of the sheep. 3 The doorkeeper
opens it for him, and the sheep hear
his voice. He calls his own sheep by
name and leads them out. 4 When
he has brought all his own outside,
he goes ahead of them. The sheep
follow him because they recognize
his voice. 5 They will never follow a
stranger; instead they will run away
from him, because they don't recognize the voice of strangers.”
6 Jesus gave them this illustration,
but they did not understand what
He was telling them.
7 So Jesus said again, “I assure you:
I am the door of the sheep. 8 All who
came before Me[B] are thieves and robbers, but the sheep didn't listen to
them. 9 I am the door. If anyone enters by Me, he will be saved and will
come in and go out and find pasture.
10 A thief comes only to steal and to
kill and to destroy. I have come so
that they may have life and have it
in abundance.
11 “I am the good shepherd. The
good shepherd lays down his life for
the sheep. 12 The hired man, since he
is not the shepherd and doesn't own
the sheep, leaves them[C] and runs
away when he sees a wolf coming.
The wolf then snatches and scatters
them. 13 This happens because he is
a hired man and doesn't care about
the sheep.
14 “I am the good shepherd. I know
My own sheep, and they know Me,
15 as the Father knows Me, and I
know the Father. I lay down My life
for the sheep. 16 But I have other
sheep that are not of this fold; I
must bring them also, and they will
listen to My voice. Then there will
be one flock, one shepherd. 17 This is
why the Father loves Me, because I
am laying down My life so I may take
it up again. 18 No one takes it from
Me, but I lay it down on My own. I
have the right to lay it down, and
I have the right to take it up again.
I have received this command from
My Father.”
19 Again a division took place
among the •Jews because of these
words. 20 Many of them were saying,
“He has a demon and He's crazy!
Why do you listen to Him?” 21 Others
were saying, “These aren't the words
of someone demon-possessed. Can a
demon open the eyes of the blind?”
22 Then the Festival of Dedication[D] took place in Jerusalem, and
it was winter. 23 Jesus was walking in
the •temple complex in Solomon's
Colonnade.[E] 24 Then the Jews sur-

[A]9:41 To *have sin* is an idiom that refers to guilt caused by sin. [B]10:8 Other mss omit *before Me* [C]10:12 Lit *leaves the sheep* [D]10:22 Or *Hanukkah*, also called *the Feast of Lights*; this festival commemorated the rededication of the temple in 164 B.C. [E]10:23 Rows of columns supporting a roof

10:1-21 Jesus introduced two more "I am" statements: **I am the door of the sheep** (v. 7) and **I am the good shepherd** (v. 11). These metaphors were clearly understood by Jesus' audience, for the sheep were important to sustaining life, providing food and clothing. When the flocks of several shepherds mingled together, the sheep still recognized the familiar voice of their own shepherd and followed him (v. 4). The shepherd also knew his sheep, not merely by a family brand but **by name** (v. 3). The shepherd fed his sheep, led them to water, and protected them, often putting himself in harm's way.

The metaphor is rich in Old Testament imagery (Ps 23:1; 79:13; 80:1; Ezk 34:15). Jesus' proclamation of Himself as "the good shepherd" is the fulfillment of Ezk 34. Like the the false shepherds described by the prophet, the religious leaders failed to lead the people faithfully.

The **other sheep that are not of this fold** is a reference to the Gentiles who were not of the "fold" of Judaism (Jn 10:16). Gentiles as well as Jews would share in the salvation He brought and would be under one Shepherd. **A hired man**, who was more concerned about his own well-being, would flee when confronted by a predator (vv. 12-13). Jesus used this analogy to show the difference between Him as the shepherd and the religious leaders, who indeed might do some good things for the sheep but would never sacrifice themselves for the sheep.

10:22-23 Solomon's Colonnade was a magnificent structure with its roof supported by rows of 40-foot high pillars. Solomon built the oldest porches on the east side. Jesus was walking on the west porches build by Herod. These porches were used for people as a place to pray and meditate and by rabbis as a place for teaching.

Occurring a few months before the Passover, **the Festival of Dedication** (*Hanukkah* or the Festival of Lights) is not mentioned in the Old Testament. It was established to commemorate the dedication of the temple by Judas Maccabaeus (*Kislev* 25, 165 B.C.) after the temple had been desecrated by Antiochus Epiphanes, the king of Syria, in 167 B.C. Antiochus tried to abolish the Jewish religion by attacking Jerusalem and profaning the temple complex with the sacrifice of swine on the altar. Judas Maccabaeus and his brothers retaliated and defeated Antiochus. They cleansed the temple, rebuilt the altar, and restored worship. This festival is still celebrated by Jews every December(*Kislev*) and lasts eight days with the lighting of a candle each day. Accordingly, the *Hanukkah* menorah has eight branches.

>WORD|*study*

10:1 The sheep pen, built from mud-bricks or local rough-hewn stones or sometimes simply a cane, had only one opening in order to protect the sheep from predators and/or a thief [Gk *kleptēs*, "deceiver or imposter"] and a robber (Gk *lēstēs*, "plunderer, bandit, revolutionary"). The slight nuances of meaning suggest in the former trickery and deceit and in the latter violent plunder. Together the dangers are vividly portrayed (Jn 10:1). Jesus used the metaphor of "the door" to emphasize that only He could provide access to God to reaffirm His willingness to lay down His life for His sheep (vv. 7-10).

rounded Him and asked, “How long
are You going to keep us in suspense?[A] If You are the •Messiah, tell
us plainly.”[B]
25 “I did tell you and you don’t believe,” Jesus answered them. “The
works that I do in My Father’s name
testify about Me. 26 But you don’t believe because you are not My sheep.[C]
27 My sheep hear My voice, I know
them, and they follow Me. 28 I give
them eternal life, and they will never perish—ever! No one will snatch
them out of My hand. 29 My Father,
who has given them to Me, is greater than all. No one is able to snatch
them out of the Father’s hand. 30 The
Father and I are one.”[D]
31 Again the Jews picked up rocks
to stone Him.
32 Jesus replied, “I have shown you
many good works from the Father.
Which of these works are you stoning Me for?”
33 “We aren’t stoning You for a
good work,” the Jews answered, “but
for blasphemy, because You—being
a man—make Yourself God.”
34 Jesus answered them, “Isn’t it
written in your scripture,[E] **I said,
you are gods**?[F] 35 If He called those
whom the word of God came to
‘gods’—and the Scripture cannot
be broken— 36 do you say, ‘You are
blaspheming’ to the One the Father
set apart and sent into the world,
because I said: I am the Son of God?
37 If I am not doing My Father’s
works, don’t believe Me. 38 But if I
am doing them and you don’t believe Me, believe the works. This way
you will know and understand[G] that
the Father is in Me and I in the Father.” 39 Then they were trying again
to seize Him, yet He eluded their
grasp.
40 So He departed again across the
Jordan to the place where John had
been baptizing earlier, and He remained there. 41 Many came to Him
and said, “John never did a sign, but
everything John said about this man
was true.” 42 And many believed in
Him there.

Jesus as the Resurrection and the Life (11:1-57)

11 Now a man was sick, Lazarus,
from Bethany, the village of
Mary and her sister Martha. 2 Mary
was the one who anointed the Lord
with fragrant oil and wiped His feet
with her hair, and it was her brother
Lazarus who was sick. 3 So the sisters sent a message to Him: “Lord,
the one You love is sick.”
4 When Jesus heard it, He said,
“This sickness will not end in death
but is for the glory of God, so that
the Son of God may be glorified
through it.” 5 Now Jesus loved Martha, her sister, and Lazarus. 6 So
when He heard that he was sick, He
stayed two more days in the place

[A]10:24 Lit *How long are you taking away our life?* [B]10:24 Or *openly*, or *publicly* [C]10:26 Other mss add *just as I told you* [D]10:30 Lit *I and the Father—We are one.* [E]10:34 Other mss read *in the scripture* [F]10:34 Ps 82:6 [G]10:38 Other mss read *know and believe*

CHARACTER PROFILE

Martha of Bethany A Dedicated Servant

Her Background	• She lived with her sister Mary and her brother Lazarus in Bethany (Jn 11:1). • She welcomed Jesus into their home (Lk 10:38).
Her Story	• She was a faithful disciple (Lk 10:39). • She gave a great confession of faith at the tomb of Lazarus (Jn 11:21-27). • She complained about Mary’s lack of help as she worked to prepare for a dinner (Lk 10:38-42). • She served Jesus at a dinner in Bethany, where her sister Mary anointed Jesus with oil (Jn 12:1-2).
Life Lesson	Martha was a spiritually-minded woman with a servant’s heart—two qualities that are not mutually exclusive.

10:24-42 The Jews challenged Jesus quite plainly about His identity. They still did not understand because they were not His “sheep” (v. 26). His sheep listened to His voice. No one could **snatch** His sheep from Him because the Father **is greater than all** (v. 29). Eternal security is one of the most wonderful blessings for those who belong to Christ (v. 28). The Greek text uses a double negative (*ou mē*, literally “not not”). *Ou* is used in questions where an affirmative response is expected, and *mē* is used in questions where a negative answer is expected. The two together carry the strongest assertion—a solemn and absolute assertion. God not only initiates salvation, but He also accomplishes that redemptive work; and believers are forever secure in the hands of both the Father and the Son.

The conclusion of Jesus’ reply was considered by the Jews to be blasphemous because Jesus declared: **the Father and I are one** (v. 30). This carefully worded answer testified to the two individual persons in the Godhead, while “one” (Gk *hen*, a neuter pronoun) affirmed the unity of nature. To refute this charge of blasphemy, Jesus quoted from Ps 82:6, which refers to evil judges as “gods.” The Jews allowed their own judges to be called gods because of the divine origin of the civil authority they wielded and the justice at the foundation of their system of jurisprudence (Jn 10:34). Since the Jews had expressed no antagonism against the Hebrew psalmist, they were on shaky ground to use this means for an attack on Jesus. Surely they were continually amazed at Jesus’ grasp of the Old Testament—even obscure passages and minute details. He knew the Scriptures, and He could explain them far and beyond any man (vv. 35-36). The point is that, if Scripture acknowledges evil judges to be authorities on earth in a limited sense, then why should He not apply the term to Himself, one who is clearly God’s unique Son.

11:1-20 John ends the first half of his book with the most dramatic of Jesus’ miracles: the raising of **Lazarus** (Hb, “one whom God helps”, a derivation from the name *Eleazer*) from the dead. Jesus had brought people back from death previously in His ministry, but this occasion was the most significant because Lazarus had been dead for **four days** (v. 17). According to Jewish tradition (*Genesis Rabbah 100*, 164a), the soul stayed near the body for only three days. That Lazarus was dead was beyond doubt.

Lazarus was a personal friend of Jesus. Jesus seemed determined to delay going to Bethany (Hb “house of figs or unripe figs” or “house of sorrow or misery or affliction”) located on the eastern slope of the Mount of Olives about **two miles away** from Jerusalem and probably within an hour's walk (11:18). The mountain blocked viewing Jerusalem and set the village apart in seclusion, perhaps making it a worthy retreat for quiet renewal and thus very useful to Jesus. Tradition associates the gathering of invalids and outcasts and thus the designation "house of suffering," despite the message concerning Lazarus's serious illness (vv. 4-6). He demonstrated His omniscience in knowing the moment of Lazarus's death and His omnipotence in knowing He would restore Lazarus to life (v. 11). Again He demonstrated His humanity (loving concern for a friend, vv. 35-36) and deity (power to raise one from the dead, v. 44). Jesus described Lazarus's death as falling **asleep**, a euphemism for death (vv. 11,14; cp. Mt 9:24; Ac 7:60; 1 Co 15:6; 1 Th 4:13).

Mary, a Greek personal name equivalent to Hb *Miriam* (meaning "bitter" from Hb *Mara*; see Ru 1:20) affirms her devotion to Christ (Jn 11:2). **Martha** (Hb "lady—as of the house") arose to the challenge of her name in managing her household and extending hospitality (Lk 10:38,40; Jn 11:20; 12:2).

11:21-28 Martha showed her familiarity with the Old Testament teaching on the resurrection (v. 24), and she affirmed her faith in Jesus' power over death (vv. 21-22). Jesus added to her understanding by declaring Himself to be **the resurrection** (v. 25)—a very important revelation for Jesus to entrust to Martha. Jesus significantly timed this fifth "I am" statement, since His mission in Bethany was to demonstrate His power to raise the dead, a meaningful foreshadowing of the guarantee that those who physically died in Him would be raised to eternal life in the future (v. 26; cp. 1Co 15:22). The only ultimate escape from death does not interrupt the physical cycle of decay that entered the world with sin, but for those who commit themselves to Christ, eternal life and bodily resurrection to join Christ are assured.

11:33-37 John, more than the other Gospel writers, revealed the deep compassion of Jesus. Jesus knew that Lazarus would be restored to life, yet still He was greatly moved. He was **angry** (Gk *enebrimēsato*, "scold, censure, warn sternly," vv. 33,38) with the sense of speaking harshly. Jesus was also **deeply moved** (Gk *etaraxen*, "stir up, disturb, unsettle") in the sense of being troubled or agitated. **Jesus wept** (Gk *edakrusen*, "shed tears," a *hapax*, a word not used elsewhere in the Gk NT). Of course, He shared the sorrow of the loss, though temporary, of a friend and the pain of seeing those whom He loved suffer, but even more than these typically human responses

CHARACTER PROFILE

Mary Of Bethany A Single-minded Disciple

Her Background	• She lived with her sister Martha and her brother Lazarus in the village of Bethany (Jn 11:1). • She regularly welcomed Jesus into their home (Lk 10:38).
Her Story	• She was a faithful disciple of Jesus (Lk 10:39). • She saw Lazarus raised to life after being dead for four days (Jn 11:28-44). • She lovingly anointed Jesus' feet with fragrant oil at a dinner in Bethany (Jn 12:1-8; Mt 26:6-13). • She was commended by Jesus for the right choice of sitting at His feet and listening to Him (Lk 10:38-42).
Life Lesson	Jesus commended Mary twice for her single-minded devotion to Him.

where He was. 7 Then after that, He
said to the disciples, "Let's go to Judea again."
8 "•Rabbi," the disciples told Him,
"just now the •Jews tried to stone
You, and You're going there again?"
9 "Aren't there 12 hours in a day?"
Jesus answered. "If anyone walks
during the day, he doesn't stumble,
because he sees the light of this
world. 10 If anyone walks during the
night, he does stumble, because the
light is not in him." 11 He said this,
and then He told them, "Our friend
Lazarus has fallen •asleep, but I'm
on My way to wake him up."
12 Then the disciples said to Him,
"Lord, if he has fallen asleep, he will
get well."
13 Jesus, however, was speaking
about his death, but they thought
He was speaking about natural sleep.
14 So Jesus then told them plainly,
"Lazarus has died. 15 I'm glad for you
that I wasn't there so that you may
believe. But let's go to him."
16 Then Thomas (called "Twin")
said to his fellow disciples, "Let's go
so that we may die with Him."
17 When Jesus arrived, He found
that Lazarus had already been in the
tomb four days. 18 Bethany was near
Jerusalem (about two miles[A] away).
19 Many of the Jews had come to Martha and Mary to comfort them about
their brother. 20 As soon as Martha
heard that Jesus was coming, she
went to meet Him. But Mary remained seated in the house.
21 Then Martha said to Jesus,
"Lord, if You had been here, my
brother wouldn't have died. 22 Yet
even now I know that whatever You
ask from God, God will give You."
23 "Your brother will rise again,"
Jesus told her.
24 Martha said, "I know that he will
rise again in the resurrection at the
last day."
25 Jesus said to her, "I am the resurrection and the life. The one who
believes in Me, even if he dies, will
live. 26 Everyone who lives and believes in Me will never die—ever. Do
you believe this?"
27 "Yes, Lord," she told Him, "I believe You are the •Messiah, the Son
of God, who comes into the world."
28 Having said this, she went back
and called her sister Mary, saying in
private, "The Teacher is here and is
calling for you."
29 As soon as she heard this, she got
up quickly and went to Him. 30 Jesus
had not yet come into the village but
was still in the place where Martha
had met Him. 31 The Jews who were
with her in the house consoling
her saw that Mary got up quickly
and went out. So they followed her,
supposing that she was going to the
tomb to cry there.
32 When Mary came to where Jesus
was and saw Him, she fell at His feet
and told Him, "Lord, if You had been

[A] **11:18** Lit *15 stadia*; 1 *stadion* = 600 feet

here, my brother would not have died!"

33 When Jesus saw her crying, and the Jews who had come with her crying, He was angry[A] in His spirit and deeply moved. 34 "Where have you put him?" He asked.

"Lord," they told Him, "come and see."

35 Jesus wept.

36 So the Jews said, "See how He loved him!" 37 But some of them said, "Couldn't He who opened the blind man's eyes also have kept this man from dying?"

38 Then Jesus, angry[B] in Himself again, came to the tomb. It was a cave, and a stone was lying against it. 39 "Remove the stone," Jesus said.

Martha, the dead man's sister, told Him, "Lord, he's already decaying.[C] It's been four days."

40 Jesus said to her, "Didn't I tell you that if you believed you would see the glory of God?"

41 So they removed the stone. Then Jesus raised His eyes and said, "Father, I thank You that You heard Me. 42 I know that You always hear Me, but because of the crowd standing here I said this, so they may believe You sent Me." 43 After He said this, He shouted with a loud voice, "Lazarus, come out!" 44 The dead man came out bound hand and foot with linen strips and with his face wrapped in a cloth. Jesus said to them, "Loose him and let him go."

45 Therefore, many of the Jews who came to Mary and saw what He did believed in Him. 46 But some of them went to the •Pharisees and told them what Jesus had done.

47 So the •chief priests and the Pharisees convened the •Sanhedrin and said, "What are we going to do since this man does many signs? 48 If we let Him continue in this way, everyone will believe in Him! Then the Romans will come and remove both our place[D] and our nation."

49 One of them, Caiaphas, who was high priest that year, said to them, "You know nothing at all! 50 You're not considering that it is to your[E] advantage that one man should die for the people rather than the whole nation perish." 51 He did not say this on his own, but being high priest that year he prophesied that Jesus was going to die for the nation, 52 and not for the nation only, but also to unite the scattered children of God. 53 So from that day on they plotted to kill Him. 54 Therefore Jesus no longer walked openly among the Jews but departed from there to the countryside near the wilderness, to a town called Ephraim. And He stayed there with the disciples.

55 The Jewish •Passover was near, and many went up to Jerusalem from the country to purify[F] themselves before the Passover. 56 They were looking for Jesus and asking one another as they stood in the •temple complex: "What do you think? He won't come to the festival, will He?" 57 The chief priests and the Pharisees had given orders that if anyone knew where He was, he should report it so they could arrest Him.

Actions in Preparation for Death (12:1-50)

Anointing at Bethany (12:1-11)

12 Six days before the •Passover, Jesus came to Bethany where

A 11:33 The Gk word is very strong and probably indicates Jesus' anger against sin's tyranny and death. B 11:38 See note at 11:33. C 11:39 Lit *he already stinks* D 11:48 The temple or possibly all of Jerusalem E 11:50 Other mss read *to our* F 11:55 The law of Moses required God's people to purify or cleanse themselves so they could celebrate the Passover. Jews often came to Jerusalem a week early to do this; Nm 9:4-11.

was recognizing the hopelessness of the people who still did not believe.

11:38-57 Although the conversation between Jesus and Martha had concluded with Martha's confession of faith (v. 27), when she arrived at the tomb of Lazarus, her lack of understanding surfaced again (v. 39), and Jesus reminded her that she would see **the glory of God** if she **believed** (v. 40). The lesson is clear: Using the right words does not necessarily mean you understand the message. What sets apart a committed follower of Christ is the determination to live so that you are "fleshing out" the words into a life of obedience to Christ, whatever the cost.

Jesus addressed the Father concerning His work, remembering His mission, **so they may believe You sent Me** (v. 42). The prayer showed His one-mindedness with the Father (vv. 41-42; see also 20:31). Jesus knew and did the will of the Father. This miracle had surpassed the others and prompted a gathering of the **Sanhedrin**, which included 70 priests and as the Jewish "supreme court" met in Jerusalem. The high priest was added to the group in order to break any tie that might occur (v. 47). They were greatly troubled by Jesus' popularity with the people, which made it difficult for them to get rid of Him.

Caiaphas, who was high priest that year and the son-in-law of Annas, who himself served as high priest and who was mentioned in connection with Jesus' trial, uttered a profound statement; and despite His own prejudices, he spoke the words of God (v. 51), not realizing that God was using Him to deliver a prophecy concerning Jesus and His redemptive purpose (v. 50). He set forth clearly the substitutionary nature of the atonement (v. 50). The word **for** (Gk *huper*) clearly means "in behalf of or in the place of." God uses even His enemies to deliver His message.

The response to Jesus' miracle was diverse. On the one hand, **many of the Jews...believed in Him** (v. 45), but **some of them went to the Pharisees** (v. 46) as spies to betray Jesus.

12:1-11 Six days before the Passover **...Martha was serving** (v. 2), and from what follows one can assume Mary was again sitting at the feet of Jesus (v. 3). Martha served without complaining, perhaps offering her service and hospitality as a gift to the Lord. While Matthew and Mark both mentioned Mary's anointing of Jesus, only John notes when the anointing took place (i.e., on the Saturday before what is now known as Palm Sunday). Mary poured on Jesus' feet a jar of perfume that was worth more than a year's wages (v. 5).

>WORD|*study*

12:1-11 For the anointing Mary used a pound of fragrant oil (Gk *murou*, "ointment, perfume, or myrrh"), an aromatic ingredient also used to embalm bodies (19:39), and nard (Gk *nardou*, "oil") or spikenard, which was a fragrant oil derived from the hair stem of a plant growing in northern India (11:3; Mk 14:3; see also Sg 1:12; 4:13-14). The "nard" was described as pure (Gk *pistikēs*, "fit to be trusted, genuine"), a fitting allusion to the holiness of God that resided in the nature of Jesus, and expensive (Gk *polutimou*, "of great worth, valuable"), which was a reminder of the precious life He would lay down in payment for the sins of the world. Judas placed on the oil a monetary value of 300 denarii, the equivalent of about a year's wages for the common laborer (Jn 11:5).

Anointing was usually for the head. Mary showed her own deep humility as she chose to pour the costly, fragrant oil over Jesus' feet. Only the lowliest servant attended the feet of guests, which would be dirty and dusty. No act could have been any more symbolic of her personal devotion to Christ and of her desire to sit at His feet to learn and to worship. The use of her hair to dry His feet was not common in the ancient world. Perhaps this act was yet another way of humbling herself by letting down her hair, usually bound or braided as customary for women in public, to complete the act of service.

Mary's actions were symbolic of preparing a body for burial. Perhaps sensing that Jesus' death was imminent, she used her most precious possession. (Nothing in the text suggests that she took the family resources to purchase an extravagant oil, but rather she was willing to give up something of value she already had.) Because the imported spices and ointments were quite costly and yet occupied little space, they were often stored as an investment or life savings.

Because Lazarus' resurrection from the dead had verified Jesus' power over death, the **chief priests** wanted **to kill** him as well as Jesus (v. 10). They were Sadducees and thus did not even believe in the resurrection of the dead. A living Lazarus would cause them to lose influence and power over the people.

Judas protested Mary's gift. Jesus knew the heart of Judas (6:20) and was well aware of his coming betrayal. Other disciples had fallen away and deserted Him, but Judas remained, perhaps hoping for financial gain or powerful position—some way to enrich himself as he had already done through his position as treasurer (v. 6). John makes clear that Judas cared nothing for **the poor** (v. 6). Caring for the poor was a command of the Old Testament (Dt 15:11). However, what Mary did was quite appropriate under the circumstances.

12:12-23 All of the Gospel writers mentioned Jesus' final entry into **Jerusalem**, but John supplements the Synoptic accounts by adding some unique details. Upon seeing Jesus' entry into Jerusalem, the Pharisees exclaimed that **the world has gone after Him!** (v. 19), a unique note from John, which prepares the way for his mention of the **Greeks** who came to Jesus. These "Greeks" may have been God-fearing men like Cornelius (Ac 10) or proselytes. The designation is one generally inclusive of Gentiles. The raising of Lazarus from the dead had far-reaching effects. Certainly these words offered a prophetic voice of what would come through Jesus' atonement for the sins of the world—Jews and Gentiles (Jn 12:32).

Lazarus[A] was, the one Jesus had
raised from the dead. 2 So they gave
a dinner for Him there; Martha was
serving them, and Lazarus was one
of those reclining at the table with
Him. 3 Then Mary took a pound of
fragrant oil—pure and expensive
nard—anointed Jesus' feet, and
wiped His feet with her hair. So the
house was filled with the fragrance
of the oil.

4 Then one of His disciples, Judas
Iscariot (who was about to betray
Him), said, 5 "Why wasn't this fragrant oil sold for 300 •denarii[B] and
given to the poor?" 6 He didn't say
this because he cared about the poor
but because he was a thief. He was in
charge of the money-bag and would
steal part of what was put in it.

7 Jesus answered, "Leave her
alone; she has kept it for the day of
My burial. 8 For you always have the
poor with you, but you do not always
have Me."

9 Then a large crowd of the Jews
learned He was there. They came
not only because of Jesus, but also
to see Lazarus the one He had raised
from the dead. 10 Therefore the •chief
priests decided to kill Lazarus also
11 because he was the reason many of
the Jews were deserting them[C] and
believing in Jesus.

Entry into Jerusalem (12:12-50)

12 The next day, when the large
crowd that had come to the festival
heard that Jesus was coming to Jerusalem, 13 they took palm branches
and went out to meet Him. They
kept shouting: "•***Hosanna!*** **He who**
comes in the name of the Lord is
the blessed One[D]—the King of Israel!"

14 Jesus found a young donkey and
sat on it, just as it is written: 15 **Fear**
no more, Daughter •Zion. Look,
your King is coming, sitting on a
donkey's colt.[E]

16 His disciples did not understand
these things at first. However, when
Jesus was glorified, then they remembered that these things had
been written about Him and that
they had done these things to Him.
17 Meanwhile, the crowd, which had
been with Him when He called Lazarus out of the tomb and raised him
from the dead, continued to testify.[F]
18 This is also why the crowd met
Him, because they heard He had
done this sign.

19 Then the •Pharisees said to one
another, "You see? You've accomplished nothing. Look—the world
has gone after Him!"

20 Now some Greeks were among
those who went up to worship at the
festival. 21 So they came to Philip,
who was from Bethsaida in Galilee,
and requested of him, "Sir, we want
to see Jesus."

22 Philip went and told Andrew;
then Andrew and Philip went and
told Jesus. 23 Jesus replied to them,
"The hour has come for the •Son of
Man to be glorified.

24 "•I assure you: Unless a grain of
wheat falls to the ground and dies,
it remains by itself. But if it dies, it
produces a large crop.[G] 25 The one
who loves his life will lose it, and the
one who hates his life in this world
will keep it for eternal life. 26 If anyone serves Me, he must follow Me.
Where I am, there My servant also
will be. If anyone serves Me, the Father will honor him.

27 "Now My soul is troubled. What
should I say—Father, save Me from
this hour? But that is why I came
to this hour. 28 Father, glorify Your
name!"[H]

Then a voice came from heaven: "I
have glorified it, and I will glorify it
again!"

29 The crowd standing there heard
it and said it was thunder. Others
said that an angel had spoken to
Him.

30 Jesus responded, "This voice
came, not for Me, but for you. 31 Now
is the judgment of this world. Now
the ruler of this •world will be cast
out. 32 As for Me, if I am lifted up[I]
from the earth I will draw all people
to Myself." 33 He said this to signify
what kind of death He was about to
die.

[A]12:1 Other mss read *Lazarus who died* [B]12:5 This amount was about a year's wages for a common worker. [C]12:11 Lit *going away* [D]12:13 Ps 118:25-26 [E]12:15 Zch 9:9 [F]12:17 Other mss read *Meanwhile the crowd, which had been with Him, continued to testify that He had called Lazarus out of the tomb and raised him from the dead.* [G]12:24 Lit *produces much fruit* [H]12:28 Other mss read *Your Son* [I]12:32 Or *exalted*

34 Then the crowd replied to Him, "We have heard from the scripture that the •Messiah will remain forever. So how can You say, 'The Son of Man must be lifted up'?[A] Who is this Son of Man?"

35 Jesus answered, "The light will be with you only a little longer. Walk while you have the light so that darkness doesn't overtake you. The one who walks in darkness doesn't know where he's going. 36 While you have the light, believe in the light so that you may become sons of light." Jesus said this, then went away and hid from them.

37 Even though He had performed so many signs in their presence, they did not believe in Him. 38 But this was to fulfill the word of Isaiah the prophet, who said:[B]

> **Lord, who has believed**
> **our message?**
> **And who has the arm**
> **of the Lord**
> **been revealed to?**[C]

39 This is why they were unable to believe, because Isaiah also said:

> 40 **He has blinded their eyes**
> **and hardened their hearts,**
> **so that they would not see**
> **with their eyes**
> **or understand**
> **with their hearts,**
> **and be converted,**
> **and I would heal them.**[D]

41 Isaiah said these things because[E] he saw His glory and spoke about Him.

42 Nevertheless, many did believe in Him even among the rulers, but because of the Pharisees they did not confess Him, so they would not be banned from the •synagogue. 43 For they loved praise from men more than praise from God.[F]

44 Then Jesus cried out, "The one who believes in Me believes not in Me, but in Him who sent Me. 45 And the one who sees Me sees Him who sent Me. 46 I have come as a light into the world, so that everyone who believes in Me would not remain in darkness. 47 If anyone hears My words and doesn't keep them, I do not judge him; for I did not come to judge the world but to save the world. 48 The one who rejects Me and doesn't accept My sayings has this as his judge:[G] The word I have spoken will judge him on the last day. 49 For I have not spoken on My own, but the Father Himself who sent Me has given Me a command as to what I should say and what I should speak. 50 I know that His command is eternal life. So the things that I speak, I speak just as the Father has told Me."

Teaching in Preparation for Death (13:1–17:26)

Servant Ministry vs. Betrayal (13:1-30)

13 Before the •Passover Festival, Jesus knew that His hour had come to depart from this world to the Father. Having loved His own who were in the world, He loved them to the end.[H]

2 Now by the time of supper, the Devil had already put it into the heart of Judas, Simon Iscariot's son, to betray Him. 3 Jesus knew that the Father had given everything into His hands, that He had come from God, and that He was going back to God. 4 So He got up from supper, laid aside His robe, took a towel, and tied it around Himself. 5 Next, He poured water into a basin and began to wash His disciples' feet and to dry them with the towel tied around Him.

6 He came to Simon Peter, who asked Him, "Lord, are You going to wash my feet?"

7 Jesus answered him, "What I'm doing you don't understand now, but afterward you will know."

8 "You will never wash my feet—ever!" Peter said.

Jesus replied, "If I don't wash you, you have no part with Me."

9 Simon Peter said to Him, "Lord, not only my feet, but also my hands and my head."

10 "One who has bathed," Jesus told him, "doesn't need to wash anything except his feet, but he is completely •clean. You are clean, but not all of you." 11 For He knew

[A]**12:34** Or *exalted* [B]**12:38** Lit *which he said* [C]**12:38** Is 53:1 [D]**12:40** Is 6:10 [E]**12:41** Other mss read *when* [F]**12:43** Lit *loved glory of men more than glory of God*; v. 41; Jn 5:41 [G]**12:48** Lit *has the one judging him* [H]**13:1** = completely or always

12:24-36 Jesus' parable about the **grain of wheat**, which **falls to the ground and dies** (v. 24), has an application through the paradox of the man who loses eternal life because of his fixation on physical life and temporal passions, while the man who has God as the first priority in his life will receive **eternal life** (vv. 25-26; cp. Mt 6:33; Lk 12:15,22). The expression **hates his life** was not meant to suggest contempt for oneself and certainly was not an allusion to a low value of life or suicidal tendencies (Jn 12:25). The climax of the parable came when Jesus emphatically stated that, in His death, He would draw **all people** to Himself (v. 32). "All people" is not a suggestion of universalism in the sense that all will be saved. However, it does provide assurance that Christ died for all and draws all without regard for ethnicity, gender, or economic status to Himself.

John's use of the phrase **lifted up** (Gk *hupsōthō*, "raise high, exalt," used exclusively by John to refer to Jesus' death, vv. 32-34; 3:14; 8:28; but elsewhere with the sense of "exalting") has a double meaning: The crucifixion of Christ will ultimately lead to His exaltation as well as to redemption (3:16). Once again, the people did not fully understand the meaning of His words (12:34). The disciples seemed to understand that Jesus' death was imminent; yet they could not comprehend that the Messiah could be "lifted up" to die (Dn 7:13-14).

13:1-30 Jesus' strong sense of identity and mission moved Him to perform this extraordinary act of service. The washing of **feet** clad only with sandals and filthy from walking miles on dusty, dirty roads was a common practice for a host to offer to those who had been guests invited for a meal (v. 5). However, the slaves or lowest-ranking servants of the house were responsible for this mundane task. None of the disciples volunteered to do what needed to be done. Jesus dramatically assumed the posture of a servant, showing in vivid reality His own humility and setting the pattern for His disciples as they would minister to one another in His absence (v. 2).

When Jesus **came to Simon Peter**, He was met first with an emphatic refusal from the impetuous disciple: **You will never wash my feet—ever!** (Gk *ou mē*, "absolutely never," v. 8), using in the grammatical construction a double negative for emphasis. Jesus replied, just as emphatically, that to be a partaker in the gospel, Peter must share this experience.

The only other mention of footwashing in the New Testament involved devout widows who were to offer hospitality and loving service to the saints, especially the poor

(1Tm 5:10). Most evangelicals do not prescribe footwashing or *pedilavium* (Lat, "foot bath") since the act is nowhere prescribed or commanded as an ordinance in the New Testament. Common observance in the early church was an act of hospitality and a way of expressing love and offering service to one another. Those who have experienced regeneration needed only to have cleansing from daily sins since regeneration was once and forever (Jn 13:10).

John set Jesus' ultimate act of love and service in stark contrast with Jesus' prediction of Judas' betrayal and Peter's denial.

John's use of veiled language would seem appropriate. Although **reclining close beside Jesus** (more literally "reclining on the bosom of Jesus") would be a natural description of the one next to Jesus since customarily all reclined around a low table during meals, but certainly a person next to Jesus would have a place of honor and would enjoy more intimate conversation with Him.

Judas, a common name, was probably from Kerioth (Hb, "cities"), once a fortified city of Moab (Jr 48:24,41; Am 2:2), which would explain the descriptor **Simon Iscariot's son** (Jn 13:2). As the keeper of the group's money, John noted that Judas had stolen a portion for himself (12:5-6). Perhaps John used the transitional phrase **it was night** (13:30) to underscore the spiritual darkness into which Judas was catapulting himself.

13:31-38 The **new command** was in contrast to the old (Lv 19:18; Lk 10:27) in the sense that Jesus introduced a new motive and dimension (Jn 13:34-35). "New" denotes a fresh and improved approach. Jesus used an affectionate vocative or familiar address, **children** (Gk *teknia*), to express His loving concern as He delivered an important admonition to His disciples (v. 33). **Peter** had genuine affection for Jesus (v. 37), but he was impetuous and impatient. Jesus knew that Peter was not yet ready to stand in the line of fire (v. 38).

Roosters were so reliable with their crowing that tradition says the Roman guards changed their shifts according to this reliable time indication, usually crowing at midnight and then at three in the morning. Jesus prophesied that Peter would deny Him **three times** before dawn.

who would betray Him. This is why He said, "You are not all clean."

12 When Jesus had washed their feet and put on His robe, He reclined[A] again and said to them, "Do you know what I have done for you? 13 You call Me Teacher and Lord. This is well said, for I am. 14 So if I, your Lord and Teacher, have washed your feet, you also ought to wash one another's feet. 15 For I have given you an example that you also should do just as I have done for you.

16 "•I assure you: A •slave is not greater than his master,[B] and a messenger is not greater than the one who sent him. 17 If you know these things, you are blessed if you do them. 18 I'm not speaking about all of you; I know those I have chosen. But the Scripture must be fulfilled: **The one who eats My bread[C] has raised his heel against Me.**[D]

19 "I am telling you now before it happens, so that when it does happen you will believe that I am He. 20 I assure you: Whoever receives anyone I send receives Me, and the one who receives Me receives Him who sent Me."

21 When Jesus had said this, He was troubled in His spirit and testified, "I assure you: One of you will betray Me!"

22 The disciples started looking at one another—uncertain which one He was speaking about. 23 One of His disciples, the one Jesus loved, was reclining close beside Jesus.[E] 24 Simon Peter motioned to him to find out who it was He was talking about. 25 So he leaned back against Jesus and asked Him, "Lord, who is it?"

26 Jesus replied, "He's the one I give the piece of bread to after I have dipped it." When He had dipped the bread, He gave it to Judas, Simon Iscariot's son.[F] 27 After Judas ate the piece of bread, Satan entered him. Therefore Jesus told him, "What you're doing, do quickly."

28 None of those reclining at the table knew why He told him this. 29 Since Judas kept the money-bag, some thought that Jesus was telling him, "Buy what we need for the festival," or that he should give something to the poor. 30 After receiving the piece of bread, he went out immediately. And it was night.

Farewell Discourse (13:31–16:33)

31 When he had gone out, Jesus said, "Now the •Son of Man is glorified, and God is glorified in Him. 32 If God is glorified in Him,[G] God will also glorify Him in Himself and will glorify Him at once.

33 "Children, I am with you a little while longer. You will look for Me, and just as I told the •Jews, 'Where I am going you cannot come,' so now I tell you.

34 "I give you a new command: Love one another. Just as I have loved you, you must also love one another. 35 By this all people will know that you are My disciples, if you have love for one another."

36 "Lord," Simon Peter said to Him, "where are You going?"

Jesus answered, "Where I am going you cannot follow Me now, but you will follow later."

37 "Lord," Peter asked, "why can't I follow You now? I will lay down my life for You!"

38 Jesus replied, "Will you lay down your life for Me? I assure you: A rooster will not crow until you have denied Me three times.

14 "Your heart must not be troubled. Believe[H] in God; believe also in Me. 2 In My Father's house are many dwelling places;[I] if not, I would have told you. I am going away to prepare a place for you. 3 If I go away and prepare a place for you, I will come back and receive you to Myself, so that where I am you may be also. 4 You know the way to where I am going."[J]

5 "Lord," Thomas said, "we don't know where You're going. How can we know the way?"

6 Jesus told him, "I am the way, the

[A] **13:12** At important meals the custom was to recline on a mat at a low table and lean on the left elbow. [B] **13:16** Or *lord* [C] **13:18** Other mss read *eats bread with Me* [D] **13:18** Ps 41:9 [E] **13:23** Lit *reclining at Jesus' breast*; that is, on His right; Jn 1:18 [F] **13:26** Other mss read *Judas Iscariot, Simon's son* [G] **13:32** Other mss omit *If God is glorified in Him* [H] **14:1** Or *You believe* [I] **14:2** The Vg used the Lat term *mansio*, a traveler's resting place. The Gk word is related to the verb *meno*, meaning *remain* or *stay*, which occurs 40 times in John. [J] **14:4** Other mss read this verse: *And you know where I am going, and you know the way*

Doctrine HOLY SPIRIT

In John 14:16-26, Jesus promised that He would give **another Counselor**, the **Holy Spirit**, who would be with them forever. Once Jesus returned to the Father, the Holy Spirit would in a sense stand in the Lord's place. He would be their helper, interpreter, witness, and revealer. The Father, Son, and Holy Spirit in their fullness will be with the believer who obeys and loves Him (Jesus).

The Greek word translated "Counselor" (*paraklētos*, "advocate, helper, intercessor, comforter") links the preposition *para* ("near or alongside") with the verb *kaleō* ("call or summon"). The Holy Spirit is called alongside believers to give help and advice:

- He is a person;
- He is God;
- He has unique functions within the divine triunity.

Fire, oil, water, and a dove are symbols used to represent the Holy Spirit's presence, as is wind or breath (Gk *pneuma*). The neuter case of this word does not justify viewing the person of the Holy Spirit merely as an impersonal power or force. The references to the Spirit affirm His intellect, emotion, and will (v. 17; 15:26; 16:7,13), and personal pronouns are appropriate and necessary in reference to Him.

"Another" (Gk *allon*, specifically "another of the same kind," 14:16) is a key word. The Holy Spirit comes from the Father, and He is commissioned by the Son (15:26). The Spirit's deity is full and not subordinated in any way; rather this "procession" testifies to the operation or function within the Godhead. Nevertheless, the Holy Spirit is not new on the scene, for the Spirit actively participated in creation (Gn 1:2), has been calling out individuals to specific tasks (Jdg 3:10; 13:25; 14:6), was as an agent in baptism (Mt 3:11; Mk 1:8; Lk 3:16; Jn 1:33), and effects the new birth (3:5). What was new after Jesus' departure was the intimate and permanent indwelling of the Spirit in the heart of every believer (15:26; cp. Ac 2:33; 5:31-32). That indwelling or baptism of the Spirit comes at the moment of conversion and never ceases.

At conversion, the Holy Spirit acts as a seal or guarantee of salvation (Eph 1:13; 4:30). In the Christian's life, the Spirit bestows the fruit of Christlike virtues (Gl 5:22-23) and distributes gifts equipping believers to do the work of the kingdom (Rm 12:3-13; 1Co 12:1-11; Eph 4:7-16; 1Pt 4:10-11). God acts through, reveals His will to, and empowers His children to do His work by means of His Holy Spirit. The Spirit's indwelling of the believer is instantaneous and permanent, but believers may pursue the "filling" of the Spirit, and from that filling comes the real power (Eph 5:18).

The work of the Holy Spirit is not as visible as that of the Father and Son, since His function is to glorify the Son, not calling attention to Himself. Still He has specific work to do

- teaching or illuminating God's Word (Jn 14:26; 16:13);
- reproving, convicting, and judging (16:8-11);
- regenerating (3:5);
- praying and interceding for believers (Rm 8:26);
- comforting (Jn 14:16);
- renewing (Ti 3:5);
- guiding into truth (Jn 16:13);
- empowering (Mt 28:19-20; Ac 1:8);
- testifying (Jn 15:26); and
- restraining evil (2Th 2:6-7).

The Holy Spirit also inspired the writers of Scripture and the prophets (2Tm 3:16; 1Pt 1:21-22; Nm 11:29; Ezk 2:2).

truth, and the life. No one comes to
the Father except through Me.
7 "If you know Me, you will also
know[A] My Father. From now on you
do know Him and have seen Him."
8 "Lord," said Philip, "show us the
Father, and that's enough for us."
9 Jesus said to him, "Have I been
among you all this time without
your knowing Me, Philip? The one
who has seen Me has seen the Father.
How can you say, 'Show us the
Father'? 10 Don't you believe that
I am in the Father and the Father
is in Me? The words I speak to you
I do not speak on My own. The Father
who lives in Me does His works.
11 Believe Me that I am in the Father
and the Father is in Me. Otherwise,
believe[B] because of the works themselves.
12 "I assure you: The one who believes
in Me will also do the works
that I do. And he will do even greater
works than these, because I am going
to the Father. 13 Whatever you
ask in My name, I will do it so that
the Father may be glorified in the
Son. 14 If you ask Me[C] anything in My
name, I will do it.[D]
15 "If you love Me, you will keep[E]
My commands. 16 And I will ask the
Father, and He will give you another
•Counselor to be with you

[A]14:7 Other mss read *If you had known Me, you would have known* [B]14:11 Other mss read *believe Me* [C]14:14 Other mss omit *Me* [D]14:14 Other mss omit all of v. 14 [E]14:15 Other mss read *If you love Me, keep* (as a command)

14:1-26 The "Farewell Discourse" or "Upper Room Discourse" has been one of the most appreciated and revered sections by believers in every era. This intimate and moving account of Jesus' instructions to His disciples took place after Jesus' last Passover meal and was recorded in detail by John. Chapters 14–17 resemble the established genre of a farewell discourse in Jewish literature. A great leader whose death was imminent might well prepare his followers for the future life, including the continuation of his work.

Sandwiched between Jesus' discussion of His departure and return (14:1-31 and 16:5-33) are His words of admonition to "remain in" Him (15:1-17) and His warning concerning the hatred of the world to be incurred by His followers (15:18–16:4). The main teaching of this entire discourse contained Christ's encouraging revelation concerning the person and work of the coming Holy Spirit, who would ultimately bring them comfort and give them courage (14:26). He would never leave them (vv. 16-17). The ultimate purpose of this discourse was to help the disciples understand Christ's death and resurrection. **The Holy Spirit** would shed further light on the person and work of Christ (v. 26).

Peter was the first to ask where Jesus was going (13:36). Jesus answered that He was returning to the Father **to prepare a place for** them (14:1-4).

The **dwelling places** (Gk *monai*, "staying place, room, abode") may be referring to places where the disciples can find peaceful living (vv. 2,23) but is probably more a reference to permanent dwelling places.

Jesus' claim that they knew **the way to where** He was going prompted **Thomas** to ask about the way (v. 5).

Thomas was skeptical and full of doubt, and he expressed those feelings honestly (v. 5). He in no way rejected Jesus, for he had already expressed a willingness to die for Him (11:16).

Jesus' answer, His sixth "I am" statement (v. 6), was startling and authoritative.

14:27-31 Peace (Gk *eirēnēn*, "tranquility, unity") is not the cessation of conflict and difficulty. Even Jesus spoke of being troubled and agitated about the existing circumstances of life (12:27), and He knew a violent and painful death awaited Him. However, in the midst of sorrow and suffering and injustice, Jesus had confidence in the Father so that He could move without fear along the journey before Him (14:27). **The ruler of the world** was a reference to the Devil (v. 30), who was continually present to sow his discord and deceit.

15:1-8 This section began with the seventh and final "I am" statement: **I am the true vine** (v. 1). Jesus uses the analogy of a vine and **branches** to teach that dependence on Him produces fruit (v. 5). Verses 1-8 present only two alternatives—either one **remains on the vine** and bears **fruit** or one does not. Those who remain are pruned so that they may become more fruitful; those who do not remain **are burned**. Those who do not remain were never really true believers. In verses 9-17, Jesus defines further what counts as "Christlike love." It is sacrificial service. In fact, fruit (v. 2) is "expressed" in sacrificial service.

In the Old Testament the vine represented Israel (Ps 80:8; Is 5:1-7; Jr 2:21), and the prophet spoke of Israel as becoming a wild and useless vineyard. Jeremiah also compared Israel to a degenerate plant, and Hosea complained about Israel as being an empty vine (Hs 10:1-15). In contrast, Jesus identifies Himself as "the true [Gk *alēthinē*, "genuine, authentic"] vine" (Jn 15:1). His **Father** is **the vineyard keeper**, and His followers are the "branches." Using the literary device of allegory, Jesus promised to produce fruit (v. 5) in the lives of believers. The branches have no life within themselves but receive life and are sustained by remaining attached to the vine. Those without fruit are either counterfeit followers or unproductive disciples (v. 4), and probably the former. Those who are false followers and fruitless are cast into the fire (v. 6). A branch apart from the vine and without the care of the keeper cannot produce fruit. The passage does not undercut the security of genuine believers but simply affirms the fate of those who are not genuine disciples. Discipleship is demonstrated by fruit-bearing.

A Christian apart from Christ and without the provision of God cannot live a Christlike life and bring glory to God. Prayer is a powerful tool for believers, and there is no difference between the presence of Christ and the impact of His words—both act as a governing force.

15:9-25 Love has ever been the motivation for obedience, and obedience in turn is a demonstration

forever. 17 He is the Spirit of truth. The •world is unable to receive Him because it doesn't see Him or know Him. But you do know Him, because He remains with you and will be[A] in you. 18 I will not leave you as orphans; I am coming to you.

19 "In a little while the world will see Me no longer, but you will see Me. Because I live, you will live too. 20 In that day you will know that I am in My Father, you are in Me, and I am in you. 21 The one who has My commands and keeps them is the one who loves Me. And the one who loves Me will be loved by My Father. I also will love him and will reveal Myself to him."

22 Judas (not Iscariot) said to Him, "Lord, how is it You're going to reveal Yourself to us and not to the world?"

23 Jesus answered, "If anyone loves Me, he will keep My word. My Father will love him, and We will come to him and make Our home with him. 24 The one who doesn't love Me will not keep My words. The word that you hear is not Mine but is from the Father who sent Me.

25 "I have spoken these things to you while I remain with you. 26 But the Counselor, the Holy Spirit—the Father will send Him in My name—will teach you all things and remind you of everything I have told you.

27 "Peace I leave with you. My peace I give to you. I do not give to you as the world gives. Your heart must not be troubled or fearful. 28 You have heard Me tell you, 'I am going away and I am coming to you.' If you loved Me, you would have rejoiced that I am going to the Father, because the Father is greater than I. 29 I have told you now before it happens so that when it does happen you may believe. 30 I will not talk with you much longer, because the ruler of the world is coming. He has no power over Me.[B] 31 On the contrary, I am going away[C] so that the world may know that I love the Father. Just as the Father commanded Me, so I do.

"Get up; let's leave this place.

15

"I am the true vine, and My Father is the vineyard keeper. 2 Every branch in Me that does not produce fruit He removes, and He prunes every branch that produces fruit so that it will produce more fruit. 3 You are already •clean because of the word I have spoken to you. 4 Remain in Me, and I in you. Just as a branch is unable to produce fruit by itself unless it remains on the vine, so neither can you unless you remain in Me.

5 "I am the vine; you are the branches. The one who remains in Me and I in him produces much fruit, because you can do nothing without Me. 6 If anyone does not remain in Me, he is thrown aside like a branch and he withers. They gather them, throw them into the fire, and they are burned. 7 If you remain in Me and My words remain in you, ask whatever you want and it will be done for you. 8 My Father is glorified by this: that you produce much fruit and prove to be[D] My disciples.

9 "As the Father has loved Me, I have also loved you. Remain in My love. 10 If you keep My commands you will remain in My love, just as I have kept My Father's commands and remain in His love.

11 "I have spoken these things to you so that My joy may be in you and your joy may be complete. 12 This is My command: Love one another as I have loved you. 13 No one has greater love than this, that someone would lay down his life for his friends. 14 You are My friends if you do what I command you. 15 I do not call you •slaves anymore, because a slave doesn't know what his master[E] is doing. I have called you friends, because I have made known to you everything I have heard from My Father. 16 You did not choose Me, but I chose you. I appointed you that you should go out and produce fruit and that your fruit should remain, so that whatever you ask the Father in My name, He will give you. 17 This is what I command you: Love one another.

18 "If the •world hates you, understand that it hated Me before it hat-

[A] **14:17** Other mss read *and is* [B] **14:30** Lit *He has nothing in Me* [C] **14:31** Probably refers to the cross [D] **15:8** Or *and become* [E] **15:15** Or *lord*

ed you. 19 If you were of the world, the world would love you as its own. However, because you are not of the world, but I have chosen you out of it, the world hates you. 20 Remember the word I spoke to you: 'A slave is not greater than his master.' If they persecuted Me, they will also persecute you. If they kept My word, they will also keep yours. 21 But they will do all these things to you on account of My name, because they don't know the One who sent Me. 22 If I had not come and spoken to them, they would not have sin.[A] Now they have no excuse for their sin. 23 The one who hates Me also hates My Father. 24 If I had not done the works among them that no one else has done, they would not have sin. Now they have seen and hated both Me and My Father. 25 But this happened so that the statement written in their scripture might be fulfilled: **They hated Me for no reason.**[B]

26 "When the •Counselor comes, the One I will send to you from the Father—the Spirit of truth who proceeds from the Father—He will testify about Me. 27 You also will testify, because you have been with Me from the beginning.

16 "I have told you these things to keep you from •stumbling. 2 They will ban you from the •synagogues. In fact, a time is coming when anyone who kills you will think he is offering service to God. 3 They will do these things because they haven't known the Father or Me. 4 But I have told you these things so that when their time[C] comes you may remember I told them to you. I didn't tell you these things from the beginning, because I was with you.

5 "But now I am going away to Him who sent Me, and not one of you asks Me, 'Where are You going?' 6 Yet, because I have spoken these things to you, sorrow has filled your heart. 7 Nevertheless, I am telling you the truth. It is for your benefit that I go away, because if I don't go away the •Counselor will not come to you. If I go, I will send Him to you. 8 When He comes, He will convict the world about sin, righteousness, and judgment: 9 About sin, because they do not believe in Me; 10 about righteousness, because I am going to the Father and you will no longer see Me; 11 and about judgment, because the ruler of this •world has been judged.

12 "I still have many things to tell you, but you can't bear them now. 13 When the Spirit of truth comes, He will guide you into all the truth. For He will not speak on His own, but He will speak whatever He hears. He will also declare to you what is to come. 14 He will glorify Me, because He will take from what is Mine and declare it to you. 15 Everything the Father has is Mine. This is why I told you that He takes from what is Mine and will declare it to you.

16 "A little while and you will no longer see Me; again a little while and you will see Me."[D]

17 Therefore some of His disciples said to one another, "What is this He tells us: 'A little while and you will not see Me; again a little while and you will see Me'; and, 'because I am going to the Father'?" 18 They said, "What is this He is saying,[E] 'A little while'? We don't know what He's talking about!"

19 Jesus knew they wanted to question Him, so He said to them, "Are you asking one another about what I said, 'A little while and you will not see Me; again a little while and you will see Me'?

20 "•I assure you: You will weep and wail, but the world will rejoice. You will become sorrowful, but your sorrow will turn to joy. 21 When a woman is in labor she has pain because her time has come. But when she has given birth to a child, she no longer remembers the suffering because of the joy that a person has been born into the world. 22 So you also have sorrow[F] now. But I will see you again. Your hearts will rejoice, and no one will rob you of your joy. 23 In that day you will not ask Me anything.

"I assure you: Anything you ask the Father in My name, He will give

of love (vv. 9-10). It is the supreme evidence (fruit) of genuine discipleship.

The Spirit is especially needed in the believer's life in times of pressure and upheaval. People who cling to **the world** oppose Christians because they **don't know** God (v. 21). Unbelievers are rebuked by the life of Jesus and His holiness, which means those who follow Him and emulate His standards will also be **hated** (v. 24).

15:18–16:4 Jesus warned His disciples that they would be hated because He was hated. Those who hate them were really without excuse. Those who had eyes to see could have witnessed Jesus' teachings and His deeds. The Spirit would give them boldness and inner strength in times of trial. Jesus was sternly warning them to be prepared for what was coming.

16:5-23 In this final section, Jesus returned to the subject of His departure. He began by further discussing the work of the Holy Spirit. Unless Jesus left, the Spirit would not come to them. The phrase **sorrow has filled your heart** (v. 6) suggests a lingering spirit of gloom and doom among the disciples, who still did not understand what would happen when Jesus departed and the Holy Spirit moved into their hearts (v. 7). The Holy Spirit **will convict the world:**

- **about sin**, namely, its ultimate manifestation, which is an individual's unbelief and the failure to place his trust in Christ (v. 9);
- **about righteousness** because Christ has returned to the Father, having conquered sin and death through His resurrection (v. 10);
- **about judgment, because the ruler of the world** [the Devil] **has been judged** in the cross and resurrection (v. 11). The Holy Spirit convicts of sins committed, righteousness forfeited, and judgment coming.

The Spirit's assignment to **guide you into all the truth** certainly applied to the writing of the New Testament documents, but the Spirit's guidance is not limited to the canon of Scripture (v. 23). God has not inspired subsequent revelation of the kind He has provided in Scripture, but the Spirit who inspired these writings is available to enable believers to understand the Scriptures and see their application in the believer's life.

16:16-24 Also in this section Jesus reminded His disciples that their grief would **turn to joy** (v. 20). His departure would bring the coming of the Holy Spirit. His resurrection would turn their sorrow into **joy** (v. 22). The vivid analogy of a woman's experience in childbirth strikes a familiar cord and is not a new image for Scripture.

[A] **15:22** To *have sin* is an idiom that refers to guilt caused by sin. [B] **15:25** Ps 69:4 [C] **16:4** Other mss read *when the time* [D] **16:16** Other mss add *because I am going to the Father* [E] **16:18** Other mss omit *He is saying* [F] **16:22** Other mss read *will have sorrow*

17:1-26 This prayer truly is the "Lord's Prayer"—for Himself, His disciples, and for all those who would believe in Him. His personal petitions consisted mainly of requests to help Him finish His mission. He spoke plainly of His pre-existence and of the glory He had before the creation of the world. He also clearly defined eternal life.

Jesus' main concern for His disciples was that they be protected from the enemy (v. 15). He prayed that they not be overpowered by the Devil but that they become sanctified, growing in the grace and knowledge of God (v. 17). Although some suggest disparagingly that Jesus was not praying for the world in this context, one must remember that this section was part of the Upper Room discourse, where Jesus was primarily concerned with preparing the Twelve for life after His departure. Therefore, these verses must be interpreted in this light. Jesus was concerned for the lost since other contexts demonstrate that clearly (see Lk 15:7,10,23,32; 19:10). His main concern in these verses, however, is for the Twelve, that those who believe His message might dwell in unity. In some profoundly mysterious way, the church reflects (or ought to reflect) the divine triunity. Believers must, by the power of the Holy Spirit, dwell in unity

Eternal life has several dimensions—purchased in the past through the Lord's atonement, keeping believers in the present from day to day, and securing the future when faith is consummated for eternity in the presence of the Lord (Jn 17:2-3). Jesus affirmed the completion of His mission and work assigned to Him by the Father, knowing that through His obedience the Father had been glorified (v. 4). Because He had been obedient to the Father's will, Christ would be exalted in the glories of heaven (v. 5).

A precious promise contained in Jesus' prayer is the assurance that **not one of them is lost** (v. 12). Some suggest that Jesus failed in the case of Judas, **the son of destruction**, but Judas perished because he rejected Christ. Even then, God's plan was accomplished and the Scripture fulfilled. Judas made his own choice, but God in His omniscience knew what that choice would be in eternity past, and that choice had personal consequences for Judas and eternal significance in God's plan for redemption.

Christians are in the world. Jesus recognized that they could live in the world without being bound to its mindset (v. 16). Jesus did pray for the protection of His children from **the evil one**, a reference to the Devil (v. 15). The disciples were needed in the world to share the good news of the gospel.

Sanctification is linked with truth (i.e., the word of God), which provides a sure and unchanging standard for life.

you. 24 Until now you have asked for
nothing in My name. Ask and you
will receive, so that your joy may be
complete.
25 "I have spoken these things to
you in figures of speech. A time is
coming when I will no longer speak
to you in figures, but I will tell you
plainly about the Father. 26 In that
day you will ask in My name. I am
not telling you that I will make requests to the Father on your behalf.
27 For the Father Himself loves you,
because you have loved Me and have
believed that I came from God.[A]
28 I came from the Father and have
come into the world. Again, I am
leaving the world and going to the
Father."
29 "Ah!" His disciples said. "Now
You're speaking plainly and not using any figurative language. 30 Now
we know that You know everything
and don't need anyone to question
You. By this we believe that You
came from God."
31 Jesus responded to them, "Do
you now believe? 32 Look: An hour is
coming, and has come, when each
of you will be scattered to his own
home, and you will leave Me alone.
Yet I am not alone, because the Father is with Me. 33 I have told you
these things so that in Me you may
have peace. You will have suffering
in this world. Be courageous! I have
conquered the world."

High Priestly Prayer (17:1-26)

17 Jesus spoke these things, looked up to heaven, and said:

Father,
the hour has come.
Glorify Your Son
so that the Son
may glorify You,
2 for You gave Him authority
over all flesh;[B]
so He may give eternal life
to all You have given Him.
3 This is eternal life:
that they may know You,
the only true God,
and the One You
have sent—Jesus Christ.
4 I have glorified You
on the earth
by completing the work
You gave Me to do.
5 Now, Father, glorify Me
in Your presence
with that glory I had with You
before the world existed.

6 I have revealed Your name
to the men You gave Me
from the world.
They were Yours,
You gave them to Me,
and they have kept Your word.
7 Now they know that all things
You have given to Me are
from You,
8 because the words that You
gave Me,
I have given them.
They have received them
and have known for certain
that I came from You.
They have believed
that You sent Me.
9 I pray[C] for them.
I am not praying
for the •world
but for those You have
given Me,
because they are Yours.
10 Everything I have is Yours,
and everything You have
is Mine,
and I have been glorified
in them.
11 I am no longer in the world,
but they are in the world,
and I am coming to You.
Holy Father,
protect[D] them by Your name
that You have given Me,
so that they may be one
as We are one.
12 While I was with them,
I was protecting them
by Your name
that You have given Me.
I guarded them and not one
of them is lost,
except the son
of destruction,[E]
so that the Scripture may be
fulfilled.
13 Now I am coming to You,

[A]16:27 Other mss read *from the Father* [B]17:2 Or *people* [C]17:9 Lit *ask* (throughout this passage) [D]17:11 Lit *keep* (throughout this passage) [E]17:12 The one destined for destruction, loss, or perdition

and I speak these things
in the world
so that they may have My joy
completed in them.
14 I have given them Your word.
The world hated them
because they are not
of the world,
as I am not of the world.
15 I am not praying
that You take them
out of the world
but that You protect them
from the evil one.
16 They are not of the world,
as I am not of the world.
17 •Sanctify[A] them by the truth;
Your word is truth.
18 As You sent Me
into the world,
I also have sent them
into the world.
19 I sanctify Myself for them,
so they also may be sanctified
by the truth.

20 I pray not only for these,
but also for those who believe
in Me
through their message.
21 May they all be one,
as You, Father, are in Me
and I am in You.
May they also be one[B] in Us,
so the world may believe
You sent Me.
22 I have given them the glory
You have given Me.
May they be one as
We are one.
23 I am in them
and You are in Me.
May they be made
completely one,
so the world may know You
have sent Me
and have loved them as
You have loved Me.
24 Father,
I desire those
You have given Me
to be with Me where I am.
Then they will see My glory,
which You have given Me
because You loved Me
before the world's foundation.
25 Righteous Father!
The world has not known You.
However, I have known You,
and these have known
that You sent Me.
26 I made Your name known
to them
and will make it known,
so the love
You have loved Me with
may be in them and I may be
in them.

Events Surrounding Jesus' Death (18:1–20:31)

Arrest, Trials, and Crucifixion (18:1–19:42)

18 After Jesus had said these
things, He went out with His
disciples across the Kidron Valley,
where there was a garden, and He
and His disciples went into it. 2 Judas, who betrayed Him, also knew
the place, because Jesus often met
there with His disciples. 3 So Judas
took a •company of soldiers and
some temple police from the •chief
priests and the •Pharisees and came
there with lanterns, torches, and
weapons.
4 Then Jesus, knowing everything
that was about to happen to Him,
went out and said to them, "Who is
it you're looking for?"
5 "Jesus the •Nazarene," they answered.
"I am He,"[C] Jesus told them.
Judas, who betrayed Him, was also
standing with them. 6 When He told
them, "I am He," they stepped back
and fell to the ground.
7 Then He asked them again, "Who
is it you're looking for?"
"Jesus the Nazarene," they said.
8 "I told you I am He," Jesus replied. "So if you're looking for Me,
let these men go." 9 This was to fulfill the words He had said: "I have
not lost one of those You have given
Me."
10 Then Simon Peter, who had
a sword, drew it, struck the high
priest's •slave, and cut off his right
ear. (The slave's name was Malchus.)
11 At that, Jesus said to Peter,
"Sheathe your sword! Am I not to
drink the cup the Father has given
Me?"
12 Then the company of soldiers,

Jesus knew the importance of being sanctified (Gk *hagiason*, "dedicated, purified") or set apart unto the Lord for His disciples, and the only way to that goal was through the working of God's word in their lives (v. 17).

Jesus not only stressed the importance of the love of believers one for the other (13:34), but He also admonished them to achieve unity (vv. 21-22), not in the sense of seeking sameness but becoming like-minded in order to present the gospel to the world in the best possible way.

18:1–19:42 Judas knew to look for Jesus in Gethsemane since Jesus often sought the quiet of this garden for prayer and meditation. Located on the lower slope of the Mount of Olives, this site is still marked by a grove of ancient olive trees (18:1).

Peter was obviously devoted to Jesus and courageous enough to risk his own life to defend Jesus against the arresting mob. He was armed and took action impulsively. Although Jesus told Peter, **"Sheathe your sword!"** there is no hint of pacifism here but rather Jesus' conscious determination to follow the Father's plan and timing (18:11). Guards from the Jewish temple were joined by a **company of soldiers** (Gk *speira*, "military cohort, a tenth of the legion"), likely a contingency of about 300 to 600 Roman soldiers, so the arrest would be legal. The troops were accompanied by a throng of religious leaders. The party seemingly evolved into an armed mob (18:3).

In the account of Jesus' passion, John to a large degree parallels the Synoptic Gospels. However, John does include some material that is not recorded in Matthew, Mark, or Luke. For instance, John notes the fact that Jesus was brought before **Annas**, the **father-in-law of Caiaphas, who was high priest that year** (18:12-14,19-24), for an informal trial. Since Jewish law claimed that the role as high priest was one held for life, Annas still exercised authority and influence.

The identity of **another disciple** (18:15) is not stated in Scripture. Some have speculated that it might have been Joseph of Arimathea, who later made his own personal tomb available for Jesus' burial, or Nicodemus, who is mentioned as helping Joseph prepare Jesus' body for burial. However, the person most often identified in this way in the book of John seems to be John himself. In any case, this individual had the distinction of being known by the high priest.

Although the Sanhedrin, the Jewish Supreme Court, had the authority to assess the death penalty, they could not carry out execution without the approval of the Roman government (18:31). **The governor's headquarters** (Gk *praitōrion*, transliterated as Praetorium, "imperial

[A] **17:17** Set apart for special use [B] **17:21** Other mss omit *one* [C] **18:5** Lit *I am*; see note at Jn 8:58.

guard") was probably located close to the palace of Herod (18:28). The Jewish religious leaders would not enter for fear they would be defiled and unable to eat the Passover meal.

From Jesus' final words, clearly love of enemies and steadfast commitment to the will of God were supreme. In Christ's death was modeled commitment to the two greatest commandments: loving God and loving neighbor, and loving them to the uttermost.

19:1-16 Pilate had Jesus **flogged** (Gk *emastigōsen*, "whip, scourge, punish"), a cruel and inhumane punishment in which the victim was bound to a post with the skin of his back fully exposed and then whipped 39 times (13 blows to the victim's chest and 26 to his back) by a soldier or some man of strength. The leather whip had pieces of bone and lead interwoven. The flesh was torn, and the ordeal served to hasten death. (For a timeline of Jesus' final week, see note on Mk 15:21-39.)

The Roman governor Pontius **Pilate** (A.D. 26-36) was procurator of Judea during Jesus' public ministry and at the time of His arrest, trial and crucifixion (Mt 27:11-26; Lk 3:1; 15:21-39; 23:1-25). He was directly accountable to the emperor Tiberius Caesar for all Roman governance in Judea. If the Jews filed a formal complaint against him, he could lose his position and perhaps his life (Jn 19:12). John recorded Pilate's verdict of "not guilty" (**I find no grounds for charging Him**, v. 4), proving that Jesus was not found guilty of any crime against Rome. Jesus did make clear that Pilate's power was temporal and limited, while Jesus' power was eternal and without limit (v. 11). Jesus also made clear the degrees of culpability. Judas, one of His inner circle, had greater knowledge and thus would bear greater guilt. There are degrees to the offensiveness of sin, and the more one knows the truth, the greater is her accountability before God.

Pilate pronounced his official decision to turn Jesus over to the Jews **in a place called the Stone Pavement** (Gk *lithostrōton*, "paved with stones"; Hb *Gabbatha*) from a raised platform outside in front of the Praetorium (v. 13). The response of the Jewish **chief priests** was astounding. They expressed their allegiance to the pagan emperor they hated and under whose governance they had long chafed (v. 15). The depth of their spiritual degradation was nowhere any more clear than in the hypocrisy of this act of betrayal (see 1:11).

19:17-42 Pilate's contempt for the Jews was evident in the title he placed over Jesus on the cross. Ironically, that title was exactly right (v. 19). The fact that its message was in **Hebrew,**

the commander, and the Jewish temple police arrested Jesus and tied Him up. 13 First they led Him to Annas, for he was the father-in-law of Caiaphas, who was high priest that year. 14 Caiaphas was the one who had advised the •Jews that it was advantageous that one man should die for the people.

15 Meanwhile, Simon Peter was following Jesus, as was another disciple. That disciple was an acquaintance of the high priest; so he went with Jesus into the high priest's courtyard. 16 But Peter remained standing outside by the door. So the other disciple, the one known to the high priest, went out and spoke to the girl who was the doorkeeper and brought Peter in.

17 Then the slave girl who was the doorkeeper said to Peter, "You aren't one of this man's disciples too, are you?"

"I am not!" he said. 18 Now the slaves and the temple police had made a charcoal fire, because it was cold. They were standing there warming themselves, and Peter was standing with them, warming himself.

19 The high priest questioned Jesus about His disciples and about His teaching.

20 "I have spoken openly to the world," Jesus answered him. "I have always taught in the •synagogue and in the •temple complex, where all the Jews congregate, and I haven't spoken anything in secret. 21 Why do you question Me? Question those who heard what I told them. Look, they know what I said."

22 When He had said these things, one of the temple police standing by slapped Jesus, saying, "Is this the way you answer the high priest?"

23 "If I have spoken wrongly," Jesus answered him, "give evidence[A] about the wrong; but if rightly, why do you hit Me?"

24 Then Annas sent Him bound to Caiaphas the high priest.

25 Now Simon Peter was standing and warming himself. They said to him, "You aren't one of His disciples too, are you?"

He denied it and said, "I am not!"

26 One of the high priest's slaves, a relative of the man whose ear Peter had cut off, said, "Didn't I see you with Him in the garden?"

27 Peter then denied it again. Immediately a rooster crowed.

28 Then they took Jesus from Caiaphas to the governor's •headquarters. It was early morning. They did not enter the headquarters themselves; otherwise they would be defiled and unable to eat the •Passover.

29 Then •Pilate came out to them and said, "What charge do you bring against this man?"

30 They answered him, "If this man weren't a criminal,[B] we wouldn't have handed Him over to you."

31 So Pilate told them, "Take Him yourselves and judge Him according to your law."

"It's not legal[C] for us to put anyone to death," the Jews declared. 32 They said this so that Jesus' words might be fulfilled signifying what kind of death He was going to die.

33 Then Pilate went back into the headquarters, summoned Jesus, and said to Him, "Are You the King of the Jews?"

34 Jesus answered, "Are you asking this on your own, or have others told you about Me?"

35 "I'm not a Jew, am I?" Pilate replied. "Your own nation and the chief priests handed You over to me. What have You done?"

36 "My kingdom is not of this •world," said Jesus. "If My kingdom were of this world, My servants[D] would fight, so that I wouldn't be handed over to the Jews. As it is, My kingdom does not have its origin here."[E]

37 "You are a king then?" Pilate asked.

"You say that I'm a king," Jesus replied. "I was born for this, and I have come into the world for this: to testify to the truth. Everyone who is of the truth listens to My voice."

38 "What is truth?" said Pilate.

After he had said this, he went out to the Jews again and told them, "I find no grounds for charging Him. 39 You have a custom that I release

[A]**18:23** Or *him, testify* [B]**18:30** Lit *an evil doer* [C]**18:31** According to Roman law [D]**18:36** Or *attendants*, or *helpers* [E]**18:36** Lit *My kingdom is not from here*

one prisoner to you at the Passover.
So, do you want me to release to you
the King of the Jews?"
40 They shouted back, "Not this
man, but Barabbas!" Now Barabbas
was a revolutionary.[A]

19 Then •Pilate took Jesus and had
Him flogged. 2 The soldiers also
twisted together a crown of thorns,
put it on His head, and threw a
purple robe around Him. 3 And they
repeatedly came up to Him and said,
"Hail, King of the Jews!" and were
slapping His face.
4 Pilate went outside again and
said to them, "Look, I'm bringing
Him outside to you to let you know I
find no grounds for charging Him."
5 Then Jesus came out wearing
the crown of thorns and the purple
robe. Pilate said to them, "Here is
the man!"
6 When the •chief priests and the
temple police saw Him, they shouted, "Crucify! Crucify!"
Pilate responded, "Take Him and
crucify Him yourselves, for I find no
grounds for charging Him."
7 "We have a law," the •Jews replied
to him, "and according to that law
He must die, because He made Himself[B] the Son of God."
8 When Pilate heard this statement, he was more afraid than ever.
9 He went back into the •headquar-
ters and asked Jesus, "Where are You
from?" But Jesus did not give him
an answer. 10 So Pilate said to Him,
"You're not talking to me? Don't
You know that I have the authority
to release You and the authority to
crucify You?"
11 "You would have no authority over Me at all," Jesus answered
him, "if it hadn't been given you
from above. This is why the one
who handed Me over to you has the
greater sin."[C]
12 From that moment Pilate made
every effort[D] to release Him. But the
Jews shouted, "If you release this
man, you are not Caesar's friend.
Anyone who makes himself a king
opposes Caesar!"
13 When Pilate heard these words,
he brought Jesus outside. He sat
down on the judge's bench in a place
called the Stone Pavement (but in
•Hebrew *Gabbatha*). 14 It was the
preparation day for the •Passover,
and it was about six in the morning.[E] Then he told the Jews, "Here
is your king!"
15 But they shouted, "Take Him
away! Take Him away! Crucify Him!"
Pilate said to them, "Should I crucify your king?"
"We have no king but Caesar!" the
chief priests answered.
16 So then, because of them, he
handed Him over to be crucified.
Therefore they took Jesus away.[F]
17 Carrying His own cross, He went
out to what is called Skull Place,
which in Hebrew is called *Golgotha*.
18 There they crucified Him and two
others with Him, one on either side,
with Jesus in the middle. 19 Pilate
also had a sign lettered and put on
the cross. The inscription was:

JESUS THE NAZARENE
THE KING OF THE JEWS.

20 Many of the Jews read this sign,
because the place where Jesus was
crucified was near the city, and it
was written in Hebrew,[G] Latin, and
Greek. 21 So the chief priests of the
Jews said to Pilate, "Don't write,
'The King of the Jews,' but that He
said, 'I am the King of the Jews.'"
22 Pilate replied, "What I have written, I have written."
23 When the soldiers crucified
Jesus, they took His clothes and
divided them into four parts, a part
for each soldier. They also took the
tunic, which was seamless, woven
in one piece from the top. 24 So they
said to one another, "Let's not tear
it, but cast lots for it, to see who
gets it." They did this to fulfill the
Scripture that says: **They divided
My clothes among themselves, and
they cast lots for My clothing.**[H] And
this is what the soldiers did.
25 Standing by the cross of Jesus
were His mother, His mother's sister, Mary the wife of Clopas, and
•Mary Magdalene. 26 When Jesus

[A]18:40 Or *robber*; see Jn 10:1,8 for the same Gk word used here [B]19:7 He claimed to be [C]19:11 To *have sin* is an idiom that refers to guilt caused by sin. [D]19:12 Lit *Pilate was trying* [E]19:14 Lit *the sixth hour*; see note at Jn 1:39; an alt time reckoning would be *about noon* [F]19:16 Other mss add *and led Him out* [G]19:20 Or *Aramaic* [H]19:24 Ps 22:18

Latin, and Greek only enhanced the importance of Jesus' death as having universal influence (v. 20). Hebrew was the language of the Jews and the common tongue for the people of Judea. Latin was the official language of the Roman Empire, and Greek was the language of the marketplace as well as the eastern provinces of the empire.

Several women remained at the cross along with **the disciple He loved**, probably John. Jesus' tender affection and sense of responsibility to His mother is nowhere more apparent than here (vv. 25-27). Jesus took seriously the responsibility of the firstborn son to provide for His mother. He assigned John to be her provider and protector.

Roman law required that criminals being crucified remain on the cross until dead, however long that might be. **The bodies** were then left to the vultures. Breaking the **legs** often hastened death (v. 31). Jewish law complicated this crucifixion scene because it required that the body be removed the same day and buried before evening, especially when **the Sabbath** was approaching (v. 31). Since Jesus was already dead, His legs were not **broken**, fulfilling another prophecy (vv. 33,36; Ps 34:20).

John is the only Gospel writer who records that Jesus' side was **pierced** while He was on the cross (19:31-37) and describes the significance of this piercing (i.e., that Scripture would be fulfilled, v. 36; see also Ps 34:20). John states quite clearly that he witnessed these things and testifies about them so that his readers might believe. Perhaps there is no better witness to the significance of the crucifixion than Jesus' words, which are contained in seven statements—three from the Gospel of John—as He hung on the cross:

- "Father, forgive them, for they do not know what they are doing" (Lk 23:34);
- "I assure you: Today you will be with me in Paradise" (Lk 23:43);
- First to Mary, **"Woman, here is your son,"** and then to John, **"Here is your mother"** (Jn 19:27);
- "My God, My God, why have you forsaken Me?" (Mk 15:34);
- **"I'm thirsty!"** (Jn 19:28);
- **"It is finished!"** (19:30);
- "Father, into your hands I entrust My spirit" (Lk 23:46).

In Greek, the last saying of Jesus on the cross, **It is finished** (Gk *tetelestai*, "accomplished, completed, fulfilled," Jn 19:30) is one word. The verb is in the perfect tense, signifying something accomplished in the past with continuing results in the present and future. With this word Jesus did not simply pronounce the end of His life but rather proclaimed the completion of His mission from the Father. Most important about the crucifixion is not the cause of death but rather the fact that Jesus did die a physical death as the substitute for all mankind (vv. 33-34).

Joseph of Arimathea is mentioned in all the Gospels (v. 38; Mt 27:57-60; Mk 15:42-46; Lk 23:50-56). He was wealthy, a member of the Sanhedrin, a God-fearing man, and in the end a follower of Christ. His daring request became a public confession of his faith in Christ (Jn 19:38). Joseph and **Nicodemus** (v. 39), as members of the Jewish "supreme court," had much more to lose than most of the other followers of Jesus. With the Jews' hostility toward Jesus, even their lives, not to mention livelihoods and reputations, were on the line.

20:1-22 John devotes more space to the resurrection account than any of the other Gospel writers. In this chapter, **Peter** and John ("the one Jesus loved") are juxtaposed. Both of them ran to **the tomb** and found it empty, but only the beloved disciple **saw, and believed** (vv. 3-10). The rest of the chapter spotlights the interaction between **Mary** and Jesus (vv. 11-18) and between **the disciples** and Jesus (vv. 19-29).

The first day of the week would have been the day after the Sabbath, beginning at sundown on Saturday and ending at sundown on Sunday (v. 1). The visit from the women occurred **early** on Sunday morning. John mentioned only **Mary Magdalene**, but others are noted in the Synoptic Gospels (v. 1; Mt 28:1; Mk 16:1; Lk 24:10). **The other disciple** (Jn 20:3) seems to be the Apostle John, who spoke of himself humbly in this way.

The Jewish custom of wrapping the dead body with long strips of cloth and then placing a napkin over the face would suggest that getting out of this mummy-like grave clothing would require a struggle and leave a disheveled mess. However, not only were the grave clothes still there, indicating the body had not been stolen, but they were neatly folded (vv. 6-7).

Fear of the Jews indicated why Joseph of Arimathea had not come forward earlier to identify himself as a disciple (19:38) as well as why the apostles were gathering behind closed doors (20:19). On the other hand, Mary Magdalene went alone to the tomb of Jesus **while it was still dark** (v. 1), while **Simon Peter** and the **one Jesus loved** waited until it was becoming daylight to go (vv. 2-8). Mary Magdalene is a wonderful example of eagerness to minister to and to honor the Lord. The risen Lord Jesus chose to send her to His brothers (v. 17) before the apostles received Christ's command. Jesus personally sent them out with the message of forgiveness in the power of **the Holy Spirit** (vv. 21-23).

saw His mother and the disciple He loved standing there, He said to His mother, "•Woman, here is your son." 27 Then He said to the disciple, "Here is your mother." And from that hour the disciple took her into his home.

28 After this, when Jesus knew that everything was now accomplished that the Scripture might be fulfilled, He said, "I'm thirsty!" 29 A jar full of sour wine was sitting there; so they fixed a sponge full of sour wine on hyssop[A] and held it up to His mouth.

30 When Jesus had received the sour wine, He said, "It is finished!" Then bowing His head, He gave up His spirit.

31 Since it was the preparation day, the Jews did not want the bodies to remain on the cross on the Sabbath (for that Sabbath was a special[B] day). They requested that Pilate have the men's legs broken and that their bodies be taken away. 32 So the soldiers came and broke the legs of the first man and of the other one who had been crucified with Him. 33 When they came to Jesus, they did not break His legs since they saw that He was already dead. 34 But one of the soldiers pierced His side with a spear, and at once blood and water came out. 35 He who saw this has testified so that you also may believe. His testimony is true, and he knows he is telling the truth. 36 For these things happened so that the Scripture would be fulfilled: **Not one of His bones will be broken.**[C] 37 Also, another Scripture says: **They will look at the One they pierced.**[D]

38 After this, Joseph of Arimathea, who was a disciple of Jesus—but secretly because of his fear of the Jews—asked Pilate that he might remove Jesus' body. Pilate gave him permission, so he came and took His body away. 39 Nicodemus (who had previously come to Him at night) also came, bringing a mixture of about 75 pounds[E] of myrrh and aloes. 40 Then they took Jesus' body and wrapped it in linen cloths with the aromatic spices, according to the burial custom of the Jews. 41 There was a garden in the place where He was crucified. A new tomb was in the garden; no one had yet been placed in it. 42 They placed Jesus there because of the Jewish preparation and since the tomb was nearby.

Resurrection (20:1-29)

20 On the first day of the week •Mary Magdalene came to the tomb early, while it was still dark. She saw that the stone had been removed[F] from the tomb. 2 So she ran to Simon Peter and to the other disciple, the one Jesus loved, and said to them, "They have taken the Lord out of the tomb, and we don't know where they have put Him!"

3 At that, Peter and the other disciple went out, heading for the tomb. 4 The two were running together, but the other disciple outran Peter and got to the tomb first. 5 Stooping down, he saw the linen cloths lying there, yet he did not go in. 6 Then, following him, Simon Peter came also. He entered the tomb and saw the linen cloths lying there. 7 The wrapping that had been on His head was not lying with the linen cloths but was folded up in a separate place by itself. 8 The other disciple, who had reached the tomb first, then entered the tomb, saw, and believed. 9 For they still did not understand the Scripture that He must rise from the dead. 10 Then the disciples went home again.

11 But Mary stood outside facing the tomb, crying. As she was crying, she stooped to look into the tomb. 12 She saw two angels in white sitting there, one at the head and one at the feet, where Jesus' body had been lying. 13 They said to her, "•Woman, why are you crying?"

"Because they've taken away my Lord," she told them, "and I don't know where they've put Him." 14 Having said this, she turned around and saw Jesus standing there, though she did not know it was Jesus.

15 "Woman," Jesus said to her, "why are you crying? Who is it you are looking for?"

Supposing He was the gardener, she replied, "Sir, if you've removed

A 19:29 Or *with hyssop* B 19:31 Lit *great* C 19:36 Ex 12:46; Nm 9:12; Ps 34:20 D 19:37 Zch 12:10 E 19:39 Lit *100 litrai*; a Roman *litrai* = 12 ounces F 20:1 Lit *She saw the stone removed*

CHARACTER PROFILE

Mary Magdalene A Devoted Follower

Her Background	• Resident of the village of Magdala • Popularly identified as a prostitute, although there is no textual evidence for that view
Her Story	• She was delivered from seven demons (Lk 8:2-3). • She financially supported Jesus' ministry. • She witnessed the crucifixion and burial of Jesus (Mt 27:55-61). • She went to the tomb early Sunday morning and reported it empty to Peter (Jn 20:1-2). • She saw two angels in the tomb and spoke with them (Jn 20:13). • She was the first to see the risen Lord (Jn 20:16-18; Mk 16:1-10). • She delivered a message to the disciples (Mt 28:10).
Life Lesson	An encounter with Jesus' mercy and forgiveness can transform a life forever.

Him, tell me where you've put Him,
and I will take Him away."
16 Jesus said, "Mary."
Turning around, she said to Him
in •Hebrew, *"Rabbouni!"*[A]—which
means "Teacher."
17 "Don't cling to Me," Jesus told
her, "for I have not yet ascended to
the Father. But go to My brothers
and tell them that I am ascending to
My Father and your Father—to My
God and your God."
18 Mary Magdalene went and announced to the disciples, "I have
seen the Lord!" And she told them
what[B] He had said to her.
19 In the evening of that first day
of the week, the disciples were gathered together with the doors locked
because of their fear of the •Jews.
Then Jesus came, stood among
them, and said to them, "Peace to
you!"
20 Having said this, He showed
them His hands and His side. So the
disciples rejoiced when they saw the
Lord.
21 Jesus said to them again, "Peace
to you! As the Father has sent Me,
I also send you." 22 After saying this,
He breathed on them and said,[C] "Receive the Holy Spirit. 23 If you forgive
the sins of any, they are forgiven
them; if you retain the sins of any,
they are retained."
24 But one of the Twelve, Thomas
(called "Twin"), was not with them
when Jesus came. 25 So the other
disciples kept telling him, "We have
seen the Lord!"
But he said to them, "If I don't see
the mark of the nails in His hands,
put my finger into the mark of the
nails, and put my hand into His side,
I will never believe!"
26 After eight days His disciples
were indoors again, and Thomas
was with them. Even though the
doors were locked, Jesus came and
stood among them. He said, "Peace
to you!"
27 Then He said to Thomas, "Put
your finger here and observe My
hands. Reach out your hand and put
it into My side. Don't be an unbeliever, but a believer."
28 Thomas responded to Him, "My
Lord and my God!"
29 Jesus said, "Because you have
seen Me, you have believed.[D] Those
who believe without seeing are
blessed."

Purpose of the Gospel (20:30-31)

30 Jesus performed many other
signs in the presence of His disciples
that are not written in this book.

[A]20:16 *Rabbouni* is also used in Mk 10:51 [B]20:18 Lit *these things* [C]20:22 Lit *He breathed and said to them* [D]20:29 Or *have you believed?* (as a question)

Mary Magdalene had the honor of being the first messenger commissioned by the risen Christ. In John, Mary was the carrier of the news about the empty tomb and the resurrected Lord to the other disciples. Perhaps the bookend effect created by the repeated wording, **because of his fear of the Jews** in 19:38 and **because of their fear of the Jews** in 20:19, is a literary touch that spotlighted this woman disciple. That wording is found elsewhere in John only in 7:13, a reference to why many Jews would not openly seek Jesus. This observation affirms the courage of Mary Magdalene, who faithfully bore her testimony in a fearful situation (20:18).

Jesus' salutation, **Woman,** was the polite way of addressing a woman. She did not recognize His voice then, but immediately when He uttered her name, she knew it was the Lord. Mary used the affectionate and respectful address ***Rabbouni*** (Aram, "my master, my teacher"). When Jesus said to Mary, **"Don't cling to Me"** (v. 17), He was not concerned about being touched since He asked Thomas to touch Him (v. 27). Rather, He wanted Mary to realize that He was there only temporarily. His return to the Father was imminent. **Brothers** included more than His siblings. The disciples now were related to Him in a new way because of His representing them to the Father (Heb 2:11-12). Jesus used **My Father and your Father** because Mary's relationship to God was different than His own (Jn 20:17).

The phrase **He breathed on them** (v. 22) again used Old Testament imagery (Gn 2:7, Ezk 37:9). Christ imparted spiritual life in the same way God gave physical life to Adam. This bestowal of the Holy Spirit on the disciples was a precursor of what would take place at Pentecost (Ac 2:1-4). God does not look to any man to decide whether or not to forgive (Jn 20:23). However, those who represent Him in sharing the gospel are recognized by forgiving or not forgiving sins, depending on whether the one who hears the message of salvation accepts or rejects Christ as Savior. Because the first two verbs are aorist tense, which implies a one-time action, and the other verbs are in perfect tense, which suggests a continuation and ongoing of the action of the former verbs, a more literal translation would be thus: "Those whose sins you forgive have already been forgiven; those whose sins you do not forgive have not been forgiven" (see note on Mt 16:13-20).

20:23-31 Thomas's confession of faith in Christ is a great spontaneous testimony of genuine belief (v. 28). **Thomas** moved from the lowest measure of faith—doubt and unbelief—to the highest confidence and faith. **My Lord** was Jesus' title used by His disciples, and **my God** was full acknowledgment of His deity.

John includes Jesus' last beatitude (v. 29) in this Gospel. Jesus pronounced a blessing on those who, unlike Thomas, would never see Him in the flesh but yet would exercise faith and believe in Him and His resurrection. Immediately following is the purpose statement of the entire Gospel (v. 31).

21:1-23 Important highlights of this section include the similarity of the miracle of the catch of **fish** and the account of the initial call of the disciples recorded in Lk 5:1-11. The action of **Simon Peter** is in character with other representations of him (Mt 16:21-23; 26:33-35; Jn 13:36-38; 18:10-11,15-18,25-27; 20:6). The reference to **sheep** closely follows the metaphor in 10:1-18, and 21:19 uses language concerning Peter that is applied to Jesus in 12:33. Another important point of this section has to do with John's desire to quell the rumor that he would not die before Christ's return.

21:15-17 John introduces a play on words in the exchange between Jesus and Peter. Jesus asked Peter, **Do you love Me?** three times. Three times Peter had denied Christ (18:16-17,25-27), and Jesus, in restoring Peter, gave Him three opportunities to affirm his love for the Lord.

Perhaps Peter was cautious in his avowal because of his bitter disappointment over having denied Jesus earlier. However, Jesus seemed to be making His point concerning the nature of Peter's love, coupling the question of love with the responsibility of ministry for Christ—i.e., **feed** (Gk *boske*, "tend") and **shepherd** [Gk *poimaine*, "guide, protect"; "nurture"] **My lambs** (Gk *arnia*) in 21:15 and **My sheep** (Gk *probata*) in verses 16 and 17. Both "lambs" and "sheep" denote tenderness and suggest care and protection. Jesus also prophesied that Peter would die as a martyr because of his commitment to follow Christ (vv. 18-19). Many interpret **stretch out your hands** as a reference to crucifixion. According to tradition, Peter was crucified in Rome between A.D. 64 and 68, and he insisted on being crucified upside down because he did not feel worthy to die as his Savior did.

31 But these are written so that you may believe Jesus is the •Messiah, the Son of God,[A] and by believing you may have life in His name.

The Reinstatement of the Disciples (21:1-23)

21 After this, Jesus revealed Himself again to His disciples by the Sea of Tiberias.[B] He revealed Himself in this way:

2 Simon Peter, Thomas (called "Twin"), Nathanael from Cana of Galilee, Zebedee's sons, and two others of His disciples were together.

3 "I'm going fishing," Simon Peter said to them.

"We're coming with you," they told him. They went out and got into the boat, but that night they caught nothing.

4 When daybreak came, Jesus stood on the shore. However, the disciples did not know it was Jesus.

5 "Men,"[C] Jesus called to them, "you don't have any fish, do you?"

"No," they answered.

6 "Cast the net on the right side of the boat," He told them, "and you'll find some." So they did,[D] and they were unable to haul it in because of the large number of fish. 7 Therefore the disciple, the one Jesus loved, said to Peter, "It is the Lord!"

When Simon Peter heard that it was the Lord, he tied his outer garment around him[E] (for he was stripped) and plunged into the sea. 8 But since they were not far from land (about 100 yards[F] away), the other disciples came in the boat, dragging the net full of fish. 9 When they got out on land, they saw a charcoal fire there, with fish lying on it, and bread.

10 "Bring some of the fish you've just caught," Jesus told them. 11 So Simon Peter got up and hauled the net ashore, full of large fish—153 of them. Even though there were so many, the net was not torn.

12 "Come and have breakfast," Jesus told them. None of the disciples dared ask Him, "Who are You?" because they knew it was the Lord. 13 Jesus came, took the bread, and gave it to them. He did the same with the fish.

14 This was now the third time[G] Jesus appeared[H] to the disciples after He was raised from the dead.

15 When they had eaten breakfast, Jesus asked Simon Peter, "Simon, son of John,[I] do you love[J] Me more than these?"

"Yes, Lord," he said to Him, "You know that I love You."

"Feed My lambs," He told him.

16 A second time He asked him, "Simon, son of John, do you love Me?"

"Yes, Lord," he said to Him, "You know that I love You."

"Shepherd My sheep," He told him.

17 He asked him the third time, "Simon, son of John, do you love Me?"

Peter was grieved that He asked him the third time, "Do you love Me?" He said, "Lord, You know everything! You know that I love You."

"Feed My sheep," Jesus said. 18 "•I assure you: When you were young, you would tie your belt and walk wherever you wanted. But when you grow old, you will stretch out your hands and someone else will tie you and carry you where you don't want to go." 19 He said this to signify by what kind of death he would glorify God.[K] After saying this, He told him, "Follow Me!"

20 So Peter turned around and saw the disciple Jesus loved following them. That disciple was the one who had leaned back against Jesus at the supper and asked, "Lord, who is the one that's going to betray You?" 21 When Peter saw him, he said to Jesus, "Lord—what about him?"

22 "If I want him to remain until I come," Jesus answered, "what is that to you? As for you, follow Me."

[A]20:31 Or *that the Messiah, the Son of God, is Jesus* [B]21:1 The Sea of Galilee; *Sea of Tiberias* is used only in John; Jn 6:1,23 [C]21:5 Lit *Children* [D]21:6 Lit *they cast* [E]21:7 Lit *he girded his garment* [F]21:8 Lit *about 200 cubits* [G]21:14 The other two are in Jn 20:19-29. [H]21:14 Lit *was revealed* (v. 1) [I]21:15-17 Other mss read *Simon, son of Jonah*; Mt 16:17; Jn 1:42 [J]21:15-17 Two synonyms are translated *love* in this conversation: *agapao*, the first 2 times by Jesus (vv. 15-16); and *phileo*, the last time by Jesus (v. 17) and all 3 times by Peter (vv. 15-17). Peter's threefold confession of love for Jesus corresponds to his earlier threefold denial of Jesus; Jn 18:15-18,25-27. [K]21:19 Jesus predicts that Peter would be martyred. Church tradition says that Peter was crucified upside down.

[23] So this report[A] spread to the
•brothers[B] that this disciple would
not die. Yet Jesus did not tell him
that he would not die, but, "If I want
him to remain until I come, what is
that to you?"

Epilogue (21:24-25)

[24] This is the disciple who testifies
to these things and who wrote them
down. We know that his testimony
is true.
[25] And there are also many other
things that Jesus did, which, if they
were written one by one, I suppose
not even the world itself could contain the books[C] that would be written.

[A]21:23 Lit *this word* [B]21:23 The word brothers refers to the late first century Christian community. [C]21:25 Lit *scroll*

21:24-25 The Epilogue contains many descriptions that suggest the author was an actual participant in the events taking place. However, in a peculiar sense these words were also penned for a people who were far removed from these events. When the Fourth Gospel was written, the New Testament literature (such as the Synoptic Gospels and perhaps some of Paul's letters) was probably already circulating and becoming well-known. John freely admitted that he recorded only a mere pittance of Jesus' words and deeds. Yet his testimony has enriched the church throughout the generations.

JOHN . . . WRITTEN ON MY *Heart*

A prayer . . .

Father, every time I pray, may I remember the costly sacrifice paid by Your Son Jesus to give me the eternal life I already enjoy in fellowship with You in the presence of Your Holy Spirit. Whenever I eat or serve a meal, may I remember that Jesus is the bread of life. Whenever I turn on a light, may I remember that Jesus is the light of the world. Whenever I go in and out of my home, may I remember that Jesus is the one doorway into relationship with You. Every time I am concerned about a need, remind me that Jesus is my shepherd—the Good Shepherd who lays down His life for me. Whenever I am tempted to fear or even to be overly concerned about temporal things, may my perspective be transformed by remembering that Jesus is the resurrection and the life, and may I freely proclaim the hope of this truth. May the message of my life leave no doubt that Jesus is indeed *the* way, *the* truth, and *the* life. Wherever I go and whatever I do, may I remember that life is worth living because Jesus is the true vine apart from whom I can do nothing. Above all, may the face of each person I see remind me of Your sacrificial love and move me to obey You in serving them as a testimony to this love found only in You. In Jesus' name, Amen.

Acts

Timeline	AD 36	AD 36–37	AD 47–49	AD 49
World Events / Biblical Events	Paul's conversion	Paul's time in Arabia	Paul's first missionary journey	Jerusalem Council on whether a Gentile has to be circumcised to be saved

"You will be My witnesses in Jerusalem, in all Judea and Samaria, and to the ends of the earth" (1:8b).

Who wrote Acts?

Although Luke never names himself, available evidence confirms him as the author. Luke and Acts have a common style, structure, and vocabulary, reaffirming that the same author produced both.

Who were the recipients?

Like the Gospel of Luke, Acts is addressed to Theophilus (Gk, "one who loves God," v. 1). The actual identity of Theophilus remains an enigma, as Luke and Acts provide the only known historical references to him. Theophilus could have been a new convert in need of full knowledge concerning the initiation and growth of Christianity, an interested Greek whom Luke hoped to convert to Christ, a high-ranking Roman official since Luke 1:3 refers to him as "most honorable Theophilus," or Luke may not have been addressing a specific individual but rather anyone who loves God.

When was Acts written?

Acts concludes with Paul's two-year imprisonment in Rome; therefore, the book must have been written during or after approximately A.D. 62.

Where did it happen?

Covering a span of 30 years, Acts recounts the expansion of the church from its Jewish roots in Jerusalem all the way to Rome, the center of the Roman Empire.

What is Acts about?

- *The spread of the early church.* Many commentators consider Ac 1:8 the theme verse. In this verse, Jesus outlines the strategy for the apostles to fulfill the "Great Commission" (Mt 28:18-20; Lk 24:46-48). The verse also provides the basic geographical outline of the spread of the gospel as depicted in Acts. The good news of the gospel was first shared in Jerusalem (chaps. 1–5), then in Judea and Samaria (chaps. 6–8), and eventually all the way to Rome and "the ends of the earth" (chaps. 13–28). Although Rome is not literally "the ends of the earth," Luke effectively shows the potency of the gospel message and its spreading via the ministry of Christ's followers who had been empowered by the Holy Spirit.
- *The power and presence of the Holy Spirit.* In the book's 28 chapters, Luke mentions the Spirit, whose activity pervades the entire book, over 50 times. The Holy Spirit, a gift to every believer (2:38), empowers believers to witness (1:8; 4:31); teaches believers (8:29; 10:19; 16:6-7); and guides the church (13:2). The Holy Spirit is also essential in both the formation and fulfillment of Scripture (1:16; 4:25). From start to finish in Acts the work of the Holy Spirit is evident. See **Doctrine**, p.1513.

Why should women read Acts?

One of the most exciting books in the New Testament, Acts is action-packed, providing relevant details on the spread of the gospel and the beginning of the Christian church. The ministries and lives of women in Acts are highlighted perhaps more than in any other New Testament book, showing the active and significant role women played in the formation of the early church. From beginning to end, Luke notes important women who played key roles in the formation of the apostolic church.

How do you read Acts?

Acts functions as the hinge between the Gospels and the Epistles or letters, and as the only historical sequel to the Gospels in the Bible. It provides the background and setting for many of the Pauline letters. If the church did not have Acts, all that is known about the beginnings of Christianity would be the bits gathered from Paul's letters. A reading of Acts enables believers to understand God's purposes and plans for the church. The book furnishes principles for revival and missionary work; it gives guidance for church government; it teaches how to disciple believers and how to grow churches; and it presents a strategy for evangelizing the world.

Outline

I. Introduction (1:1–11)
   - A. The Prologue (1:1-3)
   - B. The Promise of the Holy Spirit (1:4-8)
   - C. Jesus' Ascension (1:9-11)

II. Peter: Missionary to the Jews (1:12–12:25)
   - A. The Spread of the Gospel to Jerusalem (1:12–3:26)
   - B. The Opposition to Christianity in Jerusalem (4:1–5:42)
   - C. The Selection of the Seven Deacons (6:1–8:3)
   - D. The Spread of the Gospel in Judea, Galilee, and Samaria (8:4–9:31)
   - E. The Spread of the Gospel as Far as Phoenicia, Cyprus, and Antioch (9:32–12:25)

III. Paul: Missionary to the Gentiles (13:1–28:31)
   - A. The Spread of the Gospel Through the Region of Phrygia and Galatia (13:1–15:35)
   - B. The Spread of the Gospel into Macedonia, Achaia, and Asia (15:36–21:14)
   - C. The Spread of the Gospel to Rome (21:15–28:31)

AD 49–52	*AD 53–58*	*AD 58*	*AD 59*	*AD 60–62*
Paul's second missionary journey	Paul's third missionary journey	Paul's imprisonment in Caesarea	Paul's journey to Rome	Paul's house arrest in Rome

The Prologue (1:1-3)

1 I wrote the first narrative, Theophilus, about all that Jesus began to do and teach 2 until the day He was taken up, after He had given orders through the Holy Spirit to the apostles He had chosen. 3 After He had suffered, He also presented Himself alive to them by many convincing proofs, appearing to them during 40 days and speaking about the kingdom of God.

The Promise of the Holy Spirit (1:4-8)

4 While He was together[A] with them, He commanded them not to leave Jerusalem, but to wait for the Father's promise. "This," He said, "is what you heard from Me; 5 for John baptized with water, but you will be baptized with the Holy Spirit not many days from now."

6 So when they had come together, they asked Him, "Lord, are You restoring the kingdom to Israel at this time?"

7 He said to them, "It is not for you to know times or periods that the Father has set by His own authority. 8 But you will receive power when the Holy Spirit has come on you, and you will be My witnesses in Jerusalem, in all Judea and Samaria, and to the ends[B] of the earth."

Jesus' Ascension (1:9-11)

9 After He had said this, He was taken up as they were watching, and a cloud took Him out of their sight. 10 While He was going, they were gazing into heaven, and suddenly

[A]1:4 Or *He was eating*, or *He was lodging* [B]1:8 Lit *the end*

HARD QUESTION

What is the baptism of the Holy Spirit?

The promise of the Holy Spirit was foreshadowed by the ministry of John the Baptist. John had **baptized with water,** but the time was coming when people would **be baptized with the Holy Spirit** (1:5). Baptism with water, believer's baptism, identifies the person who has already accepted Christ with His death, burial, and resurrection. The baptism of the Holy Spirit occurs only once in a Christian's life at the point of salvation, when the Holy Spirit enters the believer to take up permanent residence (see Rm 8:9). The baptism of the Holy Spirit is an entirely divine activity that comes, like salvation itself, through grace and not by human effort. It is not a "second blessing" or some exclusive experience subsequent to conversion. Believers may be filled with the Holy Spirit again and again, but conversion is the point at which the Spirit is received as a permanent resident (see Eph 5:18). This baptism of the Spirit is different from the continuing and repeated actions of being "filled by the Spirit" (Eph 5:18) and living by the Spirit (Gl 5:25).

>WORD|*study*

1:8 The heart of Jesus' commission is the challenge to be witnesses (Gk *martures*). "Witness" is a key word in the book of Acts, used 29 times as either as a verb (*marturеō*) or a noun (*martus*). By definition, to bear witness means to testify to the truth of what you have seen, heard, or known. To be a witness for Jesus has been costly for many men and women who faithfully shared the gospel and as a result suffered torture and even death. In Acts, this was the case with both Stephen (7:59-60) and James (12:1-2). Many Christians throughout history have lost their lives for bearing a faithful witness to Christ. Eventually the Greek word for witness (*martus*) was anglicized as "martyr."

Title Acts was originally written as a sequel to the Gospel of Luke (see Lk 1:1-4; Ac 1:1-2). During the first century Acts and Luke likely circulated as a two-volume set. Early in the second century, the two works separated; and the Gospel of Luke was combined and circulated with the other three Gospels. Acts apparently did not have a fixed title until around the third century and was called "The Acts of the Apostles" or "The Acts of the Holy Spirit." Current scholars frequently shorten the title to "Acts" (Gk *praxeis*, a word often used to describe the "acts" of great men).

1:1-11 These verses serve as a bridge between the account of Jesus' life and ministry in the Gospel of Luke and the historical account of the development of the apostolic church in Acts.

1:6 Anticipating the coming of the kingdom, the apostles asked Jesus if He was **restoring the kingdom to Israel.** This question was a logical response because they linked the outpouring of the Holy Spirit with the coming of the promised kingdom (see Ezk 36; Jl 2:28–3:1; Zch 12:8-10). The apostles had not yet forsaken their belief that Jesus' goal was to establish His kingdom during their generation. They fully believed the kingdom belonged solely to Israel.

1:8 Jesus' plan for the evangelization of the world, as well as a rough outline for the book of Acts, is summarized in verse 8. Empowered by the Holy Spirit, the apostles **will be** Christ's **witnesses in Jerusalem** (chaps. 1–7), **in all Judea and Samaria** (chaps. 8–12), **and to the ends of the earth** (chaps. 13–28). The evangelization of the world would begin in Jerusalem, the very city where Jesus was crucified. This plan was strategic because Jewish pilgrims attended festivals in Jerusalem each year during Pentecost. Many of these would become seed planters for the early expansion of the church. The church would expand to Judea (the larger region in which Jerusalem was located) and Samaria (the region to the north of Judea). Eventually, the church would expand "to the ends of the earth." While some believe that this

two men in white clothes stood by them. 11 They said, "Men of Galilee, why do you stand looking up into heaven? This Jesus, who has been taken from you into heaven, will come in the same way that you have seen Him going into heaven."

The Spread of the Gospel to Jerusalem (1:12–3:26)

United in Prayer (1:12-14)

12 Then they returned to Jerusalem from the mount called the Mount of Olives, which is near Jerusalem—a Sabbath day's journey away. 13 When they arrived, they went to the room upstairs where they were staying:

> Peter, John,
> James, Andrew,
> Philip, Thomas,
> Bartholomew, Matthew,
> James the son of Alphaeus,
> Simon the Zealot,
> and Judas the son of James.

14 All these were continually united in prayer,[A] along with the women, including Mary[B] the mother of Jesus, and His brothers.

The Choice of Matthias (1:15-26)

15 During these days Peter stood up among the •brothers[C]—the number of people who were together was about 120—and said: 16 "Brothers, the Scripture had to be fulfilled that the Holy Spirit through the mouth of David spoke in advance about Judas, who became a guide to those who arrested Jesus. 17 For he was one of our number and was allotted a share in this ministry." 18 Now this man acquired a field with his unrighteous wages. He fell headfirst and burst open in the middle, and all his insides spilled out. 19 This became known to all the residents of Jerusalem, so that in their own language that field is called *Hakeldama* (that is, Field of Blood). 20 "For it is written in the Book of Psalms:

> **Let his dwelling become**
> **desolate;**
> **let no one live in it;**[D] and
> **Let someone else take**
> **his position.**[E]

21 "Therefore, from among the men who have accompanied us during the whole time the Lord Jesus went in and out among us— 22 beginning from the baptism of John until the day He was taken up from us—from among these, it is necessary that one become a witness with us of His resurrection."

23 So they proposed two: Joseph, called Barsabbas, who was also known as Justus, and Matthias. 24 Then they prayed, "You, Lord, know the hearts of all; show which of these two You have chosen 25 to take the place[F] in this apostolic service that Judas left to go to his own place." 26 Then they cast lots for them, and the lot fell to Matthias. So he was numbered with the 11 apostles.

Pentecost (2:1-13)

2 When the day of Pentecost had arrived, they were all together in one place. 2 Suddenly a sound like that of a violent rushing wind came from heaven, and it filled the whole house where they were staying. 3 And tongues, like flames of fire that were divided, appeared to them and rested on each one of them. 4 Then they were all filled with the Holy Spirit and began to speak in different •languages, as the Spirit gave them ability for speech.

5 There were Jews living in Jerusalem, devout men from every nation under heaven. 6 When this sound occurred, a crowd came together and was confused because each one heard them speaking in his own language. 7 And they were astounded and amazed, saying,[G] "Look, aren't all these who are speaking Galileans? 8 How is it that each of us can hear in our own native language? 9 Parthians, Medes, Elamites; those who live in Mesopotamia, in Judea and Cappadocia, Pontus and •Asia, 10 Phrygia and Pamphylia, Egypt and the parts of Libya near Cyrene; visitors from Rome, both Jews and •proselytes, 11 Cretans and Arabs—we hear them speaking the magnificent acts of God in our own languages." 12 They were all astounded and perplexed,

[A]**1:14** Other mss add *and petition* [B]**1:14** Or *prayer, with their wives and Mary* [C]**1:15** Other mss read *disciples* [D]**1:20** Ps 69:25 [E]**1:20** Ps 109:8 [F]**1:25** Other mss read *to share* [G]**2:7** Other mss add *to one another*

latter reference is to Rome, since Acts concluded in Rome, more likely Jesus was referring to a genuinely worldwide witness.

1:9-11 The ascension of Christ is mentioned three times in the Bible (1:9-11; Mk 16:19-20; Lk 24:50-51). These accounts note that from the Mount of Olives, Jesus lifted up His hands, blessed His disciples, and was **taken up** by a **cloud** into **heaven** (Ac 1:9) where He sat down at the right hand of God (Mk 16:19). The unique contribution of Acts to the ascension narrative concerns the details of Christ's return (vv. 10-11). Other Scriptures confirm that one day Christ will return again to the Mount of Olives to set up His earthly kingdom **in the same way** He ascended into the clouds (Dn 7:13; Mt 24:30; 26:64; Lk 21:27; Rv 1:7; 14:14).

1:12 A **Sabbath day's journey** was equal to three fourths of a mile. The disciples could have traveled this distance, and no restrictions applied because they traveled on a Thursday, 40 days after the resurrection.

1:14 The women and Jesus' **brothers** joined the 11 apostles. The presence of **Mary the mother of Jesus** among the women is the last mention of her in the New Testament. Mary Magdalene, Mary the wife of Clopas, Martha, Joanna, Susanna, and Salome, as well as others, were possibly present. These women had been a vital part of Jesus' ministry, accompanying Him when He traveled and supporting Him financially (Lk 8:1-3). Some of them followed Jesus from Galilee before His crucifixion (Lk 23:27), stood at a distance from the cross when He died (Jn 19:25), made the necessary preparations for His burial (Lk 23:55-56; 24:1), and reported the news of Jesus' resurrection to the 11 apostles (Lk 24:9-10). These faithful followers of Christ gathered in the room upstairs, or "upper room," to pray with the apostles (v. 13).

1:15-26 Over the course of the 10 days between the ascension and Pentecost, the believers in Jerusalem gathered together to pray and to discuss the vacancy left among the apostles by the departure of Judas Iscariot.

1:15 The text indicates that **Peter stood up among the brothers**. Depending on the context, the Greek word used here for "brothers" (Gk *adelphōn*, "near kinsmen or associates") can refer to men and women or to siblings. The term is not gender specific. This generic reference may well be to brothers and sisters in the family of God. Luke noted that the group numbered approximately **120**. This number may have been significant, because Jewish law required 120 men

saying to one another, "What could
this be?" 13 But some sneered and
said, "They're full of new wine!"

Peter's Sermon (2:14-36)

14 But Peter stood up with the Elev-
en, raised his voice, and proclaimed
to them: "Men of Judah and all you
residents of Jerusalem, let me explain this[A] to you and pay attention
to my words. 15 For these people are
not drunk, as you suppose, since it's
only nine in the morning.[B] 16 On the
contrary, this is what was spoken
through the prophet Joel:

17 **And it will be** in the last days,
says God,
that **I will pour out My Spirit**
on all humanity;
then your sons
and your daughters
will prophesy,
your young men will
see visions,
and your old men will
dream dreams.
18 **I will even pour out My Spirit**
on My male
and female ˙slaves
in those days,
and they will prophesy.
19 **I will display wonders**
in the heaven above
and signs on the earth below:
blood and fire and a cloud
of smoke.
20 **The sun will be turned**
to darkness
and the moon to blood
before the great and
remarkable Day of the
Lord comes.
21 **Then everyone who calls**
on the name of the Lord
will be saved.[C]

22 "Men of Israel, listen to these
words: This Jesus the ˙Nazarene was
a man pointed out to you by God
with miracles, wonders, and signs
that God did among you through
Him, just as you yourselves know.
23 Though He was delivered up according to God's determined plan
and foreknowledge, you used[D] lawless people[E] to nail Him to a cross
and kill Him. 24 God raised Him up,
ending the pains of death, because it
was not possible for Him to be held
by it. 25 For David says of Him:

I saw the Lord ever
before me;
because He is
at my right hand,
I will not be shaken.
26 **Therefore my heart was glad,**
and my tongue rejoiced.
Moreover, my flesh will rest
in hope,
27 **because You will not leave me**
in ˙Hades
or allow Your Holy One
to see decay.
28 **You have revealed**
the paths of life to me;
You will fill me with gladness
in Your presence.[F]

29 "Brothers, I can confidently
speak to you about the patriarch
David: He is both dead and buried,
and his tomb is with us to this day.
30 Since he was a prophet, he knew
that God had sworn an oath to him
to seat one of his descendants[G,H] on
his throne. 31 Seeing this in advance,
he spoke concerning the resurrection of the ˙Messiah:

He[I] was not left in Hades,
and His flesh **did not**
experience decay.[J]

32 "God has resurrected this Jesus.
We are all witnesses of this. 33 Therefore, since He has been exalted to
the right hand of God and has received from the Father the promised
Holy Spirit, He has poured out what
you both see and hear. 34 For it was
not David who ascended into the
heavens, but he himself says:

The Lord declared
to my Lord,
'Sit at My right hand
35 **until I make Your enemies**
Your footstool.'[K]

36 "Therefore let all the house of
Israel know with certainty that God
has made this Jesus, whom you crucified, both Lord and Messiah!"

to establish a community with its own council. Luke might have been asserting that the group of believers was now large enough to form its own community.

1:16-19 In Peter's speech to the 120 Jerusalem believers, he recounted Judas' death. According to Acts, **this man** [Judas] **acquired a field with his unrighteous wages.** The Gospel of Matthew provides more specific details, noting that Judas returned the money he received for betraying Jesus to the chief priests and the elders. They then bought the "Field of Blood" (Mt 27:3-9). Luke simply notes in Acts that Judas' money purchased the "Field of Blood" (Aram *Hakeldamach*). Matthew demonstrates that the purchase of the field fulfilled Scripture, while Luke shows that Judas received what he deserved—a horrible death. Luke provides the more vivid account of Judas' death. Matthew only notes that Judas hanged himself (Mt 27:5). Even though Luke omits this information, you can deduce that Judas' falling **headfirst** resulted from his being suspended. The rope either broke due to the weight of his body, or someone cut the rope. While falling, Judas' body probably struck a sharp object, causing his body to **burst open**.

1:21 The apostle was to come **from among the men**. A woman apostle was not an option, even though women had been a part of kingdom service throughout Jesus' ministry. The leadership role of an apostle belonged exclusively to men. Jesus had purposefully chosen 12 men to be His apostles and the replacement would be a man as well.

1:26 Casting **lots** was an Old Testament practice for discerning the will of God when a prophet was not available (Pr 16:33). After the outpouring of the Holy Spirit at Pentecost, this practice became unnecessary, as the Holy Spirit guides believers into all truth (Jn 16:13).

2:1-13 The day of Pentecost (Gk *pentēkostēs*, "fifty") occurred 50 days after Passover and so just over 50 days after the resurrection of Christ. "Pentecost," the Festival of Weeks or Harvest in the Old Testament, was one of three annual feasts that brought all devout Jewish men to Jerusalem (Ex 23:16; 34:22-23; Lv 23:15-21). At this gathering, though, Luke makes clear that a supernatural occurrence took place.

2:1-2 When this eventful day arrived, **they were all together in one place.** Whether this group included only the 12 apostles or the 120 believers mentioned in 1:15 is unclear. The context seems to indicate the larger number (2:6-11). The **place**, which

[A] **2:14** Lit *let this be known* [B] **2:15** Lit *it's the third hour of the day* [C] **2:17-21** Jl 2:28-32 [D] **2:23** Other mss read *you have taken* [E] **2:23** Or *used the hand of lawless ones* [F] **2:25-28** Ps 16:8-11 [G] **2:30** Other mss add *according to the flesh to raise up the Messiah* [H] **2:30** Lit *one from the fruit of his loin* [I] **2:31** Other mss read *His soul* [J] **2:31** Ps 16:10 [K] **2:34-35** Ps 110:1

is referred to as a **house**, probably located close to the temple, was most likely the room upstairs in which the believers had been gathering for prayer.

2:37-38 Peter's sermon caused many of the Jewish listeners to come **under deep conviction**. They were convinced of the truths about Jesus and convicted of their sins. In desperation they asked the apostles: **What must we do?** Peter commanded them to **repent** (Gk *metanoēsate*, a "change of direction or a change of purpose"), turning from sin to Christ, the essential beginning point for salvation. Then, they were to **be baptized**, the public declaration of their repentance and faith. Baptism is not a prerequisite for salvation but a personal choice for completing obedience to Christ with a public testimony of repentance and faith. Some controversy surrounds the inclusion of a baptismal command with the phrase **for the forgiveness of your sins**. Some people argue that both repentance and baptism are necessary for salvation. However, this view is not viable because many other verses of Scripture clearly indicate that the forgiveness of sins results from faith alone (Jn 3:16; Rm 4:1-7; 11:6; Gl 3:8-9; Eph 2:8-9). Peter himself spoke of forgiveness of sins on the basis of faith alone (Ac 5:31; 10:43; 13:38-39). Additionally, the thief on the cross next to Jesus was never baptized; yet Jesus promised him a place in paradise (Lk 23:39-43). For these reasons, baptism is not essential for salvation. Forgiveness for sins does not come as a result of baptism but rather through what baptism symbolizes—the death, burial, and resurrection of Jesus.

2:43 The **fear** (Gk *phobos*, "amazement") or reverential awe that came over everyone was a result of the realization of the power and majesty of God.

2:44-47 All the believers were together and held all things in common. Unity marked the early church. They cared for each other, giving **as anyone had a need**. This voluntary selling and sharing of goods was not compulsory but the result of their deep commitment to both God and each other.

3:1-10 The healing of the **lame** man is one of the wonders and signs performed by the apostles (2:43). The text indicates that the lame man begged **every day at the temple gate called Beautiful**, a large and ornate gate separating the court of Gentiles from the court of women inside the temple mount on the eastern side. Peter, apparently with John looking on, performed the healing **in the name of Jesus Christ the**

Forgiveness Through the Messiah (2:37-40)

37 When they heard this, they came under deep conviction[A] and said to Peter and the rest of the apostles: "Brothers, what must we do?"

38 "Repent," Peter said to them, "and be baptized, each of you, in the name of Jesus Christ for the forgiveness of your sins, and you will receive the gift of the Holy Spirit. 39 For the promise is for you and for your children, and for all who are far off,[B] as many as the Lord our God will call." 40 And with many other words he testified and strongly urged them, saying, "Be saved from this corrupt[C] generation!"

A Generous and Growing Church (2:41-47)

41 So those who accepted his message were baptized, and that day about 3,000 people were added to them. 42 And they devoted themselves to the apostles' teaching, to the fellowship, to the breaking of bread, and to the prayers.

43 Then fear came over everyone, and many wonders and signs were being performed through the apostles. 44 Now all the believers were together and held all things in common. 45 They sold their possessions and property and distributed the proceeds to all, as anyone had a need.[D] 46 Every day they devoted themselves to meeting together in the •temple complex, and broke bread from house to house. They ate their food with a joyful and humble attitude, 47 praising God and having favor with all the people. And every day the Lord added to them[E] those who were being saved.

The Healing of a Lame Man (3:1-10)

3 Now Peter and John were going up together to the •temple complex at the hour of prayer at three in the afternoon.[F] 2 And a man who was lame from birth was carried there and placed every day at the temple gate called Beautiful, so he could beg from those entering the temple complex. 3 When he saw Peter and John about to enter the temple complex, he asked for help. 4 Peter, along with John, looked at him intently and said, "Look at us." 5 So he turned to them,[G] expecting to get something from them. 6 But Peter said, "I don't have silver or gold, but what I have, I give you: In the name of Jesus Christ the •Nazarene, get up and walk!" 7 Then, taking him by the right hand he raised him up, and at once his feet and ankles became strong. 8 So he jumped up, stood, and started to walk, and he entered the temple complex with them—walking, leaping, and praising God. 9 All the people saw him walking and praising God, 10 and they recognized that he was the one who used to sit and beg at the Beautiful Gate of the temple complex. So they were filled with awe and astonishment at what had happened to him.

Preaching in Solomon's Colonnade (3:11-26)

11 While he[H] was holding on to Peter and John, all the people, greatly amazed, ran toward them in what is called Solomon's Colonnade. 12 When Peter saw this, he addressed the people: "Men of Israel, why are you amazed at this? Or why do you stare at us, as though we had made him walk by our own power or godliness? 13 The God of Abraham, Isaac, and Jacob, the God of our fathers, has glorified His Servant Jesus, whom you handed over and denied in the presence of •Pilate, when he had decided to release Him. 14 But you denied the Holy and Righteous One and asked to have a murderer given to you. 15 You killed the source[I] of life, whom God raised from the dead; we are witnesses of this. 16 By faith in His name, His name has made this man strong, whom you see and know. So the faith that comes through Him has given him this perfect health in front of all of you.

17 "And now, •brothers, I know that you did it in ignorance, just as your leaders also did. 18 But what God predicted through the mouth

A **2:37** Lit *they were pierced to the heart* B **2:39** For distant generations or perhaps Gentiles C **2:40** Or *crooked*, or *twisted* D **2:45** Or *to all, according to one's needs* E **2:47** Other mss read *to the church* F **3:1** Lit *at the ninth hour* G **3:5** Or *he paid attention to them* H **3:11** Other mss read *the lame man who was healed* I **3:15** Or *the Prince*, or *the Ruler*

of all the prophets—that His •Messiah would suffer—He has fulfilled in this way. 19 Therefore repent and turn back, so that your sins may be wiped out, that seasons of refreshing may come from the presence of the Lord,[A] 20 and that He may send Jesus, who has been appointed for you as the Messiah. 21 Heaven must welcome[B] Him until the times of the restoration of all things, which God spoke about by the mouth of His holy prophets from the beginning. 22 Moses said:[C]

The Lord your God will raise up for you a Prophet like me from among your brothers. You must listen to Him in everything He will say to you. 23 And everyone who will not listen to that Prophet will be completely cut off from the people.[D]

24 "In addition, all the prophets who have spoken, from Samuel and those after him, have also announced these days. 25 You are the sons of the prophets and of the covenant that God made with your ancestors, saying to Abraham, **And all the families of the earth will be blessed through your offspring.**[E] 26 God raised up His Servant[F] and sent Him first to you to bless you by turning each of you from your evil ways."

The Opposition to Christianity in Jerusalem (4:1–5:42)

The Arrest of Peter and John (4:1-4)

4 Now as they were speaking to the people, the priests, the commander of the temple police, and the •Sadducees confronted them, 2 because they were provoked that they were teaching the people and proclaiming the resurrection from the dead, using Jesus as the example.[G] 3 So they seized them and put them in custody until the next day, since it was already evening. 4 But many of those who heard the message believed, and the number of the men came to about 5,000.

Peter and John Before the Jewish Leadership (4:5-12)

5 The next day, their rulers, elders, and •scribes assembled in Jerusalem 6 with Annas the high priest, Caiaphas, John and Alexander, and all the members of the high-priestly family.[H] 7 After they had Peter and John stand before them, they asked the question: "By what power or in what name have you done this?"

8 Then Peter was filled with the Holy Spirit and said to them, "Rulers of the people and elders:[I] 9 If we are being examined today about a good deed done to a disabled man—by what means he was healed— 10 let it be known to all of you and to all the people of Israel, that by the name of Jesus Christ the •Nazarene—whom you crucified and whom God raised

HARD QUESTION

Is there only one way to heaven?

The importance of Acts in determining the way of salvation cannot be underestimated. Many people embrace "pluralism," believing that the world's major religions provide independent paths to a saving relationship with God. However, Acts indicates both implicitly and explicitly that salvation can only be obtained through Jesus Christ (4:12). Does this mean that devout people of other faiths will not go to heaven? Yes. For further evidence of this conclusion consider the story in Ac 8, where the Ethiopian official was instructed by Philip. First, the Ethiopian was a devout man. He traveled thousands of miles to worship in the outer areas of the Jewish synagogue. He read the prophet Isaiah as he traveled. Despite the Ethiopian's religious nature, the Holy Spirit instructed Philip to share the gospel with him. If this man were going to be saved through another religion, Philip would have had no reason to go to him in the first place. Additionally, consider the man named Cornelius (Ac 10:2). Why did he need to hear about Jesus Christ? Yet God in a vision told Peter to share the gospel with this man. Being religious is not enough. Salvation comes by grace through faith in Jesus Christ alone. Knowing that Jesus Christ is the only way should encourage every woman to be bold in sharing her faith and to take an active role in missionary efforts to spread the gospel. Every person should take seriously the gospel message of Jesus Christ.

Nazarene. To invoke the name of Jesus means to call upon His authority and power.

3:17 After confronting his Jewish **brothers** with the crucifixion of Christ, Peter acknowledged that they **did it in ignorance**, as Jesus previously stated while on the cross (Lk 23:34). The Jews alone should not be held responsible. This redemption via the cross had been predicted through the mouth of all the prophets. The death of Christ was no surprise but a fulfillment of prophecy to provide atonement for the sins of all.

4:4 Luke notes that **the number of the men** (Gk *andrōn*, "male") **came to about 5,000**, the total of believing men at the time. Since "men" is not a gender neutral term, this number would not have included the women and children who had believed.

4:5-6 The next day Peter and John stood trial before the **rulers, elders, and scribes**, or the Sanhedrin, Israel's supreme court (Mk 15:1). **Annas the high priest** was actually the former high priest (A.D. 6–15) and the father-in-law of **Caiaphas**, the current high priest (A.D. 18–36). Annas, whose power had been removed by the Romans, was still regarded by the Jews as the high priest, thus possessing considerable power. **John** is a possible reference to Jonathan, one of Annas' sons, who later replaced Caiaphas as high priest in A.D. 36. Nothing is known about **Alexander,** though he may likely have been one of the **members of the high-priestly family** in attendance at the trial. Someone in this group, likely Annas or Caiaphas, questioned Peter and John about the healing.

4:7-10 The leaders of the Sanhedrin did not question the reality of the healing because a lame man known to everyone now walked. Instead, the Sanhedrin wanted to know **by what power or in what name** the healing had been performed. Facing persecution, the power of **the Holy Spirit,** as Jesus had promised, enabled Peter to speak boldly yet succinctly in answering the questions from the Sanhedrin much as he had answered questions earlier from the crowd (3:11-26; Lk 12:11-12). The healing was accomplished by the power and in **the name of Jesus Christ the Nazarene.**

[A] **3:19** Some editors or translators put *that seasons . . . the Lord* in v. 20 [B] **3:21** Or *receive*, or *retain* [C] **3:22** Other mss add *to the fathers* [D] **3:22-23** Dt 18:15-19 [E] **3:25** Gn 12:3; 18:18; 22:18; 26:4 [F] **3:26** Other mss add *Jesus* [G] **4:2** Lit *proclaiming in Jesus the resurrection from the dead* [H] **4:6** Or *high-priestly class*, or *high-priestly clan* [I] **4:8** Other mss add *of Israel*

4:13 These fishermen were without formal training in any rabbinical schools. Nevertheless, it was apparent that **they had been with Jesus**, providing unique credentials for their task.

4:14-21 The **Sanhedrin** could not deny that the man had been healed, yet they could not afford to allow teaching and healing in Jesus' name to continue.

4:23-30 Their prayer began with an acknowledgment that God is the Creator of **heaven, the earth, and the sea, and everything in them**. As the **Master** and Creator, God controls all things. They prayed Scripture, recognizing the authority and truthfulness of the words of God that were written **through the Holy Spirit**. The gathered group of believers, praying about their current situation, could have easily been intimidated by the threats of the powerful Sanhedrin; however, they prayed for **boldness**, not protection, in speaking His word. Perhaps they remembered Jesus' words from His Sermon on the Mount (Mt 5:10-12).

4:31 After they finished praying, God displayed His presence as **the place where they were assembled was shaken**. This physical manifestation of the presence of God was not unlike what happened at Pentecost. This divine sign was not a chance occurrence. God answered their prayers and they all **began to speak God's message with boldness**. This fresh in-filling was God's refueling these believers according to their needs in a new situation.

4:36-37 A man **the apostles called Barnabas** (Aram, "son of encouragement") gave generously to the needs of others. Barnabas, a significant figure later in Acts, was named **Joseph**; but due to his righteous character and encouraging demeanor, his name was changed to Barnabas. Barnabas was a Hellenistic Jew, a Levite from Cyprus, and a kinsman of John Mark (Col 4:10).

5:1-2 A contrast is introduced by the transitional word **But**. While Barnabas provided a good example of sharing (4:36-37), **Ananias** and **Sapphira** provided a negative one. Feigning piety, the married couple **sold a piece of property** and pretended to give all of the proceeds to the church but instead **kept back part of the proceeds** for themselves. Possibly the example of Barnabas' Spirit-led generosity prompted Ananias and Sapphira to desire that same approval. In any case, the actions of Ananias and Sapphira demonstrated an improper motive in giving.

from the dead—by Him this man is standing here before you healthy. 11 This Jesus is

the stone rejected by you
builders,
which has become
the cornerstone.[A,B]

12 There is salvation in no one else, for there is no other name under heaven given to people, and we must be saved by it."

The Threat Against Peter and John (4:13-22)

13 When they observed the boldness of Peter and John and realized that they were uneducated and untrained men, they were amazed and recognized that they had been with Jesus. 14 And since they saw the man who had been healed standing with them, they had nothing to say in response. 15 After they had ordered them to leave the •Sanhedrin, they conferred among themselves, 16 saying, "What should we do with these men? For an obvious sign, evident to all who live in Jerusalem, has been done through them, and we cannot deny it! 17 However, so this does not spread any further among the people, let's threaten them against speaking to anyone in this name again." 18 So they called for them and ordered them not to preach or teach at all in the name of Jesus.

19 But Peter and John answered them, "Whether it's right in the sight of God for us to listen to you rather than to God, you decide; 20 for we are unable to stop speaking about what we have seen and heard."

21 After threatening them further, they released them. They found no way to punish them, because the people were all giving glory to God over what had been done; 22 for this sign of healing had been performed on a man over 40 years old.

A Prayer for Boldness (4:23-31)

23 After they were released, they went to their own people and reported everything the •chief priests and the elders had said to them. 24 When they heard this, they all raised their voices to God and said, "Master, You are the One who made the heaven, the earth, and the sea, and everything in them. 25 You said through the Holy Spirit, by the mouth of our father David Your servant:[C]

Why did the Gentiles rage
and the peoples plot
futile things?
26 **The kings of the earth**
took their stand
and the rulers
assembled together
against the Lord and
against His •Messiah.[D]

27 "For, in fact, in this city both •Herod and Pontius •Pilate, with the Gentiles and the people[E] of Israel, assembled together against Your holy Servant Jesus, whom You anointed, 28 to do whatever Your hand and Your plan had predestined to take place. 29 And now, Lord, consider their threats, and grant that Your •slaves may speak Your message with complete boldness, 30 while You stretch out Your hand for healing, signs, and wonders to be performed through the name of Your holy Servant Jesus." 31 When they had prayed, the place where they were assembled was shaken, and they were all filled with the Holy Spirit and began to speak God's message with boldness.

The Sharing of Believers (4:32-37)

32 Now the large group of those who believed were of one heart and mind, and no one said that any of his possessions was his own, but instead they held everything in common. 33 And the apostles were giving testimony with great power to the resurrection of the Lord Jesus, and great grace was on all of them. 34 For there was not a needy person among them, because all those who owned lands or houses sold them, brought the proceeds of the things that were sold, 35 and laid them at the apostles' feet. This was then distributed for each person's basic needs.[F]

36 Joseph, a Levite and a Cypriot by birth, the one the apostles called Barnabas, which is translated Son of Encouragement, 37 sold a field he

[A]**4:11** Lit *the head of the corner* [B]**4:11** Ps 118:22 [C]**4:25** Other mss read *through the mouth of David Your servant* [D]**4:25-26** Ps 2:1-2 [E]**4:27** Lit *peoples* [F]**4:35** Lit *person as anyone had need*

CHARACTER PROFILE

Sapphira A Deceitful Woman

Her Background	She, together with her husband Ananias, was a part of the early church.
Her Story	• They sold a piece of property, lying about their profit (5:1-2). • Ananias brought the money to Peter, who accused him of lying to the Holy Spirit and keeping part of the profit (5:3-6). • Ananias died instantly. • Three hours later Sapphira arrived, unaware of what had happened to her husband (5:7-11). • She lied also and died instantly. • Great fear came upon the small community of believers.
Life Lesson	Integrity of the heart is much more valuable to God than outward acts of worship.

owned, brought the money, and laid it at the apostles' feet.

Result of Lying to the Holy Spirit (5:1-11)

5 But a man named Ananias, with his wife Sapphira, sold a piece of property. 2 However, he kept back part of the proceeds with his wife's knowledge, and brought a portion of it and laid it at the apostles' feet.

3 Then Peter said, "Ananias, why has Satan filled your heart to lie to the Holy Spirit and keep back part of the proceeds from the field? 4 Wasn't it yours while you possessed it? And after it was sold, wasn't it at your disposal? Why is it that you planned this thing in your heart? You have not lied to men but to God!" 5 When he heard these words, Ananias dropped dead, and a great fear came on all who heard. 6 The young men got up, wrapped his body, carried him out, and buried him.

7 There was an interval of about three hours; then his wife came in, not knowing what had happened. 8 "Tell me," Peter asked her, "did you sell the field for this price?"

"Yes," she said, "for that price."

9 Then Peter said to her, "Why did you agree to test the Spirit of the Lord? Look! The feet of those who have buried your husband are at the door, and they will carry you out!"

10 Instantly she dropped dead at his feet. When the young men came in, they found her dead, carried her out, and buried her beside her husband. 11 Then great fear came on the whole church and on all who heard these things.

Apostolic Signs and Wonders (5:12-16)

12 Many signs and wonders were being done among the people through the hands of the apostles. By common consent they would all meet in Solomon's Colonnade. 13 None of the rest dared to join them, but the people praised them highly. 14 Believers were added to the Lord in increasing numbers—crowds of both men and women. 15 As a result, they would carry the sick out into the streets and lay them on cots and mats so that when Peter came by, at least his shadow might fall on some of them. 16 In addition, a large group came together from the towns surrounding Jerusalem, bringing sick people and those who were tormented by •unclean spirits, and they were all healed.

An Angel's Intervention (5:17-21a)

17 Then the high priest took action. He and all his colleagues, those who belonged to the party of the •Sadducees, were filled with jealousy. 18 So they arrested[A] the apostles and put them in the city jail. 19 But an angel of the Lord opened the doors of the jail during the night, brought them out, and said, 20 "Go and stand in the •temple complex, and tell the people

[A] 5:18 Lit *laid hands on*

5:3-4 No law required the early believers to sell their land and give it away. In fact, Ananias and Sapphira could have done what they pleased with the land. Christians are to give what they have decided in their heart to give, not reluctantly or under compulsion, "for God loves a cheerful giver" (2Co 9:7). Their failure to give would not have been sin; their sin was that they lied **to the Holy Spirit**, which was lying **to God**.

5:5-11 As a result of his sin, **Ananias dropped dead. Three hours** later, after repeating the same lie, Sapphira instantly **dropped dead**. The text does not indicate how they died, but the assumption is that they died as a result of the judgment of God since **great fear came on the whole church and on all who heard**. The same Spirit that brought God's blessing to believers also convicted believers of sin. "God is not mocked. For whatever a man sows he will also reap" (Gl 6:7). Ananias and Sapphira sowed lies and deceit, and they reaped judgment and a premature death. They wanted to appear more generous than they were. Was this sin so dreadful as to merit death? Perhaps the severity of judgment underscored the importance of keeping the church pure in these early days of its existence and reinforced the difference made by the filling of the Spirit.

5:15-16 Many more people were healed by Peter and the apostles. Luke made a distinction between those with common sicknesses and those with **unclean spirits**. Only the Gospels and Acts mention people tormented by unclean or evil spirits. The rest of the New Testament is silent about this issue. Around the time of Jesus' ministry and shortly thereafter, a proliferation of people affected with demon possession appeared. The Bible never describes believers as being tormented by unclean spirits. This condition is found only in those who do not have the Holy Spirit.

5:19-20 God sent **an angel of the Lord** to free the apostles from jail. This angel of the Lord should be distinguished from "the angel of the LORD" in the Old Testament, who was often identified as the pre-incarnate Christ (a Christophany). This jail miracle was the first of three recorded in Acts (see 12:6-10; 16:26-27).

5:21 In contrast to the previous trial of Peter and John, the entire **Sanhedrin** (i.e., **the full Senate of the sons of Israel**) was in attendance. The Sanhedrin was composed of 70 people plus the high priest, who presided over the council. These 71 men formed the ruling body of the Jewish people.

5:26 The guards **brought** the apostles **in without force** because **they were afraid the people might stone them.** The apostles did not fear stoning because they were regarded highly by the people (2:47; 5:13). Rather the captain and the temple police feared being stoned for their re-arresting the apostles.

5:29 Admitting that they had disobeyed the orders not to teach in Jesus' name, Peter and the apostles gave reason for their noncompliance: **We must obey God rather than men.** The apostles were not laying aside all laws and governmental authority. Instead they were arguing that when the laws of God come in conflict with the laws of man, they must first and foremost obey God.

5:30 By using the phrase **God of our fathers**, the apostles were identifying with Judaism. The God of whom they were speaking was not another god, but the God of Israel, the triune God who raised Jesus up and who exalted Him as Ruler and Savior.

5:33-34 The apostles' response **enraged** a majority of the Sanhedrin, to the extent that they **wanted to kill** the apostles. Although the Sanhedrin was primarily made up of Sadducees, Pharisees were members as well. **A Pharisee named Gamaliel** offered a solution and became the first man to function as the friend of Christianity in court. Gamaliel was highly respected by all the people and recognized as the greatest teacher of his day. He was the grandson of the great Rabbi Hillel and the teacher of the Apostle Paul (22:3).

5:35-39 Gamaliel wisely and in a timely manner suggested that they **be careful** and not act hastily with the apostles. Citing Jewish history, he noted two uprisings that came to nothing. **Theudas**, who is not referenced in any other historical account, with **a group of about** 400 men rallied to no avail. Likewise, **Judas the Galilean**, the founder of the Zealots, led a rebellion that failed. For this reason, Gamaliel argued that the Sanhedrin should stay away from these men, i.e., the apostles, and leave them alone. Gamaliel insightfully noted that the Sanhedrin might **even be found fighting against God**. However, given Gamaliel's comparison of Jesus to the two men, he may have thought

all about this life." 21 In obedience to this, they entered the temple complex at daybreak and began to teach.

The Apostles' Testimony (5:21b-32)

When the high priest and those who were with him arrived, they convened the •Sanhedrin—the full Senate of the sons of Israel—and sent orders to the jail to have them brought. 22 But when the temple police got there, they did not find them in the jail, so they returned and reported, 23 "We found the jail securely locked, with the guards standing in front of the doors, but when we opened them, we found no one inside!" 24 As[A] the commander of the temple police and the •chief priests heard these things, they were baffled about them, as to what could come of this.

25 Someone came and reported to them, "Look! The men you put in jail are standing in the temple complex and teaching the people." 26 Then the commander went with the temple police and brought them in without force, because they were afraid the people might stone them. 27 After they brought them in, they had them stand before the Sanhedrin, and the high priest asked, 28 "Didn't we strictly order you not to teach in this name? And look, you have filled Jerusalem with your teaching and are determined to bring this man's blood on us!"

29 But Peter and the apostles replied, "We must obey God rather than men. 30 The God of our fathers raised up Jesus, whom you had murdered by hanging Him on a tree. 31 God exalted this man to His right hand as ruler and Savior, to grant repentance to Israel, and forgiveness of sins. 32 We are witnesses of these things, and so is the Holy Spirit whom God has given to those who obey Him."

Gamaliel's Advice (5:33-42)

33 When they heard this, they were enraged and wanted to kill them. 34 A •Pharisee named Gamaliel, a teacher of the law who was respected by all the people, stood up in the Sanhedrin and ordered the men[B] to be taken outside for a little while. 35 He said to them, "Men of Israel, be careful about what you're going to do to these men. 36 Not long ago Theudas rose up, claiming to be somebody, and a group of about 400 men rallied to him. He was killed, and all his partisans were dispersed and came to nothing. 37 After this man, Judas the Galilean rose up in the days of the census and attracted a following.[C] That man also perished, and all his partisans were scattered. 38 And now, I tell you, stay away from these men and leave them alone. For if this plan or this work is of men, it will be overthrown; 39 but if it is of God, you will not be able to overthrow them. You may even be found fighting against God." So they were persuaded by him. 40 After they called in the apostles and had them flogged, they ordered them not to speak in the name of Jesus and released them. 41 Then they went out from the presence of the Sanhedrin, rejoicing that they were counted worthy to be dishonored on behalf of the Name.[D] 42 Every day in the temple complex, and in various homes, they continued teaching and proclaiming the good news that Jesus is the •Messiah.

The Selection of the Seven Deacons (6:1–8:3)

The Complaint (6:1-7)

6 In those days, as the number of the disciples was multiplying, there arose a complaint by the Hellenistic Jews[E] against the Hebraic Jews[F] that their widows were being overlooked in the daily distribution. 2 Then the Twelve summoned the whole company of the disciples and said, "It would not be right for us to give up preaching about God to handle financial matters.[G] 3 Therefore, •brothers, select from among you seven men of good reputation, full of the Spirit and wisdom, whom we can appoint to this duty. 4 But we will devote ourselves to prayer and to the preaching ministry." 5 The proposal pleased the whole com-

[A]5:24 Other mss add *the high priest and* [B]5:34 Other mss read *apostles* [C]5:37 Lit *and drew people after him* [D]5:41 Other mss add *of Jesus*, or *of Christ* [E]6:1 Jews of Gk language and culture [F]6:1 Jews of Aram or Hb language and culture [G]6:2 Or *to serve tables*

Doctrine CHURCH

Who chooses the deacons in a church? According to the pattern set forth in Ac 6, the congregation should choose from among themselves men who meet the qualifications given in 1Tm 3:8-13. Failure to meet these qualifications does not prohibit a man from ministry, but he is prohibited from holding the office of deacon. If a church takes the responsibility seriously, those not qualified to serve are prohibited from serving in this role.

What do they do? In some churches the deacons act as a board of trustees or a ruling body; however, Ac 6 indicates, as does the word "deacon" (Gk *diaconos*), that this role calls for service. The deacons are to serve, not rule, the church. The final authority for the church lies in the congregation. For example, in the Lord's Supper, the pastor usually asks these set-apart men to come to the front. The pastor then hands the elements to the "servants" or deacons, who pass out the elements to the congregation. This service in a symbolic way represents the role of deacons in a church.

pany. So they chose Stephen, a man
full of faith and the Holy Spirit, and
Philip, Prochorus, Nicanor, Timon,
Parmenas, and Nicolaus, a ˚proselyte
from Antioch. [6] They had them stand
before the apostles, who prayed and
laid their hands on them.[A]

[7] So the preaching about God
flourished, the number of the disciples in Jerusalem multiplied greatly,
and a large group of priests became
obedient to the faith.

The Accusation of Stephen (6:8-15)

[8] Stephen, full of grace and power,
was performing great wonders and
signs among the people. [9] Then
some from what is called the Freedmen's ˚Synagogue, composed of
both Cyrenians and Alexandrians,
and some from Cilicia and ˚Asia,
came forward and disputed with
Stephen. [10] But they were unable to
stand up against his wisdom and the
Spirit by whom he was speaking.

[11] Then they persuaded some men
to say, "We heard him speaking blasphemous words against Moses and
God!" [12] They stirred up the people,
the elders, and the ˚scribes; so they
came, dragged him off, and took
him to the ˚Sanhedrin. [13] They also
presented false witnesses who said,
"This man does not stop speaking blasphemous words against
this holy place and the law. [14] For
we heard him say that Jesus, this
˚Nazarene, will destroy this place
and change the customs that Moses
handed down to us." [15] And all who
were sitting in the Sanhedrin looked
intently at him and saw that his face
was like the face of an angel.

Stephen's Sermon (7:1-8)

7 "Is this true?"[B] the high priest
asked.

[2] "Brothers and fathers," he said,
"listen: The God of glory appeared
to our father Abraham when he was
in Mesopotamia, before he settled in
Haran, [3] and said to him:

Get out of your country
and away from your relatives,
and come to the land
that I will show you.[C]

[4] "Then he came out of the land of
the Chaldeans and settled in Haran.
From there, after his father died,
God had him move to this land you
now live in. [5] He didn't give him an
inheritance in it, not even a foot of
ground, but He promised to give it
to him as a possession, and to his
descendants after him, even though
he was childless. [6] God spoke in this
way:

His descendants
would be strangers
in a foreign country,
and they would enslave
and oppress them 400 years.
[7] **I will judge the nation**
that they will serve as ˚slaves,
God said.
After this, they will come out
and worship Me
in this place.[D]

[8] Then He gave him the covenant of
circumcision. After this, he fathered
Isaac and circumcised him on the
eighth day; Isaac did the same with
Jacob, and Jacob with the 12 patriarchs.

The Patriarchs in Egypt (7:9-16)

[9] "The patriarchs became jealous
of Joseph and sold him into Egypt,
but God was with him [10] and rescued
him out of all his troubles. He gave
him favor and wisdom in the sight

the teachings of Jesus would also fade away.

6:3-4 The **brothers** selected **seven men** to assist the apostles by serving tables. These men became the first deacons in the church. While it might have been easier for the apostles to select the men themselves, the apostles involved the church as a whole in making the decision, while they were guiding the process.

6:5 The seven men selected all had Greek names, implying they were Hellenistic Jews. **Nicolaus**, described as being **a proselyte**, must have been a Gentile convert to Judaism. Perhaps the choice of men who were probably Hellenists would ameliorate the conflict concerning the alleged neglect of Hellenistic widows by the Palestinian Jews who were controlling the financial resources assigned to caring for the widows. A conflict that caused the first major division in the early church had to be addressed in a timely way.

6:10-11 Frustrated by their lack of ability to debate with Stephen, these synagogue antagonists persuaded people to claim falsely that Stephen had been **speaking blasphemous words**, a serious offense punishable by death (Lv 24:16).

7:1-53 The **high priest** asked Stephen, **"Is this true?"** in reference to the charge of blasphemy. Stephen's response to this simple question formed the longest sermon in Acts. Although some have accused Stephen of historical inaccuracies, a careful study reveals his effective use of events from Israel's history and the citing of at least 22 verses from the Old Testament. Stephen turned the charges back on his accusers, indicating that they, not he, were the real blasphemers of God. Structurally, the speech falls into six sections: the promises of Abraham (vv. 2-8); the deliverance through Joseph (vv. 9-16); the deliverance through Moses (vv. 17-34); the apostasy of Israel (vv. 35-43); the real tabernacle of God (vv. 44-50); and the rejection of the Messiah (vv. 51-53).

7:8 God gave Abraham **the covenant of circumcision**, the surgical procedure performed on infant boys in which the foreskin is removed from the penis for reasons of health and hygiene, as the sign of the covenant God had made with him (Gn 17:1-14). For the Jews, this procedure was a religious ritual distinguishing the male Jew, the descendant of Abraham, from the Gentile. God had commanded that circumcision be performed as a sign of His covenant with Abraham.

7:9-16 As a continuation of the history of Israel. Stephen summarized the

[A] **6:6** The laying on of hands signified the prayer of blessing for the beginning of a new ministry.
[B] **7:1** Lit *"Are these things so?"* [C] **7:3** Gn 12:1 [D] **7:6-7** Gn 15:13-14

story of Joseph, son of Jacob, from Gn 37–46. By using the story of **Joseph**, Stephen demonstrated that throughout history God's appointed leaders had been rejected by Israel just as Jesus was. What Joseph's older brothers intended for evil, God used for good, saving the people of Israel from the **famine** (Gn 50:20). Even though Jesus was rejected by Israel, He was God's appointed One. The crucifixion, which the Jews intended for evil, God used to provide a way to save people from their sins (Rm 5:9).

7:14 Stephen alluded to **75 people in all**. In Gn 46:26, the number was recorded as 66 people, which did not include Jacob, Joseph, Manasseh, and Ephraim. All those in Jacob's household numbered 70 (Gn 46:15,18,22,25), a number symbolizing completeness or perfection and significant in representing God's complete work in preparing Israel. Stephen's figure of "75," however, most certainly comes from the Septuagint, which added to the count the five grandsons of Joseph (Ac 7:14).

7:15-16 Shechem, located on the slope of Mount Ebal in north central Palestine and an important city before the Israelites settled there, became the first capital of the northern kingdom (1Kg 12:1). **Jacob** bought land and settled in Shechem (Gn 33:18-19). The remains of Jacob and Joseph were returned to Canaan, or Shechem, for burial.

7:17-43 Along came **Moses**, the next prominent character in Israel's history. Stephen's discourse on Moses composed the longest section of his speech, probably because he was defending himself against the claim he had blasphemed Moses (Ac 6:11). He discussed all three of the major segments of Moses' life, each covering a 40-year span.

7:29 Moses fled Egypt because of his fear of the wrath of the pharaoh and because of the rejection of his people (Ex 2:14). While in **the land of Midian**, Moses married Zipporah (Hb, "small bird or sparrow"), whose father was Jethro, the priest of Midian. The couple had **two sons**, Gershom (Hb, "alien or sojourner") and Eliezer (Hb, "God helps," Ex 2:22; 18:2-4).

7:35 There are several references to the **angel** who spoke to Moses (vv. 35,38; see also v. 53; Gl 3:19; Hb 2:2). In Ex 19 the one who spoke to Moses identified Himself as the "Lord" (Hb *Yahweh*). There are two possibilities: Stephen was assuming that God was speaking to Moses via an angel, or the "angel" may well have been God Himself appearing in what has been called a

of Pharaoh, king of Egypt, who appointed him ruler over Egypt and over his whole household. 11 Then a famine and great suffering came over all of Egypt and Canaan, and our ancestors could find no food. 12 When Jacob heard there was grain in Egypt, he sent our ancestors the first time. 13 The second time, Joseph was revealed to his brothers, and Joseph's family became known to Pharaoh. 14 Joseph then invited his father Jacob and all his relatives, 75 people in all, 15 and Jacob went down to Egypt. He and our ancestors died there, 16 were carried back to Shechem, and were placed in the tomb that Abraham had bought for a sum of silver from the sons of Hamor in Shechem.

Moses, a Rejected Leader (7:17-36)

17 "As the time was drawing near to fulfill the promise that God had made to Abraham, the people flourished and multiplied in Egypt 18 until a different king who did not know Joseph ruled over Egypt.[A] 19 He dealt deceitfully with our race and oppressed our ancestors by making them leave their infants outside, so they wouldn't survive.[B] 20 At this time Moses was born, and he was beautiful in God's sight. He was cared for in his father's home three months, 21 and when he was left outside, Pharaoh's daughter adopted and raised him as her own son. 22 So Moses was educated in all the wisdom of the Egyptians and was powerful in his speech and actions.

23 "As he was approaching the age of 40, he decided[C] to visit his brothers, the Israelites. 24 When he saw one of them being mistreated, he came to his rescue and avenged the oppressed man by striking down the Egyptian. 25 He assumed his brothers would understand that God would give them deliverance through him, but they did not understand. 26 The next day he showed up while they were fighting and tried to reconcile them peacefully, saying, 'Men, you are brothers. Why are you mistreating each other?'

27 "But the one who was mistreating his neighbor pushed him[D] away, saying:

> **Who appointed you a ruler and a judge over us? 28 Do you want to kill me, the same way you killed the Egyptian yesterday?**[E]

29 "At this disclosure, Moses fled and became an exile in the land of Midian, where he fathered two sons. 30 After 40 years had passed, an angel[F] appeared to him in the wilderness of Mount Sinai, in the flame of a burning bush. 31 When Moses saw it, he was amazed at the sight. As he was approaching to look at it, the voice of the Lord came: 32 **I am the God of your fathers—the God of Abraham, of Isaac, and of Jacob.**[G] So Moses began to tremble and did not dare to look.

33 "Then the Lord said to him:

> **Remove the sandals from your feet, for the place where you are standing is holy ground. 34 I have observed the oppression of My people in Egypt; I have heard their groaning and have come down to rescue them. And now, come, I will send you to Egypt.**[H]

35 "This Moses, whom they rejected when they said, **Who appointed you a ruler and a judge?**[E]—this one God sent as a ruler and a redeemer by means of the angel who appeared to him in the bush. 36 This man led them out and performed wonders and signs in the land of Egypt, at the Red Sea, and in the wilderness 40 years.

Israel's Rebellion Against God (7:37-43)

37 "This is the Moses who said to the Israelites, **God**[I] **will raise up for you a Prophet like me from among your brothers.**[J] 38 He is the one who was in the congregation in the wilderness together with the angel who spoke to him on Mount Sinai, and with our ancestors. He received liv-

[A]**7:18** Other mss omit *over Egypt* [B]**7:19** A common pagan practice of population control by leaving infants outside to die [C]**7:23** Lit *40, it came into his heart* [D]**7:27** Moses [E]**7:27-28,35** Ex 2:14 [F]**7:30** Other mss add *of the Lord* [G]**7:32** Ex 3:6,15 [H]**7:33-34** Ex 3:5,7-8,10 [I]**7:37** Other mss read *'The Lord your God* [J]**7:37** Dt 18:15

ing oracles to give to us. 39 Our ancestors were unwilling to obey him, but pushed him away, and in their hearts turned back to Egypt. 40 They told Aaron:

Make us gods who will go before us. As for this Moses who brought us out of the land of Egypt, we don't know what's happened to him.[A]

41 They even made a calf in those days, offered sacrifice to the idol, and were celebrating what their hands had made. 42 Then God turned away and gave them up to worship the host of heaven, as it is written in the book of the prophets:

House of Israel, did you
bring Me offerings
and sacrifices
40 years in the wilderness?
43 **No, you took up**
the tent of Moloch[B]
and the star of
your god Rephan,[C]
the images that you made
to worship.
So I will deport you
beyond Babylon![D]

God's Real Tabernacle (7:44-50)

44 "Our ancestors had the tabernacle of the testimony in the wilderness, just as He who spoke to Moses commanded him to make it according to the pattern he had seen. 45 Our ancestors in turn received it and with Joshua brought it in when they dispossessed the nations that God drove out before our fathers, until the days of David. 46 He found favor in God's sight and asked that he might provide a dwelling place for the God[E] of Jacob. 47 But it was Solomon who built Him a house. 48 However, the Most High does not dwell in sanctuaries made with hands, as the prophet says:

49 **Heaven is My throne,**
and earth My footstool.
What sort of house
will you build for Me?
says the Lord,
or what is My resting place?
50 **Did not My hand make all**
these things?[F]

Resisting the Holy Spirit (7:51-53)

51 "You stiff-necked people with uncircumcised hearts and ears! You are always resisting the Holy Spirit; as your ancestors did, so do you. 52 Which of the prophets did your fathers not persecute? They even killed those who announced beforehand the coming of the Righteous One, whose betrayers and murderers you have now become. 53 You received the law under the direction of angels and yet have not kept it."

The First Christian Martyr (7:54-60)

54 When they heard these things, they were enraged in their hearts[G] and gnashed their teeth at him. 55 But Stephen, filled by the Holy Spirit, gazed into heaven. He saw God's glory, with[H] Jesus standing at the right hand of God, and he said, 56 "Look! I see the heavens opened and the •Son of Man standing at the right hand of God!"

57 Then they screamed at the top of their voices, covered their ears, and together rushed against him. 58 They threw him out of the city and began to stone him. And the witnesses laid their robes at the feet of a young man named Saul. 59 They were stoning Stephen as he called out: "Lord Jesus, receive my spirit!" 60 Then he knelt down and cried out with a loud voice, "Lord, do not charge them with this sin!" And saying this, he fell •asleep.

Saul the Persecutor (8:1-3)

8 Saul agreed with putting him to death.

On that day a severe persecution broke out against the church in Jerusalem, and all except the apostles were scattered throughout the land of Judea and Samaria. 2 Devout men buried Stephen and mourned deeply over him. 3 Saul, however, was ravaging the church. He would enter house after house, drag off men and women, and put them in prison.

A7:40 Ex 32:1,23 B7:43 Canaanite or Phoenician sky or sun god C7:43 Perhaps an Assyrian star god—the planet Saturn D7:42-43 Am 5:25-27 E7:46 Other mss read *house* F7:49-50 Is 66:1-2 G7:54 Or *were cut to the quick* H7:55 Lit *and*

Christophany—an appearance of the preincarnate Christ, the Son of God.

7:44-50 After addressing his supposed blasphemy against Moses, Stephen dealt with the accusation that he blasphemed the temple, recounting the history of it. Stephen noted that these structures could not truly contain God in all His glory. Instead, God's dwelling place, represented by His **throne**, is in **heaven** (vv. 49-50; Is 66:1-2).

7:51-53 The Sanhedrin's anger level grew with Stephen's conclusion, which applied his message directly to them.

7:55 Although the Bible normally portrays Jesus as sitting **at the right hand of God** (Ps 110:1; Rm 8:34; Col 3:1; Heb 1:3,13; 8:1; 10:12; 12:2; 1Pt 3:22), Stephen viewed Him as **standing**, perhaps signifying that Jesus was standing in Stephen's defense or that He was standing to welcome Stephen into heaven.

7:58 Violating the law, which required the authorization of the Roman government to prosecute an offense calling for capital punishment, the mob threw Stephen **out of the city** and stoned him (Jn 18:31). From the apparent immediate action of the Sanhedrin, no formal vote was taken to determine Stephen's guilt or innocence. Instead, in anger they responded to what they perceived to be outrageously blasphemous statements, which according to Jewish law were punishable by stoning (Lv 24:14-16); and yet they ignored the civil law under which they were living. In order to throw the first stones, the witnesses removed their robes and laid them **at the feet of a young man named Saul**, who, as Paul, would later become a prominent figure in the apostolic church.

7:59-60 In response to his stoning, Stephen reacted much as Jesus did on the cross. While Jesus called on the Father to receive His Spirit, Stephen called on the **Lord Jesus**, demonstrating how the early church clearly viewed Jesus as God. Additionally, Stephen asked for the forgiveness of his persecutors just as Jesus did. Even in the face of death Stephen led a life completely yielded to the Spirit of God.

8:1-3 Saul (Lat, *Paul*) was born a Roman citizen in Tarsus, the capital of Cilicia. He studied under the famous rabbi Gamaliel, becoming a scholar in Jewish tradition and in the interpretation of Scripture. As a Pharisee, Saul zealously committed himself to the teaching and practicing of Old Testament laws and traditions. He apparently led in the **severe persecution** against **the church in**

Jerusalem, imprisoning both **men and women**. Women were involved in the early church and experienced persecution.

8:5 Philip, the first missionary named and one of the seven men chosen to serve tables (6:5), went to **Samaria** (a region north of Jerusalem). They were ready to receive Philip's message of the Messiah. Many of them had possibly heard about Jesus from the Samaritan woman Jesus encountered at the well of Sychar (Jn 4).

8:9 Simon's **sorcery** (Gk *mageuōn*, "practice magic"). Simon's sorcery, also described in the Bible as magic and witchcraft, invoked demonic powers exercise control over nature and people. Simon **astounded** his contemporaries. The Jews were forbidden to be involved in any form of sorcery (Dt 18:10-14; cp. Rv 21:8).

8:18-19 Simon was impressed with the "signs and great miracles" that Philip performed (v. 13) and likely feigned belief in Christ in an attempt to gain the same **power**, which was far greater than his own demonic power. Even now the coined word "simony" refers to the buying of ecclesiastical offices in an unworthy and deceitful way. Many see this encounter as Christianity's first confrontation with the occult. Moses had warned the Israelites of this danger before they entered Canaan (Dt 18:9-14; see also Lv 20:6,27; Dt 17:2-5).

8:20-22 Peter realized that Simon did not understand God's grace or the free nature of salvation. The implication is that Simon was not a Christian, even though he had expressed belief and had been baptized. Salvation requires more than mere mental assent, for even the demons believe in God (Jms 2:19).

8:26 Gaza, approximately 50 miles southwest of Jerusalem, was one of five chief cities of the Philistines.

8:27 That the man was **Ethiopian** does not mean he was from the modern nation called Ethiopia but that he was from ancient Nubia, the region stretching from Aswan in southern Egypt to Khartoum in the Sudan. He was a **eunuch**, a man who had been castrated. Eunuchs were considered especially trustworthy and were often in charge of harems. This eunuch held a high position in Ethiopia as the one in charge of the queen's entire treasury. **Candace** was not the name of the queen but the title used by the queens of Meroe, the capital city of ancient Ethiopia. The Ethiopian was heading home after worshiping **in Jerusalem**. As a eunuch he would have been denied access to the temple (Dt 23:1).

The Spread of the Gospel in Judea, Galilee, and Samaria (8:4–9:31)

Philip in Samaria (8:4-8)

4 So those who were scattered
went on their way preaching the
message of good news. 5 Philip went
down to a[A] city in Samaria and proclaimed the •Messiah to them. 6 The
crowds paid attention with one
mind to what Philip said, as they
heard and saw the signs he was performing. 7 For •unclean spirits, crying out with a loud voice, came out
of many who were possessed, and
many who were paralyzed and lame
were healed. 8 So there was great joy
in that city.

The Response of Simon (8:9-13)

9 A man named Simon had previously practiced sorcery in that city
and astounded the •Samaritan people, while claiming to be somebody
great. 10 They all paid attention to
him, from the least of them to the
greatest, and they said, "This man
is called the Great Power of God!"[B]
11 They were attentive to him because he had astounded them with
his sorceries for a long time. 12 But
when they believed Philip, as he
preached the good news about the
kingdom of God and the name of
Jesus Christ, both men and women
were baptized. 13 Then even Simon
himself believed. And after he was
baptized, he went around constantly
with[C] Philip and was astounded
as he observed the signs and great
miracles that were being performed.

Simon's Sin (8:14-25)

14 When the apostles who were at
Jerusalem heard that Samaria had
welcomed God's message, they sent
Peter and John to them. 15 After they
went down there, they prayed for
them, so the Samaritans might receive the Holy Spirit. 16 For He had
not yet come down on[D] any of them;
they had only been baptized in the
name of the Lord Jesus. 17 Then
Peter and John laid their hands on
them, and they received the Holy
Spirit.
18 When Simon saw that the Holy[E]
Spirit was given through the laying
on of the apostles' hands, he offered
them money, 19 saying, "Give me this
power too, so that anyone I lay hands
on may receive the Holy Spirit."
20 But Peter told him, "May your
silver be destroyed with you, because
you thought the gift of God could be
obtained with money! 21 You have no
part or share in this matter, because
your heart is not right before God.
22 Therefore repent of this wickedness of yours, and pray to the Lord
that the intent of your heart may
be forgiven you. 23 For I see you are
poisoned by bitterness and bound by
iniquity."
24 "Please pray[F] to the Lord for
me," Simon replied, "so that nothing you have said may happen to
me."
25 Then, after they had testified
and spoken the message of the Lord,
they traveled back to Jerusalem,
evangelizing many villages of the
Samaritans.

The Conversion of the Ethiopian Official (8:26-40)

26 An angel of the Lord spoke to
Philip: "Get up and go south to the
road that goes down from Jerusalem
to Gaza." (This is the desert road.)[G]
27 So he got up and went. There was
an Ethiopian man, a eunuch and
high official of Candace, queen of
the Ethiopians,[H] who was in charge
of her entire treasury. He had come
to worship in Jerusalem 28 and was
sitting in his chariot on his way
home, reading the prophet Isaiah
aloud.
29 The Spirit told Philip, "Go and
join that chariot."
30 When Philip ran up to it, he
heard him reading the prophet Isaiah, and said, "Do you understand
what you're reading?"
31 "How can I," he said, "unless
someone guides me?" So he invited
Philip to come up and sit with him.
32 Now the Scripture passage he was
reading was this:

He was led like a sheep
to the slaughter,

[A]**8:5** Other mss read *the* [B]**8:10** Or *This is the power of God called Great* [C]**8:13** Or *he kept close company with* [D]**8:16** Or *yet fallen on* [E]**8:18** Other mss omit *Holy* [F]**8:24** Gk words *you* and *pray* are pl [G]**8:26** Or *is a desert place* [H]**8:27** = Nubia

CHARACTER PROFILE

Candace Queen of Ethiopia

Her Background
- "Candace" was a title used for the queens of Ethiopia.
- She had a trusted servant who came to Jerusalem to worship (8:27).

Her Story
- Her servant was reading Isaiah as he traveled (8:28).
- He met Philip, who explained the text and the gospel to him (8:31-35).
- The servant was baptized by Philip (8:36-38).
- According to tradition, the eunuch returned to Ethiopia, shared his testimony with Candace, and she was converted.

Life Lesson
This story combines the power of the written Word, the testimony of a Spirit-filled believer, and the glorious conversion of one seeking God.

and as a lamb is silent
before its shearer,
so He does not open
His mouth.
33 **In His humiliation justice**
was denied Him.
Who will describe
His generation?
For His life is taken
from the earth.[A]

34 The eunuch replied to Philip, "I
ask you, who is the prophet saying
this about—himself or another person?" 35 So Philip proceeded[B] to tell
him the good news about Jesus, beginning from that Scripture.
36 As they were traveling down the
road, they came to some water. The
eunuch said, "Look, there's water!
What would keep me from being
baptized?" [37 And Philip said, "If you
believe with all your heart you may."
And he replied, "I believe that Jesus
Christ is the Son of God."][C] 38 Then
he ordered the chariot to stop, and
both Philip and the eunuch went
down into the water, and he baptized him. 39 When they came up out
of the water, the Spirit of the Lord
carried Philip away, and the eunuch
did not see him any longer. But he
went on his way rejoicing. 40 Philip
appeared in[D] Azotus,[E] and he was
traveling and evangelizing all the
towns until he came to Caesarea.

The Damascus Road (9:1-9)

9 Meanwhile, Saul was still breathing threats and murder against
the disciples of the Lord. He went to
the high priest 2 and requested letters from him to the •synagogues in
Damascus, so that if he found any
men or women who belonged to the
Way, he might bring them as prisoners to Jerusalem. 3 As he traveled and
was nearing Damascus, a light from
heaven suddenly flashed around
him. 4 Falling to the ground, he
heard a voice saying to him, "Saul,
Saul, why are you persecuting Me?"
5 "Who are You, Lord?" he said.
"I am Jesus, the One you are persecuting," He replied. 6 "But get up
and go into the city, and you will be
told what you must do."
7 The men who were traveling
with him stood speechless, hearing
the sound but seeing no one. 8 Then
Saul got up from the ground, and
though his eyes were open, he could
see nothing. So they took him by the
hand and led him into Damascus.
9 He was unable to see for three days
and did not eat or drink.

Saul's Baptism (9:10-19a)

10 There was a disciple in Damascus named Ananias. And the Lord
said to him in a vision, "Ananias!"
"Here I am, Lord!" he said.
11 "Get up and go to the street
called Straight," the Lord said to

[A]8:32-33 Is 53:7-8 [B]8:35 Lit *Philip opened his mouth* [C]8:37 Other mss omit bracketed text [D]8:40 Or *Philip was found at*, or *Philip found himself in* [E]8:40 Or *Ashdod*

8:31-33 The Ethiopian's confusion regarding the passage in Isaiah was understandable, for even the Jewish religious experts disagreed about the meaning of Is 53:7-8. Some taught that the **sheep** led to **slaughter** represented Israel; others believed Isaiah was referring to himself, while still others rightly understood the passage to refer to the Messiah.

8:35 In Acts and throughout the rest of the New Testament, gospel presentations begin by explaining the Scriptures. Biblical exposition is the example provided by Peter, Stephen, Philip, and Paul because the "sacred Scriptures, which are able to give you wisdom for salvation through faith in Christ Jesus" (2Tm 3:15) are at the heart of this method. Gospel presentations devoid of the truths from God's Word lack power to convict and convince.

9:1 With the word **meanwhile**, Luke transitions back to **Saul** who had been ravaging the church (Ac 8:1-3). Luke uses the names *Saul* and *Paul* interchangeably.

9:2 Damascus, an important ancient city existing back to the days of Abraham (Gn 14:15), was a commercial center where caravans converged from all directions and the location of a large Jewish population. Saul realized that Christianity could spread throughout the world from Damascus because of its strategic location about 150 miles northeast of Jerusalem; therefore, he specifically sought to stop the spread of the movement to Damascus. The phrase **the Way** describes the Christian movement only in Acts (19:9,23; 22:4; 24:14,22), perhaps because Jesus referred to Himself as "the way" (Jn 14:6) or because the Christians were proclaiming "the way" of salvation (Ac 16:17).

9:3-16 Saul's conversion experience is highlighted several times in Acts as well as in his own writings (see 22:6-21; 26:4-18; 1Co 15:8; Gl 1:12-16). The three accounts in Acts, while similar, have some minor differences. These differences can be explained by considering their purposes, settings, and audiences. In Ac 9:3-19, Luke reported the historical facts of Paul's conversion. In Ac 22:6-21, Luke recounts Paul's testimony in an address to an angry mob of Jews in Jerusalem using the first person. Acts 26:4-18, in which Paul sought to persuade Agrippa to become a Christian, also was recorded in the first person as Paul's personal revelation of the change in his life. All three of these accounts originated with Paul so that minor variations are unimportant. By persecuting the church, which is the body of Christ (1Co 12:27; Eph 1:22-23), Saul had been persecuting Christ Himself (9:4).

Saul had considered himself a devout follower of God, yet he had been persecuting the very One who was God.

Not much is known about **Ananias** (9:10), who undoubtedly was one of the leaders in the Damascus church. Scripture refers to him only here. Several times in Acts God used **a vision** to communicate with His people (see also 10:1-16; 16:9-10; 18:9-10). **The street called Straight** (9:11), which still exists today, is one of the main routes through Damascus.

9:17-18 Interestingly, when Ananias entered the house, he greeted Paul as **Brother Saul**. No longer was Saul the feared persecutor of the church; he had become a brother in Christ, a member of the family of God. Although Ananias was the channel, Christ Himself commissioned Saul to be His ambassador, caused **scales** to fall **from his eyes**, and **filled** him **with the Holy Spirit**. Hence Paul later wrote that he had not received his apostolic commission from any mortal man but from the risen Christ (Gl 1:1,11-20). Additional details about Ananias's encounter with Paul are recorded in Ac 22:14-16 and 26:16-18.

9:19-20 Saul's arrival **in Damascus** had been expected, but his message was not. Instead of arresting the disciples of Jesus, Saul argued that their message about Jesus was true. The persecutor of the church joined the persecuted.

9:26-27 After narrowly escaping death, Saul went to **Jerusalem**. The disciples shunned him out of fear. **Barnabas** ("Son of Encouragement," 4:36), living up to his name, befriended Saul, introduced **him to the apostles and explained to them** Saul's conversion and total commitment to Christ. Gaining the acceptance of the apostles, namely, Peter and James (Gl 1:18-19), Saul began to minister alongside them.

9:29-30 The Hellenistic Jews were not from Jerusalem but from various parts of the Greek-speaking world. Angered by Saul's debating ability, the Jews attempted to kill him. **The brothers**, likely a reference to the disciples in general, **found out** about the plan to assassinate Saul and took him **to Caesarea,** a Mediterranean coastal city north of Jerusalem and a stopping point en route to his ultimate destination of **Tarsus** of Cilicia, located in the southeastern portion of Asia Minor in what is modern Turkey.

9:36-38 A disciple named Tabitha (Dorcas), resided in Joppa, modern Jaffe, South Tel Aviv, and the major seaport of Judea. Only here in the New Testament is a woman specifically referenced as a "disciple."

him, "to the house of Judas, and ask for a man from Tarsus named Saul, since he is praying there. 12 In a vision[A] he has seen a man named Ananias coming in and placing his hands on him so he can regain his sight."

13 "Lord," Ananias answered, "I have heard from many people about this man, how much harm he has done to Your •saints in Jerusalem. 14 And he has authority here from the •chief priests to arrest all who call on Your name."

15 But the Lord said to him, "Go! For this man is My chosen instrument to take My name to Gentiles, kings, and the Israelites. 16 I will show him how much he must suffer for My name!"

17 So Ananias left and entered the house. Then he placed his hands on him and said, "Brother Saul, the Lord Jesus, who appeared to you on the road you were traveling, has sent me so that you can regain your sight and be filled with the Holy Spirit."

18 At once something like scales fell from his eyes, and he regained his sight. Then he got up and was baptized. 19 And after taking some food, he regained his strength.

Saul's Proclamation about the Messiah (9:19b-25)

Saul was with the disciples in Damascus for some days. 20 Immediately he began proclaiming Jesus in the synagogues: "He is the Son of God."

21 But all who heard him were astounded and said, "Isn't this the man who, in Jerusalem, was destroying those who called on this name and then came here for the purpose of taking them as prisoners to the chief priests?"

22 But Saul grew more capable and kept confounding the Jews who lived in Damascus by proving that this One is the •Messiah.

23 After many days had passed, the Jews conspired to kill him, 24 but their plot became known to Saul. So they were watching the gates day and night intending to kill him, 25 but his disciples took him by night and lowered him in a large basket through an opening in the wall.

Saul in Jerusalem (9:26-31)

26 When he arrived in Jerusalem, he tried to associate with the disciples, but they were all afraid of him, since they did not believe he was a disciple. 27 Barnabas, however, took him and brought him to the apostles and explained to them how Saul had seen the Lord on the road and that He had talked to him, and how in Damascus he had spoken boldly in the name of Jesus. 28 Saul was coming and going with them in Jerusalem, speaking boldly in the name of the Lord. 29 He conversed and debated with the Hellenistic Jews,[B] but they attempted to kill him. 30 When the •brothers found out, they took him down to Caesarea and sent him off to Tarsus.

31 So the church throughout all Judea, Galilee, and Samaria had peace, being built up and walking in the •fear of the Lord and in the encouragement of the Holy Spirit, and it increased in numbers.

The Spread of the Gospel as Far as Phoenicia, Cyprus, and Antioch (9:32–12:25)

The Healing of Aeneas (9:32-35)

32 As Peter was traveling from place to place,[C] he also came down to the saints who lived in Lydda. 33 There he found a man named Aeneas, who was paralyzed and had been bedridden for eight years. 34 Peter said to him, "Aeneas, Jesus Christ heals you. Get up and make your bed,"[D] and immediately he got up. 35 So all who lived in Lydda and Sharon saw him and turned to the Lord.

Dorcas's Restoration to Life (9:36-43)

36 In Joppa there was a disciple named Tabitha, which is translated Dorcas.[E] She was always doing good works and acts of charity. 37 In those days she became sick and died. After washing her, they placed her in a room upstairs. 38 Since Lydda was near Joppa, the disciples heard that Peter was there and sent two men to him who begged him, "Don't delay in coming with us." 39 So Peter got

[A]**9:12** Other mss omit *In a vision* [B]**9:29** Lit *Hellenists*; that is, Gk-speaking Jews [C]**9:32** Lit *Peter was passing through all* [D]**9:34** Or *and get ready to eat* [E]**9:36** = Gazelle

CHARACTER PROFILE

Dorcas A Woman of Good Works

Her Background	• She was a beloved woman in the church at Joppa, near modern Tel Aviv (9:36). • Luke calls her a "disciple," meaning a committed follower of Christ (9:36).
Her Story	• She was known for her servant spirit and charitable works (9:39). • She became ill and died (9:37). • Her friends sent for Peter (9:38-39). • Peter knelt and prayed at her bedside and she was restored to life (9:40-41). • As a result, many believed in the Lord.
Life Lesson	God honors those who serve the poor and needy.

up and went with them. When he
arrived, they led him to the room
upstairs. And all the widows approached him, weeping and showing him the robes and clothes that
Dorcas had made while she was
with them. 40 Then Peter sent them
all out of the room. He knelt down,
prayed, and turning toward the body
said, "Tabitha, get up!" She opened
her eyes, saw Peter, and sat up. 41 He
gave her his hand and helped her
stand up. Then he called the saints
and widows and presented her alive.
42 This became known throughout
Joppa, and many believed in the
Lord. 43 And Peter stayed on many
days in Joppa with Simon, a leather
tanner.[A]

Cornelius's Vision (10:1-8)

10 There was a man in Caesarea
named Cornelius, a •centurion
of what was called the Italian •Regi-
ment. 2 He was a devout man and
feared God along with his whole
household. He did many charitable
deeds for the Jewish people and always prayed to God. 3 About three in
the afternoon[B] he distinctly saw in a
vision an angel of God who came in
and said to him, "Cornelius!"
4 Looking intently at him, he became afraid and said, "What is it,
lord?"
The angel told him, "Your prayers
and your acts of charity have come
up as a memorial offering before
God. 5 Now send men to Joppa and
call for Simon, who is also named
Peter. 6 He is lodging with Simon, a
tanner, whose house is by the sea."
7 When the angel who spoke to
him had gone, he called two of his
household slaves and a devout soldier, who was one of those who
attended him. 8 After explaining everything to them, he sent them to
Joppa.

Peter's Vision (10:9-16)

9 The next day, as they were traveling and nearing the city, Peter
went up to pray on the housetop
about noon.[C] 10 Then he became
hungry and wanted to eat, but while
they were preparing something, he
went into a visionary state. 11 He
saw heaven opened and an object
that resembled a large sheet coming down, being lowered by its four
corners to the earth. 12 In it were all
the four-footed animals and reptiles
of the earth, and the birds of the sky.
13 Then a voice said to him, "Get up,
Peter; kill and eat!"
14 "No, Lord!" Peter said. "For I
have never eaten anything common[D] and ritually •unclean!"
15 Again, a second time, a voice said

[A]9:43 Tanners were considered ritually •unclean because of their occupation. [B]10:3 Lit *About the ninth hour* [C]10:9 Lit *about the sixth hour* [D]10:14 Perhaps *profane*, or *non-sacred*; Jews ate distinctive food according to OT law and their traditions, similar to modern kosher or non-kosher foods.

10:1-48 Chapter 10 signified a pivotal point for the church with the spread of the gospel to the Gentiles. One might have expected Paul, the apostle to the Gentiles, to be the bearer of the good news. Instead Peter was prepared for this task. Peter spoke at Pentecost, proclaiming the gospel to the Jews. He then went to Samaria to welcome the Samaritans into the church, and in Ac 10 he opened the way for the Gentiles to enter the church. Although other Gentiles such as the Ethiopian eunuch had been saved, this encounter uniquely demonstrated that the gospel was meant for the Gentiles as well as the Jews.

10:1-2 Cornelius, a centurion, commanded a military unit of at least 100 soldiers. His unit was a part of the **Italian Regiment** (about 600 men), which was part of the Roman legion (about 6,000 men). As a God-fearer, Cornelius was a Gentile who had accepted many of the truths of the Jewish faith, but he had not become a full convert because he had not been circumcised (11:2-3). Cornelius even may have had a reserved seat in the synagogue because of his faithfulness, but he had not completed the transition to Judaism.

10:4 The male angel commended Cornelius for his **prayers** and his **acts of charity** (vv. 4,31), which had the effect of **a memorial offering before God**. The term "memorial" is reminiscent of Old Testament sacrificial language. As a God-fearer and not a Jewish convert, Cornelius would have been barred from presenting offerings to God in the Jewish temple. Nevertheless, his acts of piety were not unnoticed, a point that Luke reiterated throughout the passage (vv. 2,4,22). Although Cornelius was a pious man devoted to the one true God, he needed the knowledge of Jesus Christ to be saved (4:12).

10:10-16 The image Peter saw coming out of heaven indicated the message as sent from God. Some suggest that the **four corners** represented the ends of the earth, pointing ultimately to the worldwide mission (Rv 7:1). Both clean and unclean animals were represented. Leviticus 11 gave specific regulations about what Jewish people could and could not eat. In refusing to kill and eat, Peter attempted to be true to his Jewish faith. He had never eaten anything declared **unclean**, and he did not desire to do so now, despite his hunger. But Peter overlooked what Jesus once said. Things like food cannot defile a person, but what comes from within—evil thoughts, greed, pride, and sexual immoralities—causes defilement (Mk 7:17-23). The vision was repeated **three times**, emphasizing its importance.

10:24-26 Cornelius understood the importance of this meeting, and he wanted **his relatives and close friends** to hear this sacred message as well.

10:28-29 Although Peter's vision was of clean and unclean animals, by application God showed him that he **must not call any person common or unclean**. Although Jewish law forbade a Jewish man to associate or visit a foreigner, Peter was willing to come to the home of a Gentile **without any objection**. God had divinely prepared Peter for this moment, which would forever change the church.

10:34-48 For each major segment of the Lord's commission (1:8), an outpouring on the body of believers collectively occurred as a symbol of heaven's approval of what was happening in kingdom ministry: the spreading of the gospel abroad to the Jew (2:1-4), to the Samaritan (8:4-17), and to the Gentile (10:34-44).

10:35 The statement in verse 35 is frequently misunderstood as advocating a works-based salvation. However, if that were true, there would have been no need for Peter to come and share the gospel with Cornelius, who was already regarded as an upright and God-fearing man. Instead Peter's statement needs to be understood within the larger context of his sermon, which clearly indicated that only those who believe in the name of Jesus will receive forgiveness of sins (v. 43).

10:36 Peace (Gk *eirēnē*n, "blessing or tranquility") comes through a right relationship with Jesus Christ (Rm 5:1-11). Although the gospel message was first for the Jewish people (Rm 1:16), Jesus **is Lord of all**. He came to earth and died for Jews and Gentiles alike.

10:37-39 By utilizing the phrase **you know**, Peter assumed his audience possessed a familiarity with the events surrounding Jesus' life, beginning with **the baptism that John preached**.

to him, "What God has made •clean, you must not call common." 16 This happened three times, and then the object was taken up into heaven.

Peter's Visit to Cornelius (10:17-33)

17 While Peter was deeply perplexed about what the vision he had seen might mean, the men who had been sent by Cornelius, having asked directions to Simon's house, stood at the gate. 18 They called out, asking if Simon, who was also named Peter, was lodging there.

19 While Peter was thinking about the vision, the Spirit told him, "Three men are here looking for you. 20 Get up, go downstairs, and accompany them with no doubts at all, because I have sent them."

21 Then Peter went down to the men and said, "Here I am, the one you're looking for. What is the reason you're here?"

22 They said, "Cornelius, a centurion, an upright and God-fearing man, who has a good reputation with the whole Jewish nation, was divinely directed by a holy angel to call you to his house and to hear a message from you." 23 Peter then invited them in and gave them lodging.

The next day he got up and set out with them, and some of the brothers from Joppa went with him. 24 The following day he entered Caesarea. Now Cornelius was expecting them and had called together his relatives and close friends. 25 When Peter entered, Cornelius met him, fell at his feet, and worshiped him.

26 But Peter helped him up and said, "Stand up! I myself am also a man." 27 While talking with him, he went on in and found that many had come together there. 28 Peter said to them, "You know it's forbidden for a Jewish man to associate with or visit a foreigner. But God has shown me that I must not call any person common or unclean. 29 That's why I came without any objection when I was sent for. So I ask: Why did you send for me?"

30 Cornelius replied, "Four days ago at this hour, at three in the afternoon,[A] I was[B] praying in my house. Just then a man in a dazzling robe stood before me 31 and said, 'Cornelius, your prayer has been heard, and your acts of charity have been remembered in God's sight. 32 Therefore send someone to Joppa and invite Simon here, who is also named Peter. He is lodging in Simon the tanner's house by the sea.'[C] 33 Therefore I immediately sent for you, and you did the right thing in coming. So we are all present before God, to hear everything you have been commanded by the Lord."

Good News for the Gentiles (10:34-43)

34 Then Peter began to speak: "Now I really understand that God doesn't show favoritism, 35 but in every nation the person who fears Him and does righteousness is acceptable to Him. 36 He sent the message to the Israelites, proclaiming the good news of peace through Jesus Christ—He is Lord of all. 37 You know the events[D] that took place throughout Judea, beginning from Galilee after the baptism that John preached: 38 how God anointed Jesus of Nazareth with the Holy Spirit and with power, and how He went about doing good and healing all who were under the tyranny of the Devil, because God was with Him. 39 We ourselves are witnesses of everything He did in both the Judean country and in Jerusalem, yet they killed Him by hanging Him on a tree. 40 God raised up this man on the third day and permitted Him to be seen, 41 not by all the people, but by us, witnesses appointed beforehand by God, who ate and drank with Him after He rose from the dead. 42 He commanded us to preach to the people and to solemnly testify that He is the One appointed by God to be the Judge of the living and the dead. 43 All the prophets testify about Him that through His name everyone who believes in Him will receive forgiveness of sins."

Gentile Conversion and Baptism (10:44-48)

44 While Peter was still speaking these words, the Holy Spirit came

A 10:30 Lit *at the ninth hour* B 10:30 Other mss add *fasting and* C 10:32 Other mss add *When he arrives, he will speak to you.* D 10:37 Or *word*; lit *thing*

down on all those who heard the message. 45 The circumcised believers[A] who had come with Peter were astounded because the gift of the Holy Spirit had been poured out on the Gentiles also. 46 For they heard them speaking in other •languages and declaring the greatness of[B] God.

Then Peter responded, 47 "Can anyone withhold water and prevent these people from being baptized, who have received the Holy Spirit just as we have?" 48 And he commanded them to be baptized in the name of Jesus Christ. Then they asked him to stay for a few days.

Defense of Gentile Salvation (11:1-18)

11 The apostles and the •brothers who were throughout Judea heard that the Gentiles had welcomed God's message also. 2 When Peter went up to Jerusalem, those who stressed circumcision[C] argued with him, 3 saying, "You visited uncircumcised men and ate with them!"

4 Peter began to explain to them in an orderly sequence, saying: 5 "I was in the town of Joppa praying, and I saw, in a visionary state, an object that resembled a large sheet coming down, being lowered by its four corners from heaven, and it came to me. 6 When I looked closely and considered it, I saw the four-footed animals of the earth, the wild beasts, the reptiles, and the birds of the sky. 7 Then I also heard a voice telling me, 'Get up, Peter; kill and eat!'

8 "'No, Lord!' I said. 'For nothing common or ritually •unclean has ever entered my mouth!' 9 But a voice answered from heaven a second time, 'What God has made •clean, you must not call common.'

10 "Now this happened three times, and then everything was drawn up again into heaven. 11 At that very moment, three men who had been sent to me from Caesarea arrived at the house where we were. 12 Then the Spirit told me to accompany them with no doubts at all. These six brothers accompanied me, and we went into the man's house. 13 He reported to us how he had seen the angel standing in his house and saying, 'Send[D] to Joppa, and call for Simon, who is also named Peter. 14 He will speak a message[E] to you that you and all your household will be saved by.'

15 "As I began to speak, the Holy Spirit came down on them, just as on us at the beginning. 16 Then I remembered the word of the Lord, how He said, 'John baptized with water, but you will be baptized with the Holy Spirit.' 17 Therefore, if God gave them the same gift that He also gave to us when we believed on the Lord Jesus Christ, how could I possibly hinder God?"

18 When they heard this they became silent. Then they glorified God, saying, "So God has granted repentance resulting in life[F] even to the Gentiles!"

The Church in Antioch (11:19-26)

19 Those who had been scattered as a result of the persecution that started because of Stephen made their way as far as Phoenicia, Cyprus, and Antioch, speaking the message to no one except Jews. 20 But there were some of them, Cypriot and Cyrenian men, who came to Antioch and began speaking to the Hellenists,[G,H] proclaiming the good news about the Lord Jesus. 21 The Lord's hand was with them, and a large number who believed turned to the Lord. 22 Then the report about them was heard by the church that was at Jerusalem, and they sent out Barnabas to travel[I] as far as Antioch. 23 When he arrived and saw the grace of God, he was glad and encouraged all of them to remain true to the Lord with a firm resolve of the heart, 24 for he was a good man, full of the Holy Spirit and of faith. And large numbers of people were added to the Lord. 25 Then he[J] went to Tarsus to search for Saul, 26 and when he found him he brought him to Antioch. For a whole year they met with the church and taught large

10:44-46 Due to the similarity of this event with Pentecost, some refer to it as the "Gentile Pentecost."

10:47-48 As a result of their saving faith and subsequent gift of the Holy Spirit, Peter argued that the Gentiles should **be baptized**. Baptism came as a result of their faith.

11:18 Peter's argument proved convincing, for his former critics **became silent**. They began to understand that God had a plan for the Gentiles as well as for the circumcised. The irate crowd of circumcised believers became a group who **glorified God** for granting to the Gentiles **repentance resulting in life**, a phrase signifying salvation and highlighting the centrality of repentance in salvation. The issue of inclusion of the Gentiles in the church would reemerge at the Jerusalem Council in Ac 15 since some men continued to teach that circumcision was necessary for salvation.

11:19 Luke returns to the martyrdom of **Stephen** (8:1-2), showing how his death resulted in the scattering of the church and the spread of the gospel **as far as Phoenicia, Cyprus, and Antioch**.

11:21 In the Old Testament, **the Lord's hand** could mean two things: God's power expressed in judgment (Dt 2:15; Jos 4:24; 1Sm 5:7; 7:13) or God's power expressed in blessing (Ezr 7:9; 8:18; Neh 2:18). This instance refers to blessing because **a large number who believed turned to the Lord**. People not only believed the truths about Christ, but they turned from their sins and to the Lord. Mental belief in Christ is not enough, for even the demons believe and shudder (Jms 2:19). Saving belief is always linked to repentance.

11:22-24 As a Greek-speaking Jewish Christian and a native of Cyprus, **Barnabas** was the best person to investigate the radical church growth movement and to assist in building up the church at Antioch. Barnabas ("son of encouragement") genuinely cared about the welfare of these new believers. He desired that they live out their faith and share Christ with others daily. Initially in Acts, Luke was able to provide specific numbers, but by this point so many people had come to the Lord that they were beyond counting.

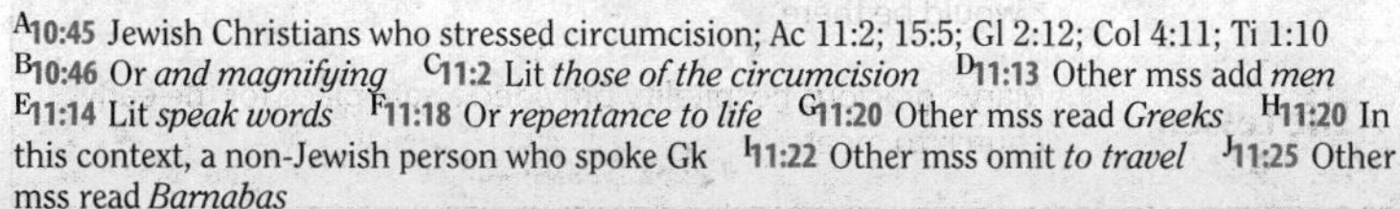

[A]**10:45** Jewish Christians who stressed circumcision; Ac 11:2; 15:5; Gl 2:12; Col 4:11; Ti 1:10
[B]**10:46** Or *and magnifying* [C]**11:2** Lit *those of the circumcision* [D]**11:13** Other mss add *men*
[E]**11:14** Lit *speak words* [F]**11:18** Or *repentance to life* [G]**11:20** Other mss read *Greeks* [H]**11:20** In this context, a non-Jewish person who spoke Gk [I]**11:22** Other mss omit *to travel* [J]**11:25** Other mss read *Barnabas*

>WORD|*study*

11:26 Luke adds that **Antioch** was the place where **the disciples were first called** Christians. The term "Christian" literally means "belonging to the party of Christ" or "little Christs." What began as a nickname and sometimes an insulting label became a means of identifying those who lived and behaved like Christ. Over a period of time the church separated from its roots of Judaism, becoming recognized as a distinct group. The Greek term *Christianous* is used only twice more in the New Testament (26:28; 1Pt 4:16).

numbers. The disciples were first
called Christians at Antioch.

Famine Relief (11:27-30)

27 In those days some prophets
came down from Jerusalem to Antioch. 28 Then one of them, named
Agabus, stood up and predicted
by the Spirit that there would be a
severe famine throughout the Roman world.[A] This took place during
the time of Claudius.[B] 29 So each of
the disciples, according to his ability, determined to send relief to the
brothers who lived in Judea. 30 They
did this, sending it to the elders by
means of Barnabas and Saul.

Persecution of James and Peter (12:1-5)

12 About that time King ·Herod
cruelly attacked some who belonged to the church, 2 and he killed
James, John's brother, with the
sword. 3 When he saw that it pleased
the Jews, he proceeded to arrest
Peter too, during the days of ·Un-
leavened Bread. 4 After the arrest, he
put him in prison and assigned four
squads of four soldiers each to guard
him, intending to bring him out to
the people after the ·Passover. 5 So
Peter was kept in prison, but prayer
was being made earnestly to God for
him by the church.

The Rescue of Peter (12:6-19)

6 On the night before Herod was to
bring him out for execution, Peter,
bound with two chains, was sleeping
between two soldiers, while the sentries in front of the door guarded the
prison. 7 Suddenly an angel of the
Lord appeared, and a light shone in
the cell. Striking Peter on the side,
he woke him up and said, "Quick,
get up!" Then the chains fell off his
wrists. 8 "Get dressed," the angel
told him, "and put on your sandals."
And he did so. "Wrap your cloak
around you," he told him, "and follow me." 9 So he went out and followed, and he did not know that
what took place through the angel
was real, but thought he was seeing
a vision. 10 After they passed the first
and second guard posts, they came
to the iron gate that leads into the
city, which opened to them by itself.
They went outside and passed one

[A]**11:28** Or *the whole world* [B]**11:28** Emperor A.D. 41–54; there was a famine A.D. 47–48.

CHARACTER PROFILE

Mary **Mother of John Mark**

Her Background	• Mary was the mother of John Mark, the author of the second Gospel (Mk 1:1; Ac 12:12; 13:13; 15:37-40; Col 4:10; 2Tm 4:11; 1Pt 5:13). • She was a woman of means, having a home large enough to accommodate a number of people and several servants (12:12-13).
Her Story	• Her home was the meeting place for the early church. • After Peter's escape from prison, he went to her house immediately, indicating he knew that his fellow believers would be there.
Life Lesson	Mary's gracious hospitality provided a safe place for the early church to meet.

11:25-26 After spending a short time with the believers in Antioch, Barnabas realized he would need help discipling the new believers. So he went to **Tarsus** to enlist the help of **Saul**. Barnabas and Saul provided some guidance for **the church**, meeting with them and teaching **large numbers**. They realized the greatest need of the church was for believers to be grounded doctrinally in the Word of God. As a result the church in Antioch flourished, eventually becoming the center from which missionaries embarked to share the gospel. Out of this predominantly Gentile congregation were sent the first international missionaries (13:1-3).

11:27 Although **Antioch** is north of Jerusalem, the prophets went **down** because Jerusalem is at a much higher elevation than Antioch. **Prophets** (Gk *prophētai*, "proclaimers, interpreters, ones who speak forth") had an important role in the early church. Under inspiration of the Holy Spirit, they not only announced future events but also revealed the will of God.

11:28 Among the prophets who came from Jerusalem was **Agabus**, mentioned here for the first time in the New Testament. He reemerges later in Acts when he comes to the assistance of Paul (21:10-11). Agabus's prediction of **severe famine** occurred around A.D. 39. Luke, who wrote about this prediction after it was fulfilled, notes that the famine came **during the time of Claudius**, the Roman emperor A.D. 41–54.

11:29 Because of the prediction, **the disciples** in Antioch decided to begin a famine **relief** program for their sister congregation in Jerusalem.

11:30 Barnabas and Saul delivered the support **to the elders** (Gk *presbuterous*) of the Jerusalem church. These elders functioned as pastors of the churches, and their primary responsibilities were preaching and teaching (1Tm 5:17). Paul notes qualifications for elders in 1Tm 3:1-7, where the terms "overseer" and "elder" are used interchangeably.

12:1-2 **King Herod** is Agrippa I, the grandson of Herod the Great. Agrippa I ruled Judea A.D. 41–44. Therefore, this narrative occurred within that time span. The mode of execution for **James**, the son of Zebedee and brother of John, is not certain. If James was executed in the Roman fashion, the phrase **with the sword** would mean he was beheaded. If Herod used the Jewish mode of execution, the sword was thrust through James' body.

12:3-4 Herod intended to kill Peter, but since it was **during the days of Unleavened Bread,** he chose to wait. Executing Peter during the religious

CHARACTER PROFILE

Rhoda Bearer of Joyful News

Her Background
- Her name means "rose."
- She was a servant in the home of Mary, mother of John Mark.

Her Story
- Peter had been imprisoned by Herod and the church was praying for his release (12:5).
- An angel miraculously freed him from prison, and he went directly to Mary's house (12:6-12).
- He knocked at the door and Rhoda answered, recognizing his voice (12:13-16).
- In her excitement she neglected to open the door and let him in.

Life Lesson
Young adults played an important role in the New Testament church.

street, and immediately the angel
left him.
11 Then Peter came to himself and
said, "Now I know for certain that
the Lord has sent His angel and
rescued me from Herod's grasp and
from all that the Jewish people expected." 12 When he realized this, he
went to the house of Mary, the mother of John Mark,[A] where many had
assembled and were praying. 13 He
knocked at the door in the gateway,
and a servant named Rhoda came
to answer. 14 She recognized Peter's
voice, and because of her joy, she did
not open the gate but ran in and announced that Peter was standing at
the gateway.
15 "You're crazy!" they told her.
But she kept insisting that it was
true. Then they said, "It's his angel!"
16 Peter, however, kept on knocking,
and when they opened the door and
saw him, they were astounded.
17 Motioning to them with his
hand to be silent, he explained to
them how the Lord had brought
him out of the prison. "Report these
things to James[B] and the •brothers,"
he said. Then he departed and went
to a different place.
18 At daylight, there was a great
commotion[C] among the soldiers as
to what could have become of Peter.
19 After Herod had searched and did
not find him, he interrogated the
guards and ordered their execution.
Then Herod went down from Judea
to Caesarea and stayed there.

Herod's Death (12:20-25)

20 He had been very angry with the
Tyrians and Sidonians.[D] Together
they presented themselves before
him. They won over Blastus, who
was in charge of the king's bedroom, and through him they asked
for peace, because their country was
supplied with food from the king's
country. 21 So on an appointed day,
dressed in royal robes and seated on
the throne, Herod delivered a public
address to them. 22 The assembled
people began to shout, "It's the voice
of a god and not of a man!" 23 At once
an angel of the Lord struck him
because he did not give the glory
to God, and he became infected
with worms and died. 24 Then God's
message flourished and multiplied.
25 After they had completed their relief mission, Barnabas and Saul returned to[E] Jerusalem, taking along
John who is called Mark.

The Spread of the Gospel Through the Region of Phrygia and Galatia (13:1–15:35)

Appointment of Missionaries (13:1-3)

13 In the church that was at Antioch there were prophets
and teachers: Barnabas, Simeon

[A]12:12 Lit *John who was called Mark* [B]12:17 This was James, the Lord's brother; Mk 6:3. This was not James the apostle; Ac 12:2. [C]12:18 Or *was no small disturbance* [D]12:20 The people of the area of modern Lebanon [E]12:25 Other mss read *from*

holiday might have offended the Jews, the exact opposite of what he wanted to achieve. Jews celebrated the Passover the evening of Nisan 14. It was followed by seven days of eating unleavened bread, ending on Nisan 21. **Four soldiers** were guarding Peter at all times. Herod took every precaution because he had heard rumors of the apostles' previous escapes from jail (5:17-21).

12:12 Peter **went to the house of Mary, the mother of John Mark,** a woman of means with servants and a house big enough for the large group of believers to gather. Since Luke did not mention her husband, she might have been a widow. She was a brave woman of faith with the gift of hospitality, and she willingly opened her home to the church even in the face of persecution. She was the aunt of Barnabas (Col 4:10) and mother of John Mark, who later became a prominent figure in the early church and the author of the Gospel of Mark. Mary's house may have served as a regular place of worship for the Jerusalem church since Peter went straight there. Peter realized that the believers would be **assembled** and **praying** for him.

12:13 A **servant** girl **named Rhoda** answered the door. The fact that Luke mentions the servant by name, as well as the fact that Rhoda **recognized Peter's voice**, indicates that Peter knew the members of Mary's household personally.

12:17 Peter asked the believers at Mary's house to **report** what had happened to him **to James and the brothers**. This James, obviously not the James martyred earlier in the chapter, was the half-brother of Jesus, who was a leader in the Jerusalem church (Gl 1:19). Scholars disagree widely about the place Peter went, since staying in Jerusalem would not have been safe. Some say Antioch, others Caesarea, while still others suggest Rome. Luke omits this detail from the text.

12:23 According to the Jewish historian Josephus, Herod suffered five days of excruciating pain before his death. No longer did the disciples in Jerusalem have to worry about this infamous persecutor of the church. After Herod's death, first Felix and then Festus ruled in his place.

12:25 Luke returns to where he left off in Ac 11:30 with **Barnabas and Saul**. Formerly they had been in Antioch gathering relief for the famine-stricken Jerusalem church. Luke notes that they returned to Jerusalem, probably the trip during which they delivered the relief supplies. Verse 25 essentially functions as an introduction to the next chapter.

13:1 The local **church that was at Antioch** was a prosperous and growing church composed largely of Gentiles. They actively sought to minister to others, demonstrated by their outreach to Gentiles in their city (11:19-36) as well as by their sending relief to the Jerusalem church (11:27-30). Luke uses the terms **prophets and teachers** to describe the five men he lists as leaders of the church, and Luke lists only men as the leaders of the church. Although women, such as Dorcas (9:36-43) and Mary the mother of John Mark (12:12), performed important ministries, their roles and assignments differed from those given to the men. Women did not function as teachers of men in the church.

13:2 The phrase **ministering** [Gk *leitourgountōn*] **to the Lord** indicates they were worshiping through service. Worship was accompanied by **fasting** (Gk *nēsteuontōn*, "going without food") as they actively sought God's guidance. Fasting could be a private spiritual discipline or a public community effort to put aside food and/or drink for a set period of time. The early church used fasting in tandem with prayer in order to determine how best to move forward the spread of the gospel and how to respond to the challenges of persecution and difficulties they faced in a world hostile to the message of Christ and to those who embraced that message.

13:4-5 **Sent** not only by the church but even more importantly **by the Holy Spirit**, Barnabas and Saul embarked from Antioch on what has been called Paul's first missionary journey. From Antioch, they traveled 16 miles to **Seleucia**, a Syrian city that functioned as Antioch's eastern port on the Mediterranean coast. From Seleucia, they sailed approximately 70 miles to the city of **Salamis**, the chief eastern port for the island of **Cyprus.**

13:6-8 Upon leaving Seleucia, they traveled approximately 90 miles across the island until they came to **Paphos,** located on the southwestern coast and the capital of Cyprus. Sergius Paulus, the proconsul of Cyprus, was apparently searching for spiritual answers. He had listened to what the Jewish sorcerer had to say, but now he wanted to hear from the two missionaries. Luke adds the sorcerer's name, **Elymas**, which was translated as "sorcerer." **Bar-Jesus**, the name previously given, means "son of Jesus." The name "Elymas" was related more to his function, with **meaning** similar to the word **sorcerer**.

13:9-12 At this point, **Saul** comes to the forefront. While Barnabas's name had always been listed first, possibly indicating that he had been the leader of the group, from this point Saul's name is listed before Barnabas (except when they were in Jerusalem and in 14:14).

who was called Niger, Lucius the Cyrenian, Manaen, a close friend of •Herod the tetrarch, and Saul.

2 As they were ministering to[A] the Lord and fasting, the Holy Spirit said, "Set apart for Me Barnabas and Saul for the work I have called them to." 3 Then after they had fasted, prayed, and laid hands on them, they sent them off.

The Mission to Cyprus (13:4-12)

4 Being sent out by the Holy Spirit, they came down to Seleucia, and from there they sailed to Cyprus. 5 Arriving in Salamis, they proclaimed God's message in the Jewish •synagogues. They also had John as their assistant. 6 When they had gone through the whole island as far as Paphos, they came across a sorcerer, a Jewish false prophet named Bar-Jesus. 7 He was with the •proconsul, Sergius Paulus, an intelligent man. This man summoned Barnabas and Saul and desired to hear God's message. 8 But Elymas the sorcerer (this is the meaning of his name) opposed them and tried to turn the proconsul away from the faith.

9 Then Saul—also called Paul—filled with the Holy Spirit, stared straight at the sorcerer 10 and said, "You son of the Devil, full of all deceit and all fraud, enemy of all righteousness! Won't you ever stop perverting the straight paths of the Lord? 11 Now, look! The Lord's hand is against you. You are going to be blind, and will not see the sun for a time." Suddenly a mist and darkness fell on him, and he went around seeking someone to lead him by the hand.

12 Then the proconsul, seeing what happened, believed and was astonished at the teaching about the Lord.

Paul's Sermon in Antioch of Pisidia (13:13-41)

13 Paul and his companions set sail from Paphos and came to Perga in Pamphylia. John, however, left them and went back to Jerusalem. 14 They continued their journey from Perga and reached Antioch in Pisidia. On the Sabbath day they went into the synagogue and sat down. 15 After the reading of the Law and the Prophets, the leaders of the synagogue sent word to them, saying, "Brothers, if you have any message of encouragement for the people, you can speak."

16 Then Paul stood up and motioned with his hand and said: "Men of Israel, and you who fear God, listen! 17 The God of this people Israel chose our ancestors, exalted the people during their stay in the land of Egypt, and led them out of it with a mighty[B] arm. 18 And for about 40 years He put up with them[C] in the wilderness; 19 then after destroying seven nations in the land of Canaan, He gave their land to them as an inheritance. 20 This all took about 450 years. After this, He gave them judges until Samuel the prophet. 21 Then they asked for a king, so God gave them Saul the son of Kish, a man of the tribe of Benjamin, for 40 years. 22 After removing him, He raised up David as their king and testified about him: '**I have found David** the son of Jesse, **a man loyal to Me,**[D] who will carry out all My will.'

23 "From this man's descendants, according to the promise, God brought the Savior, Jesus,[E] to Israel. 24 Before He came to public attention,[F] John had previously proclaimed a baptism of repentance to all the people of Israel. 25 Then as John was completing his life's work, he said, 'Who do you think I am? I am not the One. But look! Someone is coming after me, and I am not worthy to untie the sandals on His feet.'

26 "Brothers, sons of Abraham's race, and those among you who fear God, the message of this salvation has been sent to us. 27 For the residents of Jerusalem and their rulers, since they did not recognize Him or the voices of the prophets that are read every Sabbath, have fulfilled their words[G] by condemning Him. 28 Though they found no grounds for the death penalty, they asked •Pilate to have Him killed. 29 When they had fulfilled all that had been written about Him, they took Him

[A]**13:2** Or *were worshiping* [B]**13:17** Lit *with an uplifted* [C]**13:18** Other mss read *He cared for them* [D]**13:22** 1Sm 13:14; Ps 89:20 [E]**13:23** Other mss read *brought salvation* [F]**13:24** Lit *Before the face of His entrance* [G]**13:27** Lit *fulfilled them*

down from the tree and put Him in
a tomb. 30 But God raised Him from
the dead, 31 and He appeared for
many days to those who came with
Him from Galilee to Jerusalem, who
are now His witnesses to the people.
32 And we ourselves proclaim to you
the good news of the promise that
was made to our ancestors. 33 God
has fulfilled this for us, their children, by raising up Jesus, as it is
written in the second Psalm:

You are My Son;
today I have become
Your Father.[A,B]

34 Since He raised Him from the
dead, never to return to decay, He
has spoken in this way, **I will grant
you the faithful covenant bless-
ings**[C] **made to David.**[D] 35 Therefore
He also says in another passage, **You
will not allow Your Holy One to see
decay.**[E] 36 For David, after serving his
own generation in God's plan, fell
•asleep, was buried with his fathers,
and decayed. 37 But the One God
raised up did not decay. 38 Therefore,
let it be known to you, brothers, that
through this man forgiveness of sins
is being proclaimed to you, 39 and everyone who believes in Him is •justi-
fied from everything that you could
not be justified from through the
law of Moses. 40 So beware that what
is said in the prophets does not happen to you:

41 **Look, you scoffers,**
marvel and vanish away,
because I am doing a work
in your days,
a work that you will
never believe,
even if someone were
to explain it to you."[F]

Paul and Barnabas in Pisidian Antioch (13:42-52)

42 As they[G] were leaving, the people[H] begged that these matters be
presented to them the following
Sabbath. 43 After the synagogue had
been dismissed, many of the Jews
and devout •proselytes followed Paul
and Barnabas, who were speaking
with them and persuading them to
continue in the grace of God.
44 The following Sabbath almost
the whole town assembled to hear
the message of the Lord.[I] 45 But
when the Jews saw the crowds, they
were filled with jealousy and began
to oppose what Paul was saying by
insulting him.

46 Then Paul and Barnabas boldly
said: "It was necessary that God's
message be spoken to you first.
But since you reject it and consider
yourselves unworthy of eternal life,
we now turn to the Gentiles! 47 For
this is what the Lord has commanded us:

I have made you
a light for the Gentiles
to bring salvation
to the ends[J] **of the earth."**[K]

48 When the Gentiles heard this, they
rejoiced and glorified the message
of the Lord, and all who had been
appointed to eternal life believed.
49 So the message of the Lord spread
through the whole region. 50 But the
Jews incited the prominent women,
who worshiped God, and the leading men of the city. They stirred up
persecution against Paul and Barnabas and expelled them from their
district. 51 But they shook the dust
off their feet against them and went
to Iconium. 52 And the disciples were
filled with joy and the Holy Spirit.

Growth and Persecution in Iconium (14:1-7)

14 The same thing happened in
Iconium; they entered the Jewish •synagogue and spoke in such
a way that a great number of both
Jews and Greeks believed. 2 But the
Jews who refused to believe stirred
up and poisoned the minds of the
Gentiles against the brothers. 3 So
they stayed there for some time
and spoke boldly in reliance on the
Lord, who testified to the message
of His grace by granting that signs
and wonders be performed through
them. 4 But the people of the city
were divided, some siding with the
Jews and some with the apostles.

[A]13:33 Or *I have begotten You* [B]13:33 Ps 2:7 [C]13:34 Lit *faithful holy things* [D]13:34 Is 55:3 [E]13:35 Ps 16:10 [F]13:41 Hab 1:5 [G]13:42 Paul and Barnabas [H]13:42 Other mss read *they were leaving the synagogue of the Jews, the Gentiles* [I]13:44 Other mss read *of God* [J]13:47 Lit *the end* [K]13:47 Is 49:6

Paul, under the leadership of **the Holy Spirit**, confronted "the sorcerer," calling him the **son of the Devil**, in direct opposition to the sorcerer's name "son of Jesus." Paul revealed the false prophet's true character and pronounced a curse of temporary blindness that immediately took effect on him. As a result of the miracle performed by Paul through the power of the Holy Spirit, the most influential person on the island of Cyprus placed his faith in Jesus Christ.

13:13 Although not on the Mediterranean coast, the city of **Perga** could be reached by sailing seven miles up the Cestrus River. **Pamphylia** was a small province on the southern coast of Asia Minor surrounded by mountains and foothills. For unknown reasons, perhaps because of the rough terrain, the change in leadership, or the focus on converting Gentiles, **John . . . went back to Jerusalem.** Because of this desertion, Paul refused to take John Mark on a later journey, causing a disagreement between Paul and Barnabas, which resulted in their parting ways (15:36-39).

13:50 The prominent women—historians Josephus and Strabo both noted that many of the Gentile women were attracted to Judaism during the Diaspora. They attended the synagogues; some became proselytes. Religious women as well as men rejected the gospel and took part in direct opposition to the missionary efforts of the early church. Unlike Cyprus, where the most powerful person was converted, here the people of influence persecuted and kicked Paul and Barnabas out of the area.

14:1 After expulsion from Antioch of Pisida, Paul and Barnabas traveled approximately 90 miles southeast to the city of **Iconium**, located in the Galatian province and more specifically in the district of Lycaonia.

14:4 Luke calls Paul and Barnabas **apostles** (Gk *apostolois*, "ones sent as messengers"). Only here and in 14:14 does Luke call anyone other than the Twelve whom Jesus selected an apostle. Since the two were sent from the church in Antioch of Syria, they both can be called apostles or messengers in a general sense. However, only Paul and the 12 disciples were officially apostles of Jesus Christ, because they are the only ones who received their commission directly from the risen Lord. Some question whether or not Paul was an apostle in this more specific sense. From the testimony of Scripture, clearly Paul regarded himself as an apostle and frequently began his letters with that designation (Rm 1:1; 1Co 1:1; 9:1; 2Co 1:1; Gl 1:1; Eph 1:1; Col 1:1; 1Tm 1:1; 2:7; 2Tm 1:1,11; Ti 1:1).

14:5-7 This effort **to assault and stone them** was not an official sanction of the synagogue since a number of Gentiles were involved. However, perhaps the Jews instigated the assault since the official punishment for blasphemy was death through stoning. Paul and Barnabas were probably informed of the plan by one of the new believers. So they **fled** to continue their mission of **evangelizing**.

14:8 Lystra, a town surrounded by mountains, was approximately 20 miles south of Iconium. Luke does not mention a synagogue in Lystra, perhaps because the city was too small for one. However, at least some Jews, including Timothy's Jewish mother, lived there (16:1).

14:11-13 Believing the two men were gods, the people **started to call Barnabas, Zeus, and Paul, Hermes**. From Greek mythology, Zeus was the king of the gods and Hermes was the messenger god. Because Paul **was the main speaker**, the crowd confused him with Hermes. According to Lystran legend, Zeus and Hermes in disguise had once visited the town seeking food and lodging. After being rejected by everyone but an elderly couple named Philemon and Baucis, the two gods sent a flood, drowning everybody but the hospitable couple. Not wanting to repeat their ancestors' supposed mistake, the people of Lystra sought **to offer sacrifice** to the two missionaries.

14:15-17 Paul and Barnabas's method for sharing the gospel with the people of Lystra differed from their previous encounters in which their listeners at least understood the concept of God. Here they had to begin with something even more basic: the creation of the world. Paul and Barnabas told about how God created and sustained the Universe.

14:19 Those arriving from **Antioch** of Pisidia exhibited determination, in traveling over 100 miles of rough terrain to try to kill the two missionaries. Perhaps insulted by Paul and Barnabas's refusal to accept their sacrifice, the Lystran people who once attempted to worship them were now **won over** by the visiting Jews and tried to kill them. Paul undoubtedly was knocked unconscious as a result of the stoning, explaining why his attackers assumed he was dead and testifying to the brutality of the attack.

14:20 Amazingly Paul, having been stoned almost to death the previous day, left Lystra and began a walk of 60 miles southeast to **Derbe**. Paul later mentioned the stoning, along with many other persecutions (2Co 11:23-27).

5 When an attempt was made by both the Gentiles and Jews, with their rulers, to assault and stone them, 6 they found out about it and fled to the Lycaonian towns called Lystra and Derbe, and to the surrounding countryside. 7 And there they kept evangelizing.

Mistaken Identity in Lystra (14:8-20)

8 In Lystra a man without strength in his feet, lame from birth,[A] and who had never walked, sat 9 and heard Paul speaking. After observing him closely and seeing that he had faith to be healed, 10 Paul said in a loud voice, "Stand upright on your feet!" And he jumped up and started to walk around.

11 When the crowds saw what Paul had done, they raised their voices, saying in the Lycaonian language, "The gods have come down to us in the form of men!" 12 And they started to call Barnabas, Zeus, and Paul, Hermes, because he was the main speaker. 13 Then the priest of Zeus, whose temple was just outside the town, brought oxen and garlands to the gates. He, with the crowds, intended to offer sacrifice.

14 The apostles Barnabas and Paul tore their robes when they heard this and rushed into the crowd, shouting: 15 "Men! Why are you doing these things? We are men also, with the same nature as you, and we are proclaiming good news to you, that you should turn from these worthless things to the living God, **who made the heaven, the earth, the sea, and everything in them.**[B] 16 In past generations He allowed all the nations to go their own way, 17 although He did not leave Himself without a witness, since He did what is good by giving you rain from heaven and fruitful seasons and satisfying your[C] hearts with food and happiness." 18 Even though they said these things, they barely stopped the crowds from sacrificing to them.

19 Then some Jews came from Antioch and Iconium, and when they had won over the crowds and stoned Paul, they dragged him out of the city, thinking he was dead. 20 After the disciples surrounded him, he got up and went into the town. The next day he left with Barnabas for Derbe.

Church Planting (14:21-28)

21 After they had evangelized that town and made many disciples, they returned to Lystra, to Iconium, and to Antioch, 22 strengthening the[D] disciples by encouraging them to continue in the faith and by telling them, "It is necessary to pass through many troubles on our way into the kingdom of God."

23 When they had appointed elders in every church and prayed with fasting, they committed them to the Lord in whom they had believed. 24 Then they passed through Pisidia and came to Pamphylia. 25 After they spoke the message in Perga, they went down to Attalia. 26 From there they sailed back to Antioch where they had been entrusted to the grace of God for the work they had now completed. 27 After they arrived and gathered the church together, they reported everything God had done with them and that He had opened the door of faith to the Gentiles. 28 And they spent a considerable time[E] with the disciples.

Dispute in Antioch (15:1-5)

15 Some men came down from Judea and began to teach the brothers: "Unless you are circumcised according to the custom prescribed by Moses, you cannot be saved!" 2 But after Paul and Barnabas had engaged them in serious argument and debate, the church arranged for Paul and Barnabas and some others of them to go up to the apostles and elders in Jerusalem concerning this controversy. 3 When they had been sent on their way by the church, they passed through both Phoenicia and Samaria, explaining in detail the conversion of the Gentiles, and they created great joy among all the brothers.

4 When they arrived at Jerusalem, they were welcomed by the church, the apostles, and the elders, and they reported all that God had done with them. 5 But some of the believ-

[A] **14:8** Lit *from his mother's womb* [B] **14:15** Ex 20:11; Ps 146:6 [C] **14:17** Other mss read *our*
[D] **14:22** Lit *the souls of the* [E] **14:28** Or *spent no little time*

ers from the party of the •Pharisees
stood up and said, "It is necessary to
circumcise them and to command
them to keep the law of Moses!"

The Jerusalem Council (15:6-21)

6 Then the apostles and the elders
assembled to consider this matter.
7 After there had been much debate,
Peter stood up and said to them:
"Brothers, you are aware that in the
early days God made a choice among
you,[A] that by my mouth the Gentiles
would hear the gospel message and
believe. 8 And God, who knows the
heart, testified to them by giving[B]
the Holy Spirit, just as He also did
to us. 9 He made no distinction between us and them, cleansing their
hearts by faith. 10 Now then, why are
you testing God by putting a yoke on
the disciples' necks that neither our
ancestors nor we have been able to
bear? 11 On the contrary, we believe
we are saved through the grace of
the Lord Jesus in the same way they
are."

12 Then the whole assembly fell
silent and listened to Barnabas and
Paul describing all the signs and
wonders God had done through
them among the Gentiles. 13 After
they stopped speaking, James responded: "Brothers, listen to me!
14 Simeon[C] has reported how God
first intervened to take from the
Gentiles a people for His name.
15 And the words of the prophets
agree with this, as it is written:

16 **After these things**
I will return
and rebuild
David's fallen tent.
I will rebuild its ruins
and set it up again,
17 **so the rest of humanity**
may seek the Lord—
even all the Gentiles
who are called by My name,
declares the Lord who does
these things,
18 **known from long ago.**[D,E]

19 Therefore, in my judgment, we
should not cause difficulties for
those among the Gentiles who turn
to God, 20 but instead we should
write to them to abstain from things
polluted by idols, from sexual immorality, from eating anything that
has been strangled, and from blood.
21 For since ancient times, Moses has
had those who proclaim him in every city, and every Sabbath day he is
read aloud in the •synagogues."

The Letter to the Gentile Believers (15:22-29)

22 Then the apostles and the elders,
with the whole church, decided to
select men who were among them
and to send them to Antioch with
Paul and Barnabas: Judas, called
Barsabbas, and Silas, both leading
men among the brothers. 23 They
wrote this letter to be delivered by
them:[F]

From the apostles and the elders, your brothers,
To the brothers among the Gentiles in Antioch, Syria, and Cilicia:
Greetings.

24 Because we have heard that
some without our authorization went out from us and
troubled you with their words
and unsettled your hearts,[G]
25 we have unanimously decided to select men and send them
to you along with our dearly
loved Barnabas and Paul, 26 who
have risked their lives for the
name of our Lord Jesus Christ.
27 Therefore we have sent Judas
and Silas, who will personally report the same things by
word of mouth.[H] 28 For it was
the Holy Spirit's decision—and
ours—to put no greater burden on you than these necessary things: 29 that you abstain
from food offered to idols, from
blood, from eating anything
that has been strangled, and
from sexual immorality. You
will do well if you keep yourselves from these things.
Farewell.

[A] **15:7** Other mss read *us* [B] **15:8** Other mss add *them* [C] **15:14** Simon (Peter) [D] **15:17-18** Other mss read *says the Lord who does all these things. Known to God from long ago are all His works.* [E] **15:16-18** Am 9:11-12; Is 45:21 [F] **15:23** Lit *Writing by their hand:* [G] **15:24** Other mss add *by saying, "Be circumcised and keep the law,"* [H] **15:27** Lit *things through word*

15:1 Unnamed men from **Judea** came to Antioch and **began to teach** the Christians. These Judaizers, who apparently believed in Christ, taught that faith in Christ alone was not enough but must be coupled with keeping the law of Moses and circumcision.

15:2 Some others likely included Titus (Gl 2:1). This initial serious threat to the unity of the fledgling church resulted in the convening of the Jerusalem Council, a meeting of utmost importance for the church because the very nature of salvation was at stake. The issue was not whether or not Gentiles could receive salvation but rather the matter of how they were saved. Specifically, must Gentiles become circumcised proselytes (i.e., embracing all the tenets of Judaism) before they received salvation? Or did trust and faith in Jesus alone secure salvation? The discussions and conclusions from this conference would be crucial for the future of Christianity.

15:6-21 James, the half-brother of Jesus, presided over the meeting; and testimonies came from the foremost leaders of the church.

15:10 Peter referred to the Mosaic law as **a yoke**, which the Jews and their **ancestors** were not **able to bear**. See, **Hard Question**, p. 1508.

15:13 James, the pastor of the church in Jerusalem, issued a concluding statement. Jesus' half-brother, who also authored the book bearing his name, would later be martyred for his faith. He quoted Amos as representative of the prophets, who were in agreement that God would save Gentiles. James emphasized to the Jerusalem Council that Scripture did not indicate that the Gentiles had to become Jewish proselytes to enter the kingdom in the millennium; therefore, the requirement should not be imposed upon them now.

15:16 David's fallen tent is the Jerusalem temple, which, although still standing during the days of the Jerusalem Council, was destroyed approximately 20 years later in A.D. 70.

15:28-29 They desired **to put no greater burden** than **necessary** on the Gentile believers, repeating what James had previously said (15:19-20) and refuting what the unauthorized people had said. Circumcision would not be a prerequisite to salvation.

15:36 This marks the beginning of Paul's second missionary journey.

15:37-39 Barnabas wanted to take along John Mark. . . . who had deserted them on their first missionary journey in Pamphylia (13:13), but **Paul did not think it** was **appropriate** since Mark had proven unreliable in the past. In addition to this **sharp disagreement**, Paul confronted Barnabas about some hypocrisy in his life (see Gl 2:13). Likely, the rift between Paul and Barnabas was healed, because Paul later briefly referred to him in a positive light (1Co 9:6). In addition, Paul also changed his opinion about Mark, describing him as "useful to me in the ministry" and as a coworker in the kingdom of God (2Tm 4:11; Col 4:10-11).

15:40-41 Paul and **Silas** traveled by ground north through **Syria** and into the province of **Cilicia**, which is modern Turkey, **strengthening the churches** as they went. Tarsus, Paul's hometown, was located in Cilicia. They probably stopped there before crossing the Taurus mountains into southern Galatia, where Derbe and Lystra were located.

16:1-3 Derbe and Lystra, located in southern Galatia, which is now a part of modern Turkey, were cities Paul and Barnabas visited on Paul's first missionary journey. A **disciple named Timothy** was highly regarded by the disciples in Lystra and **Iconium** and was likely converted on Paul's first missionary journey. Paul spoke of him as his "true son in the faith" (1Tm 1:2). Timothy's mother Eunice was **a believing Jewish woman, but his father was a Greek.** As a result, Timothy was not circumcised according to Jewish tradition; however, he was taught the Scriptures from a young age (2Tm 3:15). **Paul wanted Timothy** to accompany him and Silas on their journey, but the fact that Timothy was not circumcised created a problem. Although the Jerusalem Council established that circumcision was not a requirement for salvation (Ac 15:6-21), its absence was still a stumbling block for some Jews. Since many people in **those places** to which they would travel knew Timothy's **father was a Greek**, Paul **circumcised him** lest he become a hindrance to the gospel.

16:9-13 The area of **Macedonia** roughly corresponds to modern northern Greece. Paul considered his vision of the Macedonian to be his mandate from God to preach the gospel in this province north of Achaia. This use of the pronoun **we** marks the addition of Luke, the author of Acts, to Paul's traveling group. **Samothrace**, an island in the Aegean Sea, was about halfway between Asia Minor and the Greek mainland. **Philippi**, a city of

CHURCH GOVERNMENT

15:28-29 *Ruling body?* No. The issue of who rules the church has been given increased attention during recent years. Many use Ac 15:6-29 to maintain that a ruling body has control over the church. However, in this passage, "the whole church" was involved in the decision-making process (15:22). The New Testament does not call for a ruling body but affirms the role of the congregation in decision-making.

What the congregation should do. First, the congregation should elect its leaders. In Ac 6 the congregation chose from among themselves their own deacons. The appointing of elders by Paul and Barnabas did not contradict this principle (Ac 14:23). Second, the congregation must discipline members. Matthew 18 outlines the steps for church discipline. The final step is to bring the matter before the church. Jesus Himself stated that the church, not a board of elders or any other ruling body, held the final authority in church discipline (see 1Co 5:4-5). Paul indicated the setting for this action was the assembly. The church is responsible for disciplining its members. Third, the congregation should embrace its members. Paul did not command but urged the "majority" of the congregation to confirm their love by accepting a disciplined member back into the body (2Co 2:6-8). From this passage and the fact that the church as a whole had a responsibility for its own purity, one can see that the congregation must have a role in accepting members.

What the congregation should not do. The congregation should not fight and bicker about matters of no importance. The color of the carpet or the type of chair in a Sunday School classroom will have little impact on the eternal destiny of lost souls. When the church turns its focus inward instead of outward, disputes occur that make congregational polity difficult. Additionally, when church discipline is not properly practiced, unregenerate members can create trouble. Church rolls overloaded with members who never attend should be purged or those members disciplined. The New Testament model is a regenerate church membership focused on fulfilling the commission of Jesus Christ to spread the gospel to the entire world.

The Outcome of the Jerusalem Letter (15:30-35)

30 Then, being sent off, they went
down to Antioch, and after gathering the assembly, they delivered
the letter. 31 When they read it, they
rejoiced because of its encouragement. 32 Both Judas and Silas, who
were also prophets themselves, encouraged the brothers and strengthened them with a long message.
33 After spending some time there,
they were sent back in peace by the
•brothers to those who had sent
them.[A,B] 35 But Paul and Barnabas,
along with many others, remained
in Antioch teaching and proclaiming the message of the Lord.

The Spread of the Gospel into Macedonia, Achaia, and Asia (15:36–21:14)

Paul's Choice of Silas (15:36-41)

36 After some time had passed,
Paul said to Barnabas, "Let's go back
and visit the brothers in every town
where we have preached the message of the Lord and see how they're
doing." 37 Barnabas wanted to take
along John Mark.[C] 38 But Paul did not
think it appropriate to take along
this man who had deserted them
in Pamphylia and had not gone on
with them to the work. 39 There was
such a sharp disagreement that they
parted company, and Barnabas took
Mark with him and sailed off to Cyprus. 40 Then Paul chose Silas and
departed, after being commended to
the grace of the Lord by the brothers. 41 He traveled through Syria and
Cilicia, strengthening the churches.

Paul's Selection of Timothy (16:1-5)

16 Then he went on to Derbe and
Lystra, where there was a disciple named Timothy, the son of a
believing Jewish woman, but his
father was a Greek. 2 The •brothers
at Lystra and Iconium spoke highly
of him. 3 Paul wanted Timothy[D] to go
with him, so he took him and circumcised him because of the Jews
who were in those places, since they
all knew that his father was a Greek.
4 As they traveled through the towns,
they delivered the decisions reached
by the apostles and elders at Jerusalem for them to observe. 5 So the
churches were strengthened in the
faith and increased in number daily.

Evangelization in Europe (16:6-10)

6 They went through the region
of Phrygia and Galatia and were
prevented by the Holy Spirit from
speaking the message in •Asia.
7 When they came to Mysia, they
tried to go into Bithynia, but the
Spirit of Jesus did not allow them.
8 So, bypassing Mysia, they came
down to Troas. 9 During the night a
vision appeared to Paul: A Macedonian man was standing and pleading

A 15:33 Other mss read *the brothers to the apostles* B 15:33 Other mss add v. 34: *But Silas decided to stay there.* C 15:37 Lit *John who was called Mark* D 16:3 Lit *wanted this one*

with him, "Cross over to Macedonia and help us!" [10]After he had seen the vision, we[A] immediately made efforts to set out for Macedonia, concluding that God had called us to evangelize them.

Lydia's Conversion (16:11-15)

[11]Then, setting sail from Troas, we ran a straight course to Samothrace, the next day to Neapolis, [12]and from there to Philippi, a Roman colony, which is a leading city of that district of Macedonia. We stayed in that city for a number of days. [13]On the Sabbath day we went outside the city gate by the river, where we thought there was a place of prayer. We sat down and spoke to the women gathered there. [14]A woman named Lydia, a dealer in purple cloth from the city of Thyatira, who worshiped God, was listening. The Lord opened her heart to pay attention to what was spoken by Paul. [15]After she and her household were baptized, she urged us, "If you consider me a believer in the Lord, come and stay at my house." And she persuaded us.

Paul and Silas in Prison (16:16-24)

[16]Once, as we were on our way to prayer, a •slave girl met us who had a spirit of prediction.[B] She made a large profit for her owners by fortune-telling. [17]As she followed Paul and us she cried out, "These men, who are proclaiming to you[C] the way of salvation, are the slaves of the Most High God." [18]And she did this for many days.

But Paul was greatly aggravated and turning to the spirit, said, "I command you in the name of Jesus Christ to come out of her!" And it came out right away.[D]

[19]When her owners saw that their hope of profit was gone, they seized Paul and Silas and dragged them into the marketplace to the authorities. [20]Bringing them before the chief magistrates, they said, "These men are seriously disturbing our city. They are Jews [21]and are promoting customs that are not legal for us as Romans to adopt or practice."

[22]Then the mob joined in the attack against them, and the chief magistrates stripped off their clothes and ordered them to be beaten with rods. [23]After they had inflicted many blows on them, they threw them in jail, ordering the jailer to keep them securely guarded. [24]Receiving such

[A]16:10 The use of we in this passage probably indicates that the author Luke is joining Paul's missionary team here. [B]16:16 Or *a spirit by which she predicted the future* [C]16:17 Other mss read *us* [D]16:18 Lit *out this hour*

HARD QUESTION

Is it okay to baptize infants?

The book of Acts contains references to "household baptisms," a phrase sometimes used to support the practice of infant baptism (16:11-15,31-34;18:8). However, a careful analysis of these passages provides no support for baptizing infants. To the contrary, belief in Christ as a prerequisite to Christian baptism is consistently stated in Acts.

Lydia and **her household were baptized** (16:15). Some have assumed that Lydia must have had children in the house and that these children would have been baptized. However, whether or not Lydia was married or had children is not stated in the text. She was a seller of purple from the city of Thyatira, about 300 miles from Philippi. Had she been married, customarily she would have worked with her husband in the business or more likely presided over the home and cared for her children. Additionally, in verse 15 she referred to **my house**, again implying that she had no husband and the house was hers alone. In verse 40, the house is referred to by Luke as **Lydia's house**. The most logical explanation is that Lydia had no husband or children. She, together with those who worked for her in her house, accepted the gospel of Jesus Christ. Thus, believers were those who understood their commitment as individuals and were thus proper candidates for baptism.

Acts 16:31-34 discusses the salvation and baptism of the Philippian jailer and his household. However, before the baptism, Paul told them, **"Believe on the Lord Jesus, and you will be saved—you and your household."** Certainly Paul did not mean that the jailer could believe and everyone would be saved but that everyone in the house could believe and each, according to the exercising of his faith, would be saved. Belief in Christ was and is a prerequisite to biblical baptism. Additionally, he "rejoiced because he had believed God with his entire household." In infancy, one does not have the intellectual development to believe, and thus, should not be baptized.

Crispus . . . believed the Lord, along with his whole household (Ac 18:8). This introductory phrase indicates that all in the household were capable of belief. Apparently no infants were present, and those who believed were baptized. Throughout Acts and the entire New Testament a consistent pattern of belief in Christ emerges first, and baptism follows. Thus, only a believer in Christ is a candidate for baptism.

considerable size, contained minimal Jewish population because there was no synagogue, which required only 10 Jewish males. Therefore, **on the Sabbath**, the group went outside the city gate by the river, where they thought there was **a place of prayer**. Although the exact location is unknown, they probably gathered at the River Gangites or at a stream that flows a short distance away from the city's west gate. A group of **women gathered** to worship, and there Paul began the evangelization of Macedonia.

16:14 Lydia was **from the city of Thyatira**, located in the Roman province of Lydda in Asia Minor and noted for its production of purple dye and dyed goods. Lydia herself was **a dealer in purple cloth**. The purple dye was made from a shellfish called a "murex" and from the root of a madder plant. It was extremely expensive and worn only by royalty and the wealthy. Lydia's business plus her ability to house the group of missionaries demonstrated that she most likely possessed wealth. Like Cornelius (10:1-8), she **worshiped God**; yet she had not converted to Judaism. See **Character Profile**, p. 1432.

16:15 Luke notes that **the Lord opened her heart** so Lydia then paid **attention** to what Paul said, obviously responded positively to Paul's message, genuinely believing that Jesus was the Messiah spoken about in the Old Testament Scriptures. Lydia became Paul's first convert in Europe. As an outward expression of her new faith in Christ, she was **baptized**, probably in the river near where they worshiped. The text also indicates that her **household**—including her servants, as well as any family members old enough to fully comprehend and respond to the grace available through Jesus Christ—were baptized.

Hospitality is an important ministry for all Christians, especially women (1Tm 5:9-10). In the ancient world, inns were often unavailable, too expensive, or too dangerous. By opening her home to the four missionaries, Lydia contributed to their ministry. At her request, Paul and his companions accepted her invitation and most likely stayed with her for the rest of their time in Philippi.

16:16 In Philippi, **a slave girl** was possessed by **a** [demonic] **spirit of prediction**; she was demon-possessed. Fortune-telling was widely practiced in the Roman Empire. The Bible strongly condemns such occult practices (Lv 19:26 and Jr 27:9). The girl's masters abused her by using her extraordinary abilities to predict the future for their personal profit. See **Character Profile**, p. 1433.

16:17-18 The slave girl often **followed Paul** and his companions. The demon-possessed girl spoke truth, even using biblical terminology. The phrase **Most High God** was an Old Testament description of the God of Israel used by Abraham, the psalmist, and Daniel (Gn 14:22; Ps 78:35; Dn 5:18). The element of truth made her more dangerous. Since the girl agreed with the missionaries, some could have assumed that she was a part of their group and been deceived, bringing harm to the cause of Christ.

16:25 Singing hymns (Gk *humnoun*, "sing hymn of praise", transliterated into English as "hymns") affirms this medium of worship and praise as a worthy testimony.

16:26 Earthquakes occurred often in this region, but the timing and results of this quake demonstrated God's hand in the situation.

16:27 The jailer knew the law. If a Roman soldier allowed a prisoner to escape, no matter the cause, he paid with his own life (12:9; 27:42). Instead of facing a humiliating prosecution and an agonizing death, the jailer **drew his sword** to commit suicide.

16:31-33 Salvation has never been attained by being a good person, by going to church, or by being baptized. Salvation comes only through belief in the Lord Jesus Christ. The jailer and **all his family** responded positively to the gospel message and **were baptized** immediately. Judaism had a rich heritage in the leadership of the husband and father in the home, and this model definitely extended to the spiritual arena; for the head of the family to lead and then be followed by others in the household who were moved by his example was a natural thing. In addition, plain language in the text suggests that Paul's teaching and preaching extended beyond the jailer to include the entire household.

16:35-37 Luke does not indicate why the **chief magistrates** changed their opinion. Perhaps the jailer pleaded for their release. When the jailer let them know that they could **go in peace**, Paul refused. For the first time in Acts, Paul revealed that he and Silas were **Roman citizens**. According to the law, Roman citizens were protected from public beatings, imprisonment, and death without a trial. By denying these men their rights, the magistrates had broken the law. Paul demanded a public apology for the sake of the church. Without a public apology, the people of the city would always believe that Paul and Silas had been guilty of a crime, which could have caused unnecessary persecution of the new believers who had been associated with them.

16:40-17:1 Paul and Silas **departed** with Timothy for **Thessalonica**.

CHARACTER PROFILE

Lydia A Believing Businesswoman

Her Background	• She had a successful business selling fine purple fabrics (16:14). • She lived in Philippi, a major city in Macedonia (16:12). • She worshiped God (16:14).
Her Story	• She attended a prayer meeting with other women on the Sabbath (16:13-14). • "The Lord opened her heart," and she listened to Paul's message (16:14). • She was baptized along with her household (Gk *oikos*), which includes family and servants (16:15). • She urged Paul and Silas to be guests in her home (16:15).
Life Lesson	The Lord reveals more truth about Himself when you are obedient to what you already know and believe.

an order, he put them into the inner prison and secured their feet in the stocks.

A Midnight Deliverance (16:25-34)

25 About midnight Paul and Silas were praying and singing hymns to God, and the prisoners were listening to them. 26 Suddenly there was such a violent earthquake that the foundations of the jail were shaken, and immediately all the doors were opened, and everyone's chains came loose. 27 When the jailer woke up and saw the doors of the prison open, he drew his sword and was going to kill himself, since he thought the prisoners had escaped.

28 But Paul called out in a loud voice, "Don't harm yourself, because all of us are here!"

29 Then the jailer called for lights, rushed in, and fell down trembling before Paul and Silas. 30 Then he escorted them out and said, "Sirs, what must I do to be saved?"

31 So they said, "Believe on the Lord Jesus, and you will be saved—you and your household." 32 Then they spoke the message of the Lord to him along with everyone in his house. 33 He took them the same hour of the night and washed their wounds. Right away he and all his family were baptized. 34 He brought them into his house, set a meal before them, and rejoiced because he had believed God with his entire household.

An Official Apology (16:35-40)

35 When daylight came, the chief magistrates sent the police to say, "Release those men!"

36 The jailer reported these words to Paul: "The magistrates have sent orders for you to be released. So come out now and go in peace."

37 But Paul said to them, "They beat us in public without a trial, although we are Roman citizens, and threw us in jail. And now are they going to smuggle us out secretly? Certainly not! On the contrary, let them come themselves and escort us out!"

38 Then the police reported these words to the magistrates. They were afraid when they heard that Paul and Silas were Roman citizens. 39 So they came and apologized to them, and escorting them out, they urged them to leave town. 40 After leaving the jail, they came to Lydia's house where they saw and encouraged the brothers, and departed.

A Short Ministry in Thessalonica (17:1-4)

17 Then they traveled through Amphipolis and Apollonia and came to Thessalonica, where there was a Jewish •synagogue. 2 As usual, Paul went to the synagogue, and on three Sabbath days reasoned with them from the Scriptures, 3 explaining and showing that the •Messiah had to suffer and rise from the dead: "This Jesus I am proclaiming to you

CHARACTER PROFILE

A Fortune-Telling Slave Girl

Her Background	• She was a demon-possessed slave, who lived in Philippi. • She was a fortune-teller. • She was exploited by her owners, providing their income (16:16).
Her Story	• She followed Paul and Silas for many days, crying out loudly and disturbing their ministry (16:17-18). • She recognized them as servants of the true God. • Paul commanded the demon to come out of her.
Life Lesson	Note the contrast between the treatment of a young slave girl in a pagan culture as opposed to the valuing of women by first-century Christians.

is the Messiah." 4 Then some of them were persuaded and joined Paul and Silas, including a great number of God-fearing Greeks, as well as a number[A] of the leading women.

Riot in the City (17:5-9)

5 But the Jews became jealous, and they brought together some scoundrels from the marketplace, formed a mob, and started a riot in the city. Attacking Jason's house, they searched for them to bring them out to the public assembly. 6 When they did not find them, they dragged Jason and some of the •brothers before the city officials, shouting, "These men who have turned the world upside down have come here too, 7 and Jason has received them as guests! They are all acting contrary to Caesar's decrees, saying that there is another king—Jesus!" 8 The Jews stirred up the crowd and the city officials who heard these things. 9 So taking a security bond from Jason and the others, they released them.

The Bereans and the Scriptures (17:10-15)

10 As soon as it was night, the brothers sent Paul and Silas off to Berea. On arrival, they went into the synagogue of the Jews. 11 The people here were more open-minded than those in Thessalonica, since they welcomed the message with eagerness and examined the Scriptures daily to see if these things were so. 12 Consequently, many of them believed, including a number of the prominent Greek women as well as men. 13 But when the Jews from Thessalonica found out that God's message had been proclaimed by Paul at Berea, they came there too, agitating and disturbing[B] the crowds. 14 Then the brothers immediately sent Paul away to go to the sea, but Silas and Timothy stayed on there. 15 Those who escorted Paul brought him as far as Athens, and after receiving instructions for Silas and Timothy to come to him as quickly as possible, they departed.

Paul in Athens (17:16-21)

16 While Paul was waiting for them in Athens, his spirit was troubled within him when he saw that the city was full of idols. 17 So he reasoned in the synagogue with the Jews and with those who worshiped God and in the marketplace every day with those who happened to be there. 18 Then also, some of the Epicurean and Stoic philosophers argued with him. Some said, "What is this pseudo-intellectual[C] trying to say?"

Others replied, "He seems to be a preacher of foreign deities"—because he was telling the good news about Jesus and the Resurrection.[D]

19 They took him and brought him to the Areopagus,[E] and said, "May we learn about this new teaching you're

They apparently left Luke behind in Philippi because the "first person" or "we" sections temporarily ceased until Paul returned to the city on his third missionary journey (20:5). Luke likely remained so that he could continue the ministry and disciple the new believers.

17:2 Luke notes that Paul was in Thessalonica **on three Sabbath days**, indicating that he ministered out of the synagogue for approximately three weeks, after which he might have based his ministry out of the house of Jason (vv. 5-9). The group of missionaries remained in Thessalonica long enough to receive an offering from the Philippians (Php 4:16) and to establish work (1Th 2:9).

17:4 The phrase **leading women** may denote women who held positions of authority in the city or women who were wives of prominent men since the phrase can also be translated "wives of the leading men." Paul did on occasion single out influential women who were converts in the congregation of Macedonia (16:14; 17:4,12), and without doubt in social and civic arenas Macedonian women did have influence as confirmed in extrabiblical sources. Again, however, whether these women had prominence of position or wealth in their own right or because they shared that influence with their husbands, the fact remains that women of influence did respond to the gospel; and, as with Lydia, they did devote their resources and energies to kingdom service. The main thrust of this passage seems to be that only **some** of the Jews were converted, while a great number of Gentile men and women were converted. Much of Paul's success came in his ministry to the Gentile population.

17:10 Berea, 45 miles west of Thessalonica, was in northern Greece and is now called Veria.

17:16-18 Athens, an ancient city settled before 3000 B.C., was named for Athena, the goddess of wisdom. It was located approximately 200 miles south of Thessalonica in the province of Achaia, five miles from the Aegean Sea. Regarded in Paul's day as the intellectual capital of the world, the city was known for its art, literature, and especially its philosophy. History's three most famous **philosophers**—Socrates, Plato, and Aristotle—called Athens home. Two other significant philosophers resided in Athens: Epicurus (341-270 B.C.)., founder of Epicureanism, and Zeno of Citium (344-262 B.C.), founder of Stoicism. These philosophies were dominant in Paul's day.

[A] **17:4** Lit *as well as not a few* [B] **17:13** Other mss omit *and disturbing* [C] **17:18** Lit *this seed picker*; = one who picks up scraps [D] **17:18** = Gk *Anastasis* [E] **17:19** Or *Mars Hill*, the oldest and most famous court in Athens with jurisdiction in moral, religious, and civil matters

17:22-31 This sermon demonstrates how Paul effectively adapted the gospel message to his audience. He did not change the truth of the gospel but rather the manner in which he presented it. When addressing the Jews or worshipers of God, Paul presented the gospel using the proofs of Scripture (13:16-41). Since this audience had no concept of God or the Old Testament, Paul told them about Jesus from a different perspective, although he still grounded his statements in Scripture. This sermon is Paul's best preserved message to a pagan audience.

17:23 Paul did not openly accuse his Athenian audience of anything wrong, such as superstition. The Athenians likely interpreted this remark as a compliment, but Paul subtly implied that their deities were evil spirits rather than gods. Paul attempted to find common ground with his audience. As he had been exploring Athens, among the many idols and **objects of . . . worship** he discovered an altar on which was inscribed: **TO AN UNKNOWN GOD**, an inscription Paul used as his basis to tell them about this God whom they did not know.

17:32-34 Paul's speech and particularly his mention of the **resurrection** prompted three responses. The first group **began to ridicule him**. It was inconceivable to them with their pagan frame of mind that a man could be raised from the dead. Paul's speech piqued the interest of the second group, and they wanted to hear more. The third group **believed**, including **Dionysius the Areopagite**, who was one of the members of the upper echelons of the Athens Council (all of whom were at least 60 years of age and had held some high government office), and **a woman named Damaris**. There is a strong tradition, noted in Eusebius, that Dionysius was the first bishop of Athens and that he died a martyr's death. Damaris does not seem to be his wife, and little is known about her. While Paul did not labor in vain, only a few people accepted Christ, and no lasting church was established. His next stop in nearby Corinth proved more fruitful.

18:1 From Athens, Paul traveled approximately 50 miles west **to Corinth**, the capital of the province of Achaia, which was strategically located at the point of convergence for land and sea trade routes. While Athens was known for its culture and learning, Corinth was known for its prosperity and immorality. Immorality so characterized the city that the verb "to Corinthianize" meant to be sexually immoral.

18:2 In Corinth, Paul encountered a Jewish couple named **Aquila** and

>WORD|*study*

17:17-18 The philosophers demeaningly dubbed Paul a pseudo-intellectual (Gk *spermologos*, "scavenger," figuratively "one who picks up scraps of knowledge or seed-picker"). The image of a seed-picker suggests a bird picking seeds indiscriminately in the barnyard. First used of birds and then of men collecting odds and ends in the market, essentially they denigrated Paul as someone who grabbed scraps of ideas here and there and then attempted to pass them off as some great knowledge but with no depth of understanding and worth no more than the trash he peddled. They could not understand Paul's talk about a bodily resurrection because the Epicureans did not believe in existence after death, and the Stoics believed only the soul survived death.

speaking of? 20 For what you say sounds strange to us, and we want to know what these ideas mean." 21 Now all the Athenians and the foreigners residing there spent their time on nothing else but telling or hearing something new.

The Areopagus Address (17:22-34)

22 Then Paul stood in the middle of the Areopagus and said: "Men of Athens! I see that you are extremely religious in every respect. 23 For as I was passing through and observing the objects of your worship, I even found an altar on which was inscribed:

TO AN UNKNOWN GOD.

Therefore, what you worship in ignorance, this I proclaim to you. 24 The God who made the world and everything in it—He is Lord of heaven and earth and does not live in shrines made by hands. 25 Neither is He served by human hands, as though He needed anything, since He Himself gives everyone life and breath and all things. 26 From one man[A] He has made every nationality to live over the whole earth and has determined their appointed times and the boundaries of where they live. 27 He did this so they might seek God, and perhaps they might reach out and find Him, though He is not far from each one of us. 28 For in Him we live and move and exist, as even some of your own poets have said, 'For we are also His offspring.'[B] 29 Being God's offspring then, we shouldn't think that the divine nature is like gold or silver or stone, an image fashioned by human art and imagination.

30 "Therefore, having overlooked the times of ignorance, God now commands all people everywhere to repent, 31 because He has set a day when He is going to judge the world in righteousness by the Man He has appointed. He has provided proof of this to everyone by raising Him from the dead."

32 When they heard about resurrection of the dead, some began to ridicule him. But others said, "We'd like to hear from you again about this." 33 Then Paul left their presence. 34 However, some men joined him and believed, including Dionysius the Areopagite, a woman named Damaris, and others with them.

Founding of the Corinthian Church (18:1-17)

18 After this, he[C] left Athens and went to Corinth, 2 where he found a Jewish man named Aquila, a native of Pontus, who had recently come from Italy with his wife Priscilla because Claudius[D] had ordered all the Jews to leave Rome. Paul came to them, 3 and being of the same occupation, stayed with them and worked, for they were tentmakers[E] by trade. 4 He reasoned in the •synagogue every Sabbath and tried to persuade both Jews and Greeks.

5 When Silas and Timothy came down from Macedonia, Paul was occupied with preaching the message[F] and solemnly testified to the Jews that Jesus is the •Messiah. 6 But when they resisted and blasphemed, he shook his robe[G] and told them, "Your blood is on your own heads! I am innocent.[H] From now on I will

A **17:26** Other mss read *one blood* B **17:28** This citation is from Aratus, a third-century B.C. Gk poet. C **18:1** Other mss read *Paul* D **18:2** Roman emperor A.D. 41–54; he expelled all Jews from Rome in A.D. 49. E **18:3** Or *leatherworkers*, or less likely *manufacturers of theatrical properties* F **18:5** Other mss read *was urged by the Spirit* G **18:6** A symbolic display of protest; Mt 10:14; Ac 13:51 H **18:6** Lit *•clean*

go to the Gentiles." 7 So he left there and went to the house of a man named Titius Justus, a worshiper of God, whose house was next door to the synagogue. 8 Crispus, the leader of the synagogue, believed the Lord, along with his whole household. Many of the Corinthians, when they heard, believed and were baptized.

9 Then the Lord said to Paul in a night vision, "Don't be afraid, but keep on speaking and don't be silent. 10 For I am with you, and no one will lay a hand on you to hurt you, because I have many people in this city." 11 And he stayed there a year and six months, teaching the word of God among them.

12 While Gallio was •proconsul of Achaia, the Jews made a united attack against Paul and brought him to the judge's bench. 13 "This man," they said, "persuades people to worship God contrary to the law!"

14 As Paul was about to open his mouth, Gallio said to the Jews, "If it were a matter of a crime or of moral evil, it would be reasonable for me to put up with you Jews. 15 But if these are questions about words, names, and your own law, see to it yourselves. I don't want to be a judge of such things." 16 So he drove them from the judge's bench. 17 Then they all[A] seized Sosthenes, the leader of the synagogue, and beat him in front of the judge's bench. But none of these things concerned Gallio.

The Return Trip to Antioch (18:18-23)

18 So Paul, having stayed on for many days, said good-bye to the •brothers and sailed away to Syria. Priscilla and Aquila were with him. He shaved his head at Cenchreae because he had taken a vow. 19 When they reached Ephesus he left them there, but he himself entered the synagogue and engaged in discussion with[B] the Jews. 20 And though they asked him to stay for a longer time, he declined, 21 but he said good-bye and stated,[C] "I'll come back to you again, if God wills." Then he set sail from Ephesus.

22 On landing at Caesarea, he went up and greeted the church[D] and went down to Antioch. 23 And after spending some time there, he set out, traveling through one place after another in the Galatian territory and Phrygia, strengthening all the disciples.

The Eloquent Apollos (18:24-28)

24 A Jew named Apollos, a native Alexandrian, an eloquent man who was powerful in the use of the Scriptures, arrived in Ephesus. 25 This man had been instructed in the way of the Lord; and being fervent in spirit,[E] he spoke and taught the things about Jesus accurately, although he knew only John's baptism. 26 He began to speak boldly in the synagogue. After Priscilla and Aquila heard him, they took him home[F] and explained the way of God to him more accurately. 27 When he

[A]18:17 Other mss read *Then all the Greeks* [B]18:19 Or *and addressed* [C]18:21 Other mss add *"By all means it is necessary to keep the coming festival in Jerusalem. But* [D]18:22 The church in Jerusalem [E]18:25 Or *in the Spirit* [F]18:26 Lit *they received him*

Priscilla. Originally from **Pontus**, Aquila had moved to Rome. Inscriptions in the catacombs in Rome hint that Priscilla was from a distinguished family of high standing in Rome where the couple likely met. The New Testament mentions Priscilla and Aquila six times (18:2,18,26; Rm 16:3; 1Co 16:19; 2Tm 4:19). Two times Aquila's name appeared before Priscilla's, and four times Priscilla is listed before Aquila. This styling of their names may be an indication of Priscilla's higher social status or that she had a more active role in the ministry or simply a gentlemanly courtesy or deference to a gracious woman. The text does not indicate one way or the other, so any conclusion is conjecture at best. In Acts, Luke always refers to Priscilla by her common name "Priscilla," while Paul preferred her more formal name, "Prisca."

As a result of an edict by **Claudius** the Roman emperor expelling all **Jews** from **Rome**, Aquila and Priscilla had recently relocated to Corinth. Historical sources indicate that this edict occurred in the ninth year of Claudius's reign around A.D. 49. Since Aquila and Priscilla arrived in Rome before Paul, he did not likely arrive in Corinth before the middle of A.D. 49.

18:24-28 After Paul left Ephesus, **a Jew named Apollos** arrived in the city. Apollos was from Alexandria, a city in northern Egypt known as a center for education and philosophy. Accordingly, Apollos was an educated man, **eloquent** and **powerful in the use of the Scriptures**. The "Scriptures," as always throughout the New Testament, denoted the Old Testament. Apollos's unique gifts enabled him to be an effective witness for Christ. Apollos had been instructed in the way of the Lord, but one great gap appeared in his knowledge. **He knew only John's baptism**. What he knew about Jesus he taught **accurately** and **boldly**, but he did not know the whole story.

BIBLICAL WOMANHOOD Priscilla's Ministry

Some cite the example of Priscilla's teaching Apollos (18:26) to support nullifying the teaching of 1Tm 2:12, which states that a woman should not "teach" or "have authority over a man." This account cannot contradict 1Tm 2:12 for several reasons:

- *Priscilla taught alongside her husband.* She was not teaching Apollos by herself but assisting her husband. The text does not indicate how this teaching was done, but clearly Priscilla and her husband taught Apollos.
- *The content of the teaching was evangelistic.* Aquila and Priscilla taught Apollos critical truths about the Christian faith. He did not have a full understanding of Christ. They explained the way to God more accurately to him.
- *The teaching occurred in a private place and not in a public service or class.* Aquila and Priscilla invited Apollos into the privacy of their home so they could help him more accurately understand the very nature of the Christian faith.

For these reasons, this account cannot be viewed as contradicting the clear teaching of other passages of Scripture.

When **Priscilla and Aquila** heard Apollos speak, they quickly recognized his fervent spirit and boldness as well as his areas of weakness. Apparently, all he knew came from the disciples of John the Baptist. Perhaps he knew that Jesus was the Messiah and something of His earthly ministry but nothing of the resurrection. Recognizing the great potential in Apollos, the Christian couple **took him home and explained the way of God to him more accurately**.

As a result of Priscilla and Aquila's instruction, Apollos was adequately equipped for mission work. With the support of the brothers in Ephesus, Apollos traveled to the city of Corinth in the province of Achaia. From Paul's frequent mention of Apollos's name in his first letter to the Corinthians, one can deduce that Apollos had an effective ministry there (1Co 3:4-6,22; 4:6; 16:12).

19:1 Luke returns to Paul and the account of the apostle's third missionary journey. After concluding his second missionary journey in Antioch, Paul ventured out again, traveling from place to place in Galatia and Phrygia, strengthening all the disciples (18:22-23). From Phrygian Galatia, **Paul** evidently continued his travel by land **through the interior regions** into the province of Asia until he **came to Ephesus**. On his way to Ephesus, Paul likely traveled through his hometown Tarsus, as well as through Derbe, Lystra, Iconium, and Antioch in Pisidia, visiting churches he had established on his first two missionary journeys. When Paul arrived in Ephesus, he found some **disciples** (Gk *mathētas*, "learners or pupils") of John the Baptist. A disciple may be at varying stages in his learning process.

19:2 Paul obviously sensed something about these men that made him question their understanding of salvation. Since John the Baptist had prophesied of the baptism of the Holy Spirit (Lk 3:16), these disciples were probably indicating that they had not heard about the Spirit's arrival. They might not have heard about the death, burial, and resurrection of Jesus. While Apollos's knowledge about Jesus possessed some gaps, these men knew very little about Jesus.

19:5 Rebaptism in the Holy Spirit is not possible. Believer's baptism is a one-time occurrence simultaneously as the Spirit comes to dwell within one who believes. This ordinance is significant because to follow Christ in baptism completes the new believer's obedience in salvation. When one is baptized for the wrong reason (i.e., when his knowledge of Christ is defective or even erroneous), the baptism is meaningless. Thus re-immersion for the right reasons

CHARACTER PROFILE

Priscilla Co-Laborer with Her Husband

Her Background	• She and her husband, Aquila, met Paul in Corinth (18:1-3). • This Jewish couple were tent makers, as was Paul. • They worked with and were trained by Paul.
Her Story	• She and her husband hosted a house church in Corinth (1Co 16:19). • They traveled with Paul to Ephesus (Ac 18:18). • They invited Apollos to their home to teach him a more accurate understanding of the gospel (18:26). • They returned to Rome, opening their home to believers there (Rm 16:3-5). • They protected Paul at their own risk.
Life Lesson	Gifted women like Priscilla can make a significant contribution to the spreading of the gospel.

wanted to cross over to Achaia, the brothers wrote to the disciples urging them to welcome him. After he arrived, he greatly helped those who had believed through grace. 28 For he vigorously refuted the Jews in public, demonstrating through the Scriptures that Jesus is the Messiah.

Twelve Disciples of John the Baptist (19:1-7)

19 While Apollos was in Corinth, Paul traveled through the interior regions and came to Ephesus. He found some disciples 2 and asked them, "Did you receive the Holy Spirit when you believed?"

"No," they told him, "we haven't even heard that there is a Holy Spirit."

3 "Then what baptism were you baptized with?" he asked them.

"With John's baptism," they replied.

4 Paul said, "John baptized with a baptism of repentance, telling the people that they should believe in the One who would come after him, that is, in Jesus."

5 When they heard this, they were baptized in the name of the Lord Jesus. 6 And when Paul had laid his hands on them, the Holy Spirit came on them, and they began to speak in other •languages and to prophesy. 7 Now there were about 12 men in all.

In the Lecture Hall of Tyrannus (19:8-10)

8 Then he entered the •synagogue and spoke boldly over a period of three months, engaging in discussion and trying to persuade them about the things of the kingdom of God. 9 But when some became hardened and would not believe, slandering the Way in front of the crowd, he withdrew from them and met separately with the disciples, conducting discussions every day in the lecture hall of Tyrannus. 10 And this went on for two years, so that all the inhabitants of •Asia, both Jews and Greeks, heard the message about the Lord.

The Defeat of Demonism in Ephesus (19:11-20)

11 God was performing extraordinary miracles by Paul's hands, 12 so that even facecloths or work aprons[A] that had touched his skin were brought to the sick, and the diseases left them, and the evil spirits came out of them.

13 Then some of the itinerant Jewish exorcists attempted to pronounce the name of the Lord Jesus over those who had evil spirits, saying, "I command you by the Jesus that Paul preaches!" 14 Seven sons of Sceva, a Jewish •chief priest, were doing this. 15 The evil spirit answered them, "I know Jesus, and I recognize Paul—but who are you?" 16 Then the

[A]19:12 Or *that also sweatbands and sweatcloths* or *handkerchiefs*

CHARACTER PROFILE

Damaris Athenian Believer

Her Background	• A prominent Athenian woman (17:33) • Perhaps one of the intellectual women who associated with philosophers and politicians (17:4) • An idol worshiper
Her Story	• She heard Paul's sermon on Mars Hill (17:22-34). • She, with others, believed in Christ.
Life Lesson	Following Christ in the face of ridicule requires courage (17:32).

man who had the evil spirit leaped
on them, overpowered them all,
and prevailed against them, so that
they ran out of that house naked
and wounded. 17 This became known
to everyone who lived in Ephesus,
both Jews and Greeks. Then fear
fell on all of them, and the name
of the Lord Jesus was magnified.
18 And many who had become believers came confessing and disclosing their practices, 19 while many of
those who had practiced magic collected their books and burned them
in front of everyone. So they calculated their value and found it to be
50,000 pieces of silver. 20 In this way
the Lord's message flourished and
prevailed.

The Riot in Ephesus (19:21-41)

21 When these events were over,
Paul resolved in the Spirit to pass
through Macedonia and Achaia and
go to Jerusalem. "After I've been
there," he said, "I must see Rome
as well!" 22 So after sending two of
those who assisted him, Timothy
and Erastus, to Macedonia, he himself stayed in Asia for a while.
23 During that time there was a
major[A] disturbance about the Way.
24 For a person named Demetrius, a
silversmith who made silver shrines
of Artemis,[B] provided a great deal of[C]
business for the craftsmen. 25 When
he had assembled them, as well as
the workers engaged in this type of
business, he said: "Men, you know
that our prosperity is derived from
this business. 26 You both see and
hear that not only in Ephesus, but
in almost all of Asia, this man Paul
has persuaded and misled a considerable number of people by saying that gods made by hand are not
gods! 27 So not only do we run a risk
that our business may be discredited, but also that the temple of the
great goddess Artemis may be despised and her magnificence come
to the verge of ruin—the very one
all of Asia and the world adore."
28 When they had heard this,
they were filled with rage and began to cry out, "Great is Artemis
of the Ephesians!" 29 So the city
was filled with confusion, and they
rushed all together into the amphitheater, dragging along Gaius
and Aristarchus, Macedonians who
were Paul's traveling companions.
30 Though Paul wanted to go in before the people, the disciples did not
let him. 31 Even some of the provincial officials of Asia, who were his
friends, sent word to him, pleading
with him not to take a chance by going[D] into the amphitheater. 32 Meanwhile, some were shouting one
thing and some another, because
the assembly was in confusion, and
most of them did not know why they
had come together. 33 Then some
of the crowd gave Alexander advice
when the Jews pushed him to the
front. So motioning with his hand,
Alexander wanted to make his defense to the people. 34 But when they
recognized that he was a Jew, a united cry went up from all of them for

is essential to complete obedience. The men at Ephesus had known only "John's baptism"; they were re-immersed immediately after accepting the gospel of the death, burial, and resurrection of Christ.

19:13-15 God's healing work through Paul was contrasted with the false ministry of the **Jewish exorcists**, who were immersed in the world of the demonic. Having observed Paul perform miraculous healings in the name of Jesus, the exorcists attempted to emulate his work, failing miserably.

19:16-20 Unlike Jesus and Paul, the Jewish exorcists possessed no power and no authority from above. The evil spirit recognized this lack of power. Both Jews and Greeks came to recognize the genuine healing power in the name of Jesus through the hands of Paul and the inability for this to be replicated by sorcery.

19:23-24 During Paul's last months in Ephesus, **a major disturbance** arose concerning **the Way**, one of the designations for Christians. So many people came to Christ, that "the Way" threatened the financial prosperity of some who made their living off of the worship of Artemis (Lat, *Diana*). Artemis of Ephesus should not be confused with the chaste huntress of Greek mythology. Instead, she was the goddess of fertility and the mother goddess of Asia Minor, who was most often depicted as a grotesque, multi-breasted woman. The Roman Empire possessed at least 33 shrines devoted to Artemis, who was one of the most widely worshiped deities. Each year pilgrims would flock to Ephesus, the focal city for her worship, to the temple of Artemis, which was documented as one of seven wonders of the ancient world.

19:29-31 The huge **amphitheater** of Ephesus held 24,000 people. **Gaius and Aristarchus,** two Christians from Macedonia, were Paul's traveling companions. When Paul heard of the riot and that they held his friends captive, he wanted to go and defend his faith, but some **disciples** and **provincial officials** prevented him.

19:33-34 **Alexander** possibly wanted to make it clear that the Jews had nothing to do with the Christians; but when the crowd realized Alexander was a monotheistic Jew, they turned on him as well. The Ephesians took great pride in their heritage, and Artemis was closely tied to their culture and livelihood.

[A] **19:23** Lit *was not a little* [B] **19:24** Artemis was the ancient Gk mother goddess believed to control all fertility. [C] **19:24** Lit *provided not a little* [D] **19:31** Lit *not to give himself*

19:35-41 The city clerk functioned as the chief administrative officer of the city and as the liaison between the city and Roman provincial administration. He sought to maintain peace because he realized that the mob at the theater could be viewed as an unscheduled and illegal gathering that could create problems with the Roman officials.

20:2-3 From Macedonia, Paul continued to **Greece**, specifically to the city of Corinth in the province of Achaia. Paul wanted to get to the Jerusalem church as quickly and safely as possible because he would be delivering the money he had collected from Gentile churches. Paul focused on this offering throughout his third missionary journey. He demonstrated its importance by mentioning it in all of his epistles written during this time (Rm 15:25-32; 1Co 16:1-4; 2Co 8-9; Gl 2:10).

20:5-6 Representatives from many of the churches accompanied Paul back to Jerusalem to help deliver the offering. Some of the delegation traveled straight to **Troas** most likely to procure a ship for their trip to Palestine, while the remainder stopped in **Philippi** (see note on 16:9-13) until after the Festival of **Unleavened Bread** (see note on 12:3-4). From Philippi, they traveled **five days** to reunite with the group in Troas. The reverse trip noted in Ac 16:11 only took two days, perhaps because of the direction of the winds. Once in Troas the entire group stayed for **seven days**, probably awaiting the departure of their ship.

20:7 The phrase **break bread** indicates Paul's traveling companions and some believers in Troas were celebrating the Lord's Supper (1Co 10:16-17; 11:17-34), which was accompanied by Paul's extensive sermon. This worship service is one of the earliest references to their celebration on Sunday instead of Saturday, according to Jewish Sabbath tradition.

20:18-35 Paul's farewell address to the Ephesian elders is the only sermon recorded from his third missionary journey and his only recorded sermon for a specifically Christian audience in Acts. As such, the message closely resembled Paul's epistles, which were addressed to Christian audiences. The sermon can be divided into three parts: a review of Paul's past ministry in Ephesus (vv. 18-21); a description of the present situation (vv. 22-27); and future responsibilities for the Ephesian elders (vv. 28-35).

20:19 Paul highlighted his **humility** even though to do so was often thought to be a sign of weakness in the Greco-Roman world. He wanted the Ephesian leaders to know the importance of

about two hours: "Great is Artemis of the Ephesians!"

35 However, when the city clerk had calmed the crowd down, he said, "Men of Ephesus! What man is there who doesn't know that the city of the Ephesians is the temple guardian of the great[A] Artemis, and of the image that fell from heaven? 36 Therefore, since these things are undeniable, you must keep calm and not do anything rash. 37 For you have brought these men here who are not temple robbers or blasphemers of our[B] goddess. 38 So if Demetrius and the craftsmen who are with him have a case against anyone, the courts are in session, and there are •proconsuls. Let them bring charges against one another. 39 But if you want something else, it must be decided in a legal assembly. 40 In fact, we run a risk of being charged with rioting for what happened today, since there is no •justification that we can give as a reason for this disorderly gathering." 41 After saying this, he dismissed the assembly.

Paul in Macedonia (20:1-6)

20 After the uproar was over, Paul sent for the disciples, encouraged them, and after saying goodbye, departed to go to Macedonia. 2 And when he had passed through those areas and exhorted them at length, he came to Greece 3 and stayed three months. When he was about to set sail for Syria, a plot was devised against him by the Jews, so a decision was made to go back through Macedonia. 4 He was accompanied[C] by Sopater son of Pyrrhus[D] from Berea, Aristarchus and Secundus from Thessalonica, Gaius from Derbe, Timothy, and Tychicus and Trophimus from •Asia. 5 These men went on ahead and waited for us in Troas, 6 but we sailed away from Philippi after the days of •Unleavened Bread. In five days we reached them at Troas, where we spent seven days.

Reviving of Eutychus at Troas (20:7-12)

7 On the first day of the week, we[E] assembled to break bread. Paul spoke to them, and since he was about to depart the next day, he extended his message until midnight. 8 There were many lamps in the room upstairs where we were assembled, 9 and a young man named Eutychus was sitting on a window sill and sank into a deep sleep as Paul kept on speaking. When he was overcome by sleep, he fell down from the third story and was picked up dead. 10 But Paul went down, fell on him, embraced him, and said, "Don't be alarmed, for his •life is in him!" 11 After going upstairs, breaking the bread, and eating, Paul conversed a considerable time until dawn. Then he left. 12 They brought the boy home alive and were greatly comforted.

Journey from Troas to Miletus (20:13-16)

13 Then we went on ahead to the ship and sailed for Assos, intending to take Paul on board there. For these were his instructions, since he himself was going by land. 14 When he met us at Assos, we took him on board and came to Mitylene. 15 Sailing from there, the next day we arrived off Chios. The following day we crossed over to Samos, and[F] the day after, we came to Miletus. 16 For Paul had decided to sail past Ephesus so he would not have to spend time in Asia, because he was hurrying to be in Jerusalem, if possible, for the day of Pentecost.

Farewell Address to the Ephesian Elders (20:17-38)

17 Now from Miletus, he sent to Ephesus and called for the elders of the church. 18 And when they came to him, he said to them: "You know, from the first day I set foot in Asia, how I was with you the whole time— 19 serving the Lord with all humility, with tears, and with the trials that came to me through the plots of the Jews— 20 and that I did not shrink back from proclaiming to you anything that was profitable or from teaching it to you in public and from house to house. 21 I testified to both Jews and Greeks about

[A] 19:35 Other mss add *goddess* [B] 19:37 Other mss read *your* [C] 20:4 Other mss add *to Asia* [D] 20:4 Other mss omit *son of Pyrrhus* [E] 20:7 Other mss read *the disciples* [F] 20:15 Other mss add *after staying at Trogyllium*

repentance toward God and faith in our Lord Jesus.

22 "And now I am on my way to Jerusalem, bound in my spirit,[A] not knowing what I will encounter there, 23 except that in town after town the Holy Spirit testifies to me that chains and afflictions are waiting for me. 24 But I count my life of no value to myself, so that I may finish my course[B] and the ministry I received from the Lord Jesus, to testify to the gospel of God's grace.

25 "And now I know that none of you will ever see my face again—everyone I went about preaching the kingdom to. 26 Therefore I testify to you this day that I am innocent[C] of everyone's blood, 27 for I did not shrink back from declaring to you the whole plan of God. 28 Be on guard for yourselves and for all the flock that the Holy Spirit has appointed you to as •overseers, to shepherd the church of God,[D] which He purchased with His own blood. 29 I know that after my departure savage wolves will come in among you, not sparing the flock. 30 And men will rise up from your own number with deviant doctrines to lure the disciples into following them. 31 Therefore be on the alert, remembering that night and day for three years I did not stop warning each one of you with tears.

32 "And now[E] I commit you to God and to the message of His grace, which is able to build you up and to give you an inheritance among all who are •sanctified. 33 I have not coveted anyone's silver or gold or clothing. 34 You yourselves know that these hands have provided for my needs and for those who were with me. 35 In every way I've shown you that by laboring like this, it is necessary to help the weak and to keep in mind the words of the Lord Jesus, for He said, 'It is more blessed to give than to receive.'"

36 After he said this, he knelt down and prayed with all of them. 37 There was a great deal of weeping by everyone. They embraced Paul and kissed him, 38 grieving most of all over his statement that they would never see his face again. Then they escorted him to the ship.

Warnings on the Journey to Jerusalem (21:1-14)

21 After we tore ourselves away from them and set sail, we came by a direct route to Cos, the next day to Rhodes, and from there to Patara. 2 Finding a ship crossing over to Phoenicia, we boarded and set sail. 3 After we sighted Cyprus, leaving it on the left, we sailed on to Syria and arrived at Tyre, because the ship was to unload its cargo there. 4 So we found some disciples and stayed there seven days. Through the Spirit they told Paul not to go to Jerusalem. 5 When our days there were over, we left to continue our journey, while all of them, with their wives and children, escorted us out of the city. After kneeling down on the beach to pray, 6 we said good-bye to one another. Then we boarded the ship, and they returned home.

7 When we completed our voyage from Tyre, we reached Ptolemais, where we greeted the •brothers and stayed with them one day. 8 The next day we left and came to Caesarea, where we entered the house of Philip the evangelist, who was one of the Seven, and stayed with him. 9 This man had four virgin daughters who prophesied.

10 While we were staying there many days, a prophet named Agabus came down from Judea. 11 He came to us, took Paul's belt, tied his own feet and hands, and said, "This is what the Holy Spirit says: 'In this way the Jews in Jerusalem will bind the man who owns this belt and deliver him into Gentile hands.'" 12 When we heard this, both we and the local people begged him not to go up to Jerusalem.

13 Then Paul replied, "What are you doing, weeping and breaking my heart? For I am ready not only to be bound but also to die in Jerusalem for the name of the Lord Jesus."

14 Since he would not be persuaded, we stopped talking and simply said, "The Lord's will be done!"

[A]20:22 Or *in the Spirit* [B]20:24 Other mss add *with joy* [C]20:26 Lit •*clean* [D]20:28 Other mss read *church of the Lord*; other mss read *church of the Lord and God* [E]20:32 Other mss add *brothers,*

humility to being Christlike (Php 2:1-11). He also recalled his **tears**—due to **trials** and misunderstandings from fellow believers. Specifically he mentioned trials related to **the plots of the Jews**, even though the only trial Luke records about Paul in Ephesus was instigated by Gentiles. Apparently Paul endured more trials than those recorded in Acts.

20:28 In the third part of Paul's address to the Ephesian elders, he delineated to them their future responsibilities **as overseers to shepherd the church of God**. Luke uses the term "overseers" interchangeably with "elders" (vv. 17,28; for more information about this office in the church, see 1Tm 3; also see **Doctrine**, p. 1557). Paul used three terms to denote pastoral leadership:

- "elders" (Gk *presbuterous*, Ac 20:17),
- "overseers" (Gk *episkopous*, "guardians, bishops," v. 28), and
- "shepherd" (Gk *poimainein*, "guide, protect, nurture," v. 28).

The latter is a verb instead of a noun as are the other terms. These terms are not suggesting levels of authority but rather diversity in function. They are used interchangeably and refer to differing responsibilities of the men who are pastors for the congregations.

21:5-6 During their seven-day stay in Tyre, Paul and his traveling companions developed a close relationship with their new-found brothers and sisters in the Lord. To portray this close relationship, Luke notes that they **all**, even **their wives and children, escorted** them **out of the city**. In one week, Paul's group made a considerable impact on the Christians in Tyre.

•**21:8-9 Philip . . . was one of the Seven** chosen to serve tables (Ac 6:1-7). Philip also ministered in Samaria and to the Ethiopian eunuch (8:4-40). Luke identifies Philip's four **daughters** as virgins, perhaps indicating their ability to devote themselves wholeheartedly to the ministry (1Co 7:25-34). That they **prophesied** was fulfillment of the prophecy quoted by Peter at Pentecost (2:17; Jl 2:28). The text provides no details about the outworking of the ministry of the four prophetesses, but other passages of Scripture provide some parameters (1Co 11:5; 14:3; 1Tm 2:12).

21:10-11 Agabus, the prophet who predicted the famine in Acts 11:28, came from Judea while Paul and his companions were staying with Philip. He predicted that Paul would be imprisoned by **the Jews in Jerusalem** and delivered **into Gentile hands**. God used these warnings to prepare Paul for what was coming. God had called him to Jerusalem; therefore, he was going.

21:18 After one night in Jerusalem, Paul and the representatives from the churches went to meet **James**, the half-brother of Jesus and leader of the church in Jerusalem, and the other **elders**.

21:20-22 The leaders rejoiced and **glorified God** at Paul's news; yet they feared the Jews' reaction. In Jerusalem a time of intense Jewish nationalism and political unrest had arisen; thus Paul's mission to the Gentiles with the gospel would not be well received by the Jewish population. Some people had accused Paul of teaching Jews **to abandon** both the law of **Moses** and the practice of circumcision. But this was not the case. While Paul did not believe circumcision necessary for salvation, he obviously did not discourage Jews from the practice since he had already had Timothy circumcised (16:3).

21:23-24 In an effort to appease the Jews and deal with the false rumors, the elders suggested that Paul perform a public act of Jewish piety. This action would help stifle the rumors because everyone would know that he was **careful about observing the law**.

21:26 The **offering** from the four men likely included two pigeons and one lamb for each person, for a total of eight pigeons and four lambs.

21:31-32 The **chaos** attracted the attention of **the commander of the regiment**, who was on guard at the Fortress of Antonia, adjacent to the temple. From the towers there, he had a view of the entire temple complex. Troops were kept in readiness during festivals for outbreaks such as this. He, along with some of his **soldiers and centurions**, responded to the commotion immediately. The commander, Claudius Lysias (23:26), was in charge of 1,000 Roman soldiers. At least 200 of them responded to this commotion, indicated by the use of the plural word centurions since a centurion commanded 100 men.

21:33-34 Taking control of the situation, **the commander . . . took** Paul **into custody**, which actually served to protect Paul. Had the Jews been left to their own devices, Paul would have been beaten to death. Unable **to get reliable information** in the chaotic situation, the commander ordered the soldiers to take Paul **into the barracks**.

21:37 Right before they took him into the barracks, Paul shocked the commander by speaking to him in the **Greek** language. Greek was the language of cultured and educated men and was not used by the common criminal Paul was wrongly assumed to be.

CHARACTER PROFILE

Daughters of Philip

Second-Generation Christians

Their Background	• Their father was Philip, one of seven disciples set apart for special service in the early church (21:7-9; cp. 6:1-7; 8:5-7). • They were unmarried.
Their Story	• Seemingly they were spiritually mature young women. • There is no indication how their gifts functioned. • They fulfilled Old Testament prophecy (Jl 2:28), which Peter had quoted in his sermon at Pentecost (Ac 2:17).
Life Lesson	Philip's daughters were "second-generation" Christians, following in the footsteps of their godly father, each contributing to the growth of the kingdom.

The Spread of the Gospel to Rome (21:15–28:31)

Conflict over the Gentile Mission (21:15-25)

15 After these days we got ready and
went up to Jerusalem. 16 Some of the
disciples from Caesarea also went
with us and brought us to Mnason,
a Cypriot and an early disciple, with
whom we were to stay.
17 When we reached Jerusalem,
the •brothers welcomed us gladly.
18 The following day Paul went in
with us to James, and all the elders
were present. 19 After greeting them,
he related in detail what God did
among the Gentiles through his
ministry.
20 When they heard it, they glorified God and said, "You see, brother,
how many thousands of Jews there
are who have believed, and they are
all zealous for the law. 21 But they
have been told about you that you
teach all the Jews who are among
the Gentiles to abandon Moses, by
telling them not to circumcise their
children or to walk in our customs.
22 So what is to be done?[A] They will
certainly hear that you've come.
23 Therefore do what we tell you: We
have four men who have obligated
themselves with a vow. 24 Take these
men, purify yourself along with
them, and pay for them to get their
heads shaved. Then everyone will
know that what they were told about
you amounts to nothing, but that
you yourself are also careful about
observing the law. 25 With regard
to the Gentiles who have believed,
we have written a letter containing
our decision that[B] they should keep
themselves from food sacrificed
to idols, from blood, from what is
strangled, and from sexual immorality."

The Riot in the Temple Complex (21:26-36)

26 Then the next day, Paul took the
men, having purified himself along
with them, and entered the temple,
announcing the completion of the
purification days when the offering
for each of them would be made.
27 As the seven days were about to
end, the Jews from •Asia saw him
in the •temple complex, stirred up
the whole crowd, and seized him,
28 shouting, "Men of Israel, help!
This is the man who teaches everyone everywhere against our people,
our law, and this place. What's more,
he also brought Greeks into the
temple and has profaned this holy
place." 29 For they had previously
seen Trophimus the Ephesian in the
city with him, and they supposed
that Paul had brought him into the
temple complex.[C]
30 The whole city was stirred up,
and the people rushed together.
They seized Paul, dragged him out
of the temple complex, and at once
the gates were shut. 31 As they were
trying to kill him, word went up to

[A] **21:22** Other mss add *A multitude has to come together, since* [B] **21:25** Other mss add *they should observe no such thing, except that* [C] **21:29** The inner temple court for Jewish men

the commander of the •regiment
that all Jerusalem was in chaos.
32 Taking along soldiers and •centu-
rions, he immediately ran down to
them. Seeing the commander and
the soldiers, they stopped beating
Paul. 33 Then the commander came
up, took him into custody, and ordered him to be bound with two
chains. He asked who he was and
what he had done. 34 Some in the
mob were shouting one thing and
some another. Since he was not able
to get reliable information because
of the uproar, he ordered him to
be taken into the barracks. 35 When
Paul got to the steps, he had to be
carried by the soldiers because of
the mob's violence, 36 for the mass of
people followed, yelling, "Take him
away!"

Paul's Defense Before the Jerusalem
Mob (21:37–22:5)

37 As he was about to be brought
into the barracks, Paul said to the
commander, "Am I allowed to say
something to you?"
He replied, "Do you know Greek?
38 Aren't you the Egyptian who
raised a rebellion some time ago and
led 4,000 Assassins[A,B] into the wilderness?"
39 Paul said, "I am a Jewish man
from Tarsus of Cilicia, a citizen of an
important city.[C] Now I ask you, let
me speak to the people."
40 After he had given permission,
Paul stood on the steps and motioned
with his hand to the people. When
there was a great hush, he addressed
22 them in the •Hebrew language:
1 "Brothers and fathers, listen
now to my defense before you."
2 When they heard that he was addressing them in the Hebrew language, they became even quieter.
3 He continued, "I am a Jewish man,
born in Tarsus of Cilicia but brought
up in this city[D] at the feet of Gamaliel and educated according to the
strict view of our patriarchal law. Being zealous for God, just as all of you
are today, 4 I persecuted this Way to
the death, binding and putting both
men and women in jail, 5 as both the
high priest and the whole council
of elders can testify about me. After
I received letters from them to the
brothers, I traveled to Damascus
to bring those who were prisoners
there to be punished in Jerusalem.

Paul's Testimony (22:6-21)

6 "As I was traveling and near
Damascus, about noon an intense
light from heaven suddenly flashed
around me. 7 I fell to the ground and
heard a voice saying to me, 'Saul,
Saul, why are you persecuting Me?'
8 "I answered, 'Who are You, Lord?'
"He said to me, 'I am Jesus the
•Nazarene, the One you are persecuting!' 9 Now those who were with
me saw the light,[E] but they did not
hear the voice of the One who was
speaking to me.
10 "Then I said, 'What should I do,
Lord?'
"And the Lord told me, 'Get up
and go into Damascus, and there
you will be told about everything
that is assigned for you to do.'
11 "Since I couldn't see because of
the brightness of that light, I was
led by the hand by those who were
with me, and came into Damascus.
12 Someone named Ananias, a devout
man according to the law, having a
good reputation with all the Jews
residing there, 13 came and stood by
me and said, 'Brother Saul, regain
your sight.' And in that very hour I
looked up and saw him. 14 Then he
said, 'The God of our fathers has appointed you to know His will, to see
the Righteous One, and to hear the
sound of His voice.[F] 15 For you will
be a witness for Him to all people of
what you have seen and heard. 16 And
now, why delay? Get up and be baptized, and wash away your sins by
calling on His name.'
17 "After I came back to Jerusalem
and was praying in the •temple complex, I went into a visionary state
18 and saw Him telling me, 'Hurry
and get out of Jerusalem quickly,
because they will not accept your
testimony about Me!'
19 "But I said, 'Lord, they know
that in •synagogue after synagogue
I had those who believed in You imprisoned and beaten. 20 And when

21:38-39 Since Paul spoke Greek, the commander then assumed that Paul was **the Egyptian who** had **raised a rebellion** against Jerusalem some years earlier. The historian Josephus recounted this event, noting that an Egyptian false prophet led men to the Mount of Olives in an effort to destroy the city walls and overthrow the Romans. Although hundreds of his followers died, the leader of the rebellion had escaped unscathed. Paul responded that he was not the Egyptian insurgent, but a **Jewish man from Tarsus of Cilicia.**

22:1 Paul began his defense as Stephen did in Ac 7, by addressing the crowd as **brothers and fathers.** This introduction identified him with his listeners and demonstrated respect.

22:2 Although there had previously been "a great hush" (21:40), the crowd grew **even quieter** when they heard him speaking **in the Hebrew language**. Paul had their full attention.

22:3-4 Under Gamaliel, Paul received the best education available to a Jew. He emphasized his close ties to Judaism, stressing that he had been **zealous for God**, just as his listeners were. Paul had once **persecuted** those who belonged to **this Way**. Although Acts repeatedly refers to "the Way," Paul used "this Way," identifying himself with the movement he once persecuted. Here Paul acknowledged his role in **the death** and imprisonment of Christians. Perhaps Stephen's stoning came to mind (7:54–8:3).

22:6-21 Acts provides three detailed accounts of Paul's conversion. The first account is told from Luke's perspective (9:1-19), while the other two accounts are told from Paul's (22:6-21; 26:4-23). He was addressing a Jewish audience, while in 26:4-23 he was talking to a predominantly Gentile audience.

22:16 Salvation comes as a result of **calling on His name**. Here, baptism is simply a metaphor for the washing **away** of **sins**. Salvation is closely aligned with baptism in the New Testament but not in the sense that baptism is necessary for a person to be saved. Paul was already a Christian, and he was calling on new believers to give testimony to their salvation by submitting themselves to the ordinance of baptism.

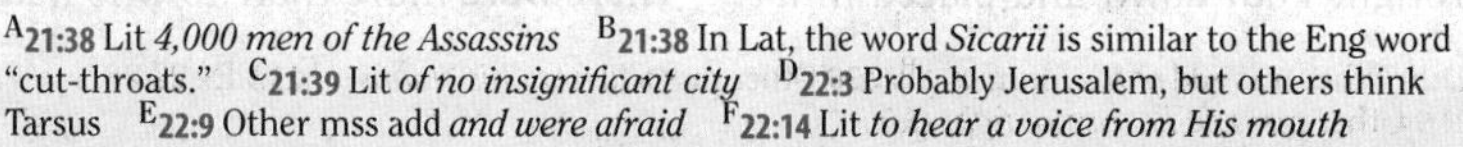

[A]**21:38** Lit *4,000 men of the Assassins* [B]**21:38** In Lat, the word *Sicarii* is similar to the Eng word "cut-throats." [C]**21:39** Lit *of no insignificant city* [D]**22:3** Probably Jerusalem, but others think Tarsus [E]**22:9** Other mss add *and were afraid* [F]**22:14** Lit *to hear a voice from His mouth*

the blood of Your witness Stephen was being shed, I was standing by and approving,[A] and I guarded the clothes of those who killed him.’

21 “Then He said to me, ‘Go, because I will send you far away to the Gentiles.’”

Paul’s Roman Protection (22:22-29)

22 They listened to him up to this word. Then they raised their voices, shouting, “Wipe this person off the earth—it’s a disgrace for him to live!”

23 As they were yelling and flinging aside their robes and throwing dust into the air, 24 the commander ordered him to be brought into the barracks, directing that he be examined with the scourge, so he could discover the reason they were shouting against him like this. 25 As they stretched him out for the lash, Paul said to the •centurion standing by, “Is it legal for you to scourge a man who is a Roman citizen and is uncondemned?”

26 When the centurion heard this, he went and reported to the commander, saying, “What are you going to do? For this man is a Roman citizen.”

27 The commander came and said to him, “Tell me—are you a Roman citizen?”

“Yes,” he said.

28 The commander replied, “I bought this citizenship for a large amount of money.”

“But I was born a citizen,” Paul said.

29 Therefore, those who were about to examine him withdrew from him at once. The commander too was alarmed when he realized Paul was a Roman citizen and he had bound him.

Paul Before the Sanhedrin (22:30–23:10)

30 The next day, since he wanted to find out exactly why Paul was being accused by the Jews, he released him[B] and instructed the •chief priests and all the •Sanhedrin to convene. Then he brought Paul down and placed him

23 before them. 1 Paul looked intently at the •Sanhedrin and said, “Brothers, I have lived my life before God in all good conscience until this day.” 2 But the high priest Ananias ordered those who were standing next to him to strike him on the mouth. 3 Then Paul said to him, “God is going to strike you, you whitewashed wall! You are sitting there judging me according to the law, and in violation of the law are you ordering me to be struck?”

4 And those standing nearby said, “Do you dare revile God’s high priest?”

5 “I did not know, brothers, that he was the high priest,” replied Paul. “For it is written, **You must not speak evil of a ruler of your people.**”[C] 6 When Paul realized that one part of them were •Sadducees and the other part were •Pharisees, he cried out in the Sanhedrin, “Brothers, I am a Pharisee, a son of Pharisees! I am being judged because of the hope of the resurrection of the dead!” 7 When he said this, a dispute broke out between the Pharisees and the Sadducees, and the assembly was divided. 8 For the Sadducees say there is no resurrection, and no angel or spirit, but the Pharisees affirm them all.

9 The shouting grew loud, and some of the •scribes of the Pharisees’ party got up and argued vehemently: “We find nothing evil in this man. What if a spirit or an angel has spoken to him?”[D] 10 When the dispute became violent, the commander feared that Paul might be torn apart by them and ordered the troops to go down, rescue him from them, and bring him into the barracks.

The Plot Against Paul (23:11-22)

11 The following night, the Lord stood by him and said, “Have courage! For as you have testified about Me in Jerusalem, so you must also testify in Rome.”

12 When it was day, the Jews formed a conspiracy and bound themselves under a curse: neither to eat nor to drink until they had killed Paul. 13 There were more than 40 who had

[A] 22:20 Other mss add *of his murder* [B] 22:30 Other mss add *from his chains* [C] 23:5 Ex 22:28
[D] 23:9 Other mss add *Let us not fight God.*

22:22-23 Everything Paul said had been tolerable to them until he brought up his ministry to the Gentiles. That God would send someone to minister to the Gentiles was a blasphemous notion to the Jews. As Paul shook the dust off his feet at Antioch of Pisidia (13:51) and out of his clothes at Corinth (18:6), the Jews did so to demonstrate their opposition to Paul.

22:24 The phrase **examined with the scourge** indicates an interrogation accompanied by a brutal flogging in an attempt to discover the reason for the Jews’ hostility towards him.

22:25-28 Right before the beating commenced, Paul brought up his **Roman** citizenship, as he had at Philippi (16:37). Although Roman citizenship could not technically be purchased, the commander indicated he had **bought** his **citizenship**, likely via a bribe, **for a large amount of money**. Possession of Roman citizenship afforded people certain rights and high status. Paul’s citizenship provided protection, giving him the right to a Roman trial, exemption from the scourging, protection from execution, and eventually the right of appeal.

23:2 Ananias, not to be confused with Annas (4:6), served as high priest from A.D. 47 to 59. Noted for his cruelty, violence, and corruptness, his own people would later kill him.

23:3 The one appointed to judge Paul according to law violated the law by ordering Paul to be struck. The phrase **God is going to strike you** was not a curse, but an acknowledgment that God would deal with Ananias justly.

23:6-10 When Paul realized he stood in front of the **Sanhedrin**, which consisted of both **Sadducees** and **Pharisees**, he used to his advantage the sharp doctrinal disagreements between these two rival parties. Paul pointed out that he was not only **a Pharisee**, but **a son of Pharisees**, indicating that both his father and grandfather had been Pharisees. Paul’s statement that he was on trial for his belief in **the hope of the resurrection** prompted the Pharisees to come quickly to his defense. Doing so, the Pharisees were not defending the resurrection of Jesus, but the concept of the resurrection and life after death. Their suggestion that **a spirit or an angel** might have spoken to Paul was a jibe against the Sadducees’ denial of that possibility (v. 8).

23:11 The following night, the Lord appeared to Paul in his prison cell. Having the Lord by his side undoubtedly comforted Paul in his difficult circumstances. The Lord provided him

formed this plot. 14 These men went
to the •chief priests and elders and
said, "We have bound ourselves under a solemn curse that we won't
eat anything until we have killed
Paul. 15 So now you, along with the
Sanhedrin, make a request to the
commander that he bring him down
to you[A] as if you were going to investigate his case more thoroughly.
However, before he gets near, we are
ready to kill him."
16 But the son of Paul's sister, hearing about their ambush, came and
entered the barracks and reported
it to Paul. 17 Then Paul called one of
the •centurions and said, "Take this
young man to the commander, because he has something to report to
him."
18 So he took him, brought him to
the commander, and said, "The prisoner Paul called me and asked me
to bring this young man to you, because he has something to tell you."
19 Then the commander took him
by the hand, led him aside, and inquired privately, "What is it you
have to report to me?"
20 "The Jews," he said, "have agreed
to ask you to bring Paul down to the
Sanhedrin tomorrow, as though
they are going to hold a somewhat
more careful inquiry about him.
21 Don't let them persuade you, because there are more than 40 of
them arranging to ambush him,
men who have bound themselves
under a curse not to eat or drink
until they kill him. Now they are
ready, waiting for a commitment
from you."
22 So the commander dismissed
the young man and instructed him,
"Don't tell anyone that you have informed me about this."

Journey to Caesarea by Night (23:23-35)

23 He summoned two of his centurions and said, "Get 200 soldiers
ready with 70 cavalry and 200 spear-
men to go to Caesarea at nine tonight.[B] 24 Also provide mounts so
they can put Paul on them and bring
him safely to Felix the governor."
25 He wrote a letter of this kind:
26 Claudius Lysias,
To the most excellent governor
Felix:
Greetings.
27 When this man had been
seized by the Jews and was
about to be killed by them, I
arrived with my troops and
rescued him because I learned
that he is a Roman citizen.
28 Wanting to know the charge
they were accusing him of, I
brought him down before their
Sanhedrin. 29 I found out that
the accusations were about
disputed matters in their law,
and that there was no charge
that merited death or chains.
30 When I was informed that
there was a plot against the
man,[C] I sent him to you right
away. I also ordered his accusers to state their case against
him in your presence.[D]

31 Therefore, the soldiers took Paul
during the night and brought him
to Antipatris as they were ordered.
32 The next day, they returned to
the barracks, allowing the cavalry
to go on with him. 33 When these
men entered Caesarea and delivered
the letter to the governor, they also
presented Paul to him. 34 After he[E]
read it, he asked what province he
was from. So when he learned he
was from Cilicia, 35 he said, "I will
give you a hearing whenever your
accusers get here too." And he ordered that he be kept under guard in
•Herod's •palace.

The Accusation Against Paul (24:1-9)

24 After five days Ananias the
high priest came down with
some elders and a lawyer[F] named
Tertullus. These men presented
their case against Paul to the governor. 2 When he was called in, Tertullus began to accuse him and said:
"Since we enjoy great peace because
of you, and reforms are taking place
for the benefit of this nation by
your foresight, 3 we acknowledge
this in every way and everywhere,
most excellent Felix, with utmost

with encouragement—commendation of Paul's past ministry in Jerusalem and a future prediction that Paul would survive the trials in Jerusalem so he could **testify** about Him **in Rome**.

23:12 The next day **the Jews** developed an assassination plan. To be **bound . . . under a curse** (Gk *anethematisan*), from which the English word "anathema" comes, is a strong verb of commitment suggesting a person's binding himself in such a way that he calls upon himself a curse if he does not fulfill his oath. Paul's would-be assassins were willing to be under a curse from God if they failed to take his life.

23:16-19 The son of Paul's sister heard about **their ambush**. This explicit reference to Paul's family members is the only one in Scripture. Fearing his uncle's safety, Paul's unnamed nephew came and entered the barracks and reported it to Paul. Since he could enter the barracks, Paul was not in solitary confinement and was afforded personal visits. Realizing the impending threat to his life, Paul got **one of the centurions** to take his nephew to Claudius Lysias, **the commander**, who used privacy to protect the identity of the informant.

23:26 Antonius **Felix** served as **governor** of Judea from A.D. 52 to 59. Felix and his brother Pallas were once slaves of Antonia, mother of the Emperor Claudius. Pallas, who was a favorite of Emperor Claudius, procured the current appointment for his brother.

23:31 Antipatris was a military post about 40 miles from Jerusalem on the way to Caesarea.

23:34-35 After reading the letter, Felix asked Paul what **province** he was from to determine if he had jurisdiction in the case. Since the Roman province of **Cilicia** fell under the authority of the Roman legate of Syria—to whom Felix reported—therefore, he possessed jurisdiction for the case.

24:1-2 After five days **Ananias** came to Caesarea along with **some elders and a lawyer named Tertullus**, who was most likely a Hellenistic Jew. He was enlisted to be the prosecutor. Whether a Jew or Roman, he was an excellent judicial orator. Tertullus diplomatically began by complimenting, no doubt insincere flattery, the judge Felix. He attributed the peace in the region to the rulership of Felix, a most desirable compliment because the primary task of rulers in that day was to maintain peace in their regions.

[A] **23:15** Other mss add *tomorrow* [B] **23:23** Lit *at the third hour tonight* [C] **23:30** Other mss add *by the Jews* [D] **23:30** Other mss add *Farewell* [E] **23:34** Other mss read *the governor* [F] **24:1** In Gk, the word *rhetor* is similar to the Eng "rhetoric." In this situation, a rhetorician who was skilled in public speaking in the Gk language was needed.

24:23 Since Paul was a Roman citizen who had not been found guilty of a crime, he was allowed **some freedom** (i.e., frequent visits from **his friends**).

24:24 Over the course of Paul's two-year imprisonment in Caesarea, he experienced frequent visits with Felix. On one occasion, Paul discussed **faith in Christ Jesus** with Felix and his third **wife**. The youngest daughter of Herod Agrippa I, **Drusilla** professed to be **Jewish**. Once married to the king of Emesa (in the province of Syria), she had been lured away by Felix, who had been struck by her beauty. At the age of 16, she married Felix and bore him a son. When Drusilla heard the good news of the gospel from Paul, she was not yet 20 years old. Approximately 20 years later, Drusilla and her son died in Pompeii during the eruption of Mount Vesuvius (A.D. 79).

24:25-26 Since Drusilla was Jewish, Paul probably reasoned with her from the Scriptures, showing how Jesus fulfilled Old Testament prophecy. **Righteousness, self-control, and the judgment to come** are sometimes called the "three tenses of salvation," beginning with how to be justified or made righteous by God, then learning to overcome temptation through self-mastery, and finally escaping the final judgment of God. Married to a woman whom he had lured away from her husband, Felix lacked both righteousness and self-control; thus, the realization that he faced judgment made him **afraid**. Although Felix was convicted of his sins, he put off making a decision for Christ. The fact that he later sought **money** in the form of a bribe from Paul, indicated that he never seriously pursued giving his life to Christ.

24:27 When Paul had been in prison for **two years**, Felix was removed from office. His removal resulted from Jewish complaints to Rome about his brutality. He would have faced severe punishment from Emperor Nero if his influential brother had not interceded in his behalf. Not much is known about Felix's **successor, Porcius Festus**, because he died two years after assuming office in A.D. 62.

25:1-3 The chief priests and the leaders of the Jews, the Sanhedrin, **presented their case against Paul** to Festus and asked that Paul be sent **to Jerusalem**, under the pretext that his case would be heard there. They planned **an ambush** to **kill him** while in transport. Two years earlier, 40 Jews planned a similar ploy, enlisting the Sanhedrin as collaborators (23:15). This time the leaders themselves planned the ambush.

CHARACTER PROFILE

Drusilla Wife of a Roman Governor

Her Background	• Jewish wife of Felix, the Roman governor (24:24) • Granddaughter of Herod the Great and daughter of Herod Agrippa, a persecutor of the early church
Her Story	• She married King Aziz of Emesa at age 15 but left him to marry Felix. • She accompanied Felix to hear Paul give his defense and present the gospel message. • Felix became afraid; there is no record of Drusilla's response. • Josephus, the Jewish historian, records that Drusilla, with her only child, died twenty years later in Pompeii when Mt. Vesuvius erupted.
Life Lesson	Drusilla's story is a reminder of the danger of hardening your heart against God's call.

gratitude. 4 However, so that I will
not burden you any further, I beg
you in your graciousness to give us
a brief hearing. 5 For we have found
this man to be a plague, an agita-
tor among all the Jews throughout
the Roman world, and a ringleader
of the sect of the •Nazarenes! 6 He
even tried to desecrate the temple,
so we apprehended him [and wanted to judge him according to our
law. 7 But Lysias the commander
came and took him from our hands
with great force, 8 commanding his
accusers to come to you.][A] By examining him yourself you will be
able to discern all these things we
are accusing him of." 9 The Jews
also joined in the attack, alleging
that these things were so.

Paul's Defense Before Felix (24:10-21)

10 When the governor motioned
to him to speak, Paul replied: "Because I know you have been a judge
of this nation for many years, I am
glad to offer my defense in what
concerns me. 11 You are able to determine that it is no more than 12
days since I went up to worship in
Jerusalem. 12 They didn't find me
disputing with anyone or causing
a disturbance among the crowd,
either in the •temple complex or
in the •synagogues or anywhere in
the city. 13 Neither can they provide
evidence to you of what they now
bring against me. 14 But I confess
this to you: I worship my fathers'
God according to the Way, which
they call a sect, believing all the
things that are written in the Law
and in the Prophets. 15 And I have
a hope in God, which these men
themselves also accept, that there is
going to be a resurrection,[B] both of
the righteous and the unrighteous.
16 I always do my best to have a clear
conscience toward God and men.
17 After many years, I came to bring
charitable gifts and offerings to my
nation, 18 and while I was doing this,
some Jews from •Asia found me ritually purified in the temple, without a
crowd and without any uproar. 19 It
is they who ought to be here before
you to bring charges, if they have
anything against me. 20 Either let
these men here state what wrongdoing they found in me when I stood
before the •Sanhedrin, 21 or about
this one statement I cried out while
standing among them, 'Today I am
being judged before you concerning
the resurrection of the dead.'"

Postponement of the Verdict (24:22-27)

22 Since Felix was accurately informed about the Way, he adjourned
the hearing, saying, "When Lysias
the commander comes down, I will
decide your case." 23 He ordered that
the •centurion keep Paul[C] under
guard, though he could have some

[A] **24:6-8** Other mss omit bracketed text [B] **24:15** Other mss add *of the dead* [C] **24:23** Lit *him*

freedom, and that he should not
prevent any of his friends from serving[A] him.
24 After some days, when Felix
came with his wife Drusilla, who
was Jewish, he sent for Paul and listened to him on the subject of faith
in Christ Jesus. 25 Now as he spoke
about righteousness, self-control,
and the judgment to come, Felix became afraid and replied, "Leave for
now, but when I find time I'll call for
you." 26 At the same time he was also
hoping that money would be given
to him by Paul.[B] For this reason he
sent for him quite often and conversed with him.
27 After two years had passed, Felix
received a successor, Porcius Festus, and because he wished to do a
favor for the Jews, Felix left Paul in
prison.

Paul's Appeal to Caesar (25:1-12)

25 Three days after Festus arrived
in the province, he went up to
Jerusalem from Caesarea. 2 Then
the •chief priests and the leaders
of the Jews presented their case
against Paul to him; and they appealed, 3 asking him to do them a
favor against Paul,[C] that he might
summon him to Jerusalem. They
were preparing an ambush along
the road to kill him. 4 However, Festus answered that Paul should be
kept at Caesarea, and that he himself was about to go there shortly.
5 "Therefore," he said, "let the men
of authority among you go down
with me and accuse him, if there is
any wrong in this man."
6 When he had spent not more
than eight or 10 days among them,
he went down to Caesarea. The next
day, seated at the judge's bench, he
commanded Paul to be brought in.
7 When he arrived, the Jews who had
come down from Jerusalem stood
around him and brought many serious charges that they were not able
to prove, 8 while Paul made the defense that, "Neither against the Jewish law, nor against the temple, nor
against Caesar have I sinned at all."
9 Then Festus, wanting to do a
favor for the Jews, replied to Paul,
"Are you willing to go up to Jerusalem, there to be tried before me on
these charges?"
10 But Paul said: "I am standing at
Caesar's tribunal, where I ought to
be tried. I have done no wrong to the
Jews, as even you can see very well.
11 If then I am doing wrong, or have
done anything deserving of death, I
do not refuse to die, but if there is
nothing to what these men accuse
me of, no one can give me up to
them. I appeal to Caesar!"
12 After Festus conferred with his
council, he replied, "You have appealed to Caesar; to Caesar you will
go!"

Visit of King Agrippa and Bernice to Festus (25:13-22)

13 After some days had passed,
King Agrippa[D] and Bernice arrived
in Caesarea and paid a courtesy call
on Festus. 14 Since they stayed there
many days, Festus presented Paul's
case to the king, saying, "There's a
man who was left as a prisoner by
Felix. 15 When I was in Jerusalem,
the chief priests and the elders of
the Jews presented their case and
asked for a judgment against him.
16 I answered them that it's not the
Romans' custom to give any man
up[E] before the accused confronts
the accusers face to face and has an
opportunity to give a defense concerning the charges. 17 Therefore,
when they had assembled here, I
did not delay. The next day I sat at
the judge's bench and ordered the
man to be brought in. 18 Concerning him, the accusers stood up and
brought no charge of the sort I was
expecting. 19 Instead they had some
disagreements with him about their
own religion and about a certain
Jesus, a dead man Paul claimed to
be alive. 20 Since I was at a loss in
a dispute over such things, I asked
him if he wished to go to Jerusalem
and be tried there concerning these
matters. 21 But when Paul appealed
to be held for trial by the Emperor,
I ordered him to be kept in custody
until I could send him to Caesar."
22 Then Agrippa said to Festus, "I
would like to hear the man myself."

[A]**24:23** Other mss add *or visiting* [B]**24:26** Other mss add *so that he might release him* [C]**25:3** Lit *asking a favor against him* [D]**25:13** Herod Agrippa II ruled Palestine A.D. 52–ca 95. [E]**25:16** Other mss add *to destruction*

25:4 Unaware of their plan, **Festus** denied their request, choosing for the time to keep Paul in **Caesarea**. Nevertheless, he invited the leaders back to Caesarea where they could air their accusations in formal court.

25:9-12 After hearing both sides, Festus realized Paul had not broken Roman law and should have acquitted him of all charges. But like Felix before him, Festus realized this action would infuriate the Jews—causing unrest throughout Judea. Bowing to pressure from the Jews, he asked Paul to go to Jerusalem to be tried again on the same charges. Although Festus intended to try the case, indicated by the phrase **before me,** Paul realized he would never receive a fair trial in Jerusalem—if he ever made it to trial. Paul argued that as a Roman citizen, he had the right to be judged at **Caesar's tribunal**. Paul exercised an ancient right of Roman citizens called *provocation*. In this case, he appealed to Caesar. After conferring **with his council**, Festus granted Paul's appeal, allowing Festus to maintain amicable relations with the Jews without incriminating an innocent man. Paul at last had the opportunity to go to Rome and share the gospel with the most powerful person in the Roman Empire.

25:13 While Paul waited to begin his journey to Rome, **King Agrippa and Bernice** (see **Character Profile**, p. 1446). came to **Caesarea** to get acquainted with the new governor **Festus**. King Agrippa (also known as Herod Agrippa II and Marcus Julius Agrippa II) and Bernice were two of the four children of Herod Agrippa I and the grandchildren of Herod the Great (Mt 2:1). Although Agrippa II never ruled over the main Jewish territory of Judea, Samaria, and Galilee as had his father, some regarded him the "king of the Jews" because he possessed the authority to appoint and remove the high priests. Twice a widow, Bernice, along with her two sons Berniceanus and Hyrancus, lived with her brother whom she never married. Rumors continually circulated about an incestuous relationship between the two siblings. Years later Bernice became the mistress of Titus, the son of Emperor Vespasian. Titus wanted to marry her, but for him to marry a Jewess would have been socially unacceptable. When he himself became emperor in A.D. 79, he abandoned his relationship with her.

25:14-21 Festus realized that King Agrippa, as king of the Jews, would have great insight into Paul's case. Since Festus was sending Paul to Rome, he had to write a letter to the emperor, similar to the one Claudius Lysias wrote to Felix (23:25-30). Because the matters related to the case dealt primarily with Jewish law, Festus sought Agrippa's opinion on the matter, and Festus presented his version of the events (25:15-21), paralleling Paul's account in 25:1-12. Festus provided a fairly accurate summary—the **Jews** wanted Paul convicted of a crime.

25:23-27 Paul's meeting before Agrippa was characterized by **great pomp** since all the important people in Caesarea were invited to the event, including the five high-ranking **commanders** of the Roman military and the **prominent men of the city**. In essence, Festus used this opportunity to honor King Agrippa.

26:1-2 Paul **stretched out his hand,** the common gesture of a first-century orator. Paul cherished every opportunity to share the gospel. Jesus predicted that the disciples would be brought before governors and kings to bear witness to the nations. He also told them not to worry about what they should speak because they would not be speaking—the Holy Spirit would speak through them (Mt 10:18-20). Paul had this assurance as he testified before Governor Festus and King Agrippa.

26:6-7 The hope of the promise made by God to the **fathers** is the resurrection, specifically the resurrection of Jesus. The reference to the 12 tribes is a way of identifying all Israel or the Jewish people.

26:10 The indication that Paul **cast** his **vote** did not necessarily mean he had been a part of the Sanhedrin. He was probably too young for service at the time; however, he may have filled the role of prosecutor for the Sanhedrin, therefore voting for the execution of imprisoned Christians.

26:12-23 This third account of Paul's conversion and commission in Acts (see also 9:1-19; 22:6-21) provides the least information, omitting the details of his temporary blindness and of his encounter with Ananias. The emphasis in this account is on his commissioning from Christ, which in the other two accounts was tied to Ananias' visit. Paul received his commission from the Lord while on the Damascus road and again humanly speaking from Ananias.

26:14 Goads were long sticks with a sharp pointed end, which were used by farmers to prod animals, particularly oxen, and point them in the right direction. The animals did not like being prodded; therefore, they would kick at the goad. Eventually the animals learned the futility of kicking and submitted to the farmer's direction. This Hebrew idiom expressed the futility of struggling against one's direction in life. In persecuting Christians, Paul had been struggling against his destiny to

CHARACTER PROFILE

Bernice Granddaughter of Herod the Great

Her Background	• She and her older sister Drusilla were daughters of Herod Agrippa. • She had a history of immorality.
Her Story	• She accompanied her brother King Agrippa to Caesarea to pay a courtesy call on Festus, who succeeded Felix (24:27). • She heard Paul's defense (25:23–26:23). • She did not believe Paul was guilty of a crime deserving the death sentence (26:30-31). • There is no record of her response to his message.
Life Lesson	You may hear the gospel with your ears but not respond with your heart.

"Tomorrow you will hear him," he
replied.

Paul before Agrippa (25:23-27)

23 So the next day, Agrippa and
Bernice came with great pomp and
entered the auditorium with the
commanders and prominent men of
the city. When Festus gave the command, Paul was brought in. 24 Then
Festus said: "King Agrippa and all
men present with us, you see this
man about whom the whole Jewish community has appealed to me,
both in Jerusalem and here, shouting that he should not live any longer. 25 Now I realized that he had not
done anything deserving of death,
but when he himself appealed to the
Emperor, I decided to send him. 26 I
have nothing definite to write to my
lord about him. Therefore, I have
brought him before all of you, and
especially before you, King Agrippa,
so that after this examination is
over, I may have something to write.
27 For it seems unreasonable to me
to send a prisoner and not to indicate the charges against him."

Paul's Defense (26:1-11)

26 Agrippa said to Paul, "It is
permitted for you to speak for
yourself."

Then Paul stretched out his hand
and began his defense: 2 "I consider
myself fortunate, King Agrippa, that
today I am going to make a defense
before you about everything I am
accused of by the Jews, 3 especially
since you are an expert in all the
Jewish customs and controversies.
Therefore I beg you to listen to me
patiently.

4 "All the Jews know my way of life
from my youth, which was spent
from the beginning among my own
nation and in Jerusalem. 5 They
had previously known me for quite
some time, if they were willing to
testify, that according to the strict-
est party of our religion I lived as a
•Pharisee. 6 And now I stand on trial
for the hope of the promise made
by God to our fathers, 7 the promise
our 12 tribes hope to attain as they
earnestly serve Him night and day.
King Agrippa, I am being accused
by the Jews because of this hope.
8 Why is it considered incredible by
any of you that God raises the dead?
9 In fact, I myself supposed it was
necessary to do many things in opposition to the name of Jesus the
•Nazarene. 10 I actually did this in
Jerusalem, and I locked up many
of the •saints in prison, since I had
received authority for that from the
•chief priests. When they were put to
death, I cast my vote against them.
11 In all the •synagogues I often tried
to make them blaspheme by punishing them. I even pursued them
to foreign cities since I was greatly
enraged at them.

Paul's Account of His Conversion and Commission (26:12-23)

12 "I was traveling to Damascus
under these circumstances with authority and a commission from the
chief priests. 13 King Agrippa, while

on the road at midday, I saw a light
from heaven brighter than the sun,
shining around me and those traveling with me. 14 We all fell to the
ground, and I heard a voice speaking to me in the •Hebrew language,
'Saul, Saul, why are you persecuting
Me? It is hard for you to kick against
the goads.'[A]
15 "Then I said, 'Who are You, Lord?'
"And the Lord replied: 'I am Jesus,
the One you are persecuting. 16 But
get up and stand on your feet. For
I have appeared to you for this purpose, to appoint you as a servant and
a witness of what you have seen[B]
and of what I will reveal to you. 17 I
will rescue you from the people and
from the Gentiles. I now send you
to them 18 to open their eyes so they
may turn from darkness to light and
from the power of Satan to God, that
by faith in Me they may receive forgiveness of sins and a share among
those who are •sanctified.'
19 "Therefore, King Agrippa, I was
not disobedient to the heavenly vision. 20 Instead, I preached to those
in Damascus first, and to those in
Jerusalem and in all the region of
Judea, and to the Gentiles, that they
should repent and turn to God, and
do works worthy of repentance.
21 For this reason the Jews seized
me in the •temple complex and were
trying to kill me. 22 To this very day, I
have obtained help that comes from
God, and I stand and testify to both
small and great, saying nothing else
than what the prophets and Moses
said would take place— 23 that the
•Messiah must suffer, and that as the
first to rise from the dead, He would
proclaim light to our people and to
the Gentiles."

Agrippa's Deliberation (26:24-32)

24 As he was making his defense
this way, Festus exclaimed in a loud
voice, "You're out of your mind,
Paul! Too much study is driving you
mad!"
25 But Paul replied, "I'm not out
of my mind, most excellent Festus.
On the contrary, I'm speaking words
of truth and good judgment. 26 For
the king knows about these matters.
It is to him I am actually speaking
boldly. For I am convinced that none
of these things escapes his notice,
since this was not done in a corner.
27 King Agrippa, do you believe the
prophets? I know you believe."
28 Then Agrippa said to Paul, "Are
you going to persuade me to become
a Christian so easily?"
29 "I wish before God," replied
Paul, "that whether easily or with
difficulty, not only you but all who
listen to me today might become as
I am—except for these chains."
30 So the king, the governor, Bernice, and those sitting with them
got up, 31 and when they had left
they talked with each other and said,
"This man is doing nothing that deserves death or chains."
32 Then Agrippa said to Festus,
"This man could have been released
if he had not appealed to Caesar."

Paul's Journey to Rome (27:1-8)

27 When it was decided that
we were to sail to Italy, they
handed over Paul and some other
prisoners to a •centurion named
Julius, of the Imperial •Regiment.
2 So when we had boarded a ship of
Adramyttium, we put to sea, intending to sail to ports along the coast
of •Asia. Aristarchus, a Macedonian
of Thessalonica, was with us. 3 The
next day we put in at Sidon, and Julius treated Paul kindly and allowed
him to go to his friends to receive
their care. 4 When we had put out to
sea from there, we sailed along the
northern coast[C] of Cyprus because
the winds were against us. 5 After
sailing through the open sea off Cilicia and Pamphylia, we reached Myra
in Lycia. 6 There the centurion found
an Alexandrian ship sailing for Italy
and put us on board. 7 Sailing slowly
for many days, we came with difficulty as far as Cnidus. Since the
wind did not allow us to approach
it, we sailed along the south side[C] of
Crete off Salmone. 8 With yet more
difficulty we sailed along the coast
and came to a place called Fair Havens near the city of Lasea.

Paul's Advice Ignored (27:9-12)

9 By now much time had passed,

[A]26:14 Sharp sticks used to prod animals, such as oxen in plowing [B]26:16 Other mss read *things in which you have seen Me* [C]27:4,7 Lit *sailed under the lee*

become one of the greatest proponents for the Christian faith.

26:20 Paul did not need to mention his missionary journeys because those areas fell beyond the jurisdiction of both Agrippa and Festus. Paul explained to his audience that the ultimate goal of his ministry was for Gentiles to **repent** [Gk *metanoein*, "undergo a change in frame of mind and feeling or change in principle and practice"] **and turn to God, and do works worthy of repentance**. The idea is reform or a change of behavior. Paul's use of "turn" (Gk *epistrephein*, "turn around, bring back, return") reinforces the meaning.

26:24 Festus proved to be an example of someone blinded by Satan. He could not understand the resurrection of Jesus. In his mind, no sane person would believe that a dead man came back to life. Therefore, Festus concluded that Paul must be **mad**.

26:26-29 The phrase **this was not done in a corner** indicated that what Paul spoke about was common knowledge throughout Palestine. Paul realized that he would have a better chance convincing **Agrippa** than Festus. Being a Jew himself and as the king of the Jews, Agrippa would have been well acquainted with Paul's teaching. He knew that if Agrippa embraced the message of the prophets, he could demonstrate how the life, death, and resurrection of Jesus were a fulfillment of the prophets. As a Jew, Agrippa could not deny his belief in **the prophets**, but he was not ready to affirm the truth of the Christian faith. Paul readily admitted his desire that Agrippa as well as everyone else believe in Christ. He wanted all to become as he was, minus the **chains**, meaning he wanted everyone to know the love of God found in Christ.

26:32 Since they deemed Paul innocent, he could have been released. Although it would not have been illegal for Festus to free Paul, he would have risked offending the emperor. For this reason Paul's appeal would still have to be heard in Rome.

27:1-2 The remainder of Acts focuses exclusively on Paul's journey to Rome and his ministry in Rome. Paul had long desired to share the gospel in Rome (19:21). Paul finally had the opportunity to go to Rome as the Lord had promised him (23:11), but as a prisoner—not as he envisioned. Luke, who reemerges in this chapter, was probably one of Paul's most frequent visitors. He accompanied Paul on the journey to Rome, providing vivid details of the voyage across the Mediterranean to **Italy**. **Adramyttium** was a city on the northwest coast of Asia Minor. **Julius**, a Roman **centurion** of the

Imperial Regiment, allowed Paul a considerable amount of freedom and even prevented others from taking Paul's life (27:3,43).

27:9 The **Fast** was probably a reference to the Day of Atonement (also known as *Yom Kippur*), occurring between late September and early October. Sailing after that time of year would have been particularly dangerous due to the unsettling weather patterns on the Mediterranean Sea.

27:14-16 The **"northeaster"** or "Euraquilo" was **fierce** (Gk *tuphōnikos*, "like a whirlwind"). Literally a typhonic wind—a whirling, cyclonic wind of hurricane force, came and hit the ship. The wind swiftly blew the ship south **of a little island called Cauda** (the modern Greek island of Gaudos), located approximately 23 miles southwest of Crete.

27:20 The fact that the **sun** and the **stars** did not appear made navigation impossible.

27:27 Luke's designation of **the Adriatic Sea** (or Sea of Adria) should not be confused with the modern Adriatic Sea between the coasts of Yugoslavia and western Italy. The ancient writers called the north-central portion of the Mediterranean Sea between Greece and Italy the "Sea of Adria." During the storm, the ship drifted approximately 475 miles from Crete to the small island Malta, south of Sicily.

27:28 A **sounding** was made by throwing a weighted, marked line into the water. When the lead hit the bottom, the sailors could tell the depth from the water marks on the rope.

27:33 For the second time Luke mentions that they had been **going without food** (27:21,33), perhaps because of seasickness, the difficulty of preparing food in the storm, or as a means of rationing the food so that it would not run out. At this point it was necessary for them to eat so that they would have strength to survive what ensued.

27:42-43 The time had come to abandon the ship. Fearing the repercussions if the prisoners escaped, the soldiers intended **to kill** them. But **the centurion** came to the rescue **because he wanted to save Paul**. Evidently Paul had garnered his respect over the course of the journey. Perhaps the centurion had even come to believe in Jesus.

28:1 Malta is a small Mediterranean island (only 16 miles long and 9 miles wide), lying approximately 60 miles south of Sicily and 180 miles north of

and the voyage was already dangerous. Since the Fast[A] was already over, Paul gave his advice 10 and told them, "Men, I can see that this voyage is headed toward damage and heavy loss, not only of the cargo and the ship but also of our lives." 11 But the centurion paid attention to the captain and the owner of the ship rather than to what Paul said. 12 Since the harbor was unsuitable to winter in, the majority decided to set sail from there, hoping somehow to reach Phoenix, a harbor on Crete open to the southwest and northwest, and to winter there.

Storm-Tossed Ship (27:13-38)

13 When a gentle south wind sprang up, they thought they had achieved their purpose. They weighed anchor and sailed along the shore of Crete. 14 But not long afterward, a fierce wind called the "northeaster"[B] rushed down from the island. 15 Since the ship was caught and was unable to head into the wind, we gave way to it and were driven along. 16 After running under the shelter of a little island called Cauda,[C] we were barely able to get control of the skiff. 17 After hoisting it up, they used ropes and tackle and girded the ship. Then, fearing they would run aground on the Syrtis,[D] they lowered the drift-anchor, and in this way they were driven along. 18 Because we were being severely battered by the storm, they began to jettison the cargo the next day. 19 On the third day, they threw the ship's gear overboard with their own hands.

20 For many days neither sun nor stars appeared, and the severe storm kept raging. Finally all hope that we would be saved was disappearing. 21 Since many were going without food, Paul stood up among them and said, "You men should have followed my advice not to sail from Crete and sustain this damage and loss. 22 Now I urge you to take courage, because there will be no loss of any of your lives, but only of the ship. 23 For this night an angel of the God I belong to and serve stood by me, 24 and said, 'Don't be afraid, Paul. You must stand before Caesar. And, look! God has graciously given you all those who are sailing with you.' 25 Therefore, take courage, men, because I believe God that it will be just the way it was told to me. 26 However, we must run aground on a certain island."

27 When the fourteenth night came, we were drifting in the Adriatic Sea,[E] and in the middle of the night the sailors thought they were approaching land.[F] 28 They took a sounding and found it to be 120 feet[G] deep; when they had sailed a little farther and sounded again, they found it to be 90 feet[H] deep. 29 Then, fearing we might run aground in some rocky place, they dropped four anchors from the stern and prayed for daylight to come.

30 Some sailors tried to escape from the ship; they had let down the skiff into the sea, pretending that they were going to put out anchors from the bow. 31 Paul said to the centurion and the soldiers, "Unless these men stay in the ship, you cannot be saved." 32 Then the soldiers cut the ropes holding the skiff and let it drop away.

33 When it was about daylight, Paul urged them all to take food, saying, "Today is the fourteenth day that you have been waiting and going without food, having eaten nothing. 34 Therefore I urge you to take some food. For this has to do with your survival, since none of you will lose a hair from your head." 35 After he said these things and had taken some bread, he gave thanks to God in the presence of all of them, and when he broke it, he began to eat. 36 They all became encouraged and took food themselves. 37 In all there were 276 of us on the ship. 38 When they had eaten enough, they began to lighten the ship by throwing the grain overboard into the sea.

Shipwreck (27:39-44)

39 When daylight came, they did not recognize the land but sighted

[A]**27:9** The Day of Atonement [B]**27:14** Lit *Euraquilo*, a violent northeast wind [C]**27:16** Or *Clauda* [D]**27:17** = sandbanks or sandbars near North Africa [E]**27:27** Part of the northern Mediterranean Sea; not the modern Adriatic Sea east of Italy [F]**27:27** Lit *thought there was land approaching them* [G]**27:28** Lit *20 fathoms* [H]**27:28** Lit *15 fathoms*

a bay with a beach. They planned to
run the ship ashore if they could.
40 After casting off the anchors, they
left them in the sea, at the same
time loosening the ropes that held
the rudders. Then they hoisted the
foresail to the wind and headed for
the beach. 41 But they struck a sand-
bar and ran the ship aground. The
bow jammed fast and remained immovable, while the stern began to
break up by the pounding of the
waves.
42 The soldiers' plan was to kill
the prisoners so that no one could
swim away and escape. 43 But the
centurion kept them from carrying
out their plan because he wanted to
save Paul, so he ordered those who
could swim to jump overboard first
and get to land. 44 The rest were to
follow, some on planks and some on
debris from the ship. In this way, everyone safely reached the shore.

Malta's Hospitality (28:1-6)

28 Once ashore, we then learned
that the island was called
Malta. 2 The local people showed us
extraordinary kindness, for they lit
a fire and took us all in, since it was
raining and cold. 3 As Paul gathered
a bundle of brushwood and put it on
the fire, a viper came out because
of the heat and fastened itself to his
hand. 4 When the local people saw
the creature hanging from his hand,
they said to one another, "This man
is probably a murderer, and though
he has escaped the sea, Justice[A] does
not allow him to live!" 5 However, he
shook the creature off into the fire
and suffered no harm. 6 They expected that he would swell up or suddenly drop dead. But after they waited a
long time and saw nothing unusual
happen to him, they changed their
minds and said he was a god.

Ministry in Malta (28:7-10)

7 Now in the area around that
place was an estate belonging to the
leading man of the island, named
Publius, who welcomed us and entertained us hospitably for three
days. 8 Publius's father was in bed
suffering from fever and dysentery.
Paul went to him, and praying and
laying his hands on him, he healed
him. 9 After this, the rest of those
on the island who had diseases also
came and were cured. 10 So they
heaped many honors on us, and
when we sailed, they gave us what
we needed.

Rome at Last (28:11-16)

11 After three months we set sail in
an Alexandrian ship that had win-
tered at the island, with the Twin
Brothers[B] as its figurehead. 12 Putting in at Syracuse, we stayed three
days. 13 From there, after making a
circuit along the coast,[C] we reached
Rhegium. After one day a south
wind sprang up, and the second
day we came to Puteoli. 14 There we
found believers[D] and were invited to
stay with them for seven days.
And so we came to Rome. 15 Now
the believers[D] from there had heard
the news about us and had come to
meet us as far as the Forum of Appius and the Three Taverns. When
Paul saw them, he thanked God and
took courage. 16 When we entered
Rome,[E] Paul was permitted to stay
by himself with the soldier who
guarded him.

Paul's Conversation with Jewish Leaders in Rome (28:17-22)

17 After three days he called together the leaders of the Jews. When
they had gathered he said to them:
"Brothers, although I have done
nothing against our people or the
customs of our ancestors, I was delivered as a prisoner from Jerusalem
into the hands of the Romans. 18 After they examined me, they wanted
to release me, since I had not committed a capital offense. 19 Because
the Jews objected, I was compelled
to appeal to Caesar; it was not as
though I had any accusation against
my nation. 20 For this reason I've
asked to see you and speak to you. In
fact, it is for the hope of Israel that
I'm wearing this chain."
21 Then they said to him, "We
haven't received any letters about
you from Judea. None of the brothers has come and reported or spoken

[A] **28:4** Gk *Dike*, a goddess of justice [B] **28:11** Gk *Dioscuri*, twin sons of Zeus [C] **28:13** Other mss read *From there, casting off,* [D] **28:14,15** Lit *brothers* [E] **28:16** Other mss add *the centurion turned the prisoners over to the military commander; but*

Libya. Settled by the Phoenicians, the island came under Roman rule in 21 B.C. Although the island had a large degree of autonomy, Rome ruled through a governor. The shipwreck occurred only three miles from the entrance of what is interestingly known today as St. Paul's Bay.

28:3 The **viper** (Gk *echidna*, "snake") was obviously a poisonous reptile. Since today Malta has no known poisonous snakes, some claim this detail to be Luke's embellishment. However, even the recorded reaction of the natives indicates the snake was poisonous. Additionally, just because no poisonous snakes exist there in this era does not mean that none existed 19 centuries ago.

28:4 Justice, (Gk *dikē*, "penalty, punishment") for the locals referred to the Greek goddess *Dike* (translated here as "Justice"), the daughter of Zeus, whom they believed watched over all human affairs and reported to Zeus all wrongdoings so the guilty could pay for their crimes.

28:7-10 The text is not clear as to whether **Publius** welcomed the entire group of 276 (which would have been difficult) or just Paul and his personal companions. The healing of Publius's father was the only occasion in Acts when both prayer and the laying on of hands accompanied healing. Although Luke does not mention the spiritual reaction of the people, many probably came to believe in Jesus, since miracles in Acts often preceded faith (3:1-10; 5:14-16; 8:6-8).

28:11 After three months on the island waiting for the bad sailing weather of winter to pass, they left on another **Alexandrian ship** headed for Rome. This ship bore the images of **the Twin Brothers as its figurehead.** Ships often carried the insignia of Castor and Pollux, the twin gods who were the sons of Leda and Zeus in Greek mythology. Represented by the constellation Gemini, people worshiped these two idols throughout Egypt. Sailors believed them to be the protectors of the sea.

28:14 Rome was a city with over a million inhabitants and the dominating power of the world for two millennia (from the second century B.C. to the eighteenth century A.D.). It served as the capital of the Roman Empire with its population of 120,000,000 and land mass extending 3,000 miles east and west and 2,000 miles north and south.

28:15 Hearing about Paul's arrival, some of the believers from Rome came **as far as the Forum of Appius** (approximately 40 miles from Rome) **and the Three Taverns** (approximately 30 miles from Rome) to meet them.

They had long anticipated Paul's arrival because years ago Paul had written a letter to the church in Rome, indicating his desire to visit them (Rm 1:11,15; 15:23).

28:16 While in Rome, the authorities permitted Paul to stay by himself in a rented house with a **soldier who guarded him**. Apparently, Paul was not deemed a flight risk; so with limited freedom he could minister fruitfully while under house arrest.

28:21-22 The Jewish leaders had not heard about the charges against Paul previously. They had not **received any letters** about him **from Judea**, nor had any of the Jews come from Jerusalem and **reported or spoken anything evil** against him. For this reason, they received Paul warmly and still desired to hear more about what he had to say. Nevertheless, they were **aware** of Christian teachings, and they realized those teachings had been rejected by Jews virtually **everywhere**.

28:23 The phrase **kingdom of God** includes not only the death and resurrection of Christ but also the eschatological significance of Christ's reign on earth. The phrase is used several times in Acts (1:3-6; 8:12; 14:22; 19:8; 20:25). Paul attempted to persuade them that Jesus was the Messiah, using the Old Testament Scriptures—**the Law of Moses and the Prophets**.

28:26-27 Paul applied the words of Is 6:9-10 to his contemporaries. Like Israel in Isaiah's day, the Jews had deafened ears, spiritually blinded eyes, and calloused hearts.

28:28-29 The news that the hope of Israel was also for **the Gentiles** angered the Roman Jews, just as it had angered the Jews in Judea. At this point **the Jews departed**, but they continued to **debate** the issue **among themselves**.

28:30-31 Luke concludes Acts with Paul's first Roman imprisonment. For **two whole years** Paul stayed **in his own rented house** with one soldier to guard him. While under house arrest, Paul remained active in the ministry. During those two years he also wrote what are frequently called the Prison Epistles: Ephesians, Colossians, Philemon, and Philippians. Paul's imprisonment did not hinder the all-powerful truth of the gospel. Even in chains, Paul's prayer was that he would be bold in sharing the gospel (Eph 6:20).

anything evil about you. 22 But we
would like to hear from you what
you think. For concerning this
sect, we are aware that it is spoken
against everywhere."

The Response to Paul's Message (28:23-29)

23 After arranging a day with him,
many came to him at his lodging.
From dawn to dusk he expounded
and witnessed about the kingdom
of God. He tried to persuade them
concerning Jesus from both the Law
of Moses and the Prophets. 24 Some
were persuaded by what he said, but
others did not believe.
25 Disagreeing among themselves,
they began to leave after Paul made
one statement: "The Holy Spirit correctly spoke through the prophet
Isaiah to your[A] ancestors 26 when He
said,

Go to these people and say:
You will listen and listen,
yet never understand;
and you will look and look,
yet never perceive.

27 **For the hearts**
of these people
have grown callous,
their ears are hard
of hearing,
and they have shut
their eyes;
otherwise they might see
with their eyes
and hear with their ears,
understand with their heart,
and be converted,
and I would heal them.[B]

28 Therefore, let it be known to you
that this saving work of God has
been sent to the Gentiles; they will
listen!" [29 After he said these things,
the Jews departed, while engaging
in a prolonged debate among themselves.][C]

Paul's Ministry Unhindered (28:30-31)

30 Then he stayed two whole years
in his own rented house. And he
welcomed all who visited him,
31 proclaiming the kingdom of God
and teaching the things concerning
the Lord Jesus Christ with full boldness and without hindrance.

[A]**28:25** Other mss read *our* [B]**28:26-27** Is 6:9-10 [C]**28:29** Other mss omit bracketed text

The book of Acts presents more than a historical account of great men and women. It presents the message of Jesus—the only name under heaven by which mankind must be saved (4:12) then and now. Thus, the commission given to the apostles remains the commission given to the church, and yet another generation filled with the Holy Spirit must proclaim the gospel to the entire world. As Paul, all must be willing to suffer—even die for Jesus' name, willing to proclaim the gospel as Paul did—while in chains "with full boldness and without hindrance" (28:31).

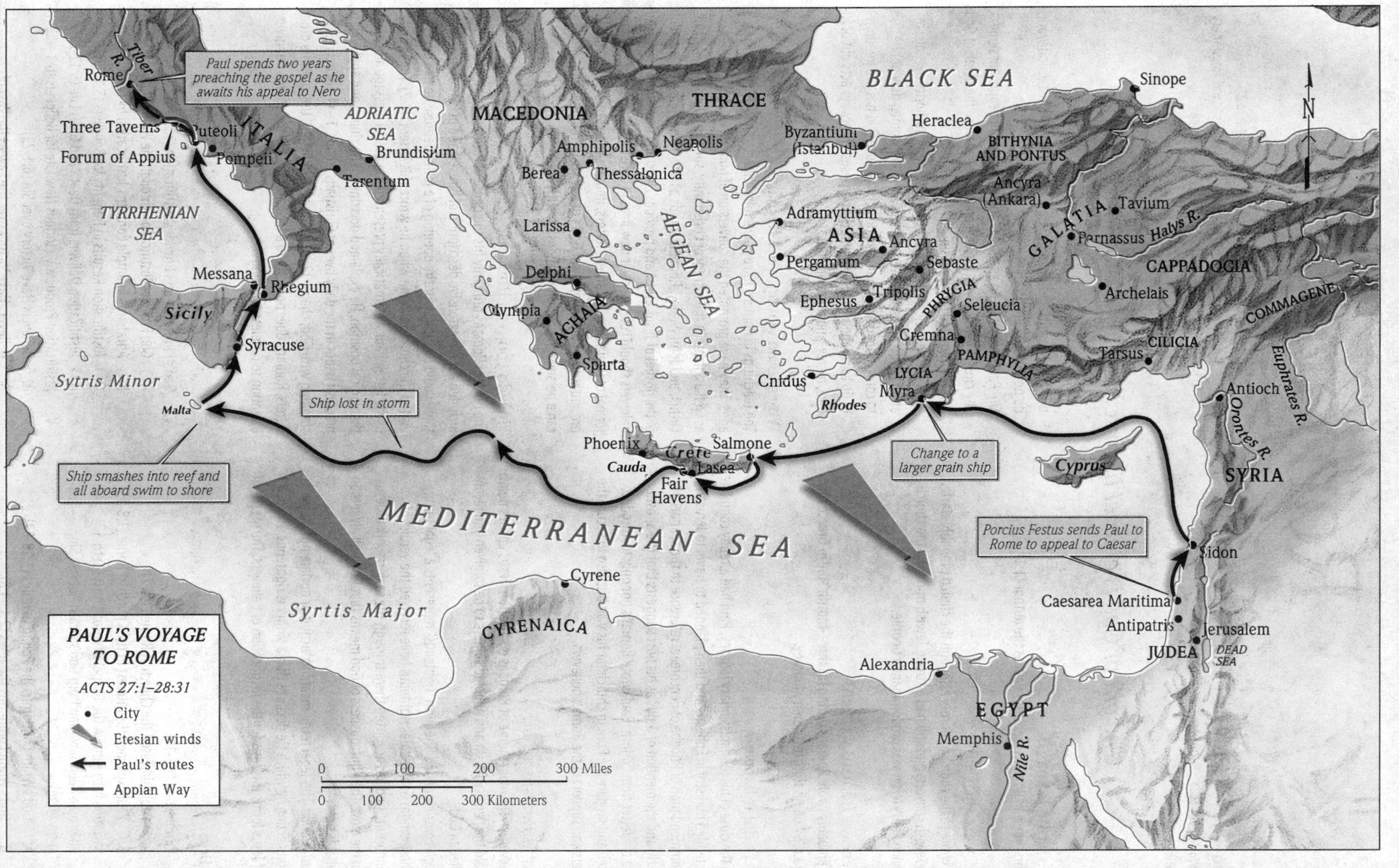
PAUL'S VOYAGE TO ROME
ACTS 27:1–28:31
City
Etesian winds
Paul's routes
Appian Way
0 100 200 300 Miles
0 100 200 300 Kilometers
Paul spends two years preaching the gospel as he awaits his appeal to Nero
Ship lost in storm
Ship smashes into reef and all aboard swim to shore
Change to a larger grain ship
Porcius Festus sends Paul to Rome to appeal to Caesar
BLACK SEA
ADRIATIC SEA
TYRRHENIAN SEA
AEGEAN SEA
MEDITERRANEAN SEA
Sytris Minor
Syrtis Major
Rome
Tiber R.
Three Taverns
Forum of Appius
Puteoli
Pompeii
ITALIA
Brundisium
Tarentum
Messana
Rhegium
Sicily
Syracuse
Malta
MACEDONIA
THRACE
Amphipolis
Neapolis
Berea
Thessalonica
Larissa
Delphi
Olympia
ACHAIA
Sparta
Byzantium (Istanbul)
Heraclea
Sinope
BITHYNIA AND PONTUS
Ancyra (Ankara)
GALATIA
Tavium
Parnassus
Halys R.
CAPPADOCIA
Archelais
Adramyttium
ASIA
Ancyra
Pergamum
Sebaste
Ephesus
Tripolis
PHRYGIA
Seleucia
Cremna
PAMPHYLIA
CILICIA
Tarsus
COMMAGENE
Euphrates R.
Cnidus
Rhodes
LYCIA
Myra
Phoenix
Crete
Salmone
Cauda
Lasea
Fair Havens
Cyprus
Antioch
Orontes R.
SYRIA
Sidon
Caesarea Maritima
Antipatris
Jerusalem
JUDEA
DEAD SEA
Cyrene
CYRENAICA
Alexandria
EGYPT
Memphis
Nile R.
N

Romans

Timeline World Events Biblical Events	*753 BC* Conjectured date for founding of Rome	*AD 36* Paul's conversion	*AD 47–49* Paul's first missionary journey	*AD 49–52* Paul's second missionary journey

"The gift of God is eternal life in Christ Jesus our Lord" (6:23b).

Who wrote Romans?

The first verse of Romans identifies Paul as the author (1:1).

Who were the recipients?

Paul wrote to the church at Rome. Although the church probably started from Jewish converts and still had a strong Jewish minority, the church receiving Paul's letter was predominantly Gentile.

When was Romans written?

Paul probably wrote Romans during his three-month stay in Greece in early A.D. 57 on his third missionary journey.

Where did it happen?

With the close of his third missionary journey, Paul had already completed an extended ministry in Ephesus and then planned to travel to Jerusalem. His commendation of Phoebe of Cenchreae, reference to the seaport of Corinth, and the mention of Gaius as his host suggests that the apostle wrote the letter from Corinth. Paul wrote Romans not only to introduce himself and prepare the Roman church for his visit but also to secure the prayers and support of the Roman believers.

What is Romans about?

- *Salvation*. The main theme of Romans is salvation. Jesus Christ's death paid the penalty for sin and enabled sinners to be forgiven and reconciled to God.
- *Righteousness of God*. The term "righteous" represents a legal term. Those whom God declares righteous have received the verdict of "innocent." God has acquitted them through the saving work of Jesus on the cross. The righteousness of God means that God will always do what is right.
- *Justification*. This legal term, meaning "acquit or declare not guilty," is God's action by which He declares that a sinner is righteous. The death of Jesus forms the basis for the justification of believers. The means of this act of acquittal is the individual's faith in Jesus Christ. Good works do not achieve justification.
- *Sin*. Paul presented sin as serious and universal. All people are sinners. The cross reveals sin in all its evil and power because the death of God's Son was required to defeat sin.
- *God's Sovereignty*. God has complete power and authority over all creation as the potter has over the clay. Men and women may not be able to comprehend how and why God acts because God has the freedom to do as He chooses to carry out His purposes. He always acts out of His love, mercy, and righteousness.

Why should women read Romans?

The teachings in Romans have powerfully impacted people across the ages. They have prompted the conversion of humble women and men, as well as giants in the history of Christianity, such as Augustine, Martin Luther, and John Wesley. Romans stands as one of the clearest statements of the gospel of Jesus Christ and provides clear, practical guidelines on how believers should conduct their new lives in Christ. As the longest and most formal of Paul's New Testament letters, Romans represents his systematic presentation of the theology of God's grace, answering the question, "How can a person have a right relationship with God?"

How do you read Romans?

The book of Romans primarily fits the genre of the personal letter. Paul included a more extensive description of himself and of his addressees than would be typical for the opening of a letter because he had never visited the church in Rome when he wrote this letter (1:1-7). In the body of the letter, Paul systematically presented the gospel message and his theological position. He explained doctrine to the church and applied it to practical issues in the daily lives of Christians (chaps. 1–11 discuss right standing with God; chaps. 12–15 present right living). Unlike Paul's other letters, Romans does not refer to a local situation of the church but gives attention to timeless teachings.

Outline

I. Introduction (1:1-15)
   A. Paul Addressed the Church at Rome (1:1-7)
   B. Paul Explained His Interest in the Church at Rome (1:8-15)

II. Salvation Is by Faith in the Gospel of Jesus Christ (1:16-17)

III. All People Need Salvation from God's Wrath Against Sin (1:18–3:20)
   A. God's Wrath Condemns the Pagan Gentiles (1:18-32)
   B. God's Wrath Condemns the Jews (2:1–3:8)
   C. God's Wrath Condemns All People (3:9-20)

IV. God's Righteousness Provides Justification (3:21–5:21)
   A. God Provides Justification Through the Work of Christ (3:21-31)
   B. Abraham's Example Confirms Justification by Faith (4:1-25)
   C. Justification Results in Benefits for Believers (5:1-11)
   D. Justification Delivers from Death and Gives Life (5:12-21)

V. Justification Produces Victorious New Life for Believers (6:1–8:39)
   A. Believers Have Victory over Sin (6:1-23)
   B. Believers Have Victory over the Law as the Way of Righteousness (7:1-25)

AD 53–58	*AD 57*	*AD 59*	*AD 60–62*	*AD 64*
Paul's third missionary journey	Paul's writing of Romans while in Corinth	Paul's journey to Rome	Paul's house arrest in Rome	Great fire in Rome, for which Nero blamed Christians

Outline (continued)

- C. Believers Have Victory over Condemnation (8:1-39)
- VI. The Problem of Israel's Unbelief Vindicates God's Righteousness (9:1–11:36)
  - A. Paul Grieved over Israel's Rejection of Christ (9:1-5)
  - B. God Displays His Sovereignty in Dealing with Israel (9:6-29)
  - C. Israel Has Responsibility for Her Rejection of Christ (9:30–10:21)
  - D. God Will Fulfill His Purposes for Israel (11:1-36)
- VII. Paul Offered Practical Instructions for Christian Living (12:1–15:13)
  - A. Believers Should Dedicate Themselves to God (12:1-2)
  - B. Believers Should Exercise Their Spiritual Gifts in Humility (12:3-8)
  - C. Believers Should Cultivate Christian Virtues (12:9-21)
  - D. Believers Should Submit to Civil Authority (13:1-7)
  - E. Believers Should Remember the Supremacy of Love (13:8-10)
  - F. Believers Should Recognize the Urgency of Christian Living (13:11-14)
  - G. Believers Should Seek to Build Up One Another (14:1–15:13)
- VIII. Paul Concluded His Letter to the Romans (15:14–16:27)
  - A. Paul Gave His Reasons for Writing (15:14-33)
  - B. Paul Commended Phoebe (16:1-2)
  - C. Paul Greeted Friends in Rome (16:3-16)
  - D. Paul Warned Against False Teachers (16:17-20)
  - E. Paul's Associates Greeted the Romans (16:21-24)
  - F. Paul Offered Glory to God (16:25-27)

Introduction (1:1-15)

Paul Addressed the Church at Rome (1:1-7)

1 Paul, a •slave of Christ Jesus,
called as an apostle[A] and singled
out for God's good news— 2 which
He promised long ago through His
prophets in the Holy Scriptures—
3 concerning His Son, Jesus Christ
our Lord, who was a descendant of
David[B] according to the flesh 4 and
who has been declared to be the
powerful Son of God by the resurrection from the dead according to
the Spirit of holiness.[C] 5 We have
received grace and apostleship
through Him to bring about[D] the
obedience of faith[E] among all the
nations,[F] on behalf of His name, 6 including yourselves who also belong
to Jesus Christ by calling:

7 To all who are in Rome, loved by
God, called as •saints.

Grace to you and peace from
God our Father and the Lord Jesus
Christ.

Paul Explained His Interest in the Church at Rome (1:8-15)

8 First, I thank my God through
Jesus Christ for all of you because
the news of your faith[G] is being reported in all the world. 9 For God,
whom I serve with my spirit in telling the good news about His Son,
is my witness that I constantly
mention you, 10 always asking in
my prayers that if it is somehow in
God's will, I may now at last succeed
in coming to you. 11 For I want very
much to see you, so I may impart to
you some spiritual gift to strengthen
you, 12 that is, to be mutually encouraged by each other's faith, both
yours and mine.

13 Now I want you to know,[H]
•brothers, that I often planned to
come to you (but was prevented until now) in order that I might have

[A]1:1 Or *Jesus, a called apostle* [B]1:3 Lit *was of the seed of David* [C]1:4 Or *the spirit of holiness*, or *the Holy Spirit* [D]1:5 Or *Him for*; lit *Him into* [E]1:5 Or *the obedience that is faith*, or *the faithful obedience*, or *the obedience that comes from faith*; Rm 16:26 [F]1:5 Or *Gentiles* [G]1:8 Or *because your faith* [H]1:13 Lit *I don't want you to be unaware*

Title: In its shortest form, the Greek title of this epistle is *pros Romaious*, "to the Romans."

1:1-7 Paul presents his qualifications. He follows the usual pattern for letter-writing by identifying himself, his readers, and then greeting them. Romans contains the longest, most formal of his letter introductions because he was writing to a church he had not yet visited and to whom he desired to make clear the content of his teaching.

1:1 Paul describes himself as **a slave of Christ Jesus**, affirming his complete loyalty to the Lord and his willingness to serve Him in obedient submission. God called him to be **an apostle**, commissioned and sent with authority.

1:9-10 Paul shares his desire to visit Rome not only because of its legendary reputation as the seat of government but also because of the reports coming about the faithful congregation of believers found there. By calling God as his **witness**, Paul affirmed the sincerity of his claim that he prayed repeatedly for the Roman Christians. Perhaps because he had not personally visited Rome, the apostle felt the need to make this solemn oath.

1:14 Greeks were the culturally elite in the Hellenistic world; **barbarians** were those not yet tutored in the Hellenistic culture. Together they represented all Gentiles, and Paul's burden was to share the gospel with all.

1:16 Paul now presents the theme of the epistle: **the gospel** (Gk *euaggelion*, lit "good message"—*eu*, "good, right" linked with *aggelion*, "message, report"), which is the heart of salvation of Jesus Christ. The apostle was ready to preach in Rome because he was **not ashamed of the gospel** of Christ. Many would have contempt for a crucified carpenter. Paul, however, gloried in the gospel even though his commitment to it had brought him suffering and grief. Salvation has a universal scope. It is for everyone, **first to the Jew** and then to the **Greek** or Gentile (i.e., to the totality of humanity). At the same time, however, this salvation has a restriction. It belongs to those who believe, to those who trust in Jesus Christ and commit their lives to Him. The power of the gospel makes it possible for people to believe.

1:17 God's **righteousness** is a central concept in Romans. It refers to God's unfathomable holiness and His intent and actions to declare righteous those who are unrighteous—those who have **faith** in His Son's atoning death. From the human side, believing God's Word has been the only way of right standing before Him (Gn 15:6).

1:18 Wrath, which is as much a part of God's character as is love, is directed against evil and includes not only displeasure with present evil but also the ultimate defeat of evil (Mt 8:12). Unrighteous men and women by their wicked lives hinder and stifle the general **truth** about God, which is available to everyone.

1:19-20 The created universe itself offers a natural revelation of the God who created it. God has given people this revelation in nature, but many have chosen to ignore or reject it and are **without excuse**.

1:21-23 The Gentile rejection of God led to their degradation. Their thinking became **senseless**, and their whole inner being became **darkened**. Those who rejected God claimed to be wise. In reality, **they became fools**. Instead of worshiping the One who is worthy of worship, they gave up the glory of the incorruptible God. They chose idolatry, worshiping the image of corruptible creatures—humans and animals—instead of the Creator.

1:24-25 Paul states the consequences of the pagan world's refusal to worship

Theological Terms

Term	Definition	References
Salvation	Deliverance from the guilt and condemnation of sin	Rm 1:16; Eph 2:8
Grace	Acceptance and loving mercy, neither deserved nor earned but given freely by God	Eph 2:8
Faith	Demonstration of total trust in and commitment to the Lord	Rm 3:28; 5:1; Php 3:9
Righteousness	"Righteous" is a legal term equal to acquittal. The word is used when the accused is declared "not guilty." Theologically, it means the state of being right with God, of being acquitted when tried by Him.	Rm 1:17; 2:13
Justification	The first aspect of salvation in which a person's relationship with God is made right through the saving work of Jesus Christ	Rm 3:21-26
Sanctification	The Holy Spirit indwells, sets apart, and works in the believer to bring about increasing Christlikeness and holiness.	1Co 6:11; Heb 2:10-12
Glorification	The culmination of salvation in which the believer is transformed into Christ's likeness	Rm 8:30; Php 3:21

a fruitful ministry[A] among you, just
as among the rest of the Gentiles.
14 I am obligated both to Greeks
and barbarians,[B] both to the wise
and the foolish. 15 So I am eager to
preach the good news to you also
who are in Rome.

Salvation Is by Faith in the Gospel of Jesus Christ (1:16-17)

16 For I am not ashamed of the gospel,[C] because it is God's power for
salvation to everyone who believes,
first to the Jew, and also to the
Greek. 17 For in it God's righteousness is revealed from faith to faith,[D]
just as it is written: **The righteous
will live by faith.**[E,F]

All People Need Salvation from God's Wrath Against Sin (1:18–3:20)

God's Wrath Condemns the Pagan Gentiles (1:18-32)

18 For God's wrath is revealed from
heaven against all godlessness and
unrighteousness of people who by
their unrighteousness suppress the
truth, 19 since what can be known[G]
about God is evident among them,
because God has shown it to them.
20 For His invisible attributes, that is,
His eternal power and divine nature,
have been clearly seen since the creation of the world, being understood
through what He has made. As a
result, people are without excuse.
21 For though they knew God, they

A1:13 Lit *have some fruit* B1:14 Or *non-Greeks* C1:16 Other mss add *of Christ* D1:17 Or *revealed out of faith into faith* E1:17 Or *The one who is righteous by faith will live* F1:17 Hab 2:4 G1:19 Or *what is known*

>WORD|*study*

1:18 God's **wrath** (Gk *orgē*, "settled displeasure or opposition, indignation"; cp. 2:5,8; 3:5; 4:5; 5:9; 9:22; 12:19; 13:4-5; Mk 3:5) also is continually being revealed. God's wrath is not like an angry human response, which often manifests itself in an uncontrolled and vindictive explosion; rather God's holy reaction is directed toward offenses that break His laws. He is always consistent and just.

did not glorify Him as God or show gratitude. Instead, their thinking became nonsense, and their senseless minds were darkened. 22 Claiming to be wise, they became fools 23 and exchanged the glory of the immortal God for images resembling mortal man, birds, four-footed animals, and reptiles.

24 Therefore God delivered them over in the cravings of their hearts to sexual impurity, so that their bodies were degraded among themselves. 25 They exchanged the truth of God for a lie, and worshiped and served something created instead of the Creator, who is praised forever. •Amen.

26 This is why God delivered them over to degrading passions. For even their females exchanged natural sexual relations[A] for unnatural ones. 27 The males in the same way also left natural relations[A] with females and were inflamed in their lust for one another. Males committed shameless acts with males and received in their own persons[B] the appropriate penalty of their error.

28 And because they did not think it worthwhile to acknowledge God, God delivered them over to a worthless mind to do what is morally wrong. 29 They are filled with all unrighteousness,[C] evil, greed, and wickedness. They are full of envy, murder, quarrels, deceit, and malice. They are gossips, 30 slanderers, God-haters, arrogant, proud, boastful, inventors of evil, disobedient to parents, 31 undiscerning, untrustworthy, unloving,[D] and unmerciful. 32 Although they know full well God's just sentence—that those who practice such things deserve to die[E]—they not only do them, but even applaud[F] others who practice them.

God's Wrath Condemns the Jews (2:1–3:8)

2 Therefore, any one of you[G] who judges is without excuse. For when you judge another, you condemn yourself, since you, the judge, do the same things. 2 We know that God's judgment on those who do such things is based on the truth. 3 Do you really think—anyone of you who judges those who do such things yet do the same—that you will escape God's judgment? 4 Or do you despise the riches of His kindness, restraint, and patience, not recognizing[H] that God's kindness is intended to lead you to repentance? 5 But because of your hardness and unrepentant heart you are storing up wrath for yourself in the day of wrath, when God's righteous judgment is revealed. 6 **He will repay each one according to his works:**[I] 7 eternal life to those who by persistence in doing good seek glory, honor, and immortality; 8 but wrath and indignation to those who are self-seeking and disobey the truth but are obeying unrighteousness; 9 affliction and distress for every human being who does evil, first to the Jew, and also to the Greek; 10 but glory, honor, and peace for everyone who does what is good, first to the Jew, and also to the Greek. 11 There is no favoritism with God.

12 All those who sinned without the law will also perish without the law, and all those who sinned under the law will be judged by the law. 13 For the hearers of the law are not righteous before God, but the doers of the law will be declared righteous.[J] 14 So, when Gentiles, who do not have the law, instinctively do what the law demands, they are a law to themselves even though they do not

[A]1:26,27 Lit *natural use* [B]1:27 Or *in themselves* [C]1:29 Other mss add *sexual immorality* [D]1:31 Other mss add *unforgiving* [E]1:32 Lit *things are worthy of death* [F]1:32 Lit *even take pleasure in* [G]2:1 Lit *Therefore, O man, every one* [H]2:4 Or *patience, because you do not recognize* [I]2:6 Ps 62:12; Pr 24:12 [J]2:13 Or *will be justified* or *acquitted*

God. God allowed them to do what they wanted to do. Immersion in their own sin became their punishment. Their sinful desires led to **sexual impurity**, and this sexual impurity led in turn to the degrading of their bodies.

1:26-27 Homosexuality and lesbianism are identified as distortions of the creation order—antithetical to the Creator's design biologically (for continuing the generations) as well as emotionally and psychologically (for the unique intimacy God planned between the man and woman). Other passages in Scripture also address homosexuality (Lv 18:22; 20:13; see especially, **Hard Question**, p. 1479).

1:28-32 The sinners Paul is describing deliberately refused to **acknowledge** God. They preferred to know other things instead. Therefore, God gave them over to the consequences of their actions, to a depraved mind. These unrighteous people knew enough of what God has revealed to know what is right and what is wrong. Yet, they still practiced these evil acts and even applauded and encouraged others who practiced such sins.

2:1 Although Paul's words are general enough to apply to Gentiles or Jews, the apostle appears to have addressed his arguments toward the Jews in this chapter. With their high moral standards, they would have thought themselves superior to the Gentiles and would have criticized them. Yet, those who pass judgment on others condemn themselves, for they are also guilty of sin.

2:2 God judges justly and fairly based on **truth**. God judges based on deeds done, not on status or nationality. Unbelieving Jews evidently felt exempt from divine judgment because of their descent from Abraham. The apostle insisted that they would not escape God's judgment. They were as guilty as the ones they judged.

2:7-8 Judgment will result in two different rewards: **eternal life** or **wrath and indignation**. Those who put their trust in God, not their own achievements, will receive that special quality of life lived in the presence of God. In contrast, those motivated by self-centeredness reject the truth and obey unrighteousness. Their reward will be wrath and anger.

2:12-13 Paul makes his first mention of the Mosaic **law** in this letter (see **Hard Question**, p. 1508). It does not matter whether or not everybody has received the law. All stand under God's condemnation. The Jews cannot plead their privileged position of having the law and hearing the law. This will not make them **righteous**.

2:14-16 Paul contends that the Gentiles have three witnesses to guide them:

- What the law requires is written on Gentile **hearts**. They have a deep conviction of the rightness of some things. Their good deeds show that something within them points to what is right.
- Their **consciences** bear witness to them of their past actions, evaluating and passing judgment on deeds already committed.
- Their conflicting **thoughts** accuse or defend them. Gentiles have what they need to guide them on the right path. They know enough to understand what they ought to do. They have no excuse when they do wrong.

2:25-29 The Jews confused privilege and responsibility by depending on **circumcision.** Circumcision distinguished the seed of Abraham from the Gentiles (Gn 17:1-11); it reminded Israel of the covenant between Abraham and God, which extended to all of his descendants (Gn 17:9-14); it represented putting away evil and being set apart (Jr 4:4). Although this outward sign was merely a testimony that the Jew was included in the covenant relationship God made with Abraham and Moses, many Jews made circumcision an end in itself. They failed to realize that the inward heart condition matters more than an outward physical sign. Paul insisted that disobeying the law is as if one becomes uncircumcised. Covenant people should live as covenant people by obeying God's commands. Otherwise, circumcision—the sign of the covenant relationship—has no meaning at all.

3:1-2 The Jews' **advantage** is that God entrusted them with His **spoken words** (i.e. the entire written revelation known as the Old Testament). This fact implies both the privilege of receiving the "words of God" and the responsibility of sharing those words with others.

3:10-18 Sin controls and brings condemnation to all who are under its power. Sin is a tyrant from whom individuals cannot free themselves. The apostle proved the universality of sin with the testimony of Scripture, primarily from the Psalms. Based on the standard of God's righteousness, both Jews and Gentiles fall short. There is no exception. Evidence shows that no one is righteous. No one even understands his lack of righteousness because he still chooses sin.

have the law. 15 They show that the
work of the law[A] is written on their
hearts. Their consciences confirm
this. Their competing thoughts
will either accuse or excuse them[B]
16 on the day when God judges what
people have kept secret, according
to my gospel through Christ Jesus.
17 Now if[C] you call yourself a Jew,
and rest in the law, boast in God,
18 know His will, and approve the
things that are superior, being instructed from the law, 19 and if you
are convinced that you are a guide
for the blind, a light to those in
darkness, 20 an instructor of the
ignorant, a teacher of the immature, having the full expression[D] of
knowledge and truth in the law—
21 you then, who teach another, don't
you teach yourself? You who preach,
"You must not steal"—do you steal?
22 You who say, "You must not commit adultery"—do you commit
adultery? You who detest idols, do
you rob their temples? 23 You who
boast in the law, do you dishonor
God by breaking the law? 24 For, as
it is written: **The name of God is
blasphemed among the Gentiles because of you.**[E]
25 For circumcision benefits you if
you observe the law, but if you are
a lawbreaker, your circumcision has
become uncircumcision. 26 Therefore if an uncircumcised man keeps
the law's requirements, will his
uncircumcision not be counted as
circumcision? 27 A man who is physically uncircumcised, but who fulfills
the law, will judge you who are a lawbreaker in spite of having the letter
of the law and circumcision. 28 For a
person is not a Jew who is one outwardly, and true circumcision is not
something visible in the flesh. 29 On
the contrary, a person is a Jew who
is one inwardly, and circumcision
is of the heart—by the Spirit, not
the letter.[F] That man's praise[G] is not
from men but from God.

3 So what advantage does the Jew
have? Or what is the benefit of
circumcision? 2 Considerable in every way. First, they were entrusted
with the spoken words of God.
3 What then? If some did not believe,
will their unbelief cancel God's
faithfulness? 4 Absolutely not! God
must be true, even if everyone is a
liar, as it is written:

> **That You may be justified**
> **in Your words**
> **and triumph**
> **when You judge.**[H]

5 But if our unrighteousness highlights[I] God's righteousness, what are
we to say? I use a human argument:[J]
Is God unrighteous to inflict wrath?
6 Absolutely not! Otherwise, how will
God judge the world? 7 But if by my
lie God's truth is amplified to His
glory, why am I also still judged as
a sinner? 8 And why not say, just as
some people slanderously claim we
say, "Let us do what is evil so that
good may come"? Their condemnation is deserved!

God's Wrath Condemns All People
(3:9-20)

9 What then? Are we any better?[K]
Not at all! For we have previously
charged that both Jews and Gentiles[L] are all under sin,[M] 10 as it is
written:[N]

> **There is no one righteous,**
> **not even one.**
> 11 **There is no one**
> **who understands;**
> **there is no one**
> **who seeks God.**
> 12 **All have turned away;**
> **all alike have become useless.**
> **There is no one who does**
> **what is good,**
> **not even one.**[O]
> 13 **Their throat is an open grave;**
> **they deceive**
> **with their tongues.**[P]
> **Vipers' venom is**
> **under their lips.**[Q]
> 14 **Their mouth is full**
> **of cursing and bitterness.**[R]

[A]**2:15** The code of conduct required by the law [B]**2:15** Internal debate, either in a person or among the pagan moralists [C]**2:17** Other mss read *Look*— [D]**2:20** Or *the embodiment* [E]**2:24** Is 52:5 [F]**2:29** Or *heart—spiritually, not literally* [G]**2:29** In Hb, the words Jew, Judah, and praise are related. [H]**3:4** Ps 51:4 [I]**3:5** Or *shows*, or *demonstrates* [J]**3:5** Lit *I speak as a man* [K]**3:9** Are we Jews any better than the Gentiles? [L]**3:9** Lit *Greeks* [M]**3:9** Under sin's power or dominion [N]**3:10** Paul constructs this charge from a chain of OT quotations, mainly from the Psalms. [O]**3:10-12** Ps 14:1-3; 53:1-3; Ec 7:20 [P]**3:13** Ps 5:9 [Q]**3:13** Ps 140:3 [R]**3:14** Ps 10:7

15 **Their feet are swift**
to shed blood;
16 **ruin and wretchedness are**
in their paths,
17 **and the path of peace**
they have not known.[A]
18 **There is no fear of God**
before their eyes.[B]

19 Now we know that whatever the
law says speaks to those who are
subject to the law,[C] so that every
mouth may be shut and the whole
world may become subject to God's
judgment.[D] 20 For no one will be
•justified[E] in His sight by the works
of the law, because the knowledge of
sin comes through the law.

God's Righteousness Provides Justification (3:21–5:21)

God Provides Justification Through the Work of Christ (3:21-31)

21 But now, apart from the law,
God's righteousness has been revealed—attested by the Law and the
Prophets[F] 22—that is, God's righteousness through faith in Jesus
Christ,[G] to all who believe, since
there is no distinction. 23 For all have
sinned and fall short of the[H] glory
of God. 24 They are justified freely
by His grace through the •redemp-
tion that is in Christ Jesus. 25 God
presented Him as a •propitiation[I]
through faith in His blood, to demonstrate His righteousness, because
in His restraint God passed over the
sins previously committed. 26 God
presented Him to demonstrate His
righteousness at the present time,
so that He would be righteous and
declare righteous[J] the one who has
faith in Jesus.
27 Where then is boasting? It is excluded. By what kind of law?[K] By one
of works? No, on the contrary, by a
law[L] of faith. 28 For we conclude that
a man is justified by faith apart from
the works of the law. 29 Or is God for
Jews only? Is He not also for Gentiles? Yes, for Gentiles too, 30 since
there is one God who will justify the
circumcised by faith and the uncircumcised through faith. 31 Do we
then cancel the law through faith?
Absolutely not! On the contrary, we
uphold the law.

Abraham's Example Confirms Justification by Faith (4:1-25)

4 What then can we say that Abraham, our physical ancestor,[M] has
found? 2 If Abraham was •justified[N]
by works, he has something to brag
about—but not before God.[O] 3 For
what does the Scripture say?

Abraham believed God,
and it was credited to him
for righteousness.[P]

4 Now to the one who works, pay
is not considered as a gift, but as
something owed. 5 But to the one
who does not work, but believes on
Him who declares the ungodly to be
righteous,[Q] his faith is credited for
righteousness.
6 Likewise, David also speaks of
the blessing of the man God credits
righteousness to apart from works:

7 **How joyful are those whose**
lawless acts are forgiven
and whose sins are covered!
8 **How joyful is the man**
the Lord will never charge
with sin![R]

9 Is this blessing only for the circumcised, then? Or is it also for the
uncircumcised? For we say, **Faith**
was credited to Abraham for righ-
teousness.[P] 10 In what way then
was it credited—while he was circumcised, or uncircumcised? Not
while he was circumcised, but uncircumcised. 11 And he received the
sign of circumcision as a seal of the
righteousness that he had by faith[S]
while still uncircumcised. This was
to make him the father of all who
believe but are not circumcised, so

3:19-20 The law gives **knowledge of sin**. No one can be put right with God or **justified** by **works of the law**. People are weak and unable to meet God's requirements. In fact, the law works by showing you your sin. The law reveals your failure and your need for the gospel.

3:21-26 This passage is central to understanding the entire Roman epistle. The reason everyone must come to God through faith in Jesus Christ is that all people are sinners. Those who believe are **justified**. This legal term means they are acquitted of the guilt and charges brought by sin. God declares these believers righteous.

Christ was a **propitiation** (Gk *hilastērion*, also translated "atonement, mercy seat"), a reconciling sacrifice. This metaphor is a reminder of the Day of Atonement when the blood of the sacrificial animal was sprinkled on the mercy seat in the most holy place as atonement for the sins of the people (Lv 16:14-16). Propitiation suggests the idea of appeasing or satisfying, and Christ's death satisfied divine justice and averted the wrath of God toward sinners. The means of Christ's propitiatory act was the shedding of His blood—His death on the cross. God's holy nature required a sacrifice, and He Himself provided it through His Son.

3:27-28 Faith makes justification effective and excludes all boasting. Salvation by grace through faith excludes all boasting by any person, not just the Jews. Any **works**-oriented religion that claims human effort and merit as a means of acceptance with God could lead to pride and boasting.

4:1-25 Paul wants to establish that faith-righteousness is not an innovation. The true understanding of the Old Testament itself points to this. He uses Abraham as the proof of his argument. The Jews looked to Abraham as the father of their nation and as one of the most righteous men who ever lived. They believed he was justified by his works, especially his circumcision. The apostle asserts, however, that Abraham was justified by his faith.

4:3 Paul quotes Gn 15:6 to show why Abraham had no reason to boast before God. Abraham put his trust in God—he was not placing faith in his own works. God **credited** (Gk *elogisthē*, an accounting term) his faith as righteousness; in essence, his spiritual books were balanced, ruling out any idea of merit on the part of Abraham because God did the crediting.

4:9-12 Abraham was justified by **faith** before circumcision.

[A] **3:15-17** Is 59:7-8 [B] **3:18** Ps 36:1 [C] **3:19** Lit *those in the law* [D] **3:19** Or *become guilty before God*, or *may be accountable to God* [E] **3:20** Or *will be declared righteous*, or *will be acquitted* [F] **3:21** When capitalized, *the Law and the Prophets* = OT [G] **3:22** Or *through the faithfulness of Jesus Christ* [H] **3:23** Or *and lack the* [I] **3:25** Or *as a propitiatory sacrifice*, or *as an offering of atonement*, or *as a mercy seat*; 2Co 5:21; Heb 9:5 [J] **3:26** Or *and justify*, or *and acquit* [K] **3:27** Or *what principle?* [L] **3:27** Or *a principle* [M] **4:1** Lit *our ancestor according to the flesh* [N] **4:2** Or *was declared righteous*, or *was acquitted* [O] **4:2** He has no reason for boasting in God's presence. [P] **4:3,9** Gn 15:6 [Q] **4:5** Or *who acquits*, or *who justifies* [R] **4:7-8** Ps 32:1-2 [S] **4:11** Lit *righteousness of faith*

4:16 Paul concludes that the promise must be by **faith** so that it can be purely a matter of God's **grace**. Promise, faith, and grace belong together. Law, works, and merit stand together in a completely different sphere. Grace guarantees God's promise to all Abraham's spiritual descendants, believing Jews (those who are of the law) and believing Gentiles (those who are of Abraham's faith). Abraham is the **father of . . . all** who believe. His example of faith demonstrates the only way to God.

4:19-20 From a human perspective, there was nothing to support Abraham's faith. How could his old body produce a child? Yet, Abraham believed in the God who promised him that his descendants would be "as numerous as the stars of the sky" (Gn 26:4), thus making him the father of many nations. Hope in God is a certainty, for God can do what people cannot do. To have God is to have hope. Abraham never became weak in his faith, even when he thought of his body as already dead (he was 100 years old) and when he considered the emptiness of **Sarah's womb** (she was 90). Instead of focusing on his own physical limitations, he focused on God and His promise.

5:1 Believers have **peace** and harmony with God as a result of Christ's work of justification. They are no longer His enemies, objects of His wrath, estranged from Him because of their sin.

5:2 For Christians, **hope** is a certainty. Now that believers have been made right with God, they can anticipate with confidence sharing in His glory.

5:3-5 The strong word **afflictions** (Gk *thlipsesin*, "tribulations") refers to being under pressure, especially the pressure that comes from being a believer in a hostile world. The meaning, however, could include any real troubles that burden believers. Such difficulties should cause rejoicing because they produce steadfast **endurance** (Gk *hupomonēn*, "living under"), a bearing up under pressure, in the life of believers. The idea is holding out, standing firm, bearing up under, putting up with. This discipline in turn produces **proven character**. This strength of character, whose testing has proven God's faithfulness, produces **hope** (Gk *elpida*, "confident assurance"). This hope does not put believers to shame because God's love has flooded their hearts in abundance through the Holy Spirit God gave them at the time of their conversion.

5:6-8 The death of Jesus Christ on the cross shows the greatness of God's love because Christ died on behalf of people who are:

that righteousness may be credited to them also. 12 And he became the father of the circumcised, who are not only circumcised but who also follow in the footsteps of the faith our father Abraham had while he was still uncircumcised.

13 For the promise to Abraham or to his descendants that he would inherit the world was not through the law, but through the righteousness that comes by faith.[A] 14 If those who are of the law are heirs, faith is made empty and the promise is canceled. 15 For the law produces wrath. And where there is no law, there is no transgression.

16 This is why the promise is by faith, so that it may be according to grace, to guarantee it to all the descendants—not only to those who are of the law[B] but also to those who are of Abraham's faith. He is the father of us all 17 in God's sight. As it is written: **I have made you the father of many nations.**[C] He believed in God, who gives life to the dead and calls things into existence that do not exist. 18 He believed, hoping against hope, so that he became **the father of many nations**[C] according to what had been spoken: **So will your descendants be.**[D] 19 He considered[E] his own body to be already dead (since he was about 100 years old) and also considered the deadness of Sarah's womb, without weakening in the faith. 20 He did not waver in unbelief at God's promise but was strengthened in his faith and gave glory to God, 21 because he was fully convinced that what He had promised He was also able to perform. 22 Therefore, **it was credited to him for righteousness.**[F] 23 Now **it was credited to him** was not written for Abraham alone, 24 but also for us. It will be credited to us who believe in Him who raised Jesus our Lord from the dead. 25 He was delivered up for[G] our trespasses and raised for[G] our justification.[H]

Justification Results in Benefits for Believers (5:1-11)

5 Therefore, since we have been declared righteous by faith, we have peace[I] with God through our Lord Jesus Christ. 2 We have also obtained access through Him by faith[J] into this grace in which we stand, and we rejoice in the hope of the glory of God. 3 And not only that, but we also rejoice in our afflictions, because we know that affliction produces endurance, 4 endurance produces proven character, and proven character produces hope. 5 This hope will not disappoint us, because God's love has been poured out in our hearts through the Holy Spirit who was given to us.

6 For while we were still helpless, at the appointed moment, Christ died for the ungodly. 7 For rarely will someone die for a just person—though for a good person perhaps someone might even dare to die. 8 But God proves His own love for us in that while we were still sinners, Christ died for us! 9 Much more then, since we have now been declared righteous by His blood, we will be saved through Him from wrath. 10 For if, while we were enemies, we were reconciled to God through the death of His Son, then how much more, having been reconciled, will we be saved by His life! 11 And not only that, but we also rejoice in God through our Lord Jesus Christ. We have now received this reconciliation through Him.

Justification Delivers from Death and Gives Life (5:12-21)

12 Therefore, just as sin entered the world through one man, and death through sin, in this way death spread to all men, because all sinned.[K] 13 In fact, sin was in the world before the law, but sin is not charged to a person's account when there is no law. 14 Nevertheless, death reigned from Adam to Moses, even over those who did not sin in the likeness of Adam's transgression. He is a prototype[L] of the Coming One.

[A] 4:13 Lit *righteousness of faith* [B] 4:16 Or *not to those who are of the law only* [C] 4:17,18 Gn 17:5 [D] 4:18 Gn 15:5 [E] 4:19 Other mss read *He did not consider* [F] 4:22 Gn 15:6 [G] 4:25 Or *because of* [H] 4:25 Or *acquittal* [I] 5:1 Other mss read *faith, let us have peace*, which can also be translated *faith, let us grasp the fact that we have peace* [J] 5:2 Other mss omit *by faith* [K] 5:12 Or *have sinned* [L] 5:14 Or *figure*, or *pattern*; = an OT person or thing that prefigures a NT person or thing

15 But the gift is not like the trespass. For if by the one man's trespass the many died, how much more
have the grace of God and the gift
overflowed to the many by the grace
of the one man, Jesus Christ. 16 And
the gift is not like the one man's
sin, because from one sin came the
judgment, resulting in condemnation, but from many trespasses
came the gift, resulting in •justi-
fication.[A] 17 Since by the one man's
trespass, death reigned through that
one man, how much more will those
who receive the overflow of grace
and the gift of righteousness reign
in life through the one man, Jesus
Christ.
18 So then, as through one trespass
there is condemnation for everyone,
so also through one righteous act
there is life-giving justification[B] for
everyone. 19 For just as through one
man's disobedience the many were
made sinners, so also through the
one man's obedience the many will
be made righteous. 20 The law came
along to multiply the trespass. But
where sin multiplied, grace multiplied even more 21 so that, just as sin
reigned in death, so also grace will
reign through righteousness, resulting in eternal life through Jesus
Christ our Lord.

Justification Produces Victorious New Life for Believers (6:1–8:39)

Believers Have Victory over Sin (6:1–23)

6 What should we say then? Should
we continue in sin so that grace
may multiply? 2 Absolutely not! How
can we who died to sin still live in
it? 3 Or are you unaware that all of
us who were baptized into Christ
Jesus were baptized into His death?
4 Therefore we were buried with Him
by baptism into death, in order that,
just as Christ was raised from the
dead by the glory of the Father, so
we too may •walk in a new way[C] of
life. 5 For if we have been joined with
Him in the likeness of His death, we
will certainly also be[D] in the likeness

Doctrine BAPTISM

Baptism illustrates the believer's union with Christ: dead to sin, alive to God (6:3-4). It is not required for salvation, but it is the public testimony of a believer to what has occurred in her life. Those who have united themselves to Christ picture this union by being plunged into the waters of baptism, showing that they have been **baptized** [Gk *ebaptisthēmen*, "immersed"] **into His death**. "Baptism" is the transliteration or anglicization of the Greek word. The idea of the Greek word is a total enveloping of one substance in another. The argument for immersion as the proper mode for baptism is clearly made with the meaning of the word, coupled with the example of Jesus and John. Paul's use of the imagery of baptism also effectively testifies to its public testimony of what transpires in conversion:

- The death, burial, and resurrection of Christ are pictured in the believer's immersion in baptismal waters and being raised out of them.
- A believer also pictures her own regeneration, dying to the old life of sin and arising to a new life with Christ.
- The believer is also declaring her confidence in her reunion with Christ at His return.

of His resurrection. 6 For we know
that our old self[E] was crucified with
Him in order that sin's dominion
over the body[F] may be abolished, so
that we may no longer be enslaved
to sin, 7 since a person who has died
is freed[G] from sin's claims.[H] 8 Now
if we died with Christ, we believe
that we will also live with Him, 9 because we know that Christ, having
been raised from the dead, will not
die again. Death no longer rules
over Him. 10 For in light of the fact
that He died, He died to sin once for
all; but in light of the fact that He
lives, He lives to God. 11 So, you too
consider yourselves dead to sin but
alive to God in Christ Jesus.[I]
12 Therefore do not let sin reign in
your mortal body, so that you obey[J]
its desires. 13 And do not offer any
parts[K] of it to sin as weapons for unrighteousness. But as those who are
alive from the dead, offer yourselves
to God, and all the parts[K] of yourselves to God as weapons for righteousness. 14 For sin will not rule
over you, because you are not under
law but under grace.
15 What then? Should we sin because we are not under law but

- **helpless** (Gk *asthenōn*—negative particle *a*-, "not, without," combined with the verb *sthenoō*, "strengthen"—"without strength, weak"; cp. 1Co 8:7,10);
- **ungodly** (Gk *asebōn*—negative particle *a*-, "not, without," combined with the verb *sebō*, "reverence"—"destitute of reverence for God; rebellious to God's authority"; cp. 4:5; 1Tm 1:9; Jd 4,15).

Christ died on behalf of individuals while they were sinners—not good, righteous people. God's actions through Christ for sinners are based on who He is, not on who a sinner is or what he has done.

6:1-2 Paul anticipates that some might think an emphasis on justification by faith could lead to sin. Paul emphatically rejects this thinking. Believers have died to sin. They no longer are bound by sin. New life in Christ releases them from sin's power in their lives.

6:6-11 Before being united with Christ, believers were slaves to sin. Now they are no longer dominated by sin. Believers may still sin, but sinning does not characterize their lives. Dying to self and uniting with Christ ends the old way of life and frees you from sin's claims and mastery. Christ died in relation to sin **once for all**. Christ Himself was sinless, and so His sacrifice was complete and sufficient. In the Old Testament, atonement for sin had to be made over and over again through sacrifices at the temple. However, Christ's sacrifice never needs to be repeated.

6:12-14 Paul appeals to Christians to become in practice what they already are in status. They have already died to sin and are justified. Sin, however, still remains in their lives. Negatively, believers are to stop letting sin rule in their mortal bodies (subject to weakness and physical death) so that they obey sin's evil desires. Positively, believers should decisively surrender themselves and all parts of their bodies to God as **weapons for righteousness**. Paul gives the promise of victory over sin to encourage Christians. **Sin will not rule over** believers, even if they struggle intensely, because sin no longer has lordship over them.

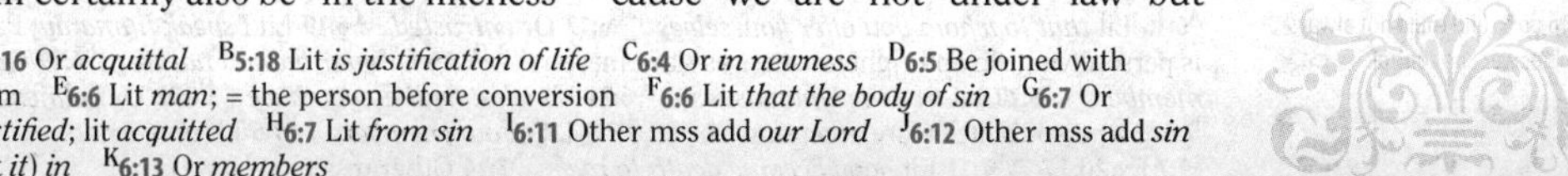

[A]**5:16** Or *acquittal* [B]**5:18** Lit *is justification of life* [C]**6:4** Or *in newness* [D]**6:5** Be joined with Him [E]**6:6** Lit *man*; = the person before conversion [F]**6:6** Lit *that the body of sin* [G]**6:7** Or *justified*; lit *acquitted* [H]**6:7** Lit *from sin* [I]**6:11** Other mss add *our Lord* [J]**6:12** Other mss add *sin* (lit *it*) *in* [K]**6:13** Or *members*

6:16-23 Paul was speaking in **human** terms to explain why he would use the metaphor of slavery to describe Christian service (v. 19). Such a strong image was necessary because of their human weakness in discerning spiritual truths. Believers are servants of righteousness, not of sin, and Paul illustrated his argument by showing that people are **slaves** to whatever master they obey. No one can serve two owners. Unbelievers are slaves to sin, for they obey its demands. Believers are slaves, obedient to God.

6:23 Paul concluded his discussion on a triumphant note. He used a new metaphor with the word **wages**, which was often used to denote the payment a general gives his soldiers. The wages of sin is death. In contrast, the **gift** (Gk *charisma*, "favor") of God is eternal life. **Eternal life** refers to both a present possession and a future consummation. Believers do nothing to earn or deserve this gift. It is completely free. This eternal life comes through the mediation of the Lord Jesus Christ and His work.

7:1-6 An **example** from marriage illustrates the binding nature of the law. A wife is **bound to her husband** by law as long as he is living. When her husband dies, the wife's legal obligation to the marriage law ceases. She is no longer a wife and is free to marry another. If the woman joins herself to another man, however, while her husband is still alive, she would be considered an adulteress because she has broken the law of marriage (Gn 2:24). The law no longer has any binding authority over believers as a way of salvation because they have died to the law by their union with the crucified Christ. The result of this freedom is the ability to serve God in a fresh, superior way as they are enabled by the Spirit.

7:7-12 The relationship of the law to sin illustrates the believer's freedom from the law. Paul denies that the law is sin. The law helps people know what sin is. Paul knew the law could not serve as a means of salvation for people, but it could produce guilt and give an awareness of sin. For an extended discussion of the purpose of the law, see **Hard Question**, p. 1508.

7:14-25 Although Paul was probably speaking autobiographically, his experience characterized that of all believers. Paul understood his moral weakness as a human being as well as sin's strength. He did not always do what he should do even when he desired to do so and could not always resist sin's power and control.

under grace? Absolutely not! 16 Don't
you know that if you offer yourselves
to someone[A] as obedient •slaves, you
are slaves of that one you obey—either of sin leading to death or of
obedience leading to righteousness?
17 But thank God that, although you
used to be slaves of sin, you obeyed
from the heart that pattern of teaching you were transferred[B] to, 18 and
having been liberated from sin, you
became enslaved to righteousness.
19 I am using a human analogy[C] because of the weakness of your flesh.[D]
For just as you offered the parts[E] of
yourselves as slaves to moral impurity, and to greater and greater
lawlessness, so now offer them as
slaves to righteousness, which results in •sanctification. 20 For when
you were slaves of sin, you were
free from allegiance to righteousness.[F] 21 So what fruit was produced[G]
then from the things you are now
ashamed of? For the end of those
things is death. 22 But now, since
you have been liberated from sin
and have become enslaved to God,
you have your fruit, which results
in sanctification[H]—and the end is
eternal life! 23 For the wages of sin is
death, but the gift of God is eternal
life in Christ Jesus our Lord.

Believers Have Victory over the Law as the Way of Righteousness (7:1-25)

7 Since I am speaking to those who
understand law, •brothers, are
you unaware that the law has authority over someone as long as he
lives? 2 For example, a married woman is legally bound to her husband
while he lives. But if her husband
dies, she is released from the law
regarding the husband. 3 So then,
if she gives herself to another man
while her husband is living, she will
be called an adulteress. But if her
husband dies, she is free from that
law. Then, if she gives herself to another man, she is not an adulteress.
4 Therefore, my brothers, you also
were put to death in relation to the
law through the crucified body of
the •Messiah, so that you may belong
to another—to Him who was raised
from the dead—that we may bear
fruit for God. 5 For when we were in
the flesh,[I] the sinful passions oper-
ated through the law in every part
of us[J] and bore fruit for death. 6 But
now we have been released from the
law, since we have died to what held
us, so that we may serve in the new
way[K] of the Spirit and not in the old
letter of the law.

7 What should we say then? Is the
law sin? Absolutely not! On the contrary, I would not have known sin if
it were not for the law. For example,
I would not have known what it is to
covet if the law had not said, **Do not
covet.**[L] 8 And sin, seizing an opportunity through the commandment,
produced in me coveting of every
kind. For apart from the law sin is
dead. 9 Once I was alive apart from
the law, but when the commandment came, sin sprang to life 10 and
I died. The commandment that was
meant for life resulted in death for
me. 11 For sin, seizing an opportunity through the commandment,
deceived me, and through it killed
me. 12 So then, the law is holy, and
the commandment is holy and just
and good.

13 Therefore, did what is good
cause my death?[M] Absolutely not!
On the contrary, sin, in order to be
recognized as sin, was producing
death in me through what is good,
so that through the commandment,
sin might become sinful beyond
measure. 14 For we know that the
law is spiritual, but I am made out
of flesh,[N] sold into sin's power. 15 For
I do not understand what I am doing, because I do not practice what
I want to do, but I do what I hate.
16 And if I do what I do not want to do,
I agree with the law that it is good.
17 So now I am no longer the one
doing it, but it is sin living in me.
18 For I know that nothing good lives
in me, that is, in my flesh. For the
desire to do what is good is with me,
but there is no ability to do it. 19 For
I do not do the good that I want to
do, but I practice the evil that I do

[A] **6:16** Lit *that to whom you offer yourselves* [B] **6:17** Or *entrusted* [C] **6:19** Lit *I speak humanly*; Paul is personifying sin and righteousness as slave masters. [D] **6:19** Or *your human nature* [E] **6:19** Or *members* [F] **6:20** Lit *free to righteousness* [G] **6:21** Lit *what fruit do you have* [H] **6:22** Or *holiness* [I] **7:5** = a person's life before accepting Christ [J] **7:5** Lit *of our members* [K] **7:6** Lit *in newness* [L] **7:7** Ex 20:17 [M] **7:13** Lit *good become death to me?* [N] **7:14** Other mss read *I am carnal*

Doctrine SIN

Both Old and New Testaments have extensive vocabulary to describe sin (7:7-12). At the root of sin is the idea of missing the mark or failing to meet God's requirements. There is no exhaustive list of sins; rather any act that misses God's perfect will is sin, separating the sinner from God. Hebrew words include these:

- *hattah*, stressing failure or mistake (Gn 4:7);
- *ᵓasham*, emphasizing guilt (Is 53:10);
- *peshaᶜ*, suggesting trespass (Pr 10:19);
- *ᶜawon*, indicating iniquity (Lv 16:21).

There are even more words in Greek:

- *hamartia*, with the nuance of going astray or being off the standard (Rm 7:13);
- *paraptōma*, with the idea of stumbling or blundering (Eph 2:5);
- *parabasis*, emphasizing crossing the boundary (Rm 5:14);
- *anomia*, meaning no law or lawlessness, an attitude of disregard for God's law (4:7);
- *asabeia*, stressing ungodliness or irreverence (5:6);
- *aselgeia*, picturing excess and used in reference to all kinds of sexual immorality (Eph 4:19);
- *asōtia*, indicating carelessness and unnecessary extravagance (Eph 5:18);
- *parakoē*, suggesting a refusal to hear (Rm 5:19).

Although this listing makes no claim of being exhaustive, it does demonstrate the overwhelming devastation that accompanies sin and its disobedience to God.

not want to do. 20 Now if I do what I do not want, I am no longer the one doing it, but it is the sin that lives in me. 21 So I discover this principle:[A] When I want to do what is good, evil is with me. 22 For in my inner self[B] I joyfully agree with God's law. 23 But I see a different law in the parts of my body,[C] waging war against the law of my mind and taking me prisoner to the law of sin in the parts of my body.[C] 24 What a wretched man I am! Who will rescue me from this dying body? 25 I thank God through Jesus Christ our Lord![D] So then, with my mind I myself am a slave to the law of God, but with my flesh, to the law of sin.

Believers Have Victory over Condemnation (8:1-39)

8 Therefore, no condemnation now exists for those in Christ Jesus,[E] 2 because the Spirit's law of life in Christ Jesus has set you[F] free from the law of sin and of death. 3 What the law could not do since it was limited[G] by the flesh, God did. He condemned sin in the flesh by sending His own Son in flesh like ours under sin's domain,[H] and as a sin offering, 4 in order that the law's requirement would be accomplished in us who do not •walk according to the flesh but according to the Spirit. 5 For those who live[I] according to the flesh think about the things of the flesh, but those who live[I] according to the Spirit, about the things of the Spirit. 6 For the mind-set of the flesh is death, but the mind-set of the Spirit is life and peace. 7 For the mind-set of the flesh is hostile to God because it does not submit itself to God's law, for it is unable to do so. 8 Those who are in the flesh cannot please God. 9 You, however, are not in the flesh, but in the Spirit, since[J] the Spirit of God lives in you. But if anyone does not have the Spirit of Christ, he does not belong to Him. 10 Now if Christ is in you, the body is dead[K] because of sin, but the Spirit[L] is life because of righteousness. 11 And if the Spirit of Him who raised Jesus from the dead lives in you, then He who raised Christ from the dead will also bring your mortal bodies to life through[M] His Spirit who lives in you.

12 So then, •brothers, we are not obligated to the flesh to live according to the flesh, 13 for if you live according to the flesh, you are going to die. But if by the Spirit you put to death the deeds of the body, you will live. 14 All those led by God's Spirit are God's sons. 15 For you did not receive a spirit of slavery to fall back into fear, but you received the Spirit of adoption, by whom we cry out, "•*Abba*, Father!" 16 The Spirit Himself testifies together with our spirit that we are God's children, 17 and if children, also heirs—heirs of God and coheirs with Christ—seeing that[J] we suffer with Him so that we may also be glorified with Him.

18 For I consider that the sufferings of this present time are not worth comparing with the glory that is

[A] **7:21** Or *law* [B] **7:22** Lit *inner man* [C] **7:23** Lit *my members* [D] **7:25** Or *Thanks be to God*—(it is done) *through Jesus Christ our Lord!* [E] **8:1** Other mss add *who do not walk according to the flesh but according to the Spirit* [F] **8:2** Other mss read *me* [G] **8:3** Or *weak* [H] **8:3** Lit *in the likeness of sinful flesh* [I] **8:5** Or *those who are* [J] **8:9,17** Or *provided that* [K] **8:10** Or *the body will die* [L] **8:10** Or *spirit* [M] **8:11** Other mss read *because of*

7:22-25 In his inmost being the apostle joyfully agreed with **God's law**. The conflict, however, was within himself. His longing for deliverance led him to thanksgiving to God through Jesus Christ the Lord. Paul had confidence he would triumph in the struggle. Jesus was his Deliverer.

8:1 Condemnation is the opposite of justification. God has acquitted believers from sin's penalty and guilt. The sentence against them no longer applies because the life-giving Holy Spirit has set them free in Christ Jesus, delivering them from the enslaving power of sin and death. The Holy Spirit within believers gives them a new power to defeat sin.

8:3-4 The **law** could not rescue people from the power of sin and death because it had to depend on the weak human nature to fulfill its demands. God had to act personally to break sin's power. He did so by sending His own Son in the likeness of sinful **flesh like ours**. Jesus was not a sinner Himself. He took the form of a man to defeat sin.

The work of the **Spirit** in believers accomplishes the law's demands. His enabling power helps believers to walk according to a standard they could never reach by themselves. See **Doctrine**, p. 1513.

8:9-11 The **Spirit** delivers believers from death. Their lower nature or flesh no longer is master of their lives. They are **in the Spirit** because God's Spirit dwells in them. He then is the controlling influence in their lives because He has taken residence in their lives. The same Spirit of God who raised Jesus from the dead lives in believers.

8:14-15 God's Spirit is not an impersonal moving force. He maintains intimate fellowship with believers as He resides within the heart of every child of God. Not only does the Holy Spirit empower, but He also guides, protects, and confirms membership in God's family. All those who are led by the Holy Spirit are **God's sons**, His children by **adoption** (Gk *huiothesias*, a term used only by Paul in the NT; cp. v. 23; 9:4; Gl 4:5; Eph 1:5). The person who is adopted into God's family receives all the rights, privileges, and responsibilities afforded to Christ. This adoption is not based on merit; it is always dependent on God's grace. As members of God's family, Christians can address the Lord in prayer in the warm, intimate terms a child would use, ***"Abba,* Father!"** The Spirit gives believers the assurance of membership in God's family by bearing witness with their inmost being that they indeed are children of God through faith in Jesus Christ.

8:19-25 Not only do Christians suffer and long for glorification, but the whole creation does also. Paul personifies creation in his description of its response—it **eagerly waits with anticipation**. This picture suggests a person leaning forward with great interest and desire.

8:26-27 The Spirit **intercedes** for believers and also **joins to help** (Gk *sunantilambanetai,* "lend a hand together, at the same time; to come to the aid of someone") weak believers—a word picture of the Spirit standing over against believers and pulling with them as they bear their burdens. **Weakness** (Gk *astheneiais,* "lack of strength, sickness, disease, timidity") can refer broadly to any area of weakness, but the context seems to point to difficulty in prayer.

8:28 God purposes **good** for believers. Paul does not say that everything happening is good in itself. Rather he recognizes that even problems and crises cannot derail a sovereign God. Because God is omnipotent and omniscient and omnipresent, He is faithful to bring ultimate good even from the most tragic happenings. He works all things together for good—not for all people in general, but for believers.

8:33 There will always be those who accuse believers. Satan himself acts in this role of adversary. Yet, no charge will stand against those whom God has chosen because **God** Himself **justifies** them. The only One who could justifiably bring an accusation (since all sin is ultimately against Him) is the One who declares believers righteous.

8:35-39 Paul lists seven things that some might think could **separate** them from Christ's love. He asserts that nothing can do that.

9:1–11:36 Why does **Israel** stand separated from the love of Christ? Paul agrees that God chose Israel. He gave them the covenants and the law. How, then, could Paul claim that the law has been set aside for something new? How can Israel reject Jesus if they are God's chosen people and if even their Scriptures teach justification by faith? Can God reject His own chosen nation? Paul probably struggled with these questions himself, and the Jews confronted him with these issues. In chapters 9–11, Paul discusses the faithfulness of God in light of the doctrine of election. (For the significance of the doctrine of election, one of the most misunderstood teachings of Scripture, see **Doctrine**, p. 1533).

HARD QUESTION

If I struggle with sin, does that mean I am not saved?

Becoming a Christian does not remove you from all sin and temptation. You will still have to struggle with sin. Paul's words in Rm 7:14-25 assure you that this is a normal part of the believer's life. Sin is a powerful force. Although this struggle will follow you throughout life, you do have hope. God promises deliverance. Victory is certain. You cannot overcome sin and temptation by your own self-determination and strength. You must look to the Lord Jesus for help. He has conquered sin once for all. He will fight by your side. Thank God, when you are in Christ Jesus, He no longer condemns you. Let Christ's enabling power through the indwelling Holy Spirit lift you to victory over sin.

going to be revealed to us. 19 For the
creation eagerly waits with anticipation for God's sons to be revealed.
20 For the creation was subjected
to futility—not willingly, but because of Him who subjected it—in
the hope 21 that the creation itself
will also be set free from the bondage of corruption into the glorious
freedom of God's children. 22 For we
know that the whole creation has
been groaning together with labor
pains until now. 23 And not only that,
but we ourselves who have the Spirit
as the •firstfruits—we also groan
within ourselves, eagerly waiting
for adoption, the •redemption of our
bodies. 24 Now in this hope we were
saved, yet hope that is seen is not
hope, because who hopes for what
he sees? 25 But if we hope for what
we do not see, we eagerly wait for it
with patience.

26 In the same way the Spirit also
joins to help in our weakness, because we do not know what to pray
for as we should, but the Spirit Himself intercedes for us[A] with unspoken
groanings. 27 And He who searches
the hearts knows the Spirit's mind-
set, because He intercedes for the
•saints according to the will of God.

28 We know that all things work together[B] for the good[C] of those who
love God: those who are called according to His purpose. 29 For those
He foreknew He also predestined to
be conformed to the image of His
Son, so that He would be the firstborn among many brothers. 30 And
those He predestined, He also called;
and those He called, He also •justi-
fied; and those He justified, He also
glorified.

31 What then are we to say
about these things?
If God is for us, who is
against us?
32 He did not even spare
His own Son
but offered Him up for us all;
how will He not also
with Him grant
us everything?
33 Who can bring an accusation
against God's elect?
God is the One who justifies.
34 Who is the one
who condemns?
Christ Jesus is the One
who died,
but even more,
has been raised;
He also is at the right hand
of God
and intercedes for us.
35 Who can separate us
from the love of Christ?
Can affliction or anguish
or persecution
or famine or nakedness
or danger or sword?
36 As it is written:
Because of You
we are being put to death
all day long;
we are counted as sheep
to be slaughtered.[D]
37 No, in all these things we are
more than victorious
through Him who loved us.
38 For I am persuaded that not
even death or life,
angels or rulers,
things present or
things to come,
hostile powers,
39 height or depth, or any other
created thing
will have the power
to separate us
from the love of God that is
in Christ Jesus our Lord!

[A]8:26 Some mss omit *for us* [B]8:28 Other mss read *that God works together in all things* [C]8:28 The ultimate good [D]8:36 Ps 44:22

>WORD|*study*

8:29-30 Five key words describe God's saving purpose for believers.

- He **foreknew** (Gk *proegnō*, lit "know before or in advance,") them. He set His heart on or chose them beforehand. (For the significance of God's "choosing" known as the doctrine of election, see **Doctrine**, p. 1533.)
- He **predestined** (Gk *proōrisen*, "decide beforehand"; cp. 1Co 2:7; Eph 1:5,11) them. God initiated everything. He set apart believers beforehand to become conformed to His Son's image so that Jesus would be the firstborn, the preeminent One, among many brothers. God planned for many children in His family.
- **Called** (Gk *ekalesen*, "invite, call by name"; cp. Mt 9:13) refers to being brought in. It is an effectual call—those called have already responded.
- **Justified** (Gk *edikaiōsen*, "render or declare righteous or just"; cp. Rm 3:24-30; Gl 3:24) refers to a right relationship with God and being treated as righteous.
- **Glorified** (Gk *edoxasen*, "praise, honor"; cp. Heb 5:5) refers to perfect conformity to the image of Christ, the ultimate state of believers when they become like Christ. Paul used the past tense of "glorified" because he was so certain that God's plan included glorification that he could speak of it as an accomplished fact. Salvation from start to finish is an amazing work.

The Problem of Israel's Unbelief Vindicates God's Righteousness (9:1–11:36)

Paul Grieved over Israel's Rejection of Christ (9:1-5)

9 I speak the truth in Christ—I am not lying; my conscience is testifying to me with the Holy Spirit[A]—
2 that I have intense sorrow and continual anguish in my heart.
3 For I could almost wish to be cursed and cut off[B] from the ·Messiah for the benefit of my ·brothers, my own flesh and blood.
4 They are Israelites, and to them belong the adoption, the glory, the covenants, the giving of the law, the temple service, and the promises.
5 The ancestors are theirs, and from them, by physical descent,[C] came the Messiah, who is God over all, praised forever.[D] ·Amen.

God Displays His Sovereignty in Dealing with Israel (9:6-29)

6 But it is not as though the word of God has failed. For not all who are descended from Israel are Israel.
7 Neither are they all children because they are Abraham's descendants.[E] On the contrary, **your ·offspring will be traced[F] through Isaac.**[G]
8 That is, it is not the children by physical descent[H] who are God's children, but the children of the promise are considered to be the offspring.
9 For this is the statement of the promise: **At this time I will come, and Sarah will have a son.**[I]
10 And not only that, but also Rebekah received a promise when she became pregnant[J] by one man, our ancestor Isaac.
11 For though her sons had not been born yet or done anything good or bad, so that God's purpose according to election might stand—
12 not from works but from the One who calls—she was told: **The older will serve the younger.**[K]
13 As it is written: **I have loved Jacob, but I have hated Esau.**[L]

14 What should we say then? Is there injustice with God? Absolutely not!
15 For He tells Moses:

I will show mercy
to whom I will show mercy,
and I will have compassion
on whom I will
have compassion.[M]

16 So then it does not depend on human will or effort[N] but on God who shows mercy.
17 For the Scripture tells Pharaoh:

I raised you up
for this reason
so that I may display
My power in you
and that My name
may be proclaimed in all
the earth.[O]

18 So then, He shows mercy to those

[A]9:1 Or *testifying with me by the Holy Spirit* [B]9:3 Lit *were anathema* [C]9:5 Lit *them, according to the flesh* [D]9:5 Or *the Messiah, the One who is over all, the God who is blessed forever*, or *Messiah. God, who is over all, be blessed forever* [E]9:7 Lit *seed* [F]9:7 Lit *called* [G]9:7 Gn 21:12 [H]9:8 Lit *children of the flesh* [I]9:9 Gn 18:10,14 [J]9:10 Or *Rebekah conceived by the one act of sexual intercourse* [K]9:12 Gn 25:23 [L]9:13 Mal 1:2-3 [M]9:15 Ex 33:19 [N]9:16 Or *on the one running*; lit *on the one willing* [O]9:17 Ex 9:16

9:1-5 Paul felt intense grief over Israel's rejection of Jesus Christ as the promised Messiah. To emphasize personal concern for his own people, Paul expresses a prayer-wish—that he himself were accursed and cut off from Christ for the sake of his brothers. He longed to take the place of his kinsmen **by physical descent** in death so that they might become Christians and claim life.

9:4-5 Paul lists seven great privileges demonstrating God's favor upon the Israelites.

9:6-9 Paul insists that all Israel did not receive God's promises. God's saving purpose never applied to the whole ethnic nation but to a smaller group within the nation. Paul developed his argument by quoting Gn 21:12 to show that not all Abraham's offspring were his true children. God made His promises to Isaac, the son of Abraham and Sarah and thus the child of promise. Mere **physical descent** from Abraham (such as Ishmael through the concubine Hagar) did not automatically mean inheriting the promises of God.

9:10-13 **Jacob** and **Esau** had the same mother and father. Even before they were born and before they had done anything good or bad, God chose Jacob for the spiritual line. He told Rebekah that the older brother would serve the younger, deliberately going against the cultural expectations of that day. God's choice of Jacob revealed His free sovereignty and demonstrated that election is not based on works. Election is based on God and His purposes, not on any human achievement. God worked out His purpose according to His own way, choosing Jacob over Esau.

9:14-15 Paul answers an imaginary objector who might have claimed God acted unjustly. This charge of **injustice** assumes some individuals are worthy of God's favor. The apostle strongly affirmed there can be no injustice with God. To act unjustly would be out of God's character (Ex 33:19).

9:17-18 Paul uses **Pharaoh** as another example. God raised this ruler up to his place in history for His own redemptive purposes. In the great events of the exodus God demonstrated His power in the face of Pharaoh's stubborn opposition. As a result of the liberation of His people from Egyptian slavery, God's name was proclaimed throughout the earth. Pharaoh refused God's way and grace. His unbelief and rebellion hardened his heart. God delivered him over to his own sin. God used Pharaoh's poor choices for His glory, but Pharaoh did what he wanted to do. God hardened him in the wrong he chose to do.

9:20-21 Paul uses the potter-and-clay image employed also by the Old Testament prophets (Is 29:15-16; Jr 18:1-6), to emphasize that God has the right and authority as the Potter to shape and use His creatures (i.e., the pots) as He desires.

9:22-23 God has patiently put up with the unbelieving Jews (objects of wrath) because He wanted to show mercy to both Jews and Gentiles.

9:24-26 Although Hs 2:23 originally applied to the rebellious 10 tribes of Israel, both Paul and Peter (1Pt 2:10) broaden the application to include the Gentiles as well.

9:27-29 God chooses to extend His mercy to **a remnant** in Israel.

9:32-33 Paul uses Is 8:14 and 28:16 to show how the very One who should have been the object of the Jews' faith became instead **the stumbling stone**.

10:1-3 Israel rejected **righteousness** based on faith. Paul shared with his Christian brothers in Rome his deep, heartfelt concern for the Jews. He prayed for their salvation.

10:9-10 Paul defines the message that calls for faith and results in salvation. People must **confess** (Gk *homologēsēs*, "say plainly, speak the same thing") with their mouths, **"Jesus is Lord"** and **believe** in their hearts **that God raised Him from the dead**. The apostle places confession before believing; and, of course, belief must precede confession. In fact, for confession to lead to salvation, one must agree with God in His judgments and in His remedy for redemption from sin. Verses 9 and 10 constitute one of the earliest confessions of faith. Belief (heart) refers to the inward aspect of faith, and confession (mouth) relates to the outward aspect.

10:11-13 Paul affirms the universal availability of salvation. **Everyone who believes** in Christ will not be disappointed. Believers **will not be put to shame** when they must give an account of themselves to God.

10:14-15 The apostle asks a series of rhetorical questions to show that calling upon the Lord for salvation does not take place apart from the proclamation of **the gospel**. He links five key actions: calling, believing, hearing, preaching, and sending.

10:16 Everybody who hears the good news, however, does not obey it. Paul was thinking of the Israelites in particular. He quotes Is 53:1 to show that this had happened throughout history. Isaiah implies that not many believed the message.

He wants to, and He hardens those
He wants to harden.
19 You will say to me, therefore,
"Why then does He still find fault?
For who can resist His will?" 20 But
who are you, a mere man, to talk
back to God? Will what is formed
say to the one who formed it, "Why
did you make me like this?" 21 Or
has the potter no right over the
clay, to make from the same lump
one piece of pottery for honor and
another for dishonor? 22 And what if
God, desiring to display His wrath
and to make His power known, endured with much patience objects of
wrath ready for destruction? 23 And
what if He did this to make known
the riches of His glory on objects of
mercy that He prepared beforehand
for glory— 24 on us, the ones He also
called, not only from the Jews but
also from the Gentiles? 25 As He also
says in Hosea:

I will call Not My People, My
People,
and she who is Unloved,
Beloved.[A]
26 **And it will be in the place**
where they were told,
you are not My people,
there they will be called sons
of the living God.[B]

27 But Isaiah cries out concerning
Israel:

Though the number
of Israel's sons
is like the sand of the sea,
only the remnant
will be saved;
28 **for the Lord will execute**
His sentence
completely and decisively
on the earth.[C,D]

29 And just as Isaiah predicted:

If the Lord of ·Hosts[E]
had not left us offspring,
we would have become
like Sodom,
and we would
have been made
like Gomorrah.[F]

Israel Has Responsibility for Her Rejection of Christ (9:30–10:21)

30 What should we say then?
Gentiles, who did not pursue righteousness, have obtained righteousness—namely the righteousness
that comes from faith. 31 But Israel,
pursuing the law for righteousness,
has not achieved the righteousness
of the law.[G] 32 Why is that? Because
they did not pursue it by faith, but as
if it were by works.[H] They stumbled
over the stumbling stone. 33 As it is
written:

Look! I am putting a stone
in ·Zion to stumble over
and a rock to trip over,
yet the one who believes
on Him
will not be put to shame.[I]

10 ·Brothers, my heart's desire
and prayer to God concerning
them[J] is for their salvation! 2 I can
testify about them that they have zeal
for God, but not according to knowledge. 3 Because they disregarded
the righteousness from God and attempted to establish their own righteousness, they have not submitted
themselves to God's righteousness.
4 For Christ is the end[K] of the law for
righteousness to everyone who believes. 5 For Moses writes about the
righteousness that is from the law:
The one who does these things will
live by them.[L] 6 But the righteousness that comes from faith speaks
like this: **Do not say in your heart,**
"Who will go up to heaven?"[M] that
is, to bring Christ down 7 or, **"Who**
will go down into the ·abyss?"[N]
that is, to bring Christ up from the
dead. 8 On the contrary, what does
it say? **The message is near you,**
in your mouth and in your heart.[O]
This is the message of faith that we
proclaim: 9 If you confess with your
mouth, "Jesus is Lord," and believe
in your heart that God raised Him
from the dead, you will be saved.
10 One believes with the heart, resulting in righteousness, and one confesses with the mouth, resulting in

[A]**9:25** Hs 2:23 [B]**9:26** Hs 1:10 [C]**9:28** Or *land* [D]**9:27-28** Is 10:22-23; 28:22; Hs 1:10 [E]**9:29** Gk *Sabaoth*; this word is a transliteration of the Hb word for *Hosts*, or *Armies*. [F]**9:29** Is 1:9 [G]**9:31** Other mss read *the law for righteousness* [H]**9:32** Other mss add *of the law* [I]**9:33** Is 8:14; 28:16 [J]**10:1** Other mss read *God for Israel* [K]**10:4** Or *goal* [L]**10:5** Lv 18:5 [M]**10:6** Dt 9:4; 30:12 [N]**10:7** Dt 30:13 [O]**10:8** Dt 30:14

salvation. 11 Now the Scripture says, **Everyone who believes on Him will not be put to shame,**[A] 12 for there is no distinction between Jew and Greek, since the same Lord of all is rich to all who call on Him. 13 For **everyone who calls on the name of the Lord will be saved.**[B]

14 But how can they call on Him they have not believed in? And how can they believe without hearing about Him? And how can they hear without a preacher? 15 And how can they preach unless they are sent? As it is written: **How beautiful**[C] **are the feet of those**[D] **who announce the gospel of good things!**[E] 16 But all did not obey the gospel. For Isaiah says, **Lord, who has believed our message?**[F] 17 So faith comes from what is heard, and what is heard comes through the message about Christ.[G] 18 But I ask, "Did they not hear?" Yes, they did:

Their voice has gone out
to all the earth,
and their words to the ends
of the inhabited world.[H]

19 But I ask, "Did Israel not understand?" First, Moses said:

I will make you jealous
of those who are not
a nation;
I will make you angry
by a nation
that lacks understanding.[I]

20 And Isaiah says boldly:

I was found
by those who were not
looking for Me;
I revealed Myself
to those who were not asking
for Me.[J]

21 But to Israel he says: **All day long I have spread out My hands to a disobedient and defiant people.**[K]

God Will Fulfill His Purposes for Israel (11:1-36)

11 I ask, then, has God rejected His people? Absolutely not! For I too am an Israelite, a descendant of Abraham, from the tribe of Benjamin. 2 God has not rejected His people whom He foreknew. Or don't you know what the Scripture says in the passage about Elijah—how he pleads with God against Israel?

3 **Lord, they have killed**
Your prophets
and torn down Your altars.
I am the only one left,
and they are trying to take
my life![L]

4 But what was God's reply to him? **I have left 7,000 men for Myself who have not bowed down to •Baal.**[M] 5 In the same way, then, there is also at the present time a remnant chosen by grace. 6 Now if by grace, then it is not by works; otherwise grace ceases to be grace.[N]

7 What then? Israel did not find what it was looking for, but the elect did find it. The rest were hardened, 8 as it is written:

God gave them a spirit
of insensitivity,[O]
eyes that cannot see
and ears that cannot hear,
to this day.[P]

9 And David says:

Let their feasting[Q] **become**
a snare and a trap,
a pitfall and a retribution
to them.
10 **Let their eyes be darkened**
so they cannot see,
and their backs be bent
continually.[R]

11 I ask, then, have they stumbled in order to fall? Absolutely not! On the contrary, by their stumbling,[S] salvation has come to the Gentiles to make Israel jealous. 12 Now if their stumbling[S] brings riches for the world, and their failure riches for the Gentiles, how much more will their full number bring!

13 Now I am speaking to you Gentiles. In view of the fact that I am an apostle to the Gentiles, I magnify

10:18 Paul responds to someone who might object that the Jews have not heard the gospel. He affirms that they had indeed heard the good news. He supports himself with the authority of Scripture (Ps 19:4). This verse speaks about the witness of God in creation.

10:19-21 Others might have objected that the Jews did not **understand** the gospel. Paul answers that objection with quotes from the Law (Dt 32:21) and the Prophets (Is 65:1).

11:1 God's purpose includes a remnant chosen by grace. God's rejection of Israel was not total. Paul gives himself as proof. He, too, was **an Israelite, a descendant of Abraham**, a member of **the tribe of Benjamin**, and a believer in Jesus Christ.

11:2-5 The apostle asserts that God's rejection of Israel was an impossibility. God has not rejected the people **whom He foreknew**. Paul gives an Old Testament example from the time of **Elijah**. The prophet felt isolated and alone as he witnessed the rejection of worship of the one true God. He felt he was **the only one** who remained faithful, and now others were seeking to kill him. God told Elijah, however, that 7,000 (a number representing perfection and completion) continued to worship Him faithfully. They had not submitted to **Baal** worship. God had preserved a faithful **remnant**. In the same way as in Elijah's day there remained a remnant of believing Jews. They proved that God had not abandoned His people or His purposes.

11:6 Only **grace** (i.e., unmerited favor) enables a person to be included in God's family and to have a right relationship with Him. If the remnant gains this relationship by grace, then the rest of the Jews must also see God's election as based on grace, not on any human effort.

11:7-10 The apostle sums up the consequences of Israel's choices. The Jews, though sincere, **did not find** the righteousness for which they were **looking** because they sought it in the wrong way, through works.

11:11-12 Despite this bleak picture of the Jews, Paul saw hope for his people. They had indeed **stumbled**. He emphatically insists, however, that they did not stumble so as to fall beyond recovery. God used their transgression for His greater purpose, to bring salvation to the Gentiles. The Gentile reception of God's blessings would make the Jews jealous and desirous of that same salvation.

11:13 Paul saw his Gentile mission as important in the purposes of God for the salvation of the Jews.

[A]**10:11** Is 28:16 [B]**10:13** Jl 2:32 [C]**10:15** Or *welcome*, or *timely* [D]**10:15** Other mss read *feet of those who announce the gospel of peace, of those* [E]**10:15** Is 52:7; Nah 1:15 [F]**10:16** Is 53:1 [G]**10:17** Other mss read *God* [H]**10:18** Ps 19:4 [I]**10:19** Dt 32:21 [J]**10:20** Is 65:1 [K]**10:21** Is 65:2 [L]**11:3** 1Kg 19:10,14 [M]**11:4** 1Kg 19:18 [N]**11:6** Other mss add *But if of works it is no longer grace; otherwise work is no longer work.* [O]**11:8** Lit *stupification* [P]**11:8** Dt 29:4; Is 29:10 [Q]**11:9** Lit *table* [R]**11:9-10** Ps 69:22-23 [S]**11:11,12** Or *transgression*

11:16-24 Paul warned the Gentile Christians not to fall into the trap of spiritual pride. He uses an allegory of **olive** trees.

11:25-32 Paul brings his discussion on the problem of Israel (chaps. 9–11) to a climactic conclusion. He refers to God's dealing with Israel as a **mystery** (Gk *mustērion*, "secret, something hidden"), something unknown previously but now revealed by God.

11:28-32 He identifies the Jews from two perspectives or relationships. **They are enemies** from the standpoint of **the gospel** because of their rejection of Jesus. God was hostile toward them. The **disobedience** of the Jews led to the conversion of the Gentiles. God worked through the Jews' faithlessness to carry out His purpose. From the standpoint of God's **election** or choice, the Jews **are loved** for the sake of the promises God made to Abraham. God's purpose does not change. He does not take back what He has given.

11:33-36 God deserves praise for His wisdom and ways. As Paul concludes his discussion on the difficult issue of Israel's unbelief, he bursts into praise of God.

12:1-2 These two verses mark the change in the letter from doctrinal instruction to practical application. Using the familiar generic address, **brothers**, he urged believers to respond with total commitment to God. The basis for Christian living centers in the mercies of God. Because of all that God has done for believers in Jesus Christ, they should willingly **present** themselves as a **sacrifice** to God. This sacrifice is **living** in contrast to the slain animals of the Jewish ritual and rises out of the new life in Christ, which is holy, dedicated to God and His will. Believers should not be **conformed** [Gk *suschēmatizesthe*, "shaped by, living after the pattern of"] **to this age** or world, which opposes God and lies under the control of Satan. On the other hand, believers should continually **be transformed** [Gk *metamorphousthe*, "changed in form"] **by the renewing** of their minds. This change is radical, working from the inside out. Believers do not think like unbelievers. They are continually renewed in their thinking by the Holy Spirit.

12:3 Paul wants believers to use their God-given gifts in humility, not thinking **more highly** of themselves than they ought. When believers recognize that their gifts come from God and can be used only in dependence upon Him, they cannot be arrogant but will have a proper opinion of themselves.

my ministry, 14 if I can somehow
make my own people[A] jealous and
save some of them. 15 For if their rejection brings reconciliation to the
world, what will their acceptance
mean but life from the dead? 16 Now
if the •firstfruits offered up are holy,
so is the whole batch. And if the root
is holy, so are the branches.

17 Now if some of the branches
were broken off, and you, though
a wild olive branch, were grafted
in among them and have come to
share in the rich root[B] of the cultivated olive tree, 18 do not brag that
you are better than those branches.
But if you do brag—you do not sustain the root, but the root sustains
you. 19 Then you will say, "Branches
were broken off so that I might be
grafted in." 20 True enough; they
were broken off by unbelief, but you
stand by faith. Do not be arrogant,
but be afraid. 21 For if God did not
spare the natural branches, He will
not spare you either. 22 Therefore,
consider God's kindness and severity: severity toward those who have
fallen but God's kindness toward
you—if you remain in His kindness. Otherwise you too will be cut
off. 23 And even they, if they do not
remain in unbelief, will be grafted
in, because God has the power to
graft them in again. 24 For if you
were cut off from your native wild
olive and against nature were grafted into a cultivated olive tree, how
much more will these—the natural
branches—be grafted into their own
olive tree?

25 So that you will not be conceited, •brothers, I do not want you to
be unaware of this •mystery: A partial hardening has come to Israel
until the full number of the Gentiles
has come in. 26 And in this way all[C]
Israel will be saved, as it is written:

The Liberator will come
from •Zion;
He will turn away
godlessness from Jacob.
27 **And this will be My covenant**
with them[D]
when I take away their sins.[E]

28 Regarding the gospel, they are
enemies for your advantage, but
regarding election, they are loved
because of the patriarchs, 29 since
God's gracious gifts and calling
are irrevocable.[F] 30 As you once disobeyed God, but now have received
mercy through their disobedience,
31 so they too have now disobeyed,
resulting in mercy to you, so that
they also now[G] may receive mercy.
32 For God has imprisoned all in
disobedience, so that He may have
mercy on all.

33 Oh, the depth of the riches
both of the wisdom
and the knowledge of God!
How unsearchable
His judgments
and untraceable His ways!
34 **For who has known the mind**
of the Lord?
Or who has been
His counselor?
35 **Or who has ever first given**
to Him,
and has to be repaid?[H]
36 For from Him and
through Him
and to Him are all things.
To Him be the glory
forever. •Amen.

Paul Offered Practical Instructions for Christian Living (12:1–15:13)

Believers Should Dedicate Themselves to God (12:1-2)

12 Therefore, •brothers, by the
mercies of God, I urge you to
present your bodies as a living sacrifice, holy and pleasing to God;
this is your spiritual worship.[I] 2 Do
not be conformed to this age, but
be transformed by the renewing of
your mind, so that you may discern
what is the good, pleasing, and perfect will of God.

Believers Should Exercise Their Spiritual Gifts in Humility (12:3-8)

3 For by the grace given to me,
I tell everyone among you not to
think of himself more highly than
he should think. Instead, think sensibly, as God has distributed a mea-

[A] **11:14** Lit *flesh* [B] **11:17** Other mss read *the root and the richness* [C] **11:26** Or *And then all* [D] **11:26-27** Is 59:20-21 [E] **11:27** Jr 31:31-34 [F] **11:29** Or *are not taken back* [G] **11:31** Other mss omit *now* [H] **11:34-35** Jb 41:11; Is 40:13; Jr 23:18 [I] **12:1** Or *your reasonable service*

sure of faith to each one. 4 Now as we have many parts in one body, and all the parts do not have the same function, 5 in the same way we who are many are one body in Christ and individually members of one another. 6 According to the grace given to us, we have different gifts:

If prophecy,
use it according to
the standard of one's[A] faith;
7 if service, in service;
if teaching, in teaching;
8 if exhorting, in exhortation;
giving, with generosity;
leading, with diligence;
showing mercy,
with cheerfulness.

Believers Should Cultivate Christian Virtues (12:9-21)

9 Love must be without hypocrisy. Detest evil; cling to what is good. 10 Show family affection to one another with brotherly love. Outdo one another in showing honor. 11 Do not lack diligence; be fervent in spirit; serve the Lord. 12 Rejoice in hope; be patient in affliction; be persistent in prayer. 13 Share with the •saints in their needs; pursue hospitality. 14 Bless those who persecute you; bless and do not curse. 15 Rejoice with those who rejoice; weep with those who weep. 16 Be in agreement with one another. Do not be proud; instead, associate with the humble. Do not be wise in your own estimation. 17 Do not repay anyone evil for evil. Try to do what is honorable in everyone's eyes. 18 If possible, on your part, live at peace with everyone. 19 Friends, do not avenge yourselves; instead, leave room for His[B] wrath. For it is written: **Vengeance belongs to Me; I will repay,**[C] says the Lord. 20 But

If your enemy is hungry,
feed him.
If he is thirsty, give him
something to drink.
For in so doing
you will be heaping
fiery coals on his head.[D]

21 Do not be conquered by evil, but conquer evil with good.

Believers Should Submit to Civil Authority (13:1-7)

13 Everyone must submit to the governing authorities, for there is no authority except from God, and those that exist are instituted by God. 2 So then, the one who resists the authority is opposing God's command, and those who oppose it will bring judgment on themselves. 3 For rulers are not a terror to good conduct, but to bad. Do you want to be unafraid of the authority? Do what is good, and you will have its approval. 4 For government is God's servant for your good. But if you do wrong, be afraid, because it does not carry the sword for no reason. For government is God's servant, an avenger that brings wrath on the one who does wrong. 5 Therefore, you must submit, not only because of wrath, but also because of your conscience. 6 And for this reason you pay taxes, since the authorities are God's public servants, continually attending to these tasks.[E] 7 Pay your obligations to everyone: taxes to those you owe taxes, tolls to those you owe tolls, respect to those you owe respect, and honor to those you owe honor.

Believers Should Remember the Supremacy of Love (13:8-10)

8 Do not owe anyone anything,[F] except to love one another, for the one who loves another has fulfilled the law. 9 The commandments:

Do not commit adultery;
do not murder;
do not steal;[G]
do not covet;[H]

and whatever other commandment—all are summed up by this: **Love your neighbor as yourself.**[I]

10 Love does no wrong to a neighbor. Love, therefore, is the fulfillment of the law.

Believers Should Recognize the Urgency of Christian Living (13:11-14)

11 Besides this, knowing the time,

12:4-8 Paul uses the human body as an analogy of the Christian community. Paul affirms that believers have **different gifts** given to them by God's **grace. Prophecy** involves proclamation of God's direct word, delivered in **faith** with dependence on God.

12:9 Without Hypocrisy (Gk *anhupokritos* where *an* ["not"] + *hupokritos*, translated "pretense, outward show") referred to an actor who would wear a mask to depict a mood or certain character. In the spiritual sense, it refers to someone who masks his true character by pretending to be something he is not.

13:1-2 Everyone, Christians and non-Christians alike, **must submit to the governing authorities.** Paul gives the reason for this: All human **authority** comes ultimately **from God.** The authority that governments possess is a delegated authority. Submission does not mean obedience in all things. Believers must obey God rather than man (Ac 5:29) if the orders of authorities directly conflict with God's commands. They must also be willing to accept the consequences of their decisions. To resist the authority of those ruling legitimately is to rebel against God's command. Those who oppose will suffer the consequences—the government's judgment or punishment. Believers must respect the state and its authority.

13:4 Paul identifies the government or its ruler as **God's servant.** These rulers may have an exalted view of themselves or their positions of power and authority, but they are in reality God's servants. They are ultimately responsible to God Himself for the lowliest of tasks. They serve His purposes. As God's servants, they enable their citizens to do good, to carry out God's will. Those who do wrong (probably referring to public acts of wrong) should continually fear because civil rulers have the authority to enforce punishment—they **carry the sword.** They serve as instruments of God's wrath to punish wrongdoing and restrain evil.

13:6-7 The government cannot function without financial undergirding. Although individual rulers may be unworthy, God has ordained the institution of government and placed these individuals in power. Christians should treat them with the dignity due them.

13:11-14 Paul presents an eschatological motivation for his exhortations on how Christians should conduct themselves, especially loving others—they know the **time.** As

[A]12:6 Or *the thing* [B]12:19 Lit *the* [C]12:19 Dt 32:35 [D]12:20 Pr 25:21-22 [E]13:6 Lit *to this very thing* [F]13:8 Or *Leave no debt outstanding to anyone* [G]13:9 Other mss add *you shall not bear false witness* [H]13:9 Ex 20:13-17; Dt 5:17-21 [I]13:9 Lv 19:18

people who belong to Christ and **the daylight**, believers are to live their lives with proper behavior. The sins Paul identifies stem from focus on self and its desires: abuse of alcohol; sexual misconduct; attitudes of self-will.

14:1-2 Paul writes to deal with the relationship between strong and **weak** Christians. The latter are not necessarily believers who are morally lax and easily susceptible to temptation, but they have a weakness in applying faith to the daily decisions of life.

14:4 Paul uses a household servant-master analogy. No one would think of criticizing someone else's **slave**. Such a servant stands accountable to his master only. It does not matter what others think, only what the master thinks. In the same way both strong and weak believers are accountable to the Lord alone.

14:13 Paul urged the strong to set examples that do not lead to sin on the part of their weaker brothers and sisters. They should consider the effect their actions have on others.

14:14 Paul agrees with the convictions of the believers considered "strong." He affirms that **nothing is unclean in itself**. Yet, he recognizes that to those who consider something unclean, to them **it is unclean**. Until they change their views on certain foods, they will violate their consciences to eat them.

15:1-3 Paul speaks directly to the **strong** and includes himself among them. The strong **have an obligation to bear the weaknesses of those without strength**. They will not act selfishly to please themselves but will work for the unity of the Christian community even if that entails partially giving up their freedom in Christ. The actions of believers must contribute to the spiritual growth of others. They must seek the good of others, not their own good. Christ is the example to follow; His commitment to do God's will and serve others brought Him suffering. As a consequence of His obedience, Jesus became the recipient of the insults of the people (Ps 69:9).

15:5-7 The apostle prayed that God would bring unity to the Roman church with its strong-weak conflicts. This unity would center in Jesus Christ, following His example. He exhorted believers—strong and weak—to accept each other (Rm 14:1) and based his exhortation on the fact that Christ has accepted them.

15:15-16 Paul confesses that he had written **boldly on some points** for the purpose of reminding these believers of truths already known or with which

it is already the hour for you[A] to wake up from sleep, for now our salvation is nearer than when we first believed. 12 The night is nearly over, and the daylight is near, so let us discard the deeds of darkness and put on the armor of light. 13 Let us •walk with decency, as in the daylight: not in carousing and drunkenness; not in sexual impurity and promiscuity; not in quarreling and jealousy. 14 But put on the Lord Jesus Christ, and make no plans to satisfy the fleshly desires.

Believers Should Seek to Build Up One Another (14:1–15:13)

14 Accept anyone who is weak in faith,[B] but don't argue about doubtful issues. 2 One person believes he may eat anything, but one who is weak eats only vegetables. 3 One who eats must not look down on one who does not eat, and one who does not eat must not criticize one who does, because God has accepted him. 4 Who are you to criticize another's household slave? Before his own Lord he stands or falls. And he will stand. For the Lord is able[C] to make him stand.

5 One person considers one day to be above another day. Someone else considers every day to be the same. Each one must be fully convinced in his own mind. 6 Whoever observes the day, observes it for the honor of the Lord.[D] Whoever eats, eats for the Lord, since he gives thanks to God; and whoever does not eat, it is for the Lord that he does not eat it, yet he thanks God. 7 For none of us lives to himself, and no one dies to himself. 8 If we live, we live for the Lord; and if we die, we die for the Lord. Therefore, whether we live or die, we belong to the Lord. 9 Christ died and came to life for this: that He might rule over both the dead and the living. 10 But you, why do you criticize your brother? Or you, why do you look down on your brother? For we will all stand before the tribunal of God.[E] 11 For it is written:

> **As I live, says the Lord,**
> **every knee will bow to Me,**
> **and every tongue will give**
> **praise to God.**[F]

12 So then, each of us will give an account of himself to God.

13 Therefore, let us no longer criticize one another. Instead decide never to put a stumbling block or pitfall in your brother's way. 14 (I know and am persuaded by the Lord Jesus that nothing is •unclean in itself. Still, to someone who considers a thing to be unclean, to that one it is unclean.) 15 For if your brother is hurt by what you eat, you are no longer •walking according to love. Do not destroy that one Christ died for by what you eat. 16 Therefore, do not let your good be slandered, 17 for the kingdom of God is not eating and drinking, but righteousness, peace, and joy in the Holy Spirit. 18 Whoever serves Christ in this way is acceptable to God and approved by men.

19 So then, we must pursue what promotes peace and what builds up one another. 20 Do not tear down God's work because of food. Everything is •clean, but it is wrong for a man to cause stumbling by what he eats. 21 It is a noble thing not to eat meat, or drink wine, or do anything that makes your brother stumble.[G] 22 Do you have a conviction?[H] Keep it to yourself before God. The man who does not condemn himself by what he approves is blessed. 23 But whoever doubts stands condemned if he eats, because his eating is not from a conviction,[I] and everything that is not from a conviction[I] is sin.

15 Now we who are strong have an obligation to bear the weaknesses of those without strength, and not to please ourselves. 2 Each one of us must please his neighbor for his good, to build him up. 3 For even the •Messiah did not please Himself. On the contrary, as it is written, **The insults of those who insult You have fallen on Me.**[J] 4 For whatever was written in the past was written for our instruction, so that we may have hope through endur-

[A]**13:11** Other mss read *for us* [B]**14:1** Or *weak in the Faith* [C]**14:4** Other mss read *For God has the power* [D]**14:6** Other mss add *but whoever does not observe the day, it is to the Lord that he does not observe it* [E]**14:10** Other mss read *of Christ* [F]**14:11** Is 45:23; 49:18 [G]**14:21** Other mss add *or offended or weakened* [H]**14:22** Lit *have faith* [I]**14:23** Or *faith* [J]**15:3** Ps 69:9

ance and through the encouragement from the Scriptures. 5 Now may the God who gives[A] endurance and encouragement allow you to live in harmony with one another, according to the command of Christ Jesus, 6 so that you may glorify the God and Father of our Lord Jesus Christ with a united mind and voice.

7 Therefore accept one another, just as the Messiah also accepted you, to the glory of God. 8 For I say that the Messiah became a servant of the circumcised[B] on behalf of God's truth, to confirm the promises to the fathers, 9 and so that Gentiles may glorify God for His mercy. As it is written:

Therefore I will praise You
among the Gentiles,
and I will sing psalms
to Your name.[C]

10 Again it says: **Rejoice, you Gentiles, with His people!**[D] 11 And again:

Praise the Lord, all
you Gentiles;
all the peoples should praise
Him![E]

12 And again, Isaiah says:

The root of Jesse will appear,
the One who rises to rule
the Gentiles;
the Gentiles will hope
in Him.[F]

13 Now may the God of hope fill you with all joy and peace as you believe in Him so that you may overflow with hope by the power of the Holy Spirit.

Paul Concluded His Letter to the Romans (15:14–16:27)

Paul Gave His Reasons for Writing (15:14-33)

14 My •brothers, I myself am convinced about you that you also are full of goodness, filled with all knowledge, and able to instruct one another. 15 Nevertheless, I have written to remind you more boldly on some points[G] because of the grace given me by God 16 to be a minister of Christ Jesus to the Gentiles, serving as a priest of God's good news. My purpose is that the offering of the Gentiles may be acceptable, •sanctified by the Holy Spirit. 17 Therefore I have reason to boast in Christ Jesus regarding what pertains to God. 18 For I would not dare say anything except what Christ has accomplished through me to make the Gentiles obedient by word and deed, 19 by the power of miraculous signs and wonders, and by the power of God's Spirit. As a result, I have fully proclaimed the good news about the Messiah from Jerusalem all the way around to Illyricum.[H] 20 My aim is to evangelize where Christ has not been named, so that I will not build on someone else's foundation, 21 but, as it is written:

Those who were not told
about Him will see,
and those who have not
heard will understand.[I]

22 That is why I have been prevented many times from coming to you. 23 But now I no longer have any work to do in these provinces,[J] and I have strongly desired for many years to come to you 24 whenever I travel to Spain.[K] For I hope to see you when I pass through, and to be assisted by you for my journey there, once I have first enjoyed your company for a while. 25 Right now I am traveling to Jerusalem to serve the •saints, 26 for Macedonia and Achaia[L] were pleased to make a contribution for the poor among the saints in Jerusalem. 27 Yes, they were pleased, and indeed are indebted to them. For if the Gentiles have shared in their spiritual benefits, then they are obligated to minister to Jews in material needs. 28 So when I have finished this and safely delivered the funds[M] to them, I will visit you on the way to Spain. 29 I know that when I come to you, I will come in the fullness of the blessing[N] of Christ.

30 Now I appeal to you, brothers, through our Lord Jesus Christ and through the love of the Spirit, to

they were confronted for the first time. Paul wrote because of God's commissioning of him as the apostle to the Gentiles (the grace given to him). He took this calling very seriously. This call included being a **minister** of Christ Jesus to the Gentiles, **serving as a priest of God's good news**. As a priest, he proclaimed the gospel. The purpose of Paul's priestly service was to present **the Gentiles** as an **offering** to God, **acceptable** and **sanctified by the Holy Spirit**.

15:17-18 Paul's mission to the Gentiles had proved successful. Yet, he did not boast in his own accomplishment but in Christ Jesus who enabled and strengthened him for this ministry. He was simply God's instrument.

15:19 The apostle's ministry had been confirmed by **miraculous signs and wonders** and enabled by the power of the Holy Spirit. He notes the extent of his proclamation in geographical terms, **from Jerusalem . . . to Illyricum**, a Roman province northwest of Macedonia on the eastern shore of the Adriatic Sea (modern Yugoslavia and Albania).

15:20-21 Paul's great ambition was to proclaim the gospel where Christ had not yet been named. He did not want to build on the **foundation** of another. Paul was not referring to competition in ministry. He usually worked with associates. He desired to see as many people as possible come to faith in Jesus Christ. Pioneer missionary labor meant going where no one else had yet gone to unreached people to plant new churches (Is 52:15).

15:22-24 Paul shared his plans to visit **Spain**. He explained that he had been prevented many times from coming to Rome because of his pressing commitment to preach to those who had not heard the gospel in the east. He had followed the Spirit's leading. Now he felt he was ready to expand his focus.

15:25-29 Presently Paul was on his way to **Jerusalem** with the relief offering the Gentile churches in **Macedonia and Achaia** had collected to help the poverty-stricken Christians in the mother church at Jerusalem. The apostle had focused on this offering during his third missionary journey. He felt this trip to be so important that he delayed his longed-for trip to Rome. He saw the relief offering as an expression of love by the Gentile believers for Jewish Christians. He hoped this effort would bring unity and fellowship between the two groups, who often disputed with each other, and would validate his Gentile mission.

[A]**15:5** Lit *God of* [B]**15:8** The Jews [C]**15:9** 2Sm 22:50; Ps 18:49 [D]**15:10** Dt 32:43 [E]**15:11** Ps 117:1 [F]**15:12** Is 11:10 [G]**15:15** Other mss add *brothers* [H]**15:19** A Roman province northwest of Greece on the eastern shore of the Adriatic Sea [I]**15:21** Is 52:15 [J]**15:23** Lit *now, having no longer a place in these parts* [K]**15:24** Other mss add *I will come to you.* [L]**15:26** The churches of these provinces [M]**15:28** Lit *delivered this fruit* [N]**15:29** Other mss add *of the gospel*

15:30-33 The apostle requested prayer from the Romans because he knew difficulties faced him in **Jerusalem** from hostile Jews and even legalistic Jewish Christians who had doubts about his work among the Gentiles. He had already had to leave that city previously because of Jewish hostility so Paul urged them to **join** together with him in prayer to God on his behalf.

16:1-16 Paul greets 26 people by name and mentions two more without using a name as well as noting several households. With the great amount of travel in the first century due to Roman peace and well-kept roads, Paul could well have known many people already in a church he had not visited. Also, since he had not yet been to Rome, the apostle was anxious to establish the fact that they already had many relationships in common. The names are a mix of Greek, Latin, and Jewish. They indicate people from all strata of society, slaves and freedmen, singles and married, men and women, Jew and Gentile. They reflect the universal extension of the gospel. The repeated words **in Christ** or **in the Lord** throughout the list of names points to the commitment of all those named to the gospel of Jesus Christ. Of the people mentioned, Paul identifies 10 women, which was truly amazing in the male-dominated culture of that time. The acceptance and importance of women and their roles in the church is clear. They all gave valuable service to the Lord and to kingdom causes.

16:1-7 Many people traveled in the first-century Roman Empire. They often carried letters of recommendation from those who had friends in the city of their destination. Paul's lengthy commendation of **Phoebe** likely indicates that she carried his letter to the Romans and delivered it to the church in the capital city. She was a believing sister, a fellow Christian, and a servant of the church at **Cenchreae**. The Greek word for **servant** (*diakonon*, "helper") definitely has the connotation of one who serves or ministers to another. It has been transliterated into English as "deacon" or "deaconess." Were women also assigned official responsibilities in such service ministries? One cannot say with any certainty. In fact, this reference to Phoebe is the only one that could be understood in that way. If understood in the New Testament sense, a deacon or deaconess certainly needs no title to find ample opportunity for service. On the other hand, if being a deacon or deaconess is viewed as official spiritual leadership and if it is considered a position of authority over the congregation, as has evolved in many modern churches, other passages penned by the apostle Paul clearly provide additional guidelines (see 1Tm

join with me in fervent prayers to
God on my behalf. 31 Pray that I may
be rescued from the unbelievers in
Judea, that the gift I am bringing
to[A] Jerusalem may be acceptable to
the saints, 32 and that, by God's will,
I may come to you with joy and be
refreshed together with you.
33 The God of peace be with all of
you. •Amen.

Paul Commended Phoebe (16:1-2)

16 I commend to you our sister
Phoebe, who is a servant[B] of the
church in Cenchreae. 2 So you should
welcome her in the Lord in a manner
worthy of the •saints and assist her
in whatever matter she may require
your help. For indeed she has been a
benefactor of many—and of me also.

Paul Greeted Friends in Rome (16:3-16)

3 Give my greetings to Prisca[C]
and Aquila, my coworkers in
Christ Jesus, 4 who risked their
own necks for my life. Not
only do I thank them, but so
do all the Gentile churches.
5 Greet also the church that
meets in their home.
Greet my dear friend
Epaenetus, who is the first
convert[D] to Christ from •Asia.[E]
6 Greet Mary,[F] who has worked
very hard for you.[G]
7 Greet Andronicus and
Junia,[H] my fellow countrymen
and fellow prisoners. They are
noteworthy in the eyes of the
apostles,[I,J] and they were also

[A]15:31 Lit *that my service for* [B]16:1 Others interpret this term in a technical sense: *deacon*, or *deaconess*, or *minister*, or *courier* [C]16:3 Traditionally, *Priscilla*, as in Ac 18:2,18,26 [D]16:5 Lit *the firstfruits* [E]16:5 Other mss read *Achaia* [F]16:6 Or *Maria* [G]16:6 Other mss read *us* [H]16:7 Either a feminine name or "Junias," a masculine name [I]16:7 Or *are outstanding among* [J]16:7 "The apostles" is not always a technical term referring to the 12; cp. 2Co 8:23; Php 2:25 where this word is translated as "messenger."

CHARACTER PROFILE

Phoebe A Servant

Her Background	• She lived in Cenchreae, a port city near Corinth (16:1-2). • She was a believer, a servant of the church. • She was a woman of status and influence.
Her Story	• She was traveling to Rome, possibly on a business trip. • She was commended by Paul for her character and the importance of her work. • She could have been the carrier of this letter.
Life Lesson	Phoebe's character, service, and quality of her work gained the respect of Paul and the early church.

CHARACTER PROFILE

Junia Co-worker in the Faith

Her Background	• This name could be an abbreviated version of the male name "Junianus," but it was also a female name. • The pairing of Junia with Adronicus suggests that they were a married couple (16:7).
Her Story	• She and Andronicus were converted before Paul. • They were in prison with him at some point and were diligent and respected coworkers in the faith.
Life Lesson	Again Paul's recognition and appreciation for faithfulness and commitment in the spreading of the gospel is apparent.

in Christ before me.
[8] Greet Ampliatus, my dear friend in the Lord.
[9] Greet Urbanus, our coworker in Christ, and my dear friend Stachys.
[10] Greet Apelles, who is approved in Christ.
Greet those who belong to the household of Aristobulus.
[11] Greet Herodion, my fellow countryman.
Greet those who belong to the household of Narcissus who are in the Lord.

2:11-15; 3:8-13). The word certainly indicates that Phoebe had a servant's heart and that she used her energies to serve within her church family in some capacity.

Phoebe was also a **benefactor** (Gk *prostatis*, "helper," lit "one standing before") for many. Lexicons define the term as "protectress, patroness, helper." The use of this word probably

Women Mentioned by Paul in Romans

Name	Reference	Comments in the Text	Application
Phoebe (Gk, "pure, radiant")	Rm 16:1-2	Probably a woman of wealth and influence and perhaps functioning in the world of commerce or government Described by Paul as: • A **sister** (Gk *adelphēn*) • **A servant** (Gk *diakonov*, transliterated into English as *deacon*) • One of **the saints** (Gk *hagiōn*, "set apart, holy, morally pure," often a reference to one who belongs to and is wholly devoted to God) • **A benefactor** (Gk *prostatis*, "helper, friend")	Even wealth, position, and influence do not relieve a woman of the responsibility of humble service.
Prisca or Priscilla (Lat, "dutiful")	Rm 16:3; Ac 18:18, 26; 1Co 16:19; 2Tm 4:19	• Described by Paul, together with her husband Aquila, as his **coworkers** (Gk *sunergous*, lit "work with") • Noted for dedication to risk their lives for the gospel • Highly esteemed by the churches • Host with her husband for church in their home	Work for Christ is woven into the warp and woof of life—in the tasks of home and marketplace.
Mary (Hb, "bitter")	Rm 16:6	Described by Paul as one **who has worked very hard**	Hard work, difficulties, and obstacles, are part of the kingdom task.
Junia (Gk feminine form). See note on 16:7.	Rm 16:7	Paul describes Andronicus and Junia together as: • **fellow countrymen,** • **fellow prisoners,** • outstanding among the apostles, • followers of Christ before Paul's conversion.	Whether male or female, God honors your work in His name.
Tryphaena (Gk, "dainty"), **Tryphosa** (Gk, "delicate")	Rm 16:12	Described by Paul as women **who have worked hard in the Lord**	Although their names could indicate frailty or physical weakness, they worked hard.
Persis	Rm 16:12	Described by Paul as: • **my dear friend** • one **who has worked very hard in the Lord**	Working hard together builds and sustains friendships.
Unnamed **mother** of **Rufus**	Rm 16:13	Described by Paul as like a mother to him	Maternal nurturing is a precious ministry to the saints.
Unnamed **sister** of **Nereus**	Rm 16:15	Worthy of greetings from Paul	Gratitude for your service for Christ is not dependent on whether or not your name is remembered or mentioned.

indicated that Phoebe was a woman of some wealth and position. She may have been a businesswoman. In any case, she was an important person. In fact, a woman would not be likely to be traveling alone in the first century. Phoebe may have been accompanied by servants from her household. Paul stated that Phoebe had helped many people, including him. He did not identify the nature of that help. Perhaps like Lydia of Philippi, Phoebe shared her material resources with those in need.

Prisca and **Aquila** were a ministry team of wife and husband. They had worked with the apostle at Corinth and at Ephesus. Paul identified them as his **coworkers** and thanked them for risking their lives for him. He also sent greetings to the church that met in their home. House churches were common among the early Christians. Few other meeting places, apart from private homes, were available to those fledging congregations (see **Biblical Womanhood**, p. 1435; **Character Profile**, p. 1436; note on Ac 18).

Andronicus and **Junia** (16:7) could have been another husband-wife ministry team. However, there is considerable debate and no consensus among evangelical scholarship as to whether Junia is male or female (the masculine form differs only slightly from the feminine). In any case, they were among the earliest believers since they came to Christ before Paul was converted. As Paul's **fellow countrymen**, they were probably Jews. Like Paul, they, too, had suffered imprisonment for the sake of the gospel. Paul describes them as **noteworthy in the eyes of the apostles** (Gk *episēmoi* ["illustrious"] *en* ["in, with, among"] *tois apostolois*). Again the text lacks clarity on the nature of apostleship as used here. "Apostle" (Gk *apostolois*, "messenger") in its most basic meaning is "one sent." The term often refers to the 12 disciples who were called and sent by Jesus. The only other instance of the word's use in this way includes Matthias, who succeeded Judas (Ac 1:26), and Paul himself (Ac 14:14). Here the word seems more logically used in its broader sense as designating those commissioned and sent out by the Lord to spread the gospel, as was Barnabas (Ac 14:14). In any case, Paul respected Junia, whether woman or man, and recognized this dedicated believer as having made a unique contribution to Christian ministry. There is no contradiction or confusion regardless of whether Junia is male or female.

16:17-18 Paul abruptly interrupts his greetings to give a strong warning

[12] Greet Tryphaena and
Tryphosa, who have worked
hard in the Lord.
Greet my dear friend Persis,
who has worked very hard in
the Lord.
[13] Greet Rufus, chosen in the
Lord; also his mother—and
mine.
[14] Greet Asyncritus, Phlegon,
Hermes, Patrobas, Hermas,
and the •brothers who are
with them.
[15] Greet Philologus and Julia,
Nereus and his sister, and
Olympas, and all the saints
who are with them.
[16] Greet one another with a
holy kiss.
All the churches of Christ
send you greetings.

Paul Warned Against False Teachers (16:17-20)

[17] Now I urge you, brothers, to
watch out for those who cause dissensions and obstacles contrary to
the doctrine you have learned. Avoid
them, [18] for such people do not serve
our Lord Christ but their own appetites.[A] They deceive the hearts of the
unsuspecting with smooth talk and
flattering words.
[19] The report of your obedience
has reached everyone. Therefore I
rejoice over you. But I want you to
be wise about what is good, yet innocent about what is evil. [20] The God
of peace will soon crush Satan under your feet. The grace of our Lord
Jesus be with you.

Paul's Associates Greeted the Romans (16:21-24)

[21] Timothy, my coworker, and Lucius, Jason, and Sosipater, my fellow
countrymen, greet you.
[22] I Tertius, who wrote this letter,
greet you in the Lord.[B]
[23] Gaius, who is host to me and
to the whole church, greets you.
Erastus, the city treasurer, and our
brother Quartus greet you.
[[24] The grace of our Lord Jesus
Christ be with you all.][C]

Paul Offered Glory to God (16:25-27)

[25] Now to Him who has power to
strengthen you according to my
gospel and the proclamation about
Jesus Christ, according to the revelation of the •mystery kept silent
for long ages [26] but now revealed and
made known through the prophetic
Scriptures, according to the command of the eternal God to advance
the obedience of faith[D] among all
nations— [27] to the only wise God,
through Jesus Christ—to Him be
the glory forever![E] •Amen.

[A] **16:18** Lit *belly* [B] **16:22** Or *letter in the Lord, greet you* [C] **16:24** Other mss omit bracketed text; cp. v. 20 [D] **16:26** Or *the obedience that is faith*, or *the faithful obedience*, or *the obedience that comes from faith*; Rm 1:5 [E] **16:25-27** Other mss have these vv. at the end of chap. 14 or 15.

Paul systematically presented the gospel message in this theologically rich letter. Praise God that though all have sinned and deserve death, through Christ, anyone can have a right relationship with God. While we were yet sinners and enemies of God, Christ died for us so we could be reconciled to Him. Anyone who confesses that Jesus is Lord and believes in her heart that God raised Him from the dead will be saved.

Paul's second missionary journey brought him to Macedonia and then to Corinth where he planted a church and stayed for eighteen months. It was from Corinth (A.D. 57) that Paul wrote the letter to Rome and dispatched it via Phoebe, a believer from Cenchreae, the eastern port city of Corinth (Rm 16:1).

about false teachers. The Romans were to **watch out** for these people, implying that they had not yet infiltrated the church, but the possibility that they might remained. Although Paul does not identify the nature of their error, these heretics did cause dissension and put up stumbling blocks contrary to the Christian teaching the Roman believers had already learned. Those whose instruction differed from the sound doctrine they knew should be avoided. Paul urges believers to keep away from such persons, not giving them any opportunity to deceive the Christians.

16:20 Despite any evil the believers would encounter, Paul confidently predicts that the God of peace (not dissension) will **crush Satan**, the initiator of evil, who seeks to sow discord among believers. God does the crushing, but Satan ends up under the feet of the Christians. They will have the victory. **The grace of our Lord Jesus be with you** is Paul's customary closing benediction.

16:21-24 The apostle's friends and associates who were with him in Corinth also sent their greetings to the Roman believers. Those sending greetings included **Tertius**, Paul's amanuensis (secretary), who wrote the letter for him.

16:25-27 The apostle ends his letter with a doxology of praise to God, which in essence summarizes the teachings of the epistle. God is able to strengthen the Roman Christians and do for them whatever they need. This empowering is according to the gospel Paul had preached and had made his own, the proclamation he faithfully delivered about Jesus Christ. The gospel had been a mystery for ages; but with the coming of Jesus Christ, God has revealed it. The gospel shows that Jesus explained and fulfilled the Old Testament Scriptures in every way according to the eternal God's commandment. This revelation is for the purpose of leading all nations to believe and obey the gospel.

1 Corinthians

Timeline World Events Biblical Events	**1000 BC** Founding of Corinth by Dorian Greeks	**550 BC** Construction of the temple of Apollo	**44 BC** Rebuilding of Corinth, by Julius Caesar, as a colony of Rome	**AD 47–49** Paul's first missionary journey

"No one should seek his own good, but the good of the other person" (10:24).

Who wrote 1 Corinthians?

Paul—the book not only is marked by his style but also bears his signature at beginning and end (1Co 1:1; 16:21).

Who were the recipients?

Paul addressed the believers in the Corinthian church, which was established about A.D. 50 during Paul's 18-month residence there in the midst of his second missionary journey (Ac 18:1-17).

When was 1 Corinthians written?

Paul probably wrote 1 Corinthians near the end of his stay in Ephesus (1Co 16:8; Ac 20:31) and before his departure for Macedonia (1Co 16:5; Ac 20:1) about A.D. 54.

Where did it happen?

Corinth was a thriving Roman colony, which, because of viable trade business, hosted a transient population and mirrored ethnic, cultural, and economic diversity.

What is 1 Corinthians about?

Doctrinal and Lifestyle Issues. With a compassionate firmness, Paul dealt with tough issues, including doctrinal errors and confusion about church order, sensualism and immorality, disunity and pride, and the abuse of Christian liberty and gifts. Consider the specific issues addressed in this book:

- Sexual immorality (5:1; 6:15),
- Struggles for power and leadership (1:1-17),
- Denial of the resurrection of the body (15:12),
- Testimony in the workplace and community (8:10; 10:25),
- Taking fellow believers to court (6:1),
- The role of women in public worship (11:2-6; 14:34),
- Confusion about the Lord's Supper (11:21),
- Misunderstanding of spiritual gifts (12:1–14:40),
- Understanding love (13:1-13), and
- Charitable offerings and gifts (16:1-4).

Why should women read 1 Corinthians?

On Paul's second missionary journey, he came to Corinth and built a strong friendship with fellow tentmakers, a Jewish couple named Aquila and Priscilla. Paul remained in Corinth about a year and a half, evangelizing and preaching in the Jewish synagogues. While God worked in mighty ways, the church struggled for purity and maturity. Paul wrote to the Corinthians, diligently teaching doctrine and carefully explaining Christian behavior. Heated questions were addressed. Of particular interest are a number of passages specifically affecting women.

How do you read 1 Corinthians?

First Corinthians is a personal letter from the Apostle Paul to the church in Corinth and follows a typical format for Greco-Roman letters of the time. However, unlike the letter to the Romans, 1 Corinthians is not a carefully crafted doctrinal treatise; rather, Paul responded personally and directly to a variety of troubling issues that had developed within the Corinthian church.

Outline

I. Paul's Greeting (1:1-9)

II. Facing the Issue of Disunity (1:10–3:23)
- A. Maturity Versus Immaturity (1:10–3:4)
- B. A Foundation in Christ (3:5-23)

III. Examining Christian Conduct (4:1–6:20)
- A. Managers of the Mysteries of God (4:1-5)
- B. Humility (4:6-13)
- C. Church Discipline (4:14–5:13)
- D. Lawsuits (6:1-11)
- E. Christian Liberty (6:12-20)

IV. Addressing Questions of the Church (7:1–10:33)
- A. Perspectives on Singleness and Marriage (7:1-40)
- B. Considerations for Dealing with Food Offered to Idols (8:1-13)
- C. A Defense of Apostleship (9:1-27)
- D. Warnings from Israel's Past (10:1-22)
- E. The Abuse of Christian Liberty (10:23-33)

V. Outlining Conduct in the Church (11:1–14:40)
- A. Head Coverings and Women (11:1-16)
- B. Self-Control and the Lord's Supper (11:17-34)
- C. Spiritual Gifts and the Body of Christ (12:1-31)
- D. Loving Others and Spiritual Maturity (13:1–14:40)

VI. Teachings About the Resurrection (15:1-58)

VII. Concluding Personal Reminders (16:1-24)
- A. The Gift for the Church in Jerusalem (16:1-4)
- B. Plans for Paul's Travel (16:5-12)
- C. A Final Exhortation from Paul (16:13-24)

AD 49	AD 49–52	AD 50–51	AD 54	AD 54
Expulsion of many Jews from Rome by the Emperor Claudius	Paul's second missionary journey	Paul's 18-month stay in Corinth while planting the church there	Writing of 1 Corinthians	Writing of 2 Corinthians

Paul's Greeting (1:1-9)

1 Paul, called as an apostle of Christ Jesus by God's will, and Sosthenes our brother:

2 To God's church at Corinth, to those who are •sanctified in Christ Jesus and called as •saints, with all those in every place who call on the name of Jesus Christ our Lord—both their Lord and ours.

3 Grace to you and peace from God our Father and the Lord Jesus Christ.

4 I always thank my God for you because of God's grace given to you in Christ Jesus, 5 that by Him you were enriched in everything—in all speech and all knowledge. 6 In this way, the testimony about Christ was confirmed among you, 7 so that you do not lack any spiritual gift as you eagerly wait for the revelation of our Lord Jesus Christ. 8 He will also strengthen you to the end, so that you will be blameless in the day of our Lord Jesus Christ. 9 God is faithful; you were called by Him into fellowship with His Son, Jesus Christ our Lord.

Facing the Issue of Disunity (1:10–3:23)

Divisions at Corinth (1:10-17)

10 Now I urge you, •brothers, in the name of our Lord Jesus Christ, that all of you agree in what you say, that there be no divisions among you, and that you be united with the same understanding and the same conviction. 11 For it has been reported to me about you, my brothers, by members of Chloe's household, that there is rivalry among you. 12 What I am saying is this: Each of you says, "I'm with Paul," or "I'm with Apollos," or "I'm with •Cephas," or "I'm with Christ." 13 Is Christ divided? Was it Paul who was crucified for you? Or were you baptized in Paul's name? 14 I thank God[A,B] that I baptized none of you except Crispus and Gaius, 15 so that no one can say you were baptized in my name. 16 I did, in fact, baptize the household of Stephanas; beyond that, I don't know if I baptized anyone else. 17 For Christ did not send me to baptize, but to evangelize—not with clever words, so that the cross of Christ will not be emptied of its effect.

Christ—the Power and Wisdom of God (1:18-25)

18 For the message of the cross is foolishness to those who are perishing, but it is God's power to us who are being saved. 19 For it is written:

I will destroy the wisdom
of the wise,
and I will set aside
the understanding
of the experts.[C]

20 Where is the philosopher?[D] Where is the scholar? Where is the debater of this age? Hasn't God made the world's wisdom foolish? 21 For since, in God's wisdom, the •world did not know God through wisdom, God was pleased to save those who believe through the foolishness of the message preached. 22 For the Jews ask for signs and the Greeks seek wisdom, 23 but we preach Christ crucified, a stumbling block to the Jews and foolishness to the Gentiles.[E] 24 Yet to those who are called, both Jews and Greeks, Christ is God's power and God's wisdom, 25 because God's foolishness is wiser than human wisdom, and God's weakness is stronger than human strength.

A **1:14** Other mss omit *God* B **1:14** Or *I am thankful* C **1:19** Is 29:14 D **1:20** Or *wise* E **1:23** Other mss read *Greeks*

Title The Greek title of the letter is *pros Korinthiogē A*, "to the Corinthians A," derived from the letter's immediate recipients.

1:1 Paul identifies himself as the author, **an apostle** commissioned by God; he often did this in his letters when his apostolic authority was being attacked.

1:2 As the political capital of Greece, **Corinth** was a seat of commerce and intellectual life with a reputation for luxury, sexual immorality, and even sacred prostitution. Its acropolis, the Acrocorinth, was used for defense and for pagan worship. On the Acrocorinth was located the temple to Aphrodite, which enticed many locals and foreigners.

1:4 Paul reminds his spiritual children of his loving concern. He expresses appreciation for them and reminds them of God's faithfulness to set a context for the chastisement he would give concerning their un-Christlike behavior.

1:10-16 Paul was concerned about the **divisions** the church was experiencing. **Rivalry** is a serious threat to unity in the church, and the word suggests a sharp challenge and contentious spirit. This letter is in response to a report Paul received from members of **Chloe's household** regarding the divisions in the church (1:10–4:21) and sexual immorality among the members (5:1–6:20).

Members of the church were taking sides and trying to associate themselves with cliques centered around **Paul**, **Apollos**, **Cephas** (Peter), and **Christ**—claiming for each leader superior wisdom over the others.

1:17-25 Paul emphasized the **power** of **the cross** to those who believe. Like the Corinthians, the people whom God addressed through the prophet Isaiah fell short in moral and ethical living (Is 29:14). In both Isaiah and 1 Corinthians, readers are reminded that even the wisest men fail in comparison to **God's wisdom** and perfection.

1:26-31 Your **calling** (Gk *klēsin*, "invitation, position, vocation") is the call from the Lord Himself to enter a personal and intimate fellowship with Him. That call is not based on your intellectual attainments, wisdom, or on your position or status but strictly on the grace of God. The problem is never with God's ability to save but with people who have become accustomed to trusting in their own abilities, positions, or resources instead of trusting the Lord. Your glory is in Christ alone.

2:1-5 This section includes critical life lessons for Christians. The power of God is not limited by human **weakness**.

2:6-9 Paul contrasts earthly wisdom and spiritual wisdom and emphasized that earthly wisdom is not eternal and will come to an end. The Greeks depended on human mental prowess and insight to unravel the mysteries of life, but Paul relied on God's revelation in Christ (1Co 1:30; Eph 1:8-9,17; 3:8-12). **Wisdom** (Gk *sophian*, "prudence, skill, knowledge") pertains more to the skillful use of intelligence and ability in living, having a sense of discernment for using what God has given—whether tangible or intangible. In the Old Testament, wisdom does not refer to intellectual ability but to "one who looks to God for instruction in living." The wise Solomon notes that wisdom begins with "the fear of the Lord" (Pr 1:7), which implies that even a very gifted individual who does not fear and reverence God is a fool (see Ps 14:1).

2:7 God's wisdom is described as a **mystery** (Gk *mustēriō*, "secret"), which in the Bible has a different nuance of describing something **hidden** from human understanding until revealed and made clear through the Holy Spirit to believers.

2:10-11 Paul affirms the Holy Spirit's work of drawing men to God and acting as a guide, teacher, and helper since Jesus is no longer physically present to minister. **The Spirit of God** is the key to unlocking God's wisdom. The Holy Spirit knows the wisdom of God because He is God (see **Doctrine**: "The Work of the Holy Spirit," p. 1513).

2:14 The **unbeliever** cannot receive the things of God because they are **foolishness** [Gk *mōria*, anglicized as *moron*] **to him**. "Foolishness" suggests dullness and tasteless mediocrity—the response of people without spiritual sensitivities to the beauty and excellence of divine truth. Spiritual things cannot be rightly judged by those with a carnal mindset. Without the Spirit of God, no one can discern and accept the things of God.

Boasting Only in the Lord (1:26-31)

[26] Brothers, consider your calling: Not many are wise from a human perspective,[A] not many powerful, not many of noble birth. [27] Instead, God has chosen what is foolish in the world to shame the wise, and God has chosen what is weak in the world to shame the strong. [28] God has chosen what is insignificant and despised in the world—what is viewed as nothing—to bring to nothing what is viewed as something, [29] so that no one[B] can boast in His presence. [30] But it is from Him that you are in Christ Jesus, who became God-given wisdom for us—our righteousness, sanctification, and •redemption, [31] in order that, as it is written: **The one who boasts must boast in the Lord.**[C]

Paul's Proclamation (2:1-5)

2 When I came to you, •brothers, announcing the testimony[D] of God to you, I did not come with brilliance of speech or wisdom. [2] For I didn't think it was a good idea to know anything among you except Jesus Christ and Him crucified. [3] I came to you in weakness, in fear, and in much trembling. [4] My speech and my proclamation were not with persuasive words of wisdom[E] but with a powerful demonstration by the Spirit, [5] so that your faith might not be based on men's wisdom but on God's power.

Spiritual Wisdom (2:6-16)

[6] However, we do speak a wisdom among the mature, but not a wisdom of this age, or of the rulers of this age, who are coming to nothing. [7] On the contrary, we speak God's hidden wisdom in a •mystery, a wisdom God predestined before the ages for our glory. [8] None of the rulers of this age knew this wisdom, for if they had known it, they would not have crucified the Lord of glory. [9] But as it is written:

> **What eye did not see and ear**
> **did not hear,**
> **and what never entered**
> **the human mind—**
> **God prepared this for those**
> **who love Him.**[F]

[10] Now God has revealed these things to us by the Spirit, for the Spirit searches everything, even the depths of God. [11] For who among men knows the thoughts[G] of a man except the spirit of the man that is in him? In the same way, no one knows the thoughts[G] of God except the Spirit of God. [12] Now we have not received the spirit of the •world, but the Spirit who comes from God, so that we may understand what has been freely given to us by God. [13] We also speak these things, not in words taught by human wisdom, but in those taught by the Spirit, explaining spiritual things to spiritual people.[H] [14] But the unbeliever[I] does not welcome what comes from God's Spirit, because it is foolishness to him; he is not able to understand it since it is evaluated[J] spiritually. [15] The spiritual person, however, can evaluate[K] everything, yet he himself cannot be evaluated[J] by anyone. [16] For

> **who has known**
> **the Lord's mind,**
> **that he may instruct Him?**[L]

But we have the mind of Christ.

The Problem of Immaturity (3:1-4)

3 •Brothers, I was not able to speak to you as spiritual people but as people of the flesh, as babies in Christ. [2] I gave you milk to drink, not solid food, because you were not yet ready for it. In fact, you are still not ready, [3] because you are still fleshly. For since there is envy and strife[M] among you, are you not fleshly and living like unbelievers?[N] [4] For whenever someone says, "I'm with Paul," and another, "I'm with Apollos," are you not unspiritual people?[O,P]

The Role of God's Servants (3:5-17)

[5] What then is Apollos? And what is Paul? They are servants through whom you believed, and each has the

[A] **1:26** Lit *wise according to the flesh* [B] **1:29** Lit *that not all flesh* [C] **1:31** Jr 9:24 [D] **2:1** Other mss read *mystery* [E] **2:4** Other mss read *human wisdom* [F] **2:9** Is 52:15; 64:4 [G] **2:11** Or *things* [H] **2:13** Or *things with spiritual words* [I] **2:14** Or *unspiritual*; lit *natural* [J] **2:14,15** Or *judged*, or *discerned* [K] **2:15** Or *judge*, or *discern* [L] **2:16** Is 40:13 [M] **3:3** Other mss add *and divisions* [N] **3:3** Lit *and walking according to man* [O] **3:4** Other mss read *are you not carnal* [P] **3:4** Lit *not just human*

>WORD|*study*

3:14 Reward (Gk *misthon*, "pay, wages, reward, or punishment") is to be understood as compensation for a task. The term may refer to monetary payment, but usually its connotation has to do with some aspect of divine evaluation of human activity. Jesus used the word several times in the Sermon on the Mount in reference to rewards that the ungodly receive in this life (Mt 5:46; 6:2,5,16; see also 2Pt 2:13,15; Jd 11) in contrast to rewards that believers will receive in heaven (Mt 5:12; 6:1; see Mk 9:41; Lk 6:23,35; 2Jn 8). Paul in 1 Corinthians used the term four times, all referring to the reward that comes from kingdom ministry.

role the Lord has given. 6 I planted,
Apollos watered, but God gave the
growth. 7 So then neither the one
who plants nor the one who waters
is anything, but only God who gives
the growth. 8 Now the one planting
and the one watering are one in purpose, and each will receive his own
reward according to his own labor.
9 For we are God's coworkers.[A] You
are God's field, God's building. 10 According to God's grace that was giv-
en to me, I have laid a foundation as
a skilled master builder, and another
builds on it. But each one must be
careful how he builds on it. 11 For
no one can lay any other foundation
than what has been laid down. That
foundation is Jesus Christ. 12 If anyone builds on that foundation with
gold, silver, costly stones, wood, hay,
or straw, 13 each one's work will become obvious, for the day[B] will disclose it, because it will be revealed
by fire; the fire will test the quality of each one's work. 14 If anyone's
work that he has built survives, he
will receive a reward. 15 If anyone's
work is burned up, it will be lost, but
he will be saved; yet it will be like an
escape through fire.[C]
16 Don't you yourselves know that
you are God's sanctuary and that the
Spirit of God lives in you? 17 If anyone destroys God's sanctuary, God
will destroy him; for God's sanctuary is holy, and that is what you are.

The Folly of Human Wisdom (3:18-23)

18 No one should deceive himself.
If anyone among you thinks he is
wise in this age, he must become
foolish so that he can become wise.
19 For the wisdom of this ·world is
foolishness with God, since it is
written: **He catches the wise in
their craftiness;**[D] 20 and again, **The
Lord knows that the reasonings of
the wise are meaningless.**[E] 21 So no
one should boast in human leaders,
for everything is yours— 22 whether
Paul or Apollos or ·Cephas or the
world or life or death or things present or things to come—everything
is yours, 23 and you belong to Christ,
and Christ belongs to God.

Examining Christian Conduct (4:1–6:20)

Managers of the Mysteries of God (4:1-5)

4 A person should consider us in
this way: as servants of Christ
and managers of God's ·mysteries.
2 In this regard, it is expected of
managers that each one of them be
found faithful. 3 It is of little importance to me that I should be evaluated by you or by any human court.[F]
In fact, I don't even evaluate myself.
4 For I am not conscious of anything
against myself, but I am not justified
by this. The One who evaluates me
is the Lord. 5 Therefore don't judge
anything prematurely, before the
Lord comes, who will both bring to
light what is hidden in darkness and
reveal the intentions of the hearts.
And then praise will come to each
one from God.

Humility (4:6-13)

6 Now, ·brothers, I have applied
these things to myself and Apollos
for your benefit, so that you may
learn from us the saying: "Nothing beyond what is written."[G] The
purpose is that none of you will
be inflated with pride in favor of
one person over another. 7 For who
makes you so superior? What do
you have that you didn't receive?
If, in fact, you did receive it, why do
you boast as if you hadn't received
it? 8 You are already full! You are

3:1-4 The Corinthians were preoccupied with wisdom, and in the process they had aligned themselves with their favorite leaders. Their human pride asserted itself in an elitist attitude.

3:5-7 Paul explains the role Christian mentors can play in a young believer's life. He was not discounting the importance of nurturing the lives of others and being grateful when others plant and water in your life, but Paul defended the truth that **only God . . . gives the growth**. God deserves credit for the growth.

3:13 On **the day** of judgment the Lord will test by fire the purity of everyone's ministry. Some will receive a reward, while others will endure loss, though not the loss of salvation. This judgment is only for Christians and takes place immediately after the church has been raptured or translated into heaven. This judgment seat of Christ (Gk *bēma*) is not the place for assigning eternal destiny to anyone but rather the time for determining and giving rewards to believers (Rm 14:10; 2Co 5:10).

3:15 Paul explains that a believer who works carelessly will still be saved but **like an escape through fire**, identifying the seriousness of investing in work that is worthless. The Roman Catholic church has appealed to this text to justify purgatory, but this "fire" is not to purge evil. It is to annihilate what is worthless.

3:16 The application here addresses the believers at Corinth, or the local church, as the most holy place or the unique dwelling place of the Spirit of God. Division within the local church (1Co 3:4) defiles the sanctuary of God and calls for His judgment.

3:18-20 To receive the wisdom of God, you **must become foolish** in your own eyes, recognizing your worthless and hopeless state without Christ.

4:1-2 Paul explains that leaders should be seen as **servants** [Gk *hupēretas*, "helpers or assistants"] **of Christ**, doing the will of the Master. He also described them as **managers** [Gk *oikonomous*, "stewards, administrators, treasurers"] **of God's mysteries**. "Managers" are those in possession of and accountable for handling a valuable commodity. "Mysteries" is a reference to the truths of God that cannot be discovered by an individual on her own. They must be, and are intended to be, revealed by God Himself. Paul considered himself a custodian of God's revealed truth.

[A] **3:9** Or *are coworkers belonging to God* [B] **3:13** The day of Christ's judgment of believers [C] **3:15** Lit *yet so as through fire* [D] **3:19** Jb 5:13 [E] **3:20** Ps 94:11 [F] **4:3** Lit *a human day* [G] **4:6** The words in quotation marks could = the OT, a Jewish maxim, or a popular proverb.

4:9 Paul uses an interesting metaphor, describing the apostles as a **spectacle** (Gk *theatron*, "play"; anglicized as "theater") to illustrate the humiliation and suffering of indignities by the apostles. God uses these displays of weakness to demonstrate His power.

4:10 Fools (Gk *mōroi*, "stupid," in the sense of being ridiculous) and **weak** and **dishonored** were descriptors of the apostles in contrast to **wise** and **strong** and **distinguished** in reference to the Corinthians.

4:11-13 The apostle moves to a lesson on how to respond to mistreatment—timely for every generation. You **bless** (Gk *eulogoumen*, "say good words," i.e., deliver a eulogy, memorializing an individual) when **reviled** (Gk *loidoroumenoi*, "insult"). You **endure** (Gk *anechometha*, "put up with, accept, bear with") when you are **persecuted** (Gk *diōkomenoi*, "pursue with malignity").

4:14-21 By calling himself their spiritual **father**, Paul was reminding the Corinthians that he had a family connection with them and desired their well-being—and because he did, he wanted their thinking and behavior to honor Christ. Like a loving father, Paul intended to guide them and take care of them. He desperately wanted to be with them, but since his coming was impossible at that time, he arranged to send **Timothy** in his place.

Paul explained that they had much correction to face, and he asked how they would like to receive correction when he came. Paul did not have in mind a physical **rod** but rather strong, corrective verbiage.

5:1-5 Sexual immorality (Gk *porneia*, "unlawful sexual intercourse, prostitution, unchastity, fornication") usually refers to sexual acts outside of marriage. Paul identified specifically one in the Corinthian congregation who was **living with his father's wife** (Gk *gunaika*, probably a reference to the stepmother of the offender). The father might have been deceased, but in any case the liaison was forbidden, and they were living together without being married (Lv 18:7-8; 20:11). Even Roman law forbade such unions.

Instead of being saddened by this behavior and dealing with it in a biblical way, the Corinthians were still **inflated with pride**, willing to overlook and tolerate this behavior.

Turn that one over to Satan most likely meant releasing the member into the world where Satan currently rules and away from the protection of the church. The phrase **destruction of the flesh** probably did not refer to physical death or disease but may have been a metaphor for rendering the fleshly nature of a man

already rich! You have begun to
reign as kings without us—and I
wish you did reign, so that we could
also reign with you! 9 For I think
God has displayed us, the apostles,
in last place, like men condemned to
die: We have become a spectacle to
the world and to angels and to men.
10 We are fools for Christ, but you are
wise in Christ! We are weak, but you
are strong! You are distinguished,
but we are dishonored! 11 Up to the
present hour we are both hungry
and thirsty; we are poorly clothed,
roughly treated, homeless; 12 we labor, working with our own hands.
When we are reviled, we bless;
when we are persecuted, we endure
it; 13 when we are slandered, we respond graciously. Even now, we are
like the world's garbage, like the dirt
everyone scrapes off their sandals.

Paul's Fatherly Care (4:14-21)

14 I'm not writing this to shame
you, but to warn you as my dear
children. 15 For you can have 10,000
instructors in Christ, but you can't
have many fathers. For I became
your father in Christ Jesus through
the gospel. 16 Therefore I urge you
to imitate me. 17 This is why I have
sent Timothy to you. He is my dearly
loved and faithful son in the Lord.
He will remind you about my ways
in Christ Jesus, just as I teach everywhere in every church. 18 Now some
are inflated with pride, as though I
were not coming to you. 19 But I will
come to you soon, if the Lord wills,
and I will know not the talk but the
power of those who are inflated with
pride. 20 For the kingdom of God is
not a matter of talk but of power.
21 What do you want? Should I come
to you with a rod, or in love and a
spirit of gentleness?

Immoral Church Members (5:1-8)

5 It is widely reported that there
is sexual immorality among you,
and the kind of sexual immorality
that is not even tolerated[A] among
the Gentiles—a man is living with
his father's wife. 2 And you are inflated with pride, instead of filled with
grief so that he who has committed
this act might be removed from your
congregation. 3 For though I am absent in body but present in spirit, I
have already decided about the one
who has done this thing as though I
were present. 4 When you are assembled in the name of our Lord Jesus
with my spirit and with the power of
our Lord Jesus, 5 turn that one over
to Satan for the destruction of the
flesh, so that his spirit may be saved
in the Day of the Lord.

6 Your boasting is not good. Don't
you know that a little yeast permeates the whole batch of dough?
7 •Clean out the old yeast so that you
may be a new batch. You are indeed
unleavened, for Christ our •Passover
has been sacrificed.[B] 8 Therefore, let
us observe the feast, not with old
yeast or with the yeast of malice and
evil but with the unleavened bread
of sincerity and truth.

HARD QUESTION

Should Christians file lawsuits?

Paul specifically addresses lawsuits among Christians, and he is forbidding Christians from filing lawsuits against other Christians (6:1-8). Paul begins with a logical explanation that when Christ returns, Christians will rule and **judge** the entire world. Based on this truth, for Christians to enter the law courts of the Gentiles and be judged by **unbelievers** is ridiculous. Paul was disheartened for two reasons:

- The church was not disciplined enough to control and train its members to observe ethical practices.
- The church, even after seeing this problem, did not deal with it wisely and promptly. Instead, they were letting unbelievers have an inside look at their problems and weaknesses. In a sense, Paul was saying, "Clean up your own act and don't give unbelievers a reason to doubt the authenticity of Christianity."

If the saints looked to civil courts, several elements would be missing, including the Spirit of God residing in the heart of the judge or arbiter, who would not have God's wisdom, as well as the judge's familiarity with anything beyond Roman law. By going outside the congregation, their witness would be tarnished, if not destroyed, in the eyes of the pagan magistrates and people of the community.

Much easier than cleaning up their own act and doing the hard work of following Christian principles or dealing with a brother according to Scripture, was letting someone else, namely a civil judge, settle the matters the Corinthians did not want to face. Greek culture, as modern society, was intrigued with litigation. Paul was not dismissing the need for justice; instead he was calling on believers to seek justice properly.

[A] 5:1 Other mss read *named* [B] 5:7 Other mss add *for us*

HARD QUESTION

Does the Bible really condemn homosexuality?

Jesus condemned religious leaders who were not prepared to address the challenges critical in their day: "You know how to read the appearance of the sky, but you can't read the signs of the times" (Mt 16:3). Without a doubt, one of the biggest questions facing the church today is what does the Bible really teach about **homosexuality** (1Co 6:9)? The culture at large will argue that homosexuality is not a choice—a person is simply born that way. Even some believers will argue that the Bible just condemns immoral homosexual relations and not those between committed individuals.

What does the Bible really say? The Bible says homosexuality is a sin. In Gn 18:20-21 and 19:3-7, it was one of the "extremely serious" sins of the cities of Sodom and Gomorrah. In the Holiness Codes in Lv 18 and 20, the writer lists many unlawful sexual relations including homosexuality (Lv 18:22; 20:13). In the New Testament, several passages address this issue (Rm 1:18-32, esp. vv. 26-27; 1Co 6:9). That being said, the church has been guilty at times in the way they have reacted to this sin—demonizing it as an unforgiveable sin.

How should Christians respond to homosexuality?

- *Flee it* if you are struggling with it (1Co 6:18)—just as with any sexual temptation, you must run from it and seek godly counsel.
- *Love people and share the truth.* You must love the sinner (since all are sinners), but you should view sin as God views it—detestable, requiring the death of His Son. If the church would truly learn to love people, more people would be open to hearing the truth of the gospel.

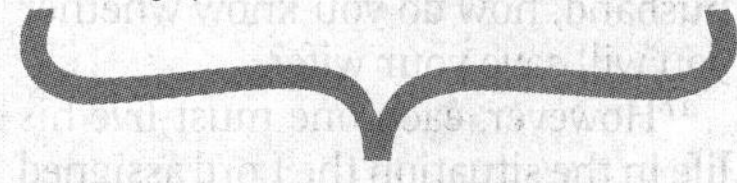

Church Discipline (5:9-12)

9 I wrote to you in a letter not to
associate with sexually immoral
people. 10 I did not mean the immoral people of this •world or the greedy
and swindlers or idolaters; otherwise you would have to leave the
world. 11 But now I am writing[A] you
not to associate with anyone who
claims to be a believer[B] who is sexually immoral or greedy, an idolater
or verbally abusive, a drunkard or a
swindler. Do not even eat with such
a person. 12 For what business is it of
mine to judge outsiders? Don't you
judge those who are inside? 13 But
God judges outsiders. **Put away
the evil person from among yourselves.**[C]

Lawsuits Among Believers (6:1-11)

6 If any of you has a legal dispute
against another, do you dare go
to court before the unrighteous,[D]
and not before the •saints? 2 Or
don't you know that the saints will
judge the •world? And if the world
is judged by you, are you unworthy to judge the smallest cases?
3 Don't you know that we will judge
angels—not to mention ordinary
matters? 4 So if you have cases pertaining to this life, do you select
those[E] who have no standing in
the church to judge? 5 I say this to
your shame! Can it be that there
is not one wise person among you
who is able to arbitrate between his
•brothers? 6 Instead, believer[F] goes
to court against believer, and that
before unbelievers!

7 Therefore, to have legal disputes
against one another is already a
moral failure for you. Why not rather put up with injustice? Why not
rather be cheated? 8 Instead, you act
unjustly and cheat—and you do this
to believers! 9 Don't you know that
the unrighteous will not inherit
God's kingdom? Do not be deceived:
No sexually immoral people, idolaters, adulterers, or anyone practicing homosexuality,[G] 10 no thieves,
greedy people, drunkards, verbally
abusive people, or swindlers will
inherit God's kingdom. 11 And some
of you used to be like this. But you
were washed, you were •sanctified,
you were •justified in the name of
the Lord Jesus Christ and by the
Spirit of our God.

Christian Liberty (6:12-20)

12 "Everything is permissible for
me,"[H] but not everything is helpful.
"Everything is permissible for me,"
but I will not be brought under the
control of anything. 13 "Food for the
stomach and the stomach for food,"
but God will do away with both of
them.[I] The body is not for sexual

A 5:11 Or *now I wrote* B 5:11 Lit *anyone named a brother* C 5:13 Dt 17:7 D 6:1 Unbelievers; v. 6 E 6:4 Or *life, appoint those* (as a command) F 6:6-8 Lit *brothers* G 6:9 Lit *adulterers, passive homosexual partners, active homosexual partners* H 6:12-13 The words in quotation marks are most likely slogans used by some Corinthian Christians and corrected by Paul. I 6:13 Lit *both it and them*

powerless. The word is used elsewhere in connection with God's judgment against sin.

5:6-8 Paul uses the culinary metaphor of **yeast** (Gk *zumē*, "leaven") to remind his readers that just as a very small amount of yeast permeates and spreads throughout the dough mixture in a short time, to ignore this problem would open the door for rapid fermentation or spoiling of the whole church. Jewish regulations concerning **Passover** emphasize this principle since all leaven, symbolic of sin, must be removed from the house in preparation for this religious feast. The illustration is one with which women could readily identify since in that day, most women spent hours preparing meals, and bread was a main staple.

5:9-13 Paul references a former **letter** (which is not in existence today) in which he had instructed the church **not to associate** with those practicing sexual immorality and clarifies this instruction. Paul explains that he does not expect them to avoid nonbelievers who live in sin, but he does encourage them to avoid anyone in the church (**who claims to be a believer**) who refuses to live a life wholly consecrated to Christ. God has called Christians to befriend and share the gospel with those who have not embraced the gospel message. To separate themselves totally from **the world** would be against God's plan for drawing people into His family through the sharing of personal testimony.

Allowing people in the family to live as pagans is against the plan of God. Paul explains that the believers should avoid those in the church whose lifestyle contradicts the name they bear. Such people should be judged, and believers should refuse **to associate** with an unrepentant brother. Paul notes the foolishness of judging those outside the church because God will do that; believers must **judge those who are inside** the church in order to keep the church pure and healthy. Paul issues a clear command to **put away the evil person** (see 5:2; Dt 13:5; 17:7,12; 21:21; 22:21). Paul had a "no tolerance" policy. Discipline is best for everyone. Discipline allows unbelievers to see a clear distinction between the world and the church and gives the sinning brother the message that his behavior is unacceptable to God.

6:9-20 Clearly this portion of the letter was not written solely to address eternal security; however, the subject matter falls right in line with passages teaching that a genuine believer cannot lose his salvation. First, those who live for themselves are obviously not surrendered to God and thus will not inherit heaven. Second, Paul acknowledges that some in the church were previously evildoers, but he also notes that they **were justified** by Jesus Christ. He is showing that God is willing to forgive and justify. Paul is also showing that once a person is justified, his behavior will change, as evidence of his salvation. He is calling into question the authenticity of salvation for one who does not live for Christ and whose life is characterized by a pattern of ongoing, habitual sin because genuine salvation is evidenced by changed behavior.

In verses 12-20 Paul apparently refers to a slogan of the Corinthians (**everything is permissible for me**) in order to address several admonitions dealing with how a believer's freedom is limited by what is helpful or profitable to the Lord. Although there is liberty in Christ, this liberty should not be used if it causes someone else to become enslaved by something.

6:15-16 Behaving immorally in the earthly **body** is like joining the holy, perfect Christ with a **prostitute**. When sexual sin is committed, the two are **joined** in the flesh, so how then can one who is joined with the Lord also be joined with someone immoral—a vile misrepresentation of the mercy of Christ.

6:18 Paul urges believers not to wait or think about what they ought to do when faced with a questionable situation but to **run from sexual immorality**, which is especially damaging because this sin cannot be separated from the body, as evidenced by many consequences such as pregnancy out of wedlock and sexually transmitted diseases. The sole purpose of "sexual immorality" is the gratification of lust, which makes this sin quite heinous because of the obvious selfishness prompting the sin as well as the inevitable damage to personal spiritual sensitivities.

6:20 He emphasizes the value of the body and soul because of the high **price** paid by Jesus' perfect life, death, and resurrection. This loving sacrifice of Jesus ought to be the motivation to live a holy and pure life.

7:1-40 Paul addresses questions about marriage raised by the Corinthians in previous correspondence. Ultimately Paul makes clear that each individual has his own gift—whether celibacy or marriage—and each is a blessing when used according to divine guidelines. The importance and value of marriage is affirmed and clear guidelines are offered to those married, expressing the idea that getting marriage right is more important than simply being married. Paul also affirms single living.

immorality but for the Lord, and the Lord for the body. 14 God raised up the Lord and will also raise us up by His power. 15 Don't you know that your bodies are a part of Christ's body? So should I take a part of Christ's body and make it part of a prostitute? Absolutely not! 16 Don't you know that anyone joined to a prostitute is one body with her? For Scripture says, **The two will become one flesh.**[A] 17 But anyone joined to the Lord is one spirit with Him.

18 Run from sexual immorality! "Every sin a person can commit is outside the body."[B] On the contrary, the person who is sexually immoral sins against his own body. 19 Don't you know that your body is a sanctuary of the Holy Spirit who is in you, whom you have from God? You are not your own, 20 for you were bought at a price. Therefore glorify God in your body.[C]

Addressing Questions of the Church (7:1–10:33)

Perspectives on Singleness and Marriage (7:1-40)

7 Now in response to the matters you wrote[D] about: "It is good for a man not to have relations with[E] a woman."[F] 2 But because sexual immorality is so common,[G] each man should have his own wife, and each woman should have her own husband. 3 A husband should fulfill his marital responsibility to his wife, and likewise a wife to her husband. 4 A wife does not have the right over her own body, but her husband does. In the same way, a husband does not have the right over his own body, but his wife does. 5 Do not deprive one another sexually—except when you agree for a time, to devote yourselves to[H] prayer. Then come together again; otherwise, Satan may tempt you because of your lack of self-control. 6 I say the following[I] as a concession, not as a command. 7 I wish that all people were just like me. But each has his own gift from God, one person in this way and another in that way.

8 I say to the unmarried and to widows: It is good for them if they remain as I am. 9 But if they do not have self-control, they should marry, for it is better to marry than to burn with desire.

10 I command the married—not I, but the Lord—a wife is not to leave[J] her husband. 11 But if she does leave, she must remain unmarried or be reconciled to her husband—and a husband is not to leave his wife. 12 But I (not the Lord)[K] say to the rest: If any brother has an unbelieving wife and she is willing to live with him, he must not leave her. 13 Also, if any woman has an unbelieving husband and he is willing to live with her, she must not leave her husband. 14 For the unbelieving husband is set apart for God by the wife, and the unbelieving wife is set apart for God by the husband.[L] Otherwise your children would be corrupt, but now they are set apart for God. 15 But if the unbeliever leaves, let him leave. A brother or a sister is not bound in such cases. God has called you[M] to live in peace. 16 For you, wife, how do you know whether you will save your husband? Or you, husband, how do you know whether you will save your wife?

17 However, each one must live his life in the situation the Lord assigned when God called him.[N] This is what I command in all the churches. 18 Was anyone already circumcised when he was called? He should not undo his circumcision. Was anyone called while uncircumcised? He should not get circumcised. 19 Circumcision does not matter and uncircumcision does not matter, but keeping God's commands does. 20 Each person should remain in the life situation[O] in which he was called. 21 Were you called while a •slave? It should not be a concern to you. But if you can

[A] **6:16** Gn 2:24 [B] **6:18** See note at 1Co 6:12-13. [C] **6:20** Other mss add *and in your spirit, which belong to God.* [D] **7:1** Other mss add *to me* [E] **7:1** Lit *not to touch* [F] **7:1** The words in quotation marks are a principle that the Corinthians wrote to Paul about to ask for his view. [G] **7:2** Lit *because of immoralities* [H] **7:5** Other mss add *fasting and to* [I] **7:6** Lit *say this*; some interpret the word as referring to v. 2, vv. 2-5, v. 5 (wholly or in part), or v. 6 [J] **7:10** Or *separate from,* or *divorce* [K] **7:12** Jesus did not address the situation of a marriage in the Gentile world where only one person is a believer. [L] **7:14** Lit *the brother* [M] **7:15** Other mss read *us* [N] **7:17** Lit *called each* [O] **7:20** Lit *in the calling*

The Marriage Dilemma 1 Corinthians 7

Current Situation	Paul's Advice	Biblical Principle
Unmarried	Marry (v. 2).	Avoid sexual immorality (vv. 2,9,36).
	Stay single (vv. 8,26-27).	Remain devoted to the Lord without distraction (vv. 32-35).
Married	"Do not deprive one another" (v. 5).	• Authority over the body is given to one's spouse in marriage (vv. 3-4). • Deprivation is an invitation to temptation (v. 5).
Married, having left spouse	Remain unmarried or be reconciled to spouse (v. 10).	The Lord commands the wife "not to leave her husband" (v. 10).
Married to unbeliever who stays	Do not leave (vv. 12-13).	The Holy Spirit works in the lives of the spouse and of the children (v. 14).
Married to unbeliever who leaves	Let him/her go (v. 15).	You are "not bound in such cases" (vv. 15-16).

become free, by all means take the
opportunity.[A] 22 For he who is called
by the Lord as a slave is the Lord's
freedman.[B] Likewise he who is called
as a free man[C] is Christ's slave. 23 You
were bought at a price; do not become slaves of men. 24 •Brothers,
each person should remain with God
in whatever situation he was called.

25 About virgins: I have no command from the Lord, but I do give
an opinion as one who by the Lord's
mercy is trustworthy. 26 Therefore I
consider this to be good because of
the present distress: It is fine for a
man to remain as he is. 27 Are you
bound to a wife? Do not seek to be
loosed. Are you loosed from a wife?
Do not seek a wife. 28 However, if you
do get married, you have not sinned,
and if a virgin marries, she has not
sinned. But such people will have
trouble in this life,[D] and I am trying
to spare you. 29 And I say this, brothers: The time is limited, so from now
on those who have wives should be
as though they had none, 30 those
who weep as though they did not
weep, those who rejoice as though
they did not rejoice, those who buy
as though they did not possess,
31 and those who use the world as
though they did not make full use of
it. For this world in its current form
is passing away.

32 I want you to be without concerns. An unmarried man is concerned about the things of the
Lord—how he may please the Lord.
33 But a married man is concerned
about the things of the world—how
he may please his wife— 34 and his
interests are divided. An unmarried woman or a virgin is concerned
about the things of the Lord, so that
she may be holy both in body and
in spirit. But a married woman is
concerned about the things of the
world—how she may please her husband. 35 Now I am saying this for your
own benefit, not to put a restraint on
you, but because of what is proper
and so that you may be devoted to
the Lord without distraction.

[A]7:21 Or *But even though you can become free, make the most of your position as a slave.*
[B]7:22 A former slave [C]7:22 A man who was never a slave [D]7:28 Lit *in the flesh*

7:3-4 Paul clarifies sexual conduct in marriage. He is encouraging healthy marriages and the right, proper, and fulfilling sexual life within God's design. Paul shares the same information with wives and husbands in a culture that generally deferred to the needs of men, underscoring Paul's attitude of concern that both men and women enjoy the blessings of God in their relationships with one another. The temptation to believe that Paul was chauvinistic in other instructions to women is thereby circumvented.

7:5-6 The mandate, **do not deprive one another** suggests that sexual abstinence within marriage should not be the norm and is contrary to the purpose and commitment in this holy union. Paul explains the conditions to be met for a husband and wife to refuse to have sexual relations: agreement on the part of both, a set **time** frame, and the purpose of devoting themselves **to prayer**. Then normal marital activities should resume. Since Jewish men often took certain vows during which they withheld themselves from the marital bed to give special time to prayer and study of the Torah, Paul was demonstrating his equal concern for wives and husbands by insisting that the husband and wife must **agree** on this matter.

There is no hint in verse 6 (nor in vv. 12,25,40) that Paul is departing from apostolic authority or Spirit-breathed transmission in order to insert his own opinions. His speaking is by **concession** or permission or under the direction of the Holy Spirit and is best understood by accepting the words within the context in which they were written. Paul has given a mandate prohibiting sexual abstinence in marriage, but then he gives a "concession" for the temporary abstinence, which is carefully defined but not mandated. Far from suggesting a lack of inspiration, Paul's use of these phrases reaffirms the extent of inspiration, underscoring that Paul would not arbitrarily insert his own opinions but speaks only what God expressly gives to him through the Holy Spirit.

7:7 Paul expresses contentment in his single state. However, he recognizes that God has given a different **gift** to each, and all should be content with the gift that God has given. Marriage is a gift, and singleness is a gift. Both are gifts with purpose, and both should be celebrated with contentment.

7:36-38 In the ancient world, fathers had control over the marital plans of their daughters, and Paul said it was fine for fathers to give permission to marry and better for daughters to marry than to disobey God's clear commands regarding sexual behavior.

7:39-40 Paul then speaks to widows. He releases the women to marry upon the death of their husbands and again affirms the importance of lifelong commitment. He leaves one requirement for remarriage. There is no exception. Christians must be committed to marrying **in the Lord**, providing the best chance for a successful home life and protecting the church. Knowing that widows had a vital ministry in the New Testament church, Paul expressed his opinion that a widow would be **happier** and more fulfilled in service if she remained single.

8:1-13 Pagan people in Corinth were afraid of evil spirits and regularly made meat sacrifices to the idols so that they would not be overcome with evil spirits. The meats were later sold in the market. Many new converts to Christianity had lived under this fear of evil spirits and idols before their conversions. All were faced with the acceptability of eating this meat because it was such an integral part of society. Wondering if it might be contaminated by evil spirits, many new converts were afraid that eating the meat would tempt them to return to idol worship. Others easily recognized that idols were totally false gods and had no power over the crucified Christ.

Paul recognized that their **knowledge**, which built them up **with pride**, was really keeping them spiritually immature. Paul wanted them instead to grow in Christian maturity and to edify others rather than building themselves up by putting inordinate values on Christian liberty. Real love for God produces genuine love for God's children, brothers and sisters in Christ.

Paul agreed that there was nothing wrong with eating the meat **offered to idols** because there is only **one** true **God**—idols were nothing (vv. 4-6).

Paul's solid grasp of truth did not keep him from recognizing those with a tender **conscience** who felt it was improper to eat of this meat. Paul pointed out that although some were right in believing that the idols were nothing, they were wrongly proud of their understanding. Even though allowed, this practice was becoming **a stumbling block to the weak** in the church with a tender conscience (v. 9).

9:11-14 Paul uses this controversy to answer questions about Christian

36 But if any man thinks he is acting improperly toward his virgin,[A] if she is past marriageable age,[B] and so it must be, he can do what he wants. He is not sinning; they can get married. 37 But he who stands firm in his heart (who is under no compulsion, but has control over his own will) and has decided in his heart to keep his own virgin, will do well. 38 So then he who marries[C] his virgin does well, but he who does not marry[D] will do better.

39 A wife is bound[E] as long as her husband is living. But if her husband dies, she is free to be married to anyone she wants—only in the Lord.[F] 40 But she is happier if she remains as she is, in my opinion. And I think that I also have the Spirit of God.

Considerations for Dealing with Food Offered to Idols (8:1-13)

8 About food offered to idols: We know that "we all have knowledge."[G] Knowledge inflates with pride, but love builds up. 2 If anyone thinks he knows anything, he does not yet know it as he ought to know it. 3 But if anyone loves God, he is known by Him.

4 About eating food offered to idols, then, we know that "an idol is nothing in the world," and that "there is no God but one." 5 For even if there are so-called gods, whether in heaven or on earth—as there are many "gods" and many "lords"—

6 yet for us there is one God,
 the Father.
All things are from Him,
 and we exist for Him.
And there is one Lord,
 Jesus Christ.
All things are through Him,
 and we exist through Him.

7 However, not everyone has this knowledge. In fact, some have been so used to idolatry up until now that when they eat food offered to an idol, their conscience, being weak, is defiled. 8 Food will not make us acceptable to God. We are not inferior if we don't eat, and we are not better if we do eat. 9 But be careful that this right of yours in no way becomes a stumbling block to the weak. 10 For if someone sees you, the one who has this knowledge, dining in an idol's temple, won't his weak conscience be encouraged to eat food offered to idols? 11 Then the weak person, the brother for whom Christ died, is ruined[H] by your knowledge. 12 Now when you sin like this against the •brothers and wound their weak conscience, you are sinning against Christ. 13 Therefore, if food causes my brother to fall, I will never again eat meat, so that I won't cause my brother to fall.

A Defense of Apostleship (9:1-27)

9 Am I not free? Am I not an apostle? Have I not seen Jesus our Lord? Are you not my work in the Lord? 2 If I am not an apostle to others, at least I am to you, for you are the seal of my apostleship in the Lord. 3 My defense to those who examine me is this: 4 Don't we have the right to eat and drink? 5 Don't we have the right to be accompanied by a Christian wife[I] like the other apostles, the Lord's brothers, and •Cephas? 6 Or do Barnabas and I alone have no right to refrain from working? 7 Who ever goes to war at his own expense? Who plants a vineyard and does not eat its fruit? Or who shepherds a flock and does not drink the milk from the flock? 8 Am I saying this from a human perspective? Doesn't the law also say the same thing? 9 For it is written in the law of Moses, **Do not muzzle an ox while it treads out grain.**[J] Is God really concerned with oxen? 10 Or isn't He really saying it for us? Yes, this is written for us, because he who plows ought to plow in hope, and he who threshes should do so in hope of sharing the crop. 11 If we have sown spiritual things for you, is it too much if we reap material benefits from you? 12 If others have this right to receive benefits from you, don't we even more?

However, we have not made use of this right; instead we endure everything so that we will not hinder the

[A] **7:36** = a man's fiancée, or his daughter, or his Levirate wife, or a celibate companion [B] **7:36** Or *virgin, if his passions are strong,* [C] **7:38** Or *marries off* [D] **7:38** Or *marry her off* [E] **7:39** Other mss add *by law* [F] **7:39** Only a believer [G] **8:1** See note at 1Co 6:12-13. [H] **8:11** Or *destroyed* [I] **9:5** Lit *a sister as a wife* [J] **9:9** Dt 25:4

gospel of Christ. 13 Don't you know
that those who perform the temple
services eat the food from the temple, and those who serve at the altar
share in the offerings of the altar?
14 In the same way, the Lord has
commanded that those who preach
the gospel should earn their living
by the gospel.
15 But I have used none of these
rights, and I have not written this to
make it happen that way for me. For
it would be better for me to die than
for anyone to deprive me of my boast!
16 For if I preach the gospel, I have no
reason to boast, because an obligation is placed on me. And woe to me
if I do not preach the gospel! 17 For
if I do this willingly, I have a reward,
but if unwillingly, I am entrusted
with a stewardship. 18 What then is
my reward? To preach the gospel and
offer it free of charge and not make
full use of my authority in the gospel.
19 Although I am a free man and
not anyone's •slave, I have made
myself a slave to everyone, in order
to win more people. 20 To the Jews I
became like a Jew, to win Jews; to
those under the law, like one under the law—though I myself am
not under the law[A]—to win those
under the law. 21 To those who are
without that law, like one without
the law—not being without God's
law but within Christ's law—to win
those without the law. 22 To the weak
I became weak, in order to win the
weak. I have become all things to all
people, so that I may by every possible means save some. 23 Now I do all
this because of the gospel, so I may
become a partner in its benefits.[B]
24 Don't you know that the runners
in a stadium all race, but only one
receives the prize? Run in such a
way to win the prize. 25 Now everyone
who competes exercises self-control
in everything. However, they do it to
receive a crown that will fade away,
but we a crown that will never fade
away. 26 Therefore I do not run like
one who runs aimlessly or box like
one beating the air. 27 Instead, I discipline my body and bring it under
strict control, so that after preaching to others, I myself will not be
disqualified.

Warnings from Israel's Past (10:1-22)

10 Now I want you to know, •broth-
ers, that our fathers were all
under the cloud, all passed through
the sea, 2 and all were baptized into
Moses in the cloud and in the sea.
3 They all ate the same spiritual food,
4 and all drank the same spiritual
drink. For they drank from a spiritual rock that followed them, and that
rock was Christ. 5 But God was not
pleased with most of them, for they
were struck down in the wilderness.
6 Now these things became examples for us, so that we will not desire evil things as they did.[C] 7 Don't
become idolaters as some of them
were; as it is written, **The people
sat down to eat and drink, and got
up to play.**[D,E] 8 Let us not commit
sexual immorality as some of them
did,[F] and in a single day 23,000 people fell dead. 9 Let us not test Christ
as some of them did[G] and were destroyed by snakes. 10 Nor should we
complain as some of them did,[H] and
were killed by the destroyer.[I] 11 Now
these things happened to them as
examples, and they were written
as a warning to us, on whom the
ends of the ages have come. 12 So,
whoever thinks he stands must be
careful not to fall. 13 No temptation
has overtaken you except what is
common to humanity. God is faithful, and He will not allow you to be
tempted beyond what you are able,
but with the temptation He will also
provide a way of escape so that you
are able to bear it.
14 Therefore, my dear friends, flee
from idolatry. 15 I am speaking as to
wise people. Judge for yourselves
what I say. 16 The cup of blessing that
we give thanks for, is it not a sharing in the blood of Christ? The bread
that we break, is it not a sharing in
the body of Christ? 17 Because there
is one bread, we who are many are
one body, for all of us share that one
bread. 18 Look at the people of Israel.[J]
Do not those who eat the sacrifices
participate in what is offered on the

[A]9:20 Other mss omit *though I myself am not under law* [B]9:23 Lit *partner of it* [C]10:6 Lit *they desired* [D]10:7 Or *to dance* [E]10:7 Ex 32:6 [F]10:8 Lit *them committed sexual immorality* [G]10:9 Lit *them tested* [H]10:10 Lit *them complained* [I]10:10 Or *the destroying angel* [J]10:18 Lit *Look at Israel according to the flesh*

liberty. He affirms his right to receive payment for his work in the ministry but explains that he personally limited his compensation when it could be a stumbling block to others and keep them from coming into a relationship with Jesus Christ.

9:21 Paul next addresses his desire to reach Gentiles or those **without the law**. He went where they lived; he ate with them. Paul explains that he would never disobey **God's law** in order to become like someone else, but he did not hesitate to relate to them and make them feel comfortable even at his own discomfort.

9:24 Paul uses the easily recognizable metaphor of a **race** to create urgency and competition and to add importance to his message. By encouraging the church to **run in such a way** as to **win**, he was telling them that they could win. This encouragement and vote of confidence must have been needed after the chiding the people had experienced under the apostle's disciplinary actions.

9:25 The Christian's eternal enjoyment of heaven will be unending. Because of this unbelievable reality, Paul urged the Corinthians to exercise **self-control**, run with purpose, and discipline the body.

10:1-5 To illustrate the point that one could be disqualified (9:27), Paul brought up the example of the Israelites (**our fathers**), God's chosen people. He reminded the people of Israel's past, showing examples of how God powerfully moved in their lives to provide for their needs and to display His power.

10:6-13 Paul did not merely mention the Israelites' mistakes; he listed them. Then, Paul explained that God did not desire to harm His children but left these **examples** of His willingness to exercise judgment if necessary. Like the Israelites of the past, the Corinthians could easily **fall**. However, he reminded the church that **God is faithful** even in temptation, providing **a way of escape** as well as His power to resist the temptation.

10:16-18 Paul explains that Christianity is wholly different from any religion by referencing what is symbolized through the Lord's Supper. Paul refers to **the cup of blessing** as **the blood of Christ** and to **the bread that we break** as **the body of Christ**, reminding all that Jesus is unlike any other religious figure, evidenced by the fact that He gave His own life to pay the sin debt of mankind. "Communion," or the Lord's Supper, for believers is a reminder of the sacrifice of Jesus and the life-saving covenant offered through His blood, prompting gratitude and thankfulness. It bears testimony to the exclusive nature of the gospel and to the impossibility of participating in communion with God while worshiping an idol.

10:20-22 Participating in or even condoning other religions is like partnering with **demons**.

10:31-33 Paul beautifully closes the argument by bringing the focus to God, not to behavior, self, or others. Pleasing God is the bottom line and should be the determining factor for behavior.

11:2-16 Paul turns to address a particular matter of church order for when the church gathers for corporate worship—regulations for men and women as they pray and prophesy in the church.

11:4-6 The ancient robes were rather androgynous. Men and women did not have the great diversity in clothing that is seen in the modern era. Since garments for both men and women were robes, the head covering became a clear distinction of gender. The verses addressing the cultural custom of head coverings explain their significance to society. This covering was a sign of a woman's submission to her husband and displayed a commitment of loyalty to him and his leadership. For a man to wear a head covering or for a woman to refuse to wear a head covering appeared to be a role reversal.

11:5 A woman who refused to cover her head was dishonoring her own

altar? 19 What am I saying then? That
food offered to idols is anything, or
that an idol is anything? 20 No, but I
do say that what they[A] sacrifice, they
sacrifice to demons and not to God.
I do not want you to participate with
demons! 21 You cannot drink the cup
of the Lord and the cup of demons.
You cannot share in the Lord's table
and the table of demons. 22 Or are we
provoking the Lord to jealousy? Are
we stronger than He?

The Abuse of Christian Liberty
(10:23-33)

23 "Everything is permissible,"[B,C]
but not everything is helpful. "Everything is permissible,"[B] but not
everything builds up. 24 No one
should seek his own good, but the
good of the other person.

25 Eat everything that is sold in the
meat market, asking no questions
for conscience' sake, 26 for **the earth
is the Lord's, and all that is in it.**[D]
27 If one of the unbelievers invites
you over and you want to go, eat everything that is set before you, without raising questions of conscience.
28 But if someone says to you, "This
is food offered to an idol," do not eat
it, out of consideration for the one
who told you, and for conscience'
sake.[E] 29 I do not mean your own
conscience, but the other person's.
For why is my freedom judged by
another person's conscience? 30 If I
partake with thanks, why am I slandered because of something I give
thanks for?

31 Therefore, whether you eat or
drink, or whatever you do, do everything for God's glory. 32 Give no offense to the Jews or the Greeks or
the church of God, 33 just as I also try
to please all people in all things, not
seeking my own profit, but the profit
of many, so that they may be saved.

Conduct in the Church (11:1–14:40)

Head Coverings and Women (11:1-16)

11 1 Imitate me, as I also imitate
Christ.

2 Now I praise you[F] because you
always remember me and keep the
traditions just as I delivered them to
you. 3 But I want you to know that
Christ is the head of every man, and
the man is the head of the woman,[G]
and God is the head of Christ. 4 Every
man who prays or prophesies with
something on his head dishonors his
head. 5 But every woman who prays
or prophesies with her head uncovered dishonors her head, since that
is one and the same as having her

[A] **10:20** Other mss read *Gentiles* [B] **10:23** Other mss add *for me* [C] **10:23** See note at 1Co 6:12-13.
[D] **10:26** Ps 24:1 [E] **10:28** Other mss add *"For the earth is the Lord's and all that is in it."*
[F] **11:2** Other mss add *brothers,* [G] **11:3** Or *the husband is the head of the wife*

Biblical Womanhood Man as the Head of Woman

In 1Co 11:3, **man** is called **the head of woman**. This does not imply inferiority of the woman or superiority of the man but makes clear the difference in the role assignment for each. God's order of creation is irrevocable and inviolable (see **Biblical Womanhood,** p. 8). The relationship between God the Father and God the Son serves as a model for husbands and wives—equality in essence (Jn 14:9) and distinction in office (Jn 14:28). Both men and women were created in the image of God, and yet He gives to each a purposeful assignment. This order comes from God. Order is not a reflection of personal worth or value but a prelude to purpose and effectiveness. Everyone wants to know his role and rank. Most jobs come with a description and chart explaining the pecking order. A lack of clarity causes more harm, confusion, and mistrust than an honest description of reality.

Paul was reminding all that order and authority are part of every area of life, including life in the Godhead. This truth should be a tremendous encouragement to all women. Christ does not shrink back from His role but clearly defines that role for the betterment of everyone. Ontologically, the three persons of the Trinity are equal in value and importance. Practically and functionally, however, their individual roles vary. If the persons of the triunity can find satisfaction and contentment in their assigned roles, then women ought to follow suit quickly. This understanding is also the basis for role differentiation among men and women in the home and in the church.

Male headship in the home and church is necessary because of its reflection of the relationship between God the Father and Jesus the Son. While men and women are both created to reflect the image of God, they are given unique assignments on how to do so.

>WORD|*study*

11:3 Head (Gk *kephalē*, "top, chief, one to whom others are subordinate") is used 11 times in verses 3-13. Although the word does not always carry the same meaning, the context clearly indicates whether the word is to be understood in the spiritual (vv. 3a,3b,4b,5b) or physical sense (vv. 4a,5a,5c,6,7,10,13). The word is best and most often understood to refer to "authority over." Colossians and Ephesians also refer to Christ as the "head" (Eph 1:22; 4:15; 5:23; Col 1:18; 2:10).

head shaved. 6 So if a woman's head[A]
is not covered, her hair should be cut
off. But if it is disgraceful for a woman to have her hair cut off or her
head shaved, she should be covered.
7 A man, in fact, should not cover
his head, because he is God's image
and glory, but woman is man's glory.
8 For man did not come from woman, but woman came from man.
9 And man was not created for woman, but woman for man. 10 This is
why a woman should have a symbol
of authority on her head, because of
the angels. 11 In the Lord, however,
woman is not independent of man,
and man is not independent of woman. 12 For just as woman came from
man, so man comes through woman, and all things come from God.
13 Judge for yourselves: Is it proper
for a woman to pray to God with her
head uncovered? 14 Does not even nature itself teach you that if a man has
long hair it is a disgrace to him, 15 but
that if a woman has long hair, it is her
glory? For her hair is given to her[B] as
a covering. 16 But if anyone wants to
argue about this, we have no other[C]
custom, nor do the churches of God.

Self-Control and the Lord's Supper (11:17-34)

17 Now in giving the following instruction I do not praise you, since
you come together not for the better but for the worse. 18 For to begin
with, I hear that when you come
together as a church there are divisions among you, and in part I
believe it. 19 There must, indeed, be
factions among you, so that those
who are approved may be recognized
among you. 20 Therefore, when you
come together, it is not really to eat
the Lord's Supper. 21 For at the meal,
each one eats his own supper ahead
of others. So one person is hungry
while another gets drunk! 22 Don't
you have houses to eat and drink in?
Or do you look down on the church
of God and embarrass those who
have nothing? What should I say to
you? Should I praise you? I do not
praise you for this!
23 For I received from the Lord
what I also passed on to you: On the
night when He was betrayed, the
Lord Jesus took bread, 24 gave thanks,
broke it, and said,[D] "This is My body,
which is[E] for you. Do this in remembrance of Me."
25 In the same way, after supper
He also took the cup and said, "This
cup is the new covenant established
by My blood. Do this, as often as you
drink it, in remembrance of Me."
26 For as often as you eat this bread

Doctrine THE LORD'S SUPPER

The Lord's Supper was instituted by Jesus Christ. He commanded its observance and asked that it be done as a **remembrance** and celebration of His sacrifice and love. Jesus ate the Last Supper with His disciples during Passover and just before He died (Mt 26:19-30). Jesus died at Passover as He became the new Passover Lamb (1Co 5:7) and instituted this memorial supper to commemorate His death (11:24-25). The annual Passover celebration marked the deliverance of the Jews from Egypt (Ex 12:24-27).

The events in the Supper continue to speak eloquently to believers. The symbolism of the **bread** as His broken **body** and **the cup** as His shed **blood** reenact in the believer's heart the vicarious death of Jesus in his behalf. Therefore, the Supper is for repentant sinners who have accepted Christ as Savior. This memorial supper is to be observed **until He comes** (1Co 11:26), looking forward always to the Lamb's Supper (Rv 19:7-9). Several distinct truths are communicated in observing the Lord's Supper:

- a memorial to the central truth in Christianity—the atonement of Christ (1Co 11:24-25),
- the fellowship within the body of Christ (v. 18),
- a diagnostic feast in which the believer examines his own walk with Christ (v. 28),
- a feast of thanksgiving for salvation (v. 24),
- an evangelistic witness to Christ's death (v. 26), and
- an eschatological feast of hope (v. 26).

head, or husband, by opposing the purpose God created her to fulfill. She was also taking value away from the importance of femininity by exclaiming that its importance was so little that it was much better simply to be like a man. The striking importance of this letter for today's readers is jolting as many men of this generation have been so squashed by the modern feminist movement that they hardly know what it means to be men or leaders. There is a lack of understanding on the part of males and females to understand and fulfill their assigned and crucially important roles, and this deficiency has very obviously harmed society.

11:6 In Paul's day the only women whose heads were **shaved** or who wore short hair were prostitutes or adulteresses.

11:7-9 Glory (Gk *doxa*, "reputation, credit, honor") speaks of adornment, beauty, or a crown indicating high rank. Creating man from the dust of the earth was a display of God's majesty and glory. In this sense, the man pointed to and gave glory to God the Father. Woman, also created by God to display His image, was created not only from the man, but for the man as a helper (Gn 2:18). She has a different purpose, namely, helping the man as a co-regent of the earth. In this way, she is a beautiful adornment to him.

11:10 There is much confusion concerning the phrase **because of the angels**. The most natural understanding for their presence in the worship services would be angels as heavenly beings created for the work of God. In this case, the presence of these exalted heavenly visitors ought to inspire these women to demonstrate their submission to their husbands and to God.

11:11-12 Knowing that this issue would be difficult for some to accept, Paul affirmed the value and importance of both men and women, who have equal opportunity to know God and experience His spiritual benefits. Both men and women are needed in the church, in life, and in marriage. Men and women need each other and cannot accomplish God's purpose alone (Gn 2:18). God has created this beneficial and challenging dichotomy, and it must be recognized as from the Lord, as beautiful, and without contention. Logically, no one should be prideful regarding his position or earthly assignment; neither should he be ashamed because each assignment, or in this case gender, comes directly from God, with intrinsic value and worth.

[A] **11:6** Lit *a woman* [B] **11:15** Other mss omit *to her* [C] **11:16** Or *no such* [D] **11:24** Other mss add "*Take, eat.* [E] **11:24** Other mss add *broken*

11:28 Paul encouraged everyone to **examine** (Gk *dokimazetō*, "put to the test, prove by testing") himself honestly before partaking in the Lord's Supper, which should be observed seriously and with reverence. The idea is to put yourself on trial, not in the sense of exposing yourself to the judgment of others but to do an intense searching of your own heart and life to find anything that is unacceptable to God.

11:30 The word **asleep** was used to refer to death.

12:4-7 Spiritual **gifts** should not be divisive and distracting. The problem is not with the Distributor of the gifts but with the recipients. The Corinthians placed too much importance on certain gifts. Paul began by clarifying the gifts and purposes. His list was not meant to be exhaustive but instructive.

12:8 Generally, **a message of wisdom** is understood to be knowing God's Word, understanding His will, and being able to make known God's wisdom to individuals in a particular situation (cp. Ac 6:1-6; 15:13-21). The **message of knowledge** indicates a sharp mind with the ability to study and understand difficult principles and truths that many cannot grasp on their own.

12:9 The gift of **faith** is an important and unusual ability to trust God, a great benefit in particularly difficult circumstances (13:2; cp. Jms 5:17-18). **Healing** is a supernatural work that has always been accomplished by God. In New Testament times, God healed through the apostles, the 70, and some associates of the apostles. Christians may freely ask God for healing but must realize that even in New Testament times, as now, some may receive healing and some may not. God may work through the medical profession or through simply willing the healing to come to pass. God is still good whatever the outcome. Even Paul could not heal indiscriminately (2Tm 4:20).

12:10 God works in commonly observed patterns that may differ from those used in **the performing of miracles**. They were a sign to show the glory of God so that people would believe in Jesus (Heb 2:3-4). **Prophecy** (Gk *prophēteia*, linking *pro*, a preposition meaning "before" with *phēmi*, a verb meaning "speak") carries a breadth of meaning from the speaking of the words of God before people to speaking about an event before it occurs.

The gift of **distinguishing between spirits** has also been called discernment and is an important gift in protecting and guiding the church because Satan is so skilled at distorting

and drink the cup, you proclaim the
Lord's death until He comes.
[27] Therefore, whoever eats the
bread or drinks the cup of the Lord
in an unworthy way will be •guilty
of sin against the body[A] and blood of
the Lord. [28] So a man should examine
himself; in this way he should eat the
bread and drink from the cup. [29] For
whoever eats and drinks without recognizing the body,[B] eats and drinks
judgment on himself. [30] This is why
many are sick and ill among you,
and many have fallen •asleep. [31] If we
were properly evaluating ourselves,
we would not be judged, [32] but when
we are judged, we are disciplined by
the Lord, so that we may not be condemned with the •world.
[33] Therefore, my •brothers, when
you come together to eat, wait for
one another. [34] If anyone is hungry,
he should eat at home, so that when
you gather together you will not
come under judgment. And I will
give instructions about the other
matters whenever I come.

Spiritual Gifts and the Body of Christ (12:1-31)

12 Now concerning what comes
from the Spirit:[C] •brothers,
I do not want you to be unaware.
[2] You know that when you were pagans, you used to be led off to the
idols that could not speak. [3] Therefore I am informing you that no one
speaking by the Spirit of God says,
"Jesus is cursed," and no one can
say, "Jesus is Lord," except by the
Holy Spirit.
[4] Now there are different gifts, but
the same Spirit. [5] There are different
ministries, but the same Lord. [6] And
there are different activities, but the
same God activates each gift in each
person.[D] [7] A demonstration of the
Spirit is given to each person to produce what is beneficial:

[8] to one is given a message
of wisdom
through the Spirit,
to another, a message
of knowledge
by the same Spirit,

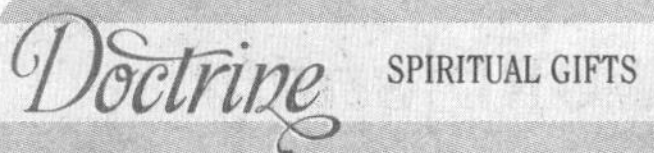

SPIRITUAL GIFTS

Paul mentions about 20 different gifts in his epistles, arranged in four passages according to purpose:

- Rm 12:6-8, discussing gifts in a general way;
- Eph 4:7-13, introducing gifts that work toward unity in the body of Christ;
- 1Pt 4:10-11, emphasizing the service rendered by the gifts;
- 1Co 12:8-10,28-30, setting forth some of the more extraordinary gifts.

These gifts are undoubtedly supernaturally endowed and not merely natural or human giftedness. The Holy Spirit gives one or more gifts to every believer (vv. 7,11), and there were clear purposes noted for these gifts:

- the common good or **what is beneficial** (v. 7);
- the proper functioning of believers within the body of Christ (vv. 14-27);
- edification and equipping of believers (14:3-12);
- affirmation of the preached word—the gospel (14:24; Ac 1:8; Heb 2:3-4);
- cooperation among believers (1Co 12:14-26).

[9] to another, faith
by the same Spirit,
to another, gifts of healing
by the one Spirit,
[10] to another, the performing
of miracles,
to another, prophecy,
to another, distinguishing
between spirits,
to another, different kinds
of •languages,
to another, interpretation
of languages.
[11] But one and the same Spirit is active in all these, distributing to each
person as He wills.
[12] For as the body is one and has
many parts, and all the parts of
that body, though many, are one
body—so also is Christ. [13] For we
were all baptized by[E] one Spirit into
one body—whether Jews or Greeks,
whether •slaves or free—and we
were all made to drink of one Spirit.
[14] So the body is not one part but
many. [15] If the foot should say, "Because I'm not a hand, I don't belong
to the body," in spite of this it still
belongs to the body. [16] And if the ear
should say, "Because I'm not an eye,
I don't belong to the body," in spite
of this it still belongs to the body. [17] If
the whole body were an eye, where

[A] **11:27** Lit *be guilty of the body* [B] **11:29** Other mss read *drinks unworthily, not discerning the Lord's body* [C] **12:1** Or *concerning spiritual things*, or *spiritual gifts* [D] **12:6** Lit *God acts all things in all* [E] **12:13** Or *with*, or *in*

would the hearing be? If the whole body were an ear, where would the sense of smell be? 18 But now God has placed each one of the parts in one body just as He wanted. 19 And if they were all the same part, where would the body be? 20 Now there are many parts, yet one body.

21 So the eye cannot say to the hand, "I don't need you!" Or again, the head can't say to the feet, "I don't need you!" 22 But even more, those parts of the body that seem to be weaker are necessary. 23 And those parts of the body that we think to be less honorable, we clothe these with greater honor, and our unpresentable parts have a better presentation. 24 But our presentable parts have no need of clothing. Instead, God has put the body together, giving greater honor to the less honorable, 25 so that there would be no division in the body, but that the members would have the same concern for each other. 26 So if one member suffers, all the members suffer with it; if one member is honored, all the members rejoice with it.

27 Now you are the body of Christ, and individual members of it. 28 And God has placed these in the church:

first apostles, second prophets,
third teachers, next miracles,
then gifts of healing, helping,
managing, various kinds
of languages.
29 Are all apostles?
Are all prophets?
Are all teachers?
Do all do miracles?
30 Do all have gifts of healing?
Do all speak
in other languages?
Do all interpret?

31 But desire the greater gifts. And I will show you an even better way.

Loving Others and Spiritual Maturity (13:1–14:40)

13 If I speak human or angelic
•languages
but do not have love,
I am a sounding gong
or a clanging cymbal.
2 If I have the gift of prophecy
and understand all •mysteries
and all knowledge,
and if I have all faith
so that I can move mountains
but do not have love,
I am nothing.
3 And if I donate all my goods
to feed the poor,
and if I give my body in order
to boast[A]
but do not have love,
I gain nothing.
4 Love is patient, love is kind.
Love does not envy,
is not boastful,
is not conceited,
5 does not act improperly,
is not selfish, is not provoked,
and does not keep a record
of wrongs.
6 Love finds no joy
in unrighteousness
but rejoices in the truth.
7 It bears all things, believes
all things,
hopes all things, endures
all things.

8 Love never ends.
But as for prophecies,
they will come to an end;
as for languages,
they will cease;
as for knowledge, it will come
to an end.
9 For we know in part,
and we prophesy in part.
10 But when the perfect comes,
the partial will come
to an end.
11 When I was a child,
I spoke like a child,
I thought like a child,
I reasoned like a child.
When I became a man,
I put aside childish things.
12 For now we see indistinctly,[B]
as in a mirror,[C]
but then face to face.
Now I know in part,
but then I will know fully,
as I am fully known.
13 Now these three remain:
faith, hope, and love.
But the greatest of these
is love.

[A]13:3 Other mss read *body to be burned* [B]13:12 Or *indirectly* [C]13:12 Ancient mirrors were normally made out of polished metals and were not as clear as modern ones.

the truth and confusing well-meaning people.

Different kinds of languages were gifts that were certainly used in New Testament churches and given by God. However, they were being misused in the Corinthian church as Paul explained in 1Co 14; he provided very clear guidelines to direct the use of this gift in church meetings.

12:11 Paul concludes the naming of the gifts by reminding his readers that the Holy **Spirit is active** and involved in all these gifts, and He determines who will receive the gift(s). And, all must realize that the Holy Spirit does not give gifts in a vacuum. They are all given to unify and build the church. Therefore, division because of gifts is in direct contradiction to God's purpose in bestowing the gifts.

12:12-27 Paul uses the human **body** as a great metaphor describing the universal and local body of Christ. Like the parts of the human body, the members of the church body must unify, work together, and efficiently learn to live in the most effective way.

12:13 At conversion the believer is **baptized by one Spirit** and simultaneously united to the body of Christ—the church (see **Hard Question**, p. 1407).

12:28 Paul uses the word **apostles** in its particular or restrictive sense to mean the Twelve (Lk 6:13), whom the Spirit inspired and empowered in unique ways. An "apostle" had to be a witness of the resurrection (cp. Ac 1:21-24). These men had no successors. However, public proclamation and teaching continue in the church today.

13:1-13 True, complete, Christlike love is the overarching theme of this epistle. Obviously, Jesus Christ is the picture of this **love** (Gk *agapē*). God Himself came to earth to exhibit perfectly all these previously unknown qualities. Jesus did not merely possess the qualities of love; He exercised them naturally and consistently. The love of which Paul speaks is so profound and life-changing that it should diminish many of the problems faced by the church, such as pride, selfishness, and division. The Corinthians were overwhelmed with self-love. Paul certainly knew about self-love. He had formerly hated and persecuted Christians. Paul knew firsthand the transforming power of Christ's love. He strongly desired that the Corinthians know and experience this love.

13:11-13 Paul uses the illustration of growing from **a child** to **a man** to explain that with knowledge and maturity comes responsibility to react the right way. As God's people learn, spiritual truth ought to shape their behavior and interaction with others.

14:1-5 Paul stresses the importance of the gift of **prophecy** because this gift, like no other, edifies, encourages, and comforts.

14:6-19 Using strong examples, Paul appealed to the people to seek order and clarity. He affirmed the gift of languages but stressed the importance of **understanding**, which would allow more people to grow. Paul, as the consummate soul-winner and spiritual father, always desired growth and maturity among his converts.

14:26-28 Paul began addressing the group as **brothers**, a generic term including men and women. He was coming, still with authority, but as a fellow heir of Christ Jesus. Paul did not forbid ecstatic utterance, but he placed limitations upon its practice.

14:34-35 This controversial section grabs the attention of women. In a sense Paul is saying, if you are really trying to build up others, why does each one of you want your own ministry showcased? The problems the church faced were not caused by women alone. However, clearly the women were out of order, misusing gifts in ways that were harmful to the church and its mission.

Paul had previously affirmed women and acknowledged that, along with men, they would receive spiritual gifts. He encouraged all believers, both male and female, to use their respective gifts in ministry within the body. However, women as well as men were required to follow guidelines in church meetings. Paul stood against disorder and disobedience.

14:34 Possible interpretations of this verse include:

- **Women** were not to **speak** at all, which would seem to contradict the earlier passages where Paul commended the women who prayed and prophesied under the headship of their respective husbands (11:5; 14:26).
- This verse was addressed only to the Corinthians and to no other church beyond them, which would seem to unravel the entire point of the letter since Paul's instructions have been carefully presented with clear theological foundations and as principles transcending time.
- Women are to **be silent** with respect to the activity under discussion, which is the judging of prophecies since this is a task of governing (14:28). The argument is that "doctrinal guardianship" is the task of men.

14 Pursue love and desire spiritual gifts, and above all that you may prophesy. [2] For the person who speaks in another •language is not speaking to men but to God, since no one understands him; however, he speaks •mysteries in the Spirit.[A] [3] But the person who prophesies speaks to people for edification, encouragement, and consolation. [4] The person who speaks in another language builds himself up, but he who prophesies builds up the church. [5] I wish all of you spoke in other languages, but even more that you prophesied. The person who prophesies is greater than the person who speaks in languages, unless he interprets so that the church may be built up.

[6] But now, •brothers, if I come to you speaking in other languages, how will I benefit you unless I speak to you with a revelation or knowledge or prophecy or teaching? [7] Even inanimate things that produce sounds—whether flute or harp—if they don't make a distinction in the notes, how will what is played on the flute or harp be recognized? [8] In fact, if the trumpet makes an unclear sound, who will prepare for battle? [9] In the same way, unless you use your tongue for intelligible speech, how will what is spoken be known? For you will be speaking into the air. [10] There are doubtless many different kinds of languages in the world, and all have meaning.[B] [11] Therefore, if I do not know the meaning of the language, I will be a foreigner[C] to the speaker, and the speaker will be a foreigner to me. [12] So also you—since you are zealous for spiritual gifts,[D] seek to excel in building up the church.

[13] Therefore the person who speaks in another language should pray that he can interpret. [14] For if I pray in another language, my spirit prays, but my understanding is unfruitful. [15] What then? I will pray with the spirit, and I will also pray with my understanding. I will sing with the spirit, and I will also sing with my understanding. [16] Otherwise, if you praise with the spirit,[E] how will the uninformed person[F] say "•Amen" at your giving of thanks, since he does not know what you are saying? [17] For you may very well be giving thanks, but the other person is not being built up. [18] I thank God that I speak in other languages more than all of you; [19] yet in the church I would rather speak five words with my understanding, in order to teach others also, than 10,000 words in another language.

[20] Brothers, don't be childish in your thinking, but be infants in regard to evil and adult in your thinking. [21] It is written in the law:

> **I will speak to these people**
> **by people of other languages**
> **and by the lips of foreigners,**
> **and even then, they will not**
> **listen to Me,**[G]

says the Lord. [22] It follows that speaking in other languages is intended as a sign,[H] not for believers but for unbelievers. But prophecy is not for unbelievers but for believers. [23] Therefore, if the whole church assembles together and all are speaking in other languages and people who are uninformed or unbelievers come in, will they not say that you are out of your minds? [24] But if all are prophesying and some unbeliever or uninformed person comes in, he is convicted by all and is judged by all. [25] The secrets of his heart will be revealed, and as a result he will fall facedown and worship God, proclaiming, "God is really among you."

[26] What then is the conclusion, brothers? Whenever you come together, each one[I] has a psalm, a teaching, a revelation, another language, or an interpretation. All things must be done for edification. [27] If any person speaks in another language, there should be only two, or at the most three, each in turn, and someone must interpret. [28] But if there is no interpreter, that person should keep silent in the church and speak to himself and to God. [29] Two or three prophets should speak, and

[A] **14:2** Or *in spirit*, or *in his spirit* [B] **14:10** Lit *and none is without a sound* [C] **14:11** Gk *barbaros* = in Eng a "barbarian." To a Gk, a *barbaros* was anyone who did not speak Gk. [D] **14:12** Lit *zealous of spirits*; *spirits* = human spirits, spiritual powers, or the Holy Spirit [E] **14:16** Or *praise by the Spirit* [F] **14:16** Lit *the one filling the place of the uninformed* [G] **14:21** Is 28:11-12 [H] **14:22** Lit *that languages are for a sign* [I] **14:26** Other mss add *of you*

the others should evaluate. 30 But if something has been revealed to another person sitting there, the first prophet should be silent. 31 For you can all prophesy one by one, so that everyone may learn and everyone may be encouraged. 32 And the prophets' spirits are under the control of the prophets, 33 since God is not a God of disorder but of peace.

As in all the churches of the •saints, 34 the women[A] should be silent in the churches, for they are not permitted to speak, but should be submissive, as the law also says. 35 And if they want to learn something, they should ask their own husbands at home, for it is disgraceful for a woman to speak in the church meeting. 36 Did the word of God originate from you, or did it come to you only?

37 If anyone thinks he is a prophet or spiritual, he should recognize that what I write to you is the Lord's command. 38 But if anyone ignores this, he will be ignored.[B] 39 Therefore, my brothers, be eager to prophesy, and do not forbid speaking in other languages. 40 But everything must be done decently and in order.

Teachings About the Resurrection (15:1-58)

15 Now •brothers, I want to clarify[C] for you the gospel I proclaimed to you; you received it and have taken your stand on it. 2 You are also saved by it, if you hold to the message I proclaimed to you—unless you believed for no purpose.[D] 3 For I passed on to you as most important what I also received:

that Christ died for our sins
according to the Scriptures,
4 that He was buried,
that He was raised
on the third day
according to the Scriptures,
5 and that He appeared
to •Cephas,
then to the Twelve.
6 Then He appeared to
over 500 brothers
at one time;
most of them are still alive,
but some have fallen •asleep.
7 Then He appeared to James,
then to all the apostles.
8 Last of all, as to one
abnormally born,[E]
He also appeared to me.

9 For I am the least of the apostles, unworthy to be called an apostle, because I persecuted the church of God. 10 But by God's grace I am what I am, and His grace toward me was not ineffective. However, I worked more than any of them, yet not I, but God's grace that was with me. 11 Therefore, whether it is I or they, so we proclaim and so you have believed.

12 Now if Christ is proclaimed as raised from the dead, how can some of you say, "There is no resurrection of the dead"? 13 But if there is no resurrection of the dead, then Christ has not been raised; 14 and if Christ has not been raised, then our proclamation is without foundation, and so is your faith.[F] 15 In addition, we are found to be false witnesses about God, because we have testified about God that He raised up Christ—whom He did not raise up if in fact the dead are not raised. 16 For if the dead are not raised, Christ has not been raised. 17 And if Christ has not been raised, your faith is worthless; you are still in your sins. 18 Therefore, those who have fallen asleep in Christ have also perished. 19 If we have put our hope in Christ for this life only, we should be pitied more than anyone.

20 But now Christ has been raised from the dead, the •firstfruits of those who have fallen asleep. 21 For since death came through a man, the resurrection of the dead also comes through a man. 22 For as in Adam all die, so also in Christ all will be made alive. 23 But each in his own order: Christ, the firstfruits; afterward, at His coming, those who belong to Christ. 24 Then comes the end, when He hands over the kingdom to God the Father, when He abolishes all rule and all authority and power. 25 For He must reign

Women speaking out of turn and critically evaluating teaching or interpretations would show an obvious lack of submission and a rebellion against God's order. Therefore, Paul instructed the women to hold their tongues and refrain from speaking out in the meetings of the congregation. This command to "be silent" does not reflect a prejudice against women. Undoubtedly, God gifts women with intellect, leadership ability, and spiritual gifts. The restriction is not based on inherent value or ability but on order.

14:35 This restriction would allow women, who previously were given no encouragement in learning, the opportunity to participate in education and to ask questions in the proper setting—one in which **their own husbands** were encouraged to teach them. By encouraging a woman to ask spiritual questions of her own husband, Paul was allowing a wife's spiritual desires to fuel the growth of her husband, who would be challenged to immerse himself in studying God's Word and prayer in order to answer the questions of his wife.

15:1-8 Paul brought the Corinthians back to the main thing: Christ and the gospel. Nowhere is there a clearer and more concise rendering of the essence of the gospel:

- **Christ died for our sins** (v. 3);
- **He was buried** (v. 4);
- He arose **on the third day** (v. 4);
- He was seen by many eyewitnesses (vv. 5-7); and
- He also **appeared to** Paul (v. 8).

15:9-11 Paul humbly notes that he was not one of the original Twelve. He also shares the failures of his former life. Had it not been for Christ's miraculous appearance to Him, Paul never would have experienced salvation or apostleship. Paul did not doubt his authority but acknowledged the power of God to forgive him and use him to advance the kingdom he had formerly resisted. God extended grace to him and was using him and others to further the gospel message.

15:12-20 Paul explains that without the resurrection the gospel is a useless message. If there will be no **resurrection of the dead**, then those who preach the resurrected **Christ** are **false witnesses**. Paul stresses that without Christ's resurrection, trusting Him to save you from your sins would be futile. If resurrection is impossible, then so is the forgiveness of sin and eternal **hope** in Jesus Christ.

In Paul's teaching on the future resurrection of believers, he describes Jesus' resurrection as **the firstfruits**. This has nothing to do with time.

[A] **14:34** Other mss read *your women* [B] **14:38** Other mss read *he should be ignored* [C] **15:1** Or *I make known* [D] **15:2** Or *believed without careful thought*, or *believed in vain* [E] **15:8** Or *one whose birth was unusual, He* [F] **15:14** Or *proclamation is useless, and your faith also is useless*, or *proclamation is empty, and your faith also is empty*

Others before Jesus were raised from the dead (see Jn 11:38-44 for one example). Jesus is first in rank. Through His triumph over death, Jesus has led the way for those who, by faith in Him, will likewise be resurrected on the day of judgment and never die again. Because of the resurrection of Christ, a believer can be confident in her own resurrection.

15:28 Paul explains that **when everything is subject to Christ** that does not change His eternal position within the Godhead. God the Father is the One who places everything under the rule of Jesus, and only the Father is not under the feet of Jesus. Jesus will deliver the earthly, millennial kingdom to the Father. While Jesus had a position and purpose different than God the Father, He continued to have equal value. He is co-eternal and co-equal with the Father.

15:29 The concept of **being baptized for the dead** is difficult to interpret and must be understood in light of other clearer passages regarding baptism. Apparently in the church at Corinth people were being baptized on behalf of believers who died without baptism. Paul points out that this practice was meaningless, especially if they did not believe in the resurrection. Nowhere does Scripture encourage a person to be baptized for a dead person. Since baptism saves no one, being baptized in the place of those who are already dead cannot be of value to anyone.

15:35-46 The glorified **body** is beyond human understanding and cannot be explained, but Paul does provide a helpful analogy. God has a plan for the earthly bodies as a gardener has a plan for his seeds and eventual harvest. The resurrected body is related to the old body in some sense, but it is also a new creation.

15:45-49 All are born like **Adam** with a natural bent toward sinning. Like Adam, all need forgiveness of that sin and a supernatural Savior. Only those who receive forgiveness of sin and accept Jesus as Savior and Lord can be reborn as heavenly or spiritual people.

15:50-52 A mystery is a revealed truth that cannot be discerned by human wisdom. Paul addresses the "mystery" that not all believers will face death. **The dead** in Christ **will be raised** before the great tribulation, and they will have received glorified bodies. Believers still living will be instantly caught up in the air and changed into their glorified bodies (cp. 1Th 4:14-17).

15:54-55 Once Christ has accomplished His work, as predicted in Is 25:8, **death**

until He puts all His enemies under
His feet. 26 The last enemy to be abolished is death. 27 For **God has put everything under His feet.**[A] But when
it says "everything" is put under
Him, it is obvious that He who puts
everything under Him is the exception. 28 And when everything is subject to Christ, then the Son Himself
will also be subject to the One who
subjected everything to Him, so that
God may be all in all.

29 Otherwise what will they do who
are being baptized for the dead? If
the dead are not raised at all, then
why are people baptized for them?[B]
30 Why are we in danger every hour?
31 I affirm by the pride in you that I
have in Christ Jesus our Lord: I die
every day! 32 If I fought wild animals
in Ephesus with only human hope,[C]
what good did that do me?[D] If the
dead are not raised, **Let us eat and
drink, for tomorrow we die.**[E] 33 Do
not be deceived: "Bad company corrupts good morals."[F] 34 Come to your
senses[G] and stop sinning, for some
people are ignorant about God. I say
this to your shame.

35 But someone will say, "How are
the dead raised? What kind of body
will they have when they come?"
36 Foolish one! What you sow does
not come to life unless it dies. 37 And
as for what you sow—you are not
sowing the future body, but only a
seed,[H] perhaps of wheat or another
grain. 38 But God gives it a body as
He wants, and to each of the seeds
its own body. 39 Not all flesh is the
same flesh; there is one flesh for
humans, another for animals, another for birds, and another for fish.
40 There are heavenly bodies and
earthly bodies, but the splendor of
the heavenly bodies is different from
that of the earthly ones. 41 There is a
splendor of the sun, another of the
moon, and another of the stars; for
one star differs from another star in
splendor. 42 So it is with the resurrection of the dead:

Sown in corruption, raised
in incorruption;
43 sown in dishonor, raised
in glory;
sown in weakness, raised
in power;
44 sown a natural body, raised
a spiritual body.

If there is a natural body, there is
also a spiritual body. 45 So it is written: **The first man Adam became a
living being;**[I] the last Adam became
a life-giving Spirit. 46 However, the
spiritual is not first, but the natural,
then the spiritual.

47 The first man was
from the earth
and made of dust;
the second man is[J]
from heaven.
48 Like the man made of dust,
so are those who are made
of dust;
like the heavenly man,
so are those who are heavenly.
49 And just as we have borne
the image of the man made
of dust,
we will also bear
the image of
the heavenly man.

50 Brothers, I tell you this: Flesh
and blood cannot inherit the kingdom of God, and corruption cannot
inherit incorruption. 51 Listen! I am
telling you a •mystery:

We will not all fall asleep,
but we will all be changed,
52 in a moment, in the blink
of an eye,
at the last trumpet.
For the trumpet will sound,
and the dead will be
raised incorruptible,
and we will be changed.
53 For this corruptible
must be clothed
with incorruptibility,
and this mortal
must be clothed
with immortality.
54 When this corruptible
is clothed
with incorruptibility,
and this mortal is clothed

[A]15:27 Ps 8:6 [B]15:29 Other mss read *for the dead* [C]15:32 Lit *Ephesus according to man* [D]15:32 Lit *what to me the profit?* [E]15:32 Is 22:13 [F]15:33 A quotation from the poet Menander, *Thais*, 218 [G]15:34 Lit *Sober up righteously* [H]15:37 Lit *but a naked seed* [I]15:45 Gn 2:7 [J]15:47 Other mss add *the Lord*

with immortality,
then the saying that is written
will take place:
Death has been swallowed up
in victory.[A]
55 **Death, where is your victory?**
Death, where is your sting?[B]
56 Now the sting of death is sin,
and the power of sin is the law.
57 But thanks be to God,
who gives us the victory
through our Lord
Jesus Christ!

58 Therefore, my dear brothers, be
steadfast, immovable, always excelling in the Lord's work, knowing that
your labor in the Lord is not in vain.

Concluding Personal Reminders (16:1-24)

The Gift for the Church in Jerusalem (16:1-4)

16 Now about the collection for
the •saints: You should do the
same as I instructed the Galatian
churches. 2 On the first day of the
week,[C] each of you is to set something aside and save in keeping with
how he prospers, so that no collections will need to be made when I
come. 3 When I arrive, I will send
with letters those you recommend
to carry your gracious gift to Jerusalem. 4 If it is suitable for me to go as
well, they can travel with me.

Plans for Paul's Travel (16:5-12)

5 I will come to you after I pass
through Macedonia—for I will be
traveling through Macedonia— 6 and
perhaps I will remain with you or
even spend the winter, so that you
may send me on my way wherever
I go. 7 I don't want to see you now
just in passing, for I hope to spend
some time with you, if the Lord allows. 8 But I will stay in Ephesus until Pentecost, 9 because a wide door
for effective ministry has opened
for me[D]—yet many oppose me. 10 If
Timothy comes, see that he has
nothing to fear from you, because
he is doing the Lord's work, just as I
am. 11 Therefore, no one should look
down on him. Send him on his way
in peace so he can come to me, for
I am expecting him with the brothers.[E]
12 About our brother Apollos: I
strongly urged him to come to you
with the brothers, but he was not at
all willing to come now. However, he
will come when he has an opportunity.

A Final Exhortation from Paul (16:13-24)

13 Be alert, stand firm in the faith,
act like a man, be strong. 14 Your every action must be done with love.
15 •Brothers, you know the household of Stephanas: They are the
•firstfruits of Achaia and have devoted themselves to serving the saints.
I urge you 16 also to submit to such
people, and to everyone who works
and labors with them. 17 I am pleased
to have Stephanas, Fortunatus, and
Achaicus present, because these
men have made up for your absence.
18 For they have refreshed my spirit
and yours. Therefore recognize such
people.
19 The churches of •Asia greet
you. Aquila and Priscilla greet you
warmly in the Lord, along with the
church that meets in their home.
20 All the brothers greet you. Greet
one another with a holy kiss.
21 This greeting is in my own
hand[F]—Paul. 22 If anyone does not
love the Lord, a curse be on him.
Marana tha that is, Lord, come![G]
23 The grace of the Lord Jesus be
with you. 24 My love be with all of
you in Christ Jesus.

will be **swallowed up** (1Co 15:54) in the **victory** of Jesus Christ. All acknowledge death as the unavoidable ultimate enemy; but Jesus will conquer even death, removing its power and **sting**. God will give His people victory over sin and death because of the sacrifice and work of Jesus Christ.

16:1-4 Since Paul was a traveling missionary, he could easily assess the needs of the churches and share news among congregations, which apparently he did regularly. Paul not only admonished the Corinthians to give to other believers who were in need, but he also told them how to give. He explained setting aside money systematically, according to the family's prosperity. The money was to be set aside before he arrived as a measure of accountability or a test for their maturity. He explained that he would make sure the gift was given to the **Jerusalem** church, which was suffering because of great persecution.

16:10-12 Paul made clear that Timothy would return and give him a report, thus providing accountability to the church for their behavior. Paul also mentioned **Apollos**, who was known to be a great preacher. Paul was able to accept the fact that God was directing Apollos, and God's timing must be trusted.

16:19-20 These verses are significant because Paul left the Corinthians with the impression that many believers were standing with them and supporting them in their efforts to become like Christ and to promote the kingdom of God. This accountability was healthy and encouraging. Paul was reminding the Corinthians that all believers are fighting an important fight.

16:22 ***Marana tha*** is a transliteration of two Aramaic words. It can be understood in two ways: either *marana tha*, meaning "Our Lord, come!" or *maran atha*, meaning "Our Lord has come!" In the New Testament this exclamation occurs only here. Since Paul had expounded on Christ's coming kingdom in chapter 15, he likely meant "Our Lord, come!"—which was an appropriate expression of joy and hope regarding Christ's return.

[A] **15:54** Is 25:8 [B] **15:55** Hs 13:14 [C] **16:2** Or *Each Sunday* [D] **16:9** Lit *for a door has opened to me, great and effective* [E] **16:11** *With the brothers* may connect with Paul or Timothy. [F] **16:21** Paul normally dictated his letters to a secretary, but signed the end of each letter himself; Rm 16:22; Gl 6:11; Col 4:18; 2Th 3:17. [G] **16:22** Or *Maran atha* (an Aram expression transliterated into Gk) = *Our Lord has come!*

WRITTEN ON MY *Heart*

1 CORINTHIANS . . . No one should seek her own good but the good of others. In the church, that means considering others before yourself and putting away those things that cause factions or that cause others to stumble. If each member would do this—put others first to build up the body—the witness of the church would burn so brightly in this dark world that it would never go out!

2 Corinthians

Timeline	1000 BC	550 BC	44 BC	AD 47–49
▶ World Events ▶ Biblical Events	Founding of Corinth by Dorian Greeks	Construction of the Temple of Apollo	Rebuilding of Corinth, by Julius Caesar, as a colony of Rome	Paul's first missionary journey

"If anyone is in Christ, he is a new creation" (5:17a).

Who wrote 2 Corinthians?

Paul is the undisputed author of this epistle, which contains many characteristics of his style and much autobiographical information (1:1; 10:1).

Who were the recipients?

Paul addressed the believers in the church he planted at Corinth during his second missionary journey (Ac 18:1-17).

When was 2 Corinthians written?

This letter was written in the year A.D. 54, not long after the writing of 1 Corinthians.

Where did it happen?

Corinth was a thriving Roman colony that mirrored ethnic, cultural, and economic diversity.

What is 2 Corinthians about?

- *Paul's apostolic authority*. Paul understood that the church's recognition of his apostolic office was closely tied to their acceptance of the gospel message.
- *False teachers*. Paul boldly warned against the deception of false teaching because the Corinthians had obviously been duped and suffered serious consequences.
- *Eternal perspective*. Looking toward heaven is a concept Paul discussed at great length in this epistle. He contrasted the earthly life with the heavenly life and offered believers an eternal perspective of a glorious future.

Why should women read 2 Corinthians?

Paul had a long and intense relationship with the Corinthians. They spent much time together, enjoyed warm fellowship in Christ, and had many confrontations. This letter was written to the church in order to prepare them for Paul's coming visit. The beginning is very positive, but the second part of the letter is strongly confrontational and straightforward as Paul defended his own authority and opposed false apostles. Paul was motivated by love to defend his ministry and thus point to Christ. His example is one from which all women can learn in order to be able lovingly to present truth and confront false teaching.

How do you read 2 Corinthians?

Second Corinthians begins with the three-part salutation typical of ancient Greco-Roman written correspondence: name of the writer, identification of the recipients, and words of greeting. Unlike other Pauline letters, these preliminaries are followed by an extended blessing (1:3-11) that introduced the nature of the epistle's contents. Paul addressed the persistent problems in the church with apostolic authority, but he had to make the case for this authority in order to be heard. His sufferings for Christ's sake proved the authenticity of his apostleship and of his genuine love for the Corinthians. Paul reiterated these themes in closing the letter and concluded with final exhortations, greeting, and benediction.

Outline

- I. Introduction (1:1-11)
  - A. Words of Greeting (1:1-2)
  - B. An Expression of Thanksgiving (1:3-11)
- II. The Defense of the Apostle (1:12–2:11)
  - A. Paul's Trustworthiness (1:12-14)
  - B. Paul's Explanation for Postponing His Visit (1:15–2:4)
  - C. Paul's Call for Forgiveness (2:5-11)
- III. The Ministry of the Apostle (2:12–6:10)
  - A. The Trip to Macedonia (2:12-13)
  - B. A Testimony of God's Sufficiency (2:14–3:6)
  - C. The Glorious New Covenant (3:7-18)
  - D. The Heart of the Gospel (4:1-6)
  - E. The Treasure of the Gospel (4:7-15)
  - F. The Eternal Perspective of the Gospel (4:16–5:21)
  - G. A Ministry Commendation (6:1-10)
- IV. The Work of the Apostle among the Corinthians (6:11–7:16)
  - A. Paul's Challenge to the Corinthians (6:11–7:1)
  - B. Paul's Response to the Corinthians (7:2-16)
- V. The Outgrowth of Paul's Ministry (8:1–9:15)
  - A. A Testimony from the Macedonians (8:1-7)
  - B. The Example of Christ (8:8-9)
  - C. An Appeal for the Collection (8:10-15)
  - D. The Response to the Collection (8:16–9:5)
  - E. Lessons Learned from Giving (9:6-15)
- VI. An Authentication of Paul's Ministry (10:1–12:13)
  - A. Paul's Authority (10:1-18)
  - B. Judging Between Genuine and False Apostles (11:1-15)
  - C. Paul's Genuine Apostleship (11:16–12:13)
- VII. Paul's Proposed Visit to Corinth (12:14-21)
- VIII. Paul's Benediction and Challenge (13:1-13)
  - A. The Apostle's Warning (13:1-4)
  - B. The Apostle's Admonition (13:5-10)
  - C. A Final Exhortation (13:11-13)

AD 49	AD 49–52	AD 50–51	AD 54	AD 54
Expulsion of many Jews from Rome by the Emperor Claudius	Paul's second missionary journey	Paul's 18-month stay in Corinth while planting the church there	Writing of 1 Corinthians	Writing of 2 Corinthians

Introduction (1:1–11)

Words of Greeting (1:1-2)

1 Paul, an apostle of Christ Jesus by God's will, and Timothy our[A] brother:

To God's church at Corinth, with all the •saints who are throughout Achaia.

2 Grace to you and peace from God our Father and the Lord Jesus Christ.

An Expression of Thanksgiving (1:3-11)

For God's comfort (1:3-7)

3 Praise the God and Father of our Lord Jesus Christ, the Father of mercies and the God of all comfort. 4 He comforts us in all our affliction,[B] so that we may be able to comfort those who are in any kind of affliction, through the comfort we ourselves receive from God. 5 For as the sufferings of Christ overflow to us, so through Christ our comfort also overflows. 6 If we are afflicted, it is for your comfort and salvation. If we are comforted, it is for your comfort, which is experienced in your endurance of the same sufferings that we suffer. 7 And our hope for you is firm, because we know that as you share in the sufferings, so you will share in the comfort.

For God's deliverance (1:8-11)

8 For we don't want you to be unaware, •brothers, of our affliction that took place in •Asia: we were completely overwhelmed—beyond our strength—so that we even despaired of life. 9 Indeed, we personally had a death sentence within ourselves, so that we would not trust in ourselves but in God who raises the dead. 10 He has delivered us from such a terrible death, and He will deliver us. We have put our hope in Him that He will deliver us again 11 while you join in helping us by your prayers. Then many will give thanks on our[C] behalf for the gift that came to us through the prayers of many.

The Defense of the Apostle (1:12–2:11)

Paul's Trustworthiness (1:12-14)

12 For this is our confidence: The testimony of our conscience is that we have conducted ourselves in the world, and especially toward you, with God-given sincerity and purity, not by fleshly[D] wisdom but by God's grace. 13 Now we are writing nothing to you other than what you can read and also understand. I hope you will understand completely— 14 as you have partially understood us—that we are your reason for pride, as you are ours, in the day of our[E] Lord Jesus.

Paul's Explanation for Postponing His Visit (1:15–2:4)

15 I planned with this confidence to come to you first, so you could have a double benefit,[F] 16 and to go on to Macedonia with your help, then come to you again from Macedonia and be given a start by you on my journey to Judea. 17 So when I planned this, was I irresponsible? Or what I plan, do I plan in a purely human[G] way so that I say "Yes, yes" and

[A]1:1 Lit *the* [B]1:4 Or *trouble*, or *tribulation*, or *trials*, or *oppression*; the Gk word has a lit meaning of being under pressure. [C]1:11 Other mss read *your* [D]1:12 The word *fleshly* (characterized by flesh) indicates that the wisdom is natural rather than spiritual. [E]1:14 Other mss omit *our* [F]1:15 Other mss read *a second joy* [G]1:17 Or *a worldly*, or *a fleshly*, or *a selfish*

Title The Greek title of the letter is *pros Korinthiogē B*, "to the Corinthians B," derived from the letter's immediate recipients.

1:3 Paul praises God as **the Father of mercies** [Gk *oiktirmōn*, "compassion, pity"; cp. Ps 103:13] **and the God of all comfort** (Gk *paraklēseōs*, "consolation, solace, encouragement"; in other contexts, "exhortation"—this word appears 16 times in the letter, cp. 1:3-7; 7:7-13). The word "comfort" suggests both the unique "consolation" of Jesus the Messiah (cp. Lk 2:25) and God's personal provision of the kind of comfort an attentive, tender-hearted mother gives her hurting or distressed child (cp. Is 66:13).

1:4 Having faced numerous hardships, Paul was familiar with **affliction** (Gk *thlipsei*, "pressure, oppression, distress, tribulation"). "Affliction" and the related verb forms occur 10 times in 2 Corinthians. The word literally suggests "pressing firmly together," particularly referring to the squeezing of grapes as in a winepress. One severe beating could forever change, perhaps even handicap, a person for life. Paul faced such beatings and more. Rather than being caught up in self-pity, he was able to delight in the **comfort** God provided. He was also able to look beyond himself and realize that his "affliction" better equipped him to minister to others.

1:5 While not enjoyable, suffering is part of the Christian life. Coming into the kingdom of Christ introduces believers to **the sufferings of Christ** as one way of being identified with Jesus. Nevertheless, Jesus is very near to those who are hurting. A believer is blessed to remember Christ, ever seated in majesty at the right hand of the Father, as He was actually standing at the martyrdom of Stephen (Ac 7:54-56) to offer immediate comfort to this precious saint at his time of greatest need.

1:6 Paul's affliction had a purpose—it gave him **comfort** and **endurance** (Gk *hupomonē*, "remaining under, patient expectation"), a word used to describe a constant "bearing up under" whatever the burden might be. In classical Greek the word was used to describe the ability of a plant to live under harsh and unfavorable conditions and even evolved to indicate a willingness on the part of a Greek mortal to die for his gods. Paul was able to focus not merely on the hardship itself but on the joy and comfort God provides.

1:22 For information on the sealing of the Holy Spirit, see note on Eph 1:13-14.

2:5-11 This section is helpful in dealing with conflicts faced by most churches. These situations are always delicate and require forgiveness. Church discipline, while required by the Bible, is difficult for churches to exercise. Paul spent time teaching the church the importance of this kind of discipline and teaching them how to carry it out. Paul realized that such discipline was not meant merely to be retributive but also to be remedial for the penitent wrongdoer.

2:6-7 Evidently, upon receiving Paul's follow-up letter, the church carried out a **punishment** that was severe. Paul encouraged them to **forgive and comfort** (Gk *parakalesai*; see 1:3) the offender, who had expressed repentance. "Forgive" (Gk *charisasthai*, "give freely, grant, cancel, remit, pardon") has as its root *charis*, "grace or unmerited favor." The idea is to be gracious in the sense of "giving a gift," which is exactly what transpires in forgiveness.

2:11 In an environment of unforgiveness, **Satan** can easily intervene and cause great damage to the church. Three times in 2 Corinthians Paul connects the work of Satan and peoples' minds: (1) Believers are **not ignorant of his** [Satan's] **schemes** to destroy them (2:11); (2) Satan blinds the "minds of . . . unbelievers" so they cannot see the light of the gospel (4:4); (3) Like Eve, who was "deceived" by Satan's "cunning," believers' minds can be "seduced" (11:3).

2:17 Paul also acknowledged that there are some who use the message of Christ not to honor God but **for profit** (Gk *kapeleuontes*, "making money by selling as retail, peddling, corrupting"), used in the LXX or Greek translation of the Old Testament for those who mix wine with water in order to cheat the buyers (Is 1:22). In classical Greek, Plato used the word to condemn those he considered to be pseudo-philosophers. Here the word refers to those who would peddle or sell God's Word for profit. Paul explains that he and Timothy, by contrast, ministered with **sincerity** (Gk *eilikrineias*, "purity, righteousness"; from *heilē*, "sunlight," and *krinō*, "examine, judge"). This word more

>WORD|*study*

1:20 Amen (Hb, "true, trustworthy"; transliterated into Gk and then anglicized) conveys firmness and reliability and is used here to affirm Paul's statement of confidence in the faithfulness of God. Jesus Himself used this word at the beginning of His utterances to affirm the authenticity and immutability of His words. The word has served as a keystone for Christian prayer, preserving the continuity of the Judeo-Christian faith (Dt 27:15; 1Ch 16:36; Ps 106:48).

"No, no" simultaneously? 18 As God is faithful, our message to you is not "Yes and no." 19 For the Son of God, Jesus Christ, who was preached among you by us—by me and Silvanus[A] and Timothy—did not become "Yes and no"; on the contrary, a final "Yes" has come in Him. 20 For every one of God's promises is "Yes" in Him. Therefore, the "•Amen" is also spoken through Him by us for God's glory. 21 Now it is God who strengthens us, with you, in Christ and has anointed us. 22 He has also sealed us and given us the Spirit as a down payment in our hearts.

23 I call on God as a witness, on my life, that it was to spare you that I did not come to Corinth. 24 I do not mean that we have control of[B] your faith, but we are workers with you for your joy, because you stand by faith.

2 1 In fact, I made up my mind about this:[C] I would not come to you on another painful visit.[D] 2 For if I cause you pain, then who will cheer me other than the one being hurt by me?[E] 3 I wrote this very thing so that when I came I wouldn't have pain from those who ought to give me joy, because I am confident about all of you that my joy will also be yours. 4 For I wrote to you with many tears out of an extremely troubled and anguished heart—not that you should be hurt, but that you should know the abundant love I have for you.

Paul's Call for Forgiveness (2:5-11)

5 If anyone has caused pain, he has caused pain not so much to me but to some degree—not to exaggerate—to all of you. 6 The punishment inflicted by the majority is sufficient for that person. 7 As a result, you should instead forgive and comfort him. Otherwise, this one may be overwhelmed by excessive grief. 8 Therefore I urge you to reaffirm your love to him. 9 I wrote for this purpose: to test your character to see if you are obedient in everything. 10 If you forgive anyone, I do too. For what I have forgiven—if I have forgiven anything—it is for you in the presence of Christ. 11 I have done this so that we may not be taken advantage of by Satan. For we are not ignorant of his schemes.

The Ministry of the Apostle (2:12–6:10)

The Trip to Macedonia (2:12-13)

12 When I came to Troas to preach the gospel of Christ, the Lord opened a door for me. 13 I had no rest in my spirit because I did not find my brother Titus, but I said goodbye to them and left for Macedonia.

A Testimony of God's Sufficiency (2:14–3:6)

14 But thanks be to God, who always puts us on display[F] in Christ[G] and through us spreads the aroma of the knowledge of Him in every place. 15 For to God we are the fragrance of Christ among those who are being saved and among those who are perishing. 16 To some we are an aroma of death leading to death, but to others, an aroma of life leading to life. And who is competent for this? 17 For we are not like the many[H] who market God's message for profit. On the contrary, we speak with sincerity in Christ, as from God and before God.

3 Are we beginning to commend ourselves again? Or do we need, like some, letters of recommendation to you or from you? 2 You yourselves are our letter, written on our hearts, recognized and read by everyone. 3 It is clear that you are

[A] **1:19** Or *Silas*; Ac 15:22-32; 16:19-40; 17:1-16 [B] **1:24** Or *we lord it over*, or *we rule over* [C] **2:1** Lit *I decided this for myself* [D] **2:1** Lit *not again in sorrow to come to you* [E] **2:2** Lit *the one pained* [F] **2:14** Or *always leads us in a triumphal procession*, or *always causes us to triumph* [G] **2:14** Lit *in the Christ*, or *in the Messiah*; 1Co 15:22; Eph 1:10,12,20; 3:11 [H] **2:17** Other mss read *the rest*

Christ's letter, produced[A] by us, not
written with ink but with the Spirit
of the living God—not on stone tablets but on tablets that are hearts of
flesh.
4 We have this kind of confidence
toward God through Christ. 5 It
is not that we are competent in[B]
ourselves to consider anything as
coming from ourselves, but our
competence is from God. 6 He has
made us competent to be ministers
of a new covenant, not of the letter,
but of the Spirit. For the letter kills,
but the Spirit produces life.

The Glorious New Covenant (3:7-18)

7 Now if the ministry of death,
chiseled in letters on stones, came
with glory, so that the Israelites
were not able to look directly at Moses' face because of the glory from
his face—a fading glory— 8 how
will the ministry of the Spirit not
be more glorious? 9 For if the ministry of condemnation had glory, the
ministry of righteousness overflows
with even more glory. 10 In fact,
what had been glorious is not glorious now by comparison because of
the glory that surpasses it. 11 For if
what was fading away was glorious,
what endures will be even more glorious.
12 Therefore, having such a hope,
we use great boldness. 13 We are not
like Moses, who used to put a veil
over his face so that the Israelites
could not stare at the end of what
was fading away, 14 but their minds
were closed.[C] For to this day, at the
reading of the old covenant, the
same veil remains; it is not lifted,
because it is set aside only in Christ.
15 Even to this day, whenever Moses
is read, a veil lies over their hearts,
16 but whenever a person turns to
the Lord, the veil is removed. 17 Now
the Lord is the Spirit, and where the
Spirit of the Lord is, there is freedom. 18 We all, with unveiled faces,
are looking as in a mirror at[D] the
glory of the Lord and are being
transformed into the same image
from glory to glory;[E] this is from the
Lord who is the Spirit.[F]

The Heart of the Gospel (4:1-6)

4 Therefore, since we have this
ministry because we were shown
mercy, we do not give up. 2 Instead,
we have renounced shameful secret
things, not •walking in deceit or
distorting God's message, but commending ourselves to every person's
conscience in God's sight by an open
display of the truth. 3 But if our gospel is veiled, it is veiled to those who
are perishing. 4 In their case, the god
of this age has blinded the minds of
the unbelievers so they cannot see
the light of the gospel of the glory
of Christ,[G] who is the image of God.
5 For we are not proclaiming ourselves but Jesus Christ as Lord, and
ourselves as your •slaves because of
Jesus. 6 For God who said, "Let light
shine out of darkness," has shone in
our hearts to give the light of the
knowledge of God's glory in the face
of Jesus Christ.

The Treasure of the Gospel (4:7-15)

7 Now we have this treasure in clay
jars, so that this extraordinary power may be from God and not from
us. 8 We are pressured in every way
but not crushed; we are perplexed
but not in despair; 9 we are persecuted but not abandoned; we are struck
down but not destroyed. 10 We always
carry the death of Jesus in our body,
so that the life of Jesus may also be
revealed in our body. 11 For we who
live are always given over to death
because of Jesus, so that Jesus' life
may also be revealed in our mortal
flesh. 12 So death works in us, but
life in you. 13 And since we have the
same spirit of faith in keeping with
what is written, **I believed, therefore I spoke,**[H] we also believe, and
therefore speak. 14 We know that the
One who raised the Lord Jesus will
raise us also with Jesus and present
us with you. 15 Indeed, everything
is for your benefit, so that grace,
extended through more and more
people, may cause thanksgiving to
increase to God's glory.

literally suggests proof that something is "unsullied" when brought into the open, under the scrutinizing rays of the sun. Paul supported himself financially so that others would not view him as one peddling the gospel for money.

3:2-3 The believers themselves were the only **letter** Paul and Timothy needed to authenticate their ministry among the Corinthian believers because the Holy Spirit within them would testify that they genuinely belonged to God.

3:7-11 Paul used this section to make an important and excellent comparison between the old covenant and the new covenant. He explained why the new covenant is superior and glorious.

3:12 Boldness (Gk *parrēsia*, "openness and frankness in speech, freedom to speak without reservation," lit "speaking all" and thus understood as "speaking openly") conveys a sense of confidence. Paul proclaimed and taught the gospel "with full boldness" (Ac 28:31), and the "boldness" of the apostles Peter and John drew attention to their having "been with Jesus" (Ac 4:13). Such courage to speak openly about Christ comes from the Spirit.

3:15-18 Paul describes the Israelites as having **a veil . . . over their hearts**. Paul acknowledges that the minds as well as the hearts of many are closed to Christ. However, **whenever a person turns to the Lord** for forgiveness and mercy, **the veil** over his heart **is removed** permanently, and he is able to display **the glory of** God.

4:6 God alone can bring **"light . . . out of darkness."** He alone can make a sinful heart pure. He alone can offer righteousness to the unrighteous. This verse is easily a description of creation when God brought light into the dark universe (Gn 1). If God is able to do all of these things, certainly He is able to bring light within the dark **hearts** of men and women.

4:7 How odd for the greatest **treasure** to be contained in weak, fragile, and common containers. Yet, the perfect God of holiness has chosen to make His sanctuary in the lives of unworthy sinners (i.e., **clay jars**).

4:8-9 In order to illustrate further the power of God in the weakness of men, Paul offers four profound examples of human weakness, which increase in severity. However, in each weakness, the power of God provided a way of escape.

4:10-12 Paul mentions **the death of Jesus** to emphasize the Savior's suffering in His earthly life and agonizing death. Paul was identifying his own hardships with the sufferings of

[A] **3:3** Lit *ministered to* [B] **3:5** Lit *from* [C] **3:14** Lit *their thoughts were hardened* [D] **3:18** Or *are reflecting* [E] **3:18** Progressive glorification or sanctification [F] **3:18** Or *from the Spirit of the Lord*, or *from the Lord, the Spirit* [G] **4:4** Or *the gospel of the glorious Christ*, or *the glorious gospel of Christ* [H] **4:13** Ps 116:10 LXX

The Eternal Perspective of the Gospel (4:16–5:21)

16 Therefore we do not give up. Even though our outer person is being destroyed, our inner person is being renewed day by day. 17 For our momentary light affliction[A] is producing for us an absolutely incomparable eternal weight of glory. 18 So we do not focus on what is seen, but on what is unseen. For what is seen is temporary, but what is unseen is eternal.

5 For we know that if our temporary, earthly dwelling[B] is destroyed, we have a building from God, an eternal dwelling[C] in the heavens, not made with hands. 2 Indeed, we groan in this body, desiring to put on our dwelling from heaven, 3 since, when we are clothed,[D] we will not be found naked. 4 Indeed, we groan while we are in this tent, burdened as we are, because we do not want to be unclothed but clothed, so that mortality may be swallowed up by life. 5 And the One who prepared us for this very purpose is God, who gave us the Spirit as a down payment.

6 So, we are always confident and know that while we are at home in the body we are away from the Lord. 7 For we •walk by faith, not by sight, 8 and we are confident and satisfied to be out of the body and at home with the Lord. 9 Therefore, whether we are at home or away, we make it our aim to be pleasing to Him. 10 For we must all appear before the tribunal of Christ, so that each may be repaid for what he has done in the body, whether good or worthless.

11 Therefore, because we know the •fear of the Lord, we seek to persuade people. We are completely open before God, and I hope we are completely open to your consciences as well. 12 We are not commending ourselves to you again, but giving you an opportunity to be proud of us, so that you may have a reply for those who take pride in the outward appearance[E] rather than in the heart. 13 For if we are out of our mind, it is for God; if we have a sound mind, it is for you. 14 For Christ's love compels[F] us, since we have reached this conclusion: If One died for all, then all died. 15 And He died for all so that those who live should no longer live for themselves, but for the One who died for them and was raised.

16 From now on, then, we do not know[G] anyone in a purely human way.[H] Even if we have known[I] Christ in a purely human way,[J] yet now we no longer know[G] Him in this way. 17 Therefore, if anyone is in Christ, he is a new creation; old things have passed away, and look, new things[K] have come. 18 Everything is from God, who reconciled us to Himself through Christ and gave us the ministry of reconciliation: 19 That is, in Christ, God was reconciling the world to Himself, not counting their trespasses against them, and He has committed the message of reconciliation to us. 20 Therefore, we are ambassadors for Christ, certain that God is appealing through

HARD QUESTION

Is there a judgment for Christians after death?

Paul's constant desire to please Christ was the direct outcome of his awareness that death would usher him into the presence of Christ. **All** will come **before the tribunal** [Gk *bēmatos*, "judge's official seat, speaker's platform"] **of Christ** (5:10). "The tribunal" in secular usage denoted the raised platform, approached by ascending steps, where the judge of a case sat, as on a throne or presiding over a tribunal. Jesus appeared before Pilate (Mt 27:19; Jn 19:13) and Paul before both secular and religious officials at the *bēmatos* (Gk). Christians, of course, will not have to worry about losing or earning their salvation, which has been won through Christ and His once-for-all atonement for sin. However, believers will be judged and rewarded for the work and ministry entrusted to them. Therefore, every Christian should be consumed with obedience to Christ and His commands. This appearance in the court of heaven will give opportunity for divine illumination of what has been hidden by darkness and is then exposed. The assessment of works and character is done, not with the determination of destiny but with the assignment of rewards. At this time the believer may suffer loss by forfeiting Christ's praise or by losing a reward that might have been given.

Jesus and believed that he and others could be so victorious in their sufferings that through the power of God, Jesus would **be revealed** (Gk *phanerōthē*, "make manifest what was hidden, exposed to view, recognized"). Paul was taking real joy in his suffering in the hope that it would bring others to Christ.

4:16-17 Paul reveals a key to the thriving Christian life. A person with a great command of the rich doctrinal truths can be **renewed** daily by the mercy and truth of God, thereby sustaining the outer body, which faces great trials. Paul had already shared the severity of the afflictions he and others faced. Yet, with this practice of daily renewal, he was able to view severe hardship as **light affliction**.

4:18 Paul concludes with more personal expressions of his theology of hope in suffering. Do not focus on the world, which is quickly fading away. Although it may seem real and tangible, focus rather on **what is unseen**, that which is truly genuine. Eternity with Christ is worth the living. Do not be confused by the fake, fading, **temporary** things of this life; instead be consumed with the real, the "unseen," and the **eternal**.

5:1-4 Paul defines the **earthly dwelling**, or the body, as **temporary**, which, while serving an important purpose, is still just temporary. Though providing some shelter, it is not permanent. Paul encourages believers to view their earthly lives and bodies as very temporary. In contrast, the **eternal** home, constructed by God, is permanent.

5:5 Christians can rest confidently in the hope to come. God has **prepared** the way and has given every believer a guarantee or **down payment** (Gk *arrabōna*, "earnest, pledge"; cp. 1:22; Eph 1:14) of what is to come, **the Spirit**. Interestingly, in modern Greek the word for "down payment" carries the meaning of an "engagement ring."

5:7 Paul observes that believers do **walk by faith**. The Lord is present not to physical eyes but to the eyes of faith.

5:11 **Fear of the Lord** is an awe and reverence for God, not a trembling, cowering fear. Paul used this concept further to support his authenticity as an apostle. He was **open** to scrutiny, both of people and of the Lord.

5:14-15 Love **compels** (Gk *sunechei*, "constrain, torment, press hard, embrace, rule, holds fast as a prisoner," a verb that implies pressure that confines and restricts as well as controls) Paul's commitment to present

[A]4:17 See note at 2Co 1:4. [B]5:1 = our present physical body [C]5:1 = our future body [D]5:3 Other mss read *stripped* [E]5:12 Lit *in face* [F]5:14 Or *For the love of Christ impels*, or *For the love of Christ controls* [G]5:16 Or *regard* [H]5:16 Lit *anyone according to the flesh* [I]5:16 Or *have regarded* [J]5:16 Lit *Christ according to the flesh* [K]5:17 Other mss read *look, all new things*

>WORD|*study*

5:18-19 Reconciled (Gk *katallazantos*, "change, exchange") referred to exchanging one thing for another as when an enemy becomes a friend. All 10 appearances of the derivatives of this Greek word in the New Testament appear in Paul's writings, and in each case **reconciliation** means the bringing together of two people or parties who were at odds with each other (see Rm 5:11; 11:15).

us. We plead on Christ's behalf, "Be
reconciled to God." [21] He made the
One who did not know sin to be sin[A]
for us, so that we might become the
righteousness of God in Him.

A Ministry Commendation (6:1-10)

6 Working together[B] with Him, we
also appeal to you, "Don't receive
God's grace in vain." [2] For He says:

I heard you in
an acceptable time,
and I helped you in the day
of salvation.[C]

Look, now is the acceptable time;
now is the day of salvation.
[3] We give no opportunity for stumbling to anyone, so that the ministry
will not be blamed. [4] But as God's
ministers, we commend ourselves
in everything:

by great endurance,
by afflictions,
by hardship, by difficulties,
5 by beatings, by imprisonments,
by riots, by labors,
by sleepless nights, by times
of hunger,
6 by purity, by knowledge,
by patience, by kindness,
by the Holy Spirit,
by sincere love,
7 by the message of truth,
by the power of God;
through weapons
of righteousness
on the right hand and the left,
8 through glory and dishonor,
through slander
and good report;
as deceivers yet true;
9 as unknown yet recognized;
as dying and look—we live;
as being disciplined
yet not killed;
10 as grieving yet
always rejoicing;
as poor yet enriching many;
as having nothing yet
possessing everything.

The Work of the Apostle Among the Corinthians (6:11–7:16)

Paul's Challenge to the Corinthians (6:11–7:1)

[11] We have spoken openly[D] to you,
Corinthians; our heart has been
opened wide. [12] You are not limited
by us, but you are limited by your
own affections. [13] I speak as to my
children. As a proper response, you
should also be open to us.
[14] Do not be mismatched with
unbelievers. For what partnership
is there between righteousness and
lawlessness? Or what fellowship does
light have with darkness? [15] What
agreement does Christ have with
Belial?[E] Or what does a believer have
in common with an unbeliever?
[16] And what agreement does God's
sanctuary have with idols? For we[F]
are the sanctuary of the living God,
as God said:

I will dwell among them
and walk among them,
and I will be their God,
and they will be My people.[G]
17 **Therefore, come out**
from among them
and be separate,
says the Lord;
do not touch
any unclean thing,
and I will welcome you.[H]
18 **I will be a Father to you,**
and you will be sons
and daughters to Me,
says the Lord Almighty.[I]

[A] **5:21** Or *be a sin offering* [B] **6:1** Or *As we work together* [C] **6:2** Is 49:8 [D] **6:11** Lit *Our mouths have been open* [E] **6:15** Or *Beliar*, a name for the Devil or antichrist in extra-biblical Jewish writings [F] **6:16** Other mss read *you* [G] **6:16** Lv 26:12; Jr 31:33; 32:38; Ezk 37:26 [H] **6:17** Is 52:11 [I] **6:18** 2Sm 7:14; Is 43:6; 49:22; 60:4; Hs 1:10

the gospel message and subsequent teaching clearly and effectively to the church for their benefit. Paul was not caught up in fads or moved by whim; he was consumed with his task because of the sacrifice of Christ.

5:16 The gospel became the lens through which Paul saw every person. No individual is excluded from the scope of redemption—God's offer of salvation is universally available though all do not accept it.

5:18-19 An individual seeking reconciliation with God does not make reconciliation happen. Rather he experiences or embraces what God has already offered through regeneration and sanctification. God reconciles His creation to Himself before they can respond to the call to be reconciled.

5:20 Believers are Christ's **ambassadors** (Gk *presbeuomen*, verb meaning "being a representative"). An ambassador is a messenger and representative. He does not speak in his own name or act on his own authority. He never communicates his own opinions or demands. Rather he delivers the message with which he has been entrusted.

6:3 While the imposters would confuse and disappoint the people, Paul said that his message and **ministry** were in line with the pure gospel and should not cause **stumbling to anyone**. Paul was concerned not merely with protecting himself but with honoring God's message and ministry.

6:4-7 Pushed into a defensive posture, Paul commended himself to the people and listed his sufferings as his credentials (vv. 4-5). Paul also considered his Christian character to be evidence of his genuine conversion and ability to lead (vv. 6-7). This insight should not be considered as arrogance but as real evidence of the Holy Spirit's work of transformation in his own life.

6:11-13 Paul did not want the Corinthians to hold back or reject his love. He wholeheartedly accepted them and hoped for the same in return. He appealed to them as family members because as their spiritual father, he had a special connection with them, one that could not easily be replaced.

6:14-18 Here Paul is addressing the temptations the Corinthians faced when they followed false apostles and false religions. Paul reminded them of the seriousness of a **partnership** as being binding and powerful. After making several strong comparisons, Paul makes his strongest argument comparing Christ and **Belial** (Gk *Beliar*, originating in Hb as "worthless" and used in extrabiblical Jewish writings to represent Satan, the prince of lawlessness and darkness and the highest enemy of God). God and Satan have nothing in common. Because of their significant differences, **a believer** should not be linked with **an unbeliever** in a partnership. The alliances Paul had in mind could have been marriage, business associations, or even social relationships (cp. 1Co 10:14). Paul combines truths from a number of Old Testament passages regarding the role of believers as the **sanctuary** or dwelling place **of the living God**.

7:5-7 Paul picks up here from his earlier discussion in chapter 2 regarding his earnest desire to meet with **Titus** and receive an update on the church and their acceptance of him. He reminded them of his unrest because of his great concern for them and due to the opposition he faced in **Macedonia**. Paul was encouraged that the people had treated Titus kindly, and he was comforted by the presence of Titus and the news he brought.

7:8 Paul references the earlier scathing **letter** he had sent the Corinthians. He recognized that his words had stung them, and he sincerely regretted hurting them. However, he was pleased that the letter accomplished the intended outcome since he was exercising tough love with the Corinthian church. While hard for parents, especially mothers, at times this display of love is necessary and greatly profitable. Although hard for Paul, he was willing to challenge them lovingly, a willingness modern parents should emulate.

7:9-12 Paul's letter produced godly **repentance** (Gk *metanoian*, "change of mind, remorse," also translated "conversion"), a word pointing to a change in thinking in contrast to simply "regret" in the sense of sorrow or grief. Such genuine repentance generates a renewed interest in spiritual matters. As vividly illustrated here in the lives of the Corinthians, repentance is not reserved for conversion but must continue even unto glorification. The godly sorrow of repentance led the Corinthians to be diligent in their service to Christ, to be determined to clear themselves of charges against them, to reject sinful behavior, to fear God, and to pursue righteousness, zeal, and vindication.

7:13 Paul commended the Corinthians for their faithful service to Titus and let them know that they had sincerely **refreshed** (Gk *anapepautai*, "allow or cause someone to stop working long enough to recover strength, provide rest") him. Titus had been blessed by his time with them. The Corinthians must have been smiling upon hearing

7 Therefore, dear friends, since
we have such promises, let us
•cleanse ourselves from every impurity of the flesh and spirit, completing our •sanctification[A] in the •fear
of God.

Paul's Response to the Corinthians (7:2-16)

Affection for them (7:2-4)

2 Accept us.[B] We have wronged no
one, corrupted no one, defrauded no
one. 3 I don't say this to condemn
you, for I have already said that you
are in our hearts, to live together
and to die together. 4 I have great
confidence in you; I have great pride
in you. I am filled with encouragement; I am overcome with joy in all
our afflictions.

Joy over their repentance (7:5-16)

5 In fact, when we came into Macedonia, we[C] had no rest. Instead, we
were troubled in every way: conflicts
on the outside, fears inside. 6 But
God, who comforts the humble,
comforted us by the arrival of Titus, 7 and not only by his arrival,
but also by the comfort he received
from you. He told us about your
deep longing, your sorrow,[D] and
your zeal for me, so that I rejoiced
even more. 8 For even if I grieved
you with my letter, I do not regret
it—even though I did regret it since
I saw that the letter grieved you, yet
only for a little while. 9 Now I rejoice, not because you were grieved,
but because your grief led to repentance. For you were grieved as God
willed, so that you didn't experience
any loss from us. 10 For godly grief
produces a repentance not to be regretted and leading to salvation, but
worldly grief produces death. 11 For
consider how much diligence this
very thing—this grieving as God
wills—has produced in you: what
a desire to clear yourselves, what
indignation, what fear, what deep
longing, what zeal, what justice! In
every way you showed yourselves
to be pure in this matter. 12 So even
though I wrote to you, it was not
because of the one who did wrong,
or because of the one who was
wronged, but in order that your diligence for us might be made plain to
you in the sight of God. 13 For this
reason we have been comforted.

In addition to our comfort, we
rejoiced even more over the joy Titus had,[E] because his spirit was refreshed by all of you. 14 For if I have
made any boast to him about you, I
have not been embarrassed; but as
I have spoken everything to you in
truth, so our boasting to Titus has
also turned out to be the truth.
15 And his affection toward you is
even greater as he remembers the
obedience of all of you, and how you
received him with fear and trembling. 16 I rejoice that I have complete confidence in you.

The Outgrowth of Paul's Ministry (8:1–9:15)

A Testimony from the Macedonians (8:1-7)

8 We want you to know, •brothers,
about the grace of God granted to
the churches of Macedonia: 2 During a severe testing by affliction,
their abundance of joy and their
deep poverty overflowed into the
wealth of their generosity. 3 I testify that, on their own, according to
their ability and beyond their ability,
4 they begged us insistently for the
privilege of sharing in the ministry
to the •saints, 5 and not just as we
had hoped. Instead, they gave themselves especially to the Lord, then
to us by God's will. 6 So we urged
Titus that just as he had begun, so
he should also complete this grace
to you. 7 Now as you excel in everything—faith, speech, knowledge,
and in all diligence, and in your love
for us[F]—excel also in this grace.

The Example of Christ (8:8-9)

8 I am not saying this as a command. Rather, by means of the diligence of others, I am testing the
genuineness of your love. 9 For you
know the grace of our Lord Jesus
Christ: Though He was rich, for your
sake He became poor, so that by His
poverty you might become rich.

An Appeal for the Collection (8:10-15)

10 Now I am giving an opinion on
this because it is profitable for you,

A7:1 Or *spirit, perfecting holiness* B7:2 Lit *Make room for us* C7:5 Lit *our flesh* D7:7 Or *lamentation*, or *mourning* E7:13 Lit *the joy of Titus* F8:7 Other mss read *in our love for you*

who a year ago began not only to
do something but also to desire it.[A]
[11] But now finish the task[B] as well,
that just as there was eagerness to
desire it, so there may also be a completion from what you have. [12] For if
the eagerness is there, it is acceptable according to what one has, not
according to what he does not have.
[13] It is not that there may be relief for
others and hardship for you, but it
is a question of equality[C]— [14] at the
present time your surplus is available for their need, so their abundance may also become available for
our need, so there may be equality.
[15] As it has been written:

The person who
gathered much
did not have too much,
and the person who
gathered little
did not have too little.[D]

The Response to the Collection (8:16–9:5)

[16] Thanks be to God who put the
same concern for you into the heart
of Titus. [17] For he accepted our urging and, being very diligent, went
out to you by his own choice. [18] We
have sent with him the brother who
is praised throughout the churches
for his gospel ministry.[E] [19] And not
only that, but he was also appointed
by the churches to accompany us
with this gift[F] that is being administered by us for the glory of the Lord
Himself and to show our eagerness
to help. [20] We are taking this precaution so no one can criticize us about
this large sum administered by us.
[21] For we are making provision for
what is right, not only before the
Lord but also before men. [22] We have
also sent with them our brother. We
have often tested him in many circumstances and found him to be diligent—and now even more diligent
because of his great confidence in
you. [23] As for Titus, he is my partner
and coworker serving you; as for our
brothers, they are the messengers
of the churches, the glory of Christ.
[24] Therefore, show them proof before
the churches of your love and of our
boasting about you.

9 Now concerning the ministry
to the •saints, it is unnecessary
for me to write to you. [2] For I know
your eagerness, and I brag about
you to the Macedonians:[G] "Achaia[H]
has been prepared since last year,"
and your zeal has stirred up most
of them. [3] But I sent the brothers so
our boasting about you in the matter would not prove empty, and so
you would be prepared just as I said.
[4] For if any Macedonians come with
me and find you unprepared, we, not
to mention you, would be embarrassed in that situation.[I] [5] Therefore
I considered it necessary to urge the
brothers to go on ahead to you and
arrange in advance the generous gift
you promised, so that it will be ready
as a gift and not as an extortion.

Lessons Learned from Giving (9:6-15)

[6] Remember this:[J] The person who
sows sparingly will also reap sparingly, and the person who sows generously will also reap generously.
[7] Each person should do as he has
decided in his heart—not reluctantly or out of necessity, for God loves
a cheerful giver. [8] And God is able to
make every grace overflow to you,
so that in every way, always having
everything you need, you may excel
in every good work. [9] As it is written:

Doctrine STEWARDSHIP

Paul emphasized the great blessings that come from giving (2Co 9:6-15). Paul emphasized the **heart** attitude, explaining that giving should not be done out of guilt, mere need, or for any other negative reason. Giving should be an expression of gratitude to God and love for others. With this godly motivation, you can cheerfully give what you have **decided**. Paul encouraged the people to think about their giving, taking time to determine the gift that would be pleasing to the Lord and then to be obedient to give. **God loves a cheerful giver**—"Cheerful" or joyful giving is the antithesis of a begrudging donation. Giving for a believer should be an act of worship, accompanied by preparation of the heart, purpose in the plan, and joy in the attitude.

Paul's compliments, and his words must have brought great pleasure and the motivation to continue in doing good.

8:1-2 The **churches of Macedonia** were new congregations in Philippi, Thessalonica, and Berea (Ac 16–17). Unlike Corinth, this area had a very poor economy and suffered much **deep poverty.**

8:6-7 Paul and Timothy had **urged Titus** to complete the collection. This collection for the great need of the Jerusalem church had probably been delayed in efforts to solve the church's greater and more immediate issues.

8:9 Christ gave up His immeasurable riches for poverty so that others could join in His riches. Once a person has tasted of wealth, it is very difficult to endure poverty, but Jesus was willing to do just that because of His great love.

8:10-12 While Paul's greatest encouragement came from the example of Christ, he did not fail to mention the commitment the Corinthians had made **a year ago** in regard to the collection. They had not been forced to make this commitment but voluntarily did so, and he indicated the importance of the fulfillment of their pledge.

8:20-23 Paul was wise to protect himself from the attacks of others and their inappropriate rumors because of **this large sum**. For accountability, Paul assigned another person to assist with the gift, thereby ensuring his own integrity. The Corinthians probably did not know this person, so Paul commended him as **diligent** and faithful and noted that he was one **we have often tested**, in the sense of proving the man's reliability.

9:1-5 Paul had previously told the Corinthians of his pride in them and his belief that they desired to add to the contribution. Although the Corinthians were not struggling financially, they were certainly struggling with unity and had probably delayed their giving in order to settle their difficult and challenging situation regarding Paul and the false prophets. Not wanting to make them feel badly about the delay, Paul gently let them know that he was sending some Christian **brothers** to expedite the collection and explained his reason for sending these men.

9:8 Paul described the character of God, whose generosity goes beyond the comprehension of His creation. God delights in giving good things to His children. If He was willing to give His only begotten Son, than surely He can make His **grace overflow** on the Christian giver, so that you have **everything you need** (Gk *autarkeian*,

[A]**8:10** Lit *to will* [B]**8:11** Lit *finish the doing* [C]**8:13** Lit *but from equality* [D]**8:15** Ex 16:18
[E]**8:18** Lit *churches, in the gospel* [F]**8:19** Or *grace* [G]**9:2** Macedonia was a Roman province in the northern area of modern Greece. [H]**9:2** Achaia was the Roman province, south of Macedonia, where Corinth was located. [I]**9:4** Or *in this confidence* [J]**9:6** Lit *And this*

"sufficiency, contentment" in the sense of a condition in which no help or support is needed; cp. 1Tm 6:6).

9:15 Paul rightly placed the emphasis on God. Those who are obedient in giving will be blessed by God. This does not mean that a person will necessarily be monetarily blessed because Paul describes the greatest blessing as an outpouring of God's grace, an **indescribable gift**. Paul was also thinking of the gift of Jesus Christ. God, in giving His Son, gave not only His best but also His all.

10:1-18 In the previous chapters, Paul was bold and straightforward regarding the recent controversy challenging his authority in the church. In this section he took a strong pastoral tone as he exerted clear leadership.

10:4-6 Paul brought a very serious message. He wanted the people to understand that they were in a spiritual battle between light and darkness. They must choose Christ, which meant accepting Paul's leadership, or follow Satan, who was represented by the false apostles. The apostle was trying to draw the lines with such clarity that there could be no mistake so that they could see for themselves that these false teachers were enemies of God.

10:8 Paul did not place weight on any human attributes but rather on the **authority** given to him by God.

10:13 God's call on Paul's life and evidence of an effective **area of ministry** (Gk *metron tou kanonos*, "measure, extent or limit of a defined sphere of activity, standard, rule or influence," vv. 13,15,16) was enough to validate his apostleship. The church should have seen that those who relied on human strength were clearly serving self and Satan rather than truth and God.

10:15-18 Wisely, Paul helped the people to think beyond their present difficulties. In their hearts, they knew God had worked powerfully among them through Paul's sharing of the gospel message. Their spiritual father wanted them to begin thinking about the further ministry God had for them, a ministry that included other regions. They had already wasted time in the confusion caused by the imposters. With unity in the gospel and obedience, they could have an **enlarged** ministry.

11:1 Paul felt forced to present his credentials yet again, though he did not desire to do this.

11:2 Paul recognized the Lord as magnificent and worthy of the Bride He desired, His church. Paul felt the Corinthians should be joined **in**

He scattered;
He gave to the poor;
His righteousness
endures forever.[A]

10 Now the One who provides seed for the sower and bread for food will provide and multiply your seed and increase the harvest of your righteousness. 11 You will be enriched in every way for all generosity, which produces thanksgiving to God through us. 12 For the ministry of this service is not only supplying the needs of the saints, but is also overflowing in many acts of thanksgiving to God. 13 They will glorify God for your obedience to the confession of[B] the gospel of Christ, and for your generosity in sharing with them and with others through the proof provided by this service. 14 And they will have deep affection for[C] you in their prayers on your behalf because of the surpassing grace of God in you. 15 Thanks be to God for His indescribable gift.

An Authentication of Paul's Ministry (10:1–12:13)

Paul's Authority (10:1-18)

10 Now I, Paul, make a personal appeal to you by the gentleness and graciousness of Christ—I who am humble among you in person but bold toward you when absent. 2 I beg you that when I am present I will not need to be bold with the confidence by which I plan to challenge certain people who think we are behaving in an unspiritual way.[D] 3 For though we live in the body,[E] we do not wage war in an unspiritual way,[F] 4 since the weapons of our warfare are not worldly,[G] but are powerful through God for the demolition of strongholds. We demolish arguments 5 and every high-minded thing that is raised up against the knowledge of God, taking every thought captive to obey Christ. 6 And we are ready to punish any disobedience, once your obedience has been confirmed.

7 Look at what is obvious.[H] If anyone is confident that he belongs to Christ, he should remind himself of this: Just as he belongs to Christ, so do we. 8 For if I boast some more about our authority, which the Lord gave for building you up and not for tearing you down, I am not ashamed. 9 I don't want to seem as though I am trying to terrify you with my letters. 10 For it is said, "His letters are weighty and powerful, but his physical presence is weak, and his public speaking is despicable." 11 Such a person should consider this: What we are in the words of our letters when absent, we will be in actions when present.

12 For we don't dare classify or compare ourselves with some who commend themselves. But in measuring themselves by themselves and comparing themselves to themselves, they lack understanding. 13 We, however, will not boast beyond measure but according to the measure of the area of ministry that God has assigned to us, which reaches even to you. 14 For we are not overextending ourselves, as if we had not reached you, since we have come to you with the gospel of Christ. 15 We are not bragging beyond measure about other people's labors. But we have the hope that as your faith increases, our area of ministry will be greatly enlarged, 16 so that we may proclaim the good news to the regions beyond you, not boasting about what has already been done in someone else's area of ministry. 17 So **the one who boasts must boast in the Lord.**[I] 18 For it is not the one commending himself who is approved, but the one the Lord commends.

Judging Between Genuine and False Apostles (11:1-15)

11 I wish you would put up with a little foolishness from me. Yes, do put up with me.[J] 2 For I am jealous over you with a godly jealousy, because I have promised you in marriage to one husband—to present a pure virgin to Christ. 3 But I fear that, as the serpent deceived Eve by his cunning, your minds may

[A] 9:9 Ps 112:9 [B] 9:13 Or *your obedient confession to* [C] 9:14 Or *will long for* [D] 10:2 Or *are living as a non-Christian*; lit *are walking according to flesh* [E] 10:3 Lit *flesh* [F] 10:3 Lit *war according to flesh* [G] 10:4 Lit *fleshly* [H] 10:7 Or *You are looking at things outwardly* [I] 10:17 Jr 9:24 [J] 11:1 Or *Yes, you are putting up with me*

be seduced from a complete and
pure[A] devotion to Christ. 4 For if a
person comes and preaches another
Jesus, whom we did not preach, or
you receive a different spirit, which
you had not received, or a different
gospel, which you had not accepted,
you put up with it splendidly!
5 Now I consider myself in no way
inferior to the "super-apostles."
6 Though untrained in public speaking, I am certainly not untrained
in knowledge. Indeed, we have always made that clear to you in everything. 7 Or did I commit a sin by
humbling myself so that you might
be exalted, because I preached the
gospel of God to you free of charge?
8 I robbed other churches by taking
pay from them to minister to you.
9 When I was present with you and
in need, I did not burden anyone, for
the brothers who came from Macedonia supplied my needs. I have kept
myself, and will keep myself, from
burdening you in any way. 10 As the
truth of Christ is in me, this boasting of mine will not be stopped[B] in
the regions of Achaia. 11 Why? Because I don't love you? God knows
I do!
12 But I will continue to do what
I am doing, in order to deny[C] the
opportunity of those who want an
opportunity to be regarded just as
our equals in what they boast about.
13 For such people are false apostles,
deceitful workers, disguising themselves as apostles of Christ. 14 And
no wonder! For Satan disguises
himself as an angel of light. 15 So it
is no great thing if his servants also
disguise themselves as servants of
righteousness. Their destiny[D] will
be according to their works.

Paul's Genuine Apostleship (11:16–12:13)

16 I repeat: No one should consider
me a fool. But if you do, at least accept me as a fool, so I too may boast
a little. 17 What I say in this matter[E]
of boasting, I don't speak as the Lord
would, but foolishly. 18 Since many
boast in an unspiritual way,[F] I will
also boast. 19 For you, being so wise,
gladly put up with fools! 20 In fact,
you put up with it if someone en-
slaves you, if someone devours you,
if someone captures you, if someone
dominates you, or if someone hits
you in the face. 21 I say this to our
shame: We have been weak.
But in whatever anyone dares to
boast—I am talking foolishly—I
also dare:

22 Are they Hebrews? So am I.
Are they Israelites? So am I.
Are they the •seed
of Abraham? So am I.
23 Are they servants of Christ?
I'm talking like a madman—
I'm a better one:
with far more labors,
many more imprisonments,
far worse beatings,
near death[G] many times.
24 Five times I received 39 lashes
from Jews.
25 Three times I was beaten
with rods by the Romans.
Once I was stoned
by my enemies.[H]
Three times
I was shipwrecked.
I have spent a night and a day
in the open sea.
26 On frequent journeys, I faced
dangers from rivers,
dangers from robbers,
dangers from my own people,
dangers from the Gentiles,
dangers in the city,
dangers in the open country,
dangers on the sea,
and dangers
among false •brothers;
27 labor and hardship,
many sleepless nights,
hunger and thirst,
often without food, cold,
and lacking clothing.

28 Not to mention[I] other things,
there is the daily pressure on me:
my care for all the churches. 29 Who
is weak, and I am not weak? Who
is made to •stumble, and I do not
burn with indignation? 30 If boasting
is necessary, I will boast about my
weaknesses. 31 The God and Father
of the Lord Jesus, who is praised
forever, knows I am not lying. 32 In

marriage to one husband. This analogy is strong, opening their eyes to the binding significance of their union.

11:3-4 Paul brought further solemnity to the situation when he compared their confusion to the deception of **Eve** in the garden. The fall of man is the most tragic event in all of history, affecting the entire world and sealing the need for redemption. Satan slipped in, and by his **cunning** (Gk *panourgia*, "craftiness, trickery, false wisdom," cp. Lk 20:23; 1Co 3:19; Eph 4:14), he **seduced** the mind of Eve. **The serpent** shared a different message with Eve. Just like Eve in the garden, the Corinthians were being confused with **a different gospel** and **a different spirit**.

11:5-7 These **"super-apostles,"** as they must have identified themselves, were obviously seeking monetary gain. Paul compared his generous conduct by identifying the foolishness of doubting his apostleship based on his refusal to accept their funding.

11:9 Paul wanted them to see that he was not seeking personal gain—he was only seeking the promotion of the gospel and the saving of souls. So committed was he, that he declined their support. He worked long hours to supply his own needs in order not to **burden anyone** and again to avoid **burdening** the Corinthians. While many might have considered him in a lower class because of his work, he made it clear that he would rather have people think of him as lowly than bring doubt upon the great gospel message.

11:12-15 In verse 12 Paul further distinguishes himself from the "super-apostles." Those with opposing messages cannot both be true. He boldly names them as **false apostles, deceitful workers, disguising themselves**. Satan **disguises himself as an angel of light**. These false teachers were not merely naïve, confused men; they were puppets of the enemy and used Satan's strategies of **disguise** and deception. Of course, these men first appeared as **servants of righteousness**, a tactic they used to gain the confidence of the Corinthians. However, Paul minces no words in explaining that their clear **destiny** is hell.

11:22-27 In previous verses Paul defended himself based on God's calling. Even though he did not feel that he should be required to defend himself with human credentials, he acquiesced to their desires, asking that they accept his defense as a final word on the issue.

[A] **11:3** Other mss omit *and pure* [B] **11:10** Or *silenced* [C] **11:12** Lit *cut off* [D] **11:15** Lit *end* [E] **11:17** Or *business*, or *confidence* [F] **11:18** Lit *boast according to the flesh* [G] **11:23** Lit *and in deaths* [H] **11:25** A common Jewish method of capital punishment; Ac 14:5 [I] **11:28** Lit *Apart from*

12:1-4 To confirm his apostleship fully to the church, Paul continued with the **revelations** and **visions** he received from God 14 years prior, referring to his salvation experience on the road to Damascus (see Ac 9:1-19). Paul **was caught up** [Gk *hērpagē*, "seized, stolen, snatched out or away"; cp. Ac 8:39; 23:10; 1Th 4:17] **into the third heaven**, a reference to **paradise**, the greatest heights of heaven.

12:5-6 Paul still was not comfortable with the idea of sharing such private information. His difficulty was apparent, and his struggle showed his humanity. He was also drawing attention to the difference between himself and his detractors. They clearly loved **to boast** about themselves. He obviously did not and was quick to relate his weaknesses.

12:7-8 God ensured that Paul remained close to the frailty of his humanity with the constant, painful pressing of the **thorn** (Gk *skolops*, "sharp, pointed piece of wood, splinter," representing an unspecified injury or ailment; a *hapax* or word used only here in the NT). Though the specific nature of the thorn is not clear (it could have been a medical issue, a spiritual issue, or could refer to the opponents to his ministry), Paul seemed to know exactly why the thorn remained. He knew the temptation of self-exaltation. While Jesus was able to defend Himself in His time of testing, the loving Father knew the limits of Paul. Although Paul obviously wanted the "thorn" to be removed, he clearly admitted that he understood its presence and agreed with its purpose.

12:9-10 The short sentence, **"My grace is sufficient for you,"** has brought untold strength to generations of Christians. In human **weaknesses**, Christ is able to perfect His strength, and if weakness meant the nearness of Christ, then Paul wanted to be the first to announce his weakness.

12:11 Paul did what they wanted—he defended his credentials. Even though they knew him well enough to affirm his apostleship, had experienced the miracles of God through his authority, and even though they should have been the ones defending his leadership, he accepted the fact that they had not.

12:12 God used **signs** and **miracles** to authenticate His message and His servants. He reminded Corinthian believers of the truth that the "signs" were given in order to bring God glory, not to bring glory to His creation.

12:13 Paul had spent a great deal of time with this church, almost more than any other church. Even with all

Damascus, the governor under King
Aretas[A] guarded the city of the Dam-
ascenes in order to arrest me, 33 so I
was let down in a basket through a
window in the wall and escaped his
hands.

12 Boasting is necessary. It is
not profitable, but I will move
on to visions and revelations of the
Lord. 2 I know a man in Christ who
was caught up into the third heaven
14 years ago. Whether he was in
the body or out of the body, I don't
know, God knows. 3 I know that this
man—whether in the body or out of
the body I don't know, God knows—
4 was caught up into paradise. He
heard inexpressible words, which a
man is not allowed to speak. 5 I will
boast about this person, but not
about myself, except of my weaknesses. 6 For if I want to boast, I will
not be a fool, because I will be telling the truth. But I will spare you,
so that no one can credit me with
something beyond what he sees in
me or hears from me, 7 especially
because of the extraordinary revelations. Therefore, so that I would not
exalt myself, a thorn in the flesh was
given to me, a messenger[B] of Satan
to torment me so I would not exalt
myself. 8 Concerning this, I pleaded
with the Lord three times to take it
away from me. 9 But He said to me,
"My grace is sufficient for you, for
power[C] is perfected in weakness."
Therefore, I will most gladly boast
all the more about my weaknesses,
so that Christ's power may reside
in me. 10 So I take pleasure in weaknesses, insults, catastrophes, persecutions, and in pressures, because of
Christ. For when I am weak, then I
am strong.

11 I have become a fool; you forced
it on me. I should have been endorsed by you, since I am not in
any way inferior to the "super-
apostles," even though I am nothing. 12 The signs of an apostle were
performed with great endurance
among you—not only signs but also
wonders and miracles. 13 So in what
way were you treated worse than the
other churches, except that I personally did not burden you? Forgive
me this wrong!

Paul's Proposed Visit to Corinth (12:14-21)

14 Now I am ready to come to you
this third time. I will not burden
you, for I am not seeking what is
yours, but you. For children are not
obligated to save up for their parents, but parents for their children.
15 I will most gladly spend and be
spent for you.[D] If I love you more,
am I to be loved less? 16 Now granted,
I have not burdened you; yet sly as I
am, I took you in by deceit! 17 Did
I take advantage of you by anyone
I sent you? 18 I urged Titus to come,
and I sent the brother with him. Did
Titus take advantage of you? Didn't
we •walk in the same spirit and in
the same footsteps?

19 You have thought all along that
we were defending ourselves to you.[E]
No, in the sight of God we are speaking in Christ, and everything, dear
friends, is for building you up. 20 For
I fear that perhaps when I come I
will not find you to be what I want,
and I may not be found by you to be
what you want;[F] there may be quarreling, jealousy, outbursts of anger,
selfish ambitions, slander, gossip,
arrogance, and disorder. 21 I fear that
when I come my God will again[G]
humiliate me in your presence, and
I will grieve for many who sinned
before and have not repented of the
moral impurity, sexual immorality,
and promiscuity they practiced.

Paul's Benediction and Challenge (13:1-13)

The Apostle's Warning (13:1-4)

13 This is the third time I am coming to you. **Every fact must be
established by the testimony[H] of two
or three witnesses.**[I] 2 I gave a warning when I was present the second
time, and now I give a warning while
I am absent to those who sinned before and to all the rest: If I come
again, I will not be lenient, 3 since
you seek proof of Christ speaking in

[A] 11:32 Aretus IV (9 B.C.–A.D. 40), a Nabatean Arab king [B] 12:7 Or *me, an angel* [C] 12:9 Other mss read *My power* [D] 12:15 Lit *for your souls*, or *for your lives* [E] 12:19 Or *Have you thought . . . to you?* [F] 12:20 Lit *be as you want* [G] 12:21 Or *come again my God will* [H] 13:1 Lit *mouth* [I] 13:1 Dt 17:6; 19:15

me. He is not weak toward you, but
powerful among you. 4 In fact, He
was crucified in weakness, but He
lives by God's power. For we also are
weak in Him, yet toward you we will
live with Him by God's power.

The Apostle's Admonition (13:5-10)

5 Test yourselves to see if you are
in the faith. Examine yourselves.
Or do you yourselves not recognize
that Jesus Christ is in you?—unless you fail the test.[A] 6 And I hope
you will recognize that we do not
fail the test. 7 Now we pray to God
that you do nothing wrong—not
that we may appear to pass the test,
but that you may do what is right,
even though we may appear to fail.
8 For we are not able to do anything
against the truth, but only for the
truth. 9 In fact, we rejoice when we
are weak and you are strong. We also
pray that you become fully mature.[B]
10 This is why I am writing these
things while absent, that when I am
there I will not use severity, in keeping with the authority the Lord gave
me for building up and not for tearing down.

A Final Exhortation (13:11-13)

11 Finally, •brothers, rejoice. Become mature, be encouraged, be of
the same mind, be at peace, and the
God of love and peace will be with
you. 12 Greet one another with a holy
kiss. All the •saints greet you.
13 The grace of the Lord Jesus
Christ, and the love of God, and the
fellowship of the Holy Spirit be with
all of you.[C]

[A] **13:5** Or *you are disqualified*, or *you are counterfeit* [B] **13:9** Or *become complete*, or *be restored* [C] **13:12-13** Some translations divide these 2 vv. into 3 vv. so that v. 13 begins with *All the saints* . . . and v. 14 begins with *The grace of* . . .

---

2 CORINTHIANS . . . WRITTEN ON MY *Heart* In Christ, we are a new creation, the old has passed and the new has come—this truth should be displayed through a changed life. Paul prayed that the Corinthians would become "fully mature," which should be the prayer of every believer. Having accepted Christ, our behavior should start reflecting our new identity in Christ.

this extra attention they received, Paul never accepted any payment or support from them. And yet, this act of sacrifice and service was actually being used against him.

12:14-18 Amid all the difficulty, Paul still desired to see them, and assured them that he was not coming to them for any personal gain nor to **take advantage of** them in any way.

12:20-21 While the rebellion against his authority was a problem, Paul realized that in the church there were many other problems, which he feared would be ignored. Paul knew that if the problems were still there upon his arrival, he would be forced to address them; so he must have encouraged the people to deal with these problems on their own. To avoid any confusion and keep the needed focus, Paul listed the sins he wanted the Corinthians to address.

13:1 Paul stressed the importance of this **third** visit by announcing it again. Paul had invested so much in this church, and he would stop at nothing to strengthen and purify it. Paul wanted them to know that he was serious about their behavior change, and he was serious about discipline.

13:3-4 Paul explained that he was modeling his behavior after the Savior. Jesus is **not weak** but **powerful**. The description and the significance of the crucifixion speaks to Christ's power and determination to set people free from sin.

13:5 The question must be addressed: Were these rebellious sinners genuine believers? Paul gave a clear answer. They must honestly **examine** (Gk *dokimazete*, "test, approve, demonstrate to be genuine"; cp. 8:8,22) their own lives to determine if they are in the faith. In other words, he was looking for evidence. Paul let them know that some might not be genuine believers if they were rejecting Christ.

13:6-8 Paul affirmed his relationship with the Lord because he had examined himself. He was not asking them to do anything he had not already done.

13:10 Paul expressed his hope that this maturity would come quickly and that their repentance would be evidenced by their own initiative. He was writing with **severity** in hopes that as pure-hearted, restored believers, they could enjoy their visit together.

Galatians

Timeline	AD 36	AD 36	AD 38	AD 47–49
■ World Events ■ Biblical Events	Paul persecutes the church.	Paul is converted to faith in Christ.	Paul goes to Jerusalem for the first time following his conversion.	Paul and Barnabas plant churches in southern Galatia.

"I no longer live, but Christ lives in me" (2:20a).

Who wrote Galatians?

Galatians is one of the first books written by the Apostle Paul (1:1; 5:2).

Who were the recipients?

The letter was addressed to the churches that Paul founded in the southern area of Galatia.

When was Galatians written?

Chapter 2 describes Paul's visit to the Jerusalem Council outlined in Acts 15 so it was written after that event. Since most scholars date the Jerusalem Council as occurring around A.D. 49, a likely date for Galatians is shortly thereafter, sometime in the early 50s.

Where did it happen?

On his first missionary journey, Paul traveled through the southern part of the Roman province of Galatia preaching and establishing churches. He wrote this letter to the group of churches established in the southern area of Galatia (Antioch, Iconium, Lystra, and Derbe; see Ac 13:14–14:23). [See map of Galatia on p.1555].

What is Galatians about?

Justification by faith. Paul vigorously defended this doctrine first from a theological standpoint in chapters 3–4 and then looked at the practical ramifications in chapters 5–6. Paul was adamant in his defense that keeping the law would not save a person—faith in Christ alone saves.

Why should women read Galatians?

Believers have no greater task than to have a proper understanding of the gospel so they may then share it with others. In this book, Paul was concerned that the Galatians were deserting the gospel that he had preached to them. A number of prominent Jewish legalists infiltrated the congregation of new believers and began teaching that faith in Christ alone was not enough to make a person right with God. Shocked by the Galatians' openness to this dangerous heresy, Paul wrote this letter to defend salvation by faith and warn these churches of the dire consequences of abandoning the essential doctrine he had faithfully taught them.

How do you read Galatians?

This letters reflects the heart of a minister who was burdened for his brothers and sisters in the faith because they were being led away by false teaching. Galatians follows a typical format for a first-century, Greco-Roman epistle, which would normally include a salutation or greeting, commendation, body, exhortation, and conclusion. However, this Pauline letter is the only one that does not contain a commendation of its readers—an obvious omission reflecting the urgency Paul felt about confronting the defection of the Galatian believers and defending the central doctrine of salvation by faith alone.

Outline

I. Paul's Introductory Greeting (1:1-5)
II. Paul's Defense of the Gospel (1:6-10)
III. Paul's Defense of His Apostleship (1:11–2:21)
  A. His Conversion and Testimony (1:11-24)
  B. His Message and Witness (2:1-21)
IV. The Doctrine of Justification Through Faith Alone (3:1–4:31)
  A. The Response of the Galatian Christians to the Gospel (3:1-5)
  B. The Example of Abraham (3:6-9)
  C. The Relationship Between the Law and the Promises of God (3:10-26)
  D. The Inheritance of Sons and Heirs (3:27–4:7)
  E. Paul's Concern for the Galatians (4:8-20)
  F. Two Covenants: Sarah Versus Hagar (4:21-31)
V. Life in the Spirit (5:1-26)
  A. The Role of Freedom (5:1-15)
  B. The Spirit Versus the Flesh (5:16-26)
VI. Concluding Exhortations (6:1-18)
  A. Carrying the Burdens of Others (6:1-5)
  B. Doing Good (6:6-10)
  C. Responding to the Cross of Christ (6:11-18)

AD 49	AD 49	AD 49	AD 49–51	AD 52
Paul and Titus participate in the Jerusalem Council.	Paul confronts Peter's hypocrisy at Antioch of Syria.	Paul writes letter to the Galatians.	Paul and Silas revisit the churches in Galatia.	Paul makes third visit to churches in Galatia.

Paul's Introductory Greeting (1:1-5)

1 Paul, an apostle—not from men
or by man, but by Jesus Christ
and God the Father who raised Him
from the dead— 2 and all the •broth-
ers who are with me:
To the churches of Galatia.[A]
3 Grace to you and peace from
God the Father and our Lord[B] Jesus
Christ, 4 who gave Himself for our
sins to rescue us from this present
evil age, according to the will of our
God and Father. 5 To whom be the
glory forever and ever. •Amen.

Paul's Defense of the Gospel (1:6-10)

6 I am amazed that you are so
quickly turning away from Him who
called you by the grace of Christ and
are turning to a different gospel—
7 not that there is another gospel,
but there are some who are troubling you and want to change the
good news[C] about the •Messiah. 8 But
even if we or an angel from heaven
should preach to you a gospel other
than what we have preached to you,
a curse be on him![D] 9 As we have said
before, I now say again: If anyone
preaches to you a gospel contrary to
what you received, a curse be on him!
10 For am I now trying to win the
favor of people, or God? Or am I
striving to please people? If I were
still trying to please people, I would
not be a •slave of Christ.

Paul's Defense of His Apostleship (1:11–2:21)

His Conversion and Testimony (1:11-24)

11 Now I want you to know, brothers, that the gospel preached by me
is not based on human thought.[E]
12 For I did not receive it from a human source and I was not taught
it, but it came by a revelation from
Jesus Christ.
13 For you have heard about my
former way of life in Judaism: I persecuted God's church to an extreme
degree and tried to destroy it. 14 I
advanced in Judaism beyond many
contemporaries among my people,
because I was extremely zealous
for the traditions of my ancestors.
15 But when God, who from my birth
set me apart and called me by His
grace, was pleased 16 to reveal His
Son in me, so that I could preach
Him among the Gentiles, I did not
immediately consult with anyone.[F]
17 I did not go up to Jerusalem to
those who had become apostles before me; instead I went to Arabia and
came back to Damascus.
18 Then after three years I did
go up to Jerusalem to get to know
•Cephas,[G] and I stayed with him 15
days. 19 But I didn't see any of the
other apostles except James, the
Lord's brother. 20 Now I am not lying in what I write to you. God is my
witness.[H]
21 Afterward, I went to the regions
of Syria and Cilicia. 22 I remained
personally unknown to the Judean
churches in Christ; 23 they simply
kept hearing: "He who formerly persecuted us now preaches the faith
he once tried to destroy." 24 And they
glorified God because of me.

A1:2 A Roman province in what is now Turkey B1:3 Other mss read *God our Father and the Lord* C1:7 Or *gospel* D1:8 Or *you, let him be condemned*, or *you, let him be condemned to hell*; Gk *anathema* E1:11 Lit *not according to man* F1:16 Lit *flesh and blood* G1:18 Other mss read *Peter* H1:20 Lit *Behold, before God*

Title The book of Galatians derives its title (Gk *pros Galatas*, "to the Galatians") from the region in Asia Minor (modern Turkey), where the churches addressed were located.

1:3 Even Paul's typical greeting attacked the false teachers' legalistic system. A salvation by works, as these legalists claimed, was not by **grace** (Gk *charis*, "unmerited favor") and could not result in **peace** (Gk *eirēnē*, "peace," indicating a sense of security due to a relationship with Christ that is unaltered by the circumstances of life).

1:6-7 The Galatians were **quickly turning away** (Gk *metatithesthe*, "transfer oneself, fall away from one person and go to another"), a word describing military desertion.

1:8 Paul makes a hypothetical point: He was calling out the most unlikely sources of false teaching—the apostle himself and holy angels. The Galatians should receive no messenger, regardless of how impeccable his credentials, if his doctrine of salvation differed in the slightest degree from God's truth.

1:11-14 The **gospel** Paul **preached** is not based on **human thought**, or it would be like all other human religions, permeated with the idea of human effort to earn salvation. Paul's gospel **came by a revelation from Jesus Christ**, a reference to the unveiling of Christ on the Damascus road where Paul received the truth of the gospel (see Ac 9:1-16). Judaism refers to the Jewish religious system of works' righteousness, based not primarily on the Old Testament but on rabbinic interpretations and traditions.

1:16-17 Undoubtedly, Paul was concerned that the false teachers would try to cast doubt on his apostleship, thereby causing the Galatian believers to call into question the message they heard from him. Paul was determined to convince the Galatians that he, and not the Judaizers (false teachers), preached the true gospel.

>WORD|*study*

2:12-13 The rest of the Jewish believers at Antioch joined [Peter's] hypocrisy (Gk *kai sunupekrithēsan autō*, "act hypocritically with"). **Even Barnabas was carried away by their hypocrisy** (Gk *hupokrisei*, "pretense, outward show," anglicized as "hypocrisy"; cp. Mt 23:28). The word referred to an actor who would wear a mask to depict a mood or certain character. In the spiritual sense, the reference is to someone who masked his true character by pretending to be something he was not.

2:1 After 14 years refers to the period of time between Paul's first visit to Jerusalem and the meeting of the Jerusalem Council, which was called to resolve the issue of how Gentiles were saved (see Ac 15:1-22). Paul did, in fact, visit Jerusalem during that 14-year period to deliver famine relief to the church there (see Ac 11:27-30), but he does not refer to that visit here since it has no bearing upon his apostolic authority. **Barnabas**, Paul's first ally, vouched for him before the apostles at Jerusalem and became Paul's traveling companion. **Titus** was a spiritual child of Paul and a coworker (Ti 1:4-5); as an uncircumcised Gentile, Titus was fitting proof of the effectiveness of Paul's ministry.

2:2 Paul went to Jerusalem **according to a revelation**. This revelation from God was the voice of the Holy Spirit. Paul refers to the divine commissioning of his visit in order to refute any suggestion by the Judaizers that they had sent Paul to Jerusalem to have the apostles correct his doctrine.

2:3 Paul states that **not even Titus . . . was compelled to be circumcised**. At the core of the Judaizers' system of works was the Mosaic prescription of circumcision. They were teaching that there could be no salvation without circumcision. Paul and the apostles denied that assertion, and it was settled at the Jerusalem Council.

2:4 The **false brothers** are the Judaizers, who pretended to be true Christians. However, because their teaching demanded circumcision and obedience to the Mosaic law as the prerequisite for salvation, it was opposed to Christianity.

2:11 Antioch in Syria was the location of the first Gentile church.

2:12-13 Peter (**Cephas**), knowing the decision of the Jerusalem Council, had been in Antioch for some time eating with Gentiles. When Judaizers came, Peter stopped eating with Gentiles. Peter had already given up all Mosaic ceremony (Ac 10:9-22). To eat with Judaizers and decline invitations to eat **with the Gentiles** meant that Peter was affirming the very dietary restrictions he knew God had abolished. Thus he was striking a blow to the gospel of grace.

2:18 The system [Paul] **tore down** alludes to the false system of salvation through legalism, abolished by the preaching of salvation by grace alone through faith alone.

2:19-20 Paul proclaims that he has **been crucified with Christ . . . Christ lives in** him. A person who

His Message and Witness (2:1-21)

2 Then after 14 years I went up
again to Jerusalem with Barnabas, taking Titus along also. 2 I
went up according to a revelation
and presented to them the gospel
I preach among the Gentiles—but
privately to those recognized as
leaders—so that I might not be running, or have run the race, in vain.
3 But not even Titus who was with
me, though he was a Greek, was
compelled to be circumcised. 4 This
issue arose because of false brothers
smuggled in, who came in secretly
to spy on the freedom that we have
in Christ Jesus, in order to enslave
us. 5 But we did not give up and submit to these people for even an hour,
so that the truth of the gospel would
be preserved for you.
6 Now from those recognized as
important (what they really were
makes no difference to me; God
does not show favoritism[A])—they
added nothing to me. 7 On the
contrary, they saw that I had been
entrusted with the gospel for the
uncircumcised, just as Peter was for
the circumcised, 8 since the One at
work in Peter for an apostleship to
the circumcised was also at work in
me for the Gentiles. 9 When James,
•Cephas,[B] and John, recognized as
pillars, acknowledged the grace that
had been given to me, they gave the
right hand of fellowship to me and
Barnabas, agreeing that we should
go to the Gentiles and they to the
circumcised. 10 They asked only that
we would remember the poor, which
I made every effort to do.
11 But when Cephas[B] came to Antioch, I opposed him to his face because he stood condemned.[C] 12 For
he regularly ate with the Gentiles
before certain men came from
James. However, when they came,
he withdrew and separated himself,
because he feared those from the
circumcision party. 13 Then the rest
of the Jews joined his hypocrisy, so
that even Barnabas was carried away
by their hypocrisy. 14 But when I saw
that they were deviating from the
truth of the gospel, I told Cephas[B] in
front of everyone, "If you, who are a
Jew, live like a Gentile and not like a
Jew, how can you compel Gentiles to
live like Jews?"[D]
15 We who are Jews by birth and
not "Gentile sinners" 16 know that
no one is •justified by the works of
the law but by faith in Jesus Christ.[E]
And we have believed in Christ Jesus
so that we might be justified by faith
in Christ[F] and not by the works of
the law, because by the works of the
law no human being will[G] be justified. 17 But if we ourselves are also
found to be "sinners" while seeking
to be justified by Christ, is Christ
then a promoter[H] of sin? Absolutely

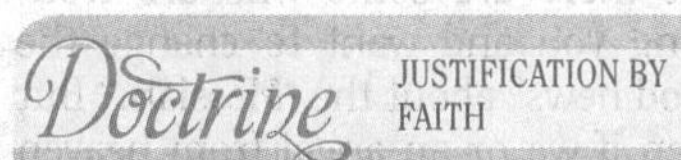

JUSTIFICATION BY FAITH

Justification (**justified**, 2:16) is a legal term referring to the acquittal of a person who has been accused of a crime (2:16). It brings to mind a picture of a judge who declares Christians as righteous when they accept Christ (see Rm 5:16-18). Christ's death on the cross accomplished an open and shut case for any person willing to accept Him as Lord and Savior. Justification takes place once for all—it is never repeated—a person cannot be accused of the crime again. For humanity, that means that once Christ has justified you of and forgiven your sin, He sees you as innocent, acquitted of your crimes. This justification is not because of your own works; it is because of **faith** in what Christ did on your behalf. Paul said that keeping **the works of the law** was not a means of salvation because the root of sinfulness is in the fallenness of a person's heart, not his actions. The law serves as a mirror to reveal sin, not as a cure for it.

[A]**2:6** Or *God is not a respecter of persons*; lit *God does not receive the face of man* [B]**2:9,11,14** Other mss read *Peter* [C]**2:11** Or *he was in the wrong* [D]**2:14** Some translations continue the quotation through v. 16 or v. 21. [E]**2:16** Or *by the faithfulness of Jesus Christ* [F]**2:16** Or *by the faithfulness of Christ* [G]**2:16** Lit *law all flesh will not* [H]**2:17** Or *servant*

not! [18]If I rebuild the system[A] I tore down, I show myself to be a lawbreaker. [19]For through the law I have died to the law, so that I might live for God. I have been crucified with Christ[B] [20]and I no longer live, but Christ lives in me. The life I now live in the body,[C] I live by faith in the Son of God, who loved me and gave Himself for me. [21]I do not set aside the grace of God, for if righteousness comes through the law, then Christ died for nothing.

The Doctrine of Justification Through Faith Alone (3:1–4:31)

The Response of the Galatian Christians to the Gospel (3:1-5)

3 You foolish Galatians! Who has hypnotized you,[D] before whose eyes Jesus Christ was vividly portrayed[E] as crucified? [2]I only want to learn this from you: Did you receive the Spirit by the works of the law or by hearing with faith?[F] [3]Are you so foolish? After beginning with the Spirit, are you now going to be made complete by the flesh?[G] [4]Did you suffer so much for nothing—if in fact it was for nothing? [5]So then, does God supply you with the Spirit and work miracles among you by the works of the law or by hearing with faith?[F]

The Example of Abraham (3:6-9)

[6]Just as Abraham **believed God, and it was credited to him for righteousness,**[H] [7]then understand that those who have faith are Abraham's sons. [8]Now the Scripture saw in advance that God would •justify the Gentiles by faith and told the good news ahead of time to Abraham, saying, **All the nations will be blessed through you.**[I] [9]So those who have faith are blessed with Abraham, who had faith.[J]

The Relationship Between the Law and the Promises of God (3:10-26)

[10]For all who rely on the works of the law are under a curse, because it is written: **Everyone who does not continue doing everything written in the book of the law is cursed.**[K] [11]Now it is clear that no one is justified before God by the law, because **the righteous will live by faith.**[L] [12]But the law is not based on faith; instead, **the one who does these things will live by them.**[M] [13]Christ has •redeemed us from the curse of the law by becoming a curse for us, because it is written: **Everyone who is hung on a tree is cursed.**[N] [14]The purpose was that the blessing of Abraham would come to the Gentiles by Christ Jesus, so that we could receive the promised Spirit through faith.

[15]•Brothers, I'm using a human illustration.[O] No one sets aside or makes additions to even a human covenant[P] that has been ratified. [16]Now the promises were spoken to Abraham and to his •seed. He does not say "and to seeds," as though referring to many, but referring to one, **and to your seed,**[Q] who is Christ. [17]And I say this: The law, which came 430 years later, does not revoke a covenant that was previously ratified by God[R] and cancel the promise. [18]For if the inheritance is from the law, it is no longer from the promise; but God granted it to Abraham through the promise.

[19]Why then was the law given? It was added because of transgressions until the Seed to whom the promise was made would come. The law was put into effect through angels by means of a mediator. [20]Now a mediator is not for just one person, but God is one. [21]Is the law therefore contrary to God's promises? Absolutely not! For if a law had been given that was able to give life, then righteousness would certainly be by the law. [22]But the Scripture has imprisoned everything under sin's power,[S] so that the promise by faith in Jesus Christ might be given to those who believe. [23]Before this faith came, we were confined under the law, imprisoned until the coming faith was revealed. [24]The law, then,

[A]2:18 Lit *rebuild those things that* [B]2:19 Other textual traditions place *I have been crucified with Christ* in v. 20. [C]2:20 Or *flesh* [D]3:1 Other mss add *not to obey the truth* [E]3:1 Other mss add *among you* [F]3:2,5 Lit *by law works or faith hearing* or *hearing the message* [G]3:3 By human effort [H]3:6 Gn 15:6 [I]3:8 Gn 12:3; 18:18 [J]3:9 Or *with believing Abraham* [K]3:10 Dt 27:26 [L]3:11 Hab 2:4 [M]3:12 Lv 18:5 [N]3:13 Dt 21:23 [O]3:15 Lit *I speak according to man* [P]3:15 Or *will, or testament* [Q]3:16 Gn 12:7; 13:15; 17:8; 24:7 [R]3:17 Other mss add *in Christ* [S]3:22 Lit *under sin*

trusts in Christ for salvation spiritually participates with the Lord in His crucifixion and receives victory over sin and death. The believer's old self is dead, having been crucified with Christ (Rm 6:3). Paul let go of all he was and all he owned in order to identify with Christ. He released the fantasy that he was somehow good or worthy in and of himself; he saw himself through God's eyes.

3:1-3 Paul repeats the word **foolish** (Gk *anoētoi*, "unintelligent"), showing how strong an appeal he was making to the Galatian believers. He was incredulous at how easily they had been duped. The notion that weak, sinful human nature could improve on the saving work of the Holy Spirit was ludicrous to Paul.

3:6-9 Paul moves to an example of Abraham who was justified by faith alone (see Gn 15:6). The phrase **Abraham's sons** refers to the truth that believing Jews and Gentiles are the true spiritual children of Abraham because they follow his example of faith. Salvation has always been by faith.

3:13 The verb **redeemed** (Gk *exēgorasen*, "bought, paid a price to recover from the power of another, ransomed"; cp. 4:5) was often used to speak of purchasing the freedom of a slave or debtor. Christ's death, because it was a death of substitution for sin, satisfied God's justice and exhausted His wrath, so that Christ actually purchased believers, delivering them from slavery to sin and from the sentence of eternal death. By bearing God's wrath for the sins of believers, Christ took upon Himself on the cross the **curse** pronounced on those who violated the law.

3:15 Brothers, a term of endearment, reveals Paul's compassionate love for the Galatians, which they may have begun to question in light of his stern rebuke. Paul then gives the Galatians an **illustration** of human covenants, which once confirmed are considered unchangeable. How much more irrevocable a covenant made by an unchanging God.

3:17 The time frame of **430 years** extended from Israel's sojourn in Egypt (Gn 46:1-4) to the giving of the law at Sinai (1445 B.C.). The law actually came 645 years after the initial promise to Abraham, but the promise was repeated to Isaac and later to Jacob. The last known reaffirmation of the Abrahamic covenant was made to Jacob (Gn 46:2-4) just before he went to Egypt—430 years before the Mosaic law was given. Paul used the length of sojourn in Egypt as recorded in Ex 12:40. The number is rounded off to 400 years elsewhere (Gn 15:13; Ac 7:6).

3:27 The verb **put on** (Gk *enedusasthe*, "dress, wear") may also be understood as "clothed with" and acts as a metaphor for what occurs when a person is no longer under the law and has been accepted in Christ. This word suggests becoming so possessed of the mind of Christ in thought, feeling, and action that a person starts resembling Him and even reproducing the life He lived.

3:29 When Paul stated **if you belong to Christ**, he was not calling into question whether or not the Galatians were true believers. Perhaps this phrase is better understood as "since you are of Christ." One becomes **Abraham's seed** and an heir to the promise by belonging to Christ and not by keeping the works of the law.

4:5 Adoption (Gk *huiothesian*, a term used only by Paul in the NT; see Rm 8:15,23; 9:4; Eph 1:5) refers to how God takes both Jews and Gentiles into His spiritual family. The person who is adopted into God's family receives all the rights, privileges, and responsibilities afforded to Christ. This adoption is not based on merit; it is always dependent on God's grace. Here in Galatians, the receiving of sonship through adoption occurs simultaneously as a person is freed from the law.

4:10 On the Jewish religious calendar the Galatians observed the **special days** marking the rituals, ceremonies, and festivals that God had given to Israel; but these were never required for the church. Paul warned the Galatians against legalistically observing them as if they were required by God or could

HARD QUESTION

What was the purpose of the law if it could not save a person?

The law reveals the utter sinfulness of every man and woman and their desperate need for a Savior—the law was never intended to be the way of salvation. Paul calls the law a **guardian** (Gk *paidagōgos*, "attendant, custodian, guide"), a term applied to a trusted slave in Greek and Roman society who was given the duty of tutoring and guiding boys of upper classes in their formative years (3:26). The *paidagōgos* was entrusted with a supervisory role that involved protecting, guarding, instructing, correcting and rebuking; he was given care over activities ranging from overseeing good hygiene to overseeing the studies of the child in his charge from his infancy to puberty. The purpose for having the law as a custodian or guardian until Christ came is made clear—**so that we could be justified by faith** (v. 24).

was our guardian[A] until Christ, so
that we could be justified by faith.
25 But since that faith has come,
we are no longer under a guardian,
26 for you are all sons of God through
faith in Christ Jesus.

The Inheritance of Sons and Heirs
(3:27–4:7)

27 For as many of you as have been
baptized into Christ have put on
Christ like a garment. 28 There is no
Jew or Greek, •slave or free, male or
female; for you are all one in Christ
Jesus. 29 And if you belong to Christ,
then you are Abraham's seed, heirs
4 according to the promise. 1 Now
I say that as long as the heir is
a child, he differs in no way from
a •slave, though he is the owner of
everything. 2 Instead, he is under
guardians and stewards until the
time set by his father. 3 In the same
way we also, when we were children,
were in slavery under the elemental
forces[B] of the world. 4 When the time
came to completion, God sent His
Son, born of a woman, born under
the law, 5 to •redeem those under the
law, so that we might receive adoption as sons. 6 And because you are
sons, God has sent the Spirit of His
Son into our[C] hearts, crying, "*•Abba*,
Father!" 7 So you are no longer a
slave but a son, and if a son, then an
heir through God.

Paul's Concern for the Galatians
(4:8-20)

8 But in the past, when you didn't
know God, you were enslaved to
things[D] that by nature are not gods.
9 But now, since you know God, or
rather have become known by God,

[A]**3:24** The word translated *guardian* in vv. 24-25 is different from the word in Gl 4:2. In our culture, we do not have a slave who takes a child to and from school, protecting the child from harm or corruption. In Gk the word *paidogogos* described such a slave. This slave was not a teacher. [B]**4:3** Or *spirits*, or *principles* [C]**4:6** Other mss read *your* [D]**4:8** Or *beings*

Biblical Womanhood The Significance of Galatians 3:28

Galatians 3:28 is one of the most debated verses concerning the role of women. In order to understand this verse properly, a person must consider its context within the book of Galatians. This verse is found in the midst of a discussion on how a person is saved—whether it is by keeping the law or through justification by faith. Paul is building a case for the Galatians to show that even in the Old Testament a person was saved by faith in the promise to come, not by keeping the law. After Christ came, a person is still saved by faith, though his faith is in the work that Christ accomplished on the cross. Whether a man or a woman, a slave or a free person, a Jew or a Gentile, a person is saved by placing his faith in Christ.

Why is it so important to establish the context of this verse? This verse has been used to argue that there are no longer distinctions in social relationships; specifically, there are no distinctions in gender roles between men and women. However, Paul was discussing the nature of salvation and not the proper social relationships of men and women in or out of the church and home. The interpretation of this passage cannot be divorced from its context or from the other letters of Paul where he clearly sets forth distinct responsibilities for husbands and wives (Eph 5:22-33; Col 3:18-19) and some distinct responsibilities for men and women in the church (1Tm 2:11-15; Ti 2:1-5).

Paul's assertion does not obliterate social or role distinctions. Rather the impartial nature of God's love is affirmed in salvation (Ac 10:34-35). Fully equal before God, women and men receive the same grace, must adhere to the same obedience, and experience the same blessing of being recipients of spiritual gifts and blessings. They are equal in worth but have received different assignments fashioned within the God-designed creation order.

how can you turn back again to the weak and bankrupt elemental forces? Do you want to be enslaved to them all over again? 10 You observe special days, months, seasons, and years. 11 I am fearful for you, that perhaps my labor for you has been wasted.

12 I beg you, •brothers: Become like me, for I also became like you. You have not wronged me; 13 you know that previously I preached the gospel to you because of a physical illness. 14 You did not despise or reject me though my physical condition was a trial for you.[A] On the contrary, you received me as an angel of God, as Christ Jesus Himself.

15 What happened to this sense of being blessed you had? For I testify to you that, if possible, you would have torn out your eyes and given them to me. 16 Have I now become your enemy by telling you the truth? 17 They[B] are enthusiastic about you, but not for any good. Instead, they want to isolate you so you will be enthusiastic about them. 18 Now it is always good to be enthusiastic about good—and not just when I am with you. 19 My children, I am again suffering labor pains for you until Christ is formed in you. 20 I would like to be with you right now and change my tone of voice, because I don't know what to do about you.

Two Covenants: Sarah Versus Hagar (4:21-31)

21 Tell me, those of you who want to be under the law, don't you hear the law? 22 For it is written that Abraham had two sons, one by a slave and the other by a free woman. 23 But the one by the slave was born according to the impulse of the flesh, while the one by the free woman was born as the result of a promise. 24 These things are illustrations,[C] for the women represent the two covenants. One is from Mount Sinai and bears children into slavery—this is Hagar. 25 Now Hagar is Mount Sinai in Arabia and corresponds to the present Jerusalem, for she is in slavery with her children. 26 But the Jerusalem above is free, and she is our mother. 27 For it is written:

> **Rejoice, childless woman,**
> **who does not give birth.**
> **Burst into song and shout,**
> **you who are not in labor,**
> **for the children**
> **of the desolate are many,**
> **more numerous than those**
> **of the woman who has**
> **a husband.**[D]

28 Now you, brothers, like Isaac, are children of promise. 29 But just as then the child born according to the flesh persecuted the one born according to the Spirit, so also now. 30 But what does the Scripture say?

> **Drive out the slave and her son, for the son of the slave will never be a coheir with the son of the free woman.**[E]

31 Therefore, brothers, we are not children of the slave but of the free woman.

Life in the Spirit (5:1-26)

The Role of Freedom (5:1-15)

5 Christ has liberated us to be free. Stand firm then and don't submit again to a yoke of slavery. 2 Take note! I, Paul, tell you that if you get yourselves circumcised, Christ will not benefit you at all. 3 Again I testify to every man who gets himself circumcised that he is obligated to keep the entire law. 4 You who are trying to be •justified by the law are alienated from Christ; you have fallen from grace. 5 For through the Spirit, by faith, we eagerly wait for the hope of righteousness. 6 For in Christ Jesus neither circumcision nor uncircumcision accomplishes anything; what matters is faith working through love.

7 You were running well. Who prevented you from obeying the truth? 8 This persuasion did not come from the One who called you. 9 A little yeast leavens the whole lump of dough. 10 I have confidence in the Lord you will not accept any other view. But whoever it is that is confusing you will pay the penalty.

earn favor with Him (see Col 2:16). Paul feared that his effort in establishing and building the Galatian churches might prove to be futile if they fell back into legalism.

4:12-20 Paul changes his approach as he moves from purely doctrinal argumentation to personal words of affection stronger than are found in any of Paul's letters. He is simply pouring out his heart in personal exhortation.

4:13 The **physical illness** Paul mentions is unknown—perhaps malaria, poor eyesight, chronic illness, or physical deformity. Whatever the condition, the Galatians welcomed Paul despite his weakness, which in no way had been a barrier to his credibility or acceptance.

4:21-31 Paul continues to contrast grace with law and faith with works, using an Old Testament story as an analogy of what he had been teaching. Specifically, he compares the **two sons** of **Abraham**, Ishmael and **Isaac** (vv. 22,28). Many years after God first promised a son to Abraham, Sarah had not yet conceived. Abraham feared that his chief servant, Eliezer of Damascus, would be his only heir, according to the custom of the day. He cried out to God in despair, and the Lord reaffirmed His original promise (Gn 15:1-4). But when after several more years Sarah still had not conceived, she persuaded Abraham to father a child by her female slave **Hagar**. The birth of that son, whose name was Ishmael, was **according to the impulse of the flesh** (Gl 4:29; cp. v. 23), not because it was physical but because the scheme for conception, devised by Sarah and carried out by Abraham, was motivated by purely selfish desires and fulfilled by purely human means. The birth of Isaac, however, was through the **promise**. His conception was supernatural, not in the sense that he was conceived directly by the Holy Spirit as Jesus was, but the Holy Spirit miraculously enabled Abraham and Sarah to produce a child despite her lifelong barrenness and the fact that she was far past normal childbearing age. The conception of Ishmael represents the way of the flesh, whereas that of Isaac represents God's way—the way of promise. The first is analogous to the way of religious self-effort and works' righteousness. The one is the way of legalism; the other is the way of grace. Ishmael symbolized those who have had only natural birth and who trusted in their own works. Isaac symbolized those who also have had spiritual birth because they have trusted in the work of Jesus Christ.

[A] **4:14** Other mss read *me* [B] **4:17** The false teachers [C] **4:24** Typology or allegory [D] **4:27** Is 54:1 [E] **4:30** Gn 21:10

5:13 In context, **flesh** refers to the sinful inclinations of fallen humanity (see v. 17).

5:16 All believers have the presence of the indwelling Holy Spirit as the personal power for living to please God. The verbal tense of **walk** indicates continuous action or a habitual lifestyle, so the verse could be understood as "make it your habit to **walk by the Spirit**." Walking also implies progress; as a believer submits to the Spirit's control, she grows in her spiritual life.

5:17-18 The flesh is not simply the physical body. It includes the mind, will, and emotions, which are all subject to sin, and refers in general to unredeemed humanity. The flesh opposes the work of the Spirit and leads the believers toward sinful behavior. Believers have a choice—they can be **led by the Spirit**, which results in righteous behavior and spiritual attitudes; or they can live by **the law**, which does not have the power to help them resist the flesh.

5:19-21 Works of the flesh—these sins characterize all the unredeemed, though not every person manifests all these sins to the same degree. The flesh manifests itself in obvious and certain ways, and Paul's list encompasses three areas of human life: sex, religion, and human relationships. The key word in Paul's warning is the verb **practice**, describing continual, habitual action. Although believers undoubtedly can commit these sins, those people whose basic character or pattern of life is summed up in the uninterrupted and unrepentant practice of these acts cannot belong to God.

5:22-23 Fruit of the Spirit refers to behavior produced by the Spirit of God. These nine characteristics or attitudes or behaviors are so inextricably linked that they are all commanded of believers throughout the New Testament. These traits are manifestations of the presence of the Holy Spirit at work in a believer and are the best evidence of the presence of the Holy Spirit living within. These characteristics are such that **there is no law** or need of one to prohibit them from being exercised in a person's life.

6:1 The word **caught** may imply the person was actually seen committing the sin, or that he was caught or snared by the sin itself. Those believers who are walking in the Spirit, filled with the Spirit, and evidencing the fruit of the Spirit, are to help restore the one who has fallen into sin. The word **restore** (Gk *katartizete*, "put in order, prepare, make sufficient") is sometimes used metaphorically of settling disputes or arguments, and it has the nuance of

>WORD|*study*

5:19 Sexual immorality (Gk *porneia*, "unlawful sexual intercourse, fornication," from which the English word "pornography" comes) refers to all illicit sexual activity, including (but not limited to) adultery, premarital sex, homosexuality, bestiality, incest, and prostitution. Promiscuity (Gk *aselgeia*, "licentiousness, sensuality, debauchery") originally referred to any excessive behavior or lack of restraint but eventually became associated with sexual excess and indulgence.

5:20 Sorcery (Gk *pharmakeia*, "magic," anglicized as "pharmacy") originally referred to medicines in general but eventually only to mood- and mind-altering drugs, as well as the occult, witchcraft, and magic. Many pagan religious practices required the use of these drugs to aid in their attempts to communicate with deities.

11 Now •brothers, if I still preach
circumcision, why am I still persecuted? In that case the offense of the
cross has been abolished. 12 I wish
those who are disturbing you might
also get themselves castrated!
13 For you were called to be free,
brothers; only don't use this freedom as an opportunity for the flesh,
but serve one another through love.
14 For the entire law is fulfilled in
one statement: **Love your neighbor
as yourself.**[A] 15 But if you bite and
devour one another, watch out, or
you will be consumed by one another.

The Spirit Versus the Flesh (5:16-26)

16 I say then, •walk by the Spirit
and you will not carry out the desire
of the flesh. 17 For the flesh desires
what is against the Spirit, and the
Spirit desires what is against the
flesh; these are opposed to each
other, so that you don't do what
you want. 18 But if you are led by the
Spirit, you are not under the law.
19 Now the works of the flesh are
obvious:[B,C] sexual immorality, moral
impurity, promiscuity, 20 idolatry,
sorcery, hatreds, strife, jealousy,
outbursts of anger, selfish ambitions, dissensions, factions, 21 envy,[D]
drunkenness, carousing, and anything similar. I tell you about these
things in advance—as I told you before—that those who practice such
things will not inherit the kingdom
of God.
22 But the fruit of the Spirit is
love, joy, peace, patience, kindness,
goodness, faith,[E] 23 gentleness, self-
control. Against such things there is
no law. 24 Now those who belong to
Christ Jesus have crucified the flesh
with its passions and desires. 25 Since
we live by the Spirit, we must also
follow the Spirit. 26 We must not become conceited, provoking one another, envying one another.

Concluding Exhortations (6:1-18)

Carrying the Burdens of Others (6:1-5)

6 •Brothers, if someone is caught
in any wrongdoing, you who are
spiritual should restore such a person with a gentle spirit, watching
out for yourselves so you also won't
be tempted. 2 Carry one another's
burdens; in this way you will fulfill
the law of Christ. 3 For if anyone
considers himself to be something
when he is nothing, he deceives
himself. 4 But each person should
examine his own work, and then he
will have a reason for boasting in
himself alone, and not in respect to
someone else. 5 For each person will
have to carry his own load.

Doing Good (6:6-10)

6 The one who is taught the message must share all his good things
with the teacher. 7 Don't be deceived:
God is not mocked. For whatever a
man sows he will also reap, 8 because
the one who sows to his flesh will
reap corruption from the flesh, but
the one who sows to the Spirit will
reap eternal life from the Spirit. 9 So
we must not get tired of doing good,
for we will reap at the proper time if
we don't give up. 10 Therefore, as we
have opportunity, we must work for
the good of all, especially for those
who belong to the household of faith.

Responding to the Cross of Christ (6:11-18)

11 Look at what large letters I use
as I write to you in my own hand-

[A] 5:14 Lv 19:18 [B] 5:19 Other mss add *adultery* [C] 5:19 Lit *obvious, which are:* [D] 5:21 Other mss add *murders* [E] 5:22 Or *faithfulness*

writing. 12 Those who want to make a good impression in the flesh are the ones who would compel you to be circumcised—but only to avoid being persecuted for the cross of Christ. 13 For even the circumcised don't keep the law themselves; however, they want you to be circumcised in order to boast about your flesh. 14 But as for me, I will never boast about anything except the cross of our Lord Jesus Christ. The •world has been crucified to me through the cross, and I to the world. 15 For[A] both circumcision and uncircumcision mean nothing; what matters instead is a new creation. 16 May peace come to all those who follow this standard, and mercy to the Israel of God!

17 From now on, let no one cause me trouble, because I bear on my body scars for the cause of Jesus. 18 Brothers, the grace of our Lord Jesus Christ be with your spirit. •Amen.

[A]6:15 Other mss add *in Christ Jesus*

GALATIANS … WRITTEN ON MY *Heart* The right understanding of and faith in the gospel of Christ will set you free from the bondage of sin. Do not think you must earn your salvation—it is freely offered to you from God if you will put your faith in Christ's death, burial, and resurrection as payment for your sins. Praise God that He empowers and enables you to live the Christian life once you have accepted Him.

mending or repairing, sometimes used of setting a broken bone or repairing a dislocated limb.

6:5 Verse 5 does not contradict verse 2. **Load** (Gk *phortion*, "cargo or burden") has no connotation of extraordinary difficulty or heavy burden but refers to life's routine obligations and each believer's ministry calling. God requires faithfulness in meeting these responsibilities.

6:8 **Corruption** (Gk *phthoran*, "deterioration, depravity, destruction") describes degeneration, as in decaying food; sin always corrupts and, when left unchecked, makes a person progressively worse in character.

6:11 Paul's expression **what large letters** can be understood as Paul's poor eyesight forcing him to use large letters or as Paul's use of the large, block letters (frequently employed in public notices) instead of the normal cursive style of writing used by professional scribes to emphasize the letter's urgent content.

Ephesians

Timeline	AD 52	AD 52	AD 54	AD 54
■ World Events ■ Biblical Events	Paul travels through Ephesus at the end of his second missionary journey.	Apollos comes to Ephesus and is mentored by Aquila and Priscilla.	Paul returns to Ephesus during his third missionary journey.	Paul teaches in the synagogue in Ephesus.

"Walk worthy of the calling you have received" (4:1b).

Who wrote Ephesians?
Paul named himself as the author of the letter (1:1; 3:1).

Who were the recipients?
The letter was addressed to the church that Paul founded in Ephesus, and likely this epistle was intended to circulate among churches in Asia Minor.

When was Ephesians written?
This letter was probably written during Paul's first imprisonment in Rome A.D. 60–62 (Ac 28:30-31).

Where did it happen?
While imprisoned in Rome, Paul wrote this letter to the believers in the church at Ephesus, the influential capital of the Roman province of Asia located on the eastern portion of the Aegean Sea in what is now Turkey.

What is Ephesians about?
- *The Church as the Body of Christ*. For the young church, this revelation was crucial to understanding God's marvelous plan of working in and through His people to accomplish His worldwide eternal purposes.
- *Unity*. Paul spent time explaining the importance of unity in the family as well as among believers in varied situations.

Why should women read Ephesians?
Many consider this epistle to hold some of the greatest Pauline theology, coupled with practical truths for living, and the brief letter continues to influence the church today. Women can especially appreciate the passage on understanding God's design for marriage found in Ephesians.

How do you read Ephesians?
The book of Ephesians is framed as a letter and, like other letters of the ancient Greco-Roman world and of the Pauline corpus, opens with the typical identification of author and recipients followed by greetings. In terms of content, the letter follows more closely the form of a sermon or homily with a greater emphasis on doctrinal and ethical issues than on particular ecclesiastical problems or issues relating to church polity.

Outline

I. Salutation (1:1-2)
II. Salvation in Christ (1:3–2:10)
  A. The Favor of the Beloved (1:3-6)
  B. The Glorious Redemption (1:7-14)
  C. Paul's Prayer for Believers (1:15-23)
  D. Those Dead in Trespasses (2:1-10)
III. Unity in the Body of Christ (2:11–4:16)
  A. Unity of the Body Through Christ's Sacrifice (2:11-22)
  B. Ministry to the Gentiles in the Body (3:1-13)
  C. Paul's Prayer (3:14-21)
  D. Unity in the Body Through the Spirit (4:1-6)
  E. Unity in the Body Through Gifts (4:7-11)
  F. Unifying of the Body Around Truth (4:12-16)
IV. Walking like Christ (4:17–5:21)
  A. A Warning Not to Walk in Your Former Life (4:17-32)
  B. An Admonition to Walk in Love (5:1-21)
V. Relationships in Christ (5:22–6:9)
  A. Between Husband and Wife (5:22-33)
  B. Between Parent and Child (6:1-4)
  C. Between Employee and Employer (6:5-9)
VI. Strength in Christ (6:10-20)
VII. Benediction (6:21-24)

AD 54–56	AD 56	AD 61	AD 62	AD 67
Paul moves from the synagogue in Ephesus to the hall of Tyrannus.	Paul leaves Ephesus for Macedonia.	Paul writes letter to the Ephesians.	Paul writes first letter to Timothy, bishop of Ephesus.	Paul writes second letter to Timothy.

Salutation (1:1-2)

1 Paul, an apostle of Christ Jesus by
God's will:
To the faithful •saints in Christ
Jesus at Ephesus.[A]
2 Grace to you and peace from
God our Father and the Lord Jesus
Christ.

Salutation in Christ (1:3–2:10)

The Favor of the Beloved (1:3-6)

3 Praise the God and Father of our
Lord Jesus Christ, who has blessed
us in Christ with every spiritual
blessing in the heavens. 4 For He
chose us in Him, before the foundation of the world, to be holy and
blameless in His sight.[B] In love[C]
5 He predestined us to be adopted
through Jesus Christ for Himself,
according to His favor and will, 6 to
the praise of His glorious grace that
He favored us with in the Beloved.

The Glorious Redemption (1:7-14)

7 We have •redemption in Him
through His blood, the forgiveness
of our trespasses, according to the
riches of His grace 8 that He lavished
on us with all wisdom and understanding. 9 He made known to us the
•mystery of His will, according to
His good pleasure that He planned
in Him 10 for the administration[D] of
the days of fulfillment[E]—to bring
everything together in the •Messiah,
both things in heaven and things on
earth in Him.
11 We have also received an inheritance[F] in Him, predestined according to the purpose of the One who
works out everything in agreement
with the decision of His will, 12 so

Doctrine THE WORK OF THE HOLY SPIRIT

God the Holy Spirit is fully God and equal to the Father and Son, yet He has a different ministry and work than either the Father or Son (1:13-14). The work or ministry of the Holy Spirit is multifaceted. He . . .

- inspires (2Pt 1:21),
- illuminates and teaches (Jn 14:26),
- convicts (Jn 16:8-11),
- regenerates (Ti 3:5),
- empowers (Ac 1:8),
- intercedes (Eph 6:18-19; Rm 8:26),
- gives assurances of salvation (Rm 8:16),
- comforts (Jn 14:16),
- gives spiritual gifts (1Co 12:28), and much more.

that we who had already put our
hope in the Messiah might bring
praise to His glory.
13 When you heard the message of
truth, the gospel of your salvation,
and when you believed in Him, you
were also sealed with the promised
Holy Spirit. 14 He is the down payment of our inheritance, for the redemption of the possession,[G] to the
praise of His glory.

Paul's Prayer for Believers (1:15-23)

15 This is why, since I heard about
your faith in the Lord Jesus and your
love for all the saints, 16 I never stop
giving thanks for you as I remember
you in my prayers. 17 I pray that the
God of our Lord Jesus Christ, the
glorious Father,[H] would give you a
spirit[I] of wisdom and revelation in
the knowledge of Him. 18 I pray that
the perception of your mind[J] may be
enlightened so you may know what
is the hope of His calling, what are
the glorious riches of His inheritance among the saints, 19 and what

[A]1:1 Other mss omit *at Ephesus* [B]1:4 Vv. 3-14 are 1 sentence in Gk. [C]1:4 Or *In His sight in love* [D]1:10 Or *dispensation*; lit *house law* (Gk *oikonomia*) [E]1:10 Lit *the fulfillment of times* [F]1:11 Or *we also were chosen as an inheritance*, or *we were also made an inheritance* [G]1:14 *The possession* could be either man's or God's [H]1:17 Or *the Father of glory* [I]1:17 Or *you the Spirit* [J]1:18 Lit *the eyes of your heart*

Title The Greek title for the epistle is *Pros Ephesious*, "To the Ephesians."

1:1 As is typical of New Testament letters, **Paul** begins by identifying himself as the author and defines his position as **an apostle of Christ Jesus**.

1:3 Paul begins with great praise by honoring **God** the **Father** and acknowledging Him as the ultimate Giver of blessings for all people.

1:4 God gives because **He chose** [Gk *exelexato*, "picked out, selected"] **us in Him, before the foundation of the world**. For the significance of the doctrine of election, see **Doctrine**, p. 1533.

1:5 For an understanding of what it means to be **adopted through Jesus Christ**, see note on Gl 4:5. For a discussion of the term **predestined**, see **Word Study**, p. 1463.

1:7 Paul calls believers to realize the incredible **redemption** (Gk *apolutrōsin*, "liberation or release upon payment of a ransom"; cp. v. 14; 4:30; Rm 3:24; 8:23; 1Co 1:30; Col 1:14) and **forgiveness** (Gk *aphesin*, "pardon, remission of penalty, release from imprisonment"; cp. Col 1:14) because of the shedding of the **blood** of Jesus. Although "redemption" and "forgiveness" are not identical, "forgiveness" of sins is a central component in "redemption." Because Christ, through his sacrifice on the cross, is able to redeem us, He can offer us forgiveness from our sins.

1:13-14 This passage in Ephesians discusses a particular ministry called the sealing of the Holy Spirit (see also 4:30; 2Co 1:22) . To be **sealed** [Gk *esphragisthēte*, "marked with a seal, certified"] **with the promised Holy Spirit** is to be authenticated, proven to belong to God. With sealing comes ownership and security; it conveys the sense of being secured from Satan, to whom the seal would identify you as off limits. The Holy Spirit is the **down payment** (Gk *arrabōn*, "earnest money, first installment, deposit, pledge that full payment will follow"; cp. 2Co 1:22; 5:5) or assurance of the **inheritance** to come and completion of the transaction.

1:22-23 Jesus is above **everything** that was, is, or will come. He is the ruler, the **head** (Gk *kephalēn*; see **Word Study**, p. 1485), and Jesus knows His purpose and position, especially in relation to His beloved church. This Scripture identifies Jesus' unbreakable union with His church.

2:1 Apart from a saving relationship with Christ, people are **dead** and without hope because of their **sins** (see **Doctrine**, p. 1461).

2:3 Paul also explains that without the shelter of a relationship with Jesus, you are **children** living **under wrath** (see **Word Study**, p. 1455). The **fleshly desires** of people draw them to do evil things, and Satan and his demons work along with the world to draw them away from God.

2:4-5 Mercy, on one hand, suggests the divine withholding of what is deserved (i.e., divine judgment); on the other hand, **grace** offers what is not deserved.

2:8-9 Salvation is a work of God, not of man. For people to imagine they are able to earn their salvation by doing good things is natural. However, Paul makes it clear that no person can do enough good **works** or live a life perfect enough to merit salvation.

2:10 God has planned for believers to do **good works** as a result and as evidence of their salvation. Other Scriptures clearly say that there is no way your "good works" can make you worthy of salvation (Gl 2:21; Php 3:9; 2Tm 1:9; Ti 3:5), but rather, "good works" should follow salvation. You are not saved *by* good works but *for* good works.

2:14-19 This section is an incredible and inspiring description of one of the mysteries of the kingdom of God—the unity brought through Jesus Christ. In Christ, **our peace**, all who are saved, both Jews and Gentiles, are with the Messiah, are included as **fellow citizens with the saints** in Christ's kingdom, are no longer foreigners and strangers, have hope, and as **members of God's household** belong to God now and for eternity.

2:14 Christ Jesus, by His once-for-all sacrifice (Heb 10:10-12) tore down the **dividing wall**. The spiritual equality for Jews and Gentiles, men and women, slaves and free was a revolutionary concept for the world and was accomplished so that **hostility** would end.

3:11-12 In the Messiah, Jesus our Lord, believers have **boldness** (Gk *parrhēsian*, "freedom to speak without reserve but openly and frankly; fearless

is the immeasurable greatness of His power to us who believe, according to the working of His vast strength.

[20] He demonstrated this power in the Messiah by raising Him from the dead and seating Him at His right hand in the heavens— [21] far above every ruler and authority, power and dominion, and every title given,[A] not only in this age but also in the one to come. [22] And **He put everything under His feet**[B] and appointed Him as head over everything for the church, [23] which is His body, the fullness of the One who fills all things in every way.

Those Dead in Trespasses (2:1-10)

2 And you were dead in your trespasses and sins [2] in which you previously •walked according to the ways of this world, according to the ruler who exercises authority over the lower heavens,[C] the spirit now working in the disobedient.[D] [3] We too all previously lived among them in our fleshly desires, carrying out the inclinations of our flesh and thoughts, and we were by nature children under wrath as the others were also. [4] But God, who is rich in mercy, because of His great love that He had for us,[E] [5] made us alive with the •Messiah even though we were dead in trespasses. You are saved by grace! [6] Together with Christ Jesus He also raised us up and seated us in the heavens, [7] so that in the coming ages He might display the immeasurable riches of His grace through His kindness to us in Christ Jesus. [8] For you are saved by grace through faith, and this is not from yourselves; it is God's gift— [9] not from works, so that no one can boast. [10] For we are His creation, created in Christ Jesus for good works, which God prepared ahead of time so that we should walk in them.

Unity in the Body of Christ (2:11–4:16)

Unity of the Body Through Christ's Sacrifice (2:11-22)

[11] So then, remember that at one time you were Gentiles in the flesh—called "the uncircumcised" by those called "the circumcised," which is done in the flesh by human hands. [12] At that time you were without the Messiah, excluded from the citizenship of Israel, and foreigners to the covenants of the promise, without hope and without God in the world. [13] But now in Christ Jesus, you who were far away have been brought near by the blood of the Messiah. [14] For He is our peace, who made both groups one and tore down the dividing wall of hostility. In His flesh, [15] He made of no effect the law consisting of commands and expressed in regulations, so that He might create in Himself one new man from the two, resulting in peace. [16] He did this so that He might reconcile both to God in one body through the cross and put the hostility to death by it.[F] [17] When the Messiah came, He proclaimed the good news of peace to you who were far away and peace to those who were near. [18] For through Him we both have access by one Spirit to the Father. [19] So then you are no longer foreigners and strangers, but fellow citizens with the •saints, and members of God's household, [20] built on the foundation of the apostles and prophets, with Christ Jesus Himself as the cornerstone. [21] The whole building, being put together by Him, grows into a holy sanctuary in the Lord. [22] You also are being built together for God's dwelling in the Spirit.

Ministry to the Gentiles in the Body (3:1-13)

3 For this reason, I, Paul, the prisoner of Christ Jesus on behalf of you Gentiles— [2] you have heard, haven't you, about the administration of God's grace that He gave to me for you? [3] The •mystery was made known to me by revelation, as I have briefly written above. [4] By reading this you are able to understand my insight about the mystery of the •Messiah. [5] This was not made known to people[G] in other generations as it is now revealed to His holy apostles and prophets by the Spirit: [6] The Gentiles are coheirs, members

[A] 1:21 Lit *every name named* [B] 1:22 Ps 8:6 [C] 2:2 Lit *ruler of the domain of the air* [D] 2:2 Lit *sons of disobedience* [E] 2:4 Lit *love with which He loved us* [F] 2:16 Or *death in Himself* [G] 3:5 Lit *to the sons of men*

of the same body, and partners of the
promise in Christ Jesus through the
gospel. 7 I was made a servant of this
gospel by the gift of God's grace that
was given to me by the working of
His power.
8 This grace was given to me—the
least of all the •saints—to proclaim
to the Gentiles the incalculable
riches of the Messiah, 9 and to shed
light for all about the administration
of the mystery hidden for ages in
God who created all things. 10 This is
so God's multi-faceted wisdom may
now be made known through the
church to the rulers and authorities
in the heavens. 11 This is according
to His eternal purpose accomplished
in the Messiah, Jesus our Lord. 12 In
Him we have boldness and confident
access through faith in Him.[A] 13 So
then I ask you not to be discouraged
over my afflictions on your behalf,
for they are your glory.

Paul's Prayer (3:14-21)

14 For this reason I kneel before
the Father[B] 15 from whom every family in heaven and on earth is named.
16 I pray that He may grant you, according to the riches of His glory, to
be strengthened with power in the
inner man through His Spirit, 17 and
that the Messiah may dwell in your
hearts through faith. I pray that you,
being rooted and firmly established
in love, 18 may be able to comprehend with all the saints what is the
length and width, height and depth
of God's love, 19 and to know the
Messiah's love that surpasses knowledge, so you may be filled with all
the fullness of God.
20 Now to Him who is able to do
above and beyond all that we ask or
think according to the power that
works in us— 21 to Him be glory in
the church and in Christ Jesus to
all generations, forever and ever.
•Amen.

Unity in the Body Through the Spirit
(4:1-6)

4 Therefore I, the prisoner for the
Lord, urge you to •walk worthy of
the calling you have received, 2 with
all humility and gentleness, with
patience, accepting[C] one another in
love, 3 diligently keeping the unity of
the Spirit with the peace that binds
us. 4 There is one body and one Spirit—just as you were called to one
hope[D] at your calling— 5 one Lord,
one faith, one baptism, 6 one God
and Father of all, who is above all
and through all and in all.

Unity in the Body Through Gifts (4:7-11)

7 Now grace was given to each one
of us according to the measure of
the •Messiah's gift. 8 For it says:

When He ascended on high,
He took prisoners
into captivity;[E]
He gave gifts to people.[F]

9 But what does "He ascended" mean
except that He[G] descended to the
lower parts of the earth?[H] 10 The One
who descended is also the One who
ascended far above all the heavens,
that He might fill[I] all things. 11 And
He personally gave some to be
apostles, some prophets, some evangelists, some pastors and teachers,

Unifying of the Body Around Truth
(4:12-16)

12 for the training of the •saints in
the work of ministry, to build up the
body of Christ, 13 until we all reach
unity in the faith and in the knowledge of God's Son, growing into a
mature man with a stature measured
by Christ's fullness. 14 Then we will
no longer be little children, tossed by
the waves and blown around by every
wind of teaching, by human cunning
with cleverness in the techniques
of deceit. 15 But speaking the truth
in love, let us grow in every way
into Him who is the head—Christ.
16 From Him the whole body, fitted
and knit together by every supporting ligament, promotes the growth
of the body for building up itself in
love by the proper working of each
individual part.

Walking like Christ (4:17–5:21)

A Warning Not to Walk in Your Former Life (4:17-32)

17 Therefore, I say this and testify

confidence"; cp. 6:19) and **access** to God because the sin that separated them has been covered by the sacrifice of Christ on the cross.

3:16-19 Paul prays for the Holy Spirit's power to strengthen **the inner man** or the deepest recesses of the hearts of believers. For **the Messiah** to **dwell** (Gk *katoikēsai*, "settle, inhabit, take up residence," from the root *oikos*, "house") in the hearts of God's people provides an incredible strength and connection with the Father and His power. The essence of Paul's powerful prayer is that believers would use the resources available to them through God.

3:20-21 God is able to do **above and beyond all that we ask or think**—this free access to God and the realization of His ability to work on behalf of believers ought to cause all to bring Him glory for generations to come.

4:1 Paul had been changed, and he had a new calling on his life. This change in a believer's life should be so profound that you no longer walk as those dead in trespasses but as those **worthy** [Gk *axiōs*, in a "fitting or suitable" manner] **of the calling**.

4:2 Paul explains the characteristics Christians are to develop with the help of the Holy Spirit. **Humility** is viewing yourself properly before God. Interestingly Paul places humility as the foundation for the Christian life and calling. The Greeks and Romans considered humility to be a great weakness, and this kind of attitude was not encouraged or appreciated.

Gentleness is a fruit of the Spirit (Gl 5:22-23) and can be characterized by self-control. The element of restraint is included in its meaning, suggesting controlled and steadfast strength rather than weakness. **Patience** suggests a patient endurance even when others have inflicted pain or suffering. In fact, in the New Testament often the word describes a reluctance to return evil for evil, a refusal to seek revenge. While easy to praise, patience can be extremely difficult to live out.

4:3 God has made **peace** with those who come to Him through His Son. **The Spirit** then indwells Christians, uniting them with the Godhead and uniting them with one another. Living in **unity** with one another in the Spirit's love is a wonderful way to show outsiders the love of Christ.

A **3:12** Or *through His faithfulness* B **3:14** Other mss add *of our Lord Jesus Christ* C **4:2** Or *tolerating* D **4:4** Lit *called in one hope* E **4:8** Or *He led the captives* F **4:8** Ps 68:18 G **4:9** Other mss add *first* H **4:9** Or *the lower parts, namely, the earth* I **4:10** Or *fulfill*; Eph 1:23

4:26-27 Paul offers a strong warning to the church about being angry (Gk *parorgismō*, "wrath, indignation, exasperation," in the sense of a violent irritation). This word is used only here in the Greek New Testament and seems to suggest the expression of harmful words or inconsiderate actions or even an antagonistic stare—any or all of which can be hidden beneath the surface as an angry mood just smoldering and waiting to erupt. Opening the door to anger can **give the Devil an opportunity**. Paul encourages believers to keep their anger in check by dealing with it daily. People should not push their anger down and let it fester into ungodliness. Anger must be confessed, dealt with, and acted upon according to Scripture.

4:30 The Spirit indwells all believers at conversion, giving the promise of eternity with God. He has **sealed** (Gk *esphragisthēte*, "marked, confirmed, certified, secured") believers (see note on Eph 1:13-14.

5:1 Most significant in this chapter is the principle that believers are to **be imitators** [Gk *mimētai*, in the sense of leaving a "mark, image, form, pattern"; see 1Th 1:6] **of God**. This vision should guide all thought and behavior.

5:3-5 Paul lists conduct that is inappropriate for a Christian. For example, being **sexually immoral** would not cause someone to lose his salvation because a person cannot lose her salvation. However, a sexually immoral pattern of life suggests that the person may not have been saved in the first place (see **Hard Question**, p. 1462; **Hard Question**, p. 1574; see note on 1Co 6:9-20).

5:7 Believing empty lies and participating in wicked behavior is likened to a partnership. A partnership has ties that bind, and Paul explains that disobedience to God is by default a partnership with darkness. Many do not realize that when they disobey God, they are partnering with Satan to produce pain, heartache, and emptiness.

5:18 Do not make choices that will lead you to disobedience, but instead fill your lives with godly things and serve the Holy Spirit. Paul specifically contrasts being **filled with the Spirit** to being **drunk with wine**. For believers, the only guiding influence in their lives should be the Spirit.

in the Lord: You should no longer walk as the Gentiles walk, in the futility of their thoughts. 18 They are darkened in their understanding, excluded from the life of God, because of the ignorance that is in them and because of the hardness of their hearts. 19 They became callous and gave themselves over to promiscuity for the practice of every kind of impurity with a desire for more and more.[A]

20 But that is not how you learned about the Messiah, 21 assuming you heard about Him and were taught by Him, because the truth is in Jesus. 22 You took off[B] your former way of life, the old self[C] that is corrupted by deceitful desires; 23 you are being renewed[D] in the spirit of your minds; 24 you put on[E] the new self, the one created according to God's likeness in righteousness and purity of the truth.

25 Since you put away lying, **Speak the truth, each one to his neighbor,**[F] because we are members of one another. 26 **Be angry and do not sin.**[G] Don't let the sun go down on your anger, 27 and don't give the Devil an opportunity. 28 The thief must no longer steal. Instead, he must do honest work with his own hands, so that he has something to share with anyone in need. 29 No foul language is to come from your mouth, but only what is good for building up someone in need,[H] so that it gives grace to those who hear. 30 And don't grieve God's Holy Spirit. You were sealed by Him[I] for the day of •redemption. 31 All bitterness, anger and wrath, shouting and slander must be removed from you, along with all malice. 32 And be kind and compassionate to one another, forgiving one another, just as God also forgave you[J] in Christ.

An Admonition to Walk in Love (5:1-21)

5 Therefore, be imitators of God, as dearly loved children. 2 And •walk in love, as the •Messiah also loved us and gave Himself for us, a sacrificial and fragrant offering to God. 3 But sexual immorality and any impurity or greed should not even be heard of[K] among you, as is proper for •saints. 4 Coarse and foolish talking or crude joking are not suitable, but rather giving thanks. 5 For know and recognize this: Every sexually immoral or impure or greedy person, who is an idolater, does not have an inheritance in the kingdom of the Messiah and of God.

6 Let no one deceive you with empty arguments, for God's wrath is coming on the disobedient[L] because of these things. 7 Therefore, do not become their partners. 8 For you were once darkness, but now you are light in the Lord. Walk as children of light— 9 for the fruit of the light[M] results in all goodness, righteousness, and truth— 10 discerning what is pleasing to the Lord. 11 Don't participate in the fruitless works of darkness, but instead expose them. 12 For it is shameful even to mention what is done by them in secret. 13 Everything exposed by the light is made clear, 14 for what makes everything clear is light. Therefore it is said:

Get up, sleeper, and rise up
from the dead,
and the Messiah will shine
on you.[N]

15 Pay careful attention, then, to how you walk—not as unwise people but as wise— 16 making the most of the time,[O] because the days are evil. 17 So don't be foolish, but understand what the Lord's will is. 18 And don't get drunk with wine, which leads to reckless actions, but be filled by the Spirit:

19 speaking to one another
in psalms, hymns,
and spiritual songs,
singing and making music
from your heart to the Lord,

[A]4:19 Lit *with greediness* [B]4:21-22 Or *Jesus. This means: take off* (as a command) [C]4:22 Lit *man*; = a person before conversion [D]4:22-23 Or *desires; renew* (as a command) [E]4:23-24 Or *minds; and put on* (as a command) [F]4:25 Zch 8:16 [G]4:26 Ps 4:4 [H]4:29 Lit *for the building up of the need* [I]4:30 Or *Spirit, by whom you were sealed* [J]4:32 Other mss read *us* [K]5:3 Or *be named* [L]5:6 Lit *sons of disobedience* [M]5:9 Other mss read *fruit of the Spirit* [N]5:14 This poem may have been an early Christian hymn based on several passages in Isaiah; Is 9:2; 26:19; 40:1; 51:17; 52:1; 60:1. [O]5:16 Lit *buying back the time*

>WORD|*study*

5:21 Submitting (Gk *hupotassomenoi*, "lining oneself up under") is in the present tense and middle voice, thus suggesting the idea of continuing in submission and clearly noting that the action is by personal choice. The word definitely expresses the idea of voluntarily giving up your own rights and bowing your own will to another. In the Greek culture, the word was often used in military terminology in the sense of soldiers standing under the authority of a commanding officer.

20 giving thanks always
for everything
to God the Father
in the name of our Lord
Jesus Christ,
21 submitting to one another
in the fear of Christ.

Relationships in Christ (5:22–6:9)

Between Husband and Wife (5:22-33)

22 Wives, submit[A] to your own husbands as to the Lord, 23 for the husband is the head of the wife as Christ
is the head of the church. He is the
Savior of the body. 24 Now as the
church submits to Christ, so wives
are to submit to their husbands
in everything. 25 Husbands, love
your wives, just as Christ loved the
church and gave Himself for her 26 to
make her holy, cleansing[B] her with
the washing of water by the word.
27 He did this to present the church
to Himself in splendor, without spot
or wrinkle or anything like that, but
holy and blameless. 28 In the same
way, husbands are to love their
wives as their own bodies. He who
loves his wife loves himself. 29 For no
one ever hates his own flesh but provides and cares for it, just as Christ
does for the church, 30 since we are
members of His body.[C]

31 **For this reason a man**
will leave
his father and mother
and be joined to his wife,
and the two will become
one flesh.[D]

32 This •mystery is profound, but
I am talking about Christ and the
church. 33 To sum up, each one of
you is to love his wife as himself, and
the wife is to respect her husband.

HARD QUESTION

Did Paul hate women?

Much has been said about the Apostle Paul's attitude toward women. In fact, some feminist theologians have reacted so strongly against Paul's words that they have simply rejected the words penned by Paul in Scripture. Feminist theologians suggest that Jesus loved women but that Paul was speaking under the influence of his own culture. In other words: Jesus spoke for God, but Paul spoke only for himself. A brief look at Paul's historical context shows that nothing could be further from the truth.

Paul undoubtedly had been immersed in an atmosphere in which the understanding was that women were not as valuable to society as men. However, this historical reality actually makes Paul's words of encouragement toward women more profound. While some interpret Paul's words toward women as pejorative, the truth is that Paul was not reflecting his culture; he was reacting against it. His strong stand on divorce (1Co 7), his encouragement of the women who ministered to and with him (Lydia, Ac 16:40; Phoebe, Rm 16:1; Priscilla, Rm 16:3), and even the way he encouraged women who were great participants and patrons for world missions (Priscilla, Ac 18)—all illustrate that Paul was bringing to his world a new way of thinking about the value of women within the context of Christianity and about their usefulness in the spreading of the gospel.

In Eph 5:25-30 Paul makes three revolutionary statements about women. First, Paul's teaching style illustrates that men and women are equal. He gives instructions to both. Second, Paul commands the men to **love their wives as their own bodies** (vv. 26,28). The verb (Gk *agapate*) indicates continuous and habitual action (5:25). Third, this love leads to a man's nourishing and cherishing his wife.

Between Parent and Child (6:1-4)

6 Children, obey your parents as
you would the Lord,[E] because
this is right. 2 **Honor your father**
and mother, which is the first commandment[F] with a promise, 3 **so**
that it may go well with you and
that you may have a long life in
the land.[G,H] 4 Fathers, don't stir up
anger in your children, but bring

5:21 Christians should always seek the betterment of others and be willing to sacrifice personal preferences for the good of the body of Christ. This **submitting to one another** should be the regular behavior of Christians. It should not be resented or avoided but done as unto the Lord.

5:31 This verse, a reference to Gn 2:24, proclaims the exclusive covenant relationship of husband and wife (see note on Gn 2:24-25).

5:32 Paul expresses awe that God created marriage in order to explain and show others about the **mystery** of the gospel. By entering into Christian marriage and behaving in marriage as **Christ** intended, Christian families are a witness of Jesus' sacrifice and acceptance of His bride. Marriage is a living example of the mystery of the gospel of Jesus Christ.

6:1-3 Paul first commands **children** to **obey** their **parents** because it is the **right** thing to do. A child's obedience to his parents is a reflection of his obedience to the Lord. Children are to **honor** (Gk *tima*, "revere, to count as valuable") their parents in the sense of treating "father and mother" as precious, an attitude of reverence with a double promise—well-being and longevity. The latter part of the promise is appropriate not as a guarantee of length of days but as a reminder that disobedience to parents is an indication of an undisciplined life, which can put a child on the fast track to sinful patterns that in themselves tend to shorten life.

6:4 The primary responsibility of leadership in the home rests upon the shoulders of the father, who must balance love and authority. Paul boldly tells **fathers** not to provoke or cause anger in their children continually but instead to bring them up in such a way that children will desire to obey and honor their parents and to be open to learning from them about the Lord.

[A]**5:22** Other mss omit *submit* [B]**5:26** Or *having cleansed* [C]**5:30** Other mss add *and of His flesh and of His bones* [D]**5:31** Gn 2:24 [E]**6:1** Lit *parents in the Lord* [F]**6:2** Or *is a preeminent commandment* [G]**6:3** Or *life on the earth* [H]**6:2-3** Ex 20:12

6:5-8 In this section Paul is not endorsing slavery but acknowledging it as a way of life at the time. Paul encourages a strong work ethic, which would make the **slave** valuable in the master's sight and an attitude that would endear him to those in authority over him. These verses are often applied to the employer/employee relationship in the modern era.

6:10-17 This passage on Christian warfare is a great encouragement since it offers a clear and honest picture of the Christian life. While many would like to believe that accepting Jesus means comfort, wealth, and blessing, the Bible offers quite a different perspective; the reality is that a Christian has many enemies in the world. Enemies can be Satan, unbelievers, your own flesh, and others.

6:13-17 Paul calls the believers to get ready for battle and **take up the full armor of God** so that they will be ready to stand against the tactics of the devil. This full armor includes a **shield**, **sword**, lance, **helmet**, and breastplate. Satan will not wait for the Christian to get her act together and dress for battle; he will start his attack when you are most vulnerable.

6:18 Just as any soldier would have to practice with weaponry to be used, so believers must learn to be comfortable with their armor; and this verse offers a great training program showing the necessity of prayer.

6:19-20 Paul closes this section by making himself and his own needs known to the people. He did not consider himself above temptation and knew troubles and suffering well. Paul was certainly on the front lines of battle and needed support from other Christians.

them up in the training and instruction of the Lord.

Between Employee and Employer (6:5-9)

5 •Slaves, obey your human[A] masters with fear and trembling, in
the sincerity of your heart, as to
Christ. 6 Don't work only while being watched, in order to please men,
but as slaves of Christ, do God's
will from your heart.[B] 7 Serve with
a good attitude, as to the Lord and
not to men, 8 knowing that whatever
good each one does, slave or free, he
will receive this back from the Lord.
9 And masters, treat your slaves
the same way, without threatening
them, because you know that both
their Master and yours is in heaven,
and there is no favoritism with Him.

Strength in Christ (6:10-20)

10 Finally, be strengthened by the
Lord and by His vast strength. 11 Put
on the full armor of God so that you
can stand against the tactics[C] of the
Devil. 12 For our battle is not against
flesh and blood, but against the rulers, against the authorities, against
the world powers of this darkness,
against the spiritual forces of evil in
the heavens. 13 This is why you must
take up the full armor of God, so
that you may be able to resist in the
evil day, and having prepared everything, to take your stand. 14 Stand,
therefore,

with truth like a belt
around your waist,
righteousness like armor
on your chest,
15 and your feet sandaled
with readiness
for the gospel of peace.[D]
16 In every situation take
the shield of faith,
and with it you will be able
to extinguish
all the flaming arrows
of the evil one.
17 Take the helmet of salvation,
and the sword of the Spirit,
which is God's word.

18 Pray at all times in the Spirit with
every prayer and request, and stay
alert in this with all perseverance
and intercession for all the •saints.
19 Pray also for me, that the message
may be given to me when I open my
mouth to make known with boldness the •mystery of the gospel.
20 For this I am an ambassador in
chains. Pray that I might be bold
enough in Him to speak as I should.

Benediction (6:21-24)

21 Tychicus, our dearly loved brother and faithful servant[E] in the Lord,
will tell you all the news about me
so that you may be informed. 22 I am
sending him to you for this very reason, to let you know how we are and
to encourage your hearts.
23 Peace to the •brothers, and love
with faith, from God the Father and
the Lord Jesus Christ. 24 Grace be
with all who have undying love for
our Lord Jesus Christ.[F,G]

[A]6:5 Lit *according to the flesh* [B]6:6 Lit *from soul* [C]6:11 Or *schemes*, or *tricks* [D]6:15 Ready to go tell others about the gospel [E]6:21 Or *deacon* [F]6:24 Other mss add *Amen.* [G]6:24 Lit *all who love our Lord Jesus Christ in incorruption*

EPHESIANS... WRITTEN ON MY *Heart*

Living out the truths of the Christian life can be difficult, but God's call to you is clear—walk in a manner worthy of your calling. He has given to believers the church, with its diverse members and gifts, in order to help all learn how to walk worthy.

Biblical Womanhood Submission in Marriage

Both men and women were created to display the image of God, and the Old and New Testaments affirm an equal value, coupled with a differentiation in roles between men and women. The idea of equal value with differing responsibility is easy to understand by looking at the example of God Himself in the triunity. While the Father, Son, and Holy Spirit are equally God, holy and perfect, each also fulfills a different function. Each member of the triunity has the same worth and importance, but each carries out a function in order to accomplish their unified purpose. For instance, Scripture notes that Jesus was totally submissive to the will of the Father (Lk 22; Jn 5). Jesus did not have an identity crisis; rather, He perfectly understood His role and the importance of His responsibility. Similarly, men and women can have equal value and importance before the Lord and still carry out different functions. Some view this principle as degrading; however, the complementarity between women and men accurately reflects the need each gender has for the other.

Submission to the Lord calls a woman to understand her role of modeling submission in the home and church, and Paul offers a clear explanation for submission. Paul is encouraging women to look beyond this life and instead consider the eternal implications of their behavior in marriage with the wife's joyful submission to her husband and a husband's love for his wife **just as Christ loved the church** (Eph 5:25). Such a marriage becomes a vibrant witness to the lost world concerning Christ's relationship to believers (5:32). Marriage is a model for the church. Jesus **Christ is the** loving **head**, or authority, **of the church** (5:23). Husbands are to represent this loving headship in their families. Wives represent the response of the church to Jesus Christ by submitting to and respecting the leadership of their respective husbands.

When a Christian woman marries, she should understand that while she is her husband's equal in personhood and in her spiritual accountability to God, she is called to submit herself willingly to her husband's leadership. Wives must yield to their husbands in love. The wife's submission is voluntary (see **Word Study**, p. 1517), not a response to the threat or demand of the husband. Just as Jesus willingly submitted Himself to the desire of the Father, so women choose submission to their own husbands over personal independence. Submission is also to a specific authority (**to your own husbands**, v. 22)—not to every man.

As Christ is the spiritual head of the church, so husbands ought to be the spiritual heads of their homes, modeled after the loving and serving Savior. Husbands are accountable to God Himself. He is a loving and protective Father who deeply cares for His daughters. A man who is under the authority of Jesus will be reminded of his own responsibility to care sacrificially for his wife. A healthy family is characterized by a husband and father who considers even his life less important than meeting the needs of his family and a wife who willingly allows her husband to lead, thus supporting the structure created by God.

Philippians

Timeline	*359 BC*	*42 BC*	*AD 49*	*AD 50*
World Events **Biblical Events**	Gold-mining town of Crenides seized by Philip II of Macedon and renamed Philippi	Battle of Philippi, a strategic turning point in Roman history	Beginning of Paul's second missionary journey	Paul plants the church in Philippi

"Make your own attitude that of Christ Jesus" (2:5).

Who wrote Philippians?

Paul named himself as the author of the letter (1:1).

Who were the recipients?

Paul wrote this letter to the believers in the city of Philippi. The Philippian church, founded by Paul on his second missionary journey in the early A.D. 50s, bears the distinction of being the first church in Europe.

When was Philippians written?

Clearly from the book itself one notes that Paul was in prison awaiting sentence when he wrote the letter (1:7,13-14,17,20,30; 2:17), and it was most likely written during Paul's first imprisonment in Rome A.D. 60–62 (Ac 28:30-31).

Where did it happen?

While imprisoned in Rome, Paul wrote this letter to the believers in the church at Philippi, a cosmopolitan city located on the plain of eastern Macedonia, about 10 miles inland from Neapolis, an important seaport.

What is Philippians about?

- *Joy.* The words "joy" and "rejoice" are found more times in this letter than in any other of Paul's letters. Paul discovered the true source of joy in Christ Himself, and Christ enabled Paul to experience joy even in suffering.
- *Unity.* Paul's emphasis on unity implies that the Philippian believers needed to be reminded that unity was essential for the church body and for the progress of the gospel in the world (1:27; 2:2-4,14; 4:2).
- *Christ.* The Christocentricity of the book is evident by the more than 50 references to Jesus, whom Paul calls "Lord," "Savior," and "Christ."

Why should women read Philippians?

When Paul arrived in Philippi, Paul found an assembly of God-fearing women, and among this group of women down by the riverside, the Philippian church was born. In this tender letter from the apostle Paul to the Philippian church, one sees Paul's heart as a mentor in the faith and as a father who deeply cared for his spiritual children. The Philippian church was beloved by Paul (1:3-8). They were a praying people (1:19), as well as loyal and liberal givers throughout Paul's ministry. Even when no one else supported him (4:15), they gave out of their own "deep poverty" (2Co 8:2) to further the gospel message. Paul yearned to see their spiritual growth; thus, he taught them the essence of the Christian life.

How do you read Philippians?

Paul's letter follows the form of ancient letters written and exchanged between friends in the Greco-Roman world. Although the letter is similar in form to ancient letters, the content is uniquely Christocentric and full of Paul's own articulation of the gospel message.

Outline

I. Introductory Matters (1:1-11)
   A. Greeting (1:1-2)
   B. Thanksgiving (1:3-8)
   C. Intercession (1:9-11)
II. The Present and Future of Paul's Imprisonment (1:12-26)
   A. Paul's Present Joy: Good Outcomes of Imprisonment (1:12-18a)
   B. Paul's Future Joy: Christ's Honor and the Philippians' Joy (1:18b-26)
III. Commission and Follow-Up (1:27–2:30)
   A. The Philippians' Commission (1:27–2:18)
   B. Paul's Follow-Up (2:19-30)
IV. The Essence of the Gospel and Life Itself (3:1–4:1)
   A. The Inadequacy of the Flesh (3:1-7)
   B. The Sufficiency of Christ (3:8-14)
   C. The Appeal (3:15–4:1)
V. Concluding Matters (4:2-23)
   A. Reiterative Exhortations (4:2-9)
   B. Appreciation (4:10-20)
   C. Closing Greeting and Benediction (4:21-23)

AD 52	AD 57	AD 59	AD 60–62	AD 62
Paul's return to Antioch, concluding his second missionary journey	Paul's likely return to Philippi to take an offering for believers in Judea	Paul's journey from Caesarea to Rome to appeal to Caesar	Paul's house arrest in Rome	Paul's letter to the Philippians

Greeting (1:1-2)

1 Paul and Timothy, slaves of Christ Jesus:
To all the •saints in Christ Jesus who are in Philippi, including the •overseers and deacons.
2 Grace to you and peace from God our Father and the Lord Jesus Christ.

Thanksgiving (1:3-8)

3 I give thanks to my God for every remembrance of you,[A] 4 always
praying with joy for all of you in my
every prayer, 5 because of your partnership in the gospel from the first
day until now. 6 I am sure of this,
that He who started a good work in
you[B] will carry it on to completion
until the day of Christ Jesus. 7 It is
right for me to think this way about
all of you, because I have you in my
heart,[C] and you are all partners with
me in grace, both in my imprisonment and in the defense and establishment of the gospel. 8 For God is
my witness, how deeply I miss all
of you with the affection of Christ
Jesus.

Intercession (1:9-11)

9 And I pray this: that your love will
keep on growing in knowledge and
every kind of discernment, 10 so that
you can approve the things that are
superior and can be pure and blameless in[D] the day of Christ, 11 filled
with the fruit of righteousness that
comes through Jesus Christ to the
glory and praise of God.

Paul's Present Joy: Good Outcomes of Imprisonment (1:12-18a)

Unbelievers and Christ (1:12-13)

12 Now I want you to know, •broth-
ers, that what has happened to me
has actually resulted in the advance of the gospel, 13 so that it
has become known throughout
the whole imperial guard,[E] and
to everyone else, that my imprisonment is in the cause of Christ.

Believers and Christ (1:14-18a)

14 Most of the brothers in the Lord
have gained confidence from my
imprisonment and dare even more
to speak the message[F] fearlessly.

A 1:3 Or *for your every remembrance of me* B 1:6 Or *work among you* C 1:7 Or *because you have me in your heart* D 1:10 Or *until* E 1:13 Lit *praetorium*, a Lat word that can also refer to a military headquarters, to the governor's palace, or to Herod's palace. F 1:14 Other mss add *of God*

Title The Greek title of the epistle is simply *pros Philippēsious*, "to the Philippians."

1:1 While **Paul** is clearly the author of the letter, he chose to include **Timothy** (Gk *Timotheos*, combining *timē*, "honor," and *theos*, "God," "honored of God") in the greeting as well. Timothy had a vested interest in the church as its co-founder (Ac 16–18) and was presently with Paul (Php 2:19).

The term **saints** (Gk *hagiois*, "holy or set apart ones") indicates the privilege of being recipients of Christ's saving work and a responsibility to live holy lives, set apart for His use (1Pt 1:15-16). The inclusion of the **overseers** [Gk *episkopois*, source of the English words "episcopate" and "Episcopal"] **and deacons** (Gk *diakonois*) in the greeting occurs only here in Paul's letters. See **Doctrine**, p. 1545, p. 1557; and note on 1Pt 5:1-4.

Philippi was a cosmopolitan city founded in 359 B.C. by Philip of Macedon (the father of Alexander the Great) and then made into a Roman military colony in 42 B.C. When Paul arrived in Philippi, he saw a "miniature Rome," made up of privileged people who were diverse in nationality and social position (see Ac 16:13-40).

1:13-19 Paul saw a beneficial outcome of his imprisonment: the opportunity to testify of the gospel of Jesus Christ in Rome. The **whole imperial guard** and **everyone else** knew why he was in chains.

BIBLICAL WOMANHOOD Praying for Your Children

In Php 1:3-11, one gets a glimpse of the deep love Paul had for the Philippian believers, whom he considered to be his spiritual children. Paul thought of them often, for they were in his heart (v. 7). And yet, Paul did not spend time merely *thinking* of his spiritual children; he spent time *praying* for them. Intercession was a natural by-product of his Godward focus, which constantly channeled his thinking about the believers into *prayers* on their behalf. God has uniquely gifted women to be nurturers and to care for their children. To think about your children is easy; this process is what it means to be a mother! Paul's example, however, causes you to ask yourself: Do I spend as much time praying for my children as I do thinking about them? And do I pray with an eye toward what God's purposes are for them (vv. 9-11)? And how often do you make your children aware of *what* you are praying for them (which encourages them to act on what you are praying)? Paul's example is a reminder that caring for your children means offering up fervent, visionary prayers on their behalf.

Most of the Roman believers had a renewed boldness in preaching Christ. One group of Roman believers understood that Paul was in prison because he had been **appointed for the defense of the gospel.** Another group of Roman believers preached Christ out of entirely different motives—apparently **out of envy and strife** and rivalry with Paul. They hoped that their preaching would cause Paul trouble in his **imprisonment**.

Although Paul most certainly was hurt by the opposition of fellow believers, he was able to rejoice because Christ was being proclaimed. His concern was the reputation of Christ, not his own. Paul's focus on Christ enabled him to choose to rejoice, even in his own difficult circumstances. His **deliverance** (Gk *sōtērian*, "salvation" in the sense of preservation from danger or destruction, v. 19) would result in vindication before God.

1:27-30 Paul turns his attention to the Philippians' spiritual walk. He commissioned them to live **worthy of the gospel**, standing united for the sake of Christ. Living in a Roman military colony, the Philippians would have understood well Paul's instruction to **live** (Gk *politeuesthe*, "conduct oneself as a citizen") worthy of the gospel. They were to conduct themselves as citizens of Christ's rule (cp. 3:20), for Christ—not Caesar—is Lord (2:11).

2:1-4 Paul knew the Philippians would have had all the resources necessary to be united in every way (note the repeated emphasis on "same" and "one"). This soul-unity starts at the individual level, with each person living out his relationships with others in **humility**, which is a mindset that acknowledges each person as equally valuable since each is made in the image of God. Rather than relating to others in selfishness (**rivalry**, cp. 1:17) and **conceit** (Gk *kenodoxian*, "seeking praise though not deserving it"), the Philippians were to put others first. Paul had already set an example for them in this (1:21-26), and he reminded them of the supreme example of humility—Christ Himself (2:5-11).

2:5 In this section, Paul directs his readers' gaze to Christ Himself, the supreme model of humility and obedience, and admonished them to **make [their] attitude that of Christ Jesus**. Paul is calling them not only to imitate what they knew of Christ's attitudes and actions, but even more, to live in accordance with the transformation Christ had already made in their minds and attitudes.

15 To be sure, some preach Christ
out of envy and strife, but others out
of good will.[A] 16 These do so out of
love, knowing that I am appointed
for the defense of the gospel; 17 the
others proclaim Christ out of rivalry, not sincerely, seeking to cause
me anxiety in my imprisonment.[B]
18 What does it matter? Just that in
every way, whether out of false motives or true, Christ is proclaimed.

Paul's Future Joy: Christ's Honor and the Philippians' Joy (1:18b-26)

And in this I rejoice. Yes, and I will
rejoice 19 because I know this will
lead to my deliverance[C] through
your prayers and help from the Spirit of Jesus Christ. 20 My eager expectation and hope is that I will not be
ashamed about anything, but that
now as always, with all boldness,
Christ will be highly honored in my
body, whether by life or by death.
21 For me, living is Christ and dying is gain. 22 Now if I live on in the
flesh, this means fruitful work for
me; and I don't know which one I
should choose. 23 I am pressured by
both. I have the desire to depart and
be with Christ—which is far better—24 but to remain in the flesh is
more necessary for you. 25 Since I
am persuaded of this, I know that I
will remain and continue with all of
you for your progress and joy in the
faith, 26 so that, because of me, your
confidence may grow in Christ Jesus
when I come to you again.

The Philippians' Commission (1:27–2:18)

Unity and Humility (1:27–2:4)

27 Just one thing: Live your life in
a manner worthy of the gospel of
Christ. Then, whether I come and
see you or am absent, I will hear
about you that you are standing
firm in one spirit, with one mind,[D]
working side by side for the faith
that comes from the gospel, 28 not
being frightened in any way by your
opponents. This is a sign of destruction for them, but of your deliverance—and this is from God. 29 For
it has been given to you on Christ's
behalf not only to believe in Him,
but also to suffer for Him, 30 having
the same struggle that you saw I had
and now hear that I have.

2 If then there is any encouragement in Christ, if any consolation
of love, if any fellowship with the
Spirit, if any affection and mercy,
2 fulfill my joy by thinking the same
way, having the same love, sharing
the same feelings, focusing on one
goal. 3 Do nothing out of rivalry or
conceit, but in humility consider
others as more important than
yourselves. 4 Everyone should look
out not only for his own interests,
but also for the interests of others.

Christlike Attitude (2:5-11)

5 Make your own attitude that of
Christ Jesus,

6 who, existing in the form
of God,
did not consider equality
with God
as something to be used
for His own advantage.[E]
7 Instead He emptied Himself
by assuming the form
of a •slave,
taking on the likeness of men.
And when He had come
as a man
in His external form,
8 He humbled Himself
by becoming obedient
to the point of death—
even to death on a cross.
9 For this reason God
highly exalted Him
and gave Him the name
that is above every name,
10 so that at the name of Jesus
every knee will bow—
of those who are in heaven
and on earth
and under the earth—
11 and every tongue
should confess
that Jesus Christ is Lord,[F]
to the glory of God the Father.

Obedience (2:12-18)

12 So then, my dear friends, just
as you have always obeyed, not only

[A]**1:15** The good will of men, or God's good will or favor [B]**1:17** Lit *sincerely, intending to raise tribulation to my bonds* [C]**1:19** Or *vindication* [D]**1:27** Lit *soul* [E]**2:6** Or *to be grasped*, or *to be held on to* [F]**2:11** Gk *kurios* = Yahweh; Is 42:8 LXX

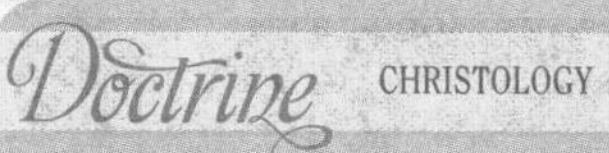

CHRISTOLOGY

Philippians 2:6-11, known as the Christ Hymn, tells the story of the person and work of Jesus Christ—His pre-existence, His incarnation, His death, and His exaltation. This hymn has been central to the Church's formation of Christology (a study of the person and work of Christ).

The first section of the hymn speaks of Christ's humiliation (vv. 6-8). Although **existing** [*always* existing; cp. Jn 1:1-3] **in the form of God**—thus, being equal with God—Christ refused to act selfishly by taking **advantage** of the rights of His Lordship. Instead He **emptied Himself** (Gk *ekenōsen*, "make empty or of no effect") voluntarily—not of His *deity*, for He was still in the form of God and equal with God, but perhaps of the *display* of His deity. This is the incarnation: the One who was fully God becoming fully man, henceforth existing as two natures (deity and humanity) in one person (Jesus Christ).

The subject changes in the second part of this hymn, Christ's exaltation (vv. 9-11). Having traced the work of God the Son, now the hymn traces the work of God the Father. Because of the Son's humble obedience, God has **highly exalted** [Gk *huperupsōsen*, "exalt to the highest degree"] **Him**. The **name that is above every name** seems to refer to **the name of Jesus**, but most likely this goes further to mean that God the Father grants Jesus the title of **Lord** (Gk *kurios*, equivalent to the Hb title, *Adonai*). One day, the lordship of Jesus will be confessed by **every tongue** on a day when **every knee will bow**. Paul displays this portrait of Jesus the Servant-King before the Philippians, so that they could see what true humility and selflessness meant.

in my presence, but now even more in my absence, work out your own salvation with fear and trembling. 13 For it is God who is working in you, enabling you both to desire and to work out His good purpose. 14 Do everything without grumbling and arguing, 15 so that you may be blameless and pure, children of God who are faultless in a crooked and perverted generation, among whom you shine like stars in the world. 16 Hold firmly to[A] the message of life. Then I can boast in the day of Christ that I didn't run or labor for nothing. 17 But even if I am poured out as a •drink offering on the sacrifice and service of your faith, I am glad and rejoice with all of you. 18 In the same way you should also be glad and rejoice with me.

Paul's Follow-Up (2:19-30)

Arrival of Timothy (2:19-24)

19 Now I hope in the Lord Jesus to send Timothy to you soon so that I also may be encouraged when I hear news about you. 20 For I have no one else like-minded who will genuinely care about your interests; 21 all seek their own interests, not those of Jesus Christ. 22 But you know his proven character, because he has served with me in the gospel ministry like a son with a father. 23 Therefore, I hope to send him as soon as I see how things go with me. 24 I am convinced in the Lord that I myself will also come quickly.

Arrival of Epaphroditus (2:25-30)

25 But I considered it necessary to send you Epaphroditus—my brother, coworker, and fellow soldier, as well as your messenger and minister to my need—26 since he has been longing for all of you and was distressed because you heard that he was sick. 27 Indeed, he was so sick that he nearly died. However, God had mercy on him, and not only on him but also on me, so that I would not have one grief on top of another. 28 For this reason, I am very eager to send him so that you may rejoice when you see him again and I may be less anxious. 29 Therefore, welcome him in the Lord with all joy and hold men like him in honor, 30 because he came close to death for the work of Christ, risking his life to make up what was lacking in your ministry to me.

The Inadequacy of the Flesh (3:1-7)

3 Finally, my •brothers, rejoice in the Lord. To write to you again about this is no trouble for me and is a protection for you.

2 Watch out for "dogs,"[B] watch out for evil workers, watch out for those who mutilate the flesh. 3 For we are the circumcision, the ones who serve by the Spirit of God, boast in Christ Jesus, and do not put confidence in the flesh—4 although I once also had confidence in the flesh. If anyone else thinks he has grounds for confidence in the flesh, I have more: 5 circumcised the eighth day; of the nation

2:12 Verse 12 has caused anxiety for many readers who think Paul was calling for attaining salvation by works. One should look at this verse in the context of Paul's other writings, however. Paul emphasizes that salvation is by grace through faith alone (3:9; Rm 3:28; Gl 2:16,21; 3:3,24; Eph 2:8-9; 2Tm 1:9, etc.). In this context, the working out of your salvation is the working out of the salvation you already have—it is merely confirmation that believers must live out the salvation they have been given. Obedience is not intended to gain God's favor; it is the result of salvation and the living out of who one is in Christ.

2:19-30 Both **Timothy** and **Epaphroditus** were prime examples of what Paul had been teaching the Philippians (vv. 19,25). Although Paul expected to see the Philippians soon, he was not able to come yet. For this reason, both men were perfect candidates to go to Philippi and follow up on their spiritual growth. Apparently Epaphroditus had been the Philippians' **messenger and minister** to Paul when they heard Paul was in prison. They sent Epaphroditus with a gift (4:18) and seemingly intended for him to stay with Paul for a time.

3:2 Not everyone rejoices in the Lord. Some rejoice in their own achievements and, even worse, teach others to do the same. Concerned that the Philippians not fall prey to this "Christ plus" gospel of the Judaizers (cp. Gl 2:1-14), Paul wrote words of warning, using irony to make his point. These Judaizers may have sounded confident in their standing before God; however, they were in fact **dogs** (a label of uncleanness the Jews reserved for the Gentiles); **evil workers** (not keepers of the law, as they claimed); and mutilators of **the flesh** (for their act of circumcision had lost its value). God's people are not constituted by circumcision of the flesh but by circumcision of the heart through faith (Dt 10:16; Jr 4:4; Rm 2:29; Gl 5:1-6; 6:15).

3:4-6 If anyone could have achieved a right standing with God based on his credentials, Paul qualified. However, when Paul encountered Christ on the Damascus road (Ac 9:1-9), those things in which he had previously put his **confidence** appeared worthless in light of the surpassing worth of Christ (see note on Acts 26:4-11).

[A]2:16 Or *Offer*, or *Hold out* [B]3:2 An expression of contempt for the unclean, those outside the people of God

3:8 At his conversion, Paul's life changed radically. Like Isaiah, who said all of one's righteous deeds are like filthy rags (Is 64:6), Paul saw that everything upon which he formerly depended for God's favor was mere **filth** (Gk *skubala*, lit "human excrement" or "trash thrown to the dogs").

3:9 Paul speaks of two different types of **righteousness.** Self-conferred righteousness looks to one's own ability to keep the law and conform to its standards, in hopes that he will become righteous. The righteousness that is from God, on the other hand, is not based on your ability to keep the law but is based on your **faith in Christ.**

3:10-11 Paul's desire to know Christ was so intense that he yearned to drink deeply even of Christ's sufferings.

3:12-14 Although **the prize** is not clearly stated, one can assume from the context of this passage that Paul looked forward most of all to being with Christ (1:21,23), knowing Him completely (3:10), and being transformed into His image at the resurrection (vv. 20-21).

3:18-19 Of these **enemies of the cross of Christ,** headed for **destruction,** Paul said **their god is their stomach.** This could be interpreted to mean that they focused on strict dietary laws, they were gluttonous, or they lived according to sensuous appetites. No matter the interpretation, clearly their deified appetites dictate their lives; thus, being egocentric, they have not made Christ their Lord.

3:20-21 Believers are to be future-oriented, with eyes toward Christ, **eagerly** awaiting Him and the day of His return, when by His power, He **will transform** frail, sinful bodies into bodies like His (cp. 1Jn 3:2).

4:2-3 For brevity, verse 2 is striking for several reasons. First, it is unusual for Paul to mention specific names in his exhortation; second, the names belong to women; third, the Greek here is verbatim to 2:2—but now with specificity, indicating that this is the crux of the unity problem in Philippi. Apparently two women in the Philippian church—**Euodia** (Gk, "pleasant, fragrant") and **Syntyche** (Gk, "lucky, fortunate")—were in disagreement on an issue about which no details are given here. Their disagreement was significant enough that word of it had reached Paul and serious enough that he felt the need to address it. The matter apparently threatened church unity (2:2-4; 3:15)—and did so because these women were of some influence. Not

CHARACTER PROFILE

Euodia and Syntyche

Their Background	They were leaders and workers in the church at Philippi (4:2-3).
Their Story	• A dispute had risen between them and was causing a disruption in the Philippian church. • Paul appealed to them to come to an agreement. He asked the other believers to intervene and help them also.
Life Lesson	A woman who insists on her own way, disregarding the feelings or opinions of others, does not honor Christ.

of Israel, of the tribe of Benjamin, a Hebrew born of Hebrews; regarding the law, a •Pharisee; 6 regarding zeal, persecuting the church; regarding the righteousness that is in the law, blameless.

7 But everything that was a gain to me, I have considered to be a loss because of Christ.

The Sufficiency of Christ (3:8-14)

8 More than that, I also consider everything to be a loss in view of the surpassing value of knowing Christ Jesus my Lord. Because of Him I have suffered the loss of all things and consider them filth, so that I may gain Christ 9 and be found in Him, not having a righteousness of my own from the law, but one that is through faith in Christ[A]—the righteousness from God based on faith. 10 My goal is to know Him and the power of His resurrection and the fellowship of His sufferings, being conformed to His death, 11 assuming that I will somehow reach the resurrection from among the dead.

12 Not that I have already reached the goal or am already fully mature, but I make every effort to take hold of it because I also have been taken hold of by Christ Jesus. 13 Brothers, I do not[B] consider myself to have taken hold of it. But one thing I do: Forgetting what is behind and reaching forward to what is ahead, 14 I pursue as my goal the prize promised by God's heavenly[C] call in Christ Jesus.

The Appeal (3:15–4:1)

15 Therefore, all who are mature should think this way. And if you think differently about anything, God will reveal this also to you. 16 In any case, we should live up to whatever truth we have attained. 17 Join in imitating me, brothers, and observe those who live according to the example you have in us. 18 For I have often told you, and now say again with tears, that many live as enemies of the cross of Christ. 19 Their end is destruction; their god is their stomach; their glory is in their shame. They are focused on earthly things, 20 but our citizenship is in heaven, from which we also eagerly wait for a Savior, the Lord Jesus Christ. 21 He will transform the body of our humble condition into the likeness of His glorious body, by the power that enables Him to subject everything to Himself.

4 So then, my •brothers, you are dearly loved and longed for—my joy and crown. In this manner stand firm in the Lord, dear friends.

Reiterative Exhortations (4:2-9)

Appeal for Unity (4:2-3)

2 I urge Euodia and I urge Syntyche to agree in the Lord. 3 Yes, I also ask you, true partner,[D] to help these women who have contended for the

[A] 3:9 Or *through the faithfulness of Christ* [B] 3:13 Other mss read *not yet* [C] 3:14 Or *upward* [D] 4:3 Or *true Syzygus*, possibly a person's name

gospel at my side, along with Clem-
ent and the rest of my coworkers
whose names are in the book of life.

Call to Be Christ-focused (4:4-7)

4 Rejoice in the Lord always. I will
say it again: Rejoice! 5 Let your
graciousness be known to everyone. The Lord is near. 6 Don't worry
about anything, but in everything,
through prayer and petition with
thanksgiving, let your requests
be made known to God. 7 And the
peace of God, which surpasses every
thought, will guard your hearts and
minds in Christ Jesus.

Goal of Obedience (4:8-9)

8 Finally brothers, whatever is true,
whatever is honorable, whatever is
just, whatever is pure, whatever is
lovely, whatever is commendable—
if there is any moral excellence and
if there is any praise—dwell on
these things. 9 Do what you have
learned and received and heard and
seen in me, and the God of peace
will be with you.

Appreciation (4:10-20)

10 I rejoiced in the Lord greatly
that once again you renewed your
care for me. You were, in fact, concerned about me but lacked the opportunity to show it. 11 I don't say
this out of need, for I have learned
to be content in whatever circumstances I am. 12 I know both how to
have a little, and I know how to have
a lot. In any and all circumstances I
have learned the secret of being content—whether well fed or hungry,
whether in abundance or in need.
13 I am able to do all things through
Him[A] who strengthens me. 14 Still,
you did well by sharing with me in
my hardship.

15 And you Philippians know that
in the early days of the gospel, when
I left Macedonia, no church shared
with me in the matter of giving and
receiving except you alone. 16 For
even in Thessalonica you sent gifts
for my need several times. 17 Not that
I seek the gift, but I seek the profit[B]
that is increasing to your account.
18 But I have received everything in
full, and I have an abundance. I am
fully supplied, having received from
Epaphroditus what you provided—a
fragrant offering, an acceptable sacrifice, pleasing to God. 19 And my God
will supply all your needs according
to His riches in glory in Christ Jesus.
20 Now to our God and Father be glory forever and ever. •Amen.

Closing Greeting and Benediction (4:21-23)

21 Greet every •saint in Christ Jesus.
Those brothers who are with me
greet you. 22 All the saints greet you,
but especially those from Caesar's
household. 23 The grace of the Lord
Jesus Christ be with your spirit.[C]

A 4:13 Other mss read *Christ* B 4:17 Lit *fruit* C 4:23 Other mss add *Amen.*

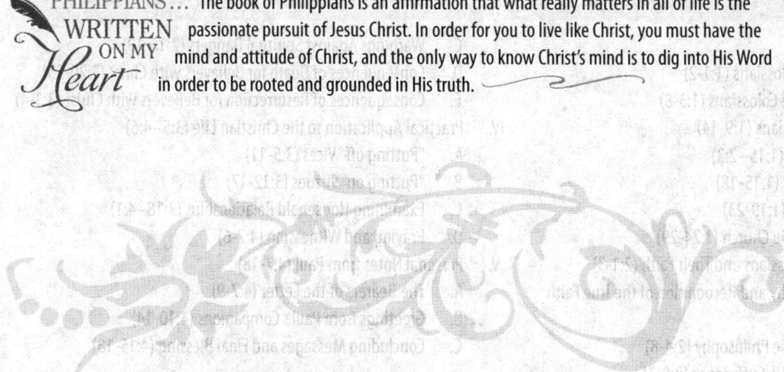

PHILIPPIANS … The book of Philippians is an affirmation that what really matters in all of life is the passionate pursuit of Jesus Christ. In order for you to live like Christ, you must have the mind and attitude of Christ, and the only way to know Christ's mind is to dig into His Word in order to be rooted and grounded in His truth.

much is known about them, except that they **contended for the gospel** with Paul. Paul's use of the Greek verb *sunēthlēsan* (a military word meaning "fight alongside"; cp. 1:27) implies that in the midst of difficult and even dangerous opposition, these women had stood firmly and bravely for the cause of the gospel. Their vigorous and ongoing partnership with Paul was not surprising, considering the involvement of Philippian women in the church since its beginning (cp. Ac 16). However, one should not exaggerate the leadership of these women beyond what the text actually says. For example, one cannot argue from this text that women held offices in the church. What *may* be said, however, is that Paul viewed women as equal partners in the ministry and as vital to the spread of the gospel. Their influence could therefore be a help—or a hindrance—to the gospel.

4:6-7 How do you stop worrying about all that concerns you? Paul says the solution is to pray about **everything**. Trusting God with one's petitions brings God's **peace** (Gk *eirēnē*, "peace," equivalent to Hb *shalom*, "wholeness, well-being"). The word **guard** actually pictures soldiers guarding a city gate from *within* the gate. So in entrusting one's petitions to God, God's peace will stand guard within the gates of your mind and heart to prevent the invasion of fear. Such peace, in the midst of trial, is so shocking that it **surpasses every thought**.

4:11-13 Paul had **learned** the secret of how **to be content** no matter the need or the circumstance. For Greek Stoics in Paul's day, contentment was a fundamental virtue. It was an indication of self-sufficiency—the ability to face any situation by your own resources. For the Christian, though, contentment comes not from self-sufficiency but from dependence on Christ and His resources.

4:14-19 The Philippians were a uniquely generous people (cp. 2Co 8:1-5), and they had a one-of-a-kind relationship with Paul (Php 4:15-16). Furthermore, their gift (apparently food) sent through **Epaphroditus** was exactly what Paul needed (v. 18). Even still, Paul's cause for rejoicing was not the meeting of his **need** (4:11). Instead, he rejoiced because their giving resulted in heavenly dividends for *them* (v. 17), as well as God's provision for their needs now (v. 19).

4:21-23 The greetings from those in **Caesar's household** are noteworthy. At the very least, this phrase suggests that there were disciples in the emperor's civil service (e.g., soldiers, government officials).

Colossians

Timeline

- **World Events**
- **Biblical Events**

430 BC	AD 7–18	AD 17	AD 54–56
The Greek historian Herodotus describes Colossae as "a great city of Phrygia."	Roman geographer Strabo describes Colossae as a small town	A destructive earthquake damages Colossae, Hierapolis, and Laodicea.	Epaphras becomes a believer under Paul's teaching in Ephesus and plants church at Colossae.

"Be careful that no one takes you captive through philosophy and empty deceit" (2:8a).

Who wrote Colossians?

According to Colossians 1:1, the Apostle Paul wrote the letter, and Timothy most probably served as Paul's *amanuensis*, a secretary or stenographer in the ancient world.

Who were the recipients?

The recipients of the book were the people of the church at Colossae. Evidence suggests that Paul had not visited Colossae at this point in time (2:1), even though he was certainly acquainted with individuals from the church.

When was Colossians written?

Paul was in prison in Rome when he wrote the letter sometime between A.D. 60–62 (Ac 28:30-31).

Where did it happen?

While imprisoned in Rome, Paul wrote this letter to the believers in the church at Colossae, a city at the base of Mount Cadmus about 120 miles east of Ephesus in the Lycus River Valley.

What is Colossians about?

- *False teaching.* Paul's letter is specifically focused upon combating some dangerous false teachings about Jesus Christ circulating in the church.
- *Christian living.* Paul desired to instruct the Colossians in how to live the Christian life based upon a true understanding of the life of Christ.

Why should women read Colossians?

Far too many women do not experience the "abundant life" that Christ came to bring them. Paul uses two words to describe the Christian life in Colossians: *freedom* and *fullness*. Followers of Jesus are free from sin because Jesus erased the certificate of debt and its obligations through His death on the cross. In the freedom found through Christ, the Christian is provided with fullness of life because she is God's chosen one, holy and loved. The truth about the person and work of Christ triumphs over deceptive heresy and teaches Christians to live in fullness and freedom through Him.

How do you read Colossians?

Read this letter as you would a letter today—not taking things out of context but with an understanding of the letter as a whole. Letters of ancient times had a particular literary form. Most ancient epistles, including this one, are in the following form: *Salutation*—References are made to the sender and to the recipient of the letter, together with a greeting. *Thanksgiving and/or Prayer*—All Paul's letters, except Galatians, where its absence is significant, include this element. *Body*—This section is typically the longest part of Paul's letters. *Exhortation*—These specific instructions are directed to the congregation, depending upon their respective situations and needs. *Conclusion*—Words calling for peace, greetings to friends, and/or closing blessings are included.

Outline

I. Introduction (1:1-14)
   A. Paul's Salutation to the Colossians (1:1-2)
   B. Paul's Thanksgiving for the Colossians (1:3-8)
   C. Paul's Prayer for the Colossians (1:9-14)

II. Christ's Work and Paul's Mission (1:15–2:3)
   A. Christ's Divine Personhood (1:15-18)
   B. Christ's Redemptive Work (1:19-23)
   C. Paul's Ministry to the Whole Church (1:24-29)
   D. Paul's Concern for the Colossians and Their Faith (2:1-3)

III. Refutation of the False Philosophy and Recognition of the True Faith (2:4–3:4)
   A. A Warning Against the False Philosophy (2:4-8)
   B. An Elaboration of Christ's All-Sufficiency (2:9-15)
   C. Warnings Against Spiritual Dangers (2:16-19)
   D. Consequences of Death for Believers with Christ (2:20-23)
   E. Consequences of Resurrection for Believers with Christ (3:1-4)

IV. Practical Application to the Christian Life (3:5–4:6)
   A. "Putting off" Vices (3:5-11)
   B. "Putting on" Virtues (3:12-17)
   C. Examining Household Relationships (3:18–4:1)
   D. Praying and Witnessing (4:2-6)

V. Personal Notes from Paul (4:7-18)
   A. The Bearers of the Letter (4:7-9)
   B. Greetings from Paul's Companions (4:10-14)
   C. Concluding Messages and Final Blessing (4:15-18)

AD 60	AD 60	AD 61	AD 61	AD 60–64
Paul is under house arrest in Rome.	Paul encounters Onesimus, a runaway slave from Colossae.	Paul writes the letter to the Colossians.	Tychicus and Onesimus travel from Rome to Colossae with the letter to the Colossians and the Laodiceans, as well as a personal letter to Philemon of Colossae.	Colossae experiences a devastating earthquake.

Introduction (1:1-14)

Paul's Salutation to the Colossians (1:1-2)

1 Paul, an apostle of Christ Jesus
by God's will, and Timothy our[A]
brother:
2 To the ·saints in Christ at Colossae, who are faithful ·brothers.
Grace to you and peace from God
our Father.[B]

Paul's Thanksgiving for the Colossians (1:3-8)

3 We always thank God, the Father
of our Lord Jesus Christ, when we
pray for you, 4 for we have heard of
your faith in Christ Jesus and of the
love you have for all the saints 5 because of the hope reserved for you
in heaven. You have already heard
about this hope in the message of
truth, the gospel 6 that has come
to you. It is bearing fruit and growing all over the world, just as it has
among you since the day you heard
it and recognized God's grace in the
truth.[C] 7 You learned this from Epaphras, our dearly loved fellow ·slave.
He is a faithful servant of the ·Mes-
siah on your[D] behalf, 8 and he has
told us about your love in the Spirit.

Paul's Prayer for the Colossians (1:9-14)

9 For this reason also, since the day
we heard this, we haven't stopped
praying for you. We are asking that
you may be filled with the knowledge of His will in all wisdom and
spiritual understanding,[E] 10 so that
you may ·walk worthy of the Lord,
fully pleasing to Him, bearing fruit
in every good work and growing in
the knowledge of God. 11 May you
be strengthened with all power, according to His glorious might, for
all endurance and patience, with
joy 12 giving thanks to the Father,
who has enabled you[F] to share in
the saints'[G] inheritance in the light.
13 He has rescued us from the domain of darkness and transferred
us into the kingdom of the Son He
loves. 14 We have ·redemption,[H] the
forgiveness of sins, in Him.

Christ's Work and Paul's Mission (1:15–2:3)

Christ's Divine Personhood (1:15-18)

15 He is the image
of the invisible God,
the firstborn
over all creation.[I]
16 For everything was created
by Him,
in heaven and on earth,
the visible and the invisible,
whether thrones
or dominions
or rulers or authorities—
all things have been created
through Him and for Him.
17 He is before all things,
and by Him all things
hold together.
18 He is also the head
of the body, the church;
He is the beginning,
the firstborn from the dead,
so that He might come
to have
first place in everything.

Christ's Redemptive Work (1:19-23)

19 For God was pleased to have
all His fullness dwell in Him,
20 and through Him to reconcile

[A]1:1 Lit *the* [B]1:2 Other mss add *and the Lord Jesus Christ* [C]1:6 Or *and truly recognized God's grace* [D]1:7 Other mss read *our* [E]1:9 Or *all spiritual wisdom and understanding* [F]1:12 Other mss read *us* [G]1:12 Or *holy ones'* [H]1:14 Other mss add *through His blood* [I]1:15 The One who is preeminent over all creation

Title Colossians was so named because its primary recipients were in the church at Colossae, a small town in western Asia Minor (modern Turkey).

1:2 Paul's use of the term **brothers** in reference to the Colossians does not mean that women were not included, for 3:18, with its instruction to "wives," indicates Paul is addressing the women of the church as well as the men. Thus, the term "brothers" is being used generically in this salutation.

1:9 Paul clearly expresses his desire for the Colossians to have spiritual intelligence, and Paul's prayer is a practical reminder for all believers to pray for one another.

1:10-12 Women often struggle with feelings of inadequacy or inferiority. These feelings can have negative effects on their efforts to live the Christian life, preventing them from experiencing the fullness of God's blessings in Christ. Colossians 1:12, though, has good news for women: You have been qualified by God to share in the **inheritance** of the saints. While before you were unworthy of God's inheritance, Jesus has made you worthy through His death and resurrection. So, what does this "inheritance" mean for you? First, a glorious reward awaits you in eternity when you are finally in the presence of the Savior. Second, you can live victoriously in this truth right now.

1:15-20 These verses make up one of the Christological passages of praise and serve as a challenge to the false teachers in the Colossian church. Jesus is **the image** of God. The Greek word *eikōn*, translated "image," also referred to likenesses placed upon coins, portraits, and statues. It communicates the concept of an equivalence to the original. When a coin was made, a piece of softened metal was stamped by an engraved tool, and the hardened metal coin would contain the exact representation of the engraving from the original stamp. The God-man Jesus Christ is the exact "stamp" of the Father's nature. In His essence, God is **invisible** to human beings, but Jesus Christ has perfectly revealed

Himself to you. Logically, since no mere creature can perfectly reveal God, then Jesus must be God Himself. The term **firstborn** refers to Jesus' rank in **creation**, not creation in time; it refers to Jesus' rank or position of authority, as both the inheritor of the universe and the ruler over it.

Saying that Jesus is **before all things** means that He is eternally existent, an attribute that belongs only to God. At the same time, Jesus sustains the universe.

Jesus is sovereign over creation as well as over the church. Jesus' position of supremacy in the church is specifically founded upon His nature as **the firstborn from the dead**. As in verse 15, "firstborn" has nothing to do with time. Others before Jesus rose from the dead (see Jn 11:38-44 for one example). Jesus is first in rank. Through His triumph over death, Jesus has led the way for those who, by faith in Him, will likewise be resurrected on the Day of Judgment and never die again. Because of the resurrection of Christ, a believer can be confident in her own resurrection (1Co 15:20-23).

1:23 The word **if** must not be misunderstood. Paul is not casting doubt on the believer's future status before God, as if her eternal salvation is dependent upon her performance here on earth. You are not saved by your steadfastness in the faith. But, you are **steadfast in the faith** because you are saved.

2:4 Paul affirms he has written **so that no one will deceive** them with **persuasive arguments** (Gk *pithanologia*, lit "pithy words"). False teaching is usually passed off as "smooth talking" that lures you away from Christ. Such teaching is craftily dressed up like a wolf in sheep's clothing: sweet and innocent on the outside but deceitful and wicked on the inside. It promises everything but delivers nothing.

2:6-7 In order to prepare for the enemy, Paul strongly encourages these Colossian believers to **walk** in their faith just as they **received Christ Jesus** in the first place. "Walk" in Paul's letters is a metaphor for "live." Essentially, he is saying, "You began your Christian life with Christ; now continue it with Christ. You began your Christian life with faith; now continue it with faith."

2:8 Even in a state of readiness and faithfulness, though, believers face the real threat of being taken **captive** by false teaching. You can, in effect, be spiritually "kidnapped" by **philosophy and empty deceit**. This warning is not a complete indictment of *all* philosophy, only against those ideologies that are full of "empty

Doctrine RECONCILIATION, THE MINISTRY OF CHRIST

Jesus is supreme over all things because all of God's **fullness** dwells in Him—Christ is fully God and fully human. There is a profound theological point in Col 1:19-20: Paul says all of God's nature dwelt bodily in Jesus Christ, and he declares that Jesus Christ was crucified for the purpose of your reconciliation with God. On the cross something truly remarkable happened: God turned His righteous anger, which human sin evoked, upon Himself in the person of His Son, thus satisfying His own anger and canceling out the sins of anyone who throws herself upon His mercy. In effect, God condemned sin and took the punishment for sin on your behalf for the purpose of reconciliation so you can have fellowship with God.

everything to Himself
by making peace
through the blood
of His cross[A]—
whether things on earth
or things in heaven.

[21] Once you were alienated and
hostile in your minds because of
your evil actions. [22] But now He has
reconciled you by His physical body[B]
through His death, to present you
holy, faultless, and blameless before Him— [23] if indeed you remain
grounded and steadfast in the faith
and are not shifted away from the
hope of the gospel that you heard.
This gospel has been proclaimed in
all creation under heaven, and I,
Paul, have become a servant of it.

Paul's Ministry to the Whole Church (1:24-29)

[24] Now I rejoice in my sufferings for
you, and I am completing in my flesh
what is lacking in Christ's afflictions
for His body, that is, the church. [25] I
have become its servant, according
to God's administration that was
given to me for you, to make God's
message fully known, [26] the •mystery
hidden for ages and generations but
now revealed to His saints. [27] God
wanted to make known among the
Gentiles the glorious wealth of this
mystery, which is Christ in you, the
hope of glory. [28] We proclaim Him,
warning and teaching everyone with
all wisdom, so that we may present
everyone mature in Christ. [29] I labor
for this, striving with His strength
that works powerfully in me.

Paul's Concern for the Colossians and Their Faith (2:1-3)

2 For I want you to know how great
a struggle I have for you, for
those in Laodicea, and for all who
have not seen me in person. [2] I want
their hearts to be encouraged and
joined together in love, so that they
may have all the riches of assured
understanding and have the knowledge of God's •mystery—Christ.[C]
[3] All the treasures of wisdom and
knowledge are hidden in Him.

Refutation of the False Philosophy and Recognition of the True Faith (2:4–3:4)

A Warning Against the False Philosophy (2:4-8)

[4] I am saying this so that no one
will deceive you with persuasive arguments. [5] For I may be absent in
body, but I am with you in spirit, rejoicing to see how well ordered you
are and the strength of your faith in
Christ.
[6] Therefore, as you have received
Christ Jesus the Lord, •walk in Him,
[7] rooted and built up in Him and
established in the faith, just as you
were taught, overflowing with gratitude.
[8] Be careful that no one takes you
captive through philosophy and
empty deceit based on human tradition, based on the elemental forces of
the world, and not based on Christ.

An Elaboration of Christ's All-Sufficiency (2:9-15)

[9] For the entire fullness of God's nature[D] dwells bodily[E] in Christ, [10] and
you have been filled by Him, who is
the head over every ruler and authority. [11] You were also circumcised
in Him with a circumcision not
done with hands, by putting off the
body of flesh, in the circumcision of
the •Messiah.[F] [12] Having been buried with Him in baptism, you were
also raised with Him through faith
in the working of God, who raised
Him from the dead. [13] And when
you were dead in trespasses and in

[A]1:20 Other mss add *through Him* [B]1:22 His body of flesh on the cross [C]2:2 Other mss read *mystery of God, both of the Father and of Christ*; other ms variations exist on this v. [D]2:9 Or *of the deity* [E]2:9 Or *nature lives in a human body* [F]2:11 = His death

the uncircumcision of your flesh, He made you alive with Him and forgave us all our trespasses. 14 He erased the certificate of debt, with its obligations, that was against us and opposed to us, and has taken it out of the way by nailing it to the cross. 15 He disarmed the rulers and authorities and disgraced them publicly; He triumphed over them by Him.[A]

Warnings Against Spiritual Dangers (2:16-19)

16 Therefore, don't let anyone judge you in regard to food and drink or in the matter of a festival or a new moon or a Sabbath day.[B] 17 These are a shadow of what was to come; the substance is[C] the Messiah. 18 Let no one disqualify you,[D] insisting on ascetic practices and the worship of angels, claiming access to a visionary realm and inflated without cause by his unspiritual[E] mind. 19 He doesn't hold on to the head, from whom the whole body, nourished and held together by its ligaments and tendons, develops with growth from God.

Consequences of Death for Believers with Christ (2:20-23)

20 If you died with the Messiah to the elemental forces of this world, why do you live as if you still belonged to the world? Why do you submit to regulations: 21 "Don't handle, don't taste, don't touch"? 22 All these regulations refer to what is destroyed by being used up; they are commands and doctrines of men. 23 Although these have a reputation of wisdom by promoting ascetic practices, humility, and severe treatment of the body, they are not of any value in curbing self-indulgence.[F]

Consequences of Resurrection for Believers with Christ (3:1-4)

3 So if you have been raised with the •Messiah, seek what is above, where the Messiah is, seated at the right hand of God. 2 Set your minds on what is above, not on what is on the earth. 3 For you have died, and your life is hidden with the Messiah in God. 4 When the Messiah, who is your[G] life, is revealed, then you also will be revealed with Him in glory.

Practical Application to the Christian Life (3:5–4:6)

"Putting off" Vices (3:5-11)

5 Therefore, put to death what belongs to your worldly nature:[H] sexual immorality, impurity, lust, evil desire, and greed, which is idolatry. 6 Because of these, God's wrath comes on the disobedient,[I] 7 and you once •walked in these things when you were living in them. 8 But now you must also put away all the following: anger, wrath, malice, slander, and filthy language from your mouth. 9 Do not lie to one another, since you have put off the old self[J] with its practices 10 and have put on the new self. You are being renewed in knowledge according to the image of your[K] Creator. 11 In Christ[L] there is not Greek and Jew, circumcision and uncircumcision, barbarian, Scythian,[M] •slave and free; but Christ is all and in all.

"Putting on" Virtues (3:12-17)

12 Therefore, God's chosen ones, holy and loved, put on heartfelt compassion, kindness, humility, gentleness, and patience, 13 accepting one another and forgiving one another if anyone has a complaint against another. Just as the Lord has forgiven you, so you must also forgive. 14 Above all, put on love—the perfect bond of unity. 15 And let the peace of the Messiah, to which you were also called in one body, control your hearts. Be thankful. 16 Let the message about the Messiah dwell richly among you, teaching and admonishing one another in all wisdom, and singing psalms, hymns, and spiritual songs, with gratitude in your hearts to God. 17 And whatever you do, in word or in deed, do everything in the name of the Lord Jesus, giving thanks to God the Father through Him.

deceit," as opposed to having the fullness of Jesus Christ (1:19; 2:9).

2:9-10 Attacks of false teaching usually focus on two major issues: (1) the person of Jesus Christ and (2) the Christian's identity in Him. False teachers may deny that Jesus Christ is God, or they may undermine His personhood as being fully human. They often propose "something more" as necessary for the completion of salvation. Quasi-Christian cults have an easily identifiable "mathematical" formula: They *subtract* from the person of Jesus Christ and *add* to the method of salvation.

2:14-15 These verses are a vivid picture of Jesus' accomplishment in forgiving your sins. **Certificate of debt** comes from Jewish business practices of the era. It was a hand-written note that recorded the various financial debts of the people. Upon payment of the debt, the note would be read aloud, declared to be fulfilled, and then destroyed. The "certificate of debt" for you and me is the violation of God's laws and rebellion against His rule. Through His death and resurrection, Jesus has **erased** the certificate of debt for those who believe in Him.

3:5-7 Based upon the believer's death and resurrection with Christ (cp. 2:20-23; 3:1-4), Paul exhorts believers to **put to death** in their lives **what belongs to your worldly nature.** This exhortation is not a reference to the careful management of sins in your lives, but it demands the complete extermination of sins from your lives.

3:5 **Sexual immorality** is from the Greek word *porneia*, referring to any kind of sexual activity outside the bonds of marriage.

3:8-10 The metaphor in verse 8 becomes one of changing clothes. The call to **put away**, followed by the charge to **put off** and **put on**, communicates a powerful idea: Believers are to discard their old habits like a set of worn-out clothes. Then they are to adorn themselves with the kind of behaviors befitting a child of God.

3:8 **Anger** (Gk *orgēn*), also translated indignation, is the slow-burning fuse of emotion that remains smoldering right below the surface, while **wrath** (Gk *thumon*, "passion, rage") is the explosive burst of emotion that rises and falls quickly, but with much intensity.

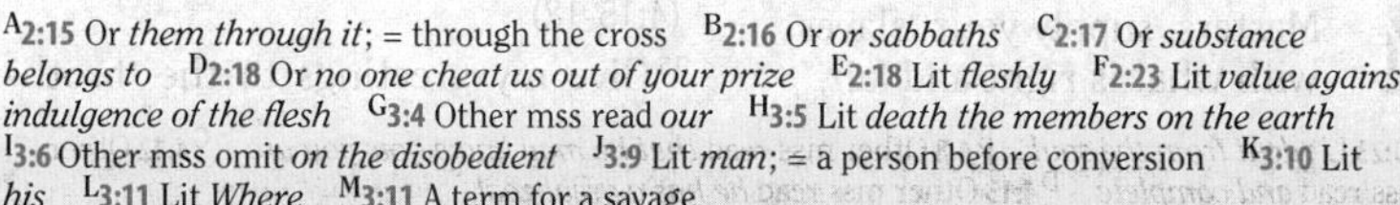
A2:15 Or *them through it*; = through the cross B2:16 Or *or sabbaths* C2:17 Or *substance belongs to* D2:18 Or *no one cheat us out of your prize* E2:18 Lit *fleshly* F2:23 Lit *value against indulgence of the flesh* G3:4 Other mss read *our* H3:5 Lit *death the members on the earth* I3:6 Other mss omit *on the disobedient* J3:9 Lit *man*; = a person before conversion K3:10 Lit *his* L3:11 Lit *Where* M3:11 A term for a savage

3:18–4:1 As Paul turns his attention to how Christian behavior is manifested in the home, see also the similar passage in Eph 5:22–6:9.

3:18 Wives are called to **be submissive** to their **husbands** (see **Biblical Womanhood**, p. 1519). Submission is not a demeaning posture for a wife to take, for Jesus is the perfect model of biblical submission. Though equal with the Father, He willingly submits to the authority of the One with whom He is equal (1Co 11:3; 15:28; Php 2:5-11). The Bible clearly teaches that a wife is equal to her husband (Gn 1:27; 1Pt 3:7). Yet, in her equality, she is to place herself voluntarily under her husband's authority. Paul says that this submission is **fitting in the Lord**. All institutions have clear lines of authority; submission as a part of God's design for the home is no different.

3:19 Husbands are not given the right to treat their wives as a vassal. Instead, each husband is to honor his wife with sacrificial **love**. This love is selfless, meeting the needs of others regardless of the personal cost. Husbands are never to use their authority in the home as an excuse to be harsh, domineering, or cruel.

3:20 Children are to **obey . . . parents in everything, for this pleases the Lord**. Jesus told His disciples that, if they loved Him, they should obey His commandments (Jn 14:15). In the same way, children must show their love for their parents by obeying them.

3:21 The authority of parents, specifically **fathers**, over their children, again is not a license for harshness. Paul encourages fathers not to **exasperate** their children. The word translated "exasperate" (Gk *erethizete*) reflects a form of bitterness caused by harassment or provocation, and the word translated **discouraged** (Gk *athumōsin*) refers to losing heart or becoming discouraged, having a broken spirit. As parents train up their children, they should seek to harness, not break, the spirits of their children. Also, fathers are warned to discipline their children with the ultimate goal of saving them from the wrath of God by leading them into a proper relationship with Christ.

3:22–4:1 This section addressing **slaves** and **masters** is quite long, compared to the section on the family, likely because of the situation in Colossae, in which the runaway slave Onesimus was returning to his master Philemon with a letter from Paul. Slavery was common in the Roman provinces of Paul's day, even in Christian homes. The church at

HARD QUESTION

Does submission lead to abuse?

Submission is meant to be a good and beautiful thing in a Christian marriage (even if it is not always easy to do!). It is important, however, for women to understand the distinction between biblical submission to a servant leader and coercion from an oppressive tyrant. Biblical submission is a voluntary choice. Submission is the willing and loving acceptance of a husband's authority and leadership in marriage. Yet, it is not the passive acceptance of physical, mental, or verbal abuse. Such behavior is oppressive, dangerous, and contemptible to God. If you or someone you know is suffering from abuse, seek help from a trusted and godly confidant, whether a pastor, counselor, or close friend. God's desire is for wives to have healthy and happy marriages. With intervention, repentance, and the grace of God, that can become a reality.

Examining Household Relationships (3:18–4:1)

18 Wives, be submissive to
your husbands, as is fitting in
the Lord.
19 Husbands, love your wives
and don't be bitter toward
them.
20 Children, obey your parents
in everything, for this pleases
the Lord.
21 Fathers, do not exasperate
your children, so they won't
become discouraged.
22 Slaves, obey your human
masters in everything.
Don't work only while
being watched, in order
to please men, but work
wholeheartedly, fearing the
Lord.
23 Whatever you do, do
it enthusiastically,[A] as
something done for the Lord
and not for men, 24 knowing
that you will receive the
reward of an inheritance from
the Lord. You serve the Lord
Christ. 25 For the wrongdoer
will be paid back for whatever
wrong he has done, and there
is no favoritism.

4 Masters, supply your •slaves
with what is right and fair,
since you know that you too
have a Master in heaven.

Praying and Witnessing (4:2-6)

2 Devote yourselves to prayer; stay
alert in it with thanksgiving. 3 At the
same time, pray also for us that God
may open a door to us for the message, to speak the •mystery of the
•Messiah, for which I am in prison,
4 so that I may reveal it as I am required to speak. 5 Act wisely toward
outsiders, making the most of the
time. 6 Your speech should always be
gracious, seasoned with salt, so that
you may know how you should answer each person.

Personal Notes from Paul (4:7-18)

The Bearers of the Letter (4:7-9)

7 Tychicus, our dearly loved brother, faithful servant, and fellow slave
in the Lord, will tell you all the news
about me. 8 I have sent him to you
for this very purpose, so that you
may know how we are[B] and so that
he may encourage your hearts. 9 He
is with Onesimus, a faithful and
dearly loved brother, who is one of
you. They will tell you about everything here.

Greetings from Paul's Companions (4:10-14)

10 Aristarchus, my fellow prisoner,
greets you, as does Mark, Barnabas's
cousin (concerning whom you have
received instructions: if he comes to
you, welcome him), 11 and so does
Jesus who is called Justus. These
alone of the circumcision are my
coworkers for the kingdom of God,
and they have been a comfort to
me. 12 Epaphras, who is one of you,
a slave of Christ Jesus, greets you.
He is always contending for you in
his prayers, so that you can stand
mature and fully assured[C] in everything God wills. 13 For I testify about
him that he works hard[D] for you, for
those in Laodicea, and for those in
Hierapolis. 14 Luke, the dearly loved
physician, and Demas greet you.

Concluding Messages and Final Blessing (4:15-18)

15 Give my greetings to the •broth-

[A] **3:23** Lit *do it from the soul* [B] **4:8** Other mss read *that he may know how you are* [C] **4:12** Other mss read *and complete* [D] **4:13** Other mss read *he has a great zeal*

ers in Laodicea, and to Nympha and
the church in her home. [16]When
this letter has been read among you,
have it read also in the church of the
Laodiceans; and see that you also
read the letter from Laodicea. [17]And
tell Archippus, "Pay attention to the
ministry you have received in the
Lord, so that you can accomplish it."
[18]This greeting is in my own
hand—Paul. Remember my imprisonment. Grace be with you.[A]

[A]**4:18** Other mss add *Amen*.

Colossae would have consisted of both slave owners and slaves. Though the spread of Christianity would eventually dismantle the Roman slave system, Paul gives instructions here for how to function as Christians within this deeply entrenched economic and social structure. For the purpose of application, the present-day relationship of employee to employer is the closest comparison to this concept of slave to master.

4:15 The case of **Nympha and the church in her home** is a reminder that, for 200 years, the early church met in homes, not "church buildings."

4:16 Apparently, a letter, which would be valuable to the Colossians as well, was sent to the **church of the Laodiceans**, but no copy of this letter exists today.

COLOSSIANS ... WRITTEN ON MY Heart **The understanding of salvation as an unearned and free gift of God is a hallmark of true biblical faith. The only way for a Christian to avoid being led astray by false teaching is by knowing the Word of God and understanding the doctrines of the faith.**

BIBLICAL WOMANHOOD Sisters in Christ

The friendships among Christian women often prove to be lifelines of truth, hope, and encouragement. As redeemed daughters of the King (1Jn 3:1-3), they are eternally "sisters in Christ." As you consider the following notes on specific men whom Paul regarded as "brothers" (Col 1:1-2; 4:7,9,15), thank the Lord for the women who have blessed your life in similar ways and pray for opportunities to be the kind of friend your "sisters" would likewise esteem. Determine to pray like Epaphras for friends who are maturing in their faith and vulnerable to a divided heart like Demas (cp. Lk 16:13).

- **Timothy** (1:1)—see Ac 16:1-3; 1Co 4:17; 1 and 2 Timothy.
- Of the Gentiles who stayed with Paul during his imprisonment, **Epaphras** (1:7) was the prayer warrior contending for his fellow believers and working hard on their behalf (4:12-13).
- **Tychicus** (4:7-8) was a trusted colleague of Paul. Originally from Asia Minor (Ac 20:4), Tychicus probably served as the carrier of the letter to the Colossians as well as the letter to the Ephesians.
- **Onesimus** (4:9) was Philemon's fugitive slave returning to Colossae (see the letter to Philemon). Apparently, he somehow encountered Paul and became a Christian under his ministry, then served him faithfully while Paul was in prison. In his letter to Philemon, Paul pleaded with Onesimus's master for his forgiveness and acceptance back into the household.
- **Aristarchus** (4:10-11) was with Paul during the Ephesian riot (Ac 19:29) and during his shipwreck (Ac 27:2; Phm 24).
- **Mark** (4:10-11) abandoned Paul on his first missionary journey but was restored to the ministry with the help of Barnabas (cp. Ac 12:25; 15:36-39; 2Tm 4:11; Phm 24).
- **Justus** was another of Paul's "coworkers for the kingdom of God" (Col 4:11). Evidently, Aristarchus, Mark, and Justus were the only Jewish believers ("of the circumcision") who were with Paul in prison. They had been "a comfort" to Paul.
- **Luke** (4:14) was a constant companion of Paul's (see Ac 16:8-10 and the rest of the book; 2Tm 4:11).
- Although **Demas** (Col 4:14; Phm 24) was at Paul's side as he wrote Colossians, he would later defect from the ministry because of his love for the world (2Tm 4:10).
- **Archippus** (Col 4:17; Phm 2,24) may have served as the pastor of the church that met in Philemon's home. In Philemon 2, Paul calls him a "fellow soldier," suggesting that his ministry was similar to Paul's.

1 Thessalonians

Timeline World Events Biblical Events	***168–103 BC*** First Jewish community in Thessalonica, émigrés from Alexandria	***146 BC*** Thessalonica, the capital of the Roman province of Macedonia, and "the Mother of Macedonia"	***42 BC*** Thessalonica declared a free city under Augustus	***AD 15*** Loss of Thessalonica's free city status during the reign of Tiberius

"This is God's will, your sanctification" (4:3a).

Who wrote 1 Thessalonians?

The Apostle Paul was the principal author. However, Timothy and Silvanus (Silas) also contributed.

Who were the recipients?

The letter was written to the church at Thessalonica, to the brothers and sisters who had come to faith in Jesus Christ as a result of Paul's brief ministry there during his second missionary journey (Ac 17:1-9).

When was 1 Thessalonians written?

First Thessalonians was written shortly after Timothy joined Paul at Corinth (3:6), bringing encouraging news about the Thessalonians' growth in Christ and their affection for Paul. He responded to Timothy's report with this letter at some point within his 18-month ministry in Corinth (A.D. 51-52; Ac 18:11).

Where did it happen?

Thessalonica, the destination of Paul's letter, was the self-governing capital of Macedonia and seat of Roman power, situated at the intersection of river trade routes and located on the *Via Egnatia,* an important Roman highway.

What is 1 Thessalonians about?

- *Persecution.* Paul wrote to encourage the church to press on in the midst of persecution.
- *Christ's return*. The return of Christ is mentioned in every chapter of this book and offers hope for Christians facing tough circumstances.
- *Christian living*. Paul responded to specific questions that may have arrived via a letter carried by Timothy. Paul recognized that the Thessalonians' lifestyle mistakes were linked to their misunderstanding of doctrinal issues. He did not simply tell them to live differently but corrected the thinking that led to those choices. The connection between *orthodoxy* ("right thinking") and *orthopraxy* ("right practice") was vital in Paul's thinking.

Why should women read 1 Thessalonians?

Women will face a variety of difficulties throughout a lifetime, but God teaches in 1 Thessalonians that a Christian's response to difficulties is diametrically opposed to the way the lost world responds. Learning how to live like Christ in a culture that is so foreign to Christian ideals is a process in which a woman allows God to mold her into His image and chip away those things that are not godly.

How do you read 1 Thessalonians?

This tender-hearted pastoral epistle follows the basic structure of other letters written during the Greco-Roman period—introduction, body, and conclusion—but in a distinctively Christian manner. The letter opens with the typical identification of the authors and recipients and Paul's unique greeting, "Grace to you and peace" (1:1); but the introductory section consists of a prayer of thanksgiving (1:2-5), and the concluding section (5:23-24) contains a benediction before the closing greetings (5:25-28).

Outline

I. Delivering a Personal Testimony (1:1–3:13)
   A. Thanksgiving for the Thessalonian Believers (1:1-10)
   B. Paul's Ministry in Thessalonica (2:1-16)
   C. Timothy's Ministry (2:17–3:13)
II. The Call to Sanctification (4:1-8)
III. Responding to Questions (4:9–5:11)
   A. On Brotherly Love (4:9-10)
   B. On Earning One's Living (4:11-12)
   C. On Those Who Die Before the Day of the Lord (4:13-18)
   D. On the Day of the Lord (5:1-11)
IV. Offering a Challenge to Christian Duty (5:12-22)
   A. Leadership in the Community (5:12-13)
   B. Fellowship in the Community (5:14-15)
   C. Submission to Christ (5:16-22)
V. Concluding Prayer, Greetings, and Blessing (5:23-28)

>WORD|*study*

1:1 The city of the Thessalonians, previously a town called Therme (Gk "hot"), was named after Thessalonike (Gk "victory in Thessaly"), the half-sister of Alexander the Great in 315 B.C. Located on the eastern coast of Macedonia, the city boasted a deep harbor and protection from dangerous winds. The climate was ideal for crops, rain was abundant, forests provided timber for construction, and the rivers provided fish. Consequently, Thessalonica was not only the largest but also a very strategic city from which to advance the gospel throughout the Roman Empire. The city's religious climate was diverse and included Judaism, the imperial cult, Greek gods Cabirus and Dionysus, and Egyptian gods. The resident Jews had established a synagogue there.

AD 36	AD 47–49	AD 49	AD 50	AD 51
Paul's conversion on the Damascus Road	Paul's first missionary journey	Beginning of Paul's second missionary journey	Paul's ministry in Thessalonica	Paul's first letter to the Thessalonians

Delivering a Personal Testimony (1:1–3:13)

Thanksgiving for the Thessalonian Believers (1:1-10)

1 Paul, Silvanus,[A] and Timothy:
To the church of the Thessalonians in God the Father and the
Lord Jesus Christ.
Grace to you and peace.[B]
2 We always thank God for all of
you, remembering you constantly
in our prayers. 3 We recall, in the
presence of our God and Father,
your work of faith, labor of love,
and endurance of hope in our Lord
Jesus Christ, 4 knowing your election, •brothers loved by God. 5 For
our gospel did not come to you in
word only, but also in power, in the
Holy Spirit, and with much assurance. You know what kind of men
we were among you for your benefit,
6 and you became imitators of us and
of the Lord when, in spite of severe
persecution, you welcomed the message with joy from the Holy Spirit.
7 As a result, you became an example
to all the believers in Macedonia
and Achaia. 8 For the Lord's message rang out from you, not only in
Macedonia and Achaia, but in every
place that your faith[C] in God has
gone out. Therefore, we don't need

ELECTION

Election (Gk *eklogē n*, "selection, choosing," 1:4) is a reminder that salvation from start to finish is the work of God; it is not based on a person's own virtue, merit, or work. Clearly it is inextricably linked to the gospel of Christ, the proclamation of the message of salvation, and the work of the Holy Spirit. The doctrine of election has been debated and misunderstood in the history of Christian thought. Election *does not mean* a person is not required to repent to come to faith in Christ. However, all those who do repent and come to faith have been elected. Election *does not mean* that Christians do not need to share the gospel. It is through the sharing of the gospel that people see their sin and need for repentance. The response to the concept of election should be gratitude to God and should encourage believers during difficult times. Just as the Thessalonian church was encouraged while facing trials, all believers should be comforted and strengthened in their trials by the knowledge that God has chosen them. Wherever a person happens to be in her understanding of election, several practical applications may serve as a reminder that you must keep the big picture in mind when you are investigating even the smallest detail in the Bible:

- Election should bring joy—God has chosen you to be an heir of salvation!
- Election should be an encouragement for evangelism and prayer and sound teaching. The same God who *chose* you also *commanded* you to go share the good news and make disciples.
- Election should encourage holiness. Elect people are to "be holy and blameless in His sight" (Eph 1:4-6; Col 3:12). The assurance of your salvation should never hinder you from allowing God to continue His work of sanctification in your life.

[A] **1:1** Or *Silas*; Ac 15:22-32; 16:19-40; 17:1-16 [B] **1:1** Other mss add *from God our Father and the Lord Jesus Christ* [C] **1:8** Or *in every place news of your faith*

>WORD|*study*

1:6 Paul consistently uses the word imitators (Gk *mimētai*, "mark, image, form, pattern") to encourage believers to follow his example or imitate his way of life (2:14; 1Co 4:16; 11:1; Eph 5:1; 2Th 3:7,9; Heb 6:12). The English word "mime" designates an actor who presents a character or concept only with movements and facial expressions that mimic, imitate, or copy those of his subject. The image of the traditional white-painted face, white-gloved mime illustrates the point Paul makes (1Th 1:5-6). A mime performs without words, and a convincing performance focuses the audience's attention on the story or message being presented. Paul emphasized the integrity of the gospel by clarifying that the good news had come to the Thessalonians not only in words but also in the Holy Spirit's power to transform lives. Paul could praise the Thessalonians for becoming "imitators" of the apostles and of the Lord because in doing so they recognized that the Holy Spirit changes the way a person acts. Authentic Christians do not present the gospel with words *alone* but also by *imitating* Christ in their lives; Christian living means acting like Jesus.

Title In the Greek New Testament the title is *pros Thessalonikeis A*, "to the Thessalonians, A." More loosely, the title might be rendered "the first letter to the Thessalonians."

1:1 Silvanus (Latin form of Silas), likely a Roman citizen (Ac 16:29), accompanied **Paul** on his second missionary journey and was one of the "leading men among the brothers" at the church in Jerusalem (Ac 15:22). Paul probably met **Timothy**, Lois, and Eunice on the first missionary journey. They may have come to faith in Christ at that time. By the time of Paul's second journey, Timothy was highly regarded in Iconium and Lystra (see note on 1Tm 1:2; cp. Ac 16:1-3). Paul chose him to be one of his companions, and Timothy accompanied the apostle on his second and third missionary journeys until Paul appointed him to stay at the church in Ephesus (1 Tm 1:3).

1:3 The memory of Christian virtues—**faith**, **hope**, and **love**—among the Thessalonians prompted Paul to prayers of thanksgiving. The believers were known by labor, which was self-sacrificing for the sake of others. They were also able to remain steadfast in the face of suffering because of their hope in the coming of the **Lord Jesus Christ**.

1:4 Paul refers to the believers as **brothers** [Gk *adelphoi*, "associates, members of the Christian community"] **loved by God**, not to exclude women but to highlight the nature of the relationship shared by believers who have been born into the family of God (Jn 1:12-13; 3:5). "Brothers" in its most basic understanding referred to near kinsmen or those "from the same womb." Paul repeatedly calls Christians "brothers"—an identity used in the early church. Believers may have been alienated from society, but they formed a new spiritual identity as children of one Father.

1:5 The message was recognized as divine because of the **power** (Gk *dunamei*, "able, mighty") of **the Holy Spirit**—the preaching of the gospel and the work of the Holy Spirit went hand in hand. The Spirit is the one who convinced the Thessalonians of the truth of the message.

1:9 For the Thessalonians to convert from idolatry meant abandoning a cult and turning from its immoral practices. The word **turned** (Gk *epestrepsate*; cp. Ac 9:35; 11:21; 14:15; 26:18,20) implies a change in attitude and action, which is necessary for true repentance.

1:10 The Thessalonians had hope in the promise that the Son would return. Their hope was manifested in their moral life and steadfastness in face of persecution. God's Son was the object of their expectation. Jesus was described in three ways:

- God's Son comes **from heaven**. Jesus' sovereignty is affirmed because He comes from the place where God is.
- He is the one **whom He** [God] **raised from the dead**—the core of Paul's message.
- He **rescues us from the coming wrath** (i.e., judgment awaiting those who violate God's law). The Thessalonian believers were assured of their liberation from this wrath.

2:2-6 God had **emboldened** them **to speak** the truth in the midst of **great opposition**. Their preaching in the midst of opposition demonstrated their pure motives. Paul's defense suggests that he and his companions had been accused of impure motives and a desire for status, fame, or financial gain.

2:7 Paul used a **nursing mother** (Gk *trophos*, "nurse") as a vivid simile to convey his tender affection for the believers. Paul fed the baby believers with the gospel, teaching them spiritual survival just as a mother **nurtures** her children, demonstrating caring activity as well as a loving attitude.

2:11 Paul employs the image of a godly father's encouragement and exhortation of **his own children** to illustrate his own commitment to teach and encourage those new to the faith. The apostle's fatherly concern drove him to insist that the Thessalonians respond with a certain course of action.

2:13-16 Paul thanked God for the Thessalonians' reception of the gospel because they had the spiritual insight to recognize it as the word of God with the power to transform believers. As a result of accepting the message, they imitated the steadfast faith and courage of Judean believers who suffered at the hands of **Jews**. Paul's strong language against the Jews because they **persecuted** (Gk *ekdiōxantōn*, "drove out, banished") believers (see Ac 17:5-9) must be read

to say anything, [9] for they themselves report[A] what kind of reception we had from you: how you turned to God from idols to serve the living and true God [10] and to wait for His Son from heaven, whom He raised from the dead—Jesus, who rescues us from the coming wrath.

Paul's Ministry in Thessalonica (2:1-16)

2 For you yourselves know, •brothers, that our visit with you was not without result. [2] On the contrary, after we had previously suffered, and we were treated outrageously in Philippi, as you know, we were emboldened by our God to speak the gospel of God to you in spite of great opposition. [3] For our exhortation didn't come from error or impurity or an intent to deceive. [4] Instead, just as we have been approved by God to be entrusted with the gospel, so we speak, not to please men, but rather God, who examines our hearts. [5] For we never used flattering speech, as you know, or had greedy motives—God is our witness— [6] and we didn't seek glory from people, either from you or from others. [7] Although we could have been a burden as Christ's apostles, instead we were gentle[B] among you, as a nursing mother nurtures her own children. [8] We cared so much for you that we were pleased to share with you not only the gospel of God but also our own lives, because you had become dear to us. [9] For you remember our labor and hardship, brothers. Working night and day so that we would not burden any of you, we preached God's gospel to you. [10] You are witnesses, and so is God, of how devoutly, righteously, and blamelessly we conducted ourselves with you believers. [11] As you know, like a father with his own children, [12] we encouraged, comforted, and implored each one of you to •walk worthy of God, who calls you into His own kingdom and glory.

[13] This is why we constantly thank God, because when you received the message about God that you heard from us, you welcomed it not as a human message, but as it truly is, the message of God, which also works effectively in you believers. [14] For you, brothers, became imitators of God's churches in Christ Jesus that are in Judea, since you have also suffered the same things from people of your own country, just as they did from the Jews [15] who killed both the Lord Jesus and the prophets and persecuted us; they displease God and are hostile to everyone, [16] hindering us from speaking to the Gentiles so that they may be saved. As a result, they are always completing the number of their sins, and wrath has overtaken them at last.[C]

Timothy's Ministry (2:17–3:13)

[17] But as for us, brothers, after we were forced to leave you for a short time (in person, not in heart), we greatly desired and made every effort to return and see you face to face. [18] So we wanted to come to you—even I, Paul, time and again—but Satan hindered us. [19] For who is our hope or joy or crown of boasting in the presence of our Lord Jesus at His coming? Is it not you? [20] For you are our glory and joy!

3 Therefore, when we could no longer stand it, we thought it was better to be left alone in Athens. [2] And we sent Timothy, our brother and God's coworker[D] in the gospel of Christ, to strengthen and encourage you concerning your faith, [3] so that no one will be shaken by these persecutions. For you yourselves know that we are appointed to[E] this. [4] In fact, when we were with you, we told you previously that we were going to

[A] **1:9** Lit *report about us* [B] **2:7** Other mss read *infants* [C] **2:16** Or *to the end* [D] **3:2** Other mss read *servant* [E] **3:3** Or *are destined for*

>WORD|*study*

2:2 Opposition (Gk *agōni*, "contest, struggle," anglicized as "agony") may refer to outward conflict or inner turmoil or anxiety. The word was used of athletes competing in the Olympic Games to describe their strenuous training or the intense effort required to defeat an opponent in a contest. The term was also used metaphorically of a person's struggle against temptation. Here, Paul speaks of tangible persecution intended to obstruct the progress of the gospel.

HARD QUESTION

Does prayer matter?

Paul's commitment to pray for the Thessalonians is a challenge to believers to participate in the sanctification of others (3:13). You can love other believers by praying for their holiness as you watch and wait for the Lord to return. Indeed, your holiness and that of other believers should be a continual concern. If so, you will be moved to pray, teach, and encourage one another toward holiness so that God may be glorified and His people fit for kingdom service.

suffer persecution, and as you know,
it happened. [5]For this reason, when
I could no longer stand it, I also sent
him to find out about your faith,
fearing that the tempter had tempted you and that our labor might be
for nothing.
[6]But now Timothy has come to
us from you and brought us good
news about your faith and love and
reported that you always have good
memories of us, wanting to see us,
as we also want to see you. [7]There-
fore, •brothers, in all our distress
and persecution, we were encouraged about you through your faith.
[8]For now we live, if you stand firm
in the Lord. [9]How can we thank God
for you in return for all the joy we
experience before our God because
of you, [10]as we pray very earnestly
night and day to see you face to face
and to complete what is lacking in
your faith?
[11]Now may our God and Father
Himself, and our Lord Jesus, direct
our way to you. [12]And may the Lord
cause you to increase and overflow
with love for one another and for
everyone, just as we also do for you.
[13]May He make your hearts blameless in holiness before our God and
Father at the coming of our Lord
Jesus with all His •saints. •Amen.[A]

The Call to Sanctification (4:1-8)

4 Finally then, •brothers, we ask
and encourage you in the Lord
Jesus, that as you have received
from us how you must •walk and
please God—as you are doing[B]—do
so even more. [2]For you know what
commands we gave you through the
Lord Jesus.
[3]For this is God's will, your •sanc-
tification: that you abstain from sexual immorality, [4]so that each of you
knows how to control his own body[C]
in sanctification and honor, [5]not

[A]3:13 Other mss omit *Amen.* [B]4:1 Lit *walking* [C]4:4 Or *to acquire his own wife*; lit *to possess his own vessel*

in light of the totality of his teaching. Paul was personally familiar with this persecution because he had previously participated in it before becoming a Christian. In Romans he demonstrates his love for his people and desire for their salvation. He also uses strong language in Romans against the Gentiles' conduct. This rebuke was in response to the persecution he and his flock received at the hands of the Jews and does not indicate anti-Semitic sentiments; rather, he is confirming that God will judge all, Jews and Gentiles alike.

4:1 As was Paul's practice, after laying a theological foundation in the first half of his letter, in the second half he turns to instruction for Christian living. The word **finally** serves as a transition marking Paul's movement to exhortation. By calling the Thessalonians **brothers** (Gk *adelphoi*), Paul reinforced the familial relationship he had shared with them.

4:3-4 Paul begins the section on practical instruction with an exhortation for **sanctification** (Gk *hagiasmos*, "consecration, holiness") or the daily process of becoming more Christlike, especially in the area of sexual matters, perhaps indicating a predominance of this type of sinful behavior in contemporary Greek society. The Christian call to **abstain from sexual immorality** (Gk *porneias*, "fornication") was radical in a culture in which marriage was not enough to prohibit men from pursuing sexual satisfaction wherever they could find it. "Sexual immorality" could refer to a broad spectrum of sexual

BIBLICAL WOMANHOOD Holiness in Sexuality

Paul made the connection between ignorance or rejection of God and succumbing to sexual immorality (4:5). The implication is that those who have identified with Christ should demonstrate their new identity through having control over their bodies, setting them apart from the ungodly who act on their sexual desires without constraint. Knowing God should result in self-control and a desire to do God's will with regard to sexuality. Paul suggests three ways in which to honor God in the area of sexuality:

- ***Abstain from sexual immorality*** (4:3). The Greek word for sexual immorality (*porneias*) includes not just sexual acts but also suggests impurity in thought, words, and actions. Abstaining from sexual immorality will have implications in what you allow yourself to think and talk about and watch and read. Believers should not think that they are being pure in this matter because they are not engaging in sexual acts.
- *Exercise **control** over your own body* (4:4). You cannot control the actions of those around you, but you can control yourself. One way to "exercise control" over your body is in the area of modesty. First Timothy 2:9-10 encourages women to dress modestly because it is fitting for one who professes to be a worshiper of God. Can a person tell even by the style of your clothing that you are different, that you are a follower of God?
- *Do not take advantage of fellow believers in the area of sexual matters* (4:6). Christians especially need to be above reproach in how they deal with members of the opposite sex. Does the way you interact with others encourage holiness, or do you tempt people to be sexually immoral in their thoughts, words, or actions?

with lustful desires, like the Gentiles who don't know God. 6 This means one must not transgress against and defraud his brother in this matter, because the Lord is an avenger of all these offenses,[A] as we also previously told and warned you. 7 For God has not called us to impurity but to sanctification. 8 Therefore, the person who rejects this does not reject man, but God, who also gives you His Holy Spirit.

Responding to Questions (4:9–5:11)

On Brotherly Love (4:9-10)

9 About brotherly love: You don't need me to write you because you yourselves are taught by God to love one another. 10 In fact, you are doing this toward all the brothers in the entire region of Macedonia. But we encourage you, brothers, to do so even more,

On Earning One's Living (4:11-12)

11 to seek to lead a quiet life, to mind your own business,[B] and to work with your own hands, as we commanded you, 12 so that you may walk properly[C] in the presence of outsiders[D] and not be dependent on anyone.[E]

On Those Who Die Before the Day of the Lord (4:13-18)

13 We do not want you to be uninformed, brothers, concerning those who are •asleep, so that you will not grieve like the rest, who have no hope. 14 Since we believe that Jesus died and rose again, in the same way God will bring with Him those who have fallen asleep through[F] Jesus. 15 For we say this to you by a revelation from the Lord:[G] We who are still alive at the Lord's coming will certainly have no advantage over[H] those who have fallen asleep. 16 For the Lord Himself will descend from heaven with a shout,[I] with the archangel's voice, and with the trumpet of God, and the dead in Christ will rise first. 17 Then we who are still alive will be caught up together with them in the clouds to meet the Lord in the air and so we will always be with the Lord. 18 Therefore encourage[J] one another with these words.

On the Day of the Lord (5:1-11)

5 About the times and the seasons: •Brothers, you do not need anything to be written to you. 2 For you yourselves know very well that the Day of the Lord will come just like a thief in the night. 3 When they say, "Peace and security," then sudden destruction comes on them, like labor pains come on a pregnant woman, and they will not escape. 4 But you, brothers, are not in the dark, for this day to overtake you like a thief. 5 For you are all sons of light and sons of the day. We do not belong to the night or the darkness. 6 So then, we must not sleep, like the rest, but we must stay awake and be serious. 7 For those who sleep, sleep at night, and those who get drunk are drunk at night. 8 But since we belong to the day, we must be serious and put the armor of faith and love on our chests, and put on a helmet of the hope of salvation. 9 For God did not appoint us to wrath, but to obtain salvation through our Lord Jesus Christ, 10 who died for us, so that whether we are awake or •asleep, we will live together with Him. 11 Therefore encourage one another and build each other up as you are already doing.

Offering a Challenge to Christian Duty (5:12-22)

Leadership in the Community (5:12-13)

12 Now we ask you, brothers, to give recognition to those who labor among you and lead you in the Lord and admonish you, 13 and to regard them very highly in love because of their work. Be at peace among yourselves.

Fellowship in the Community (5:14-15)

14 And we exhort you, brothers: warn those who are irresponsible,[K] comfort the discouraged, help the weak, be patient with everyone. 15 See to it that no one repays evil for evil to

[A] **4:6** Lit *things* [B] **4:11** Lit *to practice one's own things* [C] **4:12** Or *may live respectably* [D] **4:12** Non-Christians [E] **4:12** Or *not need anything*, or *not be in need* [F] **4:14** Or *in* [G] **4:15** Or *a word of the Lord* [H] **4:15** Or *certainly not precede* [I] **4:16** Or *command* [J] **4:18** Or *comfort* [K] **5:14** Or *who are disorderly*, or *who are undisciplined*

sin (premarital sex, extramarital sex, homosexuality, lesbianism, sodomy, incest, and bestiality).

4:13-15 Those who are asleep (Gk *koimōmenōn*, "fall asleep, die") are believers who have died. The believer goes immediately into the presence of the Lord at death (2Co 5:8). Jesus, even in the agony of His own crucifixion, had affirmed this promise to the thief on the cross (Lk 23:39-43). Perhaps members of the church had died since Paul had been with them, and the grief of those remaining left them with questions about Christ's return. The promise of Christ's coming was their hope in the midst of sadness over losing loved ones.

4:16-17 Paul teaches that Jesus Himself will return in majesty, **with the trumpet** pronouncing a divine command to rise. The **shout** (Gk *keleusmati*, "word of command, signal, summons," in the sense of a military order) and **trumpet** were evidence of triumph. The dead in Christ will have the prominence of rising first. Paul offers more reassurance as he informs believers that they will all, dead and alive, be **caught up together . . . to meet the Lord**. This idiom was used to welcome an important person upon his arrival. The leading citizens from a Hellenistic city like Thessalonica would go out to meet a visiting dignitary when he arrived and accompany him to the city.

5:1-5 Perhaps the Thessalonians' experience of persecution made urgent their need to be reassured that **the Day of the Lord** (Christ's return) would indeed come. Paul uses the imagery of **a thief** [Gk *kleptēs*, "one who comes unexpectedly"] **in the night** to teach the unexpected nature of Christ's return. However unexpected, believers should be ready. In contrast, unbelievers assume all is safe, and then "the Day of the Lord" will come unexpectedly, suddenly, and inevitably, as the process of giving birth cannot be stopped when the time comes.

5:6-10 Sleep (Gk *katheudōmen)* here is not a reference to death as in 4:13 but describes spiritual apathy characteristic of unbelievers. Believers, however, must be marked by watchfulness and circumspection in light of the Lord's imminent return.

The text seems to affirm that believers are excluded from the tribulation (i.e., the "Day of the Lord" or the "wrath" to come).

5:11 Paul ends this teaching on the Day of the Lord by reminding the Thessalonians to strengthen **one another** by their words and **build** one another up in faith. While Paul

>WORD|study

4:5 Lustful desires (Gk *pathei epithumias*, lit "hot-after passion") is a strong expression of unrestrained desires. Strength of will in controlling desires within the realm of sexuality is the fruit of knowing God.

5:14 Irresponsible (Gk *ataktous*, "lazy, disorderly, unruly, insubordinate, undisciplined") often designated a soldier who was "out of the ranks, out of order, or truant" (i.e., one who neglects his duties).

anyone, but always pursue what is good for one another and for all.

Submission to Christ (5:16-22)

16 Rejoice always!
17 Pray constantly.
18 Give thanks in everything,
for this is God's will for you
in Christ Jesus.
19 Don't stifle the Spirit.
20 Don't despise prophecies,
21 but test all things.
Hold on to what is good.
22 Stay away from every kind
of evil.

Concluding Prayer, Greetings, and Blessing (5:23-28)

23 Now may the God of peace Himself •sanctify you completely. And
may your spirit, soul, and body be
kept sound and blameless for the
coming of our Lord Jesus Christ.
24 He who calls you is faithful, who
also will do it. 25 Brothers, pray for
us also. 26 Greet all the brothers
with a holy kiss. 27 I charge you by
the Lord that this letter be read to
all the brothers. 28 The grace of our
Lord Jesus Christ be with you.

1 THESSALONIANS … WRITTEN ON MY Heart While you cannot control your circumstances, you can control your own attitude and actions. God's will and desire is that you would continue to become more like Him in your thoughts, words, and deeds—that you would be holy. In doing so, unbelievers, even those who persecute you, may come to know Him.

obviously felt some responsibility to strengthen these believers, he was instructing not just the leaders but also all the members of the church to take up this call. This injunction is to mutual edification, which he recognized they were **doing** and called them to continue.

5:12-13 Paul instructs believers **to give recognition** to their leaders **because of their work**—not because of their position, status, or personality—and to demonstrate it by love.

5:23-25 Paul concludes this letter in his usual style. He prays for the recipients of his letter that they will be sanctified thoroughly. Specifically, he prays that their whole person will be **blameless** and have integrity in all aspects of their being until the Lord returns.

5:26 The **holy kiss**, probably on the cheek, was the common, affectionate greeting of believers as they gathered for worship. It is still a custom practiced in some cultures today, especially in the Middle East.

5:27 Paul charged the Thessalonians to **read** this letter aloud. A public reading would contribute to their sense of community as they shared in Paul's commendation and exhortations. They would be left with a common commitment to sanctification, accountability, and joy.

2 Thessalonians

Timeline	168–103 BC	5 BC	5 BC	AD 15–20
➡ World Events ➡ Biblical Events	First Jewish community in Thessalonica	Jesus' birth in Bethlehem	Paul's birth in Tarsus of Cilicia	Paul's studies with Gamaliel in Jerusalem

"Don't let anyone deceive you in any way" (2:3a).

Who wrote 2 Thessalonians?

The Apostle Paul was the primary author; however, Timothy and Silvanus (Silas) were also included in the greeting (1:1).

Who were the recipients?

The letter was written to the fellowship of believers at Thessalonica.

When was 2 Thessalonians written?

Paul wrote his second letter to the Thessalonians shortly after his first letter (A.D. 51–52), and most likely from Corinth where he stayed for 18 months during his second missionary journey (Ac 18:11).

Where did it happen?

During his second missionary journey, while in Corinth. Paul wrote this letter to the believers in Thessalonica, the self-governing capital of Macedonia and seat of Roman power, located at the *Via Egnatia* at the intersection of river trade routes.

What is 2 Thessalonians about?

- *Persecution.* Paul addresses persecution and the perseverance that would be necessary to stand firm during persecution. He assured them with the promise of his prayers and the destiny of both the persecutors and the Christians.
- *End times.* Paul dealt specifically with the advent of the Day of the Lord and the man of lawlessness. The Thessalonians, by some means, were deceived into believing that the day had already come.

Why should women read 2 Thessalonians?

Second Thessalonians teaches two important truths about the Christian life—it will not be easy, and it is important to know what you believe. As women dig into this small book, they will get encouragement to stand firm in the truth even in their most difficult days. In addition, they will be reminded to know the truth of God's Word. Far too many believers do not have a firm grasp of their faith, and, as a result, they stumble when someone comes along with a false teaching. Make sure you know the Bible well enough so that you will be able to discern truth from error.

How do you read 2 Thessalonians?

Typical of correspondence in the Greco-Roman period, the letter expands on themes that Paul had addressed in 1 Thessalonians. Paul aimed to persuade the Thessalonians to choose a course of action, particularly in regard to eschatological expectations (chap. 2) and various ethical concerns (3:6-14). The tone of Paul's reproof is more authoritative in this letter than in the first, but he deftly mixed stern exhortation with loving encouragement, reiterating in the closing greeting an emphasis on peace that was much needed by the persecuted church (3:15-18).

Outline

I. Greeting (1:1-2)
II. An Expression of Thanksgiving and Prayer (1:3-12)
III. The Body of the Letter (2:1–3:15)
  A. The Coming of Jesus Christ (2:1-12)
  B. A Word of Encouragement (2:13-17)
  C. Final Instructions (3:1-15)
IV. Conclusion (3:16-18)

AD 33	AD 36	AD 51	AD 51	AD 58
Jesus' death, resurrection, and ascension	Paul's conversion on the Damascus Road	Paul's first letter to the Thessalonians	Paul's second letter to the Thessalonians	Paul delivers funds to the churches in Judea

Greeting (1:1-2)

1 Paul, Silvanus,[A] and Timothy:
To the church of the Thessa-
lonians in God our Father and the
Lord Jesus Christ.
2 Grace to you and peace from
God our Father and the Lord Jesus
Christ.

An Expression of Thanksgiving and Prayer (1:3-12)

3 We must always thank God for
you, ˚brothers. This is right, since
your faith is flourishing and the love
each one of you has for one another
is increasing. 4 Therefore, we ourselves boast about you among God's
churches—about your endurance
and faith in all the persecutions and
afflictions you endure. 5 It is a clear
evidence of God's righteous judgment that you will be counted worthy of God's kingdom, for which you
also are suffering, 6 since it is righteous for God to repay with affliction
those who afflict you 7 and to reward
with rest you who are afflicted,
along with us. This will take place
at the revelation of the Lord Jesus
from heaven with His powerful angels, 8 taking vengeance with flaming fire on those who don't know
God and on those who don't obey
the gospel of our Lord Jesus. 9 These
will pay the penalty of eternal destruction from the Lord's presence
and from His glorious strength 10 in
that day when He comes to be glorified by His ˚saints and to be admired
by all those who have believed, because our testimony among you was
believed. 11 And in view of this, we always pray for you that our God will

HARD QUESTION

How can you support the persecuted church?

Most Christians in the Western world do not experience the ongoing persecution about which Paul writes in this letter (1:4). Yet, in times when western culture affords relative ease for worshiping God, you have a responsibility to encourage, support, and pray for those who are suffering at the hands of evildoers for the sake of the gospel. Brothers and sisters in faraway lands desperately need a word of hope, prayer, and encouragement to endure. You can have a vital partnership with them through such intercession.

consider you worthy of His calling,
and will, by His power, fulfill every
desire for goodness and the work
of faith, 12 so that the name of our
Lord Jesus will be glorified by you,
and you by Him, according to the
grace of our God and the Lord Jesus
Christ.

The Body of the Letter (2:1–3:15)

The Coming of Jesus Christ (2:1-12)

2 Now concerning the coming of
our Lord Jesus Christ and our
being gathered to Him: We ask you,
˚brothers, 2 not to be easily upset in
mind or troubled, either by a spirit
or by a message or by a letter as if
from us, alleging that the Day of the
Lord[B] has come. 3 Don't let anyone
deceive you in any way. For that day
will not come unless the apostasy[C]
comes first and the man of lawlessness[D] is revealed, the son of destruction. 4 He opposes and exalts himself
above every so-called god or object

Title In the Greek New Testament the title for this letter is *pros Thessalonikeis B*, "to the Thessalonians, B," denoting "the second letter to the Thessalonians." This is the second of two letters sent by Paul to the Thessalonians and included in the Bible.

1:1 The greeting used by **Paul, Silvanus** [Silas], **and Timothy** is similar to that in 1 Thessalonians (see 1Th 1:1).

2:1 Although Paul had dealt with **the coming** (Gk *parousia*, may refer to the coming or arrival of either person or event, but most often in the NT it refers to the future coming of the Lord Jesus) of the Lord in his first letter to the Thessalonians (5:1-11), he felt the need to return to this subject. Perhaps some of Paul's communication had been misunderstood or ignored. Or perhaps his teaching had been confused with the teaching of another with a different message. As a result, this matter is the primary topic of concern in his second letter. The instruction in this letter is not comprehensive teaching on the return of Christ but assumes prior knowledge.

2:2 Paul begins by asking his brothers to be level-headed, not to be shaken off balance by sudden false teaching. Further, they are not to be **troubled** (Gk *throeisthai*, "alarmed, frightened or weighed down by worry and anxiety"). Jesus also used this expression in an eschatological discourse (see Mt 24:6; Mk 13:7). Apparently, the Thessalonians received a letter purported to be from Paul, which taught that **the Day of the Lord has come**. Paul sought to empower the Thessalonian church to withstand deception by demonstrating the inaccuracy of the anonymous letter.

2:3-4 Paul explains that the **day will not come unless** certain things are in place. First will come **apostasy** (Gk *apostasia*, "abandonment," lit "standing away from," as in the abandonment of God's law), conveying both the idea of political rebellion and religious revolt against God's authority—perhaps in opposition to civil order, or rebellion. Then **the man of lawlessness,** also called **the son of destruction,** will be

[A]**1:1** Or *Silas*; Ac 15:22-32; 16:19-40; 17:1-16 [B]**2:2** Other mss read *Christ* [C]**2:3** Or *rebellion*
[D]**2:3** Other mss read *man of sin*

revealed. This man who personifies evil and sin is to be identified with the first beast (Rv 13), the little horn (Dn 7–8), and the abomination (Mt 24:15).

2:9 Paul recognizes the power of **the lawless one** ("man of lawlessness," v. 3) by mentioning his **false miracles, signs, and wonders**. All three of these words are used in the Gospels to describe the miracles of Jesus (see also Ac 2:22; 2Co 12:12), but Paul notes here that these acts are done to deceive people into destruction. Then, as now, the counterfeit nature of these deeds is best exposed when placed alongside the work of Christ. Paul made clear that Jesus is abundantly more powerful.

2:10-12 Paul turns from discussing the man of lawlessness to emphasizing the fate of those who have followed the deceiver. Those deceived will **perish** because they are not rightly related to **the truth** (Jesus), revealing the attitude of their hearts. Therefore, they will not **be saved**—an eternal consequence—but will be **condemned**.

2:15 In light of the teaching on the man of lawlessness and the future glory, Paul told the Thessalonian believers to **stand firm** (Gk *stēkete*, "persevere, remain steadfast"). They were not to waver but to **hold to** [Gk *krateite*, "hold fast, not discard or let go"]) **the traditions**, teachings they had received from Paul in person and from his **letter**, a probable reference to 1 Thessalonians.

2:16-17 Recognizing that believers cannot accomplish what his teaching requires in their own strength, Paul prays that God will **strengthen** them. This prayer attributes deity and supreme power to Jesus Christ.

3:1 Paul asked the Thessalonians to pray continually for the apostles, recognizing that they too, were dependent on God to accomplish any good for the kingdom. He asked them to pray specifically that the gospel **message** may **spread rapidly** (Gk *trechē*), a word for describing runners in a race or of someone moving in haste. Apparently the gospel had been effective in this way with the Thessalonians. They responded quickly and **honored** God's word as they saw its impact.

3:3 The character of God is important to remember when facing any difficult situation. Paul affirms that because God is **faithful** (Gk *pistos*, "trustworthy, credible, sure, relied upon"; cp. 1Th 5:24), He will **strengthen** (Gk *stērixei*, "make stable or firm or steadfast"; cp. 2Th 2:17) and **guard** (Gk *phulaxei*, "protect, have in custody, watch, keep

of worship, so that he sits[A] in God's sanctuary,[B] publicizing that he himself is God.

5 Don't you remember that when I was still with you I told you about this? 6 And you know what currently restrains him, so that he will be revealed in his time. 7 For the •mystery of lawlessness is already at work, but the one now restraining will do so until he is out of the way, 8 and then the lawless one will be revealed. The Lord Jesus will destroy him with the breath of His mouth and will bring him to nothing with the brightness of His coming. 9 The coming of the lawless one is based on Satan's working, with all kinds of false miracles, signs, and wonders, 10 and with every unrighteous deception among those who are perishing. They perish because they did not accept the love of the truth in order to be saved. 11 For this reason God sends them a strong delusion so that they will believe what is false, 12 so that all will be condemned—those who did not believe the truth but enjoyed unrighteousness.

HARD QUESTION

Is it judgmental to tell someone she is wrong?

Paul expressed his love for the Thessalonian believers by correcting their wrong beliefs (2:10-12). He knew that their wrong thinking would result in behavior unfitting for believers, so he made every effort to instruct them more perfectly. This methodology remains an important means of expressing love for one another to this day. You can love and serve one another by continually using gentle instruction to help a sister grasp a concept of God more accurately. This responsibility is not the pastor's alone, but each member of the body is competent to minister in this way. Bible studies, discipleship groups, prayer partners, meeting over coffee, taking long walks for discussion together are some venues where this kind of love in action can take place. Asking poignant questions, listening well, and knowing Scripture in order to give wise input into a person's situation are necessary. Discipleship and correction should be an integral part of life within the body of Christ.

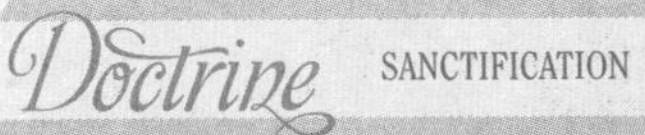

SANCTIFICATION

Sanctification (Gk *hagiasmō*, "holiness, consecration," 2:13; cp. Heb 12:14; 1Pt 1:2) indicates being set apart or dedicated to God (2:13). This progressive cleansing of soul and life is part of the salvation process whereby the Holy **Spirit** indwells, sets apart, and works in the believer to bring about increasing Christlikeness and holiness. The moment you are saved, you are justified or acquitted of your sin debt; God declares your sin debt as paid in full. God sees you as sinless, perfect, and holy because you have accepted Christ's sacrifice. However, just because you have received Christ's righteousness at the moment of your conversion, your *behavior* does not necessarily instantly change. There is a process where you become more like Christ in thought, word, and deed. This process is known as sanctification.

A Word of Encouragement (2:13-17)

13 But we must always thank God for you, brothers loved by the Lord, because from the beginning[C] God has chosen you for salvation through •sanctification by the Spirit and through belief in the truth. 14 He called you to this through our gospel, so that you might obtain the glory of our Lord Jesus Christ. 15 Therefore, brothers, stand firm and hold to the traditions you were taught, either by our message or by our letter.

16 May our Lord Jesus Christ Himself and God our Father, who has loved us and given us eternal encouragement and good hope by grace, 17 encourage your hearts and strengthen you in every good work and word.

Final Instructions (3:1-15)

3 Finally, •brothers, pray for us that the Lord's message may spread rapidly and be honored, just as it was with you, 2 and that we may be delivered from wicked and evil men, for not all have faith.[D] 3 But the Lord is faithful; He will strengthen and guard you from the evil one. 4 We have confidence in the Lord about you, that you are doing and will do what we command. 5 May the Lord direct your hearts to God's love and Christ's endurance.

6 Now we command you, brothers, in the name of our Lord Jesus Christ, to keep away from every brother who •walks irresponsibly

[A] 2:4 Other mss add *as God* [B] 2:4 Or *temple* [C] 2:13 Other mss read *because as a firstfruit* [D] 3:2 Or *for the faith is not in everyone*

and not according to the tradition received from us. [7]For you yourselves know how you must imitate us: We were not irresponsible among you; [8]we did not eat anyone's food[A] free of charge; instead, we labored and struggled, working night and day, so that we would not be a burden to any of you. [9]It is not that we don't have the right to support, but we did it to make ourselves an example to you so that you would imitate us. [10]In fact, when we were with you, this is what we commanded you: "If anyone isn't willing to work, he should not eat." [11]For we hear that there are some among you who walk irresponsibly, not working at all, but interfering with the work of others. [12]Now we command and exhort such people by the Lord Jesus Christ that quietly working, they may eat their own food.[A] [13]Brothers, do not grow weary in doing good.

[14]And if anyone does not obey our instruction in this letter, take note of that person; don't associate with him, so that he may be ashamed. [15]Yet don't treat him as an enemy, but warn him as a brother.

Conclusion (3:16-18)

[16]May the Lord of peace Himself give you peace always in every way. The Lord be with all of you. [17]This greeting is in my own hand—Paul. This is a sign in every letter; this is how I write. [18]The grace of our Lord Jesus Christ be with all of you.

A 3:8,12 Or *bread*

safe") believers **from the evil one**. They do not face difficulties alone.

3:6-11 Paul returns to another subject discussed in his first letter—irresponsible members. They were told **to keep away** or withhold fellowship **from** those who were lazy or irresponsible. Paul reminded the Thessalonians again of something they had heard earlier (1Th 5:14). **If anyone isn't willing to work**, let him **not eat**. Scripture notes the provision for one unable to do gainful work (cp. 1Co 16:1-3), but such benevolent support is not appropriate for those who can work (Ex 20:9). Some did not work at all, and worse, they interfered in the work of others.

3:17 Paul dictated his letters to a scribe. At some point toward the end of his letters, he took the pen in hand and wrote a few lines to punctuate the fact that the letter originated with him. In his own handwriting he wrote, **this is how I write**, which may have served to distinguish his letter from a letter falsely attributed to him. They could now expect any correspondence from him to bear this **sign**.

2 THESSALONIANS ... WRITTEN ON MY Heart You will face difficulties in life; nevertheless, God exhorts you to stand firm! He doesn't leave you on your own during trials, but He gives you the strength of the Holy Spirit who is working in you to help you become more like Christ. By not wavering from the truths you have learned through the Bible, you will be able to discern truth from error even in the midst of the direst of circumstances.

BIBLICAL WOMANHOOD Woman-to-Woman Mentoring

One might be put off by Paul's tendency to point to himself as an example (3:7-9; cp. 1Co 4:16, 11:1; Php 3:17; 1Th 1:6). Paul knew that the success of the gospel was related to his determination to live according to it. Surely Paul did not claim to be perfect, but as a man of integrity, he had to show congruence between what he said he believed and how he lived. Paul did not just expect this of himself, but he calls you to the same standard (1Th 2:14; 1Tm 4:12; Ti 2:7). He specifically expects this behavior of older women (Ti 2:3-6) and calls them to teach younger women through their words and example (2Th 3:7). The success of the church demands from women a willingness to love one another in this way, to be bold enough to say, "Imitate me, as I also imitate Christ" (1Co 11:1).

1 Timothy

Timeline	AD 47–49	AD 49–52	AD 50	AD 51
■ World Events ■ Biblical Events	Paul's first missionary journey	Paul's second missionary journey	Ministry of Paul, Timothy, and Silas in Philippi, Thessalonica, and Berea	Timothy and Silas in Berea after Paul's departure

"I have written so that you will know how people ought to act in God's household" (3:15b).

Who wrote 1 Timothy?

Paul identifies himself as the sender of the epistle (1:1).

Who were the recipients?

Paul addresses this letter to Timothy, his "true son in the faith" (1:2).

When was 1 Timothy written?

Paul wrote 1 Timothy sometime between A.D. 62 and 67.

Where did it happen?

During the time the Pastoral Epistles were penned, the Apostle Paul was out of prison, and he wrote this letter to Timothy who was ministering in Ephesus, a thriving commercial and religious center strategically located on the major east-west trade route near the southern coast of Asia Minor. Paul founded the church during a brief stop on his second missionary journey.

What is 1 Timothy about?

- *Church order.* In addition to giving attention to the qualifications for the leaders of the church, Paul gives instructions to believers on how they should conduct themselves in church.
- *Sound vs. false doctrine*. Throughout his epistles, Paul's primary strategy for refuting false doctrine is to state clearly sound doctrine and to demonstrate its power to change lives.
- *Lifestyle guidelines.* Paul's goal is to encourage righteous living by both leaders (3:1-13; 5:17-25; 6:11-16) and lay people (5:1-6; 6:1-2,17-19).

Why should women read 1 Timothy?

Right knowledge leads to right behavior, and the woman who wants to honor God through her life must know what God teaches about how to do this. In this book, Paul gives several important teachings for and about women—the proper lifestyle for a woman who professes to know God, how women should conduct themselves in church, how churches should care for widows, and the importance of true contentment in the life of the believer. This book offers a road map for how to live out the Christian faith within the community of faith.

How do you read 1 Timothy?

First and Second Timothy, together with a third letter written to Paul's disciple Titus, are commonly called the Pastoral Epistles since they gave instruction and encouragement to these two younger men serving in pastoral roles. This letter to Timothy serves as an instruction manual on church leadership. Paul wrote to Timothy so he would "know how people ought to act in God's household" (3:15), and this letter should be read with the understanding that the instructions apply directly to the church setting.

Outline

- I. Salutation (1:1-2)
- II. Directives Concerning Sound Doctrine (1:3-20)
  - A. False Doctrine and Its Teachers (1:3-11)
  - B. Paul's Testimony (1:12-17)
  - C. Timothy's Responsibility (1:18-20)
- III. Directives Concerning the Worship Assembly (2:1-15)
  - A. Instructions on Prayer (2:1-7)
  - B. Instructions to Men (2:8)
  - C. Instructions to Women (2:9-10)
  - D. How the Women Should Receive Instruction (2:11-15)
- IV. Directives Concerning Church Leaders (3:1-16)
  - A. Leaders or Overseers (3:1-7)
  - B. Deacons (3:8-13)
  - C. The Mystery of Godliness (3:14-16)
- V. Directives Concerning False Teachers (4:1-16)
  - A. Demonic Influence (4:1-5)
  - B. Timothy's Response to False Teachers (4:6-10)
  - C. Paul's Encouragement for More Effective Ministry (4:11-16)
- VI. Directives Concerning Various Church Members (5:1–6:10)
  - A. Admonishing Older and Younger Church Members (5:1-2)
  - B. Caring for Widows (5:3-16)
  - C. Support, Discipline, and Selection of Pastors (5:17-25)
  - D. Slaves (6:1-2a)
  - E. Exposure of Greedy False Teachers (6:2b-10)
- VII. Directives Concerning Those Who Serve Christ (6:11-21)
  - A. Exhortation for Timothy to Pursue a Godly Lifestyle (6:11-16)
  - B. Exhortation for the Wealthy to Handle Their Wealth Responsibly (6:17-19)
  - C. Exhortation for Timothy to Guard Sound Doctrine (6:20-21)

AD 51	AD 51–52	AD 52	AD 53–58	AD 54–56
Timothy and Paul in Athens	Timothy's return to minister in the church in Thessalonica	Timothy and Paul in Corinth	Paul's third missionary journey	Timothy and Paul in Ephesus

Salutation (1:1-2)

1 Paul, an apostle of Christ Jesus by the command of God our Savior and of Christ Jesus our hope:
2 To Timothy, my true son in the faith.

Grace, mercy, and peace from God the[A] Father and Christ Jesus our Lord.

Directives Concerning Sound Doctrine (1:3-20)

False Doctrine and Its Teachers (1:3-11)

3 As I urged you when I went to Macedonia, remain in Ephesus so that you may instruct certain people not to teach different doctrine 4 or to pay attention to myths and endless genealogies. These promote empty speculations rather than God's plan, which operates by faith. 5 Now the goal of our instruction is love that comes from a pure heart, a good conscience, and a sincere faith. 6 Some have deviated from these and turned aside to fruitless discussion. 7 They want to be teachers of the law, although they don't understand what they are saying or what they are insisting on. 8 But we know that the law is good, provided one uses it legitimately. 9 We know that the law is not meant for a righteous person, but for the lawless and rebellious, for the ungodly and sinful, for the unholy and irreverent, for those who kill their fathers and mothers, for murderers, 10 for the sexually immoral and homosexuals, for kidnappers,[B] liars, perjurers, and for whatever else is contrary to the sound teaching 11 based on the glorious gospel of the blessed God, which was entrusted to me.

Paul's Testimony (1:12-17)

12 I give thanks to Christ Jesus our Lord who has strengthened me, because He considered me faithful, appointing me to the ministry— 13 one who was formerly a blasphemer, a persecutor, and an arrogant man. But I received mercy because I acted out of ignorance in unbelief. 14 And the grace of our Lord overflowed, along with the faith and love that are in Christ Jesus. 15 This saying is trustworthy and deserving of full acceptance: "Christ Jesus came into the world to save sinners"—and I am the worst of them. 16 But I received mercy for this reason, so that in me, the worst of them, Christ Jesus might demonstrate His extraordinary patience as an example to those who would believe in Him for eternal life. 17 Now to the King eternal, immortal, invisible, the only[C] God, be honor and glory forever and ever. •Amen.

Timothy's Responsibility (1:18-20)

18 Timothy, my son, I am giving you this instruction in keeping with the prophecies previously made

[A]1:2 Other mss read *our* [B]1:10 Or *slave traders* [C]1:17 Other mss add *wise*

Title First Timothy (Gk *pros Timotheon A*) bears the name of its intended recipient—Timothy, Paul's "son in the faith" (1:2).

1:1 Paul identifies himself as the writer of this letter and **an apostle** called by God, a designation that would hardly be necessary if he intended only his spiritual son Timothy to read the letter. This reference to his apostolic office clarified his intention that the letter be read to the congregation since it would underscore the authority he was delegating to Timothy to carry out the changes mandated in his letter.

1:2 Paul's reference to **Timothy** is warm and personal: **my true son in the faith.** Although Paul discipled various younger men, such as Silas and Titus, Timothy seems to have held a unique place in his heart (Php 2:20-22). Timothy was from Lystra, a city in southern Asia Minor, which Paul visited on his first and second missionary journeys (Ac 14:6,21; 16:1). Timothy's father was a Gentile, but his mother and grandmother, who were Jewish, taught him the Scriptures from an early age (Ac 16:1; 2Tm 1:5; 3:15). He probably heard the gospel during Paul's first journey; and since the apostle referred to him as "my dearly loved and faithful son in the Lord" (1Co 4:17; cp. 1:2; 2Tm 2:1), he possibly led Timothy to personal faith in Christ. Timothy later traveled extensively with Paul and also was sent on missions to various churches, including Thessalonica, Corinth, and Philippi, as Paul's representative (1Co 4:17; Php 2:19-24; 1Th 3:2,6).

1:3 The events mentioned in 1 Timothy occurred after Paul was released from the Roman imprisonment (Ac 28:16-31). The letter opens with a clear statement of one aspect of Timothy's mission: He was to stop the false teachers who were causing dissension and strife and turning believers away from **God's plan, which operates by faith.** Sound teaching is central both in establishing a personal relationship with God through Jesus Christ (Eph 2:8-9) and in continuing the daily work of sanctification by Him (1Th 4:1-3).

>WORD|*study*

1:10 Sound (Gk *hugiainousē*, "healthy") is a medical term, used here metaphorically to talk about correct teaching. In the Pastoral Epistles the apostle focuses on the "healthiness" of the teaching found in the "glorious gospel" that he taught (v. 11), in contrast to the "sick interest" of the false teachers in their "disputes . . . over words" (6:4) and teachings that "will spread like gangrene" (2Tm 2:17).

about you, so that by them you may
strongly engage in battle, [19]having
faith and a good conscience. Some
have rejected these and have suffered the shipwreck of their faith.
[20]Hymenaeus and Alexander are
among them, and I have delivered
them to Satan, so that they may be
taught not to blaspheme.

Directives Concerning the Worship Assembly (2:1-15)

Instructions on Prayer (2:1-7)

2 First of all, then, I urge that petitions, prayers, intercessions,
and thanksgivings be made for everyone, [2]for kings and all those who
are in authority, so that we may
lead a tranquil and quiet life in all
godliness and dignity. [3]This is good,
and it pleases God our Savior, [4]who
wants everyone to be saved and to
come to the knowledge of the truth.

5 For there is one God
and one mediator between
God and humanity,
Christ Jesus, Himself human,
6 who gave Himself—a ransom
for all,
a testimony at the proper time.

[7]For this I was appointed a herald,
an apostle (I am telling the truth;[A] I
am not lying), and a teacher of the
Gentiles in faith and truth.

Instructions to Men (2:8)

[8]Therefore, I want the men in
every place to pray, lifting up holy
hands without anger or argument.

Instructions to Women (2:9-10)

[9]Also, the women are to dress themselves in modest clothing, with
decency and good sense, not with
elaborate hairstyles, gold, pearls, or
expensive apparel, [10]but with good
works, as is proper for women who
affirm that they worship God.

[A]2:7 Other mss add *in Christ*

1:20 Hymenaeus and Alexander, probably well-known elders, may have once confessed Christ but then turned from their confession, showing that they had never been truly converted in the first place.

2:8 Prayer is not limited to **men**, since in 1Co 11:5 women are encouraged both **to pray** and to prophesy.

2:11 The apostle states that **a woman should learn**. The verb connotes learning through instruction (Jn 7:15; 1Co 14:31; 2Tm 3:7,14) and underscores Paul's assumption that women both could and would learn. Two phrases describe the manner in which they should learn: **in silence with full submission**. The apostle is referring to a heart attitude and demeanor of "quietness" rather than to absolute silence. In the second phrase Paul directs the women to learn "with full submission." Since the context is not addressing family relationships, Paul is not likely urging the women to be submissive to their husbands, although this is taught elsewhere (Eph 5:21-22; Col 3:18). In this context of learning in the worship assembly, the object of their submission is best understood either as the pastor ("overseer" in 3:2; "elders" in 5:17) or, more likely, as sound doctrine. In light of the presence of false teachers, a combination of the two is also possible: Women were to submit themselves only to those pastors who taught sound doctrine.

2:13-14 Paul offers two reasons why the women are to receive instruction quietly and submissively in the worship assembly rather than teaching or exercising authority over men. He first

THE WORK OF CHRIST

In 1Tm 2:5-6, Paul uses three distinct terms to describe the work of Christ: **mediator**, **ransom**, and **testimony**. Jesus Christ incarnate is both fully God and perfectly human. In His role as "mediator," or intermediary, He has brought reconciliation between a holy God and sinful human beings through His atoning death on the cross (2Co 5:18-19; 1Jn 2:2). Jesus **gave Himself—a ransom for all** (Mk 10:45; Mt 20:28). "Ransom" (Gk *antilutron*) referred to the payment that Jesus made when He died on the cross (Rm 5:8) "for" (Gk *huper*, "on behalf of") all mankind as the substitute. As a result, all who receive Him are released from judgment (Rm 3:25-26), sin (Eph 1:7) and death (Rm 8:2), and they are adopted into God's family (Rm 8:15, 23; Gl 4:5; Eph 1:5). The final phrase, **a testimony at the proper time**, refers to the whole of verses 5-6. In the history of God's redemptive plan, the time has arrived for God's mercy to be shown to all people. Jesus' sacrificial death for all stands as a witness to the church.

BIBLICAL WOMANHOOD Boundaries for Women in Church Service

Paul states, **I do not allow a woman to teach or to have authority over a man** (2:12). This apostolic directive is more than his personal preference; rather it is prompted by the creation order and divine mandate. He notes two boundaries for women in church service:

- First, a woman is not "to teach" (Gk *didaskein*, "admonish, direct") a man in the worship assembly. A teacher is one who effectively gives systematic explanation of truth to others with an emphasis on its application to daily living (Mt 28:19-20). This term and its related noun are the most common New Testament words for teaching and are used almost exclusively for teaching in a public forum. Since the context is the worship assembly, he is likely forbidding the women to teach Scripture.
- Second, a woman is not to "have authority" over a man in the worship assembly. This term (Gk *authentein*, "to have/exercise/usurp authority, control") appears only here in the New Testament and is rare in existing Greek literature. The limited linguistic data available indicates that either "to exercise authority" or "to usurp authority" are possible meanings.

The apostle completes his prohibition by reiterating that a woman is "to be silent" (Gk *hēsuchia*), exactly the same phrase he uses in verse 11, and in both verses the best translation is "in quietness." By using the identical phrase at the beginning and end of this prohibition to women, Paul emphasizes his positive directive that women are to receive instruction with an inner attitude of quietness and submission to the truth of the gospel.

How Women Should Receive
Instruction (2:11-15)

11 A woman should learn in silence
with full submission. 12 I do not allow a woman to teach or to have
authority over a man; instead, she is
to be silent. 13 For Adam was created
first, then Eve. 14 And Adam was not
deceived, but the woman was deceived and transgressed. 15 But she
will be saved through childbearing,
if she continues[A] in faith, love, and
holiness, with good judgment.

Directives Concerning Church Leaders (3:1-16)

Leaders or Overseers (3:1-7)

3 This saying is trustworthy:[B] "If
anyone aspires to be an •over-
seer, he desires a noble work." 2 An
overseer, therefore, must be above
reproach, the husband of one wife,
self-controlled, sensible, respectable, hospitable, an able teacher,[C]
3 not addicted to wine, not a bully
but gentle, not quarrelsome, not
greedy— 4 one who manages his own
household competently, having his
children under control with all dignity. 5 (If anyone does not know how
to manage his own household, how
will he take care of God's church?)
6 He must not be a new convert, or
he might become conceited and fall
into the condemnation of the Devil.
7 Furthermore, he must have a good
reputation among outsiders, so that
he does not fall into disgrace and the
Devil's trap.

Doctrine THE OFFICE OF THE PASTOR

Paul establishes two offices of church leadership: pastors and deacons (3:1-7). Paul refers to a pastor as an **overseer** (Gk *episkopēs*, Ac 20:28; Ti 1:7, suggesting the role of watching over the congregation) and as an **elder** (Gk *presbuteros*, Ac 20:17; 1Tm 5:17,19; Ti 1:5, suggesting spiritual maturity); he uses these interchangeably to designate this pastoral office of church leadership. The duties include teaching, preaching, and generally giving oversight to the church (1Tm 3:1-7; 5:17).

Doctrine THE OFFICE OF A DEACON

Paul lists a number of qualifications for **deacons** (an anglicized form of Gk *diakonous*, "servants, attendants, those who execute the commands of another") more commonly translated "servant" in the New Testament (3:8-13). The Greek term can refer to either a man or woman, depending on the context. For example, Phoebe is called "a servant" (Rm 16:1), as are Timothy (1Tm 4:6) and Paul himself (Eph 3:7). However, the term also refers to people holding the office of deacon in the church. Deacon and pastor are the church leaders mentioned specifically in the New Testament (Php 1:1). While generally understood to be a position more focused on service, this fact is not explicitly stated in this passage. Although the word "deacon" is not used in Ac 6:1-6, these men handling the food distribution in the Jerusalem church are commonly understood to be the first appointed deacons.

Deacons (3:8-13)

8 Deacons, likewise, should be worthy of respect, not hypocritical, not
drinking a lot of wine, not greedy
for money, 9 holding the •mystery
of the faith with a clear conscience.
10 And they must also be tested first;
if they prove blameless, then they
can serve as deacons. 11 Wives, too,
must be worthy of respect, not
slanderers, self-controlled, faithful in everything. 12 Deacons must

[A] **2:15** Lit *if they continue* [B] **3:1** "This saying is trustworthy" could refer to 1Tm 2:15. [C] **3:2** Or *hospitable, skillful in teaching*

refers to the accounts of the creation and fall of the human race (cp. Gn 2–3). He does this by means of summary citation, a common rabbinic method for referring to the Old Testament. In other words, he uses the summary statement in verse 13 to refer to the entire section of Scripture dealing with the creation of man and woman (Gn 2:4-24), and the summary statement in verse 14 to refer to the account of the fall (Gn 3:1-15). Paul was well-trained in the rabbinic exegetical methods of his day, and he used arguments by analogy. Verse 13 implies here that Adam's chronological priority in creation carries some degree of authority. In verse 14 Paul is not saying that women are more easily deceived than men or that they are less intelligent. Rather, Paul is saying that a reversal of roles occurred in Gn 3. Scripture makes clear that God held Adam ultimately responsible for their fall into sin (Rm 5:12). Paul's analogy, then, is that just as it caused such problems in the beginning of history, so such a reversal of roles and the resulting problems should be avoided in the Ephesian church.

2:15 She will be saved through childbearing. Although multiple interpretations have been suggested for this notoriously difficult verse, it is best understood as affirming that women will receive salvation, with a focus on eschatological (future) reward, through faithfulness to their unique role, exemplified here in motherhood. This is not suggesting that a woman is saved by her works, rather that there is future reward for a woman who fulfills her unique role. A literal use of the word childbearing seems unlikely here, since not all women bear children. The term most probably serves as a figure of speech (a synecdoche, in which a part represents the whole)—i.e., "childbearing" represents the typical range of activities in a woman's life. This was an apt illustration in Paul's day, since a limited life span meant that most of a woman's adult years would be focused on marriage and motherhood.

3:2 That the elder should be married rather than single is unlikely since Paul highly valued his own celibacy (1Co 7:7-8,17). The most likely interpretation is that the elder should be faithful to his wife or be a "one-woman man."

3:12-13 Paul returns to the subject of the male deacons and says that they are to **be husbands of one wife**. This expression is exactly the same used regarding the overseers (v. 2). Also like the overseers, they are responsible for **managing their children and their own households competently** (vv. 4-5).

>WORD|*study*

3:11 The main question regarding this verse is whether or not the Greek term translated wives (Gk *gunaikas*, "women, wives") describes wives of deacons or women deacons. The qualifications of these women are very similar to those of the male deacons. The women are to be **worthy of respect**, the same word used to refer to the male deacons (v. 9). They are not to be slanderers (Gk *diabolous*), those who spread false and malicious reports about another person. They are to be self-controlled (Gk *nēphalious*, "temperate, clear-headed," the term used earlier to describe overseers and male deacons, vv. 2,8) and **faithful in everything**. Whether these women are deaconesses or wives of deacons, their ministry would certainly have been one of service and directed especially to women (Ti 2:3-5).

5:1-2 The verb **rebuke** is a strong term used metaphorically to picture a harsh verbal rebuke. Instead, Timothy should **exhort** (Gk *parakalei*, "encourage, appeal to, exhort," e.g., 1:3; 2:1) **an older man . . . as a father**, showing respect for him as a person while yet bringing needed correction. The next three groups of people are also pictured as members of God's family who at some point may need to receive correction. He should exhort the **younger men**—those around his own age or younger—**as brothers**, and the **older women as mothers**. As expected by the family analogy, Timothy was also to treat **the younger women as sisters**. Paul, however, added an important warning here: Timothy was to relate to them **with all propriety** (Gk *hagneia*, "chastity, purity"), emphasizing the need for sexual purity—an exhortation that had special relevance as he dealt with the young widows (5:11-16).

5:17 The term **leaders** is used by Paul earlier to refer to the elder's role in his household, and here it has the same meaning of leading, directing, governing, and protecting those committed to his care (3:4-5). Those who lead the church well are worthy of honor and respect, but the meaning is broader here. The church is to provide them, as the widows, with material and financial support (e.g., 1Co 9:7-14; 2Co 11:8-9; 1Th 2:7).

5:18 The apostle placed an exclamation point after his directive to support financially those elders who fulfill their ministries with excellence by giving reasons from both the Old Testament and the words of Jesus. Paul gives equal authority to the words of the Old Testament (Dt. 25:4) and the words of Jesus (Lk 10:7) and refers to both as **Scripture**.

5:19 Paul's statements on bringing disciplinary action **against an elder** or pastor are particularly relevant in light of the presence of the false teachers in the Ephesian church, some of whom were likely pastors (Ac 20:30). The apostle sought to safeguard those in authority against false accusations. The support **by two or three witnesses** was the normally accepted standard for bringing accusation against someone in the church (2Co 13:1), a custom with roots in the Mosaic law (Dt 17:6; 19:15) and affirmed by Jesus (Mt 18:16; Jn 8:17; Heb 10:28). Paul's emphasis is to protect those pastors who were innocent.

5:20 The apostle turns his attention to elders who are genuinely guilty. Timothy was to **publicly rebuke those who sin**, a reference to pastors who had established a lifestyle of sinning, not to those who, as every

be husbands of one wife, managing
their children and their own households competently. 13 For those who
have served well as deacons acquire
a good standing for themselves, and
great boldness in the faith that is in
Christ Jesus.

The Mystery of Godliness (3:14-16)

14 I write these things to you, hoping to come to you soon. 15 But if I
should be delayed, I have written
so that you will know how people
ought to act in God's household,
which is the church of the living
God, the pillar and foundation of
the truth. 16 And most certainly, the
mystery of godliness is great:

> He[A] was manifested
>   in the flesh,
> vindicated in the Spirit,
> seen by angels,
> preached among the nations,
> believed on in the world,
> taken up in glory.

Directives Concerning False Teachers (4:1-16)

Demonic Influence (4:1-5)

4 Now the Spirit explicitly says that
in later times some will depart
from the faith, paying attention to
deceitful spirits and the teachings of
demons, 2 through the hypocrisy of
liars whose consciences are seared.
3 They forbid marriage and demand
abstinence from foods that God created to be received with gratitude
by those who believe and know the
truth. 4 For everything created by
God is good, and nothing should be
rejected if it is received with thanksgiving, 5 since it is sanctified by the
word of God and by prayer.

Timothy's Response to False Teachers (4:6-10)

6 If you point these things out to
the •brothers, you will be a good servant of Christ Jesus, nourished by
the words of the faith and the good
teaching that you have followed.
7 But have nothing to do with irreverent and silly myths. Rather, train
yourself in godliness, 8 for

> the training of the body has
>   a limited benefit,
> but godliness is beneficial
>   in every way,
> since it holds promise
>   for the present life
> and also for the life to come.

9 This saying is trustworthy and deserves full acceptance. 10 In fact, we
labor and strive[B] for this, because we
have put our hope in the living God,
who is the Savior of everyone, especially of those who believe.

Paul's Encouragement for More Effective Ministry (4:11-16)

11 Command and teach these
things. 12 Let no one despise your
youth; instead, you should be an example to the believers in speech, in
conduct, in love,[C] in faith, in purity.
13 Until I come, give your attention
to public reading, exhortation, and
teaching. 14 Do not neglect the gift
that is in you; it was given to you
through prophecy, with the laying
on of hands by the council of elders.
15 Practice these things; be committed to them, so that your progress
may be evident to all. 16 Pay close attention to your life and your teaching; persevere in these things, for by
doing this you will save both yourself and your hearers.

Directives Concerning Various Church Members (5:1–6:10)

Admonishing Older and Younger Church Members (5:1-2)

5 Do not rebuke an older man, but
exhort him as a father, younger
men as brothers, 2 older women as
mothers, and with all propriety, the
younger women as sisters.

Caring for Widows (5:3-16)

3 Support[D] widows who are genuinely widows. 4 But if any widow
has children or grandchildren, they
must learn to practice godliness toward their own family first and to
repay their parents, for this pleases
God. 5 The real widow, left all alone,
has put her hope in God and continues night and day in her petitions
and prayers; 6 however, she who is
self-indulgent is dead even while
she lives. 7 Command this also, so

[A]3:16 Other mss read *God* [B]4:10 Other mss read *and suffer reproach* [C]4:12 Other mss add *in spirit* [D]5:3 Lit *Honor*

they won't be blamed. 8 But if anyone does not provide for his own,
that is his own household, he has
denied the faith and is worse than
an unbeliever.
9 No widow should be placed on
the official support list[A] unless she
is at least 60 years old, has been the
wife of one husband, 10 and is well
known for good works—that is, if
she has brought up children, shown
hospitality, washed the ˙saints' feet,
helped the afflicted, and devoted
herself to every good work. 11 But
refuse to enroll younger widows,
for when they are drawn away from
Christ by desire, they want to marry
12 and will therefore receive condemnation because they have renounced
their original pledge. 13 At the same
time, they also learn to be idle, going from house to house; they are
not only idle, but are also gossips
and busybodies, saying things they
shouldn't say. 14 Therefore, I want
younger women to marry, have children, manage their households, and
give the adversary no opportunity to
accuse us. 15 For some have already
turned away to follow Satan. 16 If
any[B] believing woman has widows
in her family, she should help them,
and the church should not be burdened, so that it can help those who
are genuinely widows.

Support, Discipline, and Selection of Pastors (5:17-25)

17 The elders who are good leaders
should be considered worthy of an
ample honorarium,[C] especially those
who work hard at preaching and
teaching. 18 For the Scripture says:

> **Do not muzzle an ox**
> **while it is treading out**
> **the grain,**[D] and,
> the worker is worthy
> of his wages.

19 Don't accept an accusation
against an elder unless it is supported by two or three witnesses.
20 Publicly rebuke those who sin,
so that the rest will also be afraid.
21 I solemnly charge you before God
and Christ Jesus and the elect angels to observe these things without prejudice, doing nothing out
of favoritism. 22 Don't be too quick
to appoint[E] anyone as an elder, and
don't share in the sins of others.
Keep yourself pure. 23 Don't continue drinking only water, but use a
little wine because of your stomach
and your frequent illnesses. 24 Some
people's sins are obvious, going before them to judgment, but the sins
of others surface[F] later. 25 Likewise,
good works are obvious, and those
that are not obvious cannot remain
hidden.

[A]**5:9** Lit *be enrolled* [B]**5:16** Other mss add *believing man or* [C]**5:17** Or *of respect and remuneration*; lit *of double honor* [D]**5:18** Dt 25:4 [E]**5:22** Lit *to lay hands on* = to ordain [F]**5:24** Lit *follow*

human being, did so occasionally. The purpose for such a public, literally "before everyone," reproof is **so that the rest will also be afraid**, perhaps a reference to the church in general or more likely primarily to the other pastors.

5:22 The apostle's third concern in this section on elders has to do with their selection. The removal of some pastors from office would logically require their replacement by others with good character. Timothy was cautioned: **Don't be too quick to appoint anyone as an elder**, a reference to setting apart and commissioning a pastor for service officially, as in Timothy's own commissioning (4:14; Ac 13:1-3). Paul urged Timothy not to "be too quick" to do this since the whole truth about the person may not be immediately apparent (5:24-25). Timothy must not **share in the sins of others** by setting apart unqualified pastors for ministry too quickly and risking becoming involved in the same sins besetting these individuals (cp. 4:12).

5:23 The risk of drinking water contaminated with parasites also could be reduced by mixing **water** with **wine**. The result would be a very diluted wine that had little potential for making anyone drunk. In fact, Paul makes clear earlier in the book that leaders in the church should not be "addicted to wine" (3:3).

Biblical Womanhood Widows

When numerous government and private safety nets are available for aging widows, the dire situation of widows in the ancient world can be misunderstood (5:1-16). The Old Testament law made special provision for those least able to protect and provide for themselves (Ex 22:22; Dt 24:17,19-21). God Himself was seen as being their champion (Ps 68:5), and through the prophet Isaiah He exhorted Israel to do the same (Is 1:17). The early church also made special provision for widows. The first major point of dissension recorded in the early church concerned the care of widows. In the daily distribution of food, the Hellenistic Jews felt their widows were being discriminated against in favor of those of Hebrew ethnicity (Ac 6:1). The early believers did what was necessary to resolve this problem (Ac 6:2-6).

Even with this understanding that the church had a primary role to play in the care of its widows, why so much attention to the needs of widows when the primary concern elsewhere in the letter was with developing godly church leadership and combating the threat of false teachers (1Tm 5:3-16)? The answer seems to lie in the clear contrast made between those widows who are older and living godly lives, and those who are **younger** and living lives of idleness and sexual promiscuity (vv. 11-13). Clearly Paul wanted the needs of those who were **genuinely widows** to be met (vv. 3-4,8,16). At the same time the apostle seemed to be using their godly lives to highlight the undesirable lifestyles of the younger ones (vv. 11-15), just as he earlier contrasted Timothy's lifestyle with that of the false teachers (4:6-16; 6:11-16). Above all, Paul did not want their behavior to be a cause of reproach to the Christian community (5:14; cp. 3:2; 5:7; 6:14).

6:1 Well over half of the people in the Greco-Roman world were **slaves**, so Paul's words would have had wide relevance in the Ephesian church. The message of the gospel is that all are liberated from the bondage of sin and are made brothers and sisters in Christ. Nevertheless, the social institution of slavery was a fact of life in the first century, and the apostle wanted to encourage the Christian slaves to relate appropriately to their masters.

6:6-8 Paul describes the great value of true **godliness**—the sort based on the gospel and the empowering of the Holy Spirit—which, when paired **with contentment**, is a means to **great gain**. Although "contentment" in the sense of "self-sufficiency," was a concept favored by the Stoic philosophers of his day, the apostle's meaning was different. He believed that true contentment involved "Christ-sufficiency," which enabled him to live beyond material abundance or lack of it (see Php 4:11, where a cognate term was used).

6:10 The love of money is not the only **root** cause **of evil** but seemed to be a central one in the Ephesian church. The false teachers, who are **craving** riches and reaching out greedily for all they can get, illustrate this premise. The results can be tragic for them personally, as well as their hearers.

6:12 Paul exhorted Timothy to **take hold of eternal life**, picturing an athlete seizing the prize of victory. Believers have eternal life the moment they receive Jesus Christ as their personal Savior and Lord (Rm 6:23). The opportunity is theirs to experience life abundantly throughout their sojourn on earth (Jn 10:10), although its fullest expression will be in His presence in heaven.

6:13 The exact nature of Christ's **good confession before Pontius Pilate** is not entirely clear. It could refer to something Jesus actually said to Pilate during His trial, or it may be a more general reference to the witness Jesus bore as He persevered both through His life and especially at His death.

6:15b-16 As he reflected on God's sovereignty and omnipotence, Paul broke out into a hymn of praise bearing similarities to his doxology in 1:17.

Slaves (6:1-2a)

6 All who are under the yoke as
•slaves must regard their own
masters[A] to be worthy of all respect,
so that God's name and His teaching will not be blasphemed. 2 Those
who have believing masters should
not be disrespectful to them because
they are •brothers, but should serve
them better, since those who benefit
from their service are believers and
dearly loved.

Exposure of Greedy False Teachers (6:2b-10)

Teach and encourage these things.
3 If anyone teaches other doctrine
and does not agree with the sound
teaching of our Lord Jesus Christ
and with the teaching that promotes
godliness, 4 he is conceited, understanding nothing, but has a sick
interest in disputes and arguments
over words. From these come envy,
quarreling, slander, evil suspicions,
5 and constant disagreement among
people whose minds are depraved
and deprived of the truth, who
imagine that godliness[B] is a way to
material gain.[C] 6 But godliness with
contentment is a great gain.

7 For we brought nothing
into the world,
and[D] we can take nothing out.
8 But if we have food
and clothing,[E]
we will be content with these.

9 But those who want to be rich
fall into temptation, a trap, and
many foolish and harmful desires,
which plunge people into ruin and
destruction. 10 For the love of money
is a root[F] of all kinds of evil, and
by craving it, some have wandered
away from the faith and pierced
themselves with many pains.

Directives Concerning Those Who Serve Christ (6:11-21)

Exhortation for Timothy to Pursue a Godly Lifestyle (6:11-16)

11 But you, man of God, run
from these things,
and pursue righteousness,
godliness, faith,
love, endurance,
and gentleness.
12 Fight the good fight
for the faith;
take hold of eternal life
that you were called to
and have made a good
confession about
in the presence of
many witnesses.

13 In the presence of God, who gives
life to all, and of Christ Jesus, who
gave a good confession before Pontius •Pilate, I charge you 14 to keep
the command without fault or failure until the appearing of our Lord
Jesus Christ. 15 God will bring this
about in His own time. He is

the blessed
and only Sovereign,
the King of kings,
and the Lord of lords,
16 the only One
who has immortality,
dwelling
in unapproachable light;
no one has seen
or can see Him,
to Him be honor
and eternal might.
•Amen.

HARD QUESTION

Is it really possible to be content?

Contentment is the ultimate acceptance of yourself, your surroundings, your past, and your future (6:6-11). Many women are full of discontent. They seek happiness from others, accumulate material possessions to find joy, move to a new home, or marry another husband in search of contentment. The Christian woman should learn to be content in Christ. Though contentment seems elusive, you can be content as you trust in God, relying on Him to provide what you need. You must be confident in yourself. You must be grateful for your family and your friends. Paul challenges you to seek **godliness** with contentment with whatever you have (v. 6). If you truly desire to follow God, He will teach you to **be content**. Godliness with contentment is **great gain**.

[A]6:1 Or *owners* [B]6:5 Referring to religion as a means of financial gain [C]6:5 Other mss add *From such people withdraw yourself.* [D]6:7 Other mss add *it is clear that* [E]6:8 Or *food and shelter* [F]6:10 Or *is the root*

Exhortation for the Wealthy to Handle Their Wealth Responsibly (6:17-19)

[17] Instruct those who are rich in
the present age not to be arrogant
or to set their hope on the uncertainty of wealth, but on God,[A] who
richly provides us with all things to
enjoy. [18] Instruct them to do what
is good, to be rich in good works,
to be generous, willing to share,
[19] storing up for themselves a good
reserve[B] for the age to come, so that
they may take hold of life that is
real.

Exhortation for Timothy to Guard Sound Doctrine (6:20-21)

[20] Timothy, guard what has been
entrusted to you, avoiding irreverent, empty speech and contradic-
tions from the "knowledge" that
falsely bears that name. [21] By professing it, some people have deviated from the faith.

Grace be with all of you.

[A] 6:17 Other mss read *on the living God* [B] 6:19 Or *foundation*

6:19 The apostle concludes this section with compelling motivation for believers' generosity. In so doing, they are **storing up for themselves a good reserve for the age to come**. He is not speaking of good works as a means to attaining salvation, which comes by grace through faith alone (Eph 2:8-9; 1Tm 1:12-17). Instead, he uses two metaphors—of "storing up" spiritual riches and of laying "a good foundation" through those riches—to emphasize the importance of amassing what Jesus called "an inexhaustible treasure in heaven" (Lk 12:33b).

6:20-21a When Paul instructs Timothy to **guard what has been entrusted to** him, he is referring to the gospel in all its fullness, including both its doctrinal structure and its practical outworking in a lifestyle of godliness.

1 TIMOTHY ... WRITTEN ON MY *Heart*

Godliness is the goal for the mature Christian—a goal that is obtained through discipline and training. Like an athlete who studies her sport and spends time preparing to be in peak physical condition, believers must know their faith and practice the principles taught in Scripture. It takes dedication, but for the believer, the prize is so much better than a medal. "We labor and strive for this [godliness], because we have put our hope in the living God, who is the Savior" (1Tm 4:10).

BIBLICAL WOMANHOOD Modesty

Throughout Scripture, God gives instruction to His children about lifestyle and behavior. Both the Old Testament and New Testament address modesty, which continues to be an important virtue to develop and discuss. The word "modesty" (Lat *modus*, lit "measure") has come to mean a measure of propriety or humility, characterized by reserve and freedom from excess. In the Bible, modesty impacts inner life as well as outer appearance. Modesty in appearance reflects godliness in character. A godly woman should develop the virtue of modesty and govern her life accordingly. While people are greatly influenced by culture, a woman's sense of modesty is to be regulated by her personal relationship with Jesus Christ and His example of purity. Paul discusses modesty in several of his letters to first-century churches. Lack of modesty in the Bible is often connected with immorality or sensuality. Therefore, the Christian woman should be modest in all ways (2:9). Paul makes the more general exhortation that they should **dress themselves in modest** [Gk *kosmein*, "well-ordered or –arranged"; cp. "respectable," 3:2] **clothing**. The apostle then singles out some items of adornment worn by the Ephesian women which he deemed especially inappropriate: **elaborate hairstyles, gold, pearls, or expensive apparel**. Some of the women may have been dressing in a more sensual manner reminiscent of their former pagan lifestyles, or more probably some of the wealthier women, who could afford to own more elaborate accessories, were dressing in a way to reflect pride in their superior social status. The emphasis is not to prohibit tasteful accessories but to enjoin modesty and propriety.

2 Timothy

Timeline	AD 47–49	AD 49–52	AD 50	AD 51
■ World Events ■ Biblical Events	Paul's first missionary journey	Paul's second missionary journey	Ministry of Paul, Timothy, and Silas in Philippi, Thessalonica, and Berea	Timothy and Silas in Berea after Paul's departure

"Fulfill your ministry" (4:5b).

Who wrote 2 Timothy?

The salutation of 2 Timothy clearly identifies the Apostle Paul as the writer of the letter.

Who were the recipients?

Paul addressed this letter to Timothy, whom he had known for approximately 20 years (ca A.D. 46–66), when he wrote this letter to his "dearly loved son" in the faith (1:2).

When was 2 Timothy written?

Paul wrote 2 Timothy sometime between A.D. 66 and 67.

Where did it happen?

Paul wrote this letter from a Roman prison where he awaited a second judicial hearing (4:16-18). Timothy received the letter in Ephesus where he served a church which had been founded by Paul but infiltrated by false teachers.

What is 2 Timothy about?

Writing to encourage Timothy in his role as a pastor, Paul emphasized several major themes.

- *Endurance of suffering and persecution*. Throughout the letter Paul refers both to his current experience of suffering and to his expectation of "difficult times" and persecution to come (3:1,12).
- *Danger of false teachers.* Much of the letter is devoted to the tasks of confronting false teachers and protecting believers from their deception (2:14-19,23-26; 3:6-9; 4:3-4; 4:14-15).
- *Hope of eternal life*. Despite Paul's impending death, he had an unshakable confidence and hope in Christ's past, present, and future glory.

Why should women read 2 Timothy?

Second Timothy is sometimes called Paul's last will and testament since he wrote it in full acceptance of his probable impending death. The letter gives women a glimpse into the heart and mind of a man who made it his goal to bring glory to God and who at the end of life could say that he had fulfilled his ministry. That should be the goal of every believer, and this letter offers insight into how to run the race of life with endurance, how to keep the faith in the midst of difficulties, and how to fulfill your ministry (your life's purpose) with a clear conscience before God.

How do you read 2 Timothy?

Second Timothy has the features of a personal letter typical of the ancient Greco-Roman world and typical of Paul with its uniquely Christian greeting and its personal closing. As one of the "Pastoral Epistles," 2 Timothy is distinguished from other New Testament letters clearly addressed to churches rather than to individuals. However, letters, like most written documents in the ancient world, were regarded as recorded speech, a substitute for the personal presence of the writer. Although 2 Timothy is personally addressed to a particular pastor, its contents provide guidance for both the pastor and the members of the church.

Outline

I. Salutation (1:1-2)

II. An Admonition to Timothy to Serve Faithfully in God's Power (1:3-18)
- A. Paul's Prayers for Timothy (1:3-5)
- B. An Exhortation to Keep Ablaze His Spiritual Gift (1:6-7)
- C. An Appeal to Join Paul in Suffering for the Gospel (1:8-12)
- D. An Exhortation to Guard the Gospel Message (1:13-14)
- E. An Example of One Who Has Served Faithfully (1:15-18)

III. An Encouragement to Timothy to Endure the Hardships That Accompany Ministry (2:1-13)
- A. An Appeal to Commit the Gospel to the Faithful (2:1-2)
- B. An Exhortation to Share in Suffering for the Gospel (2:3-7)
- C. Paul's Loyalty to Jesus Christ, the Author of Salvation (2:8-10)
- D. Christ's Enduring Faithfulness to Believers (2:11-13)

IV. A Warning to Timothy to Resist and Correct the False Teachers (2:14-26)
- A. A Warning to Avoid the False Teachers' Controversies (2:14-19)
- B. An Analogy of Household Vessels (2:20-21)
- C. An Admonition to Live Righteously and Avoid the False Teachers' Disputes (2:22-26)

V. A Plea to Timothy to Stand Firm in the Face of Inevitable Apostasy (3:1-17)
- A. Paul's Assurance that a Time of Apostasy Is Coming (3:1-9)
- B. Paul's Appeal to Timothy to Stand Firm in the Face of Persecution (3:10-17)

VI. A Solemn Charge to Timothy to Fulfill His Ministry in All Circumstances (4:1-8)
- A. A Charge to Proclaim the Gospel Consistently (4:1-5)
- B. The Victorious Completion of Paul's Ministry (4:6-8)

VII. Final Instructions to Timothy (4:9-18)
- A. Instruction to Come to Paul in Rome (4:9-15)
- B. Paul's Testimony of God's Faithfulness During His First Trial (4:16-18)

VIII. Paul's Greetings and Blessings (4:19-22)
- A. His Greetings to the Believers (4:19-21)
- B. His Final Blessing to Timothy (4:22)

AD 51	AD 51–52	AD 52	AD 53–58	AD 54–56
Timothy and Paul in Athens	Timothy's return to minister in the church in Thessalonica	Timothy and Paul in Corinth	Paul's third missionary journey	Timothy and Paul in Ephesus

Salutation (1:1-2)

1 Paul, an apostle of Christ Jesus by
God's will, for the promise of life
in Christ Jesus:
2 To Timothy, my dearly loved son.
Grace, mercy, and peace from God
the Father and Christ Jesus our Lord.

An Admonition to Timothy to Serve Faithfully in God's Power (1:3-18)

Paul's Prayers for Timothy (1:3-5)

3 I thank God, whom I serve with
a clear conscience as my ancestors
did, when I constantly remember
you in my prayers night and day.
4 Remembering your tears, I long to
see you so that I may be filled with
joy, 5 clearly recalling your sincere
faith that first lived in your grandmother Lois, then in your mother
Eunice, and that I am convinced is
in you also.

An Exhortation to Keep Ablaze His Spiritual Gift (1:6-7)

6 Therefore, I remind you to keep
ablaze[A] the gift of God that is in you
through the laying on of my hands.
7 For God has not given us a spirit[B]
of fearfulness, but one of power,
love, and sound judgment.

An Appeal to Join Paul in Suffering for the Gospel (1:8-12)

8 So don't be ashamed of the testimony about our Lord, or of me His
prisoner. Instead, share in suffering
for the gospel, relying on the power
of God.

9 He has saved us and called us
with a holy calling,
not according to our works,
but according to
His own purpose and grace,
which was given to us
in Christ Jesus
before time began.
10 This has now
been made evident
through the appearing
of our Savior Christ Jesus,
who has abolished death
and has brought life
and immortality to light
through the gospel.

11 For this gospel I was appointed a

[A]1:6 Or *to rekindle* [B]1:7 Or *us the Spirit*

CHARACTER PROFILE

Lois and Eunice **Nurturing Women**

Their Background	• Lois was Timothy's grandmother and Eunice was his mother (1:5). • His father was a Greek Gentile (Acts 16:1).
Their Story	• They taught Timothy the Scriptures when he was a young child (3:14-15). • Their genuine faith was commended by Paul.
Life Lesson	Lois and Eunice represent the countless Christian mothers and grandmothers who have diligently nurtured their children in the faith. They clearly understood the importance of teaching children God's Word at a young age.

Title Paul's second letter to Timothy is designated as such by its title in the Greek text: *pros Timotheon B*, "To Timothy, B." As the second letter in the Greek alphabet, "B" signifies the "second" of two things in a sequence.

1:2 Paul affectionately refers to **Timothy** as his **dearly loved son** (cp. 1Co 4:17). Born of a Jewish Christian mother and a Gentile father, Timothy was uniquely suited to minister with Paul in the mixed urban culture of Hellenistic Judaism and paganism. Timothy had traveled with Paul, had been sent by Paul on missions to various churches, and had assisted the apostle in writing or personally delivering several of his letters. Paul had participated in Timothy's ordination and reminded the younger pastor of the spiritual calling and gifts entrusted to him (1Tm 1:18; 4:14).

1:3 As he offered his thanks, Paul entered into the presence of **God** with assurance that he was serving Him **as my ancestors did**. Trained as a Pharisee, Paul was also ethnically Jewish and had been reared in the rich tradition of Jewish beliefs and under the influence of the Old Testament Scriptures (Php 3:5-6). The reference to his forefathers emphasizes the interconnectedness of the Old Testament and the gospel message (cp. 3:14-17).

1:5 The apostle clearly recalled Timothy's **sincere faith**. In contrast to the faith of the false teachers, Timothy's faith was "sincere" (Gk *anupokritou*, "unfeigned, undisguised, genuine," lit "not hypocritical") and was the primary cause for Paul's thankfulness as he remembered his spiritual son, for he knew that this faith would keep him faithful to the Lord Jesus despite the hardships. Timothy's faith had been nurtured in a faith-filled home environment through his mother **Eunice** and his grandmother **Lois**. Although his father was a Gentile, his mother was Jewish (Ac 16:1). "From childhood" he had been taught the Old Testament Scriptures (3:15), which shaped his thought patterns and lifestyle.

1:14 Paul exhorted Timothy to **guard** the gospel message as **that good thing entrusted to you** (see 1Tm 6:20). Knowing that such a responsibility required more than human ability, Paul emphasized that Timothy would guard the treasure of the gospel **through the Holy Spirit** indwelling both Paul and Timothy. For the third time in this opening series of exhortations, the apostle refers to the necessity of reliance on the Holy Spirit for accomplishing the work of the ministry.

1:16-18 While **Onesiphorus** was in Rome, he often **refreshed** (Gk, figuratively "was a breath of fresh air") Paul. This refreshing would certainly have been through meeting his physical needs in the prison, but it would also have included the spiritual and emotional comfort and encouragement he brought as a brother in Christ. More importantly to Paul's overall argument in this section of the letter, Onesiphorus **was not ashamed** of Paul's imprisonment. In fact, by actively seeking out Paul he had assumed great personal risk—his friendly association with a prisoner in Rome could have led to his own arrest. Paul used this man's example of faithful service, both to himself and to Christ and His gospel, as an object lesson to motivate his beloved son, Timothy, also to serve faithfully and unashamedly.

2:2 One of Paul's purposes in this letter was to urge Timothy to leave Ephesus, even though his task there had not yet been completed, and to come to him in Rome (4:9). To do so, the younger man would need to appoint leaders, **faithful men**, who could teach accurately and pastor the flock.

2:8 Descended from David, Jesus is the true Messiah who has fulfilled Old Testament prophecy.

2:9 For the gospel Paul suffered **to the point of being bound like a criminal** (Gk *kakourgos*, "evildoer"). Paul was not under the house arrest described in Ac 28. Rather, this imprisonment was dark, harsh, and involved being bound in chains like a dangerous criminal—a clear indignity for someone who was both innocent of wrongdoing and a Roman citizen. But while he, the best-known teacher of the gospel, is in chains, he victoriously declares that **God's message is not bound.** Although the prevailing government can chain the messenger, the message itself will progress unfettered (cp. Php 1:12-18).

2:15 Timothy should aspire to stand before God as one who had lived and proclaimed the gospel message as unadulterated, undistorted truth. Unlike

herald, apostle, and teacher,[A] [12]and
that is why I suffer these things. But
I am not ashamed, because I know
the One I have believed in and am
persuaded that He is able to guard
what has been entrusted to me[B] until that day.

An Exhortation to Guard the Gospel Message (1:13-14)

[13]Hold on to the pattern of sound
teaching that you have heard from
me, in the faith and love that are
in Christ Jesus. [14]Guard, through
the Holy Spirit who lives in us,
that good thing entrusted to you.

An Example of One Who Has Served Faithfully (1:15-18)

[15]This you know: All those in •Asia
have turned away from me, including Phygelus and Hermogenes.
[16]May the Lord grant mercy to the
household of Onesiphorus, because
he often refreshed me and was not
ashamed of my chains. [17]On the
contrary, when he was in Rome, he
diligently searched for me and found
me. [18]May the Lord grant that he
obtain mercy from Him on that day.
And you know very well how much
he ministered at Ephesus.

An Encouragement to Timothy to Endure the Hardships That Accompany Ministry (2:1-13)

An Appeal to Commit the Gospel to the Faithful (2:1-2)

2 You, therefore, my son, be strong
in the grace that is in Christ
Jesus. [2]And what you have heard
from me in the presence of many
witnesses, commit to faithful men
who will be able to teach others also.

An Exhortation to Share in Suffering for the Gospel (2:3-7)

[3]Share in suffering as a good soldier of Christ Jesus. [4]No one serving as a soldier gets entangled in the
concerns of civilian life; he seeks to
please the recruiter. [5]Also, if anyone
competes as an athlete, he is not
crowned unless he competes according to the rules. [6]The hardworking
farmer ought to be the first to get a
share of the crops. [7]Consider what I

THE WORK OF CHRIST

Paul highlights two purposes of Christ's ministry (1:10).

- He **has abolished** [Gk *katargēsantos*, "wiped out, set aside, broken"; cp. 1Co 15:26; Eph 2:15; 2Th 2:8] **death**. This same verb can be translated "destroyed" as in Heb 2:14 where the writer says that Jesus shared the flesh and blood of His people "so that through His death He might destroy the one holding the power of death—that is, the Devil." The penalty for sin is death in the sense of spiritual death or eternal separation from God (Rm 5:8), but Jesus, through His substitutionary atonement on the cross has paid that penalty. Death has no power over believers since they stand before God without condemnation (Rm 8:1).
- Christ **has brought life and immortality** [Gk *aphtharsian*, "incorruption, eternality"] **to light through the gospel.** The gospel alone displays the eternal life that Jesus has made available to each believer.

say, for the Lord will give you understanding in everything.

Paul's Loyalty to Jesus Christ, the Author of Salvation (2:8-10)

[8]Keep your attention on Jesus
Christ as risen from the dead and
descended from David. This is according to my gospel. [9]I suffer for
it to the point of being bound like
a criminal, but God's message is
not bound. [10]This is why I endure
all things for the elect: so that they
also may obtain salvation, which is
in Christ Jesus, with eternal glory.

Christ's Enduring Faithfulness to Believers (2:11-13)

[11]This saying is trustworthy:

For if we have died with Him,
we will also live with Him;
12 if we endure,
we will also reign with Him;
if we deny Him,
He will also deny us;
13 if we are faithless,
He remains faithful,
for He cannot deny Himself.

A Warning to Timothy to Resist and Correct the False Teachers (2:14-26)

A Warning to Avoid the False Teachers' Controversies (2:14-19)

[14]Remind them of these things,

[A]1:11 Other mss add *of the Gentiles* [B]1:12 Or *guard what I have entrusted to Him*, or *guard my deposit*

charging them before God[A] not to fight about words; this is in no way profitable and leads to the ruin of the hearers. [15] Be diligent to present yourself approved to God, a worker who doesn't need to be ashamed, correctly teaching the word of truth. [16] But avoid irreverent, empty speech, for this will produce an even greater measure of godlessness. [17] And their word will spread like gangrene; Hymenaeus and Philetus are among them. [18] They have deviated from the truth, saying that the resurrection has already taken place, and are overturning the faith of some. [19] Nevertheless, God's solid foundation stands firm, having this inscription:

The Lord knows those
who are His,[B] and
Everyone who names
the name of the Lord
must turn away
from unrighteousness.

An Analogy of Household Vessels (2:20-21)

[20] Now in a large house there are not only gold and silver bowls, but also those of wood and clay, some for honorable[C] use, some for dishonorable.[D] [21] So if anyone purifies himself from anything dishonorable,[E] he will be a special[F] instrument, set apart, useful to the Master, prepared for every good work.

An Admonition to Live Righteously and Avoid False Teachers' Disputes (2:22-26)

[22] Flee from youthful passions, and pursue righteousness, faith, love, and peace, along with those who call on the Lord from a pure heart. [23] But reject foolish and ignorant disputes, knowing that they breed quarrels. [24] The Lord's •slave must not quarrel, but must be gentle to everyone, able to teach,[G] and patient, [25] instructing his opponents with gentleness. Perhaps God will grant them repentance leading them to the knowledge of the truth. [26] Then they may come to their senses and escape the Devil's trap, having been captured by him to do his will.

A Plea to Timothy to Stand Firm in the Face of Inevitable Apostasy (3:1-17)

Paul's Assurance that a Time of Apostasy Is Coming (3:1-9)

3 But know this: Difficult times will come in the last days. [2] For people will be lovers of self, lovers of money, boastful, proud, blasphemers, disobedient to parents, ungrateful, unholy, [3] unloving, irreconcilable, slanderers, without self-control, brutal, without love for what is good, [4] traitors, reckless, conceited, lovers of pleasure rather than lovers of God, [5] holding to the form of godliness but denying its power. Avoid these people!

[6] For among them are those who worm their way into households and capture idle women burdened down with sins, led along by a variety of passions, [7] always learning and never able to come to a knowledge of the truth. [8] Just as Jannes and Jambres resisted Moses, so these also resist the truth, men who are corrupt in mind, worthless in regard to the faith. [9] But they will not make further progress, for their lack of understanding will be clear to all, as theirs[H] was also.

Paul's Appeal to Timothy to Stand Firm in the Face of Persecution (3:10-17)

[10] But you have followed my teaching, conduct, purpose, faith, patience, love, and endurance, [11] along with the persecutions and sufferings that came to me in Antioch, Iconium, and Lystra. What persecutions I endured! Yet the Lord rescued me from them all. [12] In fact, all those who want to live a godly life in Christ Jesus will be persecuted. [13] Evil people and impostors will become worse, deceiving and being deceived. [14] But as for you, continue in what you have learned and firmly believed. You know those who taught you, [15] and you know that from childhood you have known the sacred Scriptures, which are able to give you wisdom for salvation through faith in Christ Jesus. [16] All Scripture is inspired by God[I] and is

[A]2:14 Other mss read *before the Lord* [B]2:19 Nm 16:5 [C]2:20 Or *special* [D]2:20 Or *ordinary* [E]2:21 Lit *from these* [F]2:21 Or *an honorable* [G]2:24 Or *everyone, skillful in teaching* [H]3:9 = Jannes and Jambres [I]3:16 Lit *breathed out by God*; the Scripture is the product of God's Spirit working through men; 2Pt 1:20-21.

the false teachers, Timothy should be **a worker who doesn't need to be ashamed** before God because of faulty craftsmanship. Instead, he is to be one who is **correctly teaching the word of truth**.

2:17-18 Overturning the faith of some. "Overturning" (Gk *anatrepousin*, "overthrowing, destroying, upsetting, subverting"; cp. Ti 1:11) vividly describes Jesus' literal overturning of the money changers' tables in the temple (Jn 2:15). This particular heresy was not new in the life of the early church and probably came from a Hellenistic misconception that "resurrection" was a purely spiritual concept and that there would be no bodily resurrection of believers. Paul considered the resurrection of the body to be a cardinal truth of the gospel, so he urged Timothy to fight against this false teaching (1Co 15:20-28).

2:20-21 In a wealthier household, **gold and silver bowls** would be reserved for special occasions and **wood and clay** ones would be used for ordinary meals, cooking preparation, and garbage disposal. Paul uses this analogy to illustrate the need for a believer to purify himself from the contamination of false teaching and "unrighteousness" in order to be a special instrument, figuratively one of the gold or silver ones.

3:8-9 Jannes and **Jambres** were Pharaoh's chief magicians who resisted Moses (Ex 7:11-12,22; 8:7) . The apostle compares their deceptive practices with those of the false teachers. Just as the Egyptian magicians were shown to be charlatans, so the false teachers will be exposed both in their false teaching and in their lack of understanding the gospel.

3:10-12 Paul appealed to Timothy's firsthand knowledge of the **persecutions** he **endured** in the region where Timothy lived when Paul invited him to become part of his second missionary journey. The intensity of the persecution can be seen in the motivation of Paul's opponents. They walked about 100 miles, one way, from Pisidian Antioch to Lystra to do Paul great harm. They stoned Paul, and, believing him to be dead, drug him out of Lystra. Timothy either saw this or heard vivid, first-hand accounts of what was done to Paul.

3:14-15 Timothy had learned the **Scriptures** (a reference to the OT) from Paul himself, but he had been taught also **from childhood.** Although his father was a Gentile, his mother Eunice and his grandmother Lois were Jewish (2Tm 1:5), and they educated him in the Jewish Scriptures from a very young age.

4:1-8 In all of Paul's writings, a charge more solemn than this one is hard to imagine (cp. 2:14; 1Tm 5:21; 6:13) because Paul reminded Timothy he lived his life **before God.**

4:3-4 Paul explains why proclaiming God's word will be such a difficult task. A **time will come when** people will not put up with **sound doctrine**, a synonym for God's word, especially in the Pastoral Epistles (e.g., 1:13; 1Tm 1:10; 6:3), emphasizing the health and life-giving nature of the gospel. These people will **turn aside to myths** (Gk *muthous*, "fables, fictions, falsely construed stories," as the antithesis of truth; cp. 1Tm 1:4; 4:7; Ti 1:14; 2Pt 1:16). Pictured here is a lineup of false teachers, each with a slightly different emphasis that will prove new and interesting to the hearers. There can be no true satisfaction, however, because only God's word, received in humility and with a willingness to obey, can prove truly satisfying to the soul.

4:6 Paul believed he would not live much longer; he was **already being poured out as a drink offering**, a reference to the Old Testament sacrificial system. Timothy was invested with the assignment to continue where Paul left off.

4:8 Looking ahead now to his **future** life in heaven with the Lord, Paul reflected on what **is reserved** (Gk *apokeitai*, "laid away, placed in safekeeping") for him there: **the crown of righteousness**. This reference may be to a physical crown given to him because he had pursued a life of practical righteousness through the power of the indwelling Holy Spirit. It may also refer to a symbolic crown since Christ had credited His righteousness to him. **On that day** in heaven, this "crown" will be awarded to him and to **all those who have loved His appearing.** As the Apostle John later wrote, the greatest incentive for righteous living is an anticipation of Christ's return (1Jn 3:2-3).

4:9-11a Paul urged Timothy to join him soon in Rome. Little else is known of **Demas**, who deserted Paul, except that he was a coworker during Paul's previous Roman imprisonment (Col 4:14; Phm 24; see **Biblical Womanhood**, p. 1531). Demas's departure was clearly very painful to Paul, perhaps especially so because this "coworker" had chosen to embrace the world and its values rather than to remain with the apostle. Two other men had also left, but Paul likely had sent them out on assignments. **Crescens**, of whom nothing else is known, went to **Galatia** in central Asia Minor. **Titus**, whom Paul earlier sent to the church in Crete (Ti 1:5), had been in Rome with Paul and was then sent to

HARD QUESTION

Why is the Bible considered different than other books?

Paul reflects on the true character of the Scriptures and their value to him in ministry (3:16-17). That **all Scripture is inspired by God** (Gk *theopneustos*, "God-breathed," the only instance of this word in the NT) emphasizes God's initiation and control of the process of communicating His thoughts to human beings. The Holy Spirit orchestrated this process, so the original writings are without error (2Pt 1:21). God's written word is authoritative simply because it is *God's* word. It is also infallible (i.e., it cannot be broken, Jn 10:35). What God says will come to pass. Paul goes on to say that Scripture is **profitable**:

- for **teaching** (Gk *didaskalian*, "instructing" in regard to doctrine) God's truth to others—one of Timothy's primary ministry responsibilities (4:3; 1Tm 4:6,13,16; Ti 1:9; 2:1,7,10);
- for **rebuking** (Gk *elegchon*, "proof, conviction")—i.e., enabling Timothy to expose the errors of both the lifestyles and the teaching of the heretics (1Tm 5:20; 2Tm 4:2);
- for **correcting** (Gk *epanorthōsin*, "restoring to an upright position, making straight again") those who are in error and setting them on a path of restoration (Jn 17:17; 2Tm 2:25);
- for **training** [Gk *paideian*, "discipline, course of instruction" aimed at cultivation of both knowledge and character; cp. Eph 6:4; Heb 12:5-11] **in righteousness**, providing wisdom in how to develop an intimate relationship with the Lord and how to minister in the full power of the Holy Spirit.

profitable for teaching, for rebuking, for correcting, for training in righteousness, 17 so that the man of God may be complete, equipped for every good work.

A Solemn Charge to Timothy to Fulfill His Ministry in All Circumstances (4:1-8)

A Charge to Proclaim the Gospel Consistently (4:1-5)

4 I solemnly charge you before God and Christ Jesus, who is going to judge the living and the dead, and because of His appearing and His kingdom: 2 Proclaim the message; persist in it whether convenient or not; rebuke, correct, and encourage with great patience and teaching. 3 For the time will come when they will not tolerate sound doctrine, but according to their own desires, will multiply teachers for themselves because they have an itch to hear something new.[A] 4 They will turn away from hearing the truth and will turn aside to myths. 5 But as for you, be serious about everything, endure hardship, do the work of an evangelist, fulfill your ministry.

The Victorious Completion of Paul's Ministry (4:6-8)

6 For I am already being poured out as a •drink offering, and the time for my departure is close. 7 I have fought the good fight, I have finished the race, I have kept the faith. 8 There is reserved for me in the future the crown of righteousness, which the Lord, the righteous Judge, will give me on that day, and not only to me, but to all those who have loved His appearing.

Final Instructions to Timothy (4:9-18)

Instruction to Come to Paul in Rome (4:9-15)

9 Make every effort to come to me soon, 10 for Demas has deserted me, because he loved this present world, and has gone to Thessalonica. Crescens has gone to Galatia, Titus to Dalmatia. 11 Only Luke is with me. Bring Mark with you, for he is useful to me in the ministry. 12 I have sent Tychicus to Ephesus. 13 When you come, bring the cloak I left in Troas with Carpus, as well as the scrolls, especially the parchments. 14 Alexander the coppersmith did great harm to me. The Lord will repay him according to his works. 15 Watch out for him yourself because he strongly opposed our words.

Paul's Testimony of God's Faithfulness During His First Trial (4:16-18)

16 At my first defense, no one stood by me, but everyone deserted me. May it not be counted against them. 17 But the Lord stood with me and strengthened me, so that the proclamation might be fully made through me and all the Gentiles might hear. So I was rescued from the lion's mouth. 18 The Lord will rescue me from every evil work and will bring me safely into His heavenly king-

[A] **4:3** Or *to hear what they want to hear*; lit *themselves, itching in the hearing*

CHARACTER PROFILE

Claudia **Respected Friend**

Her Background	• A Gentile • A respected and influential woman
Her Story	• A convert of the gospel • A member of the Roman church • A personal friend of Timothy • An encourager to Paul and other believers
Life Lesson	In the most challenging circumstances that prompt many to lose heart (vv. 9-10), a woman who sets her heart on Christ's "heavenly kingdom" rather than on "this present world" (vv. 9,18) can be a champion for the gospel.

dom. To Him be the glory forever
and ever! •Amen.

Paul's Greetings and Blessings (4:19-22)

His Greetings to the Believers (4:19-21)

19 Greet Prisca and Aquila, and the
household of Onesiphorus. 20 Erastus has remained at Corinth; I left
Trophimus sick at Miletus. 21 Make
every effort to come before winter.
Eubulus greets you, as do Pudens,
Linus, Claudia, and all the •brothers.

His Final Blessing to Timothy (4:22)

22 The Lord be with your spirit.
Grace be with you.

2 TIMOTHY ... WRITTEN ON MY *Heart* Knowing how to handle God's word is the safest way for believers to protect themselves from being led astray with the latest fad, gimmick, or quick spiritual fix that cannot fulfill on its empty promise (2:13). Learn God's word and how to study it effectively so that you can stand before Him unashamed and with a clear conscience (1:3). Believers will face difficult days (3:1), but the Lord stands with His children, strengthening them in the midst of trials (4:17). Let Him strengthen you through His Word!

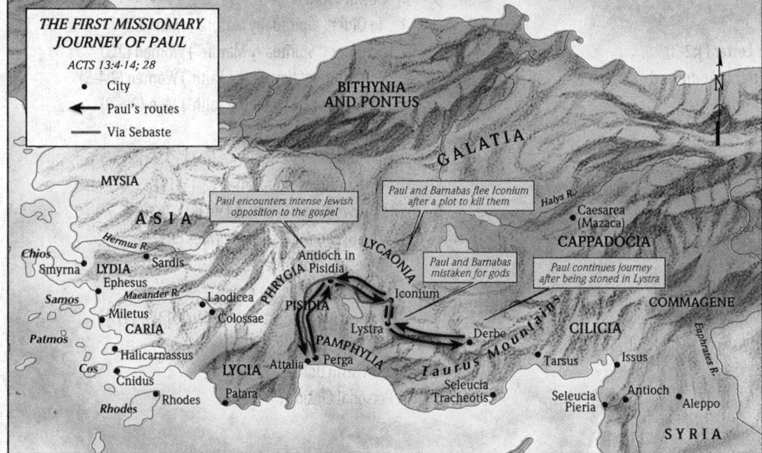

Paul probably first met Timothy on his first missionary journey as he came to Pisidian Antioch, Iconium, Lystra, and Derbe. Paul alludes (2Tm 3:10-12) to Timothy's first-hand knowledge of the apostle's sufferings where he was left for dead outside Lystra (Ac 14:19-20). On Paul's second missionary journey through Lystra, he invited Timothy to join him and Silas as the moved westward and planted the first churches in Europe (Ac 16:1–18:17). From the beginning, Timothy was aware of the cost of following Christ.

Dalmatia up the Adriatic coast. **Only Luke** remained with him.

4:11b Mark had earlier traveled with Paul and Barnabas but had left when things became too difficult (Ac 13:13). Whether or not to bring Mark on a subsequent journey became a matter of contention between Paul and Barnabas, who had taken Mark under his care and had played a key role in Mark's restoration to ministry (Ac 15:36-41).

4:12 Paul further notes that he had sent **Tychicus to Ephesus** (Eph 6:21; Col 4:7; Ti 3:12). He seems to have been the bearer of this letter and was probably the one sent to take over Timothy's responsibilities in the Ephesian church.

4:14-15 In the strongest possible words, Paul warned Timothy about **Alexander the coppersmith**, a man who **did great harm** to Paul and **strongly opposed** his **words**. Scholars have suggested that this man was the one who had facilitated Paul's arrest, especially since the word translated **did** (Gk *enedeixato*, commonly "show or point out") in secular texts can have the meaning of "inform against." Whatever the case, Paul had placed him in the Lord's hands for judgment.

4:16 The apostle updated Timothy on what had been happening to him since being imprisoned in Rome. He spoke of his **first defense**, apparently referring to a preliminary hearing, called a *prima actio* within the Roman legal system, which would have been followed later by a formal trial. A two-year delay during his earlier imprisonment under Felix (Ac 24:27) made it reasonable for Paul to assume that there would be enough time for Timothy to reach him now.

4:19 Paul concluded this letter, as he typically did, with personal words and greetings. He extended his greetings to **Prisca** (elsewhere Priscilla) and **Aquila,** close friends whom he met in Corinth on his second missionary journey (Ac 18:2). They had traveled with him (Ac 18:18) and had served in the church in Ephesus (Ac 18:26). He also greeted **the household of Onesiphorus**, who had so bravely stayed with him during his current imprisonment (1:16-18).

4:21 Since only Luke was still with him, Paul again urged Timothy to join him **before winter**, when high seas and unpredictable winds would make sailing impossible.

Titus

Timeline	AD 36	AD 47–49	AD 49	AD 49–52
➡ World Events ➡ Biblical Events	Paul's conversion on the Damascus Road	Paul's first missionary journey	Paul's attendance with Titus at the Jerusalem Council	Paul's second missionary journey

"Teach what is good" (2:3b).

Who wrote Titus?

Paul identifies himself as the sender of the epistle (1:1).

Who were the recipients?

Paul addressed this letter to his Greek convert Titus, who was ministering in Crete.

When was Titus written?

Paul wrote Titus sometime between A.D. 62 and 64.

Where did it happen?

During the time the Pastoral Epistles were penned, the Apostle Paul seemed to be on the move—at least out of prison (1Tm 1:3; 3:14; Ti 1:5). Paul's reference to an earlier visit to Crete suggests that he established a church, leaving Titus to organize the congregation and disciple the new believers.

What is Titus about?

- *Sound doctrine* is at the heart of this brief epistle (2:1-14; 3:4-7).
- *Servanthood or Christlike living* is delineated as the natural and essential outgrowth of understanding sound doctrine. Despite the pagan environment, the Cretans were held to the highest ethical standards, as is every believer.

Why should women read Titus?

One of the greatest ministries that God has given to women in the church is the opportunity to invest in the lives of other women. This small letter outlines for women the great adventure of spiritual mothering, the investment of spiritually mature women in the lives of those younger in the faith. Paul describes the character of a mentor as well as the curriculum that the mentors are to teach.

How do you read Titus?

The book is a personal letter from Paul, a trusted mentor, to his son in the faith, Titus. Although Titus was not identified as a pastor, this letter, as those written to Timothy, dealt with practical and timely issues that would have been foremost in the minds of congregants and church leaders. This letter gave Titus the authority and the encouragement to address issues of doctrine, church polity, and even the spiritual formation of the church in Crete.

Outline

I. Introduction (1:1-4)
  A. Author of the Letter (1:1)
  B. Motivation for Writing the Letter (1:2-3)
  C. Recipient to Whom the Letter Is Addressed (1:4a)
  D. Salutation and Greeting (1:4b)
II. The Appointment of Pastors (1:5-9)
  A. Consistent Patterns in Character (1:5-8)
    1. In the Family (1:5-6)
    2. In Personal Habits and Life (1:7)
    3. In Faith and Practice (1:8)
  B. Passionate Purpose in Ministry (1:9)
III. The Challenge of Combating Heresy (1:10-16)
  A. Overcoming the General Worldview (1:10-12a)
  B. Engaging the Specific Field Assignment (1:12b-16)
IV. The Instructions for Believers (2:1-10)
  A. A General Word (2:1)
  B. A Specific Word (2:2-10)
    1. To Older ("Spiritually Mature") Men (2:2)
    2. To Older ("Spiritually Mature") Women (2:3)
    3. To Younger ("New in the Faith") Women (2:4-5)
    4. To Younger ("New in the Faith") Men (2:6-8)
    5. To Slaves (2:9-10)
V. A Persuasive Reason for Obedience (2:11–3:11)
  A. The Gift of Grace in Salvation (2:11-15)
  B. The Outworking of Faith in Life (3:1-11)
    1. The Recognition of Authorities (3:1)
    2. A Respect for Others (3:2)
    3. A Call to Obedience (3:3-8)
    4. A Warning Against Disobedience (3:9-11)
VI. Conclusion (3:12-15)
  A. Final Instructions (3:12-14)
  B. A Personal Closing (3:15)

AD 52–54	AD 54	AD 59/60	AD 62	AD 64–65
Paul's ministry in Ephesus	Paul's assignment of Titus as his representative to the church at Corinth	Paul's voyage to Rome	Paul's release from house arrest after his appeal to Caesar	Visit of Paul and Silas to Crete; Paul's letter to Titus

Introduction (1:1-4)

1 Paul, a •slave of God and an
apostle of Jesus Christ, to build
up[A] the faith of God's elect and
their knowledge of the truth that
leads[B] to godliness, 2 in the hope of
eternal life that God, who cannot
lie, promised before time began.
3 In His own time He has revealed
His message in the proclamation that I was entrusted with by
the command of God our Savior:
4 To Titus, my true son in our common faith.

Grace and peace from God the Father and Christ Jesus our Savior.

The Appointment of Pastors (1:5-9)

Consistent Patterns in Character (1:5-8)

5 The reason I left you in Crete
was to set right what was left undone and, as I directed you, to appoint elders in every town: 6 one
who is blameless, the husband of
one wife, having faithful[C] children
not accused of wildness or rebellion. 7 For an •overseer, as God's
administrator, must be blameless,
not arrogant, not hot-tempered,
not addicted to wine, not a bully,
not greedy for money, 8 but hospitable, loving what is good, sensible,
righteous, holy, self-controlled,

Passionate Purpose in Ministry (1:9)

9 holding to the faithful message as
taught, so that he will be able both to
encourage with sound teaching and
to refute those who contradict it.

The Challenge of Combating Heresy (1:10-16)

Overcoming the General Worldview (1:10-12a)

10 For there are also many rebellious people, full of empty talk and
deception, especially those from
Judaism.[D] 11 It is necessary to silence them; they overthrow whole
households by teaching what they
shouldn't in order to get money
dishonestly. 12 One of their very own
prophets said,

A1:1 Or *according to* B1:1 Or *corresponds* C1:6 Or *believing* D1:10 Lit *the circumcision*

Doctrine CHURCH LEADERSHIP

Paul uses two words in Titus (1:5-7) to describe leadership—**elders** (Gk *presbuterous*, source of the English word "presbyter") and **overseer** (Gk *episkopon*, "overseer, guardian, bishop," source of the English word "episcopal"). These words are used interchangeably in Scripture in reference to pastors (Gk *poimenas*, Eph 4:11, also translated "shepherd" in other contexts). Four major passages discuss the qualifications and responsibilities of the pastor or elder or overseer (Ti 1:5-7; Ac 20:28-35; 1Tm 3:1-7; 1Pt 5:1-4). The pastors appointed were local, living among the congregants they served, and they had requirements to meet (see chart, pp. 1561-1563).

>WORD|*study*

1:1 Paul, in his salutation, describes himself as a slave (Gk *doulos*). Perhaps it is significant that this word was frequently used to describe one born into slavery, and anyone who comes into this relationship with Christ is born again, becoming a bond slave through spiritual birth. Every follower of Christ must become a slave to the Lord, dying to self and committing himself entirely unto Him (Rm 6:1-23; Gl 2:20; Eph 6:6).

Title This epistle bears the name of its recipient—Titus, the young protégé of Paul. A Greek by ethnic heritage, Titus was converted under the ministry of Paul (1:4). He chose to remain uncircumcised, perhaps as a testimony to the power of the gospel for Gentiles as well as Jews (Gl 2:3).

1:1 As an **apostle** [Gk *apostolos*, "messenger, one sent"] **of Jesus Christ**, Paul claims a unique relationship reserved for only a few selected for a particular service to Christ.

1:2 **Hope** is not to be understood as something without certainty, as the word is popularly used in modernity. Believers must know that their hope is a sure thing, based upon a settled expectation and grounded in the very person of God Himself.

1:5 Paul gave to Titus a reminder of his assignment—he was to **set right** [Gk *epidiorthōsē*, "correct"] **what was left undone** when Paul had to leave. The verb was used in medical writings in reference to setting broken limbs and could project the idea that the task was necessary and would require enduring some painful adjustment as well as heeding an urgent demand for getting it right.

1:6 The phrase **husband of one wife** does not necessarily mean that the pastor must be married, for Paul himself was single—at least at this time (whether by choice or as a widower). Rather, the emphasis is that the pastor should be a one-woman man, having taken very seriously God's plan for marriage (Gn 2:24; Mt 19:5).

1:10 The phrase **especially those from Judaism** is a reference to some of the legalistic Jews, who believed themselves to be the only real interpreters of Scripture.

1:12 The quote is from the Cretan poet Epimenides, who inhabited the island in the sixth century B.C. Interestingly, Paul was well acquainted with ancient nonbiblical literature. Perhaps here he was using that knowledge to gain a hearing from nonbelievers in Crete. Or he may simply have been using the words of a pagan poet to awaken the people to their profligate lives and thus the need for the life-changing gospel of Jesus Christ. Historically the residents of Crete had been known for their immorality.

1:14-16 Paul describes the false teaching as **Jewish myths** but does not elaborate on these. However, Jewish rabbis were known for the elevation of their own traditions to a position of importance alongside the law of God. Their legalistic interpretations often added to or even contradicted the divine law recorded in Scripture. They assumed that they could make themselves acceptable to God by their own traditions and rituals, such as their extensive and complicated dietary regulations. The false teachers were observant of religious traditions yet denied God by their works.

2:2 Paul moves from the necessity of Christlike holy living for pastors to a call for personal holiness in the lives of believers in the congregation. He begins with the **older men** (Gk *presbutas*). No age is specified, but the idea expressed seems to identify men who are mature and settled in their own homes and in their respective spiritual walks. Those addressed here were not pastors but rather the natural lay leaders of the congregation.

2:3-5 Older women (Gk *presbutidas*, "old or elderly women") can be understood as "spiritually mature" women who are usually older in years, immersed in faith, but most of all, well-versed in God's Word and saturated with His wisdom. They are directed to **teach** the **young women** (Gk *neas*, "new, fresh, young"), who are not necessarily young in years but are new to the faith.

2:6-8 Paul's admonition to the **young men**, as with the young women, is made with earnest entreaty, urging them to be **self-controlled**, a word that connotes caution and precludes self-interest. Here Paul found a natural opportunity to call for Titus to serve as an example for other young men in what he did as well as what he taught. Nothing is any more important to spiritual leadership than consistency in your character and life. What you teach must be exemplified in how you live.

2:9-10 Slaves were an essential part of the Roman society, especially its economy. Paul does not express approval of slavery in his comments on how Christian slaves were to relate to their masters. Rather the apostle addresses the matter of correct behavior for those who found themselves in slavery, concentrating

Self-Control Is the Key

The Group	The Dominant Character Trait	The Faithful Outworking
"older men" (2:2)	"worthy of respect"	• "level headed" • "sensible" • "sound in faith, love, and endurance"
"older women" (vv. 3-5)	"reverent in behavior"	• "not slanderers" • "not addicted to much wine" • teaching "what is good" • encouraging the young women
"young women" (vv. 4-5)	• lovers of their husbands • lovers of their children • "self-controlled" • "pure"	• good "homemakers" • "kind" • "submissive to their husbands"
"young men" (v. 6)	"self-controlled in everything"	
Titus—the pastor (vv. 1,6-8)	teaching with "integrity and dignity"	• "say the things that are consistent with "sound teaching" • "an example of good works" • "message" that is "sound beyond reproach"
"slaves" (vv. 9-10)	"demonstrating utter faithfulness"	• "submissive to their masters in everything" • "well-pleasing" • "not talking back" • not "stealing"

Engaging the Specific Field Assignment (1:12b-16)

Cretans are always liars,
evil beasts, lazy gluttons.[A]

13 This testimony is true. So, rebuke
them sharply, that they may be
sound in the faith 14 and may not pay
attention to Jewish myths and the
commands of men who reject the
truth.
15 To the pure, everything is pure,
but to those who are defiled and unbelieving nothing is pure; in fact,
both their mind and conscience are
defiled. 16 They profess to know God,
but they deny Him by their works.
They are detestable, disobedient, and
disqualified for any good work.

The Instructions for Believers (2:1-10)

2 But you must say the things that
are consistent with sound teaching. 2 Older men are to be level headed, worthy of respect, sensible, and
sound in faith, love, and endurance.
3 In the same way, older women are
to be reverent in behavior, not slanderers, not addicted to much wine.
They are to teach what is good,
4 so they may encourage the young
women to love their husbands and
to love their children, 5 to be self-
controlled, pure, homemakers,
kind, and submissive to their husbands, so that God's message will
not be slandered.
6 In the same way, encourage the
young men to be self-controlled 7 in

A 1:12 This saying is from the Cretan poet Epimenides (6th century B.C.).

everything. Make yourself an example of good works with integrity
and dignity[A] in your teaching. [8]Your
message is to be sound beyond reproach, so that the opponent will be
ashamed, having nothing bad to say
about us.

[9]•Slaves are to be submissive to
their masters in everything, and to
be well-pleasing, not talking back
[10]or stealing, but demonstrating utter faithfulness, so that they may
adorn the teaching of God our Savior
in everything.

A2:7 Other mss add *incorruptibility*

his energies on helping slaves—and masters—to live and act in Christlike ways. The important issue was how slaves and masters were to treat one another. All of the qualities associated with the Christian slave are just as appropriate in the right relationship between a Christian employee and her

BIBLICAL WOMANHOOD Spiritual Mothering

Spiritual Mothering. Mentoring relationships among women (2:3-5) have been God-ordained and profoundly effective, and this woman-to-woman teaching goes back to early Christianity where it was tried and proven. Paul describes the character of the spiritually mature women who will be teaching the younger women:

- **Reverent** (Gk *hieroprepeis*, "like people engaged in sacred duties, that which is suitable to holiness, temple-like"). Certainly this demeanor would be inclusive of dress, suggesting a godly modesty. The word calls for outward action as emanating from inner character. A woman's everyday activities are as if she were engaged in sacred duties, carrying into daily life the demeanor appropriate for the temple. In fact, the root for the word translated "reverent" is *hieron* (Gk, "temple").
- **Not slanderers** (Gk *diabōlous*, "prone to accuse others falsely, gossiping"; the noun form can refer to the Devil—e.g., 2Tm 2:26). Of course, the Devil is the great accuser and uses every opportunity to bring charges against the lives and character of believers. Spiritually mature women who are going to be leaders and teachers must not "gossip." Their words are to be encouraging and uplifting and instructive.
- **Not addicted** [Gk *dedoulōmenas*, "enslave, subject, bring into bondage"] **to much wine.** This phrase is not surprising in a letter concerning the Cretans, who were known for their drunkenness. Even in contemporary society, though, women who want to be teachers and mentors of other women are to be held to the highest standards.
- They are to **teach what is good**. The spiritually mature women are to instruct and teach what is good in character and life as well as to motivate those women who are new in the faith to live godly lives, incorporating what is good and Christlike into their own lives. The emphasis is not on formal instruction but upon the private counsel and encouragement given by word and example.

Paul then provides the curriculum for what the older women are to teach the younger women:

- **To love their husbands . . . to love their children.** Note two primary words used, *philandrous* (Gk "husband-loving") and *philoteknous* (Gk "children-loving"), which remind the reader that these are really two different assignments. You do indeed love husband and children, but your loving deeds and faithful service are offered to each in different ways. Because the woman was created to be a helper to the man before children ever arrived and because they as husband and wife begin their journey, and usually end it, without their children, for the first admonition to be for wives to love their husbands is quite fitting. But children are worthy of appropriate lessons in loving as well.
- **To be homemakers** (Gk *oikourous*, "working at home"). The emphasis is on a woman's efficient management of her household. The household is the basic unit of society and is interconnected with the church and even with the state. The proper ordering of the household—how husbands and wives as well as parents and children relate to one another—is essential to maintain order in the church and support lawfulness in the community.
- **To be submissive to their** [own] **husbands.** The word calling for submission is not demeaning. In fact, submission means to place yourself willingly under someone's authority. Submission is a choice, and the obedience mandated goes beyond human authority because the mandate comes from the heart of God Himself.

What is the importance of the ministry of spiritual mothering? Paul says that women are to teach in this way **so that God's message will not be slandered.** The surprise is in the choice of the Greek word *blasphēmētai*, which probably for some seems a bit strong. The word is transliterated into English as "blasphemy," a sin not to be taken lightly. The word does have the nuance of "slander" or more precisely "speak lightly of sacred and holy things" or "speak against God so that you cast through or make null and void God's word and His truths." Only by obedience to the divine mandate do you magnify the Lord and draw others to Him. Disobedience brings the gospel itself into disrepute and incites reproach against God's Word. *Dorothy Kelley Patterson*

A Persuasive Reason for Obedience (2:11–3:11)

The Gift of Grace in Salvation (2:11-15)

11 For the grace of God has appeared with salvation[A] for all people, 12 instructing us to deny godlessness and worldly lusts and to live in a sensible, righteous, and godly way in the present age, 13 while we wait for the blessed hope and appearing of the glory of our great God and Savior, Jesus Christ. 14 He gave Himself for us to •redeem us from all lawlessness and to cleanse for Himself a people for His own possession, eager to do good works.

15 Say these things, and encourage and rebuke with all authority. Let no one disregard[B] you.

The Outworking of Faith in Life (3:1-11)

3 Remind them to be submissive to rulers and authorities, to obey, to be ready for every good work, 2 to slander no one, to avoid fighting, and to be kind, always showing gentleness to all people. 3 For we too were once foolish, disobedient, deceived, enslaved by various passions and pleasures, living in malice and envy, hateful, detesting one another.

4 But when the
kindness of God our Savior
and His love
for mankind appeared,
5 He saved us—
not by works of righteousness
that we had done,
but according to His mercy—
through the washing
of regeneration
and renewal by
the Holy Spirit.
6 He poured out this Spirit
on us abundantly
through Jesus Christ
our Savior
7 so that, having been •justified
by His grace,
we may become heirs
with the hope of eternal life.

8 This saying is trustworthy. I want you to insist on these things, so that those who have believed God might be careful to devote themselves to good works. These are good and profitable for everyone. 9 But avoid foolish debates, genealogies, quarrels, and disputes about the law, for they are unprofitable and worthless. 10 Reject a divisive person after a first and second warning, 11 knowing that such a person is perverted and sins, being self-condemned.

Conclusion (3:12-15)

12 When I send Artemas or Tychicus to you, make every effort to come to me in Nicopolis, for I have decided to spend the winter there. 13 Diligently help Zenas the lawyer and Apollos on their journey, so that they will lack nothing.

14 And our people must also learn to devote themselves to good works for cases of urgent need, so that they will not be unfruitful. 15 All those who are with me greet you. Greet those who love us in the faith. Grace be with all of you.

[A] **2:11** Or *appeared, bringing salvation*; or *appeared with saving power* [B] **2:15** Or *despise*

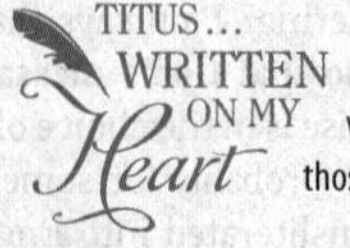

Character is written in the daily decisions you make, especially in how you are going to live your life. Do you compromise God's standards or do you champion His way as the only way for you? God urges His children to hold to what is good and teach those things that are according to sound doctrine.

employer. Excellence in the marketplace is a powerful tool for witness.

2:13 The blessed hope is the return of Jesus Christ. He came as a baby in the manger in His incarnation, assumed the form of an obedient slave, and died on a Roman cross for the redemption of man. However, when He returns, He will come in strength and victory, and that return is the next great event in redemptive history and one to which all who put their trust in Him for salvation can look with expectancy.

3:1 Again the call for submission appears, coupled with a call for obedience. If obedience to those in authority would impress earthly rulers, how much more would the heavenly Father be encouraged and glorified when believers are **submissive** and obedient to Him and His mandates. Obedience is a necessary attribute for anyone who identifies herself with Christ, and that obedience is shallow and unimpressive unless it is complete and unconditional.

3:4-7 Paul undoubtedly believed that God is the author of salvation. God initiates the process by making provision for your salvation and by drawing you to Himself. He extends His mercy; and once you accept that mercy, He completes the work of redemption. You are not saved by your own works of righteousness; rather, Christ provides His work of righteousness; and thus Paul speaks clearly, **not by works of righteousness that we had done, but according to His mercy**. Salvation, which comes through God's merciful grace, not works that come from our own imperfect and feeble efforts, makes the doing of good works possible. Good works are not possible without a right relationship to God, and a right relationship to God will produce good works as its fruit.

What then is meant by the **washing of regeneration**? David spoke of a unique kind of cleansing: "Wash away my guilt, and cleanse me from my sin" (Ps 51:2). The sweet psalmist of Israel certainly did not have reference to baptism, but his language indicates that he sought and expected to receive a cleansing from his sin. Baptismal waters, as important as they are for obedience and witness, cannot wash away sin. Rather, Jesus shed His blood on the cross, and that blood does indeed cleanse from sin.

3:10 Reject a divisive [Gk *hairetikon*, "factious, causing division"] **person.** In English the word has been transliterated as "heretical" and first came to denote self-willed opinions and eventually adapted the connotation of opinions of personal preference that produce divisions. One who decides to go his own way and in the process causes divisions may not hold false doctrine, but he does bring havoc within the assembly of believers.

3:12-13 Paul seems to indicate a changing of personnel in Crete when he calls for Titus to join him in Nicopolis, suggesting that he would send Artemis or Tychicus (see Ac 20:4; Eph 6:21; Col 4:7) to continue the work on Crete. Note the mention of the eloquent and brilliant Apollos, who had received instruction from Priscilla and Aquila in Ephesus (Ac 18:24-26).

3:14-15 Paul in his final instructions makes clear that the pastor or even a team of pastors cannot meet all the **urgent** needs of a congregation—whatever the size. He thus challenges the **people**, all believers, to arise and do **good works**. His final words are a poignant reminder to the congregation that all must be done in love and harmony, which would then draw **grace** or the unmerited favor of God Himself to all **in the faith**.

Pattern for Pastors

REQUIREMENT	INSIGHT	REFERENCE
Blameless	(Gk *anegklētos*, "irreproachable")—The word meaning "accuse" is prefixed with an alpha privative (alpha, first letter in the Greek alphabet), which negates the word. Thus, the word means non-chargeable. The pastor should stand above accusation, maintaining the highest moral character, having an untarnished reputation.	1:6
The husband of one wife	The emphasis is not that the pastor must be married, for Paul himself was single—at least at this time (whether by choice or as a widower). Rather, the emphasis is that the pastor should be a one-woman man, having taken very seriously God's plan for marriage (Gn 2:24; Mt 19:5). His marriage must also be exemplary.	v. 6
Having faithful children	(Gk *tekna echōn pista*, "having believing children")—Seemingly these children were still under their father's authority in the home. This idea was not just a physical behavior requirement but a spiritual heart condition. Above all, a pastor ought to give his energies and passion to winning his own children to faith in Christ. And his exemplary life should call forth the respect of his children.	v. 6
Not accused of wildness or rebellion	(Gk *asōtias*, "reckless living, dissipation")—This word for "wildness" was also used in Luke 15:13 to describe the lifestyle of the prodigal son. It was sometimes translated "incurable" in the sense that one was destroying his life so completely that it could not be rebuilt. "Rebellion" (Gk *anupotakta*, "undisciplined, disobedient") suggested refusal to submit to authority. Parents cannot control or dictate a child's response to God, but they are responsible for guiding the child's public behavior. It stands to reason that a child who refuses the authority of his parents or teachers would not likely honor God or submit to His mandates. No pastor should want his child's outrageous behavior to bring hurt to the church and destroy his credibility as God's servant.	v. 6
God's administrator	(Gk *oikonomon*, "steward, treasurer") — A steward managed the owner's household with responsibilities and authority assigned by the owner. The church is God's household, and pastors have been given its human oversight. They are directly accountable to God.	v. 7

(continued on next page)

Biblical Womanhood Digging Deeper into God's Word

Overwhelmingly women purchase more Bibles and more Bible study materials than men do. By all rights, just the amount of materials in the marketplace should make women the best equipped Bible students of the modern era. However, one has only to peruse those materials to see that there is a great gulf fixed between most of what is being produced by women for women and even the most basic devotional commentary. Inspirational thoughts, practical application, and systematic topical studies are all important, but women need more. Women can study the Bible in depth; they can learn to do genuine exposition or verse-by-verse interpretation of God's Word, using the best hermeneutical principles; and this study tool is a step in making available to women resources produced especially for them. Here is a clarion call to women to demand the best in biblical scholarship—even resources prepared by women and men who have been formally trained in biblical studies—and to spend the time necessary to dig deeply into God's Word and pull out its rich truths and full knowledge.

Pattern for Pastors (continued)

REQUIREMENT	INSIGHT	REFERENCE
Not arrogant	(Gk *authadē*, "self-willed, stubborn")—This compound word links the personal pronoun and the verb meaning "enjoy oneself." A pastor should be more concerned with pleasing God than himself.	v. 7
Not hot- tempered	(Gk *orgilon*, "inclined to anger")—Righteous indignation is perfectly acceptable, but there has never been a place for eruptive anger or bitter wrath, and most pastors will have many challenges that test their self-control.	v. 7
Not addicted to wine	The fermented fruit of the vine of Paul's day cannot be compared to the intoxicating alcoholic beverage of the modern-day liquor industry, which wrecks homes and takes lives. Pastors must bring even their habits into subjection to an exemplary standard.	v. 7
Not a bully	(Gk *plēktēn*, "combative person")—No believer should allow an annoyance to provoke him to violence toward another. Scripture is clear that a believer is to endure suffering with a patient spirit.	v. 7
Not greedy for money	(Gk *aischrokerdē*, "fond of dishonest gain")—Materialism grips this age, including those who serve the Lord. Doing the best for your family, providing their necessities, and working to give some extras are the happy privileges of every husband and father. However, one must guard against being pulled into a materialistic mindset where things are more important than people and God.	v. 7
Hospitable	(Gk *philoxenon*, "loving or delighting in a stranger or foreigner")—Rarely used in the New Testament, the word could be appropriate here because of the necessity for travelers to depend on local homes for accommodations, or perhaps the emphasis is on the open door such loving care would provide to share the gospel.	v. 8
Loving what is good	(Gk *philagathon*, linking the word *phileō*, "love," with the word for good)—The admonition is entreating pastors to seek and to embrace with passion the good as a springboard for all they do.	v. 8
Sensible or wise	(Gk *sōphrona*, "thoughtful, moderate, self-controlled, decent, modest")—The spiritual dimension adds to good intellectual choices a sanctifying presence that permeates all of life with wise and discerning choices of how a pastor thinks, what decisions he makes, what words he utters, and what deeds he does. No trait is more important for a pastor.	v. 8
Righteous	(Gk *dikaion*, "just")—The pastor must not only be in right standing with God, but he must also be just and fair in dealing with members of his family and congregation, whether in business or community or matters of the church.	v. 8
Holy	(Gk *hosion,* "devout, pious")—This word is not the usual New Testament word for "holy." The nuance in its meaning suggests going beyond the usual reverence for God with the idea of being accountable to God without any regulation or monitoring. How could a pastor represent God to the people if he himself is not set apart unto the Lord in a unique and all-encompassing way? His task is to model holiness and draw others to walk in the way of the Lord.	v. 8

Pattern for Pastors (continued)

REQUIREMENT	INSIGHT	REFERENCE
Self-controlled	(Gk *egkratē*, "disciplined")—Certainly a pastor must be master of himself in the sense that he commits his life and decisions to be controlled by the Holy Spirit. He moves from self-control to God-control in his own life and seeks to move all in his congregation to that model.	v. 8
Holding to the faithful message as taught	His task culminated in the mandate to cling to or hold firmly (Gk *antechomenon*, the verb meaning "have" is prefixed with the preposition "against" so that the idea is literally "to have against," suggesting that your hold is not easy but is buffeted with difficulties that are working against you). What a picture for the pastor who must hold fast and firm the teachings of Scripture in the midst of his own pressures and challenges so that he will have a "faithful message." Clearly this message is one that embodies faith and comes directly from God. It is not only free from error but imparts health and encourages growth. The apostle continues to expound on the nature of that message, using the phrase "sound teaching" (Gk *didaskalia tē hugiainousē*). The "teaching" or instruction entailed both content (OT and NT—the whole counsel of God) and action (lifestyle), and it is further described as "sound" or, more literally, "healthy." This medical term often describes someone in perfect health. No better tool could come to the pastor in his task of discounting false doctrine than to have "healthy teaching" to use in confronting error and distortions that would attack the gospel.	v. 9

Philemon

Timeline	AD 36	AD 38	AD 47	AD 50
World Events / Biblical Events	Paul's conversion on the Damascus Road	Paul's escape from death threats in Damascus and Jerusalem	Paul's narrow escape from death in Lystra	The incarceration of Paul and Silas in Philippi

"No longer as a slave, but more than a slave—as a dearly loved brother" (16a).

Who wrote Philemon?

Paul is identified as the author (v. 1).

Who were the recipients?

This semi-private letter was addressed to Philemon, a believer who opened his home as a place of worship in Colossae.

When was Philemon written?

The traditional view is that this letter was written during Paul's first incarceration in Rome A.D. 60–63 (Ac 28:30-31).

Where did it happen?

While imprisoned in Rome, Paul wrote this letter to Philemon who was living in Colossae.

What is Philemon about?

Christian fellowship. How a person treats both believers and unbelievers reflects upon the Holy Spirit who lives within and thus will affect her relationships.

Why should women read Philemon?

Even though Philemon is the shortest of Paul's letters (only 25 verses), no other epistle gives its readers a better glance at Paul's skill in handling practical problems within the family of God. A valuable lesson can be learned by studying Paul's use of tact and courtesy as he calls for Christian maturity in handling a difficult situation.

How do you read Philemon?

Paul sent the letter with Tychicus and Onesimus, a run-away slave (Col 4:7-9), to Philemon to encourage him to accept Onesimus, not as a slave but "as a dearly loved brother" (v. 16). As if you were reading a personal letter from one friend to another, you would need to understand the circumstances surrounding this personal letter in order to grasp its full significance.

Outline

I. Introductory Greeting (vv. 1-3)
II. Paul's Confidence in Philemon (vv. 4-7)
III. Paul's Intercession for Onesimus (vv. 8-22)
 A. Paul's Account of Onesimus's Conversion (vv. 8-11)
 B. Paul's Assessment of Onesimus (vv. 12-16)
 C. Paul's Solution to the Problem (vv. 17-22)
IV. Concluding Greetings (vv. 23-25)

>WORD|*study*

1 Paul identifies himself as a **prisoner** (Gk *desmios*) instead of an apostle of Christ (see Rm 1:1; 1Co 1:1; 2Co 1:1; Gl 1:1; Eph 1:1; Col 1:1, 1Tm 1:1; 2Tm 1:1) or as a slave of Christ (see Rm 1:1; Php 1:1). Only here does Paul use "prisoner" to identify himself in an epistolary greeting. By using this word or one of its derivatives four times in this short letter (vv. 1,9,10,13), clearly Paul wants to stress his present circumstances to Philemon.

1 **Coworker** (Gk *sunergō*, "helper, fellow worker"). This word is frequently used by Paul to describe those actively engaged in the ministry of the gospel.

12 Paul refers to Onesimus as **part of** himself (Gk *ta ema splagchna*, lit "my own bowels," cp. vv. 7,20). Metaphorically, Paul is describing Onesimus as his "own heart" (i.e., the source of his mercy and compassion). The apostle is asking that Onesimus be given the same reception Paul would be given if he were able to come.

15 **Permanently** (Gk *aiōnion*, "a significant period of time, illimitable duration") could also mean "eternally"—now Onesimus was his brother in Christ for the rest of eternity.

AD 54	AD 58	AD 60–62	AD 60–62	AD 62
Epaphras's planting of the church at Colossae in response to Paul's teaching in Ephesus	Paul's escape from death and subsequent imprisonment in Caesarea	Paul's house arrest in Rome, awaiting appeal to Caesar	Paul's witness to Onesimus, the runaway slave from Colossae	Tychicus and Onesimus as carriers of Paul's letters to Philemon, to the Colossians and the Laodiceans

Introductory Greeting (vv. 1-3)

Paul, a prisoner of Christ Jesus, and Timothy our brother:
To Philemon our dear friend and
coworker, 2 to Apphia our sister,[A] to
Archippus our fellow soldier, and
to the church that meets in your
home.
3 Grace to you and peace from
God our Father and the Lord Jesus
Christ.

Paul's Confidence in Philemon (vv. 4-7)

4 I always thank my God when I
mention you in my prayers, 5 because
I hear of your love and faith toward[B]
the Lord Jesus and for all the •saints.
6 I pray that your participation in the
faith may become effective through
knowing every good thing that is
in us[C] for the glory of Christ. 7 For
I have great joy and encouragement
from your love, because the hearts
of the saints have been refreshed
through you, brother.

Paul's Intercession for Onesimus (vv. 8-22)

Paul's Account of Onesimus's Conversion (vv. 8-11)

8 For this reason, although I have
great boldness in Christ to command you to do what is right, 9 I
appeal to you, instead, on the basis
of love. I, Paul, as an elderly man[D]
and now also as a prisoner of Christ
Jesus, 10 appeal to you for my son,
Onesimus.[E] I fathered[F] him while I
was in chains. 11 Once he was useless
to you, but now he is useful both to
you and to me.

Paul's Assessment of Onesimus (vv. 12-16)

12 I am sending him back to you
as a part of myself.[G,H] 13 I wanted
to keep him with me, so that in
my imprisonment for the gospel
he might serve me in your place.
14 But I didn't want to do anything

[A]2 Other mss read *our beloved* [B]5 Lit *faith that you have toward* [C]6 Other mss read *in you* [D]9 Or *an ambassador* [E]10 In Gk, Onesimus means useful. [F]10 Referring to the fact that Paul led him to Christ; 1Co 4:15 [G]12 Other mss read *him back. Receive him as a part of myself.* [H]12 Lit *you—that is, my inward parts*

CHARACTER PROFILE

Apphia Hostess for God's People

Her Background	• Mentioned with Philemon in Paul's greeting (Phm 2) • Not found elsewhere in Scripture
Her Story	• Possibly the wife of Philemon • Probably hostess for the church meeting in Philemon's home • Tradition suggests she was martyred with Onesimus, Philemon, and Archippus during the persecution of Nero
Life Lesson	A true "sister" in the faith is anchored in Christ as a fellow believer and caring friend.

Title In its shortest form, the Greek title of this epistle is *pros Philēmona*, "to Philemon." The title simply reflects the designated recipient of this letter.

2 Archippus our fellow soldier (Gk *sustratiōtē*, "comrade in arms") was a member of Philemon's household. The designation "fellow soldier" brings to mind a person who shares similar objectives and goals with another, someone who is engaged in the same conflicts and battles. Archippus may have been Philemon's son or the pastor of the church that met in Philemon's house; he was certainly prominent in the church in Colossae (see Col 4:17).

8-9 For this reason—Although Paul had certain rights that would give him great boldness to command Philemon to obey his request, he chose instead to appeal to Philemon's love for his fellow believers. Paul uses a masterful rhetorical device (see also v. 19); he tells Philemon exactly *why* he should grant his request and then tells him why he dares to deal with him so boldly—because he trusts Philemon to make the right decision. Any mother can appreciate Paul's logic and creativity in this verse. He calls himself **an elderly** [Gk *presbutēs*, "older man, aged person"] **man** and **a prisoner of Christ Jesus**, undoubtedly casting himself in a more sympathetic light through gentle self-depreciation. How could Philemon possibly say no to his request!

10 Paul appeals to Philemon on behalf of **Onesimus** whom he considered his **son** in the Lord because Paul more than likely played an instrumental role in bringing the slave to salvation. The metaphor of fatherhood expresses the endearment of Onesimus to Paul, identifying him as a son instead of a slave. Paul was teaching Philemon to renew his thinking—his slave was not only a son but also a brother in Christ. Onesimus's name was common among slaves and meant "useful or profitable."

11-14 Paul makes a play on words in saying that Onesimus was once **useless** (Gk *achrēston*, "worthless") but had become **useful** (Gk *euchrēston*, "serviceable") both to Philemon and

Paul—he could now live up to his name. By ministering to Paul, Onesimus was doing so on Philemon's behalf, and he became useful again. Paul made the generous assumption that Philemon wanted to help him; and since Philemon could not minister to Paul during his imprisonment, Onesimus could minister to him in Philemon's place.

Paul gave up his own rights and preference to give Philemon an opportunity for service. By empowering Philemon to demonstrate his maturity and love for his brothers in Christ, Paul asks Philemon to empower Onesimus with the same opportunity. To help someone make the right choice is not to enslave him but to free him.

19 Paul often used a scribe in writing his letters, but perhaps because of the deeply personal nature of this letter, he made a point to let Philemon know he wrote this letter with his **own hand**.

23 Epaphras, (per v. 23) [Gk "lovely"] **my fellow prisoner** is identified elsewhere as "our dearly loved fellow slave" (Col 1:7) and a "slave of Christ Jesus" (Col 4:12). This preacher from Colossae was instrumental in opening Colossae, Hierapolis, and Laodicea to the gospel. He was imprisoned with Paul when he came to Rome seeking Paul's help to fight against incipient Gnosticism.

24 Mark (see Ac 12:12,25; 15:37,39; Col 4:10; 2Tm 4:11; 1Pt 5:13), a Jew, was the cousin of Barnabas (Col 4:10). **Aristarchus** was a traveling companion of Paul from Macedonia (Ac 19:29). According to tradition, Nero put Aristarchus to death in Rome. **Demas**, a companion and coworker of Paul, later deserted him because Demas "loved this present world" (2Tm 4:10). **Luke**, author of the third Gospel and the book of Acts and a close friend and traveling companion of Paul's, was also with Paul shortly before his martyrdom (2Tm 4:11). Also see **Biblical Womanhood**, p. 1531.

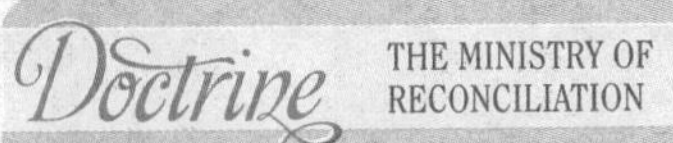

Doctrine THE MINISTRY OF RECONCILIATION

Although Paul does not state explicitly that Onesimus had run away from Philemon, this fact can be inferred through the letter's content (18). He could have faced severe punishment for his crime, yet Paul urged Philemon to exercise mercy and grace and even offered to pay any debt Onesimus owed to Philemon, setting forth a beautiful illustration of the gospel message. Paul offered to pay a debt that Onesimus could not pay in order for this slave to be reconciled with his master; Christ likewise paid sin's debt so that women and men could be reconciled with God.

without your consent, so that your
good deed might not be out of obligation, but of your own free will.
15 For perhaps this is why he was
separated from you for a brief time,
so that you might get him back permanently,
16 no longer as a •slave,
but more than a slave—as a dearly
loved brother. He is especially so to
me, but even more to you, both in
the flesh and in the Lord.[A]

Paul's Solution to the Problem (vv. 17-22)

17 So if you consider me a partner,
accept him as you would me. 18 And
if he has wronged you in any way, or
owes you anything, charge that to
my account. 19 I, Paul, write this with
my own hand: I will repay it—not
to mention to you that you owe me
even your own self. 20 Yes, brother,
may I have joy from you in the Lord;
refresh my heart in Christ. 21 Since I
am confident of your obedience, I am
writing to you, knowing that you will
do even more than I say. 22 But meanwhile,
also prepare a guest room for
me, for I hope that through your
prayers I will be restored to you.

Concluding Greetings (vv. 23-25)

23 Epaphras, my fellow prisoner
in Christ Jesus, greets you, and so
do 24 Mark, Aristarchus, Demas, and
Luke, my coworkers.

25 The grace of the Lord[B] Jesus
Christ be with your spirit.

[A] 16 Both physically and spiritually [B] 25 Other mss read *our Lord*

PHILEMON… WRITTEN ON MY *Heart* Paul's entreaty and gentle encouragement to Philemon to treat Onesimus as a brother displays a vital truth of Christianity: All believers, regardless of race, gender, social status, or economic background, are to be treated with love and respect. This small epistle echoes Christ's words, "By this all people will know that you are My disciples, if you have love for one another" (Jn 13:35).

BIBLICAL WOMANHOOD The Ministry of Hospitality

Before the third century, house churches were the most common gathering for a group of believers. Many women and men in the early church exercised the gift of hospitality to build up the body of Christ and spread the gospel.

Paul calls for Philemon's **participation** (Gk *koinōnia*, "close relationship") to be **effective** (Gk *energēs*, "powerful, efficient"; anglicized as "energetic," v. 6). "Participation" indicates both fellowship and generosity—genuine partnership.

"Effective" carries the sense of active and productive. A Christian woman's faith is infused with life and productivity as the great blessings residing in her are used for the glory of Christ, such as a ministry of hospitality. Paul identifies this faith as effective for Christ.

Paul had experienced great **joy** because of Philemon's love for his fellow Christians. He uses the word **refreshed** (Gk *anapepautai*, "cause to rest," v. 7) in regard to Philemon, a key concept appearing later in the letter as well (v. 20) and implying a time for rest or relaxation, which prepares a person to begin his labor anew. The outpouring of Philemon's great love upon his fellow believers refreshed them so that they were energized to devote themselves to the work of the kingdom. What a coveted commendation that every woman would "refresh" the hearts of fellow believers through her great love for them so that they would want to devote themselves afresh to the work of God's kingdom. Such a woman is like a cool stream in the midst of a dry desert—she has a great ministry simply because she loves her brothers and sisters as Christ would love them and she pours out her energies in ministries to them.

Hebrews

Timeline **World Events** **Biblical Events**	***2091 BC*** Abraham's response to God's call to leave his home for a land God would give him and his offspring	***2066 BC*** Sarah's pregnancy at age 90	***2046 BC*** God's test of Abraham, asking him to offer his son Isaac	***1930 BC*** Isaac's blessing of Esau and Jacob

"The Son is the radiance of God's glory and the exact expression of His nature" (1:3).

Who wrote Hebrews?

Author is anonymous with proposed writers including Paul, Luke, Apollos, Barnabas, or Silvanus.

Who were the recipients?

A persecuted group of Jewish believers were their original recipients.

When was Hebrews written?

A.D. 65–68 is the date projected.

Where did it happen?

Location for the persecuted Jewish believers addressed in the book is unknown with proposed sites Rome, Jerusalem, or Syrian Antioch.

What is Hebrews about?

- *Jesus' superiority and preeminence over everything*
- *Jesus' provision of salvation for all who believe in Him*
- *The new covenant's superiority over the old covenant*
- *The superiority of living by faith in Jesus over living by legalism*
- *The encouragement of believers to mature and persevere in their faith*

Why should women read Hebrews?

Are you ever discouraged? Do day-to-day struggles overwhelm you? Do you ever wonder, "Why is life so difficult? Why does my Christian commitment create stress? Why can't my discipleship simply consist of an easy 'to-do' list?" If you have experienced any of these attitudes, then you need to read the book of Hebrews. Its message will remind you that Jesus is God's superior answer to all of life's dilemmas. He gave Himself as a sacrifice for you and lives to intercede on your behalf. Hebrews will encourage you to persevere in faith. Above all else—don't let go of Jesus!

How do you read Hebrews?

If you understand the nature of debate, you will better understand Hebrews. In a debate, people with different, opposing opinions present their views at length and in detail. They try to persuade listeners to accept their respective positions. The author of Hebrews wrote his "message of exhortation" (13:22) or sermon to argue for the superiority of Jesus Christ over everything that came before Him. He wrote to encourage struggling Christians, some of whom had started to question the sufficiency and supremacy of Jesus.

To present his arguments most effectively, the author quoted from a reliable source—the Old Testament Scriptures. He used the Greek translation of the Old Testament, called the Septuagint (LXX). If you read your Old Testament translation to check his quotes in context, you may find some differences in wording. He also used the debate technique of arguing from the lesser to the greater (for example, from the old covenant to the new covenant). Throughout his debate the author interjected warnings about rejecting the gospel of Jesus Christ, as well as applications and exhortations to persevere in the Christian faith and to apply its truths to life's details.

Outline

I. The Superiority of the Person of Jesus (1:1–4:16)
  - A. God's Revelation Through Jesus (1:1-4)
  - B. Jesus' Superiority to the Angels (1:5-14)
  - C. Warning Against Neglecting Salvation (2:1-4)
  - D. The Glory of Jesus (2:5-18)
  - E. Jesus' Superiority to Moses (3:1–4:13)
  - F. Jesus, the High Priest (4:14-16)

II. The Superiority of the Priesthood of Jesus (5:1–10:39)
  - A. Jesus' Perfect Priesthood (5:1-10)
  - B. The Problem of Believers' Immaturity (5:11–6:20)
  - C. Jesus' Superiority to Aaron and His Likeness to Melchizedek (7:1-28)
  - D. The Superiority of Christ's New Covenant (8:1–10:39)
    1. The Nature of the New Covenant (8:1-13)
    2. The Sacrifice of the New Covenant (9:1-28)
    3. The Sufficiency of the New Covenant Sacrifice (10:1-39)

III. The Superiority of the Power of Christ (11:1–12:29)
  - A. The Great Hall of Faith (11:1-40)
  - B. A Call to Endurance (12:1-29)

IV. Concluding Remarks (13:1-25)

1859 BC	1526 BC	1446 BC	AD 33	AD 65–68
Jacob's blessing of Joseph's sons, Ephraim and Manasseh	Birth of Moses	God's covenant with Israel at Sinai	Jesus' death, resurrection, and ascension	Writing of the letter to the Hebrews

God's Revelation Through Jesus (1:1-4)

1 Long ago God spoke to the fathers by the prophets at different times and in different ways. 2 In these last days, He has spoken to us by His Son. God has appointed Him heir of all things and made the universe[A] through Him. 3 The Son is the radiance[B] of God's glory and the exact expression[C] of His nature, sustaining all things by His powerful word. After making purification for sins,[D] He sat down at the right hand of the Majesty on high.[E] 4 So He became higher in rank than the angels, just as the name He inherited is superior to theirs.

Jesus' Superiority to the Angels (1:5-14)

5 For to which of the angels did He ever say, **You are My Son; today I have become Your Father,**[F,G] or again, **I will be His Father, and He will be My Son?**[H] 6 When He again[I] brings His firstborn into the world, He says, **And all God's angels must worship Him.**[J] 7 And about the angels He says:

He makes His angels winds,[K]
and His servants[L]
a fiery flame,[M]

8 but to[N] the Son:

Your throne, God,
is forever and ever,
and the scepter
of Your kingdom
is a scepter of justice.
9 **You have loved righteousness**
and hated lawlessness;
this is why God, Your God,
has anointed You
with the oil of joy
rather than
Your companions.[O,P]

10 And:

In the beginning, Lord,
You established the earth,
and the heavens are
the works of Your hands;

[A]1:2 Lit *ages* [B]1:3 Or *reflection* [C]1:3 Or *representation*, or *copy*, or *reproduction* [D]1:3 Other mss read *for our sins by Himself* [E]1:3 Or *He sat down on high at the right hand of the Majesty* [F]1:5 Or *have begotten You* [G]1:5 Ps 2:7 [H]1:5 2Sm 7:14; 1Ch 17:13 [I]1:6 Or *And again, when He* [J]1:6 Dt 32:43 LXX; Ps 97:7 [K]1:7 Or *spirits* [L]1:7 Or *ministers* [M]1:7 Ps 104:4 [N]1:8 Or *about* [O]1:9 Or *associates* [P]1:8-9 Ps 45:6-7

>WORD|*study*

1:3 Expression (Gk *charaktēr*, "reproduction, representation," anglicized as *character*) refers to an engraved character or impression made on a seal or coin—"the very stamp." **The exact expression of His nature** means the Son's nature is the same as God the Father's (Jn 10:30).

1:3 By His Powerful word (Gk *tō rhēmati tēs dunameōs autou*) literally means "by the word of His power," specifically the spoken word, what is said with one's voice (see also 6:5; 11:3; 12:19). John's Gospel identifies Jesus as "the Word" (Gk *ho logos*) using a different noun.

1:3 Purification (Gk *katharismon*, "ceremonial cleansing") points to the defiling aspect of sin. The same word is used to describe the cleansing of lepers.

Title: Originally the letter had no title until it was given a place among collections of other apostolic letters. The oldest manuscript of the letter is titled "To the Hebrews" (Gk *pros Hebraious*).

1:1-4 This Christological passage describes the superiority of Jesus, a major theme of Hebrews. (See other Christological passages: Jn 1:1-18; Php 2:6-11; Col 1:15-20).

1:1-2 God reveals Himself to humanity and desires to be known by those whom He created. He formerly spoke, for example, through a burning bush (Ex 3:1-10), a quiet voice (1Kg 19:11-13), and visions (Nm 12:6). The prophets' ministries were important but temporary. Revelation reached its climax with the birth, life, death, and resurrection of Jesus, God's Son.

1:2-3 The author describes the greatness of Jesus, establishing the theme for the entire epistle:

- Jesus is the eternal, incarnate, and exalted Son.
- **Heir of all things**, a title of dignity, demonstrates His supreme position in the universe.
- Through Jesus **the universe** was created. God, the Creator of the world, spoke all of creation into being through the Son (Jn 1:3; 1Co 8:6; Col 1:16).
- The **Son is the radiance of God's glory**, the revelation of God's majesty. Jesus is also **the exact expression of** God's **nature**.
- Jesus sustains **all things by His powerful word**.
- Jesus made **purification for sins.** The Son came to confront the problem of humanity's sin. His priestly work in offering the ultimate sin offering forever removed the penalty of death from those who place their faith in Him.
- Sitting at God's **right hand** affirms that Jesus' saving work has been completed forever. He now occupies the seat of highest honor.

1:5-14 The writer cites seven Old Testament passages to support Jesus' superiority to the angels. He takes references originally referring to Israel's kings and applies them to Jesus, understanding Jesus as the heir to David's throne. As the **firstborn** Son of God, Jesus deserves the worship of every angel. Whereas **the angels** are God's servants, the Son is the ruler of the universe. Jesus rules with **a scepter of justice** (v. 8), a distinct characteristic of God. He despises **lawlessness** (v. 9), alluding to Jesus' earthly obedience to God. God **has anointed** His Son **with the oil of joy** (v. 9). This recalls the Old Testament ceremony in which Israel's leaders were anointed with oil as a symbol of God's presence with them as the chosen leaders of His people (see Ex 29:5-7; 1Sm 9:26–10:1). The Son created the universe and will **remain** unchanged even when creation is destroyed during the end times. The Son shares the immutable and eternal characteristics of God's nature. Jesus sits in a place of authority at the **right hand** of God. In contrast, angels are always standing or moving because they serve God. The Son has final victory over His **enemies**.

1:14 The Son reigns while angels—**ministering spirits—serve** believers. This offers hope to those enduring persecution.

2:1-4 The writer admonished his readers not to **neglect** their **great salvation** with five warning passages (3:7-19; 5:11-6:3; 10:26-31; 12:1-2,14-29). The temptation to renounce their faith and return to traditional Judaism confronted these Jewish believers. Since Jesus reigns supreme over all things, the epistle's recipients would be wise to pay careful attention to what they had learned regarding the gospel message.

2:2 The writer compares **the message spoken through angels** with the message given by the Son. If the message given by the angels **was legally binding** (Gk *bebaios*, "valid, firm, permanent, steadfast, dependable, guaranteed"), how much more respect and honor should believers give to the message delivered by God's Son? While the Old Testament does not directly state that angels were present at the giving of the Mosaic law, several New Testament passages imply it (Ac 7:53; Gl 3:19).

2:5-9 Jesus represents the ultimate fulfillment of Psalm 8. He fully satisfied God's design for human beings. Jesus is the one who was **made lower than the angels** (at the incarnation) and **crowned with glory and honor because of His suffering in death**.

2:10-11 By Jesus' humanity He is able to bring men and women **to glory**. Jesus, the source of **all things**, is **the**

>WORD|*study*

2:1 Pay even more attention (Gk *prosechein*, "care for, devote yourself to, heed, be attentive, attach oneself to, or cleave to") makes a strong admonition. The writer stresses the importance of cleaving to the gospel message and not straying from its teaching. Failure to focus on one's salvation leads to neglecting the things of God and inevitably to the temptation to sin.

11 **they will perish,**
but You remain.
They will all wear out
like clothing;
12 **You will roll them up**
like a cloak,[A]
and they will be changed
like a robe.
But You are the same,
and Your years
will never end.[B]

13 Now to which of the angels has He
ever said:

Sit at My right hand
until I make Your enemies
Your footstool?[C,D]

14 Are they not all ministering spirits
sent out to serve those who are going to inherit salvation?

Warning Against Neglecting Salvation (2:1-4)

2 We must, therefore, pay even
more attention to what we have
heard, so that we will not drift away.
2 For if the message spoken through
angels was legally binding[E] and every transgression and disobedience
received a just punishment, 3 how
will we escape if we neglect such a
great salvation? It was first spoken
by the Lord and was confirmed to
us by those who heard Him. 4 At
the same time, God also testified by
signs and wonders, various miracles,
and distributions of gifts from the
Holy Spirit according to His will.

The Glory of Jesus (2:5-18)

5 For He has not subjected to angels the world to come that we are
talking about. 6 But one has somewhere testified:

What is man
that You remember him,
or the son of man
that You care for him?
7 **You made him lower**
than the angels
for a short time;
You crowned him with glory
and honor[F]
8 **and subjected everything**
under his feet.[G]

For in **subjecting everything** to him,
He left nothing that is not subject
to him. As it is, we do not yet see
everything subjected to him. 9 But
we do see Jesus—**made lower than**
the angels for a short time so that
by God's grace He might taste death
for everyone—crowned with glory

[A]**1:12** Other mss omit *like a cloak* [B]**1:10-12** Ps 102:25-27 [C]**1:13** Or *enemies a footstool for Your feet* [D]**1:13** Ps 110:1 [E]**2:2** Or *valid*, or *reliable* [F]**2:7** Other mss add *and set him over the works of your hands* [G]**2:6-8** Ps 8:5-7 LXX

Key Old Testament Text	Explanation in Hebrews
Psalm 8:4-6	2:5-18
Psalm 95:7-11	3:7–4:13
Psalm 110:4	4:16–7:28
Jeremiah 31:31-34	8:1–10:18
Habakkuk 2:3-4	10:32–12:3
Proverbs 3:11-12	12:4-13
Exodus 19	12:18-29

>WORD|study

2:14 Shared, the word used to describe Jesus' act of sharing (Gk *meteschen* "share, participate, belong, enjoy") human nature, literally conveys the idea of "becoming partners," emphasizing that Jesus Himself, not another, became flesh on humanity's account. Jesus became partners with men and women for the purpose of saving them from the penalty of sin.

2:17 Jesus could **make propitiation** [Gk *hilaskesthai*, "make atonement for, satisfy," referring to a sacrifice that satisfies God's justice in the light of His holiness and turns away His wrath from sinners] **for the sins of the people.** As a **high priest** who shares the humanity of **His brothers**, Jesus died on the cross to provide that once-for-all atoning sacrifice. In His priestly role He displays faithfulness and mercy as He acts on believers' behalf.

and honor because of His suffering
in death.
10 For in bringing many sons to
glory, it was entirely appropriate
that God—all things exist for Him
and through Him—should make
the source[A] of their salvation perfect
through sufferings. 11 For the One
who •sanctifies and those who are
sanctified all have one Father.[B] That
is why Jesus is not ashamed to call
them •brothers, 12 saying:

I will proclaim Your name
to My brothers;
I will sing hymns to You
in the congregation.[C]

13 Again, **I will trust in Him.**[D] And
again, **Here I am with the children**
God gave Me.[E]
14 Now since the children have
flesh and blood in common, Jesus
also shared in these, so that through
His death He might destroy the one
holding the power of death—that
is, the Devil— 15 and free those who
were held in slavery all their lives
by the fear of death. 16 For it is clear
that He does not reach out to help
angels, but to help Abraham's offspring. 17 Therefore, He had to be
like His brothers in every way, so
that He could become a merciful
and faithful high priest in service[F]
to God, to make •propitiation for
the sins of the people. 18 For since
He Himself was tested and has suffered, He is able to help those who
are tested.

Jesus' Superiority to Moses (3:1–4:13)

3 Therefore, holy •brothers and
companions in a heavenly calling, consider Jesus, the apostle
and high priest of our confession;
2 He was faithful to the One who
appointed Him, just as Moses was
in all God's household. 3 For Jesus
is considered worthy of more glory
than Moses, just as the builder has
more honor than the house. 4 Now
every house is built by someone,
but the One who built everything
is God. 5 Moses was faithful as a servant in all God's household, as a testimony to what would be said in the
future. 6 But Christ was faithful as a
Son over His household. And we are
that household if we hold on to the
courage and the confidence of our
hope.[G]
7 Therefore, as the Holy Spirit
says:

Today, if you hear His voice,
8 **do not harden your hearts**
as in the rebellion,

[A]2:10 Or *pioneer*, or *leader* [B]2:11 Or *father*, or *origin*, or *all are of one* [C]2:12 Ps 22:22 [D]2:13 2Sm 22:3 LXX; Is 8:17 LXX; 12:2 LXX [E]2:13 Is 8:18 LXX [F]2:17 Lit *things* [G]3:6 Other mss add *firm to the end*

>WORD|study

3:5 Servant (Gk *therapōn*, "one who ministers willingly") is related to the verb *therapeuō*, "heal, serve," and the noun *therapeia*, "service, care," from which the English words *therapy* and *therapeutic* are derived. The term lends dignity to Moses' willing obedience to the assignments God gave him.

3:8,15 Rebellion (Gk *parapikrasmō*, "exasperate, revolt, rebel, incite one's indignation" or more literally "produce a bitter taste in the stomach," (also v. 15) is from the verb *pikrainō* and has the sense of "embitter, exasperate, make indignant, deal bitterly with, grieve." The sinful rebellion of the Israelites exasperated and grieved God. In human terms their behavior "upset His stomach."

source (Gk *archēgon*, "author, leader, ruler, prince, originator, founder, or pioneer"; see 12:2) of salvation. Jesus could lead people into salvation because He was made **perfect through sufferings**. Jesus' perfection refers to the completion of His purpose in redeeming people, reconciling them to God. By His death Jesus makes believers holy and identifies them as His brothers before the Father.

2:12-13 Three Old Testament passages support Christ's oneness with His **brothers** (v. 11). Psalm 22, a messianic psalm describing Jesus' suffering, shows Jesus' presence with the **congregation**, the gathered church. Isaiah 8:17 indicates Jesus, the Son, trusts in His Father. Isaiah 8:18 shows Jesus' union with His **children**—believers.

2:14-17 In order to deliver people from the bondage of sin, Jesus had to become **flesh and blood**. By becoming a human being, Jesus **through His death** destroyed **the one holding the power of death** that held people in captivity—**the Devil**. Similar uses of the word **destroy** (Gk *katargēsē*, "render inoperative or powerless, make ineffective, nullify, abolish, release, put an end to, do away with, deprive of power") are found in 1Co 15:24,26; Eph 2:15; 2Th 2:8; 2Tm 1:10. Death, though a reality, does not hold power over those who believe in Jesus. Death has lost its "sting" (1Co 15:55). Jesus helps **Abraham's offspring** (believers). He **does not reach out to help angels**.

2:18 Jesus **Himself** was **tested and has suffered**. He identifies with believers in their suffering and stands ready to help them when they are tested or tempted to sin and when they suffer. Jesus delivers believers from sin's power.

3:1–4:13 Judaism recognized Moses' prominence. Moses enjoyed a special relationship with God. God chose him to lead His people from Egyptian slavery into the promised land. God gave Moses the Ten Commandments and the Sinai covenant. Yet, the writer of Hebrews declares Jesus' superiority over Moses in both His person and work.

3:1 Believers should **consider**—fix their minds on—**Jesus, the apostle and high priest of our confession**. The New Testament refers to Jesus as "apostle" only in this verse. The idea that God sent Jesus on a mission, however, occurs frequently, especially in John's Gospel. The Father sent His Son as the world's Savior (1Jn 4:14). **High priest** emphasizes the sacrificial nature of that mission.

3:7-11 The author warns believers against making the same mistake the Israelites did by hardening their hearts to the Lord and acting according to their own will. He quotes Ps 95:7-11 to illustrate how the Israelites grumbled against the Lord and doubted His promise even though He had delivered them during their wilderness wanderings. As a result of their unbelief, the Israelites missed their inheritance and died outside of the promised land.

3:12-19 Brothers emphasizes that the writer is addressing believers in Jesus the Messiah. Believers must be careful to guard against an **unbelieving heart**. **Watch out** (Gk *blepete*, "see, beware") stresses the sternness of this warning. Believers are exhorted to **encourage each other daily** so that their hearts will not grow **hardened** by sin. This would help prevent the tendency to stray from God's word.

The writer describes believers as **companions** [Gk *metochoi*, "sharing in, participating with the sense of being partners or partakers"] **of the Messiah**. Christians are Christ's partners (v. 14). This privilege of serving alongside Jesus as His companion is contingent on the faithfulness of the believer. Believers must **hold firmly until the end** and not harden their hearts as the Israelites did **in the rebellion**. Unbelief kept Israel from entering God's rest. Unbelief keeps any person from entering God's rest.

4:1 Believers have **the promise** of entering God's **rest**, but they must be careful lest they **miss it** as the Israelites did. As long as the promise **remains**, people have an opportunity to enter God's rest.

4:2-3 Believers have received **the good news** (Gk *euēggelismenoi*) of future rest for God's people just as the Israelites did. This good news **did not benefit** the Israelites because of their lack of **faith**. The writer wants his readers to persevere, trusting in the promise of God, a recurring theme in Hebrews. Believers today must exercise faith in order to profit from God's promise of rest.

4:4-6 When God completed the acts of creation, He **rested** from His work (Gn 2:2-3). The writer links God's Sabbath **rest** with the "rest" that the Israelites missed in the desert. Their **disobedience** kept them from the promised rest.

4:7-11 God promises His rest to those who **do not harden** their hearts to His voice (Ps 95:7-8). Even though Joshua conquered the land promised to the Israelites, God's perfect rest still had not been fully realized. **A Sabbath rest** remains for the people of God, reached by persevering to the end and living according to His will. The writer urges believers to **make every effort**

>WORD|*study*

3:12-19 The author defines Israel's sin as having **an evil, unbelieving heart that** departs [Gk *apostēnai*, "leave someone, desert, mislead, defect, cause to rebel, fall away or withdraw from, cause to be faithless," transliterated into English as *apostasy*] **from the living God**. Some Bible scholars believe "departs" points to a departure from God by refusing to live according to His will instead of abandoning one's faith completely. God condemns and disciplines this sin. Others, however, maintain that the nature of apostasy points to unbelievers who have turned completely away from God.

on the day of testing
in the wilderness,
9 **where your fathers tested Me,**
tried Me,
and saw My works
10 **for 40 years.**
Therefore I was provoked
with that generation
and said, "They always
go astray in their hearts,
and they have not known
My ways."
11 **So I swore in My anger,**
"They will not enter
My rest."[A]

12 Watch out, brothers, so that there
won't be in any of you an evil, unbelieving heart that departs from the
living God. 13 But encourage each
other daily, while it is still called **to-**
day, so that none of you is hardened
by sin's deception. 14 For we have become companions of the •Messiah if
we hold firmly until the end the reality[B] that we had at the start. 15 As it
is said:

Today, if you hear His voice,
do not harden your hearts
as in the rebellion.[C]

16 For who heard and rebelled? Wasn't
it really all who came out of Egypt
under Moses? 17 And who was He provoked with for 40 years? Was it not
with those who sinned, whose bodies fell in the wilderness? 18 And who
did He swear to that they would not
enter His rest, if not those who disobeyed? 19 So we see that they were
unable to enter because of unbelief.

4 Therefore, while the promise to
enter His rest remains, let us
fear that none of you should miss
it.[D] 2 For we also have received the
good news just as they did; but the
message they heard did not benefit

[A] **3:7-11** Ps 95:7-11 [B] **3:14** Or *confidence* [C] **3:15** Ps 95:7-8 [D] **4:1** Or *that any of you might seem to have missed it*

Exhortations in Hebrews

Let us fear that none of you should miss [His rest].	4:1
Let us then make every effort to enter that rest.	4:11
Let us hold fast to the confession.	4:14
Let us approach the throne of grace with boldness.	4:16
Let us go on to maturity.	6:1
Let us draw near [to the sanctuary] with a true heart.	10:22
Let us hold on to the confession of our hope without wavering.	10:23
Let us be concerned about one another.	10:24
Let us lay aside every weight and the sin that so easily ensnares us.	12:1
Let us run with endurance the race that lies before us.	12:1
Let us hold on to grace.	12:28
Let brotherly love continue.	13:1
Let us then go to [Jesus] . . . bearing His disgrace.	13:13
Let us continually offer up to God a sacrifice of praise.	13:15

>WORD|study

4:1 The concept of rest (Gk *katapausin*) relates closely to its Old Testament roots. It is a reminder of the entrance of the people of Israel into Canaan (Dt 3:20; 12:10; Jos 1:13,15; 21:44; 22:4) as well as of the future rest promised to the people of God (Ps 95:11).

them, since they were not united
with those who heard it in faith[A]
3 (for we who have believed enter the
rest), in keeping with what[B] He has
said:

> **So I swore in My anger,**
> **they will not enter My rest.**[C]

And yet His works have been finished since the foundation of the
world, 4 for somewhere He has spoken about the seventh day in this
way:

> **And on the seventh day**
> **God rested**
> **from all His works.**[D]

5 Again, in that passage He says,
They will never enter My rest.[C]
6 Since it remains for some to enter
it, and those who formerly received
the good news did not enter because
of disobedience, 7 again, He specifies a certain day—**today**—speaking through David after such a long
time, as previously stated:

> **Today, if you hear His voice,**
> **do not harden your hearts.**[E]

8 For if Joshua had given them rest,
God would not have spoken later
about another day. 9 Therefore, a
Sabbath rest remains for God's
people. 10 For the person who has
entered His rest has rested from
his own works, just as God did from
His. 11 Let us then make every effort
to enter that rest, so that no one will
fall into the same pattern of disobedience.
12 For the word of God is living and
effective and sharper than any double-edged sword, penetrating as far
as the separation of soul and spirit,
joints and marrow. It is able to judge
the ideas and thoughts of the heart.
13 No creature is hidden from Him,
but all things are naked and exposed
to the eyes of Him to whom we must
give an account.

Jesus, the High Priest (4:14-16)

14 Therefore, since we have a great
high priest who has passed through
the heavens—Jesus the Son of
God—let us hold fast to the confession. 15 For we do not have a high
priest who is unable to sympathize
with our weaknesses, but One who
has been tested in every way as we
are, yet without sin. 16 Therefore
let us approach the throne of grace
with boldness, so that we may receive mercy and find grace to help
us at the proper time.

Jesus' Perfect Priesthood (5:1-10)

5 For every high priest taken from
men is appointed in service[F] to
God for the people, to offer both
gifts and sacrifices for sins. 2 He is
able to deal gently with those who
are ignorant and are going astray,
since he is also subject to weakness.
3 Because of this, he must make a sin
offering for himself as well as for the
people. 4 No one takes this honor on
himself; instead, a person is called
by God, just as Aaron was. 5 In the
same way, the •Messiah did not exalt
Himself to become a high priest, but
the One who said to Him, **You are
My Son; today I have become Your
Father,**[G] 6 also said in another passage, **You are a priest forever in the
order of Melchizedek.**[H]
7 During His earthly life,[I] He offered prayers and appeals with loud
cries and tears to the One who was
able to save Him from death, and He
was heard because of His reverence.
8 Though He was God's Son, He
learned obedience through what He

to enter that rest by believing and obeying, unlike the Israelites who fell into a **pattern of disobedience.**

4:12 The writer describes God's word as **living and effective and sharper than any double-edged sword.** Its **penetrating** power reaches the innermost part of a person's being so that it judges even **the ideas and thoughts of the heart.** God's word detects all unbelief, insincerity, and lack of faith. It is able to divide that which seems indivisible. His truth penetrates your heart, bringing sinful motives and behavior to light.

4:14-16 The writer encourages believers to approach God boldly because of what their **great high priest**—Jesus—has done for them. Jesus intercedes on their behalf and is able **to sympathize with** their **weaknesses** because He has been **tested in every way** as believers are tested. Jesus, however, was **without sin.** Unlike the priests of the Old Testament, Jesus is **the Son of God**—both human and divine. This compassionate and understanding high priest enables believers to **approach the throne of grace** confidently. God's throne is one of **grace,** extended as a result of Jesus' ultimate act of love in offering Himself as the sacrifice for sin. God gives **mercy** and grace **to help** believers **at the proper time**—when they need His help.

5:1-7 Jesus has superiority as the great **high priest** (4:14). The high priest was **called by God** (v. 4) and **taken from men** (v. 1) to serve as their representative in offering **gifts** [Gk *dōra*, "gift or present offered as an expression of honor"; cp. 8:3-4; 9:9; Mt 2:11] **and sacrifices** (Gk *thusias*; cp. Heb 7:27; 8:3; 9:9,26; 10:1,5,8,11-12,26; 11:4; 13:15-16; Eph 5:2). High priests dealt **gently** [Gk *metriopathein*, a compound of *metrios*, "measured, moderate," and *pathos*, "passion, feeling"] **with those who are ignorant and are going astray.** "Gently" conveys the picture of one who chooses not to be upset by another's errors or sins. The high priest's compassion derived from his own **weakness** (v. 2) and sin. He had to offer sacrifices first for himself before making **a sin offering** on behalf of the people (v. 3). Jesus, however, is far superior. He did not have to make an offering for His own sins, being without sin (4:15). God appointed His Son to the office of high priest, choosing Jesus to serve as the unique intercessor on behalf of all humanity **in the order of Melchizedek** (Ps 110:4). Jesus also offered prayers to God (Lk 22:39-44; 23:34-46; Jn 17) **with loud cries and tears.** God heard Him **because of His reverence,** Jesus' submission to His Father.

[A] **4:2** Other mss read *since it was not united by faith in those who heard* [B] **4:3** Or *rest), just as*
[C] **4:3,5** Ps 95:11 [D] **4:4** Gn 2:2 [E] **4:7** Ps 95:7-8 [F] **5:1** Lit *things* [G] **5:5** Ps 2:7 [H] **5:6** Gn 14:18-20; Ps 110:4 [I] **5:7** Lit *In the days of His flesh*

5:8-9 Jesus experienced the true meaning of obedience through suffering. His suffering **perfected** (Gk *teleiōtheis*, "made complete," describing the accomplishment of a goal or purpose) Him. As sinless, Jesus had no moral imperfection. He became perfect in the sense of accomplishing the purpose God had for Him. His suffering prepared Him for the role of high priest.

Jesus **became the source** [Gk *aitios*, "cause, author"] **of eternal salvation**. Salvation is eternal because it has its basis in Christ's accomplished once-for-all sacrifice, valid forever. **For all who obey Him** does not mean that believers earn their salvation by their obedience. Salvation results from faith in Christ. The outworking of that faith is obedience in daily living.

5:11-14 These verses serve as the writer's third warning to believers and concern the immaturity and sluggishness that can mark the spiritual walk. He had **a great deal to say** regarding the priesthood of Jesus (7:1–10:18). This would be **difficult to explain** because his readers had become **too lazy to understand**. He rebuked them for being so immature they were not able to teach others—that they still required **milk** instead of **solid food**. Instead of confidently holding fast to their faith in Jesus as the Messiah, they were tempted to return to the trappings of Judaism. Therefore, they needed to be trained again in **the basic principles of God's revelation**. These infants were incapable of telling others **the message about righteousness**.

6:1-2 The writer challenges his readers to press on toward spiritual **maturity** by **leaving the elementary message** about Christ. This includes six basic foundation areas.

6:9-12 Having warned them severely about of the danger of not maturing in their faith and returning to dead works, the author encourages his readers by stating his confidence in them. He trusts they will heed his warnings and persevere to the end. He reminds them that God sees their **work** and **love** and will reward them accordingly. He urges them to maintain their **diligence** as they approach **the final realization of** their **hope** and not **become lazy**. Believers can guard themselves from this danger by recalling and imitating those who have inherited the promises of God through their **faith and perseverance**.

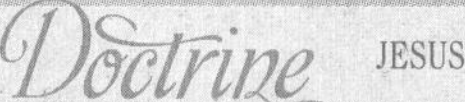

JESUS

Jesus Christ has unique qualifications to serve as High Priest. He was sinless though tempted (4:15). He was appointed by God in a different way than Aaron—after **the order of Melchizedek** (5:1,4-6). Scripture confirmed His appointment (5:4-6). Jesus **offered prayers and appeals** to God the Father (5:7). He learned obedience through suffering (5:8). He remains the source of **eternal salvation** (5:9).

suffered. 9 After He was perfected, He became the source of eternal salvation for all who obey Him, 10 and He was declared by God a high priest in the order of Melchizedek.

The Problem of Believers' Immaturity (5:11–6:20)

11 We have a great deal to say about this, and it's difficult to explain, since you have become too lazy to understand. 12 Although by this time you ought to be teachers, you need someone to teach you the basic principles of God's revelation again. You need milk, not solid food. 13 Now everyone who lives on milk is inexperienced with the message about righteousness, because he is an infant. 14 But solid food is for the mature—for those whose senses have been trained to distinguish between good and evil.

6 Therefore, leaving the elementary message about the •Messiah, let us go on to maturity, not laying again the foundation of repentance from dead works, faith in God, 2 teaching about ritual washings,[A] laying on of hands, the resurrection of the dead, and eternal judgment. 3 And we will do this if God permits.

4 For it is impossible to renew to repentance those who were once enlightened, who tasted the heavenly gift, became companions with the Holy Spirit, 5 tasted God's good word and the powers of the coming age, 6 and who have fallen away, because,[B] to their own harm, they are recrucifying the Son of God and holding Him up to contempt. 7 For ground that has drunk the rain that has often fallen on it and that produces vegetation useful to those it is cultivated for receives a bless-

[A] 6:2 Or *about baptisms* [B] 6:6 Or *while*

HARD QUESTION

Can a true Christian lose her salvation?

No. As you study Hebrews 6:4-8 within the context of the whole of Scripture, you will find that salvation in Christ is eternally secure. These verses represent the most difficult passage in Hebrews, and at least four interpretations have been offered:

- *Believers can lose their salvation*. This view contradicts other Scriptures that clearly affirm the believer's eternal security in Jesus (see Jn 5:24; 6:39,40; 10:27-29; Rm 8:28-39; Eph 4:30; 2Tm 1:12; Heb 6:19; 10:14; 1Jn 2:1; Jd 24). Salvation is God's work, not man's.
- *The writer is not addressing true believers* but people who either professed to be saved or have merely **tasted** salvation but have not actually partaken of it. However, the additional description—having **become companions** [Gk *metochoi*, "those who partake or share in"] **with the Holy Spirit**—suggests otherwise (cp. Heb 3:1,14; 12:8).
- *Believers who have **fallen away** into willful sin are in danger of losing future rewards* and becoming ineffective in their service to God.
- The writer is describing *a hypothetical situation*. In other words, *if* believers could lose their salvation, *then* it would be impossible for them to be restored to the community of faith later. Salvation is secured by Jesus' crucifixion and resurrection—an unrepeatable set of historical events (cp. Heb 6:6 and 10:12,14), and there is no salvation apart from Christ.

The imagery in Heb 6:7-8, like other biblical passages that employ similar imagery (see Mt 7:15-23; 12:33-35; 13:1-29; Jn 15:1-10; Eph 5:8-13; cp. 1Jn 1:5-10), underscores that from God's perspective, there are only two categories of people—those who have genuinely received His gift of salvation in Jesus Christ and those who have not. When you trust Christ for your salvation, you receive God's forgiveness (Eph 1:7; Col 1:14), eternal life (Jn 5:24), and His presence (the Holy Spirit; Ac 2:38; Eph 1:13); these *cannot be lost* for they are promised by God, who is faithful to keep all His promises (2Co 1:18-20).

If a woman's life produces nothing but **thorns and thistles**, genuine believers *should* help her honestly examine her spiritual status to determine whether she is an authentic Christian struggling with sin or one who has been "riding the fence"—pretending to receive the gospel but actually resisting the character-transforming power that comes with dying to self and receiving new life (see Rv 3:14-22; see **Hard Question**, p. 1462). Real Christians, who have been "born again" (another one-time event for an individual; see Jn 3:1-21) and "rescued" from sin and death (Col 1:13; cp. Ac 26:18) *eternally* belong to the Father.

>WORD|*study*

7:1-4 Melchizedek combines two Hebrew words: *melek*, "king" and *tsedeq*, "righteousness." The name means, "My king (is) righteousness," or **king of righteousness**. The Hebrew place-name Salem, like the word *shalom*, means "peace." Salem was probably an ancient name for Jerusalem. Melchizedek was also **king of peace**.

Righteousness and peace represent messianic attributes. True righteousness and peace with God come through Melchizedek's kind of priesthood. The author emphasizes Melchizedek's uniqueness by describing him as having no **genealogy**, **resembling the Son of God**, and remaining as a **priest forever**. What was said of Melchizedek applies to Jesus in a fuller, more literal sense.

ing from God. 8 But if it produces
thorns and thistles, it is worthless
and about to be cursed, and will be
burned at the end.

9 Even though we are speaking
this way, dear friends, in your case
we are confident of the better things
connected with salvation. 10 For God
is not unjust; He will not forget
your work and the love[A] you showed
for His name when you served the
•saints—and you continue to serve
them. 11 Now we want each of you to
demonstrate the same diligence for
the final realization of your hope,
12 so that you won't become lazy
but will be imitators of those who
inherit the promises through faith
and perseverance.

13 For when God made a promise
to Abraham, since He had no one
greater to swear by, He swore by
Himself:

14 **I will indeed bless you,**
and I will greatly
multiply you.[B]

15 And so, after waiting patiently,
Abraham[C] obtained the promise.
16 For men swear by something
greater than themselves, and for
them a confirming oath ends every
dispute. 17 Because God wanted to
show His unchangeable purpose
even more clearly to the heirs of
the promise, He guaranteed it with
an oath, 18 so that through two unchangeable things, in which it is impossible for God to lie, we who have
fled for refuge might have strong
encouragement to seize the hope set
before us. 19 We have this hope as an
anchor for our lives, safe and secure.
It enters the inner sanctuary behind
the curtain. 20 Jesus has entered
there on our behalf as a forerunner,
because He has become a high priest
forever in the order of Melchizedek.

Jesus' Superiority to Aaron and His Likeness to Melchizedek (7:1-28)

7 For this Melchizedek—

King of Salem, priest
of the Most High God,
who met Abraham
and blessed him
as he returned from defeating
the kings,
2 and Abraham gave him
a tenth of everything;
first, his name means
king of righteousness,
then also, king of Salem,
meaning king of peace;
3 without father, mother,
or genealogy,
having neither beginning
of days nor end of life,
but resembling the Son
of God—

remains a priest forever.

4 Now consider how great this man
was—even Abraham the patriarch
gave a tenth of the plunder to him!
5 The sons of Levi who receive the
priestly office have a command according to the law to collect a tenth
from the people—that is, from their
•brothers—though they have also
descended from Abraham.[D] 6 But
one without this[E] lineage collected
tenths from Abraham and blessed
the one who had the promises.
7 Without a doubt,[F] the inferior is
blessed by the superior. 8 In the
one case, men who will die receive
tenths, but in the other case, Scripture testifies that he lives. 9 And in

6:13-20 God's **promise to Abraham** (Gn 22:15-18) has its ultimate fulfillment in Christ and the church. God's promises have not failed. He has not changed plans. God's promise and His solemn oath—**two unchangeable things** (Heb 6:18)—confirm His purpose. God did not need to swear an **oath**. Yet, He did so to make absolutely clear to Abraham that He would fulfill the promise. God's intention constitutes a **hope**, **an anchor** that will prevent drifting away because it is **safe and secure.**

The "anchor" of a ship serves as a symbol of hope in both ancient and modern times. Hope is the anchor that holds the soul secure and enables the believer to stand firm in Christ. Such security comes in knowing that Jesus has gone before and has led the way as **a forerunner**. As priest, Jesus stepped **behind the curtain** of the inner sanctuary to intercede on **behalf** of believers.

7:1-10 The writer demonstrates how Jesus is superior to **Melchizedek** (Gn 14:18-20). He describes this man as both a **priest** and a **king**, titles also given to the Son of God. Melchizedek **blessed** Abraham, and **Abraham** responded by offering him a tithe. This encounter reinforced the superiority of Melchizedek to Abraham and thus Abraham's descendents, including **Levi**, the father of the priestly tribe and the priestly order of Aaron.

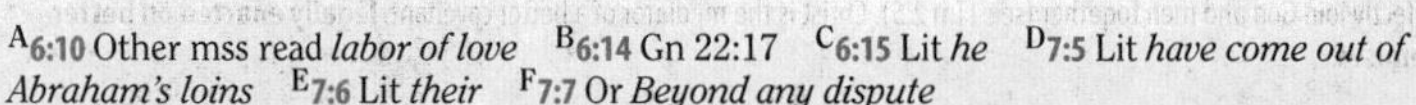

[A] 6:10 Other mss read *labor of love* [B] 6:14 Gn 22:17 [C] 6:15 Lit *he* [D] 7:5 Lit *have come out of Abraham's loins* [E] 7:6 Lit *their* [F] 7:7 Or *Beyond any dispute*

7:11-28 Christ, as a priest **in the order of Melchizedek** (vv. 11,17) and not that **of Aaron**, has a superior high priesthood beyond that of the Levitical priesthood. Jesus' work achieves **perfection** (v. 11). It is based on His **indestructible life** (v. 16) and personal character (v. 26), not upon His ancestry (vv. 11-14). The **oath** of God Himself established His priesthood (vv. 20-22,28). His priestly service is associated with a **better covenant** (v. 22). Christ's priesthood required only one priest and one sacrifice. Since **He remains forever**, He **holds His priesthood permanently** (v. 24). Jesus' superior sacrifice is **Himself** (v. 27). His **once for all** sacrifice forever met God's requirement for a blood sacrifice for sin. He saves **always** and lives eternally to **intercede** for believers (v. 25).

8:1-6 The writer demonstrates the superiority of the **true tabernacle** in heaven as compared with the tabernacle built by man. God crafted the heavenly tabernacle. The earthly tabernacle represents a **copy and shadow** of the eternal, heavenly one. The writer urges his Jewish readers to recognize the perfection of the new tabernacle. Jesus the priest offered something better than the usual **gifts and sacrifices**. He offered Himself as a sacrifice for sins. His ministry is superior. He serves as **the mediator of a better covenant**.

a sense Levi himself, who receives tenths, has paid tenths through Abraham,
10 for he was still within his ancestor[A] when Melchizedek met him.
11 If then, perfection came through the Levitical priesthood (for under it the people received the law), what further need was there for another priest to appear, said to be in the order of Melchizedek and not in the order of Aaron?
12 For when there is a change of the priesthood, there must be a change of law as well.
13 For the One these things are spoken about belonged to a different tribe. No one from it has served at the altar.
14 Now it is evident that our Lord came from Judah, and Moses said nothing about that tribe concerning priests.
15 And this becomes clearer if another priest like Melchizedek appears,
16 who did not become a priest based on a legal command concerning physical[B] descent but based on the power of an indestructible life.
17 For it has been testified:

You are a priest forever
in the order of Melchizedek.[C]

18 So the previous command is annulled because it was weak and unprofitable
19 (for the law perfected nothing), but a better hope is introduced, through which we draw near to God.
20 None of this happened without an oath. For others became priests without an oath,
21 but He became a priest with an oath made by the One who said to Him:

The Lord has sworn,
and He will not change
His mind,
You are a priest forever.[C]

22 So Jesus has also become the guarantee of a better covenant.
23 Now many have become Levitical priests, since they are prevented by death from remaining in office.
24 But because He remains forever, He holds His priesthood permanently.
25 Therefore, He is always able to save[D] those who come to God through Him, since He always lives to intercede for them.
26 For this is the kind of high priest we need: holy, innocent, undefiled, separated from sinners, and exalted above the heavens.
27 He doesn't need to offer sacrifices every day, as high priests do—first for their own sins, then for those of the people. He did this once for all when He offered Himself.
28 For the law appoints as high priests men who are weak, but the promise of the oath, which came after the law, appoints a Son, who has been perfected forever.

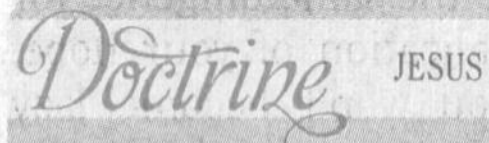

JESUS

Jesus' character qualities make Him the ideal **high priest** (7:26-28). He is **holy** (Gk *hosios*, "morally faultless or unblemished, holy, pious, devout"). He perfectly fulfills all that God requires. He can never be charged with error or impurity. Jesus is **innocent** (Gk *akakos*, "harmless; devoid of evil, guile, or guilt"). He has no guilt—unlike the Levitical priests. Jesus is **undefiled** (Gk *amiantos*, "unsoiled, stainless, untainted"). The Levitical high priest had a continuous preoccupation with ritual cleanliness. Jesus possesses total moral purity. Jesus is **separated from sinners** because He is sinless. Jesus' incomparable nature results in His exaltation above the heavens. He has been **perfected forever**.

The Superiority of Christ's New Covenant (8:1–10:39)

The Nature of the New Covenant (8:1-13)

8 Now the main point of what is being said is this: We have this kind of high priest, who sat down at

[A]7:10 Lit *still in his father's loins* [B]7:16 Or *fleshly* [C]7:17,21 Ps 110:4 [D]7:25 Or *He is able to save completely*

>WORD|*study*

8:6 Mediator (Gk *mesitēs*, "one who intervenes to restore peace or friendship, one who ratifies a covenant"; cp. 9:15; 12:24; Gl 3:19-20) is someone who stands between two parties and brings them together. While Moses, the prophets, and the priests all served as mediators between the people of Israel and God, they only reflected the true Mediator who would perfectly join God and men together (see 1Tm 2:5). Christ is the mediator of a better covenant, **legally enacted on better promises**.

the right hand of the throne of the
Majesty in the heavens, 2 a minister
of the sanctuary and the true tabernacle that was set up by the Lord
and not man. 3 For every high priest
is appointed to offer gifts and sacrifices; therefore it was necessary for
this priest also to have something to
offer. 4 Now if He were on earth, He
wouldn't be a priest, since there are
those[A] offering the gifts prescribed
by the law. 5 These serve as a copy
and shadow of the heavenly things,
as Moses was warned when he was
about to complete the tabernacle.
For God said, **Be careful that you
make everything according to the
pattern that was shown to you on
the mountain.**[B] 6 But Jesus has now
obtained a superior ministry, and to
that degree He is the mediator of a
better covenant, which has been legally enacted on better promises.
7 For if that first covenant had
been faultless, there would have
been no occasion for a second one.
8 But finding fault with His people,[C]
He says:[D]

Look, the days are coming,
says the Lord,
when I will make
a new covenant
with the house of Israel
and with the house
of Judah—
9 **not like the covenant**
that I made
with their ancestors
on the day I took them
by their hands
to lead them out of the land
of Egypt.
I disregarded them,
says the Lord,
because they did not continue
in My covenant.
10 **But this is the covenant**
that I will make
with the house of Israel
after those days,
says the Lord:
I will put My laws
into their minds
and write them
on their hearts.
I will be their God,
and they will be My people.
11 **And each person**
will not teach
his fellow citizen,[E]
and each his brother, saying,
"Know the Lord,"
because they will all
know Me,
from the least to the greatest
of them.
12 **For I will be merciful**
to their wrongdoing,
and I will never again
remember their sins.[F,G]

13 By saying, **a new covenant**, He has
declared that the first is old. And
what is old and aging is about to
disappear.

The Sacrifice of the New Covenant (9:1-28)

9 Now the first covenant also had
regulations for ministry and
an earthly sanctuary. 2 For a tabernacle was set up, and in the first
room, which is called the holy place,
were the lampstand, the table, and
the presentation loaves. 3 Behind
the second curtain, the tabernacle
was called the most holy place. 4 It
contained the gold altar of incense
and the ark of the covenant, covered with gold on all sides, in which
there was a gold jar containing the
manna, Aaron's staff that budded,
and the tablets of the covenant.
5 The •cherubim of glory were above
it overshadowing the •mercy seat. It
is not possible to speak about these
things in detail right now.
6 With these things set up this way,
the priests enter the first room repeatedly, performing their ministry.
7 But the high priest alone enters the
second room, and he does that only
once a year, and never without blood,
which he offers for himself and for
the sins of the people committed
in ignorance. 8 The Holy Spirit was
making it clear that the way into the
most holy place had not yet been disclosed while the first tabernacle was
still standing. 9 This is a symbol for
the present time, during which gifts
and sacrifices are offered that cannot
perfect the worshiper's conscience.

8:7-13 The Mosaic covenant was not wrong but limited. Jeremiah 31:31-34, quoted in verses 8-12, indicates that the people's sin caused the limitations of the Mosaic covenant and reveals the superiority of the **new covenant**. God made both old and new covenants **with the house of Israel**. Paul explains the inclusion of the Gentiles into the new covenant (Rm 11:23-24). All believers—Jews and Gentiles—receive the blessings and promises of the new covenant. The Mosaic covenant was based on the law. Its blessings depended on the people's obedience. The new covenant, however, is based on grace. The new covenant emphasizes an inward, personal relationship with God, as opposed to external rule-keeping. The Mosaic covenant was written on tablets of stone, whereas the new covenant is written on the hearts and minds of those who follow God. The new covenant provides forgiveness of sins. Consequently, the **first** covenant is **old, aging**, and **about to disappear**.

9:1-28 The author compares the **regulations** and practices of worship under the Mosaic covenant with Jesus' fulfillment in the new covenant, emphasizing the latter's superiority.

9:1-10 The writer briefly describes the **earthly. . . . tabernacle** (see details in Ex 25–40). This structure was not permanent and provided only limited access to God. The physical arrangement demonstrated the separation between God and sinners. The **high priest** alone was able to enter the most holy place **only once a year** on the Day of Atonement. He could **never** enter **without blood** offered to God for his and the people's **sins . . . committed in ignorance**. The old covenant's sacrificial system could not **perfect the worshiper's conscience**. Such inner defilement prevented fellowship with God. These external rituals and ceremonies had a place **until the time of restoration** or the time of the new covenant inaugurated through the person of Jesus.

[A]**8:4** Other mss read *priests* [B]**8:5** Ex 25:40 [C]**8:8** Lit *with them* [D]**8:8** Other mss read *finding fault, He says to them* [E]**8:11** Other mss read *neighbor* [F]**8:12** Other mss add *and their lawless deeds* [G]**8:8-12** Jr 31:31-34

9:16-23 The promise of an eternal inheritance prompted the writer of Hebrews to consider **a will** (Gk *diathēkē*, the same word rendered "covenant" in previous verses). In the legal sense Jesus wrote all believers' names in His will for eternal life. A will, however, can become effective only upon the death of the one making the will. Jesus died and paid the price with His blood for believers to inherit eternal life. The old covenant was also sealed in blood—animal's blood. A ceremony of sprinkling the sacrificial blood **inaugurated** and established the old covenant. God required **the shedding of blood** for the **forgiveness** of sin (Lv 17:11). The writer proves the superiority of the new covenant by noting it was established **with better sacrifices**.

9:24-28 Jesus, the high priest, fulfilled the new covenant when He entered once and for all the eternal sanctuary and ministered on believers' behalf, representing them before God. He does not stand in the earthly holy of holies but **in the presence of God** in heaven. Jesus' sacrifice for sin was **offered once** and does not have to be repeated.

10:1-4 If perfection had been possible under the old covenant, then the sacrifices would have ceased. Even after making sacrifices, the people still had a **consciousness of sins**. Animal sacrifices provided a provisional atonement, but individuals still possessed an unpaid debt. The Messiah and His perfect sacrifice alone could pay the debt in full.

10:5-10 The writer interprets Ps 40:6-8 as a messianic passage. It declares the ultimate ineffectiveness of sin offerings and the anticipation of One who would fulfill God's will by satisfying the payment for sin forever. The words **prepared** (Gk *katērtisō*, "made, created, put in order, restore, make sufficient, fit or shaped for") and **body** (Gk *sōma*) refer to Jesus' incarnation. As a human being, Jesus came to achieve the will of God by perfecting those who worship under the new covenant. God sent Jesus for the purpose of redeeming mankind. He completed His mission perfectly and completely.

10:11-18 Jesus' obedient sacrifice of Himself **sanctified** believers (10:10,14). This sanctification is an accomplished, completed action because Jesus **has perfected** (Gk *teteleiōken*, "made perfect or complete") believers **forever** (10:14). The Greek perfect tense of "perfected" and "sanctified" indicates an action completed in the past with ongoing effects. The sacrifices of the Levitical priests had no continuing results. Jesus' seat **at the right hand of God** signals the decisiveness of His sacrifice. The resulting **forgiveness** of sins under

10 They are physical regulations and only deal with food, drink, and various washings imposed until the time of restoration.

11 But the •Messiah has appeared, high priest of the good things that have come.[A] In the greater and more perfect tabernacle not made with hands (that is, not of this creation), 12 He entered the most holy place once for all, not by the blood of goats and calves, but by His own blood, having obtained eternal •redemption. 13 For if the blood of goats and bulls and the ashes of a young cow, sprinkling those who are defiled, sanctify for the purification of the flesh, 14 how much more will the blood of the Messiah, who through the eternal Spirit offered Himself without blemish to God, cleanse our[B] consciences from dead works to serve the living God?

15 Therefore, He is the mediator of a new covenant,[C] so that those who are called might receive the promise of the eternal inheritance, because a death has taken place for redemption from the transgressions committed under the first covenant. 16 Where a will exists, the death of the one who made it must be established. 17 For a will is valid only when people die, since it is never in force while the one who made it is living. 18 That is why even the first covenant was inaugurated with blood. 19 For when every command had been proclaimed by Moses to all the people according to the law, he took the blood of calves and goats, along with water, scarlet wool, and hyssop, and sprinkled the scroll itself and all the people, 20 saying, **This is the blood of the covenant that God has commanded for you.**[D] 21 In the same way, he sprinkled the tabernacle and all the articles of worship with blood. 22 According to the law almost everything is purified with blood, and without the shedding of blood there is no forgiveness.

23 Therefore it was necessary for the copies of the things in the heavens to be purified with these sacrifices, but the heavenly things themselves to be purified with better sacrifices than these. 24 For the Messiah did not enter a sanctuary made with hands (only a model[E] of the true one) but into heaven itself, so that He might now appear in the presence of God for us. 25 He did not do this to offer Himself many times, as the high priest enters the sanctuary yearly with the blood of another. 26 Otherwise, He would have had to suffer many times since the foundation of the world. But now He has appeared one time, at the end of the ages, for the removal of sin by the sacrifice of Himself. 27 And just as it is appointed for people to die once—and after this, judgment—28 so also the Messiah, having been offered once to bear the sins of many, will appear a second time, not to bear sin, but[F] to bring salvation to those who are waiting for Him.

The Sufficiency of the New Covenant Sacrifice (10:1-39)

10 Since the law has only a shadow of the good things to come, and not the actual form of those realities, it can never perfect the worshipers by the same sacrifices they continually offer year after year. 2 Otherwise, wouldn't they have stopped being offered, since the worshipers, once purified, would no longer have any consciousness of sins? 3 But in the sacrifices there is a reminder of sins every year. 4 For it is impossible for the blood of bulls and goats to take away sins.

5 Therefore, as He was coming into the world, He said:

You did not want sacrifice
and offering,
but You prepared a body
for Me.
6 **You did not delight**
in whole burnt offerings
and sin offerings.
7 **Then I said, "See—**
it is written about Me
in the volume of the scroll—
I have come to do Your will,
God!"[G]

8 After He says above, **You did not**

[A]9:11 Other mss read *that are to come* [B]9:14 Other mss read *your* [C]9:15 The Gk word used here and in vv. 15-18 can be translated covenant, will, or testament. [D]9:20 Ex 24:8 [E]9:24 Or *antitype*, or *figure* [F]9:28 Lit *time, apart from sin,* [G]10:5-7 Ps 40:6-8

want or delight in sacrifices and of-
ferings, whole burnt offerings and
sin offerings (which are offered according to the law), 9 He then says,
See, I have come to do Your will.[A]
He takes away the first to establish
the second. 10 By this will of God, we
have been •sanctified through the
offering of the body of Jesus Christ
once and for all.
11 Every priest stands day after day
ministering and offering the same
sacrifices time after time, which can
never take away sins. 12 But this man,
after offering one sacrifice for sins
forever, sat down at the right hand
of God. 13 He is now waiting until
His enemies are made His footstool.
14 For by one offering He has perfected forever those who are sanctified.
15 The Holy Spirit also testifies to us
about this. For after He says:

16 **This is the covenant**
I will make with them
after those days,
says the Lord:
I will put My laws
on their hearts
and write them
on their minds,

17 He adds:

I will never again remember
their sins and
their lawless acts.[B]

18 Now where there is forgiveness of
these, there is no longer an offering
for sin.
19 Therefore, •brothers, since we
have boldness to enter the sanctuary through the blood of Jesus, 20 by
a new and living way He has opened
for us through the curtain (that is,
His flesh), 21 and since we have a
great high priest over the house of
God, 22 let us draw near with a true
heart in full assurance of faith, our
hearts sprinkled •clean from an evil
conscience and our bodies washed
in pure water. 23 Let us hold on to the
confession of our hope without wavering, for He who promised is faithful. 24 And let us be concerned about
one another in order to promote
love and good works, 25 not staying
away from our worship meetings, as
some habitually do, but encouraging each other, and all the more as
you see the day drawing near.
26 For if we deliberately sin after receiving the knowledge of the truth,
there no longer remains a sacrifice
for sins, 27 but a terrifying expectation of judgment and the fury of a
fire about to consume the adversaries. 28 If anyone disregards Moses'
law, he dies without mercy, based on
the testimony of two or three witnesses. 29 How much worse punishment do you think one will deserve
who has trampled on the Son of
God, regarded as profane[C] the blood
of the covenant by which he was
sanctified, and insulted the Spirit of
grace? 30 For we know the One who
has said, **Vengeance belongs to Me,**
I will repay,[D,E] and again, **The Lord**
will judge His people.[F] 31 It is a terrifying thing to fall into the hands of
the living God!
32 Remember the earlier days
when, after you had been enlightened, you endured a hard struggle

A10:9 Other mss add *God* B10:16-17 Jr 31:33-34 C10:29 Or *ordinary* D10:30 Other mss add *says* *the Lord* E10:30 Dt 32:35 F10:30 Dt 32:36

the new covenant means no further **offering for sin** is necessary.

10:19-21 Verse 19 marks the beginning of the practical division of Hebrews. The writer concludes his discussion on the priesthood and ministry of Jesus. Now the focus turns to the implications of His work.

10:26-31 The writer issues a strong warning against the danger of apostasy. This section has parallels to 6:1-6. Those who have received **the knowledge of the truth** but who continue to sin **deliberately** can expect a **terrifying** display of **judgment**. "Deliberately" highlights the seriousness of willfully sinning. By intentionally sinning one rejects the truth of God and therefore insults the sacrifice of Jesus. Renouncing the efficacious sacrifice of Jesus removes any other sacrifice that can save one from God's ultimate judgment. If the punishment was severe under the old covenant, imagine how much more severe it is under the new covenant. This rejection results in judgment (10:27,30), punishment (10:29), and death (10:28).

Apostasy includes three indictments: trampling the Son of God, profaning His blood, and insulting the Spirit of grace. **Has trampled** (Gk *katapatēsas*, "tread upon, treat with disdain") implies insulting or spurning the Son of God. This means rebellion against God. Profaning the **blood of the covenant** signifies treating the Son's blood as common or cheap. Treating shamefully the Spirit who dispenses God's grace disregards the respect due the Holy Spirit.

10:32-39 Those who stand fast, remain true, exercise confidence in God, and press on in faith will **obtain life** from the returning Lord.

>WORD|*study*

10:13 Jesus is waiting (Gk *ekdechomenos*, "expecting, awaiting, looking for, receiving") for **His enemies** to be made His footstool (Gk *hupopodion*, lit "under foot"). The ancient conqueror demonstrated victory by placing his foot on the conquered enemy's neck. Christ will demonstrate victory over His enemies by subjecting them to His power.

10:20 The new . . . way (Gk *prosphaton*, meaning "freshly slain" or "recently made new") is used only here in the New Testament, drawing attention to the fresh access that believers have to God compared with that found in the old covenant.

10:24 To promote (Gk *paroxusmon*, "provoking, encouraging, sharp disagreement" or even "incite, urge, spur on or sharpen") implies stimulating something to action. The word suggests that individuals must work at loving others in such a way that they are stimulated to demonstrate this love in tangible ways.

11:1-3 The author defines **faith** using the words **reality** (Gk *hupostasis*, lit "that which stands under") and **proof** (Gk *elegchos*). Faith serves as the foundation for the Christian life and results in a life that persists in trusting in God. Faith is confidence in God's promises despite circumstances or consequences and results in a life of faithfulness and perseverance.

11:11-12 Abraham's wife Sarah is the first woman referenced in the "hall of faith." The writer sets her faith apart from her husband's by the words **even Sarah herself**. Well **past the age** of childbearing, Sarah believed God's promise that she would bear a child and that from him would come **offspring as numerous as the stars of heaven**. Although Sarah initially laughed upon hearing the news that she would bear a child, her disbelief eventually turned to faith before the birth of her son Isaac (Gn 18:12). Sarah evidenced a changed attitude. She shared in God's blessings with Abraham. The biblical texts revere her as a godly woman, both in her faith and submission to the Lord and in her submission to her husband.

11:13-16 By faith the Old Testament saints described in verses 4-12 **saw** the promises made to them only **from a distance.** Yet, they pressed on, desiring their heavenly inheritance. Although they did not receive the promises while they lived, they still believed these promises would be fulfilled. The patriarchs never obtained a **homeland** (Gk *patrida*, "fatherland, one's native country, permanent abode") on earth during their lifetime. Instead they considered themselves as **temporary residents** on the earth. God honored their faithfulness and **is not ashamed to be called their God**.

11:23 The writer does not give the name of the second woman mentioned among these champions of faith—Jochebed, the mother of **Moses** (Ex 6:20). He mentions the faith of **his parents** in hiding their baby because they trusted in God's protection. They walked in faith, not **fear**. God rewarded this mother's faith by arranging for Jochebed to nurse and teach Moses until he was weaned, at the age of three or four in the ancient world.

11:31 Rahab, the third woman named in the hall of faith, is especially noteworthy since she was a Gentile and a **prostitute**. This immoral woman risked her life for the people of Israel and identified herself with the God of Israel. Rahab declared her own personal faith in Israel's God to **the spies** and the conviction that the Lord God of Israel had given them the land to conquer (Jos 2:8-11). As a result, she **didn't perish** with those in Jericho.

with sufferings. 33 Sometimes you were publicly exposed to taunts and afflictions, and at other times you were companions of those who were treated that way. 34 For you sympathized with the prisoners[A] and accepted with joy the confiscation of your possessions, knowing that you yourselves have a better and enduring possession.[B] 35 So don't throw away your confidence, which has a great reward. 36 For you need endurance, so that after you have done God's will, you may receive what was promised.

37 For yet in **a very little while,**
the Coming One will come
and not delay.
38 **But My righteous one**[C]
will live by faith;
and if he draws back,
I have no pleasure in him.[D]

39 But we are not those who draw back and are destroyed, but those who have faith and obtain life.

The Great Hall of Faith (11:1-40)

11 Now faith is the reality[E] of what is hoped for, the proof[F] of what is not seen. 2 For our ancestors won God's approval by it.

3 By faith we understand that the universe was[G] created by God's command,[H] so that what is seen has been made from things that are not visible.

4 By faith Abel offered to God a better sacrifice than Cain did. By faith he was approved as a righteous man, because God approved his gifts, and even though he is dead, he still speaks through his faith.

5 By faith Enoch was taken away so he did not experience death, and **he was not to be found because God took him away.**[I] For prior to his removal he was approved, since he had pleased God. 6 Now without faith it is impossible to please God, for the one who draws near to Him must believe that He exists and rewards those who seek Him.

7 By faith Noah, after he was warned about what was not yet seen and motivated by godly fear, built an ark to deliver his family. By faith he condemned the world and became an heir of the righteousness that comes by faith.

8 By faith Abraham, when he was called, obeyed and went out to a place he was going to receive as an inheritance. He went out, not knowing where he was going. 9 By faith he stayed as a foreigner in the land of promise, living in tents with Isaac and Jacob, coheirs of the same promise. 10 For he was looking forward to the city that has foundations, whose architect and builder is God.

11 By faith even Sarah herself, when she was unable to have children, received power to conceive offspring, even though she was past the age, since she[J] considered that the One who had promised was faithful. 12 Therefore from one man—in fact, from one as good as dead—came offspring as numerous as the stars of heaven and as innumerable as the grains of sand by the seashore.

13 These all died in faith without having received the promises, but they saw them from a distance, greeted them, and confessed that they were foreigners and temporary residents on the earth. 14 Now those who say such things make it clear that they are seeking a homeland. 15 If they were thinking about where they came from, they would have had an opportunity to return. 16 But they now desire a better place—a heavenly one. Therefore God is not ashamed to be called their God, for He has prepared a city for them.

17 By faith Abraham, when he was tested, offered up Isaac. He received the promises and he was offering his unique son, 18 the one it had been said about, **Your •seed will be traced**[K] **through Isaac.**[L] 19 He considered God to be able even to raise someone from the dead, and as an illustration,[M] he received him back.

[A] **10:34** Other mss read *sympathized with my imprisonment* [B] **10:34** Other mss add *in heaven* [C] **10:38** Other mss read *the righteous one* [D] **10:37-38** Is 26:20 LXX; Hab 2:3-4 [E] **11:1** Or *assurance* [F] **11:1** Or *conviction* [G] **11:3** Or *the worlds were*, or *the ages were* [H] **11:3** Or *word* [I] **11:5** Gn 5:21-24 [J] **11:11** Or *By faith Abraham, even though he was past age—and Sarah herself was barren—received the ability to procreate since he* [K] **11:18** Lit *called* [L] **11:18** Gn 21:12 [M] **11:19** Or *a foreshadowing*, or *a parable*, or *a type*

20 By faith Isaac blessed Jacob and
Esau concerning things to come.
21 By faith Jacob, when he was dying,
blessed each of the sons of Joseph,
and **he worshiped, leaning on the
top of his staff.**[A] 22 By faith Joseph,
as he was nearing the end of his life,
mentioned the exodus of the Israelites and gave instructions concerning his bones.

23 By faith, after Moses was born,
he was hidden by his parents for
three months, because they saw
that the child was beautiful, and
they didn't fear the king's edict. 24 By
faith Moses, when he had grown
up, refused to be called the son of
Pharaoh's daughter 25 and chose to
suffer with the people of God rather
than to enjoy the short-lived pleasure of sin. 26 For he considered the
reproach because of the •Messiah to
be greater wealth than the treasures
of Egypt, since his attention was on
the reward.

27 By faith he left Egypt behind,
not being afraid of the king's anger,
for Moses persevered as one who
sees Him who is invisible. 28 By faith
he instituted the •Passover and the
sprinkling of the blood, so that the
destroyer of the firstborn might not
touch the Israelites. 29 By faith they
crossed the Red Sea as though they
were on dry land. When the Egyptians attempted to do this, they were
drowned.

30 By faith the walls of Jericho fell
down after being encircled by the Israelites for seven days. 31 By faith Rahab the prostitute received the spies
in peace and didn't perish with those
who disobeyed.

32 And what more can I say? Time
is too short for me to tell about
Gideon, Barak, Samson, Jephthah,
David, Samuel, and the prophets,
33 who by faith conquered kingdoms, administered justice, obtained
promises, shut the mouths of lions,
34 quenched the raging of fire, escaped the edge of the sword, gained
strength after being weak, became
mighty in battle, and put foreign
armies to flight. 35 Women received
their dead—they were raised to life
again. Some men were tortured,
not accepting release, so that they
might gain a better resurrection,
36 and others experienced mockings
and scourgings, as well as bonds and
imprisonment. 37 They were stoned,[B]
they were sawed in two, they died
by the sword, they wandered about
in sheepskins, in goatskins, destitute, afflicted, and mistreated. 38 The
•world was not worthy of them. They
wandered in deserts and on mountains, hiding in caves and holes in
the ground.

39 All these were approved through
their faith, but they did not receive
what was promised, 40 since God had
provided something better for us, so
that they would not be made perfect
without us.

A Call to Endurance (12:1-29)

12 Therefore, since we also have
such a large cloud of witnesses
surrounding us, let us lay aside every weight and the sin that so easily ensnares us. Let us run with
endurance the race that lies before
us, 2 keeping our eyes on Jesus,[C] the
source and perfecter[D] of our faith,
who for the joy that lay before Him[E]
endured a cross and despised the
shame and has sat down at the right
hand of God's throne.

3 For consider Him who endured
such hostility from sinners against
Himself, so that you won't grow

[A]**11:21** Gn 47:31 [B]**11:37** Other mss add *they were tempted* [C]**12:2** Or *us, looking to Jesus* [D]**12:2** Or *the founder and completer* [E]**12:2** Or *who instead of the joy lying before Him*; that is, the joy of heaven

>WORD|*study*

12:1-4 Keeping (Gk *aphorōntes*, derived from *apo*, a prefix denoting "separation," and *horaō*, "see") carries the meaning of turning one's sight *away from* what originally held the attention *to* something else. This term signifies concentrated attention, not a mere gaze. It describes an intense looking with the focus squarely on the object at hand. Believers should focus on Jesus.

12:1 The New Testament usually ascribes endurance (Gk *hupomonēs*, "steadfastness," lit the act of "remaining under") to the believer who remains undeterred from loyalty to Christ despite great trials and suffering. The purpose of endurance is to do the will of God (10:36).

James mentioned her favorably as an example to follow because her **faith** was not without works (Jms 2:25). Rahab's lineage included Boaz, the godly husband of Ruth; David, the great king of Israel; and Jesus Christ, the Savior of the world. God granted her a lasting legacy.

11:32-40 Having mentioned only faithful men and women from Genesis to Joshua, the writer begins to summarize the stories of other known heroes of the faith. He lists six more faith champions by name—four judges (**Gideon, Barak, Samson, Jephthah**), a king (**David**), and a prophet (**Samuel**)—**and the prophets**. Then the author enumerates many things they and others encountered and endured as they walked by faith in God. Some **conquered kingdoms** (David), while others **shut the mouths of lions** (Daniel). Others **were stoned** (Zechariah) for their commitment to God. The writer attested **the world was not worthy** of these heroes of the faith (v. 38). Though they were **approved through their faith**, they had not yet received what had been **promised** to them through the Messiah (v. 39). They longed for Him, believed in Him, and yet did not live to see His appearance. They would receive their rewards with Christian believers.

12:1-4 The writer exhorts his readers by comparing the Christian life to a race. The runners are surrounded by **a large crowd of witnesses** (Gk *marturōn*; source of the English word "martyr"), including the heroes of the faith identified in chapter 11, who cheer for believers as they run. These heroes are not merely spectators but are those who testify from their own experience in the Christian walk. Believers who **run with endurance** (Gk *hupomonēs*; see **Word Study** below) must take three actions. First, they must find encouragement and inspiration in the examples of the champions of faith. Second, they must **lay aside every weight and the sin that so easily ensnares** them. **Ensnares** (Gk *euperistaton*, combining *eu*, "well done"; *peri*, "around"; *histēmi*, "set, stand, establish"—"skillfully or effectively surrounding, besetting, easily encompassing") conveys the idea of taking off a long heavy robe that would prevent running. In the same way believers must remove everything—especially sin—that would hinder them from running with endurance. The author does not visualize a short sprint but a long-distance **race** requiring determined persistence to continue to the finish. Finally, believers must keep their **eyes on Jesus**.

Jesus is the ultimate example of one who ran with endurance. He displayed a life of complete faithfulness to God despite the humiliation and suffering He **endured** on the **cross.** He is **the source** [Gk *archēgon*; see 2:10] **and perfecter of our faith.** Jesus kept His eyes fixed on **the joy** set before Him. As a result of His faithful obedience, He has **sat down at the right hand of God's throne**, a phrase the writer uses several times to note Jesus' triumphant position and completed work upon the cross (1:3; 8:1; 10:12). His endurance under such circumstances should encourage believers to continue to run and not to **grow weary and lose heart**. Unlike Jesus, the readers had **not yet resisted to the point of shedding** their **blood.**

12:5-12 God uses the **suffering** of believers to **discipline** them as His children. Discipline testifies to the position of believers as members of God's family and His love for them. Those who do not receive discipline are considered **illegitimate children and not sons.** God's correcting discipline enables believers to **share His holiness** and produces **peace and righteousness** in their lives. Believers should respond toward discipline with a renewed resolve to persevere. Returning to the racing illustration, the writer exhorted his readers to **strengthen** their **tired hands and weakened knees.**

12:15 Believers should avoid any **root of bitterness.** This attitude comes from intense hostility and resentment. This bitter root produces diseased fruit, such as jealousy, anger, conflict, and immorality. A spirit of bitterness could also infect others. Recognizing God's grace in their lives helps believers overcome bitterness. Knowing they have received His forgiveness should encourage believers to extend that forgiveness to others.

12:16-17 Esau serves as an example of one who fell short of or abandoned God's grace. As an **immoral or irreverent** person, Esau showed contempt for his spiritual privileges. He forfeited his **blessing**, exchanging it for **one meal.** Immediate gratification took precedence over his privileges as the firstborn. Once he realized what he had done, it was too late. (See Gn 25:27-32.) Believers should guard against becoming bitter about their sufferings. This could result in falling short of God's grace.

12:18-24 The writer contrasts the delivery of God's law to the people of Israel to the new covenant—from shadow to reality. When discouragement comes and endurance in the race of faith seems impossible, believers find encouragement by meditating on the glories of heaven.

>WORD|*study*

12:5-13 Discipline (Gk *paideias*, referring to a child's overall "education and training—of mind, morals, and body") has the sense not only of instruction but also of correction, scolding, and of parents' punishment of their children.

weary and lose heart. 4 In struggling
against sin, you have not yet resisted
to the point of shedding your blood.
5 And you have forgotten the exhortation that addresses you as sons:

My son, do not take
the Lord's discipline lightly
or faint when you are
reproved by Him,
6 **for the Lord disciplines**
the one He loves
and punishes every son
He receives.[A]

7 Endure suffering as discipline: God
is dealing with you as sons. For what
son is there that a father does not discipline? 8 But if you are without discipline—which all[B] receive[C]—then
you are illegitimate children and
not sons. 9 Furthermore, we had
natural fathers discipline us, and we
respected them. Shouldn't we submit even more to the Father of spirits and live? 10 For they disciplined
us for a short time based on what
seemed good to them, but He does it
for our benefit, so that we can share
His holiness. 11 No discipline seems
enjoyable at the time, but painful.
Later on, however, it yields the fruit
of peace and righteousness to those
who have been trained by it.
12 Therefore strengthen your tired
hands and weakened knees, 13 and
make straight paths for your feet, so
that what is lame may not be dislocated[D] but healed instead.
14 Pursue peace with everyone, and
holiness—without it no one will see
the Lord. 15 Make sure that no one
falls short of the grace of God and
that no root of bitterness springs
up, causing trouble and by it, defiling many. 16 And make sure that
there isn't any immoral or irreverent person like Esau, who sold his
birthright in exchange for one meal.
17 For you know that later, when he
wanted to inherit the blessing, he
was rejected because he didn't find
any opportunity for repentance,
though he sought it with tears.
18 For you have not come to what
could be touched, to a blazing fire, to
darkness, gloom, and storm, 19 to the
blast of a trumpet, and the sound of
words. (Those who heard it begged
that not another word be spoken to
them, 20 for they could not bear what
was commanded: **And if even an ani-**
mal touches the mountain, it must
be stoned![E] 21 The appearance was so
terrifying that Moses said, **I am terri-**
fied and trembling.[F]) 22 Instead, you
have come to Mount •Zion, to the city
of the living God (the heavenly Jerusalem), to myriads of angels in festive
gathering, 23 to the assembly of the
firstborn whose names have been
written[G] in heaven, to God who is
the Judge of all, to the spirits of righteous people made perfect, 24 to Jesus
(mediator of a new covenant), and to
the sprinkled blood, which says better things than the blood of Abel.
25 Make sure that you do not reject
the One who speaks. For if they did
not escape when they rejected Him
who warned them on earth, even less
will we if we turn away from Him who
warns us from heaven. 26 His voice
shook the earth at that time, but
now He has promised, **Yet once more**
I will shake not only the earth but
also heaven.[H] 27 This expression, "Yet
once more," indicates the removal of
what can be shaken—that is, created
things—so that what is not shaken
might remain. 28 Therefore, since we
are receiving a kingdom that cannot
be shaken, let us hold on to grace.[I] By
it, we may serve God acceptably, with
reverence and awe, 29 for our God is a
consuming fire.

[A]**12:6** Pr 3:11-12 [B]**12:8** = Christians [C]**12:8** Lit *discipline, of which all have become participants* [D]**12:13** Or *so that the lame will not be turned aside* [E]**12:20** Ex 19:12 [F]**12:21** Dt 9:19 [G]**12:23** Or *registered* [H]**12:26** Hg 2:6 [I]**12:28** Or *let us give thanks*, or *let us have grace*

>WORD|*study*

13:2 The Greek word for hospitality, *philoxenias*, combines *philos*, "friend" (noun) or "loving" (adjective) and *xenos*, "stranger, foreigner," thus showing love to strangers, treating them as friends. "Hospitality," then, is the practice of welcoming, sheltering, and feeding those who find themselves away from home.

Concluding Remarks (13:1-25)

13 Let brotherly love continue.
[2]Don't neglect to show hospitality, for by doing this some have
welcomed angels as guests without
knowing it. [3]Remember the prisoners, as though you were in prison
with them, and the mistreated, as
though you yourselves were suffering bodily.[A] [4]Marriage must be
respected by all, and the marriage
bed kept undefiled, because God will
judge immoral people and adulterers. [5]Your life should be free from
the love of money. Be satisfied with
what you have, for He Himself has
said, **I will never leave you or forsake you.**[B] [6]Therefore, we may boldly say:

> **The Lord is my helper;**
> **I will not be afraid.**
> **What can man do to me?**[C]

[7]Remember your leaders who
have spoken God's word to you. As
you carefully observe the outcome
of their lives, imitate their faith.
[8]Jesus Christ is the same yesterday,
today, and forever. [9]Don't be led
astray by various kinds of strange
teachings; for it is good for the heart
to be established by grace and not by
foods, since those involved in them
have not benefited. [10]We have an
altar from which those who serve
the tabernacle do not have a right
to eat. [11]For the bodies of those

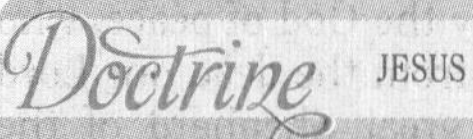

JESUS

Jesus is changeless throughout time (13:8), and only He serves as the high priest who continually intercedes in behalf of believers. His followers can rely on Him. His sacrifice to atone for humanity's sins was perfect. Just as the sin offering was **burned outside the camp**, Jesus' sacrifice also was made outside the city of Jerusalem where He sanctified **the people** with **His own blood** (13:11-12). His suffering had a purpose—to set apart believers for God. Rather than return to the trappings of Judaism, the writer encourages his readers to identify themselves completely with Jesus and His sacrifice. The writer describes Jesus as the **great Shepherd of the sheep** (13:20). He leads the flock of God. *Great* emphasizes His uniqueness. He has no equal.

animals whose blood is brought
into the most holy place by the high
priest as a sin offering are burned
outside the camp. [12]Therefore Jesus
also suffered outside the gate, so
that He might •sanctify[D] the people
by His own blood. [13]Let us then go
to Him outside the camp, bearing
His disgrace. [14]For we do not have
an enduring city here; instead, we
seek the one to come. [15]Therefore,
through Him let us continually offer up to God a sacrifice of praise,
that is, the fruit of our lips that
confess His name. [16]Don't neglect
to do what is good and to share, for
God is pleased with such sacrifices.
[17]Obey your leaders[E] and submit to
them, for they keep watch over your
souls as those who will give an account, so that they can do this with

12:25-29 The writer urges his readers not to **turn away from** God. If people **did not escape when they rejected** God who spoke from Mount Sinai, how much more must believers heed the words He speaks **from heaven**. Since believers will receive an unshakable **kingdom**, they should hold firmly to God's grace, serving Him **with reverence and awe** because God **is a consuming fire**.

13:1 **Brotherly love** (Gk *philadelphia*) is the most important Christian attribute, commanded by the Lord Jesus (Jn 13:34-35). By loving one another the persecuted readers would not only encourage one another but also serve as a witness to those around them.

13:2 Believers should practice **hospitality**. Jesus spoke of taking in a stranger and feeding and clothing him without realizing that such actions were ministering to Him (Mt 25:35-44).

13:3-6 Believers should **remember the prisoners** and their needs (see 10:34). These included fellow believers who were imprisoned because of their testimony. In their private lives believers should honor marriage, be free from the love of money, and remain **satisfied** with God's gifts and provision.

13:7,17 Believers should **remember** and follow the examples of their spiritual **leaders**, who faithfully taught them. The text implies these have already died, but believers also have a responsibility toward their current leaders (v. 17). They should **obey** and **submit** to them. Such leaders will have to give an account of their actions to God.

[A]**13:3** Or *mistreated, since you are also in a body* [B]**13:5** Dt 31:6 [C]**13:6** Ps 118:6 [D]**13:12** Or *set apart*, or *consecrate* [E]**13:17** Or *rulers*

Biblical Womanhood Marriage

God established marriage (Gn 2:24). Believers can honor marriage in a number of ways, including the mutual love and respect of a husband and wife (Heb 13:3-6). Believers should also keep the **marriage bed . . . undefiled**. This refers to sexual intercourse, an important and exclusive aspect of the marriage relationship. God will judge those who break this exclusive commitment—**immoral people** (Gk *pornous*, "fornicators, those who indulge in illicit sex") and **adulterers** (Gk *moichous*, "those who have sexual relations with someone other than their spouse"). Such people violate the sanctity of marriage.

joy and not with grief, for that would be unprofitable for you. 18 Pray for us; for we are convinced that we have a clear conscience, wanting to conduct ourselves honorably in everything. 19 And I especially urge you to pray[A] that I may be restored to you very soon.

20 Now may the God of peace, who brought up from the dead our Lord Jesus—the great Shepherd of the sheep—with the blood of the everlasting covenant, 21 equip[B] you with all that is good to do His will, working in us what is pleasing in His sight, through Jesus Christ. Glory belongs to Him forever and ever.[C] •Amen.

22 •Brothers, I urge you to receive this message of exhortation, for I have written to you briefly. 23 Be aware that our brother Timothy has been released. If he comes soon enough, he will be with me when I see you. 24 Greet all your leaders and all the •saints. Those who are from Italy greet you. 25 Grace be with all of you.

[A] **13:19** Lit *to do this* [B] **13:21** Or *perfect* [C] **13:21** Other mss omit *and ever*

HEBREWS … WRITTEN ON MY *Heart*

Hebrews calls you to mature as a believer by keeping your focus on Jesus alone. Whatever else competes for your attention, you need to remember that Christ is better. To grow in your discipleship you need to center your life on Jesus, not depend on religious traditions, not yield to sin, and not trust in your own efforts. You should not allow anything or anyone to come between you and the Lord. Jesus is sufficient and superior. He is God's perfect revelation, the final and complete sacrifice for your sins, your understanding Mediator, your Great High Priest, the Source and Perfecter of your faith, and your Great Shepherd. Cling to Jesus!

Doctrine THE ATONEMENT AND WOMEN

Believers **have boldness to enter the sanctuary** (10:19). Because of the shedding of Jesus' blood, women may enter the holy of holies—coming into the presence of God—without fear of death. The old covenant allowed only men who had been ordained to serve as priests from the tribe of Levi to enter this sanctuary. Now all people—men and women who believe in Jesus—may enter this sacred place. Jesus' blood purifies believers of their sin, enabling them to stand in the very presence of the holy God. Only through Jesus can an individual have access to God the Father (Jn 14:6). **The curtain** between the holy place and most holy place in the temple was torn from top to bottom the moment Jesus died, which symbolized the opening of access to God (Heb 10:19-20; see Mt 27:51; Mk 15:38; Lk 23:45).

Thinking of what Christ has done should lead believers to a number of specific actions.

- Believers should **draw near**. They can enter His presence by faith in Jesus' sacrifice. He has cleansed them from all of their sin and impurities. **Our bodies washed in pure water** refers to believer's baptism when a believer demonstrates outwardly what has already taken place inwardly. Believers can stand confidently before Him, not because of what they have done but because of what Jesus has done on their behalf (Heb 10:22).
- Believers should **hold on to the confession of** their **hope**. They can trust in the faithfulness of God to fulfill His promises (v. 23).
- Believers should **be concerned about one another**, attentive to the needs of fellow brothers and sisters in Christ, promoting **love and good works** (v. 24).
- Believers should not stay away from **worship meetings** (v. 25). Persecution had led some readers to neglect worship and fellowship. They needed to love and encourage one another. This loving encouragement remains important for every generation.

James

Timeline

- World Events
- Biblical Events

AD 33	*AD 37*	*AD 44*
Appearance of Jesus to His brother James following the crucifixion and resurrection	Paul's meeting with James and Peter on his first visit to Jerusalem following his conversion	Recognition of James as leader of the church at Jerusalem

"Be doers of the word and not hearers only" (1:22).

Who wrote James?

James, the brother of Jesus, is the author.

Who were the recipients?

Likely Jewish Christians living in or around Jerusalem and Antioch (1:1; 2:2) were the original recipients.

When was James written?

Between A.D. 48 and 62 (one of the oldest New Testament books*)* is the time frame.

Where did it happen?

No single geographical location is identified for the Jewish believers scattered by persecution.

What is James about?

- *How faith and works relate to one another*
- *Practical ways for Christians to live out their faith*
- *Trials and temptations*
- *The power of speech*
- *Wisdom*
- *The relationship between the poor and the rich*

Why should women read James?

If you want to know some specific ways you should act as a believer in Jesus Christ, then you need to read the book of James. This practical epistle serves as a "how-to book" in Christian living, challenging you to put your faith into action in concrete ways. You may already read and study God's word. You may think about it, but are you a *doer* of His word? Are you trusting and obeying? Genuine faith in the Lord will transform your life. James will aid you along that path of transformation and help you practice what you teach. Get ready for action!

How do you read James?

James reads like a sermon or collection of essays. At first glance the epistle appears to offer random ethical instructions. The author, however, repeats themes, providing some structure to his epistle. These themes include how to deal with trials and temptations, divine wisdom, the proper perspective on wealth and poverty, the use and abuse of speech, prayer, and putting faith into action. James does not try to develop doctrine but focuses on Christian behavior. To achieve this goal he includes many statements that echo sayings from the Old Testament wisdom literature (such as Proverbs) and the teachings of Jesus. James often tries to persuade readers of the truth of his arguments by imagining a discussion with an opponent to whom he poses a series of questions and answers. He keeps the believing community—the church—in mind at all times. He desires believers to change the way they interact with each other as God's people. He wants to remove conflict among believers and create healthy communities that live by the law of love.

As you read this epistle, imagine you are listening to a sermon. Ask yourself, "After hearing this message, what changes do I need to make in my life to put my faith into action?"

Outline

I. Address and Salutation (1:1)

II. Trials and Christian Maturity (1:2-18)
- A. The Purpose of Trials (1:2-4)
- B. Wisdom, Prayer, and Faith (1:5-8)
- C. The Paradox of Poverty and Wealth (1:9-11)
- D. The Source of Trials and Temptations (1:12-18)

III. True Christianity as Seen in its Works (1:19–2:26)
- A. Speech and Anger (1:19-21)
- B. Doers of the Word (1:22-27)
- C. The Sin of Favoritism and the Law of Love (2:1-13)
- D. Faith That Saves (2:14-26)

IV. Dissensions Within the Community (3:1–4:12)
- A. The Power of the Tongue (3:1-12)
- B. Wisdom from Above (3:13-18)
- C. A Condemnation of Evil Passions (4:1-3)
- D. A Summons to Repentance (4:4-10)
- E. A Prohibition of Critical Speech (4:11-12)

V. Implications of a Christian Worldview (4:13–5:11)
- A. A Condemnation of Arrogance (4:13-17)
- B. A Condemnation of Those Who Misuse Wealth (5:1-6)
- C. An Encouragement to Endure Patiently (5:7-11)

VI. Concluding Exhortations (5:12-20)
- A. Truthful Speech (5:12)
- B. Prayer and Healing (5:13-18)
- C. A Closing Summons to Action (5:19-20)

AD 44	AD 49	AD 62	AD 230	AD 330
Martyrdom of James, son of Zebedee and brother of John, by Herod Agrippa	Jerusalem Council (Ac 15; Gl 2:1)	Martyrdom of James (brother of Jesus) by stoning	Quotation of James in Origen's commentary on the Gospel of John	Eusebius's reference to the letter of James as Scripture

Address and Salutation (1:1)

1 James, a •slave of God and of the Lord Jesus Christ:
To the 12 tribes in the Dispersion.[A]
Greetings.

Trials and Christian Maturity (1:2-18)

The Purpose of Trials (1:2-4)

2 Consider it a great joy, my •brothers, whenever you experience various trials, 3 knowing that the testing of your faith produces endurance. 4 But endurance must do its complete work, so that you may be mature and complete, lacking nothing.

Wisdom, Prayer, and Faith (1:5-8)

5 Now if any of you lacks wisdom, he should ask God, who gives to all generously and without criticizing, and it will be given to him. 6 But let him ask in faith without doubting. For the doubter is like the surging sea, driven and tossed by the wind. 7 That person should not expect to receive anything from the Lord. 8 An indecisive[B] man is unstable in all his ways.

The Paradox of Poverty and Wealth (1:9-11)

9 The brother of humble circumstances should boast in his exaltation, 10 but the one who is rich should boast in his humiliation because he will pass away like a flower of the field. 11 For the sun rises with its scorching heat and dries up the grass; its flower falls off, and its beautiful appearance is destroyed. In the same way, the rich man will wither away while pursuing his activities.

The Source of Trials and Temptations (1:12-18)

12 A man who endures trials[C] is blessed, because when he passes the test he will receive the crown of life that God[D] has promised to those who love Him.

13 No one undergoing a trial should say, "I am being tempted by God." For God is not tempted by evil,[E] and He Himself doesn't tempt anyone. 14 But each person is tempted when he is drawn away and enticed by his own evil desires. 15 Then after desire has conceived, it gives birth to sin, and when sin is fully grown, it gives birth to death.

[A] 1:1 Jewish people scattered throughout Gentile lands who spoke Gk and were influenced by Gk culture. [B] 1:8 Or *A doubting*, or *A double-minded* [C] 1:12 Lit *trial*, used as a collective [D] 1:12 Other mss read *that the Lord* [E] 1:13 Or *evil persons*, or *evil things*

>WORD|*study*

1:1 Dispersion (Gk *diaspora*, "scattering") indicates those who are exiles in a foreign country and became the technical name for the Jewish community living outside of Palestine. Linking "dispersion" with "12" tribes almost certainly indicates that James was addressing Jewish Christians.

1:4 The goal specified, **that you may be mature** [Gk *teleioi*, "perfect, complete," in the sense of the completion of a process, an OT idea that defines perfection as a right relationship with God, unstained by worldly pursuits] **and complete** (Gk *holoklēroi*, "whole, sound, complete, blameless") is something for which the Christian must strive constantly with all her power, even though she will not attain that goal until she sees her Savior in heaven.

1:14 Drawn away (Gk *exelkomenos*, "drag away, lure away," a hunting term used to describe a trap designed to lure and catch an unsuspecting animal) and **enticed** (Gk *deleazomenos*, "lure," a term suggesting luring prey from safety to capture and even death) add intensity to the desires that pull toward sin.

Title: The Greek heading "*Iakōbos*" (the Gk form of the Hebrew *Iakōb* or Jacob, a common name among the Jews) identifies this epistle.

1:1 James characterizes himself simply as **a slave of God and of the Lord Jesus Christ**. By calling himself a "slave" (Gk *doulos*, "servant, slave, bondservant"), James shows that he considers his position to be one of humble service to his master, the Lord Jesus. He identifies the letter's recipients as the **12 tribes in the Dispersion**.

1:2-4 The command, **consider it a great joy**, suggests the need for a definite decision to take up a joyful attitude. Believers should react with joy when faced with **various trials** (Gk *peirasmois*, "test, testing") because these outward circumstances—whether suffering, troubles, or conflicts—are the means through which God works in believers to prove a perfect faith or build **endurance** (Gk *hupomonēn*, in the sense of a staying power that surpasses simply hanging in there through afflictions to include a determination to work through difficulties with purpose and focus). The **testing of your faith** is not a means of affliction and destruction but rather a way to refine and purify, to produce a deeper, stronger, more certain faith.

1:5 One of the most important virtues a Christian may lack is **wisdom** (Gk *sophias*, "knowledge, wisdom"). James refers here to wisdom as Christian enlightenment, which only comes through the work of God in a believer's life since He is the source and giver of wisdom. The idea is more than a temporary solving of difficulties. It includes learning and profiting through challenging experiences. In promising his readers that God will give wisdom to those who ask, James reflects Old Testament teaching (Pr 2:6a). He bases his confidence in God's response on His character because He **gives to all generously and without criticizing**.

1:12-15 Sin is attractive and addictive. **Desire** (Gk *epithumia*, lit "hot after") or lust, although long associated exclusively with evil and especially sexual promiscuity, is not bad in itself but simply describes a strong, deep-seated longing for anything—good or bad. When that desire grows out of control, however, and becomes a governing habit, the bent toward sinning takes charge. The fault for inappropriate desires rests entirely with the individual. God cannot be blamed. The human desire becomes so overwhelming that the person ignores the trap until she cannot turn back. **Fully grown** (Gk *apotelestheisa*, "finish, complete, perform") acknowledges completion of a goal—in this case, sin has reached its height and engulfed the sinner.

1:19-21 James bases the prohibition of unrestrained **anger** on the fact that anger **does not accomplish God's righteousness.** James uses "righteousness" to mean the righteous status that God confers on believers.

1:22-25 Those who fail to do **the word**, who are **hearers only**, are guilty of a dangerous and potentially fatal self-delusion. If the gospel, by nature, contains both saving power and summons to obedience, those who disobey have not truly embraced the gospel. Thus, people who only hear the word are **deceiving** themselves.

1:27 Orphans and widows were among the most vulnerable in ancient society. They needed protection and provision. **Pure and undefiled religion** is based on action, such as compassionate care and provision for the defenseless, and refusing the world's values.

2:1-7 James uses a hypothetical situation to condemn the sin of favoritism. He describes discrimination against a person just because he is **dressed in dirty clothes** instead of **fine clothes**. Such prejudice should not characterize a believer. Believers show the sin of favoritism by belonging to cliques, classifying people according to their economic status, showing hardness of heart to the needy, comparing people, and trying to control people because of an attitude of superiority.

2:8-9 James reminds his readers of the Lord's **royal** [Gk *basilikon*, "of, belonging to, or worthy of a king"] **law** (Gk *nomom*; cp. 1:25; 2:10-12; 4:11)—the law of love—with the command to **love your neighbor as yourself** (cp. Lv 19:18; Mt 22:39). The designation "royal" may be because the law comes from God, the King of kings or because this law is the highest authority governing human relationships. This law is superior to all others. Loving others by considering their needs first combats the sin of favoritism.

16 Don't be deceived, my dearly loved brothers. 17 Every generous act and every perfect gift is from above, coming down from the Father of lights; with Him there is no variation or shadow cast by turning. 18 By His own choice, He gave us a new birth by the message of truth[A] so that we would be the •firstfruits of His creatures.

True Christianity as Seen in Its Works (1:19–2:26)

Speech and Anger (1:19-21)

19 My dearly loved brothers, understand this: Everyone must be quick to hear, slow to speak, and slow to anger, 20 for man's anger does not accomplish God's righteousness. 21 Therefore, ridding yourselves of all moral filth and evil,[B] humbly receive the implanted word, which is able to save you.[C]

Doers of the Word (1:22-27)

22 But be doers of the word and not hearers only, deceiving yourselves. 23 Because if anyone is a hearer of the word and not a doer, he is like a man looking at his own face[D] in a mirror. 24 For he looks at himself, goes away, and immediately forgets what kind of man he was. 25 But the one who looks intently into the perfect law of freedom and perseveres in it, and is not a forgetful hearer but one who does good works—this person will be blessed in what he does.

26 If anyone[E] thinks he is religious without controlling his tongue, then his religion is useless and he deceives himself. 27 Pure and undefiled religion before our[F] God and Father is this: to look after orphans and widows in their distress and to keep oneself unstained by the •world.

The Sin of Favoritism and the Law of Love (2:1-13)

2 My •brothers, do not show favoritism as you hold on to the faith in our glorious Lord Jesus Christ. 2 For example, a man comes into your meeting wearing a gold ring and dressed in fine clothes, and a poor man dressed in dirty clothes also comes in. 3 If you look with favor on the man wearing the fine clothes and say, "Sit here in a good place," and yet you say to the poor man, "Stand over there," or, "Sit here on the floor by my footstool," 4 haven't you discriminated among yourselves and become judges with evil thoughts?

5 Listen, my dear brothers: Didn't God choose the poor in this world to be rich in faith and heirs of the kingdom that He has promised to those who love Him? 6 Yet you dishonored that poor man. Don't the rich oppress you and drag you into the courts? 7 Don't they blaspheme the noble name that was pronounced over you at your baptism?

8 Indeed, if you keep the royal law prescribed in the Scripture, **Love your neighbor as yourself**,[G] you are doing well. 9 But if you show favoritism, you commit sin and are convicted by the law as transgressors. 10 For whoever keeps the entire law, yet fails in one point, is •guilty of breaking it all. 11 For He who said, **Do not commit adultery**,[H] also said, **Do not murder.**[I] So if you do not commit adultery, but you do murder, you are a lawbreaker.

12 Speak and act as those who will be judged by the law of freedom. 13 For judgment is without mercy to the one who hasn't shown mercy. Mercy triumphs over judgment.

Faith That Saves (2:14-26)

14 What good is it, my brothers, if

[A]**1:18** = the gospel [B]**1:21** Lit *evil excess* [C]**1:21** Lit *save your souls* [D]**1:23** Lit *at the face of his birth* [E]**1:26** Other mss add *among you* [F]**1:27** Or *before the* [G]**2:8** Lv 19:18 [H]**2:11** Ex 20:14; Dt 5:18 [I]**2:11** Ex 20:13; Dt 5:17

>WORD|*study*

2:1 Favoritism (Gk *prosōpolēmpsiais*, "partiality, receiving one's face") comes from two Greek words *prosōpon*, "face," and *lambanein*, "to take or hold." This word is a form of the Hebrew idiom *panim nasa'*, "to lift up the face of a person" and so in turn to be partial to that person (cp. Rm 2:11; Eph 6:9; Col 3:25).

HARD QUESTION

Does the Bible contradict itself?

Absolutely not! At first glance Jms 2:14-26 may appear to contradict Paul's discussion in Romans 4. Was Abraham justified because he believed God, as Romans indicates, or did works justify him, as Jms 2:21 states? Paul and James use the terms "justification," "faith," and "works" differently. Paul focuses on the importance of justification when a believer initially makes her commitment to Christ. James emphasizes the believer's commitment to faith and the acceptance of its demand for obedience. Faith, for Paul, is the response of someone who has accepted Jesus as Lord. James sees two kinds of faith: genuine faith lived out with deeds and false faith. In the same manner, Paul understands "works" as acts someone would perform in order to earn God's initial acceptance or approval. James views "works" as the byproduct of a changed life. Paul expresses this concept most often with the metaphor of fruit in a believer's life. Both Paul and James see the importance of fruit or deeds in a believer's life. James admonishes his readers to live so that their lifestyle matched their profession of faith. To attempt to separate faith and works is **foolish** (2:20). Faith and works are inseparably linked in God's plan.

someone says he has faith but does not have works? Can his faith[A] save him?
15 If a brother or sister is without clothes and lacks daily food 16 and one of you says to them, "Go in peace, keep warm, and eat well," but you don't give them what the body needs, what good is it? 17 In the same way faith, if it doesn't have works, is dead by itself.
18 But someone will say, "You have faith, and I have works."[B] Show me your faith without works, and I will show you faith from my works.[C]
19 You believe that God is one; you do well. The demons also believe—and they shudder.
20 Foolish man! Are you willing to learn that faith without works is useless? 21 Wasn't Abraham our father justified by works when he offered Isaac his son on the altar?
22 You see that faith was active together with his works, and by works, faith was perfected. 23 So the Scripture was fulfilled that says, **Abraham believed God, and it was credited to him for righteousness,**[D] and he was called God's friend. 24 You see that a man is •justified by works and not by faith alone. 25 And in the same way, wasn't Rahab the prostitute also justified by works when she received the messengers and sent them out by a different route? 26 For just as the body without the spirit is dead, so also faith without works is dead.

Dissensions Within the Community (3:1–4:12)

The Power of the Tongue (3:1-12)

3 Not many should become teachers, my •brothers, knowing that we will receive a stricter judgment,
2 for we all stumble in many ways. If anyone does not stumble in what he says,[E] he is a mature man who is also able to control his whole body.[F]
3 Now when we put bits into the mouths of horses to make them obey us, we also guide the whole animal.[G]
4 And consider ships: Though very large and driven by fierce winds, they are guided by a very small rudder wherever the will of the pilot directs. 5 So too, though the tongue is a small part of the body, it boasts great things. Consider how large a forest a small fire ignites. 6 And the tongue is a fire. The tongue, a world of unrighteousness, is placed among the parts of our bodies. It pollutes the whole body, sets the course of life on fire, and is set on fire by •hell.
7 Every sea creature, reptile, bird, or animal is tamed and has been

[A]**2:14** Or *Can faith*, or *Can that faith*, or *Can such faith* [B]**2:18** The quotation may end here or after v. 18b or v. 19. [C]**2:18** Other mss read *Show me your faith from your works, and from my works I will show you my faith.* [D]**2:23** Gn 15:6 [E]**3:2** Lit *in word* [F]**3:2** Lit *to bridle the whole body* [G]**3:3** Lit *whole body*

>WORD|*study*

3:6 The Synoptic Gospels use hell (Gk *geennēs*, "the valley of Hinnom, hell, Gehenna") 11 times (all in the words of Jesus). James has the only other occurrence. The word is derived from the valley called "the Valley of the Sons of Hinnom," a ravine south of Jerusalem once used for pagan fire sacrifices (see 2Kg 23:10; Jr 7:31). This valley was also a garbage dump where trash was burned and fires were going continually. This valley eventually became linked to the idea of punishment for the wicked. By New Testament times it was synonymous with the concept of hell.

2:8-9 This passage may be viewed as a form of Hellenistic diatribe. James sets up a proposition (faith without works cannot save, v. 14), gives a rationale or proof for the proposition (vv. 15-16), confirms the proposition through use of an imaginary opponent (vv. 18-19), and amplifies the truth of the proposition through use of examples (vv. 20-26).

2:14-17 James states his proposition by asking a question that demands a negative response. Is faith that produces no works saving faith? No! James uses **works** to refer to acts of mercy and help for the poor and oppressed. For James "works" or deeds are primary in the sense that they validate the genuineness of one's faith. Works are outward manifestations of a right relationship with God expressed in relationships with others. Those whose faith is merely an emotional or intellectual acceptance of doctrine have a false understanding of faith. This kind of faith is dead and gives no evidence of genuine salvation.

2:18-19 James stresses the absurdity of true, saving faith existing as an inward commitment without any outward manifestation. **The demons** have faith, but their faith does not save.

2:20-26 James concludes that Abraham was **justified by works**, using the word "justified" in the sense of proving or giving evidence. Abraham proved the genuineness of his faith through acts of obedience.

3:1-12 James focuses on the destructive nature of the **tongue**. He uses three metaphors (**horses** and **bits**, **ships** and **rudder**, and **a small fire** and **a forest**, vv. 3-5) to illustrate the powerful force of the tongue and warn against uncontrolled speech (v. 6).

3:6 The image of the **tongue** as **a fire** would have been very familiar to the Jews (see Pr 16:27; 26:18-22). **World** (Gk *kosmos*) has a negative connotation in James' epistle (see 1:27; 2:5; 4:4), referring to the sinful world. Perhaps James considered the tongue as representative of the world. This tiny member of the body can lead to demonstrations of **unrighteousness** or wickedness. The tongue **pollutes** [Gk *spilousa*, "stain or defile"] **the whole body**. "Pollutes" has a symbolic sense of "spiritual and moral corruption." The tongue can serve as the primary means of expressing hostility to God and leading others to do the same. The tongue is also **set on fire by hell**. James links the potential evil of the tongue to hell, perhaps because of the irreparable damage done by evil speaking. Speech can be the source of wickedness that affects the entire course of a person's life.

3:13-18 James contrasts earthly wisdom with its sinful attitudes of **bitter envy** and **selfish ambition** to **the wisdom from above**. These attitudes produce **disorder and every kind of evil**.

4:6-7 A woman who humbles herself before the Lord recognizes her desperate need of God's help and submits to His will for all her life. The enjoyment of spiritual vitality and victory comes not through her independent efforts but through complete dependence on the Lord. To try to exalt herself by relying on her own abilities or status or money brings only failure and condemnation.

4:13-17 James condemns those who leave God and His values out of their way of life. He exhorts businessmen to change their boastful attitudes. James also warns about the sin of omission or neglecting to do what is right. Such sin is as serious as that of commission.

5:1-6 James continues to denounce a pursuit of **wealth** that disregards God and His purposes. He condemns any employer who treats his employees unjustly (cp. Is 3:14-15; 10:2) and promises judgment on all who oppressed the poor. The **rich people** pictured were clearly wealthy landowners, a class accused of economic exploitation and oppression from early times. James justified the condemnation of these rich landholders because they selfishly hoarded wealth, defrauded their workers, lived self-indulgently, and oppressed **the righteous**.

tamed by man, 8 but no man can tame the tongue. It is a restless evil, full of deadly poison. 9 We praise our[A] Lord and Father with it, and we curse men who are made in God's likeness with it. 10 Praising and cursing come out of the same mouth. My brothers, these things should not be this way. 11 Does a spring pour out sweet and bitter water from the same opening? 12 Can a fig tree produce olives, my brothers, or a grapevine produce figs? Neither can a saltwater spring yield fresh water.

Wisdom from Above (3:13-18)

13 Who is wise and has understanding among you? He should show his works by good conduct with wisdom's gentleness. 14 But if you have bitter envy and selfish ambition in your heart, don't brag and deny the truth. 15 Such wisdom does not come from above but is earthly, unspiritual, demonic. 16 For where envy and selfish ambition exist, there is disorder and every kind of evil. 17 But the wisdom from above is first pure, then peace-loving, gentle, compliant, full of mercy and good fruits, without favoritism and hypocrisy. 18 And the fruit of righteousness is sown in peace by those who cultivate peace.

A Condemnation of Evil Passions (4:1-3)

4 What is the source of wars and fights among you? Don't they come from the cravings that are at war within you?[B] 2 You desire and do not have. You murder and covet and cannot obtain. You fight and war. You do not have because you do not ask. 3 You ask and don't receive because you ask with wrong motives, so that you may spend it on your evil desires.

A Summons to Repentance (4:4-10)

4 Adulteresses![C,D] Don't you know that friendship with the •world is hostility toward God? So whoever wants to be the world's friend becomes God's enemy. 5 Or do you think it's without reason the Scripture says that the Spirit who lives in us yearns jealously?[E]

6 But He gives greater grace. Therefore He says:

> **God resists the proud,**
> **but gives grace**
> **to the humble.**[F]

7 Therefore, submit to God. But resist the Devil, and he will flee from you. 8 Draw near to God, and He will draw near to you. Cleanse your hands, sinners, and purify your hearts, double-minded people! 9 Be miserable and mourn and weep. Your laughter must change to mourning and your joy to sorrow. 10 Humble yourselves before the Lord, and He will exalt you.

A Prohibition of Critical Speech (4:11-12)

11 Don't criticize one another, •brothers. He who criticizes a brother or judges his brother criticizes the law and judges the law. But if you judge the law, you are not a doer of the law but a judge. 12 There is one lawgiver and judge[G] who is able to save and to destroy. But who are you to judge your neighbor?

Implications of a Christian Worldview (4:13–5:11)

A Condemnation of Arrogance (4:13-17)

13 Come now, you who say, "Today or tomorrow we will travel to such and such a city and spend a year there and do business and make a profit." 14 You don't even know what tomorrow will bring—what your life will be! For you are like smoke that appears for a little while, then vanishes. 15 Instead, you should say, "If the Lord wills, we will live and do this or that." 16 But as it is, you boast in your arrogance. All such boasting is evil. 17 So it is a sin for the person who knows to do what is good and doesn't do it.

A Condemnation of Those Who Misuse Wealth (5:1-6)

5 Come now, you rich people! Weep and wail over the miseries that are coming on you. 2 Your wealth is ruined and your clothes are motheaten. 3 Your silver and gold are corroded, and their corrosion will be a witness against you and will eat your flesh like fire. You stored up treasure

[A] **3:9** Or *praise the* [B] **4:1** Lit *war in your members* [C] **4:4** Other mss read *Adulterers and adulteresses* [D] **4:4** Or *Unfaithful people!* [E] **4:5** Or *He who caused the Spirit to live in us yearns jealously*, or *the spirit He caused to live in us yearns jealously*, or *He jealously yearns for the Spirit He made to live in us* [F] **4:6** Pr 3:34 [G] **4:12** Other mss omit *and judge*

>WORD|*study*

5:14 Sick (Gk *asthenei*) can mean weakness of any kind, moral (1Co 8:7, 11-12) or physical. The latter is the most common connotation in the New Testament and the best understanding in verse 14 (see also Mt 10:8; 25:36; Lk 9:2; Jn 4:46; 5:3; Ac 9:37; Php 2:26).

in the last days! 4 Look! The pay that you withheld from the workers who reaped your fields cries out, and the outcry of the harvesters has reached the ears of the Lord of •Hosts.[A] 5 You have lived luxuriously on the land and have indulged yourselves. You have fattened your hearts for[B] the day of slaughter. 6 You have condemned—you have murdered—the righteous man; he does not resist you.

An Encouragement to Endure Patiently (5:7-11)

7 Therefore, •brothers, be patient until the Lord's coming. See how the farmer waits for the precious fruit of the earth and is patient with it until it receives the early and the late rains. 8 You also must be patient. Strengthen your hearts, because the Lord's coming is near.

9 Brothers, do not complain about one another, so that you will not be judged. Look, the judge stands at the door!

10 Brothers, take the prophets who spoke in the Lord's name as an example of suffering and patience. 11 See, we count as blessed those who have endured.[C] You have heard of Job's endurance and have seen the outcome from the Lord. The Lord is very compassionate and merciful.

Concluding Exhortations (5:12-20)

Truthful Speech (5:12)

12 Now above all, my brothers, do not swear, either by heaven or by earth or with any other oath. Your "yes" must be "yes," and your "no" must be "no," so that you won't fall under judgment.[D]

Prayer and Healing (5:13-18)

13 Is anyone among you suffering? He should pray. Is anyone cheerful? He should sing praises. 14 Is anyone among you sick? He should call for the elders of the church, and they should pray over him after anointing him with olive oil in the name of the Lord. 15 The prayer of faith will save the sick person, and the Lord will restore him to health; if he has committed sins, he will be forgiven. 16 Therefore, confess your sins to one another and pray for one another, so that you may be healed. The urgent request of a righteous person is very powerful in its effect. 17 Elijah was a man with a nature like ours; yet he prayed earnestly that it would not rain, and for three years and six months it did not rain on the land. 18 Then he prayed again, and the sky gave rain and the land produced its fruit.

A Closing Summons to Action (5:19-20)

19 My brothers, if any among you strays from the truth, and someone turns him back, 20 let him know that whoever turns a sinner from the error of his way will save his •life from death and cover a multitude of sins.

5:14 The person who is physically sick should call on the **elders** or the leaders of his local body of believers to have them **pray over him** and anoint him with **oil**, a Jewish custom (see Is 61:3 where oil is offered as a remedy to soften sores and wounds). The Bible offers two main reasons for **anointing** a person: for medicinal or practical purposes and for symbolic reasons.

5:15-16 Save has a broad range of meanings, including saving one from physical death, saving a person from a dangerous situation, freeing someone from disease, keeping something or someone in good condition, and saving someone from eternal death. The context here indicates the term refers to physical healing. Sickness gives the Christian community an opportunity to minister to the physical needs of other members of the body. Sin can be a factor in some illnesses. The healing of the sick person and that of the community must take into account the spiritual dimensions of illness. Confession helps believers to gain spiritual wholeness. While James is speaking primarily of physical healing, believers also experience spiritual healing and unity as they confess their sins to one another.

[A]**5:4** Gk *Sabaoth*; this word is a transliteration of the Hb word for *Hosts*, or *Armies*. [B]**5:5** Or *hearts in* [C]**5:11** Or *have persevered* [D]**5:12** Other mss read *fall into hypocrisy*

JAMES... WRITTEN ON MY *Heart*

Do you recall Jesus' words, "You'll recognize them by their fruit" (Mt 7:20)? If you apply the words of James to your life, others will recognize you as a follower of the Lord Jesus Christ by what you do and what you say. Your changed life—as seen in your loving actions toward others, your controlled speech, your godly wisdom, your lack of worldly attitudes toward wealth, your lack of prejudice against the poor, and your attitude toward troubles—will draw others to Christ. What is the use of saying you are a Christian if you do not prove it by your actions? Become a doer of the word!

1 Peter

Timeline	AD 29	AD 33	AD 33	AD 33
■ World Events ■ Biblical Events	Jesus' appointment of Peter as one of His 12 apostles	Peter's denial of Jesus at his trial in the courtyard of Annas	Appearance of Jesus to Peter, following the crucifixion and resurrection; Jesus' restoration of Peter	Response of 3,000 people to Peter's sermon at the Festival of Pentecost

"You are being protected by God's power through faith . . ." (1:5).

Who wrote 1 Peter?

Peter (1:1) is the author.

Who were the recipients?

Believers scattered throughout Asia Minor (modern Turkey) are recipients.

When was 1 Peter written?

Between A.D. 62 and 64 is the time frame.

Where did it happen?

The epistle was written from Rome to believers scattered throughout Asia Minor (modern Turkey)

What is 1 Peter about?

- *God's grace*
- *Encouragement during suffering*
- *How to live in a hostile world*

Why should women read 1 Peter?

How do you live as a Christian in a world that increasingly opposes believers and the biblical truths they uphold? How can you lead a holy life when others persecute you? How should you respond to unjust criticism and ridicule? How can you resist giving up and losing hope when you are struggling? If you relate to any of these questions, you must read 1 Peter. This book will remind you that Christians may suffer for what they believe. The letter will affirm, however, that Jesus Christ is your hope in the midst of all suffering. He shows you how to endure afflictions with patience and faith. Get ready for encouragement—read 1 Peter!

How do you read 1 Peter?

First Peter is an epistle—a letter. Peter wrote it to actual believers with real problems. The Christians to whom he wrote were experiencing persecution because of their faith. Peter wrote to encourage these believers as they faced hostility and mistreatment. Peter returns to the theme of suffering throughout this letter. He wants his readers to understand their suffering in the light of God's greater purposes. He reminds Christians that they are actually "aliens" on earth because their inheritance is in heaven. The apostle wants these believers to live like heavenly people—with holy lives—to show others their true citizenship. Peter wants them to live in such a way that they can win over their pagan neighbors to the gospel. He points his readers to Jesus as their example to follow. Jesus suffered unjustly, yet He now reigns victoriously. Believers can face their own sufferings triumphantly if they rely on Christ. Their safety and security rests in God who has given them eternal life. This hope should motivate believers to serve their Lord with commitment despite the cost. As you read 1 Peter, look for Old Testament quotes and passages that echo Peter's own sermons as recorded in Acts.

Outline

I. God's Grace Is the Power of God unto Salvation (1:1–2:12)
   A. Greeting (1:1-2)
   B. A Living Hope (1:3-12)
   C. The Responsibility of Salvation (1:13–2:3)
      1. Holy Living (1:13-21)
      2. Love (1:22-25)
      3. Spiritual Growth (2:1-3)
   D. The Chosen Stone and His People (2:4-12)

II. God's Grace Is the Power of God unto Submission (2:13–3:7)
   A. Submission to Government (2:13-17)
   B. Submission in the Workplace (2:18-25)
   C. Submission in the Home (3:1-7)

III. God's Grace Is the Power of God unto Suffering and Service (3:8–5:14)
   A. Principles of Godly Living (3:8-12)
   B. Suffering for Righteousness' Sake (3:13-22)
   C. Suffering as Christ Suffered (4:1-6)
   D. Serving for God's Glory (4:7-11)
   E. Suffering for God's Glory (4:12-19)
   F. The Responsibility of Elders (5:1-4)
   G. Submission to Elders (5:5-7)
   H. A Final Warning and Farewell (5:8-14)

AD 37	AD 49	AD 66	AD 112–114
Paul's meeting with Peter and James on his first visit to Jerusalem following his conversion	Jerusalem Council (Ac 15; Gl 2:1); Paul's confrontation of Peter for refusing to eat with Gentile believers	Martyrdom of Peter in Rome during Nero's persecution of Christians	Polycarp's *Letter to Philippians*, which shows dependence on 1 Peter

>WORD|*study*

1:1-2 Foreknowledge (Gk *prognōsin*, lit "knowing beforehand") highlights an important attribute of God, for it contrasts finite human knowledge with His perfect knowledge of His creation and His desire and ability to rescue all from the penalty of death.

1:3-4 Peter uses specific words to describe the believers' inheritance. Imperishable (Gk *aphtharton*, "incorruptible, immortal") is derived from the verb *phtheirō*, "destroy or corrupt." Jews regarded the temple as "destroyed" when it was defiled or damaged in the slightest way. The adjective "imperishable" thus describes an inheritance that is not subject to decay or corruption, one that cannot perish. Uncorrupted (Gk *amianton*, "undefiled, pure") identifies the believer's inheritance as "unsoiled, stainless, untainted" (cp. Heb 7:26; 13:4; Jms 1:27). Unfading (Gk *amaranton*, "dried up or withered, wasted away") appears once, in Jms 1:11, comparing grass and flowers that have been dried up and destroyed by the sun's heat with the temporality of a rich man consumed by his pursuits.

Greeting (1:1-2)

1 Peter, an apostle of Jesus Christ:
To the temporary residents dispersed[A] in Pontus, Galatia, Cappadocia, •Asia, and Bithynia, chosen
2 according to the foreknowledge of
God the Father and set apart by the
Spirit for obedience and for sprinkling with the blood of Jesus Christ.
May grace and peace be multiplied
to you.

A Living Hope (1:3-12)

3 Praise the God and Father of our
Lord Jesus Christ. According to His
great mercy, He has given us a new
birth into a living hope through the
resurrection of Jesus Christ from the
dead 4 and into an inheritance that is
imperishable, uncorrupted, and unfading, kept in heaven for you. 5 You
are being protected by God's power
through faith for a salvation that is
ready to be revealed in the last time.
6 You rejoice in this,[B] though now for
a short time you have had to struggle
in various trials 7 so that the genuineness of your faith—more valuable

[A]**1:1** Jewish people scattered throughout Gentile lands who spoke Gk and were influenced by Gk culture [B]**1:6** Or *In this fact rejoice*

Title: The Greek words *Petrou A* identify the text as the first epistle of Peter.

1:1-2 These verses reflect the doctrine of election, as Peter recounts God's purposeful act of choosing believers to be called His children. The **chosen** (Gk *eklektois*, "selected, picked out, excellent, elect"; cp. 2:4,6,9) sojourners are sanctified—**set apart** (Gk *hagiosmō*, "consecrated, purified, separated out for God's purposes," cp. 2Th 2:13)—**by the Spirit**, because of His Son's death upon the cross.

1:4 What believers inherit as God's children is not subject to decay and cannot be destroyed or marred; it is permanent and unfading in its purity and beauty, unlike anything in the temporal world. **Kept** (Gk *tetērēmenēn*,

Teachings on Suffering in 1 Peter

Suffering . . .	Reference	Suffering . . .	Reference
is inevitable	1:6	is sometimes unjust	3:18
is short-lived, temporary	1:6; 5:10	should not be a surprise	4:12
is varied	1:6	should be cause for rejoicing	4:13
may result in praise, glory, and honor	1:7	is sharing in Christ's suffering	4:13
was experienced by Christ	1:11; 4:1	is an opportunity to glorify the name of Christ	4:16
is redemptive	1:18-19	reflects an act of commitment	4:19
is commendable before God	2:20-21	may be instigated by the Devil	5:8
brings blessing	3:14; 4:14	is experienced by all believers	5:9
may be the will of God	3:17		

"guarded, carefully attended to, taken care of, stored away") reinforces the picture of how secure the inheritance is **in heaven**.

1:10 Longing to understand all that they recorded about **salvation,** the prophets **searched** (Gk *exezētēsan*, "searched out, charge with," often applying to seeking God; cp. Heb 11:6) and **carefully investigated** (Gk *exēraunēsan*, "inquired with great care," usually reference to searching out a place such as a tent or a city) in order to find someone or something, suggesting diligent and thorough investigation.

1:11-12 Peter emphasizes that **angels desire** [Gk *epithumousin*, "long for, eagerly desire"] **to look into** salvation, but they cannot because it is reserved for mankind.

1:13-16 Desires here and elsewhere in the letter (2:11; 4:2,3) has the negative sense of sinful desires or lusts. Those who have been born anew into God's family, having willingly submitted to His authority, must no longer operate according to the sinful thought patterns, false hopes, and destructive desires that characterized their former life of ignorance.

1:17-21 A sense of reverential awe for God should characterize the Christian. What makes the difference is an accurate view of the **empty** [Gk *mataias*, "without purpose, devoid of truth"] **way of life** from which believers **were redeemed** (Gk *elutrōthēte*, "released, delivered, or liberated by payment of a ransom") and an appreciation for the inestimable value of the price paid for that redemption, the **precious** [Gk *timiō*, "of great price, very costly, especially dear"] **blood of Christ**. Peter identified Jesus with the Passover lamb, which had to be **without defect or blemish** (Ex 12:5; Heb 9:14).

1:22-25 Peter pictures believers as those who have **purified** themselves in the metaphorical sense of the ceremonial cleansing required before celebration of the Passover (Jn 11:55). To obey the **truth** means to submit one's life to Christ's lordship—forsaking the sin that is forgiven and cleansed by the blood of the sinless Lamb of God. Having been **born again** uniquely enables Christians to comply with the command to love one another earnestly from a pure heart. The love commanded is the unconditional, self-sacrificing love of Christ. **Earnestly** suggests that Christians must love each other actively, reaching outward to embrace other believers as family members. Genuine love overflows from a heart cleansed of impure motives and sinful desires, a heart ruled by Christ.

>WORD|*study*

1:13 The phrase your minds ready for action (Gk *anazōsamenoi tas osphuas*, "gird up the loins" with *tēs dianoias humōn* "of your minds, thoughts, understanding") metaphorically applies to the ancient custom of tucking in long robes around the waist for comfort and ease of movement. Of primary importance in holy living is getting thought patterns that would hinder progress in spiritual growth out of the way.

1:13 Be serious (Gk *nēphontes*, "being sober, temperate; watching, being circumspect," from the root verb *nēphō*, "free from every form of mental and spiritual drunkenness, free from excess, passion, rashness; well balanced"; cp. 4:7; 5:8) implies overall self-control—sobriety in conduct, speech, and judgment. Being holy requires a disciplined heart.

than gold, which perishes though refined by fire—may result in[A] praise, glory, and honor at the revelation of Jesus Christ. 8 You love Him, though you have not seen Him. And though not seeing Him now, you believe in Him and rejoice with inexpressible and glorious joy, 9 because you are receiving the goal of your[B] faith, the salvation of your souls.[C]

10 Concerning this salvation, the prophets who prophesied about the grace that would come to you searched and carefully investigated. 11 They inquired into what time or what circumstances[D] the Spirit of Christ within them was indicating when He testified in advance to the messianic sufferings[E] and the glories that would follow.[F] 12 It was revealed to them that they were not serving themselves but you. These things have now been announced to you through those who preached the gospel to you by the Holy Spirit sent from heaven. Angels desire to look into these things.

The Responsibility of Salvation (1:13–2:3)

Holy Living (1:13-21)

13 Therefore, with your minds ready for action,[G] be serious and set your hope completely on the grace to be brought to you at the revelation of Jesus Christ. 14 As obedient children, do not be conformed to the desires of your former ignorance. 15 But as the One who called you is holy, you also are to be holy in all your conduct; 16 for it is written, **Be holy, because I am holy.**[H]

17 And if you address as Father the One who judges impartially based on each one's work, you are to conduct yourselves in fear during the time of your temporary residence. 18 For you know that you were •redeemed from your empty way of life inherited from the fathers, not with perishable things like silver or gold, 19 but with the precious blood of Christ, like that of a lamb without defect or blemish. 20 He was chosen[I] before the foundation of the world but was revealed at the end of the times for you 21 who through Him are believers in God, who raised Him from the dead and gave Him glory, so that your faith and hope are in God.

Love (1:22-25)

22 By obedience to the truth,[J] having purified yourselves[K] for sincere love of the •brothers, love one another earnestly[L] from a pure[M] heart, 23 since you have been born again—not of perishable seed but of imperishable—through the living and enduring word of God. 24 For

All flesh is like grass,
and all its glory like a flower
of the grass.
The grass withers,
and the flower falls,
25 **but the word of the Lord**
endures forever.[N]

And this is the word that was preached as the gospel to you.

Spiritual Growth (2:1-3)

2 So rid yourselves of all malice, all deceit, hypocrisy, envy, and all slander. 2 Like newborn infants, desire the pure spiritual milk, so that you may grow by it for your salva-

A1:7 Lit *may be found for* B1:9 Other mss read *our*, or they omit the possessive pronoun C1:9 Or *your lives* D1:11 Or *inquired about the person or time* E1:11 Or *the sufferings of Christ* F1:11 Lit *the glories after that* G1:13 Lit *Therefore, when you have the loins of your mind girded* H1:16 Lv 11:44-45; 19:2; 20:7 I1:20 Or *foreknown* J1:22 Other mss add *through the Spirit* K1:22 Or *purified your souls* L1:22 Or *intensely* M1:22 Other mss omit *pure* N1:24-25 Is 40:6-8

Submission

(Gk *Hupotassō*, "Lining up under Authority")

What it does not mean	What it does mean
• Subjecting oneself to abusive tyranny • Forced obedience • Inequality in essence and worth • Selective submission, an attitude of "I'll submit when I want to submit."	• Willingly choosing to obey • Placing oneself under another's authority • Equality in essence and personhood but difference in role and assignment • Obedience in all situations and circumstances according to God's word—not choosing when you will and will not obey • An attitude of the will, void of stubbornness • Voluntary commitment of service to others

tion,[A] 3 since **you have tasted that the Lord is good.**[B]

The Chosen Stone and His People (2:4-12)

4 Coming to Him, a living stone—rejected by men but chosen and valuable to God— 5 you yourselves, as living stones, are being built into a spiritual house for a holy priesthood to offer spiritual sacrifices acceptable to God through Jesus Christ. 6 For it is contained in Scripture:

Look! I lay a stone in ˚Zion,
a chosen
and honored[C] **cornerstone,**[D]
and the one who believes
in Him
will never be put to shame![E,F]

7 So honor will come to you who believe, but for the unbelieving,

The stone that the builders
rejected—
this One has become
the cornerstone,[G]

8 and

A stone to stumble over,[H]
and a rock to trip over.[I,J]

They stumble because they disobey the message; they were destined for this.

9 But you are **a chosen race,**[K,L]
a royal priesthood,[M]
a holy nation,[N] **a people**
for His possession,[O]
so that you may proclaim
the praises[P,Q]
of the One who called you
out of darkness
into His marvelous light.
10 Once you were not a people,
but now you are God's people;
you had not received mercy,
but now you have received
mercy.

11 Dear friends, I urge you as strangers and temporary residents to abstain from fleshly desires that war against you.[R] 12 Conduct yourselves honorably among the Gentiles,[S] so that in a case where they speak against you as those who do what is evil, they will, by observing your good works, glorify God on the day of visitation.[T]

Submission to Government (2:13-17)

13 Submit to every human authority[U] because of the Lord, whether to the Emperor[V] as the supreme authority 14 or to governors as those sent out by him to punish those who do what is evil and to praise those who do what is good. 15 For it is God's will that you silence the ignorance of foolish people by doing

2:2-3 Desire could also be translated "crave." Scripture commands believers to develop an insatiable appetite for God's word (Jb 23:11-12). A believer's growth in Christ is contingent on her appetite for the word of God.

2:4-10 Peter describes Jesus as a **living stone** (v. 4), the **cornerstone** (vv. 6-7), the **rejected** stone (vv. 4,7), and a stone that causes people to **stumble** (v. 8). Peter affirms that the church is built with **living stones**, those who confess Jesus as Christ.

2:11-12 Peter begs his audience to **abstain from fleshly** [Gk *sarkikōn*, "carnal," controlled by the human nature in opposition to the Spirit] **desires** (Gk *epithumiōn*, "cravings, longings, lusts, desires for what is forbidden"). He encouraged them to live in such a way that their conduct stood as a witness. Peter stressed that a real spiritual battle continued to rage around them, seeking to attack believers at their weakest point. Peter's word choice illustrates the seriousness of this battle: **desires that war** [Gk *strateuontai*, "fight, serve in active military duty, lead an army unit into battle"] **against you**. A believer's conduct has the potential for causing others to **glorify God** as they observe their Christlike behavior.

2:13–3:7 Appropriate submission is a characteristic of believes and also their Lord Jesus. See chart, p.1601.

2:13-15 Believers should submit themselves to the civil authorities. Christians are expected to obey the law (see Mt 22:15-22; Rm 13:1-7). The government has been instituted for the purpose of punishing the wicked and protecting the good. The motivation, however, for submitting to government authorities should not be simply for the sake of avoiding punishment but rather **because of the Lord**. God expects His children to submit themselves to human government in order that their

[A] **2:2** Other mss omit *in your salvation* [B] **2:3** Ps 34:8 [C] **2:6** Or *valuable* [D] **2:6** Lit *head of the corner* [E] **2:6** Or *be disappointed* [F] **2:6** Is 28:16 LXX [G] **2:7** Ps 118:22 [H] **2:8** Or *a stone causing stumbling* [I] **2:8** Or *a rock to trip over* [J] **2:8** Is 8:14 [K] **2:9** Or *generation*, or *nation* [L] **2:9** Dt 7:6; 10:15; Is 43:20 LXX [M] **2:9** Ex 19:6; 23:22 LXX; Is 61:6 [N] **2:9** Ex 19:6; 23:22 LXX [O] **2:9** Ex 19:5; 23:22 LXX; Dt 4:20; 7:6; Is 43:21 LXX [P] **2:9** Or *the mighty deeds* [Q] **2:9** Is 42:12; 43:21 [R] **2:11** Or *against the soul* [S] **2:12** Or *among the nations*, or *among the pagans* [T] **2:12** The day when God intervenes in human history, either in grace or in judgment [U] **2:13** Or *creature* [V] **2:13** Lit *king*

excellent behavior might draw others to Him. **By doing good** believers **silence** the ignorant and foolish talk of those who falsely accused them.

2:18-20 Many masters were kind and fair, yet Peter acknowledged that some were **cruel**. Submission did not depend on a master's treatment of his slave or, in contemporary terms, on an employer's treatment of an employee.

2:21–3:4 The sacrifice of Jesus represents the most powerful **example** of submission, providing the pattern for how His children should live. Peter describes these characteristics of a godly woman as very valuable or precious in the eyes of God, as well as having an **imperishable quality** in contrast to gold, jewels, and other ornaments that will eventually fade away. The quiet and gentle woman, however, will be admired by those who observe her behavior. God approves of her for her faithfulness in living according to His pattern.

3:5-6 Peter identifies women who have exhibited such godly beauty **in the past**. He refers to them as **the holy women** who served as wives, **submitting to their own husbands**. These women **beautified** [Gk *ekosmoun*, "adorned, prepared, arranged, put in order," from which comes the anglicized "cosmetic"] **themselves** with the qualities described earlier. Peter specifically mentions Sarah, his primary example of a woman who lived in submission to her husband. She often found herself in difficult situations, yet she demonstrated the godly qualities previously described. She called Abraham **lord**, also translated *master*, as an expression of her submission to

good. 16 As God's •slaves, live as free
people, but don't use your freedom
as a way to conceal evil. 17 Honor everyone. Love the brotherhood. Fear
God. Honor the Emperor.[A]

Submission in the Workplace (2:18-25)

18 Household slaves, submit with
all fear to your masters, not only
to the good and gentle but also to
the cruel.[B] 19 For it brings favor[C] if,
mindful of God's will,[D,E] someone
endures grief from suffering unjustly. 20 For what credit is there if
you sin and are punished, and you
endure it? But when you do what is
good and suffer, if you endure it, this
brings favor with God.

21 For you were called to this,
because Christ also suffered
for you,
leaving you an example,
so that you should follow
in His steps.
22 He **did not commit sin,**
and no deceit was found
in His mouth;[F]
23 when He was reviled,
He did not revile in return;
when He was suffering,
He did not threaten
but entrusted
Himself to the One
who judges justly.
24 He Himself bore our sins
in His body on the tree,
so that, having died to sins,
we might live
for righteousness;
you have been healed
by **His wounds.**[G]
25 For you **were like sheep**
going astray,[H]
but you have now returned
to the Shepherd and Guardian[I]
of your souls.

Submission in the Home (3:1-7)

3 In the same way, wives, submit
yourselves to your own husbands
so that, even if some disobey the
Christian message, they may be won
over[J] without a message by the way
their wives live 2 when they observe
your pure, reverent lives. 3 Your
beauty should not consist of outward
things like elaborate hairstyles and
the wearing of gold ornaments[K] or
fine clothes. 4 Instead, it should consist of what is inside[L] the heart with
the imperishable quality of a gentle
and quiet spirit, which is very valuable in God's eyes. 5 For in the past,
the holy women who put their hope
in God also beautified themselves in

[A] 2:17 Lit *king* [B] 2:18 Or *unscrupulous*; lit *crooked* [C] 2:19 Other mss add *with God* [D] 2:19 Other mss read *if, because of a good conscience* [E] 2:19 Lit *if, because of conscience toward God* [F] 2:22 Is 53:9 [G] 2:24 Is 53:5 [H] 2:25 Is 53:6 [I] 2:25 Or *Overseer* [J] 3:1 Lit *may be gained* [K] 3:3 Lit *and of putting around of gold items* [L] 3:4 Lit *Instead, the hidden man of*

Biblical Womanhood Marriage

A wife is to be submissive (3:1-2), not because of any merit on her husband's part, but as an act of obedience to the Lord. Submission is an act of worship motivated by love for the Lord and a desire to follow Christ's example. It is neither a wife's escape route for avoiding unpleasant circumstances nor a tool for manipulating her husband. Biblical submission represents part of a wife's response to God in light of His love. A wife's submission to her husband also demonstrates the importance and uniqueness of the marriage relationship in which God has chosen to display His power and glory in the midst of a corrupt society. While being essentially equal to their husbands, wives are called upon, nonetheless, to submit themselves voluntarily to their husbands.

Submission involves both a woman's *outward* actions and *inward* disposition. Peter first addressed the former. Most commentators agree that women were well represented in the churches in the geographic region to which Peter originally sent this letter. Some of their husbands were not believers. Peter anticipated that these women were likely questioning the relevance of submission to their husbands because of their marital situation. The purity of a godly woman's life exercised in submission can soften her husband's heart without her speaking a word. A woman's submissive spirit serves as one of the greatest evangelistic tools in her home and community. Submission does not mean inferiority. Peter demonstrated the importance of living according to God's pattern established in Genesis. He provided both husbands and wives with principles needed to combat the effects that sin made on God's original design of male and female.

>WORD|*study*

3:1 **Submit** (Gk *hupotassomenai*, "subordinate, be subject to, yield to") was a military term for arranging troops under a commander's leadership, but it was also used for voluntarily giving in, carrying a burden, placing in a certain order, assigning a place. Elsewhere in Scripture the word describes Jesus' obedience to His parents (Lk 2:51), citizens to governing authorities (Rm 13:1; Ti 3:1), believers to church officials (1Pt 5:5), and ultimately all creation to God (Jms 4:7; Heb 12:9). Here, the verb is in the middle voice, implying an action that results from a woman's own choice.

3:4 Being **gentle** (Gk *praeōs*, "meek, humble") is a mark of strength rather than weakness. The word was frequently used in ancient literature to refer to a wild beast that had been tamed, suggesting that the characteristic is acquired rather than natural. Jesus described His own disposition as "gentle" (Mt 11:29). Gentleness is also commended as a fruit of the Spirit (Gl 5:23). Being **quiet** (Gk *hēsuchiou*) does not mean being totally silent; neither does it suggest being devoid of personality. Instead, the idea is "self-control" and "trust."

3:7 **Honor** (Gk *timēn*, "value") describes the attitude of reverence appropriate to a great treasure that is to be nurtured and protected. The word fits precisely what God ordained from the beginning in the establishment of male headship (Gn 1–2).

this way, submitting to their own
husbands, 6 just as Sarah obeyed
Abraham, calling him lord. You have
become her children when you do
what is good and are not frightened
by anything alarming.
7 Husbands, in the same way, live
with your wives with an understanding of their weaker nature[A] yet
showing them honor as coheirs of
the grace of life, so that your prayers
will not be hindered.

Principles of Godly Living (3:8-12)

8 Now finally, all of you should
be like-minded and sympathetic,
should love believers,[B] and be compassionate and humble,[C] 9 not paying
back evil for evil or insult for insult
but, on the contrary, giving a blessing, since you were called for this, so
that you can inherit a blessing.

10 For **the one who wants**
to love life
and to see good days
must keep his tongue
from evil
and his lips
from speaking deceit,
11 **and he must turn away**
from evil
and do what is good.
He must seek peace
and pursue it,
12 **because the eyes of the Lord**
are on the righteous
and His ears are open
to their request.
But the face of the Lord
is against
those who do what is evil.[D]

Suffering for Righteousness' Sake (3:13-22)

13 And who will harm[E] you if you
are deeply committed to what is
good?[F] 14 But even if you should
suffer for righteousness, you are
blessed. **Do not fear what they fear**

[A]3:7 Lit *understanding as the weaker vessel* [B]3:8 Lit *sympathetic, loving the brothers* [C]3:8 Other mss read *courteous* [D]3:10-12 Ps 34:12-16 [E]3:13 Or *mistreat*, or *do evil to* [F]3:13 Or *you are partisans for the good*; lit *you are zealots*

his leadership in their home. Sarah's reverence for her husband does not reflect subjection to a cultural view of women as inferior or a cultural mandate for wives to be subservient to their husbands without dignity. Sarah was not coerced into calling Abraham *lord* but rather willingly chose to place herself under his leadership and care. Peter identifies wives who exhibit these godly qualities and are not unsettled by trying circumstances as "daughters of Sarah," **her children**. A wife characterized by a gentle and quiet spirit is a woman of strength under control, able to avoid panic in the most difficult situations, and relying on the Holy Spirit rather than on herself.

3:7 Husbands, too, are to follow God's established pattern for them, to lead the family with the attitude of Christ. Peter exhorts husbands to offer their wives two specific gifts of love: respect (**honor**) and **understanding**. Husbands must strive to understand their wives, seeking to know them as intimately as possible—emotionally, intellectually, spiritually, and physically. Husbands are also expected to bestow honor on their wives.

Most commentators agree that **weaker nature** (or *vessel*) refers to biological differences between men and women, with women generally being

Biblical Womanhood Beauty

Peter addresses the inward appearance that also characterizes a godly woman (3:3-4). Some completely misinterpret this passage by maintaining that women are not to wear certain things or even care for their appearance. Peter does not give a legalistic code of what can and cannot be worn. Rather he affirms a woman's outward appearance is not primarily what matters to God but rather her inward character. Peter notes three aspects of biblical beauty:

- It is hidden—internal, not external.
- It is **imperishable**. Internal beauty will not fade away, unlike the fleeting beauty of one's outward appearance.
- It is **valuable** to God.

Peter used two words to describe godly beauty: gentleness and quietness.

weaker *physically.* While a woman is fully equal to a man in her essence and personhood, as well as intellectually and morally, she is physically weaker simply due to her biological nature. Peter was not demeaning women, but he was exhorting the husband to recognize that women are created differently. Husbands should honor wives as **coheirs** of **grace**. Husbands and wives have the same spiritual standing, having been chosen by Jesus Christ as His children. The husband's motivation for adhering to these commands involves his relationship to God: **so that your prayers will not be hindered**.

3:15 The inward reverence believers should have for Christ as Lord will be demonstrated in an outward readiness **to give a defense . . . for the hope that is in you**.

3:18 Peter chooses Jesus as the example of the innocent, sinless man who suffered and died in submission to God the Father.

3:19-22 Of these four explanations offered by interpreters, the latter two are more popular:

- Christ descended into Sheol (Hb "the realm of the dead," equivalent to the Gk Hades) to preach the gospel to Old Testament believers held there until their atonement had been accomplished.
- He descended into Sheol to proclaim judgment on those condemned during the Old Testament period.
- Jesus did not descend into the realm of the dead. His proclamation to the spirits in prison refers to His preaching through Noah by means of the Spirit to those in the time of Noah. On this view, "spirits in prison" refers to Noah's contemporaries awaiting the final judgment of God.
- After His death and resurrection, Christ proclaimed victory over the

>WORD|*study*

3:15 To give a defense (Gk *apologian*, "verbal defense, formal justification"), like the legal term *apologia* or "apology," is to make one's case, to provide a reasoned argument. Apologetics is a branch of theology that focuses upon defending the faith and proving the truths of Scripture. To give a defense or apology in this sense does not involve apologizing—making excuses or expressing shame for being a Christian.

4:1 Equip yourselves (Gk *hoplisasthe*, "furnish with weapons, equip, provide"; metaphorically, "take on the same mind") is a military expression. Like soldiers preparing themselves for battle, so believers must be diligent in preparing themselves for suffering.

or be disturbed,[A] [15]but honor[B] the
•Messiah[C] as Lord in your hearts.
Always be ready to give a defense to
anyone who asks you for a reason[D]
for the hope that is in you. [16]How-
ever, do this with gentleness and
respect, keeping your conscience
clear,[E,F] so that when you are accused,[G] those who denounce your
Christian life[H] will be put to shame.
[17]For it is better to suffer for doing
good, if that should be God's will,[I]
than for doing evil.

[18] For Christ also suffered
for sins once for all,[J]
the righteous
for the unrighteous,[K]
that He might bring you[L]
to God,
after being put to death
in the fleshly realm[M]
but made alive
in the spiritual realm.[N]

[19]In that state[O] He also went and
made a proclamation to the spirits
in prison[P] [20]who in the past were disobedient, when God patiently waited
in the days of Noah while an ark was
being prepared. In it a few—that is,
eight people[Q]—were saved through
water. [21]Baptism, which corresponds to this, now saves you (not
the removal of the filth of the flesh,
but the pledge[R] of a good conscience
toward God) through the resurrection of Jesus Christ. [22]Now that He
has gone into heaven, He is at God's
right hand with angels, authorities,
and powers subject to Him.

Suffering as Christ Suffered (4:1-6)

4 Therefore, since Christ suffered[S]
in the flesh,[T] equip[U] yourselves
also with the same resolve[V]—because the one who suffered in the
flesh has finished with sin[W]— [2]in

[A]3:14 Is 8:12 [B]3:15 Or *sanctify*; lit *set apart* [C]3:15 Other mss read *set God* [D]3:15 Or *who demands of you an accounting* [E]3:16 Lit *good* [F]3:16 Or *keeping a clear conscience* [G]3:16 Other mss read *when they speak against you as evildoers* [H]3:16 Lit *your good behavior in Christ* [I]3:17 Lit *if the will of God should will* [J]3:18 Other mss read *died for sins on our behalf*; other mss read *died for our sins*; other mss read *died for sins on your behalf* [K]3:18 Or *the Righteous One in the place of the unrighteous many* [L]3:18 Other mss read *us* [M]3:18 Or *in the flesh* [N]3:18 Or *in the spirit*, or *in the Spirit* [O]3:19 Or *In whom*, or *At that time*, or *In which* [P]3:19 Perhaps fallen supernatural beings or angels; 2Pt 2:4; Jd 6 [Q]3:20 Lit *souls* [R]3:21 Or *the appeal* [S]4:1 Other mss read *suffered for us* [T]4:1 The phrase "in the flesh" probably means in human experience. [U]4:1 Or *arm* [V]4:1 Or *perspective*, or *attitude* [W]4:1 Or *the one who has suffered in the flesh has ceased from sin*

Biblical Womanhood Hospitality

Peter includes hospitality in the ministry of spiritual gifts (4:9). Biblical hospitality ministers to givers as well as receivers. The Bible promotes hospitality that:

- shares with the poor (Pr 31:20);
- does not seek reward or compensation in return (Mt 6:1-4);
- puts people before things (Mt 10:42);
- shares all possessions (Ac 2:44);
- offers freedom and forgiveness (Rm 8:2);
- seeks to serve others (1Pt 4:8-9); and
- does not complain (1Pt 4:10).

Biblical hospitality is opening one's home and heart to others in Jesus' name. It involves more than elaborate menus, elegant table settings, or lavish entertaining. It includes sharing what a woman has and who she is with whomever God sends her way. Christians are to extend love and grace to friends and strangers while enjoying their fellowship.

order to live the remaining time in the flesh, no longer for human desires,[A] but for God's will. 3 For there has already been enough time spent in doing what the pagans choose to do:[B] carrying on in unrestrained behavior, evil desires, drunkenness, orgies, carousing, and lawless idolatry. 4 So they are surprised that you don't plunge with them into the same flood[C] of wild living—and they slander you. 5 They will give an account to the One who stands ready to judge the living and the dead. 6 For this reason the gospel was also preached to those who are now dead, so that, although they might be judged by men in the fleshly realm,[D] they might live by God in the spiritual realm.[E]

Serving for God's Glory (4:7-11)

7 Now the end of all things is near; therefore, be serious and disciplined for prayer. 8 Above all, maintain an intense love for each other, since **love covers a multitude of sins.**[F] 9 Be hospitable to one another without complaining. 10 Based on the gift each one has received, use it to serve others, as good managers of the varied grace of God. 11 If anyone speaks, it should be as one who speaks God's words; if anyone serves, it should be from the strength God provides, so that God may be glorified through Jesus Christ in everything. To Him belong the glory and the power forever and ever. •Amen.

Suffering for God's Glory (4:12-19)

12 Dear friends, don't be surprised when the fiery ordeal[G] comes among you to test you as if something unusual were happening to you. 13 Instead, rejoice as you share in the sufferings of the •Messiah, so that you may also rejoice with great joy at the revelation of His glory. 14 If you are ridiculed for the name of Christ, you are blessed, because the Spirit of glory and of God rests on you.[H] 15 None of you, however, should suffer as a murderer, a thief, an evildoer, or a meddler.[I] 16 But if anyone suffers as a "Christian," he should not be ashamed but should glorify God in having that name. 17 For the time has come for judgment to begin with God's household, and if it begins with us, what will the outcome be for those who disobey the gospel of God?

18 And **if a righteous person**
is saved with difficulty,
what will become
of the ungodly
and the sinner?[J]

19 So those who suffer according to God's will should, while doing what is good, entrust themselves to a faithful Creator.

The Responsibility of Shepherd's of God's Flock (5:1-4)

5 Therefore, as a fellow elder and witness to the sufferings of the •Messiah and also a participant in the glory about to be revealed, I exhort the elders among you: 2 Shepherd God's flock among you, not overseeing[K] out of compulsion but freely, according to God's will;[L] not for the money but eagerly; 3 not lording it over those entrusted to you, but being examples to the flock. 4 And when the chief Shepherd appears, you will receive the unfading crown of glory.

Submission to Elders (5:5-7)

5 In the same way, you younger men, be subject to the elders. And all of you clothe yourselves with[M] humility toward one another, because

God resists the proud
but gives grace
to the humble.[N]

6 Humble yourselves, therefore, under the mighty hand of God, so that He may exalt you at the proper time,[O] 7 casting all your care on Him, because He cares about you.

[A] **4:2** Lit *for desires of human beings* [B] **4:3** Or *Gentiles* [C] **4:4** Lit *you don't run with them into the same pouring out* [D] **4:6** Or *in the flesh* [E] **4:6** Or *in the spirit* [F] **4:8** Pr 10:12 [G] **4:12** Lit *the burning* [H] **4:14** Other mss add *He is blasphemed because of them, but He is glorified because of you.* [I] **4:15** Or *as one who defrauds others* [J] **4:18** Pr 11:31 LXX [K] **5:2** Other mss omit *overseeing* [L] **5:2** Other mss omit *according to God's will* [M] **5:5** Lit *you tie around yourselves* [N] **5:5** Pr 3:34 LXX [O] **5:6** Lit *in time*

demonic "spirits" (i.e., the fallen angels).

3:20-21 The judgment of the flood destroyed all but **eight people.** Noah and his family were saved through water. Peter compares **baptism** with the water that saved Noah and his family. As the outward testimony of a believer's decision to follow Christ, baptism pictures the destruction of the believer's sinful life and her new birth in Christ.

4:2-5 A Christian's changed identity and behavior will capture the interest of those who walk in darkness but can also provoke hostility in unbelievers as an offense to their own lifestyle. Though **they slander you** (Gk *blasphēmountes*, "blaspheme, revile, malign, speak reproachfully, give an evil report"), they will one day face **the One** who will **judge** them for their acts against God's children. No person escapes giving **an account** to God.

4:7-11 The shortness of time, in light of eternity, should motivate believers to live for and serve Jesus.

4:12-16 Peter encourages endurance in **sufferings** with Christlike faith, knowing that believers would be identified with Him. He summarized the nature of these trials believers will encounter: intense, inevitable, and testing. God uses these trials as part of the refining fire to mold and shape His children into His likeness. Trials should cause believers to **rejoice**, knowing that they are identifying with Christ's death and have the hope of seeing Him face-to-face. Peter encourages believers to consider themselves **blessed** when persecuted **for the name of Christ** (Mt 5:11).

5:1-4 Peter describes the role of pastors with three words:

- **Elders** (Gk *presbuterous*) suggests maturity and the respect and esteem due a pastor by virtue of his divinely appointed office.
- **Shepherd** (Gk *poimanate*, "tend a flock of sheep") depicts the role of a spiritual leader who must faithfully care for "God's flock" by serving them, feeding them the Word of God, guiding, leading by example, and protecting them from spiritual corruption. A pastor's flock does not ultimately belong to the shepherd but to God. The shepherd's job is to lead and care for the sheep rather than being preoccupied with financial gain.
- **Overseeing** (Gk *episkopountes*, "look at, take care, care for") emphasizes the administrative responsibilities of this leader in the congregation.

5:5-7 Peter exhorts believers to exercise

humility (Gk *tapeinophrosunēn*, "modestly," from *tapeinos*, "lowly, of low degree, low to the ground," and *phrēn*, "heart, mind, intellect, thinking") toward one another. "Humility" denotes a lowliness of mind as opposed to thinking too highly of oneself, a deep sense of one's smallness in comparison with others rather than an attitude of superiority, a sense of modesty instead of braggadocio, and opinion of oneself marked by humility rather than one of proud self-promotion. God honors humility. He lifts up the humble with His **mighty hand**. Peter encouraged believers to cast their cares upon God. This requires the deliberate release of control and the intentional placement of worries and concerns upon God.

5:8-9 Believers need to be **serious** and **alert** because they have an **adversary** [Gk *antidikos*, "enemy, opponent," particularly in a lawsuit], **the Devil**. Believers must both recognize and **resist** this enemy because he is dangerous:

- he **is prowling around like a roaring lion**, vicious and ready to attack;
- he is **looking for anyone he can devour** (Gk *katapiein*, "swallow, destroy, overwhelm").

When they sense Satan's presence, believers are commanded to resist (Gk *antistēte*, "oppose, set oneself against," see Gl 2:11; Eph 6:13; Jms 4:7) him by standing firmly in their **faith**. Believers know God is in control, cares for them, hears their prayers, and will cause Satan to flee. They can entrust themselves to His protection. Their fellow believers **throughout the world** were also suffering.

5:13 Babylon means either the literal city of Babylon on the Euphrates or a code word for Rome. In the Old Testament, "Babylon" represents those who oppose God.

A Final Warning and Farewell (5:8-14)

8 Be serious! Be alert! Your adversary the Devil is prowling around
like a roaring lion, looking for anyone he can devour. 9 Resist him and
be firm in the faith, knowing that
the same sufferings are being experienced by your fellow believers
throughout the world.
10 Now the God of all grace, who
called you to His eternal glory in
Christ Jesus, will personally[A] restore, establish, strengthen, and
support you after you have suffered
a little.[B] 11 The dominion[C] belongs to
Him forever.[D] •Amen.
12 I have written you this brief letter through Silvanus[E] (I know him
to be a faithful brother) to encourage you and to testify that this is the
true grace of God. Take your stand
in it! 13 The church in Babylon,[F] also
chosen, sends you greetings, as does
Mark, my son. 14 Greet one another
with a kiss of love. Peace to all of you
who are in Christ.[G]

[A] **5:10** Lit *Himself* [B] **5:10** Or *a little while*, or *to a small extent* [C] **5:11** Other mss read *dominion and glory*; other mss read *glory and dominion* [D] **5:11** Other mss read *forever and ever* [E] **5:12** Or *Silas*; Ac 15:22-32; 16:19-40; 17:1-16 [F] **5:13** Probably refers to Rome [G] **5:14** Other mss read *Christ Jesus. Amen.*

1 PETER… WRITTEN ON MY *Heart*

Commitment to Christ is costly. The Lord Jesus suffered for you. As His follower, you should expect the same treatment. When you are persecuted for your faith, rejoice that God has counted you worthy to suffer for Christ. God uses your trials to refine your faith. He is in control. His power will protect you and enable you by faith to have joy. Jesus has given you the pattern to follow—patient suffering, knowing that a glorious future destiny awaits you. Your temporary sufferings cannot compare to the coming eternal glory God has planned for you. Trust yourself to the God who made you. He will never fail you!

Submission

DEFINITION	METHOD	EXAMPLE	REWARDS
• An attitude of the will • More than obedience • Resting, leaning, trusting, abandoning yourself to the Lord • Void of stubbornness • Confidence that His will is best	"As to the Lord" (Eph 5:22) "To your own husbands" (Eph 5:22; 1Pt 3:1) An act of the will (1Pt 3:1-2) Extends to "everything" (Eph 5:24) Patterned after the relationship between Christ and the church (Eph 5:25-32) A response to love (Eph 5:24-25) Extends to everyone: • The church to Christ (Eph 5:24) • All believers to God (Heb 12:9; Jms 4:7) • All believers to spiritual leaders Heb 13:17) • All believers to governing authorities (Rm 13:1,5; Ti 3:1; 1Pt 2:13) • All believers to one another (Eph 5:21) • Wives to husbands (Eph 5:22,24; Col 3:18; Ti 2:5; 1Pt 3:1,5) • Children to parents (Eph 6:1-3) • Slaves to masters (Ti 2:9; 1Pt 2:18)	**Jesus:** • He had no other purpose (Heb 10:7) • To submit was joy (Ps 40:7-8) • He did not consider His own will (Jn 5:30) **Esther:** "I will go … if I perish, I perish" (Est 4:16) **Sarah:** "Sarah . . . obeyed Abraham" (1Pt 3:5-6) **Rebekah:** "I will go"(Gn 24:58) **Abigail:** "Here I am . . ." (1Sm 25:32-42) **Mary:** "May it be done to me" (Lk 1:38)	A vibrant witness (1Pt 3:1) An opportunity for glorifying God (1Pt 3:5-6) A means for teaching spiritual truths (Eph 5:25-32) A way to train children (Ti 2:3-5) The object of human love and divine protection (Eph 5:25; 1Pt 3:7) A tool to increase worth (1Pt 3:4) A means for liberating creativity (1Pt 3:7)

2 Peter

Timeline World Events Biblical Events	*2085 BC* God's rescue of Lot from the destruction of Sodom and Gomorrah	*AD 29* Jesus' appointment of Peter as one of His 12 apostles	*AD 32* Peter's confession that Jesus is the Messiah at Caesarea Philippi	*AD 33* Peter's denial of Jesus at His trial in the courtyard of Annas	*AD 33* Appearance of Jesus to Peter, following His crucifixion and resurrection

"His [Jesus'] divine power has given us everything required for life and godliness" (1:3).

Who wrote 2 Peter?
Peter (1:1) is the author.

Who were the recipients?
Probably the churches in Asia Minor identified in his first letter—Galatia, Cappadocia, Asia, and Bithynia (1Pt 1:1)—were recipients.

When was 2 Peter written?
Between A.D. 64 and 67 is the time frame.

Where did it happen?
The epistle was written from Rome to all believers everywhere.

What is 2 Peter about?
- *Growing in the knowledge of Jesus Christ*
- *Identifying false teachings*
- *Anticipating the Lord's return*

Why should women read 2 Peter?
The media sometimes popularizes a "spiritual leader" who tries to espouse his version of "salvation" with the support of a well-known celebrity. At times a bestseller becomes a must-read book—everyone seems to be extolling its claims. How do you know if these people or authors are speaking the truth—God's truth? What's the best way to discern false teaching? How can you resist the challenges presented to you by the sinful world? The best way to resist heretics and to live a life of moral excellence is to grow in the grace and knowledge of the Lord Jesus Christ. Second Peter will encourage you to be diligent in your Christian growth.

How do you read 2 Peter?
Second Peter represents the Apostle Peter's farewell speech. He knew death approached. He desired above all else for his readers to continue to grow as believers and show others their lives of holiness. He reminded them of the importance of knowing the Lord, persevering in following Him, and remembering what He taught. Peter knew false teachers had risen who would keep these Christians from their goal of spiritual growth. His description of these heretics revealed their true character of deceit and sinful lifestyles. Peter particularly attacked their denial of Christ's return by affirming the reliability and truth of God's word through the prophets or Scripture. Jesus has delayed so that more sinners will repent and turn to Him. Peter declared the certainty of His return. The Lord is coming and will judge those who reject Him and live according to their own desires.

Outline

I. A Reminder of God's Provision for Growth (1:1-21)
   A. Greeting (1:1-2)
   B. The Need for Faithful Growth in Christ (1:3-11)
   C. The Reliability of Scripture (1:12-21)
II. A Reminder of Destructive Teachers (2:1-22)
   A. The Power of Deception (2:1-3)
   B. The Doom of False Teachers (2:4-11)
   C. The Deception of False Teachers (2:12-22)
III. A Reminder of God's Promises (3:1-18)
   A. The Assurance of Jesus' Return (3:1-13)
   B. Farewell (3:14-18)

>WORD|*study*

1:2 Knowledge (Gk *epignōsei*, "certain, decisive, true knowledge") refers to the believer's "coming to know" Christ in conversion. Various forms of the word "knowledge" served as a key term for Peter (see vv. 3, 5-6, 8, 20; 2:20-21; 3:17-18; 1Pt 3:7). Knowledge of God must remain at the heart of a believer's spiritual journey (Pr 9:10; Hs 6:6)—described not merely in intellectual terms but including experiential knowledge of God. In the New Testament this knowledge of God comes through a relationship with Jesus (Jn 8:19; Col 2:2-3).

AD 33	AD 33	AD 37	AD 49	AD 49	AD 66
Jesus' restoration of Peter	Response of 3,000 people to Peter's sermon at the Festival of Pentecost	Paul's meeting with Peter and James on his first visit to Jerusalem following his conversion	Jerusalem Council (Ac 15; Gl 2:1)	Paul's confrontation of Peter for refusing to eat with Gentile believers	Martyrdom of Peter in Rome during Nero's persecution of Christians

A Reminder of God's Provision for Growth (1:1-21)

Greeting (1:1-2)

1 Simeon[A] Peter, a •slave and an apostle of Jesus Christ:

To those who have obtained a faith of equal privilege with ours[B] through the righteousness of our God and Savior Jesus Christ.

2 May grace and peace be multiplied to you through the knowledge of God and of Jesus our Lord.

The Need for Faithful Growth in Christ (1:3-11)

3 His[C] divine power has given us everything required for life and godliness through the knowledge of Him who called us by[D] His own glory and goodness. 4 By these He has given us very great and precious promises, so that through them you may share in the divine nature, escaping the corruption that is in the world because of evil desires. 5 For this very reason, make every effort to supplement your faith with goodness, goodness with knowledge, 6 knowledge with self-control, self-control with endurance, endurance with godliness, 7 godliness with brotherly affection, and brotherly affection with love. 8 For if these qualities are yours and are increasing, they will keep you from being useless or unfruitful in the knowledge of our Lord Jesus Christ. 9 The person who lacks these things is blind and shortsighted and has forgotten the cleansing from his past sins. 10 Therefore, •brothers, make every effort to confirm your calling and election, because if you do these things you will never stumble. 11 For in this way, entry into the eternal kingdom of our Lord and Savior Jesus Christ will be richly supplied to you.

The Reliability of Scripture (1:12-21)

12 Therefore I will always remind you about these things, even though you know them and are established in the truth you have. 13 I consider it right, as long as I am in this bodily tent,[E] to wake you up with a reminder, 14 knowing that I will soon lay aside my tent, as our Lord Jesus Christ has also shown me. 15 And I will also make every effort that you may be able to recall these things at any time after my departure.[F]

16 For we did not follow cleverly contrived myths when we made known to you the power and coming of our Lord Jesus Christ; instead, we were eyewitnesses of His majesty. 17 For when He received honor and glory from God the Father, a voice came to Him from the Majestic Glory:

> This is My beloved Son.[G]
> I take delight in Him![H]

18 And we heard this voice when it came from heaven while we were with Him on the holy mountain. 19 So we have the prophetic word strongly confirmed. You will do well to pay attention to it, as to a lamp shining in a dismal place, until the day dawns and the morning star rises in your hearts. 20 First of all, you should know this: No prophecy of Scripture comes from one's own interpretation, 21 because no prophecy ever came by the will of man;

[A]1:1 Other mss read *Simon* [B]1:1 Or *obtained a faith of the same kind as ours* [C]1:3 Lit *As His* [D]1:3 Or *to* [E]1:13 = Peter's body [F]1:15 Or *my death* [G]1:17 Other mss read *My Son, My Beloved* [H]1:17 = Christ's transfiguration; Mt 17:5

Title: In the earliest manuscripts, 2 Peter is entitled simply *Petrou B*, the second letter of Peter.

1:1 Peter stresses the coequality of God and Jesus Christ, perhaps in response to heretical teachings that questioned Jesus' divinity.

1:4 God's **promises** enable the believer to **share in** [Gk *genēsthe . . . koinōnoi*, "become, be made . . . partners, partakers"] **the divine nature** of God as His new creation (2Co 5:17) and to live a holy life. This does not mean that the believer will be "deified" in the sense of becoming God. Neither does it mean that the believer will be free from all sin. Instead, Peter maintains that believers will share in the nature of God by becoming like Him, as His children, at the point of conversion. This process will reach its ultimate consummation in the future when Jesus returns.

1:5-11 Peter describes eight **qualities** that should be evident and **increasing** in the believer's life as she grows in the knowledge of God. While **calling and election** are God's work in salvation, Peter emphasizes the responsibility of believers to live faithfully according to their calling as children of God. God's calling and godly living go together, contradicting the tenets of false teachers who claimed that God's grace provides license for living however one desires.

1:16-18 Peter stresses the importance of apostolic authority in discerning truth from error. True faith is founded on historical facts, which **eyewitnesses**, such as the apostles, saw with their own eyes. What Peter had taught regarding Jesus' **coming** (Gk *parousian*, "advent, arrival, presence"; cp. 1Th 2:19; 3:13; Jms 5:7-8; 1Jn 2:28) was based on what he knew to be true, what he himself had seen and **heard.** On the Mount of Transfiguration (Mt 17:1-5), Peter, James, and John had witnessed a preview of Jesus' coming **glory** as the King of kings.

1:20-21 Peter emphasizes that **no prophecy** originates with man but rather with God. On the inspiration and interpretation of **Scripture**, Peter declares:

- Scripture should not be interpreted according to an individual's private **interpretation**.
- Scripture is willed by God, not by man.
- God is the divine author of Scripture. The human authors who penned the words of Scripture were **moved** (Gk *pheromenoi*, "borne or carried along") **by the Holy Spirit**. In Acts 27:15,17 *moved* is used to describe a sailing vessel being "driven along" by the wind. Human authors were involved in the process—but only as **men** who **spoke from God**.

2:1-3 Peter compares the **false prophets** of the Old Testament to **false teachers** emerging in the early church and identified common characteristics.

2:3 Peter makes clear the nature of punishment awaiting such false teachers—utter **destruction**.

2:6-11 God delivered **Lot** from the fires that burned against the rebellious cities of Sodom and Gomorrah. To readers familiar with the biblical account of Lot's life (Gn 19), Peter's description of him as **righteous** may seem surprising. Peter explains that Lot was **distressed** [Gk *kataponoumenon*, "oppressed, afflicted, subdued, exhausted, troubled"] **by the unrestrained** [Gk *aselgeia*, "sensual, licentious"] **behavior of the immoral** (Gk *athesmōn*, "lawless, unprincipled" describing those who set aside the law in their pursuit of self-gratification) among whom he lived.

2:12-16 Peter compares false teachers to **irrational** [Gk *aloga*, "without or contrary to reasoning"] **animals** following their natural passions rather than the truth.

2:17-19 False teachers are able to bring destruction into the church because of the vulnerability of those whom they seek to destroy. They prey on those **who have barely escaped from those who live in error**. Both new believers and people who are being introduced to the gospel are vulnerable. Knowing the weakness of sinful human nature, these teachers use the sensuality of the flesh to **seduce** (Gk *deleazousin*, "allure, catch with bait, entice") others. Their coming judgment promises utter **darkness**.

instead, men spoke from God as they were moved by the Holy Spirit.

A Reminder of Destructive Teachers (2:1-22)

The Power of Deception (2:1-3)

2 But there were also false prophets among the people, just as there will be false teachers among you. They will secretly bring in destructive heresies, even denying the Master who bought them, and will bring swift destruction on themselves. 2 Many will follow their unrestrained ways, and the way of truth will be blasphemed because of them. 3 They will exploit you in their greed with deceptive words. Their condemnation, pronounced long ago, is not idle, and their destruction does not sleep.

The Doom of False Teachers (2:4-11)

4 For if God didn't spare the angels who sinned but threw them down into Tartarus[A] and delivered them to be kept in chains[B] of darkness until judgment; 5 and if He didn't spare the ancient world, but protected Noah, a preacher of righteousness, and seven others,[C] when He brought a flood on the world of the ungodly; 6 and if He reduced the cities of Sodom and Gomorrah to ashes and condemned them to ruin,[D] making them an example to those who were going to be ungodly;[E] 7 and if He rescued righteous Lot, distressed by the unrestrained behavior of the immoral 8 (for as he lived among them, that righteous man tormented himself day by day with the lawless deeds he saw and heard)— 9 then the Lord knows how to rescue the godly from trials and to keep the unrighteous under punishment until the day of judgment, 10 especially those who follow the polluting desires of the flesh and despise authority.

Bold, arrogant people! They do not tremble when they blaspheme the glorious ones; 11 however, angels, who are greater in might and power, do not bring a slanderous charge against them before the Lord.[F]

The Deception of False Teachers (2:12-22)

12 But these people, like irrational animals—creatures of instinct born to be caught and destroyed—speak blasphemies about things they don't understand, and in their destruction they too will be destroyed, 13 suffering harm as the payment for unrighteousness. They consider it a pleasure to carouse in the daytime. They are spots and blemishes, delighting in their deceptions[G] as they feast with you. 14 They have eyes full of adultery and are always looking for sin. They seduce unstable people and have hearts trained in greed. Children under a curse! 15 They have gone astray by abandoning the straight path and have followed the path of Balaam, the son of Bosor,[H] who loved the wages of unrighteousness 16 but received a rebuke for his transgression: A donkey that could not talk spoke with a human voice and restrained the prophet's irrationality.

17 These people are springs without water, mists driven by a whirlwind. The gloom of darkness has been reserved for them. 18 For by uttering boastful, empty words, they seduce, with fleshly desires and debauchery, people who have barely escaped[I] from those who live in error. 19 They promise them freedom, but they themselves are •slaves of corruption, since people are enslaved to whatever defeats them. 20 For if, having escaped the world's impurity through the knowledge of our Lord and Savior Jesus Christ, they are again entangled in these things and defeated, the last state is worse for them than the first. 21 For it would have been better for them not to have known the way of righteousness than, after knowing it, to turn back from the holy command delivered to them. 22 It has happened to them according to the true proverb: **A dog returns to its own vomit,**[J] and, "a sow, after washing itself, wallows in the mud."

A2:4 = Gk name for a place of divine punishment in the underworld. B2:4 Other mss read *in pits* C2:5 Lit *righteousness, as the eighth* D2:6 Other mss omit *to ruin* E2:6 Other mss read *an example of what is going to happen to the ungodly* F2:11 Other mss read *them from the Lord* G2:13 Other mss read *delighting in the love feasts* H2:15 Other mss read *Beor* I2:18 Or *people who are barely escaping* J2:22 Pr 26:11

A Reminder of God's Promises (3:1-18)

The Assurance of Jesus' Return (3:1-13)

3 Dear friends, this is now the second letter I have written to you; in both letters, I want to develop a genuine understanding with a reminder, 2 so that you can remember the words previously spoken by the holy prophets and the command of our Lord and Savior given through your apostles. 3 First, be aware of this: Scoffers will come in the last days to scoff, living according to their own desires, 4 saying, "Where is the promise of His coming? Ever since the fathers fell •asleep, all things continue as they have been since the beginning of creation." 5 They willfully ignore this: Long ago the heavens and the earth were brought about from water and through water by the word of God. 6 Through these waters the world of that time perished when it was flooded. 7 But by the same word, the present heavens and earth are stored up for fire, being kept until the day of judgment and destruction of ungodly men.

8 Dear friends, don't let this one thing escape you: With the Lord one day is like a thousand years, and a thousand years like one day. 9 The Lord does not delay His promise, as some understand delay, but is patient with you, not wanting any to perish but all to come to repentance.

10 But the Day of the Lord will come like a thief;[A] on that day the heavens will pass away with a loud noise, the elements will burn and be dissolved, and the earth and the works on it will be disclosed.[B] 11 Since all these things are to be destroyed in this way, it is clear what sort of people you should be in holy conduct and godliness 12 as you wait for and earnestly desire the coming[C] of the day of God. The heavens will be on fire and be dissolved because of it, and the elements will melt with the heat. 13 But based on His promise, we wait for the new heavens and a new earth, where righteousness will dwell.

Farewell (3:14-18)

14 Therefore, dear friends, while you wait for these things, make every effort to be found at peace with Him without spot or blemish. 15 Also, regard the patience of our Lord as an opportunity for salvation, just as our dear brother Paul has written to you according to the wisdom given to him. 16 He speaks about these things in all his letters in which there are some matters that are hard to understand. The untaught and unstable twist them to their own destruction, as they also do with the rest of the Scriptures.

17 Therefore, dear friends, since you know this in advance, be on your guard, so that you are not led away by the error of lawless people and fall from your own stability. 18 But grow in the grace and knowledge of our Lord and Savior Jesus Christ. To Him be the glory both now and to the day of eternity.[D] •Amen.[E]

[A] **3:10** Other mss add *in the night* [B] **3:10** Other mss read *will be burned up* [C] **3:12** Or *and speed the coming* [D] **3:18** Or *now and forever* [E] **3:18** Other mss omit *Amen.*

3:5-7 The false teachers **willfully ignore** that the earth is the Lord's. They believe that the universe must follow a natural course, meaning that Jesus' return will be impossible. Peter reminds the believers that God is Creator and has all dominion and authority over creation.

3:8-9 God has waited to bring destruction on the world because of His desire for **all to come to repentance** (Gk *metanoian*, "change of mind or purpose, remorse," see Mt 4:17; Rv 3:3). The apparent **delay** in Christ's return is not due to His indifference but rather reveals His patience and mercy. Peter is not teaching universalism, that God will save *all* mankind. God *desires* that all will be saved, knowing that many will reject Him (see 1Tm 2:4).

3:10-13 The Day of the Lord **will come** as a surprise, **like a thief**. The Lord will appear and destroy the world. The end-time events described as "the Day of the Lord" will be marked by devastation and catastrophe. The present order will be completely renewed as the new creation becomes the dwelling place of righteousness for the children of God. In light of certain, future destruction, believers should be motivated toward **holy conduct**, living Christ-centered lives set apart from the world and from false teachers with an attitude of waiting and trusting in the Lord's return.

3:15-16 Peter acknowledges that some things contained in Paul's letters are **hard to understand** and thus are misused by ignorant men who **twist** Paul's words and all of Scripture to fit their own motivations.

2 PETER… WRITTEN ON MY *Heart*

You should live each day with the expectation that Christ will return at any moment. The sinful world will continue to tempt even mature believers and challenge your faith. False teachers will claim to have the truth and demand your attention and loyalty. You need to determine that you will grow in your knowledge of Christ and reject those who have a message inconsistent with God's word. You must put forth the effort through Bible study, prayer, worship, and obedience to draw closer to Jesus, to know Him better and better. This will enable you to stand for truth and resist temptation, enabling God to produce His character in you.

1 John

Timeline World Events Biblical Events	AD 29	AD 32	AD 33	AD 44
	Jesus' appointment of John and his brother James as two of His 12 apostles	Transfiguration of Jesus witnessed by John, James, and Peter	Jesus' request from the cross for John to care for His mother Mary	Martyrdom of John's brother James

"So that you may know that you have eternal life" (5:13b).

Who wrote 1 John?

John, the beloved disciple, is the author.

Who were the recipients?

The initial recipients were possibly a congregation in Asia Minor but certainly one that knew John well, for he addressed them as "my little children" (2:1) and "dear friends" (2:7). Undoubtedly the letter was circulated and read among other churches throughout Asia Minor.

When was 1 John written?

Between A.D. 80 and 95 is the time frame.

Where did it happen?

The multiple congregations were throughout Asia Minor.

What is 1 John about?

- *Love for God expressed in obedience*
- *Love for others*
- *The historical Jesus as the Christ*
- *Light versus darkness*
- *Pure doctrine*

Why should women read 1 John?

Do you know God? Do you know Jesus? Was the historical Jesus really the Son of God? Can you sin and still be a child of God? Do you know that you have eternal life? If any of these questions has troubled you, you need to read 1 John. This book will help to dismiss doubts you may possess about God's love for sinners or about the identity of Jesus Christ. You will learn what it means to have fellowship with God. You will find assurance that God forgives you when you sin and know for certain your eternal destiny. Read 1 John and become confident in your faith!

How do you read 1 John?

First John does not have the form of a letter. It uses simple, limited vocabulary, repetition, and contrasts. Although these features make its verses easy to understand, the truths they convey are profound. At the same time, reading 1 John involves some difficulty because John did not follow a logical outline. His structure seems more a spiral than linear. John presented themes, explained why he wrote, warned against false teachers, returned to develop his themes, and finally related his themes to each other. Expect some confusion as you try to follow his argument.

Keep in mind that John wrote to refute false prophets who did not love those in need, who probably claimed that they themselves were sinless, and who said that Jesus had not come in the flesh. Consequently, the apostle gives evidence for the incarnation of Christ, explains the importance of love for fellow believers, and shows the relationship between sin and being God's children. Look for what John has to say about God as light, love, and life. These truths will comfort you and give your faith certainty.

Outline

I. The Prologue: What Is True? (1:1-4)

II. True Fellowship Is in Christ (1:5–3:10)

- A. Living in Obedience to God (1:5–2:11)
  1. Walking in the Light (1:5–2:2)
  2. Following God's Commands (2:3-11)
- B. Orientation to God and to the World (2:12–3:10)
  1. The Christian's Response to the World (2:12-17)
  2. A Warning Against Antichrists (2:18-27)
  3. The Love of God the Father (2:28–3:3)
  4. The Contrast Between Lawlessness and Godliness (3:4-10)

III. God Is Love (3:11–5:17)

- A. The Necessity of God's Love (3:11-24)
  1. Life and Death (3:11-18)
  2. Assurance of Salvation (3:19-24)
- B. Testing the Spirits (4:1-6)
- C. Loving the Fellowship (4:7-21)
- D. Being Victorious Through Faith (5:1-5)
- E. Accepting the Witness of the Spirit (5:6-13)
- F. Receiving the Bounty of Prayer (5:14-17)
- G. Conclusion: What the Believer Knows (5:18-21)

>WORD|*study*

1:3 The word fellowship (Gk *koinōnia*, "close relationship, participation") suggests that a group, corporately or with each possessing an equal part, has joint ownership of something. In this instance, all believers are equal heirs of heaven. The fellowship that believers have with one another requires their own respective individual fellowship with God.

1:9 Confess combines two Greek words, *homos*, meaning "same," and *legō*, meaning "to say." *Confession,* then, is "saying the same" or "agreeing." Believers are called to say the same thing God says about sin—to see sin as God sees it. When a believer confesses personal sin and professes faith in Christ, then God will faithfully and justly **forgive** sin and cleanse him of all unrighteousness. Confession is essential to the believer's relationship with God and to fellowship with other people.

AD 66–70	AD 70–95	AD 80–90	AD 95
John's move from Jerusalem to Ephesus	John's ministry in Ephesus	Writing of the Gospel of John	Writing of Revelation: The Apocalypse

The Prologue: What Is True (1:1-4)

1 What was from the beginning,
what we have heard,
what we have seen
with our eyes,
what we have observed
and have touched
with our hands,
concerning the Word of life—
2 that life was revealed,
and we have seen it
and we testify and declare
to you
the eternal life that was
with the Father
and was revealed to us—
3 what we have seen and heard
we also declare to you,
so that you may have
fellowship along with us;
and indeed our fellowship is
with the Father
and with His Son
Jesus Christ.
4 We are writing these things[A]
so that our[B] joy
may be complete.

Living in Obedience to God (1:5–2:11)

Walking in the Light (1:5–2:2)

5 Now this is the message we have
heard from Him and declare to you:
God is light, and there is absolutely
no darkness in Him. 6 If we say, "We
have fellowship with Him," yet we
•walk in darkness, we are lying and
are not practicing[C] the truth. 7 But if
we walk in the light as He Himself is
in the light, we have fellowship with
one another, and the blood of Jesus
His Son cleanses us from all sin. 8 If
we say, "We have no sin," we are deceiving ourselves, and the truth is
not in us. 9 If we confess our sins, He
is faithful and righteous to forgive
us our sins and to cleanse us from
all unrighteousness. 10 If we say, "We
don't have any sin," we make Him a
liar, and His word is not in us.

2 My little children, I am writing you these things so that you
may not sin. But if anyone does sin,
we have an •advocate with the Father—Jesus Christ the Righteous
One. 2 He Himself is the •propitia-
tion for our sins, and not only for
ours, but also for those of the whole
world.

Following God's Commands (2:3-11)

3 This is how we are sure that we
have come to know Him: by keeping His commands. 4 The one who
says, "I have come to know Him,"
yet doesn't keep His commands, is
a liar, and the truth is not in him.
5 But whoever keeps His word, truly

A1:4 Other mss add *to you* B1:4 Other mss read *your* C1:6 Or *not living according to*

>WORD|*study*

2:1-2 John reminds his readers that when believers sin, in Jesus they **have an** advocate (Gk *paraklēton*, more lit "one called alongside," a word found five times in the Greek New Testament, all in John's writings). Here the term refers to the intercessory ministry of Christ as He stands before God the Father on behalf of His children. The word especially denotes one who is summoned to another's aid or one who pleads another's cause in a court of law, or before a judge, somewhat like a defense attorney. Jesus thwarts the evil one's accusations of sin against God's children by being the **Righteous One** and the **propitiation for our sins**. Jesus effectively pleads the sinner's case before the Father because as the sinless Lamb of God He has fulfilled the death penalty incurred by the sinner's crimes. John's four other uses of "advocate" refer to the Holy Spirit as "Counselor" (Jn 14:16,26; 15:26; 16:7).

Title: The Greek title "*Iōannou A*" ("Of John A") reflects the letter's author, John the beloved apostle.

1:1-4 The historical man Jesus is also the Christ. John wrote a clear progression of the gospel: It **was from the beginning**; it **was revealed**; it was proclaimed by the apostles and shared with others to **complete** their **joy**. John could speak with authority about Jesus because he was a witness to the life, teachings, and actions of Jesus during His earthly ministry. John knew the Word became flesh because he had **touched** the flesh.

1:5 John defines God as **light,** a metaphor for salvation or life in Scripture. The first-century Hellenistic culture used light as a symbol of goodness and as an indication of safety. John emphasizes that God is the ultimate good, the complete source of light for Christians. In Him there is **no darkness**, one of the most graphic metaphors for evil.

1:6-7 The life of an unbeliever is characterized by lying. The life of a Christian results in:

- fellowship with other believers and
- cleansing from sin through Jesus' blood. **Cleanses** (Gk *katharizei*) is in the perfect tense, indicating that the cleansing is a completed action with continuing results.

1:8 The false teachers imported elitism into Christianity. They believed that being a Christian gave one a higher position than others. Therefore, the Christian was considered perfect. Since the Christian was viewed as perfect, all she did was flawless, meaning that even in doing things that would be sinful for others to do, she would not be sinning. John repudiated this teaching.

2:3-4 The perfect tense of **have come to know** (Gk *ginōskomen*, "perceive, understand") affirms that an action from the past has a continual effect. John used this Greek verb 25 times in the epistle with the idea of having experiential knowledge or understanding, knowing on the basis of life experience or personal observation. John might have chosen not to use *gnōsis* because of the heresy his opponents embraced. To know God in the biblical sense is to have a personal relationship with Him through forgiveness of sin, not, as the false teachers claimed, merely to achieve release from ignorance. John offered a series of tests to provide the believer with assurance of salvation, beginning with the test of obedience. Obeying God's commandments is the natural, inevitable fruit of salvation—of knowing Christ. John used the strongest possible language about the person who claims to know Him but does not obey—that person **is a liar**. On the other hand, the believer's obedience to Him gives her assurance that she has **come to know Him**.

2:7-11 John gives the second test to provide the believer with assurance of salvation—the test of active love. This command ran contrary to that of those espousing the heresy whose focus was just intellectual. Their condition was analogous to physical blindness with the result that they did not know where they were going.

2:12-14 The three groups—**children**, **fathers** and **young men**—could refer to stages of spiritual development among John's readers. The "children" are new converts. "Young men" are growing in their relationship with the Lord, looking for guidance and wisdom. The "fathers" are Christians who have an intimate relationship with the Father, resulting in greater spiritual maturity. John focuses on the young men who are engaged in daily spiritual battles and commends them for overcoming Satan.

2:15-16 The world (Gk *kosmon*), God's whole creation in rebellion against Him, has an attitude of self-serving that is characteristic of a godless society. John shows the gradual progression of what results from loving the world:

- **the lust of the flesh**, sensuality or lack of restraint in desire for food, drink, or sexual gratification;
- **the lust of the eyes**, envious or greedy, engulfed in materialism;
- **the pride in one's lifestyle**, controlled by arrogance or motivated by thinking more highly of oneself, demanding power and position.

Each of these three snares represents a corruption of one of God's good gifts—the body, the eyes, possessions, and opportunities for leadership—putting one in opposition to God (also cp. Gn 3:6).

2:18 The **last hour** refers to the time following Christ's ascension and before His return.

>WORD|*study*

2:18 The word **antichrist** (Gk *antichristos*, "adversary of the Messiah," from the prefix *anti*, meaning "against, opposite to, instead of," and *Christos* or "anointed one, Messiah") is found only in John's letters (vv. 18,22; 4:3; 2 Jn 1:7).

in him the love of God is perfected.[A]
This is how we know we are in Him:
6 The one who says he remains in
Him should •walk just as He walked.
7 Dear friends, I am not writing
you a new command but an old
command that you have had from
the beginning. The old command
is the message you have heard. 8 Yet
I am writing you a new command,
which is true in Him and in you, because the darkness is passing away
and the true light is already shining.
9 The one who says he is in the light
but hates his brother is in the darkness until now. 10 The one who loves
his brother remains in the light, and
there is no cause for stumbling in
him.[B] 11 But the one who hates his
brother is in the darkness, walks
in the darkness, and doesn't know
where he's going, because the darkness has blinded his eyes.

Orientation to God and to the World (2:12–3:10)

The Christian's Response to the World (2:12-17)

12 I am writing to you,
little children,
because your sins have
been forgiven
because of Jesus' name.
13 I am writing to you, fathers,
because you have come
to know
the One who is
from the beginning.
I am writing to you,
young men,
because you have had victory
over the evil one.
14 I have written to you,
children,
because you have come
to know the Father.
I have written to you, fathers,
because you have come
to know
the One who is
from the beginning.
I have written to you,
young men,
because you are strong,
God's word remains in you,
and you have had victory
over the evil one.

15 Do not love the •world or the
things that belong to[C] the world.
If anyone loves the world, love
for the Father is not in him. 16 For
everything that belongs to[D] the
world—the lust of the flesh, the lust
of the eyes, and the pride in one's
lifestyle—is not from the Father,
but is from the world. 17 And the
world with its lust is passing away,
but the one who does God's will remains forever.

A Warning Against Antichrists (2:18-27)

18 Children, it is the last hour. And
as you have heard, "Antichrist is
coming," even now many antichrists
have come. We know from this that
it is the last hour. 19 They went out
from us, but they did not belong to
us; for if they had belonged to us,
they would have remained with us.
However, they went out so that it
might be made clear that none of
them belongs to us.
20 But you have an anointing from
the Holy One, and all of you have
knowledge.[E] 21 I have not written
to you because you don't know the
truth, but because you do know it,
and because no lie comes from the
truth. 22 Who is the liar, if not the one
who denies that Jesus is the •Mes-
siah? This one is the antichrist: the
one who denies the Father and the
Son. 23 No one who denies the Son
can have the Father; he who confesses the Son has the Father as well.
24 What you have heard from the
beginning must remain in you. If
what you have heard from the beginning remains in you, then you

[A]2:5 Or *truly completed* [B]2:10 Or *in it* [C]2:15 Lit *things in* [D]2:16 Lit *that is in* [E]2:20 Other mss read *and you know all things*

will remain in the Son and in the Father. 25 And this is the promise that He Himself made to us: eternal life. 26 I have written these things to you about those who are trying to deceive you.

27 The anointing you received from Him remains in you, and you don't need anyone to teach you. Instead, His anointing teaches you about all things and is true and is not a lie; just as He has taught you, remain in Him.

The Love of God the Father (2:28–3:3)

28 So now, little children, remain in Him, so that when He appears we may have boldness and not be ashamed before Him at His coming. 29 If you know that He is righteous, you know this as well: Everyone who does what is right has been born of Him.

3 1 Look at how great a love[A] the Father has given us that we should be called God's children. And we are! The reason the •world does not know us is that it didn't know Him. 2 Dear friends, we are God's children now, and what we will be has not yet been revealed. We know that when He appears, we will be like Him because we will see Him as He is. 3 And everyone who has this hope in Him purifies himself just as He is pure.

The Contrast between Lawlessness and Godliness (3:4-10)

4 Everyone who commits sin also breaks the law;[B] sin is the breaking of law. 5 You know that He was revealed so that He might take away sins,[C] and there is no sin in Him. 6 Everyone who remains in Him does not sin;[D] everyone who[E] sins has not seen Him or known Him.

7 Little children, let no one deceive you! The one who does what is right is righteous, just as He is righteous. 8 The one who commits[F] sin is of the Devil, for the Devil has sinned from the beginning. The Son of God was revealed for this purpose: to destroy the Devil's works. 9 Everyone who has been born of God does not sin,[G] because His[H] seed remains in him; he is not able to sin,[I] because he has been born of God. 10 This is how God's children—and the Devil's children—are made evident.

Whoever does not do what is right is not of God, especially the one who does not love his brother.

The Necessity of God's Love (3:11-24)

Life and Death (3:11-18)

11 For this is the message you have heard from the beginning: We should love one another, 12 unlike Cain, who was of the evil one and murdered[J] his brother. And why did he murder him? Because his works were evil, and his brother's were righteous. 13 Do not be surprised, •brothers, if the world hates you. 14 We know that we have passed from death to life because we love our brothers. The one who does not love remains in death. 15 Everyone who hates his brother is a murderer, and you know that no murderer has eternal life residing in him.

16 This is how we have come to know love: He laid down His life for us. We should also lay down our lives for our brothers. 17 If anyone has this world's goods and sees his brother in need but closes his eyes to his need—how can God's love reside in him?

18 Little children, we must not love with word or speech, but with truth and action.

Assurance of Salvation (3:19-24)

19 This is how we will know we belong to the truth and will convince our conscience in His presence, 20 even if our conscience condemns us, that God is greater than our conscience, and He knows all things.

21 Dear friends, if our conscience doesn't condemn us, we have confidence before God 22 and can receive whatever we ask from Him because we keep His commands and do what is pleasing in His sight. 23 Now this is His command: that we believe in the name of His Son Jesus Christ, and love one another as He commanded us. 24 The one who keeps His commands remains in Him, and He in him. And the way we know that He

[A] **3:1** Or *at what sort of love* [B] **3:4** Or *also commits iniquity* [C] **3:5** Other mss read *our sins* [D] **3:6** Or *not keep on sinning* [E] **3:6** Or *who keeps on sinning* [F] **3:8** Or *practices* [G] **3:9** Or *not practice sin* [H] **3:9** God's [I] **3:9** Or *to keep on sinning* [J] **3:12** Or *slaughtered*

The perception of "antichrist" by John's audience was inspired by people like Gaius (Roman emperor A.D. 37–41), who set up an image of himself in Jerusalem's temple as a reminder to his Jewish faction that they were to honor him as a god. John refers to such individuals as the **many antichrists** who would precede the **Antichrist** expected at the end time.

2:20 John reminds the believers that they **have an anointing** (Gk *chrisma*, "unction, appointment," lit "anything applied by smearing, ointment"). Most likely "anointing" refers to the work of the Holy Spirit in helping the believer understand the truth of Scripture.

2:21-27 John's third test is that of doctrine. One cannot claim to know God the Father without embracing God the Son. The discernment of the Spirit should give the believer the necessary perception to differentiate between true and false teachings.

3:4-10 The words **everyone who remains in Him does not sin** appear to contradict John's earlier assertion, "If we say, 'We don't have any sin,' we make Him a liar" (1:10). John does not teach that a believer will never commit an act of sin. The sense of the verse is, "Everyone who remains or lives in Christ does not keep on habitually and continually sinning." A believer's position in Christ and the indwelling Holy Spirit enables her to overcome habitual sinning (5:18). In addition, the believer has **His seed** (Gk *sperma*, "offspring, progeny, posterity," v. 9). Whether "seed" means the word of God (see Jms 1:18; 1Pt 1:23-25) or the principles emanating from the Word or a reference to the indwelling Holy Spirit (Jn 3:5-8)—all these serve to equip and strengthen the believer to battle the evil one and to emulate Christ in her lifestyle.

3:11-14 **Cain bore** evidence of being a child of the Devil. Cain hated Abel because Abel was more **righteous** than he (cp. Gn 4:3-12). For the same reason the world hates believers. The conditional clause **if the world hates you** suggests that the world's hatred of believers is not only a present existing reality but also a condition that will continue to exist in the future.

3:15-18 Proof of eternal life is given through the believer's love for her **brothers** in Christ. John contrasts **love** for fellow believers with its opposite—hatred, even murder of one's brother.

3:18-24 The heretical teachings must have caused even genuine believers in the fellowship to question their salvation. For that reason, John provides evidence of the readers' **confidence before God**:

- Believers possess an active love that shows itself in practical, working actions.
- God knows the truth **even if our conscience condemns us**. He knows all a person has done and will do in the future and confirms her salvation. God controls salvation, not the person.
- Believers experience answered prayer. If one asks anything in God's will, she is asking in obedience, not selfish desires.
- Believers obey God's commands, especially as the result of abiding in Christ.
- Believers have the personal indwelling of the Holy **Spirit**.

4:1-3 John's readers need to be reminded of the power of demonic forces and what such forces can do to a church, as well as how to distinguish evil spirits from the Holy Spirit. Returning to the doctrine of the historical Jesus as the Christ gives believers discernment.

4:4-6 John emphasizes the power of being a child of God by reminding believers that the Holy Spirit dwells in them. Satan was created by God, and the creation cannot be greater than the Creator.

4:9-16 The perfect tense of the verb **sent** shows the work of Jesus for the believer's salvation has staying power. The believer not only should have God's love but also should display that **love**. John presents three characteristics of the believer:

- the indwelling of the Holy Spirit,
- the confessing of **Jesus** as **the Son of God**, and
- living in God's love.

4:17-21 God's **love** is the reason no one in the fellowship should fear **the day of judgment**.

5:3-5 God's **commands are not a burden**. God will provide the believer what she needs to overcome the world and will create in her a new desire to be obedient to Him. Some believers may get discouraged with the human propensity to sin and feel that they have not overcome the world, but John reminds his readers that through union with Jesus the world is defeated.

remains in us is from the Spirit He
has given us.

Testing the Spirits (4:1-6)

4 Dear friends, do not believe every spirit, but test the spirits
to determine if they are from God,
because many false prophets have
gone out into the world.
2 This is how you know the Spirit of
God: Every spirit who confesses that
Jesus Christ has[A] come in the flesh is
from God. 3 But every spirit who does
not confess Jesus[B] is not from God.
This is the spirit of the antichrist; you
have heard that he is coming, and he
is already in the world now.
4 You are from God, little children,
and you have conquered them, because the One who is in you is greater than the one who is in the world.
5 They are from the •world. Therefore
what they say is from the world, and
the world listens to them. 6 We are
from God. Anyone who knows God
listens to us; anyone who is not from
God does not listen to us. From this
we know the Spirit of truth and the
spirit of deception.

Loving the Fellowship (4:7-21)

7 Dear friends, let us love one another, because love is from God, and
everyone who loves has been born of
God and knows God. 8 The one who
does not love does not know God,
because God is love. 9 God's love was
revealed among us in this way:[C] God
sent His •One and Only Son into the
world so that we might live through
Him. 10 Love consists in this: not
that we loved God, but that He loved
us and sent His Son to be the[D] •pro-
pitiation for our sins. 11 Dear friends,
if God loved us in this way, we also
must love one another. 12 No one has
ever seen God.[E] If we love one another, God remains in[F] us and His
love is perfected in us.
13 This is how we know that we
remain in Him and He in us: He
has given assurance to us from His
Spirit. 14 And we have seen and we
testify that the Father has sent His
Son as the world's Savior. 15 Whoever
confesses[G] that Jesus is the Son of
God—God remains in him and he in
God. 16 And we have come to know
and to believe the love that God has
for us. God is love, and the one who
remains in love remains in God, and
God remains in him.
17 In this, love is perfected with us
so that we may have confidence in
the day of judgment, for we are as
He is in this world. 18 There is no fear
in love; instead, perfect love drives
out fear, because fear involves punishment.[H] So the one who fears has
not reached perfection in love. 19 We
love[I] because He first loved us.
20 If anyone says, "I love God," yet
hates his brother, he is a liar. For the
person who does not love his brother he has seen cannot love the God
he has not seen.[J] 21 And we have this
command from Him: The one who
loves God must also love his brother.

Being Victorious Through Faith (5:1-5)

5 Everyone who believes that Jesus
is the •Messiah has been born of
God, and everyone who loves the
Father also loves the one born of
Him. 2 This is how we know that we
love God's children when we love
God and obey[K] His commands. 3 For
this is what love for God is: to keep
His commands. Now His commands
are not a burden, 4 because whatever has been born of God conquers
the •world. This is the victory that
has conquered the world: our faith.
5 And who is the one who conquers
the world but the one who believes
that Jesus is the Son of God?

Accepting the Witness of the Spirit (5:6-13)

6 Jesus Christ—He is the One
who came by water and blood, not
by water only, but by water and by
blood. And the Spirit is the One who
testifies, because the Spirit is the
truth. 7 For there are three that testify:[L] 8 the Spirit, the water, and the

[A]4:2 Or *confesses Jesus to be the Christ* [B]4:3 Other mss read *confess that Jesus has come in the flesh* [C]4:9 Or *revealed in us* [D]4:10 Or *a* [E]4:12 Since God is an infinite being, no one can see Him in His absolute essential nature; Ex 33:18-23. [F]4:12 Or *remains among* [G]4:15 Or *acknowledges* [H]4:18 Or *fear has its own punishment* or *torment* [I]4:19 Other mss add *Him* [J]4:20 Other mss read *has seen, how is he able to love . . . seen?* (as a question) [K]5:2 Other mss read *keep* [L]5:7-8 Other mss (Vg and a few late Gk mss) read *testify in heaven: the Father, the Word, and the Holy Spirit, and these three are One.* [8]*And there are three who bear witness on earth:*

Love in the New Testament

Who?
- The Father loves His children (3:1).
- Believers (God's children) love the Father (2:15; 4:20).
- Believers love one another (1:7; 2:10; 3:14,23; 4:21).

Where? Believers love one another in this world (4:17).

What?
- God loved us and sent His Son to be the propitiation for our sins (4:10).
- God is love (4:16).
- Believers who love lay down their lives for fellow Christians (3:16).
- Believers demonstrate love and compassion by sharing their possessions with brothers in need (3:17).
- Believers show their love for God by keeping His commands (5:2-3).

How? Believers love:
- in deed and truth (3:18),
- by doing what is right (3:10), and
- without fear (4:18).

Why?
- Christ laid down His life for us (3:16; 4:10).
- Love is from God (4:7,10).
- God first loved us (3:1; 4:19).
- Christ commands believers to love (3:23; 4:21; 5:2).

When? Love is "present tense"—here and now (4:7-16).

blood—and these three are in agreement. 9 If we accept the testimony of men, God's testimony is greater, because it is God's testimony that He has given about His Son. 10 (The one who believes in the Son of God has this testimony within him. The one who does not believe God has made Him a liar, because he has not believed in the testimony God has given about His Son.) 11 And this is the testimony: God has given us eternal life, and this life is in His Son.

12 The one who has the Son has life. The one who doesn't have the Son of God does not have life. 13 I have written these things to you who believe in the name of the Son of God, so that you may know that you have eternal life.

Receiving the Bounty of Prayer (5:14-17)

14 Now this is the confidence we have before Him: Whenever we ask anything according to His will, He hears us. 15 And if we know that He hears whatever we ask, we know that we have what we have asked Him for.

16 If anyone sees his brother committing a sin that does not bring death, he should ask, and God[A] will give life to him—to those who commit sin that doesn't bring death. There is sin[B] that brings death. I am not saying he should pray about that. 17 All unrighteousness is sin, and there is sin that does not bring death.

Conclusion: What the Believer Knows (5:18-21)

18 We know that everyone who has been born of God does not sin, but the One[C] who is born of God keeps him,[D,E] and the evil one does not touch him.

19 We know that we are of God, and the whole world is under the sway of the evil one.

20 And we know that the Son of God has come and has given us understanding so that we may know the true One.[F] We are in the true One—that is, in His Son Jesus Christ. He is the true God and eternal life.

21 Little children, guard yourselves from idols.

[A]5:16 Lit *He* [B]5:16 Or *is a sin* [C]5:18 Jesus Christ [D]5:18 Other mss read *himself* [E]5:18 Or *the one who is born of God keeps himself* [F]5:20 Other mss read *the true God*

5:7-13 These verses are not in some of the earliest texts and were often found as side notes before they were officially added to the text in the 1520s. They confirm that the Holy **Spirit** is the testimony upon which believers should depend. John bore witness to the baptism (**water**), death (**blood**), and resurrection of Jesus. The Holy Spirit is God's witness to Jesus. God the Father also testified to the ministry of Jesus at His baptism (Mt 3:17).

5:16-17 Some scholars see the **sin** resulting in **death** as a reference to physical death, while others hold that this alludes to the spiritual death coming to those false teachers who had heard a clear presentation of the gospel but openly rejected it. The **sin that brings death** (Gk *thanaton*) was probably apostasy. The heretics were committing this sin.

1 JOHN… WRITTEN ON MY *Heart*

Sometimes you may question whether or not you have genuine saving knowledge of God. First John offers you some simple tests to assure you of your relationship with God through Jesus: Are you obeying God's commandments? Do you love others, especially fellow Christians? Do you believe that Jesus is the Christ, the Son of God, and that He came physically to the world? Then, know that God has saved you and given you eternal life. You will still sin and need to confess it, but a true believer does not make disobedience the pattern of her life. When you do sin, God forgives, and you have an Advocate with the Father—Jesus Christ the Righteous One.

2 John

Timeline ➡ **World Events** ➡ **Biblical Events**	***AD 29*** Jesus' appointment of John and his brother James as two of His 12 apostles	***AD 32*** Transfiguration of Jesus witnessed by John, James, and Peter	***AD 33*** Jesus' request from the cross for John to care for His mother Mary	***AD 44*** Martyrdom of John's brother James

"This is love: that we walk according to His commands" (v. 6).

Who wrote 2 John?

John, the beloved disciple, is the author.

Who were the recipients?

Multiple congregations throughout Asia Minor received the epistle.

When was 2 John written?

The date of composition was between A.D. 80 to 95, probably around A.D. 90.

Where did it happen?

The epistle was written from Ephesus to multiple congregations throughout Asia Minor.

What is 2 John about?

- *The truth of the gospel and Jesus Christ*
- *Love for others*
- *Warning about false teachers*

Why should women read 2 John?

Reminders help you stay "on track." The brief epistle of 2 John will help you to remain on God's course for your life by reminding you of the basics of the Christian life—truth and love. It will also warn you against helping any false teachers who distort the facts of the gospel of Jesus Christ.

How do you read 2 John?

Second John is a personal letter from John to believers he knew and loved. This epistle reflects the character of first-century Greco-Roman letters in its brevity—it had to fit on a single page of papyrus. It presents in abbreviated form the message of 1 John with its emphases on believers loving one another and the Incarnation (as opposed to the teachings of the false teachers). As you read, note what words John repeated—truth, love, walk, command, and deceiver, revealing his purpose for writing.

Itinerant missionaries were important in the spread of Christianity. Believers often provided hospitality to them in the form of room and board. That background explains John's instructions in 2 John about not welcoming false teachers into their homes. Perhaps those who had left the congregation (1 John) had now traveled to another fellowship (2 John) to spread their heresy. John did not condemn hospitality to unbelievers but to those who opposed the true teachings of the Christian faith.

Outline

I. Address and Salutation (vv. 1-3)
II. Following God's Commands (vv. 4-6)
III. The Truth Versus the Deceivers (vv. 7-11)
IV. Conclusion (vv. 12-13)

Title: In the Greek New Testament, the title is simply *"Iōannou B,"* designating it as John's second letter.

1 The **elder** (Gk *ho presbuteros*, "the presbyter or older man") in this context is a title of authority.

Truth refers to what is ultimately real and genuine—God Himself and more especially His Son Jesus who identified Himself as the truth (Jn 14:6). John uses the Greek verb **love**, *agapaō* ("value, esteem, be faithful towards"), suggesting unconditional

Address and Salutation (vv. 1-3)

The Elder:[A]
To the elect lady[B] and her
children: I love all of you in the
truth—and not only I, but also all
who have come to know the truth—
2 because of the truth that remains
in us and will be with us forever.
3 Grace, mercy, and peace will be
with us from God the Father and
from Jesus Christ, the Son of the
Father, in truth and love.

Following God's Commands (vv. 4-6)

4 I was very glad to find some of
your children •walking in the truth,

[A]1 Or *Presbyter* [B]1 Or *Kyria*, a proper name; probably a literary figure for a local church known to John; the children would be its members.

>WORD|*study*

1 Lady (Gk *kuria*) is the feminine form of *kurios*, "lord," a term showing respect for the recipient(s) of the letter. **Elect** (Gk *eklektē*, "chosen, selected, picked out") also suggests the idea of "excellence." Some scholars think the "elect lady" was an actual woman. Her name could have been *Electa, Kuria*, or *Electa Kuria*. However, through context and the frequent feminine personification of the church in the New Testament, most have concluded that the "elect lady" refers to a church. The words **her children** indicate members of the congregation.

AD 66–70	*AD 70–95*	*AD 80–90*	*AD 80–90*	*AD 95*
John's move from Jerusalem to Ephesus	John's ministry in Ephesus	Writing of 1 John	Writing of the Gospel of John	John's exile to Patmos; writing of Revelation

in keeping with a command we have received from the Father. 5 So now I urge you, dear lady—not as if I were writing you a new command, but one we have had from the beginning—that we love one another. 6 And this is love: that we walk according to His commands. This is the command as you have heard it from the beginning: you must walk in love.[A]

The Truth vs. the Deceivers (vv. 7-11)

7 Many deceivers have gone out into the world; they do not confess the coming of Jesus Christ in the flesh.[B] This is the deceiver and the antichrist. 8 Watch yourselves so you don't lose what we[C] have worked for, but that you may receive a full reward. 9 Anyone who does not remain in Christ's teaching but goes beyond it, does not have God. The one who remains in that teaching, this one has both the Father and the Son. 10 If anyone comes to you and does not bring this teaching, do not receive him into your home, and don't say, "Welcome," to him; 11 for the one who says, "Welcome," to him shares in his evil works.

Conclusion (vv. 12-13)

12 Though I have many things to write to you, I don't want to do so with paper and ink. Instead, I hope to be with you and talk face to face[D] so that our joy may be complete.

13 The children of your elect sister send you greetings.

[A]6 Lit *in it* [B]7 Or *confess Jesus Christ as coming in the flesh* [C]8 Other mss read *you* [D]12 Lit *mouth to mouth*

love, uniquely characteristic of Christ and His followers. John's inclusion of **all who have come to know the truth** also confirms that he was writing to a church.

2 John affirms that God's truth **remains in** (Gk *menousan en*, "remains, abides in, continues to be present, does not depart, lasts or endures") the believer and never leaves.

4-6 John praises the obedience of **some** of the members of the church. This implies that not all the members of the church were **walking in the truth** and love. John addressed the entire church with the words, **So now I urge you, dear lady**. He is urging the same action as in his first letter—love demonstrated in practical ways in the fellowship of believers. Those who believe the truth will walk in it by expressing love to others.

7 John warns the fellowship about **deceivers** (Gk *planoi*, "leading astray, wandering or roving") who may try to propagate false doctrine about Christ. These deceivers seem to embrace the same false knowledge, i.e., Jesus was not fully human, as the false teachers mentioned in 1 John. True believers confess the historical Jesus as the Christ. **The coming of Jesus Christ in the flesh** is a present active participle, meaning that Jesus Christ came in the flesh and continues to remain in the flesh—He never stopped being human. John labeled one advocating the heretical view as **the deceiver** [figuratively meaning wandering from the truth, designates one who "leads into error, an imposter or deceiver"] **and the antichrist** (Gk *antichristos*, one actively opposed to Christ). False teachers who peddle heretical doctrine have an inadequate understanding of Jesus.

8 The warning, **watch yourselves** (Gk *blepete*) stresses vigilance both in the negative sense (**don't lose what we have worked for**) and the positive (**you may receive a full reward**). The apostle wants those in the fellowship to be continually on alert and to avoid becoming complacent. Complacency could result in some loss, not of salvation, but of heavenly reward.

9 Promoters of the heresy that John refutes viewed themselves as superior to others because they believed their special knowledge of God made them Christians. However, their knowledge was outside of Scripture or **beyond** [Gk *proagōn*, "lead out, go before" in the sense of "running ahead"] **it**. They claimed advanced teaching but actually had moved beyond the boundaries of biblical truth. They had tried to separate God the Father from God the Son, resulting in heresy.

10-11 John does not mean that believers cannot have false teachers in their homes for the purpose of loving confrontation concerning God's truth. He warns believers not to **welcome** these deceivers into their homes for the purpose of furthering the heresy. Such a welcome could result in the believer's alignment with the deceiver—at least in public perception.

13 If the elect lady is a church, the **elect sister** (Gk *adelphēs*, "sister, fellow-believer") refers to another church under John's care.

2 JOHN… WRITTEN ON MY *Heart*

This tiny letter encourages you to study and know God's Word—the Bible, the source of truth. Then, you will be able to identify those who promote a message opposed to its teachings. You must take care that you do not align yourself with or support those who distort the truth of the gospel. This epistle also causes you to ask yourself, "Am I obeying the Lord completely by loving others? Am I putting that love into action by helping, giving, and meeting needs?"

3 John

Timeline World Events Biblical Events	*AD 29* Jesus' appointment of John and his brother James as two of His 12 apostles	*AD 32* Transfiguration of Jesus witnessed by John, James, and Peter	*AD 33* Jesus' request from the cross for John to care for His mother Mary	*AD 44* Martyrdom of John's brother James

"You are showing faithfulness by whatever you do for the brothers" (5).

Who wrote 3 John?

John, the beloved disciple, the son of Zebedee and brother of James, is the author.

Who were the recipients?

Gaius received the letter.

When was 3 John written?

The epistle was written between A.D. 80 and 95.

Where did it happen?

The epistle was written to Gaius from Ephesus.

What is 3 John about?

- *Appreciation for Gaius*
- *Rebuke of Diotrephes*
- *Commendation of Demetrius*
- *Hospitality, especially to ministers*

Why should women read 3 John?

Many women find social media fascinating as they glimpse the lives of friends, acquaintances, and even strangers. The personal, private letter of 3 John will provide a glance into the lives of three Christian men who lived in the first century. Two provide examples to imitate; one serves as a negative role model. Read to discover what you can learn from these three men.

How do you read 3 John?

When you read 3 John, you are viewing the words of a personal letter written to a specific individual, Gaius, and not to a church. Only Philemon shares this distinctive. This letter is the shortest in the New Testament. Its contents center around four personalities: John the Elder, who wrote the letter; Gaius, who received the letter; Diotrephes, who caused the letter to be written; and, Demetrius, who carried the letter from John to Gaius. Third John provides insight into the early church communities and the need for believers to extend hospitality to traveling Christians, especially approved itinerant teachers.

Outline

I. Salutation (vv. 1-4)
II. Exhortation to Gaius (vv. 5-8)
III. Diotrephes and Demetrius (vv. 9-12)
   A. Condemnation of Diotrephes (vv. 9-10)
   B. Commendation of Demetrius (vv. 11-12)
IV. Conclusion (vv. 13-14)

Three Men in 3 John

Gaius (vv. 1-8)	Diotrephes (vv. 9-10)	Demetrius (vv. 11-12)
• Name meaning "lord" (Lat) • Beloved friend of the Apostle John • Committed to the truth • Demonstrating his faith • Loving others unconditionally • Extending hospitality to friends and strangers • An example to all Christians	• Name meaning "nourished or supported by Zeus" (Gk god of the sky and ruler of the Olympian pantheon) • A prominent member of the church • Refusing to assist workers in the kingdom • Spurning the authority of John • Causing division in the church	• Name meaning "belonging to Demeter" (Gk goddess of agriculture) • A good reputation among believers • Accepting God's truth • Walking in faith • Having a testimony of faithfulness

AD 66–70	**AD 70–95**	**AD 80–90**	**AD 80–90**	**AD 95**
John's move from Jerusalem to Ephesus	John's ministry in Ephesus	Writing of 1 John	Writing of the Gospel of John	John's exile to Patmos; writing of Revelation

Salutation (vv. 1-4)

The Elder:

To my dear friend[A] Gaius: I love you in the truth.

2 Dear friend,[B] I pray that you may prosper in every way and be in good health physically just as you are spiritually.[C] 3 For I was very glad when some •brothers came and testified to your faithfulness to the truth—how you are •walking in the truth. 4 I have no greater joy than this: to hear that my children are walking in the truth.

Exhortation to Gaius (vv. 5-8)

5 Dear friend,[B] you are showing faithfulness[D] by whatever you do for the brothers, especially when they are strangers. 6 They have testified to your love in front of the church. You will do well to send them on their journey in a manner worthy of God, 7 since they set out for the sake of the Name, accepting nothing from pagans. 8 Therefore, we ought to support such men so that we can be coworkers with[E] the truth.

Diotrephes and Demetrius (vv. 9-12)

Condemnation of Diotrephes (vv. 9-10)

9 I wrote something to the church, but Diotrephes, who loves to have first place among them, does not receive us. 10 This is why, if I come, I will remind him of the works he is doing, slandering us with malicious words. And he is not satisfied with that! He not only refuses to welcome the brothers himself, but he even stops those who want to do so and expels them from the church.

Commendation of Demetrius (vv. 11-12)

11 Dear friend,[B] do not imitate what is evil, but what is good. The one who does good is of God; the one who does evil has not seen God. 12 Demetrius has a good testimony from everyone, and from the truth itself. And we also testify for him, and you know that our testimony is true.

Conclusion (vv. 13-14)

13 I have many things to write you, but I don't want to write to you with pen and ink. 14 I hope to see you soon, and we will talk face to face.[F]

Peace be with you. The friends send you greetings. Greet the friends by name.

A1 Or *my beloved* B2,5,11 Or *Beloved* C2 Lit *as your soul prospers* D5 Lit *are doing a faithful thing* E8 Or *coworkers for* F14 Lit *mouth to mouth*

3 JOHN… WRITTEN ON MY Heart

John encourages fellow Christians who walk in the truth and demonstrate kindness to others. Do you? Gaius worked faithfully and selflessly in the church, demonstrating his faith through love and hospitality. Do you? Prideful Diotrephes refused to offer hospitality and rejected rightful authority. Do you? Demetrius had a good reputation among believers and had a high regard for the truth. Do you? How would others describe your character?

Title: In the Greek New Testament the title *"Iōannou C"* designates it as John's third letter.

1-2 John refers to himself as **the Elder** (Gk *presbuteros*), providing a sense of authority for the letter. He expresses affection for **Gaius**, his **dear friend** (Gk *agapēte*, "one who is loved, beloved"). No other information is available on Gaius in Scripture. He probably occupied a position of leadership in the church. The phrase **just as you are spiritually** (lit "just as your soul [Gk *psuchē*] prospers") suggests that John was concerned for the spiritual health of Gaius as well as his physical health.

3-4 John commends Gaius for his obedience to God's commands as reported by other Christians. Gaius might have been one of John's converts since the apostles often referred to their converts as their children. John wrote of the **joy** he felt to learn that his **children are walking in the truth**.

5-8 John praises Gaius for treating the itinerant teachers with proper hospitality and respect so as to honor the Lord's **name. To send them on their journey** meant providing basic necessities—food and money needed to help them travel comfortably. To be supported by fellow believers put these teachers in contrast to the itinerant philosophers and beggar priests of pagan deities who requested compensation and favors in exchange for their instruction.

9-10 Unlike Gaius, **Diotrephes** refused to **welcome the brothers** and even prevented other members of the church from extending such hospitality. He also spurned John's authority. John describes Diotrephes as one **who loves to have first place** (Gk *philoprōteuōn*). The word expresses the ambitious desire to be above everyone else, and the present tense adds the idea of continual and habitual action.

11-12 When John wrote for Gaius to **imitate . . . what is good**, he was entreating him to continue his hospitality and walk in the truth. He commended **Demetrius** as an example of one **who has a good testimony from everyone**. Demetrius was probably John's carrier for the letter to Gaius.

Jude

Timeline	2085 BC	1446 BC	1420 BC	1406 BC
World Events / Biblical Events	Destruction of Sodom and Gomorrah	Exodus of the Israelites from Egyptian bondage	Korah's rebellion	Death of Moses

"Contend for the faith" (v. 3).

Who wrote Jude?
Jude, brother of Jesus (1:1), is the author.

Who were the recipients?
Jewish Christians in an unknown location received the letter.

When was Jude written?
The epistle was written between A.D. 65 and 80.

What is Jude about?
- *The importance of sound doctrine*
- *The danger of false teachers*
- *An exhortation to faithfulness*

Why should women read Jude?
Do you ever minimize the sinfulness of sin? Have you twisted the Bible to justify your own opinions and sinful behavior? Read Jude's epistle. This brother and servant of Jesus shouts a clear warning to avoid any false teachers and behavior that would lead you away from Christian truth and godly living.

How do you read Jude?
Jude wrote with a specific purpose in mind. False teachers had wormed their way into Jewish Christian churches. Jude targeted at least two particularly deceptive heresies, antinomianism and spiritual elitism. "Antinomianism" (Gk *anti*, "against" and *nomos*, "law") is a misinterpretation of Christian freedom as meaning to be set free from the moral imperatives of Old Testament law. Having cast off the obligation to pursue righteousness as prescribed in Scripture, those who subscribed to the heresy also cast off moral restraint in the name of freedom. Jude refers to the distinctly unchristian manifestations of this thinking in verse 4 ("turning the grace of our God into promiscuity") and his description of the "sexual immorality" that mirrored the perverted lifestyles of Sodom and Gomorrah (v. 7). Jude also countered the false teachers' claims to spiritual authority on the basis of ecstatic visions and private spiritual experience. He denounced such imposters as "not having the Spirit" at all (v. 19).

These heretics denied the Lordship of Jesus by their immoral lifestyle. They encouraged others to follow their wrong example. Jude describes these individuals and their actions in negative terms. He uses numerous examples from the Old Testament showing God's judgment on this behavior. He reminds his readers that the apostles had predicted the presence of such scoffers and how they would divide fellowships. Jude wanted these believers to defend the truth of the gospel. He assured them—and contemporary Christians as well—that God would keep them from stumbling and bring them into His presence innocent of sin and with great joy.

Outline
I. Introductory Greeting (vv. 1-2)
II. A Purpose for Writing the Letter (vv. 3-4)
III. A Reminder for the Recipients (vv. 5-11)
IV. A Description of the Intruders (vv. 12-16)
V. An Exhortation for Believers (vv. 17-23)
VI. Concluding Doxology (vv. 24-25)

>WORD|*study*

3 The Greek word for **Contend** (Gk *epagōnizesthai*, "fight") combines the prefix *epi-* ("on") and *agōnizomai* ("enter a contest; fight against adversaries; endeavor with strenuous zeal to obtain something," figuratively, "struggle with difficulties and dangers"). The word conveys the idea of agonizing effort given to defend ground (in military action) or to struggle for a prize (in an athletic competition). The root verb is the source of the English word "agonize."

3 Dear friends (Gk *agapētoi*, "beloved, worthy of love") is a warm term denoting God's love and care for His people. By using this term repeatedly, Jude reminded his readers of their relationship with Christ as Savior. In the context of the full letter, Jude linked this relationship to the last judgment. For those persevering through the difficulties of this life, the view of eternal reward and punishment was paramount.

AD 33	AD 62	AD 70	AD 96
Pentecost	Martyrdom of James, the brother of Jesus and leader of the church at Jerusalem	Destruction of Jerusalem	Appearance of Jude's grandsons before Emperor Domitian

Introductory Greeting (vv. 1-2)

Jude, a •slave of Jesus Christ and a
brother of James:
To those who are the called, loved[A]
by God the Father and kept by Jesus
Christ.
2 May mercy, peace, and love be
multiplied to you.

A Purpose for Writing the Letter (vv. 3-4)

3 Dear friends, although I was eager
to write you about the salvation we
share, I found it necessary to write
and exhort you to contend for the
faith that was delivered to the •saints
once for all. 4 For some men, who
were designated for this judgment
long ago, have come in by stealth;
they are ungodly, turning the grace of
our God into promiscuity and denying Jesus Christ, our only Master and
Lord.

A Reminder for the Recipients (vv. 5-11)

5 Now I want to remind you, though
you know all these things: The Lord[B]
first[C] saved a people out of Egypt and
later destroyed those who did not believe; 6 and He has kept, with eternal
chains in darkness for the judgment
of the great day, the angels who did
not keep their own position but deserted their proper dwelling. 7 In the
same way, Sodom and Gomorrah
and the cities around them committed sexual immorality and practiced
perversions,[D] just as angels did, and
serve as an example by undergoing
the punishment of eternal fire.
8 Nevertheless, these dreamers
likewise defile their flesh, reject
authority, and blaspheme glorious ones. 9 Yet Michael the archangel, when he was disputing with
the Devil in a debate about Moses'
body, did not dare bring an abusive condemnation against him but
said, "The Lord rebuke you!" 10 But
these people blaspheme anything
they don't understand. What they
know by instinct like unreasoning
animals—they destroy themselves
with these things. 11 Woe to them!
For they have traveled in the way of
Cain, have abandoned themselves to
the error of Balaam for profit, and
have perished in Korah's rebellion.

[A]1 Other mss read *sanctified* [B]5 Other mss read *Jesus/Joshua, God,* or *God Christ* [C]5 Other mss place *first* after *remind you* [D]7 Lit *and went after other flesh*

Title: The name of Jude (Gk *Ioudas*), a slave of Jesus Christ and a brother of James is the title.

1-2 The relationship between Jesus and His brothers during His earthly ministry was tense because they did not yet believe in Him (Mk 6:3-4; Jn 7:5). However, at some point **Jude** recognized and consequently served and worshiped Jesus as God.

3 Jude challenged the recipients of his letter **to contend for the faith that was delivered to the saints** because of the presence of false teachers in the church. Their teaching had to be confronted and corrected for the good of the fellowship.

4 These rebellious men did not blatantly proclaim their heresy, but they deceitfully infiltrated the church. Jude describes them as **ungodly** and promiscuous. Their actions denied the Lordship of Christ. Jude relates doctrine to practice. He illustrates his condemnation of the false teachers using their own behavior and practices.

5-11 Jude includes seven historical examples of those who exhibited various responses to the mercy of God. These accounts reminded Jewish believers of both good and bad choices made in the salvific history of Israel.

5 The exodus of the Israelites from Egypt and their rescue from slavery were pivotal in the history of Israel. Jude reminds his readers of God's faithfulness and warns them about the consequences of infidelity. The people of Israel rebelled against the Lord with grumbling and disbelief in the desert; therefore, they were not allowed into the promised land (Nm 14).

6 Jude refers to the pre-cosmic rebellion of Satan and his coterie of **angels** who rebelled against God (see Lk 10:18; Is 14:1-15; Ezk 28:1-19). God cast Satan and his followers out of heaven. These angels would not escape **judgment**.

7 The **sexual immorality** of **Sodom and Gomorrah** was similar to that of the intruders. Jude reminded the believers that **eternal fire** awaited all those who indulged in this sort of rebellion.

8 Jude describes the deceiving teachers as **dreamers** (Gk *enupniazomenoi*, "receive some supernatural impression or information in a dream or cherish vain opinions"). Jude was not condemning all those who dream or have ambition, but he was condemning those who based their entire lives on vain visions. Their dreams were selfish and autonomous and without respect to any **authority**, including God's.

9 According to Jewish history, the archangel **Michael** refused to rebuke **the Devil** when arguing with him over **Moses' body**. He chose to trust God to do that. Michael's example stands in contrast to those who disobeyed God.

11 Cain was the first man to commit murder—the homicide of his own brother (Gn 4:8). When God rebuked Cain for his offering, he chose to rebel by killing his brother rather than correcting his own wrongs. The **error of Balaam** rested in Balaam's defiant unwillingness to bless Israel because of his own greed (Nm 22–24; Dt 23:4-5). Korah rebelled against the leadership of Moses and Aaron (Nm 16). He did not respect the authority of God's servants. As a result, the earth consumed Korah and his allies. The false teachers confronting Jude's readers were similar to Cain, Balaam, and Korah in their defiance, greed, and insubordinate attitude toward authority. Their actions would have consequences.

12 Jude likens the false teachers to **dangerous reefs at your love feasts.** Common among the practices of the early church was the sharing of a large meal, which ended with the Lord's Supper. Reefs are large underwater rocks that cause trouble for ships because they are difficult to see. These false teachers were difficult to identify at their fellowships. As reefs cause unexpected damage and shipwreck, these false teachers also caused damage to the faith. **Waterless clouds** and **trees in late autumn** refer to the lack of depth and help found in the false teachers.

13 Jude also compares these teachers to **wild waves of the sea** and **wandering stars.** The surging waves of the sea produce sticky foam. The licentious lifestyle of these men produced shameful deeds. They were like wandering stars that provided no navigational assistance. The false teachers could not provide genuine assurance.

14-15 Although the false prophets could fool some, God knew the nature of their teaching and misdeeds. He would **execute judgment on all.**

21 Jude contrasts the impure lives of the false teachers to the proper behavior of those who truly know the Lord, urging his readers to **keep yourselves in the love of God.** The **mercy of our Lord Jesus Christ for eternal life** should motivate believers.

24-25 Jude concludes his letter with a doxology. He reminded the believers of the nature and character of God. He would keep them pure and holy for eternity.

>WORD|*study*

16 Jude also called these men **grumblers** (Gk *goggustai*, "speak privately in a low voice, mutter, utter secret and sullen discontent"). They were arrogant, selfish, and flatterers. In this sense Jude rejected his opponents on theological and moral grounds.

A Description of the Intruders (vv. 12-16)

12 These are the ones who are like
dangerous reefs[A] at your love feasts.
They feast with you, nurturing only
themselves without fear. They are
waterless clouds carried along by
winds; trees in late autumn—fruitless, twice dead, pulled out by the
roots; 13 wild waves of the sea, foam-
ing up their shameful deeds; wandering stars for whom the blackness
of darkness is reserved forever!
14 And Enoch, in the seventh generation from Adam, prophesied
about them:

Look! The Lord comes[B]
with thousands
of His holy ones
15 to execute judgment on all
and to convict them[C]
of all their ungodly acts
that they have done
in an ungodly way,
and of all the harsh things
ungodly sinners
have said against Him.

16 These people are discontented
grumblers, •walking according to
their desires; their mouths utter arrogant words, flattering people for
their own advantage.

An Exhortation for Believers (vv. 17-23)

17 But you, dear friends, remember
what was predicted by the apostles
of our Lord Jesus Christ; 18 they told
you, "In the end time there will be
scoffers walking according to their
own ungodly desires." 19 These people create divisions and are unbelievers,[D] not having the Spirit.
20 But you, dear friends, as you
build yourselves up in your most
holy faith and pray in the Holy
Spirit, 21 keep yourselves in the love
of God, expecting the mercy of our
Lord Jesus Christ for eternal life.
22 Have mercy on those who doubt;
23 save others by snatching them
from the fire; have mercy on others
but with fear, hating even the garment defiled by the flesh.

Concluding Doxology (vv. 24-25)

24 Now to Him who is able to protect you from stumbling and to make
you stand in the presence of His glory, blameless and with great joy, 25 to
the only God our Savior, through
Jesus Christ our Lord,[E] be glory, majesty, power, and authority before all
time,[F] now and forever. •Amen.

[A]12 Or *like spots* [B]14 Or *came* [C]15 Lit *convict all* [D]19 Or *natural* [E]25 Other mss omit *through Jesus Christ our Lord* [F]25 Other mss omit *before all time*

JUDE . . . WRITTEN ON MY *Heart*

Bible teachers and study materials abound. How do you know what to study and with whom to study? Jude helps you observe these teachers. What kind of lives do they live? What fruit do their ministries produce? What kind of relationships do they have? Does godliness characterize their behavior? What beliefs do these Bible study leaders hold? By trusting God, rooting and grounding yourself in Him and His truths, you will not fall prey to heretics and what they advocate. Nor will you follow their fruitless, immoral conduct.

HARD QUESTION

How do you appropriate godly authorities in your life?

For the Christian woman today, Jude's lesson concerning authority and its place in her life is of special importance. Many see relationships of authority as having no significance. Feminist ideology has taught women and men that they are completely autonomous with the right to define themselves, their world, and their God.

However, Scripture teaches that understanding authority is essential to understanding how you properly relate to God and others. Jude confronted certain men who had crept into the fellowship of believers by giving examples of others who had despised authority. He urged his readers to consider negative and positive examples of those in relationships of authority. For the Christian woman, the example of Michael is appropriate as he willingly submitted to God to take care of the Devil in His own way (vv. 8-9). Christian women also do well to obey God through submission to authority while trusting Him to take care of the outcome.

BIBLICAL WOMANHOOD Rescue the Perishing

One of the most valuable but often difficult ministries to which you may be called is confronting a sister who gives evidence of taking a wrong path. If you saw this sister in great physical danger, you would go to almost any length to stand between her and that danger. Spiritual and moral dangers have even greater consequences, although they are not as obvious.

For those in trouble with regard to their faith, Jude instructed the Jewish believers to **save** them **by snatching them from the fire** (v. 23). This phrase does not mean that they were already in the fire, but rather that they were in danger of fire. They must be admonished strongly and carefully so as to restore their faith. Others were to be shown **mercy . . . but with fear**. This mercy was not without recognition of sin's consequences. The believers were to respond lovingly to those with garments **defiled by the flesh**, while also deeply despising their sin.

Revelation

Timeline World Events Biblical Events	*AD 44* Execution of James, John's brother, by Herod Agrippa	*AD 64* Great fire in Rome, for which the emperor Nero blamed and executed Christians	*AD 66* Martyrdom of Peter in Rome	*AD 69–79* Reign of the Roman emperor Vespasian

"Look! I am coming quickly . . ." (22:12).

Who wrote Revelation?

The Apostle John (1:1,4) is the author.

Who were the recipients?

Christians in Asia Minor were facing increasing persecution because they refused to worship the emperor of Rome.

When was Revelation written?

The book was written in A.D. mid-90s.

Where did it happen?

John was on the island of Patmos when he received and recorded the revelation from God. After the letters to the churches (chaps. 2–3), what John saw included the throne room of heaven and the unfolding of future events involving both heaven and the whole earth.

What is Revelation about?

- *Division between the followers of the Lamb and the followers of "the beast"*
- *Practical obedience*
- *God's sovereign rule over the world*
- *Jesus Christ, fully divine and equal to God in nature and status*
- *Eschatology—the doctrine of last things*

Why should women read Revelation?

Do news headlines discourage you—wars, murders, weather catastrophes, and promotion of attitudes and behaviors that Christians label sin? Does wickedness seem widespread and growing stronger? Does the persecution of believers anger you? Then, you need to read the book of Revelation. Its message proclaims hope. It affirms that God is sovereign and in control. Jesus is returning to vindicate the righteous and judge the wicked. Satan and his followers, evil in every form, and those who reject Christ as Lord will be punished and defeated. Christ will reign victoriously and believers will live in God's presence forever. "Amen! Come, Lord Jesus!" (22:20).

How do you read Revelation?

Revelation presents challenges to contemporary readers because John wrote his letter as words of prophecy in the form of apocalyptic literature, similar to parts of Daniel in the Old Testament. This style of writing uses symbolic images to express its message. John interpreted the most important of the images, identifying, for example, "the great dragon" as Satan (12:9). Other images have a well-known meaning historically, such as an earthquake signifying God's judgment. View each vision as a whole without trying to identify the meaning of each detail.

As you read, remember that John saw the messages God gave him as a fulfillment of the Old Testament. You will find hundreds of allusions to the Old Testament. The last chapter of Revelation appropriately pictures a restored garden of Eden.

Keep in mind the historical setting of the first readers of Revelation. The apostle wrote to offer hope to the suffering believers as well as to warn those who were not living as Christians should. God would judge the Roman Empire. John saw the suffering of first-century churches in a broader context—the conflict between God and Satan. God would ultimately judge all people, governments, and spiritual beings who rebel against Him and cause His people to suffer.

Outline

I. The Prologue (1:1-20)
II. The Messages to Seven Churches of Asia (2:1–3:22)
III. Adoration in the Throne Room of Heaven (4:1–5:14)
IV. The Seven Seals (6:1–8:6)
V. The Seven Trumpets (8:7–11:19)
VI. Two Great Signs and Their Interpretation (12:1-18)
VII. The Two Beasts and Their Deception (13:1-18)
VIII. The Firstfruits and the Harvest (14:1-20)
IX. The Seven Last Plagues (15:1–16:21)
X. Babylon and Her Destiny (17:1–19:5)
XI. The Final Victory (19:6–20:15)
XII. The New Heaven and New Earth (21:1–22:5)
XIII. Epilogue (22:6-21)

>WORD|*study*

1:1-2 Revelation (Gk *apokalupsis*, "unveiling, uncovering, laying bare, disclosure," anglicized as *apocalypse*) indicates that the book is categorized as apocalyptic literature, comparable to the Old Testament book of Daniel. "Revelation" specifically refers to God's unveiling to John His plan for the world. More broadly, however, the message is conveyed through a genre of ancient literature characterized by the prediction of future events, accounts of visionary experiences or journeys, and vivid symbolism.

AD 70	AD 79	AD 79–81	AD 81–96	AD 95
Capture of Jerusalem by Vespasian's son Titus; destruction of the temple	Volcanic eruption of Mt. Vesuvius, burying the cities of Pompeii and Herculaneum	Reign of the Roman emperor Titus	Reign of the Roman emperor Domitian	Traditional date of John's exile to the island of Patmos

Eschatology Terms

Allegorical Interpretation	A method that looks beyond the literal sense of a historical statement for symbolic meanings of people, places, things, or events
Apocalypse (Gk *apokalupsis*, "unveiling")	The anglicized title for the New Testament book of Revelation
***Bēma* (Gk "raised platform")**	The judgment seat of God, before which every Christian must appear to give an account and to receive rewards (Rm 14:10-12; 2Co 5:10)
Eschatology (Gk *eschaton*, "end, last")	The branch of theology focusing on study of "last things, end times, or events to be fulfilled in the future"
Kingdom	In the New Testament, this word appears in various contexts: (1) Christ's earthly kingdom, (2) the Father's heavenly kingdom, or (3) the sovereign reign of Christ in a believer's heart.
Israel	Most often a reference to the literal national group called "Israel"
Millennium (Lat, "1,000 years")	A reference to the 1,000-year reign of Christ, during which Satan is imprisoned (Rv 20:1-7)
Rapture (Gk *harpagēsometha*, "catch up, snatch away, seize"; Lat *rapiemur*, "carried off")	Word used to describe the way believers will meet the Lord upon His return; removal of believers from the world when Christ returns (1Th 4:17)
Tribulation	A seven-year period of intense suffering on earth, unlike any other in history (Dn 12:1; Zph 1:15; Mt 24:21-22,29; Mk 13:19,24; Lk 21:25-26; Rv 7:14)

The Prologue (1:1-20)

The Title (1:1-3)

1 The revelation of[A] Jesus Christ
that God gave Him to show His
•slaves what must quickly[B] take
place. He sent it and signified it[C]
through His angel to His slave John,
2 who testified to God's word and to
the testimony[D] about Jesus Christ,
in all he saw.[E] 3 The one who reads
this is blessed, and those who hear
the words of this prophecy and keep[F]
what is written in it are blessed, because the time is near!

Greetings and Praise to Jesus (1:4-8)

4 John:

To the seven churches in •Asia.

Grace and peace to you from[G]
the One who is, who was, and who
is coming; from the seven spirits[H]
before His throne; 5 and from Jesus
Christ, the faithful witness, the

A1:1 Or *Revelation of*, or *A revelation of* B1:1 Or *soon* C1:1 Made it known through symbols D1:2 Or *witness* E1:2 Lit *as many as he saw* F1:3 Or *follow*, or *obey* G1:4 Other mss add *God* H1:4 Or *the sevenfold Spirit*

Title: The full title is **the revelation of Jesus Christ** (v. 1). "Revelation" suggests a great secret or mystery that human ability cannot discover. God alone must reveal such realities.

1:3 This verse represents the first of seven "blessing" statements, or beatitudes, in the book.

1:4 The seven spirits before His throne may refer to the angels of **the seven churches** (2:1,8,12,18; 3:1,7,14) or other angels (8:2). Because the number "seven" often symbolizes completion or perfection, the "seven spirits" may also represent the fullness of the Holy Spirit (see Is 11:2).

THE SEVEN CHURCHES OF REVELATION

- City
- Cities of the Seven Churches
- Major road

Patmos, the small island in the Aegean Sea off the western coast (present-day Turkey) is where John was exiled when he received and wrote the Revelation. The Romans used Patmos as a place for political exiles. Eusebius, an early church historian, wrote that John was sent to Patmos by Emperor Domitian in A.D. 95 and was released after 18 months. John was pastor in Ephesus, one of the seven cities of the book of Revelation, some 50 miles from Patmos. Marked with a symbol are the seven cities where the churches addressed in chapters 2 and 3 of Revelation were located. The messages to the seven churches have none of the normal characteristics of ancient letters; rather they are styled as prophetic oracles or messages. There is no evidence they were ever sent out independently of the book.

Doctrine of God Focus on God's Sovereign Rule

1:4,8	"The One who is, who was, and who is coming" affirms that God is always in control—past, present, and future. His omnipresent sovereignty guarantees the future fulfillment of His promises to His people.
1:8	"The Alpha and the Omega" points to divine sufficiency. God is not only in charge of the past and future but also everything in between.
1:8	"The Almighty" signifies the omnipotence of God, which ensures His ultimate triumph over the forces of evil.
4:2-3	The exalted One "seated on the throne" emphasizes His holiness and incomprehensible wisdom.
15:3	"Lord God, the Almighty . . . King of the Nations" magnifies God's rule over all nations.

firstborn from the dead and the ruler of the kings of the earth.
To Him who loves us and has set
us free[A] from our sins by His blood,
6 and made us a kingdom,[B] priests[C]
to His God and Father—the glory
and dominion are His forever and
ever. •Amen.

7 **Look! He is coming**
with the clouds,
and **every eye will see Him,**
including those
who pierced[D] **Him.**
And all the families
of the earth[E,F]
will mourn over Him.[G,H]
This is certain. Amen.

8 "I am the •Alpha and the Omega,"
says the Lord God, "the One who is,
who was, and who is coming, the Almighty."

John's Vision and Commission to Write (1:9-20)

9 I, John, your brother and partner
in the tribulation, kingdom, and
endurance that are in Jesus, was on
the island called Patmos because of
God's word and the testimony about
Jesus.[I] 10 I was in the Spirit[J,K] on the
Lord's day,[L] and I heard a loud voice
behind me like a trumpet 11 saying,
"Write on a scroll[M] what you see and
send it to the seven churches: Ephesus, Smyrna, Pergamum, Thyatira,
Sardis, Philadelphia, and Laodicea."
12 I turned to see whose voice it
was that spoke to me. When I turned
I saw seven gold lampstands, 13 and
among the lampstands was One like
the •Son of Man,[N] dressed in a long
robe and with a gold sash wrapped
around His chest. 14 His head and
hair were white like wool—white
as snow—and His eyes like a fiery flame. 15 His feet were like fine
bronze as it is fired in a furnace, and
His voice like the sound of cascading[O] waters. 16 He had seven stars
in His right hand; a sharp double-
edged sword came from His mouth,
and His face was shining like the
sun at midday.[P]
17 When I saw Him, I fell at His feet
like a dead man. He laid His right
hand on me and said, "Don't be
afraid! I am the First and the Last,
18 and the Living One. I was dead, but
look—I am alive forever and ever,
and I hold the keys of death and •Ha-
des. 19 Therefore write what you have
seen, what is, and what will take
place after this. 20 The •secret of the
seven stars you saw in My right hand
and of the seven gold lampstands is
this: The seven stars are the angels[Q]
of the seven churches, and the seven
lampstands[R] are the seven churches.

1:5 Jesus Christ is **the faithful witness** (Gk *martus*, "one who testifies, provides a testimony, or attests to the veracity of a claim," from which the English word "martyr" is derived). Revelation makes clear that God who is "King of the Nations" (15:3) has made Christ the "King of kings" (17:14; 19:16), the ruler and judge over all. Jesus **loves** (Gk *agapōnti*, "loving unconditionally and self-sacrificially) believers. He **has set** them **free** [Gk *lusanti*, "loose or release from that which binds, untie, release, break, destroy, overthrow"] **from** their **sins**.

1:7 This verse, perhaps the theme verse of Revelation, predicts the return of Christ and emphasizes the contrast between His first coming and His future return.

1:8 Alpha and **Omega**, the first and last letters of the Greek alphabet, affirm God's eternal nature.

1:9 Historical tradition indicates that the Roman Emperor Domitian exiled John to the **island called Patmos** about A.D. 95.

1:10-11 The phrase **in the Spirit** occurs three other times (4:2; 17:3; 21:10), each time meaning, "I had a vision inspired by the Spirit of God." John possibly used this phrase to organize the book around the four major visions.

1:13-15 Jesus referred to Himself with the title **Son of Man** from Dn 7:13 to identify Himself indirectly as the Messiah without awakening the inevitable misunderstanding that using the term *Messiah* would have created in the Jewish community.

A1:5 Other mss read *has washed us* B1:6 Other mss read *kings and* C1:6 Or *made us into* (or *to be*) *a kingdom of priests*; Ex 19:6 D1:7 Or *impaled* E1:7 Or *all the tribes of the land* F1:7 Gn 12:3; 28:14; Zch 14:17 G1:7 Or *will wail because of Him* H1:7 Dn 7:13; Zch 12:10 I1:9 Lit *the witness of Jesus* J1:10 Or *in spirit*; lit *I became in the Spirit* K1:10 John was brought by God's Spirit into a realm of spiritual vision. L1:10 Sunday M1:11 Or *book* N1:13 Or *like a son of man* O1:15 Lit *many* P1:16 Lit *like the sun shines in its power* Q1:20 Or *messengers* R1:20 Other mss add *that you saw*

>WORD|*study*

2:7 Jesus referred to the believer as a VICTOR (Gk *nikōnti*, "one who conquers, prevails, or is victorious over enemies"). The Greek New Testament uses the verb 28 times—24 in John's writings, including 17 in Revelation, where the word most often describes Jesus as conqueror (3:21; 5:5; 6:2; 17:14; 21:7) and saints as victors (12:11; 15:2). Twice "the beast" is the subject of the verb, only by divine permission (11:7; 13:7). Revelation contains Jesus' personal promises of rewards to those in and through whom Christ displays His complete triumph over evil (2:7,11,17,26,28; 3:5,12,21). The book thus depicts the fulfillment of Jesus' promise of victory to His disciples (Jn 16:33). The victorious ones are all those who overcome the world and its sufferings even to the point of death.

2:10 The purpose of these experiences is TO TEST (Gk *peirasthēte*, "ascertain by trial"; see 2:2; 3:10) them. The verb can be understood to have a double meaning. Satan desires to "tempt" them to apostatize, and God desires to "test" their faith.

The Messages to Seven Churches of Asia (2:1–3:22)

The Message to Ephesus (2:1-7)

2 "Write to the angel[A] of the church in Ephesus:

"The One who holds the seven stars in His right hand and who walks among the seven gold lampstands says: 2 I know your works, your labor, and your endurance, and that you cannot tolerate evil. You have tested those who call themselves apostles and are not, and you have found them to be liars. 3 You also possess endurance and have tolerated many things because of My name and have not grown weary. 4 But I have this against you: You have abandoned the love you had at first. 5 Remember then how far you have fallen; repent, and do the works you did at first. Otherwise, I will come to you[B] and remove your lampstand from its place—unless you repent. 6 Yet you do have this: You hate the practices of the Nicolaitans, which I also hate.

7 "Anyone who has an ear should listen to what the Spirit says to the churches. I will give the victor the right to eat from the tree of life, which is in[C] God's paradise.

The Message to Smyrna (2:8-11)

8 "Write to the angel of the church in Smyrna:

"The First and the Last, the One who was dead and came to life, says: 9 I know your[D] affliction and poverty, yet you are rich. I know the slander of those who say they are Jews and are not, but are a •synagogue of Satan. 10 Don't be afraid of what you are about to suffer. Look, the Devil is about to throw some of you into prison to test you, and you will have affliction for 10 days. Be faithful until death, and I will give you the crown[E] of life.

11 "Anyone who has an ear should listen to what the Spirit says to the churches. The victor will never be harmed by the second death.

The Message to Pergamum (2:12-17)

12 "Write to the angel of the church in Pergamum:

"The One who has the sharp, double-edged sword says: 13 I know[F] where you live—where Satan's throne is! And you are holding on to My name and did not deny your faith in Me,[G] even in the days of Antipas, My faithful witness who was killed among you, where Satan lives. 14 But I have a few things against you. You have some there who hold to the teaching of Balaam, who taught Balak to place a stumbling block[H] in front of the Israelites: to eat meat sacrificed to idols and to commit sexual immorality.[I] 15 In the same way, you also have those who hold to the teaching of the Nicolaitans.[J] 16 Therefore repent! Otherwise, I will come to you quickly and fight against them with the sword of My mouth.

17 "Anyone who has an ear should listen to what the Spirit says to the churches. I will give the victor some of the hidden manna.[K] I will also give him a white stone, and on the stone a new name is inscribed that

[A] **2:1** Or *messenger* here and elsewhere [B] **2:5** Other mss add *quickly* [C] **2:7** Other mss read *in the midst of* [D] **2:9** Other mss add *works and* [E] **2:10** Or *wreath* [F] **2:13** Other mss add *your works and* [G] **2:13** Or *deny My faith* [H] **2:14** Or *to place a trap* [I] **2:14** Or *commit fornication* [J] **2:15** Other mss add *which I hate* [K] **2:17** Other mss add *to eat*

2:1–3:22 The messages to the seven churches have a similar order. Each is prefaced with a charge to write to the angel of the specific church (2:1,8,12,18; 3;1,7,14). Then,

- a characteristic of Christ is described;
- a compliment of the church is given;
- a criticism of the church is made (except for the churches of Smyrna and Philadelphia);
- a command to the church is given; and
- a commitment from Christ is made to those who are obedient to Christ until death.

The messages address the practical problems of individual churches in light of the imminent return of Jesus Christ. They provide the historical background for the rest of Revelation. The themes of moral purity, overcoming evil, endurance amidst suffering, and eternal reward are threads woven throughout Revelation.

2:1-7 Ephesus (modern Kusadasi in Turkey), located on a major harbor in western Asia Minor, was one of the most powerful cities in the Roman Empire.

2:1 Because Jesus is walking among the churches, He knows what they are doing. As Head of the church, He can rightly criticize their actions and motives.

2:4 The love you had at first may refer to their love for Christ as new converts or to their lack of love for one another.

2:5-6 If the Ephesian church refused to **repent** (Gk *metanoēsēs*, "change one's mind," esp. for the better, forsaking sin; a key word in Revelation), Christ would **remove** their **lampstand from its place**. While Christ has vowed that His church will flourish worldwide (Mt 16:18), He gave no promise of permanence to any individual congregation. **The Nicolaitans** were a heretical group who appeared also in the church of Pergamum (Rv 2:14-15).

2:7 The entreaty for all to **listen to what the Spirit says to the churches** reminds readers that the messages to the churches are for all of Christ's followers. Jesus promised the Ephesians that **the victor**—the one who is faithful to Christ and His teachings unto death—will be given eternal life; see chart, p. 1647.

2:8-11 Smyrna (Hb, "myrrh, bitterness"), modern Izmir in Turkey—another harbor city known for its architectural beauty, an imposing array of pagan temples, material wealth, and civic pride—had a large Jewish

>WORD|*study*

2:17 New (Gk *kainon*, "unused, novel, unprecedented") signifies God's activity, particularly in terms of the future fulfillment of His redemptive purpose. When Christ's reign is revealed to all, the victors receive a **new name**; a "new Jerusalem" comes "down out of heaven from God" (3:12; 21:2) and is "called by a new name" (Is 62:2); the saints sing "a new song" (5:9; 14:3); and there is "a new heaven and a new earth" (21:1). The "One seated on the throne" exclaims, "Look! I am making everything new" (21:5).

2:20 Woman (Gk *gunaika*, "wife") occurs 19 times in the Greek text of Revelation. With two exceptions (Rv 9:8; 14:4), each time the word occurs a significant character in Revelation's drama is being addressed. Here the word refers to the false **prophetess** named **Jezebel**, probably metaphorically describing her character. Chapter 12 uses derivatives of the word eight times as the "great sign" in heaven portrays "a woman clothed with the sun" (12:1), who gives birth to "a Son" (12:5), a symbol of Christ. The word appears six times describing the mysterious "notorious prostitute" identified as "Babylon the Great" (17:15,18; 18:2). The final two uses are for the bride of the Lamb making herself ready for her bridegroom (19:7) and then for the bride of Christ in the eternal state (21:9).

2:22 Great tribulation refers to a general time of intense affliction, the nature of which is not known. Its use foreshadows the affliction to come upon the whole earth (3:10; 7:14).

no one knows except the one who receives it.

The Message to Thyatira (2:18-29)

18 "Write to the angel of the church in Thyatira:

"The Son of God, the One whose eyes are like a fiery flame and whose feet are like fine bronze,[A] says: 19 I know your works—your love, faithfulness,[B] service, and endurance. Your last works are greater than the first. 20 But I have this against you: You tolerate the woman Jezebel, who calls herself a prophetess and teaches and deceives My •slaves to commit sexual immorality[C] and to eat meat sacrificed to idols. 21 I gave her time to repent, but she does not want to repent of her sexual immorality.[D] 22 Look! I will throw her into a sickbed and those who commit adultery with her into great tribulation, unless they repent of her[E] practices. 23 I will kill her children with the plague.[F] Then all the churches will know that I am the One who examines minds[G] and hearts, and I will give to each of you according to your works. 24 I say to the rest of you in Thyatira, who do not hold this teaching, who haven't known the deep things[H] of Satan—as they say—I do not put any other burden on you. 25 But hold on to what you have until I come. 26 The one who is victorious and keeps My works to the end: I will give him authority over the nations—

27 **and he will shepherd[I] them**
with an iron scepter;
he will shatter them
like pottery[J]—

just as I have received this from My Father. 28 I will also give him the morning star.

29 "Anyone who has an ear should listen to what the Spirit says to the churches.

The Message to Sardis (3:1-6)

3 "Write to the angel of the church in Sardis:

"The One who has the seven spirits of God and the seven stars says: I know your works; you have a reputation[K] for being alive, but you are dead. 2 Be alert and strengthen[L] what remains, which is about to die, for I have not found your works complete before My God. 3 Remember, therefore, what you have received and heard; keep it, and repent. But if you are not alert, I will come[M] like a thief, and you have no idea at what hour I will come against you.[N] 4 But you have a few people[O] in Sardis who have not defiled[P] their clothes, and they will walk with Me in white, because they are worthy. 5 In the same way, the victor will be dressed in white clothes, and I will never erase

A2:18 Probably gleaming white hot; Rv 1:15 B2:19 Or *faith* C2:20 Or *commit fornication* D2:21 Or *her fornication* E2:22 Other mss read *their* F2:23 Or *I will surely kill her children* G2:23 Lit *kidneys* H2:24 Or *the secret things* I2:27 Or *rule*; see 19:15 J2:27 Ps 2:9 K3:1 Lit *have a name* L3:2 Other mss read *guard* M3:3 Other mss add *upon you* N3:3 Or *upon you* O3:4 Lit *few names* P3:4 Or *soiled*

population that bitterly opposed Christianity.

2:12-15 In the first century A.D., the city of Pergamum was the leading religious center of Asia Minor. Countless temples, shrines, and altars were dedicated to the many gods of the area. The temple of Asklepius, the Greek god of healing, was the most famous. The Pergamum church, however, tolerated the presence of heretics, those **who hold to the teaching of Balaam,** a Gentile prophet enlisted by **Balak,** king of Moab (Nm 22–24), to place a curse on the Israelites. The Israelites committed immorality with Moabite women and worshiped Baal (Nm 25:1-3). Apparently, the teaching of the Nicolaitans was causing similar sin among its followers in the church at Pergamum.

2:17 A white stone served as a type of ancient "ticket" into a feast or community gathering, figuratively here, the feast of the Messiah in the kingdom of God. White and black stones were also used in ancient Greek courts to indicate acquittal or condemnation, respectively, and as a means of voting in elections.

2:18 Thyatira (modern Akhisar) was a commercial town located on the Lycus River and the smallest and least important of the seven cities to whom John wrote. Although the economy and social life of most Roman cities centered around trade guilds, those of Thyatira were especially prominent, notably shoemakers, sellers of dyed cloth (such as Lydia, Ac 16:12-15), and bronzesmiths. Each guild had a patron god or goddess, and social events centered on their worship. The pressure for Christians to participate in this idolatrous, immoral lifestyle was great economically and socially.

2:20-23 The weaknesses of the Thyatiran believers, however, outweighed their strengths. They were tolerating **the woman Jezebel, who calls herself a prophetess** and who was teaching Christians **to commit sexual immorality and to eat meat sacrificed to idols.**

3:1 Sardis (modern Sart in Turkey), founded around 1200 B.C. and one of the most ancient cities in Asia Minor, was built on the slope of Mount Tmolus and thus was almost impregnable to intruders unless its walls were left unguarded. The people of Sardis, who were especially interested in death and immortality, sought after the divine in the fertility cycles of nature and the worship of Artemis, the goddess of fertility. Jesus had no words of praise for the church in Sardis. The church had many **works** and **a reputation**

for being alive, but it was spiritually **dead**.

3:7 Philadelphia (Gk "brotherly love," combining *philos*, "love," and *adelphos*, "brother, sibling"), modern Alaşehir in Turkey, was an agriculturally prosperous city on the main trade route to the east coast of Asia Minor where Mysia, Lydia, and Phrygia came together. Although the earthquake of A.D. 17 affected Sardis as well, Philadelphia was nearer the epicenter and suffered more lasting effects. Thus, the people made long-term and short-term plans with earthquakes in mind.

3:8-10 An open door offers encouragement to believers who have experienced persecution—the promise of entrance to the messianic kingdom as a reward for faithful service.

3:12-13 The **victor** will be made **a pillar in the sanctuary of My God**. The idea is one of permanence and stability, a comforting promise to people living in a region frequently stricken by earthquakes.

3:15-17 Jesus did not commend **the church in Laodicea**. They were **neither cold nor hot** but **lukewarm**. Because the Laodiceans did not have a water supply, they had to pipe in their water from a hot spring four miles away. By the time the water reached the city, it was lukewarm in contrast to water in the nearby cities of Colossae, whose waters were cold, pure, and refreshing to drink, and Hierapolis, whose hot springs were well known for their healing and therapeutic effect on the body. Christ was saying that their deeds were worthless to Him, and for that reason He was going **to vomit** them out of His **mouth**. Jesus has no use for a church that is not serving her proper purpose. Also, the Laodicean church's wealth had led to self-sufficiency, complacency, and pride. Jesus exposed the truth: they were **wretched**, **pitiful**, **poor**, **blind**, **and naked**—elements of shame and degradation in the ancient world.

3:18-20 Jesus advised three things: spiritual riches, not earthly wealth; clothing of righteousness, not earthly attire; and spiritual discernment, not earthly vision. He urged the church to **be committed** and **repent**. Christ used the illustration of standing **at the door** of the church, announcing His presence and eagerness to join them in fellowship. The person who **hears** Christ's **voice** has a personal responsibility to open the door, for Christ does not share a meal with someone who does not want Him. In Near Eastern cultures sharing a meal meant sharing a life.

>WORD|*study*

3:8-10 To **bow down** (Gk *proskunēsousin*, "worship") in Oriental custom was to kneel and bow to the floor, touching one's forehead to the ground, as an expression of reverence. The root word is *kuon*, "dog," expressing the kind of loyalty demonstrated by a dog licking its master's hand. The word generally portrays kneeling or prostrating oneself to demonstrate homage or respect to one of superior rank and therefore often denotes worship. The Old Testament taught that the Gentile nations would be forced to bow down to the Jews in the kingdom of God (Is 60:14), but here the promise was given a new meaning. Israel will have a different attitude toward the church and turn to pay homage even to Gentile believers.

3:10 The identity of **those who live on the earth** or the "earth-dwellers" is key to understanding the events described in the book of Revelation. The earth-dwellers are unbelievers (17:8), who are held responsible for the deaths of believing martyrs (6:10) and upon whom the "hour of testing" is focused (3:10). They make themselves the enemies of God by worshiping the beast and persecuting believers. The **hour of testing**, then, is the period of time preceding the return of Christ during which God will pour out His wrath upon the unbelieving world.

his name from the book of life but will acknowledge his name before My Father and before His angels.

6 "Anyone who has an ear should listen to what the Spirit says to the churches.

The Message to Philadelphia (3:7-13)

7 "Write to the angel of the church in Philadelphia:

"The Holy One, the True One, the One who has the key of David, who opens and no one will close, and closes and no one opens says: 8 I know your works. Because you have limited strength, have kept My word, and have not denied My name, look, I have placed before you an open door that no one is able to close. 9 Take note! I will make those from the •synagogue of Satan, who claim to be Jews and are not, but are lying—note this—I will make them come and bow down at your feet, and they will know that I have loved you. 10 Because you have kept My command to endure,[A] I will also keep you from the hour of testing that is going to come over the whole world to test those who live on the earth. 11 I am coming quickly. Hold on to what you have, so that no one takes your crown. 12 The victor: I will make him a pillar in the sanctuary of My God, and he will never go out again. I will write on him the name of My God and the name of the city of My God—the new Jerusalem, which comes down out of heaven from My God—and My new name.

13 "Anyone who has an ear should listen to what the Spirit says to the churches.

The Message to Laodicea (3:14-22)

14 "Write to the angel of the church in Laodicea:

"The •Amen, the faithful and true Witness, the Originator[B] of God's creation says: 15 I know your works, that you are neither cold nor hot. I wish that you were cold or hot. 16 So, because you are lukewarm, and neither hot nor cold, I am going to vomit[C] you out of My mouth. 17 Because you say, 'I'm rich; I have become wealthy and need nothing,' and you don't know that you are wretched, pitiful, poor, blind, and naked, 18 I advise you to buy from Me gold refined in the fire so that you may be rich, white clothes so that you may be dressed and your shameful nakedness not be exposed, and ointment to spread on your eyes so that you may see. 19 As many as I love, I rebuke and discipline. So be committed[D] and repent. 20 Listen! I stand at the door and knock. If anyone hears My voice and opens the door, I will come in to him and have dinner with him, and he with Me. 21 The victor: I will give him the right to sit with Me on My throne, just as I also won the victory and sat down with My Father on His throne.

22 "Anyone who has an ear should listen to what the Spirit says to the churches."

Adoration in the Throne Room of Heaven (4:1–5:14)

The Throne and its Surroundings (4:1-11)

4 After this I looked, and there in heaven was an open door. The

[A] 3:10 Lit *My word of endurance* [B] 3:14 Or *Ruler*, or *Source*, or *Beginning* [C] 3:16 Or *spit* [D] 3:19 Or *be zealous*

first voice that I had heard speaking
to me like a trumpet said, “Come up
here, and I will show you what must
take place after this.”
2 Immediately I was in the Spirit,[A]
and a throne was set there in heaven.
One was seated on the throne, 3 and
the One seated[B] looked like jasper[C]
and carnelian[D] stone. A rainbow that
looked like an emerald surrounded
the throne. 4 Around that throne
were 24 thrones, and on the thrones
sat 24 elders dressed in white clothes,
with gold crowns on their heads.
5 Flashes of lightning and rumblings
of thunder came from the throne.
Seven fiery torches were burning before the throne, which are the seven
spirits of God. 6 Something like a
sea of glass, similar to crystal, was
also before the throne. Four living
creatures covered with eyes in front
and in back were in the middle[E] and
around the throne. 7 The first living
creature was like a lion; the second
living creature was like a calf; the
third living creature had a face like a
man; and the fourth living creature
was like a flying eagle. 8 Each of the
four living creatures had six wings;
they were covered with eyes around
and inside. Day and night they never
stop,[F] saying:

Holy, holy, holy,[G]
Lord God, the Almighty,
who was, who is,
and who is coming.

9 Whenever the living creatures give
glory, honor, and thanks to the One
seated on the throne, the One who
lives forever and ever, 10 the 24 elders
fall down before the One seated on
the throne, worship the One who
lives forever and ever, cast their
crowns before the throne, and say:

11 Our Lord and God,[H]
You are worthy to receive
glory and honor and power,
because You have created
all things,
and because of Your will
they exist and were created.

The Lamb and the Seven-sealed Scroll (5:1-14)

5 Then I saw in the right hand of
the One seated on the throne a
scroll with writing on the inside
and on the back, sealed with seven
seals. 2 I also saw a mighty angel
proclaiming in a loud voice, “Who is
worthy to open the scroll and break
its seals?” 3 But no one in heaven or
on earth or under the earth was able
to open the scroll or even to look in
it. 4 And I cried and cried because no
one was found worthy to open[I] the
scroll or even to look in it.
5 Then one of the elders said to me,
“Stop crying. Look! The Lion from
the tribe of Judah, the Root of David,
has been victorious so that He may
open the scroll and[J] its seven seals.”
6 Then I saw One like a slaughtered
lamb standing between[K] the throne
and the four living creatures and
among the elders. He had seven
horns and seven eyes, which are the
seven spirits of God sent into all the
earth. 7 He came and took the scroll[L]
out of the right hand of the One
seated on the throne.
8 When He took the scroll, the four
living creatures and the 24 elders
fell down before the Lamb. Each one
had a harp and gold bowls filled with
incense, which are the prayers of the
•saints. 9 And they sang a new song:

You are worthy to take
the scroll
and to open its seals,
because You
were slaughtered,
and You •redeemed[M] people[N]
for God by Your blood
from every tribe and language
and people and nation.
10 You made them a kingdom[O]
and priests to our God,
and they will reign
on the earth.

11 Then I looked and heard the
voice of many angels around the
throne, and also of the living creatures and of the elders. Their number was countless thousands, plus

[A]4:2 Or *in spirit*; lit *I became in the Spirit* [B]4:3 Other mss omit *and the One seated* [C]4:3 A precious stone [D]4:3 A translucent red gem [E]4:6 Lit *In the middle of the throne* [F]4:8 Or *they never rest* [G]4:8 Other mss read *holy* 9 times [H]4:11 Other mss add *the Holy One*; other mss read *Lord* [I]5:4 Other mss add *and read* [J]5:5 Other mss add *loose* [K]5:6 Or *standing in the middle of* [L]5:7 Other mss exclude *the scroll* [M]5:9 Or *purchased* [N]5:9 Other mss read *us* [O]5:10 Other mss read *them kings*

4:1–5:14 Chapters 4 and 5 contain John's vision of the heavenly throne room. They highlight the God of creation (chap. 4, in which the Father is central) and the God of redemption (chap. 5, in which the Son is the focus). Worship dominates this vision.

4:1-11 Parallels to this vision of the throne are found in Ezk 1:4-28, Is 6:1-4, and Dn 7:9-14.

4:1 God would reveal to John His intended progression of events for the conclusion of redemption history.

4:2-3 Jasper is an opaque jewel found in many different colors, especially associated with the glory of God. **Carnelian stone** is fiery red and was very popular in the ancient world.

4:4 The **24 elders** are human beings, representative of the redeemed.

4:5 The **flashes of lightning and rumblings of thunder** coming from the throne recall the appearance of God to the Israelites at Mount Sinai (Ex 19:16-19).

4:6-8a Nothing in creation escapes the gaze of the **four living creatures**, who represent the noblest, strongest, wisest, and swiftest among God's living beings (see Ezk 1:5-6,10-11). Having **six wings** and **eyes around and inside** seems to combine the descriptions of the cherubim (Ezk 1; 10) and the seraphim (Is 6), representing the highest order of celestial beings who lead in worship and judgment (Rv 6:1,3,5,7).

4:8b-11 The four living creatures celebrate God's holiness, power and eternality.

5:1 The **right hand** of God symbolizes power and authority. The **scroll** (Gk *biblion*, "small book") not only includes lamentation but also God's perfect plan (symbolized by the number seven) for redeeming His creation, which will culminate in the end times. The contents of the scroll can only be revealed, however, when all seven seals affixed to the outside of the scroll are removed.

5:6-7 The victorious nature of Jesus is rooted in the fact that He was slain for the sins of the world. Yet, the sacrificial **lamb** also has **seven horns**, symbolic of the Messiah-Warrior who would lead the people of God to victory. The sevenfold Holy Spirit described as **sent** emphasizes His role in the gospel's proliferation throughout the world.

5:11-14 This hymn stresses the unity and equality of God the Father and God the Son. All created beings without exception worship God and His Son.

thousands of thousands. 12 They said with a loud voice:

The Lamb who was
slaughtered is worthy
to receive power and riches
and wisdom and strength
and honor and glory
and blessing!

13 I heard every creature in heaven, on earth, under the earth, on the sea, and everything in them say:

Blessing and honor and glory
and dominion
to the One seated
on the throne,
and to the Lamb, forever
and ever!

14 The four living creatures said, "•Amen," and the elders fell down and worshiped.

Major Old Testament Allusions in the Book of Revelation

Revelation	Old Testament
1:7	Dn 7:13-14; Zch 12:10
4:1-11	Ezk 1
6:1-8	Zch 1:8-10
6:12-17	Jl 2:30-31
9:1-12	Jl 1:1-12
10:8-11	Ezk 3:1-4
11:1-4	Ezk 40:2-5; Zch 4:11-14
12:1-6	Gn 3:15
13:1-17	Dn 7:7-8,23-25
14:17-19	Jl 3:13
17:7-14	Dn 7:23-27
18:1-24	Jr 51
20:4-10	Ezk 38–39
21:1–22:5	Is 65–66; Ezk 40–48; Gn 2:8-14

The Seven Seals (6:1–8:6)

The Opening of the First Four Seals (6:1-8)

6 Then I saw[A] the Lamb open one of the seven[B] seals, and I heard one of the four living creatures say with a voice like thunder, "Come!"[C,D] 2 I looked, and there was a white horse. The horseman on it had a bow; a crown was given to him, and he went out as a victor to conquer.[E]

3 When He opened the second seal, I heard the second living creature say, "Come!"[C,D] 4 Then another horse went out, a fiery red one, and its horseman was empowered[F] to take peace from the earth, so that people would slaughter one another. And a large sword was given to him.

5 When He opened the third seal, I heard the third living creature say, "Come!"[C,D] And I looked, and there was a black horse. The horseman on it had a set of scales in his hand. 6 Then I heard something like a voice among the four living creatures say, "A quart of wheat for a •denarius, and three quarts of barley for a denarius—but do not harm the olive oil and the wine."

7 When He opened the fourth seal, I heard the voice of the fourth living creature say, "Come!"[C,D] 8 And I looked, and there was a pale green[G] horse. The horseman on it was named Death, and •Hades was following after him. Authority was given to them[H] over a fourth of the earth, to kill by the sword, by famine, by plague, and by the wild animals of the earth.

The Opening of the Fifth Seal (6:9-11)

9 When He opened the fifth seal, I saw under the altar the people[I] slaughtered because of God's word and the testimony they had.[J] 10 They cried out with a loud voice: "Lord,[K] the One who is holy and true, how long until You judge and avenge our blood from those who live on the earth?" 11 So a white robe was given to each of them, and they were told to rest a little while longer until the number would be completed of their

[A]6:1 Lit *saw when* [B]6:1 Other mss omit *seven* [C]6:1,3,5,7 Other mss add *and see* [D]6:1,3,5,7 Or *Go!* [E]6:2 Lit *went out conquering and in order to conquer* [F]6:4 Or *was granted*; lit *was given* [G]6:8 Or *a greenish gray* [H]6:8 Other mss read *him* [I]6:9 Lit *souls* [J]6:9 Other mss add *about the Lamb* [K]6:10 Or *Master*

6:1-17 The **seven seals** (6:1-17; 8:1-6), the seven trumpets (8:7–9:21), the seven thunders (10:1-4), and the seven bowls (16:1-21) represent four series of judgments. These events form part of the great tribulation, marked by the wrath and judgment of God on a world that has rejected the Lord, the awakening of Israel's longing for the Messiah, and the preparation for Christ's return.

6:1-2 The opening of the first four seals is portrayed by four horsemen, an image taken from Zch 1:7-11, although the colors of the horses are different. Some take the **horseman** on the **white horse** as Jesus because of the similarity to Him at His return (Rv 19:11). Others state this rider cannot be Jesus since He returns as a conqueror at the end, not the beginning of the tribulation. The **bow** indicates this horseman is a soldier, and the **crown** shows he is a ruler. The phrase **given to him** emphasizes the sovereignty of God over this figure. The white horse symbolizes conquest.

6:3-4 The opening of the **second seal** revealed a second horse that is **fiery red**. The rider of this horse is given two things: a **large sword** (a sign of political power) and the power **to take peace from the earth** (civil peace). This horse represents bloodshed and war.

6:5-6 The famine and scarcity that the horseman on a **black horse** symbolizes naturally follow war. The balance **scales** reflect that food is distributed by rationed amounts in times of scarcity. **Wheat** and **barley** were the staple foods of the Roman Empire, with a quart being enough food for one person for one day. The **denarius** (a Roman coin) was the average day's wage for a laborer. With the inflation of prices during the famine, a man can barely afford to feed himself, not including his family, for a day.

6:7-8 The horse of the **fourth seal** is **pale green**, or greenish gray, the color of dead human flesh and represents **Death**. **Hades** signifies the grave.

6:9-11 The words **under the altar** and **blood** recall the Old Testament sacrificial system in which the blood of the sacrificial animal was poured at the base of the altar.

The people under the altar are martyrs, sacrifices for the cause of Christ. Their plea for vengeance does not violate Jesus' teachings of mercy and forgiveness, for this is a righteous call for divine justice mirrored elsewhere in Scripture (Ps 6:3; 74:10; 79:5: 80:4). The Lord responds to the martyrs' prayers by giving them **a white robe** and telling them to **rest a little while longer**. A white robe

fellow slaves and their •brothers,
who were going to be killed just as
they had been.

The Opening of the Sixth Seal (6:12-17)

12 Then I saw Him open[A] the sixth
seal. A violent earthquake occurred;
the sun turned black like •sackcloth
made of goat hair; the entire moon[B]
became like blood; 13 the stars[C] of
heaven fell to the earth as a fig tree
drops its unripe figs when shaken
by a high wind; 14 the sky separated
like a scroll being rolled up; and every mountain and island was moved
from its place.
15 Then the kings of the earth,
the nobles, the military commanders, the rich, the powerful, and
every •slave and free person hid
in the caves and among the rocks
of the mountains. 16 And they said
to the mountains and to the rocks,
"Fall on us and hide us from the face
of the One seated on the throne and
from the wrath of the Lamb, 17 because the great day of Their[D] wrath
has come! And who is able to stand?"

HARD QUESTION

Does God's wrath contradict His love?

The reference to the coming **wrath** [Gk *orgēs*, "violent anger, indignation"] **of the Lamb** appears to contradict divine love (6:16). Yet, the revelation of God's love necessitates the revelation of God's wrath. In His desire to redeem mankind for Himself, God sacrificed His Son, allowing Him to be humiliated, beaten, and crucified. The earth-dwellers who reject His love spurn this sacrifice of God's Son. In light of their rejection, the wickedness of their sins remains upon them, and the wrath of God is kindled against them. Although the wrath of God against sin has already been revealed in Jesus (Jn 3:36; Rm 1:18), the great day of God's wrath, called "the day of the LORD" in the Old Testament (see Is 13:9; Zph 1:14-15), is still to come.

The First Interlude Vision (7:1-8)

7 After this I saw four angels standing at the four corners of the
earth, restraining the four winds
of the earth so that no wind could
blow on the earth or on the sea or on
any tree. 2 Then I saw another angel,
who had the seal of the living God
rise up from the east. He cried out in
a loud voice to the four angels who
were empowered[E] to harm the earth
and the sea: 3 "Don't harm the earth
or the sea or the trees until we seal
the •slaves of our God on their foreheads." 4 And I heard the number of
those who were sealed:

144,000 sealed from
every tribe of the Israelites:
5 12,000 sealed from the tribe
of Judah,
12,000[F] from the tribe
of Reuben,
12,000 from the tribe of Gad,
6 12,000 from the tribe
of Asher,
12,000 from the tribe
of Naphtali,
12,000 from the tribe
of Manasseh,
7 12,000 from the tribe
of Simeon,
12,000 from the tribe of Levi,
12,000 from the tribe
of Issachar,
8 12,000 from the tribe
of Zebulun,
12,000 from the tribe
of Joseph,
12,000 sealed from the tribe
of Benjamin.

The Second Interlude Vision (7:9-17)

9 After this I looked, and there was
a vast multitude from every nation,
tribe, people, and language, which
no one could number, standing before the throne and before the Lamb.
They were robed in white with palm

[A]6:12 Lit *I saw when He opened* [B]6:12 Or *the full moon* [C]6:13 Perhaps meteors [D]6:17 Other mss read *His* [E]7:2 Lit *angels to whom it was given* [F]7:5-8 Other mss add *sealed* after each number

symbolizes the purity of the martyrs and the end-time joy awaiting them. Before the vengeance of God can be poured out upon those who live on the earth, more of God's **slaves** and the martyrs' **brothers** must be killed. In the midst of the suffering meted out by the opening of the seals, a faithful and persevering witness will be required of all believers. For their faith, some will suffer persecution and death, but in the end God will vindicate His people and avenge their blood. The promise of God's judgment for the martyrs will finally be fulfilled (19:2), and their total vindication will be shown (20:4-6,11-14).

6:12-17 The breaking of the **sixth seal** reveals cosmic, cataclysmic events: **a violent earthquake**, the **sun turned black**, the **moon became like blood**, and the **stars of heaven fell to the earth**. These catastrophes emphasize that nature will go awry between the incarnation of Christ and His return. John saw all peoples of the earth quake in terror at these disasters. The earth-dwellers would rather be buried in an avalanche of rock than face **the One seated on the throne** and the **wrath of the Lamb**. The great day of **their wrath** refers to the approaching great tribulation period in which the earth-dwellers will be tested (3:10). Although their rhetorical question, **And who is able to stand?** is intended to be answered in the negative, God's servants may stand even in the midst of these natural disasters. Even in death earth-dwellers will not escape God's judgment (20:11-14).

7:1-17 Chapter 7 provides an interlude between the opening of the sixth and seventh seals. The interlude is made up of two parts: the sealing of the **144,000** servants of God on earth and the appearance of **a vast multitude in heaven**.

7:2-3 This **seal**—whether visible or invisible, a mark, picture, or name—sets the people apart as belonging to God and covers them with His protection. The "seal" of God contrasts with the "mark" of the beast received by the earth-dwellers (13:16).

7:4-8 The **144,000** are listed in what resembles a military census (see Nm 1:3,17-46), with **12,000** present from every tribe. If taken literally, following the premillennial view, the number refers to a believing Jewish remnant, who will follow Jesus as the Messiah in the last days.

7:9-17 John did not know the identity of this **vast multitude**. The elder informed him they had come out of **the great tribulation** (v. 14) and had **washed their robes** and **made them white in the blood of the Lamb**.

>WORD|*study*

7:14 Of the 43 New Testament appearances of the word **tribulation** (Gk *thlipseōs*), often translated "tribulation" but also "affliction," "suffering," or "distress," only five to seven refer specifically to end-times events. The remaining uses relate to suffering in the Christian life (see Ac 14:22). Tribulation takes place during the course of the age (see 1:9 and 2:9-10), but unparalleled "great tribulation" occurs at the end of the age (7:14).

All followers of Jesus are made clean by His blood. After the reign of war, famine, death, and destruction over the earth, believers will **serve** God in a priestly manner **day and night in His sanctuary** (v. 15), finally finding eternal peace and comfort with their Savior, who is also their Shepherd.

8:1 The opening of the **seventh seal** brings **silence in heaven** in awe and anticipation of God's judgments about to be unleashed upon the earth.

8:2-4 Trumpets announce the arrival of events in the end times (Mt 24:31; 1Co 15:52; 1Th 4:16). The sounding of these **seven trumpets** will bring forth a judgment of plagues to fall upon the earth and its inhabitants. In the Old Testament **incense** stood both for protection of the people (Lv 16:13; Nm 16:47- 48) and for the people's prayers as they ascended before God (Ps 141:2). Here, the smoke of the incense is bearing up the **prayers of the saints.**

8:5-6 In Ezk 10:2-7 coals of fire, symbolizing fiery judgment from the throne, are scattered over the city. Here, fiery judgment about to fall upon the earth is God's direct response to the cries of His people and reflects His desire to vindicate them for their sufferings at the hands of the earth-dwellers.

8:7-13 The destruction meted out by the first four trumpets upon the world closely mirrors the plagues visited upon Egypt (Ex 7–11). In the Old Testament **wormwood** became a symbol for bitter sorrow, judgment, and death (see Pr 5:4; Jr 9:15; 23:15; Lm 3:15,19). While the first four trumpets introduce catastrophic happenings, these events are limited to nature. The next judgments, however, will strike the earth-dwellers directly.

branches in their hands. 10 And they
cried out in a loud voice:

Salvation belongs to our God,
who is seated on the throne,
and to the Lamb!

11 All the angels stood around the
throne, the elders, and the four living creatures, and they fell facedown
before the throne and worshiped
God, 12 saying:

•Amen! Blessing and glory
and wisdom
and thanksgiving and honor
and power and strength
be to our God forever
and ever. Amen.

13 Then one of the elders asked
me, "Who are these people robed
in white, and where did they come
from?"
14 I said to him, "Sir,[A] you know."
Then he told me:

These are the ones
coming out
of the great tribulation.
They washed their robes
and made them white
in the blood of the Lamb.
15 For this reason they are
before the throne of God,
and they serve Him
day and night
in His sanctuary.
The One seated on the throne
will shelter[B] them:
16 They will no longer hunger;
they will no longer thirst;
the sun will no longer
strike them,
nor will any heat.
17 For the Lamb who is
at the center of the throne
will shepherd them;
He will guide them to springs
of living waters,
and God will wipe away
every tear from their eyes.

The Opening of the Seventh Seal (8:1-6)

8 When He opened the seventh
seal, there was silence in heaven
for about half an hour. 2 Then I saw
the seven angels who stand in the
presence of God; seven trumpets
were given to them. 3 Another angel,
with a gold incense burner, came
and stood at the altar. He was given
a large amount of incense to offer
with the prayers of all the •saints on
the gold altar in front of the throne.
4 The smoke of the incense, with the
prayers of the saints, went up in the
presence of God from the angel's
hand. 5 The angel took the incense
burner, filled it with fire from the altar, and hurled it to the earth; there
were rumblings of thunder, flashes of
lightning, and an earthquake. 6 And
the seven angels who had the seven
trumpets prepared to blow them.

The Seven Trumpets (8:7–11:19)

The First Four Trumpets (8:7-13)

7 The first angel[C] blew his trumpet,
and hail and fire, mixed with blood,
were hurled to the earth. So a third
of the earth was burned up, a third
of the trees were burned up, and all
the green grass was burned up.
8 The second angel blew his trumpet, and something like a great
mountain ablaze with fire was
hurled into the sea. So a third of the
sea became blood, 9 a third of the living creatures in the sea died, and a
third of the ships were destroyed.
10 The third angel blew his trumpet, and a great star, blazing like a
torch, fell from heaven. It fell on
a third of the rivers and springs
of water. 11 The name of the star is
Wormwood, and a third of the waters became •wormwood. So, many
of the people died from the waters,
because they had been made bitter.
12 The fourth angel blew his trumpet, and a third of the sun was
struck, a third of the moon, and a
third of the stars, so that a third of
them were darkened. A third of the
day was without light, and the night
as well.
13 I looked again and heard an eagle[D] flying high overhead, crying out
in a loud voice, "Woe! Woe! Woe to
those who live on the earth, because
of the remaining trumpet blasts
that the three angels are about to
sound!"

A 7:14 Lit *My lord* B 7:15 Or *will spread His tent over* C 8:7 Other mss include *angel* D 8:13 Other mss read *angel*

>WORD|*study*

9:1-2 **Abyss** (Gk *abussou*, "bottomless, unbounded, immeasurable depth"; cp. Lk 8:31; Rm 10:7) generally refers to an underground pit considered to be a present holding place and the eventual destination for the Devil and his demons (Rv 9:1-2,11; 11:7; 17:8; 20:1,3). Angels come *down* to earth from heaven and demons come *up* to earth from the abyss. The imagery of the abyss pictures the prison for evil spirits, where angels are described as "kept with eternal chains in darkness for the judgment of the great day" (Jd 6). The final dwelling-place of wicked humans and demons is not the abyss but the lake of fire (20:14).

The Fifth Trumpet or First Woe (9:1-12)

9 The fifth angel blew his trumpet, and I saw a star that had
fallen from heaven to earth. The
key to the shaft of the •abyss was
given to him. 2 He opened the shaft
of the abyss, and smoke came up
out of the shaft like smoke from a
great[A] furnace so that the sun and
the air were darkened by the smoke
from the shaft. 3 Then locusts came
out of the smoke on to the earth,
and power[B] was given to them like
the power that scorpions have on
the earth. 4 They were told not to
harm the grass of the earth, or any
green plant, or any tree, but only
people who do not have God's seal
on their foreheads. 5 They were not
permitted to kill them but were to
torment them for five months; their
torment is like the torment caused
by a scorpion when it strikes a man.
6 In those days people will seek death
and will not find it; they will long to
die, but death will flee from them.
7 The appearance of the locusts
was like horses equipped for battle.
Something like gold crowns was
on their heads; their faces were
like men's faces; 8 they had hair like
women's hair; their teeth were like
lions' teeth; 9 they had chests like
iron breastplates; the sound of their
wings was like the sound of chariots
with many horses rushing into battle; 10 and they had tails with sting-
ers like scorpions, so that with their
tails they had the power[B] to harm
people for five months. 11 They had
as their king[C] the angel of the abyss;
his name in Hebrew is •Abaddon,[D]
and in Greek he has the name Apollyon.[E] 12 The first woe has passed.
There are still two more woes to
come after this.

The Sixth Trumpet or Second Woe (9:13-21)

13 The sixth angel blew his trumpet. From the four[F] horns of the
gold altar that is before God, I heard
a voice 14 say to the sixth angel who
had the trumpet, "Release the four
angels bound at the great river Euphrates." 15 So the four angels who
were prepared for the hour, day,
month, and year were released to
kill a third of the human race. 16 The
number of mounted troops was
200 million;[G] I heard their number. 17 This is how I saw the horses
in my vision: The horsemen had
breastplates that were fiery red,
hyacinth blue, and sulfur yellow.
The heads of the horses were like
lions' heads, and from their mouths
came fire, smoke, and sulfur. 18 A
third of the human race was killed
by these three plagues—by the fire,
the smoke, and the sulfur that came
from their mouths. 19 For the power
of the horses is in their mouths and
in their tails, for their tails, which
resemble snakes, have heads, and
they inflict injury with them.

[A]9:2 Other mss omit *great* [B]9:3,10 Or *authority* [C]9:11 Or *as king over them* [D]9:11 Or *destruction* [E]9:11 Or *destroyer* [F]9:13 Other mss omit *four* [G]9:16 Other mss read *100 million*

>WORD|*study*

9:14 The **Euphrates**, sometimes simply called "the great river," figures prominently throughout the Bible beginning as one of the rivers flowing out of the garden of Eden (Gn 2:14). It served as the eastern boundary of the promised land and later came to be associated with the Israel's enemies, such as Assyria, Babylon, and Persia, who attacked Israel by crossing over it. This judgment from the four angels of the Euphrates prepares the way for the sixth bowl (16:12) in which the river dries up completely, allowing safe passage for the "kings of the whole world" to assemble their vast armies for "the battle of the great day of God" (16:14).

9:1-12 The fifth and sixth trumpets, or the first and second woes, contain two demonic plagues, which directly attack the earth-dwellers. The Book of Joel serves as a background for these plagues (Jl 1:4-6).

9:1-2 The **star** represents an **angel** who had **fallen from heaven to earth**. Although the term "fallen" could suggest a demon, this angel has the key to the **abyss**, the home of demonic fiends (9:3,7-11). This angel later chains and locks up the Devil inside the abyss (20:1).

9:3-10 Emerging from the depths of the smoke-filled shaft are hordes of **locusts**. People of the ancient Near East feared locust plagues because of the widespread devastation wreaked on the land. In the five months spanning spring and late summer, millions of locusts could emerge from the desert, devouring all vegetation and bringing economic ruin on the region. Rather than devouring vegetation, these demonic locusts brought the earth-dwellers pain, terrorizing them without mercy. John used imagery to describe the locusts' appearance. The repeated word **like** speaks of comparison, not literalism. Their **gold crowns** are those of usurpers claiming authority and power they do not possess. God loans them temporary power to accomplish their task. The locusts' human **faces** depict intelligence, suggesting they are not inanimate objects but rather spiritual beings. Having chests **like iron breastplates** emphasizes their preparedness for battle as well as their invincibility.

9:11-12 The leader, or king, of the destructive locusts is called **the angel of the abyss**, whose name is **Abaddon** (Hb) or **Apollyon** (Gk). Both words literally mean "Destroyer." Even as the earth-dwellers persist in their worship of demons, the very objects of their worship turn on them in contempt and cruelty, eager to destroy them.

9:15-16 The **four angels**, with God's permission, are released with a singular purpose: **to kill a third of the human race** with an army of **200 million**. The timing of this massacre is within the predetermined plan of God to the very hour.

9:17-19 The three colors probably correspond to what was spewed from the horses' mouths—**fire, smoke, and sulfur**—all of which were said to be the cause of death for **a third of the human race**.

9:20-21 The chief sin of the people centers in their worship of **demons and idols**. Even with a third of the earth's population dead, they do **not repent** (see **Doctrine**, p. 1240). God's purpose in sending the plagues is for the earth-dwellers to repent and be saved.

10:1–11:14 This second interlude in Revelation (the first: 7:1-17) occurs between the sixth and seventh trumpets. It is divided into two major visions: John and the little scroll and the two witnesses who prophesy. This parenthesis highlights the role of God's people during the events described, encouraging them in light of the terrible nature of the phenomena following the trumpets' blasts.

10:8-11 The events of this section parallel the commissioning of the prophet Ezekiel (Ezk 3:1-3), while also containing allusions to Jesus' taking the scroll (Rv 5:1-8). The **little scroll** is either the same scroll as in 5:8 (now appearing *little* in the hand of the immense angel) or a different scroll. Consuming God's word, a common theme in the Old Testament (Ps 19:10; Jr 15:16), means to take Scripture's message to heart and apply it to your life. For John and all heralds of God's word, His message is pleasing to consume, yet often bitter in its delivery due to its rejection by those who refused to receive God's message. Also, while the end times hold much sweetness and promise for those who are followers of Jesus, much sorrow and bitterness will also come, especially for those followers of Christ still on the earth.

11:1-2 John was told to **measure God's sanctuary**, along with the altar and the worshipers, instructions paralleling Ezekiel's vision (Ezk 40:3,5) in which the measuring of the temple represents God's possession and protection of His people. The meaning here is similar: God will preserve those who worship Him during the great tribulation. God limits the time that the nations have to **trample the holy city** to **42 months**. God will deliver the faithful still on the earth into the hands of sinners for this period. Though they will be conquered physically (13:7), they are "sealed" by God and cannot be conquered spiritually.

11:3-6 God gives the **two witnesses** power to **prophesy** in His name for a limited time, **1,260 days**. The description of the witnesses—as two **olive trees** and **two lampstands**—connects them with a similar vision (Zch 4:2-6), in which the gold lampstand represents the Spirit of God and the olive trees represent Joshua the high priest and Zerubbabel the governor (Zch 4:14). The Holy Spirit

20 The rest of the people, who were not killed by these plagues, did not repent of the works of their hands to stop worshiping demons and idols of gold, silver, bronze, stone, and wood, which are not able to see, hear, or walk. 21 And they did not repent of their murders, their sorceries,[A] their sexual immorality, or their thefts.

HARD QUESTION

How could a good God allow the powers of darkness to commit such atrocities against a world He is supposed to love (Jn 3:16)?

Upon witnessing the spiritual decay of Israel and the nation's approaching invasion by the Babylonian Empire, the prophet Habakkuk asked: "Why do You tolerate wrongdoing?" (Hab 1:3a). The Lord answered:

- God has the right to use whatever tools He desires, even the wicked, to bring about His will (Hab 1:6-11).
- Although in God's purposes the wicked may be allowed to triumph for a time, their judgment is assuredly coming (Hab 2:2-20).

A good and just God can use demons to bring about His higher purpose just as He used the Babylonians in Habakkuk's day. While the demons are given power for a season, they eventually will take their place in the lake of fire forever.

The First Interlude Vision (10:1-11)

10 Then I saw another mighty angel coming down from heaven, surrounded by a cloud, with a rainbow over his head.[B] His face was like the sun, his legs[C] were like fiery pillars, 2 and he had a little scroll opened in his hand. He put his right foot on the sea, his left on the land, 3 and he cried out with a loud voice like a roaring lion. When he cried out, the seven thunders spoke with their voices. 4 And when the seven thunders spoke, I was about to write. Then I heard a voice from heaven, saying, "Seal up what the seven thunders said, and do not write it down!"

5 Then the angel that I had seen standing on the sea and on the land raised his right hand to heaven. 6 He swore an oath by the One who lives forever and ever, who created heaven and what is in it, the earth and what is in it, and the sea and what is in it: "There will no longer be an interval of time,[D] 7 but in the days of the sound of the seventh angel, when he will blow his trumpet, then God's •hidden plan will be completed, as He announced to His servants[E] the prophets."

8 Now the voice that I heard from heaven spoke to me again and said, "Go, take the scroll that lies open in the hand of the angel who is standing on the sea and on the land."

9 So I went to the angel and asked him to give me the little scroll. He said to me, "Take and eat it; it will be bitter in your stomach, but it will be as sweet as honey in your mouth."

10 Then I took the little scroll from the angel's hand and ate it. It was as sweet as honey in my mouth, but when I ate it, my stomach became bitter. 11 And I was told,[F] "You must prophesy again about[G] many peoples, nations, languages, and kings."

The Second Interlude Vision (11:1-14)

11 Then I was given a measuring reed like a rod,[H] with these words: "Go[I] and measure God's sanctuary and the altar, and count those who worship there. 2 But exclude the courtyard outside the sanctuary. Don't measure it, because it is given to the nations,[J] and they will trample the holy city for 42 months. 3 I will empower[K] my two witnesses, and they will prophesy for 1,260 days,[L] dressed in •sackcloth."[M] 4 These are the two olive trees and the two lampstands that stand before the Lord[N] of the earth. 5 If anyone wants to harm them, fire comes from their mouths and consumes their enemies; if anyone wants to harm them, he must be killed in this way. 6 These men have the power to close up the sky so that it does not rain during the days of their proph-

[A]**9:21** Or *magic potions, or drugs*; Gk *pharmakon* [B]**10:1** Or *a halo on his head* [C]**10:1** Or *feet* [D]**10:6** Or *be a delay* [E]**10:7** Or *slaves* [F]**10:11** Lit *And they said to me* [G]**10:11** Or *prophesy again against* [H]**11:1** Other mss add *and the angel stood up* [I]**11:1** Lit *Arise* [J]**11:2** Or *Gentiles* [K]**11:3** Lit *I will give to* [L]**11:3** = $3^1/_2$ years of 30-day months [M]**11:3** Mourning garment of coarse, often black, material [N]**11:4** Other mss read *God*

Followers

Of the Lamb		Of the Beast	
Heaven-dwellers	5:9-11; 7:9; 12:12; 19:1,6,14; 20:4,6	Earth-dwellers	3:10; 6:9-11; 8:13; 11:10; 13:8; 17:2,6,8; 18:24–19:2
Harvest of wheat	14:14-16	Harvest of grapes	14:17-20
"Bride" of Christ	19:7; 21:9	"Notorious prostitute"	17:1
New Jerusalem	21:1,10	Babylon the Great	17:5; 18:1-24
Marriage feast of the Lamb	19:9	Great supper of God	19:17-18
First resurrection (unto life)	20:6	Second resurrection (unto death)	20:12

ecy. They also have power over the
waters to turn them into blood and
to strike the earth with every plague
whenever they want.
7 When they finish their testimony, the beast[A] that comes up
out of the •abyss will make war
with them, conquer them, and kill
them. 8 Their dead bodies[B] will lie
in the public square[C] of the great
city, which prophetically[D] is called
Sodom and Egypt, where also their
Lord was crucified. 9 And representatives from[E] the peoples, tribes, languages, and nations will view their
bodies for three and a half days and
not permit their bodies to be put
into a tomb. 10 Those who live on the
earth will gloat over them and celebrate and send gifts to one another
because these two prophets brought
judgment to those who live on the
earth.
11 But after 3½ days, the breath[F]
of life from God entered them, and
they stood on their feet. So great fear
fell on those who saw them. 12 Then
they heard[G] a loud voice from heav-
en saying to them, "Come up here."
They went up to heaven in a cloud,
while their enemies watched them.
13 At that moment a violent earthquake took place, a tenth of the city
fell, and 7,000 people were killed in
the earthquake. The survivors were
terrified and gave glory to the God
of heaven. 14 The second woe has
passed. Take note: The third woe is
coming quickly!

The Seventh Trumpet or Third Woe (11:15-19)

15 The seventh angel blew his
trumpet, and there were loud voices
in heaven saying:

The kingdom of the •world
has become the kingdom
of our Lord
and of His •Messiah,
and He will reign forever
and ever!

16 The 24 elders, who were seated before God on their thrones, fell facedown and worshiped God, 17 saying:

We thank You, Lord God,
the Almighty,
who is and who was,[H]
because You have taken
Your great power
and have begun to reign.
18 The nations were angry,
but Your wrath has come.
The time has come
for the dead to be judged
and to give the reward
to Your servants the prophets,
to the •saints, and to those
who fear Your name,
both small and great,
and the time has come
to destroy
those who destroy the earth.

19 God's sanctuary in heaven was

will be upon the two witnesses as they prophesy upon the earth, proclaiming the word of God and manifesting His judgment on the earth-dwellers. The earthly ministries of Moses and Elijah serve as the background for the signs the two witnesses can perform.

11:7-10 Following their three-and-a-half-year ministry, God will allow the forces of evil to conquer the witnesses for a time by the beast that comes up out of the abyss, a character identified with the antichrist figure later in the book (13:1; 17:8). The beast is joined by the earth-dwellers in hating God's people. They celebrate and gloat over the witnesses' deaths. In the ancient world, their refusal to bury the two dead bodies indicated contempt and disrespect.

11:11-12 After 3½ days, God resurrects the two witnesses, displaying their triumph over death and the evil one. All who see the two witnesses are filled with **great fear.** The exaltation of the two witnesses teaches that while the faithful will be persecuted and killed, those who persevere to the end will be vindicated by God in due time.

11:13-14 Following the ascension of the witnesses, another **violent earthquake** strikes the earth. This outpouring of wrath evokes a desire for repentance. While the previous instances of God's judgment are met with unrepentant hearts in the earth-dwellers, apparently many are now converted to Christ.

11:15 With the sounding of the **seventh** and final **trumpet,** heavenly **voices** focus attention on what is to come: The eternal and blessed reign **of our Lord and of His Messiah.**

[A]**11:7** Or *wild animal* [B]**11:8** Lit *Their corpse* [C]**11:8** Or *lie on the broad street* [D]**11:8** Or *spiritually*, or *symbolically* [E]**11:9** Lit *And from* [F]**11:11** Or *spirit* [G]**11:12** Other mss read *Then I heard* [H]**11:17** Other mss add *and who is to come*

>WORD|*study*

12:1-2 The **woman clothed with the sun** is one of three major female characters who play a significant part in the drama of Revelation. The other two female characters are: "Babylon the Great, the Mother of Prostitutes" (17:5) and the "wife" of the Lamb (19:7). The woman of chapter 12 represents Israel, the nation through whom the Messiah would come. The Old Testament imagery of Israel as the wife of Yahweh (Jr 2:1-3; 3:6; Hs 2:19-20) seems to merge with the New Testament concept of the "bride" of Christ (Rv 19) so that by the triumphant marriage of the Lamb the two women have essentially become one (19:7). This understanding is further supported by the imagery in the new Jerusalem combining Israel and the church or the people of God described as the "wife of the Lamb" (21:9).

opened, and the ark of His covenant[A]
appeared in His sanctuary. There
were flashes of lightning, rumblings
of thunder, an earthquake,[B] and severe hail.

Two Great Signs and Their Interpretation (12:1-18)

Two Signs in Heaven: The Woman and the Dragon (12:1-6)

12 A great sign[C] appeared in heav-
en: a woman clothed with the
sun, with the moon under her feet
and a crown of 12 stars on her head.
2 She was pregnant and cried out in
labor and agony as she was about to
give birth. 3 Then another sign[D] appeared in heaven: There was a great
fiery red dragon having seven heads
and 10 horns, and on his heads were
seven diadems.[E] 4 His tail swept away
a third of the stars in heaven and
hurled them to the earth. And the
dragon stood in front of the woman
who was about to give birth, so that
when she did give birth he might devour her child. 5 But she gave birth
to a Son—a male who is going to
shepherd[F] all nations with an iron
scepter—and her child was caught
up to God and to His throne. 6 The
woman fled into the wilderness,
where she had a place prepared by
God, to be fed there[G] for 1,260 days.

The Dragon Thrown out of Heaven (12:7-17)

7 Then war broke out in heaven:
Michael and his angels fought
against the dragon. The dragon
and his angels also fought, 8 but he
could not prevail, and there was no
place for them in heaven any longer.
9 So the great dragon was thrown
out—the ancient serpent, who is
called the Devil[H] and Satan,[I] the one
who deceives the whole world. He
was thrown to earth, and his angels
with him.
10 Then I heard a loud voice in
heaven say:

The salvation and the power
and the kingdom of our God
and the authority
of His •Messiah
have now come,
because the accuser
of our •brothers
has been thrown out:
the one who accuses them
before our God day and night.
11 They conquered him
by the blood of the Lamb
and by the word
of their testimony,
for they did not love
their lives
in the face of death.
12 Therefore rejoice,
you heavens,
and you who dwell in them!
Woe to the earth and the sea,
for the Devil has come down
to you
with great fury,
because he knows he has
a short time.

13 When the dragon saw that he
had been thrown to earth, he persecuted the woman who gave birth
to the male child. 14 The woman was
given two wings of a great eagle, so
that she could fly from the serpent's
presence to her place in the wilderness, where she was fed for a time,
times, and half a time.[J] 15 From his
mouth the serpent spewed water

[A]**11:19** Other mss read *ark of the covenant of the Lord* [B]**11:19** Other mss omit *an earthquake* [C]**12:1** Or *great symbolic display*; see Rv 12:3 [D]**12:3** Or *another symbolic display* [E]**12:3** Or *crowns* [F]**12:5** Or *rule* [G]**12:6** Lit *God, that they might feed her there* [H]**12:9** In Gk, *diabolos* means slanderer. [I]**12:9** In Hb, Satan means adversary. [J]**12:14** This expression, occurring in Dn 7:25; 12:7, = 3½ years or 42 months (Rv 11:2; 13:5) or 1,260 days (Rv 11:3).

12:1-2 This **woman** represents the nation Israel, anticipating the coming Messiah.

12:3-6 The **dragon** (Gk *drakōn*, a synonym for the word translated "serpent," cp. Gn 3:1) represents Satan (Rv 12:9). The multiple **heads, horns,** and **diadems** allude to his power, wealth, and prestige. Some have suggested that **a third of the stars** refers to the angels who followed Satan in his rebellion against God and were thus cast to the earth. He is intent on destroying the child, **a Son**, the promised Messiah of Israel. This alludes to the prophecy found in Gn 3:15. Both Herod's slaughter of Bethlehem's babies and the crucifixion are examples of the Devil's attempts to annihilate the Messiah. The woman's son is going to **shepherd all nations with an iron scepter**, a reference to the messianic king of Israel (Ps 2). His use of the iron scepter refers to His judgment. Before the dragon could devour him, the Son is caught up to God and to His throne.

12:7-9 The **great dragon** will not triumph in this battle but experience defeat, as he is revealed as **the ancient serpent . . . the Devil and Satan.** This seems to refer to a future time shortly before the return of Christ when the Devil is finally excluded from *any* access to the presence of God. Up to this point, he has been allowed limited admission to heaven's throne room, where he goes to appear before God and accuse God's people (Jb 1:6-12). Yet, after this final battle between the angels of light and the angels of darkness, Satan and his demons will be cast out forever and take their last stand on the earth before being cast into the lake of fire (Rv 20:10).

12:10-12 Just as the prayers of the saints have been ascending before the throne of God, the accusations of the Devil have been going up in a similar way. For this reason Jesus' intercession for believers in heaven is important (Rm 8:34; Heb 7:25). **The blood of the Lamb** cleanses believers from sin's stain, enabling them to stand before God spotless. Because Christians are justified and forgiven in God's sight through faith, the Devil's accusations against them fail. Christians overcome the Devil through their allegiance to Christ in the midst of suffering and persecution. In response to the Devil's downfall, the heavens and those who dwell in them are called to rejoice.

12:13-17 After being cast out of heaven, the dragon now pursues the woman, hoping that he can wipe out the people of God before his time is up. Yet, God comes to the aid of the woman, giving her **two wings of a great eagle**, so that she may flee to **her place in the wilderness** and be

like a river flowing after the woman,
to sweep her away in a torrent. 16 But
the earth helped the woman. The
earth opened its mouth and swallowed up the river that the dragon
had spewed from his mouth. 17 So
the dragon was furious with the
woman and left to wage war against
the rest of her offspring[A]—those
who keep God's commands and
have the testimony about Jesus.
18 He[B] stood on the sand of the sea.[C]

The Two Beasts and Their Deception (13:1-18)

The Beast from the Sea (13:1-10)

13 And I saw a beast coming up
out of the sea. He[D] had 10 horns
and seven heads. On his horns were
10 diadems, and on his heads were
blasphemous names.[E] 2 The beast I
saw was like a leopard, his feet were
like a bear's, and his mouth was like
a lion's mouth. The dragon gave him
his power, his throne, and great authority. 3 One of his heads appeared
to be fatally wounded,[F] but his fatal
wound was healed. The whole earth
was amazed and followed the beast.[G]
4 They worshiped the dragon because he gave authority to the beast.
And they worshiped the beast, saying, "Who is like the beast? Who is
able to wage war against him?"
5 A mouth was given to him to
speak boasts and blasphemies. He
was also given authority to act[H,I] for
42 months. 6 He began to speak[J] blasphemies against God: to blaspheme
His name and His dwelling—those
who dwell in heaven. 7 And he was
permitted to wage war against the
•saints and to conquer them. He
was also given authority over every
tribe, people, language, and nation.
8 All those who live on the earth will
worship him, everyone whose name
was not written from the foundation
of the world in the book[K] of life of
the Lamb who was slaughtered.[L]
9 If anyone has an ear, he should
listen:

10 If anyone is destined
for captivity,
into captivity he goes.
If anyone is to be killed[M]
with a sword,
with a sword he will be killed.

This demands the perseverance[N] and
faith of the saints.

The Beast from the Earth (13:11-18)

11 Then I saw another beast coming up out of the earth; he had two
horns like a lamb,[O] but he sounded
like a dragon. 12 He exercises all the
authority of the first beast on his
behalf and compels the earth and
those who live on it to worship the
first beast, whose fatal wound was
healed. 13 He also performs great
signs, even causing fire to come
down from heaven to earth in front
of people. 14 He deceives those who
live on the earth because of the
signs that he is permitted to perform on behalf of the beast, telling
those who live on the earth to make
an image[P] of the beast who had the
sword wound and yet lived. 15 He was
permitted to give a spirit[Q] to the image of the beast, so that the image
of the beast could both speak and
cause whoever would not worship
the image of the beast to be killed.
16 And he requires everyone—small
and great, rich and poor, free and
•slave—to be given a mark[R] on his
right hand or on his forehead, 17 so
that no one can buy or sell unless
he has the mark: the beast's name or
the number of his name.
18 Here is wisdom:[S] The one who
has understanding must calculate[T]
the number of the beast, because it
is the number of a man.[U] His number is 666.[V]

[A]12:17 Or *seed* [B]12:18 Other mss read *I*. "He" is apparently a reference to the dragon. [C]12:18 Some translations put Rv 12:18 either in Rv 12:17 or Rv 13:1. [D]13:1 The beasts in Rv 13:1,11 are customarily referred to as "he" or "him" rather than "it." The Gk word for a beast (*therion*) is grammatically neuter. [E]13:1 Other mss read *heads was a blasphemous name* [F]13:3 Lit *be slain to death* [G]13:3 Lit *amazed after the beast* [H]13:5 Other mss read *wage war* [I]13:5 Or *to rule* [J]13:6 Lit *He opened his mouth in* [K]13:8 Or *scroll* [L]13:8 Or *written in the book of life of the Lamb who was slaughtered from the foundation of the world* [M]13:10 Other mss read *anyone kills* [N]13:10 Lit *Here is the perseverance* [O]13:11 Or *ram* [P]13:14 Or *statue*, or *likeness* [Q]13:15 Or *give breath*, or *give life* [R]13:16 Or *stamp*, or *brand* [S]13:18 Or *This calls for wisdom* [T]13:18 Or *count*, or *figure out* [U]13:18 Or *is a man's number*, or *is the number of a person* [V]13:18 Other Gk mss read *616*

protected. The wings of an eagle are also pictured in the exodus of Israel from Egypt (Ex 19:4), in both cases serving as a symbol of God's protection. Furious with his inability to destroy the woman, the dragon decides to go after the individual followers of Jesus, **the rest of her offspring**. All the offspring of the woman—whether Jew or Gentile—are those who keep God's commands and have the testimony about Jesus.

13:1-4 The **blasphemous names** on the beast's **heads** probably allude to the titles of divinity given to the Roman emperors of John's day. The water monster's description connects him to the four beasts seen by Daniel (Dn 7:4-7). This **beast** represents a composite of all the evil empires throughout human history. As a political and military leader representing a major power, the monster purposes to rival the kingdom of God in every way. For this reason, the dragon gave the beast **his power, his throne, and great authority**.

13:5-8 Although the beast cannot reach the heaven-dwellers, he can do physical harm to those Christ-followers still on the earth. The earth-dwellers will worship the beast, revealing their true nature as those whose names were **not written . . . in the book of life**.

13:9-10 The coming of the antichrist is inevitable and should be anticipated.

13:11-12 John witnessed the ascent of **another beast**, the second helper who is to implement the agenda of the first beast. This beast is characterized by deceit and purposely masks himself in the likeness of the Lord Jesus, but he speaks only the words of his true master, the Devil. The second beast mimics the activity of the Holy Spirit, for he exercises all the authority of the antichrist. As the world leader of what is an apostate religion, he compels the earth-dwellers to **worship the first beast**. John later referred to the second beast as the "false prophet" (16:13; 19:20; 20:10), a title emphasizing his role in propagating the worship of the first beast.

13:13-15 The false prophet's **great signs** mirror those of Elijah, Jesus, and the two witnesses of chapter 11. He uses them to entice the people to transfer their allegiance to the antichrist.

13:16-18 Every person on the earth must give allegiance to the antichrist by receiving the beast's **mark on his right hand** or **forehead**, a satanic parody of God's sealing of the 144,000 (7:2-4). The mark is further described as the beast's name or **the number** of his name . . . **666**.

14:1-5 Mount Zion probably represents the heavenly Jerusalem (21:10), possibly indicating that the 144,000 have now been martyred. **The Lamb** stands in solidarity with the representatives of faithful Israel, whether they are in heaven or still on the earth. The **144,000** are those **who had been redeemed** (Gk *ēgorasmenoi*, "purchased," the vocabulary of buying and selling or doing business in the marketplace) from the earth. Their description emphasizes their **blameless** (Gk *amōmoi*, "faultless; without blot, blemish, or disgrace,") character before God. The phrases **not defiled with women** and **kept their virginity** refer to the spiritual cleanness of those who are morally and ethically pure and united to the Lord Jesus. **Firstfruits** indicates that the 144,000 are a sacrificial offering to God in the last days, a guarantee of the great final harvest of all believers from the earth.

14:6-7 In light of His imminent judgment, **Fear** [Gk *phobēthēte*, "have reverence or awe for, be afraid of"] **God and give Him glory . . . Worship the Maker of heaven and earth.** The choice for all people is clear: Worship the Lamb and receive salvation, or worship the beast and receive judgment.

14:8-11 In Revelation, allusions to **Babylon** are concealed references to historical Rome, the capital of the Roman world and also the center for propagating many abominable acts, including the persecution of Christians. The angel speaks of Babylon as **fallen**. Even though the city's destruction apparently will not be complete until chapter 19, this word emphasizes the certainty of her judgment.

14:12-13 Those who **die in the Lord from now on are blessed.** Martyrdom is considered a victory over Satan throughout Revelation. In contrast to the eternal torment of unbelievers, those who persevere in their faith unto death will find rest from their labors. The rewards of **their works** will await them in eternity.

14:14-16 The **gold crown** on Christ's head indicates His royal authority. The **sharp sickle** conveys the finality and power of the last judgment. If the 144,000 are the firstfruits for God (14:4), then this gathering is the final harvest of the redeemed.

The Seven Beatitudes of Revelation

Beatitude	Reference
Blessed is "the one who reads this," and blessed are "those who hear the words of this prophecy and keep what is written in it . . . because the time is near!"	1:3
Blessed are "the dead who die in the Lord from now on."	14:13
Blessed is "the one who is alert and remains clothed."	16:15
Blessed are "those invited to the marriage feast of the Lamb."	19:9
"Blessed and holy is the one who shares in the first resurrection!"	20:6
Blessed is "the one who keeps the prophetic words of this book."	22:7
"Blessed are those who wash their robes."	22:14

The Firstfruits and the Harvest (14:1-20)

The Redeemed of the Earth (14:1-5)

14 Then I looked, and there on
Mount •Zion stood the Lamb,
and with Him were 144,000 who
had His name and His Father's
name written on their foreheads. 2 I
heard a sound[A] from heaven like the
sound of cascading waters and like
the rumbling of loud thunder. The
sound I heard was also like harpists
playing on their harps. 3 They sang[B]
a new song before the throne and
before the four living creatures and
the elders, but no one could learn
the song except the 144,000 who
had been •redeemed[C] from the earth.
4 These are the ones not defiled with
women, for they have kept their
virginity. These are the ones who
follow the Lamb wherever He goes.
They were redeemed[C,D] from the human race as the •firstfruits for God
and the Lamb. 5 No lie was found in
their mouths; they are blameless.

The Messages of Three Angels (14:6-13)

6 Then I saw another angel flying
high overhead, having the eternal
gospel to announce to the inhabitants of the earth—to every nation,
tribe, language, and people. 7 He
spoke with a loud voice: "Fear God
and give Him glory, because the
hour of His judgment has come.
Worship the Maker of heaven and
earth, the sea and springs of water."
8 A second angel[E] followed, saying:
"It has fallen, Babylon the Great has
fallen,[F] who made all nations drink
the wine of her sexual immorality,[G]
which brings wrath."
9 And a third angel[H] followed
them and spoke with a loud voice:
"If anyone worships the beast and
his image and receives a mark on
his forehead or on his hand, 10 he
will also drink the wine of God's
wrath, which is mixed full strength
in the cup of His anger. He will be
tormented with fire and sulfur in
the sight of the holy angels and in
the sight of the Lamb, 11 and the
smoke of their torment will go up

[A]**14:2** Or *voice* [B]**14:3** Other mss add *as it were* [C]**14:3,4** Or *purchased* [D]**14:4** Other mss add *by Jesus* [E]**14:8** Lit *Another angel, a second* [F]**14:8** Other mss omit the second *has fallen* [G]**14:8** Or *wine of her passionate immorality* [H]**14:9** Lit *Another angel, a third*

>WORD|*study*

14:8,10 In the ancient world wine was often used as a symbol of joyous merrymaking and of sinful decadence. In Scripture "wine" can also refer to God's wrath. Here it refers to the adulterous practices of **Babylon the Great**, which inflames all the **nations** with passion for her **immorality**. Because both Babylon and the nations share in the debauchery, they will also share in **the wine of God's wrath, which is mixed full strength**. In John's day, diluting wine with water at least by half was common. To drink wine at its full strength, without water, led to drunkenness. Those who follow after the Devil must receive the full extent of God's wrath. Their suffering goes on forever and ever.

forever and ever. There is no rest[A] day or night for those who worship the beast and his image, or anyone who receives the mark of his name. 12 This demands the perseverance[B] of the •saints, who keep God's commands and their faith in Jesus."[C]

13 Then I heard a voice from heaven saying, "Write: The dead who die in the Lord from now on are blessed."

"Yes," says the Spirit, "let them rest from their labors, for their works follow them!"

The Harvest of the Earth: Part One (14:14-16)

14 Then I looked, and there was a white cloud, and One like the Son of Man[D] was seated on the cloud, with a gold crown on His head and a sharp sickle in His hand. 15 Another angel came out of the sanctuary, crying out in a loud voice to the One who was seated on the cloud, "Use your sickle and reap, for the time to reap has come, since the harvest of the earth is ripe." 16 So the One seated on the cloud swung His sickle over the earth, and the earth was harvested.

The Harvest of the Earth: Part Two (14:17-20)

17 Then another angel who also had a sharp sickle came out of the sanctuary in heaven. 18 Yet another angel, who had authority over fire, came from the altar, and he called with a loud voice to the one who had the sharp sickle, "Use your sharp sickle and gather the clusters of grapes from earth's vineyard, because its grapes have ripened." 19 So the angel swung his sickle toward earth and gathered the grapes from earth's vineyard, and he threw them into the great winepress of God's wrath. 20 Then the press was trampled outside the city, and blood flowed out of the press up to the horses' bridles for about 180 miles.[E]

The Seven Last Plagues (15:1–16:21)

The Third Great Sign in Heaven (15:1-8)

15 Then I saw another great and awe-inspiring sign[F] in heaven: seven angels with the seven last plagues, for with them, God's wrath will be completed. 2 I also saw something like a sea of glass mixed with fire, and those who had won the victory over the beast, his image,[G] and the number of his name, were standing on the sea of glass with harps from God.[H] 3 They sang the song of God's servant Moses and the song of the Lamb:

Great and awe-inspiring are
Your works,
Lord God, the Almighty;
righteous and true are
Your ways,
King of the Nations.[I]
4 Lord, who will not fear
and glorify Your name?
Because You alone are holy,
for all the nations will come
and worship before You
because Your righteous acts
have been revealed.

5 After this I looked, and the heavenly sanctuary—the tabernacle of testimony—was opened. 6 Out of the sanctuary came the seven angels with the seven plagues, dressed in •clean, bright linen, with gold sashes wrapped around their chests. 7 One of the four living creatures gave the seven angels seven gold bowls filled with the wrath of God who lives forever and ever. 8 Then the sanctuary was filled with smoke from God's glory and from His power, and no one could enter the sanctuary until the seven plagues of the seven angels were completed.

The First Three Bowls of Wrath (16:1-7)

16 Then I heard a loud voice from the sanctuary saying to the seven angels, "Go and pour out the seven[J] bowls of God's wrath on the earth." 2 The first went and poured out his bowl on the earth, and severely painful sores[K] broke out on the people who had the mark of the beast and who worshiped his image.

3 The second[L] poured out his bowl into the sea. It turned to blood like

14:17-20 The grape harvest is a metaphor for God's judgment in the Old Testament (Is 5:5; 63:2-3; Lm 1:15; Jl 3:13). The **ripened** state of the grapes probably indicates that the full measure of sin and evil has been reached. The press is then **trampled outside the city**, probably a reference to Jerusalem. To the Jews of John's day, being executed outside the city gate meant being cut off from the covenant people of God (Heb 13:12-13). The distance covered by the **blood**, about **180 miles**, is the length of Palestine from its northern to southern borders, depicting the entire Holy Land covered in the blood of the wicked.

15:1 The third sign (see 12:1,3) appears in heaven. This sign is **seven angels** with the **seven last plagues** or bowls (16:1). These bowls are not just last in the series of sevenfold judgments, but they are also the last judgments of history. With them, God's wrath will be completed.

15:5-6 Testimony refers to the stone tablets, signifying the Ten Commandments and the covenant of God with Israel (Ex 25:16; Dt 10:1-2). The seven angels who emerge from the tabernacle with seven plagues are clothed in the **linen** garments of priests and are the instruments chosen by God to administer the final punishment to the nations.

15:7-8 The **seven gold bowls** probably allude to the golden saucers found on the table of showbread in the tabernacle (Ex 25:29) and the bowls filled with incense and the prayers of the saints (Rv 5:8; 8:3-5). Now, however, they are **filled with the wrath of God**, a response to the saints' prayers and a sacred offering to the Lord. The **smoke** symbolizes the presence of God.

16:1-3 The **loud voice from the sanctuary** probably belongs to God. All people with the mark of the beast break out in **severely painful sores** (Gk *elkos*, "an abscessed or ulcerous sore, infected wound," recalling the sixth Egyptian plague of boils; (Ex 9:9-11). The **sea** was the lifeblood of the Roman Empire, so this contamination of the waters would have spelled the ruin of their civilization, echoing the first plague on Egypt (Ex 7:14-25).

[A]14:11 Lit *They have no rest* [B]14:12 Lit *Here is the perseverance* [C]14:12 Or *and faith in Jesus*, or *and faithfulness to Jesus* [D]14:14 Or *like a son of man* [E]14:20 Lit *1,600 stadia* [F]15:1 Or *and awesome symbolic display* [G]15:2 Other mss add *his mark* [H]15:2 Or *harps of God*; = harps belonging to the service of God [I]15:3 Other mss read *ages* [J]16:1 Other mss omit *seven* [K]16:2 Lit *and a severely painful sore* [L]16:3 Other mss add *angel*

16:4-7 The third bowl is poured out on all of the fresh water sources, and they also become blood. This plague shortens the time for survival of the human race.

16:8-9 With the fourth angel's bowl, the sun's power is intensified, enabling it **to burn people with fire**. The hearts of the earth-dwellers are so hardened against the Lord that instead of turning for help to God, the One who holds the power over these plagues, they curse His name and refuse to **give Him glory**.

16:10-11 The fifth angel poured out the plague on the **throne of the beast**. The effect is that **his kingdom was plunged into darkness**, alluding first to the Egyptian plague of darkness (Ex 10:21) and also to the place of final judgment, the outer darkness where there will be "weeping and gnashing of teeth" (Mt 8:12; 22:13; 25:30; 2Pt 2:17).

16:12-14 The sixth bowl's event mirrors the drying of the Red Sea for the safe crossing of the Israelites.

16:15 Jesus Himself interrupts the flow of the narrative to issue a warning and a blessing. The one who goes naked reveals his lack of spiritual diligence. The one who remains clothed shows a state of constant readiness for Christ's return.

16:16 The kings of the earth gather at the place called **Armagedon** (Hb, "mountain or hill of Megiddo"). The ancient city of Megiddo, located in the Valley of Jezreel in northern Palestine, guards the main pass through the Carmel mountain range. Megiddo is important to Revelation's imagery as the site of many famous battles (Jdg 4–5; 5:19; 6:33–7:13; 2Kg 23:29-30).

16:17-19 With the seventh bowl God proclaims His judgment complete. **Babylon the Great** has made the nations drunk with "the wine of her sexual immorality" (14:8). God forces her to drink of **the wine of His fierce anger**. Faced with destruction of this enormity, the people still do not repent but blaspheme God for His judgment. This marks the earth-dwellers' impenitence for the third and final time.

17:1–19:5 The seventh bowl (16:17-21) pictures God's judgment on Babylon. Chapters 17 and 18 extend the bowl judgments, elaborating the last two bowls leading to the destruction of Babylon the Great, the end-times civilization that rises up in opposition to God and His Messiah.

17:1-2 **Sexual immorality** is used as a metaphor for spiritual abomination. The Old Testament prophets sometimes used the image of a **prostitute** to

a dead man's, and all life[A] in the sea died.

4 The third[B] poured out his bowl into the rivers and the springs of water, and they became blood. 5 I heard the angel of the waters say:

> You are righteous,
> who is and who was,
> the Holy One,
> for You have decided
> these things.
> 6 Because they poured out
> the blood of the •saints
> and the prophets,
> You also gave them blood
> to drink;
> they deserve it!

7 Then I heard someone from the altar say:

> Yes, Lord God, the Almighty,
> true and righteous are
> Your judgments.

The Fourth Bowl (16:8-9)

8 The fourth[B] poured out his bowl on the sun. He[C] was given the power[D] to burn people with fire, 9 and people were burned by the intense heat. So they blasphemed the name of God, who had the power[D] over these plagues, and they did not repent and give Him glory.

The Fifth Bowl (16:10-11)

10 The fifth[B] poured out his bowl on the throne of the beast, and his kingdom was plunged into darkness. People[E] gnawed their tongues because of their pain 11 and blasphemed the God of heaven because of their pains and their sores, yet they did not repent of their actions.

The Sixth Bowl (16:12-16)

12 The sixth[B] poured out his bowl on the great river Euphrates, and its water was dried up to prepare the way for the kings from the east. 13 Then I saw three unclean spirits like frogs coming from the dragon's mouth, from the beast's mouth, and from the mouth of the false prophet. 14 For they are spirits of demons performing signs, who travel to the kings of the whole world to assemble them for the battle of the great day of God, the Almighty.

15 "Look, I am coming like a thief. The one who is alert and remains clothed[F] so that he may not go around naked and people see his shame is blessed."

16 So they assembled them at the place called in Hebrew, Armagedon.[G,H]

The Seventh Bowl (16:17-21)

17 Then the seventh[B] poured out his bowl into the air,[I] and a loud voice came out of the sanctuary[J] from the throne, saying, "It is done!" 18 There were flashes of lightning and rumblings of thunder. And a severe earthquake occurred like no other since man has been on the earth—so great was the quake. 19 The great city split into three parts, and the cities of the nations[K] fell. Babylon the Great was remembered in God's presence; He gave her the cup filled with the wine of His fierce anger. 20 Every island fled, and the mountains disappeared.[L] 21 Enormous hailstones, each weighing about 100 pounds,[M] fell from the sky on people, and they blasphemed God for the plague of hail because that plague was extremely severe.

Babylon and Her Destiny (17:1–19:5)

The Vision of the Woman and the Scarlet Beast (17:1-6)

17 Then one of the seven angels who had the seven bowls came and spoke with me: "Come, I will show you the judgment of the notorious prostitute[N] who sits on many[O] waters. 2 The kings of the earth committed sexual immorality with her, and those who live on the earth became drunk on the wine of her sexual immorality." 3 So he carried me away in the Spirit[P] to a desert. I saw a woman sitting on a

[A]**16:3** Lit *and every soul of life* [B]**16:4,8,10,12,17** Other mss add *angel* [C]**16:8** Or *It* [D]**16:8,9** Or *authority* [E]**16:10** Lit *They* [F]**16:15** Or *and guards his clothes* [G]**16:16** Other mss read *Armageddon*; other mss read *Harmegedon*; other mss read *Mageddon*; other mss read *Magedon* [H]**16:16** Traditionally *the hill of Megiddo*, a great city that guarded the pass between the coast and the valley of Jezreel or Esdraelon; Jdg 5:19; 2Kg 9:27 [I]**16:17** Or *on the air* [J]**16:17** Other mss add *of heaven* [K]**16:19** Or *the Gentile cities* [L]**16:20** Lit *mountains were not found* [M]**16:21** Lit *about a talent*; talents varied in weight upwards from 75 pounds [N]**17:1** Traditionally translated *the great whore* [O]**17:1** Or *by many* [P]**17:3** Or *in spirit*

scarlet beast that was covered[A] with blasphemous names and had seven heads and 10 horns. 4 The woman was dressed in purple and scarlet, adorned with gold, precious stones, and pearls. She had a gold cup in her hand filled with everything vile and with the impurities of her[B] prostitution. 5 On her forehead a cryptic name was written:

BABYLON THE GREAT
THE MOTHER OF
PROSTITUTES
AND OF THE VILE THINGS
OF THE EARTH.

6 Then I saw that the woman was drunk on the blood of the •saints and on the blood of the witnesses to Jesus. When I saw her, I was greatly astonished.

The Angel's Interpretation of the Vision (17:7-18)

7 Then the angel said to me, "Why are you astonished? I will tell you the •secret meaning of the woman and of the beast, with the seven heads and the 10 horns, that carries her. 8 The beast that you saw was, and is not, and is about to come up from the •abyss and go to destruction. Those who live on the earth whose names have not been written in the book of life from the foundation of the world will be astonished when they see the beast that was, and is not, and will be present again.

9 "Here is the mind with wisdom:[C] The seven heads are seven mountains on which the woman is seated. 10 They are also seven kings:[D] Five have fallen, one is, the other has not yet come, and when he comes, he must remain for a little while. 11 The beast that was and is not, is himself an eighth king, yet he belongs to the seven and is going to destruction. 12 The 10 horns you saw are 10 kings who have not yet received a kingdom, but they will receive authority as kings with the beast for one hour. 13 These have one purpose, and they give their power and authority to the beast. 14 These will make war against the Lamb, but the Lamb will conquer them because He is Lord of lords and King of kings. Those with Him are called, chosen, and faithful."

15 He also said to me, "The waters you saw, where the prostitute was seated, are peoples, multitudes, nations, and languages. 16 The 10 horns you saw, and the beast, will hate the prostitute. They will make her desolate and naked, devour her flesh, and burn her up with fire. 17 For God has put it into their hearts to carry out His plan by having one purpose and to give their kingdom[E] to the beast until God's words are accomplished. 18 And the woman you saw is the great city that has an empire[F] over the kings of the earth."

The Announcement of Babylon's Fall (18:1-8)

18 After this I saw another angel with great authority coming down from heaven, and the earth was illuminated by his splendor. 2 He cried in a mighty voice:

It has fallen,[G]
Babylon the Great has fallen!
She has become a dwelling
for demons,
a haunt for
every •unclean spirit,
a haunt for
every unclean bird,
and a haunt[H] for
every unclean
and despicable beast.[I]
3 For all the nations
have drunk[J]
the wine of her
sexual immorality,
which brings wrath.
The kings of the earth
have committed
sexual immorality with her,
and the merchants
of the earth
have grown wealthy
from her excessive luxury.

4 Then I heard another voice from heaven:

[A]17:3 Lit *was filled* [B]17:4 Other mss read *of earth's* [C]17:9 Or *This calls for the mind with wisdom* [D]17:10 Some editors or translators put *They are also seven kings:* in v. 9. [E]17:17 Or *sovereignty* [F]17:18 Or *has sovereignty* or *rulership* [G]18:2 Other mss omit *It has fallen* [H]18:2 Or *prison* [I]18:2 Other mss omit the words *and a haunt for every unclean beast.* The words *and despicable* then refer to the *bird* of the previous line. [J]18:3 Some mss read *have collapsed*; other mss read *have fallen*

describe powerful cities, such as Tyre (Is 23:15-17), whose corrupt combination of politics and religion reveled in widespread injustice and oppression of the masses.

17:3-4 This prostitute is pampered by a **scarlet beast**, the beast from the sea (13:1) who represents unrestrained political power personified in the antichrist. The union of these two figures shows that the evil empire moves forward in the seduction of the nations with the aid of the antichrist's military and political might.

17:5-6 Aristocratic prostitutes of ancient Rome would place their names on the headbands they wore. In a similar way, the notorious prostitute wears a **cryptic name** on her forehead. The first title, **BABYLON THE GREAT**, reveals her connection with a rebellious and godless civilization.

17:8 The beast's false resurrection will cause the earth-dwellers to be astonished and worship him. Those who are deceived by the antichrist reveal their true nature as those whose names were not **written in the book of life from the foundation of the world**.

17:9-11 The **seven heads** of the monster are **seven mountains**. The first-century city of Rome was known as "the city on seven hills." **The woman** is enthroned upon a kingdom with the same power and prestige of ancient Rome.

17:12-14 The antichrist figure will receive support from the **10 horns**, which are **10 kings who have not yet received a kingdom**. These allied kings will wage war against the Lamb, but the Lamb will conquer them all.

17:15-18 **The waters** that the prostitute is sitting on are **peoples, multitudes, nations, and languages**. John and his readers would associate this great city, the prostitute, with Rome and its empire. Ultimately this prophecy concerns the final evil civilization of the world: a Rome-like empire established and ruled by the antichrist.

18:1-3 The glorious splendor of this **angel** with great authority reflects his being in God's presence. The angel's pronouncement recalls a similar declaration regarding ancient Babylon (Is 21:9). The final destruction of **Babylon the Great** is grounded in the eternal decrees of God. The image of unclean creatures roaming about the ruined city symbolizes the total destruction of Babylon. The **kings of the earth** and the **merchants of the earth** benefit from Babylon's idolatry, wealth, and luxury. Rome provides the historical background for this materialism. The Roman government exploited its subjects to dominate the people and build national wealth. The heavy tax burden and debts of common people prevented them from rising above poverty. As the Roman Empire expanded, the additional sources of trade made the ruling and merchant classes wealthier. Even the Roman religious cults propagated the social and economic corruption by choosing their priests from among the wealthy and powerful. God punishes materialism and economic sins (e.g., Tyre, Ezk 27–28).

18:4-5 This address to Christians mirrors several Old Testament warnings where the Israelites are ordered to flee ancient Babylon (Is 48:20; Jr 51:6,45). Here the fleeing is intended primarily in a spiritual sense, for God's method of missions in every age has been to set apart a people and call them out from the world, even though they still reside in the world. As followers of Jesus, believers are to be *in* the world but not *of* the world (Jn 17:13-16). At the end of the age, those few believers residing in the kingdom of the beast will likely flee in a literal sense from the coming destruction of Babylon the Great. God has delayed the hour of her judgment, but the time has come. **God has remembered her crimes** and will bring retribution to the great city. Elsewhere in Scripture, when God "remembers" sins, judgment is coming (see Ps 109:14; Jr 14:10; Hs 8:13; 9:9).

18:6-8 Babylon will receive exactly what her crimes deserve. The commands—to **pay her back**, to double it, and to mix a double portion for her—mean to pay her back in full measure. Babylon the Great deserves to be given torment and grief, for she **glorified herself and lived luxuriously** (Gk *estrēniasen*, "with unrestrained excess, extravagantly, immorally, sensually"). Three statements summarize Babylon's arrogance:

- **I sit as a queen**, ruling over the entire world as the finest civilization of all time.
- **I am not a widow**, for my many lovers are the kings of the earth.
- **I will never see grief**, for I am in complete control of my own destiny.

18:9-10 The first mourners over Babylon the Great are the **kings of the earth** who join her in **sexual immorality** and luxurious living. They are unwilling, however, to risk coming to her aid. Instead, they will weep and mourn while they stand far off.

>WORD|*study*

18:7 To have **glorified** (Gk *edoxasen*, "praised, honored, magnified, clothed oneself with splendor") oneself is to have claimed what rightfully belongs only to God. This Greek verb appears 23 times in the Gospel of John, and each time the one glorified is either God the Father or God the Son. Jesus refused to glorify Himself (Jn 8:54).

Come out of her, My people,
so that you will not share
in her sins
or receive any of her plagues.
5 For her sins are piled up[A]
to heaven,
and God has remembered
her crimes.
6 Pay her back the way
she also paid,
and double it
according to her works.
In the cup in which she mixed,
mix a double portion for her.
7 As much as she
glorified herself
and lived luxuriously,
give her that much torment
and grief,
for she says in her heart,
"I sit as a queen;
I am not a widow,
and I will never see grief."
8 For this reason her plagues
will come in one day[B]—
death and grief and famine.
She will be burned up
with fire,
because the Lord God
who judges her is mighty.

The World's Mourning of Babylon's Fall (18:9-20)

9 The kings of the earth who have
committed sexual immorality and
lived luxuriously with her will weep
and mourn over her when they see
the smoke of her burning. 10 They
will stand far off in fear of her torment, saying:

Woe, woe, the great city,
Babylon, the mighty city!
For in a single hour[B]
your judgment has come.

11 The merchants of the earth will
also weep and mourn over her, because no one buys their merchandise any longer— 12 merchandise
of gold, silver, precious stones, and
pearls; fine fabrics of linen, purple,
silk, and scarlet; all kinds of fragrant
wood products; objects of ivory; objects of expensive wood, brass,[C] iron,
and marble; 13 cinnamon, spice,[D,E]
incense, myrrh,[F] and frankincense;
wine, olive oil, fine wheat flour, and
grain; cattle and sheep; horses and
carriages; and slaves[G] and human
lives.[H]

14 The fruit you craved
has left you.
All your splendid
and glamorous things
are gone;
they will never
find them again.

15 The merchants of these things,
who became rich from her, will
stand far off in fear of her torment,
weeping and mourning, 16 saying:

Woe, woe, the great city,
dressed in fine linen, purple,
and scarlet,
adorned with gold,
precious stones, and pearls,
17 for in a single hour[B]
such fabulous wealth
was destroyed!

And every shipmaster, seafarer,
the sailors, and all who do business by sea, stood far off 18 as they
watched the smoke from her burning and kept crying out: "Who is like
the great city?" 19 They threw dust
on their heads and kept crying out,
weeping, and mourning:

Woe, woe, the great city,
where all those
who have ships on the sea
became rich from her wealth,
for in a single hour[B]
she was destroyed.

[A]**18:5** Or *sins have reached up* [B]**18:8,10,17,19** Suddenly [C]**18:12** Or *bronze*, or *copper* [D]**18:13** Other mss omit *spice* [E]**18:13** Or *amomum*, an aromatic plant [F]**18:13** Or *perfume* [G]**18:13** Or *bodies* [H]**18:13** Slaves; "bodies" was the Gk way of referring to slaves; "souls of men" was the Hb way.

20 Rejoice over her, heaven,
and you •saints, apostles,
and prophets,
because God has executed
your judgment on her![A]

The Finality of Babylon's Destruction (18:21-24)

21 Then a mighty angel picked up
a stone like a large millstone and
threw it into the sea, saying:

In this way, Babylon
the great city
will be thrown down violently
and never be found again.
22 The sound of harpists,
musicians,
flutists, and trumpeters
will never be heard
in you again;
no craftsman of any trade
will ever be found
in you again;
the sound of a mill
will never be heard
in you again;
23 the light of a lamp
will never shine in you again;
and the voice of a groom
and bride
will never be heard
in you again.
All this will happen
because your merchants
were the nobility of the earth,
because all the nations
were deceived
by your sorcery,[B]
24 and the blood of prophets
and saints,
and of all those slaughtered
on earth,
was found in you.[C]

The Rejoicing of Heaven (19:1-5)

19 After this I heard something
like the loud voice of a vast
multitude in heaven, saying:

•Hallelujah!
Salvation, glory, and power
belong to our God,
2 because His judgments
are true[D] and righteous,
because He has judged
the notorious prostitute
who corrupted the earth
with her sexual immorality;
and He has avenged the blood
of His •slaves
that was on her hands.

3 A second time they said:

Hallelujah!
Her smoke ascends forever
and ever!

4 Then the 24 elders and the four
living creatures fell down and worshiped God, who is seated on the
throne, saying:

•Amen! Hallelujah!

5 A voice came from the throne,
saying:

Praise our God,
all His slaves, who fear Him,
both small and great!

The Final Victory (19:6–20:15)

The Announcement of the Marriage of the Lamb (19:6-10)

6 Then I heard something like the
voice of a vast multitude, like the
sound of cascading waters, and like
the rumbling of loud thunder, saying:

Hallelujah, because
our Lord God, the Almighty,

[A]18:20 Or *God pronounced on her the judgment she passed on you*; see Rv 18:6 [B]18:23 Ancient sorcery or witchcraft often used spells and drugs. Here the term may be non-literal, that is, Babylon drugged the nations with her beauty and power. [C]18:24 Lit *in her* [D]19:2 Valid; Jn 8:16; 19:35

18:11-17a The second group of mourners are the merchants who became wealthy from trade with the great city. The merchants mourn specifically because **no one buys their merchandise any longer**. All of these items were among the most costly and coveted in the Roman Empire and, apart from the food items, possessed only by the wealthy. Like the kings of the earth, the merchants made rich from the indulgences of Babylon the Great also **stand far off in fear of her torment.**

18:17b-19 The third group in mourning for Babylon the Great are those who play a part in her sea trade. Once again, this group laments their material losses. The gesture of throwing dust on their heads refers to a common sign of mourning and sorrow in the ancient world.

18:20 Rejoicing is in order for all believers because God's judgment on Babylon the Great is the vindication of His people. The final annihilation of Babylon the Great fulfills God's promise of justice to the martyrs (6:9-11). Since the bowl judgments and the fall of Babylon the Great appear to coincide, when Babylon is punished, the earth-dwellers are punished.

18:21-24 The casting of the **millstone ... into the sea** is another enacted parable (cp. 10:8,10; Jr 51:63-64), illustrating the way the **great city** will be **thrown down violently**. Lost forever will be particulars of Babylon's civilization: the music of her debauchery, all aspects of commerce, the distinguishing marks of domestic life, and joy as shown by the absence of the **groom and bride**. The fact that the **blood of all those slaughtered** on the earth is found in the prostitute points to the way this civilization's sins transcend time. Babylon the Great embodies all of the godless and corrupt empires that have stood against the Lord since the beginning of human history.

19:6-8 The arrival of the **marriage of the Lamb** causes all people to **be glad, rejoice, and give Him glory**. Israel as the bride of Yahweh is a theme in the Old Testament (Is 54:5; 61:10; Jr 31:32; Ezk 16:7-14; Hs 2:16-20) and in the New Testament, with the church as Christ's bride (2Co 11:2; Eph 5:25-27).

>WORD|*study*

19:1-5 Hallelujah is an untranslated Hebrew word meaning, "Praise the Lord." *Hallelu* is the command form of the word "praise," while *yah* is a short form for *Yahweh*, the name of God often rendered as "LORD" in English translations. This phrase became a common expression of worship in Israel, appearing throughout the Psalms (see Pss 104–106; 146–150), but it appears in the New Testament only in Revelation (Rv 19:1,3,4,6).

19:17-18 There is a stark contrast here between the "marriage feast of the Lamb" (19:9) and the **great supper of God**. No one will be exempted from the carnage of this last battle, for the list of the dead includes **everyone, both free and slave, small and great** (see Ezk 39:17-20).

19:19-21 The satanic trinity has been preparing for this battle since the sixth bowl (16:12-16), but they prove to be no match for the rider on the white horse and His army. The fight comes to an end before even one blow is delivered. As soon as the sword comes out of the Lord's mouth, the battle is over. The **beast** and the **false prophet** are captured and immediately thrown alive into the **lake of fire that burns with sulfur**. For the first time in Scripture the place of eternal punishment for the wicked is described with this imagery, which will appear several more times (20:10,14,15; 21:8). With their leader defeated forever, the armies assembled to fight against the Lamb have no defense. They are **killed with the sword** of Christ's mouth, and the birds gorge themselves on their flesh.

20:1-3 Seizing **the ancient serpent**—who has been opposing God since the garden of Eden—the angel bound him with the iron chain and threw him into **the abyss**, the prison for evil spirits (Jd 6). The seal of God upon the abyss will ensure the imprisonment of Satan for **1,000 years**, after which the Devil will **be released for a short time.**

20:4-6 The Romans preferred beheading as a method of executing Christians of the upper class, with burning, crucifixion, and exposure to wild animals being reserved for foreigners and lower classes. Here, beheading probably serves as a summary term for all martyrdom. Those who are martyred in the great tribulation have refused to worship **the beast or his image** and are without his **mark**. After the binding of Satan, God will bring the faithful dead to life and allow them to reign with His Son **in the first resurrection**. The martyrs here are representatives of all who have remained faithful to Jesus throughout the ages. Because they refuse to serve Christ in their earthly life, **the rest of the dead** must await judgment while the saints of God throughout history participate in the first resurrection.

20:7-10 **Satan will be released from his prison** following the **1,000 years**. This release is part of God's overall plan. When the Devil is released, he will deceive the nations, apparently those who survive the tribulation (19:17-21) and children born during the millennial reign of Christ who never submitted themselves to Christ. The Devil will gather these unbelievers for another battle. **Gog** [the king of the northern

has begun to reign!
7 Let us be glad, rejoice,
and give Him glory,
because the marriage
of the Lamb has come,
and His wife
has prepared herself.
8 She was given fine linen to
wear, bright and pure.

For the fine linen represents the righteous acts of the •saints.

9 Then he[A] said to me, "Write: Those invited to the marriage feast of the Lamb are fortunate!" He also said to me, "These words of God are true." 10 Then I fell at his feet to worship him, but he said to me, "Don't do that! I am a fellow slave with you and your •brothers who have the testimony about[B] Jesus. Worship God, because the testimony about Jesus is the spirit of prophecy."[C]

The Appearance of the Victorious Messiah (19:11-16)

11 Then I saw heaven opened, and there was a white horse. Its rider is called Faithful and True, and He judges and makes war in righteousness. 12 His eyes were like a fiery flame, and many crowns[D] were on His head. He had a name written that no one knows except Himself. 13 He wore a robe stained with blood,[E] and His name is the Word of God. 14 The armies that were in heaven followed Him on white horses, wearing pure white linen. 15 A sharp[F] sword came from His mouth, so that He might strike the nations with it. He will shepherd[G] them with an iron scepter. He will also trample the winepress of the fierce anger of God, the Almighty. 16 And He has a name written on His robe and on His thigh:

KING OF KINGS
AND LORD OF LORDS.

The Destruction of the Antichrist and His Allies (19:17-21)

17 Then I saw an angel standing on[H] the sun, and he cried out in a loud voice, saying to all the birds flying high overhead, "Come, gather together for the great supper of God, 18 so that you may eat the flesh of kings, the flesh of commanders, the flesh of mighty men, the flesh of horses and of their riders, and the flesh of everyone, both free and slave, small and great."

19 Then I saw the beast, the kings of the earth, and their armies gathered together to wage war against the rider on the horse and against His army. 20 But the beast was taken prisoner, and along with him the false prophet, who had performed the signs in his presence. He deceived those who accepted the mark of the beast and those who worshiped his image with these signs. Both of them were thrown alive into the lake of fire that burns with sulfur. 21 The rest were killed with the sword that came from the mouth of the rider on the horse, and all the birds were filled with their flesh.

The Binding of Satan (20:1-3)

20 Then I saw an angel coming down from heaven with the key to the •abyss and a great chain in his hand. 2 He seized the dragon, that ancient serpent who is the Devil and Satan,[I] and bound him for 1,000 years. 3 He threw him into the abyss, closed it, and put a seal on it so that he would no longer deceive the nations until the 1,000 years were completed. After that, he must be released for a short time.

Christ's Millennial Reign (20:4-6)

4 Then I saw thrones, and people seated on them who were given authority to judge. I also saw the people[J] who had been beheaded[K] because of their testimony about Jesus and because of God's word, who had not worshiped the beast or his image, and who had not accepted the mark on their foreheads or their hands. They came to life and reigned with the •Messiah for 1,000 years. 5 The rest of the dead did not come to life until the 1,000 years were completed. This is the first resurrection. 6 Blessed and holy is the one who shares in the first resurrection!

[A]19:9 Probably an angel; Rv 17:1; 22:8-9 [B]19:10 Or *to* [C]19:10 Or *the Spirit* [D]19:12 Or *diadems* [E]19:13 Or *a robe dipped in* [F]19:15 Other mss add *double-edged* [G]19:15 Or *rule* [H]19:17 Or *in* [I]20:2 Other mss add *who deceives the whole world* [J]20:4 Lit *souls* [K]20:4 All who had given their lives for their faith in Christ

Eschatology and Interpreting the Book of Revelation

View	Definition	Interpretation of Millennium
Preterist (Lat *preter* means "past")	The events recorded in Revelation were fulfilled in the days of the first century under the emperors Nero or Domitian, particularly with the destruction of the Jewish temple in Jerusalem (A.D. 70) with little or no future fulfillment to be expected apart from the return of Christ.	The term millennium is metaphorical.
Historicist (*Post*millennial)	Revelation depicts the broad sweep of church history, from the time of the apostles to the consummation of the age. Espoused by most of the Reformers (except the Anabaptists), this view is weakened by inevitable subjectivity in its interpretation of the symbolism.	The world will become progressively "Christianized" by the spread of the gospel. When that process is complete, there will be a millennium of peace on the earth, *after* which Christ will return.
Idealist (*A*millennial)	Revelation is not to be considered an ordered presentation of actual events but a symbolic depiction of the ongoing battle between God and Satan, good and evil.	There will be *no* literal millennial reign of Christ on earth. The 1,000 years figuratively describes the period of time currently experienced by the church before the return of Christ. The binding of Satan (20:2-3) during that time period refers not to his literal imprisonment but to a limitation in his powers.
Futurist (*Pre*millennial)	The events beginning with chapter 4 are a prophecy of what is to come in the future age. The early church fathers were united, with a few exceptions, in interpreting Revelation as in some sense actual history. Anabaptists also held this view. This is the position supported by the editors of this study Bible.	Christ returns *before* the millennium, after the defeat of the antichrist (19:11-21), ushering in His literal 1,000-year reign on earth.
Synthesis	Revelation is to be interpreted as an apocalyptic prophecy primarily referring to the end times, yet speaking to the problems and needs of first-century churches, while communicating principles equally binding and applicable to hearers at any point in history until the end of the age.	

The second death has no power[A]
over them, but they will be priests
of God and of the Messiah, and they
will reign with Him for 1,000 years.

Satan's Final Destruction (20:7-10)

7 When the 1,000 years are completed, Satan will be released from
his prison 8 and will go out to deceive the nations at the four corners
of the earth, Gog and Magog, to
gather them for battle. Their number is like the sand of the sea. 9 They
came up over the surface of the
earth and surrounded the encampment of the •saints, the beloved city.
Then fire came down from heaven[B]
and consumed them. 10 The Devil
who deceived them was thrown into
the lake of fire and sulfur where
the beast and the false prophet are,
and they will be tormented day and
night forever and ever.

The Final Judgment (20:11-15)

11 Then I saw a great white throne
and One seated on it. Earth and
heaven fled from His presence, and
no place was found for them. 12 I
also saw the dead, the great and the

lands] **and Magog** (the people of Gog) come to wage war against God's people. As in Ezk 38–39 , the rebel armies are destroyed by fire. Then God turns His attention to **the Devil**. The father of lies and ruler of darkness takes his place with the rest of the satanic trinity in **the lake of fire and sulfur**, where **they will be tormented day and night forever**.

20:11-15 The **white** color of the **throne** recalls the purity and holiness of God. The fleeing of earth and heaven from God's **presence** emphasizes the grandeur and fearsomeness of His character and prepares for the new heaven and new earth (21:1).

[A] **20:6** Or *authority* [B] **20:9** Other mss add *from God*

20:12-15 At the **great white throne** of God all were **judged according to their works**. The rejection of Jesus leaves one's earthly works as the only basis of judgment (Is 64:6). Based upon the absence of their names from **the book of life** and their wicked acts in the books of their deeds, the dead are found worthy of punishment in the **lake of fire**.

21:1-4 John's observation that **the sea no longer existed** stems from the ancient Jewish belief that the sea represented all the things in opposition to the rule of God. Leviathan, for example, was an Old Testament sea monster representing the forces of evil (Ps 74:13-14; Jb 41:1; Is 27:1). Isaiah also compared the wicked to the ocean (Is 57:20). The first beast of Revelation arises from the sea (Rv 13:1). The **new Jerusalem**, the final home of the redeemed, is the new earth for all eternity. Her description as **a bride adorned** links this passage with the marriage supper of the Lamb (19:7-8) and contrasts **the Holy City** or bride (Jerusalem) with the wicked city or prostitute (Babylon the Great;17:1).

In the new Jerusalem God will dwell eternally and visibly among His people (a key OT promise—see Ex 29:45; Lv 26:11-12; Ezk 37:27; Zch 2:11). He will remove all sources of sadness. God will replace the effects of sin and suffering with joy.

21:5-8 A voice declares after the seven bowls of wrath, **"It is done!"** (16:17), but now God makes the same declaration in referring to the new Jerusalem. The believer, who is thirsty for the things of God, will be able to drink from the spring of life. This person is described as **the victor** who will be considered a son of God. Unbelievers inherit the **second death**.

21:15-17 The angel **measured the city** (cp. Ezk 40–41) as a cube, each side being **12,000 *stadia*** long (about 1,400 miles). The walls measured **144 cubits** (about 200 feet) thick. These measurements, with multiples of 10 and 12, constitute the perfect proportions of the new Jerusalem.

21:18-21 **Jasper**, possibly a bright green color, is associated with God's glory. The arrangement of 12 multi-colored precious stones would give the impression that the city rests on a shimmering rainbow. The **12 pearls** of colossal size would be at least 200 feet in diameter. Pearls were considered the most luxurious of all jewels in the ancient world (see Mt 13:45-46). The priests of Israel's ancient temple used to walk on gold floors (1Kg 6:30), but now every citizen of heaven will have that same privilege and more.

>WORD|*study*

20:14-15 The lake of fire (19:20; 20:10,14,15) is an image unique to the book of Revelation. While the background of the fiery lake is uncertain, the best corresponding New Testament concept comes from *Gehenna* (Gk, usually translated "hell" or "hellfire"; Mt 5:22,29,30; 10:28; 18:9; 23:15,33; Mk 9:43,45,47; Lk 12:5; Jms 3:6). The name was originally derived from the Valley of Hinnom on the southern slope of Jerusalem, which became notorious during the evil reigns of Ahab and Manasseh when they burned their own children there as offerings to the god Molech (2Ch 28:3; 33:6). The site of this wickedness was condemned and became a symbol for future punishment (Jr 7:30-33). In Jesus' day, this place became the city dump where garbage kept the fires constantly burning.

small, standing before the throne, and books were opened. Another book was opened, which is the book of life, and the dead were judged according to their works by what was written in the books.

13 Then the sea gave up its dead, and Death and •Hades gave up their dead; all[A] were judged according to their works. 14 Death and Hades were thrown into the lake of fire. This is the second death, the lake of fire.[B] 15 And anyone not found written in the book of life was thrown into the lake of fire.

The New Heaven and New Earth (21:1–22:5)

The New Creation (21:1-8)

21 Then I saw a new heaven and a new earth, for the first heaven and the first earth had passed away, and the sea no longer existed. 2 I also saw the Holy City, new Jerusalem, coming down out of heaven from God, prepared like a bride adorned for her husband.

3 Then I heard a loud voice from the throne:[C]

Look! God's dwelling[D] is
with humanity,
and He will live with them.
They will be His people,
and God Himself will be
with them
and be their God.[E]
4 He will wipe away every tear
from their eyes.
Death will no longer exist;
grief, crying, and pain
will exist no longer,
because the previous things[F]
have passed away.

5 Then the One seated on the throne said, "Look! I am making everything new." He also said, "Write, because these words[G] are faithful and true." 6 And He said to me, "It is done! I am the •Alpha and the Omega, the Beginning and the End. I will give water as a gift to the thirsty from the spring of life. 7 The victor will inherit these things, and I will be his God, and he will be My son. 8 But the cowards, unbelievers,[H] vile, murderers, sexually immoral, sorcerers, idolaters, and all liars—their share will be in the lake that burns with fire and sulfur, which is the second death."

The New Jerusalem (21:9-27)

9 Then one of the seven angels, who had held the seven bowls filled with the seven last plagues, came and spoke with me: "Come, I will show you the bride, the wife of the Lamb." 10 He then carried me away in the Spirit[I] to a great and high mountain and showed me the holy city, Jerusalem, coming down out of heaven from God, 11 arrayed with God's glory. Her radiance was like a very precious stone, like a jasper stone, bright as crystal. 12 The city had a massive high wall, with 12 gates. Twelve angels were at the gates; the names of the 12 tribes of Israel's sons were inscribed on the gates. 13 There were three gates on the east, three gates on the north, three gates on the south, and three gates on the west. 14 The city wall had 12 foundations, and the 12 names of the Lamb's 12 apostles were on the foundations.

15 The one who spoke with me had a gold measuring rod to measure the city, its gates, and its wall. 16 The

[A]20:13 Lit *each* [B]20:14 Other mss omit *the lake of fire* [C]21:3 Other mss read *from heaven* [D]21:3 Or *tent*, or *tabernacle* [E]21:3 Other mss omit *and be their God* [F]21:4 Or *the first things* [G]21:5 Other mss add *of God* [H]21:8 Other mss add *the sinful* [I]21:10 Or *in spirit*

Revelation's Tale of Two Cities and Two Women

Babylon the Great	Bride of Christ
• a woman (chap. 17) • a city (chaps. 16 and 18) • "dressed in purple and scarlet" (17:4)	• a woman (chap. 19) • a city (chap. 21) • clothed in "fine linen . . . bright and pure" (19:8)
pseudo-queen and consort of the beast (17:3,4; 18:7)	bride of the Lamb who is King of kings (19:7,9,16)
dwelling place for demons (18:2)	dwelling place for God (21:3,11,22-23)
"a woman sitting on a scarlet beast that was covered with blasphemous names" (17:3)	an army sitting on "white horses," clothed in "pure white linen," following Him whose names include "the Word of God" and "KING OF KINGS AND LORD OF LORDS" (19:13-14,16)
"the notorious prostitute" who kills the saints (17:1,5,6)	"vast multitude" praising God for avenging the saints' blood on "the notorious prostitute" (19:1-2)
closely related to the earth-dwellers (17:8)	the heaven-dwellers, closely related to the "vast multitude" (7:9-15; 12:12; 13:6; 19:1,6)
• "the great city" (16:19; 17:18; 18:10) • "Babylon the Great" (16:19; 17:5; 18:2)	• "the holy city" (21:2,10) • "new Jerusalem" (21:2,10)
the earth-dwellers' names are not written in "the book of life" (17:8; cp. 13:8).	No one enters whose name is not written in the "book of life" (21:27).
"She glorified herself" (18:7).	She is "arrayed with God's glory" (21:11).
"In a single hour such fabulous wealth was destroyed" (18:17).	"Her radiance was like a very precious stone" (21:11).
"The voice of a groom and bride will never be heard . . . again" (18:23).	• "the marriage feast of the Lamb" (19:9), for which the bride has made herself ready (19:7,9; 21:2) • "the bride, the wife of the Lamb . . . coming down out of heaven from God" (21:9,10)

city is laid out in a square; its length
and width are the same. He measured the city with the rod at 12,000
stadia.[A] Its length, width, and height
are equal. [17] Then he measured its
wall, 144 •cubits according to human measurement, which the angel used. [18] The building material of
its wall was jasper, and the city was
pure gold like clear glass.
[19] The foundations of the city wall
were adorned with every kind of precious stone:

the first foundation jasper,
the second sapphire,
the third chalcedony,
the fourth emerald,
20 the fifth sardonyx,
the sixth carnelian,
the seventh chrysolite,
the eighth beryl,
the ninth topaz,
the tenth chrysoprase,
the eleventh jacinth,
the twelfth amethyst.

[21] The 12 gates are 12 pearls; each
individual gate was made of a single
pearl. The broad street[B] of the city
was pure gold, like transparent
glass.
[22] I did not see a sanctuary in it,
because the Lord God the Almighty
and the Lamb are its sanctuary.
[23] The city does not need the sun or
the moon to shine on it, because
God's glory illuminates it, and its
lamp is the Lamb. [24] The nations[C]
will walk in its light, and the kings

21:22-27 In the temple of ancient Israel, the presence of God in the holy of holies made the temple sacred. In the new Jerusalem, the presence of God makes the entire city a holy of holies with no need for a **sanctuary** or temple or formal location to meet with God. The radiant **glory** of **the Lord God the Almighty and the Lamb** outshines any created light source. The sun and the moon are unnecessary.

In the new Jerusalem the gates will never close. Unlike in a typical ancient city, the inhabitants of the new Jerusalem will not fear unwelcome nightly visitors or need protection from anything profane or anyone who does what is vile or false. People characterized in this way are not in **the Lamb's book of life** and so will not be present in the new Jerusalem. Because of the safety and purity of the city, **the nations** can freely come and go, bringing glory and honor to the Lamb.

[A]**21:16** A *stadion* (sg) = about 600 feet; 12,000 *stadia* = 1,400 miles. [B]**21:21** Or *The public square*
[C]**21:24** Other mss add *of those who are saved*

22:1-2 The river of living water recalls the river that "went out from Eden" (Gn 2:10) and fulfills prophecy (Zch 14:8). The source of the river is God Himself, for it flows from His throne.

"Living water" also recalls Jesus' use of this metaphor for the Holy Spirit (cp. Jn 4:10-14; 7:38) and the Holy Spirit as "streams of living water" flowing from deep within the believer (Jn 7:38). The garden of Eden also had within it the "tree of life" (Gn 3:22). After the fall, Adam and Eve were driven from the garden so that they would not eat of the tree and find immortality in the midst of their sin. In the new Jerusalem, however, the tree of life is restored to humanity. The use of the leaves of the tree for the healing of the nations has its background in Ezk 47:12.

22:3-5 With the lifting of sin's **curse**, the **slaves** of God can faithfully **serve** Him in the city. With God ruling in the city, its inhabitants will actually **see His face**. The name of God will be on the foreheads of His servants. God and His faithful servants **reign** in the new Jerusalem **forever and ever**.

22:10-15 In Daniel's day the time was not right to reveal the plan of God for the redemption of the world (Dn 12:4), but by John's day **the time** [Gk *kairos*, "a decisive, appointed time; the right or due time or season"; cp. Jn 7:6,8] **is near**. A person's character will be revealed in his or her deeds.

In light of Christ's imminent return, the Lord emphasizes the **reward** (Gk *misthos*, "wages, payment for work completed"; cp. 11:18; 2 Jn 1:8) and punishment earned by **each person according to what he has done**. Those **who wash their robes** in Christ's blood are **blessed** because they may eat from **the tree of life** and **enter** the new Jerusalem **by the gates**. Those who are not cleansed by the Lamb will have no part of such blessings. Left **outside** the city of God are those characterized by lives of impurity, idolatry, and selfishness. These sins are not beyond God's forgiveness, but they *characterize* unrepentant people, excluded, therefore, from heaven. Throughout Scripture, **dogs** refer to various kinds of impure and unclean persons (see Php 3:2).

22:17 John offered an invitation to respond to the book's message. **Whoever desires** may freely drink of **the living water**—the eternal life offered by **the Spirit** of God and **the bride** of Christ. The gospel of Jesus Christ is offered **as a gift** (Gk *dōrean*, "freely, without payment"; see 21:6) to anyone who will receive it.

22:18-19 John included a stern message of warning. The one who **adds**

of the earth will bring their glory
into it.[A] 25 Each day its gates will
never close because it will never be
night there. 26 They will bring the
glory and honor of the nations into
it.[B] 27 Nothing profane will ever enter
it: no one who does what is vile or
false, but only those written in the
Lamb's book of life.

Eden's Restoration (22:1-5)

22 Then he showed me the river[C]
of living water, sparkling like
crystal, flowing from the throne
of God and of the Lamb 2 down the
middle of the broad street of the city.
The tree of life[D] was on both sides of
the river, bearing 12 kinds of fruit,
producing its fruit every month. The
leaves of the tree are for healing the
nations, 3 and there will no longer
be any curse. The throne of God and
of the Lamb will be in the city,[E] and
His •slaves will serve Him. 4 They
will see His face, and His name will
be on their foreheads. 5 Night will
no longer exist, and people will not
need lamplight or sunlight, because
the Lord God will give them light.
And they will reign forever and ever.

Epilogue (22:6-21)

John and the Angel (22:6-11)

6 Then he said to me, "These words
are faithful and true. And the Lord,
the God of the spirits of the prophets,[F] has sent His angel to show
His slaves what must quickly take
place."[G]
7 "Look, I am coming quickly! The
one who keeps the prophetic words
of this book is blessed."
8 I, John, am the one who heard
and saw these things. When I heard
and saw them, I fell down to worship at the feet of the angel who had
shown them to me. 9 But he said to
me, "Don't do that! I am a fellow
slave with you, your •brothers the
prophets, and those who keep the
words of this book. Worship God."
10 He also said to me, "Don't seal
the prophetic words of this book,
because the time is near. 11 Let the
unrighteous go on in unrighteousness; let the filthy go on being made
filthy; let the righteous go on in
righteousness; and let the holy go
on being made holy."

Conclusion (22:12-21)

12 "Look! I am coming quickly,
and My reward is with Me to repay
each person according to what he
has done. 13 I am the •Alpha and the
Omega, the First and the Last, the
Beginning and the End.
14 "Blessed are those who wash
their robes,[H] so that they may have
the right to the tree of life and may
enter the city by the gates. 15 Outside
are the dogs, the sorcerers, the sexually immoral, the murderers, the
idolaters, and everyone who loves
and practices lying.
16 "I, Jesus, have sent My angel to
attest these things to you[I] for the
churches. I am the Root and the Offspring of David, the Bright Morning
Star."
17 Both the Spirit and the bride say,
"Come!" Anyone who hears should
say, "Come!" And the one who is
thirsty should come. Whoever desires should take the living water as
a gift.
18 I testify to everyone who hears
the prophetic words of this book: If
anyone adds to them, God will add
to him the plagues that are written
in this book. 19 And if anyone takes
away from the words of this prophetic book, God will take away his
share of the tree of life and the holy
city, written in this book.
20 He who testifies about these
things says, "Yes, I am coming
quickly."
•Amen! Come, Lord Jesus!
21 The grace of the Lord Jesus[J] be
with all the •saints.[K] Amen.[L]

[A] **21:24** Other mss read *will bring to Him the nations' glory and honor* [B] **21:26** Other mss add *in order that they might go in* [C] **22:1** Other mss read *pure river* [D] **22:2** Or *was a tree of life*, or *was a tree that gives life* [E] **22:3** Lit *in it* [F] **22:6** Other mss read *God of the holy prophets* [G] **22:6** Or *soon* [H] **22:14** Other mss read *who keep His commands* [I] **22:16** In Gk, you is pl [J] **22:21** Other mss add *Christ* [K] **22:21** Other mss omit *the saints* [L] **22:21** Other mss omit *Amen.*

REVELATION… WRITTEN ON MY *Heart* Revelation assures you that God is in control. History is moving toward the consummation of His purposes. His plan is unfolding according to His schedule. Christ will return and win the final battle against evil and injustice and reign victoriously forever. Satan will not prevail. Sin will be punished. Believers will be rescued and live in the presence of God in a glorious, beautiful place. These certainties give you hope and strength to endure any suffering that comes your way. You must also heed the warning to root out any sin that hinders your relationship with the Lord. Only a commitment to Jesus Christ will spare you from God's coming wrath.

to or **takes away from the words of this prophetic book** will bring upon himself the judgment of God, by both receiving **the plagues** of the book and not receiving eternal life in **the holy city** of God.

22:20-21 "Yes, I am coming quickly" are the last spoken words of Jesus recorded in Scripture. The Lord put an end to any doubts about His imminent return.

Victory (Gk *nikē*) in Jesus

VICTOR	REWARD/INHERITANCE
Jesus • "the Lion from the tribe of Judah, the Root of David," 5:5; • "the Lamb [who is] . . . Lord of lords and King of kings", (17:14)	• the seat with His "Father on His throne" (3:21) • the right to "open the scroll and its seven seals" (5:5) • "a crown" (6:2)
VICTOR	**REWARD/INHERITANCE GIVEN BY CHRIST**
Believers • those who keep Christ's "works to the end," 2:26; • "those with Him [who] are called, chosen, and faithful", (17:14) • "They conquered him [Satan] by the blood of the Lamb and by the word of their testimony, for they did not love their lives in the face of death" (12:11).	• eternal life—"the right to eat from the tree of life . . ." (2:7) • eternal life—never being "harmed by the second death" (2:11) • "some of the hidden manna" (2:17) • "a white stone" with the inscription of "a new name" (2:17) • "authority over the nations" (2:26) • "white clothes" (3:5) • Jesus' promise "never [to] erase his name from the book of life" (3:5) • the honor of being acknowledged by name by Christ before His Father and the angels (3:5) • the honor of being made "a pillar in the sanctuary of . . . God" (3:12) • permanently belonging to God and His city, indicated by Christ's writing three names on the victor: "My God," "the new Jerusalem," and Christ's "new name" (3:12) • "the right to sit with" Christ on His throne (3:21) • adoption as God's son, inheriting "these things" (see 21:1-7)

>WORD|*study*

2:7 Jesus referred to the believer as a victor (Gk *nikōnti*, "one who conquers, prevails, or is victorious over enemies"), a mythological Greek goddess (Gk *Nikē*, "victory") personifying triumph and victory in both military and athletic arenas. Of the 28 times the verb is used in the Greek New Testament, 24 appear in John's writings, including 17 in Revelation. First John describes believers as those who "have had victory over the evil one (1Jn 2:13-14), who have "conquered" because Christ, in whom they have placed their faith, is "greater than "the world" (1Jn 4:4; 5:4-5). In Revelation, the word most often describes Jesus as conqueror (Rv 3:21; 5:5; 6:2; 17:14; 21:7) and saints as victors (12:11; 15:2). Only twice is "the beast" the subject of the verb and then only by divine permission (11:4-7; 13:4). The book is filled with Jesus' personal promises of rewards to those in and through whom Christ displays His complete triumph over evil (2:7,11,17,26,28; 3:5,12,21). Revelation thus depicts the fulfillment of Jesus' promise of victory to His disciples (Jn 16:33). In Revelation, the victorious ones are those who overcome the world and its sufferings even to the point of death. There is no distinction between martyrs and the rest of the church. All endure suffering, and all are victorious.

so or takes away from the words of this prophetic book will bring upon himself the judgment of God, by both receiving the plagues of the book and not receiving eternal life in the holy city of God.

22:20 23 "Yes, I am coming quickly" are the last spoken words of Jesus recorded in Scripture. The Lord put an end to any doubts about His imminent return.

REVELATION ... WRITTEN ON MY HEART: Revelation assures you that God is in control. History is moving toward the consummation of His purposes. His plan is unfolding according to His schedule. Christ will return and win the final battle against evil and injustice and reign victoriously forever. Satan will not prevail. Sin will be punished. Believers will be rescued and live in the presence of God in a glorious, beautiful place. These certainties give you hope and strength to endure any suffering that comes your way. You must also heed the warning to root out any sin that hinders your relationship with the Lord. Only a commitment to Jesus Christ will spare you from God's coming wrath.

Victory (Gk *nikē*) in Jesus

VICTOR	REWARD/INHERITANCE
Jesus • "the Lion from the tribe of Judah, the Root of David" (5:5) • "the Lamb [who is] ... Lord of lords and King of kings" (17:14)	• the seat with His "Father on His throne" (3:21) • the right to "open the scroll and its seven seals" (5:5) • "a crown" (6:2)
VICTOR	**REWARD/INHERITANCE (AS SEEN BY CHRIST)**
Believers • those who keep Christ's "works to the end" (2:26) • "those with Him [who] are called, chosen, and faithful" (17:14) • "They conquered him [Satan] by the blood of the Lamb and by the word of their testimony, for they did not love their lives in the face of death" (12:11)	• eternal life—"the right to eat from the tree of life" (2:7) • eternal life—never being "harmed by the second death" (2:11) • "some of the hidden manna" (2:17) • "a white stone" with the inscription of "a new name" (2:17) • "authority over the nations" (2:26) • "white clothes" (3:5) • Jesus' promise "never [to] erase his name from the book of life" (3:5) • the honor of being acknowledged by name by Christ before His Father and His angels (3:5) • the honor of being made "a pillar in the sanctuary of ... God" (3:12) • permanently belonging to God and His city, indicated by Christ's writing three names on the victor: "My God," "the new Jerusalem," and Christ's "new name" (3:12) • "the right to sit with" Christ on His throne (3:21) • adoption as God's son, inheriting "these things" (see 21:3-7)

WORD study

[illegible]

HCSB Bullet Notes

The HCSB Bullet Notes are one of the unique features of the Holman Christian Standard Bible®. These notes explain frequently used biblical words or terms. These "bullet" words (for example: •abyss) are marked with a bullet only on their first occurrence in a chapter of the biblical text. Other frequently used words, like •gate, are marked with bullets only where the use of the word fits the definitions given below.

Abaddon	A Hebrew word for either the grave or the realm of the dead
Abba	The Aramaic word for father
abyss	The bottomless pit or the depths (of the sea); it is the prison for Satan and the demons.
acrostic	A device in Hebrew poetry in which each verse begins with a successive letter of the Hebrew alphabet
advocate	The Greek word *parakletos* means one called alongside to help, counsel, or protect; it is used of the Holy Spirit in Jn and 1Jn.
Almighty	The Hebrew phrase is *El Shaddai*; *El* means God, but the meaning of *Shaddai* is disputed; traditionally it is translated "Almighty."
Alpha and Omega	The first and last letters of the Greek alphabet; it is used to refer to God the Father in Rv 1:8 and 21:6 and to Jesus, God the Son, in Rv 22:13.
Amen	The transliteration of a Hebrew word signifying that something is certain, valid, truthful, or faithful; it is often used at the end of biblical songs, hymns, and prayers.
annihilate(d)	During periods of war in Canaan and its neighboring countries, this was the destruction of a city, its inhabitants, and their possessions, including livestock.
Arabah	The section of the Great Rift in Palestine, extending from the Jordan Valley and the Dead Sea to the Gulf of Aqabah; the Hebrew word can also be translated as "plain," referring to any plain or to any part of the Arabah.
Asaph	A musician appointed by David to oversee the music used in worship at the Temple; 12 psalms are attributed to Asaph.
Asherah(s)/ Asherah pole(s)	A Canaanite fertility goddess who was the mother of the god Baal; also the wooden poles associated with the worship of her
Ashtoreth(s)	A Canaanite goddess of fertility, love, and war, who was the daughter of Asherah and consort of Baal; the plural form of her name in Hebrew is *Ashtaroth*.
Asia	A Roman province that is now part of modern Turkey; it did not refer to the modern continent of Asia.
asleep	A term used in reference to believers who have died
atone/ atonement	A theological term for God's provision to deal with human sin; in the OT, it primarily means purification. In some contexts forgiveness, pardon, expiation, propitiation, or reconciliation is included. The basis of atonement is substitutionary sacrifice offered in faith. The OT sacrifices were types and shadows of the great and final sacrifice of Jesus on the cross.

Baal	A fertility god who was the main god of the Canaanite religion and the god of rain and thunderstorms; it is also the Hebrew word meaning "lord," "master," "owner," or "husband."
Beelzebul	A term of slander, which was variously interpreted "lord of flies," "lord of dung," or "ruler of demons"
Bread of the Presence	Bread that was offered in Yahweh's presence, that is, in the holy place, not out on the altar (Lv 24:5-9)
brother(s)	The Greek word *adelphoi* can be used as a reference to males only or to groups that include both males and females. It is the context of each usage that determines the proper meaning.
burnt offering(s)	Or *holocaust*; an offering completely burned to ashes; it was used in connection with worship, seeking God's favor, expiating sin, or averting judgment.
cause(s) the downfall of/ cause(s) to sin	The Greek word *skandalizo* has a root meaning of snare or trap but has no real English counterpart.
centurion	A Roman officer who commanded about 100 soldiers
Cephas	The Aramaic word for rock; it is parallel to the Greek word *petros* from which the English name Peter is derived.
cherub(im)	A class of winged angels, associated with the throne of God, who function as guardians and who prevented Adam and Eve from returning to the garden of Eden
chief priest(s)	A group of Jewish temple officers that included the high priest, captain of the temple, temple overseers, and treasurers
clean	When something is clean, it is holy or acceptable to God. When it is unclean, it is unholy (such as an unclean spirit). The term can be used in a ritual sense to apply to moral standards for living.
company	Or *cohort*; a Roman military unit that numbered as many as 600 men
completely destroy	During periods of war in Canaan and its neighboring countries, this was the destruction of a city, its inhabitants, and their possessions, including livestock.
Counselor	The Greek word *parakletos* means one called alongside to help, counsel, or protect; it is used of the Holy Spirit in Jn and 1Jn.
cubit(s)	An OT measurement of distance that equaled about 18 inches
Cush/Cushite	The lands of the Nile in southern Egypt, including Nubia and Northern Sudan; also the people who lived in that region
Decapolis	Originally, it referred to a federation of 10 Gentile towns east of the Jordan River.
denarius/ denarii	A small silver Roman coin, which was equal to a day's wage for a common laborer
divination	An attempt to foresee future events or discover hidden knowledge by means of physical objects such as water, arrows, flying birds, or animal livers
drink offering(s)	An offering of a specified amount of wine or beer given along with animal sacrifices; it was poured over the sacrifice before it was burned.
engaged	Jewish engagement was a binding agreement that could only be broken by divorce.
ephod	A vest-like garment, extending below the waist and worn under the breastpiece; it was used both by the priests and by the high priest.
everyone	Literally *sons of man* or *sons of Adam*
family redeemer	A family member who had certain obligations of marriage, redeeming an estate, and punishment of a wrongdoer (kinsman redeemer)
fear(s) God or the LORD/ fear of the LORD/ fear Yahweh	No single English word conveys every aspect of the word *fear* in this phrase. The meaning includes worshipful submission, reverential awe, and obedient respect to the covenant-keeping God of Israel.

fellowship sacrifice(s) or offering(s) An animal offering was given to maintain and strengthen a person's relationship with God. It was not required as a remedy for impurity or sin but was an expression of thanksgiving for various blessings. An important function of this sacrifice was to provide meat for the priests and the participants in the sacrifice; also called the peace offering or the sacrifice of well-being.

firstfruits The agricultural products harvested first and given to God as an offering with more products to come in later harvests; it is also used as a metaphor for the first people to come to faith, for Jesus, the first person to rise from the dead, or for the Spirit, who is given to believers as the first portion (or down payment) of our salvation with more to come in eternity.

gate(s) The site of community discussions, political meetings, and trying of court cases

Gittith Perhaps an instrument, musical term, tune from Gath, or song for the grape harvest

God Almighty The Hebrew phrase is *El Shaddai*; *El* means God, but the meaning of *Shaddai* is disputed; traditionally it is translated "Almighty."

grain offering(s) An offering given along with animal sacrifices or given by itself; a portion was burnt and the priests and participant ate the remainder.

guilt/guilty The liability to be punished for a fault, a sin, an act, or an omission unless there is forgiveness or atonement; the term normally concerns an objective fact, not a subjective feeling.

Hades The Greek word for the place of the dead; it corresponds to the Hebrew word *Sheol*.

Hallelujah! Or *Praise the LORD!*; it literally means *Praise Yah!* (a shortened form of *Yahweh*).

headquarters The Latin word *Praetorium* was used by Greek writers for the residence of the Roman governor; it may also refer to military headquarters, the imperial court, or the emperor's guard.

Hebrew Or *Aramaic*; the translation of this word is debated since some claim Aramaic was commonly spoken in Palestine during NT times. More recently others claim that Hebrew was the spoken language.

hell/hellfire The Greek word is *gehenna*; it is the Aramaic term for the Valley of Hinnom on the south side of Jerusalem; formerly, it was a place of human sacrifice, and in NT times, a place for the burning of garbage; it is the place of final judgment for those rejecting Christ.

Herod Name of the Idumean family ruling Palestine from 37 B.C. to A.D. 95; the main rulers from this family mentioned in the NT are:

- **Herod I** (37 B.C.–4 B.C.) He was also known as Herod the Great; he built the great temple in Jerusalem and massacred the male babies in Bethlehem.
- **Herod Antipas** (4 B.C.–A.D. 39) The son of Herod the Great; he ruled one-fourth of his father's kingdom (Galilee and Perea); he killed John the Baptist and mocked Jesus.
- **Herod Agrippa I** (A.D. 37–44) The grandson of Herod the Great; he beheaded James the apostle and imprisoned Peter.
- **Herod Agrippa II** (A.D. 52–ca 95) The great-grandson of Herod the Great; he heard Paul's defense.

Herodians They were the political supporters of Herod the Great and his family.

hidden plan Translation of the Greek word *musterion*; it is a secret that was hidden in the past but now revealed.

Higgaion Term used for a musical notation, for a device denoting a pause in an instrumental interlude, or for a murmuring harp tone

high place(s) An ancient place of worship most often associated with pagan religions; it was usually built on an elevated location.

horn — A symbol of power based on the strength of animal horns

Hosanna — A term of praise derived from the Hebrew word for save

Host(s) — Military forces consisting of God's angels, sometimes including the sun, moon, and stars, and occasionally Israel

human race — Literally *sons of man* or *sons of Adam*

I assure you — This is a phrase used only by Jesus to testify to the certainty and importance of His words; in Mt, Mk, and Lk it is literally *Amen, I say to you*; in Jn it is literally *Amen, amen, I say to you*.

Jews — In John, the term Jews usually indicates those in Israel who were opposed to Jesus, particularly the Jewish authorities in Jerusalem who led the nation.

justification/ justify/ justified — The act of God as judge that declares sinners (who were in the wrong) to be right or righteous in His sight. God is just in doing this because Jesus died on the cross to take away their sins and to give them His own righteousness (2Co 5:21). The sinner receives this justification by faith and by grace when he trusts Christ's work.

language(s) — The Greek word *glossa* can refer to the tongue as the organ of speech (see Mk 7:33) or to language the tongue produces. In certain NT passages, scholars differ on whether the term refers to human languages or to ecstatic speech capable only of divine interpretation ("speaking in tongues").

Leviathan — Or *twisting one*; a mythological sea serpent or dragon associated with the chaos at creation; sometimes it is applied to an animal such as a crocodile.

life/lives — The same Greek word *(psyche)* can be translated life or soul.

mankind — Literally *sons of man* or *sons of Adam*

Mary Magdalene — Or *Mary of Magdala*; Magdala was probably a town on the western shore of the Sea of Galilee, north of Tiberias.

Maskil — It is from a Hebrew word meaning *to be prudent* or *to have insight*; it could also mean a contemplative, instructive, or wisdom psalm.

men — Literally *sons of man* or *sons of Adam*

mercy seat — Or *place of atonement*; it was the gold lid on the ark of the covenant that was first used in the tabernacle and later in the temple.

Messiah — Or *the Christ*; the Greek word is *Christos* and means *the anointed one*. Where the NT emphasizes *Christos* as a name of our Lord or has a Gentile context, "Christ" is used. Where the NT *Christos* has a Jewish context, the title "Messiah" is used.

Miktam — A musical term of uncertain meaning; it possibly denotes a plaintive style.

Milcom — An Ammonite god who was the equivalent of Baal, the Canaanite storm god

Molech — A Canaanite god associated with death and the underworld; the worship ritual of passing someone through the fire is connected with him. This ritual could have been either fire-walking or child sacrifice.

Most High — The Hebrew word is *Elyon*; it is often used with other names of God, such as Hebrew *El* (God) or *Yahweh* (Lord); it is used to refer to God as the supreme being.

Mount of Olives — A mountain east of Jerusalem across the Kidron Valley

mystery — Translation of the Greek word *musterion*; it is a secret that was hidden in the past but now revealed.

Nazarene — A person from Nazareth; growing up in Nazareth was an aspect of the Messiah's humble beginnings.

Negev — An arid region in the southern part of Israel; the Hebrew word means south.

offend(ed) — The Greek word *skandalizo* has a root meaning of snare or trap but has no real English counterpart.

offspring	This term is used literally or metaphorically to refer to plants or grain, sowing or harvest, male reproductive seed, human children or physical descendants, and also to spiritual children or to Christ (Gl 3:16).
One and Only	Or *one of a kind*, or *incomparable*, or *only begotten*; the Greek word can refer to someone's only child as in Lk 7:12; 8:42; 9:38. It can also refer to someone's special child as in Heb 11:17.
oracle	A prophetic speech of a threatening or menacing character; it was often against the nations.
overseer(s)	Or *elder(s)*, or *bishop(s)*
palace	The Latin word *Praetorium* was used by Greek writers for the residence of the Roman governor; it may also refer to military headquarters, the imperial court, or the emperor's guard.
Passover	The Israelite festival celebrated on the fourteenth day of the first month, in the early spring; it was a celebration of the deliverance of the Israelites from Egypt, commemorating the final plague on Egypt when the firstborn were killed.
people	Literally *sons of man*, or *sons of Adam*
perverted men	Literally *sons of Belial*; in Hebrew, the basic meaning of Belial is "worthless."
Pharisee(s)	A religious sect of Judaism that followed the whole written and oral law
Pilate	Pontius Pilate was governor of the province of Judea A.D. 26–36.
Pit	A term for either the grave or the realm of the dead
proconsul	The chief Roman government official in a senatorial province, who presided over Roman court hearings
propitiation	The removal of divine wrath; Jesus' death is the means that turns God's wrath from the sinner.
proselyte(s)	A person from another race or religion who went through a prescribed ritual to become a Jew
Rabbi	The Hebrew word means *my great one*; it is used for a recognized teacher of the Scriptures.
Rabshakeh	The title of a high-ranking Assyrian official who was the chief cupbearer to the king
Rahab	Or *boisterous one*; it is the name of a mythological sea serpent or dragon defeated at the time of creation. Scripture sometimes uses the name metaphorically to describe Egypt.
redemption/ redeemed	The deliverance from bondage by a payment or ransom (Mk 10:45; 1Pt 1:18-19)
Red Sea	Literally *Sea of Reeds*
regiment	Or *cohort*; a Roman military unit that numbered as many as 600 men
restitution offering(s)	An offering that was a penalty for unintentional sins, primarily committed in relation to the tabernacle or temple; it is traditionally translated *trespass* or *guilt offering*.
sackcloth	A garment made of poor quality material and worn as a sign of grief and mourning
sacred bread	Literally *bread of presentation*; these were 12 loaves of bread, representing the 12 tribes of Israel and put on the table in the holy place in the tabernacle and later in the temple. The priests ate the previous week's loaves.
Sadducee(s)	A religious sect of Judaism that mainly followed the first 5 books of the OT (the Torah or Pentateuch)
saint(s)/ sanctification/ sanctify/ sanctified	The work of the Holy Spirit that separates believers in Jesus from the world; at the time of saving faith in Jesus, the believer is made a saint; therefore, all believers are saints. The believer participates with the Spirit in a process of transformation that continues until glorification. The goal of sanctification is progressive conformity to the image of Jesus Christ.

Samaritan(s)	A people of mixed, Gentile/Jewish ancestry who lived between Galilee and Judea and were hated by the Jews
Sanhedrin	The supreme council of Judaism; it had 70 members and was patterned after Moses' 70 elders.
scribe(s)	A professional group in Judaism that copied the law of Moses and interpreted it, especially in legal cases
secret	Translation of the Greek word *musterion*; it is a secret that was hidden in the past but now revealed.
seed	This term is used literally or metaphorically to refer to plants or grain, sowing or harvest, male reproductive seed, human children or physical descendants, and also to spiritual children or to Christ (Gl 3:16).
Selah	A Hebrew word whose meaning is uncertain; various interpretations include: (1) a musical notation, (2) a pause for silence, (3) a signal for worshipers to fall prostrate on the ground, (4) a term for the worshipers to call out, and (5) a word meaning forever.
set apart for destruction	During periods of war in Canaan and its neighboring countries, this was the destruction of a city, its inhabitants, and their possessions, including livestock.
shekel(s)	In the OT the *shekel* is a measurement of weight that came to be used as money, either gold or silver.
Sheminith	A musical term meaning *instruments* or *on the instrument of eight strings*
Sheol	A Hebrew word for either the grave or the realm of the dead
Shinar	A land in Mesopotamia, including ancient Sumer and Babylon; it is modern Iraq.
sin offering(s)	Or *purification offering*; it was the most important OT sacrifice for cleansing from impurities. It provided purification from sin and certain forms of ceremonial uncleanness.
slave(s)	The strong Greek word *doulos* cannot be accurately translated in English as servant or bond servant; the HCSB translates this word as slave, not out of insensitivity to the legitimate concerns of modern English speakers, but out of a commitment to accurately convey the brutal reality of the Roman empire's inhumane institution as well as the ownership called for by Christ.
Son of Man	The title that Jesus most frequently used for Himself (Dn 7:13; Mt 8:20)
song of ascents	A term that probably refers to the songs pilgrims sang as they traveled the roads going up to worship in Jerusalem (Pss 120–134)
soul	The same Greek word *(psyche)* can be translated life or soul.
stumble	The Greek word *skandalizo* has a root meaning of snare or trap but has no real English counterpart.
synagogue	A place where the Jewish people met for prayer, worship, and teaching of the Scriptures
tabernacle	Or *tent*, or *shelter*; a term used for temporary housing
take offense	The Greek word *skandalizo* has a root meaning of snare or trap but has no real English counterpart.
tassel	Fringe put on the clothing of devout Jews to remind them to keep the law
temple complex	In the Jerusalem temple, the complex included the sanctuary (the holy place and the holy of holies), at least 4 courtyards (for priests, Jews, women, and Gentiles), numerous gates, and several covered walkways.
testimony	A reference either to the Mosaic law in general or to a specific section of the law, the Ten Commandments, which were written on stone tablets and placed in the ark of the covenant (also called the ark of the testimony)
Topheth	A place of human sacrifice that was located outside Jerusalem in the Hinnom Valley (Jr 7:31-32)

unclean	When something is clean, it is holy or acceptable to God. When it is unclean, it is unholy (such as an unclean spirit). The term can be used in a ritual sense to apply to moral standards for living.
Unleavened Bread	A seven-day festival celebrated in conjunction with the Passover (Ex 12:1-20)
Urim & Thummim	Two objects used by Israelite priests to determine God's will
wadi	A valley, ravine, or stream that is dry except in the rainy season
walk(ed)/ walking	A term often used in a figurative way to mean "way of life" or "behavior"
wicked men	Literally *sons of Belial*; in Hebrew, the basic meaning of Belial is "worthless."
wise men	The Greek word is *magoi*; the English word "magi" is based on a Persian word. They were eastern sages who observed the heavens for signs and omens.
woman	When used in direct address, "Woman" was not a term of disrespect but of honor.
world	The organized Satanic system that is opposed to God and hostile to Jesus and His followers; it also refers to the non-Christian culture including governments, educational systems, and businesses.
wormwood	A small shrub that was used as a medicinal herb and noted for its bitter taste
Yah/Yahweh	A translation of the Hebrew letters YHWH, traditionally translated *the* Lord; "Yah" is the shortened form. The translation "Yahweh" is used in the HCSB in places where the personal name of God is discussed (Ps 68:4) or in places of His self-identification (Is 42:8).
Zion	Originally a term for the fortified section of Jerusalem and then, by extension, used for the temple and the city of Jerusalem both in the present time and in the future

the Study Bible *for* WOMEN

The features of *The Study Bible for Women* are designed to enhance both pers

Features

Introduction

Each of the Bible's 66 books opens with an Introduction that sets the context for reading and studying the book.

Included at the beginning is a carefully selected **key verse** that captures one of the book's themes, a **timeline** situating people and main events in history, and **a content outline** that has also been merged with the biblical text itself to help make sense of the whole.

The introduction answers basic fact questions about the book, explains **what the book is about**, offers **good reasons for women to read it**, and provides **guidance for studying** it effectively.

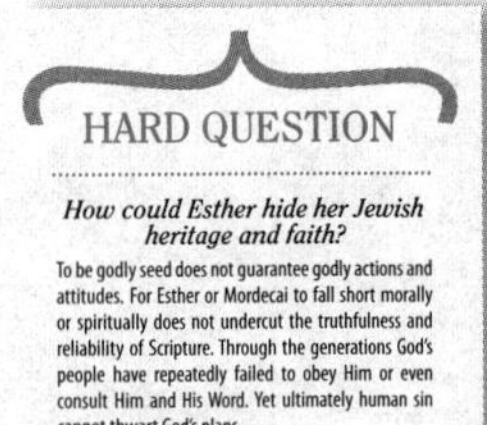

HARD QUESTION

How could Esther hide her Jewish heritage and faith?

To be godly seed does not guarantee godly actions and attitudes. For Esther or Mordecai to fall short morally or spiritually does not undercut the truthfulness and reliability of Scripture. Through the generations God's people have repeatedly failed to obey Him or even consult Him and His Word. Yet ultimately human sin cannot thwart God's plans.

Esther

Timeline World Events Biblical Events	*538 BC* Cyrus II (reigned 559–530) issued the decree permitting the Jews' return from exile.	*515 BC* The second temple was dedicated during the reign of Darius I (521–486).	*492–449 BC* Persian Wars were fought as the Greeks revolted against Persian rule.	*486–465 BC* Xerxes I (possibly Ahasuerus) ruled Persia.

"Who knows, perhaps you have come to your royal position for such a time as this." (4:14b)

Who wrote Esther?
Likely a Persian Jew well acquainted with court life as well as with the history and culture of the period

Who were the recipients?
The Jewish community living during the Diaspora since the events recorded center around the lives of Jews dwelling in exile in Persia. However, God uses the experiences of a few to speak to all future generations who face similar dangers and difficulties.

When was Esther written?
465–331 B.C.

Where did it happen?
Susa (Hb *Shushan*, lit "lily," 1:2) was the royal city and one of the capitals of the ancient Persian Empire. Its ruins are in Iran near the Iraqi border.

What is Esther about?
- the unending providence of God in His loving care for His people
- the sovereignty of God in effecting His purposes
- the free will of man to act on his own choices

Why should women read Esther?
The book of Esther bears the name of a heroine who was beautiful, brave, and brilliant. God used Esther as the primary agent to save His people, the Jews, from destruction. As a Jewess in a cruel despot's court, she risked her life while working a daring plan to deliver her people from certain death. Women are inspired by such an ordinary woman who is used of God in an extraordinary way. Women are also instructed and mentored in virtues and character traits of a woman who is not only used by God to accomplish His purposes but is also a heroine admired by her peers and future generations.

How do you read Esther?
The events recorded in Esther likely occurred during the reign of the Persian king Ahasuerus, the son of Darius I, who ruled from 486–465/64 B.C., a time within the Achaemenid period of biblical history (559–330 B.C.). The geographical setting is the royal city of Susa (Hb *Shushan*, 1:2) within a vast Persian empire described as stretching "from India [Hb *Hodu*] to Cush" (Hb), the latter being another name for Ethiopia, which is located in the region around the Nile River including Nubia and northern Sudan. Thousands of the exiles had remained in Persia despite the opportunity to return to their homeland. They retained a distinctive Jewishness instead of being completely assimilated into the Persian Empire.

The narrative in Esther is historical, as suggested from the opening words: "These events took place . . . ." The introduction of the Festival of Purim adds to the historical credibility of the book as does the fact that the book was readily admitted to the Jewish canon. Some of its statements are further confirmed by extrabiblical historical sources. The plot is woven skillfully with words carefully chosen; characters and their roles are well-developed; and a direct path leads to the denouement and memorable styling of its climactic summary. Irony, drama, suspense, intrigue, humor, and numerous literary devices are also employed in this example of redemptive history, which offers encouragement and hope for Jews and Christians from the time of these historical events until now.

The book of Esther has stirred up controversy over the years. The Jews embrace the book and accord it great honor—seeing its story as a celebration of their miraculous victory over enemies who were seeking their destruction. Others reject the book because of the absence of God's name or any specific reference to Him and His work. The book was not quoted in the New Testament and was rarely mentioned by the Church Fathers. Some find the book lacking in its moral tone and in the character of those who are identified as being God's chosen people. Yet the book is a powerful testimony to the fact that God's people do not always act in godly ways, and consequently they experience His displeasure, which may be exhibited by a veil of silence or even a temporary absence of divine activity. Nevertheless, the behavior of God's people has never changed the fact that God chose them and they are His. The free will of man on one hand and the sovereignty of God on the other effect His extraordinary purposes. Still, without explicitly mentioning God, the temple, the Torah or laws, or even prayer, the book powerfully exemplifies the providence of God, who will forever remain faithful to rescue and deliver His people.

Susa (Shushan)
Babylon
ELAM
PERSIA
BABYLONIA
Ur
Persian Gulf

Esther's World
King Ahasuerus and Queen Esther ruled the Persian Empire from Susa, the winter capital of the Empire. The territory is now in Iran. Cyrus made Susa a capital city along with Babylon, Ecbatana, and Persepolis. When Alexander the Great captured Susa, he found a large treasure that he confiscated. Archaeologists have excavated Susa largely around four areas: the royal palace, the acropolis, the royal city, and an artisan tell.

Biblical Womanhood How is fasting a spiritual discipline?

Fasting (Hb *tsum*, "abstain from food" or more lit "cover over" as preventing food from entering the mouth) was a means for depriving the body of nourishment. A fast most often lasted from sunrise to sunset (2Sm 1:12) and could mean partial or total abstinence or selective abstinence from certain food for a longer period (Ps 35:13; Dn 10:3). For some, fasting is considered a means of attaining spiritual rewards. The ascetics often starved themselves in an effort to demonstrate, through personal pain and deprivation, their devotion to God. Others make fasting a mockery by pursuing a façade of food deprivation as a ritual to be observed by onlookers, while there is no sign of personal devotion to and focus on the Lord.

Fasting in biblical times was done . . .

- to gain God's attention in behalf of someone's suffering (see 2Sm 12:16-23);
- to accompany intercession for another or for the entire nation in a time of its disobedience to God (Ezr 8:23; Neh 1:4; Dn 9:3);
- to respond in times of extreme crisis (2Ch 20:1-29) or as a national celebration, especially the Day of Atonement (Lv 16:29,31; 23:26-32; Est 9:31).

Jesus fasted for 40 days to prepare for His ministry and for the confrontation with Satan (Mt 4:1-2). He considered fasting a discipline link expected His disciples fasted to prepare for majc

Fasting in itself, just pleasure, did not move Y yourself to prayer and ı pure and uninhibited fo

>WORD|*study*

2:15 Esther (probably Persian in origin, "star"), the name used throughout the book and as it from the same root as the principal goddess of the ancient Near East, Ishtar, associated with eroticisr assumed the role of "legal guardian" or foster parent to his orphaned relative and continually demon even after she entered the king's harem (Est 2:10-11).

group Bible study. What follows is a quick overview.

483 BC	480 BC	478 BC	474 BC	473 BC
Vashti was deposed.	The Persians defeated the Greeks at the Battle of Thermopylae then lost their navy at the Battle of Salamis.	Esther became queen.	Haman solicited a royal decree for genocide of the Jewish population in the Persian Empire. Esther interceded for her people.	The Festival of Purim was celebrated.

Outline

- I. The Setting for God's Deliverance (1:1–2:23)
  - A. The Transition from Vashti to Esther (1:1–2:20)
  - B. Mordecai's Action to Save the King's Life (2:21-23)
- II. The Plot Against the Jews (3:1–4:17)
  - A. Haman's Pride and Treachery (3:1-6)
  - B. Haman's Decree for the Destruction of the Jews (3:7-15)
  - C. Mordecai's Search for an Intercessor to the King (4:1-11)
  - D. Esther's Acceptance of the Challenge (4:12-17)
- III. The Plan for Deliverance (5:1–7:10)
  - A. Esther's Approach to the King (5:1-14)
  - B. The Honoring of Mordecai by the Adversary Haman (6:1-13)
  - C. Esther's Unveiling of Haman's Wicked Plan (6:14–7:10)
- IV. The Reward of Divine Deliverance (8:1–9:32)
  - A. The Jews' Freedom to Defend Themselves (8:1-14)
  - B. The Honoring of Mordecai and Esther (8:15–9:19)
  - C. The Institution of the Festival of Purim (9:20-32)
- V. An Epilogue on Mordecai (10:1-3)

The Setting for God's Deliverance (1:1–2:23)

The Transition from Vashti to Esther (1:1–2:20)

The feast of Ahasuerus (1:1-9)

1 These events took place during the
days of Ahasuerus,[A] who ruled 127
provinces from India[B] to *Cush. 2 In
those days King Ahasuerus reigned
from his royal throne in the fortress
at Susa. 3 He held a feast in the third
year of his reign for all his officials
and staff, the army of Persia and Media, the nobles, and the officials from
the provinces. 4 He displayed the glorious wealth of his kingdom and the
magnificent splendor of his greatness
for a total of 180 days.
5 At the end of this time, the king
held a week-long banquet in the
garden courtyard of the royal palace
for all the people, from the greatest
to the least, who were present in the
fortress of Susa. 6 White and violet
linen hangings were fastened with
fine white and purple linen cords
to silver rods on marble[C] columns.
Gold and silver couches were arranged on a mosaic pavement of red
feldspar,[D] marble,[C] mother-of-pearl,
and precious stones.
7 Beverages were served in an array
of gold goblets, each with a different
design. Royal wine flowed freely, according to the king's bounty 8 and
no restraint was placed on the drinking. The king had ordered every wine
steward in his household to serve as
much as each person wanted. 9 Queen
Vashti also gave a feast for the women
of King Ahasuerus's palace.

The disobedience of Vashti and her removal from the royal court (1:10-22)

10 On the seventh day, when the
king was feeling good from the wine,
Ahasuerus commanded Mehuman,
Biztha, Harbona, Bigtha, Abagtha,
Zethar, and Carkas, the seven eunuchs who personally served him,
11 to bring Queen Vashti before him
with her royal crown. He wanted to
show off her beauty to the people
and the officials, because she was
very beautiful. 12 But Queen Vashti
refused to come at the king's command that was delivered by his eunuchs. The king became furious and
his anger burned within him.
13 The king consulted the wise men
who understood the times,[E] for it
was his normal procedure to confer
with experts in law and justice. 14 The

[A]1:1 = Xerxes; he reigned 486–465 B.C. [B]1:1 = modern Pakistan [C]1:6 Or *alabaster* [D]1:6 Or *of porphyry* [E]1:13 Or *understood propitious times*

Title: In the *Mishna*, an important Jewish collection of oral tradition, this book is called "the Roll [Hb *Megillah*, "scroll"] of Esther," since its words were written on a scroll.

1:1 Ahasuerus (Hb of Persian *Khshayarsha*, identified more commonly by the Greek name Xerxes I), reigned as king over Persia 486–465 B.C. (cp. Ezr 4:6). **Cush**, or Ethiopia, in Southern Egypt, includes Nubia, closely identified with the Nile River.

1:3-5 The author states the chronological setting for these events, **in the third year of his** [Ahasuerus's] **reign**. The Greek historian Herodotus described a war council to plan Xerxes' invasion of Greece (480–479 B.C.) during the third year of his reign. Some commentators believe this **feast** (Hb *mishteh*, "banquet," more lit, "a drinking"; cp. 1:9; 2:18; 8:17; 9:17-19,22), lasting six months, occurred in connection with this event.

1:10-12 Only **eunuchs** (castrated males) were permitted contact with the harem because of proving the legitimacy of any offspring coming from the king's wife or concubine. The detail in naming these men points to the historicity of the account.

The king's request for **Queen Vashti** to come **with her royal crown** would most naturally mean that he wanted her to appear at her best and fitting her station as queen. For **the king** to become **furious** (Hb *qatsaph*, "be full of wrath, indignant; break out into anger") is not surprising, not only

Study Notes

The study notes in the outer margins offer insights on difficult-to-understand passages and spotlight important truths.

Threads

In addition, "threads" of specialized study are woven throughout—explanations of foundational **doctrines, profiles of biblical women**, relevant discussions of **biblical womanhood**, helpful **word studies**, and **answers to hard questions** prompted by the text of Scripture.

Doctrine DIVINE APPOINTMENT

Divine appointment is never about you, but in the biblical schema you are appointed for service to God. In Esther's situation, her placement on the throne of Persia was not to make her a queen but rather to give her the opportunity to intercede for God's people.

Applications

At the end of each book is **a devotional word of application, celebration, encouragement**, or other means of allowing the Holy Spirit to write the particular truths of that book on your own heart.

ESTHER… WRITTEN ON MY Heart

Someone has noted that a veil does not necessarily cover to keep out but rather may invite the viewer to look through and see what is behind. The book of Esther, if likened to a veil, invites its readers to peer through and see the faithful providence that God has assigned to the care of His people throughout the generations.

CHARACTER PROFILE

Vashti A Deposed Queen

Her Background	• The wife of King Ahasuerus, ruler of Persia (1:9-12)
	• During a period of celebration, Vashti hosted a royal banquet for the women in the palace (1:9). • Her husband simultaneously hosted a banquet for the men, providing as much wine and food as desired (1:3-8). • On the seventh day of the feast, Ahasuerus summoned Vashti in order to show off her beauty (1:10-11). • Vashti refused to appear, was eventually deposed, and then was replaced by Esther (1:12–2:17). • The text does not indicate why Vashti refused to obey the king's command.
Life Lessons	• This dramatic story illustrates the miraculous juxtaposition between man's will and God's sovereignty. • Beauty of appearance is not the key to a happy life.

The Study Bible for Women

Index of Features

BIBLICAL WOMANHOOD

CHARACTER PROFILES

CHARTS

DOCTRINE

HARD QUESTIONS

MAPS AND RECONSTRUCTIONS

The Study Bible for Women

Acknowledgments

A project of this magnitude has involved work for many years and by many people! Sincere gratitude is expressed to many who have labored diligently "behind the scenes." Tamra Hernandez has gone far beyond her assignments as a contributor and member of the editorial committee. She has done a careful edit of content, assisted in design of charts and other graphics, and made computer entries to final drafts. Candi Finch served as her backup, especially in the early months of the project.

Special thanks is extended to others at Southwestern Baptist Theological Seminary who have supported this project including Erika Mercer, Justin Williams, Melissa Meredith, Mina Hamrokhan, Kelly King, Terri Stovall (Dean of Women's Programs), and other staff (especially presidential interns and the graphics and communications department). Appreciation is also conveyed to support staff of New Orleans Baptist Theological Seminary including Angela Reed, Taran Holland, and Natalee Morris.

It has been a joy to work with Steve Bond, editor of Bibles and Bible Reference Books, B&H Publishing Group. He has provided careful input in the entire editorial process as well as personal affirmation. We are also thankful for the continued support of the entire B&H Publishing team including Jeremy Howard, Tim Jordan, and Robin Patterson.

Our families have provided overwhelming encouragement in our commitment to develop excellent Bible study resources for women. Dorothy and Rhonda are especially grateful for their mothers, Doris Kelley and Joyce Harrington, who have prayed for them, listened to their frustrations, and loved them along the way. Dorothy is grateful for her children Armour and Rachel Patterson; Mark and Carmen Howell (and the granddaughters Abigail and Rebekah); and most of all for her husband Paige Patterson, who all through the process was willing to offer guidance and wisdom in interpreting difficult texts and who gave the loving support that made such a project possible, including the participation of Southwestern Seminary. Rhonda is grateful to her husband Chuck Kelley, who encourages her in the pursuit of her ministry calling and lovingly supports her personally. He has provided hours of theological guidance while maintaining the many responsibilities as president of the New Orleans Baptist Theological Seminary.

Citations

The Study Bible for Women has used much material from both the Old and New Testament volumes of the *Women's Evangelical Commentary*. The names of those contributors are found on the title page. We encourage every woman who wants to pursue serious study to add to this Study Bible these volumes, which deal much more extensively with the text of Scripture, and complete this trilogy of resources.

Because Patterson and Kelley were the editors for *The Woman's Study Bible* (eds. Dorothy Kelley Patterson and Rhonda Harrington Kelley, Nashville: Thomas Nelson, 1995), they have adapted some of their personal material and resources for use in this new volume.

The charts in Daniel (pp. 1130-31) were developed by Paige Patterson for teaching purposes and adapted for use here with his permission.

Section editors acknowledge the following sources:

PSALMS

Leland Ryken, James C. Wilhoit, and Tremper Longman III, eds. *Dictionary of Biblical Imagery* (Downers Grove, IL: InterVarsity Press, 1998), 685.

David C. Mitchell, "'God Will Redeem My Soul from Sheol': The Psalms of the Sons of Korah," *Journal for the Study of the Old Testament* 30 (2006): 365-84.

Note discussion on the connection between Psalm 143 and Romans 3 by Richard B. Hays, "Psalm 143 and the Logic of Romans 3," *Journal of Biblical Literature* 99 (1980): 107–15.

ECCLESIASTES

This chart on p. 829 has been compiled from references used in Robert Johnston, "Confessions of a Workaholic," *The Catholic Biblical Quarterly* 38 (1976): 14–28.

Charles C. Forman, "Koheleth's Use of Genesis," *Journal of Semitic Studies* 5 (1960): 256–263; as well as Tamra Hernandez's own research.

The quote in the note at 3:5, Robert Gordis in *Koheleth—The Man and His World: A Study of Ecclesiastes,* 3rd ed. (New York: Schocken Books, 1968), 230.

ISAIAH

James Bennett Pritchard, ed., *Ancient Near Eastern Texts* [ANET] (Princeton: Princeton University Press, 1969), 288.

JEREMIAH

J. A. Thompson, *Jeremiah,* The New International Commentary on the Old Testament (Grand Rapids: Eerdmans, 1980), 88-92.

LAMENTATIONS

Christine Mitchell Havelock, "Mourners on Greek Vases: Remarks on the Social History of Women," in *Feminism and Art History*, ed. Norma Broude and Mary D. Garrard (Philadelphia: Westminster, 1982), 44-61.

Kathleen M. O'Connor, "Lamentations," in *Women's Bible Commentary, Expanded Edition with Apocrypha*, ed. Carol A. Newsom and Sharon H. Ringe (Louisville, KY: Westminster John Knox Press), 189.

EZEKIEL

Daniel Block, *Ezekiel*, New International Commentary on the Old Testament (Grand Rapids: Eerdmans, 2000), 92, 176.

Daniel Block, "Ezekiel," *Holman Illustrated Bible Dictionary*, ed. Chad Brand, Charles Draper, and Archie England (Nashville: B&H Publishing Group, 2003), 536-37.

DANIEL

Nabonidus Chronicle," trans. A. Leo Oppenheim, in *Ancient Near Eastern Texts Relating to the Old Testament*, ed. James B. Pritchard (Princeton, NJ: Princeton University Press, 1950); cp. Albert Kirk Grayson, *Assyrian and Babylonian Chronicles* (Winona Lake, IN: Eisenbrauns, 2000).

Stephen R. Miller, *Daniel*, The New American Commentary, vol. 18 (Nashville: B &H Publishing Group, 1994), 252-57.

MATTHEW

The outline was adapted from Craig Blomberg, *Matthew*, The New American Commentary (Nashville: B&H Publishing Group, 1992), 49.

MARK

William Lane, *The Gospel According to Mark* (Grand Rapids: Eerdmans, 1974), 215.

JAMES

The outline was adapted from Douglas Moo, *James*, The Tyndale New Testament Commentaries, vol. 16 (Grand Rapids: Eerdmans, 1985), 56.

REVELATION

"Eschatology Terms," p. 1621, is adapted from *The Woman's Study Bible*, ed. by Dorothy Kelley Patterson and Rhonda Harrington Kelley (Nashville: Thomas Nelson, 1995), 1997.

RECONSTRUCTIONS

Latta, Bill, Latta Art Services, Mt. Juliet, TN: pp. 414, 1291.

Contributors

Dorothy Kelley Patterson, a homemaker, helps her husband Paige Patterson, president of Southwestern Baptist Theological Seminary, by serving as Professor of Theology in Women's Studies. With graduate and post-graduate degrees in theology, Dr. Patterson teaches, speaks, and writes for women. She is a member of the Evangelical Theological Society, serves on the Advisory Board for the Council for Biblical Manhood and Womanhood, and attends Birchman Baptist Church. The Pattersons reside in Fort Worth, Texas, but travel extensively throughout the world. Their children Armour and Rachel Patterson live in Arizona; Carmen and Mark Howell, with their daughters Abigail and Rebekah, live in Florida. (General Editor)

Rhonda Harrington Kelley is the president's wife and adjunct professor of women's ministry at New Orleans Baptist Theological Seminary. She is also a Christian author and speaker. Formerly the director of speech pathology at Ochsner Medical Center, Dr. Kelley completed advanced degrees at Baylor University and University of New Orleans. She serves as women's ministry director at First Baptist Church and lives in New Orleans, Louisiana, with her husband Chuck, president of New Orleans Baptist Theological Seminary. (Managing Editor)

Candi Finch has a Master of Divinity with a concentration in Women's Studies and is completing her Doctor of Philosophy degree in systematic theology from Southwestern Baptist Theological Seminary. She lives in Fort Worth, Texas, where she serves as an Assistant Professor of Theology in Women's Studies at Southwestern. She has a heart to see young women come to know the Lord and become mature disciples of Christ. (*Section Editor: Genesis–Deuteronomy and Acts–Philemon*)

Sharon Gritz lives in Fort Worth, Texas. She has advanced degrees from and has served as Adjunct Professor of New Testament at Southwestern Baptist Theological Seminary, where her husband, Paul, currently teaches. Dr. Gritz is a freelance writer and has written adult Bible study curriculum for LifeWay Christian Resources. She teaches Bible classes for younger children in an inner-city mission and English as a second language to adults. She also co-leads the women's prayer ministry at her church. She enjoys discussing biblical issues with her daughter, Lydia, and son-in-law, Taylor Whitley, who are students at Beeson Divinity School. (*Section Editor: Hebrews–Revelation*)

Susie Hawkins received her Master of Arts in Christian Leadership as well as a Master of Arts in Theology from Criswell College and serves as an adjunct faculty member in women's programs at Southwestern Baptist Theological Seminary. She is married to O. S. Hawkins, president of GuideStone Financial Resources of the Southern Baptist Convention, has two married daughters, and six grandchildren. She has been actively involved in teaching, speaking, and writing for women's ministry and ministry wives. (*Section Editor: Character Profiles*)

Tamra Hernandez has a Master of Divinity with Biblical Languages and is completing her dissertation for a Doctor of Philosophy degree in systematic theology at Southwestern Baptist Theological Seminary. She has one son—a cancer survivor, college student, and newlywed. They are members of Wedgwood Baptist Church in Fort Worth, Texas. (*Section Editor: Job–Song of Songs and Matthew–John)*

Lauren Johnson has a Master of Divinity from Southwestern Baptist Theological Seminary in Women's Studies. A homeschooling mom of three, Lauren and her pastor husband Chris, live in Van Buren, Arkansas, with their three children. Lauren's passion is to see women come to Christ and follow Him wholeheartedly. (*Section Editor: Hosea–Malachi)*

Stefana Dan Laing, assistant librarian for the Houston Campus of Southwestern Seminary and adjunct professor at Houston Graduate School of Theology, graduated from Southern Baptist Theological Seminary with a Master of Divinity (1997) and Doctor of Philosophy degree in Patristics/Historical Theology (2004). She and her husband, Dr. John Laing, have three children. Stefana and John teach an adult Sunday school class and are involved in discipleship training at Nassau Bay Baptist Church. They are also a military family—John has had two recent deployments as a chaplain in the Texas Army National Guard. *(Section Editor: Isaiah–Daniel)*

Katie McCoy received her Master of Divinity with a concentration in Women's Studies from Southwestern Baptist Theological Seminary in 2011 and is pursuing her Doctor of Philosophy degree in Systematic Theology from Southwestern. She is the editor of biblicalwoman.com, a women's issues website from the Women's Programs at Southwestern. Katie has a passion for connecting God's Word to contemporary culture. (*Section Editor: Joshua–Esther)*

The Editorial Committee of *The Study Bible for Women* has adapted and even added some fresh study helps from the *Women's Evangelical Commentaries: Old Testament and New Testament.*

Women's Evangelical Commentary: Old Testament Contributors

Betsy Durand
Nancy Eavenson
Candi Finch
Christa Friel
Susie Hawkins
Trish Hawley
Tamra Hernandez
Jennie Huffines
Lauren Johnson
Rhonda Harrington Kelley
Stefana Dan Laing
Kathy McReynolds
Janice Meier
Dorothy Kelley Patterson
Elizabeth Robar
Ashley Cherry Smith
Rhonda Stewart
Hayley Ann Wilton

Women's Evangelical Commentary: New Testament Contributors

Ann Bowman
Betsy Durand
Candi Finch
Christa Friel
Sharon Gritz
Trish Hawley
Tamra Hernandez
Donna Hicks
Jennie Huffines
Mary Kassian
Rhonda Harrington Kelley
Kathy McReynolds
Dorothy Kelley Patterson
Ashley Cherry Smith
Donna Thoennes
Joy White

A

Concordance

to the

Holman Christian Standard Bible

AARON
Levite, brother of Moses (Ex 4:14; 6:16-20). Spokesman for Moses (4:14-16; 7:1-2). Consecrated (Ex 29) and ordained (Lv 8) as priest (Ex 28:1; 1Ch 6:49; Heb 5:1-4; 7). Made golden calf (Ex 32). Died outside the promised land (Nm 20:1-12,22-29; 33:38-39).

ABADDON
Your faithfulness in **A**? Ps 88:11
Sheol and **A** lie open before the LORD Pr 15:11
his name in Hebrew is **A**, Rv 9:11

ABANDON
I will **a** them and hide My face Dt 31:17
certainly not **a** the LORD Jos 24:16
the LORD has **a-ed** us Jdg 6:13
LORD will not **a** His people, 1Sm 12:22
but if you **a** Him, He will **a** you. 2Ch 15:2
For You will not **a** me to Sheol; Ps 16:10
or **a** His heritage, Ps 94:14
Don't **a** wisdom, Pr 4:6
a-ed the love you had at first. Rv 2:4

ABBA
He said, "**A**, Father! Mk 14:36
we cry out, "**A**, Father!" Rm 8:15
crying, "**A**, Father!" Gl 4:6

ABEL
Shepherd, second son of Adam; brought acceptable sacrifice; was murdered (Gn 4:2-8; Mt 23:35; Heb 11:4).

ABIGAIL
Intelligent wife of the fool Nabal; pled for his life; married David after Nabal died (1Sm 25).

ABIJAH
1. Tragic son of King Jeroboam of Israel (1Kg 14:1,13).
2. Son of Rehoboam, King of Judah (2Ch 13). Also known as Abijam (1Kg 15:1-8).

ABILITY
each according to his own **a**. Mt 25:15
according to their **a** 2Co 8:3

ABIMELECH
1. King of Gerar at the time of Abraham (Gn 20:1-18; 21:22-32).
2. King of Gerar at the time of Isaac (Gn 26:1-31).
3. Son of Gideon, tried to become king of Shechem (Jdg 9).

ABLE
count the stars, if you are **a** Gn 15:5
Moses chose **a** men Ex 18:25
God is **a** to raise up children Mt 3:9
Are you **a** to drink the cup Mt 20:22
the Lord is **a** to make him stand. Rm 14:4
tempted beyond what you are **a**, 1Co 10:13
Now to Him who is **a** to do Eph 3:20
to Him who is **a** to protect you Jd 24
a to open the scroll Rv 5:3

ABNER
Saul's cousin and commander of his army (1Sm 14:50). At first supported Saul's son Ish-bosheth (2Sm 2:8-9) but defected to David (3:6-21). Killed by Joab and mourned by David (3:22-39).

ABOMINATION
Milcom, the **a** of the Ammonites. 2Kg 23:13
and set up the **a** of desolation. Dn 11:31
see the **a** that causes desolation, Mt 24:15

ABOVE
the LORD is God in heaven **a** Dt 4:39
the name that is **a** every name, Php 2:9
Set your minds on what is **a**, Col 3:2

ABRAHAM
Born Abram son of Terah in Ur, Mesopotamia; married Sarai, then lived in Haran (Gn 11:31; Ac 7:2-4). Called to Canaan and given a promise of progeny and prosperity (Gn 12:1-3). Lied to Pharaoh in Egypt about Sarai (12:10-20). Separated from his nephew Lot (Gn 13). Rescued Lot (14:1-16) and was blessed by Melchizedek (14:17-20; Heb 7:1-10). God declared him righteous because of his faith (Gn 15:6; Rm 4:3,20-22; Gl 3:6; Jms 2:23).
Fathered Ishmael by Hagar (Gn 16). Name changed (17:5); circumcised (17:9-27; Rm 4:9-12). Visited by angels (Gn 18); promised a son with Sarah (18:9-14; cp. 17:15-19). Lied to Abimelech in Gerar about Sarah (Gn 20). Fathered Isaac (21:1-7). Sent Hagar away at Sarah's request (21:8-14). Tested by God concerning Isaac (Gn 22; Heb 11:17-19; Jms 2:21-24). Buried Sarah at Machpelah (Gn 23). Sent servant to find wife for Isaac (24:1-9). Died and was buried with Sarah (25:7-11).
God promised a covenant with Abraham, then made it and confirmed it (Gn 12:1-3; 13:14-17; 15; 17; 22:15-18). It was the basis of future blessings for many people (Ex 2:24; Lv 26:42; 2Kg 13:23; Ps 105:6-11; Ac 3:25).

ABSALOM
Son of David by Maacah (2Sm 3:3). Known for his looks and hair (14:25-26). Killed Amnon for raping Tamar and was banished by David (2Sm 13). Reinstated by David at Joab's insistence (2Sm 14). Rebelled, ousted David (2Sm 15–17). Killed by Joab (18:9-15) despite David's warning (18:5). Greatly mourned by David (18:33–19:4).

ABSENT
a in body but present in spirit, 1Co 5:3
I may be **a** in body, but Col 2:5

ABSTAIN
he is to **a** from wine and beer. Nm 6:3
a from food offered to idols, Ac 15:29
a from fleshly desires 1Pt 2:11

ABUNDANCE
Seven years of great **a** Gn 41:29
bearing spices, gold in great **a**, 1Kg 10:2
have life and have it in **a**. Jn 10:10

ABUNDANTLY
He poured out this Spirit on us **a** Ti 3:6

ABUSED
a her all night Jdg 19:25

ABYSS
not to banish them to the **a**. Lk 8:31
Who will go down into the **a**? Rm 10:7

ACCEPT
Should we **a** only good from God Jb 2:10
the LORD **a-ed** Job's prayer. Jb 42:9
My son, if you **a** my words Pr 2:1
A my instruction Pr 8:10
Not everyone can **a** this saying, Mt 19:11
a one another, Rm 15:7
a-ing one another Eph 4:2; Col 3:13

ACCEPTABLE
the meditation of my heart be **a** Ps 19:14
Look, now is the **a** time; 2Co 6:2
spiritual sacrifices **a** to God 1Pt 2:5

ACCEPTANCE
what will their **a** mean Rm 11:15
and deserving of full **a**: 1Tm 1:15

ACCESS
a through Him by faith into ... grace Rm 5:2
we both have **a** by one Spirit Eph 2:18

ACCOMPANY
signs will **a** those who believe: Mk 16:17

ACCOMPLISH
it will **a** what I please Is 55:11
I watch over My word to **a** it." Jr 1:12

ACCORDING
be done for you **a** to your faith! Mt 9:29
be done to me **a** to your word. Lk 1:38
who do not walk **a** to the flesh Rm 8:4
ask anything **a** to His will, 1Jn 5:14
were judged **a** to their works Rv 20:12

ACCOUNT
a for every careless word Mt 12:36

ACCUSATION
Who can bring an **a** Rm 8:33
an **a** against an elder 1Tm 5:19

ACCUSE
He will not always **a** us Ps 103:9
standing at his right side to **a** Zch 3:1
in order to **a** Him Mt 12:10; Mk 3:2
They began to **a** Him, Lk 23:2
Your **a-r** is Moses, Jn 5:45
so that when you are **a-d**, 1Pt 3:16

ACHAIA
he wanted to cross over to **A**, Ac 18:27

ACHAN
Sinned at Jericho; stoned (Jos 7; 1Ch 2:7).

ACHISH
King of Gath before whom David feigned madness (1Sm 21:10-15). Later, he favored David (1Sm 27–29).

ACKNOWLEDGE
Then I **a-d** my sin to You Ps 32:5
I will also **a** him before My Father in heaven Mt 10:32

ACQUIT
I know You will not **a** me. Jb 9:28

ACT (N)
an outstretched arm and great **a-s** Ex 6:6
deeds and mighty **a-s** like Yours? Dt 3:24

this woman was caught in the a Jn 8:4

ACT (V)
trust in Him, and He will a, Ps 37:5
I a-ed because of My name, Ezk 20:9
these words of Mine and a-s Mt 7:24
a-ed out of ignorance in unbelief. 1Tm 1:13

ACTION
a-s are weighed by Him. 1Sm 2:3
with your minds ready for a, 1Pt 1:13
word or speech, but in truth and a. 1Jn 3:18

ACTIVE
You see that faith was a Jms 2:22

ADAM
First man. Created by God (Gn 1:26-27; 2:7). Named animals (2:18-20). Given Eve (2:21-25). Failed to obey and was evicted (1:15-17; 3:6-24; Rm 5:14; 1Co 15:22). Died at 930 years (Gn 5:3-5).

ADD
no a-ing to it or taking from it. Ec 3:14
Can any of you a a single cubit Mt 6:27
about 3,000 people were a-ed Ac 2:41

ADDICTED
not a to wine, 1Tm 3:3; Ti 1:7
not a to much wine. Ti 2:3

ADMINISTRATION
the a of the mystery Eph 3:9

ADMINISTRATOR
overseer, as God's a, must be Ti 1:7

ADMONISHING
teaching and a one another Col 3:16

ADONIJAH
Son of David (2Sm 3:4). Conspired for the throne and was executed by Solomon (1Kg 1–2).

ADOPTION
but you received the Spirit of a, Rm 8:15
to them belong the a, Rm 9:4
that we might receive a as sons. Gl 4:5

ADORN
A yourself with majesty Jb 40:10
as a bride a-s herself Is 61:10
it was a-ed with beautiful stones Lk 21:5
a the teaching of God our Savior Ti 2:10
a-ed with gold, precious stones, Rv 17:4
a bride a-ed for her husband. Rv 21:2

ADORNMENT
life for you and a for your neck. Pr 3:22

ADULTERER
both the a and the adulteress Lv 20:10
a-'s eye watches for twilight, Jb 24:15
you associate with a-s. Ps 50:18
the land is full of a-s; Jr 23:10
idolaters, a-s, male prostitutes, 1Co 6:9
judge immoral people and a-s, Heb 13:4

ADULTERESS
both the adulterer and the a Lv 20:10
an a goes after a precious life. Pr 6:26
This is the way of an a: she eats Pr 30:20
they are a-es Ezk 23:45

A-es! Don't you know Jms 4:4

ADULTEROUS
You a wife, Ezk 16:32
An evil and a generation Mt 12:39; 16:4
this a and sinful generation, Mk 8:38

ADULTERY
Do not commit a. Ex 20:14; Dt 5:18
If a man commits a Lv 20:10
already committed a with her Mt 5:28
marries another, commits a. Mt 19:9
do not commit a; do not steal; Mt 19:18
brought a woman caught in a, Jn 8:3
who said, Do not commit a, also Jms 2:11

ADVANCE
Scripture saw in a that God Gl 3:8
resulted in the a of the gospel, Php 1:12

ADVANTAGE
the a of wisdom Ec 10:10
So what a does the Jew have? Rm 3:1

ADVERSARY
I will take vengeance on My a-ies Dt 32:41
You exalt me above my a-ies; Ps 18:48
give the a no opportunity 1Tm 5:14
Your a the Devil is prowling 1Pt 5:8

ADVERSITY
life and prosperity, death and a. Dt 30:15
only good from God and not a? Jb 2:10
both a and good come from Lm 3:38

ADVICE
rejected the elders' a 2Ch 10:13
not follow the a of the wicked Ps 1:1
should have followed my a Ac 27:21

ADVISERS
with many a they succeed. Pr 15:22

ADVOCATE
we have an a with the Father 1Jn 2:1

AFFECTION
limited by your own a-s. 2Co 6:12
with the a of Christ Jesus. Php 1:8

AFFLICT
Egyptians mistreated and a-ed us, Dt 26:6
Evildoers will not a them 2Sm 7:10
He was oppressed and a-ed, Is 53:7
Though I have a-ed you, I will a you no longer. Nah 1:12
you who are a-ed, along with us. 2Th 1:7
destitute, a-ed, and mistreated. Heb 11:37

AFFLICTED (N)
He heard the outcry of the a Jb 34:28

AFFLICTION
fruitful in the land of my a. Gn 41:52
LORD saw that the a of Israel 2Kg 14:26
Consider my a and trouble, Ps 25:18
He does not enjoy bringing a Lm 3:33
she was cured of her a. Mk 5:29
a-s are waiting for me Ac 20:23
a produces endurance, Rm 5:3
momentary light a is producing 2Co 4:17

AFRAID
I was a because I was naked, Gn 3:10
not be a, Abram. I am your shield Gn 15:1
he was a to look at God. Ex 3:6
Do not be a, alarmed, or terrified Dt 20:3
Do not be a or discouraged, Jos 1:9
I am not a of the thousands Ps 3:6
of whom should I be a? Ps 27:1
When I am a, I will trust in You. Ps 56:3
She is not a for her household Pr 31:21
I will trust Him and not be a, Is 12:2
Do not be a of anyone, for I will be Jr 1:8
don't be a to take Mary Mt 1:20
Jesus told them, "Do not be a. Mt 28:10
Don't be a. Only believe. Mk 5:36
they were a of Him, Mk 11:18
they were a of the crowd Mk 11:32; 12:12
Do not be a, Mary, Lk 1:30
angel said to them, "Don't be a, Lk 2:10
they were a of the people. Lk 22:2
It is I. Don't be a! Jn 6:20
they were a of the Jews, Jn 9:22
I will not be a. What can man do Heb 13:6

AGABUS
Early church prophet (Ac 11:28; 21:10).

AGAG
Amalekite king spared by Saul, executed by Samuel (1Sm 15).

AGAINST
who is not with Me is a Me, Mt 12:30
whoever is not a us is for us. Mk 9:40
If God is for us, who is a us? Rm 8:31

AGE
already existed in the a-s before Ec 1:10
the worries of this a Mt 13:22; Mk 4:19
the sons of this a are more astute Lk 16:8

AGONY
a like a woman in labor. Jr 22:23
I am in a in this flame! Lk 16:24

AGREE
If two of you on earth a Mt 18:19
but the testimonies did not a. Mk 14:56
Why did you a to test the Spirit Ac 5:9
Saul a-d with putting him to death. Ac 8:1
I a with the law that it is good Rm 7:16
does not a with the sound teaching 1Tm 6:3

AGREEMENT
making a binding a in writing Neh 9:38
we have made an a with Sheol; Is 28:15
a does Christ have with Belial? 2Co 6:15
these three are in a. 1Jn 5:8

AGRIPPA
Herodian king who heard Paul's testimony (Ac 25–26).

AHAB
Son of Omri, king of Israel (1Kg 16:28–22:40). Married Jezebel and promoted baalism (16:31-33). Killed Naboth (21:1-14). Condemned by Elijah (18:18; 21:17-24) and other prophets (20:35-43; 22:19-28). Died in disguise in battle (22:29-40).

AHASUERUS
King of Persia, son of Darius and grandson of Cyrus. Greek name is Xerxes. Dismissed Vashti and married Esther (Est 1–2). Signed Haman's decree (Est 3) then was convinced by Esther to reverse it and hang Haman (Est

4–7) and allow the Jews to defend themselves (Est 8–9).

AHAZ
Idolatrous king of Judah (2Kg 16:2-4). Son of Jotham. Attacked by Aram and Israel (16:5-6; 2Ch 28:5-7). Refused Isaiah's advice and turned to Assyria for help (Is 7). Not buried among the kings (2Ch 28:27).

AHAZIAH
1. Son of Ahab; king of Israel (1Kg 22:40). Injured in a fall; condemned by Elijah for seeking Baal (2Kg 1:2-17).
2. Son of Jehoram; king of Judah (2Kg 8:25-27). Mortally wounded by Jehu while visiting King Joram of Israel (9:27).

AHEAD
Each creature went straight **a**. Ezk 1:9; 10:22
sending My messenger **a** of You; Mt 11:10
I will go **a** of you to Galilee. Mt 26:32
which God prepared **a** of time Eph 2:10
reaching forward to what is **a**, Php 3:13

AHIJAH
1. Priest at the time of Saul (1Sm 14:3-4,18).
2. Prophet from Shiloh to Jeroboam (1Kg 4:3; 11:29-39).

AI
Bethel on the west and **A** on the Gn 12:8
they fled from the men of **A**. Jos 7:4
Joshua burned **A** Jos 8:28

AIJALON
moon, over the Valley of **A**. Jos 10:12
A with its pasturelands, Jos 21:24

AIMLESSLY
do not run like one who runs **a** 1Co 9:26

AIR
box like one beating the **a**. 1Co 9:26
meet the Lord in the **a** 1Th 4:17
poured out his bowl into the **a**, Rv 16:17

ALABASTER
an **a** jar Mt 26:7; Mk 14:3

ALARM
sound the **a** on My holy mountain! Jl 2:1

ALARMED
and rumors of wars, don't be **a**; Mk 13:7

ALERT
be **a**, since you don't know Mt 24:42
slaves the master will find **a** Lk 12:37
Be **a**, stand firm in the faith, 1Co 16:13
stay **a** in this with all perseverance Eph 6:18
prayer; stay **a** in it Col 4:2
Be serious! Be **a**! Your adversary 1Pt 5:8

ALEXANDER
Hymenaeus and **A** 1Tm 1:20
A the coppersmith 2Tm 4:14

ALIENATED
are **a** from Christ; Gl 5:4
Once you were **a** and hostile Col 1:21

ALIVE
to keep them **a** with you. Gn 6:19
when they heard that He was **a** Mk 16:11
He also presented Himself **a** Ac 1:3
dead to sin but **a** to God Rm 6:11
in Christ all will be made **a**. 1Co 15:22
made us **a** with the Messiah Eph 2:5
He made you **a** with Him Col 2:13
Then we who are still **a** 1Th 4:17
made **a** in the spiritual realm. 1Pt 3:18
but look—I am **a** forever Rv 1:18

ALL
with **a** your heart, with **a** your soul, and with **a** your strength. Dt 6:5
search for Me with **a** your heart. Jr 29:13
love the Lord ... with **a** your heart, Lk 10:27
A have turned away, Rm 3:12
a have sinned and fall short Rm 3:23
He died to sin once for **a**; Rm 6:10
We will not **a** fall asleep, but we will **a** be changed, 1Co 15:51
the One who fills **a** things Eph 1:23
I am able to do **a** things Php 4:13
A Scripture is inspired by God 2Tm 3:16
but **a** to come to repentance. 2Pt 3:9

ALLEGIANCE
every tongue will swear **a**. Is 45:23

ALLIANCE
Solomon made an **a** with Pharaoh 1Kg 3:1
they will form an **a**, Dn 11:6

ALLOTMENT
Israel according to their **a-s**: Jos 12:7

ALLOW
will not **a** Your Faithful One to see Ps 16:10
A it for now, Mt 3:15
a Your Holy One to see decay. Ac 2:27
will not **a** you to be tempted 1Co 10:13

ALMIGHTY
I am God **A**. Gn 17:1
Isaac, and Jacob as God **A**, Ex 6:3
discover the limits of the **A**? Jb 11:7
dwells in the shadow of the **A**. Ps 91:1
was, and who is coming, the **A**. Rv 1:8
Holy, holy, holy, Lord God, the **A**, Rv 4:8
God, the **A**, has begun to reign! Rv 19:6

ALMOND
the **a** tree blossoms, Ec 12:5

ALONE
not good for the man to be **a**. Gn 2:18
man does not live on bread **a** Dt 8:3
I **a** am left, 1Kg 19:10
Against You—You **a**— Ps 51:4
the LORD **a** will be exalted Is 2:11
Man must not live on bread **a** Mt 4:4
to a remote place to be **a**. Mt 14:13
Who can forgive sins but God **a**? Mk 2:7
by works and not by faith **a**. Jms 2:24

ALPHA
the **A** and the Omega, Rv 1:8; 21:6; 22:13

ALREADY
Whatever is, has **a** been, and whatever will be, **a** is. Ec 3:15
has **a** committed adultery Mt 5:28
how I wish it were **a** set ablaze! Lk 12:49
does not believe is **a** judged, Jn 3:18
You are **a** clean Jn 15:3
You are **a** full! You are **a** rich! 1Co 4:8
Not that I have **a** reached Php 3:12
he is **a** in the world now. 1Jn 4:3

ALTAR
Noah built an **a** to the LORD. Gn 8:20
Isaac and placed him on the **a** Gn 22:9
construct the **a** of acacia wood. Ex 27:1
an **a** for the burning of incense; Ex 30:1
tear down their **a-s**, Ex 34:13
take hold of the horns of the **a**. 1Kg 1:50
I will come to the **a** of God, Ps 43:4
leave your gift ... in front of the **a**. Mt 5:24
takes an oath by the **a**, Mt 23:18
We have an **a** from which Heb 13:10
when he offered Isaac ... on the **a**? Jms 2:21
I saw under the **a** the people Rv 6:9

ALTOGETHER
reliable and **a** righteous. Ps 19:9
righteous and **a** trustworthy. Ps 119:138

ALWAYS
my sin is **a** before me. Ps 51:3
You **a** have the poor with you, Mt 26:11
I am with you **a**, Mt 28:20
Rejoice in the Lord **a**. Php 4:4
A be ready to give a defense 1Pt 3:15

AM *SEE* I AM

AMASA
David's nephew; commander of Absalom's army (2Sm 17:25). Reinstated by David (19:13). Killed by Joab (20:10).

AMAZED
a and asked, "What kind of man Mt 8:27
the crowds were **a**, Mt 9:33
He was **a** at their unbelief. Mk 6:6
they were astounded and **a**, Ac 2:7

AMAZIAH
Son of Joash; king of Judah. Defeated Edom but adopted their gods (2Ch 25:11-14). Rejected God's rebuke, challenged King Jehoash of Israel, and was defeated (26:15-24). Killed by a conspiracy (26:27).

AMBASSADOR
we are **a-s** for Christ, 2Co 5:20
For this I am an **a** in chains. Eph 6:20

AMBITION
bitter envy and selfish **a** Jms 3:14

AMBUSH
Set an **a** behind the city. Jos 8:2
set up an **a** around Gibeah. Jdg 20:29
Let's set an **a** and kill someone. Pr 1:11
40 of them arranging to **a** him, Ac 23:21

AMEN
all the people will reply, '**A**!' Dt 27:15
LORD be praised forever. **A** and **a**. Ps 89:52
will the uninformed ... say "**A**" 1Co 14:16
the "**A**" is also ... through Him 2Co 1:20
The **A**, the faithful and true Rv 3:14
A! Come, Lord Jesus! Rv 22:20

AMNON
Oldest son of David (2Sm 3:2). Raped his sister Tamar; killed by Absalom (2Sm 13).

AMON
Son of Manasseh; king of Judah; killed by his servants (2Kg 21:18-26).

AMOS
Prophet against moral decay in Israel under Jeroboam II (Am 5:24).

ANANIAS
1. Lied about gift to the church at Jerusalem and died (Ac 5:1-6).
2. Disciple in Damascus who visited Paul (Ac 9:10-19).
3. High priest at Paul's arrest (Ac 23:1-5; 24:1).

ANCESTOR
from the day their **a-s** came out 2Kg 21:15
returned to the sins of their **a-s** Jr 11:10
our **a** according to the flesh, Rm 4:1
a clear conscience as my **a-s** did, 2Tm 1:3

ANCHOR
this hope as an **a** for our lives, Heb 6:19

ANCIENT
Will you continue on the **a** path Jb 22:15
Rise up, **a** doors! Ps 24:7,9
Ask about the **a** paths: Jr 6:16
the **A** of Days took His seat. Dn 7:9
since **a** times, Moses Ac 15:21
if He didn't spare the **a** world, 2Pt 2:5
seized the dragon, that **a** serpent Rv 20:2

ANDREW
Apostle; fisherman; Peter's brother (Mt 4:18; 10:2; Mk 1:16,29; 3:18; 13:3; Lk 6:14; Jn 1:35-44; 6:8-9; 12:12; Ac 1:13).

ANGEL
two **a-s** entered Sodom Gn 19:1
A of the LORD called to him Gn 22:11
He will send His **a** before you, Gn 24:7
a-s were going up and down Gn 28:12
going to send an **a** before you Ex 23:20
A of the LORD took His stand Nm 22:22
God sent an **a** to Jerusalem 1Ch 21:15
A of the LORD encamps around Ps 34:7
He will give His **a-s** orders Ps 91:11
Praise the LORD, all His **a-s** Ps 103:20
the **a** of the LORD ... struck down Is 37:36
He sent His **a** and rescued Dn 3:28
My God sent His **a** and shut Dn 6:22
Jacob struggled with the **A** Hs 12:4
a of the Lord suddenly appeared Mt 2:13
He will give His **a-s** orders Mt 4:6
is going to come with His **a-s** Mt 16:27
their **a-s** continually view Mt 18:10
are like **a-s** in heaven. Mt 22:30
for the Devil and his **a-s**! Mt 25:41
the **a-s** began to serve Him. Mk 1:13
the **a** Gabriel was sent Lk 1:26
a said to them, "Don't be afraid Lk 2:10
the **a-s** of God ascending Jn 1:51
an **a** would go down into the pool Jn 5:4
face was like the face of an **a**. Ac 6:15
we will judge **a-s** 1Co 6:3
If I speak human or **a-ic** languages 1Co 13:1
disguises himself as an **a** of light. 2Co 11:14
even if we or an **a** from heaven Gl 1:8
the worship of **a-s**, Col 2:18
some have welcomed **a-s** as guests Heb 13:2
A-s desire to look into 1Pt 1:12
if God didn't spare the **a-s** 2Pt 2:4
Write to the **a** of the church in Rv 2–3

ANGER
until your brother's **a** subsides Gn 27:44
alone, so that My **a** can burn Ex 32:10
gracious God, slow to **a** Ex 34:6
LORD's **a** burned against Israel Jdg 2:14
His **a** may ignite at any moment. Ps 2:12
do not rebuke me in Your **a**; Ps 6:1
For His **a** lasts only a moment, Ps 30:5
I swore in My **a**, "They will not Ps 95:11
A gentle answer turns away **a**, Pr 15:1
A fool gives full vent to his **a**, Pr 29:11
compassionate, slow to **a**, Jl 2:13
jealousy, outbursts of **a**, 2Co 12:20; Gl 5:20
sun go down on your **a**, Eph 4:26
All bitterness, **a** and wrath, Eph 4:31
a, wrath, malice, slander, Col 3:8
So I swore in My **a**, Heb 3:11
slow to speak, and slow to **a**, Jms 1:19
the cup of His **a**. Rv 14:10
winepress of the fierce **a** of God, Rv 19:15

ANGRY
the Son or He will be **a** Ps 2:12
Be **a** and do not sin; Ps 4:4
An **a** man stirs up conflict, Pr 29:22
slow to become **a**, Jnh 4:2
Is it right for you to be **a**? Jnh 4:4
who is **a** with his brother Mt 5:22
Be **a** and do not sin. Eph 4:26

ANGUISH
He will see it out of His **a**, Is 53:11
in **a**, He prayed more fervently, Lk 22:44
I wrote to you with ... **a-ed** heart 2Co 2:4

ANIMAL
LORD God formed ... every wild **a** Gn 2:19
with an **a** must be put to death. Ex 22:19
may eat all these ... land **a-s**. Lv 11:2
every **a** of the forest is Mine, Ps 50:10
cares about his **a-'s** health, Pr 12:10
and the fate of **a-s** is the same. Ec 3:19
four-footed **a-s** and reptiles Ac 10:12

ANNIHILATE
a all the Jewish people Est 3:13

ANNOUNCE
I **a** them to you before they occur Is 42:9
who **a-d** beforehand the coming Ac 7:52
feet of those who **a** the gospel Rm 10:15

ANOINT
A Aaron and his sons Ex 30:30
LORD sent me to **a** you as king 1Sm 15:1
The LORD **a-ed** you king 1Sm 15:17
You **a** my head with oil; Ps 23:5
a-ed Me to bring good news Is 61:1
a-ed My body in advance Mk 14:8
a-ed Me to preach good news Lk 4:18
You didn't **a** My head with ... oil, Lk 7:46
a-ed Jesus' feet, Jn 12:3
against ... Jesus, whom You **a-ed**, Ac 4:27
pray over him after **a-ing** him Jms 5:14

ANOINTED (ADJ)
If the **a** priest sins, Lv 4:3
he will walk before My **a** one 1Sm 2:35
Do not touch My **a** ones 1Ch 16:22
against the LORD and His **A** One: Ps 2:2
Do not touch My **a** ones, Ps 105:15
an **a** guardian cherub, Ezk 28:14
These are the two **a** ones, Zch 4:14

ANOINTED (N)
lift my hand against ... Lord's **a**. 1Sm 24:6

ANOINTING (N)
an **a** from the Holy One, 1Jn 2:20
His **a** teaches you 1Jn 2:27

ANOINTING (ADJ)
spices for the **a** oil Ex 25:6

ANOTHER
Let **a** praise you, and not your Pr 27:2
I will not give My glory to **a**. Is 48:11
He will give you **a** Counselor Jn 14:16
not that there is **a** gospel, Gl 1:7

ANSWER (N)
A gentle **a** turns away anger, Pr 15:1
a of the tongue is from the Lord Pr 16:1
who gives an **a** before he listens Pr 18:13
money is the **a** for everything. Ec 10:19
were astounded at ... His **a-s**. Lk 2:47

ANSWER (V)
He **a-ed** him with fire 1Ch 21:26
but You do not **a** me; Jb 30:20
a me, for I am poor and needy Ps 86:1
Don't **a** a fool according to Pr 26:4
A a fool according to Pr 26:5
But Jesus still did not **a** Mk 15:5

ANT
Go to the **a**, you slacker! Pr 6:6
a-s are not a strong people, Pr 30:25

ANTICHRIST
heard, "**A** is coming," even now many **a-s** have come. 1Jn 2:18
is the **a**: the one who denies 1Jn 2:22
spirit of the **a**; you have heard 1Jn 4:3
This is the deceiver and the **a**. 2Jn 7

ANTIOCH
first called Christians at **A**. Ac 11:26
reached **A** in Pisidia. Ac 13:14

ANTIQUITY
origin is from **a**, from eternity. Mc 5:2

ANXIETY
A in a man's heart weighs Pr 12:25

ANXIOUS
don't be **a**. Lk 12:29

ANYTHING
Is **a** impossible for the LORD? Gn 18:14
Is **a** too difficult for Me? Jr 32:27
A you ask the Father Jn 16:23

APART
Set **a** for Me Barnabas and Saul Ac 13:2
a from the law ... righteousness has Rm 3:21
from my birth set me **a** and called Gl 1:15

APOLLOS
Alexandrian Jew, became a Christian apologist after being instructed in doctrine by Priscilla and Aquila in Ephesus (Ac 18:24-28). Was popular like Paul and Peter (1Co 1:12) but not a rival (3:5-6,22; 4:6; 16:12; Ti 3:13).

APOSTASY
a-ies will reprimand you. Jr 2:19
save them from all their **a-ies** Ezk 37:23
I will heal their **a**; Hs 14:4
unless the **a** comes first 2Th 2:3

APOSTLE
the names of the 12 **a-s**: Mt 10:2
12—He also named them **a-s** Mk 3:14
numbered with the 11 **a-s**. Ac 1:26
laid it at the **a-s'** feet. Ac 5:2
called as an **a** and singled out Rm 1:1
I am an **a** to the Gentiles, Rm 11:13
first **a-s**, second prophets, 1Co 12:28
unworthy to be called an **a**, 1Co 15:9
such people are false **a-s**, 2Co 11:13
signs of an **a** were performed 2Co 12:12
on the foundation of the **a-s** Eph 2:20
some to be **a-s**, some prophets, Eph 4:11
Jesus, the **a** and high priest Heb 3:1
12 names of the Lamb's 12 **a-s** Rv 21:14

APOSTLESHIP
We have received grace and **a** Rm 1:5
you are the seal of my **a** 1Co 9:2
Peter for an **a** to the circumcised Gl 2:8

APPEAL
I **a** to Caesar! Ac 25:11
God is **a-ing** through us. 2Co 5:20
I **a**, ... on the basis of love. Phm 9

APPEAR
the LORD **a-ed** to Abram Gn 12:7
sign of the Son of Man will **a** Mt 24:30
and **a-ed** to many. Mt 27:53
the third time Jesus **a-ed** Jn 21:14
He **a-ed** to over 500 brothers 1Co 15:6
we must all **a** before the tribunal 2Co 5:10
until the **a-ing** of our Lord 1Tm 6:14
those who have loved His **a-ing**. 2Tm 4:8
blessed hope and **a-ing** of the glory Ti 2:13
will **a** a second time, Heb 9:28

APPEARANCE
Do not look at his **a** 1Sm 16:7
no **a** that we should desire Him. Is 53:2
judging according to outward **a-s**; Jn 7:24

APPETITE
A worker's **a** works for him Pr 16:26
if you have a big **a**; Pr 23:2
yet the **a** is never satisfied. Ec 6:7
He enlarges his **a** like Sheol, Hab 2:5
Lord Christ but their own **a-s**. Rm 16:18

APPLES
is like gold **a** on a silver tray. Pr 25:11

APPLY
A yourself to discipline Pr 23:12
I **a-ied** my mind to seek Ec 1:13

APPOINT
These are the LORD's **a-ed** times, Lv 23:4
a a king to judge us 1Sm 8:5
A a king for them. 1Sm 8:22
I will **a** peace as your guard Is 60:17
A harvest is also **a-ed** for you, Hs 6:11
the LORD had **a-ed** a huge fish Jnh 1:17
God **a-ed** a worm Jnh 4:7
vision is yet for the **a-ed** time; Hab 2:3
He also **a-ed** 12 Mk 3:14
been **a-ed** for you as the Messiah. Ac 3:20
God did not **a** us to wrath, 1Th 5:9
For this I was **a-ed** a herald, 1Tm 2:7
Don't be too quick to **a** anyone 1Tm 5:22
a elders in every town: Ti 1:5
God has **a-ed** him heir of all things Heb 1:2
it is **a-ed** for people to die once Heb 9:27

APPROACH
let us **a** the throne of grace Heb 4:16

APPROPRIATE
Luxury is not **a** for a fool Pr 19:10
made everything **a** in its time. Ec 3:11

APPROVAL
our ancestors won God's **a** by it. Heb 11:2

APPROVE
was standing by and **a-ing**, Ac 22:20
and **a-d** by men. Rm 14:18
just as we have been **a-d** by God 1Th 2:4
to present yourself **a-d** to God, 2Tm 2:15

AQUILA
Husband of Priscilla; tentmaker; Jewish Christian; teacher; coworker with Paul (Ac 18:2,18,26; Rm 16:3; 1Co 16:19; 2Tm 4:19).

ARAB
Geshem the **A** Neh 2:19; 6:1
Cretans and **A-s** Ac 2:11

ARABAH
in the **A** opposite Suph, Dt 1:1
the Sea of the **A** (the Dead Sea) Jos 3:16
along the route to the **A**, 2Kg 25:4
a dry land, a wilderness, an **A**. Jr 50:12
and goes down to the **A**. Ezk 47:8

ARAM
Son of Shem (Gn 10:22). The nation named for him, perennial enemy of Israel (Jdg 3:8; 2Sm 8:6; 1Kg 11:25; 20; 22; 2Kg 6:8-24; 8:12-13; 13:3,22; 16:7).

ARAMAIC
speak to your servants in **A**, 2Kg 18:26
The letter was written in **A** Ezr 4:7
spoke to the king (**A** begins here): Dn 2:4

ARAMEAN
My father was a wandering **A**. Dt 26:5

ARARAT
on the mountains of **A**. Gn 8:4

ARAUNAH
Man whose threshing floor David bought (2Sm 24:15-25); also called Ornan (1Ch 21:15-28); threshing floor became site of the temple (1Ch 22:1; 2Ch 3:1).

ARCHANGEL
a shout, with the **a-'s** voice, 1Th 4:16
Michael the **a**, Jd 9

ARCHER
the **a-s** caught up with him 1Sm 31:3
The **a-s** shot King Josiah, 2Ch 35:23
like an **a** who wounds everyone Pr 26:10

ARCHITECT
whose **a** and builder is God. Heb 11:10

AREOPAGUS
stood in the middle of the **A** Ac 17:22

ARGUE
Let him who **a-s** with God give Jb 40:2
Pharisees ... began to **a** with Him, Mk 8:11
What were you **a-ing** about Mk 9:33
don't **a** about doubtful issues. Rm 14:1
without grumbling and **a-ing**, Php 2:14

ARGUMENT
Hear now my **a**, Jb 13:6
Then an **a** started among them Lk 9:46
We demolish **a-s** 2Co 10:4
deceive you with empty **a-s**, Eph 5:6
deceive you with persuasive **a-s**. Col 2:4
holy hands without anger or **a**. 1Tm 2:8

ARISE
God **a-s**. His enemies scatter, Ps 68:1
A, my darling. Come away, Sg 2:10
A, shine, for your light has come Is 60:1
false prophets will **a** Mt 24:24

ARK
Make ... an **a** of gofer wood. Gn 6:14
make an **a** of acacia wood, Ex 25:10
Put the tablets ... into the **a**. Ex 25:16
The **a** of God was captured, 1Sm 4:11
Nothing was in the **a** except 1Kg 8:9
a place there for the **a**, 1Kg 8:21
the day Noah boarded the **a**. Mt 24:38
built an **a** to deliver his family. Heb 11:7
while an **a** was being prepared. 1Pt 3:20
the **a** of His covenant appeared Rv 11:19

ARM
with an outstretched **a** Ex 6:6
a strong hand and an outstretched **a**, Dt 4:34
underneath are the everlasting **a-s**. Dt 33:27
Do you have an **a** like God's? Jb 40:9
a-s can bend a bow of bronze. Ps 18:34
holy **a** have won Him victory. Ps 98:1
as a seal on your **a**. Sg 8:6
taking them in My **a-s**, Hs 11:3
taking them in His **a-s**, Mk 10:16
who has the **a** of the Lord been revealed to? Jn 12:38

ARMAGEDON
place called in Hebrew, **A**. Rv 16:16

ARMOR
Saul ... had him put on **a**. 1Sm 17:38
one who puts on his **a** boast 1Kg 20:11
through the joints of his **a**. 1Kg 22:34
penetrate his double layer of **a**? Jb 41:13
put on the **a** of light. Rm 13:12
Put on the full **a** of God Eph 6:11
put the **a** of faith and love on 1Th 5:8

ARMY
chariots and his **a** into the sea; Ex 15:4
commander of the LORD's **a**. Jos 5:14
defied the **a-ies** of the living God 1Sm 17:36
a great **a**, like an **a** of God. 1Ch 12:22
Though an **a** deploys against me, Ps 27:3
king is not saved by a large **a**; Ps 33:16
Jerusalem surrounded by **a-ies**, Lk 21:20
The **a-ies** that were in heaven Rv 19:14
on the horse and against His **a**. Rv 19:19

ARREST
Herod had **a-ed** John, Mt 14:3
looking for a way to **a** Him, Mt 21:46
hold of Jesus, and **a-ed** Him. Mt 26:50
they **a-ed** the apostles Ac 5:18
he proceeded to **a** Peter too, Ac 12:3

ARROGANCE
your **a** have reached My ears, 2Kg 19:28
A leads to nothing but strife, Pr 13:10
gossip, **a**, and disorder. 2Co 12:20

you boast in your **a**. Jms 4:16

ARROGANT
For I envied the **a**; Ps 73:3
a people have attacked me; Ps 86:14
I hate **a** pride, evil conduct, Pr 8:13
an **a** spirit before a fall. Pr 16:18
Do not be **a**, but be afraid. Rm 11:20

ARROW
I will shoot three **a-s** beside it 1Sm 20:20
Elisha said, "Take the **a-s**!" 2Kg 13:18
a-s of the Almighty have pierced Jb 6:4
the **a** that flies by day, Ps 91:5
a-s in the hand of a warrior Ps 127:4
He made me like a sharpened **a**; Is 49:2
Their tongues are deadly **a-s** Jr 9:8
extinguish all the flaming **a-s** Eph 6:16

ARTAXERXES
King of Persia who allowed Ezra to rebuild the temple (Ezr 6:14; 7:1-26) and Nehemiah to rebuild the wall of Jerusalem (Neh 2:1-6).

ARTEMIS
Greek goddess (Ac 19:24-35).

ASA
Son of Abijam; king of Judah (1Kg 15:8). Instituted reforms (15:13). Rebuked for relying on Aram for military help and on doctors for healing rather than on the Lord (2Ch 16:1-12).

ASCEND
Who may **a** the mountain Ps 24:3
I will **a** to the heavens; Is 14:13
No one has **a-ed** into heaven Jn 3:13
observe the Son of Man **a-ing** Jn 6:62
not yet **a-ed** to the Father. Jn 20:17
is also the One who **a-ed** Eph 4:10

ASCENTS
song of **a**. Pss 120–134

ASCRIBE
a to the LORD glory
and strength. 1Ch 16:28; Ps 96:7
A power to God. Ps 68:34

ASENATH
Wife of Joseph (Gn 41:45,50; 46:20).

ASHAMED
All my enemies will be **a** Ps 6:10
Jacob will no longer be **a** Is 29:22
is **a** of Me and of My words Mk 8:38
I am not **a** of the gospel, Rm 1:16
don't be **a** of the testimony 2Tm 1:8
who doesn't need to be **a**, 2Tm 2:15
not **a** to call them brothers, Heb 2:11
is not **a** to be called their God, Heb 11:16
"Christian," he should not be **a** 1Pt 4:16

ASHER
Jacob's eighth son, born of Zilpah (Gn 30:13; 35:26). The tribe's territory was in the northwest on the Phoenician coast (Jos 19:24-31). Also, a town (17:7).

ASHERAH
cut down the **A** pole beside it. Jdg 6:25
and the 400 prophets of **A** 1Kg 18:19
an obscene image of **A**. 2Ch 15:16

ASHES
even though I am dust and **a** Gn 18:27
is to gather up the cow's **a** Nm 19:9
Tamar put **a** on her head 2Sm 13:19
the **a** poured from the altar, 1Kg 13:5
put on sackcloth and **a**, Est 4:1
he sat among the **a**. Jb 2:8
repent in dust and **a**. Jb 42:6
a crown of beauty instead of **a**, Is 61:3
put on sackcloth, and sat in **a**. Jnh 3:6
in sackcloth and **a** long ago! Mt 11:21
the **a** of a young cow Heb 9:13

ASIA
from speaking the message in **A**. Ac 16:6
first convert to Christ from **A**. Rm 16:5
To the seven churches in **A**. Rv 1:4

ASIDE
Do not turn **a** to the right or Dt 28:14
Jesus took the 12 disciples **a** Mt 20:17
set something **a** and save 1Co 16:2
let us lay **a** every weight Heb 12:1

ASK
When your children **a** you, Ex 12:26
When your son **a-s** you Dt 6:20
A of Me, and I will make Ps 2:8
Two things I **a** of You; Pr 30:7
sought by those who did not **a**; Is 65:1
Give to the one who **a-s** you, Mt 5:42
you need before you **a** Him. Mt 6:8
Keep **a-ing**, and it will be given Mt 7:7
you pray and **a** for—believe Mk 11:24
Holy Spirit to those who **a** Lk 11:13
Whatever you **a** in My name, Jn 14:13
a whatever you want Jn 15:7
A and you will receive, Jn 16:24
the Jews **a** for signs 1Co 1:22
lacks wisdom, he should **a** God, Jms 1:5
You **a** and don't receive because
you **a** with wrong motives, Jms 4:3
a anything according to His will, 1Jn 5:14

ASLEEP
The child is not dead but **a**. Mk 5:39
as they were sailing He fell **a**. Lk 8:23
Lazarus has fallen **a**, Jn 11:11
saying this, he fell **a**. Ac 7:60
We will not all fall **a**, 1Co 15:51
concerning those who are **a**, 1Th 4:13

ASSEMBLE
a the whole community Lv 8:3
A on the mountains of Samaria Am 3:9
to gather nations, to **a** kingdoms, Zph 3:8
a-d together against Your holy
Servant Jesus, Ac 4:27
to **a** them for the battle Rv 16:14

ASSEMBLY
sacred **a** on the first day and another
sacred **a** on the seventh day. Ex 12:16
the **a** in front of the rock, Nm 20:10
His praise in the **a** of the godly. Ps 149:1
the **a** was divided. Ac 23:7
the **a** of the firstborn Heb 12:23

ASSOCIATE
you **a** with adulterers. Ps 50:18
Don't **a** with those who drink Pr 23:20
don't **a** with rebels, Pr 24:21
a with the humble. Rm 12:16

not to **a** with anyone who claims
to be a believer 1Co 5:11
don't **a** with him, 2Th 3:14

ASSURANCE
Holy Spirit, and with much **a**. 1Th 1:5
true heart in full **a** of faith, Heb 10:22

ASSURED
stand mature and fully **a** Col 4:12

ASSYRIA
From that land he went to **A** Gn 10:11
The king of **A** deported the
Israelites to **A** 2Kg 18:11
Woe to **A**, the rod of My anger Is 10:5

ASTONISHED
crowds were **a** at His teaching, Mt 7:28
were **a** and said, "How did this Mt 13:54
they were **a** at His teaching. Mt 22:33
were **a**. "Where did this man get Mk 6:2
disciples were **a** at His words. Mk 10:24
parents saw Him, they were **a**, Lk 2:48
all **a** at the greatness of God. Lk 9:43

ASTOUNDED
were **a** at His understanding Lk 2:47

ASTRAY
led **a** to bow down to other gods Dt 30:17
who rejects correction goes **a**. Pr 10:17
We all went **a** like sheep; Is 53:6
their shepherds have led them **a**, Jr 50:6
and one of them goes **a**, Mt 18:12
lead **a**, if possible, the elect. Mk 13:22
always go **a** in their hearts, Heb 3:10
you were like sheep going **a**, 1Pt 2:25

ATHALIAH
Wife of Jehoram and mother of Ahaziah, kings of Judah; descendant of Omri (2Kg 8:26). Encouraged Baal worship (8:27). Killed heirs and ruled after her son's death (11:1-3). Jehoiada the priest executed her and crowned Josiah, the only surviving heir (11:4-20).

ATHENS
City in Greece (Ac 17; 1Th 3:1).

ATHLETE
if anyone competes as an **a**, 2Tm 2:5

ATONE
only You can **a** for our rebellions Ps 65:3
Deliver us and **a** for our sins, Ps 79:9

ATONEMENT
blood of the sin offering for **a**. Ex 30:10
priest will make **a** on their behalf, Lv 4:20
make **a** before the LORD Lv 14:31
is the Day of **A**. Lv 23:27
he ... made **a** for the Israelites. Nm 25:13

ATTACK
he may come and **a** me, Gn 32:11
I will **a** him while he is weak 2Sm 17:2
a worm that **a-ed** the plant, Jnh 4:7

ATTEMPTED
a to establish their own
righteousness, Rm 10:3
When the Egyptians **a** to do this, Heb 11:29

ATTENDANT
gave it back to the **a**, and sat — Lk 4:20

ATTENTION
to pay **a** is better than the fat — 1Sm 15:22
Pay **a** to the sound of my cry, — Ps 5:2
The God of Jacob doesn't pay **a**. — Ps 94:7
My son, pay **a** to my words; — Pr 4:20
pay **a** to the words of the wise, — Pr 22:17
pay **a** to myths and endless — 1Tm 1:4
give your **a** to public reading, — 1Tm 4:13
not pay **a** to Jewish myths — Ti 1:14
more **a** to what we have heard — Heb 2:1

ATTIRE
attendants' service and their **a**, — 1Kg 10:5

ATTITUDE
Serve with a good **a**, as to the Lord — Eph 6:7
Make your own **a** that of Christ — Php 2:5

ATTRIBUTES
His invisible **a**, — Rm 1:20

AUTHORITY
Confer some of your **a** on him — Nm 27:20
like one who had **a**, — Mt 7:29
Son of Man has **a** on earth — Mt 9:6
gave them **a** over unclean spirits — Mt 10:1
All **a** has been given to Me — Mt 28:18
You gave Him **a** over all flesh; — Jn 17:2
You would have no **a** over Me — Jn 19:11
submit to the governing **a-ies**, — Rm 13:1
there is no **a** except from God, — Rm 13:1
a symbol of **a** on her head, — 1Co 11:10
far above every ruler and **a**, — Eph 1:21
rulers, against the **a-ies**, — Eph 6:12
disarmed the rulers and **a-ies** — Col 2:15
teach or to have **a** over a man; — 1Tm 2:12
be submissive to rulers and **a-ies**, — Ti 3:1
Submit to every human **a** — 1Pt 2:13
a-ies, and powers subject to Him. — 1Pt 3:22
glory, majesty, power, and **a** — Jd 25
I will give him **a** over the nations — Rv 2:26
who were given **a** to judge. — Rv 20:4

AVENGE
He will **a** the blood — Dt 32:43
Should I not **a** Myself — Jr 5:9
do not **a** yourselves; — Rm 12:19
how long until You judge and **a** — Rv 6:10

AVENGER
cities as a refuge from the **a**, — Nm 35:12
hand him over to the **a** of blood — Dt 19:12
to silence the enemy and the **a**. — Ps 8:2
Lord is an **a** of all these offenses — 1Th 4:6

AVOID
a irreverent, empty speech — 2Tm 2:16
But **a** foolish debates, genealogies, — Ti 3:9

AWAKE
A! **A**, Deborah! — Jdg 5:12
when I **a**, I will be satisfied — Ps 17:15
or **a-n** love until — Sg 2:7; 3:5; 8:4
I **a-ned** you under the apricot tree. — Sg 8:5
He **a-ns** Me each morning;
He **a-ns** My ear to listen — Is 50:4
in the dust of the earth will **a**, — Dn 12:2
Couldn't you stay **a** one hour? — Mk 14:37
we must stay **a** and be serious. — 1Th 5:6
whether we are **a** or asleep, — 1Th 5:10

AWAY
All have turned **a**; — Ps 53:3

AWE
of the world stand in **a** of Him. — Ps 33:8
I tremble in **a** of You; — Ps 119:120
so that people will be in **a** of Him. — Ec 3:14
stand in **a** of the God of Israel. — Is 29:23
I stand in **a** of Your deeds. — Hab 3:2

AWE-INSPIRING
looked like the **a** Angel of God. — Jdg 13:6
the great and **a** God who keeps — Neh 1:5
great, mighty, and **a** God — Neh 9:32
right hand show your **a** acts. — Ps 45:4
Yahweh, the Most High, is **a**, — Ps 47:2
You answer us ... with **a** works, — Ps 65:5
His acts for humanity are **a**. — Ps 66:5
You are **a** in Your sanctuaries. — Ps 68:35
LORD—the great and **a** God — Dn 9:4
great and **a** Day of the LORD — Jl 2:31
Great and **a** are Your works, — Rv 15:3

AWESOME
What an **a** place this is! — Gn 28:17
the great, mighty, and **a** God, — Dt 10:17
glorious and **a** name—Yahweh, — Dt 28:58
great and **a** Day of the LORD — Mal 4:5

AX
iron **a** head fell into the water, — 2Kg 6:5
Does an **a** exalt itself — Is 10:15
the **a** is ready to strike — Mt 3:10; Lk 3:9

AZARIAH
1. Prophet (2Ch 15:1-8).
2. King of Judah, also called Uzziah (2Kg 15:1-7).

AZAZEL
the LORD and the other for **a**, — Lv 16:8

BAAL
Israel aligned itself with **B** of Peor, — Nm 25:3
the 450 prophets of **B** — 1Kg 18:19
knee that has not bowed to **B** — 1Kg 19:18
no longer call Me, "My **B**." — Hs 2:16
who have not bowed down to **B**. — Rm 11:4

BAASHA
King of Israel (1Kg 15:16–16:7). Exterminated Jeroboam's family (15:29).

BABY
Give the living **b** to the first — 1Kg 3:27
the **b** leaped inside her, — Lk 1:41
You will find a **b** wrapped — Lk 2:12
and the **b** who was lying in — Lk 2:16

BABYLON
Mesopotamian city; place of captivity (2Kg 24; Dn 1:1-6); symbol of wickedness (Rv 17:5).
Therefore its name is called **B**, — Gn 11:9
from a distant country, from **B**. — 2Kg 20:14
went up from **B** to Jerusalem. — Ezr 1:11
By the rivers of **B** — Ps 137:1
B has fallen, has fallen. — Is 21:9
serve the king of **B** for 70 years. — Jr 25:11
She who is in **B**, also chosen, — 1Pt 5:13
It has fallen, **B** the Great — Rv 14:8

BACK (N)
gave My **b** to those who beat Me, — Is 50:6

BACK (ADV)
looked **b** and became a pillar — Gn 19:26
ahead 10 steps or go **b** 10 steps? — 2Kg 20:9
plow and looks **b** is fit for — Lk 9:62

BAD
but a **b** tree produces **b** fruit. — Mt 7:17
B company corrupts good — 1Co 15:33

BAG
in each man's sack was his **b** of — Gn 42:35
two different weights in your **b**, — Dt 25:13
David put his hand in the **b**, — 1Sm 17:49
weeping, carrying the **b** of seed, — Ps 126:6
or **b-s** of deceptive weights? — Mc 6:11
wages into a **b** with a hole in it. — Hg 1:6

BAKE
b-d unleavened bread for them, — Gn 19:3
b-d the dough they had brought — Ex 12:39
B what you want to **b**, — Ex 16:23
a grain offering **b-d** in an oven, — Lv 2:4

BAKER
king's cupbearer and **b** — Gn 40:1

BALAAM
Prophet hired by King Balak of Moab to curse Israel (Nm 22). His donkey talked (22:21-30; 2Pt 2:16). He blessed Israel (Nm 23–24; Jos 24:10; Neh 13:2). Executed for practicing divination (Nm 31:8; Jos 13:22; 2Pt 2:15; Jd 11; Rv 2:14).

BALAK
King of Moab who hired Balaam to curse Israel (Nm 22–24).

BALANCE
You are to have honest **b-s**, — Lv 19:36
b-s and scales are the LORD's; — Pr 16:11
weighed the mountains in a **b** — Is 40:12

BALDY
chanting, "Go up, **b**! — 2Kg 2:23

BALM
Is there no **b** in Gilead? — Jr 8:22

BAN
will **b** you from the synagogues. — Jn 16:2

BANDAGE
cleansed, **b-d**, or soothed with oil. — Is 1:6
LORD **b-s** His people's injuries — Is 30:26
Look, it has not been **b-d** — Ezk 30:21
healed the sick, **b-d** the injured — Ezk 34:4
and **b-d** his wounds, — Lk 10:34

BANDIT
your need, like a **b**. — Pr 6:11; 24:34

BANISH
plans so that the one **b-ed** from Him does not remain **b-ed**. — 2Sm 14:14
not **b** me from Your presence — Ps 51:11
nations where I will **b** them. — Ezk 4:13

BANK
put my money in the **b**? — Lk 19:23

BANNER
The LORD Is My **B**. — Ex 17:15
lift the **b** in the name of our God. — Ps 20:5
as an army with **b-s** — Sg 6:4,10

BANQUET
the king held a week-long **b** Est 1:5
He brought me to the **b** hall, Sg 2:4
love the place of honor at **b-s**, Mt 23:6
a **b**, invite those who are poor, Lk 14:13

BAPTISM
Sadducees coming to ... his **b**, Mt 3:7
Where did John's **b** come from? Mt 21:25
preaching a **b** of repentance Mk 1:4
with the **b** I am baptized with? Mk 10:38
baptized with John's **b**. Lk 7:29
I have a **b** to be baptized with, Lk 12:50
he knew only John's **b**. Ac 18:25
we were buried with Him by **b** Rm 6:4
one Lord, one faith, one **b**, Eph 4:5
buried with Him in **b**, Col 2:12
B ... now saves you 1Pt 3:21

BAPTIST
In those days John the **B** came, Mt 3:1
no one greater than John the **B** Mt 11:11
Give me John the **B-'s** head Mt 14:8
Some say John the **B**; Mt 16:14
John the **B** sent us to ask You, Lk 7:20

BAPTIZE
I **b** you with water for Mt 3:11
I need to be **b-d** by You, Mt 3:14
b-ing them in the name of Mt 28:19
to be **b-d** with the baptism I Mk 10:38
and is **b-d** will be saved, Mk 16:16
Tax collectors also came to be **b-d**, Lk 3:12
Jesus also was **b-d**. Lk 3:21
b-ing more disciples than John Jn 4:1
will be **b-d** with the Holy Spirit Ac 1:5
Repent ... and be **b-d**, Ac 2:38
there's water! What would keep me from being **b-d**? Ac 8:36
who were **b-d** into Christ Jesus were **b-d** into His death? Rm 6:3
Christ did not send me to **b**, but 1Co 1:17
all were **b-d** into Moses 1Co 10:2
we were all **b-d** by one Spirit 1Co 12:13
are being **b-d** for the dead? 1Co 15:29

BARABBAS
Insurrectionist released by Pilate instead of Jesus (Mt 27:16-26; Mk 15:7-15; Lk 23:18; Jn 18:40).

BARAK
Reluctantly joined Deborah to fight Canaanites (Jdg 4–5; 1Sm 12:11; Heb 11:32).

BARBARIAN
obligated both to Greeks and **b-s**, Rm 1:14
b, Scythian, slave and free; Col 3:11

BAREFOOT
he did so, going naked and **b** Is 20:2

BARK
peeled the **b**, exposing white Gn 30:37

BARLEY
a loaf of **b** bread came tumbling Jdg 7:13
five **b** loaves and two fish Jn 6:9

BARN
gather His wheat into the **b**. Mt 3:12
sow or reap or gather into **b-s**, Mt 6:26
but store the wheat in my **b**. Mt 13:30
I'll tear down my **b-s** and build Lk 12:18

BARNABAS
Levite from Cyprus, named Joseph (Ac 4:36). Introduced Paul to Jerusalem church (9:26-27). Worked with Paul, initially as leader in Antioch (11:19-30), then on a journey (Ac 13–14), then in Jerusalem (15:1-21). Separated from Paul over whether to bring John Mark with them again (15:36-41).

BARTHOLOMEW
Apostle (Mt 10:3; Mk 3:18; Lk 6:14; Ac 1:13), possibly also called Nathanael (Jn 1:43-51).

BARUCH
Jeremiah's scribe (Jr 36).

BASED
not be **b** on men's wisdom 1Co 2:5
the law is not **b** on faith; Gl 3:12
righteousness from God **b** on faith. Php 3:9
b on the glorious gospel 1Tm 1:11
b on the testimony of two Heb 10:28
b on what seemed good to them Heb 12:10
B on the gift each one has received, 1Pt 4:10

BASHAN
the rest of Gilead and all **B**, Dt 3:13
strong ones of **B** encircle me. Ps 22:12
against all the oaks of **B**, Is 2:13
you cows of **B** Am 4:1

BASIN
Make a bronze **b** for washing Ex 30:18
he made 10 bronze **b-s** 1Kg 7:38
poured water into a **b** and began to Jn 13:5

BASKET
Three **b-s** ... were on my head. Gn 40:16
she got a papyrus **b** for him Ex 2:3
LORD showed me two **b-s** of figs Jr 24:1
A **b** of summer fruit. Am 8:1
a woman sitting inside the **b**. Zch 5:7
a lamp and puts it under a **b**, Mt 5:15
they picked up 12 **b-s** full Mt 14:20
pieces—seven large **b-s** full. Mt 15:37
how many **b-s** you collected? Mt 16:9
lowered him in a large **b** Ac 9:25

BATCH
holy, so is the whole **b**. Rm 11:16
yeast permeates the whole **b** 1Co 5:6

BATHE
he saw a woman **b-ing** 2Sm 11:2
One who has **b-d**, Jn 13:10

BATHSHEBA
Wife of Uriah the Hittite. David committed adultery with her, then married her (2Sm 11). Solomon's mother (2Sm 12; 1Kg 1–2).

BATTLE
the **b** is the LORD's. 1Sm 17:47
the **b** is not yours, but God's. 2Ch 20:15
He smells the **b** from a distance Jb 39:25
clothed me with strength for **b**; Ps 18:39
the LORD, mighty in **b**. Ps 24:8
A horse is prepared for ... **b**, Pr 21:31
or the **b** to the strong, Ec 9:11
nations against Jerusalem for **b**. Zch 14:2
our **b** is not against flesh and blood Eph 6:12
like horses equipped for **b**. Rv 9:7
the **b** of the great day of God, Rv 16:14
Magog, to gather them for **b**. Rv 20:8

BEAR (N)
Whenever a lion or a **b** came 1Sm 17:34
two female **b-s** came out 2Kg 2:24
to meet a **b** robbed of her cubs Pr 17:12
The cow and the **b** will graze, Is 11:7
He is a **b** waiting in ambush, Lm 3:10
second one, that looked like a **b**. Dn 7:5

BEAR (V)
you will **b** children in anguish. Gn 3:16
punishment is too great to **b**! Gn 4:13
wife Sarah will **b** you a son, Gn 17:19
that **b-s** its fruit in season Ps 1:3
a burden too heavy for me to **b**. Ps 38:4
He **b-s** our burdens; Ps 68:19
They will still **b** fruit in old age, Ps 92:14
He Himself **bore** our sicknesses, Is 53:4
yet He **bore** the sin of many Is 53:12
womb that **bore** You ... blessed! Lk 11:27
does not **b** his own cross Lk 14:27
but you can't **b** them now. Jn 16:12
that we may **b** fruit for God. Rm 7:4
b the weaknesses of those Rm 15:1
so that you are able to **b** it. 1Co 10:13
b-s all things, believes all 1Co 13:7
offered once to **b** the sins of Heb 9:28
He Himself **bore** our sins 1Pt 2:24
tree of life ... **b-ing** 12 kinds of fruit Rv 22:2

BEARD
shaved off half their **b-s**, 2Sm 10:4
on the **b**, running down Aaron's **b**, Ps 133:2

BEAST
Four huge **b-s** came up Dn 7:3
b that comes up out of the abyss Rv 11:7
a **b** coming up out of the sea. Rv 13:1
calculate the number of the **b**, Rv 13:18
who had the mark of the **b** Rv 16:2
who accepted the mark of the **b** Rv 19:20

BEAT
saw an Egyptian **b-ing** a Hebrew, Ex 2:11
if you **b** him with a rod, Pr 23:13
gave My back to those who **b** Me, Is 50:6
will **b** their swords into plows, Mc 4:3
they spit in His face and **b** Him; Mt 26:67
to **b** Him, saying, "Prophesy!" Mk 14:65
they stopped **b-ing** Paul. Ac 21:32
or box like one **b-ing** the air. 1Co 9:26
Three times I was **b-en** 2Co 11:25

BEATING (N)
by **b-s**, by imprisonments, by riots, 2Co 6:5

BEAUTIFIED
also **b** themselves in this way, 1Pt 3:5

BEAUTIFUL
daughters of mankind were **b**, Gn 6:2
know what a **b** woman you are. Gn 12:11
Now the girl was very **b**, Gn 24:16
Rebekah, for she is a **b** woman. Gn 26:7
but Rachel was shapely and **b**. Gn 29:17
when she saw that he was **b**, Ex 2:2
woman was intelligent and **b**, 1Sm 25:3
Let a search be made for **b** young Est 2:2
praise from the upright is **b**. Ps 33:1
How **b** you are, my darling. Sg 1:15; 4:1
How **b** on the mountains are Is 52:7
which appear **b** on the outside, Mt 23:27
used to sit and beg at the **B** Gate Ac 3:10

BEAUTY
gazing on the **b** of the LORD Ps 27:4
Zion, the perfection of **b**, Ps 50:2
Don't lust in your heart for her **b** Pr 6:25
is deceptive and **b** is fleeting, Pr 31:30
a crown of **b** instead of ashes, Is 61:3
you declared: I am perfect in **b**. Ezk 27:3
b should not consist of outward 1Pt 3:3

BED
on my **b**, I meditate on You Ps 63:6
if I make my **b** in Sheol, Ps 139:8
prepare evil plans on their **b-s**! Mc 2:1
under a basket or under a **b**? Mk 4:21
I have gone to **b**. I can't get up Lk 11:7
be in one **b**: One will be taken Lk 17:34
the marriage **b** kept undefiled, Heb 13:4

BEE
b-s with honey in the carcass. Jdg 14:8

BEELZEBUL
if I drive out demons by **B**, Mt 12:27

BEER
he is to abstain from wine and **b**. Nm 6:3
eat bread or drink wine or **b** Dt 29:6
Wine is a mocker, **b** is a brawler, Pr 20:1
or for rulers to desire **b**. Pr 31:4
Give **b** to one who is dying Pr 31:6
in the morning in pursuit of **b**, Is 5:11
who are fearless at mixing **b**, Is 5:22
they stagger, but not with **b**. Is 29:9
preach to you about wine and **b**, Mc 2:11
will never drink wine or **b**. Lk 1:15

BEER-SHEBA
place was called **B** because Gn 21:31
Abraham settled in **B**. Gn 22:19
All the Israelites from Dan to **B** Jdg 20:1
throne of David ... from Dan to **B**. 2Sm 3:10

BEFORE
B a word is on my tongue, Ps 139:4
No god was formed **b** Me, Is 43:10
Even **b** they call, I will answer; Is 65:24
messenger ... clear the way **b** Me. Mal 3:1
Father knows ... **b** you ask Him. Mt 6:8
B the rooster crows twice, Mk 14:72
B Philip called you, Jn 1:48
B Abraham was, I am. Jn 8:58
who for the joy that lay **b** Him Heb 12:2

BEG
At that time I **b-ged** the LORD: Dt 3:23
or his children **b-ging** for bread. Ps 37:25
b-ging him, 'Be patient with me Mt 18:29
I'm ashamed to **b**. Lk 16:3
Isn't this the man who sat **b-ging**? Jn 9:8

BEGGAR
a blind **b**, was sitting by Mk 10:46
formerly had seen him as a **b** Jn 9:8

BEGINNING
In the **b** God created the heavens Gn 1:1
of the LORD is the **b** of wisdom; Ps 111:10
of the LORD is the **b** of knowledge; Pr 1:7
The LORD made me at the **b** Pr 8:22
of the LORD is the **b** of wisdom, Pr 9:10
of a matter is better than its **b**; Ec 7:8
I declare the end from the **b**, Is 46:10
The **b** of the gospel of Jesus Mk 1:1
In the **b** was the Word, Jn 1:1
What was from the **b**, 1Jn 1:1
as you have heard it from the **b**: 2Jn 6
Omega, the **B** and the End. Rv 21:6

BEHEADED
had John **b** in the prison. Mt 14:10
"I **b** John," Herod said, Lk 9:9
b because of their testimony Rv 20:4

BEHEMOTH
Look at **B**, which I made Jb 40:15

BEHIND
told Peter, "Get **b** Me, Satan! Mt 16:23
Forgetting what is **b** Php 3:13

BEING
the man became a living **b**. Gn 2:7
Adam became a living **b**; 1Co 15:45

BELIEVE
Abram **b-d** the LORD, Gn 15:6
they did not **b** God or rely on Ps 78:22
inexperienced one **b-s** anything, Pr 14:15
one who **b-s** will be unshakable. Is 28:16
Who has **b-d** what we have heard? Is 53:1
Do you **b** that I can do this? Mt 9:28
of these little ones who **b** in Me Mt 18:6
if you **b**, you will receive Mt 21:22
or, 'Over here!' do not **b** it! Mt 24:23
Repent and **b** in the good news! Mk 1:15
is possible to the one who **b-s**. Mk 9:23
I do **b**! Help my unbelief. Mk 9:24
not doubt in his heart, but **b-s** Mk 11:23
b that you have received them, Mk 11:24
Don't be afraid. Only **b**, Lk 8:50
slow you are to **b** in your hearts Lk 24:25
so that all might **b** through him. Jn 1:7
so that everyone who **b-s** in Him Jn 3:16
if you **b-d** Moses, you would **b** Jn 5:46
you **b** in the One He has sent. Jn 6:29
b-s in Me will ever be thirsty Jn 6:35
who sees the Son and **b-s** in Him Jn 6:40
Anyone who **b-s** has eternal life. Jn 6:47
who **b-s** in Me, as the Scripture Jn 7:38
you don't **b** Me, **b** the works. Jn 10:38
b-s in Me will never die Jn 11:26
Lord, who has **b-d** our message? Jn 12:38
B in God; **b** also in Me. Jn 14:1
B Me that I am in the Father Jn 14:11
By this we **b** that You came Jn 16:30
world may **b** You sent Me. Jn 17:21
entered the tomb, saw, and **b-d**. Jn 20:8
seen Me, you have **b-d**. Those who
b without seeing are blessed. Jn 20:29
written so that you may **b** Jn 20:31
by **b-ing** you may have life Jn 20:31
appointed to eternal life **b-d**. Ac 13:48
B on the Lord Jesus, Ac 16:31
but others did not **b**. Ac 28:24
salvation to everyone who **b-s**, Rm 1:16
in Jesus Christ, to all who **b**, Rm 3:22
Abraham **b-d** God, and it was Rm 4:3
the father of all who **b** Rm 4:11
b in your heart that God raised Rm 10:9
b-s with the heart, resulting in Rm 10:10
call on Him they have not **b-d** in?
And how can they **b** without Rm 10:14
who has **b-d** our message? Rm 10:16
b-s all things, hopes all things, 1Co 13:7
unless you **b-d** for no purpose. 1Co 15:2
I **b-d**, therefore I spoke, 2Co 4:13
Just as Abraham **b-d** God, and it Gl 3:6
Since we **b** that Jesus died and 1Th 4:14
b-d on in the world, taken up 1Tm 3:16
especially of those who **b**. 1Tm 4:10
I know the One I have **b-d** in 2Tm 1:12
must **b** that He exists Heb 11:6
You **b** that God is one; ... The
demons also **b** Jms 2:19
Abraham **b-d** God, and it was Jms 2:23
not seeing Him now, you **b** 1Pt 1:8
do not **b** every spirit, but test 1Jn 4:1
Everyone who **b-s** that Jesus is the
Messiah has been born of God, 1Jn 5:1

BELIEVER
b goes to court against **b**, 1Co 6:6
intended as a sign, not for **b-s** 1Co 14:22
what does a **b** have in common 2Co 6:15
an example to all the **b-s** 1Th 1:7

BELLY
move on your **b** and eat dust Gn 3:14
For as Jonah was in the **b** of Mt 12:40

BELONG
that **b-s** to your neighbor. Ex 20:17
hidden things **b** to the LORD our
God, but the revealed things **b** Dt 29:29
under heaven **b-s** to Me. Jb 41:11
Salvation **b-s** to the LORD; Ps 3:8
kingship **b-s** to the LORD; Ps 22:28
the leaders of the earth **b** to God; Ps 47:9
for all the nations **b** to You. Ps 82:8
Look, every life **b-s** to Me. Ezk 18:4
forgiveness **b** to the Lord our God Dn 9:9
you may **b** to another—to Him Rm 7:4
to them **b** the adoption, the glory Rm 9:4
we live or die, we **b** to the Lord. Rm 14:8
you **b** to Christ, and Christ **b-s** to 1Co 3:23
I don't **b** to the body, 1Co 12:15
if they had **b-ed** to us, they would
have remained with us. 1Jn 2:19
Salvation **b-s** to our God, Rv 7:10

BELOVED
The LORD's **b** rests securely Dt 33:12
This is My **b** Son. I take delight Mt 3:17
My **b** in whom My soul delights; Mt 12:18
I will send my **b** son. Lk 20:13
This is My **b** Son. I take delight 2Pt 1:17

BELSHAZZAR
King of Babylon (Dn 5; 7:1; 8:1).

BELT
his sword, his bow, and his **b**. 1Sm 18:4
a leather **b** around his waist. 2Kg 1:8
with a leather **b** around his waist, Mt 3:4
took Paul's **b**, tied his own feet Ac 21:11
with truth like a **b** around your Eph 6:14

BELTESHAZZAR
Daniel's Babylonian name (Dn 1:7).

BENAIAH
Heroic warrior in charge of David's bodyguard (2Sm 8:18; 20:23; 23:20-23). Loyal to Solomon (1Kg 1; 4:4); executed Adonijah, Joab, and Shimei (2:25-46).

BENEFICIAL
but godliness is **b** in every way, 1Tm 4:8

BENEFIT
and do not forget all His **b-s**. Ps 103:2
Whatever **b** you might have Mt 15:5
What will it **b** a man if he gains Mt 16:26

you have **b-ed** from their labor. Jn 4:38
It is for your **b** that I go away, Jn 16:7
what is the **b** of circumcision? Rm 3:1
Christ will not **b** you at all. Gl 5:2

BEN-HADAD
1. King of Aram in Asa's time (1Kg 15:18-20; 2Ch 16:2-4).
2. King of Aram in Ahab's time (1Kg 20; 2Kg 6:24; 8:7-13).
3. King of Aram in Jehoash's time (2Kg 13:24-25).

BENJAMIN
Second son of Rachel, twelfth son of Jacob (Gn 35:17-18,24). Tribe with the smallest territory; Jerusalem may have originally been in it (Jos 18:16; Jdg 1:21). Nearly wiped out (Jdg 20–21). Saul and Paul were Benjaminites (1Sm 9:1; Rm 11:1; Php 3:5).

BERNICE
Wife of Agrippa (Ac 25:13,23; 26:30).

BEREA
sent Paul and Silas off to **B**. Ac 17:10

BESIDES
not have other gods **b** Me. Ex 20:3; Dt 5:7
no Savior exists **b** Me. Hs 13:4

BEST
He chose the **b** part for himself, Dt 33:21
spared ... the **b** of the sheep, 1Sm 15:9
don't recline at the **b** place, Lk 14:8

BETHANY
to **B**, and spent the night there. Mt 21:17
He led them out as far as **B**, Lk 24:50
in **B** ... where John was baptizing. Jn 1:28
Lazarus, from **B**, Jn 11:1
came to **B** where Lazarus was, Jn 12:1

BETHEL
east of **B** and pitched his tent, Gn 12:8
and named the place **B**, Gn 28:19
He set up one in **B**, 1Kg 12:29

BETHLEHEM
B Ephrathah, you are small Mc 5:2
After Jesus was born in **B** Mt 2:1
city of David, which is called **B**, Lk 2:4
Let's go straight to **B** and see Lk 2:15

BETRAY
have finished **b-ing**, they will **b** you. Is 33:1
Brother will **b** brother to death, Mt 10:21
a good opportunity to **b** Him. Mt 26:16
One of you will **b** Me. Mt 26:21
that man by whom He is **b-ed**! Lk 22:22
b-ing the Son of Man with a kiss Lk 22:48
He knew who would **b** Him. Jn 13:11
who is the one that's going to **b** Jn 21:20
the night when He was **b-ed**, 1Co 11:23

BETTER
to obey is **b** than sacrifice, 1Sm 15:22
Your faithful love is **b** than life. Ps 63:3
B a little with the fear of Pr 15:16
B a meal of vegetables where Pr 15:17
B a dry crust with peace Pr 17:1
B a poor man ... with integrity Pr 19:1
B to live on the corner of a roof Pr 21:9
B to live in a wilderness Pr 21:19
B an open reprimand Pr 27:5
b a neighbor nearby Pr 27:10
nothing **b** for man than to eat, Ec 2:24
B one handful with rest Ec 4:6
Two are **b** than one Ec 4:9
B that you do not vow Ec 5:5
good name is **b** than fine perfume Ec 7:1
The end of a matter is **b** than Ec 7:8
a live dog is **b** than a dead lion. Ec 9:4
Your love is much **b** than wine, Sg 4:10
it is **b** that you lose one of the parts Mt 5:29
b for him if a heavy millstone Mt 18:6
Are we any **b**? Not at all! Rm 3:9
it is **b** to marry than to burn 1Co 7:9
we are not **b** if we do eat. 1Co 8:8
I will show you an even **b** way. 1Co 12:31
be with Christ—which is far **b** Php 1:23
we are confident of the **b** things Heb 6:9
the guarantee of a **b** covenant. Heb 7:22
to be purified with **b** sacrifices Heb 9:23
it is **b** to suffer for doing good, 1Pt 3:17

BETWEEN
hostility **b** you and the woman, and **b** your seed and her seed. Gn 3:15
torch ... **b** the divided animals. Gn 15:17
the LORD judge **b** me and you. Gn 16:5
and to discern **b** good and evil. 1Kg 3:9
passed **b** the pieces of the calf Jr 34:19
lifted me up **b** earth and heaven Ezk 8:3
you murdered **b** the sanctuary Mt 23:35
distinction **b** Jew and Greek, Rm 10:12
one mediator **b** God and humanity, 1Tm 2:5

BEWARE
b of the yeast of the Pharisees Mt 16:6
B of the scribes ... in long robes Lk 20:46

BEYOND
not too difficult or **b** your reach. Dt 30:11
b these, my son, be warned: Ec 12:12
Nothing **b** what is written. 1Co 4:6
tempted **b** what you are able, 1Co 10:13
able to do above and **b** all Eph 3:20
in Christ's teaching, but goes **b** it, 2Jn 9

BILHAH
Rachel's slave, mother of Dan and Naphtali (Gn 30:1-7).

BIND
He **bound** his son Isaac Gn 22:9
her vows are **b-ing**, Nm 30:7
B them as a sign on your hand Dt 6:8
b them as a sign on your hands, Dt 11:18
For He crushes but also **b-s** up; Jb 5:18
and **b-s** up their wounds. Ps 147:3
Always **b** them to your heart; Pr 6:21
B up the testimony. Is 8:16
and He will **b** up our wounds. Hs 6:1
Whatever you **b** on earth is already **bound** in heaven, Mt 16:19; 18:18
I am ready not only to be **bound** Ac 21:13
A wife is **bound** as long as 1Co 7:39
but God's message is not **bound**. 2Tm 2:9
and **bound** him for 1,000 years. Rv 20:2

BIRD
every winged **b** according to its Gn 1:21
You may eat every clean **b**, Dt 14:11
b-s of the sky, and the fish of the sea Ps 8:8
in its branches the **b-s** of the air Dn 4:21
Look at the **b-s** of the sky: Mt 6:26
b-s of the sky have nests, but Mt 8:20
the **b-s** came and ate them up. Mt 13:4
worth much more than the **b-s**? Lk 12:24

BIRTH
the Rock who gave you **b**; Dt 32:18
a time to give **b** and a time to die; Ec 3:2
to a stone, "You gave **b** to me." Jr 2:27
b of Jesus Christ came about Mt 1:18
are the beginning of **b** pains. Mt 24:8
she gave **b** to her firstborn Son, Lk 2:7
a new **b** into a living hope 1Pt 1:3

BIRTHDAY
Herod's **b** celebration came, Mt 14:6

BIRTHRIGHT
First sell me your **b**. Gn 25:31
b in exchange for one meal. Heb 12:16

BIT
put **b-s** into the mouths of horses Jms 3:3

BITE
anyone who is **bitten** looks at it, Nm 21:8
In the end it **b-s** like a snake Pr 23:32
If the snake **b-s** before it is Ec 10:11
if you **b** and devour one another, Gl 5:15

BITTER
and made their lives **b** Ex 1:14
unleavened bread and **b** herbs. Ex 12:8
water at Marah because it was **b** Ex 15:23
Almighty has made me very **b**. Ru 1:20
in the end she's as **b** as wormwood Pr 5:4
wine to one whose life is **b**. Pr 31:6
who substitute **b** for sweet Is 5:20
pour out sweet and **b** water Jms 3:11

BITTERNESS
The heart knows its own **b**, Pr 14:10
All **b**, anger and wrath, Eph 4:31
that no root of **b** springs up, Heb 12:15

BLACK
the second chariot **b** horses, Zch 6:2
make a single hair white or **b**. Mt 5:36
I looked, and there was a **b** horse. Rv 6:5
the sun turned **b** like sackcloth Rv 6:12

BLAMELESS
b man You prove Yourself **b**; 2Sm 22:26
happy are those whose way is **b**, Ps 119:1
b in the day of our Lord Jesus 1Co 1:8
to be holy and **b** in His sight. Eph 1:4
so that you may be **b** and pure, Php 2:15
in the law, **b**. Php 3:6
May He make your hearts **b** 1Th 3:13
body be kept sound and **b** 1Th 5:23
b, the husband of one wife, Ti 1:6
b and with great joy, Jd 24

BLASPHEME
My name is continually **b-d** Is 52:5
He has **b-d**! Mt 26:65
He's **b-ing**! Who can forgive sins Mk 2:7
b-s against the Holy Spirit Mk 3:29
I often tried to make them **b** Ac 26:11
God is **b-d** among the Gentiles Rm 2:24
they may be taught not to **b**. 1Tm 1:20

BLASPHEMER
one who was formerly a **b**, 1Tm 1:13

BLASPHEMOUS
We heard him speaking **b** words Ac 6:11
and on his heads were **b** names. Rv 13:1

BLASPHEMY
b against the Spirit will not Mt 12:31
you've heard the **b**! Mt 26:65
stoning You ... for **b**, Jn 10:33
to speak boasts and **b-ies**. Rv 13:5

BLAZE
fire from the LORD **b-d** among Nm 11:1
mountain was **b-ing** with fire. Dt 5:23
in the morning it **b-s** like Hs 7:6

BLAZING (ADJ)
into the furnace of **b** fire. Dn 3:20

BLEMISH
he must present one without **b** Lv 3:1
offered Himself without **b** to God, Heb 9:14
a lamb without defect or **b**. 1Pt 1:19
peace with Him without spot or **b**. 2Pt 3:14

BLESS
God **b-ed** them, "Be fruitful, Gn 1:22
God **b-ed** the seventh day Gn 2:3
I will **b** you, Gn 12:2
I will **b** her; indeed, Gn 17:16
b you and make your offspring Gn 22:17
B me too, my father! Gn 27:34
let You go unless You **b** me. Gn 32:26
Yahweh **b-ed** the Sabbath day Ex 20:11
Yahweh **b** you and protect you; Nm 6:24
since He has **b-ed**, I cannot Nm 23:20
they curse, You will **b**. Ps 109:28
A generous person will be **b-ed**, Pr 22:9
b-es his neighbor with a loud Pr 27:14
the nations will be **b-ed** by Him Jr 4:2
from this day on I will **b** you. Hg 2:19
took bread, **b-ed** and broke it, Mt 26:26
He **b-ed** and broke the loaves. Mk 6:41
hands on them and **b-ed** them. Mk 10:16
b those who curse you, Lk 6:28
families of the earth will be **b-ed** Ac 3:25
B those who persecute you; **b** Rm 12:14
When we are reviled, we **b**; 1Co 4:12
nations will be **b-ed** through you. Gl 3:8
has **b-ed** us in Christ with every Eph 1:3
inferior is **b-ed** by the superior. Heb 7:7

BLESSED (ADJ)
You will be **b** in the city
and **b** in the country. Dt 28:3
May you be **b** by the LORD, Ps 115:15
He who comes in the name of
the LORD is **b**. Ps 118:26
Let your fountain be **b**, Pr 5:18
sons rise up and call her **b**. Pr 31:28
who trusts in the LORD... is **b**. Jr 17:7
The poor in spirit are **b**, Mt 5:3
He who comes in the name of
the Lord is the **b** One! Mt 21:9
You are the most **b** of women, Lk 1:42
who believe without seeing are **b**. Jn 20:29
more **b** to give than to receive. Ac 20:35
while we wait for the **b** hope Ti 2:13
A man who endures trials is **b**, Jms 1:12
for righteousness, you are **b**. 1Pt 3:14
The one who reads this is **b**, and
those who hear ... are **b**, Rv 1:3
The one who keeps the prophetic
words of this book is **b**. Rv 22:7

BLESSING (N)
you will be a **b**. Gn 12:2
deceitfully and took your **b**. Gn 27:35
set before you a **b** and a curse: Dt 11:26
He turned the curse into a **b** Dt 23:5
these **b-s** will come and overtake Dt 28:2
God turned the curse into a **b**. Neh 13:2
May the LORD's **b** be on you. Ps 129:8
B-s are on the head of the righteous, Pr 10:6
send down ... showers of **b**. Ezk 34:26
pour out a **b** for you Mal 3:10
cup of **b** that we give thanks for, 1Co 10:16
b of Abraham ... to the Gentiles Gl 3:14
blessed us ... with every spiritual **b** Eph 1:3
so that you can inherit a **b**. 1Pt 3:9
and honor and glory and **b**! Rv 5:12

BLIND (ADJ)
mute or deaf, seeing or **b**? Ex 4:11
When you present a **b** animal Mal 1:8
Woe to you, **b** guides, Mt 23:16
a **b** beggar, was sitting Mk 10:46
I was **b**, and now I can see! Jn 9:25
are wretched, pitiful, poor, **b**, Rv 3:17

BLIND (N)
block in front of the **b**, Lv 19:14
I was eyes to the **b** Jb 29:15
LORD opens the eyes of the **b**. Ps 146:8
the eyes of the **b** will be opened, Is 35:5
the **b** see, the lame walk, Mt 11:5
Can the **b** guide the **b**? Lk 6:39
you are a guide for the **b**, Rm 2:19

BLIND (V)
a bribe **b-s** the clear-sighted Ex 23:8
king of Babylon **b-ed** Zedekiah, 2Kg 25:7
deafen their ears and **b** their eyes; Is 6:10
He has **b-ed** their eyes Jn 12:40
the god of this age has **b-ed** 2Co 4:4
the darkness has **b-ed** his eyes. 1Jn 2:11

BLINK
in a moment, in the **b** of an eye, 1Co 15:52

BLOCK
I will bow down to a **b** of wood. Is 44:19
became a sinful stumbling **b** Ezk 44:12
Christ crucified, a stumbling **b** 1Co 1:23

BLOOD
Your brother's **b** cries out to Me Gn 4:10
Whoever sheds man's **b**, his **b** will
be shed by man, Gn 9:6
You are a bridegroom of **b** Ex 4:25
Nile ... will turn to **b**. Ex 7:17
see the **b**, I will pass over you. Ex 12:13
This is the **b** of the covenant Ex 24:8
must not eat any fat or any **b**. Lv 3:17
life of a creature is in the **b**, Lv 17:11
a man of war and have shed **b**. 1Ch 28:3
or drink the **b** of goats? Ps 50:13
land became polluted with **b**. Ps 106:38
I have no desire for the **b** of bulls, Is 1:11
hold you responsible for his **b**. Ezk 3:18
hold you responsible for his **b**. Ezk 33:8
moon to **b** before the great Jl 2:31
flesh and **b** did not reveal this Mt 16:17
this is My **b** ... the covenant; Mt 26:28
field has been called "**B** Field" Mt 27:8
sweat became like drops of **b** Lk 22:44
who were born, not of **b**, Jn 1:13
and drinks My **b** has eternal life, Jn 6:54
Hakeldama (that is, Field of **B**). Ac 1:19
and the moon to **b** before the great Ac 2:20
been strangled, and from **b**. Ac 15:20
through faith in His **b**, Rm 3:25
declared righteous by His **b**, Rm 5:9
is it not a sharing in the **b** 1Co 10:16
covenant established by My **b**. 1Co 11:25
Flesh and **b** cannot inherit 1Co 15:50
redemption in Him through His **b**, Eph 1:7
brought near by the **b** Eph 2:13
battle is not against flesh and **b**, Eph 6:12
by making peace through the **b** Col 1:20
not by the **b** of goats and calves,
but by His own **b**, Heb 9:12
without ... **b** there is no forgiveness Heb 9:22
with the precious **b** of Christ, 1Pt 1:19
b of Jesus His Son cleanses us 1Jn 1:7
One who came by water and **b**, 1Jn 5:6
set us free from our sins by His **b**, Rv 1:5
redeemed people ... by Your **b** Rv 5:9
the entire moon became like **b**; Rv 6:12
made them white in the **b** Rv 7:14
a third of the sea became **b**, Rv 8:8
conquered ... by the **b** of the Lamb Rv 12:11
He wore a robe stained with **b**, Rv 19:13

BLOODSHED
no one is guilty of **b**. Ex 22:2
b defiles the land, Nm 35:33
absolved of responsibility for **b**. Dt 21:8
the LORD abhors a man of **b** Ps 5:6
Save me from the guilt of **b**, Ps 51:14

BLOSSOM (N)
cups shaped like almond **b-s**, Ex 25:33
has budded, if the **b** has opened, Sg 7:12
their **b-s** will blow away like dust, Is 5:24

BLOSSOM (V)
sprouted, formed buds, **b-ed**, Nm 17:8
the almond tree **b-s**, Ec 12:5
Jacob will take root. Israel will **b** Is 27:6

BLOT
I will destroy them and **b** out Dt 9:14
b out all my guilt. Ps 51:9

BLOW
B the horn in Zion; sound the Jl 2:1
blew and pounded that house. Mt 7:25
The wind **b-s** where it pleases, Jn 3:8
b-n around by every wind Eph 4:14
seven trumpets prepared to **b** them. Rv 8:6

BOAST
who puts on his armor **b** like 1Kg 20:11
I will **b** in the LORD; Ps 34:2
We **b** in God all day long; Ps 44:8
The man who **b-s** about a gift Pr 25:14
Don't **b** about tomorrow, Pr 27:1
wise man must not **b** in his wisdom; Jr 9:23
the one who **b-s** should **b** in this, Jr 9:24
You who **b** in the law, Rm 2:23
one who **b-s** must **b** in the Lord. 1Co 1:31
if I give my body in order to **b** 1Co 13:3
gladly **b** ... about my weaknesses, 2Co 12:9
b about anything except the cross Gl 6:14
so that no one can **b**. Eph 2:9
it **b-s** great things. Jms 3:5

BOASTFUL
b cannot stand in Your presence; Ps 5:5
Love does not envy, is not **b**, 1Co 13:4

BOAT
they left the **b** and their father Mt 4:22
the **b** was being swamped Mt 8:24
climbing out of the **b**, Peter Mt 14:29

BOAZ
Husband of Ruth (Ru 4:13), kinsman redeemer (Ru 2:20; 3:1; 4:3-10,16-17). Ancestor of David (Ru 4:21-22; 1Ch 2:11-12) and Jesus (Mt 1:5; Lk 3:32).

BODY
one who comes from your own **b** Gn 15:4
He must not go near a dead **b** Nm 6:6
The eye is the lamp of the **b**. Mt 6:22
Don't fear those who kill the **b** Mt 10:28
Take and eat it; this is My **b**. Mt 26:26
the sanctuary of His **b**. Jn 2:21
let sin reign in your mortal **b**, Rm 6:12
rescue me from this dying **b**? Rm 7:24
present your **b-ies** as a living Rm 12:1
absent in **b** but present in spirit, 1Co 5:3
b-ies are a part of Christ's **b**? 1Co 6:15
know that your **b** is a sanctuary 1Co 6:19
This is My **b**, which is for you 1Co 11:24
the **b** is one and has many parts, 1Co 12:12
sown a natural **b**, raised a spiritual **b**. 1Co 15:44
out of the **b** and at home with 2Co 5:8
I bear on my **b** scars for the cause Gl 6:17
There is one **b** and one Spirit— Eph 4:4
to build up the **b** of Christ, Eph 4:12
their wives as their own **b-ies**. Eph 5:28
since we are members of His **b**. Eph 5:30
control his own **b** in sanctification 1Th 4:4
spirit, soul, and **b** be kept sound 1Th 5:23
bore our sins in His **b** on 1Pt 2:24

BODILY
God's nature dwells **b** in Christ, Col 2:9

BOIL (N)
festering **b-s** on man and beast Ex 9:9
infected Job with terrible **b-s** Jb 2:7

BOIL (V)
not **b** a ... goat in ... milk. Ex 23:19; Dt 14:21

BOLD
but **b** toward you when absent. 2Co 10:1
Pray that I might be **b** enough Eph 6:20

BOLDNESS
speak God's message with **b**. Ac 4:31
In Him we have **b** Eph 3:12
make known with **b** Eph 6:19
approach the throne ... with **b**, Heb 4:16

BOND
love—the perfect **b** of unity. Col 3:14

BONE
This one, at last, is **b** of my **b** Gn 2:23
not break any of its **b-s**. Ex 12:46
Joseph's **b-s**, ... were buried Jos 24:32
all my **b-s** are disjointed; Ps 22:14
b-s; not one of them is broken. Ps 34:20
jealousy is rottenness to the **b-s**. Pr 14:30
a gentle tongue can break a **b**. Pr 25:15
shut up in my **b-s**. Jr 20:9
valley; it was full of **b-s**. Ezk 37:1
the **b-s** came together, **b** to **b**. Ezk 37:7
are full of dead men's **b-s** Mt 23:27
Not one of His **b-s** will be Jn 19:36

BOOK
erase me from the **b** You have Ex 32:32
this **b** of the law and place it Dt 31:26
b of instruction must not depart Jos 1:8
I have found the **b** of the law 2Kg 22:8
Ezra read out of the **b** of the law of God every day, Neh 8:18
be erased from the **b** of life Ps 69:28
no end to the making of many **b-s**, Ec 12:12
seal the **b** until the time of Dn 12:4
that are not written in this **b**. Jn 20:30
could contain the **b-s** that Jn 21:25
whose names are in the **b** of life. Php 4:3
written in the Lamb's **b** of life. Rv 21:27

BOOTH
The Festival of **B-s** to the LORD Lv 23:34
dwell in **b-s** during the festival Neh 8:14

BORN
cursed the day he was **b**. Jb 3:1
I was guilty when I was **b**; Ps 51:5
I was **b** when there were no Pr 8:24
a child will be **b** for us, Is 9:6
LORD called me before I was **b**. Is 49:1
I set you apart before you were **b**. Jr 1:5
who has been **b** King of the Jews Mt 2:2
was **b** for you in the city of David. Lk 2:11
you must be **b** again. Jn 3:7
as to one abnormally **b**, 1Co 15:8
b of a woman, **b** under the law, Gl 4:4
was **b** according to ... the flesh, Gl 4:23
since you have been **b** again 1Pt 1:23
who loves has been **b** of God 1Jn 4:7

BORROW
When a man **b-s** an animal Ex 22:14
You will lend to many nations, but you will not **b**. Dt 28:12
wicked man **b-s** and does not repay Ps 37:21
the **b-er** is a slave to the lender. Pr 22:7
one who wants to **b** from you. Mt 5:42

BOUNDARY
move your neighbor's **b** marker, Dt 19:14
He set the **b-ies** of the peoples Dt 32:8
when I determined its **b-ies** Jb 38:10
set all the **b-ies** of the earth; Ps 74:17
You set a **b** they cannot cross; Ps 104:9
set the sand as the **b** of the sea, Jr 5:22

BOW (N)
placed My **b** in the clouds, Gn 9:13
arms can bend a **b** of bronze. 2Sm 22:35
I do not trust in my **b**, Ps 44:6
bent their tongues like their **b-s**; Jr 9:3

BOW (V)
May ... nations **b** down to you. Gn 27:29
and **b-ed** down to my sheaf. Gn 37:7
knee that has not **b-ed** to Baal 1Kg 19:18
Come, let us worship and **b** down; Ps 95:6
Every knee will **b** to Me, Is 45:23
coastlands of the nations will **b** Zph 2:11
every knee will **b** to Me, Rm 14:11
name of Jesus every knee will **b** Php 2:10

BOWL
the gold **b** is broken, Ec 12:6
one who dipped his hand with Me in the **b** Mt 26:23
the seven **b-s** of God's wrath Rv 16:1

BOX
or **b** like one beating the air. 1Co 9:26

BOY
some small **b-s** came out 2Kg 2:23
b here who has five barley loaves Jn 6:9

BOZRAH
Edomite city (Gn 36:33; 1Ch 1:44; Is 34:6; 63:1; Jr 49:13,22; Am 1:12).

BRANCH
B of the LORD will be beautiful Is 4:2
a **b** from his roots will bear fruit. Is 11:1
raise up a Righteous **B** of David. Jr 23:5
about to bring My servant, the **B**. Zch 3:8
a man whose name is **B**; Zch 6:12
I am the vine; you are the **b-es**. Jn 15:5
root is holy, so are the **b-es**. Rm 11:16
a wild olive **b**, were grafted in Rm 11:17

BRAWLER
Wine is a mocker, beer is a **b**, Pr 20:1

BREAD
eat **b** by the sweat of your brow Gn 3:19
Festival of Unleavened **B** Ex 12:17
b of the Presence on the table Ex 25:30
man does not live on **b** alone Dt 8:3
You provided **b** from heaven Neh 9:15
I trusted, one who ate my **b**, Ps 41:9
b eaten secretly is tasty! Pr 9:17
b on the surface of the waters, Ec 11:1
tell these stones to become **b**. Mt 4:3
Man must not live on **b** alone Mt 4:4
Give us today our daily **b**. Mt 6:11
if his son asks him for **b**, Mt 7:9
took **b**, blessed and broke it, Mt 26:26
one who is dipping **b** with Me Mk 14:20
I am the **b** of life, Jn 6:35
breaking of **b**, and to the prayers. Ac 2:42
the Lord Jesus took **b**, 1Co 11:23

BREAK *SEE ALSO* BROKEN (ADJ)
I will **b** down your strong pride. Lv 26:19
I will never **b** My covenant Jdg 2:1
will **b** them with a rod of iron; Ps 2:9
a gentle tongue can **b** a bone. Pr 25:15
three strands is not easily **broken**. Ec 4:12
He will not **b** a bruised reed, Is 42:3
long ago I **broke** your yoke; Jr 2:20
where thieves **b** in and steal. Mt 6:19
He will not **b** a bruised reed, Mt 12:20
He **broke** the loaves and gave Mt 14:19
bread, blessed and **broke** it, Mt 26:26
She **broke** the jar and poured it Mk 14:3
Not only was He **b-ing** the Sabbath Jn 5:18
the Scripture cannot be **broken** Jn 10:35
they did not **b** His legs Jn 19:33
of His bones will be **broken**. Jn 19:36
broke bread from house to house Ac 2:46
Branches were **broken** off so that Rm 11:19
gave thanks, **broke** it, 1Co 11:24
is guilty of **b-ing** it all. Jms 2:10
to open the scroll and **b** its seals? Rv 5:2
war **broke** out in heaven: Rv 12:7

BREAKERS
b and Your billows swept over me Jnh 2:3

BREAST
let her **b-s** always satisfy you; Pr 5:19
Your **b-s** are like two fawns, Sg 4:5; 7:3

BREATH
breathed the **b** of life into Gn 2:7
Remember that my life is but a **b**. Jb 7:7
the **b** entered them, Ezk 37:10
gives everyone life and **b** Ac 17:25
b of life from God entered them Rv 11:11

BREATHE
b-d the breath of life into Gn 2:7
Let everything that **b-s** praise Ps 150:6
b into these slain so that they Ezk 37:9
a loud cry and **b-d** His last. Mk 15:37
He **b-d** on them and said, Jn 20:22

BRIBE
not take a **b**, for a **b** blinds Ex 23:8
no partiality and taking no **b**. Dt 10:17
Do not accept a **b**, for it blinds Dt 16:19
the one who hates **b-s** will live. Pr 15:27
a **b** destroys the mind. Ec 7:7
love graft and chase after **b-s**. Is 1:23

BRICK
They used **b** for stone Gn 11:3
require the same quota of **b-s** Ex 5:8

BRIDE
rejoices over his **b**, so your God Is 62:5
I will remove ... the voices of the groom and the **b**, Jr 7:34
the **b** her honeymoon chamber. Jl 2:16
He who has the **b** is the groom. Jn 3:29
the **b**, the wife of the Lamb. Rv 21:9

BRIDEGROOM *SEE ALSO* GROOM
You are a **b** of blood to me! Ex 4:25

BRIGHT
B eyes cheer the heart; Pr 15:30
suddenly a **b** cloud covered Mt 17:5
dressed in clean, **b** linen, Rv 15:6
the **B** Morning Star. Rv 22:16

BRIGHTER
shining **b** and **b** until midday. Pr 4:18

BRILLIANCE
I did not come with **b** of speech 1Co 2:1

BRING
brought each to the man to see Gn 2:19
b into the ark two of all Gn 6:19
LORD who **brought** you from Ur Gn 15:7
I **brought** you out of Egypt Jdg 2:1
LORD **b-s** death and gives life; 1Sm 2:6
b an offering and enter Ps 96:8
don't know what a day might **b**. Pr 27:1
I **brought** you from the ends of Is 41:9
B My sons from far away, Is 43:6
I have spoken; so I will also **b** it Is 46:11
anointed Me to **b** good news Is 61:1
about to **b** a sword against you, Ezk 6:3
will **b** you into your own land. Ezk 36:24
B the full tenth into the storehouse Mal 3:10
I did not come to **b** peace, but Mt 10:34
brought to Him all who were sick. Mt 14:35
I came to **b** fire on the earth, Lk 12:49
b in here the poor, maimed, Lk 14:21
more will their full number **b**! Rm 11:12
b them up in the training and Eph 6:4
brought nothing into the world, 1Tm 6:7

BROAD
is **b** that leads to destruction, Mt 7:13

BROKEN (ADJ) *SEE ALSO* BREAK
sacrifice pleasing to God is a **b** spirit. God, You will not despise a **b** and humbled heart. Ps 51:17

BROKENHEARTED
The LORD is near the **b**; Ps 34:18
He heals the **b** and binds up Ps 147:3
He has sent Me to heal the **b**, Is 61:1

BRONZE
So Moses made a **b** snake Nm 21:9
The sky above you will be **b**, Dt 28:23
my arms can bend a bow of **b**. 2Sm 22:35
a third kingdom, of **b**, Dn 2:39

BROOD
B of vipers! Who warned you Mt 3:7

BROTHER
Am I my **b-'s** guardian? Gn 4:9
His **b-s** were jealous of him, Gn 37:11
When **b-s** ... and one of them dies without a son, Dt 25:5
pleasant it is when **b-s** live together Ps 133:1
a **b** is born for a difficult time. Pr 17:17
offended **b** is harder to reach Pr 18:19
friend who stays closer than a **b**. Pr 18:24
be reconciled with your **b**, Mt 5:24
B will betray **b** to death, Mt 10:21
If your **b** sins against you, Mt 18:15
forgive his **b** from his heart. Mt 18:35
Whoever does the will of God is My **b** and sister and mother. Mk 3:35
no one who has left house, **b-s** Mk 10:29
b of yours was dead and is alive Lk 15:32
my **b**, my own flesh and blood. Rm 9:3
if food causes my **b** to fall, 1Co 8:13
but warn him as a **b**. 2Th 3:15
not ashamed to call them **b-s**, Heb 2:11
for sincere love of the **b-s**, 1Pt 1:22
the one who hates his **b** is in the darkness, 1Jn 2:11
lay down our lives for our **b-s**. 1Jn 3:16

BROTHER-IN-LAW
Perform your duty as her **b** Gn 38:8
Her **b** is to take her as his wife, Dt 25:5

BRUISED
He will not break a **b** reed, Is 42:3; Mt 12:20

BUD
let's see if the vine has **b-ded**, Sg 7:12
Though the fig tree does not **b** Hab 3:17

BUILD
let us **b** ourselves a city Gn 11:4
cities that you did not **b**, Dt 6:10
So he **built** it in seven years. 1Kg 6:38
He will **b** a house for Me, 1Ch 17:12
began to **b** the LORD's temple 2Ch 3:1
appointed me to **b** Him a house Ezr 1:2
Unless the LORD **b-s** a house, Ps 127:1
Wisdom has **built** her house; Pr 9:1
wise woman **b-s** her house, Pr 14:1
to tear down and a time to **b**; Ec 3:3
B houses and live in them. Jr 29:5
who **built** his house on the rock. Mt 7:24
on this rock I will **b** My church, Mt 16:18
which is able to **b** you up Ac 20:32
for his good, to **b** him up. Rm 15:2
be careful how he **b-s** on it. 1Co 3:10
pride, but love **b-s** up. 1Co 8:1
but not everything **b-s** up. 1Co 10:23
Lord gave for **b-ing** you up 2Co 10:8
built on the foundation of the apostles and prophets, Eph 2:20
to **b** up the body of Christ, Eph 4:12
rooted and **built** up in Him Col 2:7
and **b** each other up 1Th 5:11

BUILDING (N)
Do you see these great **b-s**? Mk 13:2
You are God's field, God's **b**. 1Co 3:9
we have a **b** from God, 2Co 5:1
b, being put together by Him, Eph 2:21

BUILDER
The stone that the **b-s** rejected Ps 118:22
The stone that the **b-s** rejected Mt 21:42
whose architect and **b** is God. Heb 11:10
The stone that the **b-s** rejected 1Pt 2:7

BULL
their hands on the **b-'s** head. Ex 29:10
unblemished **b** as a sin offering Lv 4:3
Many **b-s** surround me; Ps 22:12
I will not accept a **b** from Ps 50:9
Do I eat the flesh of **b-s** Ps 50:13
no desire for the blood of **b-s**, Is 1:11
impossible for the blood of **b-s** Heb 10:4

BULLY
not a **b** but gentle, 1Tm 3:3
not a **b**, not greedy for money, Ti 1:7

BURDEN (N)
bear the **b** of the people, Nm 11:17
Cast your **b** on the LORD, Ps 55:22
Day after day He bears our **b-s**; Ps 68:19
They have become a **b** to Me; Is 1:14
no longer refer to the **b** of the LORD Jr 23:36
yoke is easy and My **b** is light. Mt 11:30
You load people with **b-s** Lk 11:46
Carry one another's **b-s**; Gl 6:2

BURDEN (V)
have **b-ed** Me with your sins; Is 43:24
you who are weary and **b-ed**, Mt 11:28
I will not **b** you, 2Co 12:14
the church should not be **b-ed**, 1Tm 5:16

BURIAL
Give me a **b** site among you Gn 23:4
does not even have a proper **b** Ec 6:3
she has prepared Me for **b**. Mt 26:12

BURN
Why isn't the bush **b-ing** up? Ex 3:3
b for **b**, bruise for bruise, Ex 21:25
b-ing on the altar continually; Lv 6:13
Israel did not **b** any of the cities Jos 11:13
to **b** their sons and daughters Jr 7:31
king not to **b** the scroll, Jr 36:25
the chaff He will **b** up with fire Mt 3:12
into the fire, and they are **b-ed**. Jn 15:6
If anyone's work is **b-ed** up, 1Co 3:15
better to marry than to **b** 1Co 7:9
a third of the earth was **b-ed** up, Rv 8:7
lake of fire that **b-s** with sulfur. Rv 19:20

BURNING (ADJ)
turned from His **b** anger. Jos 7:26
my loins are full of **b** pain, Ps 38:7
in My **b** zeal I speak against Ezk 36:5

BURNT
If his gift is a **b** offering Lv 1:3

BURST
the watery depths **b** open, Gn 7:11
about to **b** like new wineskins. Jb 32:19
the new wine will **b** the skins, Lk 5:37

He fell headfirst and **b** open Ac 1:18

BURY
be **b-ied** at a ripe old age. Gn 15:15
so that I can **b** my dead. Gn 23:4
Joseph's bones ... were **b-ied** Jos 24:32
first let me go **b** my father. Mt 8:21
let the dead **b** their own dead. Mt 8:22
were **b-ied** with Him by baptism Rm 6:4
was **b-ied**, that He was raised 1Co 15:4
b-ied with Him in baptism, Col 2:12

BUSH
the **b** was on fire but was not Ex 3:2
passage about the burning **b**, Mk 12:26
in the flame of a burning **b**. Ac 7:30

BUSINESS
to mind your own **b**, 1Th 4:11
and do **b** and make a profit. Jms 4:13

BUSYBODIES
are also gossips and **b**, 1Tm 5:13

BUTTER
churning of milk produces **b**, Pr 30:33

BUY
B—and do not sell—truth, Pr 23:23
She evaluates a field and **b-s** it; Pr 31:16
b wine and milk without money Is 55:1
drove out all those **b-ing** and Mt 21:12
for you were **bought** at a price. 1Co 6:20
You were **bought** at a price; 1Co 7:23
denying the Master who **bought** 2Pt 2:1
b from Me gold refined Rv 3:18
no one can **b** or sell unless Rv 13:17

BUYER
it's worthless!" the **b** says, Pr 20:14

CAESAREA
came to the region of **C** Philippi, Mt 16:13
a man in **C** named Cornelius, Ac 10:1
Paul should be kept at **C**, Ac 25:4

CAIAPHAS
High priest, along with his father-in-law Annas, who sentenced Jesus (Mt 23:6; Lk 3:2; Jn 18:13). Spoke prophetically (Jn 11:49-52). Threatened Peter and John (Ac 4:6).

CAIN
Firstborn of Adam and Eve; crop farmer; murdered his brother; God marked and banished him (Gn 4:1-25; Heb 11:4; 1Jn 3:12; Jd 11).

CALAMITY
will laugh at your **c**. Pr 1:26
your brother in the day of his **c**; Ob 12

CALCULATE
first sit down and **c** the cost Lk 14:28
c the number of the beast, Rv 13:18

CALEB
Judahite who scouted Canaan and, along with Joshua, recommended invasion (Nm 13:30–14:38). Entered the promised land (Dt 1:36); received Hebron (Jos 14:13).

CALF
made it into an image of a **c**. Ex 32:4
Then he made two golden **c-ves**, 1Kg 12:28
bring the fattened **c** and slaughter Lk 15:23
not by the blood of goats and **c-ves** Heb 9:12

CALL
people began to **c** on the name Gn 4:26
I **c** heaven and earth as witnesses Dt 4:26
Then the LORD **c-ed** Samuel, 1Sm 3:4
I **c-ed** to the LORD in my distress; 2Sm 22:7
c on the name of your god, and I will **c** on the name of Yahweh. 1Kg 18:24
people who are **c-ed** by My name 2Ch 7:14
C on Me in a day of trouble; Ps 50:15
I **c** to You from the ends of the earth Ps 61:2
is near all who **c** out to Him, Ps 145:18
Doesn't Wisdom **c** out? Pr 8:1
Her sons rise up and **c** her blessed. Pr 31:28
Woe to those who **c** evil good Is 5:20
c to Him while He is near. Is 55:6
Even before they **c**, I will answer; Is 65:24
everyone who **c-s** on the name of Jl 2:32
I didn't come to **c** the righteous, Mt 9:13
Why do you **c** Me 'Lord, Lord,' Lk 6:46
He **c-s** his own sheep by name Jn 10:3
You **c** Me Teacher and Lord. Jn 13:13
I do not **c** you slaves anymore, Jn 15:15
those He **c-ed**, He also justified; Rm 8:30
everyone who **c-s** on the name of Rm 10:13
God's heavenly **c** in Christ Jesus. Php 3:14
God has not **c-ed** us to impurity 1Th 4:7

CALLING (N)
God's ... and **c** are irrevocable. Rm 11:29
Brothers, consider your **c**: 1Co 1:26
walk worthy of the **c** you have Eph 4:1
confirm your **c** and election, 2Pt 1:10

CALM (N)
And there was a great **c**. Mt 8:26

CALM (V)
I have **c-ed** and quieted myself Ps 131:2
a man slow to anger **c-s** strife. Pr 15:18

CAMEL
she got down from her **c** Gn 24:64
easier for a **c** to go through the eye Mt 19:24
gnat, yet gulp down a **c**! Mt 23:24

CAMP (N)
Jacob said, "This is God's **c**." Gn 32:2
outside the **c** and slaughtered Nm 19:3
go to Him outside the **c**, Heb 13:13

CAMP (V)
c around the tent of meeting Nm 2:2

CANA
a wedding took place in **C** of Galilee. Jn 2:1

CANAAN
Son of Ham, his descendants, and the land they populated (Gn 9:18-27; 10:15-19). God promised the land to Abraham (12:4-7; 17:8; Ex 6:4; 1Ch 16:15-18).

CANAANITE
"Do not marry a **C** woman." Gn 28:6
drive out the **C-s**, Amorites, Ex 33:2
so the **C-s** lived among them Jdg 1:30
a **C** woman from that region came Mt 15:22

CANAL
among the exiles by the Chebar **C**, Ezk 1:1
I was beside the Ulai **C**. Dn 8:2

CANCEL
seven years you must **c** debts. Dt 15:1

CANOPY
made darkness a **c** around Him, 2Sm 22:12
spreading out the sky like a **c**, Ps 104:2

CAPABLE
Who can find a **c** wife? Pr 31:10

CAPERNAUM
went to live in **C** by the sea, Mt 4:13
teaching in the synagogue in **C**. Jn 6:59

CAPITALS
made two **c** of cast bronze 1Kg 7:16
Strike the **c** of the pillars Am 9:1

CAPTIVE
the king of Babylon took him **c** 2Kg 24:12
took many **c-s** to Damascus. 2Ch 28:5
to the heights, taking away **c-s**; Ps 68:18
to proclaim liberty to the **c-s** Is 61:1
to proclaim freedom to the **c-s** Lk 4:18
taking every thought **c** 2Co 10:5
Be careful that no one takes you **c** Col 2:8

CAPTIVITY
returned to Jerusalem from the **c**, Ezr 3:8
those destined for **c**, to **c**. Jr 15:2
took prisoners into **c**; He gave gifts Eph 4:8
destined for **c**, into **c** he goes. Rv 13:10

CARCASS
who touches its **c** will be unclean Lv 11:39
honey from the lion's **c**. Jdg 14:9

CARE (N)
the sheep under His **c**. Ps 95:7
I was sick and you took **c** of Me; Mt 25:36
to an inn, and took **c** of him. Lk 10:34
casting all your **c** on Him, 1Pt 5:7

CARE (V)
what is man, that You **c** for him, Ps 144:3
son of man that You **c** for him? Heb 2:6
because He **c-s** about you. 1Pt 5:7

CAREFUL
be **c** not to forget the LORD Dt 6:12
Be **c** to obey all these things Dt 12:28
c not to practice your righteousness Mt 6:1
each one must be **c** how he builds 1Co 3:10
But be **c** that this right of yours 1Co 8:9
c attention, then, to how you walk Eph 5:15

CARELESS
to account for every **c** word Mt 12:36

CARMEL
gathered the prophets at Mount **C** 1Kg 18:20

CARMI
Son of Reuben (Gn 46:9; Nm 26:6).

CAROUSING
not in **c** and drunkenness; Rm 13:13

CARPENTER
Isn't this the **c-'s** son? Mt 13:55
Isn't this the **c**, the son of Mary, Mk 6:3

CARRY
I **c-ied** you on eagles' wings Ex 19:4
God **c-ied** you as a man **c-ies** his son Dt 1:31

No one but the Levites may **c** 1Ch 15:2
shepherd them, and **c** them forever. Ps 28:9
lambs in His arms and **c-ies** them Is 40:11
and He **c-ied** our pains; Is 53:4
not **c** a load ... on the Sabbath day Jr 17:22
He Himself ... **c-ied** our diseases. Mt 8:17
Don't **c** a money-bag, traveling bag, Lk 10:4
will not **c** out the desire of the flesh. Gl 5:16
C one another's burdens; Gl 6:2

CASE
Let Baal plead his **c** Jdg 6:32
argue my **c** before God. Jb 13:3
The first to state his **c** seems right Pr 18:17
He will take up their **c** against you. Pr 23:11
let us argue our **c** together. Is 43:26
the LORD has a **c** against His people, Mc 6:2

CAST (ADJ)
Do not make **c** images of gods Ex 34:17
his **c** images are a lie; Jr 10:14; 51:17

CAST (V)
c spells, consult a medium or Dt 18:11
Joshua **c** lots for them at Shiloh Jos 18:10
He **c** the Pur (that is, the lot) Est 9:24
they **c** lots for my clothing. Ps 22:18
C your burden on the LORD, Ps 55:22
The lot is **c** into the lap, Pr 16:33
who comes to Me I will never **c** out. Jn 6:37
they **c** lots for My clothing. Jn 19:24
c-ing all your care on Him, 1Pt 5:7
c their crowns before the throne, Rv 4:10

CATCH
your sin will **c** up with you. Nm 32:23
C the foxes for us—the little foxes Sg 2:15
now on you will be **c-ing** people! Lk 5:10
brought a woman **caught** in adultery, Jn 8:3
caught up into the third heaven 2Co 12:2
be **caught** up together with them 1Th 4:17
her child was **caught** up to God Rv 12:5

CATTLE
is Mine, the **c** on a thousand hills. Ps 50:10
and no **c** in the stalls, Hab 3:17

CAUSE (N)
For You have upheld my just **c**; Ps 9:4
have persecuted me without **c**, Ps 119:161
upholds the just **c** of the poor, Ps 140:12
Don't accuse anyone without **c**, Pr 3:30

CAUSE (V)
so that I will not **c** any pain. 1Ch 4:10
and **c-s** grass to grow on the hills. Ps 147:8
Even if He **c-s** suffering, Lm 3:32
c you to follow My statutes Ezk 36:27
whoever **c-s** the downfall of one of Mt 18:6
c one of these little ones to stumble Lk 17:2

CAVE
give me the **c** of Machpelah Gn 23:9
took refuge in the **c** of Adullam. 1Sm 22:1
Then Saul left the **c** and went on 1Sm 24:7
hid them, 50 men to a **c**, 1Kg 18:4
hid in the **c-s** and among the rocks Rv 6:15

CEASE
and day and night will not **c**. Gn 8:22
there will never **c** to be poor people Dt 15:11
sin ... by **c-ing** to pray for you 1Sm 12:23
He makes wars **c** Ps 46:9
got into the boat, the wind **c-d**. Mt 14:32
otherwise grace **c-s** to be grace. Rm 11:6

as for languages, they will **c**; 1Co 13:8

CEDAR
I am living in a **c** house while 2Sm 7:2
command that **c-s** from Lebanon be 1Kg 5:6
and grow like a **c** tree in Lebanon. Ps 92:12

CELEBRATE
c it as a festival to the LORD Lv 23:41
King David dancing and **c-ing**, 1Ch 15:29
C His works among the peoples. Is 12:4

CENSUS
Take a **c** of the entire Nm 1:2; 26:2
he had taken a **c** of the troops. 2Sm 24:10

CENTURION
a **c** came to Him, pleading with Him Mt 8:5
When the **c** saw what happened, Lk 23:47
in Caesarea named Cornelius, a **c** Ac 10:1

CEPHAS
Aramaic for "Rock"; Peter (Jn 1:42; 1Co 1:12; 3:22; 9:5; 15:5; Gl 1:18; 2:9,11,14).

CERTIFICATE
he may write her a divorce **c**, Dt 24:1
He erased the **c** of debt, Col 2:14

CHAFF
were shattered and became like **c** Dn 2:35
But the **c** He will burn up with fire Mt 3:12

CHAIN
and broke their **c-s** apart. Ps 107:14
the **c-s** fell off his wrists. Ac 12:7
For this I am an ambassador in **c-s**. Eph 6:20
to be kept in **c-s** of darkness 2Pt 2:4
a great **c** in his hand. Rv 20:1

CHALDEA
Another name for the Babylonian empire (Jr 51:24; Ezk 12:13; 23:15).

CHALDEAN
Inhabitants of Chaldea (Gn 11:28). Known as sages or magicians (Dn 2:2; 4:7). Took Judah into exile (2Kg 25; 2Ch 36:17-19; Ezr 5:12; Jr 32).

CHAMBER
a groom coming from the bridal **c**; Ps 19:5
the king would bring me to his **c-s**. Sg 1:4

CHAMPION
a **c** named Goliath, from Gath, 1Sm 17:4

CHANCE
time and **c** happen to all of them. Ec 9:11

CHANGE
c-d my wages 10 times. Gn 31:7
or a son of man who **c-s** His mind Nm 23:19
does not lie or **c** His mind, 1Sm 15:29
You will **c** them like a garment, Ps 102:26
if you really **c** your ways Jr 7:5
Can the Cushite **c** his skin, Jr 13:23
Because I, Yahweh, have not **c-d**, Mal 3:6
but we will all be **c-d**, 1Co 15:51
and they will be **c-d** like a robe. Heb 1:12
and He will not **c** His mind, Heb 7:21

CHANGERS
He overturned the money **c'** tables Mt 21:12

CHANNEL
Who cuts a **c** for the flooding rain Jb 38:25

CHARACTER
you are a woman of noble **c**. Ru 3:11
c, and proven **c** produces hope. Rm 5:4

CHARGE (N)
Joseph was in **c** of the country; Gn 42:6
Above His head they put up the **c** Mt 27:37
that they could find a **c** against Him. Lk 6:7
the gospel and offer it free of **c** 1Co 9:18

CHARGE (V)
Do not **c** your brother interest Dt 23:19
man the Lord will never **c** with sin! Rm 4:8
I solemnly **c** you before God 1Tm 5:21
c-ing them before God not to fight 2Tm 2:14
c that to my account. Phm 18

CHARIOT
came back and covered the **c-s** Ex 14:28
even though they have iron **c-s** Jos 17:18
because those people had iron **c-s**. Jdg 1:19
because Jabin had 900 iron **c-s**, Jdg 4:3
Solomon accumulated 1,400 **c-s** 1Kg 10:26
a **c** of fire with horses of fire 2Kg 2:11
covered with horses and **c-s** of fire 2Kg 6:17
Some take pride in **c-s**, Ps 20:7
God's **c-s** are tens of thousands, Ps 68:17
making the clouds His **c**, Ps 104:3
saw four **c-s** coming Zch 6:1
I will cut off the **c** from Ephraim Zch 9:10

CHARITY
doing good works and acts of **c**. Ac 9:36
your acts of **c** have come up Ac 10:4

CHARM
C is deceptive and beauty is Pr 31:30

CHARMED
If the snake bites before it is **c**, Ec 10:11

CHASE
whoever **c-s** fantasies lacks sense. Pr 12:11

CHEAT
c-ed me and changed my wages Gn 31:7
Why not rather be **c-ed**? 1Co 6:7

CHEEK
My **c-s** to those who tore out My Is 50:6
Let him offer his **c** to the one Lm 3:30
if anyone slaps you on your right **c**, Mt 5:39

CHEERFUL
God loves a **c** giver. 2Co 9:7

CHEMOSH
Moab's god (Jdg 11:24; 1Kg 11:7,33).

CHERUB
Make one **c** at one end and Ex 25:19
He rode on a **c** and flew, 2Sm 22:11
The first **c-'s** height was 15 feet 1Kg 6:26
the first face was that of a **c**, Ezk 10:14

CHERUBIM
stationed the **c** and the flaming, Gn 3:24
he made two **c** 15 feet high 1Kg 6:23
You who sit enthroned on the **c**, Ps 80:1
four wheels beside the **c**, Ezk 10:9

CHEST
righteousness like armor on your **c**, Eph 6:14
armor of faith and love on our **c-s**, 1Th 5:8

CHICKS
as a hen gathers her **c** Mt 23:37; Lk 13:34

CHIEF
the **c-s** of David's warriors 1Ch 11:10
rejected by the elders, the **c** priests, Mk 8:31
when the **c** Shepherd appears, 1Pt 5:4

CHILD
quieted myself like a little weaned **c** Ps 131:2
For a **c** will be born for us, Is 9:6
and a **c** will lead them. Is 11:6
Can a woman forget her nursing **c**, Is 49:15
When Israel was a **c**, I loved him, Hs 11:1
Then He called a **c** to Him Mt 18:2
When I was a **c**, I spoke like a **c**, 1Co 13:11
give birth he might devour her **c**. Rv 12:4

CHILDBEARING
But she will be saved through **c**, 1Tm 2:15

CHILDISH
a man, I put aside **c** things. 1Co 13:11

CHILDLESS
I am **c** and the heir of my house is Gn 15:2
No woman will miscarry or be **c** Ex 23:26
who is **c** gives birth to seven, 1Sm 2:5
Rejoice, **c** one, Is 54:1
Rejoice, **c** woman, Gl 4:27

CHILDREN
you will bear **c** in anguish. Gn 3:16
When your **c** ask you, Ex 12:26
punishing the **c** for the fathers' sin, Ex 20:5
Teach them to your **c**, Dt 11:19
Fathers are not to be put to death for their **c** or **c** for their fathers; Dt 24:16
In the future, when your **c** ask you, Jos 4:6
a stronghold from the mouths of **c** Ps 8:2
Rachel weeping for her **c**, refusing to be comforted for her **c** because Jr 31:15
and the **c-'s** teeth are set on edge. Jr 31:29
and the **c-'s** teeth are set on edge Ezk 18:2
c for Abraham from these stones! Mt 3:9
how to give good gifts to your **c**, Mt 7:11
are converted and become like **c**, Mt 18:3
from the mouths of **c** and Mt 21:16
Let the little **c** come to Me. Mk 10:14
C will rise up against parents Mk 13:12
women without **c**, ... are fortunate! Lk 23:29
gave them the right to be **c** of God, Jn 1:12
testifies ... that we are God's **c**, Rm 8:16
C, obey your parents as ... the Lord, Eph 6:1
C, obey your parents in everything, Col 3:20
Fathers, do not exasperate your **c**, Col 3:21
managing their **c** and their own 1Tm 3:12
that we should be called God's **c**. 1Jn 3:1

CHINNERETH
Another name for the Sea of Galilee (Nm 34:11; Jos 13:27) and a city there (Jos 19:35).

CHOICE
I am offering you three **c-s**. 2Sm 24:12

CHOOSE *SEE ALSO* CHOSEN (ADJ)
Lot **chose** the entire Jordan Valley Gn 13:11
He will let the one He **c-s** come Nm 16:5
He **chose** their descendants Dt 4:37
LORD ... **chose** you, not because Dt 7:7
the place Yahweh your God **c-s** Dt 12:5
C life so that you Dt 30:19
c for yourselves today the one Jos 24:15
who **chose** me over your father 2Sm 6:21
the LORD has **chosen** Zion; Ps 132:13
A good name is to be **chosen** over Pr 22:1
servant, Jacob, whom I have **chosen**, Is 41:8
I **chose** you before I formed you Jr 1:5
are invited, but few are **chosen**. Mt 22:14
and He **chose** 12 of them Lk 6:13
You did not **c** Me, but I **chose** you. Jn 15:16
a remnant **chosen** by grace. Rm 11:5
He **chose** us in Him, before the Eph 1:4

CHOSEN (ADJ)
this is My **C** One; I delight in Him. Is 42:1
This is My Son, the **C** One; Lk 9:35
God's **c** ones, holy and loved, Col 3:12
a **c** and honored cornerstone, 1Pt 2:6
you are a **c** race, a royal priesthood, 1Pt 2:9

CHRIST *SEE ALSO* MESSIAH
The birth of Jesus **C** came about Mt 1:18
Messiah is coming" (... called **C**). Jn 4:25
through faith in Jesus **C**, to all Rm 3:22
we were still sinners, **C** died for us! Rm 5:8
if we died with **C**, we believe that Rm 6:8
heirs of God and co-heirs with **C** Rm 8:17
can separate us from the love of **C**? Rm 8:35
For **C** is the end of the law Rm 10:4
who are many are one body in **C** Rm 12:5
But put on the Lord Jesus **C**, Rm 13:14
but we preach **C** crucified, 1Co 1:23
and that rock was **C**. 1Co 10:4
Imitate me, as I also imitate **C**. 1Co 11:1
C is the head of every man, 1Co 11:3
you are the body of **C**, 1Co 12:27
C died for our sins according to 1Co 15:3
also in **C** all will be made alive. 1Co 15:22
Jesus **C** as Lord, and ourselves as 2Co 4:5
is in **C**, he is a new creation; 2Co 5:17
I no longer live, but **C** lives in me. Gl 2:20
except the cross of ... Jesus **C**. Gl 6:14
into Him who is the head—**C**. Eph 4:15
just as **C** loved the church Eph 5:25
living is **C** and dying is gain. Php 1:21
considered ... a loss because of **C**. Php 3:7
C is all and in all. Col 3:11
the dead in **C** will rise first. 1Th 4:16
the coming of our Lord Jesus **C** 2Th 2:1
C ... came into the world to save 1Tm 1:15
salvation, which is in **C** Jesus, 2Tm 2:10
C also suffered for sins once for all, 1Pt 3:18
ridiculed for the name of **C**, 1Pt 4:14

CHRISTIAN
were first called **C-s** at Antioch. Ac 11:26
if anyone suffers as a "**C**," 1Pt 4:16

CHURCH
on this rock I will build My **c**, Mt 16:18
no attention to them, tell the **c**. Mt 18:17
as overseers, to shepherd the **c** Ac 20:28
the **c** that meets in their home. Rm 16:5
he who prophesies builds up the **c**. 1Co 14:4
for a woman to speak in the **c** 1Co 14:35
wife as Christ is head of the **c**. Eph 5:23
regarding zeal, persecuting the **c**; Php 3:6
the head of the body, the **c**; Col 1:18
are the angels of the seven **c-es**, Rv 1:20
to the angel of the **c** in Ephesus Rv 2:1

CIRCUMCISE
your males must be **c-d**. Gn 17:10
Abraham **c-d** him, Gn 21:4
Therefore, **c** your hearts Dt 10:16
God will **c** your heart Dt 30:6
C yourselves to the LORD; Jr 4:4
they came to **c** the child Lk 1:59
you **c** a man on the Sabbath. Jn 7:22
Unless you are **c-d** according to Ac 15:1
if ... **c-d**, Christ will not benefit you Gl 5:2
c-d the eighth day; Php 3:5

CIRCUMCISION
and **c** is of the heart Rm 2:29
c and uncircumcision mean nothing; Gl 6:15
we are the **c**, the ones who serve Php 3:3
with a **c** not done with hands, Col 2:11

CIRCUMSTANCES
learned to be content in whatever **c** Php 4:11

CISTERN
may drink water from his own **c** 2Kg 18:31
Drink water from your own **c**, Pr 5:15
dug **c-s** for themselves, cracked **c-s** Jr 2:13
Jeremiah had been put into the **c**. Jr 38:7

CITIZEN
realized Paul was a Roman **c** Ac 22:29

CITIZENSHIP
I bought this **c** for a large amount Ac 22:28
but our **c** is in heaven, Php 3:20

CITY
Lot lived in the **c-ies** of the valley Gn 13:12
give **c-ies** ... for the Levites Nm 35:2
will include six **c-ies** of refuge, Nm 35:6
Select your **c-ies** of refuge, Jos 20:2
gave the Levites these **c-ies** Jos 21:3
and **c-ies** you did not build, Jos 24:13
which he named the **c** of David. 2Sm 5:9
unless the LORD watches over a **c**, Ps 127:1
her works praise her at the **c** gates. Pr 31:31
Say to the **c-ies** of Judah, "Here is your God!" Is 40:9
c situated on a hill cannot be hidden. Mt 5:14
I have many people in this **c**. Ac 18:10
he was looking forward to the **c** Heb 11:10
we do not have an enduring **c** Heb 13:14
saw the Holy **C**, new Jerusalem, Rv 21:2

CLAIM
rose up, **c-ing** to be somebody, Ac 5:36
while **c-ing** to be somebody great. Ac 8:9
C-ing to be wise, ... became fools Rm 1:22

CLAN
small among the **c-s** of Judah; Mc 5:2

CLANGING
a sounding gong or a **c** cymbal. 1Co 13:1

CLAP
C your hands, all you peoples; Ps 47:1
Let the rivers **c** their hands; Ps 98:8
trees of the field will **c** their Is 55:12

CLAY
strength is dried up like baked **c**; Ps 22:15
out of the muddy **c**, and set my feet Ps 40:2
Does **c** say to the one forming it, Is 45:9
we are the **c**, and You are our potter; Is 64:8
Just like **c** in the potter's hand, Jr 18:6
partly iron and partly fired **c**. Dn 2:33

has the potter no right over the **c**, Rm 9:21
Now we have this treasure in **c** jars, 2Co 4:7

CLEAN
of all the **c** animals, and two Gn 7:2
The one who has **c** hands and a Ps 24:4
with hyssop, and I will be **c**; Ps 51:7
create a **c** heart for me and Ps 51:10
You can make me **c**. Mt 8:2
You **c** the outside of the cup and Mt 23:25
He made all foods **c**. Mk 7:19
You are **c**, but not all of you. Jn 13:10
You are already **c** because of the Jn 15:3
God has made **c**, you must not Ac 10:15

CLEANSE
my guilt and **c** me from my sin. Ps 51:2
holy, **c-ing** her with the washing Eph 5:26
to **c** for Himself a people Ti 2:14
C your hands, sinners, and Jms 4:8
Jesus His Son **c-s** us from all sin 1Jn 1:7
to **c** us from all unrighteousness 1Jn 1:9

CLEAR
and he will **c** the way before Me Mal 3:1
and He will **c** His threshing Mt 3:12
best to have a **c** conscience Ac 24:16
the faith with a **c** conscience. 1Tm 3:9
keeping your conscience **c**, 1Pt 3:16

CLEVER
not with **c** words, so that 1Co 1:17

CLIFF
your nest is set in the **c-s**. Nm 24:21

CLIMB
I will **c** the palm tree and take Sg 7:8
he **c-ed** up a sycamore tree to see Lk 19:4
by the door but **c-s** in some other Jn 10:1

CLING
"Don't **c** to Me," Jesus told her Jn 20:17
Detest evil; **c** to what is good. Rm 12:9

CLOAK
Put your hand inside your **c**. Ex 4:6
neighbor's **c** as collateral, Ex 22:26
Spread your **c** over me, for you Ru 3:9
Wrap your **c** around you, Ac 12:8
bring the **c** I left in Troas with 2Tm 4:13
You will roll them up like a **c**, Heb 1:12

CLOSE (ADV)
who stays **c-r** than a brother. Pr 18:24

CLOSE (V)
what he opens, no one can **c**; Is 22:22
who opens and no one will **c**, Rv 3:7

CLOTH
of unshrunk **c** on an old garment Mk 2:21
Him snugly in **c** and laid Him Lk 2:7
he saw the linen **c-s** lying there, Jn 20:5

CLOTHE
and **c-d** me with gladness Ps 30:11
If that's how God **c-s** the grass of Mt 6:30
I was naked and you **c-d** Me; Mt 25:36
mortal is **c-d** with immortality, 1Co 15:54
not want to be unclothed but **c-d**, 2Co 5:4
all of you **c** yourselves with humility 1Pt 5:5
a woman **c-d** with the sun, with the Rv 12:1

CLOTHES
your **c** ... did not wear out; Dt 29:5
anointed himself, changed his **c**, 2Sm 12:20
fire and his **c** not be burned? Pr 6:27
Tear your hearts, not just your **c**, Jl 2:13
And why do you worry about **c**? Mt 6:28
get in here without wedding **c**? Mt 22:12
in fine **c**, and a poor man dressed
in dirty **c** also comes in. Jms 2:2

CLOTHING
Your **c** did not wear out, and Dt 8:4
and they cast lots for my **c**. Ps 22:18
Strength and honor are her **c**, Pr 31:25
and the body more than **c**? Mt 6:25
come to you in sheep's **c** Mt 7:15
they cast lots for My **c**. Jn 19:24
But if we have food and **c**, 1Tm 6:8

CLOUD
I have placed My bow in the **c-s**, Gn 9:13
a pillar of **c** to lead them Ex 13:21
the mountain, the **c** covered it. Ex 24:15
the **c** filled the LORD's temple, 1Kg 8:10
a **c** as small as a man's hand 1Kg 18:44
Your faithfulness reaches the **c-s**. Ps 57:10
making the **c-s** His chariot, Ps 104:3
temple was filled with the **c**, Ezk 10:4
coming with the **c-s** of heaven. Dn 7:13
a bright **c** covered them, and a
voice from the **c** said: Mt 17:5
coming on the **c-s** of heaven with Mt 24:30
coming in **c-s** with great power Mk 13:26
of Man coming in a **c** with power Lk 21:27
a **c** took Him out of their sight. Ac 1:9
fathers were all under the **c**, 1Co 10:1
in the **c-s** to meet the Lord in the 1Th 4:17
have such a large **c** of witnesses Heb 12:1
He is coming with the **c-s**, Rv 1:7

CLOUDLESS
the sun rises on a **c** morning, 2Sm 23:4

COAL
will rain burning **c-s** and sulfur Ps 11:6
will heap burning **c-s** on his head, Pr 25:22
a glowing **c** that he had taken Is 6:6
be heaping fiery **c-s** on his head. Rm 12:20

COARSE
C and foolish talking Eph 5:4

COAT
let him have your **c** as well. Mt 5:40

COFFIN
and placed him in a **c** in Egypt. Gn 50:26

COHEIRS
heirs of God and **c** with Christ Rm 8:17
The Gentiles are **c**, members of Eph 3:6
them honor as **c** of the grace of 1Pt 3:7

COIN
open its mouth you'll find a **c**. Mt 17:27
Show Me the **c** used for the tax. Mt 22:19
if she loses one **c**, Lk 15:8
widow dropping in two tiny **c-s**. Lk 21:2

COLD
is like **c** water to a parched throat. Pr 25:25
just a cup of **c** water to one Mt 10:42
the love of many will grow **c**. Mt 24:12
that you are neither **c** nor hot. Rv 3:15

COLLAPSED
a great shout, and the wall **c**. Jos 6:20
pounded that house, and it **c**. Mt 7:27

COLLECT
Don't **c** for yourselves treasures Mt 6:19
Don't **c** any more than what you Lk 3:13

COLLECTION
Now about the **c** for the saints: 1Co 16:1

COLLECTOR
even the tax **c-s** do the same? Mt 5:46
Thomas and Matthew the tax **c**; Mt 10:3
a friend of tax **c-s** and sinners! Mt 11:19
let him be like ... a tax **c** to you. Mt 18:17
Tax **c-s** and prostitutes are entering Mt 21:31
Tax **c-s** also came to be baptized, Lk 3:12
a Pharisee and the other a tax **c**. Lk 18:10
chief tax **c**, and he was rich. Lk 19:2

COLORS
made a robe of many **c** for him. Gn 37:3

COLT
on a donkey, on a **c**, the foal of Zch 9:9
a donkey, even on a **c**, the foal Mt 21:5
sitting on a donkey's **c**. Jn 12:15

COME
who **c-s** in the name of the LORD Ps 118:26
Your kingdom **c**. Your will be Mt 6:10
to another, '**C**!' and he **c-s** Mt 8:9
Are You the One who is to **c**, Mt 11:3
who **c-s** in the name of the Lord Mt 21:9
Father gives Me will **c** to Me, Jn 6:37
No one **c-s** to the Father except Jn 14:6
who is, who was, and who is **c-ing**; Rv 1:4
Spirit and the bride say, "**C**! Rv 22:17
one who is thirsty should **c**. Rv 22:17
Amen! **C**, Lord Jesus! Rv 22:20

COMFORT (N)
This is my **c** in my affliction: Ps 119:50
it is for your **c** and salvation; 2Co 1:6

COMFORT (V)
rod and Your staff—they **c** me. Ps 23:4
LORD, have helped and **c-ed** me. Ps 86:17
they have no one to **c** them. Ec 4:1
"**C**, **c** My people," says your God. Is 40:1
For the LORD has **c-ed** His people, Is 49:13
I—I am the One who **c-s** you. Is 51:12
refusing to be **c-ed** for her Jr 31:15
blessed, for they will be **c-ed**. Mt 5:4
able to **c** those who are in any kind
of affliction, through the **c** we 2Co 1:4

COMFORTERS
You are all miserable **c**. Jb 16:2
I waited ... for **c**, but found no one. Ps 69:20

COMING
can endure the day of His **c**? Mal 3:2
what is sign of Your **c** and of the Mt 24:3
still alive at the Lord's **c** 1Th 4:15
Now concerning the **c** of our Lord 2Th 2:1
be patient until the Lord's **c**. Jms 5:7
Where is the promise of His **c**? 2Pt 3:4

COMMAND (N)
who love Him and keep His **c-s**. Dt 7:9
the **c** of the LORD is radiant, Ps 19:8
I love Your **c-s** more than gold, Ps 119:127
but let your heart keep my **c-s**; Pr 3:1

who respects a **c** will be rewarded. Pr 13:13
least of these **c-s** and teaches Mt 5:19
teaching as doctrines the **c-s** of men. Mt 15:9
the greatest and most important **c.** Mt 22:38
Disregarding the **c** of God, Mk 7:8
I give you a new **c:** Jn 13:34
love Me, you will keep My **c-s.** Jn 14:15
If you keep My **c-s** you will remain Jn 15:10
This is My **c**: Love one another Jn 15:12
I write to you is the Lord's **c.** 1Co 14:37
I am not writing you a new **c** 1Jn 2:7
Now this is His **c**: that we 1Jn 3:23
love for God is: to keep His **c-s.**
Now His **c-s** are not a burden, 1Jn 5:3
saints, who keep God's **c-s** Rv 14:12

COMMAND (V)

the tree about which I **c-ed** you, Gn 3:17
everything that God had **c-ed** him. Gn 6:22
You must say whatever I **c** you; Ex 7:2
not add anything to what I **c** you Dt 4:2
so that you may **c** your children Dt 32:46
you have **c-ed** us we will do, Jos 1:16
He **c-ed**, and it came into existence Ps 33:9
for He **c-ed**, and they were created. Ps 148:5
everything I have **c-ed** you. Mt 28:20
as the Father **c-ed** Me, so I do. Jn 14:31
God ... **c-s** all people everywhere Ac 17:30
love one another as He **c-ed** us. 1Jn 3:23

COMMANDER

I have ... come as **c** of the LORD's Jos 5:14

COMMANDMENT

He wrote the Ten **C-s**, Ex 34:28
follow the Ten **C-s**, which He wrote Dt 4:13
the **c** is holy and just and good. Rm 7:12
is the first **c** with a promise Eph 6:2

COMMISSION

and **c** him in their sight. Nm 27:19
The LORD **c-ed** Joshua son of Nun, Dt 31:23

COMMIT

Do not **c** adultery. Ex 20:14; Dt 5:18
C your way to the LORD; Ps 37:5
one who **c-s** adultery lacks sense; Pr 6:32
C your activities to the LORD Pr 16:3
c-ted adultery with her in his heart. Mt 5:28
Everyone who **c-s** sin is a slave of Jn 8:34
He has **c-ted** the message ... to us. 2Co 5:19
c to faithful men who will be 2Tm 2:2
He did not **c** sin, and no deceit 1Pt 2:22

COMMON

between the holy and the **c**, Lv 10:10
and the poor have this in **c:** Pr 22:2
the oppressor have this in **c:** Pr 29:13
between the holy and the **c**, Ezk 22:26
and held all things in **c.** Ac 2:44
except what is **c** to humanity. 1Co 10:13
believer have in **c** with an 2Co 6:15

COMPANION

but a **c** of fools will suffer harm. Pr 13:20
a **c** of gluttons humiliates his father. Pr 28:7
falls, his **c** can lift him up; Ec 4:10

COMPANY

Bad **c** corrupts good morals. 1Co 15:33

COMPARE

none can **c** with You. Ps 40:5
nothing you desire **c-s** with her. Pr 3:15
nothing desirable can **c** with it. Pr 8:11
To what should I **c** this generation? Mt 11:16
What can I **c** the kingdom of God Lk 13:20
are not worth **c-ing** with the glory Rm 8:18
c-ing themselves to themselves, 2Co 10:12

COMPASSION

will have **c** on whom I will have **c.** Ex 33:19
and have **c** on His servants Dt 32:36
because of Your great **c.** Neh 9:19
according to Your abundant **c**, Ps 51:1
As a father has **c** on his children, Ps 103:13
My **c** is stirred! Hs 11:8
crowds, He felt **c** for them Mt 9:36
will have **c** on whom I will have **c.** Rm 9:15
put on heartfelt **c**, kindness Col 3:12

COMPASSIONATE

I will listen because I am **c.** Ex 22:27
the LORD your God is a **c** God. Dt 4:31
gracious and **c**, slow to anger Neh 9:17
The LORD is **c** and gracious, Ps 103:8
You are a merciful and **c** God, Jnh 4:2
And be kind and **c** to one another Eph 4:32
Lord is very **c** and merciful. Jms 5:11

COMPELS

Christ's love **c** us, since we 2Co 5:14

COMPETE

Their **c-ing** thoughts will either Rm 2:15
Now everyone who **c-s** exercises 1Co 9:25
if anyone **c-s** as an athlete, 2Tm 2:5

COMPETENCE

but our **c** is from God. 2Co 3:5

COMPETENT

not that we are **c** in ourselves 2Co 3:5
He has made us **c** to be ministers 2Co 3:6

COMPLAIN

So the people **c-ed** to Moses, Ex 17:2
All the Israelites **c-ed** about Moses Nm 14:2
Nor should we **c** as some of them 1Co 10:10
do not **c** about one another, Jms 5:9
to one another without **c-ing.** 1Pt 4:9

COMPLAINT

He has heard your **c-s** about Him. Ex 16:7
the Israelites' **c-s** that they make Nm 14:27
I will express my **c** and speak Jb 10:1
I pour out my **c** before Him; Ps 142:2
anyone has a **c** against another Col 3:13

COMPLETE (ADJ)

70 years for Babylon are **c**, Jr 29:10
So this joy of mine is **c.** Jn 3:29
in you and your joy may be **c.** Jn 15:11
that your joy may be **c.** Jn 16:24
that the man of God may be **c**, 2Tm 3:17
that you may be mature and **c**, Jms 1:4
so that our joy may be **c.** 1Jn 1:4

COMPLETE (V)

God **c-d** His work that He had done Gn 2:2
When the 70 years are **c-d**, Jr 25:12
When the 1,000 years are **c-d**, Rv 20:7

COMPLETION

carry it on to **c** until the day Php 1:6

COMPREHEND

may be able to **c** with all the Eph 3:18

CONCEAL

I did not **c** Your constant love Ps 40:10
the glory of God to **c** a matter Pr 25:2
an open reprimand than **c-ed** love. Pr 27:5
who **c-s** his sins will not prosper, Pr 28:13
For nothing is **c-ed** that won't be Lk 8:17
it was **c-ed** from them so that they Lk 9:45
use your freedom as a way to **c** evil. 1Pt 2:16

CONCEIT

So that you will not be **c-ed**, Rm 11:25
must not become **c-ed**, provoking Gl 5:26
Do nothing out of rivalry or **c**, Php 2:3
or he might become **c-ed** and fall 1Tm 3:6
he is **c-ed**, understanding nothing 1Tm 6:4

CONCEIVE

Sarai was unable to **c;** Gn 11:30
Rachel was unable to **c.** Gn 29:31
Did I **c** all these people? Nm 11:12
Manoah; his wife was unable to **c** Jdg 13:2
was sinful when my mother **c-d** me. Ps 51:5
The virgin will **c**, have a son Is 7:14
what has been **c-d** in her is by the Mt 1:20
You will **c** and give birth to a Lk 1:31
desire has **c-d**, it gives birth Jms 1:15

CONCERN (N)

Then I had **c** for My holy name, Ezk 36:21
have the same **c** for each other. 1Co 12:25

CONCERN (V)

master does not **c** himself with Gn 39:8
married man is **c-ed** about 1Co 7:33

CONCUBINES

He had 700 wives ... and 300 **c**, 1Kg 11:3

CONDEMN

my own mouth would **c** me; Jb 9:20
God will help me; who will **c** Me? Is 50:9
by your words you will be **c-ed.** Mt 12:37
can you escape being **c-ed** to hell? Mt 23:33
And they all **c-ed** Him Mk 14:64
does not believe will be **c-ed.** Mk 16:16
Do not **c**, and you will not be **c-ed.** Lk 6:37
"Neither do I **c** you," said Jesus Jn 8:11
He **c-ed** sin in the flesh by sending Rm 8:3
Who is the one who **c-s**? Rm 8:34
doubts stands **c-ed** if he eats, Rm 14:23
even if our conscience **c-s** us, 1Jn 3:20

CONDEMNATION

Their **c** is deserved! Rm 3:8
no **c** now exists for those in Rm 8:1
fall into the **c** of the Devil. 1Tm 3:6

CONDUCT (N)

shameful **c** is pleasure for a fool, Pr 10:23
are to be holy in all your **c;** 1Pt 1:15

CONDUCT (V)

knows how to **c** himself before Ec 6:8
you are to **c** yourselves in 1Pt 1:17
C yourselves honorably among the 1Pt 2:12

CONFESS

the live goat and **c** over it all Lv 16:21
But if they will **c** their sin Lv 26:40
person is to **c** the sin he has Nm 5:7
I will **c** my transgressions to Ps 32:5
If you **c** with your mouth, "Jesus Rm 10:9
tongue should **c** that Jesus Php 2:11
c your sins to one another and Jms 5:16
If we **c** our sins, He is faithful 1Jn 1:9

he who **c-es** the Son has the Father 1Jn 2:23
Every spirit who **c-es** that Jesus 1Jn 4:2

CONFESSION
good **c** ... in the presence of many 1Tm 6:12
let us hold fast to the **c**. Heb 4:14

CONFIDENCE
Lord God, my **c** from my youth. Ps 71:5
will be your **c** and will keep Pr 3:26
and do not put **c** in the flesh Php 3:3
So don't throw away your **c**, Heb 10:35

CONFIRM
to **c** the promises to the fathers Rm 15:8
every effort to **c** your calling 2Pt 1:10
the prophetic word strongly **c-ed**. 2Pt 1:19

CONFLICT
A hot-tempered man stirs up **c**, Pr 15:18

CONFORMED
predestined to be **c** to the image Rm 8:29
Do not be **c** to this age, but be Rm 12:2
being **c** to His death, Php 3:10
do not be **c** to the desires of 1Pt 1:14

CONFUSE
down there and **c** their language Gn 11:7

CONFUSION
So the city was filled with **c**, Ac 19:29

CONGREGATION
sing hymns to You in the **c**. Heb 2:12

CONQUER
I have **c-ed** the world. Jn 16:33
Do not be **c-ed** by evil, but **c** evil Rm 12:21
victory that has **c-ed** the world: 1Jn 5:4
he went out as a victor to **c**. Rv 6:2

CONSCIENCE
at night my **c** instructs me. Ps 16:7
a clear **c** toward God and men. Ac 24:16
Their **c-s** confirm this. Rm 2:15
but also because of your **c**. Rm 13:5
their **c**, being weak, is defiled. 1Co 8:7
of liars whose **c-s** are seared. 1Tm 4:2
cleanse our **c-s** from dead works to Heb 9:14
sprinkled clean from an evil **c** Heb 10:22
keeping your **c** clear, so that 1Pt 3:16

CONSECRATE
C every firstborn male to Me, Ex 13:2
c them to serve Me as priests. Ex 29:1
c it along with all its furnishings Ex 40:9
C yourselves and be holy, for I Lv 20:7
Joshua told the people, "**C** yourselves Jos 3:5
I have **c-d** this temple you have 1Kg 9:3
I have **c-d** My King on Zion, Ps 2:6

CONSECRATED (ADJ)
However, there is **c** bread, but 1Sm 21:4

CONSIDER
Have you **c-ed** My servant Job? Jb 1:8
Lord; **c** my sighing. Ps 5:1
Even a fool is **c-ed** wise when he Pr 17:28
C how the wildflowers grow: Lk 12:27
you too **c** yourselves dead to sin Rm 6:11
Brothers, **c** your calling: 1Co 1:26
but in humility **c** others as more Php 2:3
I also **c** everything to be a loss Php 3:8
she **c-ed** that the One who had Heb 11:11

C it a great joy, my brothers Jms 1:2

CONSISTENT
produce fruit **c** with repentance Mt 3:8

CONSOLATION
Christ, if any **c** of love, if any Php 2:1

CONSOLE
refused to be **c-d**, because they Mt 2:18

CONSPIRE
all of you have **c-d** against me! 1Sm 22:8
and the rulers **c** together Ps 2:2
they **c-d** to arrest Jesus Mt 26:4

CONSTANTLY
Pray **c**. 1Th 5:17

CONSULT
Saul said, "**C** a spirit for me. 1Sm 28:8
Rehoboam **c-ed** with the elders 1Kg 12:6
even **c-ed** a medium for guidance 1Ch 10:13
shouldn't a people **c** their God? Is 8:19
I will not be **c-ed** by you. Ezk 20:3,31
not immediately **c** with anyone. Gl 1:16

CONSUME
bush was on fire but was not **c-d**. Ex 3:2
so I may **c** them instantly. Nm 16:21
the Lord your God is a **c-ing** fire, Dt 4:24
fire fell and **c-d** the burnt offering 1Kg 18:38
zeal for Your house has **c-d** me, Ps 69:9
For we are **c-d** by Your anger; Ps 90:7
Zeal for Your house will **c** Me. Jn 2:17
for our God is a **c-ing** fire. Heb 12:29

CONTAIN
heaven, cannot **c** You, much less 1Kg 8:27
highest heaven cannot **c** Him? 2Ch 2:6
itself could **c** the books that Jn 21:25

CONTEMPT
some to shame and eternal **c**. Dn 12:2
things and be treated with **c**? Mk 9:12
treated Him with **c**, mocked Him Lk 23:11
of God and holding Him up to **c**. Heb 6:6

CONTEND
Will the one who **c-s** with the Jb 40:2
will **c** with the one who **c-s** with you Is 49:25
exhort you to **c** for the faith Jd 3

CONTENT
have learned to be **c** in whatever Php 4:11
we will be **c** with these. 1Tm 6:8

CONTENTMENT
godliness with **c** is a great gain 1Tm 6:6

CONTINUE
If you **c** in My word, Jn 8:31
persuading them to **c** in the grace Ac 13:43
Should we **c** in sin so that grace Rm 6:1
c in what you have learned 2Tm 3:14

CONTRARY
a gospel **c** to what you received, Gl 1:9
law therefore **c** to God's promises? Gl 3:21
whatever else is **c** to the sound 1Tm 1:10

CONTRIVED
we did not follow cleverly **c** myths 2Pt 1:16

CONTROL (N)
Spirit of the Lord took **c** of him, Jdg 14:6,19
Spirit of the Lord took **c** of David 1Sm 16:13
are under the **c** of the prophets 1Co 14:32
having his children under **c** 1Tm 3:4

CONTROL (V)
but the one who **c-s** his lips is wise. Pr 10:19
man who does not **c** his temper is Pr 25:28
is also able to **c** his whole body Jms 3:2

CONVENIENT
persist in it whether **c** or not; 2Tm 4:2

CONVERT
must not be a new **c**, or he might 1Tm 3:6

CONVERTED
unless you are **c** and become like Mt 18:3
understand ... and be **c** Jn 12:40; Ac 28:27

CONVICT
Who among you can **c** Me of sin? Jn 8:46
He will **c** the world about sin, Jn 16:8
he is **c-ed** by all and is judged by 1Co 14:24
c them of all their ungodly acts Jd 15

CONVICTION
that is not from a **c** is sin. Rm 14:23
same understanding and the same **c** 1Co 1:10

CONVINCED
fully **c** that what He had promised Rm 4:21
must be fully **c** in his own mind Rm 14:5

CONVINCING
alive to them by many **c** proofs, Ac 1:3

COPING
from foundation to **c** and from 1Kg 7:9

COPPER
whose hills you will mine **c**. Dt 8:9
and **c** is smelted from ore. Jb 28:2
All of them are **c**, tin, iron Ezk 22:18
gathers silver, **c**, iron, lead Ezk 22:20
it becomes hot and its **c** glows. Ezk 24:11
gold, silver, or **c** for your Mt 10:9
of cups, jugs, **c** utensils, and Mk 7:4

COPPERSMITH
blacksmiths and **c-s** to repair the 2Ch 24:12
Alexander the **c** did great harm 2Tm 4:14

COPY
These serve as a **c** and shadow of Heb 8:5
c-ies of the things in the heavens Heb 9:23

CORBAN
have received from me is **C** Mk 7:11

CORD
A **c** of three strands is not Ec 4:12
before the silver **c** is snapped, Ec 12:6
them with human **c-s**, with ropes Hs 11:4

CORINTH
left Athens and went to **C**, Ac 18:1

CORNELIUS
Centurion; Christian (Ac 10).

CORNER
cut off the **c** of Saul's robe. 1Sm 24:4
on the street **c-s** to be seen by people. Mt 6:5

since this was not done in a **c**. Ac 26:26
at the four **c-s** of the earth, Rv 7:1; 20:8

CORNERSTONE
rejected has become the **c**. Ps 118:22
a precious **c**, a sure foundation; Is 28:16
The **c** will come from Judah. Zch 10:4
builders rejected has become the **c**. Mt 21:42
This Jesus ... has become the **c**. Ac 4:11
Christ Jesus Himself as the **c**. Eph 2:20
in Zion, a chosen and honored **c**, 1Pt 2:6

CORPSE
The boy became like a **c**, Mk 9:26
he gave the **c** to Joseph. Mk 15:45
Where the **c** is, there also Lk 17:37

CORRECT
The one who **c-s** a mocker will Pr 9:7
rebuking, for **c-ing**, for training 2Tm 3:16
rebuke, **c**, and encourage 2Tm 4:2

CORRECTION
but one who hates **c** is stupid. Pr 12:1

CORRESPONDS
Hagar ... **c** to the present Jerusalem, Gl 4:25
Baptism, which **c** to this, now saves 1Pt 3:21

CORRUPT (N)
the earth was **c** in God's sight, Gn 6:11
all alike have become **c**. Ps 14:3
Be saved from this **c** generation! Ac 2:40

CORRUPT (V)
splendor you **c-ed** your wisdom. Ezk 28:17
Bad company **c-s** good morals. 1Co 15:33
prostitute who **c-ed** the earth with Rv 19:2

CORRUPTIBLE
For this **c** must be clothed with 1Co 15:53

CORRUPTION
set free from the bondage of **c** Rm 8:21
Sown in **c**, raised in 1Co 15:42
flesh will reap **c** from the flesh Gl 6:8
escaping the **c** that is in the 2Pt 1:4

COST
offerings that **c** me nothing. 2Sm 24:24
without money and without **c**! Is 55:1
calculate the **c** to see if he has Lk 14:28

COUNCIL
praise Him in the **c** of the elders. Ps 107:32
on of hands by the **c** of elders. 1Tm 4:14

COUNSEL
but did not seek the LORD's **c**. Jos 9:14
c and understanding are His. Jb 12:13
with My eye on you, I will give **c**. Ps 32:8
whoever listens to **c** is wise. Pr 12:15
Plans fail when there is no **c**, Pr 15:22
and no **c** will prevail against Pr 21:30
Has **c** perished from the prudent Jr 49:7

COUNSELOR
He leads **c-s** away barefoot and Jb 12:17
but with many **c-s** there is Pr 11:14
victory comes with many **c-s**. Pr 24:6
He will be named Wonderful **C**, Is 9:6
you another **C** to be with you Jn 14:16
But the **C**, the Holy Spirit—the Jn 14:26
When the **C** comes, the One I Jn 15:26
go away the **C** will not come to Jn 16:7

Or who has been His **c**? Rm 11:34

COUNT
c the stars, if you are able to **c** them. Gn 15:5
incited David to **c** the people 1Ch 21:1
of your head have all been **c-ed**. Mt 10:30
we are **c-ed** as sheep to be Rm 8:36
not **c-ing** their trespasses against 2Co 5:19
May it not be **c-ed** against them. 2Tm 4:16

COUNTRY
has no honor in his own **c**. Jn 4:44

COURAGE
Have **c**, son, your sins Mt 9:2
Have **c**! It is I. Don't be afraid. Mt 14:27
stood by him and said, "Have **c**! Ac 23:11

COURAGEOUS
Be strong and **c**; don't be Dt 31:6
Be strong and **c**, for you will Jos 1:6
be strong and **c**. Wait for the LORD Ps 27:14
Be **c**! I have conquered the world. Jn 16:33

COURSE
I may finish my **c** and the Ac 20:24

COURT
If one wanted to take Him to **c**, Jb 9:3
a day in Your **c-s** than a thousand Ps 84:10
an offering and enter His **c-s**. Ps 96:8
and His **c-s** with praise. Ps 100:4
Don't take a matter to **c** hastily. Pr 25:8
The **c** was convened, and the books Dn 7:10
you and drag you into the **c-s**? Jms 2:6

COURTYARD
make the **c** for the tabernacle. Ex 27:9
Peter was sitting outside in the **c**. Mt 26:69
Jesus into the high priest's **c**. Jn 18:15

COVENANT
I will establish My **c** with you, Gn 6:18
I am confirming My **c** with you Gn 9:9
the LORD made a **c** with Abram, Gn 15:18
carefully keep My **c**, Ex 19:5
will remember My **c** with Jacob. Lv 26:42
will never break My **c** with you. Jdg 2:1
book of the **c** that had been found 2Kg 23:2
Let us ... make a **c** before our God Ezr 10:3
I have made a **c** with my eyes. Jb 31:1
who keep His **c**, who remember Ps 103:18
I will make a new **c** with Jr 31:31
I will establish an everlasting **c** Ezk 16:60
Messenger of the **c** you desire Mal 3:1
This cup is the new **c** Lk 22:20
the adoption, the glory, the **c-s**, Rm 9:4
this will be My **c** with them Rm 11:27
This cup is the new **c** 1Co 11:25
to be ministers of a new **c**, 2Co 3:6
the women represent the two **c-s**. Gl 4:24
the guarantee of a better **c**. Heb 7:22
He is the mediator of a new **c**, Heb 9:15

COVER (N)
He spread a cloud as a **c-ing** Ps 105:39
hair is given to her as a **c-ing**. 1Co 11:15

COVER (V)
the rock and **c** you with My hand Ex 33:22
is forgiven, whose sin is **c-ed**! Ps 32:1
You **c-ed** all their sin. Ps 85:2
He will **c** you with His feathers Ps 91:4
but love **c-s** all offenses. Pr 10:12
with two he **c-ed** his face, with two Is 6:2

as the waters **c** the sea. Hab 2:14
and to the hills, '**C** us!' Lk 23:30
forgiven and whose sins are **c-ed**! Rm 4:7
if a woman's head is not **c-ed**, 1Co 11:6
man, in fact, should not **c** his head 1Co 11:7
and **c** a multitude of sins. Jms 5:20
since love **c-s** a multitude of sins 1Pt 4:8

COVET
Do not **c** your neighbor's Ex 20:17; Dt 5:21
shekels, I **c-ed** them and took them. Jos 7:21
I have not **c-ed** anyone's silver Ac 20:33
what it is to **c** if the law had not Rm 7:7
do not steal; do not **c**; Rm 13:9
You murder and **c** and cannot Jms 4:2

COW
seven other **c-s**, sickly and thin Gn 41:3
you **c-s** of Bashan who are on the Am 4:1

COWARDS
But the **c**, unbelievers, vile, Rv 21:8

CRAFTINESS
He traps the wise in their **c** Jb 5:13
He catches the wise in their **c** 1Co 3:19

CRAFTSMAN
I was a skilled **c** beside Him. Pr 8:30
business for the **c-men**. Ac 19:24

CRAVE
by **c-ing** it, some have wandered 1Tm 6:10

CRAVING (N)
come from the **c-s** that are at war Jms 4:1

CRAZY
the man is **c**," Achish said 1Sm 21:14
He has a demon and He's **c**! Jn 10:20

CREATE
In the beginning God **c-d** the heavens Gn 1:1
God **c-d** man in His own image; Gn 1:27
c a clean heart for me Ps 51:10
You who **c-d** my inward parts Ps 139:13
commanded, and they were **c-d**. Ps 148:5
who **c-d** the heavens and stretched Is 42:5
All things were **c-d** through Him, Jn 1:3
served something **c-d** instead Rm 1:25
man was not **c-d** for woman, 1Co 11:9
c-d in Christ Jesus for good works Eph 2:10
c in Himself one new man from Eph 2:15
everything was **c-d** by Him, Col 1:16
everything **c-d** by God is good, 1Tm 4:4
You have **c-d** all things, and because
of Your will they ... were **c-d**. Rv 4:11

CREATION
He rested from His work of **c**. Gn 2:3
the beginning of **c** God made them Mk 10:6
the gospel to the whole **c**. Mk 16:15
have been clearly seen since the **c** Rm 1:20
For the **c** eagerly waits with Rm 8:19
is in Christ, he is a new **c**; 2Co 5:17
we are His **c**, created in Christ Eph 2:10
the firstborn over all **c**. Col 1:15
been since the beginning of **c**. 2Pt 3:4

CREATOR
God Most High, **C** of heaven and Gn 14:22
So remember your **C** in the days Ec 12:1
created instead of the **C**, Rm 1:25
entrust themselves to a faithful **C**. 1Pt 4:19

CREATURE
and every living **c** that moves Gn 1:21
No **c** is hidden from Him, Heb 4:13
Every sea **c**, reptile, ... is tamed Jms 3:7
Four living **c-s** covered with eyes Rv 4:6

CREDIT (N)
what **c** is that to you? Lk 6:32
what **c** is there if you sin and 1Pt 2:20

CREDIT (V)
He **c-ed** it to him as righteousness. Gn 15:6
was **c-ed** to him as righteousness Ps 106:31
was **c-ed** to him for righteousness. Rm 4:3
God **c-s** righteousness to apart from Rm 4:6
will be **c-ed** to us who believe Rm 4:24
was **c-ed** to him for righteousness, Gl 3:6
was **c-ed** to him for righteousness Jms 2:23

CRETANS
prophets said, **C** are always Ti 1:12

CRETE
Island in the Mediterranean Sea. Paul assigned Titus as supervisor there (Ti 1:5) and moored there on his way to Rome (Ac 27).

CRIMINAL
as if I were a **c**, to capture Me Mt 26:55
Then two **c-s** were crucified with Mt 27:38
man weren't a **c**, we wouldn't Jn 18:30

CRIMSON
though they are as red as **c**, Is 1:18
from Edom in **c**-stained garments Is 63:1

CRITICIZE
why do you **c** your brother? Rm 14:10
who **c-s** a brother ... **c-s** the law Jms 4:11

CROOKED
with the **c** You prove 2Sm 22:27; Ps 18:26
What is **c** cannot be straightened Ec 1:15
out what He has made **c**? Ec 7:13
the **c** will become straight, Lk 3:5
faultless in a **c** and perverted Php 2:15

CROP
good ground and produced a **c**: Mt 13:8
have anywhere to store my **c-s**? Lk 12:17

CROSS (N)
doesn't take up his **c** and follow Mt 10:38
take up his **c** daily, and follow Lk 9:23
so that the **c** of Christ will not 1Co 1:17
message of the **c** is foolishness 1Co 1:18
except the **c** of our Lord Jesus Gl 6:14
death—even to death on a **c**. Php 2:8
through the blood of His **c** Col 1:20
joy ... before Him endured a **c** Heb 12:2

CROSS (V)
your God will **c** over ahead of you Dt 9:3

CROUCH
sin is **c-ing** at the door. Gn 4:7
He **c-es**; he lies down like a lion Gn 49:9

CROW
the rooster **c-s**, you will deny Me Mt 26:34
Immediately a rooster **c-ed**, Mt 26:74

CROWD
Large **c-s** followed Him Mt 4:25
He saw a huge **c**, felt compassion Mt 14:14
I have compassion on the **c**, Mt 15:32
him to Jesus because of the **c**, Mk 2:4
through the **c** and went on His Lk 4:30
stirred up the **c** and the city Ac 17:8

CROWN (N)
she will give you a **c** of beauty. Pr 4:9
wife is her husband's **c**, Pr 12:4
Gray hair is a glorious **c**; Pr 16:31
to give them a **c** of beauty Is 61:3
twisted together a **c** of thorns, Mt 27:29
to receive a **c** that will fade away 1Co 9:25
and longed for—my joy and **c**. Php 4:1
in the future the **c** of righteousness, 2Tm 4:8
receive the **c** of life that God Jms 1:12
the unfading **c** of glory. 1Pt 5:4
I will give you the **c** of life. Rv 2:10
cast their **c-s** before the throne, Rv 4:10
a **c** was given to him, and he Rv 6:2

CROWN (V)
than God and **c-ed** him with glory Ps 8:5
he is not **c-ed** unless he competes 2Tm 2:5
You **c-ed** him with glory and honor Heb 2:7

CRUCIFY *SEE ALSO* RECRUCIFYING
to be mocked, flogged, and **c-ied**, Mt 20:19
But they kept shouting, "**C** Him!" Mt 27:23
two criminals were **c-ied** with Him Mt 27:38
looking for Jesus who was **c-ied**. Mt 28:5
be **c-ied**, and rise on the third day Lk 24:7
to them, "Should I **c** your king? Jn 19:15
they **c-ied** Him and two others Jn 19:18
you **c-ied** and whom God raised Ac 4:10
our old self was **c-ied** with Him in Rm 6:6
preach Christ **c-ied**, a stumbling 1Co 1:23
would not have **c-ied** the Lord of 1Co 2:8
I have been **c-ied** with Christ Gl 2:19
Jesus have **c-ied** the flesh with Gl 5:24

CRUEL
merciful acts of the wicked are **c**. Pr 12:10

CRUSH
For He **c-es** but also binds up; Jb 5:18
He saves those **c-ed** in spirit. Ps 34:18
the bones You have **c-ed** rejoice. Ps 51:8
c-ed because of our iniquities; Is 53:5
the LORD was pleased to **c** Him Is 53:10
the poor and **c** the needy, Am 4:1
will soon **c** Satan under your feet. Rm 16:20
in every way but not **c-ed**; 2Co 4:8

CRY
Your brother's blood **c-ies** out Gn 4:10
difficult labor, and they **c-ied** out; Ex 2:23
Israelites **c-ied** out to the LORD. Jdg 3:9
attention to the sound of my **c**, Ps 5:2
His ears are open to their **c** for help Ps 34:15
My eyes are worn out from **c-ing**. Ps 88:9
A voice of one **c-ing** out: Is 40:3
the stones will **c** out from the wall, Hab 2:11
A voice of one **c-ing** out in the Mt 3:3
silent, the stones would **c** out! Lk 19:40
grief, **c-ing**, and pain will exist no Rv 21:4

CRYSTAL
a gleam like awe-inspiring **c**, Ezk 1:22
a sea of glass, similar to **c**, Rv 4:6

CUBIT
you add a single **c** to his height Mt 6:27

CUP
head with oil; my **c** overflows. Ps 23:5
gives just a **c** of cold water to Mt 10:42
to drink the **c** that I am about Mt 20:22
Then He took a **c**, and after Mt 26:27
let this **c** pass from Me. Mt 26:39
This **c** is the new covenant Lk 22:20
This **c** is the new covenant 1Co 11:25
full strength in the **c** of His anger. Rv 14:10

CUPBEARER
Egyptian king's **c** and baker Gn 40:1
I was the king's **c**. Neh 1:11

CURE
But he cannot **c** you or heal your Hs 5:13
and **c-d** those who needed healing. Lk 9:11

CURSE (N)
come and put a **c** on these people Nm 22:6
before you a blessing and a **c**: Dt 11:26
hung on a tree is under God's **c**. Dt 21:23
all these **c-s** will come Dt 28:15
an undeserved **c** goes nowhere. Pr 26:2
preached to you, a **c** be on him! Gl 1:8
redeemed us from the **c** of the law by becoming a **c** for us, Gl 3:13
Praising and **c-ing** come out of Jms 3:10

CURSE (V)
will never again **c** the ground Gn 8:21
I will **c** those who treat you Gn 12:3
Those who **c** you will be **c-d**, Gn 27:29
C God and die! Jb 2:9
and **c-d** the day he was born. Jb 3:1
Whoever **c-s** his father or mother Pr 20:20
he started to **c** and to swear Mt 26:74
fig tree that You **c-d** is withered. Mk 11:21
bless those who **c** you, pray for Lk 6:28
persecute you; bless and do not **c**. Rm 12:14
with it, and we **c** men who are Jms 3:9

CURSED (ADJ)
The ground is **c** because of you. Gn 3:17
I could almost wish to be **c** Rm 9:3
Everyone who is hung on a tree is **c**. Gl 3:13

CURTAIN
the **c** of the sanctuary was split Mt 27:51
opened for us through the **c** Heb 10:20

CUSTOM
it was Pilate's **c** to release for Mk 15:6
and are promoting **c-s** that are not Ac 16:21
or the **c-s** of our ancestors, Ac 28:17

CUT
right hand causes you to sin, **c** it off Mt 5:30
slave, and **c** off his right ear. Jn 18:10
you too will be **c** off. Rm 11:22

CYMBAL
Praise Him with resounding **c-s**; Ps 150:5
sounding gong or a clanging **c**. 1Co 13:1

CYRUS
King of Persia; used by God (Is 44:28; 45:1); permitted the exiles to return and rebuild the temple (2Ch 36:22—Ezr 1:8; 3:7; 4:3-5; 5:13–6:14).

DAGON
Philistine god (Jdg 16:23; 1Sm 5:2-7; 1Ch 10:10).

DAILY
Give us today our **d** bread. Mt 6:11
up his cross **d**, and follow Me. Lk 9:23

DAMASCUS
he traveled and was nearing **D**, Ac 9:3

DAN
Son of Jacob and Bilhah (Gn 30:4-6; 35:25). Tribe; unable to conquer allotted land west of Jerusalem and up the coast to Joppa; took land in the far north (Jos 19:40-48; Jdg 18). City (Jdg 18:29).

DANCE (N)
You turned my lament into **d-ing**; Ps 30:11
Praise Him with tambourine and **d**; Ps 150:4

DANCE (V)
David was **d-ing** with all his might 2Sm 6:14
time to mourn and a time to **d**; Ec 3:4
flute for you, but you didn't **d**; Mt 11:17
Herodias's daughter **d-d** Mt 14:6

DANGER
I fear no **d**, for You are with Ps 23:4
or nakedness or **d** or sword? Rm 8:35
d-s in the city, **d-s** in the open 2Co 11:26

DANIEL
1. Son of David (1Ch 3:1).
2. Prophet during the exile in Babylon. Called Belteshazzar (Dn 1:7); refused to eat the king's food (1:8-20); interpreted the king's dreams (Dn 3; 4) and the writing on the wall (Dn 5); thrown in the lion's den (Dn 6). Received visions (Dn 7–12).

DARE
someone might even **d** to die. Rm 5:7

DARIUS
1. The Mede, who conquered Babylon (Dn 5:31).
2. Darius I of Persia allowed the rebuilding of the temple (Ezr 4:5; 5–6; Hg 1:1; Zch 1:1).
3. Darius II of Persia (Neh 12:22).

DARK
the darkness is not **d** to You. Ps 139:12
have said in the **d** will be heard Lk 12:3

DARKEST
when I go through the **d** valley, Ps 23:4

DARKNESS
walking in **d** have seen a great Is 9:2
I form light and create **d**, Is 45:7
if the light within you is **d**—how deep is that **d**! Mt 6:23
shines in the **d**, yet the **d** did not Jn 1:5
and people loved **d** rather than Jn 3:19
fellowship does light have with **d**? 2Co 6:14
you were once **d**, but now Eph 5:8
called you out of **d** into His 1Pt 2:9
is absolutely no **d** in Him. 1Jn 1:5
but hates his brother is in the **d** 1Jn 2:9

DAUGHTER
the sons of God came to the **d-s** of Gn 6:4
sons and your **d-s** will prophesy, Jl 2:28
Rejoice greatly, **D** Zion! Zch 9:9
mother against **d**, **d** against mother Lk 12:53

DAVID
Youngest son of Jesse, anointed king by Samuel (Ru 4:17-22; 1Sm 16:1-13). Sought God's heart (1Sm 13:14; Ac 13:22). Killed Goliath (1Sm 17). Covenant of friendship with Jonathan (18:1-4; 19–20; 23:16-18). Spared Saul's life (1Sm 24; 26). Anointed king of Judah (2Sm 2:1-11) and Israel (5:1-4).
Conquered Jerusalem (5:6-9) and brought the ark there (2Sm 6). Was promised by God that He would keep his descendant on the throne (2Sm 7). Prepared for building the temple (1Ch 22–29). Psalmist, musician (Ps 23:1), and prophet (Mt 22:43; Ac 1:16; 4:25).
Committed adultery with Bathsheba and murdered Uriah, then was confronted by Nathan (2Sm 11–12). Family and political troubles followed: Amnon, Tamar, and Absalom (2Sm 13–18); Sheba (2Sm 20); punished for military census (2Sm 24; 1Ch 21); Adonijah and Solomon (1Kg 1–2).
Named Solomon as successor (1Kg 1:29-30). Died (2Sm 23:1-7; 1Kg 2:10-12). Ancestor of Jesus (Mt 1:1,6); Jesus is heir to his throne forever (Mt 12:23; 21:9; Mk 11:10; Lk 1:32; Rv 22:16).

DAWN (N)
righteousness shine like the **d**, Ps 37:6
appearance is as sure as the **d**. Hs 6:3

DAWN (V)
a light has **d-ed** on those living in Is 9:2
of death, light has **d-ed**. Mt 4:16

DAY
God called the light "**d**," Gn 1:5
he meditates on it **d** and night. Ps 1:2
pursue me all the **d-s** of my life, Ps 23:6
Teach us to number our **d-s** Ps 90:12
This is the **d** the LORD has made Ps 118:24
Creator in the **d-s** of your youth: Ec 12:1
can endure the **d** of His coming? Mal 3:2
that **d** and hour no one Mt 24:36
Give us each **d** our daily bread. Lk 11:3
will raise him up on the last **d**. Jn 6:40
now is the **d** of salvation. 2Co 6:2
time, because the **d-s** are evil. Eph 5:16
well that the **D** of the Lord will 1Th 5:2
entrusted to me until that **d**. 2Tm 1:12
one **d** is like a thousand years, 2Pt 3:8

DEACONS
D, likewise, should be 1Tm 3:8

DEAD
and let the **d** bury their own **d**. Mt 8:22
He is not the God of the **d**, Mt 22:32
'He has been raised from the **d**. Mt 28:7
looking for the living among the **d**? Lk 24:5
consider yourselves **d** to sin Rm 6:11
you were **d** in your trespasses Eph 2:1
the firstborn from the **d**, Col 1:18
and the **d** in Christ will rise 1Th 4:16
also faith without works is **d**. Jms 2:26

DEAD SEA
The end of the Jordan River, forming the southeastern border of Canaan (Nm 34:3; Jos 15:5); also called the Sea of the Arabah (Dt 3:17; Jos 3:16; 12:3; 2Kg 14:25) and the Eastern Sea (Ezk 47:18; Zch 14:8).

DEAF
makes him mute or **d**, seeing or Ex 4:11
On that day the **d** will hear the Is 29:18
the **d** hear, the dead are raised, Mt 11:5

DEATH
You put me into the dust of **d**. Ps 22:15
The **d** of His faithful ones is Ps 116:15
Rescue those being taken off to **d**, Pr 24:11
He will destroy **d** forever. Is 25:8
D, where are your barbs? Hs 13:14
will not taste **d** until they see Mt 16:28
but has passed from **d** to life. Jn 5:24
he will never see **d**—ever! Jn 8:51
d reigned from Adam to Moses, Rm 5:14
For the wages of sin is **d**, Rm 6:23
not even **d** or life, angels or rulers, Rm 8:38
D, where is your victory? 1Co 15:55
passed from **d** to life because 1Jn 3:14
I hold the keys of **d** and Hades. Rv 1:18
D and Hades were thrown into the Rv 20:14
D will no longer exist; Rv 21:4

DEBATE
Where is the **d-r** of this age? 1Co 1:20
But avoid foolish **d-s**, genealogies Ti 3:9

DEBORAH
Prophet and judge (Jdg 4–5).

DEBT
forgive us our **d-s**, as we also Mt 6:12
forgive everyone in **d** to us. Lk 11:4
He erased the certificate of **d**, Col 2:14

DEBTORS
as we also have forgiven our **d**. Mt 6:12

DECAY
allow Your Faithful One to see **d**. Ps 16:10
allow Your Holy One to see **d**. Ac 2:27
not allow Your Holy One to see **d**. Ac 13:35

DECEIT
and in whose spirit is no **d**! Ps 32:2
Israelite; no **d** is in him. Jn 1:47
quarrels, **d**, and malice. Rm 1:29
and no **d** was found in His mouth; 1Pt 2:22

DECEITFUL
heart is more **d** than anything Jr 17:9

DECEIVE
I am He,' and they will **d** many. Mk 13:6
No one should **d** himself. 1Co 3:18
Don't be **d-d**: God is not mocked Gl 6:7
Let no one **d** you with empty Eph 5:6
worse, **d-ing** and being **d-d**. 2Tm 3:13
have no sin," we are **d-ing** ourselves 1Jn 1:8

DECENCY
clothing, with **d** and good sense 1Tm 2:9

DECEPTIVE
Charm is **d** and beauty is Pr 31:30

DECISION
but its every **d** is from the LORD Pr 16:33
multitudes in the valley of **d**! Jl 3:14

DECLARE
The heavens **d** the glory of God, Ps 19:1

DECREE
In those days a **d** went out from Lk 2:1

DEDICATE
the Israelites **d-d** the Lord's 1Kg 8:63
for anyone to **d** something rashly Pr 20:25

DEED
whatever you do, in word or in **d**, Col 3:17

DEEP
D calls to **d** in the roar of Ps 42:7

DEER
As a **d** longs for streams of Ps 42:1
like those of a **d** and enables me Hab 3:19

DEFECT
No man who has any **d** is to come Lv 21:18
like that of a lamb without **d** 1Pt 1:19

DEFENSE
At my first **d**, no one stood by me, 2Tm 4:16
ready to give a **d** to anyone who 1Pt 3:15

DEFILE
that Shechem had **d-d** his daughter Gn 34:5
out of the mouth, this **d-s** a man. Mt 15:11
These are the things that **d** a man, Mt 15:20
conscience, being weak, is **d-d**. 1Co 8:7

DELIGHT (N)
his **d** is in the Lord's Ps 1:2
Take **d** in the Lord, and He will Ps 37:4
Your instruction is my **d**. Ps 119:77,174
beloved Son. I take **d** in Him! Mt 3:17
I take **d** in Him. Listen to Him! Mt 17:5

DELIGHT (V)
rescued me because He **d-ed** in me. Ps 18:19
just as a father, the son he **d-s** in. Pr 3:12
My beloved in whom My soul **d-s**; Mt 12:18

DELILAH
Philistine woman who betrayed Samson (Jdg 16:4-22).

DELIVER
let the Lord **d** him, since He Ps 22:8
the Lord **d-s** him from them all. Ps 34:19
but **d** us from the evil one. Mt 6:13
He was **d-ed** up for our trespasses Rm 4:25
has **d-ed** us from such a terrible 2Co 1:10
faith that was **d-ed** to the saints once Jd 3

DELIVERANCE
d will come to the Jewish people
from another place, Est 4:14
me with joyful shouts of **d**. Ps 32:7

DELIVERER
the Lord raised up ... a **d** to save Jdg 3:9
my fortress, and my **d**, 2Sm 22:2; Ps 18:2
You are my help and my **d**; Ps 40:17; 70:5

DELUSION
them a strong **d** so that they 2Th 2:11

DEMOLISH
We **d** arguments 2Co 10:4

DEMOLITION
for the **d** of strongholds. 2Co 10:4

DEMON
sacrificed to **d-s**, not God, Dt 32:17
drive out **d-s** in Your name Mt 7:22
and they say, 'He has a **d**!' Mt 11:18
spirits and the teachings of **d-s**, 1Tm 4:1
The **d-s** also believe—and they Jms 2:19
stop worshiping **d-s** and idols of Rv 9:20

DEMON-POSSESSED
brought ... the **d**, the epileptics, Mt 4:24
two **d** men met Him as they came Mt 8:28

DEMONSTRATE
to **d** His righteousness Rm 3:25,26

DEN
threw him into the lions' **d**. Dn 6:16
are making it a **d** of thieves! Mt 21:13

DENY
But whoever **d-ies** Me before men,
I will also **d** him before My Mt 10:33
he must **d** himself, take up Mt 16:24
you will **d** Me three times! Mt 26:34
he has **d-ied** the faith and is worse 1Tm 5:8
if we **d** Him, He will also **d** us; 2Tm 2:12
of godliness but **d-ing** its power. 2Tm 3:5
but they **d** Him by their works. Ti 1:16
d-ing the Master who bought them, 2Pt 2:1
who **d-ies** ... Jesus is the Messiah? 1Jn 2:22

DEPART
scepter will not **d** from Judah Gn 49:10
is old he will not **d** from it. Pr 22:6
on the left, '**D** from Me, you who Mt 25:41
the desire to **d** and be with Php 1:23

DEPRIVE
Do not **d** one another sexually— 1Co 7:5

DEPTH
height or **d**, or any other Rm 8:39
the **d** of the riches both of the Rm 11:33
everything, even the **d-s** of God. 1Co 2:10

DESCEND
the Spirit **d-ing** from heaven like Jn 1:32
ascending and **d-ing** on the Son of Jn 1:51
the One who **d-ed** from heaven Jn 3:13
The One who **d-ed** is also the One Eph 4:10
Himself will **d** from heaven with 1Th 4:16

DESCENDANT
So will your **d-s** be. Rm 4:18

DESERT (N)
highway for our God in the **d**. Is 40:3
rivers in the **d**, to give drink Is 43:20

DESERT (V)
disciples **d-ed** Him and ran away Mt 26:56

DESERVE
has not dealt with us as our sins **d** Ps 103:10
He has done nothing to **d** death. Lk 23:15

DESIRE (N)
Your **d** will be for your husband Gn 3:16
will give you your heart's **d-s**. Ps 37:4
my heart's **d** and prayer to God Rm 10:1
plans to satisfy the fleshly **d-s**. Rm 13:14
to marry than to burn with **d**. 1Co 7:9
carry out the **d** of the flesh. Gl 5:16
I have the **d** to depart and be Php 1:23
and enticed by his own evil **d-s**. Jms 1:14

DESIRE (V)
or **d** your neighbor's house, Dt 5:21
nothing you **d** compares with her Pr 3:15
that we should **d** Him. Is 53:2
For I **d** loyalty and not Hs 6:6
I **d** mercy and not sacrifice Mt 9:13; 12:7
I have fervently **d-d** to eat this Lk 22:15
But **d** the greater gifts. 1Co 12:31
d-ing to put on our house from 2Co 5:2
Angels **d** to look into these 1Pt 1:12

DESOLATE
your house is left to you **d**. Mt 23:38
the children of the **d** are many, Gl 4:27

DESOLATION
set up the abomination of **d**. Dn 11:31
the abomination that causes **d**, Mt 24:15
that causes **d** standing where it Mk 13:14
that its **d** has come near. Lk 21:20

DESPAIR (N)
myself over to **d** concerning all Ec 2:20
we are perplexed but not in **d**; 2Co 4:8

DESPAIR (V)
so that we even **d-ed** of life. 2Co 1:8

DESPISE
So Esau **d-d** his birthright. Gn 25:34
and she **d-d** him in her heart. 2Sm 6:16
fools **d** wisdom and discipline. Pr 1:7
He was **d-d** and rejected by men, Is 53:3
devoted to one and **d** the other. Mt 6:24
God has chosen what is ... **d-d** 1Co 1:28
Let no one **d** your youth; 1Tm 4:12
endured a cross and **d-d** the shame Heb 12:2

DESTINED
this child is **d** to cause the fall Lk 2:34

DESTITUTE
in goatskins, **d**, afflicted Heb 11:37

DESTROY
who is able to **d** both soul and Mt 10:28
Have You come to **d** us? Mk 1:24
looking for a way to **d** Him. Mk 11:18
to steal and to kill and to **d**. Jn 10:10
we are struck down but not **d-ed**. 2Co 4:9
our outer person is being **d-ed**, 2Co 4:16
if our ... earthly dwelling is **d-ed**, 2Co 5:1
who is able to save and to **d**. Jms 4:12

DESTRUCTION
set apart to the Lord for **d**. Jos 6:17
Pride comes before **d**, Pr 16:18
road is broad that leads to **d**, Mt 7:13
objects of wrath ready for **d**? Rm 9:22
Their end is **d**; their god is Php 3:19
the penalty of eternal **d** 2Th 1:9
twist them to their own **d**, 2Pt 3:16

DETERMINE
Since man's days are **d-d** and Jb 14:5
I have **d-d** that my mouth will not Ps 17:3
but the Lord **d-s** his steps. Pr 16:9
man's steps are **d-d** by the Lord, Pr 20:24
the spirits to **d** if they are 1Jn 4:1

DETEST
D evil; cling to what is good. Rm 12:9

DETESTABLE
committed all these **d** things, Lv 18:27
imitating the **d** practices 2Kg 16:3

DEVIATE
Some have **d-ed** from these and 1Tm 1:6

DEVIL
to be tempted by the **D**. Mt 4:1
enemy who sowed them is the **D**. Mt 13:39
for the **D** and his angels! Mt 25:41
Yet one of you is the **D**! Jn 6:70
don't give the **D** an opportunity Eph 4:27
against the tactics of the **D**. Eph 6:11
But resist the **D**, and he will Jms 4:7
adversary the **D** is prowling 1Pt 5:8
who is called the **D** and Satan, Rv 12:9

DEVOTED
be **d** to one and despise the other. Mt 6:24

DEVOUR
Must the sword **d** forever? 2Sm 2:26
You **d** widows' houses Mt 23:14
if you bite and **d** one another, Gl 5:15
looking for anyone he can **d**. 1Pt 5:8

DEVOUT
This man was righteous and **d**, Lk 2:25

DEW
If **d** is only on the fleece, Jdg 6:37

DICTATION
At Jeremiah's **d**, Baruch wrote on Jr 36:4

DIE
from it, you will certainly **d**. Gn 2:17
Where you **d**, I will **d**, and there I Ru 1:17
but fools **d** for lack of sense. Pr 10:21
him with a rod, he will not **d**. Pr 23:13
a time to give birth and a time to **d**; Ec 3:2
and drink, for tomorrow we **d**! Is 22:13
Even if I have to **d** with You, Mt 26:35
believes in Me will never **d** Jn 11:26
wheat falls to the ground and **d-s**, Jn 12:24
moment, Christ **d-d** for the ungodly Rm 5:6
How can we who **d-d** to sin still Rm 6:2
rescue me from this **dying** body? Rm 7:24
and if we **d**, we **d** for the Lord. Rm 14:8
that Christ **d-d** for our sins 1Co 15:3
the law I have **d-d** to the law, Gl 2:19
living is Christ and **dying** is gain. Php 1:21
for people to **d** once Heb 9:27
The dead who **d** in the Lord Rv 14:13

DIG
wells **dug** that you did not **d**, Dt 6:11
fence around it, **dug** a winepress Mt 21:33

DINAH
Daughter of Jacob and Leah (Gn 30:21). Raped by Shechem; avenged by Simeon and Levi (Gn 34).

DINNER
in to him and have **d** with him, Rv 3:20

DIP
the one who is **d-ping** bread Mk 14:20

DIRECT
He **d-s** it wherever He chooses. Pr 21:1
May the Lord **d** your hearts to 2Th 3:5

DISAPPOINT
hope will not **d** us, because God's Rm 5:5

DISARM
He **d-ed** the rulers and authorities Col 2:15

DISASTER
the wicked for the day of **d**. Pr 16:4
I make success and create **d**; Is 45:7
If a **d** occurs in a city, hasn't Am 3:6
No **d** will overtake us. Mc 3:11

DISCERN
so that you may **d** what is the Rm 12:2

DISCIPLE
Summoning His 12 **d-s**, He gave Mt 10:1
A **d** is not above his teacher, Mt 10:24
and make **d-s** of all nations, Mt 28:19
come after Me cannot be My **d**. Lk 14:27
and His **d-s** believed in Him. Jn 2:11
My word, you really are My **d-s**. Jn 8:31
and the **d** He loved Jn 19:26
d-s were first called Christians at Ac 11:26

DISCIPLINE (N)
Apply yourself to **d** and listen to Pr 23:12
Don't withhold **d** from a youth; Pr 23:13
No **d** seems enjoyable at the time Heb 12:11

DISCIPLINE (V)
Your anger or **d** me in Your wrath Ps 38:1
for the LORD **d-s** the one He loves Pr 3:12
D your son while there is hope; Pr 19:18
judged, we are **d-d** by the Lord, 1Co 11:32
for the Lord **d-s** the one He loves Heb 12:6

DISCOURAGED
Do not be afraid or **d**, Jos 1:9
pray always and not become **d**: Lk 18:1

DISCRIMINATED
haven't you **d** among yourselves Jms 2:4

DISCUSS
"Come, let us **d** this," says the Is 1:18
And they **d-ed** among themselves, Mt 16:7

DISEASE
all the terrible **d-s** of Egypt that Dt 7:15
He heals all your **d-s**. Ps 103:3
and healing every **d** and sickness Mt 4:23
weaknesses and carried our **d-s**. Mt 8:17
demons, and power to heal **d-s**. Lk 9:1

DISFIGURED
was so **d** that He did not Is 52:14

DISGRACE
When pride comes, **d** follows, Pr 11:2
but sin is a **d** to any people. Pr 14:34
has long hair it is a **d** to him, 1Co 11:14

DISGRACEFUL
But if it is **d** for a woman to 1Co 11:6
for it is **d** for a woman to speak 1Co 14:35

DISGUISE
king of Israel **d-d** himself 1Kg 22:30
Satan **d-s** himself as an angel 2Co 11:14

DISHONEST
D scales are detestable to the Pr 11:1
one who hates **d** profit prolongs Pr 28:16

DISHONOR (N)
for honor and another for **d**? Rm 9:21
sown in **d**, raised in glory; 1Co 15:43

DISHONOR (V)
her head uncovered **d-s** her head, 1Co 11:5

DISMISS
You can **d** Your slave in peace, Lk 2:29

DISOBEDIENCE
through one man's **d** the many Rm 5:19
received mercy through their **d**, Rm 11:30

DISOBEDIENT
out My hands to a **d** and defiant Rm 10:21
spirit now working in the **d**. Eph 2:2

DISORDER
is not a God of **d** but of peace. 1Co 14:33

DISPERSION
to go to the **D** among the Greeks Jn 7:35
To the 12 tribes in the **D**. Jms 1:1

DISPLAY
I will **d** My glory among the Ezk 39:21
I think God has **d-ed** us, 1Co 4:9
ages He might **d** the immeasurable Eph 2:7

DISPUTE
when he was **d-ing** with the Devil in Jd 9

DISQUALIFY
others, I myself will not be **d-ied**. 1Co 9:27
Let no one **d** you, insisting on Col 2:18

DISSENSIONS
selfish ambitions, **d**, factions, Gl 5:20

DISTINCTION
They make no **d** between the holy Ezk 22:26
believe, since there is no **d**. Rm 3:22
for there is no **d** between Jew Rm 10:12

DISTINGUISH
You must **d** between the holy and Lv 10:10
to another, **d-ing** between spirits 1Co 12:10

DISTRACTED
But Martha was **d** by her many Lk 10:40

DISTRESS
to be sorrowful and deeply **d-ed**. Mt 26:37
will be great **d** in the land Lk 21:23

DISTRIBUTE
d the land as an inheritance Jos 13:6
This was then **d-d** for each person's Ac 4:35
d-ing to each person as He wills. 1Co 12:11

DIVIDE
your hand over the sea, and **d** it Ex 14:16
They **d-d** my garments among Ps 22:18
Every kingdom **d-d** against itself Mt 12:25
Him they **d-d** His clothes Mt 27:35
my brother to **d** the inheritance Lk 12:13
Is Christ **d-d**? Was it Paul who 1Co 1:13

DIVINATION
not to practice **d** or sorcery. Lv 19:26
rebellion is like the sin of **d**, 1Sm 15:23

DIVINE
His eternal power and **d** nature, Rm 1:20
His **d** power has given us everything 2Pt 1:3
you may share in the **d** nature, 2Pt 1:4

DIVISION
No, I tell you, but rather **d**! Lk 12:51
that there be no **d-s** among you, 1Co 1:10
church there are **d-s** among you, 1Co 11:18
would be no **d** in the body, 1Co 12:25

DIVORCE
he cannot **d** her as long as he Dt 22:19
may write her a **d** certificate, Dt 24:1
given her a certificate of **d**. Jr 3:8
If he hates and **d-s** his wife, Mal 2:16
decided to **d** her secretly. Mt 1:19
must give her a written notice of **d**. Mt 5:31
permitted you to **d** your wives Mt 19:8

DIVORCED (ADJ)
marries a **d** woman commits Mt 5:32

DOCTOR
who are well don't need a **d**, Mt 9:12
proverb to Me: '**D**, heal yourself Lk 4:23

DOCTRINE
teaching as **d-s** the commands of Mt 15:9
people not to teach different **d** 1Tm 1:3
they will not tolerate sound **d**, 2Tm 4:3

DOER
But be **d-s** of the word and not Jms 1:22

DOG
The **d-s** will eat Jezebel in the 1Kg 21:23
As a **d** returns to its vomit, Pr 26:11
since a live **d** is better than a Ec 9:4
bread and throw it to the **d-s**. Mk 7:27
A **d** returns to its own vomit, 2Pt 2:22

DOMAIN
us from the **d** of darkness Col 1:13

DOMINION
His **d** is an everlasting **d** Dn 4:34; 7:14
power and **d**, and every title Eph 1:21
the glory and **d** are His forever Rv 1:6

DONKEY
the LORD opened the **d-'s** mouth, Nm 22:28
riding on a **d**, on a colt, the foal of Zch 9:9
mounted on a **d**, even on a colt Mt 21:5
A **d** that could not talk spoke 2Pt 2:16

DOOR
Rise up, ancient **d-s**! Then the King Ps 24:7
keep watch at the **d** of my lips. Ps 141:3
and the **d** will be opened to you Mt 7:7
to enter through the narrow **d**, Lk 13:24
I am the **d**. If anyone enters by Jn 10:9
the Lord opened a **d** for me. 2Co 2:12
that God may open a **d** to us for Col 4:3
you an open **d** that no one is Rv 3:8
I stand at the **d** and knock. Rv 3:20

DOORPOST
blood and put it on the two **d-s** Ex 12:7
Write them on the **d-s** of your house Dt 6:9

DOUBLE-EDGED
and as sharp as a **d** sword. Pr 5:4
and sharper than any **d** sword, Heb 4:12
sharp **d** sword came from His mouth, Rv 1:16

DOUBT
of little faith, why did you **d**? Mt 14:31
If you have faith and do not **d**, Mt 21:21
they worshiped, but some **d-ed**. Mt 28:17
whoever **d-s** stands condemned Rm 14:23
let him ask in faith without **d-ing**. Jms 1:6

DOUGH
took their **d** before it was leavened, Ex 12:34
permeates the whole batch of **d**? 1Co 5:6
leavens the whole lump of **d**. Gl 5:9

DOVE
he sent out a **d** to see whether Gn 8:8
Spirit of God descending like a **d** Mt 3:16
serpents and as harmless as **d-s**. Mt 10:16

DOWNFALL
Before his **d** a man's heart is proud Pr 18:12
causes the **d** of one of these Mt 18:6
And if your eye causes your **d**, Mt 18:9

DRAGON
And the **d** stood in front of the Rv 12:4
He seized the **d**, that ancient serpent Rv 20:2

DRAW
the Father who sent Me **d-s** him, Jn 6:44
earth I will **d** all people to Jn 12:32
let us **d** near with a true heart Heb 10:22
D near to God, and He will **d** near Jms 4:8

DREAM (N)
Joseph had a **d**. Gn 37:5
Daniel also understood ... **d-s** Dn 1:17
Daniel had a **d** with visions in Dn 7:1
your old men will have **d-s**, and Jl 2:28
appeared to Joseph in a **d**, Mt 2:13
terribly in a **d** because of Him! Mt 27:19
and your old men will dream **d-s**. Ac 2:17

DREAM (V)
he **d-ed**: A stairway was set on Gn 28:12

DREAMER
Here comes that **d**! Gn 37:19

DRESS
the women are to **d** themselves in 1Tm 2:9

DRINK
D water from your own cistern, Pr 5:15
eat and **d**, for tomorrow we die! Is 22:13
and you gave Me something to **d**; Mt 25:35
and so they all **drank** from it. Mk 14:23
Do this, as often as you **d** it, 1Co 11:25
all made to **d** of one Spirit. 1Co 12:13

DRIVE
did not **d** them out completely. Jos 17:13
He **drove** everyone out of the temple Jn 2:15
perfect love **d-s** out fear, 1Jn 4:18

DRUNK (ADJ)
And don't get **d** with wine, Eph 5:18

DRUNKARD
a glutton and a **d**, a friend of Mt 11:19
abusive, a **d** or a swindler. 1Co 5:11

DRUNKENNESS
not in carousing and **d**; Rm 13:13
envy, **d**, carousing, and anything Gl 5:21
evil desires, **d**, orgies 1Pt 4:3

DRY
and let the **d** land appear. Gn 1:9
go through the sea on **d** ground. Ex 14:16
D bones, hear the word of Ezk 37:4

DULL
D these people's minds; Is 6:10

DUST
man out of the **d** from the ground Gn 2:7
belly and eat **d** all the days Gn 3:14
offspring like the **d** of the earth, Gn 13:16
and repent in **d** and ashes. Jb 42:6
remembering that we are **d**. Ps 103:14
all come from **d**, and all return to **d**. Ec 3:20
shake the **d** off your feet when Mt 10:14
The first man was ... made of **d**; 1Co 15:47

DUTY
we've only done our **d**. Lk 17:10

DWELL
LORD, who can **d** in Your tent? Ps 15:1
and I will **d** in the house of the Ps 23:6
the Messiah may **d** in your hearts Eph 3:17
any praise—**d** on these things Php 4:8
all His fullness **d** in Him, Col 1:19
God's nature **d-s** bodily in Christ, Col 2:9

DWELLING
a place for Your **d** forever. 1Kg 8:13
house are many **d** places; Jn 14:2
being built together for God's **d** Eph 2:22

EAGLE
I carried you on **e-s'** wings and Ex 19:4
youth is renewed like the **e**. Ps 103:5
they will soar on wings like **e-s**; Is 40:31
the left, and the face of an **e**. Ezk 1:10
creature was like a flying **e**. Rv 4:7

EAR
One who shaped the **e** not hear, Ps 94:9
otherwise they ... hear with their **e-s**, Is 6:10
Anyone who has **e-s** should listen! Mt 11:15
slave, and cut off his right **e**. Jn 18:10
eye did not see and **e** did not hear, 1Co 2:9
And if the **e** should say 1Co 12:16
who has an **e** should listen to Rv 2:7

EARTH
God created the heavens and the **e**. Gn 1:1
may know the **e** belongs to Yahweh. Ex 9:29
The **e** and everything in it, Ps 24:1
sing to the LORD, all the **e**. Ps 96:1
He is coming to judge the **e**. Ps 96:13
His glory fills the whole **e**. Is 6:3
they will inherit the **e**. Mt 5:5
Heaven and **e** will pass away, Mt 24:35
and peace on **e** to people He Lk 2:14
we wait for ... a new **e**, 2Pt 3:13

EARTHLY
if our temporary, **e** dwelling 2Co 5:1
They are focused on **e** things, Php 3:19
not ... above but is **e**, unspiritual, Jms 3:15

EARTHQUAKE
but the LORD was not in the **e**. 1Kg 19:11
be famines and **e-s** in various Mt 24:7
Suddenly there was a violent **e**, Mt 28:2
was such a violent **e** that the Ac 16:26
A violent **e** occurred; Rv 6:12

EASIER
For which is **e**: to say, 'Your Mt 9:5
it is **e** for a camel to go Mt 19:24
But it is **e** for heaven and earth Lk 16:17

EAST
As far as the **e** is from the west Ps 103:12
wise men from the **e** arrived Mt 2:1

EASY
For My yoke is **e** and My burden Mt 11:30

EAT
You are free to **e** from any tree Gn 2:16
took some of its fruit and **ate** it; Gn 3:6
words were found, and I **ate** them Jr 15:16
E this scroll, then go and speak Ezk 3:1
of Man came **e-ing** and drinking, Mt 11:19
Everyone **ate** and was filled. Mt 14:20
They all **ate** and were filled. Mt 15:37
and said, "Take and **e** it; Mt 26:26
sinners and **e-s** with them! Lk 15:2
who **e-s** My flesh and drinks Jn 6:54
Get up, Peter; kill and **e**! Ac 10:13
believes he may **e** anything, Rm 14:2
whether you **e** or drink, or 1Co 10:31
work, he should not **e**. 2Th 3:10
He said to me, "Take and **e** it; Rv 10:9

EDEN
LORD God planted a garden in **E**, Gn 2:8
You were in **E**, the garden of God Ezk 28:13

EDIFICATION
speaks to people for **e**, 1Co 14:3

EDOM
is why he was also named **E**. Gn 25:30
land of Seir, the country of **E**. Gn 32:3

EFFECTIVE
is living and **e** and sharper than Heb 4:12

EFFORT
not depend on human will or **e** Rm 9:16
then make every **e** to enter that Heb 4:11
make every **e** to supplement your 2Pt 1:5

EGYPT
Abram went down to **E** to live Gn 12:10
sold Joseph in **E** to Potiphar, Gn 37:36
children went with him to **E**. Gn 46:6
lived in **E** was 430 years. Ex 12:40
out of **E** I called My son. Hs 11:1
Out of **E** I called My Son. Mt 2:15

EHUD
Benjaminite judge (Jdg 3:12-30).

ELAH
1. Valley where David fought Goliath (1Sm 17:2,19; 21:9).
2. Son of Baasha; king of Israel (1Kg 16:6-14).

ELDER
break the tradition of the **e-s**? Mt 15:2
had appointed **e-s** in every church Ac 14:23
The **e-s** who are good leaders 1Tm 5:17
accusation against an **e** unless 1Tm 5:19
call for the **e-s** of the church, Jms 5:14
thrones sat 24 **e-s** dressed in Rv 4:4

ELEAZAR
Son of Aaron; high priest (Ex 6:23; Nm 20:25-28). Helped Joshua distribute land (Jos 14:1).

ELECT
if possible, even the **e**. Mt 24:24
justice to His **e** who cry out to Lk 18:7
but the **e** did find it. Rm 11:7

ELECTION
purpose according to **e** might stand Rm 9:11
knowing your **e**, brothers loved 1Th 1:4
to confirm your calling and **e**, 2Pt 1:10

ELEMENTAL
based on the **e** forces of the Col 2:8

ELEVEN
appeared to the **E** themselves as Mk 16:14

ELI
High priest at Samuel's birth (1Sm 1–4). Blessed Hannah (1:17; 2:20). Failed to discipline his sons (2:12-17,22-36). Died when the ark was captured (4:11-18).

ELÍ
E, E, lemá sabachtháni? Mt 27:46

ELIAKIM
1. Son of Hilkiah; Hezekiah's administrator (2Kg 18:18; Is 22:20; 36:3).
2. Son of Josiah; king of Judah. Called Jehoiakim (2Kg 23:34; 2Ch 36:4).

ELIEZER
1. Abraham's servant (Gn 15:2).
2. Son of Moses (Ex 18:4; 1Ch 23:15).
3. Ancestor of Jesus (Lk 3:29).

ELIJAH
Prophet against Ahab and Ahaziah. Predicted famine (1Kg 17:1; Jms 5:17). Fed by ravens (1Kg 17:2-7); fed by widow (17:8-16; Lk 4:26); raised widow's son (1Kg 17:17-24). Defeated prophets of Baal (18:19-40). Fled Jezebel (19:1-3). Chose Elisha to succeed him (19:16,19-21); taken up into heaven (2Kg 2:1-12).
Forerunner to the Messiah, embodied in John the Baptist (Mal 4:5; Mt 11:14; 17:10-13; Lk 1:17). Appeared with Jesus (Mt 17:3-4).

ELISHA
Prophet; successor to Elijah (1Kg 19:16-21; 2Kg 2:1-18). Made bad water good (2Kg 2:19-22); called bear to punish boys (2:23-24); provided water for army (3:13-22). Provided miraculous supply of oil for widow (4:1-7); granted son to barren woman and restored him to life (4:8-37). Healed Naaman and punished Gehazi (5:1-27). Made axe head float (6:5-7). Blinded Syrian army (6:8–7:20). A man was revived by touching his dead bones (13:20-21).
Made Hazael king of Syria (8:7-15) and Jehu king of Israel (9:1-13).

ELIZABETH
Mother of John the Baptist; Mary's relative (Lk 1).

ELKANAH
Father of Samuel; husband of Hannah (1Sm 1:1).

ELOI
voice, "*E, E, lemá sabachtháni* Mk 15:34

EMBRACE
Can a man **e** fire and his clothes Pr 6:27

EMMAUS
on their way to a village called **E**, Lk 24:13

EMPTY (ADJ)
mouth will not return to Me **e**, Is 55:11
deceive you with **e** arguments, Eph 5:6

EMPTY (V)
cross of Christ will not be **e-ied** 1Co 1:17
He **e-ied** Himself by assuming Php 2:7

EMPTY-HANDED
No one is to appear before Me **e**. Ex 23:15

ENCAMPS
of the LORD **e** around those who Ps 34:7

ENCOURAGE
Therefore **e** one another with 1Th 4:18

ENCOURAGEMENT
which is translated Son of **E**, Ac 4:36
through the **e** from the Scriptures Rm 15:4
then there is any **e** in Christ, Php 2:1

END (N)
to put an **e** to every creature, Gn 6:13
and the **e-s** of the earth Your Ps 2:8
reveal to me the **e** of my life Ps 39:4
but its **e** is the way to death. Pr 14:12
The **e** of a matter is better than Ec 7:8
endures to the **e** will be delivered. Mt 10:22
endures to the **e** will be delivered. Mt 24:13
and His kingdom will have no **e**. Lk 1:33
He loved them to the **e**. Jn 13:1
and to the **e-s** of the earth. Ac 1:8
Christ is the **e** of the law for Rm 10:4
and keeps My works to the **e**: Rv 2:26
Last, the Beginning and the **E**. Rv 22:13

END (V)
Love never **e-s**. But as for 1Co 13:8

ENDURANCE
that affliction produces **e**, Rm 5:3
faith, love, **e**, and gentleness. 1Tm 6:11
Let us run with **e** the race that Heb 12:1
the testing of your faith produces **e**. Jms 1:3

ENDURE
of the LORD is pure, **e-ing** forever; Ps 19:9
May he continue while the sun **e-s** Ps 72:5
But who can **e** the day of His Mal 3:2
the one who **e-s** to the end will Mt 10:22
e-d with much patience objects of Rm 9:22
hopes all things, **e-s** all things. 1Co 13:7
if we **e**, we will also reign with 2Tm 2:12
a better and **e-ing** possession. Heb 10:34
that lay before Him **e-d** a cross Heb 12:2
the word of the Lord **e-s** forever. 1Pt 1:25

ENEMY
an **e** to your **e-ies** and a foe to Ex 23:22
me in the presence of my **e-ies**; Ps 23:5
do not let my **e-ies** gloat over me. Ps 25:2
I make Your **e-ies** Your footstool. Ps 110:1
If your **e** is hungry, give him Pr 25:21
a man's **e-ies** are the men in his own Mc 7:6
love your **e-ies** and pray for those Mt 5:44
a man's **e-ies** will be the members Mt 10:36
e who sowed them is the Devil. Mt 13:39
I put Your **e-ies** under Your feet Mt 22:44
if, while we were **e-ies**, we were Rm 5:10
But If your **e** is hungry, feed him. Rm 12:20
The last **e** He abolishes is death 1Co 15:26

world's friend becomes God's **e**. Jms 4:4

ENGAGED
to a virgin **e** to a man named Lk 1:27

ENJOY
to eat, drink, and **e** his work. Ec 2:24
provides us with all things to **e**. 1Tm 6:17

ENLIGHTENED
perception of your mind may be **e** Eph 1:18
those who were once **e**, Heb 6:4

ENOCH
Father of Methuselah (Gn 5:18-21); prophet (Jd 14); walked with God, and God took him (Gn 5:22-24; Heb 11:5).

ENSLAVE
we may no longer be **e-d** to sin, Rm 6:6
put up with it if someone **e-s** you, 2Co 11:20
want to be **e-d** to them all over again? Gl 4:9

ENSNARE
the sin that so easily **e-s** us. Heb 12:1

ENTANGLE
The ropes of Sheol **e-d** me; 2Sm 22:6
soldier gets **e-d** in the concerns 2Tm 2:4
they are again **e-d** in these things 2Pt 2:20

ENTER
anger, "They will not **e** My rest." Ps 95:11
E His gates with thanksgiving Ps 100:4
you will never **e** the kingdom of Mt 5:20
E through the narrow gate. Mt 7:13
like a little child will never **e** it. Mk 10:15
he cannot **e** the kingdom of God. Jn 3:5
just as sin **e-ed** the world through Rm 5:12
anger, "They will not **e** My rest." Heb 3:11

ENTHRONED
who is **e** above the cherubim, 2Kg 19:15
But the LORD sits **e** forever; Ps 9:7
e on the praises of Israel. Ps 22:3

ENTHUSIASTICALLY
you do, do it **e**, as something Col 3:23

ENTICE
son, if sinners **e** you, don't be Pr 1:10
drawn away and **e-d** by his own Jms 1:14

ENTRUST
Into Your hand I **e** my spirit; Ps 31:5
into Your hands I **e** My spirit. Lk 23:46
what has been **e-ed** to me until 2Tm 1:12

ENVY (N)
They are full of **e**, murder Rm 1:29
For where **e** and selfish ambition Jms 3:16

ENVY (V)
Don't let your heart **e** sinners; Pr 23:17
Don't **e** evil men or desire to be Pr 24:1
Love does not **e**, is not boastful, 1Co 13:4

EPHESUS
City in Asia Minor visited by Paul (Ac 18:19; 19:1; 1Co 16:8; Eph 1:1; Rv 2:1).

EPHOD
are to make the **e** of finely spun Ex 28:6

EPHRAIM
Son of Joseph (Gn 41:52); tribe with territory north and west of Bethel (Gn 48; Jos 14:4; 16:4-5); designation for Israel (Is 11:13; Jr 7:15; Ezk 37:16; Hs 5:13).

EPHRATHAH
Bethlehem **E**, you are small among Mc 5:2

EQUAL
making Himself **e** with God. Jn 5:18

EQUALITY
did not consider **e** with God as Php 2:6

EQUIP
be complete, **e-ped** for every good 2Tm 3:17
e you with all that is good to Heb 13:21
e yourselves ... the same resolve 1Pt 4:1

ERASE
Let them be **e-d** from the book of Ps 69:28
and I will never **e** his name from Rv 3:5

ERROR
appropriate penalty for their **e**. Rm 1:27
from the **e** of his way will Jms 5:20

ESAU
Son of Isaac; elder twin of Jacob (Gn 25:24-26); rejected by God (Mal 1:2-3; Rm 9:13); sold birthright (Gn 25:30-34; Heb 12:16); tricked out of blessing (Gn 27:1-30; Heb 11:20); reconciled with Jacob (33:4-16). Progenitor of Edomites in Seir (Dt 2:4-29).

ESCAPE (N)
He will also provide a way of **e** 1Co 10:13

ESCAPE (V)
can I go to **e** Your Spirit? Ps 139:7
that you will **e** God's judgment? Rm 2:3
how will we **e** if we neglect such Heb 2:3

ESTABLISH
But I will **e** My covenant with Gn 6:18
and I will **e** his kingdom. 2Sm 7:12
I will ... **e** your throne Ps 89:4
up in Him and **e-ed** in the faith, Col 2:7

ESTHER
Persian name of Hadassah, Mordecai's cousin (Est 2:7). Chosen queen of Persia (2:16-18); interceded at great risk to foil a plot to exterminate the Jews (Est 3–9).

ESTIMATION
Do not be wise in your own **e**. Rm 12:16

ETERNAL
for He is good. His love is **e**. Ps 136:1
must I do to have **e** life? Mt 19:16
will go away into **e** punishment,
but the righteous into **e** life. Mt 25:46
not perish but have **e** life. Jn 3:16
so He may give **e** life to all You Jn 17:2
gift of God is **e** life in Christ Rm 6:23
incomparable **e** weight of glory. 2Co 4:17
pay the penalty of **e** destruction, 2Th 1:9
Now to the King **e**, immortal 1Tm 1:17
may know that you have **e** life. 1Jn 5:13

ETERNITY
from **e** to **e**, You are God. Ps 90:2
has also put **e** in their hearts Ec 3:11

ETHIOPIAN
There was an **E** man, a eunuch Ac 8:27

EUNUCH
For there are **e-s** who were born Mt 19:12
The **e** replied to Philip, "I ask Ac 8:34

EUPHRATES
And the fourth river is the **E**. Gn 2:14

EVALUATE
but the LORD **e-s** the motives. Pr 16:2
it since it is **e-d** spiritually. 1Co 2:14
The One who **e-s** me is the Lord. 1Co 4:4

EVANGELIST
prophets, some **e-s**, some pastors Eph 4:11
the work of an **e**, fulfill your 2Tm 4:5

EVE
First woman; wife of Adam (Gn 3:20; 4:1-2,25). Gave in to temptation (3:1; 2Co 11:3; 1Tm 2:13-14).

EVERLASTING
and underneath are the **e** arms. Dt 33:27
Yahweh is the **e** God, the Creator Is 40:28
have loved you with an **e** love; Jr 31:3

EVERYTHING
you do, do **e** for God's glory. 1Co 10:31
has given us **e** required for life 2Pt 1:3

EVIL
of the knowledge of good and **e**. Gn 2:9
To fear the LORD is to hate **e**. Pr 8:13
who call **e** good and good **e**, Is 5:20
but deliver us from the **e** one. Mt 6:13
then, who are **e**, know how to Mt 7:11
an **e** man produces **e** things from Mt 12:35
protect them from the **e** one. Jn 17:15
Do not repay anyone **e** for **e**. Rm 12:17
Stay away from every kind of **e**. 1Th 5:22
is a root of all kinds of **e**, 1Tm 6:10
For God is not tempted by **e**, Jms 1:13

EVILDOER
I tell you, don't resist an **e**. Mt 5:39

EWE
one small **e** lamb that he had 2Sm 12:3

EXACT
the **e** expression of His nature, Heb 1:3

EXALT
the rock of my salvation, is **e-ed**. 2Sm 22:47
let us **e** His name together. Ps 34:3
be **e-ed** above the heavens; Ps 57:5,11
You are **e-ed** above all the gods. Ps 97:9
Righteousness **e-s** a nation, but Pr 14:34
humbles himself will be **e-ed**. Mt 23:12
God highly **e-ed** Him and gave Php 2:9
the Lord, and He will **e** you. Jms 4:10

EXAMINE
and **e-d** the Scriptures daily to see Ac 17:11
So a man should **e** himself; 1Co 11:28

EXAMPLE
given you an **e** that you also Jn 13:15
these things became **e-s** for us, 1Co 10:6
to the **e** you have in us. Php 3:17
should be an **e** to the believers 1Tm 4:12
you, but being **e-s** to the flock. 1Pt 5:3

EXASPERATE
Fathers, do not **e** your children — Col 3:21

EXCHANGE
a man give in **e** for his life? — Mt 16:26

EXCHANGED
They **e** their glory for the image — Ps 106:20
and **e** the glory of the immortal — Rm 1:23

EXCUSE
they have no **e** for their sin. — Jn 15:22
As a result, people are without **e**. — Rm 1:20

EXHORT
older man, but **e** him as a father — 1Tm 5:1

EXHORTATION
with many other **e-s**, he proclaimed — Lk 3:18

EXILE
went into **e** from its land. — 2Kg 25:21
the returned **e-s** were building — Ezr 4:1

EXILED
So Israel has been **e-d** to Assyria — 2Kg 17:23

EXIST
in his heart, "God does not **e**. — Ps 14:1; 53:1
in Him we live and move and **e**, — Ac 17:28
who, **e-ing** in the form of God, — Php 2:6
all things **e** for Him and through — Heb 2:10
believe that He **e-s** and rewards — Heb 11:6
Your will they **e** and were — Rv 4:11

EXPECT
coming at an hour you do not **e**. — Mt 24:44
and lend, **e-ing** nothing in return. — Lk 6:35

EXPECTANTLY
the LORD and wait **e** for Him; — Ps 37:7

EXPECTATION
e of the wicked comes to nothing. — Pr 10:28
but a terrifying **e** of judgment — Heb 10:27

EXPLAIN
He will **e** everything to us. — Jn 4:25

EXPOSE
so that his deeds may not be **e-d**. — Jn 3:20
darkness, but instead **e** them. — Eph 5:11
Everything **e-d** by the light is — Eph 5:13

EXPRESSION
the exact **e** of His nature, — Heb 1:3

EXTEND
would bless me, **e** my border, — 1Ch 4:10

EXTINGUISH
will be able to **e** the flaming — Eph 6:16

EYE
e for **e**, tooth for tooth — Ex 21:24; Lv 24:20
For the **e-s** of Yahweh roam — 2Ch 16:9
have made a covenant with my **e-s**. — Jb 31:1
Protect me as the pupil of Your **e**; — Ps 17:8
I lift my **e-s** toward the — Ps 121:1
they might see with their **e-s** and — Is 6:10
Your **e-s** are too pure to look on — Hab 1:13
If your right **e** causes you to — Mt 5:29
An **e** for an **e** and a tooth for — Mt 5:38
The **e** is the lamp of the body. — Mt 6:22
the speck in your brother's **e** but — Mt 7:3
And their **e-s** were opened. — Mt 9:30
see with their **e-s** and hear with — Mt 13:15
Lord and is wonderful in our **e-s**? — Mt 21:42
Then their **e-s** were opened, and — Lk 24:31
keeping our **e-s** on Jesus, — Heb 12:2
what we have seen with our **e-s**, — 1Jn 1:1
clouds, and every **e** will see Him — Rv 1:7
away every tear from their **e-s** — Rv 7:17; 21:4

EYEWITNESSES
the original **e** ... handed them down — Lk 1:2
we were **e** of His majesty. — 2Pt 1:16

EZEKIEL
Hebrew prophet at the time of the exile, writing from Babylon (2Kg 24:14-16; Ezk 1:1). Wrote about the fall of Jerusalem (Ezk 33:21) and the ultimate restoration of the city and temple (Ezk 40–48).

EZRA
Priest and teacher of the law; leader of the returning exiles, sent by King Artaxerxes of Persia to reestablish worship in the temple (Ezr 7–8). Nehemiah's colleague (Neh 8:2,6; 12:31-37). Made priests stop intermarriage with foreigners (Ezr 9–10).

FACE
I have seen God **f** to **f**, — Gn 32:30
the LORD spoke with Moses **f** to **f**, — Ex 33:11
Moses, the skin of his **f** shone! — Ex 34:30
Yahweh make His **f** shine on you — Nm 6:25
LORD, I will seek Your **f**. — Ps 27:8
I have set My **f** like flint, — Is 50:7
oil on your head, and wash your **f**, — Mt 6:17
and His **f** shone like the sun. — Mt 17:2
spit in His **f** and beat Him; — Mt 26:67
appearance of His **f** changed, — Lk 9:29
a mirror, but then **f** to **f**. — 1Co 13:12
with unveiled **f-s**, are reflecting — 2Co 3:18
But the **f** of the Lord is against — 1Pt 3:12
and His **f** was shining like the sun — Rv 1:16

FACTIONS
must, indeed, be **f** among you, — 1Co 11:19
ambitions, dissensions, **f**, — Gl 5:20

FADE
the flowers **f**, but the word of — Is 40:8
a crown that will never **f** away. — 1Co 9:25

FAIL
you that your faith may not **f**. — Lk 22:32
as though the word of God has **f-ed**. — Rm 9:6

FAILURE
and their **f** riches for the — Rm 11:12

FAINT
my body **f-s** for You in a land that — Ps 63:1
they will walk and not **f**. — Is 40:31

FAIR
'The Lord's way isn't **f**.' — Ezk 18:25; 33:17
with what is right and **f**, — Col 4:1

FAIRLY
He judges the peoples **f**. — Ps 96:10

FAITH
righteous one will live by his **f**. — Hab 2:4
Your **f** has made you well. — Mt 9:22
If you have **f** the size of a mustard — Mt 17:20
woman, "Your **f** has saved you. — Lk 7:50
to the Lord, "Increase our **f**. — Lk 17:5
will He find that **f** on earth? — Lk 18:8
that he had **f** to be healed, — Ac 14:9
is justified by **f** apart from — Rm 3:28
been declared righteous by **f**, — Rm 5:1
So **f** comes from what is heard, — Rm 10:17
if I have all **f** so that I can — 1Co 13:2
three remain: **f**, hope, and love. — 1Co 13:13
stand firm in the **f**, act like a man, — 1Co 16:13
For we walk by **f**, not by sight — 2Co 5:7
I live by **f** in the Son of God, — Gl 2:20
the righteous will live by **f**. — Gl 3:11
patience, kindness, goodness, **f**, — Gl 5:22
you are saved by grace through **f**, — Eph 2:8
one Lord, one **f**, one baptism, — Eph 4:5
situation take the shield of **f**, — Eph 6:16
righteousness from God based on **f**. — Php 3:9
the armor of **f** and love on our — 1Th 5:8
some will depart from the **f**, — 1Tm 4:1
Fight the good fight for the **f**; — 1Tm 6:12
finished the race, I have kept the **f**. — 2Tm 4:7
righteous one will live by **f**; — Heb 10:38
Now **f** is the reality of what is — Heb 11:1
By **f** we understand that the — Heb 11:3
By **f** Abel offered to God a — Heb 11:4
Now without **f** it is impossible — Heb 11:6
source and perfecter of our **f**, — Heb 12:2
f, if it doesn't have works, is dead — Jms 2:17
supplement your **f** with goodness, — 2Pt 1:5

FAITHFUL *SEE ALSO* FAITHFUL LOVE
he is **f** in all My household. — Nm 12:7
the **f** God who keeps His gracious — Dt 7:9
With the **f** You prove Yourself **f**; — 2Sm 22:26
Love the LORD, all His **f** ones. — Ps 31:23
Who then is a **f** and sensible — Mt 24:45
Well done, good and **f** slave! — Mt 25:21
God is **f**; you were called by Him — 1Co 1:9
God is **f**, and He will not allow — 1Co 10:13
He who calls you is **f**, who also — 1Th 5:24
commit to **f** men who will be able — 2Tm 2:2
He remains **f**, for He cannot deny — 2Tm 2:13
for He who promised is **f**. — Heb 10:23
entrust themselves to a **f** Creator, — 1Pt 4:19
He is **f** and righteous to forgive — 1Jn 1:9
Its rider is called **F** and True, — Rv 19:11

FAITHFUL LOVE
goodness and **f** will pursue — Ps 23:6
because Your **f** is better — Ps 63:3
will sing about the LORD's **f** forever; — Ps 89:1
to declare Your **f** in the morning — Ps 92:2
so great is His **f** toward those — Ps 103:11
slow to become angry, rich in **f**, — Jnh 4:2
because He delights in **f**. — Mc 7:18

FAITHFULNESS
to heaven, Your **f** to the clouds. — Ps 36:5
Your **f** reaches the clouds. — Ps 57:10
proclaim Your **f** to all generations — Ps 89:1
f endures through all generations. — Ps 100:5
great is Your **f**! — Lm 3:23
their unbelief cancel God's **f**? — Rm 3:3

FAITHLESS
if we are **f**, He remains faithful, — 2Tm 2:13

FALL
How the mighty have **f-en**! — 2Sm 1:19
Though he **f-s**, he will not be — Ps 37:24
Though a thousand **f** at your side — Ps 91:7
an arrogant spirit before a **f**. — Pr 16:18
a righteous man **f-s** seven times, — Pr 24:16

you have **f-en** from the heavens Is 14:12
Babylon has **f-en**, has **f-en**. Is 21:9
some seeds **fell** along the path, Mt 13:4
to cause the **f** and rise of many Lk 2:34
I watched Satan **f** from heaven Lk 10:18
grain of wheat **f-s** to the ground Jn 12:24
have sinned and **f** short of the Rm 3:23
must be careful not to **f**. 1Co 10:12
you have **f-en** from grace. Gl 5:4
and who have **f-en** away, Heb 6:6
thing to **f** into the hands Heb 10:31
a great star ... **fell** from heaven. Rv 8:10
f-en, Babylon the Great has **f-en**, Rv 14:8

FALSE

Do not give **f** testimony against Ex 20:16
Beware of **f** prophets who come Mt 7:15
do not bear **f** witness; Mt 19:18
Many **f** prophets will rise up and Mt 24:11
F messiahs and **f** prophets will Mt 24:24
whether out of **f** motives or true Php 1:18
there will be **f** teachers among you. 2Pt 2:1
the mouth of the **f** prophet. Rv 16:13

FALSEHOOD

I hate and abhor **f**, but I love Ps 119:163
Keep **f** and deceitful words far Pr 30:8

FALSELY

f say every kind of evil against you Mt 5:11
that **f** bears that name 1Tm 6:20

FAMILY

As for me and my **f**, we will Jos 24:15
All the **f-ies** of the nations will Ps 22:27
makes their **f-ies** multiply like Ps 107:41
All the **f-ies** of the earth will be Ac 3:25
he and all his **f** were baptized. Ac 16:33
from whom every **f** in heaven and Eph 3:15

FAMINE

There was a **f** in the land, Gn 12:10
seven years of **f** will take place Gn 41:30
by sword, **f**, and plague. Jr 14:12
not a **f** of bread or a thirst for Am 8:11
There will be **f-s** and earthquakes Mt 24:7
or persecution or **f** or nakedness Rm 8:35

FAR

As **f** as the east is from the Ps 103:12
yet their hearts are **f** from Me, Is 29:13
but their heart is **f** from Me. Mt 15:8
You are not **f** from the kingdom Mk 12:34
you who were **f** away have been Eph 2:13

FAST (N)

Will the **f** I choose be like this: Is 58:5
Announce a sacred **f**; Jl 1:14; 2:15

FAST (V)

baby was alive, you **f-ed** 2Sm 12:21
After He had **f-ed** 40 days and 40 Mt 4:2
Whenever you **f**, don't be sad-faced Mt 6:16
but Your disciples do not **f**? Mt 9:14
guests cannot **f** while the groom Mk 2:19
I **f** twice a week; I give a tenth Lk 18:12
after they had **f-ed**, prayed, and Ac 13:3

FASTING

so their **f** is obvious to people Mt 6:16
come out except by prayer and **f**. Mt 17:21

FAT

is better than the **f** of rams. 1Sm 15:22

FATAL

but his **f** wound was healed. Rv 13:3

FATE

there is one **f** for everyone. Ec 9:3
and who considered His **f**? Is 53:8

FATHER

a man leaves his **f** and mother Gn 2:24
become the **f** of many nations Gn 17:4
Honor your **f** and your mother so Ex 20:12
Honor your **f** and your mother, Dt 5:16
F-s are not to be put to death for Dt 24:16
Isn't He your **F** and Creator? Dt 32:6
I will be a **f** to him, and he 2Sm 7:14
today I have become Your **F**. Ps 2:7
You are my **F**, my God, the rock Ps 89:26
Listen, my son, to your **f-'s** instruction Pr 1:8
A wise son brings joy to his **f**, Pr 10:1
Eternal **F**, Prince of Peace. Is 9:6
not die for his **f-'s** iniquity. Ezk 18:17
Our **F** in heaven, Your name be Mt 6:9
who loves **f** or mother more Mt 10:37
Honor your **f** and your mother; Mt 15:4
will leave his **f** and mother and Mt 19:5
you have one **F**, who is in heaven Mt 23:9
Abba, **F**! All things are possible Mk 14:36
that I had to be in my **F-'s** house? Lk 2:49
What **f** among you, if his son asks Lk 11:11
Jesus said, "**F**, forgive them Lk 23:34
Stop turning My **F-'s** house into Jn 2:16
was even calling God His own **F**, Jn 5:18
You are of your **f** the Devil, Jn 8:44
snatch them out of the **F-'s** hand. Jn 10:29
The **F** and I are one. Jn 10:30
the **F** is in Me and I in the **F**. Jn 10:38
In My **F-'s** house are many dwelling Jn 14:2
comes to the **F** except through Jn 14:6
show us the **F**, and that's enough Jn 14:8
who has seen Me has seen the **F**. Jn 14:9
you ask the **F** in My name, Jn 15:16
by whom we cry out, "*Abba*, **F**!" Rm 8:15
I will be a **F** to you, and you 2Co 6:18
one God and **F** of all, who is Eph 4:6
Honor your **f** and mother, which Eph 6:2
F-s, don't stir up anger in Eph 6:4
F-s, do not exasperate your Col 3:21
I will be His **F**, and He will be Heb 1:5
what son is there that a **f** does not Heb 12:7
down from the **F** of lights; Jms 1:17

FATHERLESS

He executes justice for the **f** and Dt 10:18
You are a helper of the **f**. Ps 10:14
a father of the **f** and a champion Ps 68:5
and helps the **f** and the widow, Ps 146:9
don't encroach on the fields of the **f** Pr 23:10

FATTENED

Then bring the **f** calf and Lk 15:23
You have **f** your hearts for the Jms 5:5

FAULT

Cleanse me from my hidden **f-s**. Ps 19:12
Why then does He still find **f**? Rm 9:19
without **f** or failure until 1Tm 6:14

FAULTLESS

who are **f** in a crooked Php 2:15

FAVOR (N)

Noah ... found **f** in the sight of Gn 6:8
moment, but His **f**, a lifetime. Ps 30:5
and obtains **f** from the LORD, Pr 8:35
for you have found **f** with God. Lk 1:30
and in **f** with God and with Lk 2:52
God and having **f** with all the Ac 2:47
trying to win the **f** of people, Gl 1:10

FAVOR (V)

peace on earth to people He **f-s**! Lk 2:14

FAVORITISM

that God doesn't show **f**, Ac 10:34
There is no **f** with God. Rm 2:11
and there is no **f** with Him. Eph 6:9
doing nothing out of **f**. 1Tm 5:21
do not show **f** as you hold on to Jms 2:1

FEAR (N)

The **f** of the LORD is pure, Ps 19:9
and delivered me from all my **f-s**. Ps 34:4
f of the LORD is the beginning Ps 111:10
The **f** of the LORD is the beginning Pr 1:7
delight will be in the **f** of the LORD. Is 11:3
of slavery to fall back into **f**, Rm 8:15
salvation with **f** and trembling. Php 2:12
There is no **f** in love; instead,
perfect love drives out **f**, 1Jn 4:18

FEAR (V)

For now I know that you **f** God, Gn 22:12
F Yahweh your God, worship Him Dt 6:13
f-ed the LORD, but they also 2Kg 17:33
He is **f-ed** above all gods. 1Ch 16:25
f-s God and turns away from Jb 1:8; 2:3
darkest valley, I **f** no danger, for Ps 23:4
my salvation—whom should I **f**? Ps 27:1
To **f** the LORD is to hate evil. Pr 8:13
but a woman who **f-s** the LORD will Pr 31:30
f God and keep His commands, Ec 12:13
Do not **f**, for I am with you; Is 41:10
f Him who is able to destroy both Mt 10:28
town who didn't **f** God or respect Lk 18:2
So the one who **f-s** has not reached 1Jn 4:18

FEARFULNESS

has not given us a spirit of **f**, 2Tm 1:7

FEAST

I hate, I despise your **f-s**! Am 5:21
us observe the **f**, not with old 1Co 5:8
to the marriage **f** of the Lamb Rv 19:9

FEASTING (N)

than a house full of **f** with strife. Pr 17:1
than to go to a house of **f**, Ec 7:2

FEATHERS

He will cover you with His **f**; Ps 91:4

FEED

He **fed** you in the wilderness with Dt 8:16
shepherds **f** themselves rather than Ezk 34:8
your heavenly Father **f-s** them. Mt 6:26
so the one who **f-s** on Me will live Jn 6:57
"**F** My lambs," He told him. Jn 21:15
If your enemy is hungry, **f** him. Rm 12:20

FEEDING

no oxen, the **f** trough is empty, Pr 14:4
and laid Him in a **f** trough Lk 2:7

FELLOWSHIP

this is the law of the **f** sacrifice Lv 7:11
We used to have close **f**; Ps 55:14
teaching, to the **f**, to the breaking Ac 2:42
Or what **f** does light have with 2Co 6:14
and the **f** of the Holy Spirit be 2Co 13:13

we say, "We have **f** with Him" 1Jn 1:6

FEMALE
He created them male and **f**. Gn 1:27
new ... a **f** will shelter a man. Jr 31:22
beginning made them male and **f**, Mt 19:4
slave or free, male or **f**; Gl 3:28

FERVENT
and being **f** in spirit, he spoke Ac 18:25
be **f** in spirit; serve the Lord. Rm 12:11

FESTIVAL
Celebrate a **f** in My honor three Ex 23:14
"Not during the **f**," they said Mk 14:2
the matter of a **f** or a new moon Col 2:16

FESTIVE
leading the **f** procession to the Ps 42:4

FEVER
was lying in bed with a **f**, Mk 1:30

FEW
were **f** in number, very **f** indeed Ps 105:12
Let his days be **f**; let another Ps 109:8
but the workers are **f**. Mt 9:37
are invited, but **f** are chosen. Mt 22:14
are there **f** being saved? Lk 13:23

FEWEST
you were the **f** of all peoples. Dt 7:7

FIELD
Let the **f-s** and everything in them Ps 96:12
blooms like a flower of the **f**; Ps 103:15
I went by the **f** of a slacker and Pr 24:30
how the wildflowers of the **f** grow: Mt 6:28
f is the world; and the good seed Mt 13:38
out in the **f-s** and keeping watch Lk 2:8
your eyes and look at the **f-s**, Jn 4:35
You are God's **f**, God's building 1Co 3:9

FIERY
surprised when the **f** ordeal comes 1Pt 4:12

FIG
so they sewed **f** leaves together Gn 3:7
Though the **f** tree does not bud Hab 3:17
At once the **f** tree withered. Mt 21:19
F-s aren't gathered from thornbushes Lk 6:44
Can a **f** tree produce olives, Jms 3:12

FIGHT (N)
Fight the good **f** for the faith; 1Tm 6:12
I have fought the good **f**, I have 2Tm 4:7

FIGHT (V)
The Lord will **f** for you; Ex 14:14
Lord; **f** those who **f** me. Ps 35:1
F the good fight for the faith; 1Tm 6:12
God not to **f** about words; 2Tm 2:14
I have **fought** the good fight, I have 2Tm 4:7

FILL
Be fruitful, multiply, **f** the earth, Gn 1:28
glory of the Lord **f-ed** the temple. 1Kg 8:11
whole earth is **f-ed** with His glory Ps 72:19
His glory **f-s** the whole earth. Is 6:3
Do I not **f** the heavens and the Jr 23:24
and I will **f** this house with glory, Hg 2:7
Everyone ate and was **f-ed**. Mt 14:20
He will be **f-ed** with the Holy Lk 1:15
"**F** the jars with water," Jesus Jn 2:7
you ate the loaves and were **f-ed**. Jn 6:26
they were all **f-ed** with the Holy Ac 2:4
Then Peter was **f-ed** with the Holy Ac 4:8
But Stephen, **f-ed** by the Holy Ac 7:55
sight and be **f-ed** with the Holy Ac 9:17
called Paul—**f-ed** with the Holy Ac 13:9
the God of hope **f** you with all Rm 15:13
who **f-s** all things in every way. Eph 1:23
that He might **f** all things. Eph 4:10
but be **f-ed** by the Spirit: Eph 5:18
f-ed with the fruit of Php 1:11

FILTH
all things and consider them **f**, Php 3:8
of all moral **f** and evil, Jms 1:21
removal of the **f** of the flesh, 1Pt 3:21

FILTHY
was dressed with **f** clothes as he Zch 3:3
and **f** language from your mouth. Col 3:8
let the **f** go on being made **f**; Rv 22:11

FIND
If I **f** 50 righteous people Gn 18:26
you will **f** Him when you seek Dt 4:29
those who search for me **f** me. Pr 8:17
For the one who **f-s** me **f-s** life Pr 8:35
who **f-s** a wife **f-s** a good thing Pr 18:22
Who can **f** a capable wife? Pr 31:10
the Lord while He may be **found**; Is 55:6
will seek Me and **f** Me when you Jr 29:13
Keep searching, and you will **f**. Mt 7:7
and you will **f** rest for Mt 11:29
life because of Me will **f** it. Mt 16:25
whose master **f-s** him working Mt 24:46
I have **found** my lost sheep! Lk 15:6
he was lost and is **found**! Lk 15:24
And anyone not **found** written in Rv 20:15

FINISH
He said, "It is **f-ed**!" Jn 19:30
so that I may **f** my course and Ac 20:24
I have **f-ed** the race, I have kept 2Tm 4:7

FIRE
and the pillar of **f** by night Ex 13:22
a chariot of **f** with horses of **f** 2Kg 2:11
their **f** will never go out, Is 66:24
He will be like a refiner's **f** Mal 3:2
you with the Holy Spirit and **f**. Mt 3:11
burn up with **f** that never goes out. Mt 3:12
into the eternal **f** prepared for Mt 25:41
and the **f** is not quenched. Mk 9:44
I came to bring **f** on the earth, Lk 12:49
like flames of **f** that were Ac 2:3
the **f** will test the quality of 1Co 3:13
for our God is a consuming **f**. Heb 12:29
And the tongue is a **f**. Jms 3:6
second death, the lake of **f**. Rv 20:14

FIRM
Stand **f** and see the Lord's Ex 14:13
If you do not stand **f** in your faith, Is 7:9
Be alert, stand **f** in the faith 1Co 16:13
stand **f** and hold to the 2Th 2:15

FIRMLY
The world is **f** established; Ps 93:1; 96:10
are like **f** embedded nails. Ec 12:11
being rooted and **f** established Eph 3:17
if we hold **f** until the end Heb 3:14

FIRST
and then morning: the **f** day. Gn 1:5
The **f** to state his case seems Pr 18:17
I, the Lord, am the **f**, and with the Is 41:4
I am the **f** and I am the last. Is 44:6
But seek **f** the kingdom of God Mt 6:33
F take the log out of your eye, Mt 7:5
f will be last, and the last **f**. Mt 19:30
wants to be **f** among you must be Mt 20:27
F clean the inside of the cup, Mt 23:26
performed this **f** sign in Cana Jn 2:11
were **f** called Christians at Antioch. Ac 11:26
who does evil, **f** to the Jew, and Rm 2:9
The **f** man Adam became a living 1Co 15:45
the dead in Christ will rise **f**. 1Th 4:16
We love because He **f** loved us. 1Jn 4:19
I am the **F** and the Last, Rv 1:17
abandoned the love you had at **f**. Rv 2:4
for the **f** heaven and the **f** earth had Rv 21:1

FIRSTBORN
Lord struck every **f** male in Ex 12:29
Consecrate every **f** male to Me, Ex 13:2
He struck all the **f** in Egypt, Ps 78:51
she gave birth to her **f** Son, Lk 2:7
the **f** from the dead and the Rv 1:5

FIRSTFRUITS
the **f** of those who have fallen 1Co 15:20

FISH (N)
will rule the **f** of the sea, Gn 1:26
Jonah was in the **f** three days Jnh 1:17
he asks for a **f**, will give him Mt 7:10
have five loaves and two **f** here, Mt 14:17
the seven loaves and the **f**, Mt 15:36
full of large **f**—153 of them. Jn 21:11

FISH (V)
I will make you **f** for people! Mt 4:19

FISHERMEN
Then the **f** will mourn. Is 19:8
the sea, since they were **f**. Mk 1:16

FIT
looks back is **f** for the kingdom Lk 9:62

FITTING
husbands, as is **f** in the Lord. Col 3:18

FIVE
hand and chose **f** smooth stones 1Sm 17:40
For you've had **f** husbands, Jn 4:18

FIX
great chasm has been **f-ed** between Lk 16:26

FIXED (ADJ)
it is firmly **f** in heaven. Ps 119:89
If this **f** order departs from My Jr 31:36

FLAME
to him in a **f** of fire within Ex 3:2
Love's **f-s** are fiery **f-s** Sg 8:6
a fire, and its Holy One, a **f**. Is 10:17

FLAMING
cherubim and the **f**, whirling sword Gn 3:24
to extinguish all the **f** arrows of Eph 6:16

FLASH
the lightning **f-es** from horizon to Lk 17:24

FLATTER
they **f** with their tongues. Ps 5:9
A man who **f-s** his neighbor spreads Pr 29:5
f-ing people for their own advantage Jd 16

FLATTERING (ADJ)
and a **f** mouth causes ruin. Pr 26:28

FLEE
But Moses **fled** from Pharaoh and Ex 2:15
Where can I **f** from Your presence Ps 139:7
The wicked **f** when no one is Pr 28:1
dear friends, **f** from idolatry. 1Co 10:14
F from youthful passions, and 2Tm 2:22
Devil, and he will **f** from you. Jms 4:7

FLEECE
If dew is only on the **f**, Jdg 6:37

FLEETING
is deceptive and beauty is **f**, Pr 31:30
all the days of your **f** life, Ec 9:9

FLESH
bone of my bone, and **f** of my **f**; Gn 2:23
wife, and they become one **f**. Gn 2:24
yet I will see God in my **f**. Jb 19:26
and give them a heart of **f**, Ezk 11:19
and give you a heart of **f**. Ezk 36:26
f and blood did not reveal this Mt 16:17
and the two will become one **f**? Mt 19:5
is willing, but the **f** is weak. Mt 26:41
Whatever is born of the **f** is **f**, Jn 3:6
one who eats My **f** and drinks My Jn 6:56
are not in the **f**, but in the Spirit, Rm 8:9
brothers, my own **f** and blood. Rm 9:3
a thorn in the **f** was given to me 2Co 12:7
the works of the **f** are obvious: Gl 5:19
is not against **f** and blood, Eph 6:12

FLOCK
protects His **f** like a shepherd Is 40:11
You have scattered My **f**, Jr 23:2
but you do not tend the **f**. Ezk 34:3
sheep of the **f** will be scattered. Mt 26:31
watch at night over their **f**. Lk 2:8
will be one **f**, one shepherd. Jn 10:16

FLOGGED
having Jesus **f**, he handed Him Mt 27:26

FLOOD
I am bringing a **f** Gn 6:17
LORD sat enthroned at the **f**; Ps 29:10
They didn't know until the **f** came Mt 24:39
When the **f** came, the river Lk 6:48

FLOODGATES
the **f** of the sky were opened, Gn 7:11
will not open the **f** of heaven Mal 3:10

FLOODWATERS
f on the earth to destroy every Gn 6:17
Don't let the **f** sweep over me or Ps 69:15

FLOW
streams of living water **f** from Jn 7:38

FLOWER
blooms like a **f** of the field; Ps 103:15
withers, the **f-s** fade, but the word Is 40:8
withers, and the **f** falls, 1Pt 1:24

FLUTE
We played the **f** for you, but you Mt 11:17

FLY (N)
send swarms of **f-ies** against you, Ex 8:21
will whistle to the **f** that is at Is 7:18

FLY (V)
the arrow that **f-ies** by day, Ps 91:5

FOAL
on a colt, the **f** of a donkey. Zch 9:9
the **f** of a beast of burden. Mt 21:5

FOCUS
So we do not **f** on what is seen, 2Co 4:18
They are **f-ed** on earthly things, Php 3:19

FOLD (N)
sheep that are not of this **f**; Jn 10:16

FOLD (V)
little **f-ing** of the arms to rest, Pr 6:10; 24:33
but was **f-ed** up in a separate place Jn 20:7

FOLLOW
Do not **f** other gods, the gods of Dt 6:14
If Yahweh is God, **f** Him. 1Kg 18:21
F Me, … and I will make you Mt 4:19
take up his cross, and **f** Me. Mt 16:24
Anyone who **f-s** Me will never walk Jn 8:12
The sheep **f** him because they Jn 10:4
These are the ones who **f** the Lamb Rv 14:4

FOLLY
The woman **F** is rowdy; Pr 9:13

FOOD
every green plant for **f**. Gn 1:30
Every living creature will be **f** Gn 9:3
He gives **f** to every creature. Ps 136:25
feed me with the **f** I need. Pr 30:8
Isn't life more than **f** Mt 6:25
As a result, He made all **f-s** clean. Mk 7:19
My **f** is to do the will of Him Jn 4:34
Don't work for the **f** that perishes Jn 6:27
About **f** offered to idols: 1Co 8:1

FOOL
The **f** says in his heart, "God Ps 14:1; 53:1
f-s despise wisdom and discipline. Pr 1:7
A **f** despises his father's discipline, Pr 15:5
Don't answer a **f** according to Pr 26:4
whoever says to his brother, '**F**!' Mt 5:22
to be wise, they became **f-s** Rm 1:22
We are **f-s** for Christ, but you are 1Co 4:10

FOOLISH
A **f** son is grief to his father Pr 17:25
like a **f** man who built his house on Mt 7:26
of them were **f** and five were Mt 25:2
God made the world's wisdom **f**? 1Co 1:20
f Galatians! Who has hypnotized you Gl 3:1

FOOLISHNESS
but the **f** of fools produces **f**. Pr 14:24
a fool according to his **f** Pr 26:4,5
the message of the cross is **f** 1Co 1:18
of this world is **f** with God, 1Co 3:19

FOOT
Remove the sandals from your **feet**, Ex 3:5
You put everything under his **feet**: Ps 8:6
strike your **f** against a stone. Ps 91:12
is a lamp for my **feet** and a light Ps 119:105
on the mountains are the **feet** of Is 52:7
strike your **f** against a stone Mt 4:6
f causes your downfall, cut it off Mt 18:8
to wash His **feet** with her tears. Lk 7:38
showed them His hands and **feet**. Lk 24:40
began to wash His disciples' **feet** Jn 13:5
beautiful are the **feet** of those Rm 10:15
soon crush Satan under your **feet**. Rm 16:20
If the **f** should say, "Because 1Co 12:15
all His enemies under His **feet**. 1Co 15:25
and your **feet** sandaled with Eph 6:15

FOOTSTOOL
I make Your enemies Your **f**. Ps 110:1
and earth is My **f**. Is 66:1
is My throne, and earth My **f**. Ac 7:49
His enemies are made His **f**. Heb 10:13

FORBID
do not **f** speaking in other 1Co 14:39

FORBIDDEN (ADJ)
the lips of the **f** woman drip Pr 5:3

FORCE (N)
violent have been seizing it by **f**. Mt 11:12
and the **f-s** of Hades will not Mt 16:18
take Him by **f** to make Him king, Jn 6:15
the elemental **f-s** of the world. Gl 4:3
against the spiritual **f-s** of evil Eph 6:12
the elemental **f-s** of the world, Col 2:8,20

FORCE (V)
And if anyone **f-s** you to go one Mt 5:41
They **f-d** this man to carry His Mt 27:32

FORCED (ADJ)
the Canaanites serve as **f** labor Jdg 1:28

FORDS
captured the **f** of the Jordan Jdg 12:5

FOREHEAD
and as a reminder on your **f**, Ex 13:9
hit the Philistine on his **f**. 1Sm 17:49
a mark on the **f-s** of the men who Ezk 9:4
slaves of our God on their **f-s**. Rv 7:3
not have God's seal on their **f-s**. Rv 9:4
on his right hand or on his **f**, Rv 13:16
mark on their **f-s** or their hands. Rv 20:4

FOREIGN
I am a **f** resident among you. Gn 23:4
I have been a stranger in a **f** land. Ex 2:22
get rid of the **f** gods that are Jos 24:23
must not bow down to a **f** god. Ps 81:9
sing the LORD's song on **f** soil? Ps 137:4

FOREIGNER
the land where you live as a **f**, Gn 28:4
a **f** in a foreign land. Ex 2:22; 18:3
the Passover: no **f** may eat it. Ex 12:43
if you no longer oppress the **f**, Jr 7:6
by the lips of **f-s**, and even then, 1Co 14:21
are no longer **f-s** and strangers, Eph 2:19
that they were **f-s** and temporary Heb 11:13

FOREKNEW
For those He **f** He also Rm 8:29
rejected His people whom He **f**. Rm 11:2

FORERUNNER
entered there on our behalf as a **f**, Heb 6:20

FORESKIN
circumcise the flesh of your **f** Gn 17:11

FOREVER
will not remain with mankind **f**, Gn 6:3
your throne will be established **f**. 2Sm 7:16
But the LORD sits enthroned **f**; Ps 9:7
F, You are a priest like Ps 110:4

for wealth is not **f**; Pr 27:24
of this bread he will live **f**. Jn 6:51
You are a priest **f** in the order Heb 5:6
same yesterday, today, and **f**. Heb 13:8
the word of the Lord endures **f**. 1Pt 1:25
And they will reign **f** and ever. Rv 22:5

FORFEITS
whole world, yet loses or **f** himself? Lk 9:25

FORGET
be careful not to **f** the LORD who Dt 6:12
you **f-got** the God who gave birth Dt 32:18
and do not **f** all His benefits. Ps 103:2
If I **f** you, Jerusalem, may my
 right hand **f** its skill. Ps 137:5
My son, don't **f** my teaching, but Pr 3:1
Can a woman **f** her nursing child Is 49:15
F-ting what is behind Php 3:13
you have **f-gotten** the exhortation Heb 12:5
and immediately **f-s** what kind of Jms 1:24

FORGIVE
if You would only **f** their sin. Ex 32:32
f their sin, and heal their land. 2Ch 7:14
one whose transgression is **f-n**, Ps 32:1
For I will **f** their wrongdoing Jr 31:34
And **f** us our debts, as we also
 have **f-n** our debtors. Mt 6:12
Who can **f** sins but God alone? Mk 2:7
But the one who is **f-n** little, Lk 7:47
and if he repents, **f** him. Lk 17:3
Father, **f** them, because Lk 23:34
f-ing one another, just as God
 also **f-gave** you in Christ. Eph 4:32
and **f-gave** us all our trespasses. Col 2:13
committed sins, he will be **f-n**. Jms 5:15
and righteous to **f** us our sins 1Jn 1:9

FORGIVENESS
You there is **f**, so that You may Ps 130:4
shed for many for the **f** of sins. Mt 26:28
through His blood, the **f** of our Eph 1:7
have redemption, the **f** of sins, Col 1:14
shedding of blood there is no **f**. Heb 9:22

FORM (N)
He didn't have ... **f** or majesty Is 53:2
and you haven't seen His **f**. Jn 5:37
existing in the **f** of God, did not Php 2:6
holding to the **f** of godliness but 2Tm 3:5

FORM (V)
Then the LORD God **f-ed** the man out Gn 2:7
when I was **f-ed** in the depths of Ps 139:15
Will what is **f-ed** say to the
 one who **f-ed** it, Rm 9:20
you until Christ is **f-ed** in you. Gl 4:19

FORMLESS
Now the earth was **f** and empty, Gn 1:2

FORSAKE
I will not leave you or **f** you. Jos 1:5
my God, why have You **f-n** me? Ps 22:1
My God, why have You **f-n** Me? Mt 27:46
will never leave you or **f** you. Heb 13:5

FORTRESS
The LORD is my rock, my **f**, 2Sm 22:2
refuge and my **f**, my God, in whom Ps 91:2

FORTUNES
LORD restores the **f** of His people, Ps 14:7

FORWARD
and reaching **f** to what is ahead Php 3:13
he was looking **f** to the city Heb 11:10

FOUND
The LORD **f-ed** the earth by wisdom Pr 3:19

FOUNDATION
established the earth on its **f-s**; Ps 104:5
precious cornerstone, a sure **f**; Is 28:16
because its **f** was on the rock. Mt 7:25
builds on that **f** with gold, 1Co 3:12
built on the **f** of the apostles Eph 2:20
God's solid **f** stands firm, 2Tm 2:19
looking ... to the city that has **f-s**, Heb 11:10

FOUNTAIN
for with You is life's **f**. Ps 36:9
abandoned Me, the **f** of living water, Jr 2:13

FOX
F-es have dens and birds of the Mt 8:20
Go tell that **f**, 'Look! Lk 13:32

FRAGRANCE
we are the **f** of Christ among 2Co 2:15

FRAGRANT
sacrificial and **f** offering to God. Eph 5:2

FRANKINCENSE
carry gold and **f** and proclaim Is 60:6
gold, **f**, and myrrh. Mt 2:11

FREE (ADJ)
and the truth will set you **f**. Jn 8:32
Jesus has set you **f** from the law Rm 8:2
slave or **f**, male or female; Gl 3:28
Christ has liberated us to be **f**. Gl 5:1
and has set us **f** from our sins Rv 1:5

FREE (V)
The LORD **f-s** prisoners. Ps 146:7
who has died is **f-d** from sin's Rm 6:7

FREEDOM
to proclaim ... **f** to the prisoners; Is 61:1
to proclaim **f** to the captives Lk 4:18
Spirit of the Lord is, there is **f**. 2Co 3:17
don't use this **f** as an opportunity Gl 5:13
but don't use your **f** as a way to 1Pt 2:16

FREELY
our God, for He will **f** forgive. Is 55:7
are justified **f** by His grace Rm 3:24

FRESH
put new wine into **f** wineskins, Mt 9:17
saltwater spring yield **f** water. Jms 3:12

FRIEND
as a man speaks with his **f**. Ex 33:11
Now when Job's three **f-s**—Eliphaz Jb 2:11
A **f** loves at all times, Pr 17:17
but there is a **f** who stays closer Pr 18:24
wounds of a **f** are trustworthy Pr 27:6
a **f** of tax collectors and Mt 11:19
lay down his life for his **f-s**. Jn 15:13
and he was called God's **f**. Jms 2:23
be the world's **f** becomes God's Jms 4:4

FRIENDSHIP
f with the world is hostility Jms 4:4

FRONT
the **f** seats in the synagogues, Mt 23:6

FRUIT
that bears its **f** in season Ps 1:3
The **f** of the righteous is a tree Pr 11:30
produce **f** consistent with Mt 3:8
recognize them by their **f**. Mt 7:16
not drink of this **f** of the vine Mt 26:29
that does not produce **f** He removes, Jn 15:2
But the **f** of the Spirit is love, joy, Gl 5:22
bearing **f** in every good work Col 1:10
tree of life ... bearing 12 kinds of **f**, Rv 22:2

FRUITFUL
blessed them, "Be **f**, multiply, Gn 1:22
But the Israelites were **f**, Ex 1:7

FULFILL
May Yahweh **f** all your requests Ps 20:5
F what you vow. Ec 5:4
not come to destroy but to **f**. Mt 5:17
this Scripture has been **f-ed**. Lk 4:21
and the Psalms must be **f-ed**. Lk 24:44
loves another has **f-ed** the law. Rm 13:8
husband should **f** his marital 1Co 7:3
entire law is **f-ed** in one statement Gl 5:14
way you will **f** the law of Christ Gl 6:2

FULFILLMENT
therefore, is the **f** of the law. Rm 13:10

FULL
land will be as **f** of the knowledge Is 11:9
whole body will be **f** of light. Mt 6:22
from the Father, **f** of grace and Jn 1:14
You are already **f**! 1Co 4:8

FULLNESS
grace after grace from His **f**, Jn 1:16
the **f** of the One who fills all Eph 1:23
filled with all the **f** of God. Eph 3:19
have all His **f** dwell in Him, Col 1:19
entire **f** of God's nature dwells Col 2:9

FULLY
I will know **f**, as I am **f** known. 1Co 13:12

FURNACE
tested you in the **f** of affliction. Is 48:10
thrown into a **f** of blazing fire. Dn 3:6
throw them into the blazing **f** Mt 13:42

FURY
who have drunk the cup of His **f** Is 51:17
and the **f** of a fire about to Heb 10:27

FUTILE
Everything is **f**. Ec 1:2

FUTILITY
"Absolute **f**," says the Teacher. Ec 1:2
For he comes in **f** and he goes in Ec 6:4
creation was subjected to **f** Rm 8:20
in the **f** of their thoughts. Eph 4:17

FUTURE
the man of peace will have a **f**. Ps 37:37
For the evil has no **f**; Pr 24:20
to give you a **f** and a hope. Jr 29:11

GABRIEL
Angel who explained Daniel's visions (Dn 8:16; 9:21) and announced John's and Jesus' births (Lk 1:19,26).

GAD
1. Son of Jacob by Zilpah (Gn 30:9-11). Tribe with Transjordan territory north of the Dead Sea (Nm 32; Dt 3:16-17; Jos 18:7).
2. Seer at time of David (1Sm 22:5; 2Sm 24:11-19; 1Ch 21:9-19; 29:29; 2Ch 29:25).

GAIN (N)
Ill-gotten **g-s** do not profit Pr 10:2
living is Christ and dying is **g**. Php 1:21
with contentment is a great **g**. 1Tm 6:6

GAIN (V)
a man if he **g-s** the whole world Mt 16:26
benefit a man to **g** the whole world Mk 8:36
filth, so that I may **g** Christ Php 3:8

GALILEAN
You were with Jesus the **G** too. Mt 26:69

GALILEE
1. Region in northern Palestine (Jos 20:7; 21:32; 1Kg 9:11); where Jesus lived (Mt 2:22; 3:13; 21:11) and ministered (Is 9:1; Mt 4:12,15,23); where He appeared after the resurrection (Mt 26:32; Ac 1:11).
2. Sea along the Jordan (Mt 4:18; 15:29).

GALL
they gave me **g** for my food, Ps 69:21
Him wine mixed with **g** to drink. Mt 27:34

GALLOWS
he had the **g** constructed. Est 5:14

GAMALIEL
Pharisee (Ac 5:34); Paul's teacher (22:3).

GANG
a **g** of evildoers has closed in Ps 22:16

GANGRENE
their word will spread like **g**; 2Tm 2:17

GAP
and stand in the **g** before Me on Ezk 22:30

GARDEN
LORD God planted a **g** in Eden, Gn 2:8
A new tomb was in the **g**; Jn 19:41

GARDENER
Supposing He was the **g**, she Jn 20:15

GARMENT
But leaving his **g** in her hand, Gn 39:12
They divided my **g-s** among Ps 22:18
You will change them like a **g**, Ps 102:26
clothed me with the **g-s** of salvation Is 61:10
patches an old **g** with unshrunk Mt 9:16

GATE
Lift up your heads, you **g-s**! Ps 24:7
Enter His **g-s** with thanksgiving Ps 100:4
Enter through the narrow **g**. Mt 7:13
also suffered outside the **g**, Heb 13:12
Each day its **g-s** will never close Rv 21:25

GATHER
and **g** enough for that day. Ex 16:4
G My faithful ones to Me, Ps 50:5
and a time to **g** stones; Ec 3:5
He **g-s** the lambs in His arms and Is 40:11
who does not **g** with Me scatters Mt 12:30
or three are **g-ed** together in My Mt 18:20
I wanted to **g** your children together, as a hen **g-s** her chicks Mt 23:37

GAZE (N)
fix your **g** straight ahead. Pr 4:25

GAZE (V)
So I **g** on You in the sanctuary Ps 63:2
they were **g-ing** into heaven Ac 1:10

GEHAZI
Elisha's attendant (2Kg 4:11-37; 5:20-27; 8:4-5).

GENEALOGY
Now this is the **g** of Perez: Ru 4:18
Israel was registered in the **g-ies** 1Ch 9:1
to myths and endless **g-ies**. 1Tm 1:4
without father, mother, or **g**, Heb 7:3

GENERATION
to the third and fourth **g**. Ex 34:7
been our refuge in every **g**. Ps 90:1
There is a **g** that Pr 30:11
To what should I compare this **g**? Mt 11:16
adulterous **g** demands a sign, Mt 12:39
This **g** will certainly not pass Mt 24:34
from now on all **g-s** will call me Lk 1:48

GENEROSITY
giving, with **g**; Rm 12:8

GENEROUS
A **g** person will be blessed, Pr 22:9
to be **g**, willing to share, 1Tm 6:18

GENEROUSLY
who sows **g** will also reap **g**. 2Co 9:6

GENTILE
Don't even the **G-s** do the same? Mt 5:47
they will hand Him over to the **G-s** Mt 20:19
a light for revelation to the **G-s** Lk 2:32
trampled by the **G-s** until the times of the **G-s** are fulfilled. Lk 21:24
Why did the **G-s** rage Ac 4:25
been poured out on the **G-s** also. Ac 10:45
Is He not also for **G-s**? Rm 3:29
full number of the **G-s** has come Rm 11:25
he regularly ate with the **G-s** before Gl 2:12

GENTLE
A **g** answer turns away anger, Pr 15:1
a **g** tongue can break a bone. Pr 25:15
The **g** are blessed, for they Mt 5:5
because I am **g** and humble in Mt 11:29
is coming to you, **g**, and mounted Mt 21:5
peace-loving, **g**, compliant, full Jms 3:17
quality of a **g** and quiet spirit 1Pt 3:4

GENTLENESS
or in love and a spirit of **g**? 1Co 4:21
appeal to you by the **g** ... of Christ 2Co 10:1
goodness, faith, **g**, self-control. Gl 5:23
humility and **g**, with patience Eph 4:2
faith, love, endurance, and **g**. 1Tm 6:11
do this with **g** and respect, 1Pt 3:16

GENUINELY
widows who are **g** widows. 1Tm 5:3

GENUINENESS
am testing the **g** of your love. 2Co 8:8
so that the **g** of your faith 1Pt 1:7

GERASENE
sailed to the region of the **G-s**, Lk 8:26

GET
G wisdom Pr 16:16

GETHSEMANE
with them to a place called **G**, Mt 26:36

GHOST
they thought it was a **g** and cried Mk 6:49
because a **g** does not have flesh Lk 24:39

GIBEON
inhabitants of **G** heard what Jos 9:3
Sun, stand still over **G**, Jos 10:12

GIDEON
Judge (Jdg 6–8; Heb 11:32). The fleece (Jdg 6:36-40). God reduced his army (7:2-8).

GIFT
A **g** opens doors for a man and Pr 18:16
leave your **g** there in front of Mt 5:24
to give good **g-s** to your children, Mt 7:11
from me is Corban" (that is, a **g** Mk 7:11
will receive the **g** of the Holy Ac 2:38
but the **g** of God is eternal life Rm 6:23
we have different **g-s**: Rm 12:6
each has his own **g** from God, 1Co 7:7
Now there are different **g-s**, 1Co 12:4
to God for His indescribable **g**. 2Co 9:15
every perfect **g** is from above, Jms 1:17

GILEAD
Region east of the Jordan and north of Moab, allotted to Reuben, Gad, and half of Manasseh (Nm 32:40; Dt 3:12-13; Jos 13:8-31; 17:1-6).

GIRL
by the hand, and the **g** got up. Mt 9:25
Little **g**, I say to you, get up! Mk 5:41

GIVE
I will **g** this land to your offspring. Gn 12:7
The LORD **g-s**, and the LORD takes Jb 1:21
G thanks to the God of gods. Ps 136:2
if he is thirsty, **g** him water Pr 25:21
leech has two daughters: "**G**, **G**!" Pr 30:15
be born for us, a son will be **g-n** to us, Is 9:6
I will not **g** My glory to another Is 42:8
I will **g** you a new heart and Ezk 36:26
G us today our daily bread. Mt 6:11
Keep asking, and it will be **g-n** Mt 7:7
hungry and you **gave** Me Mt 25:35
G, and it will be **g-n** to you; Lk 6:38
is My body, which is **g-n** for you. Lk 22:19
He **gave** them the right to be Jn 1:12
He **gave** His One and Only Son, Jn 3:16
I **g** them eternal life, Jn 10:28
not **g** to you as the world **g-s**. Jn 14:27
since He Himself **g-s** everyone life Ac 17:25
blessed to **g** than to receive. Ac 20:35
He personally **gave** some to be Eph 4:11
gave Himself—a ransom for all 1Tm 2:6
be ready to **g** a defense to 1Pt 3:15

GIVER
for God loves a cheerful **g**. 2Co 9:7

GLAD
Let the heavens be **g** and 1Ch 16:31
let us rejoice and be **g** in it. Ps 118:24
Be **g** and rejoice, because your Mt 5:12

GLADNESS
Let me hear joy and **g**; Ps 51:8
Serve the LORD with **g**; Ps 100:2

GLASS
Something like a sea of **g**, Rv 4:6
city was pure gold like clear **g**. Rv 21:18

GLEAN
you must not **g** what is left. Dt 24:21
saw what she had **g-ed**. Ru 2:18

GLOAT
not let my enemies **g** over me. Ps 25:2

GLOOM
a day of darkness and **g**, Jl 2:2
to darkness, **g**, and storm, Heb 12:18

GLORIFY
I have **g-ied** it, and I will **g** it again! Jn 12:28
the Son of Man is **g-ied**, and
God is **g-ied** in Him. Jn 13:31
G Your Son so that the Son may **g** Jn 17:1
those He justified, He also **g-ied**. Rm 8:30
Therefore **g** God in your body. 1Co 6:20

GLORIOUS
Who is like You, **g** in holiness Ex 15:11
G things are said about you, Ps 87:3

GLORY
Please, let me see Your **g**. Ex 33:18
The **g** has departed from Israel, 1Sm 4:21
Declare His **g** among the nations 1Ch 16:24
crowned him with **g** and honor. Ps 8:5
Then the King of **g** will come in. Ps 24:7
ascribe to the LORD **g** and strength. Ps 29:1
the whole earth is filled with His **g**. Ps 72:19
ascribe to the LORD **g** and strength. Ps 96:7
His **g** fills the whole earth. Is 6:3
And the **g** of the LORD will appear, Is 40:5
the **g** of the LORD filled Ezk 43:5; 44:4
the power and the **g** forever. Mt 6:13
the Son of Man comes in His **g**, Mt 25:31
and the **g** of the Lord shone Lk 2:9
G to God in the highest heaven, Lk 2:14
We observed His **g**, the **g** as the
One and Only Son Jn 1:14
exchanged the **g** of the immortal Rm 1:23
and fall short of the **g** of God. Rm 3:23
not worth comparing with the **g** Rm 8:18
adoption, the **g**, the covenants Rm 9:4
do everything for God's **g**. 1Co 10:31
incomparable eternal weight of **g**. 2Co 4:17
Christ in you, the hope of **g**. Col 1:27
crowned him with **g** and honor Heb 2:7
worthy to receive **g** and honor Rv 4:11

GLUTTON
and the **g** will become poor Pr 23:21
they say, 'Look, a **g** and a drunkard Mt 11:19

GNASH
they **g-ed** their teeth at me. Ps 35:16
will be weeping and **g-ing** of teeth. Mt 8:12
will be weeping and **g-ing** of teeth. Mt 25:30
and **g-ed** their teeth at him. Ac 7:54

GNAT
strain out a **g**, yet gulp down Mt 23:24

GO
Let My people **g**, Ex 5:1
For wherever you **g**, I will **g**, Ru 1:16
Where can I **g** to escape Your Ps 139:7
about the way he should **g**; Pr 22:6
We all **went** astray like sheep; Is 53:6
I say to this one, '**G**!' and he **g-es**; Mt 8:9
G, therefore, and make disciples Mt 28:19
G into all the world and preach Mk 16:15
I am **g-ing** away to prepare a place Jn 14:2

GOAL
I pursue as my **g** the prize Php 3:14
receiving the **g** of your faith, 1Pt 1:9

GOAT
put them on the **g-'s** head and send Lv 16:21
bulls or drink the blood of **g-s**? Ps 50:13
separates the sheep from the **g-s**. Mt 25:32
For if the blood of **g-s** and bulls Heb 9:13

GOD
In the beginning **G** created the Gn 1:1
you will be like **G**, knowing good Gn 3:5
the sons of **G** saw that the Gn 6:2
he was a priest to **G** Most High. Gn 14:18
The **G** Who Sees, for she said Gn 16:13
saying, "I am **G** Almighty. Gn 17:1
Yahweh, the Everlasting **G**. Gn 21:33
G planned it for good to bring Gn 50:20
I am the **G** of your father, the **G** of
Abraham, the **G** of Isaac, and
the **G** of Jacob. Ex 3:6
Yahweh, the **G** of your fathers Ex 3:15
Yahweh, the **G** of the Hebrews, Ex 3:18
This is my **G**, and I will praise Him, Ex 15:2
Do not have other **g-s** besides Me. Ex 20:3
I, Yahweh your **G**, am a jealous **G**, Ex 20:5
G is not a man who lies, or a Nm 23:19
G is a consuming fire, a jealous **G**. Dt 4:24
the voice of the living **G** speaking Dt 5:26
Yahweh your **G** is **G**, the faithful **G** Dt 7:9
the LORD your **G** is the **G** of **g-s** Dt 10:17
The **G** of old is your dwelling Dt 33:27
and your **G** will be my **G**. Ru 1:16
there is no rock like our **G**. 1Sm 2:2
will know that Israel has a **G**, 1Sm 17:46
LORD **G** of Hosts was with him. 2Sm 5:10
But will **G** indeed live on earth 1Kg 8:27
G who answers with fire, He is **G** 1Kg 18:24
Their **g-s** are **g-s** of the hill 1Kg 20:23
they had worshiped other **g-s**. 2Kg 17:7
And **G** granted his request. 1Ch 4:10
Save us, **G** of our salvation; 1Ch 16:35
our **G** is greater than any of the **g-s**. 2Ch 2:5
says in his heart, "**G** does not exist." Ps 14:1
My **G**, my **G**, why have You Ps 22:1
the nation whose **G** is Yahweh Ps 33:12
G is our refuge and strength, Ps 46:1
Our **G** is a **G** of salvation, Ps 68:20
What **g** is great like **G**? Ps 77:13
For He is our **G**, and we are the Ps 95:7
Acknowledge that Yahweh is **G**. Ps 100:3
Give thanks to the **G** of **g-s**. Ps 136:2
fear **G** and keep His commands, Ec 12:13
Wonderful Counselor, Mighty **G**, Is 9:6
of Judah, "Here is your **G**!" Is 40:9
Yahweh is the everlasting **G**, Is 40:28
There is no **G** but Me. Is 44:6
I will be their **G**, and they will Jr 31:33
I am the LORD, the **G** of all flesh. Jr 32:27
people, and I will be your **G**. Ezk 36:28
Didn't one **G** create us? Mal 2:10
is translated "**G** is with us." Mt 1:23
blessed, for they will see **G**. Mt 5:8
Therefore, what **G** has joined Mt 19:6
and to **G** the things that are **G-'s**. Mt 22:21
that is, "My **G**, My **G**, why have Mt 27:46
Who can forgive sins but **G** alone? Mk 2:7
was with **G**, and the Word was **G**. Jn 1:1
For **G** loved the world in this way: Jn 3:16
G is spirit, and those who worship Jn 4:24
I said, you are **g-s**? Jn 10:34
to Him, "My Lord and my **G**!" Jn 20:28
We must obey **G** rather than men Ac 5:29
The **g-s** have come down to us in Ac 14:11
g-s made by hand are not **g-s**! Ac 19:26
G must be true, even if everyone is Rm 3:4
If **G** is for us, who is against Rm 8:31
G is the One who justifies. Rm 8:33
Be reconciled to **G**. 2Co 5:20
I will be their **G**, and they will be 2Co 6:16
that by nature are not **g-s**. Gl 4:8
one **G** and Father of all, who is Eph 4:6
who, existing in the form of **G**, Php 2:6
one **G** and one mediator between **G** 1Tm 2:5
our great **G** and Savior, Jesus Ti 2:13
for our **G** is a consuming fire. Heb 12:29
G is light, and there is 1Jn 1:5
does not know **G**, because **G** is love. 1Jn 4:8
holy, holy, Lord **G**, the Almighty, Rv 4:8
G-'s dwelling is with humanity, Rv 21:3

GODDESS
Ashtoreth, the **g** of the Sidonians, 1Kg 11:5
temple of the great **g** Artemis Ac 19:27

GOD-FEARING
centurion, an upright and **G** man, Ac 10:22

GODLESS
the hope of the **g** will perish. Jb 8:13

GODLESSNESS
heaven against all **g** and Rm 1:18
He will turn away **g** from Jacob. Rm 11:26

GODLINESS
life in all **g** and dignity. 1Tm 2:2
but **g** is beneficial in every way 1Tm 4:8
But **g** with contentment is a 1Tm 6:6
holding to the form of **g** but 2Tm 3:5
required for life and **g** 2Pt 1:3
endurance, endurance with **g**, 2Pt 1:6

GODLY
does the One seek? A **g** offspring. Mal 2:15
For **g** grief produces a 2Co 7:10
want to live a **g** life in Christ 2Tm 3:12
and **g** way in the present age, Ti 2:12

GOG
the day when **G** comes against Ezk 38:18
G and Magog, to gather them Rv 20:8

GOLD
G cannot be exchanged for it, Jb 28:15
They are more desirable than **g** Ps 19:10
more than **g**, even the purest **g**, Ps 119:127
is better than silver and **g**. Pr 22:1
is like **g** apples on a silver tray. Pr 25:11
street of the city was pure **g**, Rv 21:21

GOLGOTHA
they came to a place called **G** Mt 27:33

GOLIATH
Philistine giant from Gath killed by David (1Sm 17).

GOMER
Hosea's wife (Hs 1:3,8).

GOOD
And God saw that it was **g**. Gn 1:10
God planned it for **g** to bring about Gn 50:20
There is no one who does **g**. Ps 14:1
Taste and see that the LORD is **g**. Ps 34:8
There is no one who does **g**. Ps 53:1
withhold the **g** from those who Ps 84:11
How **g** and pleasant it is when Ps 133:1
A joyful heart is **g** medicine, Pr 17:22
who brings news of **g** things, Is 52:7
to do what is **g** on the Sabbath. Mt 12:12
Well done, **g** and faithful slave! Mt 25:21
Why do you call Me **g**? ...
No one is **g** but One—God. Mk 10:18
I am the **g** shepherd. Jn 10:11
together for the **g** of those who Rm 8:28
by evil, but conquer evil with **g**. Rm 12:21
in Christ Jesus for **g** works, Eph 2:10

GOODNESS
cause all My **g** to pass in front Ex 33:19
Only **g** and faithful love will Ps 23:6
patience, kindness, **g**, faith, Gl 5:22

GOODS
You have many **g** stored up for Lk 12:19
has this world's **g** and sees his 1Jn 3:17

GOSHEN
Region of Egypt where Israel settled (Gn 45:10; 46:28-34); the best part of the land (47:6,27); excluded from plagues (Ex 8:22; 9:26).

GOSPEL
and preach the **g** to the whole Mk 16:15
For I am not ashamed of the **g**, Rm 1:16
But if our **g** is veiled, 2Co 4:3
and are turning to a different **g** Gl 1:6
having the eternal **g** to announce Rv 14:6

GOSSIP
A **g** goes around revealing a Pr 11:13
but are also **g-s** and busybodies, 1Tm 5:13

GOVERNMENT
and the **g** will be on His shoulders. Is 9:6

GRACE
g flows from your lips. Ps 45:2
g and truth came through Jesus Jn 1:17
sin so that **g** may multiply? Rm 6:1
My **g** is sufficient for you, 2Co 12:9
you have fallen from **g**. Gl 5:4
you are saved by **g** through faith Eph 2:8
For the **g** of God has appeared Ti 2:11
having been justified by His **g**, Ti 3:7
But He gives greater **g**. Jms 4:6

GRACIOUS
I will be **g** to whom I will be **g**, Ex 33:19
Be **g** to me, God, according to Ps 51:1
are a compassionate and **g** God, Ps 86:15
Your speech should always be **g**, Col 4:6

GRAFT
wild olive branch, were **g-ed** in Rm 11:17
God has the power to **g** them in Rm 11:23

GRANDCHILDREN
G are the crown of the elderly, Pr 17:6

GRAPE
not drink any **g** juice or eat Nm 6:3
with a single cluster of **g-s**, Nm 13:23
The fathers have eaten sour **g-s**, Jr 31:29
because its **g-s** have ripened. Rv 14:18

GRASP
so that they could not **g** it, Lk 9:45
Him, yet He eluded their **g**. Jn 10:39

GRASS
As for man, his days are like **g** Ps 103:15
All humanity is **g**, and all its Is 40:6
The **g** withers, the flowers fade Is 40:7
God clothes the **g** of the field, Mt 6:30
All flesh is like **g**, and all its 1Pt 1:24
The **g** withers, and the flower 1Pt 1:24

GRASSHOPPER
To ourselves we seemed like **g-s**, Nm 13:33

GRATITUDE
with **g** in your hearts to God. Col 3:16

GRAVE
their throat is an open **g**; Ps 5:9
They made His **g** with the wicked Is 53:9
You are like unmarked **g-s**; Lk 11:44
Their throat is an open **g**; Rm 3:13

GRAY
G hair is a glorious crown; Pr 16:31

GREAT
God made the two **g** lights Gn 1:16
will make you into a **g** nation, Gn 12:2
forgive my sin, for it is **g**. Ps 25:11
LORD is a **g** God, a **g** King above all Ps 95:3
g is Your faithfulness! Lm 3:23
wants to become **g** among you Mt 20:26
because of His **g** love that He Eph 2:4
with contentment is a **g** gain. 1Tm 6:6
we neglect such a **g** salvation? Heb 2:3
Then I saw a **g** white throne and Rv 20:11

GREATER
something **g** than the temple is here! Mt 12:6
You will see **g** things than this. Jn 1:50
No one has **g** love than this, Jn 15:13
But desire the **g** gifts. 1Co 12:31
the One who is in you is **g** than the 1Jn 4:4

GREATEST
Who is **g** in the kingdom Mt 18:1
g among you will be your servant. Mt 23:11
But the **g** of these is love. 1Co 13:13

GREED
be on guard against all **g** Lk 12:15

GREEDY
A **g** person provokes conflict, Pr 28:25
thieves, **g** people, drunkards 1Co 6:10

GREEK
to the Jew, and also to the **G**. Rm 1:16
signs and the **G-s** seek wisdom, 1Co 1:22
is no Jew or **G**, slave or free Gl 3:28

GREEN
lets me lie down in **g** pastures; Ps 23:2

GRIEF
and joy may end in **g**. Pr 14:13
because your **g** led to repentance. 2Co 7:9
this with joy and not with **g**, Heb 13:17

GRIEVE
rebelled and **g-d** His Holy Spirit. Is 63:10
Peter was **g-d** that He asked him Jn 21:17
And don't **g** God's Holy Spirit. Eph 4:30
you will not **g** like the rest, 1Th 4:13

GROAN
we also **g** within ourselves, Rm 8:23

GROANING
God heard their **g**, Ex 2:24
the whole creation has been **g** Rm 8:22
intercedes for us with unspoken **g-s**. Rm 8:26

GROOM *SEE ALSO* BRIDEGROOM
as a **g** rejoices over his bride, Is 62:5
I will remove ... the voices of the
g and the bride, Jr 7:34
Let the **g** leave his bedroom, Jl 2:16
sad while the **g** is with them? Mt 9:15
Since the **g** was delayed, they Mt 25:5
He who has the bride is the **g**. Jn 3:29

GROUND
The **g** is cursed because of you. Gn 3:17
you are standing is holy **g**. Ex 3:5
Others fell on rocky **g**, Mt 13:5

GROW
He **grew** up before Him like a young Is 53:2
the wildflowers of the field **g**: Mt 6:28
boy **grew** up and became strong, Lk 2:40
let us **g** in every way into Him Eph 4:15
But **g** in the grace and knowledge 2Pt 3:18

GROWTH
but only God who gives the **g**. 1Co 3:7

GUARD (N)
The **g-s** were so shaken from fear Mt 28:4

GUARD (V)
G your heart above all else, Pr 4:23
will **g** your hearts and minds Php 4:7
g what has been entrusted to you 1Tm 6:20

GUARDIAN
Am I my brother's **g**? Gn 4:9
law, then, was our **g** until Christ, Gl 3:24
Shepherd and **G** of your souls. 1Pt 2:25

GUIDE
And if the blind **g** the blind, Mt 15:14
He will **g** you into all the truth Jn 16:13

GUILT
You took away the **g** of my sin. Ps 32:5
my sins and blot out all my **g**. Ps 51:9

GUILTY
I will not justify the **g**. Ex 23:7
I was **g** when I was born; Ps 51:5
Acquitting the **g** and condemning Pr 17:15
but is **g** of an eternal sin" Mk 3:29

HABAKKUK
Prophet in Judah before the exile (Hab 1:1).

HADES
You will go down to **H**. Mt 11:23
and the forces of **H** will not Mt 16:18
You will not leave me in **H** Ac 2:27
I hold the keys of death and **H**. Rv 1:18

HAGAR
Sarah's slave; mother of Ishmael (Gn 16; Gl 4:21-31). Sent away by Sarah (Gn 16:5-9; 21:9-21).

HAGGAI
Prophet after the exile, who encouraged rebuilding the temple (Ezr 5:1; 6:14; Hg 1–2).

HAIL
I will rain down the worst **h** that Ex 9:18
and mocked Him: "**H**, King of the Mt 27:29

HAILSTONES
LORD threw large **h** on them from Jos 10:11
Enormous **h**, each weighing about Rv 16:21

HAIR
is to let the **h** of his head grow Nm 6:5
But his **h** began to grow back Jdg 16:22
are more than the **h-s** of my head, Ps 40:12
make a single **h** white or black. Mt 5:36
But even the **h-s** of your head have Mt 10:30
and wiped His feet with her **h**, Jn 11:2
covered, her **h** should be cut off. 1Co 11:6

HAIRSTYLES
with elaborate **h**, gold, pearls, 1Tm 2:9
elaborate **h** and the wearing 1Pt 3:3

HAIRY
A **h** man with a leather belt 2Kg 1:8

HALF
give you, up to **h** my kingdom. Mk 6:23

HALLELUJAH
H! My soul, praise the LORD. Ps 146:1
multitude in heaven, saying: **H**! Rv 19:1

HAM
Son of Noah (Gn 5:32; 9:18-27). Ancestor of Cushites, Egyptians, and Canaanites (Gn 9:18-27; 10:6; Ps 78:51; 105:23,27; 106:22).

HAMAN
Nobleman of Persia at the time of Esther (Est 3:1-2); enemy of Jews (3:3-15). Hanged on his own gallows (7:9-10).

HANANIAH
1. False prophet; opposed Jeremiah (Jr 28).
2. Shadrach's original name (Dn 1:6).

HAND (N)
rock and cover you with My **h** Ex 33:22
lay their **h-s** on the bull's head Lv 4:15
they pierced my **h-s** and my feet. Ps 22:16
Sit at My right **h** until I make Ps 110:1
even there Your **h** will lead me; Ps 139:10
Whatever your **h-s** find to do, Ec 9:10
of the field will clap their **h-s**. Is 55:12
man's **h** appeared and began writing Dn 5:5
if your right **h** causes you to Mt 5:30
let your left **h** know what your right Mt 6:3
Sit at My right **h** until I put Mt 22:44
into Your **h-s** I entrust My spirit. Lk 23:46
He showed them His **h-s** and feet. Lk 24:40
will snatch them out of My **h**. Jn 10:28
Because I'm not a **h**, I don't 1Co 12:15
dwelling ... not made with **h-s**. 2Co 5:1
lifting up holy **h-s** without anger 1Tm 2:8
to fall into the **h-s** of the living Heb 10:31

HAND (V)
he **h-ed** Him over to be crucified. Mt 27:26
when He **h-s** over the kingdom to 1Co 15:24

HANDLE
Don't **h**, don't taste, don't touch Col 2:21

HANG
anyone **hung** on a tree is under Dt 21:23
Then he went and **h-ed** himself. Mt 27:5
Everyone who is **hung** on a tree Gl 3:13

HANNAH
Wife of Elkanah; mother of Samuel (1Sm 1–2).

HAPPY
How **h** is the man who does not Ps 1:1
H is the nation whose God is Ps 33:12
H is the man who has filled his Ps 127:5
H is a man who finds wisdom and Pr 3:13

HARD
It will be **h** for a rich person Mt 19:23
This teaching is **h**! Who can accept Jn 6:60
that are **h** to understand. 2Pt 3:16

HARDEN
But I will **h** his heart so that Ex 4:21
Do not **h** your hearts as at Meribah, Ps 95:8
and He **h-s** those He wants to **h**. Rm 9:18
elect did find it. The rest were **h-ed** Rm 11:7
A partial **h-ing** has come to Israel Rm 11:25
do not **h** your hearts as in the Heb 3:8

HAREM
beautiful young women to the **h** Est 2:3

HARM (N)
Don't plan any **h** against your Pr 3:29

HARM (V)
But they were planning to **h** me. Neh 6:2

HARMLESS
as serpents and as **h** as doves. Mt 10:16

HARP
praise Him with **h** and lyre. Ps 150:3
Each one had a **h** and gold bowls Rv 5:8

HARSH
but a **h** word stirs up wrath. Pr 15:1

HARVEST
earth endures, seedtime and **h**, Gn 8:22
observe the Festival of **H** with Ex 23:16
sleeps during **h** is disgraceful. Pr 10:5
The **h** is abundant, but the workers Mt 9:37
fields, for they are ready for **h**. Jn 4:35
since the **h** of the earth is ripe Rv 14:15

HASTY
Do not be **h** to speak, Ec 5:2

HATE
You who love the LORD, **h** evil! Ps 97:10
To fear the LORD is to **h** evil. Pr 8:13
will not use the rod **h-s** his son, Pr 13:24
a time to love and a time to **h**; Ec 3:8
H evil and love good; Am 5:15
I loved Jacob, but I **h-d** Esau. Mal 1:3
If he **h-s** and divorces Mal 2:16
your neighbor and **h** your enemy. Mt 5:43
do what is good to those who **h** you Lk 6:27
Me and does not **h** his own father Lk 14:26
want to do, but I do what I **h**. Rm 7:15
loved Jacob, but I have **h-d** Esau. Rm 9:13

HATRED
not harbor **h** against your brother. Lv 19:17

HAY
stones, wood, **h**, or straw, 1Co 3:12

HEAD
will strike your **h**, and you will Gn 3:15
lay their hands on the bull's **h** Lv 4:15
You anoint my **h** with oil; Ps 23:5
will heap burning coals on his **h**, Pr 25:22
Man has no place to lay His **h**. Mt 8:20
His **h** was brought on a platter Mt 14:11
Christ is the **h** of every man, and the man is the **h** of the woman, 1Co 11:3
her **h** uncovered dishonors her **h**, 1Co 11:5
husband is the **h** of the wife as Eph 5:23

HEAL
For I am Yahweh who **h-s** you. Ex 15:26
their sin, and **h** their land. 2Ch 7:14
He **h-s** the brokenhearted Ps 147:3
a time to kill and a time to **h**; Ec 3:3
and we are **h-ed** by His wounds. Is 53:5
H the sick, raise the dead Mt 10:8
it lawful to **h** on the Sabbath? Mt 12:10
Doctor, **h** yourself. Lk 4:23
converted, and I would **h** them. Jn 12:40
so that you may be **h-ed**. Jms 5:16
have been **h-ed** by His wounds. 1Pt 2:24

HEALING
will rise with **h** in its wings, Mal 4:2
gifts of **h** by the one Spirit, 1Co 12:9
the tree are for **h** the nations, Rv 22:2

HEALTHY
The **h** don't need a doctor, Lk 5:31

HEAR
may You **h** in heaven and forgive 1Kg 8:34
One who shaped the ear not **h**, Ps 94:9
with their eyes and **h** with their ears, Is 6:10
Have you not **h-d**? Has it not been Is 40:21
Dry bones, **h** the word of the LORD Ezk 37:4
You have **h-d** that it was said Mt 5:21
longed ... to **h** the things you **h** Mt 13:17
Anyone who **h-s** My word and Jn 5:24
My sheep **h** My voice, Jn 10:27
And how can they **h** without a Rm 10:14
So faith comes from what is **h-d**, Rm 10:17
did not see and ear did not **h**, 1Co 2:9
Everyone must be quick to **h**, Jms 1:19
according to His will, He **h-s** us. 1Jn 5:14
If anyone **h-s** My voice and opens Rv 3:20

HEARERS
For the **h** of the law are not Rm 2:13
of the word and not **h** only, Jms 1:22

HEARING (N)
works of the law or by **h** with faith? Gl 3:2

HEART
I will harden his **h** so that he Ex 4:21
when you seek Him with all your **h** Dt 4:29
LORD your God with all your **h**, Dt 6:5
but the LORD sees the **h**. 1Sm 16:7
meditation of my **h** be acceptable Ps 19:14
create a clean **h** for me and Ps 51:10
Your word in my **h** so that I may Ps 119:11
Search me, God, and know my **h**; Ps 139:23

Trust in the LORD with all your **h**, Pr 3:5
The **h** is more deceitful than Jr 17:9
them and write it on their **h-s**. Jr 31:33
I will give you a new **h** Ezk 36:26
The pure in **h** are blessed, Mt 5:8
there your **h** will be also. Mt 6:21
the law is written on their **h-s**. Rm 2:15
and circumcision is of the **h** Rm 2:29
believe in your **h** that God raised Rm 10:9

HEAVEN

God created the **h-s** and the earth. Gn 1:1
Most High, Creator of **h** and earth, Gn 14:19
h, the highest **h**, cannot contain 1Kg 8:27
When I observe Your **h-s**, the work Ps 8:3
The **h-s** declare the glory of God, Ps 19:1
Your faithful love reaches to **h**. Ps 36:5
Who do I have in **h** but You? Ps 73:25
Let the **h-s** be glad and the earth Ps 96:11
For as high as the **h-s** are above Ps 103:11
time for every activity under **h**: Ec 3:1
create a new **h** and a new earth; Is 65:17
coming with the clouds of **h**. Dn 7:13
the kingdom of **h** has come near! Mt 3:2
The **h-s** suddenly opened for Him, Mt 3:16
for yourselves treasures in **h**, Mt 6:20
H and earth will pass away, Mt 24:35
Who will go up to **h**? Rm 10:6
into the third **h** 14 years ago. 2Co 12:2
but our citizenship is in **h**, Php 3:20
Messiah did not enter a sanctuary ...
but into **h** itself, Heb 9:24
that day the **h-s** will pass away 2Pt 3:10
I saw a new **h** and a new earth Rv 21:1

HEAVENLY

and your **h** Father knows that you Mt 6:32
a multitude of the **h** host with Lk 2:13
There are **h** bodies and earthly 1Co 15:40
by God's **h** call in Christ Php 3:14
and companions in a **h** calling, Heb 3:1

HEBREW

came and told Abram the **H**, Gn 14:13
This is one of the **H** boys. Ex 2:6
Yahweh, the God of the **H-s**, Ex 3:18
He answered them, "I'm a **H**. Jnh 1:9
was written in **H**, Latin, and Jn 19:20
of Benjamin, a **H** born of **H-s**; Php 3:5

HEEL

and you will strike his **h**. Gn 3:15
Esau's **h** with his hand. Gn 25:26
has raised his **h** against me. Ps 41:9
has raised his **h** against Me. Jn 13:18

HEIGHT

cubit to his **h** by worrying? Mt 6:27
h or depth, or any other Rm 8:39
breadth and width, **h** and depth, Eph 3:18

HEIR

born in my house will be my **h**. Gn 15:3
if children, also **h-s**—**h-s** of God Rm 8:17
h-s according to the promise. Gl 3:29
a son, then an **h** through God. Gl 4:7
The Gentiles are co-**h-s**, members Eph 3:6
them honor as co-**h-s** of the grace 1Pt 3:7

HELL *SEE ALSO* HADES, HELLFIRE, SHEOL

to have two hands and go to **h** Mk 9:43
authority to throw people into **h** Lk 12:5

HELLFIRE

will be subject to **h**. Mt 5:22

HELMET

and a **h** of salvation on His head; Is 59:17
Take the **h** of salvation, Eph 6:17

HELP (N)

He is our **h** and shield. Ps 33:20
Where will my **h** come from? Ps 121:1
gifts of healing, **h-ing**, managing, 1Co 12:28

HELP (V)

LORD has **h-ed** us to this point 1Sm 7:12
I do believe! **H** my unbelief. Mk 9:24
He is able to **h** those who are Heb 2:18

HELPER

I will make a **h** as his complement. Gn 2:18
You are a **h** of the fatherless. Ps 10:14
a **h** who is always found in times Ps 46:1
Lord is my **h**; I will not be afraid. Heb 13:6

HELPFUL

but not everything is **h**. 1Co 6:12

HELPLESS

For while we were still **h**, Rm 5:6

HEN

as a **h** gathers her chicks under Mt 23:37

HERALD

are the feet of the **h**, who proclaims Is 52:7

HERB

unleavened bread and bitter **h-s**. Ex 12:8

HERE

"**H** I am," he answered. Ex 3:4
ran to Eli and said, "**H** I am; 1Sm 3:5
I said: **H** I am. Send me. Is 6:8

HERITAGE

Sons are indeed a **h** from the LORD, Ps 127:3

HEROD

1. The Great; King in Judea at the time of Jesus' birth; executed male babies (Mt 2).
2. Archelaus; son of 1. (Mt 2:22).
3. Philip; son of 1. (Mk 6:17).
4. Antipas; son of 1.; tetrarch of Galilee; arrested and executed John the Baptist (Mt 14:1-12).
5. Agrippa I; grandson of 1.; persecuted the church; died when he didn't give glory to God (Ac 12).
6. Agrippa II; son of 5. (Ac 25:13). Heard Paul's defense (25:22–26:32).

HERODIAS

Wife of Herod Antipas, formerly of Herod Philip; requested head of John the Baptist (Mt 14:3-11; Mk 6:17-28; Lk 3:19).

HEZEKIAH

Son of Ahaz; king of Judah (2Kg 18–20; 2Ch 29–32; Is 36–39). Reformer (2Kg 18:4; 2Ch 29–31). Healed of fatal illness (2Kg 20:1-11); showed treasuries to Babylonians (20:12-19).

HIDDEN (ADJ)

The **h** things belong to the LORD Dt 29:29
Cleanse me from my **h** faults. Ps 19:12
and nothing **h** that won't be made Mt 10:26

HIDE

they **hid** themselves from the LORD Gn 3:8
she **hid** him for three months. Ex 2:2
because she **hid** the men we sent. Jos 6:17
h me in the shadow of Your wings Ps 17:8
hid me in the shadow of His hand. Is 49:2
situated on a hill cannot be **h-den**. Mt 5:14
and went off and **hid** your talent Mt 25:25
your life is **h-den** with the Messiah Col 3:3
Fall on us and **h** us from the Rv 6:16

HIDING (ADJ)

You are my **h** place; Ps 32:7

HIGH *SEE ALSO* HIGH PLACE, HIGH PRIEST, MOST HIGH

For as **h** as the heavens are Ps 103:11
took Him to a very **h** mountain Mt 4:8

HIGH PLACE

people were sacrificing on the **h-s**, 1Kg 3:2
LORD at the **h** in Gibeon 1Ch 16:39
They enraged Him with their **h-s** Ps 78:58

HIGH PRIEST

led Him away to Caiaphas the **h**, Mt 26:57
become a merciful and faithful **h** Heb 2:17
this is the kind of **h** we need: Heb 7:26

HIGHER

so My ways are **h** than your ways Is 55:9

HIGHLY

Yahweh is great and is **h** praised; Ps 145:3
of himself more **h** than he should Rm 12:3

HIGHWAY

make a straight **h** for our God in Is 40:3
Go out into the **h-s** and lanes and Lk 14:23

HILL

the cattle on a thousand **h-s**. Ps 50:10
mountain and **h** will be leveled; Is 40:4
situated on a **h** cannot be hidden Mt 5:14
mountain and **h** will be made low Lk 3:5
and to the **h-s**, 'Cover us!' Lk 23:30

HINDER

your prayers will not be **h-ed**. 1Pt 3:7

HIP

He struck Jacob's **h** socket Gn 32:25

HIRAM

1. King of Tyre; helped David build his palace and Solomon build the temple (2Sm 5:11; 2Kg 5). Manned Solomon's fleet (1Kg 9:27).
2. Craftsman; helped build the temple and its furnishings (1Kg 7:13-14); also called Huram (2Ch 4:11) or Huram-abi (2:13; 4:16).

HIRE

the morning to **h** workers for his Mt 20:1

HIRED (ADJ)

of my father's **h** hands have more Lk 15:17
he is a **h** man and doesn't care Jn 10:13

HIT

Prophesy! Who **h** You? Lk 22:64

HITTITES
Ancient people of the promised land (Gn 10:15-18; 15:20; Jos 1:4); Abraham lived among them (Gn 23); Esau married them (26:34; 27:46; 36:2). Formerly lived in the hill country (Nm 13:29; Jos 9:1; 11:3; 12:8); dispossessed by Israel (Ex 23:23; Dt 7:1; 20:17; Jos 3:10); some remained (Jdg 1:6; 3:5; 1Kg 9:20-21); fought alongside Israel (1Sm 26:6; 2Sm 23:39; 2Kg 7:6); intermarried (2Sm 11:24-27; 1Kg 11:1).

HOLD
Your right hand **h-s** on to me. Ps 63:8
You **h** my right hand. Ps 73:23
Your heart must **h** on to my words Pr 4:4
I will **h** on to you with My Is 41:10
H firmly to the message of life. Php 2:16
by Him all things **h** together. Col 1:17
test all things. **H** on to what is 1Th 5:21
take **h** of eternal life 1Tm 6:12
Let us **h** on to the confession of Heb 10:23

HOLIDAY
It is a **h** when they send gifts Est 9:19

HOLINESS
Who is like You, glorious in **h**, Ex 15:11
in the splendor of His **h** Ps 29:2; 96:9
so that we can share His **h**. Heb 12:10

HOLY *SEE ALSO* HOLY PLACE, HOLY SPIRIT
you are standing is **h** ground. Ex 3:5
and be **h** because I am **h**. Lv 11:44
is no one **h** like the LORD. 1Sm 2:2
H, **h**, **h** is the LORD of Is 6:3
who is My equal?" asks the **H** One. Is 40:25
So then, the law is **h**, and the Rm 7:12
and called us with a **h** calling, 2Tm 1:9
is written, Be **h**, because I am **h**. 1Pt 1:16
H, **h**, **h**, Lord God, the Rv 4:8
I also saw the **H** City, new Rv 21:2

HOLY PLACE
between the **h** and the most **h**. Ex 26:33
enter the most **h** in this way: Lv 16:3
Then he made the most **h**; 2Ch 3:8
Who may stand in His **h**? Ps 24:3
standing in the **h**" (let the reader Mt 24:15
entered the most **h** once for all, Heb 9:12

HOLY SPIRIT
Third person of the Trinity, through whom God acts, reveals His will, empowers individuals, and discloses His personal presence.
or take Your **H** from me. Ps 51:11
and grieved His **H**. Is 63:10
baptize you with the **H** and fire. Mt 3:11
speaks against the **H**, it will not Mt 12:32
Father and of the Son and of the **H**, Mt 28:19
The **H** will come upon you Lk 1:35
and the **H** descended on Lk 3:22
Father give the **H** to those who ask Lk 11:13
the Counselor, the **H**, Jn 14:26
they were all filled with the **H** Ac 2:4
H had been poured out on Gentiles Ac 10:45
prevented by the **H** from Ac 16:6
Did you receive the **H** when you Ac 19:2
your body is a sanctuary of the **H** 1Co 6:19
were sealed with the promised **H**. Eph 1:13
don't grieve God's **H**, Eph 4:30
moved by the **H**, men spoke 2Pt 1:21

HOME
God provides **h-s** for those who are Ps 68:6
sparrow finds a **h**, and a swallow Ps 84:3
Go back to your **h**, and tell all Lk 8:39
to him and make Our **h** with him. Jn 14:23
is hungry, he should eat at **h**, 1Co 11:34
of the body and at **h** with the Lord. 2Co 5:8

HOMEOWNER
If the **h** had known what time the Mt 24:43

HOMETOWN
not without honor except in his **h** Mt 13:57

HOMOSEXUAL
adulterers, . . . one practicing **h-ity**, 1Co 6:9
for the sexually immoral and **h-s**, 1Tm 1:10

HONEST
How painful **h** words can be! Jb 6:25
word with an **h** and good heart, Lk 8:15

HONEY
land flowing with milk and **h** Ex 3:8
What is sweeter than **h**? Jdg 14:18
sweeter than **h**, which comes from Ps 19:10
It is not good to eat too much **h** Pr 25:27
his food was locusts and wild **h**. Mt 3:4

HONOR (N)
crowned him with glory and **h**. Ps 8:5
is not without **h** except in his Mt 13:57

HONOR (V)
H your father and your mother Ex 20:12
H the LORD with your possessions Pr 3:9
Your name be **h-ed** as holy. Mt 6:9
H your father and your mother; Mt 15:4
These people **h** Me with their Mt 15:8
if one member is **h-ed**, all the 1Co 12:26
but **h** the Messiah as Lord 1Pt 3:15

HONORABLE
whatever is **h**, whatever is just Php 4:8

HONORABLY
ourselves **h** in everything. Heb 13:18

HOPE (N)
where then is my **h**? Who can see Jb 17:15
Put your **h** in God, for I will Ps 42:5
This **h** will not disappoint Rm 5:5
Rejoice in **h**; be patient in Rm 12:12
three remain: faith, **h**, and love. 1Co 13:13
what is the **h** of His calling, Eph 1:18
Christ in you, the **h** of glory. Col 1:27
like the rest, who have no **h**. 1Th 4:13
a helmet of the **h** of salvation. 1Th 5:8
birth into a living **h** through 1Pt 1:3
reason for the **h** that is in you 1Pt 3:15
who has this **h** in Him purifies 1Jn 3:3

HOPE (V)
He kills me, I will **h** in Him. Jb 13:15
all things, **h-s** all things 1Co 13:7
the reality of what is **h-d** for, Heb 11:1

HORN
caught in the thicket by its **h-s**. Gn 22:13
My shield, the **h** of my salvation 2Sm 22:3
and it had 10 **h-s**. Dn 7:7
has raised up a **h** of salvation Lk 1:69

HORSE
has thrown the **h** and its rider into Ex 15:1
chariots, and others in **h-s**, but we Ps 20:7
The **h** is a false hope for safety Ps 33:17
and there was a white **h**. Rv 6:2
and there was a white **h**. Rv 19:11

HOSANNA
H in the highest heaven! Mt 21:9

HOSEA
Prophet in Israel near the end of the kingdom; his marriage modeled God's love and Israel's unfaithfulness (Hs 1–3).

HOSHEA
Son of Elah; last king of Israel (2Kg 15:30; 17:1-6).

HOSPITABLE
respectable, **h**, an able teacher 1Tm 3:2
Be **h** to one another without 1Pt 4:9

HOSPITALITY
in their needs; pursue **h**. Rm 12:13
neglect to show **h**, for by doing Heb 13:2

HOST
of the heavenly **h** with the angel Lk 2:13

HOSTILE
mind-set of the flesh is **h** to God Rm 8:7

HOSTILITY
I will put **h** between you and the Gn 3:15
down the dividing wall of **h**. Eph 2:14
who endured such **h** from sinners Heb 12:3
with the world is **h** toward God? Jms 4:4

HOT
you are neither cold nor **h**. Rv 3:15

HOT-TEMPERED
not **h**, not addicted to wine, Ti 1:7

HOUR
that day and **h** no one knows Mt 24:36
But an **h** is coming, and is now Jn 4:23
The **h** has come for the Son of Jn 12:23
Father, the **h** has come. Jn 17:1
keep you from the **h** of testing Rv 3:10

HOUSE
dwell in the **h** of the LORD as Ps 23:6
zeal for Your **h** has consumed me Ps 69:9
Unless the LORD builds a **h**, Ps 127:1
Wisdom has built her **h**; Pr 9:1
for My **h** will be called a **h** of prayer Is 56:7
who built his **h** on the rock. Mt 7:24
And everyone who has left **h-s**, Mt 19:29
My **h** will be called a **h** of prayer. Mt 21:13
devour widows' **h-s** and make long Mt 23:14
he was of the **h** and family line Lk 2:4
My Father's **h** into a marketplace Jn 2:16
In My Father's **h** are many Jn 14:2
builder has more honor than the **h**. Heb 3:3
into a spiritual **h** for a holy 1Pt 2:5

HOUSEHOLD
will be the members of his **h**. Mt 10:36
believed, along with his whole **h**. Jn 4:53
believed God with his entire **h**. Ac 16:34
manages his own **h** competently, 1Tm 3:4

HULDAH
Wife of Shallum; prophetess in Josiah's time (2Kg 22:14).

HUMAN
heaven on the **h** race to see if Ps 14:2
Even **h** wrath will praise You; Ps 76:10
I led them with **h** cords, with Hs 11:4
is He served by **h** hands, Ac 17:25
not depend on **h** will or effort Rm 9:16
is wiser than **h** wisdom, 1Co 1:25
is one flesh for **h-s**, another for 1Co 15:39
humanity, Jesus Christ, Himself **h**, 1Tm 2:5

HUMANITY
and all **h** together will see it Is 40:5
pour out My Spirit on all **h**; Jl 2:28
pour out My Spirit on all **h**; Ac 2:17
you except what is common to **h**. 1Co 10:13
between God and **h**, Jesus Christ, 1Tm 2:5

HUMBLE (ADJ)
Moses was a very **h** man, Nm 12:3
He leads the **h** in what is right Ps 25:9
but gives grace to the **h**. Pr 3:34
h and riding on a donkey, Zch 9:9
I am gentle and **h** in heart, Mt 11:29
but gives grace to the **h**. Jms 4:6

HUMBLE (V)
that He might **h** you and test you Dt 8:2
despise a broken and **h-d** heart. Ps 51:17
whoever **h-s** himself like this child Mt 18:4
who exalts himself will be **h-d**, Lk 14:11
He **h-d** Himself by becoming Php 2:8
H yourselves before the Lord, Jms 4:10
H yourselves, therefore, under the 1Pt 5:6

HUMBLY
and to walk **h** with your God. Mc 6:8

HUMILIATION
In His **h** justice was denied Him Ac 8:33

HUMILITY
and **h** comes before honor. Pr 15:33
but in **h** consider others as more Php 2:3
clothe yourselves with **h** toward one 1Pt 5:5

HUNGER
Those who **h** ... for righteousness Mt 5:6
They will no longer **h**; Rv 7:16

HUNGRY
If I were **h**, I would not tell Ps 50:12
and giving food to the **h**. Ps 146:7
your enemy is **h**, give him food Pr 25:21
days and 40 nights, He was **h**. Mt 4:2
For I was **h** and you gave Me Mt 25:35
You who are now **h** are blessed, Lk 6:21
who comes to Me will ever be **h**, Jn 6:35
If your enemy is **h**, feed him. Rm 12:20

HURAM *SEE* HIRAM

HURAM-ABI *SEE* HIRAM

HURRY
You are to eat it in a **h**; Ex 12:11

HURT
brother is **h** by what you eat Rm 14:15

HUSBAND
Your desire will be for your **h**, Gn 3:16
"Go call your **h**," He told her, Jn 4:16
you've had five **h-s**, and the man you
now have is not your **h**. Jn 4:18
A **h** should fulfill his marital 1Co 7:3
for the **h** is the head of the wife Eph 5:23
H-s, love your wives, just as Eph 5:25
the **h** of one wife, 1Tm 3:2
encourage ... women to love their **h-s** Ti 2:4
H-s, in the same way, live with 1Pt 3:7

HUSHAI
David's friend and spy in Absalom's court (2Sm 15:32–17:15).

HYMN
praying and singing **h-s** to God, Ac 16:25
in psalms, **h-s**, and spiritual Eph 5:19
singing psalms, **h-s**, and spiritual Col 3:16

HYPNOTIZED
Who has **h** you, before whose eyes Gl 3:1

HYPOCRISY
are full of **h** and lawlessness Mt 23:28
Love must be without **h**. Rm 12:9
without favoritism and **h**. Jms 3:17

HYPOCRITE
you must not be like the **h-s**, Mt 6:5
H! First take the log out of Mt 7:5
scribes and Pharisees, **h-s**! Mt 23:13

HYSSOP
Purify me with **h**, and I will be Ps 51:7

I AM
I WHO **I**. Ex 3:14
I the first and **I** the last. There is no Is 44:6
"**I**," said Jesus, Mk 14:62
"**I** He," Jesus told her, Jn 4:26
Before Abraham was, **I**. Jn 8:58
When He told them, "**I** He," they Jn 18:6

IDOL
Do not make an **i** for yourself, Ex 20:4
Their **i-s** are silver and gold, Ps 115:4
one offers incense, one praises an **i** Is 66:3
abstain from food offered to **i-s**, Ac 15:29
About food offered to **i-s**: 1Co 8:1
we know that "an **i** is nothing 1Co 8:4

IDOLATRY
my dear friends, flee from **i**. 1Co 10:14
i, sorcery, hatreds, strife Gl 5:20
desire, and greed, which is **i**. Col 3:5

IGNORANCE
overlooked the times of **i**, Ac 17:30
silence the **i** of foolish people 1Pt 2:15

IGNORANT
reject foolish and **i** disputes, 2Tm 2:23
those who are **i** and are going Heb 5:2

ILLEGITIMATE
then you are **i** children and not Heb 12:8

ILLNESSES
stomach and your frequent **i**. 1Tm 5:23

ILLUMINATE
my God **i-s** my darkness. Ps 18:28

IMAGE
Let Us make man in Our **i**, Gn 1:26
Whose **i** and inscription is this Mt 22:20
he is God's **i** and glory, 1Co 11:7
He is the **i** of the invisible God Col 1:15
an **i** of the beast Rv 13:14

IMITATE
I urge you to **i** me. 1Co 4:16
I me, as I also **i** Christ. 1Co 11:1
of their lives, **i** their faith. Heb 13:7
do not **i** what is evil, but what is 3Jn 11

IMITATORS
Therefore, be **i** of God, as Eph 5:1
but will be **i** of those who inherit Heb 6:12

IMMANUEL
have a son, and name him **I**. Is 7:14
they will name Him **I**, which is Mt 1:23

IMMORAL
associate with sexually **i** people 1Co 5:9
No sexually **i** people, idolaters, 1Co 6:9
Every sexually **i** or impure or Eph 5:5
there isn't any **i** or irreverent Heb 12:16
murderers, sexually **i**, sorcerers Rv 21:8

IMMORALITY
except in a case of sexual **i**, Mt 5:32
except for sexual **i**, and marries Mt 19:9
We weren't born of sexual **i**, Jn 8:41
abstain ... from sexual **i**, Ac 15:20
The body is not for sexual **i** but for 1Co 6:13
Run from sexual **i**! 1Co 6:18
Let us not commit sexual **i** as some 1Co 10:8
But sexual **i** and any impurity or Eph 5:3
that you abstain from sexual **i**, 1Th 4:3

IMMORTAL
glory of the **i** God for images Rm 1:23
the King eternal, **i**, invisible 1Tm 1:17

IMMORTALITY
mortal must be clothed with **i**. 1Co 15:53
the only One who has **i**, dwelling 1Tm 6:16
brought life and **i** to light 2Tm 1:10

IMPERISHABLE
into an inheritance that is **i**, 1Pt 1:4

IMPLANTED
humbly receive the **i** word, Jms 1:21

IMPORTANT
have neglected the more **i** matters Mt 23:23
on to you as most **i** what I also 1Co 15:3
others as more **i** than yourselves Php 2:3

IMPOSSIBLE
Is anything **i** for the LORD? Gn 18:14
It is **i** for God to do wrong, Jb 34:10
Nothing will be **i** for you. Mt 17:20
With men this is **i**, but with God Mt 19:26

IMPRISONED
For God has **i** all in disobedience, Rm 11:32
Scripture has **i** everything under Gl 3:22

IMPURE
immoral or **i** or greedy person, Eph 5:5

IMPURITY
cleanse you from all your **i-ies** Ezk 36:25
as slaves to moral **i**, Rm 6:19
and any **i** or greed should Eph 5:3

INCALCULABLE
to the Gentiles the **i** riches of Eph 3:8

INCENSE
an altar for the burning of **i**; Ex 30:1

prayer be set before You as **i**, Ps 141:2

INCITED
against Israel and **i** David to count 1Ch 21:1

INCORRUPTIBLE
and the dead will be raised **i**, 1Co 15:52

INCORRUPTION
Sown in corruption, raised in **i**; 1Co 15:42

INCREASE
If wealth **i-s**, pay no attention to it. Ps 62:10
said to the Lord, "**I** our faith." Lk 17:5
He must **i**, but I must decrease. Jn 3:30

INDICATING
Christ within them was **i** when He 1Pt 1:11

INEXPRESSIBLE
He heard **i** words, which a man is 2Co 12:4
rejoice with **i** and glorious joy 1Pt 1:8

INFANT
mouths of children and nursing **i-s** Ps 8:2
mouths of children and nursing **i-s** Mt 21:16
Like newborn **i-s**, desire the 1Pt 2:2

INFERIOR
in no way **i** to the "super-apostles" 2Co 11:5
the **i** is blessed by the superior. Heb 7:7

INFINITE
His understanding is **i**. Ps 147:5

INFLATE
Now some are **i-d** with pride, 1Co 4:18
Knowledge **i-s** with pride, but 1Co 8:1
realm and **i-d** without cause Col 2:18

INHERIT
You will **i** their land, since I Lv 20:24
the humble will **i** the land Ps 37:11
his household will **i** the wind, Pr 11:29
blameless will **i** what is good. Pr 28:10
blessed, for they will **i** the earth. Mt 5:5
must I do to **i** eternal life? Lk 10:25; 18:18
unjust will not **i** God's kingdom? 1Co 6:9

INHERITANCE
to be a people for His **i**, Dt 4:20
Levi has no **i** among his brothers,
the LORD is his **i**, Dt 18:2
We have also received an **i** in Him Eph 1:11
and into an **i** that is imperishable, 1Pt 1:4

INIQUITY
You and did not conceal my **i**. Ps 32:5
crushed because of our **i-ies**; Is 53:5
punished Him for the **i** of us all. Is 53:6

INJURY
born prematurely but there is no **i**, Ex 21:22

INJUSTICE
Is there **i** with God? Rm 9:14
Why not rather put up with **i**? 1Co 6:7

INK
to do so with paper and **i**. 2Jn 12

INN
him to an **i**, and took care Lk 10:34

INNER
our **i** person is being renewed 2Co 4:16
strengthened ... in the **i** man Eph 3:16

INNKEEPER
two denarii, gave them to the **i**, Lk 10:35

INNOCENCE
wash my hands in **i** and go around Ps 26:6
will they be incapable of **i**? Hs 8:5

INNOCENT
hands that shed **i** blood, Pr 6:17
sinned by betraying **i** blood, Mt 27:4

INSANE
pretended to be **i** in their 1Sm 21:13

INSCRIBE
tablets **i-d** by the finger of God. Ex 31:18
I have **i-d** you on the palms of My Is 49:16

INSCRIPTION
but none could read the **i** Dn 5:8
Whose image and **i** is this? Mt 22:20
on the cross. The **i** was: JESUS Jn 19:19

INSENSITIVITY
God gave them a spirit of **i**, Rm 11:8

INSIGHT
A man is praised for his **i**, Pr 12:8
to understand my **i** about the Eph 3:4

INSIST
I **i** on paying the full price, 1Ch 21:24

INSPIRED
then that David, **i** by the Spirit Mt 22:43
All Scripture is **i** by God and is 2Tm 3:16

INSTITUTED
those that exist are **i** by God. Rm 13:1

INSTRUCT
Your good Spirit to **i** them. Neh 9:20
I will **i** you and show you the Ps 32:8
A wise heart **i-s** its mouth and Pr 16:23

INSTRUCTION
This book of **i** must not depart Jos 1:8
his delight is in the LORD's **i**, Ps 1:2
The **i** of the LORD is perfect, Ps 19:7
see wonderful things from Your **i**. Ps 119:18
but I delight in Your **i**. Ps 119:70
Listen, my son, to your father's **i**, Pr 1:8
Listen to **i** and be wise; Pr 8:33
who listens to **i** will be happy. Pr 29:18
For **i** will go out of Zion and Is 2:3
For **i** will go out of Zion and Mc 4:2
in the past was written for our **i**, Rm 15:4
the goal of our **i** is love 1Tm 1:5

INSTRUCTOR
can have 10,000 **i-s** in Christ, 1Co 4:15

INSULT (N)
whoever ignores an **i** is sensible. Pr 12:16
there began to yell **i-s** at Him: Lk 23:39

INSULT (V)
of those who **i** You have fallen Ps 69:9
who mocks the poor **i-s** his Maker, Pr 17:5
blessed when they **i** and persecute Mt 5:11
of those who **i** You have fallen Rm 15:3

INTEGRITY
if you walk before Me ... with ... **i** 1Kg 9:4
He still retains his **i**, even though you Jb 2:3
You desire **i** in the inner self Ps 51:6
The **i** of the upright guides them Pr 11:3
with **i** and dignity in your teaching. Ti 2:7

INTELLIGENT
The woman was **i** and beautiful, 1Sm 25:3
The **i** person restrains his words Pr 17:27

INTENSIFY
I will **i** your labor pains; Gn 3:16

INTENTION
and reveal the **i-s** of the hearts. 1Co 4:5

INTERCEDE
But Moses **i-d** with the LORD his Ex 32:11
sins against the LORD, who can **i** 1Sm 2:25
sin of many and **i-d** for the rebels. Is 53:12
the Spirit Himself **i-s** for us with Rm 8:26
He always lives to **i** for them. Heb 7:25

INTERCESSION
perseverance and **i** for all the Eph 6:18
prayers, **i-s**, and thanksgivings 1Tm 2:1

INTERCOURSE
has sexual **i** with an animal Ex 22:19
You are not to have sexual **i** with Lv 18:9

INTEREST
you must not charge him **i**. Ex 22:25
You may charge a foreigner **i**, Dt 23:20
who does not lend his money at **i** Ps 15:5
received my money back with **i**. Mt 25:27
not only for his own **i-s**, but also Php 2:4
but has a sick **i** in disputes 1Tm 6:4

INTERMARRY
I with us; give your daughters Gn 34:9
Do not **i** with them. Dt 7:3
and **i** with the peoples who Ezr 9:14

INTERPRET
a dream, and no one can **i** it. Gn 41:15
and the ability to **i** dreams, Dn 5:12
in other languages? Do all **i**? 1Co 12:30
unless he **i-s** so that the church 1Co 14:5
and someone must **i**. 1Co 14:27

INTERPRETATION
Don't **i-s** belong to God? Gn 40:8
tell me the dream and its **i**, Dn 2:5
inscription and give me its **i**, Dn 5:16
to another, **i** of languages. 1Co 12:10
comes from one's own **i**, 2Pt 1:20

INTERPRETER
But if there is no **i**, that person 1Co 14:28

INTIMATE
Adam was **i** with his wife Eve, Gn 4:1
I have not been **i** with a man? Lk 1:34

INTIMATELY
not know her **i** until she gave Mt 1:25

INVADE
king of Assyria **i-d** the whole land 2Kg 17:5
For a nation has **i-d** My land, Jl 1:6

INVALIDATE
You completely **i** God's command Mk 7:9

INVESTIGATE
glory of kings to **i** a matter. Pr 25:2
I have carefully **i-d** everything Lk 1:3

INVISIBLE
His **i** attributes, that is, His Rm 1:20
He is the image of the **i** God, Col 1:15
immortal, **i**, the only God, 1Tm 1:17

INVITE
Then **i** Jesse to the sacrifice, 1Sm 16:3
For many are **i-d**, but few are Mt 22:14
a banquet, **i** those who are poor, Lk 14:13

INWARD
was You who created my **i** parts; Ps 139:13

INWARDLY
a person is a Jew who is one **i**, Rm 2:29

IRON
it there, and made the **i** float. 2Kg 6:6
break them with a rod of **i**; Ps 2:9
I sharpens **i**, and one man Pr 27:17
legs were **i**, ... feet were partly **i** and Dn 2:33

IRRESPONSIBLE
warn those who are **i**, comfort 1Th 5:14

IRREVERENT
the unholy and **i**, for those who 1Tm 1:9

IRREVOCABLE
gracious gifts and calling are **i**. Rm 11:29

ISAAC
Son of Abraham and Sarah; fulfillment of a promise (Gn 17:17; 21:5). God tested Abraham by asking him to sacrifice Isaac (Gn 22; Heb 11:17-19). Married Rebekah (Gn 24). Heir to Abraham's promise (Gn 25:5,11; Ps 105:9; Rm 9:7). Father of Esau and Jacob (Gn 25:21-26); blessed Jacob (Gn 27). Lied to Abimelech in Gerar about Rebekah (26:7-11). Died in Hebron (35:27-29).

ISAIAH
Son of Amoz; prophet to four kings of Judah (Is 1:1). Called (Is 6). Sons' names were symbolic (7:3; 8:3).

ISH-BOSHETH
Saul's son; tried to become king (2Sm 2:8-17; 3:6-16); was murdered (2Sm 4).

ISHMAEL
Son of Abraham and Hagar (Gn 16:11-15). Received a blessing but not the promise (17:18-21). Descendants are perpetual opponents of Israel (25:18).

ISLAND
the many coasts and **i-s** be glad. Ps 97:1

ISRAEL
Name God gave Jacob (Gn 32:28; 35:10). Also his descendants—God's chosen people—and their land (Ex 3:16; 1Sm 13:19; 15:35; 1Kg 4:1; Mt 2:6,20; Php 3:5). In the divided kingdom, the northern (1Kg 12:20).

ISRAELITE
about him, "Here is a true **I**; Jn 1:47
They are **I-s**, and to them belong Rm 9:4
For I too am an **I**, a descendant Rm 11:1
Are they **I-s**? So am I. 2Co 11:22

ISSACHAR
Son of Jacob and Leah (Gn 30:18). Tribe with territory from Jezreel to Tabor (Jos 19:17-23); its troops who rallied to David understood the times (1Ch 12:32).

ITCH
they have an **i** to hear something 2Tm 4:3

ITHAMAR
Fourth son of Aaron (Ex 6:23; 28:1; Nm 26:20; 1Ch 6:3; 24:1); took over priesthood when his brothers died (Lv 10:6,12,16; Nm 3:4; 1Ch 24:2); in charge of the Levites (Ex 38:21; Nm 4:28,33; 7:8).

IVORY
from **i** palaces harps bring you Ps 45:8
lie on beds inlaid with **i**, Am 6:4

JABEZ
Israelite who asked for and received a blessing (1Ch 4:9-10).

JABIN
A king of Canaan, whose commander Sisera was defeated by Israel (Jdg 4–5).

JACOB
Son of Isaac and Rebekah; younger twin brother of Esau (Gn 25:21-26). Took birthright (25:33); fled Esau (27:41–28:5). Received the promise (28:10-22). Worked for his wives (29:1-30). Wrestled with God (32:22-32); God changed his name to Israel (32:28; 49:2). Reconciled with Esau (33:4-16). Fathered the twelve tribes (29:21–30:24; 35:16-18). Went to Egypt (46:1-7). Died there, buried in Hebron (49:29–50:14). Ancestor of Jesus (Mt 1:2).
Even so, I loved **J**, Mal 1:2
J-'s well was there, and Jesus Jn 4:6
J I have loved, but Esau I have Rm 9:13

JAIRUS
Synagogue leader whose daughter Jesus restored (Mk 5:22-43; Lk 8:41-56).

JAMES
1. Apostle; son of Zebedee; brother of John (Mt 4:21; 10:2). At transfiguration (17:1); in Gethsemane (26:36-37). Martyred (Ac 12:2).
2. Apostle; son of Alphaeus (Mt 10:3).
3. Brother of Jesus (Mt 13:55; Gl 1:19). Believed after the resurrection (Jn 7:3; Ac 1:14; 1Co 15:7). Leader of church in Jerusalem (Ac 15; 21:18; Gl 2:9). Author (Jms 1:1).

JAPHETH
Son of Noah (Gn 5:32; 9:18-27).

JAR
in the house except a **j** of oil. 2Kg 4:2
with an alabaster **j** of pure and Mk 14:3
an alabaster **j** of fragrant oil Lk 7:37
have this treasure in clay **j-s**, 2Co 4:7

JAWBONE
He found a fresh **j** of a donkey, Jdg 15:15

JEALOUS
His brothers were **j** of him, Gn 37:11
Yahweh your God, am a **j** God, Ex 20:5
being **j** by nature, is a **j** God. Ex 34:14
is a consuming fire, a **j** God. Dt 4:24
and I will be **j** for My holy name Ezk 39:25
I will make you **j** of those who Rm 10:19
For I am **j** over you with a godly 2Co 11:2

JEALOUSLY
Spirit who lives in us yearns **j**? Jms 4:5

JEALOUSY
provoked His **j** with foreign gods Dt 32:16
For **j** enrages a husband, and he Pr 6:34
hatreds, strife, **j**, outbursts of Gl 5:20

JEBUSITES
Descendants of Canaan (Gn 10:16; 15:21; Ex 3:8; Dt 7:1; 20:17), inhabitants of Jebus (1Ch 11:4). Defeated by Judah and Benjamin, but not dispossessed (Jos 15:63; Jdg 1:8,21; 3:5); defeated by David (2Sm 5:6-9) and enslaved by Solomon (1Kg 9:20-21).

JEHOAHAZ
1. Son of Jehu; king of Israel (2Kg 13:1-9).
2. Son of Josiah; king of Judah (2Kg 23:30-34). Called Shallum (Jr 22:11).

JEHOASH
1. Alternate name of Joash son of Ahaziah, king of Judah (2Kg 12).
2. Son of Jehoahaz; king of Israel (2Kg 13:10–14:13).

JEHOIACHIN
Son of Jehoiakim; king of Judah (2Kg 24:6). Also called Jeconiah or Coniah (Jr 22:24; 24:1). Exiled (2Kg 24:10-17) but later favored (25:27-30).

JEHOIAKIM
Son of Josiah; king of Judah. Succeeded his brother Jehoahaz; name changed from Eliakim by Neco (2Kg 23:34). Burned Jeremiah's scroll (Jr 36). Became vassal of Babylon; later rebelled and was defeated (2Kg 24:1-6; Dn 1:2).

JEHORAM
1. Alternate form of Joram, son of Ahab; king of Israel (2Kg 3:1).
2. Son of Jehoshaphat; king of Judah (2Kg 8:16-24; 2Ch 21). Ahab's son-in-law (2Kg 8:18). Edom gained independence during his reign (8:20).

JEHOSHAPHAT
1. Son of Asa; king of Judah (1Kg 15:24). Initially faithful, strong, blessed (2Ch 17). Then married Ahab's daughter Athaliah and formed alliances with Ahab and Joram, kings of Israel (1Kg 22; 2Kg 3; 8:26; 2Ch 18; 20).
2. Valley of judgment (Jl 3:2,12).

JEHU
1. Son of Hanani; prophet against Baasha king of Israel (1Kg 16:1-12).
2. Son of Jehoshaphat; king of Israel. Anointed by Elisha's servant; executed Ahaziah king of Judah, Joram, Jezebel and the house of Ahab in Israel, and the worshipers of Baal (2Kg 9–10; cp. 1Kg 19:16-17).

JEPHTHAH
Gileadite judge who made rash vow affecting his daughter (Jdg 11–12; 1Sm 12:11; Heb 11:32).

JEREMIAH
Prophet to Judah in the time leading up to the exile (Jr 1:1-3). Put in stocks (20:1-3), threatened (Jr 26), opposed (Jr 28), imprisoned (32:2; 37), censured (Jr 36), and thrown into a cistern (Jr 38). Taken to Egypt against his will (Jr 43).

JERICHO
City near the Jordan River north of the Dead Sea (Nm 22:1). Spied out (Jos 2) and conquered (Jos 6; Heb 11:30) by Joshua; rebuilt by Hiel (1Kg 16:34). Visited by Jesus (Mt 20:29-34; Mk 10:46-52; Lk 18:35; 19:1-10).

JEROBOAM
1. Son of Nebat; Solomon's servant; rebelled; first king of Israel (1Kg 11:26–12:20). Judged for notorious idolatry (12:25–14:20).
2. Son of Joash, king of Israel (2Kg 14:23-29).

JERUSALEM
Formerly called Salem (Gn 14:18; Ps 76:2) or Jebus (Jos 18:28); 1Ch 11:4. David conquered it and made it his capital (2Sm 5:5-9); Solomon built temple, palace, and fortifications (1Kg 3:1). Conquered by Babylon (2Kg 24:10-12). Rebuilt and resettled after the exile (Ezr 1; Neh 12:27). Jesus visited (Mt 21:1; Jn 2:13); mourned (Mt 23:37). Important city in early church (Ac 15:4). New Jerusalem promised (Rv 3:12; 21:2,10).

in **J** he reigned 33 years over all — 2Sm 5:5
J, the city I chose for Myself to put My name there. — 1Kg 11:36
For a remnant will go out from **J**, — 2Kg 19:31
Pray for the peace of **J**: — Ps 122:6
If I forget you, **J**, may my right — Ps 137:5
Speak tenderly to **J**, and announce — Is 40:2
From ... rebuild **J** until Messiah — Dn 9:25
O **J**! **J** that kills the prophets and — Mt 23:37
say that the place to worship is in **J**. — Jn 4:20
you will be My witnesses in **J**, in all — Ac 1:8
the Holy City, new **J**, coming down — Rv 21:2

JESHUA
Son of Jozadak; high priest; returned with Zerubbabel (Ezr 3:2; Neh 7:7).

JESSE
David's father (Ru 4:17-22; 1Sm 16; 1Ch 2:12-16; Mt 1:5-6; Lk 3:32).

JESUS
Messiah and Lord (Ac 2:36; Eph 3:11; 1Pt 3:15). Born in Bethlehem (Mt 1:18-25; Lk 2:1-7) to a virgin, Mary (Mt 1:20; Lk 1:26-38). Genealogy (Mt 1:1-17; Lk 3:23-38). Raised in Nazareth (Mt 2:19-23; Lk 2:39-40). Visited the temple at age 12 (Lk 2:41-50).

Baptized by John (Mt 3:13-17; Lk 3:21). Tempted in the wilderness (Mt 4:1-11; Lk 4:1-13). Chose apostles (Lk 5:1-11; 27-28; 6:12-16; Jn 1:35-51).

Transfigured (Mt 17:1-9; Mk 9:2-10). Triumphal entry into Jerusalem (Mt 21:1-11; Lk 19:28-40). Betrayal and arrest (Mt 26:17-25,47-56; Mk 14:17-21,43-50; Lk 22:1-6,47-54), trial (Mt 26:57-66; 27:11-31; Mk 14:53-65; 15:1-20; Lk 22:66–23:25), crucifixion (Mt 27:32-56; Mk 15:21-39; Lk 23:32-49), and resurrection (Mt 28; Mk 16; Lk 24; Jn 20–21).

JETHRO
Priest of Midian; Moses' father-in-law and advisor (Ex 3:1; 4:18; 18). Also called Reuel (2:18).

JEW
He planned to destroy all ... the **J-s**, — Est 3:6
has been born King of the **J-s**? — Mt 2:2
Are You the King of the **J-s**? — Mt 27:11
How is it that You, a **J**, ask for a — Jn 4:9
salvation is from the **J-s**. — Jn 4:22
first to the **J**, and also to the — Rm 1:16
a person is a **J** who is one inwardly, — Rm 2:29
Or is God for **J-s** only? Is He not — Rm 3:29
To the **J-s** I became like a **J**, — 1Co 9:20
There is no **J** or Greek, slave or — Gl 3:28

JEWEL
She is more precious than **j-s**; — Pr 3:15

JEZEBEL
Wife of King Ahab of Israel, daughter of the king of Sidon; brought Baal worship to Israel (1Kg 16:31-33). Killed prophets and threatened Elijah (18:4,13; 19:1-2). Killed by Jehu (2Kg 9:30-37) in fulfillment of prophecy (1Kg 21). Name used as a label (Rv 2:20).

JOAB
Son of Zeruiah; David's nephew and commander of his troops (1Ch 2:16; 11:6). Killed Abner (2Sm 3:22-39), Absalom (2Sm 18), Amasa, and Sheba (2Sm 20). Sided with Adonijah (1Kg 1:7,19); David told Solomon to execute him (2:5-6,28-35).

JOASH
1. Son of Ahaziah; king of Judah (2Kg 12). Protected by Jehoiada (2Kg 11). Repaired temple (2Ch 24:4-14).
2. Alternate name of Jehoash son of Jehoahaz, king of Israel (2Kg 13:10).

JOB
Wealthy patriarch. His book tells of his testing (Jb 1–2), perseverance (Jb 3–37), rebuke (Jb 38–41), and vindication (Jb 42; Jms 5:11).

JOEL
1. Dishonest son of Samuel (2Sm 8:2).
2. Son of Pethuel; prophet who urged priests to call Judah to repentance; depicted calamities (Jl 1:1–2:11); predicted the Messiah (2:21-32; Ac 2:16).

JOHANAN
Commander; stayed in Judah and tried to protect Gedaliah (2Kg 25:23); forced Jeremiah to go to Egypt (Jr 40–43).

JOHN
1. The baptizer; Son of Zechariah; prophet. Annunciation and birth (Lk 1:5-25,57-66). Preached repentance, announced the coming Messiah (Mt 3:1-12; Mk 1:1-8; Lk 3:1-18; 7:27-28), and baptized Jesus (Mt 3:13-15; Mk 1:9; Lk 3:21-22). Fulfilled the role of Elijah (Mt 11:13-14; 17:12-13; Mk 9:12-13; Mt 3:4; cp. 2Kg 1:8). Asked Jesus to verify His identity (Mt 11:2-6; Lk 7:18-23). Beheaded by Herod Antipas (Mt 14:1-12; Mk 6:14-29; Lk 3:19-20; 9:7-9).
2. Apostle; Son of Zebedee; brother of James. Call (Mt 4:21-22; Mk 1:19-20). Among the inner three at special occasions (Mk 9:2; 14:32-33). With James, called "Sons of Thunder" (Mk 3:17); asked for places of honor (Mk 10:35-41). Often with Peter (Ac 1:13; 3:1-11; 4:13-20; 8:14); a leader in Jerusalem (Gl 2:9). In his gospel, called the disciple Jesus loved (Jn 13:23; 19:26; 20:2; 21:7,20); also wrote three letters and Revelation.
3. John Mark *see* MARK

JOIN
to house and **j** field to field — Is 5:8
Then **j** them together into a — Ezk 37:17
what God has **j-ed** together, — Mt 19:6

JOINTS
soul and spirit, **j** and marrow. — Heb 4:12

JOKING
or crude **j** are not suitable — Eph 5:4

JONAH
Son of Amittai; prophet at the time of Jeroboam II (2Kg 14:23-27). Rejected God's call to preach in Nineveh; swallowed by a great fish (Jnh 1). Prayed (Jnh 2); preached repentance in Nineveh (Jnh 3); scolded by God for his anger (Jnh 4). Used as an example (Mt 12:39-41; 16:4; Lk 11:29-32).

JONATHAN
Son of Saul; friend of David (1Sm 18:1-4; 19:1-7; 20; 23:16-18). Killed in battle (31:1-13); mourned by David (2Sm 1:17-27).

JORAM
1. Son of Ahab; king of Israel (2Kg 3). Succeeded his brother Ahaziah (1:17). Attacked Moab with the help of Judah, Edom, and Elisha (3:4-27). Wounded by Arameans (8:28); killed by Jehu (9:14-26).
2. Alternate form of Jehoram, son of Jehoshaphat; king of Judah (2Kg 8:16-24; 2Ch 21).

JORDAN
Lot chose the entire **J** Valley — Gn 13:11
the border will go down to the **J** — Nm 34:12
dry ground in the middle of the **J**, — Jos 3:17
himself in the **J** seven times, — 2Kg 5:14
Jesus came ... to John at the **J**, — Mt 3:13

JOSEPH
1. Son of Jacob and Rachel. Sold into slavery in Egypt (Gn 37); imprisoned on false accusations (Gn 39); became Pharaoh's second in command (41:39-45); sold grain to brothers (Gn 42–45); enabled his father and brothers to move to Egypt (Gn 46–47). Sons Ephraim and Manasseh each became tribes (Gn 48). Died in Egypt, buried in Canaan (50:22-26; Ex 13:19; Jos 24:32; Ac 7:16).
2. Husband of Mary; foster father of Jesus (Mt 1:16,20; Lk 2:4; 3:23: 4:22; Jn 1:45; 6:42). Carpenter (Mt 13:55). Told in a dream not to divorce Mary (Mt 1:18-25); told in a dream to flee to Egypt (2:13-23).
3. Of Arimathea; a righteous member of the Sanhedrin who sought the kingdom of God; put Jesus' body in his tomb (Mt 27:57-60; Mk 15:43-46; Lk 23:50-53; Jn 19:38-42).

JOSHUA

Son of Nun; successor to Moses as leader of Israelites. Leader of Moses' army (Ex 17:8-13); Moses' servant on Mt. Sinai (32:17). Scouted Canaan and, along with Caleb, recommended invasion (Nm 13:30–14:38). Chosen, commissioned, and encouraged by God (Nm 27:15-23; Dt 31:14-15,23; Jos 1:1-9).

Conquered Canaan (Jos 2–11) and distributed the land (Jos 12–21). Renewed the covenant and charged the people (Jos 23–24).

JOSIAH

Son of Amon; king of Judah. Became king at age 8 (2Kg 21:19–22:2). Found the book of the law and instituted reforms (2Kg 22–23; 2Ch 34–35). Died resisting Pharaoh Neco (2Kg 23:29-30; 2Ch 35:20-25).

JOTHAM

1. Son of Gideon (Jdg 9).
2. Son of Uzziah/Azariah; co-regent (2Kg 15:5), then king of Judah (15:32-38).

JOURNEY

like a man on a **j**, who left his Mk 13:34
On frequent **j-s**, I faced dangers 2Co 11:26

JOY

altar of God, to God, my greatest **j**. Ps 43:4
Restore the **j** of Your salvation Ps 51:12
A wise son brings **j** to his father, Pr 10:1
crowned with unending **j**. Is 35:10; 51:11
turn their mourning into **j**, Jr 31:13
immediately receives it with **j**. Mt 13:20
Share your master's **j**!' Mt 25:21
news of great **j** that will be for Lk 2:10
will be more **j** in heaven over Lk 15:7
but your sorrow will turn to **j**. Jn 16:20
peace, and **j** in the Holy Spirit. Rm 14:17
fruit of the Spirit is love, **j**, peace Gl 5:22
fulfill my **j** by thinking the same Php 2:2
who for the **j** that lay before Him Heb 12:2
Consider it a great **j**, my brothers Jms 1:2
inexpressible and glorious **j**, 1Pt 1:8
I have no greater **j** than this: 3Jn 4

JOYFUL

come before Him with **j** songs. Ps 100:2
A **j** heart is good medicine, Pr 17:22
In the day of prosperity be **j**, Ec 7:14
ate their food with a **j** and humble Ac 2:46
How **j** those whose lawless acts Rm 4:7

JOYFULLY

Shout **j** to God, all the earth! Ps 66:1

JUBILEE

It will be your **J**, when Lv 25:10

JUDAH

Son of Jacob and Leah (Gn 29:35); tribe with large territory west and south of Jerusalem (Jos 15:20-63). Tricked by daughter-in-law (Gn 38). Ancestor of David and Jesus (Gn 49:10; 1Sm 17:12; Mt 1:3,6,16; Rv 5:5). Name of the southern part of the divided kingdom (2Kg 12:20; 14:21; 23:27; Ezk 37:15-23) and the Persian province in the restoration (Neh 5:14; Hg 1:1).

JUDAISM

my former way of life in **J**: Gl 1:13

JUDAS

1. Iscariot; apostle (Mt 10:4); treasurer, miser, thief (Jn 12:4-6). Betrayed Jesus (Mt 26:21-25,44-50; Lk 22:3-6; Jn 13:21-30); committed suicide (Mt 27:3-10; Ac 1:16-20).
2. Son of James; apostle; called Thaddaeus (Mt 10:3; Mk 3:18; Lk 6:16; Jn 14:22).
3. Brother of Jesus (Mt 13:55; Mk 6:3); also called Jude.

JUDE

Brother of Jesus; also called Judas; author (Mt 13:55; Jd 1).

JUDEA

Another name for the territory of Judah.
Jesus was born in Bethlehem of **J** Mt 2:1
Pontius Pilate was governor of **J**, Lk 3:1
in Jerusalem, in all **J** and Samaria, Ac 1:8

JUDGE (N)

Won't the **J** of all the earth do Gn 18:25
LORD raised up **j-s**, who saved Jdg 2:16
a **j** ... who didn't fear God or Lk 18:2

JUDGE (V)

May the LORD **j** between me and Gn 16:5
He is coming to **j** the earth. 1Ch 16:33
He **j-s** the world with righteousness; Ps 9:8
There is a God who **j-s** on earth! Ps 58:11
coming to **j** the earth. He will **j** the Ps 96:13
Do not **j**, so that you won't be **j-d**. Mt 7:1
who believes in Him is not **j-d**, Jn 3:18
rather **j** according to righteous Jn 7:24
I did not come to **j** the world but Jn 12:47
that the saints will **j** the world? 1Co 6:2
who is going to **j** the living and 2Tm 4:1
who are you to **j** your neighbor? Jms 4:12
the dead were **j-d** according to Rv 20:12

JUDGMENT

the wicked will not survive the **j**, Ps 1:5
my mouth, for I hope in Your **j-s**. Ps 119:43
Teach me good **j** and discernment Ps 119:66
arrived and a **j** was given in Dn 7:22
Sodom on the day of **j** than for Mt 11:24
not come under **j** but has passed Jn 5:24
His **j-s** and untraceable Rm 11:33
eats and drinks **j** on himself. 1Co 11:29
die once—and after this, **j**— Heb 9:27
has come for **j** to begin with 1Pt 4:17
because His **j-s** are true and Rv 19:2

JUG

and the oil **j** will not run dry 1Kg 17:14

JUST

Judge of all the earth do what is **j**? Gn 18:25
is holy and **j** and good. Rm 7:12
whatever is **j**, whatever is pure Php 4:8

JUSTICE

must not deny **j** to a poor person Ex 23:6
but He gives **j** to the afflicted Jb 36:6
Evil men do not understand **j**, Pr 28:5
He will bring **j** to the nations. Is 42:1
the LORD, showing faithful love, **j**, Jr 9:24
But let **j** flow like water, Am 5:24
will proclaim **j** to the nations. Mt 12:18
kind of herb, and you bypass **j** Lk 11:42

JUSTIFICATION

and raised for our **j**. Rm 4:25
there is life-giving **j** for everyone. Rm 5:18

JUSTIFY

he had **j-ied** himself rather than God. Jb 32:2
righteous Servant will **j** many, Is 53:11
But wanting to **j** himself, he Lk 10:29
down to his house **j-ied** rather than Lk 18:14
who believes in Him is **j-ied** Ac 13:39
They are **j-ied** freely by His grace Rm 3:24
that a man is **j-ied** by faith apart Rm 3:28
and those He called, He also **j-ied**; Rm 8:30
God is the One who **j-ies**. Rm 8:33
no one is **j-ied** by the works of the Gl 2:16
we might be **j-ied** by faith in Christ Gl 2:16
that God would **j** the Gentiles by Gl 3:8
a man is **j-ied** by works and not Jms 2:24

JUSTLY

the LORD requires of you: to act **j**, Mc 6:8

KADESH

Oasis, also called Kadesh-barnea. Where Abraham fought the Amalekites (Gn 14:7). Where the Israelites camped, they sent out spies, and Moses struck the rock (Nm 13:26; 20:1,11; 27:14; 32:8; Dt 1:46; 9:23; Jdg 11:16-17). Southern limit of Judah (Nm 34:4; Jos 10:41; 15:3).

KEEP

be with me, and **k** me from harm 1Ch 4:10
is great reward in **k-ing** them. Ps 19:11
K your tongue from evil and your Ps 34:13
How can a young man **k** his way
pure? By **k-ing** Your word. Ps 119:9
K my commands and live Pr 4:4; 7:2
fear God and **k** His commands, Ec 12:13
K listening, but do not understand; Is 6:9
You will **k** ... in perfect peace Is 26:3
K asking, and it will be given Mt 7:7
"I have **kept** all these," the young Mt 19:20
hates his life in this world will **k** it Jn 12:25
loves Me, he will **k** My word. Jn 14:23
the race, I have **kept** the faith. 2Tm 4:7
whoever **k-s** the entire law, yet Jms 2:10
and unfading, **kept** in heaven for 1Pt 1:4
and those who **k** the words of Rv 22:9

KETURAH

Abraham's second wife (Gn 25:1-4).

KEY

give you the **k-s** of the kingdom Mt 16:19
and I hold the **k-s** of death and Rv 1:18
the One who has the **k** of David, Rv 3:7

KIDNAP

Whoever **k-s** a person must be put Ex 21:16

KILL

his brother Abel and **k-ed** him. Gn 4:8
Am I God, **k-ing** and giving life 2Kg 5:7
a time to **k** and a time to heal; Ec 3:3
Don't fear those who **k** the body
but are not able to **k** the soul; Mt 10:28
k-ed, and be raised the third day. Mt 16:21
way to arrest and **k** Him. Mk 14:1
Why do you want to **k** Me? Jn 7:19
You **k-ed** the source of life, Ac 3:15
For the letter **k-s**, but the Spirit 2Co 3:6

KIND (ADJ)

Love is patient, love is **k**. 1Co 13:4
And be **k** and compassionate to Eph 4:32

KIND (N)
seed in it according to their **k-s**. Gn 1:11
the birds according to their **k-s**, Gn 6:20
asked, "What **k** of man is this? Mt 8:27
is a root of all **k-s** of evil, 1Tm 6:10

KINDNESS
K to the poor is a loan to the Pr 19:17
God's **k** is intended to lead you to Rm 2:4
consider God's **k** and severity: Rm 11:22
patience, **k**, goodness, faith Gl 5:22

KING
days there was no **k** in Israel; Jdg 17:6
said, "Give us a **k** to judge us 1Sm 8:6
anointed David **k** over the house 2Sm 2:4
The **k-s** of the earth take their Ps 2:2
The LORD is **K** forever and ever; Ps 10:16
Who is this **K** of glory? Ps 24:8
It is by me that **k-s** reign and rulers Pr 8:15
the glory of **k-s** to investigate Pr 25:2
my eyes have seen the **K**, Is 6:5
the living God and eternal **K**. Jr 10:10
Look, your **K** is coming to you; Zch 9:9
who has been born **K** of the Jews? Mt 2:2
Look, your **K** is coming to you, Mt 21:5
JESUS THE **K** OF THE JEWS Mt 27:37
Now to the **K** eternal, immortal 1Tm 1:17
for **k-s** and all those who are in 1Tm 2:2
K of **k-s**, and the Lord of lords, 1Tm 6:15
K OF **K-S** AND LORD OF Rv 19:16

KINGDOM *SEE ALSO* KINGDOM OF GOD; KINGDOM OF HEAVEN
you will be My **k** of priests and Ex 19:6
Your **k** is an everlasting **k**; Ps 145:13
showed Him all the **k-s** of the world Mt 4:8
Your **k** come. Your will be done Mt 6:10
these are the sons of the **k**. Mt 13:38
I will give you the keys of the **k** Mt 16:19
nation, and **k** against **k**. Mt 24:7
will give you, up to half my **k**. Mk 6:23
But seek His **k**, and these Lk 12:31
My **k** is not of this world, Jn 18:36
transferred us into the **k** of the Son Col 1:13
The **k** of the world has become Rv 11:15

KINGDOM OF GOD (GOD'S KINGDOM)
But seek first the **k** and His Mt 6:33
for a rich person to enter the **k**. Mt 19:24
for the **k** belongs to such as these. Mk 10:14
You are not far from the **k**. Mk 12:34
you see, the **k** is among you. Lk 17:21
is born again, he cannot see the **k**. Jn 3:3
for the **k** is not eating and drinking, Rm 14:17
will not inherit **God's kingdom**? 1Co 6:9

KINGDOM OF HEAVEN
Repent, because the **k** has come near! Mt 3:2
poor in spirit ... the **k** is theirs. Mt 5:3
The **k** is like a mustard seed Mt 13:31
I will give you the keys of the **k**, Mt 16:19
k is made up of people like this. Mt 19:14

KINGSHIP
for **k** belongs to the LORD; Ps 22:28

KISS (N)
but the **k-es** of an enemy are Pr 27:6
betraying the Son of Man with a **k**? Lk 22:48
Greet one another with a holy **k**. Rm 16:16

KISS (V)
mouth that has not **k-ed** him. 1Kg 19:18
that he would **k** me with the Sg 1:2
The One I **k**, He's the One; Mt 26:48

KNEE
Every **k** will bow to Me, every Is 45:23
the Lord, every **k** will bow to Me Rm 14:11
name of Jesus every **k** will bow Php 2:10

KNEEL
let us **k** before the LORD our Ps 95:6
a stone's throw, **knelt** down, Lk 22:41
For this reason I **k** before the Eph 3:14

KNIFE
and took the **k** to slaughter his Gn 22:10

KNIT
k me together in my mother's Ps 139:13
fitted and **k** together by every Eph 4:16

KNOCK
Keep **k-ing**, and the door will be Mt 7:7
I stand at the door and **k**. Rv 3:20

KNOW
be like God, **k-ing** good and evil. Gn 3:5
For now I **k** that you fear God, Gn 22:12
Egyptians will **k** that I am Yahweh Ex 7:5
But I **k** my living Redeemer, Jb 19:25
since He **k-s** the secrets of the Ps 44:21
and **k** that I am God, Ps 46:10
The LORD **k-s** man's thoughts; Ps 94:11
You have searched me and **k-n** me. Ps 139:1
You **k** when I sit down and when I Ps 139:2
and I **k** this very well Ps 139:14
Search me, God, and **k** my heart; Ps 139:23
for you don't **k** what a day might Pr 27:1
K the LORD, for they will all **k** Me Jr 31:34
your left hand **k** what your right Mt 6:3
your Father **k-s** the things you need Mt 6:8
I never **knew** you! Depart from Me, Mt 7:23
that day and hour no one **k-s** Mt 24:36
you don't **k** what day your Lord Mt 24:42
I **k** My own sheep, and they **k** Me, Jn 10:14
We **k** that his testimony is true Jn 21:24
not for you to **k** times or Ac 1:7
For though they **knew** God, they Rm 1:21
searches the hearts **k-s** the Spirit's Rm 8:27
We **k** that all things work Rm 8:28
Now I **k** in part, but then I will **k** fully, as I am fully **k-n**. 1Co 13:12
k the Messiah's love that surpasses Eph 3:19
the surpassing value of **k-ing** Christ Php 3:8
to **k** Him and the power of His Php 3:10
your requests be made **k-n** to God. Php 4:6
I **k** the One I have believed in 2Tm 1:12
The Lord **k-s** those who are His, 2Tm 2:19
who says, "I have come to **k** Him," 1Jn 2:4
to **k** love: He laid down His life 1Jn 3:16

KNOWLEDGE
the tree of the **k** of good and evil. Gn 2:9
Can anyone teach God **k**, Jb 21:22
extraordinary **k** is beyond me. Ps 139:6
of the LORD is the beginning of **k**; Pr 1:7
The wise store up **k**, Pr 10:14
of the wisdom and the **k** of God! Rm 11:33
K inflates with pride, but love 1Co 8:1
all mysteries and all **k**, 1Co 13:2
Messiah's love that surpasses **k**, Eph 3:19
wisdom and **k** are hidden in Him. Col 2:3
from the "**k**" that falsely bears 1Tm 6:20

in the grace and **k** of our Lord 2Pt 3:18

KORAH
1. Led rebellion against Moses (Nm 16; Jd 11).
2. Kohathite Levite (Ex 6:21; 1Ch 6:22); ancestor of temple singers (2Ch 20:19; Pss 42; 44–49; 84–85; 87–88).

LABAN
Rebekah's brother (Gn 24:29); father of Leah and Rachel (Gn 29:15-30).

LABOR (N)
that your **l** in the Lord is 1Co 15:58

LABOR (V)
You are to **l** six days and do all Ex 20:9
they don't **l** or spin thread. Mt 6:28

LACK
shepherd; there is nothing I **l**. Ps 23:1
but fools die for **l** of sense. Pr 10:21
You **l** one thing: Go, sell all Mk 10:21
Now if any of you **l-s** wisdom, Jms 1:5

LAKE
were thrown alive into the **l** of fire Rv 19:20
second death, the **l** of fire. Rv 20:14

LAMB
God Himself will provide the **l** Gn 22:8
The wolf will live with the **l**, Is 11:6
He gathers the **l-s** in His arms Is 40:11
Like a **l** led to the slaughter Is 53:7
you out like **l-s** among wolves. Lk 10:3
L of God, who takes away the sin Jn 1:29
"Feed My **l-s**," He told him. Jn 21:15
like that of a **l** without defect 1Pt 1:19
L who was slaughtered is worthy Rv 5:12
the marriage feast of the **L** Rv 19:9
written in the **L-'s** book of life. Rv 21:27

LAME
Then the **l** will leap like a deer Is 35:6
the blind see, the **l** walk, Mt 11:5

LAMENT
the following **l** for Saul and his 2Sm 1:17
You turned my **l** into dancing; Ps 30:11
heard in Ramah, a **l** with bitter Jr 31:15
we sang a **l**, but you didn't Mt 11:17

LAMP
LORD, You light my **l**; Ps 18:28
Your word is a **l** for my feet and Ps 119:105
but the **l** of the wicked is put out. Pr 13:9
No one lights a **l** and puts it Mt 5:15
The eye is the **l** of the body. Mt 6:22
like 10 virgins who took their **l-s** Mt 25:1
the light of a **l** will never Rv 18:23

LAMPLIGHT
will not need **l** or sunlight, Rv 22:5

LAMPSTAND
a **l** out of pure, hammered gold. Ex 25:31
but rather on a **l**, and it gives light Mt 5:15
seven **l-s** are the seven churches. Rv 1:20
and remove your **l** from its place Rv 2:5

LAND
God called the dry **l** "earth," Gn 1:10
I will give this **l** to your Gn 12:7
a **l** flowing with milk and honey Ex 3:8
So Joshua took the entire **l**, Jos 11:23

divide this **l** as an inheritance Jos 13:7
Judah went into exile from its **l**. 2Kg 25:21
forgive their sin, and heal their **l**. 2Ch 7:14
the humble will inherit the **l** Ps 37:11
Woe to you, **l**, when your king is Ec 10:16
My flock from all the **l-s** where I Jr 23:3
and strike the **l** with a curse. Mal 4:6
those who owned **l-s** or houses sold Ac 4:34
on the sea, his left on the **l**, Rv 10:2

LANGUAGE
the whole earth had the same **l** Gn 11:1
He will speak ... in a foreign **l**. Is 28:11
they will speak in new **l-s**; Mk 16:17
began to speak in different **l-s**, Ac 2:4
in other **l-s** and declaring Ac 10:46
in other **l-s** and to prophesy. Ac 19:6
different kinds of **l-s**, to another, interpretation of **l-s**. 1Co 12:10
If I speak human or angelic **l-s** 1Co 13:1
as for **l-s**, they will cease; 1Co 13:8
person who speaks in another **l** 1Co 14:2
not forbid speaking in other **l-s** 1Co 14:39
and filthy **l** from your mouth. Col 3:8
every tribe and **l** and people Rv 5:9

LAPPED
deliver you with the 300 men who **l** Jdg 7:7

LASHES
than a hundred **l** into a fool. Pr 17:10
Five times I received 39 **l** 2Co 11:24

LAST (ADJ)
These are the **l** words of David: 2Sm 23:1
In the **l** days the mountain of Is 2:2
are first will be **l**, and the **l** first. Mt 19:30
he must be **l** of all and servant Mk 9:35
The **l** enemy He abolishes is 1Co 15:26
of an eye, at the **l** trumpet. 1Co 15:52
In these **l** days, He has spoken Heb 1:2
Children, it is the **l** hour. 1Jn 2:18

LAST (N)
He will stand on the dust at **l**. Jb 19:25
I am the first and I am the **l**. Is 44:6
I am the First and the **L**, Rv 1:17

LAST (V)
For His anger **l-s** only a moment, Ps 30:5

LATER
Lord your God in **l** days and obey Dt 4:30
that in **l** times some will depart 1Tm 4:1

LAUGH
Why did Sarah **l**, Gn 18:13
The One enthroned in heaven **l-s**; Ps 2:4
a time to weep and a time to **l**; Ec 3:4

LAUGHTER
Even in **l** a heart may be sad, Pr 14:13
Your **l** must change to mourning Jms 4:9

LAUNDERER
white as no **l** on earth could Mk 9:3

LAW
the stone tablets with the **l** Ex 24:12
Moses wrote down this **l** and gave it Dt 31:9
L after **l**, **l** after **l**, line after line, Is 28:10
assume that I came to destroy the **L** Mt 5:17
All the **L** and the Prophets depend Mt 22:40
stroke of a letter in the **l** to drop Lk 16:17
the **l** was given through Moses; Jn 1:17
are not under **l** but under grace Rm 6:14
So then, the **l** is holy, and the Rm 7:12
For Christ is the end of the **l** Rm 10:4
The **l**, then, was our guardian until Gl 3:24
For the entire **l** is fulfilled in Gl 5:14
I will put My **l-s** into their minds Heb 8:10
Since the **l** has only a shadow Heb 10:1
For whoever keeps the entire **l**, Jms 2:10
sin is the breaking of **l**. 1Jn 3:4

LAWBREAKER
Depart from Me, you **l-s**! Mt 7:23

LAWLESS
and then the **l** one will be 2Th 2:8

LAWLESSNESS
Because **l** will multiply, Mt 24:12
the mystery of **l** is already at 2Th 2:7

LAY
Look, I have **laid** a stone in Zion Is 28:16
Man has no place to **l** His head. Mt 8:20
in cloth and **laid** Him in a feeding Lk 2:7
I **l** down My life for the sheep. Jn 10:15
through the **l-ing** on of my hands 2Tm 1:6
ritual washings, **l-ing** on of hands Heb 6:2
let us **l** aside every weight and Heb 12:1
He **laid** down His life for us. 1Jn 3:16

LAZARUS
1. Poor man in Jesus' parable (Lk 16:19-31).
2. Brother of Mary and Martha; friend of Jesus (Jn 11:1-5). Died; revived by Jesus (11:3-44). Endangered because of fame (12:9-11,17).

LAZY
A **l** man doesn't roast his game, Pr 12:27
and a **l** person will go hungry. Pr 19:15
so that you won't become **l** Heb 6:12

LEAD
of cloud to **l** them on their way Ex 13:21
way of the wicked **l-s** to ruin. Ps 1:6
He **l-s** me beside quiet waters. Ps 23:2
way, Lord, and **l** me on a level Ps 27:11
L me to a rock that is high above me Ps 61:2
l me in the everlasting way. Ps 139:24
The fear of the Lord **l-s** to life; Pr 19:23
and a child will **l** them. Is 11:6
Like a lamb **led** to the slaughter Is 53:7
l astray, if possible, even the elect. Mt 24:24
and **led** Him away to crucify Him. Mt 27:31
sheep by name and **l-s** them out. Jn 10:3
is intended to **l** you to repentance? Rm 2:4
sin **l-ing** to death or of obedience Rm 6:16
All those **led** by God's Spirit are Rm 8:14
But if you are **led** by the Spirit, Gl 5:18

LEADER
He chose Judah as **l**, 1Ch 28:4
For the **l-s** of the earth belong to Ps 47:9
out of you will come a **l** who will Mt 2:6
of the synagogue **l-s**, named Jairus Mk 5:22
Obey your **l-s** and submit Heb 13:17

LEADING (ADJ)
as a number of the **l** women. Ac 17:4

LEAF
they sewed fig **l-ves** together and Gn 3:7
and whose **l** does not wither Ps 1:3
becomes tender and sprouts **l-ves**, Mt 24:32
The **l-ves** of the tree are for Rv 22:2

LEAH
Wife of Jacob; mother of Reuben, Simeon, Levi, Judah, Issachar, Zebulun, and Dinah (Gn 29:16-35; 30:14-21).

LEAN
temple, so I can **l** against them. Jdg 16:26
So he **l-ed** back against Jesus and Jn 13:25

LEAP
with my God I can **l** over a wall. Ps 18:29
greeting, the baby **l-ed** inside her Lk 1:41
walking, **l-ing**, and praising God. Ac 3:8

LEARN
will listen and **l** to fear the Lord Dt 31:13
that I could **l** Your statutes. Ps 119:71
and the inexperienced **l** a lesson; Pr 19:25
L to do what is good. Is 1:17
take up My yoke and **l** from Me, Mt 11:29
is not how you **l-ed** about the Eph 4:20
for I have **l-ed** to be content in Php 4:11
A woman should **l** in silence with 1Tm 2:11
He **l-ed** obedience through what He Heb 5:8

LEARNED (N)
these things from the wise and **l** Mt 11:25

LEASE
He **l-d** it to tenant farmers and Mt 21:33

LEAST
are by no means **l** among the Mt 2:6
will be called **l** in the kingdom Mt 5:19
you did for one of the **l** of these Mt 25:40
For I am the **l** of the apostles, 1Co 15:9

LEATHER
man with a **l** belt around his 2Kg 1:8
garment with a **l** belt around his Mt 3:4

LEAVE
This is why a man **l-s** his father Gn 2:24
I will not **l** you or forsake you Jos 1:5
Spirit of the Lord had **left** Saul, 1Sm 16:14
I alone am **left**, and they are 1Kg 19:10
do not **l** me or abandon me, Ps 27:9
l your gift there in front of Mt 5:24
won't he **l** the 99 on the Mt 18:12
we have **left** everything and Mt 19:27
reason a man will **l** his father Mk 10:7
I will not **l** you as orphans; Jn 14:18
of Hosts had not **left** us offspring, Rm 9:29
I will never **l** you or forsake Heb 13:5

LEAVENS
A little yeast **l** the whole lump Gl 5:9

LEBANON
Mountainous region of northern promised land (Dt 1:7; 11:24). Known for its cedars and lush growth (Jdg 9:15; 1Kg 5:6; 2Ch 2:8,16; Ps 72:16; 92:12; Sg 4:11,15; Is 2:13; Ezk 27:5; 31:3). God is greater (Ps 29:5-6; 104:16).

LEECH
The **l** has two daughters: "Give, Pr 30:15

LEFT
not to turn aside to the right or the **l**. Dt 5:32
Don't turn to the right or to the **l**; Pr 4:27
down on your **l** side and place Ezk 4:4
don't let your **l** hand know what Mt 6:3
right and the other on Your **l**, Mt 20:21

right, and the goats on the **l**. Mt 25:33

LEFT-HANDED
Ehud son of Gera, a **l** Benjaminite, Jdg 3:15

LEFTOVER
up 12 baskets full of **l** pieces! Mt 14:20
they collected the **l** pieces Mt 15:37
Collect the **l-s** so that nothing Jn 6:12

LEGAL
It's not **l** for us to put Jn 18:31
that are not **l** for us as Romans Ac 16:21
Is it **l** for you to scourge a Ac 22:25

LEGION
with more than 12 **l-s** of angels? Mt 26:53
"My name is **L**," he answered Him Mk 5:9

LEGS
its **l** were iron, and its feet Dn 2:33
they did not break His **l** since Jn 19:33

LEND
If you **l** money to My people Ex 22:25
who does not **l** his money at Ps 15:5
come to a man who **l-s** generously Ps 112:5
and **l**, expecting nothing in return. Lk 6:35

LENDER
borrower is a slave to the **l**. Pr 22:7

LENGTH
l of days forever and ever. Ps 21:4
Its **l**, width, and height are equal. Rv 21:16

LENGTHENING (ADJ)
I fade away like a **l** shadow; Ps 109:23

LEOPARD
and the **l** will lie down with the Is 11:6
his skin, or a **l** his spots? Jr 13:23

LESS
punished us **l** than our sins Ezr 9:13
You made him little **l** than God Ps 8:5

LESSER
the **l** light to have dominion over Gn 1:16

LET
L there be light, Gn 1:3
L the little children come to Me. Mk 10:14

LETTER
not the smallest **l** or one stroke Mt 5:18
l kills, but the Spirit produces life. 2Co 3:6
His **l-s** are weighty and powerful 2Co 10:10
Look at what large **l-s** I use Gl 6:11
these things in all his **l-s** in which 2Pt 3:16

LEVEL (ADJ)
My foot stands on **l** ground; Ps 26:12
Spirit lead me on **l** ground. Ps 143:10
The path of the righteous is **l**; Is 26:7
and rough places into **l** ground. Is 42:16

LEVEL (V)
mountain and hill will be **l-ed**; Is 40:4

LEVI
1. Son of Jacob and Leah (Gn 29:34). Ancestor of priestly tribe (Ex 32:25-29; Nm 3:11-13; Dt 10:6-9); received no allotment of land, only scattered towns and cities of refuge (Nm 18:20; 35:1-8; Jos 13:14,33); supported by tithes (Nm 18:21; Heb 7:5). Assisted descendants of Aaron in worship (Nm 3:5-9; 1Ch 6:16,31-32,49; 23:24-32; 2Ch 29:12-21); taught the word of God (2Ch 17:7-9; Neh 8:9-12).
2. Apostle, called Matthew (Mk 2:14; Lk 5:27-29; cp. Mt 9:9).

LEVIATHAN
Can you pull in **L** with a hook or Jb 41:1
You crushed the heads of **L**; Ps 74:14

LEVITICAL
came through the **L** priesthood Heb 7:11

LIAR
alarm I said, "Everyone is a **l**." Ps 116:11
he is a **l** and the father of **l-s**. Jn 8:44
be true, even if everyone is a **l**, Rm 3:4
we make Him a **l**, and His word is 1Jn 1:10
and all **l-s**—their share will Rv 21:8

LIBERATED
you have been **l** from sin and Rm 6:22
Christ has **l** us to be free. Gl 5:1

LIBERATOR
The **L** will come from Zion; Rm 11:26

LIBERTY
to proclaim **l** to the captives Is 61:1

LICK
the dogs will also **l** your blood! 1Kg 21:19
The dogs **l-ed** up his blood, 1Kg 22:38

LIE (N)
and one who utters **l-s** perishes. Pr 19:9
they prophesy a **l** to you so that Jr 27:10
exchanged the truth of God for a **l**, Rm 1:25
because no **l** comes from the truth. 1Jn 2:21

LIE (V) (PREVARICATE) *SEE ALSO* LYING
You must not ... **l** to one another. Lv 19:11
God is not a man who **l-s**, or a Nm 23:19
your heart to **l** to the Holy Spirit Ac 5:3
Do not **l** to one another, since Col 3:9

LIE (V) (RECLINE)
when you **l** down and when you get Dt 6:7
He lets me **l** down in green Ps 23:2
the leopard will **l** down with the Is 11:6
in cloth and **l-ing** in a manger. Lk 2:12

LIFE
the breath of **l** into his Gn 2:7
the tree of **l** in the middle Gn 2:9
then you must give **l** for **l**, Ex 21:23
the **l** of a creature is in the blood, Lv 17:11
Choose **l** so that you and your Dt 30:19
Remember that my **l** is but a breath. Jb 7:7
LORD is perfect, renewing one's **l**; Ps 19:7
will pursue me all the days of my **l**, Ps 23:6
the blessing—**l** forevermore. Ps 133:3
preserve my **l** from the anger Ps 138:7
Guard it, for it is your **l**. Pr 4:13
the one who finds me finds **l** Pr 8:35
presenting to you the way of **l** and the Jr 21:8
awake, some to eternal **l**, and some Dn 12:2
Don't worry about your **l**, Mt 6:25
gains whole world yet loses his **l**? Mt 16:26
to give His **l**—a ransom for many. Mt 20:28
one's **l** is not in the abundance of Lk 12:15
L was in Him, and that **l** was the light Jn 1:4
in Him will have eternal **l**. Jn 3:15
but has passed from death to **l**. Jn 5:24
"I am the bread of **l**," Jesus told Jn 6:35
that they may have **l** and have it Jn 10:10
I am the resurrection and the **l**. Jn 11:25
the way, the truth, and the **l**. Jn 14:6
too may walk in a new way of **l**. Rm 6:4
but the Spirit produces **l**. 2Co 3:6
The **l** I now live in the body, Gl 2:20
and your **l** is hidden with the Col 3:3
required for **l** and godliness 2Pt 1:3
lay down our **lives** for our brothers 1Jn 3:16
in the book of **l** of the Lamb who Rv 13:8

LIFEBLOOD
not eat meat with its **l** in it. Gn 9:4

LIFE-GIVING
last Adam became a **l** Spirit. 1Co 15:45

LIFETIME
only a moment, but His favor, a **l**. Ps 30:5

LIFT
and the One who **l-s** up my head. Ps 3:3
L up your heads, you gates! Ps 24:7
You have **l-ed** me up and have Ps 30:1
so the Son of Man must be **l-ed** up, Jn 3:14
When you **l** up the Son of Man, Jn 8:28
if I am **l-ed** up from the earth I Jn 12:32

LIGHT (N)
"Let there be **l**," and there was **l**. Gn 1:3
The LORD is my **l** and my salvation Ps 27:1
for my feet and a **l** on my path. Ps 119:105
like the **l** of dawn, shining brighter Pr 4:18
let us walk in the LORD's **l**. Is 2:5
in darkness have seen a great **l**; Is 9:2
people and a **l** to the nations Is 42:6
Arise, shine, for your **l** has come, Is 60:1
live in darkness have seen a great **l**, Mt 4:16
You are the **l** of the world. Mt 5:14
a **l** for revelation to the Gentiles Lk 2:32
I am the **l** of the world. Jn 8:12
walk in the **l** as He ... is in the **l** 1Jn 1:7

LIGHT (V)
No one **l-s** a lamp and puts it Mt 5:15
to horizon and **l-s** up the sky, Lk 17:24

LIGHTNING
was thunder and **l**, a thick cloud Ex 19:16
He hurled **l** bolts and routed them. Ps 18:14
For as the **l** comes from the east Mt 24:27
His appearance was like **l**, Mt 28:3

LIKE
you will be **l** God, knowing good Gn 3:5
I am God, and no one is **l** Me. Is 46:9
Yahweh, there is no one **l** You. Jr 10:6
What is the kingdom of God **l**, Lk 13:18
spoke **l** a child, I thought **l** a child, 1Co 13:11
He had to be **l** His brothers in Heb 2:17

LIKE-MINDED
have no one else **l** who will Php 2:20

LIKENESS
Our image, according to Our **l**. Gn 1:26
joined with Him in the **l** of His death Rm 6:5
slave, taking on the **l** of men. Php 2:7
curse men who are made in God's **l** Jms 3:9

LIMIT
when He set a **l** for the sea so Pr 8:29

LIMITED
Is the LORD's power **l**? Nm 11:23

LINE
l after **l**, **l** after **l**, a little here Is 28:10

LINEN
on his **l** robe and **l** undergarments. Lv 6:10
body, wrapped it in clean, fine **l**, Mt 27:59
tomb and saw the **l** cloths lying Jn 20:6

LINTEL
and brush the **l** and the two Ex 12:22

LION
Judah is a young **l** Gn 49:9
and the **l** will eat straw like the ox. Is 11:7
will be thrown into the **l-s'** den. Dn 6:7
prowling around like a roaring **l**, 1Pt 5:8
The **L** from the tribe of Judah, Rv 5:5

LIPS
His praise will always be on my **l**. Ps 34:1
a stranger, and not your own **l**. Pr 27:2
I am a man of unclean **l** Is 6:5
people honors Me with their **l**, Mt 15:8
and by the **l** of foreigners, 1Co 14:21

LIP-SERVICE
honor Me with **l**—yet their hearts Is 29:13

LISTEN
L, Israel: Yahweh is our God; Dt 6:4
Speak, for Your servant is **l-ing**. 1Sm 3:10
LORD, **l** and be gracious to me; Ps 30:10
For the LORD **l-s** to the needy and Ps 69:33
L, my sons, to a father's Pr 4:1
who gives an answer before he **l-s** Pr 18:13
Keep **l-ing**, but do not understand; Is 6:9
You will **l** and **l**, yet never Mt 13:14
I take delight in Him. **L** to Him! Mt 17:5
But if he won't **l**, take one or Mt 18:16
you cannot **l** to My word. Jn 8:43
and they will **l** to My voice. Jn 10:16
not from God does not **l** to us. 1Jn 4:6

LITTLE
You made him **l** less than God and Ps 8:5
Better a **l** with the fear of the Pr 15:16
are you fearful, you of **l** faith? Mt 8:26
the one who is forgiven **l**, loves **l**. Lk 7:47
I know both how to have a **l**, Php 4:12
and he had a **l** scroll opened in Rv 10:2

LIVE
for no one can see Me and **l**. Ex 33:20
man does not **l** on bread alone Dt 8:3
The LORD **l-s**—may my rock be Ps 18:46
to my God as long as I **l**. Ps 146:2
Keep my commands and **l** Pr 4:4; 7:2
on those **l-ing** in the land of darkness. Is 9:2
listen, so that you will **l**. Is 55:3
the righteous one will **l** by his faith. Hab 2:4
Man must not **l** on bread alone Mt 4:4
in Me, even if he dies, will **l**. Jn 11:25
Because I **l**, you will **l** too. Jn 14:19
in Him we **l** and move and Ac 17:28
The righteous will **l** by faith. Rm 1:17
fact that He **l-s**, He **l-s** to God. Rm 6:10
If we **l**, we **l** to the Lord; Rm 14:8
I no longer **l**, but Christ **l-s** in me. The life I now **l** in the body, I **l** by faith Gl 2:20

LIVING (ADJ)
and the man became a **l** being. Gn 2:7
the voice of the **l** God speaking Dt 5:26
But I know my **l** Redeemer, and He Jb 19:25
flesh cry out for the **l** God. Ps 84:2
let every **l** thing praise His Ps 145:21
Me, the fountain of **l** water, and dug Jr 2:13
On that day **l** water will flow Zch 14:8
Messiah, the Son of the **l** God! Mt 16:16
and He would give you **l** water. Jn 4:10
I am the **l** bread that came down Jn 6:51
your bodies as a **l** sacrifice, Rm 12:1
word of God is **l** and effective Heb 4:12
into the hands of the **l** God! Heb 10:31

LIVING (N)
God of the dead, but of the **l**. Mt 22:32
l is Christ and dying is gain. Php 1:21
to judge the **l** and the dead. 1Pt 4:5

LOAD (N)
tie up heavy **l-s** that are hard to Mt 23:4

LOAD (V)
You **l** people with burdens that Lk 11:46

LOAF
only have five **loaves** and two fish Mt 14:17
took the seven **loaves** and the fish, Mt 15:36

LOAN
to the poor is a **l** to the LORD, Pr 19:17
Don't ... put up security for **l-s**. Pr 22:26

LOCK
You **l** up the kingdom of heaven Mt 23:13

LOCUST
I will bring **l-s** into your territory. Ex 10:4
fruit of their labor to the **l**. Ps 78:46
What the devouring **l** has left, the Jl 1:4
his food was **l-s** and wild honey. Mt 3:4

LODGE
He's gone to **l** with a sinful Lk 19:7
no room for them at the **l-ing** place. Lk 2:7

LOFTY
It is **l**; I am unable to reach it. Ps 139:6
against all that is proud and **l**, Is 2:12
Lord seated on a high and **l** throne, Is 6:1

LOG
notice the **l** in your own eye Mt 7:3

LONG (ADJ)
you may have a **l** life in the land Ex 20:12
How **l** will you hesitate between 1Kg 18:21
How **l** will You hide Your face Ps 13:1
How **l**, LORD? Will You hide Ps 89:46
houses and make **l** prayers just Mt 23:14
if a man has **l** hair it is a disgrace 1Co 11:14

LONG (V)
As a deer **l-s** for streams of water, so Ps 42:1
I **l** for You in the night; Is 26:9
He **l-ed** to eat his fill from the Lk 15:16

LOOK
But his wife **l-ed** back and became Gn 19:26
he was afraid to **l** at God. Ex 3:6
Do not **l** at his appearance or 1Sm 16:7
The LORD **l-s** down from heaven on Ps 14:2
L down from heaven and see; Ps 80:14
Let your eyes **l** forward; Pr 4:25
keep **l-ing**, but do not perceive. Is 6:9
that day people will **l** to their Maker Is 17:7
that we should **l** at Him, Is 53:2
eyes are too pure to **l** on evil, Hab 1:13
will **l** at Me whom they pierced. Zch 12:10
everyone who **l-s** at a woman to Mt 5:28
because **l-ing** they do not see, Mt 13:13
the plow and **l-s** back is fit for Lk 9:62
'**L** there!' or '**L** here!' Don't Lk 17:23
L at My hands and My feet, Lk 24:39
your eyes and **l** at the fields, Jn 4:35
They will **l** at the One they Jn 19:37

LOOSE
whatever you **l** on earth is already Mt 16:19
a wife? Do not seek to be **l-d**. 1Co 7:27

LORD LD = LORD/YAHWEH *SEE ALSO* YAHWEH
For the **LD** your God is the God of gods and **L** of **l-s**, Dt 10:17
LD gives, and the **Ld** takes away. Jb 1:21
The **LD** is my shepherd; Ps 23:1
declaration of the **LD** to my **L**: Ps 110:1
Give thanks to the **L** of **l-s**. Ps 136:3
l-s other than You have ruled over Is 26:13
who says to Me, '**L**, **L**!' will enter Mt 7:21
Son of Man is **L** of the Sabbath. Mt 12:8
The **L** declared to my **L**, Mt 22:44
If David calls Him '**L**,' how then Mt 22:45
The **L** our God, The **L** is One. Mk 12:29
you call Me '**L**, **L**,' and don't do Lk 6:46
You call Me Teacher and **L**. Jn 13:13
Thomas ... "My **L** and my God!" Jn 20:28
crucified, both **L** and Messiah! Ac 2:36
with your mouth, "Jesus is **L**," Rm 10:9
are many "gods" and many "**l-s**" 1Co 8:5
one **L**, Jesus Christ. 1Co 8:6
can say, "Jesus is **L**," except by 1Co 12:3
Now the **L** is the Spirit; 2Co 3:17
one **L**, one faith, one baptism, Eph 4:5
confess that Jesus Christ is **L**, Php 2:11
King of kings, and the **L** of **l-s**, 1Tm 6:15
obeyed Abraham, calling him **l**. 1Pt 3:6
but honor the Messiah as **L** 1Pt 3:15
was in the Spirit on the **L-'s** day, Rv 1:10
KING OF KINGS AND **L** OF **L-S** Rv 19:16

LORDING
not **l** it over those entrusted to 1Pt 5:3

LOSE
finding his life will **l** it, Mt 10:39
but whoever **l-s** his life because Mt 16:25
100 sheep and **l-s** one of them, Lk 15:4
that I should **l** none of those He Jn 6:39

LOSS
everything to be a **l** in view of Php 3:8

LOST (ADJ)
I wander like a **l** sheep; Ps 119:176
and a time to count as **l**; Ec 3:6
My people are **l** sheep; Jr 50:6
go to the **l** sheep of the house Mt 10:6
sent only to the **l** sheep of the Mt 15:24
he was **l** and is found! Lk 15:24
them and not one of them is **l**, Jn 17:12
is veiled to those who are **l**. 2Co 4:3

LOST (N)
I will seek the **l**, bring back Ezk 34:16
will not seek the **l** or heal the Zch 11:16
come to seek and to save the **l**. Lk 19:10

LOT
Abraham's nephew (Gn 11:27). Separated from Abraham; settled in Sodom (13:1-13). Rescued from kings (14:1-16); from Sodom (18:16–19:29; Lk 17:28-29; 2Pt 2:7-9). Fathered Moabites and Ammonites by his daughters (Gn 19:30-38).

LOT
The land must be divided by **l**; Nm 26:55
Cast the **l** between me and my 1Sm 14:42
Pur (that is, the **l**) was cast Est 3:7
and they cast **l-s** for my clothing Ps 22:18
The **l** is cast into the lap, Pr 16:33
cast **l-s**, and the **l** singled out Jonah. Jnh 1:7
His clothes by casting **l-s**. Mt 27:35
Let's not tear it, but cast **l-s** for it, Jn 19:24
and the **l** fell to Matthias. Ac 1:26

LOUD
neighbor with a **l** voice early Pr 27:14
Jesus cried out with a **l** voice, Mt 27:46
I heard a **l** voice behind me like Rv 1:10

LOVE (N)
showing faithful **l** to a thousand Ex 20:6
rich in faithful **l** and truth, Ex 34:6
not withdraw My faithful **l** from Ps 89:33
His **l** is eternal. Ps 136:1-26
but **l** covers all offenses. Pr 10:12
your **l** is more delightful than wine. Sg 1:2
have loved you with an everlasting **l**; Jr 31:3
with human cords, with ropes of **l**. Hs 11:4
No one has greater **l** than this, Jn 15:13
God proves His own **l** for us in that Rm 5:8
L must be without hypocrisy. Rm 12:9
inflates with pride, but **l** builds up. 1Co 8:1
L is patient; **l** is kind. **L** does not 1Co 13:4
For the **l** of money is a root of 1Tm 6:10
God is **l**, 1Jn 4:16
abandoned the **l** you had at first. Rv 2:4

LOVE (V)
but **l** your neighbor as yourself; Lv 19:18
L the LORD your God with all Dt 6:5
Your God **l-d** Israel enough to 2Ch 9:8
I **l** You, LORD, my strength. Ps 18:1
He **l-s** righteousness and justice; Ps 33:5
I **l** the LORD because He has Ps 116:1
How I **l** Your instruction! Ps 119:97
LORD disciplines the one He **l-s**, Pr 3:12
I **l** those who **l** me, and those Pr 8:17
A friend **l-s** at all times, Pr 17:17
a time to **l** and a time to hate; Ec 3:8
I have **l-d** you with an everlasting Jr 31:3
When Israel was a child, I **l-d** him, Hs 11:1
Hate evil and **l** good; Am 5:15
Even so, I **l-d** Jacob, Mal 1:2
l your enemies and pray for Mt 5:44
will hate one and **l** the other, Mt 6:24
L the Lord your God with all Mt 22:37
L your neighbor as yourself. Mt 22:39
is forgiven little, **l-s** little. Lk 7:47
For God **l-d** the world in this way Jn 3:16
a new command: **L** one another. Jn 13:34
for God **l-s** a cheerful giver. 2Co 9:7
Husbands, **l** your wives, just as Eph 5:25
He who **l-s** his wife **l-s** himself. Eph 5:28
Do not **l** the world or the things 1Jn 2:15
l one another, because **l** is from God 1Jn 4:7
We **l** because He first **l-d** us. 1Jn 4:19
As many as I **l**, I rebuke and Rv 3:19

LOVELY
How **l** is Your dwelling place, Ps 84:1
I am dark ... yet **l** like the curtains of Sg 1:5
whatever is pure, whatever is **l**, Php 4:8

LOVER
will be **l-s** of self, **l-s** of money 2Tm 3:2

LOW
and hill will be made **l**; Lk 3:5

LOWER
You made him **l** than the angels Heb 2:7

LOWLY
He sets the **l** on high, Jb 5:11
thrones and exalted the **l**. Lk 1:52

LOYAL
LORD has found a man **l** to Him, 1Sm 13:14

LOYALTY
keeps His gracious covenant **l** Dt 7:9
He shows **l** to His anointed, 2Sm 22:51
Never let **l** and faithfulness Pr 3:3
For I desire **l** and not sacrifice Hs 6:6

LUKE
Companion of Paul (2Tm 4:11; Phm 24); physician (Col 4:14); author of Luke and Acts (note "we" in Ac 16:10; 28:16).

LUKEWARM
because you are **l**, and neither Rv 3:16

LUMP
leavens the whole **l** of dough. Gl 5:9

LUST (N)
the **l** of the flesh, the **l** of the eyes 1Jn 2:16

LUST (V)
looks at a woman to **l** for her has Mt 5:28

LUXURY
L is not appropriate for a fool Pr 19:10

LYDIA
First Philippian convert; seller of purple (Ac 16:12-15,40).

LYING (ADJ)
go and become a **l** spirit 1Kg 22:22
arrogant eyes, a **l** tongue, hands Pr 6:17

LYING (N)
Cursing, **l**, murder, stealing Hs 4:2
Since you put away **l**, Speak Eph 4:25

LYRE
who knows how to play the **l**. 1Sm 16:16
Praise the LORD with the **l**; Ps 33:2
we hung up our **l-s** on the poplar Ps 137:2
flute, zither, **l**, harp, drum Dn 3:5

MAACAH
1. David's wife; mother of Absalom (2Sm 3:3; 1Ch 3:2).
2. Mother of Judah's King Abijam (1Kg 15:2); promoted Asherah worship (15:13).

MAD
Too much study is driving you **m**! Ac 26:24

MADMAN
He acted like a **m** around them, 1Sm 21:13
I'm talking like a **m**— 2Co 11:23

MADNESS
and knowledge, **m** and folly; Ec 1:17

MAGDALENE *SEE* MARY 2.

MAGIC
seems like a **m** stone to its Pr 17:8
practiced **m** collected their books Ac 19:19

MAGICIAN
summoned all the **m-s** of Egypt Gn 41:8
the **m-s** of Egypt, and they also did Ex 7:11

MAGNIFICENT
our Lord, how **m** is Your name Ps 8:1
m acts of God in our own language Ac 2:11

MAGNIFY
name of the Lord Jesus was **m-ied**. Ac 19:17

MAGOG
Land ruled by Gog, an apocalyptic foe from the north (Ezk 38:2; 39:6; Rv 20:8).

MAIMED
It is better for you to enter life **m** Mt 18:8
invite those who are poor, **m**, lame, Lk 14:13

MAJESTIC
All that He does is splendid and **m**; Ps 111:3
came to Him from the **M** Glory: 2Pt 1:17

MAJESTY
Splendor and **m** are before Him; 1Ch 16:27
and the splendor and the **m** 1Ch 29:11
awesome **m** surrounds Him. Jb 37:22
He is robed in **m**; Ps 93:1
right hand of the **M** on high. Heb 1:3
we were eyewitnesses of His **m**. 2Pt 1:16

MAKE
Let Us **m** man in Our image, Gn 1:26
The sea is His; He **made** it. Ps 95:5
He **made** us, and we are His Ps 100:3
is the day the LORD has **made**; Ps 118:24
I have been ... wonderfully **made**. Ps 139:14
forming it, 'What are you **m-ing**?' Is 45:9
when I will **m** a new covenant Jr 31:31
and I will **m** you fish for people! Mt 4:19
and **m** disciples of all nations, Mt 28:19
Sabbath was **made** for man and not Mk 2:27
Why did you **m** me like this? Rm 9:20
made him lower than the angels Heb 2:7

MAKER
or a man more pure than his **M**? Jb 4:17
kneel before the LORD our **M**. Ps 95:6
Indeed, your husband is your **M** Is 54:5

MALACHI
Postexilic prophet (Mal 1:1).

MALE
He created them **m** and female. Gn 1:27
made them **m** and female, Mt 19:4
M-s committed shameless acts Rm 1:27
slave or free, **m** or female; Gl 3:28

MALICE
quarrels, deceit, and **m**. Rm 1:29
anger, wrath, **m**, slander, Col 3:8

MAN *SEE ALSO* MAN OF GOD
Let Us make **m** in Our image, Gn 1:26
God formed the **m** out of the dust Gn 2:7
for **m** sees what is visible, 1Sm 16:7
How happy is the **m** who does not Ps 1:1
what is **m** that You remember him, Ps 8:4
M is like a breath; his days are Ps 144:4
a way that seems right to a **m** Pr 14:12
Egyptians are **men**, not God; Is 31:3
that He did not look like a **m**, Is 52:14
One like a son of **m** coming with Dn 7:13
I am God and not **m**, the Holy One Hs 11:9
M must not live on bread alone Mt 4:4
will acknowledge Me before **men** Mt 10:32
as doctrines the commands of **men**. Mt 15:9
this reason a **m** will leave his Mt 19:5
will see the Son of **M** coming on Mt 24:30
for **m** and not **m** for the Sabbath Mk 2:27
You—being a **m**—make Yourself Jn 10:33
praise from **men** more than praise Jn 12:43
your young **men** will see visions, Ac 2:17
We must obey God rather than **men**. Ac 5:29
We are **men** also, with the same Ac 14:15
entered the world through one **m**, Rm 5:12
Christ is the head of every **m**, and
the **m** is the head of the woman, 1Co 11:3
as to the Lord and not to **men**, Eph 6:7
taking on the likeness of **men**. Php 2:7
What is **m**, that You remember him Heb 2:6
m-'s anger does not accomplish Jms 1:20
was One like the Son of **M** Rv 1:13
it is the number of a **m**. Rv 13:18

MAN OF GOD
blessing that Moses, the **m**, gave Dt 33:1
She said to Elijah, "**M**, what do 1Kg 17:18
When Elisha the **m** heard 2Kg 5:8
word ... came to Shemaiah, the **m**: 2Ch 11:2
as David the **m** had prescribed. Neh 12:24
you, **m**, run from these things, 1Tm 6:11
so that the **m** may be complete, 2Tm 3:17

MANAGE
one who **m-s** his own household 1Tm 3:4

MANAGING (N)
gifts of healing, helping, **m**, 1Co 12:28

MANASSEH
1. Son of Joseph and Asenath (Gn 41:50-51). Adopted by Jacob as a tribe (Gn 48); allotted half of its territory east of the Jordan from Gerasa to Mt. Hermon in the far north and half west of the Jordan to the Mediterranean from the Yarkon River to Mt. Carmel (Nm 32:33-42; Jos 13:29-31; 17).
2. Son of Hezekiah; king of Judah (2Kg 21:1-18). Wickedness brought on God's judgment (21:10-15; Jr 15:4).

MANGER
in cloth and lying in a **m**. Lk 2:12

MANIFESTATION
A **m** of the Spirit is given to each 1Co 12:7

MANIFESTED
He was **m** in the flesh, vindicated 1Tm 3:16

MANNA
Israel named the substance **m**. Ex 16:31
The **m** resembled coriander seed, Nm 11:7
the land, the **m** ceased. Jos 5:12
fathers ate the **m** in the Jn 6:31,49

MANNER
Live your life in a **m** worthy of Php 1:27

MANSLAUGHTER
could flee there who committed **m**, Dt 4:42
for the one who commits **m**, Jos 21:13-38

MANTLE
him and threw his **m** over him. 1Kg 19:19
picked up the **m** that had fallen 2Kg 2:13

MANY
give His life—a ransom for **m**. Mt 20:28
For **m** are invited, but few are Mt 22:14
way we who are **m** are one body Rm 12:5

MARANA THA
M that is, Lord, come! 1Co 16:22

MARCH
m around the city seven times, Jos 6:4

MARITAL
his **m** responsibility to his wife, 1Co 7:3

MARK, JOHN
Missionary (Ac 12:12,25); Barnabas's cousin (Col 4:10); cause of split between Paul and Barnabas (Ac 15:36-40); later apparently reconciled to Paul (Col 4:10; 2Tm 4:11; Phm 24). Also close to Peter (1Pt 5:13). Wrote the Gospel of Mark.

MARK
He placed a **m** on Cain so that Gn 4:15
If I don't see the **m** of the nails Jn 20:25
and receives a **m** on his forehead Rv 14:9
who accepted the **m** of the beast Rv 19:20

MARKET
that is sold in the meat **m** 1Co 10:25

MARKETPLACE
My Father's house into a **m**! Jn 2:16

MARRIAGE
nor are given in **m** but are like Mt 22:30
and giving in **m**, until the day Mt 24:38
M must be respected by all, Heb 13:4
the **m** of the Lamb has come, Rv 19:7

MARRIED (ADJ)
a **m** man is concerned about 1Co 7:33

MARROW
soul and spirit, joints and **m**. Heb 4:12

MARRY
who have **m-ied** foreign women Ezr 10:14
divorces ... and **m-ies** another, Mt 19:9
For all seven had **m-ied** her. Lk 20:33
the dead neither **m** nor are given Lk 20:35
it is better to **m** than to burn 1Co 7:9

MARTHA
Sister of Mary and Lazarus (Lk 10:38-42; Jn 11:1–12:2).

MARVELOUS
of darkness into His **m** light 1Pt 2:9

MARY
1. Mother of Jesus (Mt 1:16; Lk 1:26-56; 2:1-20,34-35). Present at the cross (Jn 19:25-27); among the believers (Ac 1:14).
2. Magdalene; delivered from demons (Lk 8:2); follower and supporter of Jesus (Mk 15:40-41). Witness to the crucifixion and resurrection (Mt 27:54–28:10; Mk 16:1-10; Lk 24:10; Jn 19:25–20:18).
3. Mother of James and Joseph/Joses; follower and supporter of Jesus (Mk 15:40-41). Witness to the crucifixion and resurrection (Mt 27:54–28:10; Mk 16:1-8; Lk 24:10).
4. Sister of Martha and Lazarus (Jn 11); anointed Jesus' feet (12:1-3).

MASSACRE
He gave orders to **m** all the male Mt 2:16

MASTER (N)
And if I am a **m**, where is Mal 1:6
No one can be a slave of two **m-s** Mt 6:24
is not greater than his **m**, Jn 13:16
doesn't know what his **m** is doing. Jn 15:15
obey your human **m-s** with fear Eph 6:5
m-s, treat your slaves the same way Eph 6:9

MAT
lowered the **m** ... the paralytic Mk 2:4
pick up your **m** and walk! Jn 5:8

MATERIAL
godliness is a way to **m** gain. 1Tm 6:5

MATTHEW
Apostle; former tax collector (Mt 9:9; 10:3). Also called Levi son of Alphaeus (Mk 2:14; cp. Lk 5:27-32). Wrote a gospel.

MATTHIAS
Chosen to replace Judas (Ac 1:23-26).

MATURE
speak a wisdom among the **m**, 1Co 2:6
who are **m** should think this way. Php 3:15
But solid food is for the **m** Heb 5:14

MATURITY
us go on to **m**, not laying Heb 6:1

MEAL
in exchange for one **m**. Heb 12:16

MEANINGLESS
reasonings of the wise are **m**. 1Co 3:20

MEANS
by every possible **m** save some. 1Co 9:22

MEASURE (N)
a full and honest dry **m**, Dt 25:15
and with the **m** you use, it will be Mt 7:2
a good **m**—pressed down, shaken Lk 6:38
He gives the Spirit without **m**. Jn 3:34

MEASURE (V)
Who has **m-d** the waters in the Is 40:12
He **m-d** the thickness of the Ezk 40:5
you use, it will be **m-d** to you. Mt 7:2
He **m-d** the city with the rod at Rv 21:16

MEASUREMENTS
You must not be unfair in **m** Lv 19:35
These are the city's **m**: Ezk 48:16

MEASURING (ADJ)
will make justice the **m** line Is 28:17
and a **m** rod in his hand. Ezk 40:3
was given a **m** reed like a rod Rv 11:1

MEAT
LORD will give you **m** to eat Ex 16:8
It is a noble thing not to eat **m**, Rm 14:21
I will never again eat **m**, so that I 1Co 8:13

MEDES
People of Media, conquerors of Babylon (Is 13:17; 21:2; Jr 51:11,28); Darius (Dn 5:31; 9:1; 11:1); present at Pentecost (Ac 2:9).

MEDIA
Country of the Medes, north of Elam and west of Assyria (Ezr 6:2); ally of Persia (Est 1:3; Dn 5:28; 8:20); cursed by Jeremiah (Jr 25:25).

MEDIATOR
through angels by means of a **m**. Gl 3:19
one God and one **m** between God 1Tm 2:5
He is the **m** of a better Heb 8:6

MEDICINE
A joyful heart is good **m**, Pr 17:22

MEDITATE
he **m-s** on it day and night. Ps 1:2
I will **m** on Your precepts Ps 119:15
in her heart and **m-ing** on them Lk 2:19

MEDITATION
mouth and the **m** of my heart Ps 19:14
It is my **m** all day long. Ps 119:97

MEDITERRANEAN SEA
Western border of Israel (Ex 23:31; Nm 34:6; Dt 11:24; 34:2; Jos 1:4; 23:4; Ezk 47:15-20), including several of the tribal territories (Jos 15:4,11,12,47; 16:3,8; 17:9).

MEDIUM
Do not turn to **m-s** or consult Lv 19:31
A man or a woman who is a **m** Lv 20:27
a woman at En-dor who is a **m**. 1Sm 28:7

MEET
I will **m** with you there above Ex 25:22
faithful God will come to **m** me; Ps 59:10
Israel, prepare to **m** your God! Am 4:12
in the clouds to **m** the Lord in 1Th 4:17

MEETING (N)
In the tent of **m** outside the Ex 27:21
not staying away from ... **m-s** Heb 10:25

MELCHIZEDEK
King of Salem and priest (Gn 14:18); represents undying priesthood (Ps 110:4; Heb 5:6,10; 6:20; 7).

MELT
The mountains **m** like wax at the Ps 97:5
elements will **m** with the heat. 2Pt 3:12

MEMBER
individually **m-s** of one another. Rm 12:5
one **m** suffers, all the **m-s** suffer 1Co 12:26
since we are **m-s** of His body. Eph 5:30

MEMORY
All **m** of him perishes from the Jb 18:17
let Him erase all **m** of them Ps 109:15
will also be told in **m** of her. Mt 26:13

MENAHEM
King of Israel; obtained throne by force (2Kg 15:10-16). Paid tribute to the king of Assyria (15:19-20).

MENE
inscribed: **M**, **M**, TEKEL, PARSIN Dn 5:25

MENTION
that I constantly **m** you, Rm 1:9
shameful even to **m** what is done Eph 5:12
my God when I **m** you in my Phm 4

MEPHIBOSHETH
1. Son of Jonathan; granted privilege in David's court (2Sm 4:4; 9; 16; 19).
2. Son of Saul whom David delivered to the Gibeonites (2Sm 21:1-9). His mother guarded his body until he was buried (21:10-14).

MERCIFUL
The **m** are blessed, for they will be Mt 5:7
Be **m**, just as your Father also is **m**. Lk 6:36
a **m** and faithful high priest Heb 2:17
is very compassionate and **m**. Jms 5:11

MERCY
Make a **m** seat of pure gold, Ex 25:17
in the cloud above the **m** seat. Lv 16:2
from above the **m** seat that was Nm 7:89
LORD is waiting to show you **m** Is 30:18
for His **m-ies** never end. Lm 3:22
In Your wrath remember **m**! Hab 3:2
blessed, for they will be shown **m**. Mt 5:7
I desire **m** and not sacrifice. Mt 9:13
of the law—justice, **m**, and faith. Mt 23:23
show **m** to whom I will show **m**, Rm 9:15
by the **m-ies** of God, I urge Rm 12:1
the Father of **m-ies** and the God of 2Co 1:3
But God, who is rich in **m**, Eph 2:4
it overshadowing the **m** seat. Heb 9:5
M triumphs over judgment. Jms 2:13

MESSAGE
Their **m** has gone out to all the Ps 19:4
because His **m** had authority. Lk 4:32
Lord, who has believed our **m**? Jn 12:38
believe in Me through their **m**. Jn 17:20
the **m** of the cross is foolishness 1Co 1:18
committed the **m** of reconciliation 2Co 5:19
Hold firmly to the **m** of life. Php 2:16

MESSENGER
or deaf like My **m** I am sending? Is 42:19
See, I am going to send My **m**, Mal 3:1
am sending My **m** ahead of You Mt 11:10
a **m** of Satan to torment me so 2Co 12:7

MESSIAH
until **M** the Prince will be seven Dn 9:25
You are the **M**, the Son of the Mt 16:16
False **m-s** and false prophets Mt 24:24
before he saw the Lord's **M**. Lk 2:26
told him, "We have found the **M**!" Jn 1:41
I know that **M** is coming Jn 4:25
Could this be the **M**? Jn 4:29
that you may believe Jesus is the **M** Jn 20:31
you crucified, both Lord and **M**! Ac 2:36
proving that this One is the **M**. Ac 9:22
Scriptures that Jesus is the **M**. Ac 18:28
the substance is the **M**. Col 2:17
And let the peace of the **M** Col 3:15
more will the blood of the **M** Heb 9:14
honor the **M** as Lord in your 1Pt 3:15
who denies that Jesus is the **M**? 1Jn 2:22
Jesus is the **M** has been born of God, 1Jn 5:1
kingdom of our Lord and of His **M** Rv 11:15
with the **M** for 1,000 years Rv 20:4

MICAH
1. Ephraimite idolater (Jdg 17–18).
2. Prophet to Israel and Judah in the days of kings Jotham, Ahaz, and Hezekiah of Judah (Jr 26:18; Mc 1:1).

MICAIAH
Son of Imlah; prophet against Ahab (1Kg 22:5-28; 2Ch 18:4-27).

MICHAEL
Archangel; guardian of Israel (Dn 10:13,21; 12:1). Disputed with the Devil (Jd 9); will fight the dragon (Rv 12:7).

MICHAL
Daughter of Saul (1Sm 14:49); offered to David to endanger him (18:20-29); warned David of a plot (19:11-17). Given to Palti (25:44); taken back (2Sm 3:12-16). Despised David dancing before the Lord (6:14-23; 1Ch 15:29).

MIDDLE
tree in the **m** of the garden, Gn 3:3

MIDWIFE
of Egypt said to the Hebrew **m-ves** Ex 1:15

MIGHT
and will declare Your **m** Ps 145:11
Not by strength or by **m**, but by My Zch 4:6
who are greater in **m** and power, 2Pt 2:11

MIGHTY
How the **m** have fallen! 2Sm 1:19
strong and **m**, the LORD, **m** in battle. Ps 24:8
and will proclaim Your **m** acts. Ps 145:4
Counselor, **M** God, Eternal Father Is 9:6
because the **M** One has done great Lk 1:49
Lord God who judges her is **m**. Rv 18:8

MILE
if anyone forces you to go one **m**, Mt 5:41

MILK
a land flowing with **m** and honey Ex 3:8
churning of **m** produces butter Pr 30:33
gave you **m** to drink, not solid food, 1Co 3:2
You need **m**, not solid food. Heb 5:12
desire the pure spiritual **m**, 1Pt 2:2

MILL
while the sound of the **m** fades; Ec 12:4
will be grinding at the **m**: Mt 24:41

MILLSTONE
or an upper **m** as security for a Dt 24:6
better for him if a heavy **m** were Mt 18:6

MINA
gave them 10 **m-s**, and told them Lk 19:13

MIND
a son of man who changes His **m**. Nm 23:19
is not man who changes his **m**. 1Sm 15:29
a whole heart and a willing **m**, 1Ch 28:9
or gave the **m** understanding? Jb 38:36
examine my heart and **m**. Ps 26:2
I applied my **m** to seek and Ec 1:13

Dull the **m-s** of these people; Is 6:10
will keep the **m** ... in perfect peace, Is 26:3
all your soul, and with all your **m.** Mt 22:37
them over to a worthless **m** Rm 1:28
by the renewing of your **m,** Rm 12:2
But we have the **m** of Christ. 1Co 2:16
has blinded the **m-s** of the 2Co 4:4
renewed in the spirit of your **m-s;** Eph 4:23
Set your **m-s** on what is above, Col 3:2
will put My laws into their **m-s** Heb 8:10
One who examines **m-s** and hearts, Rv 2:23

MIND-SET
For the **m** of the flesh is death Rm 8:6

MINISTER (N)
Levites to be **m-s** before the ark 1Ch 16:4
speak of you as **m-s** of our God Is 61:6
be a **m** of Christ Jesus to the Rm 15:16
as God's **m-s,** we commend 2Co 6:4
a **m** of the sanctuary and the Heb 8:2

MINISTER (V)
worn by Aaron whenever he **m-s** Ex 28:35

MINISTERING (N)
Are they not all **m** spirits sent Heb 1:14

MINISTRY
prayer and to the preaching **m.** Ac 6:4
gave us the **m** of reconciliation: 2Co 5:18
of the saints in the work of **m** Eph 4:12
an evangelist, fulfill your **m.** 2Tm 4:5
has now obtained a superior **m** Heb 8:6

MINT
pay a tenth of **m,** dill, and cumin, Mt 23:23

MIRACLE
Pharaoh tells you, 'Perform a **m,**' Ex 7:9
and do many **m-s** in Your name? Mt 7:22
For if the **m-s** that were done in Mt 11:21
was not able to do any **m-s** there, Mk 6:5
extraordinary **m-s** by Paul's hands Ac 19:11
testified by signs ... various **m-s,** Heb 2:4

MIRIAM
Sister of Moses and Aaron; daughter of Jochebed and Amram (Nm 26:59; 1Ch 6:3). Watched over baby Moses (Ex 2:4-8). Prophetess; led dancing at Red Sea (15:20-21). Struck with skin disease for criticizing Moses (Nm 12; Dt 24:9); died in Kadesh (Nm 20:1).

MIRROR
as in a **m,** but then face to face. 1Co 13:12
looking at his own face in a **m.** Jms 1:23

MISERABLE
You are all **m** comforters. Jb 16:2
Be **m** and mourn and weep. Jms 4:9

MISERY
I have observed the **m** of My people Ex 3:7

MISMATCHED
Do not be **m** with unbelievers. 2Co 6:14

MIST
Your loyalty is like the morning **m** Hs 6:4

MISTAKE
do not say ... that it was a **m.** Ec 5:6

MISTREAT
pray for those who **m** you. Lk 6:28

MISTRESS
she treated her **m** with contempt. Gn 16:4

MISUSE
Do not **m** the name of Yahweh Ex 20:7

MOABITE
No Ammonite or **M** may enter the Dt 23:3

MOABITESS
her daughter-in-law Ruth the **M.** Ru 1:22

MOCK
At noon Elijah **m-ed** them. 1Kg 18:27
Everyone who sees me **m-s** me; Ps 22:7
He **m-s** those who **m,** but gives grace Pr 3:34
down before Him and **m-ed** Him: Mt 27:29
God is not **m-ed.** For whatever a man Gl 6:7

MOCKER
or join a group of **m-s!** Ps 1:1
one who corrects a **m** will bring Pr 9:7
Wine is a **m,** beer is a brawler Pr 20:1

MODEST
dress themselves in **m** clothing, 1Tm 2:9

MOMENT
For His anger lasts only a **m,** Ps 30:5
I deserted you for a brief **m** Is 54:7
at the appointed **m,** Christ died for Rm 5:6
in a **m,** in the blink of an eye, 1Co 15:52

MOMENTARY
For our **m** light affliction is 2Co 4:17

MONEY
return each man's **m** to his sack, Gn 42:25
loves **m** is never satisfied with **m,** Ec 5:10
and **m** is the answer for everything. Ec 10:19
you without **m,** come, buy, and eat! Is 55:1
cannot be slaves of God and of **m.** Mt 6:24
overturned the **m** changers' Mt 21:12
no traveling bag, no bread, no **m;** Lk 9:3
a lot of wine, not greedy for **m,** 1Tm 3:8
For the love of **m** is a root of 1Tm 6:10
be free from the love of **m.** Heb 13:5

MONEY-BAG
Don't carry a **m,** traveling bag Lk 10:4
charge of the **m** and would steal Jn 12:6

MONSTER
all sea **m-s** and ocean depths, Ps 148:7

MONTH
it is the first **m** of your year. Ex 12:2
Each **m** they will bear fresh fruit Ezk 47:12
producing its fruit every **m.** Rv 22:2

MOON
this time the sun, **m,** and 11 stars Gn 37:9
sun stood still and the **m** stopped Jos 10:13
the **m** and the stars, which You set Ps 8:3
you by day or the **m** by night. Ps 121:6
the **m** to blood before the great Jl 2:31
and the **m** will not shed its light; Mt 24:29
the **m** to blood before the great Ac 2:20
another of the **m,** and another 1Co 15:41

MORALS
Bad company corrupts good **m.** 1Co 15:33

MORDECAI
Cousin and legal guardian of Esther (Est 2:7). Uncovered assassination plot (2:21-23). Offended Haman (3:1-7); Haman sought genocide (3:7-15); Mordecai led Esther to thwart the attempt (Est 4–5). Honored by the king (Est 6); wrote revenge edict (Est 8).

MORNING
came, and then **m:** the first day. Gn 1:5
the **m** stars sang together Jb 38:7
but there is joy in the **m.** Ps 30:5
a loud voice early in the **m** Pr 27:14
They are new every **m;** Lm 3:23
Very early in the **m,** on the first day Mk 16:2
and the **m** star rises in your hearts. 2Pt 1:19
of David, the Bright **M** Star. Rv 22:16

MORON
'You **m**!' will be subject to hellfire. Mt 5:22

MORTAL
let sin reign in your **m** body, Rm 6:12
and this **m** must be clothed with 1Co 15:53

MORTALITY
that **m** may be swallowed up 2Co 5:4

MOSES
Leader of Israel; Levite; brother of Aaron and Miriam (1Ch 6:3). Born under Egyptian oppression (Ex 1); set adrift on Nile; rescued and raised by Pharaoh's daughter (2:1-10). Killed Egyptian; fled to Midian and married Zipporah (2:11-22). Called by God from burning bush (Ex 3–4). Announced ten plagues (Ex 7–11).
Divided the Red Sea (Ex 14). Brought water from a rock (17:1-7); held up God's staff and defeated Amalek (17:8-13). Delegated judging (18:13-26).
God spoke to him at Sinai: law (Ex 19–23); tabernacle, equipment, and garments (Ex 25–28; 30); consecration of priests (Ex 29). Discovered golden calf and broke tablets (Ex 32). Saw God's glory (33:12–34:28). Ordained Aaron and his sons (Lv 8–9).
Opposed by Aaron and Miriam (Nm 12); opposed by Korah (Nm 16). Excluded from promised land for striking rock (Nm 20:1-13; 27:12-14; Dt 32:51). Made a bronze snake for healing (Nm 21:4-9; Jn 3:14). Wrote the book of the law (Jos 23:6; 2Ch 34:14). Saw promised land from a distance (Dt 3:23-27; 34:1-4); commissioned Joshua as successor (Nm 27:12-23); buried by God (34:5-8).

MOST
holy place and the **m** holy place. Ex 26:33
you are all sons of the **M** High. Ps 82:6
Jesus, Son of the **M** High God? Mk 5:7
is the **m** important of all? Mk 12:28
making the **m** of the time Eph 5:16

MOST HIGH
he was a priest to God **M.** Gn 14:18
I call to God **M,** to God who Ps 57:2
under the protection of the **M** Ps 91:1
come from the mouth of the **M**? Lm 3:38
Jesus, Son of the **M** God? Mk 5:7
called the Son of the **M,** Lk 1:32
the **M** does not dwell in sanctuaries Ac 7:48
of Salem, priest of the **M** God, Heb 7:1

MOTH
where **m** and rust destroy and Mt 6:19

MOTHER
a man leaves his father and **m** Gn 2:24
she was the **m** of all the living Gn 3:20
Honor your father and your **m** so Ex 20:12
Naked I came from my **m-'s** womb, Jb 1:21
the joyful **m** of children. Ps 113:9
don't reject your **m-'s** teaching, Pr 1:8
oracle that his **m** taught him: Pr 31:1
As a **m** comforts her son, so I Is 66:13
father or **m** more than Me is Mt 10:37
Who is My **m** and who are My Mt 12:48
Honor your father and your **m**; Mt 15:4
leave his father and **m** and be joined Mt 19:5
not hate his own father and **m** Lk 14:26
to the disciple, "Here is your **m**." Jn 19:27

MOTHER-IN-LAW
a daughter-in-law is against her **m**; Mc 7:6
a daughter-in-law against her **m**; Mt 10:35
Simon's **m** was suffering from Lk 4:38

MOTIVES
but the LORD evaluates the **m**. Pr 16:2
whether out of false **m** or Php 1:18

MOUNT (N) *SEE ALSO* CARMEL, MOUNT OF OLIVES, SINAI, ZION
The LORD came down on **M** Sinai Ex 19:20
the blessing at **M** Gerizim and Dt 11:29
M Zion on the slopes of the north is Ps 48:2
M Zion, which He loved. Ps 78:68
The **M** of Olives will be split in Zch 14:4
was sitting on the **M** of Olives, Mt 24:3
they went out to the **M** of Olives. Mt 26:30
Now Hagar is **M** Sinai in Arabia Gl 4:25

MOUNT (V)
gentle, and **m-ed** on a donkey, Mt 21:5

MOUNT OF OLIVES
The **M** will be split in half Zch 14:4
psalms, they went out to the **M**. Mt 26:30
made His way as usual to the **M**, Lk 22:39
But Jesus went to the **M**. Jn 8:1

MOUNTAIN
will be provided on the LORD's **m**. Gn 22:14
came to Horeb, the **m** of God. Ex 3:1
My King on Zion, My holy **m**. Ps 2:6
The **m-s** melt like wax at the Ps 97:5
I lift my eyes toward the **m-s**. Ps 121:1
Jerusalem—the **m-s** surround her Ps 125:2
let us go up to the **m** of the LORD, Is 2:3
beautiful on the **m-s** are the feet Is 52:7
became a great **m** and filled the Dn 2:35
to a very high **m** and showed Him Mt 4:8
up on a high **m** by themselves. Mt 17:1
will tell this **m**, 'Move from Mt 17:20
and every **m** and hill will be Lk 3:5
all faith so that I can move **m-s** 1Co 13:2

MOURN
a time to **m** and a time to dance; Ec 3:4
to comfort all who **m**, Is 61:2
will **m** for Him as one **m-s** for Zch 12:10
Those who **m** are blessed, for Mt 5:4
Be miserable and **m** and weep. Jms 4:9
of the earth will **m** over Him. Rv 1:7

MOURNING (N)
day long I go around in **m**. Ps 38:6
festive oil instead of **m**, Is 61:3
I will turn their **m** into joy, Jr 31:13

MOUTH
Who made the human **m**? Ex 4:11
from the **m-s** of children Ps 8:2
May the words of my **m** and Ps 19:14
They have **m-s** but cannot speak Ps 115:5
from His **m** come knowledge and Pr 2:6
praise you, and not your own **m** Pr 27:2
Do not let your **m** bring guilt on Ec 5:6
yet He did not open His **m**. Is 53:7
that comes from the **m** of God. Mt 4:4
If you confess with your **m** Rm 10:9
and cursing come out of the same **m**. Jms 3:10

MOVE
M-ed with compassion, Jesus Mt 20:34
so that I can **m** mountains 1Co 13:2

MUD
made some **m** from the saliva, Jn 9:6

MUDDY
out of the **m** clay, and set my feet Ps 40:2

MULTIPLY
Be fruitful, **m**, fill the earth, Gn 1:28
fruitful, increased rapidly, **m-ied**, Ex 1:7
Yet the fool **m-ies** words. Ec 10:14
The more they **m-ied**, the more they Hs 4:7
where sin **m-ied**, grace **m-ied** Rm 5:20
sin so that grace may **m**? Rm 6:1

MULTITUDE
M-s, **m-s** in the valley of decision! Jl 3:14
and cover a **m** of sins. Jms 5:20
since love covers a **m** of sins. 1Pt 4:8
there was a vast **m** from every Rv 7:9

MURDER
Do not **m**. Ex 20:13
Do not **m**, and whoever **m-s** will Mt 5:21
whom you had **m-ed** by hanging Ac 5:30
adultery, also said, Do not **m**. Jms 2:11

MURDERER
the **m** must be put to death. Nm 35:16
He was a **m** from the beginning Jn 8:44
who hates his brother is a **m**, 1Jn 3:15

MUSIC
in charge of the **m** in the LORD's 1Ch 6:31
sing and make **m** to the LORD. Ps 27:6
harp and the **m** of a lyre. Ps 92:3
house, he heard **m** and dancing. Lk 15:25
songs, singing and making **m** Eph 5:19

MUSICAL
accompanied by **m** instruments 1Ch 15:16
the **m** instruments of the LORD, 2Ch 7:6
the **m** instruments of David Neh 12:36

MUSTARD
is like a **m** seed that a man Mt 13:31
faith the size of a **m** seed, Mt 17:20

MUTE
Who makes him **m** or deaf, seeing Ex 4:11

MUTUALLY
to be **m** encouraged by each Rm 1:12

MUZZLE
Do not **m** an ox while it treads Dt 25:4
my mouth with a **m** as long as the Ps 39:1
Do not **m** an ox while it is 1Tm 5:18

MYRRH
My hands dripped with **m**, Sg 5:5
gold, frankincense, and **m**. Mt 2:11

MYSTERY
I will speak **m-ies** from the past Ps 78:2
The **m** was then revealed to Daniel Dn 2:19
I am telling you a **m**: 1Co 15:51
This **m** is profound, but I am Eph 5:32
the **m** hidden for ages and Col 1:26
holding the **m** of the faith with 1Tm 3:9
the **m** of godliness is great: 1Tm 3:16

MYTHS
pay attention to **m** and endless 1Tm 1:4
truth and will turn aside to **m**. 2Tm 4:4
contrived **m** when we made known 2Pt 1:16

NAGGING (ADJ)
share a house with a **n** wife Pr 21:9
rainy day and a **n** wife are Pr 27:15

NAGGING (N)
a wife's **n** is an endless Pr 19:13

NAHUM
Prophet against Nineveh (Nah 1:1).

NAIL (N)
finger into the mark of the **n-s** Jn 20:25

NAIL (V)
people to **n** Him to a cross Ac 2:23
the way by **n-ing** it to the cross Col 2:14

NAKED
the man and his wife were **n** Gn 2:25
Who told you that you were **n**? Gn 3:11
N I came from my mother's womb, Jb 1:21
I was **n** and you clothed Me; Mt 25:36
we will not be found **n**. 2Co 5:3

NAKEDNESS
they covered their father's **n**. Gn 9:23
or famine or **n** or danger or Rm 8:35

NAME (N)
The man gave **n-s** to all the Gn 2:20
This is My **n** forever; Ex 3:15
Do not misuse the **n** of Yahweh Ex 20:7
the place to have His **n** dwell. Dt 12:11
My people who are called by My **n** 2Ch 7:14
magnificent is Your **n** throughout Ps 8:1
we take pride in the **n** of Yahweh Ps 20:7
let us exalt His **n** together. Ps 34:3
within me, praise His holy **n**. Ps 103:1
who comes in the **n** of the LORD Ps 118:26
n of Yahweh is a strong tower; Pr 18:10
A good **n** is to be chosen over Pr 22:1
I am Yahweh, that is My **n**; Is 42:8
I had concern for My holy **n** Ezk 36:21
Your **n** be honored as holy. Mt 6:9
These are the **n-s** of the 12 Mt 10:2
that your **n-s** are written in heaven. Lk 10:20
have asked for nothing in My **n**. Jn 16:24
calls on the **n** of the Lord will Ac 2:21
there is no other **n** under heaven Ac 4:12
calls on the **n** of the Lord will Rm 10:13
the **n** that is above every **n**, Php 2:9
whose **n-s** are in the book Php 4:3

beast's **n** or the number of his **n**. Rv 13:17

NAME (V)
and you are to **n** Him Jesus, Mt 1:21

NAOMI
Ruth's mother-in-law (Ru 1:2-4).

NAPHTALI
Son of Jacob and Bilhah (Gn 30:1-8). Tribe with territory north and west of the Sea of Galilee (Jos 19:32-39); praised by Deborah (Jdg 5:18); produced Hiram the craftsman (1Kg 7:13-14).

NARROW
Enter through the **n** gate. Mt 7:13

NATHAN
Prophet to David; told David he would never fail to have a descendant on the throne (2Sm 7:4-17); confronted David about Bathsheba (12:1-15). Anointed Solomon (1Kg 1).

NATHANAEL
Apostle "in whom is no deceit"; invited by Philip; asked if anything good comes out of Nazareth (Jn 1:45-49; 21:2); possibly also called Bartholomew (Mt 10:3).

NATION
I will make you into a great **n** Gn 12:2
kingdom of priests and My holy **n**. Ex 19:6
Why do the **n-s** rebel and the Ps 2:1
Happy is the **n** whose God is Ps 33:12
Declare His glory among the **n-s** Ps 96:3
Righteousness exalts a **n**, but sin Pr 14:34
N-s will not take up the sword Is 2:4
proclaim My glory among the **n-s**. Is 66:19
For **n** will rise up against **n**, Mt 24:7
and make disciples of all **n-s** Mt 28:19
a royal priesthood, a holy **n**, 1Pt 2:9
and language and people and **n**. Rv 5:9

NATURAL
exchanged **n** sexual relations Rm 1:26
did not spare the **n** branches, Rm 11:21
sown a **n** body, raised a 1Co 15:44

NATURE
His eternal power and divine **n** Rm 1:20
and against **n** were grafted into Rm 11:24
Does not even **n** itself teach you 1Co 11:14
was a man with a **n** like ours; Jms 5:17
you may share in the divine **n** 2Pt 1:4

NAZARENE
that He will be called a **N**. Mt 2:23
"Jesus the N," they answered. Jn 18:5
of the sect of the **N-s**! Ac 24:5

NAZARETH
Hometown of Jesus (Mt 2:23; Lk 2:51; 4:16; Jn 1:45-46).

NAZIRITE
a special vow, a **N** vow, Nm 6:2
boy will be a **N** to God from Jdg 13:5

NEAR
But the message is very **n** you, Dt 30:14
The LORD is **n** all who call out Ps 145:18
call to Him while He is **n**. Is 55:6
The great Day of the LORD is **n**, Zph 1:14
kingdom of heaven has come **n**! Mt 3:2
The message is **n** you, in your Rm 10:8
The Lord is **n**. Php 4:5
Draw **n** to God, and He will draw **n** Jms 4:8
because the time is **n**. Rv 22:10

NEARER
our salvation is **n** than when we Rm 13:11

NEBUCHADNEZZAR
King of Babylon; defeated and exiled Judah (2Kg 24–25; 1Ch 6:15; 2Ch 36; Jr 39). Dreams interpreted by Daniel (Dn 2; 4); threw Shadrach, Meshach, and Abednego into the furnace (Dn 3); temporarily insane (Dn 4); praised God (2:47; 3:28; 4:34-37).

NECK
you and adornment for your **n**. Pr 3:22
Your **n** is like the tower of Sg 4:4

NEED (N)
a robber, your **n**, like a bandit. Pr 24:34
supply all your **n-s** according Php 4:19
brother in **n** but closes his eyes 1Jn 3:17

NEED (V)
Father knows the things you **n** Mt 6:8
who are well don't **n** a doctor Mt 9:12
say to the hand, "I don't **n** you!" 1Co 12:21

NEEDLE
the eye of a **n** than for a rich Mt 19:24

NEEDY
and lifts the **n** from the garbage 1Sm 2:8
I was a father to the **n**, Jb 29:16
is kind to the **n** honors Him. Pr 14:31

NEGATIVE
a **n** report about the land Nm 14:36

NEGLECT
you have **n-ed** the more important Mt 23:23
Do not **n** the gift that is in you 1Tm 4:14
we escape if we **n** such a great Heb 2:3

NEHEMIAH
Cupbearer to King Artaxerxes of Babylon (Neh 1:11); obtained permission, planned, and supervised rebuilding Jerusalem's walls despite opposition (Neh 2–6). Was appointed governor of Judah (5:14). Dedicated wall (12:27-43). Promoted reforms (Neh 8–10; 13). Prayed frequently (1:4-11; 2:4; 4:4-5,9; 5:19; 6:9,14; 13:14,22,29,31).

NEIGHBOR
false testimony against your **n**. Ex 20:16
Do not covet your **n-'s** wife, Ex 20:17
but love your **n** as yourself; Lv 19:18
better a **n** nearby than a brother Pr 27:10
one teach his **n** or his brother, Jr 31:34
to him who gives his **n-s** drink, Hab 2:15
Love your **n** and hate your enemy Mt 5:43
and love your **n** as yourself. Mt 19:19
asked Jesus, "And who is my **n**?" Lk 10:29
Love your **n** as yourself. Gl 5:14

NEST (N)
your **n** is set in the cliffs. Nm 24:21
and make your **n** among the stars Ob 4
and birds of the sky have **n-s** Mt 8:20

NEST (V)
sky come and **n** in its branches. Mt 13:32

NET
They prepared a **n** for my steps; Ps 57:6
to spread a **n** where any bird can Pr 1:17
street like an antelope in a **n**. Is 51:20
they left their **n-s** and followed Mt 4:20
Cast the **n** on the right side of Jn 21:6

NEVER
and they will **n** perish—ever! Jn 10:28
Love **n** ends. 1Co 13:8
I will **n** leave you or forsake Heb 13:5

NEW
A **n** king, who had not known Ex 1:8
Sing a **n** song to Him; Ps 33:3
He put a **n** song in my mouth, Ps 40:3
there is nothing **n** under the sun. Ec 1:9
will create a **n** heaven and a **n** earth; Is 65:17
I will make a **n** covenant with Jr 31:31
you a **n** heart and put a **n** spirit Ezk 36:26
And no one puts **n** wine into old Mt 9:17
A **n** teaching with authority! Mk 1:27
This cup is the **n** covenant Lk 22:20
I give you a **n** command: Love Jn 13:34
in Christ, he is a **n** creation; 2Co 5:17
and have put on the **n** self. Col 3:10
wait for the **n** heavens and a **n** earth 2Pt 3:13
I saw a **n** heaven and a **n** earth, Rv 21:1
I am making everything **n**. Rv 21:5

NEWBORN
Like **n** infants, desire the 1Pt 2:2

NEWS
good **n** strengthens the bones. Pr 15:30
who brings **n** of good things, Is 52:7
Then the **n** about Him spread Mt 4:24
the poor are told the good **n**. Mt 11:5
Repent and believe in the good **n**! Mk 1:15
And the good **n** must first be Mk 13:10

NICODEMUS
Pharisee and member of the Sanhedrin. Visited Jesus at night (Jn 3:1-21); defended Jesus to the Sanhedrin (7:45-52); helped prepare Jesus' body for burial (19:39).

NIGHT
and He called the darkness "**n**." Gn 1:5
on the earth 40 days and 40 **n-s** Gn 7:4
you are to recite it day and **n** Jos 1:8
he meditates on it day and **n**. Ps 1:2
not fear the terror of the **n** Ps 91:5
He had fasted 40 days and 40 **n-s** Mt 4:2
watch at **n** over their flock. Lk 2:8
man came to Him at **n** and said, Jn 3:2
come just like a thief in the **n**. 1Th 5:2
not belong to the **n** or the darkness. 1Th 5:5
N will no longer exist, and Rv 22:5

NILE
River of Egypt (Gn 41:1; Ex 1:22; 2:3; Is 7:18; 19:7-8; Ezk 29:3-10; Nah 3:8; Zch 10:11); floods periodically (Jr 46:7-8; Am 8:8; 9:5); struck by the plagues (Ex 7:20-21; 8:3).

NINE
He was **n** feet, **n** inches tall 1Sm 17:4
10 cleansed? Where are the **n**? Lk 17:17
since it's only **n** in the morning Ac 2:15

NINETY-YEAR-OLD
Can Sarah, a **n** woman, give birth? Gn 17:17

NINEVEH
Capital of Assyria (Gn 10:11-12; 2Kg 19:36; Is 37:37); Jonah preached against (Jnh 3:2-4) and the people repented (3:5-7; Mt 12:41; Lk 11:30-32); prophets condemned (Nah 1:1; Zph 2:13).

NOAH
Son of Lamech; descendant of Seth; a righteous man (Gn 5:28-29; 6:9; Ex 14:14; 2Pt 2:5; Heb 11:7). Built an ark, entered it with animals and his family, and survived the flood (Gn 6:14–8:19; 1Pt 3:20). Received God's promise (Gn 8:20–9:17). Got drunk and cursed Canaan (9:20-27). Flood a symbol of sudden judgment (Mt 24:37-38; Lk 17:26-27).

NOBLE (ADJ)
you are a woman of **n** character. Ru 3:11
My heart is moved by a **n** theme as I Ps 45:1
She has done a **n** thing for Me. Mt 26:10
powerful, not many of **n** birth. 1Co 1:26

NOBLE (N)
Do not trust in **n-s**, in man, who Ps 146:3
when your king is a son of **n-s** Ec 10:17
slaughtered all Judah's **n-s**. Jr 39:6

NOISE
Pharaoh king of Egypt was all **n**; Jr 46:17
an end to the **n** of your songs, Ezk 26:13
from Me the **n** of your songs! Am 5:23
will pass away with a loud **n** 2Pt 3:10

NORTH
the king of the **N** will come, Dn 11:15

NOSE
and twisting a **n** draws blood, Pr 30:33

NOSTRILS
the breath of life into his **n** Gn 2:7
from God remains in my **n** Jb 27:3
blast of the breath of Your **n**. Ps 18:15

NOTHING
N is too difficult for You! Jr 32:17
N will be impossible for you. Mt 17:20
you can do **n** without Me. Jn 15:5
but do not have love, I am **n**. 1Co 13:2
I didn't run or labor for **n**. Php 2:16
For we brought **n** into the world, 1Tm 6:7

NUMBER (N)
and increased in **n** daily. Ac 16:5
until the full **n** of the Gentiles Rm 11:25
it is the **n** of a man. His **n** is 666. Rv 13:18

NUMBER (V)
Teach us to **n** our days carefully Ps 90:12
God has **n-ed** the days of your Dn 5:26
who was **n-ed** among the Twelve. Lk 22:3

NURSE
that Sarah would **n** children? Gn 21:7
woman took the boy and **n-d** him. Ex 2:9

NURSING (ADJ)
mouths of children and **n** infants Ps 8:2
a woman forget her **n** child Is 49:15
mouths of children and **n** infants? Mt 21:16

OAK
live near the **o-s** of Mamre Gn 13:18
and he was as sturdy as the **o-s**; Am 2:9

OATH
The LORD swore an **o** to David, Ps 132:11
I tell you, don't take an **o** at all: Mt 5:34
by earth or with any other **o**. Jms 5:12

OBADIAH
Prophet against Edom (Ob 1).

OBEDIENCE
through the one man's **o** the many Rm 5:19
or of **o** leading to righteousness? Rm 6:16
He learned **o** through what He Heb 5:8

OBEDIENT
to Nazareth and was **o** to them. Lk 2:51
becoming **o** to the point of death Php 2:8

OBEY
to **o** is better than sacrifice, 1Sm 15:22
the winds and the sea **o** Him! Mt 8:27
unclean spirits, and they **o** Him. Mk 1:27
We must **o** God rather than men. Ac 5:29
Children, **o** your parents as Eph 6:1

OBLIGATED
are not **o** to the flesh to Rm 8:12

OBSERVE
You must **o** My Sabbaths, Ex 31:13
When I **o** Your heavens, the work Ps 8:3
teaching them to **o** everything I Mt 28:20
You **o** special days, months, Gl 4:10
will, by **o-ing** your good works, 1Pt 2:12

OBTAIN
have **o-ed** righteousness Rm 9:30

OBVIOUS
each one's work will become **o** 1Co 3:13
the works of the flesh are **o**: Gl 5:19
good works are **o**, and those that 1Tm 5:25

OFFEND
anyone is not **o-ed** because of Me Mt 11:6

OFFENSE
but love covers all **o-s**. Pr 10:12
o-s must come, but woe to that Mt 18:7
that case the **o** of the cross has Gl 5:11

OFFENSIVE
if there is any **o** way in me; Ps 139:24

OFFER
o him there as a burnt offering Gn 22:2
if you are **o-ing** your gift on Mt 5:23
once for all when He **o-ed** Himself Heb 7:27
not do this to **o** Himself many Heb 9:25

OFFERING (N) *SEE ALSO* BURNT, FELLOWSHIP
take pleasure in burnt **o-s** ... as much as in obeying the LORD? 1Sm 15:22
You do not delight in sacrifice and **o** Ps 40:6
You make Him a restitution **o** Is 53:10
of God rather than burnt **o-s**. Hs 6:6
and fragrant **o** to God. Eph 5:2
You did not want sacrifice and **o**, Heb 10:5

OFFSPRING
I will give this land to your **o**. Gn 12:7
said, 'For we are also His **o**.' Ac 17:28
I am the Root and the **O** of David, Rv 22:16

OIL
and the **o** jug did not run dry, 1Kg 17:16
You anoint my head with **o**; Ps 23:5
sensible ones took **o** in their flasks Mt 25:4

OLD
I have been young and now I am **o**, Ps 37:25
even when he is **o** he will not Pr 22:6
your **o** men will have dreams, Jl 2:28
puts new wine into **o** wineskins. Mt 9:17
and your **o** men will dream dreams Ac 2:17
o things have passed away, 2Co 5:17
have put off the **o** self with its Col 3:9

OLDER
The **o** will serve the younger. Rm 9:12

OLIVE *SEE ALSO* MOUNT OF OLIVES
was a plucked **o** leaf in her beak Gn 8:11

OMEGA
the Alpha and the **O** Rv 1:8; 21:6; 22:13

OMRI
Army commander; king of Israel; founded the city of Samaria (1Kg 16:15-28).

ONCE
He died to sin **o** for all; Rm 6:10
appointed for people to die **o** Heb 9:27

ONE *SEE* ONE AND ONLY SON
Yahweh is our God; Yahweh is **O**. Dt 6:4
Are You the **O** who is to come, Mt 11:3
the two will become **o** flesh? Mt 19:5
The Father and I are **o**. Jn 10:30
they may be **o** as We are **o**. Jn 17:11
baptized by **o** Spirit into **o** body 1Co 12:13
you are all **o** in Christ Jesus. Gl 3:28
o Lord, **o** faith, **o** baptism, Eph 4:5
For there is **o** God and **o** mediator 1Tm 2:5
You believe that God is **o**; Jms 2:19

ONE AND ONLY SON
glory as the **O** from the Father, Jn 1:14
No one has ever seen God. The **O** Jn 1:18
He gave His **O**, so that everyone Jn 3:16
not believed in the name of the **O** Jn 3:18
God sent His **O** into the world so 1Jn 4:9

OPEN
eyes will be **o-ed** and you will be Gn 3:5
O my eyes so that I may Ps 119:18
what he **o-s**, no one can close; Is 22:22
yet He did not **o** His mouth. Is 53:7
and the door will be **o-ed** to you Mt 7:7
hears My voice and **o-s** the door, Rv 3:20
Who is worthy to **o** the scroll Rv 5:2
and books were **o-ed**. Rv 20:12

OPPORTUNITY
looking for a good **o** to betray Him Mt 26:16
and don't give the Devil an **o**. Eph 4:27

OPPRESS
He was **o-ed** and afflicted, Is 53:7
to the blind, to set free the **o-ed**, Lk 4:18
Don't the rich **o** you and drag Jms 2:6

ORACLE
The **o** of Balaam son of Beor, Nm 24:3
an **o** that his mother taught him Pr 31:1
received living **o-s** to give to us. Ac 7:38

ORDAIN
the way you will **o** Aaron and his Ex 29:9
unless the Lord has **o-ed** it? Lm 3:37

ORDER
Put your affairs in **o**, 2Kg 20:1
give His angels **o-s** concerning Ps 91:11
give His angels **o-s** concerning Mt 4:6
must be done decently and in **o**. 1Co 14:40
forever in the **o** of Melchizedek. Heb 5:6

ORDINANCE
the **o-s** of the LORD are reliable Ps 19:9

ORDINATION
the ram of Aaron's **o** Ex 29:26

ORGIES
drunkenness, **o**, carousing, 1Pt 4:3

ORIGINATE
Did the word of God **o** from you, 1Co 14:36

ORNAMENT
wearing of gold **o-s** or fine clothes. 1Pt 3:3

ORNAN *SEE* ARAUNAH

ORPHANS
I will not leave you as **o**; Jn 14:18
to look after **o** and widows in Jms 1:27

OTHER
I am the LORD, and there is no **o**; Is 45:5
as you want **o-s** to do for you, Lk 6:31
gospel **o** than what we have preached Gl 1:8

OTHNIEL
Judge; defeated Arameans (Jdg 3:7-11); Caleb's nephew (Jos 15:17; Jdg 1:13).

OUTDO
O one another in showing honor. Rm 12:10

OUTER
though our **o** person is being 2Co 4:16

OUTLAWS
And He was counted among **o**. Mk 15:28

OUTRAN
other disciple **o** Peter and got Jn 20:4

OUTSIDE
You clean the **o** of the cup and Mt 23:25
person can commit is **o** the body. 1Co 6:18
Jesus also suffered **o** the gate, Heb 13:12

OUTSIDER
Act wisely toward **o-s**, Col 4:5
properly in the presence of **o-s** 1Th 4:12

OUTSTRETCHED
you with an **o** arm and great acts Ex 6:6

OUTWARD
Stop judging according to **o** Jn 7:24
should not consist of **o** things 1Pt 3:3

OUTWARDLY
person is not a Jew who is one **o**, Rm 2:28

OVERCOME
yet the darkness did not **o** it. Jn 1:5

OVERFLOW
my cup **o-s**. Ps 23:5
speaks from the **o** of the heart. Mt 12:34
to make every grace **o** to you, 2Co 9:8

OVERLOOK
having **o-ed** the times of ignorance Ac 17:30

OVERPOWER
forces of Hades will not **o** it. Mt 16:18

OVERSEE
not **o-ing** out of compulsion but 1Pt 5:2

OVERSEER
If anyone aspires to be an **o** 1Tm 3:1
an **o**, as God's administrator, must Ti 1:7

OVERSHADOW
of the Most High will **o** you. Lk 1:35

OVERTAKE
my sins have **o-n** me; Ps 40:12
so that darkness doesn't **o** you. Jn 12:35
temptation has **o-n** you except 1Co 10:13
for this day to **o** you like a thief. 1Th 5:4

OVERTURN
o-ed the money changers' tables Mt 21:12

OVERWHELM
rivers, they will not **o** you. Is 43:2

OWE
one who **o-d** 10,000 talents Mt 18:24
not ... a gift, but as something **o-d**. Rm 4:4
Do not **o** anyone anything, except Rm 13:8
you **o** me even your own self. Phm 19

OWN (ADJ)
rely on your **o** understanding; Pr 3:5
all have turned to our **o** way; Is 53:6

OWN (N)
He came to His **o**, Jn 1:11
Having loved His **o** who were in Jn 13:1
You are not your **o**, 1Co 6:19

OX
Do not muzzle an **o** while it treads Dt 25:4
not muzzle an **o** while it treads 1Co 9:9

PAIN
I will intensify your labor **p-s**; Gn 3:16
so that I will not cause any **p**. 1Ch 4:10
and He carried our **p-s**; Is 53:4
if I cause you **p**, then who will 2Co 2:2
and **p** will exist no longer, Rv 21:4

PALM
you on the **p-s** of My hands; Is 49:16
they took **p** branches and went Jn 12:13

PARABLE
He told them many things in **p-s** Mt 13:3
Why do You speak ... in **p-s**? Mt 13:10
speak anything ... without a **p** Mt 13:34
I will open My mouth in **p-s**; Mt 13:35
but to the rest it is in **p-s**, so that Lk 8:10

PARADISE
you will be with Me in **p** Lk 23:43
was caught up into **p**. 2Co 12:4

PARALYTIC
brought to Him a **p** lying on a Mt 9:2
told the **p**, "Son, your sins are Mk 2:5

PARENT
who sinned, this man or his **p-s**, Jn 9:2
evil, disobedient to **p-s**, Rm 1:30
Children, obey your **p-s** as Eph 6:1
obey your **p-s** in everything, Col 3:20
disobedient to **p-s**, ungrateful, 2Tm 3:2

PART
You who created my inward **p-s**; Ps 139:13
wash you, you have no **p** with Me. Jn 13:8
as we have many **p-s** in one body, Rm 12:4
your bodies are a **p** of Christ's 1Co 6:15
body is one and has many **p-s**, 1Co 12:12
know in **p**, and we prophesy in **p**. 1Co 13:9

PARTIAL
A **p** hardening has come to Israel Rm 11:25

PARTIALITY
Do not show **p** when deciding Dt 1:17
not good to show **p** Pr 18:5; 24:23; 28:21
You don't show **p** but teach Mk 12:14

PARTNERSHIP
For what **p** is there between 2Co 6:14
because of your **p** in the gospel Php 1:5

PASS
see the blood, I will **p** over you. Ex 12:13
when you **p** through the waters, Is 43:2
Heaven and earth will **p** away, but My words will never **p** away. Mt 24:35
let this cup **p** from Me. Mt 26:39
he **p-ed** by on the other side. Lk 10:31
but has **p-ed** from death to life. Jn 5:24
God **p-ed** over the sins previously Rm 3:25
For I **p-ed** on to you as most 1Co 15:3
old things have **p-ed** away, 2Co 5:17
we have **p-ed** from death to life 1Jn 3:14

PASSIONS
them over to degrading **p**. Rm 1:26
Flee from youthful **p**, and pursue 2Tm 2:22

PASSOVER
it is the LORD's **P**. Ex 12:11
the **P** lamb had to be sacrificed. Lk 22:7
eat this **P** with you before I suffer. Lk 22:15
Christ our **P** has been sacrificed. 1Co 5:7

PAST
Do not hold **p** sins against us; Ps 79:8
the cleansing from his **p** sins. 2Pt 1:9

PASTORS
some **p** and teachers, Eph 4:11

PASTURE
lets me lie down in green **p-s** Ps 23:2
His people, the sheep of His **p**. Ps 100:3
come in and go out and find **p**. Jn 10:9

PATCH
No one sews a **p** of unshrunk Mk 2:21

PATH
or take the **p** of sinners Ps 1:1
the right **p-s** for His name's Ps 23:3
for my feet and a light on my **p**. Ps 119:105
make His **p-s** straight! Mt 3:3
some seeds fell along the **p**, Mt 13:4

make straight **p-s** for your feet, Heb 12:13

PATIENCE
endured with much **p** objects of Rm 9:22
love, joy, peace, **p**, kindness, Gl 5:22

PATIENT
Rejoice in hope; be **p** in affliction; Rm 12:12
Love is **p**, love is kind. 1Co 13:4
able to teach, and **p**, 2Tm 2:24
but is **p** with you, not wanting any 2Pt 3:9

PATIENTLY
I waited **p** for the LORD, Ps 40:1

PATTERN
according to the **p** you have been shown on the mountain. Ex 25:40
according to the **p** that was shown Heb 8:5

PAUL
Early church missionary, theologian, and writer. Also called Saul (Ac 13:9). Citizen of Tarsus, a Benjaminite, raised in Jerusalem as a rabbinical student and Pharisee (Ac 21:39; 22:3,28; 26:5; Gl 1:14; Php 3:5). Persecuted Christians, including Stephen (Ac 8:1; 26:9-11); converted on the way to Damascus (9:1-19); began preaching Christ in Arabia and Damascus and was threatened (9:20-22; Gl 1:17; 2Co 11:32-33).

Introduced to the church at Jerusalem by Barnabas (Ac 9:26-30); carried money with Barnabas from Antioch to Judea (11:27-30). Set apart with Barnabas to go through Cyprus and Galatia as missionaries (Ac 13–14); stoned (Ac 14:19-20). Focused on Gentile evangelism (Ac 9:15; Gl 2:7; Eph 3:8). Attended Jerusalem council (Ac 15). Split with Barnabas over John Mark (15:36-39).

Traveled with Silas and Timothy through Asia Minor and Greece (15:39–16:3). Hindered by the Spirit from entering Bithynia; called to Macedonia in a vision (16:7-10). Beaten, imprisoned, and released in Philippi (16:16-40). Spoke at Areopagus in Athens (17:19-34). Preached at Corinth and Ephesus (Ac 18–19). Said farewell in Ephesus (20:17-38).

Arrested at riot in Jerusalem (21:26-36); testified before the Sanhedrin (23:1-10), Governors Felix and Festus (24:10-21; 25:1-12), and King Agrippa (Ac 26); appealed to Caesar (25:11). Shipwrecked on the way to Rome (Ac 27); ministered in Malta, then Rome (Ac 28).

PAY
until you have **paid** the last penny! Mt 5:26
Is it lawful to **p** taxes to Caesar Mt 22:17
P your obligations to everyone: Rm 13:7
not **p-ing** back evil for evil or 1Pt 3:9

PAYMENT
Spirit as a down **p** in our hearts. 2Co 1:22
gave us the Spirit as a down **p**. 2Co 5:5
He is the down **p** of our Eph 1:14

PEACE
favor on you and give you **p**. Nm 6:26
seek **p** and pursue it. Ps 34:14
Pray for the **p** of Jerusalem: Ps 122:6
time for war and a time for **p**. Ec 3:8
Eternal Father, Prince of **P**. Is 9:6
You will keep ... in perfect **p** Is 26:3
who proclaims **p**, who brings news Is 52:7
P, **p**, when there is no **p**. Jr 6:14; 8:11
I did not come to bring **p**, Mt 10:34
and **p** on earth to people He favors! Lk 2:14
P I leave with you. My **p** I give Jn 14:27
we have **p** with God through our Rm 5:1
fruit of the Spirit is love, joy, **p**, Gl 5:22
For He is our **p**, who made both Eph 2:14
And the **p** of God, which surpasses Php 4:7
by making **p** through the blood Col 1:20
to take **p** from the earth, Rv 6:4

PEACEMAKERS
The **p** are blessed, for they Mt 5:9

PEARL
or toss your **p-s** before pigs, Mt 7:6
When he found one priceless **p** Mt 13:46
gate was made of a single **p**. Rv 21:21

PEKAH
King of Israel; assassin (2Kg 15:25-31).

PEKAHIAH
Son of Menahem; king of Israel; assassinated by his captain, Pekah (2Kg 15:22-26).

PENTECOST
When the day of **P** had arrived, Ac 2:1

PEOPLE
your **p** will be my **p**, Ru 1:16
and My **p** who are called by My 2Ch 7:14
His **p**, the sheep of His pasture. Ps 100:3
but sin is a disgrace to any **p**. Pr 14:34
They will be My **p**, and I will be Jr 24:7
will save His **p** from their sins. Mt 1:21
has God rejected His **p**? Rm 11:1
God, and they will be My **p**. 2Co 6:16
God, and they will be My **p**. Heb 8:10
a holy nation, a **p** for His possession, 1Pt 2:9
and language and **p** and nation. Rv 5:9
will be His **p**, and God Himself Rv 21:3

PERCEIVE
keep looking, but do not **p**. Is 6:9
look and look, yet never **p**. Mt 13:14

PERFECT (ADJ)
The instruction of the LORD is **p**, Ps 19:7
You will keep ... in **p** peace Is 26:3
Be **p**, therefore, as your heavenly Mt 5:48
pleasing, and **p** will of God. Rm 12:2
But when the **p** comes, 1Co 13:10
and every **p** gift is from above, Jms 1:17
instead, **p** love drives out fear, 1Jn 4:18

PERFECT (V)
for power is **p-ed** in weakness. 2Co 12:9
and His love is **p-ed** in us. 1Jn 4:12

PERFECTER
the source and **p** of our faith Heb 12:2

PERISH
If I **p**, I **p**. Est 4:16
one of these little ones **p**. Mt 18:14
in Him will not **p** but have Jn 3:16
Don't work for the food that **p-es** Jn 6:27
and they will never **p**—ever! Jn 10:28
foolishness to those who are **p-ing** 1Co 1:18
not wanting any to **p** but all to 2Pt 3:9

PERISHABLE
not of **p** seed but of 1Pt 1:23

PERMISSIBLE
Everything is **p** for me, 1Co 6:12
"Everything is **p**," but not 1Co 10:23

PERPLEXED
we are **p** but not in despair; 2Co 4:8

PERSECUTE
Princes have **p-d** me without Ps 119:161
blessed when they insult and **p** you Mt 5:11
and pray for those who **p** you, Mt 5:44
they **p-d** Me, they will also **p** you. Jn 15:20
Saul, Saul, why are you **p-ing** Me? Ac 9:4
Bless those who **p** you; Rm 12:14
we are **p-d** but not abandoned; 2Co 4:9
in Christ Jesus will be **p-d**. 2Tm 3:12

PERSECUTION
When pressure or **p** comes Mt 13:21
a severe **p** broke out against Ac 8:1
or anguish or **p** or famine or Rm 8:35

PERSEVERE
p in these things, for by doing 1Tm 4:16

PERSIST
p in it whether convenient or not; 2Tm 4:2

PERSISTENCE
because of his ... **p**, he will get up Lk 11:8

PERSISTENT
be **p** in prayer. Rm 12:12

PERSUADE
Are you going to **p** me to become Ac 26:28
For I am **p-d** that not even death Rm 8:38
we seek to **p** people. 2Co 5:11
and am **p-d** that He is able 2Tm 1:12

PERSUASIVE
deceive you with **p** arguments. Col 2:4

PERVERSION
to mate with it; it is a **p**. Lv 18:23

PERVERT
Does God **p** justice? Jb 8:3

PERVERTED (ADJ)
p men of the city surrounded Jdg 19:22
in a crooked and **p** generation, Php 2:15

PESTERING
because this widow keeps **p** me, Lk 18:5

PESTILENCE
or the **p** that ravages at noon. Ps 91:6

PETER
Apostle; originally named Simon; also called Simeon (Ac 15:14) and Cephas. A fisherman in business with James and John (Lk 5:2-3,10); married, lived in Capernaum (Mk 1:21,29-30).

Walked on water (Mt 14:28-31). Confessed Jesus as Messiah (Mt 16:13-20; Mk 8:27-30; Lk 9:18-21). At transfiguration (Mt 17:1-9; Mk 9:2-8; Lk 9:28-36; 2Pt 1:16-18). Jesus predicted he would deny Him (Mt 26:31-35; Mk 14:27-31; Lk 22:31-34; Jn 13:36-38); denial (Mt 26:69-75; Mk 14:66-72; Lk 22:54-62; Jn 18:15-18,25-27); restoration to "feed My sheep" (Jn 21:15-19).

Spoke at Pentecost (Ac 2:14-40). Healed people (3:1-10; 5:15; 9:34); raised Tabitha from the dead (9:36-43). Arrested and forbidden to preach (4:1-31; 5:17-41). Saw vision: sent to Cornelius (Ac 10); reported Gentile conversions (Ac 11; 15); confronted by Paul for inconsistency (Gl 2:11-14). Imprisoned by Herod; freed by angel (Ac 12:1-19).
Focused on Jewish evangelism (Gl 2:7). Wrote two letters (1Pt 1:1; 2Pt 1:1).

PETITION
prayer and **p** with thanksgiving, Php 4:6
I urge that **p-s**, prayers, 1Tm 2:1

PHARAOH
Then **P** sent for Joseph, Gn 41:14
when I receive glory through **P**, Ex 14:18
For the Scripture tells **P**: Rm 9:17

PHARISEE
surpasses that of the scribes and **P-s** Mt 5:20
Then the **P-s** went and plotted Mt 22:15
woe to you, scribes and **P-s**, Mt 23:13
a **P** asked Him to dine with him. Lk 11:37
one a **P** and the other a tax Lk 18:10
I am a **P**, a son of **P-s**! Ac 23:6
regarding the law, a **P**; Php 3:5

PHILIP
1. Apostle (Mt 10:3; Jn 12:21-22). Invited Nathanael to "come and see" (1:43-51); questioned how to feed the 5,000 (6:5-7); asked Jesus to show them the Father (14:8-9).
2. One of the first seven deacons (Ac 6:1-6); evangelized Simon the sorcerer in Samaria (8:5-13) and an Ethiopian eunuch (8:26-39).

PHILIPPI
City in Macedonia where Paul preached (Ac 16:12; 20:6; 1Th 2:2) and to whom he wrote (Php 1:1; 4:15).

PHILISTINES
People of Philistia (Gn 10:14; 26:1). Originated in Caphtor (Jr 47:4; Am 9:7) as the Casluhim (Gn 10:14).
Enemies of Israel: Moses and Joshua did not defeat them (Ex 13:17; Jos 13:2; Jdg 3:1-3). In conflict with Shamgar (3:31); with Samson (13–16); with Samuel (1Sm 4–7); with Saul (13–14; 17; 23:27-28; 28:5,15; 31:1-6); with David (17:20-57; 18:20-27; 19:8; 23:1-5; 30:16; 2Sm 5:17-25; 8:1; 21:15-22; 23:9-13); with Jehoram (2Ch 21:16); with Uzziah (26:6-7); with Ahaz (28:18); and with Hezekiah (2Kg 18:8). David hid among them (1Sm 27:1,7,11; 29:11) but did not fight for them (27:8-12; 29:9).
Prophesied against (Is 11:14; 14:29-32; Jr 47; Ezk 25:15-17; Am 1:6-8; Ob 19; Zph 2:4-7; Zch 9:5-7).

PHILOSOPHER
Where is the **p**? Where is the 1Co 1:20

PHILOSOPHY
captive through **p** and empty Col 2:8

PHYSICIAN
Luke, the dearly loved **p**, Col 4:14

PIECE
weighed out 30 **p-s** of silver for Mt 26:15

PIERCE
they **p-d** my hands and my feet. Ps 22:16
But He was **p-d** because of our Is 53:5
will look at Me whom they **p-d**. Zch 12:10
a sword will **p** your own soul Lk 2:35
the soldiers **p-d** His side with Jn 19:34
will look at the One they **p-d**. Jn 19:37

PIG
like a gold ring in a **p-'s** snout. Pr 11:22
or toss your pearls before **p-s**, Mt 7:6
a large herd of **p-s** was feeding. Mt 8:30
him into his fields to feed **p-s**. Lk 15:15

PILATE, PONTIUS
Governor of Judea; presided over Jesus' trial and sentencing (Mt 27:11-26; Mk 15:1-15; Lk 23:1-25; Jn 18:28–19:16); warned by his wife (Mt 27:19); gave Jesus' body to Joseph of Arimathea (Mt 27:58; Mk 15:45; Lk 23:52; Jn 19:38); assigned guards to the tomb (Mt 27:65).

PILLAR
back and became a **p** of salt. Gn 19:26
p of cloud by day and the **p** of fire Ex 13:22
the **p** and foundation of the truth. 1Tm 3:15

PINNACLE
stand on the **p** of the temple, Mt 4:5; Lk 4:9

PIT
redeems your life from the **P**; Ps 103:4
blind, both will fall into a **p**. Mt 15:14

PITIED (ADJ)
we should be **p** more than anyone. 1Co 15:19

PLACE *SEE ALSO* HIGH PLACE, HOLY PLACE
Surely the LORD is in this **p**, Gn 28:16
going away to prepare a **p** for you. Jn 14:2
they now desire a better **p** Heb 11:16

PLAGUE
to send all My **p-s** against you, Ex 9:14
angels with the seven last **p-s** Rv 15:1
add to him the **p-s** that are Rv 22:18

PLAIN
and the rough places, a **p**. Is 40:4

PLAN
P-s fail when there is no Pr 15:22
A man's heart **p-s** his way, but Pr 16:9
Many **p-s** are in a man's heart, Pr 19:21
I have **p-ned** it; I will also do it. Is 46:11
Your **p** had predestined to take place Ac 4:28

PLANT (N)
will eat the **p-s** of the field. Gn 3:18
grew up before Him like a young **p** Is 53:2

PLANT (V)
LORD God **p-ed** a garden in Eden, Gn 2:8
like a tree **p-ed** beside streams Ps 1:3
a time to **p** and a time to uproot; Ec 3:2
I **p-ed**, Apollos watered, but God 1Co 3:6

PLATTER
the Baptist's head here on a **p**! Mt 14:8

PLAY
p skillfully on the strings, Ps 33:3
An infant will **p** beside the Is 11:8
p-ed the flute for you, but you Mt 11:17
eat and drink, and got up to **p**. 1Co 10:7

PLEAD
We **p** on Christ's behalf, 2Co 5:20

PLEASANT
have fallen for me in **p** places; Ps 16:6
How good and **p** it is when Ps 133:1

PLEASE
heaven and does whatever He **p-s**. Ps 115:3
does whatever He **p-s** in heaven Ps 135:6
the LORD was **p-d** to crush Him Is 53:10
it will accomplish what I **p** Is 55:11
I give it to anyone I **p**. Jr 27:5
The wind blows where it **p-s**, Jn 3:8
in the flesh cannot **p** God. Rm 8:8
the Messiah did not **p** Himself. Rm 15:3
how he may **p** his wife 1Co 7:33
as I also try to **p** all people in all 1Co 10:33
am I striving to **p** people? Gl 1:10
in order to **p** men, but Eph 6:6; Col 3:22
God was **p-d** to have all His Col 1:19
obey ... for this **p-s** the Lord. Col 3:20
it is impossible to **p** God, Heb 11:6

PLEASING (ADJ)
The sacrifice **p** to God is a Ps 51:17
May my meditation be **p** to Him; Ps 104:34
living sacrifice, holy and **p** to God; Rm 12:1
acceptable sacrifice, **p** to God. Php 4:18

PLEASURE
in Your right hand are eternal **p-s**. Ps 16:11
since He takes **p** in him. Ps 22:8
The one who loves **p** will become Pr 21:17
I take no **p** in anyone's death. Ezk 18:32
according to His good **p** Eph 1:9
lovers of **p** rather than lovers 2Tm 3:4
enjoy the short-lived **p** of sin. Heb 11:25

PLOT
and the peoples **p** in vain? Ps 2:1

PLOW (N)
swords into **p-s** and their spears Is 2:4
Beat your **p-s** into swords and Jl 3:10
his hand to the **p** and looks back Lk 9:62

PLOW (V)
If you hadn't **p-ed** with my young Jdg 14:18
he who **p-s** ought to **p** in hope, 1Co 9:10

PLUMB LINE
I am setting a **p** among My people Am 7:8

POINT
obedient to the **p** of death Php 2:8
yet fails in one **p**, is guilty Jms 2:10

POISON
evil, full of deadly **p**. Jms 3:8

POISONOUS
the LORD sent **p** snakes among Nm 21:6

POLLUTED
abstain from things **p** by idols, Ac 15:20

POOL
your eyes like **p-s** in Heshbon Sg 7:4
there is a **p**, called Bethesda Jn 5:2

POOR
there will never cease to be **p** Dt 15:11
He raises the **p** from the dust 1Sm 2:8
He raises the **p** from the dust Ps 113:7
Idle hands make one **p**, Pr 10:4
Me to bring good news to the **p**. Is 61:1
The **p** in spirit are blessed, Mt 5:3
and the **p** are told the good news Mt 11:5
You always have the **p** with you, Mt 26:11
all my goods to feed the **p** 1Co 13:3
for your sake He became **p**, 2Co 8:9

PORE
You **p** over the Scriptures Jn 5:39

PORTION
But the Lord's **p** is His people, Dt 32:9
strength of my heart, my **p** forever. Ps 73:26
Jacob's **P** is not like these Jr 10:16
The Lord is my **p**, therefore I Lm 3:24
and brought a **p** of it and laid Ac 5:2

POSSESS
to give you this land to **p**. Gn 15:7
those **p-ed** fell down before Him Mk 3:11
nothing yet **p-ing** everything. 2Co 6:10

POSSESSION
Canaan—as an eternal **p**, Gn 17:8
chosen you to be His own **p** Dt 7:6; 14:2
the ends of the earth Your **p**. Ps 2:8
Honor the Lord with your **p-s** Pr 3:9
in the abundance of his **p-s**. Lk 12:15
sold their **p-s** and property Ac 2:45
a people for His own **p**, Ti 2:14
a holy nation, a people for His **p**, 1Pt 2:9

POSSIBLE
but with God all things are **p**. Mt 19:26
If it is **p**, let this cup pass Mt 26:39
Everything is **p** to the one who Mk 9:23
If **p**, on your part, live at Rm 12:18

POTTER
we are the clay, and You are our **p**; Is 64:8
Just like clay in the **p-'s** hand, Jr 18:6
and bought the **p-'s** field with it Mt 27:7
Or has the **p** no right over the clay, Rm 9:21

POUR
after day they **p** out speech; Ps 19:2
p out your hearts before Him. Ps 62:8
I will **p** out My Spirit on your Is 44:3
I will **p** out My Spirit on all Jl 2:28
of heaven and **p** out a blessing Mal 3:10
that I will **p** out My Spirit on Ac 2:17
even if I am **p-ed** out as a drink Php 2:17

POVERTY
your **p** will come like a Pr 6:11; 24:34
Give me neither **p** nor wealth; Pr 30:8
but she out of her **p** has put in Mk 12:44
so that by His **p** you might 2Co 8:9

POWER
this purpose: to show you My **p** Ex 9:16
Ascribe **p** to God. Ps 68:34
death are in the **p** of the tongue, Pr 18:21
kingdom and the **p** and the glory Mt 6:13
the Scriptures or the **p** of God. Mt 22:29
right hand of the **P** and coming Mt 26:64
the kingdom of God come in **p**. Mk 9:1
you will receive **p** when the Holy Ac 1:8
the Holy Spirit and with **p**, Ac 10:38
it is God's **p** for salvation to Rm 1:16
His eternal **p** and divine nature Rm 1:20
or things to come, hostile **p-s**, Rm 8:38
for **p** is perfected in weakness. 2Co 12:9
the world **p-s** of this darkness Eph 6:12
know Him and the **p** of His Php 3:10
fearfulness, but one of **p**, love, 2Tm 1:7
form of godliness but denying its **p** 2Tm 3:5
His divine **p** has given us 2Pt 1:3
glory, and **p** belong to our God, Rv 19:1

POWERFUL
many **p**, not many of noble 1Co 1:26
are **p** through God for the 2Co 10:4

PRACTICE
they don't **p** what they teach. Mt 23:3
those who **p** such things Rm 1:32; Gl 5:21
and are not **p-ing** the truth 1Jn 1:6

PRAISE (N)
enthroned on the **p-s** of Israel. Ps 22:3
His **p** will always be on my lips. Ps 34:1
Sing **p** to God, sing **p**; Ps 47:6
and His courts with **p**. Ps 100:4
have prepared **p** from the mouths Mt 21:16
For they loved **p** from men more Jn 12:43
to the **p** of His glorious grace Eph 1:6
up to God a sacrifice of **p**, Heb 13:15

PRAISE (V)
This is my God, and I will **p** Him, Ex 15:2
Lord is great and highly **p-d**; 1Ch 16:25
Lord lives—may my rock be **p-d**! Ps 18:46
that breathes **p** the Lord. Ps 150:6
Let another **p** you, and not your Pr 27:2
host with the angel, **p-ing** God Lk 2:13
P the God and Father of our Lord 1Pt 1:3
We **p** our Lord and Father with it, Jms 3:9

PRAY
against the Lord by ceasing to **p** 1Sm 12:23
by My name humble themselves, **p** 2Ch 7:14
we **p-ed** to our God and stationed Neh 4:9
P for the peace of Jerusalem: Ps 122:6
and **p** for those who persecute you, Mt 5:44
you should **p** like this: Mt 6:9
the mountain by Himself to **p**. Mt 14:23
teach us to **p**, just as John Lk 11:1
I **p** for them. I am not **p-ing** for Jn 17:9
know what to **p** for as we should Rm 8:26
Every man who **p-s** or prophesies 1Co 11:4
P at all times in the Spirit, Eph 6:18
P constantly. 1Th 5:17
suffering? He should **p**. Jms 5:13

PRAYER
the Lord accepts my **p**. Ps 6:9
a house of **p** for all nations. Is 56:7
out except by **p** and fasting. Mt 17:21
will be called a house of **p**. Mt 21:13
be persistent in **p**. Rm 12:12
everything, through **p** and petition Php 4:6
which are the **p-s** of the saints. Rv 5:8

PREACH
the world and **p** the gospel to Mk 16:15
how can they **p** unless they are Rm 10:15
but we **p** Christ crucified, 1Co 1:23
p Christ out of envy and strife Php 1:15
seen by angels, **p-ed** among the 1Tm 3:16

PREACHER
how can they hear without a **p**? Rm 10:14

PRECIOUS
their lives are **p** in his sight. Ps 72:14
She is more **p** than jewels; Pr 3:15
She is far more **p** than jewels. Pr 31:10
a tested stone, a **p** cornerstone Is 28:16
but with the **p** blood of Christ, 1Pt 1:19

PREDESTINED
Your plan had **p** to take place. Ac 4:28
He also **p** to be conformed Rm 8:29
a wisdom God **p** before the ages 1Co 2:7
He **p** us to be adopted through Eph 1:5
p according to the purpose of Eph 1:11

PREGNANT
and hit a **p** woman so that her Ex 21:22
that she was **p** by the Holy Mt 1:18
will become **p** and give birth to Mt 1:23
was engaged to him and was **p**. Lk 2:5

PREPARE
You **p** a table before me in the Ps 23:5
P the way of the Lord in the Is 40:3
Israel, **p** to meet your God! Am 4:12
P the way for the Lord; Mt 3:3
he will **p** Your way before You. Mt 11:10
she has **p-d** Me for burial. Mt 26:12
going away to **p** a place for you Jn 14:2
God **p-d** this for those who love 1Co 2:9
which God **p-d** ahead of time so Eph 2:10
but You **p-d** a body for Me. Heb 10:5

PRESENCE
the bread of the **P** on the table Ex 25:30
in the **p** of my enemies; Ps 23:5
Do not banish me from Your **p** or Ps 51:11
Where can I flee from Your **p**? Ps 139:7
not only in my **p**, but now even Php 2:12
appear in the **p** of God for us. Heb 9:24

PRESENT (ADJ)
things **p** or things to come, Rm 8:38
absent in body but **p** in spirit, 1Co 5:3

PRESENT (V)
I urge you to **p** your bodies as a Rm 12:1
He did this to **p** the church to Eph 5:27
Be diligent to **p** yourself 2Tm 2:15

PRESERVE
loses his life will **p** it. Lk 17:33

PRESS
good measure—**p-ed** down, shaken Lk 6:38

PRESSURE
When **p** or persecution comes Mk 4:17

PRESSURED
We are **p** in every way but not 2Co 4:8

PREVENT
were **p-ed** by the Holy Spirit from Ac 16:6

PREVIOUSLY
over the sins **p** committed. Rm 3:25
in which you **p** walked according Eph 2:2

PRICE
I insist on paying the full **p**, 1Ch 21:24
the **p** of Him whose **p** was set by Mt 27:9
for you were bought at a **p**. 1Co 6:20
You were bought at a **p**; 1Co 7:23

PRICELESS
When he found one **p** pearl, Mt 13:46

PRIDE
When **p** comes, disgrace follows Pr 11:2
P comes before destruction, Pr 16:18

PRIEST
he was a **p** to God Most High. Gn 14:18
be My kingdom of **p-s** and My holy Ex 19:6
serve Me as **p**—Aaron, his sons Ex 28:1
You are a **p** like Melchizedek. Ps 110:4
A **p** happened to be going Lk 10:31
a great high **p** who has passed Heb 4:14
You are a **p** forever in the order Heb 5:6
but they will be **p-s** of God and Rv 20:6

PRIESTHOOD
a permanent **p** for them Ex 40:15
He holds His **p** permanently. Heb 7:24
race, a royal **p**, a holy nation 1Pt 2:9

PRINCE
P-s have persecuted me without Ps 119:161
Eternal Father, **P** of Peace. Is 9:6

PRISON
I was in **p** and you visited Me' Mt 25:36
Peter was kept in **p**, but prayer Ac 12:5
saw the doors of the **p** open, Ac 16:27
to the spirits in **p** 1Pt 3:19

PRISONER
The LORD frees **p-s**. Ps 146:7
and freedom to the **p-s**; Is 61:1
p of Christ Jesus on behalf Eph 3:1

PRIZE
but only one receives the **p**? 1Co 9:24
as my goal the **p** promised by Php 3:14

PROCLAIM
and I will **p** the name Yahweh Ex 33:19
P His salvation from day to day. 1Ch 16:23
and the sky **p-s** the work of His Ps 19:1
The heavens **p** His righteousness Ps 50:6
to **p** liberty to the captives Is 61:1
must first be **p-ed** to all nations. Mk 13:10
He has sent Me to **p** freedom to Lk 4:18
you **p** the Lord's death until He 1Co 11:26
P the message; persist in it 2Tm 4:2

PRODUCE
A good tree can't **p** bad fruit; Mt 7:18
of your faith **p-s** endurance. Jms 1:3

PROFANE
Do not **p** the name of your God; Lv 18:21

PROFESS
They **p** to know God, but they Ti 1:16

PROFIT
who hates dishonest **p** prolongs Pr 28:16
not seeking my own **p**, but the **p** 1Co 10:33
and do business and make a **p**. Jms 4:13

PROFITABLE
God and is **p** for teaching 2Tm 3:16

PROGRESS
for your **p** and joy in the faith, Php 1:25
so that your **p** may be evident to 1Tm 4:15

PROMINENT
number of the **p** Greek women Ac 17:12

PROMISCUITY
evil actions, deceit, **p**, stinginess Mk 7:22
moral impurity, **p**, Gl 5:19
turning the grace of our God into **p** Jd 4

PROMISCUOUS
Go and marry a **p** wife Hs 1:2

PROMISE (N)
not one **p** has failed. Jos 23:14
For the **p** is for you and for Ac 2:39
of God's **p-s** is "Yes" in Him. 2Co 1:20
first commandment with a **p** Eph 6:2
since it holds **p** for the present 1Tm 4:8
The Lord does not delay His **p** 2Pt 3:9

PROMISE (V)
This is the land I **p-d** Abraham, Dt 34:4
for He who **p-d** is faithful. Heb 10:23
did not receive what was **p-d**, Heb 11:39

PROMISED (ADJ)
from the Father the **p** Holy Spirit, Ac 2:33

PRONOUNCE
he could not **p** it correctly, Jdg 12:6

PROOF
to them by many convincing **p-s** Ac 1:3
the **p** of what is not seen. Heb 11:1

PROPER
Is it **p** for a woman to pray to 1Co 11:13
among you, as is **p** for saints. Eph 5:3

PROPERTY
wife Sapphira, sold a piece of **p**. Ac 5:1

PROPHECY
miracles, to another, **p**, 1Co 12:10
If I have the gift of **p** 1Co 13:2
But as for **p-ies**, they will come to 1Co 13:8
it was given to you through **p**, 1Tm 4:14
No **p** of Scripture comes from 2Pt 1:20

PROPHESY
sons and your daughters will **p**, Jl 2:28
Lord, didn't we **p** in Your name, Mt 7:22
P to us, Messiah! Who hit You? Mt 26:68
sons and your daughters will **p** Ac 2:17
and above all that you may **p**. 1Co 14:1
and they will **p** for 1,260 days, Rv 11:3

PROPHET
God will raise up for you a **p** like Dt 18:15
A **p** is not without honor except Mt 13:57
be called a **p** of the Most High, Lk 1:76
No **p** is accepted in his hometown. Lk 4:24
"Are you the **P**?" "No," Jn 1:21
first apostles, second **p-s**, 1Co 12:28
apostles, some **p-s**, some Eph 4:11
the beast and the false **p** are, Rv 20:10

PROPHETESS
There was also a **p**, Anna, Lk 2:36

PROPHETIC
known through the **p** Scriptures, Rm 16:26
we have the **p** word strongly 2Pt 1:19

PROPITIATION
Him as a **p** through faith Rm 3:25
to make **p** for the sins of the Heb 2:17
Himself is the **p** for our sins, 1Jn 2:2
Son to be the **p** for our sins. 1Jn 4:10

PROSELYTE
land and sea to make one **p** Mt 23:15
from Rome, both Jews and **p-s**, Ac 2:10

PROSPER
Whatever he does **p-s**. Ps 1:3
will **p** in what I send it to do. Is 55:11

PROSPERITY
set before you life and **p**, Dt 30:15
I saw the **p** of the wicked. Ps 73:3

PROSTITUTE
a **p** named Rahab, and stayed there. Jos 2:1
p-s are entering the kingdom Mt 21:31
and make it a part of a **p**? 1Co 6:15

PROTECT
P me as the pupil of Your eye; Ps 17:8
He **p-s** His flock like a shepherd Is 40:11
who is able to **p** you from Jd 24

PROTECTION
lives under the **p** of the Most High Ps 91:1

PROUD
LORD, my heart is not **p**; Ps 131:1
downfall a man's heart is **p**, Pr 18:12
arrogant, **p**, boastful, inventors Rm 1:30
money, boastful, **p**, blasphemers 2Tm 3:2
God resists the **p**, but gives Jms 4:6

PROVE
But God **p-s** His own love for us Rm 5:8

PROVEN
endurance produces **p** character, Rm 5:4

PROVERB
Solomon composed 3,000 **p-s**, 1Kg 4:32
The **p-s** of Solomon son of David, Pr 1:1
you will quote this **p** to Me: Lk 4:23

PROVIDE
God Himself will **p** the lamb Gn 22:8
all these things will be **p-d** for you. Mt 6:33
He will also **p** a way of escape 1Co 10:13
own flesh but **p-s** and cares for it, Eph 5:29
if anyone does not **p** for his own 1Tm 5:8
richly **p-s** us with all things 1Tm 6:17

PROVOKE
tested God and **p-d** the Holy One Ps 78:41
is not selfish, is not **p-d**, 1Co 13:5

PROWLING
the Devil is **p** around like a 1Pt 5:8

PRUNES
and He **p** every branch that Jn 15:2

PSALM
After singing **p-s**, they went out Mt 26:30
and the **P-s** must be fulfilled. Lk 24:44
each one has a **p**, a teaching 1Co 14:26
speaking to one another in **p-s**, Eph 5:19

PUBLIC
your attention to **p** reading, 1Tm 4:13

PUBLICLY
not wanting to disgrace her **p** Mt 1:19
P rebuke those who sin, so that 1Tm 5:20

PUNISH
the LORD has **p-ed** Him for the Is 53:6
and **p-es** every son He receives. Heb 12:6
if you sin and are **p-ed**, 1Pt 2:20

PUNISHMENT
My **p** is too great to bear! Gn 4:13
p for our peace was on Him, Is 53:5
son won't suffer **p** for the father's Ezk 18:20
they will go away into eternal **p**, Mt 25:46
because fear involves **p** 1Jn 4:18

PUPIL
protected him as the **p** of His eye. Dt 32:10
Protect me as the **p** of Your eye; Ps 17:8

PURCHASED
which He **p** with His own blood. Ac 20:28

PURE
The fear of the LORD is **p**, Ps 19:9
can a young man keep his way **p**? Ps 119:9
eyes are too **p** to look on evil, Hab 1:13
The **p** in heart are blessed, Mt 5:8
whatever is just, whatever is **p**, Php 4:8
To the **p**, everything is **p**, but to Ti 1:15
earnestly from a **p** heart, 1Pt 1:22

PURIFICATION
After making **p** for sins, He sat Heb 1:3

PURIFY
P me with hyssop, and I will be Ps 51:7
He will **p** the sons of Levi and Mal 3:3

PURIM
reason these days are called **P**, Est 9:26

PURITY
by **p**, by knowledge, by patience, 2Co 6:6

PURPLE
crown of thorns and the **p** robe. Jn 19:5

PURPOSE
has prepared everything for His **p** Pr 16:4
because I was sent for this **p**. Lk 4:43
are called according to His **p**. Rm 8:28
so that God's **p** according to Rm 9:11
and to work out His good **p**. Php 2:13

PURSUE
seek peace and **p** it. Ps 34:14
who did not **p** righteousness, Rm 9:30
and **p** righteousness, godliness 1Tm 6:11
P peace with everyone, and Heb 12:14
He must seek peace and **p** it, 1Pt 3:11

PURSUIT
futile, a **p** of the wind. Ec 1:14

PUT
But **p** on the Lord Jesus Christ, Rm 13:14
P on the full armor of God so Eph 6:11

QUAIL
So at evening **q** came Ex 16:13

QUAKE
earth **q-d** and the rocks were split. Mt 27:51

QUALITY
will test the **q** of each one's 1Co 3:13

QUARREL
The Lord's slave must not **q**, 2Tm 2:24

QUARRELSOME
but gentle, not **q**, not greedy 1Tm 3:3

QUEEN
The **q** of Sheba heard about 1Kg 10:1
The **q** of the south will rise up Mt 12:42

QUENCHED
not die, and the fire is not **q**. Mk 9:44

QUICK
Everyone must be **q** to hear, Jms 1:19

QUICKLY
What you're doing, do **q**. Jn 13:27
I am coming **q**. Hold on to what Rv 3:11
Yes, I am coming **q**. Rv 22:20

QUIET
He leads me beside **q** waters. Ps 23:2
a tranquil and **q** life in all 1Tm 2:2
of a gentle and **q** spirit, 1Pt 3:4

QUIVER
who has filled his **q** with them. Ps 127:5

QUOTA
require the same **q** of bricks Ex 5:8

RABBI
do not be called '**R**,' because you Mt 23:8

RABBOUNI
she said to Him in Hebrew, "*R!*" Jn 20:16

RAB-SARIS
Title of Assyrian and Babylonian officials (2Kg 18:17; Jr 39:3,13).

RACE (N)
the **r** is not to the swift, Ec 9:11
I have finished the **r**, I have kept 2Tm 4:7
endurance the **r** that lies before Heb 12:1
you are a chosen **r**, a royal 1Pt 2:9

RACE (V)
the runners in a stadium all **r**, 1Co 9:24

RACHEL
Daughter of Laban; wife and cousin of Jacob (29:10,18-30); mother of Joseph and Benjamin (30:24; 35:16-20); stole her father's household idols (31:19).
R weeping for her children; Mt 2:18

RADIANCE
The Son is the **r** of God's glory, Heb 1:3

RAGE (N)
king's **r** is like the roaring of a lion Pr 19:12

RAGE (V)
Why did the Gentiles **r** and Ac 4:25

RAHAB
Prostitute in Jericho who hid the Israelite spies (Jos 2; Heb 11:31); spared by Joshua (Jos 6:17,22-25). Mother of Boaz (Mt 1:5).

RAIN (N)
and the **r** fell on the earth 40 Gn 7:12
and sends **r** on the righteous and Mt 5:45

RAIN (V)
prayed ... that it would not **r**, Jms 5:17

RAISE
I will **r** up for them a prophet Dt 18:18
LORD **r-d** up judges, who saved Jdg 2:16
God is able to **r** up children for Mt 3:9
killed, and be **r-d** the third day. Mt 16:21
and I will **r** it up in three days. Jn 2:19
and I will **r** him up on the last Jn 6:40
and **r-d** for our justification. Rm 4:25
that He was **r-d** on the third 1Co 15:4
dead will be **r-d** incorruptible, 1Co 15:52
who **r-d** the Lord Jesus will **r** us 2Co 4:14
He also **r-d** us up and seated us Eph 2:6

RAM
and saw a **r** caught in the thicket Gn 22:13

RANK
higher in **r** than the angels Heb 1:4

RANSOM (N)
these cannot ... pay his **r** to God Ps 49:7
to give His life—a **r** for many. Mt 20:28
gave Himself—a **r** for all, a 1Tm 2:6

RANSOM (V)
for the LORD has **r-ed** Jacob and Jr 31:11

RASHLY
something **r** and later to reconsider Pr 20:25

RAVEN
he sent out a **r**. Gn 8:7
The **r-s** kept bringing him bread 1Kg 17:6
Consider the **r-s**: They don't sow Lk 12:24

READ
Sabbath day and stood up to **r**. Lk 4:16
you understand what you're **r-ing**? Ac 8:30
your attention to public **r-ing**, 1Tm 4:13
The one who **r-s** this is blessed, Rv 1:3

READY
Always be **r** to give a defense 1Pt 3:15

REAL
My flesh is **r** food and My blood Jn 6:55

REALITY
faith is the **r** of what is hoped Heb 11:1

REALLY
Did God **r** say, 'You can't eat from Gn 3:1

REAP
sow in tears will **r** with shouts Ps 126:5
the wind and **r** the whirlwind. Hs 8:7
They don't sow or **r** or gather Mt 6:26
a man sows he will also **r**, Gl 6:7
r, for the time to **r** has come, Rv 14:15

REASON (N)
They hated Me for no **r**. Jn 15:25
asks you for a **r** for the hope 1Pt 3:15

REASON (V)
So he **r-ed** in the synagogue with Ac 17:17
a child, I **r-ed** like a child. 1Co 13:11

REBEKAH
Sister of Laban; wife of Isaac (Gn 24); mother of Jacob and Esau (25:21-26). Passed off as Isaac's sister (26:6-11). Encouraged Jacob to secure Isaac's blessing (27:1-17).

REBEL
Only don't **r** against the LORD, Nm 14:9
Why do the nations **r** and the peoples Ps 2:1
but they have **r-led** against Me. Is 1:2

REBELLION
For **r** is like the sin of divination, 1Sm 15:23
the wicked increase, **r** increases Pr 29:16

REBELLIOUS
a stubborn and **r** generation, Ps 78:8
unbelieving and **r** generation! Mt 17:17

REBUILD
to go up and **r** the LORD's house Ezr 1:5
Come, let's **r** Jerusalem's wall Neh 2:17
and the ruins will be **rebuilt**. Ezk 36:33
sanctuary and **r** it in three days. Mt 26:61

REBUKE
do not **r** me in Your anger; Ps 6:1
The LORD **r** you, Satan! Zch 3:2
He got up and **r-d** the winds Mt 8:26
go and **r** him in private. Mt 18:15
Do not **r** an older man, 1Tm 5:1
Publicly **r** those who sin, 1Tm 5:20
profitable for teaching, for **r-ing**, 2Tm 3:16
r, correct, and encourage with 2Tm 4:2
him but said, "The Lord **r** you!" Jd 9
many as I love, I **r** and discipline. Rv 3:19

RECEIVE
who asks **r-s**, and the one who Mt 7:8
But to all who did **r** Him, He gave Jn 1:12
Ask and you will **r**, Jn 16:24
But you will **r** power when the Ac 1:8
is more blessed to give than to **r**. Ac 20:35
What do you have that you didn't **r**? 1Co 4:7
For I **r-d** from the Lord what I 1Co 11:23
as you have **r-d** Christ Jesus Col 2:6

RECOGNIZE
r-d his brothers, they did not **r** him Gn 42:8
opened, and they **r-d** Him, but Lk 24:31
yet the world did not **r** Him. Jn 1:10

RECONCILE
First go and be **r-d** with your Mt 5:24
Christ's behalf, "Be **r-d** to God." 2Co 5:20
that He might **r** both to God Eph 2:16
through Him to **r** everything to Col 1:20

RECONCILIATION
we have now received this **r** Rm 5:11
if their rejection brings **r** Rm 11:15
and gave us the ministry of **r**: 2Co 5:18

RECONSIDER
rashly and later to **r** his vows. Pr 20:25

RECORD
does not keep a **r** of wrongs. 1Co 13:5

RECRUCIFYING
they are **r** the Son of God Heb 6:6

RED
Don't gaze at wine because it is **r**, Pr 23:31
they are as **r** as crimson, Is 1:18
good weather because the sky is **r**. Mt 16:2
another horse went out, a fiery **r** one, Rv 6:4

RED SEA
Crossed by Israel (Ex 13:18; 14:15-31; Nm 21:14; Dt 11:4; Jos 2:10; 4:23; 24:6; Neh 9:9; Ps 106:7,9-11,22; 136:13-15; Ac 7:36; Heb 11:29); southern extent of the promised land (Ex 23:31); location of Solomon's fleet (1Kg 9:26).

REDEEM
I will **r** you with an outstretched arm Ex 6:6
to **r** a people for Himself, 2Sm 7:23
the price of **r-ing** him is too costly, Ps 49:8
He **r-s** your life from the Pit; Ps 103:4
Christ has **r-ed** us from the curse Gl 3:13
to **r** those under the law, Gl 4:5

REDEEMED (N)
Let the **r** of the LORD Ps 107:2
r of the LORD will return Is 35:10; 51:11

REDEEMER
I know my living **R**, and He will Jb 19:25
LORD, my rock and my **R**. Ps 19:14
for their **R** is strong, Pr 23:11
Your **R** is the Holy One of Israel. Is 41:14

REDEMPTION
because your **r** is near! Lk 21:28
adoption, the **r** of our bodies. Rm 8:23
have **r** in Him through His blood, Eph 1:7
We have **r**, the forgiveness of sins, Col 1:14
having obtained eternal **r**. Heb 9:12

REED
He will not break a bruised **r**, Is 42:3
A **r** swaying in the wind? Mt 11:7
He will not break a bruised **r** Mt 12:20

REFINER
For He will be like a **r-'s** fire Mal 3:2

REFLECT
are **r-ing** the glory of the Lord 2Co 3:18

REFRESHING (N)
that seasons of **r** may come Ac 3:19

REFUGE
will include six cities of **r**, Nm 35:6
whose wings you have come for **r**. Ru 2:12
God is our **r** and strength, Ps 46:1
shield to those who take **r** in Him. Pr 30:5
we who have fled for **r** might Heb 6:18

REFUSE
but the one who **r-s** to believe Jn 3:36

REFUTE
For he vigorously **r-d** the Jews in Ac 18:28

REGARD (N)
The LORD had **r** for Abel and his Gn 4:4

REGARD (V)
but we in turn **r-ed** Him stricken, Is 53:4

REGENERATION
through the washing of **r** and Ti 3:5

REGION
In the same **r**, shepherds were Lk 2:8

REGISTER
that the whole empire should be **r-ed**. Lk 2:1

REGRET
LORD **r-ted** that He had made man Gn 6:6
I **r** that I made Saul king, 1Sm 15:11

REGULATIONS
Why do you submit to **r**: Col 2:20

REHOBOAM
Son of Solomon; king of Judah (1Kg 11:43). Answered people harshly; the kingdom was divided (12:1-19; 2Ch 10:1-19).

REIGN
The LORD will **r** forever and ever! Ex 15:18
The LORD **r-s**! He is robed in Ps 93:1
The LORD **r-s** forever; Ps 146:10
who says to Zion, "Your God **r-s**!" Is 52:7
He will **r** over the house of Lk 1:33
death **r-ed** from Adam to Moses, Rm 5:14
do not let sin **r** in your mortal Rm 6:12
For He must **r** until He puts all 1Co 15:25
we will also **r** with Him; 2Tm 2:12
and He will **r** forever and ever! Rv 11:15
will **r** with Him for 1,000 years. Rv 20:6

REJECT
LORD, He has **r-ed** you as king. 1Sm 15:23
stone that the builders **r-ed** has Ps 118:22
He was despised and **r-ed** by men, Is 53:3
the builders **r-ed** has become Mt 21:42
Whoever **r-s** you **r-s** Me. Lk 10:16
has God **r-ed** His people? Rm 11:1
r-ed by men but chosen and 1Pt 2:4

REJOICE
all who take refuge in You **r**; Ps 5:11
let us **r** and be glad in it. Ps 118:24
R greatly, Daughter Zion! Zch 9:9
but **r** that your names are written Lk 10:20
R with those who **r**; Rm 12:15
but **r-s** in the truth. 1Co 13:6
R in the Lord always. I will say it again: **R**! Php 4:4
R always! 1Th 5:16

RELATIONS
males ... left natural **r** with females Rm 1:27

RELATIVE
The man is a close **r**. Ru 2:20
in his hometown, among his **r-s**, Mk 6:4

RELEASE
do you want me to **r** for you? Mt 27:21

RELENT
and **r** concerning this disaster Ex 32:12
but the LORD **r-ed** concerning 2Sm 24:16
may turn and **r** and leave a blessing Jl 2:14
so God **r-ed** from the disaster Jnh 3:10

RELIGION
and undefiled **r** before our God Jms 1:27

RELIGIOUS
are extremely **r** in every respect. Ac 17:22

RELY
He **r-ies** on the LORD; let Him Ps 22:8
do not **r** on your own understanding; Pr 3:5
What are you **r-ing** on? Is 36:4
all who **r** on the works of the law Gl 3:10

REMAIN
the word of our God **r-s** forever. Is 40:8
R in Me, and I in you. Jn 15:4
three **r**: faith, hope, and love. 1Co 13:13
they would have **r-ed** with us. 1Jn 2:19

REMARKABLE
and look at this **r** sight. Ex 3:3

REMARKABLY
been **r** and wonderfully made. Ps 139:14

REMEMBER
God **r-ed** Noah, Gn 8:1
R the Sabbath day, to keep it holy: Ex 20:8
what is man that You **r** him, Ps 8:4
made of, **r-ing** that we are dust. Ps 103:14
So **r** your Creator in the days Ec 12:1
own sake and **r** your sins no more. Is 43:25
and never again **r** their sin. Jr 31:34
R Lot's wife! Lk 17:32
asked only that we would **r** the poor Gl 2:10
R my imprisonment. Col 4:18
I will never again **r** their sins. Heb 8:12

REMEMBRANCE
there is no **r** of You in death; Ps 6:5
Do this in **r** of Me. Lk 22:19; 1Co 11:24

REMIND
r you of everything I have told you. Jn 14:26

REMINDER
there is a **r** of sins every year. Heb 10:3

REMNANT
For a **r** will go out from 2Kg 19:31
our God to preserve a **r** for us Ezr 9:8
The **r** will return, the **r** of Jacob, Is 10:21
I will gather the **r** of My flock Jr 23:3
only the **r** will be saved; Rm 9:27

REMOTE
by boat to a **r** place to be alone. Mt 14:13

REMOVAL
not the **r** of the filth of the flesh, 1Pt 3:21

REMOVE
R the sandals from your feet, Jos 5:15
so far has He **r-d** our Ps 103:12
I will **r** your heart of stone and Ezk 36:26

RENEW
He **r-s** my life; He leads me along Ps 23:3
and **r** a steadfast spirit within me. Ps 51:10
youth is **r-ed** like the eagle. Ps 103:5
the LORD will **r** their strength; Is 40:31
by the **r-ing** of your mind, Rm 12:2
person is being **r-ed** day by day. 2Co 4:16
is impossible to **r** to repentance Heb 6:4

RENEWAL
regeneration and **r** by the Holy Spirit. Ti 3:5

REPAY
Vengeance belongs to Me; I will **r**. Dt 32:35
deserve or **repaid** us according to Ps 103:10
Do not **r** anyone evil for evil. Rm 12:17
I will **r**, says the Lord. Rm 12:19
that no one **r-s** evil for evil 1Th 5:15

REPEAT
R them to your children. Dt 6:7

REPENT
and **r** in dust and ashes. Jb 42:6
R, because the kingdom of heaven Mt 3:2
one sinner who **r-s** than over 99 Lk 15:7
R ... and be baptized, Ac 2:38
all people everywhere to **r**, Ac 17:30

REPENTANCE
fruit consistent with **r**. Mt 3:8
a baptism of **r** for the forgiveness Mk 1:4
righteous, but sinners to **r**. Lk 5:32
r for forgiveness of sins will be Lk 24:47
and do works worthy of **r**. Ac 26:20
kindness is intended to lead you to **r** Rm 2:4
godly grief produces a **r** 2Co 7:10
any to perish but all to come to **r**. 2Pt 3:9

REPRIMAND
Better an open **r** than concealed Pr 27:5

REPROACH
must be above **r**, the husband of 1Tm 3:2
he considered the **r** because of Heb 11:26

REPUTATION
have a good **r** among outsiders, 1Tm 3:7
you have a **r** for being alive, Rv 3:1

REQUEST
your **r-s** be made known to God. Php 4:6

REQUIRE
what it is the LORD **r-s** of you: Mc 6:8
Much will be **r-d** of everyone Lk 12:48

REQUIREMENT
in order that the law's **r** would Rm 8:4

RESCUE
relies on the LORD; let Him **r** him; Ps 22:8
R those being taken off to death, Pr 24:11
His trust in God; let God **r** Him Mt 27:43
has **r-d** us from the domain of Col 1:13
r-s us from the coming wrath. 1Th 1:10
Lord knows how to **r** the godly 2Pt 2:9

RESIDE
Christ's power may **r** in me. 2Co 12:9
has eternal life **r-ing** in him. 1Jn 3:15

RESIDENCE
I will place My **r** among you, Lv 26:11
a place for Your **r** forever. 2Ch 6:2
flesh and took up **r** among us. Jn 1:14

RESIST
tell you, don't **r** an evildoer. Mt 5:39
are always **r-ing** the Holy Spirit; Ac 7:51
For who can **r** His will? Rm 9:19
may be able to **r** in the evil day Eph 6:13
have not yet **r-ed** to the point Heb 12:4
But **r** the Devil, and he will flee Jms 4:7

RESOUND
sea and all that fills it **r**. Ps 96:11
Praise Him with **r-ing** cymbals; Ps 150:5

RESPECT (N)
r to those you owe **r**, Rm 13:7
masters to be worthy of all **r**, 1Tm 6:1
do this with gentleness and **r**, 1Pt 3:16

RESPECT (V)
Each of you is to **r** his mother Lv 19:3
'They will **r** my son,' he said. Mt 21:37
the wife is to **r** her husband. Eph 5:33

RESPONSIBILITY
his marital **r** to his wife, 1Co 7:3

REST (N)
be a Sabbath of complete **r**, Ex 31:15
They will not enter My **r**. Ps 95:11
and find **r** for yourselves. Jr 6:16
and I will give you **r**. Mt 11:28
Sabbath **r** remains for God's people Heb 4:9

REST (V)
He **r-ed** on the seventh day Gn 2:2

RESTORE
the LORD **r-d** his prosperity and Jb 42:10
R the joy of Your salvation to me, Ps 51:12
is coming and will **r** everything, Mt 17:11
it out, and his hand was **r-d**. Mk 3:5
are You **r-ing** the kingdom to Israel Ac 1:6
spiritual should **r** such a person Gl 6:1

RESTRAIN
know what currently **r-s** him, 2Th 2:6

RESTRAINT
because in His **r** God passed over Rm 3:25

RESURRECTED
and He will be **r** on the third Mt 20:19
For He has been **r**, just as He said. Mt 28:6
He has been **r**! He is not here! Mk 16:6
God has **r** this Jesus. Ac 2:32

RESURRECTION
in the **r** ... whose wife will she be Mt 22:28
the **r** of life ... the **r** of judgment. Jn 5:29
I am the **r** and the life. Jn 11:25
if there is no **r** of the dead, 1Co 15:13
know Him and the power of His **r** Php 3:10
This is the first **r**. Rv 20:5

RETAIN
r the sins of any, they are **r-ed**. Jn 20:23

RETURN
you are dust, and you will **r** to dust. Gn 3:19
the spirit **r-s** to God who gave Ec 12:7
mouth will not **r** to Me empty, Is 55:11
Come, let us **r** to the LORD. Hs 6:1

REUBEN
Son of Jacob and Leah; eldest (Gn 29:32). Lost birthright for sleeping with father's concubine (35:22; 49:4; 1Ch 5:1). Tried to rescue Joseph (Gn 37:21-29); offered to protect Benjamin (42:37). Tribe with territory east of the Dead Sea, north of the Arnon River (Nm 32; Jos 13:15-23).

REVEAL
the arm of the LORD been **r-ed** to Is 53:1
whom the Son desires to **r** Him. Mt 11:27
blood did not **r** this to you, Mt 16:17
him and will **r** Myself to him. Jn 14:21
of his heart will be **r-ed**, 1Co 14:25

REVELATION
Without **r** people run wild, Pr 29:18
light for **r** to the Gentiles Lk 2:32
eagerly wait for the **r** of our Lord 1Co 1:7
has a psalm, a teaching, a **r**, 1Co 14:26
it came by a **r** from Jesus Gl 1:12
was made known to me by **r**, Eph 3:3

at the **r** of the Lord Jesus 2Th 1:7
at the **r** of Jesus Christ 1Pt 1:7
The **r** of Jesus Christ that God gave Rv 1:1

REVERE
descendants of Israel, **r** Him! Ps 22:23

REVERENCE
serve God acceptably, with **r** Heb 12:28

REVERENT
observe your pure, **r** lives. 1Pt 3:2

REVILE
When we are **r-d**, we bless; 1Co 4:12
He was **r-d**, He did not **r** in return; 1Pt 2:23

REVIVE
LORD is perfect, **r-ing** the soul; Ps 19:7
Will You not **r** us again so that Ps 85:6

REVOKE
You **r** God's word by your tradition Mk 7:13

REWARD (N)
there is a **r** for the righteous! Ps 58:11
from the LORD, children, a **r**. Ps 127:3
His **r** is with Him, and His gifts Is 40:10
your **r** is great in heaven. Mt 5:12
They've got their **r**! Mt 6:2,5,16
survives, he will receive a **r**. 1Co 3:14
his attention was on the **r**. Heb 11:26

REWARD (V)
He exists and **r-s** those who seek Heb 11:6

RIB
God made the **r** ... into a woman Gn 2:22

RICH
Don't wear yourself out to get **r**; Pr 23:4
in a hurry to get **r** will not Pr 28:20
hard for a **r** person to enter Mt 19:23
woe to you who are **r**, Lk 6:24
who want to be **r** fall into 1Tm 6:9
r should boast in his humiliation Jms 1:10

RICHES
and you have not requested **r** 2Ch 1:11
in her left, **r** and honor. Pr 3:16
make known the **r** of His glory Rm 9:23
Oh, the depth of the **r** Rm 11:33
immeasurable **r** of His grace Eph 2:7

RIDDLE
directly, openly, and not in **r-s**; Nm 12:8
"Let me tell you a **r**," Samson said Jdg 14:12
words of the wise, and their **r-s**. Pr 1:6

RIDE
humble and **r-ing** on a donkey, Zch 9:9

RIDER
horse and its **r** into the sea. Ex 15:1,21

RIGHT (ADJ)
So You are **r** when You pass Ps 51:4
Sit at My **r** hand until I make Ps 110:1
way that seems **r** to a man, Pr 14:12; 16:25
one on Your **r** and the other on Mt 20:21
Sit at My **r** hand until I put Mt 22:44
He will put the sheep on His **r** Mt 25:33
He also is at the **r** hand of God Rm 8:34
Sit at My **r** hand until I make Heb 1:13
sat down at the **r** hand of God. Heb 10:12

RIGHT (N)
Defend the **r-s** of the fatherless. Is 1:17
gave them the **r** to be children Jn 1:12

RIGHTEOUS (ADJ)
no one alive is **r** in Your sight. Ps 143:2
raise up a **R** Branch of David. Jr 23:5
But the **r** one will live by his faith. Hab 2:4
Joseph, being a **r** man, and not Mt 1:19
saying, "This man really was **r**!" Lk 23:47
the coming of the **R** One, Ac 7:52
is no one **r**, not even one. Rm 3:10
But My **r** one will live by faith; Heb 10:38
Jesus Christ the **R** One. 1Jn 2:1

RIGHTEOUS (N)
watches over the way of the **r** Ps 1:6
I have not seen the **r** abandoned Ps 37:25
The **r** will never be shaken, Pr 10:30
the **r** run to it and are protected. Pr 18:10
sends rain on the **r** and the Mt 5:45
I didn't come to call the **r** Mt 9:13
The **r** will live by faith. Rm 1:17
because the **r** will live by faith. Gl 3:11

RIGHTEOUSLY
He will judge the world **r** Ps 98:9

RIGHTEOUSNESS
He credited it to him as **r**. Gn 15:6
He judges the world with **r**; Ps 9:8
His **r** endures forever. Ps 111:3; 112:3
R exalts a nation, but sin is Pr 14:34
will be named: Yahweh Our **R**. Jr 23:6
hunger and thirst for **r** are blessed, Mt 5:6
kingdom of God and His **r**, Mt 6:33
apart from the law, God's **r** has Rm 3:21
it was credited to him for **r**. Rm 4:3
end of the law for **r** to everyone Rm 10:4
His **r** endures forever. 2Co 9:9
r like armor on your chest, Eph 6:14
reserved for me ... the crown of **r**, 2Tm 4:8
was credited to him for **r** Jms 2:23

RING
is like a gold **r** in a pig's snout. Pr 11:22

RISE
From the **r-ing** of the sun to its Ps 113:3
After three days I will **r** again. Mt 27:63
A great prophet has **r-n** among us, Lk 7:16
that Jesus died and **rose** again, 1Th 4:14
dead in Christ will **r** first. 1Th 4:16

RIVALRY
that there is **r** among you. 1Co 1:11
proclaim Christ out of **r** Php 1:17
Do nothing out of **r** or conceit, Php 2:3

RIVER
There is a **r**—its streams Ps 46:4
By the **r-s** of Babylon—there we Ps 137:1
make peace flow to her like a **r**, Is 66:12
were baptized by him in the Jordan **R** Mt 3:6
showed me the **r** of living water Rv 22:1

ROAD
r is broad that leads to destruction, Mt 7:13

ROAR
though its waters **r** and foam Ps 46:3
The LORD **r-s** from heaven; Jr 25:30
The LORD will **r** from Zion and Jl 3:16

ROARING (ADJ)
prowling around like a **r** lion, 1Pt 5:8

ROAST
they should eat it, **r-ed** over the fire Ex 12:8
A lazy man doesn't **r** his game, Pr 12:27

ROB
to meet a bear **r-bed** of her cubs Pr 17:12
Will a man **r** God? Yet you are Mal 3:8

ROBBER
this house ... become a den of **r-s** Jr 7:11
and fell into the hands of **r-s**. Lk 10:30

ROBE
and he made a **r** of many colors Gn 37:3
cut off the corner of Saul's **r**. 1Sm 24:4
and His **r** filled the temple. Is 6:1
If I can just touch His **r**, Mt 9:21
and his **r** was as white as snow. Mt 28:3
crown of thorns and the purple **r**. Jn 19:5
they will be changed like a **r**. Heb 1:12
He wore a **r** stained with blood, Rv 19:13

ROBED (V)
He is **r** in majesty; Ps 93:1

ROCK
when you hit the **r**, water will Ex 17:6
will put you in the crevice of the **r** Ex 33:22
and struck the **r** twice with his Nm 20:11
The LORD is my **r**, Ps 18:2
LORD, my **r** and my Redeemer. Ps 19:14
and set my feet on a **r**, Ps 40:2
and a **r** to trip over, Is 8:14
who built his house on the **r**. Mt 7:24
on this **r** I will build My church, Mt 16:18
Other seed fell on the **r**; Lk 8:6
and a **r** to trip over, Rm 9:33
drank from a spiritual **r** that followed them, and that **r** was Christ. 1Co 10:4
and a **r** to trip over. 1Pt 2:8

ROCKY
Others fell on **r** ground, where Mt 13:5

ROD
break them with a **r** of iron; Ps 2:9
Your **r** and Your staff—they Ps 23:4
not use the **r** hates his son, Pr 13:24
beat him with a **r**, he will not die. Pr 23:13

ROLL
The skies will **r** up like a scroll, Is 34:4
Who will **r** away the stone from Mk 16:3
very large—had been **r-ed** away. Mk 16:4

ROMAN
Tell me—are you a **R** citizen? Ac 22:27

ROME
Italian city, capital of the Roman Empire; represented at Pentecost (Ac 2:10); Jews expelled (18:2); Paul addressed a letter to the church there (Rm 1:7,15) and goes there (Ac 19:21; 23:11; 28:14-16; 2Tm 1:17).

ROOF
From the **r** he saw a woman 2Sm 11:2
went up on the **r** and lowered him Lk 5:19

ROOM
you pray, go into your private **r**, Mt 6:6
there was no **r** for them at the Lk 2:7

ROOSTER
before the **r** crows, you will Mt 26:34

ROOT
On that day the **r** of Jesse will Is 11:10
and like a **r** out of dry ground. Is 53:2
they had no **r**, they withered. Mt 13:6
And if the **r** is holy, so are the Rm 11:16
The **r** of Jesse will appear, Rm 15:12
r-ed and firmly established Eph 3:17
r-ed and built up in Him and Col 2:7
of money is a **r** of all kinds 1Tm 6:10
and that no **r** of bitterness Heb 12:15
of Judah, the **R** of David, Rv 5:5

ROUGH
and the **r** places, a plain. Is 40:4
straight, the **r** ways smooth, Lk 3:5

ROYAL
if you keep the **r** law prescribed Jms 2:8
a chosen race, a **r** priesthood, a 1Pt 2:9

RUIN (N)
his lips invites his own **r**. Pr 13:3
My house still lies in **r-s** Hg 1:9
desires, which plunge people into **r** 1Tm 6:9
leads to the **r** of the hearers. 2Tm 2:14

RUIN (V)
Woe is me for I am **r-ed** Is 6:5
and the skins are **r-ed**. Mt 9:17

RULE (N)
when He abolishes all **r** and all 1Co 15:24
he competes according to the **r-s**. 2Tm 2:5

RULE (V)
They will **r** the fish of the sea Gn 1:26
He **r-s** forever by His might; Ps 66:7
For sin will not **r** over you, Rm 6:14

RULER
and the **r-s** conspire together against Ps 2:2
One will come from you to be **r** Mc 5:2
know that the **r-s** of the Gentiles Mt 20:25
Now the **r** of this world will be Jn 12:31
death or life, angels or **r-s**, Rm 8:38
but against the **r-s**, against Eph 6:12
Remind them to be submissive to **r-s** Ti 3:1

RUMOR
to hear of wars and **r-s** of wars. Mt 24:6

RUN
His word **r-s** swiftly. Ps 147:15
righteous **r** to it and are protected. Pr 18:10
they will **r** and not grow weary; Is 40:31
R in such a way to win the prize. 1Co 9:24
not be **r-ning**, or have **r** ... in vain. Gl 2:2
You were **r-ning** well. Gl 5:7
Let us **r** with endurance the race Heb 12:1

RUNNER
the **r-s** in a stadium all race, but 1Co 9:24

RUSH
sound ... of a violent **r-ing** wind Ac 2:2

RUST
where moth and **r** destroy and Mt 6:19

RUTH
Moabitess; widowed daughter-in-law of Naomi (Ru 1:1-5); married Boaz; ancestor of David and Christ (4:1; Mt 1:5-6,16).

RUTHLESSLY
They worked the Israelites **r** Ex 1:13

SABBATH
Remember the **S** day to keep it Ex 20:8
through the grainfields on the **S**. Mt 12:1
The **S** was made for man and not Mk 2:27
Son of Man is Lord even of the **S**. Mk 2:28
whether He would heal him on the **S**. Mk 3:2
lawful on the **S** to do what is good Mk 3:4
a **S** rest remains for God's people Heb 4:9

SACKCLOTH
with fasting, **s**, and ashes. Dn 9:3
proclaimed a fast and dressed in **s** Jnh 3:5
would have repented in **s** and ashes Mt 11:21

SACRED
you have known the **s** Scriptures, 2Tm 3:15

SACRIFICE
is the Passover **s** to the LORD, Ex 12:27
to obey is better than **s**, 1Sm 15:22
You do not delight in **s** and offering; Ps 40:6
You do not want a **s**, or I would Ps 51:16
The **s** pleasing to God is a broken Ps 51:17
For I desire loyalty and not **s**, Hs 6:6
I desire mercy and not **s**. Mt 9:13
your bodies as a living **s**, Rm 12:1
our Passover has been **s-d**. 1Co 5:7
an acceptable **s**, pleasing to God. Php 4:18
need to offer **s-s** every day, Heb 7:27
of sin by the **s** of Himself. Heb 9:26
offer up to God a **s** of praise, Heb 13:15
offer spiritual **s-s** acceptable to 1Pt 2:5

SADDUCEES
of the yeast of the Pharisees and **S**. Mt 16:6
S, who say there is no resurrection Mt 22:23

SAD-FACED
don't be **s** like the hypocrites. Mt 6:16

SAFETY
The horse is a false hope for **s**; Ps 33:17

SAINT
intercedes for the **s-s** according Rm 8:27
His inheritance among the **s-s**, Eph 1:18
Greet every **s** in Christ Jesus. Php 4:21
to the **s-s** once for all. Jd 3
are the prayers of the **s-s**. Rv 5:8
the righteous acts of the **s-s**. Rv 19:8

SAKE
right paths for His name's **s**. Ps 23:3
not for your **s** that I will act Ezk 36:22,32

SALOME
Wife of Zebedee, mother of James and John (Mk 15:40; 16:1; cp. Mt 27:56); possibly Mary's sister (Jn 19:25).

SALT
back and became a pillar of **s**. Gn 19:26
It is a permanent covenant of **s** Nm 18:19
You are the **s** of the earth. Mt 5:13
seasoned with **s**, so that you may Col 4:6

SALVATION
Stand firm and see the LORD's **s** Ex 14:13
He has become my **s**. Ex 15:2
Proclaim His **s** from day to day. 1Ch 16:23
The God of my **s** is exalted. Ps 18:46
The LORD is my light and my **s** Ps 27:1
Restore the joy of Your **s** to me, Ps 51:12
He has become my **s**. Ps 118:14
who proclaims **s**, who says to Is 52:7
For my eyes have seen Your **s**. Lk 2:30
everyone will see the **s** of God. Lk 3:6
There is **s** in no one else, Ac 4:12
now is the day of **s**. 2Co 6:2
the helmet of **s**, and the sword Eph 6:17
work out your own **s** with fear Php 2:12
if we neglect such a great **s**? Heb 2:3
S belongs to our God, who is Rv 7:10

SAMARIA
Capital and namesake of the northern kingdom (1Kg 13:32; 16:24; 2Kg 17:24; Is 7:9; Ezk 16:46; 23:4; Hs 8:5; Ob 19; Mc 1:1); captured by Assyria (2Kg 17:6).

In NT times, region of central hill country between Judah and Galilee (Lk 17:11; Ac 1:8; 8:1,5,14), often shunned by Jews (Jn 4:4-9); home of Samaritans.

SAMARITAN
But a **S** on his journey came up Lk 10:33
thanking Him. And he was a **S**. Lk 17:16
Jews do not associate with **S-s**. Jn 4:9

SAME
Jesus Christ is the **s** yesterday, Heb 13:8

SAMSON
Son of Manoah; Danite judge. Birth announced; to be a Nazirite (Jdg 13). Rashly married a Philistine; posed a riddle (Jdg 14). Took revenge on Philistines: set fire to fields; killed 1,000 with donkey's jawbone (Jdg 15). Married Delilah; was betrayed (16:4-21). Slaughter in Dagon's temple (16:23-30; Heb 11:32-34).

SAMUEL
Son of Elkanah and Hannah; Ephraimite judge, kingmaker, priest, and prophet. Born in answer to prayer (1Sm 1:1-20); raised at Shiloh by Eli (1:25-28; 2:11); called (3:1-18). Served as military and judicial judge (1Sm 7). Warned people about the nature of a king (8:10-18; 10:25); anointed Saul (10:1); rejected Saul (13:11-14; 15:10-29). Anointed David (16:1-13); protected David from Saul (19:18-24). Death (25:1); appearance to Saul after death (28:3-19).

SANCTIFICATION
which results in **s** Rm 6:19,22
For this is God's will, your **s**: 1Th 4:3

SANCTIFY
S them by the truth; Jn 17:17
washed, you were **s-ied**, you were 1Co 6:11
the God of peace Himself **s** you 1Th 5:23

SANCTUARY
They are to make a **s** for Me Ex 25:8
up my hands toward Your holy **s**. Ps 28:2
Praise God in His **s**. Ps 150:1
and will set My **s** among them Ezk 37:26
Destroy this **s**, and I will raise Jn 2:19

that you are God's **s** 1Co 3:16
your body is a **s** of the Holy 1Co 6:19
not enter a **s** made with hands Heb 9:24
Almighty and the Lamb are its **s**. Rv 21:22

SAND

offspring like the **s** of the sea, Gn 32:12
who built his house on the **s**. Mt 7:26

SANDAL

Remove the **s-s** from your feet, Ex 3:5
Remove the **s-s** from your feet, Jos 5:15
not worthy to remove His **s-s**. Mt 3:11

SARAH

Wife and half sister of Abraham; originally named Sarai (Gn 11:29-31; 20:12); barren (11:30). Twice passed off as Abraham's sister (12:10-20; 20). Gave Hagar to Abraham, then sent her away (Gn 16; 21:9-21). Laughed when she heard the promise of a son (18:9-15). Bore Isaac (21:1-7; Heb 11:11). Died; buried at Machpelah (Gn 23; 25:10; 49:31).

SATAN

Lord asked **S**, "Where have you Jb 1:7
Jesus told him, "Go away, **S**! Mt 4:10
If **S** drives out **S**, he is divided Mt 12:26
told Peter, "Get behind Me, **S**! Mt 16:23
I watched **S** fall from heaven Lk 10:18
Then **S** entered Judas, called Lk 22:3
and from the power of **S** to God, Ac 26:18
S disguises himself as an angel 2Co 11:14
messenger of **S** to torment me so 2Co 12:7
synagogue of **S** Rv 2:9; 3:9
who is called the Devil and **S**, Rv 12:9
S will be released from his Rv 20:7

SATISFY

your wages on what does not **s**? Is 55:2

SAUL

1. First King of united Israel. Son of Kish; tall, handsome Benjaminite (1Sm 9:1-2). Met Samuel while looking for donkeys (9:3-27). Anointed privately (10:1); chosen by lot and announced publicly (10:17-24); delivered Jabesh-gilead (11:1-11); confirmed king at Gilgal (11:12-15). Rebuked and rejected (13:8-15; 15:11-30). Attempted to kill David (18:11,17,25; 19:10-17; 23:8,25; 24:2; 26:2); spared by David (1Sm 24; 26). Among the prophets (10:9-13; 19:18-24). Consulted a medium to inquire of Samuel (1Sm 28). Killed by Philistines (1Sm 31).
2. Paul's Hebrew name. *see* PAUL

SAVE

and I was **s-d** from my enemies. Ps 18:3
and **s** those stumbling toward Pr 24:11
Turn to Me and be **s-d**, all the ends Is 45:22
on the name of Yahweh will be **s-d**, Jl 2:32
Jesus, because He will **s** His people Mt 1:21
whoever wants to **s** his life will Mt 16:25
asked, "Then who can be **s-d**?" Mt 19:25
and is baptized will be **s-d**, Mk 16:16
come to seek and to **s** the lost. Lk 19:10
world might be **s-d** through Him. Jn 3:17
name of the Lord will be **s-d**. Ac 2:21
Sirs, what must I do to be **s-d**? Ac 16:30
on name of the Lord will be **s-d**. Rm 10:13
you are **s-d** by grace through faith, Eph 2:8
came into the world to **s** sinners 1Tm 1:15
wants everyone to be **s-d** 1Tm 2:4

to this, now **s-s** you (not the 1Pt 3:21

SAVIOR

They forgot God their **S**, Ps 106:21
and there is no other **S** but Me. Is 43:11
and no **S** exists besides Me. Hs 13:4
a **S**, who is Messiah the Lord, Lk 2:11
God, who is the **S** of everyone, 1Tm 4:10
appearing of our **S** Christ Jesus, 2Tm 1:10
glory of our great God and **S**, Ti 2:13
of our Lord and **S** Jesus Christ. 2Pt 3:18

SAY

who do you **s** that I am? Mt 16:15

SCALE

Dishonest **s-s** are detestable Pr 11:1
something like **s-s** fell from his Ac 9:18
had a set of **s-s** in his hand. Rv 6:5

SCARLET

Though your sins are like **s**, Is 1:18
dressed Him in a **s** military robe. Mt 27:28

SCATTER

sheep of the flock will be **s-ed**. Mt 26:31
A man **s-s** seed on the ground; Mk 4:26

SCEPTER

s will not depart from Judah Gn 49:10

SCOFFERS

S will come in the last days to 2Pt 3:3

SCORN

and **s-ed** the Rock of his salvation. Dt 32:15
s-ed by men and despised by people. Ps 22:6

SCORPION

asks for an egg, will give him a **s**? Lk 11:12

SCOUT

Send men to **s** out the land Nm 13:2

SCRIBE

authority, and not like their **s-s**. Mt 7:29
woe to you, **s-s** and Pharisees, Mt 23:13

SCRIPTURE

don't know the **S-s** or the power Mt 22:29
Today ... this **S** has been fulfilled. Lk 4:21
concerning Himself in all the **S-s**. Lk 24:27
You pore over the **S-s** because you Jn 5:39
and the **S** cannot be broken Jn 10:35
you have known the sacred **S-s**, 2Tm 3:15
All **S** is inspired by God and is 2Tm 3:16
No prophecy of **S** comes from one's 2Pt 1:20

SCROLL

Eat this **s**, then go and speak to Ezk 3:1
open the **s** and break its seals? Rv 5:2

SEA

through the **s** on dry ground, Ex 14:22
the winds and the **s** obey Him! Mt 8:27
toward them walking on the **s**. Mt 14:25
Something like a **s** of glass, Rv 4:6

SEAL (N)

Set me as a **s** on your heart, Sg 8:6
the scroll and break its **s-s**?" Rv 5:2

SEAL (V)

s the book until the time of the end. Dn 12:4
He has also **s-ed** us and given us 2Co 1:22

also **s-ed** with the promised Holy Eph 1:13
s-ed with seven seals. Rv 5:1
s the slaves ... on their foreheads. Rv 7:3

SEARCH

You have **s-ed** me and known me. Ps 139:1
S me, God, and know my heart; Ps 139:23
Me when you **s** for Me with all Jr 29:13
Keep **s-ing**, and you will find. Mt 7:7
And He who **s-es** the hearts knows Rm 8:27
for the Spirit **s-es** everything, 1Co 2:10

SEASON

that bears its fruit in **s** Ps 1:3
days, months, **s-s**, and years. Gl 4:10
About the times and the **s-s**: 1Th 5:1

SEASONED

be gracious, **s** with salt, so Col 4:6

SEAT (N)

Make a mercy **s** of pure gold, Ex 25:17
love the front **s** in the Lk 11:43

SEAT (V)

I saw the Lord **s-ed** on a high and Is 6:1
s-ed at the right hand of the Mt 26:64
us up and **s-ed** us in the heavens, Eph 2:6

SECOND

The **s** is like it: Love your Mt 22:39
This is the **s** death, the lake of Rv 20:14

SECRET

He knows the **s-s** of the heart? Ps 44:21
Father who sees in **s** will reward you. Mt 6:4
things kept **s** from the Mt 13:35
judges what people have kept **s**, Rm 2:16
The **s-s** of his heart will be 1Co 14:25
I have learned the **s** of being Php 4:12

SECRETLY

decided to divorce her **s**. Mt 1:19
but **s** because of his fear of the Jn 19:38

SECURE

anchor for our lives, safe and **s**. Heb 6:19

SEE

no one can **s** Me and live. Ex 33:20
They say, "The Lord doesn't **s** it. Ps 94:7
they might **s** with their eyes Is 6:10
darkness have **s-n** a great light, Mt 4:16
blessed, for they will **s** God. Mt 5:8
because looking they do not **s**, Mt 13:13
No one has ever **s-n** God. Jn 1:18
I was blind, and now I can **s**! Jn 9:25
who has **s-n** Me has **s-n** the Father. Jn 14:9
what we have **s-n** with our eyes, 1Jn 1:1
because we will **s** Him as He is. 1Jn 3:2

SEED

and between your **s** and her **s**. Gn 3:15
who sowed good **s** in his field. Mt 13:24
like a mustard **s** that a man took Mt 13:31
faith the size of a mustard **s**, Mt 17:20
Other **s** fell on the rock; Lk 8:6
He does not say "and to **s-s**," Gl 3:16
not of perishable **s** but of 1Pt 1:23

SEEK

when you **s** Him with all your Dt 4:29
If you **s** Him, He will be found 1Ch 28:9
pray and **s** My face, and turn 2Ch 7:14
s peace and pursue it. Ps 34:14

S the Lord while He may be found; Is 55:6
But s first the kingdom of God Mt 6:33
come to s and to save the lost. Lk 19:10
No one should s his own good, 1Co 10:24
and rewards those who s Him. Heb 11:6

SEEM
a way that s-s right to a man Pr 14:12; 16:25

SEIZE
Then they tried to s Him. Jn 7:30

SELF
put off the old s with its Col 3:9
For people will be lovers of s, 2Tm 3:2

SELF-CONTROL
you because of your lack of s. 1Co 7:5
gentleness, s. Against such Gl 5:23
knowledge with s, s with endurance, 2Pt 1:6

SELF-CONTROLLED
sensible, righteous, holy, s, Ti 1:8

SELF-INDULGENCE
not of any value in curbing s. Col 2:23

SELFISH
is not s, is not provoked, 1Co 13:5
of anger, s ambitions, slander 2Co 12:20
envy and s ambition Jms 3:14,16

SELL
and do not s—truth, wisdom Pr 23:23
You were **sold** for nothing, and you Is 52:3
joy he goes and s-s everything Mt 13:44
s all you have and give to the poor Mk 10:21
sold his birthright in exchange Heb 12:16
one can buy or s unless he has Rv 13:17

SEND
I AM has **sent** me to you. Ex 3:14
Who should I s? ... Here I am. S me. Is 6:8
of the harvest to s out workers Mt 9:38
sent out these 12 after giving Mt 10:5
Me welcomes Him who **sent** Me. Mt 10:40
has **sent** Me to proclaim freedom Lk 4:18
For God did not s His Son into Jn 3:17
the will of Him who **sent** Me. Jn 5:30; 6:38
If I go, I will s Him to you. Jn 16:7
Father has **sent** Me, I also s you. Jn 20:21
they preach unless they are **sent**? Rm 10:15
God **sent** His Son, born of a woman, Gl 4:4
He loved us and **sent** His Son to be 1Jn 4:10

SENSE
who commits adultery lacks s; Pr 6:32

SENSIBLE
who accepts correction is s. Pr 15:5
were foolish and five were s. Mt 25:2

SEPARATE (ADJ)
out from among them and be s, 2Co 6:17

SEPARATE (V)
and a gossip s-s close friends. Pr 16:28
joined together, man must not s. Mt 19:6
just as a shepherd s-s the sheep Mt 25:32
Who can s us from the love of Rm 8:35

SEPARATION
as far as the s of soul and spirit, Heb 4:12

SERIOUS
but we must stay awake and be s. 1Th 5:6
Be s! Be on the alert! 1Pt 5:8

SERPENT
Now the s was the most cunning Gn 3:1
as shrewd as s-s and as harmless Mt 10:16
as the s deceived Eve by his 2Co 11:3
the ancient s, who is called Rv 12:9

SERVANT
Speak, for Your s is listening. 1Sm 3:10
Give praise, you s-s of Yahweh Ps 135:1
This is My S; I strengthen Him, Is 42:1
See, My S will act wisely; Is 52:13
Here is My S whom I have chosen Mt 12:18
great among you must be your s, Mt 20:26
he must be last of all and s of all. Mk 9:35
Where I am, there My s also will be Jn 12:26

SERVE
S the Lord with gladness; Ps 100:2
did not come to be s-d, but to s, Mt 20:28
am among you as the One who s-s. Lk 22:27
but s one another through love. Gl 5:13
S with a good attitude, Eph 6:7

SERVICE
if s, in s; if teaching, in teaching; Rm 12:7

SET
S apart for Me Barnabas and Saul Ac 13:2
instrument, s apart, useful to 2Tm 2:21

SEVEN
march around the city s times, Jos 6:4
will be s weeks and 62 weeks. Dn 9:25
forgive him? As many as s times? Mt 18:21
To the s churches in Asia. Rv 1:4
s angels with the s last plagues, Rv 15:1

SEVENTH
By the s day, God completed His Gn 2:2
the s day is a Sabbath to Yahweh Ex 20:10
And on the s day God rested from Heb 4:4

SEVENTY *SEE ALSO* 70
S weeks are decreed about your Dn 9:24
The S returned with joy, saying, Lk 10:17

SEVERE
and s treatment of the body, Col 2:23

SEW
so they s-ed fig leaves together Gn 3:7
No one s-s a patch of unshrunk Mk 2:21

SHADE
to provide s over Jonah's Jnh 4:6
birds of the sky can nest in its s. Mk 4:32

SHADOW
Our days on earth are like a s, 1Ch 29:15
hide me in the s of Your wings Ps 17:8
man walks about like a mere s. Ps 39:6
dwells in the s of the Almighty. Ps 91:1
in darkness and the s of death, Lk 1:79
least his s might fall on some Ac 5:15
as a copy and s of the heavenly Heb 8:5

SHAKE
established; it cannot be s-n. 1Ch 16:30
of the Lord s-s the wilderness; Ps 29:8
The righteous will never be s-n, Pr 10:30
s the dust off your feet when you Mt 10:14
pressed down, s-n together, Lk 6:38
where they were assembled was s-n, Ac 4:31
once more I will s not only the Heb 12:26

SHALLUM
1. King of Israel; assassinated Zechariah; was assassinated by Menahem (2Kg 15:10-15).
2. Alternate name for Jehoahaz (2Kg 23:30-34; Jr 22:11). *see* JEHOAHAZ

SHAME
were naked, yet felt no s. Gn 2:25
hope in Me will not be put to s. Is 49:23
some to s and eternal contempt. Dn 12:2
on Him will not be put to s. Rm 9:33
what is foolish ... to s the wise, 1Co 1:27
their glory is in their s. Php 3:19
a cross and despised the s. Heb 12:2
in Him will never be put to s! 1Pt 2:6

SHAMEFUL
For it is s even to mention what Eph 5:12

SHAMELESS
Males committed s acts with males Rm 1:27

SHAMGAR
Judge; killed 600 Philistines with an oxgoad (Jdg 3:31; 5:6).

SHAPHAN
Josiah's court secretary or scribe (2Kg 22:3-14); his sons were friends of Jeremiah (Jr 26:24; 36:10; 39:14).

SHARE
S your master's joy! Mt 25:21
two shirts must s with someone Lk 3:11

SHARES
let me inherit two s of your spirit. 2Kg 2:9

SHARP
There was such a s disagreement Ac 15:39

SHARPEN
s-s iron, and one man s-s another. Pr 27:17

SHARPER
s than any double-edged sword, Heb 4:12

SHAVE
If I am s-d, my strength will leave Jdg 16:17
emissaries, s-d off half their 2Sm 10:4
for them to get their heads s-d. Ac 21:24
the same as having her head s-d. 1Co 11:5

SHEAF
shouts of joy, carrying his s-ves. Ps 126:6

SHEARER
a sheep silent before her s-s, Is 53:7
a lamb is silent before its s, Ac 8:32

SHEBA
Nation whose queen came to see Solomon (1Kg 10; 2Ch 9); also called Sabeans (Jb 1:15; Jl 3:8).

SHECHEM
1. City in the hill country of Ephraim. Simeon and Levi destroyed the city in revenge for the rape of Dinah (Gn 34); Joshua renewed the covenant there (Jos 24:1-28); served as

first capital of the Northern Kingdom (1Kg 12:25).
2. Son of Hamor; raped Dinah (Gn 34).

SHED
Whoever **s-s** man's blood, his blood Gn 9:6
My blood; it is **s** for you. Lk 22:20
without the **s-ding** of blood there Heb 9:22

SHEEP
hills like **s** without a shepherd. 1Kg 22:17
people, the **s** of His pasture. Ps 100:3
We all went astray like **s**; Is 53:6
and like a **s** silent before her Is 53:7
and the **s** will be scattered; Zch 13:7
like **s** without a shepherd. Mt 9:36
go to the lost **s** of the house of Mt 10:6
If a man has 100 **s**, and one Mt 18:12
separates the **s** from the goats. Mt 25:32
He calls his own **s** by name Jn 10:3
I lay down My life for the **s**. Jn 10:15
My **s** hear My voice, I know them, Jn 10:27
"Feed My **s**," Jesus said. Jn 21:17
was led like a **s** to the slaughter, Ac 8:32

SHEET
a large **s** coming down, Ac 10:11

SHELTER
under the **s** of Your wings. Ps 61:4

SHEOL
You will not abandon me to **S**; Ps 16:10
make my bed in **S**, You are there. Ps 139:8
Her house is the road to **S**, Pr 7:27
S and Abaddon lie open before Pr 15:11
have made an agreement with **S**; Is 28:15
S, where is your sting? Hs 13:14

SHEPHERD (N)
hills like sheep without a **s**. 1Kg 22:17
The LORD is my **s**; there is Ps 23:1
He protects His flock like a **s**; Is 40:11
prophesy against the **s-s** of Israel. Ezk 34:2
appoint over them a single **s**, Ezk 34:23
Strike the **s**, and the sheep will Zch 13:7
like sheep without a **s**. Mt 9:36
I will strike the **s**, and the sheep Mt 26:31
s-s were staying out in the fields Lk 2:8
I am the good **s**. The good **s** lays Jn 10:11
the great **S** of the sheep Heb 13:20
And when the chief **S** appears, 1Pt 5:4

SHEPHERD (V)
You will **s** My people Israel 2Sm 5:2
overseers, to **s** the church of God, Ac 20:28
S God's flock among you, not 1Pt 5:2

SHIELD
He is a **s** to all who take refuge 2Sm 22:31
LORD is my strength and my **s**; Ps 28:7
situation take the **s** of faith, Eph 6:16

SHINE
Yahweh make His face **s** on you Nm 6:25
Arise, **s**, for your light has Is 60:1
let your light **s** before men, Mt 5:16
righteous will **s** like the sun Mt 13:43
and His face **shone** like the sun. Mt 17:2
glory of the Lord **shone** around them, Lk 2:9
That light **s-s** in the darkness, Jn 1:5
and the Messiah will **s** on you. Eph 5:14

SHIPWRECK
Three times I was **s-ed**. 2Co 11:25
suffered the **s** of their faith. 1Tm 1:19

SHIRT
to sue you and take away your **s**, Mt 5:40

SHOOT
a **s** will grow from the stump Is 11:1

SHORE
daybreak came, Jesus stood on the **s**. Jn 21:4

SHORT
Is My hand too **s** to redeem? Is 50:2
the crowd, since he was a **s** man. Lk 19:3
sinned and fall **s** of the glory Rm 3:23

SHOULDERS
government will be on His **s**. Is 9:6

SHOUT
until the time I say, '**S**!' Then you Jos 6:10
S to the LORD, all the earth; Ps 98:4
S triumphantly to the LORD, Ps 100:1
they kept **s-ing**, "Crucify Him!" Mt 27:23
descend from heaven with a **s**, 1Th 4:16

SHOW
for they will be **s-n** mercy. Mt 5:7
make long prayers just for **s**. Mt 23:14
He **s-ed** them His hands and feet. Lk 24:40
s us the Father, and that's enough Jn 14:8
s mercy to whom I will **s** mercy, Rm 9:15
And I will **s** you an even better 1Co 12:31
S me your faith without works, Jms 2:18

SHOWERS
s in ... season—**s** of blessing. Ezk 34:26

SHREWD
crooked You prove Yourself **s**. Ps 18:26
Therefore be as **s** as serpents Mt 10:16

SHUDDER
also believe—and they **s**. Jms 2:19

SHUT
and they have **s** their eyes; Mt 13:15
that every mouth may be **s** Rm 3:19

SICK
need a doctor, but the **s** do. Mt 9:12
I was **s** and you took care of Me; Mt 25:36
is why many are **s** and ill among 1Co 11:30
Is anyone among you **s**? Jms 5:14

SICKLE
Swing the **s** because the harvest Jl 3:13
and a sharp **s** in His hand. Rv 14:14

SICKNESS
He Himself bore our **s-es**, Is 53:4
healing every disease and every **s**. Mt 9:35

SIDE
Though a thousand fall at your **s** Ps 91:7
If the LORD had not been on our **s** Ps 124:1
pierced His **s** with a spear, Jn 19:34
showed them His hands and His **s**. Jn 20:20

SIFT
has asked to **s** you like wheat. Lk 22:31

SIGHT
The blind receive their **s**, Lk 7:22
For we walk by faith, not by **s** 2Co 5:7

SIGN
will give you a **s**: The virgin Is 7:14
demands a **s**, but no **s** will be given to it except the **s** of ... Jonah. Mt 12:39
s of Your coming and of the end Mt 24:3
This will be the **s** for you: Lk 2:12
this first **s** in Cana of Galilee Jn 2:11
Jesus performed many other **s-s** Jn 20:30
by granting that **s-s** and wonders Ac 14:3
Jews ask for **s-s** and the Greeks 1Co 1:22
languages is intended as a **s**, 1Co 14:22

SILAS
Early church leader and prophet; also called Silvanus. Brought news from Jerusalem to Antioch (Ac 15:22,32); worked with Paul and Peter in missions and writing letters (15:40-41; 16:19-40; 17:10-15; 18:5; 2Co 1:19; 1Th 1:1; 2Th 1:1; 1Pt 5:12).

SILENCE (N)
should learn in **s** with full 1Tm 2:11
there was **s** in heaven for about Rv 8:1

SILENCE (V)
that He had **s-d** the Sadducees, Mt 22:34
said to the sea, "**S**! Be still!" Mk 4:39

SILENT
If you keep **s** at this time, Est 4:14
When I kept **s**, my bones became Ps 32:3
considered wise when he keeps **s**, Pr 17:28
and like a sheep **s** before her Is 53:7
But Jesus kept **s**. Mt 26:63
and as a lamb is **s** before its Ac 8:32
women should be **s** in the 1Co 14:34
instead, she is to be **s**. 1Tm 2:12

SILOAM
Pool in Jerusalem (Jn 9:7,11).

SILVER
my instruction instead of **s**, Pr 8:10
like gold apples on a **s** tray. Pr 25:11
30 pieces of **s** for him. Mt 26:15
I don't have **s** or gold, but Ac 3:6

SIMEON
1. Son of Jacob and Leah (Gn 29:33); with Levi, avenged Dinah's rape by Shechem (34:25-31; 49:5); held as hostage by Joseph (42:24). Tribe with territory within Judah (Jos 19:1-9; Jdg 1:3,17).
2. Devout Jew who blessed the baby Jesus (Lk 2:25-35).
3. Jewish variation of Simon (Ac 15:14; 2Pt 1:1). *see* PETER

SIMON
1. Apostle Peter's original name (Mt 4:18). *see* PETER
2. Apostle; called the Zealot (Mt 10:4; Mk 3:18; Lk 6:15; Ac 1:13).
3. Leper who hosted Jesus (Mt 26:6-13).
4. Cyrenian forced to carry Jesus' cross (Mk 15:21).
5. Sorcerer who wanted to buy the power of the Spirit (Ac 8:9-24).
6. Tanner of Joppa who hosted Peter, where Peter saw the vision (Ac 9:43).

SIN (N)
be sure your **s** will catch up with Nm 32:23
forgive their **s**, and heal their land. 2Ch 7:14

and my **s** is always before me. Ps 51:3
He forgives all your **s**; Ps 103:3
but **s** is a disgrace to any people. Pr 14:34
yet He bore the **s** of many Is 53:12
authority on earth to forgive **s-s** Mt 9:6
forgive us our **s-s**, for we Lk 11:4
takes away the **s** of the world! Jn 1:29
The one without **s** among you Jn 8:7
just as **s** entered the world Rm 5:12
For the wages of **s** is death, Rm 6:23
Christ died for our **s-s** according to 1Co 15:3
who did not know **s** to be **s** for us, 2Co 5:21
way as we are, yet without **s**. Heb 4:15
weight and the **s** that so easily Heb 12:1
confess our **s-s**, He is faithful 1Jn 1:9
say, "We don't have any **s**," we 1Jn 1:10
s is the breaking of law. 1Jn 3:4

SIN (V)

You—You alone—I have **s-ned** Ps 51:4
so that I may not **s** against You. Ps 119:11
your right eye causes you to **s**, Mt 5:29
If your brother **s-s** against you, Mt 18:15
If your brother **s-s**, rebuke him, Lk 17:3
And if he **s-s** against you seven Lk 17:4
from now on do not **s** anymore. Jn 8:11
Rabbi, who **s-ned**, this man or Jn 9:2
For all have **s-ned** and fall short Rm 3:23
so that you may not **s**. 1Jn 2:1

SINAI

Mountain where God revealed the Law (Ex 19:20; 31:18; 34:32; Lv 25:1; Ac 7:38; Gl 4:25). The wilderness region (Ex 19:1; Lv 7:38).

SINCERE

for **s** love of the brothers, 1Pt 1:22

SINFUL

I was **s** when my mother conceived Ps 51:5
into the hands of **s** men, Lk 24:7

SING

I will **s** to the LORD, for He is Ex 15:1
S to the LORD, all the earth. 1Ch 16:23
the morning stars **sang** together Jb 38:7
S praise to God, **s** praise; Ps 47:6
S a new song to the LORD Ps 96:1; 98:1
After **s-ing** psalms, they went out Mt 26:30
praying and **s-ing** hymns to God, Ac 16:25
songs, **s-ing** and making music Eph 5:19
s-ing psalms, hymns, and spiritual Col 3:16
cheerful? He should **s** praises. Jms 5:13
they **sang** a new song: You are Rv 5:9

SINGED

not a hair of their heads was **s**, Dn 3:27

SINGER

S-s lead the way, with musicians Ps 68:25

SINK

I have **sunk** in deep mud, Ps 69:2
And beginning to **s** he cried out, Mt 14:30

SINNER

or take the path of **s-s** Ps 1:1
My son, if **s-s** entice you, don't Pr 1:10
Don't let your heart envy **s-s**; Pr 23:17
to call the righteous, but **s-s**. Mt 9:13
friend of tax collectors and **s-s**! Mt 11:19
Even **s-s** do that. Lk 6:33
in heaven over one **s** who repents Lk 15:7
while we were still **s-s**, Christ died Rm 5:8
came into the world to save **s-s** 1Tm 1:15

SISTER

say you're my **s** Gn 12:13
is My brother and **s** and mother. Mt 12:50
the younger women as **s-s**. 1Tm 5:2

SIT

the LORD **s-s** enthroned forever; Ps 9:7
S at My right hand until I make Ps 110:1
You know when I **s** down and when Ps 139:2
But to **s** at My right and left is Mt 20:23
into heaven and **sat** down at the Mk 16:19
S at My right hand until I make Heb 1:13

SIX

are to labor **s** days and do all Ex 20:9

SKILL

may my right hand forget its **s**. Ps 137:5

SKIN

clothing out of **s-s** for Adam and Gn 3:21
unclean; he has a **s** disease. Lv 13:8
Naaman ... had a **s** disease. 2Kg 5:1
"S for **s**!" Satan answered Jb 2:4
Even after my **s** has been destroyed Jb 19:26
Can the Cushite change his **s**, Jr 13:23
a man with a serious **s** disease came Mt 8:2
Otherwise, the **s-s** burst, Mt 9:17
cleanse those with **s** diseases, Mt 10:8
Simon who had a serious **s** disease, Mk 14:3

SKULL

Golgotha (which means S Place), Mt 27:33

SKY

God called the expanse "**s**." Gn 1:8
good weather because the **s** is red. Mt 16:2
Son of Man will appear in the **s**, Mt 24:30
the **s** separated like a scroll Rv 6:14

SLACKER

Go to the ant, you **s**! Pr 6:6
by the field of a **s** and by the Pr 24:30

SLANDER (N)

and whoever spreads **s** is a fool. Pr 10:18
hypocrisy, envy, and all **s**. 1Pt 2:1

SLANDER (V)

who does not **s** with his tongue, Ps 15:3
are **s-ed**, we respond graciously. 1Co 4:13
to **s** no one, to avoid fighting, Ti 3:2

SLANDERER

worthy of respect, not **s-s**, 1Tm 3:11
behavior, not **s-s**, not addicted Ti 2:3

SLANDEROUSLY

as some people **s** claim we say, Rm 3:8

SLAP

if anyone **s-s** you on your right Mt 5:39

SLAUGHTER

are counted as sheep to be **s-ed**. Ps 44:22
save those stumbling toward **s**. Pr 24:11
Like a lamb led to the **s** Is 53:7
was led like a sheep to the **s**, Ac 8:32
are counted as sheep to be **s-ed**. Rm 8:36
The Lamb who was **s-ed** is worthy Rv 5:12

SLAVE

Remember that you were a **s** in Dt 5:15
borrower is a **s** to the lender. Pr 22:7
No one can be a **s** of two masters Mt 6:24
to my **s**, 'Do this!' and he does it. Mt 8:9
first among you must be your **s**; Mt 20:27
Well done, good and faithful **s**! Mt 25:21
"I am the Lord's **s**," said Mary. Lk 1:38
s-s; we've only done our duty. Lk 17:10
who commits sin is a **s** of sin. Jn 8:34
I do not call you **s-s** anymore,
because a **s** doesn't know what Jn 15:15
you used to be **s-s** of sin, Rm 6:17
no Jew or Greek, **s** or free, male Gl 3:28
by assuming the form of a **s**, Php 2:7
As God's **s-s**, live as free 1Pt 2:16

SLAVERY

out of Egypt, out of the place of **s**, Ex 13:3
you did not receive a spirit of **s** Rm 8:15
don't submit again to a yoke of **s**. Gl 5:1

SLEEP (N)

God caused a deep **s** to come over Gn 2:21
A little **s**, a little slumber, Pr 6:10; 24:33

SLEEP (V)

of Israel does not slumber or **s**. Ps 121:4
the girl isn't dead, but **s-ing**. Mt 9:24
disciples and found them **s-ing**. Mt 26:40

SLEEPER

Get up, **s**, and rise up from the Eph 5:14

SLING

Philistine with a **s** and a stone. 1Sm 17:50

SLOW

s to anger and rich in faithful Ex 34:6
to hear, **s** to speak, and **s** to anger, Jms 1:19

SLUMBER

your Protector will not **s**. Ps 121:3
A little sleep, a little **s**, Pr 6:10; 24:33

SMALL

Four things on earth are **s**, Pr 30:24
faithful in a very **s** matter, Lk 19:17

SMALLEST

It's the **s** of all the seeds, Mt 13:32

SMOKE

Sinai was ... enveloped in **s** Ex 19:18
the temple was filled with **s**. Is 6:4

SMOLDERING

He will not put out a **s** wick; Is 42:3
He will not put out a **s** wick, Mt 12:20

SMOOTH

S lips with an evil heart are Pr 26:23
the uneven ground will become **s** Is 40:4
straight, the rough ways **s**, Lk 3:5

SNAKE

the ground, and it became a **s**. Ex 4:3
made a bronze **s** and mounted it Nm 21:9
In the end it bites like a **s** Pr 23:32
for a fish, will give him a **s**? Mt 7:10
they will pick up **s-s**; Mk 16:18
the authority to trample on **s-s** Lk 10:19
as Moses lifted up the **s** in the Jn 3:14

SNARE

their gods, it will be a **s** for you. Ex 23:33
the **s-s** of death confronted me. 2Sm 22:6

will keep your foot from a **s**. Pr 3:26
The fear of man is a **s**, Pr 29:25

SNATCH
one comes and **s-es** away what was Mt 13:19
No one will **s** them out of My Jn 10:28

SNOUT
like a gold ring in a pig's **s**. Pr 11:22

SNOW
and I will be whiter than **s**. Ps 51:7
they will be as white as **s**; Is 1:18
and his robe was as white as **s**. Mt 28:3

SNUGLY
she wrapped Him **s** in cloth and Lk 2:7

SOAR
s-ing on the wings of the wind. Ps 18:10
will **s** on wings like eagles; Is 40:31

SODOM
City on the plain, where Lot settled (Gn 10:19; 13:10; 14:11-12); destroyed along with Gomorrah by God (Gn 18:20; 19:24).

SOIL
quickly since the **s** wasn't deep. Mt 13:5

SOLDIER
The **s-s** also mocked Him. Lk 23:36
No one serving as a **s** gets entangled 2Tm 2:4

SOLID
gave you milk to drink, not **s** food, 1Co 3:2
But **s** food is for the mature Heb 5:14

SOLOMON
Son of David and Bathsheba; third king of Israel (2Sm 12:24; 1Kg 1:30-40). Asked for wisdom (3:5-15); knew many proverbs and songs (4:32; Pss 72; 127; Pr 1:1; 10:1; 25:1; Sg 1:1); wisdom demonstrated in child dispute (1Kg 3:16-28) and the visit of the Queen of Sheba (10:1-13). Built and dedicated the temple (1Kg 5–8). Accumulated vast wealth (9:26-28; 10:26-29); had many wives and concubines, who influenced him toward idolatry (11:1-8).

SON *SEE ALSO* SON OF DAVID, SON OF GOD, SON OF MAN, SONS OF GOD
"Take your **s**," He said, "your only Gn 22:2
and he will be a **s** to Me. 2Sm 7:14
My **s** Absalom! My **s**, my **s** 2Sm 18:33
He said to Me, "You are My **S**; Ps 2:7
are all **s-s** of the Most High. Ps 82:6
S-s are indeed a heritage from Ps 127:3
The virgin will conceive, have a **s**, Is 7:14
born for us, a **s** will be given to us, Is 9:6
be called: **S-s** of the living God. Hs 1:10
and out of Egypt I called My **s**. Hs 11:1
Out of Egypt I called My **S**. Mt 2:15
beloved **S**. I take delight in Him! Mt 3:17
how then can the Messiah be his **S**? Mt 22:45
This man really was God's **S**! Mt 27:54
called the **S** of the Most High, Lk 1:32
you will be **s-s** of the Most High. Lk 6:35
longer worthy to be called your **s**. Lk 15:19
He gave His One and Only **S**, Jn 3:16
believes in the **S** has eternal life, Jn 3:36
by God's Spirit are God's **s-s**. Rm 8:14
conformed to the image of His **S**, Rm 8:29
He did not even spare His own **S** Rm 8:32
will be called **s-s** of the living Rm 9:26
you will be **s-s** and daughters 2Co 6:18
slave but a **s**, and if a **s**, then an heir Gl 4:7
He has spoken to us by His **S**. Heb 1:2
that addresses you as **s-s**: Heb 12:5
One and Only **S** into the world 1Jn 4:9
loved us and sent His **S** to be 1Jn 4:10
The one who has the **S** has life. 1Jn 5:12

SON OF DAVID
Have mercy on us, **S**! Mt 9:27
Perhaps this is the **S**! Mt 12:23
Hosanna to the **S**! Mt 21:9

SON OF GOD
If You are the **S**, come down Mt 27:40
will be called the **S**. Lk 1:35
Are You, then, the **S**? Lk 22:70
that He is the **S**! Jn 1:34
of the One and Only **S**. Jn 3:18
I believe that Jesus Christ is the **S**. Ac 8:37
declared to be the powerful **S** by Rm 1:4
confesses that Jesus is the **S** 1Jn 4:15
one who believes that Jesus is the **S**? 1Jn 5:5

SON OF MAN
s that You look after him? Ps 8:4
He said to me, "**S**, Ezk 2:1
I saw One like a **s** coming Dn 7:13
S has no place to lay His Mt 8:20
S coming in His kingdom. Mt 16:28
so will be the coming of the **S**. Mt 24:27
When the **S** comes in His glory, Mt 25:31
see the **S** seated at the right hand Mk 14:62
so the **S** must be lifted up, Jn 3:14
Who is this **S**? Jn 12:34
S standing at the right hand of God! Ac 7:56
One like the **S** was seated on Rv 14:14

SONG
The Lord is my strength and my **s**; Ex 15:2
Sing a new **s** to Him; Ps 33:3
He put a new **s** in my mouth, Ps 40:3
psalms, hymns, and spiritual **s-s**, Eph 5:19
psalms, hymns, and spiritual **s-s**, Col 3:16
the **s** of the Lamb: Rv 15:3

SONS OF GOD
the **s** saw that the daughters of man Gn 6:2
peacemakers ... will be called **s**. Mt 5:9
you are all **s** through faith in Christ Gl 3:26

SORCERER
But Elymas the **s** ... opposed them Ac 13:8

SORCERY
interpret omens, practice **s**, Dt 18:10
idolatry, **s**, hatreds, strife, Gl 5:20

SORROW
For with much wisdom is much **s**; Ec 1:18
and **s** and sighing will flee. Is 35:10; 51:11
My soul is swallowed up in **s** Mt 26:38
but your **s** will turn to joy. Jn 16:20
I have intense **s** and continual Rm 9:2

SOUL
with all your **s**, and with all strength. Dt 6:5
to destroy both **s** and body in hell. Mt 10:28
with all your **s**, and with all Mt 22:37
My **s** is swallowed up in sorrow Mt 26:38
a sword will pierce your own **s** Lk 2:35
Now My **s** is troubled. Jn 12:27
separation of **s** and spirit, joints Heb 4:12
the salvation of your **s-s**. 1Pt 1:9
Shepherd and Guardian of your **s-s**. 1Pt 2:25

SOUND (N)
if the trumpet makes an unclear **s**, 1Co 14:8
voice like the **s** of cascading waters. Rv 1:15

SOUND (V)
s the alarm on My holy mountain! Jl 2:1
the trumpet will **s**, and the dead 1Co 15:52

SOUR
The fathers have eaten **s** grapes, Jr 31:29
The fathers eat **s** grapes, and Ezk 18:2

SOURCE
You killed the **s** of life, Ac 3:15
s and perfecter of our faith, Heb 12:2

SOVEREIGN
He is the blessed and only **S**, 1Tm 6:15

SOW
those who **s** trouble reap the same. Jb 4:8
Those who **s** in tears will reap Ps 126:5
who **s-s** injustice will reap disaster, Pr 22:8
They don't **s** or reap or gather Mt 6:26
As he was **s-ing**, some seeds fell Mt 13:4
a man who **s-ed** good seed Mt 13:24
One **s-s** and another reaps. Jn 4:37
we have **sown** spiritual things 1Co 9:11
Sown in corruption, raised in 1Co 15:42
person who **s-s** sparingly will 2Co 9:6
whatever a man **s-s** he will also Gl 6:7

SOWER
Consider the **s** who went out to Mt 13:3
The **s** sows the word. Mk 4:14

SPARE
He did not even **s** His own Son Rm 8:32
if God didn't **s** the angels who 2Pt 2:4

SPARINGLY
person who sows **s** will also reap **s**, 2Co 9:6

SPARROW
are worth more than many **s-s**. Mt 10:31

SPEAK
He **spoke**, and it came into being; Ps 33:9
to be silent and a time to **s**; Ec 3:7
the mouth of the Lord has **spoken**. Is 40:5
worry about ... what you should **s**. Mt 10:19
We **s** what We know Jn 3:11
began to **s** in different languages, Ac 2:4
If I **s** human or angelic languages 1Co 13:1
was a child, I **spoke** like a child, 1Co 13:11
But **s-ing** the truth in love, let Eph 4:15
He has **spoken** to us by His Son. Heb 1:2
instead, men **spoke** from God 2Pt 1:21

SPEAR
their **s-s** into pruning knives. Is 2:4; Mc 4:3
your pruning knives into **s-s**. Jl 3:10
pierced His side with a **s**, Jn 19:34

SPECK
the **s** in your brother's eye Mt 7:3

SPECTACLE
We have become a **s** to the world 1Co 4:9

SPEECH
I am slow and hesitant in **s**. Ex 4:10
Day after day they pour out **s**; Ps 19:2
There is no **s**; there are no words; Ps 19:3
s should always be gracious, Col 4:6

SPEND
gladly **s** and be **spent** for you. 2Co 12:15

SPICES
cloths with the aromatic **s**, Jn 19:40

SPIN
They don't labor or **s** Mt 6:28; Lk 12:27

SPIRIT *SEE ALSO* HOLY SPIRIT, SPIRIT OF GOD, SPIRIT OF THE LORD
My S will not remain with mankind Gn 6:3
an evil **s** sent from the LORD 1Sm 16:14
Into Your hand I entrust my **s**; Ps 31:5
renew a steadfast **s** within me. Ps 51:10
or take Your Holy S from me. Ps 51:11
pleasing to God is a broken **s**. Ps 51:17
Where can I go to escape Your S? Ps 139:7
Who knows if the **s** of people rises Ec 3:21
the **s** returns to God who gave Ec 12:7
I have put My S on Him; Is 42:1
and put a new **s** within you; Ezk 36:26
pour out My S on all humanity Jl 2:28
but by My S,' says the LORD Zch 4:6
The poor in **s** are blessed, Mt 5:3
them authority over unclean **s-s**, Mt 10:1
I will put My S on Him, and He Mt 12:18
against the S will not be Mt 12:31
The **s** is willing, but the flesh Mt 26:41
open and the S descending to Him Mk 1:10
into Your hands I entrust My **s**. Lk 23:46
God is **s**, and those who worship Him must worship in **s** and truth. Jn 4:24
He is the S of truth. Jn 14:17
pour out My S on all humanity Ac 2:17
but the S of Jesus did not allow Ac 16:7
met us who had a **s** of prediction Ac 16:16
are not in the flesh, but in the S, Rm 8:9
testifies together with our **s** that we Rm 8:16
have the S as the firstfruits Rm 8:23
S ... joins to help in our weakness, Rm 8:26
different gifts, but the same S. 1Co 12:4
distinguishing between **s-s**, 1Co 12:10
the S as a down payment 2Co 1:22; 5:5
walk by the S and you will not Gl 5:16
There is one body and one S Eph 4:4
but be filled by the S: Eph 5:18
Don't stifle the S. 1Th 5:19
And may your **s**, soul, and body 1Th 5:23
separation of soul and **s**, joints Heb 4:12
proclamation to the **s-s** in prison 1Pt 3:19
not believe every **s**, but test the **s-s** 1Jn 4:1

SPIRIT OF GOD
S was hovering over the surface Gn 1:2
He saw the S descending like a dove Mt 3:16

SPIRIT OF THE LORD
S took control of David from that 1Sm 16:13
The S God is on Me, Is 61:1
S is on Me ... He has appointed Me Lk 4:18
where the S is, there is freedom. 2Co 3:17

SPIRITIST
not turn to mediums or consult **s-s**, Lv 19:31

SPIRITUAL
this is your **s** worship. Rm 12:1
explaining **s** things to **s** people. 1Co 2:13
a natural body, raised a **s** body. 1Co 15:44
who are **s** should restore such Gl 6:1
blessed us ... with every **s** blessing Eph 1:3
hymns, and **s** songs, Eph 5:19; Col 3:16
desire the pure **s** milk, 1Pt 2:2

SPIRITUALLY
since it is evaluated **s**. 1Co 2:14

SPIT
Then they **s** in His face and beat Mt 26:67
He **s** on the ground, made some mud Jn 9:6

SPLENDOR
S and majesty are before Him; 1Ch 16:27
Worship Yahweh in the **s** of Ps 29:2
are clothed with majesty and **s**. Ps 104:1
not even Solomon in all his **s** was Mt 6:29

SPLIT
He **s** the rock, and water gushed Is 48:21

SPOKESMAN
He will be your **s**, Ex 4:16

SPONGE
a **s** full of sour wine on hyssop Jn 19:29

SPOT
his skin, or a leopard his **s-s**? Jr 13:23
without **s** or wrinkle or anything Eph 5:27
with Him without **s** or blemish. 2Pt 3:14

SPRAWL
with ivory, **s-ed** out on their Am 6:4
of those who **s** out will come to Am 6:7

SPREAD
s-ing out the sky like a canopy, Ps 104:2
day long I have **s** out My hands Rm 10:21
message may **s** rapidly and 2Th 3:1

SPRING (N)
a gift ... from the **s** of life. Rv 21:6

SPRING (V)
S up, well—sing to it! Nm 21:17
they **sprang** up quickly since Mt 13:5
well of water **s-ing** up within him Jn 4:14

SPRINKLE
s it on all sides of the altar. Ex 29:16
so He will **s** many nations. Is 52:15
will also **s** clean water on you, Ezk 36:25
hearts **s-d** clean from an evil Heb 10:22
and to the **s-d** blood, which says Heb 12:24
s-ing with the blood of Jesus Christ. 1Pt 1:2

SPROUT
cause ... Branch to **s** up for David, Jr 33:15

SPY
secretly to **s** on the freedom we have Gl 2:4

SQUANDERED
he **s** his estate in foolish living. Lk 15:13

STAFF
threw down his **s** before Pharaoh Ex 7:10
s of the man I choose will sprout, Nm 17:5
rod and Your **s**—they comfort me. Ps 23:4
the manna, Aaron's **s** that budded, Heb 9:4

STAIRWAY
A **s** was set on the ground with Gn 28:12
the shadow ... on Ahaz's **s**. 2Kg 20:11

STAND
where you are **s-ing** is holy ground. Ex 3:5
place where you are **s-ing** is holy. Jos 5:15
And the sun **stood** still and Jos 10:13
s still, and see the salvation 2Ch 20:17
Who may **s** in His holy place? Ps 24:3
will be able to **s** when He appears? Mal 3:2
against itself, that house cannot **s**. Mk 3:25
into this grace in which we **s**, Rm 5:2
he **s-s** or falls. And **s** he will! For the Lord is able to make him **s**. Rm 14:4
thinks he **s-s** must be careful 1Co 10:12
so that you can **s** against the Eph 6:11
I **s** at the door and knock. Rv 3:20

STAR
God made ... as well as the **s-s**. Gn 1:16
numerous as the **s-s** of the sky Gn 22:17
the morning **s-s** sang together Jb 38:7
moon and the **s-s**, which You set Ps 8:3
we saw His **s** in the east Mt 2:2
you shine like **s-s** in the world. Php 2:15
of David, the Bright Morning S. Rv 22:16

STARTED
He who **s** a good work in you Php 1:6

STATURE
look at his appearance or his **s**, 1Sm 16:7
Jesus increased in wisdom and **s**, Lk 2:52

STAY
and **s** awake with Me. Mt 26:38

STEADFAST
me and renew a **s** spirit within Ps 51:10

STEAL
Do not **s**. Ex 20:15
or I might have nothing and **s**, Pr 30:9
where thieves break in and **s**. Mt 6:19
adultery; do not **s**; do not bear Mt 19:18
comes only to **s** and to kill and Jn 10:10
The thief must no longer **s**. Eph 4:28

STEP
but the LORD determines his **s-s**. Pr 16:9
you should follow in His **s-s**. 1Pt 2:21

STEPHEN
Foremost of the first seven deacons (Ac 6:1-7). First Christian martyr (6:8–7:60); Saul approved of his death (8:1; 22:20); start of persecution and dispersion (11:19).

STEWARDSHIP
I am entrusted with a **s**. 1Co 9:17

STIFLE
Don't **s** the Spirit. 1Th 5:19

STILL
reflect in your heart and be **s**. Ps 4:4
Silence! Be **s**!" The wind ceased Mk 4:39

STING
Sheol, where is your **s**? Hs 13:14
Death, where is your **s**? 1Co 15:55

STIR
but a harsh word **s-s** up wrath. Pr 15:1

My compassion is **s-red**! Hs 11:8
from time to time and **s** up the water. Jn 5:4

STOLEN
S water is sweet, Pr 9:17

STOMACH
passes into the **s** and is eliminated? Mt 15:17
Food for the **s** and the **s** for food, 1Co 6:13
their god is their **s**; Php 3:19
a little wine because of your **s** 1Tm 5:23

STONE (N)
s tablets inscribed by ... God. Ex 31:18
five smooth **s-s** from the wadi 1Sm 17:40
strike your foot against a **s**. Ps 91:12
The **s** that the builders rejected Ps 118:22
a time to throw **s-s** and a time to Ec 3:5
He will be a **s** to stumble over Is 8:14
I have laid a **s** in Zion, a tested **s**, Is 28:16
remove your heart of **s** and give Ezk 36:26
tell these **s-s** to become bread." Mt 4:3
strike your foot against a **s**. Mt 4:6
for bread, will give him a **s**? Mt 7:9
The **s** that the builders rejected Mt 21:42
Who will roll away the **s** from Mk 16:3
silent, the **s-s** would cry out! Lk 19:40
be the first to throw a **s** at her. Jn 8:7
stumbled over the stumbling **s**. Rm 9:32
not on **s** tablets but on tablets 2Co 3:3
to Him, a living **s**—rejected by 1Pt 2:4

STONE (V)
were **s-ing** Stephen as he called Ac 7:59

STORE
have anywhere to **s** my crops? Lk 12:17

STOREHOUSE
brings the wind from His **s-s**. Jr 10:13; 51:16
Bring the full tenth into the **s** Mal 3:10

STOREROOM
brings out of his **s** what is new and Mt 13:52

STORM
and shelter from **s** and rain. Is 4:6
such a violent **s** arose on the sea Jnh 1:4
a violent **s** arose on the sea, Mt 8:24

STRAIGHT
make a **s** highway for our God in Is 40:3
the crooked will become **s**, Lk 3:5
Make **s** the way of the Lord Jn 1:23

STRAIN
You **s** out a gnat, yet gulp down Mt 23:24

STRANGER
I was a **s** and you took Me in; Mt 25:35
no longer foreigners and **s-s**, Eph 2:19
I urge you as **s-s** 1Pt 2:11

STRANGLE
eating anything that has been **s-d**, Ac 15:20

STRAP
whose sandal **s** I'm not worthy to Jn 1:27

STRAW
go and gather **s** for themselves. Ex 5:7
costly stones, wood, hay, or **s**, 1Co 3:12

STREAM
planted beside **s-s** of water Ps 1:3
its **s-s** delight the city of God, Ps 46:4
s-s of living water flow from Jn 7:38

STREET
Wisdom calls out in the **s**; Pr 1:20
on the **s** corners to be seen by people. Mt 6:5
s of the city was pure gold, Rv 21:21

STRENGTH
The LORD is my **s** and my song; Ex 15:2
all your soul, and with all your **s**. Dt 6:5
does not prevail by his own **s**. 1Sm 2:9
I love You, LORD, my **s**. Ps 18:1
The LORD is my **s** and my shield; Ps 28:7
God is our refuge and **s**, a helper Ps 46:1
ascribe to the LORD glory and **s**. Ps 96:7
in the LORD will renew their **s**; Is 40:31
strong man must not boast in his **s**; Jr 9:23
Not by **s** or by might, but by My Zch 4:6
your mind, and with all your **s**. Mk 12:30

STRENGTHEN
have turned back, **s** your brothers. Lk 22:32
He will also **s** you to the end, 1Co 1:8
be **s-ed** by the Lord and by His Eph 6:10
things through Him who **s-s** me. Php 4:13
Lord who has **s-ed** me, 1Tm 1:12
Therefore **s** your tired hands Heb 12:12

STRICKEN
but we in turn regarded Him **s**, Is 53:4

STRIFE
a house full of feasting with **s**. Pr 17:1
there is envy and **s** among you, 1Co 3:3
sorcery, hatreds, **s**, jealousy, Gl 5:20

STRIKE
s your head, and you will **s** his heel. Gn 3:15
and **struck** the rock twice Nm 20:11
you will not **s** your foot against Ps 91:12
The sun will not **s** you by day Ps 121:6
S the shepherd, and the sheep will Zch 13:7
you will not **s** your foot against Mt 4:6
I will **s** the shepherd, and the Mt 26:31
struck down but not destroyed. 2Co 4:9

STRIP
They **s-ped** him, beat him up, Lk 10:30

STRIVE
Don't keep **s-ing** for Lk 12:29
s-ing with His strength that works Col 1:29

STROKE
or one **s** of a letter will pass from Mt 5:18
than for one **s** of a letter ... to drop Lk 16:17

STRONG
Be **s** and courageous; Dt 31:6
be **s** and very courageous Jos 1:7
LORD, **s** and mighty, the LORD, Ps 24:8
The name of Yahweh is a **s** tower; Pr 18:10
Redeemer is **s**, and He will take Pr 23:11
Their Redeemer is **s**; Yahweh Jr 50:34
can someone enter a **s** man's house Mt 12:29
The boy grew up and became **s**, Lk 2:40
Now we who are **s** have an Rm 15:1
For when I am weak, then I am **s**. 2Co 12:10

STRONGER
God's weakness is **s** than human 1Co 1:25

STRONGHOLD
David did capture the **s** of Zion, 2Sm 5:7
my salvation, my **s**, my refuge, 2Sm 22:3
the God of Jacob is our **s**. Ps 46:7,11
my rock and my salvation, my **s**; Ps 62:2,6
way of the LORD is a **s** for the Pr 10:29
for the demolition of **s-s**. 2Co 10:4

STRUGGLE
s-ing against sin, you have not Heb 12:4

STUBBORN
a **s** and rebellious generation, Ps 78:8

STUDY
and much **s** wearies the body. Ec 12:12
Too much **s** is driving you mad! Ac 26:24

STUMBLE
nothing makes them **s**. Ps 119:165
when you run, you will not **s**. Pr 4:12
be a stone to **s** over and a rock Is 8:14
cause one of these little ones to **s**. Lk 17:2
walks during the day, he doesn't **s**, Jn 11:9
They **s-d** over the **s-ing** stone. Rm 9:32
to cause **s-ing** by what he eats. Rm 14:20
We give no opportunity for **s-ing** 2Co 6:3
for we all **s** in many ways. Jms 3:2
A stone to **s** over, 1Pt 2:8
who is able to protect you from **s-ing** Jd 24

STUMBLING BLOCK
instead decide never to put a **s** Rm 14:13
Christ crucified, a **s** to the Jews 1Co 1:23
this right ... in no way becomes a **s** 1Co 8:9

STUMP
shoot will grow from the **s** of Jesse, Is 11:1

STUPID
one who hates correction is **s**. Pr 12:1

SUBDUE
fill the earth, and **s** it. Gn 1:28

SUBJECT
the creation was **s-ed** to futility Rm 8:20
when everything is **s** to Christ, 1Co 15:28
s-ed everything under his feet. Heb 2:8

SUBMISSION
learn in silence with full **s**. 1Tm 2:11

SUBMISSIVE
Wives, be **s** to your husbands, as Col 3:18
Remind them to be **s** to rulers Ti 3:1

SUBMIT
He **s-ted** Himself to death, Is 53:12
s to the governing authorities, Rm 13:1
don't **s** again to a yoke of slavery. Gl 5:1
Wives, **s** to your own husbands Eph 5:22
Why do you **s** to regulations: Col 2:20
Therefore, **s** to God. But resist Jms 4:7
S to every human authority 1Pt 2:13
s yourselves to your own husbands 1Pt 3:1

SUCCESS
He stores up **s** for the upright; Pr 2:7

SUDDENLY
you seek will **s** come to His temple, Mal 3:1

SUE
one who wants to **s** you and take Mt 5:40

SUEZ
LORD will divide the Gulf of **S**. Is 11:15

SUFFER
Son of Man must **s** many things Mk 8:31
Passover with you before I **s**. Lk 22:15
s these things and enter into His Lk 24:26
Messiah would **s** and rise from Lk 24:46
that His Messiah would **s** Ac 3:18
we **s** with Him so that we may Rm 8:17
one member **s-s**, all ... **s** with it; 1Co 12:26
share in **s-ing** for the gospel, 2Tm 1:8
obedience through what He **s-ed**. Heb 5:8
Is anyone among you **s-ing**? Jms 5:13
when you do what is good and **s**, 1Pt 2:20
Christ also **s-ed** for you, 1Pt 2:21
it is better to **s** for doing good, 1Pt 3:17
Christ also **s-ed** for sins once 1Pt 3:18

SUFFERING (N)
man of **s** who knew what sickness Is 53:3
the **s-s** of this present time are not Rm 8:18
the fellowship of His **s-s**, Php 3:10
share in the **s-s** of the Messiah 1Pt 4:13

SUFFICIENT
My grace is **s** for you, 2Co 12:9

SUMMER
it prepares its provisions in **s**; Pr 6:8
leaves, you know that **s** is near. Mt 24:32

SUN
And the **s** stood still Jos 10:13
the LORD God is a **s** and shield. Ps 84:11
s will not strike you by day Ps 121:6
there is nothing new under the **s**. Ec 1:9
The **s** will be turned to darkness Jl 2:31
the **s** of righteousness will rise Mal 4:2
For He causes His **s** to rise on Mt 5:45
The **s** will be darkened, Mt 24:29
Don't let the **s** go down on your Eph 4:26
His face was shining like the **s** Rv 1:16
not need the **s** or the moon to Rv 21:23

SUNLIGHT
will not need lamplight or **s**, Rv 22:5

SUNRISE
they went to the tomb at **s**. Mk 16:2

SUPERIOR
He inherited is **s** to theirs. Heb 1:4
inferior is blessed by the **s**. Heb 7:7

SUPPER
took the cup after **s** and said, Lk 22:20
after **s**, he also took the cup 1Co 11:25

SUPPLY
And my God will **s** all your needs Php 4:19

SUPPORT
but the LORD was my **s**. 2Sm 22:19

SUPPRESS
unrighteousness **s** the truth, Rm 1:18

SURE
be **s** your sin will catch up with Nm 32:23
cornerstone, a **s** foundation; Is 28:16

SURELY
to say to Him, "**S** not I, Lord?" Mt 26:22

SURPASS
capable, but you **s** them all! Pr 31:29
unless your righteousness **s-es** Mt 5:20
love that **s-es** knowledge, Eph 3:19
view of the **s-ing** value of knowing Php 3:8
peace of God, which **s-es** every Php 4:7

SURROUND
Many bulls **s** me; Ps 22:12
large cloud of witnesses **s-ing** us, Heb 12:1

SURVIVE
wicked will not **s** the judgment, Ps 1:5
were limited, no one would **s**. Mt 24:22
built **s-s**, he will receive a reward. 1Co 3:14

SURVIVOR
of Hosts had not left us a few **s-s**, Is 1:9

SUSTAIN
wake again because the LORD **s-s** me. Ps 3:5
establish and **s** it with justice Is 9:7
not **s** the root, but the root **s-s** you. Rm 11:18
s-ing all things by His powerful Heb 1:3

SUSTAINER
the Lord is the **s** of my life. Ps 54:4

SWALLOW
My soul is **s-ed** up in sorrow Mt 26:38
has been **s-ed** up in victory. 1Co 15:54

SWEAR
By Myself I have **sworn**, Gn 22:16
swore in My anger, "They will not Ps 95:11
LORD **swore** an oath to David, Ps 132:11
Neither should you **s** by your head, Mt 5:36
swore in My anger, "They will not Heb 3:11
to **s** by, He **swore** by Himself: Heb 6:13
Lord has **sworn**, and He will not Heb 7:21
brothers, do not **s**, either by Jms 5:12

SWEAT
eat bread by the **s** of your brow Gn 3:19
His **s** became like drops of blood Lk 22:44

SWEEP
vacant, **swept**, and put in order. Mt 12:44
not light a lamp, **s** the house, Lk 15:8

SWEET
How **s** Your word is to my taste Ps 119:103
Stolen water is **s**, Pr 9:17
it was as **s** as honey in my mouth. Ezk 3:3
Does a spring pour out **s** and bitter Jms 3:11

SWIFT
that the race is not to the **s**, Ec 9:11
Their feet are **s** to shed blood; Rm 3:15

SWINDLER
or **s-s** will inherit God's kingdom. 1Co 6:10

SWORD
whirling **s** east of the garden of Gn 3:24
not by **s** ... that the LORD saves, 1Sm 17:47
Nations will not take up the **s** against Is 2:4
Beat your plows into **s-s** Jl 3:10
will beat their **s-s** into plows, Mc 4:3
come to bring peace, but a **s**. Mt 10:34
who take up a **s** will perish by a **s**. Mt 26:52
a **s** will pierce your own soul Lk 2:35
does not carry the **s** for no reason. Rm 13:4
and the **s** of the Spirit, Eph 6:17
sharper than any double-edged **s**, Heb 4:12
a **s** came from His mouth, Rv 1:16

SYCAMORE
he climbed up a **s** tree to see Lk 19:4

SYMBOL
a **s** on your forehead Ex 13:16; Dt 6:8
should have a **s** of authority 1Co 11:10

SYMPATHIZE
a high priest who is unable to **s** Heb 4:15

SYNAGOGUE
teaching in their **s-s**, preaching Mt 4:23
He entered the **s** on the Sabbath Lk 4:16
They will ban you from the **s-s**. Jn 16:2
taught in the **s** and in the temple Jn 18:20
reasoned in the **s** every Sabbath Ac 18:4
but are a **s** of Satan. Rv 2:9

TABERNACLE
the pattern of the **t** Ex 25:9
glory of the LORD filled the **t**. Ex 40:34
I will make three **t-s** here: Mt 17:4
Jewish Festival of **T-s** was near, Jn 7:2
more perfect **t** not made with Heb 9:11

TABLE
construct a **t** of acacia wood, Ex 25:23
You prepare a **t** before me in the Ps 23:5
overturned the money changers' **t-s** Mt 21:12
and drink at My **t** in My kingdom. Lk 22:30
the Lord's **t** and the **t** of demons. 1Co 10:21

TABLET
that I may give you the stone **t-s** Ex 24:12
them on the **t** of your heart. Pr 3:3; 7:3
engraved on the **t** of their hearts Jr 17:1
not on stone **t-s** but on **t-s** 2Co 3:3

TACTICS
against the **t** of the Devil. Eph 6:11

TAKE
or **t** Your Holy Spirit from me. Ps 51:11
t up My yoke and learn from Me, Mt 11:29
deny himself, **t** up his cross, Mt 16:24
one will be **taken** and one left. Mt 24:40
T and eat it; this is My body. Mt 26:26
who **t-s** away the sin of the world! Jn 1:29
they've **taken** away my Lord, Jn 20:13
t up the full armor of God, Eph 6:13

TALENTS
To one he gave five **t**; Mt 25:15

TALK
T about them when you sit in Dt 6:7

TALL
He was nine feet, nine inches **t** 1Sm 17:4

TAMAR
1. Judah's daughter-in-law; widow of Er and Onan; mother of Judah's sons (Gn 38).
2. Daughter of David; raped by Amnon; avenged by Absalom (2Sm 13).

TAMBOURINE
Praise Him with **t** and dance; Ps 150:4

TARSHISH
Distant Mediterranean port city known for sea trade (1Kg 10:22; 22:48; Ps 48:7; 72:10; Is 2:16; 23:1,6,10,14; 66:19; Jr 10:9; Ezk

THISTLES
produce thorns and **t** for you, Gn 3:18

THOMAS
Apostle; sought evidence of resurrection; made confession of faith (Jn 20:24-29).

THORN
It will produce **t-s** and thistles Gn 3:18
fell among **t-s**, and the **t-s** came up Mt 13:7
twisted together a crown of **t-s**, Mt 27:29
t in the flesh was given to me, 2Co 12:7

THOUGHT
The LORD knows man's **t-s**; Ps 94:11
You understand my **t-s** from far Ps 139:2
My **t-s** are not your **t-s**, Is 55:8
But perceiving their **t-s**, Jesus said, Mt 9:4
a child, I **t** like a child, 1Co 13:11
taking every **t** captive to obey 2Co 10:5

THOUSAND *SEE ALSO* 1,000
his **t-s**, but David his tens of **t-s**. 1Sm 18:7
the cattle on a **t** hills. Ps 50:10
in Your sight a **t** years are like Ps 90:4
one day is like a **t** years, 2Pt 3:8

THREATEN
He was suffering, He did not **t** 1Pt 2:23

THREE
cord of **t** strands is not easily Ec 4:12
the huge fish **t** days and **t** nights, Mt 12:40
For where two or **t** are gathered Mt 18:20
you will deny Me **t** times! Mt 26:34
and rebuild it in **t** days. Mt 26:61
killed, and rise after **t** days. Mk 8:31
Now these **t** remain: faith, hope, 1Co 13:13
For there are **t** that testify: 1Jn 5:7

THRESHING FLOOR
David bought the **t** 2Sm 24:24

THROAT
their **t** is an open grave; Ps 5:9
Their **t** is an open grave; Rm 3:13

THRONE
will establish the **t** of his kingdom 2Sm 7:13
Your **t**, God, is forever and ever; Ps 45:6
seated on a high and lofty **t**, Is 6:1
He will reign on the **t** of David Is 9:7
Heaven is My **t**, and earth is My Is 66:1
heaven, because it is God's **t**; Mt 5:34
will also sit on 12 **t-s**, judging Mt 19:28
whether **t-s** or dominions or Col 1:16
Your **t**, God, is forever and Heb 1:8
let us approach the **t** of grace with Heb 4:16
cast their crowns before the **t**, Rv 4:10
great white **t** and One seated on it. Rv 20:11

THROW
He has **t-n** the horse and its rider Ex 15:1
should be the first to **t** a stone at her. Jn 8:7

THUNDERCLOUD
I answered you from the **t**. Ps 81:7

TIME
for such a **t** as this. Est 4:14
a **t** for every activity under heaven: Ec 3:1
for a **t**, **t-s**, and half a **t**. Dn 7:25; 12:7
Teacher says: My **t** is near; Mt 26:18
you will deny Me three **t-s**! Mt 26:34
My **t** has not yet arrived, Jn 7:6
It is not for you to know **t-s** Ac 1:7
making the most of the **t**. Col 4:5
About the **t-s** and the seasons: 1Th 5:1
was fed for a **t**, **t-s**, and half a **t**. Rv 12:14

TIMOTHY
Companion of Paul (Ac 16–20; Rm 16:21; 2Co 1:1; 1Th 1:1; 2Th 1:1; Php 1:1; Phm 1). Sent by Paul to Corinth (1Co 4:17); to Philippi (Php 2:19); to Thessalonica (1Th 3:2). Pastored Ephesian church (1Tm 1:3). Received two letters from Paul (1Tm 1:2; 2Tm 1:2) and a plea to come (4:9).

TIRED
must not get **t** of doing good, Gl 6:9

TITUS
Gentile coworker with Paul (2Co 8:23; Gl 2:1-3). Sent to Corinth (2Co 7:13-15; 8:16-17); in charge of church in Crete (Ti 1:5); went to Dalmatia (2Tm 4:10).

TOBIAH
Adversary against Nehemiah's efforts to rebuild Jerusalem's walls (Neh 2:10,19; 4:1-9; 6; 13:4-9).

TODAY
T, if you hear His voice: Ps 95:7
Give us **t** our daily bread. Mt 6:11
T you will be with Me in paradise. Lk 23:43
t I have become Your Father, Heb 1:5; 5:5
while it is still called **t**, Heb 3:13
T, if you hear His voice, do not Heb 3:15
same yesterday, **t**, and forever. Heb 13:8

TOLA
Issacharite judge (Jdg 10:1-2).

TOLERABLE
It will be more **t** on the day of Mt 10:15

TOLERATE
they will not **t** sound doctrine, 2Tm 4:3
and that you cannot **t** evil. Rv 2:2

TOMB
You are like whitewashed **t-s**, Mt 23:27
he placed Him in a **t** cut out of Mk 15:46
stone rolled away from the **t**. Lk 24:2
already been in the **t** four days. Jn 11:17

TOMORROW
Don't boast about **t**, for you don't Pr 27:1
Let us eat and drink, for **t** we die! Is 22:13
Therefore don't worry about **t**, Mt 6:34
us eat and drink, for **t** we die. 1Co 15:32
don't even know what **t** will bring Jms 4:14

TONGUE
Before a word is on my **t**, You Ps 139:4
death are in the power of the **t**, Pr 18:21
every **t** will swear allegiance. Is 45:23
And **t-s**, like flames of fire that Ac 2:3
and every **t** should confess that Php 2:11
but no man can tame the **t**. Jms 3:8

TOOTH
for eye, **t** for **t** Ex 21:24; Lv 24:20; Dt 19:21
for an eye and a **t** for a **t**. Mt 5:38
weeping and gnashing of **teeth**. Mt 8:12

TOP
split in two from **t** to bottom; Mt 27:51

TORCH
fire pot and a flaming **t** appeared Gn 15:17

TORMENT
come here to **t** us before the time? Mt 8:29
those **t-ed** by unclean spirits Lk 6:18
they will be **t-ed** day and night Rv 20:10

TORRENT
the **t** would have swept over us; Ps 124:4

TOSS
driven and **t-ed** by the wind. Jms 1:6

TOUCH
You must not eat it or **t** it, Gn 3:3
t-ed my mouth with it and said: Is 6:7
If I can just **t** His robe, Mt 9:21
to Him so He might **t** them, Mk 10:13
T Me and see, because a ghost Lk 24:39
Don't handle, don't taste, don't **t** Col 2:21
and have **t-ed** with our hands, 1Jn 1:1

TOWEL
took a **t**, and tied it around Himself. Jn 13:4

TOWER
a **t** with its top in the sky. Gn 11:4
name of Yahweh is a strong **t**; Pr 18:10

TOWN
and from the **t** of Bethlehem, Jn 7:42

TRADERS
When Midianite **t** passed by, Gn 37:28

TRADITION
You revoke God's word by your **t** Mk 7:13
empty deceit based on human **t**, Col 2:8
hold to the **t-s** you were taught 2Th 2:15

TRAGEDY
a sickening **t** Ec 5:13,16
here is a **t** I have observed Ec 6:1

TRAIN
who **t-s** my hands for battle and Ps 144:1
will never again **t** for war. Is 2:4; Mc 4:3

TRAINING
them up in the **t** and instruction Eph 6:4
t of the body has a limited benefit, 1Tm 4:8
correcting, for **t** in righteousness, 2Tm 3:16

TRAITOR
Judas Iscariot, who became a **t**. Lk 6:16

TRAMPLE
be thrown out and **t-d** on by men. Mt 5:13
pearls before pigs, or they will **t** Mt 7:6
Jerusalem will be **t-d** by the Lk 21:24
who has **t-d** on the Son of God, Heb 10:29

TRAMPLING (N)
you—this **t** of My courts? Is 1:12

TRANSFORM
He was **t-ed** in front of them, Mt 17:2
be **t-ed** by the renewing of your Rm 12:2
are being **t-ed** into the same image 2Co 3:18
He will **t** the body of our humble Php 3:21

TRANSGRESSION
is the one whose **t** is forgiven, Ps 32:1
has He removed our **t-s** from us. Ps 103:12

VINDICATE
wisdom is **v-d** by all her children. Lk 7:35

VINE
I am the true **v**, and My Father Jn 15:1

VINEGAR
thirst they gave me **v** to drink. Ps 69:21

VINEYARD
to hire workers for his **v**. Mt 20:1
who planted a **v**, put a fence Mt 21:33
and My Father is the **v** keeper. Jn 15:1

VIOLENCE
although He had done no **v** Is 53:9
of heaven has been suffering **v**, Mt 11:12

VIOLENT
and the **v** have been seizing it Mt 11:12

VIPER
he said to them, "Brood of **v-s**! Mt 3:7
Snakes! Brood of **v-s**! How can Mt 23:33

VIRGIN
The **v** will conceive, have a son, Is 7:14
the **v** will become pregnant and Mt 1:23
be like 10 **v-s** who took their Mt 25:1
The **v-'s** name was Mary. Lk 1:27

VISIBLE
man sees what is **v**, but the LORD 1Sm 16:7
made from things that are not **v**. Heb 11:3

VISION
and your young men will see **v-s**. Jl 2:28
your young men will see **v-s**, Ac 2:17
move on to **v-s** and revelations 2Co 12:1

VISIT
was in prison and you **v-ed** Me. Mt 25:36
God has **v-ed** His people. Lk 7:16

VIVIDLY
Jesus Christ was **v** portrayed as Gl 3:1

VOICE
after the fire there was a **v**, a soft 1Kg 19:12
Today, if you hear His **v**: Ps 95:7
A **v** of one crying out: Is 40:3
A **v** was heard in Ramah, a lament Jr 31:15
A **v** was heard in Ramah, weeping, Mt 2:18
And there came a **v** from heaven: Mt 3:17
and the sheep hear his **v**. Jn 10:3
Then a **v** came from heaven: Jn 12:28
Their **v** has gone out to all the Rm 10:18
Today, if you hear His **v**, Heb 3:7,15; 4:7
If anyone hears My **v** and opens Rv 3:20

VOMIT (N)
As a dog returns to its **v**, Pr 26:11
A dog returns to its own **v**, 2Pt 2:22

VOMIT (V)
I am going to **v** you out of My Rv 3:16

VOW (N)
makes a special **v**, a Nazirite **v**, Nm 6:2
Jephthah made this **v** to the LORD: Jdg 11:30
I will fulfill my **v-s** before those Ps 22:25
and later to reconsider his **v-s**. Pr 20:25

VOW (V)
Fulfill what you **v**. Ec 5:4

WAGE
the worker is worthy of his **w-s**. Lk 10:7
For the **w-s** of sin is death, Rm 6:23
the worker is worthy of his **w-s**. 1Tm 5:18

WAIST
a leather belt around his **w**, Mt 3:4

WAIT
W for the LORD; be strong Ps 27:14
creation eagerly **w-s** with Rm 8:19
we eagerly **w** for it with patience. Rm 8:25
as you eagerly **w** for the revelation 1Co 1:7
to **w** for His Son from heaven, 1Th 1:10

WALK
Enoch **w-ed** with God; then he was Gn 5:24
they will **w** and not faint. Is 40:31
and to **w** humbly with your God. Mc 6:8
or to say, 'Get up and **w**'? Mt 9:5
saw Him **w-ing** on the sea, Mt 14:26
pick up your mat and **w**! Jn 5:8
we too may **w** in a new way of life. Rm 6:4
we **w** by faith, not by sight 2Co 5:7
w by the Spirit and you will not Gl 5:16
W as children of light Eph 5:8
But if we **w** in the light as He 1Jn 1:7

WALL
shout, and the **w** collapsed. Jos 6:20
let's rebuild Jerusalem's **w**, Neh 2:17
down the dividing **w** of hostility. Eph 2:14
By faith the **w-s** of Jericho fell Heb 11:30

WANDER
have **w-ed** away from the faith 1Tm 6:10

WANDERER
will be a restless **w** on the earth. Gn 4:12

WAR
makes **w-s** cease throughout the Ps 46:9
a time for **w** and a time for Ec 3:8
will never again train for **w**. Is 2:4
hear of **w-s** and rumors of **w-s**. Mt 24:6
do not wage **w** in an unspiritual 2Co 10:3

WARFARE
weapons of our **w** are not worldly 2Co 10:4

WARM
lie down together, they can keep **w**; Ec 4:11

WARN
if you **w** a wicked person Ezk 3:19; 33:9
And being **w-ed** in a dream Mt 2:12,22
Who **w-ed** you to flee from the Mt 3:7
were written as a **w-ing** to us, 1Co 10:11
w-ing and teaching everyone with Col 1:28

WARRIOR
LORD is a **w**; Yahweh is His name. Ex 15:3

WASH
Go **w** seven times in the Jordan 2Kg 5:10
w me, and I will be whiter than Ps 51:7
they don't **w** their hands when Mt 15:2
began to **w** His feet with her tears. Lk 7:38
began to **w** His disciples' feet Jn 13:5
and **w** away your sins by calling Ac 22:16
But you were **w-ed**, you were 1Co 6:11
the **w-ing** of water by the word. Eph 5:26
Blessed ... who **w** their robes, Rv 22:14

WASTE
Why has this fragrant oil been **w-d**? Mk 14:4
my labor for you has been **w-d**. Gl 4:11

WATCH (N)
keeping **w** at night over their flock. Lk 2:8
for they keep **w** over your souls Heb 13:17

WATCH (V)
the LORD **w-es** over the way of Ps 1:6
unless the LORD **w-es** over a city, Ps 127:1
W! Be alert! For you don't know Mk 13:33

WATCHMAN
the **w** stays alert in vain. Ps 127:1
more than **w-men** for the morning Ps 130:6
I have made you a **w** Ezk 3:17; 33:7

WATER (N)
w covered the earth. Gn 7:6
I am poured out like **w**, Ps 22:14
He leads me beside quiet **w-s**. Ps 23:2
bread on the surface of the **w-s**, Ec 11:1
who is thirsty, come to the **w-s**; Is 55:1
abandoned ... fountain of living **w**, Jr 2:13
will also sprinkle clean **w** on you, Ezk 36:25
that day living **w** will flow out Zch 14:8
I baptize you with **w** for repentance, Mt 3:11
a cup of cold **w** to one of these Mt 10:42
Peter started walking on the **w** Mt 14:29
is born of **w** and the Spirit, Jn 3:5
and He would give you living **w**. Jn 4:10
of living **w** flow from deep Jn 7:38
the washing of **w** by the word. Eph 5:26
the One who came by **w** and blood, 1Jn 5:6
I will give **w** as a gift to the thirsty Rv 21:6

WATER (V)
I planted, Apollos **w-ed**, but God 1Co 3:6

WATERFALLS
calls to deep in the roar of Your **w**; Ps 42:7

WAVER
He did not **w** in unbelief at God's Rm 4:20
of our hope without **w-ing**, Heb 10:23

WAVES
was being swamped by the **w**. Mt 8:24
even the winds and the **w**, Lk 8:25

WAX
my heart is like **w**, melting within Ps 22:14

WAY
God—His **w** is perfect; 2Sm 22:31
watches over the **w** of the righteous Ps 1:6
Commit your **w** to the LORD; Ps 37:5
can a young man keep his **w** pure? Ps 119:9
See if there is any offensive **w** in me;
lead me in the everlasting **w**. Ps 139:24
There is a **w** that seems right Pr 14:12
youth about the **w** he should go; Pr 22:6
Prepare the **w** of the LORD in the Is 40:3
we all have turned to our own **w**; Is 53:6
and your **w-s** are not My **w-s**. Is 55:8
Prepare the **w** for the Lord; Mt 3:3
God loved the world in this **w**: Jn 3:16
I am the **w**, the truth, and the life. Jn 14:6
found any ... who belonged to the **W** Ac 9:2
will also provide a **w** of escape 1Co 10:13
will show you an even better **w**. 1Co 12:31

WEAK
spirit is willing, but the flesh is **w**. Mt 26:41

Accept anyone who is **w** in faith, Rm 14:1
God has chosen ... what is **w** 1Co 1:27
For when I am **w**, then I am 2Co 12:10

WEAKER
understanding of their **w** nature 1Pt 3:7

WEAKNESS
took our **w-es** and carried our Mt 8:17
also joins to help in our **w**, Rm 8:26
sown in **w**, raised in power; 1Co 15:43
for power is perfected in **w**. 2Co 12:9
to sympathize with our **w-es** Heb 4:15

WEALTH
They trust in their **w** Ps 49:6
W is not profitable on a day of Pr 11:4
Give me neither poverty nor **w**; Pr 30:8
wealthy man must not boast in his **w**. Jr 9:23
seduction of **w** choke the word, Mt 13:22
hard it is for those who have **w** to Mk 10:23

WEAPON
No **w** formed against you will Is 54:17
the **w-s** of our warfare are not 2Co 10:4

WEAR
about your body, what you will **w**. Mt 6:25
and the **w-ing** of gold ornaments 1Pt 3:3

WEARISOME
All things are **w**; man is unable Ec 1:8

WEARY
they will run and not grow **w**; Is 40:31
Come to Me, all of you who are **w** Mt 11:28
do not grow **w** in doing good. 2Th 3:13

WEDDING
Can the **w** guests be sad while Mt 9:15
get in here without **w** clothes?' Mt 22:12
a **w** took place in Cana of Galilee. Jn 2:1

WEEDS
w among the wheat, Mt 13:25

WEEK
Observe the Festival of **W-s** Ex 34:22
Seventy **w-s** are decreed Dn 9:24
first day of the **w** was dawning, Mt 28:1

WEEP (WEPT)
W-ing may spend the night, but Ps 30:5
wept when we remembered Zion. Ps 137:1
a time to **w** and a time to laugh; Ec 3:4
Rachel **w-ing** for her children, Jr 31:15
Rachel **w-ing** for her children; Mt 2:18
there will be **w-ing** and gnashing Mt 8:12
Jesus **wept**. Jn 11:35
who rejoice; **w** with those who **w**. Rm 12:15

WEIGH
you have been **w-ed** in the balance Dn 5:27

WEIGHT
honest balances, honest **w-s**, Lv 19:36
incomparable eternal **w** of glory. 2Co 4:17
lay aside every **w** and the sin that Heb 12:1

WELCOME
whoever **w-s** one child like this Mt 18:5

WELFARE
plans for your **w**, not for disaster, Jr 29:11

WELL
and I know this very **w**. Ps 139:14
master said to him, '**W** done, Mt 25:21

WENT *SEE* GO

WEST
far as the east is from the **w**, Ps 103:12

WHATEVER
W you ask in My name, I will do Jn 14:13
brothers, **w** is true, **w** is honorable, Php 4:8

WHEAT
sowed weeds among the **w**, Mt 13:25
has asked to sift you like **w**. Lk 22:31
Unless a grain of **w** falls to Jn 12:24

WHEEL
was like a **w** within a **w**. Ezk 1:16

WHIPPED
I will have Him **w** and Lk 23:16

WHIRLWIND
Elijah up to heaven in a **w**. 2Kg 2:1
LORD answered Job from the **w**. Jb 38:1
sow the wind and reap the **w**. Hs 8:7

WHISPER
there was a voice, a soft **w**. 1Kg 19:12
What you hear in a **w**, proclaim Mt 10:27

WHITE
scarlet, they will be as **w** as snow; Is 1:18
make a single hair **w** or black. Mt 5:36
and his robe was as **w** as snow. Mt 28:3
head and hair were **w** like wool Rv 1:14
I saw a great **w** throne and One Rv 20:11

WHITER
and I will be **w** than snow. Ps 51:7

WHITEWASH
You are like **w-ed** tombs, Mt 23:27

WHO
w do you say that I am? Mt 16:15

WHOLE
if he gains the **w** world yet loses Mt 16:26

WICK
will not put out a smoldering **w**; Is 42:3
will not put out a smoldering **w**, Mt 12:20

WICKED
does not follow the advice of the **w** Ps 1:1
They made His grave with the **w** Is 53:9
no pleasure in the death of the **w**, Ezk 33:11

WICKEDNESS
saw that man's **w** was widespread Gn 6:5

WIDE
the gate is **w** and the road is broad Mt 7:13

WIDOW
devour **w-s'** houses and make long Mt 23:14
Support **w-s** who are genuinely **w-s** 1Tm 5:3

WIFE
and mother and bonds with his **w**, Gn 2:24
Do not covet your neighbor's **w**, Ex 20:17
700 **w-ves** who ... turned his heart 1Kg 11:3
pleasure in the **w** of your youth. Pr 5:18
A man who finds a **w** finds a good Pr 18:22
Who can find a capable **w**? Pr 31:10
each man should have his own **w**, 1Co 7:2
W-ves, submit to your Eph 5:22
Husbands, love your **w-ves**, Eph 5:25
husband of one **w**, 1Tm 3:2
the bride, the **w** of the Lamb. Rv 21:9

WILD
Without revelation people run **w**, Pr 29:18
food was locusts and **w** honey. Mt 3:4
you, though a **w** olive branch, Rm 11:17
into the same flood of **w** living 1Pt 4:4

WILDERNESS
Prepare the way of the LORD in the **w** Is 40:3
voice of one crying out in the **w**: Mt 3:3
into the **w** to be tempted Mt 4:1
fathers ate the manna in the **w**, Jn 6:31,49

WILDFLOWERS
Consider how the **w** grow: Lk 12:27

WILL (N)
I delight to do Your **w**, my God; Ps 40:8
Your **w** be done on earth as it is Mt 6:10
one who does the **w** of My Father Mt 7:21
Yet not as I **w**, but as You **w**. Mt 26:39
My food is to do the **w** of Him Jn 4:34
it does not depend on human **w** Rm 9:16
the good, pleasing, and perfect **w** Rm 12:2
See, I have come to do Your **w**. Heb 10:9
ask anything according to His **w**, 1Jn 5:14

WILL (V)
say, "If the Lord **w-s**, we will Jms 4:15

WILLING (ADJ)
and give me a **w** spirit. Ps 51:12
her wings, yet you were not **w**! Mt 23:37
The spirit is **w**, but the flesh Mt 26:41
if You are **w**, take this cup away Lk 22:42

WIND
but the LORD was not in the **w**. 1Kg 19:11
soaring on the wings of the **w**. Ps 18:10
will inherit the **w**, Pr 11:29
they sow the **w** and reap the Hs 8:7
the **w-s** and the sea obey Him! Mt 8:27
The **w** blows where it pleases, Jn 3:8
around by every **w** of teaching, Eph 4:14

WINDSTORM
A fierce **w** arose, and the waves Mk 4:37

WINE
W is a mocker, beer is a brawler, Pr 20:1
and **w** to one whose life is bitter. Pr 31:6
no one puts new **w** into old Mt 9:17
water (after it had become **w**), Jn 2:9
said, "They're full of new **w**!" Ac 2:13
And don't get drunk with **w**, Eph 5:18
not addicted to **w**, 1Tm 3:3; Ti 1:7
a little **w** because of your stomach 1Tm 5:23

WINESKIN
no one puts new wine into old **w-s**. Mt 9:17

WING
I carried you on eagles' **w-s** Ex 19:4
under whose **w-s** you have come Ru 2:12
soaring on the **w-s** of the wind. 2Sm 22:11
hide me in the shadow of Your **w-s** Ps 17:8
soaring on the **w-s** of the wind. Ps 18:10

will soar on **w-s** like eagles; Is 40:31
rise with healing in its **w-s**, Mal 4:2
gathers her chicks under her **w-s**, Mt 23:37

WINTER
Pray it won't happen in **w**. Mk 13:18

WIPE
Lord GOD will **w** away the tears Is 25:8
She **w-d** His feet with the hair Lk 7:38
will **w** away every tear Rv 7:17; 21:4

WISDOM
God gave Solomon **w**, 1Kg 4:29
of the LORD is the beginning of **w**, Pr 9:10
Yet **w** is vindicated by all her Lk 7:35
both of the **w** and the knowledge Rm 11:33
I will destroy the **w** of the wise, 1Co 1:19
able to give you **w** for salvation 2Tm 3:15
Now if any of you lacks **w**, Jms 1:5
and riches and **w** and strength Rv 5:12

WISE
making the inexperienced **w**. Ps 19:7
is considered **w** when he keeps Pr 17:28
w men from the east arrived Mt 2:1
hidden these things from the **w** Mt 11:25
foolish ... to shame the **w**, 1Co 1:27

WITHER
and whose leaf does not **w**. Ps 1:3
The grass **w-s**, the flowers fade Is 40:7
they had no root, they **w-ed**. Mt 13:6
At once the fig tree **w-ed**. Mt 21:19
grass **w-s**, and the flower falls, 1Pt 1:24

WITHHOLD
have not **w-held** your only son Gn 22:12,16

WITNESS
the testimony of two or three **w-es**. Dt 19:15
two or three **w-es** every fact may Mt 18:16
many false **w-es** came forward. Mt 26:60
will be My **w-es** in Jerusalem, Ac 1:8
a good confession ... many **w-es**. 1Tm 6:12
large cloud of **w-es** surrounding Heb 12:1
from Jesus Christ, the faithful **w**, Rv 1:5
empower my two **w-es**, and they Rv 11:3

WOE
W is me for I am ruined Is 6:5
w to you, scribes and Pharisees, Mt 23:13
W to you who are now full, Lk 6:25
And **w** to me if I do not preach 1Co 9:16
W! **W**! **W** to those who live on Rv 8:13

WOLF
The **w** will live with the lamb, Is 11:6
you out like sheep among **w-ves**. Mt 10:16
savage **w-ves** will come in Ac 20:29

WOMAN (WOMEN)
this one will be called "**w**," Gn 2:23
w who fears the LORD ... praised. Pr 31:30
who looks at a **w** to lust for her Mt 5:28
There were also **w-en** looking on Mk 15:40
are the most blessed of **w-en**, Lk 1:42
brought a **w** caught in adultery Jn 8:3
not to have relations with a **w**. 1Co 7:1
the man is the head of the **w**, 1Co 11:3
w-en should be silent in the 1Co 14:34
God sent His Son, born of a **w**, Gl 4:4
I do not allow a **w** to teach 1Tm 2:12

WOMB
Two nations are in your **w**; Gn 25:23
Naked I came from my mother's **w**, Jb 1:21
me together in my mother's **w**. Ps 139:13
me from the **w** to be His Servant, Is 49:5
before I formed you in the **w**; Jr 1:5
his mother's **w** a second time Jn 3:4

WONDERFUL
My name ... since it is **w**. Jdg 13:18
tell about all His **w** works! Ps 105:2
it is **w** in our eyes. Ps 118:23
w things from Your instruction. Ps 119:18
Your works are **w**, and I know Ps 139:14
He will be named **W** Counselor, Is 9:6
and is **w** in our eyes? Mt 21:42

WONDERFULLY
been remarkably and **w** made. Ps 139:14

WONDERS
God of Israel, who alone does **w**. Ps 72:18
I will display **w** in the heaven Ac 2:19

WOOD
I will bow down to a block of **w**. Is 44:19
costly stones, **w**, hay, or straw, 1Co 3:12

WOOL
made of both **w** and linen. Dt 22:11
as crimson, they will be like **w**. Is 1:18
head and hair were white like **w** Rv 1:14

WORD
bread alone but on every **w** that Dt 8:3
the **w** of the LORD is pure. Ps 18:30
May the **w-s** of my mouth and the Ps 19:14
treasured Your **w** in my heart so Ps 119:11
Your **w** is a lamp for my feet Ps 119:105
Before a **w** is on my tongue, Ps 139:4
Every **w** of God is pure; Pr 30:5
w of our God remains forever. Is 40:8
My **w** ... not return to Me empty, Is 55:11
bread alone but on every **w** that Mt 4:4
hears these **w-s** of Mine and acts Mt 7:24
but My **w-s** will never pass away. Mt 24:35
The sower sows the **w**. Mk 4:14
beginning was the **W**, and the **W** was with God, and the **W** was God. Jn 1:1
The **W** became flesh and took up Jn 1:14
You have the **w-s** of eternal life. Jn 6:68
by the truth; Your **w** is truth. Jn 17:17
correctly teaching the **w** of truth. 2Tm 2:15
For the **w** of God is living and Heb 4:12
His name is the **W** of God. Rv 19:13
who keeps the ... **w-s** of this book Rv 22:7

WORK (N)
seventh day God completed His **w** Gn 2:2
six days and do all your **w**, Ex 20:9
heavens, the **w** of Your fingers, Ps 8:3
w-s are wonderful, and I know Ps 139:14
There is profit in all hard **w**, Pr 14:23
we all are the **w** of Your hands. Is 64:8
do even greater **w-s** than these, Jn 14:12
faith apart from the **w-s** of the law. Rm 3:28
if by grace, then it is not by **w-s**; Rm 11:6
test the quality of each one's **w**. 1Co 3:13
because by the **w-s** of the law no Gl 2:16
not from **w-s**, so that no one can Eph 2:9
in Christ Jesus for good **w-s**, Eph 2:10
started a good **w** in you will Php 1:6
equipped for every good **w**. 2Tm 3:17
has faith but does not have **w-s**? Jms 2:14

I know your **w-s** Rv 2:2,19; 3:1,8,15
judged according to their **w-s**. Rv 20:13

WORK (V)
master finds him **w-ing** when he Mt 24:46
My Father is still **w-ing**, and I Jn 5:17
Don't **w** for the food that Jn 6:27
that all things **w** together for Rm 8:28
w out your own salvation with Php 2:12
For it is God who is **w-ing** in you, Php 2:13
isn't willing to **w**, he should not eat 2Th 3:10

WORKER
abundant, but the **w-s** are few. Mt 9:37
the **w** is worthy of his wages. Lk 10:7
The **w** is worthy of his wages. 1Tm 5:18
a **w** who doesn't need to be 2Tm 2:15

WORLD
He judges the **w** with righteousness; Ps 9:8
You are the light of the **w**. Mt 5:14
gains the whole **w** yet loses his Mt 16:26
Go into all the **w** and preach the Mk 16:15
who takes away the sin of the **w**! Jn 1:29
For God loved the **w** in this way: Jn 3:16
I am the light of the **w**. Jn 8:12; 9:5
I have conquered the **w**. Jn 16:33
Do not love the **w** or the things 1Jn 2:15
greater than the one who is in the **w**. 1Jn 4:4

WORM
But I am a **w** and not a man, Ps 22:6
for their **w** will never die, Is 66:24
God appointed a **w** that attacked Jnh 4:7
where Their **w** does not die, Mk 9:44

WORMWOOD
The name of the star is **W**, Rv 8:11

WORRY
Don't **w** about your life, Mt 6:25
don't **w** beforehand what you will Mk 13:11
Don't **w** about anything, but in Php 4:6

WORSHIP
W the LORD in the splendor of 1Ch 16:29
Come, let us **w** and bow down; Ps 95:6
those who **w** Him must **w** in spirit Jn 4:24
this is your spiritual **w**. Rm 12:1

WORSHIPERS
when the true **w** will worship Jn 4:23

WORTHLESS
not been raised, your faith is **w**; 1Co 15:17

WORTHY
to the LORD, who is **w** of praise, 2Sm 22:4
and follow Me is not **w** of Me. Mt 10:38
I am not **w** to untie the strap of Lk 3:16
you to walk **w** of the calling Eph 4:1
Lamb who was slaughtered is **w** Rv 5:12

WOUND
and binds up their **w-s**. Ps 147:3
The **w-s** of a friend are trustworthy, Pr 27:6
and we are healed by His **w-s**. Is 53:5
you have been healed by His **w-s**. 1Pt 2:24
but his fatal **w** was healed. Rv 13:3

WRAP
body, **w-ped** it in clean, fine linen, Mt 27:59
and she **w-ped** Him snugly in cloth Lk 2:7

WRATH
do not discipline me in Your **w**. Ps 6:1
Even human **w** will praise You; Ps 76:10
is not profitable on a day of **w**, Pr 11:4
but a harsh word stirs up **w**. Pr 15:1
you to flee from the coming **w**? Mt 3:7
For God's **w** is revealed from Rm 1:18
were by nature children under **w**, Eph 2:3
and from the **w** of the Lamb, Rv 6:16

WRESTLED
man **w** with him until daybreak. Gn 32:24

WRETCHED
What a **w** man I am! Who will Rm 7:24
you don't know that you are **w**, Rv 3:17

WRINKLE
without spot or **w** or anything Eph 5:27

WRITE
Moses **wrote** down all the words Ex 24:4
w them on the tablet of your Pr 3:3; 7:3
within them and **w** it on their hearts. Jr 31:33
hand appeared and began **w-ing**, Dn 5:5
because he **wrote** about Me. Jn 5:46
are **w-ten** so that you may believe Jn 20:31
I will ... **w** them on their hearts. Heb 8:10

WRONG
this man has done nothing **w**. Lk 23:41
Love does no **w** to a neighbor. Rm 13:10
does not keep a record of **w-s**. 1Co 13:5

WRONGDOING
if you forgive people their **w**, Mt 6:14
if someone is caught in any **w**, Gl 6:1

YAHWEH
Divine name by which God revealed Himself to Moses (Ex 3:15-16; 6:2-8; 15:3; 34:5-6). Usually translated LORD.
Y, the God of your fathers, Ex 3:15
I did not make My name **Y** known Ex 6:3
I am **Y** your God, who brought you Ps 81:10
I am **Y**, that is My name; Is 42:8
nations will know that I am **Y** Ezk 36:23
Y-'s name must not be invoked. Am 6:10
I worship **Y**, the God of the Jnh 1:9

YEAR
The fiftieth **y** will be your Jubilee; Lv 25:11
a thousand **y-s** are like yesterday Ps 90:4
proclaim the **y** of the LORD's favor, Is 61:2
proclaim the **y** of the Lord's favor. Lk 4:19
days, months, seasons, and **y-s**. Gl 4:10
continually offer **y** after **y**. Heb 10:1
one day is like a thousand **y-s**, 2Pt 3:8
for 1,000 **y-s**. Rv 20:2,4,6

YEARN
caused to live in us **y-s** jealously? Jms 4:5

YEAST
of heaven is like **y** that a woman Mt 13:33
beware of the **y** of the Pharisees Mt 16:6
know that a little **y** permeates 1Co 5:6

YES
let your word '**y**' be '**y**,' Mt 5:37
God's promises is "**Y**" in Him. 2Co 1:20
Your "**y**" must be "**y**," and your Jms 5:12

YESTERDAY
were born only **y** and know nothing Jb 8:9
Jesus Christ is the same **y**, today, Heb 13:8

YOKE
Your father made our **y** difficult. 1Kg 12:4
take up My **y** and learn from Me, Mt 11:29
submit again to a **y** of slavery. Gl 5:1

YOUNG
How can a **y** man keep his way Ps 119:9
and your **y** men will see visions. Jl 2:28
your **y** men will see visions, Ac 2:17

YOUNGER
The older will serve the **y**. Rm 9:12
y men as brothers, 1Tm 5:1

YOUTH
Do not remember the sins of my **y** Ps 25:7
y is renewed like the eagle. Ps 103:5
take pleasure in the wife of your **y**. Pr 5:18
Teach a **y** about the way he should Pr 22:6
your Creator in the days of your **y**: Ec 12:1
Let no one despise your **y**; 1Tm 4:12

YOUTHFUL
Flee from **y** passions, 2Tm 2:22

ZACCHAEUS
Tax collector who hosted Jesus and was converted (Lk 19:2-9).

ZEAL
The **z** of the LORD of Hosts will 2Kg 19:31
z for Your house has consumed me, Ps 69:9
z is not good without knowledge, Pr 19:2
The **z** of the LORD of Hosts will Is 9:7; 37:32
Z for Your house will consume Me. Jn 2:17
that they have **z** for God, but Rm 10:2
regarding **z**, persecuting the church; Php 3:6

ZEBULUN
Son of Jacob and Leah (Gn 30:20). Tribe with territory between the Sea of Galilee and Mount Carmel (Jos 19:10-16).

ZECHARIAH
1. Son of Jeroboam II; king of Israel (2Kg 15:8-12).
2. Prophet after the exile; son of Berechiah; descendant of Iddo (Ezr 5:1; Zch 1:1).
3. Father of John the Baptist (Lk 1:5-23, 59-79).

ZEDEKIAH
Son of Josiah; last king of Judah; originally called Mattaniah; sons blinded; exiled (2Kg 24:17–25:7).

ZEPHANIAH
Prophet to Josiah; descendant of Hezekiah (Zch 1:1).

ZERUBBABEL
Leader of those returning from exile to rebuild the temple (Ezr 2:2; 4:2; 5:2; Hg 1:1). Descendant of David and Jehoiachin; ancestor of Jesus (1Ch 3:9-19; Mt 1:13; Lk 3:27).

ZIMRI
Chariot commander; killed Elah king of Israel; reigned seven days (1Kg 16:8-20).

ZION
Specifically, the stronghold in Jerusalem; also refers to the temple, hill, city, people, and heavenly city.
did capture the stronghold of **Z**, 2Sm 5:7
Mount **Z** on the slopes of the north Ps 48:2
Sing us one of the songs of **Z**. Ps 137:3
laid a stone in **Z**, a tested stone Is 28:16
Blow the horn in **Z**; sound the alarm Jl 2:1
Rejoice greatly, Daughter **Z**! Zch 9:9
Tell Daughter **Z**, "See, your King Mt 21:5
Fear no more, Daughter **Z**; Jn 12:15
a stone in **Z** to stumble over, Rm 9:33
The Liberator will come from **Z**; Rm 11:26

10 *SEE ALSO* TEN
will be like **10** virgins who took Mt 25:1
to the one who has **10** talents. Mt 25:28
Were not **10** cleansed? Lk 17:17
The **10** horns you saw are **10** kings Rv 17:12

12 *SEE ALSO* TWELVE
Jacob had **12** sons: Gn 35:22
the names of the **12** apostles: Mt 10:2
12 thrones, judging the **12** tribes Mt 19:28
When He was **12** years old, they Lk 2:42
12 foundations, and ... the **12** names of the Lamb's **12** apostles. Rv 21:14

24
on the thrones sat **24** elders Rv 4:4
and the **24** elders fell down Rv 5:8

30
my wages, **30** pieces of silver Zch 11:12
weighed out **30** pieces of silver Mt 26:15
Jesus was about **30** years old and Lk 3:23

40
rain fell ... **40** days and **40** nights. Gn 7:12
on the mountain **40** days and **40** Ex 24:18
in the wilderness for **40** years Nm 14:33
40 days to be tempted by the Devil. Lk 4:2
appearing to them during **40** days Ac 1:3

62
be seven weeks and **62** weeks. Dn 9:25

70
until **70** years were fulfilled. 2Ch 36:21
When **70** years for Babylon Jr 29:10
number of years ... would be **70**. Dn 9:2
but **70** times seven. Mt 18:22

99
Abraham was **99** years old when Gn 17:24
leave the **99** in the open field Lk 15:4

400
will be ... oppressed **400** years. Gn 15:13
enslave and oppress them **400** years. Ac 7:6

430
lived in Egypt was **430** years. Ex 12:40
which came **430** years later, Gl 3:17

500
to over **500** brothers at one 1Co 15:6

666
of a man. His number is **666**. Rv 13:18

700
He had **700** wives who were 1Kg 11:3

1,000 *SEE ALSO* THOUSAND

and bound him for **1,000** years. Rv 20:2
reign with Him for **1,000** years. Rv 20:6

1,260

they will prophesy for **1,260** days, Rv 11:3

5,000

who ate were about **5,000** men, Mt 14:21

10,000

one who owed **10,000** talents was Mt 18:24
than **10,000** words in another 1Co 14:19

144,000

144,000 sealed from every tribe Rv 7:4

600,000

about **600,000** soldiers on foot, Ex 12:37

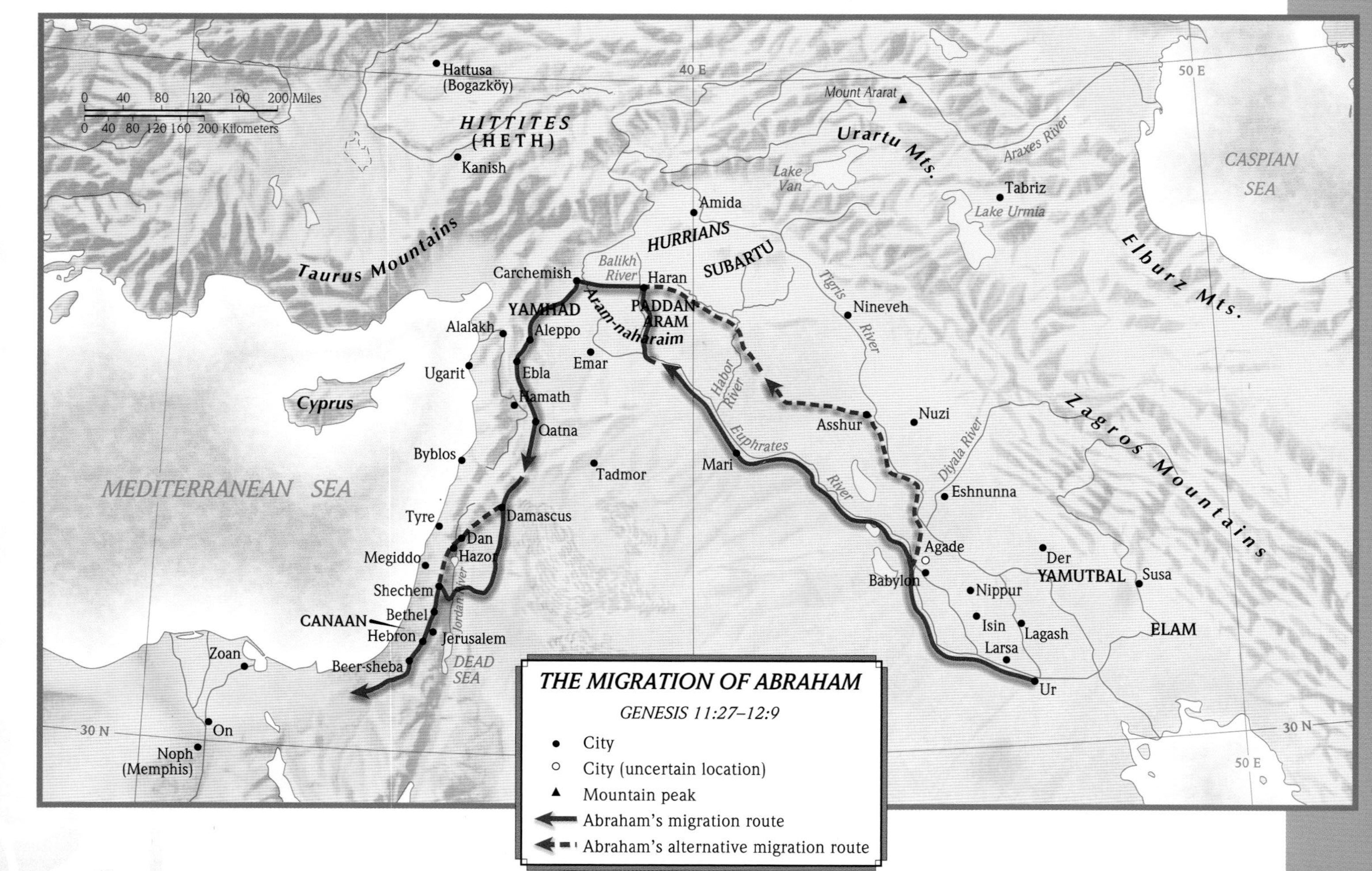
THE MIGRATION OF ABRAHAM
GENESIS 11:27–12:9
City
City (uncertain location)
Mountain peak
Abraham's migration route
Abraham's alternative migration route
0 40 80 120 160 200 Miles
0 40 80 120 160 200 Kilometers
Hattusa (Bogazköy)
HITTITES (HETH)
Kanish
Taurus Mountains
Carchemish
YAMHAD
Alalakh
Aleppo
Ugarit
Ebla
Hamath
Qatna
Byblos
Cyprus
MEDITERRANEAN SEA
Tyre
Damascus
Dan
Hazor
Megiddo
Shechem
Bethel
CANAAN
Hebron
Jerusalem
Jordan River
DEAD SEA
Beer-sheba
Zoan
On
Noph (Memphis)
30 N
40 E
50 E
Balikh River
Haran
PADDAN ARAM
Aram-naharaim
Emar
Tadmor
Amida
HURRIANS
SUBARTU
Lake Van
Mount Ararat
Urartu Mts.
Araxes River
Tabriz
Lake Urmia
CASPIAN SEA
Elburz Mts.
Tigris River
Nineveh
Habor River
Euphrates River
Mari
Asshur
Nuzi
Diyala River
Zagros Mountains
Eshnunna
Agade
Babylon
Der
YAMUTBAL
Susa
Nippur
Isin
Lagash
Larsa
ELAM
Ur

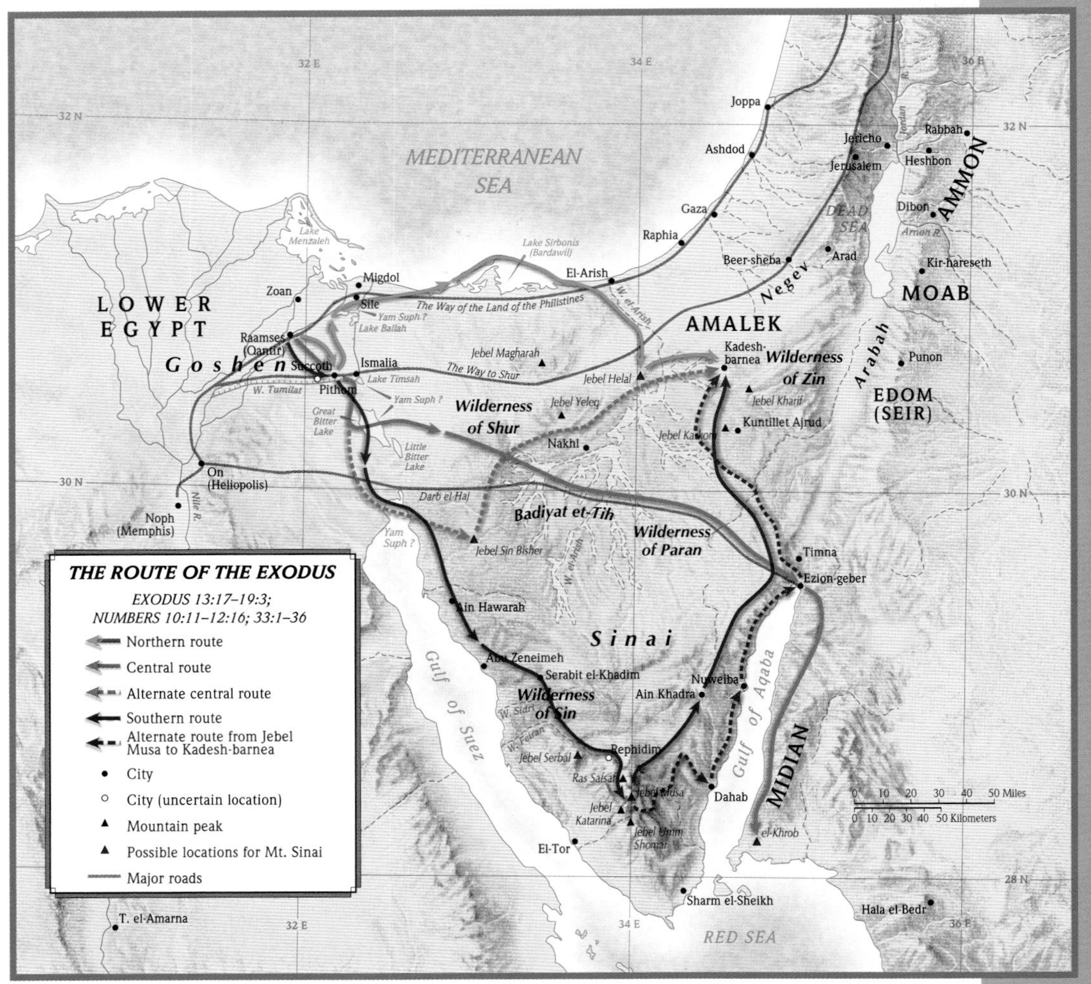

THE ROUTE OF THE EXODUS
EXODUS 13:17–19:3;
NUMBERS 10:11–12:16; 33:1–36
Northern route
Central route
Alternate central route
Southern route
Alternate route from Jebel Musa to Kadesh-barnea
City
City (uncertain location)
Mountain peak
Possible locations for Mt. Sinai
Major roads
MEDITERRANEAN SEA
LOWER EGYPT
Goshen
Zoan
Raamses (Qantir)
Succoth
Pithom
Ismalia
Migdol
Sile
Yam Suph ?
Lake Ballah
Lake Menzaleh
Lake Timsah
Great Bitter Lake
Little Bitter Lake
W. Tumilat
On (Heliopolis)
Noph (Memphis)
Nile R.
T. el-Amarna
The Way of the Land of the Philistines
The Way to Shur
Darb el-Haj
Lake Sirbonis (Bardawil)
El-Arish
W. el-Arish
Raphia
Gaza
Ashdod
Joppa
Beer-sheba
Negev
Arad
Jerusalem
Jericho
Jordan
DEAD SEA
Rabbah
Heshbon
Dibon
Arnon R.
Kir-hareseth
AMMON
MOAB
Arabah
Punon
EDOM (SEIR)
AMALEK
Kadesh-barnea
Wilderness of Zin
Jebel Kharif
Kuntillet Ajrud
Jebel Kakom
Jebel Magharah
Jebel Yeleq
Jebel Helal
Wilderness of Shur
Nakhl
Badiyat et-Tih
Wilderness of Paran
Jebel Sin Bisher
Yam Suph ?
Ain Hawarah
Abu Zeneimeh
Serabit el-Khadim
Sinai
Wilderness of Sin
W. Sidri
W. Feiran
Jebel Serbal
Rephidim
Ras Safsaf
Jebel Musa
Jebel Katarina
Jebel Umm Shomar
El-Tor
Ain Khadra
Nuweiba
Dahab
Sharm el-Sheikh
Gulf of Suez
Gulf of Aqaba
Timna
Ezion-geber
MIDIAN
el-Khrob
Hala el-Bedr
RED SEA
32 N
30 N
28 N
32 E
34 E
36 E
0 10 20 30 40 50 Miles
0 10 20 30 40 50 Kilometers

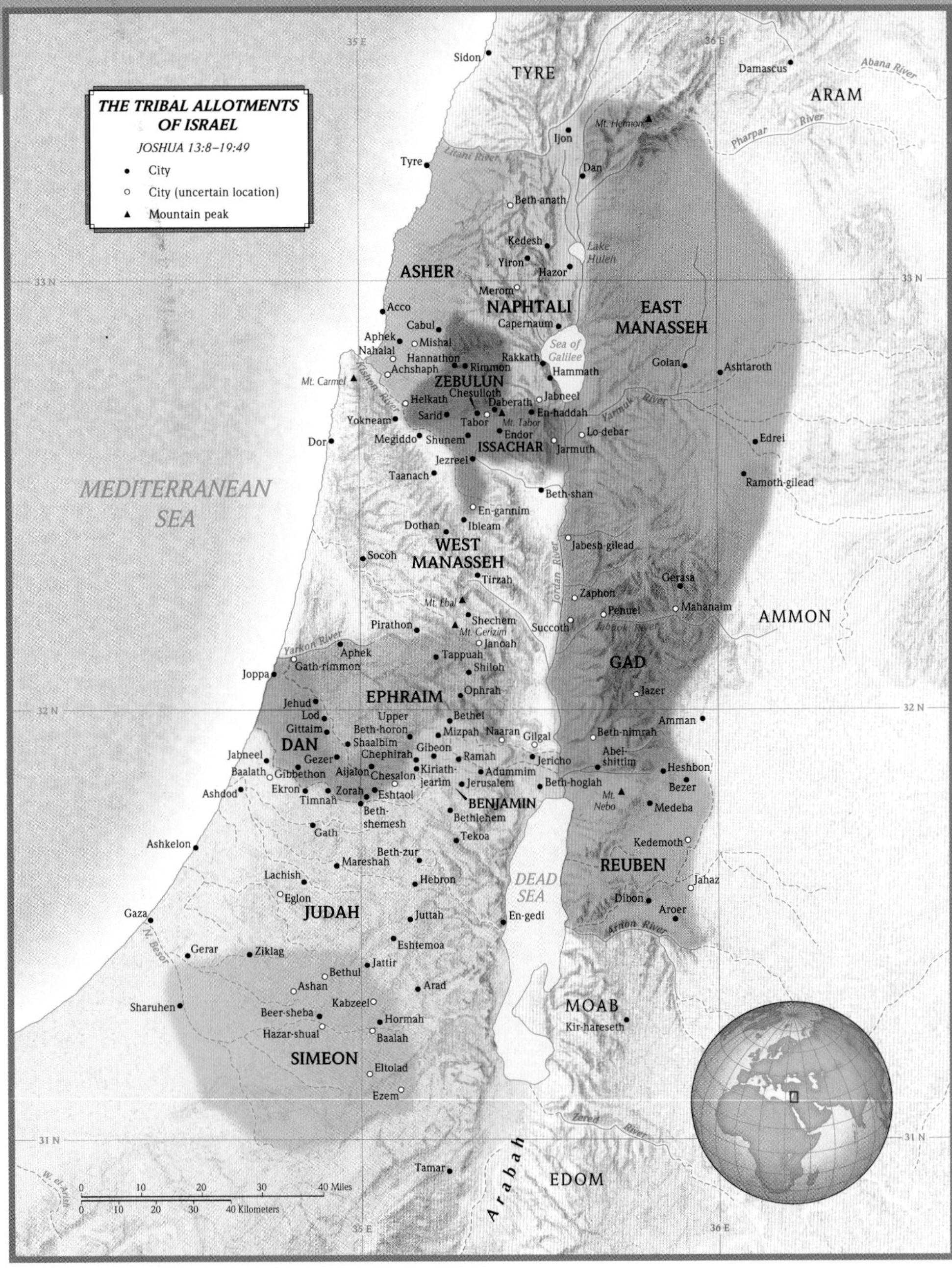

THE TRIBAL ALLOTMENTS OF ISRAEL
JOSHUA 13:8–19:49
City
City (uncertain location)
Mountain peak
MEDITERRANEAN SEA
ASHER
NAPHTALI
ZEBULUN
ISSACHAR
WEST MANASSEH
EAST MANASSEH
EPHRAIM
DAN
BENJAMIN
JUDAH
SIMEON
GAD
REUBEN
TYRE
ARAM
AMMON
MOAB
EDOM
Sidon
Tyre
Damascus
Mt. Hermon
Ijon
Dan
Beth-anath
Kedesh
Yiron
Hazor
Lake Huleh
Merom
Acco
Cabul
Capernaum
Aphek
Mishal
Nahalal
Hannathon
Rimmon
Rakkath
Sea of Galilee
Hammath
Achshaph
Mt. Carmel
Golan
Ashtaroth
Helkath
Chesulloth
Jabneel
Daberath
En-haddah
Sarid
Tabor
Mt. Tabor
Yokneam
Endor
Lo-debar
Dor
Megiddo
Shunem
Jarmuth
Edrei
Jezreel
Taanach
Beth-shan
Ramoth-gilead
En-gannim
Dothan
Ibleam
Jabesh-gilead
Socoh
Tirzah
Gerasa
Mt. Ebal
Zaphon
Shechem
Penuel
Mahanaim
Pirathon
Mt. Gerizim
Succoth
Janoah
Yarkon River
Aphek
Tappuah
Gath-rimmon
Joppa
Shiloh
Ophrah
Jazer
Jehud
Lod
Upper
Bethel
Amman
Gittaim
Beth-horon
Mizpah
Naaran
Gilgal
Beth-nimrah
Shaalbim
Gibeon
Chephirah
Ramah
Jericho
Abel-shittim
Jabneel
Gezer
Heshbon
Baalath
Gibbethon
Aijalon
Chesalon
Kiriath-jearim
Adummim
Bezer
Ekron
Jerusalem
Beth-hoglah
Ashdod
Zorah
Eshtaol
Timnah
Mt. Nebo
Medeba
Beth-shemesh
Bethlehem
Gath
Tekoa
Kedemoth
Ashkelon
Beth-zur
Mareshah
Lachish
Hebron
Jahaz
Eglon
DEAD SEA
Dibon
Aroer
Gaza
Juttah
En-gedi
Arnon River
N. Besor
Eshtemoa
Gerar
Ziklag
Jattir
Bethul
Ashan
Arad
Sharuhen
Kabzeel
Beer-sheba
Hormah
Kir-hareseth
Hazar-shual
Baalah
Eltolad
Ezem
Zered River
Tamar
Arabah
W. el-Arish
Litani River
Kishon River
Jordan River
Yarmuk River
Jabbok River
Abana River
Pharpar River
0 10 20 30 40 Miles
0 10 20 30 40 Kilometers
35 E
36 E
33 N
32 N
31 N

THE KINGDOMS OF ISRAEL AND JUDAH
1 KINGS 12
City
Capital city
City (uncertain location)
Mountain peak
Israel
Judah
International roads
Local roads
0 10 20 30 40 50 Miles
0 10 20 30 40 50 Kilometers
MEDITERRANEAN SEA
PHOENICIA
ARAM
GESHUR
ISRAEL
AMMON
PHILISTIA
JUDAH
MOAB
EDOM
Negev
Wilderness
Eastern Desert
Beirut
Sidon
Tyre
Damascus
Mt. Hermon
Ijon
Dan
Abel-beth-maacah
Jeroboam built a sanctuary
Kedesh
Hazor
Lake Huleh
Achzib
Acco
Chinnereth
Sea of Galilee
Mt. Carmel
Gath-hepher
Aphek
Ashtaroth
Mt. Tabor
Edrei
Megiddo
Dor
Jezreel
Taanach
Mt. Gilboa
Ramoth-gilead
Beth-shan
Dothan
Ibleam
Pehel
Jabesh-gilead
Socoh
Tirzah
Samaria
Political capital of Israel from Omri onward
Mt. Ebal
Shechem
Penuel
Mahanaim
Succoth
Mt. Gerizim
Aphek
Adam
Joppa
Shiloh
Jeroboam built a sanctuary
Upper Beth-horon
Lower Beth-horon
Bethel
Rabbah (Amman)
Gezer
Mizpah
Jericho
Ashdod
Aijalon
Ramah
Geba
Gibeah
Heshbon
Ekron
Jerusalem
Mt. Nebo
Gath
Azekah
Medeba
Ashkelon
Bethlehem
Beth-zur
Mareshah
Tekoa
Lachish
Hebron
Adoraim
Dibon
Gaza
Ziph
Carmel
DEAD SEA
Gerar
Maon
Arad
Beer-sheba
Kir-hareseth
King's Highway
Tamar
Bozrah
Kadesh-barnea
Litani River
Kishon River
Yarmuk River
Jordan River
Jabbok River
Yarkon River
Arnon River
Zered River
N. Besor
W. el-Arish
Int
34 E
36 E
32 N

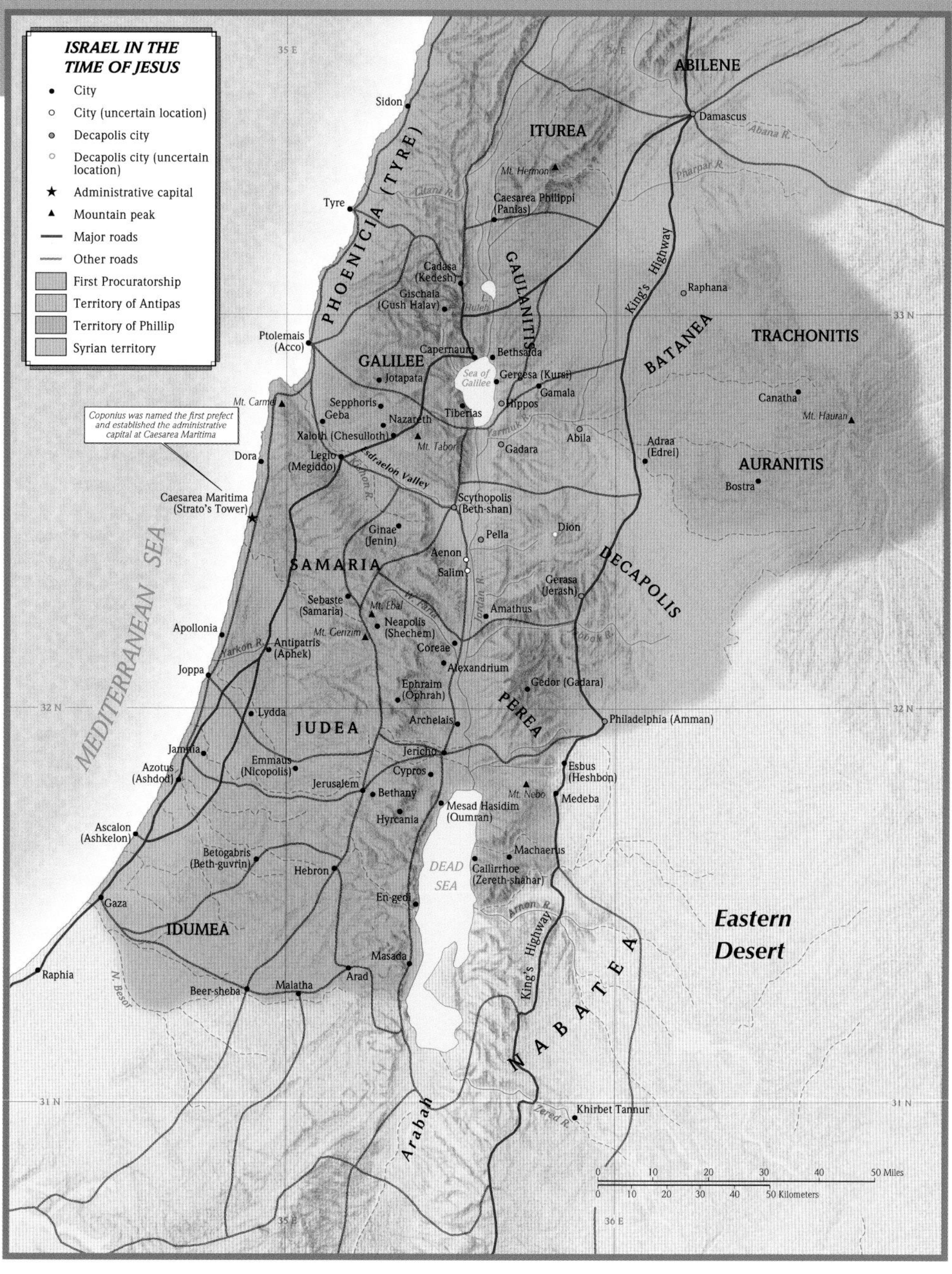

ISRAEL IN THE TIME OF JESUS
City
City (uncertain location)
Decapolis city
Decapolis city (uncertain location)
Administrative capital
Mountain peak
Major roads
Other roads
First Procuratorship
Territory of Antipas
Territory of Phillip
Syrian territory
Coponius was named the first prefect and established the administrative capital at Caesarea Maritima
ABILENE
ITUREA
PHOENICIA (TYRE)
GAULANITIS
GALILEE
BATANEA
TRACHONITIS
AURANITIS
SAMARIA
DECAPOLIS
JUDEA
PEREA
IDUMEA
NABATEA
MEDITERRANEAN SEA
Eastern Desert
Sidon
Damascus
Tyre
Caesarea Philippi (Panias)
Mt. Hermon
Cadasa (Kedesh)
Gischala (Gush Halav)
Raphana
King's Highway
Ptolemais (Acco)
Capernaum
Bethsaida
Sea of Galilee
Gergesa (Kursi)
Jotapata
Gamala
Canatha
Mt. Hauran
Mt. Carmel
Sepphoris
Geba
Nazareth
Hippos
Tiberias
Xaloth (Chesulloth)
Mt. Tabor
Abila
Gadara
Adraa (Edrei)
Dora
Legio (Megiddo)
Jezreel Valley
Bostra
Scythopolis (Beth-shan)
Caesarea Maritima (Strato's Tower)
Ginae (Jenin)
Pella
Dion
Aenon
Salim
Gerasa (Jerash)
Sebaste (Samaria)
Mt. Ebal
Neapolis (Shechem)
Mt. Gerizim
Amathus
Apollonia
Antipatris (Aphek)
Coreae
Alexandrium
Joppa
Ephraim (Ophrah)
Gedor (Gadara)
Lydda
Archelais
Philadelphia (Amman)
Jamnia
Emmaus (Nicopolis)
Jericho
Azotus (Ashdod)
Cypros
Esbus (Heshbon)
Jerusalem
Bethany
Mt. Nebo
Medeba
Mesad Hasidim (Qumran)
Hyrcania
Ascalon (Ashkelon)
Betogabris (Beth-guvrin)
Machaerus
Hebron
DEAD SEA
Callirrhoe (Zereth-shahar)
En-gedi
Gaza
Masada
Raphia
Arad
Beer-sheba
Malatha
Arabah
Khirbet Tannur
Zered R.
35 E
36 E
33 N
32 N
31 N
0 10 20 30 40 50 Miles
0 10 20 30 40 50 Kilometers

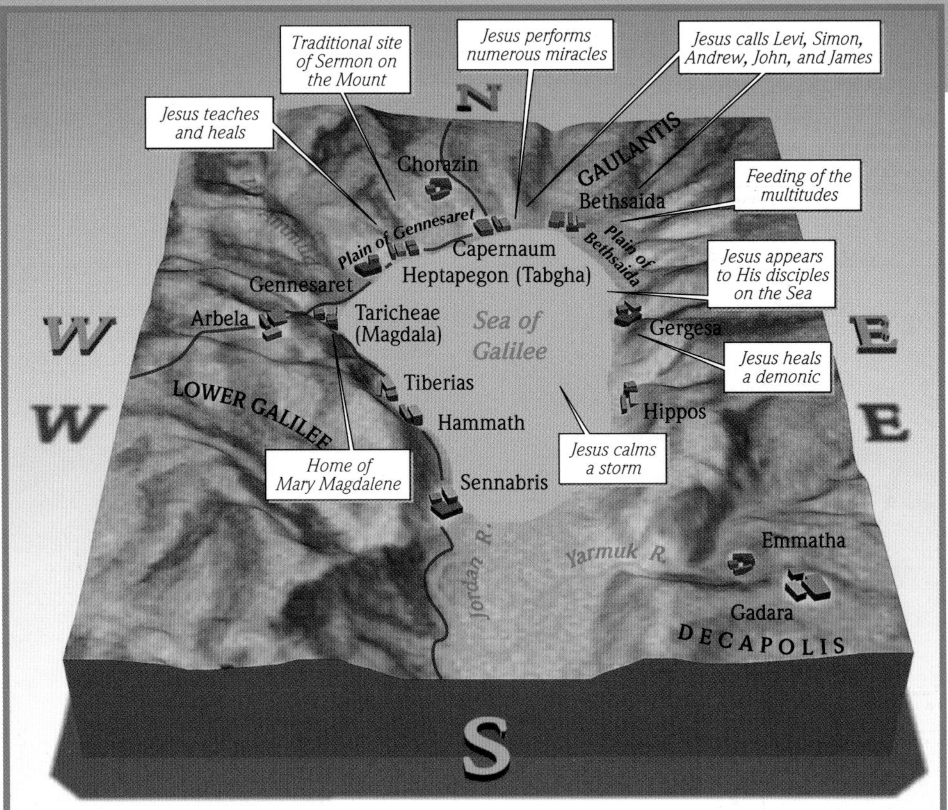

N
W
E
S

Traditional site of Sermon on the Mount
Jesus performs numerous miracles
Jesus calls Levi, Simon, Andrew, John, and James
Jesus teaches and heals
Feeding of the multitudes
Jesus appears to His disciples on the Sea
Jesus heals a demonic
Jesus calms a storm
Home of Mary Magdalene

GAULANTIS
Chorazin
Bethsaida
Plain of Gennesaret
Capernaum
Heptapegon (Tabgha)
Plain of Bethsaida
Gennesaret
Arbela
Taricheae (Magdala)
Sea of Galilee
Gergesa
Tiberias
LOWER GALILEE
Hammath
Hippos
Sennabris
Jordan R.
Yarmuk R.
Emmatha
Gadara
DECAPOLIS

THE MINISTRY OF JESUS AROUND THE SEA OF GALILEE

MATTHEW 5–7; 9:1-9
MARK 1:21-34; 2:1-14; 4:35-41; 5:1-20; 6:45-52
LUKE 7:1-10; 9:12-17
JOHN 6:1-25

City

Road